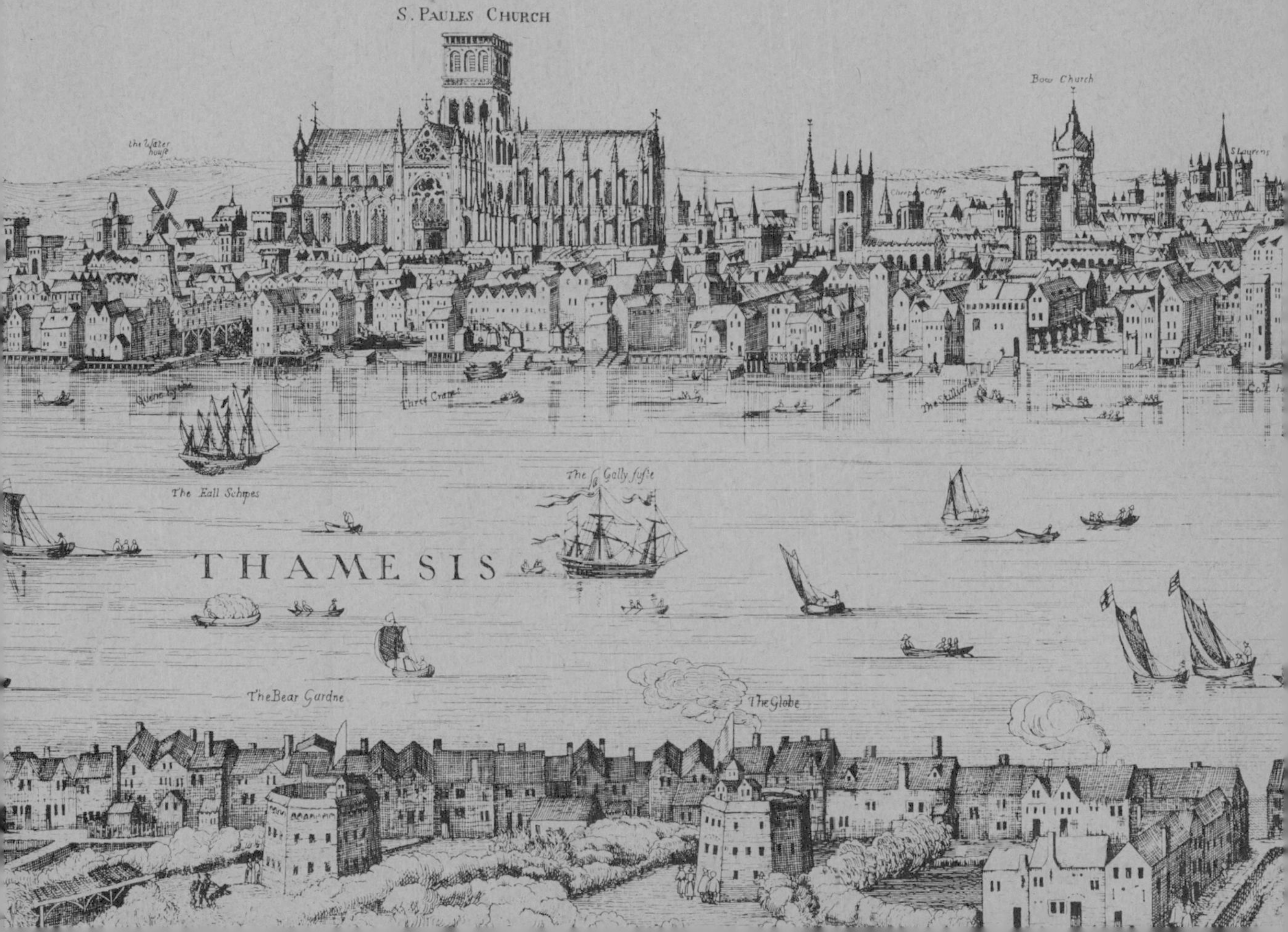
S. PAULES CHURCH
Bow Church
the Water house
The Eall Schipes
THAMESIS
The Bear Gardne
The Globe

# THE COMPLETE
# SIGNET CLASSIC
# SHAKESPEARE

# THE COMPLETE
# SIGNET CLASSIC
# SHAKESPEARE

HARCOURT BRACE JOVANOVICH, INC.

*New York    Chicago    San Francisco    Atlanta*

The endpaper illustrations are details from the Folger Shakespeare Library's copy of Claes Janszoon de Visscher's *View of London*, 1616. The two pages from the front matter of the First Folio of 1623, showing Ben Jonson's verse on the Droeshout Portrait and the title page, which includes the portrait, are from the Folger Shakespeare Library collection.

ILLUSTRATION CREDITS   The Folger Shakespeare Library, pp. 3 (top), 67 (right), 68, 79, 238, 330, 371, 404, 445, 487, 530, 566, 607, 729, 806, 845, 880, 917, 969, 1009, 1057, 1096, 1143, 1182, 1233, 1269, 1324, 1375, 1418, 1454, 1501, 1543, 1577, 1679, 1693; Shakespeare Birthplace Trust, p. 3 (bottom); University Library, Utrecht, Ms. 842, fol. 132r., p. 6; Collection of Mr. and Mrs. Paul Mellon, p. 8 (top); Guildhall Library, London, p. 8 (bottom); © the Marquess of Bath, p. 11; Dulwich College, London, p. 24; New York Public Library Picture Collection, p. 30; The Huntington Library, San Marino, California, pp. 67 (left), 290, 1626, 1714, 1715, 1719, 1730; New York Public Library, Rare Book Room, pp. 110, 152, 643, 686, 765; Bodleian Library, Oxford, and New York Public Library, Rare Book Room, p. 196

*All's Well That Ends Well* © 1965 by Sylvan Barnet; *Antony and Cleopatra* © 1964 by Barbara Everett; *As You Like It* © 1963 by Albert Gilman; *The Comedy of Errors* © 1965 by Harry Levin; *Coriolanus* © 1966 by Reuben Brower; *Cymbeline* © 1968 by Richard Hosley; *Hamlet* © 1963 by Edward Hubler; *Henry VIII* © 1967 by S. Schoenbaum; *Henry V* © 1965 by John Russell Brown; *1 Henry IV* © 1965 by Maynard Mack; *2 Henry IV* © 1965 by Norman N. Holland, Jr.; *1 Henry VI* © 1967 by Lawrence V. Ryan; *2 Henry VI* © 1967 by Arthur Freeman; *3 Henry VI* © 1968 by Milton Crane; *Julius Caesar* © 1963 by William and Barbara Rosen; *King John* © 1966 by William H. Matchett; *King Lear* © 1963 by Russell Fraser; *Love's Labor's Lost* © 1965 by John Arthos; *Macbeth* © 1963 by Sylvan Barnet; *Measure for Measure* © 1964 by S. Nagarajan; *The Merchant of Venice* © 1965 by Kenneth Myrick; *The Merry Wives of Windsor* © 1965 by William Green; *A Midsummer Night's Dream* © 1963 by Wolfgang Clemen; *Much Ado About Nothing* © 1964 by David L. Stevenson; *Othello* © 1963 by Alvin Kernan; *Pericles* © 1965 by Ernest Schanzer; *The Poems* © 1968 by William Burto, Introduction © 1968 by William Empson; *Richard II* © 1963 by Kenneth Muir; *Richard III* © 1964 by Mark Eccles; *Romeo and Juliet* © 1964 by J. A. Bryant, Jr.; *The Sonnets* © 1964 by William Burto, Introduction © 1964 by W. H. Auden; *The Taming of the Shrew* © 1966 by Robert B. Heilman; *The Tempest* © 1964 by Robert Langbaum; *Timon of Athens* © 1965 by Maurice Charney; *Titus Andronicus* © 1964 by Sylvan Barnet; *Troilus and Cressida* © 1963 by Daniel Seltzer; *Twelfth Night* © 1965 by Herschel Baker; *The Two Gentlemen of Verona* © 1964 by Bertrand Evans; *The Two Noble Kinsmen* © 1966 by Clifford Leech; *The Winter's Tale* © 1963 by Frank Kermode

Library of Congress Catalog Card Number: 71-169067

ISBN: 0-15-512610-5

PRINTED IN THE UNITED STATES OF AMERICA

# PREFACE

Because there are almost two thousand pages of great writing in this book, I hesitate to detain the reader here. Yet a few prefatory words must be said.

First, I confess my surprise that so large a book is so readable. The publisher has given the speech prefixes in full (not *Cae.* and *Cass.*, but *Caesar* and *Cassius*); has signaled footnotes by placing a bubble after each word or phrase being glossed and has put the footnotes where they belong, at the bottom of the column in which the word or phrase appears; has minimized the number of turned-over lines of poetry; and has used high-quality paper and readable type.

Second, a comment on the arrangement of the contents is called for. There are really only two possible arrangements: the plays can be arranged by genres (comedies, histories, tragedies, nondramatic works), or they can be arranged chronologically (with the nondramatic works either interspersed or grouped at the end). Although the chronology has never been exactly determined, the arrangement of this edition is chronological, partly because even if an organization by genres is used, the chronological problems must be faced in ordering the plays within each genre. Moreover, the three genres established by the editors of the first collected edition of Shakespeare's plays no longer seem entirely satisfactory. There has been a tendency to remove some of the "Comedies" and one of the "Tragedies" of the First Folio to make a fourth category, "Romances," and to treat some of the "Tragedies" as "Histories" and some of the "Histories" as "Tragedies." The day had to come when the author of an otherwise useful book on comedy would announce that of the fourteen plays called comedies in the First Folio, only five can properly be so called. And so the genres multiply. Yet another reason for using a chronological arrangement is simply that most readers find it helpful to study Shakespeare's plays, or a selection of them, in the approximate order in which they were written. The earliest plays, to be sure, are on the whole inferior to the later ones, but they are full of good things, and the reader will not be bored at the outset even if he begins with such early works as *The Comedy of Errors*, *Titus Andronicus*, and *Richard III*. Moreover, although the chronology has not been exactly determined, the main lines are clear, and today we run no such danger as that which in the eighteenth century beset James Hurdis, who argued that Shakespeare progressed from the rather free verse of *The Winter's Tale* (now established as one of Shakespeare's last plays) to the more regular verse of *The Comedy of Errors* (now established as one of the first plays).

Two pleasant tasks remain: to call attention to new features and to old debts. First, this collected edition of the Signet Classic Shakespeare contains a General Introduction that seeks to describe in some detail not only the background to Shakespeare's achievements but also something of the achievements themselves; and this edition contains a newly revised (and greatly amplified) list of Suggested References. Second, I wish to express my gratitude to the editors of the individual plays and poems, both for their original work and for the revisions which they contributed to this new edition. I wish also to thank Victor Weybright, who initiated the paperback series; Ronald Campbell, who initiated this collected edition; Richard Hosley, who provided valuable information about the Elizabethan playhouse; Frederick C. Nelson, who interpreted some statistical data; Morton Berman, Michael Bliss, and William Burto, who improved the General Introduction; Wallace MacCaffrey, who suggested some books on the Elizabethan historical background; Edward Owens, who checked the list of Suggested References; Mrs. Bernice Nunley and Mrs. Ann Parker, who typed (and at times improved) the General Introduction; and Cele Gardner, Louise Marinis, and Linda Reiman, of Harcourt Brace Jovanovich, who presided over the metamorphosis of forty paperback books into this book. The list of Suggested References is, of course, an acknowledgment of further debts.

The chief debt is to Shakespeare. But—in the words of his fellow actors who first collected his plays—"It is not our province, who only gather his works, and give them to you, to praise him. It is yours that read him."

SYLVAN BARNET, *General Editor*

# CHRONOLOGICAL TABLE OF CONTENTS

# The Poems, 1665

# The Sonnets, 1722

# Suggested References, 1759

# Index to First Lines of the Sonnets, 1775

# ALPHABETICAL
# TABLE OF CONTENTS

# CONTENTS (ALPHABETICAL)

THE COMPLETE

SIGNET CLASSIC

# SHAKESPEARE

# To the Reader.

This Figure, that thou here feeſt put,
    It vvas for gentle Shakeſpeare cut;
Wherein the Grauer had a ſtrife
    with Nature, to out-doo the life :
O, could he but haue dravvne his vvit
    As vvell in braſſe, as he hath hit
His face ; the Print vvould then ſurpaſſe
    All, that vvas euer vvrit in braſſe.
But, ſince he cannot, Reader, looke
    Not on his Picture, but his Booke.

                                B. I.

# Mr. WILLIAM
# SHAKESPEARES

## COMEDIES,
## HISTORIES, &
## TRAGEDIES.

Published according to the True Originall Copies.

Martin Droeshout sculpsit London.

# LONDON

Printed by Isaac Iaggard, and Ed. Blount. 1623.

# GENERAL INTRODUCTION

BY SYLVAN BARNET

## Shakespeare's Life

Perhaps it is well to say at the outset that there is a good deal of evidence supporting the idea that William Shakespeare of Stratford and London wrote Shakespeare's plays. Several dozen other names have been put forward, the most notable of which are Bacon, Raleigh, Marlowe, and Queen Elizabeth; perhaps the most amusing candidates are a nun named Anne Whately and an alleged illegitimate son of Queen Elizabeth. But there is no evidence to support any of these claims, all of which begin with the assumption that "the Stratford poacher" or "the Stratford butcher-boy" simply could not have written great plays and poems. A suitably learnèd or aristocratic candidate must then be found, and if the candidate has written under his own name, verbal echoes between the plays and the candidate's undisputed works must be collected. Sometimes ciphers are detected; for example, in the comically long word *honorificabilitudinitatibus* in *Love's Labor's Lost* (V.i.42), Bacon is said to have planted a Latin anagram, *Hi ludi F. Bacon nati tuiti orbi* ("These plays, offspring of F. Bacon, are preserved for the world"). It is true that a similar long word, *honorificabilitudine*, appears in a manuscript that contains some of Bacon's essays, but slight variations of this word appear elsewhere too; indeed, the word in the exact form in which it is found in *Love's Labor's Lost* had appeared in print a century before the birth of either Shakespeare or Bacon. Moreover, other anagrams can be extracted from it—for example, *Ubi Italicus ibi Danti honor fit* ("Where there is an Italian, there honor is paid to Dante").

Against all anti-Stratfordian theories stands the fact that scores of Elizabethans spoke of Shakespeare as a playwright, and no Elizabethan is on record as having believed that Shakespeare did not write the plays. If the actor William Shakespeare was a mere front for another author, how was the secret kept so well? Why, for example, was it never detected by Ben Jonson, who both in print and in conversation spoke of William Shakespeare's plays? (One answer which has been offered is that Jonson called Shakespeare the playwright because Jonson himself was the author of the plays but wished to hide his identity.) In short, if Shakespeare did not write the plays, a great many people were fooled during the thirty-five or so years between the date of the earliest plays and the publication in 1623 of the collected plays. Did the actors—some of whom worked with Shakespeare for about twenty years—never suspect that their dull colleague could not have written the plays he was passing off as his own? Or if, as another approach holds, so many people were not fooled but rather were in on the secret, how is it possible that in its own day this widely shared secret never leaked out? According to another desperate theory, which recognizes that the plays were regularly attributed to William Shakespeare but refuses to tolerate the idea of the Stratford poacher as an author, the plays were written not by William Shakespeare of Stratford but by another man of the same name. But to the charge that William Shakespeare of Stratford-upon-Avon was not William Shakespeare the actor and playwright there are many replies, at least two of which are simple and compelling: Jonson and others speak of the playwright as the "swan of Avon"; and in the Stratford man's will bequests are made to some actors in the London theatrical company who acted Shakespeare's plays, thus indisputably linking the Stratford man with the London theater. Not until 1769 was any doubt expressed about the authorship of the body of work ascribed to Shakespeare, and this doubt was founded on the *a priori* assumption that the plays must have been written by a learnèd man.

It seems reasonable, then, to believe what so many Elizabethans believed, that William Shakespeare of Stratford and London wrote the works of William Shakespeare.

Between the record of his baptism in Stratford on April 26, 1564, and the record of his burial in Stratford on April 25, 1616, many documents name Shakespeare, and many others name his parents, his children, and his grandchildren. On the whole these documents are official records of baptism, marriage, real-estate transactions, lawsuits, taxation, and death. Had Shakespeare, like Marlowe, been accused of atheism and been killed in a tavern brawl, or had he, like Jonson, killed a man, we would probably know more about him. Nonetheless, more facts are known about William Shakespeare than about any other playwright of the period except Ben Jonson. The facts should, however, be distinguished from the legends. The latter, inevitably more engaging and better known, tell us that the Stratford boy killed a calf in high style, poached deer and rabbits, and was forced to flee to London, where he held horses outside a playhouse. These legends are simply that; they may be true, but no evidence supports them, and it is well to stick to the facts—though inevitably the following account will include probabilities and conjectures as well.

Mary Arden, the dramatist's mother, was the daughter of a substantial landowner; about 1557 she married John Shakespeare, a glovemaker and trader in various farm commodities in the prosperous town of Stratford, which served as one of the market centers for farmers of the nearby villages in the county of Warwickshire. In 1557 John Shakespeare was a member of the Council (the governing body of Stratford), in 1558 a constable of the borough, in 1561 one of the two town chamberlains, in 1565 an alderman (entitling him to the appellation "Mr."), and in 1568 a high bailiff—the town's highest political office, equivalent to mayor. After 1577 John Shakespeare dropped out of local politics, perhaps because—as records of lawsuits and of property transactions suggest—he was in financial difficulties.

The birthday of William Shakespeare, the eldest son of this locally prominent man, is unrecorded; but the Stratford parish register indicates that the infant was baptized on April 26, 1564. (It is quite possible that he was born on April 23, as tradition holds, but this date has probably been assigned for three reasons: some infants were baptized when they were three days old; fifty-two years later Shakespeare died on April 23; and April 23 is the day of England's patron saint, Saint George.)

In Elizabethan England when a child was four or five years old he attended a petty (elementary) school, where he learned to memorize some prayers and passages from the Scripture and learned to write English; in the third year he began Latin. Most girls completed their formal education at seven or eight, but boys, unless their families were very poor and needed the child's labor, generally went on to the grammar school, where they remained until they were fourteen or fifteen. The school year was longer than it is today: the school week was six days long, and the school day about eight or ten hours. The Elizabethan curriculum did not include mathematics, the natural sciences, and modern languages, but it taught a good deal of Latin grammar, rhetoric, logic, and literature. The basic text was William Lily's *A Short Introduction of Grammar*, which is written largely in Latin and which Shakespeare alludes to in *Titus Andronicus*. Among the authors studied in the Elizabethan grammar school were Cicero, Plautus, Terence, Virgil, and Ovid, all of whom seem to have left their marks on Shakespeare's plays. Recitation in Latin was important, and the schoolboys performed scenes from Plautus and Terence. Outside of school they were able to see English plays performed by the professional companies of actors who occasionally played in the guildhall at Stratford.

The attendance records of the Stratford grammar school of the period are not extant, but it is reasonable to assume that the son of a local official attended the school and received substantial training in Latin. The comic scene in *The Merry Wives of Windsor* (IV.i), in which a schoolmaster asks a pupil named William to exhibit his competence in Latin, should not lead us to think that the masters were ill-trained; the two masters of the Stratford grammar

school from Shakespeare's seventh to fifteenth years held Oxford degrees. Thus the late seventeenth-century report that Shakespeare "understood Latin pretty well" is entirely credible. It is not irreconcilable with Ben Jonson's statement that Shakespeare had "small Latin and less Greek," for Jonson was an immensely learnèd poet who would inevitably have regarded anything less than expertness as "small." Whether Shakespeare knew any foreign language other than Latin—Jonson's reference to his Greek is probably as generous as his reference to his Latin is niggardly—is uncertain. A few of the sources for Shakespeare's plays exist today only in Italian, but possibly there were lost English versions; in any case, Shakespeare's knowledge of Latin would have enabled him to get the gist of an Italian story. Of his knowledge of French, a little more can be said: in *Henry V* there is an entire scene (an English lesson) in French, so it seems reasonable to assume that Shakespeare had at least a working knowledge of the language.

During Shakespeare's childhood there are several records of his father's dealings but none of the boy's doings. After the registration of his baptism, the next record that names Shakespeare are documents of November 27 and 28, 1582, recording the issuance of a marriage license to "William Shagspere . . . and Anne Hathwey." Anne Hathaway, who was eight years her husband's senior, bore a child in May 1583. Perhaps the marriage was necessary, but perhaps the couple had earlier engaged in a formal "troth plight," which would have rendered their children legitimate even if no further ceremony had been performed. In 1585 Anne Hathaway bore Shakespeare twins.

That Shakespeare was born is excellent; that he married and had children is pleasant; but that we know nothing about his departure from Stratford to London, or about the beginning of his theatrical career, is lamentable and must be admitted. We would gladly sacrifice details about his children's baptism for details about his earliest days on the stage. Perhaps the poaching episode is true (but it is first reported almost a century after Shakespeare's death), or perhaps he first left Stratford to be a schoolteacher, as another theory holds. Perhaps he was moved by

Such wind as scatters young men through the world,
To seek their fortunes farther than at home,
Where small experience grows.
                            (*The Taming of the Shrew*, I.ii.49–51)

There are no existing records of Shakespeare's activities between 1585 and 1592. One can with safety say only that at some time prior to 1592 he went to London and commenced his theatrical career. In 1592, thanks to the cantankerousness of Robert Greene, a rival playwright and a pamphleteer, the first reference—a snarling one—to Shakespeare as an actor and playwright appears. Greene warns those of his own educated friends who wrote for the theater against actors—"puppets . . . that spake from our mouths"—and particularly against one actor who had presumed to turn playwright:

There is an upstart crow, beautified with our feathers, that with his *tiger's heart wrapped in a player's hide* supposes he is as well able to bombast out a blank verse as the best of you, and being an absolute Johannes-factotum is in his own conceit the only Shake-scene in a country.

The reference to the player, as well as the allusion to a crow (which in a fable strutted in borrowed plumage, as an actor struts in fine words not his own), makes it clear that by this date Shakespeare had both acted and written. Possibly there is a charge of plagiarism here too, for the crow was sometimes used to symbolize a writer who pilfered from others. That Shakespeare is meant is indicated not only by "Shake-scene" but by the parody of a line from one of Shakespeare's plays, *3 Henry VI:* "O, tiger's heart wrapped in a woman's hide." If Shakespeare was prominent enough by 1592 to be attacked by an envious dramatist, he probably had served an apprenticeship in the theater for at least a few years. If Greene's allusion to the crow does imply plagiarism, quite possibly Shakespeare began his career as a dramatist by revising earlier plays. Certainly he was to do this later on a grand scale, in *Hamlet* and *King Lear*, for instance.

Numerous subsequent references to Shakespeare indicate that as early as 1594 he was not only an actor but also a partner in a new theatrical company, the Lord Chamberlain's Men, which soon became one of London's two chief companies. Acting was not considered a suitable profession for a gentleman, and it occasionally drew the scorn of university men, who resented writing speeches for persons less educated than themselves. But acting was respectable enough: prosperous players were in effect members of the bourgeoisie, and there is nothing to suggest that Stratford considered William Shakespeare less than a solid citizen. In 1596 the Shakespeares were granted a coat of arms. The draft of the grant, a copy, and a draft of another grant authorizing additions are preserved in the archives of the College of Heralds in London. The Shakespeares' shield is gold with a black band crossing it diagonally; on the band is a gold spear with a silver tip. Above the shield is a silver wreath on which perches a silver falcon holding a gold spear with a silver tip. The grant was made to Shakespeare's father, who as bailiff had been (in the words of an appended note) "the queen's officer," but one can conjecture that William Shakespeare—who the next year bought the second-largest house in town—had arranged the matter on his own behalf. In subsequent transactions he is usually styled a gentleman. The house he bought in 1597 was built by a man who later became Lord Mayor of London; in 1643 it was still fine enough for Queen Henrietta Maria to spend two nights there as the guest of Shakespeare's daughter and granddaughter. Records of purchases and investments in later years demonstrate both Shakespeare's prosperity and his involvement with Stratford even during his theatrical career in London.

In 1593 and 1594 Shakespeare published *Venus and Adonis* and *The Rape of Lucrece*, two narrative poems dedicated to Henry Wriothesley, Earl of Southampton, and he may well have written most or all of his sonnets in the nineties. But Shakespeare's major literary activity during this time was devoted to the theater. (It may be significant that the two narrative poems were written between the summer of 1592 and the spring of 1594, in years when the plague closed the theaters.) In 1594, as has been mentioned, he was a member of a theatrical company called the Lord Chamberlain's Men (which in 1603 changed its name to the King's Men); until he retired to Stratford (about 1611, apparently), he was with this remarkably stable company. From 1599 the company acted

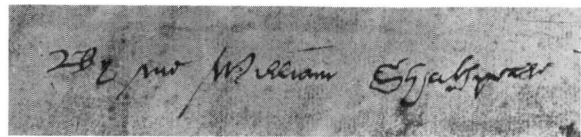

(Top) *A sketch of the Shakespeare coat of arms, probably by Ralph Brooke (1553–1625). The falcon and the tip of the spear are marked "Ar" for argent, silver; the shield "O" for or, gold; the diagonal band "S" for sable, black. "Garter" refers to Garter King-of-Arms, the official who issued the Grant of Arms.*

(Bottom) *All of Shakespeare's six undisputed signatures are in the native English angular hand rather than in the newer Italian cursive hand. Of the six, only this signature, at the end of his will, is preceded by other words in his writing, here, "By me." Possibly the writing is that of a dying man, but possibly Shakespeare, like the young Hamlet, "did hold it, as our statists do,/A baseness to write fair."*

primarily at the Globe Theatre, in which Shakespeare held a one-tenth interest. Of the more than three hundred known Renaissance English playwrights, some of whom acted as well as wrote, only Shakespeare is known to have been entitled to a share in the profits of the playhouse.

Shakespeare's first eight published plays did not bear his name, but this is not remarkable; the most popular play of the sixteenth century, Thomas Kyd's *The Spanish Tragedy*, went through many editions without naming Kyd, and Kyd's authorship is known only because a book on the profession of acting happened to quote (and attribute to Kyd) some lines on the interest of Roman emperors in the drama. What is remarkable is the fact that after 1598 Shakespeare's name commonly appears on printed plays—some of which are not his. Another indication of his popularity comes from Francis Meres' *Palladis Tamia: Wit's Treasury* (1598): in this commonplace book of anecdotes, quotations, and allusions, there is also "A Comparative Discourse of Our English Poets with the Greek, Latin, and Italian Poets," which mentions many playwrights, but Shakespeare is the only playwright whose plays are listed. Here is Meres' comment on Shakespeare:

> As the soul of Euphorbus was thought to live in Pythagoras: so the sweet witty soul of Ovid lives in mellifluous and honey-tongued Shakespeare, witness his *Venus and Adonis*, his *Lucrece*, his sugared *Sonnets* among his private friends, etc.
>
> As Plautus and Seneca are accounted the best for Comedy and Tragedy among the Latins, so Shakespeare among the English is the most excellent in both kinds for the stage; for Comedy, witness his *Gentlemen of Verona*, his *Errors*, his *Love Labor's Lost*, his *Love Labor's Won*, his *Midsummer's Night Dream* and his *Merchant of Venice*: for Tragedy his *Richard the 2*, *Richard the 3*, *Henry the 4*, *King John*, *Titus Andronicus* and his *Romeo and Juliet*.
>
> As Epius Stolo said that the Muses would speak with Plautus' tongue if they would speak Latin, so I say that the Muses would speak with Shakespeare's fine filed phrase, if they would speak English.

There is no extant play by Shakespeare titled *Love Labor's Won*. Perhaps Meres was referring to a play now known under another name, such as *The Taming of the Shrew*, which is the only Shakespearean comedy surely written before 1598 that Meres does not mention. Meres also includes Shakespeare's name in his somewhat undiscriminating lists of the best lyric poets, tragic and comic playwrights, and love poets.

> As Pindarus, Anacreon and Callimachus among the Greeks, and Horace and Catullus among the Latins are the best lyric poets, so in this faculty the best among our poets are Spenser (who excelleth in all kinds), Daniel, Drayton, Shakespeare, Breton. . . .
>
> These are our best for tragedy, the Lord Buckhurst, Doctor Leg of Cambridge, Doctor Edes of Oxford, Master Edward Ferris, the author of the *Mirror for Magistrates*, Marlowe, Peele, Watson, Kyd, Shakespeare, Drayton, Chapman, Dekker, and Benjamin Jonson. . . .
>
> The best for comedy amongst us be Edward Earl of Oxford, Doctor Gager of Oxford, Master Rowley once a rare scholar of learned Pembroke Hall in Cambridge, Master Edwards one of her Majesty's Chapel, eloquent and witty John Lily, Lodge, Gascoine, Greene, Shakespeare, Thomas Nashe, Thomas Heywood, Anthony Mundie our best plotter, Chapman, Porter, Wilson, Hathway, and Henry Chettle. . . .
>
> These are the most passionate among us to bewail and bemoan the perplexities of love, Henry Howard Earl of Surrey, Sir Thomas Wyatt the elder, Sir Francis Brian, Sir Philip Sidney, Sir Walter Raleigh, Sir Edward Dyer, Spenser, Daniel, Drayton, Shakespeare. . . .

Shakespeare probably completed his first sixteen plays by the end of 1598—in a decade or less. In the next ten years he was almost as prolific, writing perhaps thirteen or fourteen plays, including many that are his greatest. In the remaining years of his career Shakespeare seems to have slowed down a bit, writing about a play a year. Some evidence suggests that he gradually withdrew from the theater to live in Stratford. From his acting and play-writing and his share in the Globe Theatre, Shakespeare made a considerable amount of money. He put it to work, making substantial investments in Stratford real estate, although during his career he lived in London. By 1612, when a document of a London court identifies him as "William Shakespeare of Stratford-upon-Avon," he was apparently again living in Stratford. When he revised his will in 1616 (less than a month before he died), he sought to leave most of his property intact to his descendants: first to his daughter, Susanna, then to her eldest surviving son, and so on. But all four of his grandchildren died without lineal heirs, and the estate was eventually broken up. Of the small bequests made to relatives and friends (including three actors, Richard Burbage, John Heminges, and Henry Condell), the bequest to his wife of the second-best bed has provoked the most comment; perhaps it was the bed the couple had slept in, the best bed having been reserved for visitors. In any case, had Shakespeare not excepted it, the bed would have gone along with the rest of his household possessions to his daughter and her husband. Nor need we fret that Shakespeare's wife was left with only a bed. The laws of the period assured a widow of one third of the income from her husband's estate during her lifetime.

The cause of Shakespeare's death is not known, but a clergyman who settled in Stratford in 1662—almost fifty years after Shakespeare's death—recorded in his diary that "Shakespeare, Drayton, and Ben Jonson had a merry meeting, and it seems drank too hard, for Shakespeare died of a fever there contracted." This may or may not be true. In any case, on April 25, 1616, Shakespeare was buried under the floor of the chancel in the church at Stratford. An unattractive monument to his memory, placed on a wall near the grave, says he died on April 23. The monument consists of a bust flanked by columns; above the bust are Shakespeare's arms, helm, and crest, and two small figures representing Rest and Labor; the whole statue is topped by a skull. The monument was painted realistically, but the present colors are not the original ones. Carved on the slab over the grave itself are the lines, perhaps written by Shakespeare himself, that (more than his literary fame) have kept his bones undisturbed in the crowded burial ground beneath the church floor, where old bones were often dislodged to make way for new:

> Good friend, for Jesus' sake forbear
> To dig the dust enclosèd here.
> Blessed be the man that spares these stones
> And cursed be he that moves my bones.

Shakespeare's wife died on August 6, 1623; when his last descendant, a granddaughter, died in 1670, Shakespeare's large house was bequeathed outside the family.

# The Shakespeare Canon

*Edward Dowden* (handwritten)

Thirty-seven plays, one hundred fifty-four sonnets, two nondramatic poems, and one elegy constitute the Shakespeare canon, or list of accepted works. A thirty-eighth play, *The Two Noble Kinsmen*, has increasingly gained acceptance as having been written at least in part by Shakespeare. One other play in the apocrypha, or body of writing sometimes attributed to Shakespeare but not widely accepted as authentic, deserves mention. This is *Sir Thomas More*, which survives in manuscript and which includes three pages that some experts believe are in Shakespeare's handwriting. Possibly, too, some of Shakespeare's plays are lost, but probably the canon preserves all or almost all of his work.

The dates of composition of most of the works are highly uncertain, but there is often evidence of a *terminus a quo* (starting point) and/or a *terminus ad quem* (ending point) that provides a framework for intelligent guessing. For example, *Richard II* cannot have been written earlier than 1595, the publication date of some material to which it is indebted; *The Merchant of Venice* cannot have been written later than 1598, the year Francis Meres mentioned it. Sometimes arguments for a date hang on an alleged topical allusion, such as the lines about the unseasonable weather in *A Midsummer Night's Dream* (II.i.81–117); but such an allusion (if indeed it is an allusion) can be variously interpreted, and there is always the possibility that a topical allusion was inserted during a revision, years after the composition of a play. Dates are often attributed to plays on the basis of style, and although conjectures about style usually rest on other conjectures, sooner or later one must rely on one's literary sense. There is no real proof, for example, that *Othello* was not written as early as *Julius Caesar*, but one feels that *Othello* is a later play, and because the first record of its performance is 1604, one is glad enough to set its composition at that date or a little earlier and not push it back into Shakespeare's early years. The following chronology, then, is as much indebted to informed guesswork and literary sensitivity as it is to fact. The dates, necessarily imprecise, indicate what is essentially a scholarly consensus. The dates of the earliest plays are especially uncertain because it is not known when Shakespeare began writing for the stage (that his first plays were not written earlier than 1588 is only a conjecture) and because some of them show signs of having been revised several years after they were written. *Love's Labor's Lost* especially suggests an early date, perhaps 1588, and a revision in 1595 or so.

## PLAYS

| | |
|---|---|
| 1588–93 | The Comedy of Errors |
| 1588–92 | 2 Henry VI |
| 1588–92 | 3 Henry VI |
| 1588–92 | 1 Henry VI |
| 1592–93 | Richard III |
| 1592–94 | Titus Andronicus |
| 1593–94 | The Taming of the Shrew |
| 1593–94 | The Two Gentlemen of Verona |
| 1588–95 | Love's Labor's Lost |
| 1594–96 | Romeo and Juliet |
| 1595 | Richard II |
| 1594–96 | A Midsummer Night's Dream |
| 1590–97 | King John |
| 1596–97 | The Merchant of Venice |
| 1597 | 1 Henry IV |
| 1597–98 | 2 Henry IV |
| 1598–1600 | Much Ado About Nothing |
| 1598–99 | Henry V |
| 1599 | Julius Caesar |
| 1599–1600 | As You Like It |
| 1600–02 | Twelfth Night |
| 1600–01 | Hamlet |
| 1597–1601 | The Merry Wives of Windsor |
| 1601–02 | Troilus and Cressida |
| 1602–04 | All's Well That Ends Well |
| 1603–04 | Othello |
| 1604 | Measure for Measure |
| 1604–09 | Timon of Athens |
| 1605–06 | King Lear |
| 1605–06 | Macbeth |
| 1606–07 | Antony and Cleopatra |
| 1607–09 | Coriolanus |
| 1608–09 | Pericles |
| 1609–10 | Cymbeline |
| 1610–11 | The Winter's Tale |
| 1611 | The Tempest |
| 1612–13 | Henry VIII |
| 1613 | The Two Noble Kinsmen |

(handwritten annotations: "In the workshop", "In the world", "In the depths", "On the heights")

## POEMS

| | |
|---|---|
| 1592 | Venus and Adonis |
| 1593–94 | The Rape of Lucrece |
| 1593–1600 | Sonnets |
| 1600–01 | The Phoenix and the Turtle |

# Shakespeare's Theaters and Actors

A good deal of theatrical activity took place in England during Shakespeare's youth, but much of it was not performed by professionals in a theater. There was play-acting in the schools and universities; there was pageantry in the streets; there were masques at court. This section, however, is concerned only with the professional theater. (For a discussion of some of the amateur traditions behind Elizabethan drama, see pp. 12–14.)

### THE THEATERS

In Shakespeare's infancy, Elizabethan actors performed wherever they could—possibly in bearbaiting and bull-baiting arenas, and certainly in the courtyards of inns, in great halls, and at court. The innyards probably made rather unsatisfactory theaters; on some days they were unavailable because carters bringing goods to London used them as depots; when available, they had to be rented from the innkeeper. Perhaps most important, London inns were under the jurisdiction of the Common Council of London, which was not well disposed toward theatricals. In 1574 the Common Council required that plays and playing places in London be licensed. It asserted that

> sundry great disorders and inconveniences have been found to ensue to this city by the inordinate haunting of great multitudes of people, specially youth, to plays, interludes, and shows, namely occasion of frays and quarrels, evil practices of incontinency in great inns having chambers and secret places adjoining to their open stages and galleries,

and ordered that innkeepers who wished licenses to hold performances put up a bond and make contributions to the poor.

The requirement that plays and innyard theaters be licensed, along with the other drawbacks of playing at inns, probably drove James Burbage, a carpenter turned actor, to rent in 1576 a plot of land northeast of the city walls and to build there, on property outside the juris-diction of the city, England's first permanent construction designed for plays. He called it simply the Theatre. About all that is known of its construction is that it was made of wood and was in the shape of an "amphitheatrum," that is, round or approximately so, like a bearbaiting arena. Presumably Burbage erected a stage in the yard, and behind the stage a dressing room or "tiring house" from which actors could enter the stage through doorways that were perhaps fitted with hanging cloths. Such an arrangement probably resembled the curtained booths at the rear of the temporary stages that players used in the market theaters or the hall-screen in a great house that masked the doors to the pantry, kitchen, and buttery from the hall itself but allowed entrance to the hall through doorways in the hall-screen. The Theatre was probably three stories high, and the yard was partly sheltered with a roof topped by a hut,

*Arend Van Buchel's copy of Johannes De Witt's now lost drawing of the Swan, showing the theater as De Witt saw it in 1596.*

which housed suspension gear for flying effects. Burbage's Theatre soon had imitators, the most famous of which was the Globe (1599), built by Shakespeare and his fellow sharers in the Lord Chamberlain's company. The Globe was built on the Bankside, south of the Thames (again outside the city's jurisdiction), and was made from timbers of the Theatre, which had been dismantled and transported across London when Burbage's lease ran out.

There are three important sources of information about the structure of Elizabethan playhouses: drawings, a contract, and stage directions in plays. Of drawings, only the so-called De Witt drawing (about 1596) of the Swan—actually a friend's copy of De Witt's drawing—is of much significance. Although the De Witt drawing raises several questions, it gives us a good deal of information about the Elizabethan theater. It shows a circular building of three galleries, with a stage jutting from a wall into the yard formed by the surrounding galleries. The galleries are roofed, and part of the stage is covered by a roof that projects from the rear and is supported at its front by two posts. The groundlings, who paid a penny to stand in front of the stage or at its sides, were exposed to the sky. (Performances in such a playhouse were held only in the daytime; artificial illumination was not used.) At the rear of the stage are two doors in the tiring-house wall; above the stage is a gallery. That actors entered the stage through these doors seems obvious, but what is not obvious is the identity of De Witt's figures in the gallery above the stage. Probably they are spectators, but why are all the other galleries empty? (The neatest answer is that it would be difficult and tedious for the artist to populate all of the galleries.) As will be seen below, actors could use this upper area in plays that required them to be "above," but when plays did not require such action, the area was devoted entirely to spectators.

The second major source of information, the contract for the Fortune, specifies that although the Globe was to be its model, the Fortune was to be square, eighty feet outside and fifty-five inside. (The polygonal or circular theaters seem to have been larger: perhaps the interior diameter was eighty or eighty-five feet, the exterior diameter ninety-five or a hundred feet.) The stage was to be forty-three feet broad and was to extend into the middle of the yard (the platform was thus twenty-seven and a half feet deep). For patrons willing to pay more than the general admission charged the groundlings, there were to be three galleries provided with seats.

From the third chief source, stage directions, it is known that actors entered the stage by doors, presumably spaced widely apart at the rear ("*Enter one citizen at one door, and another at the other*"), and that in addition to the platform stage there was occasionally a curtained space (whether booth or alcove) that allowed for "discovery" scenes and a playing space "aloft" or "above" used to represent such areas as the top of a city's walls or the window of a room above the street. Doubtless each theater had its own peculiarities; but it is possible to talk about a "typical" Elizabethan theater if we bear in mind that no theater need exactly have fitted the description, just as no father is a typical father with 3.7 children. This hypothetical Elizabethan theater is wooden, round or polygonal (in *Henry V* Shakespeare calls it a "wooden O"), and capable of holding about three thousand spectators—perhaps two thousand standing in the yard around the projecting elevated stage and one thousand seated in the three roofed galleries. Because the spectators stood rather than sat in chairs on the ground level, and because the three galleries circled the auditorium rather than being confined to the rear (as in most proscenium-arch theaters), a large number of people could be squeezed into a relatively small building. The stage, protected by a roof, called the "cover" or "heavens," was entered by two doors. These doors may have been curtained (although curtains are not shown in the De Witt drawing of the Swan) and thus may have served as the area for "discoveries" mentioned above. Or there may have been a third opening, a curtained booth or alcove against the rear wall between these two doors. In *The Merchant of Venice*, for example, "the curtain" is opened three times to reveal Portia's three caskets. In *1 Henry IV* Falstaff hides and is later discovered "*behind the arras.*" But a door itself, without a curtain, would presumably have served as an entrance to Juliet's tomb. When Romeo "*opens the tomb,*" he probably opened a pair of double-hung doors, like those in the De Witt drawing, to reveal Juliet lying on a coffin. Surprisingly, such discovery scenes are very rare in Elizabethan drama. It is worth mentioning that usually no more than two persons are discovered at once, which suggests that the area was too small to be considered (as it sometimes is in the twentieth century) an "inner stage." After being discovered, the character or characters did not move about in the discovery space; they walked out onto the stage. Behind the stage was the "tiring house" (attiring house, or dressing room), and above the doors was a gallery that sometimes held spectators but that was also used, for example, as the bedroom window from which Romeo—according to a stage direction in one text—"*goeth down*" or as the castle wall from which young Arthur in *King John* leaps down. Some evidence suggests that a throne was lowered onto the platform stage, perhaps from the stage cover; certainly characters descended from the stage through a trap or traps into the cellar, or "hell." Sometimes this space beneath the platform was used to accommodate a sound-effects man or musician (in *Antony and Cleopatra* "*music of the hautboys is under the stage*") or an actor (in *Hamlet* the "*Ghost cries under the stage*"). Most characters simply walked on and off, but because there was no curtain at the front of the stage, corpses had to be carried off—thus an Elizabethan Hamlet had to lug Polonius' body into the adjoining room.

Such may have been the so-called public theater. There was also another kind of theater, called the "private theater" because its much greater admission charge limited its audience to the wealthy or the prodigal. This type of theater was basically a large room, entirely roofed and therefore artificially illuminated, with a stage at one end and a tiring house behind the stage. In 1576, a year before the first permanent public theater was built, such a theater was established in Blackfriars, a Dominican priory in London that had been suppressed in 1538 and confiscated by the crown and thus was not under the city's jurisdiction. All the actors in the Blackfriars theater were boys about eight to thirteen years old. This private theater had a precarious existence and ceased operations in 1584. In 1596 James Burbage, who had already made theatrical history by building the Theatre, began to construct a second Blackfriars theater. He died in 1597, and for several years this second Blackfriars was used by a troupe of boys. In 1608 two of Burbage's sons and five other actors (including Shakespeare) became joint operators of the theater, using it in the winter, when the open-air Globe was unsuitable. Perhaps such a smaller theater (its capacity was about seven hundred), roofed, artificially illuminated, and patronized by a fashionable audience, exerted an influence on Shakespeare's later plays, but it would be a mistake to think either that these later plays have fundamentally different staging needs or that they are essentially different in spirit from Shakespeare's earlier work. It should be noted, too, that Elizabethan theatrical companies were occasionally called upon to give a performance at court, on a temporary stage in a room illuminated by candles and torches. But since a play thus staged was commonly selected from the company's repertory by the queen's Master of the Revels, a performance at court was probably not vastly different from a performance in a theater.

Performances in the private theaters may well have had intermissions, during which music was played, but in the public theaters the action was probably uninterrupted, flowing from scene to scene almost without a break.

Detail of a drawing (circa 1640) by Wenceslaus Hollar showing the second Globe Theatre and the Beargarden. The first Globe had burned in 1613; the second was promptly built on the site.

Hollar (1607–77), a native of Prague, lived in England from 1637 to 1645. In 1647 his engraving of a panoramic map of London was published in Antwerp, probably based on sketches he had made while in England. The labels "Beere bayting" and "The [Second] Globe" almost surely are reversed.

Actors entered, spoke, and exited, and other actors immediately entered and established a new locale (if necessary) by a few properties and by words and gestures. Here are some samples of how Shakespeare set the place or the time of his plays:

JULIET
Wilt thou be gone? It is not yet near day.
It was the nightingale, and not the lark,
That pierced the fearful hollow of thine ear.

. . .

ROMEO
It was the lark, the herald of the morn;
No nightingale. Look, love, what envious streaks
Do lace the severing clouds in yonder East.
(*Romeo and Juliet*, III.v.1–3,6–8)

Sometimes the setting of locale is more direct:

TITUS
The hunt is up, the morn is bright and gray,
The fields are fragrant, and the woods are green.
(*Titus Andronicus*, II.ii.1–2)

DUNCAN
This castle hath a pleasant seat; the air
Nimbly and sweetly recommends itself
Unto our gentle senses.    (*Macbeth*, I.vi.1–3)

CAPTAIN
This is Illyria, lady.    (*Twelfth Night*, I.ii.2)

ROSALIND
Well, this is the Forest of Arden.
(*As You Like It*, II.iv.14)

But it is a mistake to conceive of the Elizabethan stage as bare. Although the Chorus in *Henry V* calls the stage an "unworthy scaffold" and urges the spectators to "eke out our performance with your mind," the stage façade itself was apparently richly decorated, and the underside of the cover was adorned with stars. Moreover, considerable spectacle took place on the platform stage itself. In the last act of *Macbeth*, for example, five stage directions call for "*drum and colors*," and another sort of appeal to the eye is made by the stage direction "*Enter Macduff, with Macbeth's head.*" Some scenery and properties may have been substantial: thrones, altars, and chariots may have been used, as well as mossy banks and trees. One play of the period includes this stage direction: "*Hector takes up a great piece of rock and casts at Ajax, who tears up a young tree by the roots and assails Hector.*" (See p. 69 for a further discussion of stage directions.)

## THE ACTORS

In the late Middle Ages religious plays were performed by members of various craft guilds: bakers, butchers, goldsmiths, and so forth acted in plays on biblical subjects. Amateur theatrical activity flourished (we should also keep in mind Robin Hood plays, Saint George plays, May games, and other amateur seasonal theatricals of a folkloric nature), creating a climate in which professionalism could develop. By the middle of the fifteenth century traveling troupes were staging plays throughout England. These troupes were small—usually consisting of four actors—but they must have been highly skilled, for their livelihood depended on doing better what innumerable amateurs were also doing. By the middle of the sixteenth century some traveling troupes included as many as a dozen actors, with boys playing the female roles. In their social origins these actors were generally men like Bottom the weaver and his fellows who in *A Midsummer Night's Dream* perform a play before the duke. But the ineptitude of Bottom's amateur company should not be confused with the skill of the professionals; the craftsmen who left their looms or cobbler's benches to become professional actors had to be expert in their new craft if they were to survive.

For various reasons, including the break-up of feudal households during the Wars of the Roses and the dissolution of the monasteries, Tudor England had a large number of unemployed wanderers, and laws were devised to restrain them. Because a "masterless man" was considered unnatural—the more so because there was a labor shortage—traveling actors were nominally considered the "servants" of a nobleman; but from this patron they usually got only a license or patent and payment for an occasional performance in his household on a festive day. The actors depended for their livelihood on the patronage of the general public, and the license was necessary if they were to reach that public, as is indicated by the following letter from the Duke of Lennox, addressed "to all mayors, justices of peace, sheriffs, bailiffs, constables, and all other his Highness' officers . . . to whom it shall or may in any wise appertain":

I am given to understand that you have forbidden the company of players that call themselves mine the exercise of their plays. I pray you to forebear any such course against them, and, seeing they have my license, to suffer them to continue the use of their plays; and until you receive other signification from me of them, to afford them your favor and assistance. And so I bid you heartily farewell.

When Shakespeare's company received the patronage of King James I in 1603, its license read as follows:

Know ye that We of our special grace, certain knowledge, and mere motion have licensed and authorized and by these presents do license and authorize these our servants Lawrence Fletcher, William Shakespeare, Richard Burbage, Augustine Phillips, John Heminges, Henry Condell, William Sly, Robert Armin, Richard Cowley, and the rest of their associates freely to use and exercise the art and faculty of playing comedies, tragedies, histories, interludes, moralities, pastorals, stage plays, and such others like as they have already studied or hereafter shall use or study, as well for the recreation of our loving subjects as for our solace and pleasure when we shall think good to see them, during our pleasure. And the said comedies, tragedies, histories, interludes, moralities, pastorals, stage plays, and such like to show and exercise publicly to their best commodity, when the infection of the plague shall decrease, as well within their now usual house called the Globe within our county of Surrey, as also within any town halls or moot halls or other convenient places within the liberties and freedom of any other city, university, town, or borough whatsoever within our said realms and dominions. Willing and commanding you and every of you, as you tender our pleasure, not only to permit and suffer them herein without any your hindrances or molestations during our said pleasure, but also to be aiding and assisting to them, if any wrong be to them offered. And to allow them such former courtesies as hath been given to men of their place and quality, and also that further favor you shall show to these our servants for our sake we shall take kindly at your hands.

This was doubtless a most useful document for an acting company.

By the end of the sixteenth century, despite harassment by puritanical forces, the status of actors was fairly secure: acting was recognized as a "trade" or "profession," subject not to local authorities but to the crown through the Master of the Revels and his superior, the Lord Chamberlain. Therefore, although the Revels Office censored plays and could be a powerful enemy when it suspected that a play harbored seditious ideas, it was for the most part (like the lords who lent acting companies their nominal patronage) an important ally of the players: it arranged for occasional remunerative performances at court, and more important, it stood between the players and the local bourgeois officials, who often regarded theatrical performances as a waste of time, or as indecent shows, or worst of all as vestiges of Roman Catholic activities. (It should be remembered that the old religious drama survived in some parts of England past the middle of the sixteenth century.) There is a large body of anti-theatrical writing, much of it amusing in its abusiveness, but one example, from a sermon written in 1578 by John Stockwood, should suffice:

> Will not a filthy play, with the blast of a trumpet, sooner call thither a thousand than an hour's tolling of a bell bring to the sermon a hundred? . . . If you resort to the Theatre, the Curtain, and other places of plays in the city, you shall on the Lord's day have these places, with many other that I cannot reckon, so full as possibly they can throng.

Even allowing for the exaggeration of an indignant competitor, Stockwood's comments help to indicate the magnitude of theatrical activity that took place in the period of Shakespeare's youth.

A theatrical company such as the Lord Chamberlain's Men was a substantial business enterprise. The company was formed in the summer of 1594; if Shakespeare was not a charter member, he joined the company soon after its formation, for he is specified as a member in March 1595, and he stayed with it for the remainder of his professional life. As has been mentioned, with the accession of James I in 1603, the company became the King's Men, and it endured until the Puritans closed the theaters in 1642. The company's organization was rather medieval, consisting of three groups which resembled the craft-guild hierarchy of master craftsmen, journeymen, and apprentices: (1) senior actors, such as Shakespeare, called "fellows" or "sharers" because each owned a share in the plays and the properties, and therefore shared in the profits; (2) hired men, who performed minor roles or served as musicians, prompters, doorkeepers, and so on, and did not share in the profits; and (3) boys, who were in effect apprenticed to the sharers and played most or all of the female roles. (Possibly the garrulous old Nurse in *Romeo and Juliet* was played by a man rather than by a boy.) A boy entered the company when he was about ten, trained for a while, and then acted female roles until his voice changed or he grew too tall for the part. That all the performers were male should not seem strange; all the performers in classical Greek, Chinese, and Japanese drama also were male, as were the performers in the folk plays (see p. 12). It would seem that drama, when it is still close to ceremony and not yet fully dedicated to realism, prefers men to represent women. (E. K. Chambers, in *The English Folk-Play*, quotes a man who had performed in a folk play: "Oh, you wouldn't have women in that; it's more like being in church.") Shakespeare's company expanded over the years, beginning with five sharers and ending with twelve, but it probably never had more than about two dozen actors. Even *Henry VIII*, which has forty-one speaking parts, can be performed by about a dozen actors by doubling and tripling.

Doubtless the composition of Shakespeare's company left its mark on his plays; Shakespeare knew what it could do, and he knew for whom he had to write parts. For example, because there were probably only two or three boys at any given time who could play important roles, and another two or three in training, Shakespeare's plays rarely have more than four significant female roles, though of course a larger number can be handled by doubling. The fact that so many of Shakespeare's heroines are motherless—for example, Rosalind and Celia in *As You Like It*—is probably due to the restrictions imposed by the company rather than to anything in Shakespeare's psychology. Probably, too, the availability of a good clown encouraged Shakespeare to write in a clown's part, and so on. (It might be argued with equal validity, of course, that the audience wanted a clown, and so the company made it its business to have one.) Viewed one way, Shakespeare was in bondage to his company; viewed another way, Shakespeare had the advantage of knowing what his actors could and could not do before he put pen to paper.

Actors in Shakespeare's day worked hard, and they probably worked hardest of all during those months when the plague closed the London theaters and forced the actors to tour the remote provinces. But even when they were in London, playing was not all fun. A company performed five or six times a week, giving in a season twenty-five or thirty different plays, about half of which were new in the repertory and the remainder either recent favorites or revivals of older plays. Occasionally a play was given two or three consecutive performances, but commonly the program changed every day, and the same play was rarely acted twice in one week. Thus in a month a company might perform a dozen different plays. Although no annual records for the Lord Chamberlain's Men are extant, it is possible to get an idea of its activities from the records of its rival, the Admiral's Men. Between 1594 and 1597 the Admiral's Men gave 728 performances of fifty-five plays; or to take a more microscopic view, between August 1595 and February 1596 it gave 150 performances of thirty different plays, fourteen of which were new.

Existing evidence on the style of Elizabethan acting is open to various interpretations. There are essentially two schools of thought: one sees Elizabethan acting as realistic (or natural); the other sees it as conventional (or formal). Advocates of the realistic theory point to various Elizabethan passages that praise actors as lifelike: Hamlet, for example, warns the players against ranting, and this is taken as evidence that the actors in *Hamlet* did not rant. But this very statement can also be taken as evidence that actors normally ranted, and that Shakespeare was trying to restrain his actors. Moreover, even if we agree that the actors in *Hamlet* did not rant, we need not conclude that they acted realistically. Another piece of evidence usually taken as indicating that acting was realistic is John Webster's comment on the ability of a good actor: "What we see him personate, we think truly done before us." But one can reply that every age insists that its good actors are natural. The acting in the motion pictures of the thirties, for example, seems quaint to us today, though it struck its contemporaries as thoroughly lifelike.

On the other hand, those who argue that Elizabethan acting was formal rather than natural discount Elizabethan statements about holding the mirror up to nature; they regard such statements as being of no more value than those Elizabethan testimonials that describe a tapestry—necessarily unrealistic—as the very image of life. They argue that the conditions of the stage required formal acting: performances were given in daylight, even though some scenes occurred at night; boys performed female parts; the language of the play was commonly poetry rather than daily speech. In addition, characters sometimes addressed the audience directly, breaking (it is argued) any illusion of the reality of the world on the stage. (There are comic monologues in Shakespeare that unquestionably are direct addresses to the audience. And Iago, for example, appeals to the audience when he says, "And what's he then that says I

play the villain?") Such arguments in behalf of formal acting have much merit, yet they cannot be taken as proof that Elizabethan acting was *highly* stylized and devoid of naturalism. The dialogue in the plays themselves, for example, provides evidence that characters did not silently walk across the stage, take up a position, and then declaim; they spoke while they walked, while they dressed, and so on. Probably, then, it is safest to conclude that although natural acting was highly praised and unnatural acting ridiculed, the acting of Shakespeare's day was a combination of both styles, and it was probably somewhat more naturalistic than the acting of his youth, which had come to seem bombastic. In *A Midsummer Night's Dream* Bottom is perhaps old-fashioned when he says he "will move storms" and when he yearns for "a part to tear a cat in, to make all split." A few years later Hamlet deplores actors who split the ears of the groundlings.

Not a great deal is known about the costumes that Elizabethan actors wore, but at least three points are clear: (1) many of the costumes were sumptuous versions of contemporary Elizabethan dress; (2) some attempts were made to approximate the dress of certain occupations and of antique or exotic characters such as Romans, Turks, and Jews; (3) some costumes indicated that the wearer was supernatural. Evidence for elaborate contemporary dress can be found in the many references to Elizabethan clothing (doublets, hose, and so on) in the plays themselves and in contemporary comments about the "sumptuous" players who wore the discarded clothing of noblemen, as well as in various account books which itemize such things as "a scarlet cloak with two broad gold laces, with gold buttons of the same down the sides." The attempt at approximating the dress of certain occupations and nationalities also can be documented from the plays themselves, and it derives additional confirmation from a drawing—the only extant picture of an identifiable Elizabethan stage production—

*A drawing (circa 1594) of characters in* Titus Andronicus, *showing the mixture of pseudo-Roman and contemporary costumes.*

of a scene from *Titus Andronicus*. The drawing, probably done in 1594 or 1595, shows Queen Tamora pleading for mercy. She wears a robe and a crown; Titus wears a toga and a wreath, but two soldiers behind him wear costumes fairly close to Elizabethan dress. There is, however, some conflicting evidence: in *Julius Caesar* a reference is made to Caesar's doublet, which, if taken literally, suggests that even the protagonist did not wear Roman clothing; and certainly the lesser characters, who are said to wear hats, did not wear Roman garb. But perhaps in its context the word *doublet* merely denotes a garment for the upper part of the body, not the specifically Elizabethan garment. The use of symbolic costumes for supernatural creatures is nicely illustrated by a property listed in the journal of an Elizabethan theatrical entrepreneur: "a robe for to go invisible." In *The Tempest* this stage direction appears:

"*Enter Ariel, invisible*" (III.ii). Possibly this symbolic robe was worn; possibly the stage direction is merely an instruction to the actors, but certainly in III.iii, "*Enter Ariel, like a harpy*," a symbolic costume was used. Finally, it should be mentioned that even ordinary clothing can be symbolic: Hamlet's "inky cloak," for example, sets him aside from the brightly dressed members of Claudius' court and symbolizes his mourning; the fresh clothes that are put on King Lear partly symbolize his return to sanity. This device, of course, is not confined to the tragedies. Near the end of *Much Ado About Nothing*, just before Claudio's bride is restored to him—giving him, in effect, a new life—Don Pedro says to Claudio, "Come, let us hence and put on other weeds." Claudio's reappearance, presumably in a new splendid costume, is a visual representation of his renewal.

# The Dramatic Background

As has been mentioned, a good deal of theatrical and quasi-theatrical activity took place in England in Shakespeare's youth. This activity ranged from professional productions to amateur productions in Latin and the performances of trained animals. It is not possible to discuss here such activities as jousts and tournaments, which were highly ritualized and spectacular encounters with conflict at their heart, and public executions, in which the condemned man was allowed to make a speech to the assembled crowd, but there is no doubt that such activities influenced Shakespeare's plays, as can be seen from the interrupted joust in *Richard II* (I.iii) and the report of the Thane of Cawdor's words just before he is executed in *Macbeth* (I.iv.1–11) or Othello's words just before he kills himself (V.ii.337–55). Rather, this section will be concerned with five sorts of drama, and the subsequent discussions of Shakespeare's comedies, histories, and tragedies will occasionally amplify some of the points raised here.

First, an enduring drama existed among the folk, the peasants and artisans who enacted annual playlets celebrating the renewal of the year, which had "died" in the winter and been "reborn" in the spring. Often these festive plays were transferred from the spring or summer to the Christmas festivities, for Christmas symbolized the possibility of the renewal or rebirth of fallen man. Commonly the players would visit their lord's manor house and perform their rudimentary playlet, thus in a way bringing into the household the spirit of rebirth and joy that was being enacted. The most famous of such traditional entertainments was the Saint George play, which deals with a combat, a death, and a resurrection and concludes with a blessing, or wish for prosperity. Here is the end of a version that was performed at Christmas:

I am Father Christmas! Hold, men, hold!
Be there loaf in your locker, and sheep in your fold,
A fire on the hearth, and good luck for your lot,
Money in your pocket, and a pudding in the pot!

As the discussion of Shakespeare's comedies will indicate, the overall movement is from a troubled or deathlike state (for example, at the beginning of *A Midsummer Night's Dream* if Egeus' daughter will not obey her father the law may sentence her "to death, or to a vow of single life") to a state of prosperity, fertility, and joy, symbolized by a feast, a dance, or especially, a marriage. Other common folk rituals, such as midsummer festivities, in which revelers ignited torches at a "blessing fire" and then carried them home to bring good luck to the household, also left their mark on Shakespeare's plays. Again *A Midsummer Night's Dream* affords an example: in celebrating a marriage the King and Queen of Fairies "through the house give glimmering light." Other festivities included May games, especially the Whitsun pastorals, which Shakespeare alludes to in *A Winter's Tale* (IV.iv). May Day activities involved the choice of a Queen of the May or of a Maid Marian; the Queen was given a garland and then entertained by songs, dances, and a procession, sometimes of persons disguised as the Nine Worthies, whom Shakespeare introduces in a show in *Love's Labor's Lost*. May Day invariably attracted more formal plays, such as two anonymous plays on Robin Hood, printed about 1560 and said by the publisher to be "very proper to be played in May games."

A second dramatic form, related to the folk rituals and plays because it too was probably derived from primitive celebrations of a life-giving power, was an aristocratic entertainment which the Middle Ages called a "disguising" and the Renaissance called a "masque." In these entertainments courtiers amused themselves and sought to express in allegory a high ideal—in Ben Jonson's words, to "lay hold on more removed mysteries"—by dressing up, for example, as shepherds or Moors or Russians, entering a great household, performing a dance which was sometimes interpreted by a narrator, or Presenter, and then (in a part known as "the revels") dancing with the ladies. Here too, in the movement from surprise or uncertainty to the celebration of the life-giving force of the powerful person in whose honor the masque was held, is an implication of fertility, or at least of a united society. Shakespeare never wrote a court masque, but some of his plays include scenes in which characters engage in a masque. In *Love's Labor's Lost* the king and three courtiers, intending "to parle, to court and dance," disguise themselves as Russians when they visit the ladies. *Henry VIII* includes an episode that occurred in 1530 when Henry and some of his courtiers, dressed as shepherds (but splendidly), visited Anne Bullen at Cardinal Wolsey's palace: "*Hautboys. Enter king and others, as masquers, habited like shepherds. . . . They pass directly before the cardinal, and gracefully salute him.*" The chamberlain, acting as the Presenter, explains:

Because they speak no English, thus they prayed
To tell your grace: that having heard by fame
Of this so noble and so fair assembly
This night to meet here, they could do no less
(Out of the great respect they bear to beauty)
But leave their flocks and, under your fair conduct,
Crave leave to view these ladies and entreat
An hour of revels with 'em.               (I.iv.65–72)

After the cardinal grants them their wish, the revels begin: "*Choose ladies*; *King and Anne Bullen*," and then "*Music. Dance.*" Similarly, in *Much Ado About Nothing* Don Pedro and his nobles enter masked and dance with the ladies. In *Timon of Athens* Timon, a monarch and spirit of generosity who sustains the city, presides over a masque of Amazons. After a trumpet call announces Cupid, the Presenter, who explains that Timon is much beloved, there is a "*Masque of ladies as Amazons, with lutes in their hands, dancing and playing.*" Then "*The lords rise from the table, with much adoring of Timon, and to show their love, each singles out an Amazon, and all dance, men with women, a lofty strain or two to the hautboys, and cease*" (I.ii). Closely related to these courtly disguisings were spectacular entertainments in great houses, celebrating an event such as a noble wedding. In *The Tempest* Prospero conjures up a masque of goddesses to celebrate an impending marriage. But the dissolution of this show—when Prospero remembers the plot against him and the masque abruptly vanishes—is different from the dissolution of a masque. When a court masque dissolves, the aristocratic performers join the audience, and the virtues represented in the masque are thus symbolically bestowed upon the audience; but Prospero's show abruptly dissolves, occasioning his remarks on the transience or insubstantiality of all substance (IV.i.148 ff.).

A third kind of dramatic activity that survived from the Middle Ages into Shakespeare's youth was the miracle play. (Some scholars distinguish between plays based on saints' lives and plays based on biblical episodes, calling the former miracle plays and the latter mystery plays. However, no medieval English play was in its own time called a mystery play.) By the end of the fourteenth century vast cycles of plays, performed in the streets and sponsored by the craft guilds, had developed. In a sense, a cycle is one great play, consisting of as many as forty-eight small plays performed consecutively and covering the history of the world from the Creation through the Fall of the Angels, the Creation and Fall of Man, the Incarnation, the Cruci-

fixion, the Resurrection, and Judgment Day. These cycles were performed early in June on the feast of Corpus Christi. Because the cycle aims at celebrating the entire story of Christ, from his incarnation to his redemption of fallen man, it presents on the stage a remote past which is also an eternal present. In one play, for example, Christ instructs John the Baptist to preach to sinners, and so John turns to the spectators in front of him, establishing a bond between the world on the stage and the world of the spectators. This is not very different from, say, the moment in *As You Like It* when Duke Senior says—as much to the spectators as to the characters on the stage—"This wide and universal theater/Presents more woeful pageants than the scene/Wherein we play in" (II.vii.136–38).

This tendency to see the stage as intimately related to the daily world of the audience is not the only characteristic that binds the miracle plays to the Elizabethan drama. Although the overall plot of a cycle is "comic," in that it has a happy ending, it includes apparently "tragic" material, such as the murder of Abel and the Slaughter of the Innocents. Such episodes—especially those depicting savage tyranny destroying innocence and ultimately destroying itself or being destroyed by a higher power—probably helped to establish the context of such a scene as Macbeth's slaughter of Macduff's children. Moreover, the comprehensiveness of a miracle cycle's scheme, which required it to mix comedy and tragedy, bequeathed to the Renaissance stage a tradition of mixing the genres. This tradition of mixed dramatic forms distressed those who knew something of classical drama: shortly before Shakespeare began to write for the theater, Sir Philip Sidney lamented that the playwrights of his age wrote "neither right tragedies nor right comedies" but, "mingling kings and clowns," wrote "mongrel tragicomedy." Shakespeare's comedies continued this tradition; they often include threats of death and occasionally (in some of his last plays) death itself. Similarly, his tragedies include comic bits: there are clownish rebels in *2 Henry VI*, a serious history play dealing with violent times, a comic murderer in *Richard III*, a comic gravedigger in *Hamlet*, a fool in *King Lear*, a drunken porter in *Macbeth*, and a comic rural fellow in *Antony and Cleopatra*. The murder scene in *Richard III*, I.iv, is very much in the seriocomic tradition of medieval drama. In the following speech, the Second Murderer has just told the First Murderer that he is determined to let their intended victim live:

FIRST MURDERER  I'll back to the Duke of Gloucester and tell him so.
SECOND MURDERER  Nay, I prithee stay a little. I hope this passionate humor [compassionate mood] of mine will change; it was wont to hold me but while one tells [counts to] twenty.
FIRST MURDERER  How dost thou feel thyself now?
SECOND MURDERER  Faith, some certain dregs of conscience are yet within me.
FIRST MURDERER  Remember our reward when the deed's done.
SECOND MURDERER  Zounds, he dies! I had forgot the reward.
FIRST MURDERER  Where's thy conscience now?
SECOND MURDERER  O, in the Duke of Gloucester's purse.

FIRST MURDERER  When he opens his purse to give us our reward, thy conscience flies out.

SECOND MURDERER  'Tis no matter, let it go. There's few or none will entertain it.

FIRST MURDERER  What if it come to thee again?

SECOND MURDERER  I'll not meddle with it; it makes a man a coward. A man cannot steal, but it accuseth him; a man cannot swear, but it checks him; a man cannot lie with his neighbor's wife, but it detects him. 'Tis a blushing shamefaced spirit that mutinies in a man's bosom. It fills a man full of obstacles. It made me once restore a purse of gold that, by chance, I found. It beggars any man that keeps it. It is turned out of towns and cities for a dangerous thing, and every man that means to live well endeavors to trust to himself and live without it.

And so on, until they finally murder their victim.

As a child, Shakespeare could easily have seen a cycle of miracle plays. There were plays done at nearby Coventry, for instance, until 1581, when they were suppressed by ecclesiastical authorities who feared popery. But interest in the plays was probably waning by that date, for professional troupes offered better dramatic fare than the amateur companies of guildsmen offered.

A fourth kind of drama that survived into Shakespeare's youth was the morality play, in effect a dramatized sermon, which can be traced to the late fourteenth century. The miracle-play cycles are historical, dramatizing what happened; the morality plays use allegorical figures to dramatize man's chief moral dilemmas as he struggles in a world of deceitful appearances. In *The Castle of Perseverance* (early fifteenth century), for example, a character called Mankind is guided by such figures as Good Angel and Conscience in a struggle against the World, the Flesh, the Devil, the Seven Deadly Sins, and so on. Mankind yields to sin, repents, then relapses; Death enters, but dying Mankind calls for God's mercy, and (as we are told in an epilogue) he is forgiven and allowed to go to heaven. Despite its happy ending, then, the play dramatizes suffering and death in this world and thus approaches tragedy. Like *The Castle of Perseverance*, most of the extant morality plays are concerned with the battle for a man's soul (the psychomachia), and it is not far-fetched to see their influence in Shakespeare's plays. For instance, despite the example of the saintly King Duncan, Macbeth yields to forces of evil; Othello faces on one side "the divine Desdemona" and on the other the villainous Iago, who is often associated with diabolic images: late in the play, when Othello realizes that he has been tricked by Iago into murdering Desdemona, he seeks to learn of "that demi-devil/Why he hath thus ensnared my soul and body" (V.ii.300–01). Because the morality play dramatizes God's grace, its plot is not tragic; but in its depiction of men making moral decisions and becoming aware of the possible consequences of their mistakes, it approaches tragedy. The Second Murderer's speeches in *Richard III*, quoted earlier, evoke the morality play in the Murderer's wavering between repentance and evil-doing, and in his allegorical conception of "conscience." A thoroughly comic version of such a conflict is found in *The Merchant of Venice* in Gobbo's monologue:

The fiend is at mine elbow and tempts me, saying to me, "Gobbo, Launcelot Gobbo, good Launcelot," or "good Gobbo," or "good Launcelot Gobbo—use your legs, take the start, run away." My conscience says, "No. Take heed, honest Launcelot; take heed, honest Gobbo," or as aforesaid, "honest Launcelot Gobbo, do not run. . . ." Well, my conscience hanging about the neck of my heart says very wisely to me, "My honest friend Launcelot, being an honest man's son"—or rather an honest woman's son, for indeed my father did something smack, something grow to, he had a kind of taste—Well, my conscience says, "Launcelot, budge not." "Budge," says the fiend. "Budge not," says my conscience. "Conscience," say I, "you counsel well." "Fiend," say I, "you counsel well." . . . The fiend gives the more friendly counsel. I will run, fiend; my heels are at your commandment, I will run.

(II.ii.2–30)

Although most morality plays show such an inner battle, some are concerned primarily with the coming of death (notably, *Everyman*); others are concerned with political controversy and thus bear some resemblance to Shakespeare's history plays. All the extant moralities except *Everyman* include a good deal of comedy, ranging from physical buffoonery and coarse puns to witty satire, thus continuing the miracle-play tradition of "mongrel tragicomedy." The chief trickster is the Vice, and if Iago is a tragic descendant of that seducer of mankind, the mischievous fools and clowns in Shakespeare's comedies are at least to some degree his comic descendants. In *Twelfth Night* Feste explicitly refers to the Vice:

I am gone, sir.
And anon, sir,
I'll be with you again,
In a trice,
Like to the old Vice,
Your need to sustain.
Who with dagger of lath,
In his rage and his wrath,
Cries "Ah ha" to the devil.
Like a mad lad,
"Pare thy nails, dad."
Adieu, goodman devil.               (IV.ii.122–33)

A quotation from one Ralph Willis, who was born the same year as Shakespeare, gives us a good idea of the morality plays and their impact:

In the City of Gloucester the manner is (as I think it is in other like corporations) that when players of interludes come to town, they first attend the Mayor to inform him what nobleman's servants they are, and so to get license for their public playing; and if the Mayor like the actors, or would show respect to their lord and master, he appoints them to play their first play before himself and the Aldermen and Common Council of the City; and that is called the Mayor's Play, where everyone that will comes in without money, the Mayor giving the players a reward as he thinks fit to show respect unto them. At such a play, my father took me with him, and made me stand between his legs, as he sat upon one of the benches where we saw and heard very well. The play was called *The Cradle of Security*, wherein was personated a king or some other great prince with his courtiers of several kinds, amongst which three ladies were in special grace with him; and they keeping him in delights and pleasures, drew him from his graver counsellors, hearing of sermons, and listening to good counsel, and admonitions, that in the end they got him to lie down in a cradle upon the stage, where these three ladies joining in a sweet song rocked him asleep, that he snorted again, and in the meantime closely conveyed under the cloths where withall he was covered, a vizard like a swine's snout upon his face, with three wire chains fastened thereunto, the other end whereof being held severally by those three ladies, who fall to singing again, and then discovered his face, that the spectators might see how they had transformed him, going on with their singing. While all this was acting, there came forth of another door at the farthest end of the stage two old men, the one in blue with a sergeant-at-arms his mace on his shoulder, the other in red with a drawn sword in his hand, and leaning with the other hand upon the other's shoulder, and so these two went along in a soft pace round about by the skirt of the stage till at last they came to the cradle, when all the court was in greatest jollity, and then the foremost old man with his mace struck a fearful blow upon the cradle; whereat all the courtiers with the three ladies and the vizard all vanished; and the desolate Prince starting up barefaced, and finding himself thus sent for to judgment, made a lamentable complaint of his miserable case, and so was carried away by wicked spirits. This Prince did personate in the moral the wicked of the world; the three ladies pride, covetousness, and luxury; the two old men, the end of the world and the last judgment. This sight took such impression in me that when I came towards man's estate, it was fresh in my memory as if I had seen it newly acted.

Three things of special interest should be noted here. First are Willis' opening remarks, which give us an idea of the procedures governing a theatrical company in the provinces. Second is the fact that in the punishment of a wicked "desolate Prince" the play anticipates some of the stuff of Elizabethan histories and tragedies. Third, and most important, is Willis' view of the play: today we tend to think of allegorical drama as lifeless, but it made a lasting impression on Willis, who saw it chiefly as a play about people—a king, ladies, counselors, and so on—and only in his final summary as allegory.

As Willis' account indicates, in the sixteenth century the morality play was performed by professionals. The morality play was closely related to a type called the "interlude," a short play, often with the structure, characters, and comedy of a morality play, that was performed in a great house, especially during a holiday season. Possibly the chief difference is that an interlude is usually shorter and requires fewer characters than a morality play. (The name *interlude* seems to suggest that the play was performed between two parts of a banquet.) The morality play abounds in vigorous men of this world, and it is not surprising that in the sixteenth century there were many short plays in which exuberant worldly characters are the center of interest: these plays, performed as entertainments in a banquet-hall, sometimes became essentially a dramatized joke rather than a dramatized sermon, and then of course the distinction between interlude and morality play becomes clear.

A fifth kind of theatrical activity that exerted an influence on Shakespeare was the drama of the schools and universities. In the sixteenth century students read Roman drama and occasionally performed it. Schoolmasters, with Roman plays in mind, wrote plays to help their students improve their enunciation, poise, and skill in disputation. Neo-Latin as well as English plays were written, and though no academic drama has much literary or theatrical excellence, the fact that in Shakespeare's day some university graduates wrote for the popular stage indicates that the academic drama exerted at least some influence on the popular drama. (The specific influences of Plautus and Terence on comedy, and of Seneca on tragedy, are discussed on pp. 33–34, 55–56.)

Brief mention should be made here of the professional drama of Shakespeare's immediate predecessors and contemporaries, notably John Lyly, Thomas Kyd, and Christopher Marlowe. Lyly's rather precious comedies, performed by a children's company chiefly in the 1580's, with their formal groupings and elegant witty debates and with their contrasts between scenes of delightfully absurd romantic lovers and scenes of low comedy, must have helped Shakespeare—and yet Shakespeare's comedy is distinctively his own, more humane, less allegorical, less satirical, less stiff than Lyly's, and more thoughtful and better articulated than anything on the earlier popular stage. Similarly, through about 1589 Kyd apparently gave English popular tragedy a strong sense of a coherent plot (for example, ironically juxtaposed scenes instead of more loosely connected episodes), and Marlowe from about 1589 until his death in 1593 gave English tragedy heroes who speak a splendid blank verse worthy of heroes. These two writers themselves were deeply indebted to earlier dramatic traditions, Kyd to Senecan drama and Marlowe to the morality play. Shakespeare's achievement soon became distinctive, indebted to but far outstripping his early contemporaries. The drama of Shakespeare's age is discussed in the sections on Shakespeare's comedies, tragedies, and histories, but for the moment it may be amusing to hear Stephen Gosson's puritanical attack on these genres as they existed six or eight years before Shakespeare set to work, when romances, continental short fiction (*novelle*), and chronicles provided much of the stuff of popular drama. The passages are all from Gosson's *Plays Confuted in Five Actions* (1582). First, Gosson on comedy, which he sees as immoral. Judging from the plays that survive, it may be said that Gosson grossly overstates the immorality, but he gives us a fair sense of the chief theme of much comedy:

The groundwork of comedies is love, cozenage, flattery, bawdry, sly conveyance of whoredom; the persons, cooks, queans, knaves, bawds, parasites, courtezans, lecherous old men, amorous young men. . . . Comedies so tickle our senses . . . that they make us lovers of laughter and pleasure without any mean. . . . What schooling is this?

Next, Gosson on tragedy, which he sees not as valuable but as debilitating. Again he gives us a sense of the chief action:

The beholding of troubles and miserable slaughters that are in tragedies drive us to immoderate sorrow, heaviness, womanish weeping and mourning, whereby we become lovers of dumps, and lamentation, both enemies to fortitude.

Finally, Gosson on history plays, which he sees as distortions of history and therefore vicious. His observations are surely right, though his implications are surely wrong:

> If a true history be taken in hand, it is made like our shadows, longest at the rising and falling of the sun, shortest of all at high noon. For the poets drive it most commonly unto such points as may best show the majesty of their pen in tragical speeches, or set the hearers agog with discourses of love, or paint a few antics to fit their own humors with scoffs and taunts, or wring in a show to furnish the stage when it is too bare. When the matter of itself comes short of this, they follow the practice of the cobbler, and set their teeth to the leather to pull it out. So was the history of Caesar and Pompey, and the play of the Fabii at the Theater, both amplified there, where the drums might walk or the pen ruffle. When the history swelled and ran too high for the number of the persons that should play it, the poet with Proteus [that is, Procrustes] cut the same fit to his own measure; when it afforded no pomp at all, he brought it to the rack to make it serve.

Had Gosson written again some thirty years later, when Shakespeare had completed his career, he probably would have seen no reason to alter his words. To a hostile eye, Shakespeare would only seem to be doing better what his predecessors had done (and therefore he was the more dangerous). Subsequent pages will try to call attention to his distinction.

# Style and Structure

Perhaps "style" would be enough because, if broadly and deeply conceived, it takes in everything: the choice of words and their arrangement in lines, metrics, prose rhythms, and even the choice of plots and of characters. Though style is often contrasted with content, as though it were a decorative treatment of meaning, it can be argued that style (for example, Latinate versus Anglo-Saxon diction, or the inclusion versus the exclusion of comic material in a tragic plot) is inherently part of the meaning. Cardinal Newman put it thus: "Thought and meaning are inseparable from each other. Matter and expression are parts of one: style is a thinking out into language."

Because Shakespeare was a dramatist, his style is a thinking out not only into language (which includes diction, grammar, images, meter, and rhythm) but also into costumes, sound effects, gestures, and even silences. The use of costumes as a part of the dramatist's language has already been discussed (pp. 11–12). To the examples of Hamlet's "inky cloak," which separates him from the opulently dressed courtiers, and the fresh clothing in which Lear is garbed after his madness, can be added the broader matter of disguises—for example, the monk's robe worn by Duke Vincentio in *Measure for Measure* and Rosalind's and Viola's male attire in *As You Like It* and *Twelfth Night* —which are removed at the ends of the plays, when the truth is at last revealed and the characters can again be fully themselves. In short, the removal of disguises *says* something.

Sound effects too communicate meaning. Perhaps the most obvious example is the sound of the storm in *King Lear*, which is a reflection of Lear's disordered kingdom, disordered family, and disordered mind. A little less obvious is the noise of cannon in *Hamlet*. Early in the play cannon are fired when Claudius drinks deeply, and the reverberation of the noise to the heavens suggests Claudius' power, vulgarity, and arrogance; later in the play Claudius again orders the cannon to sound, this time when he hypocritically drinks to Hamlet before the fencing match; at the end of the play the cannon are once again ordered to be fired, not by Claudius but by Fortinbras, and now in tribute to Hamlet, who has earned "the soldiers' music."

Gestures are also an important part of the dramatist's language. For example, King Lear kneels before his daughter Cordelia for a benediction (IV.vii.57–59), an act of humility that contrasts with his earlier speeches banishing her and that contrasts also with a comparable gesture, his ironic kneeling before Regan (II.iv.152). In the first act of *Coriolanus* Volumnia hopes that her son will defeat Aufidius "and tread upon his neck," but in the last act it is Aufidius who, according to the stage direction, "*stands on*" Coriolanus. *Coriolanus* also affords an example of the importance of dramatic silence; before the protagonist yields to his mother's entreaties (V.iii.182), there is this stage direction: "*Holds her by the hand, silent.*" In *Macbeth*, when Macduff learns that his wife and children have been murdered, he is silent at first, as Malcolm's speech indicates: "What, man! Ne'er pull your hat upon your brows./Give sorrow words" (IV.iii.208 ff.). In the abdication scene of *Richard II* (IV.i), Richard speaks 132 lines against Bolingbroke's fourteen, and Bolingbroke's forbidding silence—which Richard comments on when he addresses the "silent king"—is part of Bolingbroke's character and part of the meaning of the play. A playwright's language, clearly, is not simply verbal language. Even an actor's position on the stage may have meaning. In *Romeo and Juliet* (III.v) the lovers share a scene "*aloft,*" suggesting their exaltation. Romeo then "*goeth down,*" and Juliet, looking down on him, prophetically says, "Methinks I see thee, now thou art so low,/As one dead in the bottom of a tomb."

Of course, when we think of Shakespeare's style we think primarily of his language, both the poetry and the prose. Although two of the plays (*Richard II* and *King John*) have no prose at all, about half the others have at least one fourth of the dialogue in prose, and some have notably more: *Troilus and Cressida*, one third; *1 Henry IV* and *2 Henry IV*, about half; *As You Like It* and *Twelfth Night*, a little more than half; *Much Ado About Nothing*, about three fourths; and *The Merry Wives of Windsor*, about nine tenths. All these plays were probably written between 1597 and 1602, what might be called (with exaggeration, of course) Shakespeare's "prose period." During this time Shakespeare was perhaps developing as a poet, learning how to make significant rather than unvarying use of poetry, and learning how to bring his language closer to an approximation of speech.

Today we perhaps think of prose as "natural" for comedies, but Greek, Roman, and early English comedies were written in verse. In fact, prose was not generally considered a literary medium in England until the late fifteenth century; Chaucer tells even his bawdy stories in verse. By the end of the 1580's, however, prose had established itself on the English comic stage with the plays of John Lyly, comedies that used an extremely patterned and figurative prose and that were designed for a courtly rather than a popular audience. In tragedy, Marlowe had made some use of prose, not simply in the speeches of clownish servants but even in the speech of a tragic hero, Doctor Faustus. With the notable exceptions of Lyly and Marlowe, however, dramatic prose before Shakespeare is scarcely memorable. It was normally used only for special circumstances: (1) letters and proclamations, to set them off from the poetic dialogue; (2) mad characters, to indicate that normal thinking has become disordered; and (3) low comedy, or speeches uttered by clowns even when they are not being comic. Shakespeare made use of these conventions (to the second group—mad characters such as Lear, Ophelia, and Lady Macbeth—can be added Lepidus when he is drunk in *Antony and Cleopatra*), but he also went far beyond them. He sometimes used prose for (4) cynical commentary, such as Thersites' remarks in *Troilus and Cressida* or Casca's report in *Julius Caesar* of Caesar's reluctant refusal of the crown (I.ii); (5) scenes of ordinary life, such as those of Prince Hal at his ease in the tavern in *1 Henry IV*; (6) scenes of courtship, such as those between Beatrice and Benedick in *Much Ado About Nothing*, and Rosalind and Orlando (though Orlando does not realize that courtship is going on) in *As You Like It*, and even between King Henry and Katherine of France in *Henry V*. Moreover, sometimes a scene begins in prose and then shifts into verse as the emotion is heightened; or conversely, a scene shifts from verse to prose when a speaker is lowering the emotional level (as when Brutus speaks in the forum). Thus it is not enough to say that low characters speak prose, high characters speak verse; in *Richard II*, for example, the gardeners (III.iv) and the groom (V.v) speak verse, and in other plays monarchs often speak prose.

Nor is Shakespeare's prose prosaic, used only to represent ordinary conversation or to communicate necessary information. Hamlet's prose includes not only small talk with Rosencrantz and Guildenstern but princely reflections on "What a piece of work is a man" (II.ii). In conversation with Ophelia Hamlet shifts from light talk in verse to a passionate prose denunciation of women (III.ii), though the shift to prose here is perhaps intended to suggest the possibility of madness—at least Ophelia immediately concludes that Hamlet's "noble mind is here o'erthrown."

Below are examples of Shakespeare's prose, showing something of its structure and its range. The first is from Brutus' funeral oration in *Julius Caesar:*

Romans, countrymen, and lovers, hear me for my cause, and be silent, that you may hear. Believe me for mine honor, and have respect to mine honor, that you may believe. Censure me in your wisdom, and awake your senses, that you may the better judge. (III.ii.13–17)

Despite its apparent simplicity, this prose speech is elaborately constructed. Notice Brutus' use of isocolon (successive phrases or clauses of approximately equal length) in three successive sentences, each approximately equal in length and each with three clauses:

hear me for my cause,/and be silent,/that you may hear.
Believe me for mine honor,/and have respect to mine honor,/that you may believe.
Censure me in your wisdom,/and awake your senses,/that you may the better judge.

Notice, too, the rather complacent repetitions: "hear . . . hear," "mine honor . . . mine honor," "Censure . . . senses." Later in the speech there are alliterative lines: "base . . . be . . . bondman," "rude . . . Roman." The speech is fully in accord with Brutus' conception of himself as a man who balances things thoughtfully in his mind. But there is something repelling in the sixfold repetition (in forty-two words) of "me," "my," "me," "mine," "mine," "me."

Brutus' speech can be contrasted with a second passage, from *Hamlet* V.ii. When Horatio offers to make excuses if Hamlet wishes to avoid the duel with Laertes, Hamlet replies:

Not a whit, we defy augury. There is special providence in the fall of a sparrow. If it be now, 'tis not to come; if it be not to come, it will be now; if it be not now, yet it will come. The readiness is all. Since no man of aught he leaves knows, what is't to leave betimes? Let be. (V.ii.221–26)

Of the sixty-two words in the speech, only seven are of more than one syllable. On the whole the diction is colloquial (note especially "Not a whit"), but there is the solemn echo of the Bible ("special providence in the fall of a sparrow"), and the clauses are balanced. The speech is simple and meditative, yet strong-willed in the final "Let be."

There is no need here to quote examples of what are in effect comic prose monologues, such as Touchstone's speech on lying (*As You Like It*, V.iv.69–82) or Falstaff's discourse on honor (*1 Henry IV*, V.i.127–41). (A comic speech of this type—Gobbo's debate with his conscience—is quoted on p. 14.) What is especially worth noting is that although Shakespeare's characters occasionally utter the garbled chaos that is our daily talk—such as the Nurse in *Romeo and Juliet*, "Well, sir, my mistress is the sweetest lady. Lord, Lord! When 'twas a little prating thing—O, there is a nobleman in town" (II.iv.203–05)—for the most part even his lowest characters speak coherently, and each seems to speak his appropriate idiom. Here is the simple country fellow who tells Cleopatra that he has brought the asp with which she will commit suicide:

Truly I have him; but I would not be the party that should desire you to touch him, for his biting is immortal: those that do die of it do seldom or never recover.
(V.ii.245–48)

The clown has an odd idea of death, and he says "immortal" for "mortal"; yet Cleopatra *does* become immortal, and though the entire speech has an impressive coherence, it somehow conveys the clown's simplicity.

As has been mentioned, verse drama in England goes back to the Middle Ages, but truly poetic drama is probably no older than George Peele's *The Arraignment of Paris* (about 1580). For the most part the drama of the seventies presented such harrowing stuff as this passage from *Cambises* (about 1569), written in fourteeners, or pairs of rhyming lines of fourteen syllables each:

I feel myself a-dying now, of life bereft am I,
And death hath caught me with his dart, for want of blood I die.
Thus gasping here on ground I lie; for nothing do I care;
A just reward for my misdeeds my death doth plain declare.

This passage is not meant to be comic, though it sounds rather like Bottom's words when he impersonates the dying Pyramus in *A Midsummer Night's Dream* (V.i).

By Shakespeare's day, however, rhyme no longer dominated poetic drama; a finer medium, blank verse, had been adopted. But before looking at Elizabethan unrhymed verse, a few things should be said about the chief uses of rhyme in Shakespeare's plays. (1) Emotional heightening at the end of a blank-verse speech is often indicated by a couplet (a pair of rhyming lines). (2) Characters sometimes speak a couplet as they leave the stage. (3) Except in the latest plays, scenes or acts fairly often conclude with a couplet, and sometimes, as in *Richard II*, I.i.18–19, the entrance of a new character within a scene is preceded by a couplet, which wraps up the earlier portion of that scene. (4) Speeches of two characters occasionally are linked by rhyme, most notably in *Romeo and Juliet*, I.v.95–108, where the lovers speak a sonnet between them; elsewhere a taunting reply occasionally rhymes with the previous speaker's last line. (5) Speeches with sententious or gnomic remarks are sometimes in rhyme, as in the duke's speech in *Othello* (I.iii.199–206) and the king's speech in *All's Well That Ends Well* (II.iii.126–45). (6) Speeches with sardonic mockery are sometimes in rhyme—for example, Iago's speech on women in *Othello* (II.i.146–58)—and sometimes conclude with an emphatic couplet, as in Bolingbroke's speech on comforting words in *Richard II* (I.iii.301–02). (7) Some characters are associated with rhyme—for example, the fairies in *A Midsummer Night's Dream* and to a lesser degree Faulconbridge in *King John* and Apemantus in *Timon of Athens*, though because Faulconbridge and Apemantus are given to mockery their rhymes perhaps properly belong in the previous category. (8) In the early plays, especially *The Comedy of Errors* and *The Taming of the Shrew*, comic scenes which in later plays would be in prose are in jingling rhymes. (9) Prologues, choruses, plays-within-the-play, inscriptions, vows, epilogues, and so on, are often in rhyme, and of course the songs in plays are rhymed. The play-within-the-play in *Hamlet*, for example, is written in an older style to set it off from the language of the play itself:

Full thirty times hath Phoebus' cart gone round
Neptune's salt wash and Tellus' orbèd ground,
And thirty dozen moons with borrowed sheen
About the world have times twelve thirties been,
Since love our hearts, and Hymen did our hands,
Unite commutual in most sacred bands.     (III.ii.158–63)

The plays with the highest percentage of rhymed dialogue are (in decreasing order) *Love's Labor's Lost*, *A Midsummer Night's Dream*, *The Comedy of Errors*, *Richard II*, and *Romeo and Juliet*. Of these five, all but *The Comedy of Errors* were written about 1594–96, which is probably also the period during which Shakespeare wrote many of his sonnets. Most of the rhyme in Shakespeare's last plays (with the exception of *Pericles*) is not in dialogue properly speaking but in songs, choruses, or a masque (*The Tempest*). Broadly speaking, then, after the "prose period" of about 1597–1602 Shakespeare tended to use less and less rhyme in dialogue.

But it is neither prose nor rhyme that comes to mind when we first think of Shakespeare's medium: it is blank verse, unrhymed iambic pentameter (in a mechanically exact line, five feet, each foot with two syllables, every second syllable accented). The first speech in *A Midsummer Night's Dream* is an example of blank verse:

Now, fair Hippolyta, our nuptial hour
Draws on apace. Four happy days bring in
Another moon; but, O, methinks, how slow
This old moon wanes! She lingers my desires,
Like to a stepdame, or a dowager,
Long withering out a young man's revenue.     (I.i.1–6)

As this passage shows, Shakespeare's blank verse is not mechanically unvarying. Though the predominant foot is the iamb (customarily indicated by ⌣ ´), there are numerous variations. In the first line the stress can be placed on "fair," as the regular metrical pattern suggests, but it is likely that "Now" gets almost as much emphasis; probably in the second line "Draws" is more heavily emphasized than "on," giving us a trochee (indicated by ´ ⌣); and in the fourth line each word in the phrase "This old moon wanes" is probably stressed fairly heavily, conveying by two spondees (each indicated by ´ ´) the oppressive tedium that Theseus feels.

Blank verse, first printed in England in 1557 in Surrey's posthumously published translation of parts of Virgil's *Aeneid*, was first used in a play in 1561, in Thomas Sackville and Thomas Norton's *Gorboduc*. But if *Gorboduc* thus looks forward to Marlowe and Shakespeare, it also looks backward in its heavy alliteration, its tendency to use paired lines (much of it seems to be couplets without rhymes), and its formal balance, as the first speech of the play indicates:

The silent night, that brings the quiet pause
From painful travails of the weary day,

Prolongs my careful thoughts, and makes me blame
The slow Aurore, that so for love or shame
Doth long delay to show her blushing face.
And now the day renews my grieful plaint.

The first line introduces a favorite Renaissance device, a disyllabic adjective followed by a monosyllabic noun ("silent night," "quiet pause"); this device reappears in the next line ("weary day") and yet again in all but one of the following lines ("careful thoughts," "blushing face," "grieful plaint"). Elsewhere lines are often end-stopped (that is, there is a distinct syntactical pause at the end of the line), as the second speech in *Gorboduc* reveals:

My gracious lady and my mother dear,
Pardon my grief for your so grievèd mind,
To ask what cause tormenteth so your heart.

Alliteration is abundant: in the first speech "*p*ause," "*p*ainful," "*P*rolongs," "*s*low," "*s*o," "*D*oth," "*d*elay," "*d*ay," "*p*laint"; in the second speech "*g*racious," "*g*rief," "*g*rievèd." In the late 1580's Marlowe changed all this, partly by somewhat reducing the amount of alliteration and partly by joining phrases and clauses with *and* so that a sentence ran to a dozen or so lines. Most important, Marlowe was a poet, not a versifier, and he gave to blank verse a richness that inevitably drew later poets to the form.

In Shakespeare's early plays much of the poetry is end-stopped, but he later developed the ability to write iambic-pentameter verse paragraphs (rather than lines) that give the illusion of speech. His chief techniques are (1) running the thought beyond the single line; (2) occasionally substituting another foot for an iambic foot; (3) varying the position of the chief pause within a line; (4) adding an occasional unstressed syllable at the end of a line, a so-called feminine ending; (5) and beginning or ending a speech with a half-line. In addition, Shakespeare's speeches often suggest the nature of the speaker, whereas in *Gorboduc* all the speeches sound alike, as though they issued from a single undefined mouth. In *Hamlet* the king ceremoniously —that is, rather formally—addresses his court in a long sentence whose meaning is suspended until near the end:

Though yet of Hamlet our dear brother's death
The memory be green, and that it us befitted
To bear our hearts in grief, and our whole kingdom
To be contracted in one brow of woe,
Yet so far hath discretion fought with nature
That we with wisest sorrow think on him
Together with remembrance of ourselves.     (I.ii.1–7)

Later in the scene Claudius speaks more intimately:

And now, Laertes, what's the news with you?
You told us of some suit. What is't, Laertes?
You cannot speak of reason to the Dane
And lose your voice. What wouldst thou beg, Laertes,
That shall not be my offer, not thy asking?     (I.ii.42–46)

Notice the short sentences and the ingratiating repetition of the name "Laertes," to whom the speech is addressed.

Notice, too, the shift from the royal "us" in the second line to the more intimate "my" in the last line, and from "you" in the first line to the more intimate "thou" and "thy" in the last two lines.

Guildenstern's sycophantic speech to Claudius in III.iii is marked by windy repetitions ("holy and religious," "many many," "live and feed"):

Most holy and religious fear it is
To keep those many many bodies safe
That live and feed upon your majesty.     (III.iii.8–10)

Hamlet, who has several styles in the play, uses a simple style in rejecting his friends' entreaties not to follow the Ghost:

I do not set my life at a pin's fee,
And for my soul, what can it do to that,
Being a thing immortal as itself?
It waves me forth again. I'll follow it.     (I.iv.65–68)

Macbeth, distressed by the doctor's inability to cure Lady Macbeth and by the imminent battle, addresses some of his remarks to the doctor and others to the servant who is arming him. The entire speech, with its pauses, interruptions, and irresolution (in "Pull't off, I say," Macbeth orders the servant to remove the armor he has been putting on him), catches Macbeth's disintegration:

Throw physic to the dogs, I'll none of it.
Come, put mine armor on. Give me my staff.
Seyton, send out.—Doctor, the thanes fly from me.—
Come, sir, dispatch. If thou couldst, doctor, cast
The water of my land, find her disease
And purge it to a sound and pristine health,
I would applaud thee to the very echo,
That should applaud again.—Pull't off, I say.—
What rhubarb, senna, or what purgative drug,
Would scour these English hence? Hear'st thou of them?
                                        (V.iii.47–56)

Duke Frederick in *As You Like It* is disappointed to find that a young man who has performed nobly is the son of an enemy:

I would thou hadst been son to some man else.
The world esteemed thy father honorable,
But I did find him still mine enemy.
Thou shouldst have better pleased me with this deed
Hadst thou descended from another house.
But fare thee well; thou art a gallant youth;
I would thou hadst told me of another father.
                                        (I.ii.220–26)

Duke Frederick's lines are end-stopped, but the effect is not one of monotony. Rather, the regular pauses and the repetition of part of the first line in the last ("I would thou hadst") and the continual turning back ("But," "But") convey the tension of conflicting emotions and the speaker's unwillingness to let his spirit generously expand.

| | 1 | 2 | 3 | 4 | 5 | 6 |
|---|---|---|---|---|---|---|
| | Total lines | % prose | % blank | % rhyme | % run-on | % feminine endings |
| Errors | 1777 | 14 | 65 | 21 | 13 | 17 |
| 2 Henry VI | 3162 | 17 | 80 | 3 | 11 | 13 |
| 3 Henry VI | 2904 | 0.1 | 95.5 | 4.4 | 10 | 13 |
| 1 Henry VI | 2677 | 0.07 | 88 | 11.9 | 10 | 8 |
| Richard III | 3619 | 2 | 94 | 4 | 13 | 19 |
| Titus | 2523 | 2 | 93 | 5 | 12 | 9 |
| Shrew | 2647 | 23 | 71 | 6 | 8 | 20 |
| Two Gentlemen | 2292 | 28 | 66 | 6 | 12 | 18 |
| Love's Labor's | 2785 | 38 | 21 | 41 | 18 | 5 |
| Romeo | 3050 | 15 | 70 | 15 | 14 | 8 |
| Richard II | 2757 | 0 | 81 | 19 | 20 | 12 |
| Midsummer | 2174 | 23 | 37 | 40 | 13 | 8 |
| King John | 2570 | 0 | 95 | 5 | 18 | 6 |
| Merchant | 2658 | 25 | 70 | 5 | 22 | 17 |
| 1 Henry IV | 3176 | 47 | 51 | 2 | 23 | 6 |
| 2 Henry IV | 3446 | 55 | 43 | 2 | 21 | 16 |
| Much Ado | 2825 | 74 | 23 | 3 | 19 | 23 |
| Henry V | 3381 | 48 | 50 | 2 | 22 | 22 |
| Julius Caesar | 2477 | 7 | 92 | 1 | 19 | 18 |
| As You Like It | 2856 | 59 | 33 | 8 | 17 | 25 |
| Twelfth Night | 2690 | 65 | 28 | 7 | 15 | 21 |
| Hamlet | 3929 | 32 | 64 | 4 | 23 | 22 |
| Merry Wives | 3018 | 92 | 7 | 1 | 20 | 25 |
| Troilus | 3496 | 35 | 60 | 5 | 27 | 22 |
| All's Well | 2966 | 50 | 41 | 9 | 28 | 29 |
| Othello | 3316 | 21 | 76 | 3 | 20 | 27 |
| Measure | 2820 | 41 | 56 | 3 | 23 | 23 |
| Timon | 2374 | 29 | 64 | 7 | 33 | 22 |
| King Lear | 3328 | 28 | 67 | 5 | 29 | 26 |
| Macbeth | 2106 | 8 | 86 | 6 | 37 | 25 |
| Antony | 3059 | 10 | 89 | 1 | 43 | 24 |
| Coriolanus | 3406 | 24 | 75 | 1 | 46 | 28 |
| Pericles | 2393 | 23 | 67 | 10 | 12 | 19 |
| Cymbeline | 3339 | 16 | 80 | 4 | 46 | 31 |
| Winter's Tale | 3074 | 29 | 69 | 2 | 38 | 32 |
| Tempest | 2062 | 24 | 73 | 3 | 42 | 33 |
| Henry VIII | 2819 | 3 | 96 | 1 | 31 | 48 |
| Two Kinsmen | 2817 | 6 | 92 | 2 | 20 | 44 |

For the most part, the figures in the table are translations into percentages of the numbers given in E. K. Chambers, *William Shakespeare*, II, Appendix H.

*Column 1* gives the total number of lines in the play, an inexact measure, of course, because the number of prose lines differs from edition to edition, depending on the width of the page and on the editor's decision as to whether a given passage should be printed as prose or as verse. For example, certain passages printed as prose in *1 Henry IV* (such as III.i.3–11) are so rhythmic that they might be considered verse, and if printed as verse they would constitute a larger number of lines.

*Column 2* gives the percentage of the play that is in prose, *excluding* those parts of the play that are not "normal" dramatic dialogue—such as prologues, epilogues, choruses, the plays-within-the-plays in *A Midsummer Night's Dream* and *Hamlet*, and the masque in *The Tempest*. As the table shows, the percentage of prose is relatively low for the early

comedies—except for *Love's Labor's Lost*, which was probably revised six or seven years after it was written—and for the early histories. The percentage increases markedly in the later histories, written about 1597–99 (*1 and 2 Henry IV* and *Henry V*), and in the comedies written about 1598–1604. Most of the tragedies and the last plays make considerable use of prose, but not to the same extent as the later histories and comedies.

*Column 3* gives the percentage of blank-verse dialogue in the play, again excluding prologues, epilogues, and so on.

*Column 4* gives the percentage of rhymed dialogue in the play. Again, prologues, epilogues, and so on, are excluded (if such material were not excluded, many of the figures in this column would be higher). As has been mentioned (p. 18), with the exception of *The Comedy of Errors* the five plays with the highest percentage of rhymed dialogue were written in the middle nineties, which was probably also the period of the sonnets.

Finally the Nurse in *Romeo and Juliet* babbles in blank verse that Juliet will soon be fourteen years old:

> Come Lammas Eve at night shall she be fourteen.
> Susan and she (God rest all Christian souls!)
> Were of an age. Well, Susan is with God;
> She was too good for me. But, as I said,
> On Lammas Eve at night shall she be fourteen;
> That shall she, marry; I remember it well.
> 'Tis since the earthquake now eleven years;
> And she was weaned (I never shall forget it),
> Of all the days of the year, upon that day;
> For I had then laid wormwood to my dug,
> Sitting in the sun under the dovehouse wall.
> My lord and you were then at Mantua.
> Nay, I do bear a brain. (I.iii.17-29)

Blank verse, then, can be much more than unrhymed iambic pentameter, and even within a single play Shakespeare's blank verse often consists of several styles, depending on the speaker and on the speaker's emotion at the moment. Of course, much depends on the length of the speech: a speech of a single line has a different tone from a long speech, even though the metrical pattern in both is iambic.

One particular kind of dialogue, which Shakespeare used sparingly, deserves special notice. From the Roman dramatist Seneca the Elizabethans borrowed a device called stichomythia, the exchange of single lines (sometimes pairs of lines) in which the words of one speaker are picked up and tossed back by another, giving the effect of a duel with words. Stichomythia commonly makes use of figures of thought, or artful arrangements of words, such as repetition and antithesis. Here is a famous example from *Hamlet*:

QUEEN
  Hamlet, thou hast thy father much offended.
HAMLET
  Mother, you have my father much offended.
QUEEN
  Come, come, you answer with an idle tongue.
HAMLET
  Go, go, you question with a wicked tongue. (III.iv.10-13)

Another departure from logical or literal usage common in Shakespeare (and in almost all poets) is the use of tropes, or figurative language. When Iago urges Roderigo to "poison [Othello's] delight" he is not advocating the literal use of poison, and when he urges Roderigo to "plague him with flies" he is suggesting not that Roderigo open a bag of flies in Othello's presence but that he somehow distress Othello with trivial, irritating things. The words are clearly not used in their literal or normal sense.

Shakespeare's early figurative language is sometimes ostentatious. The figures often seem to be tacked on, elaborate embellishments of an idea rather than the inevitable presentation of the idea itself. For example, Queen Tamora's lover in *Titus Andronicus*, an early play, describes the queen's good fortune thus:

> Now climbeth Tamora Olympus' top,
> Safe out of fortune's shot, and sits aloft,
> Secure of thunder's crack or lightning flash,
> Advanced above pale envy's threat'ning reach.
> As when the golden sun salutes the morn,
> And having gilt the ocean with his beams,
> Gallops the zodiac in his glistering coach,
> And overlooks the highest-peering hills;
> So Tamora. (II.i.1-9)

The last five lines seem tacked on to the first four, an embellishment rather than an integral part of the speech.

Shakespeare's later figurative language appears more natural, less decorative, and more integral—though of course there are exceptions. The speech from *Titus Andronicus* quoted above is utterly different from Iago's "plague him with flies," where the figure is integral. This difference is not simply one of a short figure versus a long figure. When Othello in the last act describes himself as "one whose hand,/Like the base Judean, threw a pearl away/Richer than all his tribe" (V.ii.345-47), again the figure contains its own meaning rather than merely embellishing an earlier meaning. Othello is alluding either to Judas or to Herod, both enemies of Christ, and thereby indicates his appraisal of himself as a foe to goodness; he emphasizes the comparison a few lines later when he identifies himself with a pagan Turk. (Another text of *Othello* has "Indian" instead of "Judean," but either word implies separation from Christianity.)

Shakespeare's progress was something like Berowne's in *Love's Labor's Lost*. Near the end of the play Berowne says that he will forswear "taffeta phrases" and "Three-pile

*Column 5* gives the percentage of run-on lines found in all pentameter lines (*not* total lines) in the play. In contrast to an end-stopped line, a run-on line does not have a natural or grammatical pause at the end. In the following passage from *The Tempest* only the second line is run-on:

> Our revels now are ended. These our actors,
> As I foretold you, were all spirits and
> Are melted into air, into thin air. (IV.i.148-50)

Because readers may disagree about which lines do not reasonably call for a pause at the end, the figures are somewhat subjective. Generally speaking, the later plays have a higher percentage of run-on lines than the earlier plays, in which each line tends to be a clause or a sentence.

*Column 6* gives the percentage of verse lines with feminine endings, that is, lines concluding with an extra unstressed syllable, as in the first, fourth, and fifth lines of the following passage from *The Tempest*:

> Was Milan thrust from Milan that his issue
> Should become kings of Naples? O, rejoice
> Beyond a common joy, and set it down
> With gold on lasting pillars. In one voyage
> Did Claribel her husband find at Tunis. (V.i.205-09)

Roughly speaking, the plays written during the second half of Shakespeare's career have a notably higher percentage of feminine endings than do the earlier plays. As in the preceding column, the figures in this column show a significant increase in the later plays. This increasing freedom with the blank-verse line is demonstrated in yet another way, not indicated in the table: speeches in the early plays relatively rarely end in mid-line, but in the later plays speeches that end in this way are very common.

hyperboles, spruce affectation,/Figures pedantical" and will substitute for them "russet yeas and honest kersey noes" (homespun woolen cloth). The expression "russet yeas and honest kersey noes" of course is itself as figurative as "taffeta phrases," and Shakespeare never abandoned figures, though he curbed his exuberance.

Figures commonly add sensory content—compare "plague him with flies" with "bother him with trivialities"—but of course not all sensory words are figurative. When Othello commands the Venetians to "Keep up your bright swords," the phrase "bright swords" refers literally (rather than figuratively) to the swords they are flourishing. All such sensory words, whether figurative or literal, can be called images, though there is a tendency in criticism to concentrate on figurative rather than literal images, neglecting, for example, the abundant literal talk about blood in *Julius Caesar* while dwelling on metaphors. One can deplore the neglect of the literal, especially in the study of drama, which involves people carrying swords, holding up bloody hands, and so forth, but one can understand why critics have tended to dwell on those images involving metaphors, similes, and the host of other figurative uses of language that are enumerated in handbooks of rhetoric.

There are at least three important uses of imagery: First, it can afford delight in itself, giving a sense of the nature of things. By saying "Keep up your bright swords" rather than "Calm yourselves" or "Do not fight," Othello gives us a rich sense of the concrete world—both its singularity and its multiplicity. As Coleridge said, Shakespeare "by metaphors and figures involves in the thing considered a universe of past and possible experiences." At the end of the first scene in *Hamlet* Horatio talks of the coming of the dawn:

But look, the morn in russet mantle clad
Walks o'er the dew of yon high eastward hill.

(I.i.166–67)

Horatio's lines tell us of the time of day, but the images serve a further dramatic purpose. The scene begins at midnight, and is full of uncertainties, including two harrowing encounters with a ghost; then it becomes early morning, and the suggestion of light implies the coming of order and harmony. But the image of "in russet mantle clad" precisely qualifies this light: dawn is personified not as the bright and sunny Aurora but as a peasant in his workaday mantle of coarse grayish-brown material. The morning and the daily business of living dispel the darkness, but full light has not yet come to the shadowy tragic world. There is, then, something sharp and precisely right (and therefore delightful) about the description of this particular kind of morning. We may never have noticed such a morning, and the image serves to enrich our sense of the world.

Second, imagery can help to characterize the speaker. Not every line and image in Shakespeare does this, of course. The passage just quoted from *Hamlet* is not especially typical of Horatio's manner. If we were to look for lines that characterize Horatio, we would probably choose less "poetic" or lyrical and more ironic lines, such as his dry "a truant disposition," when Hamlet asks him why he is not at the university. Horatio's speech about the dawn exists not to reveal anything about Horatio but to tell us about the time of the day and the particular quality of the

morning, and to balance the appearance of the Ghost with a sense of nature's divinity. But innumerable images in Shakespeare do help to define character. The tragic heroes, for example, often speak in hyperbole, a figure appropriate to their greatness. Othello says that were it not for the love of Desdemona he would not confine himself "for the sea's worth"; nine months gone by are "nine moons wasted"; caves are "anters vast"; waves are "hills of seas Olympus-high." Iago says that Othello brags and tells "fantastical lies," but this is a villain's cynical view, unsupported by anything else in the play. Against Othello's hyperbolic and exotic language are Iago's figures that diminish men. Iago's allusion to flies has already been noted; other animals are commonly in his mind: a faithful servant is an "ass," Othello is "an old black ram," Desdemona is a "white ewe," their offspring will "neigh," and the lovers "are making the beast with two backs." All these words occur in the first 115 lines of the first scene. In later scenes Iago alludes to women as wildcats, to Cassio and Desdemona as "goats, . . . monkeys, . . . wolves," and to a married man as "yoked" (that is, an ox). In contrast to Othello, Iago is the sort of man who sees people chiefly as sexual or stupid beasts. Interestingly, however, once Iago has succeeded in infecting Othello's mind, Othello too begins to use such images, speaking of "goats and monkeys," "toads," "aspics' tongues," "crocodile," and "flies."

Finally, images often help to define the theme of the play. (A few words about this third use of imagery are included in the discussion of images of rising and falling in *Richard II* on pp. 50–51 and in the discussion of images of light, dark, and speed in *Romeo and Juliet* on p. 57.) In *Othello*, diabolic images ("hell," "devil," "perdition") are at first associated with Iago and then, as Othello comes under Iago's power, with Othello. As S. L. Bethell points out in *Shakespeare Survey 5*, there are sixty-four such images in Othello. Of course, not all the occurrences are of equal significance—for example, the first diabolic image, Iago's assertion that Cassio is "almost damned in a fair wife," is trivial when compared with Iago's

I have't! It is engendered! Hell and night
Must bring this monstrous birth to the world's light.

(I.iii.392–93)

But though the statistics must be interpreted with caution, they do add up to something. Here are Bethell's calculations. First, the diabolic images steadily increase from the first act to the last: the figures for the five acts are 10, 11, 13, 14, and 16, respectively. Furthermore, the disposition of these images according to speaker is interesting. As Bethell explains,

Iago has only his fair proportion of diabolic imagery, yet we undoubtedly gain the impression that in this play the theme of hell, as it were, originates with him and is passed to Othello later as Iago succeeds in dominating his mind. Statistics show this impression to be well-founded. In Act I Iago has eight diabolic images and Othello none; in Act II he has six and Othello one. The change comes in Act III, where Iago drops to three and Othello rises to nine. In Act IV Iago has only one while Othello has ten, and in Act V Iago has none and Othello six. It all begins, then, with Iago.

These images, of course, help to define the speakers: Iago is a nasty figure given (like the devil) to destructiveness; Othello is a man who at least for a while becomes his instrument. But the images also go beyond character and help to define the theme: on one level *Othello* is a domestic tragedy, a play about a man who kills his wife; on another level it is about the mysterious power of evil, of the sort associated with the devil—an evil that hates what is good (Coleridge aptly speaks of Iago's "motiveless malignity") and sometimes brings it to material and spiritual destruction. (One need not, however, argue that Othello is damned. When at the end of the play Othello reaffirms his love for Desdemona and executes justice on himself, he shows that Iago has *not* corrupted him. The play does not have a sixth act, set in the next world. But the images do help to suggest that the conflict has a spiritual dimension.)

Another example of imagery that goes beyond characterization and helps to establish theme is the storm imagery in *King Lear*. A storm literally takes place in the middle of the play, but the storm also has symbolic implications. As early as I.ii Gloucester speaks of disturbances in nature and of "all ruinous disorder"; Lear calls down "Blasts and fogs" (I.iv.301) and the "nimble lightnings" (II.iv.162) upon Goneril. As the break with his only remaining daughter, Regan, is widened and Lear is almost driven to madness, the stage direction "*Storm and tempest*" appears (II.iv.280), followed in three lines by Lear's explicit fear that he "shall go mad." Thus, as has already been mentioned, the chaos in Lear's family, the chaos in nature, and the chaos in Lear's mind are all linked. A few lines later Cornwall says that it is "a wild night," and still later we see the deranged Lear in a stormy, deranged world. Lear himself equates the macrocosm and the microcosm, the great world and the little world of man, when he speaks of "the tempest in my mind." Only a few of the storm images have been commented on here; but the more one studies the play the more one sees that the images are not decorative but integral; if they were removed from the play, and if the storm itself were removed, *King Lear* would say something entirely different.

Of course, no spectator can be fully aware of all the implications of all Shakespeare's images; nor can a reader be, unless he takes notes line by line. Shakespeare himself probably was not conscious of the patterns of images he created, and he would have been surprised by Bethell's statistics on *Othello* or by a list of the storm images in *King Lear*. But if these statistics would have surprised him, it is probably only because he did not put the images in one by one; rather, he imagined his characters and his plots and his themes so fully that the images inevitably came in the speeches. Though we may be unaware of them, the images, both figurative and literal (as for instance the blood in *Julius Caesar*), have a profound effect; they work along with the nonverbal imagery of visible stage properties, gestures, and costumes (see pp. 11–12 and 16 for a discussion of such imagery).

When we think of a play, however—unless we have been corrupted by education—we first think not of images or themes but of characters and plot. Shakespeare's powers of characterization are so great that we may sometimes feel, like Alexander Pope, that "had all the speeches been printed without the names of the persons, I believe one might have applied them with certainty to every speaker."

Of course, as we have seen, this is not always true, partly because Shakespeare was sometimes concerned not with characterization but with establishing (for example) time or locale and partly because a good many First and Second Gentlemen have no character. Moreover, sometimes part of the point is that the characters are *not* distinct. The lovers in *A Midsummer Night's Dream*, all of whom quite naturally think that their experiences are unique, often sound very much alike, and this similarity—this uniformity of which the lovers are comically unaware—is surely part of Shakespeare's meaning. On the whole, however, Shakespeare's characters do have a roundness, an identity.

What a character is depends on at least two things: what he says and does, and what other characters say about him and what they do. We have already seen how prose and verse reveal character. Relationships between characters also perform this function, as can be seen by an illustration from *Hamlet*. Like Hamlet, Laertes has lost his father. Hamlet has a chance to avenge his father's death when Claudius is praying (III.iii), but he passes it by; Laertes says that if his father's killer were within reach, he would "cut his throat i' th' church" (IV.vii); Hamlet feels "the dread of something after death" (III.i); Laertes says "Conscience and grace to the profoundest pit!/I dare damnation" (IV.v) and so on. Laertes is prone to action—but he is less scrupulous than Hamlet and he easily becomes a cat's-paw for Claudius. As he is dying Laertes confesses, "I am justly killed with mine own treachery." If Hamlet is slow to act, it is at least partly because he is more imaginative than Laertes. What Hamlet *is*, then, is partly clarified by his contrast to Laertes, a young man who is also concerned about avenging his father's death. Fortinbras, another man with whom Hamlet is contrasted, is also fatherless; indeed, his father died at the hands of Hamlet's father. Fortinbras, of course, is not an avenger, but he can fight for a worthless patch of ground, while Hamlet, with an urgent cause, delays. But Fortinbras' very willingness to sacrifice thousands of lives "even for an eggshell" undermines the importance of action. A third character, the stoical Horatio, also helps to define Hamlet. Hamlet admires Horatio's dispassionateness (III.ii); yet this very dispassionateness makes Horatio a lesser figure, a man who presumably even in Hamlet's circumstances would not feel the heroic urge to see that justice is done. In short, what Laertes, Fortinbras, and Horatio are and what they say or do help to define what Hamlet is: he is first of all someone different from them. Of course the remaining characters—most notably Polonius, Gertrude, and especially Claudius, with whom Hamlet in effect is at war—also play a part in defining Hamlet's character.

Similarly, Shakespeare's plots are commonly organized so that scenes modify one another; thus the events, to apply Bottom's words, "grow to a point." For the Elizabethans, the "plot" was the groundplan of a play, a list of scenes posted backstage so that the actors could know when they would next be needed. In this sense, "plot" is to be distinguished from "story," which is simply the gist of the narrative; thus all plays about, say, the death of Julius Caesar tell pretty much the same story, as do the history books. But a plot is the choice and arrangement of episodes. The first scene of Shakespeare's *Julius Caesar*, showing the tribunes rebuking the citizens, is not a necessary part of the story of Caesar's fall, but it is a part of

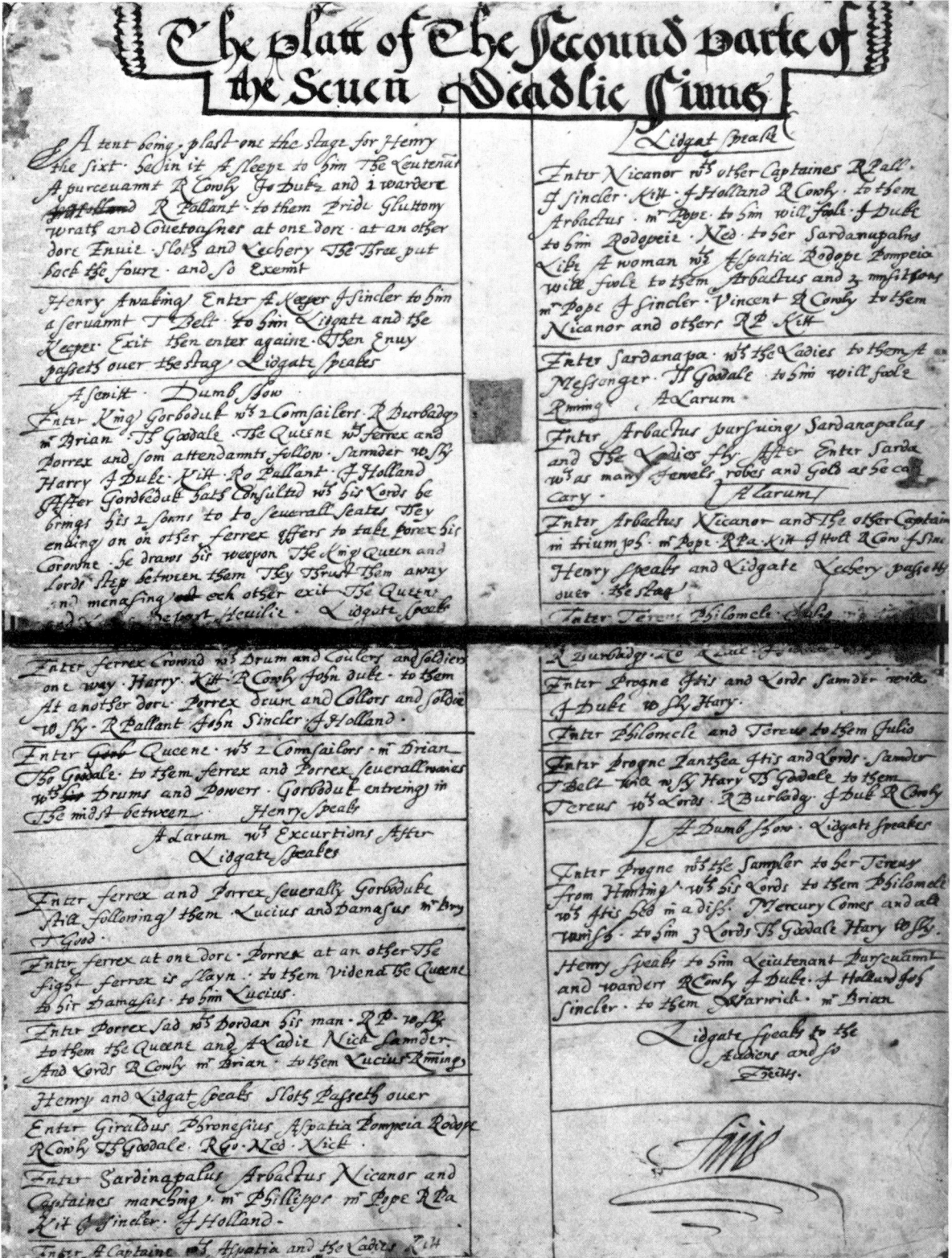

A plot, or "platt," giving a scene-by-scene outline of Richard Tarlton's now lost *Seven Deadly Sins*. The plot served to remind the actors, or the prompter, which actors performed in each scene.

THE PLATT OF THE SECOUND PARTE OF
THE SEUEN DEADLIE SINNS

A tent being plast one the stage for Henry the sixt · he in it A sleepe to him The Leutenat A purceuaunt R Cowly Jo Duke and i wardere [J Holland] R Pallant : to them Pride · Gluttony Wrath and couetousnes at one dore · at an other dore Enuie · Sloth and Lechery · The Three put back the foure · and so Exeunt

Henry Awaking Enter A Keeper J sincler · to him a seruaunt T Belt · to him Lidgate and the Keeper · Exit then enter againe · Then Enuy passeth ouer the stag · Lidgate speakes

A senitt · Dumb show ·
Enter King Gorboduk w^th 2 Counsailers · R Burbadg m^r Brian · Th Goodale · The Queene w^th ferrex and Porrex and som attendaunts follow · saunder w sly Harry J Duke · Kitt · Ro Pallant · J Holland After Gordbeduk hath Consulted w^th his Lords he brings his 2 sonns to to seuerall seates · They enuing on on other ferrex offers to take Porex his Corowne · he draws his weopon The King Queene and Lords step between them They Thrust Them away and menasing [ect] ech other exit · The Queene and L Depart Heuilie · Lidgate speaks

Enter ferrex Crownd w^th Drum and Coulers and soldiers one way · Harry · Kitt · R Cowly John duke · to them At a nother dore · Porrex drum and Collors and soldie W sly · R Pallant · John Sincler · J Holland ·

Enter [Gorb] Queene · w^th 2 Counsailors · m^r Brian Tho Goodale · to them ferrex and Porrex seuerall waies w^th [his] Drums and Powers · Gorboduk entreing in The midst between · Henry speaks

A Larum w^th Excurtions After
Lidgate speakes
Enter ferrex and Porrex seuerally Gorboduke still following them · Lucius and Damasus m^r Bry T Good ·

Enter ferrex at one dore · Porrex at an other The fight ferrex is slayn: to them Videna The Queene to hir Damasus · to him Lucius ·

Enter Porrex sad w^th Dordan his man · R P · w sly : to them the Queene and A Ladie Nick saunder And Lords R Cowly m^r Brian · to them Lucius Runing

Henry and Lidgat speaks    Sloth Passeth ouer

Enter Giraldus Phronesius Aspatia Pompeia Rodope R Cowly Th Goodale · R Go · Ned · Nick · Enter Sardina-palus Arbactus Nicanor and Captaines marching · m^r Phillipps m^r Pope R Pa Kit J sincler · J Holland ·

Enter A Captaine w^th Aspatia and the Ladies Kitt

Lidgate speake

Enter Nicanor w^th other Captaines R Pall · J sincler · Kitt · J Holland R Cowly · to them Arbactus · m^r Pope · to him will foole · J Duke to him Rodopeie · Ned · to her Sardanapalus Like A woman w^th Aspatia Rodope Pompeia will foole to them Arbactus and 3 musitions m^r Pope J sincler · Vincent R Cowly to them Nicanor and others R P · Kitt

Enter sardanapa · w^th the Ladies to them A Messenger · Th Goodale · to him will foole Runing A Larum

Enter Arbactus pursuing Sardanapalus and The Ladies fly · After Enter Sarda w^th as many Jewels robes and Gold as he ca cary ·

A larum

Enter Arbactus Nicanor and The other Captains in t^riumph · m^r Pope · R Pa · Kitt J Hall R Cow · J Sinc

Henry speaks and Lidgate Lechery passeth ouer · the stag

Enter Tereus Philomele · Julio and R Burbadg · Ro R Pall · J si

Enter Progne Jtis and Lords saunder will J Duke w sly Hary ·

Enter Philomele and Tereus to them Julio

Enter Progne Panthea Jtis and Lords · saunder T Belt will w sly Hary Th Goodale to them Tereus w^th Lords · R Burbadg · J Duk R Cowly

A Dumb show · Lidgate speakes

Enter Progne w^th the Sampler to her Tereus from Hunting · w^th his Lords to them Philomele w^th Jtis hed in a dish · Mercury Comes and all Vanish · to him 3 Lords Th Goodale Hary w sly ·

Henry speaks to him Leiutenant Purseuaunt and warders R Cowly J Duke · J Holland John sincler · to them Warwick · m^r Brian

Lidgate speaks to the
Audiens and so
Exitts ·

finis

Shakespeare's plot, for it introduces the motif of the mob's fickleness. Thus the oft-repeated notion that Shakespeare borrowed all his plots is false. He borrowed his stories, and arranged them into his own plots, selecting episodes and linking them into meaningful relationships. For example, like the first scene of *Julius Caesar*, the first scene of *Hamlet* is not essential to the story. Indeed, the talk about a possible war between Denmark and Norway proves to be a red herring, for no such war develops; and the Ghost reappears in Hamlet's presence, so it need not appear now. What function, then, does this scene have in the plot? Quite practically, of course, it gets the audience quiet before the main characters appear. In addition, the talk about the possibility of a war between Denmark and Norway introduces the web of doubt that stretches throughout the play, giving a sense of the difficulty of meaningful action in a world of uncertainty. Finally, the first appearance of the Ghost (I.i) makes us see everything in the following scene with a double vision. We listen to the assembled court, but we listen to it with a knowledge that none of the courtiers has. Thus, for example, we not only sense Hamlet's numbness when he speaks of the "weary, stale, flat, and unprofitable" world; we also know, as he does not, that a spiritual principle is active in it.

In short, each scene adds an increment to the story, but each scene also modifies all that has come before it, developing our understanding of what is happening and our understanding of the characters. As the example from *Hamlet* shows, a scene that appears to be unnecessary may contribute to the point; one is almost tempted to say that in Shakespeare when something seems to be unnecessary and therefore unimportant it must be very important indeed. *Macbeth* provides another example. When Macduff and Malcolm are at the English court (IV.iii), the action seems to stop. But this scene has several important functions: (1) Malcolm's suspicion of Macduff shows the enormous suspicion that Macbeth's tyranny has engendered; (2) Malcolm's dissembling is for a good purpose, in contrast to Macbeth's, which is for a wicked purpose; (3) Malcolm's enumeration of "the king-becoming graces," such as "justice, verity, temp'rance, stableness," tells us what Macbeth lacks; (4) the English king's miraculous healing of the sick suggests that a rightful king has a divine power that makes his country wholesome, whereas Macbeth, a usurper, has brought "disease" to Scotland (V.iii.50–52); (5) the setting in England adds breadth to the play and suggests the infusion of new forces, which are made explicit at the end of the scene, with "the pow'rs above/Put on their instruments."

The interrelationships between stories can also be seen in *A Midsummer Night's Dream*, which is much more complicated in plot than *Macbeth*. There is the story of Theseus and Hippolyta, who will be married in four days; the story of the four young lovers; the story of Bottom and his fellow craftsmen, who are rehearsing a play; and the story of the quarreling fairies. All these stories are related, and eventually come together: the lovers marry on the same day as Theseus and Hippolyta; the craftsmen perform their play at the wedding; the fairies come to witness the wedding and bless it. One of the play's themes, of course, is love, as shown in the contrasts between the stately love of Theseus and Hippolyta, the changeable romantic love of the four young Athenians, the love of Pyramus and Thisby in the play that the craftsmen are rehearsing, the quarrel between the fairy king and queen, and even Titania's infatuation with Bottom. All these stories play against one another, sometimes very subtly, and sometimes explicitly, as when Lysander, having shifted his affection from Hermia to Helena, says, "Reason says you are the worthier maid" (II.ii), and Bottom in the next scene accepts Titania's love, saying, "Reason and love keep little company together nowadays." The nature of reason is also implicitly discussed in the play, in the numerous references to "fantasy" and "fancy," or imagination. There is scarcely a scene that does not touch on the matter of the power of the imagination. In the opening scene, for example, Egeus says that Lysander has corrupted Hermia's fantasy (I.i.32), and Duke Theseus tells Hermia that she must perceive her suitors as her father perceives them. The most famous of these references is Theseus' speech on "the lunatic, the lover, and the poet" (V.i). In addition to setting the time and place, the images help to define the nature of fantasy: there is an emphasis on night and moonlight during the period of confusion, and then references to the "morning lark," "day," and so on, when Theseus (the spokesman for reason) enters the woods and the lovers are properly paired (IV.i.104 ff.). The last scene reintroduces night, and the lovers have moved from the dark wood back to the civilized world of Athens, and the night will bring them to bed. The plot of *A Midsummer Night's Dream*, then, juxtaposes speech against speech, image against image, and scene against scene, telling not simply a story but a story that "grows to something of great constancy, . . . strange and admirable."

# A Note on Shakespeare's English

## PRONUNCIATION, ACCENTS, PUNS

From the philologist's point of view at least, Shakespeare's English is Modern English. It requires footnotes, but the inexperienced reader can often comprehend a substantial passage with very little help; on the other hand, for the same reader Middle English is a foreign language.

By the beginning of the fifteenth century the chief grammatical changes in English had taken place, and the final unaccented *-e* of Middle English had been lost (though it survives even today in spelling, as in *name*); during the fifteenth century the dialect of London, the commercial and political center, gradually displaced the provincial dialects, at least in writing; by the end of the century, printing helped to regularize and stabilize the language, especially spelling. Elizabethan spelling may seem erratic to us (there were dozens of spellings of *Shakespeare*, and a simple word like *been* was also spelled *beene* or *bin*), but it had much in common with our own spelling. Elizabethan spelling was conservative in that for the most part it reflected an older pronunciation (Middle English) rather than the sound of the language as it was then spoken, just as our spelling continues to reflect medieval pronunciation —most obviously in the now-silent letters in a word such as *knight*. Elizabethan pronunciation was closer to ours than to that of the Middle Ages, but it was not identical with ours.

There are two instances in which an awareness of the difference between our pronunciation and Shakespeare's is crucial: in accent, or number of syllables (many metrically regular lines may look irregular to us), and in puns (which may not look like puns to us). Explanations of puns and of syllabification are given in the glosses to the plays, but examples of both may be useful here. Some words that were at least on occasion stressed differently from today are *aspéct*, *cómplete*, *revénue*, and *sepúlcher*. Words that had an additional syllable are *emp[e]ress*, *mon[e]th*, and *villain*; words that had one less syllable than now are *needle* (pronounced "neel") and *violet*. An example of a pun that has become obliterated by a change in pronunciation is Falstaff's reply to Prince Hal's "Come, tell us your reason" in *1 Henry IV*: "Give you a reason on compulsion? If reasons were as plentiful as blackberries, I would give no man a reason upon compulsion, I" (II.iv. 239–42). The *ea* in *reason* was pronounced rather like a long *a*, like the *ai* in *raisin*; hence the comparison with blackberries.

Puns, of course, are not merely attempts to be funny; like metaphors, they often involve bringing into a meaningful relationship areas of experience normally seen as remote. In *2 Henry IV*, III.ii.239–40, when Feeble is conscripted, he stoically says, "I care not. A man can die but once. We owe God a death," punning on *debt*, which was the way *death* was pronounced. Here an enormously significant fact of life is put into simple commercial imagery, suggesting its commonplace quality. Shakespeare used the same pun earlier in *1 Henry IV*, V.i.126, when Prince Hal says to Falstaff, "Why, thou owest God a death," and Falstaff wittily replies, "'Tis not due yet: I would be loath to pay him before his day. What need I be so forward with him that calls not on me?" Sometimes the puns reveal a delightful playfulness; sometimes they reveal aggressiveness, as when Hamlet replies to Claudius' "But now, my cousin Hamlet, and my son" with "A little more than kin, and less than kind!" (I.ii.65). These are Hamlet's first words in the play, and we already hear him warring against Claudius. Hamlet's "less than kind" probably means (1) Hamlet is not of Claudius' family or nature; (2) Hamlet is not kindly (affectionately) disposed toward Claudius; (3) Claudius is not naturally (but rather unnaturally, incestuously) Hamlet's father. The puns, evidently, were not put in as sops to the groundlings; they are an important part of Shakespeare's way of writing.

## VOCABULARY

A chief difficulty in reading Shakespeare is the fact that some of his words are no longer in common use—for example, words concerned with armor, astrology, clothing, coinage, hawking, horsemanship, law, medicine, sailing, and war. (This technical vocabulary is also glossed in the plays.) Shakespeare had an immense vocabulary—something like 17,000 words—but it was not so much a vocabulary of "big" or learnèd words as a vocabulary drawn from a wide range of life, and it is partly his ability to call upon a great body of concrete language that gives his plays the sense of being in close contact with life.

Less overtly troublesome than the technical words but more treacherous are the words that seem readily intelligible to us but whose Elizabethan meanings are not identical with their modern meanings. When Horatio describes the Ghost as an "erring spirit," he is saying not that the ghost has sinned or made an error but that it is wandering. Here is a short list of some of the most common words in Shakespeare's plays which often (but not always) have a meaning other than their most usual modern meaning:

'*a* he; *an, and* if; *accident* occurrence; *advertise* inform; *brave* fine, splendid; *censure* opinion; *cheer* (1) face (2) frame of mind; *chorus* a single person who comments on the events; *closet* small private room; *competitor* partner; *conceit* idea, imagination; *cousin* kinsman; *disaster* evil astrological influence; *doom* judgment; *entertain* receive into service; *envy* malice; *event* outcome; *excrement* outgrowth (of hair); *fact* evil deed; *fancy* (1) love (2) imagination; *fell* cruel; *fellow* (1) companion (2) low person (often an insulting term if addressed to someone of approximately equal rank); *fond* foolish; *free* (1) innocent (2) liberal, generous; *hap, haply* chance, by chance; *head* army; *humor* (1) mood (2) bodily fluid (see p. 31); *intelligence* news; *kind* natural, acting according to nature; *let* hinder; *lewd* base; *mere(ly)* utter(ly); *modern* commonplace; *natural* a fool or an idiot; *naughty* (1) wicked (2) worthless; *next* nearest; *nice* (1) trivial (2) fussy; *noise* music; *presently* immediately; *prevent* anticipate; *prove* test; *quick* alive; *sad* serious; *secure* without care, incautious; *silly* innocent; *sensible* capable of being perceived by the senses; *shrewd* sharp; *so* provided that; *starve* die; *still* always; *success* that which follows; *tall* brave; *tell* count; *tonight* last night; *wanton* playful, careless; *watch* keep awake; *will* lust; *wink* close both eyes; *wit* mind, intelligence.

All glosses, of course, are mere approximations; sometimes one of Shakespeare's words may hover between an older meaning and a modern one, and as has been seen, his words often have multiple meanings.

## ELLIPSIS, TRANSFERRED EPITHETS, HENDIADYS

Ellipsis, or the omission of words that are assumed to be understood, also causes difficulty occasionally, but most often it does not, as in "And he to England shall along with you," where "go" is understood. When read aloud an elliptical line often becomes clear. Other sources of slight difficulty are transferred epithets, as in "idle bed" for "bed of idleness," where "idle" is transferred from the person to the bed, and hendiadys, or the use of two nouns joined by a conjunction instead of a noun and a modifier, as in "with every gale and vary" for "with every varying gale" and "this . . . gentleness and course" for "this . . . gentle course."

## GRAMMAR

A few matters of grammar may be surveyed, though it should be noted at the outset that because Shakespeare was a poet he sometimes made up his own grammar. As E. A. Abbott says in *A Shakespearian Grammar*, almost any part of speech can be used as any other part of speech: a noun as a verb ("He childed as I fathered"); a verb as a noun ("She hath made compare"); or an adverb as an adjective ("a seldom pleasure"). There are hundreds, perhaps thousands, of such instances in Shakespeare's plays, many of which at first glance would not seem at all irregular and would trouble only a pedant. But here are a few broad matters. The Elizabethans thought that the -*s* genitive ending for *nouns* (as in *man's*) derived from *his*; thus the line "'Gainst the count his galleys I did some service" for "the count's galleys." By Shakespeare's time *adjectives* had lost the endings that once indicated gender, number, and case. About the only difference between Shakespeare's adjectives and ours is the use of the now-redundant *more* or *most* with the comparative or superlative: "This was the most unkindest cut of all." The greatest change was in *pronouns*. In Middle English the singular forms *thou*, *thy*, and *thee* were used among familiars and in speaking to children and inferiors; the plural forms *ye*, *your*, and *you* were used in speaking to a superior or to an equal with whom one was not familiar. Increasingly the "polite" forms were used in all direct address, regardless of rank, and the accusative *you* displaced the nominative *ye*. Shakespeare sometimes uses *ye* instead of *you*, but even in Shakespeare's day *ye* was archaic, and it occurs mostly in rhetorical appeals. *Thou*, *thy*, and *thee* were not completely displaced, however, and Shakespeare occasionally makes significant use of them, sometimes to connote familiarity or intimacy and sometimes to connote contempt. In *Twelfth Night* Sir Toby advises Sir Andrew to insult Cesario by addressing him as *thou*: "If thou thou'st him some thrice, it shall not be amiss" (III.ii.44). In *Othello* when Brabantio is addressing an unidentified voice in the dark he says, "What are you?" (I.i.91), but when the voice identifies itself as the foolish suitor Roderigo, Brabantio uses the contemptuous form, saying in line 93, "I have charged thee not to haunt about my doors." He uses this form for a while, but later in the scene, when he comes to regard Roderigo as an ally, he shifts again to the polite *you*, beginning in line 163: "What said she to you?" and so on to the end of the scene. Perhaps the most unusual use of pronouns, from our point of view, is the neuter singular. *His* was often used in place of our *its*, as in "How far that little candle throws *his* beams." But the use of a masculine pronoun for a neuter noun came to seem unnatural, and so *it* was used for the possessive as well as the nominative: "The hedge-sparrow fed the cuckoo so long/That it had it head bit off by it young." (In the late sixteenth century the possessive form *its* apparently developed by analogy with the -*s* ending used to indicate a genitive noun, as in *book's*. But *its* was not yet common usage in Shakespeare's day. It has been said that Shakespeare uses *its* only ten times, mostly in his later plays.) Other usages, such as "You have seen Cassio and she together" or the substitution of *who* for *whom*, cause no difficulty even when noticed. *Verbs* too cause almost no difficulty: the third person singular present form commonly ends in -*s*, as in Modern English, but sometimes it ends in -*eth* (Portia explains to Shylock that mercy "blesseth him that gives and him that takes"). Broadly speaking, -*eth* was old-fashioned or "literary" rather than colloquial, except for the words *doth*, *hath*, and *saith*. The -*eth* ending is very rare in Shakespeare's dramatic prose, though not surprisingly it occurs twice in the rather formal prose summary of the narrative poem *Lucrece*. Sometimes a plural subject, especially if it has collective force, takes a verb ending in -*s*, as in "My old bones aches." Some of our strong or irregular preterites (such as *broke*) have a different form in Shakespeare (*brake*); some verbs that now have a weak or regular preterite (such as *helped*) in Shakespeare have a strong or irregular preterite (*holp*). Some *adverbs* that today end in -*ly* were not inflected: "grievous sick," "wondrous strange." Finally, *prepositions* often are not the ones we expect: "We are such stuff as dreams are made on"; "I have a king here to my flatterer."

Again, none of these differences (except meanings that have substantially changed or been lost) causes much difficulty. But it must be confessed that for some elliptical passages there is no widespread agreement on meaning. The editors of the Signet Shakespeare have tried to resist saying more than they know, and when they are uncertain they have added a question mark to their gloss, inviting the reader to think of a better interpretation.

# A Note on the Intellectual Background

In *A Treatise on Money* John Maynard Keynes discusses the inflation that continued throughout Shakespeare's lifetime and gave to all but the poorest Elizabethans a sense of "buoyancy" and "exhilaration." Keynes suggests that England was "just in a financial situation to afford Shakespeare at the moment he presented himself." Like all types of historical studies, economic studies of the Renaissance have their own value and interest, but one may question whether they shed much light on Shakespeare. That Shakespeare is of the Renaissance is undisputed, but that a study of the economic, political, or religious background of the Renaissance greatly illuminates Shakespeare is arguable. A good example is the matter of the discovery of the New World and the subsequent voyages which brought great wealth to England. Although *The Tempest* is derived in part from some writings on Bermuda, the play itself is set on an island in the Mediterranean, and its real roots are in the comic traditions of Roman drama, not in contemporary pamphlets. In *Twelfth Night* a casual reference is made to "the new map with the augmentation of the Indies," and that is about it. The shipwrecks in *The Comedy of Errors, Twelfth Night,* and other plays owe more to the late Greek romances and to Roman comedies than to Elizabethan exploration. Similarly it is dangerous to relate Shakespeare closely to the religious conflicts of his age. The Puritans are spoofed in a few plays, chiefly in Falstaff's parodies of them (for example, *1 Henry IV,* I.ii.83 ff.), and the Jesuit infiltrators are briefly noted in a comic speech in *Macbeth* (II.iii.8 ff.). But we would scarcely know from Shakespeare's works how tense the religious situation actually was in his time. After the Act of Supremacy of 1534, which made the monarch the supreme head of the Church of England, the fear of Catholicism was so great that merely to harbor a priest was held to be an act of high treason; in Shakespeare's plays, however, Italy, the home of popery, is on the whole attractively presented, and a fair number of plays have benevolent friars. (People who do not understand that literature and life are not identical have tried to reconcile the apparent paradox by arguing that Shakespeare may have been a Roman Catholic.)

The attempts to relate Shakespeare closely to his age have caused difficulty on both sides. On the one hand, the allegedly typical ideas of the age, usually gathered from sermons, books on household management, and so on, are sometimes brought forth to interpret the plays, on the assumption that they help us to understand Shakespeare's attitude toward, say, Moors or Jews. But such a procedure fails to account for the possibility that Shakespeare's ideas were not commonplace. In addition, it fails to recognize that a play is not a sermon or a book on household management but an imaginative work that draws on literary conventions as well as on personal vision; that is, a play is designed to afford pleasure rather than to record facts or to move to action. Of course, an historical sense can shed some light on Shakespeare's age and can assist us in reading the plays intelligently, but our familiarity with Elizabethan treatises must ultimately be subordinated to our experience of literature as literature.

On the other hand, the plays have often been taken too seriously as historical documents. Juliet is fourteen years old, and so books on the Elizabethan period sometimes tell us that "girls often married at fourteen," but in fact Elizabethan marriage records lend almost no support to such a statement. There are some instances of betrothals between infants, but Elizabethan child marriages apparently were very rare.

Still, a few large ideas of the period do recur—with a good many modifications—in Shakespeare's works. One of these is the idea of order or degree. According to this view, everything except God has a superior. Beneath God the hierarchy is as follows: angelic creatures (pure intelligence), man (intelligence and "sense," or instinct, or feeling), animals (sense), plants (growth but no sense), inorganic matter (mere existence), and finally chaos. Within a given rank there are subhierarchies: just as God is the highest spiritual being, so the sun is the chief planet, the king is the chief human being, man is the superior of woman, the lion is the king of beasts, gold is the best metal. This idea of a hierarchical cosmos is older than Christianity, of course, but Christianity gave it additional support by sanctioning the idea of order: for example, Paul in Romans 13:1 said, "Let every soul be subject to

the higher power," and in 13:7, "Render therefore to all their dues: tribute to whom tribute is due; custom to whom custom; fear to whom fear; honor to whom honor." On a more humble level, the English rules of succession, by which even a distant cousin could succeed to a title, helped to give a sense of an enduring aristocracy.

It is evident that Elizabethan authorities were obsessed with inculcating the idea of order: sermons on the topic were officially prepared and appointed to be read in the churches, where attendance was supposed to be compulsory. Some of these sermons were very beautiful, tracing God's creation of order in the natural world ("The water above is kept and raineth down in due time and season"), in man ("Soul, heart, mind, memory, understanding, reason, speech, with all singular corporal members of his body [are] in a profitable, necessary, and pleasant order"), and in society ("Some are in high degree, some in low, . . . fathers and children, husbands and wives, rich and poor, every one have need of other, so that in all things is to be lauded and praised the goodly order of God"). When catechized, an Englishman affirmed his duty "to submit myself to all my governors, teachers, spiritual pastors and masters." Among Shakespeare's speeches on order are Luciana in *The Comedy of Errors* (II.i.16–25), Kate in *The Taming of the Shrew* (V.ii.148–81), the Gardener (III.iv.29–66) and Carlisle (IV.i.115–38) in *Richard II,* Canterbury in *Henry V* (I.ii.183–204), Ulysses in *Troilus and Cressida* (I.iii.78–136), and Menenius in *Coriolanus* (I.i.97–156). These speeches of course exist in dramatic contexts: a character preaches the doctrine of order because it suits his purpose at the moment, not necessarily because Shakespeare wished to propagandize for the status quo. Still, the idea of order appears so often in the plays that it is reasonable to say that it was much in Shakespeare's mind.

It is not really surprising that Shakespeare's plays include a good number of speeches on order. Drama is concerned with conflict, with the disruption of order—whether by tragic heroes, villains, ambitious politicians, or young people who fall in love—and its ultimate restoration. It is thus quite natural that the subject is discussed, as when the Duke of York urges Richard II not to confiscate Gaunt's estate but to let it descend in orderly fashion to Gaunt's son and heir, Harry Hereford:

Seek you to seize and gripe into your hands
The royalties and rights of banished Hereford?
Is not Gaunt dead? and doth not Hereford live?
Was not Gaunt just? and is not Harry true?
Did not the one deserve to have an heir?
Is not his heir a well-deserving son?
Take Hereford's rights away, and take from Time
His charters and his customary rights,
Let not tomorrow then ensue today;
Be not thyself. For how art thou a king
But by fair sequence and succession? (II.i.189–99)

Richard persists, and indeed disorder overcomes him. Hereford returns to claim his inheritance, and ultimately he forces Richard to abdicate the throne. But in the abdication scene the Bishop of Carlisle points out that Hereford's action too will engender consequences:

My Lord of Hereford here, whom you call king,
Is a foul traitor to proud Hereford's king;
And if you crown him, let me prophesy
The blood of English shall manure the ground,
And future ages groan for this foul act;
Peace shall go sleep with Turks and infidels,
And, in this seat of peace, tumultuous wars
Shall kin with kin, and kind with kind, confound;
Disorder, horror, fear, and mutiny
Shall here inhabit, and this land be called
The field of Golgotha and dead men's skulls.
O, if you raise this house against this house,
It will the woefullest division prove
That ever fell upon this cursèd earth!
Prevent it, resist it, let it not be so,
Lest child, child's children, cry against you woe.

(IV.i.134–49)

It is important to note, however, that conventional ideas of order are not always validated in the plays. Richard II is at times confident that the heavens will come to his aid because he is a divinely anointed king, and that such is the nature of things, but he is mistaken. Egeus in *A Midsummer Night's Dream* feels that he has the right to expect his daughter Hermia to submit to his choice of husband for her, and Duke Theseus supports Egeus. (Did not the Elizabethan catechism require a man to promise to "honor . . . my father . . . [and] to submit myself to all governors"?) Students of the Elizabethan background find support for this view from Robert Cleaver, who in *A Goodly Form of Household Governance* (1598) said that god-fearing children, having "considered what honor and obedience they do owe unto their parents and what power and authority He hath in His word sanctified unto them over their children," should "willingly submit themselves unto their [parents'] choice." But in the world of romantic comedy our sympathies are with young lovers, and the conventional idea of order here can only lead us astray if we insist that Hermia is morally culpable. To judge Hermia in *A Midsummer Night's Dream* or Jessica in *The Merchant of Venice* by Cleaver's doctrine is to value his treatise above the play, and to read the play as a treatise.

But though Duke Theseus' argument that Hermia must learn to see things as her father sees them is ultimately rejected by the play, the notion of authority and order in other forms has its truth. In large part a man's identity depends upon others: his ties to others make him what he is. A husband is not the same man that he was before he incurred the obligations and privileges of being a husband. So much is obvious. In the Renaissance, however, and in Shakespeare's plays, the idea had greater weight than we are likely to give it today. Every subject owed his allegiance to the monarch, who was also the supreme head of the Church of England, officially above statutory law, and by divine sanction the maker of law. The monarch demanded obedience; the subject confessed that obedience was his duty, and in large measure he derived his identity from this relationship. When the rebellious Essex heard the sentence of death pronounced upon him—hanging, castration, drawing, and quartering—he said that it was fitting that his "poor quarters, which have done Her Majesty true service in diverse parts of the world, should now at the last be sacrificed and disposed of at Her Majesty's

pleasure." (Essex was given a more dignified death, on the block, when he confessed his faults and died in "humility and obedience.") Along these lines too is the oft-told story of John Stubbs, who had published a book arguing against the advisability of a marriage between Queen Elizabeth and the Duke of Anjou. For his impertinent opinions Stubbs had his right hand chopped off by a cleaver struck with a mallet. William Camden, who witnessed the punishment, reports that "after his right hand was cut off, [Stubbs] put off his hat with his left; and said with a loud voice, 'God save the Queen.'" Such was the power of identifying the self with the monarch and with the principle of order. Shakespeare makes almost no use of Queen Elizabeth in connection with this idea, except at the end of *Henry VIII*, where it is suggested that the birth of Elizabeth will bestow good on everyone around her, but over and over he suggests that a man's identity depends on a figure of authority. For example, in *Henry V* the three traitors confess their crimes to the king and seem immensely relieved to identify themselves with the system that condemns them to death. In *Antony and Cleopatra* after

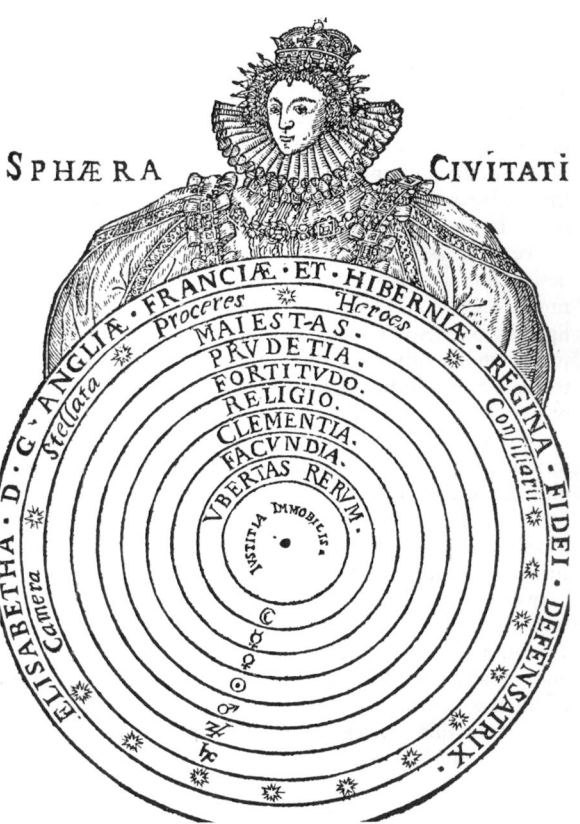

*Woodcut from John Case's* Sphaera civitatis *(1588), showing Queen Elizabeth governing the spheres of state by divine right. This image of a well-ordered state is derived from pre-Copernican astronomy, in which a vast sphere, the* primum mobile, *held a series of concentric rotating crystalline spheres, in each of which was embedded a heavenly body. The* primum mobile *imparted motion to these heavens; in the center was the earth, unmoving.*

Enobarbus deserts Antony and finds to his dismay that he no longer has any reason for living, he dies. Macbeth finds that by killing his king he had made life a horror. In the comedies, lovers gladly give themselves to their beloved, finding an identity in this new relationship by losing themselves. The idea, again, is not particularly Elizabethan, but it is perhaps more often expressed in Elizabethan than in later thought.

One particularly Elizabethan idea about man's nature—or rather, an ancient idea that lasted into the Elizabethan period but has not survived—is the doctrine of the four humors, or bodily fluids whose combination was believed to regulate a man's temperament (Latin *temperamentum* = mixture). There were four of these bodily fluids: blood, choler, phlegm, and melancholy. The Elizabethans believed that sudden changes in the mixture of fluids made a man moody, or "humorous," like Duke Frederick in *As You Like It* (I.ii.262). A person with an abundance of blood had a sanguine disposition (Latin *sanguis* = blood) and a ruddy complexion and was probably plump and cheerful. A person with an abundance of choler, or yellow bile, was choleric or bilious (irritable) and probably tall and lean. Abundant phlegm, or mucus, found in fat people, made a man phlegmatic or sluggish. Melancholy, or black bile, found in lean people, made a man introverted and gloomy. Shakespeare often alludes to this system of psychology, as, for example, when Hamlet speaks of "some complexion/Oft breaking down the pales and forts of reason" (I.iv). Similarly, Hamlet and Guildenstern discuss the king's condition in these terms after Hamlet has caught Claudius' conscience with the play-within-the-play:

GUILDENSTERN  The king, sir—
HAMLET  Ay, sir, what of him?

GUILDENSTERN  Is in his retirement marvelous distemp'red.
HAMLET  With drink, sir?
GUILDENSTERN  No, my lord, with choler.
HAMLET  Your wisdom should show itself more richer to signify this to the doctor, for for me to put him to his purgation would perhaps plunge him into more choler.
(III.ii.303–12)

The glosses to the plays provide all necessary explanations of such matters, as well as explanations of the astrological influences that were also thought to govern personality. (It is worth mentioning too that skepticism concerning astrological influences is most often voiced in the plays by cynics or villains, such as Cassius in *Julius Caesar*, Iago in *Othello*, and Edmund in *King Lear*.) Shakespeare drew upon this body of ideas, but we do not turn to Shakespeare for medical learning, or even for the medical learning of his age. We turn to him for something larger: in Ben Jonson's words, "He was not of an age, but for all time," and in Samuel Johnson's words, his plays are works

. . . exhibiting the real state of sublunary nature, which partakes of good and evil, joy and sorrow, mingled with endless variety of proportion and innumerable modes of combination; and expressing the course of the world, in which the loss of one is the gain of another; in which, at the same time, the reveller is hasting to his wine, and the mourner burying his friend; in which the malignity of one is sometimes defeated by the frolic of another; and many mischiefs and many benefits are done and hindered without design.

# Shakespeare's Comedies

### THE BACKGROUND

The First Folio edition of Shakespeare's plays prints fourteen works under the heading "Comedies"; to these we can add *Cymbeline*, printed with the tragedies, and two plays absent from the Folio, *Pericles* and *The Two Noble Kinsmen*. Some editors add an eighteenth play, *Troilus and Cressida* (here discussed with the tragedies), printed in the Folio in unnamed territory between the histories and the tragedies.

If we look at Shakespearean comedy as a whole (and overlook a good deal) we see that generally speaking it is a comedy of young lovers who encounter difficulties but who are ultimately united; the plays follow the Renaissance formula for comedy, according to which, in the words of Shakespeare's fellow playwright Thomas Heywood, "comedies begin in trouble and end in peace." Thus, in the first act of *A Midsummer Night's Dream*, Egeus appears:

Full of vexation come I, with complaint
Against my child, my daughter Hermia.   (I.i.22–23)

Egeus wants Hermia to marry Demetrius, but she is in love with Lysander, and so Egeus calls upon the law, which holds that she must follow her father's will or suffer either death or life in a cloister. The play ends with Hermia marrying her beloved Lysander, Demetrius marrying a girl who dotes upon him, and a few other happy bits. In the words of Puck, who quotes "the country proverb":

Jack shall have Jill;
Nought shall go ill;
The man shall have his mare again, and all shall be well.
(III.ii.461–63)

Similarly, at the start of *The Merchant of Venice* Antonio is mysteriously troubled, Bassanio is in financial difficulties, and Portia is unpleasantly confined by the terms of her father's will. At the end of the play all these problems are solved. The heroines of the comedies are liberated, and the plays regularly end with marriage:

> Wedding is great Juno's crown,
>   O blessed bond of board and bed!
> 'Tis Hymen peoples every town;
>   High wedlock then be honorèd.
> Honor, high honor, and renown
> To Hymen, god of every town!
>
> (*As You Like It*, V.iv.141–46)

As Northrop Frye has pointed out, Shakespeare often contrasts two worlds, not merely a world of age against a world of youth but an urban, troubled world against a more pastoral world, which Frye calls "the green world." In this world characters undergo a renewal and find what they are seeking: *A Midsummer Night's Dream* begins in Athens, the place of the quarrel between Egeus and his daughter, then moves into the moonlit forest, where wonderful transformations occur, and finally returns to Athens, which is no longer a place "full of vexation" but a "blessed" place full of "jollity." In *The Merchant of Venice* too there is a contrast (not in all details, but a contrast nevertheless) between Venice, the home of the unpleasant Shylock, and Belmont, Portia's estate, a place of music, beauty, and wooing. Like the woods outside Athens, Belmont is sometimes said to be moonlit. In *The Merchant of Venice* there is no final return to the urban world; but in those plays where there is such a return, the urban world seems to be transformed by the infusion from the green world. Corresponding to the renewal of society is the renewal of the individual; the individual usually finds what he wants and in doing so sometimes finds that he is freed from a misapprehension or constricting view. Thus at the end of *The Taming of the Shrew* Katherine discovers that she does not really wish to dominate men; at the end of *As You Like It* Duke Frederick and Oliver, finding that they do not wish to tyrannize good men, reform.

Broadly speaking, Shakespeare's comedies are romantic: they tell of the trials and the ultimate successes in love of aristocratic young people. Behind them are earlier Renaissance plays of courtship, adventure, wandering, and reunion, and behind these in turn is the medieval idea of the power of love to conquer and transform. In 1582 Stephen Gosson, a hostile critic of drama, irritably characterized the romantic plays of his age: "Sometime you shall see nothing but the adventures of an amorous knight, passing from country to country for the love of his lady, encountering many a terrible monster of brown paper. . . . What learn you by that? When the soul of your plays is either mere trifles, or Italian bawdry, or wooing of gentlewomen, what are we taught?" In *A Midsummer Night's Dream* Shakespeare himself affectionately alludes to the taste that wanted "the adventures of an amorous knight" when Francis Flute, a bellows mender, wonders if his part in the amateur theatrical will be "a wand'ring knight."

If we divide comedy into two sorts, romantic comedy (showing a dreamlike world of delightful lovers) and satiric comedy (showing a world of people who behave as we ought not to behave), Shakespeare's comedies, despite some satire of romance, belong to the former group. Even Prince Hamlet, when he hears that the players have arrived at Elsinore, thinks of the romantic type of play:

He that plays the king shall be welcome; his majesty shall have tribute of me; the adventurous knight shall use his foil and target [shield]; the lover shall not sign gratis; the humorous [eccentric] man shall end his part in peace; the clown shall make those laugh whose lungs are tickle o' th' sere [on hair trigger]; and the lady shall say her mind freely. (II.ii.327–33)

By Shakespeare's time, romantic plots—at least when handled by the better dramatists—were no longer the mere episodic adventures they had been in the seventies: daring fights against monsters of brown paper had been eliminated, but wooing continued, and the spirit of fun, surprise, and adventure remained. Shakespeare's slightly later contemporary, Ben Jonson, who preferred satiric comedy, compared romantic to satiric comedy in *Every Man Out of His Humor*. Jonson's first speaker prefers romantic comedy and rejects comedy that is "near and familiarly allied to the time," but the second speaker puts him in his place, rejecting the stuff of the popular stage and citing an ancient authority:

MITIS   The argument of his comedy might have been of some other nature, as of a duke to be in love with a countess, and that countess to be in love with the duke's son, and the son to love the lady's waiting-maid: some such cross-wooing, with a clown to their serving man, better than to be thus near and familiarly allied to the time.

CORDATUS   You say well, but I would fain hear one of these autumn-judgments define once, *Quid sit comoedia* [what is comedy]? If he cannot, let him content himself with Cicero's definition (till he have strength to propose to himself a better) who would have a comedy to be *Imitatio vitae, speculum consuetudinis, imago veritatis* [an imitation of life, a mirror of customs, the image of truth]; a thing throughout pleasant and ridiculous, and accommodated to the correction of manners.

Jonson is one with Gosson here, in the assumption that comedy teaches. His hostile description of what seemed to him a pointless chain of lovers is almost a description of Shakespeare's *Twelfth Night*, in which Orsino is in love with Olivia, Olivia is in love with Cesario (really Viola disguised as a boy), and Cesario-Viola is in love with Orsino. (There is no serving man who is a clown, but there is a clown.) Of course, within the romance there is occasional satire—satire not only of crabby impediments to love but even of love itself; yet curiously we do not think the less of the lovers for seeing their faults. When the heroine of *As You Like It*, Rosalind, disguised as a boy, learns that her beloved Orlando is nearby, she says:

Alas the day! What shall I do with my doublet and hose? What did he when thou saw'st him? What said he? How looked he? Wherein went he? What makes he here? Did he ask for me? Where remains he? How parted he with thee? And when shalt thou see him again? Answer me in one word. (III.ii.220–25)

But if we laugh *at* her, we also laugh *with* her, delighting in her wit, her gaiety, and her resourcefulness, all of which (clearly in evidence in other parts of the play when she herself mocks at love) suggest a golden world in contrast to the brazen world of satiric comedy.

When Rosalind leaves the court for the Forest of Arden, she goes to a place where "merry men . . . live like the old Robin Hood of England. They say many young gentlemen . . . fleet the time carelessly as they did in the golden world." The evocation of Robin Hood, the emphasis upon a joyous ("care-less") existence, and the reference to a golden world (Northrop Frye's "green world") suggest a life of play and a spirit of fun. Indeed, something of a holiday spirit is suggested by the very names of some of the comedies: *A Midsummer Night's Dream, Much Ado About Nothing, As You Like It,* and *Twelfth Night, or What You Will.* The festive spirit is present everywhere, even in moments of strain. When Rosalind says, "How full of briers is this working-day world," Celia replies, "They are but burrs, cousin, thrown upon thee in holiday foolery." Festivity is of course especially evident at the end of a comedy, when all has been set right, and it sometimes extends even to the spoilsport who represents a threat to happiness in the earlier parts of the play. At the end of *The Merry Wives of Windsor,* for example, Sir John Falstaff, who has been humiliated by the two women he had sought to seduce, is invited to join in the fun, and even the jealous husband Ford agrees:

> let us every one go home,
> And laugh this sport o'er by a country fire;
> Sir John and all.
>
> FORD          Let it be so.          (V.v.240–42)

Like the characters in the play, the members of the audience richly enjoy themselves and return, vivified, from the world of "holiday foolery" to the "working-day world." In its spirit, Shakespearean comedy is thus close to the medieval folk plays performed at holiday time that concluded with a sense of renewal (see p. 12).

If Shakespearean comedy is indebted for much of its spirit to festive rites, it is indebted for some of its shape to the Roman comedy of Plautus (254?–184 B.C.) and Terence (190?–159? B.C.), which itself was indebted to the New Comedy of Greece. Old Comedy, represented by Aristophanes, though phallic and ending in a *komos,* or celebration of sexual union, is primarily satirical and political. New Comedy, represented by Menander (343?–291? B.C.) is of the boy-meets-girl sort, though it is not romantic by our standards because it deals more with sex and seduction than with love. In this type of comedy a young man wants a girl—often a slave girl—and with the aid of a clever slave outwits the pander who owns her and who sometimes plans to sell her to someone less attractive than the hero. In *The Taming of the Shrew* Grumio sums it up: "See, to beguile the old folks, how the young folks lay their heads together." Terence especially was much studied in Elizabethan schools, and he gave the Elizabethan dramatists—often at second or third hand—a sense of how to organize a plot. The late medieval cycle plays, which spanned time from the Creation through the Fall to the Last Judgment, established an episodic tradition, and this tradition, along with the medieval chivalric romances that

were the sources of much romantic drama, makes most of the plays before the 1580's seem shapeless. But as the sixteenth century wore on, the professional drama became better established and came under the influence of men with considerable secular education. Had they had their way, some of these men would have turned the drama into lifeless imitations of ancient drama, and we can rejoice that the academic influence was never very great. But Roman and Italian plots helped to show dramatists how a plot might be organized. Theoreticians studying Terence developed the idea that a play has a five-act structure: in the first act there is a situation with tensions; in the second the conflict that is implicit in the first is developed; in the third the conflict is open, reaches a height, and seems to arrive at an impasse; in the fourth act things begin to clear up, and in the fifth act all knots are untied. Few if any of the English popular playwrights felt obliged to follow this formula, but the best playwrights probably did think in terms of an overall plot rather than a series of episodes. There is little that is obviously Plautine or Terentian about Shakespeare's best comedies, but this is not to say that he learned nothing from these Roman playwrights. It is quite evident from *The Comedy of Errors,* which may have been Shakespeare's first play, that he learned a good deal, though he was later to transform what he learned into something quite his own.

### THE THREE EARLIEST COMEDIES: THE COMEDY OF ERRORS, THE TAMING OF THE SHREW, THE TWO GENTLEMEN OF VERONA

It seems likely enough that Shakespeare began his career as a playwright—perhaps even before he went to London—by writing a play that closely resembles the Latin dramas that he would have read and perhaps acted in while in grammar school. *The Comedy of Errors,* though certainly more than an adaptation of Plautus, remains greatly indebted to Plautus' *Menaechmi,* a play about twins separated for most of their lives who after several episodes of mistaken identity at last meet and are reunited. Although the setting is bourgeois (an unusual setting for Shakespeare), there are elements in the play that foreshadow the later comedies. For example, the meter varies to suit the characters and the mood: about half the play is written in end-stopped blank verse (not surprising for a beginner); in addition there are prose, doggerel for the low comedy, and a few rhymed stanzaic passages, notably a lyrical (un-Plautine) passage in which Antipholus of Syracuse woos Luciana:

> Sweet mistress, what your name is else, I know not;
> Nor by what wonder you do hit of mine;
> Less in your knowledge and your grace you show not
> Than our earth's wonder, more than earth divine.
> Teach me, dear creature, how to think and speak:
> Lay open to my earthy-gross conceit,
> Smoth'red in errors, feeble, shallow, weak,
> The folded meaning of your words' deceit.
> Against my soul's pure truth why labor you
> To make it wander in an unknown field?
> Are you a god? Would you create me new?
> Transform me, then, and to your pow'r I'll yield.
>
>                                        (III.ii.29–40)

The notion that a woman is godlike and can transform a man is nothing that Plautus or any Roman comic dramatist would have thought of. Indeed, Luciana is Shakespeare's addition to Plautus' plot, an addition that enabled Shakespeare to end his play not merely with a family reunion but with the promise of a wedding.

Another important addition to Plautus is found in the first and last scenes concerning Egeon, the father of the twins. In *The Menaechmi* the father is dead; and when fathers do appear in classical comedy, it is to be outwitted, or at least to be laughed at. Drawing on the pseudo-Greek romance *Apollonius of Tyre*, which he was to use again late in his career in *Pericles*, Shakespeare began the play with a serious treatment of a despairing father sentenced to death, and concluded with the restoration of the father to his wife and children. The unanticipated appearance of the wife, who during the long separation has been an abbess, adds a hint of the miraculous or providential that is so evident in the later comedies, where it is often associated with rebirth or renewal. The motif of renewal is prepared for early in the play, when Antipholus of Syracuse says that as a lonely wanderer searching for his brother and mother he has lost his identity:

> I to the world am like a drop of water
> That in the ocean seeks another drop,
> Who, falling there to find his fellow forth,
> Unseen, inquisitive, confounds [loses] himself.
> So I, to find a mother and a brother,
> In quest of them, unhappy, lose myself.    (I.ii.35–40)

The abundant subsequent references to witchcraft, which was believed to rob a man of his identity, continue the idea. In the fifth act the members of the family find each other and renew themselves, gaining a new life and a new sense of identity; this renewal is heightened for Antipholus of Syracuse, who is not only reunited with his family but also finds a woman who will become his wife. The sense of new identity appears also (as in Plautus) in the freeing of the slave, Dromio of Ephesus. (At the end of his career Shakespeare again uses this classical convention in *The Tempest* when Prospero frees Ariel.)

If there are great differences between *The Menaechmi* and Shakespeare's play, then, there are also numerous similarities. But even the similarities are with a difference. Dr. Pinch, for example, is derived from the stock classical character of the *medicus*, but he is thoroughly Elizabethan: "a mountebank, a threadbare juggler and a fortuneteller." It is characteristic of Shakespeare to make his borrowings his own, and if some of his plays have such stock figures as the *senex*, or old father—Egeus in *A Midsummer Night's Dream* or Shylock in *The Merchant of Venice*—the *adulescens*, or young lover, the *servus*, or servant, and so on, the characters are nevertheless transformed almost beyond recognition.

Finally, there is a pervasive difference in moral tone between the two plays. Shakespeare's play has bawdry, but the moral tone is notably higher than that of *The Menaechmi*. For example, Antipholus of Ephesus visits the Courtesan only after his wife bars him from his home, and Antipholus of Syracuse offers to pay for the gold chain that the Merchant gives to him. In short, although *The Comedy of Errors* is in obvious ways close to its source, it is indisputably a very different play from its source, and with hindsight we can see in it some of the directions that Shakespeare was to take in later and greater plays.

There is a good deal of uncertainty about whether Shakespeare's *The Taming of the Shrew* is based on an earlier comedy, but it is clear that the chief plot of the play—"the taming of the shrew"—is derived ultimately from a widespread bit of folklore. To this Shakespeare added the story of Bianca and her suitors, derived from Italian Renaissance comedy, with its intriguing servant (here Tranio), its outwitted old men, and its trio of suitors. The setting is bourgeois, as in only two of Shakespeare's other comedies, *The Comedy of Errors* and *The Merry Wives of Windsor*; Petruchio sees marriage chiefly as an economic institution ("I come to wive it wealthily in Padua"), and although we may at first think that the Lucentio-Bianca plot is more romantic (the two young people fall in love at first sight), the play is not yet the sort of romantic comedy which Shakespeare was to write at the turn of the century in *The Merchant of Venice, Much Ado About Nothing, As You Like It*, and *Twelfth Night*. But this is not to say *The Taming of the Shrew* is a failure because it is not romantic; one of its chief delights is the fact that the romantic marriage of Bianca and Lucentio at the end dwindles into bickering, while the marriage of Petruchio and Katherine turns out to be (at least in sixteenth-century terms) mutually satisfactory. There is, after all, much to be said for—and much to delight in—the realistic view uttered by Petruchio's servant: "Winter tames man, woman, and beast; for it hath tamed my old master, and my new mistress, and myself." Seen thus, the taming of the shrew is not brutality but a schooling in humanity. Although Petruchio tames Katherine by humiliating her, in one important motif the play looks forward to the later comedies: he tames her by pretending that she is not shrewish but "pleasant, gamesome, passing courteous." Indeed, such is the power of the lover's imagination that the beloved is subsequently freed from the "mad and headstrong" tantrums that possess her and is transformed into Petruchio's image. She is, one can say, cured of her crippling, self-indulgent personality. Early in the play (II.i), during the course of her schooling, Katherine becomes sufficiently sensitized to protest against Petruchio's treatment of the Tailor and the Haberdasher, and finally she becomes an ideal wife. Having shaken off a constricting personality, she at last assumes her proper role in society. This theme of a change in personality, the formation of a new identity—already treated in *The Comedy of Errors*—has a comic parallel in the Induction, where Christopher Sly, a drunken tinker, is persuaded when he awakens from his stupor that he is a lord who for fifteen years has been mentally ill. Sly even changes his language for a while from prose to blank verse. This part of the play ends inconclusively with a few lines between I.i. and I.ii in which Sly continues to play the lord. His transformation cannot have the permanence of Katherine's, since romantic comedy shows moral rather than social or economic change. Perhaps there was originally an Epilogue, now lost, in which Sly resumes his workaday character (in *A Midsummer Night's Dream* Bottom is similarly transformed and "translated" back again without difficulty).

*The Two Gentlemen of Verona* approaches what was to become Shakespeare's characteristic comedy: the heart of the plot, derived from a chivalric and pastoral tale, is the story of courtly lovers who, in a romantic environment, engage in what has been called an obstacle race to the altar. The relationship between love and friendship is explored, and although the lovers are not yet very interesting, the appearance of a heroine disguised as a boy suggests the world of the romantic comedies, which (in words from *Twelfth Night*) "give a very echo to the seat/Where love is throned." Of particular interest is the spoofing of love, which in the later comedies (and in *Romeo and Juliet*) helps to define love:

VALENTINE Why, how know you that I am in love?
SPEED Marry, by these special marks: first, you have
learned, like Sir Proteus, to wreathe your arms, like a
malcontent; to relish a love song, like a robin redbreast;
to walk alone, like one that had the pestilence; to sigh,
like a schoolboy that had lost his ABC; to weep, like a
young wench that had buried her grandam. . . . When
you fasted, it was presently [immediately] after dinner;
when you looked sadly, it was for want of money. And
now you are metamorphized with a mistress, that, when
I look on you, I can hardly think you my master.
(II.i.18–33)

After listening to a conversation between Valentine and Silvia, Speed comments: "Though the chameleon love can feed on the air, I am one that am nourished by my victuals, and would fain have meat." To help show both the folly of love and the difference between courtly love and clownish love, there is a clown in love. Thinking of his beloved's virtues, the clown Launce says, "She can fetch and carry. Why, a horse can do no more: nay, a horse cannot fetch, but only carry; therefore is she better than a jade" (III.i.274–76).

Moreover, although there is an evident delight in wordplay, especially in the puns of the clownish servants, speech in *Two Gentlemen* is more closely related to character than in the earlier comedies. There are very few ornate set pieces that are almost detachable from the speakers—though we are grateful for the exquisite song "Who Is Silvia" and for Launce's comic monologue on his dog's indifference (II.iii), both of which indeed are virtually independent bits. The play also includes a host of motifs and devices that appear in later plays: a woman disguises herself as a boy, a man mistakenly trusts a false companion, the heroine and her lady-in-waiting discuss suitors (compare I.ii with *The Merchant of Venice*, I.ii), a lover is anatomized (compare II.i.19–33 with *As You Like It*, III.ii. 371–81), and characters gather in a forest or wood and are converted, thus forming a better society at the end. This last point has been touched on earlier (see p. 32), but it is worth repeating that at the heart of some of Shakespeare's comedies is a "green world" where people reach a clarification and form a regenerated society. This regenerated society is presumed to be stable, unlike the capricious, whimsical, and sometimes arbitrary and tyrannical society at the outset of the play, when lovers are inconstant or thwarted. In *The Two Gentlemen of Verona* the fickle Proteus, rightly characterized by his best friend as a "treacherous man," is presumably converted to constancy, and the play ends with "one feast, one house, one mutual happiness."

## THE ACHIEVEMENT OF POETIC COMEDY: LOVE'S LABOR'S LOST

The date of *Love's Labor's Lost* is uncertain, and it is entirely possible that the only existing text is a revision, possibly as late as 1597, of a play that Shakespeare wrote as early as 1588. In its present form the play has a splendid poetry of a sort not found in Shakespeare's earlier plays; probably the writing of his two long narrative poems, *Venus and Adonis* (1593) and *The Rape of Lucrece* (1594), and of some sonnets greatly assisted his development as a poet. There are type-characters—Berowne speaks of "the pedant, the braggart, the hedge-priest, the fool, and the boy"—and Holofernes the pedant especially is infatuated with words and with the "odoriferous flowers of fancy." But Shakespeare vitalizes the type-characters of the *commedia dell' arte* and he masters the "taffeta phrases, silken terms precise," and the "golden cadence," giving us so fine a dramatic speech as this:

KING
Let fame, that all hunt after in their lives,
Live regist'red upon our brazen tombs
And then grace us in the disgrace of death,
When, spite of cormorant devouring Time,
Th' endeavor of this present breath may buy
That honor which shall bate his scythe's keen edge
And make us heirs of all eternity.
Therefore, brave conquerors—for so you are
That war against your own affections
And the huge army of the world's desires—
Our late edict shall strongly stand in force:
Navarre shall be the wonder of the world;
Our court shall be a little academe,
Still and contemplative in living art.
You three, Berowne, Dumaine, and Longaville,
Have sworn for three years' term to live with me,
My fellow scholars, and to keep those statutes
That are recorded in this schedule here.
Your oaths are passed; and now subscribe your names,
That his own hand may strike his honor down
That violates the smallest branch herein.
If you are armed to do as sworn to do,
Subscribe to your deep oaths, and keep it too. (I.i.1–23)

One might call attention to this speech as an expression of the Renaissance awareness of the tragic brevity of life, and of the Renaissance habit of trying to win glory by a great achievement so that at least one's reputation will survive devouring Time. But the point to be made here is that the earlier Elizabethan stage had rarely heard such excellent dramatic poetry. No less excellent is the prose. A few minutes after the courtiers sign a bond to study for three years and not "to see a woman in that term," the clown Costard is brought in by Constable Dull for having been caught with a wench. Costard explains: "It is the manner of a man to speak to a woman. . . . Such is the simplicity of man to hearken after the flesh." Thus the king's fine speech is clownishly put into its proper perspective. Costard can be generous as well as exact. Later in the play he comes to the defense of Nathaniel, who like a good Elizabethan has performed in an amateur theatrical to entertain his betters but has not been able to sustain his role of Alexander in the show of the Nine Worthies:

> There, an't shall please you, a foolish mild man; an honest man, look you, and soon dashed. He is a marvelous good neighbor, faith, and a very good bowler; but for Alisander —alas! you see how 'tis—a little o'erparted. (V.ii.576–80)

One can regret the abundance of topical allusions in the play—more properly, one can regret that the allusions are now baffling—and perhaps the wit occasionally overwhelms the action, but the play is certainly not without action in the sense of a motive or theme, for it dramatizes the infirmity of idealism. Berowne early perceives the limits of idealism, remarking that "every man with his affects [passions] is born,/Not by might mastered, but by special grace," and the truth of his perception becomes apparent, as we have seen, when Constable Dull brings in Costard. In mocking the high-minded courtiers who make war against "their own affections/And the huge army of the world's desires," Shakespeare comes near to writing a satirical play, but there is something so noble in the courtiers' aspiration and something so delightful (and beautiful) in their absurdity that we do not view them with contempt. Satire diminishes the object of its attack; as Ezra Pound has said in *Literary Essays*, "Satire reminds one that certain things are not worthwhile. It draws one to consider time wasted." But in *Love's Labor's Lost* although we laugh at the courtiers, first for their efforts to forswear women and then for their efforts to win women, we also gain a glimpse of a world of delightful and high-minded rather than worthless people. We are pleased that when they finally are reconciled to the fact that "it is the manner of a man to speak to a woman" they are not crushed by their enlightenment; indeed, if we value life, we can scarcely regret that their idealism is displaced by a recognition of man's physical nature. Costard, after all, is on the side of life, as the courtiers come to see. But at the end of the play —and this is most unusual in Shakespeare's comedies—the young men are not allowed to marry the women they court. Berowne complains, "Our wooing doth not end like an old play;/Jack hath not Jill," and remarkably the last words are not about union or reunion but about separation: "You that way, we this way." The later comedies conclude more harmoniously, with the journey ending in lovers meeting, but these comedies also sometimes include a touch of melancholy or disharmony. For example, Jaques in *As You Like It* and Malvolio in *Twelfth Night* stand apart from the happiness that dominates the final scenes, complicating the vision of the play. In *Love's Labor's Lost*, the happiness that the courtiers project in their dream of an academe is dispelled, and later the happiness that they project in their roles as lovers is also dispelled by the announcement that the princess' father has died. The weddings must be postponed for a year, during which time the men must do penance. But the ending is not merely melancholy, for the implications are that the recognition of the reality of death and the performance of a year of penance will lead to marriages that are based on the fullest possible awareness of the facts of life.

## THE EARLY FESTIVE COMEDIES: A MIDSUMMER NIGHT'S DREAM, THE MERCHANT OF VENICE

With *A Midsummer Night's Dream* (written about 1594–96) Shakespeare indisputably established himself as a great writer of romantic comedy. The confusions in *The Comedy of Errors* are amusing, and they are not totally devoid of implications concerning the complexities of life and man's blindness, but the implications are sporadic, and the play is content to amuse. *A Midsummer Night's Dream*, no less amusing, goes further and deeper by adding to the story of lovers' mistaken identities the actions of the royal classical lovers, Theseus and Hippolyta; the fairy lovers of folklore, Oberon and Titania; and the lovers in the craftsmen's play, Pyramus and Thisby. This rich collaboration makes *A Midsummer Night's Dream* an unexcelled comedy, a finely plotted and beautifully lyrical exploration of the nature of love, the nature of imagination ("fantasy"), the nature of reality or truth, almost, in short, the nature of life.

Much of the play is derived from books: the story of Theseus and Hippolyta is taken from Chaucer's *The Knight's Tale*, perhaps reinforced with some details from Plutarch's *Lives*; Puck (or Robin Goodfellow) probably owes something to Reginald Scot's *Discovery of Witchcraft* as well as to old wives' tales that Shakespeare may have heard as a child in Stratford; Ovid's story of Pyramus and Thisby was studied in Elizabethan grammar schools; and the ass-headed Bottom probably owes something to an Elizabethan translation of Lucius Apuleius' *The Golden Ass*. But the play does not smell of the lamp. Rather, it appears as effortless and as richly suggestive as a dream, and no less complex, beautiful, profound, or mysterious; and not least important, it is much more funny. *A Midsummer Night's Dream* was probably written at about the same time as *Romeo and Juliet*. There are some resemblances between the two plays, most obviously in Lysander's speech ending with "quick bright things come to confusion" (I.i.141–49), which parallels abundant images in *Romeo and Juliet* of beauty quickly yielding to darkness (especially II.ii.119–20), and in the play-within-the-play concerning Pyramus and Thisby, who are in effect an ancient Romeo and Juliet. Aldous Huxley has complained that tragedy, in portraying only the single-minded, heroic strain in man, does not tell "the whole truth." No work of art tells the whole truth, of course, and it is unreasonable to judge a tragedy by such a standard. But one understands Huxley's comment: fine though *Romeo and Juliet* is, it seems a more mechanical, thinner, and less substantial exploration of life than *A Midsummer Night's Dream*.

Theseus feels that the lovers' story is "more strange than true," and at the end of the play Puck suggests that the audience can dismiss the entire play easily:

> If we shadows have offended,
> Think but this, and all is mended:
> That you have but slumb'red here,
> While these visions did appear.
> And this weak and idle theme,
> No more yielding but a dream. (V.i.422–27)

But the dreams in the play are perceptions of reality: Hermia dreams (II.ii) that Lysander does not come to her aid while a serpent eats her heart, and when she awakens she finds that Lysander is gone, his love now fastened on another woman. Bottom dreams that he is an ass. Thus it may be an error to dismiss this dreamlike play and fail to see that the comedy is a profound treatment of love as a force, sometimes creative, sometimes destructive, sometimes wonderful, and sometimes laughable, but powerful and transfiguring.

In *The Merchant of Venice* (probably written in 1596) Shakespeare broadens his presentation of human personality. Shylock and Portia, the opposed proponents of legalism and mercy, are much more fully realized characters than those in *A Midsummer Night's Dream*. But Bassanio, the male lover, is still not of very great interest. It is worth noting that Shakespeare's comic heroes are usually less witty and less resourceful, and therefore less interesting, than his heroines.

For many readers and spectators, Shylock is too interesting a character: the comic villain becomes a sympathetic and almost tragic figure, the wronged Jew towers above the petty Venetians. But such an interpretation is perhaps a misreading of the play, for it places too much weight on a few speeches in which the Venetians taunt Shylock and on other speeches in which Shylock quite rightly insists on his sufferings. The most famous instance of the latter is in III.i, when Shylock asks,

Hath not a Jew eyes? Hath not a Jew hands, organs, dimensions, senses, affections, passions?—fed with the same food, hurt with the same weapons, subject to the same diseases, healed by the same means, warmed and cooled by the same winter and summer as a Christian is? If you prick us, do we not bleed? If you tickle us, do we not laugh? If you poison us, do we not die? And if you wrong us, shall we not revenge? (III.i.56–64)

One cannot easily dismiss this powerful speech by saying that it is only a justification for revenge, not a plea for tolerance. But to argue that Shylock's speech is what *The Merchant of Venice* is about is to turn away from much of the rest of the play; it is to overlook, for example, Portia's no less wonderful speech about mercy (IV.i.183–204), in which she points out that no one's deeds are so just that he does not require mercy, and to overlook the superb unconscious irony of Shylock's reply to that speech, "My deeds upon my head! I crave the law." Law is in fact what he gets, and only mercy saves him from the death penalty that the law imposes. What the play as a whole dramatizes is not the problem of a minority group suffering at the hands of a hostile society but the conflict of two ways of life, one concerned with hoarding (Shylock's "Fast bind, fast find,/A proverb never stale in thrifty mind"), the other with generous giving (Antonio's "My purse, my person,/My extremest means/Lie all unlocked to your occasions," and Portia's "What is mine, to you and yours/Is now converted"). Almost every element in the play is arranged to set forth some such fundamental opposition, but again the characters are not pale abstractions, and Shylock is no straw man. Shakespeare gives him powerful utterances and lets us see him fully, from the inside, as in the long speech quoted above. Probably no earlier character in Shakespeare so fully evokes from the hearer the response, "I understand exactly how that man feels." But the play is not about Shylock; rather, Shylock is an important character

in a play about the triumph of generosity (love is a kind of giving), which transforms society into something more than a group of men who buy and sell and lend. The final scene is rich in intimations of a spiritually renewed society: "Let me give light," "riveted with faith unto your flesh," "my soul upon the forfeit," "you drop manna." In short, a new day is dawning ("it is almost morning")—which is not to say that sex and bawdry do not have their place, but only that this play about very human people is also a play with a great theme.

## A BOURGEOIS COMEDY: THE MERRY WIVES OF WINDSOR

The date of *The Merry Wives of Windsor* is uncertain, but as the editor's Introduction to the play suggests, a good case can be made for the spring of 1597. If that date is right, Shakespeare interrupted his work on the cycle of history plays concerning the reigns of Richard II, Henry IV, and Henry V to write a comedy centering on Falstaff, who appears in an earlier play, *1 Henry IV*. According to legend, Shakespeare wrote the comedy in two weeks in response to Queen Elizabeth's desire to see Falstaff in love. The legend gains some support from the fact that the play is not in the romantic-comic vein that Shakespeare had been working in, perhaps because it was written quickly. In the play a character named Falstaff—who only sporadically has the wit of the Falstaff of *1 Henry IV*—attempts to seduce two married women and is ignominiously defeated. Possibly Shakespeare refurbished an old play, but if he did so, readers have not forgiven him for raising their expectations by calling one of the characters Falstaff and then failing to deliver the real Falstaff. (As Dr. Johnson said, "Falstaff could not love, but by ceasing to be Falstaff.") There is a romantic plot involving a young man named Fenton, who is said to "speak holiday" and "smell April and May," but romance has only a small role in the play, which has strong affinities with Roman and Italian comedy: a braggart is humiliated, and a young man and a girl outwit the girl's parents and marry.

Whatever the source, Shakespeare's handling of the plot is uncertain: for example, at the start Falstaff's old crew, Bardolph, Pistol, and Nym, appear; but after the first act they do nothing; the first scene introduces the idea of a quarrel between Falstaff and Justice Shallow, but nothing comes of it. Curiously this play, which seems so thin, is effective on the stage, and it is of special interest to those readers who see beneath the surface to the pattern of the ritual expulsion of Misrule or Riot, for Falstaff, an embodiment of Misrule, is dumped into the river and later is pinched and singed with candles by people disguised as fairies. The locale is contemporary Windsor, but there seem to be echoes of ancient rites of purification, such as survived in the Saint George plays (see p. 12).

## THE LATER FESTIVE COMEDIES: MUCH ADO ABOUT NOTHING, AS YOU LIKE IT, TWELFTH NIGHT

Near the turn of the century—just after he had finished his second tetralogy of history plays and was nearing the great tragedies—Shakespeare wrote three comedies that for many readers and spectators are the essence of Shakespearean romantic comedy: *Much Ado About Nothing* (1598–1600), *As You Like It* (1599–1600), and *Twelfth Night* (1600–02). These plays, like *The Merchant of Venice* and to a lesser degree *A Midsummer Night's Dream* and *The Two Gentlemen of Verona*, are plays of courtship. The assumption behind them is that despite momentary absurdities and pains, love liberates, enriches, and fulfills the lovers. But each play is unique, and it is perhaps best not to insist too loudly on their resemblances.

The main plot of *Much Ado About Nothing* concerns the love of Claudio and Hero, the interruption of that love (caused by the malicious Don John, a descendant of the medieval Vice), and the restoration and completion of their love in marriage, when Hero is cleared from slander and reunited with Claudio. To this pair of lovers Shakespeare adds another, Beatrice and Benedick. They begin as witty foes, are deceived into thinking that each is loved by the other, and then find that they do indeed love each other. Thus in this parallel plot (it cannot be called a subplot because it is no less important than the plot of Claudio and Hero), lovers undergo a conversion, and the somewhat self-righteous society of the early part of the play is disabused of its illusions, thereby acquiring a new life. For example, at the start Beatrice is characterized thus:

> But Nature never framed a woman's heart
> Of prouder stuff than that of Beatrice.
> Disdain and Scorn ride sparkling in her eyes,
> Misprizing what they look on; and her wit
> Values itself so highly that to her
> All matter else seems weak. She cannot love,
> Nor take no shape nor project of affection,
> She is so self-endeared. (III.i.49–56)

Both Beatrice and Benedick are liberated from this bondage to the self, just as Claudio is liberated from his mistaken view of Hero and from his subsequent grief for Hero's supposed death. The prelude to this renewal is announced in verse, a medium that the earlier parts of the play are not rich in:

> Good morrow, masters; put your torches out.
> The wolves have preyed, and look, the gentle day,
> Before the wheels of Phoebus, round about
> Dapples the drowsy east with spots of gray. (V.iii.24–27)

Appropriately enough, the play ends with the marriage of Claudio and Hero, the promise of a marriage between Benedick and Beatrice, and finally a dance giving visual representation to the transformed and now harmonious society. Thoughts of the villainous Don John, now a prisoner, are not allowed to intrude seriously upon the new-found joy: "Think not on him till tomorrow. I'll devise thee brave punishments for him. Strike up, pipers!" The play ends with music and dancing: "All . . . sounds of woe," to quote from a song in Act II, have been converted into "hey nonny, nonny."

Finally, a point should be made concerning Dogberry and his fellows, the delightfully ignorant watchmen who through a series of blunders apprehend the malefactors. The actions of Dogberry and his fellows are one variant of the theme—recurrent in the comedies—that mistaken

beliefs or errors have fortunate consequences. Benedick and Beatrice are deceived, and the outcome is good; Claudio is deceived, and the outcome is good (presumably his love for Hero at the end is greater because he has learned that his earlier mistrust was totally without foundation). Dogberry's errors too have a happy result; moreover, his sublime self-confidence is a comic imitation of the less amiable self-confidence of others in Messina. This is not to say that we value him only because he plays an important role in the plot and because he contributes to the theme. A richly comic figure, he affords us delight, and we would value him for this even if he were irrelevant. In one of his bumbling speeches he comes closest to stating the theme of this comedy in which events happily conspire to give people more than they deserve. The play shows us a world of people, as Dogberry says, "condemned into everlasting redemption."

Like *A Midsummer Night's Dream* and *The Merchant of Venice, As You Like It* presents two worlds. *A Midsummer Night's Dream* moves from Athens, with its harsh law and its harsh father, to the moonlit woods outside of Athens, where lovers are transformed into their better selves; *The Merchant of Venice* moves from the commercial world of Venice to the moonlit world of Portia's Belmont. In *As You Like It* the movement is from the court of the usurper, Duke Frederick, to the Forest of Arden, where lovers find what they seek and where the wicked are converted. Charles the wrestler puts it quite clearly:

> There's no news at the court, sir, but the old news. That is, the old duke is banished by his younger brother the new duke, and three or four loving lords have put themselves into voluntary exile with him, whose lands and revenues enrich the new duke. . . . They say [the old duke] is already in the Forest of Arden, and a many merry men with him; and there they live like the old Robin Hood of England. They say many young gentlemen flock to him every day, and fleet the time carelessly as they did in the golden world. (I.i.97–101, 112–17)

The play is full of "holiday foolery," but the foolery is not devoid of meaning, for it embodies an enduring vision of love and of the triumph of the gifts of nature over those of fortune. Various kinds of lovers are juxtaposed: the romantic young lovers, Rosalind and Orlando and Celia and the reformed Oliver; the prettified artificial pastoral figures, hard-hearted Phebe and her mooning Silvius, who thinks no man has ever loved as he loves; the low pastoral figures, old Corin, who has forgotten the ridiculous actions that love moved him to in his youth, and the young bumpkins William and Audrey; and finally the clown Touchstone, who remembers that when he was in love he kissed "the cow's dugs that her pretty chopt [chapped] hands had milked." Love is wonderfully displayed in the "strange capers" of these figures, and it is treasured even when it is mocked—as when Rosalind realistically warns Phebe against scorning Silvius' offers, saying, "Sell when you can, you are not for all markets" or when Rosalind, concealing her love for Orlando, offers to cure him of the madness of loving Rosalind, and he replies, "I would not be cured." Nor, of course, would Rosalind or the audience want him cured. The love poems that Orlando writes are wretched (Touchstone drily offers to produce such rhymes "eight years together, dinners and suppers and sleeping hours excepted"), yet we would not have Orlando's rhymes improved; we value them for their delightful ineptitude. Rosalind herself is delightfully mocked, as in this bit of dialogue in which Celia (Aliena) prosaically reminds us that people in love can be very boring:

ROSALIND  I'll tell thee, Aliena, I cannot be out of the sight of Orlando. I'll go find a shadow, and sigh till he come.
CELIA  And I'll sleep.                                (IV.i.213–16)

In short everything in the play, including the folly, is in Celia's words "O wonderful, wonderful, and most wonderful wonderful, and yet again wonderful." Not least wonderful are the improbable conversions of Oliver and the wicked Duke Frederick; again we are grateful for these improbabilities because we would not deny to anyone the possibility of finding joy by shedding self-centeredness. These two men come late to self-knowledge and its concomitant generosity of spirit, but better late than never. The play ends with "a wedlock hymn" and other strong hints of a transfigured world. Thus the return of the exiles to the court is not a bit of cynicism discrediting their experience in the forest; rather, it brings the vitality and harmony of the forest into the court, which earlier in the play is a place of tyranny.

It is no derogation of *Twelfth Night* (probably written about 1600) to say that in it Shakespeare again uses several motifs from his earlier plays. Like *The Comedy of Errors*, it involves twins—this time a brother and sister—who have been separated by a shipwreck and who are now (unknown to each other) in the same city. As in *The Two Gentlemen of Verona*, there is a girl disguised as a boy who serves the man she loves as a page, even to the extent of courting on his behalf a woman whom he woos. Like Benedick and Beatrice, who in *Much Ado About Nothing* are tricked into thinking that they love each other, Malvolio is tricked into thinking that Olivia loves him. Other similarities include a resourceful young woman (here Viola, in *The Merchant of Venice* Portia, in *As You Like It* Rosalind); deep affection between friends (here Antonio and Sebastian, in *The Merchant of Venice* Antonio and Bassanio); a fool (here Feste, in *As You Like It* Touchstone); and a somewhat Falstaffian character, Sir Toby Belch. And in its festive spirit—for example, in its songs and mistaken identities—the play reminds us of episodes in *A Midsummer Night's Dream*, *The Merchant of Venice*, and *As You Like It*. But despite such similarities, there are important differences. For example, in *The Comedy of Errors* the mistakes which cause bewilderment are largely physical—that is, they are literal cases of mistaken identity caused by the presence of twins; but in *Twelfth Night* there are more profound mistakes as well in the failure of some of the characters to understand *themselves*. Thus Malvolio not only misunderstands Olivia; he misunderstands his own nature and his role in society. Similarly, in pining for Olivia Orsino does not see the egoism in his love, and so, for example, the love song that he calls for (II.iv) is really a song of self-love in which the lover calls attention to his pathetic fidelity. At the end of the play Orsino is freed from the torments of his own desires, which at the start pursue him "like fell and cruel hounds." Olivia, too, grieving for her dead

brother, finds that she has mistaken the depth of her grief, and she is liberated from her own "eye-offending brine." Thus despite the shipwreck and despite the trick played on Malvolio, much of the trouble is not external but is rooted in self-deception. Against egoism and self-deception —neatly summed up in Olivia's words to Malvolio, "O, you are sick of self-love"—is a liberating generosity, not only in small details, as when Antonio freely gives money to Sebastian (III.iii), but notably in Viola, who gives herself to Orsino's effort to woo Olivia even though Viola herself "would be his wife."

In *Twelfth Night*, then, although Shakespeare uses earlier plots and characters, he is saying new things, especially about the development of insight. One small index is provided by the clown Feste, who, though by profession resembling Touchstone in *As You Like It*, is very different from Touchstone in his wit and actions. Touchstone, however cynically, joins in the procession to the altar, but Feste remains unwed, and after the unregenerated Malvolio leaves and the lovers depart, Feste is left alone on the stage to sing the Epilogue, with its melancholy refrain, "For the rain it raineth every day." In *As You Like It* the melancholy Jaques stands apart from the comic resolution, but he too looks forward to a new life, perhaps to be gained through conversation with the regenerated Duke Frederick. But in *Twelfth Night* Feste—whose name suggests that he is the very incarnation of festivity—stands apart, calling attention to the hardships of life. He does not thereby deflate the romantic vision, but he does complicate it.

## THE DARK COMEDIES: ALL'S WELL THAT ENDS WELL, MEASURE FOR MEASURE

Two comedies, *All's Well That Ends Well* (1602–04?) and *Measure for Measure* (1604), are often called "dark comedies" or "problem plays." When the latter term is used, *Hamlet* (1600–01) and *Troilus and Cressida* (1601–02) are sometimes included as well. The term *problem play*, first used in the late nineteenth century to characterize some of Ibsen's work, denotes a play that examines a social problem rather than an unchanging fact of life, such as death. Thus it has been argued that *Measure for Measure* is about such problems as: Can a judge condemn a criminal for a crime that the judge himself is guilty of? May a person sin to save a life? But clearly *All's Well* and *Measure for Measure* are not primarily debates on such problems; if they are, they contain enormous amounts of irrelevant material.

The term *dark comedies*, then, is perhaps more useful: *All's Well* and *Measure for Measure* do not have the festive spirit that dominates *A Midsummer Night's Dream*, *The Merchant of Venice*, *Much Ado*, *As You Like It*, and *Twelfth Night*, and that is plentiful in some of the other comedies. Put most briefly, the lovers simply do not show as much delight as the lovers in the earlier comedies, where a spirit of playfulness abounds. *All's Well* has some close resemblances to the great romantic comedies—a resourceful heroine, disguise, coincidences, and finally a reunion between young people—but there is little of the joy of love in it. The play has the conventions but not the spirit of comedy. The nominal hero is not a young man in love;

the closest he comes to being a suitor is when he resorts to bribery in an effort to seduce a woman.

The plots of both *All's Well* and *Measure for Measure* include actions that critics, especially those in the late nineteenth century, have found unpleasant. In both plays, for example, a man thinks he is seducing a woman but is tricked into sleeping with another woman whom he has rejected. The heroines in each play have struck some readers as unamiable, the nominal heroes as detestable. (In *Troilus and Cressida* too there is a faithless woman who by virtue of her faithlessness diminishes not only herself but her lover.) Here is Dr. Johnson on the hero of *All's Well*:

I cannot reconcile my heart to Bertram; a man noble without generosity, and young without truth; who marries Helen as a coward, and leaves her as a profligate: when she is dead by his unkindness, sneaks home to a second marriage, is accused by a woman whom he has wronged, defends himself by falsehood, and is dismissed to happiness.

In both plays there is clowning, but for some readers there is too much joking about syphilis, too much comic cowardice, too much disillusionment, and too much unpleasant behavior that reveals not merely folly but vice. *As You Like It* has a usurping duke and a wicked elder brother, but we see little of them and they reform; during most of the play we are diverted by the lovers in the Forest of Arden. *Twelfth Night* has a shipwreck and the unregenerated Malvolio, but the shipwreck takes place off stage with no real harm done, and Malvolio is funny rather than criminally vicious. Of the earlier comedies, perhaps *Much Ado* comes closest to—though it is still far away from—*All's Well* and *Measure for Measure*. In *Much Ado* Don John is villainous, the hero Claudio is churlish, the witty lovers Benedick and Beatrice are on the whole satiric rather than romantic, and the setting is never varied by an excursion into a green world. But in *Much Ado* there is the sublimely bumbling Constable Dogberry, who by his ineptitude saves the situation. As one of the villains says to the wiser folk in *Much Ado*, "What your wisdoms could not discover, these shallow fools have brought to light." But in the two dark comedies evil is fended off only by vigorous effort. In *As You Like It* the characters do little more than disport themselves in the woods until the two wicked characters repent, and in *Twelfth Night* Viola relies on time to solve the problem: "O time, thou must untangle this, not I;/It is too hard a knot for me t' untie." But in *All's Well* the heroine (like a good counselor in a morality play) must energetically pursue her wayward husband, saving him from fornication by a trick in which she interposes her own body, and in *Measure for Measure* the good duke must keep bustling if the lecherous Angelo is not to have his way. Time, of course, has a role in these plays too, but in both plays the central characters must energetically make use of it, rather than, as in *Twelfth Night*, await it.

That the plays have less festivity or playfulness, and that they have potent sources of evil, is indisputable. On the other hand, if we are repelled by the "bed trick," and if we resent the fact that Bertram is "dismissed to happiness," perhaps we are deficient in a sense of playfulness. That these comedies are not festive comedies is perhaps no more significant than that they are not tragedies or histories: they are what they are, and we can be thankful for them. Nor should we characterize the plays as cynical: *All's Well* especially has honorable characters who not only utter noble sentiments but who act virtuously and effectively; *Measure for Measure* is ultimately based on the generous view that evil intentions, if unacted and repented of, do not deserve punishment, and the play concludes with contrition and forgiveness.

Finally, a point about the origin of these dark comedies should be made: readers have tended to date them near to each other (though *All's Well* often has the abundant rhyme of the earlier plays) and have assumed that around 1600 Shakespeare became pessimistic, perhaps because a mistress was unfaithful or because Essex' revolt was abortive. But Shakespeare's plays need not reflect his mental ups and downs. Rather, some elements in the plays may represent a literary fad, perhaps stimulated by Ben Jonson, whose satiric comedies regularly scourge folly: in *All's Well* Bertram and Parolles are revealed as fools; in *Measure for Measure* the ascetic Angelo betrays his ideals and is exposed. (*Troilus and Cressida* too is a thoroughly ironic play: the heroine is false, her noble lover is gulled, and Thersites and Pandarus are at least as gross as the world they comment on.) Yet even the dark comedies finally are charitable: no one is everlastingly cast out, Bertram and Angelo (like Mankind in a morality play) are redeemed, and if there are not the joyous feasts that conclude some of the earlier comedies, there is nevertheless, as the braggart Parolles in *All's Well* says, "place and means for every man alive." Parolles, in fact, is at last welcomed to Lafew's table, although Lafew was the first to see through his deceptions: "Though you are a fool and a knave," he tells Parolles, "you shall eat."

## THE ROMANCES:
## PERICLES, CYMBELINE, THE WINTER'S TALE, THE TEMPEST, THE TWO NOBLE KINSMEN

If the conjectured dates of the dark comedies are right (about 1602–04), during the next few years Shakespeare wrote only tragedies: *King Lear* (1605–06), *Macbeth* (1605–06), *Antony and Cleopatra* (1606–07), *Timon of Athens* (1604–09), and *Coriolanus* (1607–09). But he ended his career with a return to comedy, that is, with plays that end happily: *Pericles* (1608–09), *Cymbeline* (1609–10), *The Winter's Tale* (1610–11), and *The Tempest* (1611). To these can be added two plays on which he may have collaborated with John Fletcher, *Henry VIII* (1612–13) and *The Two Noble Kinsmen* (1613). *Henry VIII*, an historical play, is discussed with the histories (see p. 53), but in a broad sense it is "comic," like Dante's *Divine Comedy*, for it moves from trouble to joy, ending with the christening of the infant Elizabeth I and the promise of a joyous future.

Shakespeare's last plays are in various ways fairly closely related, and critics usually call *Pericles*, *Cymbeline*, *The Winter's Tale*, and *The Tempest* "the romances." Except for *The Tempest*, like nondramatic romances the plays are concerned with wonderful actions that cover a long period. The title page of *Pericles* calls attention to this aspect of the play: "the true relation of the whole history, adventures, and fortunes of the said prince, as also the no less strange and worthy accidents in the birth and life of his daughter Marina." A dominant motif in these four plays is the restoration of losses: Pericles regains his wife Thaisa, who had been thought dead, and his daughter Marina, who had been abducted by pirates; King Cymbeline regains his two sons, abducted in infancy; in *The Winter's Tale* friends who had quarreled are after many years reunited, and the king regains his lost daughter; in *The Tempest* an exiled duke regains his dukedom, and the King of Naples regains his son. Of course, the earlier comedies too have such restorations: in *The Comedy of Errors* a long-separated family is at last reunited; in *As You Like It* a duke regains his dukedom. But *The Comedy of Errors* is mostly about comic errors in identity, and *As You Like It* is mostly about love. In contrast, the last plays in large measure are about restoration; moreover, the restoration of losses is closely related to a sense of renewal consequent upon suffering and repentance. It is rather as though *King Lear* were given a happy ending, with Lear and Cordelia reunited. In the romances the stuff of tragedy—exile, jealousy, even death—usually takes place early (in *The Tempest* the exile of Prospero takes place before the play begins), and the plays focus on the post-tragic regeneration and reunion. In *The Winter's Tale* the first three acts are ominous, including mad and destructive jealousy, a storm, death, and the exposure of an infant to the elements, but then the scene changes to springtime and a pastoral world, and the last two acts work toward a resolution. One cannot conceive of a happy ending added to the first three acts of *King Lear* (the pre-Shakespearean play *King Leir* did restore Leir to his throne, but Leir had not gone mad on the heath). As Charles Lamb said of such a possibility,

A happy ending—as if the living martyrdoms that Lear had gone through—the flaying of his feelings alive, did not make a fair dismissal from the stage of life the only decorous thing for him. If he is to live and be happy after, if he could sustain this world's burden after, why all this pudder and preparation—why torment us with all this unnecessary sympathy? As if the childish pleasure of getting his gilt robes and scepter again could tempt him to act over again his misused station—as if at his years, and with his experience, anything was left but to die.

This is finely put; and yet the romances are concerned with a stage of life that puts great suffering into a new perspective. Pericles says to the gods, as Lear could not, "Your present kindness/Makes my past miseries sports."

Although there are deaths in *Pericles*, *Cymbeline*, *The Winter's Tale*, and *The Two Noble Kinsmen*, the plays have a serenity that separates them from the festivity of the early comedies, the stress of the dark comedies, and the agony of the tragedies. Consider the idealized and somewhat etherealized heroines in the last plays: Marina in *Pericles*, who miraculously remains unspotted though she is sold into a brothel; Imogen in *Cymbeline*; Perdita in *The Winter's Tale*; Miranda in *The Tempest*, who has seen no man other than her father and a bestial servant; and Emilia in *The Two Noble Kinsmen*. For the most part the heroines of the earlier comedies are witty and resourceful, but the later heroines, notable for their innocence, have a sort of Snow White quality.

Coupled with this emphasis on innocence and the restoration of losses is a strong sense of providence, made obvious by visible manifestations of the deity: Diana appears in *Pericles* and Jupiter appears in *Cymbeline*, Apollo's oracle is quoted in *The Winter's Tale*, and Duke Prospero has magical powers in *The Tempest*. In *The Two Noble Kinsmen* prayers are made before the altars of Mars, Venus, and Diana, and the deities respond. In these plays, to quote from *Pericles*, we strongly feel that we see "virtue preserved from fell destruction's blast,/Led on by heaven and crowned at last."

The note of innocence and the sense of providence are strengthened by the pastoral settings of some of these plays and by the images of the sea and storms, which contrast with the pastoral settings. Shakespeare used a shipwreck as early as *The Comedy of Errors*, but in the last plays the sea and the storms are under the control of providence. In *Pericles* the lovely Marina is born during a storm at sea, and when she is finally reunited with her father a "great sea of joys" rushes upon him and he says, "Though the seas threaten, they are merciful." The emphasis on innocence and providence makes the plays hover at the edge of allegory. The characters seem a bit flatter or thinner, and if we prefer the earlier more complex characters we may find in the last plays too much freedom or casualness not only in the characterization but in the plotting and the versification. The commonest reply to this is that Shakespeare deliberately used thin characters, improbable situations, unidiomatic speech, and relatively free versification in order to move beyond these elements to the transcendent post-tragic vision behind the happenings. Having written festive comedies, darker comedies that treat romantic love somewhat skeptically, and tragedies, Shakespeare ended his career with a sort of play that has elements of all the earlier types but contains a new vision. Other explanations have been offered: Shakespeare was bored with the theater and was now interested only in making experiments in poetry itself; or Shakespeare, especially after the acquisition of the indoor theater at Blackfriars in 1608, was trying to attract a more courtly audience, one that preferred spectacular, allegorical masques and plays remote from common life; or for some unknown reason at the end of his career Shakespeare was returning to the loose romantic dramas of his youth; or Shakespeare was losing his grip. In any case, these plays are related, but it is time to look at them singly.

The earliest of the romances, *Pericles*, is of uncertain date and even uncertain authorship; it was not included in the First Folio, perhaps because the compilers of the Folio believed it to be written in large part by a hand other than Shakespeare's. In any case, most critics hesitate to attribute the first two acts to Shakespeare, chiefly because the poetry in these acts is very weak. (It is hard to tell exactly how weak, because the text is badly corrupted in places.) The plot is derived from a narrative which Shakespeare used as early as *The Comedy of Errors*, when he attached to Plautus' *Menaechmi* the old tale of a family dispersed by a storm at sea and reunited after much wandering. In *Pericles* a king is reunited with his wife and daughter after abundant grief, and the story deals with "this great miracle." There are storms in *Pericles* as in *King Lear*, but in *Pericles* the storms are ultimately seen to be providential. Thaisa, thought dead, is coffined and dropped into the sea, but she is miraculously restored to Pericles; his daughter, abducted and sold to a brothel, remains a virgin and converts her potential customers; Pericles, almost dead from sorrow, is miraculously restored to life by his long-lost daughter. If we wished to find an emblem for the play's theme, we would perhaps find it in the device on the hero's shield, "a withered branch that's only green at top" (II.ii.42). The world seems a barren, deathly, tempestuous place, but for the innocent and the patient there is, at the top, the possibility of new life.

The editors of the First Folio put *Cymbeline* among the tragedies, perhaps because they felt that a play in part concerned with a Roman invasion of Britain could not with propriety be put among the comedies; nor could it be put among the histories, since it includes romance material and deals with a legendary pre-Christian Britain, whereas all the history plays deal with medieval or early Renaissance England.

Like *Pericles*, *Cymbeline* is concerned with exile and restoration; like *Pericles* too it is set in a pagan world, but with markedly Christian overtones. For example, when Jupiter says, "Whom best I love I cross; to make my gift,/The more delayed, delighted," it is not merely the word *cross* (here a verb, meaning "to thwart") that evokes a Christian framework but the whole idea that the heavenly powers chasten those whom they love (compare the Bible's "Whom the Lord loveth, He chasteneth"). Suffering is transcended, and all losses are restored: "The fingers of the pow'rs above do tune/The harmony of this peace" (V.v.466–67). But viewers and readers have found that the harmony is achieved only after a bewildering diffusion of interest. The dialogue is often obscure; characterization in general counts for less than striking theatrical situations, and because there is no central character the focus is in doubt. The play mingles three motifs: pastoral matter of princes brought up close to nature, political-historical matter of Rome's conquest of Britain, and a story of love, which includes a disguised princess who apparently dies and comes back to life. In some degree, the play is Shakespeare's fusion of the histories (there is something about England's role in the world), the tragedies (exile, war, and death), and the comedies (courtship and marriage).

Like *Pericles*, *The Winter's Tale* is derived from a prose narrative that includes much of the stuff of the Hellenistic romances: an exotic pagan setting, an abandoned infant, an oracle, a storm, a long separation, love, and ultimately a reunion between those separated. In some matters Shakespeare lessens the operations of chance; for example, in the source the young lovers by the accident of shipwreck find themselves in Sicily, where the girl is reunited with her father, but in *The Winter's Tale* they deliberately set out for Sicily. But the play as a whole has an air of the wonderful or, as in King Leontes' sudden fit of jealously (I.ii), of the unpredictable and the irrational. Against this are elements that on a casual view can be called realistic—notably the roguish peddler Autolycus and the sheep-shearing festival in Act IV, where comedy and English character-types and customs appear in remote Bohemia. More precisely, however, this pastoral "realism" is not realism at all but another variety of romance; it is the romance no longer of the exotic but of the simple or "natural," for Perdita at the shepherds' festival gives us a picture of the vitality of innocence, in a setting of fertile nature. But the play as a whole presents a very different world from that of *As You Like It*,

with its delightful Forest of Arden. The seriousness of the issues is insisted on: Leontes' jealousy at the start causes the death of his little son and of others, and it initiates sixteen years of separation from his wife and his daughter. The first three acts, in short, are a winter's tale, tragic in tone. But in III.ii, when the infant Perdita is abandoned on a stormy coast and found by shepherds, there is a turn: "Now bless thyself," one shepherd says to another, "thou met'st with things dying, I with things newborn." Act IV begins with Time, who tells us that sixteen years have passed, and soon Autolycus appears and introduces a note of spring in a song about daffodils. Ultimately, Perdita is restored to her repentant father Leontes; her mother Hermione—thought dead not only by Leontes but by the audience—is also restored. The restoration to Hermione of the lost Perdita, who is associated with the spring, is a sort of analogue to the Greek myth of the seasons, in which Proserpina is rescued from the lower world and restored to her mother Ceres in the spring. It resembles, too, the Christian pattern of redemption. At the reunion—the resurrection, we might almost say—Hermione's first words are a prayer to the gods to pour their graces upon her daughter's head, and there is the implication here, as in *The Tempest*, that the innocent love of the children redeems the errors and sins of their fathers. Like *Pericles*, the play ends happily with expressions of joy, but it cannot be grouped with the festive comedies, not only because its first half has the violence of tragedy but also because its ending is suffused with solemnity. If we must classify the play, we might take a hint from Polonius and call it tragical-comical-pastoral.

Like some of the early comedies, which are ultimately indebted in varying degrees to late Greek and Roman comedy, *The Tempest* has a shipwreck (compare *The Comedy of Errors* and *Twelfth Night*), an irritable father (compare Egeus in *A Midsummer Night's Dream*), and a character who more or less manipulates the plot (compare Rosalind in *As You Like It*). Like *The Comedy of Errors*, possibly Shakespeare's earliest comedy, it obeys the ancient traditions of unity of time and place: the play spans only a few hours and occurs in one locale. But despite these and other resemblances, the unusual amount of spectacle in *The Tempest*—and, more important, the serious tone—ties the play to Shakespeare's other last plays. The old conventions are here, but with new meanings: *The Tempest* is concerned with guilt and forgiveness, royal children, wonderful quasi-resurrections, and finally reunions. "These are not natural events, they strengthen/From strange, to stranger." The pastoral setting, implying the freshness and vitality of nature, prominent in parts of *Cymbeline* under the thin disguise of the Welsh countryside and in *The Winter's Tale* in the Bohemian shepherds' feast, is presented in *The Tempest* in the mysterious island—though this island means different things to different people: to one observer the grass looks "lush and lusty," but to another the grass is "indeed tawny." Pastoralism appears too in the masque of Ceres and Juno and the dance of nymphs and harvesters. Again there is a shipwreck, and again the results prove beneficent. Those who are cast upon the island find, strangely, that their "garments, being, as they were, drenched in the sea, hold, notwithstanding, their freshness and glosses, being rather new-dyed than stained with salt water" (II.i.64–67). This note of renewal or regeneration is variously sounded throughout the play. Suffering brings renewal: "Some kinds of baseness/Are nobly undergone, and most poor matters/Point to rich ends."

> In one voyage
> Did Claribel her husband find at Tunis,
> And Ferdinand her brother found a wife
> Where he himself was lost; Prospero his dukedom
> In a poor isle; and all of us ourselves
> When no man was his own.     (V.i.208–13)

The sense of providence, strong in the last plays, is embodied in *The Tempest* chiefly by the magician Prospero, who raises and allays the storm that helps to regenerate and reconcile. (But Prospero, though in some ways godlike, is not God; he himself must learn to pity and to forgive the wrongdoer.)

Because *The Tempest* is probably the last play that is entirely Shakespeare's (he seems to have had a collaborator for *Henry VIII* and *The Two Noble Kinsmen*), there is a tendency to see in Prospero, the magician who can call up visions but who at the end breaks his staff and abjures his "potent art," a picture of Shakespeare putting down his pen and contemplating retirement to Stratford. There is no great harm in such a reading as long as it does not reduce the play to an autobiographical scrap. It would be a pity to see in *The Tempest* only a farewell to the theater and to fail to notice that Prospero goes not to retirement but to the active role of ruling in Milan as the duke. The meaning of this play, like the meanings of Shakespeare's other plays, finally is complex. But this is not to say that the play is obscure or cryptic, although the Baconians find a cryptogram in the two lines at the end:

> As you from crimes would pardoned be,
> Let your indulgence set me free.

What was Shakespeare *really* saying at the end of his last play? The Baconian answer is that the letters in these lines can be rearranged into this message: "Tempest of Francis Bacon, Lord Verulam; do ye ne'er divulge me, ye words." Such, for some, is Shakespeare's final message; no matter that this message has three *a*'s in it and Prospero's lines only two.

There remains a postscript. *The Two Noble Kinsmen* was first published in 1634 and the title page ascribes it to John Fletcher and William Shakespeare. Readers have often disagreed with the ascription, but there is no uniformity in their disagreement; some attribute the entire play to Fletcher, some to Shakespeare. The ascription of the title page seems more reasonable than either of these extreme positions. Like the other late romances *The Two Noble Kinsmen* is rich in spectacle, which is perhaps related to the fact that Shakespeare's company was at the time using the Blackfriars theater, playing to audiences with courtly tastes. The play opens with a nuptial procession (described in some detail in the first stage direction) before the Temple of Hymen, and it contains processions to the altars of Mars, Venus, and Diana, as well as a country dance. Like *Pericles*, *Cymbeline*, and *The Winter's Tale*, *The Two Noble Kinsmen* is based on what Ben Jonson called a "mouldy tale"—in this case, the narrative romance that Chaucer's Knight tells in *The Canterbury Tales*. And like Shakespeare's other late plays, and unlike many of his earlier plays, characterization is flatter, resulting sometimes in sharp contrasts. It is occasionally so thin in this play that the effect is of characterlessness. Unlike Shakespeare's other romances, however, *The Two Noble Kinsmen* is not concerned with the regeneration of men who have sinned or erred or with the restoration of old losses, although at the end of the fifth act there are passages which strongly remind us of the other last plays:

>         O cousin,
> That we should things desire which do cost us
> The loss of our desire! That nought could buy
> Dear love but loss of dear love!     (V.iv.108–11)

And:

>         O you heavenly charmers,
> What things you make of us! For what we lack,
> We laugh; for what we have, are sorry; still
> Are children in some kind. Let us be thankful
> For that which is, and with you leave dispute
> That are above our question.     (V.iv.130–35)

But these passages are only passages, and the bulk of the dramatic action does not greatly support them. Much of *The Two Noble Kinsmen* is more mannered, more prettified, and more ceremonious but also more hollow than the romances. It has a politeness and a pointlessness that we associate with Fletcher. Possibly it is best to see *The Two Noble Kinsmen* as largely Fletcher's, with Shakespeare—not always at top form—writing perhaps Acts I and V and adding passages here and there.

# Shakespeare's History Plays

## THE BACKGROUND

There are some two hundred Elizabethan history plays, most of them written within a fairly short period, between 1588 or so and 1600. Before the defeat of the Spanish Armada in 1588 there seems not to have been a single play on English history written for the public stage, though there were dramas on biblical, classical, and legendary heroes and villains, popular entertainments dramatizing Saint George of England and Robin Hood, and, for a limited audience, some academic dramas on English history with a very heavy infusion of political morality, notably *Gorboduc* (1561). For about a decade after the defeat of the Armada, the English history play was in vogue in the public theater. Of the eighteen plays that Shakespeare wrote up to the end of 1599 nine were on English history. But he then abandoned the genre, returning to it only once, at the end of his career, about 1613.

If we include plays on classical history (*Julius Caesar, Antony and Cleopatra,* and *Coriolanus*) and on legendary British history (*King Lear, Macbeth, Cymbeline*), almost half of Shakespeare's plays can be called historical, but the editors of the First Folio, in separating the histories from the comedies and tragedies, classified as history only those ten plays that dealt with relatively recent British history. These plays they arranged chronologically by date of subject matter (not of composition), beginning with *King John* and ending with *Henry VIII.* Three of these plays had been published earlier in individual volumes as tragedies: *3 Henry VI* as *The True Tragedy of Richard, Duke of York, Richard III* as *The Tragedy of King Richard III,* and *Richard II* as *The Tragedy of King Richard the Second.* Conversely, *King Lear,* included in the Folio among the tragedies, was first published as *The True Chronicle History of the Life and Death of King Lear,* and *The Merchant of Venice,* a comedy, was first published as *The Most Excellent History of the Merchant of Venice.* The history play evidently was not (and is not) a clearly defined genre; but it is still useful to consider the ten history plays of the Folio as a group. The subject matter—political events in England—relates these plays to one another in a way that the Roman plays, for example, are not related. Though it is not quite true to say that the sole concern of the plays is politics and that the real protagonist is England (people keep breaking in). Even those plays that have a tragic shape, *Richard II* and *Richard III,* stand apart from such tragedies as *King Lear* and *Macbeth* by their primary emphasis on several characters engaged in political actions. Although political actions do occur in the tragedies, the primary emphasis is on what might be called the private matters of a central figure—for example, Lear's relations with his daughters and movement toward self-knowledge and Macbeth's relations with his conscience.

The first four plays—three on Henry VI and one on Richard III—cover a continuous period from 1422 to 1485 and so may be considered a tetralogy; four later plays—*Richard II, 1 Henry IV, 2 Henry IV,* and *Henry V*—cover an earlier continuous period from 1398 to 1422 and so may be considered a second tetralogy. The two tetralogies thus run from 1398 to 1485, when Henry VII, the first Tudor monarch and the grandfather of Queen Elizabeth, ascended the throne. These plays were presented singly, not as tetralogies, but insofar as each play looks both backward and forward and tells only a piece of a larger story, the tetralogies bear some resemblance to the great medieval cycles of miracle plays, which spanned time from the Creation to the Day of Judgment and which also allegedly presented history, showing such events as Herod's Slaughter of the Innocents and the subsequent punishment visited upon him. For example, in the first play of Shakespeare's second tetralogy, *Richard II,* Bolingbroke takes the throne from Richard, the next two plays reveal the suffering and turmoil consequent upon this act of usurpation and the working out of evil, and the last of the four plays, *Henry V,* reveals the restoration of peace and unity in England under a monarch said to be "the mirror of all Christian kings." Like the medieval cycles, Renaissance history plays were presumably not only entertaining but also instructive, for Elizabethans assumed that one learns from history how to behave. For the Elizabethans history, properly understood, was morality, as an Elizabethan schoolboy found when he read his Caesar and Sallust and Livy, for he saw that rebellion is inevitably punished. In the dedication to *A Mirror for Magistrates* (1559), a collection of narrative poems on the fall of rulers, the editor addresses "the nobility and all other in office" and informs them that "here, as in a looking glass, you shall see (if any vice be in you) how the like hath been punished in other heretofore, whereby admonished, I trust it will be a good occasion to move you to the sooner amendment." (Another aspect of this influential book is discussed in connection with Shakespeare's tragedies, pp. 54–55.) In 1592 Thomas Nashe defended the stage against puritanical attacks, by seizing on the moral implications of history plays. First, he held, they revive "our forefathers' valiant acts," serving as a "reproof to these degenerate effeminate days of ours"; second, "in plays, all cozenage, all cunning drifts over-gilded with outward holiness, all stratagems of war, all the cankerworms that breed on the rust of peace, are most lively anatomized: they show the ill success of treason, the fall of hasty climbers, the wretched end of usurpers, the misery of civil dissension, and how just God is evermore in punishing of murder."

This emphasis on history as morality serves also to link the history play to certain late morality plays which had concerned themselves with politics. Sometimes Shakespeare's plays strongly remind us of the abstractions of the old moralities, as when in *2 Henry VI* a character says,

Ah, gracious lord, these days are dangerous:
Virtue is choked with foul ambition,

And charity chased hence by rancor's hand;
Foul subornation is predominant,
And equity exiled your highness' land.     (III.i.142–46)

The political moralities, in turn, helped to give rise to a type that can be called the moral history. For example, John Bale's *King John* (1539, revised between 1558 and 1563) is indebted to the morality play for such characters as Nobility, Civil Order, Sedition, and Dissimulation, but it approaches the history play when Sedition becomes Stephen Langton, Private Wealth becomes Pandulphus, Usurper Power becomes the Pope, and so on. Moreover, King John is not deceived by evil counselors, as he would be in a morality play; rather, he is an ideal Christian and the defender of the widow England, though he is finally poisoned by Dissimulation, who has become the monk Simon of Swinstead. In some sense, then, Bale's *King John* is concerned not with the trial of a soul but with an historical failure. Only after John's death is England rescued from the wicked. In this respect Bale's play is closer to the miracle play than to the morality play; indeed, the Interpreter in the play compares John to Moses, who sought to withstand "proud Pharaoh for his poor Israel."

The Tudor history play, then, is not a period piece evoking the atmosphere of a particular age; rather, though it dramatizes the past, it is supposed to be timeless, for the sins and the political machinations of one age are very like those of another, and man (so the theory held) should learn from the past how to behave in the present. Contemporary problems of government are seen not through allegory but through episodes from the past. This idea is still with us, in such expressions as "History repeats itself" and "Those who cannot remember the past are condemned to repeat it." For the Elizabethans, parallels between reigns and between rulers readily suggested themselves. Queen Elizabeth, when reading some documents concerning Richard II (who had been deposed) is said to have angrily exclaimed, "I am Richard II." And in 1601 Essex arranged for a performance of Shakespeare's *Richard II* the day before his rebellion against Elizabeth, presumably to show the populace that a monarch might be deposed.

But though Shakespeare's history plays show the painful consequences of usurpation and tyranny, they are not sermons; a central character, representative of mankind, no longer dominates the plays, and they are filled with personalities who color or overshadow the political lessons. If the plays sometimes seem to illustrate a text in the first book of homilies, *An Exhortation Concerning Good Order and Obedience to Rulers and Magistrates* (1547)—"Take away kings . . . and such estates of God's order, no man shall sleep in his house or bed unkilled; . . . there must needs follow all mischief"—they do so not simply from a desire to urge subjects to be dutiful but from an understanding of the ways people act and react. To take a simple example: with the aid of Worcester and others Bolingbroke deposes Richard II; in the next play, *1 Henry IV*, Bolingbroke (now Henry IV) finds that he cannot trust his former allies, and Worcester finds that he cannot trust the new king, for he knows that Henry will always suspect him of feeling that he has not been sufficiently rewarded; moreover, Henry will always suspect Worcester of contemplating yet a second overthrow of a king. If there is a moral here, it is not obtrusive; the play is chiefly about people, rather than

about providence's government of the realm, though it is true that as in medieval drama there is a sense of retribution: crimes are punished.

That the plays are not overtly didactic is perhaps the more remarkable in view of their relation to the moral histories and their immediate derivation for the most part from Raphael Holinshed's *Chronicles of England, Scotland, and Ireland* (1577); second edition, used by Shakespeare, 1587). About 1501 Henry VIII, the first Tudor, brought Polydore Virgil from Italy to rewrite English history from the Tudor point of view, and Virgil's work, along with that of several successors (notably Edward Hall), was more or less incorporated into Holinshed's enormous history book. (Strictly speaking, Holinshed's own work also became incorporated into the book bearing his name because the second edition was not really his; it was produced by collaborators after his death.) As part of this rewriting of history, Richard III, for example, who was pushed from the throne by Henry VII, was made into a monster, first by Sir Thomas More and Polydore Virgil, then by Hall, who borrowed from them, and then by Holinshed, who used their material. Holinshed borrowed not only many of the details of his predecessors but also the overall view that the history of England showed the workings of God: Henry IV's usurpation of the throne led to a century of war, but God watched over England, punished the wicked, and at last placed the Tudors on the throne. Occasionally this note is heard in Shakespeare's history plays, especially in the last history, *Henry VIII*, which celebrates the birth of Queen Elizabeth and which suggests that England is again Eden. But for the most part the plays give us a picture of men forging their own destinies, though of course such a picture is not incompatible with the idea that God works in mysterious ways, leaving man's will free but finally seeing that His will is done.

## THE FIRST TETRALOGY: HENRY VI AND RICHARD III

The three plays on Henry VI, covering about fifty years from the death of Henry V (1422) to the murder of Henry VI (1471), are troublesome, and some critics claim that much in these plays was written by a hand other than Shakespeare's. (If the plays are entirely by Shakespeare, it may well be that he originated the English history play, for it is not certain that any plays of this type preceded them on the public stage, the moral histories being closer to the morality plays than to these chronicle plays.) Probably the most widely accepted view today is that the three plays are chiefly Shakespeare's, written between 1588 and 1592, and that *1 Henry VI* was written after *2 and 3 Henry VI*; possibly *1 Henry VI* is Shakespeare's revision of an older play. Of the three, *1 Henry VI* is notably the most episodic; it more or less chronicles a period, but it does not always pull the events into a unity (though of course it can be said that the play is united by its theme of the weakness of England under a vacillating king). There is some attempt to appeal to patriotism—the "brave" Talbot is an English paragon who has captured fifty French fortresses—and some attempt to warn Englishmen against disunity— Talbot is "entrapped" by "the fraud of England, not the

# Genealogical Table of the Houses of York and Lancaster

The table below traces the history of the English crown for 277 years: from 1327 when Edward III was crowned to 1603 when Elizabeth I died. The period began with the Hundred Years War (1337–1453), which saw the English gain then lose a vast French empire. Even before the French wars were concluded civil strife erupted at home. From 1455 to 1485 the bitter Wars of the Roses raged, and the crown became the plaything of the great noble families. One hundred and fifty years of fighting abroad and on their own soil had decimated the ranks of the important feudal houses of Plantagenet, York, Lancaster, and others. A new English

dynasty was founded at Bosworth where Henry Tudor, Elizabeth's grandfather, was given the crown. Nine of Shakespeare's plays (*Richard II*; *1 and 2 Henry IV*; *Henry V*; *1, 2, and 3 Henry VI*; *Richard III*; and *Henry VIII*) chronicle the events of these years. The table includes many of the characters who people the plays. The names of reigning monarchs are written in small capitals. (From *The Reader's Encyclopedia of Shakespeare*, edited by Oscar James Campbell and Edward G. Quinn. Copyright © 1966 by Thomas Y. Crowell Company. Reprinted by permission of the publisher.)

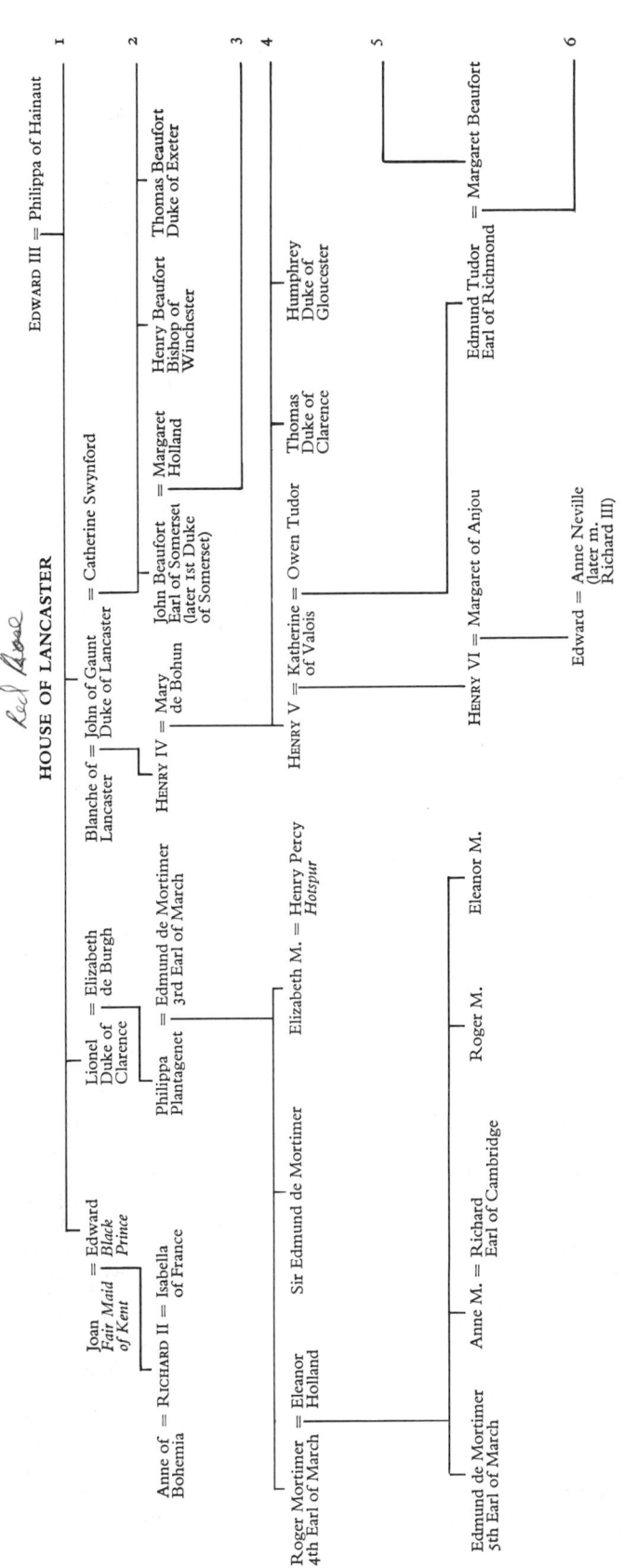

White Rose

# HOUSE OF YORK

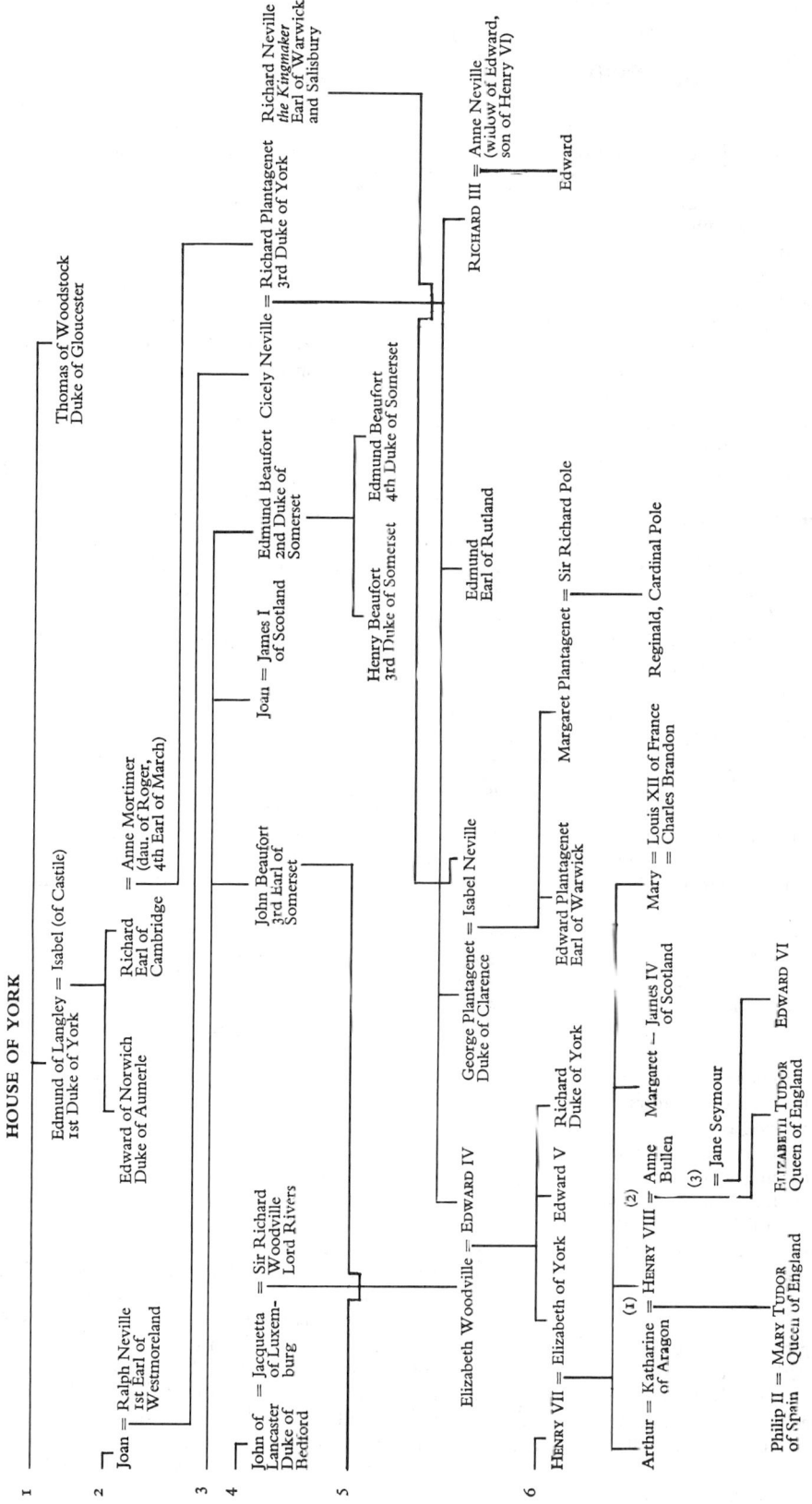

force of France" (IV.iv.36–37). On the whole, the play is a series of scenes, some of which are effective, especially in establishing antitheses (as between the heroic Talbot and the wicked Joan and between honest Humphrey Duke of Gloucester and the corrupt Bishop of Winchester), but some of which lead nowhere, chiefly, it seems, because Shakespeare did not yet have that insight into human nature that he was to achieve in his later historical plays. Something too must be forgiven a dramatist who sets out to dramatize material whose shapelessness Holinshed (Shakespeare's source) explained in this manner: "Thus oftentimes varied the chance of doubtful war."

That Shakespeare saw in the history play something other than a mere exhortation of patriotism, or a mere illustration of providence's concern for England, is revealed also in *2 and 3 Henry VI*. In *2 Henry VI* the king evokes pity but little respect; Richard Plantagenet, Duke of York, evokes horror; and Cade and his low followers evoke laughter. Only Duke Humphrey is much of a credit to England, and he is murdered halfway through the play. Like *1 Henry VI*, *2 Henry VI* contains scenes that do not lead to further action and that at first glance perhaps seem extraneous—such as Duke Humphrey's exposure of Simcox, who claims to have been miraculously cured of blindness (II.i), and the death of Thomas the armorer at the hands of his apprentice (II.iii). But these scenes are in fact relevant to the whole: the first episode helps to demonstrate the good sense that Humphrey has and that the king lacks; the second helps to demonstrate the disorder that pervades the realm, showing on a low level the chaos that exists also among the nobility. The material concerning Jack Cade's rebellion provides York with the excuse that he must bring back his army from Ireland to put down the lowly Cade, and in Cade's ignorance and cruelty there is yet another image of the horrors of civil strife engendered by the nobles. The brutality that is present throughout the play is neatly illustrated in a single sentence when Cade replies to Lord Say's self-defense: "He shall die, an it be but for pleading so well for his life." That brutality engenders further brutality is well dramatized throughout the play but perhaps nowhere more effectively than in V.ii, when young Clifford finds that his father has been slain by York:

> York not our old men spares;
> No more will I their babes: tears virginal
> Shall be to me even as the dew to fire,
> And beauty, that the tyrant oft reclaims,
> Shall to my flaming wrath be oil and flax.
> Henceforth I will not have to do with pity:
> Meet I an infant of the house of York,
> Into as many gobbets will I cut it
> As wild Medea young Absyrtus did.     (V.ii.51–59)

The mythological reference in the last line—a simile occupying exactly one end-stopped line—is a bit of gratuitously and obtrusively displayed learning, but on the whole the speech is a fine one, especially in the powerful simplicity of "Henceforth I will not have to do with pity."

*3 Henry VI* continues the dramatization of chaos from about 1455 to 1471. In the first act young Clifford fulfills

the promise he made in *2 Henry VI* not to spare "babes" when he kills York's youngest son, the Earl of Rutland. Other deaths follow in this highly episodic play, but the episodes are thematically united in their emphasis on the breadth of the destruction, as in the scene balancing a son who has killed his father against a father who has killed his son and in the death of the young Prince Edward, which is a variation on the death of young Rutland. *3 Henry VI* ends with Richard murdering Henry VI, and with the accession of Edward IV; but despite Edward's concluding line— "For here, I hope, begins our lasting joy"—the ending is not an ending, because (as Edward's feeble "I hope" almost implies) bloodshed is to continue in *Richard III*. Richard's distinctive blend of irony and cruelty is already present in the first scene of *3 Henry VI*, when instead of recounting his exploits in battle, as his brothers do, he throws down the severed head of the Duke of Somerset and says, "Speak thou for me, and tell them what I did." Richard continues this tone to the end of the play, when he holds up his bloody sword and says, "See how my sword weeps for the poor king's death." Between these speeches he vows "to catch the English crown . . ./Or hew [his] way out with a bloody ax." Richard's subsequent bloody deeds are the substance of the fourth play of the tetralogy, *Richard III*.

The Tudor chroniclers had reported Richard's enormities, and Shakespeare followed them in describing a man capable of every inhumanity. In the three plays in which Richard appears, he is compared to (in alphabetical order) a bear, a boar, a dog, a hedgehog, a lizard, a spider, a tiger, a toad, and a wolf, as well as to three mythical beasts, a basilisk, a cockatrice, and a hellhound. But why is he capable of every sort of villainy? And why is he not simply repellent to us? The answer to the first question briefly is that Richard (like Aaron in *Titus Andronicus* and Iago in *Othello*) is descended from the medieval Vice, the diabolic trickster who delighted in villainy. The answer to the second question is probably that Richard's energy and enthusiasm in his villainy offer esthetic pleasure; he continually sees himself as an actor performing the most outrageous roles, and though we deplore his atrocities we delight in his verve. We can attribute Richard's own delight in activity and power to the fact that as a hunchback he cannot know the normal satisfactions that come from respect and love, and in a long speech in *3 Henry VI* (III.ii.146–71) Richard suggests that since he is barred from normal delights he will dedicate himself to the conquest of "such as are of better person than myself." But Shakespeare sees Richard too as the unmotivated Vice; indeed, Richard sees himself as the Vice: "Thus, like the formal Vice, Iniquity,/I moralize [interpret] two meanings in one word" (III.i.82–83). (The Vice regularly deceived people by double meanings.) This aside to the audience, inviting an appreciation of Richard's theatrical skill as well as of his theatrical origin, helps us to see him as an expert performer rather than as a moral monster. (In an aside at the very end of *3 Henry VI* he invites the audience to see him as no less skilled in deception than Judas.) Thus Richard is sometimes the passionate man, defrauded by the accident of his misshapen body; but at other times (and most often) he is a spirit of deceit, given to witty asides and soliloquies, entertaining in his very mischief, and inviting the audience to delight in his resourcefulness even though his energy is misdirected:

I do the wrong, and first begin to brawl.
The secret mischiefs that I set abroach
I lay unto the grievous charge of others.

. . .

But then I sigh, and with a piece of Scripture
Tell them that God bids us do good for evil;
And thus I clothe my naked villainy
With odd old ends stol'n forth of holy writ,
And seem a saint when most I play the devil.

(I.iii.323–25, 333–37)

The most notable of Richard's successes, the winning of Lady Anne (whose husband and father he had killed), is accomplished, as he says, with no aid other than "the plain devil and dissembling looks." We deplore his immorality but we admire his theatrical skill.

Another theatrical tradition put to work in this play should be mentioned: historically Margaret played no part in the action, for she had gone to France and died there, but Shakespeare seems to use her as a Senecan Fury, a creature who moves others to vengeance and whose curses embody destiny, specifically in the form of retributive justice—though the idea of retribution is found in some miracle plays too, where such tyrants as Pharaoh and Herod come to a bad end, and also in much of *A Mirror for Magistrates*. In short, *Richard III* draws the gist of its plot from the chronicles, but it draws its understanding of the plot, and its methods, from earlier drama. (For a discussion of the medieval origins of the comic murderers in I.iv, who discuss the power of conscience, see pp. 13–14.) Superimposed on these theatrical traditions is the Tudor chronicler's view that God expressed His will in English history; England is providentially united by the victory of the rather colorless Richmond, who defeats "one that hath ever been God's enemy." The marriage of Richmond (Lancastrian) to Princess Elizabeth (Yorkist) will unite the factions of England and thus end the Wars of the Roses.

## KING JOHN

There is a good deal of uncertainty about the date of *King John* (conjectures range from 1590 to 1597) and some uncertainty about that of *Richard II* (conjectures range from 1595 to 1597). Whichever play was earlier, it is clear that having written an historical tetralogy Shakespeare decided to continue writing history plays but not to carry the story beyond where he had left it, with the accession of Henry VII in 1485. To have carried it forward would have brought him up to the sixteenth century—dangerously close to his own times. Instead he went backward, to King John (1167?–1216) and to Richard II (1367–1400). But parallels with contemporary politics were not thereby excluded: King John's rejection of the Papal Legate's authority (III.i) was often seen as an anticipation of Henry VIII's break with the Roman Catholic Church and of Elizabeth's position after the pope excommunicated her in 1569; the deposition of Richard II, as Shakespeare's company found out, was for a while taken as a comment to the effect that Elizabeth might appropriately be deposed. King John was a figure of considerable interest to the Elizabethans, but not because he signed the Magna Carta, which Shakespeare does not even mention. Because he

defied papal authority medieval chroniclers saw in John a wicked king; for the same reason, most Tudor chroniclers saw in John a Protestant martyr. When about 1536 the militant Protestant John Bale wrote an anti-Catholic political morality play, he sought to avoid anything reminiscent of the old religious drama and so went to English history and chose King John as his central figure. But unlike Bale's play, Shakespeare's *King John* is not vehemently anti-Catholic, despite the king's rebuff to the Papal Legate; nor is the play calculated to appeal throughout to an Englishman's patriotism, for John is a usurper and he is responsible for the death of his nephew Arthur, the legitimate heir. In fact, Shakespeare's King John is a mixture of the two historical traditions; he owes something to the Catholic tradition of the lawless king and something to the Protestant tradition of the nationalistic martyr. This blend of traditions is pretty far from *Richard III*, where good and evil are clearly separated; and it is also pretty far from any simple view of English history. In *King John* the historical material is used as the stuff of moral decisions, and with hindsight we can see John as an anticipation of Shakespeare's Brutus, a man whose political motives are honorable (John seeks to strengthen England) but who becomes involved in moral guilt (complicity in Arthur's death). And so John degenerates after III.ii (though he is unaccountably called "our great King John" in V.iv) and dies unheroically, while Faulconbridge, the engaging satiric commentator, rises. Faulconbridge's final speech is a patriotic address:

This England never did, nor never shall,
Lie at the proud foot of a conqueror
But when it first did help to wound itself. (V.vii.112–14)

Perhaps more interesting than this dubious assertion (which seems to have little to do with the shifting allegiances of international politics throughout the play) is the fact that Faulconbridge is a serious yet at times comic character who wittily and shrewdly comments on the passing scene. None of the earlier histories has so complex a figure; indeed, it is partly the characterization of Faulconbridge that makes the date of 1590 seem too early for this play. But Shakespeare is full of surprises.

## THE SECOND TETRALOGY:
## RICHARD II, 1 AND 2 HENRY IV, HENRY V

*Richard II* (1595), the first play of Shakespeare's second tetralogy, is very different from *King John*, partly because it is given a tragic shape. Its antecedents include those narrative poems in *A Mirror for Magistrates* and its predecessors that set forth the fall of kings, and Richard sees himself as a fit subject for such a story:

Let's talk of graves, of worms, and epitaphs,
Make dust our paper, and with rainy eyes
Write sorrow on the bosom of the earth.
Let's choose executors and talk of wills.

. . .

For God's sake let us sit upon the ground
And tell sad stories of the death of kings:

How some have been deposed, some slain in war,
Some haunted by the ghosts they have deposed,
Some poisoned by their wives, some sleeping killed,
All murdered—for within the hollow crown
That rounds the mortal temples of a king
Keeps Death his court, and there the antic sits,
Scoffing his state and grinning at his pomp,
Allowing him a breath, a little scene,
To monarchize, be feared, and kill with looks,
Infusing him with self and vain conceit,
As if this flesh which walls about our life
Were brass impregnable; and, humored thus,
Comes at the last, and with a little pin
Bores thorough his castle wall, and farewell king!

                                    (III.ii.145–48, 155–70)

Later in the play he urges his queen to "tell . . . the lamentable tale of me,/And send the hearers weeping to their beds."

With Richard's fall comes Bolingbroke's rise, giving us the first extant English play in which two characters are pitted against each other. (In Marlowe's *Edward II* the weakling protagonist, who must have influenced Shakespeare's conception of Richard, is opposed not by an individual but by a group.) Viewed one way, as the Duke of York explains to Richard (II.i.195–99), the play is the tragedy of an irresponsible king who makes the mistake of confiscating John of Gaunt's estate, thus bringing Gaunt's son Bolingbroke back to England to claim his inheritance and finally to depose and indirectly murder Richard. Viewed another way, the play is a political play exploring the nature of kingship, the duties of subjects, and the realities of political struggles. Twentieth-century critics have tended to stress the second view, but for the general reader —who is not likely to be familiar with Tudor historical writing or to have in mind the three subsequent histories (*1 Henry IV*, *2 Henry IV*, and *Henry V*) that deal with the results of the deposition—the play probably remains a tragedy; its protagonist anticipates Hamlet in his neurotic sensibility, his changeableness, and his grief—which is not to say that there are not enormous differences between Richard and Hamlet.

If *Richard II* is a tragedy, or even if it is a political play, what sort of king is Richard? Critics divide into the softhearted and the hardhearted. The first group sees Richard as a poet, a delicate and tender prince too fine for this gross world (according to W. B. Yeats, he belongs to that group of people who lack a commonplace "rough energy" but have something more precious, such as "contemplative virtue, . . . lyrical phantasy, . . . sweetness of temper"). The hardhearted group turns this view inside out and says that if Richard is a poet, he is a very bad poet, a man in love with words but indifferent to people other than himself, and ignorant of himself because he swathes his actions in such abundant metaphors that he loses sight of the actions themselves. This second view is now dominant, and much stress has been put on Richard's tendency to use highly figurative language. It should be mentioned, however, that Richard is not the only one in this play to use elaborate figures. The truth is that the play is highly figurative throughout; even the Gardener speaks metaphoric verse; and Bolingbroke, widely regarded as businesslike, describes his exile thus:

Must I not serve a long apprenticehood
To foreign passages, and in the end,
Having my freedom, boast of nothing else
But that I was a journeyman to grief?    (I.iii.270–73)

The figure of an exile as an apprentice, heightened by the pun on "*journeyman*," cautions us against speaking too easily of Richard as a man whose fault is that he plays on words, or whose strength is a sensitivity to language. Probably the truth is that Shakespeare had only recently— perhaps because he had been writing two narrative poems and dozens of sonnets—developed as a poet and was now writing not merely drama in somewhat mechanical verse but drama in highly lyrical poetry. Like *Romeo and Juliet* and *A Midsummer Night's Dream*, *Richard II* is among Shakespeare's first plays to employ iterative imagery— that is, recurring images that help to give unity to the play. The dates of these three plays are uncertain (probably all were written between 1594 and 1596); *Richard II* may indeed be Shakespeare's first play to use such imagery. There are many images, for example, comparing England to a garden. These are most obvious in III.iv, when the Gardener and his man compare *their* commonwealth, the garden itself, to Richard's garden, England. The man asks his master why they should

                    in the compass of a pale,
Keep law and form and due proportion,
Showing, as in a model, our firm estate,
When our sea-wallèd garden, the whole land,
Is full of weeds, her fairest flowers choked up,
Her fruit trees all unpruned, her hedges ruined,
Her knots disordered, and her wholesome herbs
Swarming with caterpillars?            (III.iv.40–47)

The Gardener replies, now varying the figure by seeing Richard himself as a plant:

He that hath suffered this disordered spring
Hath now himself met with the fall of leaf:
The weeds which his broad spreading leaves did shelter,
That seemed in eating him to hold him up,
Are plucked up root and all by Bolingbroke—
I mean the Earl of Wiltshire, Bushy, Green.

                                       (III.iv.48–53)

And so on. But such imagery is not confined to this scene, where it is almost inevitable. John of Gaunt earlier compares England to the Garden of Eden, and goes on to say that Richard has degraded it to a wretched farm; Bolingbroke characterizes Bushy and others as "the caterpillars of the commonwealth,/Which I have sworn to weed and pluck away"; Richard later is said to be a rightful king "planted many years," and if Bolingbroke usurps the crown "the blood of England shall manure the ground"; in his final speech Bolingbroke regrets that "blood should sprinkle me to make me grow."

Although there are manifest dangers in reading a play as though it were a short lyric poem (the spectator, after all, cannot hold each image in his mind and then relate it to the next occurrence of the image), it is clear that *Richard II* lends itself to this sort of reading. It should be noted too that some of the imagery is reinforced by the action. There are, for example, images and gestures of rising and falling (the play shows Bolingbroke's rise and Richard's fall), as in Richard's invitation to "sit upon the ground/And tell sad stories of the death of kings" and in Richard's address to Bolingbroke, who is kneeling before him: "Up, cousin, up, your heart is up, I know." In short, actions as well as images have their effect. If in *Richard II* Shakespeare was writing a *poetic* play, he was also writing a poetic *play*.

In the two plays on the reign of Henry IV and the play on the reign of Henry V Shakespeare abandoned the tragic structure that he had used to give shape to *Richard II* and returned to a looser, chronicle arrangement. He returned also to the occasional use of prose and of comedy, both of which are absent from *Richard II*. These plays, however, do not merely plod through the happenings of the reigns as Shakespeare encountered them in history books, though the titles of the plays sometimes lead a reader to think they are shapeless. *1 Henry IV* (1597), for instance, was first published under this title page (which includes the earliest extant use of the word *history* as a theatrical designation): *The History of Henry the Fourth; with the battle at Shrewsbury between the King and Lord Henry Percy, surnamed Henry Hotspur of the north. With the humourous conceits of Sir John Falstaff.* But the play is not merely a history or chronicle with a big battle and some "humorous conceits"; rather, it is largely organized by showing Henry IV visited by retribution, by juxtapositions of related characters, and by the story of the reformation of Prince Hal. (More precisely, the play is organized around the apparent reformation of Hal, since Hal even in his rakish days is never really sullied and therefore does not need to reform, though he does need to put off pleasure and to accept duty.) If one must come up with a single unifying formula, perhaps it will do to say that the play is about the revelation of Hal's political virtue. *1 Henry IV*, then, bears some resemblance to the morality plays on the motif of the Prodigal Son. To put it perhaps too simply, Hal is a figure of Mankind, tempted toward a riotous life by Falstaff; but at length he recognizes his duty and returns to help his father conquer the rebellious lords. A bit more precisely, Hal allows Falstaff to entertain him with images of riotous behavior but does his duty when required. The nature of honor is wonderfully explored, sometimes in explicit speeches about honor, as in Hotspur's rather huffing lines about plucking "bright honor from the palefaced moon" (I.iii.192–206) and in Falstaff's pragmatic catechism to the effect that honor is a mere "word, . . . air" (V.i.127–41) and again in his later comments on the "grinning honor" that the dead Sir Walter Blount has won (V.iii.32–33, 58–63). Sometimes the nature of honor is explored in actions, as when Hal defeats Hotspur and (by way of contrast) when Falstaff shams death. And of course the explicit discussions fuse with the actions: for example, a moment after Falstaff concludes that honor is only a word, Worcester dishonorably fails to tell Hotspur of "the liberal and kind offer of the king." While exploring honor, specifically in the political world, Shakespeare also explores the nature of kingship, partly by arranging his scenes so that they illuminate his themes. In the beginning of the play the king is weak and shaken, but he looks forward to a time of security when he can make a crusade to Jerusalem. News soon comes to the effect that a rebellion (recall that Henry himself had been a rebel against Richard II) prevents this

journey. This first scene alludes to Northumberland's son Hotspur, and the king, commenting on his own scapegrace son, expresses his envy of Northumberland, who has "so blest a son." The next scene shows the scapegrace with Falstaff, and in the course of the scene it becomes clear that Hal is not quite what his father thinks. The third scene, showing the king dealing with his potentially rebellious allies, brings Hotspur on the stage, and the disloyalty of the young man who a bit earlier had been praised by the king is now explicit. Such juxtapositions are the work of a dramatist, not a chronicler. Lest there be any doubt, it is worth mentioning (to take only the most obvious example) that Shakespeare made Hotspur—who in fact was thirty-nine at the Battle of Shrewsbury—much younger, pairing him off with Hal, who in fact was sixteen at Shrewsbury.

The play, then, is carefully constructed. However, it seems likely that at the start Shakespeare did not know just where he was going. Judging from the early part of the play, with its talk of rejecting Falstaff, it rather looks as though Shakespeare planned to end the play with the death of Henry IV, the coronation of Hal, and the rejection of Falstaff; but midway through the play he perhaps found that too much material remained to be fitted into the little space remaining, and so he ended with the victory at Shrewsbury and saved the additional material for another play, *2 Henry IV*, which he probably wrote shortly after.

A spectator watching *2 Henry IV* (1597–98) must start with the assumption that Hal is still unreformed and unreconciled with the king, although reformation and reconciliation take place in *1 Henry IV*. That is, this sequel again removes Hal from the tavern and reconciles him with the king. But despite this resemblance in plot, the plays are very different, for *2 Henry IV* is a darker play, and if its theme can be summed up in a word, that word is not honor or valor but justice. But it is not only that the theme is different; the world of the play is different. In *2 Henry IV* there are numerous images of diseases: Northumberland is sick (or crafty-sick); the king is sick and during the play dies; the kingdom is sick ("You perceive the body of our kingdom/How foul it is, what rank diseases grow"), and perhaps most important for our present purpose, Falstaff is sick. When we first meet him he is inquiring about the doctor's opinion of his urine (I.ii); later he says, "I am old, I am old," and the Chief Justice describes him so incisively that even Falstaff's witty retort does not obliterate the image of decrepit age:

Have you not a moist eye, a dry hand, a yellow cheek, a white beard, a decreasing leg, an increasing belly? Is not your voice broken, your wind short, your chin double, your wit single, and every part about you blasted with antiquity . . . ? (I.ii.182–86)

Moreover, in *2 Henry IV* Falstaff is associated with darker companions, the doddering and corrupt Justice Shallow, the craven braggart Pistol, and the whore Doll Tearsheet, the last two of whom have beaten a man to death. There is humor in the play, but on the whole the humor is of a different sort, tinged with darkness. In *1 Henry IV* there are delightful bouts in which Hal and Falstaff heap abundant entertaining abuse on each other, but in *2 Henry IV* Hal and Falstaff have only two scenes together: in the first of these scenes (II.iv) there is some of the old fooling, but the scene ends with Hal's brusque "Give me my sword and cloak. Falstaff, good night"; in the second scene (V.v.47 ff.) Hal rejects Falstaff, in a famous speech beginning "I know thee not, old man." The speech is justly famous, but for some critics it is notorious because Hal (in their view) callously turns off an old companion, revealing that accession to the throne has narrowed his sympathies to those of only another politic man who knows how to get ahead in the world. Against this view it can be argued that at his coronation Hal can scarcely embrace the man who represents disorder, and that in this play—as opposed to *1 Henry IV*, where he is more genial—Falstaff represents not an engaging comprehensiveness but disorder or anarchy. At least at a crucial moment, when he learns that Hal has become king, he utters a joyous yet dangerous bullying cry:

Let us take any man's horses; the laws of England are at my commandment. Blessed are they that have been my friends, and woe to my Lord Chief Justice!
(V.iii.140–43)

Falstaff's joy is undercut even more by the fact that the audience, having already seen Hal take the Lord Chief Justice as his new guide, knows that Falstaff must be rejected. In a sense, the end of the play brings us back to the beginning, when in the Prologue Rumor talks about "smooth comforts false" that help to destroy men. (Another aspect of this motif is the deceptive words by which Prince John destroys the rebels; in *1 Henry IV* heroism plays a part in putting down rebellion, but not in *2 Henry IV*.) However we take the rejection of Falstaff, whether as an indication of Hal's maturity or of his diminution, *2 Henry IV* remains a very different play from *1 Henry IV*. But to say that *2 Henry IV* is the darker of the two is not to say that it is black; despite the emphasis on sickness, corruption, and death, there is some mirth and some nobility, not least when the wretched Feeble, a conscripted recruit, says, "I will do my good will, sir. You can have no more" and, with a pun on *debt/death*, "A man can die but once. We owe God a death. I'll ne'er bear a base mind. And't be my destiny, so. And't be not, so. No man's too good to serve's prince" (III.ii.239–42).

Possibly before Shakespeare wrote *Henry V* (1598–99) he wrote *The Merry Wives of Windsor*, a comedy with Falstaff, but that play does not concern us here; for despite Falstaff's presence, *The Merry Wives* makes no use of historical materials. In *Henry V* Shakespeare finished the tetralogy that he began with *Richard II* and then developed in two plays on the reign of Henry IV. In *Henry V* he returned to the rather episodic technique of his earliest history plays, in which the chief principle of arrangement is chronology, though of course he was highly selective in what he presented. The play is usually regarded as a dramatic epic, a kind of narrative of the heroic doings of "the mirror of all Christian kings," a king who, because he is not weak like Richard or tainted like the usurper Henry IV, can lead his country to glory in a just war against France. This interpretation may be right, but it is too simple for some readers, especially readers living in an age when war is inglorious. As a result, a counterinterpretation has developed: Henry is less an ideal king than an

adept politician, a man of narrow sensibilities (had he not narrowed himself when he rejected Falstaff, saying he "despised" the life that Falstaff stood for?), at ease uttering hypocrisies and playing upon men. Yeats, whose praise of Richard II was quoted earlier, put it thus: "Having made the vessel of porcelain Richard II, Shakespeare had to make the vessel of clay Henry V. He makes him the reverse of all that Richard was. He has the gross vices, the coarse nerves, of one who is to rule among violent people." Thus Henry's lament on the treachery of Scroop, Cambridge, and Grey (II.ii.127–42), which moves him to say "I will weep for thee;/For this revolt of thine, methinks, is like/ Another fall of man," has led critics to comment sourly that Henry had betrayed Falstaff and goes on to betray his other early friends. One sympathizes with critics who find complexity here, and one cannot brush off the complexity simply by saying that it exists only in the minds of the critics, for as Robert Frost once remarked, a poet is entitled to the credit for everything that a reader finds in his work. Still, the three traitors themselves confess their treachery; nowhere is there an explicit statement that lends support to the idea that we are not to take Henry's words at face value. Similarly, though it can be said that the cowardly Pistol is a parody of Hal, deflating Hal's heroic speeches, it can be replied that Hal is Hal and that Pistol does not refute him but rather sets him off more clearly. And yet these replies do not finally convince; the impression remains that despite Henry's public virtues, the private man has something unattractive about him. He is a hero, but (we somehow feel) he is also an astute politician.

Even if there is such an ambiguity in *Henry V*, the play remains simpler than the two parts of *Henry IV*. Yet it does not lack variety: *Henry V* is not written in a single idiom, say that of "Once more unto the breach, dear friends, once more;/Or close the wall up with our English dead." There is also admirable prose, some of it in dialect, some of it bawdy, some of it so deceptively near to common speech that we must remind ourselves that its "naturalness" is no less artful than the more conspicuous "big" speeches. For example, on the eve of the Battle of Agincourt a common soldier describes Henry's show of courage thus:

He may show what outward courage he will; but I believe, as cold a night as 'tis, he could wish himself in Thames up to the neck; and so I would he were, and I by him, at all adventures, so we were quit here. (IV.i.113–17)

Possibly we can accept *Henry V* a bit more easily if we think of it as the happy final act in a four-act play (*Richard II, 1 Henry IV, 2 Henry IV, Henry V*) on the history of England from 1398 to 1415, working its way through weakness, deceit, and violence to a harmonious conclusion, "Congreeing in a full and natural close,/Like music." In fact, like a comedy the play ends with a betrothal. But the end of a comedy is assumed to be permanent, with the implication that the lovers live happily ever after. Shakespeare saw history as an unending series of ups and downs, and so at the very end of the play the Chorus reminds us that although Henry won a bride and France, "the world's best garden," Eden was again lost during the reign of Henry VI.

## THE LAST HISTORY: HENRY VIII

At the end of his career, probably around 1613, Shakespeare returned to English historical drama, which he had put aside about 1599 with the completion of *Henry V*. Possibly he felt in 1599 that he could come no closer to the present than he had already come, for in *Richard III* he had reached the Tudor period. He turned to Roman history, writing the tragedy of *Julius Caesar*, and then to a variety of comic and tragic subjects. But about the time of his retirement from the theater he returned to English history for some reason, and wrote (perhaps in collaboration with John Fletcher) another play drawn largely from his old sourcebook, Holinshed's *Chronicles*. *Henry VIII* is a curious play; it is not at all like Shakespeare's earlier histories, which (although varied) give a sense of England engaged in military conflict, working out from one reign to the next the sins and errors of previous years. But the Prologue to *Henry VIII* announces that we will not get the usual battle scenes, and we do not. *Henry VIII* relates the falls of three eminent people, Buckingham, Katherine, and Wolsey, and the near-fall of Cranmer, sometimes accompanied by declamations and interspersed with elaborate pageants.

To the extent that *Henry VIII* has more visual splendor than Shakespeare's earlier histories it has affinities with *Cymbeline*, *The Winter's Tale*, and *The Tempest*—that is, with the other plays Shakespeare wrote at the end of his career. This affinity is strengthened by the presence in *Henry VIII* of some of the themes found in the other last plays, notably the themes of patience in adversity and the innocence and vitality of a new generation. But for some readers and spectators, in *Henry VIII* these themes do not succeed in uniting the splendid episodes, which are not tightly connected by causal relationships. *Henry VIII* looks back to *A Mirror for Magistrates* in its account of the falls of illustrious people (the predominantly good Buckingham, the totally innocent Katherine, and the ambitious and scheming Wolsey), and it concludes with a burst of religiously tinged patriotism celebrating the birth and christening of the infant Elizabeth, who will introduce a new golden age. The three falls taken together involve the stuff of tragedy—innocence and guilt, intrigue, and bad luck; but these motifs are separated in the play and the effect is that of oversimplification, except insofar as we can pull the episodes together by seeing in the play a providential hand governing England. For example, in the punishment of Wolsey we can see, with a little effort, the king as dispenser of divine justice. Perhaps, too, there is a contrary ironic view, for although the play ends with Cranmer, Cromwell, and Anne Bullen high on Fortune's wheel and with the prophecy of greatness for England under Elizabeth and her successor, Shakespeare's audience knew that the first three had in turn been brought low, and it may have felt that Elizabethan glory started to fade even as Elizabeth did.

For three centuries stage history has proved that *Henry VIII* is effective in the theater, though never more so than at what probably was its premiere in 1613 when (quite literally) it brought the house down: cannon shot off in accordance with a stage direction (I.iv.49) ignited the thatched roof, and the Globe Theatre burned to the ground. England's greatest age of drama was over.

# Shakespeare's Tragedies

## THE BACKGROUND

A Renaissance dictionary defines tragedy as "a lofty kind of poetry and representing personages of great state and matter of much trouble, a great broil or stir: it beginneth prosperously, it endeth unfortunately or doubtfully, contrary to a comedy." (A comedy "beginneth sorrowfully, and endeth merrily, contrary to a tragedy.") Broadly speaking, Shakespeare's tragedies follow this pattern, except for *Hamlet*, where the hero is not "prosperous" at the beginning. For instance, at the start of the play Othello is newly married to Desdemona; Lear is almost a demigod giving away kingdoms; Macbeth has conquered on the battlefield and been elevated in rank. Moreover, all of Shakespeare's tragic heroes, with the possible exception of Romeo and Juliet, are "personages of great state," but even Romeo and Juliet are the children of important families. And each of these people "endeth unfortunately."

The idea that tragedy involves a fall from a height was commonplace in the Middle Ages, though at that time "tragedy" denoted a story rather than a play. Before reciting some narrative tragedies Chaucer's Monk defined his subject in this way:

Tragedie is to seyn a certeyn storie,
As olde bookes maken us memorie,
Of hym that stood in greet prosperitee,
And is yfallen out of heigh degree
Into myserie, and endeth wrecchedly.

I wol biwaille, in manere of tragedie,
The harm of hem that stoode in heigh degree,
And fillen so that ther nas no remedie
To brynge hem out of hir adversitee.
For certein, whan that Fortune list to flee,
Ther may no man the cours of hire withholde.
Lat no man truste on blynd prosperitee;
Be war by thise ensamples trewe and olde.

The blame for adversity is placed on Fortune, and though this goddess is sometimes conceived of as the executor of God's will, she is commonly considered capricious, turning her wheel to elevate some men and to cast down others who are aloft. Chaucer's tragic figures include men who are totally innocent, such as the noble King Peter of Cyprus, who is slain merely out of envy, the moral being that Fortune can "out of joye bring men to sorwe." But the Monk's tragic figures include Lucifer, who "fel . . . for his synne," and Adam, who for his "mysgovernaunce/ Was dryven out of hys hye prosperitee." This sort of ambiguity concerning the cause of the Fall (capricious Fortune or man's vice?) continues in later medieval thinking about tragedy, and it survives into the Renaissance. The title page of *A Mirror for Magistrates* (1559) says that the book shows "with how grievous plagues *vices* are punished; and how frail and unstable worldly prosperity is found, even of those whom *Fortune* seemeth to favor." The dedication says that the book shows "the slippery deceits of the wavering lady [Fortune] and the due reward for all kinds of vice." Sir Philip Sidney, author of the most important critical treatise of the English Renaissance, similarly observed that tragedy shows both the punishment of vice and "the uncertainty of this world, and upon how weak foundations gilden roofs are builded."

Shakespeare was familiar with the idea of Fortune as arbitrarily casting down those whom she had elevated. A poet in *Timon of Athens* says that his poem tells how "Fortune in her shift and change of mood/Spurns down her late beloved"; Richard II sees himself as a character in a book of "sad stories of the death of kings." Similarly, Wolsey in *Henry VIII* sees himself as an epitome of mankind, flourishing and then suddenly cut down, and though he goes on to attribute his fall to pride and to equate himself with Lucifer, he implies at the beginning and the end of the speech that the fault is not his:

Farewell! A long farewell to all my greatness!
This is the state of man: today he puts forth
The tender leaves of hopes; tomorrow blossoms,
And bears his blushing honors thick upon him.
The third day comes a frost, a killing frost,
And, when he thinks, good easy man, full surely
His greatness is aripening, nips his root,
And then he falls, as I do. I have ventured,
Like little wanton boys that swim on bladders,
This many summers in a sea of glory,
But far beyond my depth. My high-blown pride
At length broke under me and now has left me,
Weary and old with service, to the mercy
Of a rude stream that must forever hide me.
Vain pomp and glory of this world, I hate ye.
I feel my heart new opened. O, how wretched
Is that poor man that hangs on princes' favors!
There is betwixt that smile we would aspire to,
That sweet aspect of princes, and their ruin,
More pangs and fears than wars or women have.
And when he falls, he falls like Lucifer,
Never to hope again.　　　　　　(III.ii.351–72)

What attitude is the spectator to have toward the fall of Shakespeare's tragic heroes? J. V. Cunningham in *Woe or Wonder* convincingly suggests that our response to the tragic action should be guided by Horatio's words in *Hamlet* when he tells Fortinbras and other late arrivals what to make of the sight of the corpses on the stage:

What is it you would see?
If aught of woe or wonder, cease your search.
　　　　　　(V.ii.364–65)

"Woe," or pity and fear; "wonder," or astonishment and admiration. The spectacle is all of these, as it would not be if the hero were merely the victim of Fortune or, on the other hand, the victim of his own vice. Shakespeare's tragic heroes are not, of course, all of a kind; at one extreme are Romeo and Juliet, who are chiefly presented as victims ("star-crossed lovers"); in the middle perhaps are Lear ("more sinned against than sinning") and, somewhat more guilty, Mark Antony ("his taints and honors/Waged equal with him"); at the other extreme is Macbeth, who is unequivocally an assassin. But there is always some ambiguity: a number of passages in *Romeo and Juliet* suggest that the lovers are undone by their own haste, or to put it more negatively, by their rashness; at the opposite extreme there is at least the hint that Macbeth is beguiled into evil by the witches and is thus himself a victim of mysterious cosmic forces.

Thus the old idea that Shakespeare's heroes suffer because of a tragic "flaw" is grossly inadequate. In fact, the heroes are sometimes undone by their eminence rather than by their weakness. They have a greatness of spirit that propels them to act, and action increases a man's vulnerability, for it sets up reactions. For example, Hamlet, unable to accept the death of his father and the remarriage of his mother, which the rest of the court (including his mother) accepts easily, stands apart from the court by virtue of his heightened moral sense, and he comes to feel that "The time is out of joint" and that he must set it right. Moreover, Hamlet's death is most immediately brought about not by any fault (such as the procrastination he is often accused of) but by his noblemindedness, which does not allow him to suspect that Laertes will behave treacherously in the duel. Claudius knows that Hamlet's excellence makes him vulnerable, and he explains this to Laertes: because he is "Most generous and free from all contriving," Hamlet "Will not peruse the foils." Similarly, Othello is brought to murder Desdemona not simply because he is jealous but because he is (as Iago knows) "of a free and open nature/That thinks men honest that but seem to be so." Iago knows, too, that he can turn Desdemona's "virtue into pitch,/And out of her own goodness make the net/That shall enmesh them all." Excellence, paradoxically, plays its role in destroying the heroes, for it impels them (as ordinary men are not impelled) to perform daring actions that have woeful consequences, or it allows lesser men to prey upon them. Those puritanical critics who denounced tragedies because they were full of "killing, hewing, stabbing, dagger-drawing, fighting, butchery, treachery, villainy, etc., and all kinds of heroic evils whatever" (the words are John Greene's, in 1615) were not unfair in their descriptions of the tragic plots, and their indignation suggests not that they failed to see the moral implications of tragedy but that they clearly saw them and did not like them. It is, after all, subversive of established morality to suggest that goodness may involve one in evildoing.

As has been mentioned, in the tragic world actions have consequences that are irreversible. (In the comic world, wicked plots fail, and mistakes, such as Puck's anointing of the wrong lover's eyes, can be reversed.) Iago knows that a hero can be snared in a web of circumstances, and Rosencrantz knows that "the cess of majesty" (the death of a king) is more than the death of an individual:

The cess of majesty
Dies not alone, but like a gulf doth draw
What's near it with it; or it is a massy wheel
Fixed on the summit of the highest mount,
To whose huge spokes ten thousand lesser things
Are mortised and adjoined, which when it falls,
Each small annexment, petty consequence,
Attends the boist'rous ruin. Never alone
Did the king sigh, but with a general groan.

(*Hamlet*, III.iii.15–23)

But this tragic vision of a world in which all events are enmeshed is complemented by another vision, that of the hero as becoming progressively isolated. Before they die, Shakespeare's tragic heroes usually move away from society. Even at the start, of course, their eminence separates them in some degree from the rest of mankind, but by and large (except for Hamlet) they are attached to society: Titus, Othello, Macbeth, and Coriolanus are indispensable military leaders, and Lear is a reigning monarch. Their actions, however, propel them into a private world; thus Lear is led to "abjure all roofs" and to move to the stormy heath, and Macbeth finds that he can confide in no one, not even in his wife. Juliet, isolated from Romeo, from her parents, and from her Nurse, knows that "My dismal scene I needs must act alone." Hamlet even at the outset is estranged, and his isolation is increased by the breach between himself and Ophelia and is then made physical by the sea voyage he is sent on. This isolation normally produces in the tragic hero a new sense of identity; thrown back upon himself, he comes to see more clearly what he is. Before his journey to the heath, Lear feels his identity crumbling when, astounded by his daughters' ingratitude, he asks,

Does any here know me? This is not Lear.
Does Lear walk thus? Speak thus? Where are his eyes?

.    .    .

Who is it that can tell me who I am?    (I.iv.227–28, 231)

On the heath Lear gets to know who he is; he is one who has "ta'en/Too little care."

Poor naked wretches, wheresoe'er you are,
That bide the pelting of this pitiless storm,
How shall your houseless heads and unfed sides,
Your looped and windowed raggedness, defend you
From seasons such as these? O, I have ta'en
Too little care of this! Take physic, pomp;
Expose thyself to feel what wretches feel.    (III.iv.28–34)

Similarly, Macbeth comes to the recognition (Aristotle's term is *anagnorisis*) that his earlier actions have had a result opposite from that which he intended. He aimed at the crown, thinking it would bring him happiness, but his hopes deceived him:

I have lived long enough. My way of life
Is fall'n into the sear, the yellow leaf,
And that which should accompany old age,
As honor, love, obedience, troops of friends,
I must not look to have; but, in their stead,
Curses not loud but deep, mouth-honor, breath,
Which the poor heart would fain deny, and dare not.

(V.iii.22–28)

Othello too has his moment of recognition, and though it is monstrously painful, for it tells him that he is a murderer, it also restores his identity, for it tells him that Desdemona was innocent and that he was right to love her:

Speak of me as I am. Nothing extenuate,
Nor set down aught in malice. Then must you speak
Of one that loved not wisely, but too well;
Of one not easily jealous, but, being wrought,
Perplexed in the extreme; of one whose hand,
Like the base Judean, threw a pearl away
Richer than all his tribe.    (V.ii.341–47)

Behind this speech—and very far behind it in quality though not in date—are the confessions or addresses to the world made by characters in *A Mirror for Magistrates*.

But of course there are also dramatic traditions behind Shakespeare's tragedies. Though neither the miracle play nor the morality play (see pp. 12–15) is tragic, both forms contributed to Elizabethan tragedy. The miracle play sometimes deals with tyrants such as Pharaoh and Herod, showing their cruelty and the punishment subsequently visited upon them, and in its later development it deals also with the tribulations of saints. The morality play regularly dramatizes the conflict of vice and virtue, and it often dramatizes the coming of death, sometimes conceiving of death as retribution for sin. The villains in these plays contributed to the making of the Elizabethan villain. Biblical tyrants of the miracle plays doubtless exerted an influence on the secular tyrants of mid-sixteenth-century "conqueror" plays, and so did such a figure as the wicked prince in *The Cradle of Security* (see pp. 14–15); the innocent sufferers of the miracle plays and the representatives of fallible mankind in the morality plays also exerted an influence on the Elizabethan tragic hero, but none of these characters are Shakespearean tragic heroes.

Another dramatic tradition, derived from the Roman dramatist Seneca, helped to give Elizabethan tragedy its characteristic "woe," though as we have already seen, woe was the keynote of medieval nondramatic tragic writing. Greek tragedy was little known, but in university circles at least Seneca (4 B.C.?–65 A.D.) was widely known, though perhaps more for his moral philosophy than for his plays. Nonetheless, from about the middle of the sixteenth century onward Seneca's plays were translated; the first English translation was published in 1559, the year of the first edition of *A Mirror for Magistrates*. Academic authors sometimes imitated Seneca's plays, and these imitations exerted an influence on the popular dramatists, some of whom were university graduates and all of whom could at least read Seneca in translation. That he was read in translation is indicated by Thomas Nashe's assertion in 1589 that "English Seneca read by candlelight yields many good sentences, as 'Blood is a beggar.'" Seneca's two chief themes are tyranny and revenge (both of which appear in Shakespeare's *Titus Andronicus*, *Richard III*, *Julius Caesar*, and *Hamlet*); his characters are fiercely passionate and given to alternating between furious denunciations and stoic meditations (one thinks of Hamlet); and the prevailing atmosphere is one of horror, rather like Hamlet's "the very witching time of night,/When churchyards yawn, and hell itself breathes out/Contagion to this world." Certainly an Elizabethan playwright did not have to go to Seneca's plays for any of these themes, but the very fact that they were already a part of the English tradition perhaps made Seneca the more accessible and the more welcome: here was a classical playwright whose use of such material gave it an added dignity. Seneca helped the playwrights of the decades before Shakespeare to draw upon history and legendary history, showing the fall of tyrants and the suffering visited upon passionate heroes rather than upon the character abstractions of the morality play. Moreover, when in the 1580's—and perhaps even in the 1570's—the playwrights turned to continental stories (*novelle*) for material, they could by a somewhat Senecan treatment elevate to a tragic status these tales, which for the most part dealt either with the pathetic deaths of innocent lovers in a world of intrigue or with crime and vengeance. Again, this is not to say that Seneca was responsible for the character of Elizabethan tragedy; without the help of Seneca John Bale had already adapted the political morality play into a play showing the fall of an historical figure, King John, though Bale retained some abstractions. Even Sackville and Norton's *Gorboduc* (1561), the first English historical play with no moral abstractions, praised by Sir Philip Sidney for "climbing to the height of Seneca's his style," is deeply indebted to the morality play in its treatment of the good and wicked counselors who flank the king and its heavy emphasis on the moral implications of action. Seneca, however, did not merely provide aphorisms of the sort Nashe alluded to; he also gave a classical sanction to the depictions of great falls due not simply to Fortune but to passionate natures which in some measure destroy themselves, and to the revenge plot urged by a ghost. Of course, the Elizabethans regularly complicated this plot far more than Seneca did (his plots begin just before the catastrophe), and they often added to the revenge plot other matter—for example, comic scenes—that was un-Senecan but thoroughly in the medieval dramatic tradition. Hamlet tells us that for the players who come to Elsinore "Seneca cannot be too heavy." Seneca was, in fact, too heavy for the English popular theater, which preferred "mongrel tragicomedy," but he provided the dramatists with moral tags and motifs, and indeed with a respectable model if they cared to look for one. What they saw in Seneca, of course, was what they wanted to see. *Titus Andronicus* does not closely resemble any play by Seneca (though it quotes from him), but Shakespeare probably felt that in it he had written an appropriately classical play.

## THREE EARLY TRAGEDIES:
### TITUS ANDRONICUS, ROMEO AND JULIET, JULIUS CAESAR

Like *The Comedy of Errors* (probably Shakespeare's first comedy), *Titus Andronicus* is very much an academic play. In Ovid, the Roman nondramatic poet whom he had read in school, Shakespeare found the prettified violent story of Philomela, which is explicitly referred to in the play (IV.i.42 ff.) and which resembles parts of Shakespeare's plot. From Seneca (or from English Senecan plays such as Thomas Kyd's *The Spanish Tragedy*) Shakespeare derived the motif of revenge, and of a hero driven to madness and to feigning madness. The author of *Titus Andronicus*

advertises his bookishness not only by the numerous mythological references and declamatory passages but by an explicit reference to William Lily's Latin grammar, the text used in grammar schools throughout Elizabethan England. One of Titus' enemies says of a Latin message attached to a bundle of weapons:

> O, 'tis a verse in Horace; I know it well:
> I read it in the grammar long ago.          (IV.ii.22–23)

The rather symmetrical arrangements of the characters in *Titus*—loving brothers and quarreling brothers, a virgin and a mistress, and so on—also suggest a playwright who is anxious to do things properly. But if the characters are sometimes too neatly paired, a heritage from the morality play, and if they often seem to recite rather than to talk to each other, there is still a good deal of subtlety in the play. For example, Titus, the inflexibly honorable and somewhat simple general, is contrasted not only with Aaron, the cunning villain, but with Marcus, Titus' humane brother. There is scarcely a scene or a character that does not in some way echo or contrast with another scene or character, and although these echoes and contrasts are often a bit obvious, they are nonetheless the very stuff of tragedy, where every action has its consequences—where, as Alfred North Whitehead said, we see "the remorseless working of things." Titus believes that honor requires him to sacrifice to his dead sons a son of his enemy; he acts on this belief, and thus he inevitably evokes the enmity of the victim's mother, who retaliates with outrages upon Titus' children, thereby goading Titus into counterretaliation. The elaborate parallelisms in *Titus*, then, are not very different from those in the later and greater tragedies; they are simply more obvious. In *Hamlet*, for example, the protagonist is flanked by Laertes and Fortinbras, each of whom (like Hamlet) has lost a father; in *King Lear* the protagonist is flanked by wicked daughters and a good daughter, and Gloucester has a wicked son and a good son. But the symmetry of *Titus*, though obvious, is by no means naive, and Shakespeare never discarded the technique. Moreover, it is not wholly illegitimate to read back into *Titus* characters and scenes from *Othello* (the Machiavellian Aaron anticipates Iago in his scheming, and the honest soldier Titus anticipates Othello), from *Hamlet* (driven to revenge, Titus is both mad and playing at madness), and from *King Lear* (Titus is driven beyond the bounds of sanity). Moreover, in IV.iii the first of the clowns in Shakespeare's tragedies appears; his role is minute, but he would have been unthinkable in one of Seneca's plays, and we are grateful for this simple voice that sounds across the rhetoric of the heroic (and villainous) world. Finally, like most of Shakespeare's other tragedies, *Titus* had affinities with political concerns. It begins with matters of political succession and concludes with the suggestion that the state, which has undergone a convulsion more or less parallel to the anguish of the tragic hero, will be reunited. What does not appear in *Titus*, however, is the achievement of self-understanding characteristic of the later tragic heroes. Titus sees Rome (aptly enough) as a "wilderness of tigers," but he does not see the barbarity of his own inflexible code of honor, which Tamora accurately enough characterizes as a "cruel, irreligious piety." Titus sees only the enemy outside himself; he never enters upon the sort of prolonged examination of his own actions that leads King Lear to say, "I have ta'en/Too little care of this."

*Romeo and Juliet* (1594–96) was preceded not only by *Titus* but by some history plays with tragic aspects and, no less important for the present purpose, by at least two comedies about lovers, one of which is set in Verona. Probably, too, Shakespeare was writing his sonnets at this time. Thus he was developing as a poet of love, and it is not surprising that he then turned to a tragedy of love. More exactly, it is not surprising to us; but an Elizabethan audience was probably surprised to find lovers—rather than heroic figures—the subject of a tragedy. Love was the stuff of comedies, and only a few earlier tragedies deal with love, though continental fiction offered many tales of young lovers destroyed by a cruel world. *Romeo and Juliet* was written at about the time of *Richard II* and *A Midsummer Night's Dream* (the exact dates are unknown); like these two other plays, *Romeo and Juliet* is conspicuously lyrical. For example, there is a sonnet in the dialogue between Romeo and Juliet, and the sonnet uses the conventional poetic figure of the lover as a pilgrim:

ROMEO
If I profane with my unworthiest hand
  This holy shrine, the gentle sin is this:
My lips, two blushing pilgrims, ready stand
  To smooth that rough touch with a tender kiss.
JULIET
Good pilgrim, you do wrong your hand too much,
  Which mannerly devotion shows in this;
For saints have hands that pilgrims' hands do touch,
  And palm to palm is holy palmers' kiss.
ROMEO
Have not saints lips, and holy palmers too?
JULIET
Ay, pilgrim, lips that they must use in prayer.
ROMEO
O, then, dear saint, let lips do what hands do!
  They pray; grant thou, lest faith turn to despair.
JULIET
Saints do not move, though grant for prayers' sake.
ROMEO
Then move not while my prayer's effect I take.

[*Kisses her.*]                           (I.v.95–108)

Moreover, like its near-contemporary *Richard II*, the play is rich in iterative imagery, recurrent images that help to define its meaning. In *Romeo and Juliet* there are abundant images of a speed that soon exhausts itself and of light yielding to darkness, both of which are appropriate in a play about the early death of two ardent lovers surrounded by enmity. For example:

Although I joy in thee,
I have no joy of this contract tonight.
It is too rash, too unadvised, too sudden;
Too like the lightning, which doth cease to be
Ere one can say it lightens.          (II.ii.116–20)

Wisely and slow. They stumble that run fast.   (II.iii.94)

These violent delights have violent ends
And in their triumph die, like fire and powder,
Which, as they kiss, consume.           (II.vi.9–11)

Such imagery helps to suggest the naturalness or inevitability of the lovers' deaths. The inevitability is also directly asserted by the Chorus, which speaks of the "star-crossed lovers," and this motif is periodically repeated, as when Romeo says,

My mind misgives
Some consequence yet hanging in the stars
Shall bitterly begin his fearful date
With this night's revels.                (I.iv.106–09)

The emphasis on the feud between the families also suggests that overpowering forces surround the lovers. Thus if we can look at the tragedy as proceeding in part from the passion of the lovers, we can also look at it as proceeding in part from the forces of destiny. That is, we can see the characters as contributing to their downfall, and we can also see them as victims. Juliet's father, in the play's penultimate speech, remembering the feud that has forced the lovers to a fatal secrecy, calls them "poor sacrifices of our enmity," thus emphasizing the suggestion that Romeo and Juliet are martyred victims. Shakespeare probably saw the play as appropriately classical in spirit: Seneca's emphasis on the blows of fortune (Romeo sees himself as "fortune's fool") is translated into both dire astrological influence and chance (Romeo does not receive the letter sent to inform him that Juliet has taken a potion); and like a Senecan hero Romeo is occasionally stoical ("I defy you, stars"). Some of the hyperboles ("chain me with roaring bears") have a Senecan ring; and the long final scene, set in a tomb, with its talk of worms as Juliet's chambermaids, and with the bloody corpse of Paris lying nearby, would probably have brought approving nods from university men. On the other hand, the play is distinctly un-Senecan in its hero, in its bustle, and in its comedy. The quarreling servants at the outset give a comic treatment of the feud, suggesting its tragic possibilities; the bawdy comments of Mercutio and the Nurse are delightful in themselves (or would be, if we did not need explanatory footnotes), yet they are also integral in this play about love.

When he turned to his third tragedy, *Julius Caesar* (1599–1600), Shakespeare had already written nine plays on English history and about half a dozen comedies. In the histories Shakespeare explores the unending political developments that press on from one play to the next; on the whole the concern is with man as a political rather than moral creature, with what *happened* rather than (as in tragedy) with what *happens*. After completing *Henry V* Shakespeare may have felt that he had reached a dead end, for he had already written on the reign of Henry VI, and to continue beyond the reign of Henry VI would have brought him, in effect, to the origins of contemporary politics—in short, too close to present matters. In any case, around 1599 Shakespeare turned to Roman history, writing a play that, like those on English history, concerns political machinations; but in Brutus he explores more fully a man making a moral decision and then suffering its consequences. *Julius Caesar* owes something to the earlier history plays, which were at least occasionally concerned with the idea of retributive justice, and it of course owes something to earlier tragedies, which showed a downfall, but it differs from those tragedies in an important way: in Brutus, Shakespeare presents the fall neither of a tyrant nor of a weakling but of a noble yet flawed hero, a man who seeks to act for his country's good. The English histories are not greatly concerned with moral crises; nor do the two earlier tragedies indicate much concern of this sort. In *Romeo and Juliet* the lovers do not greatly ponder their course of action; they are overwhelmingly in love, and they are "star-crossed," but in *Julius Caesar* at least to a large degree "the fault . . . is not in our stars,/But in ourselves." Brutus tries to live according to a moral code, pondering a course of action, coming to a conclusion, acting, and then suffering the unexpected yet (to our view) inevitable consequences of the action. Ironically, too, Brutus falls into evil and ultimately into destruction largely because of his nobility: had he been less high-minded and more worldly minded, Cassius could not have manipulated him so easily. Cassius makes this point clear in a soliloquy:

> Well, Brutus, thou art noble; yet I see
> Thy honorable mettle may be wrought
> From that it is disposed; therefore it is meet
> That noble minds keep ever with their likes. (I.ii.306–09)

Cassius himself, however, is not the cunning, successful man-of-the-world that he thinks he is, for he too is destroyed, and by his own hand, when he commits suicide in the mistaken belief that the battle is lost. The successful man in the play is Antony, who is adept at manipulating people, most notably in his funeral oration in III.ii. He is not a villain, but insofar as he works on others he is an ancestor of such arch-villains as Edmund in *King Lear* and Iago in *Othello*. These later voices are anticipated in Antony's wry self-satisfied comment in the middle of the play, when he sees that he has moved the plebeians to fury:

> Now let it work: Mischief, thou art afoot,
> Take thou what course thou wilt. (III.ii.261–62)

Of course, like Brutus, Caesar too is a tragic figure. It seems clear that Shakespeare saw him as fitting the tragic formula of a man who falls from a great height. He has been blamed for his arrogance, and indeed he is unlovely, though we may wonder if we would prefer just before his assassination a less supremely confident figure, a man who (for example) eagerly clutched at Artemidorus' warning message instead of brushing it off with "What touches us ourself shall be last served." As a comparison with Plutarch's life of Caesar indicates, Shakespeare was careful to omit some of Caesar's most ignoble actions. Moreover, he gave Caesar an added dignity just prior to the assassination by virtue of his cordiality to the conspirators ("Good friends, go in and taste some wine with me"), and especially by virtue of the lies and the fawning which the conspirators engage in when they surround Caesar. Finally, there is the pathos of "Et tu, Bruté? Then fall Caesar," when the wounded leader perceives that his trust in Brutus was misplaced. The play, then, is concerned with two tragic figures (a third, if we wish to add Cassius); moreover, though it is concerned with political problems to a much greater degree than the later tragedies are, it shows Shakespeare moving toward the complexities of the later tragedies, in which the tragic characters act and then must face the ironic consequences of their actions.

## THE LATER TRAGEDIES: HAMLET, OTHELLO, KING LEAR, MACBETH, ANTONY AND CLEOPATRA, CORIOLANUS

As usual, the dates of the later tragedies are uncertain, but apparently between 1600 and 1608 Shakespeare wrote *Hamlet, Othello, King Lear, Macbeth, Antony and Cleopatra*, and *Coriolanus*. In these years, too, he probably wrote his two "dark" comedies, *All's Well That Ends Well* and *Measure for Measure*, a markedly ironic tragedy, *Troilus and Cressida*, and a play about a notorious misanthrope, *Timon of Athens*. The conjunction of these plays has sometimes caused readers to assume that Shakespeare entered a "tragic" period, a period of despair during which he poured out his heart in tragic, dark, and bitter plays while he underwent a mental crisis. The crisis has been variously identified as the failure of Essex' revolution in 1601; Shakespeare's father's death in 1601; and an unsuccessful love affair, described in the sonnets concerning the Dark Lady, on whom Shakespeare had his revenge in his portraits of Cressida and Cleopatra. (But, we might ask, how do we account for Cordelia and "the divine Desdemona"?) Such views, however, assume that an author writes tragedy when he is depressed, and they do not give adequate weight to the fact that tragedy was an established literary genre at which Shakespeare had earlier tried his hand in *Titus, Romeo and Juliet*, and *Julius Caesar*. Perhaps, then, it is best to see the great tragedies as the achievement of mastery in a genre rather than as veiled autobiography.

*Hamlet* is the most widely quoted, most often alluded to, and most often written about of Shakespeare's plays. The abundance of commentary, however, stems in part from uncertainties that are found in the play, and T. S. Eliot was not alone in suggesting that *Hamlet* is an artistic failure. Why does Hamlet delay? Because he must confirm the report of the Ghost, who may be a devil? Because he is a coward? Because his moral code disapproves of killing? Because he cannot kill the man who fulfilled Hamlet's unconscious Oedipal wish to kill his own father? Inevitably another question arises: *Does* Hamlet delay? He says he does, but some critics have argued that he merely chastises himself needlessly or, alternatively, that Shakespeare was merely creating a spurious suspense by reminding us of what still had to be done. Yet another question: Is Hamlet mad or only pretending to be? (Oscar Wilde varied the question: Are the commentators on *Hamlet* mad or only pretending to be?)

In the 1580's playwrights had linked Senecan motifs of passion and revenge with continental stories of intrigue, notably in Thomas Kyd's *The Spanish Tragedy*. Almost surely there was a play about Hamlet before Shakespeare's, perhaps by Kyd, and this Hamlet was apparently conspicuous for his cunning, his madness, and his savagery. Shakespeare's Hamlet in some degree shares these traits—enough so that George Bernard Shaw complained that Hamlet kills three people and is forever apologizing that he hasn't killed a fourth. There is something to this view. Hamlet mistakenly kills Polonius, and his chief reaction is regret that his victim was not Claudius. He forges orders so that Rosencrantz and Guildenstern will be "put to sudden death,/Not shriving time allowed," though Rosencrantz and Guildenstern are merely serving the man who they have every reason to suppose is their lawful king.

Hamlet has no regrets about dispatching these two men: "They are not near my conscience." Consider, too, his rough treatment of Ophelia and of his mother, and his desire not only to kill Claudius but to damn his soul (III.iii.73–96). But this, of course, is not the whole story, and Hamlet has not lacked for sympathizers. According to Goethe's Wilhelm Meister, Hamlet, "a lovely, pure, noble and most moral nature, without the strength of nerve which forms a hero, sinks beneath a burden which it cannot bear and must not cast away."

Perhaps both of these views, and others, have some merit; perhaps too Hamlet changes as the play goes on, from (to put it crudely) a revenger full of anguish, self-hatred, and fury to an avenger who comes to see that his job is not to set the world right or to devise a trap wherein he can catch Claudius' soul but to be an instrument of God's will. In III.ii he praises Horatio for his dispassionateness, saying that Horatio "is not passion's slave." But in III.iii, when Hamlet announces that he will delay until he can catch Claudius in a sinful act, we see clearly how hideous a *dis-passionate* revenge would be. Here, if anywhere, Hamlet repels us. But late in the play, after his return from the sea voyage, he seems to have changed: he is courteous to the gravediggers, and in V.ii he apologizes to Laertes. Most important, he has ceased to be an intriguer and is content to be an instrument: "We defy augury. There is special providence in the fall of a sparrow. . . . The readiness is all." Of course there are complications here too, and critics have sometimes wondered whether Hamlet, who at first has such trouble bringing himself to act, does not ultimately lapse into a sluggish fatalism. Possibly this is true, but even so we probably prefer a sluggish Hamlet to a scheming one, and the rest of the play—his manly duel with Laertes, his execution of justice on Claudius, Laertes' tribute to "noble Hamlet," and Fortinbras' testimonial and the military funeral—suggests that Hamlet's course is noble.

Despite the variety of interpretations, it must be agreed that Shakespeare's dramaturgy is unerring: those who want patterns of imagery (notably concerning war, sickness, the nature of action, and appearance versus reality) can find them; those who want rounded characters (sometimes established by contrasts with other characters, as Hamlet is contrasted with Laertes and Fortinbras, both of whom seek to avenge their fathers' deaths) can find them; those who want philosophic poetic speeches and earthy prose speeches can find them; and those who want suspense, and then the fulfillment of expectations, can find it: the opening scene, for example, begins—appropriately for a play that has puzzled so many—with a question, "Who's there?" The suspense is then skillfully built up, slackened, and built up again with "this thing," "this dreaded sight," and "this apparition," and finally (still only at line 39) the Ghost appears, even as a previous appearance is being described. It disappears and is discussed, and during a long speech about the uncertain military situation (which introduces a reference to Caesar's ghost) it reappears, and again vanishes as the cock crows, evoking lyrical speeches from Marcellus and Horatio that help to diminish the uncertainty by introducing thoughts of purification, partly explicitly Christian (I.i.158–61) and partly natural (I.i.166–67). And so in 170 lines the scene changes from midnight to dawn (in the first forty lines we

are told eleven times that it is night), and the play moves from a sense of fear and mysterious anguish (beginning with Francisco's "I am sick at heart") to hope. The meaning of the play may baffle us, but the artistry of the play can only convince us that Shakespeare had perfected his skill, and it is not at all surprising that he went on to write other tragedies.

*Hamlet* has a complicated plot (there is intrigue and counterintrigue, and a subplot concerning Fortinbras) and a philosophically minded protagonist who calls into doubt the nature of action. *Othello*, Shakespeare's next tragedy, is simpler on both accounts: the plot is derived from an Italian short story and can be summarized in a couple of sentences, and the nature of the events is never called into doubt. A. C. Bradley put it thus: "*Othello* has not . . . the power of dilating the imagination by vague suggestions of huge universal powers working in the world of individual fate and passion." Possibly if we are attentive to the hero's hyperboles, and to the villain's diabolical malice (see p. 14), we do hear suggestions of "universal powers," but in the main Bradley is right.

Perhaps because the play is at least superficially rather simple and its hero is said to be "noble," much twentieth-century criticism, unhappy with simplicity and nobility, has found the play wanting, or has complicated it by suggesting (for example) that Othello is not what he seems to be. The critical tendency to diminish Othello—to see him as immature and theatrical if not corrupt—is perhaps best known in T. S. Eliot's comment on Othello's penultimate speech, which Eliot characterizes as an "exposure of human weakness." Eliot's point is that the speech is not to be taken at face value; rather, Othello should be viewed as "cheering himself up. He is endeavoring to escape reality, he has ceased to think about Desdemona and is thinking about himself. . . . Othello . . . [is] adopting an *aesthetic* rather than a moral attitude." Here is the speech:

Soft you, a word or two before you go.
I have done the state some service, and they know't.
No more of that. I pray you, in your letters,
When you shall these unlucky deeds relate,
Speak of me as I am. Nothing extenuate,
Nor set down aught in malice. Then must you speak
Of one that loved not wisely, but too well;
Of one not easily jealous, but, being wrought,
Perplexed in the extreme; of one whose hand,
Like the base Judean, threw a pearl away
Richer than all his tribe; of one whose subdued eyes,
Albeit unusèd to the melting mood,
Drops tears as fast as the Arabian trees
Their med'cinable gum. Set you down this.
And say besides that in Aleppo once,
Where a malignant and a turbaned Turk
Beat a Venetian and traduced the state,
I took by th' throat the circumcisèd dog
And smote him—thus.
    [*He stabs himself.*]                    (V.ii.337–55)

Against Eliot's view it can be argued that Othello judges himself accurately and severely: he compares himself to a Turk (in this play, the enemy of Christian civilization), and he inflicts upon himself the same punishment that he inflicts on the Turkish enemy. Having fully recognized his responsibility for Desdemona's death, and having condemned and executed himself, like Romeo and Mark Antony he pays his beloved a last tribute of a kiss, affirming his faith in her value and demonstrating that Iago has not, finally, corrupted him.

It seems appropriate to move from *Hamlet* and *Othello* directly to *King Lear* (though possibly *Timon of Athens* was written between these two plays), for *Lear* seems to be displacing *Hamlet* as the play that speaks to our time. *Hamlet* was especially popular with nineteenth-century critics, who often found in the uncertain prince an image of their own doubts in a world in which belief in a benevolent divine order was collapsing under the influence of scientific materialism and bourgeois aggressiveness. Many critics in our age find in *Lear*—where "for many miles about/There's scarce a bush"—a play thoroughly in the spirit of *Waiting for Godot*, where the scenery consists of a single tree. *Lear* has the amplitude that Bradley found lacking in *Othello*, and it is terrifying. Moreover, does not Lear denounce the hypocrisy of the power structure and expose the powerlessness of the disenfranchised? "Robes and furred gowns hide all. Plate sin with gold,/And the strong lance of justice hurtless breaks;/Arm it in rags, a pygmy's straw does pierce it" (IV.vi.165–67). And so Lear strips off his clothing (III.iv) and reduces himself to "a poor, bare, forked animal," to find the essential man, "the thing itself." Is there no more? What of the gods? The characters in the play offer various comments on the government of the universe, ranging from "As flies to wanton boys, are we to th' gods,/They kill us for their sport" to "The gods are just." But perhaps the most memorable reference to the gods is not a mere comment but a comment followed by an action: learning that Cordelia is in danger, Albany cries out, "The gods defend her!" and immediately his words are mocked by Lear's entrance on the stage, with the dead Cordelia in his arms.

For Kent, a moment later, "all's cheerless, dark, and deadly," and it almost seems true. But only almost, for the interpretation of *Lear* as a revelation of the emptiness of life fails to consider at least two things. First, there is an affirmation in those passages in which Lear comes to see that he is not what he thought he was. For example:

> They flattered me . . . . When the rain came to wet me once and the wind to make me chatter; when the thunder would not peace at my bidding; there I found 'em, there I smelt 'em out. Go to, they are not men o' their words: they told me I was everything; 'tis a lie, I am not ague-proof [secure against fever].     (IV.vi.96–105)

Second, this *anagnorisis* (or recognition) is several times associated with love or charity, as when Lear with unexpected tenderness invites the Fool to enter the hovel first and then confesses his guilt in having cared too little for humanity (III.iv.26–36). And this care for humanity is seen in Cordelia, who comes—though ineffectually in the long run—to the aid of her father; it is seen too in the nameless servant who at the end of III.vii promises to apply medicine to Gloucester's eyeless sockets; it is seen even in the villainous Edmund, who in dying repents and says, "Some good I mean to do,/Despite of mine own nature" (V.iii.245–46), and who thereupon seeks, unsuccessfully, to save Cordelia. Only a Dr. Pangloss would say that these actions

turn *King Lear* into a happy vision, but it is perverse to ignore them, and to refuse to see that in this play love humanizes as surely as egoism dehumanizes.

Finally, then, *King Lear* is a profound morality play; like *Everyman*, Lear is called to account and finds that those he unthinkingly trusted—Goneril and Regan—offer him no help and that those he used most harshly—Kent and Cordelia—minister to him in his trial and present him patterns of love. This is not to say that Lear becomes a saint at the end—he can still rage—but it does suggest that if the play dramatizes man's desolation it also dramatizes the love that, while providing no protection against pain or death, makes man's life something different from the life of "a dog, a horse, a rat."

In *Macbeth*, Shakespeare forsook the double plot that he used in *King Lear* (the story of Lear and his daughters and the parallel story of Gloucester and his sons) and concentrated, as he had in *Othello*, on a single and simple plot. Like *King Lear*, however, *Macbeth* has its most immediate origin not in a short tale but in Holinshed's *Chronicles*. Like *King Lear*, too, it is reasonably classified as a tragedy rather than as a history (even though it is a descendant of the mid-sixteenth-century moral history plays) because it is a play more about people than about politics, more about what happens than about what happened. The play is chiefly concerned with Macbeth, much less so with Scottish history. Yet politics are a part of the play: it was written during the reign of James I of England, who was James VI of Scotland; perhaps it was written *for* James, who was regarded as a descendant of Banquo and who therefore is implicitly complimented in the procession of kings and Banquo in IV.i.

The political nature of the play appears too in the strong emphasis at the end on a Scotland purged of evil and guided by a rightful hand. The tragedies regularly end with the suggestion that after the tragic hero's death order is restored, though this order which the survivors form is pale when compared with the hero's greatness. Thus in *Titus Andronicus* Lucius is acclaimed "Rome's gracious governor," and he makes plans to inter the dead and to punish the villain; in *Romeo and Juliet* the feud that divides the city is concluded, though the death of the lovers may well make us feel that the vibrancy has gone out of Verona; in *Julius Caesar* Octavius pays tribute to Brutus and holds the reins of government; in *Hamlet* Fortinbras pays tribute to Hamlet and acquires the Danish throne; in *King Lear* Albany (Lear's son-in-law) invites Edgar to "Rule in this realm and the gored state sustain." Edgar accepts the responsibility, but with a backward glance at vanished greatness:

> The weight of this sad time we must obey,
> Speak what we feel, not what we ought to say.
> The oldest hath borne most: we that are young
> Shall never see so much, nor live so long.   (V.iii.325–28)

Thus it is no surprise that at the end of *Macbeth* Malcolm is placed on the throne, promising justice. But because Macbeth is a villain-hero (and because the play was probably designed in part to celebrate King James) the protagonist is unusually diminished—he is "this dead butcher"—and the happy future of the new reign is emphasized. Scotland had suffered great disorder for a while because its murderous ruler was disordered, but now its rightful monarch will order the realm:

> this, and what needful else
> That calls upon us, by the grace of Grace
> We will perform in measure, time, and place:
> So thanks to all at once and to each one,
> Whom we invite to see us crowned at Scone.
>
> (V.viii.71–75)

The choice of a villain-hero probably does not indicate that Shakespeare's sense of human guilt had deepened, and it should be noted that Macbeth is given a measure of sympathy and humanity denied to an earlier villain-hero, Richard III. Richard only briefly, at the end, suffers doubts and fears, and in doing so he becomes less of a medieval Vice figure and more of an Everyman, or simply a terrified realistic king; but Macbeth's conscience regularly reminds him of his guilt, and he is punished not only at the end by death but throughout by anxiety and sleeplessness. Even before he kills Duncan he is afflicted, and though he achieves his ambition of ascending the throne (Act III opens with "Thou hast it now: king"), he finds the prize a torment:

> Upon my head they placed a fruitless crown
> And put a barren scepter in my gripe.    (III.i.61–62)

If *King Lear* is a morality play in which Lear ultimately moves toward the good counselors Cordelia and Kent and away from the savage Goneril and Regan, *Macbeth* too is a morality play in which the tragic protagonist chooses the forces of evil rather than of good (Lady Macbeth and the witches rather than Duncan and Banquo), but he is always aware of what he has done, and this self-awareness and the guilt it engenders gain him some sympathy.

Like *Macbeth*, *Antony and Cleopatra* has political implications, but it too is very different from Shakespeare's history plays. And it is very different from *Macbeth*, not only in its much wider geographical spread and in its diffusion of interest over two central figures, but in its conception of the tragic figure. There is no moral ambiguity about Macbeth; however we may view his early heroism and his continued sufferings from his conscience, we know—as he knows—that he is a murderer, not "an honorable murderer" (Othello's description of himself) but simply a murderer. Nothing extenuates his guilt. But in *Antony and Cleopatra* the case is not so clear, and it is not easy to decide whether the two lovers are, to put it simply, mostly good or mostly bad. Shaw summed it up thus: "After giving a faithful picture of the soldier broken down by debauchery, and the typical wanton in whose arms such men perish, Shakespeare finally strains all his huge command of rhetoric and stage pathos to give a theatrical sublimity to the wretched end of the business, and to persuade foolish spectators that the world was well lost by the twain." Certainly Shakespeare does not minimize Antony's debauchery or Cleopatra's wantonness. The first line of the play speaks of Antony's "dotage," and the speech goes on to contrast the present debauched Antony—a mere heavy-breathing sensualist—with the glorious Antony who was once a military hero. Cleopatra is a gypsy—that is, not merely an Egyptian but a lecherous trickster.

Antony himself later says that Cleopatra "like a right gypsy hath at fast and loose/Beguiled me" (IV.xii.28–29). It is easy to find additional evidence for this view: Antony's military wisdom disappears, and he is foolish enough to think that Octavius Caesar may fight him in single combat (Enobarbus knows better, in III.xiii, when he says of this belief, "Caesar, thou hast subdued/His judgment too"); Antony foolishly fights at sea, though he knows Caesar has the advantage there; he lapses into hysterical sadism when he orders Thidias to be whipped; and (to cut short what could be a long list) he bungles his suicide.

But this is not the whole story. Although the Romans in the play—and Antony himself, at times—judge the new Antony by the Roman standards of duty and military valor and find a sad falling off, there is another way, a non-Roman way, of looking at Antony. The new Antony, transformed by Cleopatra, can say,

> Let Rome in Tiber melt, and the wide arch
> Of the ranged empire fall! Here is my space,
> Kingdoms are clay: our dungy earth alike
> Feeds beast as man. The nobleness of life
> Is to do thus;[1] when such a mutual pair
> And such a twain can do't.    (I.i.33–38)

In short the Roman code—especially as embodied in the cold, triumphant Caesar—itself seems unattractive when compared with some of the activities of Antony and Cleopatra. Caesar sees Antony as a reveler engaged in "lascivious wassails" and eating epicurean foods, and he contrasts him to the former Antony, who on his campaigns ate "the roughest berry on the rudest hedge." But Caesar's asceticism and hard-dealing leave no room for warm friendships or even for the kind of courteous sympathy that Antony can offer the simple Lepidus, the third but negligible triumvir. When Caesar invites Antony to visit Caesar's sister, with a view toward a political marriage, Antony says,

> Let us, Lepidus,
> Not lack your company.

And Lepidus warmly responds,

> Noble Antony,
> Not sickness should detain me.    (II.ii.170–71)

Later, Antony warns Lepidus that he is in danger:

> These quicksands, Lepidus,
> Keep off them, for you sink.    (II.vii.60–61)

Early in the play Lepidus himself gives us a vision of Antony that is an alternative to the narrow Roman view. To Caesar's assertion that Antony is "th' abstract of all faults/That all men follow" (that is, the symbol of universal weakness), Lepidus counters:

---

[1] Many editors explain "thus" by adding a stage direction, "*They kiss*," or "*They embrace*," but possibly "thus" alludes not to any specific gesture but to Antony's present way of life with Cleopatra.

I must not think there are
Evils enow to darken all his goodness;
His faults, in him, seem as the spots of heaven,
More fiery by night's blackness, hereditary
Rather than purchased [acquired], what he cannot change
Than what he chooses.                              (I.iv.10–15)

It is interesting to note that although Lepidus sees Antony's faults and describes them as darkness, he later reverses the dark-light symbolism and describes the "faults" as "the spots of heaven,/More fiery by night's blackness." Even Antony's faults, Lepidus argues, have a kind of heavenly luminosity, a shining virtue in them. For example, Antony is politically irresponsible and a sensualist, but these traits are not simply flaws in a basically good man; paradoxically, they are the qualities that help to make him glorious. (We will see something of the same paradox in Coriolanus.) Something along the same lines can be said of Cleopatra, and indeed Enobarbus says it. To Maecenas' statement that Antony must leave Cleopatra, Enobarbus replies:

Never; he will not:
Age cannot wither her, nor custom stale
Her infinite variety: other women cloy
The appetites they feed, but she makes hungry
Where most she satisfies; for vilest things
Become themselves [are becoming] in her, that the holy
    priests
Bless her when she is riggish [wanton].    (II.ii.236–42)

This sort of ambiguity runs throughout the play. Even at the end, for example, Cleopatra's suicide has its noble aspect ("Husband, I come:/Now to that name my courage prove my title"), its sensuous aspect ("The stroke of death is as a lover's pinch,/Which hurts, and is desired"), and perhaps its cowardly aspect, for she knows that Caesar plans to humiliate her publicly, and thus her death is as much an escape from Caesar as a reunion with Antony. But it has its glory—the lines persuade us of that—and this glory is only dimmed, not dispelled, by Caesar's comment:

Her physician tells me
She hath pursued conclusions infinite
Of easy ways to die.                    (V.ii.353–55)

Despite such information, the final impression must be one of grandeur, of what Horatio in Hamlet calls "wonder." Though it draws upon history, Antony and Cleopatra has only a superficial resemblance to Shakespeare's chronicle histories. With a hero who is related to Hercules and described as a "grand sea," a man "past the size of dreaming," with a heroine who is "a lass unparalleled," and with a geographical sweep and abundant cosmic imagery, Antony and Cleopatra anticipates Shakespeare's last plays, the "romances," in which tragic woe yields to a sense of wonder attendant upon the revelation of a world in which love, forgiveness, and the imagination dissolve faults and take us beyond the world of time.

Like Antony and Cleopatra, Coriolanus, Shakespeare's last tragedy, is chiefly drawn from Plutarch, but the world it depicts is utterly different. In Antony and Cleopatra Shakespeare conveys the expansiveness of the late Roman Republic, partly by the setting in Egypt but more signifi-

cantly by the imperial hero whose story transcends the political motif. Coriolanus, however, depicts a much earlier and narrower world, the days of the early Republic, and there is a continual insistence on the abrasive class conflict between the plebeians and the patricians. Coriolanus is a hero, but his heroism is unattractive, for it is exclusively military; thus we tend to judge him rather than feel for him. Despite the glorification of Coriolanus in the first part of the play, we find it difficult to be warmed by his virtue, and even Coriolanus' mother, from whom he learned his valor, tells him he is "too absolute." It is a valor that is inhuman (Coriolanus is compared to an engine, and he compares himself to a dragon), a valor that is an end in itself, unconnected with mankind, and finally an enemy of mankind: "I will fight/Against my cank'red country with the spleen/Of all the under fiends" (IV.v. 94–96). It is this valor, and not any sense of justice, that is almost the whole of Coriolanus, as he tells us in the first act, when he conveys his eagerness to fight against Tullus Aufidius, his only worthy opponent:

Were half to half the world by th' ears, and he
Upon my party, I'd revolt, to make
Only my wars with him. He is a lion
That I am proud to hunt.              (I.i.235–38)

This sense of joyous energy is briefly catching, but in the end Coriolanus remains unattractive, despite such tributes as "His nature is too noble for the world" and "He shall have a noble memory." Part of the trouble is his abundant railing, which is never quite redeemed by a noble vision, for it is too rooted in contempt of the lesser people around him. Coriolanus' rebuke of the cowardly soldiers (I.iv. 30–34), for instance, is perilously close to the invective spewed by the misanthropic Thersites in Troilus and Cressida or by Timon in the latter part of Timon of Athens. Even when Coriolanus proudly rejects Rome, "Thus I turn my back;/There is a world elsewhere," we find that the world elsewhere is not a nobler vision but only Coriolanus' insistence that he will not be other than himself. And he never perceives that what he is is not everything that is worthwhile. The idea that each of Shakespeare's heroes suffers from a tragic "flaw" was briefly discussed and rejected earlier (see p. 54), but if the idea truly applies to any of them it applies to Coriolanus. In IV.vii.35–48 Aufidius suggests that Coriolanus' fault may be "pride" or "defect of judgment." In the first act, before Coriolanus appears, two Citizens discuss him. The First Citizen says Coriolanus is "proud," to which the Second Citizen replies, "What he cannot help in his nature you account a vice in him." Perhaps it is not exactly "pride" that characterizes Coriolanus, for he is unwilling—indeed, in most of the play unable—to boast of his exploits. But this insistence on isolation, which is his nature, is almost the whole of him: "He is himself alone," "one thing," and this self or thing serves him wonderfully in war but incapacitates him in peace. When he puts off his valor there is nothing left of him:

O my mother, mother! O!
You have won a happy victory to Rome;
But, for your son—believe it, O, believe it!—
Most dangerously you have with him prevailed,
If not most mortal to him.            (V.iii.185–89)

"Mercy" has drained his "honor," and Aufidius knows that he can at last defeat Coriolanus. Coriolanus regains his identity when, stung by Aufidius' rebuke, he reminds his Volscian enemies of his earlier conquest over them; yet this outburst of pride is what destroys him, for it stirs the Volscians to murder him. Thus though his heroism is never in doubt, Shakespeare's last tragic hero has less of the complex humanity of the earlier heroes. His code, which involves abundant contempt, not only keeps us at a distance; it also blinds him—though not us—to what is going on. He sees himself as his own master, but we see, ironically, that lesser people can manipulate him.

## TWO SATIRIC TRAGEDIES: TROILUS AND CRESSIDA, TIMON OF ATHENS

Probably the term "satiric" is a little too strong to describe these two plays, for they do not really hoot at their characters. Still, the characters are seen in such an ironic light and from such a detached point of view—even in comparison with *Coriolanus*—that "satiric tragedy" may be a useful starting place.

For the Renaissance, satire and tragedy were not far apart; satire was sometimes thought to have developed from tragedy. Here is John Milton's comment on the relationship: "A Satire, as it was born out of a Tragedy, so ought to resemble his parentage, to strike high, and adventure dangerously at the most eminent vices among the greatest persons." Although *Troilus and Cressida* and *Timon of Athens* are far apart in quality and can only be crudely linked together, "eminent vices" of great men in the ancient world are found in both of them. (Renaissance admiration of the classics did not always extend to Greek legendary figures. The Elizabethans held Virgil's *Aeneid*, which is unfriendly toward the Greeks, in too high esteem to see the Greeks as shining heroes.)

*Troilus and Cressida*, incomparably the better play, is probably the earlier of the two. The difficulty of classifying it was apparent in its own day: the title page of the quarto calls it a history, the preface to the quarto says it is "comical," and the editors of the First Folio planned to put it with the tragedies, but they finally put it in unnamed territory between the histories and the tragedies, though they added the word "tragedy" to its title. It is a very strange play, and the preface's statement that it was "never staled with the stage, never clapper-clawed with the palms of the vulgar," leads us to think that it may have been written for a select audience rather than for the public theater, or that if it was written for the public theater it was found unsuitable. *Troilus* has two stories, one of politics and war concerning the Greeks who besiege Troy and who finally kill Hector, and another of love concerning Cressida's infidelity to Troilus. But despite the Prologue, which leads us to expect high military exploits, there is no heroic battle, and despite the lovers there is no joyous marriage; both stories deal with treachery and the destruction of merit by baseness. Moreover, much of the play is marked by disappointment, anticlimax, and frustration. For example, Hector argues that Helen should be returned to Menelaus, but then he withdraws his argument; Ulysses constructs an elaborate plot to get Achilles to fight, but when Achilles fights it is for a different reason;

Pandarus' plot comes to nothing; Troilus is painfully disillusioned, but he does not seem to arrive at self-knowledge; and Thersites regularly gives scathing denunciations of all activity. This is the world of tragedy, but also of satire; as Ezra Pound said, satire "draws one to consider time wasted."

Thersites, who sees only "Lechery, lechery, still wars and lechery," has a parallel in Pandarus, the commentator on the love story, but their low view of life is not the only one, and though the higher views come to nothing, their presence makes the play something other than a denunciation of mankind. Troilus has an air of the romantic lover of the comedies. If we recall Bassanio's description in *The Merchant of Venice* of Portia as a treasure to be adventured for (I.i.161–76), we can see the resemblance in these lines of Troilus':

Her bed is India; there she lies, a pearl.
Between our Ilium and where she resides
Let it be called the wild and wand'ring flood,
Ourself the merchant, and this sailing Pandar
Our doubtful hope, our convoy and our bark.
(I.i.103–07)

Still, there is something more frenetic here, as there is in Troilus' apprehensiveness that love may be

some joy too fine,
Too subtle, potent, tuned too sharp in sweetness
For the capacity of my ruder powers.
I fear it much; and I do fear besides
That I shall lose distinction [ability to distinguish] in my joys.
(III.ii.21–25)

And none of the romantic heroes in the comedies is so sensual as to explain to his beloved that "the monstruosity in love" is "that the will is infinite and the execution confined; that the desire is boundless and the act a slave to limit" (III.ii.80–82). Troilus nevertheless is a lover, and Thersites' "lechery" is not quite apt. What sharply separates this play from the comedies is not the lover's attitude but the beloved's deeds: Cressida is false, and thus Troilus' love for her is put into an ironic light as Othello's (another warrior-lover) is not. Similarly, Hector, who had nobly refused to fight the disarmed Achilles, is himself slain by Achilles' henchmen when he is unarmed. It is not quite true, then, that (as Thersites says of the war) "all the argument is a whore and a cuckold," but it is true that the noble alternatives are powerless.

*Timon of Athens* has affinities with *Troilus and Cressida*, most notably in its images of disease (especially sexual) and in the railings of Apemantus, which resemble those of Thersites, and more pervasively in the ironic view we are invited to take. But it has affinities with both *Antony and Cleopatra* and *Coriolanus* (the three plays are indebted to Plutarch) in its concern with a hero who becomes an exile from society. This concern also relates Timon to *King Lear*, and it has been suggested that before Shakespeare thoroughly revised *Timon* he set to work on *King Lear* and then, having made what use he wanted to make of a man driven to distraction by ingratitude, he found no reason to return to *Timon*.

In his Introduction to *Timon* (see p. 1367) Maurice

Charney points out that it is better to see the uniqueness of *Timon* than to compare it unfavorably to plays that it resembles; but here perhaps it is appropriate to see Timon in the context of Shakespeare's other tragedies. The chief problem is this: What are we to make of Timon's initial generosity and of his later misanthropy? Is the play the tragedy of a magnanimous man who is undone by his virtue—that is, by his high view of men, which men do not fulfill and which therefore drives him to misanthropy? Or is the play a satire of both his generosity and his misanthropy? In support of the first view, one can quote lines that praise Timon—lines that are not flattery because they are not spoken in his presence—such as the reference to "his good and gracious nature" and the assertion that "The noblest mind he carries/That ever governed man." His steward Flavius testifies on his behalf, at first in words but later in deeds when he seeks out his former master. Flavius, a follower of a fallen master, thus resembles Kent in *King Lear*. Late in the play Flavius sees Timon as a man

> brought low by his own heart,
> Undone by goodness. Strange, unusual blood,
> When man's worst sin is, he does too much good.
> Who then dares to be half so kind again?
> For bounty, that makes gods, do still mar men.
>                              (IV.ii.37–41)

Against this high view of Timon it can be argued that two technicalities suggest that the play is not a tragedy (although the Folio puts it with the tragedies): first, though Timon is said to be "brought low by his own heart," his death does not result from action (indeed, his death seems curiously irrelevant), and second, the Folio denies to *Timon* alone the word "tragedy" in the title, calling the play *The Life of Timon of Athens*. Moreover, even in the first scene Timon is not merely generous; he is also responsive to flattery, and his gifts are ostentatious and apparently a means of self-aggrandizement. When he cannot bolster himself in this way, he falls into misanthropy, seeing mankind's faults but not his own. Here a comparison with Lear may be useful. Timon and Lear are both outcasts, and both rail against society, but Timon has little of interest to say about society and nothing of interest to say about himself, whereas Lear's denunciation of society—though mad—is touched with sympathy for those who suffer injustice and with an awareness of his own faults. Lear arrives at a vision larger than the one he first held; Timon merely exchanges an exalted view of man for a base one. Alcibiades puts it thus: "The middle of humanity thou never knewest, but the extremity of both ends" (IV.iii.299–300). (This polarization, incidentally, relates *Timon* to Shakespeare's last plays, the romances, in which characters tend to be either good or bad rather than "of a mingled yarn, good and ill together.") The heroes of the great tragedies are no less extreme in their unwillingness to accept the way of the world; that is why they are heroes. But they also knew the middle of humanity; that is why we feel their sufferings as our own.

# Shakespeare's Nondramatic Works

Shakespeare's first work to appear in print was not a play but a narrative poem. Because the status of poet was higher than that of playwright in Elizabethan times—professional poets were dependent on courtly patronage, whereas most playwrights were dependent on the pennies of the general public—it is likely that Shakespeare thought, at least for a while, that his poetry rather than his plays would bring him lasting fame. This hypothesis receives some support from the fact that his two long narrative poems were published in remarkably accurate texts, with dedications by the author. Shakespeare thus apparently had a hand in the publication of these poems, but he never concerned himself with the publication of the plays, and he wrote no further dedications.

Leisure time to write the two narratives was probably afforded by the plague, which closed the London theaters from the summer of 1592 to the spring of 1594. Shakespeare's first poem, *Venus and Adonis* (1593), is an artful, erotic piece of 1194 lines that was calculated to please a noble patron, the youthful Earl of Southampton, whose taste presumably had been developed by ornate and erotic mythological pieces such as Lodge's *Scylla's Metamorphosis* (1589). Marlowe's *Hero and Leander* (1593 or earlier, although not published until 1598) belongs to the same school. *Venus and Adonis* has been much praised for its realistic passages about horses, birds, the doe, and especially the hare (lines 679–708); but however we may value these passages, which seem derived from Warwickshire memories, the poem as a whole produces the effect not of realism but of most cunning artifice. It is less a photograph than a tapestry, less a description of creatures moving in external nature than a presentation of abstract types set in a hothouse; or we can vary the figure and see the poem as Hazlitt did, when, calling attention to the frigidity of this poem about passion, he characterized it as an icehouse. But *Venus and Adonis* apparently worked for its contemporary readers: there were at least ten editions of the poem in Shakespeare's lifetime; a contemporary writer noted that "the younger sort takes much delight in Shakespeare's *Venus and Adonis*"; and in a satiric play of 1601, a foolish courtier refers to the poem, saying, "I'll worship sweet master Shakespeare, and to honor him will lay his *Venus and Adonis* under my pillow."

In 1594 Shakespeare followed this bid for noble patronage with the publication of a second poem dedicated to Southampton, *The Rape of Lucrece* (thus goes the running head; the title page simply calls the poem *Lucrece*). Again the central narrative is drawn from Ovid. In its depiction of Tarquin, who, overcome by passion, sacrifices honor and gains only self-loathing and enmity, Shakespeare touches on a tragic theme, and indeed in *Macbeth* he was later to mention Tarquin. Here is the passage from *Macbeth*, followed by a passage from *Lucrece*:

> Now o'er the one half-world
> Nature seems dead, and wicked dreams abuse
> The curtained sleep; witchcraft celebrates
> Pale Hecate's offerings; and withered murder,
> Alarumed by his sentinel, the wolf,
> Whose howl's his watch, thus with his stealthy pace,
> With Tarquin's ravishing strides, towards his design
> Moves like a ghost.     *(Macbeth*, II.i.49–56)

> Now stole upon the time the dead of night,
> When heavy sleep had closed up mortal eyes.
> No comfortable star did lend his light,
> No noise but owls, and wolves' death-boding cries;
> Now serves the season that they may surprise
>   The silly lambs: pure thoughts are dead and still,
>   While lust and murder wakes to stain and kill.
>     *(Lucrece*, lines 162–68)

In Lucrece's lamentations, and especially in Tarquin's internal debates, the stuff of tragedy is set forth in a narrative form, yet the final effect is far from tragic, for like *Venus and Adonis* the poem is so obviously ornate, so richly heraldic, so formal in its contrasts, that the manner overcomes the matter. It is a web of decorative (and sometimes very beautiful) passages; it is longer than *Venus and Adonis*, but the greater length is due not to additional action but to even greater elaboration of the little there is.

Among the nondramatic poems the sonnets have won widespread praise. They belong to a genre made famous in Italy by Petrarch (1304–74); Petrarch was imitated in England by Wyatt and by Surrey, some of whose poems were published in 1557 in a book that is usually called *Tottel's Miscellany*. But sonneteering did not become a national pastime in England until 1591, when the posthumous publication of Sir Philip Sidney's *Astrophel and Stella* started the vogue. The Italian or Petrarchan sonnet is basically a two-part poem, consisting of an octave rhyming *abbaabba* and a sestet, normally in a somewhat different tone of voice, rhyming *cdecde* or *cdcdcd*, or another variant. The English sonnet (sometimes called Shakespearean, though Shakespeare did not invent the form) is a four-part poem, consisting of three quatrains and a couplet: *abab cdcd efef gg*. The couplet normally provides a syntactically independent aphoristic summary. But the thought of the sonnet does not always follow the rhyme scheme, that is, it does not always break after each quatrain. In a good number of Shakespeare's sonnets the chief turn comes, as in an Italian sonnet, after the eighth line.

Shakespeare's *Sonnets* was not published until 1609, but surely most and possibly all of the 154 sonnets that make up the book had been written at least a decade earlier. The exact date of composition is unknown, but the early and middle nineties seems reasonable. (There are also sonnets in *Love's Labor's Lost* and *Romeo and Juliet*, plays of the middle nineties.) In 1598 Francis Meres alluded to Shakespeare's "sugared sonnets." "Sugared" is appropriate for at least some of them: there are poems that show a delight in ingenious conceits of the kind we associate with the earlier plays. But other sonnets are masterful in their apparent

simplicity of utterance which, coupled with a depth of view, makes the poems among the world's greatest. If the best sonnets were written before 1598 (rather than shortly before publication in 1609), Shakespeare achieved maturity in the sonnet more quickly than in the drama. The 154 poems do not narrate a continuous story, but there are groups of related sonnets; for example, Sonnets 1–17 are all written to a young man, urging him to marry. Although the *Sonnets* may be indebted to some contact that Shakespeare had with members of the aristocracy, they cannot be read as sheer autobiography (though of course they often ring true). The usual motifs of Elizabethan sonnets can be found—the poet eternizes his patron; the eye and the heart are at war—but there is also a new range of feeling which has affinities with *Lucrece* and therefore approaches a tragic view. For instance, in *Lucrece* Shakespeare gives us this insight into one kind of tragic experience:

> Those that much covet are with gain so fond
> That what they have not, that which they possess
> They scatter and unloose it from their bond,
> And so by hoping more they have but less;
> Or, gaining more, the profit of excess
>   Is but to surfeit, and such griefs sustain
>   That they prove bankrout in this poor rich gain.
>     (lines 134–40)

After he rapes Lucrece, Tarquin is compared to a "full-fed hound or gorgèd hawk," now loathing what he had before pursued:

> His taste delicious, in digestion souring,
> Devours his will, that lived by foul devouring.
>     (lines 699–700)

Every poem is complete in itself and ought not to be reduced or expanded to coincide with any other poem, but we can see in these passages from *Lucrece* something akin to Sonnet 129, a description of lust before, during, and after consummation.

> Th' expense of spirit[2] in a waste of shame
> Is lust in action; and, till action, lust
> Is perjured, murd'rous, bloody, full of blame,
> Savage, extreme, rude, cruel, not to trust;
> Enjoyed no sooner but despisèd straight;
> Past reason hunted, and no sooner had,
> Past reason hated as a swallowed bait
> On purpose laid to make the taker mad;
> Made[3] in pursuit, and in possession so;
> Had, having, and in quest to have, extreme;
> A bliss in proof, and proved, a very woe,
> Before, a joy proposed; behind, a dream.
>   All this the world well knows, yet none knows well
>   To shun the heaven that leads men to this hell.

Not all Shakespeare's sonnets, of course, are like this, and our interest in the tragedies ought not to lead us to concentrate on poems about lust or the destructive will to the

---

[2] "Th' expense of spirit" = the expenditure of vital power, and more specifically, of semen.
[3] "Made" is often emended to "mad," but can be taken as equivalent to "Made mad."

exclusion of, say, those celebrations of beauty that are equally impressive. In short, the sonnets are remarkably varied—disordered, some readers who cherish a consistent story would say. If we were to look for a dominant subject we would perhaps find it in time, which destroys beauty but which also engenders anew; and the poet's words re-create his subject, conferring on beauty a new existence that may at least seem to arrest the triumph of time. If this inadequate description has any truth in it, the world of the sonnets is very near to that of the great plays.

The sonnets have been much esteemed for a long while, but a short poem called *The Phoenix and the Turtle* (1601) has only relatively recently gained universal praise, probably because in the 1920's admirers of John Donne and the other "metaphysical" poets helped to educate subsequent taste to appreciate this strange funereal poem about the transcendence of human love. *Venus and Adonis* can be coupled with *Lucrece*, and each sonnet can be coupled with the remaining 153, but *The Phoenix and the Turtle* stands alone—and yet in its faith in the power of love it earns its place in a story that includes the sonnets, *Romeo and Juliet*, and *Antony and Cleopatra*.

# The Texts of Shakespeare

The printed versions of *Venus and Adonis* (1593) and *The Rape of Lucrece* (1594) were each prefaced by the author's dedication and were relatively free of printer's errors, circumstances which suggest that Shakespeare read the proofs of these two works. But Shakespeare seems never to have supervised the publication of any of his plays, although eighteen were printed during his lifetime. There is nothing unusual in this fact; when an Elizabethan playwright sold a play to a theatrical company he surrendered ownership of it. Normally a company would not publish a play because to do so meant to allow competitors to acquire the piece. Some plays, however, did get published. For example, disloyal actors sometimes relied on their memories and pieced together a play for a publisher. The result was a so-called bad quarto, which is often grossly inaccurate but which is sometimes interesting because in its stage directions it may preserve bits of stage business and may even preserve some authentic dialogue that was added when the play was in rehearsal. Such elements can perhaps be considered as part of the final version of the play, especially since Shakespeare must have been involved in its staging. (We tend to think of the last draft of a play as the author's final version, but when the author is an actor, perhaps the play as he acted in it, with cuts and last-minute additions, is his final version.) Nevertheless, the bad quartos are bad; they offer mangled versions of the plays, as can be seen by comparing Hamlet's "To be or not to be" soliloquy (III.i.56 ff.) with the bad quarto's version (see p. 67).

Not all of the quartos are bad quartos, however. Sometimes a company that was in need of money sold its manuscripts; sometimes a company sold a manuscript of a play that no longer drew audiences; and sometimes an author sold a manuscript to a company and then again to a publisher. In 1608 Thomas Heywood, Shakespeare's contemporary and an actor and playwright, insisted that such a double sale was unethical: "For though some have used a double sale of their labors, first to the stage, and after to the press, for my own part I here proclaim myself ever faithful in the first, and never guilty of the last." That Shakespeare did not publish his plays, then, is scarcely remarkable; among his contemporaries only Ben Jonson carefully supervised the publication of his own plays. Those of Shakespeare's plays that were printed during his lifetime have no dedication by the author (his name was not even on the title page of the first eight to appear in print), and they offer few aids to the reader: stage directions are irregular, and there is no list of characters. The eighteen plays published during Shakespeare's lifetime were issued one play per volume in small books called quartos. (Each sheet in a quarto is folded twice, making four leaves, or eight pages, each about 7 inches wide and 9 inches high.) The quartos, with their first dates of publication (most were reprinted), are *Titus Andronicus* (1594), *2 Henry VI* (1594), *3 Henry VI* (1595—actually an octavo rather than a quarto), *Richard II* (1597), *Richard III* (1597), *Romeo and Juliet* (1597), *1 Henry IV* (1598), *Love's Labor's Lost* (1598), *Henry V* (1600), *2 Henry IV* (1600), *Much Ado About Nothing* (1600), *A Midsummer Night's Dream* (1600), *The Merchant of Venice* (1600), *The Merry Wives of Windsor* (1602), *Hamlet* (1603), *King Lear* (1608), *Troilus and Cressida* (1609), *Pericles* (1609). A quarto of a nineteenth play, *Othello*, was published in 1622, six years after Shakespeare's death. (To this list of quartos some scholars add *King John* [1591] and *The Taming of a Shrew* [1594], but most scholars hold that these two quartos are not bad quartos of Shakespeare's plays but rather plays by other men.) The quartos of *2 Henry VI*, *3 Henry VI*, *Romeo and Juliet*, *Henry V*, *The Merry Wives of Windsor*, and *Hamlet* were bad quartos, but for two of these plays good quartos were soon published, *Romeo and Juliet* in 1599 and *Hamlet* in 1604.

In 1623, seven years after Shakespeare's death, in an effort "to keep the memory of so worthy a friend and fellow alive, as was our Shakespeare," John Heminges and Henry Condell (two senior members of Shakespeare's company who had performed with him for about twenty years) collected his plays—published and unpublished—in a large volume, commonly called the First Folio. The poems were not included. (A folio is a volume consisting of sheets that are folded once, each sheet thus making two leaves, or four pages about 8½ inches wide and 13 inches high.)

The First Folio contains thirty-six plays, consisting of all the titles listed above (except *Pericles*) and eighteen additional titles, which in approximate order of composition are *The Comedy of Errors*, *1 Henry VI*, *The Taming of the*

*Ham.* To be, or not to be, I .here's the point,
To Die, to sleepe, is that all? I all:
No, to sleepe, to dreame, I mary there it goes,
For in that dreame of death, when wee awake,
And borne before an euerlasting Iudge,
From whence no passenger euer retur'nd,
The vndiscouered country, at whose sight
The happy smile, and the accursed damn'd.
But for this, the ioyfull hope of this,
Whol'd beare the scornes and flattery of the world,
Scorned by the right rich, the rich cursed of the poore?
The widow being oppressed, the orphan wrong d,
The taste of hunger, or a tirants raigne,
And thousand more calamities besides,
To grunt and sweate vnder this weary life,
When that he may his full *Quietus* make,
With a bare bodkin, who would this indure,
But for a hope of something after death?
Which pusles the braine, and doth confound the sence,
Which makes vs rather beare those euilles we haue,
Than flie to others that we know not of.
I that, O this conscience makes cowardes of vs all,
Lady in thy orizons, be all my sinnes remembred.

*Ham.* To be, or not to be, that is the question,
Whether tis nobler in the minde to suffer
The slings and arrowes of outragious fortune,
Or to take Armes against a sea of troubles,
And by opposing, end them, to die to sleepe
No more, and by a sleepe, to say we end
The hart-ake, and the thousand naturall shocks
That flesh is heire to; tis a consumaticn
Deuoutly to be wisht to die to sleepe,
To sleepe, perchance to dreame, I there's the rub,
For in that sleepe of death what dreames may come
When we haue shuffled off this mortall coyle
Must giue vs pause, there's the respect
That makes calamitie of so long life:
For who would beare the whips and scornes of time,
Th'oppressors wrong, the proude mans contumely,
The pangs of despiz'd loue, the lawes delay,
The insolence of office, and the spurnes
That patient merrit of th'vnworthy takes,
When he himselfe might his quietas make
With a bare bodkin; who would fardels beare,
To grunt and sweat vnder a wearie life,
But that the dread of something after death,
The vndiscouer'd country, from whose borne
No trauiler returnes, puzzels the will,
And makes vs rather beare those ills we haue,
Then flie to others that we know not of.
Thus conscience dooes make cowards,
And thus the natiue hiew of resolution
Is sickled ore with the pale cast of thought,
And enterprises of great pitch and moment,
With this regard theyr currents turne awry,
And loose the name of action. Soft you now,
The faire *Ophelia*, Nimph in thy orizons
Be all my sinnes remembred.

Left, *lines from the "bad" quarto (Q1) of* Hamlet, *1603.* Right, *lines from the good quarto (Q2), 1604.*

Shrew, *The Two Gentlemen of Verona, King John, Julius Caesar, As You Like It, Twelfth Night, All's Well That Ends Well, Measure for Measure, Macbeth, Antony and Cleopatra, Timon of Athens, Coriolanus, Cymbeline, The Winter's Tale, The Tempest,* and *Henry VIII.* The thirty-six plays in the Folio, and *Pericles,* are widely regarded as canonical, and a thirty-eighth play, *The Two Noble Kinsmen,* first published in 1634, is somewhat less widely held to be Shakespeare's at least in part. The plays in the Folio are arranged in three groups, comedies (fourteen), histories (ten), and tragedies (eleven, but *Cymbeline* belongs among the comedies); between the histories and the tragedies is *Troilus and Cressida,* unpaginated and omitted from the table of contents. In an address "To the great variety of readers" Heminges and Condell suggest that the republished plays are presented in better form than in the quartos: "Before you were abused with diverse stolen and surreptitious copies, maimed and deformed by the frauds and stealths of injurious impostors that exposed them; even those are now offered to your view cured and perfect of their limbs, and all the rest absolute in their numbers, as he [Shakespeare] conceived them." Some, but not all, of the quartos deserve these harsh words.

The editor assigned to prepare the texts for publication in the First Folio seems to have taken his job seriously, yet he did not perform it with uniform care. In general, the sources of the texts seem to have been good unpublished copies or good published copies. Often, it is true, the editors of the Folio did not use the *first* edition of a quarto, which presumably was set from a manuscript that had been close to Shakespeare (such as a final draft, or a scribe's clean copy of a final draft); rather, they used a later reprint which, having been set from an earlier quarto, introduced additional printer's errors. But on the whole the editors of the Folio avoided those quartos that printed badly garbled texts. The first play in the collection, *The Tempest,* is divided into acts and scenes, has unusually full stage directions and descriptions of spectacle, and concludes with a list of characters; but the editor was not able (or willing) to present the succeeding texts so fully dressed. Later texts occasionally show signs of carelessness: in one scene of *Much Ado About Nothing* the names of actors, instead of characters, appear as speech prefixes, as they had in the quarto, which the Folio reprints; proofreading throughout the Folio is very spotty and was apparently done without reference to the printer's copy; the pagination of *Hamlet* jumps from 156 to 257.

The first decision a modern editor of Shakespeare must make is to select his copy. This is no problem if the play exists only in the Folio, but it is a considerable problem if the relationship between a quarto and the Folio—or an early quarto and a later one—is unclear. When an editor has chosen what seems to him to be the most authoritative text or texts for his copy, he is not done with making decisions. Next, he must reckon with Elizabethan spelling. If he is not producing a facsimile he will probably modernize it, but should he preserve the old forms of words that were apparently pronounced quite unlike their modern forms— for example, *lanthorn* and *alablaster*? And if he does preserve these forms, is he really preserving Shakespeare's forms or those of a compositor in the printing house? What is an editor to do when he finds "lanthorn" and "lantern" in adjacent lines? (The editors of the Signet Shakespeare have assumed that in general words should be spelled in their modern form, but some exceptions have been made—for example, to preserve rhymes or puns.) Sometimes there is even doubt as to what word the original text is spelling. In *Richard II*, III.iii.98–99, Richard says that Bolingbroke's attempt to seize the crown will bring to England war that will "bedew/Her pastors grasse with faithfull English bloud." "Pastors" is usually modernized to "pastures," but why not to "pastor's," which would convey the idea of the monarch as the shepherd of the kingdom? If Elizabethan printers had used the apostrophe to indicate the possessive, its position on one side or the other of the final -*s* in "pastors" would have been decisive (except to a quarrelsome editor).

Another problem involving an omitted apostrophe occurs in *King Lear*, V.iii.16–17. Lear tells Cordelia that they will

> take vpon's the mystery of things,
> As if we were Gods spies.

In a modernized text, should the second line be printed "As if we were God's spies," giving (to put it mildly) a Christian coloring to the line, or should it be printed "gods' spies"? In favor of "God's spies" one can argue that (1) if the plural were intended, probably the Folio's "Gods" would be preceded by "the," because "gods' spies" sounds unidiomatic, and (2) though the play is nominally set in a pagan world and the characters at various times invoke pagan deities, there are some undoubted Christian overtones, such as "a soul in bliss" (IV.vii.46). But against "God's" and for "gods'" it can be argued that except in this doubtful instance every one of the two dozen other occurrences of the word indisputably is a plural—for example, "As Flies to wanton Boyes, are we to th' Gods." Of course an audience cannot hear the difference between "God's" and "gods'," and finally the meaning of the play

does not hang on the position of this apostrophe; but its position is not totally insignificant if one is concerned about the world—pagan or Christian? or pagan almost imperceptibly becoming Christian?—in *King Lear*.

Commas too can be troubling. Macbeth rejects his wife's idea that he can wash the blood from his hand:

> no: this my Hand will rather
> The multitudinous Seas incarnardine,
> Making the Greene one, Red.        (II.ii.60–62)

Obviously an editor will remove the superfluous capitals, and he will probably alter the spelling to "incarnadine," but will he leave the comma before "red," letting Macbeth speak of the sea as "the green one," or will he (like most modern editors) remove the comma and thus have Macbeth say that his hand will make the ocean *uniformly* red?

Finally, an editor sometimes has to change more than spelling or punctuation. Macbeth says to his wife:

> I dare do all that may become a man,
> Who dares no more, is none.        (I.vii.46–47)

For two centuries editors have agreed that the second line is unsatisfactory, and have emended "no" to "do": "Who dares do more is none." It seems clear that the emendation corrects an obvious misprint.

A brief discussion of one of the most famous cruxes may give further insight into this aspect of editing Shakespeare. In the Folio text of *Henry V* Mistress Quickly, describing the death of Falstaff, says, "his Nose was as sharpe as a Pen, and a Table of greene fields" (II.iii.16–17). This seems to make no sense, and in 1726 Lewis Theobald suggested emending "Table" to "babbled," with "'a babbled" meaning "he babbled," so that Falstaff goes to his death babbling of green fields, perhaps recalling the green pastures of Psalm 23. This reading has struck most subsequent editors as right and even inspired, though Theobald himself mentioned that emendation of "Table" to "talked" rather than to "babbled" was a possibility. Indeed, "talked"

> *Hoſteſſe.* Nay ſure, hee's not in Hell : hee's in *Arthurs* Boſome, if euer man went to *Arthurs* Boſome : a made a finer end, and went away and it had beene any Chriſtome Child : a parted eu'n iuſt betweene Twelue and One, eu'n at the turning o'th' Tyde : for after I ſaw him fumble with the Sheets, and play with Flowers, and ſmile vpon his fingers end, I knew there was but one way : for his Noſe was as ſharpe as a Pen, and a Table of greene fields. How now Sir *Iohn* (quoth I?) what man? be a good cheare : ſo a cryed out, God, God, God, three or foure times : now I, to comfort him, bid him a ſhould not thinke of God; I hop'd there was no neede to trouble himſelfe with any ſuch thoughts yet : ſo a bad me lay more Clothes on his feet : I put my hand into the Bed, and felt them, and they were as cold as any ſtone : then I felt to his knees, and ſo vp-peer'd, and vpward, and all was as cold as any ſtone.

*The Folio text (1623) of the Hostess' speech,* Henry V, *II.iii.9–26.*

(presumably written "talkd" in the manuscript) could more easily than "babld" have been misread as "Table," but most editors have (perhaps sentimentally) preferred "babbled." Additional emendations of this line have been proposed, one of the most comic of which was Alexander Pope's. Pope suggested that "a Table of greene fields" was not part of the speech but an instruction to a property man named Greenfield to have a table in readiness. No less ingenious—or ingenuous—is the suggestion that the passage alludes to the Elizabethan hero Sir Richard Grenville, who died in the Azores. In this view, "Table" means "picture" or "image" (it *can* have that meaning), and for some reason Falstaff at his death is said to be the very picture of Grenville. Yet one more reading—this one requiring no emendation—may be mentioned. It holds that the "and" in "and a Table of greene fields" is elliptical for "and it was." Thus Mistress Quickly says that Falstaff's nose was as sharp as a pen and was an image, in its sickly greenness, of a pasture. This last interpretation requires no alteration of the text, but is painfully thin beside Theobald's conjecture, which the Signet editor has adopted. Still, the editors of the Signet Shakespeare have restrained themselves from making abundant emendations. In their minds they hear Dr. Johnson's words on the dangers of emending: "I have adopted the Roman sentiment, that it is more honorable to save a citizen than to kill an enemy." Some departures (in addition to spelling, punctuation, and lineation) from the copy text have of course been made, but the original readings, such as "Table" in *Henry V*, are listed in the Note on the Text preceding each play, so that the reader can evaluate them for himself.

The editors of the Signet Shakespeare, following tradition, have added line numbers and in many cases act and scene divisions. The Folio divides most of the plays into acts and some plays into scenes. Early eighteenth-century editors increased the divisions. These divisions, which provide a convenient way of referring to passages in the plays, have been retained in the Signet texts, but any division that did not appear in the text chosen as the basis for the Signet text has been enclosed in square brackets [ ] to indicate that it is an editorial addition. Similarly, although no play of Shakespeare's published during his lifetime was equipped with indications of locale at the heads of scene divisions, the Signet editors have added locales in square brackets for the convenience of the reader, who lacks the information afforded to spectators by costumes, properties, and gestures. The spectator can tell at a glance that he is in the throne room, but without an editorial indication the reader may be puzzled for a while. It should be mentioned too that there are a few authentic stage directions—perhaps Shakespeare's, perhaps a prompter's—that suggest locales, giving us a sense of the way the stage is envisioned: for example, *Enter Brutus in his orchard*, and *They go up into the senate house*. It is hoped that the bracketed additions will provide the reader with the sort of help given by these two authentic directions, but it is also hoped that the reader will remember that the Elizabethan stage was not loaded with scenery and that the action flowed continuously.

During the course of his work no editor can fail to recollect some words Heminges and Condell prefixed to the Folio:

It had been a thing, we confess, worthy to have been wished, that the author himself had lived to have set forth and overseen his own writings. But since it hath been ordained otherwise, and he by death departed from that right, we pray you do not envy his friends the office of their care and pain to have collected and published them.

Nor can an editor, after he has done his best, forget Heminges and Condell's final words: "And so we leave you to other of his friends, whom if you need can be your guides. If you need them not, you can lead yourselves, and others. And such readers we wish him."

# THE PLAYS

THE PLAYS

# THE COMEDY OF ERRORS

## EDITED BY HARRY LEVIN

## Introduction

*The Comedy of Errors* has come down to us solely through the First Folio, in a good text which seems not far removed from the author's manuscript, and which is particularly interesting for the explicitness of its stage directions. The play itself is the shortest, and may indeed be the earliest, of Shakespeare's dramatic works. As such, it is more explicitly linked to classical tradition than any of the others. In spite of a notorious gibe by Ben Jonson, it is quite evident that Shakespeare was acquainted with certain standard Latin authors. There is even an accredited rumor that, before entering the theater, he had taught in a country school, where the curriculum would have consisted of very little else. If he was to assay the range of the repertory, Seneca could not be "too heavy," in the phrase of Polonius, "nor Plautus too light." *Titus Andronicus* was Shakespeare's early experiment in the mode of Senecan tragedy; *The Comedy of Errors* marks, rather more happily, his assimilation and extension of Plautine comedy. In that case there was a specific model, the archetypal comedy of twins, the *Menaechmi* or *Two Menaechmuses*. A lively translation into Elizabethan prose by one W. W. (who is commonly identified as the minor poet William Warner) was published in 1595, some 1800 years after the appearance of Plautus' play on the Roman stage.

Whether Shakespeare could have seen an unpublished draft of this version, or whether W. W. was indebted to Shakespeare's free adaptation, has been argued back and forth by scholars. Certainly Shakespeare could have known the original at first hand, and the similar phrases used by both writers may be coincidences rather than echoes. At all events, the English *Menaechmi* offers a helpful basis of comparison whereby readers may observe for themselves how Shakespeare adapted and amplified Plautus. Such observations might well begin with W. W.'s title page: "A pleasant and fine Conceited Comedy taken out of the most excellent witty Poet Plautus, chosen purposely from out the rest as least harmful and yet delightful. . . ." In other words, both the translator and the playwright chose to work from an untypical play—untypical in its all but complete reliance on chance and not on contrivance, not on malice or mischief but sheer luck. Not that fortune, often in the most commercial sense, was ever slow to inter-

vene in the world of Greco-Roman comedy. But it was commonly sought through the profit motive on the part of the old, or sexual appetite on the part of the young, and the resultant conflicts were perennially exploited by parasites and abetted by slaves. Whereas tragedy took place in temples and palaces, the comic sphere was a round of urban shops and middle-class domiciles.

In the ancient theater the proscenium was not a picture frame but an architectural façade, whose practical doors and upper windows gave a stylized impression of a street scene in some Mediterranean seaport. By convention the side exits led to the marketplace in one direction (Shakespeare's mart) and to the harbor in the other ("from the bay"). Between them flowed the continual traffic of characters, pausing at one doorway or another to transact their business, and incidentally to inform the audience of the goings-on within. What Shakespeare calls "the stirring passage of the day" moved all the faster because it did not look beyond external appearances. Drama becomes more serious when it stresses characterization; farce, at the other extreme, tends to subordinate character to plot. Hence the *donnée* of Plautus was the very essence of the farcical: two characters sufficiently alike, so that each might fit interchangeably into the other's situation, could not afford to possess distinguishing characteristics. They are, by definition, altogether exceptional. In general, the *dramatis personae* of New Comedy—the kind of comedy that was new with Menander, yet was by no means exhausted with Molière—are stock types rather than fully characterized individuals. With many changes of costume and scenery, they continue to present object lessons in avarice, flattery, braggadocio, and other continuing deviations from sound morality.

Comedy, as Sir Philip Sidney defined it for Shakespeare's age, is "an imitation of the common errors of our life," which are represented "in the most ridiculous and scornful sort that may be, so as it is impossible that any beholder can be content to be such a one." Sidney, who was involved in the defense of poetry, may bear down too heavily for our taste upon the posture of dramatist as moralist; yet, in emphasizing the correction of error, he shifts to the enlightenment of the spectator and to that civilized overview which—through a process of confusion and clarification—we finally attain: "There, but for the grace of God, go we!" To err is proverbially human; and our tragic heroes go astray grandly by committing some single and fatal mistake. Comic figures, on the other hand, run through a whole train of petty errors, and somehow manage to extricate themselves from the final consequences. Hence it is not surprising that Shakespeare's generic title had its lost forerunners, notably a *History of Error* performed in 1577. It is recorded, too, that a gala performance of the Shakespearean *Comedy of Errors* was played by the legal gentlemen of Gray's Inn during the Christmas season of 1594 (probably two or three years after it was first publicly produced), with such crowds and attendant confusions that the festive occasion "was ever afterwards called *The Night of Errors*."

In his massive studies of Shakespeare's modest Latinity, T. W. Baldwin has shown that the poet may well have studied Plautus in the contemporaneous edition of Lambinus. There the text of the *Menaechmi* was flanked by a commentary in which each successive twist or turn of the plot is signalized by the Latin verb *errare* or the noun *error*. Thus the key word utilized by Shakespeare would seem to have had the force of a technical term. Along with it we may consider another term, introduced by that versatile literary innovator, George Gascoigne, through his English rendering of Ariosto's prose comedy, *The Supposes*. Now a "suppose," as Gascoigne defined it and applied it through a series of marginal comments on the action of the play, is "a mistaking or imagination of one thing for another," generally one person supposed to be someone else because of deception, disguise, or impersonation. It requires no plotting or counterplotting in a Machiavellian sense; the only plotter is Shakespeare or Plautus himself; and what he hatches is fobbed off upon us as a trick of fate, a freak of nature, a practical joke conceived and executed by providence. The misapprehensions that gave rise to it are not poses nor supposes nor impostures; they are, plainly and simply, errors. We are at the roulette table, not the chessboard, here.

Where tragedy individualizes its protagonists, comedy underscores those broad resemblances which make it difficult to tell people apart. The closer the similarity between them, the easier it becomes for us to confound them. Blunders are most easily committed when two differing alternatives closely resemble one another, though the resemblance be no more than skin-deep. "Two faces that are alike," Pascal remarked, "though neither of them excites laughter in itself, make me laugh when together on account of the likeness." It was this sentence of Pascal's that Bergson developed into his theory of laughter as a protest of the natural and the humane against all attempts at mechanization and regimentation. Duplication, in particular, seems an affront to human dignity (one is almost tempted to call it a loss of face)—to be always mistaken for, to be almost indistinguishable from, somebody else. A set of identical twins, leading different lives, is a possibility but not a probability; and Coleridge would invoke that classic distinction to draw a line between comedy and farce. Upon his recommendation we entertain the initial hypothesis; we verily believe it because it is absurd; for, after all, absurdity is man's lot as the Existentialists have redefined it. Plautus offered Shakespeare a basic theme for the unforced interplay of cross-purposes. Shakespeare's variations, widely echoed in their turn, would be blithely syncopated by Rodgers and Hart in their appealing musical comedy *The Boys from Syracuse*.

The improbable assumption of Plautus was complicated to the very limits of the possible when Shakespeare dared to redouble the twins, and thereby to provide his pair of protagonists with a brace of retainers. Here he was acting on a hint from another Plautine source, a play so frequently imitated that Jean Giraudoux could number his treatment *Amphitryon 38*. Its myth is that of Alcmena, wooed by Jupiter in the shape of her absent husband Amphitryon, while Jupiter's companion, Mercury, assumes the person of Sosia, the household slave. Two of Shakespeare's most effective scenes, where the homecoming master and man are turned away from their own threshold, are directly inspired by Plautus' *Amphitryon*. Consequently, since each of Shakespeare's masters has a bondservant, he does not need to attach an officious parasite to the local Menaechmus as Plautus does. Messenio, the clever servant who accompanies the Syracusan Menaechmus, warns him with a pun against Epidamnum, where no one escapes "*sine damno* (without damage)"; but the Epidamnian pitfalls turn out to be unsolicited favors, which the visitor accepts with increasing insouciance. As for the citizen-twin, he is a solid man of affairs; but, having had a falling-out with his wife (and Plautus wastes no sympathy whatsoever upon the shrewish Uxor or Roman matron), he sets aside the day's business for a night's pleasure. In the true holiday spirit, both brothers are on the town.

Shakespeare, in amplifying the wife's role, reduced the part assigned to the Courtesan. The pivotal banquet is served not at her hangout, the Porpentine, but at the home of Antipholus above his shop, the Phoenix; while he, a normally faithful husband, seeks out her company only after he has reason to suspect his wife. The latter, Adriana, inherits the Uxor's misunderstanding with her husband; but Shakespeare sublimates it to a plane of genuine, if too possessive, conjugal love. Moreover, he endows her with a sister, to be courted by the bachelor Antipholus; and Luciana proves to be a *raisonneuse*, a mouthpiece of moderation, so that the twins occupy a place in the great Shakespearean debate on marriage, along with Kate and Petruchio or Rosaline and Berowne or Beatrice and Benedick. Shakespeare's characters live, as usual, in a Christian ethos. The perplexed traveler swears, "as I am a Christian," and —approached by the Courtesan—echoes Christ bidding Satan avaunt. The change in the ethical climate may be noted by the shift from Epidamnum, which is nonetheless mentioned along the way, to Ephesus. Plautus' Syracusans fear Epidamnum because it is an emporium of sharp practice, peopled by rogues and harlots and the usual comic types. Shakespeare's Syracusans are cautious too. "They say this town is full of cozenage," the traveling Antipholus warns himself.

Notwithstanding, the Ephesians he meets are not "disguised cheaters." They are, as the traveling Dromio puts it, "a gentle nation," who "speak us fair, give us gold." Shakespeare is more in his milieu where the setting is a room in the palace—or, better still, another part of the forest—than in the mercantile zones of New Comedy. It is not coney-catching but witchcraft and sorcery that envelop Ephesus in its mysterious aura. "Here we wander in illusions." This is a place of strangers and sojourners, given to curious arts, to echo the patron saint of travelers *in partibus infidelium*, the apostle Paul. Not without pertinence, it has been suggested that Paul's Epistle to the Ephesians, with its injunctions for husbands and wives, and for servants and masters, may have been in the background of Shakespeare's mind. His far-flung romance of *Pericles*, based on the folk tale of Apollonius of Tyre as retold by John Gower, reaches its resolution in the famous Temple of Diana at Ephesus. Some of the elements of the late play are present in the early one, notably the vicissitudes of a family progressing through misadventure by sea to recognition under religious auspices. The pagan temple has its counterpart in the priory, where—instead of a goddess in the machine—the flesh-and-blood Abbess is revealed to be the long-lost wife and mother.

The framing figure of Egeon contributes an emotional tension, at the very outset, to what would otherwise have remained a two-dimensional drama. His protracted expository narration is enlivened by the awareness that it is a plea, and probably a vain one, for his life. Rightly he blames his misfortunes on hap; for nowhere else in Shakespeare can a whole pattern of incidents be so directly traceable to sheer unmitigated contingency. Egeon is hopeless and helpless because he is hapless. But this is not to be a novel by Thomas Hardy; it is a knockabout farce, where bad fortune will change soon enough into good. The next scene not only offers a hint that the new arrival is one of Egeon's sons—through the mixup of the Dromios —and that the other son is just around the corner, but virtually guarantees the ransom, since the sum mentioned in both scenes is exactly a thousand marks. Coincidence has already done its best, as well as its worst, and a happy ending has been implicit from the beginning. Meanwhile the sequence of farcical episodes has been framed by the tragicomic overplot; and Shakespeare, by enlisting our sympathies for the fate of Egeon, has charged the air with a suspense which cannot be resolved until the appointed hour of execution, five o'clock in the afternoon.

Both of the Antipholuses have appointments at that hour, one of them with the Merchant and the other with Angelo the goldsmith; and since it is noon when the Syracusan arrives, and since the Ephesian Dromio gets into his troubles over the question of dinnertime, the time scheme is firmly fixed within the course of the afternoon. There are frequent reminders of time passing, to reinforce the structure of occurrences: when Komisarjevsky produced the play at Stratford-on-Avon, his setting was dominated by a gigantic clock. Adhering to the classical unities as Shakespeare does just once again in *The Tempest*, he takes the traditional city street as his horizon, moving his characters back and forth from port to mart and in and out of the various doorways between. The play would seem to lend itself very conveniently to the simultaneous stage of a great hall, such as that of Gray's Inn, where three or four free-standing houses or so-called mansions would have corresponded to the labeled locations: the Phoenix, the Porpentine for the Courtesan, the Centaur Inn, and the ultimate abbey near the place of execution. On the other hand, the recent production at Stratford, Ontario, demonstrated how well the play could adapt to the multilevel mobility of an Elizabethan playhouse.

The problem of staging ought not to be unduly strained by the presupposition that calls for identical twins. To be sure, the difficulty raised by the twins of two sexes in *Twelfth Night*, which would have been solved in Shakespeare's day when both parts were acted by young men, is virtually insoluble in the modern theater. But, granted an approximate equivalence of stature, plus the same costuming and make-up, the Antipholuses and Dromios ought to look enough alike to confuse the other characters without confusing the audience. Is it not our premise, in viewing a comedy, that we are brighter than those who are on the stage? In the Roman theater, where the employment of masks eliminated the facial disparities, Plautus had to give a tassel to Mercury and a feather to Jupiter so that they would not be confused with Sosia and Amphitryon. At Stratford, Connecticut, in 1963, the same actor was cast as both twins, thereby combining histrionic virtuosity with artistic economy. This directorial tactic must create a bigger dilemma than the one it endeavors to solve, since the audience can never know the moment of catharsis, the visual illumination of seeing the two confusing elements discriminated from one another and exhibited side by side.

That way schizophrenia lies—which does not mean that it would be unproduceable in the Theater of the Absurd. It might turn out to be something in the vein of Pirandello, if not a dramatization of *Dr. Jekyll and Mr. Hyde*. But the actual predicament is that of two personalities forced into the same role, rather than that of one personality playing two roles, since the resident twin has the contacts and continuities, and the roving twin intercepts them, as it were. Tweedledum has got to match Tweedledee, more or less, in order to be taken for him; and yet, the less he feels like him, the more the dramatic irony. Plautus did not discriminate between his two very sharply; the discrepancies that emerged largely took the concrete form of objects which fell into the wrong hands; otherwise the interconnecting characters did not seem to notice much difference. The married Menaechmus was angry from the first, so that each new chagrin could be rationalized to his mood. The interloping Menaechmus, though considerably bewildered, had no cause for being dissatisfied with his reception. Neither of them was above the temptation to profit from the contretemps; and the interloper finally engaged in a stratagem of his own, when he joined the game and pretended to be a lunatic.

That sort of conduct is what we have agreed to label a suppose, a deception which is cultivated rather than casual. The most notable fact about Shakespeare's comedy is that it has no supposes, only errors: only mischances, and no contrivances by anybody except Shakespeare himself. There is no parallel scene of pretended madness; Shakespeare must have been saving the theme for *Hamlet*. Here the suspected madman, like Malvolio in *Twelfth Night*, protests his sanity. He does not act; he is acted upon; and Shakespeare, ever the psychologist, makes a good deal more out of the attempted diagnosis of demonic possession. He makes the exorcism so very painful, and goes so far out of his way to substitute the grim-visaged schoolmaster, Dr. Pinch, for the Plautine Medicus, that we sense a virtual obsession, possibly connected with Holofernes, the pedant of *Love's Labor's Lost*, or with some other reminiscence from Shakespeare's own teaching days. It is as if the nightmare came so close that the misunderstood hero dare not pretend to be hallucinated. Again there is a precedent in Saint Paul's Epistle to the Ephesians, where the exorcist is exorcised. The customary rhetorical questions of comedy, in these mouths, become questions of existential bewilderment or expressions of cosmic vertigo: Do I dream or wake? Do we see double? Is he drunk or sober? Is she a liar or a fool? Who is crazy? Who is sane?

Contrasted with this constant inner questioning, the caricature of Dr. Pinch seems externalized. He is the one humorous personage of the play, in the Jonsonian usage, a man of obvious quirks and eccentric aspect, the crazy psychiatrist. If the others are funny, it is because of the plights they find themselves in. No, there is one other exception, though she is peripheral, and has a greater impact in her absence than in her presence onstage. This heroine, invoked indifferently as Luce or Nell, is generically a Dowsabel or, for that matter, a Dulcinea—a kitchen maid whose formidable proportions are vividly verbalized by the wrong Dromio, her brother-in-law, who is still quaking from the shock of having been claimed by her as a husband. This is the vulgar parallel to Adriana's claim upon her brother-in-law. Dromio's description of his brother's Nell, elicited by his master's queries as straight man, is a set-piece in the manner of Launce or Launcelot Gobbo, and may well have been assigned to the same comedian. With its geographical conceits, comparing the parts of her person to foreign countries (and containing, incidentally, the sole direct allusion that Shakespeare makes to America), it might almost be a ribald reversal of Othello's traveler's tales when wooing Desdemona.

But it is by no means a far-fetched gag, since it embodies—on a more than miniature scale—the principal contrast of the play: on the one hand, extensive voyaging; on the other, intensive domesticity. In using an underplot which burlesques the main plot, Shakespeare employs a device as old as Medwall's pioneer interlude of *Fulgens and Lucres*, where the rival suitors have servants who court the mistress' maid under the diagrammatic designations of A and B. With Nell, as with the demanding Adriana, the normal approaches of courtship are reversed. The closest we come to romantic love is the sketchy relationship between her brother-in-law and her husband's sister-in-law. Yet that is a good deal closer than Plautus brings us; and though both masters are suitably mated in the end, the concluding dialogue of the servants emphasizes the pairing of twins, not spouses. Parents and children are reunited, family ties are reasserted; but Dromio of Syracuse remains a free agent. His greatest moment has been the midpoint of the play, when he acted as doorkeeper and kept out his fellow Dromio, as well as that Dromio's master, the master of the house. This is the one point before the denouement when Shakespeare permits his twins to meet and talk, and the door between them seems to keep the mutual visibility fairly obscure.

It is worth noting that their brief colloquy reverts to the doggerel style of *Ralph Roister Doister*, the oldest English imitation of Plautus, in its stichomythic interchanges of rhyming fourteeners. This is the main scene (the first of Act III) that Shakespeare borrowed from the *Amphitryon* (the first of Act I), eking out the comedy of the *Menaechmi* with the underplot of the two Sosias to complete—with a vengeance—the Elizabethan require-ments for a double plot. He develops it to the very pitch of the dramatic subversion that he has been exploiting, with the outsider inside and the insider excluded, the stranger in possession of the house and the householder cast into outer darkness. Both parties are translated, as Quince will affirm of Bottom; and they could not have been so completely translated, had they not been facsimiles to begin with. The most fundamental alteration that Shakespeare made in his Plautine material was to shift the focus from the homekeeping twin to his errant brother, whose sobriquet, Antipholus Erotes, may be a variation on Erratus or Errans. The *Menaechmi* starts out with the other twin, and with the reassurance of familiar surroundings, into which the disturbing factor will be injected. *The Comedy of Errors* starts with the newcomer, and his impressions of strangeness: the witchery of Ephesus, not the bustle of Epidamnum.

Having a head start, and having to alternate scenes with Antipholus of Ephesus, who does not appear until the third act, Antipholus of Syracuse has a much larger part: roughly 272 lines to the other's 207. The disproportion is even clearer between the parts of the two Dromios: there the score is Syracuse 233, Ephesus 162. The *Menaechmi*, though it is the shorter play, has fewer characters and longer speeches; accordingly, its Syracusan twin has 251 lines, whereas the Epidamnian twin has 300. We therefore tend to visualize what goes on in the Latin play from the denizen's standpoint, and what goes on in the English play from the alien's. Epidamnum could be any old town, where everything should be in its place, *in situ*: where everyone expects his fellow citizen, Menaechmus, to go through the round of his habitual day. No one could suspect that there was another Menaechmus, whose chance encounters would lead to incongruities and discontinuities, except for his one follower, who shares and compounds his perplexities. Ephesus is another story, however. We are put off at once by the hostile reception of Egeon; and when the two other foreigners enter, Antipholus and Dromio, they are the first of those names whom we have met.

We share their misgivings all the more readily because they too have been risking their lives, and because the object of their travels has so far eluded them. When this Antipholus gets caught up in his brother's existence, it is as new to us as it is to him. We participate in an adventure; what might be matter of fact to an Ephesian is, for him and ourselves, a fantasy out of the *Arabian Nights*. "What error drives our eyes and ears amiss?" he wonders, after Adriana accosts him, reprimands him, and invites him to dinner. And tentatively he resolves,

Until I know this sure uncertainty,
I'll entertain the offered fallacy. (II.ii.186–87)

Then, after dinner, smitten with Luciana, he asks her to unfold the mystery:

Teach me, dear creature, how to think and speak:
Lay open to my earthy-gross conceit,
Smoth'red in errors, feeble, shallow, weak,
The folded meaning of your words' deceit. (III.ii.33–36)

But the undeception does not come about until all the participants in this "sympathizèd one day's error"—for so the Abbess sums it up—have sought the illumination of sanctuary within her abbey. In that cloistered serenity, far from urban corruption, the deferred recognition scenes can coincide at long last. The confessions and counter-accusations piece together a step-by-step recapitulation of how "these errors are arose." The maternal figure of the Abbess is something of a surprise, as Bertrand Evans points out in his recent study, *Shakespeare's Comedies*. Running through all of them, Mr. Evans finds their common structural principle in what he calls a "discrepant awareness." Characteristically, the humor springs from "the exploitable gulf spread between the participants' understanding and ours."

In Shakespeare's development of this resource, *The Comedy of Errors* is primordial, since it is his single comedy where the audience knows all and all the characters are in the dark. Mr. Evans' suggestive analysis can be perfectly fitted to the *Menaechmi*. Plautus, in effect, is always saying, "I told you so." But Shakespeare is always asking, "Can such things be?" The exceptional position of the Abbess not only rounds out the recognitions; it lays the spell of wonderment again upon the concluding scene; and it reminds us, as other touches do, of Shakespeare's romances. Even within the venal and angular precincts of Latinate comedy, he can make us aware of unpathed waters, undreamed shores, and things in heaven and earth that philosophy has not fathomed. Yet philosophers can tell us much, particularly about the processes of learning; and Bergson tells us much about *The Comedy of Errors* when, in his essay on laughter, he borrows a concept from optics and writes of "the reciprocal interference of series." At length we can put our supposes or errors down in scientific terminology. "A situation is invariably comic," Bergson explains, "when it belongs simultaneously to two independent series of events, and is capable of being interpreted in two entirely different meanings at the same time."

It would be hard to conceive of a better illustration than the two different series of events in the respective days of the two Antipholuses, and the ways in which they are imperceptibly crisscrossed. Antipholus of Syracuse has no particular expectations or plans. He derives a gratuitous enjoyment from the inexplicable services rendered and favors due his brother. This interference or substitution induces a certain amnesia on the brother's part, when the bills come in and the witnesses testify; naturally, he cannot remember the items attested. As one error engenders another, suspicion is bound to mount and disgruntlement spread, rising to their climax in hot pursuit toward the madhouse or the jail, and ending at the priory. Now the brunt of these displacements is borne by Antipholus of Ephesus. Of all those discomfited, he comes nearest to being a victim of the situation, since it is his situation, in the last analysis. It is his routine which is broken up, his standing in the community undermined; his normal expectations are interfered with, and—to add insult to injury—he is expected to pay for what he has been deprived of. In short, the rug has been pulled out from under the very preconditions of his existence.

Other people's bafflement can be fun, and Plautus makes the most of it. From the heights of our spectatorial vantage point, we need not worry too much about what befalls whom. We are not playing blind man's buff, we are watching the game. But Shakespeare makes us feel what it is like to be this or that Antipholus—all the difference in the world, if we happened to start by being the other one—and the interaction of opposite numbers ends by demonstrating *a fortiori* the uniqueness of the individual. When Adriana and her husband appeal to the duke, the stories they tell of their day's experience are mutually contradictory; but the discrepancies would disappear if the shadow of the interfering Antipholus were retraced through their reciprocal patterns. (Latter-day readers or viewers may be reminded of the Japanese story or film *Rashomon*.) It has been a lesson for Adriana, brought home by the gentle rebuke of the Abbess, and penitently acknowledged. For Antipholus of Ephesus, it has been an eye-opening misadventure. Apparently, he has never felt the impetus that has incited his brother and his father to sally forth in search of him. Unconcerned with his foundling origin, he rejoices in the good graces of the duke and takes for granted the stable comforts of his Ephesian citizenship.

What greater shock for him, then, than to bring a party of fellow citizens home to his well-established household for lunch and to discover that household preempted by roistering strangers, to be shut out in the street, to have one's own door slammed in one's own face? Or is it one's own? The sense of alienation, that *Verfremdungseffekt* so characteristic of Brecht and of the twentieth-century theater, is all the greater when our image of ourselves depends for its corroboration upon a settled context, and when we come to realize—what tragedy teaches us—that it is our destiny to be displaced. When Messenio saw the two Menaechmuses together, he declared that water was not more like water. After Shakespeare has adapted the metaphor, it stands not for an easy correspondence but for an unending quest.

> I to the world am like a drop of water
> That in the ocean seeks another drop, (I.ii.35–36)

Antipholus of Syracuse confesses sadly, realizing that he is less likely to find a mother and a brother than to be irretrievably lost himself. Later, Adriana, addressing him as if he were Antipholus of Ephesus, likens their imperiled love to a drop of water into the sea; and he has a similar exchange with Luciana. The Syracusan twin is conscious that he must lose his identity in order to find it; the Ephesian twin is not; but he must, and he does. And Dromio too—both Dromios, whichever is which—must undergo their crises of identity: "Am I Dromio? Am I your man? Am I myself?"

Modern psychological fiction is haunted by doubles, sometimes as overtly as in the tales of Hoffmann, Poe, and Dostoevsky, or in "The Jolly Corner" of Henry James, where the Black Stranger is recognized as the self that might have been. The other self—best friend, worst enemy—stares back at the poets from Heine's pallid ghost ("*Du! Doppelgänger, du bleicher Geselle!*") or Baudelaire's hypocritical reader ("*mon semblable! mon frère!*"). That alter ego may be demon or devil, good angel or evil genius. It may be the retribution of conscience—Philip Drunk reprehended by Philip Sober—or, at the other extreme, the vicarious pleasure the artist enjoys through the playboy, the envy of Shem for Shaun. All this may well be a far cry from Plautine or even Shakespearean farce, to which we should be glad that we can escape from our more introspective dilemmas. There all aberrations come home to roost, and are sorted out by the happy ending; we acknowledge the error of our ways, and false suppositions are replaced by truths. No one really gets damaged in Epidamnum, and everyone enjoys a new lease of life when Egeon is ransomed and reprieved. Everything will be explained at a feast, after the conventional manner of comedy. Debts will be paid, relationships renewed, and daily routine taken up where it broke off. Having been restored once more to our familiar world, we laugh away the shudder of estrangement.

## A NOTE ON THE SOURCE

Titus Maccius Plautus, who was born during the third century B.C. and died during the second, was the most popular of the Roman playwrights. Freely adapted into the Latin vernacular from the New Comedy of the Greeks, his plays were distinguished by their broad humor, fast movement, vivid language, and nimble versification. Among the twenty-one Plautine comedies that have come down to us, the *Menaechmi* is one of the best known and the most influential, doubtless because it reduces the dilemmas of mistaken identity to an archetypal pattern. A rough but vigorous translation into Elizabethan prose, which Shakespeare may or may not have known in manuscript form, was published in 1595, presumably a few years after the first production of *The Comedy of Errors*. The initials of the translator, W. W., are generally thought to stand for William Warner, a man of letters who is sometimes remembered for his historical poem, *Albion's England*. For the underplot of the twin servants, Shakespeare is indebted to the *Amphitruo* of Plautus, particularly the opening scene and the fourth act.

## A NOTE ON THE TEXT

*The Comedy of Errors* was first published in the Folio of 1623, which provides the only authoritative text. It is possible that the copy for the Folio was Shakespeare's manuscript; the ambiguity of some names in stage directions and in speech prefixes would have been confusing in a promptbook. For example, Egeon is *Mer(chant)* in I.i., but other merchants appear in other scenes without distinctive titles. More important, *E. Dro(mio)* is, as might be expected, *Dromio of Ephesus*; but *E. Ant.* is Antipholus of Syracuse, an abbreviation of his earlier designation, *Ant. Errotis*—which is perhaps an approximation of *erraticus*, wandering. A promptbook doubtless would have clarified the nomenclature.

The Folio's text is a good one, presenting the editor with relatively few problems. In the present edition the speech prefixes and names in stage directions have been regularized, spelling and punctuation have been modernized, and obvious typographical errors have been corrected. A few passages that the Folio prints as prose are given in verse, and the positions of a few stage directions have been slightly altered. Act division (translated from the Latin) is that of the Folio; scene division is that of the Globe text. Other departures from the Folio are listed below, with the adopted reading first, in boldface, and the original reading next, in roman.

**I.i.17 at** at any  **42 the** he  **102 upon** vp  **116 bark** backe  **123 thee** they  **151 health** helpe
**I.ii.s.d. Antipholus of Syracuse** Antipholis Erotes  **4 arrival** a riuall  **30 lose** loose  **32 s.d. Exit** Exeunt  **40 unhappy** vnhappie a  **65 score** scoure  **66 clock** cooke  **93 God's** God  **94 s.d. Exit** Exeunt
**II.i.s.d. Antipholus of Ephesus** Antipholis Sereptus  **11 o' door** adore  **12 ill** thus  **45 two** too  **62 thousand** hundred  **73 errand** arrant  **108 alone, alone** alone, a loue  **113 Wear** Where  **114 But** By
**II.ii.s.d. Antipholus of Syracuse** Antipholis Errotis  **12 didst** did didst  **80 men** them  **98 tiring** trying  **102 e'en** in  **176 stronger** .stranger  **187 offered** free'd  **195 drone** Dromio  **196 am not I** am I not
**III.i.54 trow** hope  **75 you** your  **89 her** your  **91 her** your
**III.ii.s.d. Luciana** Iuliana  **1 Luciana** Iulia  **2 Antipholus,** hate Antipholus  **4 building** buildings  **16 attaint** attaine  **21 but** not  **26 wife** wise  **46 sister's** sister  **49 bed** bud; **them thee**  **57 where** when  **109 and** is  **127 chalky** chalkle  **167 here is** here's
**IV.i.17 her** their  **28 carat** charect  **47 to blame** too blame  **88 then she** then sir she
**IV.ii.6 Of** Oh  **61 'a** I
**IV.iii.1 S. Antipholus** [F omits]  **59 if you do** if do
**V.i.s.d. [another] Merchant** the Merchant  **33 God's** God  **121 death** depth  **168 Messenger** [F omits]  **246 all together** altogether  **282 s.d. abbey** Abbesse  **403 ne'er** are  **406 joy with** go with  **408 s.d. Exeunt** Exeunt omnes. Manet  **423 senior** Signior

# THE COMEDY OF ERRORS

[Dramatis Personae

SOLINUS *Duke of Ephesus*
EGEON *a merchant of Syracuse*

ANTIPHOLUS OF EPHESUS } *twin brothers, and*
ANTIPHOLUS OF SYRACUSE } *sons of Egeon and Emilia*

DROMIO OF EPHESUS } *twin brothers, and bond-*
DROMIO OF SYRACUSE } *men to the two Antipholuses*

BALTHASAR
ANGELO *a goldsmith*
A MERCHANT *friend to Antipholus of Syracuse*

ANOTHER MERCHANT *to whom Angelo is in debt*
DOCTOR PINCH *a schoolmaster*
EMILIA *an abbess at Ephesus, wife of Egeon*
ADRIANA *wife of Antipholus of Ephesus*
LUCIANA *her sister*
LUCE *or Nell, kitchen maid to Adriana*
COURTESAN
JAILER HEADSMAN OFFICERS ATTENDANTS

*Scene:* Ephesus]

## ACT I

### Scene I. [*A public place.*]

*Enter the* DUKE *of Ephesus, with* [EGEON] *the merchant of Syracusa,°* JAILER, *and other* ATTENDANTS.

EGEON
Proceed, Solinus, to procure my fall,
And by the doom° of death end woes and all.
DUKE
Merchant of Syracusa, plead no more;
I am not partial° to infringe our laws.
The enmity and discord which of late          5
Sprung from the rancorous outrage of your duke
To merchants, our well-dealing countrymen,
Who, wanting guilders° to redeem their lives,
Have sealed his rigorous statutes with their bloods,
Excludes all pity from our threat'ning looks.   10
For, since the mortal and intestine jars°
'Twixt thy seditious countrymen and us,

It hath in solemn synods been decreed,
Both by the Syracusians and ourselves,
To admit no traffic to our adverse° towns.      15
Nay more; if any born at Ephesus°
Be seen at Syracusian marts and fairs;
Again, if any Syracusian born
Come to the bay of Ephesus, he dies,
His goods confiscate to the duke's dispose,°    20
Unless a thousand marks° be levied
To quit° the penalty and to ransom him.
Thy substance, valued at the highest rate,
Cannot amount unto a hundred marks;
Therefore by law thou art condemned to die.     25
EGEON
Yet this my comfort: when your words are done,
My woes end likewise with the evening sun.
DUKE
Well, Syracusian, say, in brief, the cause
Why thou departed'st from thy native home,
And for what cause thou cam'st to Ephesus.      30
EGEON
A heavier task could not have been imposed
Than I to speak my griefs unspeakable;

---

*The decorative border above appeared on the first page of* The Comedy of Errors *in the First Folio edition of Shakespeare's plays, 1623.*

**I.i.s.d. Syracusa** Syracuse, ancient capital of Sicily   **2 doom** sentence   **4 partial** predisposed   **8 guilders** Dutch coins worth about forty cents   **11 intestine jars** internal conflicts

**15 adverse** hostile   **16 Ephesus** rich city on the coast of Asia Minor   **20 dispose** disposal   **21 marks** valued at somewhat more than three dollars   **22 quit** acquit

Yet, that the world may witness that my end
Was wrought by nature, not by vile offense,
I'll utter what my sorrow gives me leave. 35
In Syracusa was I born, and wed
Unto a woman happy but for me,
And by me, had not our hap been bad.
With her I lived in joy, our wealth increased
By prosperous voyages I often made 40
To Epidamnum,° till my factor's° death
And the great care of goods at random left
Drew me from kind embracements of my spouse;
From whom my absence was not six months old,
Before herself—almost at fainting under 45
The pleasing punishment that women bear—
Had made provision for her following me,
And soon and safe arrivèd where I was.
There had she not been long, but she became
A joyful mother of two goodly sons; 50
And, which was strange, the one so like the other,
As could not be distinguished but by names.
That very hour, and in the selfsame inn,
A mean° woman was deliverèd
Of such a burden male, twins both alike. 55
Those, for° their parents were exceeding poor,
I bought, and brought up to attend my sons.
My wife, not meanly° proud of two such boys,
Made daily motions° for our home return.
Unwilling I agreed; alas, too soon 60
We came aboard.
A league from Epidamnum had we sailed
Before the always wind-obeying deep
Gave any tragic instance° of our harm.
But longer did we not retain much hope; 65
For what obscurèd light the heavens did grant
Did but convey unto our fearful minds
A doubtful warrant° of immediate death,
Which, though myself would gladly have embraced,
Yet the incessant weepings of my wife, 70
Weeping before for what she saw must come,
And piteous plainings° of the pretty babes,
That mourned for fashion,° ignorant what to fear,
Forced me to seek delays for them and me.
And this it was—for other means was none: 75
The sailors sought for safety by our boat,
And left the ship, then sinking-ripe,° to us.
My wife, more careful for the latter-born,°
Had fast'ned him unto a small spare mast,
Such as seafaring men provide for storms; 80
To him one of the other twins was bound,
Whilst I had been like heedful of the other.
The children thus disposed, my wife and I,
Fixing our eyes on whom our care was fixed,
Fast'ned ourselves at either end the mast; 85
And floating straight, obedient to the stream,
Was carried towards Corinth,° as we thought.
At length the sun, gazing upon the earth,
Dispersed those vapors that offended us,

And, by the benefit of his wishèd° light, 90
The seas waxed calm, and we discoverèd
Two ships from far, making amain° to us:
Of Corinth that, of Epidaurus° this.
But ere they came—O, let me say no more!
Gather the sequel by that went before. 95

DUKE
Nay, forward, old man; do not break off so,
For we may pity, though not pardon thee.

EGEON
O, had the gods done so, I had not now
Worthily° termed them merciless to us.
For, ere the ships could meet by twice five leagues, 100
We were encount'red by a mighty rock,
Which being violently borne upon,
Our helpful ship° was splitted in the midst;
So that, in this unjust divorce of us,
Fortune had left to both of us alike 105
What to delight in, what to sorrow for.
Her part, poor soul, seeming as burdenèd
With lesser weight, but not with lesser woe,
Was carried with more speed before the wind;
And in our sight they three were taken up 110
By fishermen of Corinth, as we thought.
At length another ship had seized on us,
And, knowing whom it was their hap to save,
Gave healthful welcome to their shipwracked guests,
And would have reft° the fishers of their prey, 115
Had not their bark been very slow of sail;
And therefore homeward did they bend their course.
Thus have you heard me severed from my bliss,
That by misfortunes was my life prolonged
To tell sad stories of my own mishaps. 120

DUKE
And, for the sake of them thou sorrowest for,
Do me the favor to dilate° at full
What have befall'n of them and thee till now.

EGEON
My youngest boy, and yet my eldest care,
At eighteen years became inquisitive 125
After his brother, and importuned me
That his attendant—so his case was like,
Reft of his brother, but retained his name—
Might bear him company in the quest of him;
Whom whilst I labored of a love° to see, 130
I hazarded the loss of whom I loved.
Five summers have I spent in farthest Greece,
Roaming clean through the bounds of Asia,
And coasting homeward, came to Ephesus,
Hopeless to find,° yet loath to leave unsought 135
Or° that or any place that harbors men.
But here must end the story of my life;
And happy were I in my timely death,
Could all my travels° warrant me they live.

DUKE
Hapless Egeon, whom the fates have marked 140
To bear the extremity of dire mishap!

**41 Epidamnum** Adriatic seaport; **factor's** agent's **54 mean** poor **56 for** because **58 not meanly** more than a little **59 motions** proposals **64 instance** token **68 doubtful warrant** ominous sign **72 plainings** wails **73 fashion** custom **77 sinking-ripe** ready to sink **78 latter-born** but see line 124 **87 Corinth** major Greek seaport

**90 his wishèd** its wished-for **92 amain** with full speed **93 Epidaurus** ancient name for both a Greek and an Adriatic town **99 Worthily** deservedly **103 ship** the mast **115 reft** robbed **122 dilate** relate **130 of a love** out of love **135 Hopeless to find** without hope of finding **136 Or** either **139 travels** with the further implication of "travails"

Now trust me, were it not against our laws,
Against my crown, my oath, my dignity,°
Which princes, would they, may not disannul,°
My soul should sue as advocate for thee.     145
But though thou art adjudged° to the death,
And passèd sentence may not be recalled
But to our honor's great disparagement,°
Yet will I favor thee in what I can;
Therefore, merchant, I'll limit thee this day     150
To seek thy health by beneficial help.
Try all the friends thou hast in Ephesus—
Beg thou, or borrow, to make up the sum,
And live; if no, then thou art doomed to die.
Jailer, take him to thy custody.     155

JAILER
I will, my lord.

EGEON
Hopeless and helpless doth Egeon wend,
But to procrastinate° his lifeless end.     *Exeunt.*

[Scene II. *The mart.°*]

*Enter* ANTIPHOLUS [OF SYRACUSE], *a* MERCHANT, *and* DROMIO [OF SYRACUSE].

MERCHANT
Therefore, give out you are of Epidamnum,
Lest that your goods too soon be confiscate.
This very day a Syracusian merchant
Is apprehended for arrival here,
And not being able to buy out° his life,     5
According to the statute of the town,
Dies ere the weary sun set in the west.
There is your money that I had to keep.

S. ANTIPHOLUS
Go bear it to the Centaur,° where we host,°
And stay there, Dromio, till I come to thee;     10
Within this hour it will be dinnertime;
Till that, I'll view the manners of the town,
Peruse the traders, gaze upon the buildings,
And then return and sleep within mine inn;
For with long travel I am stiff and weary.     15
Get thee away.

S. DROMIO
Many a man would take you at your word,
And go indeed, having so good a mean.°
         *Exit* DROMIO.

S. ANTIPHOLUS
A trusty villain,° sir, that very oft,
When I am dull with care and melancholy,     20
Lightens my humor° with his merry jests.
What, will you walk with me about the town,
And then go to my inn and dine with me?

MERCHANT
I am invited, sir, to certain merchants,
Of whom I hope to make much benefit.     25

I crave your pardon; soon at five o'clock,
Please you, I'll meet with you upon the mart,
And afterward consort° you till bedtime.
My present business calls me from you now.

S. ANTIPHOLUS
Farewell till then. I will go lose myself,     30
And wander up and down to view the city.

MERCHANT
Sir, I commend you to your own content.     *Exit.*

S. ANTIPHOLUS
He that commends me to mine own content
Commends me to the thing I cannot get.
I to the world am like a drop of water     35
That in the ocean seeks another drop,
Who, falling there to find his fellow forth,°
Unseen, inquisitive, confounds° himself.
So I, to find a mother and a brother,
In quest of them, unhappy,° lose myself.     40

*Enter* DROMIO OF EPHESUS.

Here comes the almanac° of my true date.
What now? How chance thou art returned so soon?

E. DROMIO
Returned so soon! Rather approached too late.
The capon burns, the pig falls from the spit;
The clock hath strucken twelve° upon the bell;     45
My mistress made it one upon my cheek.
She is so hot because the meat is cold;
The meat is cold because you come not home;
You come not home because you have no stomach;°
You have no stomach, having broke your fast.     50
But we, that know what 'tis to fast and pray,
Are penitent for your default° today.

S. ANTIPHOLUS
Stop in your wind,° sir; tell me this, I pray:
Where have you left the money that I gave you?

E. DROMIO
O, sixpence, that I had o' Wednesday last,     55
To pay the saddler for my mistress' crupper?°
The saddler had it, sir, I kept it not.

S. ANTIPHOLUS
I am not in a sportive humor now.
Tell me, and dally not, where is the money?
We being strangers here, how dar'st thou trust     60
So great a charge from thine own custody?

E. DROMIO
I pray you, jest, sir, as you sit at dinner.
I from my mistress come to you in post;°
If I return, I shall be post° indeed,
For she will score° your fault upon my pate.     65
Methinks your maw,° like mine, should be your clock,
And strike you home without a messenger.

S. ANTIPHOLUS
Come, Dromio, come, these jests are out of season;

---

28 **consort** accompany   37 **find . . . forth** seek his fellow out   38 **confounds** loses   40 **unhappy** unlucky   41 **almanac** Dromio reminds Antipholus of his own age   45 **twelve** dinnertime or later   49 **stomach** appetite   52 **default** (1) sin (2) failure to appear   53 **wind** breath   56 **crupper** strap from saddle to horse's tail   63 **post** haste   64 **post** posted (to pay account, with pun meaning "beaten")   65 **score** with pun on *scour*, beat   66 **maw** stomach (ordinarily used with animals)

143 **dignity** office   144 **disannul** cancel   146 **adjudgèd** sentenced   148 **disparagement** injury   158 **procrastinate** postpone
**I.ii.s.d. mart** marketplace   5 **buy out** redeem   9 **Centaur** name and sign of an inn; **host** lodge   18 **mean** means   19 **villain** in the original sense of "bondman"   21 **humor** mood

Reserve them till a merrier hour than this.
Where is the gold I gave in charge to thee?      70

E. DROMIO
To me, Sir? Why, you gave no gold to me.

S. ANTIPHOLUS
Come on, sir knave, have done your foolishness,
And tell me how thou hast disposed thy charge.

E. DROMIO
My charge was but to fetch you from the mart
Home to your house, the Phoenix,° sir, to dinner.    75
My mistress and her sister stays for you.

S. ANTIPHOLUS
Now, as I am a Christian, answer me,
In what safe place you have bestowed° my money;
Or I shall break that merry sconce° of yours
That stands on° tricks when I am undisposed.     80
Where is the thousand marks thou hadst of me?

E. DROMIO
I have some marks of yours upon my pate,
Some of my mistress' marks upon my shoulders,
But not a thousand marks between you both.
If I should pay° your worship those again,      85
Perchance you will not bear them patiently.

S. ANTIPHOLUS
Thy mistress' marks? What mistress, slave, hast thou?

E. DROMIO
Your worship's wife, my mistress at the Phoenix;
She that doth fast till you come home to dinner,
And prays that you will hie you home to dinner.    90

S. ANTIPHOLUS
What, wilt thou flout me thus unto my face,
Being forbid? There, take you that, sir knave.

[*Beats him.*]

E. DROMIO
What mean you, sir? For God's sake, hold your hands!
Nay, and° you will not, sir, I'll take my heels.
                               *Exit* DROMIO.

S. ANTIPHOLUS
Upon my life, by some device or other,      95
The villain is o'erraught° of all my money.
They say this town is full of cozenage:°
As° nimble jugglers that deceive the eye,
Dark-working sorcerers that change the mind,
Soul-killing witches that deform the body,     100
Disguisèd cheaters, prating mountebanks,°
And many suchlike liberties° of sin.
If it prove so, I will be gone the sooner.
I'll to the Centaur, to go seek this slave.
I greatly fear my money is not safe.        *Exit.* 105

---

# ACT II

[*Scene I. The Phoenix.*]

*Enter* ADRIANA, *wife to Antipholus [of Ephesus], with*
LUCIANA, *her sister.*

ADRIANA
Neither my husband nor the slave returned,
That in such haste I sent to seek his master.
Sure, Luciana, it is two o'clock.

LUCIANA
Perhaps some merchant hath invited him,
And from the mart he's somewhere gone to dinner.   5
Good sister, let us dine, and never fret;
A man is master of his liberty.
Time is their master, and when they see time,
They'll go or come; if so, be patient, sister.

ADRIANA
Why should their liberty than ours be more?     10

LUCIANA
Because their business still° lies out o' door.

ADRIANA
Look when° I serve him so, he takes it ill.

LUCIANA
O, know he is the bridle of your will.

ADRIANA
There's none but asses will be bridled so.

LUCIANA
Why, headstrong liberty is lashed° with woe.   15
There's nothing situate under heaven's eye
But hath his bound, in earth, in sea, in sky.
The beasts, the fishes, and the wingèd fowls
Are their males' subjects, and at their controls;°
Man, more divine, the master of all these,     20
Lord of the wide world and wild wat'ry seas,
Indued with intellectual sense° and souls,
Of more preeminence than fish and fowls,
Are masters to their females, and their lords;
Then let your will attend on their accords.     25

ADRIANA
This servitude makes you to keep unwed.

LUCIANA
Not this, but troubles of the marriage bed.

ADRIANA
But, were you wedded, you would bear some
    sway.°

LUCIANA
Ere I learn love, I'll practice to obey.

ADRIANA
How if your husband start some other where?°   30

LUCIANA
Till he come home again, I would forbear.

ADRIANA
Patience unmoved! no marvel though she pause;°
They can be meek that have no other cause.°
A wretched soul, bruised with adversity,
We bid be quiet when we hear it cry;       35
But were we burd'ned with like weight of pain,

---

75 **Phoenix** house of Antipholus, denoted by the sign of his
shop   78 **bestowed** deposited   79 **sconce** head   80 **stands on**
insists upon   85 **pay** also meaning "beat"   94 **and** if   96
**o'erraught** overreached   97 **cozenage** cheating   98 **As**
such as   101 **mountebanks** quacks   102 **liberties** uninhibited
acts

**II.i.11 still** always   12 **Look when** whenever   15 **lashed**
whipped   19 **controls** commands   22 **intellectual sense** reason
28 **sway** authority   30 **start . . . where** pursue another
woman   32 **pause** delay in getting married   33 **cause** motive

As much or more we should ourselves complain:
So thou, that hast no unkind mate to grieve thee,
With urging helpless° patience would relieve me;
But, if thou live to see like right bereft,°     40
This fool-begged° patience in thee will be left.

LUCIANA
Well, I will marry one day, but to try.
Here comes your man, now is your husband nigh.

*Enter* DROMIO OF EPHESUS.

ADRIANA
Say, is your tardy master now at hand?

E. DROMIO   Nay, he's at two hands with me, and that   45
my two ears can witness.

ADRIANA
Say, didst thou speak with him? Know'st thou his mind?

E. DROMIO   Ay, ay, he told° his mind upon mine ear.
Beshrew his hand, I scarce could understand it.

LUCIANA   Spake he so doubtfully,° thou couldst not   50
feel his meaning?

E. DROMIO   Nay, he struck so plainly, I could too
well feel his blows; and withal so doubtfully, that I
could scarce understand° them.

ADRIANA
But say, I prithee, is he coming home?     55
It seems he hath great care to please his wife.

E. DROMIO   Why, mistress, sure my master is horn-
mad.

ADRIANA
Horn-mad,° thou villain!

E. DROMIO           I mean not cuckold-mad,
But sure he is stark mad.     60
When I desired him to come home to dinner,
He asked me for a thousand marks in gold.
"'Tis dinnertime," quoth I. "My gold!" quoth he.
"Your meat doth burn," quoth I. "My gold!" quoth he.
"Will you come?" quoth I. "My gold!" quoth he.   65
"Where is the thousand marks I gave thee, villain?"
"The pig," quoth I, "is burned." "My gold!" quoth he.
"My mistress, sir—" quoth I. "Hang up° thy mistress!
I know not thy mistress, out on° thy mistress!"

LUCIANA   Quoth who?     70

E. DROMIO
Quoth my master.
"I know," quoth he, "no house, no wife, no mistress."
So that my errand due unto° my tongue,
I thank him, I bare° home upon my shoulders;
For, in conclusion, he did beat me there.     75

ADRIANA
Go back again, thou slave, and fetch him home.

E. DROMIO
Go back again, and be new beaten home?
For God's sake, send some other messenger.

ADRIANA
Back, slave, or I will break thy pate across.°

E. DROMIO
And he will bless that cross with other beating;     80
Between you, I shall have a holy° head.

ADRIANA
Hence, prating peasant! Fetch thy master home.

E. DROMIO
Am I so round° with you, as you with me,
That like a football you do spurn me thus?
You spurn me hence, and he will spurn me hither;     85
If I last in this service, you must case me in leather.
                       [*Exit.*]

LUCIANA
Fie, how impatience lowereth° in your face!

ADRIANA
His company must do his minions° grace,
Whilst I at home starve° for a merry look:
Hath homely age th' alluring beauty took
From my poor cheek? Then he hath wasted it.
Are my discourses° dull? Barren my wit?
If voluble and sharp discourse be marred,
Unkindness blunts it more than marble hard.
Do their gay vestments his affections bait?°     95
That's not my fault; he's master of my state.
What ruins are in me that can be found,
By him not ruined? Then is he the ground
Of my defeatures.° My decayèd fair°
A sunny look of his would soon repair.     100
But, too unruly deer,° he breaks the pale,°
And feeds from° home; poor I am but his stale.°

LUCIANA
Self-harming jealousy! fie, beat it hence.

ADRIANA
Unfeeling fools can with such wrongs dispense.°
I know his eye doth homage otherwhere,°     105
Or else what lets° it but he would be here?
Sister, you know he promised me a chain.
Would that alone, alone he would detain,°
So he would keep fair quarter° with his bed!
I see the jewel best enamelèd     110
Will lose his° beauty; yet the gold bides still
That others touch, and often touching will
Wear gold, and no man that hath a name
But falsehood and corruption doth it shame.°
Since that my beauty cannot please his eye,     115
I'll weep what's left away, and weeping die.

LUCIANA
How many fond° fools serve mad jealousy!
                    *Exit* [*with* ADRIANA].

---

**39 helpless** unavailing   **40 like right bereft** your own rights denied   **41 fool-begged** assumed as one would assume responsibility for a fool   **48 told** with a pun on *tolled*   **50 doubtfully** uncertainly   **54 understand** pun on *stand under*   **59 Horn-mad** (1) like a mad bull (2) a cuckold   **68 Hang up** be hanged   **69 out on** angry interjection   **73 due unto** appropriate to   **74 bare** bore   **79 across** taken by Dromio as *a cross*

**81 holy** quibbling on *full of holes*   **83 round** (1) plain-spoken (2) spherical   **87 lowereth** frowns   **88 minions** paramours   **89 starve** pine away   **92 discourses** conversations   **95 bait** entice   **99 defeatures** disfigurements; **decayèd fair** impaired beauty   **101 deer** pun on *dear*; **pale** enclosure   **102 from** away from; **stale** dupe   **104 dispense** offer a dispensation   **105 otherwhere** elsewhere   **106 lets** prevents   **108 detain** keep back   **109 keep fair quarter** keep the peace   **111 his** its   **110–14 I . . . shame** through these ambiguous metaphors Adriana seems to imply that she still values her husband, though he is made less attractive by promiscuity   **117 fond** foolish

[Scene II. *The mart.*]

*Enter* ANTIPHOLUS [OF SYRACUSE].

S. ANTIPHOLUS
The gold I gave to Dromio is laid up
Safe at the Centaur, and the heedful slave
Is wand'red forth, in care to seek me out,
By computation° and mine host's report.
I could not speak with Dromio since at first          5
I sent him from the mart! See, here he comes.

*Enter* DROMIO OF SYRACUSE.

How now, sir, is your merry humor altered?
As you love strokes, so jest with me again.
You know no Centaur? You received no gold?
Your mistress sent to have me home to dinner?          10
My house was at the Phoenix? Wast thou mad,
That thus so madly thou didst answer me?

S. DROMIO
What answer, sir? When spake I such a word?

S. ANTIPHOLUS
Even now, even here, not half an hour since.

S. DROMIO
I did not see you since you sent me hence,          15
Home to the Centaur, with the gold you gave me.

S. ANTIPHOLUS
Villain, thou didst deny the gold's receipt,
And told'st me of a mistress, and a dinner;
For which, I hope, thou felt'st I was displeased.

S. DROMIO
I am glad to see you in this merry vein.          20
What means this jest? I pray you, master, tell me.

S. ANTIPHOLUS
Yea, dost thou jeer, and flout me in the teeth?°
Think'st thou, I jest? Hold, take thou that! And that!

*Beats* DROMIO.

S. DROMIO
Hold, sir, for God's sake! Now your jest is earnest.°
Upon what bargain do you give it me?          25

S. ANTIPHOLUS
Because that I familiarly sometimes
Do use you for my fool and chat with you,
Your sauciness will jest upon my love,
And make a common° of my serious hours.
When the sun shines, let foolish gnats make sport;          30
But creep in crannies, when he hides his beams.
If you will jest with me, know my aspect,°
And fashion your demeanor to my looks,
Or I will beat this method in your sconce.°

S. DROMIO  Sconce, call you it? So you would leave          35
battering, I had rather have it a head. And you use
these blows long, I must get a sconce for my head, and
ensconce° it too, or else I shall seek my wit° in my
shoulders. But, I pray, sir, why am I beaten?

S. ANTIPHOLUS
Dost thou not know?          40

S. DROMIO  Nothing, sir, but that I am beaten.

II.ii.4 **computation** calculation  **22 in the teeth** to my face
**24 earnest** (1) serious (2) a deposit  **29 common** public property  **32 aspect** attitude (astrological term for planetary
influence)  **34 sconce** (1) head (2) fortification  **38 ensconce**
screen; **wit** brains

S. ANTIPHOLUS
Shall I tell you why?

S. DROMIO  Ay, sir, and wherefore; for they say every
why hath a wherefore.

S. ANTIPHOLUS
Why, first for flouting me, and then wherefore,          45
For urging it the second time to me.

S. DROMIO
Was there ever any man thus beaten out of season,
When in the why and the wherefore is neither rhyme
    nor reason?
Well, sir, I thank you.

S. ANTIPHOLUS          Thank me, sir, for what?

S. DROMIO  Marry,° sir, for this something that you          50
gave me for nothing.

S. ANTIPHOLUS  I'll make you amends next, to give you
nothing for something. But say, sir, is it dinnertime?

S. DROMIO  No, sir. I think the meat wants that° I
have.          55

S. ANTIPHOLUS  In good time,° sir. What's that?

S. DROMIO  Basting.°

S. ANTIPHOLUS  Well, sir, then 'twill be dry.

S. DROMIO  If it be, sir, I pray you eat none of it.

S. ANTIPHOLUS  Your reason?          60

S. DROMIO  Lest it make you choleric° and purchase
me another dry° basting.

S. ANTIPHOLUS  Well, sir, learn to jest in good time;
there's a time for all things.

S. DROMIO  I durst have denied that, before you were          65
so choleric.

S. ANTIPHOLUS  By what rule, sir?

S. DROMIO  Marry, sir, by a rule as plain as the plain
bald pate of Father Time himself.

S. ANTIPHOLUS  Let's hear it.          70

S. DROMIO  There's no time for a man to recover his
hair that grows bald by nature.

S. ANTIPHOLUS  May he not do it by fine and
recovery?°

S. DROMIO  Yes, to pay a fine for a periwig and          75
recover the lost hair of another man.

S. ANTIPHOLUS  Why is Time such a niggard of hair,
being, as it is, so plentiful an excrement?°

S. DROMIO  Because it is a blessing that he bestows on
beasts: and what he hath scanted men in hair, he hath          80
given them in wit.

S. ANTIPHOLUS  Why, but there's many a man hath
more hair than wit.

S. DROMIO  Not a man of those but he hath the wit
to lose his hair.          85

S. ANTIPHOLUS  Why, thou didst conclude hairy
men plain dealers without wit.

S. DROMIO  The plainer dealer, the sooner lost; yet he
loseth it in a kind of jollity.°

S. ANTIPHOLUS  For what reason?          90

S. DROMIO  For two; and sound° ones too.

**50 Marry** mild exclamation (originally an oath, from "By the
Virgin Mary")  **54 wants that** lacks what  **56 In good time**
indeed  **57 Basting** (1) moistening meat (2) thrashing  **61
choleric** irascible (from a surplus of choler, the humor of
dryness)  **62 dry** bloodless  **73–74 fine and recovery** legal
form of conveyance (with a pun on *foin*, the fur of a polecat)
**78 excrement** outgrowth  **89 loseth . . . jollity** as a consequence of venereal disease  **91 sound** (1) cogent (2) healthy

S. ANTIPHOLUS  Nay, not sound, I pray you.

S. DROMIO  Sure ones, then.

S. ANTIPHOLUS  Nay, not sure, in a thing falsing.°

S. DROMIO  Certain ones, then.          95

S. ANTIPHOLUS  Name them.

S. DROMIO  The one, to save the money that he
spends in tiring;° the other, that at dinner they should
not drop in his porridge.

S. ANTIPHOLUS  You would all this time have proved  100
there is no time for all things.

S. DROMIO  Marry, and did, sir: namely, e'en no time
to recover hair lost by nature.

S. ANTIPHOLUS  But your reason was not substantial
why there is no time to recover.          105

S. DROMIO  Thus I mend it: Time himself is bald,
and therefore, to the world's end, will have bald
followers.

S. ANTIPHOLUS  I knew 'twould be a bald° conclusion.

*Enter* ADRIANA *and* LUCIANA.

But soft, who wafts° us yonder?          110

ADRIANA
Ay, ay, Antipholus, look strange° and frown;
Some other mistress hath thy sweet aspects.
I am not Adriana, nor thy wife.
The time was once when thou unurged wouldst vow
That never words were music to thine ear,          115
That never object pleasing in thine eye,
That never touch well welcome to thy hand,
That never meat sweet-savored in thy taste,
Unless I spake or looked or touched or carved° to thee.
How comes it now, my husband, O how comes it,          120
That thou art then estrangèd from thyself?
Thyself I call it, being strange to me,
That, undividable, incorporate,
Am better than thy dear self's better part.°
Ah, do not tear away thyself from me;          125
For know, my love, as easy mayst thou fall°
A drop of water in the breaking gulf,
And take unmingled thence that drop again
Without addition or diminishing
As take from me thyself, and not me too.          130
How dearly° would it touch thee to the quick,
Shouldst thou but hear I were licentious,
And that this body, consecrate to thee,
By ruffian lust should be contaminate!
Wouldst thou not spit at me, and spurn at me,          135
And hurl the name of husband in my face,
And tear the stained skin off my harlot brow,
And from my false hand cut the wedding ring,
And break it with a deep-divorcing vow?
I know thou canst, and therefore see thou do it.          140
I am possessed with an adulterate blot.
My blood is mingled with the crime° of lust;
For, if we two be one, and thou play false,
I do digest the poison of thy flesh,
Being strumpeted by thy contagion.          145

Keep then fair league and truce with thy true bed,°
I live distained,° thou undishonorèd.

S. ANTIPHOLUS
Plead you to me, fair dame? I know you not.
In Ephesus I am but two hours old,
As strange unto your town as to your talk;          150
Who,° every word by all my wit being scanned,
Wants wit in all one word to understand.

LUCIANA
Fie, brother, how the world is changed with you.
When were you wont to use my sister thus?
She sent for you by Dromio home to dinner.          155

S. ANTIPHOLUS
By Dromio?

S. DROMIO  By me?

ADRIANA
By thee, and this thou didst return from him:
That he did buffet thee, and in his blows
Denied my house for his, me for his wife.          160

S. ANTIPHOLUS
Did you converse, sir, with this gentlewoman?
What is the course and drift° of your compact?°

S. DROMIO
I, sir? I never saw her till this time.

S. ANTIPHOLUS
Villain, thou liest; for even her very words
Didst thou deliver to me on the mart.          165

S. DROMIO
I never spake with her in all my life.

S. ANTIPHOLUS
How can she thus then call us by our names,
Unless it be by inspiration?

ADRIANA
How ill agrees it with your gravity
To counterfeit thus grossly° with your slave,          170
Abetting him to thwart me in my mood!
Be it my wrong you are from me exempt,°
But wrong not that wrong with a more contempt.°
Come, I will fasten on° this sleeve of thine:
Thou art an elm, my husband, I a vine,          175
Whose weakness, married to thy stronger state,
Makes me with thy strength to communicate.°
If aught possess thee° from me, it is dross,
Usurping ivy, briar, or idle° moss,
Who, all for want of pruning, with intrusion          180
Infect thy sap and live on thy confusion.°

S. ANTIPHOLUS [*Aside.*]
To me she speaks, she moves me for her theme;°
What, was I married to her in my dream?
Or sleep I now, and think I hear all this?
What error drives our eyes and ears amiss?          185
Until I know this sure uncertainty,
I'll entertain the offered fallacy.°

LUCIANA
Dromio, go bid the servants spread for dinner.

146 **Keep . . . bed** if you are faithful to your marriage
147 **distained** unstained  151 **Who** refers to "I"  162 **course
and drift** general meaning; **compact** confederacy  170
**grossly** obviously  172 **exempt** cut off  173 **But . . . contempt** do not compound it by adding insult to injury  174
**fasten on** cling to  177 **communicate** share  178 **possess
thee** take you away  179 **idle** worthless  181 **confusion** ruin
182 **moves . . . theme** appeals to me as her subject  187
**fallacy** delusion

94 **falsing** deceptive  98 **tiring** hairdressing  109 **bald** with
a quibble on the sense "trivial"  110 **wafts** beckons  111
**strange** distant  119 **carved** a way of flirting at the dinner table
124 **better part** soul  126 **fall** let fall  131 **dearly** grievously
142 **crime** sin

S. DROMIO
O, for my beads!° I cross me for a sinner.
This is the fairyland. O spite of spites!          190
We talk with goblins, owls, and sprites;
If we obey them not, this will ensue:
They'll suck our breath, or pinch us black and blue.

LUCIANA
Why prat'st thou to thyself and answer'st not?
Dromio, thou drone, thou snail, thou slug, thou sot.°   195

S. DROMIO
I am transformèd, master, am not I?

S. ANTIPHOLUS
I think thou art in mind, and so am I.

S. DROMIO
Nay, master, both in mind and in my shape.

S. ANTIPHOLUS
Thou has thine own form.

S. DROMIO                        No, I am an ape.°

LUCIANA
If thou art changed to aught, 'tis to an ass.          200

S. DROMIO
'Tis true, she rides° me and I long for grass.
'Tis so, I am an ass; else it could never be
But I should know her as well as she knows me.

ADRIANA
Come, come, no longer will I be a fool,
To put the finger in the eye and weep,                 205
Whilst man and master laughs my woes to scorn.
Come, sir, to dinner. Dromio, keep the gate.
Husband, I'll dine above° with you today,
And shrive° you of a thousand idle pranks.
Sirrah,° if any ask you for your master,               210
Say he dines forth,° and let no creature enter.
Come, sister. Dromio, play the porter well.

S. ANTIPHOLUS [Aside.]
Am I in earth, in heaven, or in hell?
Sleeping or waking, mad or well-advised?°
Known unto these, and to myself disguised?            215
I'll say as they say, and persever so,
And in this mist at all adventures° go.

S. DROMIO
Master, shall I be porter at the gate?

ADRIANA
Ay, and let none enter, lest I break your pate.

LUCIANA
Come, come, Antipholus, we dine too late.  [Exeunt.]   220

# ACT III

Scene I. [Before the Phoenix.]

*Enter* ANTIPHOLUS OF EPHESUS, *his man* DROMIO,
ANGELO *the goldsmith, and* BALTHASAR *the merchant.*

E. ANTIPHOLUS
Good Signor° Angelo, you must excuse us all;
My wife is shrewish when I keep not hours.
Say that I lingered with you at your shop
To see the making of her carcanet,°
And that tomorrow you will bring it home.              5
But here's a villain that would face me down°
He met me on the mart, and that I beat him,
And charged him with a thousand marks in gold,
And that I did deny° my wife and house.
Thou drunkard, thou, what didst thou mean by this?    10

E. DROMIO
Say what you will, sir, but I know what I know—
That you beat me at the mart, I have your hand° to
    show;
If the skin were parchment and the blows you gave
    were ink,
Your own handwriting would tell you what I think.

E. ANTIPHOLUS
I think thou art an ass.

E. DROMIO                    Marry, so it doth appear   15
By the wrongs I suffer and the blows I bear.
I should kick, being kicked, and being at that pass,°
You would keep from my heels and beware of an ass.

E. ANTIPHOLUS
You're sad,° Signor Balthasar; pray God, our cheer°
May answer° my good will and your good welcome
    here.                                              20

BALTHASAR
I hold your dainties cheap, sir, and your welcome dear.

E. ANTIPHOLUS
O, Signor Balthasar, either at flesh or fish,
A tableful of welcome makes scarce one dainty dish.

BALTHASAR
Good meat, sir, is common; that every churl° affords.

E. ANTIPHOLUS
And welcome more common, for that's nothing but
    words.                                             25

BALTHASAR
Small cheer and great welcome makes a merry feast.

E. ANTIPHOLUS
Ay, to a niggardly host and more sparing guest.
But though my cates° be mean, take them in good part;
Better cheer may you have, but not with better heart.
But soft, my door is locked; go, bid them let us in.   30

E. DROMIO
Maud, Bridget, Marian, Cicely, Gillian, Ginn!

S. DROMIO [Within.]
Mome, malt-horse, capon, coxcomb, idiot, patch!°

---

189 **beads** rosary  195 **sot** dolt  199 **ape** (1) imitation (2) fool
201 **rides** teases  208 **above** upstairs (represented by the upper
stage)  209 **shrive** hear confession and absolve  210 **Sirrah**
term used in addressing inferiors  211 **forth** out  214 **well-
advise** of sound mind  217 **adventures** hazards

**III.i.1 Signor** the Italian title of respect is applied rather
broadly by Shakespeare  4 **carcanet** jeweled necklace  6 **face
me down** contradict me by declaring  9 **deny** disown
12 **hand** (1) handwriting (2) blows  17 **at that pass** in that
predicament  19 **sad** serious; **cheer** entertainment  20 **answer**
accord with  24 **churl** peasant  28 **cates** dainties  32 **Mome
. . . patch** blockhead, drudge, cuckold, fool, idiot, jester

Either get thee from the door or sit down at the hatch.°
Dost thou conjure for wenches, that thou call'st for
　such store,°
When one is one too many? Go, get thee from the door. 35

**E. DROMIO**
What patch is made our porter? My master stays in
　the street.

**S. DROMIO**
Let him walk from whence he came, lest he catch cold
　on's° feet.

**E. ANTIPHOLUS**
Who talks within there? Ho, open the door!

**S. DROMIO**
Right sir, I'll tell you when, and you'll tell me where-
　fore.

**E. ANTIPHOLUS**
Wherefore? For my dinner; I have not dined today. 40

**S. DROMIO**
Nor today here you must not; come again when you
　may.

**E. ANTIPHOLUS**
What art thou that keep'st me out from the house I
　owe?°

**S. DROMIO**
The porter for this time, sir, and my name is Dromio.

**E. DROMIO**
O villain, thou hast stol'n both mine office and my
　name.
The one ne'er got me credit, the other mickle° blame. 45
If thou hadst been Dromio today in my place,
Thou wouldst have changed thy face for a name, or
　thy name for an ass.°

*Enter* LUCE [*above*].

**LUCE**
What a coil° is there, Dromio? Who are those at the
　gate?

**E. DROMIO**
Let my master in, Luce.

**LUCE**　　　　　　　　Faith, no, he comes too late.
And so tell your master.

**E. DROMIO**　　　　　O Lord, I must laugh!　50
Have at you with a proverb:° "Shall I set in my
　staff?"°

**LUCE**
Have at you with another: that's "When? Can you
　tell?"°

**S. DROMIO**
If thy name be called Luce—Luce, thou hast answered
　him well.

**E. ANTIPHOLUS**
Do you hear, you minion?° You'll let us in, I trow?

**LUCE**
I thought to have asked you.

**S. DROMIO**　　　　　　And you said no.　55

**E. DROMIO**
So, come help! Well struck! There was blow for blow.

**E. ANTIPHOLUS**
Thou baggage, let me in.

**LUCE**　　　　　　Can you tell for whose sake?

**E. DROMIO**
Master, knock the door hard.

**LUCE**　　　　　　Let him knock till it ache.

**E. ANTIPHOLUS**
You'll cry for this, minion, if I beat the door down.

**LUCE**
What needs all that, and a pair of stocks° in the town? 60

*Enter* ADRIANA [*above*].

**ADRIANA**
Who is that at the door that keeps all this noise?

**S. DROMIO**
By my troth, your town is troubled with unruly boys.°

**E. ANTIPHOLUS**
Are you there, wife? You might have come before.

**ADRIANA**
Your wife, sir knave! Go, get you from the door.
　　　　　　　　　　　　[*Exit with* LUCE.]

**E. DROMIO**
If you went in pain, master, this knave would go sore. 65

**ANGELO**
Here is neither cheer, sir, nor welcome; we would fain
　have either.

**BALTHASAR**
In debating which was best, we shall part° with neither.

**E. DROMIO**
They stand at the door, master. Bid them welcome
　hither.

**E. ANTIPHOLUS**
There is something in the wind, that we cannot get in.

**E. DROMIO**
You would say so, master, if your garments were thin. 70
Your cake here is warm within; you stand here in the
　cold.
It would make a man mad as a buck° to be so bought
　and sold.°

**E. ANTIPHOLUS**
Go, fetch me something. I'll break ope the gate.

**S. DROMIO**
Break any breaking here, and I'll break your knave's
　pate.

**E. DROMIO**
A man may break° a word with you, sir, and words
　are but wind;°　　　　　　　　　　　　　　　75
Ay, and break it in your face, so he break it not behind.

**S. DROMIO**
It seems thou want'st breaking.° Out upon thee,° hind!°

**E. DROMIO**
Here's too much "out upon thee." I pray thee, let me
　in.

**S. DROMIO**
Ay, when fowls have no feathers, and fish have no fin.

**E. ANTIPHOLUS**
Well, I'll break in. Go borrow me a crow.°　　　　80

33 **hatch** lower part of a divided door　34 **store** abundance
37 **on's** in his　42 **owe** own　45 **mickle** much　47 **Thou
. . . ass** You would have been confused with someone else, or
been made a fool of (?)　48 **coil** turmoil　51 **proverb** they
bandy proverbial phrases; **set in my staff** move in　52 **When
. . . tell** a contemptuous retort　54 **minion** hussy

60 **stocks** device for the public confinement of offenders
62 **boys** fellows　67 **part** depart　72 **buck** male deer (with
an implication of "horn-mad"); **bought and sold** cheated
75 **break** exchange; **words . . . wind** a proverb, which
Dromio vulgarly quibbles upon　77 **breaking** beating; **Out
upon thee** a mild curse; **hind** menial　80 **crow** crowbar

E. DROMIO
A crow without feather? Master, mean you so?
For a fish without a fin, there's a fowl without a
   feather.
If a crow help us in, sirrah, we'll pluck a crow°
   together.

E. ANTIPHOLUS
Go, get thee gone, fetch me an iron crow.

BALTHASAR
Have patience, sir, O, let it not be so!                    85
Herein you war against your reputation,
And draw within the compass of suspect°
Th' unviolated honor of your wife.
Once this°—your long experience of her wisdom,
Her sober virtue, years, and modesty,                       90
Plead on her part some cause to you unknown;
And doubt not, sir, but she will well excuse°
Why at this time the doors are made° against you.
Be ruled by me, depart in patience,
And let us to the Tiger° all to dinner.                      95
And, about evening, come yourself alone,
To know the reason of this strange restraint.
If by strong hand you offer° to break in,
Now in the stirring passage° of the day,
A vulgar° comment will be made of it;                       100
And that supposèd by the common rout°
Against your yet ungallèd estimation,°
That may with foul intrusion enter in
And dwell upon your grave when you are dead;
For slander lives upon succession,°                         105
For ever housed where it gets possession.

E. ANTIPHOLUS
You have prevailed. I will depart in quiet,
And, in despite of mirth,° mean to be merry.
I know a wench of excellent discourse,
Pretty and witty; wild and yet, too, gentle;               110
There will we dine: this woman that I mean,
My wife—but, I protest, without desert—
Hath oftentimes upbraided me withal.
To her will we to dinner. [To ANGELO.] Get you
   home,
And fetch the chain; by this,° I know, 'tis made;         115
Bring it, I pray you, to the Porpentine,°
For there's the house. That chain will I bestow—
Be it for nothing but to spite my wife—
Upon mine hostess there. Good sir, make haste.
Since mine own doors refuse to entertain me,              120
I'll knock elsewhere, to see if they'll disdain me.

ANGELO
I'll meet you at that place some hour hence.

E. ANTIPHOLUS
Do so. This jest shall cost me some expense.    Exeunt.

[Scene II. Above.]

Enter LUCIANA, with ANTIPHOLUS OF SYRACUSE.

LUCIANA
And may it be that you have quite forgot
A husband's office? Shall, Antipholus, hate
Even in the spring of love thy love-springs° rot?
Shall love, in building, grow so ruinate?°
If you did wed my sister for her wealth,                    5
Then for her wealth's sake use her with more kindness;
Or, if you like elsewhere,° do it by stealth,
Muffle your false love with some show of blindness.
Let not my sister read it in your eye;
Be not thy tongue thy own shame's orator;                   10
Look sweet, speak fair, become disloyalty;°
Apparel vice like virtue's harbinger.
Bear a fair presence, though your heart be tainted,
Teach sin the carriage° of a holy saint,
Be secret-false: what need she be acquainted?              15
What simple thief brags of his own attaint?°
'Tis double wrong to truant° with your bed
And let her read it in thy looks at board.°
Shame hath a bastard fame,° well managèd;
Ill deeds is doubled with an evil word.                     20
Alas, poor women! Make us but believe,
Being compact of credit,° that you love us;
Though others have the arm, show us the sleeve;
We in your motion° turn, and you may move us.
Then, gentle brother, get you in again;                     25
Comfort my sister, cheer her, call her wife;
'Tis holy sport, to be a little vain,°
When the sweet breath of flattery conquers strife.

S. ANTIPHOLUS
Sweet mistress, what your name is else, I know not;
Nor by what wonder you do hit of° mine;                     30
Less in your knowledge and your grace you show° not
Than our earth's wonder,° more than earth divine.
Teach me, dear creature, how to think and speak:
Lay open to my earthy-gross conceit,°
Smoth'red in errors, feeble, shallow, weak,                 35
The folded° meaning of your words' deceit.
Against my soul's pure truth why labor you
To make it wander in an unknown field?
Are you a god? Would you create me new?
Transform me, then, and to your pow'r I'll yield.           40
But if that I am I, then well I know
Your weeping sister is no wife of mine,
Nor to her bed no homage do I owe;
Far more, far more, to you do I decline.°
O, train° me not, sweet mermaid, with thy note,            45
To drown me in thy sister's flood of tears.
Sing, siren, for thyself, and I will dote;
Spread o'er the silver waves thy golden hairs;

83 pluck a crow pick a bone  87 suspect suspicion  89
Once this in summary  92 excuse explain  93 made shut
95 Tiger name and sign of an inn  98 offer attempt
99 stirring passage busy traffic  100 vulgar public  101
rout multitude  102 ungallèd estimation unblemished
repute  105 succession its consequences  108 in . . . mirth
though disinclined to merriment  115 by this by this time
116 Porpentine Porcupine (name of the Courtesan's house)

III.ii.3 love-springs young plants of love  4 ruinate ruinous
7 like elsewhere have some other love  11 become disloyalty make infidelity seem becoming  14 carriage bearing
16 attaint disgrace  17 truant play truant  18 board table
19 bastard fame illegitimate honor  22 compact of credit
disposed to trust  24 in your motion by your moves
27 be . . . vain use a little flattery  30 hit of hit on  31 show
appear  32 earth's wonder these lines are sometimes taken
as a compliment to Queen Elizabeth  34 conceit apprehension
36 folded hidden  44 decline incline  45 train lure

And as a bed I'll take them, and there lie,
And, in that glorious supposition, think          50
He gains by death that hath such means to die.°
Let love, being light,° be drownèd if she sink!

LUCIANA
What, are you mad, that you do reason so?

S. ANTIPHOLUS
Not mad, but mated°—how, I do not know.

LUCIANA
It is a fault that springeth from your eye.          55

S. ANTIPHOLUS
For gazing on your beams, fair sun, being by.

LUCIANA
Gaze where you should, and that will clear your sight.

S. ANTIPHOLUS
As good to wink,° sweet love, as look on night.

LUCIANA
Why call you me love? Call my sister so.

S. ANTIPHOLUS
Thy sister's sister.

LUCIANA          That's my sister.

S. ANTIPHOLUS          No,          60
It is thyself, mine own self's better part,
Mine eye's clear eye, my dear heart's dearer heart;
My food, my fortune, and my sweet hope's aim;
My sole earth's heaven, and my heaven's claim.°

LUCIANA
All this my sister is, or else should be.          65

S. ANTIPHOLUS
Call thyself sister, sweet, for I am thee;
Thee will I love, and with thee lead my life;
Thou hast no husband yet, nor I no wife.
Give me thy hand.

LUCIANA          O, soft, sir, hold you still
I'll fetch my sister, to get her good will.          *Exit.* 70

*Enter* DROMIO OF SYRACUSE.

S. ANTIPHOLUS  Why, how now, Dromio! Where
run'st thou so fast?

S. DROMIO  Do you know me, sir? Am I Dromio?
Am I your man? Am I myself?

S. ANTIPHOLUS  Thou art Dromio, thou art my man, 75
thou art thyself.

S. DROMIO  I am an ass; I am a woman's man, and
besides myself.

S. ANTIPHOLUS  What woman's man? And how besides thyself?          80

S. DROMIO  Marry, sir, besides myself,° I am due° to
a woman: one that claims me, one that haunts me,
one that will have me.

S. ANTIPHOLUS  What claim lays she to thee?

S. DROMIO  Marry, sir, such claim as you would lay 85
to your horse; and she would have me as a beast°—
not that, I being a beast, she would have me, but that
she, being a very beastly creature, lays claim to me.

S. ANTIPHOLUS  What is she?

S. DROMIO  A very reverend body; ay, such a one as 90
a man may not speak of without he say "sir-reverence."° I have but lean luck in the match, and yet is
she a wondrous fat marriage.

S. ANTIPHOLUS  How dost thou mean a fat marriage?

S. DROMIO  Marry, sir, she's the kitchen wench, and 95
all grease;° and I know not what use to put her to, but
to make a lamp of her, and run from her by her own
light. I warrant her rags and the tallow in them will
burn a Poland winter. If she lives till doomsday, she'll
burn a week° longer than the whole world.          100

S. ANTIPHOLUS  What complexion is she of?

S. DROMIO  Swart,° like my shoe, but her face nothing like so clean kept; for why? She sweats; a man
may go over shoes° in the grime of it.

S. ANTIPHOLUS  That's a fault that water will mend.  105

S. DROMIO  No, sir, 'tis in grain;° Noah's flood could
not do it.

S. ANTIPHOLUS  What's her name?

S. DROMIO  Nell,° sir; but her name and three quarters—that's an ell° and three quarters—will not 110
measure her from hip to hip.

S. ANTIPHOLUS  Then she bears some breadth?

S. DROMIO  No longer from head to foot than from
hip to hip. She is spherical, like a globe. I could find
out countries in her.          115

S. ANTIPHOLUS  In what part of her body stands
Ireland?

S. DROMIO  Marry, sir, in her buttocks; I found it out
by the bogs.

S. ANTIPHOLUS  Where Scotland?          120

S. DROMIO  I found it by the barrenness, hard in the
palm of the hand.

S. ANTIPHOLUS  Where France?

S. DROMIO  In her forehead, armed and reverted,°
making war against her heir.°          125

S. ANTIPHOLUS  Where England?

S. DROMIO  I looked for the chalky cliffs,° but I could
find no whiteness in them. But I guess, it stood in her
chin, by the salt rheum° that ran between France and it.

S. ANTIPHOLUS  Where Spain?          130

S. DROMIO  Faith, I saw it not; but I felt it hot in her
breath.

S. ANTIPHOLUS  Where America, the Indies?

S. DROMIO  O, sir, upon her nose, all o'er embellished
with rubies, carbuncles, sapphires, declining° their 135
rich aspect to the hot breath of Spain, who sent whole
armadoes of carracks° to be ballast° at her nose.

S. ANTIPHOLUS  Where stood Belgia, the Netherlands?°

S. DROMIO  O, sir, I did not look so low. To conclude, 140

---

51 **die** with an implication of sexual fulfillment  52 **light**
(1) not heavy (2) wanton  54 **mated** (1) confounded (2) wedded
58 **wink** shut one's eyes  64 **heaven's claim** claim on heaven
81 **besides myself** (1) out of my mind (2) in addition to me;
**due** belonging  86 **a beast** Elizabethan pronunciation made
possible a pun on *abased*

91–92 **sir-reverence** save your reverence (meaning "pardon
the expression")  96 **grease** with a pun on *grace*  100 **week**
with a pun on *wick*  102 **Swart** swarthy  104 **over shoes**
shoe-deep  106 **in grain** inherent  109 **Nell** called Luce in
III.i.49  110 **ell** forty-five inches  124 **reverted** revolted  125
**heir** interpreted as a contemporary allusion to the struggle of
the Catholic League against Henry of Navarre, who succeeded
to the throne of France in 1593  127 **chalky cliffs** teeth
129 **rheum** moisture from the nose  135 **declining** inclining
137 **armadoes of carracks** fleets of galleons (with possible
reference to the Spanish Armada of 1588); **ballast** loaded
138–39 **Belgia, the Netherlands** the Low Countries

this drudge, or diviner,° laid claim to me, called me
Dromio, swore I was assured° to her, told me what
privy marks I had about me, as the mark of my
shoulder, the mole in my neck, the great wart on my
left arm, that I, amazed, ran from her as a witch.　145
　And, I think, if my breast had not been made of faith,
　　and my heart of steel,
　She had transformed me to a curtal dog,° and made
　　me turn i' th' wheel.°
S. ANTIPHOLUS
Go, hie thee presently,° post to the road,°
And if° the wind blow any way from shore,
I will not harbor° in this town tonight.　150
If any bark put forth, come to the mart,
Where I will walk till thou return to me.
If everyone knows us, and we know none,
'Tis time, I think, to trudge, pack, and begone.°
S. DROMIO
As from a bear a man would run for life,　155
So fly I from her that would be my wife.　　　Exit.
S. ANTIPHOLUS
There's none but witches do inhabit here,
And therefore 'tis high time that I were hence.
She that doth call me husband, even my soul
Doth for a wife abhor. But her fair sister,　160
Possessed with such a gentle sovereign grace,
Of such enchanting presence and discourse,
Hath almost made me traitor to myself.
But, lest myself be guilty to° self-wrong,
I'll stop mine ears against the mermaid's song.　165

Enter ANGELO with the chain.

ANGELO
Master Antipholus—
S. ANTIPHOLUS　　　Ay, that's my name.
ANGELO
I know it well, sir. Lo, here is the chain.
I thought to have ta'en you at the Porpentine.
The chain unfinished made me stay thus long.
S. ANTIPHOLUS
What is your will that I shall do with this?　170
ANGELO
What please yourself, sir; I have made it for you.
S. ANTIPHOLUS
Made it for me, sir? I bespoke° it not.
ANGELO
Not once, nor twice, but twenty times you have.
Go home with it and please your wife withal,
And soon at suppertime I'll visit you,　175
And then receive my money for the chain.
S. ANTIPHOLUS
I pray you, sir, receive the money now,
For fear you ne'er see chain nor money more.
ANGELO
You are a merry man, sir. Fare you well.　　　Exit.
S. ANTIPHOLUS
What I should think of this, I cannot tell:　180
But this I think, there's no man is so vain°

That would refuse so fair an offered chain.
I see a man here needs not live by shifts,°
When in the streets he meets such golden gifts.
I'll to the mart, and there for Dromio stay;　185
If any ship put out, then straight° away.　　　Exit.

# ACT IV

## Scene I. [The mart.]

Enter a MERCHANT, [ANGELO the] goldsmith, and an
OFFICER.

MERCHANT
You know since Pentecost° the sum is due,
And since I have not much importuned you,
Nor now I had not, but that I am bound
To Persia, and want guilders for my voyage;
Therefore make present° satisfaction,　5
Or I'll attach° you by this officer.
ANGELO
Even just the sum that I do owe to you
Is growing° to me by Antipholus,
And in the instant that I met with you
He had of me a chain. At five o'clock　10
I shall receive the money for the same.
Pleaseth° you, walk with me down to his house;
I will discharge my bond, and thank you too.

Enter ANTIPHOLUS OF EPHESUS, [and] DROMIO [OF
EPHESUS] from the Courtesan's.

OFFICER
That labor may you save. See where he comes.
E. ANTIPHOLUS
While I go to the goldsmith's house, go thou　15
And buy a rope's end;° that will I bestow
Among my wife and her confederates,
For locking me out of my doors by day.
But soft, I see the goldsmith; get thee gone,
Buy thou a rope and bring it home to me.　20
E. DROMIO
I buy a thousand pound a year! I buy a rope!°
　　　　　　　　　　　　　　Exit DROMIO.
E. ANTIPHOLUS
A man is well holp° up that trusts to you!
I promisèd your presence and the chain,
But neither chain nor goldsmith came to me.
Belike you thought our love would last too long,　25
If it were chained together, and therefore came not.
ANGELO
Saving your merry humor, here's the note
How much your chain weighs to the utmost carat,
The fineness of the gold and chargeful° fashion—
Which doth amount to three odd ducats° more　30

141 **diviner** witch　142 **assured** betrothed　147 **curtal dog** dog with docked tail; **wheel** spit　148 **presently** immediately; **road** harbor　149 **And if** if　150 **harbor** lodge　154 **trudge . . . begone** synonyms　164 **to** of　172 **bespoke** ordered　181 **vain** silly

183 **shifts** tricks　186 **straight** without delay
**IV.i.1 Pentecost** the fiftieth day after Easter　5 **present** immediate　6 **attach** arrest　8 **growing** accruing　12 **Pleaseth** may it please　16 **rope's end** for flogging　21 **I buy . . . a rope** Dromio's obscure irony seems motivated by his awareness that the rope's end could be used on him　22 **holp** helped　29 **chargeful** costly　30 **ducats** gold coins of varying origin and value

Than I stand debted to this gentleman.
I pray you, see him presently° discharged,
For he is bound to sea, and stays but for it.

E. ANTIPHOLUS
I am not furnished with the present money.
Besides, I have some business in the town.          35
Good signor, take the stranger to my house,
And with you take the chain, and bid my wife
Disburse the sum on the receipt thereof.
Perchance I will be there as soon as you.

ANGELO
Then you will bring the chain to her yourself?          40

E. ANTIPHOLUS
No, bear it with you, lest I come not time enough.°

ANGELO
Well, sir, I will. Have you the chain about you?

E. ANTIPHOLUS
And if I have not, sir, I hope you have,
Or else you may return without your money.

ANGELO
Nay, come, I pray you, sir, give me the chain:          45
Both wind and tide stays for this gentleman,
And I, to blame,° have held him here too long.

E. ANTIPHOLUS
Good Lord, you use this dalliance° to excuse
Your breach of promise to the Porpentine.
I should have chid you for not bringing it,          50
But, like a shrew,° you first begin to brawl.

MERCHANT
The hour steals on; I pray you, sir, dispatch.

ANGELO
You hear how he importunes me—the chain!

E. ANTIPHOLUS
Why, give it to my wife, and fetch your money.

ANGELO
Come, come, you know, I gave it you even now;          55
Either send the chain or send me by some token.

E. ANTIPHOLUS
Fie, now you run this humor out of breath.
Come, where's the chain? I pray you, let me see it.

MERCHANT
My business cannot brook this dalliance.
Good sir, say whe'er° you'll answer° me or no:          60
If not, I'll leave him to the officer.

E. ANTIPHOLUS
I answer you! What should I answer you?

ANGELO
The money that you owe me for the chain.

E. ANTIPHOLUS
I owe you none till I receive the chain.

ANGELO
You know I gave it you half an hour since.          65

E. ANTIPHOLUS
You gave me none; you wrong me much to say so.

ANGELO
You wrong me more, sir, in denying it.
Consider how it stands upon° my credit.

MERCHANT
Well, officer, arrest him at my suit.

OFFICER
I do,          70
And charge you in the duke's name to obey me.

ANGELO
This touches me in reputation.
Either consent to pay this sum for me,
Or I attach you by this officer.

E. ANTIPHOLUS
Consent to pay thee that I never had!          75
Arrest me, foolish fellow, if thou dar'st.

ANGELO
Here is thy fee; arrest him, officer.
I would not spare my brother in this case,
If he should scorn me so apparently.°

OFFICER
I do arrest you, sir; you hear the suit.          80

E. ANTIPHOLUS
I do obey thee, till I give thee bail.
But, sirrah, you shall buy this sport as dear
As all the metal in your shop will answer.

ANGELO
Sir, sir, I shall have law in Ephesus,
To your notorious shame, I doubt it not.          85

*Enter* DROMIO OF SYRACUSE *from the bay.*

S. DROMIO
Master, there's a bark of Epidamnum,
That stays but till her owner comes aboard,
And then she bears away. Our fraughtage,° sir,
I have conveyed aboard, and I have bought
The oil, the balsamum,° and aqua vitae.°          90
The ship is in her trim,° the merry wind
Blows fair from land; they stay for nought at all
But for their owner, master,° and yourself.

E. ANTIPHOLUS
How now! a madman? Why, thou peevish° sheep,°
What ship of Epidamnum stays for me?          95

S. DROMIO
A ship you sent me to, to hire waftage.°

E. ANTIPHOLUS
Thou drunken slave, I sent thee for a rope,
And told thee to what purpose and what end.

S. DROMIO
You sent me for a rope's end° as soon.
You sent me to the bay, sir, for a bark.          100

E. ANTIPHOLUS
I will debate this matter at more leisure,
And teach your ears to list° me with more heed.
To Adriana, villain, hie thee straight;
Give her this key, and tell her, in the desk
That's covered o'er with Turkish tapestry          105
There is a purse of ducats; let her send it.
Tell her I am arrested in the street,
And that shall bail me. Hie thee, slave, begone.
On, officer, to prison till it come.

*Exeunt [all but* DROMIO].

32 presently instantly  41 time enough in time  47 to blame blameworthy  48 dalliance tarrying  51 shrew scold (male or female)  60 whe'er whether; answer pay  68 stands upon concerns

79 apparently openly  88 fraughtage cargo  90 balsamum balm; aqua vitae brandy  91 in her trim ready to sail  93 master captain (?)  94 peevish silly; sheep with a pun on ship  96 waftage passage by sea  99 rope's end in the sense of "halter" here  102 list listen to

S. DROMIO
To Adriana—that is where we dined,                          110
Where Dowsabel° did claim me for her husband.
She is too big, I hope, for me to compass.°
Thither I must, although against my will;
For servants must their masters' minds fulfill.        *Exit.*

[Scene II. *Before the Phoenix.*]

*Enter* ADRIANA *and* LUCIANA.

ADRIANA
Ah, Luciana, did he tempt thee so?
Mightst thou perceive austerely° in his eye,
That he did plead in earnest, yea or no?
Looked he or red or pale, or sad or merrily?
What observation mad'st thou in this case                    5
Of his heart's meteors tilting° in his face?
LUCIANA
First, he denied you had in him no right.°
ADRIANA
He meant he did me none; the more my spite.°
LUCIANA
Then swore he that he was a stranger here.
ADRIANA
And true he swore, though yet forsworn he were.         10
LUCIANA
Then pleaded I for you.
ADRIANA                          And what said he?
LUCIANA
That love I begged for you he begged of me.
ADRIANA
With what persuasion did he tempt thy love?
LUCIANA
With words that in an honest° suit might move.
First he did praise my beauty, then my speech.              15
ADRIANA
Didst speak him fair?°
LUCIANA                         Have patience, I beseech.
ADRIANA
I cannot, nor I will not, hold me still.
My tongue, though not my heart, shall have his° will.
He is deformèd, crookèd, old and sere,
Ill-faced, worse bodied, shapeless° everywhere:           20
Vicious, ungentle, foolish, blunt, unkind,
Stigmatical in making,° worse in mind.
LUCIANA
Who would be jealous then of such a one?
No evil lost is wailed when it is gone.
ADRIANA
Ah, but I think him better than I say;                        25
And yet would herein others' eyes were worse.
Far from her nest the lapwing° cries away;

My heart prays for him, though my tongue do curse.

*Enter* DROMIO OF SYRACUSE.

S. DROMIO
Here, go—the desk, the purse! Sweet, now, make haste.
LUCIANA
How hast thou lost thy breath?
S. DROMIO                              By running fast.    30
ADRIANA
Where is thy master, Dromio? Is he well?
S. DROMIO
No, he's in Tartar limbo,° worse than hell:
A devil in an everlasting garment° hath him;
One whose hard heart is buttoned up with steel:
A fiend, a fairy,° pitiless and rough:                        35
A wolf, nay worse, a fellow all in buff:°
A back-friend,° a shoulder-clapper,° one that counter-
mands°
The passages of alleys, creeks,° and narrow lands;
A hound that runs counter,° and yet draws dry-foot°
well;
One that, before the Judgment, carries poor souls to     40
hell.
ADRIANA
Why, man, what is the matter?
S. DROMIO
I do not know the matter, he is 'rested° on the case.°
ADRIANA
What, is he arrested? Tell me, at whose suit.
S. DROMIO
I know not at whose suit he is arrested well,
But is in a suit of buff which 'rested him, that can I tell.  45
Will you send him, Mistress Redemption, the money
in his desk?
ADRIANA
Go fetch it, sister. This I wonder at,   *Exit* LUCIANA.
Thus he, unknown to me, should be in debt.
Tell me, was he arrested on a band?°
S. DROMIO
Not on a band, but on a stronger thing:                       50
A chain, a chain! Do you not hear it ring?
ADRIANA   What, the chain?
S. DROMIO
No, no, the bell; 'tis time that I were gone.
It was two ere I left him, and now the clock strikes one.°
ADRIANA
The hours come back! That did I never hear.                  55
S. DROMIO
O yes. If any hour° meet a sergeant, 'a° turns back for
very fear.
ADRIANA
As if time were in debt! How fondly° dost thou
reason!

111 **Dowsabel** from *douce et belle* (sweet and pretty), an
elaborate name for a heroine, ironically applied to Nell   112
**compass** (1) obtain (2) embrace
**IV.ii.2 austerely** by the austerity   6 **heart's meteors tilting**
emotions tossing   7 **denied . . . right** double negative
8 **spite** vexation   14 **honest** honorable   16 **speak him fair**
speak to him kindly   18 **his** its   20 **shapeless** unshapely
22 **Stigmatical in making,** deformed in appearance   27
**lapwing** peewit (who draws intruders away from its nest in
the manner described)

32 **Tartar limbo** prison, as well as the outskirts of hell (the
pagan Tartarus)   33 **everlasting garment** leather coat, the
police uniform   35 **fairy** malignant spirit   36 **buff** ox-hide
37 **back-friend** false friend (with a quibble on the mode of
arrest); **shoulder-clapper** bailiff; **countermands** prohibits
38 **creeks** winding alleys   39 **counter** (1) contrary (2) Counter,
a debtors' prison; **draws dry-foot** hunts by scent   42 **'rested**
arrested; **case** (1) special case at law (2) suit of clothes   49 **band**
bond   54 **one** with a pun on *on*   56 **hour** pun on *whore*; **'a**
colloquial form of *he, she,* or *it*   57 **fondly** foolishly

S. DROMIO
Time is a very bankrupt, and owes more than he's
   worth to season.°
Nay, he's a thief too: have you not heard men say,
That time comes stealing on by night and day?      60
If 'a be in debt and theft, and a sergeant in the way,
Hath he not reason to turn back an hour in a day?

*Enter* LUCIANA.

ADRIANA
Go, Dromio. There's the money, bear it straight,
And bring thy master home immediately.
Come, sister. I am pressed down with conceit:°      65
Conceit, my comfort and my injury.
                *Exit [with* LUCIANA *and* DROMIO*].*

[Scene III. *The mart.*]

*Enter* ANTIPHOLUS OF SYRACUSE.

S. ANTIPHOLUS
There's not a man I meet but doth salute me
As if I were their well-acquainted friend;
And everyone doth call me by my name.
Some tender money to me, some invite me;
Some other° give me thanks for kindnesses;      5
Some offer me commodities to buy.
Even now a tailor called me in his shop
And showed me silks that he had bought for me,
And therewithal took measure of my body.
Sure, these are but imaginary wiles,°      10
And Lapland° sorcerers inhabit here.

*Enter* DROMIO OF SYRACUSE.

S. DROMIO   Master, here's the gold you sent me for.
What, have you got the picture of old Adam° new-
appareled?
S. ANTIPHOLUS   What gold is this? What Adam dost    15
thou mean?
S. DROMIO   Not that Adam that kept the paradise,
but that Adam that keeps the prison; he that goes in
the calf's skin° that was killed for the Prodigal; he that
came behind you, sir, like an evil angel, and bid you   20
forsake your liberty.
S. ANTIPHOLUS   I understand thee not.
S. DROMIO   No? Why, 'tis a plain case:° he that went,
like a bass-viol, in a case of leather; the man, sir, that,
when gentlemen are tired gives them a sob° and 'rests   25
them; he, sir, that takes pity on decayed men, and
gives them suits of durance;° he that sets up his rest°
to do more exploits with his mace° than a morris-pike.°
S. ANTIPHOLUS   What, thou mean'st an officer?

S. DROMIO   Ay, sir, the sergeant of the band: he that   30
brings any man to answer it that breaks his band;°
one that thinks a man always going to bed, and says,
"God give you good rest!"°
S. ANTIPHOLUS   Well, sir, there rest in your foolery.
Is there any ships puts forth tonight? May we be gone?   35
S. DROMIO   Why, sir, I brought you word an hour
since that the bark° *Expedition* put forth tonight, and
then were you hind'red by the sergeant to tarry for
the hoy° *Delay.* Here are the angels° that you sent for
to deliver you.      40
S. ANTIPHOLUS
The fellow is distract, and so am I,
And here we wander in illusions.
Some blessèd power deliver us from hence!

*Enter a* COURTESAN.

COURTESAN
Well met, well met, Master Antipholus.
I see, sir, you have found the goldsmith now.      45
Is that the chain you promised me today?
S. ANTIPHOLUS
Satan, avoid!° I charge thee, tempt me not!
S. DROMIO   Master, is this Mistress Satan?
S. ANTIPHOLUS
It is the devil.
S. DROMIO   Nay, she is worse, she is the devil's dam;°   50
and here she comes in the habit° of a light° wench,
and thereof comes that the wenches say, "God damn
me." That's as much to say, "God make me a light
wench." It is written, they appear to men like angels
of light. Light is an effect of fire, and fire will burn:   55
ergo,° light wenches will burn.° Come not near her.
COURTESAN
Your man and you are marvelous merry, sir.
Will you go with me? We'll mend° our dinner here.
S. DROMIO   Master, if you do, expect spoon-meat,° or
bespeak a long spoon.      60
S. ANTIPHOLUS
Why, Dromio?
S. DROMIO   Marry, he must have a long spoon that
must eat with the devil.
S. ANTIPHOLUS
Avoid, then, fiend! What tell'st thou me of supping?
Thou art, as you are all, a sorceress.      65
I conjure° thee to leave me and be gone.
COURTESAN
Give me the ring of mine you had at dinner,
Or, for my diamond, the chain you promised,
And I'll be gone, sir, and not trouble you.
S. DROMIO
Some devils ask but the parings° of one's nail,      70
A rush, a hair, a drop of blood, a pin.

---

**58 season** occasion (?) ripen (?)   **65 conceit** imagination
**IV.iii.5 other** others   **10 imaginary wiles** tricks of the
imagination   **11 Lapland** notorious for sorcery   **13 old
Adam** the sergeant in his buff coat (?)   **18–19 goes . . .
skin** wears the leather garb (with a quibble on the fatted calf
in the parable)   **23 case** (1) situation (2) box (3) suit   **25 sob**
rest given a horse to recover its wind (with quibbles)   **27
suits of durance** durable clothing (with puns on *lawsuits* and
*imprisonment*); **sets . . . rest** stakes all   **28 mace** staff of
authority; **morris-pike** Moorish lance

**31 band** with pun on *bond*   **33 rest** with the usual pun
**37 bark** ship (allegorically named by Dromio)   **39 hoy**
coasting vessel; **angels** coins worth ten shillings (with pun)
**47 avoid** begone (Matthew 4:10)   **50 dam** mother   **51
habit** dress; **light** with implication of loose morals   **56 ergo**
it follows logically; **burn** infect with disease   **58 mend**
complete   **59 spoon-meat** soft food (introducing an allusion
to the proverb about the devil)   **66 conjure** solemnly call on
**70 parings** witchcraft requires such appurtenances in order to
cast a spell

A nut, a cherrystone;
But she, more covetous, would have a chain.
Master, be wise; and if you give it her,
The devil will shake her chain, and fright us with it.  75

COURTESAN
I pray you, sir, my ring, or else the chain.°
I hope you do not mean to cheat me so!

S. ANTIPHOLUS
Avaunt,° thou witch! Come, Dromio, let us go.

S. DROMIO
Fly pride, says the peacock.° Mistress, that you know.
                              *Exit* [*with* ANTIPHOLUS].

COURTESAN
Now, out of doubt, Antipholus is mad,  80
Else would he never so demean° himself.
A ring he hath of mine worth forty ducats,
And for the same he promised me a chain;
Both one and other he denies me now.
The reason that I gather he is mad,  85
Besides this present instance of his rage,°
Is a mad tale he told today at dinner,
Of his own doors being shut against his entrance.
Belike his wife, acquainted with his fits,
On purpose shut the doors against his way.  90
My way is now to hie home to his house,
And tell his wife that, being lunatic,
He rushed into my house and took perforce°
My ring away. This course I fittest choose,
For forty ducats is too much to lose.      [*Exit.*] 95

[Scene IV. *The same.*]

*Enter* ANTIPHOLUS OF EPHESUS, *with a* JAILER.

E. ANTIPHOLUS
Fear me not, man, I will not break away.
I'll give thee, ere I leave thee, so much money,
To warrant° thee, as I am 'rested for.
My wife is in a wayward mood today,
And will not lightly trust the messenger  5
That I should be attached° in Ephesus;
I tell you, 'twill sound harshly in her ears.

*Enter* DROMIO OF EPHESUS, *with a rope's end.*

Here comes my man, I think he brings the money.
How now, sir! Have you that I sent you for?

E. DROMIO
Here's that, I warrant you, will pay° them all.  10

E. ANTIPHOLUS
But where's the money?

E. DROMIO
Why, sir, I gave the money for the rope.

E. ANTIPHOLUS
Five hundred ducats, villain, for a rope?

E. DROMIO
I'll serve you,° sir, five hundred at the rate.

E. ANTIPHOLUS
To what end° did I bid thee hie thee home?  15

E. DROMIO
To a rope's end, sir, and to that end am I returned.

E. ANTIPHOLUS
And to that end, sir, I will welcome you.

[*Beats* DROMIO.]

OFFICER
Good sir, be patient.

E. DROMIO
Nay, 'tis for me to be patient; I am in adversity.

OFFICER
Good° now, hold thy tongue.  20

E. DROMIO  Nay, rather persuade him to hold his hands.

E. ANTIPHOLUS  Thou whoreson,° senseless villain!

E. DROMIO  I would I were senseless, sir, that I might not feel your blows.  25

E. ANTIPHOLUS  Thou art sensible° in nothing but blows, and so is an ass.

E. DROMIO  I am an ass, indeed; you may prove it by my long ears.° I have served him from the hour of my nativity to this instant, and have nothing at his hands  30 for my service but blows. When I am cold, he heats me with beating; when I am warm, he cools me with beating. I am waked with it when I sleep, raised with it when I sit, driven out of doors with it when I go from home, welcomed home with it when I return;  35 nay, I bear it on my shoulders, as a begger wont° her brat; and, I think, when he hath lamed me, I shall beg with it from door to door.

*Enter* ADRIANA, LUCIANA, COURTESAN, *and a schoolmaster called* PINCH.

E. ANTIPHOLUS
Come, go along; my wife is coming yonder.

E. DROMIO  Mistress, "respice finem,"° respect your  40 end; or rather, the prophecy like the parrot,° "beware the rope's end."

E. ANTIPHOLUS
Wilt thou still talk?

*Beats* DROMIO.

COURTESAN
How say you now? Is not your husband mad?

ADRIANA
His incivility confirms no less.  45
Good Doctor Pinch, you are a conjurer;°
Establish him in his true sense again,
And I will please° you what you will demand.

LUCIANA
Alas, how fiery and how sharp he looks!

COURTESAN
Mark how he trembles in his ecstasy!°  50

75 chain cf. Revelation 20:1–2  78 Avaunt away  79 peacock emblem of pride, which was also personified by a harlot  81 demean behave  86 rage madness  93 perforce by force
IV.iv.3 warrant secure  6 attached arrested  10 pay with a beating  14 serve you supply you with

15 end purpose (on which Dromio quibbles)  20 Good used vocatively  23 whoreson bastard  26 sensible (1) reasonable (2) sensitive  29 ears pun on *years*  36 wont habitually does  40 respice finem this proverbial phrase, which Dromio translates, was sometimes punningly altered to "respice funem," remember the rope  41 parrot parrots were taught to cry "rope"  46 conjurer who can exorcise evil spirits (also called "Doctor" because of his learning)  48 please satisfy  50 ecstasy frenzy

PINCH
Give me your hand, and let me feel your pulse.

[ANTIPHOLUS *strikes him.*]

E. ANTIPHOLUS
There is my hand, and let it feel your ear!

PINCH
I charge thee, Satan, housed within this man,
To yield possession to my holy prayers,
And to thy state of darkness hie thee straight;     55
I conjure thee by all the saints in heaven.

E. ANTIPHOLUS
Peace, doting wizard, peace; I am not mad.

ADRIANA
O, that thou wert not, poor distressèd soul!

E. ANTIPHOLUS
You minion,° you, are these your customers?
Did this companion° with the saffron° face     60
Revel and feast it at my house today,
Whilst upon me the guilty doors were shut,
And I denied° to enter in my house?

ADRIANA
O, husband, God doth know you dined at home,
Where would you had remained until this time,     65
Free from these slanders and this open shame!

E. ANTIPHOLUS
Dined at home! Thou villain, what sayest thou?

E. DROMIO
Sir, sooth to say, you did not dine at home.

E. ANTIPHOLUS
Were not my doors locked up, and I shut out?

E. DROMIO
Perdie,° your doors were locked, and you shut out.     70

E. ANTIPHOLUS
And did not she herself revile me there?

E. DROMIO
Sans fable,° she herself reviled you there.

E. ANTIPHOLUS
Did not her kitchen maid rail, taunt, and scorn
    me?

E. DROMIO
Certes,° she did; the kitchen vestal° scorned you.

E. ANTIPHOLUS
And did not I in rage depart from thence?     75

E. DROMIO
In verity, you did; my bones bears witness,
That since have felt the vigor of his rage.

ADRIANA
Is't good to soothe° him in these contraries?

PINCH
It is no shame; the fellow finds his vein,
And yielding to him humors well his frenzy.     80

E. ANTIPHOLUS
Thou hast suborned° the goldsmith to arrest me.

ADRIANA
Alas, I sent you money to redeem you,
By Dromio here, who came in haste for it.

E. DROMIO
Money by me? Heart and goodwill you might,
But, surely, master, not a rag° of money.     85

E. ANTIPHOLUS
Went'st not thou to her for a purse of ducats?

ADRIANA
He came to me, and I delivered it.

LUCIANA
And I am witness with her that she did.

E. DROMIO
God and the ropemaker bear me witness
That I was sent for nothing but a rope.     90

PINCH
Mistress, both man and master is possessed;
I know it by their pale and deadly looks.
They must be bound, and laid in some dark room.

E. ANTIPHOLUS
Say, wherefore didst thou lock me forth° today,
And why dost thou deny the bag of gold?     95

ADRIANA
I did not, gentle husband, lock thee forth.

E. DROMIO
And, gentle master, I received no gold;
But I confess, sir, that we were locked out.

ADRIANA
Dissembling villain, thou speak'st false in both.

E. ANTIPHOLUS
Dissembling harlot, thou art false in all,     100
And art confederate° with a damnèd pack°
To make a loathsome abject scorn of me;
But with these nails I'll pluck out these false eyes
That would behold in me this shameful sport.

*Enter three or four, and offer to bind him. He strives.*

ADRIANA
O, bind him, bind him, let him not come near me!     105

PINCH
More company! The fiend is strong within him.

LUCIANA
Ay me,° poor man, how pale and wan he looks.

E. ANTIPHOLUS
What, will you murder me? Thou jailer, thou,
I am thy prisoner; wilt thou suffer them
To make a rescue?°

OFFICER                Masters, let him go.     110
He is my prisoner, and you shall not have him.

PINCH
Go, bind this man, for he is frantic too.

ADRIANA
What wilt thou do, thou peevish° officer?
Hast thou delight to see a wretched man
Do outrage and displeasure° to himself?     115

OFFICER
He is my prisoner; if I let him go,
The debt he owes will be required of me.

ADRIANA
I will discharge° thee ere I go from thee.
Bear me forthwith unto his creditor,

---

59 minion harlot   60 companion low fellow; saffron yellow
63 denied not allowed   70 Perdie by God (*par Dieu*)   72
Sans fable without lying (French)   74 Certes certainly;
kitchen vestal so called, as Dr. Johnson pointed out, because
she kept the fire burning, like the vestal virgins of Rome
78 soothe humor   81 suborned colluded with

85 rag slang for farthing   94 forth out   101 confederate
in conspiracy; pack gang of rogues   107 Ay me expression
of sympathy   110 rescue deliverance by force   113 peevish
stupid   115 displeasure offense   118 discharge pay

And, knowing how the debt grows, I will pay it. 120
Good Master Doctor, see him safe conveyed
Home to my house. O most unhappy° day!

E. ANTIPHOLUS
O most unhappy strumpet!

E. DROMIO
Master, I am here ent'red in bond for you.

E. ANTIPHOLUS
Out on thee, villain! Wherefore dost thou mad° me? 125

E. DROMIO
Will you be bound for nothing? Be mad, good master;
Cry, "The devil!"

LUCIANA
God help, poor souls, how idly° do they talk!

ADRIANA
Go bear him hence. Sister, go you with me.

> Exeunt [PINCH and others with ANTIPHOLUS OF
> EPHESUS and DROMIO OF EPHESUS]. Manet°
> OFFICER, ADRIANA, LUCIANA, COURTESAN.

Say now, whose suit is he arrested at? 130

OFFICER
One Angelo, a goldsmith, do you know him?

ADRIANA
I know the man. What is the sum he owes?

OFFICER
Two hundred ducats.

ADRIANA                    Say, how grows° it due?

OFFICER
Due for a chain your husband had of him.

ADRIANA
He did bespeak a chain for me, but had it not. 135

COURTESAN
Whenas your husband, all in rage, today
Came to my house, and took away my ring—
The ring I saw upon his finger now—
Straight after did I meet him with a chain.

ADRIANA
It may be so, but I did never see it. 140
Come, jailer, bring me where the goldsmith is;
I long to know the truth hereof at large.

> Enter ANTIPHOLUS OF SYRACUSE, with his rapier
> drawn, and DROMIO OF SYRACUSE.

LUCIANA
God for thy mercy, they are loose again.

ADRIANA
And come with naked° swords. Let's call more help
To have them bound again.

OFFICER                    Away, they'll kill us! 145

> Run all out. Exeunt omnes as fast as may be, frighted.

S. ANTIPHOLUS
I see these witches are afraid of swords.

S. DROMIO
She that would be your wife now ran from you.

S. ANTIPHOLUS
Come to the Centaur; fetch our stuff° from thence.

I long that we were safe and sound aboard.

S. DROMIO   Faith, stay here this night; they will surely 150
do us no harm. You saw they speak us fair, give us
gold. Methinks they are such a gentle nation that, but
for the mountain of mad flesh that claims marriage of
me, I could find in my heart to stay here still,° and
turn witch. 155

S. ANTIPHOLUS
I will not stay tonight for all the town:
Therefore away, to get our stuff aboard.        Exeunt.


# ACT V

## Scene I. [Before the Phoenix.]

> Enter [another] MERCHANT and [ANGELO] the goldsmith.

ANGELO
I am sorry, sir, that I have hind'red you;
But I protest he had the chain of me,
Though most dishonestly he doth deny it.

MERCHANT
How is the man esteemed here in the city?

ANGELO
Of very reverend reputation, sir, 5
Of credit infinite, highly beloved,
Second to none that lives here in the city.
His word might bear° my wealth at any time.

MERCHANT
Speak softly; yonder, as I think, he walks.

> Enter ANTIPHOLUS and DROMIO OF SYRACUSE
> again.

ANGELO
'Tis so; and that self° chain about his neck, 10
Which he forswore° most monstrously to have.
Good sir, draw near to me; I'll speak to him.
Signor Antipholus, I wonder much
That you would put me to this shame and trouble,
And not without some scandal to yourself, 15
With circumstance° and oaths so to deny
This chain which now you wear so openly.
Beside the charge,° the shame, imprisonment,
You have done wrong to this my honest friend,
Who, but for staying on our controversy, 20
Had hoisted sail and put to sea today.
This chain you had of me, can you deny it?

S. ANTIPHOLUS
I think I had; I never did deny it.

MERCHANT
Yes, that you did, sir, and forswore it too.

S. ANTIPHOLUS
Who heard me to deny it or forswear it? 25

MERCHANT
These ears of mine, thou know'st, did hear thee.
Fie on thee, wretch! 'Tis pity that thou liv'st
To walk where any honest men resort.

---

122 **unhappy** unfortunate  125 **mad** madden  128 **idly**
foolishly  129 **s.d. Manet** remains (Latin; third person singular,
but common with a plural subject)  133 **grows** comes
144 **naked** drawn  148 **stuff** baggage

154 **still** always
**V.i.8 bear** command the support of  10 **self** same  11
**forswore** denied on oath  16 **circumstance** detailed argument
18 **charge** expense

S. ANTIPHOLUS
Thou art a villain to impeach° me thus.
I'll prove mine honor and mine honesty      30
Against thee presently,° if thou dar'st stand.°

MERCHANT
I dare, and do defy thee for a villain!

*They draw.* Enter ADRIANA, LUCIANA, COURTESAN,
*and others.*

ADRIANA
Hold, hurt him not, for God's sake! He is mad.
Some get within him,° take his sword away.
Bind Dromio too, and bear them to my house.      35

S. DROMIO
Run, master, run; for God's sake, take a house!°
This is some priory. In, or we are spoiled.
                              *Exeunt to the priory.*

Enter Lady ABBESS.

ABBESS
Be quiet, people. Wherefore throng you hither?

ADRIANA
To fetch my poor distracted husband hence.
Let us come in, that we may bind him fast,      40
And bear him home for his recovery.

ANGELO
I knew he was not in his perfect wits.

MERCHANT
I am sorry now that I did draw on him.

ABBESS
How long hath this possession° held the man?

ADRIANA
This week he hath been heavy, sour, sad,      45
And much different from the man he was;
But till this afternoon his passion
Ne'er brake into extremity of rage.

ABBESS
Hath he not lost much wealth by wrack of sea?°
Buried some dear friend? Hath not else his eye      50
Strayed° his affection in unlawful love—
A sin prevailing much in youthful men,
Who give their eyes the liberty of gazing?
Which of these sorrows is he subject to?

ADRIANA
To none of these, except it be the last,      55
Namely, some love that drew him oft from home.

ABBESS
You should for that have reprehended him.

ADRIANA
Why, so I did.

ABBESS               Ay, but not rough enough.

ADRIANA
As roughly as my modesty would let me.

ABBESS
Haply, in private.

ADRIANA               And in assemblies too.      60

ABBESS
Ay, but not enough.

ADRIANA
It was the copy° of our conference.
In bed he slept not for° my urging it;
At board he fed not for my urging it;
Alone, it was the subject of my theme:      65
In company I often glancèd° it;
Still° did I tell him it was vile and bad.

ABBESS
And thereof came it that the man was mad.
The venom° clamors of a jealous woman
Poisons more deadly than a mad dog's tooth.      70
It seems his sleeps were hind'red by thy railing,
And thereof comes it that his head is light.
Thou say'st his meat was sauced with thy upbraidings;
Unquiet meals make ill digestions;
Thereof the raging fire of fever bred—      75
And what's a fever but a fit of madness?
Thou sayest his sports were hind'red by thy brawls;
Sweet recreation barred, what doth ensue
But moody and dull melancholy,
Kinsman to grim and comfortless despair,      80
And at her heels a huge infectious troop
Of pale distemperatures° and foes to life?
In food, in sport, and life-preserving rest
To be disturbed, would mad° or man or beast.
The consequence is, then, thy jealous fits      85
Hath scared thy husband from the use of wits.

LUCIANA
She never reprehended him but mildly,
When he demeaned° himself rough, rude, and wildly.
Why bear you these rebukes and answer not?

ADRIANA
She did betray me to my own reproof.°      90
Good people, enter and lay hold on him.

ABBESS
No, not a creature enters in my house.

ADRIANA
Then, let your servants bring my husband forth.

ABBESS
Neither. He took this place for sanctuary,°
And it shall privilege him° from your hands      95
Till I have brought him to his wits again,
Or lose my labor in assaying° it.

ADRIANA
I will attend my husband, be his nurse,
Diet his sickness, for it is my office,
And will have no attorney° but myself;      100
And therefore let me have him home with me.

ABBESS
Be patient, for I will not let him stir
Till I have used the approvèd° means I have,
With wholesome syrups, drugs, and holy prayers,
To make of him a formal° man again.      105
It is a branch and parcel° of mine oath,
A charitable duty of my order;
Therefore depart, and leave him here with me.

29 **impeach** accuse  31 **presently** at once; **stand** prepare to fight  34 **within him** inside his guard  36 **take a house** get inside  44 **possession** by evil spirits  49 **wrack of sea** shipwreck  51 **Strayed** led astray

62 **copy** topic  63 **for** because of  66 **glanced** touched on  67 **Still** continually  69 **venom** venomous  82 **distemperatures** disorders  84 **mad** madden  88 **demeaned** conducted  90 **my own reproof** self-accusation  94 **sanctuary** right of asylum  95 **privilege him** grant him immunity  97 **assaying** attempting  100 **attorney** agent  103 **approved** tested  105 **formal** normal  106 **branch and parcel** part and parcel

**ADRIANA**
I will not hence, and leave my husband here;
And ill it doth beseem your holiness                    110
To separate the husband and the wife.

**ABBESS**
Be quiet and depart, thou shalt not have him. [*Exit.*]

**LUCIANA**
Complain unto the duke of this indignity.

**ADRIANA**
Come, go. I will fall prostrate at his feet,
And never rise until my tears and prayers              115
Have won his grace to come in person hither,
And take perforce my husband from the abbess.

**MERCHANT**
By this, I think, the dial points at five:
Anon, I'm sure, the duke himself in person
Comes this way to the melancholy vale,                 120
The place of death and sorry° execution,
Behind the ditches of the abbey here.

**ANGELO**
Upon what cause?

**MERCHANT**
To see a reverend Syracusian merchant,
Who put unluckily into this bay                        125
Against the laws and statutes of this town,
Beheaded publicly for his offense.

**ANGELO**
See, where they come. We will behold his death.

**LUCIANA**
Kneel to the duke before he pass the abbey.

*Enter the* DUKE *of Ephesus and* [EGEON] *the merchant of Syracuse,* barehead, *with the* HEADSMAN *and other* OFFICERS.

**DUKE**
Yet once again proclaim it publicly,                   130
If any friend will pay the sum for him,
He shall not die; so much we tender° him.

**ADRIANA**
Justice, most sacred duke, against the abbess!

**DUKE**
She is a virtuous and a reverend lady.
It cannot be that she hath done thee wrong.            135

**ADRIANA**
May it please your grace, Antipholus, my husband,
Who I made lord of me and all I had
At your important° letters, this ill day
A most outrageous fit of madness took him:
That° desp'rately he hurried through the street,       140
With him his bondman° all as mad as he,
Doing displeasure° to the citizens
By rushing in their houses, bearing thence
Rings, jewels, anything his rage did like.
Once did I get him bound, and sent him home,           145
Whilst to take order° for the wrongs I went,
That here and there his fury had committed.
Anon, I wot° not by what strong° escape,
He broke from those that had the guard of him,
And with his mad attendant and himself,                150

Each one with ireful passion, with drawn swords,
Met us again and, madly bent on us,
Chased us away, till, raising of more aid,
We came again to bind them. Then they fled
Into this abbey, whither we pursued them;              155
And here the abbess shuts the gates on us,
And will not suffer us to fetch him out,
Nor send him forth that we may bear him hence.
Therefore, most gracious duke, with thy command,
Let him be brought forth and borne hence for help.     160

**DUKE**
Long since thy husband served me in my wars;
And I to thee engaged a prince's word,
When thou didst make him master of thy bed,
To do him all the grace and good I could.
Go, some of you, knock at the abbey gate,              165
And bid the Lady Abbess come to me.
I will determine this before I stir.

*Enter a* MESSENGER.

**MESSENGER**
O mistress, mistress, shift and save yourself.
My master and his man are both broke loose,
Beaten the maids arow,° and bound the doctor,          170
Whose beard they have singed off with brands of fire,
And ever as it blazed, they threw on him
Great pails of puddled° mire to quench the hair.
My master preaches patience to him, and the while
His man with scissors nicks him like a fool;°          175
And, sure, unless you send some present help,
Between them they will kill the conjurer.

**ADRIANA**
Peace, fool, thy master and his man are here,
And that is false thou dost report to us.

**MESSENGER**
Mistress, upon my life, I tell you true;               180
I have not breathed almost° since I did see it.
He cries for you and vows, if he can take you,
To scorch your face and to disfigure you.

*Cry within.*

Hark, hark! I hear him, mistress. Fly, begone.

**DUKE**
Come, stand by me; fear nothing. Guard with
    halberds!°                                          185

**ADRIANA**
Ay me, it is my husband! Witness you,
That he is borne about invisible.
Even now we housed him° in the abbey here,
And now he's there, past thought of human reason.

*Enter* ANTIPHOLUS *and* DROMIO OF EPHESUS.

**E. ANTIPHOLUS**
Justice, most gracious duke! O, grant me justice,      190
Even for the service that long since I did thee,
When I bestrid° thee in the wars, and took
Deep scars to save thy life; even for the blood
That then I lost for thee, now grant me justice.

121 **sorry** sorrowful  132 **tender** regard  138 **important** pressing  140 **That** so that  141 **bondman** slave  142 **displeasure** harm  146 **take order** settle  148 **wot** know; **strong** violent  170 **arow** one after another  173 **puddled** muddied  175 **fool** Elizabethan fools had their hair cut off  181 **not breathed almost** hardly breathed  185 **halberds** poles with heads like battle-axes  188 **housed him** pursued him to shelter  192 **bestrid** defended by standing over

EGEON
Unless the fear of death doth make me dote,    195
I see my son Antipholus and Dromio.

E. ANTIPHOLUS
Justice, sweet prince, against that woman there!
She whom thou gav'st to me to be my wife;
That hath abusèd and dishonored me,
Even in the strength and height° of injury:    200
Beyond imagination is the wrong
That she this day hath shameless thrown on me.

DUKE
Discover° how, and thou shalt find me just.

E. ANTIPHOLUS
This day, great duke, she shut the doors upon me,
While she with harlots° feasted in my house.    205

DUKE
A grievous fault. Say, woman, didst thou so?

ADRIANA
No, my good lord. Myself, he, and my sister
Today did dine together; so befall my soul
As this is false he burdens me withal.°

LUCIANA
Ne'er may I look on day, nor sleep on night,°    210
But she tells to your highness simple truth.

ANGELO
O perjured woman! They are both forsworn.
In this the madman justly chargest them.

E. ANTIPHOLUS
My liege, I am advisèd° what I say,
Neither disturbed with the effect of wine,    215
Nor heady-rash, provoked with raging ire,
Albeit my wrongs might make one wiser mad.
This woman locked me out this day from dinner.
That goldsmith there, were he not packed° with her,
Could witness it; for he was with me then,    220
Who parted with me to go fetch a chain,
Promising to bring it to the Porpentine,
Where Balthasar and I did dine together.
Our dinner done, and he not coming thither,
I went to seek him. In the street I met him,    225
And in his company that gentleman.
There did this perjured goldsmith swear me down
That I this day of him received the chain,
Which, God he knows, I saw not; for the which,
He did arrest me with an officer.    230
I did obey, and sent my peasant° home
For certain ducats; he with none returned.
Then fairly I bespoke° the officer
To go in person with me to my house.
By th' way we met    235
My wife, her sister, and a rabble more
Of vile confederates. Along with them
They brought one Pinch, a hungry lean-faced villain;
A mere anatomy,° a mountebank,
A threadbare juggler° and a fortuneteller,    240
A needy, hollow-eyed, sharp-looking wretch;

A living dead man. This pernicious slave,
Forsooth, took on him as° a conjurer;
And, gazing in mine eyes, feeling my pulse,
And with no face, as 'twere, out-facing me,    245
Cries out, I was possessed. Then all together
They fell upon me, bound me, bore me thence,
And in a dark and dankish vault at home
There left me and my man, both bound together,
Till gnawing with my teeth my bonds in sunder,°    250
I gained my freedom; and immediately
Ran hither to your grace, whom I beseech
To give me ample satisfaction
For these deep shames and great indignities.

ANGELO
My lord, in truth, thus far I witness with him:    255
That he dined not at home, but was locked out.

DUKE
But had he such a chain of thee, or no?

ANGELO
He had, my lord, and when he ran in here
These people saw the chain about his neck.

MERCHANT
Besides, I will be sworn these ears of mine    260
Heard you confess you had the chain of him,
After you first forswore it on the mart;
And, thereupon, I drew my sword on you;
And then you fled into this abbey here,
From whence, I think, you are come by miracle.    265

E. ANTIPHOLUS
I never came within these abbey walls,
Nor ever didst thou draw thy sword on me.
I never saw the chain, so help me heaven!
And this is false you burden me withal.

DUKE
Why, what an intricate impeach° is this!    270
I think you all have drunk of Circe's cup.°
If here you housed him, here he would have been;
If he were mad, he would not plead so coldly.°
You say he dined at home, the goldsmith here
Denies that saying. Sirrah, what say you?    275

E. DROMIO
Sir, he dined with her there at the Porpentine.

COURTESAN
He did, and from my finger snatched that ring.

E. ANTIPHOLUS
'Tis true, my liege, this ring I had of her.

DUKE
Saw'st thou him enter at the abbey here?

COURTESAN
As sure, my liege, as I do see your grace.    280

DUKE
Why, this is strange. Go call the abbess hither.
I think you are all mated,° or stark mad.
                   *Exit one to the abbey.*

EGEON
Most mighty duke, vouchsafe me° speak a word.
Haply° I see a friend will save my life,
And pay the sum that may deliver me.    285

---

200 in . . . height to the strongest degree  203 Discover reveal  205 harlots rascals  208–09 so . . . withal I stake my soul that what he charges me with is false  210 on night at night  214 advisèd well aware of  219 packed conspiring  231 peasant bondman  233 fairly I bespoke politely I addressed  239 mere anatomy sheer skeleton  240 juggler sorcerer

243 took . . . as assumed the part of  250 in sunder asunder  270 impeach accusation  271 Circe's cup potion which, in Greek mythology, turns men into beasts  273 coldly rationally  282 mated confounded  283 vouchsafe me allow me to  284 Haply perchance

DUKE
Speak freely, Syracusian, what thou wilt.

EGEON
Is not your name, sir, called Antipholus?
And is not that your bondman Dromio?

E. DROMIO
Within this hour I was his bondman, sir,
But he, I thank him, gnawed in two my cords.          290
Now am I Dromio, and his man, unbound.

EGEON
I am sure you both of you remember me.

E. DROMIO
Ourselves we do remember, sir, by you;
For lately we were bound° as you are now.
You are not Pinch's patient, are you, sir?          295

EGEON
Why look you strange on me? You know me well.

E. ANTIPHOLUS
I never saw you in my life till now.

EGEON
O, grief hath changed me since you saw me last,
And careful° hours with time's deformèd hand
Have written strange defeatures° in my face.          300
But tell me yet, dost thou not know my voice?

E. ANTIPHOLUS  Neither.

EGEON
Dromio, nor thou?

E. DROMIO          No, trust me, sir, nor I.

EGEON
I am sure thou dost!

E. DROMIO  Ay, sir, but I am sure I do not; and what-  305
soever a man denies, you are now bound° to believe
him.

EGEON
Not know my voice! O, time's extremity,
Hast thou so cracked and splitted my poor tongue
In seven short years, that here my only son          310
Knows not my feeble key of untuned cares?°
Though now this grainèd° face of mine be hid
In sap-consuming winter's drizzled snow,
And all the conduits of my blood froze up,
Yet hath my night of life some memory;          315
My wasting lamps° some fading glimmer left;
My dull deaf ears a little use to hear.
All these old witnesses—I cannot err—
Tell me thou art my son Antipholus.

E. ANTIPHOLUS
I never saw my father in my life.          320

EGEON
But seven years since, in Syracusa, boy,
Thou know'st we parted; but perhaps, my son,
Thou sham'st to acknowledge me in misery.

E. ANTIPHOLUS
The duke and all that know me in the city
Can witness with me that it is not so.          325
I ne'er saw Syracusa in my life.

DUKE
I tell thee, Syracusian, twenty years

Have I been patron to Antipholus,
During which time he ne'er saw Syracusa.
I see thy age and dangers make thee dote.          330

*Enter the* ABBESS *with* ANTIPHOLUS OF SYRACUSE
*and* DROMIO OF SYRACUSE.

ABBESS
Most mighty duke, behold a man much wronged.

*All gather to see them.*

ADRIANA
I see two husbands, or mine eyes deceive me.

DUKE
One of these men is genius° to the other;
And so of these, which is the natural man,
And which the spirit? Who deciphers them?          335

S. DROMIO
I, sir, am Dromio; command him away.

E. DROMIO
I, sir, am Dromio; pray let me stay.

S. ANTIPHOLUS
Egeon art thou not, or else his ghost?

S. DROMIO
O, my old master! Who hath bound him here?

ABBESS
Whoever bound him, I will loose his bonds,          340
And gain a husband by his liberty.
Speak, old Egeon, if thou beest the man
That hadst a wife once called Emilia,
That bore thee at a burden° two fair sons!
O, if thou beest the same Egeon, speak;          345
And speak unto the same Emilia.

DUKE [*Aside.*]
Why, here begins his morning story right:
These two Antipholus', these two so like,
And these two Dromios, one in semblance,°
Besides her urging° of her wrack at sea;          350
These are the parents to these children,
Which accidentally are met together.

EGEON
If I dream not, thou art Emilia.
If thou art she, tell me where is that son
That floated with thee on the fatal raft?          355

ABBESS
By men of Epidamnum, he and I
And the twin Dromio, all were taken up;
But by and by rude fishermen of Corinth
By force took Dromio and my son from them,
And me they left with those of Epidamnum.          360
What then became of them I cannot tell;
I to° this fortune that you see me in.

DUKE
Antipholus, thou cam'st from Corinth first.

S. ANTIPHOLUS
No, sir, not I; I came from Syracuse.

DUKE
Stay, stand apart; I know not which is which.          365

E. ANTIPHOLUS
I came from Corinth, my most gracious lord.

294 **bound** pun on being a bondservant and being literally
bound as a madman  299 **careful** full of care  300 **defeatures**
disfigurements  306 **bound** a further quibble  311 **feeble
. . . cares** voice enfeebled by discordant cares  312 **grainèd**
furrowed  316 **wasting lamps** dimming eyes

333 **genius** attendant spirit  344 **burden** birth  349 **semblance** appearance  350 **urging** account  362 **I to** I came to

E. DROMIO
And I with him.

E. ANTIPHOLUS
Brought to this town by that most famous warrior,
Duke Menaphon, your most renownèd uncle.

ADRIANA
Which of you two did dine with me today?     370

S. ANTIPHOLUS
I, gentle mistress.

ADRIANA          And are not you my husband?

E. ANTIPHOLUS
No, I say nay to that.

S. ANTIPHOLUS
And so do I, yet did she call me so;
And this fair gentlewoman, her sister here,
Did call me brother. What I told you then     375
I hope I shall have leisure to make good,
If this be not a dream I see and hear.

ANGELO
That is the chain, sir, which you had of me.

S. ANTIPHOLUS
I think it be, sir; I deny it not.

E. ANTIPHOLUS
And you, sir, for this chain arrested me.     380

ANGELO
I think I did, sir. I deny it not.

ADRIANA
I sent you money, sir, to be your bail,
By Dromio; but I think he brought it not.

E. DROMIO
No, none by me.

S. ANTIPHOLUS
This purse of ducats I received from you,     385
And Dromio, my man, did bring them me.
I see we still° did meet each other's man,
And I was ta'en for him, and he for me,
And thereupon these errors are arose.

E. ANTIPHOLUS
These ducats pawn I for my father here.     390

DUKE
It shall not need; thy father hath his life.

COURTESAN
Sir, I must have that diamond from you.

E. ANTIPHOLUS
There, take it, and much thanks for my good cheer.

ABBESS
Renownèd duke, vouchsafe to take the pains
To go with us into the abbey here,     395
And hear at large discoursèd all our fortunes;

**387 still** repeatedly

And all that are assembled in this place,
That by this sympathizèd° one day's error
Have suffered wrong, go, keep us company,
And we shall make full satisfaction.     400
Thirty-three years have I but gone in travail°
Of you, my sons, and till this present hour
My heavy burden ne'er delivered.
The duke, my husband, and my children both,
And you the calendars° of their nativity,     405
Go to a gossips'° feast, and joy with me
After so long grief such nativity.°

DUKE
With all my heart I'll gossip° at this feast.
          *Exeunt [all except] the two* DROMIOS *and
                 two brothers* [ANTIPHOLUSES].

S. DROMIO
Master, shall I fetch your stuff from shipboard?

E. ANTIPHOLUS
Dromio, what stuff of mine hast thou embarked?     410

S. DROMIO
Your goods that lay at host,° sir, in the Centaur.

S. ANTIPHOLUS
He speaks to me. I am your master, Dromio.
Come, go with us; we'll look to that anon.
Embrace thy brother there; rejoice with him.
          *Exit [with* ANTIPHOLUS OF EPHESUS].

S. DROMIO
There is a fat friend at your master's house,     415
That kitchened° me for you today at dinner;
She now shall be my sister, not my wife.

E. DROMIO
Methinks you are my glass, and not my brother;
I see by you I am a sweet-faced° youth.
Will you walk in to see their gossiping?     420

S. DROMIO
Not I, sir, you are my elder.

E. DROMIO
That's a question; how shall we try it?

S. DROMIO  We'll draw cuts for the senior; till then,
lead thou first.

E. DROMIO
Nay, then, thus:     425
We came into the world like brother and brother:
And now let's go hand in hand, not one before
another.          *Exeunt.*

**398 sympathizèd** shared  **401 travail** childbirth (with a pun on *travel*)  **405 calendars** the Dromios mark the age of the Antipholus'  **406 gossips'** godparents  **407 nativity** a christening party (suggested emendations are "festivity" and "felicity")  **408 gossip** make merry  **411 at host** in the care of the host  **416 kitchened** entertained in the kitchen  **419 sweet-faced** good-looking

# THE FIRST PART OF

# HENRY THE SIXTH

EDITED BY LAWRENCE V. RYAN

## Introduction

*Henry VI, Part One* is a play with many imperfections, so many, indeed, that editors and critics have often been reluctant to attribute the greater part of it to Shakespeare. "That Drum-and-Trumpet Thing," the eighteenth-century critic Maurice Morgann called it in his essay on Sir John Falstaff, "written doubtless, or rather exhibited, long before *Shakespeare* was born, tho' afterwards repaired, I think, and furbished up by him with here and there a little sentiment and diction."

Such reluctance of ascription has led to the expenditure of much scholarly energy on attempts to isolate as undeniably Shakespearean a few scenes, in particular the finely managed quarrel of the Yorkists and Lancastrians in the Temple garden (II.iv), and to assign the bulk of the work to various teams of collaborators, among them Christopher Marlowe, George Peele, Thomas Nashe, and Robert Greene. Another consequence has been an exceptional tentativeness in much of the critical speculation about *1 Henry VI*, though several fine studies have been made of its significance in Shakespeare's evolution from apprentice playwright to master dramatist.

Arguments against Shakespeare's authorship, or primacy within a group of collaborators, have focused mainly upon resemblances in the text to patterns of diction and versification characteristic of other Elizabethan playwrights. The evidence amassed has been considerable, though sometimes contradictory; at times impressive, but never conclusive. For it is likely enough that a Shakespeare who was just setting out on his literary career would have tended to imitate the stylistic mannerisms of already established dramatists. Even Allison Gaw, among the champions of multiple authorship one of the most sensitive to the potential and actual virtues of the play, failed to associate the unusual effort to integrate historical theme and dramatic structure in a theatrically meaningful way with the designing hand of Shakespeare.

Against the collaborationist theory, however, have stood a number of commentators, among them Charles Knight and Hermann Ulrici in the nineteenth century and Peter Alexander, J. P. Brockbank, Leo Kirschbaum, Hereward Price, and E. M. W. Tillyard in our own time. These critics perceive the three dramas on the reign of Henry VI as of one piece, and regard the case for denying the Shakespearean authorship of any part as not proved. It would be rash to assert categorically that *1 Henry VI* as printed in the Folio of 1623 is entirely by Shakespeare, or that no version involving extensive collaboration with others ever did exist. But an approach to the play through the relationship between theme and dramatic design, rather than through its stylistic echoes of various contemporary writers, does considerably strengthen the argument that Shakespeare played the major, if not an exclusive, role in its composition.

Any reader or spectator coming to *1 Henry VI* after exposure to the chronicle plays of other Elizabethan authors is suddenly aware that here he is being asked not simply to observe the pageant of history but to ponder the meaning of man's role in history. Most other works of the period in this dramatic kind are, even more evidently than the civic and national chronicles upon which they are based, mere strings of episodes in sequence of time, governed, if by any sense of theme at all, by the notion of the capriciousness of the goddess Fortune. Very few are concerned with seeking any other guiding principle in history or with the dramatic interaction of personalities within the pattern of historical events. Very few are concerned with the meaning of history at all, their authors often preferring instead, like a certain kind of modern historical novelist, to invent romantic situations involving historical personages within a bare framework of actual events.

The theme that runs throughout the tetralogy of plays composed by Shakespeare on the reigns of Henry VI and Richard III, and in fact throughout all of his dramatizations of English history, is the individual's, and a people's, response to the continuing alternations of order and disorder allowed by divine providence in the political life of a nation. A strong and heroic king whose regime brings glory and harmony to the commonwealth is succeeded by a monarch lacking, through extreme youth or defect of character, in the virtues necessary for unifying all the diverse constituents of society. The ineptitude or negligence of the sovereign looses the restraints on ambitious and unscrupulous subjects, whose schemes and counter-schemes for self-aggrandizement promote faction, public disorder, and eventually civil war. As E. M. W. Tillyard has noted in his *Shakespeare's History Plays*, in the struggle for domination degree, or acknowledgment of one's proper place in the hierarchically constituted political, and even cosmic, order, is forgotten. "Vaulting ambition" causes men to o'erleap themselves and drag the rest of society with them to the brink of chaos. Finally, when a ruler appears who is powerful and virtuous enough to triumph over the contending parties and restore degree and order, the hallmarks to the Elizabethan mind of good political economy, the wheel comes full circle.

Like the sixteenth-century chronicler Edward Hall, Shakespeare seems, officially at least, to have regarded the larger cycle of order emerging from disorder as having come round fully with the rise of the Tudor dynasty. Hall, whose book is entitled *The Union of the Two Noble and Illustre Families of Lancaster and York*, believed that the cause of the civil warfare which plagued England intermittently throughout the fifteenth century had been removed by the coronation of Henry VIII, whose father was connected with the Lancastrian, or Red Rose, branch of the royal family, and whose mother was the daughter and heir of the Yorkist, or White Rose, King Edward IV. For Shakespeare and his contemporaries, the full benefit of this restoration of harmony and degree after the near-anarchy of the Wars of the Roses was manifest in the long and prosperous reign of their virgin queen. "This royal infant," prophesies Archbishop Cranmer of the just-christened Elizabeth in the final scene of *Henry the Eighth*,

> Though in her cradle, yet now promises
> Upon this land a thousand thousand blessings
> Which time shall bring to ripeness.        (V.v.18–21)

Nor will the maiden queen's death, continues Cranmer (how unprophetic the playwright here becomes of later Stuart history!), set the old cycle in motion again, because phoenix-like her "blessedness" will be reborn in her successor.

But Shakespeare was more concerned with presenting the ill effects of disrupted order than with depicting the glories of successful monarchs. Of all his plays on British historical or pseudohistorical subjects, only one, *Henry V*, concentrates on the personality of an all-prosperous ruler and an undeniably glorious moment in England's past. Despite the good fortune of the kingdom during most of Elizabeth's reign, he apparently brooded about the possibility that the cycle might recur, especially if men should ignore the lessons taught by history. Within the larger cycle described by Hall and accepted as complete by many writers of his age, Shakespeare saw smaller cycles or undulations of order and chaos that should have reminded men how precarious any state of equilibrium is in their moral and political lives.

This is not to suggest that in his earliest years as a playwright he had already blocked out in his mind a whole series of dramas to illustrate the pattern and point the historical lessons for his audiences. The order of composition of his various "chronicle histories" should dispel any such assumption. The later-written tetralogy on the troubled history of England toward the end of the Middle Ages—*Richard II, Henry IV, Parts I and II, and Henry V*—

deals with events that antedate those of the three *Henry VI* plays and *Richard III*. There also exists some possibility that the second and third parts of *Henry VI* were composed before and provided suggestions for the first. Even the earlier tetralogy, therefore, hints at a gradually emerging and changing conception in Shakespeare's mind of what his subject signified and how that significance might be rendered in dramatic terms.

The breakdown of good order, manifest in the undermining of ancient chivalric ideals that had earlier held society together, has its origins for Shakespeare in the events leading to the deposition of King Richard II at the close of the fourteenth century. Richard, a minor at his accession and as an adult deficient in the private and public virtues requisite in a king, is forced to abdicate by his cousin Henry Bolingbroke, whom he has wronged. Bolingbroke, reigning as King Henry IV, is haunted by the rebellions consequent upon Richard's death; his own success in violating degree has ironically given rise to ambition in others. His son Henry V, however, brings to the throne a clearer conscience and the qualities needed for effective rule. His triumphant kingship marks the close of one of the smaller historical cycles, and is epitomized in his ability to control the anarchical forces in society and weld its different elements into the efficient little army that defeats the French at Agincourt (1415).

Yet this brief period of glory is only an interval in the larger pattern. The hero-king has scotched, not killed, "civil dissension," the "viperous worm/That gnaws the bowels of the commonwealth" (*1 Henry VI*, III.i.72–73). The opening scene of *1 Henry VI* is shrewdly designed to give warning of the impending disorder. At the funeral of Henry V the four speeches by the king's brothers and uncles convey an awesome sense of cosmic upheaval and heavy finality. Their foreboding is immediately justified, for within less than three dozen lines the lamentations dissolve into a quarrel between the Duke of Gloucester and the Bishop of Winchester. This altercation symbolizes the release of disruptive forces within a society deprived of its main source of unity. Bedford, the new king's uncle, in fact responds to the quarrel with a desperate invocation, asking Henry V's spirit, as his living presence had done, to

> Prosper this realm, keep it from civil broils,
> Combat with adverse planets in the heavens!    (I.i.53–54)

Nor does the playwright waste any further time before showing how disastrous has been the untimely death of this "king of so much worth." Bedford's prayer is interrupted by the entrance of a courier, who rushes in unceremoniously with news of English reversals in France. He is succeeded by two others, each arriving with worse tidings, worst of all being the account of Lord Talbot's capture. The remarkable economy of the scene is evident from the impact made by this trio of messengers. Their accounts project to the audience the importance for England's success in France of the efforts of such leaders as Salisbury, Talbot, and Bedford, who reacts to the news by preparing to go immediately to the aid of the others. Through this sequence of speeches the dramatist focuses attention on the three warriors, who stand for the ideals that have caused English arms until now to prosper. Yet all three worthy nobles are represented as advanced in years and fated to die later in the play. They carry with them to their graves not only the hopes of England's monarchs for possessing the crown of France, but also the chivalric ideals of a more innocent and masculine era. Their kind will be displaced, at least temporarily, by a self-seeking breed of new "risers," the Winchesters, the Suffolks, and the Yorks.

In spite of Bedford's resolve, there can be no doubt as the scene concludes that all coherence is already gone, that the downturn in England's fortunes has begun. With a real instinct for symmetrical design, the author concludes the scene by repeating the pattern of its opening. The royal brothers and uncles take their leave in precisely the order in which they have been introduced as speakers. As each goes his way to carry out his separate function in governing the realm, there is a momentary feeling that if they can work to one end, all may yet be well. Lest the audience presume, however, that shared grief and determination to act will lead to an effective coalition, the sense of division, of a pilotless ship of state, is emphasized by the words and pageantry of the departures. When all the rest are gone, there remains the unscrupulous politician Winchester, whose earlier altercation with Gloucester has already struck the note of discord, and who regards his nephew's death as an opportunity for him to seize control "And sit at chiefest stern of public weal."

The masterful construction of this introductory scene is more evident in theatrical performance than from silent reading. For it wants, as does the play on the whole, that poetic fire one is accustomed to look for in the work of Shakespeare. But as has often been remarked about his career, he seems to have developed a keen feeling for construction and for what is theatrically right before he evolved a poetic style that can thrill the auditor with its justness for the occasion or discriminate for the sensitive ear subtle differences of mood and character.

Symmetry and purposefulness of design, unlike the formlessness of most Elizabethan chronicle plays, are indeed the keynotes of this work, and of the Lancaster-York tetralogy as a whole. If later—beginning with *Richard II* and *Henry IV* and at length most impressively in *King Lear* and *Macbeth*—Shakespeare learned to portray characters helping to shape as well as enduring history or growing in perception and self-knowledge from their interaction with events, in *1 Henry VI* he is not yet ready for such an achievement. Here the problem of man's role in history is reduced to simpler terms: a dramatic personage responds in a particular way to events and to other persons involved in the action because he has a fixed character, rather than the possibility of an evolving one. This simple consistency is, in a way, true even of the heroicomical portrayal of Joan of Arc. Although she gives an impression at the outset of being admirably eloquent, efficient, and patriotic, and then of degenerating into wantonness and diabolism, the unsavory side of her character is hinted at in her very first scene. If we are disturbed by the seemingly inconsistent and finally unchivalrous treatment of the Maid of Orleans, we should remind ourselves that in Shakespeare's day she had not yet been canonized or become the subject of more sympathetic characterizations by dramatists like Schiller, Shaw, and Anouilh. Character in Shakespeare's play is conceived broadly, flatly; the peculiar quality of every personage is unequivocally represented.

The solution for him, consequently, was to develop his dramatic theme mainly through formal structure; that is, through symbolically parallel and contrasting episodes, and through confrontations between characters representing sharply defined ethical and political values.

The first clue to this intention is the extremely cavalier handling of chronology, a disruption of time-sequence far beyond that in any of Shakespeare's other plays based on chronicles. Rather than demonstrating an ignorance of history or indifference to order, the rearrangement of events indicates a sense on the author's part that dramatic logic and the historical lesson are better served by recreating than by retelling what happened in the past. Thus, while *1 Henry VI* is grounded upon chronicle materials, it employs them so freely that one is not always certain how much indebted to the sources a given scene may be, or even, except in manifest instances, whether the principal inspiration is the work of Edward Hall or that of Raphael Holinshed.

The play also includes totally fictional scenes, among them the dispute in the Temple garden and Talbot's encounter with the Countess of Auvergne. Unlike the arbitrarily invented episodes common in other history plays of the age, those in *1 Henry VI* serve to clarify the meaning of actual events, far more effectively than anything available to the author in his historical sources. The disjointing of time, moreover, enables him to achieve striking dramatic and didactic effects. The episodes cover a period of more than thirty years, from the beginning of Henry VI's reign in 1422 to the death of the Talbots near Bordeaux in 1453, but from the opening lines incidents are juxtaposed that were in actuality separated by a number of years. Thus, the siege of Orleans (1428-29) is already taking place during the funeral of Henry V seven years earlier. The dramaturgical reason is evident: to introduce immediately the main conflict, between Joan of France and Talbot of England. In Act V, the capture of Joan (1430) is succeeded directly and without even a scene division by Suffolk's fictitious capture and wooing of Margaret of Anjou, though the negotiations for the king's marriage did not actually take place until 1444. Finally, the death of the Talbots, chronologically the last in the long series of events here dramatized, precedes these other carefully paired episodes. Apparently this dislocation was made in order to maintain as long as possible the symbolical conflict between the mirror of English chivalry and the diabolically assisted Joan, and also to imply that Margaret is about to arise from Joan's ashes to carry on the scourging of England in the remainder of the trilogy.

Divine providence allows England to be plagued by infernal as well as political enemies because her people have sinned. How the nation might have remained true to itself is signified by the words and deeds of Talbot. What she is in danger of becoming is signified in the shortcomings of the French, failings that crop up increasingly among Englishmen as the action of the play proceeds. The dissension that breaks out at home in the opening lines begins immediately to sap the English strength abroad, for it is accompanied by the decay of feudal loyalties and forgetfulness of degree. Also manifest are an English decline toward French effeminacy and the beginning of reliance on fraud and cunning rather than manly courage and straightforward knightly virtue.

In the second scene, which shifts to Orleans, the playwright quickly sketches in the defective moral character of Frenchmen, as epitomized in the behavior of the Dauphin. A braggart like his counterpart in Shakespeare's *Henry V*, he begins a sortie against the English with the cry to his followers,

> Him I forgive my death that killeth me
> When he sees me go back one foot or fly.    (I.ii.20–21)

Some moments later, his forces are beaten back, and he excuses his retreat in words a Talbot or a Salisbury would have died rather than utter:

> I would ne'er have fled,
> But that they left me 'midst my enemies.    (I.ii.23–24)

Nothing they can do as men, it is apparent from the ensuing conversation among the French leaders, can overcome these dogged Englishmen.

At this point Joan comes on stage, and the Dauphin's conversation with her brings out two grave defects of Frenchmen that also begin gradually to taint the characters of Englishmen in the play. After bowing to her in single combat, Charles woos Joan in the language not of her royal prince but of the fashionable courtly lover, asking to be her "servant and not sovereign," and imploring her "mercy" (that is, the favor of her love) as her "prostrate thrall." Such domination by the female is obviously scorned by an audience of Tudor Englishmen; it confirms their prejudices against Gallic dandyism and effeminacy. For in spite of Joan's high-sounding claims and self-assertive dash, one's admiration of her must stop far short of the Dauphin's; she is, after all, no more than a shepherd's daughter from Lorraine. The comedy of the scene is also obvious. From the number of double entendres in the Ovidian tradition of lovemaking as armed combat, the audience can scarcely be expected to take seriously Joan's claims to divine inspiration and vow to maintain her virginity while Englishmen remain on her country's soil.

All doubt about the tenor of the scene is dispelled by Charles' final ecstatic response to her messianic claims:

> Was Mahomet inspirèd with a dove?
> Thou with an eagle art inspirèd then.
> Helen, the mother of great Constantine,
> Nor yet Saint Philip's daughters, were like thee.
> Bright star of Venus, fall'n down on the earth,
> How may I reverently worship thee enough?
>                                             (I.ii.140–45)

Not only are the allusions to other lofty examples of divine inspiration too characteristic of the Dauphin's lack of moderation to be taken seriously, but their very extravagance is a strong hint that Joan's pretensions are false. When Charles climaxes his apostrophe with the words "Bright star of Venus," the imagery of courtly wooing and the bawdy overtones of the earlier part of the scene intrude themselves again. Besides, "star of

Venus, fall'n down on the earth," calls to mind not only the goddess of profane love, but also Lucifer, that brightest of angelic stars tumbled out of the heavens for his aspiration to divinity. Feminine wiles are thus linked by the epithet with diabolical fraud and deception. Charles is blameworthy for allowing himself to be dominated by a woman—a peasant girl at that!—and for resorting to preternatural aid in his efforts to rid his country of the English. "Coward of France!" exclaims Bedford,

> how much he wrongs his fame,
> Despairing of his own arm's fortitude,
> To join with witches and the help of hell.    (II.i.16–18)

The rest of the scenes in France are fashioned to contrast the reprehensible behavior of Joan and the Dauphin, as well as of Englishmen whose characters become similarly stained as the moral fiber of their leaderless country weakens, with that of the upright Talbot. These contrasts are effectively brought out through patterns, as Ernest Talbert calls them, of "intensified repetition." One such pattern is the strategic paralleling of episodes either to heighten the opposition between worthy and reprehensible forms of behavior or to point up symbolical relationships between apparently unconnected incidents. The playwright is also fond of grouping characters and episodes in climactic triads to underscore several of the main themes of the play.

Thus, since Talbot is the standard by which the measure of the other characters is taken, his first meeting with Henry VI is presented as an idealized interview between an unselfishly devoted vassal and his sovereign. For his loyal service and recovery in France of

> fifty fortresses,
> Twelve cities, and seven wallèd towns of strength,
> Beside five hundred prisoners of esteem,    (III.iv.6–8)

Talbot is created Earl of Shrewsbury. But the episode distinctly recalls the first scene of the same act, where the already scheming Richard Plantagenet is made Duke of York without having done anything to merit his elevation and pledges his fealty to the king with a hollow heart. Again, in the opening scene of Act IV Talbot tears the garter from Sir John Falstaff's[1] leg for cowardice in battle and delivers a speech on what it means to bear "the sacred name of knight." His action is a clear example of how noblemen, in helping the monarch to maintain true order and degree, should deal with the presumptions of their subordinates.

As soon as Talbot departs, however, Vernon and Basset disrupt the coronation scene with their demands for trial by combat in behalf of their respective masters, York and Somerset. In order to further their own ambitions, Henry's nobles are obviously willing to let faction breed rather than suppress their contentious retainers. Toward the end of the scene York even appears to be on the point of exclaiming to Warwick (IV.i.180) that he would prefer to have the

---

[1] Not the famous fat knight of *Henry IV*, whose death is described in *Henry V*, but rather a character based on the historical Sir John Fastolfe (c. 1378–1459), a prominent retainer of the Duke of Bedford and, according to the chronicles, one of the most valiant captains in the regent's armies.

king himself take sides against him since he might then turn it to his own advantage. This is but one of several scenes in which Talbot's conduct is sharply contrasted with that of other characters. The dramatist's intentions are unmistakable: Talbot is the ideal, the centripetal force of order that gradually gives way to the centrifugal forces of chaos represented by York and others of the rising new breed.

Dramatic triads appear in many places in *1 Henry VI* from the opening scene onward: the sense of climactic urgency in the arrival of the three messengers hot on one another's heels; the trio of ambitious nobles—Winchester, York, Suffolk; the focusing on the three stout but aging generals—Salisbury, Bedford, and Talbot—each of whose deaths is a more discouraging blow, the last the final blow, to English dynastic ambitions in France. Talbot opposes the French and their sorceress champion on all three of these occasions: at Orleans, where Salisbury is shot; at Rouen, where Bedford dies; and finally near Bordeaux, where he and his son meet their heroic end.

In each incident, fraud at first succeeds, not force of arms, and the placing of blame in each indicates progressive deterioration on the English side. At Orleans, Salisbury is killed by chance and Talbot is temporarily set back, to his complete bewilderment, by Joan's "art and baleful sorcery." His martial enterprise and trust in God, however, in contrast with the Frenchmen's lax discipline and reliance on "the help of hell," win the day for him when he returns to the attack. At Rouen (III.ii) Joan gains entrance by means of a stratagem historically employed by the English on another occasion, according to Holinshed, and transferred in the play to the French as an instance of their treachery. Eventually, Talbot overcomes again, while Bedford watches the struggle from "his litter sick." But now it is not only the French who are cowardly, who, as Talbot complains,

keep the walls
And dare not take up arms like gentlemen.  (III.ii.69–70)

Just before the victory is assured and Bedford dies content, Falstaff again shows the white feather, this time on stage instead of in a messenger's report, and runs like a Frenchman from the battle scene. It is this defection that provides the occasion for Talbot later to tear the badge of the Order of the Garter from his leg at Henry's coronation in Paris.

At Bordeaux, where the audience might expect a final confrontation between Talbot and Joan, none is provided, nor does Joan make use of any cunning device to gain advantage over the English. The dramatist's reasons are clear enough. They are placed in the mouth of Sir William Lucy as he vainly begs York and Somerset to come to Talbot's relief. It is "the vulture of sedition" and "Sleeping neglection" that are causing the loss of Henry V's conquests:

The fraud of England, not the force of France,
Hath now entrapped the noble-minded Talbot.
(IV.iv.36–37)

Malice and cunning deceit are beginning to corrupt even the highest English nobility, and Talbot is the sacrifice to their dissension. Yet even against the forces of hell and the wily allurements of womankind, England might have stood fast, if only all her noblemen had been like her stoutest champion. But when men place their self-interest ahead of the common good, the old ideals are readily forgotten. Joan's cunning becomes no longer necessary; the English are now their own worst enemies, having succumbed to the vices of the French.

This eroding of English virtue is nowhere more skillfully depicted than in the triad of scenes involving the first appearances of each of the three evil-designing Frenchwomen (interestingly enough, the only feminine characters in the play!). The scenes in question are Joan's introduction to the Dauphin, Talbot's reception by the Countess of Auvergne (II.iii), and Suffolk's wooing of Margaret of Anjou (V.iii). All three women represent a threat to English fortunes; the manner in which the three men respond to them neatly dramatizes the lesson.

Earlier it was pointed out that not only the Dauphin's accepting the demoniacally inspired assistance of Joan but also his self-debasement to servant-lover of a peasant girl, is conduct inexcusable in a prince. And even if his behavior were not a burlesque of courtly traditions, it runs counter to the ruggedly heroic ideal represented by Talbot. Not that Talbot is a boor: he does know how to treat a lady as becomes a worthy English chevalier. The Dauphin's involvement with Joan is a breaking of degree and serves, moreover, to unhinge her judgment of herself even beyond what traffic with fiends has done. When she is finally on her way to the stake, this peasant maiden who has been graced with sovereignty over her infatuated monarch pretends to "noble birth" and "gentler blood" than that of her shepherd father. Even the phrase with which she rejects the old man—"Decrepit miser!"—accentuates her disdain for her lowly origins; *miser* is the worst term of opprobrium in the vocabulary of the courtly tradition.

But the true measure of the Dauphin's folly is the scene between Talbot and the fictional countess. This lady too plots evil to the English through her ruse for capturing "the terror of the French." There is even a suggestion that she, like Joan, may have resorted to witchcraft by practicing sympathetic magic on her guest's portrait:

Long time thy shadow hath been thrall to me,
For in my gallery thy picture hangs.
But now the substance shall endure the like.  (II.iii.36–38)

The resourceful Talbot, however, outwits her by a simple counterstratagem and, refusing like a true and valiant gentleman to avenge himself on so weak an adversary, asks only honest entertainment for himself and his men before they take their leave.

Obviously if all of Talbot's compatriots had been thus immune to the allure of scheming Frenchwomen, all might have remained well enough for England. But the third encounter of this kind, that between Suffolk and Reignier's daughter Margaret, shows that Englishmen no longer are men of true honor, who, in contrast with the French, place their country's interests above their own selfish desires. Suffolk is dazzled, almost bewitched, by Margaret's beauty when he first gazes on her. And while he is the active, she almost entirely the passive, agent in this scene, from the course taken by the remaining action there can be little doubt that this woman will supplant Joan as the punishment for the sins of faction and ambition among Englishmen. Having Joan's and Margaret's captures occur in the same scene, in another of those symbolically meaningful parallelings of seemingly unconnected episodes, is theatrically most effective. And even though Joan's final scenes are far different in tone from Margaret's entry into the action, they serve a twofold function in helping to knit up the events of 1 Henry VI and to anticipate the subsequent development of the trilogy.

In defiance of historical fact, but with excellent dramatic sense, York is made to be Joan's captor and judge. But even as he is mercilessly taunting his prisoner about her past affairs with the Dauphin and his nobles, another game of man and woman is being played that will prove his undoing. The parting curses of Joan are not the impotent ragings of a "fell banning hag"; they are prophecies of ambitious York's own downfall and of the miserable years for England that are being engendered in the dalliance of Suffolk with Margaret of Anjou.

Suffolk would enjoy this lady's love and use her to further his own ends at the sacrifice of English interests in France. Worse still, his "wondrous rare description" of Margaret's beauty serves to corrupt King Henry's mind and causes him to break his pre-contract of marriage with the daughter of the Earl of Armagnac. That the choice is both impolitic and immoral is clear from the king's own inner turmoil in the last moments of the play: the "sharp dissension" that he feels within makes him "sick with working of my thoughts," and he finally departs in a state of "grief" rather than expectant elation at "This sudden execution of my will."

The threat latent in Henry's impending marriage to Margaret, with whose arrival in England the second part of the trilogy opens, is brilliantly suggested by a pair of images in the last scene of 1 Henry VI. The king compares his infatuation to a tempest, driving his soul against its more settled inclinations like a ship against the tide:

So am I driven by breath of her renown
Either to suffer shipwreck or arrive
Where I may have fruition of her love.    (V.v.7–9)

The sudden intrusion here of the conventional figure of the lover as a vessel in danger of shipwreck on the stormy seas of passion calls to mind the dangers that Petrarch (Passa la nave mia colma d'oblio) and his imitator Sir Thomas Wyatt ("My galley charged with forgetfulness") lamented as besetting the soul of the man tossed by sexual desire. For a king to make such an admission, and then to overrule good counsel and follow the inclination of his will rather than reasons of state, is a most unregal kind of behavior.

Most disturbing of all, however, are the verses with which the drama concludes. If restoration of order were implied at the end of the action, according to the usual Shakespearean closing formula there would be a speech explicitly saying so. But here the final words, coming after the king's confused withdrawal, are left for Suffolk, who exults in his success and departs for Anjou

As did the youthful Paris once to Greece,
With hope to find the like event in love,
But prosper better than the Trojan did.    (V.v.104–06)

The image could hardly be lost on an Elizabethan audience, whose own mythmaking historians traced the ancestry of the British race to Troy. French Margaret will bring disaster to England as certainly as Spartan Helen brought ruin to "the topless towers of Ilium."

The remainder of the trilogy portrays Margaret, though she is in neither play the solely dominating figure, as an evil influence in England's domestic affairs. In 2 Henry VI it is she and her lover Suffolk, along with the malevolent Winchester, who engineer the downfall of the Duke of Gloucester. In 3 Henry VI, her monstrous treatment of her archrival York is the climax of her role as England's scourge. Eventually, in Richard III, this figure of nemesis who for long has borne a "tiger's heart wrapped in a woman's hide," becomes inactive though not silent, an unheeded Cassandra warning the now-dominant House of York of its own impending doom.

Though not a great poetic drama, 1 Henry VI is by no means a failure as a play for theatrical performance. It exhibits a thoughtful design through which important themes are vigorously, if somewhat crudely, realized in the completed action. Nor is the affair of Margaret and Suffolk, as some critics would have it, only an afterthought. Strange as the final act and scene divisions in the Folio may be, the matter of these last episodes is not something inexpertly tacked onto what was originally conceived as an independent tragedy of Talbot simply because the author, or reviser, needed a way to patch together a trilogy. All that previously transpires is too carefully articulated with the concluding scenes for that. Act V is the logical conclusion to the events set in motion at the play's beginning, and at the same time an effective opening-out to the even greater disorder and calamities of 2 and 3 Henry VI. The close is nearly symmetrical with the opening, and far more ominous though more restrained and economical in its language. A nation that is leaderless because its king is an infant as the play begins, is still leaderless, or subject to dangerous misguidance, as the action ends because its now-grown king has succumbed to a destructive passion. And the unscrupulous new risers have now found an instrument for gaining the illicit power to which they aspire.

The bad news from Orleans that marked the downturn of England's fortunes in France is superseded by bad news from Angiers that will lead to misery on England's soil itself. All this the maker of 1 Henry VI was capable of rendering theatrically effective. By 1592 Shakespeare may not yet have been a supreme dramatic craftsman, but neither was he a mere botcher of other men's work, a snapper-up of other playwrights' unconsidered trifles.

## A NOTE ON THE SOURCES

For the plot of Henry VI, Part One Shakespeare drew upon at least four English chronicle histories. His chief sources were Edward Hall's The Union of the Two Noble and Illustre Families of Lancaster and York (1548) and the second edition of Raphael Holinshed's Chronicles of England, Scotland, and Ireland (1587). For a few details not found in Hall or Holinshed he also consulted the Chronicles of Robert Fabyan (1516) and Richard Grafton (1569), the latter substantially a reprint of Hall. Some of the best scenes in the play, however, such as the quarrel of the roses in the Temple garden, appear to have been invented by the playwright himself.

Although Geoffrey Bullough in his *Narrative and Dramatic Sources of Shakespeare* inclines to Hall as the principal source, in many scenes *1 Henry VI* appears to follow more closely Holinshed's account, which is largely derived from Hall without the latter's invented orations, amplification of detail, and attempts at an eloquence commensurate with the grandeur of his theme. But since Shakespeare improvised so freely upon his source materials, in most episodes of the play it is not possible to determine whether his immediate inspiration is Hall or Holinshed.

In view of this uncertainty, the reader interested in consulting the sources would be well advised to compare the two chronicles. He should definitely refer to Hall, however, for the account of Talbot's death in order to gain some idea of the elevated style of the source upon which Shakespeare obviously relied for this heroically pitched and moving episode.

## A NOTE ON THE TEXT

*Henry VI, Part One* is preserved only in the Folio of 1623, the basis of the present edition. Though acted infrequently after Shakespeare's lifetime, apparently the drama was originally well received. In the Epilogue to Shakespeare's *Henry V*, the Chorus asks the spectators to applaud this more recent work by reminding them of the company's earlier dramatizations of the reign of Henry VI:

> Which oft our stage hath shown; and for their sake,
> In your fair minds let this acceptance take.    (Epi.13–14)

It is even likely that in its earliest production *1 Henry VI* was the theatrical hit of the year. On March 3, 1592, the producer Philip Henslowe recorded in his diary that the first performance of a new (or refurbished) play called "harey the vj." had grossed £3.16s.8d., a sum indicating an exceptionally profitable opening. Over the next ten months this work was acted at least fourteen, perhaps fifteen, additional times. It may be that the patriotic theme appealed strongly to a London audience still exulting over the debacle of the Spanish Armada; for the heroic death of Lord Talbot in the fourth act, as Thomas Nashe wrote during the same year in *Pierce Penniless*, had been found deeply moving by "ten thousand spectators at least (at several times), who, in the tragedian that represents his person, imagine they behold him fresh bleeding."

The entry in Henslowe's diary and Nashe's allusion in his pamphlet to "Talbot (the terror of the French)" suggest that the play in question may have been *1 Henry VI*. Still, some doubt must remain whether this particular version was the same as that printed in the Folio, and whether Shakespeare had participated in its composition. With few exceptions, however, modern Shakespearean critics have assumed that *1 Henry VI* as we know it does come, along with the second and third parts of the trilogy, from Shakespeare's apprentice years as a playwright. In the absence of any positive evidence to the contrary, it thus seems reasonable to declare for late 1591 or early 1592 as the likeliest date of original composition for the play printed in the Folio and to presume that it is substantially, perhaps entirely, from the hand of Shakespeare.

The Folio is the only authority and affords a remarkably clear text, apart from a few baffling words and some apparently mangled lines of verse. In the present edition, therefore, the temptation to amend the original has been resisted as much as possible. Only two words to fill apparent lacunae have been supplied from consultation with the later Folios. These are "*Nero*" (I.iv.95) and "*sir*" (II.iv.132). Both of these are bracketed in the text and their sources given in the notes below. Without editorial comment, punctuation and spelling have been modernized (though "Dolphin" is retained in the dialogue), names prefixed to speeches and appearing in stage directions expanded and regularized, act and scene divisions translated where the Folio gives them in Latin, and obvious typographical errors corrected.

In the few instances where lines of verse are improperly divided in the Folio, they have been rearranged; all such corrections are noted in the table below. Occasionally when the printers of the Folio may seem to have divided a single line into two verses, it is quite clear that the line was too long for the space available, and was simply broken at a clause, rather than at the end of the column. Because the stage directions in the original are on the whole clear and amply descriptive, they have been reproduced with a minimum of emendations and additions; wherever changes have been made, they are enclosed in square brackets. In dividing acts and scenes the Folio is deficient: no scene divisions are given for Acts I and II; Act III is correctly divided into four scenes; Act IV is not only too long—since nothing but the final scene is left for Act V—but within it the scenes are also inaccurately divided. The act and scene divisions of the present edition are therefore those of the Globe text; wherever they differ from those of the Folio, they are enclosed in square brackets. The table that follows includes emendations and corrections of the Folio text. The altered reading appears first in boldface; the original follows, in roman. Where a Folio reading is retained, but seems extremely dubious, the word is given in roman, and commentary or suggested emendation is placed within square brackets.

**I.i.94 Reignier** Reynold    **96 crownèd** crown'd    **132 vanward** Vau ward
**I.ii.30 bred** breed    **99** fine [so F, but later editors, following mention in Holinshed's *Chronicles* of a pattern of "five" fleurs-de-lis on the sword, emend to *five*; conceivably the *n* in F is a mistakenly inverted *u* (i.e., for *v*)]    **103 s.d. la** de    **113 rites** rights    **132 enterèd** entred
**I.iii.29 Humphrey** Vmpheir
**I.iv.10** Went [so F, but Tyrwhitt's conjecture *Wont* is accepted by some modern editors]    **16–18** [two lines in F, but perhaps should be printed as three, divided after *watched*, *them*, and *longer*]    **29 ransomèd** ransom'd    **69 s.d. fall** falls    **95 Nero** [not in F; conjectured by Malone from the Second Folio reading "and *Nero* like will" for "and like thee"]    **101 la** de
**I.v.s.d. la** de
**I.vi.3 la** de    **6 garden** [so F, but *were* in line **7** suggests that the intended reading may have been *gardens*]    **29 la** de
**II.i.7 s.d. drums . . . march** [so F, but sounding drums seems a most peculiar way of beginning a surprise attack]    **29 all together** altogether    **77** [F reads *Exeunt* here, but the following stage direction renders the word superfluous]    **77 s.d. an** a
**II.ii.6 center** Centure    **20 Arc** Acre    **59 Whispers** [printed at end of line in F]

II.iii.11–12 [printed as one line in F]
II.iv.s.d. **Vernon, and another Lawyer** and others 117 whipped [so F, but Second Folio and all subsequent editions read *wiped*] 132 **sir** [not in F; supplied by Second Folio]
II.v.121 s.d. **Exeunt . . . Mortimer** Exit 129 will [so F, though modern editors, following Theobald, conjecture *ill* (i.e., turn my injuries to my benefit)]
III.i.52–53 [most modern editions reassign line 52 to Somerset and line 53 to Warwick] 164 all [so F, but the word is superfluous for both sense and meter] 200 **lose** loose
III.ii.50–51 [printed as three (metrically defective) lines in F, divided after *graybeard*, *death*, and *chair*] 59 s.d. **The English** They 103 s.d. **Exeunt . . . Attendants** Exit 123 **gleeks** glikes
IV.i.s.d. **Exeter . . . Paris** and Gouernor Exeter 173 s.d. **Flourish** [apparently misplaced in F in s.d. that follows line 181]

IV.ii **Before Bordeaux** [supplied by s.d. in F] 3 **calls** call 34 **due** dew 50 **moody-mad** moodie mad
IV.iii.16 s.d. **Lucy** 2 Mes. (throughout) 20 **waist** waste
IV.iv.16 regions [so F, but most modern editors amend to *legions*]
IV.vi.18 **encountered** encountred
IV.vii.96 s.d. **Exeunt** Exit
V.i. **Scene I** Scena secunda
V.ii. **Scene II** Scena Tertia
V.iii.s.d. **la** de 44 **comest** comst 57 **her** his 179 **modestly** modestie 184 s.d. **Kisses** Kisse 188, 195 **mayst** mayest 190 **wondrous** wonderous 192 **And** Mad
V.iv.s.d. **and others** Shepheard, Pucell [who obviously enter after line 1] 49 **Arc** Aire 58 **shortenèd** shortned 60 **discover** discouet 93 s.d. [placed in F after line 91]
V.v. **Scene V** Actus Quintus

# THE FIRST PART OF
# HENRY THE SIXTH

[Dramatis Personae

KING HENRY THE SIXTH
HUMPHREY *Duke of Gloucester, uncle to the king, and Protector*
JOHN *Duke of Bedford, uncle to the king, and Regent of France*
THOMAS BEAUFORT *Duke of Exeter, great-uncle to the king*
HENRY BEAUFORT *Bishop of Winchester, afterward Cardinal, great-uncle to the king*
JOHN BEAUFORT *Earl, afterward Duke, of Somerset*
RICHARD PLANTAGENET *afterward Duke, of York, son of Richard, late Earl of Cambridge*
EARL OF WARWICK
EARL OF SALISBURY
WILLIAM DE LA POLE *Earl of Suffolk*
LORD TALBOT *afterward Earl of Shrewsbury*
JOHN TALBOT *Lord Lisle, his son*
EDMUND MORTIMER *Earl of March*
SIR JOHN FALSTAFF°
SIR WILLIAM LUCY
SIR WILLIAM GLANSDALE
SIR THOMAS GARGRAVE
MAYOR OF LONDON
WOODVILLE *Lieutenant of the Tower*
VERNON *of the White Rose or York faction*

BASSET *of the Red Rose or Lancaster faction*
A LAWYER
MORTIMER'S JAILERS
A PAPAL LEGATE
CHARLES *Dauphin, afterward King, of France*
REIGNIER *Duke of Anjou, and titular King of Naples*
DUKE OF BURGUNDY
DUKE OF ALENÇON
BASTARD OF ORLEANS
GOVERNOR OF PARIS
MASTER GUNNER OF ORLEANS
HIS SON
GENERAL *of the French forces in Bordeaux*
A FRENCH SERGEANT
A PORTER
AN OLD SHEPHERD *father to Joan la Pucelle*
MARGARET *daughter to Reignier, afterward married to King Henry*
COUNTESS OF AUVERGNE
JOAN LA PUCELLE *commonly called Joan of Arc*
LORDS AMBASSADORS WARDERS OF THE TOWER HERALDS OFFICERS SOLDIERS MESSENGERS ATTENDANTS
FIENDS *appearing to la Pucelle*

*Scene:* England; France]

# ACT I

### Scene I. [*Westminster Abbey.*]

*Dead march.° Enter the funeral of King Henry the Fifth,
attended on by the Duke of* BEDFORD, *Regent of France;
the Duke of* GLOUCESTER, *Protector; the Duke of*
EXETER, WARWICK, *the Bishop of* WINCHESTER, *and
the Duke of* SOMERSET, [*with* ATTENDANTS].

BEDFORD

Hung be the heavens with black,° yield day to night!
Comets, importing change of times and states,°
Brandish your crystal° tresses in the sky,
And with them scourge the bad revolting stars
That have consented unto° Henry's death!
King Henry the Fifth, too famous to live long!      5
England ne'er lost a king of so much worth.

GLOUCESTER

England ne'er had a king until his time.
Virtue he had, deserving to command;
His brandished sword did blind men with his°
     beams;
His arms spread wider than a dragon's wings;      10
His sparkling eyes, replete with wrathful fire,
More dazzled and drove back his enemies
Than midday sun fierce bent against their faces.
What should I say? His deeds exceed all speech:
He ne'er lift° up his hand but conquerèd.      15

EXETER

We mourn in black; why mourn we not in blood?°
Henry is dead and never shall revive.
Upon a wooden° coffin we attend,
And death's dishonorable victory
We with our stately presence glorify,      20
Like captives bound to a triumphant car.°
What! shall we curse the planets of mishap°
That plotted thus our glory's overthrow?
Or shall we think the subtle-witted French
Conjurers and sorcerers that, afraid of him,      25
By magic verses have contrived his end?

WINCHESTER

He was a king blessed of the King of Kings.
Unto the French the dreadful Judgment Day
So dreadful will not be as was his sight.
The battles of the Lord of Hosts he fought;      30
The church's prayers made him so prosperous.

GLOUCESTER

The church! Where is it? Had not churchmen
     prayed,
His thread of life had not so soon decayed.
None do you like but an effeminate prince,
Whom, like a schoolboy, you may overawe.      35

WINCHESTER

Gloucester, whate'er we like, thou art protector°
And lookest° to command the prince and realm.
Thy wife is proud; she holdeth thee in awe
More than God or religious churchmen may.      40

GLOUCESTER

Name not religion, for thou lov'st the flesh,
And ne'er throughout the year to church thou go'st
Except it be to pray against thy foes.

BEDFORD

Cease, cease these jars° and rest your minds in peace;
Let's to the altar. Heralds, wait on us.      45
Instead of gold, we'll offer up our arms,°
Since arms avail not now that Henry's dead.
Posterity, await for wretched years,
When at their mothers' moistened eyes babes shall suck,
Our isle be made a nourish° of salt tears,      50
And none but women left to wail the dead.
Henry the Fifth, thy ghost I invocate:
Prosper this realm, keep it from civil broils,°
Combat with adverse planets in the heavens!
A far more glorious star thy soul will make      55
Than Julius Caesar° or bright—

*Enter a* MESSENGER.

MESSENGER

My honorable lords, health to you all!
Sad tidings bring I to you out of France,
Of loss, of slaughter, and discomfiture:
Guienne, Champagne, Rheims, Orleans,      60
Paris, Guysors, Poictiers, are all quite lost.

BEDFORD

What say'st thou, man, before dead Henry's corse?°
Speak softly, or the loss of those great towns
Will make him burst his lead° and rise from death.

GLOUCESTER

Is Paris lost? Is Rouen yielded up?      65
If Henry were recalled to life again,
These° news would cause him once more yield the
     ghost.

EXETER

How were they lost? What treachery was used?

MESSENGER

No treachery, but want of men and money.
Amongst the soldiers this is mutterèd,      70
That here you maintain several factions,°
And whilst a field should be dispatched and fought,
You are disputing of your generals:
One would have ling'ring wars with little cost;
Another would fly swift, but wanteth wings;      75
A third thinks, without expense at all,
By guileful fair words peace may be obtained.
Awake, awake, English nobility!
Let not sloth dim your honors new begot;°

---

*The decorative border on page 110 appeared on the first page of*
3 Henry VI *in* The Whole Contention betweene the Two
Famous Houses, Lancaster and Yorke, 1619.

**Dram. Pers. Falstaff** see note, Introduction, p. 105
**I.i.s.d. Dead march** a solemn piece of music for a funeral procession  **1 black** i.e., as a stage was draped in black for a
tragedy  **2 Comets . . . states** the appearance of comets
portending some misfortune  **3 crystal** bright  **5 consented
unto** conspired to bring about  **10 his** its  **16 lift** lifted  **17
in blood** by shedding blood, probably of the French in
order to avenge the king's death (see lines 25–27)  **19
wooden** unfeeling  **22 car** chariot  **23 of mishap** causing
misfortune

**37 protector** governor of the realm during the king's minority
**38 lookest** expect  **44 jars** quarrels  **46 arms** weapons  **50
nourish** nurse  **53 broils** disorders  **56 Julius Caesar**
whose soul, according to Ovid, *Metamorphoses*, XV.843–51,
became a star in the heavens after his assassination  **62 corse**
corpse  **64 lead** lining of the coffin  **67 These** since *news* was
originally plural  **71 factions** trisyllabic (the endings -*ion* and
-*ions* are often pronounced as two syllables in Shakespeare)
**79 new begot** recently obtained

Cropped are the flower-de-luces° in your arms;                80
Of England's coat° one half is cut away.

EXETER
Were our tears wanting° to this funeral,
These tidings would call forth her° flowing tides.

BEDFORD
Me they concern; regent° I am of France.
Give me my steelèd coat; I'll fight for France.               85
Away with these disgraceful wailing robes!
Wounds will I lend the French, instead of eyes,
To weep their intermissive° miseries.

*Enter to them another* MESSENGER.

SECOND MESSENGER
Lords, view these letters full of bad mischance.
France is revolted from the English quite,                    90
Except some petty towns of no import.°
The Dolphin° Charles is crownèd king in Rheims;
The Bastard of Orleans with him is joined;
Reignier, Duke of Anjou, doth take his part;
The Duke of Alençon flieth to his side.          *Exit.* 95

EXETER
The Dolphin crownèd king? All fly to him?
O, whither shall we fly from this reproach?°

GLOUCESTER
We will not fly, but to our enemies' throats.
Bedford, if thou be slack, I'll fight it out.

BEDFORD
Gloucester, why doubt'st thou of my forwardness?             100
An army have I mustered in my thoughts,
Wherewith already France is overrun.

*Enter another* MESSENGER.

THIRD MESSENGER
My gracious lords, to add to your laments,
Wherewith you now bedew° King Henry's hearse,
I must inform you of a dismal fight                          105
Betwixt the stout Lord Talbot and the French.

WINCHESTER
What? Wherein Talbot overcame, is't so?

THIRD MESSENGER
O no, wherein Lord Talbot was o'erthrown.
The circumstance I'll tell you more at large.°
The tenth of August last, this dreadful lord,               110
Retiring from the siege of Orleans,
Having full° scarce six thousand in his troop,
By three and twenty thousand of the French
Was round encompassèd and set upon.
No leisure had he to enrank° his men;                       115
He wanted pikes° to set before his archers;

Instead whereof, sharp stakes plucked out of hedges
They pitchèd in the ground confusedly,
To keep the horsemen off° from breaking in.
More than three hours the fight continuèd;                  120
Where valiant Talbot, above human thought,
Enacted wonders with his sword and lance.
Hundreds he sent to hell, and none durst stand him;
Here, there, and everywhere, enraged he slew.
The French exclaimed the devil was in arms;                 125
All the whole army stood agazed° on him.
His soldiers, spying his undaunted spirit,
"A Talbot! a Talbot!" cried out amain,°
And rushed into the bowels of the battle.
Here had the conquest fully been sealed up,                 130
If Sir John Falstaff had not played the coward.
He, being in the vanward,° placed behind
With purpose to relieve and follow them,
Cowardly fled, not having struck one stroke.
Hence grew the general wrack and massacre:                  135
Enclosèd were they with their enemies.
A base Walloon,° to win the Dolphin's grace,
Thrust Talbot with a spear into the back,
Whom all France, with their chief assembled strength,
Durst not presume to look once in the face.                 140

BEDFORD
Is Talbot slain then? I will slay myself
For living idly here in pomp and ease
Whilst such a worthy leader, wanting aid,
Unto his dastard foemen is betrayed.

THIRD MESSENGER
O no, he lives, but is took prisoner,                       145
And Lord Scales with him and Lord Hungerford;
Most of the rest slaughtered or took likewise.

BEDFORD
His ransom there is none but I shall pay.
I'll hale the Dolphin headlong from his throne;
His crown shall be the ransom of my friend;                 150
Four of their lords I'll change for one of ours.
Farewell, my masters, to my task will I;
Bonfires in France forthwith I am to make
To keep our great Saint George's feast° withal.°
Ten thousand soldiers with me I will take,                  155
Whose bloody deeds shall make all Europe quake.

THIRD MESSENGER
So you had need, for Orleans is besieged;
The English army is grown weak and faint;
The Earl of Salisbury craveth supply
And hardly keeps his men from mutiny                        160
Since they, so few, watch such a multitude.

EXETER
Remember, lords, your oaths to Henry sworn:
Either to quell° the Dolphin utterly
Or bring him in obedience to your yoke.

BEDFORD
I do remember it and here take my leave                     165
To go about my preparation.°         *Exit* BEDFORD.

80 **flower-de-luces** fleurs-de-lis, or lilies of France (heraldic
symbol of the French monarchs)   81 **coat** coat of arms (the
English royal family, as a sign of its pretensions to the throne
of France, included the fleur-de-lis in its coat of arms from
the fourteenth through the eighteenth centuries)   82 **wanting**
lacking   83 **her** England's   84 **regent** ruler in the king's
absence   88 **intermissive** coming at intervals   91 **import**
importance   92 **Dolphin** Dauphin (title of the heir to the
French throne)   97 **reproach** disgrace   104 **bedew** moisten
109 **The . . . large** I shall tell you the details at greater
length   112 **full** all told (?)   115 **enrank** set in ranks   116
**pikes** stakes with sharpened iron points, set in the ground to
impale the enemy's horses if the mounted troops charged
the archers

119 **off** apparently redundant, and inserted for metrical purposes   126 **agazed** astounded (probably a variant of *aghast*)
128 **amain** with all their might   132 **vanward** vanguard
137 **Walloon** inhabitant of the region between northeastern
France and the Netherlands   154 **Saint George's feast** April
23; **withal** with   163 **quell** destroy   166 **preparation** five
syllables

GLOUCESTER
I'll to the Tower° with all the haste I can
To view th' artillery and munition,
And then I will proclaim young Henry king.
                                         *Exit* GLOUCESTER.

EXETER
To Eltham will I, where the young king is,          170
Being ordained his special governor,
And for his safety there I'll best devise.          *Exit.*

WINCHESTER
Each hath his place and function to attend;
I am left out; for me nothing remains.
But long I will not be Jack out of office.°          175
The king from Eltham I intend to send
And sit at chiefest stern of public weal.°
                                   *Exit [with* ATTENDANTS*].*


[Scene II. *France. Before Orleans.*]

*Sound a flourish.° Enter Charles [the* DAUPHIN*],*
ALENÇON, *and* REIGNIER, *marching with drum and*
SOLDIERS.

DAUPHIN
Mars his° true moving, even as in the heavens,
So in the earth, to this day is not known.
Late did he shine upon the English side;
Now we are victors; upon us he smiles.
What towns of any moment° but we have?          5
At pleasure here we lie near Orleans;
Otherwhiles° the famished English, like pale ghosts,
Faintly besiege us one hour in a month.

ALENÇON
They want their porridge and their fat bull-beeves:°
Either they must be dieted° like mules          10
And have their provender° tied to their mouths,
Or piteous they will look, like drownèd mice.

REIGNIER
Let's raise the siege; why live we idly here?
Talbot is taken, whom we wont° to fear;
Remaineth none but mad-brained Salisbury,          15
And he may well in fretting spend his gall;°
Nor° men nor money hath he to make war.

DAUPHIN
Sound, sound alarum!° we will rush on them.
Now for the honor of the forlorn French!
Him I forgive my death that killeth me          20
When he sees me go back one foot or fly.          *Exeunt.*

*Here alarum; they are beaten back by the* ENGLISH *with
great loss. Enter Charles [the* DAUPHIN*],* ALENÇON,
*and* REIGNIER.

DAUPHIN
Who ever saw the like? What men have I?
Dogs! cowards! dastards! I would ne'er have fled,
But that they left me 'midst my enemies.

REIGNIER
Salisbury is a desperate homicide;          25
He fighteth as one weary of his life.
The other lords, like lions wanting food,
Do rush upon us as their hungry prey.°

ALENÇON
Froissart,° a countryman of ours, records
England all Olivers and Rowlands° bred          30
During the time Edward the Third did reign.
More truly now may this be verified,
For none but Samsons and Goliases°
It sendeth forth to skirmish. One to ten!
Lean raw-boned rascals!° who would e'er suppose          35
They had such courage and audacity?

DAUPHIN
Let's leave this town, for they are harebrained slaves,
And hunger will enforce° them to be more eager.°
Of old I know them; rather with their teeth
The walls they'll tear down than forsake the siege.          40

REIGNIER
I think, by some odd gimmors° or device
Their arms are set, like clocks, still to strike on;
Else ne'er could they hold out so as they do.
By my consent, we'll even let them alone.

ALENÇON   Be it so.          45

*Enter the* BASTARD *of Orleans.*

BASTARD
Where's the Prince Dolphin? I have news for him.

DAUPHIN
Bastard of Orleans, thrice welcome to us.

BASTARD
Methinks your looks are sad, your cheer appaled.°
Hath the late overthrow wrought this offense?
Be not dismayed, for succor is at hand:          50
A holy maid hither with me I bring,
Which by a vision sent to her from heaven
Ordainèd is to raise this tedious siege
And drive the English forth° the bounds of France.
The spirit of deep prophecy she hath,          55
Exceeding the nine sibyls° of old Rome:
What's past and what's to come she can descry.
Speak, shall I call her in? Believe my words,
For they are certain and unfallible.°

DAUPHIN
Go, call her in. [*Exit* BASTARD.] But first, to try her
   skill,          60
Reignier, stand thou as Dolphin in my place;
Question her proudly; let thy looks be stern:
By this means shall we sound° what skill she hath.

*Enter [the* BASTARD *of Orleans, with] Joan [la]*
PUCELLE.°

167 **Tower** Tower of London   175 **Jack . . . office** a person
deprived of official function   177 **And . . . weal** and maintain control of the government
**I.ii.s.d. flourish** fanfare of trumpets   1 **Mars his** Mars'   5
**moment** importance   7 **Otherwhiles** at times   9 **bull-beeves**
eating of bull beef was believed to give one courage   10 **dieted**
fed   11 **provender** food   14 **wont** were accustomed   16 **gall**
bitterness of spirit   17 **Nor** neither   18 **alarum** call to arms

28 **their hungry prey** prey for which they hunger   29
**Froissart** chronicler of fourteenth-century French, English,
and Spanish affairs   30 **Olivers and Rowlands** Oliver and
Rowland were the heroes of the French medieval epic *La
Chanson de Roland*   33 **Goliases** Goliaths   35 **rascals** lean,
inferior deer   38 **enforce** compel; **eager** (1) hungry (2) fierce
41 **gimmors** connecting parts for transmitting motion (variant
of *gimmals*)   48 **cheer appaled** countenance pale with fear
54 **forth** beyond   56 **nine sibyls** nine books of prophetic
utterances offered to King Tarquin of Rome by the sibyl at
Cumae   59 **unfallible** infallible   63 **sound** test; **s.d. la
Pucelle** the virgin

REIGNIER
Fair maid, is't thou wilt do these wondrous feats?

PUCELLE
Reignier, is't thou that thinkest to beguile me?          65
Where is the Dolphin? Come, come from behind;
I know thee well, though never seen before.
Be not amazed, there's nothing hid from me;
In private will I talk with thee apart.
Stand back, you lords, and give us leave awhile.          70

REIGNIER
She takes upon her bravely at first dash.°

PUCELLE
Dolphin, I am by birth a shepherd's daughter,
My wit° untrained in any kind of art.
Heaven and our Lady° gracious hath it pleased
To shine on my contemptible estate.          75
Lo, whilst I waited on my tender lambs,
And to sun's parching heat displayed my cheeks,
God's mother deignèd to appear to me
And in a vision full of majesty
Willed me to leave my base vocation°          80
And free my country from calamity.
Her aid she promised and assured success;
In complete glory she revealed herself;
And, whereas I was black and swart° before,
With those clear rays which she infused° on me          85
That beauty am I blessed with which you may see.
Ask me what question thou canst possible,
And I will answer unpremeditated;
My courage try by combat, if thou dar'st,
And thou shalt find that I exceed my sex.          90
Resolve on this,° thou shalt be fortunate
If thou receive me for thy warlike mate.°

DAUPHIN
Thou hast astonished me with thy high terms;°
Only this proof I'll of thy valor make,
In single combat thou shalt buckle° with me,          95
And if thou vanquishest, thy words are true;
Otherwise I renounce all confidence.

PUCELLE
I am prepared: here is my keen-edged sword,
Decked with fine flower-de-luces on each side,
The which at Touraine, in Saint Katherine's church-
     yard,          100
Out of a great deal of old iron I chose forth.

DAUPHIN
Then come, a° God's name, I fear no woman.

PUCELLE
And while I live, I'll ne'er fly from a man.

*Here they fight, and Joan la* PUCELLE *overcomes.*

DAUPHIN
Stay, stay thy hands! thou art an Amazon
And fightest with the sword of Deborah.°          105

PUCELLE
Christ's mother helps me, else I were too weak.

DAUPHIN
Whoe'er helps thee, 'tis thou that must help me:
Impatiently I burn with thy desire;
My heart and hands thou hast at once subdued.
Excellent Pucelle, if thy name be so,°          110
Let me thy servant° and not sovereign be;
'Tis the French Dolphin sueth to° thee thus.

PUCELLE
I must not yield to any rites of love,
For my profession's sacred from above;
When I have chasèd all thy foes from hence,          115
Then will I think upon a recompense.

DAUPHIN
Meantime look gracious on thy prostrate thrall.°

REIGNIER
My lord, methinks, is very long in talk.

ALENÇON
Doubtless he shrives this woman to her smock;°
Else ne'er could he so long protract his speech.          120

REIGNIER
Shall we disturb him, since he keeps no mean?°

ALENÇON
He may mean more than we poor men do know:
These women are shrewd tempters with their tongues.

REIGNIER
My lord, where are you? What devise you on?°
Shall we give o'er Orleans, or no?          125

PUCELLE
Why, no, I say, distrustful recreants!°
Fight till the last gasp; I'll be your guard.

DAUPHIN
What she says I'll confirm: we'll fight it out.

PUCELLE
Assigned am I to be the English scourge.
This night the siege assuredly I'll raise;          130
Expect Saint Martin's summer,° halcyon's days,°
Since I have enterèd into these wars.
Glory is like a circle in the water,
Which never ceaseth to enlarge itself
Till by broad spreading it disperse to nought.          135
With Henry's death the English circle ends;
Dispersèd are the glories it included.
Now am I like that proud insulting° ship
Which Caesar and his fortune bare° at once.

DAUPHIN
Was Mahomet inspirèd with a dove?          140
Thou with an eagle° art inspirèd then.
Helen,° the mother of great Constantine,
Nor yet Saint Philip's daughters,° were like thee.
Bright star of Venus, fall'n down on the earth,

---

71 **She . . . dash** She acts bravely at the first encounter
73 **wit** mind   74 **our Lady** the Virgin Mary   80 **vocation**
occupation   84 **swart** dark-complexioned   85 **infused** shed
91 **Resolve on this** be assured of this   92 **mate** (1) comrade
(2) sweetheart (?)   93 **high terms** mastery of the grand
rhetorical style   95 **buckle** (1) grapple (2) embrace as lovers
102 **a** in   105 **Deborah** prophetess who delivered Israel from
oppression by the Canaanites (Judges 4:5)

110 **if . . . so** if you really are a virgin   111 **servant** lover
112 **sueth to** woos   117 **thrall** slave   119 **shrives . . . smock**
(1) questions her closely (2) hears her confession to the most
minute detail   121 **keeps no mean** does not control himself
124 **devise you on** are you deliberating   126 **recreants**
cowards   131 **Saint Martin's summer** Indian summer
(named after the feast of Saint Martin of Tours, November
11); **halcyon's days** peaceful times (the ancients believed
that the bird called the halcyon nested on the sea and that
the waters remained calm during its breeding season)   138
**insulting** insolently triumphant   139 **bare** bore   141 **eagle**
like Saint John the Evangelist, with the highest source of
inspiration   142 **Helen** Saint Helena, inspired by a vision
to find the cross of Jesus   143 **Saint Philip's daughters**
who had the gift of prophecy (see Acts 21:9)

How may I reverently worship thee enough? 145
**ALENÇON**
Leave off delays, and let us raise the siege.
**REIGNIER**
Woman, do what thou canst to save our honors;
Drive them from Orleans and be immortalized.
**DAUPHIN**
Presently° we'll try. Come, let's away about it;
No prophet will I trust, if she prove false. *Exeunt.* 150


[Scene III. *London. Before the Tower.*]

*Enter* GLOUCESTER, *with his* SERVINGMEN [*in blue coats*°].

**GLOUCESTER**
I am come to survey° the Tower this day:
Since Henry's death, I fear, there is conveyance.°
Where be these warders,° that they wait not here?
Open the gates; 'tis Gloucester° that calls.
**FIRST WARDER** [*Within.*]
Who's there that knocks so imperiously? 5
**GLOUCESTER'S FIRST** [SERVING]MAN
It is the noble Duke of Gloucester.
**SECOND WARDER** [*Within.*]
Whoe'er he be, you may not be let in.
**GLOUCESTER'S FIRST** [SERVING]MAN
Villains, answer you so the Lord Protector?
**FIRST WARDER** [*Within.*]
The Lord protect him! so we answer him;
We do no otherwise than we are willed. 10
**GLOUCESTER**
Who willèd you? Or whose will stands but mine?
There's none protector of the realm but I.
Break up the gates, I'll be your warrantize;°
Shall I be flouted thus by dunghill grooms?°

*Gloucester's* MEN *rush at the Tower gates, and* WOODVILLE *the lieutenant speaks within.*

**WOODVILLE**
What noise is this? What traitors have we here? 15
**GLOUCESTER**
Lieutenant, is it you whose voice I hear?
Open the gates; here's Gloucester that would enter.
**WOODVILLE**
Have patience, noble duke, I may not open;
The Cardinal of Winchester forbids:
From him I have express commandment° 20
That thou nor none of thine shall be let in.
**GLOUCESTER**
Faint-hearted Woodville, prizest him 'fore me?°
Arrogant Winchester, that haughty prelate,
Whom Henry, our late sovereign, ne'er could brook?°
Thou art no friend to God or to the king; 25
Open the gates, or I'll shut thee out shortly.

**SERVINGMEN**
Open the gates unto the Lord Protector,
Or we'll burst them open, if that° you come not
quickly.

*Enter to the* PROTECTOR *at the Tower gates* WINCHESTER *and his* MEN *in tawny coats.*°

**WINCHESTER**
How now, ambitious Humphrey, what means this?
**GLOUCESTER**
Peeled° priest, dost thou command me to be shut out? 30
**WINCHESTER**
I do, thou most usurping proditor,°
And not protector, of the king or realm.
**GLOUCESTER**
Stand back, thou manifest conspirator,
Thou that contriv'dst to murder our dead lord,
Thou that giv'st whores indulgences° to sin; 35
I'll canvas thee in thy broad cardinal's hat,°
If thou proceed in this thy insolence.
**WINCHESTER**
Nay, stand thou back, I will not budge a foot;
This be Damascus,° be thou cursèd Cain,
To slay thy brother° Abel, if thou wilt. 40
**GLOUCESTER**
I will not slay thee, but I'll drive thee back;
Thy scarlet robes as a child's bearing cloth°
I'll use to carry thee out of this place.
**WINCHESTER**
Do what thou dar'st, I beard° thee to thy face.
**GLOUCESTER**
What! am I dared and bearded to my face? 45
Draw, men, for all this privilegèd place,°
Blue coats to tawny coats. Priest, beware your beard;
I mean to tug it, and to cuff you soundly.
Under my feet I stamp thy cardinal's hat;
In spite of pope or dignities of church,° 50
Here by the cheeks I'll drag thee up and down.
**WINCHESTER**
Gloucester, thou wilt answer this before the pope.
**GLOUCESTER**
Winchester goose,° I cry, a rope!° a rope!
Now beat them hence; why do you let them stay?
Thee I'll chase hence, thou wolf in sheep's array. 55
Out, tawny coats! out, scarlet° hypocrite!

*Here Gloucester's* MEN *beat out the Cardinal's* MEN, *and enter in the hurly-burly*° *the* MAYOR *of London and his* OFFICERS.

**28 if that** if; **s.d. tawny coats** servants of churchmen traditionally wore tawny, or brownish-yellow, coats **30 Peeled** tonsured, bald **31 proditor** traitor **35 indulgences** the brothels near the theaters on the south bank of the Thames were within the jurisdiction of the Bishops of Winchester **36 canvas . . . hat** toss you in your wide-brimmed ecclesiastical hat as if it were a blanket **39 Damascus** supposed to have been built in the place where Cain killed Abel **40 brother** Winchester was half-brother to Gloucester's father, King Henry IV **42 bearing cloth** christening robe **44 beard** defy **46 for . . . place** even though drawing of weapons is forbidden under pain of death in royal residences **50 dignities of church** your high ecclesiastical rank **53 Winchester goose** (1) venereal infection (2) prostitute (see note to line 35); **rope** hangman's cord **56 scarlet** a derisive allusion to the red robes of the cardinal; **s.d. hurly-burly** tumult

**149 Presently** immediately
**I.iii.s.d. blue coats** blue clothing was customary for servants **1 survey** inspect **2 conveyance** underhand dealing **3 warders** guards **4 Gloucester** trisyllabic here and often, for metrical purposes, elsewhere in the play **13 warrantize** pledge of security **14 dunghill grooms** vile servingmen **20 commandment** trisyllabic; spelled *commandement* in the Folio **22 prizest . . . me** rank him above me **24 brook** endure

MAYOR
Fie, lords! that you, being supreme magistrates,°
Thus contumeliously° should break the peace!

GLOUCESTER
Peace, mayor! thou know'st little of my wrongs:
Here's Beaufort, that regards nor God nor king,            60
Hath here distrained° the Tower to his use.

WINCHESTER
Here's Gloucester, a foe to citizens,
One that still motions° war and never peace,
O'ercharging your free purses with large fines,°
That seeks to overthrow religion                           65
Because he is protector of the realm,
And would have armor here out of the Tower
To crown himself king and suppress° the prince.

GLOUCESTER
I will not answer thee with words, but blows.

*Here they skirmish again.*

MAYOR
Nought rests for me in this tumultuous strife             70
But to make open proclamation.
Come, officer, as loud as e'er thou canst,
Cry.
[OFFICER]   All manner of men assembled here in arms
this day against God's peace and the king's, we charge   75
and command you, in his highness' name, to repair°
to your several° dwelling places; and not to wear,
handle, or use any sword, weapon, or dagger henceforward, upon pain° of death.

GLOUCESTER
Cardinal, I'll be no breaker of the law,                  80
But we shall meet, and break our minds at large.°

WINCHESTER
Gloucester, we'll meet to thy cost, be sure:
Thy heart-blood I will have for this day's work.

MAYOR
I'll call for clubs,° if you will not away.
This cardinal's more haughty than the devil.              85

GLOUCESTER
Mayor, farewell; thou dost but what thou mayst.

WINCHESTER
Abominable Gloucester, guard thy head,
For I intend to have it ere long.            *Exeunt.*

MAYOR
See the coast cleared, and then we will depart.
Good God, these nobles should such stomachs bear!°        90
I myself fight not once in forty year.        *Exeunt.*

57 **magistrates** administrators of the kingdom 58 **con-
tumeliously** insolently 61 **distrained** seized 63 **still motions**
always proposes 64 **O'ercharging . . . fines** overburden-
ing you with excessive special taxes 68 **suppress** depose
76 **repair** return 77 **several** own 79 **pain** penalty 81 **break
. . . large** reveal our thoughts fully 84 **call for clubs**
summon the apprentices of the city to come with clubs and
assist the officers in putting down the riot 90 **these . . . bear**
that these noblemen should have such quarrelsome tempers

[Scene IV. *Orleans.*]

*Enter the* MASTER GUNNER *of Orleans and his* BOY.

MASTER GUNNER
Sirrah,° thou know'st how Orleans is besieged,
And how the English have the suburbs won.

BOY
Father, I know, and oft have shot at them,
Howe'er, unfortunate, I missed my aim.

MASTER GUNNER
But now thou shalt not. Be thou ruled by me:               5
Chief master gunner am I of this town;
Something I must do to procure me grace.°
The prince's espials° have informèd me
How the English, in the suburbs close intrenched,
Went through a secret grate of iron bars                  10
In yonder tower to overpeer° the city
And thence discover how with most advantage
They may vex us with shot or with assault.
To intercept° this inconvenience,
A piece of ordnance° 'gainst it I have placed,            15
And even these three days have I watched
If I could see them. Now do thou watch,
For I can stay no longer.
If thou spy'st any, run and bring me word,
And thou shalt find me at the governor's.     *Exit.* 20

BOY
Father, I warrant you, take you no care;
I'll never trouble you, if I may spy them.    *Exit.*

*Enter* SALISBURY *and* TALBOT *on the turrets, with* [*Sir
William* GLANSDALE, *Sir Thomas* GARGRAVE, *and*]
*others.*

SALISBURY
Talbot, my life, my joy, again returned!
How wert thou handled, being prisoner?
Or by what means gots thou° to be released?               25
Discourse,° I prithee,° on this turret's top.

TALBOT
The Earl of Bedford had a prisoner
Called the brave Lord Ponton de Santrailles;
For him was I exchanged and ransomèd.
But with a baser° man of arms by far                      30
Once in contempt they would have bartered me;
Which I disdaining scorned and craved death
Rather than I would be so pilled-esteemed.°
In fine,° redeemed I was as I desired.
But O! the treacherous Falstaff wounds my heart,          35
Whom with my bare fists I would execute,
If I now had him brought into my power.

SALISBURY
Yet tell'st thou not how thou wert entertained.

TALBOT
With scoffs and scorns and contumelious taunts,
In open marketplace produced they me,                     40
To be a public spectacle to all:
Here, said they, is the terror of the French,

I.iv.1 **Sirrah** a term used in addressing children or inferiors
7 **grace** favor 8 **espials** spies 11 **overpeer** look down upon
14 **intercept** stop 15 **piece of ordnance** cannon 25 **gots
thou** did you manage 26 **Discourse** relate; **prithee**
pray thee 30 **baser** less wellborn 33 **pilled-esteemed**
poorly valued 34 **In fine** finally

The scarecrow that affrights° our children so.
Then broke I from the officers that led me,
And with my nails digged stones out of the ground    45
To hurl at the beholders of my shame.
My grisly° countenance made others fly;
None durst come near for fear of sudden death.
In iron walls they deemed me not secure;
So great fear of my name 'mongst them were spread    50
That they supposed I could rend bars of steel
And spurn in pieces posts of adamant.°
Wherefore a guard of chosen shot° I had
That walked about me every minute while,°
And if I did but stir out of my bed,    55
Ready they were to shoot me to the heart.

*Enter the* BOY *with a linstock.°*

SALISBURY
I grieve to hear what torments you endured,
But we will be revenged sufficiently.
Now it is suppertime in Orleans;
Here, through this grate, I count each one    60
And view the Frenchmen how they fortify;
Let us look in; the sight will much delight thee.
Sir Thomas Gargrave, and Sir William Glansdale,
Let me have your express° opinions
Where is best place to make our batt'ry° next.    65
GARGRAVE
I think at the north gate, for there stands lords.
GLANSDALE
And I, here, at the bulwark° of the bridge.
TALBOT
For aught I see, this city must be famished,
Or with light skirmishes enfeeblèd.°

*Here they shoot, and* SALISBURY [*and* GARGRAVE] *fall down.*

SALISBURY
O Lord, have mercy on us, wretched sinners!    70
GARGRAVE
O Lord, have mercy on me, woeful man!
TALBOT
What chance is this that suddenly hath crossed° us?
Speak, Salisbury; at least, if thou canst speak,
How far'st thou, mirror of° all martial men?
One of thy eyes and thy cheek's side struck off!    75
Accursèd tower! accursèd fatal hand°
That hath contrived this woeful tragedy!
In thirteen battles Salisbury o'ercame;
Henry the Fifth he first trained to the wars;
Whilst any trump° did sound, or drum struck up,    80
His sword did ne'er leave striking in the field.
Yet liv'st thou, Salisbury? Though thy speech doth fail,
One eye thou hast, to look to heaven for grace.
The sun with one eye vieweth all the world.
Heaven, be thou gracious to none alive    85
If Salisbury wants° mercy at thy hands!

Bear hence his body; I will help to bury it.
Sir Thomas Gargrave, hast thou any life?
Speak unto Talbot; nay, look up to him.
Salisbury, cheer thy spirit with this comfort:    90
Thou shalt not die whiles°—
He beckons with his hand and smiles on me,
As who° should say, "When I am dead and gone,
Remember to avenge me on the French."
Plantagenet,° I will; and like thee, [Nero,]    95
Play on the lute, beholding the towns burn.
Wretched shall France be only in° my name.

*Here an alarum, and it thunders and lightens.*

What stir° is this? What tumult's in the heavens?
Whence cometh this alarum, and the noise?

*Enter a* MESSENGER.

MESSENGER
My lord, my lord, the French have gathered head:°    100
The Dolphin, with one Joan la Pucelle joined,
A holy prophetess new risen up,
Is come with a great power to raise the siege.

*Here* SALISBURY *lifteth himself up and groans.*

TALBOT
Hear, hear how dying Salisbury doth groan!
It irks his heart he cannot be revenged.    105
Frenchmen, I'll be a Salisbury to you.
Pucelle or pussel,° Dolphin or dogfish,
Your hearts I'll stamp out with my horse's heels,
And make a quagmire of your mingled brains.
Convey me° Salisbury into his tent,    110
And then we'll try what these dastard Frenchmen dare.
                              *Alarum. Exeunt.*

[*Scene V. Orleans.*]

*Here an alarum again, and* TALBOT *pursueth the* DAU-
PHIN, *and driveth him. Then enter Joan la* PUCELLE,
*driving* ENGLISHMEN *before her* [*and exit after them*].
*Then* [*re-*]*enter* TALBOT.

TALBOT
Where is my strength, my valor, and my force?
Our English troops retire, I cannot stay them;
A woman clad in armor chaseth them.

*Enter* [*la*] PUCELLE.

Here, here she comes. I'll have a bout with thee;
Devil or devil's dam,° I'll conjure thee:°    5
Blood will I draw on thee,° thou art a witch,
And straightway give thy soul to him thou serv'st.
PUCELLE
Come, come, 'tis only° I that must disgrace thee.

---

**91 whiles** until   **93 As who** as if he   **95 Plantagenet** though Salisbury's name was Thomas Montacute, he was related to the royal family, which adopted the name Plantagenet in the fifteenth century   **97 only in** merely at the sound of (?)   **98 stir** commotion   **100 gathered head** raised forces   **107 pussel** lewd woman, strumpet   **110 Convey me** carry   **I.v.5 dam** (1) mistress (2) mother; **conjure thee** i.e., back to hell whence you came   **6 Blood . . . thee** whoever could draw blood from a witch was free of her power   **8 only** with no other assistance

43 affrights frightens   47 grisly grim   52 adamant in-destructible material   53 chosen shot picked marksmen   54 every minute while incessantly   56 s.d. linstock staff to hold the match for lighting a cannon   64 express precise   65 make our batt'ry direct our fire   67 bulwark fortification   69 enfeeblèd weakened   72 crossed thwarted   74 mirror of model for   76 fatal hand hand of fate   80 trump trumpet   86 wants lacks

*Here they fight.*

TALBOT
Heavens, can you suffer hell so to prevail?
My breast I'll burst with straining of my courage     10
And from my shoulders crack my arms asunder,
But I will chastise this high-minded° strumpet.

*They fight again.*

PUCELLE
Talbot, farewell; thy hour is not yet come;
I must go victual° Orleans forthwith.°

*A short alarum. Then enter the town with* SOLDIERS.

O'ertake me if thou canst; I scorn thy strength.     15
Go, go, cheer up thy hungry-starvèd men;
Help Salisbury to make his testament;
This day is ours, as many more shall be.     *Exit.*

TALBOT
My thoughts are whirlèd like a potter's wheel;
I know not where I am, nor what I do.     20
A witch, by fear, not force, like Hannibal,°
Drives back our troops and conquers as she lists;°
So bees with smoke and doves with noisome stench
Are from their hives and houses driven away.
They called us for our fierceness English dogs;     25
Now, like to whelps,° we crying run away.

*A short alarum.*

Hark, countrymen! either renew the fight,
Or tear the lions° out of England's coat;
Renounce your soil,° give sheep in lions' stead:
Sheep run not half so treacherous° from the wolf,     30
Or horse or oxen from the leopard,
As you fly from your oft-subduèd slaves.

*Alarum. Here another skirmish.*

It will not be. Retire into your trenches.
You all consented unto Salisbury's death,
For none would strike a stroke in his revenge.     35
Pucelle is entered into Orleans
In spite of us or aught that we could do.
O, would I were to die with Salisbury!
The shame hereof will make me hide my head.
*Exit* TALBOT. *Alarum. Retreat.°*


[Scene VI. *Orleans.*]

*Flourish. Enter on the walls* [la] PUCELLE, DAUPHIN,
REIGNIER, ALENÇON, *and* SOLDIERS.

PUCELLE
Advance° our waving colors on the walls;
Rescued is Orleans from the English.
Thus Joan la Pucelle hath performed her word.

DAUPHIN
Divinest creature, Astraea's daughter,°
How shall I honor thee for this success?     5
Thy promises are like Adonis'° garden
That one day bloomed and fruitful were the next.
France, triumph in thy glorious prophetess!
Recovered is the town of Orleans;
More blessèd hap° did ne'er befall our state.     10

REIGNIER
Why ring not out the bells aloud throughout the
town?
Dolphin, command the citizens make bonfires
And feast and banquet in the open streets
To celebrate the joy that God hath given us.

ALENÇON
All France will be replete with mirth and joy     15
When they shall hear how we have played the men.°

DAUPHIN
'Tis Joan, not we, by whom the day is won;
For which I will divide my crown with her,
And all the priests and friars in my realm
Shall in procession sing her endless praise.     20
A statelier pyramis° to her I'll rear
Than Rhodope's° or Memphis' ever was.
In memory of her when she is dead,
Her ashes, in an urn more precious
Than the rich-jeweled coffer of Darius,°     25
Transported shall be at high festivals
Before the kings and queens of France.
No longer on Saint Denis° will we cry,
But Joan la Pucelle shall be France's saint.
Come in, and let us banquet royally,     30
After this golden day of victory.     *Flourish. Exeunt.*


# ACT II

Scene I. [*Orleans.*]

*Enter a* [French] SERGEANT *of a band, with two* SEN-
TINELS.

SERGEANT
Sirs, take your places and be vigilant;
If any noise or soldier you perceive
Near to the walls, by some apparent sign
Let us have knowledge at the court of guard.°

SENTINEL
Sergeant, you shall. [*Exit* SERGEANT.] Thus are poor     5
servitors,°
When others sleep upon their quiet beds,
Constrained to watch in darkness, rain, and cold.

---

**12 high-minded** arrogant   **14 victual** bring provisions into;
**forthwith** immediately   **21 Hannibal** who terrified the
Romans by driving among them oxen with lighted torches
fixed to their horns   **22 lists** pleases   **26 whelps** puppies
**28 lions** heraldic royal symbol of England   **29 soil** possibly a
misprint for *style*; the line appears to mean "replace the lions
in your royal coat of arms with sheep"   **30 treacherous**
fearfully   **39 s.d. Retreat** signal for withdrawal from battle
**I.vi.1 Advance** raise

**4 Astraea's daughter** daughter of the goddess of justice
(cf. "Deborah," I.ii.105)   **6 Adonis'** of the youth loved by
Venus (for a description of his garden, see Edmund Spenser,
*Faerie Queene,* III.vi.29–50)   **10 hap** good fortune   **16 played
the men** proved our courage   **21 pyramis** pyramid   **22
Rhodope's** according to legend, the famous Greek courtesan
Rhodopis built the third pyramid   **25 coffer of Darius** the
Persian monarch's jewel chest (said to have been used by
Alexander the Great to hold a copy of Homer)   **28 Saint
Denis** patron saint of France
**II.i.4 court of guard** headquarters of the guard   **5 servitors**
soldiers

*Enter* TALBOT, BEDFORD, *and* BURGUNDY, [*and*
FORCES,] *with scaling ladders, their drums beating a dead
march.*

TALBOT
Lord Regent, and redoubted° Burgundy,
By whose approach° the regions of Artois,
Wallon, and Picardy° are friends to us,
This happy night the Frenchmen are secure,°      10
Having all day caroused and banqueted;
Embrace we° then this opportunity
As fitting best to quittance° their deceit
Contrived by art° and baleful° sorcery.      15

BEDFORD
Coward of France! how much he wrongs his fame,
Despairing of his own arm's fortitude,
To join with witches and the help of hell.

BURGUNDY
Traitors have never other company.
But what's that Pucelle whom they term so pure?      20

TALBOT
A maid, they say.

BEDFORD          A maid? And be so martial?

BURGUNDY
Pray God she prove not masculine° ere long,
If underneath the standard of the French
She carry armor as she hath begun.

TALBOT
Well, let them practice° and converse with spirits.      25
God is our fortress, in whose conquering name
Let us resolve to scale their flinty° bulwarks.

BEDFORD
Ascend, brave Talbot; we will follow thee.

TALBOT
Not all together: better far, I guess,
That we do make our entrance several° ways;      30
That, if it chance the one of us do fail,
The other yet may rise against their force.

BEDFORD
Agreed; I'll to yond° corner.

BURGUNDY          And I to this.

TALBOT
And here will Talbot mount, or make his grave.
Now, Salisbury, for thee, and for the right      35
Of English Henry, shall this night appear
How much in duty I am bound to both.

SENTINEL
Arm! arm! the enemy doth make assault!

[*The* ENGLISH, *scaling the walls,*] *cry,* "St. George! a
Talbot!" [*and enter the town*].

*The* FRENCH *leap o'er the walls in their shirts. Enter
several ways* BASTARD, ALENÇON, REIGNIER, *half
ready,° and half unready.*

ALENÇON
How now, my lords! what, all unready so?

BASTARD
Unready? Ay, and glad we 'scaped so well.      40

REIGNIER
'Twas time, I trow,° to wake and leave our beds,
Hearing alarums at our chamber doors.

ALENÇON
Of all exploits since first I followed arms,
Ne'er heard I of a warlike enterprise
More venturous or desperate than this.      45

BASTARD
I think this Talbot be a fiend of hell.

REIGNIER
If not of hell, the heavens, sure, favor him.

ALENÇON
Here cometh Charles; I marvel how he sped.°

*Enter Charles* [*the* DAUPHIN] *and Joan* [*la* PUCELLE].

BASTARD
Tut, holy Joan was his defensive guard.

DAUPHIN
Is this thy cunning,° thou deceitful dame?      50
Didst thou at first, to flatter us withal,°
Make us partakers of a little gain,
That now our loss might be ten times so much?

PUCELLE
Wherefore is Charles impatient with his friend?
At all times will you have my power alike?      55
Sleeping or waking must I still° prevail,
Or will you blame and lay the fault on me?
Improvident° soldiers! had your watch been good,
This sudden mischief never could have fall'n.

DAUPHIN
Duke of Alençon, this was your default,°      60
That, being captain of the watch tonight,
Did look no better to that weighty charge.°

ALENÇON
Had all your quarters been as safely kept
As that whereof I had the government,°
We had not been thus shamefully surprised.      65

BASTARD
Mine was secure.

REIGNIER          And so was mine, my lord.

DAUPHIN
And, for myself, most part of all this night,
Within her quarter° and mine own precinct°
I was employed in passing to and fro,
About relieving of the sentinels.      70
Then how or which way should they first break in?

PUCELLE
Question, my lords, no further of the case,
How or which way; 'tis sure they found some place
But weakly guarded, where the breach was made.
And now there rests no other shift° but this,      75

**8 redoubted** distinguished  **9 approach** presence  **9–10
Artios . . . Picardy** provinces in northeastern France, parts
of which are now in Belgium  **11 secure** careless  **13
Embrace we** let us seize  **14 quittance** repay  **15 art** (black)
magic; **baleful** harmful  **22 prove not masculine** (1) does
not turn out to be a man (?) (2) does not become pregnant
with a male child  **25 practice** conjure  **27 flinty** rugged
**30 several** by separate  **33 yond** yonder  **38 s.d. ready**
dressed

**41 trow** think  **48 marvel . . . sped** wonder how he fared
**50 cunning** craftiness  **51 to . . . withal** in order to deceive
us  **56 still** always  **58 Improvident** unwary  **60 default**
fault  **62 weighty charge** important responsibility  **64
government** command  **68 quarter** (1) assigned area for
defense (2) chamber; **precinct** area of command  **75 shift**
expedient, stratagem

To gather our soldiers, scattered and dispersed,
And lay new platforms to endamage them.°

*Alarum. Enter an [English] SOLDIER, crying, "A Talbot!
a Talbot!" They fly, leaving their clothes behind.*

SOLDIER
I'll be so bold to take what they have left.
The cry of Talbot serves me for a sword,
For I have loaden me° with many spoils,            80
Using no other weapon but his name.        *Exit.*

[Scene II. *Orleans. Within the town.*]

*Enter TALBOT, BEDFORD, BURGUNDY, [a CAPTAIN,
and others].*

BEDFORD
The day begins to break, and night is fled,
Whose pitchy° mantle overveiled the earth.
Here sound retreat, and cease our hot pursuit. *Retreat.*

TALBOT
Bring forth the body of old Salisbury,
And here advance it° in the marketplace,            5
The middle center of this cursèd town.
Now have I paid my vow unto his soul;
For every drop of blood was drawn from him
There hath at least five Frenchmen died tonight.
And that hereafter ages may behold            10
What ruin happened in revenge of him,
Within their chiefest temple° I'll erect
A tomb, wherein his corpse shall be interred;
Upon the which, that everyone may read,
Shall be engraved the sack° of Orleans,            15
The treacherous manner of his mournful death,
And what a terror he had been to France.
But, lords, in all our bloody massacre,
I muse° we met not with the Dolphin's grace,°
His new-come champion, virtuous Joan of Arc,            20
Nor any of his false confederates.°

BEDFORD
'Tis thought, Lord Talbot, when the fight began,
Roused on the sudden from their drowsy beds,
They did amongst the troops of armèd men
Leap o'er the walls for refuge in the field.            25

BURGUNDY
Myself, as far as I could well discern
For° smoke and dusky vapors of the night,
Am sure I scared the Dolphin and his trull,°
When arm in arm they both came swiftly running,
Like to a pair of loving turtledoves            30
That could not live asunder day or night.
After that things are set in order here,
We'll follow them with all the power we have.

*Enter a MESSENGER.*

MESSENGER
All hail, my lords! Which of this princely train°
Call ye the warlike Talbot, for his acts            35
So much applauded through the realm of France?

TALBOT
Here is the° Talbot; who would speak with him?

MESSENGER
The virtuous lady, Countess of Auvergne,
With modesty admiring thy renown,
By me entreats, great lord, thou wouldst vouchsafe°            40
To visit her poor castle where she lies,°
That she may boast she hath beheld the man
Whose glory fills the world with loud report.

BURGUNDY
Is it even so? Nay, then, I see our wars
Will turn unto a peaceful comic sport,            45
When ladies crave to be encountered° with.
You may not, my lord, despise her gentle suit.°

TALBOT
Ne'er trust me then; for when a world of men
Could not prevail with all their oratory,
Yet hath a woman's kindness overruled;°            50
And therefore tell her I return great thanks
And in submission° will attend on her.
Will not your honors bear me company?

BEDFORD
No, truly, 'tis more than manners will,°
And I have heard it said, unbidden° guests            55
Are often welcomest when they are gone.

TALBOT
Well then, alone, since there's no remedy,
I mean to prove this lady's courtesy.°
Come hither, captain. (*Whispers.*) You perceive my
    mind?°

CAPTAIN
I do, my lord, and mean accordingly.        *Exeunt.* 60

[Scene III. *Auvergne. The countess' castle.*]

*Enter COUNTESS [and her PORTER].*

COUNTESS
Porter, remember what I gave in charge,°
And when you have done so, bring the keys to me.

PORTER
Madam, I will.        *Exit.*

COUNTESS
The plot is laid; if all things fall out right,
I shall as famous be by this exploit            5
As Scythian Tomyris° by Cyrus' death.
Great is the rumor° of this dreadful knight,
And his achievements of no less acount;

---

77 **lay . . . them** make new plans to harm the English  80
**loaden me** burdened myself
II.ii.2 **pitchy** dark  5 **advance it** raise it up  12 **chiefest
temple** cathedral  15 **sack** plundering  19 **muse** wonder why;
**the Dolphin's grace** his grace, the Dauphin  21 **confederates** companions  27 **For** because of  28 **trull** concubine, harlot

34 **princely train** noble company  37 **the** used with the
surname to designate the head of a family or clan  40
**vouchsafe** condescend  41 **lies** resides  46 **encountered** met
(for an amatory interview)  47 **gentle suit** mannerly request
50 **overruled** prevailed  52 **in submission** deferentially  54
**will** require  55 **unbidden** uninvited  58 **prove . . . courtesy**
try out this lady's hospitality  59 **perceive my mind**
understand my plan
II.iii.1 **gave in charge** instructed you to do  6 **Tomyris**
queen of a fierce Central Asian people who slew Cyrus the
Great in battle  7 **rumor** reputation

Fain° would mine eyes be witness with mine ears,
To give their censure° of these rare reports.          10

*Enter* MESSENGER *and* TALBOT.

MESSENGER
Madam,
According as your ladyship desired,
By message craved,° so is Lord Talbot come.
COUNTESS
And he is welcome. What! is this the man?
MESSENGER
Madam, it is.
COUNTESS    Is this the scourge of France?          15
Is this the Talbot, so much feared abroad
That with his name the mothers still° their babes?
I see report is fabulous° and false.
I thought I should have seen some Hercules,
A second Hector, for his grim aspect°          20
And large proportion of his strong-knit° limbs.
Alas, this is a child, a silly° dwarf!
It cannot be this weak and writhled° shrimp
Should strike such terror to his enemies.
TALBOT
Madam, I have been bold to trouble you,          25
But since your ladyship is not at leisure,
I'll sort° some other time to visit you.
COUNTESS
What means he now? Go ask him whither he goes.
MESSENGER
Stay, my Lord Talbot, for my lady craves
To know the cause of your abrupt departure.          30
TALBOT
Marry,° for that° she's in a wrong belief,
I go to certify° her Talbot's here.

*Enter* PORTER *with keys.*

COUNTESS
If thou be he, then art thou prisoner.
TALBOT
Prisoner! to whom?
COUNTESS                To me, bloodthirsty lord;
And for that cause I trained° thee to my house.          35
Long time thy shadow hath been thrall to me,
For in my gallery thy picture° hangs.
But now the substance shall endure the like,
And I will chain these legs and arms of thine
That hast by tyranny these many years          40
Wasted our country, slain our citizens,
And sent our sons and husbands captivate.°
TALBOT    Ha, ha, ha!
COUNTESS
Laughest thou, wretch? Thy mirth shall turn to moan.
TALBOT
I laugh to see your ladyship so fond°          45
To think that you have aught but Talbot's shadow
Whereon to practice your severity.°

COUNTESS
Why, art not thou the man?
TALBOT                    I am indeed.
COUNTESS
Then have I substance too.
TALBOT
No, no, I am but shadow of myself:          50
You are deceived, my substance is not here,
For what you see is but the smallest part
And least proportion of humanity.
I tell you, madam, were the whole frame° here,
It is of such a spacious lofty pitch,°          55
Your roof were not sufficient to contain't.
COUNTESS
This is a riddling merchant° for the nonce;°
He will be here, and yet he is not here.
How can these contrarieties° agree?
TALBOT
That will I show you presently.          60

*Winds° his horn; drums strike up; a peal of ordnance;°
enter* SOLDIERS.

How say you, madam? Are you now persuaded
That Talbot is but shadow of himself?
These are his substance, sinews, arms, and strength,
With which he yoketh° your rebellious necks,
Razeth your cities and subverts° your towns,          65
And in a moment makes them desolate.
COUNTESS
Victorious Talbot, pardon my abuse;
I find thou art no less than fame hath bruited°
And more than may be gathered by thy shape.
Let my presumption not provoke thy wrath,          70
For I am sorry that with reverence°
I did not entertain thee as thou art.
TALBOT
Be not dismayed, fair lady, nor misconster°
The mind of Talbot, as you did mistake
The outward composition° of his body.          75
What you have done hath not offended me,
Nor other satisfaction do I crave,
But only, with your patience, that we may
Taste of your wine and see what cates° you have,
For soldiers' stomachs always serve them well.          80
COUNTESS
With all my heart, and think me honorèd
To feast so great a warrior in my house.    *Exeunt.*

---

9 **Fain** gladly   10 **censure** judgment   13 **craved** invited
17 **still** silence   18 **fabulous** merely fictional   20 **aspect**
countenance   21 **strong-knit** well-muscled   22 **silly** feeble
23 **writhled** wrinkled   27 **sort** choose   31 **Marry** why; **for
that** because   32 **certify** inform   35 **trained** lured   37 **picture**
possibly implying that the countess was trying to practice
witchcraft on him   42 **captivate** captive   45 **fond** foolish
47 **severity** cruelty

54 **frame** structure   55 **pitch** stature   57 **riddling merchant**
enigmatic fellow;   **for the nonce** for the occasion (merely
a line-filler)   59 **contrarieties** contradictions   60 s.d. **Winds**
blows;   **peal of ordnance** salute of guns   64 **yoketh** brings
into subjection   65 **subverts** overthrows   68 **bruited** reported
71 **reverence** respect   73 **misconster** misunderstand   75
**composition** form   79 **cates** choice foods

[Scene IV. *London. The Temple garden.*°]

*Enter Richard* PLANTAGENET, WARWICK, SOMER-
SET, [*William de la*] *Pole* [*Earl of* SUFFOLK, VERNON,
*and another* LAWYER].

PLANTAGENET
Great lords and gentlemen, what means this silence?
Dare no man answer in a case of truth?

SUFFOLK
Within the Temple hall we were too loud;
The garden here is more convenient.

PLANTAGENET
Then say at once if I maintained the truth;                          5
Or else was wrangling° Somerset in th' error?

SUFFOLK
Faith,° I have been a truant° in the law,
And never yet could frame° my will to it,
And therefore frame° the law unto my will.

SOMERSET
Judge you, my Lord of Warwick, then, between us.   10

WARWICK
Between two hawks, which flies the higher pitch;
Between two dogs, which hath the deeper mouth;°
Between two blades, which bears the better temper;
Between two horses, which doth bear him° best;
Between two girls, which hath the merriest eye—       15
I have perhaps some shallow spirit° of judgment;
But in these nice sharp quillets° of the law,
Good faith, I am no wiser than a daw.°

PLANTAGENET
Tut, tut, here is a mannerly forbearance.
The truth appears so naked on my side                       20
That any purblind° eye may find it out.

SOMERSET
And on my side it is so well appareled,°
So clear, so shining, and so evident,
That it will glimmer through a blind man's eye.

PLANTAGENET
Since you are tongue-tied and so loath to speak,        25
In dumb significants° proclaim your thoughts:
Let him that is a true-born gentleman
And stands upon° the honor of his birth,
If he suppose that I have pleaded truth,
From off this brier pluck a white rose with me.          30

SOMERSET
Let him that is no coward nor no flatterer,
But dare maintain the party of the truth,
Pluck a red rose from off this thorn with me.

WARWICK
I love no colors;° and without all color
Of base insinuating flattery                                          35
I pluck this white rose with Plantagenet.

SUFFOLK
I pluck this red rose with young Somerset
And say withal° I think he held the right.

VERNON
Stay, lords and gentlemen, and pluck no more
Till you conclude that he upon whose side                  40
The fewest roses are cropped° from the tree
Shall yield the other in the right opinion.

SOMERSET
Good Master Vernon, it is well objected;°
If I have fewest, I subscribe in silence.

PLANTAGENET     And I.                                              45

VERNON
Then for the truth and plainness of the case,
I pluck this pale and maiden° blossom here,
Giving my verdict on the white rose side.

SOMERSET
Prick not your finger as you pluck it off,
Lest bleeding you do paint the white rose red            50
And fall on my side so against your will.

VERNON
If I, my lord, for my opinion bleed,
Opinion shall be surgeon to my hurt
And keep me on the side where still I am.

SOMERSET
Well, well, come on, who else?                                   55

LAWYER
Unless my study and my books be false,
The argument you held was wrong in you;
In sign whereof I pluck a white rose too.

PLANTAGENET
Now, Somerset, where is your argument?

SOMERSET
Here is my scabbard, meditating° that                       60
Shall dye your white rose in a bloody red.

PLANTAGENET
Meantime your cheeks do counterfeit° our roses,
For pale they look with fear, as witnessing
The truth on our side.

SOMERSET                     No, Plantagenet,
'Tis not for fear, but anger that thy cheeks              65
Blush for pure shame to counterfeit our roses,
And yet thy tongue will not confess thy error.

PLANTAGENET
Hath not thy rose a canker,° Somerset?

SOMERSET
Hath not thy rose a thorn, Plantagenet?

PLANTAGENET
Ay, sharp and piercing, to maintain his truth          70
Whiles thy consuming canker eats his falsehood.

SOMERSET
Well, I'll find friends to wear my bleeding roses,
That shall maintain what I have said is true
Where false Plantagenet dare not be seen.

PLANTAGENET
Now, by this maiden blossom in my hand,                 75
I scorn thee and thy fashion,° peevish boy.

---

**II.iv.s.d. Temple garden** the Inner and Middle Temples
were residences for students of the common law   **6 wrangling**
quarrelsome   **7 Faith** in truth; **truant** lazy student   **8
frame** dispose   **9 frame** twist   **12 mouth** bark, bay   **14
bear him** behave himself   **16 shallow spirit** small amount
**17 nice sharp quillets** precise and subtle distinctions   **18 daw**
simpleton   **21 purblind** nearly blind   **22 appareled** (1) dressed
(2) ordered   **26 In dumb significants** by mute signs   **28
stands upon** takes pride in   **34 colors** (1) pretenses (2)
adornments of speech

**38 withal** thereby   **41 cropped** plucked   **43 objected** proposed   **47 maiden** flawless   **60 meditating** planning   **62
counterfeit** imitate   **68 canker** (1) disease (2) caterpillar
larva   **76 fashion** (1) manner of behavior (2) faction (?)

**SUFFOLK**
Turn not thy scorns this way, Plantagenet.

**PLANTAGENET**
Proud Pole, I will, and scorn both him and thee.

**SUFFOLK**
I'll turn my part thereof into thy throat.

**SOMERSET**
Away, away, good William de la Pole!     80
We grace the yeoman° by conversing with him.

**WARWICK**
Now, by God's will, thou wrong'st him, Somerset;
His grandfather° was Lionel Duke of Clarence,
Third son to the third Edward King of England:
Spring crestless° yeomen from so deep a root?     85

**PLANTAGENET**
He bears him on the place's privilege,°
Or durst not, for his craven heart, say thus.

**SOMERSET**
By him that made me, I'll maintain my words
On any plot of ground in Christendom.
Was not my father, Richard Earl of Cambridge,     90
For treason executed in our late king's days?
And, by his treason, stand'st not thou attainted,
Corrupted, and exempt from ancient gentry?°
His trespass° yet lives guilty in thy blood,
And, till thou be restored, thou art a yeoman.°     95

**PLANTAGENET**
My father was attachèd,° not attainted,
Condemned to die for treason, but no traitor;
And that I'll prove° on better men than Somerset,
Were growing time once ripened to my will.°
For your partaker° Pole and you yourself,     100
I'll note you in my book of memory
To scourge you for this apprehension.°
Look to it well and say you are well warned.

**SOMERSET**
Ah, thou shalt find us ready for thee still,
And know us by these colors for thy foes,     105
For these my friends in spite of thee shall wear.

**PLANTAGENET**
And, by my soul, this pale and angry rose,
As cognizance° of my blood-drinking° hate,
Will I forever and my faction wear
Until it wither with me to my grave     110
Or flourish to the height of my degree.°

**SUFFOLK**
Go forward and be choked with thy ambition!
And so farewell until I meet thee next.     *Exit.*

**SOMERSET**
Have with thee,° Pole. Farewell, ambitious Richard.
    *Exit.*

**PLANTAGENET**
How I am braved° and must perforce° endure it!     115

**WARWICK**
This blot that they object against your house
Shall be whipped° out in the next parliament
Called for the truce of Winchester and Gloucester,
And if thou be not then created York,°
I will not live to be accounted° Warwick.     120
Meantime, in signal of my love to thee,
Against proud Somerset and William Pole,
Will I upon thy party° wear this rose.
And here I prophesy: this brawl° today,
Grown to this faction in the Temple garden,     125
Shall send, between the red rose and the white,
A thousand souls to death and deadly night.

**PLANTAGENET**
Good Master Vernon, I am bound to you
That you on my behalf would pluck a flower.

**VERNON**
In your behalf still will I wear the same.     130

**LAWYER**
And so will I.

**PLANTAGENET**
Thanks, gentle [sir].
Come, let us four to dinner: I dare say
This quarrel will drink blood° another day.     *Exeunt.*

[Scene V. *The Tower of London.*]

*Enter* MORTIMER, *brought in a chair, and* JAILERS.

**MORTIMER**
Kind keepers of my weak decaying age,
Let dying Mortimer here rest himself.
Even like a man new halèd from the rack,°
So fare my limbs with long imprisonment,
And these gray locks, the pursuivants° of death,     5
Nestor-like° agèd in an age of care,
Argue° the end of Edmund Mortimer.
These eyes, like lamps whose wasting° oil is spent,
Wax° dim, as drawing to their exigent;°
Weak shoulders, overborne with burthening° grief,     10
And pithless° arms, like to a withered vine
That droops his sapless branches to the ground.
Yet are these feet, whose strengthless stay° is numb,
Unable to support this lump of clay,
Swift-winged with desire to get a grave,     15
As witting I no other comfort have.
But tell me, keeper, will my nephew come?

**FIRST JAILER**
Richard Plantagenet, my lord, will come:
We sent unto the Temple, unto his chamber,
And answer was returned that he will come.     20

---

81 **grace the yeoman** dignify this commoner   83 **grandfather** great-great-grandfather   85 **crestless** not having the right to a coat of arms   86 **privilege** of sanctuary (since the Temple was founded as a religious house)   92–93 **attainted . . . gentry** legal penalties by which the heirs of a person convicted of treason were prevented from inheriting his property and titles   94 **trespass** crime   95 **And . . . yeoman** therefore, you shall remain a commoner until your titles are legally restored   96 **attachèd** arrested   98 **prove** establish through trial by combat   99 **Were . . . will** if I should ever be restored to the nobility   100 **partaker** partisan   102 **apprehension** notion, display of wit   108 **cognizance** a badge; **blood-drinking** bloodthirsty   111 **to . . . degree** until I regain my high rank   114 **Have with thee** I'll go with you

115 **braved** defied; **perforce** necessarily   117 **whipped** quickly stricken   119 **York** Duke of York   120 **accounted** considered   123 **upon thy party** in support of you   124 **brawl** quarrel   134 **drink blood** result in bloodshed   II.v.3 **new . . . rack** just released from the torturer's rack   5 **pursuivants** heralds   6 **Nestor-like** the Greek king Nestor, in Homer's *Iliad*, is a type of old age   7 **Argue** foretell   8 **wasting** consuming   9 **Wax** grow; **exigent** end   10 **burthening** disyllabic; burdensome   11 **pithless** strengthless   13 **stay** support

MORTIMER

Enough; my soul shall then be satisfied.
Poor gentleman! his wrong doth equal mine.
Since Henry Monmouth° first began to reign,
Before whose glory I was great in arms,
This loathsome sequestration° have I had;                    25
And even since then hath Richard been obscured,°
Deprived of honor and inheritance.
But now the arbitrator of despairs,
Just death, kind umpire° of men's miseries,
With sweet enlargement° doth dismiss me hence.              30
I would his° troubles likewise were expired,
That so he might recover what was lost.

*Enter Richard* [PLANTAGENET].

FIRST JAILER

My lord, your loving nephew now is come.

MORTIMER

Richard Plantagenet, my friend, is he come?

PLANTAGENET

Ay, noble uncle, thus ignobly used,                         35
Your nephew, late despisèd° Richard, comes.

MORTIMER

Direct mine arms I may° embrace his neck
And in his bosom spend my latter gasp.°
O, tell me when my lips do touch his cheeks,
That I may kindly give one fainting kiss.                   40
And now declare, sweet stem from York's great stock,°
Why didst thou say, of late thou wert despised?

PLANTAGENET

First, lean thine agèd back against mine arm,
And, in that ease, I'll tell thee my disease.°
This day, in argument upon a case,                          45
Some words there grew 'twixt Somerset and me;
Among which terms he used his lavish° tongue
And did upbraid° me with my father's death:
Which obloquy° set bars before my tongue,
Else with the like I had requited° him.                     50
Therefore, good uncle, for my father's sake,
In honor of a true Plantagenet,
And for alliance' sake, declare the cause°
My father, Earl of Cambridge, lost his head.

MORTIMER

That cause, fair nephew, that imprisoned me                 55
And hath detained me all my flow'ring° youth
Within a loathsome dungeon, there to pine,
Was cursèd instrument of his decease.

PLANTAGENET

Discover° more at large what cause that was,
For I am ignorant and cannot guess.                         60

MORTIMER

I will, if that my fading breath permit
And death approach not ere my tale be done.
Henry the Fourth, grandfather to this king,

Deposed his nephew° Richard, Edward's son,
The first-begotten and the lawful heir                      65
Of Edward king, the third of that descent:°
During whose reign the Percies° of the north,
Finding his usurpation most unjust,
Endeavored my advancement to the throne.
The reason moved° these warlike lords to this               70
Was, for that—young° Richard thus removed,
Leaving no heir begotten of his body—
I was the next by birth and parentage:
For by my mother° I derivèd° am
From Lionel Duke of Clarence, third son                     75
To King Edward the Third; whereas he
From John of Gaunt doth bring his pedigree,
Being but fourth of that heroic line.
But mark:° as in this haughty° great attempt
They labored to plant the rightful heir,                    80
I lost my liberty and they their lives.
Long after this, when Henry the Fifth,
Succeeding his father Bolingbroke, did reign,
Thy father, Earl of Cambridge, then derived
From famous Edmund Langley, Duke of York,                   85
Marrying my sister that thy mother was,
Again, in pity of my hard distress,
Levied an army, weening to redeem
And have installed me in the diadem;°
But, as the rest, so fell that noble earl                   90
And was beheaded. Thus the Mortimers,
In whom the title rested, were suppressed.

PLANTAGENET

Of which, my lord, your honor is the last.

MORTIMER

True; and thou see'st that I no issue have
And that my fainting words do warrant° death.               95
Thou art my heir; the rest I wish thee gather,°
But yet be wary in thy studious care.°

PLANTAGENET

Thy grave admonishments prevail with me,
But yet, methinks, my father's execution
Was nothing less than bloody tyranny.                       100

MORTIMER

With silence, nephew, be thou politic:
Strong-fixèd is the house of Lancaster,
And like a mountain, not to be removed.
But now thy uncle is removing hence,
As princes do their courts, when they are cloyed°           105
With long continuance in a settled place.

PLANTAGENET

O, uncle, would some part of my young years
Might but redeem the passage° of your age!

64 **nephew** cousin   64–66 **Edward's . . . descent** Richard II, son of Edward the Black Prince and grandson of King Edward III   67 **Percies** noble family of Northumberland   70 **moved** that provoked   71 **young** Richard was actually over thirty at the time of his deposition   74 **mother** actually, grandmother; **derivèd** descended   79 **mark** listen attentively; **haughty** lofty   88–89 **Levied . . . diadem** raised an army, with the intention of rescuing me and having me crowned king   95 **warrant** give assurance of   96 **the . . . gather** (1) I want you to conclude for yourself (2) I hope that you may gain all that is rightfully yours   97 **But . . . care** but always be careful even as you take pains in this enterprise   105 **cloyed** satiated   108 **redeem the passage** buy back the passing

23 **Henry Monmouth** King Henry V   25 **sequestration** imprisonment   26 **obscured** degraded   29 **umpire** arbitrator   30 **enlargement** release   31 **his** Plantagenet's   36 **late despisèd** just insulted   37 **I may** so that I may   38 **spend . . . gasp** draw my last breath   41 **stock** trunk (i.e., lineage)   44 **disease** source of my discomfort   47 **lavish** licentious, unrestrained   48 **upbraid** insult   49 **obloquy** reproach   50 **requited** repaid   53 **the cause** for what reason   56 **flow'ring** vigorous, flourishing   59 **Discover** explain

**MORTIMER**

Thou dost then wrong me, as that slaughterer doth
Which giveth many wounds when one will kill.    110
Mourn not, except thou sorrow for my good;
Only give order° for my funeral.
And so farewell, and fair be all thy hopes,
And prosperous be thy life in peace and war!    *Dies.*

**PLANTAGENET**

And peace, no war, befall thy parting soul!    115
In prison hast thou spent a pilgrimage°
And like a hermit overpassed° thy days.
Well, I will lock his counsel in my breast,
And what I do imagine, let that rest.
Keepers, convey him hence, and I myself    120
Will see his burial better than his life.°

     [*Exeunt* JAILERS *with the body of Mortimer.*]

Here dies the dusky° torch of Mortimer,
Choked with ambition of the meaner sort.°
And for those wrongs, those bitter injuries
Which Somerset hath offered to my house,    125
I doubt not but with honor to redress.°
And therefore haste I to the parliament,
Either to be restorèd to my blood,
Or make my will th' advantage of my good.°    *Exit.*


# ACT III

Scene I. [*London. The parliament house.*]

*Flourish. Enter* KING, EXETER, GLOUCESTER,
WINCHESTER, WARWICK, SOMERSET, SUFFOLK,
*Richard* PLANTAGENET. GLOUCESTER *offers to put up
a bill;*° WINCHESTER *snatches it, tears it.*

**WINCHESTER**

Com'st thou with deep premeditated lines,°
With written pamphlets studiously devised?
Humphrey of Gloucester, if thou canst accuse
Or aught intend'st to lay unto my charge,
Do it without invention,° suddenly,    5
As I with sudden and extemporal° speech
Purpose to answer what thou canst object.

**GLOUCESTER**

Presumptuous priest! this place commands my
     patience,
Or thou shouldst find thou hast dishonored me.
Think not, although in writing I preferred°    10
The manner of thy vile outrageous crimes,

That therefore I have forged,° or am not able
Verbatim to rehearse the method of my pen.°
No, prelate, such is thy audacious wickedness,
Thy lewd, pestiferous, and dissentious pranks,°    15
As very° infants prattle of thy pride.
Thou art a most pernicious usurer,°
Froward° by nature, enemy to peace,
Lascivious, wanton, more than well beseems°
A man of thy profession and degree.    20
And for thy treachery, what's more manifest?
In that thou laid'st a trap to take my life,
As well at London Bridge as at the Tower.
Beside, I fear me, if thy thoughts were sifted,°
The king, thy sovereign, is not quite exempt    25
From envious malice of thy swelling° heart.

**WINCHESTER**

Gloucester, I do defy thee. Lords, vouchsafe
To give me hearing what I shall reply.
If I were covetous, ambitious, or perverse,
As he will have me,° how am I so poor?    30
Or how haps it° I seek not to advance
Or raise myself, but keep my wonted calling?°
And for dissension, who preferreth peace
More than I do?—except I be provoked.
No, my good lords, it is not that offends;    35
It is not that that hath incensed° the duke:
It is, because no one should sway° but he,
No one but he should be about the king,
And that engenders thunder in his breast
And makes him roar these accusations forth.    40
But he shall know I am as good—

**GLOUCESTER**      As good?

Thou bastard° of my grandfather!

**WINCHESTER**

Ay, lordly° sir; for what are you, I pray,
But one imperious° in another's throne?

**GLOUCESTER**

Am I not protector, saucy priest?    45

**WINCHESTER**

And am not I a prelate of the church?

**GLOUCESTER**

Yes, as an outlaw in a castle keeps
And useth it to patronage° his theft.

**WINCHESTER**

Unreverent Gloucester!

**GLOUCESTER**      Thou art reverent
Touching thy spiritual function,° not thy life.    50

**WINCHESTER**

Rome shall remedy this.

**WARWICK**      Roam thither, then.
My lord, it were your duty to forbear.

---

112 **give order** make arrangements   116 **pilgrimage** full life's journey   117 **overpassed** lived out   121 **Will . . . life** will see that he receives the honor in his funeral that was denied him during his lifetime   122 **dusky** gloomy   123 **Choked . . . sort** stifled by the ambition of men of inferior birth (i.e., the house of Lancaster)   126 **redress** remedy   129 **will . . . good** determination of purpose the means of achieving my ambition (see A Note on the Text, p. 109)   **III.i.s.d. offers . . . bill** attempts to post a statement of accusations   1 **deep premeditated lines** statements carefully thought out in advance   5 **invention** seeking out the grounds for argument in the manner of a rhetorician or a lawyer trained in oratory   6 **extemporal** extemporaneous   10 **preferred** set forth

12 **forged** fabricated lies   13 **rehearse . . . pen** repeat the contents of what I have written   15 **lewd . . . pranks** wicked, mischievous, and quarrelsome offenses   16 **As very** that even   17 **pernicious usurer** alluding to Winchester's reputation for gaining riches through extortions and loans made at exorbitant rates of interest   18 **Froward** inclined to evil   19 **beseems** is fitting to   24 **sifted** closely examined   26 **swelling** proud   30 **have me** make me out to be   31 **haps it** does it happen   32 **calling** religious vocation   36 **incensed** enraged   37 **sway** rule   42 **bastard** Winchester was an illegitimate son of John of Gaunt, Duke of Lancaster   43 **lordly** haughty   44 **imperious** ruling   48 **patronage** defend   50 **Touching . . . function** only in respect of your high ecclesiastical office

SOMERSET
Ay, see the bishop be not overborne.°
Methinks my lord° should be religious
And know the office° that belongs to such.      55

WARWICK
Methinks his lordship° should be humbler;
It fitteth not a prelate so to plead.

SOMERSET
Yes, when his holy state is touched so near.°

WARWICK
State holy or unhallowed,° what of that?
Is not his grace° protector to the king?      60

PLANTAGENET [Aside.]
Plantagenet, I see, must hold his tongue,
Lest it be said, "Speak, sirrah, when you should;
Must your bold verdict° enter talk with lords?"
Else would I have a fling at° Winchester.

KING
Uncles of Gloucester and of Winchester,      65
The special watchmen° of our English weal,°
I would prevail, if prayers might prevail,
To join your hearts in love and amity.
O, what a scandal is it to our crown,
That two such noble peers as ye should jar!      70
Believe me, lords, my tender years can tell
Civil dissension is a viperous worm°
That gnaws the bowels of the commonwealth.

*A noise within*, "Down with the tawny coats!"

What tumult's this?

WARWICK            An uproar, I dare warrant,°
Begun through malice of the bishop's men.      75

*A noise again*, "Stones! stones!" *Enter* MAYOR.

MAYOR
O my good lords, and virtuous Henry,
Pity the city of London, pity us!
The bishop° and the Duke of Gloucester's men,
Forbidden late° to carry any weapon,
Have filled their pockets full of pebble stones      80
And banding themselves in contrary parts°
Do pelt so fast at one another's pate°
That many have their giddy° brains knocked out.
Our windows are broke down in every street,
And we for fear compelled to shut our shops.      85

*Enter* [SERVINGMEN *of Gloucester and Winchester*] *in skirmish, with bloody pates.*

KING
We charge you, on allegiance to ourself,
To hold your slaught'ring hands and keep the peace.
Pray, uncle Gloucester, mitigate° this strife.

FIRST SERVINGMAN   Nay, if we be forbidden stones,
we'll fall to it with our teeth.      90

SECOND SERVINGMAN   Do what ye dare, we are as resolute.

*Skirmish again.*

GLOUCESTER
You of my household, leave this peevish broil
And set this unaccustomed° fight aside.

THIRD SERVINGMAN
My lord, we know your grace to be a man      95
Just and upright; and, for your royal birth,
Inferior to none but to his majesty,
And ere that we will suffer° such a prince,
So kind a father of the commonweal,
To be disgracèd by an inkhorn mate,°      100
We and our wives and children all will fight
And have our bodies slaughtered by thy foes.

FIRST SERVINGMAN
Ay, and the very parings of our nails
Shall pitch a field° when we are dead.      *Begin again.*

GLOUCESTER                         Stay, stay, I say!
And if you love me, as you say you do,      105
Let me persuade you to forbear awhile.

KING
O, how this discord doth afflict my soul!
Can you, my Lord of Winchester, behold
My sighs and tears and will not once relent?
Who should be pitiful, if you be not?      110
Or who should study° to prefer a peace,
If holy churchmen take delight in broils?

WARWICK
Yield, my Lord Protector; yield, Winchester,
Except° you mean with obstinate repulse°
To slay your sovereign and destroy the realm.      115
You see what mischief and what murder too
Hath been enacted through your enmity;
Then be at peace, except ye thirst for blood.

WINCHESTER
He shall submit, or I will never yield.

GLOUCESTER
Compassion on the king commands me stoop;      120
Or I would see his heart out ere the priest
Should ever get that privilege° of me.

WARWICK
Behold, my Lord of Winchester, the duke
Hath banished moody discontented fury,
As by his smoothèd brows it doth appear:      125
Why look you still so stern and tragical?°

GLOUCESTER
Here, Winchester, I offer thee my hand.

KING
Fie, uncle Beaufort! I have heard you preach
That malice was a great and grievous sin,
And will not you maintain the thing you teach,      130
But prove a chief offender in the same?

WARWICK
Sweet king! the bishop hath a kindly gird.°

---

53 **overborne** prevailed over  54 **lord** Gloucester  55 **office** respect  56 **lordship** Winchester  58 **holy . . . near** ecclesiastical office is so directly involved  59 **holy or unhallowed** ecclesiastical or secular  60 **grace** Gloucester  63 **bold verdict** presumptuous opinion  64 **have a fling at** reprove  66 **watchmen** guardians; **weal** state  72 **worm** serpent  74 **warrant** swear  78 **bishop** bishop's  79 **late** recently  81 **parts** parties  82 **pate** head  83 **giddy** foolish  88 **mitigate** appease

94 **unaccustomed** indecorous  98 **suffer** permit  100 **inkhorn mate** scribbling fellow (an unlettered person's disparaging allusion to the literacy of clergymen)  104 **pitch a field** serve as stakes in a pitched battlefield  111 **study** make it his aim  114 **Except** unless; **repulse** refusal  122 **privilege** advantage yielded  126 **tragical** gloomy  132 **kindly gird** fitting gibe

For shame, my Lord of Winchester, relent!
What, shall a child instruct you what to do?

WINCHESTER
Well, Duke of Gloucester, I will yield to thee    135
Love for thy love, and hand for hand I give.

GLOUCESTER [*Aside.*]
Ay, but, I fear me, with a hollow° heart.

[*Aloud.*]

See here, my friends and loving countrymen;
This token° serveth for a flag of truce
Betwixt ourselves and all our followers.    140
So help me God, as I dissemble not!

WINCHESTER [*Aside.*]
So help me God, as I intend it not!

KING
O loving uncle, kind Duke of Gloucester,
How joyful am I made by this contract!°
Away, my masters! trouble us no more,    145
But join in friendship, as your lords have done.

FIRST SERVINGMAN
Content; I'll to the surgeon's.

SECOND SERVINGMAN     And so will I.

THIRD SERVINGMAN   And I will see what physic° the
tavern affords.°       *Exeunt.*

WARWICK
Accept this scroll,° most gracious sovereign,    150
Which in the right of Richard Plantagenet
We do exhibit to your majesty.

GLOUCESTER
Well urged, my Lord of Warwick: for, sweet prince,
And if° your grace mark° every circumstance,
You have great reason to do Richard right,    155
Especially for those occasions°
At Eltham Place I told your majesty.

KING
And those occasions, uncle, were of force.
Therefore, my loving lords, our pleasure is
That Richard be restorèd to his blood.°    160

WARWICK
Let Richard be restorèd to his blood;
So shall his father's wrongs be recompensed.

WINCHESTER
As will the rest, so willeth Winchester.

KING
If Richard will be true, not that all alone
But all the whole inheritance I give    165
That doth belong unto the house of York,
From whence you spring by lineal descent.

PLANTAGENET
Thy humble servant vows obedience
And humble service till the point of death.

KING
Stoop then and set your knee against my foot,    170
And in reguerdon° of that duty done,
I girt° thee with the valiant sword of York.
Rise, Richard, like a true Plantagenet,
And rise created princely Duke of York.

PLANTAGENET
And so thrive Richard as thy foes may fall!    175
And as my duty springs, so perish they
That grudge one thought° against your majesty!

ALL
Welcome, high prince, the mighty Duke of York!

SOMERSET [*Aside.*]
Perish, base prince, ignoble Duke of York!

GLOUCESTER
Now will it best avail your majesty    180
To cross the seas and to be crowned in France:
The presence of a king engenders love
Amongst his subjects and his loyal friends,
As it disanimates° his enemies.

KING
When Gloucester says the word, King Henry goes,    185
For friendly counsel cuts off many foes.

GLOUCESTER
Your ships already are in readiness.
     *Sennet.° Flourish. Exeunt. Manet° EXETER.*

EXETER
Ay, we may march in England or in France,
Not seeing what is likely to ensue.
This late dissension grown betwixt the peers    190
Burns under feignèd ashes of forgèd° love
And will at last break out into a flame;
As festered members° rot but by degree°
Till bones and flesh and sinews fall away,
So will this base and envious discord breed.    195
And now I fear that fatal prophecy
Which in the time of Henry named the Fifth
Was in the mouth of every sucking° babe,
That Henry born at Monmouth should win all
And Henry born at Windsor lose all:    200
Which is so plain that Exeter doth wish
His days may finish ere that hapless time.     *Exit.*

[Scene II. *France. Before Rouen.*]

*Enter* [la] PUCELLE, *disguised, with four* SOLDIERS *with
sacks upon their backs.*

PUCELLE
These are the city gates, the gates of Rouen,
Through which our policy° must make a breach.
Take heed, be wary how you place your words;
Talk like the vulgar° sort of market men°
That come to gather money for their corn.°    5
If we have entrance, as I hope we shall,
And that we find the slothful watch but weak,
I'll by a sign give notice to our friends
That Charles the Dolphin may encounter° them.

SOLDIER
Our sacks shall be a mean° to sack the city,    10

---

137 **hollow** insincere   139 **token** handclasp   144 **contract**
agreement   148 **physic** remedy   149 **affords** provides   150
**scroll** document   154 **And if** if; **mark** take notice of   156
**occasions** reasons   160 **blood** title and rights of nobility
171 **reguerdon** ample reward   172 **girt** gird

177 **grudge one thought** entertain one grudging thought
184 **disanimates** disheartens   187 **s.d. Sennet** trumpet signal
for the exit of an important personage; **Manet** remains (Latin)
191 **forged** pretended   193 **members** parts of the body; **by
degree** little by little, gradually   198 **sucking** nursing
III.ii.2 **policy** stratagem   4 **vulgar** common; **market men**
people going to market   5 **corn** grain   9 **encounter** assail
10 **mean** means

And we be lords and rulers over Rouen;
Therefore we'll knock.

*Knock.*

WATCHMAN [*Within.*]    Qui est là?°
PUCELLE
Paysans là, pauvres gens de France:°
Poor market folks that come to sell their corn.                    15
WATCHMAN
Enter, go in, the market bell is rung.
PUCELLE
Now, Rouen, I'll shake thy bulwarks to the ground.
                                                    *Exeunt.*

*Enter Charles [the DAUPHIN], BASTARD, ALENÇON,
[REIGNIER, and FORCES].*

DAUPHIN
Saint Denis bless this happy stratagem,
And once again we'll sleep secure in Rouen!
BASTARD
Here entered Pucelle and her practisants.°                         20
Now she is there, how will she specify:
Here is the best and safest passage in?
REIGNIER
By thrusting out a torch from yonder tower,
Which, once discerned, shows that her meaning is:
No way to° that, for weakness, which she entered.      25

*Enter [la] PUCELLE on the top, thrusting out a torch
burning.*

PUCELLE
Behold, this is the happy wedding torch
That joineth Rouen unto her countrymen,
But burning fatal to the Talbonites!°              [*Exit.*]
BASTARD
See, noble Charles, the beacon of our friend,
The burning torch, in yonder turret stands.                        30
DAUPHIN
Now shine it° like a comet of revenge,
A prophet to the fall of all our foes!
REIGNIER
Defer° no time, delays have dangerous ends;
Enter and cry, "The Dolphin!" presently,
And then do execution on the watch.                                35
                                        *Alarum. [Exeunt.]*

*An alarum. TALBOT in an excursion.°*

TALBOT
France, thou shalt rue this treason with thy tears,
If Talbot but survive thy treachery.
Pucelle, that witch, that damnèd sorceress,
Hath wrought this hellish mischief unawares,
That hardly we escaped the pride° of France.    *Exit.* 40

*An alarum: excursions. BEDFORD, brought in sick in a
chair. Enter TALBOT and BURGUNDY without: within
[la] PUCELLE, Charles [the DAUPHIN], BASTARD,
[ALENÇON,] and REIGNIER on the walls.*

PUCELLE
Good morrow, gallants!° Want ye corn for bread?
I think the Duke of Burgundy will fast
Before he'll buy again at such a rate.
'Twas full of darnel;° do you like the taste?
BURGUNDY
Scoff on, vile fiend and shameless courtesan!°                     45
I trust ere long to choke thee with thine own
And make thee curse the harvest of that corn.
DAUPHIN
Your grace may starve perhaps before that time.
BEDFORD
O, let no words, but deeds, revenge this treason!
PUCELLE
What will you do, good graybeard? Break a lance,                  50
And run atilt at° death within a chair?
TALBOT
Foul fiend of France, and hag of all despite,°
Encompassed° with thy lustful paramours!°
Becomes it thee to taunt his valiant age
And twit° with cowardice a man half dead?                         55
Damsel,° I'll have a bout with you again,
Or else let Talbot perish with this shame.
PUCELLE
Are ye so hot,° sir? Yet, Pucelle, hold thy peace;
If Talbot do but thunder, rain will follow.

*[The ENGLISH] whisper together in council.*

God speed the parliament! who shall be the speaker?°              60
TALBOT
Dare ye come forth and meet us in the field?
PUCELLE
Belike° your lordship takes us then for fools,
To try if that our own be ours or no.
TALBOT
I speak not to that railing Hecate,°
But unto thee, Alençon, and the rest.                             65
Will ye, like soldiers, come and fight it out?
ALENÇON    Signior,° no.
TALBOT
Signior, hang! base muleters° of France!
Like peasant footboys° do they keep the walls
And dare not take up arms like gentlemen.                          70
PUCELLE
Away, captains! let's get us from the walls;
For Talbot means no goodness by his looks.
Good-by, my lord! we came but to tell you
That we are here.            *Exeunt from the walls.*
TALBOT
And there will we be too, ere it be long,                          75
Or else reproach be Talbot's greatest fame.
Vow, Burgundy, by honor of thy house,
Pricked on° by public wrongs sustained in France,
Either to get the town again or die.

---

13 **Qui est là** Who is there? 14 **Paysans . . . France**
peasants here, poor folk of France 20 **practisants** companions
in the stratagem 25 **to** comparable to 28 **Talbonites**
followers of Talbot 31 **shine it** may it shine 33 **Defer** waste
35 **s.d. excursion** sortie 40 **pride** finest warriors

41 **gallants** gentlemen 44 **darnel** weeds 45 **courtesan**
prostitute 50–51 **Break . . . at** joust, combat 52 **of all
despite** full of malice 53 **Encompassed** surrounded;
**paramours** lovers 55 **twit** chide 56 **Damsel** girl 58 **hot**
(1) angry (2) sexually aroused 60 **speaker** presiding officer
62 **Belike** perhaps 64 **railing Hecate** abusive witch (after
Hecate, goddess of sorcery) 67 **Signior** sir 68 **muleters**
mule-drivers 69 **footboys** boy-servants 78 **Pricked on**
provoked

And I, as sure as English Henry lives     80
And as his father here was conqueror,
As sure as in this late-betrayèd town
Great Cordelion's° heart was buried,
So sure I swear to get° the town or die.

BURGUNDY
My vows are equal partners with thy vows.     85

TALBOT
But, ere we go, regard° this dying prince,
The valiant Duke of Bedford. Come, my lord,
We will bestow you in some better place,
Fitter for sickness and for crazy° age.

BEDFORD
Lord Talbot, do not so dishonor me;     90
Here will I sit before the walls of Rouen
And will be partner of your weal or woe.°

BURGUNDY
Courageous Bedford, let us now persuade you.

BEDFORD
Not to be gone from hence, for once I read
That stout Pendragon° in his litter° sick     95
Came to the field and vanquishèd his foes.
Methinks I should revive the soldiers' hearts,
Because I ever found them as myself.

TALBOT
Undaunted spirit in a dying breast!
Then be it so: heavens keep old Bedford safe!     100
And now no more ado, brave Burgundy,
But gather we our forces out of hand
And set upon our boasting enemy.

[*Exeunt all but* BEDFORD *and his* ATTENDANTS.]

*An alarum: excursions.*° *Enter Sir John* FALSTAFF *and a*
CAPTAIN.

CAPTAIN
Whither away, Sir John Falstaff, in such haste?

FALSTAFF
Whither away? To save myself by flight;     105
We are like to have the overthrow° again.

CAPTAIN
What! Will you fly, and leave Lord Talbot?

FALSTAFF               Ay,
All the Talbots in the world, to save my life.    *Exit.*

CAPTAIN
Cowardly knight, ill fortune follow thee!    *Exit.*

*Retreat. Excursions.* [La] PUCELLE, ALENÇON, *and*
*Charles* [*the* DAUPHIN *enter and*] *fly.*

BEDFORD
Now, quiet soul, depart when heaven please,     110
For I have seen our enemies' overthrow.
What is the trust or strength of foolish man?
They that of late were daring with their scoffs
Are glad and fain° by flight to save themselves.

    BEDFORD *dies and is carried in by two in his chair.*

*An alarum. Enter* TALBOT, BURGUNDY, *and the rest*
[*of their* MEN].

TALBOT
Lost, and recovered in a day again!     115
This is a double honor, Burgundy;
Yet heavens have glory for this victory!

BURGUNDY
Warlike and martial Talbot, Burgundy
Enshrines thee in his heart and there erects
Thy noble deeds as valor's monuments.     120

TALBOT
Thanks, gentle duke. But where is Pucelle now?
I think her old familiar° is asleep.
Now where's the Bastard's braves,° and Charles his
    gleeks?°
What, all amort?° Rouen hangs her head for grief
That such a valant company are fled.     125
Now will we take some order° in the town,
Placing therein some expert° officers,
And then depart to Paris to the king,
For there young Henry with his nobles lie.°

BURGUNDY
What wills Lord Talbot pleaseth Burgundy.     130

TALBOT
But yet, before we go, let's not forget
The noble Duke of Bedford, late deceased,
But see his exequies° fulfilled in Rouen.
A braver soldier never couchèd° lance,
A gentler° heart did never sway° in court.     135
But kings and mightiest potentates must die,
For that's the end of human misery.    *Exeunt.*

Scene III. [*The plains near Rouen.*]

*Enter Charles* [*the* DAUPHIN], BASTARD, ALENÇON,
[*la*] PUCELLE, [*and* FORCES].

PUCELLE
Dismay not, princes, at this accident,
Nor grieve that Rouen is so recoverèd.
Care is no cure, but rather corrosive,°
For things that are not to be remedied.
Let frantic° Talbot triumph for a while     5
And like a peacock sweep along his tail;
We'll pull° his plumes and take away his train,°
If Dolphin and the rest will be but ruled.°

DAUPHIN
We have been guided by thee hitherto
And of thy cunning had no diffidence;°     10
One sudden foil° shall never breed distrust.

BASTARD
Search out thy wit° for secret policies,
And we will make thee famous through the world.

ALENÇON
We'll set thy statue in some holy place,

---

83 **Cordelion's** King Richard the Lionhearted's  84 **get** retake  86 **regard** behold  89 **crazy** infirm, decrepit  92 **weal or woe** good or bad fortune  95 **Pendragon** Uther Pendragon, father of King Arthur; **litter** stretcher bed  103 **s.d. excursions** entries and exits of skirmishing troops  106 **have the overthrow** be defeated  114 **fain** eager

122 **familiar** servant demon  123 **braves** boasts; **gleeks** jests, scoffs  124 **amort** dejected  126 **take some order** restore order  127 **expert** experienced  129 **lie** reside  133 **exequies** funeral ceremonies  134 **couchèd** leveled for the assault  135 **gentler** nobler; **sway** prevail
III.iii.3 **corrosive** a caustic drug  5 **frantic** raging  7 **pull** pluck; **train** (1) followers (2) equipment for battle  8 **ruled** guided (by Joan)  10 **diffidence** lack of confidence  11 **foil** defeat  12 **Search . . . wit** examine your mind

And have thee reverenced like a blessèd saint.                              15
Employ thee° then, sweet virgin, for our good.

PUCELLE
Then thus it must be; this doth Joan devise:°
By fair persuasions mixed with sugared° words
We will entice the Duke of Burgundy
To leave the Talbot and to follow us.                                       20

DAUPHIN
Ay, marry, sweeting,° if we could do that,
France were no place for Henry's warriors,
Nor should that nation boast it so with° us,
But be extirpèd° from our provinces.

ALENÇON
Forever should they be expulsed° from France                                25
And not have title of° an earldom here.

PUCELLE
Your honors shall perceive how I will work
To bring this matter to the wishèd end.

*Drum sounds afar off.*

Hark! by the sound of drum you may perceive
Their powers are marching unto Paris-ward.°                                  30

*Here sound an English march.*

There goes the Talbot, with his colors spread,°
And all the troops of English after him.

*French march.* [*Enter the Duke of* BURGUNDY *and*
FORCES.]

Now in the rearward comes the duke and his;
Fortune in favor° makes him lag behind.
Summon a parley; we will talk with him.                                     35

*Trumpets sound a parley.*

DAUPHIN
A parley with the Duke of Burgundy!

BURGUNDY
Who craves a parley with the Burgundy?

PUCELLE
The princely Charles of France, thy countryman.

BURGUNDY
What say'st thou, Charles? For I am marching hence.

DAUPHIN
Speak, Pucelle, and enchant him with thy words.                             40

PUCELLE
Brave Burgundy, undoubted hope of France!
Stay, let thy humble handmaid speak to thee.

BURGUNDY
Speak on, but be not overtedious.

PUCELLE
Look on thy country, look on fertile France,
And see the cities and the towns defaced                                    45
By wasting ruin of the cruel foe,
As looks the mother on her lowly babe
When death doth close his tender-dying° eyes.
See, see the pining° malady of France;

Behold the wounds, the most unnatural wounds,                               50
Which thou thyself has given her woeful breast.
O, turn thy edgèd° sword another way;
Strike those that hurt, and hurt not those that help.
One drop of blood drawn from thy country's bosom
Should grieve thee more than streams of foreign gore.                       55
Return thee therefore with a flood of tears,
And wash away thy country's stainèd° spots.

BURGUNDY
Either she hath bewitched me with her words,
Or nature makes me suddenly relent.

PUCELLE
Besides, all French and France exclaims on° thee,                           60
Doubting thy birth and lawful progeny.°
Who join'st thou with, but with a lordly° nation
That will not trust thee but for profit's sake?
When Talbot hath set footing° once in France
And fashioned thee° that instrument of ill,                                 65
Who then but English Henry will be lord,
And thou be thrust out like a fugitive?
Call we to mind, and mark but this for proof:
Was not the Duke of Orleans thy foe?
And was he not in England prisoner?                                         70
But when they heard he was thine enemy,
They set him free without his ransom paid,
In spite of Burgundy and all his friends.
See then, thou fight'st against thy countrymen
And join'st with them will be thy slaughtermen.°                            75
Come, come, return; return, thou wandering lord;
Charles and the rest will take thee in their arms.

BURGUNDY
I am vanquishèd; these haughty° words of hers
Have battered me like roaring cannon-shot,
And made me almost yield upon my knees.                                     80
Forgive me, country, and sweet countrymen,
And, lords, accept this hearty kind° embrace.
My forces and my power of men° are yours.
So farewell, Talbot; I'll no longer trust thee.

PUCELLE [*Aside.*]
Done like a Frenchman: turn and turn again!°                                85

DAUPHIN
Welcome, brave duke! thy friendship makes us fresh.°

BASTARD
And doth beget new courage in our breasts.

ALENÇON
Pucelle hath bravely played her part in this,
And doth deserve a coronet° of gold.

DAUPHIN
Now let us on, my lords, and join our powers,                               90
And seek how we may prejudice° the foe.          *Exeunt.*

---

**16 Employ thee** apply your efforts **17 devise** determine
**18 sugared** sweet-sounding **21 sweeting** sweetheart **23
boast . . . with** lord it over **24 extirpèd** rooted out **25
expulsed** driven out **26 title of** claim to **30 unto Paris-
ward** toward Paris **31 colors spread** banners unfurled
**34 in favor** to our advantage **48 tender-dying** prematurely
dying **49 pining** consuming

**52 edgèd** sharp **57 stainèd** disgraceful **60 exclaims on**
cries out against **61 lawful progeny** legitimate parentage
**62 lordly** imperious, disdainful **64 set footing** entered **65
fashioned thee** made you into **75 slaughtermen** executioners
**78 haughty** loftily brave **82 kind** (1) friendly (2) of a kinsman
**83 my . . . men** (1) my full complement of troops (?) (2)
command over my troops **85 turn . . . again** change sides
frequently **86 makes us fresh** renews our spirits **89
coronet** a small crown worn on state occasions by members
of the nobility **91 prejudice** damage

Scene IV. [*Paris. The palace.*]

*Enter the* KING, GLOUCESTER, WINCHESTER,
YORK, SUFFOLK, SOMERSET, WARWICK, EXETER,
[VERNON, BASSET, *and others*]. *To them, with his*
SOLDIERS, TALBOT.

TALBOT
My gracious prince, and honorable peers,
Hearing of your arrival in this realm,
I have awhile given truce unto my wars
To do my duty to my sovereign.
In sign whereof, this arm, that hath reclaimed°    5
To your obedience fifty fortresses,
Twelve cities, and seven wallèd towns of strength,
Beside five hundred prisoners of esteem,°
Lets fall his sword before your highness' feet,
And with submissive loyalty of heart    10
Ascribes the glory of his conquest got
First to my God and next unto your grace.
KING
Is this the Lord Talbot, uncle Gloucester,
That hath so long been resident in France?
GLOUCESTER
Yes, if it please your majesty, my liege.°    15
KING
Welcome, brave captain and victorious lord!
When I was young (as yet I am not old)
I do remember° how my father said
A stouter champion never handled sword.
Long since we were resolvèd of your truth,°    20
Your faithful service, and your toil in war;
Yet never have you tasted our reward
Or been reguerdoned° with so much as thanks,
Because till now we never saw your face.
Therefore, stand up, and for these good deserts    25
We here create you Earl of Shrewsbury,
And in our coronation take your place.
*Sennet. Flourish. Exeunt. Manet*° VERNON *and* BASSET.
VERNON
Now, sir, to you, that were so hot° at sea,
Disgracing of° these colors that I wear
In honor of my noble Lord of York—    30
Dar'st thou maintain the former words thou spak'st?
BASSET
Yes, sir, as well as you dare patronage°
The envious barking of your saucy tongue
Against my lord the Duke of Somerset.
VERNON
Sirrah, thy lord I honor as he is.    35
BASSET
Why, what is he? As good a man as York.
VERNON
Hark ye, not so: in witness,° take ye that.

*Strikes him.*

BASSET
Villain, thou knowest the law of arms is such
That whoso draws a sword,° 'tis present° death,
Or else this blow should broach° thy dearest blood.    40
But I'll unto his majesty and crave°
I may have liberty to venge° this wrong,
When thou shalt see I'll meet thee to thy cost.
VERNON
Well, miscreant,° I'll be there as soon as you,
And, after, meet you sooner than you would. *Exeunt.*    45

# ACT IV

Scene I. [*Paris. A hall of state.*]

*Enter* KING, GLOUCESTER, WINCHESTER, YORK,
SUFFOLK, SOMERSET, WARWICK, TALBOT,
EXETER, GOVERNOR [*of Paris, and others*].

GLOUCESTER
Lord Bishop, set the crown upon his head.
WINCHESTER
God save King Henry, of that name the sixth!
GLOUCESTER
Now, Governor of Paris, take your oath,
That you elect no other king but him;
Esteem none friends but such as are his friends,    5
And none your foes but such as shall pretend°
Malicious practices° against his state:
This shall ye do, so help you righteous God!

*Enter* FALSTAFF.

FALSTAFF
My gracious sovereign, as I rode from Calais
To haste unto your coronation,    10
A letter was delivered to my hands,
Writ to your grace from th' Duke of Burgundy.
TALBOT
Shame to the Duke of Burgundy and thee!
I vowed, base knight, when I did meet thee next,
To tear the garter° from thy craven's° leg,    15

[*Plucking it off.*]

Which I have done, because unworthily
Thou wast installèd in that high degree.°
Pardon me, princely Henry, and the rest:
This dastard, at the battle of Poictiers,°
When but in all I was six thousand strong    20
And that the French were almost ten to one,
Before we met or that a stroke was given,
Like to a trusty squire° did run away.
In which assault we lost twelve hundred men;
Myself and divers gentlemen beside    25
Were there surprised and taken prisoners.

---

**III.iv.5 reclaimed** subdued  **8 esteem** good reputation in battle and high birth (thus likely to command a profitable ransom)  **15 liege** sovereign lord  **18 remember** but Henry VI was only nine months old when his father died  **20 resolvèd ... truth** convinced of your loyalty  **23 reguerdoned** repaid  **27 s.d. Manet** remains (the Latin singular with a plural subject is common in Elizabethan stage directions)  **28 hot** passionate  **29 Disgracing of** disparaging  **32 patronage** (1) maintain (2) defend  **37 in witness** as proof

**39 draws a sword** i.e., in a royal residence; **present** immediate  **40 broach** draw as with a tap  **41 crave** beg  **42 venge** avenge  **44 miscreant** coward
**IV.i.6 pretend** purpose  **7 practices** stratagems  **15 garter** badge of the Order of the Garter, England's highest degree of knighthood; **craven's** coward's  **17 degree** dignity  **19 Poictiers** Patay (1429)  **23 trusty squire** used contemptuously: person of inferior character

Then judge, great lords, if I have done amiss,
Or whether that such cowards ought to wear
This ornament of knighthood, yea or no.

GLOUCESTER
To say the truth, this fact° was infamous 30
And ill beseeming any common man,
Much more a knight, a captain, and a leader.

TALBOT
When first this order was ordained, my lords,
Knights of the Garter were of noble birth,
Valiant and virtuous, full of haughty° courage, 35
Such as were grown to credit° by the wars;
Not fearing death, nor shrinking for distress,°
But always resolute in most extremes.°
He then that is not furnished in this sort°
Doth but usurp the sacred name of knight, 40
Profaning this most honorable order,
And should (if I were worthy to be judge)
Be quite degraded, like a hedge-born swain°
That doth presume to boast of gentle blood.

KING
Stain to thy countrymen, thou hear'st thy doom!° 45
Be packing,° therefore, thou that wast a knight:
Henceforth we banish thee on pain of death.
                              [Exit FALSTAFF.]
And now, Lord Protector, view the letter
Sent from our uncle Duke of Burgundy.

GLOUCESTER
What means his grace, that he hath changed his style?° 50
No more but plain and bluntly, "To the king!"
Hath he forgot he is his sovereign?
Or doth this churlish superscription
Pretend° some alteration in good will?
What's here? "I have, upon especial cause, 55
Moved with compassion of my country's wrack,°
Together with the pitiful complaints
Of such as your oppression feeds upon,
Forsaken your pernicious faction
And joined with Charles, the rightful King of France." 60
O monstrous treachery! can this be so,
That in alliance, amity, and oaths,
There should be found such false dissembling guile?

KING
What! doth my uncle Burgundy revolt?

GLOUCESTER
He doth, my lord, and is become your foe. 65

KING
Is that the worst this letter doth contain?

GLOUCESTER
It is the worst, and all, my lord, he writes.

KING
Why, then, Lord Talbot there shall talk with him
And give him chastisement for this abuse.
How say you, my lord; are you not content? 70

TALBOT
Content, my liege? Yes, but that I am prevented,°
I should have begged I might have been employed.

KING
Then gather strength, and march unto him straight;
Let him perceive how ill we brook° his treason
And what offense it is to flout his friends. 75

TALBOT
I go, my lord, in heart desiring still
You may behold confusion of your foes.          [Exit.]

Enter VERNON and BASSET.

VERNON
Grant me the combat,° gracious sovereign.

BASSET
And me, my lord, grant me the combat too.

YORK
This is my servant; hear him, noble prince. 80

SOMERSET
And this is mine; sweet Henry, favor him.

KING
Be patient, lords, and give them leave to speak.
Say, gentlemen, what makes you thus exclaim,
And wherefore crave you combat? Or with whom?

VERNON
With him, my lord, for he hath done me wrong. 85

BASSET
And I with him, for he hath done me wrong.

KING
What is that wrong whereof you both complain?
First let me know, and then I'll answer you.

BASSET
Crossing the sea from England into France,
This fellow here, with envious carping° tongue, 90
Upbraided° me about the rose I wear,
Saying, the sanguine° color of the leaves
Did represent my master's blushing cheeks,
When stubbornly he did repugn° the truth
About a certain question in the law 95
Argued betwixt the Duke of York and him;
With other vile and ignominious terms;
In confutation of which rude reproach
And in defense of my lord's worthiness,
I crave the benefit of law of arms.° 100

VERNON
And that is my petition, noble lord:
For though he seem with forgèd quaint conceit°
To set a gloss upon° his bold intent,
Yet know, my lord, I was provoked by him,
And he first took exceptions at° this badge 105
Pronouncing that the paleness of this flower
Bewrayed° the faintness of my master's heart.

YORK
Will not this malice, Somerset, be left?

SOMERSET
Your private grudge, my Lord of York, will out,
Though ne'er so cunningly you smother it. 110

KING
Good Lord, what madness rules in brainsick men,
When for so slight and frivolous a cause

---

30 **fact** deed   35 **haughty** high   36 **credit** honorable reputation   37 **distress** adversity   38 **in most extremes** in the most difficult situations   39 **furnished . . . sort** possessed of such qualities   43 **hedge-born swain** low peasant   45 **doom** judgment, condemnation   46 **Be packing** begone   50 **style** form of address   54 **Pretend** signify   56 **wrack** misfortune   71 **prevented** anticipated

74 **brook** bear with   78 **combat** trial by arms   90 **carping** fault-finding   91 **Upbraided** reproached   92 **sanguine** blood-red   94 **repugn** resist   100 **benefit . . . arms** privilege of trial by combat   102 **forgèd quaint conceit** crafty manner of expression   103 **set . . . upon** veil in specious language   105 **took exceptions at** disapproved of   107 **Bewrayed** revealed

Such factious emulations° shall arise!
Good cousins both, of York and Somerset,
Quiet yourselves, I pray, and be at peace.     115

YORK
Let this dissension first be tried by fight,
And then your highness shall command a peace.

SOMERSET
The quarrel toucheth° none but us alone;
Betwixt ourselves let us decide it, then.

YORK
There is my pledge;° accept it, Somerset.     120

VERNON
Nay, let it rest where it began at first.

BASSET
Confirm it so, mine honorable lord.

GLOUCESTER
Confirm it so? Confounded be your strife!
And perish ye with your audacious prate!°
Presumptuous vassals, are you not ashamed     125
With this immodest° clamorous outrage
To trouble and disturb the king and us?
And you, my lords, methinks you do not well
To bear with their perverse objections,
Much less to take occasion from their mouths     130
To raise a mutiny betwixt yourselves.
Let me persuade you take a better course.

EXETER
It grieves his highness. Good my lords, be friends.

KING
Come hither, you that would be combatants:
Henceforth I charge you, as you love our favor,     135
Quite to forget this quarrel and the cause.
And you, my lords, remember where we are:
In France, amongst a fickle wavering nation;
If they perceive dissension in our looks
And that within ourselves we disagree,     140
How will their grudging stomachs° be provoked
To willful disobedience, and rebel!
Beside, what infamy will there arise,
When foreign princes shall be certified°
That for a toy,° a thing of no regard,     145
King Henry's peers and chief nobility
Destroyed themselves and lost the realm of France!
O, think upon the conquest of my father,
My tender years, and let us not forgo
That for a trifle that was bought with blood!     150
Let me be umpire in this doubtful strife.
I see no reason, if I wear this rose,

[Putting on a red rose.]

That anyone should therefore be suspicious
I more incline to Somerset than York;
Both are my kinsmen, and I love them both.     155
As well they may upbraid me with my crown
Because, forsooth,° the King of Scots is crowned.
But your discretions° better can persuade
Than I am able to instruct or teach,

And therefore, as we hither came in peace,     160
So let us still continue peace and love.
Cousin of York, we institute your grace
To be our regent in these parts of France;
And, good my Lord of Somerset, unite
Your troops of horsemen with his bands of foot,     165
And, like true subjects, sons of your progenitors,
Go cheerfully together and digest
Your angry choler° on your enemies.
Ourself, my Lord Protector, and the rest
After some respite will return to Calais;     170
From thence to England, where I hope ere long
To be presented, by your victories,
With Charles, Alençon, and that traitorous rout.°

*Flourish. Exeunt. Manet* YORK, WARWICK,
                         EXETER, VERNON.

WARWICK
My Lord of York, I promise you, the king
Prettily, methought, did play the orator.     175

YORK
And so he did, but yet I like it not,
In that he wears the badge of Somerset.

WARWICK
Tush, that was but his fancy, blame him not;
I dare presume, sweet prince, he thought no harm.

YORK
And if—I wish—he did. But let it rest;     180
Other affairs must now be managèd.

*Exeunt. Manet* EXETER.

EXETER
Well didst thou, Richard, to suppress thy voice;
For, had the passions of thy heart burst out,
I fear we should have seen deciphered° there
More rancorous spite, more furious raging broils,     185
Than yet can be imagined or supposed.
But howsoe'er, no simple man that sees
This jarring discord of nobility,
This shouldering° of each other in the court,
This factious bandying° of their favorites,     190
But that it doth presage some ill event.°
'Tis much° when scepters are in children's hands,
But more when envy breeds unkind division;°
There comes the ruin, there begins confusion.    *Exit.*

[Scene II.] *Before Bordeaux.*

*Enter* TALBOT, *with trump and drum.*

TALBOT
Go to the gates of Bordeaux, trumpeter;
Summon their general unto the wall.

[Trumpet] *sounds. Enter* GENERAL *aloft* [with others].

English John Talbot, captains, calls you forth,
Servant in arms to Harry King of England,
And thus he would: open your city gates,
Be humble to us, call my sovereign yours     5

---

131 **emulations** contentions  118 **toucheth** concerns
120 **pledge** challenge (made by casting down one's glove)
124 **prate** chatter  126 **immodest** arrogant  141 **grudging
stomachs** resentful dispositions  144 **certified** informed
145 **toy** trifle  157 **forsooth** in truth (used derisively)  158
**discretions** lordships, judgments

168 **choler** bile (according to earlier physiology, the cause
of anger or hot temper)  173 **rout** crowd  184 **deciphered**
revealed  189 **shouldering** jostling  190 **bandying** contention
191 **presage . . . event** predict some evil outcome  192
**much** difficult  193 **unkind division** unnatural disunion

And do him homage as obedient subjects,
And I'll withdraw me and my bloody power.
But, if you frown upon this proffered peace,
You tempt the fury of my three attendants,          10
Lean famine, quartering° steel, and climbing fire,
Who in a moment even° with the earth
Shall lay your stately and air-braving° towers,
If you forsake the offer of their love.

GENERAL
Thou ominous and fearful owl of death,°          15
Our nation's terror and their bloody scourge!
The period° of thy tyranny approacheth.
On us thou canst not enter but by death,
For, I protest, we are well fortified
And strong enough to issue out and fight.          20
If thou retire, the Dolphin, well appointed,°
Stands with the snares of war to tangle thee.
On either hand° thee there are squadrons pitched
To wall thee from the liberty of flight,
And no way canst thou turn thee for redress,°          25
But death doth front° thee with apparent spoil,°
And pale destruction meets thee in the face.
Ten thousand French have ta'en the sacrament°
To rive° their dangerous artillery
Upon no Christian soul but English Talbot.          30
Lo, there thou stand'st, a breathing valiant man,
Of an invincible unconquered spirit!
This is the latest° glory of thy praise
That I, thy enemy, due° thee withal,
For ere the glass that now begins to run          35
Finish the process of his sandy hour,
These eyes, that see thee now well colorèd,°
Shall see thee withered, bloody, pale, and dead.

*Drum afar off.*

Hark! hark! The Dolphin's drum, a warning bell,
Sings heavy° music to thy timorous soul,          40
And mine shall ring thy dire departure out.
                        *Exit [with his* FOLLOWERS].

TALBOT
He fables not,° I hear the enemy;
Out, some light° horsemen, and peruse their wings.°
O, negligent and heedless discipline!
How are we parked and bounded in a pale,°          45
A little herd of England's timorous deer,
Mazed with° a yelping kennel of French curs!
If we be English deer, be then in blood,°
Not rascal-like° to fall down with a pinch,°
But rather moody-mad;° and, desperate stags,          50
Turn on the bloody° hounds with heads of steel
And make the cowards stand aloof at bay.

Sell every man his life as dear as mine,
And they shall find dear° deer of us, my friends.
God and Saint George, Talbot and England's right,          55
Prosper our colors in this dangerous fight!   [*Exeunt.*]

[*Scene III. Plains in Gascony.*]

*Enter a* MESSENGER *that meets York. Enter* YORK *with trumpet and many* SOLDIERS.

YORK
Are not the speedy scouts returned again
That dogged° the mighty army of the Dolphin?

MESSENGER
They are returned, my lord, and give it out°
That he is marched to Bordeaux with his power
To fight with Talbot. As he marched along,          5
By your espials° were discoverèd
Two mightier troops than that the Dolphin led,
Which joined with him and made their march for
   Bordeaux.

YORK
A plague upon that villain Somerset,
That thus delays my promisèd supply          10
Of horsemen that were levied for this siege!
Renownèd Talbot doth expect° my aid,
And I am louted° by a traitor villain
And cannot help the noble chevalier.°
God comfort him in this necessity!          15
If he miscarry,° farewell wars in France.

*Enter another messenger [Sir William* LUCY].

LUCY
Thou princely leader of our English strength,
Never so needful on the earth of France,
Spur to the rescue of the noble Talbot,
Who now is girdled with a waist of iron          20
And hemmed about with grim destruction.
To Bordeaux, warlike duke! to Bordeaux, York!
Else, farewell Talbot, France, and England's honor.

YORK
O God, that Somerset, who in proud heart
Doth stop my cornets,° were in Talbot's place!          25
So should we save a valiant gentleman
By forfeiting a traitor and a coward.
Mad ire and wrathful fury makes me weep,
That thus we die, while remiss traitors sleep.

LUCY
O, send some succor to the distressed lord!          30

YORK
He dies, we lose; I break my warlike word;
We mourn, France smiles; we lose, they daily get;
All long° of this vile traitor Somerset.

LUCY
Then God take mercy on brave Talbot's soul,
And on his son young John, who two hours since          35
I met in travel toward his warlike father!

IV.ii.11 **quartering** that cuts men into quarters  12 **even** level  13 **air-braving** skyscraping  15 **owl of death** alluding to the owl as a supposed harbinger of death or misfortune  17 **period** end  21 **appointed** equipped  23 **hand** side of  25 **redress** relief  26 **front** confront; **apparent spoil** obvious destruction  28 **ta'en the sacrament** confirmed their oaths by receiving Holy Communion  29 **rive** burst  33 **latest** final  34 **due** endue  37 **well colorèd** of healthy complexion  40 **heavy** doleful  42 **fables not** does not speak falsely  43 **light** lightly armed; **peruse their wings** scout their flanks  45 **parked . . . pale** surrounded and hemmed in by a fence  47 **Mazed with** terrified by  48 **in blood** (1) in full vigor (2) in temper  49 **rascal-like** like inferior deer; **pinch** nip  50 **moody-mad** furious in mood  51 **bloody** bloodthirsty

54 **dear** costly
IV.iii.2 **dogged** tracked, closely pursued  3 **give it out** report  6 **espials** spies  12 **expect** await  13 **louted** mocked  14 **chevalier** knight  16 **miscarry** be destroyed  25 **stop my cornets** withhold my squadrons of cavalry  33 **long** on account

This seven years did not Talbot see his son,
And now they meet where both their lives are done.

YORK

Alas, what joy shall noble Talbot have
To bid his young son welcome to his grave?   40
Away! vexation almost stops my breath,
That sundered° friends greet in the hour of death.
Lucy, farewell, no more my fortune can°
But curse the cause° I cannot aid the man.
Maine, Blois, Poictiers, and Tours are won away,  45
Long all° of Somerset and his delay.

      *Exit [with his* SOLDIERS].

LUCY

Thus, while the vulture of sedition
Feeds in the bosom of such great commanders,
Sleeping neglection° doth betray to loss
The conquest of our scarce-cold° conqueror,  50
That ever living man of memory,
Henry the Fifth. Whiles they each other cross,
Lives, honors, lands, and all hurry to loss.

[Scene IV. *Other plains in Gascony.*]

*Enter* SOMERSET *with his* ARMY, [*a* CAPTAIN *of Talbot's with him*].

SOMERSET

It is too late, I cannot send them now;
This expedition was by York and Talbot
Too rashly plotted. All our general° force
Might with a sally° of the very° town
Be buckled with. The overdaring Talbot  5
Hath sullied all his gloss° of former honor
By this unheedful, desperate, wild adventure;
York set him on to fight and die in shame,
That, Talbot dead, great York might bear the name.

CAPTAIN

Here is Sir William Lucy, who with me  10
Set from our o'ermatched° forces forth for aid.

SOMERSET

How now, Sir William! whither were you sent?

LUCY

Whither, my lord? from bought and sold Lord Talbot;
Who, ringed about with bold adversity,°
Cries out for noble York and Somerset  15
To beat assailing death from his weak regions;°
And whiles the honorable captain there
Drops bloody sweat from his war-wearied limbs,
And in advantage ling'ring° looks for rescue,
You, his false hopes, the trust of England's honor, 20
Keep off aloof with worthless emulation.°
Let not your private discord keep away
The levied succors° that should lend him aid
While he, renownèd noble gentleman,
Yield up his life unto a world of odds;  25

Orleans the Bastard, Charles, Burgundy,
Alençon, Reignier compass him about,
And Talbot perisheth by your default.

SOMERSET

York set him on, York should have sent him aid.

LUCY

And York as fast upon your grace exclaims,  30
Swearing that you withhold his levied host,
Collected for this expedition.

SOMERSET

York lies; he might have sent and had the horse!
I owe him little duty, and less love,
And take° foul scorn to fawn on him by sending. 35

LUCY

The fraud of England, not the force of France,
Hath now entrapped the noble-minded Talbot;
Never to England shall he bear his life,
But dies betrayed to fortune by your strife.

SOMERSET

Come, go; I will dispatch the horsemen straight; 40
Within six hours they will be at his aid.

LUCY

Too late comes rescue, he is ta'en or slain,
For fly he could not, if he would have fled,
And fly would Talbot never though he might.

SOMERSET

If he be dead, brave Talbot, then adieu!  45

LUCY

His fame lives in the world, his shame in you.

         *Exeunt.*

[Scene V. *The English camp near Bordeaux.*]

*Enter* TALBOT *and his son* [JOHN].

TALBOT

O young John Talbot! I did send for thee
To tutor thee in stratagems of war,
That Talbot's name might be in thee revived
When sapless° age and weak unable° limbs
Should bring thy father to his drooping chair.° 5
But, O malignant and ill-boding stars!
Now thou art come unto a feast of death,
A terrible and unavoided° danger:
Therefore, dear boy, mount on my swiftest horse,
And I'll direct thee how thou shalt escape  10
By sudden flight. Come, dally not, be gone.

JOHN

Is my name Talbot? And am I your son?
And shall I fly? O, if you love my mother,
Dishonor not her honorable name,
To make a bastard and a slave of me.  15
The world will say, he is not Talbot's blood,
That basely fled when noble Talbot stood.

TALBOT

Fly, to revenge my death, if I be slain.

JOHN

He that flies so will ne'er return again.

---

42 **sundered** separated 43 **fortune can** circumstances enable me to do 44 **cause** reason why 46 **Long all** because 49 **neglection** negligence 50 **scarce-cold** barely dead
**IV.iv.3 general** whole 4 **sally** sudden outrush; **very** itself 6 **gloss** luster 11 **o'ermatched** outnumbered 14 **bold adversity** confident opponents 16 **regions** places 19 **in advantage ling'ring** (1) desperately clinging to every advantage (?) (2) while holding out on advantageous ground (?) 21 **emulation** rivalry 23 **succors** reinforcements

35 **take** submit to
**IV.v.4 sapless** withered; **unable** powerless 5 **drooping chair** decline from vigor 8 **unavoided** unavoidable

TALBOT
If we both stay, we both are sure to die.                    20
JOHN
Then let me stay, and, father, do you fly:
Your loss is great, so your regard should be;
My worth unknown, no loss is known in me.
Upon my death the French can little boast;
In yours they will, in you all hopes are lost.               25
Flight cannot stain the honor you have won,
But mine it will, that no exploit have done;
You fled for vantage,° everyone will swear,
But, if I bow,° they'll say it was for fear.
There is no hope that ever I will stay                       30
If the first hour I shrink and run away.
Here on my knee I beg mortality,°
Rather than life preserved with infamy.
TALBOT
Shall all thy mother's hopes lie in one tomb?
JOHN
Ay, rather than I'll shame my mother's womb.                 35
TALBOT
Upon my blessing, I command thee go.
JOHN
To fight I will, but not to fly the foe.
TALBOT
Part of thy father may be saved in thee.
JOHN
No part of him but will be shame to me.
TALBOT
Thou never hadst renown, nor canst not lose it.              40
JOHN
Yes, your renownèd name: shall flight abuse it?
TALBOT
Thy father's charge° shall clear thee from that stain.
JOHN
You cannot witness for me, being slain.
If death be so apparent, then both fly.
TALBOT
And leave my followers here to fight and die?               45
My age was never tainted with such shame.
JOHN
And shall my youth be guilty of such blame?
No more can I be severed from your side
Than can yourself yourself in twain° divide.
Stay, go, do what you will, the like do I;                  50
For live I will not, if my father die.
TALBOT
Then here I take my leave of thee, fair son,
Born to eclipse° thy life this afternoon.
Come, side by side together live and die;
And soul with soul from France to heaven fly.               55
                              *Exit* [*with* JOHN].

[Scene VI. *A field of battle.*]

*Alarum: excursions, wherein Talbot's son* [JOHN] *is hemmed about, and* TALBOT *rescues him.*

TALBOT
Saint George and victory! fight, soldiers, fight!
The regent hath with Talbot broke his word
And left us to the rage of France his sword.
Where is John Talbot? Pause, and take thy breath;
I gave thee life and rescued thee from death.                5
JOHN
O, twice my father, twice am I thy son!
The life thou gav'st me first was lost and done,
Till with thy warlike sword, despite of° fate,
To my determined° time thou gav'st new date.
TALBOT
When from the Dolphin's crest thy sword struck fire,         10
It warmed thy father's heart with proud desire
Of bold-faced victory. Then leaden° age,
Quickened° with youthful spleen° and warlike rage,
Beat down Alençon, Orleans, Burgundy,
And from the pride of Gallia° rescued thee.                  15
The ireful Bastard Orleans, that drew blood
From thee, my boy, and had the maidenhood
Of thy first fight, I soon encounterèd,
And interchanging blows I quickly shed
Some of his bastard blood; and in disgrace                   20
Bespoke him thus: "Contaminated, base,
And misbegotten blood I spill of thine,
Mean and right poor, for that pure blood of mine
Which thou didst force from Talbot, my brave boy."
Here,° purposing the Bastard to destroy,                     25
Came in strong rescue. Speak, thy father's care,
Art thou not weary, John? How dost thou fare?
Wilt thou yet leave the battle, boy, and fly,
Now thou art sealed° the son of chivalry?
Fly, to revenge my death when I am dead;                     30
The help of one stands me in little stead.
O, too much folly is it, well I wot,°
To hazard° all our lives in one small boat!
If I today die not with Frenchmen's rage,
Tomorrow I shall die with mickle° age.                       35
By me they nothing gain and if I stay;
'Tis but the short'ning of my life one day.
In thee thy mother dies, our household's name,
My death's revenge, thy youth, and England's fame:
All these and more we hazard by thy stay;                    40
All these are saved if thou wilt fly away.
JOHN
The sword of Orleans hath not made me smart;
These words of yours draw lifeblood from my heart.
On that advantage, bought with such a shame,
To save a paltry life and slay bright fame,                  45
Before young Talbot from old Talbot fly,
The coward horse that bears me fall and die!
And like° me to the peasant boys of France,
To be shame's scorn and subject of mischance!°

IV.vi.8 **despite of** in spite of  **9 determined** predestined, fated  **12 leaden** spiritless  **13 Quickened** animated; **spleen** high spirits, courage  **15 Gallia** France  **25 Here** here I  **29 sealed** authenticated (by his deeds)  **32 wot** know  **33 hazard** gamble  **35 mickle** much, advanced  **48 like** compare  **49 subject of mischance** an example of unhappy fate

28 **for vantage** to gain a tactical advantage  **29 bow** flee  **32 mortality** death  **42 charge** attack  **49 twain** two  **53 eclipse** end

Surely, by all the glory you have won, 　　　　　50
And if I fly, I am not Talbot's son.
Then talk no more of flight, it is no boot;°
If son to Talbot, die at Talbot's foot.

TALBOT
Then follow thou thy desperate sire of Crete,°
Thou Icarus; thy life to me is sweet; 　　　　　55
If thou wilt fight, fight by thy father's side;
And, commendable proved, let's die in pride.°

　　　　　　　　　　　　　　*Exit [with* JOHN].


[Scene VII. *Another part of the field.*]

*Alarum: excursions. Enter old* TALBOT, *led [by a* SER-
VANT].

TALBOT
Where is my other life? Mine own is gone.
O, where's young Talbot? Where is valiant John?
Triumphant death, smeared with captivity,°
Young Talbot's valor makes me smile at thee.
When he perceived me shrink° and on my knee, 　　5
His bloody sword he brandished over me,
And like a hungry lion did commence
Rough deeds of rage and stern impatience,
But when my angry guardant° stood alone,
Tend'ring° my ruin and assailed of° none, 　　　10
Dizzy-eyed° fury and great rage of heart
Suddenly made him from my side to start
Into the clust'ring battle° of the French,
And in that sea of blood my boy did drench
His overmounting° spirit and there died, 　　　15
My Icarus, my blossom, in his pride.

*Enter [*SOLDIERS,*] with* JOHN *Talbot, borne.*

SERVANT
O my dear lord, lo, where your son is borne!

TALBOT
Thou antic° death, which laugh'st us here to scorn,
Anon,° from thy insulting tyranny,
Coupled in bonds of perpetuity,° 　　　　　　20
Two Talbots, wingèd through the lither° sky,
In thy despite shall 'scape mortality.
O thou, whose wounds become hard-favored° death,
Speak to thy father ere thou yield thy breath!
Brave death by speaking, whether he will or no; 　25
Imagine him a Frenchman and thy foe.
Poor boy! he smiles, methinks, as who should say,°
"Had death been French, then death had died today."
Come, come and lay him in his father's arms;
My spirit can no longer bear these harms. 　　　30

Soldiers, adieu! I have what I would have,
Now my old arms are young John Talbot's grave.

　　　　　　　　　　　　　　　　　　*Dies.*

*Enter Charles [the* DAUPHIN], ALENÇON, BUR-
GUNDY, BASTARD, *and [la]* PUCELLE, *[with*
FORCES].

DAUPHIN
Had York and Somerset brought rescue in,
We should have found a bloody day of this.

BASTARD
How the young whelp of Talbot's, raging wood,° 　35
Did flesh his puny-sword° in Frenchmen's blood!

PUCELLE
Once I encountered him and thus I said:
"Thou maiden youth, be vanquished by a maid."
But, with a proud majestical high scorn,
He answered thus: "Young Talbot was not born 　40
To be the pillage° of a giglot° wench."
So, rushing in the bowels° of the French,
He left me proudly, as unworthy fight.°

BURGUNDY
Doubtless he would have made a noble knight.
See, where he lies inhearsèd° in the arms 　　　45
Of the most bloody nurser° of his harms!

BASTARD
Hew them to pieces, hack their bones asunder,
Whose life was England's glory, Gallia's wonder.

DAUPHIN
O no, forbear! for that which we have fled
During the life, let us not wrong it dead. 　　　50

*Enter* LUCY, *[attended by a French* HERALD].

LUCY
Herald, conduct me to the Dolphin's tent,
To know who hath obtained the glory of the day.

DAUPHIN
On what submissive message art thou sent?

LUCY
Submission, Dolphin! 'Tis a mere French word;
We English warriors wot not° what it means. 　55
I come to know what prisoners thou hast ta'en
And to survey the bodies of the dead.

DAUPHIN
For prisoners ask'st thou? Hell our prison is.°
But tell me whom thou seek'st.

LUCY
But where's the great Alcides° of the field, 　　60
Valiant Lord Talbot, Earl of Shrewsbury,
Created, for his rare success in arms,
Great Earl of Washford, Waterford, and Valence,
Lord Talbot of Goodrig and Urchinfield,
Lord Strange of Blackmere, Lord Verdun of Alton, 　65
Lord Cromwell of Wingfield, Lord Furnival of
　　Sheffield,
The thrice-victorious Lord of Falconbridge,

---

**52 boot** use　**54 sire of Crete** Daedalus (who made wings of
feathers and wax on which he and his son Icarus attempted to
escape from King Minos of Crete)　**57 pride** glory
**IV.vii.3 captivity** the blood of your captives (?)　**5 shrink**
give way　**9 guardant** protector　**10 Tend'ring** tenderly
caring for me in; **of** by　**11 Dizzy-eyed** giddy　**13 clust'ring
battle** close-grouped battle formation　**15 overmounting** too
highly aspiring　**18 antic** (1) grinning (2) buffoon　**19 Anon**
immediately　**20 of perpetuity** eternal　**21 lither** yielding,
pliant　**23 hard-favored** ugly-looking　**27 who should say**
as if saying

**35 wood** mad　**36 flesh his puny-sword** initiate his untried
sword in battle　**41 pillage** plunder; **giglot** wanton　**42
bowels** midst　**43 unworthy fight** not worthy of fighting
with　**45 inhearsèd** enclosed as in a hearse　**46 nurser** fosterer
**55 wot not** do not know　**58 Hell . . . is** We kill all our
enemies　**60 Alcides** Hercules

Knight of the noble order of Saint George,
Worthy Saint Michael, and the Golden Fleece,°
Great Marshal to Henry the Sixth                                70
Of all his wars within the realm of France?

PUCELLE
Here's a silly stately style° indeed!
The Turk,° that two and fifty kingdoms hath,
Writes not so tedious a style as this.
Him that thou magnifi'st with all these titles        75
Stinking and fly-blown lies here at our feet.

LUCY
Is Talbot slain, the Frenchmen's only scourge,
Your kingdom's terror and black Nemesis?
O, were mine eyeballs into bullets turned,
That I in rage might shoot them at your faces!     80
O, that I could but call these dead to life,
It were enough to fright the realm of France!
Were but his picture left amongst you here,
It would amaze° the proudest of you all.
Give me their bodies, that I may bear them hence   85
And give them burial as beseems their worth.

PUCELLE
I think this upstart is old Talbot's ghost,
He speaks with such a proud commanding spirit.
For God's sake, let him have him; to keep them
    here,
They would but stink and putrefy the air.             90

DAUPHIN
Go, take their bodies hence.

LUCY
I'll bear them hence, but from their ashes shall be
    reared
A phoenix° that shall make all France afeard.°

DAUPHIN
So we be rid of them, do with him what thou wilt.
And now to Paris, in this conquering vein:°        95
All will be ours, now bloody Talbot's slain.   *Exeunt.*

# ACT V

[Scene I. *London. The palace.*]

*Sennet. Enter* KING, GLOUCESTER, *and* EXETER.

KING
Have you perused the letters from the pope,
The emperor, and the Earl of Armagnac?

GLOUCESTER
I have, my lord, and their intent is this:
They humbly sue unto your excellence
To have a godly peace concluded of                    5
Between the realms of England and of France.

KING
How doth your grace affect° their motion?

GLOUCESTER
Well, my good lord, and as the only means
To stop effusion of our Christian blood
And stablish° quietness on every side.                10

KING
Ay, marry, uncle, for I always thought
It was both impious and unnatural
That such immanity° and bloody strife
Should reign among professors of° one faith.

GLOUCESTER
Beside, my lord, the sooner to effect               15
And surer bind this knot of amity,
The Earl of Armagnac, near knit° to Charles,
A man of great authority in France,
Proffers his only daughter to your grace
In marriage, with a large and sumptuous dowry.   20

KING
Marriage, uncle! alas, my years are young,
And fitter is my study and my books
Than wanton dalliance with a paramour.°
Yet call th' ambassadors, and, as you please,
So let them have their answers every one:         25
I shall be well content with any choice
Tends to God's glory and my country's weal.

*Enter* WINCHESTER [*in cardinal's habit*], *and three*
AMBASSADORS, [*one of them a* LEGATE°].

EXETER
What! is my Lord of Winchester installed,
And called unto a cardinal's degree?
Then I perceive that will be verified             30
Henry the Fifth did sometime° prophesy:
"If once he come to be a cardinal,
He'll make his cap° co-equal with the crown."

KING
My lords ambassadors, your several suits°
Have been considered and debated on.              35
Your purpose is both good and reasonable,
And therefore are we certainly resolved,
To draw conditions of a friendly peace,
Which by my Lord of Winchester we mean
Shall be transported presently to France.         40

GLOUCESTER
And for the proffer of my lord your master,°
I have informed his highness so at large
As° liking of the lady's virtuous gifts,
Her beauty and the value of her dower,°
He doth intend she shall be England's queen.      45

KING
In argument and proof of which contract,
Bear her this jewel, pledge of my affection.
And so, my Lord Protector, see them guarded
And safely brought to Dover, wherein shipped,°
Commit them to the fortune of the sea.            50
    *Exeunt [all but* WINCHESTER *and the* LEGATE].

68–69 **Saint George . . . Saint Michael . . . Golden Fleece** chivalric orders of England, France, and the Holy Roman Empire respectively  72 **stately style** imposing title  73 **the Turk** the sultan  84 **amaze** stupefy, terrify  93 **phoenix** in mythology, an Arabian bird that is resurrected from the ashes of its own funeral pyre; **afeard** afraid  95 **vein** mood
**V.i.7 affect** like

10 **stablish** establish  13 **immanity** monstrous cruelty  14 **professors of** believers in  17 **near knit** closely bound by blood relationship  23 **wanton . . . paramour** lascivious sport with a mistress  27 **s.d. Legate** representative of the pope  31 **sometime** once  33 **cap** cardinal's skullcap  34 **several suits** individual requests  41 **master** the Count of Armagnac  43 **As** that  44 **dower** marriage settlement  49 **shipped** embarked

WINCHESTER
Stay, my Lord Legate; you shall first receive
The sum of money which I promisèd
Should be delivered to his holiness
For clothing me in these grave ornaments.°
LEGATE
I will attend upon your lordship's leisure.          55
WINCHESTER [*Aside.*]
Now Winchester will not submit, I trow,
Or be inferior to the proudest peer.
Humphrey of Gloucester, thou shalt well perceive
That, neither in birth or for authority,
The bishop will be overborne by thee.          60
I'll either make thee stoop and bend thy knee,
Or sack this country with a mutiny.°          *Exeunt.*


[*Scene II. France. Plains in Anjou.*]

*Enter Charles* [*the* DAUPHIN], BURGUNDY, ALIN-
ÇON, BASTARD, REIGNIER, *and Joan* [*la* PUCELLE,
*with* FORCES].

DAUPHIN
These news, my lords, may cheer our drooping spirits:
'Tis said the stout Parisians do revolt
And turn again unto the warlike French.
ALENÇON
Then march to Paris, royal Charles of France.
And keep not back your powers in dalliance.°          5
PUCELLE
Peace be amongst them, if they turn to us;
Else, ruin combat with their palaces!

*Enter* SCOUT.

SCOUT
Success unto our valiant general,
And happiness to his accomplices!
DAUPHIN
What tidings send our scouts? I prithee, speak.          10
SCOUT
The English army, that divided was
Into two parties, is now conjoined° in one,
And means to give you battle presently.
DAUPHIN
Somewhat too sudden, sirs, the warning is,
But we will presently provide for them.          15
BURGUNDY
I trust the ghost of Talbot is not there;
Now he is gone, my lord, you need not fear.
PUCELLE
Of all base passions, fear is most accursed.
Command the conquest, Charles, it shall be thine;
Let Henry fret and all the world repine.°          20
DAUPHIN
Then on, my lords, and France be fortunate!          *Exeunt.*

[*Scene III. Before Angiers.*]

*Alarum. Excursions. Enter Joan la* PUCELLE.

PUCELLE
The regent° conquers, and the Frenchmen fly.
Now help, ye charming° spells and periapts,°
And ye choice° spirits that admonish° me
And give me signs of future accidents.°

*Thunder.*

You speedy helpers, that are substitutes          5
Under the lordly monarch of the north,°
Appear and aid me in this enterprise.

*Enter* FIENDS.

This speedy and quick appearance argues proof
Of your accustomed diligence to me.
Now, ye familiar spirits, that are culled°          10
Out of the powerful regions under earth,
Help me this once, that France may get° the field.

*They walk, and speak not.*

O, hold me not with silence overlong!
Where I was wont to feed you with my blood,
I'll lop a member° off and give it you          15
In earnest° of a further benefit,
So you do condescend to help me now.

*They hang their heads.*

No hope to have redress? My body shall
Pay recompense if you will grant my suit.

*They shake their heads.*

Cannot my body nor blood-sacrifice          20
Entreat you to your wonted furtherance?°
Then take my soul; my body, soul, and all,
Before that England give the French the foil.°
          *They depart.*
See, they forsake me! Now the time is come
That France must vail° her lofty plumèd crest          25
And let her head fall into England's lap.
My ancient° incantations are too weak,
And hell too strong for me to buckle with.
Now, France, thy glory droopeth to the dust.          *Exit.*

*Excursions.* BURGUNDY *and* YORK *fight hand to hand.*
FRENCH *fly,* [*pursued.* YORK *returns with la* PUCELLE
*captive*].

YORK
Damsel of France, I think I have you fast;          30
Unchain your spirits now with spelling° charms
And try if they can gain your liberty.
A goodly prize, fit for the devil's grace!

---

54 **grave ornaments** symbols of high rank  62 **mutiny**
rebellion
**V.ii.**5 **dalliance** idleness  12 **conjoined** united  20 **repine**
complain

**V.iii.**1 **regent** York  2 **charming** exercising magic power;
**periapts** amulets  3 **choice** excellent; **admonish** inform  4
**accidents** events  6 **monarch . . . north** the devil (evil spirits
were traditionally thought to dwell in the regions of the
north)  10 **culled** gathered  12 **get** win  15 **member** part
of the body  16 **earnest** pledge  21 **furtherance** assistance
23 **the foil** defeat, repulse  25 **vail** lower or take off in
token of submission  27 **ancient** former  31 **spelling** spell-
casting

See, how the ugly witch doth bend her brows,
As if, with Circe,° she would change my shape!          35
PUCELLE
Changed to a worser shape thou canst not be.
YORK
O, Charles the Dolphin is a proper man;
No shape but his can please your dainty° eye.
PUCELLE
A plaguing° mischief light on Charles and thee!
And may ye both be suddenly surprised          40
By bloody hands, in sleeping on your beds!
YORK
Fell banning° hag, enchantress, hold thy tongue!
PUCELLE
I prithee, give me leave to curse awhile.
YORK
Curse, miscreant, when thou comest to the stake.

*Exeunt.*

*Alarum. Enter* SUFFOLK, *with* MARGARET *in his hand.*

SUFFOLK
Be what thou wilt, thou art my prisoner.          45

*Gazes on her.*

O fairest beauty, do not fear nor fly!
For I will touch thee but with reverent° hands;
I kiss these fingers for eternal peace
And lay them gently on thy tender side.
Who art thou? Say, that I may honor thee.          50
MARGARET
Margaret my name, and daughter to a king,
The King of Naples, whosoe'er thou art.
SUFFOLK
An earl I am, and Suffolk am I called.
Be not offended, nature's miracle,
Thou art allotted° to be ta'en by me:          55
So doth the swan her downy cygnets save,
Keeping them prisoner underneath her wings.
Yet if this servile usage° once offend,
Go and be free again as Suffolk's friend.

*She is going.*

O, stay! [*Aside.*] I have no power to let her pass;          60
My hand would free her, but my heart says no.
As plays the sun upon the glassy° streams,
Twinkling another counterfeited° beam,
So seems this gorgeous beauty to mine eyes.
Fain would I woo her, yet I dare not speak;          65
I'll call for pen and ink, and write my mind.
Fie, de la Pole! disable° not thyself.
Hast not a tongue? Is she not here?
Wilt thou be daunted by a woman's sight?
Ay, beauty's princely majesty is such,          70
Confounds the tongue and makes the senses rough.°
MARGARET
Say, Earl of Suffolk, if thy name be so,

What ransom must I pay before I pass?
For I perceive I am thy prisoner.
SUFFOLK [*Aside.*]
How canst thou tell she will deny thy suit,          75
Before thou make a trial of her love?
MARGARET
Why speak'st thou not? What ransom must I pay?
SUFFOLK [*Aside.*]
She's beautiful and therefore to be wooed;
She is a woman, therefore to be won.
MARGARET
Wilt thou accept of ransom, yea or no?          80
SUFFOLK [*Aside.*]
Fond man, remember that thou hast a wife;
Then how can Margaret be thy paramour?
MARGARET
I were best to leave him, for he will not hear.
SUFFOLK [*Aside.*]
There all is marred; there lies a cooling card.°
MARGARET
He talks at random; sure, the man is mad.          85
SUFFOLK [*Still aside, but more loudly.*]
And yet a dispensation° may be had.
MARGARET
And yet I would that you would answer me.
SUFFOLK [*Aside.*]
I'll win this Lady Margaret. For whom?
Why, for my king. [*Somewhat more loudly.*] Tush,
    that's a wooden° thing!
MARGARET
He talks of wood: it° is some carpenter.          90
SUFFOLK [*Aside.*]
Yet so my fancy may be satisfied
And peace establishèd between these realms.
But there remains a scruple° in that too:
For though her father be the King of Naples,
Duke of Anjou and Maine, yet is he poor,          95
And our nobility will scorn the match.
MARGARET
Hear ye, captain, are you not at leisure?
SUFFOLK [*Aside.*]
It shall be so, disdain they ne'er so much:
Henry is youthful and will quickly yield.

[*Aloud.*]

Madam, I have a secret to reveal.          100
MARGARET [*Aside.*]
What though I be enthralled?° he seems a knight,
And will not any way dishonor me.
SUFFOLK
Lady, vouchsafe to listen what I say.
MARGARET [*Aside.*]
Perhaps I shall be rescued by the French,
And then I need not crave his courtesy.          105
SUFFOLK
Sweet madam, give me hearing in a cause.
MARGARET [*Aside.*]
Tush, women have been captivate ere now.

35 with Circe like Circe (the sorceress in the *Odyssey* who transformed men into beasts)   38 dainty fastidious   39 plaguing tormenting   42 Fell banning evil cursing   47 reverent respectful   55 allotted fated   58 servile usage unworthy treatment   62 glassy smooth   63 counterfeited reflected   67 disable disparage   71 rough dull

84 cooling card something to cool my ardor   86 dispensation annulment of a previous marriage   89 wooden dull   90 it he   93 scruple difficulty   101 enthralled captured

SUFFOLK
Lady, wherefore talk you so?

MARGARET
I cry you mercy,° 'tis but quid for quo.°

SUFFOLK
Say, gentle princess, would you not suppose          110
Your bondage happy, to be made a queen?

MARGARET
To be a queen in bondage is more vile
Than is a slave in base servility,
For princes should be free.

SUFFOLK                          And so shall you,
If happy England's royal king be free.              115

MARGARET
Why, what concerns his freedom unto me?

SUFFOLK
I'll undertake to make thee Henry's queen,
To put a golden scepter in thy hand
And set a precious crown upon thy head,
If thou wilt condescend to be my—

MARGARET                         What?          120

SUFFOLK   His love.

MARGARET
I am unworthy to be Henry's wife.

SUFFOLK
No, gentle madam, I unworthy am
To woo so fair a dame to be his wife,
And have no portion in° the choice myself.          125
How say you, madam, are ye so content?

MARGARET
And if my father please, I am content.

SUFFOLK
Then call our captains and our colors forth.
And, madam, at your father's castle walls
We'll crave a parley, to confer with him.           130

Sound [a parley]. Enter REIGNIER on the walls.

See, Reignier, see, thy daughter prisoner!

REIGNIER
To whom?

SUFFOLK   To me.

REIGNIER          Suffolk, what remedy?
I am a soldier and unapt° to weep
Or to exclaim on fortune's fickleness.

SUFFOLK
Yes, there is remedy enough, my lord:               135
Consent, and for thy honor give consent,
Thy daughter shall be wedded to my king,
Whom° I with pain° have wooed and won thereto,
And this her easy-held imprisonment
Hath gained thy daughter princely liberty.          140

REIGNIER
Speaks Suffolk as he thinks?

SUFFOLK                       Fair Margaret knows
That Suffolk doth not flatter, face,° or feign.

REIGNIER
Upon thy princely warrant, I descend
To give thee answer to thy just demand.     [Exit.]

SUFFOLK
And here I will expect° thy coming.                 145

Trumpets sound. Enter REIGNIER.

REIGNIER
Welcome, brave earl, into our territories;
Command in Anjou what your honor pleases.

SUFFOLK
Thanks, Reignier, happy for° so sweet a child,
Fit to be made companion with a king.
What answer makes your grace unto my suit?         150

REIGNIER
Since thou dost deign to woo her little worth°
To be the princely bride of such a lord,
Upon condition I may quietly
Enjoy mine own, the country Maine and Anjou,
Free from oppression or the stroke of war,         155
My daughter shall be Henry's, if he please.

SUFFOLK
That is her ransom; I deliver her,
And those two countries I will undertake
Your grace shall well and quietly enjoy.

REIGNIER
And I again, in Henry's royal name,                160
As deputy° unto that gracious king,
Give thee her hand, for sign of plighted faith.°

SUFFOLK
Reignier of France, I give thee kingly thanks
Because this is in traffic° of a king.

[Aside.]

And yet, methinks, I could be well content          165
To be mine own attorney° in this case.

[Aloud.]

I'll over then to England with this news,
And make this marriage to be solemnized.
So farewell, Reignier; set this diamond safe
In golden palaces, as it becomes.                  170

REIGNIER
I do embrace thee, as I would embrace
The Christian prince, King Henry, were he here.

MARGARET
Farewell, my lord; good wishes, praise, and prayers
Shall Suffolk ever have of Margaret.

She is going.

SUFFOLK
Farewell, sweet madam; but hark you, Margaret:      175
No princely commendations to my king?

MARGARET
Such commendations as becomes a maid,
A virgin, and his servant, say to him.

SUFFOLK
Words sweetly placed and modestly directed.°
But, madam, I must trouble you again:               180
No loving token to his majesty?

---

**109 cry you mercy** beg your pardon; **quid for quo** even
exchange, tit for tat  **125 no portion in** (1) no share in (2)
nothing to gain by  **133 unapt** not ready  **138 Whom**
Margaret; **pain** much effort  **142 face** deceive

**145 expect** await  **148 for** in having  **151 her little worth**
a lady of such modest rank and fortune  **161 deputy** Suffolk
**162 plighted faith** promise to marry  **164 in traffic** in
negotiation  **166 attorney** pleader  **179 directed** uttered

MARGARET
Yes, my good lord, a pure unspotted heart,
Never yet taint with love,° I send the king.

SUFFOLK
And this withal.

*Kisses her.*

MARGARET
That for thyself; I will not so presume                    185
To send such peevish tokens° to a king.
                    [*Exeunt* REIGNIER *and* MARGARET.]

SUFFOLK
O, wert thou for myself! But, Suffolk, stay;
Thou mayst not wander in that labyrinth;
There minotaurs° and ugly treasons lurk.
Solicit° Henry with her wondrous praise;                   190
Bethink thee on her virtues that surmount,
And natural graces that extinguish° art;
Repeat their semblance° often on the seas,
That, when thou com'st to kneel at Henry's feet,
Thou mayst bereave° him of his wits with wonder.          195
                                              *Exit.*


[Scene IV. *Camp of the Duke of York in Anjou.*]

*Enter* YORK, WARWICK, [*and others*].

YORK
Bring forth that sorceress condemned to burn.

[*Enter la* PUCELLE, *guarded, and a* SHEPHERD.]

SHEPHERD
Ah, Joan, this kills thy father's heart outright!
Have I sought° every country far and near,
And now° it is my chance to find thee out,
Must I behold thy timeless° cruel death?                   5
Ah, Joan, sweet daughter Joan, I'll die with thee!

PUCELLE
Decrepit miser!° base ignoble wretch!
I am descended of a gentler blood.
Thou art no father nor no friend of mine.

SHEPHERD
Out, out!° My lords, and° please you, 'tis not so.        10
I did beget her, all the parish knows;
Her mother liveth yet, can testify
She was the first fruit of my bachelorship.°

WARWICK
Graceless! wilt thou deny thy parentage?

YORK
This argues what her kind of life hath been,              15
Wicked and vile, and so her death concludes.

SHEPHERD
Fie, Joan, that thou wilt be so obstacle!°
God knows thou art a collop° of my flesh,
And for thy sake have I shed many a tear.
Deny me not, I prithee, gentle Joan.                       20

PUCELLE
Peasant, avaunt!° You have suborned° this man
Of purpose to obscure° my noble birth.

SHEPHERD
'Tis true, I gave a noble° to the priest
The morn that I was wedded to her mother.
Kneel down and take my blessing, good my girl.            25
Wilt thou not stoop? Now cursèd be the time
Of thy nativity! I would the milk
Thy mother gave thee when thou suck'dst her
    breast
Had been a little ratsbane° for thy sake!
Or else, when thou didst keep my lambs afield,            30
I wish some ravenous wolf had eaten thee!
Dost thou deny thy father, cursèd drab?°
O, burn her, burn her! hanging is too good.     *Exit.*

YORK
Take her away, for she hath lived too long,
To fill the world with vicious qualities.                 35

PUCELLE
First, let me tell you whom you have condemned:
Not me begotten of a shepherd swain
But issued from the progeny of kings;
Virtuous and holy, chosen from above,
By inspiration of celestial grace,                        40
To work exceeding miracles on earth.
I never had to do with wicked spirits,
But you, that are polluted with your lusts,
Stained with the guiltless blood of innocents,
Corrupt and tainted with a thousand vices,                45
Because you want the grace that others have,
You judge it straight a thing impossible
To compass° wonders but by help of devils.
No, misconceivèd!° Joan of Arc hath been
A virgin from her tender infancy,                         50
Chaste and immaculate in very thought,
Whose maiden blood, thus rigorously effused,°
Will cry for vengeance at the gates of heaven.

YORK
Ay, ay; away with her to execution!

WARWICK
And hark ye, sirs: because she is a maid,                 55
Spare for no° faggots, let there be enow;°
Place barrels of pitch upon the fatal stake,
That so her torture may be shortenèd.

PUCELLE
Will nothing turn your unrelenting hearts?
Then, Joan, discover thine infirmity,°                     60
That warranteth by law to be thy privilege.
I am with child, ye bloody homicides;

---

**183 taint with love** tinged with immodest desire **186
peevish tokens** foolish signs of affection **189 minotaurs**
alluding to the mythological monster of Crete, half-bull and
half-man, who was slain by Theseus **190 Solicit** allure **192
extinguish** obscure by greater brilliancy **193 Repeat their
semblance** remind yourself of their appearance **195 bereave**
dispossess
**V.iv.3 sought** searched **4 now** now that **5 timeless** untimely
**7 miser** old wretch **10 Out, out** alas; **and** if it **13 first
. . . bachelorship** begotten out of wedlock (but the shepherd
apparently is confused about the meaning of *bachelorship*)

**17 obstacle** obstinate (a malapropism) **18 collop** piece **21
avaunt** begone; **suborned** bribed **22 obscure** conceal
**23 noble** gold coin worth about ten shillings **29 ratsbane**
rat poison **32 drab** prostitute **48 compass** accomplish **49
misconceivèd** deceived person **52 rigorously effused**
cruelly shed **56 Spare for no** do not spare; **enow** enough
**60 discover thine infirmity** reveal your bodily unfitness

Murder not then the fruit within my womb,
Although ye hale° me to a violent death.

YORK

Now heaven forfend!° the holy maid with child!          65

WARWICK

The greatest miracle that e'er ye wrought.
Is all your strict preciseness° come to this?

YORK

She and the Dolphin have been juggling;°
I did imagine° what would be her refuge.°

WARWICK

Well, go to;° we'll have no bastards live,               70
Especially since Charles must father it.

PUCELLE

You are deceived, my child is none of his,
It was Alençon that enjoyed my love.

YORK

Alençon! that notorious Machiavel!°
It dies, and if it had a thousand lives.                 75

PUCELLE

O, give me leave, I have deluded you:
'Twas neither Charles nor yet the duke I named,
But Reignier, King of Naples, that prevailed.°

WARWICK

A married man! that's most intolerable.

YORK

Why, here's a girl!° I think she knows not well,         80
There were so many, whom she may accuse.

WARWICK

It's sign she hath been liberal and free.°

YORK

And yet, forsooth,° she is a virgin pure.
Strumpet, thy words condemn thy brat and thee.
Use no entreaty, for it is in vain.                      85

PUCELLE

Then lead me hence; with whom I leave my curse:
May never glorious sun reflex° his beams
Upon the country where you make abode,
But darkness and the gloomy shade of death
Environ you, till mischief and despair                   90
Drive you to break your necks or hang yourselves!
                                        Exit [guarded].

YORK

Break thou in pieces and consume to ashes,
Thou foul accursèd minister° of hell.

*Enter Cardinal [Beaufort, Bishop of* WINCHESTER].

WINCHESTER

Lord Regent, I do greet your excellence
With letters of commission from the king.                95
For know, my lords, the states of Christendom,
Moved with remorse of° these outrageous broils,
Have earnestly implored a general peace
Betwixt our nation and the aspiring French,

And here at hand the Dolphin and his train°            100
Approacheth, to confer about some matter.

YORK

Is all our travail° turned to this effect?
After the slaughter of so many peers,
So many captains, gentlemen, and soldiers,
That in this quarrel have been overthrown              105
And sold their bodies for their country's benefit,
Shall we at last conclude effeminate peace?
Have we not lost most part of all the towns,
By treason, falsehood, and by treachery,
Our great progenitors had conquerèd?                   110
O, Warwick, Warwick! I foresee with grief
The utter loss of all the realm of France.

WARWICK

Be patient, York; if we conclude a peace,
It shall be with such strict and severe covenants°
As little shall the Frenchmen gain thereby.            115

*Enter Charles [the* DAUPHIN], ALENÇON, BASTARD,
REIGNIER, [*and others*].

DAUPHIN

Since, Lord of England, it is thus agreed
That peaceful truce shall be proclaimed in France,
We come to be informèd by yourselves
What the conditions of that league must be.

YORK

Speak, Winchester, for boiling choler chokes          120
The hollow passage of my poisoned° voice
By sight of these our baleful enemies.

WINCHESTER

Charles, and the rest, it is enacted thus:
That, in regard King Henry gives consent,
Of° mere compassion and of lenity,                     125
To ease your country of distressful war
And suffer you to breathe in fruitful peace,
You shall become true liegemen° to his crown.
And, Charles, upon condition thou wilt swear
To pay him tribute, and submit thyself,                130
Thou shalt be placed as viceroy under him,
And still enjoy thy regal dignity.

ALENÇON

Must he be then as shadow of himself?
Adorn his temples with a coronet,
And yet, in substance and authority,                   135
Retain but privilege of a private man?
This proffer is absurd and reasonless.

DAUPHIN

'Tis known already that I am possessed
With more than half the Gallian territories,
And therein reverenced for° their lawful king:        140
Shall I, for lucre° of the rest unvanquished,
Detract so much from that prerogative°
As to be called but viceroy of the whole?
No, Lord Ambassador, I'll rather keep
That which I have than, coveting for more,             145
Be cast° from possibility of all.

---

64 **hale** drag  65 **forfend** forbid  67 **preciseness** pretense
of scrupulousness  68 **juggling** playing tricks  69 **imagine**
wonder; **refuge** excuse  70 **go to** come, come  74 **Machiavel**
intriguer (after Niccolò Machiavelli, author of *The Prince*)
78 **prevailed** gained her love  80 **girl** wench  82 **liberal
and free** used ironically, since a lady was supposed to have
these qualities, without Joan's implied wantonness  83 **forsooth**
in truth  87 **reflex** reflect  93 **minister** agent  97 **remorse
of** sorrow at

100 **train** retinue  102 **travail** labor, trouble  114 **covenants**
conditions  121 **poisoned** sickened as though with poison
125 **Of** out of  128 **liegemen** vassals  140 **reverenced for**
honored as  141 **lucre** gain  142 **prerogative** preeminence
(as king)  146 **cast** driven

YORK
Insulting Charles! hast thou by secret means
Used intercession to obtain a league,°
And, now the matter grows to compromise,
Stand'st thou aloof upon comparison?°           150
Either accept the title thou usurp'st,
Of° benefit proceeding from our king
And not of any challenge of desert,°
Or we will plague thee with incessant wars.

REIGNIER
My lord, you do not well in obstinacy          155
To cavil° in the course of this contract:
If once it be neglected, ten to one
We shall not find like opportunity.

ALENÇON
To say the truth, it is your policy
To save your subjects from such massacre       160
And ruthless slaughters as are daily seen
By our proceeding in hostility;
And therefore take this compact of° a truce—

[Aside.]

Although you break it when your pleasure serves.

WARWICK
How say'st thou, Charles? Shall our condition stand? 165

DAUPHIN
It shall;
Only reserved, you claim no interest
In any of our towns of garrison.

YORK
Then swear allegiance to his majesty,
As thou art knight, never to disobey            170
Nor be rebellious to the crown of England,
Thou, nor thy nobles, to the crown of England.

[The DAUPHIN and French NOBLES give signs of fealty.]

So, now dismiss your army when ye please;
Hang up your ensigns,° let your drums be still,
For here we entertain° a solemn peace.    Exeunt. 175


[Scene V. London. The royal palace.]

Enter SUFFOLK in conference with the KING,
GLOUCESTER, and EXETER.

KING
Your wondrous rare description, noble earl,
Of beauteous Margaret hath astonished me.
Her virtues, gracèd with external gifts,
Do breed love's settled passions in my heart,
And like as rigor° of tempestuous gusts          5
Provokes° the mightiest hulk° against the tide,
So am I driven by breath° of her renown
Either to suffer shipwreck or arrive
Where I may have fruition of her love.

SUFFOLK
Tush, my good lord, this superficial° tale        10
Is but a preface of her worthy praise.
The chief perfections of that lovely dame,
Had I sufficient skill to utter them,
Would make a volume of enticing lines,
Able to ravish any dull conceit;°                15
And, which is more, she is not so divine,
So full replete with choice of all delights,
But with as humble lowliness of mind
She is content to be at your command;
Command, I mean, of virtuous chaste intents,°    20
To love and honor Henry as her lord.

KING
And otherwise will Henry ne'er presume.
Therefore, my Lord Protector, give consent
That Margaret may be England's royal queen.

GLOUCESTER
So should I give consent to flatter° sin.         25
You know, my lord, your highness is betrothed
Unto another lady° of esteem.
How shall we then dispense with that contract,
And not deface your honor with reproach?

SUFFOLK
As doth a ruler with unlawful oaths,             30
Or one that, at a triumph° having vowed
To try his strength, forsaketh yet the lists°
By reason of his adversary's odds.°
A poor earl's daughter is unequal odds,
And therefore may be broke° without offense.     35

GLOUCESTER
Why, what, I pray, is Margaret more than that?
Her father is no better than an earl,
Although in glorious titles he excel.

SUFFOLK
Yes, my lord, her father is a king,
The King of Naples and Jerusalem,               40
And of such great authority in France
As his alliance will confirm our peace
And keep the Frenchmen in allegiance.

GLOUCESTER
And so the Earl of Armagnac may do
Because he is near kinsman unto Charles.          45

EXETER
Beside, his wealth doth warrant a liberal dower,
Where Reignier sooner will receive than give.

SUFFOLK
A dower, my lords! disgrace not so your king,
That he should be so abject, base, and poor,
To choose for wealth and not for perfect love.    50
Henry is able to enrich his queen
And not to seek a queen to make him rich.
So worthless peasants bargain for their wives,
As market men for oxen, sheep, or horse.
Marriage is a matter of more worth                55
Than to be dealt in by attorneyship;°
Not whom we will, but whom his grace affects,

---

148 **league** alliance  150 **upon comparison** weighing the odds  152 **Of** through  153 **challenge of desert** claim that it is yours by right  156 **cavil** find fault without good reason  163 **compact of** mutual agreement for  174 **ensigns** banners  175 **entertain** accept
**V.v.5 rigor** violence  6 **Provokes** drives on; **hulk** ship  7 **breath** utterance

10 **superficial** touching only the surface  15 **ravish . . . conceit** enchant even the dullest imagination  20 **intents** intentions  25 **flatter** condone  27 **another lady** the daughter of the Earl of Armagnac  31 **triumph** tournament  32 **lists** tournament ground  33 **odds** inferiority  35 **broke** the pledge of marriage may be broken  56 **attorneyship** proxy

Must be companion of his nuptial bed.
And therefore, lords, since° he affects her most,
Most of all these reasons bindeth us,                               60
In our opinions she should be preferred.
For what is wedlock forcèd but a hell,
An age of discord and continual strife?
Whereas the contrary bringeth bliss,
And is a pattern of celestial peace.                                65
Whom should we match with Henry, being a king,
But Margaret, that is daughter to a king?
Her peerless feature,° joinèd with her birth,
Approves° her fit for none but for a king.
Her valiant courage and undaunted spirit,                           70
More than in women commonly is seen,
Will answer our hope in issue of a king;
For Henry, son unto a conqueror,
Is likely to beget more conquerors,
If with a lady of so high resolve                                   75
As is fair Margaret he be linked in love.
Then yield, my lords, and here conclude with me
That Margaret shall be queen, and none but she.
KING
Whether it be through force of your report,
My noble Lord of Suffolk, or for that                               80
My tender youth was never yet attaint°
With any passion of inflaming love,
I cannot tell; but this I am assured,
I feel such sharp dissension in my breast,
Such fierce alarums both of hope and fear,                          85

59 **since** the fact that   68 **feature** comeliness   69 **Approves**
proves   81 **attaint** stained

As I am sick with working of my thoughts.
Take, therefore, shipping; post, my lord, to France;
Agree to any covenants, and procure
That Lady Margaret do vouchsafe to come
To cross the seas to England and be crowned                         90
King Henry's faithful and anointed queen.
For your expenses and sufficient charge,°
Among the people gather up a tenth.°
Be gone, I say, for, till you do return,
I rest° perplexèd with a thousand cares.                            95
And you, good uncle, banish all offense;
If you do censure° me by what you were,
Not what you are, I know it will excuse
This sudden execution° of my will.
And so, conduct me where, from company,                             100
I may revolve and ruminate° my grief.          *Exit.*
GLOUCESTER
Ay, grief, I fear me, both at first and last.
          *Exit* GLOUCESTER [*with* EXETER].
SUFFOLK
Thus Suffolk hath prevailed, and thus he goes,
As did the youthful Paris once to Greece,
With hope to find the like event° in love,                          105
But prosper better than the Trojan did.
Margaret shall now be queen, and rule the king;
But I will rule both her, the king, and realm.     *Exit.*

92 **sufficient charge** adequate money to meet costs   93 **tenth**
a levy of a tenth of the value of personal property (collected to
meet unusual expenses, such as a royal marriage)   95 **rest**
remain   97 **censure** judge   99 **execution** carrying into
effect   101 **revolve and ruminate** consider and meditate
upon   105 **event** result

# THE SECOND PART OF
# HENRY THE SIXTH

EDITED BY ARTHUR FREEMAN

## Introduction

Shakespeare's *Henry VI, Part Two* may be his earliest surviving work; it may be the first adaptation by anyone of English history for the Elizabethan stage; and if it is neither, it still certainly remains among the three or four earliest both of the career and the genre, and as such the object of curious examination for centuries. But has the play value beyond curiosity and "importance," or virtues beyond nuggets of promise and flashes of the characteristic "easiness of expression and fluency of numbers" we identify in the body of Shakespeare's work? Rarely, we observe, does *Henry VI*—singly, doubly, or triply—come on the stage, and scarcely more often does a single part recommend itself to the modern reader who is not simply covering or re-covering *all* of Shakespeare, like an obstacle course. How good is the play? And more pointedly, perhaps, from what particular strengths does its excellence, if any, arise?

Unquestionably the poetry of *2 Henry VI* is no strong point. It ranges from inflated extreme:

The gaudy, blabbing, and remorseful day
Is crept into the bosom of the sea,
And now loud-howling wolves arouse the jades
That drag the tragic melancholy night        (IV.i.1–4)

to slack plateau:

And had I twenty times so many foes,
And each of them had twenty times their power,
All these could not procure me any scathe,
So long as I am loyal, true, and crimeless        (II.iv.60–63)

embracing along the way all sorts of weakness appropriate to the neophyte versifier: flatness, extravagance, redundancy, and unassimilated imitation. When Margaret lamely laments her enforced parting from the Duke of Suffolk, and the imminent death of Cardinal Beaufort,

Ay me! What is this world! What news are these!
But wherefore grieve I at an hour's poor loss,
Omitting Suffolk's exile, my soul's treasure?
Why only, Suffolk, mourn I not for thee,
And with the southern clouds contend in tears
        (III.ii.380–84)

her rhetoric is heavily indebted to Thomas Kyd's; likewise the "jades" are Marlowe's, and the "twenty . . . twenty" hyperbole a well-worn piece of stock from the Kyd-Marlowe-Greene warehouse of formulaic clichés. Often, indeed, *2 Henry VI* sounds so unlike the later Shakespeare and so much like his predecessors and mentors that scholars have sought another's hand in the text—either as collaborator, or as the unwitting source of Shakespeare's flagrant plagiary. Yet few would deny to Shakespeare the fine intensity of Young Clifford's battlefield imprecations (V.ii.31–65), the emotional accuracy of the bulk of III.ii, Margaret's farewell to Suffolk, or the wily and succinct logic of Warwick's apology for the commons, and the warning to King Henry (III.ii.242–69); and what seems less than the best in the play may easily be explained in terms of uncertainty and inexperience as of fragmentary authorship. We cannot demand of Shakespeare in his twenties the consistency, control, and ease of the seasoned professional he was rapidly to become.

But what emerges preeminently from the play is the sure sense of theater, dramatic design, and skill in characterization which are such inalienable hallmarks of Shakespeare's genius that even bardolatrous theatergoers of 1796 could without hesitation hiss a travesty like *Vortigern* (forged by W. H. Ireland) from the stage—not for its mawkish language and already tainted reputation, but for the lack of those attributes absolutely characteristic of the Genuine Remains. Ragged and faltering though its verse may occasionally be, *Henry VI* exemplifies the dramatic virtues of construction—continuity, tension, proportion, pace—which no playwright before Shakespeare had succeeded in uniting with a good sense of what interests an audience. Thinking of *2 Henry VI* as a playwright's play—an embryonic, germinal type—we can single out from it virtues of dramaturgy, aspects of craftsmanship which may illuminate for us what Shakespeare the playwright "began with" at the outset of a career in Elizabethan theater.

The peculiar problem facing a playwright who attempts a play based on chronicle history is that no very extravagant changes in plot may be introduced. All the more pressing are the demands on the playwright's skill as a

146

shaper of story, selector of detail, imputer of motives; all the more difficult his task of making an arbitrary tract of historical time appear complete and self-sufficient, artistically independent from the events-leading-up and the sequel. Given the limitations of the source, the exigencies of factual history, as well as the prescribed slants Tudor chroniclers imposed on their material (King John a victim of papal interference, Richard III—the last Plantagenet—an ignominious tyrant, Richard II's overthrow fundamentally unjustified) and the necessity for treading lightly where political or social issues come into question, how does Shakespeare's artistry shape, structure, and implement the twenty-year history his play intends to convey? Most obviously, and first, by a compression of time, and a conflation of events. Facts remain facts, but their order may justifiably be varied: Eleanor's attainture may be laid to Queen Margaret's influence, although in fact it took place four years before the royal marriage; Peter's combat with his master Thomas the armorer may be relocated at the time of York's displacement as regent of France, and associated—as in the chronicles it is not—with York's treason. Likewise, the long and repetitious subversion of Salisbury and Warwick, among other members of the nobility, which drags over years in Hall and Holinshed, may be reduced to a single scene (II.ii) and left firmly settled rather than tentative; and the long-smoldering hostilities between King Henry and York, all their intermittent battles, truces, accords, and new outbreaks, may be altered to a single continuing action in Act V, with a conclusion more "final" than history suggests. Thus twenty years of fits and starts in the Lancaster-York troubles appear all part of one rational sequence of events, impelled forward by the force of hindsight, the implied teleology of history itself, stripped of "irrelevant" excursions, like York's in and out of Ireland, and framed artificially by emphasis on fulfilled prophecy and culminatory violence. Like any dramatist restricted to a small repertory cast, Shakespeare dwells on individual confrontations rather than spectacular, massive, and realistic encounters to embody the historical action. Chosen pairs of antagonists, like chosen events, stand for the struggle at large: York duels anachronistically with old Clifford as a representative of all the loyal nobility, and the company of factious schemers of I.i dwindles from eight to a soliloquizing York, as if to symbolize the disintegration of English union into rival, baronial interests. Another dramatic device ensuring the illusion of continuity is Shakespeare's imputation of motives in certain matters the chroniclers agree to leave haphazard: only a hint in Hall provides the suggestion, fully implemented by Shakespeare, of an intrigue between Suffolk and the queen; and the ensuing suggestion that Somerset fills the same office is merely extrapolated from the first: there is no source for this in written history. Nor do the chroniclers provide any connection between Cade's uprising and the policy of York, whereas the play quite plausibly links Cade to the main action specifically as York's factor in Kent.

The illusion that history, in *2 Henry VI*, is self-contained and independent, that a "just period" has been imposed on the events described, once more is a function of dramatic management. We watch the Duke of York alter from a silent, politic, and guarded rival claimant, whose primary mode of self-expression is the ironic "aside" and the soliloquy (I.i., III.i), to an outspoken enemy of the crown who dares fling his defiance in the face of the Presence: the play thus provides a kind of emotional catharsis for York not wholly warranted by the chronicles, one which gives the impression of a retaliatory anger coming full circle from the implied past outrage and house-curse of Richard II's deposition. Paired against York's rise to action is King Henry's degeneration into helpless passivity: never martial, nor even authoritative in his office, he does flare up once in righteous fury against Suffolk, following the murder of Duke Humphrey—even if Warwick's unsubtle pressure must goad him to a firm stand—but by IV.ix, in the face of Yorkist defiance, he has reached a nadir of despair and incompetence:

> Come, wife, let's in, and learn to govern better;
> For yet may England curse my wretched reign.
>
> (IV.ix.48–49)

By the end of Act V he remains scarcely a man, let alone king (QUEEN What are you made of? You'll nor fight nor fly), and his death in the play's sequel seems a foregone conclusion. While York's forces, around Salisbury and Warwick, have snowballed into an irresistible front, King Henry's counselors, like the provinces of France, have fallen from him one by one; until like Lear alone on the heath with his fool, stripped of his entourage, king and queen must flee the lost battle at the prompting of no more than the young Clifford, last of the loyalists, bitter, pitiless, and a little mad. A more deliberate device, perhaps, for setting the just period on events in the play, is the satisfaction of a second of three prophecies made late in Act I: Somerset's death under the sign of the Castle, an alehouse in Saint Albans, seems to even up the score between Gloucester's family and their assailants—Suffolk for Gloucester (IV.i), and now Somerset for Eleanor.

Within the measure of the play, the period of the whole action, lodges a rhythmic pattern of interlocked impugnments—fortuitous falls, medieval "tragedies," if we wish, or inevitable consequences of one fatal, preliminary mistake. "The three *Henry VI* plays, and *Richard III*," writes Irving Ribner, "may be viewed as virtually a series of successive waves, in each of which one hero falls and another rises to replace him. The most significant of the falls are displayed as divine retribution for sin, but there are some also which seem to illustrate only an arbitrary and capricious fortune." Within *2 Henry VI* a parallel series may be distinguished: first Eleanor, then Humphrey, then Suffolk, then Lord Say, and finally Somerset are impugned, attainted, and done away with, as the barriers between King Henry and the raw malice of York one by one come down. Successive objects of blame for the loss of France—Humphrey by the peers, York by Somerset and Suffolk, Suffolk by Warwick, Salisbury, and the commons, Say by Jack Cade and his rebels, and Salisbury by York—suggest the harried administration of a losing enterprise firing manager after manager. And all comes about through the "fatal marriage" of Henry with Margaret, the "haught-stomached" mannish queen of the chronicles, the amorous impatient designer of *2 Henry VI*s the bloody avenger of *3 Henry VI*, and the hideou, Cassandra of *Richard III*. As France forms the unseen background for the historical tragedy, in Elizabethan terms, of Henry VI's reign, so France in the person of Margaret and the responsibility for mismanaging the wars forms the pretext of all the succeeding failures of the play. For the want of Anjou and Maine, Normandy is lost, for the want of Normandy, Gascony, for the want of all France, English popular solidarity and loyalty; and by all these interlocked disasters falls King Henry. France and its "blood-bespotted Neapolitan" queen lurk like a Senecan curse behind the action of *2 Henry VI*, *3 Henry VI*, and *Richard III*, a trilogy linked by themes of retribution and revenge, by generations of guilt accumulated by Lancastrians and Yorkists, until Henry Tudor can wipe clean the slate at Bosworth Field. But the triggering event of the chain, in *2 Henry VI*, is the unsuitable, expensive marriage of French Margaret with English Henry, and the hateful articles thereby concluded.

A play lives in its characters. Samuel Johnson selected from *2 Henry VI* King Henry, Queen Margaret, Warwick, and Gloucester; but there are bits as well—Peter, Eleanor, Walter Whitmore, Cade—which an actor can render memorable. At the outset of the action, a triangle of major figures—Henry, Margaret, and Humphrey—dominates our attention, Margaret and the protector vying for control of the pietistic, unworldly figurehead of a king. Now Humphrey, by sixteenth-century convention, is portrayed as charitable to a fault ("to dine at Duke Humphrey's table," an Elizabethan expression for "to go hungry," reflects the supposed self-impoverishment Gloucester's generosity drew upon himself), high-minded, confident, as Hall has it, in "his strong truth," and in "indifferent justice"—a victimized heifer or partridge, in Warwick's image, an unweaned calf, in Henry's, and a shepherd in Gloucester's own, to the lamblike king. Queen Margaret, again at Hall's suggestion, is equal in vehement ambition to the calm majesty and accustomed authority of her rival; and the traditional character of King Henry as a man "of a meek spirit, and a simple wit, preferring peace before war, rest before business, honesty before profit, and quietness before labor," is implemented by Shakespeare in scriptural terms, by larding the king's discourse with holy aphorisms, and revealing him ever more willing to comment helplessly upon an event—with eyes upraised, and hands clasped, as the adult portrait in the National Portrait Gallery depicts him—than to demand action. The interrelationship of these three main figures is never better exposed than in II.i, at the spurious miracle of cured blindness in Saint Albans. To a townsman's announcement of "A miracle!" Henry reacts immediately with full credulity: "Now God be praised," etc., and with a homely and pious *caveat*:

Great is his comfort in this earthly vale,
Although by sight his sin be multiplied.          (II.i.70–71)

Gloucester, meanwhile, seasons his admiration with the skepticism of a good judge. Interrogation confirms his suspicions, and with a bit of low comedy he administers an unmasking. Now that Simpcox is revealed an impostor, the king speaks again: "O God, see'st thou this, and bearest so long?" (II.i.153). Whereas Queen Margaret, in a reflection superbly revealing of her hardening nature, comments: "It made me laugh to see the villain run" (II.i.154). Given

the king's ineffectuality, it of course falls to Gloucester to prescribe punishment; and as the case does not warrant mercy (Simpcox's wife's plea, "Alas, sir, we did it for pure need," appeals merely for pity, in a stoical sense) Gloucester's sentence is not unsevere. "By this may be seen," says Foxe, "how Duke Humphrey had not only an head to discern and dissever truth from forged and feigned hypocrisy, but study also and diligence likewise was in him to reform that which was amiss." Shakespeare has retained the main point of the *exemplum*, but simultaneously seized upon the occasion to underscore his portraits of Henry and Margaret as well.

After the elimination of Gloucester, the "crutch" of the king, our attention is shifted to those auguries of disintegration, the wrangling peers, the scheming Yorkists, pirates, and the anarchic rebels of Jack Cade. From the decorum of the first scene, a courtly reception of the new queen, to the bloody holocaust of Act V, culminating in the emergence of a new order of violent young men—York's savage sons, the "foul, indigested lump" Richard, and furious Clifford Junior—we are led by way of dissident nobles and lawless commoners to an end no better than what precedes it, but certainly less weak. After Gloucester's death the focus of characterization moves freely among the representative types of imperial decay, pausing once for a curiously affecting last interview between Margaret and the Duke of Suffolk (III.ii.300 ff.). Prior to this parting we have had little or no sympathy for either party, but in the space of a hundred lines our antagonism is severely shaken. It is a crude and unprepared reversal, perhaps, but there are few examples in the English drama before 1590 of anything at all like Shakespeare's "shading" of characterization, or of his insistence on keeping our judgment on the ultimate worth of a man suspended until the tension of the action involving him has relaxed. We have been encouraged to dislike Suffolk, but with III.ii we are not permitted to despise him; we are asked to reconsider our earlier censure of both queen and lover, and to imagine, for a moment, the action of the play, favorable and unfavorable to them, through their own eyes, as it affects them, rather than as they affect it. This is a remarkable achievement, in a somewhat primitive form, for a short unexpected exchange. Analogous to it perhaps is the pity evoked in us by the sight of Eleanor humbled—we may think of Kent in the stocks or the dead Hotspur—or our grudging admiration for the impolitic and noble arrogance with which Suffolk meets his end; but these are simpler dramatic formulas.

In its own time, and possibly in ours, the main attraction of the play as staged may well have been the comical prose scenes of Cade's rebellion. Action is not lacking in *2 Henry VI*, nor spectacle, what with witchcraft, trial by combat, a false miracle, alarums and excursions, and the excitement generated by York's open defiance and Gloucester's bristling temper against Beaufort's; but the Cade scenes bring to the stage as well an element, especially trenchant for Elizabethans, of sociopolitical commentary. Shakespeare's audiences were accustomed to read into plays on past history lessons for the present, and indeed contemporary playwrights were not blind to the implications their histories raised. *Gorboduc* warned of the evils of dividing a kingdom; *Richard II* of the hazards of weak kingship (after Essex' rebellion in 1601, and the ill-advised performance of *Richard II* on the eve of the uprising, the queen angrily remarked to William Lambarde, "I am Richard II, know ye not that?"); and *2 Henry VI* contains an action if anything more provocative than either of those. Presupposing a popular audience to watch a play dealing with popular revolt—one in particular in which the rabble bears all before it for some time—and considering that London in the early 1590's was racked by insubordination and riot, one may imagine how determined the authorities might be to assure themselves that no matter or opinion expressed in such a scene of such a play be "dangerous," and to be certain that any moral extrapolated from the conclusion be perfectly in accord with law, order, and the present regime. Thus episodes like Cade's rebellion and the rising of the masses in *Sir Thomas More*, putatively revised by Shakespeare himself, were composed under strict scrutiny, and carefully reviewed by the Master of the Revels or his staff before production could be permitted. Change a scene, omit a scene, and shorten an address, "and not otherwise, at your own perils," warns Edmund Tilney in his holograph comment extant on the manuscript of *Sir Thomas More:* the recommendations of the authorities are specific, censorious, and peremptory.

Nothing in Shakespeare's career or works suggests that he might find conscientious compliance with such strictures difficult. In fact the implicit conservatism of his political attitudes, so far as we can isolate them (a dangerous attempt, when speech and character must sometimes be separated), made him ideal for the job of rewriting a questioned passage of *More*, and evidently quite at ease in the matter of Cade. In line either with official policy, or his own predilections, or both, Shakespeare's Cade scarcely resembles the "youngman of goodly stature and pregnant wit," the "subtle captain," and audacious field-general Hall portrays; rather he stands for rampant ignorance, executing a clerk for his ability to read and write, and Lord Say, as much as for anything, for his cultural accomplishment—whereas Hall's Cade took advantage of sophistical doctrine, "teachers," and "privy schoolmasters" to suborn the men of Kent to his side in the struggle, and was witty enough to perceive the "dilatory plea" of Lord Say, to be tried by his peers—rather than anxious to kill him before his words might win away followers. True, in his curious fashion Hall does give a conflicting impression of Cade—as "covetous," a "mischievous head," and "a cruel tyrant"—almost in counterpoint with his more respectful estimate, but Shakespeare unquestionably was in command of information about Cade's nature which he chose not to use. Likewise, the character of Lord Say, which in Hall is made shifty and not a little cowardly, in Shakespeare is held up as maligned virtue and honesty personified, a very test case of Cade's anarchic administration, urging us to particular repugnance toward civil disobedience. And for reasons, at last, of leaving no loophole in the morality of rebellion, Shakespeare has also introduced the otherwise gratuitous episode of Iden's garden, a scene which well may bear cutting in a modern production. Iden himself remains an annoyingly loose end among disparate new faces in the last act: the man who pronounces himself loath to "live turmoilèd in the court" when he "may enjoy such quiet walks as these" in Kent (IV.x.17-18) seems within a few lines overjoyed to attend henceforth on King Henry at court: "May Iden live to merit such a bounty!"

"As narratives in verse," sums up Dr. Johnson, the *Henry VI* plays "are more happily conceived and more accurately finished than those of *King John*, *Richard II*, or the tragic scenes of *Henry IV* and *V*"—this "without regard to characters and incidents," in which they presumably are deficient; and of the three, adds Johnson, "I think the second the best." Taste since 1765 has perhaps downgraded the *Henry VI* plays, and scholarship has fastened so firmly on the bibliographical labyrinths they offer to explore that seldom are they spoken of as literature, hence seldom staged, and hence seldom read. But it is almost fair to assert that the least of Shakespeare is better than all but the best of his early theatrical contemporaries, and *2 Henry VI*—a little clumsy and uneven, but fresh, and at times brilliant—deserves nowadays more than its canonical or compulsive moiety of readership.

## A NOTE ON THE DATE AND SOURCES

*The Date.* Despite the consecutive titles provided by the Folio editors for *Henry VI, Parts One, Two,* and *Three,* it is probable that *2 and 3 Henry VI* originally constituted a two-part play, and that *1 Henry VI* had an independent conception and existence in the contemporary repertory. Early quartos (see A Note on the Text, below) designated *2 Henry VI* as *The First Part of the Contention between the Two Famous Houses of York and Lancaster,* and *3 Henry VI* as *The True Tragedy of Richard, Duke of York;* and subsequently a piratical quarto of 1619 combined the two (still ignoring *1 Henry VI*) as *The Whole Contention.*

Scholarly opinion, however, is divided on the question of precedence: did the composition proceed chronologically, with *1 Henry VI* first, followed by a double play on subsequent events, or was *1 Henry VI*, with its emphasis on action and adventure, worked up *after 2 and 3 Henry VI*, to capitalize upon their evident popularity? Certain inconsistencies of plot and characterization suggest, if anything, the latter alternative—much as *The First Part of Jeronimo,* or "Spain's Comedy," evidently postdated the immensely popular *Spanish Tragedy* of Thomas Kyd—but all we can be moderately sure of is that the three parts do not constitute an intentional trilogy. And as it is not certain that *1 Henry VI* preceded the two-part play, we can accept as established that *2 Henry VI* is the earliest definitely datable play of Shakespeare and, as such, a monument of precocious accomplishment.

Because of Robert Greene's attack (September, 1592) on the new actor-playwright Shakespeare (see the General Introduction, pp. 2–3), playing on a phrase of *3 Henry VI*, and our knowledge of a plague inhibition during the summer, we can date the composition and performance of *2 and 3 Henry VI* earlier than June 23, 1592. The publication of the second edition of Holinshed's *Chronicles* (1587) may provide an early limit of date; but apparent echoes of *3 Henry VI* in an especially allusive history play, *The Troublesome Reign of King John* (published 1591), tend to set back the date of *2 and 3 Henry VI* to 1591 or 1590 or even earlier. Hence, whether *1 Henry VI* or *2 and 3 Henry VI* are what Henslowe terms "harey the vi" in March, 1592, has little effect on our dating estimate of *2 and 3 Henry VI;* 1590–91 is a good enough guess, and possibly thus renders *2 Henry VI* the earliest known "modern" play concerned primarily with English history.

*The Sources.* Shakespeare's main source appears to have been either the York-Lancaster chronicle of Edward Hall (1542; 1548; 1550), or of Hall's publisher Richard Grafton (*A Chronicle at Large*, 1569), which are often indistinguishable, due to Grafton's cheerful and extensive plagiarism of his predecessors. Raphael Holinshed's *Chronicles* (second edition, 1587), which Shakespeare certainly knew, may also have contributed some supplementary matter, or transmitted portions of Hall's text (for like Grafton, Holinshed borrowed liberally and literally). The story of Simpcox appears first in Sir Thomas More's *Dialogue . . . of the Veneration and Worship of Images* (1529), subsequently in Grafton, but is also to be found in the extremely popular *Acts and Monuments* of the martyrologist John Foxe (1563; 1570; 1576; 1583; quoted here from the 1583 edition). Traces of Robert Fabyan's *Chronicle* (1516 *et seq.*), the versified *Mirror for Magistrates* (1559 edition, for the death of Suffolk), and John Hardyng's verse *Chronicle* (1543, another of Grafton's "sources") may or may not be identifiable in Shakespeare's text; but the primary original, in one form or another, remains Hall (see Lucille King, "The Use of Hall's Chronicles in the Folio and Quarto Texts of *Henry VI*," *Philological Quarterly*, XIII [1934], 321–32).

A most interesting analogue to the Cade scenes is found in the supposedly Shakespearean revision of Anthony Munday's *Sir Thomas More* (?1593–?1601), a play surviving only in manuscript, crabbed and partially defective, and unpublished until 1844. A passage involving rebellious commoners and a paternalistic, "reasonable" More has frequently been ascribed to Shakespeare on stylistic and paleographic grounds, many scholars considering this scrap of manuscript to be holograph, and the only extant specimen, thus, save signatures, of Shakespeare's own handwriting. (For a summary of the controversy, see R. C. Bald, "The Booke of Sir Thomas More and Its Problems," *Shakespeare Survey 2* [1949], pp. 44–61.) Only in the Cade sequence of *2 Henry VI* and in *Sir Thomas More*, if indeed both are his work, did Shakespeare treat at large the issues raised by popular insurrection—a most ticklish subject for any playwright to explore (as the heavy censorship of *More* testifies), and one most topical in the disturbed early 1590's. The political point of view, at once conservative and considerate, inherent in More's pacification of the unruly mob and in the Cade episodes of *Henry VI* seems suggestively consistent.

## A NOTE ON THE TEXT

In 1594 appeared an anonymous quarto (Q) entitled "THE/First part of the Con-/tention betwixt the two famous Houses of Yorke/and Lancaster, with the death of the good/Duke Humphrey:/And the banishment and death of the Duke of/*Suffolke*, and the Tragicall end of the proud Cardinall/of *Winchester*, with the notable Rebel-/lion/of *Iacke Cade*:/And the Duke of Yorkes first claime unto the/Crowne," consisting of some 2200 lines which parallel closely and occasionally match the 1623 Folio (F) text of *2 Henry VI*. Considered as an independent play, Q is shorter, cruder, and vastly inferior in language

and characterization to F, but its relationship to the "finished" work offers an interesting problem. As early as 1734 it was theorized, by Lewis Theobald, that Q represents a primitive version of the play later revised by Shakespeare and published. In 1787 Edmond Malone, taking Greene's famous slur on the "upstart crow" (see the General Introduction, pp. 2–3) to imply plagiarism on Shakespeare's part, suggested that Greene, and Peele, or possibly (1821) Marlowe, were the original authors of *The Contention* and its companion piece, *The True Tragedie of Richard Duke of Yorke* (1595), which bears a similar relation to *3 Henry VI*.

In the late 1920's, however, with the studies of Peter Alexander (*Shakespeare's Henry VI and Richard III*, 1929) and Madeleine Doran (*Henry VI*, 1928), a different explanation was advanced: that Q is actually a mutilated and wholly derivative "bad" version of the "good" text preserved in the Folio; that it derives, like many other unauthorized Elizabethan quartos, from a memorial reconstruction of the acted play—possibly by the bit-player who took the parts of the Armorer, the Spirit, the Mayor, Vaux, and Scales. In support of this explanation it has been shown that Q contains frequent echoes of unrelated contemporary plays such as Marlowe's *Edward II*, and *Arden of Feversham*, as if the "reporter" who furnished the copy to the typesetter were fleshing out what he had memorized imperfectly with scraps of the rest of his repertory. The F text is relatively free of such contaminations.

Some modern scholars (Feuillerat, Prouty, J. D. Wilson) argue for a return to the "revision" theory, but the consensus opposes them. Good summaries of the conflicting evidence, and a discussion of the complications compounded by the third quarto (1619) of *The Contention*, may be found in G. B. Evans' review of Prouty's "*The Contention*" and Shakespeare's "*2 Henry VI*" (*JEGP*, LIII [1954], 628–37) and J. G. McManaway, "The Contention and *2 Henry VI*," *Wiener Beiträge zur Englischen Philologie*, LXV (1957), 143–54.

As a "bad" quarto, the textual utility of Q is slight, except in its stage directions, which are frequently fuller than those of F (for example, I.i.51 s.d., which occurs only in Q). In some passages, however (for example, II.i.124 ff., II.iii.58 s.d. ff.), the F editors appear to have used slices of Q as printer's copy, possibly when the holograph script they employed primarily was defective or illegible; and in such instances the F text is likely to be mediocre, or misaligned (I.i.62–63), and Q readings may be preferable. Basically the copy for F seems to have been an author's manuscript or "foul papers," but there is evidence as well of a theatrical bookkeeper's interpolations and cuts.

This edition follows F except where indicated in the following; stage directions derived from Q are so designated. Editorial additions are set off in square brackets; spelling, punctuation, and capitalization have been modernized; and names in speech prefixes and stage directions (for example, Duke Humphrey *alias* Gloucester, Winchester *alias* Beaufort *alias* Cardinal) regularized. In a few instances verse has been slightly rearranged. The following list of significant departures from F gives the reading of the present text in boldface, followed by a bracketed [Q] if the quarto provides the reading, and the F text, *literatim*, in roman.

**I.i.s.d. Enter . . . Warwick** [Q] Enter King, Duke Humfrey, Salisbury, Warwicke, and Beauford on the one side. The Queene, Suffolke, Yorke, Somerset, and Buckingham, on the other **51 s.d.** [Q] F omits **57** duchies [Q gives "Duches"] Dutchesse **62–63 create thee/First** [Q] create thee the first **72 s.d. Gloucester . . . rest** [Q] Manet the rest **91** had hath **176** protector [Q] Protectors **249** surfeit in the surfetting in **254** in [Q] in in
**I.ii.60 s.d.** follows line 59 [F, Q] **69 s.d. Hum** [Q and chronicles] Hume
**I.iii.13 For** To **31 That . . . was?** That my Mistresse was? **32 usurer** Vsurper **33–34** [Q] F omits **102 s.d. Sound** Exit. Sound **102 s.d. Enter . . . Winchester** [Q] Enter the King, Duke Humfrey, Cardinall, Buckingham, Yorke, Salisbury, Warwicke, and the Duchesse **144 I'd** [Q] I could **152 fury** Fume
**I.iv.25 Asnath** Asmath **36–38** Q prints as prose; probably a corruption of original octosyllabic couplets **41 s.d. He . . . again** [Q] Exit Spirit **53 s.d.** [Q] F omits **62–63 Aio . . . posse** Aio Aeacida Romanos vincere posso **70–71 hard . . . understood** [Hibbard conj.] hardly attain'd,/And hardly vnderstood
**II.i.s.d. with . . . fist** [Q] F omits **25–26 Good . . . holiness?** [Cairncross conj.] Good Vnkle hide such mallice:/With such Holynesse can you doe it? **30 lord protectorship** Lords Protectorship **39–40** between these lines Q inserts the following: "*Humphrey*. Dare. I tell thee Priest, Plantagenets could neuer brooke the dare./*Card*. I am Plantagenet as well as thou, and sonne to Iohn of Gaunt./*Humph*. In Bastardie./*Cardin*. I scorne thy words" **46–48** F gives all these lines to Gloucester **71 by sight** by his sight **91 Simpcox** Symon **107 Alban** Albones **125–32** Q gives as prose; F, following the text of Q, aligns haphazardly as verse **130** his [Q] it **140–51** here F again follows the Q copy, which is aligned roughly as verse, yet prints these lines as prose. Probably they were verse originally, but so corrupt now that no plausible restoration of arrangement can be attempted
**II.ii.35 Philippa** Phillip **47 son, the son** Sonnes Sonne **50 Philippa** Phillip
**II.iii.s.d. Enter . . . Warwick** [Q] Enter the King and State, with Guard, to banish the Duchesse **3 sins** sinne **66 i' faith I'll** [Q] yfaith, and Ile **69 afeared** [Q] afraid **70–72 Second Prentice . . . a quart for me** [Q] F omits; and as F provides only two prentices, Second Prentice speaks the line here given to Third Prentice **75–77 I thank . . . my apron** [Q] I thanke you all: drinke, and pray for me, I pray you, for I thinke I haue taken my last Draught in this World. Here *Robin*, and if I dye, I giue thee my Aporne; and *Will*, thou shalt haue my Hammer **88–93 Here's . . . Ascapart** [Q] Masters, I am come hither as it were vpon my Mans instigation, to proue him a Knaue, and my selfe an honest man: and touching the Duke of Yorke, I will take my death, I neuer meant him any ill, nor the King, nor the Queene: and therefore Peter haue at thee with a downe-right blow **95 s.d.** [Q] F omits
**II.iv.16 s.d. Enter . . . halberds** [Q] Enter the Duchesse in a white Sheet, and a Taper burning in her hand, with the Sherife and Officers **73 s.d.** [Q] F omits
**III.i.222 s.d. Exit . . . Warwick** [Q] Exit
**III.ii.s.d. Enter . . . Gloucester** [F] Here Q actually stages the murder on the inner stage, where Gloucester's body, concealed by curtains, remains throughout the scene: "Then the Curtaines being drawne, Duke *Humphrey* is discouered in his bed, and two men lying on his brest and smothering him in his bed. And then enter the Duke of *Suffolke* to them." But the F stage directions here, and at III.ii.148 below, appear to intend eliminating this use of the inner stage: thus "Bed put forth" rather than "*Warwicke* drawes the curtaines and showes Duke *Humphrey* in his bed," and the lines of explanatory dialogue (III.ii.1–4) not found in Q. The Q staging, however, seems more efficient and theatrical, and has been partially retained in this text **14 s.d. Buckingham** [Q] Suffolke **26 Meg** Nell **79 Margaret** Elianor **100 Margaret** Elianor **116 witch** watch **120 Margaret** Elinor **121 s.d. Salisbury** [Q] F omits **148 s.d. Warwick . . . bed** [Q] Bed put forth [following line 146 in F] **202 s.d. Exit Cardinal** [Q] F omits **265 whe'r** where **288 s.d. Exit Salisbury** [Q] F omits **299 Exit . . . Suffolk** [Q] Exit **366 to** no **409 s.d. She kisseth him** [Q] F omits **413 s.d. Exit Suffolk . . . Exit Queen** [Q] Exeunt [follows 413 in F]
**III.iii.s.d. and then . . . mad** [Q] to the Cardinal in bed [for the III.ii.s.d. discrepancy compare above] **10 whe'r** [Q whether] where **28 s.d. The Cardinal dies** [Q] F omits
**IV.i.s.d. And then . . . Whitmore** [Q with emendation from "Captaine" to 'Lieutenant'] Enter Lieutenant, Suffolke, and others **6 Clip** Cleape **48 Jove . . . I** [Q] F omits **50 Obscure . . . blood** F assigns this line to the Lieutenant; Q to Suffolk **70 Poole . . . Poole** [Q] Lieu[tenant]. Poole, Sir Poole? Lord **77 shalt** shall **85 mother's bleeding** Mother-bleeding **93 are** and **113 Ay . . . soon** [Q] F omits **116 Whitmore** Lieu. Water: W **117 Pene** Pine **132 Come . . . can** F assigns to the Lieutenant
**IV.ii.37 fall** faile **85 Chatham** [Q Chattam] Chartam **102 an** a
**IV.iv.24 wouldest** would'st **58 be betrayed** betraid
**IV.v.2–6 No . . . rebels** F and Q print as verse
**IV.vi.s.d. sword** [Q] staffe **9 Smith** But[cher] [i.e., Dick]
**IV.vii.26 serge** Surge **47 on** [Q] in **71 But Kent** **91 caudle** Candle
**IV.viii.13 rebel** rabble **65 s.d. He . . . away** [Q] Exit
**IV.ix.33 calmed** calme
**IV.x.21 waning** warning **27 Ah** a **59 God** [Q] Ioue **60 s.d. They . . . down** [Q] Heere they Fight
**V.i.109 these** thee **111 sons** sonne **113 for** of **122 s.d. and his son** [Q] F omits **124 s.d. (Kneels to King.)** [Q] F omits **194 or** and
**V.ii.27 s.d. Alarums . . . Clifford** [Q] F omits **28 œuvres** eumenes **30 s.d. Exit York** [Q] F omits **65 s.d. Exit . . . father** [Q] F omits **65 s.d. Enter . . . Albans** [Q] Enter Richard, and Somerset to fight **71 s.d. Exit** [Q] F omits
**V.iii.15 Now . . . today** F assigns to Salisbury

# THE SECOND PART OF
# HENRY THE SIXTH

[Dramatis Personae

KING HENRY THE SIXTH
HUMPHREY *Duke of Gloucester, uncle to the king,*
*and Protector*
CARDINAL BEAUFORT *Bishop of Winchester,*
*great-uncle to the king*
RICHARD PLANTAGENET *Duke of York*
EDWARD
RICHARD *afterward Richard III* } *his sons*
DUKE OF SOMERSET
HUMPHREY *Duke of Buckingham*
WILLIAM DE LA POLE *Marquess, afterward*
*Duke, of Suffolk*
EARL OF SALISBURY
RICHARD *Earl of Warwick, his son*
LORD CLIFFORD
YOUNG CLIFFORD *his son*
LORD SAY
LORD SCALES
SIR HUMPHREY STAFFORD
SIR WILLIAM STAFFORD *his brother*
SIR JOHN STANLEY
SIR MATTHEW GOFFE
VAUX
LIEUTENANT
MASTER
MASTER'S MATE
WALTER WHITMORE

TWO GENTLEMEN *prisoners with Suffolk*
JOHN HUM
JOHN SOUTHWELL } *priests*
ROGER BOLINGBROKE *a conjuror*
A SPIRIT
THOMAS HORNER *an armorer*
PETER THUMP *his apprentice*
MAYOR OF SAINT ALBANS
CLERK OF CHATHAM
ALEXANDER IDEN *a Kentish landowner*
SAUNDER SIMPCOX *an impostor*
JACK CADE
GEORGE BEVIS
JOHN HOLLAND
DICK THE BUTCHER } *followers of Cade*
SMITH THE WEAVER
MICHAEL
TWO MURDERERS
QUEEN MARGARET
ELEANOR *Duchess of Gloucester*
MARGERY JOURDAIN *a witch*
WIFE OF SIMPCOX
TWO PETITIONERS  BEADLE  HERALD
  SHERIFF  ALDERMEN  THREE NEIGHBORS
  OF HORNER  THREE PRENTICES
  FALCONERS  CITIZENS  GUARDS
  SOLDIERS  MESSENGERS  ATTENDANTS
  *Scene:* England]

# ACT I

### Scene I. [*London. The palace.*]

*Flourish° of trumpets: then hautboys.° Enter at one door*
KING *Henry the Sixth, and* Humphrey, *Duke of*
GLOUCESTER, *the Duke of* SOMERSET, *the Duke of*
BUCKINGHAM, CARDINAL *Beaufort, and others.*
*Enter at the other door the Duke of* YORK, *and the Marquess*
*of* SUFFOLK, *and* QUEEN *Margaret, and the Earls of*
SALISBURY *and* WARWICK.

SUFFOLK
As by your high imperial majesty
I had in charge at my depart for France,
As procurator° to your excellence,
To marry Princess Margaret for your grace,
So in the famous ancient city, Tours,          5
In presence of the Kings of France and Sicil,
The Dukes of Orleans, Calaber,° Bretagne and Alençon,
Seven earls, twelve barons, and twenty reverend
    bishops,
I have performed my task and was espoused,
And humbly now upon my bended knee,          10
In sight of England and her lordly peers,
Deliver up my title in the queen
To your most gracious hands, that are the substance
Of that great shadow I did represent—
The happiest° gift that ever the marquess gave,          15
The fairest queen that ever king received.

KING
Suffolk, arise. Welcome, Queen Margaret:
I can express no kinder sign of love
Than this kind° kiss. O Lord, that lends me life,
Lend me a heart replete with thankfulness!          20
For thou hast given me in this beauteous face
A world of earthly blessings to my soul,
If sympathy of love unite our thoughts.

QUEEN
Great King of England and my gracious lord,
The mutual conference° that my mind hath had,          25
By day, by night, waking, and in my dreams,
In courtly company or at my beads,
With you mine alderliefest° sovereign,
Makes me the bolder to salute my king
With ruder terms, such as my wit° affords          30
And overjoy of heart doth minister.°

KING
Her sight did ravish, but her grace in speech,
Her words yclad° with wisdom's majesty,
Makes me from wond'ring fall to weeping joys,
Such is the fullness of my heart's content.          35
Lords, with one cheerful voice welcome my love.

ALL (*Kneel.*)
Long live Queen Margaret, England's happiness!

*The decorative border on page 152 appeared on the first page of*
*2 Henry VI in* The Whole Contention betweene the Two
Famous Houses, Lancaster and Yorke, *1619.*
**I.i.s.d. Flourish** fanfare; **hautboys** oboes **3 procurator**
deputy **7 Calaber** location uncertain, but evidently *not*
Calabria **15 happiest** most fortunate **18–19 kinder . . .**
**kind** more natural . . . affectionate **25 mutual conference**
intimate conversation **28 alderliefest** dearest of all **30 wit**
intelligence, understanding **31 minister** provide **33 yclad**
clad (archaic)

QUEEN
We thank you all.

*Flourish.*

SUFFOLK
My Lord Protector, so it please your grace,
Here are the articles of contracted peace          40
Between our sovereign and the French king Charles,
For eighteen months concluded by consent.

GLOUCESTER (*Reads.*)
"Imprimis,° It is agreed between the French king
Charles, and William de la Pole, Marquess of Suffolk,
ambassador for Henry King of England, that the said          45
Henry shall espouse the Lady Margaret, daughter unto
Reignier King of Naples, Sicilia, and Jerusalem, and
crown her Queen of England ere the thirtieth of May
next ensuing. Item, That the duchy of Anjou and the
county of Maine shall be released and delivered to          50
the king her father"—

GLOUCESTER *lets it fall.*

KING
Uncle, how now?

GLOUCESTER          Pardon me, gracious lord;
Some sudden qualm hath struck me at the heart,
And dimmed mine eyes, that I can read no further.

KING
Uncle of Winchester, I pray read on.          55

CARDINAL [*Reads.*]
"Item, It is further agreed between them, that the
duchies of Anjou and Maine shall be released and
delivered over to the king her father, and she sent
over of the King of England's own proper° cost and
charges, without having any dowry."          60

KING
They please us well.
Lord Marquess, kneel down: we here create thee
First Duke of Suffolk, and girt thee with the sword.
Cousin of York, we here discharge your grace
From being regent i' th' parts of France,          65
Till term of eighteen months be full expired.
Thanks, uncle Winchester, Gloucester, York,
Buckingham, Somerset, Salisbury, and Warwick;
We thank you all for this great favor done,
In entertainment° to my princely queen.          70
Come, let us in, and with all speed provide
To see her coronation be performed.
                    *Exit* KING, QUEEN, *and* SUFFOLK; *and*
                        GLOUCESTER *stays all the rest.*

GLOUCESTER
Brave peers of England, pillars of the state,
To you Duke Humphrey must unload his grief—
Your grief, the common grief of all the land.          75
What! Did my brother Henry spend his youth,
His valor, coin, and people, in the wars?
Did he so often lodge in open field,
In winter's cold, and summer's parching heat,
To conquer France, his true inheritance?°          80

**43 Imprimis** in the first place **59 proper** personal **70**
**entertainment** welcome **80 inheritance** by his marriage
with Katherine of Valois (see *Henry V*, V.ii.333)

And did my brother Bedford° toil his wits,
To keep by policy° what Henry got?
Have you yourselves, Somerset, Buckingham,
Brave York, Salisbury, and victorious Warwick,
Received deep scars in France and Normandy?          85
Or hath mine uncle Beaufort and myself,
With all the learnèd council° of the realm,
Studied so long, sat in the council house
Early and late, debating to and fro
How France and Frenchmen might be kept in awe,          90
And had his highness in his infancy
Crownèd in Paris in despite of foes?
And shall these labors and these honors die?
Shall Henry's conquest, Bedford's vigilance,
Your deeds of war, and all our counsel die?          95
O peers of England, shameful is this league!
Fatal this marriage, canceling your fame,
Blotting your names from books of memory,
Razing the characters° of your renown,
Defacing monuments of conquered France,          100
Undoing all, as all had never been.

CARDINAL
Nephew, what means this passionate discourse,
This peroration with such circumstance?°
For France, 'tis ours; and we will keep it still.

GLOUCESTER
Ay, uncle, we will keep it, if we can;          105
But now it is impossible we should.
Suffolk, the new-made duke that rules the roast,°
Hath given the duchy of Anjou and Maine
Unto the poor Reignier, whose large style
Agrees° not with the leanness of his purse.          110

SALISBURY
Now, by the death of Him that died for all,
These counties were the keys of Normandy!
But wherefore weeps Warwick, my valiant son?

WARWICK
For grief that they are past recovery:
For, were there hope to conquer them again,          115
My sword should shed hot blood, mine eyes no tears.
Anjou and Maine! myself did win them both;
Those provinces these arms of mine did conquer:
And are the cities that I got with wounds
Delivered up again with peaceful words?          120
Mort Dieu!°

YORK
For Suffolk's duke, may he be suffocate
That dims the honor of this warlike isle!
France should have torn and rent my very heart
Before I would have yielded to this league.          125
I never read but England's kings have had
Large sums of gold and dowries with their wives;
And our King Henry gives away his own,
To match with her that brings no vantages.°

GLOUCESTER
A proper jest, and never heard before,          130

That Suffolk should demand a whole fifteenth°
For costs and charges in transporting her!
She should have stayed in France, and sterved° in
     France,
Before—

CARDINAL
My Lord of Gloucester, now ye grow too hot:          135
It was the pleasure of my lord the king.

GLOUCESTER
My Lord of Winchester, I know your mind;
'Tis not my speeches that you do mislike,
But 'tis my presence that doth trouble ye.
Rancor will out: proud prelate, in thy face          140
I see thy fury. If I longer stay,
We shall begin our ancient bickerings.
Lordings, farewell, and say, when I am gone,
I prophesied France will be lost ere long.
                    *Exit* GLOUCESTER.

CARDINAL
So, there goes our protector in a rage.          145
'Tis known to you he is mine enemy—
Nay more, an enemy unto you all,
And no great friend, I fear me, to the king.
Consider, lords, he is the next of blood,
And heir apparent to the English crown:          150
Had Henry got an empire by his marriage,
And all the wealthy kingdoms of the west,
There's reason he should be displeased at it.
Look to it, lords: let not his smoothing words
Bewitch your hearts, be wise and circumspect.          155
What though the common people favor him,
Calling him "Humphrey, the good Duke of Glouces-
     ter,"
Clapping their hands, and crying with loud voice,
"Jesu maintain your royal excellence!"
With "God preserve the good Duke Humphrey!"          160
I fear me, lords, for all this flattering gloss,
He will be found a dangerous protector.

BUCKINGHAM
Why should he then protect our sovereign,
He being of age to govern of himself?
Cousin of Somerset, join you with me,          165
And altogether with the Duke of Suffolk,
We'll quickly hoise° Duke Humphrey from his seat.

CARDINAL
This weighty business will not brook° delay;
I'll to the Duke of Suffolk presently.°
                    *Exit* CARDINAL.

SOMERSET
Cousin of Buckingham, though Humphrey's pride          170
And greatness of his place° be grief to us,
Yet let us watch the haughty cardinal.
His insolence is more intolerable
Than all the princes' in the land beside.
If Gloucester be displaced, he'll be protector.          175

BUCKINGHAM
Or thou or° I, Somerset, will be protector,
Despite Duke Humphrey or the cardinal.
                    *Exit* BUCKINGHAM *and* SOMERSET.

81 **Bedford** John, Duke of Bedford, the second of Henry IV's three sons  82 **policy** political craft, statesmanship  87 **council** the privy council  99 **Razing the characters** effacing the written letters  103 **peroration . . . circumstance** rhetorical discourse with so many details or illustrations  107 **rules the roast** domineers (from the proverbial expression "to rule the roast after one's own diet")  110 **Agrees** accords  121 **Mort Dieu** By God's death!  129 **vantages** profit

131 **fifteenth** tax of one-fifteenth part levied on property  133 **sterved** (1) died (2) starved  167 **hoise** hoist  168 **brook** tolerate  169 **presently** immediately  171 **place** position  176 **Or thou or** either thou or

SALISBURY

Pride went before, ambition follows him.
While these do labor for their own preferment,
Behoves° it us to labor for the realm.                                    180
I never saw but Humphrey Duke of Gloucester
Did bear him like a noble gentleman.
Oft have I seen the haughty cardinal,
More like a soldier than a man o' th' church,
As stout° and proud as he were lord of all,                               185
Swear like a ruffian and demean himself
Unlike the ruler of a commonweal.
Warwick, my son, the comfort of my age,
Thy deeds, thy plainness, and thy housekeeping,°
Hath won the greatest favor of the commons,                               190
Excepting none but good Duke Humphrey:
And, brother York, thy acts in Ireland,
In bringing them to civil discipline,
Thy late exploits done in the heart of France,
When thou wert regent for our sovereign,                                  195
Have made thee feared and honored of the people:
Join we together for the public good,
In what we can, to bridle and suppress
The pride of Suffolk and the cardinal,
With Somerset's and Buckingham's ambition;                                200
And, as we may, cherish Duke Humphrey's deeds,
While they do tend° the profit of the land.

WARWICK

So God help Warwick, as he loves the land,
And common profit of his country!

YORK

And so says York—[aside] for he hath greatest cause.   205

SALISBURY

Then let's make haste away, and look unto the main.°

WARWICK

Unto the main! O father, Maine is lost,
That Maine which by main force Warwick did win,
And would have kept so long as breath did last!
Main chance, father, you meant, but I meant Maine,      210
Which I will win from France, or else be slain.
            Exit WARWICK and SALISBURY; manet° YORK.

YORK

Anjou and Maine are given to the French;
Paris is lost; the state of Normandy
Stands on a tickle point° now° they are gone:
Suffolk concluded on the articles,                      215
The peers agreed, and Henry was well pleased
To change two dukedoms for a duke's fair daughter.
I cannot blame them all—what is't to them?
'Tis thine they give away, and not their own.
Pirates may make cheap pennyworths of their pillage,°   220
And purchase friends, and give to courtesans,
Still reveling like lords till all be gone;
While as the silly° owner of the goods
Weeps over them and wrings his hapless hands,
And shakes his head and trembling stands aloof,         225
While all is shared and all is borne away,
Ready to sterve and dare not touch his own:

So York must sit, and fret, and bite his tongue,
While his own lands are bargained for and sold.
Methinks the realms of England, France, and Ireland    230
Bear that proportion to my flesh and blood
As did the fatal brand Althaea° burned
Unto the prince's heart of Calydon.°
Anjou and Maine both given unto the French?
Cold news for me, for I had hope of France,             235
Even as I have of fertile England's soil.
A day will come when York shall claim his own;
And therefore I will take the Nevils' parts
And make a show of love to proud Duke Humphrey,
And, when I spy advantage, claim the crown,             240
For that's the golden mark I seek to hit.
Nor shall proud Lancaster° usurp my right,
Nor hold the scepter in his childish fist,
Nor wear the diadem upon his head,
Whose churchlike humors° fits not for a crown.         245
Then, York, be still awhile, till time do serve:
Watch thou and wake, when others be asleep,
To pry into the secrets of the state;
Till Henry surfeit in the joys of love
With his new bride and England's dear-bought queen,     250
And Humphrey with the peers be fall'n at jars:°
Then will I raise aloft the milk-white rose,
With whose sweet smell the air shall be perfumed,
And in my standard bear the arms of York,
To grapple with the house of Lancaster;                 255
And, force perforce,° I'll make him yield the crown,
Whose bookish° rule hath pulled fair England down.
                                        Exit YORK.


[Scene II. The Duke of Gloucester's house.]

Enter GLOUCESTER and his wife [DUCHESS] Eleanor.

DUCHESS

Why droops my lord, like overripened corn
Hanging the head at Ceres'° plenteous load?
Why doth the great Duke Humphrey knit his brows,
As frowning at the favors of the world?
Why are thine eyes fixed to the sullen° earth,          5
Gazing on that which seems to dim thy sight?
What see'st thou there? King Henry's diadem,
Enchased° with all the honors of the world?
If so, gaze on, and grovel on thy face,
Until thy head be circled with the same.                10
Put forth thy hand, reach at the glorious gold.
What, is't too short? I'll lengthen it with mine;
And, having both together heaved it up,
We'll both together lift our heads to heaven,
And never more abase our sight so low                   15
As to vouchsafe one glance unto the ground.

232 Althaea Althaea caused the death of her son, Meleager,
Prince of Calydon, by temperamentally burning a brand
(log) upon which the Fates had told her his life would
depend   233 prince's . . . Calydon the Prince of Calydon's
heart   242 Lancaster Henry VI   245 humors temperament
251 at jars to quarreling   256 force perforce willy-nilly
257 bookish scholarly (i.e., inactive)
I.ii.2 Ceres the goddess of the harvest   5 sullen dull   8
Enchased adorned

180 Behoves behooves   185 stout fierce, arrogant   189 housekeeping hospitality   202 tend foster   206 main main chance
(a gambling term for the most important thing at stake)
211 s.d. manet remains (Latin)   214 on . . . point in an
unstable position; now now that   220 make . . . pillage
squander recklessly what they steal   223 silly pitiful

**GLOUCESTER**
O Nell, sweet Nell, if thou dost love thy lord,
Banish the canker of ambitious thoughts:
And may that thought, when I imagine ill
Against my king and nephew, virtuous Henry,          20
Be my last breathing in this mortal world!
My troublous dreams this night° doth make me sad.

**DUCHESS**
What dreamed my lord? Tell me, and I'll requite it
With sweet rehearsal of my morning's dream.°

**GLOUCESTER**
Methought this staff, mine office badge in court,          25
Was broke in twain: by whom, I have forgot,
But as I think, it was by th' cardinal;
And on the pieces of the broken wand
Were placed the heads of Edmund Duke of Somerset,
And William de la Pole, first Duke of Suffolk.          30
This was my dream: what it doth bode, God knows.

**DUCHESS**
Tut, this was nothing but an argument
That he that breaks a stick of Gloucester's grove
Shall lose his head for his presumption.
But list to me, my Humphrey, my sweet duke:          35
Methought I sat in seat of majesty
In the cathedral church of Westminster,
And in that chair where kings and queens were
    crowned;
Where Henry and Dame Margaret kneeled to me,
And on my head did set the diadem.          40

**GLOUCESTER**
Nay, Eleanor, then must I chide outright:
Presumptuous dame, ill-nurtured Eleanor,
Art thou not second woman in the realm,
And the protector's wife, beloved of him?
Hast thou not worldly pleasure at command          45
Above the reach or compass of thy thought?
And wilt thou still be hammering° treachery,
To tumble down thy husband and thyself
From top of honor to disgrace's feet?
Away from me, and let me hear no more!          50

**DUCHESS**
What, what, my lord! Are you so choleric°
With Eleanor, for telling but her dream?
Next time I'll keep my dreams unto myself,
And not be checked.

**GLOUCESTER**
Nay, be not angry; I am pleased again.          55

*Enter* MESSENGER.

**MESSENGER**
My Lord Protector, 'tis his highness' pleasure
You do prepare to ride unto Saint Albans,
Where as° the king and queen do mean to hawk.°

**GLOUCESTER**
I go. Come, Nell, thou wilt ride with us?

**DUCHESS**
Yes, my good lord, I'll follow presently.°          60
            *Exit* GLOUCESTER [*and* MESSENGER].

Follow I must; I cannot go before,
While Gloucester bears this base and humble mind.
Were I a man, a duke, and next of blood,°
I would remove these tedious stumbling blocks
And smooth my way upon their headless necks;          65
And, being a woman, I will not be slack
To play my part in fortune's pageant.
Where are you there, Sir John? Nay, fear not, man,
We are alone; here's none but thee and I.

*Enter* HUM.

**HUM**
Jesus preserve your royal majesty!          70

**DUCHESS**
What say'st thou, "majesty"? I am but grace.

**HUM**
But, by the grace of God, and Hum's advice,
Your grace's title shall be multiplied.°

**DUCHESS**
What say'st thou, man? Hast thou as yet conferred
With Margery Jourdain, the cunning witch,          75
With Roger Bolingbroke, the conjuror?
And will they undertake to do me good?

**HUM**
This they have promisèd, to show your highness
A spirit raised from depth of underground,
That shall make answer to such questions          80
As by your grace shall be propounded him.

**DUCHESS**
It is enough: I'll think upon the questions.
When from Saint Albans we do make return,
We'll see these things effected to the full.
Here, Hum, take this reward; make merry, man,          85
With thy confederates in this weighty cause.
            *Exit* [DUCHESS] *Eleanor.*

**HUM**
Hum must make merry with the duchess' gold;
Marry,° and shall. But how now, Sir John Hum!
Seal up your lips, and give no words but mum:
The business asketh° silent secrecy.          90
Dame Eleanor gives gold to bring the witch:
Gold cannot come amiss, were she a devil.
Yet have I gold flies from another coast°—
I dare not say, from the rich cardinal
And from the great and new-made Duke of Suffolk.          95
Yet I do find it so—for, to be plain,
They, knowing Dame Eleanor's aspiring humor,°
Have hirèd me to undermine the duchess
And buzz these conjurations° in her brain.
They say, "A crafty knave does need no broker";          100
Yet am I Suffolk and the cardinal's broker.°
Hum, if you take not heed, you shall go near
To call them both a pair of crafty knaves.
Well, so it stands; and thus, I fear, at last
Hum's knavery will be the duchess' wrack,°          105
And her attainture° will be Humphrey's fall.
Sort how it will, I shall have gold for all.          *Exit.*

**63 next of blood** the successor to the crown, if Henry VI dies
without issue **73 Your . . . multiplied** a play on 1 Peter
1:2, "Grace and peace be multiplied unto you" **88 Marry** a
mild oath, from "By the Virgin Mary" **90 asketh** requires
**93 coast** quarter **97 humor** temperament **99 conjurations**
incantations **101 broker** agent, go-between **105 wrack** ruin
**106 attainture** incrimination

**22 this night** last night **24 morning's dream** morning dreams
were reputed true **47 hammering** devising **51 choleric**
angry **58 Where as** where; **hawk** hunt with hawks **60
presently** immediately

[Scene III. *The palace.*]

*Enter three or four* PETITIONERS; [PETER] *the armorer's man, being one.*

FIRST PETITIONER   My masters, let's stand close: my Lord Protector will come this way by and by, and then we may deliver our supplications in the quill.°

SECOND PETITIONER   Marry, the Lord protect him, for he's a good man, Jesu bless him!     5

*Enter* SUFFOLK *and* QUEEN.

PETER   Here 'a° comes, methinks, and the queen with him. I'll be the first, sure.

SECOND PETITIONER   Come back, fool! this is the Duke of Suffolk, and not my Lord Protector.

SUFFOLK   How now, fellow! wouldst anything with   10 me?

FIRST PETITIONER   I pray, my lord, pardon me: I took ye for my Lord Protector.

QUEEN   For my Lord Protector! Are your supplications to his lordship? Let me see them: what is thine?    15

FIRST PETITIONER   Mine is, and't please your grace, against John Goodman, my Lord Cardinal's man,° for keeping my house, and lands, and wife and all, from me.

SUFFOLK   Thy wife too! that's some wrong, indeed.   20 What's yours? What's here? [*Reads.*] "Against the Duke of Suffolk, for enclosing the commons° of Melford." How now, sir knave!

SECOND PETITIONER   Alas, sir, I am but a poor petitioner of our whole township.     25

PETER   [*Giving his petition.*] Against my master, Thomas Horner, for saying that the Duke of York was rightful heir to the crown.

QUEEN   What say'st thou? did the Duke of York say he was rightful heir to the crown?     30

PETER   That my master was? No, forsooth: my master said that he was, and that the king was an usurer.

QUEEN   An usurper, thou wouldst say.

PETER   Ay, forsooth, an usurper.

SUFFOLK   Who is there? (*Enter* SERVANT.) Take this   35 fellow in, and send for his master with a pursuivant° presently. We'll hear more of your matter before the king.       *Exit* [SERVANT, *with* PETER].

QUEEN
And as for you, that love to be protected
Under the wings of our protector's grace,     40
Begin your suits anew, and sue to him.

*Tear[s] the supplication.*

Away, base cullions!° Suffolk, let them go.

ALL
Come, let's be gone.            *Exit.*

QUEEN
My Lord of Suffolk, say, is this the guise,°
Is this the fashions in the court of England?    45
Is this the government of Britain's isle,
And this the royalty of Albion's° king?

What! Shall King Henry be a pupil still
Under the surly Gloucester's governance?
Am I a queen in title and in style,°      50
And must be made a subject to a duke?
I tell thee, Pole, when in the city Tours
Thou ran'st atilt° in honor of my love
And stol'st away the ladies' hearts of France,
I thought King Henry had resembled thee    55
In courage, courtship, and proportion:°
But all his mind is bent to holiness,
To number Ave-Maries on his beads;°
His champions° are the prophets and apostles,
His weapons holy saws° of sacred writ,     60
His study is his tilt yard, and his loves
Are brazen images of canonized saints.
I would the college of the cardinals
Would choose him pope and carry him to Rome,
And set the triple crown° upon his head:    65
That were a state fit for his holiness.

SUFFOLK
Madam, be patient: as I was cause
Your highness came to England, so will I
In England work your grace's full content.

QUEEN
Beside the haughty protector, have we Beaufort   70
The imperious churchman, Somerset, Buckingham,
And grumbling York; and not the least of these
But can do more in England than the king.

SUFFOLK
And he of these that can do most of all
Cannot do more in England than the Nevils:   75
Salisbury and Warwick are no simple peers.

QUEEN
Not all these lords do vex me half so much
As that proud dame, the Lord Protector's wife:
She sweeps it through the court with troops of ladies,
More like an empress than Duke Humphrey's wife.   80
Strangers° in court do take her for the queen:
She bears a duke's revenues on her back,
And in her heart she scorns our poverty.
Shall I not live to be avenged on her?
Contemptuous° base-born callet° as she is,    85
She vaunted 'mongst her minions° t' other day,
The very train of her worst wearing gown
Was better worth than all my father's lands,
Till Suffolk gave two dukedoms for his daughter.

SUFFOLK
Madam, myself have limed a bush° for her,    90
And placed a quire° of such enticing birds
That she will light to listen to the lays,°
And never mount to trouble you again.
So let her rest: and, madam, list to me,
For I am bold to counsel you in this:      95

---

50 **style** name   53 **ran'st atilt** competed in a tourney   56 **proportion** shape   58 **number . . . beads** say rosaries   59 **champions** warriors chosen to represent him (chivalric term)   60 **saws** maxims, platitudes   65 **triple crown** the papal tiara   81 **Strangers** foreigners   85 **Contemptuous** contemptible; **callet** trull   86 **minions** effeminate or female retainers (contemptuous)   90 **limed a bush** small birds were trapped by smearing bird lime (a sticky preparation of holly bark) over the twigs of bushes   91 **quire** (1) group (2) choir   92 **lays** songs

---

I.iii.3 **in the quill** in succession (?)   6 **'a** he   17 **man** agent, protégé   22 **enclosing the commons** fencing off the public pasture   36 **pursuivant** warrant officer   42 **cullions** rascals   44 **guise** custom   47 **Albion's** England's

Although we fancy not the cardinal,
Yet must we join with him and with the lords,
Till we have brought Duke Humphrey in disgrace.
As for the Duke of York, this late complaint°
Will make but little for his benefit.                                    100
So, one by one, we'll weed them all at last,
And you yourself shall steer the happy° helm.

*Sound a sennet.° Enter* KING *Henry, and the Duke of*
YORK *and the Duke of* SOMERSET *on both sides of the*
KING, *whispering with him; and enter* GLOUCESTER,
*Dame* [DUCHESS] *Eleanor, the Duke of* BUCKINGHAM,
SALISBURY, *the Earl of* WARWICK, *and the* CARDINAL
*of Winchester.*

KING
For my part, noble lords, I care not which:
Or Somerset or York, all's one to me.
YORK
If York have ill demeaned himself in France,            105
Then let him be denayed° the regentship.
SOMERSET
If Somerset be unworthy of the place,
Let York be regent; I will yield to him.
WARWICK
Whether your grace be worthy, yea or no,
Dispute not that: York is the worthier.                     110
CARDINAL
Ambitious Warwick, let thy betters speak.
WARWICK
The cardinal's not my better in the field.
BUCKINGHAM
All in this presence are thy betters,° Warwick.
WARWICK
Warwick may live to be the best of all.
SALISBURY
Peace, son; and show some reason, Buckingham,       115
Why Somerset should be preferred in this.°
QUEEN
Because the king, forsooth, will have it so.
GLOUCESTER
Madam, the king is old enough himself
To give his censure.° These are no women's matters.
QUEEN
If he be old enough, what needs your grace              120
To be protector of his excellence?
GLOUCESTER
Madam, I am protector of the realm,
And at his pleasure will resign my place.
SUFFOLK
Resign it then and leave thine insolence.
Since thou wert king—as who is king but thou?—      125
The commonwealth hath daily run to wrack,
The Dolphin° hath prevailed beyond the seas,
And all the peers and nobles of the realm
Have been as bondmen° to thy sovereignty.
CARDINAL
The commons hast thou racked; the clergy's bags    130
Are lank and lean with thy extortions.

SOMERSET
Thy sumptuous buildings and thy wife's attire
Have cost a mass of public treasury.
BUCKINGHAM
Thy cruelty in execution
Upon offenders hath exceeded law,                            135
And left thee to the mercy of the law.
QUEEN
Thy sale of offices and towns in France,
If they were known, as the suspect° is great,
Would make thee quickly hop without thy head.
                                        *Exit* GLOUCESTER.

[*The* QUEEN *drops her fan.*]

Give me my fan! What, minion, can ye not?            140

*She gives the* DUCHESS *a box on the ear.*

I cry you mercy,° madam; was it you?
DUCHESS
Was't I! Yea, I it was, proud Frenchwoman:
Could I come near your beauty with my nails,
I'd set my ten commandments in your face.°
KING
Sweet aunt, be quiet;° 'twas against her will.°        145
DUCHESS
Against her will, good king? Look to't, in time
She'll hamper thee, and dandle thee like a baby.
Though in this place most master° wear no breeches,
She shall not strike Dame Eleanor unrevenged.
                                        *Exit* [DUCHESS] *Eleanor.*
BUCKINGHAM
Lord Cardinal, I will follow Eleanor,                          150
And listen after Humphrey, how he proceeds.
She's tickled° now; her fury needs no spurs,
She'll gallop far enough to her destruction.
                                        *Exit* BUCKINGHAM.

*Enter* GLOUCESTER.

GLOUCESTER
Now, lords, my choler being overblown
With walking once about the quadrangle,                 155
I come to talk of commonwealth affairs.
As for your spiteful false objections,°
Prove them, and I lie open to the law:
But God in mercy so deal with my soul,
As I in duty love my king and country!                   160
But to the matter that we have in hand:
I say, my sovereign, York is meetest° man
To be your regent in the realm of France.
SUFFOLK
Before we make election, give me leave
To show some reason, of no little force,                    165
That York is most unmeet of any man.
YORK
I'll tell thee, Suffolk, why I am unmeet:
First, for I cannot flatter thee in pride;°

99 this late complaint Peter's  102 happy fortunate; s.d. sennet phrase on the trumpet  106 denayed old form of *denied* 113 betters superiors in rank  116 preferred in this promoted to this position  119 censure opinion, judgment  127 Dolphin Dauphin, eldest son of the King of France  129 bondmen slaves, serfs

138 suspect suspicion  141 cry you mercy beg your pardon 144 set . . . face mark with fingernails  145 quiet calm; against her will unwittingly  148 most master the greatest master (i.e., here the wife rules the house)  152 tickled provoked, touchd  157 objections accusations  162 meetest most suitable  168 for . . . pride because I cannot entertain you sumptuously

Next, if I be appointed for the place,
My Lord of Somerset will keep me here,          170
Without discharge,° money, or furniture,°
Till France be won into the Dolphin's hands.
Last time, I danced attendance on his will
Till Paris was besieged, famished, and lost.

WARWICK
That can I witness; and a fouler fact°          175
Did never traitor in the land commit.

SUFFOLK
Peace, headstrong Warwick!

WARWICK
Image° of pride, why should I hold my peace?

*Enter [HORNER the] armorer and [PETER] his man [both guarded].*

SUFFOLK
Because here is a man accused of treason.
Pray God the Duke of York excuse himself!          180

YORK
Doth anyone accuse York for° a traitor?

KING
What mean'st thou, Suffolk? Tell me, what are these?

SUFFOLK
Please it your majesty, this is the man
That doth accuse his master of high treason.
His words were these: that Richard Duke of York          185
Was rightful heir unto the English crown,
And that your majesty was an usurper.

KING
Say, man, were these thy words?

HORNER   And't shall please your majesty, I never said
nor thought any such matter! God is my witness,   190
I am falsely accused by the villain.

PETER   By these ten bones,° my lords, he did speak
them to me in the garret one night, as we were
scouring my Lord of York's armor.

YORK
Base dunghill villain and mechanical,°          195
I'll have thy head for this thy traitor's speech!
I do beseech your royal majesty,
Let him have all the rigor of the law.

HORNER   Alas, my lord, hang me if ever I spake the
words! My accuser is my prentice,° and when I did   200
correct him for his fault° the other day, he did vow
upon his knees he would be even with me: I have
good witness of this; therefore I beseech your majesty,
do not cast away an honest man for a villain's
accusation.          205

KING
Uncle, what shall we say to this in law?

GLOUCESTER
This doom,° my lord, if I may judge:
Let Somerset be regent o'er the French,
Because in York this breeds suspicion.°
And let these have a day appointed them          210

For single combat,° in convenient° place,
For he hath witness of his servant's malice.
This is the law, and this Duke Humphrey's doom.

SOMERSET
I humbly thank your royal majesty.

HORNER
And I accept the combat willingly.          215

PETER   Alas, my lord, I cannot fight; for God's sake,
pity my case! The spite of man prevaileth against
me. O Lord, have mercy upon me! I shall never be
able to fight a blow. O Lord, my heart!

GLOUCESTER
Sirrah,° or you must fight, or else be hanged.          220

KING   Away with them to prison; and the day of combat shall be the last of the next month. Come,
Somerset, we'll see thee sent away.     *Flourish; exeunt.*

[Scene IV. *A garden outside Gloucester's house.
Before a tower.*]

*Enter the witch [MARGERY JOURDAIN], the two
priests [HUM and SOUTHWELL], and BOLINGBROKE
[the conjuror].*

HUM   Come, my masters; the duchess, I tell you, expects performance of your promises.

BOLINGBROKE   Master Hum, we are therefore provided:° will her ladyship behold and hear our
exorcisms?°          5

HUM   Ay, what else? Fear° you not her courage.

BOLINGBROKE   I have heard her reported to be a
woman of an invincible spirit: but it shall be convenient, Master Hum, that you be by her aloft,
while we be busy below; and so, I pray you, go,   10
in God's name, and leave us. (*Exit* HUM.) Mother
Jourdain, be you prostrate and grovel on the earth;
John Southwell, read you; and let us to our work.

*Enter DUCHESS aloft, [HUM following].*

DUCHESS   Well said, my masters; and welcome all.
To this gear,° the sooner the better.          15

BOLINGBROKE
Patience, good lady; wizards know their times.
Deep night, dark night, the silent° of the night,
The time of night when Troy was set on fire,
The time when screech owls cry, and ban-dogs° howl,
And spirits walk, and ghosts break up their graves—   20
That time best fits the work we have in hand.
Madam, sit you, and fear not: whom we raise
We will make fast within a hallowed verge.°

*Here [they] do the ceremonies belonging, and make the
circle;* BOLINGBROKE *or* SOUTHWELL *reads,* "Conjuro
te, etc."° *It thunders and lightens° terribly; then the*
SPIRIT *riseth.*

211 **single combat** a duel; **convenient** appropriate   220
**Sirrah** contemptuous term of address
**I.iv.3–4 therefore provided** equipped for that   **5 exorcisms**
ceremonies for expelling the devil (but here a malapropism
for *raising* the devil)   **6 Fear** doubt   **15 gear** business   **17
silent** silent time   **19 ban-dogs** fierce dogs chained up   **23
hallowed verge** charmed circle; **s.d. Conjuro te, etc.**
beginning of the incantation "I conjure you . . ."; **s.d.
lightens** makes lightning

**171 discharge** payment of what he owes; **furniture** equipment
(for war)   **175 fact** evil deed   **178 Image** embodiment,
epitome   **181 for** as   **192 ten bones** fingers   **195 mechanical**
manual laborer (i.e., drudge)   **200 prentice** apprentice   **201
fault** mistake   **207 doom** sentence   **209 breeds suspicion**
suggests doubt (of his loyalty)

SPIRIT  Adsum.°

MARGERY JOURDAIN
Asnath,°                                                                          25
By the eternal God, whose name and power
Thou tremblest at, answer that I shall ask:
For till thou speak, thou shalt not pass from hence.

SPIRIT
Ask what thou wilt. That I had said and done!

BOLINGBROKE [Consulting a paper.]
First of the king: what shall of him become?                  30

SPIRIT
The duke yet lives that Henry shall depose,
But him outlive, and die a violent death.°

[SOUTHWELL writes out the questions and answers.]

BOLINGBROKE
What fates await the Duke of Suffolk?

SPIRIT
By water shall he die, and take his end.

BOLINGBROKE
What shall befall the Duke of Somerset?                        35

SPIRIT
Let him shun castles:
Safer shall he be upon the sandy plains
Than where castles mounted stand.
Have done, for more I hardly can endure.

BOLINGBROKE
Descend to darkness and the burning lake!                     40
False fiend, avoid!°

*Thunder and lightning; he sinks down again.*

*Enter the Duke of* YORK *and the Duke of* BUCKINGHAM
*with their* GUARD *and break in.*

YORK
Lay hands upon these traitors and their trash.
Beldam, I think we watched you at an inch.°
What, madam, are you there? The king and com-
    monweal
Are deeply indebted for this piece of pains.°              45
My Lord Protector will, I doubt it not,
See you well guerdoned° for these good deserts.

DUCHESS
Not half so bad as thine to England's king,
Injurious° duke, that threatest where's no cause.

BUCKINGHAM
True, madam, none at all: what call you this?              50
Away with them! Let them be clapped up close,
And kept asunder. You, madam, shall with us.
Stafford, take her to thee.

*Exit* DUCHESS *above [and* HUM, *guarded].*
We'll see your trinkets° here all forthcoming.
All, away!                                                              55

*Exit [*MARGERY JOURDAIN, SOUTHWELL, *and*
BOLINGBROKE, *with the rest of the* GUARD].

YORK
Lord Buckingham, methinks you watched her well:
A pretty plot, well chosen to build upon!
Now, pray, my lord, let's see the devil's writ.
What have we here?

*Reads.*

"The duke yet lives that Henry shall depose;               60
But him outlive, and die a violent death."
Why, this is just "Aio te Acacida,
Romanos vincere posse."° Well, to the rest:
"Tell me what fate awaits the Duke of Suffolk?
By water shall he die, and take his end.                       65
What shall betide the Duke of Somerset?
Let him shun castles;
Safer shall he be upon the sandy plains
Than where castles mounted stand."
Come, come, my lords, these oracles are hard,           70
Hardly attained, and hardly° understood.
The king is now in progress towards Saint Albans;
With him, the husband of this lovely° lady.
Thither goes these news, as fast as horse can carry
    them—
A sorry breakfast for my Lord Protector.                   75

BUCKINGHAM
Your grace shall give me leave, my Lord of York,
To be the post,° in hope of his reward.

YORK
At your pleasure, my good lord. Who's within there,
    ho!

*Enter a* SERVINGMAN.

Invite my Lords of Salisbury and Warwick
To sup with me tomorrow night. Away!    *Exeunt.*  80

# [ ACT II ]

## [Scene I. *Saint Albans.*]

*Enter the* KING, QUEEN, *with a hawk on her fist,*
GLOUCESTER, CARDINAL, *and* SUFFOLK, *with*
FALCONERS *hallooing.*

QUEEN
Believe me, lords, for flying at the brook,°
I saw not better sport these seven years' day:
Yet, by your leave, the wind was very high;
And, ten to one, old Joan had not gone out.°

KING
But what a point,° my lord, your falcon made,           5
And what a pitch° she flew above the rest!

---

24 **Adsum** here I am  25 **Asnath** obscure; possibly an
anagram for *Sathan*  31–32 **The . . . death** a typically cryptic
and ambiguous prophecy: either "The duke who will depose
Henry is now living" or "The duke Henry will depose is now
living" (see lines 62–63)  41 **avoid** go hence  43 **at an inch**
closely (enough)  45 **piece of pains** masterpiece of service
(ironic)  47 **guerdoned** rewarded  49 **Injurious** abusive  54
**trinkets** the conjuring apparatus, including Southwell's written
record

62–63 **Aio . . . posse** from Ennius, the ambiguous response
of the Pythian oracle Apollo to King Pyrrhus, when Pyrrhus
asked if he would conquer Rome: either "I affirm that you,
descendant of Aeacus, can conquer the Romans" or "I affirm
that the Romans can conquer you, etc."  70–71 **hard . . .
Hardly . . . hardly** obscure . . . with difficulty . . . scarcely
to be  73 **lovely** lovable  77 **post** messenger
**II.i.1 at the brook** at waterfowl  4 **ten . . . out** the odds
were against this hawk (the queen's?) flying  5 **point** position
from which to swoop  6 **pitch** altitude

To see how God in all his creatures works!
Yea, man and birds are fain of climbing high.

SUFFOLK
No marvel, and it like your majesty,
My Lord Protector's hawks do tow'r so well: 10
They know their master loves to be aloft,
And bears his thoughts above his falcon's pitch.

GLOUCESTER
My lord, 'tis but a base ignoble mind
That mounts no higher than a bird can soar.

CARDINAL
I thought as much: he would be above the clouds. 15

GLOUCESTER
Ay, my Lord Cardinal, how think you by that?
Were it not good your grace could fly to heaven?

KING
The treasury of everlasting joy.

CARDINAL
Thy heaven is on earth; thine eyes and thoughts
Beat on° a crown, the treasure of thy heart. 20
Pernicious protector, dangerous peer,
That smooth'st it° so with king and commonweal!

GLOUCESTER
What, cardinal, is your priesthood grown peremp-
tory?°
Tantaene animis coelestibus irae!°
Churchmen so hot? Good uncle, can you dote,° 25
To hide such malice with such holiness?

SUFFOLK
No malice, sir; no more than well becomes
So good a quarrel and so bad a peer.

GLOUCESTER
As who, my lord?

SUFFOLK Why, as you, my lord,
An't like your lordly lord protectorship. 30

GLOUCESTER
Why, Suffolk, England knows thine insolence.

QUEEN
And thy ambition, Gloucester.

KING I prithee peace,
Good queen, and whet not on these furious peers,
For blessèd are the peacemakers on earth. 35

CARDINAL
Let me be blessèd for the peace I make,
Against this proud protector, with my sword!

GLOUCESTER [Aside.]
Faith, holy uncle, would 'twere come to that!

CARDINAL [Aside.]
Marry, when thou dar'st.

GLOUCESTER [Aside.]
Make up no factious numbers for the matter;° 40
In thine own person answer thy abuse.

CARDINAL [Aside.]
Ay, where thou dar'st not peep: and if° thou
dar'st,
This evening, on the east side of the grove.

KING
How now, my lords!

CARDINAL Believe me, cousin Gloucester,
Had not your man° put up the fowl° so suddenly, 45
We had had more sport. [Aside.] Come with thy
two-hand sword.

GLOUCESTER True, uncle.

CARDINAL [Aside.]
Are ye advised?° The east side of the grove?

GLOUCESTER [Aside.]
Cardinal, I am with you.

KING Why, how now, uncle Gloucester!

GLOUCESTER
Talking of hawking; nothing else, my lord.

[Aside.] 50

Now, by God's mother, priest, I'll shave your crown
for this.
Or all my fence° shall fail.

CARDINAL [Aside.]
Medice, teipsum°—
Protector, see to't well, protect yourself.

KING
The winds grow high, so do your stomachs,° lords.
How irksome is this music to my heart! 55
When such strings jar, what hope of harmony?
I pray, my lords, let me compound° this strife.

*Enter one [TOWNSMAN] crying, "A miracle!"*

GLOUCESTER
What means this noise?
Fellow, what miracle dost thou proclaim?

[TOWNSMAN] 60
A miracle! a miracle!

SUFFOLK
Come to the king and tell him what miracle.

[TOWNSMAN]
Forsooth, a blind man at Saint Alban's shrine,
Within this half hour hath received his sight—
A man that ne'er saw in his life before.

KING 65
Now, God be praised, that to believing souls
Gives light in darkness, comfort in despair!

*Enter the MAYOR of Saint Albans and his BRETHREN,
bearing the man [Saunder SIMPCOX] between two in a
chair, [Simpcox' WIFE following].*

CARDINAL
Here comes the townsmen, on° procession,
To present your highness with the man.

KING
Great is his comfort in this earthly vale,
Although by sight his sin be multiplied.° 70

GLOUCESTER
Stand by, my masters: bring him near the king:
His highness' pleasure is to talk with him.

---

**20 Beat on** harp on **22 smooth'st it** flatters **23 peremptory**
overbearing **24 Tantaene . . . irae** *Aeneid*, I.11: "So much
anger in heavenly souls?" **25 can you dote** are you so much
a fool (as to attempt) **40 Make . . . matter** bring none of
your own faction into the quarrel **42 and if** if

**45 your man** disrespectfully suggests King Henry; **put . . .
fowl** flushed the game **48 advised** agreed **52 fence** skill
at swordplay **53 Medice, teipsum** "Physician, [cure] thyself"
**55 stomachs** tempers **58 compound** compose **68 on** in
**71 Although . . . multiplied** cf. John 9:41: "If ye were
blind, ye would have no sin, but now ye say, We see: therefore
your sin remaineth"

KING
Good fellow, tell us here the circumstance,
That we for thee may glorify the Lord.                    75
What, hast thou been long blind, and now restored?

SIMPCOX
Born blind, and't please your grace.

WIFE
Ay, indeed, was he.

SUFFOLK
What woman is this?

WIFE
His wife, and't like your worship.                        80

GLOUCESTER
Hadst thou been his mother, thou couldst have better
   told.

KING
Where wert thou born?

SIMPCOX
At Berwick in the north, and't like your grace.

KING
Poor soul, God's goodness hath been great to thee:
Let never day nor night unhallowed pass,                  85
But still° remember what the Lord hath done.

QUEEN
Tell me, good fellow, cam'st thou here by chance,
Or of devotion, to this holy shrine?

SIMPCOX
God knows, of pure devotion, being called
A hundred times and oftener, in my sleep,                 90
By good Saint Alban; who said, "Simpcox, come,
Come, offer at my shrine, and I will help thee."

WIFE
Most true, forsooth; and many time and oft
Myself have heard a voice to call him so.

CARDINAL
What, art thou lame?

SIMPCOX                    Ay, God Almighty help me.       95

SUFFOLK
How cam'st thou so?

SIMPCOX                    A fall off of a tree.

WIFE
A plum tree, master.

GLOUCESTER                How long hast thou been blind?

SIMPCOX
O, born so, master.

GLOUCESTER                What, and wouldst climb a tree?

SIMPCOX
But that° in all my life, when I was a youth.

WIFE
Too true, and bought his climbing very dear.              100

GLOUCESTER
'Mass,° thou lov'dst plums well, that wouldst venture
   so.

SIMPCOX
Alas, good master, my wife desired some damsons,
And made me climb, with danger of my life.

GLOUCESTER [Aside.]
A subtle knave! But yet it shall not serve.
Let me see thine eyes: wink° now, now open them.          105
In my opinion yet thou see'st not well.

SIMPCOX
Yes, master, clear as day, I thank God and Saint Alban.

GLOUCESTER
Say'st thou me so? What color is this cloak of?

SIMPCOX
Red, master; red as blood.

GLOUCESTER
Why, that's well said. What color is my gown of?          110

SIMPCOX
Black, forsooth, coal black, as jet.

KING
Why, then, thou know'st what color jet is of?

SUFFOLK
And yet, I think, jet did he never see.

GLOUCESTER
But cloaks and gowns, before this day, a many.

WIFE
Never, before this day, in all his life!                  115

GLOUCESTER
Tell me, sirrah, what's my name?

SIMPCOX
Alas, master, I know not.

GLOUCESTER    What's his name?

SIMPCOX    I know not.

GLOUCESTER    Nor his?                                     120

SIMPCOX
No, indeed, master.

GLOUCESTER
What's thine own name?

SIMPCOX
Saunder Simpcox, and if it please you, master.

GLOUCESTER    Then, Saunder, sit there, the lying'st
knave in Christendom. If thou hadst been born blind,       125
thou mightst as well have known all our names as
thus to name the several colors we do wear. Sight
may distinguish of colors, but suddenly to nominate°
them all, it is impossible. My lords, Saint Alban here
hath done a miracle—and would ye not think his            130
cunning to be great that could restore this cripple
to his legs again?

SIMPCOX
O master, that you could!

GLOUCESTER
My masters of Saint Albans,
Have you not beadles° in your town,                       135
And things called whips?

MAYOR
Yes, my lord, if it please your grace.

GLOUCESTER
Then send for one presently.

MAYOR
Sirrah, go fetch the beadle hither straight.
                              Exit [an ATTENDANT].
GLOUCESTER    Now fetch me a stool hither by and by.       140
[They bring one.] Now, sirrah, if you mean to save
yourself from whipping, leap me° over this stool
and run away.

SIMPCOX
Alas, master, I am not able to stand alone:

---

86 still always    99 But that only once    101 'Mass by the
mass    105 wink close them

128 nominate give them names    135 beadles minor parish
officials, entrusted with keeping order in church and punishing
petty offenders    142 leap me leap for me

You go about to torture me in vain.    145

*Enter a* BEADLE *with whips.*

GLOUCESTER    Well, sir, we must have you find your
legs. Sirrah beadle, whip him till he leap over that
same stool.

BEADLE    I will, my lord. Come on, sirrah: off with
your doublet quickly.    150

SIMPCOX    Alas, master, what shall I do? I am not able
to stand.

*After the* BEADLE *hath hit him once, he leaps over the
stool and runs away; and they follow and cry,* "A miracle!"

KING
O God, see'st thou this, and bearest so long?

QUEEN
It made me laugh to see the villain run.

GLOUCESTER
Follow the knave, and take this drab° away.    155

WIFE
Alas, sir, we did it for pure need.

GLOUCESTER
Let them be whipped through every market town
Till they come to Berwick, from whence they came.
                *Exit* [MAYOR, BEADLE, WIFE, *etc.*].

CARDINAL
Duke Humphrey has done a miracle today.

SUFFOLK
True—made the lame to leap and fly away.    160

GLOUCESTER
But you have done more miracles than I:
You made in a day, my lord, whole towns to fly.°

*Enter* BUCKINGHAM.

KING
What tidings with our cousin Buckingham?

BUCKINGHAM
Such as my heart doth tremble to unfold:
A sort of naughty persons, lewdly bent,°    165
Under the countenance and confederacy°
Of Lady Eleanor, the protector's wife,
The ringleader and head of all this rout,
Have practiced dangerously against your state,
Dealing with witches and with conjurors,    170
Whom we have apprehended in the fact,°
Raising up wicked spirits from under ground,
Demanding of° King Henry's life and death,
And other of your highness' privy council,
As more at large your grace shall understand.    175

CARDINAL [*Aside.*]
And so, my Lord Protector, by this means
Your lady is forthcoming° yet at London.
This news, I think, hath turned your weapon's edge;
'Tis like, my lord, you will not keep your hour.°

GLOUCESTER [*Aside.*]
Ambitious churchman, leave to afflict my heart:    180
Sorrow and grief have vanquished all my powers;

And, vanquished as I am, I yield to thee,
Or to the meanest groom.

KING
O God, what mischiefs work the wicked ones,
Heaping confusion on their own heads thereby!    185

QUEEN
Gloucester, see here the tainture° of thy nest.
And look thyself be faultless, thou wert best.

GLOUCESTER
Madam, for myself, to heaven I do appeal,
How I have loved my king and commonweal!
And for my wife, I know not how it stands.    190
Sorry I am to hear what I have heard;
Noble she is; but if she have forgot
Honor and virtue and conversed with such
As, like to pitch, defile nobility,
I banish her my bed and company,    195
And give her as a prey to law and shame,
That hath dishonored Gloucester's honest name.

KING
Well, for this night we will repose us here:
Tomorrow toward London back again,
To look into this business thoroughly,    200
And call these foul offenders to their answers;
And poise the cause in justice' equal scales,
Whose beam stands sure, whose rightful cause prevails.°
                *Flourish. Exeunt.*

[Scene II. *London. The Duke of York's garden.*]

*Enter* YORK, SALISBURY, *and* WARWICK.

YORK
Now, my good Lords of Salisbury and Warwick,
Our simple supper ended, give me leave,
In this close walk,° to satisfy myself
In craving your opinion of my title,
Which is infallible, to England's crown.    5

SALISBURY
My lord, I long to hear it at full.

WARWICK
Sweet York, begin: and if thy claim be good,
The Nevils are thy subjects to command.

YORK
Then thus:
Edward the Third, my lords, had seven sons:    10
The first, Edward the Black Prince, Prince of Wales;
The second, William of Hatfield; and the third,
Lionel Duke of Clarence; next to whom
Was John of Gaunt, the Duke of Lancaster;
The fifth was Edmund Langley, Duke of York;    15
The sixth was Thomas of Woodstock, Duke of
   Gloucester;
William of Windsor was the seventh and last.
Edward the Black Prince died before his father,
And left behind him Richard, his only son,
Who after Edward the Third's death reigned as king;    20
Till Henry Bolingbroke, Duke of Lancaster,
The eldest son and heir of John of Gaunt,

---

155 **drab** whore   162 **You . . . fly** by presenting them to the
King of France   165 **sort . . . bent** group of worthless persons,
wickedly inclined   166 **countenance and confederacy**
patronage and participation   171 **in the fact** in the act
173 **Demanding of** inquiring about   177 **forthcoming** due
for trial   179 **hour** appointment

186 **tainture** defilement   202–03 **poise . . . prevails** balance
the testimony in the scales of justice to see which weighs more
**II.ii.3 close walk** private or concealed pathway

Crowned by the name of Henry the Fourth,
Seized on the realm, deposed the rightful king,
Sent his poor queen to France, from whence she
  came,                                              25
And him to Pomfret; where, as all you know,
Harmless Richard was murdered traitorously.

WARWICK
Father, the duke hath told the truth;
Thus got the house of Lancaster the crown.

YORK
Which now they hold by force and not by right:     30
For Richard, the first son's heir, being dead,
The issue of the next son should have reigned.

SALISBURY
But William of Hatfield died without an heir.

YORK
The third son, Duke of Clarence, from whose line
I claim the crown, had issue, Philippa, a daughter,  35
Who married Edmund Mortimer, Earl of March;
Edmund had issue, Roger Earl of March;
Roger had issue, Edmund, Anne, and Eleanor.

SALISBURY
This Edmund, in the reign of Bolingbroke,
As I have read, laid claim unto the crown;          40
And, but for Owen Glendower, had been king,
Who kept him in captivity till he died.
But to the rest.

YORK                His eldest sister, Anne,
My mother, being heir unto the crown,
Married Richard Earl of Cambridge,                  45
Who was to Edmund Langley,
Edward the Third's fifth son, the son.
By her I claim the kingdom: she was heir
To Roger of March, who was the son
Of Edmund Mortimer, who married Philippa,           50
Sole daughter unto Lionel Duke of Clarence:
So, if the issue of the elder son
Succeed before the younger, I am king.

WARWICK
What plain proceedings° is more plain than this?
Henry doth claim the crown from John of Gaunt,      55
The fourth son; York claims it from the third.
Till Lionel's issue fails, his should not reign:
It fails not yet, but flourishes in thee,
And in thy sons, fair slips° of such a stock.
Then, father Salisbury, kneel we together,          60
And in this private plot be we the first
That shall salute our rightful sovereign
With honor of his birthright to the crown.

BOTH [Kneeling.]
Long live our sovereign Richard, England's king!

YORK
We thank you, lords. But I am not your king         65
Till I be crowned and that my sword be stained
With heart-blood of the house of Lancaster;
And that's not suddenly to be performed,
But with advice° and silent secrecy.
Do you as I do in these dangerous days:             70
Wink at° the Duke of Suffolk's insolence,

At Beaufort's pride, at Somerset's ambition,
At Buckingham and all the crew of them,
Till they have snared the shepherd of the flock,
That virtuous prince, the good Duke Humphrey:       75
'Tis that they seek, and they in seeking that
Shall find their deaths, if York can prophesy.

SALISBURY
My lord, break we off; we know your mind at full.

WARWICK
My heart assures me that the Earl of Warwick
Shall one day make the Duke of York a king.         80

YORK
And, Nevil, this I do assure myself:
Richard shall live to make the Earl of Warwick
The greatest man in England but the king.    Exeunt.


[Scene III. A hall of justice.]

Sound trumpets. Enter KING Henry, and the QUEEN,
GLOUCESTER, the Duke of SUFFOLK, and the Duke
of BUCKINGHAM, the CARDINAL, and the DUCHESS
of Gloucester, [MARGERY JOURDAIN, HUM, SOUTH-
WELL, and BOLINGBROKE,] led with the OFFICERS;
and then enter to them the Duke of YORK and the Earls
of SALISBURY and WARWICK.

KING
Stand forth, Dame Eleanor Cobham, Gloucester's
  wife.
In sight of God and us, your guilt is great:
Receive the sentence of the law for sins
Such as by God's book are adjudged to death.°
You four, from hence to prison back again;           5
From thence unto the place of execution:
The witch in Smithfield° shall be burnt to ashes,
And you three shall be strangled on the gallows.
You, madam, for you are more nobly born,
Despoilèd of your honor in your life,               10
Shall, after three days' open penance done,
Live in your country here in banishment,
With Sir John Stanley, in the Isle of Man.

DUCHESS
Welcome is banishment, welcome were my death.

GLOUCESTER
Eleanor, the law thou see'st hath judgèd thee:      15
I cannot justify whom the law condemns.
            [Exeunt the DUCHESS and the
                      other PRISONERS, guarded.]
Mine eyes are full of tears, my heart of grief.
Ah, Humphrey, this dishonor in thine age
Will bring thy head with sorrow to the ground!
I beseech your majesty, give me leave to go;        20
Sorrow would° solace, and mine age would ease.

KING
Stay, Humphrey Duke of Gloucester: ere thou go,
Give up thy staff: Henry will to himself
Protector be; and God shall be my hope,
My stay, my guide, and lanthorn° to my feet.        25

54 **proceedings** order of events (in the pedigree)  59 **slips** shoots, cuttings  69 **advice** deliberation  71 **Wink at** close your eyes to

II.iii.4 **God's . . . death** Exodus 22:18: "Thou shalt not suffer a witch to live"  7 **Smithfield** a place of public execution in east-central London, now the site of the wholesale meat markets  21 **would** desires  25 **lanthorn** lantern (old form)

And go in peace, Humphrey, no less beloved
Than when thou wert protector to thy king.

QUEEN
I see no reason why a king of years
Should be° to be protected like a child.
God and King Henry govern England's realm!          30
Give up your staff, sir, and the king his realm.

GLOUCESTER
My staff? Here, noble Henry, is my staff:
As willingly do I the same resign
As e'er thy father Henry made it mine;
And even as willingly at thy feet I leave it          35
As others would ambitiously receive it.
Farewell, good king: when I am dead and gone,
May honorable peace attend thy throne.
                                    *Exit* GLOUCESTER.

QUEEN
Why, now is Henry king, and Margaret queen;
And Humphrey Duke of Gloucester scarce himself,     40
That bears so shrewd a maim:° two pulls° at once:
His lady banished, and a limb lopped off.
This staff of honor raught,° there let it stand
Where it best fits to be, in Henry's hand.

SUFFOLK
Thus droops this lofty pine and hangs his sprays;    45
Thus Eleanor's pride dies in her youngest days.

YORK
Lords, let him go. Please it your majesty,
This is the day appointed for the combat,
And ready are the appellant and defendant,
The armorer and his man, to enter the lists,         50
So please your highness to behold the fight.

QUEEN
Ay, good my lord: for purposely therefore
Left I the court, to see this quarrel tried.

KING
A° God's name, see the lists and all things fit:
Here let them end it; and God defend the right!      55

YORK
I never saw a fellow worse bested,°
Or more afraid to fight, than is the appellant,
The servant of this armorer, my lords.

*Enter at one door* [HORNER] *the armorer, and his* NEIGH-
BORS, *drinking to him so much that he is drunk; and he
enters with a drum before him and his staff with a sandbag
fastened to it;° and at the other door his man* [PETER],
*with a drum and sandbag, and* PRENTICES *drinking to
him.*

FIRST NEIGHBOR   Here, neighbor Horner, I drink
to you in° a cup of sack:° and fear not, neighbor, you   60
shall do well enough.

SECOND NEIGHBOR   And here, neighbor, here's a
cup of charneco.°

THIRD NEIGHBOR   And here's a pot of good double°
beer, neighbor: drink, and fear not your man.          65

HORNER   Let it come; i' faith I'll pledge you all, and a
fig for Peter!

FIRST PRENTICE   Here, Peter, I drink to thee: and be
not afeared.

SECOND PRENTICE   Here, Peter, here's a pint of     70
claret wine for thee.

THIRD PRENTICE   And here's a quart for me; be
merry, Peter, and fear not thy master: fight for credit
of the prentices.

PETER   I thank you all, but I'll drink no more. Here,   75
Robin, and if I die, here I give thee my hammer;
and Will, thou shalt have my apron; and here,
Tom, take all the money that I have. O Lord bless
me, I pray God, for I am never able to deal with
my master, he hath learnt so much fence already.     80

SALISBURY   Come, leave your drinking, and fall to
blows. Sirrah, what's thy name?

PETER   Peter, forsooth.

SALISBURY   Peter? What more?

PETER   Thump.                                         85

SALISBURY   Thump! then see thou thump thy master
well.

HORNER   Here's to thee, neighbor; fill all the pots
again, for before we fight, look you, I will tell you my
mind: for I am come hither, as it were, of my man's   90
instigation, to prove myself an honest man, and Peter
a knave: and so have at you, Peter, with downright
blows, as Bevis of Southampton fell upon Ascapart.°

YORK
Dispatch; this knave's tongue begins to double.°
Sound trumpets; alarum to the combatants!°           95

*They fight, and* PETER *strikes him down.*

HORNER   Hold, Peter, hold! I confess, I confess treason.
                                         *He dies.*

YORK   Take away his weapon. Fellow, thank God, and
the good wine in thy master's way.

PETER   O God, have I overcome mine enemies in this
presence?° O Peter, thou hast prevailed in right!    100

KING
Go, take hence that traitor from our sight;
For by his death we do perceive his guilt:
And God in justice hath revealed to us
The truth and innocence of this poor fellow,
Which he had thought to have murdered wrongfully.   105
Come, fellow, follow us for thy reward.
                          *Sound a flourish; exeunt.*

[Scene IV. *A street.*]

*Enter* GLOUCESTER *and his* [SERVING]MEN, *in
mourning cloaks.*

GLOUCESTER
Thus sometimes hath the brightest day a cloud;
And after summer evermore succeeds
Barren winter with his wrathful nipping cold:

28–29 king . . . be a king should be of age  41 shrewd a
maim sharp or painful a mutilation; pulls pluckings (as of
fruit, or a branch)  43 raught attained (by us)  54 A  56
worse bested in worse circumstances  58 s.d. staff . . . it a
mock weapon used in sporting combat  60 in with; sack
sweet sherry  63 charneco a kind of port wine  64 double
extra strong

93 Bevis . . . Ascapart a legendary English knight and his
adversary, a giant thirty feet high; a pun may have been
intended on the name of an actor, Bevis, playing the part of
Horner  94 double stutter  95 Sound . . . combatants
given as York's line in F (Q omits) but possibly intended as a
stage direction  100 presence of the king

So cares and joys abound, as seasons fleet.
Sirs, what's o'clock?

SERVANT                    Ten, my lord.                    5

GLOUCESTER
Ten is the hour that was appointed me
To watch the coming of my punished duchess:
Uneath° may she endure the flinty streets,
To tread them with her tender-feeling feet.
Sweet Nell, ill can thy noble mind abrook°          10
The abject° people gazing on thy face
With envious° looks, laughing at thy shame,
That erst° did follow thy proud chariot wheels
When thou didst ride in triumph through the streets.
But, soft!° I think she comes, and I'll prepare          15
My tear-stained eyes to see her miseries.

*Enter* DUCHESS *of Gloucester barefoot, and a white
sheet about her, with a wax candle in her hand, and verses
written on her back and pinned on; and accompanied with
the* SHERIFF *of London and Sir John* STANLEY, *and*
OFFICERS, *with bills and halberds.°*

SERVANT
So please your grace, we'll take her from the sheriff.

GLOUCESTER
No, stir not, for your lives; let her pass by.

DUCHESS
Come you, my lord, to see my open shame?
Now thou dost penance too. Look how they gaze!          20
See how the giddy multitude do point,
And nod their heads, and throw their eyes on thee!
Ah, Gloucester, hide thee from their hateful looks,
And, in thy closet pent up, rue my shame,
And ban° thine enemies, both mine and thine.          25

GLOUCESTER
Be patient, gentle Nell; forget this grief.

DUCHESS
Ah, Gloucester, teach me to forget myself!
For whilst I think I am thy married wife
And thou a prince, protector of this land,
Methinks I should not thus be led along,          30
Mailed° up in shame, with papers on my back,
And followed with a rabble that rejoice
To see my tears and hear my deep-fet° groans.
The ruthless flint doth cut my tender feet,
And when I start, the envious° people laugh          35
And bid me be advisèd how I tread.
Ah, Humphrey, can I bear this shameful yoke?
Trowest thou that e'er I'll look upon the world
Or count them happy that enjoys the sun?
No; dark shall be my light and night my day;          40
To think upon my pomp shall be my hell.
Sometime I'll say, I am Duke Humphrey's wife,
And he a prince, and ruler of the land:
Yet so he ruled and such a prince he was
As he stood by whilst I, his forlorn duchess,          45
Was made a wonder and a pointing-stock
To every idle rascal follower.

But be thou mild and blush not at my shame,
Nor stir at nothing, till the ax of death
Hang over thee, as, sure, it shortly will;          50
For Suffolk—he that can do all in all
With her that hateth thee and hates us all—
And York, and impious Beaufort, that false priest,
Have all limed bushes° to betray thy wings;
And fly thou how thou canst, they'll tangle thee.          55
But fear not thou, until thy foot be snared,
Nor never seek prevention° of thy foes.

GLOUCESTER
Ah, Nell, forbear! Thou aimest all awry.
I must offend before I be attainted;°
And had I twenty times so many foes,          60
And each of them had twenty times their power,
All these could not procure me any scathe,°
So long as I am loyal, true, and crimeless.
Wouldst have me rescue thee from this reproach?
Why, yet thy scandal were not wiped away,          65
But I in danger for the breach of law.
Thy greatest help is quiet, gentle Nell:
I pray thee, sort° thy heart to patience;
These few days' wonder° will be quickly worn.

*Enter a* HERALD.

HERALD
I summon your grace to his majesty's parliament,          70
Holden at Bury the first of this next month.

GLOUCESTER
And my consent ne'er asked herein before?
This is close° dealing. Well, I will be there.
                                        *Exit* HERALD.
My Nell, I take my leave: and, master sheriff,
Let not her penance exceed the king's commission.          75

SHERIFF
And't please your grace, here my commission stays,
And Sir John Stanley is appointed now
To take her with him to the Isle of Man.

GLOUCESTER
Must you, Sir John, protect my lady here?

STANLEY
So am I given in charge, may't please your grace.          80

GLOUCESTER
Entreat her not the worse in that I pray
You use her well. The world may laugh again;
And I may live to do you kindness if
You do it her: and so, Sir John, farewell.

DUCHESS
What, gone, my lord, and bid me not farewell?          85

GLOUCESTER
Witness my tears, I cannot stay to speak.
                    *Exit* GLOUCESTER [*and* SERVINGMEN].

DUCHESS
Art thou gone too? All comfort go with thee!
For none abides with me: my joy is death—
Death, at whose name I oft have been afeared,
Because I wished this world's eternity.          90
Stanley, I prithee go, and take me hence;

---

II.iv.8 **Uneath** with difficulty 10 **abrook** tolerate 11
**abject** despicable 12 **envious** malicious 13 **erst** formerly
15 **soft** stay, hold (exclamation) 16 s.d. **bills and halberds**
long, ax-headed weapons 25 **ban** curse 31 **Mailed** wrapped
(hawking term) 33 **deep-fet** deep-fetched, profound 35
**envious** malicious

54 **limed bushes** smeared with a sticky substance (a means of
catching birds) 57 **prevention** remedy by anticipation 59
**attainted** condemned 62 **scathe** damage 68 **sort** adapt
69 **few days' wonder** spectacle, sensation 73 **close** secret

I care not whither, for I beg no favor;
Only convey me where thou art commanded.

STANLEY
Why, madam, that is to the Isle of Man,
There to be used according to your state.                    95

DUCHESS
That's bad enough, for I am but reproach:
And shall I then be used reproachfully?

STANLEY
Like to a duchess, and Duke Humphrey's lady:
According to that state° you shall be used.

DUCHESS
Sheriff, farewell, and better than I fare,°             100
Although thou hast been conduct° of my shame.

SHERIFF
It is my office; and madam, pardon me.

DUCHESS
Ay, ay, farewell; thy office is discharged.
Come, Stanley, shall we go?

STANLEY
Madam, your penance done, throw off this sheet,        105
And go we to attire you for our journey.

DUCHESS
My shame will not be shifted° with my sheet:
No, it will hang upon my richest robes,
And show itself, attire me how I can.
Go, lead the way; I long to see my prison.    *Exeunt.* 110

# [ ACT III ]

[Scene I. *The abbey at Bury Saint Edmunds.*]

*Sound a sennet. Enter* KING, QUEEN, CARDINAL,
SUFFOLK, YORK, BUCKINGHAM, SALISBURY, *and*
WARWICK [*and* ATTENDANTS] *to the parliament.*

KING
I muse my Lord of Gloucester is not come:
'Tis not his wont to be the hindmost man,
Whate'er occasion keeps him from us now.

QUEEN
Can you not see? Or will ye not observe
The strangeness of his altered countenance?             5
With what a majesty he bears himself,
How insolent of late he is become,
How proud, how peremptory, and unlike himself?
We know the time since he was mild and affable,
And if we did but glance a far-off look,                10
Immediately he was upon his knee,
That all the court admired him for submission.
But meet him now, and, be it in the morn,
When everyone will give the time of day,
He knits his brow and shows an angry eye                15
And passeth by with stiff unbowèd knee,
Disdaining duty that to us belongs.
Small curs are not regarded when they grin,°

But great men tremble when the lion roars;
And Humphrey is no little man in England.               20
First note that he is near you in descent,
And should you fall, he is the next will mount.
Me seemeth then it is no policy,
Respecting° what a rancorous mind he bears,
And his advantage following your decease,               25
That he should come about your royal person
Or be admitted to your highness' council.
By flattery hath he won the commons' hearts,
And when he please to make commotion,
'Tis to be feared they all will follow him.             30
Now 'tis the spring, and weeds are shallow-rooted;
Suffer them now, and they'll o'ergrow the garden,
And choke the herbs for want of husbandry.
The reverent care I bear unto my lord
Made me collect° these dangers in the duke.            35
If it be fond,° call it a woman's fear—
Which fear if better reasons can supplant,
I will subscribe,° and say I wronged the duke.
My Lord of Suffolk, Buckingham, and York,
Reprove° my allegation, if you can,                    40
Or else conclude my words effectual.°

SUFFOLK
Well hath your highness seen into this duke;
And had I first been put to speak my mind,
I think I should have told your grace's tale.
The duchess by his subornation,                         45
Upon my life, began her devilish practices:
Or if he were not privy to° those faults,
Yet, by reputing of his high descent,
As next the king he was successive heir,
And such high vaunts of his nobility,                   50
Did instigate the bedlam° brainsick duchess
By wicked means to frame our sovereign's fall.
Smooth runs the water where the brook is deep,
And in his simple show he harbors treason.
The fox barks not when he would steal the lamb.        55
No, no, my sovereign; Gloucester is a man
Unsound yet, and full of deep deceit.

CARDINAL
Did he not, contrary to form of law,
Devise strange deaths for small offenses done?

YORK
And did he not, in his protectorship,                   60
Levy great sums of money through the realm
For soldiers' pay in France, and never sent it?
By means whereof the towns each day revolted.

BUCKINGHAM
Tut, these are petty faults to faults unknown,
Which time will bring to light in smooth Duke
   Humphrey.                                            65

KING
My lords, at once the care you have of us,
To mow down thorns that would annoy our foot,
Is worthy praise: but, shall I speak my conscience,
Our kinsman Gloucester is as innocent
From meaning treason to our royal person               70
As is the sucking lamb or harmless dove.

---

**99 state** dignity  **100 better . . . fare** fare better than I  **101
conduct** guide  **107 shifted** play on *shift* (i.e., smock, what
Eleanor is wearing)
**III.i.18 grin** bare their teeth

**23–24 no policy, Respecting** unwise, considering  **35 collect**
as if by weeding  **36 fond** foolish  **38 subscribe** agree  **40
Reprove** disprove  **41 effectual** pertinent, conclusive  **47
privy to** acquainted with  **51 bedlam** crazy

The duke is virtuous, mild, and too well given
To dream on evil, or to work my downfall.

QUEEN

Ah, what's more dangerous than this fond affiance!°
Seems he a dove? His feathers are but borrowed,          75
For he's disposèd as the hateful raven.
Is he a lamb? His skin is surely lent him,
For he's inclined as is the ravenous wolves.
Who cannot steal a shape, that means deceit?
Take heed, my lord: the welfare of us all          80
Hangs on the cutting short that fraudful man.

*Enter* SOMERSET.

SOMERSET

All health unto my gracious sovereign!

KING

Welcome, Lord Somerset. What news from France?

SOMERSET

That all your interest in those territories
Is utterly bereft you: all is lost.          85

KING

Cold news, Lord Somerset: but God's will be done!

YORK [*Aside.*]

Cold news for me; for I had hope of France
As firmly as I hope for fertile England.°
Thus are my blossoms blasted in the bud,
And caterpillars eat my leaves away;          90
But I will remedy this gear° ere long,
Or sell my title for a glorious grave.

*Enter* GLOUCESTER.

GLOUCESTER

All happiness unto my lord the king!
Pardon, my liege, that I have stayed° so long.

SUFFOLK

Nay, Gloucester, know that thou come too soon,          95
Unless thou wert more loyal than thou art:
I do arrest thee of high treason here.

GLOUCESTER

Well, Suffolk, thou shalt not see me blush,
Nor change my countenance for this arrest:
A heart unspotted is not easily daunted.          100
The purest spring is not so free from mud
As I am clear from treason to my sovereign.
Who can accuse me? Wherein am I guilty?

YORK

'Tis thought, my lord, that you took bribes of France,°
And, being protector, stayed the soldiers' pay;          105
By means whereof his highness hath lost France.

GLOUCESTER

Is it but thought so? What are they that think it?
I never robbed the soldiers of their pay,
Nor ever had one penny bribe from France.
So help me God, as I have watched the night,          110
Ay, night by night, in studying good for England!
That doit° that e'er I wrested from the king,
Or any groat I hoarded to my use,
Be brought against me at my trial day!

No; many a pound of mine own proper store,°          115
Because I would not tax the needy commons,
Have I dispursèd° to the garrisons,
And never asked for restitution.

CARDINAL

It serves you well, my lord, to say so much.

GLOUCESTER

I say no more than truth, so help me God!          120

YORK

In your protectorship you did devise
Strange tortures for offenders, never heard of,
That° England was defamed by tyranny.

GLOUCESTER

Why, 'tis well known that whiles I was protector
Pity was all the fault that was in me:          125
For I should melt at an offender's tears,
And lowly words were ransom for their fault.
Unless it were a bloody murderer,
Or foul felonious thief that fleeced poor passengers,°
I never gave them condign° punishment.          130
Murder indeed, that bloody sin, I tortured
Above the felon or what° trespass else.

SUFFOLK

My lord, these faults are easy, quickly answered;
But mightier crimes are laid unto your charge,
Whereof you cannot easily purge yourself.          135
I do arrest you in his highness' name,
And here commit you to my Lord Cardinal
To keep, until your further time of trial.

KING

My Lord of Gloucester, 'tis my special hope
That you will clear yourself from all suspense.°          140
My conscience tells me you are innocent.

GLOUCESTER

Ah, gracious lord, these days are dangerous:
Virtue is choked with foul ambition,
And charity chased hence by rancor's hand;
Foul subornation is predominant,          145
And equity exiled your highness' land.
I know their complot° is to have my life,
And if my death might make this island happy,
And prove the period° of their tyranny,
I would expend it with all willingness.          150
But mine is made the prologue to their play:
For thousands more, that yet suspect no peril,
Will not conclude their plotted tragedy.
Beaufort's red sparkling eyes blab his heart's malice,
And Suffolk's cloudy brow his stormy hate;          155
Sharp Buckingham unburthens with his tongue
The envious load that lies upon his heart;
And doggèd York, that reaches at the moon,
Whose overweening arm I have plucked back,
By false accuse doth level at° my life.          160
And you, my sovereign lady, with the rest,
Causeless have laid disgraces on my head,
And with your best endeavor have stirred up
My liefest° liege to be mine enemy.
Ay, all of you have laid your heads together—          165

74 **fond affiance** foolish trust  87–88 **Cold . . . England** almost a literal repetition of I.i.235–36  91 **gear** business  94 **stayed** delayed  104 **France** the King of France  112 **doit** Dutch coin of minimal value

115 **proper store** personal possession  117 **dispursèd** disbursed  123 **That** so that  129 **passengers** travelers  130 **condign** deserved  132 **what** whatever  140 **suspense** suspicion  147 **complot** plot  149 **period** end, limit  160 **level at** aim at  164 **liefest** dearest

Myself had notice of your conventicles°—
And all to make away my guiltless life.
I shall not want° false witness to condemn me,
Nor store of treasons to augment my guilt;
The ancient proverb will be well effected:     170
"A staff is quickly found to beat a dog."

CARDINAL
My liege, his railing is intolerable.
If those that care to keep your royal person
From treason's secret knife and traitors' rage
Be thus upbraided, chid, and rated at,°     175
And the offender granted scope of speech,
'Twill make them cool in zeal unto your grace.

SUFFOLK
Hath he not twit our sovereign lady here
With ignominious words, though clerkly couched,°
As if she had subornèd some to swear     180
False allegations to o'erthrow his state?

QUEEN
But I can give the loser leave to chide.

GLOUCESTER
Far truer spoke than meant: I lose indeed;
Beshrew the winners, for they played me false!
And well such losers may have leave to speak.     185

BUCKINGHAM
He'll wrest the sense° and hold us here all day.
Lord Cardinal, he is your prisoner.

CARDINAL
Sirs, take away the duke, and guard him sure.

GLOUCESTER
Ah, thus King Henry throws away his crutch
Before his legs be firm to bear his body.     190
Thus is the shepherd beaten from thy side,
And wolves are gnarling° who shall gnaw thee first.
Ah, that my fear were false! Ah, that it were!
For, good King Henry, thy decay° I fear.
            *Exit* GLOUCESTER [*guarded*].

KING
My lords, what to your wisdoms seemeth best,     195
Do or undo, as if ourself were here.

QUEEN
What, will your highness leave the parliament?

KING
Ay, Margaret; my heart is drowned with grief,
Whose flood begins to flow within mine eyes,
My body round engirt with misery:     200
For what's more miserable than discontent?
Ah, uncle Humphrey, in thy face I see
The map of honor, truth, and loyalty;
And yet, good Humphrey, is the hour to come
That e'er I proved thee false or feared thy faith?     205
What louring star now envies thy estate,
That these great lords, and Margaret our queen
Do seek subversion° of thy harmless life?
Thou never didst them wrong, nor no man wrong:
And as the butcher takes away the calf,     210
And binds the wretch, and beats it when it strays,
Bearing it to the bloody slaughterhouse,

Even so remorseless have they borne him hence;
And as the dam runs lowing up and down,
Looking the way her harmless young one went,     215
And can do nought but wail her darling's loss,
Even so myself bewails good Gloucester's case
With sad unhelpful tears, and with dimmed eyes
Look after him and cannot do him good,
So mighty are his vowèd enemies.     220
His fortunes I will weep, and 'twixt each groan
Say, "Who's a traitor? Gloucester he is none."
        *Exit* KING, SALISBURY, *and* WARWICK.

QUEEN
Free° lords, cold snow melts with the sun's hot beams.
Henry my lord is cold in great affairs,
Too full of foolish pity; and Gloucester's show°     225
Beguiles him as the mournful crocodile
With sorrow snares relenting passengers,°
Or as the snake, rolled in a flow'ring bank,
With shining checkered slough, doth sting a child
That for the beauty thinks it excellent.     230
Believe me, lords, were none more wise than I—
And yet herein I judge mine own wit good—
This Gloucester should be quickly rid the world,
To rid us from the fear we have of him.

CARDINAL
That he should die is worthy policy,°     235
But yet we want a color° for his death:
'Tis meet° he be condemned by course of law.

SUFFOLK
But in my mind that were no policy:
The king will labor still to save his life,
The commons haply rise, to save his life;     240
And yet we have but trivial argument,
More than mistrust, that shows him worthy death.

YORK
So that, by this, you would not have him die.

SUFFOLK
Ah, York, no man alive so fain° as I!

YORK [*Aside*.]
'Tis York that hath more reason for his death.     245

[*Aloud*.]
But my Lord Cardinal, and you, my Lord of Suffolk,
Say as you think, and speak it from your souls:
Were't not all one, an empty eagle were set
To guard the chicken from a hungry kite,°
As place Duke Humphrey for the king's protector?     250

QUEEN
So,° the poor chicken should be sure of death.

SUFFOLK
Madam, 'tis true; and were't not madness, then,
To make the fox surveyor° of the fold?
Who being° accused a crafty murderer,
His guilt should be but idly posted over,°     255
Because his purpose is not executed.°
No: let him die, in that he is a fox,

---

166 **conventicles** meetings   168 **want** lack   175 **rated at** inveighed against   179 **ignominious . . . couched** infamous words, although learnedly (i.e., cleverly) phrased   186 **wrest the sense** distort the meaning (of what we say)   192 **gnarling** snarling   194 **decay** downfall   208 **subversion** overthrow   223 **Free** noble, magnanimous   225 **show** outward appearance   227 **passengers** travelers   235 **is worthy policy** deserves shrewd planning   236 **color** pretext (perhaps punning on *collar*, i.e., hangman's noose)   237 **meet** appropriate   244 **fain** willingly   249 **kite** bird of prey   251 **So** if so   253 **surveyor** overseer   254 **Who being** whoever has been   255 **posted over** hurried past   256 **executed** accomplished

By nature proved an enemy to the flock.
Before his chaps° be stained with crimson blood,
As Humphrey proved by reasons to my liege.° 260
And do not stand on quillets° how to slay him:
Be it by gins,° by snares, by subtlety,
Sleeping or waking, 'tis no matter how,
So he be dead; for that is good deceit
Which mates° him first that first intends deceit. 265

QUEEN
Thrice-noble Suffolk, 'tis resolutely spoke.

SUFFOLK
Not resolute, except so much° were done;
For things are often spoke and seldom meant:
But that my heart accordeth with my tongue,
Seeing the deed is meritorious,° 270
And to preserve my sovereign from his foe,
Say but the word, and I will be his priest.°

CARDINAL
But I would have him dead, my Lord of Suffolk,
Ere you can take due orders for a priest:
Say you consent and censure well° the deed, 275
And I'll provide his executioner;
I tender so° the safety of my liege.

SUFFOLK
Here is my hand, the deed is worthy doing.

QUEEN
And so say I.

YORK
And I: and now we three have spoke it, 280
It skills not greatly who impugns our doom.°

*Enter a* POST.

POST
Great lords, from Ireland am I come amain,°
To signify that rebels there are up,°
And put the Englishmen unto the sword.
Send succors, lords, and stop the rage betime,° 285
Before the wound do grow uncurable;
For, being green,° there is great hope of help.

CARDINAL
A breach that craves a quick expedient stop!
What counsel give you in this weighty cause?

YORK
That Somerset be sent as regent thither. 290
'Tis meet that lucky ruler be employed;
Witness the fortune he hath had in France.

SOMERSET
If York, with all his far-fet° policy,
Had been the regent there instead of me,
He never would have stayed in France so long. 295

YORK
No, not to lose it all, as thou hast done.
I rather would have lost my life betimes°
Than bring a burden of dishonor home

By staying there so long till° all were lost.
Show me one scar charactered° on thy skin: 300
Men's flesh preserved so whole do seldom win.

QUEEN
Nay then, this spark will prove a raging fire,
If wind and fuel be brought to feed it with!
No more, good York; sweet Somerset, be still:
Thy fortune, York, hadst thou been regent there, 305
Might happily° have proved far worse than his.

YORK
What, worse than nought? Nay, then a shame take all!

SOMERSET
And in the number thee, that wishest shame!

CARDINAL
My Lord of York, try what your fortune is.
Th' uncivil kerns° of Ireland are in arms 310
And temper° clay with blood of Englishmen.
To Ireland will you lead a band of men,
Collected choicely, from each county some,
And try your hap against the Irishmen?

YORK
I will, my lord, so please his majesty. 315

SUFFOLK
Why, our authority is his consent,
And what we do establish he confirms:
Then, noble York, take thou this task in hand.

YORK
I am content: provide me soldiers, lords,
Whiles I take order for mine own affairs. 320

SUFFOLK
A charge, Lord York, that I will see performed.
But now return we to the false Duke Humphrey.

CARDINAL
No more of him; for I will deal with him
That henceforth he shall trouble us no more.
And so break off: the day is almost spent; 325
Lord Suffolk, you and I must talk of that event.

YORK
My Lord of Suffolk, within fourteen days
At Bristow° I expect my soldiers;
For there I'll ship them all for Ireland.

SUFFOLK
I'll see it truly done, my Lord of York. 330
*Exeunt. Manet* YORK [*alone*].

YORK
Now, York, or never, steel thy fearful thoughts,
And change misdoubt to resolution:
Be that thou hop'st to be, or what thou art
Resign to death; it is not worth th' enjoying.
Let palefaced fear keep with the mean-born man, 335
And find no harbor in a royal heart.
Faster than springtime show'rs comes thought on
thought,
And not a thought but thinks on dignity.°
My brain more busy than the laboring spider
Weaves tedious° snares to trap mine enemies. 340
Well, nobles, well: 'tis politicly done,
To send me packing with an host of men:

---

259 **chaps** jaws  260 **As . . . liege** above, lines 191–94
261 **quillets** fine distinctions, quibbles  262 **gins** traps
265 **mates** checkmates, suppresses  267 **except so much**
unless as much  270 **meritorious** worthy reward (especially
in a religious sense, from God)  272 **be his priest** kill him
275 **censure well** approve of  277 **I tender so** I am so solicitous of  281 **It . . . doom** It matters little who disapproves
of our decision  282 **amain** in haste  283 **up** up in arms
285 **betime** in time, rapidly  287 **green** fresh  293 **far-fet**
far-fetched (i.e., deep)  297 **betimes** early

299 **staying . . . till** delaying or temporizing there until  300
**charactered** inscribed  306 **happily** by chance  310 **kerns**
light-armed Irish foot-soldiers  311 **temper** moisten (as with
mortar)  328 **Bristow** Bristol  338 **dignity** rank  340 **tedious**
laborious, intricate

I fear me you but warm the starvèd snake,
Who, cherished in your breasts, will sting your hearts.
'Twas men I lacked, and you will give them me:    345
I take it kindly; yet be well assured
You put sharp weapons in a madman's hands.
Whiles I in Ireland nourish a mighty band,
I will stir up in England some black storm
Shall blow ten thousand souls to heaven or hell;    350
And this fell° tempest shall not cease to rage
Until the golden circuit° on my head,
Like to the glorious sun's transparent beams,
Do calm the fury of this mad-bred flaw.°
And, for a minister of my intent,    355
I have seduced a headstrong Kentishman,
John Cade of Ashford,
To make commotion, as full well he can,
Under the title of John Mortimer.
In Ireland have I seen this stubborn Cade    360
Oppose himself against a troop of kerns,
And fought so long, till that his thighs with darts
Were almost like a sharp-quilled porpentine;°
And, in the end being rescued, I have seen
Him caper upright like a wild Morisco,°    365
Shaking the bloody darts as he° his bells.
Full often, like a shag-haired crafty kern,
Hath he conversèd with the enemy,
And undiscovered come to me again
And given me notice of their villainies.    370
This devil here shall be my substitute;
For that John Mortimer, which now is dead,
In face, in gait, in speech, he doth resemble:
By this I shall perceive the commons' mind,
How they affect° the house and claim of York.    375
Say he be taken, racked, and torturèd:
I know no pain they can inflict upon him
Will make him say I moved him to those arms.
Say that he thrive, as 'tis great like he will:
Why, then from Ireland come I with my strength    380
And reap the harvest which that rascal sowed.
For Humphrey being dead, as he shall be,
And Henry put apart, the next for me.     *Exit.*

[Scene II. *Bury Saint Edmunds. A room of state.*]

*Enter two or three* [MURDERERS] *running over the stage,
from the murder of Gloucester.*

FIRST MURDERER
Run to my Lord of Suffolk; let him know
We have dispatched the duke, as he commanded.
SECOND MURDERER
O that it were to do! What have we done?
Didst ever hear a man so penitent?

*Enter* SUFFOLK.

FIRST MURDERER
Here comes my lord.    5

SUFFOLK
Now, sirs, have you dispatched this thing?
FIRST MURDERER
Ay, my good lord, he's dead.
SUFFOLK
Why, that's well said. Go, get you to my house;
I will reward you for this venturous deed.
The king and all the peers are here at hand.    10
Have you laid fair the bed? Is all things well,
According as I gave directions?
FIRST MURDERER
'Tis, my good lord.
SUFFOLK
Away, be gone.     *Exeunt* [MURDERERS].

*Sound trumpets. Enter the* KING, *the* QUEEN, CARDINAL,
BUCKINGHAM, SOMERSET, *with* ATTENDANTS.

KING
Go, call our uncle to our presence straight;    15
Say we intend to try his grace today,
If he be guilty as 'tis publishèd.
SUFFOLK
I'll call him presently, my noble lord.     *Exit.*
KING
Lords, take your places; and I pray you all,
Proceed no straiter° 'gainst our uncle Gloucester    20
Than from true evidence of good esteem,
He be approved° in practice culpable.
QUEEN
God forbid any malice should prevail,
That faultless may condemn a nobleman!
Pray God he may acquit him of suspicion!    25
KING
I thank thee, Meg; these words content me much.

*Enter* SUFFOLK.

How now! Why look'st thou pale? Why tremblest
   thou?
Where is our uncle? What's the matter, Suffolk?
SUFFOLK
Dead in his bed, my lord; Gloucester is dead.
QUEEN
Marry, God forfend!°    30
CARDINAL
God's secret judgment: I did dream tonight
The duke was dumb and could not speak a word.

KING *sounds.*°

QUEEN
How fares my lord? Help, lords, the king is dead!
SOMERSET
Rear up his body; wring° him by the nose.
QUEEN
Run, go, help, help! O Henry, ope thine eyes!    35
SUFFOLK
He doth revive again; madam, be patient.
KING
O heavenly God!
QUEEN         How fares my gracious lord?

---

351 **fell** evil    352 **circuit** circle (crown)    354 **flaw** squall of wind    363 **porpentine** porcupine    365 **Morisco** Moorish, or morris, dancer; the dance is performed in grotesque attire with bells attached to the legs    366 **he** the dancer    375 **affect** favor, approve

III.ii.20 **straiter** more strictly    22 **approved** proven    30 **forfend** forbid    32 **s.d. sounds** swoons    34 **wring** squeeze (a method of restoring circulation)

SUFFOLK
Comfort, my sovereign; gracious Henry, comfort.

KING
What, doth my Lord of Suffolk comfort me?
Came he right now to sing a raven's note,                          40
Whose dismal tune bereft my vital pow'rs,
And thinks he that the chirping of a wren,
By crying comfort from a hollow breast,
Can chase away the first-conceivèd sound?
Hide not thy poison with such sugared words;                       45
Lay not thy hands on me; forbear, I say!
Their touch affrights me as a serpent's sting.
Thou baleful messenger, out of my sight!
Upon thy eyeballs murderous tyranny
Sits in grim majesty to fright the world.                          50
Look not upon me, for thine eyes are wounding.
Yet do not go away; come, basilisk,°
And kill the innocent gazer with thy sight:
For in the shade of death I shall find joy,
In life but double death, now Gloucester's dead.                   55

QUEEN
Why do you rate° my Lord of Suffolk thus?
Although the duke was enemy to him,
Yet he most Christian-like laments his death:
And for myself, foe as he was to me,
Might liquid tears or heart-offending groans                       60
Or blood-consuming sighs recall his life,
I would be blind with weeping, sick with groans,
Look pale as primrose with blood-drinking sighs,
And all to have the noble duke alive.
What know I how the world may deem of me?                           65
For it is known we were but hollow friends:
It may be judged I made the duke away;
So shall my name with slander's tongue be wounded,
And princes' courts be filled with my reproach.
This get I by his death; ay me, unhappy!                            70
To be a queen, and crowned with infamy!

KING
Ah, woe is me for Gloucester, wretched man!

QUEEN
Be woe for me, more wretched than he is.
What, dost thou turn away and hide thy face?
I am no loathsome leper; look on me.                                75
What! Art thou, like the adder, waxen° deaf?
Be poisonous too, and kill thy forlorn queen.
Is all thy comfort shut in Gloucester's tomb?
Why, then, Dame Margaret was ne'er thy joy.
Erect his statuë and worship it,                                    80
And make my image but an alehouse sign.
Was I for this nigh wracked upon the sea
And twice by awkward° wind from England's bank
Drove back again unto my native clime?
What boded this, but well forewarning wind                          85
Did seem to say, "Seek not a scorpion's nest,
Nor set no footing on this unkind shore"?
What did I then, but cursed the gentle gusts
And he that loosed them forth their brazen° caves,
And bid them blow towards England's blessèd shore,                  90
Or turn our stern upon a dreadful rock?
Yet Aeolus° would not be a murderer,
But left that hateful office unto thee.
The pretty vaulting° sea refused to drown me,
Knowing that thou wouldst have me drowned on
    shore                                                           95
With tears as salt as sea, through thy unkindness;
The splitting rocks cow'red in the sinking sands,
And would not dash me with their ragged sides,
Because thy flinty heart, more hard than they,
Might in thy palace perish Margaret.                               100
As far as I could ken° thy chalky cliffs,
When from thy shore the tempest beat us back,
I stood upon the hatches in the storm,
And when the dusky sky began to rob
My earnest-gaping sight of thy land's view,                        105
I took a costly jewel from my neck—
A heart° it was, bound in with diamonds—
And threw it towards thy land: the sea received it,
And so I wished thy body might my heart:
And even with this I lost fair England's view,                     110
And bid mine eyes be packing with my heart,
And called them blind and dusky spectacles,°
For losing ken of Albion's wishèd coast.
How often have I tempted Suffolk's tongue,
The agent of thy foul inconstancy,                                 115
To sit and witch° me, as Ascanius did
When he to madding° Dido would unfold
His father's acts, commenced in burning Troy!
Am I not witched like her? Or thou not false like him?
Ay me, I can° no more! Die, Margaret,                              120
For Henry weeps that thou dost live so long.

*Noise within. Enter* WARWICK, SALISBURY, *and many*
COMMONS.

WARWICK
It is reported, mighty sovereign,
That good Duke Humphrey traitorously is murdered
By Suffolk and the Cardinal Beaufort's means.
The commons, like an angry hive of bees                            125
That want their leader, scatter up and down,
And care not who they sting in his revenge.
Myself have calmed their spleenful° mutiny,
Until they hear the order of his death.

KING
That he is dead, good Warwick, 'tis too true;                      130
But how he died God knows, not Henry.
Enter his chamber, view his breathless corpse,
And comment then upon his sudden death.

WARWICK
That shall I do, my liege. Stay, Salisbury,
With the rude multitude till I return.                             135
        [*Exeunt* WARWICK *to the inner chamber,*° *and*
                SALISBURY *with the* COMMONS.]

KING
O Thou that judgest all things, stay my thoughts,
My thoughts, that labor to persuade my soul
Some violent hands were laid on Humphrey's life!
If my suspect° be false, forgive me, God,

---

52 **basilisk** a mythical reptile, supposedly able to kill with its
eyes  56 **rate** berate  76 **waxen** grown  83 **awkward** adverse
89 **brazen** extremely strong  92 **Aeolus** god of winds

94 **vaulting** bounding  101 **ken** discern  107 **heart** heart-
shaped gemstone  112 **spectacles** organs of sight, or instruments, like spyglasses  116 **witch** bewitch  117 **madding**
becoming mad  120 **can** am capable of  128 **spleenful** eager,
angry  135 **s.d. inner chamber** see A Note on the Text,
p. 151  139 **suspect** suspicion

For judgment only doth belong to thee.     140
Fain would I go to chafe his paly° lips
With twenty thousand kisses, and to drain
Upon his face an ocean of salt tears,
To tell my love unto his dumb deaf trunk,
And with my fingers feel his hand unfeeling:     145
But all in vain are these mean obsequies;
And to survey his dead and earthy image,
What were it but to make my sorrow greater?

WARWICK [*from within*] *draws the curtains and shows*
*Gloucester in his bed.*

WARWICK
Come hither, gracious sovereign, view this body.

KING
That is to see how deep my grave is made;     150
For with his soul fled all my worldly solace,
For, seeing him, I see my life in death.

WARWICK
As surely as my soul intends to live
With that dread King that took our state upon him
To free us from His Father's wrathful curse,     155
I do believe that violent hands were laid
Upon the life of this thrice-famèd duke.

SUFFOLK
A dreadful oath, sworn with a solemn tongue!
What instance gives Lord Warwick for his vow?

WARWICK
See how the blood is settled in his face.     160
Oft have I seen a timely parted ghost,°
Of ashy semblance, meager,° pale, and bloodless,
Being° all descended to the laboring heart,
Who,° in the conflict that it holds with death,
Attracts the same° for aidance 'gainst the enemy;     165
Which° with the heart there cools, and ne'er returneth
To blush and beautify the cheek again.
But see, his face is black and full of blood,
His eyeballs further out than when he lived,
Staring full ghastly like a strangled man;     170
His hair upreared, his nostrils stretched with struggling;
His hands abroad displayed, as one that grasped
And tugged for life, and was by strength subdued.
Look, on the sheets his hair, you see, is sticking;
His well-proportioned beard made rough and
rugged,     175
Like to the summer's corn by tempest lodged.°
It cannot be but he was murdered here:
The least of all these signs were probable.°

SUFFOLK
Why, Warwick, who should do the duke to death?
Myself and Beaufort had him in protection;     180
And we, I hope, sir, are no murderers.

WARWICK
But both of you were vowed Duke Humphrey's foes.
And you, forsooth, had the good duke to keep:
'Tis like you would not feast him like a friend,
And 'tis well seen he found an enemy.     185

QUEEN
Then you, belike, suspect these noblemen
As guilty of Duke Humphrey's timeless° death?

WARWICK
Who finds the heifer dead, and bleeding fresh,
And sees fast by a butcher with an ax,
But will suspect 'twas he that made the slaughter?     190
Who finds the partridge in the puttock's° nest,
But may imagine how the bird was dead,
Although the kite soar with unbloodied beak?
Even so suspicious is this tragedy.

QUEEN
Are you the butcher, Suffolk? Where's your knife?     195
Is Beaufort termed a kite? Where are his talons?

SUFFOLK
I wear no knife to slaughter sleeping men;
But here's a vengeful sword, rusted with ease,
That shall be scourèd in his rancorous heart
That slanders me with murder's crimson badge.     200
Say, if thou dar'st, proud Lord of Warwickshire,
That I am faulty in Duke Humphrey's death.

            *Exit* CARDINAL [*and others*].

WARWICK
What dares Warwick, if false Suffolk dare him?

QUEEN
He dares not calm his contumelious° spirit
Nor cease to be an arrogant controller,°     205
Though Suffolk dare him twenty thousand times.

WARWICK
Madam, be still—with reverence may I say—
For every word you speak in his behalf
Is slander to your royal dignity.

SUFFOLK
Blunt-witted lord, ignoble in demeanor!     210
If ever lady wronged her lord so much,
Thy mother took her into her blameful bed
Some stern° untutored churl; and noble stock
Was graft with crabtree slip, whose fruit thou art,
And never of the Nevils' noble race.     215

WARWICK
But that the guilt of murder bucklers° thee,
And I should rob the deathsman of his fee,
Quitting thee thereby of ten thousand shames,
And that my sovereign's presence makes me mild,
I would, false murd'rous coward, on thy knee     220
Make thee beg pardon for thy passèd speech,
And say it was thy mother that thou meant'st,
That thou thyself wast born in bastardy;
And after all this fearful homage done,
Give thee thy hire and send thy soul to hell,     225
Pernicious bloodsucker of sleeping men!

SUFFOLK
Thou shalt be waking while I shed thy blood,
If from this presence thou dar'st go with me.

WARWICK
Away even now, or I will drag thee hence:
Unworthy though thou art, I'll cope with thee,     230
And do some service to Duke Humphrey's ghost.

         *Exeunt* [SUFFOLK *and* WARWICK].

---

141 **paly** pale   161 **timely parted ghost** dead man who died
naturally   162 **meager** thin   163 **Being** the blood being
164 **Who** the heart   165 **the same** the blood   166 **Which**
the blood   176 **lodged** beaten flat   178 **probable** indicative
(of murder)

187 **timeless** untimely   191 **puttock's** kite's   204 **con-**
**tumelious** slanderous   205 **controller** censorious critic,
detractor   213 **stern** rough   216 **bucklers** shields

KING
What stronger breastplate than a heart untainted!
Thrice is he armed that hath his quarrel just,
And he but naked, though locked up in steel,
Whose conscience with injustice is corrupted.            235

*A noise within.*

QUEEN
What noise is this?

*Enter* SUFFOLK *and* WARWICK, *with their weapons drawn.*

KING
Why, how now, lords! Your wrathful weapons
     drawn
Here in our presence? Dare you be so bold?
Why, what tumultuous clamor have we here?

SUFFOLK
The trait'rous Warwick, with the men of Bury,        240
Set all upon me, mighty sovereign.

*Enter* SALISBURY.

SALISBURY [*To the* COMMONS *without.*]
Sirs, stand apart: the king shall know your mind.
Dread lord, the commons send you word by me,
Unless Lord Suffolk straight be done to death,
Or banishèd fair England's territories,            245
They will by violence tear him from your palace,
And torture him with grievous ling'ring death.
They say, by him the good Duke Humphrey died;
They say, in him they fear your highness' death;
And mere° instinct of love and loyalty,            250
Free from a stubborn opposite° intent,
As being thought to contradict your liking,
Makes them thus forward in his banishment.
They say, in care of your most royal person,
That if your highness should intend to sleep,        255
And charge that no man should disturb your rest
In pain of your dislike, or pain of death,
Yet, notwithstanding such a strait° edict,
Were there a serpent seen, with forkèd tongue,
That slyly glided towards your majesty,            260
It were but necessary you were waked;
Lest, being suffered° in that harmful slumber,
The mortal worm° might make the sleep eternal.
And therefore do they cry, though you forbid,
That they will guard you, whe'r° you will or no,    265
From such fell° serpents as false Suffolk is;
With whose envenomèd and fatal sting
Your loving uncle, twenty times his worth,
They say, is shamefully bereft of life.
COMMONS *Within.*
An answer from the king, my Lord of Salisbury!        270
SUFFOLK
'Tis like° the commons, rude unpolished hinds,°
Could send such message to their sovereign:
But you, my lord, were glad to be employed,
To show how quaint° an orator you are.
But all the honor Salisbury hath won            275

Is, that he was the Lord Ambassador
Sent from a sort° of tinkers to the king.
[COMMONS] *Within.*
An answer from the king, or we will all break in!
KING
Go, Salisbury, and tell them all from me,
I thank them for their tender loving care;        280
And had I not been cited° so by them,
Yet did I purpose as they do entreat;
For sure, my thoughts do hourly prophesy
Mischance unto my state by Suffolk's means.
And therefore, by His majesty I swear,            285
Whose far unworthy deputy I am,
He shall not breathe infection in this air
But three days longer, on the pain of death.
                         *Exit* SALISBURY.
QUEEN
O Henry, let me plead for gentle° Suffolk!
KING
Ungentle° queen, to call him gentle Suffolk!        290
No more, I say: if thou dost plead for him,
Thou wilt but add increase unto my wrath.
Had I but said, I would have kept my word;
But when I swear, it is irrevocable.

     [*To* SUFFOLK.]

If after three days' space thou here be'st found    295
On any ground that I am ruler of,
The world shall not be ransom for thy life.
Come, Warwick, come, good Warwick, go with me;
I have great matters to impart to thee.
                         *Exit* KING *and* WARWICK.
                         *Manet* QUEEN *and* SUFFOLK.
QUEEN
Mischance and sorrow go along with you!            300
Heart's discontent and sour affliction
Be playfellows to keep you company!
There's two of you; the devil make a third!
And threefold vengeance tend upon your steps!
SUFFOLK
Cease, gentle queen, these execrations,            305
And let thy Suffolk take his heavy leave.
QUEEN
Fie, coward woman and softhearted wretch!
Hast thou not spirit to curse thine enemy?
SUFFOLK
A plague upon them! Wherefore should I curse them?
Would curses kill, as doth the mandrake's groan,°    310
I would invent as bitter searching° terms,
As curst, as harsh, and horrible to hear,
Delivered strongly through my fixèd teeth,
With full as many signs of deadly hate,
As lean-faced envy in her loathsome cave.            315
My tongue should stumble in mine earnest words;
Mine eyes should sparkle like the beaten flint;
Mine hair be fixed an° end, as one distract;°

---

**250 mere** pure   **251 opposite** antagonistic   **258 strait** strict   **262 suffered** allowed to continue   **263 mortal worm** deadly snake   **265 whe'r** whether   **266 fell** cruel   **271 like** likely; **hinds** boors   **274 quaint** clever, fine

**277 sort** group   **281 cited** incited, urged   **289 gentle** noble   **290 Ungentle** unkind, harsh   **310 mandrake's groan** the mandrake is a poisonous plant, its forked root shaped like two human legs; when uprooted it supposedly groaned like a human, the sound being fatal to any hearer   **311 searching** cutting, lancing (as in surgery)   **318 an** on; **distract** distracted, mad

Ay, every joint should seem to curse and ban:°
And even now my burdened heart would break, 320
Should I not curse them. Poison be their drink!
Gall, worse than gall, the daintiest that they taste!
Their sweetest shade a grove of cypress° trees!
Their chiefest prospect murd'ring basilisks!°
Their softest touch as smart as lizards' stings! 325
Their music frightful as the serpent's hiss,
And boding screech owls make the consort° full!
All the foul terrors in dark-seated hell—

QUEEN
Enough, sweet Suffolk; thou torment'st thyself;
And these dread curses, like the sun 'gainst glass, 330
Or like an overchargèd gun, recoil,
And turn the force of them upon thyself.

SUFFOLK
You bade me ban, and will you bid me leave?
Now, by the ground that I am banishèd from,
Well could I curse away a winter's night, 335
Though standing naked on a mountain top,
Where biting cold would never let grass grow,
And think it but a minute spent in sport.

QUEEN
O, let me entreat thee cease. Give me thy hand,
That I may dew it with my mournful tears; 340
Nor let the rain of heaven wet this place,
To wash away my woeful monuments.
O, could this kiss be printed in thy hand,
That thou mightst think upon these° by the seal,
Through whom a thousand sighs are breathed for
    thee! 345
So, get thee gone, that I may know my grief;
'Tis but surmised whiles thou art standing by,
As one that surfeits thinking on a want.
I will repeal thee, or, be well assured,
Adventure° to be banishèd myself: 350
And banishèd I am, if but from thee.
Go, speak not to me; even now be gone.
O, go not yet! Even thus two friends condemned
Embrace and kiss and take ten thousand leaves,
Loather a hundred times to part than die. 355
Yet now farewell, and farewell life with thee!

SUFFOLK
Thus is poor Suffolk ten times banishèd;
Once by the king, and three times thrice by thee.
'Tis not the land I care for, wert thou thence;
A wilderness is populous enough, 360
So Suffolk had thy heavenly company:
For where thou art, there is the world itself,
With every several° pleasure in the world,
And where thou art not, desolation.
I can no more: live thou to joy thy life; 365
Myself to joy in nought but that thou liv'st.

*Enter* VAUX.

QUEEN
Whither goes Vaux so fast? What news, I prithee?

VAUX
To signify unto his majesty
That Cardinal Beaufort is at point of death;
For suddenly a grievous sickness took him, 370
That makes him gasp, and stare, and catch the air,
Blaspheming God, and cursing men on earth.
Sometime he talks as if Duke Humphrey's ghost
Were by his side; sometime he calls the king,
And whispers to his pillow, as to him, 375
The secrets of his overchargèd soul:
And I am sent to tell his majesty
That even now he cries aloud for him.

QUEEN
Go tell this heavy message to the king. *Exit* [VAUX].
Ay me! What is this world! What news are these! 380
But wherefore grieve I at an hour's poor loss,
Omitting Suffolk's exile, my soul's treasure?
Why only, Suffolk, mourn I not for thee,
And with the southern clouds contend in tears,
Theirs for the earth's increase,° mine for my sorrows? 385
Now get thee hence: the king, thou know'st, is
    coming;
If thou be found by me, thou art but dead.

SUFFOLK
If I depart from thee I cannot live;
And in thy sight to die, what were it else
But like a pleasant slumber in thy lap? 390
Here could I breathe my soul into the air,
As mild and gentle as the cradle babe
Dying with mother's dug between its lips;
Where, from thy sight, I should be raging mad,
And cry out for thee to close up mine eyes, 395
To have thee with thy lips to stop my mouth:
So shouldst thou either turn my flying soul,
Or I should breathe it so into thy body,
And then it lived in sweet Elysium.
To die by thee were but to die in jest; 400
From thee to die were torture more than death:
O, let me stay, befall what may befall!

QUEEN
Away! Though parting be a fretful corrosive,°
It is applied to a deathful wound.
To France, sweet Suffolk: let me hear from thee; 405
For wheresoe'er thou art in this world's globe,
I'll have an Iris° that shall find thee out.

SUFFOLK   I go.

QUEEN
And take my heart with thee.

*She kisseth him.*

SUFFOLK
A jewel, locked into the woefull'st cask 410
That ever did contain a thing of worth.
Even as a splitted bark, so sunder we:
This way fall I to death.     *Exit* SUFFOLK.

QUEEN        This way for me.
                        *Exit* QUEEN.

---

**319 curse and ban** formally excommunicate **323 cypress** traditionally grown in graveyards **324 basilisks** mythical reptiles thought to kill by a glance **327 consort** group of musicians **344 these** these lips **350 Adventure** venture **363 several** single

**385 increase** fruition **403 corrosive** caustic remedy **407 Iris** Juno's messenger, and goddess of the rainbow

[Scene III. *A bedchamber.*]

*Enter the* KING, SALISBURY, *and* WARWICK; *and then the curtains be drawn, and the* CARDINAL *is discovered in his bed, raving and staring as if he were mad.*

KING
How fares my lord? Speak, Beaufort, to thy sovereign.

CARDINAL
If thou be'st death, I'll give thee England's treasure,
Enough to purchase such another island,
So thou wilt let me live, and feel no pain.

KING
Ah, what a sign it is of evil life,                                    5
Where death's approach is seen so terrible!

WARWICK
Beaufort, it is thy sovereign speaks to thee.

CARDINAL
Bring me unto my trial when you will.
Died he not in his bed? Where should he die?
Can I make men live, whe'r they will or no?         10
O, torture me no more! I will confess.
Alive again? Then show me where he is:
I'll give a thousand pound to look upon him.
He hath no eyes, the dust hath blinded them.
Comb down his hair; look, look! It stands upright,   15
Like lime twigs° set to catch my wingèd soul.
Give me some drink, and bid the apothecary
Bring the strong poison that I bought of him.

KING
O thou Eternal Mover of the heavens,
Look with a gentle eye upon this wretch!              20
O, beat away the busy meddling fiend
That lays strong siege unto this wretch's soul,
And from his bosom purge this black despair!

WARWICK
See how the pangs of death do make him grin.°

SALISBURY
Disturb him not, let him pass peaceably.              25

KING
Peace to his soul, if God's good pleasure be.
Lord Cardinal, if thou think'st on heaven's bliss,
Hold up thy hand, make signal of thy hope.
                            *The* CARDINAL *dies.*
He dies, and makes no sign. O God, forgive him!

WARWICK
So bad a death argues° a monstrous life.             30

KING
Forbear to judge, for we are sinners all.
Close up his eyes and draw the curtain close;
And let us all to meditation.              *Exeunt.*

---

[ **ACT IV** ]

[Scene I. *The coast of Kent.*]

*Alarum. Fight at sea. Ordnance goes off. And then enter the* LIEUTENANT *of the ship, and the* MASTER, *and the master's* MATE, *and the Duke of* SUFFOLK, *disguised, and others* [GENTLEMEN] *with him, and Walter* WHITMORE.

LIEUTENANT°
The gaudy, blabbing, and remorseful day
Is crept into the bosom of the sea,
And now loud-howling wolves arouse the jades°
That drag the tragic melancholy night;
Who, with their drowsy, slow, and flagging wings      5
Clip° dead men's graves, and from their misty jaws
Breathe foul contagious darkness in the air.
Therefore bring forth the soldiers of our prize,
For whilst our pinnace anchors in the Downs°
Here shall they make their ransom on the sand,        10
Or with their blood stain this discolored shore.
Master, this prisoner freely give I thee;
And thou that art his mate, make boot of° this;
The other, Walter Whitmore, is thy share.

FIRST GENTLEMAN
What is my ransom, master? Let me know.               15

MASTER
A thousand crowns, or else lay down your head.

MATE
And so much shall you give, or off goes yours.

[*The* PRISONERS *react adversely.*]

LIEUTENANT
What! Think you much to pay two thousand crowns,
And bear the name and port° of gentlemen?
Cut both the villains' throats; for die you shall:     20
The lives of those which we have lost in fight
Be counterpoised with such a petty sum!

FIRST GENTLEMAN
I'll give it, sir; and therefore spare my life.

SECOND GENTLEMAN
And so will I, and write home for it straight.

WHITMORE [*To* SUFFOLK.]
I lost mine eye in laying the prize aboard,            25
And therefore to revenge it shalt thou die;
And so should these, if I might have my will.

LIEUTENANT
Be not so rash: take ransom, let him live.

SUFFOLK
Look on my George;° I am a gentleman.
Rate me at what thou wilt, thou shalt be paid.         30

WHITMORE
And so am I: my name is Walter Whitmore.
How now! Why starts thou? What, doth death affright?

SUFFOLK
Thy name affrights me, in whose sound is death.

IV.i.1 **Lieutenant** "Captain" in Q (i.e., the military commander of the pirate ship)  **3 jades** horses (contemptuous)  **6 Clip** embrace, hover over  **9 Downs** bay area off the Kentish coast  **13 make boot of** profit by  **19 port** style, stature  **29 George** insignia or badge of the Order of the Garter, showing Saint George on horseback

---

III.iii.16 **lime twigs** twigs smeared with bird lime   **24 grin** bare his teeth, grimace   **30 argues** suggests, betokens

A cunning man did calculate my birth,°
And told me that by "water"° I should die:    35
Yet let not this make thee be bloody-minded;
Thy name is Gaultier, being rightly sounded.

WHITMORE
Gaultier or Walter, which it is I care not.
Never yet did base dishonor blur our name,
But with our sword we wiped away the blot.    40
Therefore, when merchantlike I sell revenge,
Broke be my sword, my arms torn and defaced,
And I proclaimed a coward through the world!

SUFFOLK
Stay, Whitmore, for thy prisoner is a prince,
The Duke of Suffolk, William de la Pole.    45

WHITMORE
The Duke of Suffolk, muffled up in rags?

SUFFOLK
Ay, but these rags are no part of the duke:
Jove sometime went disguised, and why not I?

LIEUTENANT
But Jove was never slain, as thou shalt be.

SUFFOLK
Obscure and lousy swain, King Henry's blood,    50
The honorable blood of Lancaster,
Must not be shed by such a jaded groom.°
Hast thou not kissed thy hand and held my stirrup?
Bareheaded plodded by my footcloth° mule,
And thought thee happy when I shook my head?    55
How often hast thou waited at my cup,
Fed from my trencher, kneeled down at the board,
When I have feasted with Queen Margaret?
Remember it, and let it make thee crestfall'n,
Ay, and allay this thy abortive° pride:    60
How in our voiding lobby° hast thou stood
And duly waited for my coming forth.
This hand of mine hath writ in thy behalf,
And therefore shall it charm thy riotous tongue.

WHITMORE
Speak, captain, shall I stab the forlorn swain?°    65

LIEUTENANT
First let my words stab him, as he hath me.

SUFFOLK
Base slave, thy words are blunt, and so art thou.

LIEUTENANT
Convey him hence and on our long-boat's side
Strike off his head.

SUFFOLK          Thou dar'st not, for thy own.

LIEUTENANT
Yes, Poole!

SUFFOLK    Poole?°    70

LIEUTENANT
Ay, kennel,° puddle, sink, whose filth and dirt
Troubles the silver spring where England drinks.
Now will I dam up this thy yawning mouth
For swallowing the treasure of the realm;

Thy lips, that kissed the queen, shall sweep the ground;    75
And thou that smil'dst at good Duke Humphrey's
   death
Against the senseless winds shalt grin in vain,
Who in contempt shall hiss at thee again.
And wedded be thou to the hags of hell,
For daring to affy° a mighty lord    80
Unto the daughter of a worthless king,
Having neither subject, wealth, nor diadem.
By devilish policy art thou grown great
And like ambitious Sylla° overgorged
With gobbets of thy mother's bleeding heart.    85
By thee Anjou and Maine were sold to France,
The false revolting Normans thorough° thee
Disdain to call us lord, and Picardy
Hath slain their governors, surprised our forts,
And sent the ragged soldiers wounded home.    90
The princely Warwick, and the Nevils all,
Whose dreadful swords were never drawn in vain,
As hating thee, are rising up in arms;
And now the house of York, thrust from the crown
By shameful murder of a guiltless king    95
And lofty proud encroaching tyranny,
Burns with revenging fire, whose hopeful colors
Advance our half-faced sun,° striving to shine,
Under the which is writ "Invitis nubibus."°
The commons here in Kent are up in arms;    100
And, to conclude, reproach and beggary
Is crept into the palace of our king,
And all by thee. Away! Convey him hence.

SUFFOLK
O that I were a god, to shoot forth thunder
Upon these paltry, servile, abject drudges!    105
Small things make base men proud: this villain here,
Being captain of a pinnace, threatens more
Than Bargulus the strong Illyrian pirate.°
Drones suck not eagles' blood, but rob beehives:
It is impossible that I should die    110
By such a lowly vassal as thyself.
Thy words move rage and not remorse in me.

LIEUTENANT
Ay, but my deeds shall stay thy fury soon.

SUFFOLK
I go of message from the queen to France;°
I charge thee waft me safely 'cross the Channel.    115

WHITMORE
Come, Suffolk, I must waft thee to thy death.

SUFFOLK
Pene gelidus timor occupat artus:° it is thee I fear.

WHITMORE
Thou shalt have cause to fear before I leave thee.
What, are ye daunted now? Now will ye stoop?

---

**34 calculate my birth** cast my horoscope   **35 water** "Walter"
is pronounced "water," and occasionally so spelled in Q and F
**52 groom** low, ignoble fellow   **54 footcloth** ornamented
with elaborate hangings, as in processions and tourneys   **60
abortive** monstrous, untimely   **61 voiding lobby** waiting
room   **65 forlorn swain** wretched (1) fellow (2) lover (of the
queen)   **70 Poole . . . Poole** puns on *to poll* (shave the head,
as for execution), *pool* (cesspool), and *pole* (de la Pole)   **71
kennel** gutter

**80 affy** betroth   **84 Sylla** Sulla, dictator of Rome, who
proscribed and persecuted followers of his rival Marius; Rome
(and for Suffolk, England) is represented as the "mother,"
and the victims (e.g., Gloucester) as "gobbets"   **87 thorough**
through (old form)   **93 Advance . . . sun** raise high our
insignia, the sun emerging from clouds (Edward III's personal
badge)   **99 Invitis nubibus** "in spite of the clouds"   **108
Bargulus . . . pirate** Bargalus or Bardulis, a pirate in Greek
waters mentioned by Cicero   **114 France** the King of France
**117 Pene . . . artus** "Chill fear almost seizes my limbs"
(source unidentified; possibly a corrupt recollection of *Aeneid*,
VII.446)

FIRST GENTLEMAN
My gracious lord, entreat him, speak him fair.          120
SUFFOLK
Suffolk's imperial tongue is stern and rough,
Used to command, untaught to plead for favor.
Far be it we should honor such as these
With humble suit: no, rather let my head
Stoop to the block than these knees bow to any,          125
Save to the God of heaven, and to my king;
And sooner dance upon a bloody pole
Than stand uncovered to the vulgar groom.
True nobility is exempt from fear:
More can I bear than you dare execute.          130
LIEUTENANT
Hale him away, and let him talk no more.
SUFFOLK
Come, soldiers, show what cruelty ye can,
That this my death may never be forgot.
Great men oft die by vile besonians:°
A Roman sworder° and banditto slave          135
Murdered sweet Tully;° Brutus' bastard hand°
Stabbed Julius Caesar; savage islanders
Pompey the Great; and Suffolk dies by pirates.
          *Exit Walter* [WHITMORE], *with* SUFFOLK.
LIEUTENANT
And as for these whose ransom we have set,
It is our pleasure one of them depart:          140
Therefore come you with us and let him go.
          *Exit* LIEUTENANT, *and the rest;*
          *manet the* FIRST GENTLEMAN.

*Enter Walter* [WHITMORE] *with the body* [*of Suffolk*].

WHITMORE
There let his head and lifeless body lie,
Until the queen his mistress bury it.
          *Exit Walter* [WHITMORE].
FIRST GENTLEMAN
O barbarous and bloody spectacle!
His body will I bear unto the king:          145
If he revenge it not, yet will his friends;
So will the queen, that living held him dear.
          [*Exit, with Suffolk's body.*]


[Scene II. *Blackheath.*]

*Enter* BEVIS *and John* HOLLAND.°

BEVIS   Come, and get thee a sword, though made of a
lath:° they have been up° these two days.
HOLLAND   They have the more need to sleep now,
then.
BEVIS   I tell thee, Jack Cade the clothier means to 5
dress the commonwealth, and turn it, and set a new
nap upon it.
HOLLAND   So he had need, for 'tis threadbare. Well,
I say, it was never merry world in England since
gentlemen came up.°          10
BEVIS   O miserable age! virtue is not regarded in
handicraftsmen.
HOLLAND   The nobility think scorn to go in leather
aprons.
BEVIS   Nay, more, the king's council are no good 15
workmen.
HOLLAND   True: and yet it is said, "Labor in thy
vocation"; which is as much to say as, "Let the magis-
trates° be laboring men"; and therefore should we
be magistrates.          20
BEVIS   Thou hast hit it: for there's no better sign of a
brave mind than a hard hand.
HOLLAND   I see them! I see them! There's Best's son,
the tanner of Wingham.
BEVIS   He shall have the skins of our enemies, to make 25
dog's leather° of.
HOLLAND   And Dick the butcher.
BEVIS   Then is sin struck down like an ox, and
iniquity's throat cut like a calf.
HOLLAND   And Smith the weaver.          30
BEVIS   Argo,° their thread of life is spun.
HOLLAND   Come, come, let's fall in with them.

*Drum. Enter* CADE, DICK [*the*] *butcher*, SMITH *the*
*weaver, and a* SAWYER, *with infinite numbers.*

CADE   We John Cade, so termed of our supposed
father—
DICK [*Aside.*]   Or rather, of stealing a cade° of her- 35
rings.
CADE   For our enemies shall fall° before us, inspired
with the spirit of putting down kings and princes.
. . . Command silence.
DICK   Silence!          40
CADE   My father was a Mortimer—
DICK [*Aside.*]   He was an honest man, and a good
bricklayer.
CADE   My mother a Plantagenet—
DICK [*Aside.*]   I knew her well; she was a midwife.          45
CADE   My wife descended of the Lacies—
DICK [*Aside.*]   She was indeed a peddler's daughter,
and sold many laces.
SMITH [*Aside.*]   But now of late, not able to travel with
her furred pack,° she washes bucks° here at home.          50
CADE   Therefore am I of an honorable house.
DICK [*Aside.*]   Ay, by my faith, the field is honorable;
and there was he born, under a hedge: for his father
had never a house but the cage.°
CADE   Valiant I am.          55
SMITH [*Aside.*]   'A must needs, for beggary is valiant.
CADE   I am able to endure much.
DICK [*Aside.*]   No question of that; for I have seen him
whipped three market days together.
CADE   I fear neither sword nor fire.          60

134 besonians base fellows, wretches   135 sworder gladiator
136 Tully Cicero; Brutus' bastard hand a false tradition held
that Brutus was Caesar's bastard son
IV.ii.s.d. Bevis . . . Holland actors in the company (see note
to II.iii.93)   1–2 sword . . . lath a mock weapon, as employed
by soldier-clowns in the early Tudor plays   2 up up in arms
10 came up came into fashion   18–19 magistrates rulers,
administrators   26 dog's leather leather for gloves   31 Argo
corruption of Latin *ergo* = therefore   35 cade barrel of five
hundred   37 fall pun on Latin sense of Cade (*cadere* = to fall)
49–50 travel . . . pack (1) travel with a fur knapsack, as a
peddler (2) labor as a prostitute   50 washes bucks (1) does
rough laundry (2) absolves cuckolds (by making them "even"
with their wives)   54 cage a temporary prison for vagabonds
and harlots, commonly set up in marketplaces

SMITH [*Aside*.]   He need not fear the sword, for his coat is of proof.°

DICK [*Aside*.]   But methinks he should stand in fear of fire, being burnt i' th' hand° for stealing of sheep.

CADE   Be brave, then; for your captain is brave, and 65 vows reformation. There shall be in England seven halfpenny loaves sold for a penny; the three-hooped pot shall have ten hoops;° and I will make it felony to drink small beer. All the realm shall be in common,° and in Cheapside° shall my palfry go to grass; 70 and when I am king, as king I will be—

ALL   God save your majesty!

CADE   I thank you, good people—there shall be no money; all shall eat and drink on my score;° and I will apparel them all in one livery, that they may 75 agree like brothers, and worship me their lord.

DICK   The first thing we do, let's kill all the lawyers.

CADE   Nay, that I mean to do. Is not this a lamentable thing, that of the skin of an innocent lamb should be made parchment? That parchment, being scrib- 80 bled o'er, should undo a man? Some say the bee stings; but I say, 'tis the bee's wax: for I did but seal once to a thing, and I was never mine own man° since. How now! who's there?

*Enter a* CLERK [*led by others.*]

SMITH   The clerk of Chatham: he can write and read, 85 and cast accompt.°

CADE   O monstrous!

SMITH   We took him setting of boys' copies.°

CADE   Here's a villain!

SMITH   H' as a book in his pocket with red letters in't. 90

CADE   Nay, then, he is a conjuror.

DICK   Nay, he can make obligations,° and write court hand.°

CADE   I am sorry for't: the man is a proper man, of mine honor; unless I find him guilty, he shall not 95 die. Come hither, sirrah, I must examine thee: what is thy name?

CLERK   Emmanuel.

DICK   They use to write it on the top of letters:° 'twill go hard with you. 100

CADE   Let me alone. Dost thou use to write thy name? Or hast thou a mark° to thyself, like an honest plain-dealing man?

CLERK   Sir, I thank God, I have been so well brought up that I can write my name. 105

ALL   He hath confessed: away with him! He's a villain and a traitor.

CADE   Away with him, I say! Hang him with his pen and inkhorn about his neck. *Exit one with the* CLERK.

*Enter* MICHAEL.

MICHAEL   Where's our general? 110

CADE   Here I am, thou particular° fellow.

MICHAEL   Fly, fly, fly! Sir Humphrey Stafford and his brother are hard by, with the king's forces.

CADE   Stand, villain, stand, or I'll fell thee down. He shall be encountered with a man as good as himself: 115 he is but a knight, is 'a?

MICHAEL   No.

CADE   To equal him, I will make myself a knight presently. [*Kneels.*] Rise up Sir John Mortimer. [*Rises.*] Now have at him! 120

*Enter Sir Humphrey* STAFFORD *and his* BROTHER, *with* [*a* HERALD,] *drum, and* SOLDIERS.

STAFFORD
Rebellious hinds, the filth and scum of Kent,
Marked for the gallows: lay your weapons down.
Home to your cottages, forsake this groom!
The king is merciful, if you revolt.°

BROTHER
But angry, wrathful, and inclined to blood, 125
If you go forward: therefore yield, or die.

CADE
As for these silken-coated slaves, I pass° not.
It is to you, good people, that I speak,
Over whom, in time to come, I hope to reign:
For I am rightful heir unto the crown. 130

STAFFORD
Villain, thy father was a plasterer,
And thou thyself a shearman,° art thou not?

CADE
And Adam was a gardener.

BROTHER
And what of that?

CADE
Marry, this: Edmund Mortimer, Earl of March, 135
Married the Duke of Clarence' daughter, did he not?

STAFFORD   Ay, sir.

CADE
By her he had two children at one birth.

BROTHER   That's false.

CADE
Ay, there's the question; but I say, 'tis true: 140
The elder of them, being put to nurse,
Was by a beggar woman stol'n away,
And, ignorant of his birth and parentage,
Became a bricklayer when he came to age:
His son am I; deny it, if you can. 145

DICK
Nay, 'tis too true; therefore he shall be king.

SMITH   Sir, he made a chimney in my father's house, and the bricks are alive at this day to testify it; therefore deny it not.

STAFFORD
And will you credit this base drudge's words, 150
That speaks he knows not what?

ALL
Ay, marry, will we: therefore get ye gone.

BROTHER
Jack Cade, the Duke of York hath taught you this.

---

**62 of proof** (1) reliable (2) well-worn   **64 burnt . . . hand** with the letter T, for *thief*   **67–68 three-hooped . . . hoops** the quart measure will contain three quarts   **69–70 in common** held communally   **70 Cheapside** elegant commercial district of London   **74 on my score** at my expense   **83–84 mine own man** my own master   **86 accompt** account   **88 setting . . . copies** teaching schoolchildren to write   **92 obligations** bonds   **93 court hand** formal legal script   **99 They . . . letters** Emmanuel ("God with us") was often prefixed to formal letters, deeds, etc.   **102 mark** an X

**111 particular** private (pun on *general*)   **124 revolt** turn (against Cade)   **127 pass** care   **132 shearman** worker with cloth

CADE [*Aside.*]
He lies, for I invented it myself.—Go to, sirrah, tell
the king from me, that, for his father's sake, Henry 155
the Fifth, in whose time boys went to span-counter°
for French crowns, I am content he shall reign;
but I'll be protector over him.

DICK  And furthermore, we'll have the Lord Say's
head for selling the dukedom of Maine. 160

CADE  And good reason: for thereby is England
mained,° and fain to go with a staff, but that my
puissance holds it up. Fellow kings, I tell you that
that Lord Say hath gelded the commonwealth, and
made it an eunuch: and more than that, he can 165
speak French; and therefore he is a traitor.

STAFFORD
O gross and miserable ignorance!

CADE  Nay, answer, if you can: the Frenchmen are our
enemies; go to, then, I ask but this: can he that
speaks with the tongue of an enemy be a good 170
counselor, or no?

ALL  No, no, and therefore we'll have his head.

BROTHER
Well, seeing gentle words will not prevail,
Assail them with the army of the king.

STAFFORD
Herald, away; and throughout every town 175
Proclaim them traitors that are up with Cade;
That those which fly before the battle ends
May, even in their wives' and children's sight,
Be hanged up for example at their doors:
And you that be the king's friends, follow me. 180
                    *Exit* [STAFFORDS *and their* FORCES].

CADE
And you that love the commons, follow me.
Now show yourselves men; 'tis for liberty.
We will not leave one lord, one gentleman:
Spare none but such as go in clouted shoon;°
For they are thrifty honest men and such 185
As would, but that they dare not, take our parts.

DICK  They are all in order and march toward us.

CADE  But then are we in order when we are most out
of order. Come, march forward. [*Exeunt.*]

[Scene III. *Another part of Blackheath.*]

*Alarums to the fight, wherein both the* STAFFORDS *are
slain. Enter* CADE *and the rest.*

CADE  Where's Dick, the butcher of Ashford?

DICK  Here, sir.

CADE  They fell before thee like sheep and oxen, and
thou behav'dst thyself as if thou hadst been in thine
own slaughterhouse: therefore thus will I reward 5
thee, the Lent shall be as long again as it is; and
thou shalt have a license to kill° for a hundred lacking
one.°

---

156 **span-counter** a game played with marbles close up to the
opponents; figuratively, close combat  162 **mained** maimed
(variant spelling)  184 **clouted shoon** hobnailed boots
**IV.iii.7 license to kill** only infirm persons were permitted to
eat meat during Lent, and favored butchers specially licensed to
kill for them  **7–8 hundred lacking one** ninety-nine years, the
usual term of a lease

---

DICK  I desire no more.

CADE  And, to speak truth, thou deserv'st no less. [*He* 1
*puts on Sir Humphrey's armor.*] This monument
of the victory will I bear; and the bodies shall be
dragged at my horse heels till I do come to London,
where we will have the mayor's sword borne before
us. 1

DICK  If we mean to thrive and do good, break open
the jails and let out the prisoners.

CADE  Fear not that, I warrant thee. Come, let's march
towards London. *Exeunt.*

[Scene IV. *London. The palace.*]

*Enter the* KING *with a supplication, and the* QUEEN *with
Suffolk's head, the Duke of* BUCKINGHAM, *and the
Lord* SAY.

QUEEN [*Aside.*]
Oft have I heard that grief softens the mind
And makes it fearful and degenerate:
Think therefore on revenge, and cease to weep.
But who can cease to weep and look on this?
Here may his head lie on my throbbing breast; 5
But where's the body that I should embrace?

BUCKINGHAM  What answer makes your grace to the
rebels' supplication?

KING
I'll send some holy bishop to entreat;
For God forbid so many simple souls 1
Should perish by the sword! And I myself,
Rather than bloody war shall cut them short,
Will parley with Jack Cade their general.
But stay, I'll read it over once again.

QUEEN [*Aside.*]
Ah, barbarous villains! Hath this lovely face 1
Ruled like a wandering planet° over me,
And could it not enforce them to relent,
That were unworthy to behold the same?

KING
Lord Say, Jack Cade hath sworn to have thy head.

SAY
Ay, but I hope your highness shall have his. 20

KING
How now, madam!
Still lamenting and mourning for Suffolk's death?
I fear me, love, if that I had been dead,
Thou wouldest not have mourned so much for me.

QUEEN
No, my love, I should not mourn, but die for thee. 2

*Enter a* MESSENGER.

KING
How now! What news? Why com'st thou in such
haste?

MESSENGER
The rebels are in Southwark: fly, my lord!
Jack Cade proclaims himself Lord Mortimer,
Descended from the Duke of Clarence' house,
And calls your grace usurper openly, 30

---

**IV.iv.16 wandering planet** the star under which one is born,
astrologically

And vows to crown himself in Westminster.
His army is a ragged multitude
Of hinds and peasants, rude and merciless:
Sir Humphrey Stafford and his brother's death
Hath given them heart and courage to proceed.    35
All scholars, lawyers, courtiers, gentlemen,
They call false caterpillars° and intend their death.

KING
O graceless men! They know not what they do.

BUCKINGHAM
My gracious lord, retire to Killingworth,°
Until a power be raised to put them down.    40

QUEEN
Ah, were the Duke of Suffolk now alive,
These Kentish rebels would soon be appeased!

KING
Lord Say, the traitors hateth thee;
Therefore away with us to Killingworth.

SAY
So might your grace's person be in danger.    45
The sight of me is odious in their eyes:
And therefore in this city will I stay,
And live alone as secret as I may.

*Enter another* MESSENGER.

SECOND MESSENGER
Jack Cade hath gotten London Bridge!
The citizens fly and forsake their houses;    50
The rascal people, thirsting after prey,
Join with the traitor, and they jointly swear
To spoil° the city and your royal court.

BUCKINGHAM
Then linger not, my lord; away, take horse.

KING
Come, Margaret: God, our hope, will succor us.    55

QUEEN
My hope is gone, now Suffolk is deceased.°

KING
Farewell, my lord: trust not the Kentish rebels.

BUCKINGHAM
Trust nobody, for fear you be betrayed.

SAY
The trust I have is in mine innocence,
And therefore am I bold and resolute.     *Exeunt.* 60

[Scene V. *London. The Tower.*]

*Enter Lord* SCALES *upon the Tower, walking. Then
enters two or three* CITIZENS *below.*

SCALES
How now! Is Jack Cade slain?

FIRST CITIZEN   No, my lord, nor likely to be slain;
for they have won the Bridge, killing all those that
withstand them: the Lord Mayor craves aid of your
honor from the Tower to defend the city from the   5
rebels.

SCALES
Such aid as I can spare you shall command,

But I am troubled here with them myself:
The rebels have assayed to win the Tower.
But get you to Smithfield, and gather head,    10
And thither I will send you Matthew Goffe.
Fight for your king, your country, and your lives;
And so farewell, for I must hence again.     *Exeunt.*

[Scene VI. *London. Cannon Street.*]

*Enter Jack* CADE *and the rest, and strikes his sword on
London Stone.*

CADE   Now is Mortimer lord of this city. And here,
sitting upon London Stone, I charge and command
that, of the city's cost, the pissing conduit° run
nothing but claret wine this first year of our reign.
And now henceforward it shall be treason for any   5
that calls me other than Lord Mortimer.

*Enter a* SOLDIER, *running.*

SOLDIER   Jack Cade! Jack Cade!
CADE   Knock him down there.

*They kill him.*

SMITH   If this fellow be wise, he'll never call ye Jack
Cade more: I think he hath a very fair warning.    10
DICK   My lord, there's an army gathered together in
Smithfield.
CADE   Come, then, let's go fight with them: but first,
go and set London Bridge on fire; and if you can,
burn down the Tower too. Come, let's away.    15

                            *Exeunt omnes.*

[Scene VII. *London. Smithfield.*]

*Alarums. Matthew* GOFFE *is slain, and all the rest. Then
enter Jack* CADE, *with his* COMPANY.

CADE   So, sirs: now go some and pull down the
Savoy; others to th' Inns of Court: down with them
all.
DICK   I have a suit unto your lordship.
CADE   Be it a lordship, thou shalt have it for that   5
word.
DICK   Only that the laws of England may come out
of your mouth.
HOLLAND [*Aside.*]   'Mass, 'twill be sore law, then; for
he was thrust in the mouth with a spear, and 'tis not   10
whole yet.
SMITH [*Aside.*]   Nay, John, it will be stinking law; for
his breath stinks with eating toasted cheese.
CADE   I have thought upon it; it shall be so. Away,
burn all the records of the realm: my mouth shall   15
be the parliament of England.
HOLLAND [*Aside.*]   Then we are like to have biting°
statutes, unless his teeth be pulled out.
CADE   And henceforward all things shall be in
common.    20

*Enter a* MESSENGER.

37 **caterpillars** parasites (a common figure for capitalistic
oppressors)   39 **Killingworth** Kenilworth Castle   53 **spoil**
despoil   56 **My . . . deceased** a possible "aside"

IV.vi.3 **pissing conduit** an open gutter of drinking water in
London, derisively so termed
IV.vii.17 **biting** severe

MESSENGER  My lord, a prize, a prize! Here's the Lord Say, which sold the towns in France; he that made us pay one and twenty fifteens,° and one shilling to the pound, the last subsidy.

*Enter GEORGE, with the Lord SAY.*

CADE  Well, he shall be beheaded for it ten times. Ah, 25 thou say, thou serge, nay, thou buckram° lord, now art thou within point blank of our jurisdiction regal! What canst thou answer to my majesty for giving up of Normandy unto Mounsieur Basimecu,° the Dolphin of France? Be it known unto thee by these 30 presence,° even the presence of Lord Mortimer, that I am the besom° that must sweep the court clean of such filth as thou art. Thou hast most traitorously corrupted the youth of the realm in erecting a grammar school: and whereas before, our forefathers had no 35 other books but the score and the tally, thou hast caused printing to be used, and contrary to the king, his crown and dignity, thou hast built a paper mill.° It will be proved to thy face that thou hast men about thee that usually talk of a noun and a verb, and such 40 abhominable° words as no Christian ear can endure to hear. Thou hast appointed justices of peace, to call poor men before them about matters they were not able to answer. Moreover, thou hast put them in prison, and because they could not read° thou hast 45 hanged them, when, indeed, only for that cause they have been most worthy to live. Thou dost ride on a footcloth,° dost thou not?

SAY  What of that?

CADE  Marry, thou ought'st not to let thy horse wear 50 a cloak, when honester men than thou go in their hose and doublets.

DICK  And work in their shirt too as myself, for example, that am a butcher.

SAY  You men of Kent—    55

DICK  What say you of Kent?

SAY  Nothing but this: 'tis bona terra, mala gens.°

CADE  Away with him, away with him! He speaks Latin.

SAY

Hear me but speak, and bear me where you will.    60
Kent, in the *Commentaries* Caesar writ,
Is termed the civil'st place of all this isle:
Sweet is the country, because full of riches;
The people liberal, valiant, active, wealthy;
Which makes me hope you are not void of pity.    65
I sold not Maine, I lost not Normandy,
Yet to recover them would lose my life.

Justice with favor have I always done;
Prayers and tears have moved me, gifts could never.
When have I aught exacted at your hands,    70
But to maintain the realm, and you?
Large gifts have I bestowed on learnèd clerks,°
Because my book° preferred me to the king,
And seeing ignorance is the curse of God,
Knowledge the wing wherewith we fly to heaven,    75
Unless you be possessed with devilish spirits,
You cannot but forbear to murder me:
This tongue hath parleyed unto foreign kings
For your behoof°—

CADE  Tut, when struck'st thou one blow in the 80 field?

SAY

Great men have reaching hands: oft have I struck
Those that I never saw, and struck them dead.

GEORGE  O monstrous coward! What, to come behind folks?    85

SAY

These cheeks are pale for watching for your good.

CADE  Give him a box o' th' ear and that will make 'em red again.

SAY

Long sitting to determine poor men's causes
Hath made me full of sickness and diseases.    90

CADE  Ye shall have a hempen caudle then and the help of hatchet.°

DICK  Why dost thou quiver, man?

SAY

The palsy, and not fear, provokes me.

CADE  Nay, he nods at us, as who should say, "I'll be 95 even with you." I'll see if his head will stand steadier on a pole, or no: take him away, and behead him.

SAY

Tell me: wherein have I offended most?
Have I affected wealth or honor? Speak!
Are my chests filled up with extorted gold?    100
Is my apparel sumptuous to behold?
Whom have I injured, that ye seek my death?
These hands are free from guiltless bloodshedding,°
This breast from harboring foul deceitful thoughts.
O, let me live!    105

CADE [*Aside.*]  I feel remorse in myself with his words; but I'll bridle it: he shall die, and it be but for pleading so well for his life.—Away with him! He has a familiar° under his tongue; he speaks not a° God's name. Go, take him away, I say, and strike 110 off his head presently; and then break into his son-in-law's house, Sir James Cromer, and strike off his head, and bring them both upon two poles hither.

ALL  It shall be done.

SAY

Ah, countrymen! If when you make your prayers,    115
God should be so obdurate as yourselves,
How would it fare with your departed souls?
And therefore yet relent, and save my life.

**23 one . . . fifteens** taxes (a gross exaggeration)  **26 say . . . serge . . . buckram** puns on Lord Say's name: say is a silk cloth, resembling serge; serge a serviceable but less elegant material; and buckram a coarse linen stiffened with glue, commonly used in making theatrical properties  **29 Basimecu** pseudo-French pun on *baise mon cul* = kiss my backside  **30–31 Be . . . presence** play on the formal beginning of documents, *Noverint universi per praesentes* (Be it known unto all by these presents)  **32 besom** broom  **37–38 printing . . . mill** flagrant anachronisms, perhaps intentionally humorous  **41 abhominable** possibly a pun on *ad hominem*  **45 because . . . read** refers to the legal exemption from hanging and other penalties ("benefit of clergy") which Latin-reading offenders could claim  **48 footcloth** horse or mule decorated for a procession  **57 bona . . . gens** good land, bad inhabitants

**72 clerks** scholars  **73 book** learning  **79 behoof** behalf  **91–92 Ye . . . hatchet** You will be first hanged (a caudle is a curative gruel; a hempen caudle a euphemism for hanging) and then beheaded  **103 guiltless bloodshedding** shedding guiltless blood  **109 familiar** demonic attendant of a witch  **110 a** in

CADE  Away with him! And do as I command ye.

[SAY *is led away*.]

The proudest peer in the realm shall not wear a 120
head on his shoulders, unless he pay me tribute;
there shall not a maid be married, but she shall pay
to me her maidenhead ere they have it; men shall
hold me in capite;° and we charge and command
that their wives be as free as heart can wish or tongue 125
can tell.

DICK  My lord, when shall we go to Cheapside and
take up commodities upon our bills?°

CADE  Marry, presently.

ALL  O, brave!                                     130

*Enter one with the heads.*

CADE  But is not this braver? Let them kiss one another, for they loved well when they were alive.
Now part them again, lest they consult about the
giving up of some more towns in France. Soldiers,
defer the spoil of the city until night: for with these 135
borne before us, instead of maces, will we ride
through the streets; and at every corner have them
kiss. Away!                              *Exit* [*All*].

[Scene VIII. *Southwark*.]

*Alarum and retreat. Enter again* CADE *and all his rabblement.*

CADE  Up Fish Street! Down Saint Magnus' Corner!
Kill and knock down! Throw them into Thames!
(*Sound a parley.*) What noise is this I hear? Dare
any be so bold to sound retreat or parley, when I
command them kill?                                  5

*Enter* BUCKINGHAM *and old* CLIFFORD.

BUCKINGHAM
Ay, here they be that dare and will disturb thee:
Know, Cade, we come ambassadors from the king
Unto the commons whom thou hast misled,
And here pronounce free pardon to them all
That will forsake thee and go home in peace.        10

CLIFFORD
What say ye, countrymen? Will ye relent,
And yield to mercy whilst 'tis offered you,
Or let a rebel lead you to your deaths?
Who loves the king and will embrace his pardon,
Fling up his cap, and say, "God save his majesty!"  15
Who hateth him and honors not his father,
Henry the Fifth, that made all France to quake,
Shake he his weapon at us and pass by.

ALL  God save the king! God save the king!

CADE  What, Buckingham and Clifford, are ye so 20
brave? And you, base peasants, do ye believe him?
Will you needs be hanged with your pardons about
your necks? Hath my sword therefore broke through
London gates, that you should leave me at the White
Hart° in Southwark? I thought ye would never 25

have given out these arms till you had recovered your
ancient freedom: but you are all recreants and dastards,
and delight to live in slavery to the nobility. Let them
break your backs with burdens, take your houses
over your heads, ravish your wives and daughters 30
before your faces. For me, I will make shift for one;
and so, God's curse light upon you all!

ALL  We'll follow Cade, we'll follow Cade!

CLIFFORD
Is Cade the son of Henry the Fifth,
That thus you do exclaim you'll go with him?        35
Will he conduct you through the heart of France,
And make the meanest of you earls and dukes?
Alas, he hath no home, no place to fly to;
Nor knows he how to live but by the spoil,
Unless by robbing of your friends and us.           40
Were't not a shame, that whilst you live at jar,°
The fearful French, whom you late vanquishèd,
Should make a start o'er seas and vanquish you?
Methinks already in this civil broil
I see them lording it in London streets,             45
Crying "Villiago!"° unto all they meet.
Better ten thousand base-born Cades miscarry
Than you should stoop unto a Frenchman's mercy.
To France, to France! and get what you have lost:
Spare England, for it is your native coast.          50
Henry hath money, you are strong and manly;
God on our side, doubt not of victory.

ALL  A Clifford! A Clifford! We'll follow the king
and Clifford.

CADE  Was ever feather so lightly blown to and fro as 55
this multitude? The name of Henry the Fifth hales
them to an hundred mischiefs and makes them
leave me desolate. I see them lay their heads together to surprise me. My sword make way for me,
for here is no staying: in despite of the devils and 60
hell, have through the very middest of you! And
heavens and honor be witness that no want of resolution in me, but only my followers' base and
ignominious treasons, makes me betake me to my
heels.                                              65

*He runs through them with his staff, and flies away.*

BUCKINGHAM
What, is he fled? Go some, and follow him;
And he that brings his head unto the king
Shall have a thousand crowns for his reward.
*Exeunt some of them.*
Follow me, soldiers: we'll devise a mean
To reconcile you all unto the king.   *Exeunt omnes.* 70

[Scene IX. *Kenilworth Castle*.]

*Sound trumpets. Enter* KING, QUEEN, *and* SOMERSET,
*on the terrace.*

KING
Was ever king that joyed an earthly throne,
And could command no more content than I?
No sooner was I crept out of my cradle
But I was made a king, at nine months old.

124 in capite in chief, the legal term for holding a property
direct from the king, at the "head" of the state  128 take . . .
bills (1) borrow money from usurers with promissory notes
(2) pillage property with our weapons
IV.viii. 24–25 White Hart inn where Cade lodged (puns on
pale, or cowardly, heart)

41 at jar quarreling  46 Villiago villain, coward (Spanish or
Italian)

Was never subject longed to be a king        5
As I do long and wish to be a subject.

*Enter* BUCKINGHAM *and* [*old*] CLIFFORD.

BUCKINGHAM
Health and glad tidings to your majesty!
KING
Why, Buckingham, is the traitor Cade surprised?
Or is he but retired to make him strong?

*Enter multitudes, with halters about their necks.*

CLIFFORD
He is fled, my lord, and all his powers do yield,        10
And humbly thus, with halters° on their necks,
Expect your highness' doom, of life or death.
KING
Then, heaven, set ope thy everlasting gates,
To entertain° my vows of thanks and praise!
Soldiers, this day have you redeemed your lives        15
And showed how well you love your prince and
    country:
Continue still in this so good a mind,
And Henry, though he be infortunate,
Assure yourselves, will never be unkind:
And so, with thanks and pardon to you all,        20
I do dismiss you to your several countries.°
ALL
God save the king! God save the king!

*Enter a* MESSENGER.

MESSENGER
Please it your grace to be advertisèd°
The Duke of York is newly come from Ireland,
And with a puissant and a mighty power        25
Of gallowglasses° and stout kerns°
Is marching hitherward in proud array,
And still proclaimeth, as he comes along,
His arms are only to remove from thee
The Duke of Somerset, whom he terms a traitor.        30
KING
Thus stands my state, 'twixt Cade and York distressed,
Like to a ship, that having 'scaped a tempest,
Is straightway calmed, and boarded with° a pirate.
But now is Cade driven back, his men dispersed;
And now is York in arms to second him.        35
I pray thee, Buckingham, go and meet him,
And ask him what's the reason of these arms.
Tell him I'll send Duke Edmund to the Tower,
And, Somerset, we will commit thee thither,
Until his army be dismissed from him.        40
SOMERSET
My lord,
I'll yield myself to prison willingly,
Or unto death, to do my country good.
KING
In any case, be not too rough in terms,
For he is fierce, and cannot brook hard language.        45

BUCKINGHAM
I will, my lord; and doubt not so to deal
As all things shall redound unto your good.
KING
Come, wife, let's in, and learn to govern better;
For yet may England curse my wretched reign.
                                        *Flourish. Exeunt.*

[Scene X. *Kent. Iden's garden.*]

*Enter* CADE.

CADE  Fie on ambitions! Fie on myself, that have a
sword, and yet am ready to famish! These five days
have I hid me in these woods and durst not peep
out, for all the country is laid° for me; but now
am I so hungry that if I might have a lease of my        5
life for a thousand years I could stay no longer.
Wherefore, on a brick wall have I climbed into this
garden, to see if I can eat grass, or pick a sallet°
another while, which is not amiss to cool a man's
stomach° this hot weather. And I think this word°        10
"sallet" was born to do me good: for many a time,
but for a sallet, my brainpan had been cleft with
a brown bill;° and many a time, when I have been
dry and bravely marching, it hath served me instead of a quart pot to drink in; and now the word        15
"sallet" must serve me to feed on.

*Enter* [*Alexander*] IDEN.

IDEN
Lord, who would live turmoilèd in the court,
And may enjoy such quiet walks as these?
This small inheritance my father left me
Contenteth me, and worth° a monarchy.        20
I seek not to wax great by others' waning,
Or gather wealth, I care not with what envy:
Sufficeth that I have maintains my state,
And sends the poor well pleasèd from my gate.
CADE  Here's the lord of the soil come to seize me for        25
a stray, for entering his fee-simple without leave.°
Ah, villain, thou wilt betray me, and get a thousand
crowns of the king by carrying my head to him:
but I'll make thee eat iron like an ostrich, and swallow
my sword like a great pin, ere thou and I part.        30
IDEN
Why, rude companion,° whatsoe'er thou be,
I know thee not; why then should I betray thee?
Is't not enough to break into my garden,
And like a thief to come to rob my grounds,
Climbing my walls in spite of me the owner,        35
But thou wilt brave° me with these saucy terms?
CADE  Brave thee! Ay, by the best blood that ever
was broached, and beard thee° too. Look on me

---

IV.x.4 **laid** set with traps    8 **sallet** (1) salad (2) iron helmet
9–10 **cool . . . stomach** (1) satisfy a man's hunger and thirst
(2) pacify a man's anger    10 **word** pun on *wort* (i.e., medicinal
or edible herb)    13 **brown bill** halberd used by constables    20
**worth** is worth    25–26 **Here's . . . leave** the absolute owner
("lord of the soil") of an estate ("fee-simple") was entitled to
impound any stray animal which wandered accidentally over
the bounds of the property    31 **companion** fellow (derogatory)    36 **brave** challenge    38 **beard thee** defy you to your
face

---

IV.ix.11 **halters** nooses (a symbol of complete submission)
14 **entertain** receive    21 **countries** counties, areas    23
**advertisèd** informed    26 **gallowglasses** heavily armed Irish
foot-soldiers; **kerns** light-armed troops    33 **with** by

well: I have eat no meat these five days; yet, come
thou and thy five men, and if I do not leave you 40
all as dead as a doornail, I pray God I may never
eat grass more.

IDEN

Nay, it shall ne'er be said, while England stands,
That Alexander Iden, an esquire of Kent,
Took odds° to combat a poor famished man.      45
Oppose thy steadfast-gazing eyes to mine,
See if thou canst outface me with thy looks;
Set limb to limb, and thou art far the lesser:
Thy hand is but a finger to my fist,
Thy leg a stick comparèd with this truncheon;      50
My foot shall fight with all the strength thou hast;
And if mine arm be heavèd in the air,
Thy grave is digged already in the earth.
As for words, whose greatness answers words,
Let this my sword report what speech forbears.      55

CADE   By my valor, the most complete champion that
ever I heard! Steel, if thou turn the edge, or cut
not out the burly-boned clown in chines° of beef
ere thou sleep in thy sheath, I beseech God on my
knees thou mayst be turned to hobnails. *They fight,* 60
*and* CADE *falls down.* O, I am slain! Famine and no
other hath slain me: let ten thousand devils come
against me, and give me but the ten meals I have lost,
and I'd defy them all. Wither, garden, and be henceforth a burying place to all that do dwell in this 65
house, because the unconquered soul of Cade is fled.

IDEN

Is't Cade that I have slain, that monstrous traitor?
Sword, I will hallow thee for this thy deed,
And hang thee o'er my tomb when I am dead:
Ne'er shall this blood be wipèd from thy point,      70
But thou shalt wear it as a herald's coat,
To emblaze° the honor that thy master got.

CADE   Iden, farewell, and be proud of thy victory.
Tell Kent from me, she hath lost her best man,
and exhort all the world to be cowards: for I, that 75
never feared any, am vanquished by famine, not
by valor.                          *Dies.*

IDEN

How much thou wrong'st me, heaven be my judge.
Die, damnèd wretch, the curse of her that bare thee:
And as I thrust thy body in with my sword,      80
So wish I I might thrust thy soul to hell.
Hence will I drag thee headlong° by the heels
Unto a dunghill which shall be thy grave,
And there cut off thy most ungracious head,
Which I will bear in triumph to the king,      85
Leaving thy trunk for crows to feed upon.      *Exit.*

# [ACT V]

[Scene I. *Fields between London and Saint Albans.*]

*Enter* YORK, *and his* ARMY *of Irish, with drum and
colors.*

YORK

From Ireland thus comes York to claim his right,
And pluck the crown from feeble Henry's head.
Ring, bells, aloud; burn, bonfires, clear and bright,
To entertain great England's lawful king.
Ah, sancta majestas!° Who would not buy thee dear?   5
Let them obey that knows not how to rule;
This hand was made to handle nought but gold.
I cannot give due action to my words,
Except a sword or scepter balance it:
A scepter shall it have, have I a soul,      10
On which I'll toss the fleur-de-luce° of France.

*Enter* BUCKINGHAM.

Whom have we here? Buckingham, to disturb me?
The king hath sent him, sure: I must dissemble.

BUCKINGHAM

York, if thou meanest well, I greet thee well.

YORK

Humphrey of Buckingham, I accept thy greeting.    15
Art thou a messenger, or come of pleasure?

BUCKINGHAM

A messenger from Henry, our dread liege,
To know the reason of these arms in peace;
Or why thou, being a subject as I am,
Against thy oath and true allegiance sworn,      20
Should raise so great a power without his leave,
Or dare to bring thy force so near the court.

YORK [*Aside.*]

Scarce can I speak, my choler is so great.
O, I could hew-up rocks and fight with flint,
I am so angry at these abject° terms;      25
And now, like Ajax Telamonius,
On sheep or oxen could I spend my fury.°
I am far better born than is the king,
More like a king, more kingly in my thoughts:
But I must make fair weather yet awhile,      30
Till Henry be more weak and I more strong.

[*Aloud.*]

Buckingham, I prithee, pardon me,
That I have given no answer all this while;
My mind was troubled with deep melancholy.
The cause why I have brought this army hither    35
Is to remove proud Somerset from the king,
Seditious to his grace, and to the state.

BUCKINGHAM

That is too much presumption on thy part:
But if thy arms be to no other end,
The king hath yielded unto thy demand:      40
The Duke of Somerset is in the Tower.

---

V.i.5 **sancta majestas** holy majesty (Ovid)    11 **fleur-de-luce**
fleur-de-lis, the heraldic emblem of French kings    25 **abject**
degrading    26–27 **Ajax . . . fury** Ajax, son of Telamon,
in a mad rage over being denied an honor, slaughtered a flock of
sheep and then killed himself

45 **Took odds** relied on help    58 **chines** portion of flesh
surrounding the backbone    72 **emblaze** emblazon, set forth
(as in a coat of arms)    82 **headlong** head downwards

**YORK**
Upon thine honor, is he prisoner?
**BUCKINGHAM**
Upon mine honor, he is prisoner.
**YORK**
Then, Buckingham, I do dismiss my pow'rs.
Soldiers, I thank you all; disperse yourselves;          45
Meet me tomorrow in Saint George's Field,
You shall have pay and everything you wish.
And let my sovereign, virtuous Henry,
Command my eldest son, nay, all my sons,
As pledges of my fealty and love;          50
I'll send them all as willing as I live:
Lands, goods, horse, armor, anything I have,
Is his to use, so° Somerset may die.
**BUCKINGHAM**
York, I commend this kind° submission:
We twain will go into his highness' tent.          55

*Enter KING and ATTENDANTS.*

**KING**
Buckingham, doth York intend no harm to us,
That thus he marcheth with thee arm in arm?
**YORK**
In all submission and humility
York doth present himself unto your highness.
**KING**
Then what intends these forces thou dost bring?          60
**YORK**
To heave the traitor Somerset from hence,
And fight against that monstrous rebel Cade,
Who since I heard to be discomfited.

*Enter IDEN, with Cade's head.*

**IDEN**
If one so rude and of so mean condition
May pass into the presence of a king,          65
Lo, I present your grace a traitor's head,
The head of Cade, whom I in combat slew.
**KING**
The head of Cade! Great God, how just art thou!
O, let me view his visage, being dead,
That living wrought me such exceeding trouble.          70
Tell me, my friend, art thou the man that slew him?
**IDEN**
I was, an't like your majesty.
**KING**
How art thou called? And what is thy degree?
**IDEN**
Alexander Iden, that's my name;
A poor esquire of Kent, that loves his king.          75
**BUCKINGHAM**
So please it you, my lord, 'twere not amiss
He were created knight for his good service.
**KING**
Iden, kneel down. [*He kneels.*] Rise up a knight.
We give thee for reward a thousand marks,
And will that thou henceforth attend on us.          80
**IDEN**
May Iden live to merit such a bounty,
And never live but true unto his liege!

53 **so** provided that   54 **kind** natural, proper

*Enter QUEEN and SOMERSET.*

**KING**
See, Buckingham, Somerset comes with th' queen:
Go, bid her hide him quickly from the duke.
**QUEEN**
For thousand Yorks he shall not hide his head,          85
But boldly stand and front° him to his face.
**YORK**
How now! Is Somerset at liberty?
Then, York, unloose thy long-imprisoned thoughts,
And let thy tongue be equal with thy heart.
Shall I endure the sight of Somerset?          90
False king, why hast thou broken faith with me,
Knowing how hardly° I can brook abuse?
King did I call thee? No, thou art not king,
Not fit to govern and rule multitudes,
Which dar'st not, no, nor canst not rule a traitor.          95
That head of thine doth not become a crown;
Thy hand is made to grasp a palmer's staff,°
And not to grace an awful princely scepter.
That gold must round engirt these brows of mine,
Whose smile and frown, like to Achilles' spear,          100
Is able with the change to kill and cure.°
Here is a hand to hold a scepter up
And with the same to act controlling laws.
Give place: by heaven, thou shalt rule no more
O'er him whom heaven created for thy ruler.          105
**SOMERSET**
O monstrous traitor! I arrest thee, York,
Of capital treason 'gainst the king and crown:
Obey, audacious traitor; kneel for grace.
**YORK**
Wouldst have me kneel? First let me ask of these,°
If they can brook I bow a knee to man.          110
Sirrah, call in my sons to be my bail:
[*Exit ATTENDANT.*]
I know ere they will have me go to ward,°
They'll pawn their swords for my enfranchisement.
**QUEEN**
Call hither Clifford; bid him come amain,
To say if that the bastard boys of York          115
Shall be the surety for their traitor father.
[*Exit ATTENDANT.*]
**YORK**
O blood-bespotted Neapolitan,°
Outcast of Naples, England's bloody scourge!
The sons of York, thy betters in their birth,
Shall be their father's bail; and bane to those          120
That for my surety will refuse the boys!

*Enter EDWARD and RICHARD.*

See where they come: I'll warrant they'll make it
good.

*Enter CLIFFORD and [YOUNG CLIFFORD] his son.*

86 **front** confront   92 **how hardly** with what difficulty   97
**palmer's staff** insignia of the returned pilgrim, hence emblem
of piety   100–01 **like . . . cure** Telephus, wounded by
Achilles' spear, was supposedly cured by the application of its
rust   109 **these** the troops   112 **to ward** into custody   117
**Neapolitan** traditionally murderous and fond of intrigue;
although Margaret was French, her father claimed the throne of
Naples (cf. I.i.47)

QUEEN
And here comes Clifford to deny their bail.

CLIFFORD [Kneels to KING.]
Health and all happiness to my lord the king!

YORK
I thank thee, Clifford: say, what news with thee?  125
Nay, do not fright us with an angry look:
We are thy sovereign, Clifford, kneel again;
For thy mistaking so, we pardon thee.

CLIFFORD
This is my king, York, I do not mistake;
But thou mistakes me much to think I do.  130
To Bedlam° with him! Is the man grown mad?

KING
Ay, Clifford; a bedlam° and ambitious humor
Makes him oppose himself against his king.

CLIFFORD
He is a traitor; let him to the Tower,
And chop away that factious pate of his.  135

QUEEN
He is arrested, but will not obey;
His sons, he says, shall give their words for him.

YORK
Will you not, sons?

EDWARD
Ay, noble father, if our words will serve.

RICHARD
And if words will not, then our weapons shall.  140

CLIFFORD
Why, what a brood of traitors have we here!

YORK
Look in a glass, and call thy image so.
I am thy king, and thou a false-heart traitor.
Call hither to the stake my two brave bears,
That with the very shaking of their chains  145
They may astonish° these fell-lurking° curs:
Bid Salisbury and Warwick come to me.

Enter the Earls of WARWICK and SALISBURY.

CLIFFORD
Are these thy bears? We'll bait thy bears to death,
And manacle the bear'ard° in their chains,
If thou dar'st bring them to the baiting place.  150

RICHARD
Oft have I seen a hot o'erweening cur
Run back and bite, because he was withheld;
Who, being suffered,° with° the bear's fell paw
Hath clapped his tail between his legs and cried:
And such a piece of service will you do,  155
If you oppose yourselves to match Lord Warwick.

CLIFFORD
Hence, heap of wrath, foul indigested° lump,
As crooked in thy manners as thy shape!

YORK
Nay, we shall heat you thoroughly anon.

CLIFFORD
Take heed, lest by your heat you burn yourselves.  160

KING
Why, Warwick, hath thy knee forgot to bow?
Old Salisbury, shame to thy silver hair,
Thou mad misleader of thy brainsick son!
What, wilt thou on thy deathbed play the ruffian,
And seek for sorrow with thy spectacles?°  165
O, where is faith? O, where is loyalty?
If it be banished from the frosty head,
Where shall it find a harbor in the earth?
Wilt thou go dig a grave to find out war,
And shame thine honorable age with blood?  170
Why art thou old, and want'st° experience?
Or wherefore dost abuse° it, if thou hast it?
For shame! In duty bend thy knee to me,
That bows unto the grave with mickle° age.

SALISBURY
My lord, I have considered with myself  175
The title of this most renownèd duke,
And in my conscience do repute his grace
The rightful heir to England's royal seat.

KING
Hast thou not sworn allegiance unto me?

SALISBURY  I have.  180

KING
Canst thou dispense with° heaven for such an oath?

SALISBURY
It is great sin to swear unto a sin,
But greater sin to keep a sinful oath.
Who can be bound by any solemn vow
To do a murd'rous deed, to rob a man,  185
To force a spotless virgin's chastity,
To reave° the orphan of his patrimony,
To wring the widow from her customed right,°
And have no other reason for this wrong
But that he was bound by a solemn oath?  190

QUEEN
A subtle traitor needs no sophister.°

KING
Call Buckingham, and bid him arm himself.

YORK
Call Buckingham, and all the friends thou hast,
I am resolved for death or dignity.

CLIFFORD
The first I warrant thee, if dreams prove true.  195

WARWICK
You were best to go to bed and dream again,
To keep thee from the tempest of the field.

CLIFFORD
I am resolved to bear a greater storm
Than any thou canst conjure up today;
And that I'll write upon thy burgonet,°  200
Might I but know thee by thy housèd badge.°

WARWICK
Now, by my father's badge, old Nevil's crest,
The rampant bear chained to the ragged staff,
This day I'll wear aloft my burgonet,
As on a mountain top the cedar shows  205

131 **Bedlam** Bethlehem Hospital in London, where insane persons were confined  132 **bedlam** crazy  146 **astonish** terrify;  **fell-lurking** balefully skulking  149 **bear'ard** bear ward, the keeper of bears intended for baiting in the ring  153 **suffered** loosed;  **with** stuck with  157 **indigested** shapeless

165 **spectacles** organs of sight  171 **want'st** lack  172 **abuse** misuse  174 **mickle** much, great  181 **dispense with** come to terms with  187 **reave** bereave, rob  188 **customed right** i.e., of part of her husband's estate for life  191 **sophister** cunning spokesman  200 **burgonet** helmet  201 **housèd badge** emblem of the family

That keeps his leaves in spite of any storm,
Even to affright thee with the view thereof.

CLIFFORD
And from thy burgonet I'll rend thy bear
And tread it under foot with all contempt,
Despite the bear'ard that protects the bear.          210

YOUNG CLIFFORD
And so to arms, victorious father,
To quell the rebels and their complices.

RICHARD
Fie! Charity, for shame! Speak not in spite,
For you shall sup with Jesu Christ tonight.

YOUNG CLIFFORD
Foul stigmatic,° that's more than thou canst tell.          215

RICHARD
If not in heaven, you'll surely sup in hell.          *Exeunt.*

[Scene II. *Saint Albans.*]

*Enter* WARWICK.

WARWICK
Clifford of Cumberland, 'tis Warwick calls:
And if thou dost not hide thee from the bear,
Now, when the angry trumpet sounds alarum,
And dead men's cries do fill the empty air,
Clifford, I say, come forth and fight with me!          5
Proud northern lord, Clifford of Cumberland,
Warwick is hoarse with calling thee to arms.

*Enter* YORK.

How now, my noble lord! What, all afoot?

YORK
The deadly handed Clifford slew my steed,
But match to match I have encountered him,          10
And made a prey for carrion kites and crows
Even of the bonny beast he loved so well.

*Enter* CLIFFORD.

WARWICK
Of one or both of us the time is come.

YORK
Hold, Warwick, seek thee out some other chase,°
For I myself must hunt this deer to death.          15

WARWICK
Then, nobly, York; 'tis for a crown thou fight'st.
As I intend, Clifford, to thrive today,
It grieves my soul to leave thee unassailed.
          *Exit* WARWICK.

CLIFFORD
What see'st thou in me, York? Why dost thou pause?

YORK
With thy brave bearing should I be in love,          20
But that thou art so fast mine enemy.

CLIFFORD
Nor should thy prowess want praise and esteem,
But that 'tis shown ignobly, and in treason.

YORK
So let it help me now against thy sword,
As I in justice and true right express it.          25

CLIFFORD
My soul and body on the action both!

YORK
A dreadful lay!° Address° thee instantly.

*Alarums, and they fight, and* YORK *kills* CLIFFORD.

CLIFFORD   La fin couronne les œuvres.°          [*Dies.*]

YORK
Thus war hath given thee peace, for thou art still.
Peace with his soul, heaven, if it be thy will!          30
          *Exit* YORK.

*Enter* YOUNG CLIFFORD.

YOUNG CLIFFORD
Shame and confusion! All is on the rout;
Fear frames disorder, and disorder wounds
Where it should guard. O war, thou son of hell,
Whom angry heavens do make their minister,
Throw in the frozen bosoms of our part          35
Hot coals of vengeance! Let no soldier fly.
He that is truly dedicate to war
Hath no self-love; nor he that loves himself
Hath not essentially, but by circumstance,°
The name of valor. [*Sees his dead father.*] O, let the
   vile world end,          40
And the premisèd° flames of the last day
Knit earth and heaven together!
Now let the general trumpet blow his blast,
Particularities° and petty sounds
To cease! Wast thou ordained, dear father,          45
To lose thy youth in peace, and to achieve
The silver livery of advisèd age,
And, in thy reverence and thy chair days, thus
To die in ruffian battle? Even at this sight
My heart is turned to stone: and while 'tis mine,          50
It shall be stony. York not our old men spares;
No more will I their babes: tears virginal
Shall be to me even as the dew to fire,
And beauty, that the tyrant oft reclaims,
Shall to my flaming wrath be oil and flax.          55
Henceforth I will not have to do with pity:
Meet I an infant of the house of York,
Into as many gobbets will I cut it
As wild Medea young Absyrtus did:°
In cruelty will I seek out my fame.          60
Come, thou new ruin of old Clifford's house:
As did Aeneas old Anchises bear,
So bear I thee upon my manly shoulders;
But then Aeneas bare a living load,
Nothing so heavy as these woes of mine.          65
          *Exit* YOUNG CLIFFORD *with his father.*

*Enter the Duke of* SOMERSET *and* RICHARD *fighting,*
*and* RICHARD *kills him under the sign of the Castle,*
*in Saint Albans.*

RICHARD
So, lie thou there;

215 **stigmatic** branded criminal, hence a deformed person
(branded by God, as if in punishment)
**V.ii.14 chase** game

27 **lay** wager; **Address** prepare   28 **La . . . œuvres** The end
crowns the work   39 **not . . . circumstance** not by nature,
but by accident   41 **premisèd** predestined   44 **Particularities**
trifles   59 **As . . . did** Medea, fleeing with Jason from Colchis,
murdered her brother Absyrtus and cut the body into pieces,
so that her father would be delayed in his pursuit

For underneath an alehouse' paltry sign,
The Castle in Saint Alban's, Somerset
Hath made the wizard famous in his death.
Sword, hold thy temper; heart, be wrathful still:                70
Priests pray for enemies, but princes kill.                *Exit.*

*Fight. Excursions.° Enter* KING, QUEEN, *and others.*

QUEEN
Away, my lord! You are slow; for shame, away!
KING
Can we outrun the heavens? Good Margaret, stay.
QUEEN
What are you made of? You'll nor fight nor fly:
Now is it manhood, wisdom, and defense,                75
To give the enemy way, and to secure us
By what we can, which can no more but fly.

*Alarum afar off.*

If you be ta'en, we then should see the bottom
Of all our fortunes: but if we haply 'scape—
As well we may, if not through your neglect—                80
We shall to London get, where you are loved
And where this breach now in our fortunes made
May readily be stopped.

*Enter* [YOUNG] CLIFFORD.

YOUNG CLIFFORD
But that my heart's on future mischief set,
I would speak blasphemy ere bid you fly:                85
But fly you must; uncurable discomfit°
Reigns in the hearts of all our present parts.
Away, for your relief, and we will live
To see their day and them our fortune give.
Away, my lord, away!                *Exeunt.* 90

[Scene III. *Fields near Saint Albans.*]

*Alarum. Retreat. Enter* YORK, RICHARD, WARWICK,
*and* SOLDIERS, *with drum and colors.*

YORK
Of Salisbury, who can report of him,
That winter lion, who in rage forgets

---

71 s.d. **Excursions** turbulent action    86 **discomfit** defeat

---

Agèd contusions and all brush of time,
And, like a gallant in the brow of youth,
Repairs him with occasion?° This happy day                5
Is not itself, nor have we won one foot,
If Salisbury be lost.
RICHARD                My noble father,
Three times today I holp° him to his horse,
Three times bestrid° him; thrice I led him off,
Persuaded him from any further act:                10
But still, where danger was, still there I met him;
And like rich hangings in a homely house,
So was his will in his old feeble body.
But, noble as he is, look where he comes.

*Enter* SALISBURY.

Now, by my sword, well hast thou fought today.                15
SALISBURY
By th' mass, so did we all. I thank you, Richard:
God knows how long it is I have to live,
And it hath pleased him that three times today
You have defended me from imminent death.
Well, lords, we have not got that which we have:°                20
'Tis not enough our foes are this time fled,
Being opposites of such repairing nature.°
YORK
I know our safety is to follow them;
For, as I hear, the king is fled to London,
To call a present court of parliament.                25
Let us pursue him ere the writs go forth.
What says Lord Warwick? Shall we after them?
WARWICK
After them! Nay, before them, if we can.
Now, by my hand, lords, 'twas a glorious day:
Saint Albans battle won by famous York                30
Shall be eternized in all age to come.
Sound drum and trumpets, and to London all:
And more such days as these to us befall!                *Exeunt.*

---

V.iii.5 **Repairs . . . occasion** revives with opportunity
8 **holp** helped    9 **bestrid** straddled (to defend)    20 **we . . .
have** we have not secured what we have acquired    22 **repairing
nature** powers of recovery

# THE THIRD PART OF
# HENRY THE SIXTH

EDITED BY MILTON CRANE

## Introduction

From 1642 until late in the nineteenth century no performances of the uncontaminated Shakespearean dramas [2 and 3 Henry VI] seem to have taken place; and then only in one revival in London of Part Two and one at Stratford of both parts. In the present century they met with similar neglect. In America the plays have suffered even more nearly total oblivion.[1]

Thus wrote C. B. Young, as recently as 1952. But the whirligig of Time, as Malvolio among others discovered, brings in his revenges. In the past several years more persons have seen the three parts of Henry VI than had ever seen any one of the plays in all the centuries of their existence. The British Broadcasting Corporation has twice filmed and exhibited these plays (once in a cycle with Richard II, Richard III, 1–2 Henry IV, and Henry V, under the general title An Age of Kings; and once with Richard III alone). Both these cycles have been shown widely in Great Britain, Canada, and the United States. In addition, Henry VI, in parts or as a trilogy, has been performed at Stratford-upon-Avon, at Stratford, Ontario, and at Stratford, Connecticut, and was performed at the two latter festivals as recently as the summer of 1966.

How is one to explain so striking a revival of interest? Or, more strictly speaking, how is one to explain this unprecedented wave of enthusiasm for plays that historically have had many more detractors than admirers—for plays, indeed, that have only in recent years been generally accepted as Shakespeare's? The Henry VI cycle has been roundly criticized, over the centuries, as 'prentice work, a primitive and violent chronicle of blood, of interest only to scholars. Not that anything like a critical consensus can be said to exist—Richard III, which has often been deplored by the judicious for its bloody melodrama, has even more often run a close second in popularity to Hamlet. Nor should this be a cause for astonishment; Richard III, like 3 Henry VI, shares many of the most notorious (and popular) qualities of television drama.

For, though the framework of Henry VI is serious, moral, and didactic—a history, on the one hand, of France's efforts to free herself from English domination and, on the other, of the hideous social and political convulsions that we call the Wars of the Roses—these annals of an age of anarchy are full of thrilling and gruesome details calculated to delight the heart of a groundling: the rise and fall of the witch Joan of Arc; the rebellion and death of Jack Cade; the sorcery of the Duchess of Gloucester; the baiting and murder of the Duke of York, the young Earl of Rutland, the Prince of Wales, and the unfortunate King Henry himself. And, of course, the whole bloody feud of York and Lancaster is Shakespeare's inspired anticipation of the Western movie. One must not, therefore, be astonished that Shakespeare's Grand Guignol has retained its power to charm, particularly younger spectators.

Obviously the history plays are by no means alone in appealing to the audience's appetite for violence and excitement. 3 Henry VI is hardly more gratifying in this respect than Macbeth or King Lear, not to speak of the matchless Titus Andronicus, in many respects Shakespeare's most shocking creation. Shakespeare pays a high price, however, for the monstrous effects that he lovingly devises for the latter play: it is the danger that the audience's frisson may dissolve into helpless laughter, as when Titus enjoins the mutilated Lavinia, "Bear thou my hand, sweet wench, between thy teeth."

Titus Andronicus and 3 Henry VI are alike in another important respect: until recent years, they were little known to either the common reader or the common play-goer. Granted that neither is a great monument of Shakespeare's art, both are nevertheless consistently interesting and lively works by a gifted professional playwright; their structure is clear and straightforward, and they provide gratifying roles for leading actors and actresses. For the more sophisticated, 3 Henry VI reserves yet another reward—that of watching the early development of a major character, Richard III, from his beginnings as a strong, courageous, admittedly brutal, but not yet frankly villainous figure to the monster who will meet deserved destruction on Bosworth Field.

[1] "The Stage History of King Henry VI, Parts II and III," The Third Part of King Henry VI, The New Cambridge Shakespeare, ed. John Dover Wilson (1952), pp. xxxix–xl.

Civil war is, as it were, the expression in political terms of the anarchic, heedless, and all but suicidal rage that consumes, at one time or another, most of the leading characters of these plays. The scene in which Henry overhears the monologues of the son who has killed his father and of the father who has killed his son, ending in their formal but deeply moving lament, has been often and justly praised; in its terrible anonymity, this masque of death seems to come straight out of a morality play. The fact that these miserable men have unwittingly murdered and robbed their own kin is but another manifestation of the infernal forces that the Yorkists and Lancastrians have ignorantly loosed upon an appalled and helpless populace.[2]

Willard Farnham has brilliantly summarized the cumulative impact of the three parts of *Henry VI*:

Throughout the trilogy we follow the ill-fated kingship of Henry, but the most constant theme is England torn by civil war. Coming and going upon the scene are men and women who hope to profit by the bitter animosities of the struggle, who have their little day of rising ambition and success, and who quickly fall. The civil war is a forced draft fanning all those fires of worldly aspiration which the ascetic tragedy of the Middle Ages sought to quench. It favors all the criminal propensities in ambitious humanity. England as pictured under its influence is very much like the world pictured by medieval Contempt, a trackless forest filled with wild beasts and robbers, where the struggle for place is merely madness with horrible

accompaniments Sometimes the good man falls (Humphrey, Duke of Gloucester); sometimes the evil (Suffolk, destroyer of Gloucester). Henry himself is in it all, yet not of it all. He is a spiritual opposite to those around him who have lusts for power and domination; he loves peace and he has manly pity for suffering. He is hardly drawn as a weak man, and he is certainly not drawn as basely or miserably weak. He is simply a king who cannot use the strong hand of domination because brutality repels him. The ironical result is that cruel things happen in his realm which might never have happened if he had been willing to use cruelty on his own account in taking the reins of government—Duke Humphrey's murder, for example.[3]

Although, to be sure, mankind throughout its history has denounced all war as a plague, civil war has by common consent been the form most deeply dreaded—as *3 Henry VI* makes clear—for setting fathers, brothers, and sons against one another. Moreover, not only does all semblance of reason vanish when every man sets his face against every other man, but the fear persists (and experience seems to bear it out) that whatever peace may be concluded will be at best illusory and of short duration.

A kind of war that violates all normal expectations may well lead, not illogically, to the destruction of the very fabric of society. Even among warlords—perhaps one should say, especially among warlords—the one virtue that is most greatly honored is loyalty. It is the supreme political virtue. But in the world of Henry VI loyalty is the exception, not the rule. *3 Henry VI* begins with Henry's pusillanimous acceptance of the Duke of York as his heir apparent (provided that Henry is permitted to occupy the throne in peace as long as he lives) in place of his legitimate son and heir, the Prince of Wales. Here the theme of betrayal is sounded, and most disgracefully, with a father's cowardly disinheritance of his blameless son. Shakespeare is skillfully preparing us for the ever-increasing violence of Margaret's mood and her determination to wreak a terrible revenge on the Yorkists.

---

[2] This celebrated scene merits our attention for other reasons as well. It seems clear that it bears a significant relation to Sackville and Norton's *Gorboduc* (1561), one of the most explicit warnings directed to Elizabeth and designed to persuade her to take steps to avoid the danger of civil war. Miss Joan Rees has with justice pointed out (in "A Passage in *Henry VI, Part 3*," *Notes and Queries*, 199 [May, 1954], 195–96) that the traditional attribution to Hall's *Chronicle* of the major influence on Shakespeare in the composition of this scene ("This conflict was in maner vnnaturall, for in it the sonne fought against the father, the brother against the brother, the nephew against the vncle, and the tenaũt against his lord . . ." [Hall, p. 256]) probably requires drastic modification. In the concluding and summarizing speech of Eubulus in *Gorboduc*, the following passage appears:

All right and lawe shall cease . . .
The wiues shall suffer rape, the maides defloured,
And children fatherlesse shall weepe and waile.
With fire and sworde thy natiue folke shall perishe.
One kinsman shall bereaue an-others life;
The father shall vnwitting slay the sonne;
The sonne shall slay the sire and know it not.
(V.ii.204, 209–14)

Miss Rees goes on to say:

Amongst the touches which give to the last two acts of *Gorboduc* a greater vitality than is to be found in the first three, is a passage in Eubulus' speech in Act V scene 2 l. 180 to the end . . . in which he describes, with an almost lyrical intensity, the horrors of civil war. This passage . . . stands out even today and it is obvious that, because of its passionate realisation of its subject, it would be even more potent to an audience for whom the danger of civil war loomed large. . . . It may be that Hall's chronicle is at the back of this speech but the treatment of the theme in *Gorboduc* because it is so vividly realised is perhaps more likely to have stirred an imaginative response in Shakespeare than the cooler record of the chronicle. More elements of Shakespeare's scene are present in the *Gorboduc* lines than in the Hall passage: the double episode of father killing son and son father; the idea that they acted in ignorance (Shakespeare's line 69, the son's words, "Pardon me, God, I knew not what I did!" echo "The sonne shall slay the sire and

know it not"); the emphasis on the personal tragedy in the lives affected which the *Gorboduc* speech goes on to stress further and which Hall subordinates to consideration of "the puyssance of thys realme". In addition, the whole context of the passage in *Gorboduc*, with its bitter recognition that:

These are the plages, when murder is the meane
To make new heires unto the royall crowne

is close to the theme of the Henry VI trilogy and might therefore be of especial interest to Shakespeare.

It might also be noted that the situation described in Eubulus' lines and in Shakespeare's scene has no parallel in *Gorboduc* as a whole. The moralizing and generalizing message of this *raisonneur's* speech, directed at Elizabeth, is a warning against civil war, not a definition of the dangerous consequences of failing to name an heir in time.

Finally, despite the admitted importance of Hall's influence on Shakespeare's history plays, is it not highly probable that Shakespeare, in his early days as a tragic dramatist and a writer of history plays, should have looked back three decades to the honorable ancestor of all English tragedies and history plays? From this time forth, *Gorboduc* will be restricted to academic interest, at best; but for a moment it provided the young Shakespeare with a valuable suggestion.

[3] *The Medieval Heritage of Elizabethan Tragedy* (1936), pp. 385–86.

Betrayal is soon heaped on betrayal. In I.ii, a few short speeches by Richard suffice to persuade his father, the Duke of York, to break his oath to Henry and to prepare a conspiracy to unseat him. But before the duke can begin to organize his plot, he learns that Margaret with twenty thousand men intends to besiege him in his castle; and so he is relieved of any moral dilemma that may have troubled him. In due course, the captured duke is murdered by Margaret and Young Clifford, after they have tormented him with a paper crown and a handkerchief dipped in his son Rutland's blood. "*Vae victis!*" is the only principle of war that these ferocious antagonists recognize. York's death, strictly speaking, proceeds immediately from unspeakable brutality, though ultimately from treachery; but the distinction can interest only a logician. The savagery with which each party uses the other is such as to call in question the pretensions to chivalric ideals of all these gently born butchers.

The baiting and slaughter of York is paralleled in II.vi by that of Clifford, who falls into the hands of the Yorkists moments before he dies of the wounds he has received at Towton. But his enemies, not yet aware that he is dead, play out a grisly comedy in which they threaten the dead man with torture, mockingly call on him to repent, and at last cut off his head to fix on York gates in place of their father's.

Meanwhile the problem of loyalty is elaborated in III.i. Henry is recognized and taken prisoner by two keepers, who pride themselves on their loyalty to Edward:

> You are the king King Edward hath deposed;
> And we his subjects sworn in all allegiance
> Will apprehend you as his enemy.    (III.i.69–71)

Henry attempts, unsuccessfully, to argue himself free:

> I was anointed king at nine months old;
> My father and my grandfather were kings,
> And you were sworn true subjects unto me:
> And tell me, then, have you not broke your oaths?
>    (III.i.76–79)

The First Keeper knows an argument worth two of Henry's:

>       No;
> For we were subjects but while you were king.
>    (III.i.80–81)

The futility and absurdity of this disputation are expressed in Henry's rueful conclusion: "Such is the lightness of you common men" (III.i.89), though the unspoken point is clear enough: the keepers attempt to find ways to rationalize their yielding to the rule of might, whereas their betters (with rare exceptions) feel no compunctions whatever.

Richard's great set piece (III.ii.124–95) announces his grand design to win the crown for himself once he has seen "the lustful Edward's titles buried" and has disposed of

> Clarence, Henry, and his son young Edward,
> And all the unlooked-for issue of their bodies.

He concludes with a self-revelation for which nothing thus far in the trilogy has prepared us:

> Why, I can smile, and murder whiles I smile,
> And cry, "Content" to that which grieves my heart,
> And wet my cheeks with artificial tears,
> And frame my face to all occasions.
> I'll drown more sailors than the mermaid shall;
> I'll slay more gazers than the basilisk;
> I'll play the orator as well as Nestor,
> Deceive more slily than Ulysses could,
> And, like a Sinon, take another Troy.
> I can add colors to the chameleon,
> Change shapes with Proteus for advantages,
> And set the murderous Machiavel to school.
> Can I do this, and cannot get a crown?
> Tut, were it farther off, I'll pluck it down.    (III.ii.182–95)

Richard is the incomparable symbol of treachery and deceit in all forms: cant, hypocrisy, corruption, secret murder, usurpation. His last act in *3 Henry VI*, after murdering Henry in the Tower, is to give his brother Edward's infant son what he himself calls a Judas kiss.

In this world of traitors Richard is supreme but by no means unique. In III.iii Warwick arrives at the French court to negotiate the marriage of Edward with Bona, King Lewis' sister. But Warwick has been betrayed by the womanizer Edward, whose passions have triumphed over his sense of *realpolitik* and have led him to marry Lady Elizabeth Grey; furious at his loss of face, Warwick promptly changes sides, and Lewis avenges the slight to his sister by according Margaret the aid she has so far sought in vain.

As the play approaches its climax, the Lancastrian forces move up under their leaders: Oxford, Montague, Somerset, and Clarence. "Wind-changing Warwick" confidently awaits Clarence's formal greeting, but now the most dramatic moment of treachery arrives: Warwick's son-in-law, subverted by Richard, contemptuously takes the red rose from his hat and throws it at Warwick, proclaiming his return to the Yorkist party. But worse lies ahead. Edward, in his triumph, proclaims an amnesty for Prince Edward, and there seems to be no reason to doubt the sincerity of this chivalrous offer. The young prince, however, tactlessly speaks his mind to his enemies, and, before the eyes of Margaret, is stabbed to death by Edward, Richard, and Clarence, precisely as young Rutland was stabbed by Clifford, and York by Clifford and Margaret. Each step in this blood feud proceeds inexorably from the preceding one. The anguished Margaret, witnessing her son's death, entreats Richard: "O, kill me too!" and Richard seems of a mind to grant her request. But Edward, belatedly aware of what he has done, stays him: "Hold, Richard, hold; for we have done too much" (V.v.43).

Meanwhile Richard, who has left the scene of carnage with a berserker's cry: "The Tower! The Tower!", is ensuring that Henry, who has of course long since ceased to play any but a choric role in the descending action of the tragedy, will not live to see his prophecies fulfilled. Richard, in the full exercise of his powers as king-maker and king-destroyer, affords us a foretaste of his masterworks of villainy in *Richard III*. What the audience does not yet know is that the demidevil Richard—whose great speeches of self-revelation in *3 Henry VI* are stylistically and dramatically of a piece with the fantastic unmasking speech of Aaron the Moor in *Titus Andronicus*—will presently reveal himself to be one of Shakespeare's most remarkable and most accomplished humorists. Indeed, one can hardly account for the popularity of *Richard III*, and particularly for the allure of Richard himself, except by invoking the hero-villain's devastating charm, which is compounded of enchanting audacity and a disarming and cynical refusal to take himself altogether seriously. In this, as in all else, he is a master dissembler and actor, and as such fittingly inherits not only the crown but the play itself.

Perhaps inevitably, one is inclined to think of the three parts of *Henry VI* as forming a whole, unified by themes, characters, and structural devices. The degree of unity in these plays is, however, dangerously easy to exaggerate. The characters whose lives and fortunes link the three parts —King Henry, Margaret, and Richard, Duke of Gloucester —play significant roles in each of the parts, but their personalities change and develop. Thus Henry begins as an immature, saintly, love-besotted figure; becomes more saintly and more ineffectual; and dies a victim of the fiendlike Richard after making some abortive efforts to regain command of the Lancastrian forces. He is a consistent character, whose life and death set a standard of Christian charity and idealism that permits us to judge the savagery and brutality of the world into which he has been unfortunate enough to be born. On the other hand, the fact that the reign of Henry was an unmitigated disaster was perfectly clear to every Tudor historian and moralist, and men who lived in the last decade—or, indeed, any decade—of Elizabeth's reign had no difficulty in applying the meaning of this disaster to their own situation. (The queen herself was by no means the last to draw such historical parallels. "Know ye not that I am Richard the Second?" she demanded, after Essex' followers had caused Shakespeare's *Richard II* to be revived on the eve of their leader's ill-fated rebellion.)

Henry's pitiful efforts to exculpate himself in *3 Henry VI* (I.i) when his enemies the Yorkists taunt him for having lost the lands won by his heroic father, the great Henry V, recall that terrible piece of folk wisdom from *Ecclesiastes*: "Woe to thee, O land, when thy king is a child!" Admittedly it was not the infant Henry but his protector, the "good Duke" Humphrey of Gloucester, who bore the responsibility for the loss of France. But the judgment of history, however unfairly, inevitably seeks the nearest scapegoat; and the judgment is found against Henry, in whose name the follies were committed. (Henry passes in silence, of course, over his wedding gift of Anjou and Maine to his father-in-law Reignier [René], King of Naples. These provinces, much more than the lands lost by war, were fresh affronts in the minds of the Yorkists and the chief subject of their reproaches to Henry.)

Henry's queen, Margaret, likewise undergoes transformation in the course of the trilogy. She appears first in *1 Henry VI*, in one of the concluding scenes of the play, as the prisoner of Suffolk, whom she has already bewitched. She is a little too practical and matter-of-fact to be entirely believable as the demure and lovely maid that she seems to her infatuated captor; she already suggests something of the judgment that Hall was to pass on her:

> This woman excelled all others as well in beautie and fauor, as in wit and pollicie, and was of stomack and corage. more like to a man, then a woman.[4]

And she finds little difficulty in accommodating herself to her situation as the captive of the apologetic Suffolk: "Tush, women have been captivate ere now" (V.iii.107). In fact, the entire interview between Margaret and Suffolk often seems to hesitate on the edge of comedy.

The Margaret of *2 Henry VI*, on the other hand, is a virago and a meddler in matters of state, who shamelessly takes Suffolk as her lover and contrives the downfall of the Duchess of Gloucester and the murder of the duke. In *3 Henry VI* she becomes the infernal Ate in good apparel, a murderess who with her own hand plunges the sword into the captive York. The order of nature being so violently disturbed, it follows that Margaret's punishment must be equally terrible. This is the measure of what has happened to England in the course of Shakespeare's trilogy: the weakness, uncertainty, and confusion of *1 Henry VI* give way to the deep social disorders signaled by the peasant rebellion of *2 Henry VI* and ultimately to the total anarchy of *3 Henry VI*. Now the time is near for the inferno over which Richard III will reign until he is overthrown by Richmond, who will rule as Henry VII. Hall thus sums up the restoration of order by the first Tudor:

> Although by this eleccion of wyse and graue councellers all thinges semed to be brought to a good & perfight conclusion, yet there lacked a wrest to the harpe to set all the strynges in a monacorde and tune which was the matrimony to be fineshed betwene the kynge and the lady Elizabeth daughter to kyng Edward, which lyke a good prynce accordyng to his othe and promes, he did both solempnise and cōsummate in brief tyme after, that is to saye on the xviij daye of Ianuary. By reason of whiche mariage peace was thought to discende oute of heaũe into England, consideryng that the lynes of Lancastre & Yorke, being both noble families equivalēt in ryches, fame and honour, were now brought into one knot and connexed together, of whose two bodyes one heyre might succede, which after their tyme should peaceably rule and enioye the whole monarchy and realme of Englanc.[5]

Such, then, was the fragile peace and unity that emerged from the "long jars" (Ben Jonson's words) of York and Lancaster. Small wonder that Shakespeare, like many another Elizabethan, was far more deeply impressed and dismayed, in retrospect, by the holocaust of the Wars of the Roses than by its resolution. Small wonder, too, that Elizabeth thought nothing more important than the avoidance, by policy, trimming, or coercion, of such civil wars as Shakespeare has memorably re-created in this trilogy of *Henry VI*.

---

[4] Hall, *Chronicle*, ed Sir Henry Ellis (1809), p. 205.
[5] *Ibid.*, pp. 424–25.

## A NOTE ON THE SOURCES

Shakespeare drew on two principal sources for *Henry VI, Part Three*, as he had done earlier for *Henry VI, Parts One and Two*. These were two of the major historical works of sixteenth-century England: Edward Hall's chronicle *The Union of the Two Noble and Illustre Families of Lancaster & Yorke* . . . (1548); modern edition, H. Ellis (1809); and the second edition (1587) of Raphael Holinshed's *Chronicles of England, Scotlande, and Irelande;* modern edition, H. Ellis (six volumes, 1807–08), and several abridged editions, notably W. G. Boswell-Stone, *Shakspere's Holinshed* (1896) and Allardyce and Josephine Nicoll, eds., *Holinshed's Chronicle as Used in Shakespeare's Plays* (1927). Shakespeare's indebtedness to Holinshed has of course long been recognized, but modern scholarship has tended to emphasize ever more strongly the importance of Hall's work, both as a direct influence on Shakespeare and as an indirect influence through Holinshed.

All the chroniclers are, to say the least, exceedingly casual about borrowing from one another's work; and when they copy hastily or carelessly, as they not infrequently do, the modern reader's best hope of recovering his author's original meaning is to compare the text with that of an earlier chronicle. Students of Shakespeare are likely to find most interesting and helpful, among the earlier chronicles, *The Brut or the Chronicles of England*, ed. Friedrich W. D. Brie, Part I, Early English Text Society, Original Series 131 (1906; reprinted 1960), and Part II, Original Series 136 (1908); Polydore Vergil's *English History* (Henry VI, Edward IV, and Richard III), ed. Sir Henry Ellis, The Camden Society, Volume 21 (1844); and Ranulph Higden's *Polychronicon*, translated by John Trevisa (the chronicle completed to 1461 by William Caxton, who published the *Polychronicon* in 1482); modern edition, Churchill Babington and Reverend J. R. Lumby (nine volumes; 1865–86).

"Hall's chief importance," E. M. W. Tillyard has well observed, "is that he is the first English chronicle writer to show in all its completeness that new moralising of history which came in with the waning of the Middle Ages, the weakening of the Church, and the rise of nationalism. And the special literary importance of this feat is to have introduced a sense of drama into his manner of expression . . . the sense of the moral concatenation of great events: moral as against psychological drama."[6] The subject of Hall's chronicle was the union of the houses of Lancaster and York, a union which was achieved only after England had suffered the convulsions of civil war, the memory and fear of which haunt Shakespeare's plays as they haunted Elizabethan Englishmen. Disunion came in with Henry Bolingbroke; union was restored by Henry VII and Henry VIII (Hall calls the latter "the vndubitate flower and very heire of both the sayd linages"). The history of the intervening years, as Tillyard and others have noted, may be read in the titles of Hall's chapters:

    i. The vnquiet tyme of kyng Hēry the Fowerth.
    ii. The victorious actes of kyng Henry the v.
    iii. The troubleous season of kyng Henry the vi.
    iiii. The prosperous reigne of kyng Edward the iiij.

    v. The pitifull life of kyng Edward the v.
    vi. The tragicall doynges of kyng Richard the iij.
    vii. The politike gouernaunce of kyng Henry the vij.
    viii. The triumphant reigne of king Henry the viij.[7]

Throughout his history plays Shakespeare repeatedly expounded these few essential ideas: that evil must be punished and expiated, that goodness will be rewarded, that piety cannot prevail unless conjoined with strength (thus the ineffectual saintliness of Henry VI is sharply contrasted with the more muscular Christianity of Henry V). Both Hall and Holinshed provided Shakespeare with clear and vivid portraits of his principal characters; and Shakespeare, as usual, missed no significant hint, no illuminating detail, in the chronicles. At the same time, he adroitly combined and abridged his materials so as to heighten dramatic effect. Thus, both Hall and Holinshed describe how Clifford caused a paper crown to be set on the severed head of Richard, Duke of York. Shakespeare, in contrast, makes the scene in which Queen Margaret, Clifford, and the other Lancastrians actually torment and kill York (I.iv) one of the most powerful episodes of this harrowing play.

## A NOTE ON THE TEXT

*Henry VI, Part Three* has come down to us in two major texts: the so-called "bad quarto" (actually a "bad octavo"), called Q—*The true Tragedie of Richard/Duke of Yorke, and the death of/good King Henrie the Sixt,/with the whole contention betweene/the two Houses Lancaster/and Yorke, as it was sundrie times/acted by the Right Honoura-/ble the Earle of Pem-/brooke his seruants*—and the First Folio of 1623 (called F). Q, which is about two thirds the length of F and imperfect in numerous respects, was published in 1595 by P[eter] S[hort] for Thomas Millington. The copy was not entered in the Stationers' Register. Q was long considered (principally on the authority of the noted eighteenth-century editor Edmond Malone) to be the source of Shakespeare's play; but in the past four decades there has come into fairly general acceptance the view that Q represents a reported version (perhaps by the actors who played Warwick and Clifford) of the text of an early production of the play that was later printed as F. Such, at any rate, is the opinion of the most important modern editors of the play (A. S. Cairncross, John Dover Wilson, George Lyman Kittredge, and Peter Alexander, among others). The technical studies that were largely responsible for tipping the balance in favor of this view include J. S. Smart, *Shakespeare: Truth and Tradition* (1928); Madeleine Doran, *Henry VI, Parts II and III* (1928); and Peter Alexander, *Shakespeare's Henry VI and Richard III* (1929). A. S. Cairncross' introductions to his Arden editions of *Henry VI, Part Two* and *Henry VI, Part Three* summarize much useful information bearing on the relation between *Henry VI, Part Two* and *The First Part of the Contention betwixt the two famous Houses of Yorke and Lancaster* . . . and between *Henry VI, Part Three* and *The true Tragedie of Richard Duke of Yorke*. Apart from the initial "*Actus Primus. Scœna Prima,*"

[6] *Shakespeare's History Plays* (1944), p. 42.

[7] Hall's *Chronicle* (1809 edition), p. viii.

no act or scene divisions appear in F, and none at all appear in Q. The act and scene divisions in the present edition are those of the Globe edition. All divisions and stage directions that have been added are enclosed in square brackets.

A number of the stage directions in Q, like stage directions in other Shakespeare quartos, reflect stage business in actual performance, for example:

Enter *Richard* Duke of Yorke, The Earle of *Warwicke*, *The Duke of* Norffolke, *Marquis Montague, Edward Earle of March, Crookeback Richard,* and the yong *Earle of Rutland,* with Drumme and Souldiers, with white Roses in their hats.[8]

Sound a Parlie, and *Richard* and *Clarence* whispers togither, and then Clarence takes his red Rose out of his hat, and throws it at *Warwike.*[9]

Alarmes to the battell, *Yorke* flies, then the chambers be discharged. Then enter the king, *Cla. & Glo.* & the rest, & make a great shout, and crie, for *Yorke,* for *Yorke,* and then the *Queene* is taken, & the prince, & *Oxf. & Sum.* and then found and enter all againe.[10]

In the second direction quoted above, some effort has obviously been made to motivate Clarence's betrayal of Warwick—for which F does nothing to prepare us—and the stage business here echoes the accounts in the chronicles. Another stage direction of interest is at III.i, which reads: "Enter Sinklo, and Humfrey, with Crosse-bowes in their hands." (The quarto reads: "Enter two keepers with bow and arrowes.") The names Sinklo and Humfrey appear

[8] W. W. Greg, ed., *The True Tragedy of Richard Duke of York (Henry the Sixth, Part III),* Shakespeare Quarto Facsimiles No. 11 (1958), Sig. A2.
[9] *Ibid.,* Sig. E2.
[10] *Ibid.,* Sig. E4.

to be those of actors in Shakespeare's company—John Sincler, and Humphrey Jeffes—incorporated into the text by error. Possibly Shakespeare wrote the names as he composed, possibly a prompter added them to the company's copy. "Gabriel" in the stage direction at I.ii.47 is probably a similar error, naming the actor Gabriel Spencer.

Speech prefixes have been silently regularized, and the position of a few stage directions slightly altered. The following list includes emendations and corrections of F. In each case, the altered reading appears first, in boldface; the original reading follows, in roman. When the alteration is derived from Q, that fact is indicated.

I.i.69 **Exeter** [Q] Westm.   105 **Thy** [Q] My   259 **stay with** [Q] stay   261 **from** [Q] to   273 **s.d. Exeunt** Exit
I.ii.47 **Enter [a Messenger]** [Q] Enter   75 **s.d. Exeunt** Exit
I.iv.180 **Exeunt** Exit
II.i.113 **Ard . . . thought** [Q; F omits]   131 **an idle** [Q] a lazie   158 **makes** make   182 **amain** [Q; F omits]
II.ii.89–92 **Since . . . in** [F assigns to Clarence]   133 **Richard** [Q] War.   172 **deniest** [Q] denied'st
II.v.119 **Even** Men
II.vi.43 **See who it is** [Q; F gives to Richard]   58 **his** [Q] is
III.i.s.d. **Enter [two keepers]** [Q] Enter Sinklo, and Humfrey   12 **Second Keeper** Sink. [i.e., First Keeper]   17 **wast** was   24 **thee, sour adversity** the sower Aduersaries   55 **thou that** [Q] thou
III.ii.123 **honorably** [Q] honourable
III.iii.124 **eternal** [Q] externall   156 **peace** [added in F2]   228 **I'll** [Q] I
IV.i.89–90 [three lines in F, ending **thee, words, them**]   93 **thy** [Q] the
IV.ii.15 **towns** Towne
IV.iii.64 **s.d. Exeunt** exit
IV.iv.17 **wean** waine
IV.v.4 **stands** stand   8 **Comes** Come   21 **ship** shipt
IV.vi.55 **be confiscate** confiscate
IV.viii.s.d. **Exeter** Somerset
V.i.75 **s.d.** (see note in text)   78 **an** in
V.v.s.d. **Clarence . . . prisoners** Queene, Clarence, Oxford, Somerset   77 **butcher** butcher Richard   90 **s.d. Exeunt** Exit
V.vii.5 **renowned** [Q] Renowne   30 **King Edward** Cla.;   **Thanks** [Q] Thanke   38 **Reignier** Reynard

# THE THIRD PART OF
# HENRY THE SIXTH

[Dramatis Personae

KING HENRY THE SIXTH
EDWARD *Prince of Wales, his son*
LEWIS XI *King of France*
DUKE OF SOMERSET
DUKE OF EXETER
EARL OF OXFORD
EARL OF NORTHUMBERLAND
EARL OF WESTMORELAND
LORD CLIFFORD
RICHARD PLANTAGENET *Duke of York*
EDWARD *Earl of March, afterward King Edward IV*
EDMUND *Earl of Rutland*
GEORGE *afterward Duke of Clarence*
RICHARD *afterward Duke of Gloucester*

} *his sons*

DUKE OF NORFOLK
EARL OF WARWICK
MARQUESS OF MONTAGUE
EARL OF PEMBROKE
LORD HASTINGS
LORD STAFFORD
SIR JOHN MORTIMER
SIR HUGH MORTIMER

} *uncles to the Duke of York*

HENRY *Earl of Richmond, a youth*
LORD RIVERS *brother to Lady Grey*
SIR WILLIAM STANLEY
SIR JOHN MONTGOMERY
SIR JOHN SOMERVILLE
TUTOR *to Rutland*
MAYOR OF YORK
ALDERMEN
MAYOR OF COVENTRY
LIEUTENANT OF THE TOWER
A NOBLEMAN
TWO KEEPERS
A HUNTSMAN
A SON *that has killed his father*
A FATHER *that has killed his son*
THE FRENCH ADMIRAL
QUEEN MARGARET
LADY ELIZABETH GREY *afterward queen to Edward IV*
BONA *sister to the French Queen*
SOLDIERS ATTENDANTS MESSENGERS WATCHMEN ETC.

*Scene:* England and France]

# ACT I

Scene I. [London. *The parliament house.*]

*Alarum.*° *Enter Plantagenet [the Duke of* YORK],
EDWARD, RICHARD, NORFOLK, MONTAGUE,
WARWICK, *and* SOLDIERS.

WARWICK
I wonder how the king escaped our hands?

YORK
While we pursued the horsemen of the north,
He slily stole away, and left his men;
Whereat the great Lord of Northumberland
Whose warlike ears could never brook° retreat,      5
Cheered up the drooping army; and himself,
Lord Clifford, and Lord Stafford all abreast
Charged our main battle's° front, and, breaking in,
Were by the swords of common soldiers slain.

EDWARD
Lord Stafford's father, Duke of Buckingham,      10
Is either slain or wounded dangerous.°
I cleft his beaver° with a downright blow;
That this is true, father, behold his blood.

[*Shows his bloody sword.*]

MONTAGUE
And, brother, here's the Earl of Wiltshire's blood,
Whom I encountered as the battles joined.      15

RICHARD
Speak thou for me, and tell them what I did.

[*Throws down the Duke of Somerset's head.*]

YORK
Richard hath best deserved of all my sons.
But is your grace dead, my Lord of Somerset?

NORFOLK
Such hope have all the line of John of Gaunt!°

RICHARD
Thus do I hope to shake King Henry's head.      20

WARWICK
And so do I, victorious Prince of York.
Before I see thee seated in that throne
Which now the house of Lancaster usurps,
I vow by heaven these eyes shall never close.
This is the palace of the fearful° king,      25
And this the regal seat. Possess it, York;
For this is thine and not King Henry's heirs'.

YORK
Assist me, then, sweet Warwick, and I will;
For hither we have broken in by force.

NORFOLK
We'll all assist you. He that flies shall die.      30

YORK
Thanks, gentle Norfolk; stay by me, my lords;
And, soldiers, stay and lodge by me this night.

*They go up.*°

*The decorative border on page 196 appeared on the first page of the
quarto edition of 3 Henry VI, 1595.*

**I.i.s.d. Alarum** trumpet call to arms   **5 brook** endure   **8
battle's** army's   **11 dangerous** dangerously   **12 beaver** visor
**19 Such . . . Gaunt** May all of the line of John of Gaunt
have such hope! (ironical; though emendation of "hope" to
"hap" [fate] is plausible)   **25 fearful** timorous   **32 s.d. go up**
to the chair of state, presumably toward the rear of the stage

WARWICK
And when the king comes, offer him no violence,
Unless he seek to thrust you out perforce.

YORK
The queen this day here holds her parliament,      35
But little thinks we shall be of her council.
By words or blows here let us win our right.

RICHARD
Armed as we are, let's stay within this house.

WARWICK
The bloody parliament shall this be called,
Unless Plantagenet, Duke of York, be king,      40
And bashful Henry deposed, whose cowardice
Hath made us bywords to our enemies.

YORK
Then leave me not, my lords. Be resolute;
I mean to take possession of my right.

WARWICK
Neither the king, nor he that loves him best,      45
The proudest he that holds up° Lancaster,
Dares stir a wing, if Warwick shake his bells.°
I'll plant Plantagenet, root him up who dares.
Resolve thee, Richard; claim the English crown.

[YORK *seats himself in the throne.*]

*Flourish.*° *Enter* KING HENRY, CLIFFORD, NORTHUM-
BERLAND, WESTMORELAND, EXETER, *and the rest.*

KING HENRY
My lords, look where the sturdy rebel sits,      50
Even in the chair of state. Belike° he means,
Backed by the power of Warwick, that false peer,
To aspire unto the crown and reign as king.
Earl of Northumberland, he slew thy father,
And thine, Lord Clifford; and you both have vowed
  revenge      55
On him, his sons, his favorites, and his friends.

NORTHUMBERLAND
If I be not, heavens be revenged on me!

CLIFFORD
The hope thereof makes Clifford mourn in steel.°

WESTMORELAND
What, shall we suffer° this? let's pluck him down.
My heart for anger burns; I cannot brook° it.      60

KING HENRY
Be patient, gentle° Earl of Westmoreland.

CLIFFORD
Patience is for poltroons,° such as he.
He durst not sit there, had your father lived.
My gracious lord, here in the parliament
Let us assail the family of York.      65

NORTHUMBERLAND
Well hast thou spoken, cousin.° Be it so.

KING HENRY
Ah, know you not the city favors them,
And they have troops of soldiers at their beck?

EXETER
But when the duke is slain, they'll quickly fly.

KING HENRY
Far be the thought of this from Henry's heart,      70

**46 holds up** supports   **47 bells** falcon's bells   **49 s.d. Flourish**
trumpet fanfare   **51 Belike** apparently   **58 steel** armor   **59
suffer** allow   **60 brook** endure   **61 gentle** noble   **62
poltroons** cowards   **66 cousin** kinsman

To make a shambles° of the parliament house!
Cousin of Exeter, frowns, words, and threats
Shall be the war that Henry means to use.
Thou factious° Duke of York, descend my throne,
And kneel for grace and mercy at my feet. 75
I am thy sovereign.

YORK                    I am thine.

EXETER
For shame, come down; he made thee Duke of York.

YORK
It was my inheritance, as the earldom was.

EXETER
Thy father was a traitor to the crown.

WARWICK
Exeter, thou art a traitor to the crown 80
In following this usurping Henry.

CLIFFORD
Whom should he follow but his natural king?

WARWICK
True, Clifford; that's Richard Duke of York.

KING HENRY
And shall I stand, and thou sit in my throne?

YORK
It must and shall be so: content thyself. 85

WARWICK
Be Duke of Lancaster; let him be king.

WESTMORELAND
He is both king and Duke of Lancaster;
And that the Lord of Westmoreland shall maintain.

WARWICK
And Warwick shall disprove it. You forget
That we are those which chased you from the field 90
And slew your fathers, and with colors° spread
Marched through the city to the palace gates.

NORTHUMBERLAND
Yes, Warwick, I remember it to my grief,
And, by his soul, thou and thy house shall rue it.

WESTMORELAND
Plantagenet, of thee and these thy sons, 95
Thy kinsmen and thy friends, I'll have more lives
Than drops of blood were in my father's veins.

CLIFFORD
Urge it no more, lest that, instead of words,
I send thee, Warwick, such a messenger
As shall revenge his° death before I stir. 100

WARWICK
Poor Clifford; how I scorn his worthless threats!

YORK
Will you we show our title° to the crown?
If not, our swords shall plead° it in the field.

KING HENRY
What title hast thou, traitor, to the crown?
Thy father was, as thou art, Duke of York; 105
Thy grandfather, Roger Mortimer, Earl of March.
I am the son of Henry the Fifth,
Who made the Dolphin° and the French to stoop°
And seized upon their towns and provinces.

WARWICK
Talk not of France, sith° thou hast lost it all. 110

KING HENRY
The Lord Protector° lost it, and not I.
When I was crowned I was but nine months old.

RICHARD
You are old enough now, and yet° methinks you lose.
Father, tear the crown from the usurper's head.

EDWARD
Sweet father, do so; set it on your head. 11

MONTAGUE
Good brother, as thou lov'st and honorest arms,
Let's fight it out and not stand° caviling thus.

RICHARD
Sound drums and trumpets, and the king will fly.

YORK
Sons, peace!

KING HENRY
Peace, thou! and give King Henry leave to speak. 12

WARWICK
Plantagenet shall speak first. Hear him, lords;
And be you silent and attentive too,
For he that interrupts him shall not live.

KING HENRY
Think'st thou that I will leave my kingly throne,
Wherein my grandsire and my father sat? 12
No: first shall war unpeople this my realm;
Ay, and their colors, often borne in France,
And now in England to our heart's great sorrow,
Shall be my winding-sheet. Why faint° you, lords?
My title's good, and better far than his. 13

WARWICK
Prove it, Henry, and thou shalt be king.

KING HENRY
Henry the Fourth by conquest got the crown.

YORK
'Twas by rebellion against his king.

KING HENRY [Aside.]
I know not what to say; my title's weak—
Tell me, may not a king adopt an heir? 13

YORK
What then?

KING HENRY
And if° he may, then am I lawful king;
For Richard, in the view of many lords,
Resigned the crown to Henry the Fourth,
Whose heir my father was, and I am his. 14

YORK
He rose against him, being his sovereign,
And made him to resign his crown perforce.

WARWICK
Suppose, my lords, he did it unconstrained,
Think you 'twere prejudicial to his crown?

EXETER
No; for he could not so resign his crown 14
But that the next heir should succeed and reign.

KING HENRY
Art thou against us, Duke of Exeter?

EXETER
His is the right, and therefore pardon me.

YORK
Why whisper you, my lords, and answer not?

71 shambles slaughterhouse 74 factious rebellious 91 colors flags 100 his my father's 102 title legal right 103 plead defend 108 Dolphin Dauphin; stoop yield 110 sith since

111 Lord Protector Humphrey Duke of Gloucester 113 yet even now 117 stand waste time 129 faint lose heart 137 And if if

EXETER
My conscience tells me he is lawful king. 150

KING HENRY [*Aside.*]
All will revolt from me, and turn to him.

NORTHUMBERLAND
Plantagenet, for all the claim thou lay'st,
Think not that Henry shall be so deposed.

WARWICK
Deposed he shall be, in despite of all.

NORTHUMBERLAND
Thou art deceived. 'Tis not thy southern power,° 155
Of Essex, Norfolk, Suffolk, nor of Kent,
Which makes thee thus presumptuous and proud,
Can set the duke up in despite of me.

CLIFFORD
King Henry, be thy title right or wrong,
Lord Clifford vows to fight in thy defense: 160
May that ground gape and swallow me alive,
Where I shall kneel to him that slew my father!

KING HENRY
O Clifford, how thy words revive my heart!

YORK
Henry of Lancaster, resign thy crown.
What mutter you, or what conspire you, lords? 165

WARWICK
Do right unto this princely Duke of York,
Or I will fill the house with armèd men,
And over the chair of state, where now he sits,
Write up his title with usurping blood.

*He stamps with his foot, and the* SOLDIERS *show themselves.*

KING HENRY
My Lord of Warwick, hear but one word: 170
Let me for this my lifetime reign as king.

YORK
Confirm the crown to me and to mine heirs,
And thou shalt reign in quiet while thou liv'st.

KING HENRY
I am content. Richard Plantagenet,
Enjoy the kingdom after my decease. 175

CLIFFORD
What wrong is this unto the prince your son?

WARWICK
What good is this to England and himself!

WESTMORELAND
Base, fearful, and despairing Henry!

CLIFFORD
How hast thou injured both thyself and us!

WESTMORELAND
I cannot stay to hear these articles.° 180

NORTHUMBERLAND
Nor I.

CLIFFORD
Come, cousin, let us tell the queen these news.

WESTMORELAND
Farewell, faint-hearted and degenerate king,
In whose cold blood no spark of honor bides.

NORTHUMBERLAND
Be thou a prey unto the house of York, 185
And die in bands° for this unmanly deed!

CLIFFORD
In dreadful war mayst thou be overcome,
Or live in peace abandoned and despised!
        [*Exeunt* NORTHUMBERLAND, CLIFFORD, *and*
                  WESTMORELAND.]

WARWICK
Turn this way, Henry, and regard them not.

EXETER
They seek revenge, and therefore will not yield. 190

KING HENRY
Ah, Exeter!

WARWICK   Why should you sigh, my lord?

KING HENRY
Not for myself, Lord Warwick, but my son,
Whom I unnaturally shall disinherit.
But be it as it may. [*To* YORK.] I here entail° 195
The crown to thee and to thine heirs for ever;
Conditionally, that here thou take an oath
To cease this civil war; and, whilst I live,
To honor me as thy king and sovereign;
And neither by treason nor hostility 200
To seek to put me down and reign thyself.

YORK
This oath I willingly take and will perform.

[*Comes from the throne.*]

WARWICK
Long live King Henry! Plantagenet, embrace him.

KING HENRY
And long live thou and these thy forward° sons!

YORK
Now York and Lancaster are reconciled.

EXETER
Accursed be he that seeks to make them foes! 205

*Sennet.° Here they come down.*

YORK
Farewell, my gracious lord; I'll to my castle.

WARWICK
And I'll keep London with my soldiers.

NORFOLK
And I to Norfolk with my followers.

MONTAGUE
And I unto the sea from whence I came.
[*Exeunt* YORK *and his* SONS, WARWICK, NORFOLK, *and*
MONTAGUE, *with their* SOLDIERS, *and* ATTENDANTS.]

KING HENRY
And I with grief and sorrow to the court. 210

*Enter the* QUEEN [MARGARET *and Edward* PRINCE *of
Wales*].

EXETER
Here comes the queen, whose looks bewray° her
   anger.
I'll steal away.

KING HENRY   Exeter, so will I.

QUEEN MARGARET
Nay, go not from me. I will follow thee.

KING HENRY
Be patient, gentle queen, and I will stay.

**155 power** army   **180 articles** terms of agreement   **186 bands**
bonds

**194 entail** settle, bestow (as property)   **203 forward** eager
**205 s.d. Sennet** trumpet call signaling the approach or
departure of processions   **211 bewray** reveal

QUEEN MARGARET
Who can be patient in such extremes?                    215
Ah, wretched man! Would I had died a maid,
And never seen thee, never borne thee son,
Seeing thou hast proved so unnatural a father!
Hath he deserved to lose his birthright thus?
Hadst thou but loved him half so well as I,          220
Or felt that pain which I did for him once,
Or nourished him as I did with my blood,
Thou wouldst have left thy dearest heart-blood there,
Rather than have made that savage duke thine heir
And disinherited thine only son.                        225
PRINCE
Father, you cannot disinherit me.
If you be king, why should not I succeed?
KING HENRY
Pardon me, Margaret. Pardon me, sweet son.
The Earl of Warwick and the duke enforced me.
QUEEN MARGARET
Enforced thee? Art thou king, and wilt be forced?   230
I shame to hear thee speak. Ah, timorous wretch!
Thou hast undone thyself, thy son, and me;
And giv'n unto the house of York such head°
As thou shalt reign but by their sufferance.°
To entail him and his heirs unto the crown,          235
What is it, but to make thy sepulcher,
And creep into it far before thy time?
Warwick is chancellor and the Lord of Calais;
Stern Falconbridge commands the Narrow Seas;°
The duke is made protector of the realm;            240
And yet shalt thou be safe? Such safety finds
The trembling lamb environèd with wolves.
Had I been there, which am a silly° woman,
The soldiers should have tossed me on their pikes
Before I would have granted° to that act.            245
But thou preferr'st thy life before thine honor:
And seeing thou dost, I here divorce myself
Both from thy table, Henry, and thy bed,
Until that act of parliament be repealed
Whereby my son is disinherited.                         250
The northern lords, that have forsworn thy colors,
Will follow mine, if once they see them spread;
And spread they shall be, to thy foul disgrace
And utter ruin of the house of York.
Thus do I leave thee. Come, son, let's away.         255
Our army is ready; come, we'll after them.
KING HENRY
Stay, gentle Margaret, and hear me speak.
QUEEN MARGARET
Thou hast spoke too much already; get thee gone.
KING HENRY
Gentle son Edward, thou wilt stay with me?
QUEEN MARGARET
Ay, to be murdered by his enemies.                     260
PRINCE
When I return with victory from the field,
I'll see your grace: till then I'll follow her.
QUEEN MARGARET
Come, son, away; we may not linger thus.
[Exeunt QUEEN MARGARET and the PRINCE.]

KING HENRY
Poor queen! how love to me and to her son
Hath made her break out into terms of rage!        265
Revenged may she be on that hateful duke,
Whose haughty spirit, wingèd with desire,
Will cost° my crown, and like an empty eagle
Tire° on the flesh of me and of my son!
The loss of those three lords torments my heart.    270
I'll write unto them and entreat them fair.°
Come, cousin, you shall be the messenger.
EXETER
And I, I hope, shall reconcile them all.      Exeunt.

[Scene II. *Sandal Castle, near Wakefield,
in Yorkshire.*]

*Flourish. Enter* RICHARD, EDWARD, *and* MONTAGUE.
RICHARD
Brother, though I be youngest, give me leave.
EDWARD
No, I can better play the orator.
MONTAGUE
But I have reasons strong and forcible.

*Enter the Duke of* YORK.

YORK
Why, how now, sons and brother! at a strife?
What is your quarrel? How began it first?            5
EDWARD
No quarrel, but a slight contention.°
YORK
About what?
RICHARD
About that which concerns your grace and us—
The crown of England, father, which is yours.
YORK
Mine, boy? Not till King Henry be dead.            10
RICHARD
Your right depends not on his life or death.
EDWARD
Now you are heir; therefore enjoy it now.
By giving the house of Lancaster leave to breathe,
It will outrun you, father, in the end.
YORK
I took an oath that he should quietly reign.       15
EDWARD
But for a kingdom any oath may be broken.
I would break a thousand oaths to reign one year.
RICHARD
No; God forbid your grace should be forsworn.°
YORK
I shall be, if I claim by open war.
RICHARD
I'll prove the contrary, if you'll hear me speak.   20
YORK
Thou canst not, son; it is impossible.
RICHARD
An oath is of no moment, being not took
Before a true and lawful magistrate,

233 **head** advantage 234 **sufferance** permission 239
**Narrow Seas** English Channel 243 **silly** helpless 245
**granted** assented

268 **cost** with pun on **coast** (i.e., attack) 269 **Tire** prey or feed
ravenously upon 271 **entreat them fair** treat them courteously
**I.ii.6 contention** dispute **18 forsworn** perjured

That hath authority over him that swears:
Henry had none, but did usurp the place;          25
Then, seeing 'twas he that made you to depose,°
Your oath, my lord, is vain and frivolous.°
Therefore, to arms! And, father, do but think
How sweet a thing it is to wear a crown,
Within whose circuit is Elysium          30
And all that poets feign° of bliss and joy.
Why do we linger thus? I cannot rest
Until the White Rose that I wear be dyed
Even in the lukewarm blood of Henry's heart.

YORK
Richard, enough; I will be king, or die.          35
Brother, thou shalt to London presently,°
And whet on Warwick to this enterprise.
Thou, Richard, shalt to the Duke of Norfolk,
And tell him privily of our intent.
You, Edward, shall unto my Lord Cobham,          40
With whom the Kentishmen will willingly rise.
In them I trust; for they are soldiers,
Witty,° courteous, liberal,° full of spirit.
While you are thus employed, what resteth° more,
But that I seek occasion how to rise,          45
And yet the king not privy to my drift,°
Nor any of the house of Lancaster?

*Enter [a MESSENGER] Gabriel.°*

But stay! What news? Why com'st thou in such
     post?°
MESSENGER
The queen with all the northern earls and lords
Intend here to besiege you in your castle:          50
She is hard by with twenty thousand men;
And therefore fortify your hold,° my lord.
YORK
Ay, with my sword. What! think'st thou that we
     fear them?
Edward and Richard, you shall stay with me;
My brother Montague shall post to London.          55
Let noble Warwick, Cobham, and the rest,
Whom we have left protectors of the king,
With pow'rful policy° strengthen themselves,
And trust not simple Henry nor his oaths.
MONTAGUE
Brother, I go. I'll win them, fear° it not:          60
And thus most humbly I do take my leave.
                    *Exit MONTAGUE.*

*Enter [SIR JOHN] Mortimer and [SIR HUGH] his brother.*

YORK
Sir John and Sir Hugh Mortimer, mine uncles,
You are come to Sandal in a happy° hour;
The army of the queen mean to besiege us.
SIR JOHN
She shall not need, we'll meet her in the field.          65
YORK
What, with five thousand men?

RICHARD
Ay, with five hundred, father, for a need.°
A woman's general. What should we fear?

*A march afar off.*

EDWARD
I hear their drums: let's set our men in order,
And issue forth and bid them battle straight.°          70
YORK
Five men to twenty! Though the odds be great,
I doubt not, uncle, of our victory.
Many a battle have I won in France,
When as the enemy hath been ten to one.
Why should I not now have the like success?          75
                    *Alarum. Exeunt.*

[Scene III. *Field of battle between Sandal Castle
and Wakefield.*]

*Enter RUTLAND and his TUTOR.*

RUTLAND
Ah, whither shall I fly to 'scape their hands?
Ah, tutor, look where bloody Clifford comes!

*Enter CLIFFORD [and SOLDIERS].*

CLIFFORD
Chaplain, away! thy priesthood saves thy life.
As for the brat of this accursèd duke,
Whose father slew my father, he shall die.          5
TUTOR
And I, my lord, will bear him company.
CLIFFORD
Soldiers, away with him!
TUTOR
Ah, Clifford, murder not this innocent child,
Lest thou be hated both of God and man!
               *Exit [dragged off by SOLDIERS].*
CLIFFORD
How now! Is he dead already? Or is it fear          10
That makes him close his eyes? I'll open them.
RUTLAND
So looks the pent-up lion o'er the wretch
That trembles under his devouring paws;
And so he walks, insulting° o'er his prey,
And so he comes, to rend his limbs asunder.          15
Ah, gentle Clifford, kill me with thy sword
And not with such a cruel threat'ning look.
Sweet Clifford, hear me speak before I die.
I am too mean° a subject for thy wrath;
Be thou revenged on men, and let me live.          20
CLIFFORD
In vain thou speak'st, poor boy; my father's blood
Hath stopped the passage where thy words should
     enter.
RUTLAND
Then let my father's blood open it again.
He is a man, and, Clifford, cope with him.

26 **depose** take an oath  27 **vain and frivolous** worthless and
insufficient  31 **feign** relate in fiction  36 **presently** at once
43 **Witty** wise; **liberal** generous, gentlemanly  44 **resteth**
remains  46 **drift** aim  47 s.d. **Gabriel** probably not the name
of the messenger, but of Gabriel Spencer, the actor who
played the part  48 **post** haste  52 **hold** stronghold  58
**policy** secret plans  60 **fear** doubt  63 **happy** fortunate

67 **for a need** if necessary (i.e., if so many are needed)
**straight** at once  I.iii.14 **insulting** exulting  19 **mean** unworthy

CLIFFORD
Had I thy brethren here, their lives and thine                          25
Were not revenge sufficient° for me;
No, if I digged up thy forefathers' graves
And hung their rotten coffins up in chains,
It could not slake mine ire, nor ease my heart.
The sight of any of the house of York                                   30
Is as a Fury to torment my soul;
And till I root out their accursèd line
And leave not one alive, I live in hell.
Therefore—

RUTLAND
O, let me pray before I take my death!                                  35
To thee I pray. Sweet Clifford, pity me!

CLIFFORD
Such pity as my rapier's point affords.

RUTLAND
I never did thee harm. Why wilt thou slay me?

CLIFFORD
Thy father hath.

RUTLAND                But 'twas ere I was born.
Thou hast one son. For his sake pity me,                                40
Lest in revenge thereof, sith° God is just,
He be as miserably slain as I.
Ah, let me live in prison all my days;
And when I give occasion of offense,
Then let me die, for now thou hast no cause.                            45

CLIFFORD
No cause?
Thy father slew my father. Therefore die.

[Stabs him.]

RUTLAND
Di faciant laudis summa sit ista tuae!°              [Dies.]

CLIFFORD
Plantagenet! I come, Plantagenet!
And this thy son's blood cleaving to my blade                           50
Shall rust upon my weapon, till thy blood,
Congealed with this, do make me wipe off both.

                                                        Exit.


[Scene IV. Another part of the field.]

Alarum. Enter Richard, Duke of YORK.

YORK
The army of the queen hath got° the field:
My uncles both are slain in rescuing me;
And all my followers to the eager foe
Turn back° and fly, like ships before the wind
Or lambs pursued by hunger-starvèd wolves.                              5
My sons, God knows what hath bechancèd° them:
But this I know, they have demeaned° themselves
Like men born to renown by life or death.
Three times did Richard make a lane to me,
And thrice cried, "Courage, father! fight it out!"                      10
And full as oft came Edward to my side,

With purple° falchion,° painted to the hilt
In blood of those that had encountered him:
And when the hardiest warriors did retire,
Richard cried, "Charge! and give no foot of ground!"                    15
And cried, "A crown, or else a glorious tomb!
A scepter, or an earthly sepulcher!"
With this, we charged again: but out,° alas!
We budged° again, as I have seen a swan
With bootless° labor swim against the tide                              20
And spend her strength with overmatching waves.

A short alarum within.

Ah, hark! The fatal° followers do pursue,
And I am faint, and cannot fly their fury.
And were I° strong, I would not shun their fury.
The sands are numbered that makes° up my life.                          25
Here must I stay, and here my life must end.

Enter the QUEEN [MARGARET], CLIFFORD, NORTHUM-
BERLAND, the young PRINCE [of Wales], and SOLDIERS.

Come, bloody Clifford, rough Northumberland,
I dare your quenchless fury to more rage.
I am your butt,° and I abide° your shot.

NORTHUMBERLAND
Yield to our mercy, proud Plantagenet.                                  30

CLIFFORD
Ay, to such mercy as his ruthless arm
With downright payment showed unto my father.
Now Phaëthon hath tumbled from his car,°
And made an evening at the noontide prick.°

YORK
My ashes, as the phoenix, may bring forth                               35
A bird that will revenge upon you all;
And in that hope I throw mine eyes to heaven,
Scorning whate'er you can afflict me with.
Why come you not? what? multitudes, and fear?

CLIFFORD
So cowards fight when they can fly no further;                          40
So doves do peck the falcon's piercing talons;
So desperate thieves, all hopeless of their lives,
Breathe out invectives 'gainst the officers.

YORK
O Clifford, but bethink thee once again,
And in thy thought o'errun° my former time;                             45
And, if thou canst for blushing, view this face,
And bite thy tongue,° that slanders him with coward-
  ice
Whose frown hath made thee faint and fly ere this!

CLIFFORD
I will not bandy with thee word for word,
But buckler° with thee blows, twice two for one.                        50

QUEEN MARGARET
Hold, valiant Clifford! For a thousand causes

26 sufficient as often in Shakespeare, -ient is here disyllabic
41 sith since   48 Di . . . tuae Ovid, Heroides ii.66 (Phyllis to
Demophoon): The gods grant that this may be the peak of
thy glory!
I.iv.1 got won   4 Turn back turn their backs   6 bechancèd
happened to   7 demeaned behaved

12 purple red (i.e., with blood); falchion curved sword  18
out interjection expressing regret  19 budged flinched  20
bootless unavailing  22 fatal destined  24 And were I if I
were  25 makes the singular form of the verb is often used
with a plural subject  29 butt a mark set up for archers to
shoot at; abide endure  33 Phaëthon . . . car the son of
Phoebus Apollo was killed while trying to drive his father's
chariot  34 noontide prick mark on a sundial face indicating
noon  45 o'errun review  47 bite thy tongue keep silent
50 buckler grapple in combat

I would prolong awhile the traitor's life.
Wrath makes him deaf: speak thou, Northumberland.

NORTHUMBERLAND
Hold, Clifford! Do not honor him so much
To prick thy finger, though to wound his heart.           55
What valor were it, when a cur doth grin,°
For one to thrust his hand between his teeth,
When he might spurn° him with his foot away?
It is war's prize to take all vantages;°
And ten to one is no impeach of° valor.                   60

*[They lay hands on* YORK, *who struggles.]*

CLIFFORD
Ay, ay, so strives the woodcock with the gin.°

NORTHUMBERLAND
So doth the cony° struggle in the net.

YORK
So triumph° thieves upon their conquered booty;
So true men yield, with robbers so o'ermatched.

NORTHUMBERLAND
What would your grace have done unto him now?            65

QUEEN MARGARET
Brave warriors, Clifford and Northumberland,
Come, make him stand upon this molehill here
That raught° at mountains with outstretchèd arms,
Yet parted but the shadow with his hand.
What, was it you that would be England's king?           70
Was't you that reveled in our parliament,
And made a preachment of your high descent?
Where are your mess° of sons to back you now?
The wanton Edward, and the lusty George?
And where's that valiant crookback prodigy,°             75
Dicky your boy, that with his grumbling voice
Was wont to cheer his dad in mutinies?
Or, with the rest, where is your darling, Rutland?
Look, York, I stained this napkin° with the blood
That valiant Clifford, with his rapier's point,          80
Made issue from the bosom of the boy;
And if thine eyes can water for his death,
I give thee this to dry thy cheeks withal.
Alas, poor York! but that I hate thee deadly,
I should lament thy miserable state.                      85
I prithee grieve, to make me merry, York.
What, hath thy fiery heart so parched thine entrails°
That not a tear can fall for Rutland's death?
Why art thou patient, man? Thou shouldst be mad;
And I, to make thee mad, do mock thee thus.              90
Stamp, rave, and fret, that I may sing and dance.
Thou wouldst be fee'd,° I see, to make me sport.
York cannot speak, unless he wears a crown.
A crown for York! and, lords, bow low to him.
Hold you his hands whilst I do set it on.                95

*[Puts a paper crown on his head.]*

Ay, marry,° sir, now looks he like a king!
Ay, this is he that took King Henry's chair

And this is he was his adopted heir.
But how is it that great Plantagenet
Is crowned so soon, and broke his solemn oath?          100
As I bethink me, you should not be king
Till our King Henry had shook hands with death.
And will you pale° your head in Henry's glory,
And rob his temples of the diadem,
Now in his life, against your holy oath?                105
O, 'tis a fault too too unpardonable!
Off with the crown, and with the crown his head!
And whilst we breathe, take time to do him dead.

CLIFFORD
That is my office, for my father's sake.

QUEEN MARGARET
Nay, stay. Let's hear the orisons he makes.            110

YORK
She-wolf of France, but worse than wolves of France,
Whose tongue more poisons than the adder's tooth!
How ill-beseeming is it in thy sex
To triumph like an Amazonian trull°
Upon their woes whom fortune captivates!              115
But that thy face is vizardlike,° unchanging,
Made impudent with use of evil deeds,
I would assay, proud queen, to make thee blush.
To tell thee whence thou cam'st, of whom derived,
Were shame enough to shame thee, wert thou not
     shameless.                                        120
Thy father bears the type° of King of Naples,
Of both the Sicils° and Jerusalem,
Yet not so wealthy as an English yeoman.
Hath that poor monarch taught thee to insult?
It needs not, nor it boots° thee not, proud queen,     125
Unless the adage must be verified,
That beggars mounted run their horse to death.
'Tis beauty that doth oft make women proud;
But God he knows thy share thereof is small.
'Tis virtue that doth make them most admired;          130
The contrary doth make thee wondered at.
'Tis government° that makes them seem divine;
The want thereof makes thee abominable.
Thou art as opposite to every good
As the Antipodes are unto us,                          135
Or as the South to the Septentrion.°
O tiger's heart wrapped in a woman's hide!°
How couldst thou drain the lifeblood of the child,
To bid the father wipe his eyes withal,
And yet be seen to bear a woman's face?                140
Women are soft, mild, pitiful, and flexible;
Thou stern, obdurate, flinty, rough, remorseless.
Bid'st thou me rage? Why, now thou hast thy wish.
Wouldst have me weep? Why, now thou hast thy
     will.
For raging wind blows up incessant showers,           145
And when the rage allays the rain begins.
These tears are my sweet Rutland's obsequies,
And every drop cries vengeance for his death,
'Gainst thee, fell° Clifford, and thee, false French-
     woman.

---

**56 grin** show his teeth  **58 spurn** kick  **59 vantages**
opportunities  **60 impeach** of detraction from  **61 gin** trap
**62 cony** rabbit (metaphorically, a gull or dupe)  **63 triumph**
exult  **68 raught** reached  **73 mess** set of four  **75 prodigy**
monster  **79 napkin** handkerchief  **87 entrails** thought of as
the seat of sympathy  **92 fee'd** paid  **96 marry** a mild oath
(from "By the Virgin Mary")

**103 pale** enclose, encircle  **114 trull** prostitute  **116 vizard-**
**like** masklike  **121 type** title  **122 both the Sicils** Naples and
Sicily  **125 boots** avails  **132 government** self-control  **136**
**Septentrion** North  **137 O . . . hide** parodied by Robert
Greene in *A Groatsworth of Wit* (1592)  **149 fell** fierce, savage

**NORTHUMBERLAND**
Beshrew° me, but his passions move me so          150
That hardly can I check my eyes from tears.
**YORK**
That face of his the hungry cannibals
Would not have touched, would not have stained
    with blood;
But you are more inhuman, more inexorable,
O, ten times more, than tigers of Hyrcania.°          155
See, ruthless queen, a hapless father's tears:
This cloth thou dipp'dst in blood of my sweet boy,
And I with tears do wash the blood away.
Keep thou the napkin, and go boast of this;
And if thou tell'st the heavy story right,          160
Upon my soul, the hearers will shed tears;
Yea, even my foes will shed fast-falling tears
And say, "Alas, it was a piteous deed!"
There, take the crown, and, with the crown, my
    curse;
And in thy need such comfort come to thee          165
As now I reap at thy too cruel hand!
Hardhearted Clifford, take me from the world.
My soul to heaven, my blood upon your heads!
**NORTHUMBERLAND**
Had he been slaughterman to all my kin,
I should not for my life but weep with him          170
To see how inly° sorrow gripes° his soul.
**QUEEN MARGARET**
What! weeping-ripe,° my Lord Northumberland?
Think but upon the wrong he did us all,
And that will quickly dry thy melting tears.
**CLIFFORD**
Here's for my oath! here's for my father's death!          175

[*Stabs him.*]

**QUEEN MARGARET**
And here's to right our gentlehearted king!

[*Stabs him.*]

**YORK**
Open thy gate of mercy, gracious God!
My soul flies through these wounds to seek out thee.
                                    [*Dies.*]
**QUEEN MARGARET**
Off with his head, and set it on York gates,
So York may overlook the town of York.          180
                        *Flourish. Exeunt.*

150 **Beshrew** curse   155 **Hyrcania** region of the Caspian Sea
171 **inly** inwardly; **gripes** grieves   172 **weeping-ripe** ready
to weep

# [ A C T   I I ]

*A march. Enter* EDWARD, RICHARD, *and their* POWER.°

**EDWARD**
I wonder how our princely father 'scaped,
Or whether he be 'scaped away or no
From Clifford's and Northumberland's pursuit.
Had he been ta'en, we should have heard the news;
Had he been slain, we should have heard the news;          5
Or had he 'scaped, methinks we should have heard
The happy tidings of his good escape.
How fares my brother? Why is he so sad?°
**RICHARD**
I cannot joy, until I be resolved°
Where our right valiant father is become.°          10
I saw him in the battle range about
And watched him how he singled Clifford forth.°
Methought° he bore him in the thickest troop
As doth a lion in a herd of neat,°
Or as a bear, encompassed round with dogs,          15
Who having pinched° a few and made them cry,
The rest stand all aloof, and bark at him.
So fared our father with his enemies;
So fled his enemies my warlike father:
Methinks 'tis prize enough to be his son.          20
See how the morning opes her golden gates,
And takes her farewell of the glorious sun!
How well resembles it the prime of youth,
Trimmed like a younker° prancing to his love!
**EDWARD**
Dazzle mine eyes,° or do I see three suns?          25
**RICHARD**
Three glorious suns, each one a perfect sun;
Not separated with the racking° clouds,
But severed in a pale clear-shining sky.
See, see! they join, embrace, and seem to kiss,
As if they vowed some league inviolable:
Now are they but one lamp, one light, one sun.          30
In this the heaven figures° some event.
**EDWARD**
'Twas wondrous strange, the like yet never heard of.
I think it cites° us, brother, to the field,
That we, the sons of brave Plantagenet,
Each one already blazing by our meeds,°          35
Should notwithstanding join our lights together
And overshine the earth as this the world.
Whate'er it bodes, henceforward will I bear
Upon my target° three fair-shining suns.°          40
**RICHARD**
Nay, bear three daughters. By your leave I speak it,
You love the breeder° better than the male.

*Enter one* [MESSENGER] *blowing* [*a horn*].

**II.i.s.d. power** army   **8 sad** serious   **9 resolved** freed from
doubt   **10 is become** has gone   **12 singled . . . forth**
selected (for hunting)   **13 Methought** it seemed to me   **14
neat** cattle   **16 pinched** nipped   **24 younker** young man
**25 Dazzle mine eyes** are my eyes dazzled   **27 racking**
driving   **32 figures** prefigures   **34 cites** calls   **36 meeds**
merits   **40 target** shield; **suns** pun on *sons*   **42 breeder**
childbearer

But what art thou, whose heavy looks foretell
Some dreadful story hanging on thy tongue?

MESSENGER
Ah, one that was a woeful looker-on                                    45
Whenas the noble Duke of York was slain,
Your princely father and my loving lord!

EDWARD
O, speak no more, for I have heard too much.

RICHARD
Say how he died, for I will hear it all.

MESSENGER
Environèd he was with many foes,                                      50
And stood against them, as the hope of Troy°
Against the Greeks that would have entered Troy.
But Hercules himself must yield to odds;
And many strokes, though with a little ax,
Hews down and fells the hardest-timbered oak.                         55
By many hands your father was subdued;
But only slaughtered by the ireful arm
Of unrelenting Clifford and the queen,
Who crowned the gracious duke in high despite,°
Laughed in his face, and when with grief he wept,                     60
The ruthless queen gave him, to dry his cheeks,
A napkin steepèd in the harmless blood
Of sweet young Rutland, by rough Clifford slain;
And after many scorns, many foul taunts,
They took his head, and on the gates of York                          65
They set the same; and there it doth remain,
The saddest spectacle that e'er I viewed.

EDWARD
Sweet Duke of York, our prop to lean upon,
Now thou art gone, we have no staff, no stay.°
O Clifford, boist'rous° Clifford! thou hast slain                     70
The flow'r of Europe for his chivalry;
And treacherously hast thou vanquished him,
For hand to hand he would have vanquished thee.
Now my soul's palace is become a prison.
Ah, would she break from hence, that this my body                     75
Might in the ground be closèd up in rest!
For never henceforth shall I joy again;
Never, O never, shall I see more joy.

RICHARD
I cannot weep; for all my body's moisture
Scarce serves to quench my furnace-burning heart;                     80
Nor can my tongue unload my heart's great burden,
For selfsame wind° that I should speak withal
Is kindling coals that fires all my breast,
And burns me up with flames that tears would quench.
To weep is to make less the depth of grief.                           85
Tears, then, for babes; blows and revenge for me!
Richard, I bear thy name; I'll venge thy death,
Or die renownèd by attempting it.

EDWARD
His name that valiant duke hath left with thee;
His dukedom and his chair with me is left.                            90

RICHARD
Nay, if thou be that princely eagle's bird,°
Show thy descent by gazing 'gainst the sun:

For chair and dukedom, throne and kingdom say;
Either that is thine, or else thou wert not his.

*March. Enter* WARWICK, *Marquess* MONTAGUE, *and
their* ARMY.

WARWICK
How now, fair lords! What fare?° What news abroad?°   95

RICHARD
Great Lord of Warwick, if we should recompt°
Our baleful news, and at each word's deliverance
Stab poniards in our flesh till all were told,
The words would add more anguish than the wounds.
O valiant lord, the Duke of York is slain!           100

EDWARD
O Warwick, Warwick! that Plantagenet
Which held thee dearly as his soul's redemption,
Is by the stern Lord Clifford done to death.

WARWICK
Ten days ago I drowned these news in tears,
And now, to add more measure° to your woes,          105
I come to tell you things sith° then befall'n.
After the bloody fray at Wakefield fought,
Where your brave father breathed his latest gasp,
Tidings, as swiftly as the posts° could run,
Were brought me of your loss and his depart.         110
I, then in London, keeper of the king,
Mustered my soldiers, gathered flocks of friends,
And very well appointed,° as I thought,
Marched toward Saint Albans to intercept the queen,
Bearing the king in my behalf° along;°               115
For by my scouts I was advertisèd°
That she was coming with a full intent
To dash° our late decree in parliament
Touching King Henry's oath and your succession.
Short tale to make, we at Saint Albans met,          120
Our battles° joined, and both sides fiercely fought:
But whether 'twas the coldness of the king,
Who looked full gently on his warlike queen,
That robbed my soldiers of their heated spleen;°
Or whether 'twas report of her success;              125
Or more than common fear of Clifford's rigor,°
Who thunders to his captives blood and death,
I cannot judge: but, to conclude with truth,
Their weapons like to lightning came and went;
Our soldiers', like the night owl's lazy flight,     130
Or like an idle thresher with a flail,
Fell gently down, as if they struck their friends.
I cheered them up with justice of our cause,
With promise of high pay and great rewards;
But all in vain; they had no heart to fight,         135
And we in them no hope to win the day;
So that we fled; the king unto the queen;
Lord George your brother, Norfolk, and myself,
In haste, posthaste, are come to join with you;
For in the marches° here we heard you were,          140
Making another head° to fight again.

51 **the hope of Troy** Hector  59 **high despite** haughty
contempt  69 **stay** support  70 **boist'rous** savage  82 **wind**
breath  91 **bird** child (the eagle, king of birds, was said to
gaze at the sun)

95 **What fare** What cheer?; **abroad** in the world  96
**recompt** recount  105 **measure** quantity  106 **sith** since
109 **posts** messengers  113 **appointed** equipped  115 **in my
behalf** for my advantage; **along** stretched out  116 **advertised**
informed  118 **dash** frustrate  121 **battles** main forces  124
**spleen** passion  126 **rigor** cruelty  140 **marches** borderlands
(of Wales)  141 **Making another head** gathering another force

EDWARD
Where is the Duke of Norfolk, gentle Warwick?
And when came George from Burgundy to England?
WARWICK
Some six miles off the duke is with the soldiers;
And for your brother, he was lately sent          145
From your kind aunt, Duchess of Burgundy,
With aid of soldiers to this needful war.
RICHARD
'Twas odds,° belike, when valiant Warwick fled.
Oft have I heard his praises in pursuit,
But ne'er till now his scandal of retire.°          150
WARWICK
Nor now my scandal, Richard, dost thou hear;
For thou shalt know this strong right hand of mine
Can pluck the diadem from faint Henry's head,
And wring the awful° scepter from his fist,
Were he as famous and as bold in war          155
As he is famed for mildness, peace, and prayer.
RICHARD
I know it well, Lord Warwick. Blame me not.
'Tis love I bear thy glories makes me speak.
But in this troublous time what's to be done?
Shall we go throw away our coats of steel,          160
And wrap our bodies in black mourning gowns,
Numb'ring our Ave-Maries° with our beads?
Or shall we on the helmets of our foes
Tell° our devotion with revengeful arms?
If for the last, say ay, and to it, lords.          165
WARWICK
Why, therefore Warwick came to seek you out,
And therefore comes my brother Montague.
Attend° me, lords. The proud insulting queen,
With Clifford and the haught° Northumberland,
And of their feather many moe° proud birds,          170
Have wrought the easy-melting king like wax.
He swore consent to your succession,
His oath enrollèd° in the parliament;
And now to London all the crew are gone,
To frustrate both his oath and what beside          175
May make against the house of Lancaster.
Their power, I think, is thirty thousand strong.
Now, if the help of Norfolk and myself,
With all the friends that thou, brave Earl of March,
Amongst the loving Welshmen canst procure,          180
Will but amount to five and twenty thousand,
Why, via!° to London will we march amain,
And once again bestride our foaming steeds,
And once again cry, "Charge!" upon our foes,
But never once again turn back and fly.          185
RICHARD
Ay, now methinks I hear great Warwick speak.
Ne'er may he live to see a sunshine day
That cries, "Retire," if Warwick bid him stay.
EDWARD
Lord Warwick, on thy shoulder will I lean,
And when thou fail'st—as God forbid the hour!—          190
Must Edward fall, which peril heaven forfend!°

148 odds inequality (of forces)   150 scandal of retire disgraceful imputation of retreat   154 awful awe-inspiring
162 Ave-Maries prayers   164 Tell count   168 Attend hear
169 haught haughty   170 moe more (old form)   173
enrollèd recorded on a parchment roll   182 via away   191
forfend forbid

WARWICK
No longer Earl of March, but Duke of York.
The next degree° is England's royal throne;
For King of England shalt thou be proclaimed
In every borough as we pass along;          195
And he that throws not up his cap for joy
Shall for the fault° make forfeit of his head.
King Edward, valiant Richard, Montague,
Stay we no longer, dreaming of renown,
But sound the trumpets, and about our task.          200
RICHARD
Then, Clifford, were thy heart as hard as steel,
As thou hast shown it flinty by thy deeds,
I come to pierce it, or to give thee mine.
EDWARD
Then strike up, drums! God and Saint George for us!

*Enter a* MESSENGER.

WARWICK
How now? What news?          205
MESSENGER
The Duke of Norfolk sends you word by me,
The queen is coming with a puissant° host;
And craves your company for speedy counsel.
WARWICK
Why then it sorts.° Brave warriors, let's away.
                                        *Exeunt omnes.*°

[Scene II. *Before York.*]

*Flourish. Enter the* KING [HENRY], *the* QUEEN
[MARGARET], CLIFFORD, NORTHUMBERLAND, *and*
[the] young PRINCE [of Wales], *with drum and trumpets.*

QUEEN MARGARET
Welcome, my lord, to this brave° town of York.
Yonder's the head of that archenemy
That sought to be encompassed with your crown.
Doth not the object° cheer your heart, my lord?
KING HENRY
Ay, as the rocks cheer them that fear their wrack.°          5
To see this sight, it irks my very soul.
Withhold revenge, dear God! 'Tis not my fault,
Nor wittingly have I infringed my vow.
CLIFFORD
My gracious liege, this too much lenity
And harmful pity must be laid aside.          10
To whom do lions cast their gentle looks?
Not to the beast that would usurp their den.
Whose hand is that the forest bear doth lick?
Not his that spoils° her young before her face.
Who 'scapes the lurking serpent's mortal sting?          15
Not he that sets his foot upon her back.
The smallest worm will turn, being trodden on.
And doves will peck in safeguard of their brood.
Ambitious York did level° at thy crown,
Thou smiling while he knit his angry brows:          20
He, but a duke, would have his son a king,
And raise his issue like a loving sire;

193 degree step   197 fault offense   207 puissant powerful
209 it sorts it is fitting; s.d. omnes all (Latin)
II.ii.1 brave splendid   4 object sight   5 wrack shipwreck
14 spoils carries off   19 level aim

Thou, being a king, blest with a goodly son,
Didst yield consent to disinherit him,
Which argued° thee a most unloving father.    25
Unreasonable° creatures feed their young;
And though man's face be fearful to their eyes,
Yet, in protection of their tender° ones,
Who hath not seen them, even with those wings
Which sometime they have used with fearful flight,    30
Make war with him that climbed unto their nest,
Offering their own lives in their young's defense?
For shame, my liege! Make them your precedent!
Were it not pity that this goodly boy
Should lose his birthright by his father's fault,    35
And long hereafter say unto his child,
"What my great-grandfather and grandsire got
My careless father fondly° gave away"?
Ah, what a shame were this! Look on the boy;
And let his manly face, which promiseth    40
Successful fortune, steel thy melting heart
To hold thine own and leave thine own with him.

KING HENRY
Full well hath Clifford played the orator,
Inferring° arguments of mighty force.
But, Clifford, tell me, didst thou never hear    45
That things ill got had ever bad success?°
And happy always was it for that son
Whose father for his hoarding went to hell?
I'll leave my son my virtuous deeds behind;
And would my father had left me no more!    50
For all the rest is held at such a rate
As brings a thousandfold more care to keep
Than in possession any jot of pleasure.
Ah, cousin York, would thy best friends did know
How it doth grieve me that thy head is here!    55

QUEEN MARGARET
My lord, cheer up your spirits; our foes are nigh,
And this soft courage° makes your followers faint.
You promised knighthood to our forward son.
Unsheathe your sword, and dub him presently.°
Edward, kneel down.    60

KING HENRY
Edward Plantagenet, arise a knight;
And learn this lesson: Draw thy sword in right.

PRINCE
My gracious father, by your kingly leave,
I'll draw it as apparent° to the crown,
And in that quarrel use it to the death.    65

CLIFFORD
Why, that is spoken like a toward° prince.

*Enter a* MESSENGER.

MESSENGER
Royal commanders, be in readiness;
For with a band of thirty thousand men
Comes Warwick, backing of the Duke of York,
And in the towns, as they do march along,    70
Proclaims him king, and many fly to him.
Darraign° your battle, for they are at hand.

CLIFFORD
I would your highness would depart the field.
The queen hath best success when you are absent.

QUEEN MARGARET
Ay, good my lord, and leave us to our fortune.    75

KING HENRY
Why, that's my fortune too; therefore I'll stay.

NORTHUMBERLAND
Be it with resolution, then, to fight.

PRINCE
My royal father, cheer these noble lords
And hearten those that fight in your defense:
Unsheathe your sword, good father; cry, "Saint
George!"    80

*March. Enter* EDWARD, WARWICK, RICHARD,
CLARENCE,° NORFOLK, MONTAGUE, *and* SOLDIERS.

EDWARD
Now, perjured Henry, wilt thou kneel for grace,
And set thy diadem upon my head,
Or bide the mortal fortune of the field?

QUEEN MARGARET
Go rate° thy minions, proud insulting boy!
Becomes it thee to be thus bold in terms    85
Before thy sovereign and thy lawful king?

EDWARD
I am his king, and he should bow his knee.
I was adopted heir by his consent;
Since when, his oath is broke; for, as I hear,
You, that are king, though he do wear the crown,    90
Have caused him, by new act of parliament,
To blot out me, and put his own son in.

CLIFFORD
And reason too!
Who should succeed the father but the son?

RICHARD
Are you there, butcher? O, I cannot speak!    95

CLIFFORD
Ay, crookback, here I stand to answer thee,
Or any he the proudest of thy sort.

RICHARD
'Twas you that killed young Rutland, was it not?

CLIFFORD
Ay, and old York, and yet not satisfied.

RICHARD
For God's sake, lords, give signal to the fight.    100

WARWICK
What say'st thou, Henry? Wilt thou yield the
crown?

QUEEN MARGARET
Why, how now, long-tongued Warwick! Dare you
speak?
When you and I met at Saint Albans last,
Your legs did better service than your hands.

WARWICK
Then 'twas my turn to fly, and now 'tis thine.    105

CLIFFORD
You said so much before, and yet you fled.

WARWICK
'Twas not your valor, Clifford, drove me thence.

---

25 **argued** proved  26 **Unreasonable** not endowed with
reason  28 **tender** young, beloved  38 **fondly** foolishly  44
**Inferring** adducing  46 **success** outcome  57 **soft courage**
faintheartedness  59 **presently** immediately  64 **apparent**
heir apparent  66 **toward** bold  72 **Darraign** set in order

80 **s.d.** thus the Folio; in fact, George is not created Duke of
Clarence until II.vi.103  84 **rate** drive away by chiding

**NORTHUMBERLAND**
No, nor your manhood that durst make you stay.

**RICHARD**
Northumberland, I hold thee reverently.
Break off the parley; for scarce I can refrain          110
The execution of my big-swol'n heart
Upon that Clifford, that cruel child-killer.

**CLIFFORD**
I slew thy father. Call'st thou him a child?

**RICHARD**
Ay, like a dastard and a treacherous coward,
As thou didst kill our tender brother Rutland;          115
But ere sun set I'll make thee curse the deed.

**KING HENRY**
Have done with words, my lords, and hear me speak.

**QUEEN MARGARET**
Defy them then, or else hold close thy lips.

**KING HENRY**
I prithee, give no limits to my tongue:
I am a king, and privileged to speak.          120

**CLIFFORD**
My liege, the wound that bred this meeting here
Cannot be cured by words. Therefore be still.

**RICHARD**
Then, executioner, unsheathe thy sword.
By Him that made us all, I am resolved°
That Clifford's manhood lies upon his tongue.          125

**EDWARD**
Say, Henry, shall I have my right, or no?
A thousand men have broke their fasts today
That ne'er shall dine unless thou yield the crown.

**WARWICK**
If thou deny, their blood upon thy head!
For York in justice puts his armor on.          130

**PRINCE**
If that be right which Warwick says is right,
There is no wrong, but everything is right.

**RICHARD**
Whoever got° thee, there thy mother stands;
For well I wot thou hast thy mother's tongue.

**QUEEN MARGARET**
But thou art neither like thy sire nor dam,          135
But like a foul misshapen stigmatic,°
Marked by the destinies to be avoided,
As venom toads, or lizards' dreadful stings.

**RICHARD**
Iron of Naples, hid with English gilt,
Whose father bears the title of a king—          140
As if a channel° should be called the sea—
Sham'st thou not, knowing whence thou art ex-
    traught,°
To let thy tongue detect° thy base-born heart?

**EDWARD**
A wisp of straw were worth a thousand crowns,
To make this shameless callet° know herself.          145
Helen of Greece was fairer far than thou,
Although thy husband may be Menelaus;
And ne'er was Agamemnon's brother wronged
By that false woman as this king by thee.

His father reveled in the heart of France,          150
And tamed the king, and made the Dolphin° stoop;°
And had he matched according to his state,
He might have kept that glory to this day;
But when he took a beggar to his bed,
And graced thy poor sire with his bridal day,          155
Even then that sunshine brewed a show'r for him,
That washed his father's fortunes forth of° France,
And heaped sedition on his crown at home.
For what hath broached° this tumult but thy pride?
Hadst thou been meek, our title still° had slept;          160
And we, in pity of the gentle king,
Had slipped° our claim until another age.

**CLARENCE**
But when we saw our sunshine made thy spring,
And that thy summer bred us no increase,
We set the ax to thy usurping root;          165
And though the edge hath something hit ourselves,
Yet, know thou, since we have begun to strike,
We'll never leave till we have hewn thee down,
Or bathed thy growing with our heated bloods.

**EDWARD**
And, in this resolution, I defy thee;          170
Not willing any longer conference,°
Since thou deniest the gentle king to speak.
Sound trumpets! Let our bloody colors wave!
And either victory, or else a grave.

**QUEEN MARGARET**
Stay, Edward.          175

**EDWARD**
No, wrangling woman, we'll no longer stay.
These words will cost ten thousand lives this day.
                              *Exeunt omnes.*

[Scene III. *A field of battle between Towton and
        Saxton in Yorkshire.*]

*Alarum. Excursions. Enter* WARWICK.

**WARWICK**
Forspent° with toil, as runners with a race,
I lay me down a little while to breathe;°
For strokes received, and many blows repaid,
Have robbed my strong-knit sinews of their strength,
And spite of spite° needs must I rest awhile.          5

*Enter* EDWARD, *running.*

**EDWARD**
Smile, gentle heaven! or strike, ungentle° death!
For this world frowns, and Edward's sun is clouded.

**WARWICK**
How now, my lord! What hap? What hope of good?

*Enter* CLARENCE.

**CLARENCE**
Our hap° is loss, our hope but sad despair;
Our ranks are broke, and ruin follows us.          10
What counsel give you? Whither shall we fly?

---

124 **resolved** convinced   133 **got** begot   136 **stigmatic**
deformed one   141 **channel** gutter   142 **extraught** descended
143 **detect** reveal   145 **callet** scold, trull

151 **Dolphin** Dauphin; **stoop** yield   157 **forth of** out of
159 **broached** started   160 **still** always   162 **slipped** not
asserted   171 **longer conference** further discussion
II.iii.1 **Forspent** exhausted   2 **breathe** rest   5 **spite of spite**
come what may   6 **ungentle** ignoble   9 **hap** (1) fortune (2)
hope

EDWARD

Bootless° is flight. They follow us with wings,
And weak we are and cannot shun pursuit.

*Enter* RICHARD.

RICHARD

Ah, Warwick, why hast thou withdrawn thyself?
Thy brother's blood the thirsty earth hath drunk,    15
Broached° with the steely point of Clifford's lance;
And in the very pangs of death he cried,
Like to a dismal° clangor heard from far,
"Warwick, revenge! Brother, revenge my death!"
So, underneath the belly of their steeds,    20
That stained their fetlocks in his smoking° blood,
The noble gentleman gave up the ghost.

WARWICK

Then let the earth be drunken with our blood!
I'll kill my horse, because I will not fly.
Why stand we like softhearted women here,    25
Wailing our losses, whiles the foe doth rage,
And look upon,° as if the tragedy
Were played in jest by counterfeiting actors?
Here on my knee I vow to God above,
I'll never pause again, never stand still,    30
Till either death hath closed these eyes of mine
Or fortune given me measure of revenge.

EDWARD

O Warwick, I do bend my knee with thine
And in this vow do chain my soul to thine!
And ere my knee rise from the earth's cold face,    35
I throw my hands, mine eyes, my heart to thee,
Thou setter-up and plucker-down of kings,
Beseeching thee (if with thy will it stands°)
That to my foes this body must be prey,
Yet that thy brazen gates of heaven may ope,    40
And give sweet passage to my sinful soul!
Now, lords, take leave until we meet again,
Where'er it be, in heaven or in earth.

RICHARD

Brother, give me thy hand; and, gentle Warwick,
Let me embrace thee in my weary arms.    45
I, that did never weep, now melt with woe
That winter should cut off our springtime so.

WARWICK

Away, away! Once more, sweet lords, farewell.

CLARENCE

Yet let us all together to our troops,
And give them leave to fly that will not stay,    50
And call them pillars that will stand to us;
And, if we thrive, promise them such rewards
As victors wear at the Olympian games:
This may plant courage in their quailing breasts;
For yet is hope of life and victory.    55
Forslow° no longer! Make we hence amain! *Exeunt.*

[Scene IV. *Another part of the field.*]

*Excursions. Enter* RICHARD *and* CLIFFORD.

RICHARD

Now, Clifford, I have singled thee alone.
Suppose this arm is for the Duke of York,
And this for Rutland, both bound to revenge
Wert thou environed with a brazen wall.

CLIFFORD

Now, Richard, I am with thee here alone.    5
This is the hand that stabbed thy father York,
And this the hand that slew thy brother Rutland;
And here's the heart that triumphs° in their death
And cheers these hands that slew thy sire and brother
To execute the like upon thyself;    10
And so have at thee!°

*They fight.* WARWICK *comes.* CLIFFORD *flies.*

RICHARD

Nay, Warwick, single out some other chase.
For I myself will hunt this wolf to death.     *Exeunt.*

[Scene V. *Another part of the field.*]

*Alarum. Enter* KING HENRY *alone.*

KING HENRY

This battle fares like to the morning's war,
When dying clouds contend with growing light,
What time the shepherd, blowing of his nails,°
Can neither call it perfect day nor night.
Now sways it this way, like a mighty sea    5
Forced by the tide to combat with the wind.
Now sways it that way, like the selfsame sea
Forced to retire by fury of the wind.
Sometime the flood prevails, and then the wind;
Now one the better, then another best;    10
Both tugging to be victors, breast to breast,
Yet neither conqueror nor conquerèd:
So is the equal poise° of this fell war.
Here on this molehill will I sit me down.
To whom God will, there be the victory!    15
For Margaret my queen, and Clifford too,
Have chid me from the battle, swearing both
They prosper best of all when I am thence.
Would I were dead, if God's good will were so!
For what is in this world but grief and woe?    20
O God! methinks it were a happy life,
To be no better than a homely swain;°
To sit upon a hill, as I do now,
To carve out dials quaintly,° point by point,
Thereby to see the minutes how they run—    25
How many makes the hour full complete,
How many hours brings about° the day,
How many days will finish up the year,
How many years a mortal man may live;
When this is known, then to divide the times—    30
So many hours must I tend my flock,

12 **Bootless** useless   16 **Broached** pierced   18 **dismal** boding disaster   21 **smoking** steaming   27 **look upon** look on   38 **stands** agrees   56 **Forslow** delay

**II.iv.8** triumphs exults   11 **have at thee** defend yourself
**II.v.3 of his nails** on his fingers   13 **poise** weight (as in the scales of a balance)   22 **swain** shepherd   24 **quaintly** ingeniously   27 **brings about** completes

So many hours must I take my rest,
So many hours must I contemplate,
So many hours must I sport myself,
So many days my ewes have been with young,          35
So many weeks ere the poor fools will ean,°
So many years ere I shall shear the fleece.
So minutes, hours, days, months, and years,
Passed over to the end they were created,
Would bring white hairs unto a quiet grave.          40
Ah, what a life were this! how sweet! how lovely!
Gives not the hawthorn bush a sweeter shade
To shepherds looking on their silly° sheep,
Than doth a rich embroidered canopy
To kings that fear their subjects' treachery?          45
O, yes, it doth! a thousandfold it doth!
And to conclude, the shepherd's homely curds,
His cold thin drink out of his leather bottle,
His wonted sleep under a fresh tree's shade,
All which secure° and sweetly he enjoys,          50
Is far beyond a prince's delicates,°
His viands sparkling in a golden cup,
His body couchèd in a curious° bed,
When care, mistrust, and treason waits on him.

*Alarum. Enter a* SON *that hath killed his father, at one
door; and* [later] *a* FATHER *that hath killed his son at
another door.*

SON
Ill blows the wind that profits nobody.          55
This man, whom hand to hand I slew in fight,
May be possessèd with some store of crowns;
And I, that haply° take them from him now,
May yet, ere night, yield both my life and them
To some man else, as this dead man doth me.          60
Who's this? O God! it is my father's face,
Whom in this conflict I, unwares,° have killed.
O heavy times, begetting such events!
From London by the king was I pressed forth;
My father, being the Earl of Warwick's man,          65
Came on the part° of York, pressed by his master;
And I, who at his hands received my life,
Have by my hands of life bereavèd him.
Pardon me, God! I knew not what I did.
And pardon, father, for I knew not thee!          70
My tears shall wipe away these bloody marks;
And no more words till they have flowed their fill.

KING HENRY
O piteous spectacle! O bloody times!
Whiles lions war and battle for their dens,
Poor harmless lambs abide their enmity.          75
Weep, wretched man! I'll aid thee tear for tear;
And let our hearts and eyes, like civil war,
Be blind with tears, and break o'ercharged with grief.

*Enter* FATHER, *bearing of his son.*

FATHER
Thou that so stoutly hath resisted me,
Give me thy gold, if thou hast any gold;          80
For I have bought it with an hundred blows.

But let me see: is this our foeman's face?
Ah, no, no, no! It is mine only son!
Ah, boy, if any life be left in thee,
Throw up thine eye! See, see what show'rs arise,          85
Blown with the windy tempest of my heart
Upon thy wounds, that kills mine eye and heart!
O, pity, God, this miserable age!
What stratagems,° how fell, how butcherly,
Erroneous,° mutinous, and unnatural,          90
This deadly quarrel doth beget!
O boy, thy father gave thee life too soon,
And hath bereft thee of thy life too late!°
KING HENRY
Woe above woe! grief more than common grief!
O that my death would stay these ruthful° deeds!          95
O, pity, pity, gentle heaven, pity!
The red rose and the white are on his face,
The fatal colors of our striving houses:
The one his purple blood right well resembles;
The other his pale cheeks, methinks, presenteth:          100
Wither one rose, and let the other flourish!
If you contend, a thousand lives must wither.
SON
How will my mother for a father's death
Take on with me and ne'er be satisfied!
FATHER
How will my wife for slaughter of my son          105
Shed seas of tears and ne'er be satisfied!
KING HENRY
How will the country for these woeful chances
Misthink° the king and not be satisfied!
SON
Was ever son so rued a father's death?
FATHER
Was ever father so bemoaned his son?          110
KING HENRY
Was ever king so grieved for subject's woe?
Much is your sorrow; mine ten times so much.
SON
I'll bear thee hence, where I may weep my fill.
                    [*Exit with the body.*]
FATHER
These arms of mine shall be thy winding-sheet;
My heart, sweet boy, shall be thy sepulcher,          115
For from my heart thine image ne'er shall go;
My sighing breast shall be thy funeral bell;
And so obsequious° will thy father be,
Even for the loss of thee, having no more,
As Priam was for all his valiant sons.          120
I'll bear thee hence; and let them fight that will,
For I have murdered where I should not kill.
                    *Exit* [*with the body*].
KING HENRY
Sad-hearted men, much overgone° with care,
Here sits a king more woeful than you are.

*Alarums. Excursions. Enter the* QUEEN [MARGARET],
*the* PRINCE [*of Wales*], *and* EXETER.

**36 ean** bring forth lambs  **43 silly** helpless  **50 secure** free
from care  **51 delicates** delicacies  **53 curious** exquisite  **58
haply** by chance  **62 unwares** unawares  **66 part** party, side

**89 stratagems** violent deeds  **90 Erroneous** criminal  **93
late** recently  **95 ruthful** lamentable  **108 Misthink** think
ill of  **118 obsequious** dutiful (particularly toward the dead)
**123 overgone** overcome

PRINCE

Fly, father, fly! for all your friends are fled    125
And Warwick rages like a chafèd bull:
Away! for death doth hold us in pursuit.

QUEEN MARGARET

Mount you, my lord, towards Berwick post amain.°
Edward and Richard, like a brace of greyhounds
Having the fearful flying hare in sight,    130
With fiery eyes sparkling for very wrath,
And bloody steel grasped in their ireful hands,
Are at our backs; and therefore hence amain!°

EXETER

Away! for vengeance comes along with them:
Nay, stay not to expostulate; make speed!    135
Or else come after. I'll away before.

KING HENRY

Nay, take me with thee, good sweet Exeter.
Not that I fear to stay, but love to go
Whither the queen intends. Forward, away!    *Exeunt.*

[Scene VI. *Another part of the field.*]

*A loud alarum. Enter* CLIFFORD, *wounded.*

CLIFFORD

Here burns my candle out; ay, here it dies,
Which, whiles it lasted, gave King Henry light.
O Lancaster! I fear thy overthrow
More than my body's parting with my soul.
My love and fear glued° many friends to thee,    5
And now I fall, thy tough commixtures° melts,
Impairing Henry, strength'ning misproud° York.
And whither fly the gnats but to the sun?
And who shines now but Henry's enemies?
O Phoebus, hadst thou never given consent    10
That Phaëton should check thy fiery steeds,
Thy burning car never had scorched the earth!
And, Henry, hadst thou swayed° as kings should do,
Or as thy father and his father did,
Giving no ground unto the house of York,    15
They never then had sprung like summer flies;
I and ten thousand in this luckless realm
Had left no mourning widows for our death;
And thou this day hadst kept thy chair in peace.
For what doth cherish weeds but gentle air?    20
And what makes robbers bold but too much lenity?
Bootless are plaints, and cureless are my wounds;
No way to fly, nor strengthen to hold out flight;
The foe is merciless, and will not pity;
For at their hands I have deserved no pity.    25
The air hath got into my deadly wounds,
And much effuse° of blood doth make me faint.
Come, York and Richard, Warwick and the rest;
I stabbed your fathers' bosoms; split my breast.

[*Faints.*]

*Alarum and retreat. Enter* EDWARD, WARWICK,
RICHARD, *and* SOLDIERS; MONTAGUE *and* CLAR-
ENCE.

EDWARD

Now breathe we,° lords: good fortune bids us pause,    30
And smooth the frowns of war with peaceful looks.
Some troops pursue the bloody-minded queen,
That led calm Henry, though he were a king,
As doth a sail, filled with a fretting gust,
Command° an argosy° to stem the waves.    35
But think you, lords, that Clifford fled with them?

WARWICK

No, 'tis impossible he should escape;
For, though before his face I speak the words,
Your brother Richard marked him for the grave:
And whereso'er he is, he's surely dead.    40

     CLIFFORD *groans [and dies].*

EDWARD

Whose soul is that which takes her heavy leave?

RICHARD

A deadly groan, like life and death's departing.°

EDWARD

See who it is: and, now the battle's ended,
If friend or foe, let him be gently used.

RICHARD

Revoke that doom° of mercy, for 'tis Clifford;    45
Who not contented that he lopped the branch
In hewing Rutland when his leaves put forth,
But set his murdering knife unto the root
From whence that tender spray did sweetly spring:
I mean our princely father, Duke of York.    50

WARWICK

From off the gates of York fetch down the head,
Your father's head, which Clifford placèd there;
Instead whereof let this supply the room:°
Measure for measure must be answerèd.

EDWARD

Bring forth that fatal screech owl to our house,    55
That nothing sung but death to us and ours.
Now death shall stop his dismal threat'ning sound
And his ill-boding tongue no more shall speak.

WARWICK

I think his understanding is bereft.°
Speak, Clifford, dost thou know who speaks to thee?    60
Dark cloudy death o'ershades his beams of life,
And he nor sees nor hears us what we say.

RICHARD

O, would he did! and so perhaps he doth:
'Tis but his policy to counterfeit,
Because he would avoid such bitter taunts    65
Which in the time of death he gave our father.

CLARENCE

If so thou think'st, vex° him with eager° words.

RICHARD

Clifford, ask mercy and obtain no grace.

EDWARD

Clifford, repent in bootless penitence.

WARWICK

Clifford, devise excuses for thy faults.    70

CLARENCE

While we devise fell tortures for thy faults.

128, 133 **amain** with full speed
**II.vi.5 My . . . glued** both love and fear of me attached
**6 commixtures** compound   **7 misproud** arrogant   13
**swayed** ruled   **27 effuse** pouring out

**30 Now breathe we** now let us rest   **35 Command** compel;
**argosy** merchant vessel of the largest size and burden   **42
departing** separation   **45 doom** sentence   **53 room** place
**59 his understanding is bereft** he is deprived of his understanding   **67 vex** torment; **eager** sharp

**RICHARD**
Thou didst love York, and I am son to York.

**EDWARD**
Thou pitied'st Rutland, I will pity thee.

**CLARENCE**
Where's Captain Margaret, to fence° you now?

**WARWICK**
They mock thee, Clifford. Swear as thou wast wont. 75

**RICHARD**
What! not an oath? Nay, then the world goes hard
When Clifford cannot spare his friends an oath.
I know by that he's dead; and, by my soul,
If this right hand would buy two hours' life,
That I in all despite might rail at him,                    80
This hand should chop it off, and with the issuing
    blood
Stifle the villain whose unstanchèd thirst
York and young Rutland could not satisfy.

**WARWICK**
Ay, but he's dead. Off with the traitor's head,
And rear° it in the place your father's stands.            85
And now to London with triumphant march,
There to be crownèd England's royal king:
From whence shall Warwick cut the sea to France,
And ask the Lady Bona for thy queen.
So shalt thou sinew both these lands together;            90
And, having France thy friend, thou shalt not dread
The scattered foe that hopes to rise again;
For though they cannot greatly sting to hurt,
Yet look to have them buzz to offend thine ears.
First will I see the coronation.                           95
And then to Brittany I'll cross the sea,
To effect this marriage, so it please my lord.

**EDWARD**
Even as thou wilt, sweet Warwick, let it be;
For in thy shoulder do I build my seat,
And never will I undertake the thing                      100
Wherein thy counsel and consent is wanting.
Richard, I will create thee Duke of Gloucester;
And George, of Clarence: Warwick, as ourself,°
Shall do and undo as him pleaseth best.

**RICHARD**
Let me be Duke of Clarence, George of Gloucester; 105
For Gloucester's dukedom is too ominous.°

**WARWICK**
Tut, that's a foolish observation.
Richard, be Duke of Gloucester. Now to London,
To see these honors in possession.          *Exeunt.*

# [ ACT III ]

[*Scene I. A forest in the north of England.*]

*Enter [two* KEEPERS*] with crossbows in their hands.*

**FIRST KEEPER**
Under this thick-grown brake° we'll shroud° our-
    selves;
For through this laund° anon the deer will come,
And in this covert° will we make our stand,°
Culling° the principal of all the deer.

**SECOND KEEPER**
I'll stay above the hill, so both may shoot.               5

**FIRST KEEPER**
That cannot be; the noise of thy crossbow
Will scare the herd, and so my shoot is lost.
Here stand we both, and aim at the best;°
And, for° the time shall not seem tedious,
I'll tell thee what befell me on a day                    10
In this self° place where now we mean to stand.

**SECOND KEEPER**
Here comes a man, let's stay till he be past.

*Enter the* KING *[*HENRY, *disguised], with a prayerbook.*

**KING HENRY**
From Scotland am I stol'n, even of pure love,
To greet mine own land with my wishful sight.
No, Harry, Harry, 'tis no land of thine;                  15
Thy place is filled, thy scepter wrung from thee,
Thy balm washed off wherewith thou wast anointed:
No bending knee will call thee Caesar now,
No humble suitors press to speak for right,
No, not a man comes for redress of° thee;                 20
For how can I help them, and not myself?

**FIRST KEEPER**
Ay, here's a deer whose skin's a keeper's fee!
This is the quondam° king; let's seize upon him.

**KING HENRY**
Let me embrace thee, sour adversity,
For wise men say it is the wisest course.                 25

**SECOND KEEPER**
Why linger we? let us lay hands upon him.

**FIRST KEEPER**
Forbear awhile; we'll hear a little more.

**KING HENRY**
My queen and son are gone to France for aid;
And, as I hear, the great commanding Warwick
Is thither gone, to crave the French king's sister        30
To wife for Edward. If this news be true,
Poor queen and son, your labor is but lost;
For Warwick is a subtle orator,
And Lewis a prince soon won with moving words.
By this account, then, Margaret may win him;             35
For she's a woman to be pitied much.
Her sighs will make a batt'ry° in his breast;
Her tears will pierce into a marble heart;
The tiger will be mild whiles she doth mourn;
And Nero will be tainted with remorse                     40

---

**74 fence** protect  **85 rear** erect  **103 ourself** note the royal
"we"  **106 For . . . ominous** refers to the disgrace and
murder of Humphrey Duke of Gloucester, Lord Protector
see *2 Henry VI*)

**III.i.1 brake** thicket; **shroud** conceal  **2 laund** glade  **3
covert** thicket; **stand** hiding place  **4 Culling** picking out
**8 at the best** as well as we can  **9 for** so that  **11 self** same
**20 of** from  **23 quondam** former  **37 batt'ry** bombardment

To hear and see her plaints, her brinish tears.
Ay, but she's come to beg, Warwick, to give;
She on his left side, craving aid for Henry,
He on his right, asking a wife for Edward.
She weeps, and says her Henry is deposed;                    45
He smiles, and says his Edward is installed;
That she (poor wretch) for grief can speak no more;
Whiles Warwick tells his title, smooths the wrong,
Inferreth arguments of mighty strength,
And in conclusion wins the king from her,                    50
With promise of his sister, and what else,
To strengthen and support King Edward's place.
O Margaret, thus 'twill be; and thou (poor soul)
Art then forsaken, as thou went'st forlorn!

SECOND KEEPER
Say, what art thou that talk'st of kings and queens?          55

KING HENRY
More than I seem, and less than I was born to:
A man at least, for less I should not be;
And men may talk of kings, and why not I?

SECOND KEEPER
Ay, but thou talk'st as if thou wert a king.

KING HENRY
Why, so I am (in mind) and that's enough.                    60

SECOND KEEPER
But, if thou be a king, where is thy crown?

KING HENRY
My crown is in my heart, not on my head;
Not decked with diamonds and Indian stones,
Nor to be seen. My crown is called content:
A crown it is that seldom kings enjoy.                       65

SECOND KEEPER
Well, if you be a king crowned with content,
Your crown content and you must be contented
To go along with us; for (as we think)
You are the king King Edward hath deposed;
And we his subjects sworn in all allegiance                  70
Will apprehend you as his enemy.

KING HENRY
But did you never swear, and break an oath?

SECOND KEEPER
No, never such an oath; nor will not now.

KING HENRY
Where did you dwell when I was King of England?

SECOND KEEPER
Here in this country, where we now remain.                   75

KING HENRY
I was anointed king at nine months old;
My father and my grandfather were kings,
And you were sworn true subjects unto me:
And tell me, then, have you not broke your oaths?

FIRST KEEPER
No;                                                          80
For we were subjects but while you were king.

KING HENRY
Why, am I dead? Do I not breathe a man?
Ah, simple men, you know not what you swear!
Look, as I blow this feather from my face,
And as the air blows it to me again,                         85
Obeying with my wind when I do blow,
And yielding to another when it blows,
Commanded always by the greater gust—
Such is the lightness of you common men.

But do not break your oaths; for of that sin                 90
My mild entreaty shall not make you guilty.
Go where you will, the king shall be commanded;
And be you kings, command, and I'll obey.

FIRST KEEPER
We are true subjects to the king, King Edward.

KING HENRY
So would you be again to Henry,                              95
If he were seated as King Edward is.

FIRST KEEPER
We charge you, in God's name, and the king's,
To go with us unto the officers.

KING HENRY
In God's name, lead. Your king's name be obeyed:
And what God will, that let your king perform;               100
And what he will, I humbly yield unto.          Exeunt.

[Scene II. London. The palace.]

Enter KING EDWARD, [RICHARD, Duke of] Gloucester,
[George, Duke of] CLARENCE, LADY GREY.

KING EDWARD
Brother of Gloucester, at Saint Albans Field
This lady's husband, Sir Richard Grey, was slain,
His land then seized on by the conqueror.
Her suit is now to repossess those lands;
Which we in justice cannot well deny,°
Because in quarrel of the house of York                       5
The worthy gentleman did lose his life.

RICHARD
Your highness shall do well to grant her suit;
It were dishonor to deny it her.

KING EDWARD
It were no less; but yet I'll make a pause.

RICHARD [Aside to CLARENCE.]                                  10
Yea, is it so?
I see the lady hath a thing to grant,
Before the king will grant her humble suit.

CLARENCE [Aside to RICHARD.]
He knows the game: how true he keeps the wind!°

RICHARD [Aside to CLARENCE.]
Silence!                                                      15

KING EDWARD
Widow, we will consider of your suit;
And come some other time to know our mind.

LADY GREY
Right gracious lord, I cannot brook° delay:
May it please your highness to resolve me now,
And what your pleasure is shall satisfy me.                   20

RICHARD [Aside to CLARENCE.]
Ay, widow? then I'll warrant° you all your lands,
And if what pleases him shall pleasure you.
Fight closer, or, good faith, you'll catch a blow.

CLARENCE [Aside to RICHARD.]
I fear her not, unless she chance to fall.

RICHARD [Aside to CLARENCE.]
God forbid that! for he'll take vantages.°                    25

KING EDWARD
How many children hast thou, widow? tell me.

III.ii.5 deny refuse   14 keeps the wind keeps to the windward side of the game (metaphor from hunting)   18 brook
endure   21 warrant guarantee   25 take vantages take
advantage of opportunities

CLARENCE [*Aside to* RICHARD.]
I think he means to beg a child of her.

RICHARD [*Aside to* CLARENCE.]
Nay then, whip me: he'll rather give her two.

LADY GREY
Three, my most gracious lord.

RICHARD [*Aside to* CLARENCE.]
You shall have four, if you'll be ruled by him.      30

KING EDWARD
'Twere pity they should lose their father's lands.

LADY GREY
Be pitiful, dread lord, and grant it then.

KING EDWARD
Lords, give us leave: I'll try this widow's wit.°

RICHARD [*Aside to* CLARENCE.]
Ay, good leave have you; for you will have leave,
Till youth take leave and leave you to the crutch.°      35
[RICHARD *and* CLARENCE *withdraw.*]

KING EDWARD
Now tell me, madam, do you love your children?

LADY GREY
Ay, full as dearly as I love myself.

KING EDWARD
And would you not do much to do them good?

LADY GREY
To do them good, I would sustain some harm.

KING EDWARD
Then get your husband's lands, to do them good.      40

LADY GREY
Therefore I came unto your majesty.

KING EDWARD
I'll tell you how these lands are to be got.

LADY GREY
So shall you bind me to your highness' service.

KING EDWARD
What service wilt thou do me, if I give them?

LADY GREY
What you command, that rests in me° to do.      45

KING EDWARD
But you will take exceptions to my boon.°

LADY GREY
No, gracious lord, except I cannot do it.

KING EDWARD
Ay, but thou canst do what I mean to ask.

LADY GREY
Why, then I will do what your grace commands.

RICHARD [*Aside to* CLARENCE.]
He plies her hard; and much rain wears the marble.      50

CLARENCE [*Aside to* RICHARD.]
As red as fire! Nay, then her wax must melt.

LADY GREY
Why stops my lord? shall I not hear my task?

KING EDWARD
An easy task; 'tis but to love a king.

LADY GREY
That's soon performed, because I am a subject.

KING EDWARD
Why, then, thy husband's lands I freely give thee.      55

LADY GREY
I take my leave with many thousand thanks.

RICHARD [*Aside to* CLARENCE.]
The match is made; she seals it with a curtsy.

KING EDWARD
But stay thee, 'tis the fruits of love I mean.

LADY GREY
The fruits of love I mean, my loving liege.

KING EDWARD
Ay, but, I fear me, in another sense.      60
What love, think'st thou, I sue so much to get?

LADY GREY
My love till death, my humble thanks, my prayers;
That love which virtue begs and virtue grants.

KING EDWARD
No, by my troth, I did not mean such love.

LADY GREY
Why, then you mean not as I thought you did.      65

KING EDWARD
But now you partly may perceive my mind.

LADY GREY
My mind will never grant what I perceive
Your highness aims at, if I aim aright.

KING EDWARD
To tell thee plain, I aim to lie with thee.

LADY GREY
To tell you plain, I had rather lie in prison.      70

KING EDWARD
Why, then thou shalt not have thy husband's lands.

LADY GREY
Why, then mine honesty° shall be my dower;
For by that loss I will not purchase them.

KING EDWARD
Therein thou wrong'st thy children mightily.

LADY GREY
Herein your highness wrongs both them and me.      75
But, mighty lord, this merry inclination
Accords not with the sadness of my suit.°
Please you dismiss me, either with "ay" or "no."

KING EDWARD
Ay, if thou wilt say "ay" to my request;
No, if thou dost say "no" to my demand.      80

LADY GREY
Then, no, my lord. My suit is at an end.

RICHARD [*Aside to* CLARENCE.]
The widow likes him not, she knits her brows.

CLARENCE [*Aside to* RICHARD.]
He is the bluntest wooer in Christendom.

KING EDWARD [*Aside.*]
Her looks doth argue her replete with modesty;
Her words doth show her wit incomparable;      85
All her perfections challenge° sovereignty:
One way or other, she is for a king;
And she shall be my love, or else my queen—

[*Aloud.*]
Say that King Edward take thee for his queen?

LADY GREY
'Tis better said than done, my gracious lord:      90
I am a subject fit to jest withal,
But far unfit to be a sovereign.

KING EDWARD
Sweet widow, by my state I swear to thee

---

**33 wit** intelligence   **34–35 for . . . crutch** for you will take liberties until youth departs and leaves you infirm   **45 rests in me** is in my power   **46 boon** favor

**72 honesty** chastity   **77 sadness of my suit** seriousness of my request   **86 challenge** lay claim to

I speak no more than what my soul intends;
And that is, to enjoy thee for my love.                    95

LADY GREY
And that is more than I will yield unto.
I know I am too mean° to be your queen,
And yet too good to be your concubine.

KING EDWARD
You cavil, widow: I did mean, my queen.

LADY GREY
'Twill grieve your grace my sons should call you
    father.                                               100

KING EDWARD
No more than when my daughters call thee mother.
Thou art a widow, and thou hast some children;
And, by God's mother, I, being but a bachelor,
Have other some:° why, 'tis a happy° thing
To be the father unto many sons.                          105
Answer no more, for thou shalt be my queen.

RICHARD [Aside to CLARENCE.]
The ghostly° father now hath done his shrift.

CLARENCE [Aside to RICHARD.]
When he was made a shriver, 'twas for shift.°

KING EDWARD
Brothers, you muse what chat we two have had.

RICHARD
The widow likes it not, for she looks very sad.           110

KING EDWARD
You'd think it strange if I should marry her.

CLARENCE
To who, my lord?

KING EDWARD                    Why, Clarence, to myself.

RICHARD
That would be ten days' wonder at the least.

CLARENCE
That's a day longer than a wonder lasts.°

RICHARD
By so much is the wonder in extremes.                     115

KING EDWARD
Well, jest on, brothers. I can tell you both
Her suit is granted for her husband's lands.

*Enter a* NOBLEMAN.

NOBLEMAN
My gracious lord, Henry your foe is taken,
And brought your prisoner to your palace gate.

KING EDWARD
See that he be conveyed unto the Tower:                   120
And go we, brothers, to the man that took him,
To question of his apprehension.°
Widow, go you along. Lords, use her honorably.
                    *Exeunt. Manet°* RICHARD.

RICHARD
Ay, Edward will use women honorably.
Would he were wasted, marrow, bones, and all,            125
That from his loins no hopeful branch may spring,
To cross me from the golden time I look for!
And yet, between my soul's desire and me—
The lustful Edward's title burièd—

Is Clarence, Henry, and his son young Edward,            130
And all the unlooked-for° issue of their bodies,
To take their rooms, ere I can place myself:
A cold premeditation for my purpose!
Why then, I do but dream on sovereignty;
Like one that stands upon a promontory,                  135
And spies a far-off shore where he would tread,
Wishing his foot were equal with his eye,
And chides the sea that sunders him from thence,
Saying, he'll lade° it dry to have his way:
So do I wish the crown, being so far off;                140
And so I chide the means that keeps me from it;
And so (I say) I'll cut the causes off,
Flattering me with impossibilities.
My eye's too quick, my heart o'erweens too much,°
Unless my hand and strength could equal them.           145
Well, say there is no kingdom then for Richard:
What other pleasure can the world afford?
I'll make my heaven in a lady's lap,
And deck my body in gay ornaments
And witch° sweet ladies with my words and looks.        150
O miserable thought! and more unlikely
Than to accomplish° twenty golden crowns!
Why, love forswore° me in my mother's womb:
And, for° I should not deal in her soft laws,
She did corrupt frail nature with some bribe,            155
To shrink mine arm up like a withered shrub;
To make an envious° mountain on my back,
Where sits deformity to mock my body;
To shape my legs of an unequal size;
To disproportion me in every part,                       160
Like to a chaos,° or an unlicked bear whelp
That carries no impression like the dam.
And am I then a man to be beloved?
O monstrous fault,° to harbor such a thought!
Then, since this earth affords no joy to me,             165
But to command, to check, to o'erbear such
As are of better person° than myself,
I'll make my heaven to dream upon the crown,
And, whiles I live, t' account this world but hell,
Until my misshaped trunk that bears this head           170
Be round impalèd with a glorious crown.
And yet I know not how to get the crown,
For many lives stand between me and home:°
And I—like one lost in a thorny wood,
That rends the thorns and is rent with the thorns,       175
Seeking a way and straying from the way,
Not knowing how to find the open air,
But toiling desperately to find it out—
Torment myself to catch the English crown:
And from that torment I will free myself,                180
Or hew my way out with a bloody ax.
Why, I can smile, and murder whiles I smile,
And cry, "Content" to that which grieves my heart,
And wet my cheeks with artificial tears,
And frame my face to all occasions.                      185
I'll drown more sailors than the mermaid shall;

---

97 **mean** low in rank  104 **other some** others; **happy**
fortunate  107 **ghostly** spiritual  108 **for shift** (1) to serve a
purpose (2) for a woman's undergarment  114 **That's . . .
lasts** proverbially a wonder lasts only nine days  122
**apprehension** arrest  123 s.d. **Manet** remains (Latin)

131 **unlooked-for** (1) unforeseen (2) undesired  139 **lade** bail
144 **o'erweens too much** is too presumptuous  150 **witch**
bewitch  152 **accomplish** obtain  153 **forswore** abjured
154 **for** so that  157 **envious** spiteful  161 **chaos** shapeless
mass  164 **fault** error  167 **person** appearance  173 **home**
my goal

I'll slay more gazers than the basilisk;°
I'll play the orator as well as Nestor,
Deceive more slily than Ulysses could,
And, like a Sinon,° take another Troy. 190
I can add colors to the chameleon,
Change shapes with Proteus° for advantages,
And set the murderous Machiavel° to school.
Can I do this, and cannot get a crown?
Tut, were it farther off, I'll pluck it down. *Exit.* 195

[*Scene III. France. The king's palace.*]

*Flourish. Enter* LEWIS *the French king, his sister* BONA, *his* ADMIRAL, *called Bourbon;* PRINCE *Edward,* QUEEN MARGARET, *and the Earl of* OXFORD. LEWIS *sits, and riseth up again.*

KING LEWIS
Fair Queen of England, worthy Margaret,
Sit down with us: it ill befits thy state
And birth, that thou shouldst stand while Lewis
  doth sit.
QUEEN MARGARET
No, mighty King of France: now Margaret
Must strike her sail° and learn awhile to serve 5
Where kings command. I was (I must confess)
Great Albion's° queen in former golden days;
But now mischance hath trod my title down,
And with dishonor laid me on the ground;
Where I must take like seat unto my fortune, 10
And to my humble seat conform myself.
KING LEWIS
Why, say, fair queen, whence springs this deep
  despair?
QUEEN MARGARET
From such a cause as fills mine eyes with tears
And stops my tongue, while heart is drowned in cares.
KING LEWIS
Whate'er it be, be thou still like thyself, 15
And sit thee by our side. (*Seats her by him.*) Yield not
  thy neck
To fortune's yoke, but let thy dauntless mind
Still ride in triumph over all mischance.
Be plain, Queen Margaret, and tell thy grief;
It shall be eased, if France can yield relief. 20
QUEEN MARGARET
Those gracious words revive my drooping thoughts
And give my tongue-tied sorrows leave to speak.
Now, therefore, be it known to noble Lewis,
That Henry, sole possessor of my love,
Is of a king become a banished man, 25
And forced to live in Scotland a forlorn;°
While proud ambitious Edward, Duke of York,
Usurps the regal title and the seat
Of England's true-anointed lawful king.

This is the cause that I, poor Margaret, 30
With this my son, Prince Edward, Henry's heir,
Am come to crave thy just and lawful aid;
And if thou fail us, all our hope is done.
Scotland hath will to help, but cannot help;
Our people and our peers are both misled, 35
Our treasure seized, our soldiers put to flight,
And, as thou see'st, ourselves in heavy° plight.
KING LEWIS
Renownèd queen, with patience calm the storm,
While we bethink a means to break it off.°
QUEEN MARGARET
The more we stay, the stronger grows our foe. 40
KING LEWIS
The more I stay,° the more I'll succor thee.
QUEEN MARGARET
O, but impatience waiteth on° true sorrow.
And see where comes the breeder of my sorrow!

*Enter* WARWICK.

KING LEWIS
What's he approacheth boldly to our presence?
QUEEN MARGARET
Our Earl of Warwick, Edward's greatest friend. 45
KING LEWIS
Welcome, brave Warwick! What brings thee to
  France?

*He descends. She ariseth.*

QUEEN MARGARET [*Aside.*]
Ay, now begins a second storm to rise,
For this is he that moves both wind and tide.
WARWICK
From worthy Edward, King of Albion,
My lord and sovereign, and thy vowèd friend, 50
I come, in kindness and unfeignèd love,
First, to do greetings to thy royal person;
And then to crave a league of amity;
And lastly, to confirm that amity
With nuptial knot, if thou vouchsafe to grant 55
That virtuous Lady Bona, thy fair sister,
To England's king in lawful marriage.
QUEEN MARGARET [*Aside.*]
If that go forward, Henry's hope is done.
WARWICK (*Speaking to* BONA.)
And, gracious madam, in our king's behalf,
I am commanded, with your leave and favor,° 60
Humbly to kiss your hand, and with my tongue
To tell the passion° of my sovereign's heart;
Where fame,° late ent'ring at his heedful ears,
Hath placed thy beauty's image and thy virtue.
QUEEN MARGARET
King Lewis and Lady Bona, hear me speak, 65
Before you answer Warwick. His demand
Springs not from Edward's well-meant honest love,
But from deceit, bred by necessity;
For how can tyrants° safely govern home,
Unless abroad they purchase° great alliance? 70

187 **basilisk** fabulous reptile, said to kill by its look and breath
190 **Sinon** Greek warrior who devised the stratagem of the
wooden horse, by which the Greeks ultimately captured
and destroyed Troy 192 **Proteus** sea deity who assumed
various forms 193 **Machiavel** Niccolò Machiavelli, author
of *The Prince* (1513), whose name became synonymous with
sinister intrigue and the worship of power
**III.iii.5 strike her sail** humble herself 7 **Albion** ancient
name of Britain 26 **a forlorn** a forlorn man

37 **heavy** sad 39 **break it off** end it 41 **stay** with pun on
the meaning "support" 42 **waiteth on** accompanies 60
**leave and favor** kind permission 62 **passion** suffering 63
**fame** rumor 69 **tyrants** usurpers 70 **purchase** obtain

To prove him tyrant this reason may suffice,
That Henry liveth still; but were he dead,
Yet here Prince Edward stands, King Henry's son.
Look, therefore, Lewis, that by this league and
   marriage
Thou draw not on thy danger and dishonor; 75
For though usurpers sway the rule awhile,
Yet heavens are just, and time suppresseth wrongs.

WARWICK
Injurious Margaret!

PRINCE          And why not queen?

WARWICK
Because thy father Henry did usurp;
And thou no more art prince than she is queen. 80

OXFORD
Then Warwick disannuls° great John of Gaunt,
Which did subdue the greatest part of Spain;
And, after John of Gaunt, Henry the Fourth,
Whose wisdom was a mirror° to the wisest;
And, after that wise prince, Henry the Fifth, 85
Who by his prowess conquerèd all France:
From these our Henry lineally descends.

WARWICK
Oxford, how haps it, in this smooth discourse,
You told not how Henry the Sixth hath lost
All that which Henry the Fifth had gotten? 90
Methinks these peers of France should smile at that.
But for the rest: you tell° a pedigree
Of threescore and two years—a silly° time
To make prescription° for a kingdom's worth.

OXFORD
Why, Warwick, canst thou speak against thy liege, 95
Whom thou obeyèd'st thirty and six years,
And not bewray° thy treason with a blush?

WARWICK
Can Oxford, that did ever fence° the right,
Now buckler° falsehood with a pedigree?
For shame! leave Henry, and call Edward king. 100

OXFORD
Call him my king by whose injurious doom°
My elder brother, the Lord Aubrey Vere,
Was done to death? and more than so, my father,
Even in the downfall of his mellowed years,
When nature brought him to the door of death? 105
No, Warwick, no; while life upholds this arm,
This arm upholds the house of Lancaster.

WARWICK
And I the house of York.

KING LEWIS
Queen Margaret, Prince Edward, and Oxford,
Vouchsafe, at our request, to stand aside, 110
While I use further conference with Warwick.

*They stand aloof.*

QUEEN MARGARET
Heavens grant that Warwick's words bewitch him
   not!

KING LEWIS
Now, Warwick, tell me, even upon thy conscience,

Is Edward your true king? for I were loath
To link with him that were not lawful chosen. 115

WARWICK
Thereon I pawn my credit and mine honor.

KING LEWIS
But is he gracious° in the people's eye?

WARWICK
The more that Henry was unfortunate.

KING LEWIS
Then, further, all dissembling set aside,
Tell me for truth the measure of his love 120
Unto our sister Bona.

WARWICK       Such it seems
As may beseem a monarch like himself.
Myself have often heard him say and swear
That this his love was an eternal plant,
Whereof the root was fixed in virtue's ground, 125
The leaves and fruit maintained with beauty's sun,
Exempt from envy, but not from disdain,
Unless the Lady Bona quit° his pain.

KING LEWIS
Now, sister, let us hear your firm resolve.

BONA
Your grant, or your denial, shall be mine: 130
Yet I confess that often ere this day

*(Speaks to WARWICK.)*

When I have heard your king's desert recounted,
Mine ear hath tempted judgment to desire.

KING LEWIS
Then, Warwick, thus: our sister shall be Edward's;
And now forthwith shall articles be drawn 135
Touching the jointure° that your king must make,
Which with her dowry shall be counterpoised.
Draw near, Queen Margaret, and be a witness
That Bona shall be wife to the English king.

PRINCE
To Edward, but not to the English king. 140

QUEEN MARGARET
Deceitful Warwick! it was thy device
By this alliance to make void my suit:
Before thy coming Lewis was Henry's friend.

KING LEWIS
And still is friend to him and Margaret:
But if your title to the crown be weak, 145
As may appear by Edward's good success,
Then 'tis but reason that I be released
From giving aid which late I promisèd.
Yet shall you have all kindness at my hand
That your estate requires and mine can yield. 150

WARWICK
Henry now lives in Scotland at his ease,
Where having nothing, nothing can he lose.
And as for you yourself, our quondam° queen,
You have a father able to maintain you,
And better 'twere you troubled him than France. 155

QUEEN MARGARET
Peace, impudent and shameless Warwick, peace,
Proud setter-up and puller-down of kings!
I will not hence, till with my talk and tears

81 **disannuls** again cancels  84 **mirror** model  92 **tell** (1)
relate (2) count  93 **silly** scanty  94 **prescription** claim  97
**bewray** reveal  98 **fence** defend  99 **buckler** shield  101
**injurious doom** unjust sentence

117 **gracious** favored, popular  128 **quit** requite  136
**jointure** marriage settlement  153 **quondam** former

(Both full of truth) I make King Lewis behold
Thy sly conveyance° and thy lord's false love;                    160
For both of you are birds of selfsame feather.

POST *blowing a horn within.*

KING LEWIS
Warwick, this is some post to us or thee.

*Enter the* POST.

POST (*Speaks to* WARWICK.)
My Lord Ambassador, these letters are for you,
Sent from your brother, Marquess Montague;

(*To* LEWIS.)

These from our king unto your majesty;                            165

(*To* MARGARET.)

And, madam, these for you; from whom I know not.

*They all read their letters.*

OXFORD
I like it well that our fair queen and mistress
Smiles at her news, while Warwick frowns at his.
PRINCE
Nay, mark how Lewis stamps, as he were nettled.
I hope all's for the best.                                        170
KING LEWIS
Warwick, what are thy news? and yours, fair queen?
QUEEN MARGARET
Mine, such as fill my heart with unhoped joys.
WARWICK
Mine, full of sorrow and heart's discontent.
KING LEWIS
What! has your king married the Lady Grey?
And now, to soothe your forgery and his,                          175
Sends me a paper to persuade me patience?
Is this th' alliance that he seeks with France?
Dare he presume to scorn us in this manner?
QUEEN MARGARET
I told your majesty as much before:
This proveth Edward's love and Warwick's honesty!                 180
WARWICK
King Lewis, I here protest, in sight of heaven,
And by the hope I have of heavenly bliss,
That I am clear from this misdeed of Edward's,
No more my king, for he dishonors me,
But most himself, if he could see his shame.                      185
Did I forget that by the house of York
My father came untimely to his death?
Did I let pass th' abuse done to my niece?
Did I impale° him with the regal crown?
Did I put Henry from his native right?                            190
And am I guerdoned° at the last with shame?
Shame on himself! for my desert is honor:
And to repair my honor lost for him,
I here renounce him and return to Henry.
My noble queen, let former grudges pass,                          195
And henceforth I am thy true servitor:
I will revenge his wrong to Lady Bona
And replant Henry in his former state.

QUEEN MARGARET
Warwick, these words have turned my hate to love;
And I forgive and quite forget old faults,                        200
And joy that thou becom'st King Henry's friend.
WARWICK
So much his friend, ay, his unfeignèd friend,
That, if King Lewis vouchsafe to furnish us
With some few bands of chosen soldiers,
I'll undertake to land them on our coast                          205
And force the tyrant from his seat by war.
'Tis not his new-made bride shall succor him:
And as for Clarence, as my letters tell me,
He's very likely now to fall from him,
For matching° more for wanton lust than honor,                    210
Or than for strength and safety of our country.
BONA
Dear brother, how shall Bona be revenged
But by thy help to this distressèd queen?
QUEEN MARGARET
Renownèd prince, how shall poor Henry live,
Unless thou rescue him from foul despair?                         215
BONA
My quarrel and this English queen's are one.
WARWICK
And mine, fair Lady Bona, joins with yours.
KING LEWIS
And mine with hers, and thine, and Margaret's.
Therefore at last I firmly am resolved
You shall have aid.                                               220
QUEEN MARGARET
Let me give humble thanks for all at once.
KING LEWIS
Then, England's messenger, return in post,°
And tell false Edward, thy supposèd king,
That Lewis of France is sending over masquers°
To revel it with him and his new bride:                           225
Thou see'st what's passed, go fear° thy king withal.
BONA
Tell him, in hope he'll prove a widower shortly,
I'll wear the willow garland° for his sake.
QUEEN MARGARET
Tell him, my mourning weeds° are laid aside,
And I am ready to put armor on.                                   230
WARWICK
Tell him from me that he hath done me wrong,
And therefore I'll uncrown him ere't be long.
There's thy reward. Be gone.               *Exit* POST.
KING LEWIS                          But, Warwick,
Thou and Oxford, with five thousand men,
Shall cross the seas, and bid false Edward battle;                235
And, as occasion serves,° this noble queen
And prince shall follow with a fresh supply.
Yet, ere thou go, but answer me one doubt,
What pledge have we of thy firm loyalty?
WARWICK
This shall assure my constant loyalty,                            240
That if our queen and this young prince agree,
I'll join mine eldest daughter and my joy
To him forthwith in holy wedlock bands.

---

**160 conveyance** (1) transfer of property (here, Lewis' promise
of aid) (2) trickery   **189 impale** encircle   **191 guerdoned**
rewarded

**210 matching** marrying   **222 post** haste   **224 masquers**
performers   **226 fear** frighten   **228 willow garland** sign of
disappointed love   **229 weeds** garments   **236 serves** is
opportune

QUEEN MARGARET
Yes, I agree, and thank you for your motion.°
Son Edward, she is fair and virtuous,                    245
Therefore delay not, give thy hand to Warwick;
And, with thy hand, thy faith irrevocable,
That only Warwick's daughter shall be thine.

PRINCE
Yes, I accept her, for she well deserves it;
And here, to pledge my vow, I give my hand.          250

*He gives his hand to* WARWICK.

KING LEWIS
Why stay we now? These soldiers shall be levied,
And thou, Lord Bourbon, our high admiral,
Shall waft them over with our royal fleet.
I long till Edward fall° by war's mischance,
For mocking marriage with a dame of France.          255
                              *Exeunt. Manet°* WARWICK.

WARWICK
I came from Edward as ambassador,
But I return his sworn and mortal foe:
Matter of marriage was the charge he gave me,
But dreadful war shall answer his demand.°
Had he none else to make a stale° but me?             260
Then none but I shall turn his jest to sorrow.
I was the chief that raised him to the crown,
And I'll be chief to bring him down again;
Not that I pity Henry's misery,
But seek revenge on Edward's mockery.      *Exit.* 265

# [ A C T   I V ]

## [Scene I. *London. The palace.*]

*Enter* RICHARD, CLARENCE, SOMERSET, *and* MON-
TAGUE.

RICHARD
Now tell me, brother Clarence, what think you
Of this new marriage with the Lady Grey?
Hath not our brother made a worthy choice?

CLARENCE
Alas, you know 'tis far from hence to France!
How could he stay till Warwick made return?          5

SOMERSET
My lords, forbear this talk; here comes the king.

RICHARD
And his well-chosen bride.

CLARENCE
I mind to tell him plainly what I think.

*Flourish. Enter* KING EDWARD, *Lady Grey* [*as* QUEEN],
PEMBROKE, STAFFORD, HASTINGS, [*and others*].
*Four stand on one side and four on the other.*

KING EDWARD
Now, brother of Clarence, how like you our choice,
That you stand pensive, as half malcontent?°          10

CLARENCE
As well as Lewis of France, or the Earl of Warwick,
Which are so weak of courage and in judgment
That they'll take no offense at our abuse.°

KING EDWARD
Suppose they take offense without a cause:
They are but Lewis and Warwick; I am Edward,          15
Your king and Warwick's, and must have my will.

RICHARD
And shall have your will, because our king.
Yet hasty marriage seldom proveth well.

KING EDWARD
Yea, brother Richard, are you offended too?

RICHARD
Not I.                                                  20
No, God forbid that I should wish them severed
Whom God hath joined together; ay, and 'twere pity
To sunder them that yoke so well together.

KING EDWARD
Setting your scorns and your mislike aside,
Tell me some reason why the Lady Grey                  25
Should not become my wife and England's queen.
And you too, Somerset and Montague,
Speak freely what you think.

CLARENCE
Then this is mine opinion, that King Lewis
Becomes your enemy for mocking him                     30
About the marriage of the Lady Bona.

RICHARD
And Warwick, doing what you gave in charge,
Is now dishonorèd by this new marriage.

KING EDWARD
What if both Lewis and Warwick be appeased
By such invention as I can devise?                     35

MONTAGUE
Yet, to have joined with France in such alliance
Would more have strengthened this our common-
        wealth
'Gainst foreign storms than any homebred marriage.

HASTINGS
Why, knows not Montague that of itself
England is safe, if true within itself?                40

MONTAGUE
But the safer when 'tis backed with France.

HASTINGS
'Tis better using France than trusting France:
Let us be backed with God and with the seas
Which He hath given for fence impregnable,
And with their helps only° defend ourselves;          45
In them and in ourselves our safety lies.

CLARENCE
For this one speech Lord Hastings well deserves
To have the heir of the Lord Hungerford.

KING EDWARD
Ay, what of that? It was my will and grant;
And for this once my will shall stand for law.          50

RICHARD
And yet methinks your grace hath done not well,
To give the heir and daughter of Lord Scales
Unto the brother of your loving bride.
She better would have fitted me or Clarence;
But in your bride you bury brotherhood.                55

**244 motion** offer   **254 long . . . fall** am impatient for
Edward to fall   **255 s.d. Manet** remains   **259 demand** request
**260 stale** (1) dupe (2) tool
**IV.i.10 malcontent** discontented, dissatisfied

**13 abuse** deceit   **45 only** alone

**CLARENCE**
Or else you would not have bestowed the heir
Of the Lord Bonville on your new wife's son,
And leave your brothers to go speed° elsewhere.

**KING EDWARD**
Alas, poor Clarence! Is it for a wife
That thou art malcontent? I will provide thee.      60

**CLARENCE**
In choosing for yourself, you showed your judgment,
Which being shallow, you shall give me leave
To play the broker° in mine own behalf;
And to that end I shortly mind to leave you.

**KING EDWARD**
Leave me or tarry, Edward will be king,      65
And not be tied unto his brother's will.

**QUEEN ELIZABETH**
My lords, before it pleased his majesty
To raise my state to title of a queen,
Do me but right, and you must all confess
That I was not ignoble of descent;      70
And meaner° than myself have had like fortune.
But as this title honors me and mine,
So your dislikes, to whom I would be pleasing,
Doth cloud my joys with danger and with sorrow.

**KING EDWARD**
My love, forbear to fawn upon their frowns.      75
What danger or what sorrow can befall' thee,
So long as Edward is thy constant friend
And their true sovereign, whom they must obey?
Nay, whom they shall obey, and love thee too,
Unless they seek for hatred at my hands;      80
Which if they do, yet will I keep thee safe,
And they shall feel the vengeance of my wrath.

**RICHARD** [*Aside.*]
I hear, yet say not much, but think the more.

*Enter a* POST.

**KING EDWARD**
Now, messenger, what letters or what news
From France?      85

**POST**
My sovereign liege, no letters; and few words,
But such as I, without your special pardon,°
Dare not relate.

**KING EDWARD**
Go to,° we pardon thee. Therefore, in brief,
Tell me their words as near as thou canst guess them.      90
What answer makes King Lewis unto our letters?

**POST**
At my depart, these were his very words:
"Go tell false Edward, thy supposèd king,
That Lewis of France is sending over masquers
To revel it with him and his new bride."      95

**KING EDWARD**
Is Lewis so brave?° Belike he thinks me Henry.
But what said Lady Bona to my marriage?

**POST**
These were her words, uttered with mild disdain:
"Tell him, in hope he'll prove a widower shortly,
I'll wear the willow garland for his sake."      100

**KING EDWARD**
I blame not her, she could say little less;
She had the wrong. But what said Henry's queen?
For I have heard that she was there in place.

**POST**
"Tell him," quoth she, "my mourning weeds are done,
And I am ready to put armor on."      105

**KING EDWARD**
Belike she minds to play the Amazon.
But what said Warwick to these injuries?°

**POST**
He, more incensed against your majesty
Than all the rest, discharged me with these words:
"Tell him from me that he hath done me wrong,      110
And therefore I'll uncrown him ere't be long."

**KING EDWARD**
Ha! durst the traitor breathe out so proud words?
Well, I will arm me, being thus forewarned.
They shall have wars and pay for their presumption.
But say, is Warwick friends with Margaret?      115

**POST**
Ay, gracious sovereign. They are so linked in friendship
That young Prince Edward marries Warwick's
daughter.

**CLARENCE**
Belike° the elder; Clarence will have the younger.
Now, brother king, farewell, and sit you fast,
For I will hence to Warwick's other daughter,      120
That, though I want° a kingdom, yet in marriage
I may not prove inferior to yourself.
You that love me and Warwick, follow me.

*Exit* CLARENCE, *and* SOMERSET *follows.*

**RICHARD** [*Aside.*]
Not I:
My thoughts aim at a further matter. I      125
Stay not for the love of Edward, but the crown.

**KING EDWARD**
Clarence and Somerset both gone to Warwick!
Yet am I armed against the worst can happen;
And haste is needful in this desp'rate case.
Pembroke and Stafford, you in our behalf      130
Go levy men, and make prepare for war.
They are already, or quickly will be, landed.
Myself in person will straight follow you.

*Exeunt* PEMBROKE *and* STAFFORD.

But, ere I go, Hastings and Montague,
Resolve my doubt. You twain, of all the rest,      135
Are near to Warwick by blood and by alliance.
Tell me if you love Warwick more than me.
If it be so, then both depart to him;
I rather wish you foes than hollow friends.
But if you mind to hold your true obedience,      140
Give me assurance with some friendly vow,
That I may never have you in suspect.

**MONTAGUE**
So God help Montague as he proves true!

**HASTINGS**
And Hastings as he favors Edward's cause!

**KING EDWARD**
Now, brother Richard, will you stand by us?      145

---

**58 speed** prosper   **63 play the broker** act as go-between
**71 meaner** persons of lower rank   **87 pardon** permission   **89
Go to** exclamation of impatience   **96 brave** defiant

**107 injuries** insults   **118 Belike** probably   **121 want** lack

RICHARD
Ay, in despite of all that shall withstand you.

KING EDWARD
Why, so! then am I sure of victory.
Now therefore let us hence, and lose no hour,
Till we meet Warwick with his foreign pow'r.
                            *Exeunt.*

[Scene II. *A plain in Warwickshire.*]

*Enter* WARWICK *and* OXFORD *in England, with French* SOLDIERS.

WARWICK
Trust me, my lord, all hitherto° goes well;
The common people by numbers swarm to us.

*Enter* CLARENCE *and* SOMERSET.

But see where Somerset and Clarence comes!
Speak suddenly,° my lords, are we all friends?

CLARENCE
Fear not that,° my lord.                       5

WARWICK
Then, gentle Clarence, welcome unto Warwick;
And welcome, Somerset: I hold it cowardice
To rest° mistrustful where a noble heart
Hath pawned° an open hand in sign of love.
Else might I think that Clarence, Edward's brother,    10
Were but a feignèd friend to our proceedings:
But welcome, sweet Clarence; my daughter shall be
    thine.
And now what rests but, in night's coverture,°
Thy brother being carelessly encamped,
His soldiers lurking in the towns about,           15
And but attended by a simple guard,
We may surprise and take him at our pleasure?
Our scouts have found the adventure very easy:
That as Ulysses and stout° Diomede
With sleight° and manhood stole to Rhesus' tents,    20
And brought from thence the Thracian fatal steeds,°
So we, well covered with the night's black mantle,
At unawares may beat down Edward's guard
And seize himself. I say not, slaughter him,
For I intend but only to surprise him.          25
You that will follow me to this attempt,
Applaud the name of Henry with your leader.

*They all cry,* "Henry!"

Why, then, let's on our way in silent sort.°
For Warwick and his friends, God and Saint George!
                            *Exeunt.*

[Scene III. *Edward's camp, near Warwick.*]

*Enter three* WATCHMEN, *to guard the king's tent.*

FIRST WATCHMAN
Come on, my masters, each man take his stand.
The king by this° is set him down to sleep.

SECOND WATCHMAN
What, will he not to bed?

FIRST WATCHMAN
Why, no; for he hath made a solemn vow
Never to lie and take his natural rest          5
Till Warwick or himself be quite suppressed.

SECOND WATCHMAN
Tomorrow then belike shall be the day,
If Warwick be so near as men report.

THIRD WATCHMAN
But say, I pray, what nobleman is that
That with the king here resteth in his tent?      10

FIRST WATCHMAN
'Tis the Lord Hastings, the king's chiefest friend.

THIRD WATCHMAN
O, is it so? But why commands the king
That his chief followers lodge in towns about him,
While he himself keeps° in the cold field?

SECOND WATCHMAN
'Tis the more honor, because more dangerous.    15

THIRD WATCHMAN
Ay, but give me worship° and quietness;
I like it better than a dangerous honor.
If Warwick knew in what estate he° stands,
'Tis to be doubted° he would waken him.

FIRST WATCHMAN
Unless our halberds° did shut up his passage.    20

SECOND WATCHMAN
Ay, wherefore else guard we his royal tent,
But to defend his person from night foes?

*Enter* WARWICK, CLARENCE, OXFORD, SOMERSET, *and French* SOLDIERS, *silent all.*

WARWICK
This is his tent; and see where stand his guard.
Courage, my masters! honor now or never!
But follow me, and Edward shall be ours.      25

FIRST WATCHMAN
Who goes there?

SECOND WATCHMAN
Stay, or thou diest!

WARWICK *and the rest cry all,* "Warwick! Warwick!" *and set upon the* GUARD, *who fly, crying,* "Arm! arm!", WARWICK *and the rest following them.*

*The drum playing and trumpet sounding, enter* WARWICK, SOMERSET, *and the rest, bringing the* KING *out in his gown, sitting in a chair.* RICHARD *and* HASTINGS *flies over the stage.*

SOMERSET
What are they that fly there?

WARWICK
Richard and Hastings. Let them go. Here is the duke.

IV.ii.1 **hitherto** thus far   **4 suddenly** at once   **5 Fear not that** do not doubt it   **8 rest** remain   **9 pawned** pledged   **13 in night's coverture** under cover of night   **19 stout** valiant   **20 sleight** trickery   **19–21 That . . . steeds** *Iliad*, X (because an oracle had said that Troy could not be taken if Rhesus' horses grazed on Trojan plains, the Greeks sent Ulysses and Diomede to capture the horses before they reached Troy)   **28 in silent sort** silently

IV.iii.2 **by this** by this time   **14 keeps** lives   **16 worship** ease and dignity   **18 he** the king   **19 doubted** suspected   **20 halberds** battle-axes on poles

**KING EDWARD**
The duke! Why, Warwick, when we parted,    30
Thou call'dst me king.
**WARWICK**                    Ay, but the case is altered:
When you disgraced me in my embassade,°
Then I degraded you from being king,
And come now to create you Duke of York.
Alas, how should you govern any kingdom,    35
That know not how to use ambassadors,
Nor how to be contented with one wife,
Nor how to use your brothers brotherly,
Nor how to study for the people's welfare,
Nor how to shroud yourself from enemies?    40
**KING EDWARD**
Yea, brother of Clarence, art thou here too?
Nay, then I see that Edward needs must down.
Yet, Warwick, in despite of all mischance,
Of thee thyself and all thy complices,
Edward will always bear himself as king:    45
Though Fortune's malice overthrow my state,°
My mind exceeds the compass° of her wheel.
**WARWICK**
Then, for his mind,° be Edward England's king:

*Takes off his crown.*

But Henry now shall wear the English crown,
And be true king indeed, thou but the shadow.    50
My Lord of Somerset, at my request,
See that forthwith Duke Edward be conveyed
Unto my brother, Archbishop of York.
When I have fought with Pembroke and his fellows,
I'll follow you, and tell what answer    55
Lewis and the Lady Bona send to him.
Now, for a while farewell, good Duke of York.
                    *They lead him out forcibly.*
**KING EDWARD**
What fates impose, that men must needs abide;
It boots not to resist both wind and tide.    *Exeunt.*
**OXFORD**
What now remains, my lords, for us to do    60
But march to London with our soldiers?
**WARWICK**
Ay, that's the first thing that we have to do,
To free King Henry from imprisonment
And see him seated in the regal throne.    *Exeunt.*

[Scene IV. *London. The palace.*]

*Enter* RIVERS *and Lady Grey* [*as* QUEEN].

**RIVERS**
Madam, what makes you in this sudden change?°
**QUEEN ELIZABETH**
Why, brother Rivers, are you yet to learn
What late misfortune is befall'n King Edward?
**RIVERS**
What, loss of some pitched battle against Warwick?
**QUEEN ELIZABETH**
No, but the loss of his own royal person.    5

**RIVERS**
Then is my sovereign slain?
**QUEEN ELIZABETH**
Ay, almost slain, for he is taken prisoner,
Either betrayed by falsehood° of his guard
Or by his foe surprised at° unawares;
And, as I further have to understand,    10
Is new committed to the Bishop of York,
Fell Warwick's brother and by that our foe.
**RIVERS**
These news, I must confess, are full of grief;
Yet, gracious madam, bear it as you may:
Warwick may lose, that now hath won the day.    15
**QUEEN ELIZABETH**
Till then fair hope must hinder life's decay.
And I the rather wean me from despair
For love of Edward's offspring in my womb.
This is it that makes me bridle passion
And bear with mildness my misfortune's cross.    20
Ay, ay, for this I draw in many a tear
And stop the rising of bloodsucking sighs,
Lest with my sighs or tears I blast or drown
King Edward's fruit, true heir to th' English crown.
**RIVERS**
But, madam, where is Warwick then become?°    25
**QUEEN ELIZABETH**
I am informèd that he comes towards London,
To set the crown once more on Henry's head.
Guess thou the rest; King Edward's friends must down.
But, to prevent° the tyrant's violence—
For trust not him that hath once broken faith—    30
I'll hence forthwith unto the sanctuary,
To save at least the heir of Edward's right.
There shall I rest secure from force and fraud.
Come, therefore, let us fly while we may fly.
If Warwick take us we are sure to die.    *Exeunt.* 35

[Scene V. *A park near Middleham Castle in
Yorkshire.*]

*Enter* RICHARD, *Lord* HASTINGS, *and Sir William*
STANLEY.

**RICHARD**
Now, my Lord Hastings and Sir William Stanley,
Leave off to wonder why I drew you hither,
Into this chiefest thicket of the park.
Thus stands the case: you know our king, my brother,
Is prisoner to the bishop here, at whose hands    5
He hath good usage and great liberty,
And often but attended with weak guard,
Comes hunting this way to disport himself.
I have advertised° him by secret means
That if about this hour he make this way    10
Under the color° of his usual game,
He shall here find his friends with horse and men
To set him free from his captivity.

*Enter* KING EDWARD *and a* HUNTSMAN *with him.*

32 **embassade** ambassadorial errand  46 **state** sovereignty
47 **compass** range  48 **for his mind** in Edward's mind (but
not otherwise)
**IV.iv.1 Madam . . . change** What is the cause of this sudden
change in you?

8 **falsehood** treachery  9 **surprised at** captured  25 **where
. . . become** what has become of Warwick  29 **prevent**
forestall
**IV.v.9 advertised** informed  11 **color** pretext

HUNTSMAN
This way, my lord, for this way lies the game.°

KING EDWARD
Nay, this way, man! See where the huntsmen stand. 15
Now, brother of Gloucester, Lord Hastings, and the
     rest,
Stand you thus close,° to steal the bishop's deer?

RICHARD
Brother, the time and case requireth haste:
Your horse stands ready at the park corner.

KING EDWARD
But whither shall we then?

HASTINGS             To Lynn, my lord,     20
And ship from thence to Flanders.

RICHARD
Well guessed, believe me; for that was my meaning.

KING EDWARD
Stanley, I will requite thy forwardness.°

RICHARD
But wherefore stay° we? 'tis no time to talk.

KING EDWARD
Huntsman, what say'st thou? wilt thou go along?    25

HUNTSMAN
Better do so than tarry and be hanged.

RICHARD
Come then, away; let's ha' no more ado.

KING EDWARD
Bishop, farewell. Shield thee from Warwick's frown
And pray that I may repossess the crown.     *Exeunt.*

[Scene VI. *London. The Tower.*]

*Flourish. Enter* KING HENRY *the Sixth,* CLARENCE,
WARWICK, SOMERSET, *young Henry [Earl of* RICH-
MOND], OXFORD, MONTAGUE, *and* LIEUTENANT
[*of the Tower*].

KING HENRY
Master Lieutenant, now that God and friends
Have shaken Edward from the regal seat
And turned my captive state to liberty,
My fear to hope, my sorrows unto joys,
At our enlargement° what are thy due fees?     5

LIEUTENANT
Subjects may challenge° nothing of their sovereigns;
But, if an humble prayer may prevail,
I then crave pardon of your majesty.

KING HENRY
For what, lieutenant? for well using me?
Nay, be thou sure I'll well requite thy kindness    10
For that it made my imprisonment a pleasure;
Ay, such a pleasure as incagèd birds
Conceive when after many moody thoughts
At last by notes of household harmony
They quite forget their loss of liberty.     15
But, Warwick, after God, thou set'st me free,
And chiefly therefore I thank God and thee;
He was the author, thou the instrument.
Therefore, that I may conquer fortune's spite

By living low,° where fortune cannot hurt me,    20
And that the people of this blessèd land
May not be punished with my thwarting stars,°
Warwick, although my head still wear the crown,
I here resign my government to thee,
For thou art fortunate in all thy deeds.     25

WARWICK
Your grace hath still° been famed for° virtuous;
And now may seem as wise as virtuous,
By spying and avoiding fortune's malice,
For few men rightly temper° with the stars:
Yet in this one thing let me blame your grace,    30
For choosing me when Clarence is in place.°

CLARENCE
No, Warwick, thou art worthy of the sway,°
To whom the heavens in thy nativity°
Adjudged an olive branch and laurel crown,
As likely to be blest in peace and war;     35
And therefore I yield thee my free consent.

WARWICK
And I choose Clarence only for protector.

KING HENRY
Warwick and Clarence, give me both your hands:
Now join your hands, and with your hands your
     hearts,
That no dissension hinder government:     40
I make you both protectors of this land,
While I myself will lead a private life,
And in devotion spend my latter days,
To sin's rebuke and my Creator's praise.

WARWICK
What answers Clarence to his sovereign's will?    45

CLARENCE
That he consents, if Warwick yield consent,
For on thy fortune I repose myself.°

WARWICK
Why, then, though loath, yet must I be content:
We'll yoke together, like a double shadow
To Henry's body, and supply his place;     50
I mean, in bearing weight of government,
While he enjoys the honor and his ease.
And, Clarence, now then it is more than needful
Forthwith that Edward be pronounced a traitor,
And all his lands and goods be confiscate.     55

CLARENCE
What else? And that succession be determined.

WARWICK
Ay, therein Clarence shall not want his part.°

KING HENRY
But, with the first of all your chief affairs,
Let me entreat (for I command no more)
That Margaret your queen and my son Edward    60
Be sent for, to return from France with speed;
For, till I see them here, by doubtful fear
My joy of liberty is half eclipsed.

CLARENCE
It shall be done, my sovereign, with all speed.

---

14 **game** quarry   17 **close** concealed   23 **forwardness** zeal
24 **stay** delay
IV.vi.5 **enlargement** liberation   6 **challenge** demand

20 **low** humbly   22 **thwarting stars** ill fortune   26 **still**
always; **famed for** reputed   29 **temper** blend, accord   31 **in**
**place** present   32 **sway** power   33 **nativity** horoscope   47
**repose myself** rely   57 **want his part** lack his share

**KING HENRY**
My Lord of Somerset, what youth is that,                    65
Of whom you seem to have so tender care?

**SOMERSET**
My liege, it is young Henry, Earl of Richmond.

**KING HENRY**
Come hither, England's hope. (*Lays his hand on his
    head.*) If secret powers
Suggest but truth to my divining thoughts,
This pretty lad will prove our country's bliss.            70
His looks are full of peaceful majesty,
His head by nature framed to wear a crown,
His hand to wield a scepter, and himself
Likely in time to bless a regal throne.
Make much of him, my lords, for this is he                 75
Must help you more than you are hurt by me.

*Enter a* POST.

**WARWICK**
What news, my friend?

**POST**
That Edward is escapèd from your brother,
And fled, as he hears since, to Burgundy.

**WARWICK**
Unsavory news! but how made he escape?                     80

**POST**
He was conveyed° by Richard Duke of Gloucester
And the Lord Hastings, who attended° him
In secret ambush on the forest side
And from the bishop's huntsmen rescued him;
For hunting was his daily exercise.                        85

**WARWICK**
My brother was too careless of his charge.
But let us hence, my sovereign, to provide
A salve for any sore that may betide.
            *Exeunt. Manet*° SOMERSET, RICHMOND, *and*
                                            OXFORD.

**SOMERSET**
My lord, I like not of this flight of Edward's,
For doubtless Burgundy will yield him help,                90
And we shall have more wars before't be long.
As Henry's late presaging prophecy
Did glad my heart with hope of this young Richmond,
So doth my heart misgive me, in these conflicts
What may befall him, to his harm and ours:                 95
Therefore, Lord Oxford, to prevent the worst,
Forthwith we'll send him hence to Brittany,
Till storms be past of civil enmity.

**OXFORD**
Ay, for if Edward repossess the crown,
'Tis like that Richmond with the rest shall down.         100

**SOMERSET**
It shall be so; he shall to Brittany.
Come, therefore, let's about it speedily.      *Exeunt.*

---

[Scene VII. *Before York.*]

*Flourish. Enter* [KING] EDWARD, RICHARD, HASTINGS,
*and* SOLDIERS.

**KING EDWARD**
Now, brother Richard, Lord Hastings, and the rest,
Yet thus far Fortune maketh us amends,
And says that once more I shall interchange
My wanèd state for Henry's regal crown.
Well have we passed and now repassed the seas              5
And brought desirèd help from Burgundy.
What then remains, we being thus arrived
From Ravenspurgh haven before the gates of York,
But that we enter, as into our dukedom?

**RICHARD**
The gates made fast! Brother, I like not this.            10
For many men that stumble at the threshold
Are well foretold that danger lurks within.

**KING EDWARD**
Tush, man, abodements° must not now affright us:
By fair or foul means we must enter in,
For hither will our friends repair° to us.                 15

**HASTINGS**
My liege, I'll knock once more to summon them.

*Enter, on the walls, the* MAYOR *of York and his*
BRETHREN.

**MAYOR**
My lords, we were forewarnèd of your coming,
And shut the gates for safety of ourselves;
For now we owe allegiance unto Henry.

**KING EDWARD**
But, Master Mayor, if Henry be your king,                 20
Yet Edward at the least is Duke of York.

**MAYOR**
True, my good lord; I know you for no less.

**KING EDWARD**
Why, and I challenge nothing but my dukedom,
As being well content with that alone.

**RICHARD**
But when the fox hath once got in his nose,               25
He'll soon find means to make the body follow.

**HASTINGS**
Why, Master Mayor, why stand you in a doubt?
Open the gates; we are King Henry's friends.

**MAYOR**
Ay, say you so? the gates shall then be opened.
                    *He descends* [*with the* ALDERMEN].

**RICHARD**
A wise stout° captain, and soon persuaded!                30

**HASTINGS**
The good old man would fain that all were well,
So 'twere not long of° him; but being entered,
I doubt not, I, but we shall soon persuade
Both him and all his brothers unto reason.

*Enter the* MAYOR *and two* ALDERMEN [*below*].

**KING EDWARD**
So, Master Mayor: these gates must not be shut             35
But in the night or in the time of war.

---

81 **conveyed** stolen away  82 **attended** waited for  88 **s.d.**
**Manet** remains (the Latin singular is often used in Elizabethan
directions with a plural subject)

IV.vii.13 **abodements** omens  15 **repair** come  30 **stout**
valiant (here ironic)  32 **long of** because of

What! fear not, man, but yield me up the keys;

*Takes his keys.*

For Edward will defend the town and thee,
And all those friends that deign to follow me.

*March. Enter* MONTGOMERY, *with* DRUM[MER] *and*
SOLDIERS.

RICHARD
Brother, this is Sir John Montgomery,                         40
Our trusty friend, unless I be deceived.
KING EDWARD
Welcome, Sir John! But why come you in arms?
MONTGOMERY
To help King Edward in his time of storm,
As every loyal subject ought to do.
KING EDWARD
Thanks, good Montgomery. But we now forget          45
Our title to the crown and only claim
Our dukedom till God please to send the rest.
MONTGOMERY
Then fare you well, for I will hence again:
I came to serve a king and not a duke.
Drummer, strike up, and let us march away.              50

*The* DRUM[MER] *begins to march.*

KING EDWARD
Nay, stay, Sir John, awhile, and we'll debate
By what safe means the crown may be recovered.
MONTGOMERY
What talk you of debating? in few words,
If you'll not here proclaim yourself our king,
I'll leave you to your fortune and be gone             55
To keep them back that come to succor you.
Why shall we fight, if you pretend° no title?
RICHARD
Why, brother, wherefore stand you on nice points?°
KING EDWARD
When we grow stronger, then we'll make our claim;
Till then, 'tis wisdom to conceal our meaning.         60
HASTINGS
Away with scrupulous wit! Now arms must rule.
RICHARD
And fearless minds climb soonest unto crowns.
Brother, we will proclaim you out of hand;
The bruit° thereof will bring you many friends.
KING EDWARD
Then be it as you will; for 'tis my right,             65
And Henry but usurps the diadem.
MONTGOMERY
Ay, now my sovereign speaketh like himself;
And now will I be Edward's champion.
HASTINGS
Sound trumpet; Edward shall be here proclaimed.
Come, fellow-soldier, make thou proclamation.          70

*Flourish. Sound.*

SOLDIER  Edward the Fourth, by the grace of God,
King of England and France, and Lord of Ireland, etc.°

MONTGOMERY
And whosoe'er gainsays King Edward's right,
By this I challenge him to single fight.

*Throws down his gauntlet.*

ALL
Long live Edward the Fourth!                           75
KING EDWARD
Thanks, brave Montgomery; and thanks unto you
    all:
If fortune serves me, I'll requite this kindness.
Now, for this night, let's harbor here in York;
And when the morning sun shall raise his car°
Above the border of this horizon,                      80
We'll forward towards Warwick and his mates;
For well I wot° that Henry is no soldier.
Ah, froward° Clarence! how evil it beseems thee,
To flatter Henry and forsake thy brother!
Yet, as we may, we'll meet both thee and Warwick.      85
Come on, brave soldiers. Doubt not of the day,
And, that once gotten, doubt not of large pay.
                                                *Exeunt.*

[Scene VIII. *London.*
*The Bishop of London's palace.*]

*Flourish. Enter the* KING [HENRY], WARWICK,
MONTAGUE, CLARENCE, OXFORD, *and* EXETER.

WARWICK
What counsel, lords? Edward from Belgia,
With hasty Germans and blunt° Hollanders,
Hath passed in safety through the Narrow Seas,
And with his troops doth march amain° to London;
And many giddy people flock to him.                    5
KING HENRY
Let's levy men, and beat him back again.
CLARENCE
A little fire is quickly trodden out;
Which, being suffered,° rivers cannot quench.
WARWICK
In Warwickshire I have true-hearted friends,
Not mutinous in peace, yet bold in war;                10
Those will I muster up: and thou, son Clarence,
Shalt stir up in Suffolk, Norfolk and in Kent,
The knights and gentlemen to come with thee.
Thou, brother Montague, in Buckingham,
Northampton, and in Leicestershire shalt find          15
Men well inclined to hear what thou command'st.
And thou, brave Oxford, wondrous well beloved,
In Oxfordshire shalt muster up thy friends.
My sovereign, with the loving citizens,
Like to his island girt in with the ocean,             20
Or modest Dian° circled with her nymphs,
Shall rest in London till we come to him.
Fair lords, take leave and stand not to reply.
Farewell, my sovereign.
KING HENRY
Farewell, my Hector, and my Troy's true hope.          25

---

**57 pretend** claim   **58 nice points** subtle distinctions
**64 bruit** rumor   **71–72 Edward . . . etc.** the only prose
passage in the play; the use of prose here represents the language
of proclamations, official documents, and formal statements

**79 car** chariot (of Phoebus Apollo)   **82 wot** know   **83 froward**
rebellious
**IV.viii.2 blunt** rude   **4 amain** with full speed   **8 suffered**
allowed (to grow)   **21 Dian** Diana, goddess of chastity

CLARENCE
In sign of truth, I kiss your highness' hand.

KING HENRY
Well-minded° Clarence, be thou fortunate!

MONTAGUE
Comfort, my lord! and so I take my leave.

OXFORD
And thus I seal my truth and bid adieu.

KING HENRY
Sweet Oxford, and my loving Montague,                    30
And all at once, once more a happy farewell.

WARWICK
Farewell, sweet lords; let's meet at Coventry.
            *Exeunt [all but* KING HENRY *and* EXETER].

KING HENRY
Here at the palace will I rest awhile.
Cousin of Exeter, what thinks your lordship?
Methinks the power that Edward hath in field       35
Should not be able to encounter mine.

EXETER
The doubt° is that he will seduce the rest.

KING HENRY
That's not my fear. My meed° hath got me fame.
I have not stopped mine ears to their demands,
Nor posted off° their suits with slow delays.             40
My pity hath been balm to heal their wounds,
My mildness hath allayed their swelling griefs,
My mercy dried their water-flowing tears.
I have not been desirous of their wealth
Nor much oppressed them with great subsidies,°        45
Nor forward of° revenge, though they much erred.
Then why should they love Edward more than me?
No, Exeter, these graces challenge grace;°
And when the lion fawns upon the lamb,
The lamb will never cease to follow him.                   50

*Shout within,* "A Lancaster! A Lancaster!"°

EXETER
Hark, hark, my lord! what shouts are these?

*Enter [*KING*] EDWARD, [*RICHARD,*] and his* SOLDIERS.

KING EDWARD
Seize on the shamefaced° Henry, bear him hence;
And once again proclaim us King of England.
You are the fount that makes small brooks to flow.
Now stops thy spring; my sea shall suck them dry       55
And swell so much the higher by their ebb.
Hence with him to the Tower. Let him not speak.
                    *Exit [some] with* KING HENRY.
And, lords, towards Coventry bend we our course,
Where peremptory° Warwick now remains:
The sun shines hot; and, if we use delay,                  60
Cold biting winter mars our hoped-for hay.

RICHARD
Away betimes, before his forces join,
And take the great-grown traitor unawares.
Brave warriors, march amain° towards Coventry.
                                        *Exeunt.*

27 **Well-minded** well-disposed   37 **doubt** fear   38 **meed**
merit, worth   40 **posted off** postponed   45 **subsidies** taxes
46 **forward of** eager for   48 **graces challenge grace** virtues
claim favor   50 s.d. **A . . . Lancaster!** so in F; many editors
read "A York! A York!" as signalizing the entrance of King
Edward   52 **shamefaced** modest, bashful   59 **peremptory**
overbearing   64 **amain** swiftly

[**ACT V**]

[Scene I. *Coventry.*]

*Enter* WARWICK, *the* MAYOR *of Coventry, two*
MESSENGERS, *and others upon the walls.*

WARWICK
Where is the post that came from valiant Oxford?
How far hence is thy lord, mine honest fellow?

FIRST MESSENGER
By this° at Dunsmore, marching hitherward.

WARWICK
How far off is our brother Montague?
Where is the post that came from Montague?             5

SECOND MESSENGER
By this° at Daintry, with a puissant troop.

*Enter [Sir John]* SOMERVILLE.

WARWICK
Say, Somerville, what says my loving son?
And, by thy guess, how nigh is Clarence now?

SOMERVILLE
At Southam I did leave him with his forces,
And do expect him here some two hours hence.         10

[*Drum heard.*]

WARWICK
Then Clarence is at hand; I hear his drum.

SOMERVILLE
It is not his, my lord. Here Southam lies.
The drum your honor hears marcheth from Warwick.

WARWICK
Who should that be? Belike, unlooked-for friends.

SOMERVILLE
They are at hand, and you shall quickly know.          15

*March. Flourish. Enter [*KING*]* EDWARD, RICHARD,
*and* SOLDIERS.

KING EDWARD
Go, trumpet,° to the walls, and sound a parle.

RICHARD
See how the surly Warwick mans the wall!

WARWICK
O unbid spite! Is sportful° Edward come?
Where slept our scouts, or how are they seduced,
That we could hear no news of his repair?°              20

KING EDWARD
Now, Warwick, wilt thou ope the city gates,
Speak gentle words, and humbly bend thy knee,
Call Edward king, and at his hands beg mercy?
And he shall pardon thee these outrages.

WARWICK
Nay, rather, wilt thou draw thy forces hence,           25
Confess who set thee up and plucked thee down,
Call Warwick patron, and be penitent?
And thou shalt still remain the Duke of York.

RICHARD
I thought, at least, he would have said "the king";
Or did he make the jest against his will?                   30

V.i.3,6 **By this** by this time   16 **trumpet** trumpeter   18
**sportful** wanton   20 **repair** return

**WARWICK**
Is not a dukedom, sir, a goodly gift?

**RICHARD**
Ay, by my faith, for a poor earl to give!
I'll do thee service for so good a gift.

**WARWICK**
'Twas I that gave the kingdom to thy brother.

**KING EDWARD**
Why then 'tis mine, if but by Warwick's gift.    35

**WARWICK**
Thou art no Atlas for so great a weight;
And, weakling, Warwick takes his gift again,
And Henry is my king, Warwick his subject.

**KING EDWARD**
But Warwick's king is Edward's prisoner;
And, gallant Warwick, do but answer this:    40
What is the body when the head is off?

**RICHARD**
Alas, that Warwick had no more forecast,°
But, whiles he thought to steal the single ten,°
The king was slily fingered from the deck!
You left poor Henry at the bishop's palace,    45
And ten to one you'll meet him in the Tower.

**KING EDWARD**
'Tis even so. Yet you are Warwick still.

**RICHARD**
Come, Warwick, take the time.° Kneel down, kneel
   down!
Nay, when?° Strike° now, or else the iron cools.

**WARWICK**
I had rather chop this hand off at a blow,    50
And with the other fling it at thy face,
Than bear so low a sail to strike to thee.°

**KING EDWARD**
Sail how thou canst, have wind and tide thy friend,
This hand, fast wound about thy coal black hair,
Shall, whiles thy head is warm and new cut off,    55
Write in the dust this sentence with thy blood,
"Wind-changing Warwick now can change no
   more."

*Enter* OXFORD, *with drum and colors.*

**WARWICK**
O cheerful colors! see where Oxford comes!

**OXFORD**
Oxford, Oxford, for Lancaster!

*[He and his* FORCES *enter the city.]*

**RICHARD**
The gates are open, let us enter too.    60

**KING EDWARD**
So other foes may set upon our backs.
Stand we in good array, for they no doubt
Will issue out again and bid us battle.
If not, the city being but of small defense,
We'll quickly rouse° the traitors in the same.    65

**WARWICK**
O, welcome, Oxford! for we want thy help.

*Enter* MONTAGUE, *with drum and colors.*

**MONTAGUE**
Montague, Montague, for Lancaster!

*[He and his* FORCES *enter the city.]*

**RICHARD**
Thou and thy brother both shall buy this treason
Even with the dearest blood your bodies bear.

**KING EDWARD**
The harder matched, the greater victory:    70
My mind presageth happy gain and conquest.

*Enter* SOMERSET, *with drum and colors.*

**SOMERSET**
Somerset, Somerset, for Lancaster!

*[He and his* FORCES *enter the city.]*

**RICHARD**
Two of thy name, both Dukes of Somerset,
Have sold their lives unto the house of York;
And thou shalt be the third, if this sword hold.    75

*Enter* CLARENCE, *with drum and colors.*°

**WARWICK**
And lo, where George of Clarence sweeps along,
Of force enough to bid his brother battle;
With whom an upright zeal to right prevails
More than the nature of a brother's love!
Come, Clarence, come! Thou wilt, if Warwick call.    80

**CLARENCE**
Father of Warwick, know you what this means?

*[Takes his red rose out of his hat.°]*

Look here, I throw my infamy at thee.
I will not ruinate my father's house,
Who gave his blood to lime° the stones together,
And set up Lancaster. Why, trowest thou,° Warwick,    85
That Clarence is so harsh, so blunt, unnatural,
To bend the fatal instruments of war
Against his brother and his lawful king?
Perhaps thou wilt object° my holy oath.
To keep that oath were more impiety    90

**75 s.d.** at this point Q introduces the following dialogue and
business:

**WARWICK**
And loe where George of Clarence sweepes
Along, of power enough to bid his brother battell.
**CLARENCE**
Clarence, Clarence, for Lancaster.
**EDWARD**
Et tu Brute, wilt thou stab Caesar too?
A parlie sirra to George of Clarence.

*Sound a Parlie, and* RICHARD *and* CLARENCE *whispers togither,
and then* CLARENCE *takes his red Rose out of his hat and throwes
it at* WARWIKE.

This passage, and especially the stage direction, follows closely
the account in the chronicles of both Hall and Holinshed of
Clarence's final change of allegiance.
**81 s.d. Takes . . . hat** removes the symbol of his allegiance to
the house of Lancaster   **84 lime** join with mortar   **85 trowest
thou** do you think   **39 object** invoke

**42 forecast** foresight   **43 single ten** mere ten (not a court
card)   **48 take the time** seize the opportunity   **49 when**
exclamation of impatience; **Strike** (1) act (i.e., while the iron
is hot) (2) yield   **52 bear . . . thee** be so humble as to surrender to you   **65 rouse** flush (as an animal from its lair)

Than Jephthah, when he sacrificed his daughter.°
I am so sorry for my trespass made
That, to deserve well at my brother's hands,
I here proclaim myself thy mortal foe,
With resolution, wheresoe'er I meet thee          95
(As I will meet thee, if thou stir abroad)
To plague thee for thy foul misleading me.
And so, proud-hearted Warwick, I defy thee,
And to my brother turn my blushing cheeks.
Pardon me, Edward! I will make amends;          100
And, Richard, do not frown upon my faults,
For I will henceforth be no more unconstant.

KING EDWARD
Now welcome more, and ten times more beloved,
Than if thou never hadst deserved our hate.

RICHARD
Welcome, good Clarence! This is brotherlike.          105

WARWICK
O passing° traitor, perjured and unjust!

KING EDWARD
What, Warwick, wilt thou leave the town, and fight?
Or shall we beat the stones about thine ears?

WARWICK
Alas, I am not cooped° here for defense!
I will away towards Barnet presently,°          110
And bid thee battle, Edward, if thou dar'st.

KING EDWARD
Yes, Warwick, Edward dares, and leads the way.
Lords, to the field. Saint George and victory!
          *Exeunt* [KING EDWARD *and his* COMPANY].
          *March.* WARWICK *and his* COMPANY *follows.*

[Scene II. *A field of battle near Barnet.*]

*Alarum and excursions. Enter* [KING] EDWARD, *bringing
forth* WARWICK *wounded.*

KING EDWARD
So, lie thou there! Die thou, and die our fear!
For Warwick was a bug° that feared° us all.
Now, Montague, sit fast!° I seek for thee,
That Warwick's bones may keep thine company.

WARWICK
Ah, who is nigh? Come to me, friend or foe,          5
And tell me who is victor, York or Warwick.
Why ask I that? My mangled body shows,
My blood, my want of strength, my sick heart shows,
That I must yield my body to the earth
And, by my fall, the conquest to my foe.          10
Thus yields the cedar to the ax's edge,
Whose arms gave shelter to the princely eagle,
Under whose shade the ramping° lion slept,
Whose top branch overpeered Jove's spreading tree°
And kept low shrubs from winter's pow'rful wind.          15
These eyes, that now are dimmed with death's black
     veil,
Have been as piercing as the midday sun
To search the secret treasons of the world.
The wrinkles in my brows, now filled with blood,

Were likened oft to kingly sepulchers;          20
For who lived king but I could dig his grave?
And who durst smile when Warwick bent his brow?
Lo, now my glory smeared in dust and blood!
My parks, my walks, my manors that I had,
Even now forsake me, and of all my lands          25
Is nothing left me but my body's length.
Why, what is pomp, rule, reign, but earth and dust?
And, live we how we can, yet die we must.

*Enter* OXFORD *and* SOMERSET.

SOMERSET
Ah, Warwick, Warwick, wert thou as we are,
We might recover all our loss again!          30
The queen from France hath brought a puissant power.
Even now we heard the news. Ah, couldst thou fly!

WARWICK
Why, then I would not fly. Ah, Montague,
If thou be there, sweet brother, take my hand,
And with thy lips keep in my soul awhile!          35
Thou lov'st me not; for, brother, if thou didst,
Thy tears would wash this cold congealèd blood
That glues my lips and will not let me speak.
Come quickly, Montague, or I am dead.

SOMERSET
Ah, Warwick! Montague hath breathed his last,          40
And to the latest gasp cried out for Warwick
And said, "Commend me to my valiant brother."
And more he would have said, and more he spoke,
Which sounded like a cannon in a vault,
That mought° not be distinguished; but at last          45
I well might hear, delivered with a groan,
"O, farewell, Warwick!"

WARWICK
Sweet rest his soul! Fly, lords, and save yourselves;
For Warwick bids you all farewell, to meet in heaven.
          [*Dies.*]

OXFORD
Away, away, to meet the queen's great power!          50
          *Here they bear away his body. Exeunt.*

[Scene III. *Another part of the field.*]

*Flourish. Enter* KING EDWARD *in* triumph, *with*
RICHARD, CLARENCE, *and the rest.*

KING EDWARD
Thus far our fortune keeps an upward course
And we are graced with wreaths of victory.
But, in the midst of this bright-shining day
I spy a black, suspicious, threat'ning cloud
That will encounter with our glorious sun°          5
Ere he attain his easeful western bed.
I mean, my lords, those powers that the queen
Hath raised in Gallia have arrived° our coast,
And, as we hear, march on to fight with us.

CLARENCE
A little gale will soon disperse that cloud          10
And blow it to the source from whence it came.
Thy very beams will dry those vapors up,
For every cloud engenders not a storm.

---

91 Jephthah . . . daughter see Judges 11:30   106 passing
extreme   109 cooped prepared   110 presently immediately
V.ii.2 bug bugbear; feared terrified   3 sit fast watch out
13 ramping rearing   14 Jove's spreading tree the oak

45 mought might
V.iii.5 sun badge of York   8 arrived landed on

RICHARD

The queen is valued° thirty thousand strong,
And Somerset, with Oxford, fled to her:      15
If she have time to breathe, be well assured
Her faction will be full as strong as ours.

KING EDWARD

We are advertised° by our loving friends
That they do hold their course toward Tewksbury.
We, having now the best at Barnet field,      20
Will thither straight,° for willingness rids way;°
And, as we march, our strength will be augmented
In every county as we go along.
Strike up the drum. Cry, "Courage!" and away.
                                        *Exeunt.*

[Scene IV. *Plains near Tewksbury.*]

*Flourish. March. Enter the* QUEEN [MARGARET], *young*
[PRINCE] *Edward,* SOMERSET, OXFORD, *and* SOLDIERS.

QUEEN MARGARET

Great lords, wise men ne'er sit and wail their loss,
But cheerly seek how to redress their harms.
What though the mast be now blown overboard,
The cable broke, the holding-anchor° lost,
And half our sailors swallowed in the flood?      5
Yet lives our pilot still. Is't meet° that he
Should leave the helm, and like a fearful lad
With tearful eyes add water to the sea,
And give more strength to that which hath too much,
Whiles, in his moan, the ship splits on the rock,      10
Which industry° and courage might have saved?
Ah, what a shame! ah, what a fault were this!
Say Warwick was our anchor. What of that?
And Montague our topmast. What of him?
Our slaughtered friends the tackles; what of these?      15
Why, is not Oxford here another anchor?
And Somerset another goodly mast?
The friends of France our shrouds and tacklings?
And, though unskillful, why not Ned and I
For once allowed the skillful pilot's charge?°      20
We will not from the helm to sit and weep,
But keep our course (though the rough wind say no)
From shelves and rocks that threaten us with wrack.
As good to chide the waves as speak them fair.
And what is Edward but a ruthless sea?      25
What Clarence but a quicksand of deceit?
And Richard but a ragged fatal rock?
All these the enemies to our poor bark.
Say you can swim—alas, 'tis but a while!
Tread on the sand—why, there you quickly sink!      30
Bestride the rock—the tide will wash you off,
Or else you famish: that's a threefold death.
This speak I, lords, to let you understand,
If case some one of you would fly from us,
That there's no hoped-for mercy with the brothers      35
More than with ruthless waves, with sands and rocks.
Why, courage then! What cannot be avoided
'Twere childish weakness to lament or fear.

PRINCE

Methinks a woman of this valiant spirit
Should, if a coward heard her speak these words,      40
Infuse his breast with magnanimity,
And make him, naked,° foil a man at arms.
I speak not this as doubting any here;
For did I but suspect a fearful man,
He should have leave to go away betimes,      45
Lest in our need he might infect another
And make him of like spirit to himself.
If any such be here (as God forbid!)
Let him depart before we need his help.

OXFORD

Women and children of so high a courage,      50
And warriors faint! why, 'twere perpetual shame.
O brave young prince! thy famous grandfather°
Doth live again in thee: long mayst thou live
To bear his image° and renew his glories!

SOMERSET

And he that will not fight for such a hope,      55
Go home to bed, and, like the owl by day,
If he arise, be mocked and wondered at.

QUEEN MARGARET

Thanks, gentle Somerset. Sweet Oxford, thanks.

PRINCE

And take his thanks that yet hath nothing else.

*Enter a* MESSENGER.

MESSENGER

Prepare you, lords, for Edward is at hand,      60
Ready to fight; therefore be resolute.

OXFORD

I thought no less: it is his policy°
To haste thus fast, to find us unprovided.

SOMERSET

But he's deceived: we are in readiness.

QUEEN MARGARET

This cheers my heart, to see your forwardness.      65

OXFORD

Here pitch our battle; hence we will not budge.

*Flourish and march. Enter* [KING] EDWARD, RICHARD,
CLARENCE, *and* SOLDIERS.

KING EDWARD

Brave followers, yonder stands the thorny wood,
Which, by the heavens' assistance and your strength,
Must by the roots be hewn up yet ere night.
I need not add more fuel to your fire,      70
For well I wot ye blaze to burn them out.
Give signal to the fight, and to it, lords!

QUEEN MARGARET

Lords, knights, and gentlemen, what I should say
My tears gainsay; for every word I speak,
Ye see I drink the water of my eye.      75
Therefore, no more but this: Henry, your sovereign,
Is prisoner to the foe; his state usurped,
His realm a slaughterhouse, his subjects slain,
His statutes canceled, and his treasure spent;
And yonder is the wolf that makes this spoil.°      80
You fight in justice. Then, in God's name, lords,
Be valiant, and give signal to the fight.
                          *Alarum. Retreat. Excursions. Exeunt.*

14 **valued** estimated   18 **advertised** informed   21 **straight**
at once; **rids way** covers ground quickly
**V.iv.4 holding-anchor** sheet anchor (largest of ship's anchors)
6 **Is't meet** is it suitable   11 **industry** labor   20 **charge** duty
42 **naked** unarmed   52 **grandfather** Henry V   54 **image**
likeness   62 **policy** craft   80 **spoil** destruction

[Scene V. *Another part of the field.*]

*Flourish. Enter* [KING] EDWARD, RICHARD, CLARENCE, [*and* SOLDIERS, *with*] QUEEN [MARGARET], OXFORD, SOMERSET [*as prisoners*].

KING EDWARD
Now here a period of° tumultuous broils.
Away with Oxford to Hames Castle straight.°
For Somerset, off with his guilty head.
Go bear them hence. I will not hear them speak.

OXFORD
For my part, I'll not trouble thee with words.                    5

SOMERSET
Nor I, but stoop with patience to my fortune.
            *Exeunt* [OXFORD *and* SOMERSET, *guarded*].

QUEEN MARGARET
So part we sadly in this troublous world,
To meet with joy in sweet Jerusalem.

KING EDWARD
Is proclamation made, that who finds Edward
Shall have a high reward, and he his life?                       10

RICHARD
It is: and lo, where youthful Edward comes!

KING EDWARD
Bring forth the gallant, let us hear him speak.

*Enter the* PRINCE [*Edward*].

What! Can so young a thorn begin to prick?
Edward, what satisfaction° canst thou make
For bearing arms, for stirring up my subjects,                  15
And all the trouble thou hast turned me to?

PRINCE
Speak like a subject, proud ambitious York!
Suppose that I am now my father's mouth;
Resign thy chair, and where I stand kneel thou,
Whilst I propose the selfsame words to thee,                    20
Which, traitor, thou wouldst have me answer to.

QUEEN MARGARET
Ah, that thy father had been so resolved!

RICHARD
That you might still have worn the petticoat,
And ne'er have stol'n the breech° from Lancaster.

PRINCE
Let Aesop fable in a winter's night;                            25
His currish° riddles sorts not with this place.

RICHARD
By heaven, brat, I'll plague ye for that word.

QUEEN MARGARET
Ay, thou wast born to be a plague to men.

RICHARD
For God's sake, take away this captive scold.

PRINCE
Nay, take away this scolding crookback rather.                  30

KING EDWARD
Peace, willful boy, or I will charm° your tongue.

CLARENCE
Untutored lad, thou art too malapert.°

V.v.1 **a period of** an end to   2 **straight** immediately   14
**satisfaction** amends   24 **breech** breeches   26 **currish**
because Aesop was sometimes thought to be a hunchback,
because the fables talk of animals, and because their morality
resembles that of Cynic (from a Greek word for "dog")
philosophy   31 **charm** silence   32 **malapert** impudent

PRINCE
I know my duty; you are all undutiful:
Lascivious Edward, and thou perjured George,
And thou misshapen Dick, I tell ye all                          35
I am your better, traitors as ye are:
And thou usurp'st my father's right and mine.

KING EDWARD
Take that, the likeness of this railer here.

*Stabs him.*

RICHARD
Sprawl'st thou? Take that, to end thy agony.

*Richard stabs him.*

CLARENCE
And there's for twitting me with perjury.                       40

*Clarence stabs him.*

QUEEN MARGARET
O, kill me too!

RICHARD
Marry,° and shall.

*Offers to kill her.*

KING EDWARD
Hold, Richard, hold; for we have done too much.

RICHARD
Why should she live, to fill the world with words?

KING EDWARD
What! doth she swoon? use means for her recovery.               45

RICHARD
Clarence, excuse me to the king my brother;
I'll hence to London on a serious matter:
Ere ye come there, be sure to hear some news.

CLARENCE
What? what?

RICHARD
The Tower, the Tower!                           *Exit.*   50

QUEEN MARGARET
O Ned, sweet Ned! speak to thy mother, boy!
Canst thou not speak? O traitors! murderers!
They that stabbed Caesar shed no blood at all,
Did not offend, nor were not worthy blame,
If this foul deed were by to equal it.                          55
He was a man; this (in respect°) a child,
And men ne'er spend their fury on a child.
What's worse than murderer, that I may name it?
No, no, my heart will burst, and if I speak!
And I will speak, that so my heart may burst.                   60
Butchers and villains! bloody cannibals!
How sweet a plant have you untimely cropped!
You have no children, butchers! If you had,
The thought of them would have stirred up remorse:
But if you ever chance to have a child,                         65
Look in his youth to have him so cut off
As, deathsmen, you have rid this sweet young prince!

KING EDWARD
Away with her! Go bear her hence perforce.

QUEEN MARGARET
Nay, never bear me hence! Dispatch me here.
Here sheathe thy sword, I'll pardon thee my death:             70
What, wilt thou not? Then, Clarence, do it thou.

42 **Marry** indeed (light oath, from "By Mary")   56 **in respect**
in comparison

**CLARENCE**
By heaven, I will not do thee so much ease.

**QUEEN MARGARET**
Good Clarence, do! Sweet Clarence, do thou do it!

**CLARENCE**
Didst thou not hear me swear I would not do it?

**QUEEN MARGARET**
Ay, but thou usest to forswear thyself.    75
'Twas sin before, but now 'tis charity.
What wilt thou not? Where is that devil's butcher,
Hard-favored° Richard? Richard, where art thou?
Thou art not here. Murder is thy alms-deed.
Petitioners for blood thou ne'er put'st back.°    80

**KING EDWARD**
Away, I say. I charge ye bear her hence.

**QUEEN MARGARET**
So come to you and yours, as to this prince!
                      *Exit* QUEEN.

**KING EDWARD**
Where's Richard gone?

**CLARENCE**
To London, all in post;° and, as I guess,
To make a bloody supper in the Tower.    85

**KING EDWARD**
He's sudden° if a thing comes in his head.
Now march we hence, discharge the common sort
With pay and thanks, and let's away to London,
And see our gentle queen how well she fares:
By this,° I hope, she hath a son for me.    *Exeunt.* 90

[Scene VI. *London. The Tower.*]

*Enter* [KING] HENRY *the Sixth and* RICHARD, *with the*
LIEUTENANT [*of the Tower*], *on the walls.*

**RICHARD**
Good day, my lord. What, at your book so hard?

**KING HENRY**
Ay, my good lord—"my lord," I should say rather.
'Tis sin to flatter. "Good" was little better.
"Good Gloucester" and "good devil" were alike,
And both preposterous;° therefore, not "good lord."    5

**RICHARD**
Sirrah,° leave us to ourselves: we must confer.
                  [*Exit* LIEUTENANT.]

**KING HENRY**
So flies the reckless shepherd from the wolf;
So first the harmless sheep doth yield his fleece,
And next his throat unto the butcher's knife.
What scene of death hath Roscius° now to act?    10

**RICHARD**
Suspicion always haunts the guilty mind;
The thief doth fear each bush an officer.

**KING HENRY**
The bird that hath been limèd° in a bush,
With trembling wings misdoubteth° every bush;

And I, the hapless male to one sweet bird,    15
Have now the fatal object in my eye,
Where my poor young was limed, was caught and
   killed.°

**RICHARD**
Why, what a peevish fool was that of Crete,
That taught his son the office° of a fowl!
And yet, for all his wings, the fool was drowned.    20

**KING HENRY**
I, Daedalus; my poor boy, Icarus;
Thy father, Minos, that denied our course;°
The sun that seared the wings of my sweet boy
Thy brother Edward, and thyself the sea
Whose envious gulf° did swallow up his life.    25
Ah, kill me with thy weapon, not with words!
My breast can better brook thy dagger's point
Than can my ears that tragic history.
But wherefore dost thou come? Is't for my life?

**RICHARD**
Think'st thou I am an executioner?    30

**KING HENRY**
A persecutor I am sure, thou art:
If murdering innocents be executing,
Why, then thou art an executioner.

**RICHARD**
Thy son I killed for his presumption.

**KING HENRY**
Hadst thou been killed when first thou didst presume,    35
Thou hadst not lived to kill a son of mine.
And thus I prophesy, that many a thousand,
Which now mistrust no parcel of my fear,
And many an old man's sigh and many a widow's,
And many an orphan's water-standing° eye—    40
Men for their sons, wives for their husbands,
Orphans for their parents' timeless° death—
Shall rue the hour that ever thou wast born.
The owl shrieked at thy birth—an evil sign;
The night-crow cried, aboding° luckless time;    45
Dogs howled, and hideous tempest shook down trees;
The raven rooked her° on the chimney's top,
And chatt'ring pies° in dismal discords sung.
Thy mother felt more than a mother's pain,
And yet brought forth less than a mother's hope,    50
To wit, an indigested and deformèd lump,
Not like the fruit of such a goodly tree.
Teeth hadst thou in thy head when thou wast born,
To signify thou cam'st to bite the world;
And, if the rest be true which I have heard,    55
Thou cam'st—

**RICHARD**
I'll hear no more. Die, prophet, in thy speech.

*Stabs him.*

For this, amongst the rest, was I ordained.

**KING HENRY**
Ay, and for much more slaughter after this.
O God forgive my sins, and pardon thee!    *Dies.* 60

---

78 **Hard-favored** ugly   80 **put'st back** refuse   84 **all in post** in haste   86 **sudden** swift in action   90 **By this** by this time   V.vi.5 **preposterous** an inversion of the natural order   6 **Sirrah** form of address used to an inferior   10 **Roscius** great Roman actor (d. 62 B.C.)   13 **limèd** caught with bird lime (a sticky substance smeared on twigs)   14 **misdoubteth** mistrusts   15–17 **And . . . killed** I, the father of one sweet child, have in my eye the death-dealing substance by which my son was trapped and slain   19 **office** function   22 **denied our course** barred our way   25 **gulf** whirlpool   40 **water-standing** flooded with tears   42 **timeless** untimely   45 **aboding** foreboding   47 **rooked her** squatted   48 **pies** magpies

RICHARD

What? Will the aspiring blood of Lancaster
Sink in the ground? I thought it would have mounted.
See how my sword weeps for the poor king's death!
O may such purple tears be always shed
From those that wish the downfall of our house!          65
If any spark of life be yet remaining,
Down, down to hell; and say I sent thee thither—

*Stabs him again.*

I, that have neither pity, love, nor fear.
Indeed, 'tis true that Henry told me of;
For I have often heard my mother say          70
I came into the world with my legs forward.
Had I not reason, think ye, to make haste
And seek their ruin that usurped our right?
The midwife wondered, and the women cried,
"O Jesus bless us, he is born with teeth!"          75
And so I was, which plainly signified
That I should snarl and bite and play the dog.
Then, since the heavens have shaped my body so,
Let hell make crook'd my mind to answer° it.
I have no brother, I am like no brother;          80
And this word "love," which graybeards call divine,
Be resident in men like one another
And not in me: I am myself alone.
Clarence, beware. Thou keep'st me from the light;
But I will sort a pitchy day for thee;°          85
For I will buzz abroad° such prophecies
That Edward shall be fearful of his life,
And then, to purge his fear, I'll be thy death.
King Henry and the prince his son are gone:
Clarence, thy turn is next, and then the rest,          90
Counting myself but bad till I be best.
I'll throw thy body in another room
And triumph, Henry, in thy day of doom.
                              *Exit [with the body].*

[Scene VII. *London. The palace.*]

*Flourish. Enter* KING [EDWARD], QUEEN [ELIZABETH],
CLARENCE, RICHARD, HASTINGS, [*a*] NURSE [*with
the young* PRINCE], *and* ATTENDANTS.

KING EDWARD

Once more we sit in England's royal throne,
Repurchased with the blood of enemies.
What valiant foemen, like to autumn's corn,
Have we mowed down in tops of all their pride!
Three Dukes of Somerset, threefold renowned          5
For hardy and undoubted champions;
Two Cliffords, as° the father and the son,

And two Northumberlands—two braver men
Ne'er spurred their coursers° at the trumpet's sound;
With them, the two brave bears,° Warwick and
    Montague,          10
That in their chains fettered the kingly lion
And made the forest tremble when they roared.
Thus have we swept suspicion° from our seat
And made our footstool of security.
Come hither, Bess, and let me kiss my boy.          15
Young Ned, for thee, thine uncles and myself
Have in our armors watched° the winter's night,
Went all afoot in summer's scalding heat,
That thou mightst repossess the crown in peace.
And of our labors thou shalt reap the gain.          20

RICHARD [*Aside.*]

I'll blast his harvest, if your head were laid,°
For yet I am not looked on in the world.
This shoulder was ordained so thick to heave,
And heave it shall some weight, or break my back.
Work thou the way, and that shalt execute.          25

KING EDWARD

Clarence and Gloucester, love my lovely queen;
And kiss your princely nephew, brothers both.

CLARENCE

The duty that I owe unto your majesty
I seal upon the lips of this sweet babe.

KING EDWARD

Thanks, noble Clarence; worthy brother, thanks.          30

RICHARD

And, that I love the tree from whence thou sprang'st,
Witness the loving kiss I give the fruit.

[*Aside.*]

To say the truth, so Judas kissed his master,
And cried, "All hail!" whenas he meant all harm.

KING EDWARD

Now am I seated as my soul delights,          35
Having my country's peace and brothers' loves.

CLARENCE

What will your grace have done with Margaret?
Reignier, her father, to the King of France
Hath pawned the Sicils and Jerusalem,
And hither have they sent it for her ransom.          40

KING EDWARD

Away with her, and waft her hence to France!
And now what rests° but that we spend the time
With stately triumphs,° mirthful comic shows,
Such as befits the pleasure of the court?
Sound drums and trumpets! Farewell sour annoy!          45
For here, I hope, begins our lasting joy.
                              *Exeunt omnes.*

79 **answer** correspond to   85 **I . . . thee** I shall arrange a
black future for you   86 **buzz abroad** spread
**V.vii.7 as** namely

9 **coursers** horses   10 **bears** alluding to the family emblem
13 **suspicion** anxiety   17 **watched** stayed awake   21 **laid** in
the grave   42 **rests** remains   43 **triumphs** public processions

# THE TRAGEDY OF
# RICHARD THE THIRD

EDITED BY MARK ECCLES

## Introduction

*Richard III* is above all a play for the stage. It was Shakespeare's first great success, a sudden leap up from his three plays on the reign of Henry VI. Richard Burbage made his reputation by playing Richard III; so did David Garrick when he conquered London in the eighteenth century. *Richard III* was the first Shakespeare play acted professionally in America, in 1750; it was a favorite of Lincoln, who knew by heart "Now is the winter of our discontent"; and the Shakespeare Festival of Canada opened with a brilliant production. Sir Laurence Olivier has brought Richard to life again on the stage and on the screen.

When Shakespeare wrote this play, about 1592 or 1593, his audiences were eager for plays on English history. Such plays were like mirrors in which they could see what had happened to England in past crises and what might happen to themselves in the near future after the death of Queen Elizabeth. Would their next ruler be one who could unite his people, like Henry V or Henry VII, or one who would bring on civil war, like Henry VI or Richard III? The most popular plays on English history had dramatized wars and struggles for power: *The Famous Victories of Henry V*, *The Troublesome Reign of King John*, and the one great historical tragedy before Shakespeare's, Marlowe's *The Troublesome Reign and Lamentable Death of Edward II, King of England, with the Tragical Fall of Proud Mortimer*. Shakespeare emphasized as leading ideas of his English history plays the danger of division and the necessity of union: "United we stand, divided we fall."

*Richard III* is a tragedy of crimes punished by divine justice. Both branches of the royal Plantagenets, Lancaster and York, had committed cruel murders. Queen Margaret, the "she-wolf of France," had beheaded Richard, Duke of York; in revenge York's sons murdered her son, Prince Edward, and her husband, Henry VI. The murderers of Clarence tell him that he deserves God's vengeance for stabbing Prince Edward and for breaking his oath to God to fight for King Henry. Richard III must pay with his life for causing the deaths of his brother, his nephews, his wife, and his best friends. The demands for vengeance made by Queen Margaret are fulfilled; for, as Holinshed expressed the traditional religious view of history, "such is

God's justice, to leave no unrepentant wickedness unpunished." God used Richard as a scourge to punish the sins of others; the "high All-seer" then raised up Richmond to cancel Richard, "One that hath ever been God's enemy."

Yet it is one of Shakespeare's paradoxes that God's enemy is so much more fascinating than the puppet Richmond, who speaks with no voice of his own. Richard is alive; he is himself alone; he is what part of ourselves would like to be, free from the censor conscience. He can win women; he can win power; he can enjoy using his power to destroy, to do whatever he wants to do. We know he will not get away with it in the end; but meanwhile, what fun he is having! His gay soliloquies make us share his enjoyment:

> Was ever woman in this humor wooed?
> Was ever woman in this humor won?
> I'll have her, but I will not keep her long.     (I.ii.227–29)

Richard is the actor making up his part as he goes along, and making sure that it is the leading part.

How did Shakespeare create an acting role which has held so many audiences spellbound? For one thing, he made Richard a devil masked as a man: able to put on in turn the masks of the loyal brother, the impassioned lover, the kindly uncle, the self-sacrificing king. The masks are both tragic and comic; they hide death, and they mock at human folly. We pity Richard's victims, but we feel superior to them; we, of course, would never be taken in. For another thing, Richard is the underdog who fights his way to the top, one man against the world, with everything against him. The climb to power is a treacherous one, dangerous to Richard, deadly to anyone who blocks his path; he climbs over their bodies till he stands, though not for long, where he had determined to stand. This triumph of will is exciting theater; at the same time it is sharply ironic—so many years to rise, to fall in one day.

Richard dominates the play; he appears in fourteen out of twenty-five scenes, and his shadow hangs over the rest. It is the longest of Shakespeare's history plays, and longer than any other of Shakespeare's except *Hamlet*. Richard himself speaks more than a fourth of the lines, and five of his ten soliloquies come in the first three scenes, so that we see him at once take the center of the stage. His opening speech is masterly. Winter is now summer, the killing is over, it is time to live and love, but not for Richard; his keenest pleasures are to come, and the first will be to destroy his brother. Shakespeare had shown Richard's will to power in *Henry VI, Part Three:*

> How sweet a thing it is to wear a crown,
> Within whose circuit is Elysium
> And all that poets feign of bliss and joy.     (I.ii.29–31)

In III.ii of the same play Richard had planned his strategy for winning the crown:

> Why, I can smile, and murder whiles I smile,
> And cry, "Content" to that which grieves my heart,
> And wet my cheeks with artificial tears,
> And frame my face to all occasions.
>
>                  . . .
>
> I can add colors to the chameleon,
> Change shapes with Proteus for advantages,
> And set the murderous Machiavel to school.
> Can I do this, and cannot get a crown?
>                   (III.ii.182–85, 191–94)

And in V.vi, after stabbing King Henry in the Tower, he had promised that Clarence would be next:

> I have no brother, I am like no brother;
> And this word "love," which graybeards call divine,
> Be resident in men like one another
> And not in me: I am myself alone.     (V.vi.80–83)

In the first scene of *Richard III* he is in high spirits as he speaks with and without the mask: "your imprisonment shall not be long," to Clarence, and then, to himself, "I do love thee so/That I will shortly send thy soul to heaven." Richard Crookback has a crooked but original sense of humor.

Why did Shakespeare invent the famous scene of Richard's wooing of Lady Anne? The soliloquy which ends the scene provides, I think, the key to Shakespeare's purpose. Richard took up the challenge of a task that seemed impossible; if he could succeed against such odds, for him nothing would be impossible:

> What! I that killed her husband and his father
> To take her in her heart's extremest hate
>
>                  . . .
>
> And yet to win her, all the world to nothing!
>                   (I.ii.230–31, 237)

He chose a time which presented the greatest obstacles, so that he could overcome them: a time when she was calling for vengeance upon him as the murderer of King Henry and of her husband. He provoked her to attack him with words and then gave her a chance to act, to kill him with his own sword. His will proved stronger than hers. Her change is sudden, but Shakespeare means it to be. Theatrically, he achieves the shock of surprise; dramatically, he convinces us that Richard will find hardly any difficulty too great for him to master.

Shakespeare created most of the first act from his own imagination; and such history as he used he rearranged for dramatic effect. He read in Holinshed that Richard, in 1471, murdered Henry VI, whose body was brought to Saint Paul's and then buried at Chertsey; Shakespeare imagined the scene between Richard and Anne. In 1478 Edward IV had Clarence condemned to death by parliament and drowned in wine at the Tower; Shakespeare made Richard plot his brother's death, and he invented the whole vivid scene of Clarence's dream and murder. Queen Margaret had left England to live in France; Shakespeare brought her into the third scene to prophesy retribution for the house of York and especially for Richard. Margaret, Clarence, Edward IV, and Hastings were omitted from the acting version by Colley Cibber which held the stage from 1700 to 1877, a travesty of the play which contained more Cibber than Shakespeare. All are essential to Shakespeare's drama. Margaret, for example, invokes the justice of God to punish the crimes of her enemies. Recalling the bloody past, she calls for the future to pay blood for blood. As York's dread curse had prevailed with heaven to make her suffer the loss of her husband, her son, and her kingdom, so she prays that her rival Elizabeth may "Die neither mother, wife, nor England's queen." Richard deserves to suffer the worst plagues of all: the worm of conscience, suspicion and betrayal, and the terror of tormenting dreams. Shakespeare makes Margaret no ghost crying for revenge, but a bitter, passionate woman. Yet he gives her a major function in the play: to thunder with the power of a prophetess, sent to warn that no sinner can escape his doom.

The first doom fell upon Clarence. Nothing in his life became him like the dream of his death, for while he slept, his conscience was awake. If he escaped the Tower, he feared he would find himself in hell, facing the father-in-law he had betrayed and the king's son he had stabbed to death. His repentance was genuine, but it came too late to save his life; when he warned his murderers of God's vengeance, they reminded him that he himself was a murderer. Shakespeare packs the scene with tragic irony: Clarence supposing that Richard caused his death in the dream by chance, not by design, and assuring the murderers that Richard would reward them for saving his life. The reluctant Second Murderer might still have saved him by listening to the dregs of conscience; he tried, perhaps, to warn him by crying "Look behind you, my lord!" and immediately afterward he wished he could wash his hands of the murder. Shakespeare ends the first act with Richard one step closer to the crown.

After Act I Shakespeare dramatizes the history of only two years, from the death of Edward IV in 1483 to the battle of Bosworth Field in 1485. Again and again he heightens the dramatic effect of events already full of drama. He brings Richard to the deathbed of Edward in II.i to play-act the lover of peace and then to explode the news of Clarence's death and blame "the guilty kindred of the queen," when he alone is guilty. No sooner does Richard mount the throne in IV.ii than Shakespeare shows him trying to incite Buckingham to murder the princes, with the result that he drives his strongest supporter into rebellion. Above all, in V.iii Shakespeare changes Richard's dream of "images like terrible devils," as Holinshed calls them, into a vision of the souls of all whom he has murdered, crying out "Despair and die!" Here Shakespeare makes Richard look into himself with fear and horror and see how he has cut himself off from mankind:

> I shall despair. There is no creature loves me;
> And if I die, no soul will pity me.          (V.iii.201–02)

Though no one pities Richard, Shakespeare builds up recurring scenes of pity for those who suffer during this reign of terror. In II.ii he shows three generations—mother, wife, and children—left desolate by the loss of Edward and of Clarence. In IV.i the old Duchess of York longs for peace in the grave; Anne, who has had no rest with Richard, wishes that her crown were red-hot steel; and Queen Elizabeth, thinking only of her children, seeks pity for them from the stones of the Tower. The murderers of the two boys tell their death's sad story (IV.iii); and the next scene rises to a chorus of grief in the laments of their mother, of their grandmother, and of Queen Margaret. Each of these scenes intensifies emotion by a threefold pattern, as though the sorrow were too great to be expressed by only one person, and even Tyrrel shares the remorse of Dighton and Forrest. The killing of the princes is a massacre of the innocents, and their mother is like Rachel weeping for her children.

Shakespeare secures a more complex response in scenes which present characters of mixed good and evil, persons who suffer for their sins and yet who call forth pity for their suffering. Hastings and Buckingham, together with Clarence and the shadowy Rivers, Grey, and Vaughan, are neither ruthless tyrants nor innocent children. Hastings is shown hoping for revenge upon his enemies, the queen's kinsmen (I.i), hiding his hate under a vow of love for Rivers and Dorset (II.i), and then rejoicing at the execution of Rivers and the rest (III.ii). When he is condemned to die the same day (III.iv), he repents his too triumphant joy that his enemies were butchered and admits that Margaret's curse, for standing by when her son was murdered, has lighted on his head. On the other hand, he dies for loyalty to the true king, for refusing to help Richard usurp the throne. Shakespeare brings out the drama of his sudden fall when he least expects it, and the irony of his overconfident belief that Richard loves him well and that the boar will use him kindly. His last words, "They smile at me who shortly shall be dead," foretell a parallel fall for Buckingham, who mocked at Hastings and yet still trusts Richard. Blinded by infatuation, Buckingham has already disregarded Margaret's warning to beware of Richard (I.iii). He digs a pit for himself when he prays in II.i. that if ever he harms Queen Elizabeth or her family God may punish him with hate where he most expects love, and yet becomes Richard's right-hand man to plot against her and her sons. Hesitating only at murder, he gains a crown for Richard and death for himself, and in V.i he acknowledges the justice of his death. As with Hastings, he is both sinning and sinned against, and his tragic recognition of his errors leads in the end to pity for his fall.

The blank verse in *Richard III* marches to a strong, emphatic rhythm. The pause at the end of the line, or sometimes of two lines (as in I.i.1–4, 10–13), lets the actor dwell on the meaning with clarity and force. Shakespeare, who constructs his sonnets with three quatrains and a couplet, likes to build dramatic monologues also in groups of four lines. Richard's first speech is composed in quatrains, expanded twice to five lines and once to six. The second scene begins and ends with monologues which contain many quatrains, as well as groups of three or five lines. The dialogues show more variety, but Shakespeare makes striking use of stichomythia, which sets single line against single line, in Richard's duels of words with Anne in I.ii, York in III.i, and Queen Elizabeth in IV.iv. The verse of *Richard III* is far from subtle, but its careful design contributes to its power.

Shakespeare heightens the dramatic effect of speech by an extraordinary range of rhetoric. The opening scene is rich in antitheses, between war and peace, the lover and the villain, true Edward and treacherous Richard and simple, plain Clarence. Anne expresses the intensity of her grief by figures of repetition and parallelism: "Set down, set down," "bloodless . . . blood," "O cursèd . . . Cursèd," "If ever he have child . . . If ever he have wife." Queen Margaret gives force to her prophetic curse in I.iii.187 ff. by pouring forth questions and exclamations, by reiterating key words like "curse," "heaven," and "death," and by emphasizing parallel constructions: "Edward thy son, that now is Prince of Wales,/For Edward our son, that was Prince of Wales," or "Thyself a queen, for me that was a queen." All these and more appear in IV.iv: paradoxical antithesis in "Dead life, blind sight, poor mortal living ghost," repeated questions like "Where is thy husband now? Where be thy brothers?" and emphatic parallels, as in lines 20–21, 40–46, and 98–104. The conscious eloquence of the orations in V.iii contrasts with the more intense rhetoric which expresses fear and despair in Richard's soliloquy. *Richard III* shows Shakespeare rejoicing in his mastery over language, though he has not yet learned the art of concealing his art.

The play is not merely a melodrama, although it tends toward melodrama in its exaggeration of Richard's villainy. It is the tragedy of a man, of a family, and of a nation. The tragedy is ironic in that Richard, by destroying others, brings destruction upon himself. Right does not triumph without probability, as in melodrama, but as a probable result of human actions. Richard rises steadily until he orders the murder of his nephews (IV.ii); from that moment he turns friends into enemies, till "He hath no friends but what are friends for fear" (V.ii). But he does not have the inner conflict of Macbeth, who inspires pity as well as fear. Retributive justice strikes down not only Richard but the whole family of Plantagenet. The sons of York pay for the murder of Henry VI and his son by their own deaths and the murder of Edward's sons. Finally, Shakespeare shows how the people of England suffered from tyranny and civil war, when "The brother blindly shed the brother's blood." He ends the play with a heartfelt prayer that his country, united, may now live in peace.

## A NOTE ON THE SOURCES

Shakespeare found the fullest account of Richard in Raphael Holinshed's *Chronicles* (second edition, 1587). Holinshed reprinted most of Sir Thomas More's *History of King Richard the Third* (written about 1514, printed in 1557) and wove in further information from Polydore

Vergil's *Anglica Historia* (1534), Edward Hall's *The Union of the Two Noble and Illustre Families of Lancaster and York* (1548), and Richard Grafton's *Chronicles* of 1543 and 1569. Shakespeare added a few points from his own reading of Hall or Grafton, and a few from "The Tragedy of Clarence" in *The Mirror for Magistrates* (1559). The rest he drew from Holinshed or invented for himself.

The historical Richard was not so black as he was painted; it is still an unsolved question whether he committed any of the murders charged against him by his enemies. But Shakespeare was dramatizing the Richard of the Tudor historians, and they had no doubt that Richard was a murderer and a tyrant. More wrote that he "spared no man's death whose life withstood his purpose"; Hall declared that if he had not usurped the throne, he would have been "much praised and beloved, as he is now abhorred and vilipended." By the time Shakespeare wrote, Richard had already been staged as a Senecan villain in *Richardus Tertius*, a Latin play acted at Cambridge, and in *The True Tragedy of Richard the Third*, which Shakespeare quotes in *Hamlet*. More's vivid history, however, furnished the chief stimulus to Shakespeare's imagination.

### A NOTE ON THE TEXT

*Richard III*, one of Shakespeare's most popular plays, appeared in eight quarto editions, more than any other Shakespeare play except *Henry IV, Part One*. The first quarto (Q1) was entered for publication on October 20, 1597, as *The tragedie of kinge Richard the Third with the death of the Duke of Clarence*. The actors of Shakespeare's company who reconstructed this text from memory left out over two hundred lines and made many changes, but they preserved some lines omitted in the Folio, especially IV.ii.98–115. Printers added errors in each of the later quartos, dated 1598, 1602 (Q3), 1605, 1612, 1622 (Q6), 1629, and 1634.

The best text of the play appeared in 1623 in the First Folio (F). The printer, William Jaggard, had his compositors set up *Richard III* from a quarto marked with many corrections from an authentic manuscript. It used to be believed that this quarto was Q6, supplemented by an uncorrected quarto, Q3. In 1955, however, J. K. Walton, in *The Copy for the Folio Text of Richard III*, concluded that Q3, corrected, was the only quarto used for F. My collation of all variants in the first six quartos supports this conclusion. It is possible that both Q3 and Q6 were used, but that remains to be proved.

The present edition follows the readings of the First Folio except for the changes listed below. These changes have been made for definite reasons. First, the part of the Folio text containing III.i.1–168 seems to have been printed from Q3 without any correction from a manuscript, and the Folio text from V.iii.49 to the end of the play makes very few corrections. These few corrections have been accepted, but the rest of the text in these passages is based on Q1, from which Q3 and F are here derived. For example, the right reading "as" in III.i.123 appears in Q1, while "as, as," in F derives from the misprint "as, as," in Q3. Second, the reading of Q1 is also preferred, in any part of the play, to a different reading which F merely reprints from Q3. Third, the present text accepts thirty

lines from Q1 which are not in F. Finally, I have corrected errors and have made a few emendations.

The divisions into acts and scenes include all those in the Folio, translated from Latin, and these further scenes as marked in modern editions: III.v–vii, IV.iii, and V.iii–v. Brackets set off these and other editorial additions. Spelling, punctuation, and capitalization are modernized, and speech prefixes are regularized. In the following list of significant changes from the Folio, and from Q1, where it is the basic text, the reading of the present text is given in boldface and the alternative reading of the Folio, or of Q1 or Q3, in roman.

**I.i.26 spy** [Q1] see   **41 s.d. Clarence, guarded, and Brakenbury** Clarence, and Brakenbury, guarded   **45 the** [Q1] th'   **52 for** [Q1] but   **65 tempers him to this** [Q1] tempts him to this harsh   **75 to her for his** [Q1] for her   **103 I** [Q1] I do   **124 the** [Q1] this [Q3]   **133 prey** [Q1] play   **142 What** [Q1] Where
**I.ii.27 life** death (cf. IV.i.75)   **39 stand** [Q1] Stand'st   **60 deed** [Q1] Deeds   **78 a man** [Q1] man   **80 accuse** curse   **154 aspect** [Q1] Aspects   **195 was man** [Q1] man was [Q3]   **201 Richard** [Q1, not in F]   **202 Anne. To take . . . give** [Q1, not in F]   **225 Richard. Sirs . . . corse** [Q1, not in F]   **235 at all** [Q1] withall [Q3]
**I.iii.s.d. Queen** [Q1] the Queene Mother   **17 come the Lords** [Q1] comes the Lord   **108 s.d. Enter old Queen Margaret** [after 109]   **113 Tell . . . said** [Q1, not in F]   **114 avouch** [Q1] auouch't   **308 Queen Elizabeth** [Q1 Qu.] Mar.   **341, 349, 354 First Murderer** Vil.   **354 s.d. Exeunt** [Q1 after 353, not in F]
**I.iv.13 Thence** [Q1] There   **86 First Murderer** 2 Mur.   **89 Second Murderer** 1   **122 Faith** [Q1, not in F]   **126 Zounds** [Q1] Come   **147 Zounds** [Q1, not in F]   **192–93 to have . . . sins** [Q1] for any goodnesse   **240 And charged . . . other** [Q1, not in F]   **266–70 Which . . . distress** [not in Q; F inserts after 259]
**II.i.5 in** [Q1] to   **7 Rivers and Hastings** [Q1] Dorset and Riuers   **39 God** [Q1] heauen   **40 zeal** [Q1] loue   **57 unwittingly** [Q1] vnwillingly   **59 By** [Q1] To   **109 at** [Q1] and
**II.ii.1 Boy** [Q1] Edw.   **3 do you** [Q1] do   **47 have I** [Q1] haue   **83 weep** [Q1] weepes   **84–85 and so . . . Edward weep** [Q1, not in F]   **142, 154 Ludlow** [Q1] London   **145 Queen and Duchess of York. With all our hearts** [Q1, not in F]
**II.iii.43 Ensuing** [Q1] Pursuing (catchword "Ensuing")
**II.iv.1 hear** [Q1] heard [Q3]   **21 Archbishop** [Q1 Car.] Yor.   **65 death** [Q1] earth
**III.i.s.d. with others** [F] &c [Q1]   **9 Nor** [Q1] No   **40 God in heaven** [Q1] God [Q3]   **43 deep** [Q1] great [Q3]   **56 ne'er** [F] neuer [Q1]   **57 o'errule** [F] ouerrule [Q1]   **60 s.d. Exit** [not in Q1; after 59 in Q3 and F]   **63 seems** [Q1] thinkst [Q3]   **78 all-ending** [Q1] ending [Q3]   **79 ne'er** neuer [Q1, F]   **87 this** [Q3] his [Q3]   **94 s.d. and Cardinal** [F] Cardinall [Q1]   **96 loving** [Q1] noble [Q3]   **97 dread** [Q1] deare [Q3]   **120 heavy** [Q1] weightie [Q3]   **123 as** [Q1] as as [Q3]   **141 needs will** [Q1] will [Q3]   **145 grandam** [F] Granam [Q1]   **149 with** [Q1] and with [Q3]   **150 s.d. A sennet** [F, not in Q1]; **Hastings** Hast. Dors [Q1] Hastings, and Dorset [F]; **and Catesby** [F, not in Q1]   **154 parlous** perillous [Q1, F]   **160 knowest** [Q1] know'st   **161 thinkest** [Q1] think'st   **167 thinkest** [Q1] think'st; **What will he?** [Q1] Will not hee?
**III.ii.110 s.d. He whispers in his ear** [Q1] Priest. Ile wait vpon your Lordship [cf. line 121]
**III.iv.78 s.d. Exeunt** [after 77]   **81 rase** [Q1] rowse
**III.v.4 wert** [Q1] were   **104 Penker** Peuker   **105 s.d. Exeunt** Exit   **109 s.d. Exit** [Q1] Exeunt
**III.vii.218 Zounds, I'll** [Q1] we will   **219 Richard. O . . . Buckingham** [Q1, not in F]   **223 stone** Stones   **246 cousin** [Q1] Cousins
**IV.i.s.d. Enter . . . another door** Enter the Queene, Anne Duchesse of Gloucester, the Duchesse of Yorke, and Marquesse Dorset   **103 sorrow** Sorrowes
**IV.ii.71 there** [Q1] then   **89 Hereford** [Q1] Hertford   **97 Perhaps, perhaps** [Q1] perhaps   **98–115 Buckingham. My lord . . . vein today** [Q1, not in F]
**IV.iii.15 once** [Q1] one   **31 at** [Q1] and
**IV.iv.10 unblown** [Q1] vnblowed   **39 Tell o'er . . . mine** Tell

ouer . . . mine [Q1, not in F]  **45 holp'st** hop'st  **52 That excellent . . . earth** [after 53]  **64 Thy** [Q1] The  **118 nights . . . days** [Q1] night . . . day [Q3]  **128 intestate** [Q1] intestine  **141 Where** [Q1] Where't  **200 moe** [Q1] more [Q3]  **268 would I** [Q1] I would [Q3]  **274 sometimes** [Q1] sometime [Q3]  **284 this is** [Q1] this  **323 loan** Loue  **348 wail** [Q1] vaile  **364 Harp . . . past** [after 365]  **377 God . . . God's** [Q1] Heauen . . . Heanens (so misprinted)  **392 in** [Q1] with  **396 o'erpast** [Q1] repast  **417 peevish-fond** peeuish found  **423 I'll** I  **430 s.d. Exit Queen** [after 429]  **431 s.d. Enter Ratcliffe** [after "newes"]  **444 Ratcliffe** Catesby

**IV.v.10 Harfordwest** [Q1] Hertford-west [Q3]

**V.i.11 It is, my lord** [Q1] It is

**V.ii.11 center** [Q1] Centry

**V.iii.28 you** your  **54 sentinels** [F] centinell [Q1]  **58 Catesby** [Q1] Ratcliffe  **59 Catesby** Rat. [Q1]  **68 Saw'st thou** [Q1] Saw'st  **80 sit** [Q3] set [Q1]  **83 loving** [Q1] noble [Q3]  **90 the** [Q1] th'  **101 sund'red** [F] sundried [Q1]  **105 thoughts** [Q1] noise  **108 s.d. Manet Richmond** [F, not in Q1]  **113 The** [Q1] Th'  **115 the** [Q1] thy [Q3]  **118 s.d. Enter . . . Sixth** [F] Enter the ghost of young Prince Edward, sonne Harry the sixt, to Ri. [Q1]  **126 deadly holes** [Q1] holes [Q3]  **131 thy sleep** [Q1] sleepe  **132 sit** [Q3] set [Q1]  **139 s.d. and Vaughan** [F] Vaughan [Q1]  **140 Rivers** [Q3]  **146 Will** [Q3] Wel [Q1]  **146 s.d.–151 Enter . . . sake** [Q3; after line 159 in Q1]  **146 s.d. Hastings** [Q1] L. Hastings [Q3]  **152 Ghosts** [F] Ghost [Q1]  **153 lead** [Q1] laid [Q3]  **155 souls bid** [Q1] soule bids  **159 s.d. Lady Anne** [Q1] Anne  **162 perturbations** [Q3] preturbations [Q1]  **177 falls** [Q1] fall  **177 s.d. starteth up out**

of a dream [Q1] starts out of his dreame  **181 now** [Q1] not [Q3]  **184 I am** I [Q3] I and I [Q1]  **197 Perjury, perjury** [Q1] Periurie [Q3];  **highest** [Q1] high'st  **198 direst** [Q1] dyr'st  **200 to the** [Q1] all to'th'  **202 will** [Q1] shall [Q3]  **203 Nay** [F] And [Q1]  **209 Zounds, who is** [Q1] Who's  **213-15 King Richard. O Ratcliffe . . . my lord** [Q1, not in F]  **223 see** [Q1] heare [Q3]  **223 s.d. Exeunt Richard and Ratcliffe** [F] Exeunt [Q1];  **Enter . . . in his tent** [F] Enter the Lordes to Richmond [Q1]  **224 Lords** [Lo. Q1] Richm.  **233 heart** [F] soule [Q1]  **251 foil** [Q1] soile [Q3]  **256 sweat** [Q1] sweare [Q3]  **271 s.d. Ratcliffe, and** [Rat. &c Q1] Ratcliffe, and Catesby  **276 s.d. The clock striketh** [Q1] Clocke strikes  **283 not** [Q3] nor [Q1]  **294 drawn out all** [Q1] drawne [Q3]  **298 this** [Q1] the [Q3]  **302 boot** [Q3] bootes [Q1]  **304 s.d. He . . . paper** [Q1, not in F]  **308 unto** [Q1] to  **310 Conscience is but** [Q1] For Conscience is  **313 to it** [Q1] too't  **314 s.d. His . . . army** [Q1, not in F]  **320 ventures** aduentures [Q1]  **321 to you** [Q1] you to [Q3]  **323 distrain** restraine [Q1]  **336 in** [Q1] on [Q3]  **339 Fight, gentlemen** [Q1] Right Gentlemen [Q3],  **bold** [Q1] boldly [Q3]  **342 s.d. Enter a Messenger** [F, not in Q1]  **352 helms** [Q1] helpes [Q3]  **352 s.d. Exeunt** [Q1, not in F]

**V.iv.6 s.d. Alarums.** [F, not in Q1]

**V.v.s.d. Retreat . . . Lords** [F] then retrait being sounded. Enter Richmond, Darby, bearing the crowne, with other Lords, &c [Q1]  **4 this . . . royalty** [Q1] these . . . Royalties  **7 Wear it, enjoy it** [Q1] Weare it [Q3]  **11 if it please you, we may now** [Q1] (if you please) we may  **13 Stanley** [Der. F, not in Q1]  **32 their** [Q1] thy [Q3]  **41 s.d. Exeunt** [F, not in Q1]

# THE TRAGEDY OF
# RICHARD THE THIRD

[Dramatis Personae

KING EDWARD IV
EDWARD *Prince of Wales, afterward King Edward V* }
RICHARD *Duke of York* } *sons of the king*
GEORGE *Duke of Clarence*
RICHARD *Duke of Gloucester, afterward King Richard III* } *brothers of the king*
A YOUNG SON *of Clarence (Edward)*
HENRY *Earl of Richmond, afterward King Henry VII*
CARDINAL BOURCHIER *Archbishop of Canterbury*
THOMAS ROTHERHAM *Archbishop of York*
JOHN MORTON *Bishop of Ely*
DUKE OF BUCKINGHAM
DUKE OF NORFOLK
EARL OF SURREY *his son*
ANTHONY WOODVILLE *Earl Rivers, brother of Queen Elizabeth*
MARQUIS OF DORSET } *sons of Queen Elizabeth*
LORD GREY }
EARL OF OXFORD
LORD STANLEY *called also Earl of Derby*
LORD HASTINGS
LORD WOODVILLE
LORD SCALES
LORD LOVELL

SIR ROBERT BRAKENBURY *Lieutenant of the Tower*
SIR THOMAS VAUGHAN
SIR RICHARD RATCLIFFE
SIR JAMES TYRREL
SIR JAMES BLUNT
SIR WALTER HERBERT
SIR WILLIAM BRANDON
WILLIAM CATESBY
LORD MAYOR OF LONDON
CHRISTOPHER URSWICK *a chaplain*
TRESSEL } *gentlemen attending on Lady Anne*
BARKLEY }
QUEEN ELIZABETH *wife of King Edward IV*
QUEEN MARGARET *widow of King Henry VI*
DUCHESS OF YORK *mother of King Edward IV, Clarence, and Gloucester*
LADY ANNE *widow of Edward Prince of Wales, son of King Henry VI; afterward married to Richard*
A YOUNG DAUGHTER *of Clarence (Margaret)*
GHOSTS *of Richard's victims* LORDS *and other* ATTENDANTS BISHOPS PRIEST SHERIFF KEEPER TWO MURDERERS PURSUIVANT SCRIVENER PAGE CITIZENS MESSENGERS SOLDIERS ETC.

*Scene:* England]

238

# ACT I

Scene I. [*London. A street.*]

*Enter* RICHARD, *Duke of Gloucester, solus.*°

RICHARD
Now is the winter of our discontent
Made glorious summer by this sun° of York;
And all the clouds that loured upon our house
In the deep bosom of the ocean buried.
Now are our brows bound with victorious wreaths,   5
Our bruisèd arms hung up for monuments,°
Our stern alarums° changed to merry meetings,
Our dreadful marches to delightful measures.°
Grim-visaged war hath smoothed his wrinkled
    front,°
And now, instead of mounting barbèd° steeds    10
To fright the souls of fearful adversaries,
He capers nimbly in a lady's chamber
To the lascivious pleasing of a lute.
But I, that am not shaped for sportive tricks
Nor made to court an amorous looking glass;    15
I, that am rudely stamped, and want° love's majesty
To strut before a wanton ambling nymph;
I, that am curtailed of this fair proportion,
Cheated of feature° by dissembling Nature,
Deformed, unfinished, sent before my time    20
Into this breathing world scarce half made up,
And that so lamely and unfashionable
That dogs bark at me as I halt° by them;
Why, I, in this weak piping time° of peace,
Have no delight to pass away the time,    25
Unless to spy my shadow in the sun
And descant° on mine own deformity.
And therefore, since I cannot prove a lover
To entertain° these fair well-spoken days,
I am determinèd to prove a villain    30
And hate the idle pleasures of these days.
Plots have I laid, inductions° dangerous,
By drunken prophecies, libels, and dreams,
To set my brother Clarence and the king
In deadly hate the one against the other;    35
And if King Edward be as true and just
As I am subtle, false, and treacherous,
This day should Clarence closely be mewed up°
About a prophecy which says that G
Of Edward's heirs the murderer shall be.    40
Dive, thoughts, down to my soul. Here Clarence
    comes.

*Enter* CLARENCE, *guarded, and* BRAKENBURY [*Lieutenant of the Tower*].

Brother, good day. What means this armèd guard
That waits upon your grace?

CLARENCE               His majesty,
Tend'ring° my person's safety, hath appointed
This conduct° to convey me to the Tower.    45
RICHARD
Upon what cause?
CLARENCE          Because my name is George.
RICHARD
Alack, my lord, that fault is none of yours;
He should for that commit your godfathers.
O, belike° his majesty hath some intent
That you should be new christ'ned in the Tower.    50
But what's the matter, Clarence? May I know?
CLARENCE
Yea, Richard, when I know; for I protest
As yet I do not. But, as I can learn,
He harkens after prophecies and dreams,
And from the crossrow° plucks the letter G,    55
And says a wizard told him that by G
His issue disinherited should be;
And, for° my name of George begins with G,
It follows in his thought that I am he.
These (as I learn) and suchlike toys° as these    60
Hath moved his highness to commit me now.
RICHARD
Why, this it is when men are ruled by women.
'Tis not the king that sends you to the Tower.
My Lady Grey his wife, Clarence, 'tis she
That tempers° him to this extremity.°    65
Was it not she, and that good man of worship,°
Anthony Woodeville° her brother there,
That made him send Lord Hastings to the Tower,
From whence this present day he is deliverèd?
We are not safe, Clarence, we are not safe.    70
CLARENCE
By heaven, I think there is no man secure
But the queen's kindred, and nightwalking heralds°
That trudge betwixt the king and Mistress Shore.°
Heard you not what an humble suppliant
Lord Hastings was to her for his delivery?    75
RICHARD
Humbly complaining to her deity
Got my Lord Chamberlain his liberty.
I'll tell you what, I think it is our way,
If we will keep in favor with the king,
To be her men and wear her livery.    80
The jealous o'erworn widow° and herself,
Since that our brother dubbed them gentlewomen,
Are mighty gossips° in our monarchy.
BRAKENBURY
I beseech your graces both to pardon me.
His majesty hath straitly° given in charge    85
That no man shall have private conference,
Of what degree° soever, with your brother.

---

*The decorative border on page 238 appeared on the title page of the
first quarto edition of Richard III, 1597.*
**I.i.s.d. solus** alone   **2 sun** (1) emblem of King Edward (2) son
**6 monuments** memorials **7 alarums** calls to arms **8
measures** dances **9 front** forehead **10 barbèd** armored
**16 want** lack **19 feature** good shape **23 halt** limp **24
piping time** time when shepherds play their pipes **27 descant**
comment **29 entertain** while away **32 inductions** first
steps **38 mewed up** caged in prison

**44 Tend'ring** taking care of   **45 conduct** escort   **49
belike** probably   **55 crossrow** alphabet   **58 for** because   **60
toys** trifles **65 tempers** persuades; **extremity** extreme
severity **66 good . . . worship** play on *goodman*, common
man, raised to *worship*, honor, as Earl Rivers   **67 Woodeville**
trisyllabic; play on *would evil*   **72 heralds** king's messengers
(ironic) **73 Mistress Shore** Jane Shore, wife of a London
citizen; Edward IV's mistress   **81 widow** Queen Elizabeth,
widow of Sir John Grey   **83 gossips** chattering women,
busybodies **85 straitly** strictly **87 degree** rank

**RICHARD**
Even so? And° please your worship, Brakenbury,
You may partake of anything we say.
We speak no treason, man; we say the king      90
Is wise and virtuous, and his noble queen
Well struck° in years, fair, and not jealous;
We say that Shore's wife hath a pretty foot,
A cherry lip, a bonny eye, a passing pleasing tongue;
And that the queen's kindred are made gentlefolks.   95
How say you, sir? Can you deny all this?

**BRAKENBURY**
With this, my lord, myself have nought to do.

**RICHARD**
Naught° to do with Mistress Shore! I tell thee, fellow,
He that doth naught with her, excepting one,
Were best to do it secretly alone.             100

**BRAKENBURY**
What one, my lord?

**RICHARD**
Her husband, knave. Wouldst thou betray me?

**BRAKENBURY**
I beseech your grace to pardon me, and withal°
Forbear your conference with the noble duke.

**CLARENCE**
We know thy charge, Brakenbury, and will obey.   105

**RICHARD**
We are the queen's abjects,° and must obey.
Brother, farewell. I will unto the king;
And whatsoe'er you will employ me in,
Were it to call King Edward's widow sister,
I will perform it to enfranchise° you.         110
Meantime, this deep disgrace in brotherhood
Touches me deeper than you can imagine.

**CLARENCE**
I know it pleaseth neither of us well.

**RICHARD**
Well, your imprisonment shall not be long;
I will deliver you, or else lie for° you.      115
Meantime, have patience.

**CLARENCE**                I must perforce. Farewell.

*Exit* CLARENCE, [*with* BRAKENBURY *and* GUARD].

**RICHARD**
Go tread the path that thou shalt ne'er return.
Simple plain Clarence, I do love thee so
That I will shortly send thy soul to heaven,
If heaven will take the present at our hands.   120
But who comes here? The new-delivered Hastings!

*Enter Lord* HASTINGS.

**HASTINGS**
Good time of day unto my gracious lord.

**RICHARD**
As much unto my good Lord Chamberlain.
Well are you welcome to the open air.
How hath your lordship brooked° imprisonment?   125

**HASTINGS**
With patience, noble lord, as prisoners must.

But I shall live, my lord, to give them thanks
That were the cause of my imprisonment.

**RICHARD**
No doubt, no doubt; and so shall Clarence too,
For they that were your enemies are his         130
And have prevailed as much on him as you.

**HASTINGS**
More pity that the eagles should be mewed
Whiles kites° and buzzards prey at liberty.

**RICHARD**
What news abroad?

**HASTINGS**
No news so bad abroad as this at home:         135
The king is sickly, weak, and melancholy,
And his physicians fear° him mightily.

**RICHARD**
Now, by Saint John, that news is bad indeed.
O, he hath kept an evil diet° long
And overmuch consumed his royal person.        140
'Tis very grievous to be thought upon.
What, is he in his bed?

**HASTINGS**  He is.

**RICHARD**
Go you before, and I will follow you.

*Exit* HASTINGS.
He cannot live, I hope, and must not die       145
Till George be packed with post horse° up to heaven.
I'll in to urge his hatred more to Clarence
With lies well steeled° with weighty arguments;
And, if I fail not in my deep intent,
Clarence hath not another day to live.          150
Which done, God take King Edward to his mercy
And leave the world for me to bustle in!
For then I'll marry Warwick's youngest daughter.°
What though I killed her husband and her father?°
The readiest way to make the wench amends       155
Is to become her husband and her father.
The which will I, not all so much for love
As for another secret close intent
By marrying her which I must reach unto.
But yet I run before my horse to market.        160
Clarence still breathes, Edward still lives and reigns;
When they are gone, then must I count my gains.

*Exit.*

Scene II. [*A street.*]

*Enter the corse° of Henry the Sixth, with* HALBERDS°
*to guard it, Lady* ANNE *being the mourner.*

**ANNE**
Set down, set down your honorable load—
If honor may be shrouded in a hearse—
Whilst I awhile obsequiously° lament
Th' untimely fall of virtuous Lancaster.

[*The* BEARERS *set down the hearse.*]

88 And if it  92 struck advanced  98 Naught evil  103
withal moreover  106 abjects abject slaves  110 enfranchise
set free  115 lie for (1) go to prison instead of (2) tell lies
about  125 brooked endured

133 kites birds of the hawk family  137 fear fear for  139
diet way of living  146 packed . . . horse sent off in a hurry
148 steeled reinforced  153 Warwick's youngest daughter
Lady Anne  154 father father-in-law (Henry VI)
I.ii.s.d. corse corpse; halberds guards armed with long
poleaxes  3 obsequiously like a mourner at a funeral

Poor key-cold figure of a holy king,                               5
Pale ashes of the house of Lancaster,
Thou bloodless remnant of that royal blood,
Be it lawful that I invocate thy ghost
To hear the lamentations of poor Anne,
Wife to thy Edward, to thy slaught'red son,                       10
Stabbed by the selfsame hand that made these wounds!
Lo, in these windows that let forth thy life
I pour the helpless° balm of my poor eyes.
O, cursèd be the hand that made these holes!
Cursèd the heart that had the heart to do it!                     15
Cursèd the blood that let this blood from hence!
More direful hap betide° that hated wretch
That makes us wretched by the death of thee
Than I can wish to wolves, to spiders, toads,
Or any creeping venomed thing that lives!                         20
If ever he have child, abortive be it,
Prodigious,° and untimely brought to light,
Whose ugly and unnatural aspect
May fright the hopeful mother at the view,
And that be heir to his unhappiness!°                             25
If ever he have wife, let her be made
More miserable by the life of him
Than I am made by my young lord and thee!
Come, now towards Chertsey with your holy load,
Taken from Paul's° to be interrèd there;                          30

[*The* BEARERS *take up the hearse.*]

And still as° you are weary of this weight,
Rest you, whiles I lament King Henry's corse.

*Enter* RICHARD, *Duke of Gloucester.*

RICHARD
Stay, you that bear the corse, and set it down.
ANNE
What black magician conjures up this fiend
To stop devoted charitable deeds?                                 35
RICHARD
Villains, set down the corse, or, by Saint Paul,
I'll make a corse of him that disobeys.
GENTLEMAN
My lord, stand back and let the coffin pass.
RICHARD
Unmannered dog, stand° thou when I command!
Advance thy halberd higher than my breast,                        40
Or, by Saint Paul, I'll strike thee to my foot
And spurn° upon thee, beggar, for thy boldness.

[*The* BEARERS *set down the hearse.*]

ANNE
What, do you tremble? Are you all afraid?
Alas, I blame you not, for you are mortal,
And mortal eyes cannot endure the devil.                          45
Avaunt,° thou dreadful minister of hell!
Thou hadst but power over his mortal body,
His soul thou canst not have; therefore, begone.
RICHARD
Sweet saint, for charity, be not so curst.°

ANNE
Foul devil, for God's sake hence, and trouble us not,   50
For thou hast made the happy earth thy hell,
Filled it with cursing cries and deep exclaims.
If thou delight to view thy heinous deeds,
Behold this pattern° of thy butcheries.
O gentlemen, see, see dead Henry's wounds               55
Open their congealed mouths and bleed afresh!
Blush, blush, thou lump of foul deformity,
For 'tis thy presence that exhales° this blood
From cold and empty veins where no blood dwells.
Thy deed inhuman and unnatural                          60
Provokes this deluge most unnatural.
O God, which this blood mad'st, revenge his death!
O earth, which this blood drink'st, revenge his death!
Either heav'n, with lightning strike the murd'rer dead,
Or earth, gape open wide and eat him quick,°            65
As thou dost swallow up this good king's blood
Which his hell-governed arm hath butcherèd!
RICHARD
Lady, you know no rules of charity,
Which renders good for bad, blessings for curses.
ANNE
Villain, thou know'st nor law of God nor man.           70
No beast so fierce but knows some touch of pity.
RICHARD
But I know none, and therefore am no beast.
ANNE
O wonderful, when devils tell the truth!
RICHARD
More wonderful, when angels are so angry.
Vouchsafe, divine perfection of a woman,                75
Of these supposèd crimes to give me leave
By circumstance° but to acquit myself.
ANNE
Vouchsafe, diffused° infection of a man,
Of these known evils but to give me leave
By circumstance to accuse thy cursèd self.              80
RICHARD
Fairer than tongue can name thee, let me have
Some patient leisure to excuse myself.
ANNE
Fouler than heart can think thee, thou canst make
No excuse current° but to hang thyself.
RICHARD
By such despair I should accuse myself.                 85
ANNE
And by despairing shalt thou stand excusèd
For doing worthy vengeance on thyself
That didst unworthy slaughter upon others.
RICHARD
Say that I slew them not?
ANNE                          Then say they were not slain.
But dead they are, and, devilish slave, by thee.        90
RICHARD
I did not kill your husband.
ANNE                          Why, then he is alive.
RICHARD
Nay, he is dead, and slain by Edward's hands.

13 **helpless** unavailing  17 **hap betide** fortune happen to
22 **Prodigious** monstrous  25 **unhappiness** wickedness  30
**Paul's** Saint Paul's Cathedral  31 **still as** whenever  39
**stand** halt  42 **spurn** trample  46 **Avaunt** begone  49 **curst**
sharp-tongued

54 **pattern** example  58 **exhales** causes to flow  65 **quick**
alive  77 **By circumstance** in detail  78 **diffused** shapeless
84 **current** genuine

ANNE
In thy foul throat thou li'st! Queen Margaret saw
Thy murd'rous falchion° smoking in his blood;
The which thou once didst bend against her breast, 95
But that thy brothers beat aside the point.

RICHARD
I was provokèd by her sland'rous tongue,
That laid their guilt upon my guiltless shoulders.

ANNE
Thou wast provokèd by thy bloody mind,
That never dream'st on aught but butcheries. 100
Didst thou not kill this king?

RICHARD                              I grant ye.

ANNE
Dost grant me, hedgehog? Then God grant me too
Thou mayst be damnèd for that wicked deed!
O, he was gentle, mild, and virtuous!

RICHARD
The better for the King of Heaven that hath him. 105

ANNE
He is in heaven, where thou shalt never come.

RICHARD
Let him thank me that holp° to send him thither;
For he was fitter for that place than earth.

ANNE
And thou unfit for any place but hell.

RICHARD
Yes, one place else, if you will hear me name it. 110

ANNE
Some dungeon.

RICHARD            Your bedchamber.

ANNE
Ill rest betide the chamber where thou liest!

RICHARD
So will it, madam, till I lie with you.

ANNE
I hope so.

RICHARD I know so. But, gentle Lady Anne,
To leave this keen encounter of our wits 115
And fall something into a slower method,
Is not the causer of the timeless° deaths
Of these Plantagenets, Henry and Edward,
As blameful as the executioner?

ANNE
Thou wast the cause and most accursed effect.° 120

RICHARD
Your beauty was the cause of that effect;
Your beauty, that did haunt me in my sleep
To undertake the death of all the world,
So I might live one hour in your sweet bosom.

ANNE
If I thought that, I tell thee, homicide, 125
These nails should rend that beauty from my cheeks.

RICHARD
These eyes could not endure that beauty's wrack.°
You should not blemish it if I stood by.
As all the world is cheerèd by the sun,
So I by that; it is my day, my life. 130

ANNE
Black night o'ershade thy day, and death thy life!

RICHARD
Curse not thyself, fair creature; thou art both.

ANNE
I would I were, to be revenged on thee.

RICHARD
It is a quarrel most unnatural
To be revenged on him that loveth thee. 135

ANNE
It is a quarrel just and reasonable
To be revenged on him that killed my husband.

RICHARD
He that bereft thee, lady, of thy husband,
Did it to help thee to a better husband.

ANNE
His better doth not breathe upon the earth. 140

RICHARD
He lives that loves thee better than he could.

ANNE
Name him.

RICHARD  Plantagenet.

ANNE                    Why, that was he.

RICHARD
The selfsame name, but one of better nature.

ANNE
Where is he?

RICHARD      Here. [She] spits at him.
                    Why dost thou spit at me?

ANNE
Would it were mortal poison for thy sake! 145

RICHARD
Never came poison from so sweet a place.

ANNE
Never hung poison on a fouler toad.
Out of my sight! Thou dost infect mine eyes.

RICHARD
Thine eyes, sweet lady, have infected mine.

ANNE
Would they were basilisks° to strike thee dead! 150

RICHARD
I would they were, that I might die at once;°
For now they kill me with a living death.
Those eyes of thine from mine have drawn salt tears,
Shamed their aspect° with store of childish drops,
These eyes which never shed remorseful° tear, 155
No, when my father York and Edward wept
To hear the piteous moan that Rutland° made
When black-faced° Clifford shook his sword at him,
Nor when thy warlike father, like a child,
Told the sad story of my father's death 160
And twenty times made pause to sob and weep,
That all the standers-by had wet their cheeks
Like trees bedashed with rain. In that sad time
My manly eyes did scorn an humble tear;
And what these sorrows could not thence exhale 165
Thy beauty hath, and made them blind with weeping.
I never sued to friend nor enemy;
My tongue could never learn sweet smoothing° word;
But now thy beauty is proposed my fee,

---

94 **falchion** curved sword  107 **holp** helped  117 **timeless**
untimely  120 **effect** effective agent  127 **wrack** destruction
150 **basilisks** fabulous monsters believed to kill by a look
151 **at once** once and for all  154 **aspect** appearance  155
**remorseful** pitying  157 **Rutland** a young brother of
Richard (see 3 *Henry VI*, I.iii)  158 **black-faced** cruel-looking
168 **smoothing** flattering

My proud heart sues, and prompts my tongue to
   speak.                                                                    170

*She looks scornfully at him.*

Teach not thy lip such scorn, for it was made
For kissing, lady, not for such contempt.
If thy revengeful heart cannot forgive,
Lo, here I lend thee this sharp-pointed sword;
Which if thou please to hide in this true breast          175
And let the soul forth that adoreth thee,
I lay it naked to the deadly stroke
And humbly beg the death upon my knee.

*He lays his breast open. She offers at [it] with his sword.*

Nay, do not pause, for I did kill King Henry,
But 'twas thy beauty that provokèd me.                   180
Nay, now dispatch; 'twas I that stabbed young Edward,
But 'twas thy heavenly face that set me on.

*She falls° the sword.*

Take up the sword again, or take up me.
ANNE
Arise, dissembler; though I wish thy death,
I will not be thy executioner.                           185
RICHARD
Then bid me kill myself, and I will do it.
ANNE
I have already.
RICHARD       That was in thy rage.
Speak it again, and even with the word
This hand, which for thy love did kill thy love,
Shall for thy love kill a far truer love.                190
To both their deaths shalt thou be accessary.°
ANNE
I would I knew thy heart.
RICHARD
'Tis figured° in my tongue.
ANNE
I fear me both are false.
RICHARD
Then never was man true.                                 195
ANNE
Well, well, put up your sword.
RICHARD
Say, then, my peace is made.
ANNE
That shalt thou know hereafter.
RICHARD
But shall I live in hope?
ANNE
All men, I hope, live so.                                200
RICHARD
Vouchsafe° to wear this ring.
ANNE
To take is not to give.

[RICHARD *puts the ring on her finger.*]

RICHARD
Look how° my ring encompasseth thy finger,

Even so thy breast encloseth my poor heart.
Wear both of them, for both of them are thine.           205
And if thy poor devoted servant may
But beg one favor at thy gracious hand,
Thou dost confirm his happiness forever.
ANNE   What is it?
RICHARD
That it may please you leave these sad designs           210
To him that hath most cause to be a mourner,
And presently° repair to Crosby House,
Where, after I have solemnly interred
At Chertsey monast'ry this noble king
And wet his grave with my repentant tears,               215
I will with all expedient° duty see you.
For divers unknown° reasons, I beseech you,
Grant me this boon.
ANNE
With all my heart; and much it joys me too
To see you are become so penitent.                       220
Tressel and Barkley, go along with me.
RICHARD
Bid me farewell.
ANNE          'Tis more than you deserve;
But since you teach me how to flatter you,
Imagine I have said farewell already.
                    *Exit two with* ANNE.
RICHARD
Sirs, take up the corse.
GENTLEMEN        Towards Chertsey, noble lord?   225
RICHARD
No, to Whitefriars; there attend° my coming.
       *Exit* [BEARERS *and* GENTLEMEN, *with*] *corse.*
Was ever woman in this humor° wooed?
Was ever woman in this humor won?
I'll have her, but I will not keep her long.
What! I that killed her husband and his father          230
To take her in her heart's extremest hate,
With curses in her mouth, tears in her eyes,
The bleeding witness of my hatred by,
Having God, her conscience, and these bars against
   me,
And I no friends to back my suit at all                  235
But the plain devil and dissembling looks,
And yet to win her, all the world to nothing!
Ha!
Hath she forgot already that brave prince,
Edward her lord, whom I, some three months since,       240
Stabbed in my angry mood at Tewkesbury?°
A sweeter and a lovelier gentleman,
Framed in the prodigality° of nature,
Young, valiant, wise, and, no doubt, right royal,
The spacious world cannot again afford.°                245
And will she yet abase her eyes on me,
That cropped the golden prime° of this sweet prince
And made her widow to a woeful bed?
On me, whose all not equals Edward's moi'ty?°
On me, that halts and am misshapen thus?                250

---

182 s.d. **falls** lets fall  191 **accessary** sharing in guilt  193
**figured** pictured  201 **Vouchsafe** consent  203 **Look how**
just as

212 **presently** immediately  216 **expedient** speedy  217
**unknown** secret  226 **attend** await  227 **humor** mood  241
**Tewkesbury** scene of a Yorkist victory  243 **prodigality**
lavishness  245 **afford** supply  247 **prime** springtime  249
**moi'ty** half

My dukedom to a beggarly denier,°
I do mistake my person all this while.
Upon my life, she finds, although I cannot,
Myself to be a marv'lous proper° man.
I'll be at charges for° a looking glass                    255
And entertain° a score or two of tailors
To study fashions to adorn my body.
Since I am crept in favor with myself,
I will maintain it with some little cost.
But first I'll turn yon fellow in° his grave,             260
And then return lamenting to my love.
Shine out, fair sun; till I have bought a glass
That I may see my shadow as I pass.            *Exit.*

Scene III. [*The palace.*]

*Enter* QUEEN [ELIZABETH,] LORD RIVERS, [DORSET,]
*and Lord* GREY.

RIVERS
Have patience, madam; there's no doubt his majesty
Will soon recover his accustomed health.

GREY
In that you brook° it ill, it makes him worse.
Therefore for God's sake entertain good comfort
And cheer his grace with quick and merry eyes.            5

QUEEN ELIZABETH
If he were dead, what would betide on° me?

GREY
No other harm but loss of such a lord.

QUEEN ELIZABETH
The loss of such a lord includes all harms.

GREY
The heavens have blessed you with a goodly son
To be your comforter when he is gone.                     10

QUEEN ELIZABETH
Ah, he is young, and his minority
Is put unto the trust of Richard Gloucester,
A man that loves not me, nor none of you.

RIVERS
Is it concluded he shall be protector?

QUEEN ELIZABETH
It is determined, not concluded° yet;                     15
But so it must be if the king miscarry.°

*Enter* BUCKINGHAM *and* [STANLEY *Earl of*] *Derby.*

GREY
Here come the Lords of Buckingham and Derby.

BUCKINGHAM
Good time of day unto your royal grace!

STANLEY
God make your majesty joyful as you have been!

QUEEN ELIZABETH
The Countess Richmond,° good my Lord of Derby,           20
To your good prayer will scarcely say, "Amen."

Yet, Derby, notwithstanding she's your wife
And loves not me, be you, good lord, assured
I hate not you for her proud arrogance.

STANLEY
I do beseech you, either not believe                      25
The envious slanders of her false accusers,
Or, if she be accused on true report,
Bear with her weakness, which I think proceeds
From wayward sickness and no grounded malice.

QUEEN ELIZABETH
Saw you the king today, my Lord of Derby?                 30

STANLEY
But now° the Duke of Buckingham and I
Are come from visiting his majesty.

QUEEN ELIZABETH
What likelihood of his amendment, lords?

BUCKINGHAM
Madam, good hope; his grace speaks cheerfully.

QUEEN ELIZABETH
God grant him health! Did you confer with him?           35

BUCKINGHAM
Ay, madam; he desires to make atonement°
Between the Duke of Gloucester and your brothers,
And between them and my Lord Chamberlain,°
And sent to warn° them to his royal presence.

QUEEN ELIZABETH
Would all were well! But that will never be.             40
I fear our happiness is at the height.

*Enter* RICHARD [*and* HASTINGS].

RICHARD
They do me wrong, and I will not endure it!
Who is it that complains unto the king
That I, forsooth, am stern, and love them not?
By holy Paul, they love his grace but lightly            45
That fill his ears with such dissentious rumors.
Because I cannot flatter and look fair,
Smile in men's faces, smooth, deceive, and cog,°
Duck with French nods and apish courtesy,
I must be held a rancorous enemy.                        50
Cannot a plain man live and think no harm
But thus his simple truth must be abused
With silken, sly, insinuating Jacks?°

GREY
To who in all this presence speaks your grace?

RICHARD
To thee, that hast nor honesty nor grace.°               55
When have I injured thee? When done thee wrong?
Or thee? Or thee? Or any of your faction?
A plague upon you all! His royal grace—
Whom God preserve better than you would wish!—
Cannot be quiet scarce a breathing while°               60
But you must trouble him with lewd° complaints.

QUEEN ELIZABETH
Brother of Gloucester, you mistake the matter.
The king on his own royal disposition,
And not provoked by any suitor else,
Aiming, belike, at your interior hatred                  65

251 **denier** French coin worth a tenth of an English penny
254 **marv'lous proper** wonderfully handsome  255 **at
charges for** at the expense of  256 **entertain** engage  260
**in** into
**I.iii.3 brook** endure  6 **betide on** happen to  15 **determined, not concluded** decided, not finally decreed  16
**miscarry** die  20 **Countess Richmond** Margaret Tudor,
mother of the Earl of Richmond (later Henry VII) and wife
of Lord Stanley

31 **But now** just now  36 **atonement** reconciliation  38
**Lord Chamberlain** Hastings  39 **warn** summon  48 **cog**
fawn  53 **Jacks** knaves  55 **grace** virtue  60 **breathing while**
time to take a breath  61 **lewd** wicked

That in your outward action shows itself
Against my children, brothers, and myself,
Makes° him to send that he may learn the ground.

RICHARD
I cannot tell; the world is grown so bad
That wrens make prey where eagles dare not perch. 70
Since every Jack became a gentleman,
There's many a gentle° person made a Jack.

QUEEN ELIZABETH
Come, come, we know your meaning, brother
    Gloucester.
You envy my advancement and my friends'.
God grant we never may have need of you! 75

RICHARD
Meantime, God grants that I have need of you.
Our brother is imprisoned by your means,
Myself disgraced, and the nobility
Held in contempt, while great promotions
Are daily given to ennoble those 80
That scarce, some two days since, were worth a
    noble.°

QUEEN ELIZABETH
By Him that raised me to this careful° height
From that contented hap° which I enjoyed,
I never did incense his majesty
Against the Duke of Clarence, but have been 85
An earnest advocate to plead for him.
My lord, you do me shameful injury
Falsely to draw me in° these vile suspects.°

RICHARD
You may deny that you were not the mean
Of my Lord Hastings' late imprisonment. 90

RIVERS
She may, my lord, for—

RICHARD
She may, Lord Rivers! Why, who knows not so?
She may do more, sir, than denying that:
She may help you to many fair preferments,°
And then deny her aiding hand therein 95
And lay those honors on your high desert.
What may she not? She may, ay, marry,° may she!

RIVERS
What, marry, may she?

RICHARD
What, marry, may she! Marry with a king,
A bachelor and a handsome stripling too. 100
Iwis° your grandam had a worser match.

QUEEN ELIZABETH
My Lord of Gloucester, I have too long borne
Your blunt upbraidings and your bitter scoffs.
By heaven, I will acquaint his majesty
Of those gross taunts that oft I have endured. 105
I had rather be a country servant maid
Than a great queen with this condition,
To be so baited,° scorned, and stormèd at.

*Enter old* QUEEN MARGARET, [*behind*].

Small joy have I in being England's queen.

QUEEN MARGARET [*Aside.*]
And less'ned be that small, God I beseech him! 110
Thy honor, state, and seat is due to me.

RICHARD
What! Threat you me with telling of the king?
Tell him and spare not. Look what° I have said
I will avouch in presence of the king.
I dare adventure to be sent to th' Tow'r. 115
'Tis time to speak; my pains° are quite forgot.

QUEEN MARGARET [*Aside.*]
Out, devil! I do remember them too well.
Thou kill'dst my husband Henry in the Tower
And Edward, my poor son, at Tewkesbury.

RICHARD
Ere you were queen, ay, or your husband king, 120
I was a packhorse in his great affairs,
A weeder-out of his proud adversaries,
A liberal rewarder of his friends;
To royalize his blood I spent mine own.

QUEEN MARGARET [*Aside.*]
Ay, and much better blood than his or thine. 125

RICHARD
In all which time you and your husband Grey
Were factious for the house of Lancaster;
And, Rivers, so were you. Was not your husband
In Margaret's battle° at Saint Albans slain?
Let me put in your minds, if you forget, 130
What you have been ere this, and what you are;
Withal, what I have been, and what I am.

QUEEN MARGARET [*Aside.*]
A murd'rous villain, and so still thou art.

RICHARD
Poor Clarence did forsake his father° Warwick;
Ay, and forswore himself—which Jesu pardon!— 135

QUEEN MARGARET [*Aside.*]
Which God revenge!

RICHARD
To fight on Edward's party for the crown;
And for his meed,° poor lord, he is mewèd up.
I would to God my heart were flint like Edward's,
Or Edward's soft and pitiful like mine. 140
I am too childish-foolish for this world.

QUEEN MARGARET [*Aside.*]
Hie thee to hell for shame and leave this world,
Thou cacodemon!° There thy kingdom is.

RIVERS
My Lord of Gloucester, in those busy days
Which here you urge to prove us enemies, 145
We followed then our lord, our sovereign king.
So should we you, if you should be our king.

RICHARD
If I should be! I had rather be a peddler.
Far be it from my heart, the thought thereof!

QUEEN ELIZABETH
As little joy, my lord, as you suppose 150
You should enjoy were you this country's king,
As little joy you may suppose in me
That I enjoy, being the queen thereof.

---

68 **Makes** the subject has shifted from "The king" to "your
interior hatred"  72 **gentle** wellborn  81 **noble** coin worth a
third of a pound  82 **careful** care-filled  83 **hap** fortune  88
**in** into; **suspects** suspicions  94 **preferments** promotions
97 **marry** indeed (from "By the Virgin Mary")  101 **Iwis**
certainly  108 **baited** tormented

113 **Look what** whatever  116 **pains** efforts  129 **battle**
army  134 **father** father-in-law  138 **meed** reward  143
**cacodemon** evil spirit

QUEEN MARGARET [*Aside.*]
A little joy enjoys the queen thereof;
For I am she, and altogether joyless.                        155
I can no longer hold me patient.

[*Comes forward.*]

Hear me, you wrangling pirates, that fall out
In sharing that which you have pilled° from me!
Which of you trembles not that looks on me?
If not, that I am queen, you bow like subjects,            160
Yet that,° by you deposed, you quake like rebels.
Ah, gentle° villain, do not turn away!

RICHARD
Foul wrinkled witch, what mak'st thou° in my sight?

QUEEN MARGARET
But repetition of what thou hast marred;
That will I make before I let thee go.                      165

RICHARD
Wert thou not banishèd on pain of death?

QUEEN MARGARET
I was; but I do find more pain in banishment
Than death can yield me here by my abode.
A husband and a son thou ow'st to me;
And thou a kingdom; all of you allegiance.                  170
This sorrow that I have, by right is yours,
And all the pleasures you usurp are mine.

RICHARD
The curse my noble father laid on thee
When thou didst crown his warlike brows with
    paper
And with thy scorns drew'st rivers from his eyes           175
And then to dry them gav'st the duke a clout°
Steeped in the faultless blood of pretty Rutland,
His curses then from bitterness of soul
Denounced against thee are all fall'n upon thee;
And God, not we, hath plagued thy bloody deed.             180

QUEEN ELIZABETH
So just is God to right the innocent.

HASTINGS
O, 'twas the foulest deed to slay that babe
And the most merciless that e'er was heard of!

RIVERS
Tyrants themselves wept when it was reported.

DORSET
No man but prophesied revenge for it.                       185

BUCKINGHAM
Northumberland, then present, wept to see it.

QUEEN MARGARET
What! Were you snarling all before I came,
Ready to catch each other by the throat,
And turn you all your hatred now on me?
Did York's dread curse prevail so much with heaven         190
That Henry's death, my lovely Edward's death,
Their kingdom's loss, my woeful banishment,
Should all but answer° for that peevish° brat?
Can curses pierce the clouds and enter heaven?
Why then, give way, dull clouds, to my quick°
    curses!                                                 195

Though not by war, by surfeit die your king,
As ours by murder, to make him a king!
Edward thy son, that now is Prince of Wales,
For Edward our son, that was Prince of Wales,
Die in his youth by like untimely violence!                200
Thyself a queen, for me that was a queen,
Outlive thy glory like my wretched self!
Long mayst thou live to wail thy children's death
And see another, as I see thee now,
Decked in thy rights as thou art stalled° in mine!         205
Long die thy happy days before thy death,
And, after many length'nèd hours of grief,
Die neither mother, wife, nor England's queen!
Rivers and Dorset, you were standers-by,
And so wast thou, Lord Hastings, when my son              210
Was stabbed with bloody daggers. God I pray him
That none of you may live his natural age,
But by some unlooked accident cut off!

RICHARD
Have done thy charm,° thou hateful withered hag!

QUEEN MARGARET
And leave out thee? Stay, dog, for thou shalt hear me.     215
If heaven have any grievous plague in store
Exceeding those that I can wish upon thee,
O, let them keep it till thy sins be ripe
And then hurl down their indignation
On thee, the troubler of the poor world's peace!          220
The worm of conscience still begnaw thy soul!
Thy friends suspect for traitors while thou liv'st,
And take deep traitors for thy dearest friends!
No sleep close up that deadly eye of thine,
Unless it be while some tormenting dream                   225
Affrights thee with a hell of ugly devils!
Thou elvish-marked,° abortive, rooting hog!°
Thou that wast sealed° in thy nativity
The slave of nature and the son of hell!
Thou slander of thy heavy° mother's womb!                  230
Thou loathèd issue of thy father's loins!
Thou rag of honor! Thou detested—

RICHARD
Margaret.

QUEEN MARGARET    Richard!

RICHARD                              Ha?

QUEEN MARGARET                I call thee not.

RICHARD
I cry thee mercy° then, for I did think
That thou hadst called me all these bitter names.          235

QUEEN MARGARET
Why, so I did, but looked for no reply.
O, let me make the period° to my curse!

RICHARD
'Tis done by me, and ends in "Margaret."

QUEEN ELIZABETH
Thus have you breathed your curse against yourself.

QUEEN MARGARET
Poor painted° queen, vain flourish° of my fortune,         240
Why strew'st thou sugar on that bottled° spider

158 pilled plundered 160–61 that . . . that because . . .
because 162 gentle (1) wellborn (2) kindly (ironic) 163
mak'st thou are you doing 176 clout piece of cloth 193
but answer only pay back; peevish foolish 195 quick full
of life

205 stalled installed 214 charm spell, curse 227 elvish-
marked disfigured by evil fairies; hog the boar was
Richard's emblem 228 sealed marked 230 heavy sorrowful
234 cry thee mercy beg your pardon 237 period end
240 painted unreal; vain flourish useless decoration 241
bottled swollen

Whose deadly web ensnareth thee about?
Fool, fool, thou whet'st a knife to kill thyself.
The day will come that thou shalt wish for me
To help thee curse this poisonous bunch-backed
    toad.     245

HASTINGS
False-boding woman, end thy frantic curse,
Lest to thy harm thou move our patience.

QUEEN MARGARET
Foul shame upon you! You have all moved mine.

RIVERS
Were you well served, you would be taught your duty.

QUEEN MARGARET
To serve me well, you all should do me duty,    250
Teach me to be your queen and you my subjects.
O, serve me well and teach yourselves that duty!

DORSET
Dispute not with her; she is lunatic.

QUEEN MARGARET
Peace, Master Marquis, you are malapert.°
Your fire-new stamp° of honor is scarce current.    255
O, that your young nobility could judge
What 'twere to lose it and be miserable!
They that stand high have many blasts to shake them,
And if they fall, they dash themselves to pieces.

RICHARD
Good counsel, marry! Learn it, learn it, marquis.    260

DORSET
It touches you, my lord, as much as me.

RICHARD
Ay, and much more; but I was born so high.
Our aerie° buildeth in the cedar's top
And dallies with the wind and scorns the sun.

QUEEN MARGARET
And turns the sun to shade, alas! alas!    265
Witness my son, now in the shade of death,
Whose bright outshining beams thy cloudy wrath
Hath in eternal darkness folded up.
Your aerie buildeth in our aerie's nest.
O God, that see'st it, do not suffer it!    270
As it is won with blood, lost be it so!

BUCKINGHAM
Peace, peace, for shame, if not for charity.

QUEEN MARGARET
Urge neither charity nor shame to me.
Uncharitably with me have you dealt,
And shamefully my hopes by you are butchered.    275
My charity is outrage, life my shame,
And in that shame still live my sorrow's rage!

BUCKINGHAM
Have done, have done.

QUEEN MARGARET
O princely Buckingham, I'll kiss thy hand
In sign of league and amity with thee.    280
Now fair befall thee and thy noble house!
Thy garments are not spotted with our blood,
Nor thou within the compass of my curse.

BUCKINGHAM
Nor no one here; for curses never pass
The lips of those that breathe them in the air.    285

QUEEN MARGARET
I will not think but they ascend the sky
And there awake God's gentle-sleeping peace.
O Buckingham, take heed of yonder dog!
Look when° he fawns he bites; and when he bites
His venom tooth will rankle to the death.    290
Have not to do with him, beware of him.
Sin, death, and hell have set their marks on him
And all their ministers attend on him.

RICHARD
What doth she say, my Lord of Buckingham?

BUCKINGHAM
Nothing that I respect,° my gracious lord.    295

QUEEN MARGARET
What, dost thou scorn me for my gentle counsel
And soothe the devil that I warn thee from?
O, but remember this another day,
When he shall split thy very heart with sorrow,
And say poor Margaret was a prophetess.    300
Live each of you the subjects to his hate,
And he to yours, and all of you to God's!    *Exit.*

BUCKINGHAM
My hair doth stand on end to hear her curses.

RIVERS
And so doth mine. I muse° why she's at liberty.

RICHARD
I cannot blame her. By God's holy mother,    305
She hath had too much wrong, and I repent
My part thereof that I have done to her.

QUEEN ELIZABETH
I never did her any to my knowledge.

RICHARD
Yet you have all the vantage of her wrong:
I was too hot to do somebody good    310
That is too cold in thinking of it now.
Marry, as for Clarence, he is well repaid;
He is franked up° to fatting for his pains.
God pardon them that are the cause thereof!

RIVERS
A virtuous and a Christianlike conclusion,    315
To pray for them that have done scathe° to us.

RICHARD
So do I ever—[*speaks to himself*] being well advised;
For had I cursed now, I had cursed myself.

*Enter* CATESBY.

CATESBY
Madam, his majesty doth call for you;
And for your grace; and yours, my gracious lord.    320

QUEEN ELIZABETH
Catesby, I come. Lords, will you go with me?

RIVERS
We wait upon your grace.
        *Exeunt all but* [RICHARD *Duke of* ] *Gloucester.*

RICHARD
I do the wrong, and first begin to brawl.
The secret mischiefs that I set abroach°
I lay unto the grievous charge of others.    325
Clarence, who I indeed have cast in darkness,

---

254 **malapert** impudent  255 **fire-new stamp** newly coined
title  263 **aerie** brood of eagles    289 **Look when** whenever  295 **respect** pay heed to  304
**muse** wonder  313 **franked up** shut up (like an animal to be
slaughtered)  316 **scathe** harm  324 **set abroach** originate

I do beweep to many simple gulls,°
Namely to Derby, Hastings, Buckingham,
And tell them 'tis the queen and her allies°
That stir the king against the duke my brother.          330
Now they believe it, and withal whet me
To be revenged on Rivers, Dorset, Grey.
But then I sigh, and with a piece of Scripture
Tell them that God bids us do good for evil;
And thus I clothe my naked villainy                      335
With odd old ends stol'n forth of holy writ,
And seem a saint when most I play the devil.

*Enter two* MURDERERS.

But soft! Here come my executioners.
How now, my hardy, stout-resolvèd mates!
Are you now going to dispatch this thing?                340

FIRST MURDERER
We are, my lord, and come to have the warrant
That we may be admitted where he is.

RICHARD
Well thought upon; I have it here about me.

[*Gives the warrant.*]

When you have done, repair to Crosby Place.
But, sirs, be sudden in the execution,                   345
Withal obdurate, do not hear him plead;
For Clarence is well-spoken, and perhaps
May move your hearts to pity if you mark him.

FIRST MURDERER
Tut, tut, my lord, we will not stand to prate.
Talkers are no good doers; be assured                    350
We go to use our hands and not our tongues.

RICHARD
Your eyes drop millstones when fools' eyes fall° tears.
I like you, lads; about your business straight.°
Go, go, dispatch.

FIRST MURDERER  We will, my noble lord.  *Exeunt.*

Scene IV. [*The Tower.*]

*Enter* CLARENCE *and* KEEPER.

KEEPER
Why looks your grace so heavily° today?

CLARENCE
O, I have passed a miserable night,
So full of fearful dreams, of ugly sights,
That, as I am a Christian faithful man,
I would not spend another such a night                    5
Though 'twere to buy a world of happy days,
So full of dismal terror was the time.

KEEPER
What was your dream, my lord? I pray you tell me.

CLARENCE
Methoughts° that I had broken from the Tower
And was embarked to cross to Burgundy,                    10
And in my company my brother Gloucester,
Who from my cabin tempted me to walk
Upon the hatches. Thence we looked toward England
And cited up a thousand heavy times,

During the wars of York and Lancaster,                    15
That had befall'n us. As we paced along
Upon the giddy footing of the hatches,
Methought that Gloucester stumbled, and in falling
Struck me (that thought to stay° him) overboard
Into the tumbling billows of the main.°                   20
O Lord, methought what pain it was to drown!
What dreadful noise of water in mine ears!
What sights of ugly death within mine eyes!
Methoughts I saw a thousand fearful wracks;
A thousand men that fishes gnawed upon;                   25
Wedges of gold, great anchors, heaps of pearl,
Inestimable stones, unvaluèd° jewels,
All scatt'red in the bottom of the sea.
Some lay in dead men's skulls, and in the holes
Where eyes did once inhabit there were crept,             30
As 'twere in scorn of eyes, reflecting gems
That wooed the slimy bottom of the deep
And mocked the dead bones that lay scatt'red by.

KEEPER
Had you such leisure in the time of death
To gaze upon these secrets of the deep?                   35

CLARENCE
Methought I had; and often did I strive
To yield the ghost, but still the envious flood
Stopped in my soul and would not let it forth
To find the empty, vast, and wand'ring air,
But smothered it within my panting bulk,°                 40
Who almost burst to belch it in the sea.

KEEPER
Awaked you not in this sore agony?

CLARENCE
No, no, my dream was lengthened after life.
O, then began the tempest to my soul!
I passed, methought, the melancholy flood,                45
With that sour ferryman° which poets write of,
Unto the kingdom of perpetual night.
The first that there did greet my stranger soul
Was my great father-in-law, renownèd Warwick,
Who spake aloud, "What scourge for perjury                50
Can this dark monarchy afford false Clarence?"
And so he vanished. Then came wand'ring by
A shadow like an angel, with bright hair
Dabbled in blood, and he shrieked out aloud,
"Clarence is come, false, fleeting,° perjured Clarence,   55
That stabbed me in the field by Tewkesbury.
Seize on him, Furies, take him unto torment!"
With that, methought, a legion of foul fiends
Environed me and howlèd in mine ears
Such hideous cries that with the very noise               60
I, trembling, waked, and for a season after
Could not believe but that I was in hell,
Such terrible impression made my dream.

KEEPER
No marvel, lord, though it affrighted you.
I am afraid, methinks, to hear you tell it.               65

CLARENCE
Ah, keeper, keeper, I have done these things
That now give evidence against my soul
For Edward's sake, and see how he requites me!

---

327 **gulls** dupes  329 **allies** kindred  352 **fall** let fall  353
**straight** at once
I.iv.1 **heavily** sadly  9 **Methoughts** it seemed to me

19 **stay** support  20 **main** ocean  27 **unvaluèd** priceless  40
**bulk** body  46 **ferryman** Charon, who ferried the dead across
the Styx  55 **fleeting** fickle

O God! If my deep pray'rs cannot appease thee,
But thou wilt be avenged on my misdeeds,     70
Yet execute thy wrath in me alone.
O, spare my guiltless wife and my poor children!
Keeper, I prithee sit by me awhile.
My soul is heavy, and I fain would sleep.

KEEPER
I will, my lord. God give your grace good rest!    75

[CLARENCE *sleeps*.]

*Enter* BRAKENBURY, *the lieutenant*.

BRAKENBURY
Sorrow breaks seasons and reposing hours,
Makes the night morning and the noontide night.
Princes have but their titles for their glories,
An outward honor for an inward toil,
And for unfelt imaginations°             80
They often feel a world of restless cares;
So that between their titles and low name
There's nothing differs but the outward fame.

*Enter two* MURDERERS.

FIRST MURDERER   Ho! Who's here?
BRAKENBURY
What wouldst thou, fellow? And how cam'st thou
    hither?                                 85
FIRST MURDERER   I would speak with Clarence, and
I came hither on my legs.
BRAKENBURY   What, so brief?
SECOND MURDERER   'Tis better, sir, than to be
tedious. Let him see our commission, and talk no more. 90

[BRAKENBURY] *reads* [*it*].

BRAKENBURY
I am in this commanded to deliver
The noble Duke of Clarence to your hands.
I will not reason what is meant hereby,
Because I will be guiltless from the meaning.
There lies the duke asleep, and there the keys.      95
I'll to the king and signify to him
That thus I have resigned to you my charge.
FIRST MURDERER   You may, sir, 'tis a point of
wisdom. Fare you well.
                 *Exit* [BRAKENBURY, *with* KEEPER].
SECOND MURDERER   What, shall we stab him as he   100
sleeps?
FIRST MURDERER   No, he'll say 'twas done cowardly
when he wakes.
SECOND MURDERER   Why, he shall never wake until
the great Judgment Day.                 105
FIRST MURDERER   Why, then he'll say we stabbed
him sleeping.
SECOND MURDERER   The urging of that word
"judgment" hath bred a kind of remorse in me.
FIRST MURDERER   What, art thou afraid?      110
SECOND MURDERER   Not to kill him, having a
warrant; but to be damned for killing him, from the
which no warrant can defend me.
FIRST MURDERER   I thought thou hadst been resolute.
SECOND MURDERER   So I am—to let him live.    115
FIRST MURDERER   I'll back to the Duke of Gloucester
and tell him so.

SECOND MURDERER   Nay, I prithee stay a little. I
hope this passionate humor° of mine will change; it
was wont to hold me but while one tells° twenty.    120
FIRST MURDERER   How dost thou feel thyself now?
SECOND MURDERER   Faith, some certain dregs of
conscience are yet within me.
FIRST MURDERER   Remember our reward when the
deed's done.                             125
SECOND MURDERER   Zounds,° he dies! I had forgot
the reward.
FIRST MURDERER   Where's thy conscience now?
SECOND MURDERER   O, in the Duke of Gloucester's
purse.                                130
FIRST MURDERER   When he opens his purse to give
us our reward, thy conscience flies out.
SECOND MURDERER   'Tis no matter, let it go. There's
few or none will entertain it.
FIRST MURDERER   What if it come to thee again?    135
SECOND MURDERER   I'll not meddle with it; it makes
a man a coward. A man cannot steal, but it accuseth
him; a man cannot swear, but it checks him; a man
cannot lie with his neighbor's wife, but it detects
him. 'Tis a blushing shamefaced spirit that mutinies   140
in a man's bosom. It fills a man full of obstacles.
It made me once restore a purse of gold that, by
chance, I found. It beggars any man that keeps it.
It is turned out of towns and cities for a dangerous
thing, and every man that means to live well en-   145
deavors to trust to himself and live without it.
FIRST MURDERER   Zounds, 'tis even now at my
elbow, persuading me not to kill the duke.
SECOND MURDERER   Take the devil in thy mind, and
believe him° not. He would insinuate with thee but   150
to make thee sigh.
FIRST MURDERER   I am strong-framed; he cannot
prevail with me.
SECOND MURDERER   Spoke like a tall° man that
respects thy reputation. Come, shall we fall to work?   155
FIRST MURDERER   Take him on the costard° with the
hilts of thy sword, and then throw him into the
malmsey butt° in the next room.
SECOND MURDERER   O excellent device! And make
a sop° of him.                            160
FIRST MURDERER   Soft, he wakes.
SECOND MURDERER   Strike!
FIRST MURDERER   No, we'll reason° with him.
CLARENCE
Where art thou, keeper? Give me a cup of wine.
SECOND MURDERER
You shall have wine enough, my lord, anon.    165
CLARENCE
In God's name, what art thou?
FIRST MURDERER
A man, as you are.
CLARENCE
But not as I am, royal.
FIRST MURDERER
Nor you as we are, loyal.

---

**119 passionate humor** compassionate mood   **120 tells** counts
**126 Zounds** an oath (from "By God's wounds")   **150 him**
conscience   **154 tall** brave   **156 costard** head   **158 malmsey
butt** cask of malmsey, a Greek wine   **160 sop** piece of bread
soaked in wine   **163 reason** talk

**80 unfelt imaginations** pleasures imagined but not felt

CLARENCE
Thy voice is thunder, but thy looks are humble.                    170
FIRST MURDERER
My voice is now the king's, my looks mine own.
CLARENCE
How darkly and how deadly dost thou speak!
Your eyes do menace me. Why look you pale?
Who sent you hither? Wherefore do you come?
SECOND MURDERER  To, to, to—                                       175
CLARENCE
To murder me?
BOTH  Ay, ay.
CLARENCE
You scarcely have the hearts to tell me so,
And therefore cannot have the hearts to do it.
Wherein, my friends, have I offended you?                          180
FIRST MURDERER
Offended us you have not, but the king.
CLARENCE
I shall be reconciled to him again.
SECOND MURDERER
Never, my lord; therefore prepare to die.
CLARENCE
Are you drawn forth among a world of men
To slay the innocent? What is my offense?                          185
Where is the evidence that doth accuse me?
What lawful quest° have given their verdict up
Unto the frowning judge? Or who pronounced
The bitter sentence of poor Clarence' death?
Before I be convict by course of law,                              190
To threaten me with death is most unlawful.
I charge you, as you hope to have redemption
By Christ's dear blood shed for our grievous sins,
That you depart, and lay no hands on me.
The deed you undertake is damnable.°                               195
FIRST MURDERER
What we will do, we do upon command.
SECOND MURDERER
And he that hath commanded is our king.
CLARENCE
Erroneous vassals! The great King of Kings
Hath in the table of his law commanded
That thou shalt do no murder. Will you then                        200
Spurn at his edict and fulfill a man's?
Take heed; for he holds vengeance in his hand
To hurl upon their heads that break his law.
SECOND MURDERER
And that same vengeance doth he hurl on thee
For false forswearing and for murder too.                          205
Thou didst receive the sacrament to fight
In quarrel of the house of Lancaster.
FIRST MURDERER
And like a traitor to the name of God
Didst break that vow, and with thy treacherous blade
Unrip'st the bowels of thy sov'reign's son.                        210
SECOND MURDERER
Whom thou wast sworn to cherish and defend.
FIRST MURDERER
How canst thou urge God's dreadful law to us
When thou hast broke it in such dear° degree?

CLARENCE
Alas! For whose sake did I that ill deed?
For Edward, for my brother, for his sake.                          215
He sends you not to murder me for this,
For in that sin he is as deep as I.
If God will be avengèd for the deed,
O, know you yet he doth it publicly.
Take not the quarrel from his pow'rful arm.                        220
He needs no indirect or lawless course
To cut off those that have offended him.
FIRST MURDERER
Who made thee then a bloody minister
When gallant-springing brave Plantagenet,
That princely novice,° was struck dead by thee?                    225
CLARENCE
My brother's love, the devil, and my rage.
FIRST MURDERER
Thy brother's love, our duty, and thy faults
Provoke us hither now to slaughter thee.
CLARENCE
If you do love my brother, hate not me.
I am his brother, and I love him well.                             230
If you are hired for meed,° go back again,
And I will send you to my brother Gloucester,
Who shall reward you better for my life
Than Edward will for tidings of my death.
SECOND MURDERER
You are deceived; your brother Gloucester hates you.               235
CLARENCE
O, no, he loves me and he holds me dear.
Go you to him from me.
FIRST MURDERER                    Ay, so we will.
CLARENCE
Tell him, when that our princely father York
Blessed his three sons with his victorious arm
And charged us from his soul to love each other,                   240
He little thought of this divided friendship.
Bid Gloucester think on this, and he will weep.
FIRST MURDERER
Ay, millstones, as he lessoned° us to weep.
CLARENCE
O, do not slander him, for he is kind.
FIRST MURDERER
Right as° snow in harvest. Come, you deceive your-
self.                                                              245
'Tis he that sends us to destroy you here.
CLARENCE
It cannot be, for he bewept my fortune
And hugged me in his arms and swore with sobs
That he would labor° my delivery.
FIRST MURDERER
Why so he doth, when he delivers you                               250
From this earth's thralldom to the joys of heaven.
SECOND MURDERER
Make peace with God, for you must die, my lord.
CLARENCE
Have you that holy feeling in your souls
To counsel me to make my peace with God,
And are you yet to your own souls so blind                         255
That you will war with God by murd'ring me?

187 **quest** jury  195 **damnable** one which will damn your
souls  213 **dear** high

225 **princely novice** young prince  231 **meed** reward  243
**lessoned** taught  245 **Right as** just like  249 **labor** work for

O, sirs, consider, they that set you on
To do this deed will hate you for the deed.
SECOND MURDERER
What shall we do?
CLARENCE            Relent, and save your souls.
FIRST MURDERER
Relent! No. 'Tis cowardly and womanish.     260
CLARENCE
Not to relent is beastly, savage, devilish.

[To SECOND MURDERER.]

My friend, I spy some pity in thy looks.
O, if thine eye be not a flatterer,
Come thou on my side and entreat for me.
A begging prince what beggar pities not?     265
Which of you, if you were a prince's son,
Being pent from liberty as I am now,
If two such murderers as yourselves came to you,
Would not entreat for life? As you would beg,
Were you in my distress—     270
SECOND MURDERER
Look behind you, my lord!
FIRST MURDERER
Take that! And that! (Stabs him.) If all this will not do,
I'll drown you in the malmsey butt within.
                 Exit [with the body].
SECOND MURDERER
A bloody deed and desperately dispatched!
How fain, like Pilate, would I wash my hands     275
Of this most grievous murder!

Enter FIRST MURDERER.

FIRST MURDERER
How now? What mean'st thou that thou help'st me
    not?
By heaven, the duke shall know how slack you have
    been.
SECOND MURDERER
I would he knew that I had saved his brother!
Take thou the fee, and tell him what I say,     280
For I repent me that the duke is slain.     Exit.
FIRST MURDERER
So do not I. Go, coward as thou art.
Well, I'll go hide the body in some hole
Till that the duke give order for his burial;
And when I have my meed, I will away,     285
For this will out, and then I must not stay.     Exit.

# ACT II

## Scene I. [The palace.]

Flourish.° Enter the KING [EDWARD], sick, the QUEEN
[ELIZABETH], Lord Marquis DORSET, [GREY,] RIVERS,
HASTINGS, CATESBY, BUCKINGHAM, WOODVILLE,
[and SCALES].

KING EDWARD
Why, so. Now have I done a good day's work.
You peers, continue this united league.
I every day expect an embassage
From my Redeemer to redeem me hence;
And more in peace my soul shall part to heaven,     5
Since I have made my friends at peace on earth.
Rivers and Hastings, take each other's hand;
Dissemble° not your hatred, swear your love.
RIVERS
By heaven, my soul is purged from grudging hate,
And with my hand I seal my true heart's love.     10
HASTINGS
So thrive I as I truly swear the like!
KING EDWARD
Take heed you dally° not before your king,
Lest he that is the supreme King of Kings
Confound your hidden falsehood and award
Either of you to be the other's end.     15
HASTINGS
So prosper I as I swear perfect love!
RIVERS
And I as I love Hastings with my heart!
KING EDWARD
Madam, yourself is not exempt from this;
Nor you, son Dorset; Buckingham, nor you;
You have been factious one against the other.     20
Wife, love Lord Hastings, let him kiss your hand,
And what you do, do it unfeignedly.
QUEEN ELIZABETH
There, Hastings. I will never more remember
Our former hatred, so thrive I and mine!
KING EDWARD
Dorset, embrace him; Hastings, love Lord Marquis.     25
DORSET
This interchange of love, I here protest,
Upon my part shall be inviolable.
HASTINGS
And so swear I.
KING EDWARD
Now, princely Buckingham, seal thou this league
With thy embracements to my wife's allies,     30
And make me happy in your unity.
BUCKINGHAM [To the QUEEN.]
Whenever Buckingham doth turn his hate
Upon your grace, but° with all duteous love
Doth cherish you and yours, God punish me
With hate in those where I expect most love!     35
When I have most need to employ a friend,
And most assurèd that he is a friend,
Deep, hollow, treacherous, and full of guile

II.i.s.d. Flourish fanfare of trumpets   8 Dissemble disguise
by false pretense   12 dally trifle   33 but the meaning calls
for "and not"

Be he unto me! This do I beg of God,
When I am cold in zeal to you or yours.                              40

*Embrace.*

KING EDWARD
A pleasing cordial, princely Buckingham,
Is this thy vow unto my sickly heart.
There wanteth now our brother Gloucester here
To make the blessèd period° of this peace.

BUCKINGHAM
And in good time,                                                   45
Here comes Sir Richard Ratcliffe and the duke.

*Enter* RATCLIFFE *and* [RICHARD *Duke of*] *Gloucester.*

RICHARD
Good morrow to my sovereign king and queen;
And, princely peers, a happy time of day!

KING EDWARD
Happy indeed, as we have spent the day.
Gloucester, we have done deeds of charity,                          50
Made peace of enmity, fair love of hate,
Between these swelling wrong-incensèd peers.

RICHARD
A blessèd labor, my most sovereign lord.
Among this princely heap° if any here
By false intelligence or wrong surmise                              55
Hold me a foe;
If I unwittingly, or in my rage,
Have aught committed that is hardly borne°
By any in this presence, I desire
To reconcile me to his friendly peace.                              60
'Tis death to me to be at enmity;
I hate it, and desire all good men's love.
First, madam, I entreat true peace of you,
Which I will purchase with my duteous service;
Of you, my noble cousin Buckingham,                                 65
If ever any grudge were lodged between us;
Of you and you, Lord Rivers and of Dorset,
That all without desert° have frowned on me;
Of you, Lord Woodville, and, Lord Scales,° of you;
Dukes, earls, lords, gentlemen; indeed, of all.                     70
I do not know that Englishman alive
With whom my soul is any jot at odds
More than the infant that is born tonight.
I thank my God for my humility.

QUEEN ELIZABETH
A holy day shall this be kept hereafter.                            75
I would to God all strifes were well compounded.°
My sovereign lord, I do beseech your highness
To take our brother Clarence to your grace.

RICHARD
Why, madam, have I off'red love for this,
To be so flouted in this royal presence?                            80
Who knows not that the gentle duke is dead?

*They all start.*

You do him injury to scorn his corse.

KING EDWARD
Who knows not he is dead! Who knows he is?

QUEEN ELIZABETH
All-seeing heaven, what a world is this!

BUCKINGHAM
Look I so pale, Lord Dorset, as the rest?                           85

DORSET
Ay, my good lord; and no man in the presence
But his red color hath forsook his cheeks.

KING EDWARD
Is Clarence dead? The order was reversed.

RICHARD
But he, poor man, by your first order died,
And that a wingèd Mercury did bear;                                 90
Some tardy cripple bare the countermand,
That came too lag° to see him buried.
God grant that some, less noble and less loyal,
Nearer in bloody thoughts, and° not in blood,
Deserve not worse than wretched Clarence did,                       95
And yet go current from° suspicion!

*Enter* [*Lord* STANLEY] *Earl of Derby.*

STANLEY
A boon, my sovereign, for my service done!

KING EDWARD
I prithee peace. My soul is full of sorrow.

STANLEY
I will not rise unless your highness hear me.

KING EDWARD
Then say at once what is it thou requests.                          100

STANLEY
The forfeit, sovereign, of my servant's life,°
Who slew today a riotous gentleman
Lately attendant on the Duke of Norfolk.

KING EDWARD
Have I a tongue to doom my brother's death,
And shall that tongue give pardon to a slave?                       105
My brother killed no man, his fault was thought,
And yet his punishment was bitter death.
Who sued to me for him? Who, in my wrath,
Kneeled at my feet and bid me be advised?°
Who spoke of brotherhood? Who spoke of love?                        110
Who told me how the poor soul did forsake
The mighty Warwick and did fight for me?
Who told me, in the field at Tewkesbury
When Oxford had me down, he rescued me
And said, "Dear brother, live, and be a king"?                      115
Who told me, when we both lay in the field
Frozen almost to death, how he did lap° me
Even in his garments, and did give himself
All thin and naked, to the numb-cold night?
All this from my remembrance brutish wrath                          120
Sinfully plucked, and not a man of you
Had so much grace to put it in my mind.
But when your carters or your waiting vassals
Have done a drunken slaughter and defaced
The precious image of our dear Redeemer,                            125
You straight are on your knees for "Pardon, pardon!"
And I, unjustly too, must grant it you.

[STANLEY *rises.*]

---

44 **period** conclusion   54 **heap** company, group   58 **hardly
borne** resented   68 **all without desert** wholly without my
deserving it   69 **Lord Woodville . . . Scales** historically,
these are both other titles of Anthony Woodville, Earl Rivers
76 **compounded** settled

92 **lag** late   94 **and** if   96 **go current from** are taken at face
value without   101 **forfeit . . . life** forfeited life   109 **be
advised** consider carefully   117 **lap** wrap

But for my brother not a man would speak,
Nor I, ungracious, speak unto myself
For him, poor soul. The proudest of you all     130
Have been beholding to him in his life;
Yet none of you would once beg for his life.
O God, I fear thy justice will take hold
On me and you, and mine and yours, for this!
Come, Hastings, help me to my closet.° Ah, poor
   Clarence!       *Exeunt some with* KING *and* QUEEN. 135

RICHARD
This is the fruits of rashness. Marked you not
How that the guilty kindred of the queen
Looked pale when they did hear of Clarence' death?
O, they did urge it still unto the king!
God will revenge it. Come, lords, will you go     140
To comfort Edward with our company?

BUCKINGHAM
We wait upon your grace.          *Exeunt.*

Scene II. [*The palace.*]

*Enter the old* DUCHESS OF YORK, *with the two*
CHILDREN *of Clarence.*

BOY
Good grandam, tell us, is our father dead?
DUCHESS OF YORK  No, boy.
DAUGHTER
Why do you weep so oft, and beat your breast,
And cry, "O Clarence, my unhappy son"?
BOY
Why do you look on us, and shake your head,     5
And call us orphans, wretches, castaways,
If that our noble father were alive?
DUCHESS OF YORK
My pretty cousins,° you mistake me both.
I do lament the sickness of the king,
As loath to lose him, not your father's death.     10
It were lost sorrow to wail one that's lost.
BOY
Then you conclude, my grandam, he is dead.
The king mine uncle is too blame° for it.
God will revenge it, whom I will importune
With earnest prayers all to that effect.     15
DAUGHTER
And so will I.
DUCHESS OF YORK
Peace, children, peace! The king doth love you well.
Incapable° and shallow innocents,
You cannot guess who caused your father's death.
BOY
Grandam, we can; for my good uncle Gloucester     20
Told me the king, provoked to it by the queen,
Devised impeachments° to imprison him;
And when my uncle told me so, he wept,
And pitied me, and kindly kissed my cheek;
Bade me rely on him as on my father,     25
And he would love me dearly as a child.

DUCHESS OF YORK
Ah, that deceit should steal such gentle shape°
And with a virtuous visor° hide deep vice!
He is my son, ay, and therein my shame;
Yet from my dugs he drew not this deceit.     30
BOY
Think you my uncle did dissemble, grandam?
DUCHESS OF YORK  Ay, boy.
BOY
I cannot think it. Hark! What noise is this?

*Enter the* QUEEN [ELIZABETH], *with her hair about her*
*ears,* RIVERS *and* DORSET *after her.*

QUEEN ELIZABETH
Ah, who shall hinder me to wail and weep,
To chide my fortune, and torment myself?     35
I'll join with black despair against my soul
And to myself become an enemy.
DUCHESS OF YORK
What means this scene of rude impatience?
QUEEN ELIZABETH
To make an act of tragic violence.
Edward, my lord, thy son, our king, is dead!     40
Why grow the branches when the root is gone?
Why wither not the leaves that want their sap?
If you will live, lament; if die, be brief,
That our swift-wingèd souls may catch the king's,
Or like obedient subjects follow him     45
To his new kingdom of ne'er-changing night.
DUCHESS OF YORK
Ah, so much interest° have I in thy sorrow
As I had title° in thy noble husband!
I have bewept a worthy husband's death,
And lived with looking on his images;°     50
But now two mirrors of his princely semblance°
Are cracked in pieces by malignant death,
And I for comfort have but one false glass
That grieves me when I see my shame in him.
Thou art a widow, yet thou art a mother     55
And hast the comfort of thy children left;
But death hath snatched my husband from mine arms
And plucked two crutches from my feeble hands,
Clarence and Edward. O, what° cause have I,
Thine being but a moi'ty of my moan,°     60
To overgo thy woes and drown thy cries!
BOY
Ah, aunt, you wept not for our father's death.
How can we aid you with our kindred tears?
DAUGHTER
Our fatherless distress was left unmoaned;
Your widow-dolor likewise be unwept!     65
QUEEN ELIZABETH
Give me no help in lamentation;
I am not barren to bring forth complaints.
All springs reduce° their currents to mine eyes,
That I, being governed by the watery moon,
May send forth plenteous tears to drown the world.     70
Ah for my husband, for my dear lord Edward!

---

135 **closet** private room
**II.ii.8 cousins** relatives   13 **too blame** too blameworthy
18 **Incapable** unable to understand  22 **impeachments**
accusations

27 **shape** disguise  28 **visor** mask  **47 interest** share  **48
title** legal right  **50 images** children  **51 semblance**
appearance  **59 what** how much  **60 moi'ty . . . moan**
half of my grief  **68 reduce** bring

**CHILDREN**
Ah for our father, for our dear Lord Clarence!

**DUCHESS OF YORK**
Alas for both, both mine, Edward and Clarence!

**QUEEN ELIZABETH**
What stay° had I but Edward? And he's gone.

**CHILDREN**
What stay had we but Clarence? And he's gone.       75

**DUCHESS OF YORK**
What stays had I but they? And they are gone.

**QUEEN ELIZABETH**
Was never widow had so dear a loss.

**CHILDREN**
Were never orphans had so dear a loss.

**DUCHESS OF YORK**
Was never mother had so dear a loss.
Alas, I am the mother of these griefs!       80
Their woes are parceled,° mine is general.
She for an Edward weeps, and so do I;
I for a Clarence weep, so doth not she.
These babes for Clarence weep, and so do I;
I for an Edward weep, so do not they.       85
Alas, you three on me, threefold distressed,
Pour all your tears! I am your sorrow's nurse,
And I will pamper it with lamentation.

**DORSET**
Comfort, dear mother; God is much displeased
That you take with unthankfulness his doing.       90
In common worldly things 'tis called ungrateful
With dull unwillingness to repay a debt
Which with a bounteous hand was kindly lent;
Much more to be thus opposite with° heaven
For° it requires the royal debt it lent you.       95

**RIVERS**
Madam, bethink you like a careful mother
Of the young prince your son. Send straight for
him;
Let him be crowned; in him your comfort lives.
Drown desperate sorrow in dead Edward's grave
And plant your joys in living Edward's throne.       100

*Enter* RICHARD, BUCKINGHAM, [STANLEY *Earl of*]
*Derby,* HASTINGS, *and* RATCLIFFE.

**RICHARD**
Sister, have comfort. All of us have cause
To wail the dimming of our shining star;
But none can help our harms by wailing them.
Madam, my mother, I do cry you mercy;
I did not see your grace. Humbly on my knee       105
I crave your blessing.

**DUCHESS OF YORK**
God bless thee, and put meekness in thy breast,
Love, charity, obedience, and true duty!

**RICHARD**
Amen! [*Aside.*] And make me die a good old man!
That is the butt-end of a mother's blessing;       110
I marvel that her grace did leave it out.

**BUCKINGHAM**
You cloudy princes and heart-sorrowing peers
That bear this heavy mutual load of moan,
Now cheer each other in each other's love.
Though we have spent our harvest of this king,       115
We are to reap the harvest of his son,
The broken rancor of your high-swol'n hates,
But lately splintered,° knit, and joined together,
Must gently be preserved, cherished, and kept.°
Me seemeth° good that with some little train       120
Forthwith from Ludlow the young prince be fet°
Hither to London, to be crowned our king.

**RIVERS**
Why with some little train, my Lord of Buckingham?

**BUCKINGHAM**
Marry, my lord, lest by a multitude
The new-healed wound of malice should break out,       125
Which would be so much the more dangerous
By how much the estate is green° and yet ungoverned.
Where every horse bears his commanding rein
And may direct his course as please himself,
As well the fear of harm as harm apparent,°       130
In my opinion, ought to be prevented.

**RICHARD**
I hope the king made peace with all of us;
And the compact is firm and true in me.

**RIVERS**
And so in me; and so (I think) in all.
Yet, since it is but green, it should be put       135
To no apparent likelihood of breach,
Which haply° by much company might be urged.
Therefore I say with noble Buckingham
That it is meet° so few should fetch the prince.

**HASTINGS**
And so say I.       140

**RICHARD**
Then be it so; and go we to determine
Who they shall be that straight shall post to Ludlow.
Madam, and you, my sister, will you go
To give your censures° in this business?

**QUEEN AND DUCHESS OF YORK**
With all our hearts.       145
*Exeunt. Manet°* BUCKINGHAM *and* RICHARD.

**BUCKINGHAM**
My lord, whoever journeys to the prince,
For God sake let not us two stay at home;
For by the way I'll sort occasion,°
As index° to the story we late talked of,
To part the queen's proud kindred from the prince.       150

**RICHARD**
My other self, my counsel's consistory,°
My oracle, my prophet, my dear cousin,
I, as a child, will go by thy direction.
Toward Ludlow then, for we'll not stay behind.
*Exeunt.*

118 **splintered** set in splints   119 **Must . . . kept** the subject has shifted from "rancor" to its opposite   120 **Me seemeth** it seems to me   121 **fet** fetched   127 **estate is green** regime is new   130 **apparent** seen clearly   137 **haply** perhaps   139 **meet** fitting   144 **censures** judgments   145 s.d. **Manet** Latin for "remains" (the third person plural is *manent*, but the Elizabethans commonly used the third person singular—like *exit*—for the plural)   148 **sort occasion** contrive opportunity   149 **index** preface   151 **consistory** council chamber

## Scene III. [*A street.*]

*Enter one* CITIZEN *at one door and another at the other.*

FIRST CITIZEN
Good morrow, neighbor. Whither away so fast?

SECOND CITIZEN
I promise you, I scarcely know myself.
Hear you the news abroad?

FIRST CITIZEN                    Yes, that the king is dead.

SECOND CITIZEN
Ill news, by'r Lady; seldom comes the better.°
I fear, I fear 'twill prove a giddy world.                    5

*Enter another* CITIZEN.

THIRD CITIZEN
Neighbors, Godspeed!

FIRST CITIZEN                    Give you good morrow, sir.

THIRD CITIZEN
Doth the news hold of good King Edward's death?

SECOND CITIZEN
Ay, sir, it is too true, God help the while!

THIRD CITIZEN
Then, masters, look to see a troublous world.

FIRST CITIZEN
No, no; by God's good grace his son shall reign.          10

THIRD CITIZEN
Woe to that land that's governed by a child!

SECOND CITIZEN
In him there is a hope of government,
Which in his nonage counsel° under him,
And, in his full and ripened years, himself,
No doubt shall then and till then govern well.            15

FIRST CITIZEN
So stood the state when Henry the Sixth
Was crowned in Paris but at nine months old.

THIRD CITIZEN
Stood the state so? No, no, good friends, God wot!°
For then this land was famously enriched
With politic grave counsel; then the king                 20
Had virtuous uncles to protect his grace.

FIRST CITIZEN
Why, so hath this, both by his father and mother.

THIRD CITIZEN
Better it were they all came by his father,
Or by his father there were none at all;
For emulation° who shall now be nearest                   25
Will touch us all too near, if God prevent not.
O, full of danger is the Duke of Gloucester,
And the queen's sons and brothers haught° and
      proud!
And were they to be ruled,° and not to rule,
This sickly land might solace° as before.                 30

FIRST CITIZEN
Come, come, we fear the worst. All will be well.

THIRD CITIZEN
When clouds are seen, wise men put on their cloaks;
When great leaves fall, then winter is at hand;
When the sun sets, who doth not look for night?

Untimely storms makes men expect a dearth.°             35
All may be well; but if God sort° it so,
'Tis more than we deserve or I expect.

SECOND CITIZEN
Truly, the hearts of men are full of fear.
You cannot reason,° almost, with a man
That looks not heavily and full of dread.                 40

THIRD CITIZEN
Before the days of change, still is it so.
By a divine instinct men's minds mistrust
Ensuing danger, as by proof° we see
The water swell before a boist'rous storm.
But leave it all to God. Whither away?                    45

SECOND CITIZEN
Marry, we were sent for to the justices.

THIRD CITIZEN
And so was I. I'll bear you company.          *Exeunt.*

## Scene IV. [*The palace.*]

*Enter* [*the*] ARCHBISHOP [*of York*], [*the*] *young* [*Duke of*]
YORK, *the* QUEEN [ELIZABETH], *and the* DUCHESS
[OF YORK].

ARCHBISHOP
Last night, I hear, they lay at Stony Stratford;
And at Northampton they do rest tonight;
Tomorrow or next day they will be here.

DUCHESS OF YORK
I long with all my heart to see the prince.
I hope he is much grown since last I saw him.             5

QUEEN ELIZABETH
But I hear no; they say my son of York
Has almost overta'en him in his growth.

YORK
Ay, mother, but I would not have it so.

DUCHESS OF YORK
Why, my good cousin? It is good to grow.

YORK
Grandam, one night as we did sit at supper,               10
My uncle Rivers talked how I did grow
More than my brother. "Ay," quoth my uncle
      Gloucester,
"Small herbs have grace,° great weeds do grow
      apace."°
And since, methinks, I would not grow so fast,
Because sweet flow'rs are slow and weeds make haste.      15

DUCHESS OF YORK
Good faith, good faith, the saying did not hold
In him that did object° the same to thee.
He was the wretched'st thing when he was young,
So long a-growing and so leisurely,
That, if his rule were true, he should be gracious.°      20

ARCHBISHOP
And so no doubt he is, my gracious madam.

DUCHESS OF YORK
I hope he is; but yet let mothers doubt.

YORK
Now, by my troth, if I had been rememb'red,°

---

II.iii.4 **seldom . . . better** change for the better is rare (a
proverb)  **12–13 In . . . counsel** there is hope of good rule
in him, during whose minority advisers  **18 wot** knows  **25
emulation** rivalry  **28 haught** haughty  **29 were . . . ruled**
if they could be controlled  **30 solace** take comfort

**35 dearth** famine  **36 sort** arrange  **39 reason** talk  **43 proof**
experience
II.iv.**13 grace** virtue; **apace** quickly  **17 object** bring as a
reproach  **20 gracious** virtuous  **23 been rememb'red** thought

I could have given my uncle's grace a flout°
To touch his growth nearer than he touched mine.     25
DUCHESS OF YORK
How, my young York? I prithee let me hear it.
YORK
Marry, they say, my uncle grew so fast
That he could gnaw a crust at two hours old.
'Twas full two years ere I could get a tooth.
Grandam, this would have been a biting jest.     30
DUCHESS OF YORK
I prithee, pretty York, who told thee this?
YORK
Grandam, his nurse.
DUCHESS OF YORK
His nurse! Why, she was dead ere thou wast born.
YORK
If 'twere not she, I cannot tell who told me.
QUEEN ELIZABETH
A parlous° boy! Go to, you are too shrewd.°     35
DUCHESS OF YORK
Good madam, be not angry with the child.
QUEEN ELIZABETH
Pitchers have ears.°

*Enter a* MESSENGER.

ARCHBISHOP
Here comes a messenger. What news?
MESSENGER
Such news, my lord, as grieves me to report.
QUEEN ELIZABETH
How doth the prince?
MESSENGER                 Well, madam, and in health.     40
DUCHESS OF YORK
What is thy news?
MESSENGER
Lord Rivers and Lord Grey are sent to Pomfret,
And with them Sir Thomas Vaughan, prisoners.
DUCHESS OF YORK
Who hath committed them?
MESSENGER                          The mighty dukes,
Gloucester and Buckingham.
ARCHBISHOP                          For what offense?     45
MESSENGER
The sum of all I can I have disclosed.
Why or for what the nobles were committed
Is all unknown to me, my gracious lord.
QUEEN ELIZABETH
Ay me! I see the ruin of my house.
The tiger now hath seized the gentle hind;°     50
Insulting tyranny begins to jut°
Upon the innocent and aweless° throne.
Welcome destruction, blood, and massacre!
I see, as in a map, the end of all.
DUCHESS OF YORK
Accursèd and unquiet wrangling days,     55
How many of you have mine eyes beheld!
My husband lost his life to get the crown,
And often up and down my sons were tossed

For me to joy and weep their gain and loss;
And being seated, and domestic broils°
Clean overblown, themselves, the conquerors,     60
Make war upon themselves, brother to brother,
Blood to blood, self against self. O preposterous°
And frantic outrage, end thy damnèd spleen,°
Or let me die, to look on death no more!
QUEEN ELIZABETH     65
Come, come, my boy; we will to sanctuary.°
Madam, farewell.
DUCHESS OF YORK     Stay, I will go with you.
QUEEN ELIZABETH
You have no cause.     70
ARCHBISHOP [*To the* QUEEN.] My gracious lady, go,
And thither bear your treasure and your goods.
For my part, I'll resign unto your grace
The seal I keep; and so betide to me
As well I tender° you and all of yours!
Go, I'll conduct you to the sanctuary.     *Exeunt.*

# ACT III

## Scene I. [*A street.*]

*The trumpets sound. Enter* [*the*] *young* PRINCE[EDWARD],
*the Dukes of* GLOUCESTER *and* BUCKINGHAM, *Lord*
CARDINAL, [*and* CATESBY,] *with others.*

BUCKINGHAM
Welcome, sweet prince, to London, to your chamber.°
RICHARD
Welcome, dear cousin, my thoughts' sovereign.
The weary way hath made you melancholy.
PRINCE EDWARD
No, uncle, but our crosses° on the way
Have made it tedious, wearisome, and heavy.     5
I want° more uncles here to welcome me.
RICHARD
Sweet prince, the untainted virtue of your years
Hath not yet dived into the world's deceit;
Nor more can you distinguish of a man
Than of his outward show, which, God he knows,     10
Seldom or never jumpeth° with the heart.
Those uncles which you want were dangerous;
Your grace attended to their sug'red words
But looked not on the poison of their hearts.
God keep you from them, and from such false friends!     15
PRINCE EDWARD
God keep me from false friends! But they were none.
RICHARD
My lord, the Mayor of London comes to greet you.

*Enter* LORD MAYOR [*and* CITIZENS].

LORD MAYOR
God bless your grace with health and happy days!

---

**24 flout** taunt   **35 parlous** terribly quick-witted; **shrewd**
sharp-tongued   **37 Pitchers have ears** Small pitchers have
great ears (a proverb)   **50 hind** doe   **51 jut** encroach   **52
aweless** inspiring no awe

**60 domestic broils** civil wars   **63 preposterous** inverting
natural order   **64 spleen** malice   **66 sanctuary** refuge on
church property   **72 tender** care for
**III.i.1 chamber** capital   **4 crosses** vexations   **6 want** (1) lack
(2) wish for   **11 jumpeth** agrees

PRINCE EDWARD
I thank you, good my lord, and thank you all.

[MAYOR *and* CITIZENS *stand aside.*]

I thought my mother and my brother York                                20
Would long ere this have met us on the way.
Fie, what a slug° is Hastings that he comes not
To tell us whether they will come or no!

*Enter Lord* HASTINGS.

BUCKINGHAM
And in good time here comes the sweating lord.
PRINCE EDWARD
Welcome, my lord. What, will our mother come?        25
HASTINGS
On what occasion° God he knows, not I,
The queen your mother and your brother York
Have taken sanctuary. The tender prince
Would fain have come with me to meet your grace,
But by his mother was perforce° withheld.                  30
BUCKINGHAM
Fie, what an indirect and peevish° course
Is this of hers! Lord Cardinal, will your grace
Persuade the queen to send the Duke of York
Unto his princely brother presently?°
If she deny, Lord Hastings, go with him                      35
And from her jealous° arms pluck him perforce.
CARDINAL
My Lord of Buckingham, if my weak oratory
Can from his mother win the Duke of York,
Anon expect him here; but if she be obdurate
To mild entreaties, God in heaven forbid                     40
We should infringe the holy privilege
Of blessèd sanctuary! Not for all this land
Would I be guilty of so deep a sin.
BUCKINGHAM
You are too senseless-obstinate, my lord,
Too ceremonious° and traditional.                              45
Weigh it but with the grossness° of this age,
You break not sanctuary in seizing him.
The benefit thereof is always granted
To those whose dealings have deserved the place
And those who have the wit to claim the place.          50
This prince hath neither claimed it nor deserved it,
And therefore, in mine opinion, cannot have it.
Then, taking him from thence that is not there,
You break no privilege nor charter there.
Oft have I heard of sanctuary men,                            55
But sanctuary children ne'er till now.
CARDINAL
My lord, you shall o'errule my mind for once.
Come on, Lord Hastings, will you go with me?
HASTINGS
I go, my lord.
PRINCE EDWARD
Good lords, make all the speedy haste you may.       60
                    *Exit* CARDINAL *and* HASTINGS.
Say, uncle Gloucester, if our brother come,
Where shall we sojourn till our coronation?

RICHARD
Where it seems best unto your royal self.
If I may counsel you, some day or two
Your highness shall repose you at the Tower;          65
Then where you please, and shall be thought most fit
For your best health and recreation.
PRINCE EDWARD
I do not like the Tower, of any place.°
Did Julius Caesar build that place, my lord?
BUCKINGHAM
He did, my gracious lord, begin that place,             70
Which since succeeding ages have re-edified.°
PRINCE EDWARD
Is it upon record, or else reported
Successively from age to age, he built it?
BUCKINGHAM
Upon record, my gracious lord.
PRINCE EDWARD
But say, my lord, it were not regist'red,                   75
Methinks the truth should live from age to age,
As 'twere retailed° to all posterity,
Even to the general all-ending day.
RICHARD [*Aside.*]
So wise so young, they say do ne'er live long.
PRINCE EDWARD
What say you, uncle?                                               80
RICHARD
I say, without characters° fame lives long.

[*Aside.*]

Thus, like the formal° Vice,° Iniquity,
I moralize° two meanings in one word.
PRINCE EDWARD
That Julius Caesar was a famous man.
With what° his valor did enrich his wit,                   85
His wit set down to make his valor live.
Death makes no conquest of this conqueror,
For now he lives in fame, though not in life.
I'll tell you what, my cousin Buckingham—
BUCKINGHAM
What, my gracious lord?                                          90
PRINCE EDWARD
And if I live until I be a man,
I'll win our ancient right in France again
Or die a soldier as I lived a king.
RICHARD [*Aside.*]
Short summers lightly have a forward spring.°

*Enter [the] young [Duke of]* YORK, HASTINGS, *and*
CARDINAL.

BUCKINGHAM
Now in good time here comes the Duke of York.     95
PRINCE EDWARD
Richard of York, how fares our loving brother?
YORK
Well, my dread° lord—so must I call you now.

---

**22 slug** sluggard  **26 On what occasion** for what cause  **30
perforce** by force  **31 indirect and peevish** devious and
obstinate  **34 presently** at once  **36 jealous** suspicious  **45
ceremonious** punctilious  **46 grossness** coarseness

**68 of any place** of all places  **71 re-edified** rebuilt  **77
retailed** reported  **81 characters** written letters  **82 formal**
careful to observe forms (i.e., hypocritical); **Vice** mischiefmaker in a morality play  **83 moralize** interpret  **85 With
what** that with which  **94 Short . . . spring** The short-lived
are usually ("lightly") precocious  **97 dread** revered

PRINCE EDWARD
Ay, brother, to our grief, as it is yours.
Too late° he died that might have kept that title,
Which by his death hath lost much majesty.                    100
RICHARD
How fares our cousin, noble Lord of York?
YORK
I thank you, gentle uncle. O, my lord,
You said that idle° weeds are fast in growth.
The prince my brother hath outgrown me far.
RICHARD
He hath, my lord.
YORK                    And therefore is he idle?        105
RICHARD
O my fair cousin, I must not say so.
YORK
Then he is more beholding to you than I.
RICHARD
He may command me as my sovereign,
But you have power in me as in a kinsman.
YORK
I pray you, uncle, give me this dagger.                    110
RICHARD
My dagger, little cousin? With all my heart.
PRINCE EDWARD
A beggar, brother?
YORK
Of my kind uncle, that I know will give,
And being but a toy,° which is no grief to give.
RICHARD
A greater gift than that I'll give my cousin.              115
YORK
A greater gift? O, that's the sword to it.
RICHARD
Ay, gentle cousin, were it light enough.
YORK
O, then I see you will part but with light° gifts!
In weightier things you'll say a beggar nay.
RICHARD
It is too heavy for your grace to wear.                    120
YORK
I weigh° it lightly, were it heavier.
RICHARD
What, would you have my weapon, little lord?
YORK
I would, that I might thank you as you call me.
RICHARD  How?
YORK  Little.                                                125
PRINCE EDWARD
My Lord of York will still be cross° in talk.
Uncle, your grace knows how to bear with him.
YORK
You mean, to bear me, not to bear with me.
Uncle, my brother mocks both you and me;
Because that I am little, like an ape,                     130
He thinks that you should bear me on your shoulders.°
BUCKINGHAM [Aside.]
With what a sharp, provided° wit he reasons!
To mitigate the scorn he gives his uncle

He prettily and aptly taunts himself.
So cunning and so young is wonderful.                      135
RICHARD
My lord, will't please you pass along?
Myself and my good cousin Buckingham
Will to your mother, to entreat of her
To meet you at the Tower and welcome you.
YORK
What, will you go unto the Tower, my lord?                 140
PRINCE EDWARD
My Lord Protector needs will have it so.
YORK
I shall not sleep in quiet at the Tower.
RICHARD
Why, what should you fear?
YORK
Marry, my uncle Clarence' angry ghost.
My grandam told me he was murd'red there.                  145
PRINCE EDWARD
I fear no uncles dead.
RICHARD
Nor none that live, I hope.
PRINCE EDWARD
And if they live, I hope I need not fear.
But come, my lord; with a heavy heart,
Thinking on them, go I unto the Tower.                     150
        A sennet.° Exeunt PRINCE [EDWARD], YORK,
        HASTINGS, [CARDINAL, and others]. Manet
        RICHARD, BUCKINGHAM, and CATESBY.
BUCKINGHAM
Think you, my lord, this little prating York
Was not incensèd° by his subtle mother
To taunt and scorn you thus opprobriously?
RICHARD
No doubt, no doubt. O, 'tis a parlous boy,
Bold, quick, ingenious, forward, capable:                  155
He is all the mother's, from the top to toe.
BUCKINGHAM
Well, let them rest. Come hither, Catesby.
Thou art sworn as deeply to effect° what we intend
As closely to conceal what we impart.
Thou knowest our reasons urged upon the way.              160
What thinkest thou? Is it not an easy matter
To make William Lord Hastings of our mind
For the installment° of this noble duke
In the seat royal of this famous isle?
CATESBY
He for his father's sake so loves the prince               165
That he will not be won to aught against him.
BUCKINGHAM
What thinkest thou then of Stanley? What will he?
CATESBY
He will do all in all as Hastings doth.
BUCKINGHAM
Well then, no more but this: go, gentle Catesby,
And, as it were far off, sound thou Lord Hastings         170
How he doth stand affected° to our purpose,
And summon him tomorrow to the Tower
To sit° about the coronation.

---

99 **late** recently   103 **idle** useless   114 **toy** trifle   118 **light**
slight   121 **weigh** value   126 **still be cross** always be contrary
131 **bear . . . shoulders** carry me on your hunchback   132
**provided** ready

150 s.d. **sennet** trumpet signal   152 **incensèd** stirred up   158
**effect** carry out   163 **installment** installation as a king   171
**affected** inclined   173 **sit** meet with the council

If thou dost find him tractable to us,
Encourage him, and tell him all our reasons.          175
If he be leaden, icy-cold, unwilling,
Be thou so too, and so break off the talk,
And give us notice of his inclination;
For we tomorrow hold divided councils,°
Wherein thyself shalt highly be employed.             180

RICHARD
Commend me to Lord William. Tell him, Catesby,
His ancient knot° of dangerous adversaries
Tomorrow are let blood at Pomfret Castle,
And bid my lord, for joy of this good news,
Give Mistress Shore one gentle kiss the more.         185

BUCKINGHAM
Good Catesby, go effect this business soundly.

CATESBY
My good lords both, with all the heed I can.

RICHARD
Shall we hear from you, Catesby, ere we sleep?

CATESBY
You shall, my lord.

RICHARD
At Crosby House, there shall you find us both.        190
                                        Exit CATESBY.

BUCKINGHAM
Now, my lord, what shall we do if we perceive
Lord Hastings will not yield to our complots?°

RICHARD
Chop off his head. Something we will determine.
And look when° I am king, claim thou of me
The earldom of Hereford and all the movables°        195
Whereof the king my brother was possessed.

BUCKINGHAM
I'll claim that promise at your grace's hand.

RICHARD
And look° to have it yielded with all kindness.
Come, let us sup betimes,° that afterwards
We may digest° our complots in some form. Exeunt. 200


Scene II. [Before Lord Hastings' house.]

Enter a MESSENGER to the door of Hastings.

MESSENGER
My lord! My lord!

HASTINGS [Within.]
Who knocks?

MESSENGER
One from the Lord Stanley.

HASTINGS [Within.]
What is't o'clock?

MESSENGER
Upon the stroke of four.                               5

Enter Lord HASTINGS.

HASTINGS
Cannot my Lord Stanley sleep these tedious nights?

MESSENGER
So it appears by that I have to say:
First, he commends him to your noble self.

HASTINGS
What then?

MESSENGER
Then certifies your lordship that this night          10
He dreamt the boar had rasèd off his helm.°
Besides, he says there are two councils kept,
And that may be determined at the one
Which may make you and him to rue at th' other.
Therefore he sends to know your lordship's pleasure,  15
If you will presently take horse with him
And with all speed post with him toward the north
To shun the danger that his soul divines.

HASTINGS
Go, fellow, go return unto thy lord;
Bid him not fear the separated council.               20
His honor and myself are at the one,
And at the other is my good friend Catesby;
Where nothing can proceed that toucheth us
Whereof I shall not have intelligence.
Tell him his fears are shallow, without instance;°    25
And for his dreams, I wonder he's so simple
To trust the mock'ry of unquiet slumbers.
To fly the boar before the boar pursues
Were to incense the boar to follow us
And make pursuit where he did mean no chase.          30
Go bid thy master rise and come to me,
And we will both together to the Tower,
Where he shall see the boar will use us kindly.

MESSENGER
I'll go, my lord, and tell him what you say.    Exit.

Enter CATESBY.

CATESBY
Many good morrows to my noble lord!                   35

HASTINGS
Good morrow, Catesby; you are early stirring.
What news, what news, in this our tott'ring state?

CATESBY
It is a reeling world indeed, my lord,
And I believe will never stand upright
Till Richard wear the garland of the realm.           40

HASTINGS
How! Wear the garland! Dost thou mean the crown?

CATESBY
Ay, my good lord.

HASTINGS
I'll have this crown of mine cut from my shoulders
Before I'll see the crown so foul misplaced.
But canst thou guess that he doth aim at it?           45

CATESBY
Ay, on my life, and hopes to find you forward
Upon his party° for the gain thereof;
And thereupon he sends you this good news,
That this same very day your enemies,
The kindred of the queen, must die at Pomfret.        50

HASTINGS
Indeed I am no mourner for that news,

179 divided councils meetings of the council in two separate
groups   182 ancient knot long-standing clique   192 complots plots   194 look when whenever   195 movables goods
198 look expect   199 betimes early   200 digest arrange

III.ii.11 boar . . . helm Richard had cut off his head   25
instance cause   47 party side

Because they have been still my adversaries;
But that I'll give my voice on Richard's side
To bar my master's heirs in true descent,
God knows I will not do it, to the death!                    55

CATESBY
God keep your lordship in that gracious° mind!

HASTINGS
But I shall laugh at this a twelvemonth hence,
That they which brought me in my master's hate,
I live to look upon their tragedy.
Well, Catesby, ere a fortnight make me older,          60
I'll send some packing° that yet think not on't.

CATESBY
'Tis a vile thing to die, my gracious lord,
When men are unprepared and look not for it.

HASTINGS
O monstrous, monstrous! And so falls it out
With Rivers, Vaughan, Grey; and so 'twill do          65
With some men else that think themselves as safe
As thou and I, who, as thou know'st, are dear
To princely Richard and to Buckingham.

CATESBY
The princes both make high account of you—

[Aside.]

For they account his head upon the Bridge.°          70

HASTINGS
I know they do, and I have well deserved it.

Enter Lord STANLEY.

Come on, come on! Where is your boarspear, man?
Fear you the boar, and go so unprovided?

STANLEY
My lord, good morrow; good morrow, Catesby.
You may jest on, but, by the holy rood,°               75
I do not like these several° councils, I.

HASTINGS
My lord, I hold my life as dear as yours,°
And never in my days, I do protest,
Was it so precious to me as 'tis now.
Think you, but that I know our state° secure,          80
I would be so triumphant as I am?

STANLEY
The lords at Pomfret, when they rode from London,
Were jocund and supposed their states were sure,
And they indeed had no cause to mistrust;
But yet you see how soon the day o'ercast.              85
This sudden stab of rancor I misdoubt.°
Pray God, I say, I prove a needless coward!
What, shall we toward the Tower? The day is
    spent.°

HASTINGS
Come, come, have with you. Wot° you what, my
    lord?
Today the lords you talk of are beheaded.              90

STANLEY
They, for their truth,° might better wear their heads

Than some that have accused them wear their hats.
But come, my lord, let's away.

Enter a PURSUIVANT.°

HASTINGS
Go on before. I'll talk with this good fellow.
                Exit Lord STANLEY, and CATESBY.
How now, sirrah?° How goes the world with thee?     95

PURSUIVANT
The better that your lordship please to ask.

HASTINGS
I tell thee, man, 'tis better with me now
Than when thou met'st me last where now we meet.
Then was I going prisoner to the Tower
By the suggestion° of the queen's allies;              100
But now I tell thee—keep it to thyself—
This day those enemies are put to death,
And I in better state than e'er I was.

PURSUIVANT
God hold it, to your honor's good content!

HASTINGS
Gramercy,° fellow; there, drink that for me.          105

Throws him his purse.

PURSUIVANT
I thank your honor.                    Exit PURSUIVANT.

Enter a PRIEST.

PRIEST
Well met, my lord; I am glad to see your honor.

HASTINGS
I thank thee, good Sir° John, with all my heart.
I am in your debt for your last exercise;°
Come the next Sabbath, and I will content° you.      110

He whispers in his ear.

Enter BUCKINGHAM.

BUCKINGHAM
What, talking with a priest, Lord Chamberlain?
Your friends at Pomfret, they do need the priest;
Your honor hath no shriving° work in hand.

HASTINGS
Good faith, and when I met this holy man
The men you talk of came into my mind.               115
What, go you toward the Tower?

BUCKINGHAM
I do, my lord, but long I cannot stay there.
I shall return before your lordship thence.

HASTINGS
Nay, like enough, for I stay dinner there.

BUCKINGHAM [Aside.]
And supper too, although thou know'st it not.         120
Come, will you go?

HASTINGS                    I'll wait upon your lordship.
                                        Exeunt.

---

56 gracious virtuous  61 send some packing get rid of some
70 the Bridge London Bridge (where traitors' heads were
displayed)  75 rood cross  76 several separate  77 as yours
as you do yours  80 state position  86 misdoubt have misgivings about  88 spent wasted  89 Wot know  91 truth
loyalty

93 s.d. Pursuivant royal messenger with power to execute
warriors  95 sirrah common form of address to an inferior
100 suggestion instigation  105 Gramercy much thanks
108 Sir used for a priest, as well as for a knight  109 exercise
sermon  110 content reward  113 shriving confessing

## Scene III. [*Pomfret Castle.*]

*Enter Sir Richard* RATCLIFFE, *with* HALBERDS,
*carrying the nobles* [RIVERS, GREY, *and* VAUGHAN] *to
death at Pomfret.*

RIVERS
Sir Richard Ratcliffe, let me tell thee this:
Today shalt thou behold a subject die
For truth, for duty, and for loyalty.

GREY
God bless the prince from all the pack of you!
A knot you are of damnèd bloodsuckers.                    5

VAUGHAN
You live that shall cry woe for this hereafter.

RATCLIFFE
Dispatch; the limit of your lives is out.

RIVERS
O Pomfret, Pomfret! O thou bloody prison,
Fatal and ominous to noble peers!
Within the guilty closure° of thy walls                   10
Richard the Second here was hacked to death;
And, for more slander° to thy dismal seat,
We give to thee our guiltless blood to drink.

GREY
Now Margaret's curse is fall'n upon our heads,
When she exclaimed on Hastings, you, and I,              15
For standing by when Richard stabbed her son.

RIVERS
Then cursed she Richard, then cursed she Buck-
    ingham,
Then cursed she Hastings. O, remember, God,
To hear her prayer for them, as now for us!
And for my sister and her princely sons,                  20
Be satisfied, dear God, with our true blood,
Which, as thou know'st, unjustly must be spilt.

RATCLIFFE
Make haste; the hour of death is expiate.°

RIVERS
Come, Grey, come, Vaughan, let us here embrace.
Farewell, until we meet again in heaven.    *Exeunt.* 25

## Scene IV. [*The Tower.*]

*Enter* BUCKINGHAM, [*Lord* STANLEY *Earl of*] *Derby,*
HASTINGS, BISHOP OF ELY, NORFOLK, RATCLIFFE,
LOVELL, *with others, at a table.*

HASTINGS
Now, noble peers, the cause why we are met
Is to determine of the coronation.
In God's name, speak, when is the royal day?

BUCKINGHAM
Is all things ready for the royal time?

STANLEY
It is, and wants but nomination.°                          5

BISHOP OF ELY
Tomorrow then I judge a happy day.

BUCKINGHAM
Who knows the Lord Protector's mind herein?
Who is most inward° with the noble duke?

BISHOP OF ELY
Your grace, we think, should soonest know his
    mind.

BUCKINGHAM
We know each other's faces; for our hearts,              10
He knows no more of mine than I of yours;
Or I of his, my lord, than you of mine.
Lord Hastings, you and he are near in love.

HASTINGS
I thank his grace, I know he loves me well;
But for his purpose in the coronation                     15
I have not sounded him, nor he delivered
His gracious pleasure any way therein.
But you, my honorable lords, may name the time,
And in the duke's behalf I'll give my voice,
Which I presume he'll take in gentle part.               20

*Enter* [RICHARD *Duke of*] *Gloucester.*

BISHOP OF ELY
In happy time here comes the duke himself.

RICHARD
My noble lords and cousins all, good morrow.
I have been long a sleeper, but I trust
My absence doth neglect° no great design
Which by my presence might have been concluded.         25

BUCKINGHAM
Had you not come upon your cue, my lord,
William Lord Hastings had pronounced your part,
I mean your voice for crowning of the king.

RICHARD
Than my Lord Hastings no man might be bolder.
His lordship knows me well and loves me well.            30
My Lord of Ely, when I was last in Holborn
I saw good strawberries in your garden there.
I do beseech you send for some of them.

BISHOP OF ELY
Marry, and will, my lord, with all my heart.
                                       *Exit* BISHOP.

RICHARD
Cousin of Buckingham, a word with you.                   35

[*Takes him aside.*]

Catesby hath sounded Hastings in our business
And finds the testy gentleman so hot
That he will lose his head ere give consent
His master's child, as worshipfully° he terms it,
Shall lose the royalty of England's throne.              40

BUCKINGHAM
Withdraw yourself awhile. I'll go with you.
                    *Exeunt* [RICHARD *and* BUCKINGHAM].

STANLEY
We have not yet set down this day of triumph.
Tomorrow, in my judgment, is too sudden;
For I myself am not so well provided
As else I would be, were the day prolonged.°            45

---

III.iii.10 closure circuit  12 slander disgrace  23 expiate
come for suffering
III.iv.5 nomination naming

*Enter the* BISHOP OF ELY.

BISHOP OF ELY
Where is my lord the Duke of Gloucester?
I have sent for these strawberries.

HASTINGS
His grace looks cheerfully and smooth this morning;
There's some conceit° or other likes° him well
When that he bids good morrow with such spirit.        50
I think there's never a man in Christendom
Can lesser hide his love or hate than he,
For by his face straight shall you know his heart.

STANLEY
What of his heart perceive you in his face
By any livelihood° he showed today?                    55

HASTINGS
Marry, that with no man here he is offended;
For were he, he had shown it in his looks.

*Enter* RICHARD *and* BUCKINGHAM.

RICHARD
I pray you all, tell me what they deserve
That do conspire my death with devilish plots
Of damnèd witchcraft, and that have prevailed          60
Upon my body with their hellish charms.

HASTINGS
The tender love I bear your grace, my lord,
Makes me most forward in this princely presence
To doom th' offenders, whosoe'er they be.
I say, my lord, they have deservèd death.              65

RICHARD
Then be your eyes the witness of their evil.
Look how I am bewitched. Behold, mine arm
Is like a blasted sapling withered up;
And this is Edward's wife, that monstrous witch,
Consorted with that harlot strumpet Shore,             70
That by their witchcraft thus have markèd me.

HASTINGS
If they have done this deed, my noble lord—

RICHARD
If! Thou protector of this damnèd strumpet,
Talk'st thou to me of ifs? Thou art a traitor.
Off with his head! Now by Saint Paul I swear           75
I will not dine until I see the same.
Lovell and Ratcliffe, look that it be done.
The rest that love me, rise and follow me.
      *Exeunt. Manet* LOVELL *and* RATCLIFFE, *with
                          the Lord* HASTINGS.

HASTINGS
Woe, woe for England, not a whit for me!
For I, too fond,° might have prevented this.           80
Stanley did dream the boar did rase our helms,
And I did scorn it and disdain to fly.
Three times today my footcloth horse° did stumble,
And started when he looked upon the Tower,
As loath to bear me to the slaughterhouse.             85
O, now I need the priest that spake to me!
I now repent I told the pursuivant,
As too triumphing, how mine enemies
Today at Pomfret bloodily were butchered,

And I myself secure in grace and favor.                90
O Margaret, Margaret, now thy heavy curse
Is lighted on poor Hastings' wretched head!

RATCLIFFE
Come, come, dispatch; the duke would be at dinner.
Make a short shrift;° he longs to see your head.

HASTINGS
O momentary grace° of mortal men,                      95
Which we more hunt for than the grace of God!
Who builds his hope in air of your good looks
Lives like a drunken sailor on a mast,
Ready with every nod to tumble down
Into the fatal bowels of the deep.                     100

LOVELL
Come, come, dispatch; 'tis bootless° to exclaim.

HASTINGS
O bloody Richard! Miserable England!
I prophesy the fearful'st time to thee
That ever wretched age hath looked upon.
Come, lead me to the block; bear him my head.          105
They smile at me who shortly shall be dead.   *Exeunt.*


[Scene V. *The Tower walls.*]

*Enter* RICHARD [*Duke of Gloucester*] *and* BUCK-
INGHAM, *in rotten° armor, marvelous ill-favored.°*

RICHARD
Come, cousin, canst thou quake and change thy color,
Murder thy breath in middle of a word,
And then again begin, and stop again,
As if thou wert distraught and mad with terror?

BUCKINGHAM
Tut, I can counterfeit the deep tragedian;             5
Speak and look back, and pry on every side,
Tremble and start at wagging of a straw,
Intending° deep suspicion. Ghastly looks
Are at my service, like enforcèd smiles;
And both are ready in their offices°                   10
At any time to grace my stratagems.
But what, is Catesby gone?

RICHARD
He is; and see, he brings the mayor along.

*Enter the* MAYOR *and* CATESBY.

BUCKINGHAM
Lord Mayor—

RICHARD
Look to the drawbridge there!                          15

BUCKINGHAM
Hark! A drum.

RICHARD
Catesby, o'erlook° the walls.

BUCKINGHAM
Lord Mayor, the reason we have sent—

RICHARD
Look back, defend thee! Here are enemies.

49 **conceit** idea; **likes** pleases   55 **livelihood** liveliness   80
**fond** foolish   83 **footcloth horse** richly decorated horse

94 **shrift** confession   95 **grace** favor   101 **bootless** useless
III.v.s.d. **rotten** worn-out; **ill-favored** bad-looking   8
**Intending** pretending   10 **offices** functions   17 **o'erlook**
watch over

BUCKINGHAM
God and our innocency defend and guard us!    20

*Enter* LOVELL *and* RATCLIFFE, *with Hastings' head.*

RICHARD
Be patient, they are friends, Ratcliffe and Lovell.

LOVELL
Here is the head of that ignoble traitor,
The dangerous and unsuspected Hastings.

RICHARD
So dear I loved the man that I must weep:
I took him for the plainest harmless creature    25
That breathed upon the earth a Christian;
Made him my book,° wherein my soul recorded
The history of all her secret thoughts.
So smooth he daubed° his vice with show of virtue
That, his apparent open guilt omitted,    30
I mean his conversation° with Shore's wife,
He lived from all attainder of suspects.°

BUCKINGHAM
Well, well, he was the covert'st° shelt'red traitor
That ever lived.
Would you imagine, or almost believe,    35
Were't not that by great preservation
We live to tell it, that the subtle traitor
This day had plotted, in the council house,
To murder me and my good Lord of Gloucester?

MAYOR
Had he done so?    40

RICHARD
What! Think you we are Turks or infidels?
Or that we would, against the form of law,
Proceed thus rashly in the villain's death
But that the extreme peril of the case,
The peace of England, and our persons' safety    45
Enforced us to this execution?

MAYOR
Now fair befall you! He deserved his death,
And your good graces both have well proceeded
To warn false traitors from the like attempts.

BUCKINGHAM
I never looked for better at his hands    50
After he once fell in with Mistress Shore.
Yet had we not determined he should die
Until your lordship came to see his end,
Which now the loving haste of these our friends,
Something against our meanings, have prevented;°    55
Because, my lord, I would have had you heard
The traitor speak, and timorously confess
The manner and the purpose of his treasons,
That you might well have signified the same
Unto the citizens, who haply may    50
Misconster° us in him and wail his death.

MAYOR
But, my great lord, your grace's words shall serve
As well as I had seen and heard him speak;
And do not doubt, right noble princes both,

But I'll acquaint our duteous citizens    65
With all your just proceedings in this case.

RICHARD
And to that end we wished your lordship here,
T' avoid the censures of the carping world.

BUCKINGHAM
Which,° since you come too late of° our intent,
Yet witness what you hear we did intend.    70
And so, my good Lord Mayor, we bid farewell.
                     *Exit* MAYOR.

RICHARD
Go after, after, cousin Buckingham.
The mayor towards Guildhall° hies him in all post.°
There, at your meetest° vantage of the time,
Infer° the bastardy of Edward's children.    75
Tell them how Edward put to death a citizen
Only for saying he would make his son
Heir to the crown, meaning indeed his house,
Which by the sign thereof was termed so.
Moreover, urge his hateful luxury°    80
And bestial appetite in change of lust,
Which stretched unto their servants, daughters, wives,
Even where his raging eye or savage heart,
Without control, lusted to make a prey.
Nay, for a need, thus far come near my person:    85
Tell them, when that my mother went with child
Of that insatiate Edward, noble York
My princely father then had wars in France,
And by true computation of the time
Found that the issue was not his begot;    90
Which well appeared in his lineaments,
Being nothing like the noble duke my father.
Yet touch this sparingly, as 'twere far off,
Because, my lord, you know my mother lives.

BUCKINGHAM
Doubt not, my lord, I'll play the orator    95
As if the golden fee for which I plead
Were for myself; and so, my lord, adieu.

RICHARD
If you thrive well, bring them to Baynard's Castle,
Where you shall find me well accompanied
With reverend fathers and well-learnèd bishops.    100

BUCKINGHAM
I go; and towards three or four o'clock
Look for the news that the Guildhall affords.
                   *Exit* BUCKINGHAM.

RICHARD
Go, Lovell, with all speed to Doctor Shaw.

[*To Catesby.*]

Go thou to Friar Penker. Bid them both
Meet me within this hour at Baynard's Castle.    105
       *Exeunt* [LOVELL, CATESBY, *and* RATCLIFFE].
Now will I go to take some privy order°
To draw the brats of Clarence out of sight,
And to give order that no manner° person
Have any time recourse unto the princes.    *Exit.*

---

27 **book** notebook   29 **daubed** whitewashed   31 **conversation** intercourse   32 **from . . . suspects** free from all stain of suspicions   33 **covert'st** most secret   55 **prevented** forestalled 61 **Misconster** misjudge

69 **Which** as to which; **of** for   73 **Guildhall** the city hall of London; **post** haste   74 **meetest** fittest   75 **Infer** bring forward as an argument   80 **luxury** lechery   106 **privy order** secret arrangement   108 **no manner** no sort of

[Scene VI. *A street.*]

*Enter a* SCRIVENER [*with a paper in his hand*].

SCRIVENER
Here is the indictment of the good Lord Hastings,
Which in a set° hand fairly is engrossed°
That it may be today read o'er in Paul's.°
And mark how well the sequel hangs together:
Eleven hours I have spent to write it over,      5
For yesternight by Catesby was it sent me;
The precedent° was full as long a-doing;
And yet within these five hours Hastings lived,
Untainted,° unexamined, free, at liberty.
Here's a good world the while! Who is so gross°   10
That cannot see this palpable device?°
Yet who so bold but says he sees it not?
Bad is the world, and all will come to nought
When such ill dealing must be seen in thought.° *Exit.*

[Scene VII. *Baynard's Castle.*]

*Enter* RICHARD [*Duke of Gloucester*] *and* BUCK-
INGHAM *at several° doors.*

RICHARD
How now, how now? What say the citizens?
BUCKINGHAM
Now, by the holy Mother of our Lord,
The citizens are mum, say not a word.
RICHARD
Touched you the bastardy of Edward's children?
BUCKINGHAM
I did, with his contract with Lady Lucy°        5
And his contract by deputy° in France;
Th' unsatiate greediness of his desire
And his enforcement of the city wives;
His tyranny for trifles; his own bastardy,
As being got,° your father then in France,       10
And his resemblance,° being not like the duke.
Withal I did infer your lineaments,
Being the right idea° of your father
Both in your form and nobleness of mind;
Laid open all your victories in Scotland,         15
Your discipline in war, wisdom in peace,
Your bounty, virtue, fair humility;
Indeed, left nothing fitting for your purpose
Untouched or slightly handlèd in discourse;
And when my oratory drew toward end,             20
I bid them that did love their country's good
Cry, "God save Richard, England's royal king!"
RICHARD
And did they so?
BUCKINGHAM
No, so God help me, they spake not a word,

But like dumb statues° or breathing stones        25
Stared each on other and looked deadly pale.
Which when I saw, I reprehended them
And asked the mayor what meant this willful silence.
His answer was, the people were not usèd
To be spoke to but by the recorder.°              30
Then he was urged to tell my tale again:
"Thus saith the duke, thus hath the duke inferred";
But nothing spoke in warrant from himself.
When he had done, some followers of mine own
At lower end of the hall hurled up their caps,    35
And some ten voices cried, "God save King Richard!"
And thus I took the vantage of those few:
"Thanks, gentle citizens and friends," quoth I.
"This general applause and cheerful shout
Argues your wisdom and your love to Richard";     40
And even here brake off and came away.
RICHARD
What tongueless blocks were they! Would they not
   speak?
Will not the mayor then and his brethren come?
BUCKINGHAM
The mayor is here at hand. Intend° some fear;
Be not you spoke with but by mighty suit;°        45
And look you get a prayer book in your hand
And stand between two churchmen, good my lord,
For on that ground° I'll make a holy descant;°
And be not easily won to our requests.
Play the maid's part: still answer nay,° and take it.  50
RICHARD
I go; and if you plead as well for them
As I can say nay to thee for myself,
No doubt we bring it to a happy issue.
BUCKINGHAM
Go, go up to the leads.° The Lord Mayor knocks.
                              [*Exit* RICHARD.]

*Enter the* MAYOR, *and* CITIZENS.

Welcome, my lord. I dance attendance here.        55
I think the duke will not be spoke withal.°

*Enter* CATESBY.

Now, Catesby, what says your lord to my request?
CATESBY
He doth entreat your grace, my noble lord,
To visit him tomorrow or next day.
He is within, with two right reverend fathers,    60
Divinely bent to meditation,
And in no worldly suits would he be moved
To draw him from his holy exercise.°
BUCKINGHAM
Return, good Catesby, to the gracious duke.
Tell him, myself, the mayor and aldermen,         65
In deep designs, in matter of great moment,
No less importing than our general good,
Are come to have some conference with his grace.
CATESBY
I'll signify so much unto him straight.        *Exit.*

III.vi.2 **set** formal; **fairly is engrossed** is written clearly  **3**
**Paul's** Saint Paul's  **7 precedent** original draft  **9 Untainted**
not accused  **10 gross** dull  **11 palpable device** obvious
trick  **14 in thought** in silence
III.vii.s.d. **several** separate  **5 Lady Lucy** Elizabeth Lucy
(whose betrothal to Edward was never proved)  **6 by deputy**
Edward had sent Warwick to arrange a French marriage
**10 got** begotten  **11 resemblance** appearance  **13 right idea**
exact image

25 **statues** pronounced "stat-u-es"  **30 recorder** chief legal
official of the city  **44 Intend** pretend  **45 suit** petition
**48 ground** (1) melody (2) basis; **descant** (1) musical
variation (2) argument  **50 still answer nay** always say no (a
proverb)  **54 leads** flat roof covered with lead  **56 withal**
with  **63 exercise** act of devotion

**BUCKINGHAM**
Ah ha, my lord, this prince is not an Edward!    70
He is not lulling° on a lewd love-bed,
But on his knees at meditation;
Not dallying with a brace of courtesans,
But meditating with two deep divines;
Not sleeping, to engross° his idle body,    75
But praying, to enrich his watchful soul.
Happy were England, would this virtuous prince
Take on his grace the sovereignty thereof;
But sure I fear we shall not win him to it.

**MAYOR**
Marry, God defend° his grace should say us nay!    80

**BUCKINGHAM**
I fear he will. Here Catesby comes again.

*Enter* CATESBY.

Now, Catesby, what says his grace?

**CATESBY**
He wonders to what end you have assembled
Such troops of citizens to come to him,
His grace not being warned thereof before.    85
He fears, my lord, you mean no good to him.

**BUCKINGHAM**
Sorry I am my noble cousin should
Suspect me that I mean no good to him.
By heaven, we come to him in perfect love;
And so once more return and tell his grace.    90
                   *Exit* [CATESBY].
When holy and devout religious men
Are at their beads, 'tis much° to draw them thence,
So sweet is zealous contemplation.

*Enter* RICHARD *aloft, between two* BISHOPS. [CATESBY
*returns.*]

**MAYOR**
See where his grace stands 'tween two clergymen!

**BUCKINGHAM**
Two props of virtue for a Christian prince,    95
To stay him from the fall° of vanity;
And see, a book of prayer in his hand—
True ornaments to know a holy man.
Famous Plantagenet, most gracious prince,
Lend favorable ear to our requests,    100
And pardon us the interruption
Of thy devotion and right Christian zeal.

**RICHARD**
My lord, there needs no such apology.
I do beseech your grace to pardon me,
Who, earnest in the service of my God,    105
Deferred the visitation of my friends.
But, leaving this, what is your grace's pleasure?

**BUCKINGHAM**
Even that, I hope, which pleaseth God above
And all good men of this ungoverned isle.

**RICHARD**
I do suspect I have done some offense    110
That seems disgracious° in the city's eye,
And that you come to reprehend my ignorance.

**BUCKINGHAM**
You have, my lord. Would it might please your grace,
On our entreaties, to amend your fault!

**RICHARD**
Else wherefore breathe I in a Christian land?    115

**BUCKINGHAM**
Know then it is your fault that you resign
The supreme seat, the throne majestical,
The scept'red office of your ancestors,
Your state° of fortune and your due of birth,
The lineal glory of your royal house,    120
To the corruption of a blemished stock;
Whiles, in the mildness of your sleepy thoughts,
Which here we waken to our country's good,
The noble isle doth want his proper limbs;
His face defaced with scars of infamy,    125
His royal stock graft° with ignoble plants,
And almost should'red in° the swallowing gulf
Of dark forgetfulness and deep oblivion.
Which to recure,° we heartily solicit
Your gracious self to take on you the charge    130
And kingly government of this your land;
Not as protector, steward, substitute,
Or lowly factor° for another's gain,
But as successively,° from blood to blood,
Your right of birth, your empery,° your own.    135
For this, consorted with the citizens,
Your very worshipful and loving friends,
And by their vehement instigation,
In this just cause come I to move your grace.

**RICHARD**
I cannot tell if to depart in silence    140
Or bitterly to speak in your reproof
Best fitteth my degree° or your condition.°
If not to answer, you might haply think
Tongue-tied ambition, not replying, yielded
To bear the golden yoke of sovereignty    145
Which fondly you would here impose on me.
If to reprove you for this suit of yours,
So seasoned° with your faithful love to me,
Then, on the other side, I checked° my friends.
Therefore, to speak, and to avoid the first,    150
And then, in speaking, not to incur the last,
Definitively° thus I answer you.
Your love deserves my thanks, but my desert
Unmeritable shuns your high request.
First, if all obstacles were cut away    155
And that my path were even° to the crown
As the ripe revenue and due of birth,
Yet so much is my poverty of spirit,°
So mighty and so many my defects,
That I would rather hide me from my greatness,    160
Being a bark to brook° no mighty sea,
Than in my greatness covet to be hid
And in the vapor of my glory smothered.

---

119 **state** high position   126 **graft** grafted   127 **should'red
in** jostled into   129 **recure** remedy   133 **factor** agent   134
**successively** by inheritance   135 **empery** supreme power
142 **degree** rank; **condition** status   148 **seasoned** given
relish   149 **checked** should be rebuking   152 **Definitively**
once and for all   156 **even** clear   158 **poverty of spirit**
lack of self-confidence   161 **bark to brook** small ship able to
endure

---

71 **lulling** lounging   75 **engross** make fat   80 **defend** forbid
92 **much** hard   96 **fall** falling into sin   111 **disgracious**
displeasing

But, God be thanked, there is no need of me,
And much I need° to help you, were there need.            165
The royal tree hath left us royal fruit,
Which, mellowed by the stealing hours of time,
Will well become the seat of majesty
And make, no doubt, us happy by his reign.
On him I lay that you would lay on me,                     170
The right and fortune of his happy stars,
Which God defend° that I should wring from him!

BUCKINGHAM
My lord, this argues conscience in your grace,
But the respects thereof are nice° and trivial,
All circumstances well consider̀èd.                          175
You say that Edward is your brother's son.
So say we too, but not by Edward's wife;
For first was he contract to Lady Lucy—
Your mother lives a witness to his vow—
And afterward by substitute betrothed                      180
To Bona, sister to the King of France.
These both put off, a poor petitioner,
A care-crazed mother to a many sons,
A beauty-waning and distressèd widow,
Even in the afternoon of her best days,                    185
Made prize and purchase° of his wanton eye,
Seduced the pitch° and height of his degree
To base declension° and loathed bigamy.
By her, in his unlawful bed, he got
This Edward, whom our manners call the prince.             190
More bitterly could I expostulate,
Save that for reverence to some alive
I give a sparing limit to my tongue.
Then, good my lord, take to your royal self
This proffered benefit of dignity;°                        195
If not to bless us and the land withal,
Yet to draw forth your noble ancestry
From the corruption of abusing times
Unto a lineal true-derivèd course.

MAYOR
Do, good my lord; your citizens entreat you.               200

BUCKINGHAM
Refuse not, mighty lord, this proffered love.

CATESBY
O, make them joyful, grant their lawful suit!

RICHARD
Alas, why would you heap this care on me?
I am unfit for state and majesty.
I do beseech you take it not amiss,                        205
I cannot nor I will not yield to you.

BUCKINGHAM
If you refuse it, as in love and zeal
Loath to depose the child, your brother's son—
As well we know your tenderness of heart
And gentle, kind, effeminate remorse,°                     210
Which we have noted in you to your kindred
And egally° indeed to all estates—
Yet know, whe'r° you accept our suit or no,
Your brother's son shall never reign our king,

But we will plant some other in the throne                 215
To the disgrace and downfall of your house;
And in this resolution here we leave you.
Come, citizens. Zounds, I'll entreat no more!

RICHARD
O, do not swear, my lord of Buckingham.
          Exeunt [BUCKINGHAM, MAYOR, and CITIZENS].

CATESBY
Call him again, sweet prince, accept their suit.           220
If you deny them, all the land will rue it.

RICHARD
Will you enforce me to a world of cares?
Call them again. I am not made of stone,
But penetrable to your kind entreaties,
Albeit against my conscience and my soul.                  225

Enter BUCKINGHAM and the rest.

Cousin of Buckingham, and sage grave men,
Since you will buckle Fortune on my back,
To bear her burden, whe'r I will or no,
I must have patience to endure the load;
But if black scandal or foul-faced reproach                230
Attend the sequel of your imposition,°
Your mere enforcement° shall acquittance° me
From all the impure blots and stains thereof;
For God doth know, and you may partly see,
How far I am from the desire of this.                      235

MAYOR
God bless your grace! We see it and will say it.

RICHARD
In saying so you shall but say the truth.

BUCKINGHAM
Then I salute you with this royal title:
Long live King Richard, England's worthy king!

ALL
Amen.                                                      240

BUCKINGHAM
Tomorrow may it please you to be crowned?

RICHARD
Even when you please, for you will have it so.

BUCKINGHAM
Tomorrow then we will attend your grace,
And so most joyfully we take our leave.

RICHARD [To the BISHOPS.]
Come, let us to our holy work again.                       245
Farewell, my cousin; farewell, gentle friends.   Exeunt.


# ACT IV

Scene I. [Before the Tower.]

Enter the QUEEN [ELIZABETH], the DUCHESS OF
YORK, and Marquis [of] DORSET [at one door]; ANNE
Duchess of Gloucester, [with Clarence's DAUGHTER, at
another door].

---

165 need lack   172 defend forbid   174 respects . . . nice
considerations about it are too scrupulous   186 purchase
booty   187 pitch high point (of a hawk's flight)   188 base
declension a noble falling low   195 benefit of dignity gift of
greatness   210 effeminate remorse softhearted pity   212
egally equally   213 whe'r whether

231 imposition laying on the burden   232 Your mere enforcement the simple fact of your compulsion; acquittance
release

DUCHESS OF YORK
Who meets us here? My niece° Plantagenet,
Led in the hand of her kind aunt of Gloucester!
Now, for my life, she's wand'ring to the Tower
On pure heart's love to greet the tender prince.
Daughter, well met.

ANNE            God give your graces both    5
A happy and a joyful time of day!

QUEEN ELIZABETH
As much to you, good sister! Whither away?

ANNE
No farther than the Tower, and, as I guess,
Upon the like devotion° as yourselves,
To gratulate° the gentle princes there.    10

QUEEN ELIZABETH
Kind sister, thanks. We'll enter all together.

*Enter the* LIEUTENANT [*Brakenbury*].

And in good time here the lieutenant comes.
Master Lieutenant, pray you, by your leave,
How doth the prince, and my young son of York?

LIEUTENANT
Right well, dear madam. By your patience,    15
I may not suffer you to visit them;
The king hath strictly charged the contrary.

QUEEN ELIZABETH
The king? Who's that?

LIEUTENANT          I mean the Lord Protector.

QUEEN ELIZABETH
The Lord protect him from that kingly title!
Hath he set bounds between their love and me?    20
I am their mother; who shall bar me from them?

DUCHESS OF YORK
I am their father's mother; I will see them.

ANNE
Their aunt I am in law, in love their mother.
Then bring me to their sights; I'll bear thy blame
And take thy office° from thee on my peril.    25

LIEUTENANT
No, madam, no; I may not leave° it so.
I am bound by oath, and therefore pardon me.
                    *Exit* LIEUTENANT.

*Enter* STANLEY [*Earl of Derby*].

STANLEY
Let me but meet you, ladies, one hour hence,
And I'll salute your grace of York as mother
And reverend looker-on of two fair queens.    30

[*To* ANNE.]

Come, madam, you must straight to Westminster,
There to be crownèd Richard's royal queen.

QUEEN ELIZABETH
Ah, cut my lace° asunder,
That my pent heart may have some scope to beat,
Or else I swoon with this dead-killing news!    35

ANNE
Despiteful° tidings! O unpleasing news!

DORSET
Be of good cheer; mother, how fares your grace?

QUEEN ELIZABETH
O Dorset, speak not to me, get thee gone!
Death and destruction dogs thee at thy heels;
Thy mother's name is ominous to children.    40
If thou wilt outstrip death, go cross the seas
And live with Richmond, from° the reach of hell.
Go hie thee, hie thee from this slaughterhouse,
Lest thou increase the number of the dead
And make me die the thrall° of Margaret's curse,    45
Nor mother, wife, nor England's counted queen.°

STANLEY
Full of wise care is this your counsel, madam.
Take all the swift advantage of the hours.
You shall have letters from me to my son°
In your behalf, to meet you on the way.    50
Be not ta'en tardy° by unwise delay.

DUCHESS OF YORK
O ill-dispersing° wind of misery!
O my accursèd womb, the bed of death!
A cockatrice° hast thou hatched to the world,
Whose unavoided eye is murderous.    55

STANLEY
Come, madam, come; I in all haste was sent.

ANNE
And I with all unwillingness will go.
O, would to God that the inclusive verge°
Of golden metal that must round° my brow
Were red-hot steel to sear me to the brains!    60
Anointed let me be with deadly venom
And die ere men can say, "God save the queen!"

QUEEN ELIZABETH
Go, go, poor soul! I envy not thy glory.
To feed my humor° wish thyself no harm.

ANNE
No? Why, when he that is my husband now    65
Came to me as I followed Henry's corse,
When scarce the blood was well washed from his
   hands
Which issuèd from my other angel husband
And that dear saint which then I weeping followed—
O, when I say, I looked on Richard's face,    70
This was my wish: "Be thou," quoth I, "accursed
For making me, so young, so old a widow!°
And when thou wed'st, let sorrow haunt thy bed;
And be thy wife, if any be so mad,
More miserable by the life of thee    75
Than thou hast made me by my dear lord's death!"
Lo, ere I can repeat this curse again,
Within so small a time, my woman's heart
Grossly grew captive to his honey words
And proved the subject of mine own soul's curse,    80
Which hitherto hath held mine eyes from rest;
For never yet one hour in his bed
Did I enjoy the golden dew of sleep,

---

IV.i.1 **niece** granddaughter   9 **devotion** purpose   10
**gratulate** greet with joy   25 **take thy office** take over your
duty   26 **leave** abandon   33 **lace** bodice string   36 **Despiteful** cruel

42 **from** away from   45 **thrall** slave   46 **England's counted
queen** regarded as Queen of England   49 **son** his wife's son,
Richmond   51 **ta'en tardy** caught napping   52 **ill-dispersing**
scattering evil   54 **cockatrice** fabulous monster, basilisk
(see I.ii.150)   58 **inclusive verge** enclosing rim   59 **round**
encircle   64 **feed my humor** satisfy my mood   72 **so . . .
widow** a widow so aged by grief

But with his timorous dreams was still° awaked.
Besides, he hates me for my father Warwick,    85
And will, no doubt, shortly be rid of me.

QUEEN ELIZABETH
Poor heart, adieu! I pity thy complaining.

ANNE
No more than with my soul I mourn for yours.

DORSET
Farewell, thou woeful welcomer of glory!

ANNE
Adieu, poor soul that tak'st thy leave of it!    90

DUCHESS OF YORK [*To* DORSET.]
Go thou to Richmond, and good fortune guide thee!

[*To* ANNE.]

Go thou to Richard, and good angels tend thee!

[*To* QUEEN ELIZABETH.]

Go thou to sanctuary, and good thoughts possess thee!
I to my grave, where peace and rest lie with me!
Eighty odd years of sorrow have I seen,    95
And each hour's joy wracked° with a week of teen.°

QUEEN ELIZABETH
Stay, yet look back with me unto the Tower.
Pity, you ancient stones, those tender babes
Whom envy hath immured within your walls,
Rough cradle for such little pretty ones!    100
Rude ragged nurse, old sullen playfellow
For tender princes, use my babies well!
So foolish sorrow bids your stones farewell.    *Exeunt.*


Scene II. [*The palace.*]

*Sound a sennet. Enter* RICHARD, *in pomp,* BUCK-
INGHAM, CATESBY, RATCLIFFE, LOVELL, [*a* PAGE,
*and others*].

KING RICHARD
Stand all apart. Cousin of Buckingham!

BUCKINGHAM
My gracious sovereign?

KING RICHARD
Give me thy hand. *Sound.* [*He ascends the throne.*]
           Thus high, by thy advice
And thy assistance, is King Richard seated.
But shall we wear these glories for a day?    5
Or shall they last, and we rejoice in them?

BUCKINGHAM
Still live they, and forever let them last!

KING RICHARD
Ah, Buckingham, now do I play the touch°
To try if thou be current gold indeed.
Young Edward lives—think now what I would speak.    10

BUCKINGHAM
Say on, my loving lord.

KING RICHARD
Why, Buckingham, I say I would be king.

BUCKINGHAM
Why, so you are, my thrice-renownèd lord.

KING RICHARD
Ha! Am I king? 'Tis so; but Edward lives.

BUCKINGHAM
True, noble prince.

KING RICHARD    O bitter consequence,°    15
That Edward still should live true noble prince!
Cousin, thou wast not wont to be so dull.
Shall I be plain? I wish the bastards dead,
And I would have it suddenly performed.
What say'st thou now? Speak suddenly, be brief.    20

BUCKINGHAM
Your grace may do your pleasure.

KING RICHARD
Tut, tut, thou art all ice, thy kindness freezes.
Say, have I thy consent that they shall die?

BUCKINGHAM
Give me some little breath, some pause, dear lord,
Before I positively speak in this.    25
I will resolve° you herein presently.
                *Exit* BUCKINGHAM.

CATESBY [*Aside to another.*]
The king is angry. See, he gnaws his lip.

KING RICHARD
I will converse° with iron-witted° fools
And unrespective° boys. None are for me
That look into me with considerate° eyes.    30
High-reaching Buckingham grows circumspect.
Boy!

PAGE
My lord?

KING RICHARD
Know'st thou not any whom corrupting gold
Will tempt unto a close exploit° of death?    35

PAGE
I know a discontented gentleman
Whose humble means match not his haughty spirit.
Gold were as good as twenty orators
And will, no doubt, tempt him to anything.

KING RICHARD
What is his name?

PAGE    His name, my lord, is Tyrrel.    40

KING RICHARD
I partly know the man. Go call him hither, boy.
                *Exit* [PAGE].
The deep-revolving witty° Buckingham
No more shall be the neighbor to my counsels.
Hath he so long held out° with me, untired,
And stops he now for breath? Well, be it so.    45

*Enter* STANLEY [*Earl of Derby*].

How now, Lord Stanley? What's the news?

STANLEY    Know, my loving lord,
The Marquis Dorset, as I hear, is fled
To Richmond in the parts where he abides.

[*Stands aside.*]

---

84 **still** continually   96 **wracked** ruined; **teen** grief
**IV.ii.8 touch** touchstone (used to test gold)

15 **consequence** sequel   26 **resolve** answer   28 **converse**
keep company; **iron-witted** dull-witted   29 **unrespective**
heedless   30 **considerate** thoughtful   35 **close exploit** secret
deed   42 **deep-revolving witty** deeply pondering clever
44 **held out** kept up

KING RICHARD
Come hither, Catesby. Rumor it abroad
That Anne my wife is very grievous sick;    50
I will take order for her keeping close.
Inquire me out some mean poor gentleman,
Whom I will marry straight to Clarence' daughter.
The boy is foolish,° and I fear not him.
Look how thou dream'st! I say again, give out    55
That Anne my queen is sick and like to die.
About it; for it stands me much upon°
To stop all hopes whose growth may damage me.
                              [*Exit* CATESBY.]
I must be married to my brother's daughter,
Or else my kingdom stands on brittle glass.    60
Murder her brothers and then marry her!
Uncertain way of gain! But I am in
So far in blood that sin will pluck on sin.
Tear-falling pity dwells not in this eye.

*Enter* TYRREL.

Is thy name Tyrrel?    65
TYRREL
James Tyrrel, and your most obedient subject.
KING RICHARD
Art thou indeed?
TYRREL               Prove me, my gracious lord.
KING RICHARD
Dar'st thou resolve to kill a friend of mine?
TYRREL
Please° you;
But I had rather kill two enemies.    70
KING RICHARD
Why, there thou hast it! Two deep enemies,
Foes to my rest and my sweet sleep's disturbers,
Are they that I would have thee deal upon.
Tyrrel, I mean those bastards in the Tower.
TYRREL
Let me have open means to come to them,    75
And soon I'll rid you from the fear of them.
KING RICHARD
Thou sing'st sweet music. Hark, come hither, Tyrrel.
Go, by this token. Rise, and lend thine ear.

*Whispers.*

There is no more but so. Say it is done,
And I will love thee and prefer° thee for it.    80
TYRREL
I will dispatch it straight.            *Exit.*

*Enter* BUCKINGHAM.

BUCKINGHAM
My lord, I have considered in my mind
The late request that you did sound me in.
KING RICHARD
Well, let that rest. Dorset is fled to Richmond.
BUCKINGHAM
I hear the news, my lord.    35
KING RICHARD
Stanley, he is your wife's son. Well, look unto it.

BUCKINGHAM
My lord, I claim the gift, my due by promise,
For which your honor and your faith is pawned:°
Th' earldom of Hereford and the movables
Which you have promised I shall possess.    90
KING RICHARD
Stanley, look to your wife; if she convey
Letters to Richmond, you shall answer it.
BUCKINGHAM
What says your highness to my just request?
KING RICHARD
I do remember me, Henry the Sixth
Did prophesy that Richmond should be king    95
When Richmond was a little peevish° boy.
A king! Perhaps, perhaps.
BUCKINGHAM
My lord!
KING RICHARD
How chance the prophet could not at that time
Have told me, I being by, that I should kill him?    100
BUCKINGHAM
My lord, your promise for the earldom!
KING RICHARD
Richmond! When last I was at Exeter,
The mayor in courtesy showed me the castle,
And called in Rugemont; at which name I started,
Because a bard of Ireland told me once    105
I should not live long after I saw Richmond.
BUCKINGHAM
My lord!
KING RICHARD
Ay, what's o'clock?
BUCKINGHAM
I am thus bold to put your grace in mind
Of what you promised me.
KING RICHARD            Well, but what's o'clock?    110
BUCKINGHAM
Upon the stroke of ten.
KING RICHARD            Well, let it strike.
BUCKINGHAM
Why let it strike?
KING RICHARD
Because that like a Jack° thou keep'st the stroke°
Betwixt thy begging and my meditation.
I am not in the giving vein today.    115
BUCKINGHAM
May it please you to resolve me in my suit.
KING RICHARD
Thou troublest me; I am not in the vein.
           *Exit* [KING RICHARD, *and all but* BUCKINGHAM].
BUCKINGHAM
And is it thus? Repays he my deep service
With such contempt? Made I him king for this?
O, let me think on Hastings, and be gone    120
To Brecknock while my fearful head is on!    *Exit.*

---

**54 foolish** an idiot   **57 stands . . . upon** is very important to
me   **69 Please** if it pleases   **80 prefer** advance

**88 pawned** pledged   **96 peevish** childish   **113 Jack** (1) figure
of a man on a clock, striking the hour (2) knave; **thou . . .
stroke** you keep on making a noise

[Scene III. *The palace*.]

*Enter* TYRREL.

TYRREL
The tyrannous and bloody act is done,
The most arch° deed of piteous massacre
That ever yet this land was guilty of.
Dighton and Forrest, who I did suborn
To do this piece° of ruthful° butchery,                                5
Albeit they were fleshed° villains, bloody dogs,
Melted with tenderness and mild compassion,
Wept like to children in their death's sad story.
"O thus," quoth Dighton, "lay the gentle babes."
"Thus, thus," quoth Forrest, "girdling one another          10
Within their alabaster innocent arms.
Their lips were four red roses on a stalk
And in their summer beauty kissed each other.
A book of prayers on their pillow lay,
Which once," quoth Forrest, "almost changed my
    mind;                                                                          15
But O, the devil"—there the villain stopped;
When Dighton thus told on: "We smotherèd
The most replenishèd° sweet work of Nature
That from the prime° creation e'er she framèd."
Hence both are gone with conscience and remorse       20
They° could not speak; and so I left them both,
To bear this tidings to the bloody king.

*Enter* [KING] RICHARD.

And here he comes. All health, my sovereign lord!

KING RICHARD
Kind Tyrrel, am I happy in thy news?

TYRREL
If to have done the thing you gave in charge               25
Beget° your happiness, be happy then,
For it is done.

KING RICHARD            But didst thou see them dead?

TYRREL
I did, my lord.

KING RICHARD            And buried, gentle Tyrrel?

TYRREL
The chaplain of the Tower hath buried them;
But where (to say the truth) I do not know.                  30

KING RICHARD
Come to me, Tyrrel, soon at aftersupper,°
When thou shalt tell the process° of their death.
Meantime, but think how I may do thee good
And be inheritor of thy desire.
Farewell till then.

TYRREL                    I humbly take my leave.    [*Exit*.] 35

KING RICHARD
The son of Clarence have I pent up close;
His daughter meanly have I matched in marriage;
The sons of Edward sleep in Abraham's bosom,°
And Anne my wife hath bid this world good night.
Now, for° I know the Britain° Richmond aims               40
At young Elizabeth, my brother's daughter,

And by that knot° looks proudly on the crown,
To her go I, a jolly thriving wooer.

*Enter* RATCLIFFE.

RATCLIFFE
My lord!

KING RICHARD
Good or bad news, that thou com'st in so bluntly?       45

RATCLIFFE
Bad news, my lord. Morton is fled to Richmond,
And Buckingham, backed with the hardy Welshmen,
Is in the field, and still his power increaseth.

KING RICHARD
Ely with Richmond troubles me more near
Than Buckingham and his rash-levied° strength.          50
Come, I have learned that fearful commenting°
Is leaden servitor to dull delay;
Delay leads impotent and snail-paced beggary.°
Then fiery expedition° be my wing,
Jove's Mercury, and herald for a king!                        55
Go muster men. My counsel is my shield;
We must be brief when traitors brave the field.
                                                                       *Exeunt*.

Scene [IV. *The palace*.]

*Enter old* QUEEN MARGARET.

QUEEN MARGARET
So now prosperity begins to mellow
And drop into the rotten mouth of death.
Here in these confines slily have I lurked
To watch the waning of mine enemies.
A dire induction° am I witness to,                                5
And will to France, hoping the consequence°
Will prove as bitter, black, and tragical.
Withdraw thee, wretched Margaret. Who comes
    here?                                                          [*Retires*.]

*Enter* DUCHESS [OF YORK] *and* QUEEN [ELIZABETH].

QUEEN ELIZABETH
Ah, my poor princes, ah, my tender babes!
My unblown° flow'rs, new-appearing sweets!               10
If yet your gentle souls fly in the air
And be not fixed in doom perpetual,
Hover about me with your airy wings
And hear your mother's lamentation!

QUEEN MARGARET [*Aside*.]
Hover about her, say that right for right                      15
Hath dimmed your infant morn to agèd night.

DUCHESS OF YORK
So many miseries have crazed° my voice
That my woe-wearied tongue is still and mute.
Edward Plantagenet, why art thou dead?

QUEEN MARGARET [*Aside*.]
Plantagenet doth quit° Plantagenet,                           20
Edward for Edward pays a dying debt.

---

IV.iii.2 **arch** extreme  **5 piece** masterpiece; **ruthful** piteous
**6 fleshed** experienced  **18 replenishèd** complete  **19 prime**
first  **21 They** which they  **26 Beget** cause  **31 aftersupper**
late supper  **32 process** story  **38 Abraham's bosom** paradise
**40 for** because; **Britain** Breton

**42 knot** marriage tie  **50 rash-levied** hastily raised  **51 fearful commenting** timorous meditating  **53 beggary** bankruptcy
**54 expedition** speed
IV.iv.**5 induction** opening scene  **6 consequence** following
part  **10 unblown** unblossomed  **17 crazed** cracked  **20 quit**
make up for

QUEEN ELIZABETH
Wilt thou, O God, fly from such gentle lambs
And throw them in the entrails of the wolf?
When didst thou sleep when such a deed was done?

QUEEN MARGARET [*Aside.*]
When holy Harry died, and my sweet son.    25

DUCHESS OF YORK
Dead life, blind sight, poor mortal living ghost,
Woe's scene, world's shame, grave's due by life
   usurped,
Brief abstract° and record of tedious days,
Rest thy unrest on England's lawful earth,

[*Sits down.*]

Unlawfully made drunk with innocent blood!    30

QUEEN ELIZABETH
Ah that thou wouldst as soon afford a grave
As thou canst yield a melancholy seat!
Then would I hide my bones, not rest them here.
Ah, who hath any cause to mourn but we?

[*Sits down by her.*]

QUEEN MARGARET [*Comes forward.*]
If ancient sorrow be most reverend,    35
Give mine the benefit of seniory°
And let my griefs frown on the upper hand.°
If sorrow can admit society,

[*Sits down with them.*]

Tell° o'er your woes again by viewing mine.
I had an Edward, till a Richard killed him;    40
I had a husband, till a Richard killed him.
Thou hadst an Edward, till a Richard killed him;
Thou hadst a Richard, till a Richard killed him.

DUCHESS OF YORK
I had a Richard too, and thou didst kill him;
I had a Rutland too, thou holp'st° to kill him.    45

QUEEN MARGARET
Thou hadst a Clarence too, and Richard killed him.
From forth the kennel of thy womb hath crept
A hellhound that doth hunt us all to death.
That dog that had his teeth before his eyes
To worry lambs and lap their gentle blood,    50
That foul defacer of God's handiwork,
That excellent grand° tyrant of the earth
That reigns in gallèd° eyes of weeping souls,
Thy womb let loose to chase us to our graves.
O upright, just, and true-disposing° God,    55
How do I thank thee that this carnal° cur
Preys on the issue of his mother's body
And makes her pewfellow° with others' moan!

DUCHESS OF YORK
O Harry's wife, triumph not in my woes!
God witness with me I have wept for thine.    60

QUEEN MARGARET
Bear with me; I am hungry for revenge,
And now I cloy me with beholding it.
Thy Edward he is dead, that killed my Edward;

Thy other Edward dead, to quit my Edward;
Young York he is but boot,° because both they    65
Matched not the high perfection of my loss.
Thy Clarence he is dead that stabbed my Edward,
And the beholders of this frantic play,
Th' adulterate° Hastings, Rivers, Vaughan, Grey,
Untimely smothered in their dusky graves.    70
Richard yet lives, hell's black intelligencer,°
Only reserved their factor° to buy souls
And send them thither. But at hand, at hand,
Ensues his piteous and unpitied end.
Earth gapes, hell burns, fiends roar, saints pray,    75
To have him suddenly conveyed from hence.
Cancel his bond of life, dear God, I pray.
That I may live and say, "The dog is dead."

QUEEN ELIZABETH
O, thou didst prophesy the time would come
That I should wish for thee to help me curse    80
That bottled spider, that foul bunch-backed toad!

QUEEN MARGARET
I called thee then vain flourish of my fortune;
I called thee then poor shadow, painted queen,
The presentation of but° what I was,
The flattering index° of a direful pageant,°    85
One heaved a-high° to be hurled down below,
A mother only mocked with two fair babes,
A dream of what thou wast, a garish° flag
To be the aim of every dangerous shot,
A sign of dignity, a breath, a bubble,    90
A queen in jest, only to fill the scene.
Where is thy husband now? Where be thy brothers?
Where be thy two sons? Wherein dost thou joy?
Who sues and kneels and says, "God save the queen"?
Where be the bending peers that flatterèd thee?    95
Where be the thronging troops that followèd thee?
Decline° all this, and see what now thou art:
For happy wife, a most distressèd widow;
For joyful mother, one that wails the name;
For one being sued to, one that humbly sues;    100
For queen, a very caitiff° crowned with care;
For she that scorned at me, now scorned of me;
For she being feared of all, now fearing one;
For she commanding all, obeyed of none.
Thus hath the course of justice whirled about    105
And left thee but a very prey to time,
Having no more but thought of what thou wast
To torture thee the more, being what thou art.
Thou didst usurp my place, and dost thou not
Usurp the just proportion° of my sorrow?    110
Now thy proud neck bears half my burdened yoke,
From which even here I slip my wearied head
And leave the burden of it all on thee.
Farewell, York's wife, and queen of sad mischance!
These English woes shall make me smile in France.    115

QUEEN ELIZABETH
O thou well skilled in curses, stay awhile
And teach me how to curse mine enemies!

**QUEEN MARGARET**
Forbear to sleep the nights, and fast the days;
Compare dead happiness with living woe;
Think that thy babes were sweeter than they were      120
And he that slew them fouler than he is.
Bett'ring° thy loss makes the bad causer worse;
Revolving° this will teach thee how to curse.

**QUEEN ELIZABETH**
My words are dull; O, quicken° them with thine!

**QUEEN MARGARET**
Thy woes will make them sharp and pierce like mine.  125

*Exit* [QUEEN] MARGARET.

**DUCHESS OF YORK**
Why should calamity be full of words?

**QUEEN ELIZABETH**
Windy attorneys to their client's woes,°
Airy succeeders of intestate joys,°
Poor breathing orators of miseries,
Let them have scope! Though what they will impart   130
Help nothing else, yet do they ease the heart.

**DUCHESS OF YORK**
If so, then be not tongue-tied. Go with me
And in the breath of bitter words let's smother
My damnèd son that thy two sweet sons smothered.
The trumpet sounds. Be copious in exclaims.         135

*Enter* KING RICHARD *and his* TRAIN, [*marching with drums and trumpets*].

**KING RICHARD**
Who intercepts me in my expedition?°

**DUCHESS OF YORK**
O, she that might have intercepted thee,
By strangling thee in her accursèd womb,
From all the slaughters, wretch, that thou hast done!

**QUEEN ELIZABETH**
Hid'st thou that forehead with a golden crown        140
Where should be branded, if that right were right,
The slaughter of the prince that owed° that crown
And the dire death of my poor sons and brothers?
Tell me, thou villain-slave, where are my children?

**DUCHESS OF YORK**
Thou toad, thou toad, where is thy brother Clarence? 145
And little Ned Plantagenet, his son?

**QUEEN ELIZABETH**
Where is the gentle Rivers, Vaughan, Grey?

**DUCHESS OF YORK**
Where is kind Hastings?

**KING RICHARD**
A flourish, trumpets! Strike alarum, drums!
Let not the heavens hear these telltale women         150
Rail on the Lord's anointed. Strike, I say!

*Flourish. Alarums.*

Either be patient and entreat me fair,°
Or with the clamorous report of war
Thus will I drown your exclamations.

**DUCHESS OF YORK**
Art thou my son?                                      155

**KING RICHARD**
Ay, I thank God, my father, and yourself.

**DUCHESS OF YORK**
Then patiently hear my impatience.

**KING RICHARD**
Madam, I have a touch of your condition°
That cannot brook the accent of reproof.

**DUCHESS OF YORK**
O, let me speak!

**KING RICHARD** Do then; but I'll not hear.         160

**DUCHESS OF YORK**
I will be mild and gentle in my words.

**KING RICHARD**
And brief, good mother, for I am in haste.

**DUCHESS OF YORK**
Art thou so hasty? I have stayed° for thee,
God knows, in torment and in agony.

**KING RICHARD**
And came I not at last to comfort you?                165

**DUCHESS OF YORK**
No, by the holy rood, thou know'st it well,
Thou cam'st on earth to make the earth my hell.
A grievous burden was thy birth to me;
Tetchy° and wayward was thy infancy;
Thy schooldays frightful, desp'rate, wild, and furious;  170
Thy prime of manhood daring, bold, and venturous;
Thy age confirmed,° proud, subtle, sly, and bloody,
More mild, but yet more harmful, kind in hatred.
What comfortable hour canst thou name
That ever graced me with thy company?                 175

**KING RICHARD**
Faith, none but Humphrey Hour,° that called your
  grace
To breakfast once forth of my company.
If I be so disgracious° in your eye,
Let me march on and not offend you, madam.
Strike up the drum.

**DUCHESS OF YORK**   I prithee hear me speak.        180

**KING RICHARD**
You speak too bitterly.

**DUCHESS OF YORK**   Hear me a word;
For I shall never speak to thee again.

**KING RICHARD**
So.

**DUCHESS OF YORK**
Either thou wilt die by God's just ordinance
Ere from this war thou turn° a conqueror,             185
Or I with grief and extreme age shall perish
And never more behold thy face again.
Therefore take with thee my most grievous curse,
Which in the day of battle tire thee more
Than all the complete armor that thou wear'st!        190
My prayers on the adverse party fight!
And there the little souls of Edward's children
Whisper the spirits of thine enemies
And promise them success and victory!
Bloody thou art, bloody will be thy end;              195
Shame serves thy life and doth thy death attend. *Exit.*

---

122 **Bett'ring** magnifying   123 **Revolving** meditating on
124 **quicken** give life to   127 **attorneys . . . woes** spokesmen
for the griefs of the one who employs them (i.e., words)   128
**succeeders . . . joys** successors of joys which died without
leaving a will   136 **expedition** (1) campaign (2) haste   142
**owed** owned   152 **entreat me fair** treat me courteously

158 **condition** disposition   163 **stayed** waited   169 **Tetchy**
fretful   172 **age confirmed** maturity   176 **Humphrey
Hour** apparently the name of a man, chosen for the play on
"*comfortable hour*"   178 **disgracious** displeasing   185 **turn**
return

QUEEN ELIZABETH
Though far more cause, yet much less spirit to curse
Abides in me. I say amen to her.
KING RICHARD
Stay, madam; I must talk a word with you.
QUEEN ELIZABETH
I have no moe° sons of the royal blood     200
For thee to slaughter. For my daughters, Richard,
They shall be praying nuns, not weeping queens;
And therefore level° not to hit their lives.
KING RICHARD
You have a daughter called Elizabeth,
Virtuous and fair, royal and gracious.     205
QUEEN ELIZABETH
And must she die for this? O, let her live,
And I'll corrupt her manners,° stain her beauty,
Slander myself as false to Edward's bed,
Throw over her the veil of infamy;
So she may live unscarred of bleeding slaughter,     210
I will confess she was not Edward's daughter.
KING RICHARD
Wrong not her birth; she is a royal princess.
QUEEN ELIZABETH
To save her life, I'll say she is not so.
KING RICHARD
Her life is safest only in her birth.
QUEEN ELIZABETH
And only in that safety died her brothers.     215
KING RICHARD
Lo, at their birth good stars were opposite.
QUEEN ELIZABETH
No, to their lives ill friends were contrary.
KING RICHARD
All unavoided° is the doom° of destiny.
QUEEN ELIZABETH
True, when avoided grace° makes destiny.
My babes were destined to a fairer death     220
If grace had blessed thee with a fairer life.
KING RICHARD
You speak as if that I had slain my cousins!
QUEEN ELIZABETH
Cousins indeed, and by their uncle cozened°
Of comfort, kingdom, kindred, freedom, life.
Whose hand soever lanced their tender hearts,     225
Thy head (all indirectly°) gave direction.
No doubt the murd'rous knife was dull and blunt
Till it was whetted on thy stone-hard heart
To revel in the entrails of my lambs.
But that still use° of grief makes wild grief tame,     230
My tongue should to thy ears not name my boys
Till that my nails were anchored in thine eyes;
And I, in such a desp'rate bay of death,
Like a poor bark of sails and tackling reft,
Rush all to pieces on thy rocky bosom.     235
KING RICHARD
Madam, so thrive I in my enterprise
And dangerous success° of bloody wars

As I intend more good to you and yours
Than ever you and yours by me were harmed!
QUEEN ELIZABETH
What good is covered with the face of heaven,     240
To be discovered, that can do me good?
KING RICHARD
Th' advancement of your children, gentle lady.
QUEEN ELIZABETH
Up to some scaffold, there to lose their heads!
KING RICHARD
Unto the dignity and height of fortune,
The high imperial type° of this earth's glory.     245
QUEEN ELIZABETH
Flatter my sorrow with report of it.
Tell me, what state, what dignity, what honor
Canst thou demise° to any child of mine?
KING RICHARD
Even all I have—ay, and myself and all
Will I withal° endow a child of thine,     250
So in the Lethe° of thy angry soul
Thou drown the sad remembrance of those wrongs
Which thou supposest I have done to thee.
QUEEN ELIZABETH
Be brief, lest that the process° of thy kindness
Last longer telling than thy kindness' date.°     255
KING RICHARD
Then know that from my soul I love thy daughter.
QUEEN ELIZABETH
My daughter's mother thinks it with her soul.
KING RICHARD
What do you think?
QUEEN ELIZABETH
That thou dost love my daughter from° thy soul.
So from thy soul's love didst thou love her brothers,     260
And from my heart's love I do thank thee for it.
KING RICHARD
Be not so hasty to confound my meaning.
I mean that with my soul I love thy daughter
And do intend to make her Queen of England.
QUEEN ELIZABETH
Well then, who dost thou mean shall be her king?     265
KING RICHARD
Even he that makes her queen. Who else should be?
QUEEN ELIZABETH
What, thou?
KING RICHARD      Even so. How think you of it?
QUEEN ELIZABETH
How canst thou woo her?
KING RICHARD      That would I learn of you,
As one being best acquainted with her humor.°
QUEEN ELIZABETH
And wilt thou learn of me?
KING RICHARD      Madam, with all my heart.     270
QUEEN ELIZABETH
Send to her by the man that slew her brothers
A pair of bleeding hearts; thereon engrave
"Edward" and "York." Then haply will she weep;
Therefore present to her—as sometimes° Margaret
Did to thy father, steeped in Rutland's blood—     275

---

200 **moe** more (in number)   203 **level** aim   207 **manners**
habits   218 **unavoided** inevitable; **doom** decree   219 **avoided**
**grace** the rejection of God's grace (by Richard)   223 **cozened**
defrauded   226 **indirectly** underhandedly   230 **still use**
continued habit   237 **success** result

245 **type** symbol   248 **demise** convey legally   250 **withal**
with   251 **Lethe** river of oblivion   254 **process** story   255
**date** duration   259 **from** apart from (i.e., not with)   269
**humor** disposition   274 **sometimes** once

A handkerchief, which, say to her, did drain
The purple sap from her sweet brother's body,
And bid her wipe her weeping eyes withal.°
If this inducement move her not to love,
Send her a letter of thy noble deeds:                             280
Tell her thou mad'st away her uncle Clarence,
Her uncle Rivers; ay, and for her sake
Mad'st quick conveyance° with her good aunt Anne.

KING RICHARD
You mock me, madam; this is not the way
To win your daughter.

QUEEN ELIZABETH     There is no other way,               285
Unless thou couldst put on some other shape
And not be Richard that hath done all this.

KING RICHARD
Say that I did all this for love of her.

QUEEN ELIZABETH
Nay, then indeed she cannot choose but hate thee,
Having bought love with such a bloody spoil.°           290

KING RICHARD
Look what° is done cannot be now amended.
Men shall deal unadvisedly° sometimes,
Which afterhours gives leisure to repent.
If I did take the kingdom from your sons,
To make amends I'll give it to your daughter.          295
If I have killed the issue of your womb,
To quicken your increase° I will beget
Mine issue of your blood upon your daughter.
A grandam's name is little less in love
Than is the doting title of a mother;                      300
They are as children but one step below,
Even of your metal,° of your very blood,
Of all one pain, save for a night of groans
Endured of° her for whom you bid° like sorrow.
Your children were vexation to your youth,              305
But mine shall be a comfort to your age.
The loss you have is but a son being king,
And by that loss your daughter is made queen.
I cannot make you what amends I would;
Therefore accept such kindness as I can.                310
Dorset your son, that with a fearful soul
Leads discontented steps in foreign soil,
This fair alliance° quickly shall call home
To high promotions and great dignity.
The king that calls your beauteous daughter wife      315
Familiarly shall call thy Dorset brother.
Again shall you be mother to a king,
And all the ruins of distressful times
Repaired with double riches of content.
What! We have many goodly days to see.                 320
The liquid drops of tears that you have shed
Shall come again, transformed to orient° pearl,
Advantaging their loan with interest
Of ten times double gain of happiness.
Go then, my mother, to thy daughter go;                325
Make bold her bashful years with your experience;
Prepare her ears to hear a wooer's tale.

Put in her tender heart th' aspiring flame
Of golden sovereignty; acquaint the princess
With the sweet silent hours of marriage joys.          330
And when this arm of mine hath chastisèd
The petty rebel, dull-brained Buckingham,
Bound with triumphant garlands will I come
And lead thy daughter to a conqueror's bed;
To whom I will retail° my conquest won,                335
And she shall be sole victoress, Caesar's Caesar.

QUEEN ELIZABETH
What were I best to say? Her father's brother
Would be her lord? Or shall I say her uncle?
Or he that slew her brothers and her uncles?
Under what title shall I woo for thee                      340
That God, the law, my honor, and her love
Can make seem pleasing to her tender years?

KING RICHARD
Infer° fair England's peace by this alliance.

QUEEN ELIZABETH
Which she shall purchase with still-lasting war.

KING RICHARD
Tell her the king, that may command, entreats.         345

QUEEN ELIZABETH
That at her hands which the king's King forbids.

KING RICHARD
Say she shall be a high and mighty queen.

QUEEN ELIZABETH
To wail the title, as her mother doth.

KING RICHARD
Say I will love her everlastingly.

QUEEN ELIZABETH
But how long shall that title "ever" last?             350

KING RICHARD
Sweetly in force unto her fair life's end.

QUEEN ELIZABETH
But how long fairly shall her sweet life last?

KING RICHARD
As long as heaven and nature lengthens it.

QUEEN ELIZABETH
As long as hell and Richard likes of it.

KING RICHARD
Say I, her sovereign, am her subject low.             355

QUEEN ELIZABETH
But she, your subject, loathes such sovereignty.

KING RICHARD
Be eloquent in my behalf to her.

QUEEN ELIZABETH
An honest tale speeds best being° plainly told.

KING RICHARD
Then plainly to her tell my loving tale.

QUEEN ELIZABETH
Plain and not honest is too harsh° a style.           360

KING RICHARD
Your reasons are too shallow and too quick.

QUEEN ELIZABETH
O no, my reasons are too deep and dead;
Too deep and dead, poor infants, in their graves.

KING RICHARD
Harp not on that string, madam; that is past.

---

278 **withal** with (it)   283 **conveyance** (1) carrying off (2)
underhand dealing   290 **spoil** destruction   291 **Look what**
whatever   292 **shall deal unadvisedly** are bound to act
thoughtlessly   297 **quicken your increase** give life to your
offspring   302 **metal** substance   304 **of** by; **bid** suffered   313
**alliance** marriage   322 **orient** shining

335 **retail** recount   343 **Infer** bring forward as an argument
358 **speeds best being** succeeds best when it is   360 **harsh**
discordant

QUEEN ELIZABETH
Harp on it still shall I till heartstrings break. 365
KING RICHARD
Now, by my George, my garter,° and my crown—
QUEEN ELIZABETH
Profaned, dishonored, and the third usurped.
KING RICHARD
I swear—
QUEEN ELIZABETH  By nothing, for this is no oath:
Thy George, profaned, hath lost his lordly honor;
Thy garter, blemished, pawned his knightly virtue; 370
Thy crown, usurped, disgraced his kingly glory.
If something thou wouldst swear to be believed,
Swear then by something that thou hast not wronged.
KING RICHARD
Then by myself—
QUEEN ELIZABETH  Thyself is self-misused.
KING RICHARD
Now by the world—
QUEEN ELIZABETH  'Tis full of thy foul wrongs. 375
KING RICHARD
My father's death—
QUEEN ELIZABETH  Thy life hath it dishonored.
KING RICHARD
Why then, by God—
QUEEN ELIZABETH  God's wrong is most of all.
If thou didst fear to break an oath with him,
The unity the king my husband made
Thou hadst not broken, nor my brothers died. 380
If thou hadst feared to break an oath by him,
Th' imperial metal circling now thy head
Had graced the tender temples of my child,
And both the princes had been breathing here,
Which now, two tender bedfellows for dust, 385
Thy broken faith hath made the prey for worms.
What canst thou swear by now?
KING RICHARD  The time to come.
QUEEN ELIZABETH
That thou hast wrongèd in the time o'erpast;
For I myself have many tears to wash
Hereafter° time, for time past wronged by thee. 390
The children live whose fathers thou hast slaughtered,
Ungoverned° youth, to wail it in their age;
The parents live whose children thou hast butchered,
Old barren plants, to wail it with their age.
Swear not by time to come, for that thou hast 395
Misused ere used, by times ill-used o'erpast.
KING RICHARD
As I intend to prosper and repent,
So thrive I in my dangerous affairs
Of hostile arms! Myself myself confound!°
Heaven and fortune bar me happy hours! 400
Day, yield me not thy light, nor, night, thy rest!
Be opposite all planets of good luck
To my proceeding if, with dear heart's love,
Immaculate devotion, holy thoughts,
I tender° not thy beauteous princely daughter! 405
In her consists my happiness and thine;
Without her, follows to myself and thee,

Herself, the land, and many a Christian soul,
Death, desolation, ruin, and decay.
It cannot be avoided but by this; 410
It will not be avoided but by this.
Therefore, dear mother—I must call you so—
Be the attorney of my love to her.
Plead what I will be, not what I have been;
Not my deserts, but what I will deserve. 415
Urge the necessity and state of times,°
And be not peevish-fond° in great designs.
QUEEN ELIZABETH
Shall I be tempted of the devil thus?
KING RICHARD
Ay, if the devil tempt you to do good.
QUEEN ELIZABETH
Shall I forget myself to be myself?° 420
KING RICHARD
Ay, if yourself's remembrance wrong yourself.
QUEEN ELIZABETH
Yet thou didst kill my children.
KING RICHARD
But in your daughter's womb I'll bury them,
Where in that nest of spicery° they will breed
Selves of themselves, to your recomforture.° 425
QUEEN ELIZABETH
Shall I go win my daughter to thy will?
KING RICHARD
And be a happy mother by the deed.
QUEEN ELIZABETH
I go. Write to me very shortly,
And you shall understand from me her mind.
KING RICHARD
Bear her my truelove's kiss; and so farewell. 430
                    *Exit* QUEEN [ELIZABETH].
Relenting fool, and shallow, changing woman!

*Enter* RATCLIFFE, [CATESBY *following*].

How now! What news?
RATCLIFFE
Most mighty sovereign, on the western coast
Rideth a puissant° navy; to our shores
Throng many doubtful hollow-hearted friends, 435
Unarmed, and unresolved° to beat them back.
'Tis thought that Richmond is their admiral;
And there they hull,° expecting° but the aid
Of Buckingham to welcome them ashore.
KING RICHARD
Some lightfoot friend post° to the Duke of Norfolk: 440
Ratcliffe, thyself—or Catesby; where is he?
CATESBY
Here, my good lord.
KING RICHARD  Catesby, fly to the duke.
CATESBY
I will, my lord, with all convenient° haste.
KING RICHARD
Ratcliffe, come hither. Post to Salisbury.

366 George . . . garter insignia of the Order of the Garter
(a figure of Saint George and a velvet ribbon) 390 Hereafter
future 392 Ungoverned unguided 399 confound ruin 405
tender look after tenderly

416 state of times condition of affairs 417 peevish-fond
obstinately foolish 420 myself . . . myself that I am I
424 nest of spicery alludes to the nest of the phoenix, a bird
that periodically returned to its fragrant nest, where it was
consumed in flame and arose renewed 425 recomforture
consolation 434 puissant powerful 436 unresolved
irresolute 438 hull drift with the wind; expecting awaiting
440 post hasten 443 convenient appropriate

When thou com'st thither—[*To* CATESBY.] Dull un-          445
  mindful villain,
Why stay'st thou here and go'st not to the duke?

CATESBY
First, mighty liege, tell me your highness' pleasure,
What from your grace I shall deliver to him.

KING RICHARD
O, true, good Catesby. Bid him levy straight
The greatest strength and power that he can make          450
And meet me suddenly at Salisbury.

CATESBY
I go.                                                *Exit.*

RATCLIFFE
What, may it please you, shall I do at Salisbury?

KING RICHARD
Why, what wouldst thou do there before I go?

RATCLIFFE
Your highness told me I should post before.              455

KING RICHARD
My mind is changed.

*Enter Lord* STANLEY [*Earl of Derby*].
                   Stanley, what news with you?

STANLEY
None good, my liege, to please you with the hearing,
Nor none so bad but well may be reported.

KING RICHARD
Hoyday, a riddle! Neither good nor bad!
What need'st thou run so many miles about                460
When thou mayest tell thy tale the nearest way?
Once more, what news?

STANLEY                    Richmond is on the seas.

KING RICHARD
There let him sink, and be the seas on him!
White-livered runagate,° what doth he there?

STANLEY
I know not, mighty sovereign, but by guess.              465

KING RICHARD
Well, as you guess?

STANLEY
Stirred up by Dorset, Buckingham, and Morton,
He makes for England, here to claim the crown.

KING RICHARD
Is the chair empty? Is the sword unswayed?
Is the king dead, the empire unpossessed?                470
What heir of York is there alive but we?
And who is England's king but great York's heir?
Then tell me, what makes he upon the seas?

STANLEY
Unless for that, my liege, I cannot guess.

KING RICHARD
Unless for that he comes to be your liege,               475
You cannot guess wherefore the Welshman comes.
Thou wilt revolt and fly to him, I fear.

STANLEY
No, my good lord; therefore mistrust me not.

KING RICHARD
Where is thy power then to beat him back?
Where be thy tenants and thy followers?                  480
Are they not now upon the western shore,
Safe-conducting the rebels from their ships?

STANLEY
No, my good lord, my friends are in the north.

KING RICHARD
Cold friends to me! What do they in the north
When they should serve their sovereign in the west?      485

STANLEY
They have not been commanded, mighty king.
Pleaseth your majesty to give me leave,
I'll muster up my friends and meet your grace
Where and what time your majesty shall please.

KING RICHARD
Ay, thou wouldst be gone to join with Richmond.          490
But I'll not trust thee.

STANLEY                    Most mighty sovereign,
You have no cause to hold my friendship doubtful.
I never was nor never will be false.

KING RICHARD
Go then and muster men; but leave behind
Your son George Stanley. Look your heart be firm,        495
Or else his head's assurance° is but frail.

STANLEY
So deal with him as I prove true to you.
                                        *Exit* STANLEY.

*Enter a* MESSENGER.

FIRST MESSENGER
My gracious sovereign, now in Devonshire,
As I by friends am well advertisèd,°
Sir Edward Courtney and the haughty prelate,             500
Bishop of Exeter, his elder brother,
With many moe confederates, are in arms.

*Enter another* MESSENGER.

SECOND MESSENGER
In Kent, my liege, the Guilfords are in arms,
And every hour more competitors°
Flock to the rebels, and their power grows strong.       505

*Enter another* MESSENGER.

THIRD MESSENGER
My lord, the army of great Buckingham—

KING RICHARD
Out on ye, owls! Nothing but songs of death?

*He striketh him.*

There, take thou that, till thou bring better news.

THIRD MESSENGER
The news I have to tell your majesty
Is that by sudden floods and fall of waters              510
Buckingham's army is dispersed and scattered,
And he himself wand'red away alone,
No man knows whither.

KING RICHARD              I cry thee mercy.
There is my purse to cure that blow of thine.
Hath any well-advisèd friend proclaimed                  515
Reward to him that brings the traitor in?

THIRD MESSENGER
Such proclamation hath been made, my lord.

*Enter another* MESSENGER.

FOURTH MESSENGER
Sir Thomas Lovell and Lord Marquis Dorset,

---

**464 runagate** fugitive

**496 assurance** security  **499 advertisèd** informed  **504
competitors** associates

'Tis said, my liege, in Yorkshire are in arms.
But this good comfort bring I to your highness:　520
The Britain° navy is dispersed by tempest.
Richmond in Dorsetshire sent out a boat
Unto the shore to ask those on the banks
If they were his assistants, yea or no;
Who answered him they came from Buckingham　525
Upon his party. He, mistrusting them,
Hoised° sail and made his course again for Britain.°

KING RICHARD
March on, march on, since we are up in arms,
If not to fight with foreign enemies,
Yet to beat down these rebels here at home.　530

*Enter* CATESBY.

CATESBY
My liege, the Duke of Buckingham is taken.
That is the best news. That the Earl of Richmond
Is with a mighty power landed at Milford
Is colder news, but yet they must be told.

KING RICHARD
Away towards Salisbury! While we reason here,　535
A royal battle might be won and lost.
Someone take order Buckingham be brought
To Salisbury; the rest march on with me.
　　　　　　　　　　　　　　　*Flourish. Exeunt.*

Scene [V. *Lord Stanley's house.*]

*Enter* [*Lord* STANLEY *Earl of*] *Derby, and Sir*
CHRISTOPHER [*Urswick, a chaplain*].

STANLEY
Sir Christopher, tell Richmond this from me:
That in the sty of the most deadly boar
My son George Stanley is franked up in hold;°
If I revolt, off goes young George's head;
The fear of that holds off my present aid.　5
So get thee gone; commend me to thy lord.
Withal say that the queen hath heartily consented
He should espouse Elizabeth her daughter.
But tell me, where is princely Richmond now?

CHRISTOPHER
At Pembroke or at Harfordwest° in Wales.　10

STANLEY
What men of name resort to him?

CHRISTOPHER
Sir Walter Herbert, a renownèd soldier,
Sir Gilbert Talbot, Sir William Stanley,
Oxford, redoubted Pembroke, Sir James Blunt,
And Rice ap Thomas, with a valiant crew,　15
And many other of great name and worth;
And towards London do they bend their power,
If by the way they be not fought withal.

STANLEY
Well, hie thee to thy lord. I kiss his hand;
My letter will resolve° him of my mind.　20

[*Gives letter.*]

Farewell.　　　　　　　　　　　　　　*Exeunt.*

# A C T　V

### Scene I. [*Salisbury. An open place.*]

*Enter* BUCKINGHAM *with* [SHERIFF *and*] HALBERDS,°
*led to execution.*

BUCKINGHAM
Will not King Richard let me speak with him?

SHERIFF
No, my good lord; therefore be patient.

BUCKINGHAM
Hastings, and Edward's children, Grey and Rivers,
Holy King Henry and thy fair son Edward,
Vaughan, and all that have miscarrièd　5
By underhand corrupted foul injustice,
If that your moody discontented souls
Do through the clouds behold this present hour,
Even for revenge mock my destruction!
This is All Souls' Day, fellow, is it not?　10

SHERIFF
It is, my lord.

BUCKINGHAM
Why, then All Souls' Day is my body's doomsday.
This is the day which in King Edward's time
I wished might fall on me when I was found
False to his children and his wife's allies.　15
This is the day wherein I wished to fall
By the false faith of him whom most I trusted.
This, this All Souls' Day to my fearful soul
Is the determined respite of my wrongs.°
That high All-seer which I dallied with　20
Hath turned my feignèd prayer on my head
And given in earnest what I begged in jest.
Thus doth he force the swords of wicked men
To turn their own points in their masters' bosoms.
Thus Margaret's curse falls heavy on my neck:　25
"When he," quoth she, "shall split thy heart with
　　sorrow,
Remember Margaret was a prophetess."
Come lead me, officers, to the block of shame;
Wrong hath but wrong, and blame the due of blame.
　　　　　　　*Exeunt* BUCKINGHAM *with* OFFICERS.

### Scene II. [*Camp near Tamworth.*]

*Enter* RICHMOND, OXFORD, BLUNT, HERBERT, *and
others, with drum and colors.*

RICHMOND
Fellows in arms and my most loving friends,
Bruised underneath the yoke of tyranny,
Thus far into the bowels° of the land
Have we marched on without impediment;
And here receive we from our father Stanley　5
Lines of fair comfort and encouragement.
The wretched, bloody, and usurping boar,
That spoiled your summer fields and fruitful vines,
Swills your warm blood like wash, and makes his
　　trough

**521 Britain** Breton　**527 Hoised** hoisted; **Britain** Brittany
**IV.v.3 franked . . . hold** penned up in custody (*frank* = sty)
**10 Harfordwest** Haverfordwest　**20 resolve** inform

**V.i.s.d. halberds** guards armed with long poleaxes　**19**
**determined . . . wrongs** end of reprieve for my unjust acts
**V.ii.3 bowels** center

In your emboweled° bosoms, this foul swine    10
Is now even in the center of this isle,
Near to the town of Leicester, as we learn.
From Tamworth thither is but one day's march.
In God's name cheerly on, courageous friends,
To reap the harvest of perpetual peace    15
By this one bloody trial of sharp war.

OXFORD
Every man's conscience is a thousand men
To fight against this guilty homicide.

HERBERT
I doubt not but his friends will turn to us.

BLUNT
He hath no friends but what are friends for fear,    20
Which in his dearest need will fly from him.

RICHMOND
All for our vantage. Then in God's name march!
True hope is swift and flies with swallow's wings;
Kings it makes gods, and meaner creatures kings.
                                   *Exeunt omnes.*


[Scene III. *Bosworth Field.*]


*Enter* KING RICHARD *in arms, with* NORFOLK, RAT-
CLIFFE, *and the Earl of* SURREY, [*and* SOLDIERS].

KING RICHARD
Here pitch our tent, even here in Bosworth field.
My Lord of Surrey, why look you so sad?

SURREY
My heart is ten times lighter than my looks.

KING RICHARD
My Lord of Norfolk!

NORFOLK                    Here, most gracious liege.

KING RICHARD
Norfolk, we must have knocks; ha, must we not?    5

NORFOLK
We must both give and take, my loving lord.

KING RICHARD
Up with my tent! Here will I lie tonight;

[SOLDIERS *begin to set up the king's tent.*]

But where tomorrow? Well, all's one for that.
Who hath descried the number of the traitors?

NORFOLK
Six or seven thousand is their utmost power.    10

KING RICHARD
Why, our battalia° trebles that account;
Besides, the king's name is a tower of strength,
Which they upon the adverse faction want.°
Up with the tent! Come, noble gentlemen,
Let us survey the vantage of the ground.    15
Call for some men of sound direction.°
Let's lack no discipline, make no delay,
For, lords, tomorrow is a busy day.        *Exeunt.*

*Enter* RICHMOND, *Sir William* BRANDON, OXFORD,
*and* DORSET, [HERBERT, *and* BLUNT].

RICHMOND
The weary sun hath made a golden set

And by the bright tract° of his fiery car°    20
Gives token of a goodly day tomorrow.
Sir William Brandon, you shall bear my standard.
Give me some ink and paper in my tent.
I'll draw the form and model of our battle,
Limit° each leader to his several charge,    25
And part in just proportion our small power.
My Lord of Oxford, you, Sir William Brandon,
And you, Sir Walter Herbert, stay with me.
The Earl of Pembroke keeps° his regiment;
Good Captain Blunt, bear my good-night to him,    30
And by the second hour in the morning
Desire the earl to see me in my tent.
Yet one thing more, good captain, do for me:
Where is Lord Stanley quartered, do you know?

BLUNT
Unless I have mista'en his colors much,    35
Which well I am assured I have not done,
His regiment lies half a mile at least
South from the mighty power of the king.

RICHMOND
If without peril it be possible,
Sweet Blunt, make some good means to speak with him    40
And give him from me this most needful note.

BLUNT
Upon my life, my lord, I'll undertake it;
And so God give you quiet rest tonight!

RICHMOND
Good night, good Captain Blunt. [*Exit* BLUNT.]
   Come, gentlemen,
Let us consult upon tomorrow's business.    45
Into my tent; the dew is raw and cold.
                      *They withdraw into the tent.*

*Enter,* [*to his tent,* KING] RICHARD, RATCLIFFE,
NORFOLK, *and* CATESBY.

KING RICHARD
What is't o'clock?

CATESBY              It's suppertime, my lord;
It's nine o'clock.

KING RICHARD I will not sup tonight.
Give me some ink and paper.
What, is my beaver° easier than it was?    50
And all my armor laid into my tent?

CATESBY
It is, my liege; and all things are in readiness.

KING RICHARD
Good Norfolk, hie thee to thy charge;
Use careful watch, choose trusty sentinels.

NORFOLK
I go, my lord.    55

KING RICHARD
Stir with the lark tomorrow, gentle Norfolk.

NORFOLK
I warrant you, my lord.                  *Exit.*

KING RICHARD
Catesby!

CATESBY
My lord?

KING RICHARD       Send out a pursuivant-at-arms°

---

**10 emboweled** ripped up
**V.iii.11 battalia** army  **13 want** lack  **16 direction** ability
to give orders

**20 tract** track; **car** chariot  **25 Limit** assign  **29 keeps** stays
with  **50 beaver** face guard of a helmet  **59 pursuivant-at-
arms** minor herald

To Stanley's regiment; bid him bring his power　60
Before sunrising, lest his son George fall
Into the blind cave of eternal night. [*Exit* CATESBY.]
Fill me a bowl of wine. Give me a watch.°
Saddle white Surrey° for the field tomorrow.
Look that my staves° be sound and not too heavy.　65
Ratcliffe!

RATCLIFFE
My lord?

KING RICHARD
Saw'st thou the melancholy Lord Northumberland?

RATCLIFFE
Thomas the Earl of Surrey and himself,
Much about cockshut time,° from troop to troop　70
Went through the army, cheering up the soldiers.

KING RICHARD
So, I am satisfied. Give me a bowl of wine.
I have not that alacrity of spirit
Nor cheer of mind that I was wont to have.

[*Wine brought.*]

Set it down. Is ink and paper ready?　75

RATCLIFFE
It is, my lord.

KING RICHARD
Bid my guard watch. Leave me. Ratcliffe,
About the mid of night come to my tent
And help to arm me. Leave me, I say.
　　　　　*Exit* RATCLIFFE. [KING RICHARD *sleeps.*]

*Enter* [STANLEY *Earl of*] *Derby, to* RICHMOND *in his
tent,* [LORDS *and* GENTLEMEN *attending*].

STANLEY
Fortune and victory sit on thy helm!　80

RICHMOND
All comfort that the dark night can afford
Be to thy person, noble father-in-law!
Tell me, how fares our loving mother?

STANLEY
I by attorney bless thee from thy mother,
Who prays continually for Richmond's good.　85
So much for that. The silent hours steal on
And flaky° darkness breaks within the east.
In brief, for so the season° bids us be,
Prepare thy battle early in the morning
And put thy fortune to the arbitrament　90
Of bloody strokes and mortal-staring° war.
I, as I may—that which I would I cannot—
With best advantage° will deceive the time°
And aid thee in this doubtful shock of arms.
But on thy side I may not be too forward,　95
Lest, being seen, thy brother, tender George,
Be executed in his father's sight.
Farewell; the leisure° and the fearful time
Cuts off the ceremonious vows of love
And ample interchange of sweet discourse　100
Which so long sund'red friends should dwell
　　upon.

God give us leisure for these rites of love!
Once more adieu; be valiant, and speed well.

RICHMOND
Good lords, conduct him to his regiment.
I'll strive with° troubled thoughts to take a nap,　105
Lest leaden slumber peise° me down tomorrow
When I should mount with wings of victory.
Once more, good night, kind lords and gentlemen.
　　　　　　　　*Exeunt. Manet* RICHMOND.
O thou whose captain I account myself,
Look on my forces with a gracious eye!　110
Put in their hands thy bruising irons of wrath,
That they may crush down with a heavy fall
The usurping helmets of our adversaries!
Make us thy ministers of chastisement,
That we may praise thee in the victory!　115
To thee I do commend my watchful soul
Ere I let fall the windows° of mine eyes.
Sleeping and waking, O defend me still!

*Sleeps.*

*Enter the* GHOST *of Prince Edward, son to Henry the
Sixth.*

GHOST (*To* RICHARD.)
Let me sit heavy on thy soul tomorrow!
Think how thou stab'st me in my prime of youth　120
At Tewkesbury. Despair therefor° and die!

(*To* RICHMOND.)

Be cheerful, Richmond; for the wrongèd souls
Of butchered princes fight in thy behalf.
King Henry's issue,° Richmond, comforts thee.
　　　　　　　　　　　　　　　　[*Exit.*]

*Enter the* GHOST *of Henry the Sixth.*

GHOST (*To* RICHARD.)
When I was mortal, my anointed body　125
By thee was punchèd full of deadly holes.
Think on the Tower and me. Despair and die!
Harry the Sixth bids thee despair and die!

(*To* RICHMOND.)

Virtuous and holy, be thou conqueror!
Harry, that prophesied thou shouldst be king,　130
Doth comfort thee in thy sleep. Live and flourish!
　　　　　　　　　　　　　　　　[*Exit.*]

*Enter the* GHOST *of Clarence.*

GHOST [*To* RICHARD.]
Let me sit heavy in thy soul tomorrow,
I that was washed to death with fulsome wine,
Poor Clarence, by thy guile betrayed to death.
Tomorrow in the battle think on me,　135
And fall° thy edgeless sword. Despair and die!

(*To* RICHMOND.)

Thou offspring of the house of Lancaster,
The wrongèd heirs of York do pray for thee.
Good angels guard thy battle! Live and flourish!
　　　　　　　　　　　　　　　　[*Exit.*]

---

63 **watch** timepiece　64 **Surrey** the name of a horse　65
**staves** lances　70 **cockshut time** twilight　87 **flaky** streaked
with light　88 **season** time　91 **mortal-staring** fatally glaring
93 **advantage** opportunity; **the time** the people of this time
98 **leisure** time available

105 **with** against　106 **peise** weigh　117 **windows** eyelids
121 **therefor** because of that　124 **issue** offspring　136 **fall**
let fall

*Enter the ghosts of* RIVERS, GREY, *and* VAUGHAN.

RIVERS [*To* RICHARD.]
Let me sit heavy in thy soul tomorrow,                    140
Rivers, that died at Pomfret! Despair and die!
GREY
Think upon Grey, and let thy soul despair!
VAUGHAN
Think upon Vaughan and with guilty fear
Let fall thy lance: despair, and die!
ALL (*To* RICHMOND.)
Awake, and think our wrongs in Richard's bosom           145
Will conquer him! Awake, and win the day!
                                        [*Exeunt.*]

*Enter the* GHOST *of Hastings.*

GHOST [*To* RICHARD.]
Bloody and guilty, guiltily awake,
And in a bloody battle end thy days!
Think on Lord Hastings. Despair and die!

(*To* RICHMOND.)

Quiet untroubled soul, awake, awake!                     150
Arm, fight, and conquer for fair England's sake!
                                        [*Exit.*]

*Enter the* GHOSTS *of the two young princes.*

GHOSTS (*To* RICHARD.)
Dream on thy cousins smotherèd in the Tower.
Let us be lead within thy bosom, Richard,
And weigh thee down to ruin, shame, and death.
Thy nephews' souls bid thee despair and die!             155

(*To* RICHMOND.)

Sleep, Richmond, sleep in peace and wake in joy.
Good angels guard thee from the boar's annoy!°
Live, and beget a happy race of kings!
Edward's unhappy sons do bid thee flourish. [*Exeunt.*]

*Enter the* GHOST *of Lady Anne his wife.*

GHOST (*To* RICHARD.)
Richard, thy wife, that wretched Anne thy wife,          160
That never slept a quiet hour with thee,
Now fills thy sleep with perturbations.
Tomorrow in the battle think on me,
And fall thy edgeless sword. Despair and die!

(*To* RICHMOND.)

Thou quiet soul, sleep thou a quiet sleep.               165
Dream of success and happy victory!
Thy adversary's wife doth pray for thee.      [*Exit.*]

*Enter the* GHOST *of Buckingham.*

GHOST (*To* RICHARD.)
The first was I that helped thee to the crown;
The last was I that felt thy tyranny.
O, in the battle think on Buckingham,                    170
And die in terror of thy guiltiness!
Dream on, dream on, of bloody deeds and death;
Fainting, despair; despairing, yield thy breath!

(*To* RICHMOND.)

I died for hope° ere I could lend thee aid;
But cheer thy heart and be thou not dismayed.            175
God and good angels fight on Richmond's side,
And Richard falls in height of all his pride.    [*Exit.*]

RICHARD *starteth up out of a dream.*

KING RICHARD
Give me another horse! Bind up my wounds!
Have mercy, Jesu! Soft! I did but dream.
O coward conscience, how dost thou afflict me!           180
The lights burn blue. It is now dead midnight.
Cold fearful drops stand on my trembling flesh.
What do I fear? Myself? There's none else by.
Richard loves Richard: that is, I am I.
Is there a murderer here? No. Yes, I am.                 185
Then fly. What, from myself? Great reason why!
Lest I revenge. What, myself upon myself?
Alack, I love myself. Wherefore? For any good
That I myself have done unto myself?
O no! Alas, I rather hate myself                         190
For hateful deeds committed by myself.
I am a villain. Yet I lie, I am not.
Fool, of thyself speak well. Fool, do not flatter.
My conscience hath a thousand several° tongues,
And every tongue brings in a several tale,               195
And every tale condemns me for a villain.
Perjury, perjury in the highest degree,
Murder, stern murder in the direst degree,
All several sins, all used in each degree,
Throng to the bar, crying all, "Guilty! Guilty!"        200
I shall despair. There is no creature loves me;
And if I die, no soul will pity me.
Nay, wherefore should they, since that I myself
Find in myself no pity to myself?
Methought the souls of all that I had murdered           205
Came to my tent, and every one did threat
Tomorrow's vengeance on the head of Richard.

*Enter* RATCLIFFE.

RATCLIFFE
My lord!
KING RICHARD
Zounds, who is there?
RATCLIFFE
Ratcliffe, my lord; 'tis I. The early village cock       210
Hath twice done salutation to the morn.
Your friends are up and buckle on their armor.
KING RICHARD
O Ratcliffe, I have dreamed a fearful dream!
What think'st thou, will our friends prove all true?
RATCLIFFE
No doubt, my lord.
KING RICHARD        O Ratcliffe, I fear, I fear!         215
RATCLIFFE
Nay, good my lord, be not afraid of shadows.
KING RICHARD
By the apostle Paul, shadows tonight
Have struck more terror to the soul of Richard
Than can the substance of ten thousand soldiers
Armèd in proof° and led by shallow Richmond.            220

157 **annoy** disturbance

174 **for hope** because of hope (to help)   194 **several** separate
220 **proof** tested armor

'Tis not yet near day. Come, go with me.
Under our tents I'll play the easedropper°
To see if any mean to shrink from me.
                    *Exeunt* RICHARD *and* RATCLIFFE.

*Enter the* LORDS *to* RICHMOND *sitting in his tent.*

LORDS
Good morrow, Richmond.
RICHMOND
Cry mercy,° lords and watchful gentlemen,                225
That you have ta'en a tardy sluggard here.
LORDS
How have you slept, my lord?
RICHMOND
The sweetest sleep and fairest-boding dreams
That ever ent'red in a drowsy head
Have I since your departure had, my lords.               230
Methought their souls whose bodies Richard mur-
    dered
Came to my tent and cried° on victory.
I promise you my heart is very jocund
In the remembrance of so fair a dream.
How far into the morning is it, lords?                   235
LORDS
Upon the stroke of four.
RICHMOND
Why, then 'tis time to arm and give direction.

*His oration to his soldiers.*

More than I have said, loving countrymen,
The leisure and enforcement of the time
Forbids to dwell upon; yet remember this:                240
God and our good cause fight upon our side;
The prayers of holy saints and wrongèd souls,
Like high-reared bulwarks, stand before our faces.
Richard except, those whom we fight against
Had rather have us win than him they follow.             245
For what is he they follow? Truly, gentlemen,
A bloody tyrant and a homicide;
One raised in blood and one in blood established;
One that made means° to come by what he hath,
And slaughterèd those that were the means to help
    him;                                                 250
A base foul stone, made precious by the foil°
Of England's chair, where he is falsely set;
One that hath ever been God's enemy.
Then if you fight against God's enemy,
God will in justice ward° you as his soldiers;          255
If you do sweat to put a tyrant down,
You sleep in peace, the tyrant being slain;
If you do fight against your country's foes,
Your country's fat° shall pay your pains the hire;
If you do fight in safeguard of your wives,              260
Your wives shall welcome home the conquerors;
If you do free your children from the sword,
Your children's children quits° it in your age.
Then in the name of God and all these rights,
Advance your standards, draw your willing swords.        265
For me, the ransom° of my bold attempt

Shall be this cold corpse on the earth's cold face;
But if I thrive, the gain of my attempt
The least of you shall share his part thereof.
Sound drums and trumpets boldly and cheerfully;          270
God and Saint George! Richmond and victory!
                                        [*Exeunt.*]

*Enter* KING RICHARD, RATCLIFFE, *and* [SOLDIERS].

KING RICHARD
What said Northumberland as touching Richmond?
RATCLIFFE
That he was never trainèd up in arms.
KING RICHARD
He said the truth; and what said Surrey then?
RATCLIFFE
He smiled and said, "The better for our purpose."        275
KING RICHARD
He was in the right, and so indeed it is.

*The clock striketh.*

Tell° the clock there. Give me a calendar.
Who saw the sun today?
RATCLIFFE                           Not I, my lord.
KING RICHARD
Then he disdains to shine; for by the book
He should have braved° the east an hour ago.             280
A black day will it be to somebody.
Ratcliffe!
RATCLIFFE
My lord?
KING RICHARD   The sun will not be seen today;
The sky doth frown and lour upon our army.
I would these dewy tears were from the ground.           285
Not shine today! Why, what is that to me
More than to Richmond? For the selfsame heaven
That frowns on me looks sadly upon him.

*Enter* NORFOLK

NORFOLK
Arm, arm, my lord; the foe vaunts in the field.
KING RICHARD
Come, bustle, bustle  Caparison my horse.                290
Call up Lord Stanley, bid him bring his power.
I will lead forth my soldiers to the plain,
And thus my battle shall be orderèd:
My foreward shall be drawn out all in length,
Consisting equally of horse and foot;                    295
Our archers shall be placèd in the midst;
John Duke of Norfolk, Thomas Earl of Surrey,
Shall have the leading of this foot and horse.
They thus directed,° we will follow
In the main battle, whose puissance° on either side      300
Shall be well wingèd with our chiefest horse.
This, and Saint George to boot!° What think'st thou,
    Norfolk?
NORFOLK
A good direction, warlike sovereign.
This found I on my tent this morning.

*He showeth him a paper.*

222 **easedropper** eavesdropper   225 **Cry mercy** (I) beg pardon
232 **cried** called aloud   249 **made means** contrived ways
251 **foil** setting for a gem   255 **ward** protect   259 **fat**
abundance   263 **quits** repays   266 **the ransom** the price paid
(if defeated)

277 **Tell** count   280 **braved** made glorious   299 **directed**
arranged   300 **puissance** power   302 **to boot** to our help

"Jockey° of Norfolk, be not so bold,                          305
For Dickon thy master is bought and sold."°
KING RICHARD
A thing devisèd by the enemy.
Go, gentlemen, every man unto his charge.
Let not our babbling dreams affright our souls;
Conscience is but a word that cowards use,                    310
Devised at first to keep the strong in awe;
Our strong arms be our conscience, swords our law!
March on, join bravely, let us to it pell-mell,
If not to heaven, then hand in hand to hell.

*His oration to his army.*

What shall I say more than I have inferred?                    315
Remember whom you are to cope withal,
A sort° of vagabonds, rascals, and runaways,
A scum of Britains and base lackey peasants,
Whom their o'ercloyèd country vomits forth
To desperate ventures and assured destruction.               320
You sleeping safe, they bring to you unrest;
You having lands, and blest with beauteous wives,
They would distrain° the one, distain° the other.
And who doth lead them but a paltry fellow,
Long kept in Britain° at our mother's cost,                    325
A milksop, one that never in his life
Felt so much cold as over shoes in snow?
Let's whip these stragglers o'er the seas again,
Lash hence these overweening rags of France,
These famished beggars, weary of their lives,                  330
Who, but for dreaming on this fond° exploit,
For want of means, poor rats, had hanged themselves.
If we be conquerèd, let men conquer us,
And not these bastard Britains, whom our fathers
Have in their own land beaten, bobbed, and thumped,           335
And in record left them the heirs of shame.
Shall these enjoy our lands? Lie with our wives?
Ravish our daughters? (*Drum afar off.*) Hark! I hear
   their drum.
Fight, gentlemen of England! Fight, bold yeomen!
Draw, archers, draw your arrows to the head!                   340
Spur your proud horses hard and ride in blood!
Amaze the welkin° with your broken staves!

*Enter a* MESSENGER.

What says Lord Stanley? Will he bring his power?
MESSENGER
My lord, he doth deny to come.
KING RICHARD
Off with his son George's head!                               345
NORFOLK
My lord, the enemy is past the marsh.
After the battle let George Stanley die.
KING RICHARD
A thousand hearts are great within my bosom.
Advance our standards, set upon our foes!
Our ancient word of courage, fair Saint George,              350
Inspire us with the spleen° of fiery dragons!
Upon them! Victory sits on our helms.           *Exeunt.*

[Scene IV. *Bosworth Field.*]

*Alarum; excursions.*° *Enter* CATESBY [*and* NORFOLK].
CATESBY
Rescue, my Lord of Norfolk, rescue, rescue!
The king enacts more wonders than a man,
Daring an opposite° to every danger.
His horse is slain, and all on foot he fights,
Seeking for Richmond in the throat of death.                   5
Rescue, fair lord, or else the day is lost!

*Alarums. Enter* [KING] RICHARD.

KING RICHARD
A horse! A horse! My kingdom for a horse!
CATESBY
Withdraw, my lord; I'll help you to a horse.
KING RICHARD
Slave, I have set my life upon a cast,°
And I will stand the hazard° of the die.                      10
I think there be six Richmonds in the field;
Five have I slain today instead of him.
A horse! A horse! My kingdom for a horse!
                                              [*Exeunt.*]

[Scene V. *Bosworth Field.*]

*Alarum. Enter* [KING] RICHARD *and* RICHMOND; *they
fight;* RICHARD *is slain. Retreat*° *and flourish. Enter*
RICHMOND, [STANLEY *Earl of*] Derby, *bearing the
crown, with divers other* LORDS.

RICHMOND
God and your arms be praised, victorious friends!
The day is ours; the bloody dog is dead.
STANLEY
Courageous Richmond, well hast thou acquit thee.
Lo, here this long-usurpèd royalty
From the dead temples of this bloody wretch                    5
Have I plucked off, to grace thy brows withal.
Wear it, enjoy it, and make much of it.
RICHMOND
Great God of Heaven, say amen to all!
But tell me, is young Stanley living?
STANLEY
He is, my lord, and safe in Leicester town,                   10
Whither, if it please you, we may now withdraw us.
RICHMOND
What men of name° are slain on either side?
STANLEY
John Duke of Norfolk, Walter Lord Ferrers,
Sir Robert Brakenbury, and Sir William Brandon.
RICHMOND
Inter their bodies as become their births.                    15
Proclaim a pardon to the soldiers fled
That in submission will return to us;
And then, as we have ta'en the sacrament,°
We will unite the White Rose and the Red.

---

305 **Jockey** nickname for John  306 **bought and sold**
betrayed for a bribe  317 **sort** set  323 **distrain** confiscate;
**distain** dishonor  325 **Britain** Brittany  331 **fond** foolish
342 **welkin** sky  351 **spleen** fierce spirit

V.iv.s.d. **excursions** sallies  3 **opposite** opponent  9 **cast**
throw (of dice)  10 **hazard** chance
V.v.s.d. **Retreat** trumpet signal to recall troops  12 **name**
high rank  18 **ta'en the sacrament** taken a solemn oath
(to marry Elizabeth when he won the crown)

Smile heaven upon this fair conjunction,°     20
That long have frowned upon their enmity!
What traitor hears me and says not amen?
England hath long been mad and scarred herself;
The brother blindly shed the brother's blood,
The father rashly slaughtered his own son,     25
The son, compelled, been butcher to the sire.
All this divided York and Lancaster,
Divided in their dire division,
O, now let Richmond and Elizabeth,
The true succeeders of each royal house,     30

By God's fair ordinance conjoin together!
And let their heirs, God, if thy will be so,
Enrich the time to come with smooth-faced peace,
With smiling plenty, and fair prosperous days!
Abate the edge° of traitors, gracious Lord,     35
That would reduce° these bloody days again
And make poor England weep in streams of blood!
Let them not live to taste this land's increase
That would with treason wound this fair land's peace!
Now civil wounds are stopped, peace lives again;     40
That she may long live here, God say amen! *Exeunt.*

**20 conjunction** joining in marriage

**35 Abate the edge** blunt the sharp point    **36 reduce** bring back

# THE TRAGEDY OF
# TITUS ANDRONICUS

### EDITED BY SYLVAN BARNET

## Introduction

*Titus Andronicus* has had few admirers and numerous detractors. T. S. Eliot states the detractors' case as directly as any: *Titus* is "one of the stupidest and most uninspired plays ever written, a play in which it is incredible that Shakespeare had any hand at all, a play in which the best passages would be too highly honored by the signature of Peele." Unlike Eliot's notably original view that *Hamlet* "so far from being Shakespeare's masterpiece . . . is most certainly an artistic failure," his remark on *Titus* is a commonplace: Dr. Johnson, Hazlitt, Coleridge, and the editor of the Yale edition denied Shakespeare's authorship of most of the play; the editor of the New Cambridge edition gives much of it to Peele and saves some of the Shakespearean passages only by the desperate expedient of claiming that they are not really bad but are a clever burlesque of bad writing.

The idea that *Titus* may not be entirely Shakespeare's is at least as old as 1687, when Thomas Ravenscroft, who had recently given the stage his adaptation of the play, recorded that he had been told that Shakespeare "only gave some master touches to one or two of the principal parts or characters." But the evidence that Shakespeare wrote *Titus* is weighty. In 1598 Francis Meres listed it as one of Shakespeare's plays, and in 1623 Heminges and Condell, who had acted with Shakespeare for some twenty years, included *Titus* in the Folio collection of his plays. However displeased we may be by part or all of *Titus*, there is no evidence that it is not his.

There are, of course, some inconsistencies that have been offered as proof that Shakespeare was revising an older play. We are told in II.iii.86 that Tamora's infidelity to the emperor has "made him noted [notorious] long," although Tamora and the emperor have been married only one night. But such an inconsistency proves no more about dual authorship than the similar treatment of time in *Othello*, or the apparently contradictory remarks about Macbeth's children. More serious is the shift of the villain's role from Tamora to Aaron, but again it does not prove that Shakespeare is revising an earlier play; probably he found the Moor Aaron coming to life as he worked on him, and Tamora simply fell into the background until the last act, when her part is stronger.

There is no sense trying to dissociate Shakespeare from *Titus;* all the available evidence insists that it is canonical. But neither is there any sense in emphasizing, as has recently been done, its connection with Shakespeare's early historical plays or with his later Roman tragedies. A good deal has been written about the Elizabethan history play as a dramatized sermon on the wounds of civil war, a sermon of special interest to Englishmen whose monarch was an aging and heirless queen. The later Roman plays, too, are seen to have political subjects. It is true, of course, that *Julius Caesar*, *Antony and Cleopatra*, and *Coriolanus* are all concerned in part with civil war, but it is hard to believe that while witnessing a performance of, say, *Antony and Cleopatra*, Shakespeare's audience fretted about the possibility that England would find itself the battlefield of triumvirs; rather it must have been watching with interest a story in which political themes are subordinated to the doings of a "lass unparalleled" and a general who becomes "the noble ruin of her magic." *Titus* does indeed concern itself, in part of the first scene, with establishing the succession in Rome; Titus is asked (I.i.186) to "help to set a head on headless Rome." But thereafter the motif fades from view until the fifth act, when Lucius, one of Titus' sons, leads an army against the vicious emperor whom Titus in the first scene helped to establish. In V.iii.67 ff. there is a speech stressing the horror of civil war, but it can scarcely be said to be closely related to what preceded it, and its ascription to a nameless "Roman Lord" suggests that it may well have been an afterthought. There is, furthermore, a curious bit of evidence that Shakespeare regarded the play as less political than did the earliest recorded interpreter, the printer or editor of the second quarto (1600). The first quarto (1594) concludes— as presumably Shakespeare concluded—with some lines about the deceased wicked queen:

As for that ravenous tiger, Tamora,
No funeral rite, nor man in mourning weed,
No mournful bell shall ring her burial;
But throw her forth to beasts and birds to prey.
Her life was beastly and devoid of pity,
And being dead, let birds on her take pity.

When a second edition was called for, it was apparently set up from a copy that had suffered some damage to the foot of the last leaf of text; the person overseeing the publication seems to have mistakenly thought that some lines had been lost at the foot, though in fact nothing was lost but "Finis the Tragedy of Titus Andronicus." He added four lines:

See justice done on Aaron, that damned Moor,
By whom our heavy haps had their beginning;
Then afterwards to order well the state,
That like events may ne'er it ruinate.

The last two lines, though bad, are appropriate enough and have their parallels in later plays when rather colorless characters assure their fellows that some sort of order is returning to the state, but certainly neither these lines nor the first scene should turn our minds from characters and passions to politics. Shakespeare himself ended the play by calling attention not to political concerns but to the pitiless queen whose body will be left for scavenging birds.

To say that Shakespeare ended his play with a comment on the queen and not on the state is not to deny that there are substantial passages devoted to the state. But the final lines emphasize the central concern of the play—the passions and deeds that are the stuff of tragedy. Critics tend to suggest that we go to a tragedy so that we may draw political and ethical conclusions, but the tragic dramatists tend to emphasize deeds of horror and passionate responses to these deeds. Even at the end of a play, the emphasis is not on drawing conclusions but on experiencing emotions. Nobody who witnesses Hamlet can feel that the entrance of Fortinbras shifts attention from tragic experiences to ethics and politics; attention is kept on the catastrophic happenings in Denmark.

AMBASSADOR                The sight is dismal;
And our affairs from England come too late.
The ears are senseless that should give us hearing.

HORATIO
But since, so jump upon this bloody question,
You from the Polack wars, and you from England,
Are here arrived, give order that these bodies
High on a stage be placèd to the view,
And let me speak to th' yet unknowing world
How these things came about. So shall you hear
Of carnal, bloody, and unnatural acts,
Of accidental judgments, casual slaughters,
Of deaths put on by cunning and forced cause,
And, in this upshot, purposes mistook
Fall'n on th' inventors' heads.
(Hamlet V.ii.369-71, 377-87)

The violence of Titus has often aroused condemnation, as though tragedy did not customarily dramatize violence. It is true that Titus has more than its share, but if, for example, we find especially abhorrent the introduction of the severed heads of two of Titus' sons, it is perhaps because we have forgotten (since directors customarily omit the business) a stage direction in the last act of Macbeth, "Enter Macduff, with Macbeth's head." Repulsive

happenings are not something Shakespeare dramatized in his youth and then outgrew; Hamlet concludes with four corpses (there would be a fifth if Horatio had his way), to say nothing of the earlier deaths or the skulls the grave-diggers unearth; King Lear calls for Gloucester to be blinded before the audience, and it concludes with the (to modern taste) gratuitous introduction of the corpses of Goneril and Regan, who have had the grace to die offstage. The dozen or so deaths in Titus are about double the number in Lear, and the rape and cannibalism in Titus are unparalleled elsewhere in Shakespeare, but they are not incompatible with the idea of tragedy. Nor are they mere Elizabethan sensationalism. If we recall Clytemnestra exulting over her slaughtered husband, or the incestuous Oedipus entering on the stage with bloody eyeless sockets, or the lecherous Pentheus, whose mother will in a frenzy exult over his severed head, we remember that none of the world's four great tragic dramatists shrinks from dramatizing the demonic and the horrible. We tend, especially if we are readers rather than spectators, to emphasize the wisdom and patience that are allegedly achieved through heroic suffering, but surely we ought to recall, for example, that Hamlet in the last act forces poison down Claudius' throat. Again, we can talk of purgation and reconciliation in King Lear, but we must recall that the cries and horrors do not disappear toward the end of the play; it is only seventy-five lines before the end that Lear enters with the dead Cordelia in his arms ("Howl, howl, howl, howl"), and the play closes with a dead march.

Of Shakespeare's early tragedies—Richard III, Titus, Richard II, and Romeo and Juliet—Titus is certainly the poorest, but it alone has a protagonist who is both noble and flawed, and thus it looks forward to Julius Caesar and to the greater tragedies. Romeo and Juliet, perhaps the best of Shakespeare's early tragedies, is an incomparably finer piece of work than Titus, but its vision of star-crossed lovers is quite different from the tragic vision of Hamlet, Othello, Lear, Macbeth, Antony and Cleopatra, and Coriolanus, whose protagonists in a significant way resemble Titus. In Romeo and Juliet the lack of any vigorous presentation of evil (in most of the greater tragedies Shakespeare did not hesitate to draw potent villains), the decisive role played by chance, the youth and innocence of the lovers, and the emphasis on reconciliation at the end, all work together to produce a tragedy that strikes us as substantially different from the later tragedies. Of course one can say that the lovers are in some measure responsible for their fates—if they had not loved they might have outlived their parents —but the overall impression is one of innocence destroyed by destiny and released from this transitory world to a timeless realm. Titus is something else; in it, as in the great tragedies, deeds recoil on the head of the doers and even well-intentioned deeds may have their painful consequences. Titus offers up Alarbus as a sacrifice to the souls of the dead, and he thereby incurs the hatred of Tamora. Declining to accept the title of emperor, Titus helps to establish Saturninus, who quickly proves to be his foe. Titus nominates Saturninus apparently because he is the elder son—a reasonable basis—but the first two speeches of the play suggest to the hearer that Bassianus rather than Saturninus is the fitter. What Shakespeare is doing, of course, is dramatizing what seems to be an essential tragic fact—a man doing something according to his best lights and according to an impressive but, as it proves, mistaken code. In his dealings with his sons, as well as with Tamora and Saturninus, Titus prefigures the great tragic heroes: Titus' inflexible conception of honor alienates him even from those he loves. He moves, a Titan, in a world of his own, at times heroically silent when lesser men would weep, at times loudly lamenting to the stones when lesser men would be silent. At the start it is said of him,

> A nobler man, a braver warrior,
> Lives not this day within the city walls. (I.i.25–26)

His nobility, his bravery, sets him off from others, even from his own sons, and (like Othello's high vision of Desdemona that leads him to kill her when he thinks her unchaste) Titus' virtues themselves become oppressive. His code of honor sets him apart from other men; he becomes increasingly aware of a painful isolation, and he speaks of it grandly, as a tragic hero should. Juliet comes to realize that her "dismal scene [she] needs must act alone"; Macbeth, plotting Banquo's death, keeps even his wife "innocent of the knowledge"; Hamlet speaks "wild and whirling words" and is markedly detached from Horatio, as well as from Claudius, Gertrude, and Ophelia; Lear will "abjure all roofs"; Coriolanus, told that he is banished from Rome, will reply "I banish you." Titus, the earliest of these protagonists, says of himself:

> For now I stand as one upon a rock,
> Environed with a wilderness of sea,
> Who marks the waxing tide grow wave by wave,
> Expecting ever when some envious surge
> Will in his brinish bowels swallow him.
> This way to death my wretched sons are gone,
> Here stands my other son, a banished man,
> And here my brother weeping at my woes:
> But that which gives my soul the greatest spurn
> Is dear Lavinia, dearer than my soul. (III.i.93–102)

Like Shakespeare's other tragic figures, he wears the shirt of Nessus and gives vent to his feelings. The speech is a little too self-conscious, the assonance, alliteration, and other repetitions are a little too insistent (*waxing, wave by wave; expecting, ever, envious; brinish bowels; stands, son; weeping, woes; soul, spurn, dear, dearer, soul*), but one would be hard pressed to point to a better passage in the work of any of Shakespeare's early contemporaries other than Marlowe.

Shakespeare must have felt that his chief problem was one of style, not of plot: what sort of rhetoric could effectively present the bloody and unnatural horrors that were the substance of Elizabethan tragedy and of classical tragedy as he knew it? There was, of course, no question of presenting tragic happenings "realistically"; tragedy was concerned with unusual people in unusual situations; its medium was verse, not prose. *Titus* contains a few brief exchanges in prose, and indeed the Clown's prose is notable ("God forbid, I should be so bold to press to heaven in my young days"), but when he wrote *Titus*, Shakespeare must have been unable to conceive of the significant role that prose might play in his tragedies. Even half a century or so after Shakespeare's great achievements in tragic prose, England's best dramatic critic of the time believed

that because tragedy shows us "nature wrought up to a higher pitch" it ought to be in verse. (Dryden advocated heroic couplets, however, not blank verse.) The verse drama of Shakespeare's infancy and much of that of his youth was rhymed, heavily alliterative, and rich in laments built on apostrophes, rhetorical questions, and exclamations. To us it seems stiff and foolish, even in the hands of, say, George Gascoigne, who was educated at Cambridge, and who wrote some lyric and satiric verse of considerable merit. Here is a passage from Gascoigne's tragedy *Jocasta*, produced at Gray's Inn in 1566:

ANTIGONE
> O doleful day, wherein my sorry sire
> Was born, and yet O more unhappy hour
> When he was crownèd king of stately Thebes.
> The Hymenei, in unhappy bed
> And wicked wedlock, wittingly did join
> The guiltless mother with her guilty son,
> Out of which root we be the branches born
> To bear the scourge of their so foul offense.

If a passage with less narrative content is wanted, the following will do to show the tragic lament full-blown:

ANTIGONE
> O weary life, why bid'st thou in my breast
> And I contented be that these mine eyes
> Should see her die that gave to me this life,
> And I not 'venge her death by loss of life?
> Who can me give a fountain made of moan,
> That I may weep as much as is my will,
> To souse this sorrow up in swelling tears?

Finally:
OEDIPUS
> O wife, O mother, O both woeful names,
> O woeful mother, and O woeful wife,
> O would to God, alas, O would to God
> Thou ne'er had been my mother, nor my wife.

That Gascoigne is translating does not obscure the kind or the quality of his verse. Shakespeare must have been very familiar with this sort of writing; in *A Midsummer Night's Dream* he neatly parodies (through Bottom's speech) the lament of the previous generation:

> But stay, O spite!
> But mark, poor knight,
> What dreadful dole is here!
> Eyes, do you see?
> How can it be?
> O dainty duck! O dear!
> Thy mantle good,
> What, stained with blood!
> Approach, ye Furies fell!
> O Fates, come, come,
> Cut thread and thrum;
> Quail, crush, conclude, and quell! (V.i.274–85)

More subtle, Hotspur's dying words in *1 Henry IV* have a touch of the same absurd apostrophe and alliteration that marked the older drama and that are appropriate to this anachronistic young knight:

> O Harry, thou hast robbed me of my youth!
> I better brook the loss of brittle life
> Than those proud titles thou hast won of me.
> They wound my thoughts worse than thy sword my flesh.
> But thoughts, the slaves of life, and life, time's fool. . . .
> (V.iv.75–79)

In *Titus* there is a good deal of alliteration, balance, and parallelism, especially in the first two acts:

> Patient yourself, madam, and pardon me. (I.i.121)
> Rome's readiest champions, repose you here in rest (I.i.151)
> Clear up, fair queen, that cloudy countenance.
> Though chance of war hath wrought this change of cheer (I.i.263–64)
> And curtained with a counsel-keeping cave (II.iii.24)

On the whole the impression is not that of naiveté; or if there is a suggestion of naiveté, it is that of a highly talented writer infatuated with his medium and occasionally forgetful of the dramatic ends that every speech ought to serve. Despite the abundant (almost comically frequent) horrors, the atmosphere is more that of the hothouse than the slaughterhouse; the horrors exist in elegant luxuriance, and though the groundlings probably were delighted, the author must have felt he was creating a drama that would appeal also to the cultivated, who knew Seneca and Ovid.

The Latin quotations that dot the play are the most apparent sign of the lamp, but the fifty-odd mythological allusions are scarcely less apparent. Despite the classical setting, Shakespeare did not have to strew his play with references to Pyramus, Vulcan, Cerberus, Prometheus, Hecuba, the Styx, Dido and Aeneas, Priam, Virginius, and a host of others. *Julius Caesar* has only a tenth as many mythological allusions, but when he wrote *Titus*, Shakespeare evidently was aiming at something quite different from the spare style he was to use in *Julius Caesar*. In *Titus* he seeks to capture grandeur by abundance. Here is a sample:

> Now climbeth Tamora Olympus' top,
> Safe out of fortune's shot, and sits aloft,
> Secure of thunder's crack or lightning flash,
> Advanced above pale envy's threat'ning reach.
> As when the golden sun salutes the morn,
> And having gilt the ocean with his beams,
> Gallops the zodiac in his glistering coach,
> And overlooks the highest-peering hills;
> So Tamora:
> Upon her wit doth earthly honor wait,
> And virtue stoops and trembles at her frown. (II.i.1–11)

The simile beginning in line 5 is markedly introduced by the prominent position that "As" occupies in the line, and it is markedly concluded by the similarly prominent

"So" in line 9; the explicit allusion to Olympus and the only barely less explicit allusion to Phoebus suggest that Shakespeare is attempting to climb, in Sidney's phrase, to "the height of Seneca his style." (Before the speech is over there will be a reference to Prometheus, and another to Semiramis.) Sidney was speaking, about 1585, of *Gorboduc* (1562), but his words apply to the infinitely superior *Titus*: "it is full of stately speeches and well-sounding phrases."

This heightened style, as well as the conception of a tragic hero pushed beyond the limits of endurance, surely owes something to Seneca, but Ovid, too, helped shape *Titus*. The grisly business of cooking Chiron and Demetrius and serving them as a meat pie to a parent is Ovidian as well as Senecan; Seneca's *Thyestes* includes such a feast, but so too does Ovid's tale of Procne in *Metamorphoses*. In a sense, the stories are inseparable; in *Thyestes*, Atreus himself compares the feast to that in the legend of Procne, and the basic idea of a parent dining on the flesh of his offspring (a vestige of rituals in which the father killed his son as his son became a competitor?) exists in various myths. In *Titus*, Shakespeare quotes—rather misquotes—bits of Seneca, but he alludes directly not only to the legend of Procne but to its rendition in the *Metamorphoses*. The strong Ovidian influence on Shakespeare's early writing, especially on the narrative poems, is beyond all doubt; Francis Meres said in 1598 what must have seemed commonplace: "The sweet witty soul of Ovid lives in mellifluous and honey-tongued Shakespeare; witness his *Venus and Adonis*, his *Lucrece*, his sugared sonnets." In *Love's Labor's Lost* a pedant, Holofernes, speaks of Ovid, and though Holofernes can scarcely be regarded as a reliable mouthpiece, here he seems to be voicing Shakespeare's opinion, though perhaps a little bumptiously: "For the elegancy, facility, and golden cadence of poesy, . . . Ovidius Naso was the man" (IV.ii.123–25).

Ovid's elegancy, facility, and golden cadence had been famous even in antiquity (Quintilian said Ovid was unable to curb his luxuriance—even as Ben Jonson was later to say that Shakespeare "flowed with that facility that sometime it was necessary he should be stopped"), and to English playwrights in the latter part of the sixteenth century Ovid must have seemed with Seneca to be the man to add dignity to the blatant huffings of earlier English tragedy. The earlier tragedies with their abundant "O's" were notably direct; Ovid is often equally direct, but he is also rich in comparisons. Philomela's severed tongue "writhed convulsively," a recent translation says, "like a snake's tail when it has been newly cut off and, dying, tried to reach its mistress' feet." In Arthur Golding's version of Ovid, which Shakespeare surely knew, the passage runs thus:

> And with a pair of pinsons fast did catch her by the tongue,
> And with his sword did cut it off. The stump thereon it hung
> Did patter still. The tip fell down, and quivering on the ground
> As though that it had murmured it made a certain sound,
> And as an adder's tail cut off doth skip a while, even so
> The tip of Philomela's tongue did wriggle to and fro,
> And nearer to her mistressward in dying still did go.

Here is Ovid's description (in Golding's words) of Pyramus' wound: Pyramus drew

>His sword, the which among his guts he thrust, and by and by
>Did draw it from the bleeding wound beginning for to die,
>And cast himself upon his back. The blood did spin on high
>As when a conduit pipe is cracked, the water bursting out
>Doth shoot itself a great way off and pierce the air about.

Probably Shakespeare felt that his description of the mutilated Lavinia was in the best Ovidian manner:

>                    Why dost not speak to me?
>Alas, a crimson river of warm blood,
>Like to a bubbling fountain stirred with wind,
>Doth rise and fall between thy rosèd lips,
>Coming and going with thy honey breath.   (II.iv.21–25)

In *Lucrece*, probably written in 1593, within three or four years of *Titus* and possibly within the same year, Shakespeare wrote:

>And from the purple fountain Brutus drew
>   The murd'rous knife, and as it left the place,
>   Her blood, in poor revenge, held it in chase.
>                                   (lines 1734–36)

To defend *Lucrece* would be even more difficult than to defend *Titus*, but it ought to be evident that Shakespeare is attempting to make art out of violence. For naked violence we must turn, say, to *Lear*, where a woman plucks an old man's beard, urges her husband to gouge out the old man's eyes, and stabs a servant in the back. In *Titus* the horror is for the most part elevated, or at least veiled by ingenuity.

This is not to say that Shakespeare's treatment of horror is successful in *Titus*: the testimony of generations of readers (few playgoers have had the chance to see *Titus*) strongly suggests that it is unsuccessful. The elaborate treatment occasionally disgusts us, though perhaps it was meant to distance the horror and thereby make it acceptable. But in its day, and for a couple of decades after, the play was popular; as late as 1614 Ben Jonson grumbled that *Titus* still had its admirers. It is a remarkable achievement, superior in character, in plot, and in language to *The Spanish Tragedy*, and it rivals Marlowe, whose plays are the only other major plays of the period. Its exuberance, though in places distressing, is a sign of imaginative fertility that was later to be splendidly husbanded. It is, of course, a play that is of its age, but if we strongly have this impression, is it not partly because Shakespeare went on to write plays that are not of an age but for all time?

### A NOTE ON THE SOURCE

Those Shakespeareans who are embarrassed by *Titus* (but who cannot overlook the strong evidence that he wrote it) sometimes assume that it represents his reworking of an older, and presumably worse, play. No such play has come to light, and though it is possible that Shakespeare's source was a play now extant only in Shakespeare's revision, it is more than possible—even likely—that his source was a prose tale regarded as history. The Folger Shakespeare Library has a unique copy of a mid-eighteenth-century booklet entitled *The History of Titus Andronicus*, which contains a prose narrative and a ballad. The ballad is a short metrical version of the prose narrative, but this latter seems to be a reprint of a much older piece—possibly of a late-sixteenth-century version that may have been Shakespeare's source. Certainly the prose narrative is not indebted to the play: it makes no reference to Shakespeare —as it surely would if it had been written in the eighteenth century—and it includes a good deal of alleged history that Shakespeare does not. Furthermore, some of its characters are unnamed; if the narrative were based on the play, Aaron, for example, would doubtless be mentioned by name, but he is merely called "the wicked Moor."

Put it this way: the extant *History of Titus Andronicus* is almost surely a reprint of a much older piece, quite possibly a reprint of the tale that Shakespeare dramatized. There is no opposing evidence.

The prose tale, like almost all fictions, draws upon earlier fictions: Lavinia calls attention to the parallel between her plight and Philomela's in Ovid's *Metamorphoses;* the banquet of human flesh is referred to in Ovid, and is an important part of Seneca's *Thyestes*. If Shakespeare did use the prose tale, he did not have to turn to Ovid or Seneca, but he surely knew some of their work at first hand anyway. But the source of the play is not simply in specific books. The play is indebted to an Elizabethan idea of what a classical tragedy ought to be—richly ornamented, with a hero overwhelmed by passion and driven to seek revenge. The villainous Aaron, however, is derived from another dramatic tradition, that of the native morality play, which offered (in the Vice) models of ingenious, unpitying villainy. The Senecan and Ovidian influences— first-hand or through the prose tale—are real, but they have been discussed almost too much; this native influence has been almost neglected except for the good study by Bernard Spivack, *Shakespeare and the Allegory of Evil*. (For a full discussion of the possible debts to numerous books, see Geoffrey Bullough, *Narrative and Dramatic Sources of Shakespeare*, Vol. VI.)

### A NOTE ON THE TEXT

There is an allusion to a Roman hero named Titus in *A Knack To Know a Knave*, acted in June 1592. Though the allusion may, of course, be to an earlier play on the subject rather than to Shakespeare's play, there is no need to multiply entities; Shakespeare's *Titus Andronicus* may have been on the stage before 1592. The next bit of evidence is a reference of January 23, 1594, in Henslowe's *Diary* to the effect that Sussex's men acted a new piece, "titus & ondronicus." If the allusion in *A Knave* is not to Shakespeare's play, quite possibly *Titus Andronicus* was indeed new in 1594, but it is equally possible that it was "new" only to Sussex's company, or that it had been newly revised. On February 6, 1594, the Stationers' Register entered "a book intituled a Noble Roman Historye of

Titus Andronicus." Perhaps this entry alludes to the play, which indeed was published in 1594, though possibly the entry is to some other piece on the same subject. In 1614 Ben Jonson, in the Induction to *Bartholomew Fair*, mentions that Andronicus was seen on the stage as long ago as "fiue and twentie or thirtie yeeres"; strictly, Jonson's reference would date the play 1584–89, though probably he is speaking loosely and his evidence surely does not prohibit a date in the early nineties. The date widely favored is 1592–94, but there is no compelling reason to believe that *Titus* could not have been written in the late eighties.

Only one copy of the first quarto (1594) is known to be extant. Apparently the first quarto (Q1) was printed from Shakespeare's manuscript or from a copy of it; a number of stage directions—such as "*Enter . . . as many as can be*"—suggest an author's hand. In 1600 a second quarto (Q2) was issued. It omits a few lines, adds some, and alters a good deal of punctuation. There is no reason to believe that the alterations represent Shakespeare's revisions; probably all the revisions are a compositor's tamperings. Q3, issued in 1611, was set up from Q2 and therefore has no authority. The version in the First Folio (F) is based on Q3 but makes numerous small alterations (especially in stage directions) and adds an entire scene (III.ii). The new scene is of sufficient excellence to be Shakespeare's, and though the other changes in F do not suggest that great effort was made to give the play in a version much different from that of Q3, the new scene shows that the editors had access to some unpublished material. The present edition is based on Q1, except for III.ii, which is, of course, based on F. It regularizes speech prefixes (for example, Q1's "Saturnine," "Saturninus," "King," "Satur," are all given here as "Saturninus"); it slightly alters the position of a few stage directions, and it modernizes spelling and punctuation. The act divisions were first established by F; the scene divisions are the work of later editors and though of no authenticity they provide a convenient device for reference. Departures from Q1, other than those mentioned above and corrections of obvious typographical errors, are listed below, the adopted reading first, in boldface, followed by the original reading in roman. If the adopted reading is from Q2, Q3, or F, that fact is indicated in a bracket following the reading. If there is no such indication, the adopted reading is an editor's conjecture.

**I.i.35** [for the three and a half lines that follow these words in Q1 see footnote to the line] **69 s.d. her three sons** her two sonnes **98 manes** manus **226 Titan's** [Q2] Tytus **242 Pantheon** Pathan **264 chance** [Q2] change **280 cuique** cuiqum **317 Phoebe** Thebe **358 s.d. speak** speakes **369 Martius** 3. Sonne **370 Quintus** 2. Sonne **372 Quintus** 2. sonne **391** [Q1 follows with s.d.: "*Exit all but Marcus and Titus*," and the other early texts also indicate an exit] **399 Yes . . . remunerate** [F; omitted in the quartos]
**II.i.110 than** this
**II.ii.1 morn** [F] Moone
**II.iii.69 try** [Q2] trie thy **72 swart** swartie **160 ears** [Q3] yeares **210 unhallowed** [F] vnhollow **222 berayed** bereaud **231 Pyramus** [Q2] Pramus **236 Cocytus** Ocitus
**II.iv.27 him** them **30 three** their
**III.i.146 his true** her true
**III.ii** [this scene is found only in F] **39 complainer** complayne **52 thy knife** knife **53 fly** Flys **55 are cloyed** cloi'd **72 myself** my selfes
**IV.i.50 quotes** [Q2] coats **88 hope** [Q2] hop [or "I op"]
**IV.ii.95 Alcides** [Q2] Alciades
**IV.iii.57 Saturn** Saturnine **78 News** [Q2] Clowne. Newes
**IV.iv.5 know, as know** know **48 By** be **98 ears** [F] yeares
**V.ii.52 murd'rers** murder; **caves** cares **56 Hyperion's** Epeons **65 worldly** [Q2] worldie
**V.iii.125 cause** course **144 adjudged** [F] adiudge **154 blood-stained** blood slaine **163 Sung** [Q2] Song

# THE TRAGEDY OF
# TITUS ANDRONICUS

[Dramatis Personae

SATURNINUS *son to the late Emperor of Rome, afterward emperor*
BASSIANUS *brother to Saturninus*
TITUS ANDRONICUS *a noble Roman*
MARCUS ANDRONICUS *tribune, and brother to Titus*
LUCIUS
QUINTUS
MARTIUS } *sons to Titus Andronicus*
MUTIUS
YOUNG LUCIUS *a boy, son to Lucius*
PUBLIUS *son to Marcus Andronicus*
SEMPRONIUS
CAIUS } *kinsmen to Titus Andronicus*
VALENTINE

AEMILIUS *a noble Roman*
ALARBUS
DEMETRIUS } *sons to Tamora*
CHIRON
AARON *a Moor, beloved by Tamora*
A CAPTAIN
A MESSENGER
A CLOWN
TAMORA *Queen of the Goths*
LAVINIA *daughter to Titus Andronicus*
NURSE *and a blackamoor* INFANT
ROMANS GOTHS SENATORS TRIBUNES
  OFFICERS SOLDIERS ATTENDANTS

*Scene:* Rome, and the countryside near it]

## [ ACT I ]

[Scene I. *Rome. Before the Capitol.*]

[*Flourish.°*] *Enter the* TRIBUNES *and* SENATORS *aloft; and then enter* SATURNINUS *and his* FOLLOWERS *at one door, and* BASSIANUS *and his* FOLLOWERS [*at the other,*] *with drums and trumpets.*

SATURNINUS
Noble patricians, patrons of my right,
Defend the justice of my cause with arms;
And, countrymen, my loving followers,
Plead my successive title° with your swords.
I am his first-born son that was the last          5
That ware the imperial diadem of Rome;
Then let my father's honors live in me,
Nor wrong mine age° with this indignity.

*The decorative border above appeared on the title page of the second quarto edition of* Titus Andronicus, *1600.*

**I.i.s.d. Flourish** trumpet fanfare   **4 successive title** right to the succession   **8 age** seniority

BASSIANUS
Romans, friends, followers, favorers of my right,
If ever Bassianus, Caesar's son,               10
Were gracious° in the eyes of royal Rome,
Keep° then this passage to the Capitol,
And suffer not dishonor to approach
The imperial seat, to virtue consecrate,
To justice, continence,° and nobility;          15
But let desert in pure election shine,
And, Romans, fight for freedom in your choice.
MARCUS (*With the crown.*)
Princes, that strive by factions and by friends
Ambitiously for rule and empery,°
Know that the people of Rome, for whom we stand   20
A special party, have by common voice,
In election for the Roman empery,
Chosen Andronicus, surnamèd Pius
For many good and great deserts to Rome.

**11 gracious** acceptable   **12 Keep** guard   **15 continence** restraint   **19 empery** dominion (but in line 22 *empery* = emperor)

290

A nobler man, a braver warrior, 25
Lives not this day within the city walls.
He by the senate is accited° home
From weary wars against the barbarous Goths;
That with his sons, a terror to our foes,
Hath yoked° a nation strong, trained up in arms. 30
Ten years are spent since first he undertook
This cause of Rome, and chastisèd with arms
Our enemies' pride: five times he hath returned
Bleeding to Rome, bearing his valiant sons
In coffins from the field.° 35
And now at last, laden with honor's spoils,
Returns the good Andronicus to Rome,
Renownèd Titus, flourishing in arms.
Let us entreat, by honor of his name,
Whom worthily you would have now succeed, 40
And in the Capitol and senate's right,°
Whom you pretend° to honor and adore,
That you withdraw you and abate your strength,
Dismiss your followers, and, as suitors should,
Plead your deserts in peace and humbleness. 45

SATURNINUS
How fair° the tribune speaks to calm my thoughts!

BASSIANUS
Marcus Andronicus, so I do affy°
In thy uprightness and integrity,
And so I love and honor thee and thine,
Thy noble brother Titus and his sons, 50
And her to whom my thoughts are humbled all,
Gracious Lavinia, Rome's rich ornament,
That I will here dismiss my loving friends;
And to my fortunes and the people's favor
Commit my cause in balance to be weighed. 55
               *Exit [his]* SOLDIERS.

SATURNINUS
Friends, that have been thus forward in my right,
I thank you all, and here dismiss you all,
And to the love and favor of my country
Commit myself, my person, and the cause.°
               [*Exeunt his* FOLLOWERS.]
Rome, be as just and gracious unto me 60
As I am confident and kind° to thee.
Open the gates and let me in.

BASSIANUS
Tribunes, and me, a poor competitor.°
           [*Flourish.*] *They go up into the senate house.*

*Enter a* CAPTAIN.

CAPTAIN
Romans, make way! The good Andronicus,
Patron° of virtue, Rome's best champion, 65

Successful in the battles that he fights,
With honor and with fortune is returned
From where he circumscribèd with his sword
And brought to yoke the enemies of Rome.

*Sound drums and trumpets, and then enter two of Titus'*
SONS, *and then two* MEN *bearing a coffin covered with
black, then two other* SONS, *then* TITUS *Andronicus, and
then* TAMORA, *the Queen of Goths, and her three sons*
[ALARBUS,] CHIRON, *and* DEMETRIUS, *with* AARON
*the Moor, and others as many as can be; then set down the
coffin, and* TITUS *speaks.*

TITUS
Hail, Rome, victorious in thy mourning weeds!° 70
Lo, as the bark that hath discharged his fraught°
Returns with precious lading to the bay
From whence at first she weighed her anchorage,°
Cometh Andronicus, bound with laurel boughs,
To resalute his country with his tears, 75
Tears of true joy for his return to Rome.
Thou° great defender of this Capitol,
Stand gracious to the rites that we intend!
Romans, of five and twenty valiant sons,
Half of the number that King Priam had, 80
Behold the poor remains, alive and dead!
These that survive let Rome reward with love;
These that I bring unto their latest° home,
With burial amongst their ancestors.
Here Goths have given me leave to sheathe my sword. 85
Titus, unkind° and careless of thine own,
Why suffer'st thou thy sons, unburied yet,
To hover on the dreadful shore of Styx?°
Make way to lay them by their brethren.°

*They open the tomb.*

There greet in silence, as the dead are wont, 90
And sleep in peace, slain in your country's wars!
O sacred receptacle of my joys,
Sweet cell of virtue and nobility,
How many sons hast thou of mine in store,
That thou wilt never render to me more! 95

LUCIUS
Give us the proudest prisoner of the Goths,
That we may hew his limbs, and on a pile
Ad manes fratrum° sacrifice his flesh,
Before this earthy prison of their bones,
That so the shadows be not unappeased, 100
Nor we disturbed with prodigies° on earth.

TITUS
I give him you, the noblest that survives,
The eldest son of this distressèd queen.

TAMORA
Stay, Roman brethren! Gracious conqueror,
Victorious Titus, rue the tears I shed, 105
A mother's tears in passion° for her son:
And if thy sons were ever dear to thee,

---

27 **accited** summoned   30 **yoked** subjugated   35 **field**
this word is followed by "and at this day/to the monument of that Andronici/Done sacrifice of expiation,/And
slain the noblest prisoner of the Goths." (These lines, omitted
from the second and third quartos and from the Folio, are
inconsistent with the ensuing action, in which Alarbus is
sacrificed; perhaps Shakespeare neglected to cancel them in the
manuscript after deciding to make Alarbus' execution part of
the action)   41 **the . . . right** the right of the Capitol and
the senate   42 **pretend** claim   46 **fair** courteously   47 **affy**
trust   59 **cause** affair   61 **confident and kind** trusting and
natural(ly devoted)   63 **competitor** candidate   65 **Patron**
representative

70 **weeds** apparel   71 **his fraught** its freight   73 **anchorage**
anchors   77 **Thou** Jupiter   83 **latest** last   86 **unkind** unnatural   88 **Styx** river surrounding Hades   89 **brethren**
trisyllabic here and occasionally elsewhere ("breth-e-ren")
98 **Ad manes fratrum** to the ghosts of our brothers (Latin)
101 **prodigies** ominous disturbances   106 **passion** violent
emotion

O, think my son to be as dear to me!
Sufficeth not that we are brought to Rome,
To beautify thy triumphs° and return,                          110
Captive to thee and to thy Roman yoke,
But must my sons be slaughtered in the streets,
For valiant doings in their country's cause?
O, if to fight for king and commonweal
Were piety in thine, it is in these.                           115
Andronicus, stain not thy tomb with blood.
Wilt thou draw near the nature of the gods?
Draw near them then in being merciful;
Sweet mercy is nobility's true badge.
Thrice-noble Titus, spare my first-born son.                   120

TITUS
Patient° yourself, madam, and pardon me.
These are their brethren, whom your Goths beheld
Alive and dead, and for their brethren slain
Religiously they ask a sacrifice.
To this your son is marked, and die he must,                   125
T' appease their groaning shadows that are gone.

LUCIUS
Away with him! And make a fire straight,
And with our swords, upon a pile of wood,
Let's hew his limbs till they be clean consumed.
                    *Exit Titus'* SONS *with* ALARBUS.

TAMORA
O cruel, irreligious piety!                                    130

CHIRON
Was never Scythia° half so barbarous.

DEMETRIUS
Oppose° not Scythia to ambitious Rome.
Alarbus goes to rest, and we survive
To tremble under Titus' threat'ning look.
Then, madam, stand resolved, but hope withal°                  135
The selfsame gods that armed the Queen of Troy°
With opportunity of sharp revenge
Upon the Thracian tyrant in his tent
May favor Tamora, the Queen of Goths,
(When Goths were Goths and Tamora was queen)                   140
To quit° the bloody wrongs upon her foes.

*Enter the* SONS *of Andronicus again.*

LUCIUS
See, lord and father, how we have performed
Our Roman rites! Alarbus' limbs are lopped,
And entrails feed the sacrificing fire,
Whose smoke like incense doth perfume the sky.                 145
Remaineth naught but to inter our brethren,
And with loud 'larums° welcome them to Rome.

TITUS
Let it be so, and let Andronicus
Make this his latest farewell to their souls.

*Sound trumpets, and lay the coffin in the tomb.*

In peace and honor rest you here, my sons,                     150
Rome's readiest champions, repose you here in rest,

Secure from worldly chances and mishaps!
Here lurks no treason, here no envy° swells,
Here grow no damnèd drugs,° here are no storms,
No noise, but silence and eternal sleep:                       155
In peace and honor rest you here, my sons!

*Enter* LAVINIA.

LAVINIA
In peace and honor live Lord Titus long,
My noble lord and father, live in fame!
Lo, at this tomb my tributary° tears
I render for my brethren's obsequies,                          160
And at thy feet I kneel, with tears of joy
Shed on this earth for thy return to Rome.
O, bless me here with thy victorious hand,
Whose fortunes Rome's best citizens applaud.

TITUS
Kind Rome, that hast thus lovingly reserved                    165
The cordial° of mine age to glad my heart!
Lavinia, live, outlive thy father's days
And fame's eternal date,° for virtue's praise!

[*Enter above* MARCUS *Andronicus,* SATURNINUS,
BASSIANUS, *and others.*]

MARCUS
Long live Lord Titus, my belovèd brother,
Gracious triumpher in the eyes of Rome!                        170

TITUS
Thanks, gentle tribune, noble brother Marcus.

MARCUS
And welcome, nephews, from successful wars,
You that survive, and you that sleep in fame!
Fair lords, your fortunes are alike in all,
That in your country's service drew your swords,               175
But safer triumph is this funeral pomp,
That hath aspired° to Solon's happiness°
And triumphs over chance in honor's bed.
Titus Andronicus, the people of Rome,
Whose friend in justice thou hast ever been,                   180
Send thee by me, their tribune and their trust,
This palliament° of white and spotless hue,
And name thee in election for the empire
With these our late-deceasèd emperor's sons:
Be candidatus° then, and put it on,                            185
And help to set a head on headless Rome.

TITUS
A better head her glorious body fits
Than his that shakes for age and feebleness:
What° should I don this robe and trouble you?
Be chosen with proclamations today,                            190
Tomorrow yield up rule, resign my life,
And set abroad new business for you all?
Rome, I have been thy soldier forty years,
And led my country's strength successfully,
And buried one and twenty valiant sons,                        195
Knighted in field, slain manfully in arms,
In right and service of their noble country:

---

110 **triumphs** triumphal processions   121 **Patient** calm
131 **Scythia** a region in southern Russia noted for its savage
inhabitants   132 **Oppose** compare   135 **withal** with this
136 **Queen of Troy** Hecuba (who murdered the sons of
Polymnestor—"the Thracian tyrant"—of line 138—in revenge
for his murder of her son)   141 **quit** requite, repay   147
**'larums** alarums, calls to arms

153 **envy** malice   154 **drugs** poisonous plants   159 **tributary**
given as tribute   166 **cordial** comfort (literally, "stimulant to
the heart")   168 **date** duration   177 **aspired** risen; **Solon's
happiness** Solon said, "Call no man happy until he is dead"
182 **palliament** robe   185 **candidatus** candidate (Latin;
literally, "clad in white")   189 **What** why

Give me a staff of honor for mine age,
But not a scepter to control the world.
Upright he held it, lords, that held it last.          200
MARCUS
Titus, thou shalt obtain and ask° the empery.
SATURNINUS
Proud and ambitious tribune, canst thou tell?
TITUS
Patience, Prince Saturninus.
SATURNINUS          Romans, do me right.
Patricians, draw your swords and sheathe them not
Till Saturninus be Rome's emperor.          205
Andronicus, would thou were shipped to hell
Rather than rob me of the people's hearts.
LUCIUS
Proud Saturnine, interrupter of the good
That noble-minded Titus means to thee!
TITUS
Content thee, prince, I will restore to thee          210
The people's hearts, and wean them from themselves.
BASSIANUS
Andronicus, I do not flatter thee,
But honor thee, and will do till I die.
My faction if thou strengthen with thy friends,
I will most thankful be, and thanks to men          215
Of noble minds is honorable meed.°
TITUS
People of Rome, and people's tribunes here,
I ask your voices and your suffrages:
Will ye bestow them friendly on Andronicus?
TRIBUNES
To gratify the good Andronicus,          220
And gratulate° his safe return to Rome,
The people will accept whom he admits.°
TITUS
Tribunes, I thank you, and this suit I make,
That you create our emperor's eldest son,
Lord Saturnine; whose virtues will, I hope,          225
Reflect on Rome as Titan's° rays on earth,
And ripen justice in this commonweal:
Then, if you will elect by my advice,
Crown him and say, "Long live our emperor!"
MARCUS
With voices and applause of every sort,          230
Patricians and plebeians, we create
Lord Saturninus Rome's great emperor,
And say, "Long live our Emperor Saturnine!"

[A long flourish till they come down.]

SATURNINUS
Titus Andronicus, for thy favors done
To us in our election° this day,          235
I give thee thanks in° part of thy deserts,
And will with deeds requite thy gentleness:°
And for an onset,° Titus, to advance
Thy name and honorable family,
Lavinia will I make my empress,°          240

Rome's royal mistress, mistress of my heart,
And in the sacred Pantheon° her espouse.
Tell me, Andronicus, doth this motion° please thee?
TITUS
It doth, my worthy lord, and in this match
I hold me highly honored of your grace,          245
And here in sight of Rome to Saturnine,
King and commander of our commonweal,
The wide world's emperor, do I consecrate
My sword, my chariot, and my prisoners,
Presents well worthy Rome's imperious° lord.          250
Receive them then, the tribute that I owe,
Mine honor's ensigns° humbled at thy feet.
SATURNINUS
Thanks, noble Titus, father of my life!
How proud I am of thee and of thy gifts
Rome shall record, and when I do forget          255
The least of these unspeakable deserts,
Romans, forget your fealty° to me.
TITUS [To TAMORA.]
Now, madam, are you prisoner to an emperor,
To him that, for your honor and your state,
Will use you nobly and your followers.          260
SATURNINUS [Aside.]
A goodly lady, trust me, of the hue
That I would choose, were I to choose anew.

[Aloud.]

Clear up, fair queen, that cloudy countenance.
Though chance of war hath wrought this change of cheer,°
Thou com'st not to be made a scorn in Rome.          265
Princely shall be thy usage every way.
Rest on my word, and let not discontent
Daunt all your hopes. Madam, he° comforts you
Can make you greater than the Queen of Goths.
Lavinia, you are not displeased with this?          270
LAVINIA
Not I, my lord, sith° true nobility
Warrants° these words in princely courtesy.
SATURNINUS
Thanks, sweet Lavinia. Romans, let us go.
Ransomless here we set our prisoners free.
Proclaim our honors, lords, with trump and drum.          275
BASSIANUS
Lord Titus, by your leave, this maid is mine.
TITUS
How, sir! Are you in earnest then, my lord?
BASSIANUS
Ay, noble Titus, and resolved withal
To do myself this reason and this right.
MARCUS
Suum cuique° is our Roman justice.          280
This prince in justice seizeth but his own.
LUCIUS
And that he will, and shall, if Lucius live.

201 obtain and ask obtain if you ask for   216 meed reward
221 gratulate rejoice at   222 admits approves   226 Titan's
the sun god's   235 election here, as often in Shakespeare, -ion
is disyllabic   236 in as   237 gentleness nobility   238 onset
beginning   240 empress here, and often elsewhere in Titus,
trisyllabic ("em-per-es")

242 Pantheon temple dedicated to all the gods   243 motion
proposal   250 imperious imperial   252 ensigns tokens   257
fealty loyalty   264 cheer countenance   268 he he who   271
sith since   272 Warrants justifies   280 Suum cuique to
each his own (Latin)

**TITUS**
Traitors, avaunt!° Where is the emperor's guard?
Treason, my lord! Lavinia is surprised!°

**SATURNINUS**
Surprised! By whom?

**BASSIANUS**                    By him that justly may        285
Bear his betrothed from all the world away.
   [*Exeunt* MARCUS *and* BASSIANUS, *with* LAVINIA.]

**MUTIUS**
Brothers, help to convey her hence away,
And with my sword I'll keep this door° safe.
   [*Exeunt* LUCIUS, QUINTUS, *and* MARTIUS.]

**TITUS**
Follow, my lord, and I'll soon bring her back.
   [*During the fray, exeunt* SATURNINUS, TAMORA,
      DEMETRIUS, CHIRON, *and* AARON.]

**MUTIUS**
My lord, you pass not here.        290

**TITUS**
What, villain boy! Barr'st me my way in Rome?

   [*He stabs* MUTIUS.]

**MUTIUS** [*Dying.*]
Help, Lucius, help!

   [*Enter* LUCIUS.]

**LUCIUS**
My lord, you are unjust; and more than so,
In wrongful quarrel you have slain your son.

**TITUS**
Nor thou, nor he, are any sons of mine:        295
My sons would never so dishonor me.
Traitor, restore Lavinia to the emperor.

**LUCIUS**
Dead if you will, but not to be his wife
That is another's lawful promised love.        [*Exit.*]

*Enter aloft the emperor* [SATURNINUS] *with* TAMORA
*and her two* SONS *and* AARON *the Moor.*

**SATURNINUS**
No, Titus, no; the emperor needs her not,        300
Nor her, nor thee, nor any of thy stock:
I'll trust by leisure° him that mocks me once;
Thee never, nor thy traitorous haughty sons,
Confederates all thus to dishonor me.
Was none in Rome to make a stale°        305
But Saturnine? Full well, Andronicus,
Agree these deeds with that proud brag of thine,
That saidst I begged the empire at thy hands.

**TITUS**
O monstrous! What reproachful words are these?

**SATURNINUS**
But go thy ways, go, give that changing piece°        310
To him that flourished for her with his sword:
A valiant son-in-law thou shalt enjoy,
One fit to bandy° with thy lawless sons,
To ruffle° in the commonwealth of Rome.

**TITUS**
These words are razors to my wounded heart.        315

**SATURNINUS**
And therefore, lovely Tamora, Queen of Goths,
That like the stately Phoebe° 'mongst her nymphs
Dost overshine the gallant'st dames of Rome,
If thou be pleased with this my sudden choice,
Behold, I choose thee, Tamora, for my bride,        320
And will create thee Empress of Rome.
Speak, Queen of Goths, dost thou applaud my
   choice?
And here I swear by all the Roman gods,
Sith priest and holy water are so near,
And tapers burn so bright, and everything        325
In readiness for Hymenaeus° stand,
I will not resalute the streets of Rome,
Or climb my palace, till from forth this place
I lead espoused my bride along with me.

**TAMORA**
And here in sight of heaven to Rome I swear,        330
If Saturnine advance the Queen of Goths,
She will a handmaid be to his desires,
A loving nurse, a mother to his youth.

**SATURNINUS**
Ascend, fair queen, Pantheon. Lords, accompany
Your noble emperor and his lovely bride,        335
Sent by the heavens for Prince Saturnine,
Whose wisdom hath her fortune conquerèd.
There shall we consummate our spousal rites.
   *Exeunt omnes*° [*except* TITUS].

**TITUS**
I am not bid° to wait upon this bride.
Titus, when wert thou wont to walk alone,        340
Dishonored thus and challengèd° of wrongs?

*Enter* MARCUS *and Titus' sons* [LUCIUS, QUINTUS,
*and* MARTIUS].

**MARCUS**
O Titus, see, O, see, what thou hast done!
In a bad quarrel slain a virtuous son.

**TITUS**
No, foolish tribune, no; no son of mine,
Nor thou, nor these, confederates in the deed        345
That hath dishonored all our family,
Unworthy brother, and unworthy sons!

**LUCIUS**
But let us give him burial as becomes;°
Give Mutius burial with our brethren.

**TITUS**
Traitors, away! He rests not in this tomb:        350
This monument five hundred years hath stood,
Which I have sumptuously re-edified:°
Here none but soldiers and Rome's servitors
Repose in fame; none basely slain in brawls.
Bury him where you can, he comes not here.        355

**MARCUS**
My lord, this is impiety in you.
My nephew Mutius' deeds do plead for him;
He must be buried with his brethren.

*Titus' two* SONS *speak.*

---

283 **avaunt** be gone   284 **surprised** suddenly taken   288
**door** disyllabic   302 **by leisure** slowly   305 **stale** laughingstock   310 **changing piece** fickle wench   313 **bandy** contend,
bicker   314 **ruffle** brawl

317 **Phoebe** Diana, goddess of the moon   326 **Hymenaeus**
god of marriage   338 **s.d. omnes** all (Latin)   339 **bid** asked
341 **challengèd** accused   348 **becomes** is fitting   352 **re-
edified** rebuilt

[QUINTUS AND MARTIUS]
And shall, or him we will accompany.
TITUS
And shall? What villain was it spake that word?    360

*Titus'* SON *speaks.*

[QUINTUS]
He that would vouch it in any place but here.
TITUS
What, would you bury him in my despite?°
MARCUS
No, noble Titus, but entreat of thee
To pardon Mutius and to bury him.
TITUS
Marcus, even thou hast stroke upon my crest,    365
And with these boys mine honor thou hast wounded.
My foes I do repute° you every one,
So trouble me no more, but get you gone.
MARTIUS
He is not with himself; let us withdraw.
QUINTUS
Not I, till Mutius' bones be buried.    370

*The brother [MARCUS] and the* SONS *kneel.*

MARCUS
Brother, for in that name doth nature plead—
QUINTUS
Father, and in that name doth nature speak—
TITUS
Speak thou no more, if all the rest will speed.°
MARCUS
Renownèd Titus, more than half my soul—
LUCIUS
Dear father, soul and substance of us all—    375
MARCUS
Suffer° thy brother Marcus to inter
His noble nephew here in virtue's nest,
That died in honor and Lavinia's cause.
Thou art a Roman, be not barbarous:
The Greeks upon advice° did bury Ajax°    380
That slew himself; and wise Laertes' son°
Did graciously plead for his funerals:
Let not young Mutius then, that was thy joy,
Be barred his entrance here.
TITUS               Rise, Marcus, rise.
The dismal'st day is this that e'er I saw,    385
To be dishonored by my sons in Rome!
Well, bury him, and bury me the next.

*They put him in the tomb.*

LUCIUS
There lie thy bones, sweet Mutius, with thy friends,
Till we with trophies do adorn thy tomb.

*They all kneel and say:*

[ALL]
No man shed tears for noble Mutius,    390
He lives in fame that died in virtue's cause.

MARCUS
My lord, to step out of these dreary dumps,°
How comes it that the subtle Queen of Goths
Is of a sudden thus advanced in Rome?
TITUS
I know not, Marcus, but I know it is    395
(Whether° by device° or no, the heavens can tell).
Is she not then beholding° to the man
That brought her for this high good turn so far?
Yes, and will nobly him remunerate.

*Enter the emperor [SATURNINUS], TAMORA, and her
two SONS, with [AARON] the Moor, at one door. Enter
at the other door BASSIANUS and LAVINIA, with
others.*

SATURNINUS
So Bassianus, you have played your prize:°    400
God give you joy, sir, of your gallant bride!
BASSIANUS
And you of yours, my lord! I say no more,
Nor wish no less, and so I take my leave.
SATURNINUS
Traitor, if Rome have law, or we have power,
Thou and thy faction shall repent this rape.    405
BASSIANUS
Rape, call you it, my lord, to seize my own,
My true-betrothèd love, and now my wife?
But let the laws of Rome determine all;
Meanwhile am I possessed of that is mine.
SATURNINUS
'Tis good, sir; you are very short with us,    410
But if we live we'll be as sharp with you.
BASSIANUS
My lord, what I have done, as best I may
Answer I must, and shall do with my life.
Only thus much I give your grace to know—
By all the duties that I owe to Rome,    415
This noble gentleman, Lord Titus here,
Is in opinion° and in honor wronged,
That, in the rescue of Lavinia,
With his own hand did slay his youngest son,
In zeal to you, and highly moved to wrath    420
To be controlled° in that he frankly° gave.
Receive him then to favor, Saturnine,
That hath expressed himself in all his deeds
A father and a friend to thee and Rome.
TITUS
Prince Bassianus, leave to plead° my deeds;    425
'Tis thou and those that have dishonored me.
Rome and the righteous heavens be my judge,
How I have loved and honored Saturnine!
TAMORA
My worthy lord, if ever Tamora
Were gracious in those princely eyes of thine,    430
Then hear me speak indifferently° for all;
And at my suit, sweet, pardon what is past.

---

362 **in my despite** in spite of me   367 **repute** consider   373
**if . . . speed** if the rest is to go well (?) if the rest of you wish
to live (?)   376 **Suffer** allow   380 **advice** deliberation; **Ajax**
when Achilles' arms were given to Odysseus, Ajax in a fury
stabbed himself   381 **Laertes' son** Odysseus   392 **dumps** blues, melancholy state   396 **Whether** probably
pronounced "where"; **device** plot   397 **beholding** beholden,
indebted   400 **played your prize** won your contest   417
**opinion** reputation   421 **controlled** opposed; **frankly**
generously   425 **leave to plead** cease pleading   431 **indifferently** impartially

**SATURNINUS**

What, madam! Be dishonored openly,
And basely put it up° without revenge?

**TAMORA**

Not so, my lord, the gods of Rome forfend°        435
I should be author° to dishonor you!
But on mine honor dare I undertake°
For good Lord Titus' innocence in all,
Whose fury not dissembled speaks his griefs:
Then at my suit look graciously on him;        440
Lose not so noble a friend on vain suppose,°
Nor with sour looks afflict his gentle heart.

[*Aside.*]

My lord, be ruled by me, be won at last,
Dissemble all your griefs and discontents—
You are but newly planted in your throne—        445
Lest then the people, and patricians too,
Upon a just survey, take Titus' part,
And so supplant you for ingratitude,
Which Rome reputes to be a heinous sin.
Yield at entreats:° and then let me alone.°        450
I'll find a day to massacre them all,
And race° their faction and their family,
The cruel father and his traitorous sons,
To whom I suèd for my dear son's life;
And make them know what 'tis to let a queen        455
Kneel in the streets and beg for grace in vain.

[*Aloud.*]

Come, come, sweet emperor—come, Andronicus—
Take up this good old man, and cheer the heart
That dies in tempest of thy angry frown.

**SATURNINUS**

Rise, Titus, rise, my empress hath prevailed.        460

**TITUS**

I thank your majesty, and her, my lord.
These words, these looks, infuse new life in me.

**TAMORA**

Titus, I am incorporate in Rome,
A Roman now adopted happily,
And must advise the emperor for his good.        465
This day all quarrels die, Andronicus.
And let it be mine honor, good my lord,
That I have reconciled your friends and you.
For you, Prince Bassianus, I have passed
My word and promise to the emperor        470
That you will be more mild and tractable.
And fear not, lords, and you, Lavinia;
By my advice, all humbled on your knees,
You shall ask pardon of his majesty.

[**LUCIUS**]

We do, and vow to heaven, and to his highness,        475
That what we did was mildly as we might,°
Tend'ring° our sister's honor and our own.

**MARCUS**

That on mine honor here do I protest.

**SATURNINUS**

Away, and talk not, trouble us no more.

**TAMORA**

Nay, nay, sweet emperor, we must all be friends.        480
The tribune and his nephews kneel for grace.
I will not be denied. Sweet heart, look back.

**SATURNINUS**

Marcus, for thy sake, and thy brother's here,
And at my lovely Tamora's entreats,
I do remit these young men's heinous faults.        485
Stand up.
Lavinia, though you left me like a churl,
I found a friend, and sure as death I swore
I would not part° a bachelor from the priest.
Come, if the emperor's court can feast two brides,        490
You are my guest, Lavinia, and your friends.
This day shall be a love-day,° Tamora.

**TITUS**

Tomorrow, and° it please your majesty
To hunt the panther and the hart with me,
With horn and hound we'll give your grace bonjour.°        495

**SATURNINUS**

Be it so, Titus, and gramercy° too.
*Exeunt. Sound trumpets. Manet°* [AARON *the*] *Moor.*

# [ ACT II ]

[Scene I. *Rome. Before the palace.*]

[AARON *alone.*]

**AARON**

Now climbeth Tamora Olympus'° top,
Safe out of fortune's shot, and sits aloft,
Secure of° thunder's crack or lightning flash,
Advanced above pale envy's° threat'ning reach.
As when the golden sun salutes the morn,        5
And having gilt the ocean with his beams,
Gallops° the zodiac in his glistering coach,
And overlooks° the highest-peering hills;
So Tamora:
Upon her wit doth earthly honor wait,        10
And virtue stoops and trembles at her frown.
Then, Aaron, arm thy heart, and fit thy thoughts
To mount aloft with thy imperial mistress,
And mount her pitch,° whom thou in triumph long
Hast prisoner held, fettered in amorous chains,        15
And faster bound to Aaron's charming° eyes
Than is Prometheus° tied to Caucasus.
Away with slavish weeds° and servile thoughts!

**489 part** depart    **492 love-day** day appointed to settle disputes (with a pun on *day for love*)    **493 and** if    **495 bonjour** good morning (French)    **496 gramercy** thanks; **s.d. Manet** remains (Latin); clearly this and the next scene are continuous: the Folio's incorrect division into acts is retained merely to facilitate reference
**II.i.1 Olympus'** Mount Olympus' (reputed home of the gods)    **3 of** from    **4 envy's** hate's    **7 Gallops** gallops through    **8 overlooks** looks down upon    **14 mount her pitch** rise to the highest point of her flight (a term from falconry)    **16 charming** spellbinding    **17 Prometheus** a Titan fettered to a rock in the Caucasus because he stole fire from heaven    **18 weeds** apparel

**434 put it up** the figure is of putting up, or sheathing, a sword    **435 forfend** forbid    **436 author** agent    **437 undertake** assert    **441 vain suppose** empty supposition    **450 at entreats** to entreaties; **let me alone** leave it to me    **452 race** root out    **476 mildly . . . might** as mild as we might do    **477 Tend'ring** having regard for

I will be bright and shine in pearl and gold
To wait upon this new-made empress.      20
To wait, said I? To wanton with this queen,
This goddess, this Semiramis,° this nymph,
This siren, that will charm Rome's Saturnine
And see his shipwrack and his commonweal's.
Hollo! What storm is this?      25

*Enter* CHIRON *and* DEMETRIUS, *braving.*°

DEMETRIUS
Chiron, thy years wants° wit, thy wits wants edge,
And manners, to intrude where I am graced,°
And may for aught thou knowest affected° be.

CHIRON
Demetrius, thou dost overween° in all,
And so in this, to bear down me with braves.°      30
'Tis not the difference of a year or two
Makes me less gracious,° or thee more fortunate;
I am as able and as fit as thou
To serve, and to deserve my mistress' grace;
And that my sword upon thee shall approve,°      35
And plead my passions for Lavinia's love.

AARON
Clubs, clubs!° These lovers will not keep the peace.

DEMETRIUS
Why, boy, although our mother, unadvised,°
Gave you a dancing-rapier° by your side,
Are you so desperate grown, to threat your friends?      40
Go to; have your lath° glued within your sheath,
Till you know better how to handle it.

CHIRON
Meanwhile, sir, with the little skill I have,
Full well shalt thou perceive how much I dare.

*They draw.*

DEMETRIUS
Ay, boy, grow ye so brave?

AARON            Why, how now, lords!      45
So near the emperor's palace dare ye draw,
And maintain such a quarrel openly?
Full well I wot° the ground of all this grudge.
I would not for a million of gold
The cause were known to them it most concerns,      50
Nor would your noble mother for much more
Be so dishonored in the court of Rome.
For shame, put up.°

DEMETRIUS            Not I, till I have sheathed
My rapier in his bosom, and withal
Thrust those reproachful speeches down his throat,      55
That he hath breathed in my dishonor here.

CHIRON
For that I am prepared and full resolved,
Foul-spoken coward, that thund'rest with thy tongue
And with thy weapon nothing dar'st perform.

AARON
Away, I say!      60
Now, by the gods that warlike Goths adore,
This petty brabble° will undo us all.
Why, lords, and think you not how dangerous
It is to jet° upon a prince's right?
What, is Lavinia then become so loose,      65
Or Bassianus so degenerate,
That for her love such quarrels may be broached
Without controlment, justice, or revenge?
Young lords, beware! And should the empress know
This discord's ground,° the music would not please.      70

CHIRON
I care not, I, knew she and all the world:
I love Lavinia more than all the world.

DEMETRIUS
Youngling, learn thou to make some meaner° choice.
Lavinia is thine elder brother's hope.

AARON
Why, are ye mad? Or know ye not, in Rome      75
How furious and impatient they be,
And cannot brook competitors in love?
I tell you, lords, you do but plot your deaths
By this device.

CHIRON            Aaron, a thousand deaths
Would I propose° to achieve her whom I love.      80

AARON
To achieve her how?

DEMETRIUS            Why makes thou it so strange?°
She is a woman, therefore may be wooed;
She is a woman, therefore may be won;
She is Lavinia, therefore must be loved.
What, man! More water glideth by the mill      85
Than wots the miller of, and easy it is
Of a cut loaf to steal a shive,° we know:
Though Bassianus be the emperor's brother,
Better than he have worn Vulcan's badge.°

AARON [*Aside.*]
Ay, and as good as Saturninus may.      90

DEMETRIUS
Then why should he despair that knows to court it
With words, fair looks, and liberality?
What, hast not thou full often stroke a doe,
And borne her cleanly by the keeper's nose?

AARON
Why then, it seems, some certain snatch° or so      95
Would serve your turns.

CHIRON            Ay, so the turn were served.

DEMETRIUS
Aaron, thou hast hit it.

AARON            Would you had hit it too,
Then should not we be tired with this ado.
Why, hark ye, hark ye! And are you such fools
To square° for this? Would it offend you then      100
That both should speed?°

**22 Semiramis** legendary Assyrian queen, noted for her lust and beauty   **25 s.d. braving** challenging   **26 wants** the ending *-s* is frequently found with a plural subject   **27 graced** favored   **28 affected** loved   **29 overween** arrogantly presume   **30 braves** threats   **32 gracious** acceptable   **35 approve** prove   **37 Clubs, clubs** the cry raised to call the watch to separate brawlers in London   **38 unadvised** unwisely   **39 dancing-rapier** ornamental light sword   **41 lath** wooden (stage) sword   **48 wot** know   **53 put up** sheathe your weapons

**62 brabble** brawl   **64 jet** encroach   **70 ground** reason (with a pun on the musical meaning: bass to a descant)   **73 meaner** lower   **80 propose** be willing to meet   **81 Why . . . strange** Why do you seem surprised?   **87 shive** slice   **89 Vulcan's badge** the horns of cuckoldry (Vulcan's wife, Venus, deceived him with Mars)   **95 snatch** catch (the likelihood that there is also a sexual meaning here is increased by "turns" in the next line, a word often denoting sexual acts)   **100 square** quarrel   **101 speed** prosper

CHIRON                     Faith, not me.

DEMETRIUS

Nor me, so I were one.

AARON

For shame, be friends, and join for that you jar.°
'Tis policy° and stratagem must do
That you affect,° and so must you resolve,                    105
That what you cannot as you would achieve,
You must perforce° accomplish as you may.
Take this of me, Lucrece° was not more chaste
Than this Lavinia, Bassianus' love.
A speedier course than ling'ring languishment          110
Must we pursue, and I have found the path.
My lords, a solemn° hunting is in hand.
There will the lovely Roman ladies troop:
The forest walks are wide and spacious,
And many unfrequented plots° there are                    115
Fitted by kind° for rape and villainy.
Single° you thither then this dainty doe,
And strike her home by force, if not by words:
This way, or not at all, stand you in hope.
Come, come, our empress, with her sacred wit          120
To villainy and vengeance consecrate,
Will we acquaint withal what we intend,
And she shall file our engines° with advice,
That will not suffer you to square yourselves,
But to your wishes' height advance you both.          125
The emperor's court is like the House of Fame,°
The palace full of tongues, of eyes, and ears:
The woods are ruthless,° dreadful, deaf, and dull;
There speak, and strike, brave boys, and take your
    turns,
There serve your lust shadowed from heaven's eye,    130
And revel in Lavinia's treasury.

CHIRON

Thy counsel, lad, smells of no cowardice.

DEMETRIUS

Sit fas aut nefas,° till I find the stream
To cool this heat, a charm to calm these fits,
Per Stygia, per manes vehor.°               Exeunt. 135

[Scene II. *A forest near Rome*.]

Enter TITUS *Andronicus and his three* SONS [*and* MARC-
US], *making a noise with hounds and horns.*

TITUS

The hunt is up, the morn is bright and gray,°
The fields are fragrant, and the woods are green:
Uncouple° here, and let us make a bay,°
And wake the emperor and his lovely bride,

---

103 for . . . jar to get what you quarrel over  104 policy
cunning  105 affect desire  107 perforce necessarily  108
Lucrece Roman lady noted for her chastity; she killed herself
when Sextus Tarquinius raped her  112 solemn ceremonious
115 unfrequented plots unvisited areas  116 kind nature
117 Single single out (a hunting term)  123 file our engines
sharpen our minds  126 House of Fame Ovid and Chaucer
have notable poems on it; fame = rumor, and the House of
Fame is full of gossip  128 ruthless pitiless  133 Sit . . . nefas
be it right or wrong (Latin)  135 Per . . . vehor I am carried
through Stygian (infernal) regions, through ghosts (Latin;
derived from Seneca's *Hippolytus*, line 1177)
II.ii.1 gray sky blue (?)  3 Uncouple unleash the hounds;
make a bay keep up the cry of the hounds

---

And rouse the prince, and ring a hunter's peal,          5
That all the court may echo with the noise.
Sons, let it be your charge, as it is ours,
To attend the emperor's person carefully:
I have been troubled in my sleep this night,
But dawning day new comfort hath inspired.          10

*Here a cry° of hounds, and wind horns in a peal: then enter*
SATURNINUS, TAMORA, BASSIANUS, LAVINIA,
CHIRON, DEMETRIUS, *and their* ATTENDANTS.

Many good morrows to your majesty!
Madam, to you as many and as good!
I promisèd your grace a hunter's peal.

SATURNINUS

And you have rung it lustily, my lords,
Somewhat too early for new-married ladies.          15

BASSIANUS

Lavinia, how say you?

LAVINIA                          I say, no;
I have been broad awake two hours and more.

SATURNINUS

Come on then, horse and chariots let us have,
And to our sport. [*To* TAMORA.] Madam, now shall
    ye see
Our Roman hunting.

MARCUS                          I have dogs, my lord,          20
Will rouse the proudest panther in the chase,
And climb the highest promontory top.

TITUS

And I have horse will follow where the game
Makes way and runs like swallows o'er the plain.

DEMETRIUS

Chiron, we hunt not, we, with horse nor hound,          25
But hope to pluck a dainty doe to ground.    *Exeunt.*

[Scene III. *The forest*.]

Enter AARON *alone* [*with a bag of gold*].

AARON

He that had wit would think that I had none,
To bury so much gold under a tree
And never after to inherit° it.
Let him that thinks of me so abjectly°
Know that this gold must coin a stratagem,          5
Which, cunningly effected, will beget
A very excellent piece of villainy.
And so repose, sweet gold, for their unrest,
That have their alms out of the empress' chest.

[*Hides the gold*.]

Enter TAMORA *alone to the Moor*.

TAMORA

My lovely Aaron, wherefore look'st thou sad          10
When every thing doth make a gleeful boast?°
The birds chaunt melody on every bush,
The snakes lies rolled in the cheerful sun,
The green leaves quiver with the cooling wind,
And make a checkered shadow on the ground:          15

---

10 s.d. cry deep barking
II.iii.3 inherit possess  4 abjectly contemptuously  11 boast
display

Under their sweet shade, Aaron, let us sit,
And whilst the babbling echo mocks the hounds,
Replying shrilly to the well-tuned horns
As if a double hunt were heard at once,
Let us sit down and mark their yellowing° noise: 20
And after conflict such as was supposed
The wandering prince and Dido° once enjoyed,
When with a happy storm they were surprised
And curtained with a counsel-keeping cave,
We may, each wreathèd in the other's arms, 25
(Our pastimes done) possess a golden slumber,
Whiles hounds and horns and sweet melodious birds
Be unto us as is a nurse's song
Of lullaby to bring her babe asleep.

AARON
Madam, though Venus govern your desires, 30
Saturn is dominator° over mine:
What signifies my deadly standing° eye,
My silence and my cloudy melancholy,
My fleece of woolly hair that now uncurls
Even as an adder when she doth unroll 35
To do some fatal execution?
No, madam, these are no venereal° signs:
Vengeance is in my heart, death in my hand,
Blood and revenge are hammering in my head.
Hark, Tamora, the empress of my soul, 40
Which never hopes more heaven than rests in thee,
This is the day of doom for Bassianus:
His Philomel° must lose her tongue today,
Thy sons make pillage of her chastity,
And wash their hands in Bassianus' blood. 45
See'st thou this letter? Take it up, I pray thee,
And give the king this fatal-plotted scroll.
Now question me no more; we are espied.
Here comes a parcel of our hopeful booty,°
Which dreads not yet their lives' destruction. 50

*Enter BASSIANUS and LAVINIA.*

TAMORA
Ah, my sweet Moor, sweeter to me than life!
AARON
No more, great empress, Bassianus comes.
Be cross with him, and I'll go fetch thy sons
To back thy quarrels whatsoe'er they be. [*Exit.*]
BASSIANUS
Who have we here? Rome's royal empress, 55
Unfurnished of° her well-beseeming troop?
Or is it Dian, habited° like her,
Who hath abandonèd her holy groves
To see the general hunting in this forest?
TAMORA
Saucy controller° of my private steps! 60
Had I the power that some say Dian had,

Thy temples should be planted presently°
With horns, as was Actaeon's,° and the hounds
Should drive upon thy new-transformèd limbs,
Unmannerly intruder as thou art! 65
LAVINIA
Under your patience, gentle empress,
'Tis thought you have a goodly gift in horning,°
And to be doubted° that your Moor and you
Are singled forth to try experiments:
Jove shield your husband from his hounds today! 70
'Tis pity they should take him for a stag.
BASSIANUS
Believe me, queen, your swart Cimmerian°
Doth make your honor of his body's hue,
Spotted,° detested, and abominable.
Why are you sequest'red from all your train, 75
Dismounted from your snow-white goodly steed,
And wand'red hither to an obscure plot,
Accompanied but with a barbarous Moor,
If foul desire had not conducted you?
LAVINIA
And, being intercepted in your sport, 80
Great reason that my noble lord be rated°
For sauciness. I pray you, let us hence,
And let her joy° her raven-colored love;
This valley fits the purpose passing well.
BASSIANUS
The king my brother shall have notice° of this. 85
LAVINIA
Ay, for these slips have made him noted° long.
Good king, to be so mightily abused!
TAMORA
Why, I have patience to endure all this.

*Enter CHIRON and DEMETRIUS.*

DEMETRIUS
How now, dear sovereign, and our gracious mother,
Why doth your highness look so pale and wan? 90
TAMORA
Have I not reason, think you, to look pale?
These two have ticed° me hither to this place,
A barren detested vale, you see it is;
The trees, though summer, yet forlorn and lean,
Overcome with moss and baleful mistletoe: 95
Here never shines the sun; here nothing breeds,
Unless the nightly owl or fatal raven:
And when they showed me this abhorrèd pit,
They told me, here, at dead time of the night
A thousand fiends, a thousand hissing snakes, 100
Ten thousand swelling toads, as many urchins,°
Would make such fearful and confusèd cries,
As any mortal body hearing it
Should straight fall mad, or else die suddenly.
No sooner had they told this hellish tale, 105
But straight they told me they would bind me here
Unto the body of a dismal yew,

20 yellowing loudly calling  22 The . . . Dido Aeneas and the Queen of Carthage (see Virgil's *Aeneid*, IV)  31 Saturn is dominator the planet Saturn (whose influence allegedly caused sluggishness) dominates  32 deadly standing fixed in a deathlike stare (?)  37 venereal erotic  43 Philomel Philomela was ravished by Tereus, who then cut out her tongue; later she communicated her plight by weaving the story into a tapestry (see II.iv.26–27, 38–43; IV.i.47–48; V.ii.194)  49 parcel . . . booty part of the victims we hope for  56 Unfurnished of unaccompanied by  57 habited dressed  60 controller critic

62 presently immediately  63 Actaeon legendary hunter who spied on Diana bathing; she transformed him into a stag and his own hounds killed him  67 horning an unfaithful wife was said to give her husband horns  68 doubted suspected  72 Cimmerian dweller in darkness  74 Spotted infected  81 rated berated, rebuked  83 joy enjoy  85 notice monosyllabic; pronounced "notes"  86 noted notorious  92 ticed enticed  101 urchins hedgehogs

And leave me to this miserable death.
And then they called me foul adulteress,
Lascivious Goth,° and all the bitterest terms    110
That ever ear did hear to such effect.
And, had you not by wondrous fortune come,
This vengeance on me had they executed:
Revenge it, as you love your mother's life,
Or be ye not henceforth called my children.    115

DEMETRIUS
This is a witness that I am thy son.

*Stab[s] him.*

CHIRON
And this for me, struck home to show my strength.

[*Stabs* BASSIANUS.]

LAVINIA
Ay come, Semiramis, nay, barbarous Tamora!
For no name fits thy nature but thy own!

TAMORA
Give me the poniard! You shall know, my boys,    120
Your mother's hand shall right your mother's wrong.

DEMETRIUS
Stay, madam; here is more belongs to her.
First thrash the corn, then after burn the straw.
This minion stood upon° her chastity,
Upon her nuptial vow, her loyalty,    125
And with that painted° hope braves your mightiness:
And shall she carry this unto her grave?

CHIRON
And if she do, I would I were an eunuch.
Drag hence her husband to some secret hole,
And make his dead trunk pillow to our lust.    130

TAMORA
But when ye have the honey we desire,
Let not this wasp outlive us both to sting.

CHIRON
I warrant you, madam, we will make that sure.
Come, mistress, now perforce we will enjoy
That nice-preservèd honesty° of yours.    135

LAVINIA
O Tamora! Thou bearest a woman's face—

TAMORA
I will not hear her speak; away with her.

LAVINIA
Sweet lords, entreat her hear me but a word.

DEMETRIUS
Listen, fair madam, let it be your glory
To see her tears, but be your heart to them    140
As unrelenting flint to drops of rain.

LAVINIA
When did the tiger's young ones teach the dam?°
O, do not learn° her wrath; she taught it thee.
The milk thou suck'st from her did turn to marble;
Even at thy teat thou hadst thy tyranny.    145
Yet every mother breeds not sons alike,

[*To* CHIRON.]

Do thou entreat her show a woman's pity.

CHIRON
What! Wouldst thou have me prove myself a bastard?

LAVINIA
'Tis true; the raven doth not hatch a lark:
Yet have I heard—O could I find it now!—    150
The lion, moved with pity, did endure
To have his princely paws pared all away.
Some say that ravens foster forlorn children,
The whilst their own birds famish in their nests:
O, be to me, though thy hard heart say no,    155
Nothing so kind but something pitiful!°

TAMORA
I know not what it means; away with her!

LAVINIA
O, let me teach thee for my father's sake,
That gave thee life when well he might have slain thee.
Be not obdurate, open thy deaf ears.    160

TAMORA
Hadst thou in person ne'er offended me,
Even for his sake am I pitiless.
Remember, boys, I poured forth tears in vain
To save your brother from the sacrifice,
But fierce Andronicus would not relent.    165
Therefore away with her, and use her as you will;
The worse to her, the better loved of me.

LAVINIA
O Tamora, be called a gentle queen,
And with thine own hands kill me in this place!
For 'tis not life that I have begged so long;    170
Poor I was slain when Bassianus died.

TAMORA
What begg'st thou then? Fond° woman, let me go.

LAVINIA
'Tis present death I beg, and one thing more
That womanhood denies° my tongue to tell.
O, keep me from their worse than killing lust,    175
And tumble me into some loathsome pit,
Where never man's eye may behold my body.
Do this, and be a charitable murderer.

TAMORA
So should I rob my sweet sons of their fee.
No, let them satisfice their lust on thee.    180

DEMETRIUS
Away! For thou hast stayed us here too long.

LAVINIA
No grace? No womanhood? Ah beastly creature!
The blot and enemy to our general name!°
Confusion° fall—

CHIRON
Nay, then I'll stop your mouth. Bring thou her
    husband.    185
This is the hole where Aaron bid us hide him.

[DEMETRIUS *throws the corpse into a pit and then covers
it with branches. Exeunt* DEMETRIUS *and* CHIRON,
    *dragging* LAVINIA.]

TAMORA
Farewell, my sons, see that you make her sure.
Ne'er let my heart know merry cheer indeed
Till all the Andronici be made away.°

---

110 **Goth** possibly a pun on *goat*, an animal believed to be
lascivious   124 **minion stood upon** hussy made a fuss about
126 **painted** specious, unreal   135 **nice-preservèd honesty**
fastidiously guarded chastity   142 **dam** mother   143 **learn**
teach

156 **Nothing . . . pitiful** not so kind as the raven, but
somewhat pitying   172 **Fond** foolish   174 **denies** forbids   183
**our general name** womankind   184 **Confusion** destruction
189 **made away** killed

Now will I hence to seek my lovely Moor,          190
And let my spleenful° sons this trull° deflower. [*Exit.*]

*Enter* AARON *with two of Titus' sons* [QUINTUS *and*
MARTIUS].

[AARON]
Come on, my lords, the better foot before!
Straight will I bring you to the loathsome pit
Where I espied the panther fast asleep.
QUINTUS
My sight is very dull, whate'er it bodes.          195
MARTIUS
And mine, I promise you. Were it not for shame,
Well could I leave our sport to sleep awhile.

[*He falls into the pit.*]

QUINTUS
What, art thou fallen? What subtle hole is this,
Whose mouth is covered with rude-growing briers,
Upon whose leaves are drops of new-shed blood          200
As fresh as morning dew distilled on flowers?
A very fatal place it seems to me.
Speak, brother, hast thou hurt thee with the fall?
MARTIUS
O, brother, with the dismal'st object hurt
That ever eye with sight made heart lament.          205
AARON [*Aside.*]
Now will I fetch the king to find them here,
That he thereby may have a likely guess
How these were they that made away his brother.
                                        *Exit.*

MARTIUS
Why dost not comfort me and help me out
From this unhallowed and bloodstainèd hole?          210
QUINTUS
I am surprisèd° with an uncouth° fear,
A chilling sweat o'erruns my trembling joints;
My heart suspects more than mine eye can see.
MARTIUS
To prove thou hast a true-divining heart,
Aaron and thou look down into this den          215
And see a fearful sight of blood and death.
QUINTUS
Aaron is gone, and my compassionate heart
Will not permit mine eyes once to behold
The thing whereat it trembles by surmise.
O, tell me who it is, for ne'er till now          220
Was I a child to fear I know not what.
MARTIUS
Lord Bassianus lies berayed° in blood,
All on a heap, like to a slaughtered lamb,
In this detested, dark, blood-drinking pit.
QUINTUS
If it be dark, how dost thou know 'tis he?          225
MARTIUS
Upon his bloody finger he doth wear
A precious ring that lightens all this hole,
Which, like a taper in some monument,
Doth shine upon the dead man's earthy cheeks,
And shows the ragged entrails° of this pit:          230

So pale did shine the moon on Pyramus,
When he by night lay bathed in maiden blood.
O brother, help me with thy fainting hand—
If fear hath made thee faint, as me it hath—
Out of this fell° devouring receptacle,          235
As hateful as Cocytus'° misty mouth.
QUINTUS
Reach me thy hand, that I may help thee out;
Or, wanting° strength to do thee so much good,
I may be plucked into the swallowing womb
Of this deep pit, poor Bassianus' grave.          240
I have no strength to pluck thee to the brink.
MARTIUS
Nor I no strength to climb without thy help.
QUINTUS
Thy hand once more; I will not loose again
Till thou art here aloft or I below:
Thou canst not come to me; I come to thee.          245

[*Falls in.*]

*Enter the emperor* [SATURNINUS] *and* AARON *the
Moor.*

SATURNINUS
Along with me! I'll see what hole is here,
And what he is that now is leaped into it.
Say, who art thou, that lately didst descend
Into this gaping hollow of the earth?
MARTIUS
The unhappy sons of old Andronicus,          250
Brought hither in a most unlucky hour,
To find thy brother Bassianus dead.
SATURNINUS
My brother dead! I know thou dost but jest:
He and his lady both are at the lodge,
Upon the north side of this pleasant chase;          255
'Tis not an hour since I left them there.
MARTIUS
We know not where you left them all alive,
But, out alas! Here have we found him dead.

*Enter* TAMORA, [TITUS] *Andronicus, and* LUCIUS.

TAMORA
Where is my lord the king?
SATURNINUS
Here, Tamora, though grieved with killing grief.          260
TAMORA
Where is thy brother, Bassianus?
SATURNINUS
Now to the bottom dost thou search° my wound;
Poor Bassianus here lies murderèd.
TAMORA
Then all too late I bring this fatal writ,
The complot° of this timeless° tragedy;          265
And wonder greatly that man's face can fold°
In pleasing smiles such murderous tyranny.

*She giveth Saturnine a letter.*

SATURNINUS (*Reads the letter.*)
"And if° we miss to meet him handsomely°—

191 **spleenful** lustful; **trull** strumpet   211 **surprisèd** dum-
founded; **uncouth** strange   222 **berayed** defiled   230 **ragged
entrails** rugged interior

235 **fell** savage   236 **Cocytus** river in Hades   238 **wanting**
lacking   262 **search** probe   265 **complot** plot; **timeless**
untimely   266 **fold** hide (in the creases of a hypocritical smile)
268 **And if** if; **handsomely** handily

Sweet huntsman, Bassianus 'tis we mean—
Do thou so much as dig the grave for him.          270
Thou know'st our meaning. Look for thy reward
Among the nettles at the elder tree
Which overshades the mouth of that same pit
Where we decreed to bury Bassianus.
Do this and purchase us thy lasting friends."       275
O, Tamora! Was ever heard the like?
This is the pit, and this the elder tree.
Look, sirs, if you can find the huntsman out
That should° have murdered Bassianus here.

AARON
My gracious lord, here is the bag of gold.          280

SATURNINUS [*To* TITUS.]
Two of thy whelps, fell° curs of bloody kind,°
Have here bereft my brother of his life.
Sirs, drag them from the pit unto the prison,
There let them bide until we have devised
Some never-heard-of torturing pain for them.       285

TAMORA
What, are they in this pit? O wondrous thing!
How easily murder is discoverèd!

TITUS
High emperor, upon my feeble knee
I beg this boon, with tears not lightly shed,
That this fell fault of my accursèd sons,           290
Accursèd, if the faults be proved in them—

SATURNINUS
If it be proved! You see, it is apparent.°
Who found this letter? Tamora, was it you?

TAMORA
Andronicus himself did take it up.

TITUS
I did, my lord, yet let me be their bail,            295
For by my father's reverend tomb I vow
They shall be ready at your highness' will
To answer their suspicion° with their lives.

SATURNINUS
Thou shalt not bail them; see thou follow me.
Some bring the murdered body, some the murderers.  300
Let them not speak a word; the guilt is plain,
For by my soul were there worse end than death,
That end upon them should be executed.

TAMORA
Andronicus, I will entreat the king.
Fear not° thy sons; they shall do well enough.      305

TITUS
Come, Lucius, come, stay not to talk with them.
                                           [*Exeunt.*]


[Scene IV. *The forest.*]

*Enter the empress'* SONS *with* LAVINIA, *her hands cut
off, and her tongue cut out, and ravished.*

DEMETRIUS
So, now go tell, and if° thy tongue can speak,
Who 'twas that cut thy tongue and ravished thee.

CHIRON
Write down thy mind, bewray° thy meaning so,
And if thy stumps will let thee play the scribe.

DEMETRIUS
See how with signs and tokens she can scrowl.°        5

CHIRON
Go home, call for sweet° water, wash thy hands.

DEMETRIUS
She hath no tongue to call nor hands to wash,
And so let's leave her to her silent walks.

CHIRON
And 'twere my cause,° I should go hang myself.

DEMETRIUS
If thou hadst hands to help thee knit the cord.      10
            *Exeunt* [CHIRON *and* DEMETRIUS].

*Enter* MARCUS *from hunting.*

MARCUS
Who is this? My niece, that flies away so fast!
Cousin,° a word, where is your husband?
If I do dream, would all my wealth would wake me!
If I do wake, some planet strike me down,
That I may slumber an eternal sleep!                 15
Speak, gentle niece, what stern ungentle hands
Hath lopped and hewed and made thy body bare
Of her two branches, those sweet ornaments,
Whose circling shadows kings have sought to sleep in,
And might not gain so great a happiness              20
As half thy love? Why dost not speak to me?
Alas, a crimson river of warm blood,
Like to a bubbling fountain stirred with wind,
Doth rise and fall between thy rosèd lips,
Coming and going with thy honey breath.              25
But, sure, some Tereus° hath deflowered thee,
And, lest thou shouldst detect° him, cut thy tongue.
Ah, now thou turn'st away thy face for shame!
And, notwithstanding all this loss of blood,
As from a conduit with three issuing spouts,         30
Yet do thy cheeks look red as Titan's° face
Blushing to be encount'red with a cloud.
Shall I speak for thee? Shall I say 'tis so?
O, that I knew thy heart, and knew the beast,
That I might rail at him to ease my mind!            35
Sorrow concealèd, like an oven stopped,
Doth burn the heart to cinders where it is.
Fair Philomela, why she but lost her tongue,
And in a tedious sampler° sewed her mind:
But lovely niece, that mean is cut from thee;        40
A craftier Tereus, cousin, hast thou met,
And he hath cut those pretty fingers off,
That could have better sewed than Philomel.
O, had the monster seen those lily hands
Tremble like aspen leaves upon a lute,               45
And make the silken strings delight to kiss them,
He would not then have touched them for his life!
Or, had he heard the heavenly harmony
Which that sweet tongue hath made,

---

279 **should** was to   281 **fell** savage; **kind** nature   292
**apparent** obvious   298 **their suspicion** the suspicion they are
under   305 **Fear not** do not fear for
**II.iv.1 and if** if (as in line 4)

3 **bewray** reveal   5 **scrowl** scrawl (with a possible pun on
*scroll*)   6 **sweet** perfumed   9 **cause** case   12 **Cousin** commonly
used of any near relative other than a parent, child, or sibling
26 **Tereus** ravisher of Philomela (see note to II.iii.43)   27
**detect** expose   31 **Titan's** the sun god's   39 **tedious sampler**
laboriously executed tapestry

He would have dropped his knife, and fell asleep    50
As Cerberus° at the Thracian poet's feet.
Come, let us go and make thy father blind,
For such a sight will blind a father's eye.
One hour's storm will drown the fragrant meads;
What will whole months of tears thy father's eyes?    55
Do not draw back, for we will mourn with thee:
O, could our mourning ease thy misery!     *Exeunt.*


# [ A C T   I I I ]

[Scene I. *Rome. A street.*]

*Enter the* JUDGES *and* SENATORS *with Titus' two*
SONS *bound, passing on the stage to the place of execution,*
*and* TITUS *going before, pleading.*

TITUS
Hear me, grave fathers! Noble tribunes, stay!
For pity of mine age, whose youth was spent
In dangerous wars, whilst you securely slept;
For all my blood in Rome's great quarrel shed,
For all the frosty nights that I have watched,    5
And for these bitter tears, which now you see
Filling the agèd wrinkles in my cheeks,
Be pitiful to my condemnèd sons,
Whose souls is not corrupted as 'tis thought.
For two and twenty sons I never wept,    10
Because they died in honor's lofty bed;

[TITUS] *Andronicus lieth down° and the* JUDGES *pass*
*by him.*

For these, tribunes, in the dust I write
My heart's deep languor° and my soul's sad tears:
Let my tears staunch° the earth's dry appetite;
My sons' sweet blood will make it shame and blush.    15
O earth, I will befriend thee more with rain,
That shall distill from these two ancient ruins,
Than youthful April shall with all his show'rs:
In summer's drought I'll drop upon thee still,°
In winter with warm tears I'll melt the snow,    20
And keep eternal springtime on thy face,
So° thou refuse to drink my dear sons' blood.

*Enter* LUCIUS, *with his weapon drawn.*

O reverend tribunes! O gentle agèd men!
Unbind my sons, reverse the doom° of death,
And let me say, that never wept before,    25
My tears are now prevailing orators.

LUCIUS
O noble father, you lament in vain,
The tribunes hear you not, no man is by,
And you recount your sorrows to a stone.

TITUS
Ah, Lucius, for thy brothers let me plead.    30
Grave tribunes, once more I entreat of you.

LUCIUS
My gracious lord, no tribune hears you speak.
TITUS
Why, 'tis no matter, man, if they did hear
They would not mark me, if they did mark
They would not pity me, yet plead I must,    35
And bootless° unto them.
Therefore I tell my sorrows to the stones,
Who though they cannot answer my distress,
Yet in some sort they are better than the tribunes,
For that they will not intercept° my tale:    40
When I do weep they humbly at my feet
Receive my tears and seem to weep with me;
And were they but attirèd in grave weeds,°
Rome could afford no tribunes like to these.
A stone is soft as wax, tribunes more hard than stones:    45
A stone is silent and offendeth not,
And tribunes with their tongues doom men to death.
But wherefore stand'st thou with thy weapon drawn?
LUCIUS
To rescue my two brothers from their death,
For which attempt the judges have pronounced    50
My everlasting doom of banishment.
TITUS
O happy man! They have befriended thee.
Why, foolish Lucius, dost thou not perceive
That Rome is but a wilderness of tigers?
Tigers must prey, and Rome affords no prey    55
But me and mine. How happy art thou then,
From these devourers to be banishèd!
But who comes with our brother Marcus here?

*Enter* MARCUS *with* LAVINIA.

MARCUS
Titus, prepare thy agèd eyes to weep,
Or if not so, thy noble heart to break.    60
I bring consuming sorrow to thine age.
TITUS
Will it consume me? Let me see it then.
MARCUS
This was thy daughter.
TITUS               Why, Marcus, so she is.
LUCIUS
Ay me! This object° kills me!
TITUS
Fainthearted boy, arise, and look upon her.    65
Speak, Lavinia, what accursèd hand
Hath made thee handless in thy father's sight?
What fool hath added water to the sea,
Or brought a faggot to bright-burning Troy?
My grief was at the height before thou cam'st,    70
And now like Nilus° it disdaineth bounds.
Give me a sword, I'll chop off my hands too,
For they have fought for Rome, and all in vain;
And they have nursed this woe, in feeding life;
In bootless prayer have they been held up,    75
And they have served me to effectless use.
Now all the service I require of them
Is that the one will help to cut the other.
'Tis well, Lavinia, that thou hast no hands,
For hands to do Rome service is but vain.    80

---

**51 Cerberus** three-headed dog who guarded the entrance
to Hades; he was lulled by Orpheus, "the Thracian poet"
**III.i.11 s.d. lieth down** prostrates himself  **13 languor** grief
**14 staunch** satisfy, satiate  **19 still** continuously  **22 So** provided that  **24 doom** judgment

**36 bootless** in vain  **40 intercept** interrupt  **43 grave weeds**
solemn apparel  **64 object** sight  **71 Nilus** the Nile

LUCIUS
Speak, gentle sister, who hath mart'red° thee?
MARCUS
O, that delightful engine° of her thoughts,
That blabbed° them with such pleasing eloquence,
Is torn from forth that pretty hollow cage,
Where like a sweet melodious bird it sung          85
Sweet varied notes, enchanting every ear!
LUCIUS
O, say thou for her, who hath done this deed?
MARCUS
O, thus I found her, straying in the park,
Seeking to hide herself, as doth the deer
That hath received some unrecuring° wound.         90
TITUS
It was my dear, and he that wounded her
Hath hurt me more than had he killed me dead:
For now I stand as one upon a rock,
Environed with a wilderness of sea,
Who marks the waxing tide grow wave by wave,       95
Expecting ever when some envious° surge
Will in his brinish bowels swallow him.
This way to death my wretched sons are gone,
Here stands my other son, a banished man,
And here my brother weeping at my woes:           100
But that which gives my soul the greatest spurn°
Is dear Lavinia, dearer than my soul.
Had I but seen thy picture in this plight,
It would have madded me: what shall I do
Now I behold thy lively° body so?                 105
Thou hast no hands to wipe away thy tears,
Nor tongue to tell me who hath mart'red thee.
Thy husband he is dead, and for his death
Thy brothers are condemned, and dead by this.°
Look, Marcus! Ah, son Lucius, look on her!        110
When I did name her brothers, then fresh tears
Stood on her cheeks, as doth the honey dew
Upon a gath'red lily almost withered.
MARCUS
Perchance she weeps because they killed her husband,
Perchance because she knows them innocent.        115
TITUS
If they did kill thy husband, then be joyful,
Because the law hath ta'en revenge on them.
No, no, they would not do so foul a deed;
Witness the sorrow that their sister makes.
Gentle Lavinia, let me kiss thy lips,             120
Or make some sign how I may do thee ease.°
Shall thy good uncle, and thy brother Lucius,
And thou, and I, sit round about some fountain,
Looking all downwards, to behold our cheeks
How they are stained, like meadows yet not dry    125
With miry slime left on them by a flood?
And in the fountain shall we gaze so long
Till the fresh taste be taken from that clearness,°
And made a brine pit with our bitter tears?
Or shall we cut away our hands, like thine?       130
Or shall we bite our tongues, and in dumb shows°

Pass the remainder of our hateful days?
What shall we do? Let us, that have our tongues,
Plot some device of further misery,
To make us wondered at in time to come.           135
LUCIUS
Sweet father, cease your tears, for at your grief
See how my wretched sister sobs and weeps.
MARCUS
Patience, dear niece. Good Titus, dry thine eyes.
TITUS
Ah, Marcus, Marcus! Brother, well I wot
Thy napkin° cannot drink a tear of mine,          140
For thou, poor man, hast drowned it with thine
  own.
LUCIUS
Ah, my Lavinia, I will wipe thy cheeks.
TITUS
Mark, Marcus, mark! I understand her signs:
Had she a tongue to speak, now would she say
That to her brother which I said to thee:         145
His napkin, with his true tears all bewet,
Can do no service on her sorrowful cheeks.
O, what a sympathy° of woe is this!
As far from help as Limbo is from bliss!

*Enter* AARON *the Moor alone.*

AARON
Titus Andronicus, my lord the emperor            150
Sends thee this word, that, if thou love thy sons,
Let Marcus, Lucius, or thyself, old Titus,
Or any one of you, chop off your hand
And send it to the king: he for the same
Will send thee hither both thy sons alive,        155
And that shall be the ransom for their fault.
TITUS
O, gracious emperor! O, gentle Aaron!
Did ever raven sing so like a lark,
That gives sweet tidings of the sun's uprise?
With all my heart, I'll send the emperor my hand. 160
Good Aaron, wilt thou help to chop it off?
LUCIUS
Stay, father! For that noble hand of thine
That hath thrown down so many enemies
Shall not be sent; my hand will serve the turn.
My youth can better spare my blood than you,      165
And therefore mine shall save my brothers' lives.
MARCUS
Which of your hands hath not defended Rome
And reared aloft the bloody battle-ax,
Writing destruction on the enemy's castle?
O, none of both but are of high desert:           170
My hand hath been but idle; let it serve
To ransom my two nephews from their death,
Then have I kept it to a worthy end.
AARON
Nay, come, agree whose hand shall go along,
For fear they die before their pardon come.       175
MARCUS
My hand shall go.
LUCIUS               By heaven, it shall not go.

---

81 **mart'red** mutilated   82 **engine** instrument   83 **blabbed**
freely spoke   90 **unrecuring** incurable   96 **envious** malicious
101 **spurn** thrust   105 **lively** living   109 **by this** by this time
121 **do thee ease** bring you relief   128 **clearness** clear pool
131 **dumb shows** silent signs

140 **napkin** handkerchief   148 **sympathy** agreement

**TITUS**
Sirs, strive no more; such with'red herbs as these
Are meet° for plucking up, and therefore mine.

**LUCIUS**
Sweet father, if I shall be thought thy son,
Let me redeem my brothers both from death.    180

**MARCUS**
And, for our father's sake and mother's care,
Now let me show a brother's love to thee.

**TITUS**
Agree between you; I will spare my hand.

**LUCIUS**
Then I'll go fetch an ax.

**MARCUS**
But I will use the ax.    *Exeunt* [LUCIUS *and* MARCUS].  185

**TITUS**
Come hither, Aaron. I'll deceive them both;
Lend me thy hand, and I will give thee mine.

**AARON** [*Aside.*]
If that be called deceit, I will be honest,
And never whilst I live deceive men so:
But I'll deceive you in another sort,    190
And that you'll say, ere half an hour pass.

*He cuts off Titus' hand.*
*Enter* LUCIUS *and* MARCUS *again.*

**TITUS**
Now stay your strife, what shall be is dispatched.
Good Aaron, give his majesty my hand;
Tell him it was a hand that warded° him
From thousand dangers; bid him bury it;    195
More hath it merited, that let it have.
As for my sons, say I account of them
As jewels purchased at an easy price,
And yet dear too because I bought mine own.

**AARON**
I go, Andronicus, and for thy hand    200
Look by and by to have thy sons with thee.

[*Aside.*]
Their heads, I mean. O, how this villainy
Doth fat° me with the very thoughts of it!
Let fools do good, and fair men call for grace,
Aaron will have his soul black like his face.    *Exit.* 205

**TITUS**
O, here I lift this one hand up to heaven,
And bow this feeble ruin to the earth.
If any power pities wretched tears,
To that I call! [*To* LAVINIA.] What, wouldst thou
   kneel with me?
Do then, dear heart, for heaven shall hear our prayers, 210
Or with our sighs we'll breathe the welkin dim,°
And stain the sun with fog, as sometime clouds
When they do hug him in their melting bosoms.

**MARCUS**
O brother, speak with possibility,
And do not break into these deep extremes.    215

**TITUS**
Is not my sorrow deep, having no bottom?
Then be my passions° bottomless with them.

**MARCUS**
But yet let reason govern thy lament.

**TITUS**
If there were reason for these miseries,
Then into limits could I bind my woes:    220
When heaven doth weep, doth not the earth o'erflow?
If the winds rage, doth not the sea wax mad,
Threat'ning the welkin with his big-swoll'n face?
And wilt thou have a reason for this coil?°
I am the sea; hark, how her sighs doth flow!    225
She is the weeping welkin, I the earth:
Then must my sea be movèd with her sighs,
Then must my earth with her continual tears
Become a deluge, overflowed and drowned,
For why° my bowels° cannot hide her woes,    230
But like a drunkard must I vomit them.
Then give me leave, for losers will have leave
To ease their stomachs° with their bitter tongues.

*Enter a* MESSENGER, *with two heads and a hand.*

**MESSENGER**
Worthy Andronicus, ill art thou repaid
For that good hand thou sent'st the emperor.    235
Here are the heads of thy two noble sons,
And here's thy hand in scorn to thee sent back;
Thy grief their sports, thy resolution mocked:
That° woe is me to think upon thy woes,
More than remembrance of my father's death. [*Exit.*] 240

**MARCUS**
Now let hot Etna cool in Sicily,
And be my heart an ever-burning hell!
These miseries are more than may be borne!
To weep with them that weep doth ease some deal,°
But sorrow flouted at is double death.    245

**LUCIUS**
Ah, that this sight should make so deep a wound,
And yet detested life not shrink° thereat!
That ever death should let life bear his name,°
Where life hath no more interest but to breathe!

[LAVINIA *kisses* TITUS.]

**MARCUS**
Alas, poor heart, that kiss is comfortless    250
As frozen water to a starvèd° snake.

**TITUS**
When will this fearful slumber° have an end?

**MARCUS**
Now, farewell, flatt'ry, die, Andronicus,
Thou dost not slumber: see thy two sons' heads,
Thy warlike hand, thy mangled daughter here,    255
Thy other banished son with this dear° sight
Struck pale and bloodless, and thy brother, I,
Even like a stony image cold and numb.
Ah! Now no more will I control thy griefs:
Rend off thy silver hair, thy other hand    260
Gnawing with thy teeth, and be this dismal sight

---

178 **meet** fit   194 **warded** guarded   203 **fat** delight (literally, "nourish")   211 **breathe . . . dim** becloud the heavens with our breath   217 **passions** outbursts

224 **coil** fuss   230 **For why** because; **bowels** thought to be the seat of compassion; akin to the modern use of *heart* 233 **stomachs** feeling   239 **That** so that   244 **some deal** somewhat   247 **shrink** slip away   248 **bear his name** be called "life"   251 **starvèd** numbed   252 **fearful slumber** nightmare existence   256 **dear** heartfelt

The closing up of our most wretched eyes:
Now is a time to storm; why art thou still?
TITUS    Ha, ha, ha!
MARCUS
Why dost thou laugh? It fits not with this hour.    265
TITUS
Why, I have not another tear to shed.
Besides, this sorrow is an enemy,
And would usurp upon my wat'ry eyes
And make them blind with tributary° tears;
Then which way shall I find revenge's cave?    270
For these two heads do seem to speak to me,
And threat me I shall never come to bliss
Till all these mischiefs be returned again,
Even in their throats that hath committed them.
Come, let me see what task I have to do.    275
You heavy° people, circle me about,
That I may turn me to each one of you,
And swear unto my soul to right your wrongs.
The vow is made. Come, brother, take a head;
And in this hand the other will I bear.    280
And Lavinia, thou shalt be employed in these arms,
Bear thou my hand, sweet wench, between thy teeth:°
As for thee, boy, go, get thee from my sight.
Thou art an exile, and thou must not stay.
Hie to the Goths, and raise an army there,    285
And, if ye love me, as I think you do,
Let's kiss and part, for we have much to do.
                    *Exeunt* [*all but* LUCIUS].
LUCIUS
Farewell, Andronicus, my noble father,
The woefull'st man that ever lived in Rome!
Farewell, proud Rome, till Lucius come again;    290
He loves his pledges dearer than his life.
Farewell, Lavinia, my noble sister;
O, would thou wert as thou tofore° hast been!
But now nor Lucius nor° Lavinia lives
But in oblivion and hateful griefs.    295
If Lucius live, he will requite your wrongs,
And make proud Saturnine and his empress
Beg at the gates, like Tarquin° and his queen.
Now will I to the Goths and raise a pow'r,
To be revenged on Rome and Saturnine.    300
                    *Exit* LUCIUS.


[Scene II. *Rome. Within Titus' house.*]

*A banket.° Enter* [TITUS] *Andronicus,* MARCUS,
LAVINIA, *and the* BOY [*Lucius*].

TITUS
So, so, now sit, and look you eat no more
Than will preserve just so much strength in us
As will revenge these bitter woes of ours.

Marcus, unknit that sorrow-wreathen knot:°
Thy niece and I, poor creatures, want our hands,    5
And cannot passionate° our tenfold grief
With folded arms. This poor right hand of mine
Is left to tyrannize upon my breast;
Who, when my heart all mad with misery
Beats in this hollow prison of my flesh,    10
Then thus I thump it down.

[*To* LAVINIA.]

Thou map° of woe, that thus dost talk in signs,
When thy poor heart beats with outrageous beating,
Thou canst not strike it thus to make it still.
Wound it with sighing,° girl, kill it with groans;    15
Or get some little knife between thy teeth,
And just against thy heart make thou a hole,
That all the tears that thy poor eyes let fall
May run into that sink,° and, soaking in,
Drown the lamenting fool° in sea-salt tears.    20
MARCUS
Fie, brother, fie! Teach her not thus to lay
Such violent hands upon her tender life.
TITUS
How now! Has sorrow made thee dote already?
Why, Marcus, no man should be mad but I.
What violent hands can she lay on her life!    25
Ah, wherefore dost thou urge the name of hands,
To bid Aeneas° tell the tale twice o'er,
How Troy was burnt and he made miserable?
O, handle not the theme, to talk of hands,
Lest we remember still that we have none.    30
Fie, fie, how franticly I square° my talk,
As if we should forget we had no hands,
If Marcus did not name the word of hands!
Come, let's fall to; and, gentle girl, eat this.
Here is no drink? Hark, Marcus, what she says—    35
I can interpret all her martyred signs—
She says she drinks no other drink but tears,
Brewed with her sorrow, meshed° upon her cheeks.
Speechless complainer, I will learn thy thought;
In thy dumb action will I be as perfect°    40
As begging hermits in their holy prayers:
Thou shalt not sigh, nor hold thy stumps to heaven,
Nor wink,° nor nod, nor kneel, nor make a sign,
But I of these will wrest an alphabet,
And by still° practice learn to know thy meaning.    45
BOY
Good grandsire, leave these bitter deep laments.
Make my aunt merry with some pleasing tale.
MARCUS
Alas, the tender boy, in passion moved,
Doth weep to see his grandsire's heaviness.
TITUS
Peace, tender sapling, thou art made of tears,    50
And tears will quickly melt thy life away.

---

269 **tributary** paid as tribute  276 **heavy** sad  282 **teeth**
possibly Shakespeare intended to delete "teeth" from the manuscript, and substituted the less grotesque "arms" above it; if so,
the compositor mistakenly took "arms" to be part of the
previous line, and to make sense of it he perhaps altered something like "employed in this" to "employed in these arms"
293 **tofore** formerly  294 **nor . . . nor** neither . . . nor
298 **Tarquin** Roman king whose rule was overthrown when
his son (of the same name) raped Lucrece
**III.ii.s.d. banket** light meal

4 **knot** Marcus' folded arms, a sign of heavy thoughts  6
**passionate** passionately express  12 **map** picture  15 **wound
. . . sighing** sighing was believed to shorten life  19 **sink**
sewer  20 **fool** here, as often, implying affection and pity
27 **Aeneas** see Virgil's *Aeneid*, II.2  31 **square** shape  38
**meshed** mashed, brewed  40 **perfect** fully knowing  43
**wink** shut the eyes  45 **still** constant

MARCUS *strikes the dish with a knife.*

What dost thou strike at, Marcus, with thy knife?

**MARCUS**
At that that I have killed, my lord—a fly.

**TITUS**
Out on thee, murderer! Thou kill'st my heart;
Mine eyes are cloyed with view of tyranny:    55
A deed of death done on the innocent
Becomes not Titus' brother. Get thee gone;
I see thou art not for my company.

**MARCUS**
Alas, my lord, I have but killed a fly.

**TITUS**
"But"! How, if that fly had a father and mother?    60
How would he hang his slender gilded wings,
And buzz lamenting doings in the air!
Poor harmless fly,
That, with his pretty buzzing melody,
Came here to make us merry! And thou hast killed
    him.    65

**MARCUS**
Pardon me, sir; it was a black ill-favored° fly,
Like to the empress' Moor. Therefore I killed him.

**TITUS**
O, O, O,
Then pardon me for reprehending thee,
For thou hast done a charitable deed.    70
Give me thy knife, I will insult on° him,
Flattering myself, as if it were the Moor,
Come hither purposely to poison me.

[*He strikes at it.*]

There's for thyself, and that's for Tamora.
Ah, sirrah!°    75
Yet I think we are not brought so low
But that between us we can kill a fly
That comes in likeness of a coal-black Moor.

**MARCUS**
Alas, poor man! Grief has so wrought on him,
He takes false shadows for true substances.    80

**TITUS**
Come, take away.° Lavinia, go with me:
I'll to thy closet,° and go read with thee
Sad stories chancèd° in the times of old.
Come, boy, and go with me; thy sight is young,
And thou shalt read when mine begin to dazzle.    85
                          *Exeunt.*

# [ A C T   I V ]

### [Scene I. *Rome. Before Titus' house.*]

*Enter Lucius'* SON *and* LAVINIA *running after him; and
the* BOY *flies from her with his books under his arm. Enter*
TITUS *and* MARCUS.

**BOY**
Help, grandsire, help! My aunt Lavinia
Follows me everywhere, I know not why.
Good uncle Marcus, see how swift she comes.
Alas, sweet aunt, I know not what you mean.

**MARCUS**
Stand by me, Lucius, do not fear thine aunt.    5

**TITUS**
She loves thee, boy, too well to do thee harm.

**BOY**
Ay, when my father was in Rome she did.

**MARCUS**
What means my niece Lavinia by these signs?

**TITUS**
Fear her not, Lucius. Somewhat doth she mean.
See, Lucius, see, how much she makes of thee:    10
Somewhither would she have thee go with her.
Ah, boy, Cornelia° never with more care
Read to her sons than she hath read to thee
Sweet poetry and Tully's *Orator.*°
Canst thou not guess wherefore she plies thee thus?    15

**BOY**
My lord, I know not, I, nor can I guess,
Unless some fit or frenzy do possess her:
For I have heard my grandsire say full oft,
Extremity of griefs would make men mad;
And I have read that Hecuba of Troy    20
Ran mad for sorrow. That made me to fear,
Although, my lord, I know my noble aunt
Loves me as dear as e'er my mother did,
And would not, but in fury,° fright my youth,
Which made me down to throw my books and fly,    25
Causeless perhaps. But pardon me, sweet aunt:
And, madam, if my uncle Marcus go,
I will most willingly attend° your ladyship.

**MARCUS**
Lucius, I will.

**TITUS**
How now, Lavinia? Marcus, what means this?    30
Some book there is that she desires to see.
Which is it, girl, of these? Open them, boy.
But thou art deeper read, and better skilled.
Come, and take choice of all my library,
And so beguile thy sorrow, till the heavens    35
Reveal the damned contriver of this deed.
Why lifts she up her arms in sequence thus?

**MARCUS**
I think she means that there were more than one
Confederate in the fact.° Ay, more there was,
Or else to heaven she heaves them for revenge.    40

**TITUS**
Lucius, what book is that she tosseth° so?

**BOY**
Grandsire, 'tis Ovid's *Metamorphosis;*°
My mother gave it me.

**MARCUS**              For love of her that's gone,
Perhaps she culled it from among the rest.

**IV.i.12 Cornelia** mother of the Gracchi, two famous tribunes
**14 Tully's *Orator*** Cicero's *De oratore* (or his *Orator ad M.
Brutum*) **24 but in fury** except in madness **28 attend** wait on
**39 fact** crime **41 tosseth** turns the pages of **42 *Metamorphosis*** so spelled in the title of an Elizabethan translation by
Golding, with which Shakespeare was familiar; properly
*Metamorphoses*

---

**66 ill-favored** ugly   **71 insult on** exult over   **75 sirrah**
common term of address to an inferior   **81 take away** clear
the table   **82 closet** private room   **83 chancèd** that happened

**TITUS**

Soft! So busily she turns the leaves!                              45
Help her! What would   she find? Lavinia, shall I
  read?
This is the tragic tale of Philomel,
And treats of Tereus' treason and his rape;
And rape, I fear, was root of thy annoy.

**MARCUS**

See, brother, see, note how she quotes° the leaves.      50

**TITUS**

Lavinia, wert thou thus surprised, sweet girl,
Ravished and wronged, as Philomela was,
Forced in the ruthless, vast,° and gloomy woods?
See, see!
Ay, such a place there is, where we did hunt—            55
O, had we never, never hunted there—
Patterned by° that the poet here describes,
By nature made for murders and for rapes.

**MARCUS**

O, why should nature build so foul a den,
Unless the gods delight in tragedies?                     60

**TITUS**

Give signs, sweet girl, for here are none but friends,
What Roman lord it was durst do the deed:
Or slunk not Saturnine, as Tarquin erst,°
That left the camp to sin in Lucrece' bed?

**MARCUS**

Sit down, sweet niece: brother, sit down by me.          65
Apollo, Pallas, Jove, or Mercury,
Inspire me, that I may this treason find!
My lord, look here: look here, Lavinia.

*He writes his name with his staff, and guides it with feet
and mouth.*

This sandy plot is plain;° guide if thou canst,
This after me.° I have writ my name                       70
Without the help of any hand at all.
Cursed be that heart that forced us to this shift!°
Write thou, good niece, and here display at last
What God will have discovered° for revenge.
Heaven guide thy pen to print thy sorrows plain,         75
That we may know the traitors and the truth!

*She takes the staff in her mouth and guides it with her
stumps and writes.*

O, do ye read, my lord, what she hath writ?

[**TITUS**]

"Stuprum.° Chiron. Demetrius."

**MARCUS**

What, what! The lustful sons of Tamora
Performers of this heinous, bloody deed?                  80

**TITUS**

Magni Dominator poli,
Tam lentus audis scelera? tam lentus vides?°

**MARCUS**

O, calm thee, gentle lord! Although I know
There is enough written upon this earth
To stir a mutiny in the mildest thoughts,                 85

And arm the minds of infants to exclaims.°
My lord, kneel down with me; Lavinia, kneel;
And kneel, sweet boy, the Roman Hector's° hope;
And swear with me, as, with the woeful fere°
And father of that chaste dishonored dame,               90
Lord Junius Brutus° sware for Lucrece' rape,
That we will prosecute by good advice°
Mortal revenge upon these traitorous Goths,
And see their blood, or die with this reproach.

**TITUS**

'Tis sure enough, and you knew how,                       95
But if you hunt these bear-whelps, then beware:
The dame will wake; and if she wind ye° once,
She's with the lion deeply still in league,
And lulls him whilst she playeth on her back,
And when he sleeps will she do what she list.°          100
You are a young huntsman, Marcus, let alone;
And, come, I will go get a leaf of brass,
And with a gad° of steel will write these words,
And lay it by. The angry northern wind
Will blow these sands like Sibyl's leaves° abroad,      105
And where's our lesson then? Boy, what say you?

**BOY**

I say, my lord, that if I were a man,
Their mother's bedchamber should not be safe
For these base bondmen to the yoke of Rome.

**MARCUS**

Ay, that's my boy! Thy father hath full oft             110
For his ungrateful country done the like.

**BOY**

And, uncle, so will I, and if I live.

**TITUS**

Come, go with me into mine armory:
Lucius, I'll fit thee, and withal my boy
Shall carry from me to the empress' sons                115
Presents that I intend to send them both.
Come, come; thou'lt do my message, wilt thou not?

**BOY**

Ay, with my dagger in their bosoms, grandsire.

**TITUS**

No, boy, not so; I'll teach thee another course.
Lavinia, come. Marcus, look to my house.                120
Lucius and I'll go brave it° at the court;
Ay, marry,° will we, sir; and we'll be waited on.°
                                        *Exeunt.*

**MARCUS**

O heavens, can you hear a good man groan,
And not relent, or not compassion him?
Marcus, attend him in his ecstasy,°                     125
That hath more scars of sorrow in his heart
Than foemen's marks upon his batt'red shield,
But yet so just that he will not revenge.
Revenge the heavens° for old Andronicus!    *Exit.*

**50 quotes** examines  **53 vast** desolate  **57 Patterned by**
after the pattern  **63 erst** once  **69 plain** fit  **70 after me**
as I do  **72 shift** device  **74 discovered** revealed  **78 Stuprum**
rape (Latin)  **81–82 Magni . . . vides** Ruler of the great
heavens, are you so slow to hear and to see crimes? (Latin;
derived from Seneca's *Hippolytus*, lines 668–69)

**86 exclaims** exclamations  **88 the Roman Hector's**
Andronicus (Titus is compared to Hector, Troy's champion)
**89 fere** spouse  **91 Junius Brutus** chief of those who drove
the Tarquins from Rome  **92 by good advice** after careful
deliberation  **97 and . . . ye** if she get wind of (smell) you
**100 list** please  **103 gad** spike, stylus  **105 Sibyl's**
**leaves** leaves on which the Sibyl wrote prophecies  **121 brave it**
behave defiantly  **122 marry** an interjection (from "By the
Virgin Mary");  **be waited on** not be ignored  **125 ecstasy**
fit of madness  **129 Revenge the heavens** may the heavens
take revenge

[Scene II. *Rome. Within the palace.*]

*Enter* AARON, CHIRON, *and* DEMETRIUS, *at one door, and at the other door young* LUCIUS *and another, with a bundle of weapons and verses writ upon them.*

CHIRON
Demetrius, here's the son of Lucius,
He hath some message to deliver us.

AARON
Ay, some mad message from his mad grandfather.

BOY
My lords, with all the humbleness I may,
I greet your honors from Andronicus.     5

[*Aside.*]

And pray the Roman gods confound° you both.

DEMETRIUS
Gramercy,° lovely Lucius, what's the news?

BOY [*Aside.*]
That you are both deciphered, that's the news,
For villains marked with rape. [*Aloud.*] May it please
   you,
My grandsire, well-advised,° hath sent by me     10
The goodliest weapons of his armory
To gratify your honorable youth,
The hope of Rome; for so he bid me say;
And so I do, and with his gifts present
Your lordships; whenever you have need,     15
You may be armèd and appointed° well.
And so I leave you both, [*aside*] like bloody villains.
                           *Exit.*

DEMETRIUS
What's here? A scroll, and written round about?
Let's see:
      Integer vitae, scelerisque purus,
      Non eget Mauri jaculis, nec arcu.°     20

CHIRON
O, 'tis a verse in Horace; I know it well:
I read it in the grammar long ago.

AARON
Ay, just; a verse in Horace; right, you have it.

[*Aside.*]

Now, what a thing it is to be an ass!
Here's no sound jest! The old man hath found their     25
   guilt,
And sends them weapons wrapped about with lines
That wound, beyond their feeling, to the quick.
But were our witty° empress well afoot,
She would applaud Andronicus' conceit.°     30
But let her rest in her unrest awhile.

[*Aloud.*]

And now, young lords, was't not a happy star
Led us to Rome, strangers, and more than so,
Captives, to be advancèd to this height?
It did me good, before the palace gate     35
To brave the tribune in his brother's hearing.

DEMETRIUS
But me more good, to see so great a lord
Basely insinuate° and send us gifts.

AARON
Had he not reason, Lord Demetrius?
Did you not use his daughter very friendly?     40

DEMETRIUS
I would we had a thousand Roman dames
At such a bay,° by turn to serve our lust.

CHIRON
A charitable wish and full of love.

AARON
Here lacks but your mother for to say amen.

CHIRON
And that would she for twenty thousand more.     45

DEMETRIUS
Come, let us go, and pray to all the gods
For our belovèd mother in her pains.

AARON [*Aside.*]
Pray to the devils, the gods have given us over.

*Trumpets sound.*

DEMETRIUS
Why do the emperor's trumpets flourish thus?

CHIRON
Belike,° for joy the emperor hath a son.     50

DEMETRIUS
Soft! Who comes here?

*Enter* NURSE *with a blackamoor* CHILD.

NURSE               God morrow, lords.
O, tell me, did you see Aaron the Moor?

AARON
Well, more or less, or ne'er a whit at all,
Here Aaron is; and what with Aaron now?

NURSE
O gentle Aaron, we are all undone!     55
Now help, or woe betide thee evermore!

AARON
Why, what a caterwauling dost thou keep!
What dost thou wrap and fumble° in thy arms?

NURSE
O, that which I would hide from heaven's eye,
Our empress' shame and stately Rome's disgrace!     60
She is delivered, lords, she is delivered.

AARON
To whom?

NURSE         I mean, she is brought abed.

AARON
Well, God give her good rest! What hath he sent her?

NURSE
A devil.

AARON   Why, then she is the devil's dam;°
A joyful issue.     65

NURSE
A joyless, dismal, black, and sorrowful issue!
Here is the babe, as loathsome as a toad
Amongst the fair-faced breeders of our clime.
The empress sends it thee, thy stamp, thy seal,
And bids thee christen it with thy dagger's point.     70

---

**IV.ii.6 confound** destroy   **7 Gramercy** thanks   **10 well-advised** in sound mind   **16 appointed** equipped   **20–21 Integer . . . arcu** The man of upright life and free from crime has no need of a Moor's javelins or bow (Latin; from Horace, *Odes*, I.xxii.1–2)   **29 witty** wise   **30 conceit** idea, design

**38 insinuate** curry favor   **42 At . . . bay** thus cornered   **50 Belike** probably   **58 fumble** clumsily bundle up   **64 dam** mother

AARON
Zounds,° ye whore! Is black so base a hue?
Sweet blowse,° you are a beauteous blossom, sure.

DEMETRIUS
Villain, what has thou done?

AARON
That which thou canst not undo.

CHIRON
Thou hast undone our mother.                                    75

AARON
Villain, I have done° thy mother.

DEMETRIUS
And therein, hellish dog, thou hast undone her.
Woe to her chance,° and damned her loathèd choice!
Accursed the offspring of so foul a fiend!

CHIRON
It shall not live.                                              80

AARON
It shall not die.

NURSE
Aaron, it must; the mother wills it so.

AARON
What, must it, nurse? Then let no man but I
Do execution on my flesh and blood.

DEMETRIUS
I'll broach° the tadpole on my rapier's point.                 85
Nurse, give it me; my sword shall soon dispatch it.

AARON
Sooner this sword shall plow thy bowels up.
Stay, murderous villains! Will you kill your brother?
Now, by the burning tapers of the sky,
That shone so brightly when this boy was got,°                 90
He dies upon my scimitar's sharp point
That touches this my first-born son and heir!
I tell you, younglings, not Enceladus,°
With all his threat'ning band of Typhon's brood,
Nor great Alcides,° nor the god of war,                        95
Shall seize this prey out of his father's hands.
What, what, ye sanguine,° shallow-hearted boys!
Ye white-limed walls!° Ye alehouse painted signs!
Coal black is better than another hue;
In that it scorns to bear another hue,                         100
For all the water in the ocean
Can never turn the swan's black legs to white,
Although she lave° them hourly in the flood.
Tell the empress from me, I am of age
To keep mine own, excuse it how she can.                       105

DEMETRIUS
Wilt thou betray thy noble mistress thus?

AARON
My mistress is my mistress, this my self,
The vigor and the picture of my youth:
This before all the world do I prefer;
This mauger° all the world will I keep safe,                   110
Or some of you shall smoke° for it in Rome.

DEMETRIUS
By this our mother is forever shamed.

CHIRON
Rome will despise her for this foul escape.°

NURSE
The emperor in his rage will doom her death.

CHIRON
I blush to think upon this ignomy.°                            115

AARON
Why, there's the privilege your beauty bears:
Fie, treacherous hue, that will betray with blushing
The close enacts° and counsels of thy heart!
Here's a young lad framed of another leer:°
Look, how the black slave smiles upon the father,             120
As who should say, "Old lad, I am thine own."
He is your brother, lords, sensibly fed
Of that self blood° that first gave life to you,
And from your womb where you imprisoned were
He is enfranchisèd and come to light:                          125
Nay, he is your brother by the surer side,°
Although my seal be stampèd in his face.

NURSE
Aaron, what shall I say unto the empress?

DEMETRIUS
Advise thee, Aaron, what is to be done,
And we will all subscribe° to thy advice:                      130
Save thou the child, so° we may all be safe.

AARON
Then sit we down and let us all consult.
My son and I will have the wind of you:°
Keep there; now talk at pleasure of your safety.

DEMETRIUS
How many women saw this child of his?                          135

AARON
Why, so, brave lords! When we join in league,
I am a lamb: but if you brave the Moor,
The chafèd° boar, the mountain lioness,
The ocean swells not so as Aaron storms.
But say again, how many saw the child?                         140

NURSE
Cornelia the midwife, and myself,
And no one else but the delivered empress.

AARON
The empress, the midwife, and yourself:
Two may keep counsel when the third's away.
Go to the empress, tell her this I said.                       145

*He kills her.*

Wheak, wheak!
So cries a pig preparèd to the spit.

DEMETRIUS
What mean'st thou, Aaron? Wherefore didst thou
this?

AARON
O, Lord, sir, 'tis a deed of policy!°
Shall she live to betray this guilt of ours?                   150

---

71 **Zounds** an interjection (from "By God's wounds") 72 **blowse** ruddy wench (here, ironic) 76 **done** had sexual intercourse with 78 **chance** luck 85 **broach** impale 90 **got** begat 93 **Enceladus** one of the Titans (sons of Typhon) who fought the Olympians 95 **Alcides** Hercules 97 **sanguine** pink-cheeked 98 **white-limed walls** perhaps a reference to the "whited sepulchers" of Matthew 23:27 103 **lave** wash 110 **mauger** in spite of 111 **smoke** suffer

113 **escape** escapade 115 **ignomy** ignominy 118 **close enacts** secret resolutions 119 **leer** complexion 122–23 **sensibly . . . blood** his body draws on the same blood 126 **the surer side** the mother's side 130 **subscribe** agree 131 **so** provided that 133 **have . . . you** keep you safely in our view (as game is watched, downwind) 138 **chafèd** enraged 149 **policy** cunning

A long-tongued babbling gossip? No, lords, no.
And now be it known to you my full intent.
Not far one Muliteus my countryman
His° wife but yesternight was brought to bed;
His child is like to her, fair as you are.     155
Go pack° with him, and give the mother gold,
And tell them both the circumstance of all,°
And how by this their child shall be advanced,
And be receivèd for the emperor's heir,
And substituted in the place of mine,     160
To calm this tempest whirling in the court;
And let the emperor dandle him for his own.
Hark ye, lords; you see I have given her physic,°
And you must needs bestow her funeral;
The fields are near, and you are gallant grooms.     165
This done, see that you take no longer days,°
But send the midwife presently to me.
The midwife and the nurse well made away,
Then let the ladies tattle what they please.

CHIRON
Aaron, I see thou wilt not trust the air     170
With secrets.

DEMETRIUS   For this care of Tamora,
Herself and hers are highly bound to thee.     *Exeunt.*

AARON
Now to the Goths, as swift as swallow flies,
There to dispose this treasure in mine arms,
And secretly to greet the empress' friends.     175
Come on, you thick-lipped slave, I'll bear you hence;
For it is you that puts us to°our shifts.°
I'll make you feed on berries and on roots,
And feed on curds and whey, and suck the goat,
And cabin° in a cave, and bring you up     180
To be a warrior and command a camp.     *Exit.*

[Scene III. *Rome. A street.*]

*Enter* TITUS, *old* MARCUS, [*his son* PUBLIUS,] *young*
LUCIUS, *and other* GENTLEMEN, *with bows; and* TITUS
*bears the arrows with letters on the ends of them.*

TITUS
Come, Marcus, come; kinsmen, this is the way.
Sir boy, let me see your archery;
Look ye draw home° enough, and 'tis there straight.
Terras Astraea reliquit.°
Be you rememb'red,° Marcus: she's gone, she's fled.     5
Sirs, take you to your tools. You, cousins, shall
Go sound the ocean, and cast your nets;
Happily° you may catch her in the sea;
Yet there's as little justice as at land:
No, Publius and Sempronius, you must do it;     10
'Tis you must dig with mattock and with spade,
And pierce the inmost center of the earth:
Then, when you come to Pluto's region,°

I pray you deliver him this petition:
Tell him, it is for justice and for aid,     15
And that it comes from old Andronicus,
Shaken with sorrows in ungrateful Rome.
Ah, Rome! Well, well; I made thee miserable
What time° I threw the people's suffrages
On him that thus doth tyrannize o'er me.     20
Go, get you gone, and pray be careful all,
And leave you not a man of war unsearched:
This wicked emperor may have shipped her hence,
And, kinsmen, then we may go pipe for° justice.

MARCUS
O, Publius, is not this a heavy case,     25
To see thy noble uncle thus distract?

PUBLIUS
Therefore, my lords, it highly us concerns
By day and night t' attend him carefully,
And feed his humor° kindly as we may,
Till time beget some careful remedy.     30

MARCUS
Kinsmen, his sorrows are past remedy.
But° . . .
Join with the Goths, and with revengeful war
Take wreak° on Rome for this ingratitude,
And vengeance on the traitor Saturnine.     35

TITUS
Publius, how now! How now, my masters!
What, have you met with her?

PUBLIUS
No, my good lord, but Pluto sends you word,
If you will have revenge from hell, you shall:
Marry, for justice, she is so employed,     40
He thinks, with Jove in heaven, or somewhere else,
So that perforce you must needs stay a time.

TITUS
He doth me wrong to feed me with delays.
I'll dive into the burning lake below,
And pull her out of Acheron° by the heels.     45
Marcus, we are but shrubs, no cedars we,
No big-boned men framed of the Cyclops'° size;
But metal, Marcus, steel to the very back,
Yet wrung with wrongs more than our backs can bear:
And sith° there's no justice in earth nor hell,     50
We will solicit heaven, and move the gods
To send down justice for to wreak° our wrongs.
Come, to this gear.° You are a good archer, Marcus.

*He gives them the arrows.*

Ad Jovem, that's for you: here, Ad Apollinem:
Ad Martem,° that's for myself:     55
Here, boy, to Pallas: here, to Mercury:
To Saturn, Caius, not to Saturnine;
You were as good to shoot° against the wind.
To it, boy! Marcus, loose when I bid.
Of my word, I have written to effect;     60
There's not a god left unsolicited.

---

153–54 **countryman His** countryman's   156 **pack** conspire
157 **circumstance of all** all the details   163 **physic** medicine
166 **days** time   177 **puts . . . shifts** causes us to use stratagems   180 **cabin** dwell
IV.iii.3 **home** fully   4 **Terras Astraea reliquit** Astraea
(goddess of justice) has left the earth (Latin; from Ovid,
*Metamorphoses*, I.150)   5 **Be you remcmb'red** remember
8 **Happily** perhaps   13 **Pluto's region** Hades

19 **What time** when   24 **pipe for** whistle vainly for   29
**humor** mood, caprice   32 **But** a catchword indicates that
the line begins "But," though the line itself was omitted
34 **wreak** vengeance   45 **Acheron** river in Hades   47 **Cyclops'**
giants (in Homer's *Odyssey*)   50 **sith** since   52 **wreak** avenge
53 **gear** affair   54–55 **Ad Jovem . . . Ad Apollinem: Ad
Martem** to Jove . . . to Apollo; to Mars (Latin)   58 **You . . .
shoot** you would do as much good by shooting

MARCUS
Kinsmen, shoot all your shafts into the court:
We will afflict the emperor in his pride.

TITUS
Now, masters, draw. O, well said, Lucius!
Good boy, in Virgo's° lap; give it Pallas.                    65

MARCUS
My lord, I aim a mile beyond the moon;
Your letter is with Jupiter by this.

TITUS   Ha, ha!
Publius, Publius, what hast thou done!
See, see, thou hast shot off one of Taurus' horns.           70

MARCUS
This was the sport, my lord: when Publius shot,
The bull, being galled, gave Aries such a knock
That down fell both the ram's horns in the court,
And who should find them but the empress' villain?
She laughed, and told the Moor he should not choose          75
But give them to his master for a present.

TITUS
Why, there it goes! God give his lordship joy!

*Enter the* CLOWN,° *with a basket and two pigeons in it.*

News, news from heaven! Marcus, the post is come.
Sirrah, what tidings? Have you any letters?
Shall I have justice? What says Jupiter?                     80

CLOWN   Ho, the gibbet maker!° He says that he hath
taken them down again, for the man must not be
hanged till the next week.

TITUS   But what says Jupiter, I ask thee?

CLOWN   Alas, sir, I know not Jubiter; I never drank          85
with him in all my life.

TITUS   Why, villain, art not thou the carrier?

CLOWN   Ay, of my pigeons, sir, nothing else.

TITUS   Why, didst thou not come from heaven?

CLOWN   From heaven? Alas, sir, I never came there!          90
God forbid, I should be so bold to press to heaven in
my young days. Why, I am going with my pigeons
to the tribunal plebs,° to take up a matter of brawl
betwixt my uncle and one of the emperal's° men.

MARCUS   Why, sir, that is as fit as can be to serve for     95
your oration; and let him deliver the pigeons to the
emperor from you.

TITUS   Tell me, can you deliver an oration to the
emperor with a grace?

CLOWN   Nay, truly, sir, I could never say grace in all     100
my life.

TITUS
Sirrah, come hither: make no more ado,
But give your pigeons to the emperor:
By me thou shalt have justice at his hands.
Hold, hold, meanwhile, here's money for thy charges.°        105
Give me pen and ink. Sirrah, can you with a grace
    deliver up a supplication?

CLOWN   Ay, sir.

TITUS   Then here is a supplication for you. And when
you come to him, at the first approach you must            110

kneel, then kiss his foot, then deliver up your pigeons,
and then look for your reward. I'll be at hand, sir!
See you do it bravely.°

CLOWN   I warrant you, sir, let me alone.

TITUS
Sirrah, hast thou a knife? Come, let me see it.             115
Here, Marcus, fold it in the oration,
For thou hast made it like an humble suppliant.
And when thou hast given it to the emperor,
Knock at my door, and tell me what he says.

CLOWN   God be with you, sir; I will.           *Exit.*      120

TITUS   Come, Marcus, let us go. Publius, follow me.
                                              *Exeunt.*

[Scene IV. *Rome. Before the palace.*]

*Enter emperor* [SATURNINUS] *and empress* [TAMORA]
*and her two* SONS. *The emperor* [SATURNINUS] *brings
the arrows in his hand that Titus shot at him.*

SATURNINUS
Why, lords, what wrongs are these! Was ever seen
An emperor in Rome thus overborne,
Troubled, confronted thus, and for the extent°
Of egal° justice used in such contempt?
My lords, you know, as know the mightful gods,               5
However these disturbers of our peace
Buzz in the people's ears, there naught hath passed
But even° with law against the willful sons
Of old Andronicus. And what and if
His sorrows have so overwhelmed his wits,                   10
Shall we be thus afflicted in his wreaks,°
His fits, his frenzy, and his bitterness?
And now he writes to heaven for his redress!
See, here's to Jove, and this to Mercury,
This to Apollo, this to the god of war.                     15
Sweet scrolls to fly about the streets of Rome!
What's this but libeling against the senate,
And blazoning° our injustice everywhere?
A goodly humor, is it not, my lords?
As who would say, in Rome no justice were.                  20
But if I live, his feignèd ecstasies°
Shall be no shelter to these outrages,
But he and his shall know that justice lives
In Saturninus' health; whom, if he sleep,
He'll so awake, as he in fury shall                         25
Cut off the proud'st conspirator that lives.

TAMORA
My gracious lord, my lovely Saturnine,
Lord of my life, commander of my thoughts,
Calm thee, and bear the faults of Titus' age,
Th' effects of sorrow for his valiant sons,                 30
Whose loss hath pierced him deep and scarred his
    heart,
And rather comfort his distressèd plight
Than prosecute the meanest or the best
For these contempts. [*Aside.*] Why, thus it shall become
High-witted Tamora to gloze° with all.                      35
But, Titus, I have touched thee to the quick,

---

65 **Virgo's** the Virgin's (sign of the zodiac, as are *Taurus*—the
bull—in line 70, and *Aries*—the ram—in line 72)   **77 s.d.
Clown** rustic fellow   **81 gibbet maker** apparently "Jupiter"
—which in the original text is spelled "Jubiter"—was pronounced rather like "gibbeter" (i.e., gibbet maker)   **93 tribunal
plebs** malapropism for *tribunus plebis*, "tribune of the plebs"
**94 emperal's** another malapropism   **105 charges** pigeons

113 **bravely** well

IV.iv.**3 extent** exercise   **4 egal** equal   **8 even** agreeing
**11 wreaks** vengeful acts   **18 blazoning** proclaiming   **21
ecstasies** fits of madness   **35 gloze** use specious words

Thy lifeblood out:° if Aaron now be wise,
Then is all safe, the anchor in the port.

*Enter* CLOWN.

How now, good fellow? Wouldst thou speak with us?

CLOWN
Yea, forsooth, and your mistress-ship be emperial.  40

TAMORA
Empress I am, but yonder sits the emperor.

CLOWN  'Tis he. God and Saint Stephen give you
godden.° I have brought you a letter and a couple of
pigeons here.

*He* [SATURNINUS] *reads the letter.*

SATURNINUS
Go, take him away, and hang him presently.  45

CLOWN  How much money must I have?

TAMORA  Come, sirrah, you must be hanged.

CLOWN  Hanged! By Lady,° then I have brought up a
neck° to a fair end.          *Exit* [*with* GUARDS].

SATURNINUS
Despiteful and intolerable wrongs!  50
Shall I endure this monstrous villainy?
I know from whence this same device proceeds.
May this be borne as if his traitorous sons,
That died by law for murder of our brother,
Have by my means been butchered wrongfully.  55
Go, drag the villain hither by the hair,
Nor age nor honor shall shape privilege:°
For this proud mock I'll be thy slaughterman—
Sly frantic wretch, that holp'st to make me great,
In hope thyself should govern Rome and me.  60

*Enter nuntius,*° AEMILIUS.

What news with thee, Aemilius?

AEMILIUS
Arm, my lords. Rome never had more cause.
The Goths have gathered head,° and with a power°
Of high-resolvèd men, bent to the spoil,
They hither march amain, under conduct°  65
Of Lucius, son to old Andronicus;
Who threats, in course of this revenge, to do
As much as ever Coriolanus° did.

SATURNINUS
Is warlike Lucius general of the Goths?
These tidings nip me, and I hang the head  70
As flowers with frost or grass beat down with storms.
Ay, now begins our sorrows to approach:
'Tis he the common people love so much;
Myself hath often heard them say,
When I have walkèd like a private man,  75
That Lucius' banishment was wrongfully,
And they have wished that Lucius were their emperor.

TAMORA
Why should you fear? Is not your city strong?

SATURNINUS
Ay, but the citizens favor Lucius,
And will revolt from me to succor him.  80

TAMORA
King, be thy thoughts imperious, like thy name.
Is the sun dimmed, that gnats do fly in it?
The eagle suffers little birds to sing
And is not careful° what they mean thereby,
Knowing that with the shadow of his wings  85
He can at pleasure stint° their melody:
Even so mayst thou the giddy men of Rome.
Then cheer thy spirit: for know, thou emperor,
I will enchant the old Andronicus
With words more sweet, and yet more dangerous,  90
Than baits to fish, or honey stalks° to sheep;
Whenas the one is wounded with the bait,
The other rotted with delicious feed.

SATURNINUS
But he will not entreat his son for us.

TAMORA
If Tamora entreat him, then he will:  95
For I can smooth, and fill his agèd ears
With golden promises, that, were his heart
Almost impregnable, his old ears deaf,
Yet should both ear and heart obey my tongue.

[*To* AEMILIUS.]

Go thou before to be our ambassador:  100
Say that the emperor requests a parley
Of warlike Lucius, and appoint the meeting
Even at his father's house, the old Andronicus.

SATURNINUS
Aemilius, do this message honorably,
And if he stand in° hostage for his safety,  105
Bid him demand what pledge will please him best.

AEMILIUS
Your bidding shall I do effectually.          *Exit.*

TAMORA
Now will I to that old Andronicus,
And temper° him with all the art I have,
To pluck proud Lucius from the warlike Goths.  110
And now, sweet emperor, be blithe again,
And bury all thy fear in my devices.

SATURNINUS
Then go successantly,° and plead to him.     *Exeunt.*

# [ ACT V ]

[Scene I. *A plain near Rome.*]

*Enter* LUCIUS, *with an army of* GOTHS, *with drums and*
SOLDIERS.

LUCIUS
Approved° warriors, and my faithful friends,
I have received letters from great Rome,
Which signifies what hate they bear their emperor,

---

**37 Thy lifeblood out** when your blood is out  **43 godden**
good evening  **48 By Lady** an interjection (from "By
Our Lady")  **49 neck** possibly with a pun on *knack*, which
means "deceitful trick"  **57 shape privilege** provide immunity  **60 s.d. nuntius** messenger (Latin)  **63 gathered
head** raised an army; **power** army  **65 conduct** leadership
**68 Coriolanus** the Roman hero who became Rome's enemy
is the protagonist in Shakespeare's last tragedy

**84 careful** worried  **86 stint** stop  **91 honey stalks** clover
**105 stands in** insist upon  **109 temper** work upon  **113
successantly** one after the other (?)
**V.i.1 Approved** tested

And how desirous of our sight they are.
Therefore, great lords, be, as your titles witness,    5
Imperious, and impatient of your wrongs;
And wherein Rome hath done you any scath,°
Let him make treble satisfaction.

GOTH

Brave slip,° sprung from the great Andronicus,
Whose name was once our terror, now our comfort,    10
Whose high exploits and honorable deeds
Ingrateful Rome requites with foul contempt,
Be bold° in us: we'll follow where thou lead'st,
Like stinging bees in hottest summer's day,
Led by their master to the flow'red fields,    15
And be avenged on cursèd Tamora.

[OTHER GOTHS]

And as he saith, so say we all with him.

LUCIUS

I humbly thank him, and I thank you all.
But who comes here, led by a lusty Goth?

*Enter a* GOTH, *leading of* AARON *with his* CHILD *in his arms.*

GOTH

Renownèd Lucius, from our troops I strayed    20
To gaze upon a ruinous monastery,
And, as I earnestly did fix mine eye
Upon the wasted° building, suddenly
I heard a child cry underneath a wall.
I made unto the noise, when soon I heard    25
The crying babe controlled with this discourse:
"Peace, tawny° slave, half me and half thy dame.°
Did not thy hue bewray° whose brat° thou art,
Had nature lent thee but thy mother's look,
Villain, thou mightst have been an emperor:    30
But where the bull and cow are both milk-white,
They never do beget a coal-black calf.
Peace, villain, peace!" Even thus he rates° the babe,
"For I must bear thee to a trusty Goth,
Who, when he knows thou art the empress' babe,    35
Will hold thee dearly for thy mother's sake."
With this, my weapon drawn, I rushed upon him,
Surprised him suddenly, and brought him hither,
To use as you think needful of the man.

LUCIUS

O worthy Goth, this is the incarnate devil    40
That robbed Andronicus of his good hand.
This is the pearl that pleased your empress' eye,
And here's the base fruit of her burning lust.
Say, walleyed° slave, whither wouldst thou convey
This growing image of thy fiendlike face?    45
Why dost not speak? What, deaf? Not a word?
A halter, soldiers! Hang him on this tree,
And by his side his fruit of bastardy.

AARON

Touch not the boy; he is of royal blood.

LUCIUS

Too like the sire for ever being good.    50
First hang the child, that he may see it sprawl—
A sight to vex the father's soul withal.

AARON

Get me a ladder.° Lucius, save the child,
And bear it from me to the empress.
If thou do this, I'll show thee wondrous things    55
That highly may advantage thee to hear.
If thou wilt not, befall what may befall,
I'll speak no more but "Vengeance rot you all!"

LUCIUS

Say on, and if it please me which thou speak'st,
Thy child shall live, and I will see it nourished.    60

AARON

And if it please thee! Why, assure thee, Lucius,
'Twill vex thy soul to hear what I shall speak;
For I must talk of murders, rapes, and massacres,
Acts of black night, abominable deeds,
Complots of mischief, treason, villainies    65
Ruthful° to hear, yet piteously performed:°
And this shall all be buried in my death,
Unless thou swear to me my child shall live.

LUCIUS

Tell on thy mind, I say thy child shall live.

AARON

Swear that he shall, and then I will begin.    70

LUCIUS

Who should I swear by? Thou believest no god:
That granted, how canst thou believe an oath?

AARON

What if I do not? As indeed I do not;
Yet, for I know thou art religious,
And hast a thing within thee callèd conscience,    75
With twenty popish tricks and ceremonies,
Which I have seen thee careful to observe,
Therefore I urge thy oath; for that I know
An idiot holds his bauble° for a god,
And keeps the oath which by that god he swears,    80
To that I'll urge him: therefore thou shalt vow
By that same god, what god soe'er it be,
That thou adorest and hast in reverence,
To save my boy, to nourish and bring him up;
Or else I will discover naught to thee.    85

LUCIUS

Even by my god I swear to thee I will.

AARON

First know thou, I begot him on the empress.

LUCIUS

O most insatiate and luxurious° woman!

AARON

Tut, Lucius, this was but a deed of charity
To° that which thou shalt hear of me anon.    90
'Twas her two sons that murdered Bassianus;
They cut thy sister's tongue and ravished her,
And cut her hands, and trimmed her as thou sawest.

LUCIUS

O detestable villain! Call'st thou that trimming?

AARON

Why, she was washed, and cut, and trimmed, and
'twas    95
Trim sport for them which had the doing of it.

---

7 **scath** harm    9 **slip** offshoot    13 **bold** confident    23 **wasted** ruined    27 **tawny** black; **dame** mother    28 **bewray** reveal; **brat** young offspring    33 **rates** berates    44 **walleyed** glaring (literally, "having a whitish iris")

53 **Get . . . ladder** Hang me rather than the child    66 **Ruthful** pitiful; **piteously performed** performed, which excites pity    79 **bauble** carved head at the end of a court fool's stick    88 **luxurious** lustful    90 **To** in comparison with

LUCIUS
O barbarous, beastly villains, like thyself!

AARON
Indeed, I was their tutor to instruct them.
That codding° spirit had they from their mother,
As sure a card as ever won the set.°      100
That bloody mind, I think, they learned of me,
As true a dog as ever fought at head.°
Well, let my deeds be witness of my worth.
I trained° thy brethren to that guileful hole,
Where the dead corpse of Bassianus lay;      105
I wrote the letter that thy father found,
And hid the gold within that letter mentioned,
Confederate with the queen and her two sons;
And what not done, that thou hast cause to rue,
Wherein I had no stroke of mischief in it?      110
I played the cheater° for thy father's hand,
And when I had it drew myself apart,
And almost broke my heart with extreme laughter.
I pried me through the crevice of a wall,
When for his hand he had his two sons' heads;      115
Beheld his tears and laughed so heartily
That both mine eyes were rainy like to his:
And when I told the empress of this sport,
She sounded° almost at my pleasing tale,
And for my tidings gave me twenty kisses.      120

GOTH
What, canst thou say all this and never blush?

AARON
Ay, like a black dog, as the saying is.

LUCIUS
Art thou not sorry for these heinous deeds?

AARON
Ay, that I had not done a thousand more.
Even now I curse the day—and yet, I think,      125
Few come within the compass of my curse—
Wherein I did not some notorious ill:
As kill a man or else devise his death,
Ravish a maid or plot the way to do it,
Accuse some innocent and forswear° myself,      130
Set deadly enmity between two friends,
Make poor men's cattle break their necks,
Set fire on barns and haystalks in the night,
And bid the owners quench them with their tears.
Oft have I digged up dead men from their graves      135
And set them upright at their dear friends' door,
Even when their sorrows almost was forgot,
And on their skins, as on the bark of trees,
Have with my knife carvèd in Roman letters,
"Let not your sorrow die, though I am dead."      140
But, I have done a thousand dreadful things
As willingly as one would kill a fly,
And nothing grieves me heartily indeed,
But that I cannot do ten thousand more.

LUCIUS
Bring down the devil, for he must not die      145
So sweet a death as hanging presently.

AARON
If there be devils, would I were a devil,
To live and burn in everlasting fire,
So I might have your company in hell,
But to torment you with my bitter tongue!      150

LUCIUS
Sirs, stop his mouth, and let him speak no more.

*Enter* AEMILIUS.

GOTH
My lord, there is a messenger from Rome
Desires to be admitted to your presence.

LUCIUS
Let him come near.
Welcome, Aemilius, what's the news from Rome?      155

AEMILIUS
Lord Lucius, and you princes of the Goths,
The Roman emperor greets you all by me;
And, for he understands you are in arms,
He craves a parley at your father's house,
Willing you to demand your hostages,      160
And they shall be immediately delivered.

GOTH
What says our general?

LUCIUS
Aemilius, let the emperor give his pledges
Unto my father and my uncle Marcus,
And we will come. March away.      [*Exeunt.*]    165

[Scene II. *Rome. Before Titus' house.*]

*Enter* TAMORA *and her two* SONS, *disguised* [*as Revenge
attended by Rape and Murder*].

TAMORA
Thus, in this strange and sad habiliment,°
I will encounter with Andronicus,
And say I am Revenge, sent from below
To join with him and right his heinous wrongs.
Knock at his study, where, they say, he keeps°      5
To ruminate strange plots of dire revenge;
Tell him Revenge is come to join with him,
And work confusion° on his enemies.

*They knock, and* TITUS [*above*] *opens his study door.*

TITUS
Who doth molest my contemplation?
Is it your trick to make me ope the door,      10
That so my sad decrees may fly away,
And all my study be to no effect?
You are deceived; for what I mean to do
See here in bloody lines I have set down.
And what is written shall be executed.      15

TAMORA
Titus, I am come to talk with thee.

TITUS
No, not a word. How can I grace my talk,
Wanting a hand to give that accord?°
Thou hast the odds of° me, therefore no more.

99 **codding** lustful   100 **set** game   102 **at head** a courageous bulldog went for the bull's nose   104 **trained** lured   111 **cheater** officer appointed to look after escheats, or property forfeited to the crown   119 **sounded** swooned   130 **forswear** perjure

V.ii.1 **sad habiliment** dismal apparel   5 **keeps** dwells   8 **confusion** destruction   18 **give that accord** provide appropriate gestures   19 **odds of** advantage over

TAMORA
If thou didst know me, thou wouldst talk with me.   20
TITUS
I am not mad, I know thee well enough.
Witness this wretched stump, witness these crimson
   lines,
Witness these trenches made by grief and care,
Witness the tiring day and heavy night,
Witness all sorrow, that I know thee well   25
For our proud empress, mighty Tamora:
Is not thy coming for my other hand?
TAMORA
Know thou, sad man, I am not Tamora;
She is thy enemy, and I thy friend.
I am Revenge, sent from th' infernal kingdom   30
To ease the gnawing vulture of thy mind,
By working wreakful° vengeance on thy foes.
Come down and welcome me to this world's light;
Confer with me of murder and of death:
There's not a hollow cave or lurking place,   35
No vast obscurity or misty vale,
Where bloody murder or detested rape
Can couch° for fear, but I will find them out,
And in their ears tell them my dreadful name,
Revenge, which makes the foul offender quake.   40
TITUS
Art thou Revenge? And art thou sent to me,
To be a torment to mine enemies?
TAMORA
I am, therefore come down and welcome me.
TITUS
Do me some service ere I come to thee.
Lo, by thy side where Rape and Murder stands;   45
Now give some surance° that thou art Revenge;
Stab them, or tear them on thy chariot wheels;
And then I'll come and be thy wagoner,
And whirl along with thee about the globes.
Provide thee two proper palfreys,° black as jet,   50
To hale thy vengeful wagon swift away,
And find out murd'rers in their guilty caves:
And when thy car° is loaden with their heads,
I will dismount, and by thy wagon wheel
Trot like a servile footman all day long,   55
Even from Hyperion's° rising in the east,
Until his very downfall in the sea.
And day by day I'll do this heavy task,
So° thou destroy Rapine° and Murder there.
TAMORA
These are my ministers and come with me.   60
TITUS
Are they thy ministers? What are they called?
TAMORA
Rape and Murder; therefore callèd so,
'Cause they take vengeance of such kind of men.
TITUS
Good Lord, how like the empress' sons they are!
And you the empress! But we worldly° men   65
Have miserable, mad, mistaking eyes.

O sweet Revenge, now do I come to thee:
And, if one arm's embracement will content thee,
I will embrace thee in it by and by.   [Exit above.]
TAMORA
This closing° with him fits his lunacy.   70
Whate'er I forge° to feed his brainsick humors,
Do you uphold and maintain in your speeches,
For now he firmly takes me for Revenge,
And, being credulous in this mad thought,
I'll make him send for Lucius his son;   75
And, whilst I at a banket hold him sure,
I'll find some cunning practice° out of hand,°
To scatter and disperse the giddy Goths,
Or at the least make them his enemies.
See, here he comes, and I must ply my theme.   80

[Enter TITUS.]

TITUS
Long have I been forlorn, and all for thee.
Welcome, dread Fury, to my woeful house:
Rapine and Murder, you are welcome too:
How like the empress and her sons you are!
Well are you fitted, had you but a Moor:   85
Could not all hell afford you such a devil?
For well I wot the empress never wags°
But in her company there is a Moor;
And, would you represent our queen aright,
It were convenient° you had such a devil:   90
But welcome, as you are. What shall we do?
TAMORA
What wouldst thou have us do, Andronicus?
DEMETRIUS
Show me a murderer, I'll deal with him.
CHIRON
Show me a villain that hath done a rape,
And I am sent to be revenged on him.   95
TAMORA
Show me a thousand that hath done thee wrong,
And I will be revengèd on them all.
TITUS
Look round about the wicked streets of Rome,
And when thou find'st a man that's like thyself,
Good Murder, stab him; he's a murderer.   100
Go thou with him, and when it is thy hap°
To find another that is like to thee,
Good Rapine, stab him; he is a ravisher.
Go thou with them, and in the emperor's court
There is a queen attended by a Moor;   105
Well shalt thou know her by thine own proportion,
For up and down she doth resemble thee:
I pray thee, do on them some violent death;
They have been violent to me and mine.
TAMORA
Well hast thou lessoned us; this shall we do.   110
But would it please thee, good Andronicus,
To send for Lucius, thy thrice-valiant son,
Who leads towards Rome a band of warlike Goths,
And bid him come and banquet at thy house:
When he is here, even at thy solemn° feast,   115

---

32 **wreakful** avenging   38 **couch** lie hidden   46 **surance** assurance   50 **proper palfreys** excellent horses   53 **car** chariot   56 **Hyperion's** the sun god's   59 **So** provided that; **Rapine** Rape   65 **worldly** mortal, of this world

70 **closing** agreement   71 **forge** invent   77 **practice** scheme; **out of hand** on the spur of the moment   87 **wags** moves   90 **convenient** fitting   101 **hap** chance   115 **solemn** ceremonious

I will bring in the empress and her sons,
The emperor himself, and all thy foes,
And at thy mercy shall they stoop and kneel,
And on them shalt thou ease thy angry heart.
What says Andronicus to this device?                        120

TITUS
Marcus, my brother! 'Tis sad Titus calls.

*Enter* MARCUS.

Go, gentle Marcus, to thy nephew Lucius;
Thou shalt inquire him out among the Goths.
Bid him repair° to me and bring with him
Some of the chiefest princes of the Goths:                  125
Bid him encamp his soldiers where they are;
Tell him the emperor and the empress too
Feast at my house, and he shall feast with them.
This do thou for my love, and so let him,
As he regards his agèd father's life.                       130

MARCUS
This will I do, and soon return again.          [*Exit.*]

TAMORA
Now will I hence about thy business,
And take my ministers along with me.

TITUS
Nay, nay, let Rape and Murder stay with me,
Or else I'll call my brother back again,                    135
And cleave to no revenge but Lucius.

TAMORA [*Aside to her* SONS.]
What say you, boys? Will you abide with him,
Whiles I go tell my lord the emperor
How I have governed our determined jest?°
Yield to his humor, smooth and speak him fair,°             140
And tarry with him till I turn again.

TITUS [*Aside.*]
I knew them all, though they supposed me mad;
And will o'erreach them in their own devices,
A pair of cursèd hellhounds and their dame.

DEMETRIUS
Madam, depart at pleasure, leave us here.                   145

TAMORA
Farewell, Andronicus: Revenge now goes
To lay a complot° to betray thy foes.

TITUS
I know thou dost; and, sweet Revenge, farewell.
                                   [*Exit* TAMORA.]

CHIRON
Tell us, old man, how shall we be employed?

TITUS
Tut, I have work enough for you to do.                      150
Publius, come hither, Caius, and Valentine!

[*Enter* PUBLIUS *and others.*]

PUBLIUS
What is your will?

TITUS
Know you these two?

PUBLIUS
The empress' sons, I take them: Chiron, Demetrius.

TITUS
Fie, Publius, fie! Thou art too much deceived:              155

The one is Murder, and Rape is the other's name:
And therefore bind them, gentle Publius:
Caius and Valentine, lay hands on them:
Oft have you heard me wish for such an hour,
And now I find it: therefore bind them sure;                160
And stop their mouths if they begin to cry.       [*Exit.*]

CHIRON
Villains, forbear! We are the empress' sons.

PUBLIUS
And therefore do we what we are commanded.
Stop close their mouths, let them not speak a word:
Is he sure bound? Look that you find them fast.             165

*Enter* TITUS *Andronicus with a knife, and* LAVINIA *with
a basin.*

TITUS
Come, come, Lavinia; look, thy foes are bound.
Sirs, stop their mouths, let them not speak to me,
But let them hear what fearful words I utter.
O villains, Chiron and Demetrius!
Here stands the spring whom you have stained with
    mud,                                                    170
This goodly summer with your winter mixed.
You killed her husband, and for that vile fault
Two of her brothers were condemned to death,
My hand cut off and made a merry jest:
Both her sweet hands, her tongue, and that more
    dear                                                    175
Than hands or tongue, her spotless chastity,
Inhuman traitors, you constrained and forced.
What would you say if I should let you speak?
Villains, for shame you could not beg for grace.
Hark, wretches, how I mean to martyr you.                   180
This one hand yet is left to cut your throats,
Whiles that Lavinia 'tween her stumps doth hold
The basin that receives your guilty blood.
You know your mother means to feast with me,
And calls herself Revenge, and thinks me mad:               185
Hark, villains, I will grind your bones to dust,
And with your blood and it I'll make a paste,
And of the paste a coffin° I will rear,
And make two pasties of your shameful heads,
And bid that strumpet, your unhallowed dam,                 190
Like to the earth, swallow her own increase.°
This is the feast that I have bid her to,
And this the banket she shall surfeit on;
For worse than Philomel you used my daughter,
And worse than Progne° I will be revenged.                  195
And now prepare your throats. Lavinia, come,
Receive the blood; and when that they are dead,
Let me go grind their bones to powder small,
And with this hateful liquor temper° it,
And in that paste let their vile heads be baked.            200
Come, come, be every one officious°
To make this banket, which I wish may prove
More stern and bloody than the centaurs' feast.°

188 coffin pie crust  191 increase offspring  195 Progne
wife of Tereus (Tereus raped and mutilated Progne's sister,
Philomela, and in revenge Progne slaughtered Tereus'—and
her own—son and served him to Tereus)  199 temper mix
201 officious busy  203 centaurs' feast a battle followed
the marriage feast to which the Lapiths invited the centaurs

124 repair come  139 governed . . . jest managed the jest
we agreed ("determined") upon  140 smooth . . . fair
flatter and speak courteously to him  147 complot plot

*He cuts their throats.*

So, now bring them in, for I'll play the cook,
And see them ready against° their mother comes.          205
                                        *Exeunt.*

[Scene III. *Rome. Within Titus' house.*]

*Enter* LUCIUS, MARCUS, *and the* GOTHS [*with*
AARON *a prisoner, and an* ATTENDANT *bearing Aaron's*
CHILD].

LUCIUS
Uncle Marcus, since 'tis my father's mind
That I repair° to Rome, I am content.
GOTH
And ours with thine, befall what fortune will.
LUCIUS
Good uncle, take you in this barbarous Moor,
This ravenous tiger, this accursèd devil;          5
Let him receive no sust'nance, fetter him,
Till he be brought unto the empress' face
For testimony of her foul proceedings:
And see the ambush of our friends be strong;
I fear the emperor means no good to us.          10
AARON
Some devil whisper curses in my ear,
And prompt me, that my tongue may utter forth
The venomous malice of my swelling heart!
LUCIUS
Away, inhuman dog! Unhallowed slave!
Sirs, help our uncle to convey him in.          15

[GOTHS *lead* AARON *in. Trumpets sound.*]

The trumpets show the emperor is at hand.

*Sound trumpets. Enter emperor* [SATURNINUS] *and*
*empress* [TAMORA], *with* TRIBUNES *and others.*

SATURNINUS
What, hath the firmament mo° suns than one?
LUCIUS
What boots° it thee to call thyself a sun?
MARCUS
Rome's emperor, and nephew, break the parle;°
These quarrels must be quietly debated.          20
The feast is ready, which the careful° Titus
Hath ordained to an honorable end,
For peace, for love, for league, and good to Rome.
Please you, therefore, draw nigh, and take your places.
SATURNINUS
Marcus, we will.          25

*Trumpets sounding, enter* TITUS, *like a cook, placing the*
*dishes, and* LAVINIA *with a veil over her face,* [*young*
LUCIUS, *and others*].

TITUS
Welcome, my lord; welcome, dread queen;
Welcome, ye warlike Goths; welcome, Lucius;
And welcome, all: although the cheer° be poor,
'Twill fill your stomachs; please you eat of it.

SATURNINUS
Why art thou thus attired, Andronicus?          30
TITUS
Because I would be sure to have all well,
To entertain your highness and your empress.
TAMORA
We are beholding to you, good Andronicus.
TITUS
And if your highness knew my heart, you were.
My lord the emperor, resolve° me this:          35
Was it well done of rash Virginius
To slay his daughter with his own right hand,
Because she was enforced,° stained, and deflow'red?
SATURNINUS
It was, Andronicus.
TITUS
Your reason, mighty lord!          40
SATURNINUS
Because the girl should not survive her shame,
And by her presence still renew his sorrows.
TITUS
A reason mighty, strong, and effectual,
A pattern, precedent, and lively warrant,
For me, most wretched, to perform the like.          45
Die, die, Lavinia, and thy shame with thee,
And with thy shame thy father's sorrow die!

[*He kills her.*]

SATURNINUS
What hast thou done, unnatural and unkind?°
TITUS
Killed her for whom my tears have made me
    blind.
I am as woeful as Virginius was,          50
And have a thousand times more cause than he
To do this outrage, and it now is done.
SATURNINUS
What, was she ravished? Tell who did the deed.
TITUS
Will't please you eat? Will't please your highness
    feed?
TAMORA
Why hast thou slain thine only daughter thus?          55
TITUS
Not I; 'twas Chiron and Demetrius:
They ravished her and cut away her tongue;
And they, 'twas they, that did her all this wrong.
SATURNINUS
Go, fetch them hither to us presently.
TITUS
Why, there they are, both bakèd in this pie,          60
Whereof their mother daintily hath fed,
Eating the flesh that she herself hath bred.
'Tis true, 'tis true; witness my knife's sharp point.

*He stabs the empress* [TAMORA].

SATURNINUS
Die, frantic wretch, for this accursèd deed.

[*Kills* TITUS.]

205 **against** in preparation for the time when
**V.iii.2 repair** return  **17 mo** more  **18 boots** avails  19
**break the parle** interrupt the talk (i.e., cease quarreling)  21
**careful** full of sorrow  **28 cheer** hospitality

35 **resolve** answer  **38 enforced** forced, raped  **48 unkind**
(1) unnatural (2) cruel

LUCIUS

Can the son's eye behold his father bleed? 65
There's meed for meed,° death for a deadly deed.

[*Kills* SATURNINUS.]

MARCUS

You sad-faced men, people and sons of Rome,
By uproars severed, as a flight of fowl
Scattered by winds and high tempestuous gusts,
O, let me teach you how to knit again 70
This scattered corn into one mutual sheaf,
These broken limbs again into one body.

ROMAN LORD

Let Rome herself be bane° unto herself,
And she whom mighty kingdoms curtsy to,
Like a forlorn and desperate castaway, 75
Do shameful execution on herself,
But if° my frosty signs and chaps of age,°
Grave witnesses of true experience,
Cannot induce you to attend my words.

[*To* LUCIUS.]

Speak, Rome's dear friend, as erst° our ancestor,° 80
When with his solemn tongue he did discourse
To lovesick Dido's sad attending° ear
The story of that baleful° burning night,
When subtle Greeks surprised King Priam's Troy;
Tell us what Sinon° hath bewitched our ears, 85
Or who hath brought the fatal engine in
That gives our Troy, our Rome, the civil wound.
My heart is not compact° of flint nor steel;
Nor can I utter all our bitter grief,
But floods of tears will drown my oratory 90
And break my utt'rance, even in the time
When it should move ye to attend me most,
And force you to commiseration.
Here's Rome's young captain, let him tell the tale,
While I stand by and weep to hear him speak. 95

LUCIUS

Then, gracious auditory, be it known to you
That Chiron and the damned Demetrius
Were they that murd'red our emperor's brother;
And they it were that ravishèd our sister.
For their fell° faults our brothers were beheaded, 100
Our father's tears despised, and basely cozened°
Of that true hand that fought Rome's quarrel out
And sent her enemies unto the grave.
Lastly, myself unkindly banishèd,
The gates shut on me, and turned weeping out, 105
To beg relief among Rome's enemies,
Who drowned their enmity in my true tears
And oped their arms to embrace me as a friend:
I am the turned-forth, be it known to you,
That have preserved her welfare in my blood, 110
And from her bosom took the enemy's point,
Sheathing the steel in my advent'rous body.
Alas, you know I am no vaunter,° I;

My scars can witness, dumb although they are,
That my report is just and full of truth. 115
But, soft!° Methinks, I do digress too much,
Citing my worthless praise. O, pardon me,
For when no friends are by, men praise themselves.

MARCUS

Now is my turn to speak. Behold the child:
Of this was Tamora deliverèd, 120
The issue of an irreligious Moor,
Chief architect and plotter of these woes:
The villain is alive in Titus' house,
And as he is to witness, this is true.
Now judge what cause had Titus to revenge 125
These wrongs, unspeakable, past patience,
Or more than any living man could bear.
Now have you heard the truth. What say you,
   Romans?
Have we done aught amiss, show us wherein,
And, from the place where you behold us pleading, 130
The poor remainder of Andronici
Will, hand in hand, all headlong hurl ourselves
And on the ragged° stones beat forth our souls,
And make a mutual closure° of our house.
Speak, Romans, speak, and if you say we shall, 135
Lo, hand in hand, Lucius and I will fall.

AEMILIUS

Come, come, thou reverend man of Rome,
And bring our emperor gently in thy hand,
Lucius our emperor; for well I know
The common voice do cry it shall be so. 140

MARCUS

Lucius, all hail, Rome's royal emperor!

[*To* SOLDIERS.]

Go, go into old Titus' sorrowful house,
And hither hale that misbelieving Moor,
To be adjudged some direful slaught'ring death,
As punishment for his most wicked life. 145
                              [*Exeunt* ATTENDANTS.]
Lucius, all hail, Rome's gracious governor!

[*Cries of approval.*]

LUCIUS

Thanks, gentle Romans: may I govern so,
To heal Rome's harms and wipe away her woe!
But, gentle people, give me aim° awhile,
For nature puts me to a heavy task. 150
Stand all aloof; but, uncle, draw you near
To shed obsequious° tears upon this trunk.
O, take this warm kiss on thy pale cold lips,
These sorrowful drops upon thy bloodstained face,
The last true duties of thy noble son! 155

MARCUS

Tear for tear and loving kiss for kiss
Thy brother Marcus tenders on thy lips:
O, were the sum of these that I should pay
Countless and infinite, yet would I pay them!

LUCIUS

Come hither, boy; come, come, and learn of us 160
To melt in showers. Thy grandsire loved thee well;

---

66 **meed for meed** measure for measure   73 **bane** destruction   77 **But if** unless; **frosty . . . age** white hair and cracked (wrinkled) skin   80 **erst** formerly;   **our ancestor** Aeneas   82 **sad attending** seriously listening   83 **baleful** injurious   85 **Sinon** Greek who persuaded the Trojans to admit the wooden horse   88 **compact** composed   100 **fell** savage   101 **cozened** cheated   113 **vaunter** braggart

116 **soft** hold (a common interjection)   133 **ragged** rugged   134 **mutual closure** common end   149 **give me aim** assist me   152 **obsequious** mourning

Many a time he danced thee on his knee,
Sung thee asleep, his loving breast thy pillow;
Many a story hath he told to thee,
And bid thee bear his pretty tales in mind,          165
And talk of them when he was dead and gone.

MARCUS
How many thousand times hath these poor lips,
When they were living, warmed themselves on thine!
O, now, sweet boy, give them their latest° kiss.
Bid him farewell; commit him to the grave;          170
Do them° that kindness, and take leave of them.

BOY
O, grandsire, grandsire! Ev'n with all my heart
Would I were dead, so you did live again!
O Lord, I cannot speak to him for weeping;
My tears will choke me if I ope my mouth.          175

[*Enter* ATTENDANTS *with* AARON.]

ROMAN
You sad Andronici, have done with woes;
Give sentence on this execrable wretch
That hath been breeder of these dire events.

LUCIUS
Set him breast-deep in earth and famish him;

There let him stand and rave and cry for food:          180
If anyone relieves or pities him,
For the offense he dies. This is our doom.°
Some stay, to see him fast'ned in the earth.

AARON
Ah, why should wrath be mute, and fury dumb?
I am no baby, I, that with base prayers          185
I should repent the evils I have done:
Ten thousand worse than ever yet I did
Would I perform, if I might have my will:
If one good deed in all my life I did,
I do repent it from my very soul.          190

LUCIUS
Some loving friends convey the emperor hence,
And give him burial in his father's grave:
My father and Lavinia shall forthwith
Be closèd in our household's monument.
As for that ravenous tiger, Tamora,          195
No funeral rite, nor man in mourning weed,
No mournful bell shall ring her burial;
But throw her forth to beasts and birds to prey.
Her life was beastly and devoid of pity,
And being dead, let birds on her take pity.     *Exeunt.*  200

169 **latest** last   171 **them** "these poor lips" of line 167          182 **doom** sentence

# THE TAMING OF THE SHREW

### EDITED BY ROBERT B. HEILMAN

## Introduction

At a number of points critics of *The Taming of the Shrew* are in general agreement. No one doubts that Christopher Sly is skillfully characterized—in his coarseness, his liveliness, his unaffectedness, his candor, his partial yielding to illusion, his incongruous mixture of two styles of life, his difficulty in acting the gentleman and attending to even a rather popular brand of theatrical fare. No one doubts that Petruchio and Kate are made, if not altogether well-rounded characters, at least human beings of vitality and imaginativeness, so that they have an interest and plausibility that stereotypes would not have. Each first acts in a way that suggests a rather single-ply, rigid nature, and then reveals a capacity for crucial action of another quality and value. No one doubts that the Bianca plot is of secondary interest, that it turns on a conventional love story, that it has in it more of intrigue than of the romantic intensity that Shakespeare would later develop in his lovers, and that, despite its manifest limitations, Shakespeare has pumped theatrical life into it by the multiplication of candidates for Bianca's hand and by a brisk representation of their schemes and styles. No one doubts that the suitors are effectively distinguished from each other—Gremio, the clownish overage lover; Tranio, the virtuoso quasi-competitor who loves to play the gentleman; Hortensio, who can settle for an unromantic down-to-earth arrangement like a sensible man in Restoration comedy; and Lucentio, the straight man and winner. No one doubts that the lesser characters are, in brief space, endowed with much individuality and substance—Baptista, the worried and well-meaning father; Grumio, the spirited servant who finds histrionic pleasure in opposite roles, whether taking it from Petruchio or dishing it out to other servants; Biondello, the lively-talking aide-de-camp in the war of love; the conscientious and frustrated Tailor; the earnest Pedant, grimly determined to succeed in his role as Lucentio's helpful father; the actual Vincentio, driven into a temper by successive experiences of being put upon.

No one doubts, finally, that all these materials from diverse sources (see A Note on the Sources, p. 327) have been combined with so much ingenuity that the play has a convincing air of unity. The play-within-a-play is an old

device: no one feels any hiatus between the audience (Sly and the Lord's household) and the performers of a play (the actors presenting the two love affairs). The taming plot and the relatively straight love plot are brought together mechanically by the fact that the two women are sisters and that the marriage of one depends on that of the other; by the fact that Bianca's suitors collaborate in finding a suitor for Kate and, even more than that, in assisting him in his suit; by the fact that Petruchio first aids Hortensio and that Hortensio later plays along with Petruchio's game as wife-tamer; and by the fact that the final wedding celebration is a joint affair. The two actions are held together organically by the fact that the women wooed, the wooers, and their methods of wooing are in contrast, not only esthetically but, by implication, morally; and by the still more striking fact that the apparent contrast, which seems so obvious at first, is reversed in the final act. When Kate and Bianca undergo a partial change of roles at the end, we see them, not simply as ending parallel plots, but as ironically revealing different aspects of one fundamental situation—the relations of husbands and wives.

Within the last decade critics have begun to detect a still subtler form of unity, one that considerably raises the esthetic status of the play. This is "the unity of 'supposes.'" When Lucentio is made to use the phrase "counterfeit supposes" (V.i.115), Shakespeare is alluding,[1] it is assumed, to his source, Gascoigne's play *Supposes;* in this title Gascoigne is Englishing the title of his source play, Ariosto's *I Suppositi*. The idea behind these words is that of "posing," of assuming identities other than one's own. From Gascoigne Shakespeare got the Bianca plot, which is of course full of assumed or "supposed" identities: Hortensio as Litio, Lucentio as Cambio, Tranio as Lucentio, and the Pedant as Vincentio; and then the true Vincentio is accused of being someone else posing as Vincentio. But recent criticism has observed that "supposes" are not limited either to physical identity or to the Bianca plot. Within the Bianca plot, Bianca and the widow are both "supposed"

[1] There is a similar allusion in Tranio's decision that "supposed Lucentio must get a father, called 'supposed Vincentio'" (II.i. 400–01).

to be agreeable women who will be accommodating wives. That is, the dramatic treatment encourages us to see that beyond the mere putting on of a false name and a false social or professional identity may lie the putting on of a personality or moral identity (whether as a long-lasting habit or as a short-term device to secure a given end).

Once given such hints, the reader sees quickly a new and closer tie between the Bianca plot and the Sly plot (the Induction): in each, the basic mechanism is the use of "supposed" identities. The Lord and members of his household pretend to be Sly's servants and his wife. But we have hardly noted this when we see, also, that the mainspring of the Induction is a subtler alteration of identity: Sly is persuaded, or at least half-persuaded, that he is a lord. The Lord and his men have voluntarily changed identity in order to cause Sly involuntarily to change identity (just as Bianca's lovers, so to speak, have voluntarily changed identity in order to cause Bianca to accept them). From here it is only a quick step to the remarkable kinship that the main Petruchio-Kate plot has with the other two: Petruchio voluntarily assumes an identity ("poses" as a contrary, willful, autocratic, irrational man, a "shrew") in order to cause Kate involuntarily to change identity, to give up shrewishness and become a charming, cooperative wife. In three plots a "supposition" or impersonation is the means of inducing a person to act in a certain way: a man accepts a "wife" and two women accept husbands. "Acting" is the means of moving people toward a desired feeling and role; in this sense *The Taming* anticipates the much-quoted line in *As You Like It*, "All the world's a stage. . . ."

But there is a still subtler element in the functional identity of parts which creates the unity of the play. The "supposed" servants of Sly not only tell him he is a lord but hold before him verbal pictures—of omnipotence, luxury, pleasures—that move him in their own way toward imaginative acceptance of his high role. At least he accepts the external circumstances in which he finds himself; perhaps he even accepts the idea of a lordly personality in himself. The further he goes in this direction, the more fully the Induction anticipates the taming plot. For a part of Petruchio's method (by no means all of it) is to hold before Kate a picture of what she potentially is and may become if she will but cease resisting it—a "most patient, sweet, and virtuous wife" (III.ii.194). It is possible to assume that she imaginatively accepts this picture of herself and, under the stimulus of Petruchio's love, makes it come true. If this interpretation is valid, then the play—not only one of Shakespeare's earliest but a farcical one—has advanced remarkably at least to the edge of a philosophical realm. For it induces us to reflect on the belief in the primacy of the idea, on the creative powers of the imagination, on the view that, in Hamlet's phrase that has become a cliché, "Thinking makes it so." Hence *The Taming*, never thought one of Shakespeare's high achievements, moves up into the company of the truly Shakespearean, in which, however stereotyped the exterior and however obvious the popular appeal, there is a heart of profound meaningfulness and hence enduring excellence. It is possible that a once underrated play may be in danger of being overrated.

So far we have been summarizing the main grounds of

agreement among critics, especially the grounds on which *The Taming* has been praised. However, the argument for unity depends somewhat on how we understand the change in Kate—transformation, acceptance of discipline, discovery of true nature, rejection of an assumed role? This is not so demonstrable as is the tight interweaving of plots at the level of overt action. When it is asserted that the play uncovers Bianca as the real shrew, and reveals that Kate is not a shrew at all or else was only pretending to be a shrew to serve her own ends, surely we come into the realm of the arguable. There is something of the arguable about *The Taming;* indeed there has been, alongside the areas of unanimity, considerable difference of opinion about it. We can profitably change our course, then, and approach the play from the other side—in terms of the disagreements, or at least the changes of opinion, about it.

One argument grows out of sheer factual uncertainty: did Shakespeare, or did he not, keep Sly in the play for occasional comments in the later acts, and for an epilogue completing the dramatic "frame"? In *The Taming of a Shrew*, a play related to this one (see A Note on the Sources, p. 327), Sly stayed on. Hence, what about *The Shrew*? There are various opinions: (1) Shakespeare forgot about Sly; (2) Shakespeare originally wrote a Sly epilogue, but it dropped out; (3) the loss of Sly, though not a major blot, is unfortunate; (4) the loss of Sly is fortunate, and shows Shakespeare's artistry. If Shakespeare did originally give Sly the closing lines, and if these did disappear—from an acting script and hence from the printer's copy—the only compelling reason for this (in the opinion of the present editor) was not esthetic but practical: it simplified production problems such as size of cast. There is no merit in the argument that the elimination of Sly prevented an anticlimax, for this begs the question whether a Sly epilogue would inevitably be anticlimactic. There is likewise little merit in the argument that the Sly story comes to its logical end when Sly takes himself for a lord and thus in anticipation parallels Kate's transformation into a lady. For, while Kate can, with effort, retain her new moral identity, Sly cannot, with any amount of effort, retain his new moral identity. Hence it is possible to visualize a very effective Sly epilogue which would work by contrast, making us note the discrepancy between an imaginable change of being and a temporary change of status, between a hypnotism for the therapy of the subject and the imposition of a dream for the fun of the observers. We can imagine, also, the use of Sly for a cynical irony such as we know in "black comedy": the end of his new lordship might hint the diminution of Kate's new ladyship. Or, in a lighter vein, Sly might entertain, as he does in *A Shrew*, visions of being a wife-tamer, and thus introduce an implicit contrast between those who can pull off such an exploit and those who cannot. Well, the imagining of alternative endings serves only one purpose: showing that the present one is not necessarily ideal. Surely most readers feel spontaneously that, in the treatment of Sly in *The Shrew*, something is left uncomfortably hanging, and many stage directors borrow additional Sly materials from *A Shrew*.

While Petruchio and Kate, as we have noted, are admired as lively and charming creatures, forerunners of Benedick and Beatrice in *Much Ado About Nothing*, there is lack of agreement on their natures and on the nature of the transactions between them. No one doubts, of course, that they come to love each other; the problem is what they bring to that love and how they exercise it. The older view was that Petruchio was a very skillful psychologist, one who really knew how to handle a difficult woman. On the other hand, many commentators, especially in the nineteenth century, tended to feel that Petruchio's methods were not civilized and that, though they may once have been countenanced, they would never do in modern life. That sense of real life, of what it is and should be, which repeatedly infiltrates literary judgments, appears in estimates of Petruchio: there have been editors who get on the bandwagon and declare him out of date and yet rather wistfully intimate that it is too bad he has gone out of date while the world still has need of him. But in repudiating Petruchio's methods, critics have had to find ways of redeeming Petruchio, since the play obviously does not make him an intolerable man. So it has been said that he is not so much "taming" Kate as leading her to a needed discipline; that in no essential does he pass the bounds of gentlemanliness; that he simply offers Kate a picture of male strength that can elicit the respect without which she cannot love; that the heart of his method is a love which begets love. Here we have Petruchio transmuted from the relentless and mechanical taskmaster, required by a monstrous female, into a remarkably gifted gentleman-lover who simply brings out the best in an extraordinary woman—a best that, as it comes out, totally displaces a worst that had once seemed pretty much the whole story. This view is much more in tune with modern views of the right relations between men and women. But this interpretation too, if not utterly replaced, has been given a new twist and all but turned upside down by a still more "modern" view. In this most recent reading of the play, Petruchio, far from "taming" or subtly having a beneficent influence on a woman, is in reality tamed by her. While having the illusion of conquering, he is con- quered by her; when she says what he wants to hear, she is being ironic, undermining him with a show of acquies- cence and virtually a wink to the audience. In this view, Shakespeare wrote *What Every Woman Knows* over three hundred years before Barrie.

Kate, of course, has been done over in the same way. Once she was naturally and unquestionably taken to be a shrew, that is, a type of woman widely known in life and constantly represented in song and story. Then critics began to contend that Kate differed from the stereotype: that instead of being simply aggressive and contentious, she was ripe for love, wanted love, and really suffered from the fact that, inside the family and out, Bianca more readily attracted affection. Here is the move toward seeing Kate, not as an allegorical abstraction, a figure of shrew- ishness, but as an actual human being with impulses and motives experienced by all of us. This move goes still further. In one modern view (that of Nevill Coghill and the late Professor Goddard), Kate's disagreeableness of manner is not a primary fact of personality but is caused by lack of affection at home: Baptista, a "family tyrant," has petted and spoiled Bianca, and Kate is the unhappy by-product of parental irresponsibility and stupidity ("gross partiality" toward Bianca). In this view, Kate is very much like a modern problem child. But the distin- guished director of Shakespeare, Margaret Webster, offers us a still different Kate. To Miss Webster, Kate is a strong, intelligent, independent woman who is stuck in a stuffy household, "despises" her father and her "horrid little sister," thinks the local boys "beneath contempt," and finds in her fresh and vehement style the only available outlet for the talents and energy of a superior woman. Here we have the feminist's Kate, the modern woman whom it is perilous to hold back from self-expression and leadership —a far cry from the nagging Xanthippe that every now and then, from the beginning of time, would afflict a husband doomed, unless he took strong measures, to be ridiculed for his misfortune. But Goddard and Miss Webster agree in one thing: it is really Kate who takes over Petruchio, takes him over by simulating an obedience that is a paradoxical mastery. Her last long speech, then, is only a prolonged ironic commentary on the subordination of wives, and could be taken literally only by naïve believers in male supremacy.

As might be expected, critics differ on where Shake- speare stood. The most widely held assumption is that Shakespeare believed in the subordination of wives, and that in his age he could hardly do otherwise. While some readers accept this as calmly as most people accept what has happened long ago, others regret that Shakespeare was so little in accord with modern views; as early as 1897, even G. B. Shaw could insist that "the last scene is alto- gether disgusting to modern sensibility." The reader with a severe case of "modern sensibility" can either join Shaw in slapping Shakespeare's wrist or else go him one better by arguing that Shakespeare was really a modern at heart. The unspoken assumption here is that the "divine Shake- speare" could not possibly disagree with our answers to fundamental problems, especially those we have come to more recently. So various commentators say flatly that Shakespeare did *not* believe in the subordination of wives. Of Kate's long speech on the duty of wives (V.ii.138– 181), Goddard, amazed at three centuries of acceptance, exclaims, "as if Shakespeare could ever have meant it!" But only Miss Webster faced the fact that to make Shake- speare modern, one had to do something better with the wifely-duty speech than ignore it or just assert that, though the longest speech in the play, it doesn't count. So she went whole hog and treated the speech as Kate's choicest joke of all on Petruchio, who from now on, we judge, will be simply a complacent husband, happy in the laugh- able illusion that he has an obedient wife.

It is doubtful that we can know "what Shakespeare thought," and in a sense it does not matter; what is im- portant is how the play is to be taken (it is by no means impossible that the play "believes" something other than what Shakespeare as a man may have "believed"). All the aspects of it that have been taken now in one way, now in another, come together pretty well in the issue of what the play is to be called. By many critics it is called a "farce" and is discussed as a farce; yet there are those who deny vigorously that it is a farce. This difference of opinion is caused by a loose use of the term *farce*. Some people take farce as simply hurly-burly theater, with much slapstick, roughhouse (Petruchio with a whip, in the older productions), pratfalls, general confusion, trickery, uproar, gags, and so on. Yet such characteristics, which do appear generally in farce, are surface manifestations. What we need to identify is the "spirit of farce" which lies behind them. We may then be able to get away from insisting either that *The Shrew* is farce or that it is not farce, and to get on to seeing what it does with the genre of farce.

A genre is a conventionalized way of dealing with actuality, and different genres represent different habits of the human mind, or minister to the capacity for finding pleasure in different styles of representation. "Romance," for instance, is the genre that conceives of obstacles, dangers, and threats, especially those of an unusual or spectacular kind, as yielding to human ingenuity, spirit, or just good luck. On the other hand, "naturalism," as a literary mode, conceives of man as overcome by the pressure of outer forces, especially those of a dull, glacier-like, grinding persistence. The essential procedure of farce is to deal with people as if they lack, largely or totally, the physical, emotional, intellectual, and moral sensitivity that we think of as "normal." The enormous popularity of farce for several thousand years indicates that, though "farce" is often a term of disparagement, a great many people, no doubt all of us at times, take pleasure in seeing human beings acting as if they were very limited human beings. Farce offers a spectacle that resembles daily actuality but lets us participate without feeling the responsibilities and liabilities that the situation would normally evoke. Perhaps we feel superior to the diminished men and women in the plot; perhaps we harmlessly work off aggressions (since verbal and physical assaults are frequent in farce). Participation in farce is easy on us; in it we escape the full complexity of our own natures and cut up without physical or moral penalties. Farce is the realm without pain or conscience. Farce offers a holiday from vulnerability, consequences, costs. It is the opposite of all the dramas of disaster in which a man's fate is too much for him. It carries out our desire to simplify life by a selective anesthetizing of the whole person; man retains all his energy yet never gets really hurt. The give-and-take of life becomes a brisk skirmishing in which one needs neither health insurance nor liability insurance; when one is on the receiving end and has to take it, he bounces back up resiliently, and when he dishes it out, his pleasure in conquest is never undercut by the guilt of inflicting injury.

In farce, the human personality is without depth. Hence action is not slowed down by thought or by the friction of competing motives. Everything goes at high speed, with dash, variety, never a pause for stock-taking, and ever an athlete's quick glance ahead at the action coming up next. No sooner do the players come in than the Lord plans a show to help bamboozle Sly. As soon as Baptista appears with his daughters and announces the marriage priority, other lovers plan to find a man for Kate, Lucentio falls in love with Bianca and hits on an approach in disguise, Petruchio plans to go for Kate, Bianca's lovers promise him support, Petruchio begins his suit and introduces Hortensio into the scramble of disguised lovers. Petruchio rushes through the preliminary business with Baptista and the main business with Kate, and we have a marriage. The reader is hurried over to the rivalries of Bianca's lovers, making bids to Baptista and appealing directly to the girl herself, back to Kate's wedding-day scandals and out into the country for the postmarital welter of disturbances; then we shift back and forth regularly from rapid action in the Kate plot to almost equally rapid action in the Bianca plot. And so on. The driving pace made possible, and

indeed necessitated by, the absence of depth is brilliantly managed.

In the absence of depth one is not bothered by distractions; in fact, what are logically distractions are not felt as such if they fit into the pattern of carefree farcical hammer and tongs, cut and thrust. At Petruchio's first appearance, the "knocking at the gate" confusion is there for fun, not function (I.ii.5–43). The first hundred lines (in IV.i) between Grumio and Curtis are a lively rattle, full of the verbal and physical blows of farce, but practically without bearing on the action. Kate is virtually forgotten for sixty lines (in IV.iii) as Petruchio and Grumio fall into their virtuoso game of abusing the Tailor. Furthermore, action without depth has a mechanical, automatic quality: when two Vincentios appear (V.i), the characters do not reason about the duplication but, frustrated by confusion and bluffing, quickly have recourse to blows and insults, accusations of madness and chicanery, and threats of arrest —standard procedures in farce from Plautus on. Vincentio's "thus strangers may be halèd and abused" is not a bad description of the manners of farce. Mechanical action, in turn, often tends to symmetrical effects (shown most clearly in *The Comedy of Errors*, in which Shakespeare has two pairs of identical twins): the lovers of Kate and Bianca first bargain with Baptista, then approach the girls; Hortensio and Tranio (as Lucentio) resign their claims to Bianca in almost choral fashion; Bianca and the Widow respond identically to the requests of their husbands. In this final scene we have striking evidence of the manipulation of personality in the interest of symmetrical effect. Shakespeare unmistakably wants a double reversal of roles at the end, a symmetry of converse movements. The new Kate has developed out of a shrew, so the old Bianca must develop into a shrew. The earlier treatment of her hardly justifies her sudden transformation, immediately after marriage, into a cool, offhand, challenging, and even contemptuous near-bitch. Like many another character in farce, she succumbs to the habits of the generic form. Yet by some modern critics she is treated as harshly as if from the start she were a particularly obnoxious female.

All these effects come from a certain arbitrarily limited sense of personality. Those who have this personality are not really hurt, do not think much, are not much troubled by scruples. Farce often turns on practical jokes, in which the sadistic impulse is not restrained by any sense of injury to the victim. It would never occur to anyone that Sly might be pained or humiliated by letting himself act as a lord and then being let down. No one hesitates to make rough jokes about Kate (even calling her "fiend of hell") in her hearing. No one putting on a disguise to dupe others has any ethical inhibitions; the end always justifies the means. When Kate "breaks the lute to" Hortensio, farce requires that he act terrified; but it does not permit him to be injured or really resentful or grieved by the loss of the lute, as a man in a nonfarcical world might well be. Verbal abuse is almost an art form; it does not hurt, as it would in ordinary life. No one supposes that the victims of Petruchio's manhandling and tantrums—the priest and sexton at the wedding, the servants and tradesmen at his home—really feel the outrageous treatment that they get. When Petruchio and Hortensio call "To her" to Kate and the Widow, it is like starting a dogfight or cockfight. Petruchio's order to Kate to bring out the other wives is like having a trained dog retrieve a stick. The scene is possible because both husbands and all wives are not endowed with full human personalities; if they were, they could not function as trainer, retriever, and sticks.

In identifying the farcical elements in *The Shrew*, we have gradually shifted from the insensitivity that the characters must have to the mechanicalness of their responses. These people rarely think, hesitate, deliberate, or choose; they act just as quickly and unambiguously as if someone had pressed a control button. Farce simplifies life by making it painless and automatic; indeed the two qualities come together in the concept of man as machine. (The true opposite of farce is Čapek's *R. U. R.*, in which man-like robots actually begin to feel.) There is a sense in which we might legitimately call the age of computers a farcical one, for it lets us feel that basic choices are made without mental struggle or will or anxiety, and as speedily and inevitably as a series of human ninepins falling down one after another on the stage when each is bumped by the one next to it. "Belike you mean," says Kate to Petruchio, "to make a puppet of me" (IV.iii.104). It is what farce does to all characters. Now the least obvious illustration of the farcical view of life lies, not in some of the peripheral goings-on that we have been observing, but in the title action itself: the taming of the shrew. Fundamentally—we will come shortly to the necessary qualifications—Kate is conceived of as responding automatically to a certain kind of calculated treatment, as automatically as an animal to the devices of a skilled trainer. Petruchio not only uses the word *tame* more than once, but openly compares his method to that used in training falcons (IV.i.180 ff.). There is no reason whatever to suppose that this was not meant quite literally. Petruchio is not making a great jest or developing a paradoxical figure but describing a process taken at face value. He tells exactly what he has done and is doing—withholding food and sleep until the absolute need of them brings assent. (We hardly note that up to a point the assumptions are those of the "third degree" and of the more rigorous "cures" of bad habits: making it more unprofitable to assert one's will or one's bad habits than to act differently.) Before he sees Kate, he announces his method: he will assert as true the opposite of whatever she says and does and is, that is to say, will frustrate the manifestations of her will and establish the dominance of his own. Without naming them, he takes other steps that we know to be important in animal training. From the beginning he shows that he will stop at nothing to achieve his end, that he will not hesitate for a second to do anything necessary—to discard all dignity, or carry out any indecorous act or any outrageousness that will serve. He creates an image of utter invincibility, of having no weakness through which he can be appealed to. He does not use a literal whip, such as stage Petruchios were once addicted to, but he unmistakably uses a symbolic whip. Like a good trainer, however, he uses the carrot, too—not only marriage, but a new life, a happier personality for Kate. Above all, he offers love; in the end, the trainer succeeds best who makes the trainee feel the presence of something warmer than technique, rigor, and invincibility. Not that Petruchio fakes love, but that love has its part, ironically, in a process that is farcically conceived and that never wholly loses the markings of farce. Only in farce could we conceive of the occurrence,

almost in a flash, of that transformation of personality which, as known only too well in modern experience, normally requires a long, gradual, painstaking application of psychotherapy. True, conversion is believable and does happen, but even as a secular experience it requires a prior development of readiness, or an extraordinary revelatory shock, or both. (In the romantic form of this psychic event, an old hag, upon marriage to the knight, suddenly turns into a beautiful maiden.) Kate is presented initially as a very troubled woman; aggressiveness and tantrums are her way of feeling a sense of power. Though very modern, the argument that we see in her the results of paternal unkindness is not very impressive. For one thing, recent research on infants—if we may risk applying heavy science to light farce—suggests that basic personality traits precede, and perhaps influence, parental attitudes to children. More important, the text simply does not present Baptista as the overbearing and tyrannical father that he is sometimes said to be. Kate has made him almost as unhappy as she is, and driven him toward Bianca; nevertheless, when he heavily handicaps Bianca in the matrimonial sweepstakes, he is trying to even things up for the daughter that he naturally thinks is a poor runner. Nor is he willing to marry her off to Petruchio simply to get rid of her; "her love," he says, "is all in all." On her wedding day he says, kindly enough, "I cannot blame thee now to weep," and at the risk of losing husbands for both daughters he rebukes Petruchio (III.ii.96 ff.). (The Baptista that some commentators describe would surely have said nothing but "What do you expect, you bitch?") We cannot blacken Baptista to save Kate. Shakespeare presents her binding and beating Bianca (II.i.1 ff.) to show that he is really committed to a shrew; such episodes make it hard to defend the view that she is an innocent victim or is posing as a shrew out of general disgust. To sum up: in real life her disposition would be difficult to alter permanently, but farce secures its pleasurable effect by assuming a ready and total change in response to the stimuli applied by Petruchio, as if he were going through an established and proved routine. On the other hand, only farce makes it possible for Petruchio to be so skillful a tamer, that is, so unerring, so undeviating, so mechanical an enforcer of the rules for training in falconry. If Petruchio were by nature the disciplinarian that he acts for a while, he would hardly change after receiving compliance; and if he were, in real life, the charming and affectionate gentleman that he becomes in the play, he would find it impossible so rigorously to play the falcon-tamer, to outbully the bully, especially when the bully lies bleeding on the ground, for this role would simply run afoul of too much of his personality. The point here is not that the play is "unrealistic" (this would be a wholly irrelevant criticism) but that we can understand how a given genre works by testing it against the best sense of reality that we can bring to bear. It is the farcical view of life that makes possible the treatment of both Kate and Petruchio.

But this picture, of course, is incomplete; for the sake of clarity we have been stressing the purely generic in *The Shrew*, and gliding over the specific variations. Like any genre, farce is a convention, not a straitjacket; it is a fashion, capable of many variations. Genre provides a perspective, which in the individual work can be used narrowly or inclusively: comedy of manners, for instance, can move toward the character studies of James's novels or toward the superficial entertainments of Terence Rattigan. Shakespeare hardly ever uses a genre constrictively. In both *The Comedy of Errors* and *The Taming of the Shrew*, the resemblances between which are well known, Shakespeare moves away from the limited conception of personality that we find in "basic farce" such as that of Plautus, who influences both these plays. True, he protects both main characters in *The Shrew* against the expectable liabilities that would make one a less perfect reformer, and the other less than a model reformee, but he is unwilling to leave them automatons, textbook types of reformer and reformee. So he equips both with a good deal of intelligence and feeling that they would not have in elementary farce. Take sex, for instance. In basic farce, sex is purely a mechanical response, with no more overtones of feeling than ordinary hunger and thirst; the normal "love affair" is an intrigue with a courtesan. Like virtually all Renaissance lovers, Petruchio tells Kate candidly that he proposes to keep warm "in thy bed" (II.i.260). But there is no doubt that Petruchio, in addition to wanting a good financial bargain and enjoying the challenge of the shrew, develops real warmth of feeling for Kate as an individual —a warmth that makes him strive to bring out the best in her, keep the training in a tone of jesting, well-meant fantasy, provide Kate with face-saving devices (she is "curst . . . for policy" and only "in company"—II.i.285, 298), praise her for her virtues (whether she has them or not) rather than blame her for her vices, never fall into boorishness, repeatedly protest his affection for her, and by asking a kiss at a time she thinks unsuitable show that he really wants it. Here farce expands toward comedy of character by using a fuller range of personality. Likewise with Kate. The fact that she is a shrew does not mean that she cannot have hurt feelings, as it would in a plainer farce; indeed a shrew may be defined—once she develops beyond a mere stereotype—as a person who has an excess of hurt feelings and is taking revenge on the world for them. We do not, because we dislike the revenge, deny the painful feelings that may lie behind. Shakespeare has chosen to show some of those feelings, not making Kate an insentient virago on the one hand, or a pathetic victim on the other. She is jealous of Bianca and her lovers, she accuses Baptista of favoritism (in the opinion of the present editor, without justification); on her wedding day she suffers real anguish rather than simply an automatic, conventionally furious resolve for retaliation. The painful emotions take her way beyond the limitations of the essentially pain-free personality of basic farce. Further, she is witty, though, truth to tell, the first verbal battle between her and Petruchio, like various other such scenes, hardly goes beyond verbal farce, in which words are mechanical jokes or blows rather than an artistic game that delights by its quality, and in which all the speed of the short lines hardly conceals the heavy labors of the dutiful but uninspired punster (the best jokes are the bawdy ones). Kate has imagination. It shows first in a new human sympathy when she defends the servants against Petruchio (IV.i.145, 158–59). Then it develops into a gay, inspired gamesomeness that rivals Petruchio's own. When he insists, "It shall be what o'clock I say it is" (IV.iii.194) and "[The sun] shall be moon or star or what I list" (IV.v.7), he is at one level saying again that he will stop at nothing, at

no irrationality, as tamer; but here he moves the power game into a realm of fancy in which his apparent willfulness becomes the acting of the creative imagination. He is a poet, and he asks her, in effect, less to kiss the rod than to join in the game of playfully transforming ordinary reality. It is the final step in transforming herself. The point here is that, instead of not catching on or simply sulking, Kate has the dash and verve to join in the fun, and to do it with skill and some real touches of originality.

This scene on the road to Padua (IV.v.1–78) is the high point of the play. From here on, it tends to move back closer to the boundaries of ordinary farce. When Petruchio asks a kiss, we do have human beings with feelings, not robots; but the key line in the scene, which is sometimes missed, is Petruchio's "Why, then let's home again./Come sirrah, let's away" (V.i.145–46). Here Petruchio is making the same threat that he made at IV.v.8–9, that is, not playing an imaginative game but hinting the symbolic whip, even though the end is a compliance that she is inwardly glad to give. The whole wager scene, as we have already noted, falls essentially within the realm of farce: the responses are largely mechanical, as is their symmetry. Kate's final long speech on the obligations and fitting style of wives (V.ii.138–81) we can think of as a more or less automatic statement of a generally held doctrine. The easiest way to deal with it is to say that we no longer believe in it, just as we no longer believe in the divine right of kings which is an important dramatic element in many Shakespeare plays. But to some interpreters, Kate has become such a charming heroine that they cannot stand her being anything less than a modern feminist. Hence the claim that she is speaking ironically. There are two arguments against this interpretation. One is that a careful reading of the lines will show that most of them have to be taken literally; only the last seven or eight lines can be read with ironic overtones, but this means, at most, a return to the imaginative gamesomeness of IV.v, rather than a denial of the doctrine formally asserted. The second is that forty-five lines of straight irony would be too much to be borne; it would be inconsistent with the straightforwardness of most of the play, and it would really turn Kate back into a hidden shrew whose new technique was sarcastic indirection, sidemouthing at the audience while her not very intelligent husband, bamboozled, cheered her on. It would be a poor triumph. If one has to modernize the speech of the obedient wife, a better way to do it is to develop a hint of Professor Goddard's: that behind a passé doctrine lies a continuing truth. That truth is that there are real differences between the sexes, and that they are to be kept in mind. That view at least does not strain the spirit of Kate's speech.

The Katolatry which has developed in recent years reveals the romantic tendency to create heroes and heroines by denying the existence of flaws in them and by imputing all sorts of flaws in their families and other associates. We have already seen how the effort to save Kate at the beginning has resulted in an untenable effort to make Baptista into a villainous, punitive father and Bianca into a calculating little devil whose inner shrewishness slowly comes out. But it is hard to see why, if we are to admire Kate's spirit of open defiance at the beginning, and her alleged ironic defiance at the end, we should not likewise admire the spirit of Bianca and Hortensio's widow at the end. It is equally hard to see why we should admire Kate's quiet, ironic, what-every-woman-knows victory, as some would have it, over an attractive man at the end, but should not admire Petruchio's open victory over a very unattractive woman earlier. In fact, it is a little difficult to know just what Kate's supposed victory consists in. The play gives no evidence that from now on she will be twisting her husband around her finger. The evidence is rather that she will win peace and quiet and contentment by giving in to his wishes, and that her willingness will entirely eliminate unreasonable and autocratic wishes in him. But after all, the unreasonable and the autocratic are his strategy, not his nature; he gives up an assumed vice, while Kate gives up a real one. The truth is that Kate's great victory is, with Petruchio's help, over herself; she has come to accept herself as having enough merits so that she can be content without having the last word and scaring everybody off. To see this means to acknowledge that she was originally a shrew, whatever virtues may also have been latent in her personality.

What Shakespeare has done is to take an old, popular farcical situation and turn it into a well-organized, somewhat complex, fast-moving farce of his own. He has worked with the basic conceptions of farce—mainly that of a somewhat limited personality that acts and responds in a mechanical way and hence moves toward a given end with a perfection not likely if all the elements in human nature were really at work. So the tamer never fails in his technique, and the shrew responds just as she should. Now this situation might have tempted the dramatist to let his main characters be flat automatons—he a dull and rough whipwielder, and she a stubborn intransigent until beaten into insensibility (as in the ballad that was perhaps a Shakespearean source). Shakespeare, however, makes a gentleman and lady of his central pair. As tamer, Petruchio is a gay and witty and precocious artist and, beyond that, an affectionate man; and hence, a remarkable therapist. In Kate, Shakespeare has imagined, not merely a harridan who is incurable or a moral stepchild driven into a misconduct by mistreatment, but a difficult woman—a shrew, indeed—who combines willfulness with feelings that elicit sympathy, with imagination, and with a latent cooperativeness that can bring this war of the sexes to an honorable settlement. To have started with farce, to have stuck to the main lines of farce, and yet to have got so much of the supra-farcical into farce—this is the achievement of The Taming of the Shrew, and the source of the pleasure that it has always given.

## A NOTE ON THE SOURCES

Some time ago it was a rather generally held opinion that The Taming of the Shrew was Shakespeare's reworking of an anonymous play, The Taming of a Shrew (the conventional shorter form of a much longer title), published in 1594. There were at least two variations of the basic theory—one, that A Shrew itself was based on an earlier play; the other (and more widely held), that there was an intermediate play between A Shrew and Shakespeare's The Shrew. Such speculations were ways of explaining the similarities and dissimilarities between the two plays, and

to some extent, also, the apparent inconsistencies within the plays. The latter led likewise, it may be added, to much theorizing about authorship: A Shrew was attributed to various contemporary dramatists whose styles were supposedly recognizable in it, and The Shrew was believed to reveal the hand, not only of Shakespeare, but of a less gifted collaborator.

Another theory of the relationship between The Shrew and A Shrew was that they were siblings—different offspring of a single parent-play (either by Shakespeare or by someone else). Another theory of authorship was that Shakespeare himself had helped write A Shrew. Long before the putting forward of these hypotheses, Alexander Pope (1725) attributed A Shrew entirely to Shakespeare, and in his History of English Poetry (1895-1910) W. J. Courthope expressed the same conviction, though it ran counter to orthodox views at the time. The justification for mentioning these points of view here is that, in different ways and in different measure, they anticipate what is apparently the prevailing view at the present time—namely, that Shakespeare's The Shrew is the prior play and that A Shrew in some way derives from it. (The first expression of this view was Samuel Hickson's essay of 1850 on The Shrew.) One theory is that A Shrew is a "memorial reconstruction" of The Shrew, that is, an acting company's effort to put together from memory a script perhaps sold to another company. This explains parts of A Shrew that sound like badly remembered parts of The Shrew, but it hardly explains the larger extent of the Christopher Sly framework plot in A Shrew, the addition of a third daughter for Baptista, or the changing of the names of all the characters. To deal with these problems there is the hypothesis that, though A Shrew is based on The Shrew, it is a conscious revision, for whatever reasons, rather than a reassembling from memory. Obviously, much is still left unexplained. But that is true of all these theories, most of which are based on assumptions and likelihoods rather than on very hard evidence. In the end, we do not really know what the relation between the two plays is.

Scholars who believed that The Shrew was the later play tended to date it after 1595. Those who accept it as the prior play date it 1592 or 1593.

If The Shrew is the prior play, the problem of sources is simplified, for we need not consider the differences between the two plays. The Shrew is usually admired for its ingenious merging of three different bodies of material—the Christopher Sly business in the Induction, the taming plot, and the straight love story involving rival lovers (Bianca, Lucentio, and so on)—that are all, so to speak, old stories.

The story of the trick played upon the sleeper when he awakes is at least as old as the Arabian Nights (collected about 1450), in which Harun al-Rashid victimizes Abu Hassan. One scholar theorizes that ambassadors from the East may have told this story to Philip the Good (1396-1467), Duke of Burgundy, who is said to have played the trick upon a drunken man in Brussels. An officer of the duke told it to the theologian and educator Juan Luis Vives (1492-1540), who reported it in a letter (Epistolarum . . . Farrago, Antwerp, 1556). From him it passed to Heuterus, whose version in De rebus burgundicis (1584) is the most probable immediate source for Shakespeare (from Heuterus the story went via France into other English works later than *The Shrew*). Shakespeare may also have known the story in Richard Edwards' 1570 version, one of a collection of prose tales now lost.

In the taming plot Shakespeare utilized another old story of which there were versions in many countries. A possible immediate source is a long ballad (over 1100 lines) published in mid-sixteenth century, *A Merry Jest of a Shrewd and Curst Wife Lapped in Morel's Skin for Her Good Behavior*, but this is a cruder story of a rough and unsubtle husband ("Morel's Skin" is the salt hide of an old horse that the husband kills). Shakespeare, as Professor Hosley has shown, follows the humanist tradition embodied in, and perhaps derives some details from, Erasmus' colloquy, *A Merry Dialogue Declaring the Properties of Shrewd Shrews and Honest Wives* (1557). Several features of the Shakespeare story had appeared in Don Juan Manuel's *El Conde Lucanor*, a fourteenth-century collection of tales of which there was a sixteenth-century edition. Sisters somewhat like Baptista's daughters are contrasted in a tale in Giovanni Straparola's *Piacevoli notti* (1553).

Of the three main elements in *The Shrew*, the Bianca story is the only one whose source may be securely identified. That source is George Gascoigne's *Supposes* (acted 1566, published 1573; alluded to in *The Shrew*, V.i.115). Gascoigne's play, in turn, is a translation of an Italian play, Ariosto's *I Suppositi* (first acted at Ferrara in 1509). Ariosto, in turn, makes use of comic conventions that derive from the Romans Plautus and Terence and the Athenian Menander. The names *Tranio* and *Grumio* both come from Plautus. The Latin lesson may derive from a scene in R. W.'s *Three Lords and Three Ladies of London* (about 1590).

The farcical elements in *The Shrew* seem to have inspired revisers to outdo the farce of the original; Shakespeare's play is high comedy in contrast with versions of it that held the stage from mid-seventeenth to mid-nineteenth century. In 1667 Pepys saw an adaptation by John Lacy called *Sauny the Scot:* this magnifies Grumio's part (in *A Shrew*, the Grumio character was named Sander) and gives Grumio (that is, Sauny) a Scots accent. Garrick's *Catherine and Petruchio* (1756), which cut out the Sly and Bianca parts, was popular for over a century; indeed, toward the end of the nineteenth century Shaw was attacking Garrick for this commercialistic version that was still competing with Shakespeare's play. In the 1920's Fritz Lieber mounted a production in which Grumio was a Negro comic in a bellhop's uniform, and Grumio and Petruchio rode motorcycles. In 1948 Cole Porter wrote the musical *Kiss Me, Kate*, which is only nominally related to the original. However, modern productions tend, with variations, to produce *The Taming of the Shrew* in the 1623 version; the return to this began in 1844, with J. R. Planché's production at the Haymarket in London (under the sponsorship of Ben Webster, an ancestor of Margaret Webster, the modern director of Shakespeare). For more details of the stage history, see the entry under "Harold Child" in the Suggested References.

## A NOTE ON THE TEXT

The authority for the present text is the Folio of 1623 (F). Based on it were the quarto of 1631 and three later folios. These introduce a number of errors of their own but also make some corrections and some changes accepted by most subsequent editors. The present text adheres as closely as possible to F, accepting standard emendations only when F seems clearly erroneous. These emendations come mainly from such early editors as Rowe, Theobald, and Capell.

F's incomplete division into acts is almost universally altered by modern editors, and the present text conforms to standard practice. F has "*Actus primus. Scoena* [*sic*] *Prima*" at the beginning, whereas in modern practice approximately the first 275 lines are placed in an "Induction" with two scenes. F lacks a designation for Act II. F's "*Actus Tertia* [*sic*]," beginning with Lucentio's "Fiddler, forbear, etc.," is universally accepted. F's "*Actus Quartus. Scena Prima*" generally becomes modern IV.iii, and F's "*Actus Quintus*," modern V.ii.

F makes a number of erroneous or unclear speech assignments (at one time naming an actor, Sincklo, instead of the character). These are at Ind.i.88; III.i.47 ff.; IV.ii.4 ff. They are specifically listed below. Names of speakers, nearly always abbreviated in F, are regularly spelled out in the present edition. Speakers in F designated *Beggar*, *Lady*, and *Man* are given as *Sly*, *Page*, and *Servingman*, respectively.

F is not consistent in the spelling of some proper names. In the stage directions, the shrew, for instance, appears as *Katerina*, *Katherina*, *Katherine* (sometimes with *a* in the second syllable), and *Kate;* she is spoken to and of as *Katherine* and *Kate;* her speeches are headed *Ka*, *Kat*, and *Kate*. Since *Kate* is the most frequent form, this edition uses it throughout and does not include the change in the following list. In F, the name adopted by Hortensio when he pretends to be a music teacher appears three times as *Litio*, which we use here, and four times as *Lisio*. Many editors follow F2 and Rowe in emending to *Licio*.

Editors vary in the treatment of F's short lines, sometimes letting a short line stand independently, and sometimes joining several short lines into a quasi-pentameter. The latter practice is generally followed in the present edition. Modern editors are quite consistent in identifying as verse a few passages set as prose in F, and vice versa.

Errors in foreign languages in F are allowed to stand if they are conceivably errors made by the speaker, for example, errors in Latin and Spanish. Spellings of English words are corrected and modernized. The punctuation is modern. Obvious typographical errors, of which there are a great many, are corrected silently. The following materials, lacking in F, are given in square brackets in this edition: cast of characters, missing act and scene designations, indications of place of action, certain stage directions (F has an unusually copious supply of stage directions, some of which make interesting references to properties).

The following list includes all significant variations from F. The reading in the present text is in boldface, followed by the F reading in roman.

Ind.i.s.d. **Hostess and beggar** Begger and Hostes  12 **third-borough** Head-borough  17 **Broach** Brach  82 **A Player** 2. Player  88 **Second Player** Sincklo
Ind.ii.2 **lordship** Lord  18 **Sly's** Sies  136 **play it. Is** play, it is
I.i.13 **Vincentio** Vincentio's  25 **Mi perdonato** Me Pardonato  47 s.d. **suitor** sister  73 **master** Mr  162 **captum** captam  207 **colored** Conlord  243 **your** you
I.ii.13 **master** Mr  17 s.d. **wrings** rings  18 **masters** mistris

**24 Con . . . trovato** Contutti le core bene trobatto   **25 ben** bene; **26 molto** multo   **45 this's** this   **69, 89 shrewd** shrow'd   **70 Xanthippe** Zentippe   **72 she** she is   **120 me and other** me. Other   **171 help me** helpe one   **189 Antonio's** Butonios   **212 ours** yours   **265 feat** seeke

**II.i.3 gawds** goods   **8 charge thee** charge   **73 Backare** Bacare **75–76 wooing. Neighbor,** wooing neighbors:   **79 unto you this** vnto this   **104 Pisa; by report** Pisa by report   **158 vile** vilde **186 bonny** bony   **241 askance** a sconce   **323 in me**

**III.i.28 Sigeia** Sigeria (also in 32, 42)   **47 [Aside]** Luc.   **50 Bianca** [F omits] **51 Lucentio** Bian.   **53 Bianca** Hort.   **74 B mi** Beeme   **80 change** charge; **odd** old   **81 Messenger** Nicke

**III.ii.29 of thy** of   **30 such old** such   **33 hear** heard   **55 swayed** Waid   **56 half-cheeked** halfe-chekt   **127 to her love** sir, Loue **129 As I** As

**IV.i.23 Curtis** Grumio   **96 s.d. Enter . . . Servingmen** [F

places after 95]   **169 s.d.** [in F, after 170]   **193 reverent** reuerend **IV.ii.4 Hortensio** Luc.   **6 Lucentio** Hor.   **8 Lucentio** Hor. **13 none** me   **31 her** them   **63 mercatante** Marcantant   **71 Take in** Par. Take me

**IV.iii.63 Haberdasher** Fel.   **82 is a** is   **89 like a** like   **180 account'st** accountedst

**IV.iv.1 Sir** Sirs   **5** [in F, Tranio's speech begins here]   **9 s.d.** [F places after 7]   **19 Signior** Tra. Signior   **68** [F adds s.d., Enter Peter]   **91 except** expect

**IV.v.18 is** in   **35 make a** make the   **37 Whither** whether; **where** whether   **40 Allots** A lots   **47 reverend** reuerent (also in 60)   **77 she be** she

**V.i.6 master's** mistris   **52 master's** Mistris   **107 s.d.** [F places after 105]   **144 No** Mo

**V.ii.2 done** come   **37 thee, lad** the lad   **45 bitter** better   **65 for** sir

# THE TAMING OF THE SHREW

[Dramatis Personae

**Induction (and ending of Act I, Scene i)**

CHRISTOPHER SLY *a tinker*
HOSTESS *of an alehouse*
A LORD
HUNTSMEN *and* SERVANTS *of the Lord*
PLAYERS *in a traveling company*
BARTHOLOMEW *a page*

**Acts I–V**

BAPTISTA MINOLA *of Padua, father of Kate and Bianca*
KATE *the shrew*
BIANCA
PETRUCHIO *of Verona, suitor of Kate*
LUCENTIO (*Cambio*)
GREMIO *a pantaloon* } *suitors of Bianca*
HORTENSIO (*Litio*)

VINCENTIO *of Pisa, father of Lucentio*
A PEDANT (*impersonating Vincentio*)
TRANIO (*later impersonating Lucentio*)
BIONDELLO } *servants of Lucentio*
GRUMIO
CURTIS
NATHANIEL
NICHOLAS } *servants of Petruchio*
JOSEPH
PHILIP
PETER
A TAILOR
A HABERDASHER
A WIDOW
SERVANTS *of Baptista and Lucentio*

*Scene:* Warwick (Induction);
Padua; the country near Verona]

## [INDUCTION]

Scene I. [*Outside a rural alehouse.*]

*Enter* HOSTESS *and beggar Christophero* SLY.

SLY  I'll pheeze° you, in faith.
HOSTESS  A pair of stocks,° you rogue!
SLY  Y'are a baggage, the Slys are no rogues. Look in the chronicles: we came in with Richard° Conqueror. Therefore, paucas pallabris;° let the world slide.° 5 Sessa!°

*The decorative border above appeared on the first page of* The Taming of the Shrew *in the First Folio edition of Shakespeare's plays, 1623.*

**Ind.i.1 pheeze** do for (cf. *faze*)  **2 stocks** threatened punishment  **4 Richard** he means William  **5 paucas pallabris** few words (Spanish *pocas palabras*); **slide** go by (proverb; cf. Ind.ii.142)  **6 Sessa** scram (?) shut up (?)

HOSTESS  You will not pay for the glasses you have burst?
SLY  No, not a denier.° Go, by Saint Jeronimy,° go to thy cold bed and warm thee. 10
HOSTESS  I know my remedy: I must go fetch the thirdborough.° [*Exit.*]
SLY  Third or fourth or fifth borough, I'll answer him by law. I'll not budge an inch, boy;° let him come and kindly.° 15

*Falls asleep.*

*Wind° horns. Enter a* LORD *from hunting, with his* TRAIN.

**9 denier** very small coin (cf. *a copper*); **Jeronimy** Sly's oath inaccurately reflects a line in Kyd's *Spanish Tragedy*  **12 thirdborough** constable  **14 boy** wretch  **15 kindly** by all means  **15 s.d. Wind** blow

330

LORD
Huntsman, I charge thee, tender° well my hounds.
Broach° Merriman—the poor cur is embossed°—
And couple Clowder with the deep-mouthed brach.°
Saw'st thou not, boy, how Silver made it good
At the hedge-corner in the coldest fault?°           20
I would not lose the dog for twenty pound.

FIRST HUNTSMAN
Why, Bellman is as good as he, my lord;
He cried upon it at the merest loss°
And twice today picked out the dullest scent.
Trust me, I take him for the better dog.             25

LORD
Thou art a fool. If Echo were as fleet,
I would esteem him worth a dozen such.
But sup them well and look unto them all.
Tomorrow I intend to hunt again.

FIRST HUNTSMAN
I will, my lord.                                      30

LORD
What's here? One dead or drunk? See, doth he
    breathe?

SECOND HUNTSMAN
He breathes, my lord. Were he not warmed with ale,
This were a bed but cold to sleep so soundly.

LORD
O monstrous beast, how like a swine he lies!
Grim death, how foul and loathsome is thine image! 35
Sirs, I will practice on° this drunken man.
What think you, if he were conveyed to bed,
Wrapped in sweet clothes, rings put upon his fingers,
A most delicious banquet by his bed,
And brave° attendants near him when he wakes—      40
Would not the beggar then forget himself?

FIRST HUNTSMAN
Believe me, lord, I think he cannot choose.

SECOND HUNTSMAN
It would seem strange unto him when he waked.

LORD
Even as a flatt'ring dream or worthless fancy.
Then take him up and manage well the jest.           45
Carry him gently to my fairest chamber
And hang it round with all my wanton° pictures;
Balm° his foul head in warm distillèd waters
And burn sweet wood to make the lodging sweet.
Procure me music ready when he wakes                 50
To make a dulcet° and a heavenly sound;
And if he chance to speak, be ready straight°
And with a low submissive reverence
Say, "What is it your honor will command?"
Let one attend him with a silver basin               55
Full of rose water and bestrewed with flowers;
Another bear the ewer, the third a diaper,°
And say, "Will't please your lordship cool your
    hands?"
Some one be ready with a costly suit

And ask him what apparel he will wear,               60
Another tell him of his hounds and horse
And that his lady mourns at his disease.
Persuade him that he hath been lunatic,
And when he says he is,° say that he dreams,
For he is nothing but a mighty lord.                 65
This do, and do it kindly,° gentle sirs.
It will be pastime passing excellent
If it be husbanded with modesty.°

FIRST HUNTSMAN
My lord, I warrant you we will play our part
As° he shall think by our true diligence             70
He is no less than what we say he is.

LORD
Take him up gently and to bed with him,
And each one to his office° when he wakes.
                            [SLY is carried out.]

*Sound trumpets.*

Sirrah,° go see what trumpet 'tis that sounds.
                            [*Exit* SERVINGMAN.]
Belike° some noble gentleman that means,             75
Traveling some journey, to repose him here.

*Enter* SERVINGMAN.

How now? Who is it?
SERVINGMAN            An't° please your honor, players
That offer service to your lordship.

*Enter* PLAYERS.

LORD
Bid them come near. Now, fellows, you are welcome.
PLAYERS
We thank your honor.                                 80
LORD
Do you intend to stay with me tonight?
A PLAYER
So please your lordship to accept our duty.°
LORD
With all my heart. This fellow I remember
Since once he played a farmer's eldest son;
'Twas where you wooed the gentlewoman so well.       85
I have forgot your name, but sure that part
Was aptly fitted° and naturally performed.
SECOND PLAYER
I think 'twas Soto° that your honor means.
LORD
'Tis very true; thou didst it excellent.
Well, you are come to me in happy° time,             90
The rather for° I have some sport in hand
Wherein your cunning° can assist me much.
There is a lord will hear you play tonight.
But I am doubtful of your modesties,°
Lest overeyeing° of his odd behavior—               95
For yet his honor never heard a play—

---

16 **tender** look after   17 **Broach** bleed, i.e., medicate (some editors emend to "Breathe"); **embossed** foaming at the mouth   18 **brach** hunting bitch   20 **fault** lost ("cold") scent   23 **cried . . . loss** gave cry despite complete loss (of scent)   36 **practice on** play a trick on   40 **brave** well dressed   47 **wanton** gay   48 **Balm** bathe   51 **dulcet** sweet   52 **straight** without delay   57 **diaper** towel

64 **is** is "lunatic" now   66 **kindly** naturally   68 **husbanded with modesty** carried out with moderation   70 **As** so that   73 **office** assignment   74 **Sirrah** term of address used to inferiors   75 **Belike** likely   77 **An't** if it   82 **duty** respectful greeting   87 **aptly fitted** well suited (to you)   88 **Soto** in John Fletcher's *Women Pleased* (1620); reference possibly inserted here later   90 **in happy** at the right   91 **The rather for** especially because   92 **cunning** talent   94 **modesties** self-restraint   95 **overeyeing** seeing

You break into some merry passion°
And so offend him, for I tell you, sirs,
If you should smile he grows impatient.

A PLAYER
Fear not, my lord, we can contain ourselves       100
Were he the veriest antic° in the world.

LORD
Go, sirrah, take them to the buttery°
And give them friendly welcome every one.
Let them want° nothing that my house affords.

                    *Exit one with the* PLAYERS.
Sirrah, go you to Barthol'mew my page            105
And see him dressed in all suits° like a lady.
That done, conduct him to the drunkard's chamber
And call him "madam"; do him obeisance.
Tell him from me—as he will° win my love—
He bear himself with honorable action           110
Such as he hath observed in noble ladies
Unto their lords, by them accomplishèd.°
Such duty to the drunkard let him do
With soft low tongue and lowly courtesy,
And say, "What is't your honor will command      115
Wherein your lady and your humble wife
May show her duty and make known her love?"
And then, with kind embracements, tempting kisses,
And with declining head into his bosom,
Bid him shed tears, as being overjoyed           120
To see her noble lord restored to health
Who for this seven years hath esteemèd him
No better than a poor and loathsome beggar.
And if the boy have not a woman's gift
To rain a shower of commanded tears,             125
An onion will do well for such a shift,°
Which in a napkin° being close conveyed°
Shall in despite° enforce a watery eye.
See this dispatched with all the haste thou canst;
Anon° I'll give thee more instructions.          130
                    *Exit a* SERVINGMAN.
I know the boy will well usurp° the grace,
Voice, gait, and action of a gentlewoman.
I long to hear him call the drunkard husband,
And how my men will stay themselves from laughter
When they do homage to this simple peasant.      135
I'll in to counsel them; haply° my presence
May well abate the overmerry spleen°
Which otherwise would grow into extremes.
                    [*Exeunt.*]


[Scene II. *Bedroom in the Lord's house.*]

*Enter aloft*° *the drunkard* [SLY] *with* ATTENDANTS—
*some with apparel, basin, and ewer, and other appurtenances*
*—and* LORD.

SLY  For God's sake, a pot of small° ale!
FIRST SERVINGMAN
Will't please your lordship drink a cup of sack?°
SECOND SERVINGMAN
Will't please your honor taste of these conserves?°
THIRD SERVINGMAN
What raiment will your honor wear today?
SLY  I am Christophero Sly; call not me "honor" nor    5
"lordship." I ne'er drank sack in my life, and if you
give me any conserves, give me conserves of beef.°
Ne'er ask me what raiment I'll wear, for I have no
more doublets° than backs, no more stockings than
legs nor no more shoes than feet—nay, sometime      10
more feet than shoes or such shoes as my toes look
through the overleather.
LORD
Heaven cease this idle humor° in your honor!
O that a mighty man of such descent,
Of such possessions and so high esteem,            15
Should be infusèd with so foul a spirit!
SLY  What, would you make me mad? Am not I
Christopher Sly, old Sly's son of Burton-heath,° by    *Pro*
birth a peddler, by education a cardmaker,° by trans-
mutation a bearherd,° and now by present profession    20
a tinker? Ask Marian Hacket, the fat alewife of
Wincot,° if she know me not. If she say I am not
fourteen pence on the score° for sheer ale,° score me
up for the lying'st knave in Christendom. What, I am
not bestraught!° Here's—                            25
THIRD SERVINGMAN
O, this it is that makes your lady mourn.
SECOND SERVINGMAN
O, this is it that makes your servants droop.
LORD
Hence comes it that your kindred shuns your house
As beaten hence by your strange lunacy.
O noble lord, bethink thee of thy birth,           30
Call home thy ancient thoughts° from banishment
And banish hence these abject lowly dreams.
Look how thy servants do attend on thee,
Each in his office ready at thy beck.
Wilt thou have music? Hark, Apollo° plays,         35

*Music.*

And twenty cagèd nightingales do sing.
Or wilt thou sleep? We'll have thee to a couch
Softer and sweeter than the lustful bed
On purpose trimmed up for Semiramis.°
Say thou wilt walk, we will bestrow° the ground.   40
Or wilt thou ride? Thy horses shall be trapped,°
Their harness studded all with gold and pearl.
Dost thou love hawking? Thou hast hawks will soar

---

97 **merry passion** fit of merriment  101 **antic** odd person
102 **buttery** liquor pantry, bar  104 **want** lack  106 **suits**
respects (with pun)  109 **as he will** if he wishes to  112 **by
them accomplishèd** as carried out by the ladies  126 **shift**
purpose  127 **napkin** handkerchief; **close conveyed** secretly
carried  128 **Shall in despite** can't fail to  130 **Anon** then
131 **usurp** take on  136 **haply** perhaps  137 **spleen** spirit
**Ind.ii.s.d. aloft** on balcony above stage at back

1 **small** thin, diluted (inexpensive)  2 **sack** imported sherry
(costly)  3 **conserves** of fruit  7 **conserves of beef** salt beef
9 **doublets** close-fitting jackets  13 **idle humor** unreasonable
fantasy  18 **Burton-heath** probably Barton-on-the-Heath,
south of Stratford  19 **cardmaker** maker of cards, or combs,
for arranging wool fibers before spinning  20 **bearherd** leader
of a tame bear  22 **Wincot** village near Stratford (some
Hackets lived there)  23 **score** charge account; **sheer ale** ale
alone (?) undiluted ale (?)  25 **bestraught** distraught, crazy
31 **ancient thoughts** original sanity  35 **Apollo** here, god
of music  39 **Semiramis** mythical Assyrian queen, noted
for beauty and sexuality (cf. *Titus Andronicus*, II.i.22, II.iii.118)
40 **bestrow** cover  41 **trapped** decorated

Above the morning lark. Or wilt thou hunt?
Thy hounds shall make the welkin° answer them          45
And fetch shrill echoes from the hollow earth.

FIRST SERVINGMAN
Say thou wilt course,° thy greyhounds are as swift
As breathèd° stags, ay, fleeter than the roe.°

SECOND SERVINGMAN
Dost thou love pictures? We will fetch thee straight
Adonis° painted by a running brook                     50
And Cytherea all in sedges° hid,
Which seem to move and wanton° with her breath
Even as the waving sedges play with wind.

LORD
We'll show thee Io° as she was a maid
And how she was beguilèd and surprised,                55
As lively° painted as the deed was done.

THIRD SERVINGMAN
Or Daphne° roaming through a thorny wood,
Scratching her legs that one shall swear she bleeds,
And at that sight shall sad Apollo weep,
So workmanly the blood and tears are drawn.           60

LORD
Thou art a lord and nothing but a lord.
Thou hast a lady far more beautiful
Than any woman in this waning° age.

FIRST SERVINGMAN
And till the tears that she hath shed for thee
Like envious floods o'errun her lovely face,          65
She was the fairest creature in the world,
And yet° she is inferior to none.

SLY
Am I a lord, and have I such a lady?
Or do I dream? Or have I dreamed till now?
I do not sleep: I see, I hear, I speak,               70
I smell sweet savors and I feel soft things.
Upon my life, I am a lord indeed
And not a tinker nor Christopher Sly.
Well, bring our lady hither to our sight,
And once again a pot o' th' smallest° ale.            75

SECOND SERVINGMAN
Will't please your mightiness to wash your hands?
O, how we joy to see your wit° restored!
O, that once more you knew but what you are!
These fifteen years you have been in a dream,
Or when you waked so waked as if you slept.           80

SLY
These fifteen years! By my fay,° a goodly nap.
But did I never speak of° all that time?

FIRST SERVINGMAN
O yes, my lord, but very idle words,
For though you lay here in this goodly chamber,
Yet would you say ye were beaten out of door         85
And rail upon the hostess of the house°
And say you would present her at the leet°

Because she brought stone jugs and no sealed° quarts.
Sometimes you would call out for Cicely Hacket.

SLY
Ay, the woman's maid of the house.                    90

THIRD SERVINGMAN
Why, sir, you know no house nor no such maid
Nor no such men as you have reckoned up,
As Stephen Sly° and old John Naps of Greece,°
And Peter Turph and Henry Pimpernell,
And twenty more such names and men as these          95
Which never were nor no man ever saw.

SLY
Now, Lord be thankèd for my good amends!°

ALL   Amen.

*Enter [the PAGE, as a] lady, with ATTENDANTS.*

SLY
I thank thee; thou shalt not lose by it.

PAGE
How fares my noble lord?                             100

SLY
Marry,° I fare well, for here is cheer enough.
Where is my wife?

PAGE
Here, noble lord. What is thy will with her?

SLY
Are you my wife and will not call me husband?
My men should call me "lord"; I am your goodman.°    105

PAGE
My husband and my lord, my lord and husband,
I am your wife in all obedience.

SLY   I know it well. What must I call her?

LORD   Madam.

SLY   Al'ce madam or Joan madam?                      110

LORD
Madam and nothing else. So lords call ladies.

SLY
Madam wife, they say that I have dreamed
And slept above some fifteen year or more.

PAGE
Ay, and the time seems thirty unto me,
Being all this time abandoned° from your bed.        115

SLY
'Tis much. Servants, leave me and her alone.
                              [*Exeunt* SERVANTS.]
Madam, undress you and come now to bed.

PAGE
Thrice noble lord, let me entreat of you
To pardon me yet for a night or two
Or, if not, so until the sun be set.                 120
For your physicians have expressly charged,
In peril to incur° your former malady,
That I should yet absent me from your bed.
I hope this reason stands for my excuse.

SLY   Ay, it stands so° that I may hardly tarry so long, 125
but I would be loath to fall into my dreams again. I

---

45 **welkin** sky   47 **course** hunt hares   48 **breathèd** having
good wind; **roe** small deer   50 **Adonis** young hunter
loved by Venus (Cytherea) and killed by a wild boar
51 **sedges** grasslike plant growing in marshy places   52
**wanton** sway sinuously   54 **Io** mortal loved by Zeus and
changed into a heifer   56 **lively** lifelike   57 **Daphne** nymph
loved by Apollo and changed into laurel to evade him   63
**waning** decadent   67 **yet** now, still   75 **smallest** weakest   77
**wit** mind   81 **fay** faith   82 **of** in   86 **house** inn   87 **present**
. . . **leet** accuse her at the court under lord of a manor

88 **sealed** marked by a seal guaranteeing quantity   93 **Stephen
Sly** Stratford man (Naps, etc., may also be names of real
persons); **Greece** the Green (?) Greet, hamlet not far from
Stratford (?)   97 **amends** recovery   101 **Marry** in truth
(originally, "By the Virgin Mary")   105 **goodman** husband
115 **abandoned** excluded   122 **In . . . incur** because of the
danger of a return of   125 **stands so** will do (with phallic pun,
playing on *reason*, which was pronounced much like *raising*)

will therefore tarry in despite of the flesh and the blood.

*Enter a* MESSENGER.

MESSENGER
Your honor's players, hearing your amendment,
Are come to play a pleasant comedy.
For so your doctors hold it very meet,                                    130
Seeing too much sadness hath congealed your blood,
And melancholy is the nurse of frenzy.°
Therefore they thought it good you hear a play
And frame your mind to mirth and merriment,
Which bars a thousand harms and lengthens life.          135
SLY   Marry, I will let them play it. Is not a comontie°
a Christmas gambold° or a tumbling trick?
PAGE
No, my good lord, it is more pleasing stuff.
SLY   What, household stuff?°
PAGE   It is a kind of history.                                          140
SLY   Well, we'll see't. Come, madam wife, sit by my
side and let the world slip.° We shall ne'er be younger.

# [ A C T   I ]

[Scene I. *Padua. A street.*]

*Flourish.° Enter* LUCENTIO *and his man*° TRANIO.

LUCENTIO
Tranio, since for the great desire I had
To see fair Padua,° nursery of arts,
I am arrived for fruitful Lombardy,
The pleasant garden of great Italy,
And by my father's love and leave am armed                  5
With his good will and thy good company,
My trusty servant, well approved° in all,
Here let us breathe and haply institute
A course of learning and ingenious° studies.
Pisa, renownèd for grave citizens,                                10
Gave me my being and my father first,°
A merchant of great traffic° through the world,
Vincentio, come of the Bentivolii.
Vincentio's son, brought up in Florence,
It shall become to serve° all hopes conceived,             15
To deck his fortune with his virtuous deeds;
And therefore, Tranio, for the time I study,
Virtue and that part of philosophy
Will I apply° that treats of happiness
By virtue specially to be achieved.                               20
Tell me thy mind, for I have Pisa left
And am to Padua come, as he that leaves
A shallow plash° to plunge him in the deep
And with satiety seeks to quench his thirst.
TRANIO
Mi perdonato,° gentle master mine,                           25

I am in all affected° as yourself,
Glad that you thus continue your resolve
To suck the sweets of sweet philosophy.
Only, good master, while we do admire
This virtue and this moral discipline,                            30
Let's be no stoics nor no stocks,° I pray,
Or so devote° to Aristotle's checks°
As° Ovid° be an outcast quite abjured.
Balk logic° with acquaintance that you have
And practice rhetoric in your common talk.                 35
Music and poesy use to quicken° you.
The mathematics and the metaphysics,
Fall to them as you find your stomach° serves you.
No profit grows where is no pleasure ta'en.
In brief, sir, study what you most affect.°                     40
LUCENTIO
Gramercies,° Tranio, well dost thou advise.
If, Biondello, thou wert come ashore,
We could at once put us in readiness
And take a lodging fit to entertain
Such friends as time in Padua shall beget.                   45
But stay awhile, what company is this?
TRANIO
Master, some show to welcome us to town.

*Enter* BAPTISTA *with his two daughters,* KATE *and*
BIANCA; GREMIO, *a pantaloon;*° [*and*] HORTENSIO,
*suitor to Bianca.* LUCENTIO [*and*] TRANIO *stand by.*°

BAPTISTA
Gentlemen, importune me no farther,
For how I firmly am resolved you know,
That is, not to bestow my youngest daughter                50
Before I have a husband for the elder.
If either of you both love Katherina,
Because I know you well and love you well,
Leave shall you have to court her at your pleasure.
GREMIO
To cart° her rather. She's too rough for me.                 55
There, there, Hortensio, will you any wife?
KATE
I pray you, sir, is it your will
To make a stale° of me amongst these mates?°
HORTENSIO
Mates, maid? How mean you that? No mates for you
Unless you were of gentler, milder mold.                      60
KATE
I' faith, sir, you shall never need to fear:
Iwis° it° is not halfway to her° heart.
But if it were, doubt not her care should be
To comb your noddle with a three-legged stool
And paint° your face and use you like a fool.               65
HORTENSIO
From all such devils, good Lord deliver us!

---

**132 frenzy** mental illness   **136 comontie** comedy (as pronounced by Sly)   **137 gambold** gambol (game, dance, frolic)
**139 stuff** with sexual innuendo (see Eric Partridge, *Shakespeare's Bawdy*)   **142 slip** go by
**I.i.s.d. Flourish** fanfare of trumpets; **man** servant   **2 Padua** noted for its university   **7 approved** proved, found reliable
**9 ingenious** mind-training   **11 first** before that   **12 traffic** business   **15 serve** work for   **19 apply** apply myself to   **23 plash** pool   **25 Mi perdonato** pardon me

**26 affected** inclined   **31 stocks** sticks (with pun on *Stoics*)
**32 devote** devoted; **checks** restraints   **33 As** so that; **Ovid** Roman love poet (cf. III.i.28–29, IV.ii.8)   **34 Balk logic** engage in arguments   **36 quicken** make alive   **38 stomach** taste, preference   **40 affect** like   **41 Gramercies** many thanks
**47 s.d. pantaloon** laughable old man (a stock character with baggy pants in Italian Renaissance comedy); **by** nearby
**55 cart** drive around in an open cart (a punishment for prostitutes)   **58 stale** (1) laughingstock (2) prostitute; **mates** low fellows (with pun on *stalemate* and leading to pun on *mate* = husband)   **62 Iwis** certainly; **it** getting a mate; **her** Kate's
**65 paint** red with blood

GREMIO
And me too, good Lord!

TRANIO [*Aside.*]
Husht, master, here's some good pastime toward.°
That wench is stark mad or wonderful froward.°

LUCENTIO [*Aside.*]
But in the other's silence do I see                               70
Maid's mild behavior and sobriety.
Peace, Tranio.

TRANIO [*Aside.*]
Well said, master. Mum, and gaze your fill.

BAPTISTA
Gentlemen, that I may soon make good
What I have said: Bianca, get you in,                             75
And let it not displease thee, good Bianca,
For I will love thee ne'er the less, my girl.

KATE
A pretty peat!° It is best
Put finger in the eye,° and° she knew why.

BIANCA
Sister, content you in my discontent.                            80
Sir, to your pleasure humbly I subscribe.
My books and instruments shall be my company,
On them to look and practice by myself.

LUCENTIO [*Aside.*]
Hark, Tranio, thou mayst hear Minerva° speak.

HORTENSIO
Signior Baptista, will you be so strange?°                       85
Sorry am I that our good will effects
Bianca's grief.

GREMIO           Why will you mew° her up,
Signior Baptista, for this fiend of hell
And make her bear the penance of her tongue?

BAPTISTA
Gentlemen, content ye. I am resolved.                            90
Go in, Bianca.                              [*Exit* BIANCA.]
And for° I know she taketh most delight
In music, instruments, and poetry,
Schoolmasters will I keep within my house,
Fit to instruct her youth. If you, Hortensio,                    95
Or Signior Gremio, you, know any such,
Prefer° them hither; for to cunning° men
I will be very kind, and liberal
To mine own children in good bringing up.
And so, farewell. Katherina, you may stay,                      100
For I have more to commune with° Bianca.        *Exit.*

KATE
Why, and I trust I may go too, may I not?
What, shall I be appointed hours, as though, belike,°
I knew not what to take and what to leave? Ha! *Exit.*

GREMIO  You may go to the devil's dam;° your gifts 105
are so good, here's none will hold you. Their love is
not so great,° Hortensio, but we may blow our nails
together° and fast it fairly out. Our cake's dough on
both sides.° Farewell. Yet for the love I bear my sweet

Bianca, if I can by any means light on a fit man to 110
teach her that wherein she delights, I will wish° him
to her father.

HORTENSIO  So will I, Signior Gremio. But a word, I
pray. Though the nature of our quarrel yet never
brooked parle,° know now, upon advice,° it toucheth° 115
us both—that we may yet again have access to our
fair mistress and be happy rivals in Bianca's love—to
labor and effect one thing specially.

GREMIO  What's that, I pray?

HORTENSIO  Marry, sir, to get a husband for her sister. 120

GREMIO  A husband! A devil.

HORTENSIO  I say, a husband.

GREMIO  I say, a devil. Think'st thou, Hortensio,
though her father be very rich, any man is so very° a
fool to° be married to hell?                                    125

HORTENSIO  Tush, Gremio, though it pass your
patience and mine to endure her loud alarums,° why,
man, there be good fellows in the world, and° a man
could light on them, would take her with all faults,
and money enough.                                               130

GREMIO  I cannot tell, but I had as lief° take her
dowry with this condition, to be whipped at the high
cross° every morning.

HORTENSIO  Faith, as you say, there's small choice in
rotten apples. But come, since this bar in law° makes 135
us friends, it shall be so far forth° friendly maintained,
till by helping Baptista's eldest daughter to a husband,
we set his youngest free for a husband, and then have
to't° afresh. Sweet Bianca! Happy man be his dole!°
He that runs fastest gets the ring. How say you, 140
Signior Gremio?

GREMIO  I am agreed, and would I had given him the
best horse in Padua to begin his wooing, that° would
thoroughly woo her, wed her, and bed her and rid
the house of her. Come on.                                      145
        *Exeunt ambo.° Manet°* TRANIO *and* LUCENTIO.

TRANIO
I pray, sir, tell me, is it possible
That love should of a sudden take such hold?

LUCENTIO
O Tranio, till I found it to be true
I never thought it possible or likely,
But see, while idly I stood looking on,                         150
I found the effect of love-in-idleness°
And now in plainness do confess to thee,
That art to me as secret° and as dear
As Anna° to the Queen of Carthage was,
Tranio, I burn, I pine, I perish, Tranio,                       155
If I achieve not this young modest girl.

---

111 **wish** commend  115 **brooked parle** allowed negotiation;
**advice** consideration; **toucheth** concerns  124 **very** thorough
125 **to** as to  127 **alarums** outcries  128 **and** if  131 **had as
lief** would as willingly  132–33 **high cross** market cross
(prominent spot)  135 **bar in law** legal action of preventive sort
136 **so far forth** so long  138–39 **have to't** renew our competition  139 **Happy . . . dole** Let being a happy man be his
(the winner's) destiny  143 **that** antecedent is "his"  145
**s.d. ambo** both; **Manet** remain (though the Latin plural is
properly *manent*, the singular with a plural subject is common
in Elizabethan texts)  151 **love-in-idleness** popular name for
pansy (believed to have mysterious power in love; cf.
*Midsummer Night's Dream*, II.i.165 ff.)  153 **to . . . secret**
as much in my confidence  154 **Anna** sister and confidante
of Queen Dido

---

68 **toward** coming up  69 **froward** willful  78 **peat** pet (cf.
*teacher's pet*)  79 **Put . . . eye** cry; and if  84 **Minerva**
goddess of wisdom  85 **strange** rigid  87 **mew** cage (falconry
term)  92 **for** because  97 **Prefer** recommend; **cunning**
talented  101 **commune with** communicate to  103 **belike**
it seems likely  105 **dam** mother (used of animals)  107
**great** important  107–08 **blow . . . together** wait patiently
108–09 **Our . . . sides** We've both failed (proverbial)

Counsel me, Tranio, for I know thou canst.
Assist me, Tranio, for I know thou wilt.

TRANIO
Master, it is no time to chide you now.
Affection is not rated° from the heart.
If love have touched you, naught remains but so,°
"Redime te captum, quam queas minimo."°            160

LUCENTIO
Gramercies,° lad, go forward. This contents.
The rest will comfort, for thy counsel's sound.

TRANIO
Master, you looked so longly° on the maid,            165
Perhaps you marked not what's the pith of all.°

LUCENTIO
O yes, I saw sweet beauty in her face,
Such as the daughter of Agenor° had,
That made great Jove to humble him to her hand
When with his knees he kissed the Cretan strond.°   170

TRANIO
Saw you no more? Marked you not how her sister
Began to scold and raise up such a storm
That mortal ears might hardly endure the din?

LUCENTIO
Tranio, I saw her coral lips to move
And with her breath she did perfume the air.         175
Sacred and sweet was all I saw in her.

TRANIO
Nay, then, 'tis time to stir him from his trance.
I pray, awake, sir. If you love the maid,
Bend thoughts and wits to achieve her. Thus it stands:
Her elder sister is so curst and shrewd°             180
That till the father rid his hands of her,
Master, your love must live a maid at home;
And therefore has he closely mewed° her up,
Because° she will not be annoyed with suitors.

LUCENTIO
Ah, Tranio, what a cruel father's he!                185
But art thou not advised° he took some care
To get her cunning° schoolmasters to instruct her?

TRANIO
Ay, marry, am I, sir—and now 'tis plotted!°

LUCENTIO
I have it, Tranio!

TRANIO                    Master, for° my hand,
Both our inventions° meet and jump in one.°          190

LUCENTIO
Tell me thine first.

TRANIO                    You will be schoolmaster
And undertake the teaching of the maid.
That's your device.

LUCENTIO                    It is. May it be done?

TRANIO
Not possible, for who shall bear° your part

And be in Padua here Vincentio's son?                195
Keep house and ply his book, welcome his friends,
Visit his countrymen and banquet them?

LUCENTIO
Basta,° content thee, for I have it full.°
We have not yet been seen in any house,
Nor can we be distinguished by our faces             200
For man or master. Then it follows thus:
Thou shalt be master, Tranio, in my stead,
Keep house and port° and servants as I should.
I will some other be—some Florentine,
Some Neapolitan, or meaner° man of Pisa.             205
'Tis hatched and shall be so. Tranio, at once
Uncase° thee, take my colored° hat and cloak.
When Biondello comes he waits on thee,
But I will charm° him first to keep his tongue.

TRANIO
So had you need.                                     210
In brief, sir, sith° it your pleasure is
And I am tied° to be obedient—
For so your father charged me at our parting;
"Be serviceable to my son," quoth he,
Although I think 'twas in another sense—             215
I am content to be Lucentio
Because so well I love Lucentio.

LUCENTIO
Tranio, be so, because Lucentio loves,
And let me be a slave, t' achieve that maid
Whose sudden sight hath thralled° my wounded eye.    220

*Enter* BIONDELLO.

Here comes the rogue. Sirrah, where have you been?

BIONDELLO
Where have I been? Nay, how now, where are you?
Master, has my fellow Tranio stol'n your clothes,
Or you stol'n his, or both? Pray, what's the news?

LUCENTIO
Sirrah, come hither. 'Tis no time to jest,           225
And therefore frame your manners to the time.°
Your fellow Tranio, here, to save my life,
Puts my apparel and my count'nance° on,
And I for my escape have put on his,
For in a quarrel since I came ashore                 230
I killed a man and fear I was descried.°
Wait you on him, I charge you, as becomes,
While I make way from hence to save my life.
You understand me?

BIONDELLO              I, sir? Ne'er a whit.

LUCENTIO
And not a jot of Tranio in your mouth.               235
Tranio is changed into Lucentio.

BIONDELLO
The better for him. Would I were so too.

TRANIO
So could I, faith, boy, to have the next wish after,
That Lucentio indeed had Baptista's youngest daughter.

---

**160 rated** scolded  **161 so** to act thus  **162 Redime . . . minimo** ransom yourself, a captive, at the smallest possible price (from Terence's play *The Eunuch*, as quoted inaccurately in Lily's *Latin Grammar*)  **163 Gramercies** many thanks  **165 longly** (1) longingly (2) interminably  **166 pith of all** heart of the matter  **168 daughter of Agenor** Europa, loved by Jupiter, who, in the form of a bull, carried her to Crete  **170 strond** strand, shore  **180 curst and shrewd** sharp-tempered and shrewish  **183 mewed** caged  **184 Because** so that  **186 advised** informed  **187 cunning** knowing  **188 'tis plotted** I've a scheme  **189 for** I bet  **190 inventions** schemes; **jump in one** are identical  **194 bear** act

**198 Basta** enough (Italian); **full** fully (worked out)  **203 port** style  **205 meaner** of lower rank  **207 Uncase** undress; **colored** masters dressed colorfully; servants wore dark blue  **209 charm** exercise power over (he tells him a fanciful tale, lines 225–34)  **211 sith** since  **212 tied** obligated  **220 thralled** enslaved  **226 frame . . . time** adjust your conduct to the situation  **228 count'nance** demeanor  **231 descried** seen, recognized

But, sirrah, not for my sake but your master's, I advise 240
You use your manners discreetly in all kind of com-
  panies.
When I am alone, why, then I am Tranio,
But in all places else your master, Lucentio.

LUCENTIO
Tranio, let's go.
One thing more rests,° that thyself execute°— 245
To make one among these wooers. If thou ask me why,
Sufficeth my reasons are both good and weighty.
                        *Exeunt.*

*The* PRESENTERS° *above speaks.*

FIRST SERVINGMAN
My lord, you nod; you do not mind° the play.
SLY
Yes, by Saint Anne, do I. A good matter, surely.
Comes there any more of it? 250
PAGE
My lord, 'tis but begun.
SLY
'Tis a very excellent piece of work, madam lady.
Would 'twere done!

*They sit and mark.°*


[Scene II. *Padua. The street in front of*
*Hortensio's house.*]

*Enter* PETRUCHIO° *and his man* GRUMIO.

PETRUCHIO
Verona, for a while I take my leave
To see my friends in Padua, but of all
My best belovèd and approvèd friend,
Hortensio, and I trow° this is his house.
Here, sirrah Grumio, knock, I say. 5
GRUMIO  Knock, sir? Whom should I knock? Is there
  any man has rebused° your worship?
PETRUCHIO  Villain, I say, knock me here° soundly.
GRUMIO  Knock you here, sir? Why, sir, what am I,
  sir, that I should knock you here, sir? 10
PETRUCHIO
Villain, I say, knock me at this gate°
And rap me well or I'll knock your knave's pate.°
GRUMIO
My master is grown quarrelsome. I should knock you
  first,
And then I know after who comes by the worst.
PETRUCHIO
Will it not be? 15
Faith, sirrah, and° you'll not knock, I'll ring° it;
I'll try how you can sol, fa,° and sing it.

*He wrings him by the ears.*

GRUMIO
Help, masters, help! My master is mad.
PETRUCHIO
Now, knock when I bid you, sirrah villain.

*Enter* HORTENSIO.

HORTENSIO  How now, what's the matter? My old 20
friend Grumio, and my good friend Petruchio! How
do you all at Verona?
PETRUCHIO
Signior Hortensio, come you to part the fray?
Con tutto il cuore ben trovato,° may I say.
HORTENSIO
Alla nostra casa ben venuto, 25
Molto honorato signior mio Petruchio.°
Rise, Grumio, rise. We will compound° this quarrel.
GRUMIO  Nay, 'tis no matter, sir, what he 'leges° in
Latin.° If this be not a lawful cause for me to leave
his service—look you, sir, he bid me knock him and 30
rap him soundly, sir. Well, was it fit for a servant to
use his master so, being perhaps, for aught I see,
two-and-thirty, a peep out?°
Whom would to God I had well knocked at first,
Then had not Grumio come by the worst. 35
PETRUCHIO
A senseless villain! Good Hortensio,
I bade the rascal knock upon your gate
And could not get him for my heart° to do it.
GRUMIO  Knock at the gate? O heavens! Spake you
not these words plain, "Sirrah, knock me here, rap 40
me here, knock me well, and knock me soundly"?
And come you now with "knocking at the gate"?
PETRUCHIO
Sirrah, be gone or talk not, I advise you.
HORTENSIO
Petruchio, patience, I am Grumio's pledge.
Why, this's a heavy chance° 'twixt him and you, 45
Your ancient, trusty, pleasant servant Grumio.
And tell me now, sweet friend, what happy gale
Blows you to Padua here from old Verona?
PETRUCHIO
Such wind as scatters young men through the world
To seek their fortunes farther than at home, 50
Where small experience grows. But in a few,°
Signior Hortensio, thus it stands with me:
Antonio my father is deceased,
And I have thrust myself into this maze,°
Happily° to wive and thrive as best I may. 55
Crowns in my purse I have and goods at home
And so am come abroad to see the world.
HORTENSIO
Petruchio, shall I then come roundly° to thee
And wish thee to a shrewd ill-favored° wife?

---

245 **rests** remains; **execute** are to perform  247 s.d. **Presenters** commentators, actors thought of collectively, hence the
singular verb  248 **mind** pay attention to  253 s.d. **mark**
observe
I.ii.s.d. **Petruchio** correct form is *Petrucio*, with *c* pronounced
*tch*  4 **trow** think  7 **rebused** Grumio means *abused*  8 **knock
me here** knock here for me (Grumio plays a game of misunderstanding, taking "me here" as "my ear")  11 **gate** door
12 **pate** head  16 **and** if; **ring** pun on *wring*  17 **sol, fa** go
up and down the scales (possibly with puns on meanings
now lost)

24 **Con . . . trovato** with all (my) heart well found (i.e.,
welcome)  25–26 **Alla . . . Petruchio** Welcome to our
house, my much honored Signior Petruchio  27 **compound** settle  28 **'leges** alleges  29 **Latin** as if he were
English, Grumio does not recognize Italian  33 **two-and-
thirty . . . out** (1) an implication that Petruchio is aged (2) a
term from cards, slang for drunk (*peep* is an old form of *pip*, a
marking on a card)  38 **heart** life  45 **heavy chance** sad
happening  51 **few** words  54 **maze** traveling; uncertain
course  55 **Happily** haply, perchance  58 **come roundly**
talk frankly  59 **shrewd ill-favored** shrewish, poorly qualified

Thou'ldst thank me but a little for my counsel— 60
And yet I'll promise thee she shall be rich,
And very rich—but thou'rt too much my friend,
And I'll not wish thee to her.

PETRUCHIO
Signior Hortensio, 'twixt such friends as we
Few words suffice; and therefore if thou know 65
One rich enough to be Petruchio's wife—
As wealth is burthen° of my wooing dance—
Be she as foul° as was Florentius'° love,
As old as Sibyl,° and as curst and shrewd
As Socrates' Xanthippe° or a worse, 70
She moves me not, or not removes, at least,
Affection's edge in me, were she as rough
As are the swelling Adriatic seas.
I come to wive it wealthily in Padua;
If wealthily, then happily in Padua. 75

GRUMIO    Nay, look you, sir, he tells you flatly what
his mind is. Why, give him gold enough and marry
him to a puppet or an aglet-baby° or an old trot° with
ne'er a tooth in her head, though she have as many
diseases as two-and-fifty horses. Why, nothing comes 80
amiss so money comes withal.°

HORTENSIO
Petruchio, since we are stepped thus far in,
I will continue that° I broached in jest.
I can, Petruchio, help thee to a wife
With wealth enough and young and beauteous, 85
Brought up as best becomes a gentlewoman.
Her only fault—and that is faults enough—
Is that she is intolerable curst°
And shrewd and froward,° so beyond all measure
That were my state° far worser than it is, 90
I would not wed her for a mine of gold.

PETRUCHIO
Hortensio, peace. Thou know'st not gold's effect.
Tell me her father's name, and 'tis enough,
For I will board° her though she chide as loud
As thunder when the clouds in autumn crack.° 95

HORTENSIO
Her father is Baptista Minola,
An affable and courteous gentleman.
Her name is Katherina Minola,
Renowned in Padua for her scolding tongue.

PETRUCHIO
I know her father though I know not her, 100
And he knew my deceasèd father well.
I will not sleep, Hortensio, till I see her,
And therefore let me be thus bold with you,
To give you over° at this first encounter
Unless you will accompany me thither. 105

GRUMIO    I pray you, sir, let him go while the humor°

lasts. A° my word, and° she knew him as well as I do,
she would think scolding would do little good° upon
him. She may perhaps call him half a score knaves or
so—why, that's nothing. And he begin once, he'll 110
rail in his rope-tricks.° I'll tell you what, sir, and she
stand° him but a little, he will throw a figure in her
face and so disfigure her with it that she shall have no
more eyes to see withal than a cat. You know him
not, sir. 115

HORTENSIO
Tarry, Petruchio, I must go with thee,
For in Baptista's keep° my treasure is.
He hath the jewel of my life in hold,°
His youngest daughter, beautiful Bianca,
And her withholds from me and other more, 120
Suitors to her and rivals in my love,
Supposing it a thing impossible,
For° those defects I have before rehearsed,
That ever Katherina will be wooed.
Therefore this order° hath Baptista ta'en, 125
That none shall have access unto Bianca
Till Katherine the curst have got a husband.

GRUMIO
Katherine the curst!
A title for a maid of all titles the worst.

HORTENSIO
Now shall my friend Petruchio do me grace° 130
And offer° me, disguised in sober robes,
To old Baptista as a schoolmaster
Well seen° in music, to instruct Bianca,
That so I may, by this device, at least
Have leave and leisure to make love to her 135
And unsuspected court her by herself.

*Enter* GREMIO, *and* LUCENTIO *disguised [as a school-master, Cambio].*

GRUMIO    Here's no knavery! See, to beguile the old
folks, how the young folks lay their heads together!
Master, master, look about you. Who goes there, ha?

HORTENSIO
Peace, Grumio. It is the rival of my love. 140
Petruchio, stand by awhile.

*[They eavesdrop.]*

GRUMIO
A proper stripling,° and an amorous!

GREMIO
O, very well, I have perused the note.°
Hark you, sir, I'll have them very fairly bound—
All books of love, see that at any hand,° 145
And see you read no other lectures° to her.
You understand me. Over and beside
Signior Baptista's liberality,

---

**67 burthen** burden (musical accompaniment)    **68 foul** homely;
**Florentius** knight in Gower's *Confessio Amantis* (cf. Chaucer's
Wife of Bath's Tale: knight marries hag who turns into
beautiful girl)    **69 Sibyl** prophetess in Greek and Roman
myth    **70 Xanthippe** Socrates' wife, legendarily shrewish
**78 aglet-baby** small female figure forming metal tip of cord
or lace (French *aiguillette* = point); **trot** hag    **81 withal**
with it    **83 that** what    **88 intolerable curst** intolerably
sharp-tempered    **89 froward** willful    **90 state** estate, revenue
**94 board** naval term, with double sense: (1) accost (2) go
on board    **95 crack** make explosive roars    **104 give you
over** leave you    **106 humor** mood

**107 A** on; **and** if (also at lines 110 and 111)    **108 do little
good** have little effect    **111 rope-tricks** (1) Grumio's
version of *rhetoric*, going with *figure* just below (2) rascally
conduct, deserving hanging (3) possible sexual innuendo, as in
following lines    **112 stand** withstand    **117 keep** heavily
fortified inner tower of castle    **118 hold** stronghold    **123
For** because of    **125 order** step    **130 grace** a favor    **131 offer**
present, introduce    **133 seen** trained    **142 proper stripling**
handsome youth (sarcastic comment on Gremio)    **143 note**
memorandum (reading list for Bianca)    **145 at any hand** in
any case    **146 read . . . lectures** assign no other readings

I'll mend it with a largess.° Take your paper° too
And let me have them° very well perfumed,                                         150
For she is sweeter than perfume itself
To whom they go to. What will you read to her?

LUCENTIO
Whate'er I read to her, I'll plead for you
As for my patron, stand you so assured,
As firmly as° yourself were still in place°—                                     155
Yea, and perhaps with more successful words
Than you unless you were a scholar, sir.

GREMIO
O this learning, what a thing it is!

GRUMIO [Aside.]
O this woodcock,° what an ass it is!

PETRUCHIO
Peace, sirrah!                                                                   160

HORTENSIO
Grumio, mum! [Coming forward.] God save you,
   Signior Gremio.

GREMIO
And you are well met, Signior Hortensio.
Trow° you whither I am going? To Baptista Minola.
I promised to inquire carefully
About a schoolmaster for the fair Bianca,                                        165
And, by good fortune, I have lighted well
On this young man—for° learning and behavior
Fit for her turn,° well read in poetry
And other books, good ones I warrant ye.

HORTENSIO
'Tis well. And I have met a gentleman                                            170
Hath promised me to help me to° another,
A fine musician to instruct our mistress.
So shall I no whit be behind in duty
To fair Bianca, so beloved of me.

GREMIO
Beloved of me, and that my deeds shall prove.                                    175

GRUMIO [Aside.]
And that his bags° shall prove.

HORTENSIO
Gremio, 'tis now no time to vent° our love.
Listen to me, and if you speak me fair,
I'll tell you news indifferent° good for either.
Here is a gentleman whom by chance I met,                                        180
Upon agreement from us to his liking,°
Will undertake° to woo curst Katherine,
Yea, and to marry her if her dowry please.

GREMIO
So said, so done, is well.
Hortensio, have you told him all her faults?                                     185

PETRUCHIO
I know she is an irksome, brawling scold;
If that be all, masters, I hear no harm.

GREMIO
No, say'st me so, friend? What countryman?

PETRUCHIO
Born in Verona, old Antonio's son.
My father dead, my fortune lives for me,                                         190
And I do hope good days and long to see.

GREMIO
O, sir, such a life with such a wife were strange.
But if you have a stomach,° to't a° God's name;
You shall have me assisting you in all.
But will you woo this wildcat?

PETRUCHIO                                           Will I live?                  195

GRUMIO [Aside.]
Will he woo her? Ay, or I'll hang her.

PETRUCHIO
Why came I hither but to that intent?
Think you a little din can daunt mine ears?
Have I not in my time heard lions roar?
Have I not heard the sea, puffed up with winds,                                  200
Rage like an angry boar chafèd with sweat?
Have I not heard great ordnance° in the field
And heaven's artillery thunder in the skies?
Have I not in a pitchèd battle heard
Loud 'larums,° neighing steeds, and trumpets' clang?                             205
And do you tell me of a woman's tongue,
That gives not half so great a blow to hear
As will a chestnut in a farmer's fire?
Tush, tush, fear° boys with bugs.°

GRUMIO [Aside.]                               For he fears none.

GREMIO
Hortensio, hark.                                                                 210
This gentleman is happily arrived,
My mind presumes, for his own good and ours.

HORTENSIO
I promised we would be contributors
And bear his charge of° wooing, whatsoe'er.

GREMIO
And so we will, provided that he win her.                                        215

GRUMIO [Aside.]
I would I were as sure of a good dinner.

*Enter* TRANIO *brave*° [*as Lucentio*] *and* BIONDELLO.

TRANIO
Gentlemen, God save you. If I may be bold,
Tell me, I beseech you, which is the readiest way
To the house of Signior Baptista Minola?

BIONDELLO
He that has the two fair daughters? Is't he you
   mean?                                                                         220

TRANIO
Even he, Biondello.

GREMIO
Hark you, sir. You mean not her to—

TRANIO
Perhaps, him and her, sir. What have you to do?°

PETRUCHIO
Not her that chides, sir, at any hand,° I pray.

TRANIO
I love no chiders, sir. Biondello, let's away.                                   225

149 mend . . . largess add a gift of money to it; paper
note (line 143) 150 them the books 155 as as if you;
in place present 159 woodcock bird easily trapped, so
considered silly 163 Trow know 167 for in 168 turn
situation (with unconscious bawdy pun on the sense of "copulation") 171 help me to (1) find (2) become (Hortensio's jest)
176 bags of money 177 vent express 179 indifferent equally
181 Upon . . . liking if we agree to his terms (paying costs)
182 undertake promise

193 stomach inclination; a in 202 ordnance cannon 205
'larums calls to arms, sudden attacks 209 fear frighten;
bugs bugbears 214 his charge of the cost of his 216 s.d.
brave elegantly attired 223 to do to do with this 224 at
any hand in any case

LUCENTIO [*Aside.*]
Well begun, Tranio.

HORTENSIO          Sir, a word ere you go.
Are you a suitor to the maid you talk of, yea
   or no?

TRANIO
And if I be, sir, is it any offense?

GREMIO
No, if without more words you will get you
   hence.

TRANIO
Why, sir, I pray, are not the streets as free          230
For me as for you?

GREMIO          But so is not she.

TRANIO
For what reason, I beseech you?

GREMIO
For this reason, if you'll know,
That she's the choice° love of Signior Gremio.

HORTENSIO
That she's the chosen of Signior Hortensio.          235

TRANIO
Softly, my masters! If you be gentlemen,
Do me this right: hear me with patience.
Baptista is a noble gentleman
To whom my father is not all unknown,
And were his daughter fairer than she is,          240
She may more suitors have, and me for one.
Fair Leda's daughter° had a thousand wooers;
Then well one more may fair Bianca have.
And so she shall. Lucentio shall make one,
Though Paris° came° in hope to speed° alone.          245

GREMIO
What, this gentleman will out-talk us all.

LUCENTIO
Sir, give him head. I know he'll prove a jade.°

PETRUCHIO
Hortensio, to what end are all these words?

HORTENSIO
Sir, let me be so bold as ask you,
Did you yet ever see Baptista's daughter?          250

TRANIO
No, sir, but hear I do that he hath two,
The one as famous for a scolding tongue
As is the other for beauteous modesty.

PETRUCHIO
Sir, sir, the first's for me; let her go by.

GREMIO
Yea, leave that labor to great Hercules,          255
And let it be more than Alcides'° twelve.

PETRUCHIO
Sir, understand you this of me in sooth:°
The youngest daughter, whom you hearken° for,
Her father keeps from all access of suitors
And will not promise her to any man          260
Until the elder sister first be wed.
The younger then is free, and not before.

TRANIO
If it be so, sir, that you are the man
Must stead° us all, and me amongst the rest,
And if you break the ice and do this feat,          265
Achieve° the elder, set the younger free
For our access, whose hap° shall be to have her
Will not so graceless be to be ingrate.°

HORTENSIO
Sir, you say well, and well you do conceive,°
And since you do profess to be a suitor,          270
You must, as we do, gratify° this gentleman
To whom we all rest° generally beholding.°

TRANIO
Sir, I shall not be slack, in sign whereof,
Please ye we may contrive° this afternoon
And quaff carouses° to our mistress' health          275
And do as adversaries° do in law,
Strive mightily but eat and drink as friends.

GRUMIO AND BIONDELLO
O excellent motion! Fellows, let's be gone.

HORTENSIO
The motion's good indeed, and be it so.
Petruchio, I shall be your ben venuto.°          *Exeunt.*  280

# [ A C T   I I ]

[Scene I. *In Baptista's house.*]

*Enter* KATE *and* BIANCA [*with her hands tied*].

BIANCA
Good sister, wrong me not nor wrong yourself
To make a bondmaid and a slave of me.
That I disdain. But for these other gawds,°
Unbind my hands, I'll pull them off myself,
Yea, all my raiment, to my petticoat,          5
Or what you will command me will I do,
So well I know my duty to my elders.

KATE
Of all thy suitors, here I charge thee, tell
Whom thou lov'st best. See thou dissemble not.

BIANCA
Believe me, sister, of all the men alive          10
I never yet beheld that special face
Which I could fancy more than any other.

KATE
Minion,° thou liest. Is't not Hortensio?

BIANCA
If you affect° him, sister, here I swear
I'll plead for you myself but you shall have him.          15

KATE
O then, belike,° you fancy riches more:
You will have Gremio to keep you fair.°

---

234 **choice** chosen  242 **Leda's daughter** Helen of Troy
245 **Paris** lover who took Helen to Troy (legendary cause of
Trojan War); **came** should come; **speed** succeed  247 **prove
a jade** soon tire (cf. *jaded*)  256 **Alcides** Hercules (after
Alcaeus, a family ancestor)  257 **sooth** truth  258 **hearken**
long

264 **stead** aid  266 **Achieve** succeed with  267 **whose hap**
the man whose luck  268 **to be ingrate** as to be ungrateful
269 **conceive** put the case  271 **gratify** compensate  272
**rest** remain; **beholding** indebted  274 **contrive** pass  275
**quaff carouses** empty our cups  276 **adversaries** attorneys
280 **ben venuto** welcome (i.e., host)
**II.i.3 gawds** adornments  13 **Minion** impudent creature
14 **affect** like  16 **belike** probably  17 **fair** in fine clothes

**BIANCA**
Is it for him you do envy° me so?
Nay, then you jest, and now I well perceive
You have but jested with me all this while.     20
I prithee, sister Kate, untie my hands.

**KATE**
If that be jest then all the rest was so.

*Strikes her.*

*Enter* BAPTISTA.

**BAPTISTA**
Why, how now, dame, whence grows this insolence?
Bianca, stand aside. Poor girl, she weeps.
Go ply thy needle; meddle not with her.     25
For shame, thou hilding° of a devilish spirit,
Why dost thou wrong her that did ne'er wrong thee?
When did she cross thee with a bitter word?

**KATE**
Her silence flouts me and I'll be revenged.

*Flies after* BIANCA.

**BAPTISTA**
What, in my sight? Bianca, get thee in.     30
                              *Exit* [BIANCA].

**KATE**
What, will you not suffer° me? Nay, now I see
She is your treasure, she must have a husband;
I must dance barefoot on her wedding day,°
And, for your love to her, lead apes in hell.°
Talk not to me; I will go sit and weep     35
Till I can find occasion of revenge.     [*Exit.*]

**BAPTISTA**
Was ever gentleman thus grieved as I?
But who comes here?

*Enter* GREMIO, LUCENTIO *in the habit of a mean*° *man*
[*Cambio*], PETRUCHIO, *with* [HORTENSIO *as a music
teacher, Litio, and*] TRANIO [*as Lucentio*], *with his boy*
[BIONDELLO] *bearing a lute and books.*

**GREMIO**  Good morrow, neighbor Baptista.

**BAPTISTA**  Good morrow, neighbor Gremio. God    40
save you, gentlemen.

**PETRUCHIO**
And you, good sir. Pray, have you not a daughter
Called Katherina, fair and virtuous?

**BAPTISTA**
I have a daughter, sir, called Katherina.

**GREMIO** [*Aside.*]
You are too blunt; go to it orderly.°     45

**PETRUCHIO** [*Aside.*]
You wrong me, Signior Gremio, give me leave.

[*To* BAPTISTA.]

I am a gentleman of Verona, sir,
That, hearing of her beauty and her wit,
Her affability and bashful modesty,
Her wondrous qualities and mild behavior,     50
Am bold to show myself a forward° guest

Within your house, to make mine eye the witness
Of that report which I so oft have heard.
And, for an entrance to° my entertainment,°
I do present you with a man of mine,     55

[*Presenting* HORTENSIO.]

Cunning in music and the mathematics,
To instruct her fully in those sciences,
Whereof I know she is not ignorant.
Accept of him, or else you do me wrong.
His name is Litio, born in Mantua.     60

**BAPTISTA**
Y'are welcome, sir, and he for your good sake.
But for my daughter Katherine, this I know,
She is not for your turn,° the more my grief.

**PETRUCHIO**
I see you do not mean to part with her,
Or else you like not of my company.     65

**BAPTISTA**
Mistake me not; I speak but as I find.
Whence are you, sir? What may I call your name?

**PETRUCHIO**
Petruchio is my name, Antonio's son,
A man well known throughout all Italy.

**BAPTISTA**
I know him well. You are welcome for his sake.     70

**GREMIO**
Saving° your tale, Petruchio, I pray,
Let us, that are poor petitioners, speak too.
Backare,° you are marvelous° forward.

**PETRUCHIO**
O pardon me, Signior Gremio, I would fain° be doing.°

**GREMIO**
I doubt it not, sir, but you will curse your wooing.     75
Neighbor, this is a gift very grateful,° I am sure of it.
To express the like kindness myself, that° have been
more kindly beholding to you than any, freely give
unto you this young scholar [*presenting* LUCENTIO]
that hath been long studying at Rheims—as cunning     80
in Greek, Latin, and other languages, as the other in
music and mathematics. His name is Cambio.° Pray
accept his service.

**BAPTISTA**  A thousand thanks, Signior Gremio. Welcome, good Cambio. [*To* TRANIO.] But, gentle sir,     85
methinks you walk like° a stranger. May I be so bold
to know the cause of your coming?

**TRANIO**
Pardon me, sir, the boldness is mine own,
That,° being a stranger in this city here,
Do make myself a suitor to your daughter,     90
Unto Bianca, fair and virtuous.
Nor is your firm resolve unknown to me
In the preferment of° the eldest sister.
This liberty is all that I request,
That, upon knowledge of my parentage,     95

---

18 **envy** hate  26 **hilding** base wretch  31 **suffer** permit
(i.e., to deal with you)  33 **dance . . . day** expected of
older maiden sisters  34 **lead . . . hell** proverbial occupation of old maids (cf. *Much Ado About Nothing*, II.i.41)  38
s.d. **mean** lower class  45 **orderly** gradually  51 **forward**
eager  54 **entrance to** price of admission for; **entertainment** reception  63 **turn** purpose (again, with bawdy pun)  71 **Saving**
with all respect for  73 **Backare** back (proverbial quasi-Latin);
**marvelous** very  74 **would fain** am eager to; **doing** with
a sexual jest  76 **grateful** worthy of gratitude  77 **myself,
that** I myself, who  82 **Cambio** exchange (Italian)  86 **walk
like** have the bearing of  89 **That** who  93 **preferment of**
giving priority to

I may have welcome 'mongst the rest that woo
And free access and favor° as the rest.
And, toward the education of your daughters
I here bestow a simple instrument,°
And this small packet of Greek and Latin books.  100
If you accept them, then their worth is great.

BAPTISTA [*Looking at books.*]
Lucentio is your name. Of whence, I pray?

TRANIO
Of Pisa, sir, son to Vincentio.

BAPTISTA
A mighty man of Pisa; by report
I know him° well. You are very welcome, sir.  105

[*To* HORTENSIO.]

Take you the lute, [*to* LUCENTIO] and you the set of
    books;
You shall go see your pupils presently.°
Holla, within!

*Enter a* SERVANT.

            Sirrah, lead these gentlemen
To my daughters and tell them both
These are their tutors; bid them use them well.  110
    [*Exit* SERVANT, *with* LUCENTIO, HORTENSIO,
            *and* BIONDELLO *following.*]
We will go walk a little in the orchard°
And then to dinner. You are passing° welcome,
And so I pray you all to think yourselves.

PETRUCHIO
Signior Baptista, my business asketh haste,
And every day I cannot come to woo.  115
You knew my father well, and in him me,
Left solely heir to all his lands and goods,
Which I have bettered rather than decreased.
Then tell me, if I get your daughter's love
What dowry shall I have with her to wife?  120

BAPTISTA
After my death the one half of my lands,
And in possession° twenty thousand crowns.

PETRUCHIO
And, for that dowry, I'll assure her of
Her widowhood,° be it that she survive me,
In all my lands and leases whatsoever.  125
Let specialties° be therefore drawn between us
That covenants may be kept on either hand.

BAPTISTA
Ay, when the special thing is well obtained,
That is, her love, for that is all in all.

PETRUCHIO
Why, that is nothing, for I tell you, father,  130
I am as peremptory° as she proud-minded.
And where two raging fires meet together
They do consume the thing that feeds their fury.
Though little fire grows great with little wind,
Yet extreme gusts will blow out fire and all.  135

So I to her, and so she yields to me,
For I am rough and woo not like a babe.

BAPTISTA
Well mayst thou woo, and happy be thy speed!°
But be thou armed for some unhappy words.

PETRUCHIO
Ay, to the proof,° as mountains are for winds  140
That shakes not, though they blow perpetually.

*Enter* HORTENSIO *with his head broke.*

BAPTISTA
How now, my friend, why dost thou look so pale?

HORTENSIO
For fear, I promise you, if I look pale.

BAPTISTA
What, will my daughter prove a good musician?

HORTENSIO
I think she'll sooner prove a soldier.  145
Iron may hold with her,° but never lutes.

BAPTISTA
Why, then thou canst not break° her to the lute?

HORTENSIO
Why, no, for she hath broke the lute to me.
I did but tell her she mistook her frets°
And bowed° her hand to teach her fingering,  150
When, with a most impatient devilish spirit,
"Frets, call you these?" quoth she; "I'll fume with
    them."
And with that word she stroke° me on the head,
And through the instrument my pate made way.
And there I stood amazèd for a while  155
As on a pillory,° looking through the lute,
While she did call me rascal, fiddler,
And twangling Jack,° with twenty such vile terms
As° had she studied° to misuse me so.

PETRUCHIO
Now, by the world, it is a lusty° wench!  160
I love her ten times more than e'er I did.
O how I long to have some chat with her!

BAPTISTA [*To* HORTENSIO.]
Well, go with me, and be not so discomfited.
Proceed in practice° with my younger daughter;
She's apt° to learn and thankful for good turns.  165
Signior Petruchio, will you go with us
Or shall I send my daughter Kate to you?
        *Exit* [BAPTISTA, *with* GREMIO, TRANIO, *and*
            HORTENSIO]. *Manet* PETRUCHIO.°

PETRUCHIO
I pray you do. I'll attend° her here
And woo her with some spirit when she comes.
Say that she rail,° why then I'll tell her plain  170
She sings as sweetly as a nightingale.
Say that she frown, I'll say she looks as clear
As morning roses newly washed with dew.

---

97 **favor** countenance, acceptance  99 **instrument** the lute
105 **him** his name  107 **presently** at once  111 **orchard**
garden  112 **passing** very  122 **possession** at the time of
marriage  124 **widowhood** estate settled on a widow (Johnson)  126 **specialties** special contracts  131 **peremptory**
resolved

138 **speed** progress  140 **to the proof** in tested steel armor
146 **hold with her** stand her treatment  147 **break** train
149 **frets** ridges where strings are pressed  150 **bowed** bent
153 **stroke** struck  156 **pillory** with a wooden collar (old
structure for public punishment)  158 **Jack** term of contempt
159 **As** as if; **studied** prepared  160 **lusty** spirited  164
**practice** instruction  165 **apt** disposed  167 **s.d.** is in the F
position, which need not be changed; Petruchio speaks to the
departing Baptista  168 **attend** wait for  170 **rail** scold, scoff

Say she be mute and will not speak a word,
Then I'll commend her volubility                        175
And say she uttereth piercing eloquence.
If she do bid me pack,° I'll give her thanks
As though she bid me stay by her a week.
If she deny° to wed, I'll crave the day
When I shall ask the banns° and when be marrièd.        180
But here she comes, and now, Petruchio, speak.

*Enter* KATE.

Good morrow, Kate, for that's your name, I hear.

KATE
Well have you heard,° but something hard of hearing.
They call me Katherine that do talk of me.

PETRUCHIO
You lie, in faith, for you are called plain Kate,        185
And bonny° Kate, and sometimes Kate the curst.
But, Kate, the prettiest Kate in Christendom,
Kate of Kate Hall,° my super-dainty Kate,
For dainties° are all Kates,° and therefore, Kate,
Take this of me, Kate of my consolation.                 190
Hearing thy mildness praised in every town,
Thy virtues spoke of, and thy beauty sounded°—
Yet not so deeply as to thee belongs—
Myself am moved to woo thee for my wife.

KATE
Moved! In good time,° let him that moved you hither  195
Remove you hence. I knew you at the first
You were a movable.°

PETRUCHIO                    Why, what's a movable?

KATE
A joint stool.°

PETRUCHIO    Thou hast hit it; come sit on me.

KATE
Asses are made to bear° and so are you.

PETRUCHIO
Women are made to bear° and so are you.                  200

KATE
No such jade° as you, if me you mean.

PETRUCHIO
Alas, good Kate, I will not burden thee,
For, knowing thee to be but young and light—

KATE
Too light for such a swain° as you to catch
And yet as heavy as my weight should be.                 205

PETRUCHIO
Should be!° Should—buzz!

KATE                    Well ta'en, and like a buzzard.°

PETRUCHIO
O slow-winged turtle,° shall a buzzard take° thee?

KATE
Ay, for a turtle, as he takes a buzzard.°

PETRUCHIO
Come, come, you wasp, i' faith you are too angry.

KATE
If I be waspish, best beware my sting.                   210

PETRUCHIO
My remedy is then to pluck it out.

KATE
Ay, if the fool could find it where it lies.

PETRUCHIO
Who knows not where a wasp does wear his sting?
In his tail.

KATE            In his tongue.

PETRUCHIO                    Whose tongue?

KATE
Yours, if you talk of tales,° and so farewell.           215

PETRUCHIO
What, with my tongue in your tail? Nay, come again.
Good Kate, I am a gentleman—

KATE                            That I'll try.

*She strikes him.*

PETRUCHIO
I swear I'll cuff you if you strike again.

KATE
So may you lose your arms:°
If you strike me you are no gentleman,                   220
And if no gentleman, why then no arms.

PETRUCHIO
A herald,° Kate? O, put me in thy books.°

KATE
What is your crest?° A coxcomb?°

PETRUCHIO
A combless° cock, so° Kate will be my hen.

KATE
No cock of mine; you crow too like a craven.°           225

PETRUCHIO
Nay, come, Kate, come, you must not look so sour.

KATE
It is my fashion when I see a crab.°

PETRUCHIO
Why, here's no crab, and therefore look not sour.

KATE
There is, there is.

PETRUCHIO
Then show it me.

KATE                    Had I a glass° I would.            230

PETRUCHIO
What, you mean my face?

KATE                        Well aimed of° such a young one.

---

177 **pack** go away  179 **deny** refuse  180 **banns** public announcement in church of intent to marry  183 **heard** pun: pronounced like *hard*  186 **bonny** big, fine (perhaps with pun on *bony*, the F spelling)  188 **Kate Hall** possible topical reference; several places have been proposed  189 **dainties** delicacies; **Kates** *cates* (delicacies)  192 **sounded** (1) measured (effect of *deeply*) (2) spoken of (pun)  195 **In good time** indeed  197 **movable** article of furniture (with pun)  198 **joint stool** stool made by a joiner (standard term of disparagement)  199 **bear** carry  200 **bear** bear children (with second sexual meaning in Petruchio's "I will not burden thee")  201 **jade** worn-out horse (Kate has now called him both "ass" and "sorry horse")  204 **swain** country boy  206 **be** pun on *bee*; hence *buzz* = scandal (i.e., about "light" woman); **buzzard** hawk unteachable in falconry (hence idiot)

207 **turtle** turtledove, noted for affectionateness; **take** capture (with pun, "mistake for," in next line)  208 **buzzard** buzzing insect (hence "wasp," line 209)  215 **of tales** idle tales (leading to bawdy pun on *tail* = pudend)  219 **arms** pun on *coat of arms*  222 **herald** one skilled in heraldry; **books** registers of heraldry (with pun on *in your good books*)  223 **crest** heraldic device; **coxcomb** identifying feature of court fool's cap  the cap itself  224 **combless** unwarlike; **so** if  225 **craven** defeated cock  227 **crab** crab apple  230 **glass** mirror  231 **Well aimed of** a good shot (in the dark)

PETRUCHIO
Now, by Saint George, I am too young for you.
KATE
Yet you are withered.
PETRUCHIO                'Tis with cares.
KATE                                    I care not.
PETRUCHIO
Nay, hear you, Kate, in sooth° you scape° not so.
KATE
I chafe° you if I tarry. Let me go.                    235
PETRUCHIO
No, not a whit. I find you passing gentle.
'Twas told me you were rough and coy° and sullen,
And now I find report a very liar,
For thou art pleasant, gamesome, passing courteous,
But slow in speech, yet sweet as springtime flowers.    240
Thou canst not frown, thou canst not look askance,
Nor bite the lip as angry wenches will,
Nor hast thou pleasure to be cross in talk,
But thou with mildness entertain'st thy wooers,
With gentle conference,° soft and affable.              245
Why does the world report that Kate doth limp?
O sland'rous world! Kate like the hazel-twig
Is straight and slender, and as brown in hue
As hazelnuts and sweeter than the kernels.
O, let me see thee walk. Thou dost not halt.°          250
KATE
Go, fool, and whom thou keep'st° command.
PETRUCHIO
Did ever Dian° so become a grove
As Kate this chamber with her princely gait?
O, be thou Dian and let her be Kate,
And then let Kate be chaste and Dian sportful!°        255
KATE
Where did you study all this goodly speech?
PETRUCHIO
It is extempore, from my mother-wit.°
KATE
A witty mother! Witless else° her son.
PETRUCHIO
Am I not wise?
KATE                Yes,° keep you warm.
PETRUCHIO
Marry, so I mean, sweet Katherine, in thy bed.         260
And therefore, setting all this chat aside,
Thus in plain terms: your father hath consented
That you shall be my wife, your dowry 'greed on,
And will you, nill° you, I will marry you.
Now, Kate, I am a husband for your turn,°              265
For, by this light, whereby I see thy beauty—
Thy beauty that doth make me like thee well—
Thou must be married to no man but me.

*Enter* BAPTISTA, GREMIO, TRANIO.

For I am he am born to tame you, Kate,

And bring you from a wild Kate° to a Kate             270
Conformable° as other household Kates.
Here comes your father. Never make denial;
I must and will have Katherine to my wife.
BAPTISTA
Now, Signior Petruchio, how speed° you with my
    daughter?
PETRUCHIO
How but well, sir? How but well?                      275
It were impossible I should speed amiss.
BAPTISTA
Why, how now, daughter Katherine, in your dumps?°
KATE
Call you me daughter? Now, I promise° you
You have showed a tender fatherly regard
To wish me wed to one half lunatic,                   280
A madcap ruffian and a swearing Jack
That thinks with oaths to face° the matter out.
PETRUCHIO
Father, 'tis thus: yourself and all the world
That talked of her have talked amiss of her.
If she be curst it is for policy,°                    285
For she's not froward but modest as the dove.
She is not hot° but temperate as the morn;
For patience she will prove a second Grissel°
And Roman Lucrece° for her chastity.
And to conclude, we have 'greed so well together      290
That upon Sunday is the wedding day.
KATE
I'll see thee hanged on Sunday first.
GREMIO
Hark, Petruchio, she says she'll see thee hanged first.
TRANIO
Is this your speeding?° Nay, then good night our part!
PETRUCHIO
Be patient, gentlemen, I choose her for myself.       295
If she and I be pleased, what's that to you?
'Tis bargained 'twixt us twain, being alone,
That she shall still be curst in company.
I tell you, 'tis incredible to believe
How much she loves me. O, the kindest Kate,           300
She hung about my neck, and kiss on kiss
She vied° so fast, protesting oath on oath,
That in a twink° she won me to her love.
O, you are novices. 'Tis a world° to see
How tame, when men and women are alone,               305
A meacock° wretch can make the curstest shrew.
Give me thy hand, Kate. I will unto Venice
To buy apparel 'gainst° the wedding day.
Provide the feast, father, and bid the guests;
I will be sure my Katherine shall be fine.°           310
BAPTISTA
I know not what to say, but give me your hands.
God send you joy, Petruchio! 'Tis a match.

234 sooth truth; scape escape   235 chafe (1) annoy (2) warm up   237 coy offish   245 conference conversation   250 halt limp   251 whom thou keep'st your servants   252 Dian Diana, goddess of hunting and virginity   255 sportful i.e., in the game of love   257 mother-wit natural intelligence   258 else otherwise would be   259 Yes yes, just enough to (refers to a proverbial saying)   264 nill won't   265 turn advantage (with bawdy second meaning)

270 wild Kate pun on *wildcat*   271 Conformable submissive   274 speed get on   277 dumps low spirits   278 promise tell   282 face brazen   285 policy tactics   287 hot intemperate   288 Grissel Griselda (patient wife in Chaucer's Clerk's Tale)   289 Lucrece killed herself after Tarquin raped her   294 speeding success   302 vied made higher bids (card-playing term), i.e., kissed more frequently   303 twink twinkling   304 world wonder   306 meacock timid   308 'gainst in preparation for   310 fine well dressed

GREMIO AND TRANIO
Amen, say we. We will be witnesses.

PETRUCHIO
Father, and wife, and gentlemen, adieu.
I will to Venice; Sunday comes apace.    315
We will have rings and things and fine array,
And, kiss me, Kate, "We will be married a Sunday."°
                              *Exit* PETRUCHIO *and* KATE.

GREMIO
Was ever match clapped° up so suddenly?

BAPTISTA
Faith, gentlemen, now I play a merchant's part
And venture madly on a desperate mart.°    320

TRANIO
'Twas a commodity° lay fretting° by you;
'Twill bring you gain or perish on the seas.

BAPTISTA
The gain I seek is quiet in the match.

GREMIO
No doubt but he hath got a quiet catch.
But now, Baptista, to your younger daughter;    325
Now is the day we long have lookèd for.
I am your neighbor and was suitor first.

TRANIO
And I am one that love Bianca more
Than words can witness or your thoughts can guess.

GREMIO
Youngling, thou canst not love so dear as I.    330

TRANIO
Graybeard, thy love doth freeze.

GREMIO                              But thine doth fry.
Skipper,° stand back, 'tis age that nourisheth.

TRANIO
But youth in ladies' eyes that flourisheth.

BAPTISTA
Content you, gentlemen; I will compound° this strife.
'Tis deeds must win the prize, and he of both°    335
That can assure my daughter greatest dower°
Shall have my Bianca's love.
Say, Signior Gremio, what can you assure her?

GREMIO
First, as you know, my house within the city
Is richly furnishèd with plate and gold,    340
Basins and ewers to lave° her dainty hands;
My hangings all of Tyrian° tapestry;
In ivory coffers I have stuffed my crowns,
In cypress chests my arras counterpoints,°
Costly apparel, tents,° and canopies,    345
Fine linen, Turkey cushions bossed° with pearl,
Valance° of Venice gold in needlework,
Pewter and brass, and all things that belongs
To house or housekeeping. Then, at my farm
I have a hundred milch-kine to the pail,°    350

Six score fat oxen standing in my stalls
And all things answerable to this portion.°
Myself am struck° in years, I must confess,
And if I die tomorrow, this is hers,
If whilst I live she will be only mine.    355

TRANIO
That "only" came well in. Sir, list to me.
I am my father's heir and only son.
If I may have your daughter to my wife,
I'll leave her houses three or four as good,
Within rich Pisa walls, as any one    360
Old Signior Gremio has in Padua,
Besides two thousand ducats° by the year
Of° fruitful land, all which shall be her jointure.°
What, have I pinched° you, Signior Gremio?

GREMIO [*Aside.*]
Two thousand ducats by the year of land!    365
My land amounts not to so much in all.

[*To others.*]
That she shall have besides an argosy°
That now is lying in Marcellus' road.°
What, have I choked you with an argosy?

TRANIO
Gremio, 'tis known my father hath no less    370
Than three great argosies, besides two galliasses°
And twelve tight° galleys. These I will assure her
And twice as much, whate'er thou off'rest next.

GREMIO
Nay, I have off'red all. I have no more,
And she can have no more than all I have.    375
If you like me, she shall have me and mine.

TRANIO
Why, then the maid is mine from all the world
By your firm promise. Gremio is outvied.°

BAPTISTA
I must confess your offer is the best,
And let your father make her the assurance,°    380
She is your own; else you must pardon me.
If you should die before him, where's her dower?

TRANIO
That's but a cavil.° He is old, I young.

GREMIO
And may not young men die as well as old?

BAPTISTA
Well, gentlemen,    385
I am thus resolved. On Sunday next, you know,
My daughter Katherine is to be married.
Now on the Sunday following shall Bianca
Be bride to you if you make this assurance;
If not, to Signior Gremio.    390
And so I take my leave and thank you both.    *Exit.*

GREMIO
Adieu, good neighbor. Now I fear thee not.
Sirrah° young gamester,° your father were° a fool

---

**317 We . . . Sunday** line from a ballad    **318 clapped** fixed
**320 mart** "deal"    **321 commodity** here a coarse term for
women (see Partridge, *Shakespeare's Bawdy*); **fretting** decaying
in storage (with pun)    **332 Skipper** skipping (irresponsible)
fellow    **334 compound** settle    **335 he of both** the one of
you two    **336 dower** man's gift to bride    **341 lave** wash
**342 Tyrian** purple    **344 arras counterpoints** counterpanes
woven in Arras    **345 tents** bed tester (hanging cover)    **346
bossed** embroidered    **347 Valance** bed fringes and drapes
**350 milch-kine . . . pail** cows producing milk for human
use

**352 answerable . . . portion** corresponding to this settlement
(?)    **353 struck** advanced    **362 ducats** Venetian gold coins
**363 Of** from; **jointure** settlement    **364 pinched** put the
screws on    **367 argosy** largest type of merchant ship    **368
Marcellus' road** Marseilles' harbor    **371 galliasses** large
galleys    **372 tight** watertight    **378 outvied** outbid    **380
assurance** guarantee    **383 cavil** small point    **393 Sirrah**
used contemptuously; **gamester** gambler; **were** would be

To give thee all and in his waning age
Set foot under thy table.° Tut, a toy!°                          395
An old Italian fox is not so kind, my boy.          *Exit.*
TRANIO
A vengeance on your crafty withered hide!
Yet I have faced it with a card of ten.°
'Tis in my head to do my master good.
I see no reason but supposed Lucentio                            400
Must get° a father, called "supposed Vincentio,"
And that's a wonder. Fathers commonly
Do get their children, but in this case of wooing
A child shall get a sire if I fail not of my cunning.
                                                    *Exit.*

# ACT III

[Scene I. *Padua. In Baptista's house.*]

*Enter* LUCENTIO [*as Cambio*], HORTENSIO [*as Litio*],
*and* BIANCA.

LUCENTIO
Fiddler, forbear. You grow too forward, sir.
Have you so soon forgot the entertainment°
Her sister Katherine welcomed you withal?
HORTENSIO
But, wrangling pedant, this is
The patroness of heavenly harmony.
Then give me leave to have prerogative,°                          5
And when in music we have spent an hour,
Your lecture° shall have leisure for as much.
LUCENTIO
Preposterous° ass, that never read so far
To know the cause why music was ordained!                        10
Was it not to refresh the mind of man
After his studies or his usual pain?°
Then give me leave to read° philosophy,
And while I pause, serve in your harmony.
HORTENSIO
Sirrah, I will not bear these braves° of thine.                   15
BIANCA
Why, gentlemen, you do me double wrong
To strive for that which resteth in my choice.
I am no breeching° scholar° in the schools.
I'll not be tied to hours nor 'pointed times,
But learn my lessons as I please myself.                          20
And, to cut off all strife, here sit we down.

[*To* HORTENSIO.]

Take you your instrument, play you the whiles;°
His lecture will be done ere you have tuned.
HORTENSIO
You'll leave his lecture when I am in tune?

LUCENTIO
That will be never. Tune your instrument.                         25
BIANCA   Where left we last?
LUCENTIO   Here, madam:
    Hic ibat Simois, hic est Sigeia tellus,
    Hic steterat Priami regia celsa senis.°
BIANCA   Conster° them.                                           30
LUCENTIO   Hic ibat, as I told you before, Simois, I am
Lucentio, hic est, son unto Vincentio of Pisa, Sigeia
tellus, disguised thus to get your love, Hic steterat,
and that Lucentio that comes a-wooing, Priami, is
my man Tranio, regia, bearing my port,° celsa senis,              35
that we might beguile the old pantaloon.°
HORTENSIO [*Breaks in.*]   Madam, my instrument's in
tune.
BIANCA   Let's hear. O fie, the treble jars.°
LUCENTIO   Spit in the hole, man, and tune again.                 40
BIANCA   Now let me see if I can conster it. Hic ibat
Simois, I know you not, hic est Sigeia tellus, I trust you
not, Hic steterat Priami, take heed he hear us not, regia,
presume not, celsa senis, despair not.
HORTENSIO [*Breaks in again.*]
    Madam, 'tis now in tune.
LUCENTIO                       All but the bass.                   45
HORTENSIO
The bass is right; 'tis the base knave that jars.

[*Aside.*]

How fiery and forward our pedant is!
Now, for my life, the knave doth court my love.
Pedascule,° I'll watch you better yet.
BIANCA
In time I may believe, yet I mistrust.                            50
LUCENTIO
Mistrust it not, for sure Aeacides
Was Ajax,° called so from his grandfather.
BIANCA
I must believe my master; else, I promise you,
I should be arguing still upon that doubt.
But let it rest. Now, Litio, to you.                              55
Good master, take it not unkindly, pray,
That I have been thus pleasant° with you both.
HORTENSIO [*To* LUCENTIO.]
You may go walk and give me leave° a while.
My lessons make no music in three parts.°
LUCENTIO
Are you so formal, sir? [*Aside.*] Well, I must wait              60
And watch withal,° for but° I be deceived,
Our fine musician groweth amorous.
HORTENSIO
Madam, before you touch the instrument,
To learn the order of my fingering,
I must begin with rudiments of art                                65
To teach you gamut° in a briefer sort,

395 **Set . . . table** be dependent on you; **a toy** a joke  398
**faced . . . ten** bluffed with a ten-spot  401 **get** beget
**III.i.2 entertainment** "pillorying" him with the lute  6
**prerogative** priority  8 **lecture** instruction  9 **Preposterous**
putting later things (*post-*) first (*pre-*)  12 **pain** labor  13 **read**
give a lesson in  15 **braves** defiances  18 **breeching** (1) in
breeches (young) (2) whippable; **scholar** schoolboy  22 **the
whiles** meanwhile

28–29 **Hic . . . senis** Here flowed the Simois, here is the
Sigeian (Trojan) land,/Here had stood old Priam's high palace
(Ovid)  30 **Conster** construe  35 **bearing my port** taking on
my style  36 **pantaloon** Gremio (see I.i.47 s.d. note)  38
**treble jars** highest tone is off  49 **Pedascule** little pedant
(disparaging quasi-Latin)  51–52 **Aeacides Was Ajax** Ajax,
Greek warrior at Troy, was grandson of Aeacus (Lucentio
comments on next passage in Ovid)  57 **pleasant** merry
58 **give me leave** leave me alone  59 **in three parts** for three
voices  61 **withal** besides; **but** unless  66 **gamut** the scale

More pleasant, pithy, and effectual,
Than hath been taught by any of my trade;
And there it is in writing, fairly drawn.

BIANCA
Why, I am past my gamut long ago.    70

HORTENSIO
Yet read the gamut of Hortensio.

BIANCA [*Reads.*]
    Gamut I am, the ground° of all accord.°
    A re, to plead Hortensio's passion:
    B mi, Bianca, take him for thy lord,
    C fa ut, that loves with all affection;    75
    D sol re, one clef, two notes have I:
    E la mi, show pity or I die.
Call you this gamut? Tut, I like it not.
Old fashions please me best; I am not so nice°
To change true rules for odd inventions.    80

*Enter a* MESSENGER.

MESSENGER
Mistress, your father prays you leave your books
And help to dress your sister's chamber up.
You know tomorrow is the wedding day.

BIANCA
Farewell, sweet masters both, I must be gone.
       [*Exeunt* BIANCA *and* MESSENGER.]

LUCENTIO
Faith, mistress, then I have no cause to stay.    [*Exit.*] 85

HORTENSIO
But I have cause to pry into this pedant.
Methinks he looks as though he were in love.
Yet if thy thoughts, Bianca, be so humble
To cast thy wand'ring eyes on every stale,°
Seize thee that list.° If once I find thee ranging,°    90
Hortensio will be quit with thee by changing.°    *Exit.*


[*Scene II. Padua. The street in front of
Baptista's house.*]


*Enter* BAPTISTA, GREMIO, TRANIO [*as Lucentio*],
KATE, BIANCA, [LUCENTIO *as Cambio*] *and others,*
ATTENDANTS.

BAPTISTA [*To* TRANIO.]
Signior Lucentio, this is the 'pointed day
That Katherine and Petruchio should be marrièd,
And yet we hear not of our son-in-law.
What will be said? What mockery will it be
To want° the bridegroom when the priest attends    5
To speak the ceremonial rites of marriage!
What says Lucentio to this shame of ours?

KATE
No shame but mine. I must, forsooth, be forced
To give my hand opposed against my heart
Unto a mad-brain rudesby,° full of spleen,°    10
Who wooed in haste and means to wed at leisure.
I told you, I, he was a frantic fool,

Hiding his bitter jests in blunt behavior.
And to be noted for° a merry man,
He'll woo a thousand, 'point the day of marriage,    15
Make friends, invite,° and proclaim the banns,
Yet never means to wed where he hath wooed.
Now must the world point at poor Katherine
And say, "Lo, there is mad Petruchio's wife,
If it would please him come and marry her."    20

TRANIO
Patience, good Katherine, and Baptista too.
Upon my life, Petruchio means but well,
Whatever fortune stays° him from his word.
Though he be blunt, I know him passing° wise;
Though he be merry, yet withal he's honest.    25

KATE
Would Katherine had never seen him though!
     *Exit weeping* [*followed by* BIANCA *and others*].

BAPTISTA
Go, girl, I cannot blame thee now to weep.
For such an injury would vex a very saint,
Much more a shrew of thy impatient humor.°

*Enter* BIONDELLO.

BIONDELLO   Master, master, news! And such old°   30
news as you never heard of!

BAPTISTA   Is it new and old too? How may that be?

BIONDELLO   Why, is it not news to hear of Petruchio's
coming?

BAPTISTA   Is he come?    35

BIONDELLO   Why, no, sir.

BAPTISTA   What then?

BIONDELLO   He is coming.

BAPTISTA   When will he be here?

BIONDELLO   When he stands where I am and sees you   40
there.

TRANIO   But, say, what to thine old news?

BIONDELLO   Why, Petruchio is coming in a new hat
and an old jerkin;° a pair of old breeches thrice turned;°
a pair of boots that have been candle-cases,° one   45
buckled, another laced; an old rusty sword ta'en out
of the town armory, with a broken hilt and chapeless;°
with two broken points;° his horse hipped° (with an
old mothy saddle and stirrups of no kindred°), besides,
possessed with the glanders° and like to mose in the   50
chine,° troubled with the lampass,° infected with the
fashions,° full of windgalls,° sped with spavins,°
rayed° with the yellows,° past cure of the fives,° stark
spoiled with the staggers,° begnawn with the bots,°

72 **ground** beginning, first note; **accord** harmony    79 **nice**
whimsical    89 **stale** lure (as in hunting)    90 **Seize . . . list** let
him who likes capture you; **ranging** going astray    91 **changing** sweethearts
**III.ii.5 want** be without    10 **rudesby** uncouth fellow;
**spleen** caprice

14 **noted for** reputed    16 **Make friends, invite** some editors
emend to "Make feast, invite friends"    23 **stays** keeps    24
**passing** very    29 **humor** temper    30 **old** strange    44 **jerkin**
short outer coat; **turned** inside out (to conceal wear and tear)
45 **candle-cases** worn-out boots used to keep candle ends in
47 **chapeless** lacking the metal mounting at end of scabbard
48 **points** laces to fasten hose to garment above; **hipped**
with dislocated hip    49 **of no kindred** not matching    50
**glanders** bacterial disease affecting mouth and nose    50–51
**mose . . . chine** (1) glanders (2) nasal discharge    51 **lampass**
swollen mouth    52 **fashions** tumors (related to glanders);
**windgalls** swellings on lower leg; **spavins** swellings on upper
hind leg    53 **rayed** soiled; **yellows** jaundice
(swelling of submaxillary glands)    54 **staggers** nervous disorder causing loss of balance; **begnawn . . . bots** gnawed by
parasitic worms (larvae of the botfly)

swayed° in the back, and shoulder-shotten;° near- 55
legged before,° and with a half-cheeked° bit and a
head-stall° of sheep's leather,° which, being restrained°
to keep him from stumbling, hath been often burst and
now repaired with knots; one girth° six times pieced,°
and a woman's crupper° of velure,° which hath two 60
letters for her name fairly set down in studs,° and here
and there pieced with packthread.°

BAPTISTA   Who comes with him?

BIONDELLO   O sir, his lackey, for all the world
caparisoned° like the horse: with a linen stock° on one 65
leg and a kersey boot-hose° on the other, gart'red
with a red and blue list;° an old hat, and the humor
of forty fancies° pricked° in't for a feather—a monster,
a very monster in apparel, and not like a Christian
footboy° or a gentleman's lackey. 70

TRANIO
'Tis some odd humor° pricks° him to this fashion,
Yet oftentimes he goes but mean-appareled.

BAPTISTA   I am glad he's come, howsoe'er he comes.

BIONDELLO   Why, sir, he comes not.

BAPTISTA   Didst thou not say he comes? 75

BIONDELLO   Who? That Petruchio came?

BAPTISTA   Ay, that Petruchio came.

BIONDELLO   No, sir, I say his horse comes, with him
on his back.

BAPTISTA   Why, that's all one.° 80

BIONDELLO [Sings.]
    Nay, by Saint Jamy,
    I hold° you a penny,
    A horse and a man
    Is more than one
    And yet not many. 85

Enter PETRUCHIO and GRUMIO.

PETRUCHIO
Come, where be these gallants?° Who's at home?

BAPTISTA
You are welcome, sir.

PETRUCHIO              And yet I come not well.

BAPTISTA
And yet you halt° not.

TRANIO   Not so well appareled as I wish you were.

PETRUCHIO
Were it better,° I should rush in thus. 90
But where is Kate? Where is my lovely bride?
How does my father? Gentles,° methinks you frown.

And wherefore gaze this goodly company
As if they saw some wondrous monument,°
Some comet or unusual prodigy?° 95

BAPTISTA
Why, sir, you know this is your wedding day.
First were we sad, fearing you would not come,
Now sadder that you come so unprovided.°
Fie, doff this habit,° shame to your estate,°
An eyesore to our solemn festival. 100

TRANIO
And tell us what occasion of import°
Hath all so long detained you from your wife
And sent you hither so unlike yourself.

PETRUCHIO
Tedious it were to tell and harsh to hear.
Sufficeth, I am come to keep my word 105
Though in some part enforcèd to digress,°
Which, at more leisure, I will so excuse
As you shall well be satisfied with all.
But where is Kate? I stay too long from her.
The morning wears, 'tis time we were at church. 110

TRANIO
See not your bride in these unreverent robes.
Go to my chamber; put on clothes of mine.

PETRUCHIO
Not I, believe me; thus I'll visit her.

BAPTISTA
But thus, I trust, you will not marry her.

PETRUCHIO
Good sooth,° even thus; therefore ha' done with
    words. 115
To me she's married, not unto my clothes.
Could I repair what she will wear° in me
As I can change these poor accouterments,
'Twere well for Kate and better for myself.
But what a fool am I to chat with you 120
When I should bid good morrow to my bride
And seal the title° with a lovely° kiss.
                    Exit [with GRUMIO].

TRANIO
He hath some meaning in his mad attire.
We will persuade him, be it possible,
To put on better ere he go to church. 125

BAPTISTA
I'll after him and see the event° of this.
            Exit [with GREMIO and ATTENDANTS].

TRANIO
But to her love concerneth us to add
Her father's liking, which to bring to pass,
As I before imparted to your worship,
I am to get a man—whate'er he be 130
It skills° not much, we'll fit him to our turn°—
And he shall be Vincentio of Pisa,
And make assurance° here in Padua
Of greater sums than I have promisèd.

---

55 **swayed** sagging; **shoulder-shotten** with dislocated shoulder   55–56 **near-legged before** with forefeet knocking together; **half-cheeked** wrongly adjusted to bridle and affording less control   57 **head-stall** part of bridle which surrounds head; **sheep's leather** weaker than pigskin; **restrained** pulled back   59 **girth** saddle strap under belly; **pieced** patched   60 **crupper** leather loop under horse's tail to help steady saddle; **velure** velvet   61 **studs** large-headed nails of brass or silver   62 **pieced with packthread** tied together with coarse thread   65 **caparisoned** outfitted; **stock** stocking   66 **kersey boot-hose** coarse stocking worn with riding boot   67 **list** strip of discarded border-cloth   67–68 **humor . . . fancies** fanciful decoration (in place of feather)   68 **pricked** pinned   70 **footboy** page in livery   71 **humor** mood, fancy; **pricks** incites   80 **all one** the same thing   82 **hold** bet   86 **gallants** men of fashion   88 **halt** limp (pun on *come*, meaning "walk")   90 **Were it better** even if I were better   92 **Gentles** sirs

94 **monument** warning sign   95 **prodigy** marvel   98 **unprovided** ill-outfitted   99 **habit** costume; **estate** status   101 **of import** important   106 **enforcèd to digress** forced to depart (perhaps from his plan to "buy apparel 'gainst the wedding day," II.i.308)   115 **Good sooth** yes indeed   117 **wear** wear out   122 **title** as of ownership; **lovely** loving   126 **event** upshot, outcome   131 **skills** matters; **turn** purpose   133 **assurance** guarantee

So shall you quietly enjoy your hope                            135
And marry sweet Bianca with consent.
LUCENTIO
Were it not that my fellow schoolmaster
Doth watch Bianca's steps so narrowly,
'Twere good, methinks, to steal our marriage,°
Which once performed, let all the world say no,     140
I'll keep mine own despite of all the world.
TRANIO
That by degrees we mean to look into
And watch our vantage° in this business.
We'll overreach° the graybeard, Gremio,
The narrow-prying father, Minola,                              145
The quaint° musician, amorous Litio—
All for my master's sake, Lucentio.

*Enter* GREMIO.

Signior Gremio, came you from the church?
GREMIO
As willingly as e'er I came from school.
TRANIO
And is the bride and bridegroom coming home?      150
GREMIO
A bridegroom say you? 'Tis a groom° indeed,
A grumbling groom, and that the girl shall find.
TRANIO
Curster than she? Why, 'tis impossible.
GREMIO
Why, he's a devil, a devil, a very fiend.
TRANIO
Why, she's a devil, a devil, the devil's dam.°      155
GREMIO
Tut, she's a lamb, a dove, a fool to° him.
I'll tell you, Sir Lucentio, when the priest
Should ask, if Katherine should be his wife,
"Ay, by goggs woones!"° quoth he and swore so loud
That, all amazed, the priest let fall the book,         160
And as he stooped again to take it up,
This mad-brained bridegroom took° him such a cuff
That down fell priest and book and book and priest.
"Now, take them up," quoth he, "if any list."°
TRANIO
What said the wench when he rose again?              165
GREMIO
Trembled and shook, for why° he stamped and swore
As if the vicar meant to cozen° him.
But after many ceremonies done
He calls for wine. "A health!" quoth he as if
He had been aboard, carousing° to his mates        170
After a storm; quaffed off the muscadel°
And threw the sops° all in the sexton's face,
Having no other reason
But that his beard grew thin and hungerly,°
And seemed to ask him sops as he was drinking.    175

This done, he took the bride about the neck
And kissed her lips with such a clamorous smack
That at the parting all the church did echo,
And I, seeing this, came thence for very shame.
And after me, I know, the rout° is coming.           180
Such a mad marriage never was before.
Hark, hark, I hear the minstrels play.

*Music plays. Enter* PETRUCHIO, KATE, BIANCA,
HORTENSIO [*as Litio*], BAPTISTA [*with* GRUMIO *and
others*].

PETRUCHIO
Gentlemen and friends, I thank you for your pains.
I know you think to dine with me today
And have prepared great store of wedding cheer,°   185
But so it is, my haste doth call me hence
And therefore here I mean to take my leave.
BAPTISTA
Is't possible you will away tonight?
PETRUCHIO
I must away today, before night come.
Make it no wonder;° if you knew my business,       190
You would entreat me rather go than stay.
And, honest company, I thank you all
That have beheld me give away myself
To this most patient, sweet, and virtuous wife.
Dine with my father, drink a health to me,            195
For I must hence, and farewell to you all.
TRANIO
Let us entreat you stay till after dinner.
PETRUCHIO
It may not be.
GREMIO              Let me entreat you.
PETRUCHIO
It cannot be.
KATE                Let me entreat you.
PETRUCHIO
I am content.
KATE                Are you content to stay?          200
PETRUCHIO
I am content you shall entreat me stay,
But yet not stay, entreat me how you can.
KATE
Now if you love me, stay.
PETRUCHIO                           Grumio, my horse!°
GRUMIO  Ay, sir, they be ready; the oats have eaten
the horses.°                                                              205
KATE
Nay then,
Do what thou canst, I will not go today,
No, nor tomorrow, not till I please myself.
The door is open, sir, there lies your way.
You may be jogging whiles your boots are green;°   210
For me, I'll not be gone till I please myself.
'Tis like you'll prove a jolly° surly groom,
That take it on you° at the first so roundly.°

---

139 **steal our marriage** elope  143 **vantage** advantage
144 **overreach** get the better of  146 **quaint** artful  151
**groom** menial (i.e., coarse fellow)  155 **dam** mother  156
**fool to** harmless person compared with  159 **by goggs
woones** by God's wounds (a common oath)  162 **took** gave
164 **list** pleases to  166 **for why** because  167 **cozen** cheat
170 **carousing** calling "Bottoms up"  171 **muscadel** sweet
wine, conventionally drunk after marriage service  172 **sops**
pieces of cake soaked in wine; dregs  174 **hungerly** as if
poorly nourished

180 **rout** crowd  185 **cheer** food and drink  190 **Make . . .
wonder** don't be surprised  203 **horse** horses  204–05 **oats
. . . horses** (1) a slip of the tongue or (2) an ironic jest  210
**You . . . green** proverbial way of suggesting departure
to a guest (*green* = new, cleaned)  212 **jolly** domineering
213 **take . . . you** do as you please; **roundly** roughly

PETRUCHIO
O Kate, content thee; prithee,° be not angry.

KATE
I will be angry. What hast thou to do?°                    215
Father, be quiet; he shall stay my leisure.°

GREMIO
Ay, marry, sir, now it begins to work.

KATE
Gentlemen, forward to the bridal dinner.
I see a woman may be made a fool
If she had not a spirit to resist.                         220

PETRUCHIO
They shall go forward, Kate, at thy command.
Obey the bride, you that attend on her.
Go to the feast, revel and domineer,°
Carouse full measure to her maidenhead,
Be mad and merry, or go hang yourselves.                   225
But for my bonny Kate, she must with me.
Nay, look not big,° nor stamp, nor stare,° nor fret;
I will be master of what is mine own.
She is my goods, my chattels; she is my house,
My household stuff, my field, my barn,                     230
My horse, my ox, my ass, my anything,°
And here she stands. Touch her whoever dare,
I'll bring mine action° on the proudest he
That stops my way in Padua. Grumio,
Draw forth thy weapon, we are beset with thieves.          235
Rescue thy mistress, if thou be a man.
Fear not, sweet wench; they shall not touch thee, Kate.
I'll buckler° thee against a million.
          *Exeunt* PETRUCHIO, KATE [*and* GRUMIO].

BAPTISTA
Nay, let them go, a couple of quiet ones.

GREMIO
Went they not quickly, I should die with laughing.         240

TRANIO
Of all mad matches never was the like.

LUCENTIO
Mistress, what's your opinion of your sister?

BIANCA
That being mad herself, she's madly mated.

GREMIO
I warrant him, Petruchio is Kated.

BAPTISTA
Neighbors and friends, though bride and bridegroom
     wants°                                                245
For to supply the places at the table,
You know there wants no junkets° at the feast.

[*To* TRANIO.]

Lucentio, you shall supply the bridegroom's place,
And let Bianca take her sister's room.

TRANIO
Shall sweet Bianca practice how to bride it?               250

BAPTISTA
She shall, Lucentio. Come, gentlemen, let's go.
                                            *Exeunt.*

---

# [ ACT IV ]

[*Scene I. Petruchio's country house.*]

*Enter* GRUMIO.

GRUMIO   Fie, fie, on all tired jades,° on all mad masters,
and all foul ways!° Was ever man so beaten? Was
ever man so rayed?° Was ever man so weary? I am sent
before to make a fire, and they are coming after to
warm them. Now were not I a little pot and soon hot,°    5
my very lips might freeze to my teeth, my tongue to
the roof of my mouth, my heart in my belly, ere I
should come by a fire to thaw me. But I with blowing
the fire shall warm myself, for considering the weather,
a taller° man than I will take cold. Holla, ho, Curtis!  10

*Enter* CURTIS [*a servant*].

CURTIS   Who is that calls so coldly?

GRUMIO   A piece of ice. If thou doubt it, thou mayst
slide from my shoulder to my heel with no greater a
run° but my head and my neck. A fire, good Curtis.

CURTIS   Is my master and his wife coming, Grumio?       15

GRUMIO   O ay, Curtis, ay, and therefore fire, fire;
cast on no water.°

CURTIS   Is she so hot a shrew as she's reported?

GRUMIO   She was, good Curtis, before this frost, but
thou know'st winter tames man, woman, and beast;        20
for it hath tamed my old master, and my new mistress,
and myself, fellow Curtis.

CURTIS   Away, you three-inch° fool! I am no beast.

GRUMIO   Am I but three inches? Why, thy horn° is a
foot, and so long am I at the least. But wilt thou make  25
a fire, or shall I complain on thee to our mistress, whose
hand—she being now at hand—thou shalt soon feel,
to thy cold comfort, for being slow in thy hot office?°

CURTIS   I prithee, good Grumio, tell me, how goes
the world?                                               30

GRUMIO   A cold world, Curtis, in every office but
thine, and therefore, fire. Do thy duty and have thy
duty,° for my master and mistress are almost frozen to
death.

CURTIS   There's fire ready, and therefore, good        35
Grumio, the news.

GRUMIO   Why, "Jack boy, ho boy!"° and as much
news as wilt thou.

CURTIS   Come, you are so full of cony-catching.°

GRUMIO   Why therefore fire, for I have caught extreme  40
cold. Where's the cook? Is supper ready, the house
trimmed, rushes strewed,° cobwebs swept, the
servingmen in their new fustian,° the white stockings,
and every officer° his wedding garment on? Be the

---

214 **prithee** I pray thee   215 **What . . . do** What do you have
to do with it?   216 **stay my leisure** await my willingness
223 **domineer** cut up in a lordly fashion   227 **big** challenging;
**stare** swagger   231 **My . . . anything** echoing Tenth
Commandment   233 **action** lawsuit   238 **buckler** shield
245 **wants** are lacking   247 **junkets** sweetmeats, confections

**IV.i.1 jades** worthless horses   **2 foul ways** bad roads   **3
rayed** befouled   **5 little . . . hot** proverbial for small
person of short temper   **10 taller** sturdier (with allusion to
"little pot")   **14 run** running start   **17 cast . . . water** alters
"Cast on more water" in a well-known round   **23 three-
inch** (1) another allusion to Grumio's small stature (2) a phallic
jest, the first of several   **24 horn** symbol of cuckold   **28 hot
office** job of making a fire   **32–33 thy duty** what is due thee
**37 Jack . . . boy** from another round or catch   **39 cony-
catching** rabbit-catching (i.e., tricking simpletons); with pun
on *catch* = the song)   **42 strewed** on the floor (for special
occasion)   **43 fustian** coarse cloth (cotton and flax)   **44
officer** servant

jacks° fair within, the jills° fair without, the carpets° 45
laid and everything in order?

CURTIS   All ready, and therefore, I pray thee, news.

GRUMIO   First, know my horse is tired, my master and
mistress fall'n out.

CURTIS   How?       50

GRUMIO   Out of their saddles into the dirt—and
thereby hangs a tale.

CURTIS   Let's ha't, good Grumio.

GRUMIO   Lend thine ear.

CURTIS   Here.       55

GRUMIO   There.

[Strikes him.]

CURTIS   This 'tis to feel a tale, not to hear a tale.

GRUMIO   And therefore 'tis called a sensible° tale, and
this cuff was but to knock at your ear and beseech
list'ning. Now I begin. Imprimis,° we came down a 60
foul° hill, my master riding behind my mistress—

CURTIS   Both of° one horse?

GRUMIO   What's that to thee?

CURTIS   Why, a horse.

GRUMIO   Tell thou the tale. But hadst thou not 65
crossed° me thou shouldst have heard how her horse
fell and she under her horse. Thou shouldst have heard
in how miry a place, how she was bemoiled,° how he
left her with the horse upon her, how he beat me
because her horse stumbled, how she waded through 70
the dirt to pluck him off me; how he swore, how she
prayed that never prayed before; how I cried, how the
horses ran away, how her bridle was burst, how I lost
my crupper, with many things of worthy memory
which now shall die in oblivion, and thou return 75
unexperienced° to thy grave.

CURTIS   By this reck'ning° he is more shrew than she.

GRUMIO   Ay, and that thou and the proudest of you
all shall find when he comes home. But what° talk
I of this? Call forth Nathaniel, Joseph, Nicholas, 80
Philip, Walter, Sugarsop, and the rest. Let their heads
be slickly° combed, their blue° coats brushed, and
their garters of an indifferent° knit. Let them curtsy
with their left legs and not presume to touch a hair
of my master's horsetail till they kiss their hands. Are 85
they all ready?

CURTIS   They are.

GRUMIO   Call them forth.

CURTIS   Do you hear, ho? You must meet my master
to countenance° my mistress.       90

GRUMIO   Why, she hath a face of her own.

CURTIS   Who knows not that?

GRUMIO   Thou, it seems, that calls for company to
countenance her.

CURTIS   I call them forth to credit° her.       95

GRUMIO   Why, she comes to borrow nothing of them.

*Enter our for five* SERVINGMEN.

NATHANIEL   Welcome home, Grumio!

PHILIP   How now, Grumio?

JOSEPH   What, Grumio!

NICHOLAS   Fellow Grumio!       100

NATHANIEL   How now, old lad!

GRUMIO   Welcome, you; how now, you; what, you;
fellow, you; and thus much for greeting. Now, my
spruce companions, is all ready and all things neat?

NATHANIEL   All things is ready. How near is our 105
master?

GRUMIO   E'en at hand, alighted by this,° and therefore
be not—Cock's° passion, silence! I hear my master.

*Enter* PETRUCHIO *and* KATE.

PETRUCHIO
Where be these knaves? What, no man at door
To hold my stirrup nor to take my horse?       110
Where is Nathaniel, Gregory, Philip?

ALL SERVINGMEN   Here, here, sir, here, sir.

PETRUCHIO
Here, sir, here sir, here, sir, here, sir!
You loggerheaded° and unpolished grooms!
What, no attendance? No regard? No duty?       115
Where is the foolish knave I sent before?

GRUMIO
Here, sir, as foolish as I was before.

PETRUCHIO
You peasant swain!° You whoreson° malt-horse
drudge!°
Did I not bid thee meet me in the park°
And bring along these rascal knaves with thee?       120

GRUMIO
Nathaniel's coat, sir, was not fully made
And Gabriel's pumps were all unpinked° i' th' heel.
There was no link° to color Peter's hat,
And Walter's dagger was not come from sheathing.°
There were none fine but Adam, Rafe, and Gregory; 125
The rest were ragged, old, and beggarly.
Yet, as they are, here are they come to meet you.

PETRUCHIO
Go, rascals, go, and fetch my supper in.

*Exeunt* SERVANTS.

[*Sings.*]

"Where is the life that late I led?"°
Where are those°—sit down, Kate, and welcome. 130
Soud,° soud, soud, soud!

*Enter* SERVANTS *with supper.*

Why, when,° I say?—Nay, good sweet Kate, be
merry.—
Off with my boots, you rogues, you villains! When?

---

45 **jacks** (1) menservants (2) half-pint leather drinking cups;
**jills** (1) maids (2) gill-size metal drinking cups; **carpets**
table covers   58 **sensible** (1) rational (2) "feel"-able   60
**Imprimis** first   61 **foul** muddy   62 **of** on   66 **crossed**
interrupted   68 **bemoiled** muddied   76 **unexperienced**
uninformed   77 **reck'ning** account   79 **what** why   82 **slickly**
smoothly; **blue** usual color of servants' clothing   83
**indifferent** matching (?) appropriate (?)   90 **countenance**
show respect to (with puns following)   95 **credit** honor

107 **this** now   108 **Cock's** God's (i.e., Christ's)   114 **logger-
headed** blockheaded   118 **swain** bumpkin; **whoreson**
bastardly; **malt-horse drudge** slow horse on brewery tread-
mill   119 **park** country-house grounds   122 **unpinked**
lacking embellishment made by pinking (making small holes
in leather)   123 **link** torch, providing blacking   124 **sheathing**
repairing scabbard   129 **Where . . . led** from an old ballad
130 **those** servants   131 **Soud** exclamation variously explained; some editors emend to "Food"   132 **when** exclamation of annoyance, as in next line

*[Sings.]*

"It was the friar of orders gray,
As he forth walkèd on his way"°—    135
Out, you rogue, you pluck my foot awry!
Take that, and mend° the plucking of the other.

*[Strikes him.]*

Be merry, Kate. Some water here! What ho!

*Enter one with water.*

Where's my spaniel Troilus? Sirrah, get you hence
And bid my cousin Ferdinand come hither—    140
                    *[Exit* SERVANT.*]*
One, Kate, that you must kiss and be acquainted with.
Where are my slippers? Shall I have some water?
Come, Kate, and wash, and welcome heartily.
You whoreson villain, will you let it fall?

*[Strikes him.]*

KATE
Patience, I pray you. 'Twas a fault unwilling.    145
PETRUCHIO
A whoreson, beetle-headed,° flap-eared knave!
Come, Kate, sit down; I know you have a stomach.°
Will you give thanks,° sweet Kate, or else shall I?
What's this? Mutton?
FIRST SERVINGMAN   Ay.
PETRUCHIO                    Who brought it?
PETER                                                    I.
PETRUCHIO
'Tis burnt, and so is all the meat.    150
What dogs are these! Where is the rascal cook?
How durst you, villains, bring it from the dresser,°
And serve it thus to me that love it not?
There, take it to you, trenchers,° cups, and all,

*[Throws food and dishes at them.]*

You heedless joltheads° and unmannered slaves!    155
What, do you grumble? I'll be with° you straight.°
KATE
I pray you, husband, be not so disquiet.
The meat was well if you were so contented.°
PETRUCHIO
I tell thee, Kate, 'twas burnt and dried away,
And I expressly am forbid to touch it,    160
For it engenders choler,° planteth anger,
And better 'twere that both of us did fast—
Since of ourselves, ourselves are choleric°—
Than feed it° with such overroasted flesh.
Be patient. Tomorrow't shall be mended,°    165
And for this night we'll fast for company.°
Come, I will bring thee to thy bridal chamber.
                                        *Exeunt.*

*Enter* SERVANTS *severally.*

NATHANIEL   Peter, didst ever see the like?
PETER   He kills her in her own humor.°

*Enter* CURTIS, *a servant.*

GRUMIO   Where is he?    170
CURTIS   In her chamber, making a sermon of continency to her,
And rails and swears and rates,° that she, poor soul,
Knows not which way to stand, to look, to speak,
And sits as one new-risen from a dream.    175
Away, away, for he is coming hither.    *[Exeunt.]*

*Enter* PETRUCHIO.

PETRUCHIO
Thus have I politicly° begun my reign,
And 'tis my hope to end successfully.
My falcon° now is sharp° and passing empty,
And till she stoop° she must not be full gorged,°    180
For then she never looks upon her lure.°
Another way I have to man° my haggard,°
To make her come and know her keeper's call,
That is, to watch° her as we watch these kites
That bate and beat° and will not be obedient.    185
She eat° no meat today, nor none shall eat.
Last night she slept not, nor tonight she shall not.
As with the meat, some undeservèd fault
I'll find about the making of the bed,
And here I'll fling the pillow, there the bolster,°    190
This way the coverlet, another way the sheets.
Ay, and amid this hurly° I intend°
That all is done in reverent care of her,
And in conclusion she shall watch° all night.
And if she chance to nod I'll rail and brawl    195
And with the clamor keep her still awake.
This is a way to kill a wife with kindness,°
And thus I'll curb her mad and headstrong humor.
He that knows better how to tame a shrew,°
Now let him speak—'tis charity to show.    *Exit.*    200

[Scene II. *Padua. The street in front of
Baptista's house.*]

*Enter* TRANIO [*as Lucentio*] *and* HORTENSIO [*as Litio*].

TRANIO
Is't possible, friend Litio, that Mistress Bianca
Doth fancy° any other but Lucentio?
I tell you, sir, she bears me fair in hand.°

---

**134–35 It . . . way** from another old song    **137 mend**
improve    **146 beetle-headed** mallet-headed    **147 stomach**
(1) hunger (2) irascibility    **148 give thanks** say grace    **152
dresser** sideboard    **154 trenchers** wooden platters    **155 jolt-
heads** boneheads (*jolt* is related to *jaw* or *jowl*)    **156 with**
even with; **straight** directly    **158 so contented** willing to see
it as it was    **161 choler** bile, the "humor" (fluid) supposed to
produce anger    **163 choleric** bilious (i.e., hot-tempered)
**164 it** their choler    **165 shall be mended** will be better
**166 for company** together

**169 kills . . . humor** conquers her by using her own
disposition    **173 rates** scolds    **177 politicly** with a calculated
plan    **179 falcon** hawk trained for hunting (falconry figures
continue for seven lines); **sharp** pinched with hunger    **180
stoop** (1) obey (2) swoop to the lure; **full gorged** fully fed
**181 lure** device used in training a hawk to return from flight
**182 man** (1) tame (2) be a man to; **haggard** hawk captured
after reaching maturity    **184 watch** keep from sleep; **kites**
type of small hawk    **185 bate and beat** flap and flutter
(i.e., in jittery resistance to training)    **186 eat** ate (pronounced
*et*, as still in Britain)    **190 bolster** cushion extending width
of bed as under-support for pillows    **192 hurly** disturbance;
**intend** profess    **194 watch** stay awake    **197 kill . . .kindness**
ironic allusion to proverb on ruining a wife by pampering
**199 shrew** rhymes with *show*
**IV.ii.2 fancy** like    **3 bears . . . hand** leads me on

HORTENSIO
Sir, to satisfy you in what I have said,
Stand by and mark the manner of his teaching.          5
[*They eavesdrop.*]

*Enter* BIANCA [*and* LUCENTIO *as Cambio*].

LUCENTIO
Now mistress, profit you in what you read?
BIANCA
What, master, read you? First resolve° me that.
LUCENTIO
I read that° I profess,° the Art to Love.°
BIANCA
And may you prove, sir, master of your art.
LUCENTIO
While you, sweet dear, prove mistress of my heart.          10

[*They court.*]

HORTENSIO
Quick proceeders,° marry!° Now, tell me, I pray,
You that durst swear that your mistress Bianca
Loved none in the world so well as Lucentio.
TRANIO
O despiteful° love! Unconstant womankind!
I tell thee, Litio, this is wonderful.°          15
HORTENSIO
Mistake no more. I am not Litio,
Nor a musician, as I seem to be,
But one that scorn to live in this disguise,
For such a one as leaves a gentleman
And makes a god of such a cullion.°          20
Know, sir, that I am called Hortensio.
TRANIO
Signior Hortensio, I have often heard
Of your entire affection to Bianca,
And since mine eyes are witness of her lightness,°
I will with you, if you be so contented,          25
Forswear° Bianca and her love forever.
HORTENSIO
See, how they kiss and court! Signior Lucentio,
Here is my hand and here I firmly vow
Never to woo her more, but do forswear her,
As one unworthy all the former favors°          30
That I have fondly° flattered her withal.
TRANIO
And here I take the like unfeignèd oath,
Never to marry with her though she would entreat.
Fie on her! See how beastly° she doth court him.
HORTENSIO
Would all the world but he had quite forsworn.°          35
For me, that I may surely keep mine oath,
I will be married to a wealthy widow
Ere three days pass, which° hath as long loved me
As I have loved this proud disdainful haggard.°
And so farewell, Signior Lucentio.          40

Kindness in women, not their beauteous looks,
Shall win my love, and so I take my leave
In resolution as I swore before.          [*Exit.*]
TRANIO
Mistress Bianca, bless you with such grace
As 'longeth to a lover's blessèd case.          45
Nay, I have ta'en you napping,° gentle love,
And have forsworn you with Hortensio.
BIANCA
Tranio, you jest. But have you both forsworn me?
TRANIO
Mistress, we have.
LUCENTIO          Then we are rid of Litio.
TRANIO
I' faith, he'll have a lusty° widow now,          50
That shall be wooed and wedded in a day.
BIANCA
God give him joy!
TRANIO
Ay, and he'll tame her.
BIANCA          He says so, Tranio.
TRANIO
Faith, he is gone unto the taming school.
BIANCA
The taming school! What, is there such a place?          55
TRANIO
Ay, mistress, and Petruchio is the master,
That teacheth tricks eleven and twenty long°
To tame a shrew and charm her chattering tongue.

*Enter* BIONDELLO.

BIONDELLO
O master, master, I have watched so long
That I am dog-weary, but at last I spied          60
An ancient angel° coming down the hill
Will serve the turn.°
TRANIO          What° is he, Biondello?
BIONDELLO
Master, a mercatante° or a pedant,°
I know not what, but formal in apparel,
In gait and countenance° surely like a father.          65
LUCENTIO
And what of him, Tranio?
TRANIO
If he be credulous and trust my tale,
I'll make him glad to seem Vincentio,
And give assurance to Baptista Minola
As if he were the right Vincentio.          70
Take in your love and then let me alone.
[*Exeunt* LUCENTIO *and* BIANCA.]

*Enter a* PEDANT.

PEDANT
God save you, sir.
TRANIO          And you, sir. You are welcome.
Travel you far on, or are you at the farthest?

**7 resolve** answer  **8 that** what; **profess** avow, practice; **Art to Love** Ovid's *Ars Amandi*  **11 proceeders** pun on idiom "proceed Master of Arts" (cf. line 9); **marry** by Mary (mild exlamation)  **14 despiteful** spiteful  **15 wonderful** causing wonder  **20 cullion** low fellow (literally, testicle)  **24 lightness** cf. *light woman*  **26 Forswear** "swear off"  **30 favors** marks of esteem  **31 fondly** foolishly  **34 beastly** unashamedly  **35 Would . . . forsworn** Would she had only one lover  **38 which** who  **39 haggard** cf. IV.i.182

**46 ta'en you napping** seen you "kiss and court" (line 27)  **50 lusty** lively  **57 tricks . . . long** (1) many tricks (2) possibly an allusion to card game "thirty-one" (cf. I.ii.33)  **61 ancient angel** man of good old stamp (*angel* = coin; cf. *gentleman of the old school*)  **62 Will . . . turn** who will do for our purposes; **What** what kind of man  **63 mercatante** merchant; **pedant** schoolmaster  **65 gait and countenance** bearing and style

PEDANT
Sir, at the farthest for a week or two,
But then up farther and as far as Rome,                    75
And so to Tripoli if God lend me life.

TRANIO
What countryman,° I pray?

PEDANT                                    Of Mantua.

TRANIO
Of Mantua, sir? Marry, God forbid!
And come to Padua, careless of your life?

PEDANT
My life, sir? How, I pray? For that goes hard.°           80

TRANIO
'Tis death for anyone in Mantua
To come to Padua. Know you not the cause?
Your ships are stayed° at Venice and the duke,
For private quarrel 'twixt your duke and him,
Hath published and proclaimed it openly.                  85
'Tis marvel, but that you are but newly come,
You might have heard it else proclaimed about.

PEDANT
Alas, sir, it is worse for me than so,°
For I have bills for money by exchange
From Florence and must here deliver them.                 90

TRANIO
Well, sir, to do you courtesy,
This will I do and this I will advise° you.
First tell me, have you ever been at Pisa?

PEDANT
Ay, sir, in Pisa have I often been—
Pisa, renownèd for grave citizens.                        95

TRANIO
Among them, know you one Vincentio?

PEDANT
I know him not but I have heard of him—
A merchant of incomparable wealth.

TRANIO
He is my father, sir, and, sooth to say,
In count'nance somewhat doth resemble you.                100

BIONDELLO [Aside.] As much as an apple doth an
oyster, and all one.°

TRANIO
To save your life in this extremity,
This favor will I do you for his sake,
And think it not the worst of all your fortunes           105
That you are like to Sir Vincentio.
His name and credit° shall you undertake,°
And in my house you shall be friendly lodged.
Look that you take upon you° as you should.
You understand me, sir? So shall you stay                 110
Till you have done your business in the city.
If this be court'sy, sir, accept of it.

PEDANT
O sir, I do, and will repute° you ever
The patron of my life and liberty.

TRANIO
Then go with me to make the matter good.                  115
This, by the way,° I let you understand:

My father is here looked for every day
To pass assurance° of a dower in marriage
'Twixt me and one Baptista's daughter here.
In all these circumstances I'll instruct you.             120
Go with me to clothe you as becomes you.    Exeunt.

[Scene III. In Petruchio's house.]

Enter KATE and GRUMIO.

GRUMIO
No, no, forsooth, I dare not for my life.

KATE
The more my wrong,° the more his spite appears.
What, did he marry me to famish me?
Beggars that come unto my father's door,
Upon entreaty have a present° alms;                        5
If not, elsewhere they meet with charity.
But I, who never knew how to entreat
Nor never needed that I should entreat,
Am starved for meat,° giddy for lack of sleep,
With oaths kept waking and with brawling fed.             10
And that which spites me more than all these wants,
He does it under name of perfect love,
As who should say,° if I should sleep or eat
'Twere deadly sickness or else present death.
I prithee go and get me some repast,                      15
I care not what, so° it be wholesome food.

GRUMIO
What say you to a neat's° foot?

KATE
'Tis passing good; I prithee let me have it.

GRUMIO
I fear it is too choleric° a meat.
How say you to a fat tripe finely broiled?                20

KATE
I like it well. Good Grumio, fetch it me.

GRUMIO
I cannot tell, I fear 'tis choleric.
What say you to a piece of beef and mustard?

KATE
A dish that I do love to feed upon.

GRUMIO
Ay, but the mustard is too hot a little.                  25

KATE
Why then, the beef, and let the mustard rest.

GRUMIO
Nay then, I will not. You shall have the mustard
Or else you get no beef of Grumio.

KATE
Then both or one, or anything thou wilt.

GRUMIO
Why then, the mustard without the beef.                   30

KATE
Go, get thee gone, thou false deluding slave,

Beats him.

That feed'st me with the very name° of meat.

77 **What countryman** a man of what country   **80 goes hard**
cf. *is rough*   **83 stayed** held   **88 than so** than it appears so far
**92 advise** explain to   **102 all one** no difference   **107 credit**
standing; **undertake** adopt   **109 take upon you** assume your
role   **113 repute** esteem   **116 by the way** as we walk along

**118 pass assurance** give a guarantee
**IV.iii.2 The . . . wrong** the greater the wrong done me   **5
present** prompt   **9 meat** food   **13 As . . . say** as if to say
**16 so** as long as   **17 neat's** ox's or calf's   **19 choleric** temper-
producing   **32 very name** name only

Sorrow on thee and all the pack of you
That triumph thus upon my misery.
Go, get thee gone, I say.                                                    35

*Enter* PETRUCHIO *and* HORTENSIO *with meat.*

PETRUCHIO
How fares my Kate? What, sweeting, all amort?°
HORTENSIO
Mistress, what cheer?°
KATE                        Faith, as cold° as can be.
PETRUCHIO
Pluck up thy spirits; look cheerfully upon me.
Here, love, thou see'st how diligent I am
To dress thy meat° myself and bring it thee.                                 40
I am sure, sweet Kate, this kindness merits thanks.
What, not a word? Nay then, thou lov'st it not,
And all my pains is sorted to no proof.°
Here, take away this dish.
KATE                        I pray you, let it stand.
PETRUCHIO
The poorest service is repaid with thanks,                                   45
And so shall mine before you touch the meat.
KATE
I thank you, sir.
HORTENSIO
Signior Petruchio, fie, you are to blame.
Come, Mistress Kate, I'll bear you company.
PETRUCHIO [*Aside.*]
Eat it up all, Hortensio, if thou lovest me;                                 50
Much good do it unto thy gentle heart.
Kate, eat apace. And now, my honey love,
Will we return unto thy father's house
And revel it as bravely° as the best,
With silken coats and caps and golden rings,                                 55
With ruffs° and cuffs and fardingales° and things,
With scarfs and fans and double change of brav'ry,°
With amber bracelets, beads, and all this knav'ry.°
What, hast thou dined? The tailor stays thy leisure°
To deck thy body with his ruffling° treasure.                                60

*Enter* TAILOR.

Come, tailor, let us see these ornaments.

*Enter* HABERDASHER.

Lay forth the gown. What news with you, sir?
HABERDASHER
Here is the cap your worship did bespeak.°
PETRUCHIO
Why, this was molded on a porringer°—
A velvet dish. Fie, fie, 'tis lewd° and filthy.                              65
Why, 'tis a cockle° or a walnut shell,
A knack,° a toy, a trick,° a baby's cap.
Away with it! Come, let me have a bigger.

KATE
I'll have no bigger. This doth fit the time,°
And gentlewomen wear such caps as these.                                     70
PETRUCHIO
When you are gentle you shall have one too,
And not till then.
HORTENSIO [*Aside.*]   That will not be in haste.
KATE
Why, sir, I trust I may have leave to speak,
And speak I will. I am no child, no babe.                                    75
Your betters have endured me say my mind,
And if you cannot, best you stop your ears.
My tongue will tell the anger of my heart,
Or else my heart, concealing it, will break,
And rather than it shall I will be free                                      80
Even to the uttermost, as I please, in words.
PETRUCHIO
Why, thou say'st true. It is a paltry cap,
A custard-coffin,° a bauble, a silken pie.°
I love thee well in that thou lik'st it not.
KATE
Love me or love me not, I like the cap,                                      85
And it I will have or I will have none.
                                    [*Exit* HABERDASHER.]
PETRUCHIO
Thy gown? Why, ay. Come, tailor, let us see't.
O mercy, God! What masquing° stuff is here?
What's this? A sleeve? 'Tis like a demi-cannon.°
What, up and down,° carved like an apple tart?                               90
Here's snip and nip and cut and slish and slash,
Like to a censer° in a barber's shop.
Why, what, a° devil's name, tailor, call'st thou this?
HORTENSIO [*Aside.*]
I see she's like to have neither cap nor gown.
TAILOR
You bid me make it orderly and well,                                         95
According to the fashion and the time.
PETRUCHIO
Marry, and did, but if you be rememb'red,
I did not bid you mar it to the time.°
Go, hop me over every kennel° home,
For you shall hop without my custom, sir.                                    100
I'll none of it. Hence, make your best of it.
KATE
I never saw a better-fashioned gown,
More quaint,° more pleasing, nor more commendable.
Belike° you mean to make a puppet of me.
PETRUCHIO
Why, true, he means to make a puppet of thee.                                105
TAILOR
She says your worship means to make a puppet of her.
PETRUCHIO
O monstrous arrogance!
Thou liest, thou thread, thou thimble,
Thou yard, three-quarters, half-yard, quarter, nail!°

---

**36 all amort** depressed, lifeless (cf. *mortified*)   **37 what cheer**
how are things; **cold** cf. *not so hot*; "cold comfort," IV.i.28
**40 To . . . meat** in fixing your food   **43 sorted . . . proof**
have come to nothing   **54 bravely** handsomely dressed
**56 ruffs** stiffly starched, wheel-shaped collars; **fardingales**
farthingales, hooped skirts of petticoats   **57 brav'ry** handsome
clothes   **58 knav'ry** girlish things   **59 stays thy leisure**
awaits your permission   **60 ruffling** gaily ruffled   **63 bespeak**
order   **64 porringer** soup bowl   **65 lewd** vile   **66 cockle**
shell of a mollusk   **67 knack** knickknack; **trick** plaything

**69 doth . . . time** is in fashion   **83 custard-coffin** custard
crust; **pie** meat pie   **88 masquing** for masquerades or actors'
costumes   **89 demi-cannon** big cannon   **90 up and down**
entirely   **92 censer** incense burner with perforated top   **93 a**
in the   **98 to the time** for all time (cf. line 96, in which "the
time" is "the contemporary style")   **99 kennel** gutter (canal)
**103 quaint** skillfully made   **104 Belike** no doubt   **109 nail**
one-sixteenth of a yard

Thou flea, thou nit,° thou winter cricket thou!    110
Braved° in mine own house with° a skein of
    thread!
Away, thou rag, thou quantity,° thou remnant,
Or I shall so bemete° thee with thy yard
As thou shalt think on prating° whilst thou liv'st.
I tell thee, I, that thou hast marred her gown.    115

TAILOR
Your worship is deceived. The gown is made
Just as my master had direction.°
Grumio gave order how it should be done.

GRUMIO    I gave him no order; I gave him the stuff.

TAILOR
But how did you desire it should be made?    120

GRUMIO    Marry, sir, with needle and thread.

TAILOR
But did you not request to have it cut?

GRUMIO    Thou hast faced° many things.

TAILOR    I have.

GRUMIO    Face° not me. Thou hast braved° many men;    125
brave° not me. I will neither be faced nor braved. I
say unto thee, I bid thy master cut out the gown, but
I did not bid him cut it to pieces. Ergo,° thou liest.

TAILOR    Why, here is the note° of the fashion to
testify.    130

PETRUCHIO    Read it.

GRUMIO    The note lies in's throat° if he° say I said so.

TAILOR    "Imprimis,° a loose-bodied gown."°

GRUMIO    Master, if ever I said loose-bodied gown,
sew me in the skirts of it and beat me to death with a    135
bottom° of brown thread. I said, a gown.

PETRUCHIO    Proceed.

TAILOR    "With a small compassed° cape."

GRUMIO    I confess the cape.

TAILOR    "With a trunk° sleeve."    140

GRUMIO    I confess two sleeves.

TAILOR    "The sleeves curiously° cut."

PETRUCHIO    Ay, there's the villainy.

GRUMIO    Error i' th' bill,° sir, error i' th' bill. I commanded the sleeves should be cut out and sewed up    145
again, and that I'll prove upon° thee, though thy little
finger be armed in a thimble.

TAILOR    This is true that I say. And° I had thee in
place where,° thou shouldst know it.

GRUMIO    I am for° thee straight.° Take thou the bill,°    150
give me thy mete-yard,° and spare not me.

HORTENSIO    God-amercy, Grumio, then he shall have
no odds.

PETRUCHIO    Well, sir, in brief, the gown is not for me.

GRUMIO    You are i' th' right, sir; 'tis for my mistress.    155

PETRUCHIO    Go, take it up unto° thy master's use.°

GRUMIO    Villain, not for thy life! Take up my mistress'
gown for thy master's use!

PETRUCHIO    Why sir, what's your conceit° in that?

GRUMIO
O sir, the conceit is deeper than you think for.    160
Take up my mistress' gown to his master's use!
O, fie, fie, fie!

PETRUCHIO [Aside.]
Hortensio, say thou wilt see the tailor paid.

[To TAILOR.]

Go take it hence; be gone and say no more.

HORTENSIO
Tailor, I'll pay thee for thy gown tomorrow;    165
Take no unkindness of his hasty words.
Away, I say, commend me to thy master.
                                    Exit TAILOR.

PETRUCHIO
Well, come, my Kate, we will unto your father's,
Even in these honest mean habiliments.°
Our purses shall be proud, our garments poor,    170
For 'tis the mind that makes the body rich,
And as the sun breaks through the darkest clouds
So honor peereth° in the meanest habit.°
What, is the jay more precious than the lark
Because his feathers are more beautiful?    175
Or is the adder better than the eel
Because his painted skin contents the eye?
O no, good Kate, neither art thou the worse
For this poor furniture° and mean array.
If thou account'st it shame, lay° it on me,    180
And therefore frolic. We will hence forthwith
To feast and sport us at thy father's house.

[To GRUMIO.]

Go call my men, and let us straight to him;
And bring our horses unto Long-lane end.
There will we mount, and thither walk on foot.    185
Let's see, I think 'tis now some seven o'clock,
And well we may come there by dinnertime.°

KATE
I dare assure you, sir, 'tis almost two,
And 'twill be suppertime ere you come there.

PETRUCHIO
It shall be seven ere I go to horse.    190
Look what° I speak or do or think to do,
You are still crossing° it. Sirs, let 't alone:
I will not go today, and ere I do,
It shall be what o'clock I say it is.

HORTENSIO [Aside.]
Why, so this gallant will command the sun. [Exeunt.]    195

---

110 **nit** louse's egg  111 **Braved** defied; **with** by  112
**quantity** fragment  113 **bemete** (1) measure (2) beat  114
**think on prating** remember your silly talk  117 **had
direction** received orders  123 **faced** trimmed  125 **Face**
challenge; **braved** equipped with finery  126 **brave** defy
128 **Ergo** therefore  129 **note** written notation  132 **in's
throat** from the heart, with premeditation; **he** it  133
**Imprimis** first; **loose-bodied gown** worn by prostitutes,
with "loose" in pun  136 **bottom** spool  138 **compassed**
with circular edge  140 **trunk** full (cf. line 89)  142 **curiously**
painstakingly  144 **bill** the "note"  146 **prove upon** test by
dueling with  148 **And** if  149 **place where** the right place
150 **for** ready for; **straight** right now; **bill** (1) written order
(2) long-handled weapon  151 **mete-yard** yardstick

156 **up unto** away for; **use** in whatever way he can; Grumio
uses these words for a sex joke  159 **conceit** idea  169
**habiliments** clothes  173 **peereth** is recognized; **habit** clothes
179 **furniture** outfit  180 **lay** blame  187 **dinnertime**
midday  191 **Look what** whatever  192 **crossing** obstruc-
ting, going counter to

[Scene IV. *Padua. The street in front
of Baptista's house.*]

*Enter* TRANIO [*as Lucentio*] *and the* PEDANT *dressed like
Vincentio.*

TRANIO
Sir, this is the house. Please it you that I call?

PEDANT
Ay, what else? And but° I be deceived,
Signior Baptista may remember me
Near twenty years ago in Genoa,
Where we were lodgers at the Pegasus.°     5

TRANIO
'Tis well, and hold your own° in any case
With such austerity as 'longeth to a father.

PEDANT
I warrant° you. But sir, here comes your boy;
'Twere good he were schooled.°

*Enter* BIONDELLO.

TRANIO
Fear you not him. Sirrah Biondello,     10
Now do your duty throughly,° I advise you.
Imagine 'twere the right Vincentio.

BIONDELLO
Tut, fear not me.

TRANIO
But hast thou done thy errand to Baptista?

BIONDELLO
I told him that your father was at Venice     15
And that you looked for him this day in Padua.

TRANIO
Th' art a tall° fellow. Hold thee that° to drink.
Here comes Baptista. Set your countenance, sir.

*Enter* BAPTISTA *and* LUCENTIO [*as Cambio*]. PEDANT
*booted and bareheaded.*°

Signior Baptista, you are happily met.

[*To the* PEDANT.]

Sir, this is the gentleman I told you of.     20
I pray you, stand good father to me now,
Give me Bianca for my patrimony.

PEDANT
Soft,° son.
Sir, by your leave. Having come to Padua
To gather in some debts, my son Lucentio     25
Made me acquainted with a weighty cause°
Of love between your daughter and himself.
And—for the good report I hear of you,
And for the love he beareth to your daughter,
And she to him—to stay° him not too long,     30
I am content, in a good father's care,
To have him matched. And if you please to like°

No worse than I, upon some agreement
Me shall you find ready and willing
With one consent to have her so bestowed,     35
For curious° I cannot be with you,
Signior Baptista, of whom I hear so well.

BAPTISTA
Sir, pardon me in what I have to say.
Your plainness and your shortness° please me well.
Right true it is, your son Lucentio here     40
Doth love my daughter and she loveth him—
Or both dissemble deeply their affections—
And therefore, if you say no more than this,
That like a father you will deal with him
And pass° my daughter a sufficient dower,     45
The match is made, and all is done.
Your son shall have my daughter with consent.

TRANIO
I thank you, sir. Where, then, do you know° best
We be affied° and such assurance ta'en
As shall with either part's° agreement stand?     50

BAPTISTA
Not in my house, Lucentio, for you know
Pitchers have ears, and I have many servants.
Besides, old Gremio is heark'ning still,°
And happily° we might be interrupted.

TRANIO
Then at my lodging and it like° you.     55
There doth my father lie,° and there this night
We'll pass° the business privately and well.
Send for your daughter by your servant here;
My boy shall fetch the scrivener° presently.
The worst is this, that at so slender warning°     60
You are like to have a thin and slender pittance.°

BAPTISTA
It likes° me well. Cambio, hie you home
And bid Bianca make her ready straight,
And, if you will, tell what hath happenèd:
Lucentio's father is arrived in Padua,     65
And how she's like to be Lucentio's wife.

[*Exit* LUCENTIO.]

BIONDELLO
I pray the gods she may with all my heart!     *Exit.*

TRANIO
Dally not with the gods, but get thee gone.
Signior Baptista, shall I lead the way?
Welcome, one mess° is like to be your cheer.°     70
Come, sir, we will better it in Pisa.

BAPTISTA
I follow you.     *Exeunt.*

*Enter* LUCENTIO [*as Cambio*] *and* BIONDELLO.

BIONDELLO   Cambio!
LUCENTIO   What say'st thou, Biondello?
BIONDELLO   You saw my master° wink and laugh     75
upon you?

**IV.iv.2 but** unless   **3–5 Signior . . . Pegasus** the Pedant is
practicing as Vincentio   **5 Pegasus** common English inn name
(after mythical winged horse symbolizing poetic inspiration)
**6 hold your own** act your role   **8 warrant** guarantee   **9
schooled** informed (about his role)   **11 throughly** thoroughly
**17 tall** excellent; **Hold thee that** take this tip   **18 s.d. booted
and bareheaded** arriving from a journey and courteously
greeting Baptista   **23 Soft** take it easy   **26 weighty cause**
important matter   **30 stay** delay   **32 like** i.e., the match

**36 curious** overinsistent on fine points   **39 shortness** conciseness   **45 pass** legally settle upon   **48 know** think   **49
affied** formally engaged   **50 part's** party's   **53 heark'ning
still** listening constantly   **54 happily** perchance   **55 and it
like** if it please   **56 lie** stay   **57 pass** settle   **59 scrivener**
notary   **60 slender warning** short notice   **61 pittance** meal
**62 likes** pleases   **70 mess** dish; **cheer** entertainment   **75
my master** Tranio (cf. line 59)

LUCENTIO  Biondello, what of that?

BIONDELLO  Faith, nothing, but has° left me here behind to expound the meaning or moral of his signs and tokens.                                                    80

LUCENTIO  I pray thee, moralize° them.

BIONDELLO  Then thus. Baptista is safe, talking with the deceiving father of a deceitful son.

LUCENTIO  And what of him?

BIONDELLO  His daughter is to be brought by you to 85 the supper.

LUCENTIO  And then?

BIONDELLO  The old priest at Saint Luke's church is at your command at all hours.

LUCENTIO  And what of all this?                            90

BIONDELLO  I cannot tell, except they are busied about a counterfeit assurance.° Take you assurance° of her, "cum previlegio ad impremendum solem."° To th' church! Take the priest, clerk, and some sufficient honest witnesses.                                          95
If this be not that you look for, I have no more to say,
But bid Bianca farewell forever and a day.

LUCENTIO  Hear'st thou, Biondello?

BIONDELLO  I cannot tarry. I knew a wench married in an afternoon as she went to the garden for parsley 100 to stuff a rabbit. And so may you, sir. And so adieu, sir. My master hath appointed me to go to Saint Luke's, to bid the priest be ready to come against you come° with your appendix.°                    *Exit.*

LUCENTIO
I may, and will, if she be so contented.           105
She will be pleased; then wherefore should I doubt?
Hap what hap may, I'll roundly° go about° her.
It shall go hard if Cambio go without her.      *Exit.*


[Scene V. *The road to Padua.*]

*Enter* PETRUCHIO, KATE, HORTENSIO [*with* SERVANTS.]

PETRUCHIO
Come on, a° God's name, once more toward our father's.
Good Lord, how bright and goodly shines the moon.

KATE
The moon? The sun. It is not moonlight now.

PETRUCHIO
I say it is the moon that shines so bright.

KATE
I know it is the sun that shines so bright.        5

PETRUCHIO
Now, by my mother's son, and that's myself,
It shall be moon or star or what I list,°
Or ere° I journey to your father's house.

[*To* SERVANTS.]

Go on and fetch our horses back again.
Evermore crossed and crossed, nothing but crossed!° 10

HORTENSIO [*To* KATE.]
Say as he says or we shall never go.

KATE
Forward, I pray, since we have come so far,
And be it moon or sun or what you please.
And if you please to call it a rush-candle,°
Henceforth I vow it shall be so for me.              15

PETRUCHIO
I say it is the moon.

KATE                          I know it is the moon.

PETRUCHIO
Nay, then you lie. It is the blessèd sun.

KATE
Then God be blessed, it is the blessèd sun.
But sun it is not when you say it is not,
And the moon changes even as your mind.          20
What you will have it named, even that it is,
And so it shall be so for Katherine.

HORTENSIO [*Aside.*]
Petruchio, go thy ways. The field is won.

PETRUCHIO
Well, forward, forward! Thus the bowl° should run
And not unluckily against the bias.°               25
But soft,° company° is coming here.

*Enter* VINCENTIO.

[*To* VINCENTIO.]
Good morrow, gentle mistress; where away?
Tell me, sweet Kate, and tell me truly too,
Hast thou beheld a fresher° gentlewoman?
Such war of white and red within her cheeks!       30
What stars do spangle heaven with such beauty
As those two eyes become that heavenly face?
Fair lovely maid, once more good day to thee.
Sweet Kate, embrace her for her beauty's sake.

HORTENSIO [*Aside.*]
'A° will make the man mad, to make a woman of him. 35

KATE
Young budding virgin, fair and fresh and sweet,
Whither away, or where is thy abode?
Happy the parents of so fair a child!
Happier the man whom favorable stars
Allots thee for his lovely bedfellow!             40

PETRUCHIO
Why, how now, Kate, I hope thou are not mad.
This is a man, old, wrinkled, faded, withered,
And not a maiden, as thou say'st he is.

KATE
Pardon, old father, my mistaking eyes
That have been so bedazzled with the sun          45
That everything I look on seemeth green.°
Now I perceive thou art a reverend father;
Pardon, I pray thee, for my mad mistaking.

PETRUCHIO
Do, good old grandsire, and withal make known

---

78 **has** he has  81 **moralize** "expound"  92 **assurance** betrothal document; **Take you assurance** make sure  93 **cum . . . solem** Biondello's version of *cum privilegio ad imprimendum solum,* "with right of sole printing," a licensing phrase, with sexual pun in *imprimendum,* literally "pressing upon"  103–04 **against you come** in preparing for your coming  104 **appendix** (1) servant (2) wife (another metaphor from printing)  107 **roundly** directly; **about** after  IV.v.1 **a** in  7 **list** please  8 **Or ere** before

10 **crossed** opposed, challenged  14 **rush-candle** rush dipped in grease and used as candle  24 **bowl** bowling ball  25 **against the bias** not in the planned curving route, made possible by a lead insertion (bias) weighting one side of the ball  26 **soft** hush; **company** someone  29 **fresher** more radiant  35 **'A** he  46 **green** young

Which way thou travelest. If along with us,     50
We shall be joyful of thy company.

VINCENTIO
Fair sir, and you my merry mistress,
That with your strange encounter° much amazed me,
My name is called Vincentio, my dwelling Pisa,
And bound I am to Padua, there to visit     55
A son of mine which long I have not seen.

PETRUCHIO
What is his name?

VINCENTIO         Lucentio, gentle sir.

PETRUCHIO
Happily met, the happier for thy son.
And now by law as well as reverend age,
I may entitle thee my loving father.     60
The sister to my wife, this gentlewoman,
Thy son by this° hath married. Wonder not
Nor be not grieved. She is of good esteem,
Her dowry wealthy, and of worthy birth;
Beside, so qualified° as may beseem°     65
The spouse of any noble gentleman.
Let me embrace with old Vincentio
And wander we to see thy honest son,
Who will of thy arrival be full joyous.

VINCENTIO
But is this true, or is it else your pleasure,     70
Like pleasant° travelers, to break a jest
Upon the company you overtake?

HORTENSIO
I do assure thee, father, so it is.

PETRUCHIO
Come, go along, and see the truth hereof,
For our first merriment hath made thee jealous.°     75

*Exeunt [all but* HORTENSIO].

HORTENSIO
Well, Petruchio, this has put me in heart.
Have to° my widow, and if she be froward,°
Then hast thou taught Hortensio to be untoward.°

*Exit.*

# [ ACT V ]

[Scene I. *Padua. The street in front of
Lucentio's house.*]

*Enter* BIONDELLO, LUCENTIO [*as Cambio*], *and*
BIANCA; GREMIO *is out before.*°

BIONDELLO Softly and swiftly, sir, for the priest is
ready.

LUCENTIO I fly, Biondello. But they may chance to
need thee at home; therefore leave us.

*Exit [with* BIANCA].

BIONDELLO Nay, faith, I'll see the church a your     5
back,° and then come back to my master's as soon as I
can.            [*Exit.*]

GREMIO
I marvel Cambio comes not all this while.

*Enter* PETRUCHIO, KATE, VINCENTIO, [*and*]
GRUMIO, *with* ATTENDANTS.

PETRUCHIO
Sir, here's the door, this is Lucentio's house.
My father's bears° more toward the marketplace;     10
Thither must I, and here I leave you, sir.

VINCENTIO
You shall not choose but drink before you go.
I think I shall command your welcome here,
And by all likelihood some cheer is toward.°

*Knock.*

GREMIO They're busy within. You were best knock     15
louder.

PEDANT [*as Vincentio*] *looks out of the window* [*above*].

PEDANT What's° he that knocks as he would beat
down the gate?

VINCENTIO Is Signior Lucentio within, sir?

PEDANT He's within, sir, but not to be spoken withal.°     20

VINCENTIO What if a man bring him a hundred
pound or two, to make merry withal?

PEDANT Keep your hundred pounds to yourself; he
shall need none so long as I live.

PETRUCHIO Nay, I told you your son was well     25
beloved in Padua. Do you hear, sir? To leave frivolous
circumstances,° I pray you tell Signior Lucentio that
his father is come from Pisa and is here at the door to
speak with him.

PEDANT Thou liest. His father is come from Padua°     30
and here looking out at the window.

VINCENTIO Art thou his father?

PEDANT Ay sir, so his mother says, if I may believe
her.

PETRUCHIO [*To* VINCENTIO.] Why how now,     35
gentleman? Why this is flat° knavery, to take upon
you another man's name.

PEDANT Lay hands on the villain. I believe 'a° means
to cozen° somebody in this city under my countenance.°     40

*Enter* BIONDELLO.

BIONDELLO I have seen them in the church together;
God send 'em good shipping!° But who is here?
Mine old master, Vincentio! Now we are undone°
and brought to nothing.°

VINCENTIO Come hither, crack-hemp.°     45

BIONDELLO I hope I may choose,° sir.

53 **encounter** mode of address   62 **this** now   65 **so qualified**
having qualities; **beseem** befit   71 **pleasant** addicted to
pleasantries   75 **jealous** suspicious   77 **Have to** on to;
**froward** fractious   78 **untoward** difficult
**V.i.s.d. out before** precedes, and does not see, the others

5–6 **a your back** on your back (see you enter the church?
or, married?)   10 **bears** les   14 **toward** at hand   17 **What's**
who is   20 **withal** with   26–27 **frivolous circumstances**
trivial matters   30 **Padua** perhaps Shakespeare's slip of the
pen for *Pisa*, home of the real Vincentio, or *Mantua*, where the
Pedant comes from (cf. IV.ii.77)   36 **flat** unvarnished   38 **'a** he
39 **cozen** defraud   39–40 **countenance** identity   42 **shipping**
journey   43 **undone** defeated   44 **brought to nothing** cf.
*annihilated*   45 **crack-hemp** rope-stretcher (i.e., subject for
hanging)   46 **choose** have some choice (in the matter)

VINCENTIO  Come hither, you rogue. What, have
you forgot me?

BIONDELLO  Forgot you? No, sir. I could not forget
you, for I never saw you before in all my life.                    50

VINCENTIO  What, you notorious° villain, didst thou
never see thy master's father, Vincentio?

BIONDELLO  What, my old worshipful old master?
Yes, marry, sir, see where he looks out of the window.

VINCENTIO  Is't so, indeed?                                       55

*He beats* BIONDELLO.

BIONDELLO  Help, help, help! Here's a madman will
murder me.                                              [*Exit.*]

PEDANT  Help, son! Help, Signior Baptista!
                                          [*Exit from above.*]

PETRUCHIO  Prithee, Kate, let's stand aside and see the
end of this controversy.              [*They stand aside.*]  60

*Enter* PEDANT [*below*] *with* SERVANTS, BAPTISTA,
[*and*] TRANIO [*as Lucentio*].

TRANIO  Sir, what are you that offer° to beat my
servant?

VINCENTIO  What am I, sir? Nay, what are you, sir?
O immortal gods! O fine° villain! A silken doublet,
a velvet hose, a scarlet cloak, and a copatain° hat! O, I  65
am undone, I am undone! While I play the good
husband° at home, my son and my servant spend all
at the university.

TRANIO  How now, what's the matter?

BAPTISTA  What, is the man lunatic?                              70

TRANIO  Sir, you seem a sober ancient gentleman by
your habit,° but your words show you a madman.
Why sir, what 'cerns° it you if I wear pearl and gold?
I thank my good father, I am able to maintain it.

VINCENTIO  Thy father! O villain, he is a sailmaker in  75
Bergamo.

BAPTISTA  You mistake, sir, you mistake, sir. Pray,
what do you think is his name?

VINCENTIO  His name! As if I knew not his name! I
have brought him up ever since he was three years old,  80
and his name is Tranio.

PEDANT  Away, away, mad ass! His name is Lucentio,
and he is mine only son and heir to the lands of me,
Signior Vincentio.

VINCENTIO  Lucentio! O he hath murd'red his master.  85
Lay hold on him, I charge you in the duke's name.
O my son, my son! Tell me, thou villain, where is
my son Lucentio?

TRANIO  Call forth an officer.

[*Enter an* OFFICER.]

Carry this mad knave to the jail. Father Baptista, I  90
charge you see that he be forthcoming.°

VINCENTIO  Carry me to the jail!

GREMIO  Stay, officer. He shall not go to prison.

BAPTISTA  Talk not, Signior Gremio. I say he shall go
to prison.                                                       95

GREMIO  Take heed, Signior Baptista, lest you be
cony-catched° in this business. I dare swear this is the
right Vincentio.

PEDANT  Swear, if thou dar'st.

GREMIO  Nay, I dare not swear it.                              100

TRANIO  Then thou wert best° say that I am not
Lucentio.

GREMIO  Yes, I know thee to be Signior Lucentio.

BAPTISTA  Away with the dotard,° to the jail with
him!                                                            105

VINCENTIO  Thus strangers may be haled° and abused.
O monstrous villain!

*Enter* BIONDELLO, LUCENTIO, *and* BIANCA.

BIONDELLO  O we are spoiled°—and yonder he is.
Deny him, forswear him, or else we are all undone.
              *Exit* BIONDELLO, TRANIO, *and* PEDANT
                                          *as fast as may be.*

LUCENTIO
Pardon, sweet father.    *Kneel.*

VINCENTIO              Lives my sweet son?         110

BIANCA
Pardon, dear father.

BAPTISTA              How hast thou offended?
Where is Lucentio?

LUCENTIO              Here's Lucentio,
Right son to the right Vincentio,
That have by marriage made thy daughter mine
While counterfeit supposes° bleared thine eyne.°   115

GREMIO
Here's packing,° with a witness,° to deceive us all!

VINCENTIO
Where is that damnèd villain Tranio
That faced and braved° me in this matter so?

BAPTISTA
Why, tell me, is not this my Cambio?

BIANCA
Cambio is changed into Lucentio.                       120

LUCENTIO
Love wrought these miracles. Bianca's love
Made me exchange my state with Tranio
While he did bear my countenance° in the town,
And happily I have arrived at the last
Unto the wishèd haven of my bliss.                     125
What Tranio did, myself enforced him to.
Then pardon him, sweet father, for my sake.

VINCENTIO  I'll slit the villain's nose that would have
sent me to the jail.

BAPTISTA  [*To* LUCENTIO.]  But do you hear, sir?  130
Have you married my daughter without asking my
good will?

VINCENTIO  Fear not, Baptista; we will content you,
go to.° But I will in, to be revenged for this villainy.
                                                        *Exit.*

BAPTISTA  And I, to sound the depth° of this knavery.  135
                                                        *Exit.*

51 **notorious** extraordinary  61 **offer** attempt  64 **fine** well
dressed  65 **copatain** high conical  67 **husband** manager
72 **habit** manner  73 **'cerns** concerns  91 **forthcoming**
available (for trial)

97 **cony-catched** fooled  101 **thou wert best** maybe
you'll dare  104 **dotard** old fool  106 **haled** pulled about
108 **spoiled** ruined  115 **supposes** pretendings (evidently an
allusion to Gascoigne's play *Supposes*, one of Shakespeare's
sources); **eyne** eyes  116 **packing** plotting; **with a witness**
outright, unabashed  118 **faced and braved** impudently
challenged and defied  123 **bear my countenance** take on
my identity  134 **go to** mild remonstrance (cf. *go on, come,
come, don't worry*)  135 **sound the depth** get to the bottom of

LUCENTIO  Look not pale, Bianca. Thy father will not
frown.           *Exeunt* [LUCENTIO *and* BIANCA].

GREMIO
My cake is dough,° but I'll in among the rest
Out of hope of all but my share of the feast.    [*Exit.*]

KATE  Husband, let's follow, to see the end of this ado. 140

PETRUCHIO  First kiss me, Kate, and we will.

KATE  What, in the midst of the street?

PETRUCHIO  What, art thou ashamed of me?

KATE  No sir, God forbid, but ashamed to kiss.

PETRUCHIO
Why, then let's home again.          145

[*To* GRUMIO.]
Come sirrah, let's away.

KATE
Nay, I will give thee a kiss. Now pray thee, love, stay.

PETRUCHIO
Is not this well? Come, my sweet Kate.
Better once° than never, for never too late.°   *Exeunt.*

[*Scene II. Padua. In Lucentio's house.*]

*Enter* BAPTISTA, VINCENTIO, GREMIO, *the* PEDANT,
LUCENTIO, *and* BIANCA, [PETRUCHIO, KATE,
HORTENSIO,] TRANIO, BIONDELLO, GRUMIO,
*and* WIDOW; *the* SERVINGMEN *with* TRANIO
*bringing in a banquet.*°

LUCENTIO
At last, though long,° our jarring notes agree,
And time it is, when raging war is done,
To smile at 'scapes and perils overblown.°
My fair Bianca, bid my father welcome
While I with selfsame kindness welcome thine.    5
Brother Petruchio, sister Katherina,
And thou, Hortensio, with thy loving widow,
Feast with the best and welcome to my house.
My banquet is to close our stomachs° up
After our great good cheer.° Pray you, sit down,   10
For now we sit to chat as well as eat.

PETRUCHIO
Nothing but sit and sit, and eat and eat.

BAPTISTA
Padua affords this kindness, son Petruchio.

PETRUCHIO
Padua affords nothing but what is kind.

HORTENSIO
For both our sakes I would that word were true.   15

PETRUCHIO
Now, for my life, Hortensio fears° his widow.

WIDOW
Then never trust me if I be afeard.°

PETRUCHIO
You are very sensible and yet you miss my sense:
I mean Hortensio is afeard of you.

WIDOW
He that is giddy thinks the world turns round.   20

PETRUCHIO
Roundly° replied.

KATE             Mistress, how mean you that?

WIDOW
Thus I conceive by° him.

PETRUCHIO
Conceives by° me! How likes Hortensio that?

HORTENSIO
My widow says, thus she conceives her tale.°

PETRUCHIO
Very well mended. Kiss him for that, good widow.   25

KATE
"He that is giddy thinks the world turns round."
I pray you, tell me what you meant by that.

WIDOW
Your husband, being troubled with a shrew,
Measures° my husband's sorrow by his° woe,
And now you know my meaning.          30

KATE
A very mean° meaning.

WIDOW          Right, I mean you.

KATE
And I am mean° indeed, respecting you.

PETRUCHIO
To her, Kate!

HORTENSIO
To her, widow!

PETRUCHIO
A hundred marks, my Kate does put her down.°   35

HORTENSIO
That's my office.°

PETRUCHIO
Spoke like an officer. Ha'° to thee, lad.

*Drinks to* HORTENSIO.

BAPTISTA
How likes Gremio these quick-witted folks?

GREMIO
Believe me, sir, they butt° together well.

BIANCA
Head and butt!° An hasty-witted body   40
Would say your head and butt were head and horn.°

VINCENTIO
Ay, mistress bride, hath that awakened you?

BIANCA
Ay, but not frighted me; therefore I'll sleep again.

PETRUCHIO
Nay, that you shall not. Since you have begun,
Have at you° for a bitter° jest or two.   45

BIANCA
Am I your bird?° I mean to shift my bush,

138 cake is dough project hasn't worked out (proverbial; cf.
I.i.108–09)   149 once at some time; Better . . . late Better
late than never
V.ii.s.d. banquet dessert  1 At . . . long at long last  3
overblown that have blown over  9 stomachs with pun on
the sense of "irascibility" (cf. IV.i.147)  10 cheer reception at
Baptista's  16 fears is afraid of (the Widow puns on the
meaning "frightens")  17 afeard (1) frightened (2) suspected

21 Roundly outspokenly  22 conceive by understand  23
Conceives by is made pregnant by  24 conceives her tale
understands her statement (with another pun)  29 Measures
estimates; his his own  31 mean paltry  32 am mean (1) am
moderate (2) have a low opinion  35 put her down defeat
her (with sexual pun by Hortensio)  36 office job  37 Ha'
here's, hail  39 butt perhaps also but (i.e., argue or differ)  40
butt with pun on bottom  41 horn (1) butting instrument
(2) symbol of cuckoldry (3) phallus  45 Have at you let's
have; bitter biting (but good-natured)  46 bird prey

And then pursue me as you draw your bow.
You are welcome all.

*Exit* BIANCA [*with* KATE *and* WIDOW.]

PETRUCHIO
She hath prevented me.° Here, Signior Tranio,
This bird you aimed at, though you hit her not;          50
Therefore a health to all that shot and missed.

TRANIO
O sir, Lucentio slipped° me, like his greyhound,
Which runs himself and catches for his master.

PETRUCHIO
A good swift° simile but something currish.

TRANIO
'Tis well, sir, that you hunted for yourself;          55
'Tis thought your deer° does hold you at a bay.°

BAPTISTA
O, O, Petruchio, Tranio hits you now.

LUCENTIO
I thank thee for that gird,° good Tranio.

HORTENSIO
Confess, confess, hath he not hit you here?

PETRUCHIO
'A has a little galled° me, I confess,          60
And as the jest did glance away from me,
'Tis ten to one it maimed you two outright.

BAPTISTA
Now, in good sadness,° son Petruchio,
I think thou hast the veriest° shrew of all.

PETRUCHIO
Well, I say no. And therefore, for assurance,°          65
Let's each one send unto his wife,
And he whose wife is most obedient
To come at first when he doth send for her
Shall win the wager which we will propose.

HORTENSIO
Content. What's the wager?

LUCENTIO                    Twenty crowns.          70

PETRUCHIO
Twenty crowns!
I'll venture so much of° my hawk or hound,
But twenty times so much upon my wife.

LUCENTIO
A hundred then.

HORTENSIO        Content.°

PETRUCHIO                    A match,° 'tis done.

HORTENSIO
Who shall begin?

LUCENTIO        That will I.          75
Go, Biondello, bid your mistress come to me.

BIONDELLO  I go.                              *Exit.*

BAPTISTA
Son, I'll be your half,° Bianca comes.

LUCENTIO
I'll have no halves; I'll bear it all myself.

*Enter* BIONDELLO.

How now,° what news?

BIONDELLO          Sir, my mistress sends you word     80
That she is busy and she cannot come.

PETRUCHIO
How?° She's busy and she cannot come?
Is that an answer?

GREMIO              Ay, and a kind one too.
Pray God, sir, your wife send you not a worse.

PETRUCHIO  I hope, better.                          85

HORTENSIO  Sirrah Biondello, go and entreat my
wife to come to me forthwith.°     *Exit* BIONDELLO.

PETRUCHIO  O ho, entreat her! Nay, then she must
needs come.

HORTENSIO  I am afraid, sir, do what you can, yours    90
will not be entreated.

*Enter* BIONDELLO.

Now where's my wife?

BIONDELLO
She says you have some goodly jest in hand.
She will not come. She bids you come to her.

PETRUCHIO
Worse and worse. She will not come. O vile,          95
Intolerable, not to be endured!
Sirrah Grumio, go to your mistress; say
I command her come to me.          *Exit* [GRUMIO].

HORTENSIO
I know her answer.

PETRUCHIO          What?

HORTENSIO                    She will not.

PETRUCHIO
The fouler fortune mine, and there an end.          100

*Enter* KATE.

BAPTISTA
Now, by my holidame,° here comes Katherina.

KATE
What is your will, sir, that you send for me?

PETRUCHIO
Where is your sister and Hortensio's wife?

KATE
They sit conferring° by the parlor fire.

PETRUCHIO
Go fetch them hither. If they deny° to come,
Swinge° me them soundly° forth unto their husbands.  105
Away, I say, and bring them hither straight.

[*Exit* KATE.]

LUCENTIO
Here is a wonder, if you talk of a wonder.

HORTENSIO
And so it is. I wonder what it bodes.

PETRUCHIO
Marry, peace it bodes, and love, and quiet life,
An awful° rule and right supremacy;          110
And, to be short, what not° that's sweet and happy.

BAPTISTA
Now fair befall° thee, good Petruchio.
The wager thou hast won, and I will add

**49 prevented me** beaten me to it  **52 slipped** unleashed  **54
swift** quick-witted  **56 deer** (1) doe (2) dear; **at a bay** at bay
(i.e., backed up at a safe distance)  **58 gird** gibe  **60 galled**
chafed  **63 sadness** seriousness  **64 veriest** most genuine  **65
assurance** proof  **72 of** on  **74 Content** agreed; **A match**
(it's) a bet  **78 be your half** assume half your bet

**80 How now** mild exclamation (cf. *well*)  **82 How** what  **87
forthwith** right away  **101 holidame** holy dame (some editors
emend to "halidom" = sacred place or relic)  **104 conferring**
conversing  **105 deny** refuse  **106 Swinge** thrash; **soundly**
thoroughly (cf. *sound beating*)  **111 awful** inspiring respect
**112 what not** everything  **113 fair befall** good luck to

Unto their losses twenty thousand crowns, 115
Another dowry to another daughter,
For she is changed as she had never been.

PETRUCHIO
Nay, I will win my wager better yet
And show more sign of her obedience,
Her new-built virtue and obedience. 120

*Enter* KATE, BIANCA, *and* WIDOW.

See where she comes and brings your froward° wives
As prisoners to her womanly persuasion.
Katherine, that cap of yours becomes you not.
Off with that bauble, throw it under foot.

[*She throws it.*]

WIDOW
Lord, let me never have a cause to sigh 125
Till I be brought to such a silly pass.°

BIANCA
Fie, what a foolish—duty call you this?

LUCENTIO
I would your duty were as foolish too.
The wisdom of your duty, fair Bianca,
Hath cost me five hundred° crowns since suppertime. 130

BIANCA
The more fool you for laying° on my duty.

PETRUCHIO
Katherine, I charge thee, tell these headstrong women
What duty they do owe their lords and husbands.

WIDOW
Come, come, you're mocking. We will have no
telling.

PETRUCHIO
Come on, I say, and first begin with her. 135

WIDOW
She shall not.

PETRUCHIO
I say she shall—and first begin with her.

KATE
Fie, fie, unknit that threatening unkind° brow
And dart not scornful glances from those eyes
To wound thy lord, thy king, thy governor. 140
It blots thy beauty as frosts do bite the meads,
Confounds thy fame° as whirlwinds shake° fair buds,
And in no sense is meet or amiable.
A woman moved° is like a fountain troubled,
Muddy, ill-seeming, thick, bereft of beauty, 145
And while it is so, none so dry or thirsty
Will deign to sip or touch one drop of it.
Thy husband is thy lord, thy life, thy keeper,
Thy head, thy sovereign—one that cares for thee,
And for thy maintenance commits his body 150

To painful labor both by sea and land,
To watch° the night in storms, the day in cold,
Whilst thou li'st warm at home, secure and safe;
And craves no other tribute at thy hands
But love, fair looks, and true obedience: 155
Too little payment for so great a debt.
Such duty as the subject owes the prince,
Even such a woman oweth to her husband,
And when she is froward, peevish, sullen, sour,
And not obedient to his honest° will, 160
What is she but a foul contending rebel
And graceless traitor to her loving lord?
I am ashamed that women are so simple°
To offer war where they should kneel for peace,
Or seek for rule, supremacy, and sway, 165
When they are bound to serve, love, and obey.
Why are our bodies soft and weak and smooth,
Unapt to° toil and trouble in the world,
But that our soft conditions° and our hearts
Should well agree with our external parts? 170
Come, come, you froward and unable worms,°
My mind hath been as big° as one of yours,
My heart as great, my reason haply more,
To bandy word for word and frown for frown.
But now I see our lances are but straws, 175
Our strength as weak, our weakness past compare,
That seeming to be most which we indeed least are.
Then vail your stomachs,° for it is no boot,°
And place your hands below your husband's foot,
In token of which duty, if he please, 180
My hand is ready, may it° do him ease.

PETRUCHIO
Why, there's a wench! Come on and kiss me, Kate.

LUCENTIO
Well, go thy ways, old lad, for thou shalt ha't.

VINCENTIO
'Tis a good hearing° when children are toward.°

LUCENTIO
But a harsh hearing when women are froward. 185

PETRUCHIO
Come, Kate, we'll to bed.
We three are married, but you two are sped.°
'Twas I won the wager, [*to* LUCENTIO] though you
hit the white,°
And, being a winner, God give you good night.
*Exit* PETRUCHIO [*with* KATE].

HORTENSIO
Now, go thy ways; thou hast tamed a curst shrew. 190

LUCENTIO
'Tis a wonder, by your leave, she will be tamed so.
[*Exeunt.*]

---

121 **froward** uncooperative　126 **pass** situation　130 **five hundred** (1) Lucentio makes it look worse than it is, or (2) he made several bets, or (3) the text errs (some editors emend to "a hundred," assuming that the manuscript's "a" was misread as the Roman numeral v)　131 **laying** betting　138 **unkind** hostile　142 **Confounds thy fame** spoils people's opinion of you; **shake** shake off　144 **moved** i.e., by ill temper

152 **watch** stay awake, be alert during　160 **honest** honorable　163 **simple** silly　168 **Unapt to** unfitted for　169 **conditions** qualities　171 **unable worms** weak, lowly creatures　172 **big** inflated (cf. *think big*)　178 **vail your stomachs** fell your pride; **no boot** useless, profitless　181 **may it** (1) I hope it may (2) if it may　184 **hearing** thing to hear; report; **toward** tractable　187 **sped** done for　188 **white** (1) bull's eye (2) *Bianca* means white

# THE TWO GENTLEMEN
# OF VERONA

EDITED BY BERTRAND EVANS

## Introduction

Perhaps more than any other work of Shakespeare's, *The Two Gentlemen of Verona* needs to be taken for what it is: a product of its time written by a young poet-dramatist seeking his way in what was for him a new genre. So understood, it requires no defense and no apology.

The genre was romantic comedy, in the sense we mean when we mention the masterpieces that would follow in quick succession—*The Merchant of Venice, Much Ado About Nothing, As You Like It*, and *Twelfth Night*. The date of *The Two Gentlemen of Verona* is uncertain; the play may have been written as early as 1590–91, or as late as 1594–95. Most likely it was written in about 1592–93. But however late or early, within these extremes, it was for Shakespeare the first of a kind. Probably the only comedy he had written before it was *The Comedy of Errors*, a generally more satisfactory work than this, but one of an essentially different species, which gave him little practice toward the new kind that he was attempting. For *The Comedy of Errors* he had a model, a good one, made by a master craftsman of Latin comedy, Plautus. Though Shakespeare injected certain romantic elements into this model, or grafted them onto it, the finished work remained rather more Plautine than Shakespearean, more a succession of farcical incidents than a pattern woven of romance elements.

And in the unlikely event that *The Two Gentlemen of Verona* followed rather than preceded *Love's Labor's Lost*[1] and *The Taming of the Shrew*, it must yet be said that Shakespeare gained from these very little practice toward his new genre. *Love's Labor's Lost* was aimed satirically at fashionable but outlandish excesses in courtly language, manners, and ideas, and to the exploitation of these excesses the elements of romance were only incidental. The main plot of *The Shrew*, that of the taming, had no place at all for romance, in either atmosphere or action; it was hilarious farce, done in burlesque proportions. Nor did the secondary plot, that of the competition for Bianca, offer happy accommodation to the spirit and mood of romance; it turned upon a game of "supposes," in which only the attitudes of farce could be at home.

Whether before or after *Love's Labor's Lost* and *The Taming of the Shrew*, then, it was with *The Two Gentlemen of Verona* that Shakespeare found the way that led to the ultimate *Twelfth Night*. The basic stuff of romance, of course, lay around him everywhere, in prose and verse, in English, French, Spanish, and Italian, in medieval and in contemporary tellings and retellings. Long before *The Two Gentlemen of Verona* was written, the materials of romance had grown enamored of specific themes and encrusted with specific conventions. The theme of conflict between friendship and love was one that Chaucer had used and that was used again and again, in various forms of romantic tale and in various countries; indeed, Shakespeare's own sonnets play variations upon this theme, in the shadowy outline of a story that they tell of friendship between young men, of jealousy and separation occasioned by love of a third person, and finally of reconciliation. Lyly in his *Euphues*, Sidney in his *Arcadia*, less well-known contemporary romancers and translators all contributed to make the matters of romance, their themes and conventions, familiar to everyone who read or listened, familiar enough, indeed, that in any "new" romance, how a friend or lover, hero or heroine would behave in a given situation might be foretold with considerable accuracy.

What Shakespeare undertook in *The Two Gentlemen of Verona* was the experimental task of adapting the materials, themes, and conventions of meandering narrative romance (or of lyric verse) to dramatic form—to create action that might be contained in two hours, characters sufficiently credible that they might be represented by corporeal actors on a stage, a "world" of sufficient density to sustain both the action and the characters. For what he attempted there was nothing like a satisfactory precedent. For *The Comedy of Errors* he had had Plautus' *Menaechmi*; for the new genre of romantic comedy, he had nothing more suitable than, say, Lyly's *Endimion*, which was useful in every way except the one way that was needed; instead of being dramatically solid, *Endimion* was as watery as the tides governed by the moon.

For his principal story he turned to the tale of her life

---

[1] For an argument to the contrary, suggesting that *Love's Labor's Lost* may be as early as 1588, see Alfred Harbage, "*Love's Labor's Lost* and the Early Shakespeare," *Philological Quarterly*, XLI (1962), 18–36.

told by the shepherdess Felismena, in the *Diana Enamorada* of Jorge de Montemayor. But in fact the whole reservoir of romance served him, inevitably, whether he would or no. Its conventions, intruding, have made three centuries of critics of *The Two Gentlemen of Verona* wince. How could Proteus have been so dastardly as to betray, in an instant, his beloved, his friend, and his royal host—not to mention his own honor? How could Valentine so abruptly forgive his disloyal friend all his trespasses? How could he as quickly proffer his beloved Silvia to the miscreant Proteus, who only a moment before threatened to rape her? How could Silvia—the daughter of a duke—stand by without a word during this base interchange? How could Julia, after this exhibition of general dastardliness, on the second or third bounce, welcome back her errant lover?

Indeed, very nearly the sole good thing that critics have found it appropriate to say about *The Two Gentlemen of Verona* is that it was a kind of "dry run" for its great successors, anticipating in many of its details the incidents, persons, and relationships the more masterful delineation of which distinguishes the later romantic comedies. It is impossible to do other than concur—in part—with this view of the play as proving ground for the later, greater works; in fact, we have already gone somewhat beyond concurrence by flatly stating that in this play Shakespeare found the way to *Twelfth Night*. That alone should be praise enough, for it allows to *The Two Gentlemen of Verona* the same kind and degree of significance that we allow to *Julius Caesar* when we say that in it Shakespeare first worked out the basic pattern of order and relationships that we have in mind when we speak of "Shakespearean" tragedy.

It is appropriate, therefore, that we review some of the ways in which this first of the romantic comedies prepared for those to come. Perhaps it is just to say that in most cases it furnished no more than an artist's preliminary sketches for the fuller, finished portraits of character, incident, and "world" that would come after. But at the same time that we review these, we should consider whether anything contains merit and deserves praise for itself, aside from being a "first."

A good place to begin is with the heroine. Shakespeare did not invent the bright, daring girl of the comedies who, for one reason or another, casts off the outward signs of her sex and personal identity and goes a-masquerading in the world as a man; she existed already in the romances, both in those on which he directly drew for plot and in others which exercised a pervasive influence merely by existing. But in the romances she is a shadowy, pale, and bloodless abstraction that does not come alive enough to be visualized; she would never do on any stage. Shakespeare's creation, in Julia, of the flesh-and-blood heroine who set a great line going was a tremendous achievement. The world of the romantic comedies is a woman's world, and it is dominated by this recurrent figure who masquerades as a man while all of her womanliness is apparent to the audience, which is always aware of her secret. While each belongs to the line, each superlative heroine also has a life that is peculiarly her own. Portia of *The Merchant of Venice*, Rosalind of *As You Like It*, Viola of *Twelfth Night*—these can properly be likened to one another only in the common role they play, in specific recurrent situations in which they take part, and in a kind

of brilliance they share that marks them as extraordinary human beings: yet this very brilliance varies markedly in its quality, showing in one as a grand and dignified capability, in another as a mischievous brightness, and in another as a gently feminine and utterly disarming subtlety.

No doubt each of these represents as much of an improvement on Julia as Julia does upon the nebulous female of the prose romances. Nearly every incident in which Julia takes part will be repeated in richer detail by one or more of the later heroines, and just because we are so busy noting the resemblances of the first version to the later ones, and mentally comparing the earlier —to its disadvantage, of course—with the later, we may overlook the peculiar charm of this first heroine herself as she plays her part. Thus in I.ii, Julia's review of the "fair resort of gentlemen" who "every day with parle encounter me" appears a puny forerunner of Portia's review, with Nerissa, of her suitors at Belmont; for one reason, in the latter version Shakespeare knew to give the witty descriptive lines to Portia, not Nerissa, whereas in this first sketch Julia merely asks the questions and it is Lucetta who furnishes the witty replies. But it is in the incident of the letter—an incident that is *not* repeated and thereby shamed by later versions—that we come suddenly upon the fresh and ingratiating charm by which Julia bursts out of the conventions among which the insipid heroines of prose romance move, and comes quite alive; no doubt, this was the first glimpse afforded by the English stage of a new and magnificent creature, the heroine of romantic comedy. The incident immediately follows the review of potential suitors. Lucetta presents a letter from Proteus, and Julia stretches to the tiptoes of indignation in upbraiding her:

> Now, by my modesty, a goodly broker!
> Dare you presume to harbor wanton lines?
> To whisper and conspire against my youth?
> Now, trust me, 'tis an office of great worth,
> And you an officer fit for the place.
> There, take the paper; see it be returned,
> Or else return no more into my sight. (I.ii.41–47)

This show of spunk is itself worth a good deal; the pale heroine of romance could never have risen to it. Yet the heroine of Shakespearean romantic comedy is not truly born until the next instant, after Lucetta has left the stage; then, thus she speaks:

> And yet I would I had o'erlooked the letter.
> It were a shame to call her back again,
> And pray her to a fault for which I chid her.
> What fool is she, that knows I am a maid,
> And would not force the letter to my view! (I.ii.50–54)

Shakespeare could definitely have stopped the incident at this; it would have been enough to establish a new institution. But he goes on: Julia calls back Lucetta, takes the letter from her, and, in a simply superb demonstration of the chastity of mind appropriate to highborn ladies in the presence of their lessers, tears it all to bits. Shakespeare could have stopped here, too; it would have been more than enough. But once more he goes on: Lucetta is again dismissed—and in an instant Julia is down on the floor, scrambling to reassemble the pieces:

Be calm, good wind, blow not a word away
Till I have found each letter in the letter,
Except mine own name: that some whirlwind bear
Unto a ragged, fearful-hanging rock,
And throw it thence into the raging sea!    (I.ii.118–22)

In later scenes Julia repeatedly breaks the way for her great successors. In II.vii, she takes the plunge for all of them: she decides to go to Milan, to check on her—of course!—completely faithful Proteus; but not in her own identity:

Not like a woman, for I would prevent
The loose encounters of lascivious men.
Gentle Lucetta, fit me with such weeds
As may beseem some well-reputed page.    (II.vii.40–43)

This was a fateful step. Soon Portia would say to Nerissa,

I'll hold thee any wager,
When we are both accoutered like young men,
I'll prove the prettier fellow of the two
            (*Merchant of Venice*, III.iv.62–64)

Rosalind would say to Celia,

Were it not better,
Because that I am more than common tall,
That I did suit me all points like a man?
A gallant curtle-ax upon my thigh,
A boar-spear in my hand    (*As You Like It*, I.iii.113–17)

and Viola would say to the Captain, who fished her out of the deep,

Conceal me what I am, and be my aid
For such disguise as haply shall become
The form of my intent. I'll serve this duke
            (*Twelfth Night*, I.ii.53–55)

The parallels of this kind are numerous. Like all three of her famed successors, Julia talks with her loved one, who knows her not. Like Viola, she is sent as an envoy of love by her truelove to *his* love. Like Portia, she receives from his finger the ring that she gave him. Like Rosalind, she all but gives away her sex by swooning at a crucial time. And like all the others, she gets her love at last on terms of uncompromising surrender:

What is in Silvia's face, but I may spy
More fresh in Julia's with a constant eye?
            . . .
Bear witness, heaven, I have my wish forever.
            (V.iv.115–16, 120)

In every parallel incident, she suffers from the inevitable comparison, and it is only in the rare moments when we catch her, so to speak, alone, doing something uniquely hers, not "trying out" something that her successors would perfect, that she has a chance to shine. So she does in the incident of the letter, and so, for example, she does in

IV.ii, when, wearing boy's clothes and accompanied by the Host, she eavesdrops on Proteus' serenade of Silvia. Here, though the song is all Silvia's, the dramatic center is all Julia's:

HOST   How do you, man? The music likes you not.
JULIA   You mistake; the musician likes me not.
HOST   Why, my pretty youth?
JULIA   He plays false, father.    (IV.ii.55–59)

She is great here not merely for the emotional impact of her moment of heartbreak, but for her resilience. The pallid heroine of prose romance would have crawled away to bleed in secret; but Julia asks of the Host, "Where lies Sir Proteus?" Her mind has already conceived a device by which she can keep an eye on him until such time as she can capture him for once and all.

It is almost certain that Proteus and Valentine suffer less by comparison with their successors than does Julia. This will appear a startling statement, particularly with reference to Proteus, who has a long and virtually undeviating history of being abominated by critics. It is nevertheless essentially true, and the reason it is so is not hard to find. The fact is that the heroes of the romantic comedies—unlike the heroines, whose power to dazzle the eye and the imagination makes a beginning with Julia and at once thereafter becomes blinding—never do come to amount to very much. Proteus and Valentine, therefore, look about as good as any.

Between them, these two gentlemen define both of the emphases of which the one or the other dominates the later heroes. It is not strictly accurate to classify Shakespeare's romantic young males to two "types"—one wicked, the other stupid—but it is fair to say that each of them evinces a *tendency* in one or the other direction, and that two of them even tend toward both directions at the same time. To say that they exhibit a tendency toward wickedness or toward stupidity is not to say that they are wicked or stupid, but is to suggest that if they went somewhat farther along the road their qualities point them in, they would indeed be downright wicked or downright stupid. It should be added at once that though this view of the heroes is hardly flattering, surely none of us could seriously wish any one of the heroes changed in the slightest; each is perfect for the thing he is, perfect for the particular dramatic "world" of which he is part—and, what is most important, in each case the brilliant heroine loves the fellow either just as he stands or just as she has made him be by the end of the play.

Valentine is the simpler case, in more ways than one, and we should look at him before we deal with Proteus. Valentine looks ahead to the hero who is best represented by Orlando of *As You Like It*. The main thing to be said of this kind of hero is that there is nothing in the least "wrong" with him. He has nothing but virtues—all the virtues that anyone can name, except brilliance. He is kind, brave, loyal, generous, modest, forgiving—anything and everything as you like it; but any passing remark can make him look like a wonderful simpleton in an instant: "I found him under a tree," says Celia of Orlando, "like a dropped acorn." If Valentine is not quite up to Orlando in the kind that he is, he is nevertheless very nearly his equal, both in the sterling qualities of romantic young manhood that his kind of hero stands for and in the lack of intellectual keenness (especially around heroines) that he also stands for. Valentine is the perfect exemplar of friendship; he would never violate friendship even for love —and he is entirely true to his kind when, in the end, without needing to go through the painful process of thinking about it, he cheerfully offers Silvia—for whom he would just as cheerfully die—to Proteus. He could not do otherwise and be what he is; and because Shakespeare has been entirely clear in showing us what he is, it is we who are at fault if we so much as imagine that he should do otherwise. Valentine shares with Orlando, and not particularly with any of Shakespeare's other heroes of romantic comedy, a certain exaggeratedly heroic valor. Orlando hurls a professional wrestler to the ground, breaking his bones, and deals just as directly, and with no sweat, with a "sucked and hungry" lioness. But he best sums up all the qualities of his kind of romantic hero in a single incident and a single posture when, seeking food for old Adam, he pops into the clearing where the exiled duke and his followers are at table and, mistaking them all for savages who have never been out of the woods, demands with drawn sword that they "Forbear, and eat no more" until his needs are served. Here, in a stroke, he is heroic on the grand scale, great-hearted, nobly unselfish for his old servant—and, quite unconsciously, just a little ludicrous for having so much misjudged the situation.

With such a stroke, Shakespeare imparted a kind of flavor that transformed the romance hero, somewhat as he transformed the vapid romance heroine by adding some special feminine touches, including spunk. Bassanio of *The Merchant of Venice* exhibits the added quality very well when—of all people—he, the golden-fleece hunter, coolly reasons his way past the gold casket and the silver casket and takes the lead one; and he exhibits it again when, in the court scene, after Portia has pinned Shylock to the wall and has him quite at her mercy, he fails to perceive how completely the tables have turned and continues to rush forward, nobly generous, with bags of ducats—Portia's own—to buy off his friend. And this very way of surrounding his hero's grimly stalwart attitude with a tongue-in-cheek attitude Shakespeare first explored in Valentine, notably at his first encounter with the out-laws, upon whom he makes such a favorable impression that they invite him to be "king for our wild faction" after two minutes of conversation. Surely, this is an incident to the abruptness of which critics should take no such exception as some have; like Orlando's heroic-ludicrous posture at the duke's banquet, and like Valentine's own quick offer to surrender Silvia to Proteus, and like Bassanio's straight-faced choice of the leaden casket, it hints of what Shakespeare did to romance to make it romantic *comedy*.

Thus the attitude of comedy within which the actions of the Valentine-Orlando kind of hero are framed is not limited to the more obvious situations in which the comic potentialities of the hero's intellectual equipment are exploited—as in the case of Valentine's penning a love note for Silvia and not understanding, while the simple Speed is appalled by his obtuseness, that her "secret nameless friend" is himself—but extends to his most heroic and high-minded moments. On both counts, Valentine is more nearly a finished portrait than a first sketch.

At least as much may be said of Proteus, first of those who represent a contrary emphasis in the heroic character. Valentine, Bassanio, Orlando are innocent and good-hearted; none of them could ever be imagined as "going bad" under any circumstances. Proteus not only could but temporarily does go bad, and so do those who follow in his line, namely, Claudio of *Much Ado About Nothing* and—stepping just over the boundary into the "dark comedies"—Bertram of *All's Well That Ends Well*.

These heroes are clearly not so much like one another as are those of the other line, who might almost be said to be interchangeable. Claudio, in particular, shares with the Valentine-Orlando hero a certain congenital unaware-ness of situation; but, curiously, while this appears a lovable fault in the others and endears them to us as well as to the heroines, in Claudio it is odious. A callow princox of a youth, Claudio looks from the outset like one who could mistake a situation and become nasty about it, as indeed he does. If he is "cured" in the end, when the truth of the situation has been made apparent, yet he remains the same callow princox still, and one supposes that he would be capable of dastardly conduct again tomorrow or the next day if the right set of circumstances invited him. Bertram and Claudio differ most notably in that, while each is capable of dastardly conduct, Claudio's worst exhibition of contemptible qualities is based on his initial misunderstanding of situation, whereas Bertram's involvement in such unheroic activities as illicit pursuits and outright lying is quite deliberate. If Claudio is capable of contemptible behavior only when he misunderstands, Bertram is most capable of it when he understands very well.

As a hero of his kind, therefore, not being in competition with the Valentine-Orlando kind, but compared with Claudio and Bertram, Proteus looks remarkably good. As a dramatic character he is certainly as well drawn as they are, and as a man he is hardly worse than they. Proteus is like Bertram in needing no misunderstanding of situation to start him on a wayward course. It has been remarked of Macbeth that of all Shakespeare's tragic heroes he alone knowingly embraces evil as his good, and it may as well be said of Proteus and Bertram that they alone of the comic heroes knowingly take to the crooked paths of dishonor. Bertram rejects the wife of inferior birth who was forced on him; lies to her; pursues, with the intention of corrupting, for no reason but lust, a virgin of Florence; is prevented from committing adultery only by his wife's shrewd intervention; and thereafter, confronted with his deeds, lies, slanders others, and abandons all dignity and honor in an exhibition of squirming and twisting; and after his disgraceful wallowing, he is abruptly forgiven all his trespasses and welcomed home as a worthy subject, son, and husband.

Against Bertram's record as a hero, Proteus' fairly shines. He does not choose to leave his Julia, but is sent away by his father. Neither does he choose to fall in love with Silvia, any more than Romeo chooses to fall in love with Juliet (and many details of the play prove that Shakespeare had Brooke's *Romeus and Juliet* in mind as he wrote). Here, in reducing the odium of Proteus' initial fault, Shakespeare has been characteristically shrewd, for he has made Silvia irresistible, with both an inward and an outward beauty. If, lest she put Julia in the shade, he had made her only an ordinary beauty, Proteus' "three-fold perjury" committed in pursuit of her would have been difficult to understand and all but impossible to forgive. But on Silvia he has lavished all his superlatives, made her dazzling, wholly worthy of the song with which she is serenaded in Act IV and which is itself incomparable. All things considered, Silvia being as she is and what she is, who can blame Proteus?

In two other ways, also, Shakespeare goes farther toward explaining and extenuating Proteus' fault than he was to do with the faults of Claudio and Bertram. In the first scene of the play, Proteus is shown to be both a faithful friend and a faithful lover; but also the point is made evident that in a crisis of conflict between friendship and love, love would claim him:

> He after honor hunts, I after love.
> He leaves his friends to dignify them more,
> I leave myself, my friends, and all, for love.    (I.i.63–65)

He is love's votary; as it has been with Julia, so will it be with Silvia when the time comes: he will leave himself, his true friend, and all else, for love. Second, as he does not do for Claudio and Bertram, Shakespeare does Proteus the credit of allowing him to debate the right and wrong of his multiple perjury before he commits it, to debate the question, in fact, twice, in II.iv.192–214, and in II.vi.1–43. Claudio and Bertram, one notes, engage in no self-debate; they directly announce their bad intentions without troubling with any such preliminaries. Even though his decision is "wrong," Proteus at least undergoes the formality of weighing right and wrong. It is true that his self-debate involves no agonizing soul struggle such as Angelo of *Measure for Measure* undergoes in a roughly comparable situation, when flesh and the spirit are at war in him; Shakespeare quite rightly keeps Proteus' "struggle" light, superficial, artificial, well within the tone and the terms appropriate to romantic comedy:

> And ev'n that pow'r which gave me first my oath
> Provokes me to this threefold perjury:
> Love bade me swear, and love bids me forswear.
>                                              (II.vi.4–6)

Surely, this is as far as a proper hero of romantic comedy dare go in soul struggle, and critics who deplore the too-easy entrance of Proteus into treachery—even as they deplore his too-easy return from it—would do well to remember that the moral ponderings of a Hamlet, an Angelo, or a Macbeth at this point would crash out of and destroy the very genre that this particular romantic hero helped to create.

But all this is not to suggest that Proteus is a blameless hero; if he were so, he would not belong with Claudio and Bertram, but with Valentine and Orlando. It is rather to insist that of the specific kind he represents, he runs true to form and measures up extremely well. Launce identifies him and his kind clearly enough: "I am but a fool, look you, and yet I have the wit to think my master is a kind of a knave." Is he any worse than that? For only a moment he seems to be, when he threatens Silvia with violence in the forest, and here perhaps Shakespeare did indeed go too far. But whether he would actually

attack Silvia we neither know nor need to know; the fact is that he does not attack her, and we are quite aware that, with Valentine at hand, watching every move, there never was any real danger in the situation. He is guilty of nothing more than a thoroughly wicked intent, which is thwarted while it is only an impulse. A wicked impulse is not punishable, and in the world of romantic comedy is not even to be thought on too seriously.

Julia and Silvia, Valentine and Proteus are the most notable human fixtures in the special world of romantic comedy that was born with *The Two Gentlemen of Verona*. They are light but durable fixtures, as that world requires. If they are not wholly credible, yet they are more credible than were their forbears in the romances, and they are credible enough, palpable enough, one may say, for the world of romantic comedy, the nature of which would be altered if it were made to sustain creatures more solid. They are of a kind with this special world.

The world of romantic comedy, both as it was first drawn in this play and as it was re-created in each of the masterpieces that followed, of course includes other features besides the heroes and the heroines who invariably inhabit it. It includes, for example, clowns and fools. Speed and Launce stand rather uncertainly between the twin Dromios, the bewildered but witty slaves of *The Comedy of Errors*, before them, and the magnificent creations that came after, like Launcelot Gobbo of *The Merchant of Venice* and Touchstone of *As You Like It*. They are not as gifted as these—if Launcelot Gobbo, a great dunce, may be said to be gifted—and they talk too long with one another and with their masters. With the exception of Launce's long exhortation to his dog to be a better dog, their appearances are likely to be found tedious in both the theater and the study. But if they are not at all well and functionally fitted into the plot of the play—and the fact is that they are almost always purely interruptive—yet Shakespeare's introduction of them into romance helped to bring romantic comedy into being: the oozy world of romance needed their dryness. Their presence does not particularly help to make this incredible world more credible; but it does what is just as good—namely, helps to make the point that this world does not *have* to be perfectly credible, helps to render its very incredibility acceptable. In such a world as they inhabit, how can we reasonably balk at such a turn as the sudden redemption of Proteus or Valentine's magnanimous offer of Silvia? They are reminders that we are to keep our perspective and not consider things too seriously; annoying as they have proved for many critics, with their dreary stretches of low-grade quibbles and mental horseplay, they nevertheless serve the important perspective-giving function implied by Feste's refrain at the end of *Twelfth Night:* "the rain it raineth every day."

Like the heroes and the heroines, the clowns and fools, and the incidents that take extravagant turns, the dramatic verse of *The Two Gentlemen of Verona* needs also to be taken for what it is and does within the world of romantic comedy. No passages and almost no single lines in this play (setting aside the whole of the song to Silvia) are particularly memorable. If one sets, for instance, the poetic language of Julia's interviews (in disguise) with Proteus and with Silvia beside that of Viola-Cesario's interviews with Orsino and Olivia in *Twelfth Night*—a fair comparison, involving similar characters in virtually identical situations—the contrast is obvious enough; yet it is not shocking. Here is Julia-Sebastian speaking to Silvia:

> She hath been fairer, madam, than she is.
> When she did think my master loved her well,
> She, in my judgment, was as fair as you.
> But since she did neglect her looking glass,
> And threw her sun-expelling mask away,
> The air hath starved the roses in her cheeks
> And pinched the lily-tincture of her face,
> That now she is become as black as I. (IV.iv.149–56)

And here is Viola-Cesario, telling how she-he would woo Olivia:

> Make me a willow cabin at your gate,
> And call upon my soul within the house;
> Write loyal cantons of contemnèd love
> And sing them loud even in the dead of night;
> Halloo your name to the reverberate hills
> And make the babbling gossip of the air
> Cry out, "Olivia!" (*Twelfth Night*, I.v.266–72)

There is a resonance, a throaty vibrance in the music of the great poetic passages of *Twelfth Night*:

> She never told her love,
> But let concealment, like a worm i' th' bud,
> Feed on her damask cheek. She pined in thought,
> And with a green and yellow melancholy
> She sat, like Patience on a monument,
> Smiling at grief (II.iv.110–15)

to which at best *The Two Gentlemen of Verona* never once attains, unless in the single line so much praised by Logan Pearsall Smith (*Shakespeare*, p. 74): "but it is only in the *Two Gentlemen of Verona*, with the song 'Who is Silvia,' with the line 'The uncertain glory of an April day,' and the passage about the brook that makes sweet music as it strays, that his power over words becomes a magic power, and his golden mastery of speech begins to almost blind us with its beauty."

Though it is easy to assent to the glory of this single line, no one would be likely to claim particular distinction for all the poetry of the play. What is here asserted, instead, is that the poetic language is "right" for the play, that it helps in the same way that the heroes and heroines and the extravagant incidents do to create the "world" of romantic comedy. This poetry has a good deal of chaff in it; it is sometimes glittering chaff, but chaff it is. It is light and usually frivolous; even when deep ideas are asserted, they are not asserted profoundly. The speakers habitually play along the surface of things:

PROTEUS
  So, by your circumstance, you call me fool.
VALENTINE
  So, by your circumstance, I fear you'll prove.
PROTEUS
  'Tis Love you cavil at. I am not Love.

VALENTINE
  Love is your master, for he masters you;
  And he that is so yokèd by a fool,
  Methinks, should not be chronicled for wise.
PROTEUS
  Yet writers say, as in the sweetest bud
  The eating canker dwells, so eating Love
  Inhabits in the finest wits of all.
VALENTINE
  And writers say . . . (I.i.36–45)

This is as typical an example as any of the poetic talk that fills the play, and in filling it defines its kind. It is both superficial and artificial, if one will, but "right" for the kind of world in which it is spoken and which it creates in being spoken, just as, for the same reason, the principal characters and incidents are also "right." There is an attitude of frivolity about this world which is figured forth in language, character, and incident.

Viewed thus, for what it is in part and whole, the play needs no apology, and certainly it does not deserve the harsh criticism that it has received from many who have not been content to take it for what it is. It transformed romance to romantic comedy, and it founded a great line. But, viewed as we have viewed it, it need not depend for its whole credit upon the fact that it was an important "first." It would be what it is if there were no *Twelfth Night*—indeed, it would no doubt look much better if there were no *Twelfth Night*.

## A NOTE ON THE SOURCE

Both because its plot is filled with well-known romance elements and because its poetic style is laden with rhetorical devices fashionable at the time it was written, *The Two Gentlemen of Verona* appears inevitably to owe an unusual number of debts to a wide variety of materials. In its conventions as well as in its basic materials and their manner of use, it is as deeply embedded in the literary life of its time as any work of Shakespeare's.

The central theme of the play—conflict between the duties of friendship and love—had been used by Boccaccio in *La Teseide*, by Chaucer in *The Knight's Tale*, and by Lyly in *Euphues: The Anatomy of Wit* and *Endimion*; but, indeed, this theme is ancient and widespread, and Shakespeare would have encountered it in any event. Specific incidents and motifs in the play, such as Julia's disguise as a boy, may have been suggested by Sidney's pastoral romance of *Arcadia*; the abrupt election of Valentine as captain of the outlaws may derive from the same source. Many echoes of Brooke's *Romeus and Juliet*, the narrative poem which Shakespeare followed in *Romeo and Juliet*, occur in the play, perhaps the most notable being the device of the rope ladder which figures prominently in both plays.

In poetic manner and attitude, the play shows the pervasive influence of Lyly, the fashionable stylist of courtly language and the master of dramatic artifice in dialogue, scene, and character. Long stretches of wit duels between servant and servant, servant and master, lady and attendant, filled with quips and quirks and turns of phrase, mark the play as Lylyan in its most basic conception. In *The Two Gentlemen of Verona* the artifices of Lyly are more than superficial ornamentation; they are organic.

For the core of the play, however, which is the love story of Julia and Proteus, Shakespeare went to a prose romance originally written in Spanish, the *Diana Enamorada*, by the Portuguese Jorge de Montemayor, published in 1542. How Shakespeare came to know this work is uncertain, for though it was translated into English by Bartholomew Yonge about 1582, the translation was not published until 1598—some four to six years after the play was written. It has been suggested that Shakespeare could have become acquainted with the *Diana* through a French translation made before 1590; that he may have seen Yonge's manuscript before it was published; or that the story was represented in a play now lost.

## A NOTE ON THE TEXT

*The Two Gentlemen of Verona* was first printed in the First Folio of 1623, which is the authority for the present text. In the Folio it is the second play, standing between *The Tempest* and *The Merry Wives of Windsor*, the title of the latter play mistakenly appearing at the top of the final two pages. Names of characters who participate in each scene are grouped at the head of the scene, without notice made of the point of their entrance. The present edition deletes these names, and provides them, in square

brackets, at the appropriate places later in the scenes. The Folio gives "Protheus" for "Proteus" and places the dramatis personae at the end of the text. Certain irregularities occur in place names, as though Shakespeare had changed his mind or become confused about principal locations; thus in II.v Padua rather than Milan is identified as the place of action by Speed, and in III.i the Duke of Milan speaks of a lady "in Verona here." In the present edition, speech prefixes have been regularized, spelling and punctuation have been modernized, and obvious typographical errors have been corrected. Added material (stage directions, and so on) is set in brackets. Act and scene divisions are those of the Folio, translated from Latin into English. The relatively few emendations of the Folio text are indicated below: the present reading is given in boldface, followed by the Folio reading in roman.

I.i.65 **leave** loue   78 **a sheep** Sheepe   145–46 **testerned** cestern'd
I.ii.88 **your** you
I.iii.91 **Exeunt** Exeunt. Finis
II.iii.27 **wood** would
II.iv.50 **father's in** father is in   108 **mistress** a Mistresse   166 **makes** make   196 **Is . . . eye** It is mine   214 **Exit** Exeunt
II.v.37 **that my** that that my
III.i.281 **master's ship** Mastership   318 **kissed fasting** fasting   378 s.d. **Exit** Exeunt
IV.i.10 **he's** he is   35 **miserable** often miserable   50 **An** And; **near** Neece
IV.ii.113 **his** her
IV.iii.18 **abhors** abhor'd
IV.iv.70 **thou** thee   74 **to leave** not leaue   205 **Exit** Exeunt
V.ii.18 **your peace** you peace   32 **Sir Eglamour** Eglamoure   56 **Exit** Exeunt

# THE TWO GENTLEMEN
# OF VERONA

## The Names of All the Actors

DUKE [OF MILAN] *father to Silvia*
VALENTINE } *the two gentlemen*
PROTEUS
ANTONIO *father to Proteus*
THURIO *a foolish rival to Valentine*
EGLAMOUR *agent for Silvia in her escape*
HOST *where Julia lodges*
OUTLAWS *with Valentine*

SPEED *a clownish servant to Valentine*
LAUNCE *the like to Proteus*
PANTHINO *servant to Antonio*
JULIA *beloved of Proteus*
SILVIA *beloved of Valentine*
LUCETTA *waiting-woman to Julia*
[SERVANTS MUSICIANS]

[*Scene:* Verona; Milan; a forest]

## ACT I

### Scene I. [*Verona. An open place.*]

[*Enter*] VALENTINE [*and*] PROTEUS.

VALENTINE
Cease to persuade, my loving Proteus:
Home-keeping youth have ever homely wits.
Were't not affection chains thy tender days
To the sweet glances of thy honored love,
I rather would entreat thy company          5
To see the wonders of the world abroad,
Than, living dully sluggardized at home,
Wear out thy youth with shapeless idleness.
But since thou lov'st, love still, and thrive therein,
Even as I would, when I to love begin.          10
PROTEUS
Wilt thou be gone? Sweet Valentine, adieu!
Think on thy Proteus when thou haply° see'st
Some rare noteworthy object in thy travel:
Wish me partaker in thy happiness
When thou dost meet good hap;° and in thy danger,          15
If ever danger do environ thee,

Commend thy grievance to my holy prayers,
For I will be thy beadsman,° Valentine.
VALENTINE
And on a love-book° pray for my success?
PROTEUS
Upon some book I love I'll pray for thee.          20
VALENTINE
That's on some shallow story of deep love:
How young Leander° crossed the Hellespont.
PROTEUS
That's a deep story of a deeper love,
For he was more than over shoes in love.
VALENTINE
'Tis true, for you are over boots in love,          25
And yet you never swum the Hellespont.
PROTEUS
Over the boots? Nay, give me not the boots.°
VALENTINE
No, I will not, for it boots° thee not.
PROTEUS                    What?
VALENTINE
To be in love—where scorn is bought with groans,

18 **beadsman** one who contracts to pray in behalf of another 19 **love-book** instead of a prayer book 22 **Leander** legendary Greek youth who nightly swam the Hellespont to visit his beloved Hero and, one night, was drowned 27 **give . . . boots** don't jest with me 28 **boots** benefits (with pun on preceding line)

---

*The decorative border above appeared on the first page of* The Two Gentlemen of Verona *in the First Folio edition of Shakespeare's plays, 1623.*

**I.i.12 haply** by chance **15 hap** luck

Coy looks with heartsore sighs, one fading moment's
   mirth                                                              30
With twenty watchful, weary, tedious nights;
If haply won, perhaps a hapless° gain;
If lost, why then a grievous labor won;
However,° but a folly bought with wit,
Or else a wit by folly vanquishèd.                                   35

PROTEUS
So, by your circumstance,° you call me fool.

VALENTINE
So, by your circumstance, I fear you'll prove.

PROTEUS
'Tis Love you cavil at. I am not Love.

VALENTINE
Love is your master, for he masters you;
And he that is so yokèd by a fool,                                   40
Methinks, should not be chronicled° for wise.

PROTEUS
Yet writers say, as in the sweetest bud
The eating canker° dwells, so eating Love
Inhabits in the finest wits of all.

VALENTINE
And writers say, as the most forward° bud                            45
Is eaten by the canker ere it blow,°
Even so by love the young and tender wit
Is turned to folly, blasting° in the bud,
Losing his verdure even in the prime,°
And all the fair effects of future hopes.                            50
But wherefore waste I time to counsel thee,
That art a votary to fond desire?
Once more adieu! My father at the road°
Expects my coming, there to see me shipped.

PROTEUS
And thither will I bring° thee, Valentine.                           55

VALENTINE
Sweet Proteus, no; now let us take our leave.
To Milan let me hear from thee by letters
Of thy success° in love, and what news else
Betideth here in absence of thy friend,
And I likewise will visit thee with mine.                            60

PROTEUS
All happiness bechance to thee in Milan!

VALENTINE
As much to you at home! And so, farewell.   *Exit.*

PROTEUS
He after honor hunts, I after love.
He leaves his friends to dignify them more,
I leave myself, my friends, and all, for love.                       65
Thou, Julia, thou hast metamorphized me,
Made me neglect my studies, lose my time,
War with good counsel, set the world at nought,
Made wit with musing weak, heart sick with thought.

[*Enter* SPEED.]

SPEED   Sir Proteus, save you!° Saw you my master?   70
PROTEUS   But now he parted hence, to embark for
Milan.

SPEED
Twenty to one, then, he is shipped already,
And I have played the sheep° in losing him.

PROTEUS
Indeed, a sheep doth very often stray,                               75
And if° the shepherd be awhile away.

SPEED   You conclude that my master is a shepherd,
then, and I a sheep?
PROTEUS   I do.
SPEED   Why then, my horns are his horns,° whether I   80
wake or sleep.
PROTEUS   A silly answer, and fitting well a sheep.
SPEED   This proves me still a sheep.
PROTEUS   True, and thy master a shepherd.
SPEED   Nay, that I can deny by a circumstance.°        85
PROTEUS   It shall go hard but I'll prove it by
another.
SPEED   The shepherd seeks the sheep, and not the
sheep the shepherd; but I seek my master, and my
master seeks not me. Therefore I am no sheep.
PROTEUS   The sheep for fodder follow the shepherd;   90
the shepherd for food follows not the sheep; thou for
wages followest thy master, thy master for wages
follows not thee. Therefore thou art a sheep.
SPEED   Such another proof will make me cry "baa."
PROTEUS   But, dost thou hear? Gav'st thou my letter   95
to Julia?
SPEED   Ay, sir: I, a lost mutton, gave your letter to
her, a laced mutton,° and she, a laced mutton, gave
me, a lost mutton, nothing for my labor.
PROTEUS   Here's too small a pasture for such store of   100
muttons.
SPEED   If the ground be overcharged,° you were best
stick° her.
PROTEUS   Nay, in that you are astray; 'twere best
pound° you.                                                          105
SPEED   Nay, sir, less than a pound shall serve me for
carrying your letter.
PROTEUS   You mistake. I mean the pound—a pinfold.
SPEED
From a pound to a pin? Fold it over and over,
'Tis threefold too little for carrying a letter to your
   lover.                                             110
PROTEUS   But what said she?
SPEED [*Nodding.*]   Ay.
PROTEUS   Nod—ay. Why, that's noddy.°
SPEED   You mistook, sir. I say she did nod; and you
ask me if she did nod, and I say, "Ay."               115
PROTEUS   And that set together is noddy.
SPEED   Now you have taken the pains to set it together,
take it for your pains.
PROTEUS   No, no. You shall have it for bearing the
letter.                                                              120
SPEED   Well, I perceive I must be fain to bear with
you.
PROTEUS   Why, sir, how do you bear with me?

---

**32 hapless** luckless   **34 However** in either case   **36 by your
circumstance** by your argument (in the next line the same
phrase means "in your condition [of love]")   **41 chronicled**
written down   **43 canker** cankerworm   **45 most forward**
earliest   **46 blow** bloom   **48 blasting** withering   **49 prime**
spring   **53 road** harbor   **55 bring** accompany   **58 success**
fortune (good or bad)   **70 save you** a greeting

**74 sheep** pun on *ship*   **76 And if** if   **80 my . . . his horns** my
(sheep's) horns belong to him (making him a cuckold)   **85
circumstance** logical proof   **97–98 lost mutton . . . laced
mutton** lost sheep . . . laced courtesan (probably *lost* and *laced*
were similarly pronounced)   **102 overcharged** overgrazed
**103 stick** stab (slaughter)   **105 pound** impound (with pun)
**113 noddy** fool

SPEED  Marry,° sir, the letter, very orderly; having
nothing but the word "noddy" for my pains.    125
PROTEUS  Beshrew° me, but you have a quick wit.
SPEED  And yet it cannot overtake your slow purse.
PROTEUS  Come, come, open the matter in brief.
What said she?
SPEED  Open your purse, that the money and the    130
matter may be both at once delivered.
PROTEUS  Well, sir, here is for your pains. What said
she?
SPEED  Truly, sir, I think you'll hardly win her.
PROTEUS  Why, couldst thou perceive so much from    135
her?
SPEED  Sir, I could perceive nothing at all from her;
no, not so much as a ducat for delivering your letter.
And being so hard to me that brought your mind,
I fear she'll prove as hard to you in telling your    140
mind. Give her no token but stones;° for she's as
hard as steel.
PROTEUS  What said she? Nothing?
SPEED  No, not so much as "Take this for thy pains."
To testify your bounty, I thank you, you have tes-    145
terned me;° in requital whereof, henceforth carry
your letters yourself. And so, sir, I'll commend you
to my master.
PROTEUS
Go, go, be gone, to save your ship from wrack,
Which cannot perish, having thee aboard,
Being destined to a drier death on shore.°    150
                    [Exit SPEED.]
I must go send some better messenger;
I fear my Julia would not deign my lines,
Receiving them from such a worthless post.°    Exit.


Scene II. [Verona. Julia's house.]

Enter JULIA and LUCETTA.

JULIA
But say, Lucetta, now we are alone,
Wouldst thou, then, counsel me to fall in love?
LUCETTA
Ay, madam; so you stumble not unheedfully.
JULIA
Of all the fair resort of gentlemen°
That every day with parle° encounter me,    5
In thy opinion which is worthiest love?
LUCETTA
Please you repeat their names, I'll show my mind
According to my shallow simple skill.
JULIA
What think'st thou of the fair Sir Eglamour?
LUCETTA
As of a knight well-spoken, neat, and fine;    10
But, were I you, he never should be mine.

JULIA
What think'st thou of the rich Mercatio?
LUCETTA
Well of his wealth; but of himself, so so.
JULIA
What think'st thou of the gentle Proteus?
LUCETTA
Lord, Lord! To see what folly reigns in us!    15
JULIA
How now! What means this passion° at his name?
LUCETTA
Pardon, dear madam; 'tis a passing° shame
That I, unworthy body as I am,
Should censure° thus on lovely gentlemen.
JULIA
Why not on Proteus, as of all the rest?    20
LUCETTA
Then thus: of many good I think him best.
JULIA
Your reason?
LUCETTA
I have no other but a woman's reason:
I think him so because I think him so.
JULIA
And wouldst thou have me cast my love on him?    25
LUCETTA
Ay, if you thought your love not cast away.
JULIA
Why, he, of all the rest, hath never moved° me.
LUCETTA
Yet he, of all the rest, I think, best loves ye.
JULIA
His little speaking shows his love but small.
LUCETTA
Fire that's closest kept burns most of all.    30
JULIA
They do not love that do not show their love.
LUCETTA
O, they love least that let men know their love.
JULIA
I would I knew his mind.
LUCETTA
Peruse this paper, madam.
JULIA
"To Julia."—Say, from whom?    35
LUCETTA
That the contents will show.
JULIA
Say, say, who gave it thee?
LUCETTA
Sir Valentine's page; and sent, I think, from Proteus.
He would have given it you; but I, being in the way,
Did in your name receive it. Pardon the fault, I pray.    40
JULIA
Now, by my modesty, a goodly broker!°
Dare you presume to harbor wanton lines?
To whisper and conspire against my youth?
Now, trust me, 'tis an office of great worth,
And you an officer fit for the place.    45
There, take the paper; see it be returned,
Or else return no more into my sight.

124 **Marry** a casual oath (from "By the Virgin Mary")  126
**Beshrew** curse (used casually)  141 **stones** in addition to
punning on its meanings of "jewels" and "worthless gifts,"
Speed may be punning on another meaning, "testicle"
145–46 **testerned me** given me a testern (sixpence)  151
**Being . . . shore** being destined to hang  154 **post** messenger
I.ii.4 **resort of gentlemen** crowd of suitors  5 **parle** parley

16 **passion** emotion  17 **passing** surpassing  19 **censure** pass
judgment  27 **moved** proposed to  41 **broker** go-between

LUCETTA
To plead for love deserves more fee than hate,
JULIA
Will ye be gone?
LUCETTA                    That you may ruminate.    *Exit.*
JULIA
And yet I would I had o'erlooked° the letter.    50
It were a shame to call her back again,
And pray her to° a fault for which I chid her.
What fool is she, that knows I am a maid,
And would not force the letter to my view!
Since maids, in modesty, say "no" to that    55
Which they would have the profferer construe "ay."
Fie, fie, how wayward is this foolish love,
That, like a testy° babe, will scratch the nurse,
And presently,° all humbled, kiss the rod!
How churlishly I chid Lucetta hence,    60
When willingly I would have had her here!
How angerly I taught my brow to frown,
When inward joy enforced my heart to smile!
My penance is to call Lucetta back
And ask remission for my folly past.    65
What, ho! Lucetta!

*Enter* LUCETTA.

JUCETTA                    What would your ladyship?
LULIA
Is't near dinnertime?
LUCETTA                    I would it were;
That you might kill your stomach° on your meat,
And not upon your maid.°
JULIA
What is't that you took up so gingerly?    70
LUCETTA
Nothing.
JULIA
Why didst thou stoop, then?
LUCETTA
To take a paper up that I let fall.
JULIA
And is that paper nothing?
LUCETTA
Nothing concerning me.    75
JULIA
Then let it lie for those that it concerns.
LUCETTA
Madam, it will not lie where it concerns,°
Unless it have a false interpreter.
JULIA
Some love of yours hath writ to you in rhyme.
LUCETTA
That I might sing it, madam, to a tune.    80
Give me a note: your ladyship can set.°
JULIA
As little by such toys° as may be possible.
Best sing it to the tune of "Light o' love."°

LUCETTA
It is too heavy for so light a tune.
JULIA
Heavy! Belike it hath some burden,° then?    85
LUCETTA
Ay, and melodious were it, would you sing it.
JULIA
And why not you?
LUCETTA                    I cannot reach so high.
JULIA
Let's see your song. [*Takes the letter.*] How now,
    minion!
LUCETTA
Keep tune there still, so you will sing it out:
And yet methinks I do not like this tune.    90
JULIA
You do not?
LUCETTA    No, madam; 'tis too sharp.
JULIA
You, minion, are too saucy.
LUCETTA
Nay, now you are too flat,
And mar the concord with too harsh a descant.°
There wanteth but a mean° to fill your song.    95
JULIA
The mean is drowned with your unruly bass.
LUCETTA
Indeed, I bid the base° for Proteus.
JULIA
This babble shall not henceforth trouble me.
Here is a coil with protestation!°

[*Tears the letter.*]

Go get you gone, and let the papers lie;    100
You would be fing'ring them, to anger me.
LUCETTA
She makes it strange;° but she would be best pleased
To be so ang'red with another letter.    [*Exit.*]
JULIA
Nay, would I were so ang'red with the same!
O hateful hands, to tear such loving words!    105
Injurious wasps, to feed on such sweet honey,
And kill the bees, that yield it, with your stings!
I'll kiss each several° paper for amends.
Look, here is writ "kind Julia." Unkind Julia!
As in revenge of thy ingratitude,    110
I throw thy name against the bruising stones,
Trampling contemptuously on thy disdain.
And here is writ "love-wounded Proteus."
Poor wounded name! My bosom, as a bed,
Shall lodge thee, till thy wound be throughly° healed;    115
And thus I search° it with a sovereign kiss.
But twice or thrice was "Proteus" written down.
Be calm, good wind, blow not a word away
Till I have found each letter in the letter,
Except mine own name: that some whirlwind bear    120

50 **o'erlooked** perused   52 **pray her to** apologize to her for
58 **testy** irritable   59 **presently** immediately   68 **kill your
stomach** (1) allay your vexation (2) appease your hunger
68–69 **meat . . . maid** pun on *mate*   77 **lie . . . concerns**
express its content falsely (with quibble on preceding line)
81 **set** set to music   82 **toys** trifles   83 **Light o' love** a
contemporary popular ditty

85 **burden** bass refrain (with pun)   94 **descant** improvised
harmony   95 **wanteth . . . mean** lacks a tenor part (Proteus?)
97 **bid the base** in the game of prisoner's base, a challenge to
a test of speed (with pun)   99 **coil with protestation** much
ado made up of lover's protestations   102 **makes it strange**
pretends that it is nothing to her   108 **several** separate   115
**throughly** thoroughly   116 **search** probe (as in cleaning a
wound)

Unto a ragged, fearful-hanging rock,
And throw it thence into the raging sea!
Lo, here in one line is his name twice writ,
"Poor forlorn Proteus, passionate Proteus,
To the sweet Julia." That I'll tear away.— 125
And yet I will not, sith° so prettily
He couples it to his complaining names.
Thus will I fold them one upon another.
Now kiss, embrace, contend, do what you will.

[*Enter* LUCETTA.]

LUCETTA
Madam, 130
Dinner is ready, and your father stays.
JULIA
Well, let us go.
LUCETTA
What, shall these papers lie like telltales here?
JULIA
If you respect them, best to take them up.
LUCETTA
Nay, I was taken up for laying them down; 135
Yet here they shall not lie, for catching cold.
JULIA
I see you have a month's mind° to them.
LUCETTA
Ay, madam, you may say what sights you see;
I see things too, although you judge I wink.°
JULIA
Come, come; will't please you go?     *Exeunt.* 140

Scene III. [*Verona. Antonio's house.*]

*Enter* ANTONIO *and* PANTHINO.

ANTONIO
Tell me, Panthino, what sad° talk was that
Wherewith my brother held you in the cloister?
PANTHINO
'Twas of his nephew Proteus, your son.
ANTONIO
Why, what of him?
PANTHINO                 He wond'red that your lordship
Would suffer him to spend his youth at home, 5
While other men, of slender reputation,°
Put forth their sons to seek preferment out:
Some to the wars, to try their fortune there,
Some to discover islands far away,
Some to the studious universities. 10
For any, or for all these exercises,
He said that Proteus your son was meet,°
And did request me to importune you
To let him spend his time no more at home,
Which would be great impeachment° to his age, 15
In having known no travel in his youth.
ANTONIO
Nor need'st thou much importune me to that
Whereon this month I have been hammering.°

I have considered well his loss of time,
And how he cannot be a perfect man, 20
Not being tried and tutored in the world.
Experience is by industry achieved,
And perfected° by the swift course of time.
Then, tell me, whither were I best to send him?
PANTHINO
I think your lordship is not ignorant 25
How his companion, youthful Valentine,
Attends the emperor° in his royal court.
ANTONIO
I know it well.
PANTHINO
'Twere good, I think, your lordship sent him thither.
There shall he practice tilts and tournaments, 30
Hear sweet discourse, converse with noblemen,
And be in eye of° every exercise
Worthy his youth and nobleness of birth.
ANTONIO
I like thy counsel; well hast thou advised.
And that thou mayst perceive how well I like it, 35
The execution of it shall make known.
Even with the speediest expedition°
I will dispatch him to the emperor's court.
PANTHINO
Tomorrow, may it please you, Don Alphonso,
With other gentlemen of good esteem, 40
Are journeying to salute the emperor,
And to commend their service to his will.
ANTONIO
Good company; with them shall Proteus go.
And—in good time! Now will we break with° him.

[*Enter* PROTEUS.]

PROTEUS
Sweet love! Sweet lines! Sweet life! 45
Here is her hand, the agent of her heart.
Here is her oath for love, her honor's pawn.°
O, that our fathers would applaud our loves,
To seal our happiness with their consents!
O heavenly Julia! 50
ANTONIO
How now! What letter are you reading there?
PROTEUS
May't please your lordship, 'tis a word or two
Of commendations° sent from Valentine,
Delivered by a friend that came from him.
ANTONIO
Lend me the letter; let me see what news. 55
PROTEUS
There is no news, my lord, but that he writes
How happily he lives, how well beloved
And daily graced by the emperor,
Wishing me with him, partner of his fortune.
ANTONIO
And how stand you affected to his wish? 60
PROTEUS
As one relying on your lordship's will,
And not depending on his friendly wish.

___

126 **sith** since   137 **month's mind** lasting desire   139 **wink** have my eyes shut, see nothing
I.iii.1 **sad** serious   6 **slender reputation** unimportant place   12 **meet** fitted   15 **impeachment** detriment   18 **hammering** pondering

23 **perfected** accented on first syllable   27 **emperor** Duke (of Milan)   32 **be . . . of** have sight of   37 **expedition** haste   44 **break with** break the news to   47 **pawn** pledge   53 **commendations** greetings

ANTONIO
My will is something sorted° with his wish.
Muse not that I thus suddenly proceed,
For what I will, I will, and there an end.
I am resolved that thou shalt spend some time   65
With Valentinus in the emperor's court.
What maintenance he from his friends receives,
Like exhibition° thou shalt have from me.
Tomorrow be in readiness to go.   70
Excuse it not,° for I am peremptory.°

PROTEUS
My lord, I cannot be so soon provided.
Please you, deliberate a day or two.

ANTONIO
Look what° thou want'st shall be sent after thee.
No more of stay! Tomorrow thou must go.   75
Come on, Panthino; you shall be employed
To hasten on his expedition.
                    [Exeunt ANTONIO and PANTHINO.]

PROTEUS
Thus have I shunned the fire for fear of burning,
And drenched me in the sea, where I am drowned.
I feared to show my father Julia's letter,   80
Lest he should take exceptions to my love;
And with the vantage of mine own excuse
Hath he excepted most against my love.°
O, how this spring of love resembleth
The uncertain glory of an April day,   85
Which now shows all the beauty of the sun,
And by and by a cloud takes all away!

[Enter PANTHINO.]

PANTHINO
Sir Proteus, your father calls for you.
He is in haste; therefore, I pray you, go.

PROTEUS
Why, this it is: my heart accords thereto,   90
And yet a thousand times it answers "no."   Exeunt.


# ACT II

Scene I. [Milan. The duke's palace.]

Enter VALENTINE [and] SPEED.

SPEED   Sir, your glove.
VALENTINE   Not mine; my gloves are on.
SPEED   Why, then, this may be yours, for this is but
one.°
VALENTINE
Ha, let me see. Ay, give it me, it's mine.   5
Sweet ornament that decks a thing divine!
Ah, Silvia, Silvia!
SPEED   Madam Silvia! Madam Silvia!

VALENTINE   How now, sirrah?°
SPEED   She is not within hearing, sir.   10
VALENTINE   Why, sir, who bade you call her?
SPEED   Your worship, sir, or else I mistook.
VALENTINE   Well, you'll still° be too forward.
SPEED   And yet I was last chidden for being too slow.
VALENTINE   Go to, sir. Tell me, do you know Madam   15
Silvia?
SPEED   She that your worship loves?
VALENTINE   Why, how know you that I am in love?
SPEED   Marry, by these special marks: first, you have
learned, like Sir Proteus, to wreathe your arms, like   20
a malcontent; to relish a love song, like a robin redbreast; to walk alone, like one that had the pestilence;
to sigh, like a schoolboy that had lost his A B C; to
weep, like a young wench that had buried her grandam; to fast, like one that takes diet; to watch,° like   25
one that fears robbing; to speak puling,° like a beggar
at Hallowmas.° You were wont, when you laughed,
to crow like a cock; when you walked, to walk like
one of the lions; when you fasted, it was presently after
dinner; when you looked sadly, it was for want of   30
money. And now you are metamorphized with a
mistress, that,° when I look on you, I can hardly think
you my master.
VALENTINE   Are all these things perceived in me?
SPEED   They are all perceived without ye.°   35
VALENTINE   Without me? They cannot.
SPEED   Without you? Nay, that's certain, for, without°
you were so simple, none else would. But you are
so without these follies, that these follies are within
you, and shine through you like the water in an   40
urinal, that not an eye that sees you but is a physician
to comment on your malady.
VALENTINE   But tell me, dost thou know my lady
Silvia?
SPEED   She that you gaze on so as she sits at supper?   45
VALENTINE   Hast thou observed that? Even she, I
mean.
SPEED   Why, sir, I know her not.
VALENTINE   Dost thou know her by my gazing on
her, and yet know'st her not?   50
SPEED   Is she not hard-favored,° sir?
VALENTINE   Not so fair, boy, as well-favored.
SPEED   Sir, I know that well enough.
VALENTINE   What dost thou know?
SPEED   That she is not so fair as, of you, well favored.   55
VALENTINE   I mean that her beauty is exquisite, but
her favor° infinite.
SPEED   That's because the one is painted, and the other
out of all count.°
VALENTINE   How painted? And how out of count?   60
SPEED   Marry, sir, so painted, to make her fair, that
no man counts of° her beauty.
VALENTINE   How esteem'st thou me? I account of her
beauty.

63 **something sorted** somewhat in accord   **69 exhibition**
allowance   **71 Excuse it not** offer no excuses; **peremptory**
determined   **74 Look what** whatever   **82–83 with . . .**
**love** he took advantage of my own device (the pretended
letter from Valentine) to strike the heaviest blow to my affair
of love (with Julia)
**II.i.2–4 on . . . one** a pun in Elizabethan speech

9 **sirrah** common form of address to inferiors   **13 still** always
**25 watch** lie awake   **26 puling** whiningly   **27 at Hallowmas** on
All Saints' Day (when beggars vied for special treats)   **32 that**
so that   **35 without ye** by external signs (here begins a series
of quibbles)   **37 without** unless   **51 hard-favored** homely
**57 favor** charm, graciousness   **59 out . . . count** beyond
counting   **62 counts of** takes account of

SPEED  You never saw her since she was deformed.° 65

VALENTINE  How long hath she been deformed?

SPEED  Ever since you loved her.

VALENTINE  I have loved her ever since I saw her;
and still I see her beautiful.

SPEED  If you love her, you cannot see her.     70

VALENTINE  Why?

SPEED  Because love is blind. O, that you had mine
eyes; or your own eyes had the lights they were wont
to have when you chid at Sir Proteus for going
ungartered!°     75

VALENTINE  What should I see then?

SPEED  Your own present folly, and her passing°
deformity. For he, being in love, could not see to
garter his hose; and you, being in love, cannot see
to put on your hose.     80

VALENTINE  Belike, boy, then, you are in love; for
last morning you could not see to wipe my shoes.

SPEED  True, sir; I was in love with my bed. I thank
you, you swinged° me for my love which makes me
the bolder to chide you for yours.     85

VALENTINE  In conclusion, I stand affected to her.

SPEED  I would you were set,° so your affection would
cease.

VALENTINE  Last night she enjoined me to write
some lines to one she loves.     90

SPEED  And have you?

VALENTINE  I have.

SPEED  Are they not lamely writ?

VALENTINE  No, boy, but as well as I can do them.
Peace! Here she comes.     95

SPEED [Aside.]  O excellent motion! O exceeding
puppet! Now will he interpret° to her.

[Enter SILVIA.]

VALENTINE  Madam and mistress, a thousand good
morrows.

SPEED [Aside.]  O, give ye good ev'n! Here's a million 100
of manners.

SILVIA  Sir Valentine and servant,° to you two
thousand.

SPEED [Aside.]  He should give her interest, and she
gives it him.     105

VALENTINE
As you enjoined me, I have writ your letter
Unto the secret nameless friend of yours,
Which I was much unwilling to proceed in,
But for my duty to your ladyship.

SILVIA
I thank you, gentle servant; 'tis very clerkly° done.     110

VALENTINE
Now trust me, madam, it came hardly off;
For, being ignorant to whom it goes,
I writ at random, very doubtfully.

SILVIA
Perchance you think too much of so much pains?

VALENTINE
No, madam; so it stead° you, I will write,     115
Please you command, a thousand times as much.
And yet—

SILVIA
A pretty period!° Well, I guess the sequel;
And yet I will not name it; and yet I care not;
And yet take this again; and yet I thank you,     120
Meaning henceforth to trouble you no more.

SPEED [Aside.]
And yet you will; and yet another "yet."

VALENTINE
What means your ladyship? Do you not like it?

SILVIA
Yes, yes: the lines are very quaintly° writ;
But since unwillingly, take them again.     125
Nay, take them.

VALENTINE          Madam, they are for you.

SILVIA
Ay, ay. You writ them, sir, at my request;
But I will none of them; they are for you;
I would have had them writ more movingly.

VALENTINE
Please you, I'll write your ladyship another.     130

SILVIA
And when it's writ, for my sake read it over,
And if it please you, so; if not, why, so.

VALENTINE
If it please me, madam, what then?

SILVIA
Why, if it please you, take it for your labor;
And so, good morrow, servant.     Exit SILVIA.  135

SPEED
O jest unseen, inscrutable, invisible,
As a nose on a man's face, or a weathercock on a
steeple!
My master sues to her, and she hath taught her suitor,
He being her pupil, to become her tutor.
O excellent device! Was there ever heard a better,     140
That my master, being scribe, to himself should write
the letter?

VALENTINE
How now, sir? What are you reasoning with yourself?

SPEED  Nay, I was rhyming; 'tis you that have the
reason.

VALENTINE  To do what?     145

SPEED  To be a spokesman from Madam Silvia.

VALENTINE  To whom?

SPEED  To yourself. Why, she woos you by a figure.°

VALENTINE  What figure?

SPEED  By a letter, I should say.     150

VALENTINE  Why, she hath not writ to me?

SPEED  What need she, when she hath made you write
to yourself? Why, do you not perceive the jest?

VALENTINE  No, believe me.

SPEED  No believing you, indeed, sir. But did you     155
perceive her earnest?°

VALENTINE  She gave me none, except an angry word.

SPEED  Why, she hath given you a letter.

---

65 **deformed** distorted by your lover's view  74–75 **going
ungartered** a sure sign that one is in love (see *As You Like It,*
III.ii.376)  77 **passing** surpassing, extreme  84 **swinged** beat
87 **set** seated (quibble on *stand*)  96–97 **motion . . . puppet
. . . interpret** the puppeteer's voice "interprets" for the
figures in the puppet play, or "motion"  102 **servant** gallant
lover (alludes not to Speed but to Valentine)  110 **clerkly**
scholarly

115 **stead** be useful to  118 **period** full stop  124 **quaintly**
ingeniously  148 **by a figure** by indirect means  156 **earnest**
(1) seriousness (2) token payment

VALENTINE  That's the letter I writ to her friend.

SPEED  And that letter hath she delivered, and there 160
an end.

VALENTINE  I would it were no worse.

SPEED  I'll warrant you, 'tis as well;
For often have you writ to her, and she, in modesty,
Or else for want of idle time, could not again reply; 165
Or fearing else some messenger that might her mind
    discover,°
Herself hath taught her love himself to write unto her
    lover.
All this I speak in print,° for in print I found it.
Why muse you, sir? 'Tis dinnertime.

VALENTINE  I have dined.                                    170

SPEED  Ay, but hearken, sir; though the chameleon
love can feed on the air,° I am one that am nourished
by my victuals, and would fain have meat. O, be not
like your mistress; be moved, be moved.     *Exeunt.*

### Scene II. [*Verona. Julia's house.*]

*Enter* PROTEUS [*and*] JULIA.

PROTEUS
Have patience, gentle Julia.

JULIA
I must, where is no remedy.

PROTEUS
When possibly I can, I will return.

JULIA
If you turn° not, you will return the sooner.
Keep this remembrance for thy Julia's sake.          5

[*Giving a ring.*]

PROTEUS
Why, then, we'll make exchange; here, take you this.

JULIA
And seal the bargain with a holy kiss.

PROTEUS
Here is my hand for my true constancy;
And when that hour o'erslips me in the day
Wherein I sigh not, Julia, for thy sake,             10
The next ensuing hour some foul mischance
Torment me for my love's forgetfulness!
My father stays° my coming; answer not;
The tide is now—nay, not thy tide of tears;
That tide will stay me longer than I should.         15
Julia, farewell! [*Exit* JULIA.] What, gone without a
    word?
Ay, so true love should do: it cannot speak;
For truth hath better deeds than words to grace it.

[*Enter* PANTHINO.]

PANTHINO
Sir Proteus, you are stayed for.

PROTEUS
Go; I come, I come.                                  20
Alas! This parting strikes poor lovers dumb.    *Exeunt.*

### Scene III. [*Verona. A street.*]

*Enter* LAUNCE [*leading a dog*].

LAUNCE  Nay, 'twill be this hour ere I have done weeping; all the kind of the Launces have this very fault.
I have received my proportion,° like the prodigious°
son, and am going with Sir Proteus to the imperial's
court. I think Crab my dog be the sourest-natured dog  5
that lives. My mother weeping, my father wailing,
my sister crying, our maid howling, our cat wringing
her hands, and all our house in a great perplexity,
yet did not this cruel-hearted cur shed one tear.
He is a stone, a very pebble stone, and has no more    10
pity in him than a dog. A Jew would have wept to
have seen our parting. Why, my grandam, having no
eyes, look you, wept herself blind at my parting. Nay,
I'll show you the manner of it. This shoe is my father;
no, this left shoe is my father. No, no, this left shoe is 15
my mother; nay, that cannot be so neither. Yes, it is
so, it is so, it hath the worser sole. This shoe, with the
hole in it, is my mother, and this my father; a vengeance
on't! There 'tis. Now, sir, this staff is my sister, for,
look you, she is as white as a lily, and as small as a    20
wand. This hat is Nan, our maid. I am the dog. No,
the dog is himself, and I am the dog. Oh! The dog is
me, and I am myself; ay, so, so. Now come I to my
father: Father, your blessing. Now should not the
shoe speak a word for weeping: now should I kiss my   25
father: well, he weeps on. Now come I to my mother.
Oh, that she could speak now like a wood woman!°
Well, I kiss her; why, there 'tis. Here's my mother's
breath up and down.° Now come I to my sister; mark
the moan she makes. Now the dog all this while sheds  30
not a tear, nor speaks a word; but see how I lay the
dust with my tears.

[*Enter* PANTHINO.]

PANTHINO  Launce, away, away, aboard! Thy master
is shipped, and thou art to post after with oars. What's
the matter? Why weep'st thou, man? Away, ass!        35
You'll lose the tide, if you tarry any longer.

LAUNCE  It is no matter if the tied were lost; for it is
the unkindest tied that ever any man tied.

PANTHINO  What's the unkindest tide?

LAUNCE  Why, he that's tied here, Crab, my dog.       40

PANTHINO  Tut, man, I mean thou'lt lose the flood,°
and, in losing the flood, lose thy voyage, and, in
losing thy voyage, lose thy master, and, in losing thy
master, lose thy service, and, in losing thy service—
Why dost thou stop my mouth?                         45

LAUNCE  For fear thou shouldst lose thy tongue.

PANTHINO  Where should I lose my tongue?

LAUNCE  In thy tale.

PANTHINO  In thy tail!

LAUNCE  Lose the tide, and the voyage, and the master, 50
and the service, and the tied! Why, man, if the river
were dry, I am able to fill it with my tears; if the wind
were down, I could drive the boat with my sighs.

166 **discover** reveal  168 **speak in print** quote  171–72
**chameleon . . . air** the chameleon was thought to eat nothing
but air (see also II.iv.25–28 and *Hamlet*, III.ii.93)
II.ii.4 **turn** change your affection (perhaps with the additional
meaning of "engage in sexual acts")  13 **stays** waits for

II.iii.3 **proportion** Launce's blunder for *portion*; **prodigious**
blunder for *prodigal*  27 **Oh . . . woman** Launce laments that
his (wooden) shoe is not really his mother, madly distressed
(wood) as she was at parting  29 **up and down** identically
41 **flood** full tide

PANTHINO  Come, come away, man; I was sent to call thee. 55

LAUNCE  Sir, call me what thou dar'st.

PANTHINO  Wilt thou go?

LAUNCE  Well, I will go.       *Exeunt.*

### Scene IV. [*Milan. The duke's palace.*]

*Enter* VALENTINE, SILVIA, THURIO, [*and*] SPEED.

SILVIA  Servant!

VALENTINE  Mistress?

SPEED  Master, Sir Thurio frowns on you.

VALENTINE  Ay, boy, it's for love.

SPEED  Not of you. 5

VALENTINE  Of my mistress, then.

SPEED  'Twere good you knocked him.     [*Exit.*]

SILVIA  Servant, you are sad.

VALENTINE  Indeed, madam, I seem so.

THURIO  Seem you that you are not? 10

VALENTINE  Haply I do.

THURIO  So do counterfeits.

VALENTINE  So do you.

THURIO  What seem I that I am not?

VALENTINE  Wise. 15

THURIO  What instance of the contrary?

VALENTINE  Your folly.

THURIO  And how quote° you my folly?

VALENTINE  I quote it in your jerkin.

THURIO  My jerkin is a doublet.° 20

VALENTINE  Well, then, I'll double your folly.

THURIO  How?

SILVIA  What, angry, Sir Thurio! Do you change color?

VALENTINE  Give him leave, madam; he is a kind of 25 chameleon.

THURIO  That hath more mind to feed on your blood than live in your air.

VALENTINE  You have said, sir.

THURIO  Ay, sir, and done too, for this time. 30

VALENTINE  I know it well, sir; you always end ere you begin.

SILVIA  A fine volley of words, gentlemen, and quickly shot off.

VALENTINE  'Tis indeed, madam; we thank the giver. 35

SILVIA  Who is that, servant?

VALENTINE  Yourself, sweet lady; for you gave the fire. Sir Thurio borrows his wit from your ladyship's looks, and spends what he borrows kindly in your company. 40

THURIO  Sir, if you spend word for word with me, I shall make your wit bankrupt.

VALENTINE  I know it well, sir. You have an exchequer of words, and, I think, no other treasure to give your followers, for it appears by their bare° liveries that 45 they live by your bare words.

SILVIA  No more, gentlemen, no more—here comes my father.

[*Enter* DUKE.]

DUKE  Now, daughter Silvia, you are hard beset. Sir Valentine, your father's in good health. 50 What say you to a letter from your friends Of much good news?

VALENTINE       My lord, I will be thankful To any happy messenger° from thence.

DUKE  Know ye Don Antonio, your countryman?

VALENTINE  Ay, my good lord, I know the gentleman 55 To be of worth, and worthy estimation, And not without desert so well reputed.

DUKE  Hath he not a son?

VALENTINE  Ay, my good lord, a son that well deserves The honor and regard of such a father. 60

DUKE  You know him well?

VALENTINE  I know him as myself; for from our infancy We have conversed and spent our hours together; And though myself have been an idle truant, Omitting the sweet benefit of time 65 To clothe mine age with angellike perfection, Yet hath Sir Proteus, for that's his name, Made use and fair advantage of his days; His years but young, but his experience old; His head unmellowed, but his judgment ripe. 70 And, in a word, for far behind his worth Comes all the praises that I now bestow, He is complete in feature and in mind With all good grace to grace a gentleman.

DUKE  Beshrew me, sir, but if he make this good, 75 He is as worthy for an empress' love As meet° to be an emperor's counselor. Well, sir, this gentleman is come to me With commendation from great potentates, And here he means to spend his time awhile. 80 I think 'tis no unwelcome news to you.

VALENTINE  Should I have wished a thing, it had been he.

DUKE  Welcome him, then, according to his worth. Silvia, I speak to you, and you, Sir Thurio; For Valentine, I need not cite° him to it. 85 I will send him hither to you presently.     [*Exit.*]

VALENTINE  This is the gentleman I told your ladyship Had come along with me, but that his mistress Did hold his eyes locked in her crystal looks.

SILVIA  Belike that now she hath enfranchised them, 90 Upon some other pawn for fealty.°

VALENTINE  Nay, sure, I think she holds them prisoners still.

SILVIA  Nay, then, he should be blind; and, being blind, How could he see his way to seek out you?

---

**II.iv.18 quote** observe (pronounced "coat")   **20 doublet** close-fitting jacket   **45 bare** threadbare   **53 happy messenger** bringer of good news   **77 meet** fitted   **85 cite** incite, urge   **91 pawn for fealty** pledge for loyalty

VALENTINE
Why, lady, love hath twenty pair of eyes.                    95
THURIO
They say that love hath not an eye at all.
VALENTINE
To see such lovers, Thurio, as yourself.
Upon a homely object love can wink.
                                      [*Exit* THURIO.]
SILVIA
Have done, have done; here comes the gentleman.

[*Enter* PROTEUS.]

VALENTINE
Welcome, dear Proteus! Mistress, I beseech you,           100
Confirm his welcome with some special favor.
SILVIA
His worth is warrant for his welcome hither,
If this be he you oft have wished to hear from.
VALENTINE
Mistress, it is. Sweet lady, entertain° him
To be my fellow servant to your ladyship.                   105
SILVIA
Too low a mistress for so high a servant.
PROTEUS
Not so, sweet lady, but too mean° a servant
To have a look of such a worthy mistress.
VALENTINE
Leave off discourse of disability.°
Sweet lady, entertain him for your servant.                 110
PROTEUS
My duty will I boast of, nothing else.
SILVIA
And duty never yet did want his meed.°
Servant, you are welcome to a worthless mistress.
PROTEUS
I'll die on° him that says so but yourself.
SILVIA
That you are welcome?
PROTEUS                      That you are worthless.         115

[*Enter* THURIO.]

THURIO
Madam, my lord your father would speak with you.
SILVIA
I wait upon his pleasure. Come, Sir Thurio,
Go with me. Once more, new servant, welcome.
I'll leave you to confer of home affairs.
When you have done, we look to hear from you.
PROTEUS                                                      120
We'll both attend upon your ladyship.
                        [*Exeunt* SILVIA *and* THURIO.]
VALENTINE
Now, tell me, how do all from whence you came?
PROTEUS
Your friends are well, and have them much com-
mended.°
VALENTINE
And how do yours?
PROTEUS                      I left them all in health.

VALENTINE
How does your lady? And how thrives your love?             125
PROTEUS
My tales of love were wont to weary you;
I know you joy not in a love discourse.
VALENTINE
Ay, Proteus, but that life is altered now.
I have done penance for contemning Love,
Whose high imperious thoughts have punished me             130
With bitter fasts, with penitential groans,
With nightly tears, and daily heartsore sighs;
For, in revenge of my contempt of Love,
Love hath chased sleep from my enthrallèd eyes,
And made them watchers of mine own heart's sorrow.         135
O gentle Proteus, Love's a mighty lord,
And hath so humbled me, as° I confess
There is no woe to° his correction,
Nor to his service no such joy on earth.
Now no discourse, except it be of love;                     140
Now can I break my fast, dine, sup, and sleep
Upon the very naked name of love.
PROTEUS
Enough; I read your fortune in your eye.
Was this the idol that you worship so?
VALENTINE
Even she; and is she not a heavenly saint?                  145
PROTEUS
No; but she is an earthly paragon.
VALENTINE
Call her divine.
PROTEUS                      I will not flatter her.
VALENTINE
O, flatter me, for love delights in praises.
PROTEUS
When I was sick, you gave me bitter pills,
And I must minister the like to you.                        150
VALENTINE
Then speak the truth by her; if not divine,
Yet let her be a principality,
Sovereign to all the creatures on the earth.
PROTEUS
Except my mistress.
VALENTINE                      Sweet, except not any,
Except thou wilt except against° my love.                   155
PROTEUS
Have I not reason to prefer mine own?
VALENTINE
And I will help thee to prefer° her too.
She shall be dignified with this high honor—
To bear my lady's train, lest the base earth
Should from her vesture chance to steal a kiss,            160
And, of so great a favor growing proud,
Disdain to root the summer-swelling flow'r,
And make rough winter everlastingly.
PROTEUS
Why, Valentine, what braggardism is this?
VALENTINE
Pardon me, Proteus. All I can is nothing                    165
To her, whose worth makes other worthies nothing;
She is alone.

___

104 **entertain** welcome  107 **mean** low, humble  109
**Leave . . . disability** Cease this modest talk  112 **want his
meed** lack its reward  114 **die on** fight to the death  123 **have
. . . commended** themselves to you

137 **as** that  138 **to** like unto  155 **Except . . . against** unless
you will take exception to  157 **prefer** advance

PROTEUS     Then let her alone.

VALENTINE
Not for the world. Why, man, she is mine own,
And I as rich in having such a jewel
As twenty seas, if all their sand were pearl,     170
The water nectar, and the rocks pure gold.
Forgive me that I do not dream on° thee,
Because thou see'st me dote upon my love.
My foolish rival, that her father likes
Only for his possessions are so huge,     175
Is gone with her along; and I must after,
For love, thou know'st, is full of jealousy.

PROTEUS
But she loves you?

VALENTINE
Ay, and we are betrothed; nay, more, our marriage
    hour,
With all the cunning manner of our flight,     180
Determined of: how I must climb her window,
The ladder made of cords, and all the means
Plotted and 'greed on for my happiness.
Good Proteus, go with me to my chamber,
In these affairs to aid me with thy counsel.     185

PROTEUS
Go on before; I shall inquire you forth.
I must unto the road, to disembark
Some necessaries that I needs must use,
And then I'll presently attend you.

VALENTINE
Will you make haste?     190

PROTEUS
I will.     Exit [VALENTINE].
Even as one heat another heat expels,
Or as one nail by strength drives out another,
So the remembrance of my former love
Is by a newer object quite forgotten.     195
Is it mine eye, or Valentine's praise,
Her true perfection, or my false transgression,
That makes me reasonless° to reason thus?
She is fair; and so is Julia, that I love—
That I did love, for now my love is thawed,     200
Which, like a waxen image 'gainst a fire,
Bears no impression of the thing it was.
Methinks my zeal to Valentine is cold,
And that I love him not as I was wont.
O, but I love his lady too too much!     205
And that's the reason I love him so little.
How shall I dote on her with more advice,°
That thus without advice begin to love her!
'Tis but her picture° I have yet beheld,
And that hath dazzled my reason's light;     210
But when I look on her perfections,
There is no reason° but I shall be blind.
If I can check my erring love, I will;
If not, to compass° her I'll use my skill.     Exit.

Scene V. [Milan. A street.]

Enter SPEED and LAUNCE [meeting].

SPEED     Launce! By mine honesty, welcome to Padua!°
LAUNCE     Forswear° not thyself, sweet youth; for I am
not welcome. I reckon this always—that a man is
never undone till he be hanged, nor never welcome
to a place till some certain shot° be paid, and the     5
hostess say, "Welcome!"
SPEED     Come on, you madcap, I'll to the alehouse with
you presently, where, for one shot of fivepence,
thou shalt have five thousand welcomes. But, sirrah,
how did thy master part with Madam Julia?     10
LAUNCE     Marry, after they closed in earnest,° they
parted very fairly in jest.
SPEED     But shall she marry him?
LAUNCE     No.
SPEED     How, then? Shall he marry her?     15
LAUNCE     No, neither.
SPEED     What, are they broken?
LAUNCE     No, they are both as whole as a fish.
SPEED     Why, then, how stands the matter with them?
LAUNCE     Marry, thus: when it stands well with him,     20
it stands well with her.
SPEED     What an ass art thou! I understand thee not.
LAUNCE     What a block art thou, that thou canst not!
My staff understands me.
SPEED     What thou sayest?     25
LAUNCE     Ay, and what I do too. Look thee, I'll but
lean, and my staff understands me.
SPEED     It stands under thee, indeed.
LAUNCE     Why, stand-under and under-stand is all one.
SPEED     But tell me true, will't be a match?     30
LAUNCE     Ask my dog. If he say ay, it will; if he say
no, it will; if he shake his tail and say nothing, it will.
SPEED     The conclusion is, then, that it will.
LAUNCE     Thou shalt never get such a secret from me
but by a parable.°     35
SPEED     'Tis well that I get it so. But, Launce, how
sayest thou,° that my master is become a notable
lover?
LAUNCE     I never knew him otherwise.
SPEED     Than how?     40
LAUNCE     A notable lubber, as thou reportest him to be.
SPEED     Why, thou whoreson ass, thou mistak'st me.
LAUNCE     Why fool, I meant not thee; I meant thy
master.
SPEED     I tell thee, my master is become a hot lover.     45
LAUNCE     Why, I tell thee, I care not though he burn
himself in love. If thou wilt, go with me to the
alehouse; if not, thou art an Hebrew, a Jew, and not
worth the name of a Christian.
SPEED     Why?     50
LAUNCE     Because thou hast not so much charity in
thee as to go to the ale with a Christian.° Wilt thou
go?
SPEED     At thy service.     Exeunt.

II.v.1 Padua apparently Shakespeare forgot that his characters
are in Milan  2 Forswear perjure  5 shot alehouse bill
11 closed in earnest (1) formally agreed (2) embraced  35 by a
parable by indirect affirmation  36–37 how sayest thou what
do you think about this  52 go . . . Christian attend a
church-benefit festivity

172 on of  198 reasonless without justification  207 advice
careful thought  209 picture her visible being, outward
appearance  212 reason question  214 compass get,
achieve

Scene VI. [*Milan. The duke's palace.*]

*Enter* PROTEUS *solus.°*

PROTEUS
To leave my Julia shall I be forsworn;
To love fair Silvia shall I be forsworn;
To wrong my friend, I shall be much forsworn;
And ev'n that pow'r which gave me first my oath
Provokes me to this threefold perjury:                    5
Love bade me swear, and love bids me forswear.
O sweet-suggesting Love, if thou hast sinned,
Teach me, thy tempted subject, to excuse it!
At first I did adore a twinkling star,
But now I worship a celestial sun.                        10
Unheedful vows may heedfully be broken;
And he wants° wit that wants resolvèd will
To learn° his wit t' exchange the bad for better.
Fie, fie, unreverend tongue! To call her bad,
Whose sovereignty so oft thou hast preferred            15
With twenty thousand soul-confirming oaths.
I cannot leave to love, and yet I do;
But there I leave to love where I should love.
Julia I lose, and Valentine I lose.
If I keep them, I needs must lose myself;                20
If I lose them, thus find I by their loss
For Valentine, myself, for Julia, Silvia.
I to myself am dearer than a friend,
For love is still most precious in itself;
And Silvia—witness heaven, that made her fair!—         25
Shows Julia but a swarthy Ethiope.
I will forget that Julia is alive,
Rememb'ring that my love to her is dead;
And Valentine I'll hold an enemy,
Aiming at Silvia as a sweeter friend.                    30
I cannot now prove constant to myself,
Without some treachery used to Valentine.
This night he meaneth with a corded ladder
To climb celestial Silvia's chamber window,
Myself in counsel, his competitor.°                      35
Now presently I'll give her father notice
Of their disguising and pretended° flight;
Who, all enraged, will banish Valentine;
For Thurio, he intends, shall wed his daughter.
But, Valentine being gone, I'll quickly cross           40
By some sly trick blunt Thurio's dull proceeding.
Love, lend me wings to make my purpose swift,
As thou hast lent me wit to plot this drift!°   *Exit.*

Scene VII. [*Verona. Julia's house.*]

*Enter* JULIA *and* LUCETTA.

JULIA
Counsel, Lucetta; gentle girl, assist me;
And, ev'n in kind love, I do conjure thee,
Who art the table° wherein all my thoughts
Are visibly charactered and engraved,
To lesson me, and tell me some good mean,                 5

How, with my honor,° I may undertake
A journey to my loving Proteus.
LUCETTA
Alas, the way is wearisome and long!
JULIA
A true-devoted pilgrim is not weary
To measure kingdoms with his feeble steps;               10
Much less shall she that hath love's wings to fly—
And when the flight is made to one so dear,
Of such divine perfection, as Sir Proteus.
LUCETTA
Better forbear till Proteus make return.
JULIA
O, know'st thou not his looks are my soul's food?        15
Pity the dearth that I have pinèd in
By longing for that food so long a time.
Didst thou but know the inly° touch of love,
Thou wouldst as soon go kindle fire with snow
As seek to quench the fire of love with words.           20
LUCETTA
I do not seek to quench your love's hot fire,
But qualify° the fire's extreme rage,
Lest it should burn above the bounds of reason.
JULIA
The more thou damm'st it up, the more it burns.
The current that with gentle murmur glides,              25
Thou know'st, being stopped, impatiently doth
    rage;
But when his fair course is not hinderèd,
He makes sweet music with th' enameled° stones,
Giving a gentle kiss to every sedge
He overtaketh in his pilgrimage;                         30
And so by many winding nooks he strays,
With willing sport, to the wild ocean.
Then let me go, and hinder not my course.
I'll be as patient as a gentle stream,
And make a pastime of each weary step,                   35
Till the last step have brought me to my love;
And there I'll rest, as after much turmoil
A blessèd soul doth in Elysium.
LUCETTA
But in what habit° will you go along?
JULIA
Not like a woman, for I would prevent                    40
The loose encounters of lascivious men.
Gentle Lucetta, fit me with such weeds°
As may beseem some well-reputed page.
LUCETTA
Why, then, your ladyship must cut your hair.
JULIA
No, girl; I'll knit it up in silken strings             45
With twenty odd-conceited° truelove knots.
To be fantastic may become a youth
Of greater time° than I shall show to be.
LUCETTA
What fashion, madam, shall I make your breeches?
JULIA
That fits as well as, "Tell me, good my lord,            50

---

**II.vi.s.d. solus** alone (Latin)  **12 wants** lacks  **13 learn** teach
**35 competitor** accomplice  **37 pretended** intended  **43 drift**
device
**II.vii.3 table** tablet

**6 with my honor** preserving my honor  **18 inly** inward
**22 qualify** mitigate  **28 enameled** shiny  **39 habit** costume
**42 weeds** garments  **46 odd-conceited** ingeniously devised
**48 Of greater time** older

What compass° will you wear your farthingale?"°
Why, ev'n what fashion thou best likes, Lucetta.
LUCETTA
You must needs have them with a codpiece,°
   madam.
JULIA
Out, out,° Lucetta! That will be ill-favored.
LUCETTA
A round hose, madam, now's not worth a pin,     55
Unless you have a codpiece to stick pins on.
JULIA
Lucetta, as thou lov'st me, let me have
What thou think'st meet, and is most mannerly.
But tell me, wench, how will the world repute me
For undertaking so unstaid° a journey?     60
I fear me, it will make me scandalized.
LUCETTA
If you think so, then stay at home, and go not.
JULIA
Nay, that I will not.
LUCETTA
Then never dream on infamy, but go.
If Proteus like your journey when you come,     65
No matter who's displeased when you are gone:
I fear me, he will scarce be pleased withal.°
JULIA
That is the least, Lucetta, of my fear.
A thousand oaths, an ocean of his tears,
And instances of infinite° of love     70
Warrant me welcome to my Proteus.
LUCETTA
All these are servants to deceitful men.
JULIA
Base men, that use them to so base effect!
But truer stars did govern Proteus' birth.
His words are bonds, his oaths are oracles;     75
His love sincere, his thoughts immaculate;
His tears pure messengers sent from his heart;
His heart as far from fraud as heaven from earth.
LUCETTA
Pray heav'n he prove so, when you come to him!
JULIA
Now, as thou lov'st me, do him not that wrong,     80
To bear a hard opinion of his truth.
Only deserve my love by loving him,
And presently go with me to my chamber
To take a note of what I stand in need of
To furnish me upon my longing° journey.     85
All that is mine I leave at thy dispose,
My goods, my lands, my reputation;
Only, in lieu thereof, dispatch me hence.
Come, answer not, but to it presently!
I am impatient of my tarriance.     *Exeunt.* 90

# ACT III

Scene I. [*Milan. The duke's palace.*]

*Enter* DUKE, THURIO, [*and*] PROTEUS.

DUKE
Sir Thurio, give us leave, I pray, awhile;
We have some secrets to confer about.
                 [*Exit* THURIO.]
Now, tell me, Proteus, what's your will with me?
PROTEUS
My gracious lord, that which I would discover°
The law of friendship bids me to conceal;     5
But when I call to mind your gracious favors
Done to me, undeserving as I am,
My duty pricks me on to utter that
Which else no worldly good should draw from me.
Know, worthy prince, Sir Valentine, my friend,     10
This night intends to steal away your daughter.
Myself am one made privy to the plot.
I know you have determined to bestow her
On Thurio, whom your gentle daughter hates,
And should she thus be stol'n away from you,     15
It would be much vexation to your age.
Thus, for my duty's sake, I rather chose
To cross my friend in his intended drift
Than, by concealing it, heap on your head
A pack of sorrows which would press you down,     20
Being unprevented, to your timeless° grave.
DUKE
Proteus, I thank thee for thine honest care,
Which to requite, command me while I live.
This love of theirs myself have often seen,
Haply when they have judged me fast asleep;     25
And oftentimes have purposed to forbid
Sir Valentine her company and my court.
But, fearing lest my jealous° aim might err,
And so, unworthily disgrace the man,
A rashness that I ever yet have shunned,     30
I gave him gentle looks; thereby to find
That which thyself hast now disclosed to me.
And, that thou mayst perceive my fear of this,
Knowing that tender youth is soon suggested,°
I nightly lodge her in an upper tow'r,     35
The key whereof myself have ever kept;
And thence she cannot be conveyed away.
PROTEUS
Know, noble lord, they have devised a mean
How he her chamber window will ascend,
And with a corded ladder fetch her down;     40
For which the youthful lover now is gone,
And this way comes he with it presently,
Where, if it please you, you may intercept him.
But, good my lord, do it so cunningly
That my discovery be not aimed at;°     45
For love of you, not hate unto my friend,
Hath made me publisher of this pretense.°
DUKE
Upon mine honor, he shall never know
That I had any light from thee of this.

51 **compass** circumference; **farthingale** hooped petticoat
53 **codpiece** pocket or bag at front of men's breeches ("round
hose," line 55), often fashionably exaggerated   54 **Out, out**
fie, fie   60 **unstaid** unbecoming   67 **withal** with it   70
**infinite** infinity   85 **longing** occasioned by my longing

III.i.4 **discover** disclose   21 **timeless** untimely   28 **jealous**
suspicious   34 **suggested** tempted, prompted   45 **aimèd at**
guessed   47 **pretense** intention

PROTEUS
Adieu, my lord; Sir Valentine is coming.    [*Exit.*] 50

[*Enter* VALENTINE.]

DUKE
Sir Valentine, whither away so fast?
VALENTINE
Please it your grace, there is a messenger
That stays to bear my letters to my friends,
And I am going to deliver them.
DUKE
Be they of much import?    55
VALENTINE
The tenor of them doth but signify
My health and happy being at your court.
DUKE
Nay then, no matter; stay with me awhile.
I am to break with thee of some affairs
That touch me near, wherein thou must be secret.    60
'Tis not unknown to thee that I have sought
To match my friend Sir Thurio to my daughter.
VALENTINE
I know it well, my lord; and, sure, the match
Were rich and honorable; besides, the gentleman
Is full of virtue, bounty, worth, and qualities    65
Beseeming such a wife as your fair daughter.
Cannot your grace win her to fancy him?
DUKE
No, trust me; she is peevish, sullen, froward,°
Proud, disobedient, stubborn, lacking duty,
Neither regarding that she is my child    70
Nor fearing me as if I were her father.
And, may I say to thee, this pride of hers,
Upon advice,° hath drawn° my love from her;
And, where I thought the remnant of mine age
Should have been cherished by her childlike duty,    75
I now am full resolved to take a wife,
And turn her out to who will take her in.
Then let her beauty be her wedding dow'r,
For me and my possessions she esteems not.
VALENTINE
What would your grace have me to do in this?    80
DUKE
There is a lady in Verona here°
Whom I affect; but she is nice° and coy,
And nought esteems my agèd eloquence.
Now, therefore, would I have thee to my tutor—
For long agone I have forgot to court;    85
Besides, the fashion of the time is changed—
How and which way I may bestow° myself,
To be regarded in her sun-bright eye.
VALENTINE
Win her with gifts, if she respect not words.
Dumb jewels often in their silent kind°    90
More than quick words do move a woman's mind.
DUKE
But she did scorn a present that I sent her.

VALENTINE
A woman sometimes scorns what best contents her.
Send her another; never give her o'er;
For scorn at first makes after-love the more.    95
If she do frown, 'tis not in hate of you,
But rather to beget more love in you.
If she do chide, 'tis not to have you gone;
For why, the fools are mad, if left alone.
Take no repulse, whatever she doth say;    100
For "get you gone," she doth not mean "away!"
Flatter and praise, commend, extol their graces;
Though ne'er so black, say they have angels' faces.
That man that hath a tongue, I say, is no man,
If with his tongue he cannot win a woman.    105
DUKE
But she I mean is promised by her friends
Unto a youthful gentleman of worth,
And kept severely from resort of men,
That no man hath access by day to her.
VALENTINE
Why, then, I would resort to her by night.    110
DUKE
Ay, but the doors be locked, and keys kept safe,
That no man hath recourse to her by night.
VALENTINE
What lets° but one may enter at her window?
DUKE
Her chamber is aloft, far from the ground,
And built so shelving° that one cannot climb it    115
Without apparent hazard of his life.
VALENTINE
Why, then, a ladder, quaintly made of cords,
To cast up, with a pair of anchoring hooks,
Would serve to scale another Hero's tow'r,
So bold Leander would adventure it.    120
DUKE
Now, as thou art a gentleman of blood,°
Advise me where I may have such a ladder.
VALENTINE
When would you use it? Pray, sir, tell me that.
DUKE
This very night; for love is like a child,
That longs for everything that he can come by.    125
VALENTINE
By seven o'clock I'll get you such a ladder.
DUKE
But, hark thee; I will go to her alone.
How shall I best convey the ladder thither?
VALENTINE
It will be light, my lord, that you may bear it
Under a cloak that is of any length.    130
DUKE
A cloak as long as thine will serve the turn?
VALENTINE
Ay, my good lord.
DUKE                    Then let me see thy cloak.
I'll get me one of such another length.
VALENTINE
Why, any cloak will serve the turn, my lord.
DUKE
How shall I fashion me to wear a cloak?    135

---

68 peevish . . . froward obstinate . . . willful    73 advice consideration; drawn withdrawn    81 in Verona here some editors emend "in" to "of," but probably Shakespeare forgot his characters are now in Milan    82 nice fastidious    87 bestow conduct    90 kind nature

113 lets prevents    115 shelving steeply sloping    121 of blood of noble blood

I pray thee, let me feel thy cloak upon me.

[*Opens Valentine's cloak.*]

What letter is this same? What's here? "To Silvia"—
And here an engine° fit for my proceeding.
I'll be so bold to break the seal for once.

[*Reads.*]

"My thoughts do harbor with my Silvia nightly;          140
    And slaves they are to me, that send them flying.
O, could their master come and go as lightly,
    Himself would lodge where senseless they are lying!
My herald thoughts in thy pure bosom rest them,
    While I, their king, that thither them importune,     145
Do curse the grace that with such grace hath blessed
        them,
    Because myself do want my servants' fortune.
I curse myself, for they are sent by me,
That they should harbor where their lord should be."
What's here?                                            150
"Silvia, this night I will enfranchise thee."
'Tis so; and here's the ladder for the purpose.
Why, Phaethon—for thou art Merops' son—
Wilt thou aspire to guide the heavenly car,
And with thy daring folly burn the world?°             155
Wilt thou reach stars, because they shine on thee?
Go, base intruder! Overweening slave!
Bestow thy fawning smiles on equal mates,
And think my patience, more than thy desert,
Is privilege for thy departure hence.                   160
Thank me for this more than for all the favors
Which all too much I have bestowed on thee.
But if thou linger in my territories
Longer than swiftest expedition°
Will give thee time to leave our royal court,           165
By heaven, my wrath shall far exceed the love
I ever bore my daughter or thyself.
Be gone! I will not hear thy vain excuse;
But, as thou lov'st thy life, make speed from hence.
                                                  [*Exit.*]

VALENTINE
And why not death rather than living torment?           170
To die is to be banished from myself;
And Silvia is myself. Banished from her
Is self from self: a deadly banishment!
What light is light, if Silvia be not seen?
What joy is joy, if Silvia be not by?—                  175
Unless it be to think that she is by,
And feed upon the shadow° of perfection.
Except I be by Silvia in the night,
There is no music in the nightingale;
Unless I look on Silvia in the day,                     180
There is no day for me to look upon.
She is my essence, and I leave° to be,
If I be not by her fair influence°
Fostered, illumined, cherished, kept alive.
I fly not death, to fly his deadly doom:                185

Tarry I here, I but attend on death;
But, fly I hence, I fly away from life.

[*Enter* PROTEUS *and* LAUNCE.]

PROTEUS    Run, boy, run, run, and seek him out.
LAUNCE    Soho, soho!
PROTEUS    What see'st thou?                              190
LAUNCE    Him we go to find. There's not a hair° on's
    head but 'tis a Valentine.°
PROTEUS    Valentine?
VALENTINE    No.
PROTEUS    Who then? His spirit?                          195
VALENTINE    Neither.
PROTEUS    What then?
VALENTINE    Nothing.
LAUNCE    Can nothing speak? Master, shall I strike?
PROTEUS    Who wouldst thou strike?                       200
LAUNCE    Nothing.
PROTEUS    Villain, forbear.
LAUNCE    Why, sir, I'll strike nothing. I pray you—
PROTEUS    Sirrah, I say, forbear. Friend Valentine, a
    word.                                                205
VALENTINE
My ears are stopped, and cannot hear good news,
So much of bad already hath possessed them.
PROTEUS
Then in dumb silence will I bury mine,
For they are harsh, untunable, and bad.
VALENTINE
Is Silvia dead?                                          210
PROTEUS
No, Valentine.
VALENTINE
No Valentine, indeed, for sacred Silvia.
Hath she forsworn me?
PROTEUS
No, Valentine.
VALENTINE
No Valentine, if Silvia have forsworn me.               215
What is your news?
LAUNCE
Sir, there is a proclamation that you are vanished.
PROTEUS
That thou art banishèd—O, that's the news!—
From hence, from Silvia, and from me thy friend.
VALENTINE
O, I have fed upon this woe already,                    220
And now excess of it will make me surfeit.
Doth Silvia know that I am banishèd?
PROTEUS
Ay, ay, and she hath offered to the doom—
Which, unreversed, stands in effectual force—
A sea of melting pearl, which some call tears:          225
Those at her father's churlish feet she tendered;
With them, upon her knees, her humble self;
Wringing her hands, whose whiteness so became them
As if but now they waxèd pale for woe.
But neither bended knees, pure hands held up,           230
Sad sighs, deep groans, nor silver-shedding tears,
Could penetrate her uncompassionate sire;

---

138 engine contrivance (here, the ladder)  153–55 Phaethon
... world Phaethon's father, Phoebus—not Merops, who was
his mother's husband—let the youth drive the horses of the sun
across the sky, with dire results  164 expedition speed  177
shadow mere image  182 leave cease  183 influence like that
of the stars (see especially Sonnet 15)

191 hair with pun on *hare*, prepared by preceding "Soho," a
hunting cry  192 Valentine with pun, as in lines 211–215 below

But Valentine, if he be ta'en, must die.
Besides, her intercession chafed him so,
When she for thy repeal was suppliant,          235
That to close prison he commanded her,
With many bitter threats of biding° there.

VALENTINE
No more; unless the next word that thou speak'st
Have some malignant power upon my life.
If so, I pray thee, breathe it in mine ear,       240
As ending anthem° of my endless dolor.

PROTEUS
Cease to lament for that thou canst not help,
And study help for that which thou lament'st.
Time is the nurse and breeder of all good.
Here if thou stay, thou canst not see thy love;    245
Besides, thy staying will abridge thy life.
Hope is a lover's staff; walk hence with that,
And manage it against despairing thoughts.
Thy letters may be here, though thou art hence;
Which, being writ to me, shall be delivered       250
Even in the milk-white bosom of thy love.
The time now serves not to expostulate.
Come, I'll convey thee through the city gate,
And, ere I part with thee, confer at large
Of all that may concern thy love affairs.         255
As thou lov'st Silvia, though not for thyself,
Regard thy danger, and along with me!

VALENTINE
I pray thee, Launce, and if° thou see'st my boy,
Bid him make haste, and meet me at the Northgate.

PROTEUS
Go, sirrah, find him out. Come, Valentine.         260

VALENTINE
O my dear Silvia! Hapless Valentine!
                    [Exeunt VALENTINE and PROTEUS.]

LAUNCE  I am but a fool, look you, and yet I have the
wit to think my master is a kind of a knave. But
that's all one, if he be but one knave. He lives not
now that knows me to be in love, yet I am in love;  265
but a team of horse shall not pluck that from me,
nor who 'tis I love, and yet 'tis a woman; but what
woman, I will not tell myself, and yet 'tis a milkmaid;
yet 'tis not a maid, for she hath had gossips;° yet 'tis a
maid, for she is her master's maid, and serves for 270
wages. She hath more qualities than a water spaniel—
which is much in a bare Christian. [Pulling out a
paper.] Here is the cate-log of her condition. "Imprimis:°
She can fetch and carry." Why, a horse can do no
more: nay, a horse cannot fetch, but only carry; 275
therefore is she better than a jade.° "Item: She can
milk"; look you, a sweet virtue in a maid with clean
hands.

Enter SPEED.

SPEED  How now, Signior Launce! What news with
your mastership?                                   280
LAUNCE  With my master's ship? Why, it is at sea.
SPEED  Well, your old vice still; mistake the word.
What news, then, in your paper?

LAUNCE  The black'st news that ever thou heard'st.
SPEED  Why, man, how black?                        285
LAUNCE  Why, as black as ink.
SPEED  Let me read them.
LAUNCE  Fie on thee, jolthead!° Thou canst not read.
SPEED  Thou liest; I can.
LAUNCE  I will try thee. Tell me this: who begot thee? 290
SPEED  Marry, the son of my grandfather.
LAUNCE  O illiterate loiterer! It was the son of thy
grandmother. This proves that thou canst not read.
SPEED  Come, fool, come; try me in thy paper.
LAUNCE  There; and Saint Nicholas° be thy speed!°    295
SPEED [Reads.]  "Imprimis: She can milk."
LAUNCE  Ay, that she can.
SPEED  "Item: She brews good ale."
LAUNCE  And thereof comes the proverb: "Blessing
of your heart, you brew good ale."                 300
SPEED  "Item: She can sew."
LAUNCE  That's as much as to say, "Can she so?"
SPEED  "Item: She can knit."
LAUNCE  What need a man care for a stock° with a
wench when she can knit him a stock?               305
SPEED  "Item: She can wash and scour."
LAUNCE  A special virtue; for then she need not be
washed and scoured.
SPEED  "Item: She can spin."
LAUNCE  Then may I set the world on wheels,° when   310
she can spin for her living.
SPEED  "Item: She hath many nameless virtues."
LAUNCE  That's as much as to say, bastard virtues—
that, indeed, know not their fathers, and therefore
have no names.                                     315
SPEED  "Here follow her vices."
LAUNCE  Close at the heels of her virtues.
SPEED  "Item: She is not to be kissed fasting, in
respect of her breath."
LAUNCE  Well, that fault may be mended with a      320
breakfast. Read on.
SPEED  "Item: She hath a sweet mouth."°
LAUNCE  That makes amends for her sour breath.
SPEED  "Item: She doth talk in her sleep."
LAUNCE  It's no matter for that, so she sleep not in  325
her talk.
SPEED  "Item: She is slow in words."
LAUNCE  O villain, that set this down among her
vices! To be slow in words is a woman's only virtue.
I pray thee, out with't, and place it for her chief  330
virtue.
SPEED  "Item: She is proud."
LAUNCE  Out with that too; it was Eve's legacy, and
cannot be ta'en from her.
SPEED  "Item: She hath no teeth."                  335
LAUNCE  I care not for that neither, because I love
crusts.
SPEED  "Item: She is curst."°
LAUNCE  Well, the best is, she hath no teeth to bite.
SPEED  "Item: She will often praise her liquor."    340
LAUNCE  If her liquor be good, she shall; if she will
not, I will, for good things should be praised.

---

237 **biding** permanent incarceration  241 **ending anthem**
funeral hymn  258 **and if** if  269 **gossips** godparents (for her
own child)  273 **Imprimis** in the first place  276 **jade** nag
288 **jolthead** blockhead  295 **Saint Nicholas** patron saint of
scholars (among others); **speed** aid  304 **stock** dowry (pun
follows)  310 **set . . . wheels** take life easy  322 **hath . . .**
**mouth** likes sweets  338 **curst** shrewish

SPEED  "Item: She is too liberal."
LAUNCE  Of her tongue she cannot, for that's writ
down she is slow of; of her purse she shall not, for 345
that I'll keep shut. Now, of another thing she may,
and that cannot I help. Well, proceed.
SPEED  "Item: She hath more hair than wit, and more
faults than hairs, and more wealth than faults."
LAUNCE  Stop there: I'll have her. She was mine, and 350
not mine, twice or thrice in that last article. Rehearse
that once more.
SPEED  "Item: She hath more hair than wit"—
LAUNCE  More hair than wit? It may be; I'll prove it.
The cover of the salt° hides the salt, and therefore 355
it is more than the salt; the hair that covers the wit is
more than the wit, for the greater hides the less. What's
next?
SPEED  "And more faults than hairs"—
LAUNCE  That's monstrous. O, that that were out!     360
SPEED  "And more wealth than faults."
LAUNCE  Why, that word makes the faults gracious.
Well, I'll have her; and if it be a match, as nothing is
impossible—
SPEED  What then?                                    365
LAUNCE  Why, then will I tell thee—that thy master
stays for thee at the Northgate?
SPEED  For me?
LAUNCE  For thee! Ay, who art thou? He hath stayed
for a better man than thee.                          370
SPEED  And must I go to him?
LAUNCE  Thou must run to him, for thou hast stayed
so long that going° will scarce serve the turn.
SPEED  Why didst not tell me sooner? Pox of° your
love letters!                          [Exit.] 375
LAUNCE  Now will he be swinged for reading my
letter—an unmannerly slave, that will thrust himself
into secrets! I'll after, to rejoice in the boy's correction.
[Exit.]

Scene II. [Milan. The duke's palace.]

Enter DUKE [and] THURIO.

DUKE
Sir Thurio, fear not but that she will love you,
Now Valentine is banished from her sight.
THURIO
Since his exile she hath despised me most,
Forsworn my company, and railed at me,
That I am desperate of obtaining her.              5
DUKE
This weak impress° of love is as a figure
Trenchèd in ice, which with an hour's heat
Dissolves to water, and doth lose his form.
A little time will melt her frozen thoughts,
And worthless Valentine shall be forgot.           10

[Enter PROTEUS.]

How now, Sir Proteus! Is your countryman,
According to our proclamation, gone?

PROTEUS
Gone, my good lord.
DUKE
My daughter takes his going grievously.
PROTEUS
A little time, my lord, will kill that grief.       15
DUKE
So I believe, but Thurio thinks not so.
Proteus, the good conceit° I hold of thee—
For thou hast shown some sign of good desert—
Makes me the better to confer with thee.
PROTEUS
Longer than I prove loyal to your grace,           20
Let me not live to look upon your grace.
DUKE
Thou know'st how willingly I would effect
The match between Sir Thurio and my daughter.
PROTEUS
I do, my lord.
DUKE
And also, I think, thou art not ignorant            25
How she opposes her against my will.
PROTEUS
She did, my lord, when Valentine was here.
DUKE
Ay, and perversely she persevers so.
What might we do to make the girl forget
The love of Valentine, and love Sir Thurio?         30
PROTEUS
The best way is to slander Valentine
With falsehood, cowardice, and poor descent,
Three things that women highly hold in hate.
DUKE
Ay, but she'll think that it is spoke in hate.
PROTEUS
Ay, if his enemy deliver it;                         35
Therefore it must with circumstance° be spoken
By one whom she esteemeth as his friend.
DUKE
Then you must undertake to slander him.
PROTEUS
And that, my lord, I shall be loath to do.
'Tis an ill office for a gentleman,                  40
Especially against his very friend.
DUKE
Where your good word cannot advantage him,
Your slander never can endamage him;
Therefore the office is indifferent,°
Being entreated to it by your friend.               45
PROTEUS
You have prevailed, my lord. If I can do it
By aught that I can speak in his dispraise,
She shall not long continue love to him.
But say this weed her love from Valentine,
It follows not that she will love Sir Thurio.        50
THURIO
Therefore, as you unwind her love from him,
Lest it should ravel and be good to none,
You must provide to bottom° it on me;

---

355 **salt** saltcellar   **373 going** merely walking   **374 Pox of**
plague (literally, syphilis) on
**III.ii.6 impress** impression (dent, groove)

17 **conceit** opinion   36 **circumstance** circumstantial detail
44 **indifferent** neutral in effect   53 **bottom** anchor, tie (as
a weaver's thread)

Which must be done by praising me as much
As you in worth dispraise Sir Valentine.　　　55
DUKE
And, Proteus, we dare trust you in this kind,°
Because we know, on Valentine's report,
You are already Love's firm votary
And cannot soon revolt and change your mind.
Upon this warrant shall you have access　　　60
Where you with Silvia may confer at large;
For she is lumpish, heavy, melancholy,
And, for your friend's sake, will be glad of you;
Where you may temper° her by your persuasion
To hate young Valentine and love my friend.　　65
PROTEUS
As much as I can do, I will effect.
But you, Sir Thurio, are not sharp enough;
You must lay lime to tangle° her desires
By wailful sonnets, whose composèd rhymes
Should be full-fraught with serviceable vows.°　70
DUKE
Ay, much is the force of heaven-bred poesy.
PROTEUS
Say that upon the altar of her beauty
You sacrifice your tears, your sighs, your heart.
Write till your ink be dry, and with your tears
Moist it again, and frame some feeling line　　75
That may discover such integrity.°
For Orpheus' lute was strung with poets' sinews,
Whose golden touch could soften steel and stones,
Make tigers tame, and huge leviathans
Forsake unsounded deeps to dance on sands.°　80
After your dire-lamenting elegies,
Visit by night your lady's chamber window
With some sweet consort;° to their instruments
Tune a deploring dump.° The night's dead silence
Will well become such sweet-complaining grievance.　85
This, or else nothing, will inherit° her.
DUKE
This discipline° shows thou hast been in love.
THURIO
And thy advice this night I'll put in practice.
Therefore, sweet Proteus, my direction-giver,
Let us into the city presently　　　　　　90
To sort° some gentlemen well skilled in music.
I have a sonnet that will serve the turn
To give the onset° to thy good advice.
DUKE
About it, gentlemen!
PROTEUS
We'll wait upon your grace till after supper,　　95
And afterward determine our proceedings.
DUKE
Even now about it! I will pardon you.　　*Exeunt.*

---

56 kind an affair of this nature　64 temper make pliant, shape
68 lime to tangle bird lime to ensnare (bird lime is a sticky
substance spread on branches to catch birds)　70 full-fraught
. . . vows loaded with vows to serve faithfully　76 discover
such integrity exhibit such devotion　77–80 Orpheus' . . .
sands cf. *Merchant of Venice*, V.i, for a simpler tribute to the
musician of Thrace　83 sweet consort company of musicians
84 deploring dump doleful ditty　86 inherit obtain　87
discipline instruction　91 sort sort out, select　93 give the
onset make a beginning

# ACT IV

## Scene I. [*A forest.*]

*Enter certain* OUTLAWS.

FIRST OUTLAW
Fellows, stand fast; I see a passenger.°
SECOND OUTLAW
If there be ten, shrink not, but down with 'em.

[*Enter* VALENTINE *and* SPEED.]

THIRD OUTLAW
Stand, sir, and throw us that° you have about ye.
If not, we'll make you sit, and rifle you.
SPEED
Sir, we are undone; these are the villains　　　5
That all the travelers do fear so much.
VALENTINE
My friends—
FIRST OUTLAW
That's not so, sir; we are your enemies.
SECOND OUTLAW
Peace! We'll hear him.
THIRD OUTLAW
Ay, by my beard, will we, for he's a proper° man.　10
VALENTINE
Then know that I have little wealth to lose.
A man I am crossed with adversity.
My riches are these poor habiliments,
Of which if you should here disfurnish° me,
You take the sum and substance that I have.　　15
SECOND OUTLAW
Whither travel you?
VALENTINE
To Verona.
FIRST OUTLAW
Whence came you?
VALENTINE
From Milan.
THIRD OUTLAW
Have you long sojourned there?　　　　　　20
VALENTINE
Some sixteen months, and longer might have stayed
If crooked fortune had not thwarted me.
FIRST OUTLAW
What, were you banished thence?
VALENTINE　I was.
SECOND OUTLAW
For what offense?　　　　　　　　　　25
VALENTINE
For that which now torments me to rehearse:
I killed a man, whose death I much repent;
But yet I slew him manfully in fight,
Without false vantage° or base treachery.
FIRST OUTLAW
Why, ne'er repent it, if it were done so.　　　30
But were you banished for so small a fault?
VALENTINE
I was, and held me glad of such a doom.°

---

IV.i.1 passenger pedestrian　3 that that which　10 proper
handsome　14 disfurnish deprive　29 false vantage such
advantage as is gained by deceit　32 doom sentence

SECOND OUTLAW
Have you the tongues?°

VALENTINE
My youthful travel therein made me happy,°
Or else I often had been miserable.                          35

THIRD OUTLAW
By the bare scalp of Robin Hood's fat friar,
This fellow were a king for our wild faction!

FIRST OUTLAW
We'll have him. Sirs, a word.

SPEED   Master, be one of them; it's an honorable kind
of thievery.                                                 40

VALENTINE   Peace, villain!

SECOND OUTLAW   Tell us this: have you anything to
take to?°

VALENTINE   Nothing but my fortune.

THIRD OUTLAW
Know, then, that some of us are gentlemen,                    45
Such as the fury of ungoverned youth
Thrust from the company of awful° men:
Myself was from Verona banishèd
For practicing° to steal away a lady,
An heir, and near allied unto the duke.                      50

SECOND OUTLAW
And I from Mantua, for a gentleman
Who, in my mood, I stabbed unto the heart.

FIRST OUTLAW
And I for suchlike petty crimes as these.
But to the purpose—for we cite our faults,
That they may hold excused our lawless lives;                55
And partly, seeing you are beautified
With goodly shape, and by your own report
A linguist, and a man of such perfection
As we do in our quality much want°—

SECOND OUTLAW
Indeed, because you are a banished man,                       60
Therefore, above the rest, we parley to you.
Are you content to be our general,
To make a virtue of necessity,
And live, as we do, in this wilderness?

THIRD OUTLAW
What say'st thou? Wilt thou be of our consort?                65
Say ay, and be the captain of us all.
We'll do thee homage and be ruled by thee,
Love thee as our commander and our king.

FIRST OUTLAW
But if thou scorn our courtesy, thou diest.

SECOND OUTLAW
Thou shalt not live to brag what we have offered.            70

VALENTINE
I take your offer, and will live with you,
Provided that you do no outrages
On silly° women or poor passengers.

THIRD OUTLAW
No, we detest such vile base practices.
Come, go with us; we'll bring thee to our crews              75
And show thee all the treasure we have got,
Which, with ourselves, all rest at thy dispose. *Exeunt.*

Scene II. [*Milan. Beneath Silvia's window.*]

*Enter* PROTEUS.

PROTEUS
Already have I been false to Valentine,
And now I must be as unjust to Thurio.
Under the color° of commending him,
I have access my own love to prefer.°
But Silvia is too fair, too true, too holy                    5
To be corrupted with my worthless gifts.
When I protest true loyalty to her,
She twits me with my falsehood to my friend;
When to her beauty I commend my vows,
She bids me think how I have been forsworn                   10
In breaking faith with Julia whom I loved.
And notwithstanding all her sudden quips,
The least whereof would quell a lover's hope,
Yet, spaniellike, the more she spurns my love,
The more it grows, and fawneth on her still.                 15
But here comes Thurio; now must we to her window
And give some evening music to her ear.

[*Enter* THURIO *and* MUSICIANS.]

THURIO
How now, Sir Proteus, are you crept before us?

PROTEUS
Ay, gentle Thurio, for you know that love
Will creep in service where it cannot go.°                   20

THURIO
Ay, but I hope, sir, that you love not here.

PROTEUS
Sir, but I do; or else I would be hence.

THURIO   Who? Silvia?

PROTEUS   Ay, Silvia, for your sake.

THURIO
I thank you for your own. Now, gentlemen,                    25
Let's tune, and to it lustily awhile.

[*Enter, at a distance,* HOST, *and* JULIA *in boy's clothes.*]

HOST
Now, my young guest, methinks you're allycholly.°
I pray you, why is it?

JULIA
Marry, mine host, because I cannot be merry.

HOST   Come, we'll have you merry. I'll bring you            30
where you shall hear music, and see the gentleman
that you asked for.

JULIA   But shall I hear him speak?

HOST   Ay, that you shall.

JULIA   That will be music.                                   35

[*Music plays.*]

HOST   Hark, hark!

JULIA   Is he among these?

HOST   Ay, but, peace! Let's hear 'em.

                    *Song.*
        Who is Silvia, what is she,
          That all our swains commend her?                   40
        Holy, fair, and wise is she;
            The heaven such grace did lend her,
        That she might admirèd be.

33 Have . . . tongues? Do you know foreign languages?   34
happy fortunate   42–43 anything to take to any trade to
take up   47 awful deeply respectful (but possibly a printer's
slip for *lawful*)   49 practicing plotting   59 in . . . want
much lack in our profession   73 silly defenseless

IV.ii.3 color pretense   4 prefer advance   20 go walk upright
27 allycholly melancholy

Is she kind as she is fair?
　　For beauty lives with kindness. 45
Love doth to her eyes repair,
　　To help him of his blindness,
And, being helped, inhabits there.

Then to Silvia let us sing,
　　That Silvia is excelling; 50
She excels each mortal thing
　　Upon the dull earth dwelling.
To her let us garlands bring.

HOST  How now! Are you sadder than you were
before? How do you, man? The music likes° you 55
not.

JULIA  You mistake; the musician likes me not.

HOST  Why, my pretty youth?

JULIA  He plays false, father.

HOST  How? Out of tune on the strings? 60

JULIA  Not so; but yet so false that he grieves my
very heartstrings.

HOST  You have a quick ear.

JULIA  Ay, I would I were deaf; it makes me have a
slow° heart. 65

HOST  I perceive you delight not in music.

JULIA  Not a whit, when it jars so.

HOST  Hark, what fine change° is in the music!

JULIA  Ay, that change is the spite.

HOST  You would have them always play but one 70
thing?

JULIA  I would always have one play but one thing.
But, host, doth this Sir Proteus that we talk on
Often resort unto this gentlewoman?

HOST  I tell you what Launce, his man, told me—he 75
loved her out of all nick.°

JULIA  Where is Launce?

HOST  Gone to seek his dog, which tomorrow, by his
master's command, he must carry for a present to his
lady. 80

JULIA  Peace! Stand aside. The company parts.

PROTEUS
Sir Thurio, fear not you. I will so plead
That you shall say my cunning drift excels.

THURIO
Where meet we?

PROTEUS　　　At Saint Gregory's well.

THURIO　　　　　　　Farewell.

[Exeunt THURIO and MUSICIANS.]

[Enter SILVIA above.]

PROTEUS
Madam, good even to your ladyship. 85

SILVIA
I thank you for your music, gentlemen.
Who is that that spake?

PROTEUS
One, lady, if you knew his pure heart's truth,
You would quickly learn to know him by his voice.

SILVIA
Sir Proteus, as I take it. 90

PROTEUS
Sir Proteus, gentle lady, and your servant.

SILVIA
What's your will?

PROTEUS　　　　　That I may compass yours.

SILVIA
You have your wish; my will is even this:
That presently you hie you home to bed.
Thou subtle, perjured, false, disloyal man! 95
Think'st thou I am so shallow, so conceitless,°
To be seducèd by thy flattery,
That hast deceived so many with thy vows?
Return, return, and make thy love amends.
For me, by this pale queen of night I swear, 100
I am so far from granting thy request
That I despise thee for thy wrongful suit,
And by and by intend to chide myself
Even for this time I spend in talking to thee.

PROTEUS
I grant, sweet love, that I did love a lady; 105
But she is dead.

JULIA [Aside.]　'Twere false, if I should speak it,
For I am sure she is not burièd.

SILVIA
Say that she be; yet Valentine thy friend
Survives, to whom, thyself art witness,
I am betrothed. And art thou not ashamed 110
To wrong him with thy importunacy?

PROTEUS
I likewise hear that Valentine is dead.

SILVIA
And so suppose am I, for in his grave
Assure thyself my love is burièd.

PROTEUS
Sweet lady, let me rake it from the earth. 115

SILVIA
Go to thy lady's grave, and call hers thence;
Or, at the least, in hers sepulcher thine.

JULIA [Aside.]
He heard not that.

PROTEUS
Madam, if your heart be so obdurate,
Vouchsafe° me yet your picture for my love, 120
The picture that is hanging in your chamber.
To that I'll speak, to that I'll sigh and weep;
For since the substance of your perfect self
Is else devoted,° I am but a shadow,
And to your shadow° will I make true love. 125

JULIA [Aside.]
If 'twere a substance, you would, sure, deceive it,
And make it but a shadow, as I am.

SILVIA
I am very loath to be your idol, sir;
But since your falsehood shall become you well
To worship shadows and adore false shapes, 130
Send to me in the morning, and I'll send it.
And so, good rest.

PROTEUS　　　　As wretches have o'ernight
That wait for execution in the morn.

[Exeunt PROTEUS and SILVIA severally.]

---

55 likes pleases   65 slow heavy   68 change modulation (in
the next line Julia puns, alluding to the change in Proteus'
affections)   76 out . . . nick beyond measure

96 conceitless witless   120 Vouchsafe grant   124 else
devoted vowed to someone else   125 shadow portrait

JULIA Host, will you go?

HOST By my halidom,° I was fast asleep.    135

JULIA Pray you, where lies° Sir Proteus?

HOST Marry, at my house. Trust me, I think 'tis almost day.

JULIA

Not so; but it hath been the longest night
That e'er I watched, and the most heaviest.    [*Exeunt.*] 140

Scene III. [*Milan. Beneath Silvia's window.*]

*Enter* EGLAMOUR.

EGLAMOUR

This is the hour that Madam Silvia
Entreated me to call and know her mind.
There's some great matter she'd employ me in.
Madam, madam!

[*Enter* SILVIA *above.*]

SILVIA

Who calls?

EGLAMOUR Your servant and your friend,    5
One that attends your ladyship's command.

SILVIA

Sir Eglamour, a thousand times good morrow.

EGLAMOUR

As many, worthy lady, to yourself.
According to your ladyship's impose,°
I am thus early come to know what service    10
It is your pleasure to command me in.

SILVIA

O Eglamour, thou art a gentleman—
Think not I flatter, for I swear I do not—
Valiant, wise, remorseful,° well accomplished.
Thou art not ignorant what dear good will    15
I bear unto the banished Valentine,
Nor how my father would enforce me marry
Vain Thurio, whom my very soul abhors.
Thyself hast loved, and I have heard thee say
No grief did ever come so near thy heart    20
As when thy lady and thy true love died,
Upon whose grave thou vow'dst pure chastity.
Sir Eglamour, I would to Valentine,
To Mantua, where I hear he makes abode;
And, for the ways are dangerous to pass,    25
I do desire thy worthy company,
Upon whose faith and honor I repose.
Urge not my father's anger, Eglamour,
But think upon my grief, a lady's grief,
And on the justice of my flying hence    30
To keep me from a most unholy match,
Which heaven and fortune still rewards with plagues.
I do desire thee, even from a heart
As full of sorrows as the sea of sands,
To bear me company, and go with me:    35
If not, to hide what I have said to thee,
That I may venture to depart alone.

EGLAMOUR

Madam, I pity much your grievances,

Which since I know they virtuously are placed,
I give consent to go along with you,    40
Recking as little what betideth me
As much I wish all good befortune you.
When will you go?

SILVIA    This evening coming.

EGLAMOUR Where shall I meet you?    45

SILVIA At Friar Patrick's cell, where I intend holy confession.

EGLAMOUR I will not fail your ladyship. Good morrow, gentle lady.

SILVIA Good morrow, kind Sir Eglamour.    50
*Exeunt* [*severally*].

Scene IV. [*Milan. Beneath Silvia's window.*]

*Enter* LAUNCE [*with his dog*].

LAUNCE When a man's servant shall play the cur with him, look you, it goes hard: one that I brought up of° a puppy; one that I saved from drowning, when three or four of his blind brothers and sisters went to it! I have taught him, even as one would say precisely,    5 "thus I would teach a dog." I was sent to deliver him as a present to Mistress Silvia from my master, and I came no sooner into the dining chamber, but he steps me to her trencher° and steals her capon's leg. O, 'tis a foul thing when a cur cannot keep° himself in all    10 companies! I would have, as one should say, one that takes upon him to be a dog indeed, to be as it were, a dog at all things. If I had not had more wit than he, to take a fault upon me that he did, I think verily he had been hanged for't; sure as I live, he had suffered    15 for't. You shall judge. He thrusts me himself into the company of three or four gentlemanlike dogs under the duke's table; he had not been there—bless the mark!— a pissing while, but all the chamber smelt him. "Out with the dog!" says one. "What cur is that?" says    20 another. "Whip him out," says the third. "Hang him up," says the duke. I, having been acquainted with the smell before, knew it was Crab, and goes me to the fellow that whips the dogs. "Friend," quoth I, "you mean to whip the dog?" "Ay, marry, do I,"    25 quoth he. "You do him the more wrong," quoth I; "'twas I did the thing you wot° of." He makes me no more ado, but whips me out of the chamber. How many masters would do this for his servant? Nay, I'll be sworn, I have sat in the stocks for puddings°    30 he hath stol'n; otherwise he had been executed. I have stood on the pillory for geese he hath killed; otherwise he had suffered for't. Thou think'st not of this now. Nay, I remember the trick you served me when I took my leave of Madam Silvia. Did not I    35 bid thee still mark me, and do as I do? When didst thou see me heave up my leg, and make water against a gentlewoman's farthingale? Didst thou ever see me do such a trick?

[*Enter* PROTEUS *and* JULIA.]

135 **halidom** sacred relic (a mild oath)  136 **lies** lodges
IV.iii.9 **impose** command  14 **remorseful** compassionate

IV.iv.3 **of** from  9 **trencher** wooden plate  10 **keep** control
27 **wot** know  30 **puddings** sausages

**PROTEUS**
Sebastian is thy name? I like thee well,                               40
And will employ thee in some service presently.

**JULIA**   In what you please. I'll do what I can.

**PROTEUS**
I hope thou wilt. [*To* LAUNCE.] How now, you
  whoreson peasant!
Where have you been these two days loitering?

**LAUNCE**   Marry, sir, I carried Mistress Silvia the dog 45
you bade me.

**PROTEUS**   And what says she to my little jewel?

**LAUNCE**   Marry, she says your dog was a cur, and
tells you currish thanks is good enough for such a
present.                                                               50

**PROTEUS**   But she received my dog?

**LAUNCE**   No, indeed, did she not. Here have I
brought him back again.

**PROTEUS**   What, didst thou offer her this from me?

**LAUNCE**   Ay, sir. The other squirrel° was stol'n from 55
me by the hangman's boys° in the market place, and
then I offered her mine own, who is a dog as big as
ten of yours, and therefore the gift the greater.

**PROTEUS**
Go get thee hence and find my dog again,
Or ne'er return again into my sight.                                   60
Away, I say! Stayest thou to vex me here?
                                                    [*Exit* LAUNCE.]
A slave, that still an end° turns me to shame!
Sebastian, I have entertainèd° thee
Partly that° I have need of such a youth
That can with some discretion do my business,                          65
For 'tis no trusting to yond foolish lout;
But chiefly for thy face and thy behavior,
Which, if my augury deceive me not,
Witness good bringing up, fortune, and truth.
Therefore, know thou, for this I entertain thee.                       70
Go presently, and take this ring with thee;
Deliver it to Madam Silvia.
She loved me well delivered it to me.

**JULIA**
It seems you loved not her, to leave her token.
She is dead, belike?

**PROTEUS**            Not so; I think she lives.              75

**JULIA**
Alas!

**PROTEUS**
Why dost thou cry, "Alas"?

**JULIA**                      I cannot choose
But pity her.

**PROTEUS**   Wherefore shouldst thou pity her?

**JULIA**
Because methinks that she loved you as well
As you do love your lady Silvia.                                       80
She dreams on him that has forgot her love;
You dote on her that cares not for your love.
'Tis pity love should be so contrary;
And thinking on it makes me cry, "Alas!"

**PROTEUS**
Well, give her that ring, and therewithal                              85

---

**55 squirrel** little dog   **56 hangman's boys** boys who will
surely belong to the hangman (hang) at last   **62 still an end**
forevermore   **63 entertainèd** retained   **64 Partly that** in part
because

---

This letter. That's her chamber. Tell my lady
I claim the promise for her heavenly picture.
Your message done, hie home unto my chamber,
Where thou shalt find me, sad and solitary.   [*Exit.*]

**JULIA**
How many women would do such a message?               90
Alas, poor Proteus! Thou hast entertained
A fox to be the shepherd of thy lambs.
Alas, poor fool! Why do I pity him
That with his very heart despiseth me?
Because he loves her, he despiseth me;                 95
Because I love him, I must pity him.
This ring I gave him when he parted from me,
To bind him to remember my good will;
And now am I, unhappy messenger,
To plead for that which I would not obtain,            100
To carry that which I would have refused,
To praise his faith which I would have dispraised.
I am my master's true-confirmèd love,
But cannot be true servant to my master
Unless I prove false traitor to myself.                105
Yet will I woo for him, but yet so coldly
As, heaven it knows, I would not have him speed.°

[*Enter* SILVIA, *attended.*]

Gentlewoman, good day! I pray you, be my mean
To bring me where to speak with Madam Silvia.

**SILVIA**
What would you with her, if that I be she?             110

**JULIA**
If you be she, I do entreat your patience
To hear me speak the message I am sent on.

**SILVIA**
From whom?

**JULIA**
From my master, Sir Proteus, madam.

**SILVIA**
O, he sends you for a picture.                         115

**JULIA**
Ay, madam.

**SILVIA**
Ursula, bring my picture there.
Go give your master this. Tell him, from me,
One Julia, that his changing thoughts forget,
Would better fit his chamber than this shadow.        120

**JULIA**
Madam, please you peruse this letter—
Pardon me, madam; I have unadvised°
Delivered you a paper that I should not.
This is the letter to your ladyship.

**SILVIA**
I pray thee, let me look on that again.                125

**JULIA**
It may not be; good madam, pardon me.

**SILVIA**
There, hold!
I will not look upon your master's lines.
I know they are stuffed with protestations,
And full of new-found oaths which he will break        130
As easily as I do tear his paper.

**JULIA**
Madam, he sends your ladyship this ring.

---

**107 speed** prosper, succeed   **122 unadvised** unintentionally

SILVIA
The more shame for him that he sends it me,
For I have heard him say a thousand times
His Julia gave it him at his departure.                               135
Though his false finger have profaned the ring,
Mine shall not do his Julia so much wrong.

JULIA
She thanks you.

SILVIA
What say'st thou?

JULIA
I thank you, madam, that you tender her.°                             140
Poor gentlewoman! My master wrongs her much.

SILVIA
Dost thou know her?

JULIA
Almost as well as I do know myself.
To think upon her woes, I do protest
That I have wept a hundred several° times.                            145

SILVIA
Belike she thinks that Proteus hath forsook her.

JULIA
I think she doth; and that's her cause of sorrow.

SILVIA
Is she not passing° fair?

JULIA
She hath been fairer, madam, than she is.
When she did think my master loved her well,                          150
She, in my judgment, was as fair as you.
But since she did neglect her looking glass,
And threw her sun-expelling mask away,
The air hath starved the roses in her cheeks
And pinched the lily-tincture of her face,                            155
That now she is become as black° as I.

SILVIA
How tall was she?

JULIA
About my stature: for, at Pentecost,°
When all our pageants of delight were played,
Our youth got me to play the woman's part,                            160
And I was trimmed in Madam Julia's gown,
Which servèd me as fit, by all men's judgments,
As if the garment had been made for me.
Therefore I know she is about my height.
And at that time I made her weep agood,°                              165
For I did play a lamentable part.
Madam, 'twas Ariadne° passioning
For Theseus' perjury and unjust flight,
Which I so lively acted with my tears
That my poor mistress, movèd therewithal,                             170
Wept bitterly; and would I might be dead
If I in thought felt not her very sorrow!

SILVIA
She is beholding° to thee, gentle youth.
Alas, poor lady, desolate and left!
I weep myself to think upon thy words.                                175

Here, youth, there is my purse. I give thee this
For thy sweet mistress' sake, because thou lov'st her.
Farewell.          [Exit SILVIA, with ATTENDANTS.]

JULIA
And she shall thank you for't, if e'er you know her.
A virtuous gentlewoman, mild and beautiful!                           180
I hope my master's suit will be but cold,
Since she respects my mistress' love so much.
Alas, how love can trifle with itself!
Here is her picture: let me see; I think,
If I had such a tire,° this face of mine                              185
Were full as lovely as is this of hers.
And yet the painter flattered her a little,
Unless I flatter with myself too much.
Her hair is auburn, mine is perfect yellow:
If that be all the difference in his love,                            190
I'll get me such a colored periwig.
Her eyes are gray as glass, and so are mine:
Ay, but her forehead's low, and mine's as high.
What should it be that he respects in her,
But I can make respective° in myself,                                 195
If this fond Love° were not a blinded god?
Come, shadow, come, and take this shadow up,°
For 'tis thy rival. O thou senseless form,
Thou shalt be worshiped, kissed, loved, and adored!
And, were there sense in his idolatry,                                200
My substance should be statue in thy stead.
I'll use thee kindly for thy mistress' sake,
That used me so; or else, by Jove I vow,
I should have scratched out your unseeing eyes,
To make my master out of love with thee!          Exit.   205

# ACT V

### Scene I. [*Milan. An abbey.*]

*Enter* EGLAMOUR.

EGLAMOUR
The sun begins to gild the western sky,
And now it is about the very hour
That Silvia, at Friar Patrick's cell, should meet me.
She will not fail, for lovers break not hours,
Unless it be to come before their time,
So much they spur their expedition.
See where she comes.

[*Enter* SILVIA.]

                                   Lady, a happy evening!

SILVIA
Amen, amen! Go on, good Eglamour,
Out at the postern° by the abbey wall.
I fear I am attended° by some spies.                                  10

EGLAMOUR
Fear not; the forest is not three leagues off.
If we recover° that, we are sure enough.          *Exeunt.*

140 **tender her** have a care for her interest  145 **several** separate  148 **passing** surpassingly  156 **black** i.e., from the sun  158 **Pentecost** Whitsunday (seventh Sunday after Easter), an occasion for morris dances, "pageants of delight," and such outdoor festivities  165 **agood** aplenty  167 **Ariadne** daughter of King Minos, who aided Theseus' flight from the Cretan labyrinth, only to be abandoned on the isle of Naxos  173 **beholding** indebted

185 **tire** headdress  195 **respective** worthy of respect  196 **fond Love** foolish Cupid  197 **Come . . . up** come, shadow (of my former self), and "take on" this other shadow (Silvia's portrait)
V.i.9 **postern** small door at side or rear  10 **attended** followed  12 **recover** reach

Scene II. [*Milan. The duke's palace.*]

*Enter* THURIO, PROTEUS, [*and*] JULIA.

THURIO
Sir Proteus, what says Silvia to my suit?
PROTEUS
O, sir, I find her milder than she was;
And yet she takes exceptions at your person.
THURIO
What, that my leg is too long?
PROTEUS
No; that it is too little.                                                    5
THURIO
I'll wear a boot, to make it somewhat rounder.
JULIA [*Aside.*]
But love will not be spurred° to what it loathes.
THURIO
What says she to my face?
PROTEUS
She says it is a fair one.
THURIO
Nay then, the wanton lies; my face is black.          10
PROTEUS
But pearls are fair; and the old saying is,
Black men are pearls in beauteous ladies' eyes.
JULIA [*Aside.*]
'Tis true, such pearls as put out ladies' eyes;
For I had rather wink than look on them.
THURIO
How likes she my discourse?°                                 15
PROTEUS
Ill, when you talk of war.
THURIO
But well, when I discourse of love and peace?
JULIA [*Aside.*]
But better, indeed, when you hold your peace.
THURIO
What says she to my valor?
PROTEUS
O, sir, she makes no doubt of that.                         20
JULIA [*Aside.*]
She needs not, when she knows it cowardice.
THURIO
What says she to my birth?
PROTEUS
That you are well derived.
JULIA [*Aside.*]
True, from a gentleman to a fool.
THURIO
Considers she my possessions?                                25
PROTEUS
O, ay, and pities them.
THURIO
Wherefore?
JULIA [*Aside.*]
That such an ass should owe° them.
PROTEUS
That they are out by lease.°

JULIA
Here comes the duke.                                              30

[*Enter* DUKE.]

DUKE
How now, Sir Proteus! How now, Thurio!
Which of you saw Sir Eglamour of late?
THURIO
    Not I.
PROTEUS  Nor I.
DUKE                    Saw you my daughter?
PROTEUS                                            Neither.
DUKE
Why then,
She's fled unto that peasant Valentine,                   35
And Eglamour is in her company.
'Tis true; for Friar Laurence met them both
As he in penance wandered through the forest.
Him he knew well, and guessed that it was she,
But, being masked, he was not sure of it;               40
Besides, she did intend confession
At Patrick's cell this even, and there she was not.
These likelihoods confirm her flight from hence.
Therefore, I pray you, stand not to discourse,
But mount you presently, and meet with me          45
Upon the rising of the mountain foot°
That leads toward Mantua, whither they are fled.
Dispatch, sweet gentlemen, and follow me.       [*Exit.*]
THURIO
Why, this it is to be a peevish girl
That flies her fortune when it follows her.             50
I'll after, more to be revenged on Eglamour
Than for the love of reckless Silvia.                  [*Exit.*]
PROTEUS
And I will follow, more for Silvia's love
Than hate of Eglamour, that goes with her.      [*Exit.*]
JULIA
And I will follow, more to cross that love             55
Than hate for Silvia, that is gone for love.      [*Exit.*]

Scene III. [*A forest.*]

[*Enter*] SILVIA [*and*] OUTLAWS.

FIRST OUTLAW
Come, come,
Be patient; we must bring you to our captain.
SILVIA
A thousand more mischances than this one
Have learned me how to brook° this patiently.
SECOND OUTLAW
Come, bring her away.                                             5
FIRST OUTLAW
Where is the gentleman that was with her?
THIRD OUTLAW
Being nimble footed, he hath outrun us,
But Moyses and Valerius follow him.
Go thou with her to the west end of the wood;
There is our captain. We'll follow him that's fled;  10
The thicket is beset;° he cannot 'scape.

V.ii.7 **spurred** with reference to preceding "boot" **15
discourse** conversational ability **28 owe** own **29 out by
lease** because Thurio is such a fool, he will surely hold onto
his possessions only temporarily

**46 rising . . . foot** foothill
**V.iii.4 learned . . . brook** taught me how to endure **11
beset** surrounded

FIRST OUTLAW
Come, I must bring you to our captain's cave.
Fear not; he bears an honorable mind,
And will not use a woman lawlessly.

SILVIA
O Valentine, this I endure for thee!          *Exeunt.* 15

Scene IV. [*Another part of the forest.*]

*Enter* VALENTINE.

VALENTINE
How use° doth breed a habit in a man!
This shadowy desert,° unfrequented woods,
I better brook than flourishing peopled towns.
Here can I sit alone, unseen of any,
And to the nightingale's complaining notes          5
Tune my distresses and record my woes.
O thou that dost inhabit in my breast,
Leave not the mansion so long tenantless,
Lest, growing ruinous, the building fall,
And leave no memory of what it was!          10
Repair me with thy presence, Silvia;
Thou gentle nymph, cherish thy forlorn swain!

[*Noise within.*]

What halloing and what stir is this today?
These are my mates, that make their wills their law,
Have° some unhappy passenger in chase.          15
They love me well; yet I have much to do
To keep them from uncivil outrages.
Withdraw thee, Valentine. Who's this comes here?
          [*Retires.*]

[*Enter* PROTEUS, SILVIA, *and* JULIA.]

PROTEUS
Madam, this service I have done for you—
Though you respect not aught your servant doth—          20
To hazard life, and rescue you from him
That would have forced your honor and your love.
Vouchsafe me, for my meed, but one fair look;
A smaller boon than this I cannot beg,
And less than this, I am sure, you cannot give.          25

VALENTINE [*Aside.*]
How like a dream is this I see and hear!
Love, lend me patience to forbear awhile.

SILVIA
O miserable, unhappy that I am!

PROTEUS
Unhappy were you, madam, ere I came;
But by my coming I have made you happy.          30

SILVIA
By thy approach thou mak'st me most unhappy.

JULIA [*Aside.*]
And me, when he approacheth to your presence.

SILVIA
Had I been seized by a hungry lion,
I would have been a breakfast to the beast
Rather than have false Proteus rescue me.          35
O, heaven be judge how I love Valentine

Whose life's as tender° to me as my soul!
And full as much, for more there cannot be,
I do detest false perjured Proteus.
Therefore be gone; solicit me no more.          40

PROTEUS
What dangerous action, stood it next to death,
Would I not undergo for one calm look!
O, 'tis the curse in love, and still approved,°
When women cannot love where they're beloved!

SILVIA
When Proteus cannot love where he's beloved!          45
Read over Julia's heart, thy first, best love,
For whose dear sake thou didst then rend thy faith
Into a thousand oaths; and all those oaths
Descended into perjury, to love me.
Thou hast no faith left now, unless thou'dst two,          50
And that's far worse than none; better have none
Than plural faith, which is too much by one.
Thou counterfeit to thy true friend!

PROTEUS                              In love,
Who respects friend?

SILVIA                    All men but Proteus.

PROTEUS
Nay, if the gentle spirit of moving words          55
Can no way change you to a milder form,
I'll woo you like a soldier, at arms' end,
And love you 'gainst the nature of love—force ye.

SILVIA
O heaven!

PROTEUS    I'll force thee yield to my desire.

VALENTINE [*Advancing.*]
Ruffian, let go that rude uncivil touch,          60
Thou friend of an ill fashion!°

PROTEUS                              Valentine!

VALENTINE
Thou common° friend, that's without faith or love—
For such is a friend now; treacherous man!
Thou hast beguiled my hopes; nought but mine eye
Could have persuaded me. Now I dare not say          65
I have one friend alive; thou wouldst disprove me.
Who should be trusted, when one's right hand
Is perjured to the bosom? Proteus,
I am sorry I must never trust thee more,
But count the world a stranger for thy sake.          70
The private° wound is deepest. O time most accurst,
'Mongst all foes that a friend should be the worst!

PROTEUS
My shame and guilt confounds° me.
Forgive me, Valentine. If hearty sorrow
Be a sufficient ransom for offense,          75
I tender't here; I do as truly suffer
As e'er I did commit.°

VALENTINE                    Then I am paid;°
And once again I do receive thee honest.°
Who by repentance is not satisfied
Is nor of heaven nor earth, for these are pleased.          80

37 **tender** precious  43 **still approved** perennially proved true
61 **friend . . . fashion** false friend  62 **common** no better
than the ordinary  71 **private** intimate (here, given by a
friend)  73 **confounds** destroys  76–77 **I do . . . commit** I
do indeed suffer. as truly as I did commit the fault  77 **paid**
satisfied  78 **receive thee honest** accept you as being honorable

**V.iv.1 use** custom  **2 shadowy desert** wild place inhabited
only with shadows (of trees)  **15 Have** who have

By penitence th' Eternal's wrath's appeased;
And, that my love may appear plain and free,
All that was mine in Silvia I give thee.

JULIA   O me unhappy! [*Swoons.*]

PROTEUS   Look to the boy.                                        85

VALENTINE   Why, boy! Why, wag! How now!
What's the matter? Look up; speak.

JULIA   O good sir, my master charged me to deliver a
ring to Madam Silvia, which, out of my neglect, was
never done.                                                       90

PROTEUS   Where is that ring, boy?

JULIA   Here 'tis; this is it.

PROTEUS
How! Let me see.
Why, this is the ring I gave to Julia.

JULIA
O, cry you mercy,° sir, I have mistook.                           95
This is the ring you sent to Silvia.

PROTEUS   But how cam'st thou by this ring? At my
depart I gave this unto Julia.

JULIA
And Julia herself did give it me;
And Julia herself hath brought it hither.                         100

PROTEUS   How! Julia!

JULIA
Behold her that gave aim to° all thy oaths,
And entertained 'em deeply in her heart.
How oft hast thou with perjury cleft the root!
O Proteus, let this habit° make thee blush!                       105
Be thou ashamed that I have took upon me
Such an immodest raiment, if shame live
In a disguise of love.°
It is the lesser blot, modesty finds,
Women to change their shapes than men their minds.                110

PROTEUS
Than men their minds! 'Tis true. O heaven, were man
But constant, he were perfect! That one error
Fills him with faults, makes him run through all th'
   sins:
Inconstancy falls off ere it begins.°
What is in Silvia's face, but I may spy                           115
More fresh in Julia's with a constant eye?

VALENTINE
Come, come, a hand from either.
Let me be blest to make this happy close;°
'Twere pity two such friends should be long foes.

PROTEUS
Bear witness, heaven, I have my wish forever.                     120

JULIA
And I mine.

[*Enter* OUTLAWS, *with* DUKE *and* THURIO.]

OUTLAWS
A prize, a prize, a prize!

VALENTINE
Forbear, forbear, I say! It is my lord the duke.

Your grace is welcome to a man disgraced,
Banished Valentine.

DUKE               Sir Valentine!                                 125

THURIO
Yonder is Silvia, and Silvia's mine.

VALENTINE
Thurio, give back,° or else embrace thy death.
Come not within the measure° of my wrath.
Do not name Silvia thine; if once again,
Verona° shall not hold thee. Here she stands.                     130
Take but possession of her with a touch:
I dare thee but to breathe upon my love.

THURIO
Sir Valentine, I care not for her, I.
I hold him but a fool that will endanger
His body for a girl that loves him not.                           135
I claim her not, and therefore she is thine.

DUKE
The more degenerate and base art thou,
To make such means for° her as thou hast done,
And leave her on such slight conditions.
Now, by the honor of my ancestry,                                 140
I do applaud thy spirit, Valentine,
And think thee worthy of an empress' love.
Know, then, I here forget all former griefs,
Cancel all grudge, repeal° thee home again,
Plead a new state in thy unrivaled merit,°                        145
To which I thus subscribe: Sir Valentine,
Thou art a gentleman, and well derived;
Take thou thy Silvia, for thou hast deserved her.

VALENTINE
I thank your grace; the gift hath made me happy.
I now beseech you, for your daughter's sake,                      150
To grant one boon that I shall ask of you.

DUKE
I grant it, for thine own, whate'er it be.

VALENTINE
These banished men that I have kept withal°
Are men endued° with worthy qualities.
Forgive them what they have committed here,                       155
And let them be recalled from their exile:
They are reformèd, civil, full of good,
And fit for great employment, worthy lord.

DUKE
Thou hast prevailed; I pardon them and thee.
Dispose of them as thou know'st their deserts.                    160
Come, let us go. We will include all jars°
With triumphs, mirth, and rare solemnity.°

VALENTINE
And, as we walk along, I dare be bold
With our discourse to make your grace to smile.
What think you of this page, my lord?                             165

DUKE
I think the boy hath grace in him; he blushes.

---

95 **cry you mercy** I beg your pardon   102 **gave aim to** was
the object (target) of   105 **habit** her boy's garb   107–08
**if . . . love** if it can be shameful to disguise oneself for the sake
of love   114 **Inconstancy . . . begins** The inconstant man
proves false even before he begins to love   118 **close** joining
of hands

127 **give back** back off   128 **measure** range, reach   130
**Verona** Milan (see note to III.i.81)   138 **means for** efforts to
win   144 **repeal** recall (from banishment)   145 **Plead . . .
merit** the general sense appears to be one of the following:
(1) plead to be restored to your good graces, having formerly
misjudged them (2) proclaim that you are elevated to a new
place in my favor, earned by your unrivaled merit   153
**kept withal** lived with   154 **endued** endowed   161 **include
all jars** conclude all discords   162 **triumphs . . . solemnity**
celebrations . . . festivity

VALENTINE
  I warrant you, my lord, more grace than boy.
DUKE
  What mean you by that saying?
VALENTINE
  Please you, I'll tell you as we pass along,
  That you will wonder what hath fortunèd.°                      170

**170 fortunèd** chanced

Come, Proteus; 'tis your penance but° to hear
The story of your loves discoverèd.°
That done, our day of marriage shall be yours;
One feast, one house, one mutual happiness.    *Exeunt.*

**171 'tis . . . but** your only penance is  **172 discoverèd**
revealed

# LOVE'S LABOR'S LOST

EDITED BY JOHN ARTHOS

## Introduction

*Love's Labor's Lost* is one of Shakespeare's earliest and happiest comedies. It is excellently formed, moving easily toward its conclusion in a masque and a song, at the end recapitulating in all the stage's beauty the courting warfare of the young noblemen and ladies that has made up the chief part of the play, the sparrings and the surrenders and the victories. The play makes the point the theater seems to live to make, that sooner or later love conquers all, and although the title tells us that love's labor is lost, this we know is joking: the happy outcome is certain, and love and long life—as we learn at the end from what G. L. Kittredge called one of the best songs in the world—define the happy prospect.

In this Boccaccio-like setting another comic action plays its part, a comedy about the falsely learnèd and the grotesquely loving, partly contrasting with and partly parallel to the main story. The king and his lords, moved by the love of philosophy and virtue, have fallen into a most unphilosophical absurdity in supposing that the claims of love can easily be put aside. The foolish scholars light up the folly of the wise ones in still other ways, even as their own courting is mocked by the lovemaking of the others. As in so many of the later plays, it is all there—the multiple plot, the ranging between high and low minds, and love's challenge to every power in the world. All there, and as fluent in its display as in a dance.

The date of the play's composition must be guessed. The 1598 quarto title page mentions a performance of the play before her highness "this last Christmas," and it adds the phrase, "Newly corrected and augmented." This, taken along with the evidence of revisions in the text, and with the known dates of certain historical occurrences, leads to pretty substantial arguments for the composition of the play in 1593 or 1594. It should be said, however, that in the past the play was thought to be earlier than this; Coleridge, for example, believed it to be Shakespeare's first play because he thought Shakespeare was bringing into it part of the life he had just left, exploiting his experience as a schoolmaster while the memory of it was still fresh to him. This might push the writing back as far as 1589, and recently Alfred

Harbage[1] has returned to a similar line of reasoning. Likenesses to Lyly's plays in the 1580's and certain considerations making for the possibility that the play was produced by child actors in either a private or public theater, lead him to suggest 1589 or even earlier as the time of performance.

The arguments for a later date point to a general friendliness in England for Henry of Navarre until he reverted to the Church of Rome in July 1593; the beginning of the investigation in 1594 into the atheism of men associated with Sir Walter Raleigh, a group perhaps identified in the play (in IV.iii.252) as "the school of night"; the use of language that suggests the *Venus and Adonis* of 1593, the *Lucrece* of 1594, and sonnets of presumably the same period. And, of course, a number of topical allusions.[2]

The occasion of the play's first production is not known, but it was surely meant for a private performance—the house of the Earl of Southampton has been suggested—perhaps in 1593. As such it would have been part of festivities in which music and dancing would naturally be called for. The first printed text of the play alludes to a performance before the queen at Christmas, either in 1597 or 1598, and the play's immediately succeeding stage history establishes the special suitability of the work for a courtly audience. The substance of the play also makes this clear enough—the initiating idea of learnèd gentlemen in the company of their monarch retiring from the life of power, the better to perfect their lives; the abjuring the society of women in serious as well as fantastic aspiration, following the directions of the most fashionable writers out of Italy; the mockery of literary men and most particularly of courtiers with ambitions in literature; the battles between the sexes conducted with the most elaborate and sensitive protocol. In large and small matters alike the play seems to be taking something directly out of the life of the court of Elizabeth (wisely enough under another name),

---

[1] "*Love's Labor's Lost* and the Early Shakespeare," *Philological Quarterly*, XLI (1962), 18–36.
[2] The basic discussion of the date of the play's composition is H. B. Charlton's "The Date of *Love's Labour's Lost*," *Modern Language Review*, XIII (1918), 257–66; 387–400.

making what it takes into something more than life-size. It gives the audience of lords and ladies a mirror in which they will see themselves in all the wit, imagining, beauty and fun they are absorbed in.

The idea of nobility sets the tone for it all. It begins in the king's first speech, it is taken up more than once by the princess, and, ironically, it is fully triumphant in Berowne, the railer at both love and philosophy, so dangerously close in his disposition to the discarding of all values, himself in the end the defender of an aspiration as passionately felt as it is truly thought.

When the king speaks of retiring to the learnèd academy, we feel the genuine love of learning and of virtue in his words:

> Navarre shall be the wonder of the world;
> Our court shall be a little academe,
> Still and contemplative in living art.     (I.i.12–14)

And the chief critic of the idea is no philistine. He is high-spirited and he is tired of going to school, but he has his wisdom, too, and we judge he has the experience to support it:

> So study evermore is overshot.
> While it doth study to have what it would,
> It doth forget to do the thing it should.     (I.i.141–43)

And so we immediately perceive that in the conflicts that are to rage in the play the sparks of thought will be flying everywhere. The issue is to be granted its proper dignity, whatever the comic emphasis, and in the end love will be allowed to break up the academy not only because it is strong but because it may claim a special worth, and because the temper of these noble persons is deeply founded in the cultivation of the best of everything the world offers.

The princess' first scene gives us so beautiful a picture of a woman that it carries all before it as if it were the very praise of womankind. The first words to tell us this come from one of her lords, advising her on her approach to the king:

> Be now as prodigal of all dear grace
> As Nature was in making graces dear
> When she did starve the general world beside,
> And prodigally gave them all to you.     (II.i.9–12)

On the other side, the king is acknowledged as "the sole inheritor/Of all perfections that a man may owe" (II.i. 5–6). The bounty of the woman and the perfection of the man, these are the qualities that set the tone, and these are the persons to lead the dancing interplay, the parryings and the reversals and the resolutions that are to come. They themselves are the matter of love's labors, the union of nobility and bounty, like some splendid foreshadowing of the masque of Ceres in *The Tempest*.

Nature has its austerity, and love has its temperance, and the princess' chiding of the busy old Lord Boyet for his flattery is a still more telling criticism of the affectations and grossness of another kind of courtly love:

> my beauty, though but mean,
> Needs not the painted flourish of your praise.     (II.i.13–14)

Armado with his affectations brought from Spain and Italy and the courtiers with their sonnets are abusing "the heart's still rhetoric" (II.i.229). False speaking conforms to warped natures, and the play never loses sight of the idea of inherent excellence in manhood and womanhood and of the importance of true expression in love. Whatever the follies of the great as well as lesser characters, and whatever the ironies whereby nobility and the taking of oaths are made to seem like tinder before the fires of love, the decorum of the truly courtly prevails as the basis of the play's beauty.

The comic ideas also are as alive with intellectuality as the play's most serious affirmations. When the ladies call to mind and comment on the lords who accompany the king—men in the past they had encountered only briefly—praising them as it appears they deserve to be praised, we discover that all of them are in love before they know it. The audience enters into a kind of conspiracy with Shakespeare, schooled, as we are certain he was, by literature and the conventions of the stage, agreeing in advance that the great and noble always love the beautiful, and the beautiful the brave. Since this is the stage, we know that all these must be paired no matter what the claims of study. And so, won not only by the beauty and youth but by the wit of the ladies, we anticipate with pleasure the defeat of the men. We have seen the signs of love in the first words of each of the women as she sizes up her choice, and while we know enough of the men to know they will put up a kind of fight, we cannot be sorry at the prospect of a surrender they themselves will not regret.

The intermingling of the two plots is as expert as the rest. After the king has announced the program he means to follow and Berowne has had his say about it, we meet a clown, Costard, and a fop, Armado. They are showing off, and Shakespeare mocks both the clown's wenching and the fop's romancing. The scene is dramatically focused when the two confront each other in the presence of the one they are both taken with, the country maid, Jaquenetta. Costard, who has been misbehaving, is put into the custody of Armado, who is to guarantee his good behavior. The contrast is in itself pleasing—the fool who from time to time blunders into sense, and the most affected of courtiers who is yet not all fool. And in their folly as in their sense we see that they are being made to pose different versions of the questions the other characters are also asking— what has learning to do with love? and what has love to do with learning? As the plots proceed, the various lovers fall into many absurdities, but the questions themselves continually receive thoughtful answers, or thoughtful mockery. The varieties of the questioning, from such different kinds of lovers, require and get complex and significant answers, and the confusions of Costard and Armado prepare for the resolution Berowne will finally discover.

Meanwhile, the lords about the king are made to show their folly. One after another, subdued to his lady, takes to poetry, and one after another passes across the stage, sonnet in hand, or under his hat, or tucked into his belt— a snow of sonnets. The mockery is so lavish it adds the beauty of a pageant to the absurdity. The noble lords demean themselves in becoming poets, and they glory in their humiliation since they imagine it is pleasing to the ladies. This is indeed what the ladies require of those they favor, but they also require more than words. They require, as Rosaline says of her own lover, "That he should be my fool, and I his fate" (V.ii.68). The play will spell this out. Subjecting themselves to such cruel and whimsical tyrants, the men become as funny as Armado and Moth. Shakespeare lays it on with a trowel:

> To see a king transforméd to a gnat!
> To see great Hercules whipping a gig,
> And profound Solomon to tune a jig,
> And Nestor play at push-pin with the boys,
> And critic Timon laugh at idle toys!      (IV.iii.163–67)

At the end they will endure still greater transformations, but already they are well schooled in the doctrine that love is madness, and that that madness redeems all. As the song jubilantly declares of one lady:

> Thou for whom Jove would swear
> Juno but an Ethiop were.      (IV.iii.114–15)

The beautiful lyric is part of the singing of the whole play, the beauty love worships is the beauty the play is celebrating. All the changes it is ringing on the courting of high and low, on absurdity and exaggeration, on grossness and refinement, are subdued to the grave and splendid beauty that conquers even Jove.

The secondary plot continues the mockery of false ideas of learning and it also brings before us the sight of other kinds of lovemaking. The most obvious point to the mockery of pedantry is as an abuse of what the academy stands for. Holofernes, the walking dictionary, may represent John Florio, or Thomas Harriot. The name Armado brings the Spanish Armada to mind, and so it has been argued that Armado is a portrayal of Sir Walter Raleigh, the man who defeated the Armada. (If this were to be substantiated, it might strengthen the argument of those who think the play was produced shortly after the defeat of the Armada in 1588.) Or the character may be thought to represent a quite different person, the arrogant and tedious Gabriel Harvey. Moth may be Thomas Nashe. But however much the possibility of such identifications causes the characters to jump out of their parts, the parts they do play are plainly so much more interesting to the audience for the comments they provide on the characters in the main action. The characters of the minor plot are strangers to the nobility of the others, and in their ambitions and pretensions they are illustrating not only the follies of the court but its essential superiority. The king values learning because it serves the noblest purposes in life; the ideas of the pedants are ignoble. For them it is always the letter at the expense of the spirit, and pride in learning at the expense of its good use.

The point is also being made that the abuse of learning is like the stupidity of affectation in love. The true power of love as well as the true worth of learning is lost upon the low characters, not only in their grossness but in their false refinement too. In the fun Shakespeare is making of them he strikes at everyone, but most of all he means to preserve our esteem for the truer men. They want glory for learning, for the academy, glory that will outlast death, because they want learning to be a light for those who will come after them. It is such men, no mere inkpots,

who are love's true targets. In different ways, then, both plots are reinforcing the teaching that love belongs properly to the gentle heart.

Heightening and enriching this doctrine is the idea of the divinity of love. Character after character speaks of love as if it were a presence as well as a power. The play's title names love as the power at work in the play, and in every turn of the story we are shown events as if they were indeed the manipulations of a god—Eros, although unseen, yet surely directing and effecting all, showing his strength and enforcing his laws. As much as in *All's Well That Ends Well*, those who strive against him strive in vain.

Love's "labor" is a bringing to birth. The remembrances of ancient meetings come fast upon the courtiers and the ladies—"Did not I dance with you in Brabant once?" (II.i.114)—and in one after the other the seed burgeons. Part of the poetry as well as the comedy is that this growing of love goes on as it were in isolation. Cutting themselves off from so much of society, from the cares of power as well as from the entanglements with women, the lords are the more defenseless in their idleness. The king himself, treating of the matter the princess has come to negotiate on behalf of her sick father, even as he begins to talk of business finds that his heart is moved. Boyet notes this instantly:

> Why, all his behaviors did make their retire
> To the court of his eye, peeping thorough desire.
> His heart, like an agate with your print impressed,
> Proud with his form, in his eye pride expressed.
>      (II.i.234–37)

Already love is at work, in the highest as in the lowest, sometimes beautifully and sometimes grotesquely, but always irresistibly.

This leads to the truly inspired idea in the extraordinary, not to say unlikely, happenings presumably only to be accounted for by a god's workings—that all the lovers should from the beginning have had no doubt who were to be their partners. In the masquing, the ladies switched their lords' favors in order to trick their lovers into another perjury, like Portia and Nerissa in *The Merchant of Venice*, merry in forging other chains for their slaves. So this time the lords will swear again, but to the wrong partners— as if another Puck were at work—and the ladies can mock the men until, as Berowne says, they are "dry-beaten" (V.ii.264)—the very blood leaves their faces. They are driven off, and it is no comfort to them to learn finally that they have now forsworn themselves twice. Shakespeare has had his fun with the idea of inexorable destiny in love at first sight, and he makes more fun of it still by asking another question: What is it that love sees?

Love's working and love's presence—a very god— come into full sight in Berowne's great speech, wherein the railer at love and wisdom, himself now enslaved, mocks himself:

> O, and I, forsooth, in love!
> I, that have been love's whip,
> A very beadle to a humorous sigh,
> A critic, nay, a night-watch constable,
> A domineering pedant o'er the boy,

Than whom no mortal so magnificent!
This wimpled, whining, purblind, wayward boy,
This senior-junior, giant-dwarf, Dan Cupid,
Regent of love rhymes, lord of folded arms,
Th' anointed sovereign of sighs and groans

And I to be a corporal of his field!      (III.i.172–81, 186)

To make it worse, he is in love with the one he says is the least beautiful of the ladies, the most wanton, the one who would escape a guardian with a hundred eyes. But he accepts his fate: "Some men must love my lady, and some Joan" (III.i.204). This time Touchstone is a gentleman, and so somewhat more love's fool. But finally he will say more in praise of love than any other will, and however light in touch his words substantiate what the others must now acknowledge:

From women's eyes this doctrine I derive.

They are the books, the arts, the academes,
That show, contain, and nourish all the world;
Else none at all in aught proves excellent.
                                    (IV.iii.347, 349–51)

With this conclusion the play moves toward its end. The haughty must change their tactics. There is the call to arms and the embrace of battle: "Advance your standards, and upon them, lords!" (IV.iii.364). And so they dance, recapitulating in their motions the warring that has made the play, the advances and retreats, the defeats and victories, the strivings and capitulations, and the final treaties.

For the play's last words there is a song sung by allegorical personages, Spring and Winter, fantastic figures out of the world of musical entertainment and Renaissance allegory. It speaks of flowers and countrymaids and ploughmen, of love and marriage and cuckoldry, of spring and winter, of idleness and of hard work, of nature when it is kind and when it is cruel, of life by the hearth. It is a song about love making peace with life, with things as they are. It provides the most brilliant of comments on all that has been fanciful in the beauty of the play and in the ideas of these fine people. In the perfection and balance of the contrast with all that has gone before, this song sung by the personifications of time is the true culmination of the play, the marriage of sophistication and reality, of the stage and its glory and the strength of love's endurance outside it. The song celebrates the poetry of life as it is, and it is one of Shakespeare's most glorious inspirations that he has it sung by the deities of "curds and flowers," magnificently adorned, without doubt, as the Renaissance imagined gods would be.

The song follows the princess' farewell as she and the ladies leave Navarre, postponing the marriages. The lords are meanwhile to prove themselves by the most strenuous and demanding discipline, for the courtship has been

A time, methinks, too short
To make a world-without-end bargain in.   (V.ii.786–87)

The words of wisdom are indeed harsh after the music of the god of poetry, as the comment that ends the play says, words that may be given to Armado. They are words that sustain us as the play sustains us, and as the marvelous song does. And the reflection to which the last scene leads us is that love, like learning, is but a part of life, and what the whole of it is there is no one to say—there is only the testing, and good hope.

## A NOTE ON THE SOURCES

No source for the plot of Love's Labor's Lost is known to exist, but it is often supposed that Shakespeare was building upon reports of historic events. The very names of Navarre and the lords,[3] the matter of property disputes involving the King of France, the existence of a learnèd academy favored by the French nobility, and accounts of political negotiations in which certain court ladies were involved, all these point to incidents in recent French history which were reported upon at the time. So far no record has been found of any single happening that is plainly the original of the episodes of the play. It is only in the sum of the reports of similar incidents that the idea that Shakespeare is building upon historical matters comes to seem truly likely.

The play, whether meant originally for performance at a great house, or at a children's theater, exploited these historical events presumably because they treated matters in which the audience was also interested. English court circles were also drawn to the idea of learnèd academies and were involved in disputes centering on Platonic theories of love. Upon reflection, the treatment of certain episodes in France would have served as comment upon the life of the court in England. Quite as naturally Shakespeare could work into the main story all sorts of allusions to the life of letters and introduce subsidiary plotting to expand upon the story of the aristocratic academicians. So the play directs particular satire against specific English fashions—euphuism, for instance—as well as the universal extravagances of humanists and pedants and actors. Here, too, the references seem again and again to point to particular persons and to specific incidents, and scholars have therefore argued that Shakespeare took some of his contemporaries as models for the characters in his comic plot, and the characters that were in part borrowed from the commedia dell'arte from time to time present themselves in the guise of Thomas Nashe, Sir Walter Raleigh, John Florio, and perhaps others. To J. D. Wilson these matters become so important that he is convinced that the play "was written as a topical play." But G. L. Kittredge, and others after him, have thought it "merely whimsical" to identify Armado and Holofernes and the others in any such way.

On particular points it is seldom possible to resolve this dispute, most especially if the supposed allusions are studied primarily in the light of literary history. But the direction of much modern literary scholarship is to give precedence in the consideration of the elements of a work of art to a study of their relation to the work itself as an imaginative entity, and the effect of such an emphasis is to

[3] The Marshal de Biron (Berowne) and Longueville were close associates of Henry, not Ferdinand, of Navarre. The Duc de Mayenne (Dumaine?) was once his enemy but later an ally. Boyet and Marcadé are the names of historical persons.

work in opposition to any theory that regards the work primarily as a historical record. In short, the impression of topical allusion is inescapable, but if one takes the play as substantially summed up by its title, the topicality seems to be absorbed in the imaginative and the fanciful, and in all the charm of the play's poetic and theatrical effects.

The historical documents that are most often cited in presenting analogues to certain incidents in the play are *The Chronicles of Enguerrand de Monstrelet, 1440–1516;* Pierre de la Primaudaye, *The French Academie;* H. C. Davila, *The History of the Civil Wars of France; Gesta Grayorum: or The History of the High and Mighty Prince Henry, Prince of Purpoole . . . Who Reigned and Died,* A.D. *1594.* The relevant sections can be found in the first volume of Geoffrey Bullough's *Narrative and Dramatic Sources of Shakespeare.* There are of course no documents that in any substantial way support the ascriptions of topicality.

### A NOTE ON THE TEXT

This edition is based upon the quarto of 1598, which, it is generally agreed, was printed from a manuscript in Shakespeare's own hand. The title page reads: "A/Pleasant/ Conceited Comedie/Called,/Loues labors lost./As it was presented before her Highnes/this last Christmas./Newly corrected and augmented/By W. Shakespere./Imprinted at London by W. W./for Cutbert Burby./1598."

Although here there may be a reference to a previous printing, there is no trace of an earlier edition. "Newly corrected and augmented" probably refers to revisions in the manuscript, some of which, as it happens, may be detected in examining the printed text. (See notes to IV.iii.293 and V.ii.815–20.)

The printing of the 1623 Folio is based upon the quarto. It corrects some errors of the quarto and adds a number of its own. It provides act divisions (mistakenly heading the fifth act *Actus Quartus*), but the scene divisions as well as the list of the names of the persons in the play are the contributions of later editors.

Apart from a considerable number of misreadings the most noteworthy confusions in the quarto are in the speech headings. It is not merely that occasionally "Nathaniel" stands for "Holofernes," that the king is sometimes "Navarre" and sometimes "Ferdinand" in the early part of the second act, and that in the same part of the play Rosaline and Katherine are confused. In the next act the character previously identified as Armado becomes "Braggart," Moth, the page, becomes "Boy," Holofernes becomes "Pedant," Costard becomes "Clown." Later Sir Nathaniel becomes "Curate" and "Constable" becomes "Dull." The use of the generic names to take the place of the individual ones may be evidence of Shakespeare's revisions. In the present edition the speech headings have been made consistent, but the later substitutions are made evident by the supplementary stage directions indicating the entrances of the various characters.

The revision of the manuscript has left a couple of other obvious confusions. Berowne's speech in IV.iii contains lines that belong to an earlier version, and some of these should have been canceled. If lines 293–314 were omitted,

the speech would continue connectedly and without obvious repetitions. It also seems that the exchange between Berowne and Rosaline in V.ii.815–20 was meant to be struck out. In the present edition these passages are retained, but enclosed in square brackets.

The text of this edition is based upon the Heber-Daniel copy of the quarto in the British Museum; the spelling and punctuation have been modernized, obvious misspellings and wrong speech headings corrected, and the quotations from foreign languages regularized. Other departures from the quarto text are listed below: the adopted reading is given first in boldface, followed immediately by the quarto reading in roman.

**I.i.24 three** thee  **31 pomp** pome  **62 feast** fast  **104 an** any  **114 swore** sworne  **127–31** [Q gives to Longaville]  **127 gentility** gentletie  **130 public** publibue  **131 possibly** possible  **218 welkin's vicegerent** welkis Vizgerent  **240 preposterous** propostrous  **276 worst** wost  **288 King** Ber.  **307 prosperity** prosperie
**I.ii.14 epitheton** apethaton  **99 blushing** blush-in  **141 Dull** Clo.
**II.i.32 Importunes** Importuous  **34 visaged** visage  **44 parts peerelsse  88 unpeopled** vnpeeled  **115–26** [the lines here given to Rosaline are in Q given to Katharine]  **130 half of an** halfe of, of an  **140 friendship** faiendship  **142 demand** pemaund  **144 On** One  **179 mine own** my none  **195 Katharine** Rosalin  **210 Rosaline** Katherin  **221** [Q gives to *La.*]  **222–23** [Q gives to *Lad.*]  **224** [Q gives to *La.*]  **236 agate** Agot  **246 quote** coate  **254** [Q gives to *Lad.*]  **255** [Q gives to *Lad.* 2]  **256** [Q gives to *Lad.* 3]  **257** [Q gives to *Lad.*]  **258** [Q gives to *Lad.*]
**III.i.14 throat as if** throate, if  **15–16 through the nose** through: nose  **18 thin-belly** thinbellies  **24–25 note me?—that** note men that  **27 penny** penne  **66 voluble** volable  **73 the mail** thee male; **plain** plaine  **134 ounce** ouce  **137 remuneration** remuration  **138 One penny** i.d.  **174 beadle** Bedell  **175 critic** Crietick  **179 senior-junior** signior *Iunios*  **183 plackets** Placcats  **185 paritors** Parrators  **189 German clock** Iermane Cloake  **195 whitely** whitly  **203 sue** shue
**IV.i.6 On** Ore  **33 heart** hart  **71–72 saw . . . saw** See . . . see  **72 overcame** couercame  **77 king's** King  **110 suitor . . . suitor** shooter . . . shooter  **122 Pepin** Pippen  **125 Guinever** Guinouer  **132 hit it** hit  **134 mete** meate  **136 ne'er** neare  **138 pin** is in  **140 too** to  **146 to th' one** ath toothen  **149 o' t' other** atother  **150 a most** most  **150 s.d. Shout** Shoot  **151 Exit** Exeunt
**IV.ii.5 coelo** Celo  **8 epithets** epythithes  **30 we of taste we** taste  **31 indiscreet** indistreell  **37 Dictynna . . . Dictynna** Dictisima . . . dictisima  **38 Dictynna** dictima  **52 ignorant, I call** ignorault cald  **55 scurrility** squirilitie  **57 preyful** prayfull  **61 sores—o' sorel** sores o sorell  **66–150** [all speech prefixes of Holofernes and Nathaniel are reversed in Q, except at 107]  **70 pia mater** primater  **72 those in whom** those whom  **78 ingenious** ingenous  **80 sapit** sapis  **84 pierce-one** Person  **87 likest** liklest  **94–95 Fauste . . . ruminat** Facile precor gellida, quando pecas omnia sub vmbra ruminat  **98–99 Venetia . . . pretia** vemchie, vencha, que non te vnde, que non te perreche  **122 canzonet** cangenet  **136 writing** written  **138 Sir Nathaniel** Ped. Sir Holofernes  **159 ben** bien
**IV.iii.13]  14 melancholy** mallicholie  **46 King** Long.  **50 triumviry** triumpherie  **72 idolatry** ydotarie  **84 quoted** coted  **90 And I mine** And mine  **96 ode** Odo  **105 Wished Wish  109 thorn** throne  **127 o'erheard** ore-hard  **152 coaches** couches  **158 mote . . . mote** Moth . . . Moth  **177 men like you, men** men like men  **179 Joan** Ione  **245 wood** word  **256 painting and usurping** painting vsurping  **257 doters** dooters  **310 woman's** womas  **313–14** [between these lines Q has: With our selues]  **320 beauty's** beautis  **356 authors** authour  **358 Let us** Lets vs  **380 Allons! Allons!** Alone alone  **382 forsworn** forsorne
**V.i.9 hominem** hominum  **26 insanie** infamie  **28 bone** bene  **29 Bone? Bone for bene! Priscian** Bome boon for boon prescian  **32 gaudeo** gaudio  **34 Quare** Quari  **48 pueritia** puericia  **49 silly** seely  **56 wave** wane; **Mediterranean** meditaranium  **57 venew** vene we  **66 manu** vnū  **75 dunghill**

dungil **76 Dunghill** dunghel **96 importunate** importunt
**106 secrecy** secretie **115 Nathaniel** Holofernes **117 rend'red**
rended **148 Allons** Alone
**V.ii.13 ne'er** neare **17 ha' been a grandam** a bin Grandam **43
'Ware pencils, ho!** Ware pensalls, How? **53 pearls** Pearle
**65 hests** deuice **74 wantonness** wantons be **80 stabbed**
stable **89 sycamore** Siccamone **93 Warily** warely **95 overheard** ouer hard **96 they** thy **122 parley, court** parlee, to
court **134 too** two **148 her** his **152 e'er** ere **159** [Q gives to
Berowne] **163 ever** euen **175 strangers** stranges **217** [Q
gives to Rosaline] **225 Price** Prise **243–56** [Q gives "Maria"
for "Katharine"] **298 vailing** varling **300 woo** woe **310 run**
runs **324 too** to **329 ushering** hushering **342 Construe**

Consture **353 unsullied** vnsallied **375 wit** wits **408 affectation** affection **461 on't** ant **464 zany** saine **483 manage**
nuage **502 they** thy **515 least** best **529 de la guerra** delaguar
**562 this** his **582** [Q has "Exit Curat"] **596 proved** proud **644
gilt** gift **687 Stir them on, stir** stir them, or stir **748 wholesome** holdsome **776 the ambassadors** embassadours **780
this in our** this our **784 quote** cote **805 instant** instance **810
entitled** intiled **814 hermit** herrite **816 rank** rackt **822 A
wife?** [included in following speech in Q] **826 smooth-faced**
smothfast **893–94** [these lines transposed in Q] **912 foul** full
**924–25 The words . . . Apollo** [printed in larger type in Q without
any speech-heading; F adds *You that way: we this way,* and
heading *Brag.*]

# LOVE'S LABOR'S LOST

# [ A C T   I ]

[Scene I. *The park of the King of Navarre.*]

*Enter Ferdinand* KING *of Navarre,* BEROWNE, LONG-
AVILLE, *and* DUMAINE.

KING
Let fame, that all hunt after in their lives,
Live regist'red upon our brazen tombs
And then grace us in the disgrace° of death,
When, spite of cormorant° devouring Time,
Th' endeavor of this present breath may buy          5
That honor which shall bate° his scythe's keen edge
And make us heirs of all eternity.
Therefore, brave conquerors—for so you are
That war against your own affections
And the huge army of the world's desires—          10
Our late edict shall strongly stand in force:
Navarre shall be the wonder of the world;

Our court shall be a little academe,°
Still and contemplative in living art.°
You three, Berowne, Dumaine, and Longaville,          15
Have sworn for three years' term to live with me,
My fellow scholars, and to keep those statutes
That are recorded in this schedule here.
Your oaths are passed; and now subscribe your names,
That his own hand may strike his honor down          20
That violates the smallest branch herein.
If you are armed° to do as sworn to do,
Subscribe to your deep oaths, and keep it too.

LONGAVILLE
I am resolved. 'Tis but a three years' fast.
The mind shall banquet though the body pine.          25
Fat paunches have lean pates, and dainty bits
Make rich the ribs, but bankrout° quite the wits.

DUMAINE
My loving lord, Dumaine is mortified.°
The grosser manner of these world's delights
He throws upon the gross world's baser slaves.          30

---

*The decorative border above appeared on the title page of the quarto edition of Love's Labor's Lost, 1598.*

**I.i.3 disgrace** degradation  **4 cormorant** ravenous  **6 bate** make dull

**13 academe** academy  **14 Still . . . art** continually study-ing the art of living  **22 armed** resolved  **27 bankrout** bankrupt  **28 mortified** dead to worldly pleasures

To love, to wealth, to pomp, I pine and die,
With all these living in philosophy.

**BEROWNE**
I can but say their protestation over°—
So much, dear liege, I have already sworn,
That is, to live and study here three years.    35
But there are other strict observances:
As not to see a woman in that term—
Which I hope well is not enrollèd there;
And one day in a week to touch no food,
And but one meal on every day beside—    40
The which I hope is not enrollèd there;
And then to sleep but three hours in the night,
And not be seen to wink of° all the day
(When I was wont to think no harm all night
And make a dark night too of half the day)—    45
Which I hope well is not enrollèd there.
O, these are barren tasks, too hard to keep,
Not to see ladies, study, fast, not sleep!

**KING**
Your oath is passed, to pass away from these.

**BEROWNE**
Let me say no, my liege, and if° you please.    50
I only swore to study with your grace
And stay here in your court for three years' space.

**LONGAVILLE**
You swore to that, Berowne, and to the rest.

**BEROWNE**
By yea and nay,° sir, then I swore in jest.
What is the end of study, let me know?    55

**KING**
Why, that to know which else we should not know.

**BEROWNE**
Things hid and barred, you mean, from common
     sense?

**KING**
Ay, that is study's godlike recompense.

**BEROWNE**
Come on then, I will swear to study so,
To know the thing I am forbid to know:    60
As thus—to study where I well may dine
When I to feast expressly am forbid;
Or study where to meet some mistress fine
When mistresses from common sense are hid;
Or having sworn too hard-a-keeping oath,    65
Study to break it and not break my troth.°
If study's gain be thus, and this be so,
Study knows that which yet it doth not know.
Swear me to this, and I will ne'er say no.

**KING**
These be the stops° that hinder study quite    70
And train° our intellects to vain delight.

**BEROWNE**
Why, all delights are vain, but that most vain
Which, with pain purchased, doth inherit pain:
As, painfully to pore upon a book,
To seek the light of truth, while truth the while    75
Doth falsely° blind the eyesight of his look.

Light seeking light doth light of light beguile;°
So, ere you find where light in darkness lies,
Your light grows dark by losing of your eyes.
Study me how to please the eye indeed    80
By fixing it upon a fairer eye,
Who dazzling so, that eye shall be his heed°
And give him light that it was blinded by.
Study is like the heaven's glorious sun,
That will not be deep-searched with saucy looks.    85
Small have continual plodders ever won
Save base authority from others' books.
These earthly godfathers° of heaven's lights,
That give a name to every fixèd star
Have no more profit of their shining nights    90
Than those that walk and wot° not what they are.
Too much to know is to know nought but fame;°
And every godfather can give a name.

**KING**
How well he's read to reason against reading!

**DUMAINE**
Proceeded° well, to stop all good proceeding!    95

**LONGAVILLE**
He weeds the corn,° and still lets grow the weeding.°

**BEROWNE**
The spring is near, when green geese° are a-breeding.

**DUMAINE**
How follows that?

**BEROWNE**        Fit in his place and time.

**DUMAINE**
In reason nothing.

**BEROWNE**        Something then in rhyme.

**KING**
Berowne is like an envious sneaping° frost    100
That bites the first-born infants of the spring.

**BEROWNE**
Well, say I am! Why should proud summer boast
Before the birds have any cause to sing?
Why should I joy in an abortive birth?
At Christmas I no more desire a rose    105
Than wish a snow in May's new-fangled shows,
But like of each thing that in season grows.
So you—to study now it is too late—
Climb o'er the house to unlock the little gate.

**KING**
Well, sit you out. Go home, Berowne. Adieu.    110

**BEROWNE**
No, my good lord, I have sworn to stay with you;
And though I have for barbarism° spoke more
Than for that angel knowledge you can say,
Yet confident I'll keep what I have swore,
And bide the penance of each three years' day.°    115
Give me the paper, let me read the same,
And to the strictest decrees I'll write my name.

**KING**
How well this yielding rescues thee from shame!

---

33 **say . . . over** repeat their solemn declarations   43 **wink of** close the eyes during   50 **and if** if   54 **By . . . nay** in all earnestness   66 **troth** faith   70 **stops** obstructions   71 **train** entice   76 **falsely** treacherously

77 **Light . . . beguile** eyes in seeking truth lose their sight in too much seeking   82 **heed** protector   88 **earthly godfathers** astronomers   91 **wot** know   92 **fame** report   95 **Proceeded** took a degree at the university   96 **corn** wheat; **weeding** weeds   97 **green geese** geese born the previous autumn   100 **sneaping** nipping (Berowne's "rhyme" is taken as *rime*, or frost)   112 **barbarism** philistinism   115 **each . . . day** each day of the three years

BEROWNE [*Reads.*]   "Item. That no woman shall come within a mile of my court—" Hath this been pro- 120 claimed?

LONGAVILLE   Four days ago.

BEROWNE   Let's see the penalty. [*Reads.*] "—on pain of losing her tongue." Who devised this penalty?

LONGAVILLE
Marry,° that did I.

BEROWNE                Sweet lord, and why?        125

LONGAVILLE
To fright them hence with that dread penalty.

BEROWNE
A dangerous law against gentility!°
[*Reads.*] "Item. If any man be seen to talk with a woman within the term of three years, he shall endure such public shame as the rest of the court can 130 possibly devise."
This article, my liege, yourself must break;
For well you know here comes in embassy
The French king's daughter with yourself to speak,
A maid of grace and complete majesty,        135
About surrender up of Aquitaine
To her decrepit, sick, and bedrid father.
Therefore this article is made in vain,
Or vainly comes th' admirèd princess hither.

KING
What say you, lords? Why, this was quite forgot.   140

BEROWNE
So study evermore is overshot.°
While it doth study to have what it would,
It doth forget to do the thing it should;
And when it hath the thing it hunteth most,
'Tis won as towns with fire°—so won, so lost.    145

KING
We must of force° dispense with this decree.
She must lie° here on mere° necessity.

BEROWNE
Necessity will make us all forsworn
Three thousand times within this three years' space:
For every man with his affects° is born,        150
Not by might mast'red, but by special grace.
If I break faith, this word shall speak for me,
I am forsworn "on mere necessity."
So to the laws at large I write my name;

[*Subscribes.*]

And he that breaks them in the least degree     155
Stands in attainder of° eternal shame.
Suggestions° are to other as to me,
But I believe, although I seem so loath,°
I am the last that will last keep his oath.
But is there no quick recreation granted?       160

KING
Ay, that there is. Our court, you know, is haunted
With a refinèd traveler of Spain,
A man in all the world's new fashion planted,
That hath a mint of phrases in his brain;
One who the music of his own vain tongue        165

Doth ravish like enchanting harmony;
A man of complements,° whom right and wrong
Have chose as umpire of their mutiny.
This child of fancy, that Armado hight,°
For interim° to our studies shall relate         170
In highborn words the worth of many a knight
From tawny Spain, lost in the world's debate.
How you delight, my lords, I know not, I,
But, I protest, I love to hear him lie,
And I will use him for my minstrelsy.°           175

BEROWNE
Armado is a most illustrious wight,
A man of fire-new° words, fashion's own knight.

LONGAVILLE
Costard the swain° and he shall be our sport;
And so to study three years is but short.

*Enter* [DULL] *a constable, with* COSTARD [*a clown*], *with a letter.*

DULL   Which is the duke's own person?        180

BEROWNE   This, fellow. What wouldst?

DULL   I myself reprehend° his own person, for I am his grace's farborough.° But I would see his own person in flesh and blood.

BEROWNE   This is he.                            185

DULL   Signior Arm—Arm—commends you. There's villainy abroad. This letter will tell you more.

COSTARD   Sir, the contempts° thereof are as touching me.

KING   A letter from the magnificent Armado.    190

BEROWNE   How low soever the matter, I hope in God for high words.

LONGAVILLE   A high hope for a low heaven. God grant us patience!

BEROWNE   To hear, or forbear hearing?          195

LONGAVILLE   To hear meekly, sir, and to laugh moderately, or to forbear both.

BEROWNE   Well, sir, be it as the style shall give us cause to climb in the merriness.

COSTARD   The matter is to me, sir, as concerning 200 Jaquenetta. The manner of it is, I was taken with the manner.°

BEROWNE   In what manner?

COSTARD   In manner and form following, sir—all those three: I was seen with her in the manorhouse, 205 sitting with her upon the form,° and taken following her into the park; which, put together, is, in manner and form, following. Now, sir, for the manner—it is the manner of a man to speak to a woman. For the form—in some form.                            210

BEROWNE   For the following, sir?

COSTARD   As it shall follow in my correction,° and God defend the right!

KING   Will you hear this letter with attention?

BEROWNE   As we would hear an oracle.          215

COSTARD   Such is the simplicity of man to hearken after the flesh.

---

**125 Marry** By Mary (mild oath)   **127 gentility** good manners
**141 overshot** wide of the mark   **145 won . . . fire** destroyed
in being won   **146 of force** of necessity   **147 lie** lodge; **mere**
simple   **150 affects** passions   **156 in attainder of** to be
condemned to   **157 Suggestions** temptations   **158 loath**
reluctant

**167 complements** formal manners   **169 hight** is named
**170 interim** interruption   **175 minstrelsy** court entertainer
**177 fire-new** fresh from the mint   **178 swain** countryman
**182 reprehend** Dull means to say *represent*   **183 farborough**
petty constable   **188 contempts** Costard means the *contents*
of the letter   **201–02 with the manner** in the act   **206 form**
bench   **212 correction** punishment

KING [*Reads.*] "Great deputy, the welkin's vicegerent,° and sole dominator of Navarre, my soul's earth's God, and body's fost'ring patron—"                    220

COSTARD  Not a word of Costard yet.

KING  "So it is—"

COSTARD  It may be so; but if he say it is so, he is, in telling true, but so.°

KING  Peace!                    225

COSTARD  Be to me and every man that dares not fight.

KING  No words!

COSTARD  Of other men's secrets, I beseech you.

KING [*Reads.*] "So it is, besieged with sable-colored  230 melancholy, I did commend the black-oppressing humor° to the most wholesome physic° of thy health-giving air; and, as I am a gentleman, betook myself to walk. The time When? About the sixth hour; when beasts most graze, birds best peck, and men sit down to  235 that nourishment which is called supper. So much for the time When. Now for the ground Which? Which, I mean, I walked upon. It is ycleped° thy park. Then for the place Where? Where, I mean, I did encounter that obscene and most preposterous event, that  240 draweth from my snow-white pen° the ebon-colored ink, which here thou viewest, beholdest, surveyest, or see'st. But to the place Where? It standeth north-north-east and by east from the west corner of thy curious-knotted° garden. There did I see that low-  245 spirited swain, that base minnow of thy mirth—"

COSTARD  Me?

KING  "that unlettered° small-knowing soul—"

COSTARD  Me?

KING  "that shallow vassal°—"                    250

COSTARD  Still me!

KING  "which, as I remember, hight° Costard—"

COSTARD  O me!

KING  "sorted and consorted, contrary to thy established proclaimed edict and continent canon,° which  255 with—O, with—but with this I passion to say wherewith—"

COSTARD  With a wench.

KING  "with a child of our grandmother Eve, a female; or, for thy more sweet understanding, a woman.  260 Him I (as my ever-esteemed duty pricks° me on) have sent to thee, to receive the meed° of punishment, by thy sweet grace's officer, Anthony Dull, a man of good repute, carriage, bearing, and estimation."

DULL  Me, an't shall please you: I am Anthony Dull.  265

KING  "For Jaquenetta (so is the weaker vessel° called), which I apprehended with the aforesaid swain, I keep her as a vessel of thy law's fury, and shall, at the least of thy sweet notice,° bring her to trial. Thine in all

compliments of devoted and heartburning heat of  270 duty,

Don Adriano de Armado."

BEROWNE  This is not so well as I looked for, but the best that ever I heard.

KING  Ay, the best for the worst. But, sirrah,° what  275 say you to this?

COSTARD  Sir, I confess the wench.

KING  Did you hear the proclamation?

COSTARD  I do confess much of the hearing it, but little of the marking of it.                    280

KING  It was proclaimed a year's imprisonment to be taken with a wench.

COSTARD  I was taken with none, sir; I was taken with a damsel.

KING  Well, it was proclaimed "damsel."                    285

COSTARD  This was no damsel neither, sir, she was a virgin.

KING  It is so varied° too, for it was proclaimed "virgin."

COSTARD  If it were, I deny her virginity. I was taken  290 with a maid.

KING  This maid will not serve your turn, sir.

COSTARD  This maid will serve my turn,° sir.

KING  Sir, I will pronounce your sentence: you shall fast a week with bran and water.                    295

COSTARD  I had rather pray a month with mutton and porridge.

KING
And Don Armado shall be your keeper.
My Lord Berowne, see him delivered o'er.
And go we, lords, to put in practice that                    300
Which each to other hath so strongly sworn.
                    [*Exeunt* KING, LONGAVILLE, *and* DUMAINE.]

BEROWNE
I'll lay° my head to any good man's hat,
These oaths and laws will prove an idle scorn.
Sirrah, come on.

COSTARD  I suffer for the truth, sir, for true it is I was  305 taken with Jaquenetta, and Jaquenetta is a true° girl. And therefore welcome the sour cup of prosperity! Affliction may one day smile again, and till then sit thee down, sorrow!                    *Exeunt.*

[Scene II. *The park.*]

*Enter* ARMADO *and* MOTH,° *his page.*

ARMADO  Boy, what sign is it when a man of great spirit grows melancholy?

MOTH  A great sign, sir, that he will look sad.

ARMADO  Why, sadness is one and the selfsame thing, dear imp.                    5

MOTH  No, no, O Lord, sir, no!

ARMADO  How canst thou part° sadness and melancholy, my tender juvenal?°

---

218 **welkin's vicegerent** deputy-ruler of heaven  224 **but so** not worth much  231–32 **black-oppressing humor** fluid in the body that causes melancholy  232 **physic** treatment  238 **ycleped** called  241 **snow-white pen** goose-quill  245 **curious-knotted** flower beds and paths in intricate patterns  248 **unlettered** illiterate  250 **vassal** underling  252 **hight** called  255 **continent canon** the decree restraining the members of the Academy  261 **pricks** spurs  262 **meed** reward  266 **weaker vessel** general phrase for womankind  268–69 **at . . . notice** at the slightest indication of thy concern

275 **sirrah** term of address used to an inferior  288 **varied** distinguished  293 **turn** Costard uses the word in a bawdy sense  302 **lay** bet  306 **true** honest  I.ii.s.d. **Moth** probably pronounced, and with the meaning of, *mote* or speck  7 **part** distinguish between  8 **juvenal** youth (it may also signify *Juvenal*, the Roman satirist, and allude to the nickname of Thomas Nashe, Elizabethan writer)

MOTH  By a familiar demonstration of the working, my tough signor.°  10

ARMADO  Why tough signor? Why tough signor?

MOTH  Why tender juvenal? Why tender juvenal?

ARMADO  I spoke it, tender juvenal, as a congruent epitheton° appertaining to thy young days, which we may nominate tender.  15

MOTH  And I, tough signor, as an appertinent title to your old time, which we may name tough.

ARMADO  Pretty and apt.

MOTH  How mean you, sir? I pretty, and my saying apt? Or I apt and my saying pretty?  20

ARMADO  Thou pretty, because little.

MOTH  Little pretty, because little. Wherefore apt?

ARMADO  And therefore apt because quick.

MOTH  Speak you this in my praise, master?

ARMADO  In thy condign° praise.  25

MOTH  I will praise an eel with the same praise.

ARMADO  What, that an eel is ingenious?

MOTH  That an eel is quick.

ARMADO  I do say thou art quick in answers. Thou heat'st my blood.  30

MOTH  I am answered, sir.

ARMADO  I love not to be crossed.

MOTH [Aside.]  He speaks the mere contrary—crosses° love not him.

ARMADO  I have promised to study three years with 35 the duke.

MOTH  You may do it in an hour, sir.

ARMADO  Impossible.

MOTH  How many is one thrice told?

ARMADO  I am ill at reck'ning—it fitteth the spirit of 40 a tapster.°

MOTH  You are a gentleman and a gamester, sir.

ARMADO  I confess both. They are both the varnish° of a complete man.

MOTH  Then I am sure you know how much the gross 45 sum of deuce-ace amounts to.

ARMADO  It doth amount to one more than two.

MOTH  Which the base vulgar do call three.

ARMADO  True.

MOTH  Why, sir, is this such a piece of study? Now 50 here is three studied ere ye'll thrice wink; and how easy it is to put "years" to the word "three," and study three years in two words, the dancing horse° will tell you.

ARMADO  A most fine figure.°  55

MOTH [Aside.]  To prove you a cipher.

ARMADO  I will hereupon confess I am in love, and as it is base for a soldier to love, so am I in love with a base wench. If drawing my sword against the humor° of affection would deliver me from the 60 reprobate thought of it, I would take desire prisoner and ransom him to any French courtier for a new-devised cursy.° I think scorn° to sigh: methinks I

should outswear° Cupid. Comfort me, boy. What great men have been in love?  65

MOTH  Hercules, master.

ARMADO  Most sweet Hercules! More authority, dear boy, name more; and, sweet my child, let them be men of good repute and carriage.

MOTH  Samson, master—he was a man of good carriage, 70 great carriage, for he carried the town gates on his back like a porter, and he was in love.

ARMADO  O well-knit Samson, strong-jointed Samson! I do excel thee in my rapier as much as thou didst me in carrying gates. I am in love too. Who was 75 Samson's love, my dear Moth?

MOTH  A woman, master.

ARMADO  Of what complexion?°

MOTH  Of all the four,° or the three, or the two, or one of the four.  80

ARMADO  Tell me precisely of what complexion.

MOTH  Of the sea-water green, sir.

ARMADO  Is that one of the four complexions?

MOTH  As I have read, sir, and the best of them too.

ARMADO  Green° indeed is the color of lovers. But to 85 have a love of that color, methinks Samson had small reason for it. He surely affected her for her wit.°

MOTH  It was so, sir, for she had a green wit.

ARMADO  My love is most immaculate white and red.

MOTH  Most maculate° thoughts, master, are masked 90 under such colors.

ARMADO  Define, define, well-educated infant.

MOTH  My father's wit, and my mother's tongue, assist me!

ARMADO  Sweet invocation of a child, most pretty 95 and pathetical.

MOTH

If she be made of white and red,
    Her faults will ne'er be known,
For blushing cheeks by faults are bred,
    And fears by pale white shown.  100
Then if she fear or be to blame,
    By this you shall not know,
For still her cheeks possess the same
    Which native° she doth owe.°

A dangerous rhyme, master, against the reason of 105 white and red.

ARMADO  Is there not a ballet,° boy, of the King and the Beggar?

MOTH  The world was very guilty of such a ballet some three ages since. But I think now 'tis not to be 110 found, or if it were, it would neither serve for the writing nor the tune.

ARMADO  I will have that subject newly writ o'er, that I may example my digression° by some mighty precedent. Boy, I do love that country girl that I 115 took in the park with the rational hind,° Costard. She deserves well.

MOTH [Aside.]  To be whipped—and yet a better love than my master.

---

10 **signor** with a pun on *senior*  13–14 **congruent epitheton** appropriate adjective  25 **condign** well-deserved  33 **crosses** coins (so named for the crosses engraved on them)  41 **tapster** bartender  43 **varnish** outward gloss  53 **dancing horse** a performing horse well known for beating out numbers  55 **figure** figure of speech  60 **humor** innate disposition  62–63 **new-devised cursy** novel mannerism  63 **think scorn** disdain

64 **outswear** forswear  78 **complexion** disposition  79 **all the four** the four humors or fluids of the body: blood, phlegm, bile, black bile  85 **Green** immature  87 **wit** mind  90 **maculate** spotted  104 **native** by nature; **owe** possess  107 **ballet** ballad  114 **digression** Armado means to say *transgression*  116 **rational hind** intelligent yokel

ARMADO   Sing, boy. My spirit grows heavy in love.   120
MOTH   And that's great marvel, loving a light wench.
ARMADO   I say, sing.
MOTH   Forbear till this company be past.

*Enter* [COSTARD *the*] *clown,* [DULL *the*] *constable, and*
[JAQUENETTA, *a*] *wench.*

DULL   Sir, the duke's pleasure is that you keep Costard
safe, and you must suffer him to take no delight nor   125
no penance,° but 'a° must fast three days a week. For
this damsel, I must keep her at the park—she is allowed
for the day-woman.° Fare you well.
ARMADO   I do betray myself with blushing. Maid!
JAQUENETTA   Man?   130
ARMADO   I will visit thee at the lodge.
JAQUENETTA   That's hereby.
ARMADO   I know where it is situate.
JAQUENETTA   Lord, how wise you are!
ARMADO   I will tell thee wonders.   135
JAQUENETTA   With that face?
ARMADO   I love thee.
JAQUENETTA   So I heard you say.
ARMADO   And so farewell.
JAQUENETTA   Fair weather after you!   140
DULL   Come, Jaquenetta, away!
                *Exeunt* [DULL *and* JAQUENETTA].
ARMADO   Villain, thou shalt fast for thy offenses ere
thou be pardoned.
COSTARD   Well, sir, I hope when I do it I shall do it
on a full stomach.°   145
ARMADO   Thou shalt be heavily punished.
COSTARD   I am more bound to you than your fellows,°
for they are but lightly rewarded.
ARMADO   Take away this villain. Shut him up.
MOTH   Come, you transgressing slave, away!   150
COSTARD   Let me not be pent up, sir. I will fast, being
loose.
MOTH   No, sir, that were fast and loose.° Thou shalt
to prison.
COSTARD   Well, if ever I do see the merry days of   155
desolation that I have seen, some shall see.
MOTH   What shall some see?
COSTARD   Nay, nothing, Master Moth, but what they
look upon. It is not for prisoners to be too silent in
their words,° and therefore I will say nothing. I thank   160
God I have as little patience as another man, and
therefore I can be quiet.          *Exit* [*with* MOTH].
ARMADO   I do affect° the very ground (which is base)
where her shoe (which is baser) guided by her foot
(which is basest) doth tread. I shall be forsworn   165
(which is a great argument of falsehood) if I love.
And how can that be true love which is falsely attempted? Love is a familiar;° Love is a devil. There
is no evil angel but Love. Yet was Samson so tempted,
and he had an excellent strength; yet was Solomon so   170
seduced, and he had a very good wit. Cupid's butt-
shaft° is too hard for Hercules' club, and therefore too

much odds for a Spaniard's rapier. The first and
second cause° will not serve my turn; the passado° he
respects not, the due lo° he regards not. His disgrace   175
is to be called boy, but his glory is to subdue men.
Adieu, valor; rust, rapier; be still, drum; for your
manager is in love; yea, he loveth. Assist me some
extemporal god of rhyme,° for I am sure I shall turn
sonnet.° Devise, wit; write, pen; for I am for whole   180
volumes in folio.          *Exit.*

# [ ACT II ]

### [Scene I. *The park.*]

*Enter the* PRINCESS *of France, with three attending ladies*
[MARIA, KATHARINE, ROSALINE] *and three* LORDS,
[*one named* BOYET].

BOYET
Now, madam, summon up your dearest spirits.°
Consider who the king your father sends,
To whom he sends, and what's his embassy:
Yourself, held precious in the world's esteem,
To parley with the sole inheritor°                         5
Of all perfections that a man may owe,°
Matchless Navarre; the plea of no less weight
Than Aquitaine, a dowry for a queen.
Be now as prodigal of all dear grace
As Nature was in making graces dear°                      10
When she did starve the general world beside,
And prodigally gave them all to you.
PRINCESS
Good Lord Boyet, my beauty, though but mean,
Needs not the painted flourish° of your praise.
Beauty is bought by judgment of the eye,                  15
Not utt'red by base sale of chapmen's tongues.°
I am less proud to hear you tell my worth
Than you much willing to be counted wise
In spending your wit in the praise of mine.
But now to task the tasker:° good Boyet,                  20
You are not ignorant all-telling fame
Doth noise abroad Navarre hath made a vow,
Till painful study shall outwear three years,
No woman may approach his silent court.
Therefore to's seemeth it a needful course,               25
Before we enter his forbidden gates,
To know his pleasure; and in that behalf,
Bold of your worthiness,° we single you
As our best-moving° fair solicitor.
Tell him the daughter of the King of France,             30
On serious business, craving quick dispatch,

173–74 **first . . . cause** referring to rules governing the conduct
of a duel  174 **passado** forward thrust  175 **duello** correct
way of dueling  179 **extemporal . . . rhyme** god of rhymes
written on the spur of the moment  179–80 **turn sonnet**
compose a sonnet
**II.i.1 dearest spirits** best intelligence  **5 inheritor** possessor
**6 owe** own  **10 graces dear** beauty scarce  **14 painted
flourish** elaborate ornament  **16 utt'red . . . tongues** put up
for sale by huckster  **20 task the tasker** set a task to the
one who sets tasks  **28 Bold . . . worthiness** confident of
your worth  **29 best-moving** most persuasive

126 **penance** perhaps Dull means to say *pleasance,* meaning
pleasure; **'a** he  **127–28 allowed . . . day-woman** admitted
as the dairy maid  **145 on . . . stomach** bravely  **147
fellows** servants  **153 fast and loose** not playing fairly
**160 words** probably with pun on *wards* = cells  **163 affect**
love  **168 familiar** attendant spirit  **171–72 butt-shaft** unbarbed arrow

Importunes personal conference with his grace.
Haste, signify so much while we attend
Like humble-visaged suitors his high will.

BOYET
Proud of employment, willingly I go.    *Exit* BOYET. 35

PRINCESS
All pride is willing pride, and yours is so.
Who are the votaries,° my loving lords,
That are vow-fellows with this virtuous duke?

LORD
Longaville is one.

PRINCESS                    Know you the man?

MARIA
I know him, madam. At a marriage feast          40
Between Lord Perigort and the beauteous heir
Of Jacques Falconbridge solemnizèd
In Normandy saw I this Longaville.
A man of sovereign parts° he is esteemed,
Well fitted in arts, glorious in arms.          45
Nothing becomes him ill that he would well.°
The only soil of his fair virtue's gloss—
If virtue's gloss will stain with any soil—
Is a sharp wit matched with too blunt a will,
Whose edge hath power to cut, whose will still wills  50
It should none spare that come within his power.

PRINCESS
Some merry mocking lord, belike—is't so?

MARIA
They say so most that most his humors know.

PRINCESS
Such short-lived wits do wither as they grow.
Who are the rest?                               55

KATHARINE
The young Dumaine, a well-accomplished youth,
Of all that virtue love for virtue loved;
Most power to do most harm, least knowing ill,
For he hath wit to make an ill shape good,
And shape to win grace though he had no wit.    60
I saw him at the Duke Alençon's once;
And much too little° of that good I saw
Is my report to° his great worthiness.

ROSALINE
Another of these students at that time
Was there with him, if I have heard a truth.    65
Berowne they call him; but a merrier man,
Within the limit of becoming mirth,
I never spent an hour's talk withal.°
His eye begets occasion° for his wit;
For every object that the one doth catch        70
The other turns to a mirth-moving jest,
Which his fair tongue (conceit's expositor°)
Delivers in such apt and gracious words,
That agèd ears play truant at his tales,
And younger hearings are quite ravishèd,        75
So sweet and voluble is his discourse.

PRINCESS
God bless my ladies! Are they all in love,

That every one her own hath garnishèd
With such bedecking ornaments of praise?

LORD
Here comes Boyet.    *Enter* BOYET.

PRINCESS                    Now, what admittance,° lord?  80

BOYET
Navarre had notice of your fair approach;
And he and his competitors° in oath
Were all addressed° to meet you, gentle lady,
Before I came. Marry, thus much I have learnt;
He rather means to lodge you in the field,       85
Like one that comes here to besiege his court,
Than seek a dispensation for his oath
To let you enter his unpeopled house.

[*The* LADIES *mask.*]

*Enter* [KING *of*] *Navarre,* LONGAVILLE, DUMAINE,
*and* BEROWNE, [*with* ATTENDANTS].

Here comes Navarre.

KING    Fair princess, welcome to the court of Navarre.  90

PRINCESS    "Fair" I give you back again; and "welcome" I have not yet. The roof of this court is too
high to be yours, and welcome to the wide fields too
base to be mine.

KING
You shall be welcome, madam, to my court.        95

PRINCESS
I will be welcome, then. Conduct me thither.

KING
Hear me, dear lady—I have sworn an oath.

PRINCESS
Our Lady help my lord! He'll be forsworn.

KING
Not for the world, fair madam, by my will.

PRINCESS
Why, will shall break it, will, and nothing else.  100

KING
Your ladyship is ignorant what it is.

PRINCESS
Were my lord so, his ignorance were wise,
Where now his knowledge must prove ignorance.
I hear your grace hath sworn out housekeeping.°
'Tis deadly sin to keep that oath, my lord,       105
And sin to break it.
But pardon me, I am too sudden-bold;
To teach a teacher ill beseemeth me.
Vouchsafe to read the purpose of my coming,
And suddenly resolve me° in my suit.             110

[*Gives a paper.*]

KING
Madam, I will, if suddenly I may.

PRINCESS
You will the sooner that I were away,
For you'll prove perjured if you make me stay.

BEROWNE
Did not I dance with you in Brabant once?

ROSALINE
Did not I dance with you in Brabant once?        115

---

37 **votaries** those who have sworn a vow   44 **sovereign
parts** lordly qualities   46 **Nothing . . . well** Nothing that
he values is unbecoming to him   62 **much too little** far short
63 **to** compared to   68 **withal** with   69 **begets occasion**
finds opportunity   72 **conceit's expositor** one who explains
an ingenious notion

80 **admittance** permission to enter   82 **competitors** partners
83 **addressed** ready   104 **sworn out housekeeping** sworn
not to keep house or offer hospitality   110 **suddenly resolve
me** quickly give me a decision

BEROWNE
I know you did.
ROSALINE          How needless was it then
To ask the question!
BEROWNE                    You must not be so quick.
ROSALINE
'Tis long° of you that spur me with such questions.
BEROWNE
Your wit's too hot, it speeds too fast, 'twill tire.
ROSALINE
Not till it leave the rider in the mire.          120
BEROWNE
What time o' day?
ROSALINE
The hour that fools should ask.
BEROWNE
Now fair befall° your mask!
ROSALINE
Fair fall the face it covers!
BEROWNE
And send you many lovers!          125
ROSALINE
Amen, so you be none.
BEROWNE
Nay, then will I be gone.
KING
Madam, your father here doth intimate°
The payment of a hundred thousand crowns,
Being but the one half of an entire sum          130
Disbursèd by my father in his wars.
But say that he, or we (as neither have),
Received that sum, yet there remains unpaid
A hundred thousand more, in surety of the
     which,
One part of Aquitaine is bound to us,          135
Although not valued to the money's worth.
If then the king your father will restore
But that one half which is unsatisfied,
We will give up our right in Aquitaine,
And hold fair friendship with his majesty.          140
But that, it seems, he little purposeth,
For here he doth demand to have repaid
A hundred thousand crowns; and not demands,
On payment of a hundred thousand crowns,
To have his title live in Aquitaine;          145
Which we much rather had depart withal,°
And have the money by our father lent,
Than Aquitaine, so gelded° as it is.
Dear princess, were not his requests so far
From reason's yielding, your fair self should make          150
A yielding 'gainst some reason in my breast,
And go well satisfied to France again.
PRINCESS
You do the king my father too much wrong,
And wrong the reputation of your name,
In so unseeming° to confess receipt          155
Of that which hath so faithfully been paid.
KING
I do protest I never heard of it;

And if you prove it, I'll repay it back
Or yield up Aquitaine.
PRINCESS          We arrest your word.°
Boyet, you can produce acquittances°          160
For such a sum from special officers
Of Charles his father.
KING                    Satisfy me so.
BOYET
So please your grace, the packet° is not come
Where that and other specialties° are bound.
Tomorrow you shall have a sight of them.          165
KING
It shall suffice me—at which interview
All liberal reason I will yield unto.
Meantime, receive such welcome at my hand
As honor (without breach of honor) may
Make tender of° to thy true worthiness.          170
You may not come, fair princess, within my gates;
But here without you shall be so received
As you shall deem yourself lodged in my heart,
Though so denied fair harbor in my house.
Your own good thoughts excuse me, and farewell.          175
Tomorrow shall we visit you again.
PRINCESS
Sweet health and fair desires consort° your grace.
KING
Thy own wish wish I thee in every place.
                    Exit [KING and his TRAIN].
BEROWNE  Lady, I will commend you to mine own
heart.          180
ROSALINE  Pray you, do my commendations, I would
be glad to see it
BEROWNE  I would you heard it groan.
ROSALINE  Is the fool sick?
BEROWNE  Sick at the heart.          185
ROSALINE
Alack, let it blood!°
BEROWNE
Would that do it good?
ROSALINE
My physic says ay.
BEROWNE
Will you prick't with your eye?
ROSALINE
No point,° with my knife.          190
BEROWNE
Now, God save thy life!
ROSALINE
And yours from long living!
BEROWNE
I cannot stay thanksgiving.°          Exit.

Enter DUMAINE.

DUMAINE
Sir, I pray you a word. What lady is that same?
BOYET
The heir of Alençon, Katharine her name.          195

118 long because  123 fair befall good luck to  128 intimate
make known  146 depart withal give up  148 gelded cut up
155 unseeming not appearing

159 arrest your word take your word as security  160
acquittances receipts  163 packet package  164 specialties
particular legal documents  170 Make tender of offer  177
consort accompany  186 let it blood bleed him  190 No
point not at all  193 stay thanksgiving stay long enough
to give you proper thanks (for your unkind remark)

DUMAINE
A gallant lady. Monsieur, fare you well.          *Exit.*

[*Enter* LONGAVILLE.]

LONGAVILLE
I beseech you a word. What is she in the white?

BOYET
A woman sometimes, and° you saw her in the light.

LONGAVILLE
Perchance light in the light.° I desire her name.

BOYET
She hath but one for herself. To desire that were a shame.  200

LONGAVILLE
Pray you, sir, whose daughter?

BOYET
Her mother's, I have heard.

LONGAVILLE
God's blessing on your beard!

BOYET
Good sir, be not offended.
She is an heir of Falconbridge.                    205

LONGAVILLE
Nay, my choler° is ended.
She is a most sweet lady.

BOYET
Not unlike, sir; that may be.     *Exit* LONGAVILLE.

*Enter* BEROWNE.

BEROWNE
What's her name in the cap?

BOYET
Rosaline, by good hap.                             210

BEROWNE
Is she wedded or no?

BOYET
To her will, sir, or so.°

BEROWNE
O, you are welcome, sir! Adieu.

BOYET
Farewell to me, sir, and welcome to you.
                                *Exit* BEROWNE.

MARIA
That last is Berowne, the merry madcap lord.      215
Not a word with him but a jest.

BOYET                     And every jest but a word.

PRINCESS
It was well done of you to take him at his word.

BOYET
I was as willing to grapple as he was to board.

KATHARINE
Two hot sheeps, marry!

BOYET                     And wherefore not ships?
No sheep, sweet lamb, unless we feed on your lips.  220

KATHARINE
You sheep, and I pasture. Shall that finish the jest?

BOYET
So you grant pasture for me.    [*Offers to kiss her.*]

KATHARINE                     Not so, gentle beast.
My lips are no common,° though several° they be.

BOYET
Belonging to whom?

KATHARINE                  To my fortunes and me.

PRINCESS
Good wits will be jangling; but, gentles, agree.   225
This civil war of wits were much better used
On Navarre and his book-men, for here 'tis abused.

BOYET
If my observation (which very seldom lies)
By the heart's still rhetoric disclosèd with eyes
Deceive me not now, Navarre is infected.          230

PRINCESS   With what?

BOYET
With that which we lovers entitle "affected."°

PRINCESS   Your reason?

BOYET
Why, all his behaviors° did make their retire
To the court° of his eye, peeping thorough desire.  235
His heart, like an agate° with your print impressed,°
Proud with his form, in his eye pride expressed.
His tongue, all impatient to speak and not see,°
Did stumble with haste in his eyesight to be;
All senses to that sense did make their repair,    240
To feel only looking on fairest of fair.°
Methought all his senses were locked in his eye,
As jewels in crystal for some prince to buy;
Who, tend'ring° their own worth from where they
     were glassed,°
Did point° you to buy them, along as you passed.   245
His face's own margent did quote such amazes
That all eyes saw his eyes enchanted with gazes.°
I'll give you Aquitaine, and all that is his,
And° you give him for my sake but one loving kiss.

PRINCESS
Come to our pavilion. Boyet is disposed.           250

BOYET
But to speak that in words which his eye hath disclosed.
I only have made a mouth of his eye
By adding a tongue which I know will not lie.

ROSALINE
Thou art an old love-monger, and speakest skillfully.

MARIA
He is Cupid's grandfather, and learns news of him.  255

KATHARINE
Then was Venus like her mother, for her father is but
     grim.

BOYET
Do you hear, my mad wenches?

ROSALINE                          No.

BOYET                     What then? Do you see?

ROSALINE
Ay, our way to be gone.

BOYET                     You are too hard for me.
                                *Exeunt omnes.*°

232 **affected** impassioned  234 **behaviors** expression of his feelings  235 **court** watch-post  236 **agate** stone used for the engraving of images; **impressed** imprinted  238 **His . . . see** his tongue, vexed at having the power of speaking without having the power of seeing  241 **To . . . fair** sight is translated into feeling in regarding her  244 **tend'ring** offering; **glassed** enclosed in glass  245 **point** urge  246–47 **His face's . . . gazes** The amazement in Navarre's face drew attention, like comments in a book's margin, to the love in his eyes  249 **And** if  258 **s.d. omnes** all (Latin)

198 **and** if  199 **light . . . light** wanton if rightly perceived  206 **choler** wrath  212 **or so** something like that  223 **no common** not like pasture held in common; **several** two (the word also, in this context, signifies "private property")

# [ACT III]

## [Scene I. *The park.*]

*Enter* [ARMADO *the*] *braggart and* [MOTH,] *his boy.*

ARMADO  Warble, child, make passionate my sense of hearing.

MOTH  [*Sings.*]  Concolinel.°

ARMADO  Sweet air! Go, tenderness of years,° take this key, give enlargement° to the swain, bring him 5 festinately° hither. I must employ him in a letter to my love.

MOTH  Master, will you win your love with a French brawl?°

ARMADO  How meanest thou? Brawling in French? 10

MOTH  No, my complete master; but to jig off a tune at the tongue's end, canary to it° with your feet, humor it with turning up your eyelids, sigh a note and sing a note, sometime through the throat as if you swallowed love with singing love, sometime through 15 the nose as if you snuffed up love by smelling love, with your hat penthouselike o'er the shop of your eyes, with your arms crossed° on your thin-belly doublet° like a rabbit on a spit, or your hands in your pocket like a man after the old painting; and keep 20 not too long in one tune, but a snip° and away. These are complements,° these are humors, these betray nice wenches (that would be betrayed without these), and make them men of note—do you note me?—that most are affected to° these. 25

ARMADO  How hast thou purchased this experience?

MOTH  By my penny of observation.

ARMADO  But O—but O—

MOTH  "The hobbyhorse is forgot."°

ARMADO  Call'st thou my love "hobbyhorse"? 30

MOTH  No, master. The hobbyhorse is but a colt, and your love perhaps a hackney.° But have you forgot your love?

ARMADO  Almost I had.

MOTH  Negligent student, learn her by heart. 35

ARMADO  By heart, and in heart, boy.

MOTH  And out of heart, master. All those three I will prove.

ARMADO  What wilt thou prove?

MOTH  A man, if I live; and this, by, in, and without, 40 upon the instant. By heart you love her, because your heart cannot come by her; in heart you love her, because your heart is in love with her; and out of heart you love her, being out of heart that you cannot enjoy her. 45

ARMADO  I am all these three.

MOTH  [*Aside.*]  And three times as much more, and yet nothing at all.

ARMADO  Fetch hither the swain. He must carry me a letter. 50

MOTH  A message well sympathized°—a horse to be ambassador for an ass.

ARMADO  Ha, ha, what sayest thou?

MOTH  Marry, sir, you must send the ass upon the horse, for he is very slow-gaited. But I go. 55

ARMADO  The way is but short. Away!

MOTH  As swift as lead, sir.

ARMADO
The meaning, pretty ingenious?
Is not lead a metal heavy, dull, and slow?

MOTH
Minime,° honest master; or rather, master, no. 60

ARMADO
I say, lead is slow.

MOTH               You are too swift, sir, to say so.
Is that lead slow which is fired from a gun?

ARMADO
Sweet smoke of rhetoric!
He reputes me a cannon; and the bullet, that's he:
I shoot thee at the swain.

MOTH               Thump, then, and I flee. 65
                                        [*Exit.*]

ARMADO
A most acute juvenal,° voluble and free of grace!
By thy favor, sweet welkin,° I must sigh in thy face:
Most rude melancholy, valor gives thee place.°
My herald is returned.

*Enter* [MOTH *the*] *page and* [COSTARD *the*] *clown.*

MOTH
A wonder, master! Here's a costard° broken in a shin. 70

ARMADO
Some enigma, some riddle. Come, thy l'envoy°—
    begin.

COSTARD  No egma, no riddle, no l'envoy; no salve° in the mail,° sir. O, sir, plantain,° a plain plantain. No l'envoy, no l'envoy, no salve, sir, but a plantain.

ARMADO  By virtue, thou enforcest laughter; thy 75 silly thought, my spleen;° the heaving of my lungs provokes me to ridiculous smiling. O, pardon me, my stars! Doth the inconsiderate° take salve for l'envoy, and the word l'envoy for a salve?

MOTH
Do the wise think them other? Is not l'envoy a salve? 80

ARMADO
No, page; it is an epilogue, or discourse to make plain
Some obscure precedence° that hath tofore been sain.°
I will example it:
        The fox, the ape, and the humblebee
        Were still at odds, being but three. 85
There's the moral. Now the l'envoy.

MOTH  I will add the l'envoy. Say the moral again.

---

III.i.3 **Concolinel** perhaps the name of a song  **4 tenderness of years** affected talk for *young fellow*  **5 enlargement** freedom  **6 festinately** quickly  **8–9 French brawl** French dance  **12 canary to it** dance in a lively way  **18 arms crossed** a sign of melancholy  **18–19 thin-belly doublet** garment unpadded in the lower part (across your thin belly)  **21 snip** snatch  **22 complements** accompaniments  **25 affected to** taken with  **29 The . . . forgot** perhaps a phrase from an old song  **31–32 hobbyhorse . . . colt . . . hackney** slang words for *whore*

**51 well sympathized** in proper accord  **60 Minime** by no means (Latin)  **66 juvenal** in two senses: young fellow, satirist  **67 welkin** heaven  **68 gives thee place** gives place to you  **70 costard** apple, or head  **71 l'envoy** words ending a composition by way of leave-taking  **72 salve** with a pun on *salve*, the Latin word for salute  **73 mail** bag, container; **plantain** tree whose leaves were used for healing  **76 spleen** mirth  **78 inconsiderate** unthinking  **82 precedence** preceding statement; **tofore been sain** been said before

ARMADO
The fox, the ape, and the humblebee
Were still at odds, being but three.

MOTH
Until the goose came out of door,                                90
And stayed the odds by adding four.°
Now will I begin your moral, and do you follow with
my l'envoy.
The fox, the ape, and the humblebee
Were still at odds, being but three.                             95

ARMADO
Until the goose came out of door,
Staying the odds by adding four.

MOTH    A good l'envoy, ending in the goose. Would
you desire more?

COSTARD
The boy hath sold him a bargain,° a goose—that's flat.   100
Sir, your pennyworth is good, and° your goose be fat.
To sell a bargain well is as cunning as fast and loose.°
Let me see: a fat l'envoy—ay, that's a fat goose.

ARMADO
Come hither, come hither. How did this argument
begin?

MOTH
By saying that a costard was broken in a shin.          105
Then called you for the l'envoy.

COSTARD
True, and I for a plantain; thus came your argument in;
Then the boy's fat l'envoy, the goose that you bought,
And he ended the market.

ARMADO    But tell me, how was there a costard broken   110
in a shin?

MOTH    I will tell you sensibly.°

COSTARD    Thou hast no feeling of it, Moth. I will
speak that l'envoy:
I, Costard, running out, that was safely within,        115
Fell over the threshold and broke my shin.

ARMADO    We will talk no more of this matter.

COSTARD    Till there be more matter° in the shin.

ARMADO    Sirrah Costard, I will enfranchise° thee.

COSTARD    O, marry me to one Frances! I smell some    120
l'envoy, some goose, in this.

ARMADO    By my sweet soul, I mean setting thee at
liberty, enfreedoming thy person. Thou wert immured,
restrained, captivated, bound.

COSTARD    True, true, and now you will be my        125
purgation and let me loose.

ARMADO    I give thee thy liberty, set thee from
durance, and in lieu thereof, impose on thee nothing
but this. [Gives a letter.] Bear this significant° to the
country maid Jaquenetta. [Gives a coin.] There is      130
remuneration; for the best ward° of mine honor is
rewarding my dependents. Moth, follow.

MOTH
Like the sequel, I. Signior Costard, adieu.
                    Exit [ARMADO, followed by MOTH].

COSTARD
My sweet ounce of man's flesh, my incony° Jew!

—Now will I look to his remuneration. Remunera-   135
tion? O that's the Latin word for three farthings. Three
farthings—remuneration. "What's the price of this
inkle?"° "One penny." "No, I'll give you a remuneration." Why, it carries it! Remuneration! Why, it
is a fairer name than French crown.° I will never buy   140
and sell out of this word.

Enter BEROWNE.

BEROWNE    O my good knave Costard, exceedingly
well met.

COSTARD    Pray you, sir, how much carnation°
ribbon may a man buy for a remuneration?              145

BEROWNE    O, what is a remuneration?

COSTARD    Marry, sir, halfpenny farthing.

BEROWNE    O, why then, three-farthing-worth of silk.

COSTARD    I thank your worship. God be wi' you!

BEROWNE
O stay, slave, I must employ thee.                      150
As thou wilt win my favor, good my knave,
Do one thing for me that I shall entreat.

COSTARD    When would you have it done, sir?

BEROWNE    O, this afternoon.

COSTARD    Well, I will do it, sir. Fare you well.     155

BEROWNE    O, thou knowest not what it is.

COSTARD    I shall know, sir, when I have done it.

BEROWNE    Why, villain, thou must know first.

COSTARD    I will come to your worship tomorrow
morning.                                                160

BEROWNE
It must be done this afternoon. Hark, slave, it is but this:
The princess comes to hunt here in the park,
And in her train there is a gentle lady;
When tongues speak sweetly, then they name her name,
And Rosaline they call her. Ask for her,                165
And to her white hand see thou do commend
This sealed-up counsel. [Gives him a letter and a shilling.]
    There's thy guerdon.° Go.

COSTARD    Gardon, O sweet gardon! Better than
remuneration—a 'levenpence farthing better. Most
sweet gardon! I will do it, sir, in print.° Gardon!     170
Remuneration!                                    Exit.

BEROWNE
O, and I, forsooth, in love!
I, that have been love's whip,
A very beadle° to a humorous sigh,
A critic, nay, a night-watch constable,                 175
A domineering pedant o'er the boy,
Than whom no mortal so magnificent!
This wimpled,° whining, purblind,° wayward boy,
This senior-junior, giant-dwarf, Dan° Cupid,
Regent of love rhymes, lord of folded arms,            180
Th' anointed sovereign of sighs and groans,
Liege° of all loiterers and malcontents,
Dread prince of plackets,° king of codpieces,°

91 stayed . . . four turned them into evens by adding a fourth
100 sold . . . bargain made a fool of him  101 and if  102 fast
and loose cheating  112 sensibly with feeling  118 matter
pus  119 enfranchise set free  129 significant letter  131
ward protection  134 incony darling

138 inkle band of linen  140 French crown in two senses:
a coin, and the baldness caused by syphilis, the so-called French
disease  144 carnation flesh-colored  167 guerdon reward
170 in print most carefully  174 beadle parish constable
178 wimpled covered with a muffler; purblind completely
blind  179 Dan don, a derivation of dominus = lord  182
Liege lord  183 plackets slits in petticoats (vulgar term for
women); codpieces cloth covering the opening in men's
breeches

Sole imperator and great general
Of trotting paritors°—O my little heart!—                    185
And I to be a corporal of his field,°
And wear his colors like a tumbler's° hoop!
What? I love? I sue? I seek a wife?
A woman that is like a German clock,
Still a-repairing, ever out of frame,°                       190
And never going aright, being a watch,
But being watched that it may still go right!
Nay, to be perjured, which is worst of all;
And, among three, to love the worst of all,
A whitely° wanton with a velvet brow,                        195
With two pitch balls stuck in her face for eyes.
Ay, and, by heaven, one that will do the deed,°
Though Argus° were her eunuch and her guard!
And I to sigh for her, to watch for her,
To pray for her! Go to, it is a plague                       200
That Cupid will impose for my neglect
Of his almighty dreadful little might.
Well, I will love, write, sigh, pray, sue, groan.
Some men must love my lady, and some Joan. [*Exit.*]

# [ A C T   I V ]

## [Scene I. *The park.*]

*Enter the* PRINCESS, *a* FORESTER, *her* LADIES, *and her*
LORDS.

PRINCESS
Was that the king, that spurred his horse so hard
Against the steep uprising of the hill?
FORESTER
I know not, but I think it was not he.
PRINCESS
Whoe'er 'a° was, 'a showed a mounting mind.°
Well, lords, today we shall have our dispatch;            5
On Saturday we will return to France.
Then, forester, my friend, where is the bush
That we must stand and play the murderer in?
FORESTER
Hereby, upon the edge of yonder coppice,°
A stand where you may make the fairest shoot.            10
PRINCESS
I thank my beauty, I am fair that shoot,
And thereupon thou speak'st the fairest shoot.
FORESTER
Pardon me, madam, for I meant not so.
PRINCESS
What, what? First praise me, and again say no?

O short-lived pride! Not fair? Alack for woe!            15
FORESTER
Yes, madam, fair.
PRINCESS                   Nay, never paint° me now!
Where fair is not, praise cannot mend the brow.°
Here, good my glass,° take this for telling true—

[*Gives him money.*]

Fair payment for foul words is more than due.
FORESTER
Nothing but fair is that which you inherit.              20
PRINCESS
See, see—my beauty will be saved by merit!°
O heresy in fair,° fit for these days!
A giving hand, though foul, shall have fair praise.
But come, the bow! Now mercy goes to kill,°
And shooting well is then accounted ill.                 25
Thus will I save my credit in the shoot:
Not wounding, pity would not let me do't;
If wounding, then it was to show my skill,
That more for praise than purpose meant to kill.
And out of question so it is sometimes,                  30
Glory° grows guilty of detested crimes,
When, for fame's sake, for praise, an outward part,
We bend to that the working of the heart;
As I for praise alone now seek to spill
The poor deer's blood that my heart means no ill.        35
BOYET
Do not curst° wives hold that self-sovereignty
Only for praise' sake, when they strive to be
Lords o'er their lords?
PRINCESS
Only for praise, and praise we may afford
To any lady that subdues a lord.                         40

*Enter* [COSTARD *the*] *clown.*

BOYET
Here comes a member of the commonwealth.°
COSTARD  God dig-you-den° all! Pray you, which is
the head lady?
PRINCESS  Thou shalt know her, fellow, by the rest
that have no heads.                                      45
COSTARD  Which is the greatest lady, the highest?
PRINCESS  The thickest and the tallest.
COSTARD  The thickest and the tallest—it is so. Truth
is truth.
And° your waist, mistress, were as slender as my wit,    50
One o' these maids' girdles for your waist should be fit.
Are not you the chief woman? You are the thickest
here.
PRINCESS  What's your will, sir? What's your will?
COSTARD  I have a letter from Monsieur Berowne to
one Lady Rosaline.                                       55

---

185 **paritors** officers of the Ecclesiastical Court who serve summonses for certain, often sexual, offenses 186 **corporal . . . field** aide to a general 187 **tumbler's** acrobat's 190 **frame** order 195 **whitely** pale 197 **do the deed** perform the act of coition 198 **Argus** ancient mythological being with a hundred eyes
IV.i.4 **'a** he; **mounting mind** lofty spirit (with pun on *mountain*) 9 **coppice** undergrowth of small trees

16 **paint** flatter 17 **mend the brow** make the brow more beautiful 18 **good my glass** my fine mirror 21 **saved by merit** saved by what I truly deserve 22 **heresy in fair** heresy with respect to beauty 24 **mercy . . . kill** the merciful huntsman goes forth to kill—instead of leaving the prey wounded—but such killing is not well regarded 31 **Glory** i.e., ambition for glory 36 **curst** peevish 41 **member . . . commonwealth** one of our group 42 **God dig-you-den** God give you good evening 50 **And** if

**PRINCESS**
O thy letter, thy letter! He's a good friend of mine.
Stand aside, good bearer. Boyet, you can carve°—
Break up this capon.°

**BOYET**                    I am bound to serve.
This letter is mistook; it importeth° none here.
It is writ to Jaquenetta.

**PRINCESS**                    We will read it, I swear.    60
Break the neck° of the wax, and every one give ear.

**BOYET** (*Reads.*)   "By heaven, that thou art fair is most
infallible; true that thou art beauteous; truth itself
that thou art lovely. More fairer than fair, beautiful
than beauteous, truer than truth itself, have com-   65
miseration on thy heroical vassal. The magnanimous
and most illustrate° King Cophetua set eye upon the
pernicious and indubitate° beggar Zenelophon,° and
he it was that might rightly say veni, vidi, vici; which
to annothanize° in the vulgar (O base and obscure   70
vulgar!) videlicet,° he came, saw, and overcame. He
came, one; saw, two; overcame, three. Who came?
The king. Why did he come? To see. Why did he
see? To overcome. To whom came he? To the beggar.
What saw he? The beggar. Who overcame he? The   75
beggar. The conclusion is victory. On whose side?
The king's. The captive is enriched. On whose side?
The beggar's. The catastrophe is a nuptial. On whose
side? The king's. No—on both in one, or one in both.
I am the king, for so stands the comparison, thou the   80
beggar, for so witnesseth thy lowliness. Shall I command thy love? I may. Shall I enforce thy love? I
could. Shall I entreat thy love? I will. What shalt thou
exchange for rags? Robes. For tittles?° Titles. For
thyself? Me. Thus, expecting thy reply, I profane my   85
lips on thy foot, my eyes on thy picture, and my
heart on thy every part.
                    Thine in the dearest design of industry,°
                         *Don Adriano de Armado.*

Thus dost thou hear the Nemean lion° roar   90
   'Gainst thee, thou lamb, that standest as his prey.
Submissive fall his princely feet before,
   And he from forage° will incline to play.
But if thou strive, poor soul, what art thou then?
Food for his rage, repasture° for his den."   95

**PRINCESS**
What plume of feathers is he that indited° this letter?
What vane?° What weathercock?° Did you ever hear
   better?

**BOYET**
I am much deceived but I remember the style.

**PRINCESS**
Else your memory is bad, going o'er it erewhile.

**BOYET**
This Armado is a Spaniard that keeps here in court;   100

A phantasime,° a Monarcho,° and one that makes sport
To the prince and his book-mates.

**PRINCESS**                    Thou fellow, a word.
Who gave thee this letter?

**COSTARD**                    I told you—my lord.

**PRINCESS**
To whom shouldst thou give it?

**COSTARD**                    From my lord to my lady.

**PRINCESS**
From which lord to which lady?   105

**COSTARD**
From my Lord Berowne, a good master of mine,
To a lady of France that he called Rosaline.

**PRINCESS**
Thou hast mistaken° his letter. Come, lords, away.
Here, sweet, put up this; 'twill be thine another day.
         [*Exeunt* PRINCESS *and* TRAIN. BOYET *remains.*]

**BOYET**
Who is the suitor?° Who is the suitor?

**ROSALINE**                    Shall I teach you to know?   110

**BOYET**
Ay, my continent° of beauty.

**ROSALINE**                    Why, she that bears the bow.
Finely put off!°

**BOYET**
My lady goes to kill horns, but, if thou marry,
Hang me by the neck if horns that year miscarry.°
Finely put on!°   115

**ROSALINE**
Well then, I am the shooter.

**BOYET**                    And who is your deer?

**ROSALINE**
If we choose by the horns, yourself. Come not near.
Finely put on indeed!

**MARIA**
You still wrangle with her, Boyet, and she strikes at
   the brow.°

**BOYET**
But she herself is hit lower. Have I hit her now?   120

**ROSALINE**   Shall I come upon thee with an old saying
that was a man when King Pepin of France was a little
boy, as touching the hit it?°

**BOYET**   So I may answer thee with one as old, that
was a woman when Queen Guinever of Britain was a   125
little wench, as touching the hit it.

**ROSALINE**   "Thou canst not hit it, hit it, hit it,
         Thou canst not hit it, my good man.

**BOYET**       "And° I cannot, cannot, cannot,
         And I cannot, another can."   130
                    *Exit* [ROSALINE *with* KATHARINE].

**COSTARD**
By my troth, most pleasant, how both did fit it!

**MARIA**
A mark marvelous well shot, for they both did hit it.

---

**57 carve** with pun on the sense "flirt"  **58 Break . . .
capon** (1) Carve this chicken (2) Open this love-letter  **59
importeth** concerns  **61 Break the neck** still referring to the
capon  **67 illustrate** illustrious  **68 indubitate** undoubted;
**Zenelophon** character in the ballad of King Cophetua and the
Beggar  **70 annothanize** anatomize or a mock-Latin word to
mean "annotate"  **71 videlicet** namely (Latin)  **84 tittles**
small jottings in ink  **88 industry** faithful service  **90 Nemean
lion** lion killed by Hercules  **93 from forage** turning away
from feeding  **95 repasture** food  **96 indited** wrote  **97 vane**
weather vane; **weathercock** ostentatious thing

**101 phantasime** person of wild imaginings; **Monarcho** nickname of a crazy Italian at the court of Elizabeth  **108 mistaken**
taken to the wrong person  **110 suitor** pronounced "shooter"
**111 continent** container  **112 put off** repulsed  **114 if . . .
miscarry** if someone is not made a cuckold  **115 put on** lay
on, as a blow  **119 strikes . . . brow** takes careful aim (with
an allusion to the cuckold's horns)  **123 hit it** name of a dance
tune (leading to pun on the sense of *hit* = to copulate)  **129
And** if

**BOYET**
A mark! O, mark but that mark!° A mark, says my
    lady!
Let the mark have a prick° in't, to mete° at if it may be.

**MARIA**
Wide o' the bow hand!° I' faith, your hand is out.    135

**COSTARD**
Indeed 'a must shoot nearer, or he'll ne'er hit the
    clout.°

**BOYET**
And if my hand be out, then belike your hand is in.

**COSTARD**
Then will she get the upshoot° by cleaving the pin.°

**MARIA**
Come, come, you talk greasily;° your lips grow foul.

**COSTARD**
She's too hard for you at pricks, sir. Challenge her to
    bowl.    140

**BOYET**
I fear too much rubbing.° Good night, my good owl.
                                    [*Exeunt* BOYET *and* MARIA.]

**COSTARD**
By my soul, a swain,° a most simple clown!
Lord, lord, how the ladies and I have put him down!
O' my troth,° most sweet jests, most incony° vulgar
    wit.
When it comes so smoothly off, so obscenely as it
    were, so fit!    145
Armado to th' one side—O, a most dainty man!
To see him walk before a lady, and to bear her fan!
To see him kiss his hand, and how most sweetly 'a will
    swear!
And his page o' t' other side, that handful of wit,
Ah, heavens, it is a most pathetical nit!°    150

*Shout within.*

Sola,° sola!                                    [*Exit.*]

[Scene II. *The park.*]

*Enter* DULL, HOLOFERNES *the pedant, and* NATHANIEL.

**NATHANIEL**  Very reverend sport, truly, and done in
the testimony° of a good conscience.
**HOLOFERNES**  The deer was, as you know, sanguis, in
blood; ripe as the pomewater,° who now hangeth like
a jewel in the ear of coelo, the sky, the welkin, the    5
heaven; and anon falleth like a crab° on the face of
terra, the soil, the land, the earth.
**NATHANIEL**  Truly, Master Holofernes, the epithets
are sweetly varied, like a scholar at the least. But sir,
I assure ye it was a buck of the first head.°    10

**HOLOFERNES**  Sir Nathaniel, haud credo.°
**DULL**  'Twas not a haud credo, 'twas a pricket.°
**HOLOFERNES**  Most barbarous intimation!° Yet a kind
of insinuation, as it were, in via, in way, of explication;° facere,° as it were, replication,° or rather,    15
ostentare, to show, as it were, his inclination—after
his undressed, unpolished, uneducated, unpruned,
untrained, or, rather, unlettered, or, ratherest, unconfirmed fashion—to insert again my haud credo
for a deer.    20
**DULL**  I said the deer was not a haud credo, 'twas a
pricket.
**HOLOFERNES**
Twice-sod° simplicity, bis coctus!°
O thou monster ignorance, how deformed dost thou
    look!
**NATHANIEL**
Sir, he hath never fed of the dainties that are bred in a
    book.    25
He hath not eat paper, as it were, he hath not drunk
ink. His intellect is not replenished. He is only an
animal, only sensible in the duller parts.
And such barren plants are set before us that we
    thankful should be,
Which we of taste and feeling are, for those parts that
    do fructify° in us more than he.    30
For as it would ill become me to be vain, indiscreet,
    or a fool,
So were there a patch° set on learning, to see him in a
    school.
But, omne bene,° say I, being of an old father's mind,
Many can brook° the weather that love not the wind.
**DULL**
You two are book-men. Can you tell me by your wit    35
What was a month old at Cain's birth that's not five
    weeks old as yet?
**HOLOFERNES**
Dictynna,° goodman Dull. Dictynna, goodman Dull.
**DULL**  What is Dictynna?
**NATHANIEL**
A title to Phoebe, to Luna, to the moon.
**HOLOFERNES**
The moon was a month old when Adam was no more,    40
And raught° not to five weeks when he came to
    fivescore.
Th' allusion holds in the exchange.°
**DULL**  'Tis true indeed; the collusion° holds in the
exchange.
**HOLOFERNES**  God comfort thy capacity! I say th'    45
allusion holds in the exchange.
**DULL**  And I say the pollution holds in the exchange,
for the moon is never but a month old; and I say
beside that 'twas a pricket that the princess killed.

---

133 **mark** (1) target (2) pudend  134 **prick** mark within the
target (with additional bawdy suggestion); **mete** aim  135
**Wide . . . hand** far from the target on the bow-hand side
136 **clout** nail in the center of the target  138 **upshoot** best
shot; **cleaving the pin** (1) striking the center of the target
(2) causing emission in the male  139 **greasily** indecently
141 **rubbing** bowling balls striking each other (with sexual
innuendo)  142 **swain** herdsman  144 **O' my troth** by my
faith; **incony** fine  150 **nit** small thing (louse)  151 **Sola** a
hunting cry
IV.ii.2 **testimony** approval  4 **pomewater** variety of
sweet apple  6 **crab** crabapple  10 **buck . . . head** full-grown
buck

11 **haud credo** I do not believe it (Latin); in the next line, Dull
apparently takes the words as *old gray doe*  12 **pricket** two-
year-old red deer  13 **intimation** a pedantic substitute for
*insinuation*  14-15 **explication** explanation  15 **facere** to
make; **replication** unfolding, revelation  23 **Twice-sod**
soaked twice (again and again); **bis coctus** cooked twice
30 **fructify** bear fruit  32 **patch** fool  33 **omne bene** all
is well  34 **brook** endure  37 **Dictynna** Diana, the moon
41 **raught** attained  42 **Th' allusion . . . exchange** The
riddle serves for Adam as well as for Cain  43 **collusion** a
pedantic misunderstanding

HOLOFERNES   Sir Nathaniel, will you hear an extem- 50
poral° epitaph on the death of the deer? And, to
humor the ignorant, I call the deer the princess killed,
a pricket.

NATHANIEL   Perge,° good Master Holofernes, perge,
so it shall please you to abrogate scurrility.°   55

HOLOFERNES
I will something affect the letter° for it argues facility.
The preyful° princess pierced and pricked a pretty
    pleasing pricket;
Some say a sore,° but not a sore till now made sore
    with shooting.
The dogs did yell. Put L° to sore, then sorel° jumps
    from thicket;
Or pricket, sore, or else sorel. The people fall a hooting. 60
If sore be sore, then L to sore makes fifty sores—o'
    sorel.
Of one sore I an hundred make by adding but one
    more L.

NATHANIEL   A rare talent!°

DULL   If a talent be a claw, look how he claws° him
with a talent.   65

HOLOFERNES   This is a gift that I have, simple, simple;
a foolish extravagant spirit, full of forms, figures,
shapes, objects, ideas, apprehensions, motions, revolutions. These are begot in the ventricle° of memory,
nourished in the womb of pia mater,° and delivered 70
upon the mellowing of occasion.° But the gift is good
in those in whom it is acute, and I am thankful
for it.

NATHANIEL   Sir, I praise the Lord for you, and so may
my parishioners, for their sons are well tutored by 75
you, and their daughters profit very greatly under
you. You are a good member of the commonwealth.

HOLOFERNES   Mehercle,° if their sons be ingenious,
they shall want no instruction; if their daughters be
capable, I will put it to them. But vir sapit qui pauca 80
loquitur.° A soul feminine saluteth us.

*Enter* JAQUENETTA *and* [COSTARD] *the clown.*

JAQUENETTA   God give you good morrow, Master
Parson.

HOLOFERNES   Master Parson, quasi° pierce-one? And
if one should be pierced, which is the one?   85

COSTARD   Marry, Master Schoolmaster, he that is
likest to a hogshead.°

HOLOFERNES   Of piercing a hogshead!° A good luster
of conceit° in a turf° of earth, fire enough for a flint,
pearl enough for a swine. 'Tis pretty; it is well.   90

JAQUENETTA   Good Master Parson, be so good as
read me this letter. It was given me by Costard, and
sent me from Don Armado. I beseech you read it.

HOLOFERNES   Fauste, precor, gelida quando pecus
omne sub umbra ruminat,° and so forth. Ah, good old 95
Mantuan. I may speak of thee as the traveler doth of
Venice:

    Venetia, Venetia,
    Chi non ti vede, non ti pretia.°

Old Mantuan, old Mantuan! Who understandeth 100
thee not, loves thee not. Ut, re, sol, la, mi, fa. Under
pardon, sir, what are the contents? Or, rather, as
Horace says in his—What, my soul, verses?

NATHANIEL   Ay, sir, and very learned.

HOLOFERNES   Let me hear a staff,° a stanze, a verse. 105
Lege, domine.°

[NATHANIEL *Reads.*]
"If love make me forsworn, how shall I swear to love?
    Ah, never faith could hold if not to beauty vowed!
Though to myself forsworn, to thee I'll faithful prove;
    Those thoughts to me were oaks, to thee like osiers
        bowed.   110
Study his bias leaves° and makes his book thine eyes,
    Where all those pleasures live that art would
        comprehend.
If knowledge be the mark, to know thee shall suffice:
    Well learnèd is that tongue that well can thee
        commend,
All ignorant that soul that sees thee without wonder;
    Which is to me some praise, that I thy parts admire.
Thy eye Jove's lightning bears, thy voice his dreadful 115
        thunder,
    Which, not to anger bent, is music and sweet fire.
Celestial as thou art, O pardon love this wrong,
That sings heaven's praise with such an earthly
    tongue!"   120

HOLOFERNES   You find not the apostrophus,° and so
miss the accent. Let me supervise the canzonet.° Here
are only numbers ratified;° but, for the elegancy,
facility, and golden cadence of poesy, caret.° Ovidius
Naso was the man; and why indeed "Naso"° but for 125
smelling out the odoriferous flowers of fancy, the
jerks of invention?° Imitari° is nothing. So doth the
hound his master, the ape his keeper, the tired horse
his rider. But, damosella virgin, was this directed to
you?   130

JAQUENETTA   Ay, sir, from one Monsieur Berowne,
one of the strange° queen's lords.

HOLOFERNES   I will overglance the superscript.° "To
the snow-white hand of the most beauteous Lady
Rosaline." I will look again on the intellect° of the 135
letter for the nomination° of the party writing to the
person written unto. "Your ladyship's, in all desired
employment, Berowne." Sir Nathaniel, this Berowne
is one of the votaries° with the king; and here he hath

50–51 extemporal on the spur of the moment   54 Perge continue   55 abrogate scurrility put aside foul talk   56 affect
the letter alliterate   57 preyful killing much prey   58 sore
four-year-old buck   59 L the Roman numeral fifty; sorel
young buck   63 talent talon   64 claws flatters   69 ventricle
part of the brain containing the memory   70 pia mater
membrane enclosing the brain   71 mellowing of occasion
fit time   78 Mehercle By Hercules   80–81 vir . . . loquitur
the man is wise who speaks little   84 quasi as if   87
hogshead fathead   88 piercing a hogshead getting drunk
88–89 luster of conceit brilliant idea   89 turf clod

94–95 Fauste . . . ruminat I pray thee, Faustus, when all the
cattle ruminate beneath the cool shade (a quotation from a
Latin poem by Mantuan, an Italian Renaissance poet)   98–99
Venetia . . . pretia Venice, Venice, only those who do not
see thee do not value thee (Italian)   105 staff stanza   106
Lege, domine Read, master   111 Study . . . leaves the
student leaves his favorite studies   121 apostrophus mark of
punctuation taking the place of a vowel   122 canzonet song
123 numbers ratified rhythm regularized   124 caret it is
deficient   125 Naso nose   127 jerks of invention clever
strokes of wit;  Imitari to imitate   132 strange foreign   133
superscript address   135 intellect purport   136 nomination
name   139 votaries persons who have taken a vow

framed° a letter to a sequent° of the stranger queen's, 140
which accidentally, or by the way of progression,°
hath miscarried. Trip and go,° my sweet, deliver this
paper into the royal hand of the king; it may concern
much. Stay not thy compliment;° I forgive thy duty.
Adieu.                                                        145

JAQUENETTA  Good Costard, go with me. Sir, God
save your life.

COSTARD  Have with thee, my girl.
                                    Exit [with JAQUENETTA].

NATHANIEL  Sir, you have done this in the fear of
God very religiously; and as a certain father saith—   150

HOLOFERNES  Sir, tell not me of the father, I do fear
colorable colors.° But to return to the verses—did they
please you, Sir Nathaniel?

NATHANIEL  Marvelous well for the pen.°

HOLOFERNES  I do dine today at the father's of a  155
certain pupil of mine, where, if before repast it shall
please you to gratify the table with a grace, I will, on
my privilege I have with the parents of the foresaid
child or pupil, undertake your ben venuto;° where I
will prove those verses to be very unlearned, neither  160
savoring of poetry, wit, nor invention. I beseech
your society.

NATHANIEL  And thank you too, for society (saith the
text) is the happiness of life.

HOLOFERNES  And, certes,° the text most infallibly  165
concludes it. [To DULL.] Sir, I do invite you too; you
shall not say me nay. Pauca verba.° Away! The
gentles are at their game, and we will to our recreation.
                                                    Exeunt.


[Scene III. The park.]

Enter BEROWNE with a paper in his hand, alone.

BEROWNE  The king he is hunting the deer; I am
coursing° myself. They have pitched a toil;° I am
toiling in a pitch—pitch that defiles. Defile—a foul
word! Well, set thee down, sorrow, for so they say the
fool said, and so say I, and I the fool. Well proved, 5
wit! By the Lord, this love is as mad as Ajax:° it
kills sheep; it kills me—I a sheep. Well proved again
o' my side! I will not love; if I do, hang me! I' faith,
I will not. O but her eye! By this light, but for her
eye, I would not love her—yes, for her two eyes. 10
Well, I do nothing in the world but lie, and lie in my
throat. By heaven, I do love, and it hath taught me to
rhyme, and to be melancholy; and here is part of my
rhyme, and here my melancholy. Well, she hath one
o' my sonnets already. The clown bore it, the fool 15
sent it, and the lady hath it—sweet clown, sweeter
fool, sweetest lady! By the world, I would not care

a pin if the other three were in. Here comes one with
a paper. God give him grace to groan!

He stands aside.

The KING ent'reth [with a paper].

KING  Ay me!                                                 20

BEROWNE  [Aside.]  Shot, by heaven! Proceed, sweet
Cupid. Thou hast thumped him with thy bird-bolt°
under the left pap.° In faith, secrets!

KING  [Reads.]
"So sweet a kiss the golden sun gives not
    To those fresh morning drops upon the rose,        25
As thy eye-beams when their fresh rays have smote
    The night of dew that on my cheeks down flows.
Nor shines the silver moon one half so bright
    Through the transparent bosom of the deep
As doth thy face, through tears of mine, give light.    30
    Thou shin'st in every tear that I do weep;
No drop but as a coach doth carry thee.
    So ridest thou triumphing in my woe.
Do but behold the tears that swell in me,
    And they thy glory through my grief will show.      35
But do not love thyself—then thou will keep
My tears for glasses° and still make me weep.
O queen of queens, how far dost thou excel
No thought can think, nor tongue of mortal tell!"
How shall she know my griefs? I'll drop the paper.       40
Sweet leaves, shade folly. Who is he comes here?

Enter LONGAVILLE [with a paper]. The KING steps aside.

What, Longaville, and reading! Listen, ear.

BEROWNE
Now, in thy likeness, one more fool appear!

LONGAVILLE
Ay me, I am forsworn.

BEROWNE
Why, he comes in like a perjure,° wearing papers.°     45

KING
In love, I hope—sweet fellowship in shame!

BEROWNE
One drunkard loves another of the name.

LONGAVILLE
Am I the first that have been perjured so?

BEROWNE
I could put thee in comfort—not by two that I know.
Thou makest the triumviry,° the corner-cap° of
    society,                                              50
The shape of love's Tyburn,° that hangs up simplicity.

LONGAVILLE
I fear these stubborn lines lack power to move.
O sweet Maria, empress of my love!
These numbers will I tear, and write in prose.

BEROWNE
O, rhymes are guards° on wanton Cupid's hose;           55
Disfigure not his shop.°

LONGAVILLE                 This same shall go.

140 framed devised; sequent follower  141 by . . . progression on its way  142 Trip and go phrase used of a morris
dancer  144 Stay . . . compliment do not wait on ceremony
152 colorable colors plausible excuses  154 pen penmanship,
or style of writing  159 ben venuto welcome (Italian)  165
certes certainly  167 Pauca verba Few words
IV.iii.2 coursing chasing; pitched a toil set a snare  6
Ajax ancient Greek warrior who, going mad, killed sheep,
believing them his enemies

22 bird-bolt arrow for shooting birds  23 pap breast  37
glasses mirrors  45 perjure perjurer; wearing papers a
punishment for perjury, to wear a paper on the head as a
public shame (presumably Longaville has a sonnet in his hat-
band)  50 triumviry triumvirate; corner-cap cap with
corners (worn by divines, judges, and scholars)  51 Tyburn
place of execution (the triangular-shaped gallows bears a
resemblance to a corner-cap)  55 guards ornaments  56 shop
organ of generation, or codpiece

*He reads the sonnet.*

"Did not the heavenly rhetoric of thine eye,
　'Gainst whom the world cannot hold argument,
Persuade my heart to this false perjury?
　Vows for thee broke deserve not punishment.      60
A woman I forswore, but I will prove,
　Thou being a goddess, I forswore not thee.
My vow was earthly, thou a heavenly love;
　Thy grace, being gained, cures all disgrace in me.
Vows are but breath, and breath a vapor is;      65
　Then thou, fair sun, which on my earth dost shine,
Exhal'st this vapor-vow; in thee it is.
　If broken then, it is no fault of mine;
If by me broke, what fool is not so wise
To lose an oath to win a paradise?"      70

BEROWNE
This is the liver-vein,° which makes flesh a deity,
A green goose° a goddess. Pure, pure idolatry.
God amend us, God amend! We are much out o' th'
　way.°

*Enter* DUMAINE [*with a paper*].

LONGAVILLE
By whom shall I send this?—Company? Stay.

[*Steps aside.*]

BEROWNE
All hid,° all hid—an old infant play.      75
Like a demigod here sit I in the sky,
And wretched fools' secrets heedfully o'ereye.
More sacks to the mill°—O heavens, I have my wish!
Dumaine transformed! Four woodcocks° in a dish!

DUMAINE
O most divine Kate!      80

BEROWNE
O most profane coxcomb!

DUMAINE
By heaven, the wonder in a mortal eye!

BEROWNE
By earth, she is not, corporal.° There you lie!

DUMAINE
Her amber hairs for foul hath amber quoted.°

BEROWNE
An amber-colored raven was well noted.      85

DUMAINE
As upright as the cedar.

BEROWNE                              Stoop,° I say—
Her shoulder is with child.°

DUMAINE                              As fair as day.

BEROWNE
Ay, as some days; but then no sun must shine.

DUMAINE
O that I had my wish!

LONGAVILLE                    And I had mine!

KING
And I mine too, good Lord!      90

BEROWNE
Amen, so I had mine! Is not that a good word?

DUMAINE
I would forget her, but a fever she
Reigns in my blood, and will rememb'red be.

BEROWNE
A fever in your blood? Why, then incision
Would let her out in saucers. Sweet misprision!°      95

DUMAINE
Once more I'll read the ode that I have writ.

BEROWNE
Once more I'll mark how love can vary wit.

DUMAINE *reads his sonnet.*

DUMAINE "On a day—alack the day!—
　　Love, whose month is ever May,
　　Spied a blossom passing fair      100
　　Playing in the wanton air.
　　Through the velvet leaves the wind,
　　All unseen, can passage find;
　　That the lover, sick to death,
　　Wished himself the heaven's breath.      105
　　Air, quoth he, thy cheeks may blow;
　　Air, would I might triumph so!
　　But, alack, my hand is sworn
　　Ne'er to pluck thee from thy thorn.
　　Vow, alack, for youth unmeet,      110
　　Youth so apt to pluck a sweet!
　　Do not call it sin in me,
　　That I am forsworn for thee;
　　Thou for whom Jove would swear
　　Juno but an Ethiop° were,      115
　　And deny himself for Jove,
　　Turning mortal for thy love."
This will I send, and something else more plain,
That shall express my true love's fasting pain.°
O, would the king, Berowne, and Longaville      120
Were lovers too! Ill, to example ill,
Would from my forehead wipe a perjured note,°
For none offend where all alike do dote.

LONGAVILLE [*Advancing.*]
Dumaine, thy love is far from charity,
That in love's grief desir'st society.      125
You may look pale, but I should blush, I know,
To be o'erheard and taken napping so.

KING [*Advancing.*]
Come, sir, you blush! As his your case is such;
You chide at him, offending twice as much.
You do not love Maria! Longaville      130
Did never sonnet for her sake compile,
Nor never lay his wreathèd arms athwart
His loving bosom to keep down his heart.
I have been closely shrouded in this bush,
And marked you both, and for you both did blush.      135
I heard your guilty rhymes, observed your fashion,
Saw sighs reek° from you, noted well your passion.

**71 liver-vein** vein coming from the liver (the place of the origin of love) **72 green goose** goose born the previous autumn (and so, a young girl) **73 out . . . way** on the wrong track **75 All hid** formula from a child's game **78 More . . . mill** more yet to do **79 woodcocks** silly birds **83 corporal** officer (with a pun on the word for bodily, human) **84 Her . . . quoted** Her amber-colored hair made amber look ugly by contrast **86 Stoop** stooped **87 with child** rounded

**95 misprision** mistake **115 Ethiop** black person **119 fasting pain** pain caused by deprivation **121–22 Ill . . . note** wickedness, not liking to make itself an example, would remove from me the papers I bear as the punishment for perjury **137 reek** exhale

"Ay me!" says one; "O Jove!" the other cries.
One, her hairs were gold; crystal, the other's eyes.

[*To* LONGAVILLE.]

You would for paradise break faith and troth,          140

[*To* DUMAINE.]

And Jove, for your love, would infringe an oath.
What will Berowne say when that he shall hear
Faith infringèd, which such zeal did swear?
How will he scorn, how will he spend his wit!
How will he triumph, leap and laugh at it!          145
For all the wealth that ever I did see,
I would not have him know so much by me.°
BEROWNE [*Advancing.*]
Now step I forth to whip hypocrisy.
Ah, good my liege, I pray thee pardon me.
Good heart, what grace hast thou, thus to reprove          150
These worms for loving, that art most in love?
Your eyes do make no coaches;° in your tears
There is no certain princess that appears.
You'll not be perjured, 'tis a hateful thing.
Tush, none but minstrels like of sonneting!          155
But are you not ashamed? Nay, are you not,
All three of you, to be thus much o'ershot?°
You found his mote, the king your mote did see;
But I a beam° do find in each of three.
O what a scene of fool'ry have I seen,          160
Of sighs, of groans, of sorrow, and of teen!°
O me, with what strict patience have I sat,
To see a king transformèd to a gnat!
To see great Hercules whipping a gig,°
And profound Solomon to tune a jig,          165
And Nestor° play at push-pin° with the boys,
And critic Timon° laugh at idle toys!
Where lies thy grief? O, tell me, good Dumaine.
And, gentle Longaville, where lies thy pain?
And where my liege's? All about the breast.          170
A caudle,° ho!
KING                    Too bitter is thy jest.
Are we betrayed thus to thy overview?
BEROWNE
Not you by me, but I betrayed to you;
I that am honest, I that hold it sin
To break the vow I am engagèd in,          175
I am betrayed by keeping company
With men like you, men of inconstancy.
When shall you see me write a thing in rhyme?
Or groan for Joan? Or spend a minute's time
In pruning° me? When shall you hear that I          180
Will praise a hand, a foot, a face, an eye,
A gait, a state, a brow, a breast, a waist,
A leg, a limb—
KING                    Soft!° Whither away so fast?
A true° man or a thief, that gallops so?

BEROWNE
I post° from love. Good lover, let me go.          185

*Enter* JAQUENETTA *and* [COSTARD *the*] *clown.*

JAQUENETTA
God bless the king!
KING                    What present hast thou there?
COSTARD
Some certain treason.
KING                    What makes° treason here?
COSTARD
Nay, it makes nothing, sir.
KING                         If it mar nothing neither,
The treason and you go in peace away together.
JAQUENETTA
I beseech your grace let this letter be read.          190
Our parson misdoubts° it; 'twas treason, he said.
KING   Berowne, read it over.

*He* [BEROWNE] *reads the letter.*

Where hadst thou it?
JAQUENETTA   Of Costard.
KING   Where hadst thou it?          195
COSTARD   Of Dun Adramadio, Dun Adramadio.

[BEROWNE *tears the letter.*]

KING
How now, what is in you? Why dost thou tear it?
BEROWNE
A toy, my liege, a toy. Your grace needs not fear it.
LONGAVILLE
It did move him to passion, and therefore let's hear it.
DUMAINE [*Gathering up the pieces.*]
It is Berowne's writing, and here is his name.          200
BEROWNE [*To* COSTARD.]
Ah, you whoreson loggerhead,° you were born to do
   me shame!
Guilty, my lord, guilty. I confess, I confess.
KING   What?
BEROWNE
That you three fools lacked me fool to make up the
   mess.°
He, he, and you—and you, my liege, and I,          205
Are pick-purses in love, and we deserve to die.
O dismiss this audience, and I shall tell you more.
DUMAINE
Now the number is even.
BEROWNE                    True, true, we are four.
Will these turtles° be gone?
KING                         Hence, sirs, away!
COSTARD
Walk aside the true folk, and let the traitors stay.          210
          [*Exeunt* COSTARD *and* JAQUENETTA.]
BEROWNE
Sweet lords, sweet lovers, O let us embrace!
As true we are as flesh and blood can be.
The sea will ebb and flow, heaven show his face;
Young blood doth not obey an old decree.

---

**147 by me** concerning me   **152 coaches** for love to ride in (as in line 32)   **157 o'ershot** wide of the mark   **158–59 mote . . . beam** the contrast is between small and large faults (see Matthew 7:3–5; Luke 6:41–42)   **161 teen** grief   **164 gig** top   **166 Nestor** ancient Greek sage; **push-pin** child's game   **167 critic Timon** Greek misanthrope   **171 caudle** healing drink for an invalid   **180 pruning** preening   **183 Soft** Wait a minute! (an exclamation)   **184 true** honest

**185 post** ride in haste   **187 makes** does   **191 misdoubts** mistrusts   **201 whoreson loggerhead** rascally blockhead   **204 mess** party of four at table   **209 turtles** turtledoves, lovers

We cannot cross° the cause why we were born;                    215
Therefore of all hands must we be forsworn.

KING
What, did these rent° lines show some love of thine?

BEROWNE
Did they? quoth you. Who sees the heavenly Rosaline,
That, like a rude and savage man of Inde
At the first op'ning of the gorgeous East,                       220
Bows not his vassal head and, strooken blind,
Kisses the base ground with obedient breast!
What peremptory° eagle-sighted eye
Dares look upon the heaven of her brow
That is not blinded by her majesty?                              225

KING
What zeal, what fury, hath inspired thee now?
My love, her mistress, is a gracious moon;
She, an attending star, scarce seen a light.

BEROWNE
My eyes are then no eyes, nor I Berowne.
O, but for my love, day would turn to night!                    230
Of all complexions the culled sovereignty°
Do meet, as at a fair, in her fair cheek,
Where several worthies° make one dignity,
Where nothing wants° that want itself doth seek.
Lend me the flourish° of all gentle tongues—                    235
Fie, painted rhetoric!° O, she needs it not!
To things of sale° a seller's praise belongs:
She passes praise; then praise too short doth blot.
A withered hermit, fivescore winters worn,
Might shake off fifty, looking in her eye.                       240
Beauty doth varnish° age as if new-born,
And gives the crutch the cradle's infancy.
O, 'tis the sun that maketh all things shine.

KING
By heaven, thy love is black as ebony!

BEROWNE
Is ebony like her? O wood divine!                                245
A wife of such wood were felicity.
O, who can give an oath? Where is a book?
That I may swear beauty doth beauty lack
If that she learn not of her eye to look.
No face is fair that is not full so black.                       250

KING
O paradox! Black is the badge of hell,
The hue of dungeons, and the school of night;°
And beauty's crest becomes the heavens well.°

BEROWNE
Devils soonest tempt, resembling spirits of light.
O, if in black my lady's brows be decked,                        255
It mourns that painting and usurping° hair
Should ravish doters with a false aspect;°
And therefore is she born to make black fair.

Her favor° turns the fashion of the days,
For native blood° is counted painting now;                       260
And therefore red that would avoid dispraise
Paints itself black to imitate her brow.

DUMAINE
To look like her are chimney sweepers black.

LONGAVILLE
And since her time are colliers° counted bright.

KING
And Ethiops of their sweet complexion crack.°                    265

DUMAINE
Dark needs no candles now, for dark is light.

BEROWNE
Your mistresses dare never come in rain,
For fear their colors should be washed away.

KING
'Twere good yours did; for, sir, to tell you plain,
I'll find a fairer face not washed today.                        270

BEROWNE
I'll prove her fair or talk till doomsday here.

KING
No devil will fright thee then so much as she.

DUMAINE
I never knew man hold vile stuff so dear.

LONGAVILLE
Look, here's thy love; [showing his shoe] my foot° and
    her face see.

BEROWNE
O, if the streets were pavèd with thine eyes,                    275
Her feet were much too dainty for such tread.

DUMAINE
O vile! Then, as she goes, what upward lies
The street should see as she walked overhead.

KING
But what of this? Are we not all in love?

BEROWNE
O, nothing so sure, and thereby all forsworn.                    280

KING
Then leave this chat, and, good Berowne, now prove
Our loving lawful and our faith not torn.

DUMAINE
Ay marry, there, some flattery for this evil!

LONGAVILLE
O, some authority how to proceed!
Some tricks, some quillets,° how to cheat the devil!             285

DUMAINE
Some salve for perjury.

BEROWNE                        O, 'tis more than need!
Have at you, then, affection's men-at-arms!°
Consider what you first did swear unto.
To fast, to study, and to see no woman—
Flat treason 'gainst the kingly state of youth.                  290
Say, can you fast? Your stomachs are too young,
And abstinence engenders maladies.
[And where that° you have vowed to study, lords,

---

215 **cross** thwart   217 **rent** damaged   223 **peremptory** resolute   231 **culled sovereignty** chosen as the best   233 **worthies** good qualities   234 **wants** lacks   235 **flourish** adornment   236 **painted rhetoric** extravagant speech   237 **of sale** for sale   241 **varnish** lend freshness   252 **school of night** some editors emend "school" to "suit" or to "shade," but perhaps the term means a place for learning dark things   253 **beauty's . . . well** true beauty, which is bright, is heavenly, but if blackness is taken as the sign of beauty, it would be ironic to link beauty with heaven, which is the source of light   256 **usurping** false   257 **aspect** appearance

259 **favor** complexion   260 **native blood** naturally red complexion   264 **colliers** coalmen   265 **crack** boast   274 **my foot** he is wearing black shoes   285 **quillets** subtleties   287 **affection's men-at-arms** love's warriors   293 **where that** whereas (after writing lines 293-314, here bracketed, Shakespeare apparently decided he could do better, and rewrote the passage in the ensuing lines, but the printer mistakenly printed both versions)

In that each of you have forsworn his book,
Can you still dream and pore and thereon look?    295
For when would you, my lord, or you, or you,
Have found the ground of study's excellence
Without the beauty of a woman's face?
From women's eyes this doctrine I derive:
They are the ground, the books, the academes,°    300
From whence doth spring the true Promethean fire.°
Why, universal plodding poisons° up
The nimble spirits in the arteries,
As motion and long-during° action tires
The sinewy vigor of the traveler.    305
Now for not looking on a woman's face,
You have in that forsworn the use of eyes,
And study too, the causer of your vow;
For where is any author in the world
Teaches such beauty as a woman's eye?    310
Learning is but an adjunct to ourself,
And where we are our learning likewise is.
Then when ourselves we see in ladies' eyes,
Do we not likewise see our learning there?]
O, we have made a vow to study, lords,    315
And in that vow we have forsworn our books;
For when would you, my liege, or you, or you,
In leaden contemplation have found out
Such fiery numbers° as the prompting eyes
Of beauty's tutors have enriched you with?    320
Other slow arts entirely keep the brain,
And therefore, finding barren practisers,
Scarce show a harvest of their heavy toil;
But love, first learnèd in a lady's eyes,
Lives not alone immurèd in the brain,    325
But with the motion of all elements,°
Courses as swift as thought in every power,
And gives to every power a double power
Above their functions and their offices.
It adds a precious seeing to the eye:    330
A lover's eyes will gaze an eagle blind.
A lover's ear will hear the lowest sound,
When the suspicious head of theft° is stopped.
Love's feeling is more soft and sensible
Than are the tender horns of cockled° snails.    335
Love's tongue proves dainty Bacchus gross in taste.
For valor, is not love a Hercules,
Still climbing trees in the Hesperides?°
Subtle as Sphinx; as sweet and musical
As bright Apollo's lute, strung with his hair.    340
And when love speaks, the voice of all the gods
Make heaven drowsy with the harmony.
Never durst poet touch a pen to write
Until his ink were temp'red with love's sighs.
O, then his lines would ravish savage ears    345
And plant in tyrants mild humility.
From women's eyes this doctrine I derive.
They sparkle still the right Promethean fire;
They are the books, the arts, the academes,

That show, contain, and nourish all the world;    350
Else none at all in aught proves excellent.
Then fools you were these women to forswear,
Or, keeping what is sworn, you will prove fools.
For wisdom's sake, a word that all men love,
Or for love's sake, a word that loves all men,    355
Or for men's sake, the authors of these women,
Or women's sake, by whom we men are men—
Let us once lose our oaths to find ourselves,
Or else we lose ourselves to keep our oaths.
It is religion to be thus forsworn,    360
For charity itself fulfills the law,°
And who can sever love from charity?

KING
Saint Cupid then! And, soldiers, to the field!

BEROWNE
Advance your standards, and upon them, lords!
Pell-mell, down with them! But be first advised,    365
In conflict that you get the sun of them.°

LONGAVILLE
Now to plain-dealing. Lay these glozes° by.
Shall we resolve to woo these girls of France?

KING
And win them too! Therefore let us devise
Some entertainment for them in their tents.    370

BEROWNE
First from the park let us conduct them thither;
Then homeward every man attach the hand
Of his fair mistress. In the afternoon
We will with some strange pastime solace them,
Such as the shortness of the time can shape;    375
For revels, dances, masks, and merry hours
Forerun fair love, strewing her way with flowers.

KING
Away, away! No time shall be omitted
That will be time,° and may by us be fitted.

BEROWNE
Allons!° Allons! Sowed cockle reaped no corn,°    380
And justice always whirls in equal measure.
Light wenches may prove plagues to men forsworn;
If so, our copper buys no better treasure.      [Exeunt.]


# [ACT V]

## [Scene I. The park.]

*Enter* [HOLOFERNES] *the pedant,* [NATHANIEL] *the
curate, and* DULL [*the constable*].

HOLOFERNES   Satis quid sufficit.°
NATHANIEL   I praise God for you, sir. Your reasons°
at dinner have been sharp and sententious,° pleasant
without scurrility, witty without affection,° audacious

---

300 **academes** academies   301 **Promethean fire** fire stolen from heaven by Prometheus   302 **poisons** some editors emend to "prisons"   304 **long-during** long-lasting   319 **fiery numbers** passionate verses   326 **with . . . elements** with the force of all the components of the universe   333 **the . . . theft** a thief's hearing, suspicious of every sound   335 **cockled** in shells   338 **Hesperides** garden where Hercules picked the golden apples

361 **charity . . . law** Romans 13:8, "He that loveth another hath fulfilled the law"   366 **get . . . them** approach when the sun is in their eyes   367 **glozes** trivial comments   379 **be time** come to pass   380 **Allons** Let's go! (French); **Sowed . . . corn** if weeds are sown, wheat is not reaped   V.i.1 **Satis quid sufficit** Enough is as good as a feast   2 **reasons** discourses   3 **sententious** full of meaning   4 **affection** affectation

without impudency, learned without opinion,° and 5
strange without heresy. I did converse this quondam°
day with a companion of the king's, who is intituled,
nominated, or called, Don Adriano de Armado.

HOLOFERNES  Novi hominem tanquam te.° His
humor is lofty, his discourse peremptory,° his tongue 10
filed,° his eye ambitious, his gait majestical, and his
general behavior vain, ridiculous, and thrasonical.°
He is too picked,° too spruce, too affected, too odd,
as it were, too peregrinate,° as I may call it.

NATHANIEL  A most singular and choice epithet.  15

*Draws out his table-book.*°

HOLOFERNES  He draweth out the thread of his
verbosity finer than the staple° of his argument. I
abhor such fanatical phantasimes,° such insociable°
and point-devise° companions; such rackers° of
orthography as to speak "dout" fine when he should 20
say "doubt," "det" when he should pronounce
"debt"—d, e, b, t, not d, e, t. He clepeth° a calf
"cauf," half "hauf," neighbor vocatur° "nebor,"
neigh abbreviated "ne." This is abhominable, which
he would call "abominable." It insinuateth me of 25
insanie.° Ne intelligis, domine?° To make frantic,
lunatic.

NATHANIEL  Laus Deo bone intelligo.°

HOLOFERNES  Bone?° Bone for bene! Priscian° a little
scratched;° 'twill serve.  30

*Enter* [ARMADO *the*] *braggart,* [MOTH, *his*] *boy,* [*and*
COSTARD *the clown*].

NATHANIEL  Videsne quis venit?°

HOLOFERNES  Video, et gaudeo.°

ARMADO [*To* MOTH.]  Chirrah!°

HOLOFERNES  Quare° "chirrah," not "sirrah"?

ARMADO  Men of peace, well encount'red.  35

HOLOFERNES  Most military sir, salutation.

MOTH [*Aside to* COSTARD.]  They have been at a great
feast of languages and stol'n the scraps.

COSTARD  O, they have lived long on the alms-
basket° of words. I marvel thy master hath not eaten 40
thee for a word; for thou art not so long by the head
as honorificabilitudinitatibus.° Thou art easier swallowed than a flapdragon.°

MOTH  Peace! The peal° begins.

ARMADO  Monsieur, are you not lett'red?°  45

MOTH  Yes, yes! He teaches boys the hornbook.° What
is a, b, spelled backward with the horn on his head?

HOLOFERNES  Ba, pueritia,° with a horn added.

MOTH  Ba, most silly sheep with a horn. You hear his
learning.  50

HOLOFERNES  Quis,° quis, thou consonant?

MOTH  The last of the five vowels, if you repeat
them; or the fifth, if I.

HOLOFERNES  I will repeat them: a, e, i—

MOTH  The sheep. The other two concludes it—o, u.  55

ARMADO  Now, by the salt wave of the Mediterranean,
a sweet touch, a quick venew° of wit! Snip, snap,
quick and home! It rejoiceth my intellect. True wit!

MOTH  Offered by a child to an old man—which is
wit-old.°  60

HOLOFERNES  What is the figure?° What is the figure?

MOTH  Horns.

HOLOFERNES  Thou disputes like an infant. Go whip
thy gig.°

MOTH  Lend me your horn to make one, and I will 65
whip about your infamy manu cita.° A gig of a
cuckold's horn.

COSTARD  And° I had but one penny in the world,
thou shouldst have it to buy gingerbread. Hold,
there is the very remuneration I had of thy master, 70
thou halfpenny purse of wit, thou pigeon-egg of
discretion. O, and the heavens were so pleased that
thou wert but my bastard, what a joyful father
wouldest thou make me! Go to, thou hast it ad
dunghill,° at the fingers' ends, as they say.  75

HOLOFERNES  O, I smell false Latin! "Dunghill" for
unguem.

ARMADO  Arts-man,° preambulate.° We will be
singled from the barbarous. Do you not educate youth
at the charge-house° on the top of the mountain?  80

HOLOFERNES  Or mons, the hill.

ARMADO  At your sweet pleasure, for the mountain.

HOLOFERNES  I do, sans question.

ARMADO  Sir, it is the king's most sweet pleasure and
affection to congratulate the princess at her pavilion 85
in the posteriors° of this day, which the rude multitude
call the afternoon.

HOLOFERNES  The posterior of the day, most generous
sir, is liable, congruent, and measurable° for the
afternoon. The word is well culled, chose, sweet and 90
apt, I do assure you, sir, I do assure.

ARMADO  Sir, the king is a noble gentleman, and my
familiar,° I do assure ye, very good friend. For what
is inward° between us, let it pass. I do beseech thee,
remember thy courtesy.° I beseech thee apparel thy 95
head. And among other importunate and most

**opinion** dogmatism  **6 quondam** former  **9 Novi . . . te**
I know the man as well as I know you  **10 peremptory**
decisive  **11 filed** polished  **12 thrasonical** boastful
**13 picked** refined  **14 peregrinate** foreign in manner
**15 s.d. table-book** tablet (stage directions are often, as here,
in the imperative)  **17 staple** fiber  **18 phantasimes** wild
imaginers; **insociable** impossible to associate with  **19 point-
devise** perfectly correct; **rackers** torturers  **22 clepeth** calls
**23 vocatur** is called  **25–26 insinuateth . . . insanie** suggests
insanity to me  **26 Ne intelligis, domine** Do you not understand, sir?  **28 Laus . . . intelligo** Praise be to God, I well
understand  **29 Bone** probably a mixture of Latin *bene* and
French *bon*; **Priscian** Latin grammarian of sixth century
A.D.  **30 scratched** damaged  **31 Videsne quis venit** Do
you see who is coming?  **32 Video, et gaudeo** I see, and I
rejoice  **33 Chirrah** dialect form for *sirrah*  **34 Quare** why
**39–40 alms-basket** basket used at feasts to collect scraps from
the table for the poor  **42 honorificabilitudinitatibus** Latin
tongue twister, thought to be the longest word known  **43
flapdragon** burning raisin or plum floating in liquor, and so
drunk  **44 peal** of bells  **45 lett'red** man of letters

**46 hornbook** parchment with alphabet and numbers, covered
with transparent horn, for teaching spelling and counting
**48 pueritia** childishness  **51 Quis** who  **57 venew** thrust
**60 wit-old** mentally feeble (with pun on *wittol* = cuckold)
**61 figure** figure of speech  **64 gig** top  **66 manu cita** with a
swift hand  **68 And** if  **74–75 ad dunghill** perhaps a schoolboy's corruption of the proverb *ad unguem* = to the fingernail,
meaning "precisely"  **78 Arts-man** learned man; **preambulate** walk forth  **80 charge-house** school (perhaps an allusion
to a specific school on a hill, mentioned by Erasmus)  **86
posteriors** hind parts  **89 liable, congruent, measurable**
all synonyms for *suitable*  **93 familiar** close friend  **94 inward**
private  **95 remember thy courtesy** possibly, remove your
hat when the king's name is mentioned

serious designs, and of great import indeed, too—
but let that pass; for I must tell thee, it will please his
grace, by the world, sometime to lean upon my poor
shoulder, and with his royal finger thus dally with 100
my excrement,° with my mustachio—but, sweet
heart, let that pass. By the world, I recount no fable!
Some certain special honors it pleaseth his greatness to
impart to Armado, a soldier, a man of travel, that hath
seen the world—but let that pass. The very all of all 105
is (but, sweet heart, I do implore secrecy) that the
king would have me present the princess (sweet
chuck) with some delightful ostentation, or show,
or pageant, or antic,° or firework. Now, understanding that the curate and your sweet self are good 110
at such eruptions and sudden breaking out of mirth,
as it were, I have acquainted you withal, to the end to
crave your assistance.

HOLOFERNES  Sir, you shall present before her the
Nine Worthies.° Sir Nathaniel, as concerning some 115
entertainment of time, some show in the posterior of
this day, to be rend'red by our assistance, the king's
command, and this most gallant, illustrate, and
learned gentleman, before the princess—I say, none so
fit as to present the Nine Worthies. 120

NATHANIEL  Where will you find men worthy
enough to present them?

HOLOFERNES  Joshua, yourself; myself; and this
gallant gentleman, Judas Maccabaeus; this swain,
because of his great limb or joint, shall pass° Pompey 125
the Great; the page, Hercules—

ARMADO  Pardon, sir—error! He is not quantity
enough for that Worthy's thumb; he is not so big as
the end of his club.

HOLOFERNES  Shall I have audience?° He shall present 130
Hercules in minority.° His enter and exit shall be
strangling a snake; and I will have an apology° for
that purpose.

MOTH  An excellent device! So if any of the audience
hiss, you may cry, "Well done, Hercules! Now thou 135
crushest the snake!" That is the way to make an
offense gracious, though few have the grace to do it.

ARMADO  For the rest of the Worthies?

HOLOFERNES  I will play three myself.

MOTH  Thrice-worthy gentleman! 140

ARMADO  Shall I tell you a thing?

HOLOFERNES  We attend.

ARMADO  We will have, if this fadge° not, an antic.
I beseech you, follow.

HOLOFERNES  Via,° goodman Dull! Thou hast 145
spoken no word all this while.

DULL  Nor understood none neither, sir.

HOLOFERNES  Allons, we will employ thee.

DULL  I'll make one in a dance, or so; or I will play on
the tabor° to the Worthies, and let them dance the hay.° 150

HOLOFERNES  Most dull, honest Dull! To our sport,
away!      *Exeunt.*

---

**101 excrement** that which grows out (such as hair, nails,
feathers) **109 antic** fanciful pageant. **115 Nine Worthies**
traditionally, Hector, Caesar, Joshua, David, Judas Maccabaeus,
Alexander, King Arthur, Charlemagne, Godfrey of Boulogne;
here Hercules and Pompey are included **125 pass** represent
**130 have audience** be heard **131 minority** early youth
**132 apology** justification **143 fadge** succeed **145 Via** come on
(Italian) **150 tabor** small drum; **hay** country dance

---

[Scene II. *The park.*]

*Enter the ladies* [*the* PRINCESS, KATHARINE, ROSA-
LINE, *and* MARIA].

PRINCESS
Sweet hearts, we shall be rich ere we depart
If fairings° come thus plentifully in.
A lady walled about with diamonds!
Look you what I have from the loving king.

ROSALINE
Madam, came nothing else along with that? 5

PRINCESS
Nothing but this? Yes, as much love in rhyme
As would be crammed up in a sheet of paper,
Writ o' both sides the leaf, margent° and all,
That he was fain° to seal on Cupid's wax.

ROSALINE
That was the way to make his godhead wax,° 10
For he hath been five thousand year a boy.

KATHARINE
Ay, and a shrowd° unhappy gallows° too.

ROSALINE
You'll ne'er be friends with him: 'a killed your sister.

KATHARINE
He made her melancholy, sad, and heavy;
And so she died. Had she been light, like you, 15
Of such a merry, nimble, stirring spirit,
She might ha' been a grandam ere she died.
And so may you, for a light heart lives long.

ROSALINE
What's your dark meaning, mouse, of this light word?

KATHARINE
A light condition in a beauty dark. 20

ROSALINE
We need more light to find your meaning out.

KATHARINE
You'll mar the light by taking it in snuff;°
Therefore, I'll darkly end the argument.

ROSALINE
Look what° you do, you do it still i' th' dark.

KATHARINE
So do not you, for you are a light wench. 25

ROSALINE
Indeed I weigh° not you, and therefore light.

KATHARINE
You weigh me not? O, that's you care not for me!

ROSALINE
Great reason, for past care is still past cure.

PRINCESS
Well bandied° both! A set of wit well played.
But Rosaline, you have a favor too— 30
Who sent it? And what is it?

ROSALINE      I would you knew.
And if my face were but as fair as yours,
My favor were as great. Be witness this.
Nay, I have verses too, I thank Berowne;
The numbers° true, and, were the numb'ring° too, 35

---

**V.ii.2 fairings** presents **8 margent** margin **9 fain** eager
**10 wax** grow (and with a pun on *sealing wax*) **12 shrowd**
accursed; **gallows** one fit to be hanged **22 taking . . . snuff**
being annoyed **24 Look what** whatever **26 weigh** value at
a certain rate **29 bandied** hit back and forth (figure from
tennis) **35 numbers** meter; **numb'ring** estimate

I were the fairest goddess on the ground.
I am compared to twenty thousand fairs.°
O, he hath drawn my picture in his letter!
PRINCESS  Anything like?
ROSALINE  Much in the letters, nothing in the praise. 40
PRINCESS  Beauteous as ink—a good conclusion.
KATHARINE  Fair as a text B in a copybook.
ROSALINE
'Ware° pencils, ho! Let me not die your debtor,
My red dominical,° my golden letter.
O, that your face were not so full of O's!°            45
PRINCESS
A pox of° that jest, and I beshrow all shrows!°
But Katharine, what was sent to you from fair
    Dumaine?
KATHARINE
Madam, this glove.
PRINCESS                Did he not send you twain?
KATHARINE
Yes, madam; and moreover,
Some thousand verses of a faithful lover.             50
A huge translation of hypocrisy,
Vilely compiled, profound simplicity.°
MARIA
This, and these pearls, to me sent Longaville.
The letter is too long by half a mile.
PRINCESS
I think no less. Dost thou not wish in heart          55
The chain were longer and the letter short?
MARIA
Ay, or I would these hands might never part.
PRINCESS
We are wise girls to mock our lovers so.
ROSALINE
They are worse fools to purchase mocking so.
That same Berowne I'll torture ere I go.              60
O that I knew he were but in by th' week!°
How I would make him fawn, and beg, and seek,
And wait the season, and observe the times,
And spend his prodigal wits in bootless rhymes,
And shape his service wholly to my hests,°            65
And make him proud to make me proud that jests!
So pertauntlike° would I o'ersway his state°
That he should be my fool, and I his fate.
PRINCESS
None are so surely caught, when they are catched,
As wit turned fool. Folly, in wisdom hatched,         70
Hath wisdom's warrant and the help of school
And wit's own grace to grace a learnèd fool.
ROSALINE
The blood of youth burns not with such excess
As gravity's revolt to wantonness.
MARIA
Folly in fools bears not so strong a note             75
As fool'ry in the wise when wit doth dote;
Since all the power thereof it doth apply
To prove, by wit, worth in simplicity.

*Enter* BOYET.

PRINCESS
Here comes Boyet, and mirth is in his face.
BOYET
O, I am stabbed with laughter! Where's her grace?     80
PRINCESS
Thy news, Boyet?
BOYET                Prepare, madam, prepare!
Arm, wenches, arm! Encounters mounted are
Against your peace. Love doth approach disguised,
Armèd in arguments; you'll be surprised.
Muster your wits; stand in your own defense,          85
Or hide your heads like cowards and fly hence.
PRINCESS
Saint Denis° to Saint Cupid! What are they
That charge their breath against us? Say, scout, say.
BOYET
Under the cool shade of a sycamore
I thought to close mine eyes some half an hour,       90
When, lo, to interrupt my purposed rest,
Toward that shade I might behold addrest°
The king and his companions! Warily
I stole into a neighbor thicket by,
And overheard what you shall overhear—                95
That, by and by, disguised they will be here.
Their herald is a pretty knavish page
That well by heart hath conned his embassage.°
Action and accent did they teach him there:
"Thus must thou speak, and thus thy body bear."       100
And ever and anon they made a doubt°
Presence majestical would put him out;
"For," quoth the king, "an angel shalt thou see,
Yet fear not thou, but speak audaciously."
The boy replied, "An angel is not evil;               105
I should have feared her had she been a devil."
With that all laughed and clapped him on the shoulder,
Making the bold wag by their praises bolder.
One rubbed his elbow thus, and fleered,° and swore
A better speech was never spoke before.               110
Another, with his finger and his thumb,
Cried, "Via, we will do't, come what will come!"
The third he capered and cried, "All goes well!"
The fourth turned on the toe,° and down he fell.
With that they all did tumble on the ground           115
With such a zealous laughter, so profound,
That in this spleen° ridiculous appears,
To check their folly, passion's solemn tears.
PRINCESS
But what, but what? Come they to visit us?
BOYET
They do, they do, and are apparelled thus—            120
Like Muscovites or Russians, as I guess.
Their purpose is to parley,° court, and dance,
And every one his love-feat° will advance
Unto his several mistress, which they'll know
By favors several which they did bestow.              125

---

37 **fairs** beautiful women   43 **'Ware** beware   44 **red dominical** red S (for Sunday, the Lord's Day)   45 **O's** smallpox scars
46 **A pox of** may a plague strike; **beshrow all shrows**
curse all shrews   52 **simplicity** simple-mindedness   61 **in . . .
week** trapped   65 **hests** commands   67 **pertauntlike** like a
winning hand (*Pair-taunt*) in a certain card game; **o'ersway
his state** overrule his power

87 **Saint Denis** patron saint of France   92 **addrest** approaching   98 **conned his embassage** learned his commission
101 **made a doubt** expressed a fear   109 **fleered** grinned
114 **turned . . . toe** danced for happiness   117 **spleen** excess
of mirth   122 **parley** hold a conference   123 **love-feat** exploit
prompted by love

PRINCESS
And will they so? The gallants shall be tasked;°
For, ladies, we will every one be masked,
And not a man of them shall have the grace,
Despite of suit,° to see a lady's face.
Hold, Rosaline, this favor thou shalt wear,                    130
And then the king will court thee for his dear.
Hold, take thou this, my sweet, and give me thine;
So shall Berowne take me for Rosaline.
And change you favors too; so shall your loves
Woo contrary, deceived by these removes.°                    135
ROSALINE
Come on, then; wear the favors most in sight.°
KATHARINE
But in this changing what is your intent?
PRINCESS
The effect of my intent is to cross° theirs.
They do it but in mockery merriment,
And mock for mock is only my intent.                    140
Their several counsels they unbosom° shall
To loves mistook and so be mocked withal
Upon the next occasion that we meet,
With visages displayed, to talk and greet.
ROSALINE
But shall we dance if they desire us to't?                    145
PRINCESS
No, to the death° we will not move a foot,
Nor to their penned speech render we no grace,
But while 'tis spoke each turn away her face.
BOYET
Why, that contempt will kill the speaker's heart,
And quite divorce his memory from his part.                    150
PRINCESS
Therefore I do it, and I make no doubt
The rest will e'er come in if he be out.
There's no such sport as sport by sport o'erthrown,
To make theirs ours, and ours none but our own.
So shall we stay, mocking intended game,°                    155
And they, well mocked, depart away with shame.

*Sound trumpet.*

BOYET
The trumpet sounds. Be masked—the maskers come.

[*The* LADIES *mask.*]

*Enter* BLACKAMOORS *with music;* [MOTH] *the boy,*
*with a speech, and* [*the* KING, BEROWNE, *and*] *the rest*
*of the* LORDS [*in Russian dress and*] *disguised.*

MOTH
"All hail, the richest beauties on the earth!"
BOYET
Beauties no richer than rich taffeta.
MOTH
"A holy parcel of the fairest dames,                    160

*The* LADIES *turn their backs to him.*

That ever turned their backs to mortal views!"
BEROWNE   "Their eyes," villain, "their eyes"!

MOTH
"That ever turned their eyes to mortal views!
Out—"
BOYET   True. "Out" indeed!                    165
MOTH
"Out of your favors, heavenly spirits, vouchsafe
Not to behold"—
BEROWNE   "Once to behold," rogue!
MOTH
"Once to behold with your sunbeamèd eyes,
—with your sunbeamèd eyes"—                    170
BOYET
They will not answer to that epithet.
You were best call it "daughter-beamèd eyes."
MOTH
They do not mark me, and that brings° me out.
BEROWNE
Is this your perfectness? Be gone, you rogue!
                    [*Exit* MOTH.]
ROSALINE
What would these strangers? Know their minds,
    Boyet.                    175
If they do speak our language, 'tis our will
That some plain man recount their purposes.
Know what they would.
BOYET
What would you with the princess?
BEROWNE
Nothing but peace and gentle visitation.                    180
ROSALINE
What would they, say they?
BOYET
Nothing but peace and gentle visitation.
ROSALINE
Why, that they have, and bid them so be gone.
BOYET
She says you have it and you may be gone.
KING
Say to her, we have measured many miles,                    185
To tread a measure° with her on this grass.
BOYET
They say that they have measured many a mile,
To tread a measure with you on this grass.
ROSALINE
It is not so. Ask them how many inches
Is in one mile. If they have measured many,                    190
The measure then of one is eas'ly told.
BOYET
If to come hither you have measured miles,
And many miles, the princess bids you tell
How many inches doth fill up one mile.
BEROWNE
Tell her we measure them by weary steps.                    195
BOYET
She hears herself.
ROSALINE          How many weary steps,
Of many weary miles you have o'ergone,
Are numb'red in the travel of one mile?
BEROWNE
We number nothing that we spend for you.
Our duty is so rich, so infinite,                    200

---

126 **tasked** tested   129 **Despite of suit** in spite of his pleading
135 **removes** changes   136 **most in sight** conspicuously
138 **cross** thwart   141 **unbosom** confide   146 **to the
death** as long as we live   155 **game** sport

173 **brings** puts   186 **measure** stately dance

That we may do it still without accompt.°
Vouchsafe to show the sunshine of your face,
That we like savages may worship it.

ROSALINE
My face is but a moon, and clouded too.

KING
Blessèd are clouds, to do as such clouds do.          205
Vouchsafe, bright moon, and these thy stars, to shine
(Those clouds removed) upon our watery eyne.°

ROSALINE
O vain petitioner, beg a greater matter!
Thou now requests but moonshine in the water.°

KING
Then in our measure do but vouchsafe one change.°     210
Thou bid'st me beg; this begging is not strange.°

ROSALINE
Play, music then. Nay, you must do it soon.

[*The* MUSICIANS *play.*]

Not yet? No dance! Thus change I like the moon.

KING
Will you not dance? How come you thus estrangèd?

ROSALINE
You took the moon at full, but now she's changèd.     215

KING
Yet still she is the moon, and I the man.
The music plays; vouchsafe some motion to it.

ROSALINE
Our ears vouchsafe it.

KING                          But your legs should do it.

ROSALINE
Since you are strangers and come here by chance,
We'll not be nice.° Take hands. We will not dance.    220

KING
Why take we hands then?

ROSALINE                          Only to part friends.
Curtsy, sweet hearts. And so the measure ends.

KING
More measure of this measure! Be not nice.

ROSALINE
We can afford no more at such a price.

KING
Price you yourselves. What buys your company?        225

ROSALINE
Your absence only.

KING                          That can never be.

ROSALINE
Then cannot we be bought; and so adieu—
Twice to your visor,° and half once to you.

KING
If you deny to dance, let's hold more chat.

ROSALINE
In private then.

KING                          I am best pleased with that.    230

[*They converse apart.*]

BEROWNE
White-handed mistress, one sweet word with thee.

PRINCESS
Honey, and milk, and sugar—there is three.

BEROWNE
Nay then, two treys,° an if° you grow so nice,
Metheglin,° wort,° and malmsey.° Well run, dice!
There's half a dozen sweets.

PRINCESS                          Seventh sweet, adieu.    235
Since you can cog,° I'll play no more with you.

BEROWNE
One word in secret.

PRINCESS                          Let it not be sweet.

BEROWNE
Thou grievest my gall.°

PRINCESS                          Gall! Bitter.

BEROWNE                                    Therefore meet.°

[*They converse apart.*]

DUMAINE
Will you vouchsafe with me to change° a word?

MARIA
Name it.

DUMAINE   Fair lady—

MARIA                          Say you so? Fair lord.    240
Take that for your "fair lady."

DUMAINE                                    Please it you,
As much in private, and I'll bid adieu.

[*They converse apart.*]

KATHARINE
What, was your vizard° made without a tongue?

LONGAVILLE
I know the reason, lady, why you ask.

KATHARINE
O for your reason! Quickly, sir, I long.              245

LONGAVILLE
You have a double tongue° within your mask
And would afford my speechless vizard half.

KATHARINE
"Veal,"° quoth the Dutchman. Is not "veal" a calf?

LONGAVILLE
A calf, fair lady?

KATHARINE                          No, a fair lord calf.

LONGAVILLE
Let's part the word.

KATHARINE                          No, I'll not be your half.   250
Take all and wean it, it may prove an ox.

LONGAVILLE
Look how you butt yourself in these sharp mocks.
Will you give horns,° chaste lady? Do not so.

KATHARINE
Then die a calf before your horns do grow.

LONGAVILLE
One word in private with you ere I die.               255

KATHARINE
Bleat softly then. The butcher hears you cry.

[*They converse apart.*]

201 **accompt** reckoning  207 **eyne** eyes  209 **moonshine
. . . water** a mere nothing  210 **change** round of dancing
211 **not strange** not unsuitably foreign  220 **nice** fastidious
228 **visor** mask

233 **treys** threes (at dice); **an if** if  234 **Metheglin** drink
mixed with honey; **wort** unfermented beer; **malmsey** a
Mediterranean wine  236 **cog** cheat  238 **gall** sore spot;
**meet** fitting  239 **change** exchange  243 **vizard** mask  246
**double tongue** an inner projection or tongue held in the
mouth to keep the mask in place  248 **Veal** Dutch or German
pronunciation of *well*  253 **give horns** prove unfaithful

BOYET
The tongues of mocking wenches are as keen
As is the razor's edge invisible,
Cutting a smaller hair than may be seen,
Above the sense° of sense; so sensible                    260
Seemeth their conference,° their conceits° have wings
Fleeter than arrows, bullets, wind, thought, swifter
    things.

ROSALINE
Not one word more, my maids, break off, break off.

BEROWNE
By heaven, all dry-beaten° with pure scoff!

KING
Farewell, mad wenches. You have simple wits.                    265
    *Exeunt* [KING, LORDS, *and* BLACKAMOORS].

PRINCESS
Twenty adieus, my frozen Muscovits.
Are these the breed of wits so wondered at?

BOYET
Tapers they are, with your sweet breaths puffed out.

ROSALINE
Well-liking° wits they have; gross, gross; fat, fat.

PRINCESS
O poverty in wit, kingly-poor flout!°                    270
Will they not, think you, hang themselves tonight?
Or ever but in vizards show their faces?
This pert Berowne was out of count'nance quite.

ROSALINE
They were all in lamentable cases.°
The king was weeping-ripe° for a good word.                    275

PRINCESS
Berowne did swear himself out of all suit.°

MARIA
Dumaine was at my service, and his sword.
"No point,"° quoth I; my servant straight was mute.

KATHARINE
Lord Longaville said I came o'er his heart;
And trow° you what he called me?

PRINCESS                    Qualm,° perhaps.                    280

KATHARINE
Yes, in good faith.

PRINCESS                    Go, sickness as thou art!

ROSALINE
Well, better wits have worn plain statute-caps.°
But will you hear? The king is my love sworn.

PRINCESS
And quick Berowne hath plighted faith to me.

KATHARINE
And Longaville was for my service born.                    285

MARIA
Dumaine is mine as sure as bark on tree.

BOYET
Madam, and pretty mistresses, give ear.
Immediately they will again be here

In their own shapes, for it can never be
They will digest this harsh indignity.                    290

PRINCESS
Will they return?

BOYET                    They will, they will, God knows,
And leap for joy though they are lame with blows.
Therefore change° favors, and when they repair,°
Blow° like sweet roses in this summer air.

PRINCESS
How blow? How blow? Speak to be understood.                    295

BOYET
Fair ladies masked are roses in their bud;
Dismasked, their damask° sweet commixture shown,
Are angels vailing° clouds, or roses blown.

PRINCESS
Avaunt, perplexity!° What shall we do
If they return in their own shapes to woo?                    300

ROSALINE
Good madam, if by me you'll be advised,
Let's mock them still, as well known as disguised.
Let us complain to them what fools were here,
Disguised like Muscovites in shapeless gear;°
And wonder what they were, and to what end                    305
Their shallow shows and prologue vilely penned,
And their rough carriage so ridiculous,
Should be presented at our tent to us.

BOYET
Ladies, withdraw. The gallants are at hand.

PRINCESS
Whip to our tents, as roes run o'er land.                    310
    *Exeunt* [PRINCESS *and* LADIES].

*Enter the* KING *and the rest* [BEROWNE, LONGAVILLE,
*and* DUMAINE, *all in their proper habits*].

KING
Fair sir, God save you. Where's the princess?

BOYET
Gone to her tent. Please it your majesty
Command me any service to her thither?

KING
That she vouchsafe me audience for one word.

BOYET
I will; and so will she, I know, my lord.                    *Exit.*    315

BEROWNE
This fellow pecks up wit, as pigeons peas,
And utters it again when God doth please.
He is wit's peddler, and retails his wares
At wakes° and wassails,° meetings, markets, fairs;
And we that sell by gross, the Lord doth know,                    320
Have not the grace to grace it with such show.
This gallant pins the wenches° on his sleeve.
Had he been Adam, he had tempted Eve.
'A can carve° too, and lisp. Why, this is he
That kissed his hand away in courtesy.                    325
This is the ape of form,° Monsieur the Nice,°
That, when he plays at tables,° chides the dice

---

260 **Above the sense** above the reach  261 **conference** conferring; **conceits** witticisms  264 **dry-beaten** beaten with blood being drawn  269 **Well-liking** plump, sleek  270 **kingly-poor flout** a poor jest for a king  274 **cases** with pun on the sense "masks" or "costumes"  275 **weeping-ripe** about to weep  276 **out . . . suit** beyond all reasonableness  278 **No point** not at all  280 **trow** know; **Qualm** sudden sickness  282 **statute-caps** caps apprentices were required to wear

293 **change** exchange; **repair** come again  294 **Blow** blossom  297 **damask** red and white (like the Damascus rose)  298 **vailing** letting fall  299 **Avaunt, perplexity** Away, confusion!  304 **gear** outfit  319 **wakes** vigils and feastings; **wassails** revelry  322 **pins the wenches** wears maidens' favors  324 **carve** make gestures of courtship  326 **form** etiquette; **Nice** exquisite  327 **at tables** backgammon

In honorable terms. Nay, he can sing
A mean° most meanly; and in ushering
Mend° him who can. The ladies call him sweet.          330
The stairs, as he treads on them, kiss his feet.
This is the flow'r that smiles on every one,
To show his teeth as white as whale's-bone;
And consciences that will not die in debt
Pay him the due of "honey-tongued Boyet."             335

KING
A blister on his sweet tongue, with my heart,
That put Armado's page out of his part!

*Enter [the* PRINCESS *and] the* LADIES [*with* BOYET].

BEROWNE
See where it comes! Behavior, what wert thou
Till this madman showed thee, and what art thou
    now?

KING
All hail, sweet madam, and fair time of day.           340

PRINCESS
"Fair" in "all hail"° is foul, as I conceive.

KING
Construe my speeches better, if you may.

PRINCESS
Then wish me better, I will give you leave.

KING
We came to visit you, and purpose now
To lead you to our court. Vouchsafe it then.          345

PRINCESS
This field shall hold me, and so hold your vow.
Nor God nor I delights in perjured men.

KING
Rebuke me not for that which you provoke.
The virtue° of your eye must break my oath.

PRINCESS
You nickname° virtue. "Vice" you should have spoke;   350
For virtue's office never breaks men's troth.
Now, by my maiden honor, yet as pure
As the unsullied lily, I protest,
A world of torments though I should endure,
I would not yield to be your house's guest,           355
So much I hate a breaking cause° to be
Of heavenly oaths, vowed with integrity.

KING
O, you have lived in desolation here,
Unseen, unvisited, much to our shame.

PRINCESS
Not so, my lord. It is not so, I swear.                360
We have had pastimes here and pleasant game.
A mess° of Russians left us but of late.

KING
How, madam? Russians?

PRINCESS                        Ay, in truth, my lord;
Trim gallants, full of courtship and of state.

ROSALINE
Madam, speak true. It is not so, my lord.             365
My lady, to the manner of the days,°
In courtesy gives undeserving praise.

We four indeed confronted were with four
In Russian habit.° Here they stayed an hour
And talked apace; and in that hour, my lord,          370
They did not bless us with one happy° word.
I dare not call them fools, but this I think,
When they are thirsty, fools would fain have drink.

BEROWNE
This jest is dry to me. Gentle sweet,
Your wit makes wise things foolish. When we greet     375
With eyes best seeing heaven's fiery eye,°
By light we lose light. Your capacity
Is of that nature that to your huge store
Wise things seem foolish and rich things but poor.

ROSALINE
This proves you wise and rich, for in my eye—         380

BEROWNE
I am a fool, and full of poverty.

ROSALINE
But that you take what doth to you belong,
It were a fault to snatch words from my tongue.

BEROWNE
O, I am yours, and all that I possess.

ROSALINE
All the fool mine?

BEROWNE            I cannot give you less.               385

ROSALINE
Which of the vizards was it that you wore?

BEROWNE
Where, when, what vizard? Why demand you this?

ROSALINE
There, then, that vizard, that superfluous case°
That hid the worse, and showed the better face.

KING
We were descried. They'll mock us now downright.      390

DUMAINE
Let us confess, and turn it to a jest.

PRINCESS
Amazed, my lord? Why looks your highness sad?

ROSALINE
Help! Hold his brows! He'll sound.° Why look you
    pale?
Seasick, I think, coming from Muscovy.

BEROWNE
Thus pour the stars down plagues for perjury.         395
Can any face of brass° hold longer out?
Here stand I, lady, dart thy skill at me.
Bruise me with scorn, confound me with a flout,
Thrust thy sharp wit quite through my ignorance,
Cut me to pieces with thy keen conceit,°              400
And I will wish thee never more to dance,
Nor never more in Russian habit wait.
O, never will I trust to speeches penned,
Nor to the motion of a schoolboy's tongue,
Nor never come in vizard to my friend,               405
Nor woo in rhyme, like a blind harper's song!
Taffeta phrases,° silken terms precise,
Three-piled° hyperboles, spruce affectation,
Figures° pedantical—these summer flies

---

329 **mean** intermediate part  330 **Mend** surpass  341 **hail**
with a pun on the meaning "sleet"  349 **virtue** power  350
**nickname** name by mistake  356 **breaking cause** cause for
breaking off  362 **mess** group of four  366 **to . . . days**
according to the fashion of the time

369 **habit** dress  371 **happy** appropriate  376 **heaven's
fiery eye** the sun  388 **case** covering  393 **sound** swoon
396 **face of brass** brazen manner  400 **conceit** imagination
407 **Taffeta phrases** fine speech  408 **Three-piled** the finest
weight velvet  409 **Figures** figures of speech

Have blown° me full of maggot ostentation.                    410
I do forswear them; and I here protest
By this white glove (how white the hand, God knows!)
Henceforth my wooing mind shall be expressed
In russet° yeas and honest kersey° noes.
And to begin, wench—so God help me, law!—        415
My love to thee is sound, sans° crack or flaw.

ROSALINE
Sans "sans," I pray you.

BEROWNE                    Yet I have a trick°
Of the old rage. Bear with me, I am sick.
I'll leave it by degrees. Soft, let us see—
Write "Lord have mercy on us"° on those three.        420
They are infected, in their hearts it lies;
They have the plague, and caught it of your eyes.
These lords are visited;° you are not free,°
For the Lord's tokens° on you do I see.

PRINCESS
No, they are free that gave these tokens to us.        425

BEROWNE
Our states° are forfeit. Seek not to undo us.

ROSALINE
It is not so, for how can this be true,
That you stand forfeit, being those that sue?

BEROWNE
Peace! for I will not have to do with you.

ROSALINE
Nor shall not if I do as I intend.        430

BEROWNE
Speak for yourselves. My wit is at an end.

KING
Teach us, sweet madam, for our rude transgression
Some fair excuse.

PRINCESS                    The fairest is confession.
Were not you here but even now disguised?

KING
Madam, I was.

PRINCESS                    And were you well advised?        435

KING
I was, fair madam.

PRINCESS                    When you then were here,
What did you whisper in your lady's ear?

KING
That more than all the world I did respect her.

PRINCESS
When she shall challenge this, you will reject her.

KING
Upon mine honor, no.

PRINCESS                    Peace, peace, forbear!        440
Your oath once broke, you force not° to forswear.

KING
Despise me when I break this oath of mine.

PRINCESS
I will, and therefore keep it. Rosaline,
What did the Russian whisper in your ear?

ROSALINE
Madame, he swore that he did hold me dear        445

As precious eyesight, and did value me
Above this world; adding thereto, moreover,
That he would wed me or else die my lover.

PRINCESS
God give thee joy of him. The noble lord
Most honorably doth uphold his word.        450

KING
What mean you, madam? By my life, my troth,
I never swore this lady such an oath.

ROSALINE
By heaven you did! And to confirm it plain,
You gave me this, but take it, sir, again.

KING
My faith and this the princess I did give.        455
I knew her by this jewel on her sleeve.

PRINCESS
Pardon me, sir, this jewel did she wear,
And Lord Berowne, I thank him, is my dear.
What! Will you have me, or your pearl again?

BEROWNE
Neither of either, I remit both twain.        460
I see the trick on't. Here was a consent,
Knowing aforehand of our merriment,
To dash° it like a Christmas comedy.
Some carry-tale, some please-man,° some slight zany,°
Some mumble-news,° some trencher-knight,° some
Dick°        465
That smiles his cheek in years,° and knows the trick
To make my lady laugh when she's disposed,
Told our intents before; which once disclosed,
The ladies did change favors, and then we,
Following the signs, wooed but the sign of she.        470
Now, to our perjury to add more terror,
We are again forsworn, in will and error.
Much upon this 'tis.° [To BOYET.] And might not you
Forestall our sport, to make us thus untrue?
Do not you know my lady's foot by th' squier,°        475
And laugh upon the apple of her eye?°
And stand between her back, sir, and the fire,
Holding a trencher,° jesting merrily?
You put our page out.° Go, you are allowed.°
Die when you will, a smock° shall be your shroud.        480
You leer upon me, do you? There's an eye
Wounds like a leaden sword.

BOYET                    Full merrily
Hath this brave manage,° this career,° been run.

BEROWNE
Lo, he is tilting straight.° Peace! I have done.

Enter [COSTARD the] clown.

Welcome, pure wit! Thou part'st a fair fray.        485

COSTARD
O Lord, sir, they would know
Whether the three Worthies shall come in or no.

---

410 blown filled   414 russet characteristic red-brown color of peasants' clothes; kersey plain wool cloth   416 sans without   417 trick trace   420 Lord . . . us inscription posted on the doors of houses harboring the plague   423 visited attacked by plague; free free of infection   424 the Lord's tokens plague spots   426 states estates   441 force not do not think it wrong

463 dash ridicule   464 please-man toady; zany buffoon   465 mumble-news prattler; trencher-knight brave man at the table; Dick fellow   466 smiles . . . years laughs his face into wrinkles   473 Much . . . 'tis It is very much like this   475 by th' squier by the rule (i.e., have her measure)   476 laugh . . . eye laugh, looking closely into her eyes   478 trencher wooden plate   479 put . . . out take him out of his part; allowed permitted (licensed, like a court fool)   480 smock woman's garment   483 manage display of horsemanship; career charge   484 tilting straight already jousting

BEROWNE
What, are there but three?

COSTARD                         No, sir, but it is vara° fine,
For every one pursents° three.

BEROWNE                         And three times thrice is nine.

COSTARD
Not so, sir, under correction, sir, I hope, it is not so.   490
You cannot beg us,° sir, I can assure you, sir; we know
what we know.
I hope, sir, three times thrice, sir—

BEROWNE                         Is not nine?

COSTARD   Under correction, sir, we know whereuntil
it doth amount.

BEROWNE   By Jove, I always took three threes for 495
nine.

COSTARD   O Lord, sir, it were pity you should get
your living by reck'ning, sir.

BEROWNE   How much is it?

COSTARD   O Lord, sir, the parties themselves, the 500
actors, sir, will show whereuntil it doth amount. For
mine own part, I am, as they say, but to parfect° one
man in one poor man—Pompion° the Great, sir.

BEROWNE   Art thou one of the Worthies?

COSTARD   It pleased them to think me worthy of 505
Pompey the Great. For mine own part, I know not the
degree° of the Worthy, but I am to stand for him.

BEROWNE   Go, bid them prepare.

COSTARD
We will turn it finely off, sir; we will take some
care.                                    Exit.

KING
Berowne, they will shame us. Let them not approach.   510

BEROWNE
We are shame-proof, my lord; and 'tis some policy°
To have one show worse than the king's and his
company.

KING
I say they shall not come.

PRINCESS
Nay, my good lord, let me o'errule you now.
That sport best pleases that doth least know how,   515
Where zeal strives to content, and the contents
Dies in the zeal of that which it presents.°
Their form confounded makes most form in mirth°
When great things laboring perish in their birth.

BEROWNE
A right description of our sport, my lord.           520

*Enter [ARMADO the] braggart.*

ARMADO   Anointed, I implore so much expense of
thy royal sweet breath as will utter a brace° of words.

[*Converses apart with the KING, and delivers a paper to
him.*]

PRINCESS   Doth this man serve God?

BEROWNE   Why ask you?

PRINCESS   'A speaks not like a man of God his making.   525

ARMADO   That is all one, my fair, sweet, honey
monarch; for, I protest, the schoolmaster is exceeding
fantastical; too-too vain, too-too vain; but we will
put it, as they say, to *fortuna de la guerra.*° I wish you
the peace of mind, most royal couplement!°      *Exit.*   530

KING   Here is like to be a good presence of Worthies.
He presents Hector of Troy; the swain, Pompey the
Great; the parish curate, Alexander; Armado's page,
Hercules; the pedant, Judas Maccabaeus:
And if these four Worthies in their first show thrive,   535
These four will change habits° and present the other
five.

BEROWNE   There is five in the first show.

KING   You are deceivèd, 'tis not so.

BEROWNE
The pedant, the braggart, the hedge-priest,° the fool,
and the boy—
Abate throw at novum,° and the whole world again   540
Cannot pick out five such, take each one in his vein.°

KING
The ship is under sail, and here she comes amain.°

*Enter [COSTARD, for] Pompey.*

COSTARD
"I Pompey am—"

BEROWNE                    You lie, you are not he!

COSTARD
"I Pompey am—"

BOYET                      With libbard's head° on knee.

BEROWNE
Well said, old mocker. I must needs be friends with
thee.                                                    545

COSTARD
"I Pompey am, Pompey surnamed the Big—"

DUMAINE   The "Great."

COSTARD
It is "Great," sir—"Pompey surnamed the Great,
That oft in field, with targe° and shield, did make my
foe to sweat,
And traveling along this coast I here am come by
chance,                                                   550
And lay my arms before the legs of this sweet lass of
France."
If your ladyship would say, "Thanks, Pompey," I had
done.

PRINCESS   Great thanks, great Pompey.

COSTARD   'Tis not so much worth, but I hope I was
perfect. I made a little fault in "Great."                555

BEROWNE   My hat to a halfpenny, Pompey proves
the best Worthy.

*Enter [NATHANIEL the] curate, for Alexander.*

NATHANIEL
"When in the world I lived, I was the world's commander;

---

488 **vara** northern pronunciation of *very*   489 **pursents**
represents   491 **beg us** prove us fools   502 **parfect** play the
part of   503 **Pompion** pumpkin (for Pompey)   507 **degree**
rank   511 **policy** crafty device   516–17 **contents . . . presents**
the substance is destroyed by the excessive zeal in presenting
it   518 **Their . . . mirth** art that is confused is most laughable entertainment   522 **brace** pair

529 **fortuna . . . guerra** fortune of war (Italian)   530
**couplement** pair   536 **habits** costumes   539 **hedge-priest**
unlearnèd priest   540 **Abate . . . novum** except for the
throw at nine (in a game of dice)   541 **vein** characteristic
way   542 **amain** swiftly   544 **libbard's head** heraldic
painting of leopard   549 **targe** shield

By east, west, north, and south, I spread my conquering
  might;
My scutcheon° plain declares that I am Alisander—"   560

**BOYET**
Your nose says, no, you are not; for it stands too right.°

**BEROWNE**
Your nose smells "no" in this, most tender-smelling
  knight.

**PRINCESS**
The conqueror is dismayed. Proceed, good Alexander.

**NATHANIEL**
"When in the world I lived, I was the world's commander—"

**BOYET** Most true, 'tis right—you were so, Alisander.   565

**BEROWNE** Pompey the Great—

**COSTARD** Your servant, and Costard.

**BEROWNE** Take away the conqueror, take away
Alisander.

**COSTARD** [*To* NATHANIEL.] O, sir, you have over-   570
thrown Alisander the conqueror! You will be scraped
out of the painted cloth° for this. Your lion that holds
his pole-ax° sitting on a close-stool° will be given to
Ajax.° He will be the ninth Worthy. A conqueror,
and afeard to speak? Run away for shame, Alisander.   575
[NATHANIEL *stands aside.*] There, an't° shall please
you, a foolish mild man; an honest man, look you,
and soon dashed. He is a marvelous good neighbor,
faith, and a very good bowler; but for Alisander—
alas! you see how 'tis—a little o'erparted.° But there   580
are Worthies a-coming will speak their mind in some
other sort.

**PRINCESS** Stand aside, good Pompey.

[COSTARD *stands aside.*]

*Enter* [HOLOFERNES *the*] *pedant, for Judas, and* [MOTH]
*the boy, for Hercules.*

**HOLOFERNES**
"Great Hercules is presented by this imp,°
Whose club killed Cerberus, that three-headed canus;°   585
And when he was a babe, a child, a shrimp,
Thus did he strangle serpents in his manus.°
Quoniam° he seemeth in minority,°
Ergo° I come with this apology."
Keep some state° in thy exit, and vanish.   590
               *Exit* [MOTH *the*] *boy* [*to one side*].
"Judas I am—"

**DUMAINE** A Judas?

**HOLOFERNES** Not Iscariot, sir.
"Judas I am, ycleped° Maccabaeus."°

**DUMAINE** Judas Maccabaeus clipt° is plain Judas.   595

**BEROWNE** A kissing traitor. How, art thou proved
Judas?

**HOLOFERNES**
"Judas I am—"

**DUMAINE** The more shame for you, Judas.

**HOLOFERNES** What mean you, sir?   600

**BOYET** To make Judas hang himself.

**HOLOFERNES** Begin, sir; you are my elder.

**BEROWNE** Well followed: Judas was hanged on an
elder.°

**HOLOFERNES** I will not be put out of countenance.   605

**BEROWNE** Because thou hast no face.

**HOLOFERNES** What is this?

**BOYET** A cittern-head.°

**DUMAINE** The head of a bodkin.°

**BEROWNE** A death's face in a ring.°   610

**LONGAVILLE** The face of an old Roman coin, scarce
seen.

**BOYET** The pommel of Caesar's falchion.°

**DUMAINE** The carved-bone face on a flask.

**BEROWNE** Saint George's half-cheek° in a brooch.   615

**DUMAINE** Ay, and in a brooch of lead.°

**BEROWNE**
Ay, and worn in the cap of a toothdrawer.
And now forward, for we have put thee in counte-
nance.

**HOLOFERNES** You have put me out of countenance.°

**BEROWNE** False. We have given thee faces.   620

**HOLOFERNES** But you have outfaced them all.

**BEROWNE** And° thou wert a lion, we would do so.

**BOYET**
Therefore as he is an ass, let him go.
And so adieu, sweet Jude. Nay, why dost thou stay?

**DUMAINE** For the latter end of his name.   625

**BEROWNE**
For the ass to the Jude? Give it him. Jud-as, away!

**HOLOFERNES**
This is not generous, not gentle, not humble.

**BOYET**
A light for Monsieur Judas! It grows dark, he may
stumble.

[HOLOFERNES *stands aside.*]

**PRINCESS**
Alas, poor Maccabaeus, how hath he been baited!°

*Enter* [ARMADO *the*] *braggart,* [*for Hector*].

**BEROWNE** Hide thy head, Achilles! Here comes   630
Hector° in arms.

**DUMAINE** Though my mocks come home by me, I
will now be merry.

**KING** Hector was but a Troyan in respect of this.

**BOYET** But is this Hector?   635

**KING** I think Hector was not so clean-timbered.°

**LONGAVILLE** His leg is too big for Hector's.

**DUMAINE** More calf, certain.

**BOYET** No; he is best indued in the small.°

**BEROWNE** This cannot be Hector.   640

**DUMAINE** He's a god or a painter; for he makes faces.

---

**560 scutcheon** coat of arms   **561 right** straight (Alexander's
neck was a little awry)   **572 painted cloth** wall-hanging
**573 pole-ax** battle-ax (and penis); **close-stool** commode
**574 Ajax** Greek warrior (with a pun on *jakes* = privy)
**576 an't** if it   **580 o'erparted** having too difficult a part
**584 imp** child   **585 canus** dog (from Latin *canis*)   **587 manus**
hand   **588 Quoniam** since; **in minority** under age   **589
Ergo** therefore   **590 state** dignity   **594 ycleped** called;
**Maccabaeus** Hebrew warrior   **595 clipt** (1) cut (2) embraced

**604 elder** a kind of tree   **608 cittern-head** head of a stringed
musical instrument   **609 bodkin** long hairpin   **610 death's
. . . ring** finger ring with the carving of a skull   **613 falchion**
sword   **615 half-cheek** profile   **616 brooch of lead** ornament worn in a cap as badge of dentist's trade   **619 out of
countenance** disconcerted   **622 And** if   **629 baited** tormented
**630–31 Achilles . . . Hector** the Greek and Trojan champions
**636 clean-timbered** clean-limbed   **639 small** lower part of
the leg

ARMADO
"The armipotent° Mars, of lances the almighty,
Gave Hector a gift—"
DUMAINE    A gilt nutmeg.°
BEROWNE    A lemon.    645
LONGAVILLE    Stuck with cloves.
DUMAINE    No, cloven.
ARMADO    Peace!
"The armipotent Mars, of lances the almighty,
Gave Hector a gift, the heir of Ilion;    650
A man so breathed° that certain he would fight, yea
From morn till night, out of his pavilion.°
I am that flower—"
DUMAINE    That mint.
LONGAVILLE    That columbine.
ARMADO    Sweet Lord Longaville, rein thy tongue.
LONGAVILLE    I must rather give it the rein, for it runs    655
against Hector.
DUMAINE    Ay, and Hector's a greyhound.
ARMADO    The sweet war-man is dead and rotten.
Sweet chucks, beat not the bones of the buried. When
he breathed, he was a man. But I will forward with    660
my device. [To the PRINCESS.] Sweet royalty, bestow
on me the sense of hearing.

BEROWNE steps forth [to whisper to COSTARD].

PRINCESS    Speak, brave Hector; we are much de-
lighted.
ARMADO    I do adore thy sweet grace's slipper.    665
BOYET [Aside to DUMAINE.]    Loves her by the foot.
DUMAINE [Aside to BOYET.]    He may not by the yard.°
ARMADO
"This Hector far surmounted Hannibal—"
The party is gone.°
COSTARD    Fellow Hector, she is gone.° She is two    670
months on her way.
ARMADO    What meanest thou?
COSTARD    Faith, unless you play the honest Troyan,
the poor wench is cast away. She's quick;° the child
brags in her belly already. 'Tis yours.    675
ARMADO    Dost thou infamonize° me among poten-
tates? Thou shalt die.
COSTARD    Then shall Hector be whipped for Jaque-
netta that is quick by him, and hanged for Pompey
that is dead by him.    680
DUMAINE    Most rare Pompey!
BOYET    Renowned Pompey!
BEROWNE    Greater than great. Great, great, great
Pompey! Pompey the Huge!
DUMAINE    Hector trembles.    685
BEROWNE    Pompey is moved. More Ates,° more Ates!
Stir them on, stir them on!
DUMAINE    Hector will challenge him.
BEROWNE    Ay, if 'a have no more man's blood in his
belly than will sup a flea.    690
ARMADO    By the North Pole, I do challenge thee.
COSTARD    I will not fight with a pole, like a northern

man. I'll slash; I'll do it by the sword. I bepray you,
let me borrow my arms again.
DUMAINE    Room for the incensed Worthies!    695
COSTARD    I'll do it in my shirt.
DUMAINE    Most resolute Pompey!
MOTH    Master, let me take you a buttonhole lower.°
Do you not see, Pompey is uncasing° for the combat?
What mean you? You will lose your reputation.    700
ARMADO    Gentlemen and soldiers, pardon me. I will
not combat in my shirt.
DUMAINE    You may not deny it. Pompey hath made
the challenge.
ARMADO    Sweet bloods, I both may and will.    705
BEROWNE    What reason have you for't?
ARMADO    The naked truth of it is, I have no shirt. I go
woolward° for penance.
BOYET    True, and it was enjoined° him in Rome for
want of linen; since when, I'll be sworn he wore none    710
but a dishclout of Jaquenetta's, and that 'a wears next
his heart for a favor.

Enter a messenger, Monsieur MARCADE.

MARCADE
God save you, madam.
PRINCESS
Welcome, Marcade,
But that thou interrupt'st our merriment.    715
MARCADE
I am sorry, madam, for the news I bring
Is heavy in my tongue. The king your father—
PRINCESS
Dead, for my life!
MARCADE
Even so. My tale is told.
BEROWNE
Worthies, away! The scene begins to cloud.    720
ARMADO    For mine own part, I breathe free breath.
I have seen the day of wrong through the little hole
of discretion, and I will right myself like a soldier.
                            Exeunt WORTHIES.
KING
How fares your majesty?
PRINCESS
Boyet, prepare. I will away tonight.    725
KING
Madam, not so. I do beseech you, stay.
PRINCESS
Prepare, I say. I thank you, gracious lords,
For all your fair endeavors, and entreat
Out of a new-sad soul that you vouchsafe
In your rich wisdom to excuse, or hide    730
The liberal opposition of our spirits,
If overboldly we have borne ourselves
In the converse of breath.° Your gentleness
Was guilty of it. Farewell, worthy lord.
A heavy heart bears not a humble° tongue.    735
Excuse me so, coming too short of thanks
For my great suit so easily obtained.

---

642 armipotent powerful in arms  644 gilt nutmeg with
special icing  651 breathed well-exercised  652 pavilion
tent for a champion at a tournament  667 yard slang word for
male organ  669 The . . . gone Armado is referring to Hector
670 she is gone she is pregnant  674 quick pregnant  676
infamonize defame  686 Ates goddess of mischief

698 take . . . lower take you down a peg  699 uncasing
removing his coat  707–08 go woolward wearing wool next
to the skin  709 enjoined commanded  733 converse of
breath conversation  735 humble civil, tactful

KING
The extreme parts of time extremely forms
All causes to the purpose of his speed,°
And often at his very loose° decides       740
That which long process could not arbitrate.
And though the mourning brow of progeny°
Forbid the smiling courtesy of love
The holy suit which fain it would convince,°
Yet, since love's argument was first on foot,       745
Let not the cloud of sorrow justle it
From what it purposed; since to wail friends lost
Is not by much so wholesome-profitable
As to rejoice at friends but newly found.
PRINCESS
I understand you not. My griefs are double.       750
BEROWNE
Honest plain words best pierce the ear of grief;
And by these badges° understand the king.
For your fair sakes have we neglected time,
Played foul play with our oaths. Your beauty, ladies,
Hath much deformed us, fashioning our humors       755
Even to the opposèd end of our intents;
And what in us hath seemed ridiculous—
As love is full of unbefitting strains,
All wanton as a child, skipping and vain,
Formed by the eye and therefore, like the eye,       760
Full of straying shapes, of habits and of forms,
Varying in subjects as the eye doth roll
To every varied object in his glance;
Which parti-coated° presence of loose love
Put on by us, if, in your heavenly eyes,       765
Have misbecomed our oaths and gravities,
Those heavenly eyes that look into these faults
Suggested° us to make. Therefore, ladies,
Our love being yours, the error that love makes
Is likewise yours. We to ourselves prove false,       770
By being once false forever to be true
To those that make us both—fair ladies, you.
And even that falsehood, in itself a sin,
Thus purifies itself and turns to grace.
PRINCESS
We have received your letters, full of love;       775
Your favors, the ambassadors of love;
And in our maiden council rated° them
At courtship, pleasant jest, and courtesy,
As bombast° and as lining to the time.
But more devout than this in our respects       780
Have we not been, and therefore met your loves
In their own fashion, like a merriment.
DUMAINE
Our letters, madam, showed much more than jest.
LONGAVILLE
So did our looks.
ROSALINE            We did not quote° them so.
KING
Now, at the latest minute of the hour       785
Grant us your loves.

PRINCESS            A time, methinks, too short
To make a world-without-end bargain in.
No, no, my lord, your grace is perjured much,
Full of dear guiltiness; and therefore this—
If for my love (as there is no such cause)       790
You will do aught, this shall you do for me:
Your oath I will not trust, but go with speed
To some forlorn and naked hermitage,
Remote from all the pleasures of the world;
There stay until the twelve celestial signs°       795
Have brought about the annual reckoning.
If this austere insociable life
Change not your offer made in heat of blood—
If frosts and fasts, hard lodging and thin weeds,°
Nip not the gaudy blossoms of your love,       800
But that it bear this trial, and last love—
Then, at the expiration of the year,
Come challenge me, challenge me by these deserts,
And, by this virgin palm now kissing thine,
I will be thine; and till that instant, shut       805
My woeful self up in a mourning house,
Raining the tears of lamentation
For the remembrance of my father's death.
If this thou do deny, let our hands part,
Neither entitled in the other's heart.       810
KING
If this, or more than this, I would deny,
To flatter up° these powers of mine with rest,
The sudden hand of death close up mine eye!
Hence hermit then—my heart is in thy breast.
[BEROWNE
And what to me, my love? and what to me?       815
ROSALINE
You must be purged, too, your sins are rank,
You are attaint° with faults and perjury;
Therefore, if you my favor mean to get,
A twelvemonth shall you spend, and never rest,
But seek the weary beds of people sick.]°       820
DUMAINE
But what to me, my love? But what to me?
A wife?
KATHARINE     A beard, fair health, and honesty;
With threefold love I wish you all these three.
DUMAINE
O, shall I say "I thank you, gentle wife"?
KATHARINE
Not so, my lord. A twelvemonth and a day       825
I'll mark no words that smooth-faced wooers say.
Come when the king doth to my lady come;
Then, if I have much love, I'll give you some.
DUMAINE
I'll serve thee true and faithfully till then.
KATHARINE
Yet swear not, lest ye be forsworn again.       830
LONGAVILLE
What says Maria?
MARIA          At the twelvemonth's end
I'll change my black gown for a faithful friend.

---

**738–39 The . . . speed** time, as it runs out, directs everything toward its conclusion   **740 at . . . loose** in the act of letting go   **742 progeny** descendants   **744 convince** prove   **752 badges** tokens   **764 parti-coated** fool's motley   **768 Suggested** tempted   **777 rated** valued   **779 bombast** padding   **784 quote** regard

**795 twelve celestial signs** of the Zodiac   **799 weeds** garments   **812 flatter up** pamper   **817 attaint** charged   **815–20** lines 821–32 duplicate this passage in an expanded form; probably Shakespeare failed to indicate clearly that these six lines had been superseded

**LONGAVILLE**
I'll stay with patience, but the time is long.

**MARIA**
The liker° you! Few taller are so young.

**BEROWNE**
Studies my lady? Mistress, look on me.                          835
Behold the window of my heart, mine eye,
What humble suit attends thy answer there.
Impose some service on me for thy love.

**ROSALINE**
Oft have I heard of you, my Lord Berowne,
Before I saw you, and the world's large tongue      840
Proclaims you for a man replete with mocks,
Full of comparisons and wounding flouts,°
Which you on all estates° will execute
That lie within the mercy of your wit.
To weed this wormwood° from your fructful° brain, 845
And therewithal to win me, if you please,
Without the which I am not to be won,
You shall this twelvemonth term from day to day
Visit the speechless sick, and still° converse
With groaning wretches; and your task shall be      850
With all the fierce endeavor of your wit
To enforce the painèd impotent to smile.

**BEROWNE**
To move wild laughter in the throat of death?
It cannot be; it is impossible;
Mirth cannot move a soul in agony.                       855

**ROSALINE**
Why, that's the way to choke a gibing spirit,
Whose influence is begot of that loose grace
Which shallow laughing hearers give to fools.
A jest's prosperity lies in the ear
Of him that hears it, never in the tongue            860
Of him that makes it. Then, if sickly ears,
Deafed with the clamors of their own dear groans,
Will hear your idle scorns, continue then,
And I will have you and that fault withal;
But if they will not, throw away that spirit,         865
And I shall find you empty of that fault,
Right joyful of your reformation.

**BEROWNE**
A twelvemonth? Well, befall what will befall,
I'll jest a twelvemonth in an hospital.

**PRINCESS** [*To the* KING.]
Ay, sweet my lord, and so I take my leave.           870

**KING**
No, madam, we will bring you on your way.

**BEROWNE**
Our wooing doth not end like an old play;
Jack hath not Jill. These ladies' courtesy
Might well have made our sport a comedy.

**KING**
Come, sir, it wants a twelvemonth and a day,         875
And then 'twill end.

**BEROWNE**          That's too long for a play.

*Enter* [ARMADO *the*] *braggart.*

**ARMADO**  Sweet majesty, vouchsafe me—
**PRINCESS**  Was not that Hector?

**DUMAINE**  The worthy knight of Troy.
**ARMADO**  I will kiss thy royal finger, and take leave.  880
I am a votary;° I have vowed to Jaquenetta to hold
the plough for her sweet love three year. But, most
esteemed greatness, will you hear the dialogue that
the two learned men have compiled in praise of the
owl and the cuckoo? It should have followed in the  885
end of our show.
**KING**  Call them forth quickly; we will do so.
**ARMADO**  Holla! Approach.

*Enter all.*

This side is Hiems, Winter; this Ver, the Spring; the
one maintained by the owl, th' other by the cuckoo.  890
Ver, begin.

                    *The Song.*

[SPRING]  When daisies pied° and violets blue
            And lady-smocks° all silver-white
          And cuckoo-buds° of yellow hue
            Do paint the meadows with delight,      895
          The cuckoo then, on every tree,
          Mocks married men; for thus sings he,
                              "Cuckoo!
          Cuckoo, cuckoo!" O word of fear,
          Unpleasing to a married ear!

          When shepherds pipe on oaten straws,       900
            And merry larks are ploughmen's clocks,
          When turtles tread,° and rooks, and daws,
            And maidens bleach their summer smocks,
          The cuckoo then, on every tree,
          Mocks married men; for thus sings he,      905
                              "Cuckoo!
          Cuckoo, cuckoo!" O word of fear,
          Unpleasing to a married ear!

WINTER  When icicles hang by the wall,
            And Dick the shepherd blows his nail,°
          And Tom bears logs into the hall,          910
            And milk comes frozen home in pail,
          When blood is nipped, and ways be foul,
          Then nightly sings the staring owl, "Tu-whit,
          Tu-who!" a merry note,
          While greasy Joan doth keel° the pot.      915

          When all aloud the wind doth blow,
            And coughing drowns the parson's saw,°
          And birds sit brooding in the snow,
            And Marian's nose looks red and raw,
          When roasted crabs° hiss in the bowl,      920
          Then nightly sings the staring owl, "Tu-whit,
          Tu-who!" a merry note,
          While greasy Joan doth keel the pot.

[ARMADO]  The words of Mercury are harsh after the
songs of Apollo.° [You that way, we this way.         925
                              *Exeunt omnes.*]

834 **liker** more like   842 **wounding flouts** painful jokes   843 **all estates** men of all kinds   845 **wormwood** bitterness; **fructful** fruitful   849 **still** always

881 **votary** sworn follower   892 **pied** parti-colored   893 **lady-smocks** watercresses, or cuckoo flowers   894 **cuckoo-buds** crowfoot, or buttercup   902 **turtles tread** turtledoves mate   909 **blows his nail** blows on his fingernails to warm them (and so, waiting patiently)   915 **keel** cool, by stirring or skimming   917 **saw** wise saying   920 **crabs** crabapples   924–25 **The . . . Apollo** Let us end with the songs, because clever words of the god Mercury would come harshly after the songs of Apollo, the god of poetry

# THE TRAGEDY OF
# KING RICHARD THE SECOND

EDITED BY KENNETH MUIR

## Introduction

*Richard II*, at least in its present form, was written and performed in 1595, after the publication of Samuel Daniel's *Civil Wars* (which was registered in October 1594) and before December 9, when there was a private performance before Sir Edward Hoby and his friends. The play was a popular one. According to Elizabeth I, by 1601 it had been played "forty" times; but when the Essex conspirators asked Shakespeare's company to put on a special performance on the eve of the rebellion, because they thought that the deposition of Richard would be good propaganda, the players protested that it was "so old and so long out of use" that it would attract only a small audience. The conspirators therefore subsidized the performance.

Shakespeare had already dealt with the remote effects of Bolingbroke's usurpation in *Henry VI* and *Richard III*, and his obvious model in the present play was *Edward II*, a play in which Christopher Marlowe had brilliantly dramatized the deposition and murder of Richard of Bordeaux's great-grandfather. There were already at least two plays on the reign of Richard II, *Jack Straw* and *Woodstock*, and it has been argued by Professor John Dover Wilson (in his edition of *Richard II*) that Shakespeare's tragedy was based on a lost play by the author of *The Troublesome Reign of King John*, the source of Shakespeare's *King John*. The main arguments that have been advanced in support of this theory are (1) the presence of various details in the play that presuppose knowledge on the part of the audience; (2) the presence of "fossil" rhymes in blank verse speeches, which seem to indicate that the speeches were originally in rhymed verse; (3) the badness of certain scenes (for example, V.iii) which, it is supposed, Shakespeare borrowed from the source play; (4) the use by Shakespeare, either directly or indirectly, of facts available only in two or three French chronicles that were still in manuscript. The last of these points is discussed in A Note on the Sources (p. 441). On the other three, I agree with most scholars that the existence of the source play has not been proved. I can see no resemblance between the style of *The Troublesome Reign* and that of the suspected scenes of *Richard II;* Shakespeare himself may have revised his own play, turning some rhymed verse into blank verse; the obscurities, which in any case are unnoticed in performance, may be explained by sheer carelessness in introducing facts that Shakespeare remembered from his reading; and it is not positively necessary to find a scapegoat for the feeble passages of rhymed verse in Act V. It will be remembered that in the other plays written about this time—*A Midsummer Night's Dream* and *Romeo and Juliet*—there is a considerable amount of rhyme, more than there had been in previous plays. These three plays have another characteristic in common—they are the first in which Shakespeare uses patterns of imagery for dramatic purposes.[1] The reasons for the rhymed verse are not far to seek. Shakespeare completed his second narrative poem in 1594, and he was still writing sonnets in 1595. Blank verse, moreover, was still a comparatively new medium for drama. Marlowe had led his audiences away from "jigging veins of rhyming mother wits" only seven years previously. The academic dramatists—Daniel and Greville—still used rhyme in their plays. Peele had used it in some scenes of *The Arraignment of Paris* and Kyd, though he had used blank verse for *The Spanish Tragedy*, reverted to rhyme in his *Cornelia*. The Countess of Pembroke was known to favor it. Apart from Marlowe's, very little good blank verse had been written, and the best nondramatic poets— Spenser, Sidney, Daniel, Drayton—all stuck to rhyme. Looking back, we can see that Wilton, where the countess lived, was the home of lost causes; but to Shakespeare, to whom rhyme came easily, the matter was not so obvious. After all, his early blank verse was comparatively artificial and certainly rhetorical. He did not suffer from Mr. Eliot's fear that the audience would realize that it was listening to poetry. The acting, too, in these early years, had a strong element of formality: the delivery of the verse was more important than the realistic portrayal of character. Shakespeare was only just beginning to portray character by varying the verse. He did this brilliantly with Juliet's Nurse and in the contrast between Richard and Bolingbroke in the abdication scene. But his touch was still uncertain. The Gardener scene (III.iv) was admirably conceived as a commentary by the common man on the state of England, and as a parabolic statement, which links up with Gaunt's

[1] See Richard D. Altick's analysis of the play and the works by Van Doren, Clemen, and Stirling listed in the Suggested References.

description of England as "this other Eden." But the execution of the scene falls far short of the conception. The Gardener, speaking in formal blank verse, indistinguishable from that used by royal and aristocratic characters, never really emerges from his role as a chorus. It would have been better, perhaps, to have written the scene in prose; but, for some reason, Shakespeare avoided prose altogether. Perhaps he was trying to please his new aristocratic friends.

Whatever the reasons, Shakespeare introduced a considerable amount of rhymed verse into *Richard II*. Some of it is successful, as in Bolingbroke's couplets in the third scene of the play (I.iii.144–47). But one scene (V.iii.73–135) is so bad that critics would like to believe that Shakespeare did not write it; or that, if he wrote it at all, it must belong to a much earlier version of the play, left inadvertently or ill-advisedly unrevised. As we have seen, however, Shakespeare hardly used rhyme at all in some of his early plays, so that the scene was probably written at the same period as the rest of the play. Swinburne, in *A Study of Shakespeare*, called the scene "the last hysterical struggle of rhyme to maintain its place in tragedy." The situation is farcical, with York, the Duchess, and Aumerle on their knees at once, and York actually urging the execution of his son. Shakespeare must have been aware of the absurdity, but he seems to have miscalculated the effect of the scene.

*Richard II* can be regarded either as a history play, the first of the tetralogy that includes the two parts of *Henry IV* and *Henry V*, or as a tragedy complete in itself. There are several indications in the play that Shakespeare had already planned to continue the story—for example, the Bishop of Carlisle's prophecy, Richard's own prophecy about Northumberland, the references to Prince Hal and Glendower, and the introduction of Hotspur—but when the play was first printed it was entitled *The Tragedy of Richard II*. Although it is a political tragedy, since we are as much concerned with the fate of England as with the fate of the hero, Richard has a more central role than Henry VI in three earlier histories or Henry IV in the next two histories.

The critics have been very much divided on the amount of sympathy we should extend to Richard. Some find him wholly admirable, and others regard him as wholly contemptible. To Kreyssig,

> he affords us the shocking spectacle of an absolute bankruptcy, mental and spiritual no less than in the world of outward affairs, caused by one condition only: that nature has given him the character of a Dilettante, and called him to a position which, more than any other, demands the Artist.[2]

To Walter Pater, writing a few years later, Richard seemed to be "an exquisite poet." Swinburne, in *Three Plays of Shakespeare*, declared that the third scene

> reveals the protagonist of the play as so pitifully mean and cruel a weakling that no future action or suffering can lift him above the level which divides and purifies pity from contempt.

[2] Quoted by A. P. Rossiter, *"Angel with Horns" and Other Shakespeare Lectures*, ed. Graham Storey (1961), p. 39.

Later in his essay, Swinburne accused Richard of "callous cruelty" and "heartless hypocrisy," remarking that "the histrionic young tyrant" was removed

> once for all beyond reach of manly sympathy or compassion unqualified by scorn. If we can ever be sorry for anything that befalls so vile a sample of royalty, our sorrow must be so diluted and adulterated by recollection of his wickedness and baseness that the tribute could hardly be acceptable to any but the most pitiable example or exception of mankind.

Walter Raleigh, however, remarked in *Shakespeare* that "It is difficult to condemn Richard without taking sides against poetry"; and two recent poets have sprung to Richard's defense, as they would have defended a minor poet of our own day, whose life had been a failure in the eyes of the world. W. B. Yeats, in *Ideas of Good and Evil*, passed lightly over the king's faults, and declared that Shakespeare

> made his king fail, a little because he lacked some qualities that were doubtless common among his scullions, but more because he had certain qualities that are uncommon in all ages. To suppose that Shakespeare preferred the man who deposed his king is to suppose that Shakespeare judged men with the eyes of a Municipal Councilor weighing the merits of a Town Clerk; and that had he been by when Verlaine cried out from his bed, "Sir, you have been made by the stroke of a pen, but I have been made by the breath of God," he would have thought the Hospital Superintendent the better man.

John Masefield, obviously much influenced by Yeats' essay, declares in *William Shakespeare* that Richard fails because he is not common:

> The tragedy of the sensitive soul, always acute, becomes terrible when that soul is made king here by one of the accidents of life.

John Bailey, irritated by Yeats and Masefield, retorted tartly in *The Continuity of Letters*:

> Fools such critics are. . . . For their own choice Mr. Yeats and Mr. Masefield are free. Only they must not father it upon Shakespeare. No man has ever known the theater better than he; and if he had meant us to admire Richard and despise Henry [Henry V, not Henry IV] we should most assuredly not have escaped doing it; but there is no audience from his day to ours which has not instantly and instinctively worshiped Henry and pitied Richard.

We may note in passing that many good critics have had reservations about Henry V, and modern audiences (except in time of war) have been less enthusiastic about him than Bailey appears to be, and more sympathetic to Richard, especially when the part was played by Sir John Gielgud. But the debate continues. A. P. Rossiter, to give a last example, unkindly suggests that there is "something in Richard which calls out the latent homosexuality of critics"; and to Pater's claim that Richard's nature is "that of a poet," he replies: "If so, surely a very *bad* poet."

Some of Richard's sympathetic critics seem to forget that he is depicted as a murderer; and those who find no redeeming features in his character ignore or misinterpret the changes brought about by suffering. Shakespeare's model for his play (as we have seen) was *Edward II*. Marlowe's method was to concentrate on Edward's misgovernment in the opening acts of the play and to arouse sympathy for him after his deposition, partly by stressing the unscrupulousness of his opponents, partly by showing that Edward was beloved by his favorites, and partly by a detailed presentation of his sufferings. Shakespeare's method is similar. In the first two acts he gives a vivid portrayal of Richard's misgovernment, which is brought home to us particularly by the patriotic indignation of Gaunt's dying speeches. In the later acts, although we are shown again and again Richard's weaknesses of character, Shakespeare arouses sympathy for him by the poetic beauty of his long arias, by his tragic isolation, by the pathos of his leave-taking from his queen, by the account of his entry into London, and by the episode of the loyal groom. Yet Shakespeare's method differs in several respects from Marlowe's. Richard's initial guilt is greater than Edward's, his suffering is mental rather than physical, and his character is purged by it. Although some critics believe that his scene with the queen and his soliloquy in prison reveal that he is still an incorrigible sentimentalist, turning everything, like Ophelia, to favor and to prettiness, there are signs that he has acquired a greater self-awareness and a recognition of his faults: "I wasted time, and now doth Time waste me" (V.v.49). But the greatest difference between the attitudes of the two dramatists is that Marlowe never mentions, while Shakespeare continually stresses, the divine right of kings. We are warned over and over again that Richard's deposition is a sin which will be punished by the horrors of civil war. It was to stress this point that Shakespeare deviated from his sources in giving the Bishop of Carlisle his eloquent prophecy just before the deposition scene.

Professor J. Dover Wilson has called *Richard II* "a Tudor passion play," a description which fits in with the frequent references to Scripture by which Shakespeare achieves its particular tone and atmosphere. Some of Richard's speeches are lamentations on the fall of princes, a recognition of the mortality of man and of the peculiar vulnerability of those called to high estate, which read like transmutations of Lydgate's *Fall of Princes* or of *A Mirror for Magistrates*. These link up with the medieval conception of tragedy as a fall from greatness into misery. But the scriptural references are mainly designed to emphasize the sin of rebellion against an anointed king, and they show that Shakespeare was steeped in the teaching of the *Homilies*, with whatever reservations he may have had about it. Richard compares his treacherous friends to Judas and those who show an outward pity at his fall to Pilate. He imagines that Bolingbroke will tremble at his sin; he boasts that the deputy elected by the Lord cannot be deposed by the breath of worldly men, that angels will fight on his side, and that the unborn children of the rebels will be struck by pestilence. Bolingbroke, for having broken his oath of allegiance, is damned in the book of heaven. England, rent by civil war, will be called Golgotha. The Bishop of Carlisle warns Bolingbroke not to set house against house; and Bolingbroke himself compares Richard's

murderer to Cain. In prison Richard meditates on two Gospel texts.

Richard's own biblical references are an appeal for Christian compassion. It is possible, indeed, that Shakespeare had in mind the whole problem of charity and pity; but Professor Peter Alexander, who makes this suggestion in *Shakespeare's Life and Art*, goes on to complain that

the fallen king's insistence on his own position . . . is incompatible with the self-forgetfulness which is as essential to the tragic as to the Christian hero. For this is not the waking as from a dream of some disinterested heart to the self-seeking of society, but the long lament of one who gave short shrift to a dying Gaunt; and this contrast between Richard's indifference to others and exquisite sensibility for himself makes tragedy impossible.

Even if we could believe in the self-forgetfulness of Hamlet, Lear, or Othello, we may well feel that Professor Alexander does not make allowances for the development of Richard's character in the course of the play, nor for the Elizabethan convention by which a character comments on his own situation. When Lear talks of his own pitiful state, or when Othello or Antony makes his final apologia, these characters are not meant to be indulging in self-pity or vanity: they are used by the dramatist to guide the feelings of the audience. In the mature tragedies, it is true, we do not get the self-comparison of a character to Christ; but the method is largely justified in Richard's case by the central importance in the play of the concept of divine right. The same consideration justifies the strong element of ritual in the play.

We are presented throughout the play with the contrast between Richard and his successor. Richard, the anointed king, is unfit to rule, in spite of his good qualities, and in spite of his belated acquisition of self-knowledge. Henry Bolingbroke is a born ruler, but his reign is doomed to misery because he is a usurper. The contrast is brought out in other ways. Richard is frivolous, witty, eloquent, and poetic, a man of words who wears his heart upon his sleeve, one who is continually playing a part, to whom, as John Palmer says in *Political Characters*, "nothing has interest or significance but what concerns himself." He loses his crown not because he stops the duel at Coventry—an action which he takes with the approval of his council, and which can hardly be regarded as an example of his love of play-acting—but because of his murder of Gloucester before the beginning of the play, because of his confiscation of Gaunt's estates, because his return from Ireland is delayed by contrary winds, and because he despairs on his arrival in England. This last point, which is usually taken as a prime example of his refusal to face realities, could as plausibly be used to prove that he was more realistic than his supporters. He is brought to his ruin, as all Shakespeare's tragic heroes are, by a combination of fate and faults of character.

Henry is a contrast in every respect. He is generally taciturn, although he can turn on his charm like a tap, as is apparent from the way even Northumberland is captivated by it. The account given in I.iv of his triumphant journey into exile, although put into the mouth of an enemy, is corroborated by what he himself admits in *I Henry IV*:

And then I stole all courtesy from heaven,
And dressed myself in such humility
That I did pluck allegiance from men's hearts,
Loud shouts and salutations from their mouths,
Even in the presence of the crownèd king.   (III.ii.50–54)

The same calculated behavior is described in Hotspur's account of their first meeting. Bolingbroke, like Claudius, is a "king of smiles," a "fawning greyhound" who proffered Hotspur "a candy deal of courtesy." We do not see Henry in any personal relationship, except with his father in the first act, and in his complaints about his son in the last. We see him as a politician (in the Elizabethan sense of the term, "unscrupulous self-seeker") who subordinates everything to his ambition. He obtains the crown, as he confesses on his deathbed, by "bypaths and indirect crook'd ways." Shakespeare presents the character with a masterly ambiguity. As John Palmer points out:

Bolingbroke gives no sign of his purpose—and for an excellent reason. He is that most dangerous of climbing politicians, the man who will go further than his rivals because he never allows himself to know where he is going. Every step in his progress toward the throne is dictated by circumstances, and he never permits himself to have a purpose till it is more than half fulfilled.

The same point is made by Brents Stirling:

Three times—at the end of III.iii, at the end of the deposition scene, and in the Exton scenes at the end of the play—Henry has taken, if it may be so called, a decisive step. Each time the move he has made has been embodied in a terse statement, and each time someone else has either evoked it from him or stated its implications for him.

The characterization, apart from that of Richard and Bolingbroke, is less effective than that of the minor characters in Richard III. But it is not so bad as is sometimes pretended. Swinburne, with customary exaggeration, attacked what he regarded as Shakespeare's incompetence:

The poet was not yet dramatist enough to feel for each of his characters an equal or proportionate regard; to divide and disperse his interest among the various crowd of figures which claim each in its place . . . a fair and adequate share of their creator's attention and sympathy. His present interest was wholly concentrated on the single figure of Richard; . . . the subordinate figures became to him but heavy and vexatious encumbrances, to be shifted on and off the stage with as much haste and as little of labor as might be possible to an impatient and uncertain hand. . . . Even after a lifelong study of this as of all other plays of Shakespeare, it is for me at least impossible to determine what I doubt the poet could himself have clearly defined—the main principle, the motive and the meaning of such characters as York, Norfolk, and Aumerle. The Gaveston and the Mortimer of Marlowe are far more solid and definite figures than these; yet none after Richard is more important to the scheme of Shakespeare. They are fitful, shifting, vaporous; their outlines change, withdraw, dissolve, and leave not a rack behind.

Swinburne's views were influenced by his assumption that the play was one of Shakespeare's earliest. If he had realized that the poet was not a novice when he wrote it, but the author of nine or ten other plays, he might have been less anxious to complain of its immaturity. Even in Shakespeare's greatest plays, the minor characters are little more than sketches; and it must be said that York, Mowbray, and Aumerle are not really as important to the scheme of the play as Gaveston and Mortimer are in Edward II. The three characters, moreover, are not really as indeterminate and vague as Swinburne pretends. York, for example, whom Swinburne described as

an incomparable, an incredible, an unintelligible and a monstrous nullity . . . a living and driveling picture of hysterical impotence on the downward grade to dotage and distraction,

is, in fact, a perfectly credible portrait of a man torn between conflicting loyalties. He deplores Richard's behavior but he is chosen to be Lord Governor because the king realizes that his criticisms were disinterested: "For he is just, and always loved us well" (II.i.221). York tried to be faithful to his trust; but it is clear from II.ii that he is muddled, incompetent, and powerless. Both here, and in later scenes, Shakespeare extracts some humor from York's bumbling inefficiency. In II.iii his loyalty to the king, his sympathy with Bolingbroke's wrongs, and his shortage of troops combine to paralyze him. He begins by calling Bolingbroke a traitor; before long he admits, "I have had feeling of my cousin's wrongs" (II.iii.140). He confesses that his forces are too weak for him to arrest the traitor, and follows a declaration of neutrality by extending an invitation to the rebels to spend the night in the castle. Before the end of the scene he has half agreed to go with the rebels to Bristol, where Bolingbroke intends to execute the king's favorites. York has become a traitor almost without knowing it. Far from being incredible, the character is very shrewdly drawn.

Once Richard's downfall is assured, York becomes a wholehearted supporter of the new regime. Characteristically, York is full of pity for Richard; he remonstrates with Northumberland for leaving out his title (III.iii.8), and, although he is chosen to escort the king to his deposition, he movingly describes the entrance of Bolingbroke and Richard into London. His new loyalty is soon tested. When he finds that Aumerle has plotted to kill Bolingbroke, it never enters his head to be ashamed of his own coat-turning: he rushes off to Windsor to beg for his son's death. This is partly prudence—he has agreed to be pledge for Aumerle's "lasting fealty to the new-made king"—but partly the genuine zeal of a convert. The scene in which he goes on his knees to Bolingbroke, absurd as it is, is not out of character.

A similar defense could be made of Aumerle, who is deeply attached to Richard and loyal to him after his fall. He submits to Bolingbroke only when his carelessness has put his life in danger. Shakespeare tells us enough about him for the purposes of the play—his dislike of Bolingbroke revealed in his account of his leave-taking and in the accusations leveled against him in IV.i, his love for Richard shown by his tears in III.iii, and by his conspiracy against the usurper. There are some indications of irresponsibility in his character, but Shakespeare deliberately leaves unsettled whether or not he was implicated in Gloucester's murder. The scene at the beginning of Act IV where he is accused was described by Swinburne as "a morally chaotic introduction of incongruous causes, inexplicable plaintiffs, and incomprehensible defendants." But the question of which side is telling the truth is irrelevant to the effect which Shakespeare wishes to give. Aumerle has to be attacked, not because of his guilt, but because he is an opponent of the usurper.

The third character of whom Swinburne complains, Thomas Mowbray, Duke of Norfolk, appears only in two scenes of the first act. Shakespeare could rely on most of his audience knowing that Richard himself was ultimately responsible for Gloucester's murder—and those who did not know were plainly informed by Gaunt in the second scene—and they would therefore appreciate that Bolingbroke's attack on Mowbray was aimed at the king, or at least at his favorites. Richard can only banish Bolingbroke if he consents to the perpetual banishment of Mowbray. If these facts are understood, Mowbray's conduct becomes intelligible. He tries to defend himself without betraying Richard, and he is bitterly surprised at his sentence of banishment. Some critics have thought that a character with such a doubtful past should not have been given the sympathetic lines in which he expresses his patriotism, and that he should not have been given so fine an epitaph as Carlisle's speech (IV.i.91 ff.). But there are no black and no white characters in *Richard II*. We need be no more surprised at Mowbray fighting "For Jesu Christ in glorious Christian field" (IV.i.93) than that Bolingbroke should intend to expiate his responsibility for Richard's death by making a pilgrimage to the Holy Land.

Sometimes, it must be admitted, Shakespeare does not fully succeed in making his characters live. In the second scene of the play, for example, he tries to give reality to the portrait of the Duchess of Gloucester by making her forget what she was going to say:

Commend me to thy brother, Edmund York.
Lo! this is all: nay, yet depart not so;
Though this be all, do not so quickly go.
I shall remember more. Bid him—Ah! what?
With all good speed at Plashy visit me.     (I.ii.62–66)

Here the effect is blurred by the rigidity of the verse and the intrusive rhyme.

It has been necessary to defend the reality of the minor characters in the play because the conflict between Richard and Bolingbroke does not take place in a dramatic and political vacuum. The background is filled in economically and well: and the patriotism of Gaunt, the loyalty of Aumerle, the oscillation of York, the prophetic fervor of the Bishop of Carlisle are all essential to the effect of the tragedy.

In *Titus Andronicus* and *Richard III* Shakespeare had submerged tragedy in melodrama; in *Romeo and Juliet* the tragedy is brought about by accident rather than by defect of character; in *Richard II* the tragedy is firmly based on character and, as in *King Lear*, the character of the hero acquires greater depth as his fortunes decline. It may therefore be said that, in spite of its obvious weaknesses, and in spite of its inferiority in some respects to *Richard III*—it contains finer poetry and greater complexity but is usually less effective in the theater—it is closer to mature Shakespearean tragedy than any of the previous plays had been.

## A NOTE ON THE SOURCES

The following have been suggested as possible sources of the play:

1.  *The Chronicles* of Raphael Holinshed (1587), pp. 493–540.
2.  *The Union of the Two Noble and Illustre Famelies of Lancastre and Yorke* by Edward Hall (1548).
3.  *The Cronycles of Englande* by Sir John Froissart, translated by Lord Berners (1525).
4.  J. Créton's *Histoire du Roy d'Angleterre.*
5.  *Chronicque de la Traïson et Mort de Richart Deux.*
6.  Le Beau's *Chronique de Richard II depuis l'an 1377 jusques à l'an 1399.*
    (Numbers 4, 5, and 6 were in manuscript until the nineteenth century.)
7.  *Thomas of Woodstock* (anonymous play).
8.  *The First Fowre Bookes of the Civile Wars* by Samuel Daniel (1595).
9.  *A Myrroure for Magistrates* (1559).
10. A lost play.

As we have seen, Professor J. Dover Wilson believed that the main source was this lost play, the author of which used numbers 1–6 of the works listed above. The theory presupposes that this unknown dramatist displayed a historical erudition beyond Shakespeare's customary range, although there are few signs of erudition in his companion piece, *The Troublesome Reign of King John*. As it is known that Shakespeare did in other plays combine several different sources, it is easier to believe that he followed the same practice in *Richard II* than that some unknown hack writer went to the same trouble.

If, then, we are skeptical of the existence of the lost play we can examine briefly the evidence for Shakespeare's use of the remaining nine hypothetical sources. There is no doubt that he had read parts of Holinshed, Hall, and *A Mirror for Magistrates;* almost certainly he knew Berners' Froissart and Daniel's poem; and there are enough apparent echoes of *Woodstock* to make it highly probable that he knew it, probably in the theater. Whether he had read the three French manuscripts or not is much more dubious.

It is significant that Shakespeare begins his play with the quarrel between Mowbray and Bolingbroke, for this is the point at which Hall begins his story; but, apart from this, the influence of Hall is apparently very slight.

It has been argued by Professor J. Dover Wilson (following Paul Reyher) that Shakespeare's characterization of John of Gaunt was suggested by Froissart, who, in his chapter on "How the Duke of Lancaster Died," speaks of his grief at his son's banishment, and at the king's misgovernment:

For he saw well that if he long persevered and were suffered to continue, the realm was likely to be utterly lost. With these imaginations and other, the Duke fell sick, whereon he died.

Froissart also mentions Richard's joy at Gaunt's death, and in an earlier passage he makes Gaunt say:

> Our nephew, the King of England, will shame all ere he cease. He believeth too lightly evil counsel who shall destroy him; and simply, if he live long, he will lose his realm, and that hath been gotten with much cost and travail by our predecessors and by us.

Froissart, too, but not Holinshed, mentions the rumor that Richard was not the son of the Black Prince. This is found also in *Traïson*.

Mr. A. P. Rossiter, however, thought that the character of Gaunt could have been derived from *Woodstock*, Stow, and Hall. There is no doubt that Shakespeare was acquainted with *Woodstock*, for he echoes it in a number of places. For example, compare Gaunt's accusation that Richard had become England's landlord (II.i.57–60, 113) with the following lines from *Woodstock*:

> Rent out our kingdom like a pelting farm
>
> . . .
>
> And thou no king, but landlord now become.

It is not possible to prove that Shakespeare read the three French manuscript chronicles, but they were not entirely inaccessible. Holinshed, Hall, and Daniel all used Créton's poem, and Holinshed refers to *Traïson* as "an old French pamphlet belonging to Jŏhn Stow." If Shakespeare had wished to follow up Holinshed's references, the chances are that he could have done so, although the evidence that he actually did so has not convinced many scholars.

A messenger in Créton's poem describes the way people of all ages flocked to Bolingbroke's standard:

> Then might you have beheld young and old, the feeble and the strong, make a clamor, and regarding neither right nor wrong stir themselves up with one accord . . . they began to flee towards the Duke . . . he brings young and old under subjection.

So Scroop (III.ii.112 ff.), after describing the whitebeards and boys who have joined Bolingbroke, adds "both young and old rebel." In the same scene, Richard's appeals to heaven, the use of Salisbury as a messenger of evil tidings, and the account of successive disasters—

> you may be sure he was not fain to smile, for, on all sides, one after another, came pouring in upon him mischief and trouble—

are all to be found in the corresponding scene of the play. The most striking parallel, however, is the comparison of Richard's betrayal and suffering to that of Christ. In the prose section of Créton's account, he compares the rejection of Richard by the people to the rejection of Christ by the Jews:

> Then spake Duke Henry quite aloud to the commons of the said city. "Fair sirs, behold your king! consider what you will do with him!" And they made answer with a loud voice, "We will have him taken to Westminster." And so he delivered him unto them. At this hour did he remind me of Pilate, who caused our Lord Jesus Christ to be scourged

at the stake, and afterwards had him brought before the multitude of the Jews, saying, "Fair Sirs, behold your king!" who replied, "let him be crucified!" Then Pilate washed his hands of it, saying, "I am innocent of the just blood." And so he delivered our Lord unto them. Much in the like manner did Duke Henry, when he gave up his rightful lord to the rabble of London, in order that, if they should put him to death, he might say, "I am innocent of this deed."

In *Traïson* there are several similar passages. The author compares Northumberland to Judas; and a few pages later Richard compares himself to Christ, who was likewise "undeservedly sold and given into the hands of his enemies." Although Holinshed refers to a prelate as a Pilate, and although Shakespeare elsewhere associates treachery with Judas, the emphasis on the Christ parallel is to be found only in Créton, *Traïson*, and Shakespeare. There are a few minor parallels with *Traïson*. "Daring-hardy" (I.iii.43) may translate *hardie* in precisely the same context, and "base court" (III.iii.175) may likewise translate *basse cour*. There seems, therefore, to be a slight balance of probability that Shakespeare had read both Créton's poem and *Traïson*, but there is less probability that he had read Le Beau's chronicle.

About seventy parallels have been listed with Daniel's *Civil Wars*. Some of these, however, are not peculiar to Daniel's poem, and others may be explained by the fact that both poets amplified their sources independently. But enough parallels remain to convince all recent editors (Dover Wilson, Black, Ure) that Shakespeare was influenced by Daniel, especially in II.i, IV.i, V.i, and V.ii. Shakespeare and Daniel both altered the age of the queen, making her a woman instead of a child; Shakespeare was clearly indebted to Daniel for the account of the entry of Richard and Bolingbroke into London; and Gaunt's speech on England (II.i.31–68) clearly echoes the following lines from Daniel's *Civil Wars*:

> Why Neptune hast thou made us stand alone
> Divided from the world, for this say they?
>
> A place there is where proudly raised there stands
> A huge aspiring rock neighboring the skies
> Whose surly brow imperiously commands
> The sea his bounds that at his proud feet lies:
> And spurns the waves that in rebellious bands
> Assault his empire and against him rise:
>
> . . .
>
> With what contagion France didst thou infect
> The land by thee made proud to disagree?

Although we have argued that Shakespeare consulted a number of different sources, there is little doubt that the great bulk of his material came from Holinshed. The only scenes that did not largely derive from the *Chronicles* are the following:

I.ii. No direct source has been discovered
II.i.1–152. Partly based on Froissart and Daniel
II.ii. Largely invention
III.iv. No source
V.i. Possibly suggested by Daniel
V.ii.1–40. Probably suggested by Daniel

It should be noted that Shakespeare sometimes combines widely separated facts for a single scene, that he telescopes events, and that on occasion he rearranges the order of historical happenings.

Of telescoping perhaps the best example is II.i. Bolingbroke had been banished in September 1398; his father died in the following February; Richard left for Ireland in May; and Bolingbroke landed at Ravenspurgh in July. But in Shakespeare's scene Gaunt is dying immediately after his son's banishment—in I.iv we have a description of Bolingbroke's leave-taking and of Gaunt's illness—but before the end of the scene we are told that Bolingbroke has already sailed from Brittany. A period of nine months elapses in the course of the scene. By this telescoping Shakespeare is able to link the death of Gaunt with the banishment of Bolingbroke, to link the confiscation of his estates with the necessities of the Irish campaign, and to link the support Bolingbroke receives with Richard's conduct and with the patriotic admonitions of Gaunt. The scene is dramatically effective on the stage, in spite of the impossibilities revealed in the study; and the fact that Bolingbroke is returning to England before he can have heard of the confiscation of his estates, and yet pretends later that this was his motive for returning from exile, is an example of the deliberate ambiguity with which the character is presented.

The fourth act provides a good example of Shakespeare's rearrangement of historical facts, although there is no essential distortion of historical truth. Bagot's accusation of Aumerle took place on October 16, Fitzwater's accusation two days later; Carlisle's speech (which was not, as in the play, associated with Bolingbroke's claim of the crown) was a week later, on October 23; the abdication took place in the Tower (not in Westminster Hall) on September 29; and the Abbot of Westminster's entertainment of the conspirators was not until December 17. Although Swinburne complained that the quarrel at the beginning of the scene was "a morally chaotic introduction of incongruous causes, inexplicable plaintiffs, and incomprehensible defendants," it reminds us, just before the abdication, of Gloucester's death, its ultimate cause; and it provides Aumerle with a motive for rebellion. Carlisle's speech, one of the most significant moments in the whole tetralogy, is much more dramatic in its place as a warning to the characters in the play and to us of the results of Bolingbroke's usurpation at the moment of its happening. It is obviously more dramatic for Richard to go through the ritual of his abdication in public than before the commissioners in the Tower; and the Abbot's plot is properly introduced at a moment when our sympathies have been fully aroused for Richard, especially when we realize that the plot to restore him to the throne is the direct cause of his murder. Some details of the scene may have been suggested by other sources—Froissart, Hall, Daniel, *A Mirror for Magistrates*, the *Homilies*, and even *Traïson*.

Finally, an example may be given of Shakespeare's omissions. In Holinshed's account, Northumberland persuades Richard to leave Conway Castle, ambushing him on the way to Flint, and conveying him to Flint Castle as a prisoner. Shakespeare omits this incident, following Froissart, who merely says that Richard rode to Flint, and prepared to defend the castle there.

## A NOTE ON THE TEXT

*Richard II* was first published in 1597, after August 29, when it was registered. The first quarto (Q1) appeared with the following title page: "THE/Tragedie of King Ri-/charē the se-/cond./*As it hath beene publikely acted/by the right Honourable the/Lorde Chamberlaine his Ser-/uants./* LONDON/Printed by Valentine Simmes for Andrew Wise, and/are to be sold at his shop in Paules church yard at/the signe of the Angel./1597."

The play is thought to have been printed from a transcript of Shakespeare's manuscript, but it may preserve some of his spelling and punctuation. Some critics (Cairncross, Brooks, Ure) think that the text is memorially contaminated in a few places (that is, the transcriber introduced mistakes through his memory of other lines of the play and also of *Richard III*). The first quarto forms the basis of the present edition, except for the abdication scene, which was omitted from the first three quartos and included in the fourth (1608). The play was included in the First Folio (1623), probably from a corrected text of Q5 (1615). The Folio text (F) enables us to correct Q1 in a number of places, and it provides the best text of the abdication scene; but many of its readings are "sophistications"—unnecessary alterations—for which Shakespeare was not responsible.

The present edition modernizes spelling and punctuation, amplifies abbreviations and regularizes speech prefixes, corrects obvious typographical errors, adjusts the position of stage directions, and in a few cases alters the lineation. Q1 is not divided into acts or scenes; the present edition uses the divisions established by the Globe editors, who used those of F but who added one at V.iv. F indicates the divisions in Latin; they are translated here. Other deviations from Q1 (and for the abdication scene from F) are listed below. The adopted reading is given in boldface; if it is not taken from F a note in a bracket explains that it is taken (for example) from Q5 or (again, for example) from an editor's emendation—indicated by [ed.]. Next is given the original reading in roman.

**I.i.118 my scepter's** scepters   **139 But** Ah but   **152 gentlemen** Gentleman   **162 When . . . when** When Harry? when obedience bids   **192 parle** parlee
**I.ii.47 sit** set   **58 it** is
**I.iii.26 demand of** [ed.] ask   **33 comest** [Q5] comes   **84 innocency** [ed.] innocence   **172 then but** but   **180 you owe** y'owe   **221 night** nightes   **238 had it** [ed.] had't
**I.iv.1 s.d. Bagot** [ed.] Bushie   **20 cousin, cousin** Coosens Coosin   **23 Bagot . . . Green** [Q6] [Q1] omits; F has "heere Bagot and Greene"]   **53 Bushy, what news?** [Q1 omits, but prints the s.d. "Enter Bushie with newes"]   **65 All** [ed.; Q and F omit]
**II.i.18 fond** [ed.] found [the emendation to "fond" is plausible; but it is possible that "found" was an error caused by the similar endings of adjacent lines—"soundes" and "sound"—or that a line was omitted by mistake]   **48 as as** as   **102 incagèd** inraged   **113 not** [ed.] not, not   **124 brother** [Q2] brothers   **156 kernes** kerne   **177 the** a   **232 that that** [ed.] that   **257 king's** King   **280 The . . . Arundel** [ed.; Q and F omit]   **283 Thomas Ramston** [Holinshed] Iohn Ramston   **284 Quoint** Coines
**II.ii.16 eye** eyes   **25 more's** more is   **31 though** thought   **53 Henry** H   **88 cold** [ed.] they are cold   **112 Th' one** Tone   **137 The . . . will** [ed.] Will the hateful commons
**II.iii.36 Hereford** Herefords   **98 the lord** lord
**III.ii.32 succor** [ed.] succors   **38 and** [ed.] that   **40 boldly** [ed.] bouldy   **72 O'erthrows** Ouerthrowes
**III.iii.13 with you to** to   **17 mis-take** [ed.] mistake   **30 lord** Lords   **59 waters—on** [ed.] water's on   **118 prince and** [ed.] princesse

**III.iv.11 joy** [ed.] griefe **21 good.** good? **26 pins** pines **57 We at** [ed.] at **80 Cam'st** Canst
**IV.i.22 him** them **54 As** [ed.] As it **55 sun to sun** [ed.] sinne to sinne **76 my bond** bond **154–319** [for this passage, here printed from F, Q1 has only "Let it be so, and loe on wednesday next,/We solemnly proclaime our Coronation,/Lords be ready all"] **182 and on** [Q4] on; **yours** [Q4] thine **250 and** [Q4] a **254 Nor** [Q4] No, nor **275 the** [Q4] that **284 Was** [Q5] Is; that [Q4] which **285 And** [Q4] That **288 a** [Q4] an **295 manners** [Q4] manner **332 I will** [ed.] Ile
**V.i.25 stricken** throwne

**V.ii.55 prevent me** [ed.] preuent **78 life, my** [ed.] life, by my **116 And** An
**V.iii.10 While** [ed.] Which **20 but yet** [ed.] yet **35 that I** that **67 And an** **110 Bolingbroke** Yorke **134–35 With . . . him** [ed.] I pardon him with al my heart **143 cousin, too** [Q6] cousin
**V.iv.1 s.d. Enter** Manet
**V.v.27 sit** set **79 bestrid** bestride
**V.vi.8 Salisbury . . . Blunt** Oxford, Salisbury, Blunt **12 s.d. Fitzwater** [Q6] Fitzwaters **43 thorough** [ed.] through [Q] through the [F]

# THE TRAGEDY OF
# KING RICHARD THE SECOND

[Dramatis Personae

KING RICHARD THE SECOND
EDMUND *Duke of York*
JOHN OF GAUNT *Duke of Lancaster* } *his uncles*
HENRY BOLINGBROKE *Gaunt's son*
DUKE OF AUMERLE *York's son*
THOMAS MOWBRAY *Duke of Norfolk*
EARL OF SALISBURY
EARL OF BERKELEY
SIR JOHN BUSHY
SIR WILLIAM BAGOT
SIR HENRY GREEN } *Richard's favorites*
EARL OF NORTHUMBERLAND
HARRY PERCY *his son*
LORD ROSS
LORD WILLOUGHBY

BISHOP OF CARLISLE
SIR STEPHEN SCROOP
LORD FITZWATER
DUKE OF SURREY
ABBOT OF WESTMINSTER
SIR PIERCE OF EXTON
LORD MARSHAL
WELSH CAPTAIN
QUEEN ISABEL *Richard's second wife*
DUCHESS OF GLOUCESTER *Gaunt's sister-in-law*
DUCHESS OF YORK
LADIES *attending on the Queen*
GARDENERS  A KEEPER  A GROOM
  LORDS  HERALDS  OFFICERS  SOLDIERS
  ATTENDANTS  SERVANTS

*Scene:* England and Wales]

## [ ACT I ]

### [Scene I. *Windsor Castle.*]

*Enter King* RICHARD, *John of* GAUNT, *with other*
NOBLES *and* ATTENDANTS.

RICHARD
Old John of Gaunt, time-honored Lancaster,
Hast thou according to thy oath and band°
Brought hither Henry Hereford,° thy bold son,
Here to make good the boist'rous late appeal,°
Which then our° leisure would not let us hear, 5
Against the Duke of Norfolk, Thomas Mowbray?
GAUNT
I have, my liege.

RICHARD
Tell me, moreover, hast thou sounded him,
If he appeal° the duke on ancient malice,
Or worthily,° as a good subject should, 10
On some known ground of treachery in him?
GAUNT
As near as I could sift° him on that argument,°
On some apparent° danger seen in him
Aimed at your highness, no inveterate malice.
RICHARD
Then call them to our presence: face to face, 15
And frowning brow to brow, ourselves will hear
The accuser and the accusèd freely speak.
High-stomached° are they both, and full of ire,
In rage, deaf as the sea, hasty as fire.

*Enter* BOLINGBROKE *and* MOWBRAY.

---

*The decorative border above appeared on the first page of* Richard II
*in the First Folio edition of Shakespeare's plays, 1623.*

**I.i.2 band** bond  **3 Hereford** pronounced "Herford"  **4
appeal** accusation of treason  **5 our** the royal plural

**9 appeal** accuse  **10 worthily** according to desert  **12 sift**
examine thoroughly;  **argument** subject  **13 apparent**
obvious  **18 High-stomached** high-spirited

BOLINGBROKE°
Many years of happy days befall                              20
My gracious sovereign, my most loving liege!
MOWBRAY
Each day still better other's happiness,
Until the heavens, envying earth's good hap,
Add an immortal title to your crown!
RICHARD
We thank you both; yet one but flatters us,                   25
As well appeareth by the cause you come,
Namely to appeal each other of high treason.
Cousin of Hereford, what dost thou object
Against the Duke of Norfolk, Thomas Mowbray?
BOLINGBROKE
First—heaven be the record of my speech!—              30
In the devotion of a subject's love,
Tend'ring° the precious safety of my prince,
And free from other misbegotten hate,
Come I appellant° to this princely presence.
Now, Thomas Mowbray, do I turn to thee,                   35
And mark my greeting° well: for what I speak,
My body shall make good upon this earth,
Or my divine soul answer it in heaven.
Thou art a traitor and a miscreant,°
Too good to be so, and too bad to live;                      40
Since the more fair and crystal is the sky,
The uglier seem the clouds that in it fly.
Once more, the more to aggravate the note,°
With a foul traitor's name stuff I thy throat,
And wish—so please my sovereign—ere I move,         45
What my tongue speaks my right-drawn° sword may
    prove.
MOWBRAY
Let not my cold words here accuse my zeal:°
'Tis not the trial of a woman's war,
The bitter clamor of two eager° tongues,
Can arbitrate this cause betwixt us twain;                    50
The blood is hot that must be cooled for this.
Yet can I not of such tame patience boast,
As to be hushed, and naught at all to say.
First, the fair reverence of° your highness curbs me
From giving reins and spurs to my free speech,            55
Which else would post° until it had returned
These terms of treason doubled down his throat.
Setting aside his high blood's royalty,
And let him be° no kinsman to my liege,
I do defy him, and I spit at him,                              60
Call him a slanderous coward and a villain;
Which to maintain, I would allow him odds,
And meet him were I tied° to run afoot
Even to the frozen ridges of the Alps,
Or any other ground inhabitable,°                             65
Where ever Englishman durst set his foot.
Meantime, let this° defend my loyalty:
By all my hopes° most falsely doth he lie.

BOLINGBROKE
Pale trembling coward, there I throw my gage,
Disclaiming here the kindred of the king,°                    70
And lay aside my high blood's royalty,
Which fear, not reverence, makes thee to except.°
If guilty dread have left thee so much strength
As to take up mine honor's pawn,° then stoop.
By that, and all the rites of knighthood else,               75
Will I make good against thee, arm to arm,
What I have spoke, or thou canst worse devise.
MOWBRAY
I take it up; and by that sword I swear,
Which gently laid my knighthood on my shoulder,
I'll answer thee in any fair degree°                           80
Or chivalrous design of knightly trial;
And when I mount, alive may I not light,°
If I be traitor or unjustly fight.
RICHARD
What doth our cousin lay to Mowbray's charge?
It must be great that can inherit us°                         85
So much as of a thought of ill in him.
BOLINGBROKE
Look what° I speak, my life shall prove it true:
That Mowbray hath received eight thousand nobles°
In name of lendings° for your highness' soldiers,
The which he hath detained for lewd° employments,   90
Like a false traitor and injurious villain.
Besides, I say, and will in battle prove,
Or° here, or elsewhere to the furthest verge
That ever was surveyed by English eye,
That all the treasons for these eighteen years            95
Complotted and contrivèd in this land
Fetch° from false Mowbray, their first head and spring.
Further, I say and further will maintain
Upon his bad life to make all this good,
That he did plot the Duke of Gloucester's° death,       100
Suggest° his soon-believing adversaries,
And, consequently,° like a traitor coward,
Sluiced out his innocent soul through streams of
    blood;
Which blood, like sacrificing Abel's, cries
Even from the tongueless caverns of the earth          105
To me for justice and rough chastisement:
And, by the glorious worth of my descent,
This arm shall do it, or° this life be spent.
RICHARD
How high a pitch° his resolution soars!
Thomas of Norfolk, what say'st thou to this?           110
MOWBRAY
O! let my sovereign turn away his face,
And bid his ears a little while be deaf,
Till I have told this slander of his blood
How God and good men hate so foul a liar.

---

20 **Bolingbroke** pronounced and spelled "Bullingbrooke" in Shakespeare's time  32 **Tend'ring** cherishing  34 **appellant** accuser  36 **greeting** address  39 **miscreant** unbeliever, villain  43 **note** reproach  46 **right-drawn** drawn to defend the right  47 **accuse my zeal** make me seem unzealous  49 **eager** sharp  54 **fair reverence of** respect due to  56 **post** speed  59 **let him be** suppose him to be  63 **tied** obliged  65 **inhabitable** uninhabitable  67 **this** his sword  68 **hopes** i.e., of heaven

70 **Disclaiming . . . king** referring to Mowbray's words, lines 58–59  72 **except** use as excuse  74 **pawn** pledge (this glove or hood, which he throws down)  80 **degree** manner  82 **light** dismount  85 **inherit us** make us have  87 **what** whatever  88 **nobles** gold coins  89 **lendings** money on trust  90 **lewd** base  93 **Or either**  97 **Fetch** derive  100 **Gloucester** Thomas of Woodstock, who had been murdered at Richard's orders  101 **Suggest** incite  102 **consequently** afterward  108 **or** before  109 **pitch** peak of a falcon's flight (the king is uneasy that his own guilt will come to light)

RICHARD
Mowbray, impartial are our eyes and ears.    115
Were he my brother, nay, my kingdom's heir,
As he is but my father's brother's son,
Now by my scepter's awe I make a vow,
Such neighbor nearness to our sacred blood
Should nothing privilege him nor partialize°    120
The unstooping firmness of my upright soul.
He is our subject, Mowbray, so art thou:
Free speech and fearless I to thee allow.

MOWBRAY
Then, Bolingbroke, as low as to thy heart,
Through the false passage of thy throat, thou liest.    125
Three parts of that receipt I had° for Calais
Disbursed I duly to his highness' soldiers;
The other part reserved I by consent,
For that my sovereign liege was in my debt
Upon remainder of a dear account,°    130
Since last I went to France to fetch his queen.
Now swallow down that lie. For Gloucester's death,
I slew him not; but, to my own disgrace,
Neglected my sworn duty° in that case.
For you, my noble Lord of Lancaster,    135
The honorable father of my foe,
Once did I lay an ambush for your life,
A trespass that doth vex my grievèd soul;
But, ere I last received the sacrament,
I did confess it, and exactly begged    140
Your grace's pardon, and I hope I had it.
This is my fault: as for the rest appealed,
It issues from the rancor of a villain,
A recreant° and most degenerate traitor;
Which in myself I boldly will defend,    145
And interchangeably° hurl down my gage
Upon this overweening traitor's foot,
To prove myself a loyal gentleman
Even in the best blood chambered in his bosom.
In haste whereof, most heartily I pray    150
Your highness to assign our trial day.

RICHARD
Wrath-kindled gentlemen, be ruled by me.
Let's purge this choler° without letting blood:°
This we prescribe, though no physician;
Deep malice makes too deep incision;    155
Forget, forgive, conclude, and be agreed;
Our doctors say this is no month to bleed.
Good uncle, let this end where it begun:
We'll calm the Duke of Norfolk, you your son.

GAUNT
To be a make-peace shall become my age:    160
Throw down, my son, the Duke of Norfolk's gage.

RICHARD
And Norfolk, throw down his.

GAUNT                        When,° Harry, when?
Obedience bids I should not bid again.

RICHARD
Norfolk, throw down; we bid—there is no boot.°

MOWBRAY
Myself I throw, dread sovereign, at thy foot.    165
My life thou shalt command, but not my shame:
The one my duty owes; but my fair name
Despite of death that lives upon my grave,
To dark dishonor's use thou shalt not have.
I am disgraced, impeached,° and baffled° here,    170
Pierced to the soul with slander's venomed spear,
The which no balm can cure but his heart-blood
Which breathed this poison.

RICHARD                        Rage must be withstood.
Give me his gage; lions make leopards tame.°

MOWBRAY
Yea, but not change his spots.° Take but my shame,    175
And I resign my gage. My dear dear lord,
The purest treasure mortal times afford
Is spotless reputation—that away,
Men are but gilded loam, or painted clay.
A jewel in a ten-times-barred-up chest    180
Is a bold spirit in a loyal breast;
Mine honor is my life, both grow in one;
Take honor from me, and my life is done;
Then, dear my liege, mine honor let me try;
In that I live, and for that will I die.    185

RICHARD
Cousin, throw up° your gage; do you begin.

BOLINGBROKE
O, God defend my soul from such deep sin!
Shall I seem crestfallen in my father's sight?
Or with pale beggar-fear° impeach my height°
Before this outdared dastard? Ere my tongue    190
Shall wound my honor with such feeble wrong,°
Or sound so base a parle,° my teeth shall tear
The slavish motive° of recanting fear,
And spit it bleeding in his high disgrace,
Where shame doth harbor, even in Mowbray's face.    195
[Exit GAUNT.°]

RICHARD
We were not born to sue, but to command:
Which since we cannot do to make you friends,
Be ready, as your lives shall answer it,
At Coventry upon Saint Lambert's Day.°
There shall your swords and lances arbitrate    200
The swelling difference of your settled hate:
Since we cannot atone° you, we shall see
Justice design the victor's chivalry.°
Lord Marshal, command our officers-at-arms
Be ready to direct these home alarms.    205
Exit [RICHARD with others].

---

120 **partialize** make partial  126 **that . . . had** what I received  130 **dear account** private or expensive debt  134 **duty** either to kill Gloucester, or to reveal the murder  144 **recreant** renegade  146 **interchangeably** in exchange  153 **choler** anger; **letting blood** pun on bleeding medicinally and bloodshed  162 **When** exclamation of impatience  164 **boot** remedy

170 **impeached** accused; **baffled** treated with infamy  174 **lions . . . tame** alluding to the rampant lion in the king's royal arms and the standing beast in Mowbray's  175 **spots** alluding to the proverb and punning on the meaning "stains"  186 **throw up** perhaps to the upper stage on which Richard sits  189 **beggar-fear** appropriate to a beggar; **height** rank  191 **feeble wrong** a wrong so grave that the man who submits to it exhibits himself as feeble  192 **parle** parley, truce  193 **motive** moving organ (i.e., tongue)  195 **s.d. Exit Gaunt** Gaunt begins Scene II, and therefore according to stage convention must leave the stage before the end of Scene I  199 **Saint Lambert's Day** September 17  202 **atone** reconcile  203 **design . . . chivalry** indicate whose prowess will win the victory (i.e., the victor will be vindicated)

[Scene II. *London. Gaunt's house.*]

*Enter John of* GAUNT *with the* DUCHESS *of Gloucester.*

GAUNT

Alas, the part I had in Woodstock's° blood
Doth more solicit me than your exclaims°
To stir against the butchers of his life;
But since correction lieth in those hands°
Which made the fault that we cannot correct,       5
Put we our quarrel to the will of heaven,
Who, when they° see the hours° ripe on earth,
Will rain hot vengeance on offenders' heads.

DUCHESS

Finds brotherhood in thee no sharper spur?
Hath love in thy old blood no living fire?       10
Edward's seven sons, whereof thyself art one,
Were as seven vials of his sacred blood,
Or seven fair branches springing from one root.
Some of those seven are dried by nature's course,
Some of those branches by the destinies cut:       15
But Thomas, my dear lord, my life, my Gloucester,
One vial full of Edward's sacred blood,
One flourishing branch of his most royal root,
Is cracked, and all the precious liquor spilt,
Is hacked down, and his summer leaves all faded       20
By envy's hand and murder's bloody ax.
Ah! Gaunt, his blood was thine; that bed, that womb,
That metal,° that self° mold that fashioned thee,
Made him a man: and though thou livest and breathest,
Yet art thou slain in him; thou dost consent       25
In some large measure to thy father's death,
In that thou see'st thy wretched brother die,
Who was the model° of thy father's life.
Call it not patience, Gaunt, it is despair:
In suff'ring° thus thy brother to be slaught'red,       30
Thou showest the naked pathway° to thy life,
Teaching stern murder how to butcher thee.
That which in mean men we entitle patience
Is pale cold cowardice in noble breasts.
What shall I say? To safeguard thine own life,       35
The best way is to venge my Gloucester's death.

GAUNT

God's is the quarrel; for God's substitute,
His deputy° anointed in His sight,
Hath caused his death, the which if wrongfully,
Let heaven revenge, for I may never lift       40
An angry arm against His minister.

DUCHESS

Where, then, alas, may I complain myself?°

GAUNT

To God, the widow's champion and defense.

DUCHESS

Why, then, I will. Farewell, old Gaunt,
Thou goest to Coventry, there to behold       45
Our cousin° Hereford and fell° Mowbray fight.

O! sit my husband's wrongs on Hereford's spear,
That it may enter butcher Mowbray's breast;
Or if misfortune° miss the first careęr,°
Be Mowbray's sins so heavy in his bosom,       50
That they may break his foaming courser's back,
And throw the rider headlong in the lists,
A caitiff recreant° to my cousin Hereford.
Farewell, old Gaunt; thy sometimes° brother's wife
With her companion, grief, must end her life.       55

GAUNT

Sister, farewell, I must to Coventry:
As much good stay with thee, as go with me.

DUCHESS

Yet one word more: grief boundeth where it falls,
Not with the empty hollowness, but weight.°
I take my leave before I have begun,       60
For sorrow ends not when it seemeth done.
Commend me to thy brother, Edmund York.°
Lo! this is all: nay, yet depart not so;
Though this be all, do not so quickly go.
I shall remember more. Bid him—Ah! what?       65
With all good speed at Plashy° visit me.
Alack! and what shall good old York there see
But empty lodgings and unfurnished walls,
Unpeopled offices,° untrodden stones,
And what hear there for welcome but my groans?       70
Therefore commend me, let him not come there,
To seek out sorrow that dwells everywhere.
Desolate, desolate will I hence and die!
The last leave of thee takes my weeping eye. *Exeunt.*

[Scene III. *The lists at Coventry.*]

*Enter Lord* MARSHAL *and the Duke* AUMERLE.

MARSHAL

My Lord Aumerle, is Harry Hereford armed?

AUMERLE

Yea, at all points, and longs to enter in.

MARSHAL

The Duke of Norfolk, sprightfully° and bold,
Stays but the summons of the appellant's trumpet.

AUMERLE

Why, then, the champions are prepared, and stay       5
For nothing but his majesty's approach.

*The trumpets sound, and the king* [RICHARD] *enters with
his* NOBLES [*including* GAUNT, BUSHY, BAGOT,
GREEN]. *When they are set, enter* [MOWBRAY] *the
Duke of Norfolk, in arms, defendant,* [*and a* HERALD].

RICHARD

Marshal, demand of yonder champion
The cause of his arrival here in arms;
Ask him his name; and orderly proceed
To swear him in the justice of his cause.       10

MARSHAL

In God's name and the king's, say who thou art

---

I.ii.1 **Woodstock** Gloucester, Gaunt's brother   2 **exclaims**
outcries   4 **those hands** the king's   7 **they** God and his
angels; **hours** disyllabic   23 **metal** stuff; **self** same   28 **model**
copy   30 **suff'ring** allowing   31 **naked pathway** open road
(for his murderers)   38 **deputy** the idea that the king, however
unworthy, is God's deputy is stressed throughout the play   42
**Where . . . myself** To whom shall I complain?   46 **cousin**
kinsman; **fell** ruthless

49 **misfortune** disaster (to Mowbray); **career** encounter   53
**caitiff recreant** captive coward   54 **sometimes** sometime,
former   58–59 **grief . . . weight** my grief returns because it
is heavy, not like a ball   62 **York** Duke of York   66 **Plashy**
in Essex   69 **offices** kitchens, servants' quarters, etc.
I.iii.3 **sprightfully** full of spirit

And why thou comest thus knightly clad in arms,
Against what man thou com'st, and what thy quarrel.
Speak truly on thy knighthood and thy oath,
As so defend thee heaven and thy valor.                          15

MOWBRAY
My name is Thomas Mowbray, Duke of Norfolk,
Who hither come engagèd by my oath—
Which God defend° a knight should violate!
Both to defend my loyalty and truth
To God, my king, and my succeeding issue,                        20
Against the Duke of Hereford that appeals° me;
And by the grace of God, and this mine arm,
To prove him in defending of myself
A traitor to my God, my king, and me;
And as I truly° fight, defend me, heaven!                         25

*The trumpets sound. Enter* [BOLINGBROKE] *Duke of
Hereford, appellant, in armor.*

RICHARD
Marshal, demand of yonder knight in arms,
Both who he is, and why he cometh hither
Thus plated° in habiliments of war,
And formally, according to our law,
Depose° him in the justice of his cause.                          30

MARSHAL
What is thy name? And wherefore com'st thou hither
Before King Richard in his royal lists?
Against whom comest thou? And what's thy quarrel?
Speak like a true knight, so defend thee heaven.

BOLINGBROKE
Harry of Hereford, Lancaster and Derby                            35
Am I, who ready here do stand in arms
To prove by God's grace, and my body's valor
In lists, on Thomas Mowbray, Duke of Norfolk,
That he is a traitor, foul and dangerous,
To God of heaven, King Richard and to me:                         40
And as I truly fight, defend me, heaven!

MARSHAL
On pain of death, no person be so bold
Or daring-hardy° as to touch the lists,
Except the marshal and such officers
Appointed to direct these fair designs.                           45

BOLINGBROKE
Lord Marshal, let me kiss my sovereign's hand,
And bow my knee before his majesty;
For Mowbray and myself are like two men
That vow a long and weary pilgrimage:
Then let us take a ceremonious leave                              50
And loving farewell of our several friends.

MARSHAL
The appellant in all duty greets your highness,
And craves to kiss your hand and take his leave.

RICHARD
We will descend and fold him in our arms.
Cousin of Hereford, as thy cause is right,                        55
So be thy fortune in this royal fight:
Farewell, my blood, which if today thou shed,
Lament we may, but not revenge thee dead.

BOLINGBROKE
O, let no noble eye profane a tear

For me, if I be gored with Mowbray's spear:                       60
As confident as is the falcon's flight
Against a bird, do I with Mowbray fight.
My loving lord, I take my leave of you;
Of you, my noble cousin, Lord Aumerle,
Not sick, although I have to do with death,                       65
But lusty, young, and cheerly° drawing breath.
Lo! as at English feasts, so I regreet°
The daintiest last, to make the end most sweet.
O thou, the earthly author of my blood,
Whose youthful spirit in me regenerate°                           70
Doth with a twofold vigor lift me up
To reach at victory above my head,
Add proof° unto mine armor with thy prayers,
And with thy blessings steel my lance's point,
That it may enter Mowbray's waxen° coat                           75
And furbish new the name of John a° Gaunt
Even in the lusty havior° of his son.

GAUNT
God in thy good cause make thee prosperous;
Be swift like lightning in the execution,
And let thy blows doubly redoubled                                80
Fall like amazing° thunder on the casque
Of thy adverse° pernicious enemy:
Rouse up thy youthful blood, be valiant and live.

BOLINGBROKE
Mine innocency and Saint George to thrive!

MOWBRAY
However God or fortune cast my lot,                               85
There lives or dies, true to King Richard's throne,
A loyal, just, and upright gentleman.
Never did captive with a freer heart
Cast off his chains of bondage, and embrace
His golden, uncontrolled enfranchisement°                        90
More than my dancing soul doth celebrate
This feast of battle with mine adversary.
Most mighty liege, and my companion peers,
Take from my mouth the wish of happy years;
As gentle and as jocund as to jest°                               95
Go I to fight: truth hath a quiet breast.

RICHARD
Farewell, my lord; securely° I espy
Virtue with valor couchèd° in thine eye.
Order the trial, marshal, and begin.

MARSHAL
Harry of Hereford, Lancaster and Derby,                          100
Receive thy lance, and God defend the right.

BOLINGBROKE
Strong as a tower in hope,° I cry Amen.

MARSHAL
Go bear this lance to Thomas, Duke of Norfolk.

FIRST HERALD
Harry of Hereford, Lancaster, and Derby,
Stands here for God, his sovereign, and himself,                 105
On pain to be° found false and recreant,
To prove the Duke of Norfolk, Thomas Mowbray,

66 **cheerly** cheerfully 67 **regreet** greet 70 **regenerate**
reborn 73 **proof** invulnerability 75 **waxen** soft 76 **a** of
77 **havior** behavior 81 **amazing** stupefying 82 **adverse**
placed opposite 90 **enfranchisement** liberation 95 **jest**
sport 97 **securely** confidently 98 **couchèd** lying hidden
102 **Strong . . . hope** cf. Psalms 61:3 106 **On . . . be** at
the risk of being

18 **defend** forbid 21 **appeals** accuses 25 **truly** with truth
on my side 28 **plated** in plate armor 30 **Depose** examine on
oath 43 **daring-hardy** reckless

A traitor to his God, his king, and him,
And dares him to set forward to the fight.

SECOND HERALD
Here standeth Thomas Mowbray, Duke of Norfolk,   110
On pain to be found false and recreant,
Both to defend himself, and to approve°
Henry of Hereford, Lancaster, and Derby,
To God, his sovereign, and to him disloyal,
Courageously and with a free desire   115
Attending but the signal to begin.

MARSHAL
Sound trumpets; and set forward combatants!

[*A charge sounded.*]

Stay, the king hath thrown his warder° down.

RICHARD
Let them lay by their helmets and their spears
And both return back to their chairs° again.   120
Withdraw with us, and let the trumpets sound,
While we return these dukes what we decree.

[*A long flourish.°*]

Draw near,
And list° what with our council we have done.
For that our kingdom's earth should not be soiled   125
With that dear blood which it hath fostered;
And for our eyes do hate the dire aspect
Of civil wounds plowed up with neighbor's sword,
And for we think the eagle-wingèd pride
Of sky-aspiring and ambitious thoughts   130
With rival-hating envy set on you
To wake our peace, which in our country's cradle
Draws the sweet infant breath of gentle sleep,
Which so roused up with boist'rous untuned drums,
With harsh-resounding trumpets' dreadful bray,   135
And grating shock of wrathful iron arms,
Might from our quiet confines fright fair peace,
And make us wade even in our kindred's blood;
Therefore we banish you our territories:
You, cousin Hereford, upon pain of life,   140
Till twice five summers have enriched our fields,
Shall not regreet° our fair dominions,
But tread the stranger° paths of banishment.

BOLINGBROKE
Your will be done: this must my comfort be,
That sun that warms you here shall shine on me,   145
And those his golden beams to you here lent
Shall point on me, and gild my banishment.

RICHARD
Norfolk, for thee remains a heavier doom
Which I with some unwillingness pronounce:
The sly slow hours shall not determinate°   150
The dateless° limit of thy dear° exile;
The hopeless word° of "Never to return"
Breathe I against thee, upon pain of life.

MOWBRAY
A heavy sentence,° my most sovereign liege,

And all unlooked for from your highness' mouth:   155
A dearer merit,° not so deep a maim
As to be cast forth in the common air
Have I deservèd at your highness' hands!
The language I have learnt these forty years,
My native English, now I must forgo,   160
And now my tongue's use is to me no more
Than an unstringèd viol or a harp,
Or like a cunning° instrument cased up,
Or being open, put into his hands
That knows no touch to tune the harmony.   165
Within my mouth you have enjailed my tongue,
Doubly portcullised° with my teeth and lips,
And dull unfeeling barren ignorance
Is made my jailer to attend on me.
I am too old to fawn upon a nurse,   170
Too far in years to be a pupil now;
What is thy sentence then but speechless death,
Which robs my tongue from breathing native breath?

RICHARD
It boots° thee not to be compassionate:°
After our sentence, plaining comes too late.   175

MOWBRAY
Then thus I turn me from my country's light,
To dwell in solemn shades of endless night.

[*Turns to go.*]

RICHARD
Return again, and take an oath with thee.
Lay on our royal sword your banished hands;
Swear by the duty that you owe to God—   180
Our part therein we banish with yourselves°—
To keep the oath that we administer:
You never shall—so help you truth and God!—
Embrace each other's love in banishment,
Nor never look upon each other's face,   185
Nor never write, regreet, nor reconcile
This louring tempest of your homebred hate,
Nor never by advisèd° purpose meet
To plot, contrive, or complot° any ill
'Gainst us, our state, our subjects, or our land.   190

BOLINGBROKE
I swear.

MOWBRAY   And I, to keep all this.

BOLINGBROKE
Norfolk, so far as to mine enemy—
By this time, had the king permitted us,
One of our souls had wandered in the air,
Banished this frail sepulcher° of our flesh,   195
As now our flesh is banished from this land:
Confess thy treasons ere thou fly the realm;
Since thou hast far to go, bear not along
The clogging burden of a guilty soul.

MOWBRAY
No, Bolingbroke, if ever I were traitor,   200
My name be blotted from the book of life,

---

112 **approve** prove   118 **warder** truncheon (a signal to stop the combat)   120 **chairs** on which the combatants sat before mounting   122 s.d. **flourish** trumpet call   124 **list** hear   142 **regreet** greet again   143 **stranger** foreign   150 **determinate** put a limit to   151 **dateless** endless; **dear** severe   152 **word** utterance   154 **sentence** punning on "word" in line 152

156 **dearer merit** better reward   163 **cunning** ingenious and requiring skill in the playing   167 **portcullised** a portcullis was a grating which could be let down in the gateway of a castle to block it   174 **boots** avails; **compassionate** expressing passionate feeling   181 **Our . . . yourselves** we absolve you from allegiance to us   188 **advised** deliberate   189 **complot** plot with others   195 **sepulcher** here accented on second syllable

And I from heaven banished as from hence!
But what thou art, God, thou, and I, do know,
And all too soon, I fear, the king shall rue.
Farewell, my liege, now no way can I stray:    205
Save back to England all the world's my way.    *Exit.*

RICHARD
Uncle, even in the glasses° of thine eyes
I see thy grievèd heart: thy sad aspect°
Hath from the number of his banished years
Plucked four away. [*To* BOLINGBROKE.] Six frozen
   winters spent,    210
Return with welcome home from banishment.

BOLINGBROKE
How long a time lies in one little word.
Four lagging winters and four wanton° springs
End in a word—such is the breath of kings.

GAUNT
I thank my liege that in regard to me    215
He shortens four years of my son's exile,
But little vantage° shall I reap thereby:
For ere the six years that he hath to spend
Can change their moons and bring their times° about,
My oil-dried lamp and time-bewasted light    220
Shall be extinct with age and endless night;
My inch of taper will be burnt and done,
And blindfold death° not let me see my son.

RICHARD
Why! uncle, thou hast many years to live.

GAUNT
But not a minute, king, that thou canst give;    225
Shorten my days thou canst with sullen sorrow
And pluck nights from me, but not lend a morrow;
Thou canst help time to furrow me with age,
But stop no wrinkle in his pilgrimage:
Thy word is current° with him for my death,    230
But dead, thy kingdom cannot buy my breath.

RICHARD
Thy son is banished upon good advice,
Whereto thy tongue a party-verdict° gave:
Why at our justice seem'st thou then to lour?

GAUNT
Things sweet to taste prove in digestion sour.    235
You urged me as a judge, but I had rather
You would have bid me argue like a father.
O, had it been a stranger, not my child,
To smooth his fault I should have been more mild:
A partial slander° sought I to avoid,    240
And in the sentence my own life destroyed.
Alas! I looked when some of you should say
I was too strict to make mine own away;
But you gave leave to my unwilling tongue
Against my will to do myself this wrong.    245

RICHARD
Cousin, farewell, and uncle, bid him so;
Six years we banish him, and he shall go.
[*Flourish.*] *Exit* [*King* RICHARD, *with his* TRAIN].

AUMERLE
Cousin, farewell; what presence must not know,°
From where you do remain let paper show.

MARSHAL
My lord, no leave take I, for I will ride    250
As far as land will let me by your side.

GAUNT
O, to what purpose dost thou hoard thy words,
That thou returnest no greeting to thy friends?

BOLINGBROKE
I have too few to take my leave of you,
When the tongue's office should be prodigal°    255
To breathe the abundant dolor of the heart.

GAUNT
Thy grief° is but thy absence for a time.

BOLINGBROKE
Joy absent, grief is present for that time.

GAUNT
What is six winters? They are quickly gone.

BOLINGBROKE
To men in joy; but grief makes one hour ten.    260

GAUNT
Call it a travel that thou tak'st for pleasure.

BOLINGBROKE
My heart will sigh when I miscall it so,
Which finds it an enforcèd pilgrimage.

GAUNT
The sullen passage of thy weary steps
Esteem as foil° wherein thou art to set    265
The precious jewel of thy home return.

BOLINGBROKE
Nay, rather, every tedious stride I make
Will but remember° me what a deal of world
I wander from the jewels that I love.
Must I not serve a long apprenticehood    270
To foreign passages,° and in the end,
Having my freedom,° boast of nothing else
But that I was a journeyman° to grief?°

GAUNT
All places that the eye of heaven° visits
Are to a wise man ports and happy havens.    275
Teach thy necessity to reason thus:
There is no virtue° like necessity.
Think not the king did banish thee,
But thou the king. Woe doth the heavier sit
Where it perceives it is but faintly° borne.    280
Go, say I sent thee forth to purchase honor,
And not the king exiled thee; or suppose
Devouring pestilence hangs in our air,
And thou art flying to a fresher clime.
Look what° thy soul holds dear, imagine it    285
To lie that way thou goest, not whence thou com'st.
Suppose the singing birds musicians,

207 **glasses** eyes were thought to reflect the heart   208 **aspect** accent on second syllable   213 **wanton** luxuriant   217 **vantage** advantage   219 **times** seasons   223 **blindfold death** death is thought of as eyeless, like a skull, and also as Atropos, Milton's "blind fury with the abhorred shears," cutting short human lives   230 **current** valid   233 **party-verdict** one person's share of a joint verdict   240 **partial slander** imputation of partiality

248 **what . . . know** perhaps "as I cannot have your news from you in person," or "what you cannot say in present company" (Aumerle is anxious to know Bolingbroke's intentions)   255 **prodigal** lavish   257 **grief** (1) grievance (2) sorrow   265 **foil** setting (metal leaf serving as a background)   268 **remember** remind   271 **passages** experiences   272 **Having my freedom** at the end of his apprenticeship and of his exile   273 **journeyman** (1) artisan (2) traveler; **journeyman to grief** employee of grief (instead of his own master)   274 **eye of heaven** sun (as in Ovid)   277 **virtue** efficacy   280 **faintly** faintheartedly   285 **Look what** whatever

The grass whereon thou tread'st the presence strewed,°
The flowers fair ladies, and thy steps no more
Than a delightful measure or a dance;                                290
For gnarling° sorrow hath less power to bite
The man that mocks at it and sets it light.

BOLINGBROKE

O, who can hold a fire in his hand
By thinking on the frosty Caucasus?
Or cloy the hungry edge of appetite                                  295
By bare imagination of a feast?
Or wallow naked in December snow
By thinking on fantastic° summer's heat?
O, no! the apprehension of the good
Gives but the greater feeling to the worse.                          300
Fell° sorrow's tooth doth never rankle° more
Than when he bites, but lanceth° not the sore.

GAUNT

Come, come, my son, I'll bring thee on thy way.
Had I thy youth and cause, I would not stay.°

BOLINGBROKE

Then England's ground, farewell; sweet soil, adieu;                  305
My mother and my nurse that bears° me yet!
Where'er I wander, boast of this I can:
Though banished, yet a true-born Englishman.

                                                      *Exeunt.*

[Scene IV. *The Court.*]

*Enter the king* [RICHARD] *with* BAGOT, [GREEN], &c.
*at one door, and the Lord* AUMERLE *at another.*

RICHARD

We did observe.° Cousin Aumerle,
How far brought you high Hereford on his way?

AUMERLE

I brought high Hereford, if you call him so,
But to the next high way, and there I left him.

RICHARD

And say, what store of parting tears were shed?                        5

AUMERLE

Faith, none for me,° except the northeast wind,
Which then blew bitterly against our faces,
Awaked the sleeping rheum, and so by chance
Did grace our hollow parting with a tear.

RICHARD

What said our cousin when you parted with him?                        10

AUMERLE

"Farewell."
And for my heart disdainèd that my tongue
Should so profane the word, that taught me craft
To counterfeit oppression of such grief
That words seemed buried in my sorrow's grave.                        15
Marry, would the word "Farewell" have length'ned
   hours
And added years to his short banishment,

He should have had a volume of farewells;
But since it would not, he had none of me.

RICHARD

He is our cousin,° cousin, but 'tis doubt,                            20
When time shall call him home from banishment,
Whether our kinsman come to see his friends.
Ourself and Bushy, Bagot here and Green,
Observed his courtship to the common people,
How he did seem to dive into their hearts                             25
With humble and familiar courtesy,
What reverence he did throw away on slaves,
Wooing poor craftsmen with the craft of smiles
And patient underbearing of his fortune,
As 'twere to banish their affects with him.                          30
Off goes his bonnet to an oyster-wench;
A brace of draymen bid God speed him well,
And had the tribute of his supple knee,
With "Thanks, my countrymen, my loving friends";
As were our England in reversion his,                                35
And he our subjects' next degree in hope.

GREEN

Well, he is gone, and with him go these thoughts.
Now for the rebels which stand out in Ireland;
Expedient manage° must be made, my liege,
Ere further leisure yield them further means                         40
For their advantage and your highness' loss.

RICHARD

We will ourself in person to this war,
And for our coffers with too great a court
And liberal largess are grown somewhat light,
We are enforced to farm° our royal realm,                            45
The revenue whereof shall furnish us
For our affairs in hand. If that come short,
Our substitutes at home shall have blank charters;°
Whereto, when they shall know what men are rich,
They shall subscribe them for large sums of gold,                    50
And send them after to supply our wants,
For we will make for Ireland presently.

*Enter* BUSHY.

Bushy, what news?

BUSHY

Old John of Gaunt is grievous sick, my lord,
Sudden taken, and hath sent posthaste                                55
To entreat your majesty to visit him.

RICHARD

Where lies he?

BUSHY

At Ely House.

RICHARD

Now put it, God, in the physician's mind
To help him to his grave immediately!                                60
The lining° of his coffers shall make coats
To deck our soldiers for these Irish wars.
Come, gentlemen, let's all go visit him;
Pray God we may make haste and come too late!

ALL

Amen!                                                    *Exeunt.*    65

---

**288 presence strewed** royal presence chamber strewn with
rushes   **291 gnarling** snarling (with perhaps a suggestion of
the twisting effects of sorrow)   **298 fantastic** imaginary   **301
Fell** fierce; **rankle** fester   **302 lanceth** cuts with a surgeon's
knife   **304 I . . . stay** i.e., away from England   **306 bears**
(1) gives birth to (2) supports me; for a discussion of these
speeches see K. Muir, *Review of English Studies*, X (1959),
283–86
**I.iv.1 We did observe** continuing a conversation   **6 for me**
for my part

**20 cousin** Richard, Aumerle, and Bolingbroke were cousins
**39 manage** management   **45 farm** lease (Richard leased the
crown lands and customs dues to his favorites for £7000 a
month)   **48 blank charters** documents given to Richard's
agents, with power to insert what sums they pleased for the
rich to pay   **61 lining** contents (with pun on "coats")

# [ ACT II ]

[Scene I. *London. Ely House.*]

*Enter John of* GAUNT, *sick, with the Duke of* YORK,
[*the Earl of* NORTHUMBERLAND, ATTENDANTS], &c.

GAUNT
Will the king come, that I may breathe my last
In wholesome counsel to his unstaid° youth?

YORK
Vex not yourself, nor strive not with your breath,
For all in vain comes counsel to his ear.

GAUNT
O, but they say the tongues of dying men     5
Enforce attention like deep harmony:
Where words are scarce they are seldom spent in vain,
For they breathe truth that breathe their words in pain;
He that no more must say is listened more
Than they whom youth and ease have taught to glose;° 10
More are men's ends marked than their lives before;
The setting sun, and music at the close,°
As the last taste of sweets is sweetest last,°
Writ in remembrance more than things long past:
Though Richard my life's counsel would not hear,   15
My death's sad tale° may yet undeaf his ear.

YORK
No, it is stopped with other flattering sounds:
As praises—of whose taste the wise° are fond—
Lascivious meters, to whose venom° sound
The open ear of youth doth always listen;      20
Report of fashions in proud Italy
Whose manners still° our tardy-apish° nation
Limps after in base imitation.°
Where doth the world thrust forth a vanity—
So it be new, there's no respect how vile—    25
That is not quickly buzzed into his ears?
Then all too late comes counsel to be heard,
Where will° doth mutiny with wit's regard.°
Direct not him whose way himself will choose:
'Tis breath thou lack'st, and that breath wilt thou lose. 30

GAUNT
Methinks I am a prophet new inspired,
And thus expiring° do foretell of him:
His rash fierce blaze of riot° cannot last,
For violent fires soon burn out themselves.
Small showers last long, but sudden storms are short; 35
He tires betimes that spurs too fast betimes;°
With eager feeding, food doth choke the feeder.
Light vanity, insatiate cormorant,°
Consuming means, soon preys upon itself.
This royal throne of kings, this scept'red isle,    40
This earth of majesty, this seat of Mars,
This other Eden, demi-paradise,

This fortress built by Nature for herself
Against infection° and the hand of war,
This happy breed° of men, this little world,°    45
This precious stone set in the silver sea
Which serves it in the office of a wall,
Or as a moat defensive to a house,
Against the envy of less happier lands,
This blessed plot, this earth, this realm, this England, 50
This nurse, this teeming womb of royal kings,
Feared by their breed, and famous by their birth,
Renownèd for their deeds as far from home,
For Christian service° and true chivalry,
As is the sepulcher in stubborn° Jewry      55
Of the world's ransom, blessed Mary's son,
This land of such dear souls, this dear dear land—
Dear for her reputation through the world—
Is now leased out—I die pronouncing it—
Like to a tenement° or pelting° farm.°      60
England, bound in with the triumphant sea,
Whose rocky shore beats back the envious siege°
Of wat'ry Neptune, is now bound in with shame,
With inky blots, and rotten parchment bonds.
That England that was wont to conquer others   65
Hath made a shameful conquest of itself.
Ah! would the scandal vanish with my life,
How happy then were my ensuing death!

*Enter King* [RICHARD] *and* QUEEN, &c. [AUMERLE,
BUSHY, GREEN, BAGOT, ROSS, *and* WILLOUGHBY].

YORK
The king is come; deal mildly with his youth,
For young hot colts being raged° do rage the more. 70

QUEEN
How fares our noble uncle, Lancaster?

RICHARD
What comfort, man? How is't with aged Gaunt?

GAUNT
O, how that name befits my composition!
Old Gaunt indeed, and gaunt in being old!
Within me grief hath kept a tedious fast;     75
And who abstains from meat that is not gaunt?
For sleeping England long time have I watched:
Watching breeds leanness, leanness is all gaunt.
The pleasure that some fathers feed upon
Is my strict fast°—I mean my children's looks—   80
And therein fasting hast thou made me gaunt;
Gaunt am I for the grave, gaunt as a grave°
Whose hollow womb inherits° naught but bones.

RICHARD
Can sick men play so nicely° with their names?

GAUNT
No, misery makes sport to mock itself:      85
Since thou dost seek to kill my name in me,°
I mock my name, great king, to flatter thee.

II.i.2 **unstaid** unrestrained   10 **glose** utter pleasing words
12 **close** conclusion of a musical phrase   13 **last** because it
comes last   16 **My . . . tale** my solemn dying words   18 **the
wise** even the wise (see A Note on the Text, p. 443)   19
**venom** venomous   22 **still** always; **tardy-apish** imitative,
but behind the fashion   23 **imitation** five syllables; complaints of the aping of foreign fashions were common in
Elizabethan England (for this speech and the next see K. Muir,
*Review of English Studies*, X (1959), 286–89   28 **will** desire;
**wit's regard** what intelligence ought to regard   31–32
**inspired . . . expiring** pun   33 **riot** profligacy   36 **betimes**
(1) soon (2) early   38 **cormorant** glutton (from the bird)

44 **infection** moral infection   45 **happy breed** fortunate
race; **little world** a world by itself   54 **Christian service** the
Crusades   55 **stubborn** because they rejected Christ   40–60
**This . . . farm** the verb comes in line 59   60 **tenement**
leased land or property; **pelting** paltry   62 **siege** perhaps a
partial pun on *surge*   70 **raged** enraged   80 **Is . . . fast** I must
go without   73–82 **name . . . grave** Coleridge defended the
psychological truth of these puns   83 **inherits** the grave will
get only bones because Gaunt is wasted away   84 **nicely** subtly
and prettily   86 **kill . . . me** i.e., by banishing my son and heir

RICHARD
Should dying men flatter with those that live?
GAUNT
No, no, men living flatter those that die.
RICHARD
Thou, now a-dying, sayest thou flatterest me.          90
GAUNT
O no, thou diest, though I the sicker be.
RICHARD
I am in health, I breathe, and see thee ill.
GAUNT
Now He that made me knows I see thee ill;
Ill in myself to see, and in thee seeing ill.°
Thy deathbed is no lesser than thy land,               95
Wherein thou liest in reputation sick;
And thou, too careless patient° as thou art,
Commit'st thy anointed body to the cure
Of those physicians that first wounded thee.
A thousand flatterers sit within thy crown,            100
Whose compass is no bigger than thy head,
And yet incagèd in so small a verge°
The waste° is no whit lesser than thy land.
O, had thy grandsire° with a prophet's eye
Seen how his son's son should destroy his sons,°       105
From forth thy reach he would have laid thy shame,
Deposing thee before thou wert possessed,
Which art possessed° now to depose thyself.
Why, cousin,° wert thou regent of the world,
It were a shame to let this land by lease;             110
But for thy world° enjoying but this land
Is it not more than shame to shame it so?
Landlord of England art thou now, not king;
Thy state of law° is bondslave to the law,
And thou—
RICHARD [Interrupting.]
A lunatic, lean-witted fool,                           115
Presuming on an ague's privilege,
Darest with thy frozen° admonition
Make pale our cheek, chasing the royal blood
With fury from his native residence.°
Now, by my seat's° right-royal majesty,                120
Wert thou not brother to great Edward's son,
This tongue that runs so roundly° in thy head
Should run thy head from thy unreverent shoulders.
GAUNT
O, spare me not, my brother Edward's son,
For that I was his father Edward's son,                125
That blood already like the pelican°
Hast thou tapped out and drunkenly caroused:
My brother Gloucester, plain well-meaning soul—
Whom fair befall in heaven 'mongst happy souls!—

May be a precedent and witness good                    130
That thou respect'st not spilling Edward's blood.
Join with the present sickness that I have,
And thy unkindness be like crooked° age
To crop at once a too-long-withered flower.
Live in thy shame, but die not shame with thee;        135
These words hereafter thy tormentors be.
Convey me to my bed, then to my grave;
Love they to live that love and honor have.
                Exit [GAUNT, borne by ATTENDANTS,
                            and NORTHUMBERLAND].
RICHARD
And let them die that age and sullens° have,
For both hast thou, and both become the grave.         140
YORK
I do beseech your majesty, impute his words
To wayward sickliness and age in him:
He loves you, on my life, and holds you dear
As Harry, Duke of Hereford, were he here.
RICHARD
Right, you say true, as Hereford's love, so his,       145
As theirs, so mine; and all be as it is.°

[Enter NORTHUMBERLAND.]

NORTHUMBERLAND
My liege, old Gaunt commends him to your majesty.
RICHARD
What says he?
NORTHUMBERLAND    Nay, nothing, all is said;
His tongue is now a stringless instrument;
Words, life, and all, old Lancaster hath spent.        150
YORK
Be York the next that must be bankrout° so!
Though death be poor, it ends a mortal woe.
RICHARD
The ripest fruit first falls, and so doth he;
His time is spent, our pilgrimage must be;
So much for that.° Now for our Irish wars.             155
We must supplant those rough rug-headed kernes°
Which live like venom, where no venom° else,
But only they, have privilege to live.
And for these great affairs do ask some charge,
Towards our assistance we do seize to us               160
The plate, coin, revenues, and movables
Whereof our uncle Gaunt did stand possessed.
YORK
How long shall I be patient? Ah, how long
Shall tender duty make me suffer wrong?
Not Gloucester's death, nor Hereford's banishment,     165
Nor Gaunt's rebukes,° nor England's private
   wrongs,°
Nor the prevention of poor Bolingbroke°

94 Ill . . . ill (1) bad eyesight (2) evil  97 careless patient
one who does not take proper steps to cure himself
102 verge limit (and possibly area within a radius of twelve
miles around the court)  103 waste (1) destruction of landlord's
property by tenant (2) useless expense (3) wide space  104
grandsire Edward III  105 sons Gloucester and Gaunt
107–08 possessed . . . possessed (1) possessed of the crown
(2) possessed with devils  109 cousin kinsman  111 world
cf. line 45  114 state of law legal status  117 frozen (1)
frigid in style (2) prompted by ague (3) cold, and so cooling me
119 residence his cheek  120 seat's throne's  122 roundly
bluntly  126 pelican thought to wound its breast to feed its
young with its blood—a symbol both of parental self-sacrifice
and filial ingratitude

133 crooked bent (and suggesting Time with a scythe; cf. line
134)  139 sullens sulks  146 and . . . is let what will be, be
151 bankrout bankrupt  153–55 The . . . that cf. Bolingbroke's equally callous reception of Mowbray's death,
IV.i.103–04; he also changes the subject in the middle of a
line  156 rug-headed kernes shag-haired light-armed Irish
foot soldiers  157 venom reptiles (alluding to the tradition
that Saint Patrick expelled snakes from Ireland)  166 Gaunt's
rebukes rebukes suffered by Gaunt; private wrongs wrongs
suffered by private citizens  167 prevention . . . Bolingbroke Richard prevented Bolingbroke's marriage in exile to
the French king's cousin

About his marriage, nor my own disgrace,°
Have ever made me sour° my patient cheek,
Or bend one wrinkle° on my sovereign's face.                    170
I am the last of noble Edward's sons,
Of whom thy father, Prince of Wales, was first:
In war was never lion raged more fierce,
In peace was never gentle lamb more mild,
Than was that young and princely gentleman.                     175
His face thou hast, for even so looked he,
Accomplished with the number of thy hours;°
But when he frowned it was against the French,
And not against his friends; his noble hand
Did win what he did spend, and spent not that                   180
Which his triumphant father's hand had won;
His hands were guilty of no kindred blood,
But bloody with the enemies of his kin.
O, Richard, York is too far gone with grief,
Or else he never would compare between—                         185

RICHARD
Why, uncle, what's the matter?

YORK                                        O my liege,
Pardon me, if you please; if not, I pleased
Not to be pardoned, am content withal.
Seek you to seize and gripe° into your hands
The royalties° and rights of banished Hereford?                 190
Is not Gaunt dead? and doth not Hereford live?
Was not Gaunt just? and is not Harry true?
Did not the one deserve to have an heir?
Is not his heir a well-deserving son?
Take° Hereford's rights away, and take from Time                195
His charters and his customary rights,
Let not tomorrow then ensue° today;
Be not thyself. For how art thou a king
But by fair sequence and succession?°
Now afore God—God forbid I say true—                            200
If you do wrongfully seize Hereford's rights,
Call in the letters patents that he hath
By his attorneys-general to sue
His livery,° and deny° his off'red homage,
You pluck a thousand dangers on your head,                      205
You lose a thousand well-disposèd hearts,
And prick my tender patience to those thoughts
Which honor and allegiance cannot think.

RICHARD
Think what you will, we seize into our hands
His plate, his goods, his money, and his lands.                 210

YORK
I'll not be by° the while. My liege, farewell.
What will ensue hereof there's none can tell:
But by° bad courses may be understood
That their events° can never fall out good.          *Exit.*

RICHARD
Go, Bushy, to the Earl of Wiltshire° straight;                  215

Bid him repair to us to Ely House,
To see this business. Tomorrow next
We will for Ireland—and 'tis time, I trow;
And we create in absence of ourself
Our uncle York Lord Governor of England,                        220
For he is just, and always loved us well.°
Come on, our queen, tomorrow must we part;
Be merry, for our time of stay is short.
        [*Flourish.*] *Exeunt King* [RICHARD] *and* QUEEN.
        *Manet*° NORTHUMBERLAND [*with* WILLOUGHBY
                                        *and* ROSS].

NORTHUMBERLAND
Well, lords, the Duke of Lancaster is dead.

ROSS
And living too, for now his son is duke.                        225

WILLOUGHBY
Barely in title, not in revenues.

NORTHUMBERLAND
Richly in both, if justice had her right.

ROSS
My heart is great, but it must break with silence
Ere't be disburdened with a liberal° tongue.

NORTHUMBERLAND
Nay, speak thy mind, and let him ne'er speak more               230
That speaks thy words again to do thee harm.

WILLOUGHBY
Tends that that thou wouldst speak to the Duke of
    Hereford?
If it be so, out with it boldly, man;
Quick is mine ear to hear of good towards him.

ROSS
No good at all that I can do for him,                           235
Unless you call it good to pity him,
Bereft, and gelded of his patrimony.

NORTHUMBERLAND
Now, afore God, 'tis shame such wrongs are borne
In him a royal prince and many moe°
Of noble blood in this declining land!                          240
The king is not himself, but basely led
By flatterers; and what they will inform
Merely in hate 'gainst any of us all,
That will the king severely prosecute
'Gainst us, our lives, our children, and our heirs.             245

ROSS
The commons hath he pilled° with grievous taxes
And quite lost their hearts. The nobles hath he fined
For ancient quarrels and quite lost their hearts.

WILLOUGHBY
And daily new exactions are devised,
As blanks,° benevolences,° and I wot not what:                  250
But what, a° God's name, doth become of this?

NORTHUMBERLAND
Wars hath not wasted it, for warred he hath not,
But basely yielded upon compromise
That which his noble ancestors achieved with blows:
More hath he spent in peace than they in wars.                  255

ROSS
The Earl of Wiltshire hath the realm in farm.

---

168 **my own disgrace** unexplained; possibly we should accept the equally difficult original reading of Q1, "his own disgrace," corrected in all copies save one   169 **sour** make sour   170 **wrinkle** frown   177 **Accomplished . . . hours** when he was your age   189 **gripe** clutch   190 **royalties** gifts from the king   195 **Take** if you take   197 **ensue** follow upon   199 **succession** four syllables   202–04 **Call . . . livery** if you revoke the royal letters patent that enable his attorneys to obtain for him his father's lands   204 **deny** refuse   211 **by** near   213 **by** concerning   214 **events** outcomes   215 **Wiltshire** William le Scrope, treasurer of England

221 **For . . . well** in spite of York's criticisms of his conduct, Richard apparently appreciates his honesty   223 **s.d. Manet** remains   229 **liberal** free   239 **moe** more   246 **pilled** plundered   250 **blanks** cf. I.iv.48; **benevolences** forced loans (an anachronism, as they were introduced in 1473)   251 **a** in

WILLOUGHBY
The king's grown bankrout like a broken man.

NORTHUMBERLAND
Reproach and dissolution hangeth over him.

ROSS
He hath not money for these Irish wars,
His burdenous taxations notwithstanding,                260
But by the robbing of the banished duke.

NORTHUMBERLAND
His noble kinsman—most degenerate king!
But, lords, we hear this fearful tempest sing,
Yet seek no shelter to avoid the storm:
We see the wind sit sore upon our sails,                265
And yet we strike° not, but securely perish.

ROSS
We see the very wrack° that we must suffer,
And unavoided is the danger now,
For suffering so the causes of our wrack.

NORTHUMBERLAND
Not so; even through the hollow eyes of death       270
I spy life peering, but I dare not say
How near the tidings of our comfort is.

WILLOUGHBY
Nay, let us share thy thoughts, as thou dost ours.

ROSS
Be confident to speak, Northumberland;
We three are but thyself, and speaking so             275
Thy words are but as thoughts: therefore be bold.

NORTHUMBERLAND
Then thus: I have from le Port Blanc, a bay
In Brittaine,° received intelligence
That Harry, Duke of Hereford, Rainold, Lord
   Cobham,
[The son of Richard, Earl of Arundel,°]                280
That late broke° from the Duke of Exeter,
His brother, Archbishop, late of Canterbury,
Sir Thomas Erpingham, Sir Thomas Ramston,
Sir John Norbery, Sir Robert Waterton, and Francis
   Quoint—
All these well furnished by the Duke of Brittaine   285
With eight tall ships, three thousand men of war,°
Are making hither with all due expedience,°
And shortly mean to touch our northern shore.
Perhaps they had ere this, but that they stay
The first departing of the king for Ireland.         290
If then we shall shake off our slavish yoke,
Imp out° our drooping country's broken wing,
Redeem from broking pawn° the blemished
   crown,
Wipe off the dust that hides our scepter's gilt,°
And make high majesty look like itself,              295
Away with me in post° to Ravenspurgh;
But if you faint, as fearing to do so,
Stay, and be secret, and myself will go.

ROSS
To horse, to horse, urge doubts to them that fear.

WILLOUGHBY
Hold out my horse,° and I will first be there.  *Exeunt.*   300

[Scene II. *Windsor Castle.*]

*Enter the* QUEEN, BUSHY, BAGOT.

BUSHY
Madam, your majesty is too much sad.
You promised, when you parted with the king,
To lay aside life-harming heaviness,
And entertain a cheerful disposition.

QUEEN
To please the king I did: to please myself            5
I cannot do it; yet I know no cause
Why I should welcome such a guest as grief,
Save bidding farewell to so sweet a guest
As my sweet Richard. Yet again methinks
Some unborn sorrow ripe in Fortune's womb           10
Is coming towards me; and my inward soul
With nothing trembles—at something it grieves
More than with parting from my lord the king.

BUSHY
Each substance of a grief hath twenty shadows,°
Which shows like grief itself, but is not so;         15
For sorrow's eye, glazèd with blinding tears,
Divides one thing entire to many objects,
Like perspectives° which, rightly gazed upon,
Show nothing but confusion; eyed awry,
Distinguish form. So your sweet majesty,              20
Looking awry upon your lord's departure,
Find° shapes of grief more than himself to wail,°
Which looked on as it is, is nought but shadows
Of what it is not; then, thrice-gracious queen,
More than your lord's departure weep not: more's not
   seen,                                              25
Or if it be, 'tis with false sorrow's eye,
Which for things true weeps° things imaginary.

QUEEN
It may be so; but yet my inward soul
Persuades me it is otherwise. Howe'er it be,
I cannot but be sad—so heavy sad,                     30
As, though on thinking on no thought I think,°
Makes me with heavy nothing faint and shrink.

BUSHY
'Tis nothing but conceit,° my gracious lady.

QUEEN
'Tis nothing less:° conceit is still derived
From some forefather grief; mine is not so,          35
For nothing hath begot my something grief,
Or something hath the nothing that I grieve:°

---

266 **strike** a pun on striking sails and striking blows  **267
wrack** wreck  **278 Brittaine** Brittany  **280 The . . .
Arundel** some such line, necessary for the sense, is lacking,
possibly because an Earl of Arundel was executed in October
1595  **281 broke** escaped  **286 men of war** soldiers  **287
expedience** speed  **292 Imp out** engraft new feathers  **293
broking pawn** lending money upon pawns, which was
fraudulent (cf. II.i.113)  **294 gilt** pun on *guilt*  **296 in post**
with speed, with relays of horses

**300 Hold . . . horse** if my horse holds out
**II.ii.14 shadows** illusory griefs  **18 perspectives** pictures
constructed so that they look distorted when viewed directly
("rightly"), and intelligible when viewed from the side
("awry")  **22 Find** the subject "you" is understood from
"majesty"; **wail** bewail  **27 weeps** weeps for  **31 though
. . . think** though I try to think about nothing  **33 conceit**
fancy  **34 'Tis nothing less** it's anything except mere fancy
**37 something . . . grieve** the nothing that I grieve hath
something in it

'Tis in reversion that I do possess,°
But what it is that is not yet known what,
I cannot name; 'tis nameless woe I wot.°      40

[*Enter* GREEN.]

GREEN
God save your majesty! and well met, gentlemen.
I hope the king is not yet shipped for Ireland.

QUEEN
Why hopest thou so? 'Tis better hope he is,
For his designs crave° haste, his haste good hope:
Then wherefore dost thou hope he is not shipped?      45

GREEN
That he our hope might have retired his power
And driven into despair an enemy's hope,
Who strongly° hath set footing in this land:
The banished Bolingbroke repeals° himself,
And with uplifted arms is safe arrived      50
At Ravenspurgh.

QUEEN            Now God in heaven forbid!

GREEN
Ah, madam! 'tis too true; and that° is worse,
The Lord Northumberland, his son, young Henry
    Percy,°
The Lords of Ross, Beaumond, and Willoughby,
With all their powerful friends are fled to him.      55

BUSHY
Why have you not proclaimed Northumberland
And all the rest° revolted faction, traitors?

GREEN
We have: whereupon the Earl of Worcester°
Hath broken his staff, resigned his stewardship,
And all the household servants fled with him      60
To Bolingbroke.

QUEEN
So, Green, thou art the midwife to my woe,
And Bolingbroke, my sorrow's dismal heir;°
Now hath my soul brought forth her prodigy,°
And I, a gasping, new-delivered mother,      65
Have woe to woe, sorrow to sorrow, joined.

BUSHY
Despair not, madam.

QUEEN            Who shall hinder me?
I will despair and be at enmity
With cozening hope: he is a flatterer,
A parasite, a keeper-back of death,      70
Who gently would dissolve the bands° of life
Which false hope lingers° in extremity.

[*Enter the Duke of* YORK.]

GREEN
Here comes the Duke of York.

QUEEN
With signs of war° about his aged neck.

O, full of careful business° are his looks!
Uncle, for God's sake, speak comfortable° words.      75

YORK
Should I do so, I should belie my thoughts.
Comfort's in heaven, and we are on the earth,
Where nothing lives but crosses, cares, and grief.
Your husband, he is gone to save far off,      80
Whilst others come to make him lose at home.
Here am I left to underprop his land,
Who, weak with age, cannot support myself.
Now comes the sick hour that his surfeit° made;
Now shall he try his friends that flattered him.      85

[*Enter* SERVINGMAN.]

SERVINGMAN
My lord, your son was gone before I came.

YORK
He was? Why so, go all which way it will.
The nobles, they are fled, the commons cold,
And will, I fear, revolt on Hereford's side.
Sirrah, get thee to Plashy to my sister° Gloucester;      90
Bid her send me presently a thousand pound.
Hold, take my ring.

SERVINGMAN
My lord, I had forgot to tell your lordship:
Today as I came by I callèd there—
But I shall grieve you to report the rest.      95

YORK
What is't, knave?

SERVINGMAN
An hour before I came the duchess died.°

YORK
God for his mercy, what a tide of woes
Comes rushing on this woeful land at once.
I know not what to do. I would to God—      100
So my untruth° had not provoked him to it—
The king had cut off my head with my brother's.
What! are there no posts dispatched for Ireland?
How shall we do for money for these wars?
Come, sister—cousin, I would say—pray pardon me.      105
Go fellow, get thee home, provide some carts,
And bring away the armor that is there.
                     [*Exit* SERVINGMAN.]
Gentlemen, will you go muster men?
If I know how or which way to order these affairs,
Thus disorderly thrust into my hands,      110
Never believe me. Both are my kinsmen.
Th' one is my sovereign, whom both my oath
And duty bids defend; t' other again
Is my kinsman, whom the king hath wronged,
Whom conscience and my kindred bids to right.      115
Well, somewhat we must do. Come, cousin,
I'll dispose of° you. Gentlemen, go muster up your
    men,
And meet me presently at Berkeley.
I should to Plashy too,

---

**38 'Tis . . . possess** I am heir to it, and I shall know what it is when I experience it   **40 wot** know   **44 crave** demand   **48 strongly** with a strong force   **49 repeals** recalls   **52 that** what   **53 young Henry Percy** these words are repeated in the next scene, and either "Henry" or "his son" may be spurious here   **57 rest** remaining   **58 Worcester** Northumberland's brother, and the Lord Steward of the king's household   **63 heir** offspring   **64 prodigy** monster   **71 dissolve the bands** unloose the bonds   **72 lingers** causes to linger   **74 signs of war** York is wearing throat armor

**75 careful business** anxious preoccupation   **76 comfortable** comforting (the phrase "comfortable words" is used in the Anglican communion service)   **84 surfeit** overindulgence   **90 sister** sister-in-law   **97 died** in fact she died later; but Shakespeare wishes to give the effect of a succession of woes   **101 untruth** disloyalty   **117 dispose of** make arrangements for

But time will not permit. All is uneven,                          120
And everything is left at six and seven.°
      *Exeunt Duke [of* YORK], QUEEN. *Manent*
                BUSHY, [BAGOT,] GREEN.

BUSHY
The wind sits° fair for news to go for Ireland,
But none returns. For us to levy power
Proportionable° to the enemy
Is all unpossible.                                                125

GREEN
Besides, our nearness to the king in love
Is near the hate of those love not the king.

BAGOT
And that is the wavering commons, for their love
Lies in their purses, and whoso empties them
By so much fills their hearts with deadly hate.                   130

BUSHY
Wherein the king stands generally condemned.

BAGOT
If judgment lie in° them, then so do we,
Because we ever have been near the king.

GREEN
Well, I will for refuge straight to Bristow° Castle.
The Earl of Wiltshire is already there.                           135

BUSHY
Thither will I with you, for little office
The hateful commons will perform for us,
Except like curs to tear us all to pieces.
Will you go along with us?

BAGOT
No, I will to Ireland to his majesty.                             140
Farewell; if heart's presages be not vain,
We three here part that ne'er shall meet again.

BUSHY
That's as York thrives to beat back Bolingbroke.

GREEN
Alas, poor duke, the task he undertakes
Is numb'ring sands, and drinking oceans dry:                      145
Where one on his side fights, thousands will fly.
Farewell at once, for once, for all, and ever.

BUSHY
Well, we may meet again.

BAGOT                    I fear me, never. [*Exeunt.*]


            [Scene III. *In Gloucestershire.*]


*Enter [*BOLINGBROKE *Duke of*] *Hereford, [and]*
NORTHUMBERLAND [*with* SOLDIERS].

BOLINGBROKE
How far is it, my lord, to Berkeley now?

NORTHUMBERLAND
Believe me, noble lord,
I am a stranger here in Gloucestershire.
These high wild hills and rough uneven ways
Draws out our miles and makes them wearisome;                     5
And yet your fair discourse hath been as sugar,
Making the hard way sweet and delectable.°
But I bethink me what a weary way

From Ravenspurgh to Cotshall° will be found
In Ross and Willoughby, wanting your company,                     10
Which I protest hath very much beguiled
The tediousness and process° of my travel:
But theirs is sweet'ned with the hope to have
The present benefit which I possess;
And hope to joy is little less in joy                             15
Than hope enjoyed. By this the weary lords
Shall make their way seem short as mine hath done,
By sight of what I have, your noble company.

BOLINGBROKE
Of much less value is my company
Than your good words. But who comes here?                         20

*Enter Harry* PERCY.

NORTHUMBERLAND
It is my son, young Harry Percy,
Sent from my brother Worcester whencesoever.°
Harry, how fares your uncle?

PERCY
I had thought, my lord, to have learned his health of
    you.

NORTHUMBERLAND
Why, is he not with the queen?                                    25

PERCY
No, my good lord, he hath forsook the court,
Broken his staff of office, and dispersed
The household of the king.

NORTHUMBERLAND          What was his reason?
He was not so resolved when last we spake together.

PERCY
Because your lordship was proclaimèd traitor;                     30
But he, my lord, is gone to Ravenspurgh
To offer service to the Duke of Hereford,
And sent me over by Berkeley to discover
What power the Duke of York had levied there,
Then with directions to repair to Ravenspurgh.                    35

NORTHUMBERLAND
Have you forgot the Duke of Hereford, boy?

PERCY
No, my good lord, for that is not forgot
Which ne'er I did remember. To my knowledge
I never in my life did look on him.

NORTHUMBERLAND
Then learn to know him now—this is the duke.                      40

PERCY
My gracious lord, I tender you my service,
Such as it is, being tender, raw, and young,
Which elder days shall ripen and confirm
To more approvèd service and desert.

BOLINGBROKE
I thank thee, gentle Percy, and be sure                           45
I count myself in nothing else so happy
As in a soul remem'bring my good friends;
And as my fortune ripens with thy love,
It shall be still thy true love's recompense:
My heart this covenant makes, my hand thus seals it.              50

NORTHUMBERLAND
How far is it to Berkeley, and what stir
Keeps good old York there with his men of war?

---

121 **six and seven** i.e., in confusion   122 **sits** blows   124
**Proportionable** proportional   132 **lie in** depends on   134
**Bristow** old form of Bristol
II.iii.7 **delectable** accents on first and third syllables

9 **Cotshall** Cotswold   12 **tediousness and process** tedious
process   22 **whencesoever** from wherever he is

PERCY
There stands the castle by yon tuft of trees,
Manned with three hundred men, as I have heard,
And in it are the Lords of York, Berkeley, and
    Seymour,                                                    55
None else of name and noble estimate.

[*Enter* ROSS *and* WILLOUGHBY.]

NORTHUMBERLAND
Here come the Lords of Ross and Willoughby,
Bloody with spurring, fiery red with haste.

BOLINGBROKE
Welcome, my lords, I wot your love pursues
A banished traitor. All my treasury                            60
Is yet but unfelt° thanks, which more enriched
Shall be your love° and labor's recompense.

ROSS
Your presence makes us rich, most noble lord.

WILLOUGHBY
And far surmounts our labor to attain it.

BOLINGBROKE
Evermore thank's the exchequer of the poor,                    65
Which till my infant° fortune comes to years
Stands for my bounty. But who comes here?

[*Enter* BERKELEY.]

NORTHUMBERLAND
It is my Lord of Berkeley, as I guess.

BERKELEY
My Lord of Hereford, my message is to you.

BOLINGBROKE
My lord, my answer is—to Lancaster;°                           70
And I am come to seek that name in England;
And I must find that title in your tongue
Before I make reply to aught you say.

BERKELEY
Mistake me not, my lord; 'tis not my meaning
To race one title° of your honor out.                          75
To you, my lord, I come—what lord you will—
From the most gracious regent of this land,
The Duke of York, to know what pricks you on
To take advantage of the absent time,°
And fright our native peace with self-borne° arms?            80

[*Enter* YORK, *attended.*]

BOLINGBROKE
I shall not need transport my words by you:
Here comes his grace in person. My noble uncle!

[*Kneels.*]

YORK
Show me thy humble heart, and not thy knee,
Whose duty is deceivable° and false.

BOLINGBROKE
My gracious uncle—                                             85

YORK
Tut, tut! Grace me no grace, nor uncle me no uncle;

I am no traitor's uncle, and that word "grace"
In an ungracious mouth is but profane.
Why have those banished and forbidden legs
Dared once to touch a dust of England's ground?               90
But then, more "why?" Why have they dared to
    march
So many miles upon her peaceful bosom,
Frighting her palefaced villages with war,
And ostentation of despised° arms?
Com'st thou because the anointed king is hence?               95
Why, foolish boy, the king is left behind,
And in my loyal bosom lies his power.
Were I but now the lord of such hot youth
As when brave Gaunt, thy father, and myself
Rescued the Black Prince, that young Mars of men,            100
From forth the ranks of many thousand French,
O, then, how quickly should this arm of mine,
Now prisoner to the palsy, chastise thee,
And minister correction to thy fault!

BOLINGBROKE
My gracious uncle, let me know my fault:                      105
On what condition stands it, and wherein?

YORK
Even in condition of the worst degree,
In gross rebellion and detested treason.
Thou art a banished man, and here art come
Before the expiration of thy time,                            110
In braving arms against thy sovereign.

BOLINGBROKE
As I was banished, I was banished Hereford,
But as I come, I come for Lancaster.
And, noble uncle, I beseech your grace,
Look on my wrongs with an indifferent° eye.                   115
You are my father, for methinks in you
I see old Gaunt alive. O, then, my father,
Will you permit that I shall stand condemned,
A wandering vagabond, my rights and royalties
Plucked from my arms perforce, and given away                120
To upstart unthrifts?° Wherefore was I born?
If that my cousin king be King in England,
It must be granted I am Duke of Lancaster.
You have a son, Aumerle, my noble cousin:
Had you first died, and he been thus trod down,              125
He should have found his uncle Gaunt a father,
To rouse his wrongs and chase them to the bay.°
I am denied to sue my livery here,
And yet my letters patents give me leave.
My father's goods are all distrained and sold,              130
And these, and all, are all amiss employed.
What would you have me do? I am a subject;
And° I challenge law, attorneys are denied me;
And therefore personally I lay my claim
To my inheritance of free descent.                            135

NORTHUMBERLAND
The noble duke hath been too much abused.

ROSS
It stands your grace upon° to do him right.

WILLOUGHBY
Base men by his endowments are made great.

---

61 **unfelt** intangible   62 **love** love's   66 **infant** and so unable
to possess property   70 **to Lancaster** Bolingbroke is about
to reply, but in the middle of the sentence he changes his
mind, to say that he will answer only in the name of Lancaster
75 **race one title** erase one title (with pun on "title")   79 **absent
time** time of the king's absence   80 **self-borne** borne for
one's own cause   84 **deceivable** deceptive

94 **despisèd** despicable   115 **indifferent** impartial   121
**unthrifts** prodigals   127 **bay** quarry's last stand   133 **And** if
137 **It . . . upon** it behooves your grace

YORK
My lords of England, let me tell you this:
I have had feeling of my cousin's wrongs,                    140
And labored all I could to do him right;
But in this kind to come in braving arms,
Be his own carver,° and cut out his way,
To find out right with wrong—it may not be:
And you that do abet him in this kind                        145
Cherish rebellion, and are rebels all.

NORTHUMBERLAND
The noble duke hath sworn his coming is
But for his own; and for the right of that
We all have strongly sworn to give him aid:
And let him never see joy that breaks that oath.             150

YORK
Well, well, I see the issue of these arms.
I cannot mend it, I must needs confess,
Because my power is weak and all ill left:°
But if I could, by Him that gave me life,
I would attach° you all, and make you stoop                  155
Unto the sovereign mercy of the king.
But since I cannot, be it known unto you
I do remain as neuter.° So fare you well—
Unless you please to enter in the castle,
And there repose you for this night.                         160

BOLINGBROKE
An offer, uncle, that we will accept.
But we must win your grace to go with us
To Bristow Castle, which they say is held
By Bushy, Bagot, and their complices,°
The caterpillars of the commonwealth,°                       165
Which I have sworn to weed and pluck away.

YORK
It may be I will go with you, but yet I'll pause,
For I am loath to break our country's laws.
Nor friends, nor foes, to me welcome you are.
Things past redress are now with me past care.              170
                                    *Exeunt.*

[Scene IV. *In Wales.*]

*Enter Earl of* SALISBURY, *and a Welsh* CAPTAIN.°

CAPTAIN
My Lord of Salisbury, we have stayed ten days
And hardly keep our countrymen together,
And yet° we hear no tidings from the king;
Therefore we will disperse ourselves. Farewell.

SALISBURY
Stay yet another day, thou trusty Welshman;                  5
The king reposeth all his confidence in thee.

CAPTAIN
'Tis thought the king is dead: we will not stay.
The bay trees in our country are all withered,
And meteors fright the fixèd stars of heaven,
The palefaced moon looks bloody on the earth,               10

And lean-looked° prophets whisper fearful change;
Rich men look sad, and ruffians dance and leap,
The one in fear to lose what they enjoy,°
The other to enjoy by rage° and war.
These signs forerun the death or fall of kings.             15
Farewell; our countrymen are gone and fled,
As well assured Richard their king is dead.   [*Exit.*]

SALISBURY
Ah, Richard! With the eyes of heavy mind
I see thy glory like a shooting star
Fall to the base earth from the firmament;                  20
Thy sun sets weeping in the lowly west,
Witnessing storms to come, woe and unrest;°
Thy friends are fled to wait upon thy foes,
And crossly° to thy good all fortune goes.    [*Exit.*]

# [ A C T   I I I ]

[Scene I. *Bristol. Before the castle.*]

*Enter* [BOLINGBROKE] *Duke of Hereford,* YORK,
NORTHUMBERLAND, [*other* LORDS, SOLDIERS,]
BUSHY *and* GREEN *prisoners.*

BOLINGBROKE
Bring forth these men.
Bushy and Green, I will not vex your souls,
Since presently° your souls must part° your bodies,
With too much urging your pernicious lives,
For 'twere no charity; yet, to wash your blood              5
From off my hands, here in the view of men,
I will unfold some causes of your deaths.
You have misled a prince, a royal king,
A happy° gentleman in blood and lineaments,
By you unhappied and disfigured clean;                      10
You have in manner with your sinful hours
Made a divorce° betwixt his queen and him,
Broke the possession of a royal bed,
And stained the beauty of a fair queen's cheeks
With tears, drawn from her eyes by your foul wrongs.°       15
Myself a prince, by fortune of my birth,
Near to the king in blood, and near in love
Till you did make him misinterpret me,
Have stooped my neck under your injuries,
And sighed my English breath in foreign clouds,            20
Eating the bitter bread of banishment,
Whilst you have fed upon my signories,°
Disparked° my parks, and felled my forest woods,
From my own windows torn my household coat,°

11 **lean-looked** lean-looking   13 **enjoy** possess   14 **enjoy by
rage** in hope of enjoying by violent action   21–22 **sun . . .
unrest** Richard's badge was a sun obscured by or breaking
from clouds   24 **crossly** adversely
III.i.3 **presently** immediately; **part** part from   9 **happy**
fortunate   11–12 **in . . . divorce** you have made a kind of
divorce   11–15 **You . . . wrongs** there is no suggestion elsewhere in the play that Richard was estranged from his queen,
though Holinshed does refer to his adultery (if the accusation
is one of homosexuality, it may echo Marlowe's *Edward II*;
and in *Woodstock* Queen Ann complains of Richard's favorites;
but Bolingbroke is making a propaganda speech)   22 **signories**
estates   23 **Disparked** thrown open   24 **From . . . coat**
broke the coat of arms in stained glass

143 **Be . . . carver** be a law to himself   153 **ill left** left inadequate (?) left in disorder (?)   155 **attach** arrest   158 **neuter**
neutral   164 **complices** accomplices   165 **The . . . commonwealth** common Elizabethan expression, ultimately biblical,
for those who preyed on society
**II.iv.s.d. Captain** possibly Owen Glendower, mentioned in
III.i.43   3 **yet** so far

Raced out my impresse,° leaving me no sign,　　25
Save men's opinions and my living blood,
To show the world I am a gentleman.°
This and much more, much more than twice all this,
Condemns you to the death. See them delivered over
To execution and the hand of death.　　　30

BUSHY
More welcome is the stroke of death to me
Than Bolingbroke to England. Lords, farewell.

GREEN
My comfort is that heaven will take our souls
And plague injustice with the pains of hell.

BOLINGBROKE
My Lord Northumberland, see them dispatched.°　　35
[Exit NORTHUMBERLAND, with BUSHY and GREEN.]
Uncle, you say the queen is at your house;
For God's sake, fairly let her be intreated.°
Tell her I send to her my kind commends;°
Take special care my greetings be delivered.

YORK
A gentleman of mine I have dispatched　　40
With letters of your love to her at large.°

BOLINGBROKE
Thanks, gentle uncle. Come, lords, away
To fight with Glendower° and his complices;
A while to work, and after holiday.　　　Exeunt.

[Scene II. The coast of Wales, near Barkloughly Castle.]

Enter the king [RICHARD], AUMERLE, [the Bishop of]
CARLISLE, &c. [Drums, flourish, and colors.]

RICHARD
Barkloughly Castle call they this at hand?

AUMERLE
Yea, my lord. How brooks° your grace the air
After your late tossing on the breaking seas?

RICHARD
Needs must I like it well. I weep for joy
To stand upon my kingdom once again.　　5
Dear earth, I do salute° thee with my hand,
Though rebels wound thee with their horses' hoofs.
As a long-parted mother with her child
Plays fondly with her tears and smiles in meeting,
So weeping, smiling, greet I thee, my earth,　　10
And do thee favors with my royal hands.
Feed not thy sovereign's foe, my gentle earth,
Nor with thy sweets comfort his ravenous sense;
But let thy spiders, that suck up thy venom,
And heavy-gaited toads lie in their way,　　15
Doing annoyance to the treacherous feet
Which with usurping steps do trample thee;
Yield stinging nettles to mine enemies;
And when they from thy bosom pluck a flower,
Guard it, I pray thee, with a lurking adder　　20

Whose double tongue may with a mortal° touch
Throw death upon thy sovereign's enemies.
Mock not my senseless° conjuration, lords:
This earth shall have a feeling, and these stones
Prove armèd soldiers, ere her native king　　25
Shall falter under foul rebellion's arms.

CARLISLE
Fear not, my lord; that power that made you king
Hath power to keep you king in spite of all.
The means that heavens yield must be embraced
And not neglected. Else heaven would,　　30
And we will not:° heaven's offer we refuse,
The proffered means of succor and redress.

AUMERLE
He means, my lord, that we are too remiss,
Whilst Bolingbroke through our security
Grows strong and great in substance and in power.　　35

RICHARD
Discomfortable° cousin, know'st thou not
That when the searching eye of heaven is hid
Behind the globe° and lights the lower world,°
Then thieves and robbers range abroad unseen
In murders and in outrage boldly here:　　40
But when from under this terrestrial ball
He fires the proud tops of the eastern pines
And darts his light through every guilty hole,
Then murders, treasons, and detested sins,
The cloak of night being plucked from off their backs,　45
Stand bare and naked, trembling at themselves?
So when this thief, this traitor, Bolingbroke,
Who all this while hath reveled in the night
Whilst we were wand'ring with the Antipodes,
Shall see us rising in our throne, the east,　　50
His treasons will sit blushing in his face,
Not able to endure the sight of day,
But self-affrighted tremble at his sin.
Not all the water in the rough rude sea
Can wash the balm° off from an anointed king;　　55
The breath of worldly° men cannot depose
The deputy elected by the Lord.
For every man that Bolingbroke hath pressed°
To lift shrewd° steel against our golden crown,
God for his Richard hath in heavenly pay　　60
A glorious angel;° then, if angels fight,
Weak men must fall, for heaven still guards the right.

Enter SALISBURY.

Welcome, my lord. How far off lies your power?°

SALISBURY
Nor near, nor farther off, my gracious lord,
Than this weak arm. Discomfort guides my tongue,　　65
And bids me speak of nothing but despair.
One day too late, I fear me, noble lord,
Hath clouded all thy happy days on earth.
O, call back yesterday, bid time return,
And thou shalt have twelve thousand fighting men.　　70

25 Raced . . . impresse erased my impresa (emblem)  16–27
Myself . . . gentleman Bolingbroke's real complaint (he
does not mention the forced loans and the farming of the
land)  35 dispatched executed  37 intreated treated  38
commends commendations, greetings  41 at large in full
43 Glendower cf. note to II.iv.s.d.; perhaps Bolingbroke does
not know that the Welsh army has disbanded
III.ii.2 brooks enjoys  6 salute greet with a gesture

21 mortal deadly  23 senseless addressed to senseless things
30–31 Else . . . not otherwise we go against the will of
heaven  36 Discomfortable discomforting  38 globe earth;
lower world Antipodes  55 balm cf. IV.i.206  56 worldly
earthly  58 pressed conscripted  59 shrewd sharp  59–61
crown . . . angel possibly a pun on these two coins  63 power
army

Today, today, unhappy day too late,
O'erthrows thy joys, friends, fortune, and thy state;
For all the Welshmen, hearing thou wert dead,
Are gone to Bolingbroke, dispersed and fled.

AUMERLE
Comfort, my liege, why looks your grace so pale?   75

RICHARD
But now the blood of twenty thousand men
Did triumph in my face, and they are fled;
And till so much blood thither come again,
Have I not reason to look pale and dead?
All souls that will be safe fly from my side,   80
For Time hath set a blot upon my pride.

AUMERLE
Comfort, my liege, remember who you are.

RICHARD
I had forgot myself: am I not king?
Awake, thou coward majesty! Thou sleepest.
Is not the king's name twenty thousand names?   85
Arm, arm, my name! a puny subject strikes
At thy great glory. Look not to the ground,
Ye favorites of a king, are we not high?
High° be our thoughts. I know my uncle York
Hath power enough to serve our turn. But who comes
     here?   90

*Enter* SCROOP.

SCROOP
More health and happiness betide my liege
Than can my care-tuned° tongue deliver him.

RICHARD
Mine ear is open, and my heart prepared;
The worst is worldly loss thou canst unfold.
Say, is my kingdom lost? Why, 'twas my care,   95
And what loss is it to be rid of care?
Strives Bolingbroke to be as great as we?
Greater he shall not be; if he serve God,
We'll serve Him too, and be his fellow so.
Revolt our subjects? That we cannot mend:   100
They break their faith to God as well as us.
Cry woe, destruction, ruin, and decay:
The worst is death, and death will have his day.

SCROOP
Glad am I that your highness is so armed
To bear the tidings of calamity.   105
Like an unseasonable stormy day
Which makes the silver rivers drown their shores
As if the world were all dissolved to tears,
So high above his limits swells the rage
Of Bolingbroke, covering your fearful land   110
With hard bright steel and hearts harder than steel.
White beards have armed their thin and hairless scalps
Against thy majesty; boys with women's voices
Strive to speak big,° and clap their female° joints
In stiff unwieldy arms against thy crown;   115
Thy very beadsmen° learn to bend their bows
Of double-fatal° yew against thy state;
Yea, distaff-women manage° rusty bills°

Against thy seat: both young and old rebel,
And all goes worse than I have power to tell.   120

RICHARD
Too well, too well thou tell'st a tale so ill.
Where is the Earl of Wiltshire? Where is Bagot?
What is become of Bushy? Where is Green?
That they have let the dangerous enemy
Measure our confines with such peaceful° steps?   125
If we prevail, their heads shall pay for it.
I warrant they have° made peace with Bolingbroke.

SCROOP
Peace have they made with him indeed, my lord.

RICHARD
O, villains, vipers, damned without redemption!
Dogs easily won to fawn on any man!   130
Snakes in my heart-blood warmed that sting my
     heart!
Three Judases, each one thrice worse than Judas!
Would they make peace? Terrible hell
Make war upon their spotted° souls for this!

SCROOP
Sweet love, I see, changing his property,°   135
Turns to the sourest and most deadly hate.
Again uncurse their souls: their peace is made
With heads and not with hands; those whom you
     curse
Have felt the worst of death's destroying wound,
And lie full low, graved in the hollow ground.   140

AUMERLE
Is Bushy, Green, and the Earl of Wiltshire dead?

SCROOP
Ay, all of them at Bristow lost their heads.

AUMERLE
Where is the duke, my father, with his power?°

RICHARD
No matter where—of comfort no man speak.
Let's talk of graves, of worms, and epitaphs,   145
Make dust our paper, and with rainy eyes
Write sorrow on the bosom of the earth.
Let's choose executors and talk of wills:
And yet not so, for what can we bequeath
Save our deposèd bodies to the ground?   150
Our lands, our lives, and all are Bolingbroke's,
And nothing can we call our own, but death
And that small model° of the barren earth
Which serves as paste and cover° to our bones.
For God's sake let us sit upon the ground   155
And tell sad stories of the death of kings:
How some have been deposed, some slain in war,
Some haunted by the ghosts they have deposed,
Some poisoned by their wives, some sleeping killed,
All murdered—for within the hollow° crown   160
That rounds the mortal temples of a king
Keeps Death his court, and there the antic° sits,
Scoffing his state and grinning at his pomp,
Allowing him a breath, a little scene,
To monarchize,° be feared, and kill with looks,   165

**89 High** high in name and place   **92 care-tuned** tuned to the key of sorrow   **114 speak big** assume men's voices; **female** weak, effeminate   **116 beadsmen** pensioners who pray for their benefactors   **117 double-fatal** the berry is poisonous and the wood used for bows   **118 manage** wield; **bills** wooden shafts with spiked blades

**125 peaceful** unopposed   **127 they have** pronounced "they've"   **134 spotted** sinful   **135 property** distinctive quality   **143 power** army   **153 model** variously explained as mold, grave mound, and microcosm   **154 paste and cover** an image taken from pie crust, since this was sometimes called a coffin   **160 hollow** empty circle, vain, transitory   **162 antic** clown   **165 monarchize** play the monarch

Infusing him with self and vain conceit,°
As if this flesh which walls about our life
Were brass impregnable; and, humored° thus,
Comes at the last, and with a little pin
Bores thorough° his castle wall, and farewell king!    170
Cover your heads, and mock not flesh and blood
With solemn reverence; throw away respect,
Tradition, form, and ceremonious duty;
For you have but mistook me all this while:
I live with bread like you, feel want,    175
Taste grief, need friends—subjected° thus,
How can you say to me, I am a king?

CARLISLE
My lord, wise men ne'er sit and wail their woes,
But presently° prevent the ways to wail.
To fear the foe, since fear oppresseth strength,    180
Gives in your weakness strength unto your foe;
And so your follies fight against yourself.
Fear and be slain, no worse can come to fight,°
And fight and die is death destroying death,
Where fearing dying pays death servile breath.°    185

AUMERLE
My father hath a power; inquire of him,
And learn to make a body of a limb.°

RICHARD
Thou chid'st me well. Proud Bolingbroke, I come
To change° blows with thee for our day of doom.
This ague fit of fear is overblown;°    190
An easy task it is to win our own.
Say, Scroop, where lies our uncle with his power?°
Speak sweetly, man, although thy looks be sour.

SCROOP
Men judge by the complexion of the sky
The state and inclination of the day;    195
So may you by my dull and heavy eye.
My tongue hath but a heavier tale to say.
I play the torturer by small and small°
To lengthen out the worst that must be spoken:
Your uncle York is joined with Bolingbroke,    200
And all your northern castles yielded up,
And all your southern gentlemen in arms
Upon his party.°

RICHARD          Thou hast said enough.
Beshrew thee,° cousin, which° didst lead me forth
Of that sweet way° I was in to despair.    205
What say you now? What comfort have we now?
By heaven, I'll hate him everlastingly
That bids me be of comfort any more.
Go to Flint Castle: there I'll pine away;
A king, woe's slave, shall kingly woe obey.    210
That power I have, discharge, and let them go
To ear the land that hath some hope to grow,°
For I have none. Let no man speak again
To alter this, for counsel is but vain.

166 self . . . conceit empty estimate of self  168 humored
perhaps "Death thus amused" or "the king thus indulged"
170 thorough through  176 subjected made a subject and
subject to the ordinary needs of man  179 presently immediately  183 to fight by fighting  185 pays . . . breath makes
us slaves to death  187 body . . . limb make a whole out
of a part  189 change exchange  190 overblown blown
over  192 power army  198 small and small little by little
203 Upon his party on his side  204 Beshrew thee ill befall
you; which who  205 way path, habit  212 To . . . grow
to cultivate the fertile ground (i.e., desert to Bolingbroke)

AUMERLE
My liege, one word.

RICHARD          He does me double wrong    215
That wounds me with the flatteries of his tongue.
Discharge my followers, let them hence away,
From Richard's night to Bolingbroke's fair day.
          [Exeunt.]


[Scene III. *Wales. Before Flint Castle.*]

*Enter* [*with drum and colors*] BOLINGBROKE, YORK,
NORTHUMBERLAND, [ATTENDANTS, *and*
SOLDIERS].

BOLINGBROKE
So that by this intelligence we learn
The Welshmen are dispersed, and Salisbury
Is gone to meet the king, who lately landed
With some few private friends upon this coast.

NORTHUMBERLAND
The news is very fair and good, my lord;    5
Richard not far from hence hath hid his head.

YORK
It would beseem the Lord Northumberland
To say "King Richard." Alack, the heavy day
When such a sacred king should hide his head.

NORTHUMBERLAND
Your grace mistakes; only to be brief    10
Left I his title out.

YORK          The time hath been
Would you have been so brief° with him, he would
Have been so brief with you, to shorten you,
For taking so the head,° your whole head's length.

BOLINGBROKE
Mistake° not, uncle, further than you should.    15

YORK
Take not, good cousin, further than you should,
Lest you mis-take:° the heavens are over our heads.

BOLINGBROKE
I know it, uncle, and oppose not myself
Against their will. But who comes here?

*Enter* PERCY.

Welcome, Harry. What, will not this castle yield?    20

PERCY
The castle royally is manned, my lord,
Against thy entrance.

BOLINGBROKE          Royally!
Why, it contains no king?

PERCY          Yes, my good lord,
It doth contain a king: King Richard lies
Within the limits of yon lime and stone;    25
And with him are the Lord Aumerle, Lord Salisbury,
Sir Stephen Scroop, besides a clergyman
Of holy reverence—who, I cannot learn.

NORTHUMBERLAND
O, belike it is the Bishop of Carlisle.

III.iii.11–12 The . . . brief there was a time when if you had
been so curt  14 taking . . . head (1) chopping off the title
(2) acting without restraint  15 Mistake take amiss  17 mistake transgress, take what is not yours (i.e., the crown)

BOLINGBROKE

Noble lord,    30
Go to the rude ribs° of that ancient castle,
Through brazen trumpet send the breath of parley
Into his ruined ears, and thus deliver:
Henry Bolingbroke
On both his knees doth kiss King Richard's hand,    35
And sends allegiance and true faith of heart
To his most royal person; hither come
Even at his feet to lay my arms and power,
Provided that my banishment repealed,
And lands restored again be freely granted;    40
If not, I'll use the advantage of my power,
And lay the summer's dust with showers of blood
Rained from the wounds of slaughtered Englishmen—
The which,° how far off from the mind of Bolingbroke
It is such crimson tempest should bedrench    45
The fresh green lap of fair King Richard's land,
My stooping duty tenderly° shall show.
Go, signify as much, while here we march
Upon the grassy carpet of this plain.
Let's march without the noise of threat'ning drum,    50
That from this castle's tattered° battlements
Our fair appointments° may be well perused.
Methinks King Richard and myself should meet
With no less terror than the elements
Of fire and water,° when their thund'ring shock    55
At meeting tears the cloudy cheeks of heaven.
Be he the fire, I'll be the yielding water;
The rage be his, whilst on the earth I rain°
My waters—on the earth, and not on him.
March on, and mark King Richard how he looks.    60

*The trumpets sound [parle without, and answer within;
then a flourish].* RICHARD *appeareth on the walls [with
the Bishop of* CARLISLE, AUMERLE, SCROOP, *and*
SALISBURY].

See, see, King Richard doth himself appear,
As doth the blushing discontented sun
From out the fiery portal of the East,
When he perceives the envious clouds are bent
To dim his glory, and to stain the track    65
Of his bright passage to the Occident.

YORK

Yet looks he like a king: behold his eye,
As bright as is the eagle's, lightens forth°
Controlling majesty. Alack, alack for woe,
That any harm should stain so fair a show.    70

RICHARD [*To* NORTHUMBERLAND.]

We are amazed, and thus long have we stood
To watch the fearful bending of thy knee,
Because we thought ourself thy lawful king:
And if we be, how dare thy joints forget
To pay their awful° duty to our presence?    75
If we be not, show us the hand of God
That hath dismissed us from our stewardship;
For well we know no hand of blood and bone
Can gripe the sacred handle of our scepter,

Unless he do profane, steal, or usurp;    80
And though you think that all, as you have done,
Have torn their souls by turning° them from us,
And we are barren and bereft of friends,
Yet know, my master, God omnipotent,
Is mustering in his clouds on our behalf    85
Armies of pestilence, and they shall strike
Your children yet unborn and unbegot
That lift your vassal hands against my head,
And threat the glory of my precious crown.
Tell Bolingbroke—for yon methinks he stands—    90
That every stride he makes upon my land
Is dangerous treason. He is come to open
The purple testament of bleeding war;
But ere the crown he looks for live in peace
Ten thousand bloody crowns° of mothers' sons    95
Shall ill become the flower of England's face,
Change the complexion of her maid-pale peace
To scarlet indignation, and bedew
Her pastor's° grass with faithful English blood.

NORTHUMBERLAND

The King of Heaven forbid our lord the king    100
Should so with civil and uncivil arms
Be rushed upon. Thy thrice-noble cousin,
Harry Bolingbroke, doth humbly kiss thy hand,
And by the honorable tomb he swears
That stands upon your royal grandsire's bones,    105
And by the royalties of both your bloods—
Currents that spring from one most gracious
    head—
And by the buried hand of warlike Gaunt,
And by the worth and honor of himself,
Comprising all that may be sworn or said,    110
His coming hither hath no further scope°
Than for his lineal royalties,° and to beg
Infranchisement° immediate on his knees;
Which on thy royal party° granted once,
His glittering arms he will commend to rust,    115
His barbèd° steeds to stables, and his heart
To faithful service of your majesty.
This swears he, as he is a prince and just;
And, as I am a gentleman, I credit him.

RICHARD

Northumberland, say thus the king returns,°    120
His noble cousin is right welcome hither,
And all the number of his fair demands
Shall be accomplished without contradiction.
With all the gracious utterance thou hast
Speak to his gentle hearing kind commends.°    125

[*To* AUMERLE.]

We° do debase ourselves, cousin, do we not,
To look so poorly° and to speak so fair?
Shall we call back Northumberland, and send
Defiance to the traitor and so die?

31 **ribs** protecting walls    44 **The which** as to which    47
**tenderly** solicitously    51 **tattered** crenelated, dilapidated
52 **appointments** arms and equipment    55 **fire and water**
lightning and rain clouds    58 **rain** pun on *reign*    68 **lightens
forth** flashes    75 **awful** reverential

82 **torn . . . turning** pun    95 **crowns** punning on "crown"
in line 94    99 **pastor's** the king was the shepherd of his kingdom    111 **scope** aim    112 **lineal royalties** hereditary rights
113 **Infranchisement** recall from banishment and restitution
of his lands    114 **party** side    116 **barbèd** armored    120
**returns** answers    125 **commends** greetings    126 **We** the
speech prefix is repeated in the quarto, perhaps because a line
of Northumberland's has dropped out    127 **poorly** abjectly

AUMERLE

No, good my lord; let's fight with gentle words,          130
Till time lend friends, and friends their helpful swords.

RICHARD

O God! O God! that e'er this tongue of mine,
That laid the sentence of dread banishment
On yon proud man, should take it off again
With words of sooth!° O, that I were as great          135
As is my grief, or lesser than my name!°
Or that I could forget what I have been!
Or not remember what I must be now!
Swell'st thou, proud heart? I'll give thee scope to beat,
Since foes have scope to beat both thee and me.          140

AUMERLE

Northumberland comes back from Bolingbroke.

RICHARD

What must the king do now? Must he submit?
The king shall do it. Must he be deposed?
The king shall be contented. Must he lose
The name of king? a° God's name, let it go.          145
I'll give my jewels for a set of beads;°
My gorgeous palace for a hermitage;
My gay apparel for an almsman's gown;
My figured° goblets for a dish of wood;
My scepter for a palmer's° walking-staff;          150
My subjects for a pair of carvèd saints;
And my large kingdom for a little grave,
A little, little grave, an obscure grave;
Or I'll be buried in the king's highway,
Some way of common trade,° where subjects' feet          155
May hourly trample on their sovereign's head;
For on my heart they tread now whilst I live,
And buried once, why not upon my head?
Aumerle, thou weep'st, my tender-hearted cousin:
We'll make foul weather with despisèd tears;          160
Our sighs and they shall lodge° the summer corn,
And make a dearth in this revolting land:
Or shall we play the wantons° with our woes
And make some pretty match with shedding tears,
As thus, to drop them still° upon one place,          165
Till they have fretted° us a pair of graves
Within the earth; and, therein laid, "there lies
Two kinsmen digged their graves with weeping eyes":
Would not this ill do well? Well, well, I see
I talk but idly, and you laugh at me.          170
Most mighty prince, my Lord Northumberland,
What says King Bolingbroke? Will his majesty
Give Richard leave to live till Richard die?
You make a leg,° and Bolingbroke says "Ay."

NORTHUMBERLAND

My lord, in the base court° he doth attend          175
To speak with you; may it please you to come down?

RICHARD

Down, down I come, like glist'ring Phaethon,°
Wanting the manage° of unruly jades.

In the base court. Base court where kings grow base,
To come at traitors' calls, and do them grace:          180
In the base court, come down: down court, down king,
For night owls shriek where mounting larks should
      sing.

BOLINGBROKE

What says his majesty?

NORTHUMBERLAND     Sorrow and grief of heart
Makes him speak fondly° like a frantic man;
Yet he is come.

[*Enter King* RICHARD *and* ATTENDANTS, *below.*]

BOLINGBROKE     Stand all apart,          185
And show fair duty to his majesty.

*He kneels down.*

My gracious lord.

RICHARD

Fair cousin, you debase your princely knee
To make the base earth proud with kissing it.
Me rather° had my heart might feel your love,          190
Than my unpleased eye see your courtesy.
Up, cousin, up, your heart is up, I know,
Thus high° at least, although your knee be low.

BOLINGBROKE

My gracious lord, I come but for mine own.

RICHARD

Your own is yours, and I am yours, and all.          195

BOLINGBROKE

So far be mine, my most redoubted° lord,
As my true service shall deserve your love.

RICHARD

Well you deserve: they well deserve to have
That know the strong'st and surest way to get.
Uncle, give me your hands; nay, dry your eyes;          200
Tears show their love, but want their remedies.°
Cousin, I am too young to be your father,
Though you are old enough to be my heir.
What you will have, I'll give, and willing too,
For do we must what force will have us do.          205
Set on towards London, cousin, is it so?

BOLINGBROKE

Yea, my good lord.

RICHARD                    Then I must not say no.
                              [*Flourish. Exeunt.*]

[*Scene IV. The Duke of York's garden.*]

*Enter the* QUEEN *with* [*two* LADIES,] *her attendants.*

QUEEN

What sport shall we devise here in this garden,
To drive away the heavy thought of care?

LADY

Madame,° we'll play at bowls.

---

135 **sooth** flattery   136 **name** i.e., king   145 **a** in   146 **set of beads** rosary   149 **figured** ornamented   150 **palmer's** pilgrim's   155 **trade** coming and going   161 **lodge** beat down   163 **play the wantons** be unrestrained   165 **still** always   166 **fretted** worn   174 **make a leg** curtsy   175 **base court** basse cour, the lower and outer courtyard   177 **Phaethon** he drove the sun chariot of his father, Apollo, and was struck by Zeus' thunderbolt   178 **manage** art of managing horses

184 **fondly** foolishly   190 **Me rather** I would sooner   193 **Thus high** pointing to his crown   196 **redoubted** dreaded   201 **want their remedies** cannot provide a cure for themselves or for the grief which causes them
**III.iv.3 Madame** spelled thus in the quarto, possibly to suggest that the ladies came with the queen from France

**QUEEN**
'Twill make me think the world is full of rubs,°
And that my fortune runs against the bias.°                    5

**LADY**
Madame, we'll dance.

**QUEEN**
My legs can keep no measure in delight,
When my poor heart no measure° keeps in grief:
Therefore no dancing, girl; some other sport.

**LADY**
Madame, we'll tell tales.                                     10

**QUEEN**
Of sorrow, or of joy?

**LADY**                            Of either, madame.

**QUEEN**
Of neither, girl.
For if of joy, being altogether wanting,
It doth remember° me the more of sorrow;
Or if of grief, being altogether had,                         15
It adds more sorrow to my want of joy:
For what I have I need not to repeat,
And what I want it boots° not to complain.

**LADY**
Madame, I'll sing.

**QUEEN**                        'Tis well that thou hast cause;
But thou shouldst please me better, wouldst thou weep. 20

**LADY**
I could weep, madame, would it do you good.

**QUEEN**
And I could sing, would weeping do me good,
And never borrow any tear of thee.

*Enter* GARDENERS [*one the master, the other two his men*].

But stay, here come the gardeners.
Let's step into the shadow of these trees.                    25
My wretchedness unto a row of pins,
They will talk of state,° for every one doth so
Against a change;° woe is forerun with woe.

**GARDENER** [*To one* SERVANT.]
Go, bind thou up young dangling apricocks,°
Which like unruly children make their sire                    30
Stoop with oppression° of their prodigal° weight;
Give some supportance° to the bending twigs.

[*To the other* SERVANT.]

Go thou, and like an executioner
Cut off the heads of too fast growing sprays
That look too lofty in our commonwealth:                      35
All must be even in our government.
You thus employed, I will go root away
The noisome weeds which without profit suck
The soil's fertility from wholesome flowers.

**MAN**
Why should we, in the compass of a pale,°                     40
Keep law and form and due proportion,

Showing, as in a model,° our firm estate,
When our sea-wallèd garden, the whole land,
Is full of weeds, her fairest flowers choked up,
Her fruit trees all unpruned, her hedges ruined,             45
Her knots° disordered, and her wholesome herbs
Swarming with caterpillars?°

**GARDENER**                          Hold thy peace.
He that hath suffered this disordered spring
Hath now himself met with the fall of leaf:
The weeds which his broad spreading leaves did
    shelter,                                                   50
That seemed in eating him to hold him up,
Are plucked up root and all by Bolingbroke—
I mean the Earl of Wiltshire, Bushy, Green.

**MAN**
What, are they dead?

**GARDENER**                      They are; and Bolingbroke
Hath seized the wasteful king. O, what pity is it            55
That he had not so trimmed and dressed° his land
As we this garden! We at time of year
Do wound the bark, the skin of our fruit trees,
Lest being overproud in sap and blood
With too much riches it confound itself;                      60
Had he done so to great and growing men,
They might have lived to bear, and he to taste
Their fruits of duty. Superfluous branches
We lop away, that bearing boughs may live:
Had he done so, himself had borne the crown,                 65
Which waste of idle hours hath quite thrown down.

**MAN**
What, think you the king shall be deposed?

**GARDENER**
Depressed° he is already, and deposed
'Tis doubt he will be. Letters came last night
To a dear friend of the good Duke of York's,                 70
That tell black tidings.

**QUEEN**                        O, I am pressed to death
Through want of speaking!°

[*Comes forward.*]

Thou, old Adam's likeness, set to dress this garden,
How dares thy harsh rude tongue sound this unpleasing
    news?
What Eve, what serpent hath suggested° thee                  75
To make a second fall of cursèd man?
Why dost thou say King Richard is deposed?
Dar'st thou, thou little better thing than earth,
Divine his downfall? Say, where, when, and how
Cam'st thou by this ill tidings? Speak, thou wretch.         80

**GARDENER**
Pardon me, madam; little joy have I
To breathe this news, yet what I say is true:
King Richard he is in the mighty hold°
Of Bolingbroke. Their fortunes both are weighed:
In your lord's scale is nothing but himself                   85
And some few vanities that make him light;
But in the balance of great Bolingbroke
Besides himself are all the English peers,

---

**4 rubs** obstacles by which bowls were diverted from their proper course  **5 bias** the form of the bowl which imparts an oblique motion  **7–8 measure . . . measure** (1) time to music (2) a stately dance (3) moderation  **14 remember** remind  **18 boots** avails  **27 state** the realm  **28 Against a change** when a change is expected  **29 apricocks** apricots  **31 oppression** weighing down; **prodigal** wasteful  **32 supportance** support  **40 pale** fenced-in land

**42 as in a model** in miniature  **46 knots** laid-out flower beds  **47 caterpillars** cf. II.iii.165  **56 dressed** tended  **68 Depressed** lowered in fortune  **71–72 O . . . speaking** referring to the torture of pressing to death administered to prisoners who refused to speak  **75 suggested** tempted  **83 hold** custody

And with that odds he weighs King Richard down.
Post you to London, and you will find it so;                                90
I speak no more than everyone doth know.
QUEEN
Nimble mischance, that art so light of foot,
Doth not thy embassage belong to me,
And am I last that knows it? O, thou thinkest
To serve me last that I may longest keep                                    95
Thy sorrow in my breast! Come, ladies, go
To meet at London London's king in woe.
What, was I born to this, that my sad look
Should grace the triumph of great Bolingbroke?
Gard'ner, for telling me these news of woe,                                 100
Pray God, the plants thou graft'st may never grow.
                                        *Exit* [*with* LADIES].
GARDENER
Poor queen, so that thy state might be no worse,
I would my skill were subject to thy curse.
Here did she fall a tear; here in this place
I'll set a bank of rue, sour herb of grace;                                 105
Rue even for ruth° here shortly shall be seen,
In the remembrance of a weeping queen.          *Exeunt.*


# [ A C T   I V ]

### [Scene I. *Westminster Hall.*]

*Enter* BOLINGBROKE, *with the Lords* [AUMERLE,
NORTHUMBERLAND, PERCY, FITZWATER, SURREY,
*the Bishop of* CARLISLE, *the* ABBOT *of Westminster,
another* LORD, HERALD, *and* OFFICERS] *to parliament.*

BOLINGBROKE
Call forth Bagot.

*Enter* BAGOT [*with* OFFICERS].

Now, Bagot, freely speak thy mind,
What thou dost know of noble Gloucester's death,
Who wrought it with° the king, and who performed
The bloody office of his timeless° end.                                      5
BAGOT
Then set before my face the Lord Aumerle.
BOLINGBROKE
Cousin, stand forth, and look upon that man.
BAGOT
My Lord Aumerle, I know your daring tongue
Scorns to unsay what once it hath delivered.
In that dead time° when Gloucester's death was
    plotted,                                                                10
I heard you say, "Is not my arm of length,
That reacheth from the restful English court
As far as Callice° to mine uncle's head?"
Amongst much other talk that very time
I heard you say that you had rather refuse                                   15
The offer of an hundred thousand crowns
Than Bolingbroke's return to England;

Adding withal, how blest this land would be
In this your cousin's death.
AUMERLE                               Princes and noble lords,
What answer shall I make to this base man?                                   20
Shall I so much dishonor my fair stars
On equal terms° to give him chastisement?
Either I must, or have mine honor soiled
With the attainder° of his slanderous lips.
There is my gage, the manual° seal of death,                                 25
That marks thee out for hell: I say thou liest,
And will maintain what thou hast said is false
In thy heart-blood, though being all too base
To stain the temper° of my knightly sword.
BOLINGBROKE
Bagot, forbear, thou shalt not take it up.                                   30
AUMERLE
Excepting one, I would he were the best
In all this presence that hath moved me so.°
FITZWATER
If that thy valor stand on sympathy,°
There is my gage, Aumerle, in gage° to thine;
By that fair sun which shows me where thou stand'st,     35
I heard thee say, and vauntingly thou spak'st it,
That thou wert cause of noble Gloucester's death.
If thou deniest it twenty times, thou liest,
And I will turn thy falsehood to thy heart,
Where it was forged, with my rapier's point.                                40
AUMERLE
Thou dar'st not, coward, live to see that day.
FITZWATER
Now, by my soul, I would it were this hour!
AUMERLE
Fitzwater, thou art damned to hell for this.
PERCY
Aumerle, thou liest, his honor is as true
In this appeal as thou art all unjust;                                       45
And that thou art so, there I throw my gage,
To prove it on thee to the extremest point
Of mortal breathing;° seize it if thou dar'st.
AUMERLE
And if° I do not, may my hands rot off,
And never brandish more revengeful steel                                     50
Over the glittering helmet of my foe.
ANOTHER LORD
I task the earth to the like,° forsworn Aumerle,
And spur thee on with full as many lies
As may be hollowed° in thy treacherous ear
From sun to sun:° there is my honor's pawn;                                  55
Engage° it to the trial if thou darest.
AUMERLE
Who sets me else?° By heaven, I'll throw° at all!

---

106 ruth pity
IV.i.4 wrought it with persuaded   5 timeless untimely (or
everlasting)   10 dead time variously interpreted: past time,
deadly time, midnight hour   13 Callice Calais

22 On equal terms Aumerle was Bagot's superior and could
therefore refuse to fight with him   24 attainder accusation
25 manual by my own hand (punning on a seal fixed to
a document and his glove)   29 temper i.e., excellence   31–32
Excepting . . . so I wish I had been angered by the
highest in rank present, except Bolingbroke   33 stand on
sympathy depends on correspondence of rank   34 in gage
in pledge   47–48 extremest . . . breathing to the death
49 And if if indeed   52 task . . . like lay on the earth the
task of bearing another gage   54 hollowed shouted   55 sun
to sun sunrise to sunset   56 Engage pun on gage and engage
57 Who . . . else Who else puts up a stake against me?;
throw metaphor from dicing

I have a thousand spirits in one breast
To answer twenty thousand such as you.

SURREY

My Lord Fitzwater, I do remember well                                          60
The very time Aumerle and you did talk.

FITZWATER

'Tis very true; you were in presence° then,
And you can witness with me this is true.

SURREY

As false, by heaven, as heaven itself is true!

FITZWATER

Surrey, thou liest.

SURREY                    Dishonorable boy,                                     65
That lie shall lie so heavy on my sword,
That it shall render vengeance and revenge,
Till thou, the lie-giver, and that lie do lie
In earth as quiet as thy father's skull.
In proof whereof, there is my honor's pawn;                                     70
Engage it to the trial if thou dar'st.

FITZWATER

How fondly° dost thou spur a forward° horse!
If I dare eat, or drink, or breathe, or live,
I dare meet Surrey in a wilderness,
And spit upon him, whilst I say he lies,                                        75
And lies, and lies. There is my bond of faith,
To tie thee to my strong correction.°
As I intend to thrive in this new world,°
Aumerle is guilty of my true appeal.
Besides, I heard the banished Norfolk say                                       80
That thou, Aumerle, didst send two of thy men
To execute the noble Duke at Callice.

AUMERLE

Some honest Christian trust me with a gage.°
That Norfolk lies, here do I throw down this,
If he may be repealed to try his honor.                                         85

BOLINGBROKE

These differences shall all rest under gage°
Till Norfolk be repealed; repealed he shall be,
And, though mine enemy, restored again
To all his lands and signories.° When he is
    returned,
Against Aumerle we will inforce his trial.                                      90

CARLISLE

That honorable day shall never be seen.
Many a time hath banished Norfolk fought
For Jesu Christ in glorious Christian field,
Streaming° the ensign of the Christian cross
Against black pagans, Turks, and Saracens;                                      95
And, toiled° with works of war, retired himself
To Italy, and there at Venice gave
His body to that pleasant country's earth,
And his pure soul unto his captain, Christ,
Under whose colors he had fought so long.                                       100

BOLINGBROKE

Why, bishop, is Norfolk dead?

CARLISLE

As surely as I live, my lord.

BOLINGBROKE

Sweet peace conduct his sweet soul to the bosom
Of good old Abraham!° Lords appellants,°
Your differences shall all rest under gage,                                     105
Till we assign you to your days of trial.

*Enter* YORK.

YORK

Great Duke of Lancaster, I come to thee
From plume-plucked° Richard, who with willing soul
Adopts thee heir, and his high scepter yields
To the possession of thy royal hand.                                            110
Ascend his throne, descending now from him,
And long live Henry, fourth of that name!

BOLINGBROKE

In God's name, I'll ascend the regal throne.

CARLISLE

Marry,° God forbid!
Worst° in this royal presence may I speak,                                      115
Yet best beseeming me to speak the truth.
Would God that any in this noble presence
Were enough noble to be upright judge
Of noble Richard. Then true noblesse would
Learn° him forbearance from so foul a wrong.                                    120
What subject can give sentence on his king?
And who sits here that is not Richard's subject?
Thieves are not judged, but they are by to hear,
Although apparent° guilt be seen in them;
And shall the figure° of God's majesty,                                         125
His captain, steward, deputy elect,°
Anointed, crownèd, planted many years,
Be judged by subject° and inferior breath,
And he himself not present? O, forfend° it, God,
That in a Christian climate souls refined°                                      130
Should show so heinous, black, obscene° a deed!
I speak to subjects and a subject speaks,
Stirred up by God thus boldly for his king.
My Lord of Hereford here, whom you call king,
Is a foul traitor to proud Hereford's king;                                     135
And if you crown him, let me prophesy
The blood of English shall manure the ground,
And future ages groan for this foul act;
Peace shall go sleep with Turks and infidels,
And, in this seat of peace, tumultuous wars                                     140
Shall kin with° kin, and kind° with kind, confound;
Disorder, horror, fear, and mutiny
Shall here inhabit, and this land be called
The field of Golgotha° and dead men's skulls.
O, if you raise this house against this house,°                                 145
It will the woefullest division prove
That ever fell upon this cursèd earth!°
Prevent it, resist it, let it not be so,
Lest child, child's children, cry against you woe.

62 in presence present (or in attendance at court)   72 fondly
foolishly;   forward willing   77 correction punishment
78 new world of the new reign   83 Some . . . gage he has
used both his own gloves   86 under gage prorogued   89
signories estates   94 Streaming flying   96 toiled exhausted
with toil

104 Abraham cf. Luke 16:22;   appellants those who are
appealing or accusing each other   108 plume-plucked
humbled   114 Marry a light oath (from "By the Virgin
Mary")   115 Worst least in rank or competence   120 Learn
teach   124 apparent manifest   125 figure image   126 elect
chosen   128 subject of a subject   129 forfend avert   130
refined purified by the Christian environment   131 obscene
offensive   141 with by means of;   kind race   144 Golgotha
cf. Mark 15:22, "a place of dead men's skulles" (Bishops'
Bible)   145 O . . . house cf. Mark 3:25   147 cursèd earth
earth cursed by civil war

NORTHUMBERLAND
Well have you argued, sir; and for your pains        150
Of capital treason we arrest you here.
My Lord of Westminster, be it your charge
To keep him safely till his day of trial.
May it please you, lords, to grant the commons' suit?°

BOLINGBROKE
Fetch hither Richard, that in common view        155
He may surrender; so we shall proceed
Without suspicion.

YORK                I will be his conduct.°        *Exit.*

BOLINGBROKE
Lords, you that here are under our arrest,
Procure your sureties for your days of answer.
Little are we beholding to your love,        160
And little looked for at your helping hands.

*Enter* RICHARD *and* YORK.

RICHARD
Alack, why am I sent for to a king,
Before I have shook off the regal thoughts
Wherewith I reigned? I hardly yet have learned
To insinuate,° flatter, bow, and bend my knee.        165
Give Sorrow leave a while to tutor me
To this submission.   Yet I well remember
The favors° of these men: were they not mine?
Did they not sometime cry "All hail!" to me?
So Judas° did to Christ: but he in twelve°        170
Found truth in all but one; I, in twelve thousand,
        none.
God save the king! Will no man say "Amen"?
Am I both priest and clerk?° Well, then, amen.
God save the king, although I be not he;
And yet amen, if heaven do think him me.        175
To do what service am I sent hither?

YORK
To do that office° of thine own good will,
Which tired majesty did make thee offer:
The resignation of thy state and crown
To Henry Bolingbroke.

RICHARD                Give me the crown.        180
Here, cousin, seize the crown. Here, cousin,
On this side my hand, and on that side yours.
Now is this golden crown like a deep well
That owes° two buckets, filling one another,
The emptier ever dancing in the air,        185
The other down, unseen, and full of water.
That bucket down and full of tears am I,
Drinking my griefs, whilst you mount up on high.

BOLINGBROKE
I thought you had been willing to resign.

RICHARD
My crown I am, but still my griefs are mine:        190
You may my glories and my state depose,
But not my griefs; still am I king of those.

BOLINGBROKE
Part of your cares you give me with your crown.

RICHARD
Your cares° set up, do not pluck my cares down.
My care is loss of care, by old care done;        195
Your care is gain of care, by new care won.°
The cares I give, I have, though given away;
They 'tend° the crown, yet still with me they stay.

BOLINGBROKE
Are you contented to resign the crown?

RICHARD
Ay, no; no, ay: for I must nothing be.        200
Therefore no, no, for I resign to thee.
Now, mark me how I will undo° myself.
I give this heavy weight from off my head,
And this unwieldy scepter from my hand,
The pride of kingly sway from out my heart;        205
With mine own tears I wash away my balm,°
With mine own hands I give away my crown,
With mine own tongue deny my sacred state,
With mine own breath release all duteous oaths;
All pomp and majesty I do forswear;        210
My manors, rents, revenues,° I forgo;
My acts, decrees, and statutes I deny:
God pardon all oaths that are broke to me,
God keep all vows unbroke are° made to thee.
Make me, that nothing have, with nothing grieved,        215
And thou with all pleased, that hast all achieved.
Long mayst thou live in Richard's seat to sit,
And soon lie Richard in an earthy pit.
God save King Henry, unkinged Richard says,
And send him many years of sunshine days.        220
What more remains?

NORTHUMBERLAND No more, but that you read
These accusations, and these grievous crimes,
Committed by your person and your followers,
Against the state and profit of this land:
That by confessing them, the souls of men        225
May deem that you are worthily° deposed.

RICHARD
Must I do so? and must I ravel out°
My weaved-up follies? Gentle Northumberland,
If thy offenses were upon record,°
Would it not shame thee, in so fair a troop,°        230
To read a lecture of them?° If thou wouldst,
There shouldst thou find one heinous article,
Containing the deposing of a king,
And cracking the strong warrant of an oath,
Marked with a blot, damned in the book of heaven.        235
Nay, all of you that stand and look upon me,
Whilst that my wretchedness doth bait myself,
Though some of you, with Pilate,° wash your hands,
Showing an outward pity: yet you Pilates
Have here delivered me to my sour° cross,        240
And water cannot wash away your sin.

**194 cares** the word is used in several different senses in lines
194–97—sorrows, responsibilities, diligence or carefulness,
anxiety **195–96 My . . . won** My sorrow is loss of responsibility by failing to take pains; your anxiety is gain of responsibility won by your new carefulness **198 'tend** attend on
**202 undo** (1) strip (2) ruin **206 balm** anointing ointment
used at coronation **211 revenues** accent on second syllable
**214 are** that are **226 worthily** deservedly **227 ravel out**
unweave **229 record** accent on second syllable **230 troop**
assembly **231 read . . . them** read them aloud **238 Pilate**
cf. Matthew 27:24 **240 sour** bitter

**154 suit** that the charges against the king should be published
**157 conduct** conductor **165 insinuate** progress by devious
ways **168 favors** (1) faces (2) benefits **170 Judas** cf. Matthew
26:49; **twelve** the apostles **173 clerk** employed to utter
responses to the priest's prayers **177 office** York corrects
Richard's "service" **184 owes** owns

NORTHUMBERLAND
My lord, dispatch,° read o'er these articles.
RICHARD
Mine eyes are full of tears, I cannot see:
And yet salt water blinds them not so much,
But they can see a sort° of traitors here.                       245
Nay, if I turn mine eyes upon myself,
I find myself a traitor with the rest;
For I have given here my soul's consent
T' undeck the pompous° body of a king;
Made glory base, and sovereignty a slave,                        250
Proud majesty a subject, state a peasant.
NORTHUMBERLAND
My lord—
RICHARD
No lord of thine, thou haught,° insulting man,
Nor no man's lord: I have no name, no title,
No, not that name was given me at the font                       255
But 'tis usurped.° Alack, the heavy day!
That I have worn so many winters out,
And know not now what name to call myself.
O, that I were a mockery king of snow,
Standing before the sun of Bolingbroke,                          260
To melt myself away in water drops!
Good king, great king—and yet not greatly good—
And if my word be sterling° yet in England,
Let it command a mirror hither straight,
That it may show me what a face I have,                          265
Since it is bankrout° of his majesty.
BOLINGBROKE
Go some of you, and fetch a looking-glass.
                                   [Exit ATTENDANT.]
NORTHUMBERLAND
Read o'er this paper while the glass doth come.
RICHARD
Fiend, thou torments me, ere I come to hell.
BOLINGBROKE
Urge it no more, my Lord Northumberland.                         270
NORTHUMBERLAND
The commons will not then be satisfied.
RICHARD
They shall be satisfied: I'll read enough,
When I do see the very book indeed,
Where all my sins are writ,° and that's myself.

*Enter one with a glass.*

Give me the glass, and therein will I read.                      275
No deeper wrinkles yet? Hath Sorrow struck
So many blows upon this face of mine,
And made no deeper wounds? O, flatt'ring glass!
Like to my followers in prosperity,
Thou dost beguile me. Was this face the face                     280
That every day under this household roof
Did keep ten thousand men? Was this the face
That, like the sun,° did make beholders wink?
Was this the face that faced° so many follies,
And was at last outfaced by Bolingbroke?                         285

A brittle glory shineth in this face,
As brittle as the glory is the face,

[*Throws glass down.*]

For there it is, cracked in a hundred shivers.
Mark, silent king, the moral of this sport:
How soon my sorrow hath destroyed my face.                       290
BOLINGBROKE
The shadow° of your sorrow hath destroyed
The shadow° of your face.
RICHARD                           Say that again.
"The shadow of my sorrow"? Ha, let's see.
'Tis very true, my grief lies all within,
And these external manners of laments                            295
Are merely shadows to the unseen grief
That swells with silence in the tortured soul.°
There lies the substance: and I thank thee, king,
For thy great bounty, that not only giv'st
Me cause to wail, but teachest me the way                        300
How to lament the cause. I'll beg one boon,
And then be gone, and trouble you no more.
Shall I obtain it?
BOLINGBROKE   Name it, fair cousin.
RICHARD
Fair cousin? I am greater than a king:
For when I was a king, my flatterers                             305
Were then but subjects; being now a subject,
I have a king here to° my flatterer.
Being so great, I have no need to beg.
BOLINGBROKE
Yet ask.
RICHARD
And shall I have?                                                310
BOLINGBROKE
You shall.
RICHARD
Then give me leave to go.
BOLINGBROKE
Whither?
RICHARD
Whither you will, so I were from your sights.
BOLINGBROKE
Go some of you, convey him to the Tower.                         315
RICHARD
O, good! "Convey"! Conveyers° are you all,
That rise thus nimbly by a true king's fall.
        [*Exeunt* RICHARD, *some* LORDS, *and* GUARDS.]
BOLINGBROKE
On Wednesday next we solemnly set down°
Our coronation: lords, prepare yourselves.
        *Exeunt. Manent* [*the* ABBOT *of* ] *Westminster,*
            [*the Bishop of* ] CARLISLE, AUMERLE.
ABBOT
A woeful pageant have we here beheld.                            320
CARLISLE
The woe's to come; the children yet unborn
Shall feel this day as sharp to them as thorn.

---

242 **dispatch** hurry up   245 **sort** group, pack   249 **pompous**
splendid   253 **haught** haughty   255–56 **No . . . usurped**
Richard was rumored to be a bastard   263 **sterling** current
266 **bankrout** bankrupt   273–74 **book . . . writ** cf. Psalms
139:16   283 **sun** cf. III.ii.50   284 **faced** brazened out, countenanced

291 **shadow** outward show   292 **shadow** reflection   294–97
**my . . . soul** Bolingbroke had implied that Richard was
putting on an act; Richard replies that his visible grief is a
reflection of a deeper grief he is feeling   307 **to** for   316
**Conveyers** thieves (*convey* was a euphemism for "steal")   318
**set down** appoint

AUMERLE

You holy clergymen, is there no plot
To rid the realm of this pernicious blot?

ABBOT

My lord,                                                      325
Before I freely speak my mind herein,
You shall not only take the sacrament
To bury mine intents,° but also to effect
Whatever I shall happen to devise.
I see your brows are full of discontent,          330
Your hearts of sorrow, and your eyes of tears.
Come home with me to supper: I will lay
A plot shall show us all a merry day.         *Exeunt.*


# [ A C T   V ]

[Scene I. *London. A street.*]

*Enter the* QUEEN *with her* ATTENDANTS.

QUEEN

This way the king will come, this is the way
To Julius Caesar's ill-erected Tower,°
To whose flint bosom my condemnèd lord
Is doomed a prisoner by proud Bolingbroke.
Here let us rest, if this rebellious earth                5
Have any resting for her true king's queen.

*Enter* RICHARD [*and* GUARD].

But soft, but see, or rather do not see
My fair rose wither; yet look up, behold,
That you in pity may dissolve to dew,
And wash him fresh again with truelove tears.    10
Ah, thou the model where old Troy did stand!°
Thou map of honor, thou King Richard's tomb,
And not King Richard, thou most beauteous inn,
Why should hard-favored grief be lodged in thee,
When triumph is become an alehouse° guest?    15

RICHARD

Join not with grief, fair woman, do not so,
To make my end too sudden; learn, good soul,
To think our former state a happy dream,
From which awaked, the truth of what we are
Shows us but this: I am sworn brother, sweet,    20
To grim necessity, and he and I
Will keep a league till death. Hie thee to France,
And cloister thee in some religious house:°
Our holy lives must win a new world's crown,
Which our profane hours here have stricken down.°  25

QUEEN

What! is my Richard both in shape and mind
Transformed and weakened? Hath Bolingbroke
Deposed thine intellect? Hath he been in thy heart?

The lion dying thrusteth forth his paw
And wounds the earth, if nothing else, with rage    30
To be o'erpow'red, and wilt thou, pupil-like,
Take the correction mildly, kiss the rod,
And fawn on rage with base humility,
Which art a lion and the king of beasts?

RICHARD

A king of beasts indeed: if aught but beasts,     35
I had been still a happy king of men.
Good sometimes° queen, prepare thee hence for France.
Think I am dead, and that even here thou takest
As from my deathbed thy last living leave.
In winter's tedious nights sit by the fire         40
With good old folks, and let them tell thee tales
Of woeful ages long ago betid;°
And ere thou bid good night, to quite their griefs°
Tell thou the lamentable tale of me,
And send the hearers weeping to their beds.       45
For why,° the senseless brands will sympathize°
The heavy accent of thy moving tongue,
And in compassion weep the fire out:
And some° will mourn in ashes, some coal-black,
For the deposing of a rightful king.              50

*Enter* NORTHUMBERLAND.

NORTHUMBERLAND

My lord, the mind of Bolingbroke is changed:
You must to Pomfret,° not unto the Tower.
And, madam, there is order ta'en° for you:
With all swift speed you must away to France.

RICHARD

Northumberland, thou ladder wherewithal          55
The mounting Bolingbroke ascends my throne,
The time shall not be many hours of age
More than it is, ere foul sin, gathering head,°
Shall break into corruption. Thou shalt think,
Though he divide the realm and give thee half,    60
It is too little, helping him° to all;
He shall think that thou which knowest the way
To plant unrightful kings, wilt know° again,
Being ne'er so little urged another way,
To pluck him headlong from the usurped throne.    65
The love of wicked men converts° to fear,
That fear to hate, and hate turns one or both
To worthy° danger and deservèd death.

NORTHUMBERLAND

My guilt be on my head, and there an end.°
Take leave and part, for you must part° forthwith.  70

RICHARD

Doubly divorced! Bad men, you violate
A twofold marriage: 'twixt my crown and me,
And then betwixt me and my married wife.
Let me unkiss the oath 'twixt thee and me—
And yet not so, for with a kiss 'twas made.       75
Part us, Northumberland; I towards the north,

---

328 **bury mine intents** conceal my plans
**V.i.2 Tower** the Tower of London was built, according to
legend, by Julius Caesar ("ill-erected" because it was used as a
prison)  **11 model . . . stand** outline of the walls where
Troy once stood (i.e., ruined majesty—suggested by London's
old name of Trinovantum, New Troy)  **15 alehouse** Bolingbroke (contrasted with Richard, the "beauteous inn")  **23
religious house** convent  **25 our . . . down** our careless
lives have endangered our hopes of heaven

**37 sometimes** sometime, former  **42 betid** happened  **43
quite their griefs** requite, or cap. their tragic stories  **46 For
why** because of this; **sympathize** correspond to  **49 some** of
the brands  **52 Pomfret** Pontefract Castle, in Yorkshire  **53
there . . . ta'en** arrangements have been made  **58 gathering
head** metaphor from a boil  **61 helping him** seeing that you
helped him  **63 know** know how  **66 converts** changes
**68 worthy** deserved  **69 there an end** that's all I have to say
**70 part . . . part** part from your queen, for you must depart

Where shivering cold and sickness pines° the clime;
My wife to France, from whence, set forth in pomp,
She came adornèd hither like sweet May,
Sent back like Hallowmas,° or short'st of day.°                    80

QUEEN
And must we be divided? Must we part?

RICHARD
Ay, hand from hand, my love, and heart from heart.

QUEEN
Banish us both, and send the king with me.

RICHARD
That were some love, but little policy.

QUEEN
Then whither he goes, thither let me go.                    85

RICHARD
So two together weeping make one woe.
Weep thou for me in France, I for thee here;
Better far off than, near, be ne'er the near.°
Go count thy way with sighs, I mine with groans.

QUEEN
So longest way shall have the longest moans.                    90

RICHARD
Twice for one step I'll groan, the way being short,
And piece the way out° with a heavy heart.
Come, come, in wooing sorrow, let's be brief,
Since, wedding it, there is such length in grief.°
One kiss shall stop our mouths, and dumbly part:                    95
Thus give I mine, and thus take I thy heart.

QUEEN
Give me mine own again, 'twere no good part
To take on me to keep and kill thy heart.
So now I have mine own again, be gone,
That I may strive to kill it with a groan.                    100

RICHARD
We make woe wanton° with this fond delay:
Once more adieu, the rest let sorrow say.
                    *Exeunt [different ways].*

[Scene II. *The Duke of York's palace.*]

*Enter Duke of* YORK *and the* DUCHESS.

DUCHESS
My lord, you told me you would tell the rest,
When weeping made you break the story off,
Of our two cousins' coming into London.

YORK
Where did I leave?

DUCHESS                    At that sad stop, my lord,
Where rude misgoverned° hands from windows' tops   5
Threw dust and rubbish on King Richard's head.

YORK
Then, as I said, the duke, great Bolingbroke,
Mounted upon a hot and fiery steed,
Which his aspiring rider seemed to know,°
With slow but stately pace kept on his course,                    10

Whilst all tongues cried, "God save thee, Boling-
    broke!"
You would have thought the very windows spake:
So many greedy looks of young and old
Through casements darted their desiring eyes
Upon his visage; and that all the walls                    15
With painted imagery° had said at once,
"Jesu preserve thee! Welcome, Bolingbroke!"
Whilst he, from the one side to the other turning,
Bareheaded, lower than his proud steed's neck,
Bespake them thus: "I thank you, countrymen."                    20
And thus still doing, thus he passed along.

DUCHESS
Alack, poor Richard! Where rode he the whilst?

YORK
As in a theater the eyes of men,
After a well-graced° actor leaves the stage,
Are idly° bent on him that enters next,                    25
Thinking his prattle to be tedious;
Even so, or with much more contempt, men's eyes
Did scowl on gentle Richard; no man cried, "God
    save him!"
No joyful tongue gave him his welcome home,
But dust was thrown upon his sacred head;                    30
Which with such gentle° sorrow he shook off,
His face still combating with tears and smiles,
The badges° of his grief and patience,
That had not God for some strong purpose steeled
The hearts of men, they must perforce° have melted,   35
And barbarism itself have pitied him.
But heaven hath a hand in these events,
To whose high will we bound our calm contents.°
To Bolingbroke are we sworn subjects now,
Whose state and honor I for aye° allow.                    40

[*Enter* AUMERLE.]

DUCHESS
Here comes my son, Aumerle.

YORK                    Aumerle that was,
But that is lost for being Richard's friend;
And, madam, you must call him Rutland now.
I am in parliament pledge for his truth°
And lasting fealty to the new-made king.                    45

DUCHESS
Welcome, my son; who are the violets° now
That strew the green lap of the new-come spring?

AUMERLE
Madam, I know not, nor I greatly care not.
God knows I had as lief° be none as one.

YORK
Well, bear you well in this new spring of time,                    50
Lest you be cropped before you come to prime.
What news from Oxford?° Do these jousts and
    triumphs hold?°

AUMERLE
For aught I know, my lord, they do.

77 **pines** causes to pine  80 **Hallowmas** November 1;
**short'st of day** December 22  88 **ne'er the near** never the
nearer (proverbial)  92 **piece . . . out** lengthen (with possible
pun on *pace*)  94 **Since . . . grief** We are wedded to sorrow
till death and shall have plenty of time to grieve  101 **wanton**
unrestrained (with secondary sense of promiscuous)
**V.ii.5 rude misgoverned** uncivilized and wrongly directed
9 **rider . . . know** seemed to know his rider

16 **painted imagery** painted cloths, resembling tapestry
24 **well-graced** accomplished  25 **idly** without interest  31
**gentle** noble  33 **badges** signs  35 **perforce** inevitably  38
**bound . . . contents** limit our wishes to calm content  40 **aye**
ever  44 **truth** loyalty  46 **violets** favorites in the new court
49 **had as lief** would find it as pleasant  52 **Oxford** cf. line
99; Aumerle would give a start; **Do . . . hold** Will these
tournaments and triumphal celebrations be held?

YORK
You will be there, I know.

AUMERLE
If God prevent me not, I purpose so.     55

YORK
What seal° is that that hangs without thy bosom?
Yea, look'st thou pale? Let me see the writing.

AUMERLE
My lord, 'tis nothing.

YORK            No matter, then, who see it.
I will be satisfied: let me see the writing.

AUMERLE
I do beseech your grace to pardon me:     60
It is a matter of small consequence,
Which for some reasons I would not have seen.

YORK
Which for some reasons, sir, I mean to see.
I fear, I fear—

DUCHESS      What should you fear?
'Tis nothing but some band° that he is ent'red into     65
For gay apparel 'gainst° the triumph day.

YORK
Bound to himself? What doth he with a bond
That he is bound to? Wife, thou art a fool.
Boy, let me see the writing.

AUMERLE
I do beseech you, pardon me. I may not show it.     70

YORK
I will be satisfied. Let me see it, I say!

*He plucks it out of his bosom and reads it.*

Treason, foul treason, villain, traitor, slave!

DUCHESS
What is the matter, my lord?

YORK
Ho, who is within there? Saddle my horse.
God for his mercy!° What treachery is here!     75

DUCHESS
Why, what is it, my lord?

YORK
Give me my boots, I say! Saddle my horse!
Now, by mine honor, by my life, my troth,
I will appeach° the villain.

DUCHESS          What is the matter?

YORK
Peace, foolish woman.     80

DUCHESS
I will not peace. What is the matter, Aumerle?

AUMERLE
Good mother, be content; it is no more
Than my poor life must answer.

DUCHESS         Thy life answer?

YORK
Bring me my boots: I will unto the king.

*His* MAN *enters with his boots.*

DUCHESS
Strike him, Aumerle. Poor boy, thou art amazed.°     85
Hence, villain, never more come in my sight.

YORK
Give me my boots, I say.

DUCHESS
Why, York, what wilt thou do?
Wilt thou not hide the trespass of thine own?
Have we more sons? Or are we like to have?     90
Is not my teeming date° drunk up with time?
And wilt thou pluck my fair son from mine age?
And rob me of a happy mother's name?
Is he not like thee? Is he not thine own?

YORK
Thou fond,° mad woman,     95
Wilt thou conceal this dark conspiracy?
A dozen of them here have ta'en the sacrament
And interchangeably° set down their hands
To kill the king at Oxford.

DUCHESS         He shall be none;
We'll keep him here. Then what is that to him?     100

YORK
Away, fond woman, were he twenty times my son,
I would appeach him.

DUCHESS        Hadst thou groaned for him
As I have done, thou wouldst be more pitiful.
But now I know thy mind; thou dost suspect
That I have been disloyal to thy bed,     105
And that he is a bastard, not thy son:
Sweet York, sweet husband, be not of that mind;
He is as like thee as a man may be,
Not like to me, or any of my kin,
And yet I love him.

YORK           Make way, unruly woman. *Exit.* 110

DUCHESS
After, Aumerle! Mount thee upon his horse;
Spur, post,° and get before him to the king,
And beg thy pardon ere he do accuse thee.
I'll not be long behind; though I be old,
I doubt not but to ride as fast as York;     115
And never will I rise up from the ground
Till Bolingbroke have pardoned thee. Away! Be
    gone!               *[Exeunt.]*

[Scene III. *Windsor Castle.*]

*Enter* [BOLINGBROKE, *now*] *the king, with his* NOBLES
[PERCY *and others*].

BOLINGBROKE
Can no man tell me of my unthrifty° son?°
'Tis full three months since I did see him last.
If any plague° hang over us, 'tis he.
I would to God, my lords, he might be found:
Inquire at London, 'mongst the taverns there,     5
For there, they say, he daily doth frequent
With unrestrainèd loose companions,
Even such, they say, as stand in narrow lanes,
And beat our watch° and rob our passengers;°
While he, young wanton and effeminate° boy,     10

**56 seal** which would be hanging from the document on an attached strip of parchment    **65 band** bond    **66 'gainst** in preparation for    **75 God . . . mercy** Lord have mercy upon us    **79 appeach** peach, inform against    **85 amazed** dazed

**91 teeming date** time of childbearing    **95 fond** foolish    **98 interchangeably** reciprocally    **112 post** hasten    **V.iii.1 unthrifty** prodigal; **son** Prince Hal of *Henry IV*    **3 plague** he is thinking of the prophecies of Richard and Carlisle    **9 watch** watchmen; **passengers** wayfarers    **10 effeminate** voluptuous

Takes on the point of honor° to support
So dissolute a crew.

PERCY
My lord, some two days since I saw the prince,
And told him of those triumphs held at Oxford.

BOLINGBROKE
And what said the gallant?                                15

PERCY
His answer was, he would unto the stews,°
And from the commonest creature pluck a glove,
And wear it as a favor, and with that
He would unhorse the lustiest challenger.

BOLINGBROKE
As dissolute as desperate; but yet                       20
Through both° I see some sparks of better hope,
Which elder years may happily bring forth.
But who comes here?

*Enter* AUMERLE, *amazed.*

AUMERLE                    Where is the king?

BOLINGBROKE                             What means
Our cousin, that he stares and looks so wildly?

AUMERLE
God save your grace! I do beseech your majesty          25
To have some conference° with your grace alone.

BOLINGBROKE
Withdraw yourselves, and leave us here alone.
                        [*Exeunt* PERCY *and* LORDS.]
What is the matter with our cousin now?

AUMERLE
For ever may my knees grow to the earth,

[*Kneels.*]

My tongue cleave to my roof within my mouth,            30
Unless a pardon° ere I rise or speak.

BOLINGBROKE
Intended, or committed, was this fault?
If on the first,° how heinous e'er it be,
To win thy after-love I pardon thee.

AUMERLE
Then give me leave that I may turn the key,             35
That no man enter till my tale be done.

BOLINGBROKE
Have thy desire.

[AUMERLE *locks the door.*] *The Duke of* YORK *knocks at the door and crieth.*

YORK [*Within.*]
My liege, beware, look to thyself:
Thou hast a traitor in thy presence there.

BOLINGBROKE
Villain, I'll make thee safe.°                          40

[*Draws his sword.*]

AUMERLE
Stay thy revengeful hand; thou hast no cause to fear.

YORK
Open the door, secure,° foolhardy king!

Shall I for love speak treason° to thy face?
Open the door, or I will break it open.

[BOLINGBROKE *opens. Enter* YORK.]

BOLINGBROKE
What is the matter, uncle? Speak.                       45

[*He relocks door.*]

Recover breath. Tell us, how near is danger,
That we may arm us to encounter it.

YORK
Peruse this writing here, and thou shalt know
The treason that my haste forbids° me show.

AUMERLE
Remember, as thou read'st, thy promise passed.°         50
I do repent me, read not my name there;
My heart is not confederate with my hand.

YORK
It was, villain, ere thy hand did set it down.
I tore it from the traitor's bosom, king:
Fear, and not love, begets his penitence.               55
Forget° to pity him, lest thy pity prove
A serpent that will sting thee to the heart.

BOLINGBROKE
O heinous, strong,° and bold conspiracy!
O loyal father of a treacherous son!
Thou sheer immaculate and silver fountain,              60
From whence this stream, through muddy passages,
Hath held his° current, and defiled himself,°
Thy overflow of good converts° to bad;
And thy abundant goodness shall excuse
This deadly blot in thy digressing° son.                65

YORK
So shall my virtue be his vice's bawd,
And he shall spend mine honor with his shame,
As thriftless sons their scraping° fathers' gold.
Mine honor lives when his dishonor dies,
Or my shamed life in his dishonor lies.                 70
Thou kill'st me in his life, giving him breath;
The traitor lives, the true man's put to death.

DUCHESS [*Within.*]
What ho! My liege, for God's sake, let me in!

BOLINGBROKE
What shrill-voiced suppliant makes this eager cry?

DUCHESS
A woman, and thy aunt, great king—'tis I.               75
Speak with me, pity me, open the door;
A beggar begs that never begged before.

BOLINGBROKE
Our scene is alt'red from a serious thing,
And now changed to "The Beggar and the King."°
My dangerous cousin, let your mother in:                80
I know she is come to pray for your foul sin.

[AUMERLE *unlocks door during York's speech.*]

YORK
If thou do pardon, whosoever pray,°

11 Takes . . . honor undertakes as a point of honor  16 stews brothels  21 both dissoluteness and desperateness  26 conference conversation  31 Unless a pardon unless I have a pardon  33 on the first of the former kind  40 safe harmless (by killing him)  42 secure overconfident  43 treason by calling him a fool  49 haste forbids because he is out of breath  50 passed given  56 Forget forget your promise  58 strong dangerous  62 his its; himself itself  63 converts changes  65 digressing transgressing  68 scraping parsimonious  79 The . . . King referring to the title, but not to the contents, of the ballad about King Cophetua and the Beggar Maid  82 whosoever pray whoever prays

More sins for this forgiveness prosper may.

[*Enter* DUCHESS.]

This fest'red joint cut off, the rest rest° sound;
This let alone will all the rest confound.    85

DUCHESS
O king, believe not this hardhearted man:
Love loving not itself, none other can.°

YORK
Thou frantic woman, what dost thou make here?
Shall thy old dugs once more a traitor rear?°

DUCHESS
Sweet York, be patient. Hear me, gentle liege.    90

[*Kneels.*]

BOLINGBROKE
Rise up, good aunt.

DUCHESS           Not yet, I thee beseech.
For ever will I walk upon my knees,
And never see day that the happy sees,
Till thou give joy—until thou bid me joy—
By pardoning Rutland, my transgressing boy.    95

AUMERLE
Unto my mother's prayers I bend my knee.

[*Kneels.*]

YORK
Against them both my true joints bended be;

[*Kneels.*]

Ill mayst thou thrive, if thou grant any grace.

DUCHESS
Pleads he in earnest? Look upon his face.
His eyes do drop no tears, his prayers are in jest;    100
His words come from his mouth, ours from our breast;
He prays but faintly, and would be denied;
We pray with heart and soul, and all beside;
His weary joints would gladly rise, I know;
Our knees still kneel till to the ground they grow;    105
His prayers are full of false hypocrisy,
Ours of true zeal and deep integrity;
Our prayers do outpray his—then let them have
That mercy which true prayer ought to have.

BOLINGBROKE
Good aunt, stand up.

DUCHESS        Nay, do not say "Stand up";    110
Say "Pardon" first, and afterwards "Stand up";
And if I were thy nurse thy tongue to teach,
"Pardon" should be the first word of thy speech.
I never longed to hear a word till now.
Say "Pardon," king; let pity teach thee how.    115
The word is short, but not so short as sweet:
No word like "pardon" for kings' mouths so meet.

YORK
Speak it in French, king; say "Pardonne moy."°

DUCHESS
Dost thou teach pardon pardon to destroy?
Ah, my sour husband, my hardhearted lord!    120

That sets the word itself against the word.
Speak "Pardon" as 'tis current in our land:
The chopping° French we do not understand.
Thine eye begins to speak; set thy tongue there,
Or in thy piteous heart plant thou thine ear,    125
That hearing how our plaints and prayers do pierce,
Pity may move thee "Pardon" to rehearse.°

BOLINGBROKE
Good aunt, stand up.

DUCHESS          I do not sue to stand.
Pardon is all the suit° I have in hand.

BOLINGBROKE
I pardon him as God shall pardon me.    130

DUCHESS
O, happy vantage of a kneeling knee!
Yet° am I sick for fear; speak it again.
Twice saying "Pardon" doth not pardon twain,°
But makes one pardon strong.

BOLINGBROKE          With all my heart
I pardon him.

DUCHESS [*Standing.*]    A god on earth° thou art.    135

[YORK *and* AUMERLE *rise.*]

BOLINGBROKE
But for our trusty° brother-in-law,° and the abbot,
With all the rest of that consorted crew,
Destruction straight shall dog them at the heels.
Good uncle, help to order several powers
To Oxford, or where'er these traitors are;    140
They shall not live within this world, I swear,
But I will have them if I once know where.
Uncle, farewell, and cousin, too, adieu.
Your mother well hath prayed, and prove you true.°

DUCHESS
Come, my old° son, I pray God make thee new.    145
                      *Exeunt.*

[Scene IV. *Windsor Castle.*]

*Enter Sir Pierce* EXTON *and* [*a* MAN].

EXTON
Didst thou not mark the king, what words he spake?
"Have I no friend will rid me of this living fear?"
Was it not so?

MAN        These were his very words.

EXTON
"Have I no friend?" quoth he: he spake it twice,
And urged it twice together, did he not?    5

MAN
He did.

EXTON
And speaking it, he wishtly° looked on me,

---

123 **chopping** changing the meaning of words   127 **rehearse** repeat (a perfect rhyme with *pierce* in the sixteenth century) 129 **suit** (1) suit of cards (2) petition   132 **Yet** still   133 **twain** (1) two people (2) divide   135 **god on earth** the *Homilies* taught this; and, as Portia says, "earthly power doth then show likest God's/When mercy seasons justice"   136 **trusty** ironical; **brother-in-law** Duke of Exeter, Richard's half-brother, who had married Bolingbroke's sister   144 **true** loyal   145 **old** unregenerate
**V.iv.7 wishtly** probably "wishfully," with an undertone of "wistly" (i.e., intently)

---

84 **rest rest** those that remain stay   87 **Love . . . can** If he does not love his son he cannot love anyone, even you   89 **rear** raise him to life (with a pun on the usual sense)   118 **Pardonne moy** pray excuse me (i.e., "no"); "moy" rhymes with *destroy*

As who should say, "I would thou wert the man
That would divorce this terror from my heart"—
Meaning the king at Pomfret. Come, let's go:          10
I am the king's friend, and will rid his foe.   [*Exeunt.*]

[*Scene V. Pomfret Castle.*]

*Enter* RICHARD *alone.*

RICHARD
I have been studying how I may compare
This prison where I live unto the world:
And for because the world is populous,
And here is not a creature but myself,
I cannot do it. Yet I'll hammer it out:               5
My brain I'll prove the female to my soul,
My soul the father, and these two beget
A generation° of still-breeding° thoughts;
And these same thoughts people this little world,
In humors° like the people of this world,             10
For no thought is contented. The better sort,
As thoughts of things divine are intermixed
With scruples,° and do set the word itself
Against the word;° as thus: "Come, little ones";°
And then again,                                        15
"It is as hard to come as for a camel
To thread the postern of a small needle's° eye."°
Thoughts tending to ambition, they do plot
Unlikely wonders: how these vain weak nails
May tear a passage thorough the flinty ribs           20
Of this hard world, my ragged° prison walls;
And, for° they cannot, die in their own pride.°
Thoughts tending to content flatter themselves
That they are not the first of fortune's slaves,
Nor shall not be the last, like seely° beggars        25
Who sitting in the stocks refuge° their shame,
That many have, and others must, sit there;
And in this thought they find a kind of ease,
Bearing their own misfortunes on the back
Of such as have before endured the like.              30
Thus play I in one person many people,
And none contented; sometimes am I king,
Then treasons make me wish myself a beggar,
And so I am. Then crushing penury
Persuades me I was better when a king.                35
Then am I kinged again and, by and by,
Think that I am unkinged by Bolingbroke,
And straight am nothing. But whate'er I be,
Nor I, nor any man that but man is,
With nothing shall be pleased, till he be eased       40
With being nothing.° *The music plays.*
                    Music do I hear.
Ha—ha! Keep time! How sour sweet music is
When time is broke, and no proportion° kept;
So is it in the music of men's lives:

And here have I the daintiness of ear                 45
To check° time broke in a disordered° string,
But for the concord of my state and time,°
Had not an ear to hear my true time broke.
I wasted time,° and now doth Time° waste me:
For now hath Time made me his numb'ring° clock;       50
My thoughts are minutes, and with sighs they jar°
Their watches° on unto mine eyes, the outward watch°
Whereto my finger, like a dial's point,°
Is pointing still,° in cleansing them from tears.
Now, sir, the sound that tells what hour it is        55
Are clamorous groans which strike upon my heart,
Which is the bell. So sighs, and tears, and groans,
Show minutes, times, and hours; but my time
Runs posting on in Bolingbroke's proud joy,
While I stand fooling here, his jack-of-the-clock.°   60
This music mads me: let it sound no more.
For though it have holp° madmen to their wits,
In me it seems it will make wise men mad.
Yet blessing on his heart that gives it me,
For 'tis a sign of love; and love to Richard          65
Is a strange brooch° in this all-hating world.

*Enter a* GROOM *of the stable.*

GROOM
Hail, royal prince!
RICHARD                Thanks, noble° peer!
The cheapest of us is ten groats too dear.
What art thou? And how comest thou hither,
Where no man never comes, but that sad dog            70
That brings me food to make misfortune live?°
GROOM
I was a poor groom of thy stable, king,
When thou wert king, who, traveling towards York,
With much ado at length have gotten leave
To look upon my sometimes° royal master's face.      75
O, how it erned° my heart, when I beheld
In London streets, that coronation day,
When Bolingbroke rode on roan Barbary,°
That horse that thou so often hast bestrid,
That horse that I so carefully have dressed.°         80
RICHARD
Rode he on Barbary? Tell me, gentle° friend,
How went he under him?
GROOM
So proudly as if he disdained the ground.
RICHARD
So proud that Bolingbroke was on his back!
That jade hath eat bread from my royal hand;          85

---

V.v.8 **generation** offspring; **still-breeding** constantly breeding   10 **humors** psychological characteristics   13 **scruples** doubts   14 **word** passage of Scripture; **Come, little ones** Matthew 19:14 ff.   17 **needle's** monosyllabic   16–17 **It . . . eye** Matthew 19:24 ff.   21 **ragged** rugged   22 **for** because; **pride** prime   25 **seely** (silly) simple-minded   26 **refuge** protect themselves from   39–41 **nor any . . . being nothing** man is never content until he is no more   43 **proportion** musical time

46 **check** rebuke; **disordered** out of its place, a bar wrong   47 **time** the times   49 **time** measured duration; **Time** Father Time   50 **numb'ring** counting hours and minutes   51 **jar** tick (of a clock), making a discord   52 **watches** intervals of time; **outward watch** dial (with pun on a man keeping watch)   53 **dial's point** hand of clock   54 **still** continually   60 **jack-of-the-clock** mannikin to strike the hours   62 **holp** helped   66 **strange brooch** rare jewel   67 **royal . . . noble** a royal was worth ten shillings; a noble, six shillings and eightpence; a groat, fourpence (Richard is saying that to call him "royal" now is to price him too high, since he is now the peer, the equal, of the groom)   71 **make misfortune live** perpetuate my unfortunate life   75 **sometimes** former   76 **erned** grieved   78 **Barbary** here the name of the horse, as well as the breed   80 **dressed** groomed   81 **gentle** implying groom is of gentle birth

This hand hath made him proud with clapping° him.
Would he not stumble? Would he not fall down,
Since pride must have a fall, and break the neck
Of that proud man that did usurp his back?
Forgiveness, horse! Why do I rail on thee,                90
Since thou created to be awed by man
Wast born to bear? I was not made a horse,
And yet I bear a burden like an ass,
Spurred, galled,° and tired by jauncing° Bolingbroke.

*Enter one [a* KEEPER] *to* RICHARD *with meat.*

KEEPER
Fellow, give place; here is no longer stay.              95
RICHARD
If thou love me, 'tis time thou wert away.
GROOM
What my tongue dares not, that my heart shall say.
                                        *Exit* GROOM.
KEEPER
My lord, wilt please you to fall to?°
RICHARD
Taste° of it first, as thou art wont to do.
KEEPER
My lord, I dare not; Sir Pierce of Exton                100
Who lately came from the king, commands the con-
   trary.
RICHARD
The devil take Henry of Lancaster, and thee!
Patience is stale, and I am weary of it.
KEEPER  Help, help, help!

*The murderers* [EXTON *and* SERVANTS] *rush in.*

RICHARD
How now! What means death in this rude assault?°       105
Villain, thy own hand yields thy death's instrument.

*[Snatches a weapon and kills one.]*

Go thou, and fill another room° in hell!

*[He kills another.] Here* EXTON *strikes him down.*

That hand shall burn in never-quenching fire
That staggers° thus my person. Exton, thy fierce hand
Hath with the king's blood stained the king's own land. 110
Mount, mount, my soul; thy seat is up on high,
Whilst my gross flesh sinks downward here to die.
                                        [*Dies.*]
EXTON
As full of valor as of royal blood!
Both have I spilled. O, would the deed were good!
For now the devil that told me I did well                115
Says that this deed is chronicled in hell.
This dead king to the living king I'll bear.
Take hence the rest, and give them burial here.
                          [*Exeunt with the bodies.*]

[Scene VI. *Windsor Castle.*]

[*Flourish.*] *Enter* BOLINGBROKE *with the Duke of*
YORK [*and other* LORDS *and* ATTENDANTS].
BOLINGBROKE
Kind uncle York, the latest news we hear
Is that the rebels have consumed with fire
Our town of Ciceter° in Gloucestershire,
But whether they be ta'en or slain we hear not.

*Enter* NORTHUMBERLAND.

Welcome, my lord; what is the news?                       5
NORTHUMBERLAND
First, to thy sacred state wish I all happiness;
The next° news is, I have to London sent
The heads of Salisbury, Spencer, Blunt, and Kent.°
The manner of their taking may appear
At large discoursèd in this paper here.                  10
BOLINGBROKE
We thank thee, gentle Percy, for thy pains,
And to thy worth will add right worthy gains.°

*Enter Lord* FITZWATER.

FITZWATER
My lord, I have from Oxford sent to London
The heads of Brocas° and Sir Bennet Seely,
Two of the dangerous consorted° traitors                 15
That sought at Oxford thy dire overthrow.
BOLINGBROKE
Thy pains, Fitzwater, shall not be forgot:
Right noble is thy merit well I wot.

*Enter Henry* PERCY [*and the Bishop of* CARLISLE].

PERCY
The grand conspirator, Abbot of Westminster,
With clog of conscience and sour melancholy,           20
Hath yielded up his body to the grave;
But here is Carlisle living, to abide
Thy kingly doom, and sentence of his pride.
BOLINGBROKE
Carlisle, this is your doom:
Choose out some secret place, some reverend room°      25
More than thou hast,° and with it joy° thy life.
So° as thou liv'st in peace, die free from strife;
For though mine enemy thou hast ever been,
High sparks of honor in thee have I seen.

*Enter* EXTON *with* [ATTENDANTS *bearing*] *the coffin.*

EXTON
Great king, within this coffin I present               30
Thy buried fear:° herein all breathless lies
The mightiest of thy greatest enemies,
Richard of Bordeaux,° by me hither brought.
BOLINGBROKE
Exton, I thank thee not, for thou hast wrought

86 clapping patting  94 galled made sore; jauncing making the horse prance (and perhaps himself prancing and triumphant) 98 fall to start eating  99 Taste he suspects poison  105 What . . . assault What does death mean by assaulting me so violently?  107 room place  109 staggers makes to stagger

V.vi.3 Ciceter Cirencester  7 next most important  8 Spencer . . . Kent Lord Spencer, formerly Earl of Gloucester; Sir Thomas Blunt; Earl of Kent  12 right worthy gains well-deserved reward  14 Brocas Sir Leonard (or Bernard) Brocas  15 consorted associated  25 reverend room place of religious retirement  26 More . . . hast more religious and less political; joy enjoy  27 So provided that  31 buried fear cf. "living fear," V.iv.2  33 Bordeaux Richard's birthplace

A deed of slander with thy fatal hand                    35
Upon my head and all this famous land.
EXTON
From your own mouth, my lord, did I this deed.
BOLINGBROKE
They love not poison that do poison need,
Nor do I thee; though I did wish him dead,
I hate the murderer, love him murderèd.
The guilt of conscience take thou for thy labor,    40
But neither my good word, nor princely favor.
With Cain go wander thorough shades of night,
And never show thy head by day nor light.
                                    [*Exit* EXTON.]
Lords, I protest, my soul is full of woe,            45
That blood should sprinkle me to make me grow.
Come, mourn with me for what I do lament,
And put on sullen black incontinent.°
I'll make a voyage to the Holy Land,
To wash this blood off from my guilty hand.         50
March sadly after; grace my mournings here,
In weeping after this untimely bier.    [*Exeunt.*]

48 **incontinent** forthwith

# THE TRAGEDY OF
# ROMEO AND JULIET

EDITED BY J. A. BRYANT, JR.

## Introduction

*Romeo and Juliet*, even in the mutilated versions that Restoration and eighteenth-century audiences knew, has always been one of Shakespeare's most popular plays. Since 1845, when Charlotte and Susan Cushman finally brought a version approaching Shakespeare's original back to the stage, it has been a coveted vehicle among actors and actresses alike, on both sides of the Atlantic; and some of the theater's greatest names have been associated with it. In recent years audiences have also been enjoying it in film versions and on television. Among professional scholars the play has sparked less enthusiasm. In this quarter one hears praise for the ingenuity of the language, for the brilliance of the characterizations, and for the portrayal of young love; but such praise is frequently qualified by the uneasy admission that *Romeo and Juliet* resists measurement by the rules conventionally applied to Shakespeare's later tragedies. More than one scholarly critic has expressed misgivings about the emphasis on pathos, the absence of ethical purpose, and what appears to be a capricious shifting of tone, particularly between the first two acts and the last three.

Such misgivings among modern readers are understandable, but one may question whether the Elizabethans would have felt or even understood them. Apparently most of Shakespeare's contemporaries still considered an ending in death the principal requirement for tragedy; and since *Romeo and Juliet* offered six deaths, five of them on stage and two of them the deaths of protagonists, audiences in those days probably thought it more tragic than many plays so labeled. Elizabethan audiences would have found equally strange the objection that the play lacks ethical purpose. They knew by training what to think of impetuous young lovers who deceived their parents and sought advice from friars. Arthur Brooke, whose *Tragicall Historye of Romeus and Juliet* (1562) was most likely Shakespeare's only source, had spelled it all out as follows:

To this ende (good Reader) is this tragicall matter written, to describe unto thee a coople of unfortunate lovers, thralling themselves to unhonest desire, neglecting the authoritie and advise of parents and frendes, conferring their principall counsels with dronken gossyppes, and

superstitious friers (the naturally fitte instrumentes of unchastitie) attemptyng all adventures of peryll, for thattaynyng of their wished lust, usying auriculer confession (the kay of whoredome, and treason) for furtheraunce of theyre purpose, abusyng the honorable name of lawefull mariage, the cloke the shame of stolne contractes, finallye, by all means of unhonest lyfe, hastyng to most unhappy deathe.

In addition, Elizabethans also knew that suicide was the devil's business and usually meant damnation; in their view, therefore, *Romeo and Juliet* must have had automatically an abundance of ethical import. Shakespeare probably should be given some kind of credit for not challenging these deep-seated convictions of his contemporary auditors and readers; for, ironically, the modern feeling that his play is ethically deficient stems partly from the modern ability to see that Shakespeare has really approved the love of Romeo and Juliet, condoned their deceptions, and laid the blame for their deaths, even though by suicide, upon their elders.

A better explanation for the modern reader's uneasiness about ranking *Romeo and Juliet* with the so-called major tragedies lies in the widespread assumption that Shakespeare meant the play to be deterministic. Shakespeare seems to invite such a view when he promises in the Prologue to show the "misadventured piteous overthrows" of "a pair of star-crossed lovers" and thereafter lets the principals make references to fate and the stars and has them express various kinds of premonition. Romeo, for example, says in Act I that his "mind misgives/Some consequence yet hanging in the stars" (I.iv.106–07); Friar Lawrence tries to reassure himself with uneasy prayers but soon observes that "violent delights have violent ends" (II.vi.9); and Juliet, on taking leave of her husband, cries, "O Fortune, Fortune! All men call thee fickle" (III.v.60). These and other references make it easy to argue that the characters are, as they themselves sometimes imply, little better than puppets, pitiful perhaps but ethically uninteresting and scarcely due the fearful respect that one gives to the heroes of Shakespeare's later tragedies. Actually, the text as a whole gives little justification for such a view. It is true that Romeo says, as he is about to enter the Capulets' great hall,

> my mind misgives
> Some consequence yet hanging in the stars
> Shall bitterly begin his fearful date
> With this night's revels and expire the term
> Of a despisèd life, closed in my breast,
> By some vile forfeit of untimely death.    (I.iv.106–11)

But he immediately adds, "he that hath the steerage of my course/Direct my sail!" The first part of this quotation is typical of what we find—and find not so often as some imagine—in *Romeo and Juliet:* premonitions, prayers, misgivings, references to Fortune, all uttered much as we ourselves utter such things, without necessarily implying real belief in astral influence. Sometimes the character's premonition is confirmed by later events; sometimes not, as is true of the auspicious part of Romeo's dream on the night before his suicide. The second part of the quotation is typical, too; for almost as often as these characters speak of fate they speak of a superior Providence, mysteriously directing but never absolutely determining human destiny. Moreover, accident-prone as Romeo and Juliet may occasionally seem, they are really no more so than Hamlet, who also has his share of premonitions; and their actions are no more clearly determined by supernatural influence than those of Macbeth. Like its successors, *Romeo and Juliet* takes place in a universe where there is a special providence in the fall of a sparrow and where what will be, assuredly will be. All that is asked of the inhabitants of this Shakespearean world of tragedy is that they achieve readiness or ripeness for what is to come, and in this tragedy as in the others they are allowed and expected to do that much for themselves. The things to consider are whether or not the protagonists have succeeded in meeting this requirement and, if it appears they have failed, whether one had any right to suppose they would do otherwise.

A final source of uneasiness for contemporary readers of *Romeo and Juliet* is the impression, got mainly from the first two acts, that Verona is really a part of the world of comedy. Many things contribute to this impression. An amusing street fight and a masked ball in the first act, a lovers' meeting in the orchard in the second, a doting young man carrying courtly conventions to laughable excess, parents who would be custom-bound to interfere if they only knew of the affair going on under their noses, an affected troublemaker bent on vindicating honor to the letter in duels conducted with precious precision, a bawdy nurse and an even bawdier friend—such things as these in an Elizabethan play ordinarily lead to the triumph of young love and a marriage or two, with forgiveness and feasting all around. In this play, however, the familiar dream of courtly comedy shatters when Mercutio is slain, and from that point on the lightness quickly dissolves. Romeo is banished, the "comfortable" Friar falls back on desperate remedies, old Capulet grows testy and intolerant, Lady Capulet calls for blood, the amusing Nurse suggests bigamy as a practical course, and Juliet, who has scarcely known life, prepares to be familiar with death. Even the weather adapts itself to the shift in tone: it suddenly gets hot in Act III, and in Act IV it rains; the sky is still overcast as the play comes to an end.

The contrast that Shakespeare gets here between the tone of the first two acts and that of the remaining three is probably intentional and, in any case, more apparent than real. Unless a reader is genuinely sophisticated, his response to literature is always at least partly a matter of habit; he laughs and shudders on signal. Thus there will always be those who find the first two acts of *Romeo and Juliet* mainly laughable, just as there will always be some who consider *Othello* the tragedy of a handkerchief, a farce with unfortunate consequences. Shakespeare must not be held responsible for responses of this kind. The first two acts of *Romeo and Juliet* will appear to be consistently comic only if we read them in the limited light of other, very different things—second-rate farces, dramatic and nondramatic, hack work generally, certain comic strips, even—in which the same conventions have been used. The corrective is to pay attention, for Shakespeare allows us to carry any initial impression of comedy we may have got only so far as the climax of the street brawl in I.i. At that point, while the servants are still battling, Tybalt still fighting with Benvolio, Capulet yelling for a long sword, and his wife telling him to call for a crutch instead, he brings us up sharply with the Prince's words:

> What, ho! You men, you beasts,
> That quench the fire of your pernicious rage
> With purple fountains issuing from your veins!
>     (I.i.86–88)

Comedy can thrive indefinitely on beasts that pass for men, but it cannot long tolerate a reminder of original sin such as lurks in "pernicious rage" or a reminder of royal humanity's self-destructiveness like "purple fountains"; and it is with these in our ears that we pass on to the rest of the Prince's dignified rebuke and thence to the speeches of Benvolio and the Montagues which express their human concern for a youthful friend and son, the absent Romeo. When Romeo himself appears, later in the same scene, juggling words in a fashionable euphuistic manner and complaining of the contradictions of love, we are more cautious with our laughter. Laugh as we may, Romeo clearly lives in a world where folly can have serious and irrevocable consequences; and we are no longer confident that the conventions of comedy will save him from those consequences or spare us the pain of seeing him destroyed.

The remaining scenes in Acts I and II contain much that confirms our uneasiness. For example, Capulet, who has been very funny calling for his long sword, says tenderly of his daughter in I.ii:

> too soon marred are those so early made.
> Earth hath swallowèd all my hopes but she;
> She is the hopeful lady of my earth.    (I.ii.13–15)

These three lines are enough to establish him as a dramatic figure who will probably invite our sympathy as readily as he has provoked our ridicule. They also prepare us for Juliet, who never has much of the comic about her and least of all when she disturbs us with a prophetic "My grave is like to be my wedding bed" (I.v.137). Mercutio's bawdiness is perhaps the best argument for taking these two acts as comic, but an attentive listener will receive it all with the long Queen Mab speech still in mind, see that

Mercutio's bawdiness and fancy are simply complementary aspects of a single creative and remarkably perceptive imagination, and be prepared to recognize that Verona's one hope of restoration without tragedy has vanished when he dies.

In any case, a feeling that the play represents relatively mature work has disposed most scholars to seek a late date for it. The latest that can reasonably be given is 1596, since the first edition appeared early in 1597 and described the play as having been performed by "Lord Hunsdon's servants," a title that Shakespeare's company held only from July 1596 until the following March. The preferred date seems to be 1595, which is also the preferred date for *Richard II* and *A Midsummer Night's Dream*. The reason usually given for putting these plays in the same year is that the same intense lyricism characterizes all three, but it has also been suggested that *A Midsummer Night's Dream*, in its special concern with the difficulties of young love, reveals itself to be a product of the same mood or preoccupation that caused Shakespeare to write *Romeo and Juliet*. Some interesting parallels have been noted. For example, in the first scene of *A Midsummer Night's Dream* Lysander says:

Brief as the lightning in the collied night,
That, in a spleen, unfolds both heaven and earth,
And ere a man hath power to say, "Behold!"
The jaws of darkness do devour it up:
So quick bright things come to confusion.    (I.i.145-49)

To this Hermia replies, "If then true lovers have been ever crossed,/It stands as an edict in destiny." This exchange has been related plausibly both to Juliet's "too rash, too unadvised, too sudden;/Too like the lightning, which doth cease to be/Ere one can say it lightens" (II.ii.118-20) and to the "star-crossed lovers" of the Prologue. But beyond the realm of the plausible in this matter we cannot go. Those who regard the play as immature usually prefer an earlier date, insisting that the Nurse's " 'Tis since the earthquake now eleven years" (I.iii.23), by which she remembers the time of Juliet's weaning, refers to a famous earthquake which struck England in 1580 and that Shakespeare meant to date his play 1591 by having the Nurse mention something that everyone in the audience could date precisely. Against this view one might argue that there were two other earthquakes in England during the 1580's and at least one on the Continent; Shakespeare could easily have referred to one of these or just as easily to no earthquake at all. Moreover, while it is certainly reasonable to suppose that in mentioning an earthquake he would have thought of some earthquake he knew, it is hardly reasonable to think he would have bothered to fix as contemporary the date of a play that apparently had nothing to gain by being considered topical. Everything taken into account, the play seems to come after plays like *The Two Gentlemen of Verona* and *Love's Labor's Lost* and before *The Merchant of Venice* and the Henry IV plays. The most likely date, therefore, is still 1595.

Whatever the date, the style of *Romeo and Juliet* places it at a point which marks the poet's achievement of self-awareness and confidence in his mastery over the medium. The play is rich in set pieces and memorable scenes, so much so in fact that insensitive producers have sometimes turned it into a collection of dramatic recitals. Yet Shakespeare's virtuosity, intrinsically interesting as it is whenever we choose to isolate some specimen of it, never fails to function as a part of the general action of the play; and that is as true in this work, where he seems to be rejoicing openly in his creative power, as it is in the later tragedies, where the power is felt rather than seen. Nothing in *Romeo and Juliet* really stands alone, not even a startling passage like the Queen Mab speech, which almost immediately proves to be an indispensable part of Mercutio's complex personality, just as Mercutio with all his complexity ultimately proves indispensable to the meaning of the play. The creativity displayed in this passage is Shakespeare's, to be sure, but his greatest achievement is in making it credibly Mercutio's. Equally remarkable is the much-admired lyrical quality of the next scene, in which Romeo meets Juliet for the first time; but this scene is remarkable for another reason. Here we have two young people who presumably have had no opportunity to develop any special gift for language. Juliet's talk up to this point has commanded no particular attention; and Romeo's, best displayed perhaps in his first exchange with Benvolio (I.i), has been characterized by extravagant paradoxes and an occasional fortuitous couplet. Suddenly, with Juliet in sight, he begins to make something like poetry:

O, she doth teach the torches to burn bright!
It seems she hangs upon the cheek of night
As a rich jewel in an Ethiop's ear—
Beauty too rich for use, for earth too dear!    (I.v.46-49)

Capulet and Tybalt briefly obscure the young man from view, but as these move aside, we see that he has not only taken Juliet by the hand but has begun spinning sonnets with her; and even before the Nurse interrupts, we have sensed the rightness of this unexpected attachment and its potential for permanence. We are thus prepared for the orchard, or balcony, scene of Act II and for the lovely *aubade* that the two perform at the parting in Act III—both among the memorable scenes in Shakespeare because without any formal patterning they achieve a unity all their own and still serve the larger function of suggesting the integrity that love can confer briefly upon two young people who, apart from each other, will remain children to the end.

In characterization Shakespeare had always been able to make language work for him, but with *Romeo and Juliet* he mastered it so completely that the play almost became a gallery of individuals. The language of the extremes in the social scale must have been easiest to catch, with the banter of servingmen at one end and the formal periods of Prince Escalus at the other; but in between the extremes we get the Nurse's peasant speech, most noticeably of peasant origin when she tries to imitate her betters, beautifully contrasted with the self-assured and warmly healthy country-gentry talk of old Capulet; Mercutio's mature command of language at all levels and Tybalt's narrow range of sharp insolence; Friar Lawrence's moralizing, formal and sententious but never tedious, and the tiny voice of the complaisant Apothecary. Some of these characters change attitude as external circumstances require, but in general their personalities simply unfold in the language that establishes them. This is also true of Benvolio, Paris, and Lady Capulet. Romeo and Juliet, however, undergo development, and he undergoes more than she. From her first appearance the younger Juliet is more mature than her lover. Romeo is fertile in figures and can occasionally invent fresh things like "Night's candles are burnt out, and jocund day/Stands tiptoe on the misty mountaintops" (III.v.9–10); but it is always Juliet who leads the talk in their two great scenes together, and it is also she who knows what language cannot do:

> Conceit, more rich in matter than in words,
> Brags of his substance, not of ornament.
> They are but beggars that can count their worth;
> But my true love is grown to such excess
> I cannot sum up sum of half my wealth.     (II.vi.30–34)

Her best lines are those in which she draws upon language to invent for her the images of death which she must confront before Romeo can be permanently hers (IV.iii.14–58); yet when she wakes to find Romeo lifeless, she can muster no language capable of helping her in such an extremity and quickly joins her lover in death. By contrast, Romeo's best speech is perhaps the one he delivers in the tomb; with it he gives dignity, meaning, and finality to the one act he plans and executes, however unwisely, without the help of friends, Friar, or Juliet. His language here, like the deed, is his own, as the courtly conventions and fashionable euphuism of many of his earlier scenes were not. His paradoxes, his puns, even his lamentations in the Friar's cell, are borrowed things, as his mature friends know; yet Romeo's "misshapen chaos of well-seeming forms" is catalyzed into inchoate poetry whenever Juliet comes upon the scene, and in the end he achieves in her presence a man's power to act if not a man's gift of discretion.

If *Romeo and Juliet* fails to achieve the highest rank of tragedy, the reason for that failure must be sought in the protagonists themselves and not in some extraterrestrial power or agency. The reason Romeo and Juliet do not stand out clearly as protagonists in a great tragedy is simply that Shakespeare created them to be protagonists in a different kind of play, one which has many of the circumstances that we find in the other tragedies but which lacks at the center a figure capable of achieving the terrible but satisfying perception of man's involvement in the mystery of creation. "Failure" is an inappropriate word for such an achievement. The notable thing about Romeo and Juliet is not that they fail to reach a Hamlet's degree of awareness but that as very young people they behave better and mature more rapidly in that direction than we have any right to expect them to. They learn that Verona is flawed, but they do not dream that the whole world is flawed in the same way. They discover that some actions are good and some bad, but never achieve the Friar's catholic view that only will can make an action bad and only grace can redeem it. They confront imperfection courageously; they fail to see in it an image of themselves. Death overtakes them in their innocence and their unknowing; and we remember them not as we remember tragic heroes, in pity and fear, but in admiration for their loveliness, as we remember dead children.

All things considered, the Verona which serves as their testing ground is not a bad place. The Prologue refers darkly to "the continuance of their parents' rage,/Which, but their children's end, naught could remove"; but as H. B. Charlton has observed, the old people in the play seem to have little interest in continuing a quarrel. Apart from the ancient rift, one might describe the city as a reservoir of high spirits and good will, full of attractive people like the witty Mercutio, Benvolio and Paris, the wise and tolerant Friar, and the young ladies who brighten the evenings in Capulet's great hall. Yet the Prologue is right. The rift created by the old people's almost forgotten rage is still there, wide enough for irresponsible young servingmen to see and make a game of and wide enough, too, for irresponsible young noblemen, like Tybalt, to aggravate into a civic crisis. One might say of it, as Mercutio says of his death wound, "'Tis not so deep as a well, nor so wide as a church door; but 'tis enough, 'twill serve." In the end it has served as a conduit for some of the best blood in the city, including Mercutio's own, and for the tears of all the rest.

Apart from the two protagonists, the people of Verona, or rather those that Shakespeare has presented to us, may be arranged in two groups. The first of these, by far the larger, includes all the supernumeraries, such minor characters as Peter and the Apothecary, and a few relatively important figures like Tybalt, the Capulets, the Nurse, Paris, and Benvolio. These are the static or "flat" characters, who are "by nature" what they are; and their functions are to present the limited range of values they embody and to make the plot go. Tybalt, for example, is by nature choleric and determined to pick quarrels; Benvolio, by nature the opposite, is equally determined to avoid them. There are no surprises in either, even when Tybalt precipitates the climactic crisis of the play, just as there are no surprises in Paris and should be none in the Nurse. The latter is interesting to us precisely because Shakespeare's detailed unfolding of her reveals a consistent personality, yet she too is static. From the beginning, she is garrulous, corruptible, and insensitive; and as long as nothing requires her to be otherwise, she can also be amusing. At her crisis, when Juliet asks her to be wise, the Nurse can only suggest bigamy, a course quite in keeping with the values she herself is made of. Here the Nurse is no longer funny, but she has not changed. It is Juliet who has done that. The other characters in this group do not change either. They may be said to represent the abiding conditions of human intercourse in any representative community; and a lesser playwright, assembling a similar collection, would probably have included the same kind of servants and dignitaries, a Nurse or someone like her, Tybalts and Benvolios, all performing essentially the same functions as Shakespeare's and exhibiting many of the same qualities. The unique excellence of the static characters in *Romeo and Juliet* comes from Shakespeare's having particularized them so deftly that, like the protagonists in the play, we hopefully take them at first for people of larger dimensions. Their vitality tempts us to expect them to be more than they are and to give more than they have any capacity for giving. Thus when Tybalt fails to respond to Romeo's generous appeal and Lady Capulet proves blind to her daughter's need for sympathy, we feel the disappointment as sharply as if we were discovering for ourselves the limitations of common humanity.

The second group consists of three characters who give a doubly strong impression of life because they include among their qualities some degree of perception or understanding. Prince Escalus, slight as he is, is one of these, and Friar Lawrence another. Normally we should expect a magistrate to belong to the group of static or flat characters, but Shakespeare has given his magistrate a conscience and a growing presentiment of what must happen to everyone in Verona if the wound in the civil body cannot be healed. Others want to keep the peace, too, but mainly because they have a perfunctory sense of duty or perhaps because they dislike fighting. Escalus knows from the beginning that keeping the peace here is a matter of life or death, and in the end he readily takes his share of responsibility for the bloody sacrifice he has failed to avert:

> Capulet, Montague,
> See what a scourge is laid upon your hate,
> That heaven finds means to kill your joys with love.
> And I, for winking at your discords too,
> Have lost a brace of kinsmen. All are punished.
>
> (V.iii.292–96)

The Friar is included in this "all"; and the Friar, moreover, has preceded the Prince in accepting blame:

> if aught in this
> Miscarried by my fault, let my old life
> Be sacrificed some hour before his time
> Unto the rigor of severest law. (V.iii.267–70)

Like the Prince, the Friar has had from the start a clear perception of the danger latent in the old quarrel, and like the Prince he has taken steps appropriate to his position to mend the differences and restore order. Yet whereas the Prince by nature has moved openly and erred in not moving vigorously enough, Friar Lawrence by nature works in secret and his secrecy does him in. Actually his much-criticized plan for ending the quarrel is sound enough in principle. Any faithful son of the church, accustomed to cementing alliances with the sacrament of matrimony, would naturally have considered the young people's sudden affection for each other an opportunity sent by heaven. Friar Lawrence's error lies all in the execution of the thing, in letting a heaven-made marriage remain an affair of secret messages, rope ladders, and unorthodox sleeping potions, a clandestine remedy doomed to miscarriage long before the thwarted message determines the shape of the inevitable catastrophe. What was desperately needed in this case was a combination of virtues, the forthrightness of the Prince and the vigor and ingenuity of the Friar; and these virtues were combined only in Mercutio, who fell victim to the deficiencies of both in that he confronted a needlessly active Tybalt at a disadvantage caused in part by bumbling Romeo's adherence to the Friar's secret plot.

Mercutio, who is the third member of this more perceptive group, stands next to Romeo and Juliet in importance in the play. In fact, some critics who consider him more interesting than the two protagonists have suggested that Shakespeare finished him off in Act III out of necessity. This is almost as absurd as the view that Shakespeare wrote Falstaff out of *Henry V* because the fat man had become unmanageable. Others have found Mercutio's wit embarrassing and tried to relieve Shakespeare of the responsibility for some parts of it, but this is absurd too. An edited Mercutio becomes either sentimental or obscene; he also becomes meaningless, and without him the play as a whole reverts to the condition of melodrama that it had in Shakespeare's source. Consider for a moment the climax of the play, which is almost solely Shakespeare's invention. In Brooke the matter is relatively simple: Tybalt provokes Romeo, and Romeo slays him. Shakespeare has it that Tybalt deliberately sought to murder Romeo and Romeo so badly underestimated his challenger that he declined to defend himself; whereupon Mercutio, in defense of both Romeo's honor and his person, picked up the challenge and would have killed Tybalt but for Romeo's intervention. Tybalt then killed Mercutio, and Romeo killed Tybalt in revenge. But, one should ask, what if Romeo had not intervened? Tybalt would have been slain, surely, and Mercutio would have survived to receive the Prince's rebuke; at most, however, he would have been punished only slightly, for Mercutio was of the Prince's line and not of the feuding families. The feud thus would have died with Tybalt, and in time Capulet and Montague might have been reconciled openly, as Friar Lawrence hoped. In short, Mercutio was on the point of bringing to pass what neither civil authority nor well-intentioned but misplaced ingenuity had been able to accomplish, and Romeo with a single sentimental action ("I thought all for the best," he says) destroyed his only hope of averting tragedy long enough to achieve the maturity he needed in order to avoid it altogether.

Many critics have commented on the breathless pace of this play, and no wonder. Shakespeare has made it the story of a race against time. What Romeo needs most of all is a teacher, and the only one capable of giving him instruction worth having and giving it quickly is Mercutio. All the rest are unavailable, or ineffectual, like Benvolio, or unapt for dealing practically with human relations. Mercutio, however, for all his superficial show of irresponsibility, is made in the image of his creator; he is a poet, who gives equal value to flesh and spirit, sees them as inseparable aspects of total being, and accepts each as the necessary mode of the other. His first line in the play, discharged at a young fool who is playing the ascetic for love, is revealing: "Nay, gentle Romeo, we must have you dance" (I.iv.13). And when gentle Romeo persists in daydreaming, he says, "Be rough with love," declares that love is a mire and that dreamers are often liars. The long fairy speech which follows dignifies idle dreams by marrying them to earth; its intent is to compel Romeo to acknowledge his senses and to bring him to an honest and healthy confession of what he is really looking for, but Romeo is too wrapped up in self-deception to listen. In Act II Mercutio tries harder, speaks more plainly, but prompts from his pupil only the fatuous "He jests at scars that never felt a wound." Later still, in the battle of wits (II.iv), Mercutio imagines briefly that he has succeeded: "Why, is not this better now than groaning for love? Now art thou sociable, now art thou Romeo; now art thou what thou art, by art as well as by nature" (II.iv.91–94). There are no wiser words in the whole play, and none more ironic; for Romeo even here has not found his identity and is never really to find it except for those fleeting moments when Juliet is there to lead him by the hand.

Time runs out for both principals in this play, but it is Juliet who makes the race exciting. Her five-day maturation is a miracle which only a Shakespeare could have made credible; yet at the end she is still a fourteen-year-old girl, and she succumbs to an adolescent's despair. Mercutio might have helped had he been available, but Mercutio is dead. All the others have deserted her—parents, Nurse, the Friar, who takes fright at the crucial moment, and Romeo, who lies dead at her feet. She simply has not lived long enough in her wisdom to stand entirely alone. This is really the source of pathos in *Romeo and Juliet*. One hears much about the portrayal of young love here, about the immortality of the lovers and the eternality of their love; but such talk runs toward vapid sentimentality and does an injustice to Shakespeare. No one has more poignantly described the beauty of young love than he, and no one has portrayed more honestly than he the destructiveness of any love which ignores the mortality of those who make it. Romeo struggled toward full understanding but fell far short of achievement, leaving a trail of victims behind him. Juliet came much closer than we had any right to expect, but she too failed. Both have a legitimate claim to our respect, she more than he; and the youth of both relieves them of our ultimate censure, which falls not on the stars but on all those whose thoughtlessness denied them the time they so desperately needed.

## A NOTE ON THE SOURCE

The story of Romeo and Juliet was popular in Elizabethan times, and Shakespeare could have got his working outline of it from a number of places. Belleforest's *Histoires Tragiques* had a version, as did William Painter's *Palace of Pleasure;* and there had apparently been a play on the subject. Arthur Brooke, in an address "To the Reader" prefaced to his long narrative poem *The Tragicall Historye of Romeus and Juliet*, mentioned seeing "the same argument lately set foorth on stage"; but there is no evidence that Shakespeare worked from an older play or even that he consulted Belleforest or Painter, though he undoubtedly knew their works. All the evidence indicates that he worked directly from Brooke's poem, which Richard Tottell had printed in 1562 and Robert Robinson had reissued in 1587, shortly before the time that Shakespeare must have begun writing for the London stage.

Actually the story was popular, on the Continent at least, well before Elizabeth's time. Leaving out of account such obvious but distant analogues as the stories of Hero and Leander, Aeneas and Dido, Pyramus and Thisbe, and Troilus and Cressida, the first version of the story was one that appeared in Masuccio Salernitano's *Il Novellino* in 1476. This version had the clandestine lovers, the accommodating friar, the killing that led to the young man's banishment, the rival suitor, sleeping potion, thwarted messenger, and unhappy conclusion, but no suicides. It might have passed into oblivion had it not been for Luigi da Porto's *Istoria novellamente ritrovata di due Nobili Amanti* (published about 1530), which laid the scene in Verona and identified the feuding families as Montecchi

and Capelletti and the lovers as Romeo and Giulietta. Da Porto's story also named the friar Lorenzo and the slain man Thebaldo Capelletti and introduced the ball, the balcony scene, and the double suicide at the tomb. It was da Porto, moreover, who first named a minor character Marcuccio and gave him the icy hands that subsequent tellers of the tale regularly mentioned until Shakespeare discarded the detail and replaced it with a distinctive personality. Da Porto is also remembered for having Giulietta commit suicide by holding her breath—a detail which fortunately no one bothered to perpetuate.

Da Porto's tale was widely imitated both in Italy and in France, but the version of most importance to readers of Shakespeare was that of Matteo Bandello, who put the story into his *Novelle* (1554). Of all the versions before Shakespeare's, Bandello's is generally considered the best. It is a plain, straightforward narrative, unmarred by the sentimentality and moralizing that characterized the work of some of his adapters. In Bandello's story the masking appears; Peter is there (but as Romeo's servant), the Nurse has a significant part in the plot, and the rope ladder comes into play. Almost as important is the version of Pierre Boaistuau (1559), adapted from Bandello, which was included in Belleforest's *Histoires Tragiques*. Boaistuau made Romeo go to the ball in the hope of seeing his indifferent lady (the Rosaline of Shakespeare's play), worked out the business of the Capulets' restraint at discovering Romeo's presence, and developed the dilemma that Juliet finds herself in when she first hears of Tybalt's death; he also developed the character of the Apothecary. All these things went into Painter's version (1567), which was a translation of Boaistuau, and into Brooke's, which was based on Boaistuau. The line of transmission from Masuccio to Shakespeare thus includes da Porto, Bandello, Boaistuau, and Brooke, in that order, with Painter standing unconsulted to one side. Shakespeare, however, used only Brooke directly and thus derived from the tradition only as much as Brooke passed on to him; but he borrowed freely from the great wealth of detail that Brooke himself had added.

Anyone interested in consulting Brooke's version for himself will find it in the first volume of Geoffrey Bullough's *Narrative and Dramatic Sources of Shakespeare* (1957). In spite of the tedious poulter's measure (iambic couplets in which the first line has twelve syllables and the second fourteen) the poem is not entirely dull; and no other single source gave Shakespeare so much that was immediately useful. Readers should recognize at once the character and function of Benvolio (though Brooke neglected to give him a name), the Capulet that stormed at what he took to be his daughter's willful disobedience and threatened her with incarceration and endless misery, the garrulous, amoral Nurse and her conversations with the young lovers, and the needy Apothecary. They will even find the clue to Mercutio's character (which Brooke did not develop) in the lines "Even as a Lyon would emong the lambes be bolde,/Such was emong the bashfull maydes, Mercutio to beholde." Numerous such hints, together with bits of business, suggestions for metaphors, and passages of dialogue, catch the eye as one scans Brooke's lines, not so much because they are arresting in themselves but because they call to mind the use Shakespeare has made of them. And if one gets safely past Brooke's "Address to the

Reader," with its heavy-handed condemnation of lust, disobedience, and superstitious friars, one finds that Brooke too treated the lovers with sympathy and allowed his friar the best of intentions. In fact, Brooke, having discharged himself of his Protestant moralizing in the "Address," tended to make Fortune responsible for most things in the story; and Shakespeare, as we know, took Brooke's Fortune along with all the rest.

What Shakespeare did with Brooke's clean but relatively inert story was to add complication and focus, intensify it by drastic compression, and establish the intricate relationship of part to part in a texture of language that functions admirably as dialogue even as it creates the unity of a dramatic poem. In this transformation he made it possible for us to tolerate the Nurse, love Capulet, and pity the Apothecary. He relieved the Friar of the tedium that Brooke had encumbered him with, and he changed Escalus into a man who genuinely suffers and commands sympathy. In bringing Tybalt to the ball and making him the discoverer of Romeo's presence there, he gave real point to the disastrous street fight in Act III; he also enlarged Paris' part in the story and ennobled his character, and he created Mercutio. More important, he made all three of these serve as foils to a Romeo who develops and matures in response to the challenges they present and who, before the end, has ironically become responsible for the deaths of all three. Shakespeare's real miracle, however, was Juliet, transformed from an adolescent arrogantly eager to outdo her elders to an appealing child-woman, barely fourteen, who learns to mix courage with her innocence, yet falls victim to a world that only briefly and unintentionally but fatally treats her as a plaything.

## A NOTE ON THE TEXT

The first quarto (Q1) of *Romeo and Juliet* was printed in 1597 without previous entry in the Stationers' Register. It bore the following title page: "An/EXCELLENT/conceited Tragedie/OF/Romeo and Iuliet./As it hath been often (with great applause)/plaid publiquely, by the right Ho-/nourable the L. of *Hunsdon*/his Seruants./LONDON,/ Printed by Iohn Danter./1597." Until the present century, editors frequently assumed that this text, curtailed and manifestly corrupt, represented an early draft of the play. Most now agree that Q1, like the other "bad" Shakespeare quartos, is a memorial reconstruction; that is, a version which some of the actors (accusing fingers have been pointed at those who played Romeo and Peter) put together from memory and gave to the printer. The second quarto (Q2) was printed in 1599 with the following title page: "THE/MOST/EX-/cellent and lamentable/Tragedie, of Romeo/and *Iuliet./Newly corrected, augmented, and/ amended:* As it hath bene sundry times publiquely acted, by the/right Honourable the Lord Chamberlaine/his Seruants./London/Printed by Thomas Creede, for Cuthbert Burby, and are to/be sold at his shop neare the Exchange./ 1599." Apparently Q2 derives directly from the same acting version that is imperfectly reflected in the memorially reconstructed Q1, but it is based on a written script of the play rather than on actors' memories. Q2, however, is the product of careless or hasty printing and does not

inspire complete confidence. Lines that the author doubtless had canceled are sometimes printed along with the lines intended to replace them, and occasionally notes about staging appear which are probably the prompter's, or possibly Shakespeare's. Vexing matters like these, together with the fact that some speeches in Q2 are clearly based on Q1 (possibly the manuscript that provided the copy for most of Q2 was illegible in places), have caused editors to make at least limited use of Q1. The other texts of *Romeo and Juliet* have no claim to authority. The second quarto provided the basis for a third quarto (1609), which in turn served as copy for an undated fourth quarto and for the text in the Folio of 1623. A fifth quarto, based on the fourth, appeared in 1637.

None of these texts—including the second quarto, upon which the present edition is based—makes any real division of the play into acts and scenes. (The last third of Q1 does have a rough indication of scene division in the form of strips of ornamental border across the page, and the Folio has at the beginning *Actus Primus. Scena Prima*, but nothing further.) The division used here, like that in most modern texts, derives from the Globe edition, as do the dramatis personae and the various indications of place. Spelling and punctuation have been modernized, a number of stage directions have been added (in square brackets), and speech prefixes have been regularized. This last change will be regretted by those who feel, perhaps rightly, that at least some of the speech prefixes of Q2 show how Shakespeare thought of the character at each moment of the dialogue. Lady Capulet, for example, is variously designated in the speech prefixes of Q2 as "Wife," "Lady," and sometimes "Mother"; Capulet is occasionally referred to as "Father," and Balthasar as "Peter"; the First Musician of the present text (IV.v) is once called "Fidler" in Q2 and several times "Minstrel" or "Minstrels." Other deviations (apart from obvious typographical errors) from Q2 are listed in the textual notes below. There the adopted reading is given first, in boldface, followed by a note in square brackets if the source of the reading is Q1; this is followed by the rejected reading in roman. Absence of a note in square brackets indicates that the adopted reading has been taken from some other source and represents guesswork at best. Apparently the editors of F as well as of Q3 and Q4 had no access to any authentic document.

In dealing with the troublesome stage direction at the end of I.iv, I have followed the solution adopted by H. R. Hoppe in his Crofts Classics edition (1947); and I have adopted the reading of "eyes' shot" for the customary "eyes shut" at III ii.49 from the Pelican edition of John E. Hankins (1960), which presents a good argument for retaining the reading of Q2 with the addition of an apostrophe.

I.i.29 **in sense** [Q1] sense  34 **comes two** [Q1] comes  65 **swashing** washing  123 **drave** driue  150 **his** is  156 **sun** same  182 **well-seeming** [Q1] welseeing  205 **Bid a sick** [Q1] A sicke; **make** [Q1] makes  206 **Ah** [Q1] A
I.ii.32 **on** one  64–72 **Signior . . . Helena** [prose in Qq and F]  91 **fires** fier
I.iii.2–76 [Q2 prints Nurse's speeches in prose]  66, 67 **honor** [Q1] houre  99 **make it** [Q1] make
I.iv.7–8 **Nor . . . entrance** [added from Q1]  23 **Mercutio** Horatio  39 **done** [Q1] dum  42 **Of this sir-reverence** [Q1] or saue you reuerence  45 **like** lights  47 **five** fine  53–91 **O . . . bodes** [verse from Q1; Q2 has prose]  57 **atomies** ottamie

**63 film** Philome  **66 maid** [Q1] man  **113 sail** [Q1] sute  **114 s.d. They . . . and** [Q2 combines with s.d. used here at beginning of I.v]
**I.v.s.d.** [Q2 adds "Enter Romeo"]  **1, 4, 7, 12 First Servingman . . . Second Servingman . . . First Servingman . . . Second Servingman** [Q2 has "Ser.," "1.," "Ser.," and "Ser."]  **97 ready** [Q1] did readie  **144 What's this? What's this?** Whats tis? whats tis
**II.i.9 one** [Q1] on  **10 pronounce** [Q1] prouaunt; **dove** [Q1] day  **12 heir** [Q1] her  **38 et cetera** [Q1] or
**II.ii.16 do** to  **20 eyes** eye  **45 were** wene  **83 washed** washeth  **99 havior** [Q1] behauior  **101 more cunning** [Q1] coying  **163 than mine** then  **168 sweet** Neece  **187 Romeo** [Q1] Iu.
**188–89** [between these lines Q2 has "The grey eyde morne smiles on the frowning night,/Checkring the Easterne Clouds with streaks of light,/And darknesse fleckted like a drunkard reeles,/From forth daies pathway, made by *Tytans* wheeles," lines nearly identical with those given to the Friar at II.iii.1–4; presumably Shakespeare first wrote the lines for Romeo, then decided to use them in Friar Lawrence's next speech, but neglected to delete the first version, and the printer mistakenly printed it]
**II.iii.2 Check'ring** Checking  **3 fleckèd** [Q1] fleckeld  **74 ring yet** [Q1] yet ringing
**II.iv.19 Benvolio** [Q1] Ro.  **30 fantasticoes** [Q1] phantacies  **213 Ah** A
**II.v.11 three** there
**II.vi.27 music's** musicke
**III.i.2 are** [Q1; Q2 omits]  **91 s.d. Tybalt . . . flies** [Q1; Q2 has "Away Tybalt"]  **110 soundly too. Your** soundly, to your  **124 Alive** [Q1] He gan  **126 eyed** [Q1] end  **168 agile** [Q1] aged  **190 hate's** [Q1] hearts  **194 I** It
**III.ii.51 determine of** determine  **60 one** on  **72–73** [Q2 gives line 72 to Juliet, line 73 to Nurse]  **76 Dove-feathered** Rauenous doue-featherd  **79 damnèd** dimme
**III.iii.s.d. Enter Friar** [Q1] Enter Frier and Romeo  **40 But . . . banishèd** [in Q2 this line is preceded by one line, "This may flyes do, when I from this must flie," which is substantially the same as line 41, and by line 43, which is probably misplaced]  **52 Thou** [Q1] Then  **61 madmen** [Q1] mad man  **73 s.d. Knock** knocke  **75 s.d. Knock** Slud knock  **108 s.d. He . . . away** Q1; Q2 omits]  **117 lives** lies  **143 misbehaved** mishaued

**162 s.d. Nurse . . . again** [Q1; Q2 omits]  **168 disguised** disguise
**III.v.13 exhales** [Q1] exhale  **36 s.d. Enter Nurse** [Q1] Enter Madame and Nurse  **42 s.d. He goeth down** [Q1; Q2 omits]  **54 Juliet** Ro.  **83 pardon him** padon  **140 gives** giue  **182 trained** [Q1] liand
**IV.i.7 talked** talke  **72 slay** [Q1] stay  **83 chapless** chapels  **85 his shroud** his  **98 breath** [Q1] breast  **100 wanny** many  **110 In** Is [after this line Q2 has "Be borne to buriall in thy kindreds graue"; presumably as soon as Shakespeare wrote these words he decided he could do better, and expressed the gist of the idea in the next two lines, but the canceled line was erroneously printed]  **111 shalt** shall  **116 waking** walking
**IV.iii.49 wake** walke  **58 Romeo, I drink** [after "Romeo" Q2 has "heeres drinke," which is probably a stage direction printed in error]  **58 s.d. She . . . curtains** [Q1; Q2 omits]
**IV.iv.21 faith** [Q1] father
**IV.v.65 cure** care  **82 fond** some  **95 s.d. casting . . . curtains** [Q1; Q2 omits]  **99 by** [Q1] my; **amended** amended. Exit omnes  **99 s.d. Peter** [Q2 has "Will Kemp," the name of the actor playing the role]  **126 grief** [Q1] griefes  **127 And . . . oppress** [Q1; Q2 omits]  **133, 136 Pretty** [Q1] prates
**V.i.11 s.d. booted** [detail from Q1]  **15 fares my** [Q1] doth my Lady  **24 e'en** [Q1 "euen"] in; **defy** [Q1] denie  **50 And** An  **76 pay** [Q1] pray
**V.iii.s.d. with . . . water** [Q1; Q2 omits]  **3 yew** [Q1] young  **21 s.d. and Balthasar . . . iron** [Q1; Q2 has "Enter Romeo and Peter," and gives lines 40 and 43 to Peter instead of to Balthasar]  **48 s.d. Romeo . . . tomb** [Q1; Q2 omits]  **68 conjurations** [Q1] commiration  **71 Page** [Q2 omits this speech prefix]  **102 fair** [Q2 follows with "I will beleeue," presumably words that Shakespeare wrote, then rewrote in the next line, but neglected to delete]  **108 again. Here** [between these words Q2 has the following material, which Shakespeare apparently neglected to delete: "come lye thou in my arme,/Heer's to thy health, where ere thou tumblest in./O true Appothecarie/Thy drugs are quicke. Thus with a kisse I die./Depart againe"]  **137 yew** yong  **188 too** too too  **190 s.d. Enter . . . wife** [Q2 places after line 202, with "Enter Capels" at line 190]  **191 shrieked** [Q1] shrike  **200 slaughtered** Slaughter  **210 more early** [Q1] now earling

# THE TRAGEDY OF
# ROMEO AND JULIET

[Dramatis Personae

CHORUS
ESCALUS *Prince of Verona*
PARIS *a young count, kinsman to the Prince*
MONTAGUE
CAPULET
AN OLD MAN *of the Capulet family*
ROMEO *son to Montague*
MERCUTIO *kinsman to the Prince and friend to Romeo*
BENVOLIO *nephew to Montague and friend to Romeo*
TYBALT *nephew to Lady Capulet*
FRIAR LAWRENCE ⎱ *Franciscans*
FRIAR JOHN ⎰
BALTHASAR *servant to Romeo*

SAMPSON ⎱ *servants to Capulet*
GREGORY ⎰
PETER *servant to Juliet's Nurse*
ABRAM *servant to Montague*
AN APOTHECARY
THREE MUSICIANS
AN OFFICER
LADY MONTAGUE *wife to Montague*
LADY CAPULET *wife to Capulet*
JULIET *daughter to Capulet*
NURSE *to Juliet*
CITIZENS *of Verona* GENTLEMEN *and* GENTLEWOMEN *of both houses* MASKERS TORCHBEARERS PAGES GUARDS WATCHMEN SERVANTS ATTENDANTS

*Scene:* Verona; Mantua]

## THE PROLOGUE

[*Enter* CHORUS.]

CHORUS
Two households, both alike in dignity,°
  In fair Verona, where we lay our scene,
From ancient grudge break to new mutiny,°
  Where civil blood makes civil hands unclean.
From forth the fatal loins of these two foes    5
  A pair of star-crossed° lovers take their life;
Whose misadventured piteous overthrows
  Doth with their death bury their parents' strife.
The fearful passage of their death-marked love,
  And the continuance of their parents' rage,    10

Which, but their children's end, naught could remove,
  Is now the two hours' traffic of our stage;°
The which if you with patient ears attend,
What here shall miss, our toil shall strive to mend.
                   [*Exit.*]

## [ACT I]

[*Scene I. Verona. A public place.*]

*Enter* SAMPSON *and* GREGORY, *with swords and bucklers,° of the house of Capulet.*

SAMPSON Gregory, on my word, we'll not carry coals.°

---

*The decorative border above appeared on the title page of the 1597 quarto of* Romeo and Juliet.

**Pro.1 dignity** rank  **3 mutiny** violence  **6 star-crossed** fated to disaster

**12 two . . . stage** the business of our play
**I.i.s.d. bucklers** small shields  **1–2 carry coals** endure insults

GREGORY    No, for then we should be colliers.°

SAMPSON    I mean, and° we be in choler, we'll draw.°

GREGORY    Ay, while you live, draw your neck out of 5
collar.

SAMPSON    I strike quickly, being moved.

GREGORY    But thou art not quickly moved to strike.

SAMPSON    A dog of the house of Montague moves me.

GREGORY    To move is to stir, and to be valiant is to 10
stand. Therefore, if thou art moved, thou run'st away.

SAMPSON    A dog of that house shall move me to
stand. I will take the wall° of any man or maid of
Montague's.

GREGORY    That shows thee a weak slave; for the 15
weakest goes to the wall.°

SAMPSON    'Tis true; and therefore women, being the
weaker vessels, are ever thrust to the wall.° Therefore
I will push Montague's men from the wall and thrust
his maids to the wall.                                20

GREGORY    The quarrel is between our masters and us
their men.

SAMPSON    'Tis all one. I will show myself a tyrant.
When I have fought with the men, I will be civil with
the maids—I will cut off their heads.                25

GREGORY    The heads of the maids?

SAMPSON    Ay, the heads of the maids or their maidenheads. Take it in what sense thou wilt.

GREGORY    They must take it in sense that feel it.

SAMPSON    Me they shall feel while I am able to stand; 30
and 'tis known I am a pretty piece of flesh.

GREGORY    'Tis well thou art not fish; if thou hadst,
thou hadst been Poor John.° Draw thy tool!° Here
comes two of the house of Montagues.

*Enter two other servingmen* [ABRAM *and* BALTHASAR].

SAMPSON    My naked weapon is out. Quarrel! I will 35
back thee.

GREGORY    How? Turn thy back and run?

SAMPSON    Fear me not.

GREGORY    No, marry.° I fear thee!

SAMPSON    Let us take the law of our sides;° let them 40
begin.

GREGORY    I will frown as I pass by, and let them take
it as they list.

SAMPSON    Nay, as they dare. I will bite my thumb° at
them, which is disgrace to them if they bear it.    45

ABRAM    Do you bite your thumb at us, sir?

SAMPSON    I do bite my thumb, sir.

ABRAM    Do you bite your thumb at us, sir?

SAMPSON [*Aside to* GREGORY.]    Is the law of our side
if I say ay?                                       50

GREGORY [*Aside to* SAMPSON.]    No.

SAMPSON    No, sir, I do not bite my thumb at you, sir;
but I bite my thumb, sir.

GREGORY    Do you quarrel, sir?

ABRAM    Quarrel, sir? No, sir.                     55

SAMPSON    But if you do, sir, I am for you. I serve as
good a man as you.

ABRAM    No better.

SAMPSON    Well, sir.

*Enter* BENVOLIO.

GREGORY    Say "better." Here comes one of my 60
master's kinsmen.

SAMPSON    Yes, better, sir.

ABRAM    You lie.

SAMPSON    Draw, if you be men. Gregory, remember
thy swashing° blow.                                65

*They fight.*

BENVOLIO
Part, fools!
Put up your swords. You know not what you do.

*Enter* TYBALT.

TYBALT
What, art thou drawn among these heartless hinds?°
Turn thee, Benvolio; look upon thy death.

BENVOLIO
I do but keep the peace. Put up thy sword,          70
Or manage it to part these men with me.

TYBALT
What, drawn, and talk of peace? I hate the word
As I hate hell, all Montagues, and thee.
Have at thee, coward!

[*They fight.*]

*Enter* [*an* OFFICER, *and*] *three or four* CITIZENS *with
clubs or partisans.*

OFFICER    Clubs, bills, and partisans!° Strike! Beat them 75
down! Down with the Capulets! Down with the
Montagues!

*Enter old* CAPULET *in his gown, and his wife* [LADY
CAPULET].

CAPULET
What noise is this? Give me my long sword, ho!

LADY CAPULET
A crutch, a crutch! Why call you for a sword?

CAPULET
My sword, I say! Old Montague is come           80
And flourishes his blade in spite° of me.

*Enter old* MONTAGUE *and his wife* [LADY MONTAGUE].

MONTAGUE
Thou villain Capulet!—Hold me not; let me go.

LADY MONTAGUE
Thou shalt not stir one foot to seek a foe.

*Enter* PRINCE *Escalus, with his* TRAIN.

PRINCE
Rebellious subjects, enemies to peace,
Profaners of this neighbor-stainèd steel—         85
Will they not hear? What, ho! You men, you beasts,
That quench the fire of your pernicious rage

---

**3 colliers** coal venders (this leads to puns on *choler* = anger,
and *collar* = hangman's noose)    **4 and** if; **draw** draw swords
**13 take the wall** take the preferred place on the walk
**16 goes . . . wall** is pushed to the rear    **18 thrust . . . wall**
assaulted against the wall    **33 Poor John** hake salted and dried
(poor man's fare); **tool** weapon (with bawdy innuendo)    **39
marry** an interjection (from "By the Virgin Mary")    **40 take
. . . sides** keep ourselves in the right    **44 bite my thumb**
make a gesture of contempt

**65 swashing** slashing    **68 heartless hinds** cowardly rustics
**75 bills, and partisans** varieties of halberd, a combination
spear and battle-ax    **81 spite** defiance

With purple fountains issuing from your veins!
On pain of torture, from those bloody hands
Throw your mistempered° weapons to the ground    90
And hear the sentence of your movèd prince.
Three civil brawls, bred of an airy word
By thee, old Capulet, and Montague,
Have thrice disturbed the quiet of our streets
And made Verona's ancient citizens    95
Cast by their grave beseeming° ornaments
To wield old partisans, in hands as old,
Cank'red with peace, to part your cank'red° hate.
If ever you disturb our streets again,
Your lives shall pay the forfeit of the peace.    100
For this time all the rest depart away.
You, Capulet, shall go along with me;
And, Montague, come you this afternoon,
To know our farther pleasure in this case,
To old Freetown, our common judgment place.    105
Once more, on pain of death, all men depart.
     *Exeunt [all but* MONTAGUE, LADY MONTAGUE,
                    *and* BENVOLIO].

MONTAGUE
Who set this ancient quarrel new abroach?°
Speak, nephew, were you by when it began?
BENVOLIO
Here were the servants of your adversary
And yours, close fighting ere I did approach.    110
I drew to part them. In the instant came
The fiery Tybalt, with his sword prepared;
Which, as he breathed defiance to my ears,
He swung about his head and cut the winds,
Who, nothing hurt withal,° hissed him in scorn.    115
While we were interchanging thrusts and blows,
Came more and more, and fought on part and part,°
Till the prince came, who parted either part.
LADY MONTAGUE
O, where is Romeo? Saw you him today?
Right glad I am he was not at this fray.    120
BENVOLIO
Madam, an hour before the worshiped sun
Peered forth the golden window of the East,
A troubled mind drave me to walk abroad;
Where, underneath the grove of sycamore
That westward rooteth from this city side,    125
So early walking did I see your son.
Towards him I made, but he was ware° of me
And stole into the covert of the wood.
I, measuring his affections by my own,
Which then most sought where most might not be
     found,°    130
Being one too many by my weary self,
Pursued my humor not pursuing his,°
And gladly shunned who gladly fled from me.
MONTAGUE
Many a morning hath he there been seen,
With tears augmenting the fresh morning's dew,    135

Adding to clouds more clouds with his deep sighs;
But all so soon as the all-cheering sun
Should in the farthest East begin to draw
The shady curtains from Aurora's° bed,
Away from light steals home my heavy° son    140
And private in his chamber pens himself,
Shuts up his windows, locks fair daylight out,
And makes himself an artificial night.
Black and portentous must this humor° prove
Unless good counsel may the cause remove.    145
BENVOLIO
My noble uncle, do you know the cause?
MONTAGUE
I neither know it nor can learn of him.
BENVOLIO
Have you importuned him by any means?
MONTAGUE
Both by myself and many other friends;
But he, his own affections' counselor,    150
Is to himself—I will not say how true—
But to himself so secret and so close,
So far from sounding° and discovery,
As is the bud bit with an envious° worm
Ere he can spread his sweet leaves to the air    155
Or dedicate his beauty to the sun.
Could we but learn from whence his sorrows grow,
We would as willingly give cure as know.

*Enter* ROMEO.

BENVOLIO
See, where he comes. So please you step aside;
I'll know his grievance, or be much denied.    160
MONTAGUE
I would thou wert so happy° by thy stay
To hear true shrift.° Come, madam, let's away.
     *Exeunt [*MONTAGUE *and* LADY MONTAGUE].
BENVOLIO
Good morrow,° cousin.
ROMEO              Is the day so young?
BENVOLIO
But new struck nine.
ROMEO            Ay me! Sad hours seem long.
Was that my father that went hence so fast?    165
BENVOLIO
It was. What sadness lengthens Romeo's hours?
ROMEO
Not having that which having makes them short.
BENVOLIO   In love?
ROMEO   Out—
BENVOLIO   Of love?    170
ROMEO
Out of her favor where I am in love.
BENVOLIO
Alas that love, so gentle in his view,°
Should be so tyrannous and rough in proof!
ROMEO
Alas that love, whose view is muffled still,°

90 **mistempered** (1) ill-made (2) used with ill will   **96 grave beseeming** dignified and appropriate   **98 Cank'red . . . cank'red** rusted . . . malignant   **107 new abroach** newly open   **115 withal** thereby   **117 on part and part** some on one side, some on another   **127 ware** aware   **130 most sought . . . found** wanted most to be alone   **132 Pursued . . . his** followed my own inclination by not inquiring into his mood

**139 Aurora's** Aurora was the goddess of the dawn   **140 heavy** melancholy, moody   **144 humor** mood   **153 So . . . sounding** so far from measuring the depth of his mood   **154 envious** malign   **161 happy** lucky   **162 true shrift** Romeo's confession of the truth   **163 morrow** morning   **172 gentle . . . view** mild in appearance   **174 muffled still** always blindfolded

Should without eyes see pathways to his will!                              175
Where shall we dine? O me! What fray was here?
Yet tell me not, for I have heard it all.
Here's much to do with hate, but more with love.°
Why then, O brawling love, O loving hate,
O anything, of nothing first created!°                                     180
O heavy lightness, serious vanity,
Misshapen chaos of well-seeming forms,
Feather of lead, bright smoke, cold fire, sick health,
Still-waking sleep, that is not what it is!
This love feel I, that feel no love in this.                               185
Dost thou not laugh?
BENVOLIO                    No, coz,° I rather weep.
ROMEO
  Good heart, at what?
BENVOLIO                  At thy good heart's oppression.
ROMEO
  Why, such is love's transgression.
  Griefs of mine own lie heavy in my breast,
  Which thou wilt propagate, to have it prest°                             190
  With more of thine. This love that thou hast shown
  Doth add more grief to too much of mine own.
  Love is a smoke made with the fume of sighs;
  Being purged, a fire sparkling in lovers' eyes;
  Being vexed, a sea nourished with loving tears.                         195
  What is it else? A madness most discreet,°
  A choking gall, and a preserving sweet.
  Farewell, my coz.
BENVOLIO            Soft!° I will go along.
  And if° you leave me so, you do me wrong.
ROMEO
  Tut! I have lost myself; I am not here;                                 200
  This is not Romeo, he's some other where.
BENVOLIO
  Tell me in sadness,° who is that you love?
ROMEO
  What, shall I groan and tell thee?
BENVOLIO                    Groan? Why, no;
  But sadly° tell me who.
ROMEO
  Bid a sick man in sadness° make his will.                              205
  Ah, word ill urged to one that is so ill!
  In sadness, cousin, I do love a woman.
BENVOLIO
  I aimed so near when I supposed you loved.
ROMEO
  A right good markman. And she's fair I love.
BENVOLIO
  A right fair mark,° fair coz, is soonest hit.                           210
ROMEO
  Well, in that hit you miss. She'll not be hit
  With Cupid's arrow. She hath Dian's wit,°
  And, in strong proof° of chastity well armed,

From Love's weak childish bow she lives uncharmed.
She will not stay° the siege of loving terms,                             215
Nor bide° th' encounter of assailing eyes,
Nor ope her lap to saint-seducing gold.
O, she is rich in beauty; only poor
That, when she dies, with beauty dies her store.°
BENVOLIO
  Then she hath sworn that she will still° live chaste?                  220
ROMEO
  She hath, and in that sparing make huge waste;
  For beauty, starved with her severity,
  Cuts beauty off from all posterity.
  She is too fair, too wise, wisely too fair,
  To merit bliss° by making me despair.                                  225
  She hath forsworn to love, and in that vow
  Do I live dead that live to tell it now.
BENVOLIO
  Be ruled by me; forget to think of her.
ROMEO
  O, teach me how I should forget to think!
BENVOLIO
  By giving liberty unto thine eyes.                                     230
  Examine other beauties.
ROMEO                        'Tis the way
  To call hers, exquisite, in question° more.
  These happy masks that kiss fair ladies' brows,
  Being black puts us in mind they hide the fair.
  He that is strucken blind cannot forget                                235
  The precious treasure of his eyesight lost.
  Show me a mistress that is passing fair:
  What doth her beauty serve but as a note°
  Where I may read who passed that passing fair?
  Farewell. Thou canst not teach me to forget.                          240
BENVOLIO
  I'll pay that doctrine, or else die in debt.°      Exeunt.

[Scene II. A street.]

Enter CAPULET, County PARIS, and the clown [his
SERVANT].

CAPULET
  But Montague is bound° as well as I,
  In penalty alike; and 'tis not hard, I think,
  For men so old as we to keep the peace.
PARIS
  Of honorable reckoning° are you both,
  And pity 'tis you lived at odds so long.                                 5
  But now, my lord, what say you to my suit?
CAPULET
  But saying o'er what I have said before:
  My child is yet a stranger in the world,
  She hath not seen the change of fourteen years;
  Let two more summers wither in their pride                              10
  Ere we may think her ripe to be a bride.
PARIS
  Younger than she are happy mothers made.

**178 more with love** i.e., the combatants enjoyed their fighting
**180 O . . . created** Romeo here relates his own succession
of witty paradoxes to the dogma that God created everything
out of nothing  **186 coz** cousin (relative)  **190 Which . . .
prest** which griefs you will increase by burdening my breast
**196 discreet** discriminating  **198 Soft** hold on  **199 And if**
if  **202 in sadness** in all seriousness  **204 sadly** seriously
**205 in sadness** (1) in seriousness (2) in unhappiness at the prospect of death  **210 fair mark** target easily seen  **212 Dian's
wit** the cunning of Diana, huntress and goddess of chastity
**213 proof** tested power

**215 stay** submit to  **216 bide** abide (put up with)  **219 with
. . . store** she will leave no progeny to perpetuate her beauty
**220 still** always  **225 merit bliss** win heavenly bliss  **232
To . . . question** to keep bringing her beauty to mind  **238
note** written reminder  **241 I'll . . . debt** I will teach you
or else die trying
**I.ii.1 bound** under bond  **4 reckoning** reputation

CAPULET
And too soon marred are those so early made.
Earth hath swallowèd all my hopes° but she;
She is the hopeful lady of my earth.
But woo her, gentle Paris, get her heart;
My will to her consent is but a part.
And she agreed,° within her scope of choice°
Lies my consent and fair according° voice.
This night I hold an old accustomed° feast,                    20
Whereto I have invited many a guest,
Such as I love; and you among the store,
One more, most welcome, makes my number more.
At my poor house look to behold this night
Earth-treading stars° that make dark heaven light.             25
Such comfort as do lusty young men feel
When well-appareled April on the heel
Of limping winter treads, even such delight
Among fresh fennel° buds shall you this night
Inherit° at my house. Hear all, all see,                       30
And like her most whose merit most shall be;
Which, on more view of many, mine, being one,
May stand in number,° though in reck'ning none.°
Come, go with me.

[To SERVANT, giving him a paper.]

                 Go, sirrah,° trudge about
Through fair Verona; find those persons out            35
Whose names are written there, and to them say
My house and welcome on their pleasure stay.°
                    Exit [with PARIS].
SERVANT  Find them out whose names are written
here? It is written that the shoemaker should meddle
with his yard and the tailor with his last, the fisher with    40
his pencil and the painter with his nets;° but I am sent
to find those persons whose names are here writ, and
can never find° what names the writing person hath
here writ. I must to the learned. In good time!°

Enter BENVOLIO and ROMEO.

BENVOLIO
Tut, man, one fire burns out another's burning;              45
   One pain is less'ned by another's anguish;°
Turn giddy, and be holp by backward turning;°
   One desperate grief cures with another's languish.
Take thou some new infection to thy eye,
And the rank poison of the old will die.                     50
ROMEO
Your plantain leaf is excellent for that.
BENVOLIO
For what, I pray thee?
ROMEO             For your broken° shin.

BENVOLIO
Why, Romeo, art thou mad?
ROMEO
Not mad, but bound more than a madman is;
Shut up in prison, kept without my food,                     55
Whipped and tormented and—God-den,° good fellow.
SERVANT  God gi' go-den. I pray, sir, can you read?
ROMEO
Ay, mine own fortune in my misery.
SERVANT  Perhaps you have learned it without book.
But, I pray, can you read anything you see?                  60
ROMEO
Ay, if I know the letters and the language.°
SERVANT  Ye say honestly. Rest you merry.°
ROMEO  Stay, fellow; I can read.

He reads the letter.

"Signior Martino and his wife and daughters;
County Anselm and his beauteous sisters;                     65
The lady widow of Vitruvio;
Signior Placentio and his lovely nieces;
Mercutio and his brother Valentine;
Mine uncle Capulet, his wife and daughters;
My fair niece Rosaline; Livia;                               70
Signior Valentio and his cousin Tybalt;
Lucio and the lively Helena."
A fair assembly. Whither should they come?
SERVANT  Up.
ROMEO  Whither? To supper?                                   75
SERVANT  To our house.
ROMEO  Whose house?
SERVANT  My master's.
ROMEO
Indeed I should have asked you that before.
SERVANT  Now I'll tell you without asking. My          80
master is the great rich Capulet; and if you be not of
the house of Montagues, I pray come and crush a cup°
of wine. Rest you merry.             [Exit.]
BENVOLIO
At this same ancient° feast of Capulet's
Sups the fair Rosaline whom thou so loves;                   85
With all the admirèd beauties of Verona.
Go thither, and with unattainted° eye
Compare her face with some that I shall show,
And I will make thee think thy swan a crow.
ROMEO
When the devout religion of mine eye                         90
   Maintains such falsehood, then turn tears to fires;
And these, who often drowned, could never die,
   Transparent° heretics, be burnt for liars!
One fairer than my love? The all-seeing sun
Ne'er saw her match since first the world begun.             95
BENVOLIO
Tut! you saw her fair, none else being by,
Herself poised° with herself in either eye;
But in that crystal scales° let there be weighed
Your lady's love against some other maid

---

14 **hopes** children  18 **And she agreed** if she agrees; **within
. . . choice** among those she favors  19 **according** agreeing
20 **accustomed** established by custom  25 **Earth-treading
stars** young girls  29 **fennel** flowering herb  30 **Inherit** have
33 **stand in number** constitute one of the crowd; **in reck'-
ning none** not worth special consideration  34 **sirrah** a term
of familiar address  37 **stay** wait  39–41 **shoemaker . . .
nets** one should stick to what one knows how to do (but
the servant, being illiterate, reverses the proverbial expressions)
43 **find** understand  44 **In good time** i.e., here come some
learned ones  46 **another's anguish** the pain of another  47
**be . . . turning** be helped by turning in the opposite direction
52 **broken** scratched

56 **God-den** good evening (good afternoon)  61 **if . . .
language** if I already know what the writing says  62 **Rest
you merry** May God keep you merry  82 **crush a cup** have
a drink  84 **ancient** established by custom  87 **unattainted**
impartial  93 **Transparent** obvious  97 **poised** balanced  98
**crystal scales** Romeo's eyes

That I will show you shining at this feast,                                    100
And she shall scant° show well that now seems best.

ROMEO
I'll go along, no such sight to be shown,
But to rejoice in splendor of mine own.°        [*Exeunt.*]


[Scene III. *A room in Capulet's house.*]

*Enter Capulet's wife* [LADY CAPULET], *and* NURSE.

LADY CAPULET
Nurse, where's my daughter? Call her forth to me.

NURSE
Now, by my maidenhead at twelve year old,
I bade her come. What,° lamb! What, ladybird!
God forbid, where's this girl? What, Juliet!

*Enter* JULIET.

JULIET
How now? Who calls?

NURSE                    Your mother.

JULIET                                Madam, I am here. 5
What is your will?

LADY CAPULET
This is the matter.—Nurse, give leave awhile;
We must talk in secret. Nurse, come back again.
I have rememb'red me; thou's° hear our counsel.
Thou knowest my daughter's of a pretty age.        10

NURSE
Faith, I can tell her age unto an hour.

LADY CAPULET
She's not fourteen.

NURSE                I'll lay fourteen of my teeth—
And yet, to my teen° be it spoken, I have but four—
She's not fourteen. How long is it now
To Lammastide?°

LADY CAPULET   A fortnight and odd days.        15

NURSE
Even or odd, of all days in the year,
Come Lammas Eve at night shall she be fourteen.
Susan and she (God rest all Christian souls!)
Were of an age.° Well, Susan is with God;
She was too good for me. But, as I said,        20
On Lammas Eve at night shall she be fourteen;
That shall she, marry; I remember it well.
'Tis since the earthquake° now eleven years;
And she was weaned (I never shall forget it),
Of all the days of the year, upon that day;        25
For I had then laid wormwood to my dug,
Sitting in the sun under the dovehouse wall.
My lord and you were then at Mantua.
Nay, I do bear a brain.° But, as I said,
When it did taste the wormwood on the nipple        30
Of my dug and felt it bitter, pretty fool,
To see it tetchy° and fall out with the dug!
Shake, quoth the dovehouse!° 'Twas no need, I trow,°

To bid me trudge.
And since that time it is eleven years,        35
For then she could stand high-lone;° nay, by th'
   rood,°
She could have run and waddled all about;
For even the day before, she broke her brow;
And then my husband (God be with his soul!
'A° was a merry man) took up the child.        40
"Yea," quoth he, "dost thou fall upon thy face?
Thou wilt fall backward when thou hast more wit;
Wilt thou not, Jule?" and, by my holidam,°
The pretty wretch left crying and said, "Ay."
To see now how a jest shall come about!        45
I warrant, and I should live a thousand years,
I never should forget it. "Wilt thou not, Jule?" quoth
   he,
And, pretty fool, it stinted° and said, "Ay."

LADY CAPULET
Enough of this. I pray thee hold thy peace.

NURSE
Yes, madam. Yet I cannot choose but laugh        50
To think it should leave crying and say, "Ay."
And yet, I warrant, it had upon it° brow
A bump as big as a young cock'rel's stone;
A perilous knock; and it cried bitterly.
"Yea," quoth my husband, "fall'st upon thy face?        55
Thou wilt fall backward when thou comest to age,
Wilt thou not, Jule?" It stinted and said, "Ay."

JULIET
And stint thou too, I pray thee, nurse, say I.

NURSE
Peace, I have done. God mark thee to his grace!
Thou wast the prettiest babe that e'er I nursed.        60
And I might live to see thee married once,
I have my wish.

LADY CAPULET
Marry,° that "marry" is the very theme
I came to talk of. Tell me, daughter Juliet,
How stands your disposition to be married?        65

JULIET
It is an honor that I dream not of.

NURSE
An honor? Were not I thine only nurse,
I would say thou hadst sucked wisdom from thy teat.

LADY CAPULET
Well, think of marriage now. Younger than you,
Here in Verona, ladies of esteem,        70
Are made already mothers. By my count,
I was your mother much upon these years°
That you are now a maid. Thus then in brief:
The valiant Paris seeks you for his love.

NURSE
A man, young lady! Lady, such a man        75
As all the world.—Why, he's a man of wax.°

LADY CAPULET
Verona's summer hath not such a flower.

NURSE
Nay, he's a flower, in faith—a very flower.

---

101 **scant** scarcely   103 **splendor . . . own** my own lady's splendor
**I.iii.3 What** an impatient call   9 **thou's** thou shalt   13 **teen** sorrow   15 **Lammastide** August 1   19 **of an age** the same age   23 **earthquake** see Introduction, p. 481   29 **I . . . brain** my mind is still good   32 **tetchy** irritable   33 **Shake . . . dovehouse** the dovehouse (which the Nurse personifies) began to tremble; **trow** believe

36 **high-lone** alone; **rood** cross   40 **'A** he   43 **holidam** holy thing, relic   48 **stinted** stopped   52 **it** its   63 **Marry** indeed   72 **much . . . years** the same length of time   76 **man of wax** man of perfect figure

**LADY CAPULET**
What say you? Can you love the gentleman?
This night you shall behold him at our feast.    80
Read o'er the volume of young Paris' face,
And find delight writ there with beauty's pen;
Examine every married lineament,°
And see how one another lends content;°
And what obscured in this fair volume lies    85
Find written in the margent° of his eyes.
This precious book of love, this unbound° lover,
To beautify him only lacks a cover.°
The fish lives in the sea, and 'tis much pride
For fair without the fair within to hide.°    90
That book in many's eyes doth share the glory,
That in gold clasps locks in the golden story;
So shall you share all that he doth possess,
By having him making yourself no less.

**NURSE**
No less? Nay, bigger! Women grow by men.    95

**LADY CAPULET**
Speak briefly, can you like of° Paris' love?

**JULIET**
I'll look to like, if looking liking move;
But no more deep will I endart mine eye
Than your consent gives strength to make it fly.

*Enter* SERVINGMAN.

**SERVINGMAN** Madam, the guests are come, supper   100
served up, you called, my young lady asked for, the
nurse cursed° in the pantry, and everything in extremity. I must hence to wait.° I beseech you follow
straight.°                     [*Exit.*]

**LADY CAPULET**
We follow thee. Juliet, the county stays.°    105

**NURSE**
Go, girl, seek happy nights to happy days.    *Exeunt.*


[Scene IV. *A street.*]

*Enter* ROMEO, MERCUTIO, BENVOLIO, *with five or
six other* MASKERS; TORCHBEARERS.

**ROMEO**
What, shall this speech be spoke for our excuse?°
Or shall we on without apology?

**BENVOLIO**
The date is out of such prolixity.°
We'll have no Cupid hoodwinked° with a scarf,
Bearing a Tartar's painted bow of lath,    5
Scaring the ladies like a crowkeeper;°

Nor no without-book prologue,° faintly spoke
After the prompter, for our entrance;
But, let them measure° us by what they will,
We'll measure them a measure° and be gone.    10

**ROMEO**
Give me a torch. I am not for this ambling.
Being but heavy, I will bear the light.

**MERCUTIO**
Nay, gentle Romeo, we must have you dance.

**ROMEO**
Not I, believe me. You have dancing shoes
With nimble soles; I have a soul of lead    15
So stakes me to the ground I cannot move.

**MERCUTIO**
You are a lover. Borrow Cupid's wings
And soar with them above a common bound.°

**ROMEO**
I am too sore enpiercèd with his shaft
To soar with his light feathers; and so bound    20
I cannot bound a pitch° above dull woe.
Under love's heavy burden do I sink.

**MERCUTIO**
And, to sink in it, should you burden love—
Too great oppression for a tender thing.

**ROMEO**
Is love a tender thing? It is too rough,    25
Too rude, too boist'rous, and it pricks like thorn.

**MERCUTIO**
If love be rough with you, be rough with love;
Prick love for pricking,° and you beat love down.
Give me a case to put my visage in.
A visor for a visor! What care I    30
What curious eye doth quote deformities?°
Here are the beetle brows° shall blush° for me.

**BENVOLIO**
Come, knock and enter; and no sooner in
But every man betake him to his legs.°

**ROMEO**
A torch for me! Let wantons light of heart    35
Tickle the senseless rushes° with their heels;
For I am proverbed with a grandsire phrase,°
I'll be a candleholder° and look on;
The game was ne'er so fair, and I am done.°

**MERCUTIO**
Tut! Dun's the mouse, the constable's own
word!°                        40
If thou art Dun,° we'll draw thee from the mire

---

**83 married lineament** harmonious feature   **84 one . . .
content** all enhance one another   **86 margent** marginal
commentary   **87 unbound** (1) without cover (2) uncaught
**88 only . . . cover** only a wife is lacking   **89–90 The . . .
hide** The fair sea is made even fairer by hiding fair fish
within it   **96 like of** be favorable to   **101–02 the nurse cursed**
i.e., because she is not helping   **103 to wait** to serve   **104
straight** straightway   **105 the county stays** the count is
waiting
**I.iv.1 shall . . . excuse** shall we introduce ourselves with the
customary prepared speech   **3 date . . . prolixity** such
wordiness is out of fashion   **4 hoodwinked** blindfolded   **6
crowkeeper** boy set to scare crows away

**7 without-book prologue** memorized speech   **9 measure**
judge   **10 measure . . . measure** dance one dance with them
**18 bound** (1) leap (2) limit   **21 pitch** height (as in a falcon's
soaring)   **28 Prick . . . pricking** give love the spur in return
**29–31 Give . . . deformities** Give me a bag for my mask. A
mask for a mask. What do I care who notices my ugliness?
**32 beetle brows** bushy eyebrows (?); **blush** be red (i.e., be
grotesque)   **34 betake . . . legs** begin dancing   **36 rushes**
used for floor covering   **37 grandsire phrase** old saying   **38
candleholder** attendant   **39 The . . . done** I'll give up
dancing, now that I have enjoyed it as much as I ever shall
**40 Dun's . . . word** Mercutio puns on Romeo's last clause,
saying in effect "You are not done (i.e., *dun* = dark, by extension, silent) but the mouse is, and it's time to be quiet"
**41 Dun** a common name for a horse, used in an old game,
"Dun is in the mire," in which the players try to haul a heavy
log

Of this sir-reverence° love, wherein thou stickest
Upon to the ears. Come, we burn daylight,° ho!

ROMEO
Nay, that's not so.

MERCUTIO                    I mean, sir, in delay
We waste our lights° in vain, like lights by day.          45
Take our good meaning, for our judgment sits
Five times in that° ere once in our five wits.

ROMEO
And we mean well in going to this masque,
But 'tis no wit° to go.

MERCUTIO                    Why, may one ask?

ROMEO
I dreamt a dream tonight.°

MERCUTIO                    And so did I.          50

ROMEO
Well, what was yours?

MERCUTIO                    That dreamers often lie.

ROMEO
In bed asleep, while they do dream things true.

MERCUTIO
O, then I see Queen Mab° hath been with you.
She is the fairies' midwife, and she comes
In shape no bigger than an agate stone          55
On the forefinger of an alderman,
Drawn with a team of little atomies°
Over men's noses as they lie asleep;
Her wagon spokes made of long spinners'° legs,
The cover, of the wings of grasshoppers;          60
Her traces, of the smallest spider web;
Her collars, of the moonshine's wat'ry beams;
Her whip, of cricket's bone; the lash, of film;°
Her wagoner, a small gray-coated gnat,
Not half so big as a round little worm          65
Pricked from the lazy finger of a maid;°
Her chariot is an empty hazelnut,
Made by the joiner squirrel or old grub,°
Time out o' mind the fairies' coachmakers.
And in this state° she gallops night by night          70
Through lovers' brains, and then they dream of love;
On courtiers' knees, that dream on curtsies straight;
O'er lawyers' fingers, who straight dream on fees;
O'er ladies' lips, who straight on kisses dream,
Which oft the angry Mab with blisters plagues,          75
Because their breath with sweetmeats tainted are.
Sometime she gallops o'er a courtier's nose,
And then dreams he of smelling out a suit;°
And sometime comes she with a tithe pig's° tail
Tickling a parson's nose as 'a lies asleep,          80
Then he dreams of another benefice.°
Sometime she driveth o'er a soldier's neck,

And then dreams he of cutting foreign throats,
Of breaches, ambuscadoes, Spanish blades,
Of healths° five fathom deep; and then anon          85
Drums in his ear, at which he starts and wakes,
And being thus frighted, swears a prayer or two
And sleeps again. This is that very Mab
That plats the manes of horses in the night
And bakes the elflocks° in foul sluttish hairs,          90
Which once untangled much misfortune bodes.
This is the hag,° when maids lie on their backs,
That presses them and learns them first to bear,
Making them women of good carriage.°
This is she—

ROMEO                    Peace, peace, Mercutio, peace!          95
Thou talk'st of nothing.

MERCUTIO                    True, I talk of dreams;
Which are the children of an idle brain,
Begot of nothing but vain fantasy;°
Which is as thin of substance as the air,
And more inconstant than the wind, who woos          100
Even now the frozen bosom of the North
And, being angered, puffs away from thence,
Turning his side to the dewdropping South.

BENVOLIO
This wind you talk of blows us from ourselves.
Supper is done, and we shall come too late.          105

ROMEO
I fear, too early; for my mind misgives
Some consequence° yet hanging in the stars
Shall bitterly begin his fearful date°
With this night's revels and expire the term
Of a despisèd life, closed in my breast,          110
By some vile forfeit of untimely death.°
But he that hath the steerage of my course
Direct my sail! On, lusty gentlemen!

BENVOLIO    Strike, drum.
      *They march about the stage, and [retire to one side].*

[Scene V. *A hall in Capulet's house.*]

SERVINGMEN *come forth with napkins.°*

FIRST SERVINGMAN    Where's Potpan, that he helps
not to take away? He shift a trencher!° He scrape a
trencher!

SECOND SERVINGMAN    When good manners shall lie
all in one or two men's hands, and they unwashed too,          5
'tis a foul thing.

FIRST SERVINGMAN    Away with the join-stools,°
remove the court cupboard,° look to the plate. Good
thou, save me a piece of marchpane,° and, as thou

---

42 **sir-reverence** save your reverence (an apologetic expression, used to introduce indelicate expressions; here used humorously with the word "love")    43 **burn daylight** delay    45 **lights** (1) torches (2) mental faculties    47 **that** our good meaning    49 **'tis no wit** it shows no discretion    50 **tonight** last night    53 **Queen Mab** Fairy Queen (Celtic)    57 **atomies** tiny creatures    59 **spinners'** spiders'    63 **film** fine filament of some kind    65–66 **worm . . . maid** lazy maids were said to have worms breeding in their fingers    68 **joiner . . . grub** both woodworkers and adept at hollowing out nuts    70 **state** stately array    78 **suit** i.e., a petitioner, who may be induced to pay for the courtier's influence    79 **tithe pig's** tenth pig's (considered part of the parson's tithe)    81 **benefice** income, living

85 **healths** toasts    90 **elflocks** hair tangled by elves    92 **hag** nightmare or incubus    94 **carriage** (1) posture (2) capacity for carrying children    98 **fantasy** fancy    107 **consequence** future event    108 **date** duration (of the consequence or event)    109–11 **expire . . . death** the event is personified here as one who deliberately lends in expectation that the borrower will have to forfeit at great loss

**·I.v.s.d.** although for reference purposes this edition employs the conventional post-Elizabethan divisions into scenes, the reader is reminded that they are merely editorial; in the quarto this stage direction is part of the preceding one    2 **trencher** wooden plate    7 **join-stools** stools fitted together by a joiner    8 **court cupboard** sideboard, displaying plate    9 **marchpane** marzipan, a confection made of sugar and almonds

loves me, let the porter let in Susan Grindstone and    10
Nell. Anthony, and Potpan!

SECOND SERVINGMAN  Ay, boy, ready.

FIRST SERVINGMAN  You are looked for and called
for, asked for and sought for, in the great chamber.

THIRD SERVINGMAN  We cannot be here and there    15
too. Cheerly, boys! Be brisk awhile, and the longer
liver take all.                                    *Exeunt.*

*Enter* [CAPULET, LADY CAPULET, JULIET, TYBALT,
NURSE, *and*] *all the* GUESTS *and* GENTLEWOMEN *to
the* MASKERS.

CAPULET
Welcome, gentlemen! Ladies that have their toes
Unplagued with corns will walk a bout° with you.
Ah, my mistresses, which of you all                 20
Will now deny° to dance? She that makes dainty,°
She I'll swear hath corns. Am I come near ye now?
Welcome, gentlemen! I have seen the day
That I have worn a visor and could tell
A whispering tale in a fair lady's ear,             25
Such as would please. 'Tis gone, 'tis gone, 'tis gone.
You are welcome, gentlemen! Come, musicians, play.

*Music plays, and they dance.*

A hall,° a hall! Give room! And foot it, girls.
More light, you knaves, and turn the tables up,
And quench the fire; the room is grown too hot.     30
Ah, sirrah, this unlooked-for sport° comes well.
Nay, sit; nay, sit, good cousin Capulet;
For you and I are past our dancing days.
How long is't now since last yourself and I
Were in a mask?                                     35

SECOND CAPULET  By'r Lady, thirty years.

CAPULET
What, man? 'Tis not so much, 'tis not so much;
'Tis since the nuptial of Lucentio,
Come Pentecost as quickly as it will,
Some five-and-twenty years, and then we masked.

SECOND CAPULET
'Tis more, 'tis more. His son is elder, sir;        40
His son is thirty.

CAPULET              Will you tell me that?
His son was but a ward° two years ago.

ROMEO [*To a* SERVINGMAN.]
What lady's that which doth enrich the hand
Of yonder knight?

SERVINGMAN  I know not, sir.                         45

ROMEO
O, she doth teach the torches to burn bright!
It seems she hangs upon the cheek of night
As a rich jewel in an Ethiop's ear—
Beauty too rich for use, for earth too dear!
So shows a snowy dove trooping with crows           50
As yonder lady o'er her fellows shows.
The measure done, I'll watch her place of stand
And, touching hers, make blessèd my rude° hand.
Did my heart love till now? Forswear it, sight!
For I ne'er saw true beauty till this night.        55

TYBALT
This, by his voice, should be a Montague.
Fetch me my rapier, boy. What! Dares the slave
Come hither, covered with an antic face,°
To fleer° and scorn at our solemnity?
Now, by the stock and honor of my kin,              60
To strike him dead I hold it not a sin.

CAPULET
Why, how now, kinsman? Wherefore storm you so?

TYBALT
Uncle, this is a Montague, our foe,
A villain, that is hither come in spite°
To scorn at our solemnity this night.               65

CAPULET
Young Romeo is it?

TYBALT                'Tis he, that villain Romeo.

CAPULET
Content thee, gentle coz, let him alone.
'A bears him like a portly° gentleman,
And, to say truth, Verona brags of him
To be a virtuous and well-governed youth.           70
I would not for the wealth of all this town
Here in my house do him disparagement.
Therefore be patient; take no note of him.
It is my will, the which if thou respect,
Show a fair presence and put off these frowns,      75
An ill-beseeming semblance for a feast.

TYBALT
It fits when such a villain is a guest.
I'll not endure him.

CAPULET              He shall be endured.
What, goodman° boy! I say he shall. Go to!°
Am I the master here, or you? Go to!                80
You'll not endure him, God shall mend my soul!°
You'll make a mutiny° among my guests!
You will set cock-a-hoop.° You'll be the man!

TYBALT
Why, uncle, 'tis a shame.

CAPULET              Go to, go to!
You are a saucy boy. Is't so, indeed?               85
This trick may chance to scathe° you. I know what.
You must contrary me! Marry, 'tis time—
Well said, my hearts!—You are a princox°—go!
Be quiet, or—More light, more light!—For shame!
I'll make you quiet. What!—Cheerly, my hearts!      90

TYBALT
Patience perforce° with willful choler° meeting
Makes my flesh tremble in their different greeting.
I will withdraw; but this intrusion shall,
Now seeming sweet, convert to bitt'rest gall.    *Exit.*

ROMEO
If° I profane with my unworthiest hand              95
  This holy shrine,° the gentle sin is this:°

---

19 **walk a bout** dance a turn   21 **deny** refuse; **makes dainty**
seems to hesitate   28 **A hall** clear the floor   31 **unlooked-for
sport** they had not expected maskers   42 **ward** minor   53
**rude** rough

58 **antic face** fantastic mask   59 **fleer** jeer   64 **in spite**
insultingly   68 **portly** of good deportment   79 **goodman** a
term applied to someone below the rank of gentleman; **Go
to** impatient exclamation   81 **God . . . soul** roughly
equivalent to our "Indeed"   82 **mutiny** disturbance   83 **set
cock-a-hoop** be cock of the walk   86 **scathe** hurt, harm
88 **princox** impertinent youngster   91 **Patience perforce**
enforced self-control; **choler** anger   95 **If** here begins an
English, or Shakespearean, sonnet   96 **shrine** i.e., Juliet's hand;
**gentle . . . this** this is the sin of well-bred people

My lips, two blushing pilgrims, ready stand
    To smooth that rough touch with a tender kiss.
JULIET
Good pilgrim, you do wrong your hand too much,
    Which mannerly devotion shows in this;                                      100
For saints have hands that pilgrims' hands do touch,
    And palm to palm is holy palmers'° kiss.
ROMEO
Have not saints lips, and holy palmers too?
JULIET
Ay, pilgrim, lips that they must use in prayer.
ROMEO
O, then, dear saint, let lips do what hands do!                                  105
They pray; grant thou, lest faith turn to despair.
JULIET
Saints do not move,° though grant for prayers' sake.
ROMEO
Then move not while my prayer's effect I take.
Thus from my lips, by thine my sin is purged.

[Kisses her.]

JULIET
Then have my lips the sin that they have took.                                   110
ROMEO
Sin from my lips? O trespass sweetly urged!
Give me my sin again.    [Kisses her.]
JULIET                                    You kiss by th' book.°
NURSE
Madam, your mother craves a word with you.
ROMEO
What is her mother?
NURSE                          Marry, bachelor,
Her mother is the lady of the house,                                             115
And a good lady, and a wise and virtuous.
I nursed her daughter that you talked withal.°
I tell you, he that can lay hold of her
Shall have the chinks.°
ROMEO                          Is she a Capulet?
O dear account! My life is my foe's debt.°                                       120
BENVOLIO
Away, be gone; the sport is at the best.
ROMEO
Ay, so I fear; the more is my unrest.
CAPULET
Nay, gentlemen, prepare not to be gone;
We have a trifling foolish banquet towards.°
Is it e'en so?° Why then, I thank you all.                                       125
I thank you, honest gentlemen. Good night.
More torches here! Come on then; let's to bed.
Ah, sirrah, by my fay,° it waxes late;
I'll to my rest.    [Exeunt all but JULIET and NURSE.]
JULIET
Come hither, nurse. What is yond gentleman?                                      130
NURSE
The son and heir of old Tiberio.

JULIET
What's he that now is going out of door?
NURSE
Marry, that, I think, be young Petruchio.
JULIET
What's he that follows here, that would not dance?
NURSE  I know not.                                                               135
JULIET
Go ask his name.—If he is marrièd,
My grave is like to be my wedding bed.
NURSE
His name is Romeo, and a Montague,
The only son of your great enemy.
JULIET
My only love, sprung from my only hate!                                          140
Too early seen unknown, and known too late!
Prodigious° birth of love it is to me
That I must love a loathèd enemy.
NURSE
What's this? What's this?
JULIET                                    A rhyme I learnt even now
Of one I danced withal.                                                          145

One calls within, "Juliet."

NURSE                                    Anon,° anon!
Come, let's away; the strangers all are gone.    Exeunt.


# [ACT II]

# [PROLOGUE]

[Enter] CHORUS.

CHORUS
Now old desire doth in his deathbed lie,
    And young affection gapes° to be his heir;
That fair° for which love groaned for and would die,
    With tender Juliet matched, is now not fair.
Now Romeo is beloved and loves again,                                            5
    Alike bewitchèd° by the charm of looks;
But to his foe supposed he must complain,°
    And she steal love's sweet bait from fearful hooks.
Being held a foe, he may not have access
    To breathe such vows as lovers use to° swear,                             10
And she as much in love, her means much less
    To meet her new belovèd anywhere;
But passion lends them power, time means, to meet,
    Temp'ring extremities with extreme sweet.°    [Exit.]

---

102 palmers' religious pilgrims' (the term originally signified one who carried a palm branch; here it is used as a pun meaning one who holds another's hand)  107 do not move (1) do not initiate action (2) stand still  112 You . . . book You take my words literally to get more kisses  117 withal with  119 the chinks plenty of money  120 My life . . . debt My foe now owns my life  124 towards in preparation  125 Is . . . so the maskers insist on leaving  128 fay faith

142 Prodigious (1) monstrous (2) of evil portent  146 Anon at once
II.Pro.2 young affection gapes the new love is eager  3 That fair Rosaline  6 Alike bewitchèd both are bewitched  7 complain address his lover's suit  10 use to customarily  14 Temp'ring . . . sweet softening difficulties with extraordinary delights

[Scene I. *Near Capulet's orchard.*]

*Enter* ROMEO *alone.*

ROMEO
Can I go forward when my heart is here?
Turn back, dull earth, and find thy center out.°

*Enter* BENVOLIO *with* MERCUTIO. [ROMEO *retires.*]

BENVOLIO
Romeo! My cousin Romeo! Romeo!
MERCUTIO                  He is wise
And, on my life, hath stol'n him home to bed.
BENVOLIO
He ran this way and leapt this orchard wall.      5
Call, good Mercutio.
MERCUTIO           Nay, I'll conjure too.
Romeo! Humors! Madman! Passion! Lover!
Appear thou in the likeness of a sigh;
Speak but one rhyme, and I am satisfied!
Cry but "Ay me!" pronounce but "love" and "dove";    10
Speak to my gossip° Venus one fair word,
One nickname for her purblind° son and heir,
Young Abraham Cupid,° he that shot so true
When King Cophetua loved the beggar maid!°
He heareth not, he stirreth not, he moveth not;      15
The ape is dead,° and I must conjure him.
I conjure thee by Rosaline's bright eyes,
By her high forehead and her scarlet lip,
By her fine foot, straight leg, and quivering thigh,
And the demesnes° that there adjacent lie,      20
That in thy likeness thou appear to us!
BENVOLIO
And if° he hear thee, thou wilt anger him.
MERCUTIO
This cannot anger him. 'Twould anger him
To raise a spirit in his mistress' circle°
Of some strange nature, letting it there stand      25
Till she had laid it and conjured it down.
That were some spite;° my invocation
Is fair and honest:° in his mistress' name,
I conjure only but to raise up him.
BENVOLIO
Come, he hath hid himself among these trees      30
To be consorted° with the humorous° night.
Blind is his love and best befits the dark.
MERCUTIO
If love be blind, love cannot hit the mark.
Now will he sit under a medlar tree
And wish his mistress were that kind of fruit      35
As maids call medlars° when they laugh alone.

O, Romeo, that she were, O that she were
An open et cetera, thou a pop'rin pear!
Romeo, good night. I'll to my truckle bed;°
This field bed is too cold for me to sleep.      40
Come, shall we go?
BENVOLIO           Go then, for 'tis in vain
To seek him here that means not to be found.
                 *Exit* [*with others*].

[Scene II. *Capulet's orchard.*]

ROMEO [*Coming forward.*]
He jests at scars that never felt a wound.

[*Enter* JULIET *at a window.*]

But soft! What light through yonder window breaks?
It is the East, and Juliet is the sun!
Arise, fair sun, and kill the envious moon,
Who is already sick and pale with grief
That thou her maid° art far more fair than she.      5
Be not her maid, since she is envious.
Her vestal livery° is but sick and green,°
And none but fools do wear it. Cast it off.
It is my lady! O, it is my love!
O, that she knew she were!      10
She speaks, yet she says nothing. What of that?
Her eye discourses; I will answer it.
I am too bold; 'tis not to me she speaks.
Two of the fairest stars in all the heaven,      15
Having some business, do entreat her eyes
To twinkle in their spheres° till they return.
What if her eyes were there, they in her head?
The brightness of her cheek would shame those stars
As daylight doth a lamp; her eyes in heaven      20
Would through the airy region stream so bright
That birds would sing and think it were not night.
See how she leans her cheek upon her hand!
O, that I were a glove upon that hand,
That I might touch that cheek!
JULIET              Ay me!
ROMEO                 She speaks.      25
O, speak again, bright angel, for thou art
As glorious to this night, being o'er my head,
As is a wingèd messenger of heaven
Unto the white-upturnèd wond'ring eyes
Of mortals that fall back to gaze on him      30
When he bestrides the lazy puffing clouds
And sails upon the bosom of the air.
JULIET
O Romeo, Romeo! Wherefore art thou Romeo?
Deny thy father and refuse thy name;
Or, if thou wilt not, be but sworn my love,      35
And I'll no longer be a Capulet.
ROMEO [*Aside.*]
Shall I hear more, or shall I speak at this?

**II.i.1–2 Can . . . out** Romeo refuses to pass Capulet's house, commanding his body, or "earth" to stop and join its proper soul, or "center" (i.e., Juliet)   **11 gossip** crony   **12 purblind** quite blind   **13 Abraham Cupid** the phrase may mean "ancient youth" or, since *abram man* was slang for *trickster,* "rascally Cupid"   **14 King . . . maid** reference to an old familiar ballad   **16 ape is dead** Romeo plays dead, like a performing ape   **20 demesnes** domains   **22 And if** if   **24 circle** conjurers worked within a magic circle, but there is also a bawdy innuendo, as in "stand," "laid," "down," and "raise" in lines 25–29   **27 spite** vexation   **28 fair and honest** respectable   **31 consorted** associated; **humorous** (1) damp (2) moody   **36 medlars** applelike fruit, eaten when decayed (like "pop'rin" in line 38, the word was often used to refer to sexual organs)

**39 I'll . . . bed** I'll go to my trunkle bed, or baby bed (i.e., I'm innocent in affairs of this kind)
**II.ii.6 her maid** the moon is here thought of as Diana, goddess and patroness of virgins   **8 vestal livery** virginity; **sick and green** sickly, bearing the characteristics of greensickness, the virgin's malady   **17 spheres** orbits

JULIET
'Tis but thy name that is my enemy.
Thou art thyself, though not° a Montague.
What's Montague? It is nor hand, nor foot,          40
Nor arm, nor face. O, be some other name
Belonging to a man.
What's in a name? That which we call a rose
By any other word would smell as sweet.
So Romeo would, were he not Romeo called,          45
Retain that dear perfection which he owes°
Without that title. Romeo, doff thy name;
And for thy name, which is no part of thee,
Take all myself.
ROMEO              I take thee at thy word.
Call me but love, and I'll be new baptized;          50
Henceforth I never will be Romeo.
JULIET
What man art thou, that, thus bescreened in night,
So stumblest on my counsel?
ROMEO                          By a name
I know not how to tell thee who I am.
My name, dear saint, is hateful to myself          55
Because it is an enemy to thee.
Had I it written, I would tear the word.
JULIET
My ears have yet not drunk a hundred words
Of thy tongue's uttering, yet I know the sound.
Art thou not Romeo, and a Montague?          60
ROMEO
Neither, fair maid, if either thee dislike.°
JULIET
How camest thou hither, tell me, and wherefore?
The orchard walls are high and hard to climb,
And the place death, considering who thou art,
If any of my kinsmen find thee here.          65
ROMEO
With love's light wings did I o'erperch° these walls;
For stony limits cannot hold love out,
And what love can do, that dares love attempt.
Therefore thy kinsmen are no stop to me.
JULIET
If they do see thee, they will murder thee.          70
ROMEO
Alack, there lies more peril in thine eye
Than twenty of their swords! Look thou but sweet,
And I am proof° against their enmity.
JULIET
I would not for the world they saw thee here.
ROMEO
I have night's cloak to hide me from their eyes;          75
And but° thou love me, let them find me here.
My life were better ended by their hate
Than death proroguèd,° wanting of thy love.
JULIET
By whose direction found'st thou out this place?
ROMEO
By Love, that first did prompt me to inquire.          80
He lent me counsel, and I lent him eyes.
I am no pilot; yet, wert thou as far

As that vast shore washed with the farthest sea,
I should adventure° for such merchandise.
JULIET
Thou knowest the mask of night is on my face;          85
Else would a maiden blush bepaint my cheek
For that which thou hast heard me speak tonight.
Fain would I dwell on form—fain, fain deny
What I have spoke; but farewell compliment!°
Dost thou love me? I know thou wilt say "Ay";          90
And I will take thy word. Yet, if thou swear'st,
Thou mayst prove false. At lovers' perjuries,
They say Jove laughs. O gentle Romeo,
If thou dost love, pronounce it faithfully.
Or if thou thinkest I am too quickly won,          95
I'll frown and be perverse and say thee nay,
So thou wilt woo; but else, not for the world.
In truth, fair Montague, I am too fond,°
And therefore thou mayst think my havior° light;
But trust me, gentleman, I'll prove more true          100
Than those that have more cunning to be strange.°
I should have been more strange, I must confess,
But that thou overheard'st, ere I was ware,
My truelove passion. Therefore pardon me,
And not impute this yielding to light love,          105
Which the dark night hath so discoverèd.°
ROMEO
Lady, by yonder blessèd moon I vow,
That tips with silver all these fruit-tree tops—
JULIET
O, swear not by the moon, th' inconstant moon,
That monthly changes in her circle orb,          110
Lest that thy love prove likewise variable.
ROMEO
What shall I swear by?
JULIET                          Do not swear at all;
Or if thou wilt, swear by thy gracious self,
Which is the god of my idolatry,
And I'll believe thee.
ROMEO                          If my heart's dear love—          115
JULIET
Well, do not swear. Although I joy in thee,
I have no joy of this contract tonight.
It is too rash, too unadvised, too sudden;
Too like the lightning, which doth cease to be
Ere one can say it lightens. Sweet, good night!          120
This bud of love, by summer's ripening breath,
May prove a beauteous flow'r when next we meet.
Good night, good night! As sweet repose and rest
Come to thy heart as that within my breast!
ROMEO
O, wilt thou leave me so unsatisfied?          125
JULIET
What satisfaction canst thou have tonight?
ROMEO
Th' exchange of thy love's faithful vow for mine.
JULIET
I gave thee mine before thou didst request it;
And yet I would it were to give again.
ROMEO
Wouldst thou withdraw it? For what purpose, love?          130

___

**39 though not** even if you were not  **46 owes** owns  **61
dislike** displeases  **66 o'erperch** fly over  **73 proof** protected
**76 but** if only  **78 proroguèd** deferred

**84 adventure** risk the journey  **89 compliment** formal
courtesy  **98 fond** (1) affectionate (2) foolishly tender  **99
havior** behavior  **101 strange** aloof  **106 discoverèd** revealed

JULIET
But to be frank° and give it thee again.
And yet I wish but for the thing I have.
My bounty° is as boundless as the sea,
My love as deep; the more I give to thee,
The more I have, for both are infinite.          135
I hear some noise within. Dear love, adieu!

[NURSE *calls within.*]

Anon, good nurse! Sweet Montague, be true.
Stay but a little, I will come again.          [*Exit.*]
ROMEO
O blessèd, blessèd night! I am afeard,
Being in night, all this is but a dream,          140
Too flattering-sweet to be substantial.

[*Enter* JULIET *again.*]

JULIET
Three words, dear Romeo, and good night indeed.
If that thy bent° of love be honorable,
Thy purpose marriage, send me word tomorrow,
By one that I'll procure to come to thee,          145
Where and what time thou wilt perform the rite;
And all my fortunes at thy foot I'll lay
And follow thee my lord throughout the world.
[NURSE *Within.*]     Madam!
JULIET
I come anon.—But if thou meanest not well,          150
I do beseech thee—
[NURSE *Within.*]
Madam!
JULIET     By and by° I come.—
To cease thy strife° and leave me to my grief.
Tomorrow will I send.
ROMEO                    So thrive my soul—
JULIET
A thousand times good night!          [*Exit.*] 155
ROMEO
A thousand times the worse, to want thy light!
Love goes toward love as schoolboys from their
     books;
But love from love, toward school with heavy looks.

*Enter* JULIET *again.*

JULIET
Hist! Romeo, hist! O for a falc'ner's voice
To lure this tassel gentle° back again!          160
Bondage is hoarse° and may not speak aloud,
Else would I tear the cave where Echo lies
And make her airy tongue more hoarse than mine
With repetition of "My Romeo!"
ROMEO
It is my soul that calls upon my name.          165
How silver-sweet sound lovers' tongues by night,
Like softest music to attending° ears!
JULIET
Romeo!
ROMEO     My sweet?

JULIET                    What o'clock tomorrow
Shall I send to thee?
ROMEO                    By the hour of nine.
JULIET
I will not fail. 'Tis twenty years till then.          170
I have forgot why I did call thee back.
ROMEO
Let me stand here till thou remember it.
JULIET
I shall forget, to have thee still stand there,
Rememb'ring how I love thy company.
ROMEO
And I'll still stay, to have thee still forget,          175
Forgetting any other home but this.
JULIET
'Tis almost morning. I would have thee gone—
And yet no farther than a wanton's° bird,
That lets it hop a little from his hand,
Like a poor prisoner in his twisted gyves,°          180
And with a silken thread plucks it back again,
So loving-jealous of his liberty.
ROMEO
I would I were thy bird.
JULIET                    Sweet, so would I.
Yet I should kill thee with much cherishing.
Good night, good night! Parting is such sweet sorrow          185
That I shall say good night till it be morrow.° [*Exit.*]
ROMEO
Sleep dwell upon thine eyes, peace in thy breast!
Would I were sleep and peace, so sweet to rest!°
Hence will I to my ghostly friar's° close cell,
His help to crave and my dear hap° to tell.          *Exit.* 190

[Scene III. *Friar Lawrence's cell.*]

*Enter* FRIAR [*Lawrence*] *alone, with a basket.*

FRIAR
The gray-eyed morn smiles on the frowning night,
Check'ring the eastern clouds with streaks of light;
And fleckèd° darkness like a drunkard reels
From forth day's path and Titan's burning wheels.°
Now, ere the sun advance his burning eye          5
The day to cheer and night's dank dew to dry,
I must upfill this osier cage° of ours
With baleful° weeds and precious-juicèd flowers.
The earth that's Nature's mother is her tomb.
What is her burying grave, that is her womb;          10
And from her womb children of divers kind
We sucking on her natural bosom find,
Many for many virtues excellent,
None but for some, and yet all different.

178 **wanton's** capricious child's 180 **gyves** fetters 186
**morrow** morning 188 **rest** the four lines that follow in the
quarto are here deleted because they are virtually identical
with the first four lines of the next scene (see A Note on the
Text, p. 486); apparently Shakespeare wrote them and then
decided to use them at the start of the next scene but forgot to
delete their first occurrence 189 **ghostly friar's** spiritual
father's (i.e., confessor's) 190 **dear hap** good fortune
II.iii.3 **fleckèd** spotted 4 **Titan's burning wheels** wheels of
the sun's chariot 7 **osier cage** willow basket 8 **baleful** (1)
evil (2) poisonous

131 **frank** generous 133 **bounty** capacity for giving 143
**bent** aim 152 **By and by** at once 153 **strife** efforts 160
**tassel gentle** tercel gentle, male falcon 161 **Bondage is
hoarse** being surrounded by "protectors," I cannot cry loudly
167 **attending** attentive

O, mickle° is the powerful grace that lies                    15
In plants, herbs, stones, and their true qualities;
For naught so vile that on the earth doth live
But to the earth some special good doth give;
Nor aught so good but, strained° from that fair use,
Revolts from true birth,° stumbling on abuse.                 20
Virtue itself turns vice, being misapplied,
And vice sometime by action dignified.°

*Enter* ROMEO.°

Within the infant rind° of this weak flower
Poison hath residence and medicine° power;
For this, being smelt, with that part cheers each part;°  25
Being tasted, stays all senses with the heart.
Two such opposèd kings encamp them still°
In man as well as herbs—grace and rude will;
And where the worser is predominant,
Full soon the canker° death eats up that plant.             30

ROMEO
Good morrow, father.

FRIAR                    Benedicite!°
What early tongue so sweet saluteth me?
Young son, it argues a distemperèd head°
So soon to bid good morrow to thy bed.
Care keeps his watch in every old man's eye,               35
And where care lodges, sleep will never lie;
But where unbruisèd youth with unstuffed° brain
Doth couch his limbs, there golden sleep doth reign.
Therefore thy earliness doth me assure
Thou art uproused with some distemp'rature;                40
Or if not so, then here I hit it right—
Our Romeo hath not been in bed tonight.

ROMEO
That last is true. The sweeter rest was mine.

FRIAR
God pardon sin! Wast thou with Rosaline?

ROMEO
With Rosaline, my ghostly father? No.                      45
I have forgot that name and that name's woe.

FRIAR
That's my good son! But where hast thou been then?

ROMEO
I'll tell thee ere thou ask it me again.
I have been feasting with mine enemy,
Where on a sudden one hath wounded me                      50
That's by me wounded. Both our remedies
Within thy help and holy physic° lies.
I bear no hatred, blessèd man, for, lo,
My intercession° likewise steads° my foe.

FRIAR
Be plain, good son, and homely in thy drift.°              55
Riddling confession finds but riddling shrift.°

**15 mickle** much   **19 strained** diverted   **20 Revolts . . . birth** falls away from its real purpose   **22 dignified** made worthy   **22 s.d. *Enter* Romeo** the entry of Romeo at this point, unseen by the Friar, emphasizes the appropriateness of the remaining eight lines of the Friar's speech, not only to the flower but to Romeo   **23 infant rind** tender bark, skin   **24 medicine** medicinal   **25 For . . . part** being smelled, this flower stimulates every part of the body   **27 still** always   **30 canker** cankerworm, larva that feeds on leaves   **31 Benedicite** Bless you!   **33 distemperèd head** troubled mind   **37 unstuffed** untroubled   **52 physic** medicine   **54 intercession** entreaty; **steads** helps   **55 homely . . . drift** plain in your talk   **56 shrift** absolution

ROMEO
Then plainly know my heart's dear love is set
On the fair daughter of rich Capulet;
As mine on hers, so hers is set on mine,
And all combined,° save what thou must combine            60
By holy marriage. When and where and how
We met, we wooed, and made exchange of vow,
I'll tell thee as we pass; but this I pray,
That thou consent to marry us today.

FRIAR
Holy Saint Francis! What a change is here!                65
Is Rosaline, that thou didst love so dear,
So soon forsaken? Young men's love then lies
Not truly in their hearts, but in their eyes.
Jesu Maria! What a deal of brine
Hath washed thy sallow cheeks for Rosaline!               70
How much salt water thrown away in waste
To season° love, that of it doth not taste!
The sun not yet thy signs from heaven clears,
Thy old groans ring yet in mine ancient ears.
Lo, here upon thy cheek the stain doth sit                75
Of an old tear that is not washed off yet.
If e'er thou wast thyself, and these woes thine,
Thou and these woes were all for Rosaline.
And art thou changed? Pronounce this sentence then:
Women may fall° when there's no strength° in men.         80

ROMEO
Thou chid'st me oft for loving Rosaline.

FRIAR
For doting, not for loving, pupil mine.

ROMEO
And bad'st me bury love.

FRIAR                        Not in a grave
To lay one in, another out to have.

ROMEO
I pray thee chide me not. Her I love now                  85
Doth grace° for grace and love for love allow.
The other did not so.

FRIAR                    O, she knew well
Thy love did read by rote, that could not spell.°
But come, young waverer, come go with me.
In one respect° I'll thy assistant be;                    90
For this alliance may so happy prove
To turn your households' rancor to pure love.

ROMEO
O, let us hence! I stand on° sudden haste.

FRIAR
Wisely and slow. They stumble that run fast. *Exeunt.*

[Scene IV. *A street.*]

*Enter* BENVOLIO *and* MERCUTIO.

MERCUTIO
Where the devil should this Romeo be?
Came he not home tonight?

BENVOLIO
Not to his father's. I spoke with his man.

**60 combined** (1) brought into unity (2) settled   **72 season** (1) preserve (2) flavor   **80 may fall** may be expected to be fickle; **strength** constancy   **86 grace** favor   **88 did . . . spell** said words without understanding them   **90 In one respect** with respect to one particular   **93 stand on** insist on

MERCUTIO
Why, that same pale hardhearted wench, that Rosaline,
Torments him so that he will sure run mad.                                5

BENVOLIO
Tybalt, the kinsman to old Capulet,
Hath sent a letter to his father's house.

MERCUTIO    A challenge, on my life.

BENVOLIO    Romeo will answer it.

MERCUTIO    Any man that can write may answer a    10
letter.

BENVOLIO    Nay, he will answer the letter's master,
how he dares, being dared.

MERCUTIO    Alas, poor Romeo, he is already dead:
stabbed with a white wench's black eye; run through    15
the ear with a love song; the very pin° of his heart cleft
with the blind bow-boy's butt-shaft;° and is he a man
to encounter Tybalt?

BENVOLIO    Why, what is Tybalt?

MERCUTIO    More than Prince of Cats.° O, he's the    20
courageous captain of compliments.° He fights as you
sing pricksong°—keeps time, distance, and proportion;
he rests his minim rests,° one, two, and the third in
your bosom! The very butcher of a silk button,° a
duelist, a duelist! A gentleman of the very first house,°    25
of the first and second cause.° Ah, the immortal
passado!° The punto reverso!° The hay!°

BENVOLIO    The what?

MERCUTIO    The pox of such antic, lisping, affecting
fantasticoes°—these new tuners of accent! "By Jesu,    30
a very good blade! A very tall° man! A very good
whore!" Why, is not this a lamentable thing, grandsir,
that we should be thus afflicted with these strange flies,
these fashionmongers, these pardon-me's,° who stand
so much on the new form° that they cannot sit at ease    35
on the old bench? O, their bones,° their bones!

*Enter* ROMEO.

BENVOLIO    Here comes Romeo! Here comes Romeo!

MERCUTIO    Without his roe,° like a dried herring. O
flesh, flesh, how art thou fishified! Now is he for the
numbers° that Petrarch flowed in. Laura,° to his    40
lady, was a kitchen wench (marry, she had a better
love to berhyme her), Dido° a dowdy,° Cleopatra a
gypsy,° Helen and Hero° hildings° and harlots, Thisbe°

a gray eye° or so, but not to the purpose. Signior
Romeo, bonjour! There's a French salutation to your
French slop.° You gave us the counterfeit fairly last
night.                                                            45

ROMEO    Good morrow to you both. What counterfeit
did I give you?

MERCUTIO    The slip,° sir, the slip. Can you not con-    50
ceive?

ROMEO    Pardon, good Mercutio. My business was
great, and in such a case as mine a man may strain
courtesy.

MERCUTIO    That's as much as to say, such a case° as    55
yours constrains a man to bow in the hams.

ROMEO    Meaning, to curtsy.

MERCUTIO    Thou hast most kindly hit° it.

ROMEO    A most courteous exposition.

MERCUTIO    Nay, I am the very pink° of courtesy.    60

ROMEO    Pink for flower.

MERCUTIO    Right.

ROMEO    Why, then is my pump° well-flowered.°

MERCUTIO    Sure wit, follow me this jest now till thou
hast worn out thy pump, that, when the single sole    65
of it is worn, the jest may remain, after the wearing,
solely singular.°

ROMEO    O single-soled jest, solely singular for the
singleness!

MERCUTIO    Come between us, good Benvolio! My    70
wits faint.

ROMEO    Swits° and spurs, swits and spurs; or I'll cry
a match.°

MERCUTIO    Nay, if our wits run the wild-goose
chase,° I am done; for thou hast more of the wild    75
goose in one of thy wits than, I am sure, I have in my
whole five. Was I with you there for the goose?°

ROMEO    Thou wast never with me for anything when
thou wast not there for the goose.°

MERCUTIO    I will bite thee by the ear for that jest.    80

ROMEO    Nay, good goose, bite not!°

MERCUTIO    Thy wit is a very bitter sweeting;° it is a
most sharp sauce.

ROMEO    And is it not, then, well served in to a sweet
goose?°                                                          85

MERCUTIO    O, here's a wit of cheveril,° that stretches
from an inch narrow to an ell broad!°

ROMEO    I stretch it out for that word "broad," which,
added to the goose, proves thee far and wide a broad°
goose.                                                          90

MERCUTIO    Why, is not this better now than groaning

---

**II.iv.16 pin** center (of a target)    **17 blind bow-boy's butt-
shaft** Cupid's blunt arrow    **20 Prince of Cats** Tybalt's name,
or some variant of it, was given to the cat in medieval stories of
Reynard the Fox    **21 compliments** formal courtesies    **22
sing pricksong** (1) sing from a text (2) sing with attention to
accuracy    **23 he . . . rests** he scrupulously observes every
formality (literally, "he observes even the shortest rests in the
notation")    **24 button** on his opponent's shirt    **25 first
house** first rank    **26 first . . . cause** dueling terms, meaning
formal grounds for taking offense and giving a challenge
**27 passado** lunge;    **punto reverso** backhanded stroke;    **hay**
home thrust (Italian *hai*)    **30 fantasticoes** fops    **31 tall** brave
**34 pardon-me's** persons who affect foreign phrases (cf.
Italian *perdona mi*)    **35 form** (1) fashion (2) bench    **36 bones**
pun on French *bon*    **38 Without his roe** (1) emaciated like a
fish that has spawned or (2) stripped of "Ro," leaving only
"me-o" (a sigh)    **40 numbers** verses;    **Laura** Petrarch's
beloved    **42 Dido** Queen of Carthage, enamored of Aeneas;
**dowdy** a drab woman    **43 gypsy** a deceitful woman (gypsies
were commonly believed to be Egyptians);    **Helen and Hero**
beloved respectively of Paris and Leander;    **hildings** good-for-
nothings;    **Thisbe** beloved of Pyramus in a story analogous
to that of Romeo and Juliet

**44 gray eye** gleam in the eye    **46 slop** loose breeches    **50 slip**
(1) escape (2) counterfeit coin    **55 case** (1) situation (2) physical
condition    **58 most kindly hit** most politely interpreted    **60
pink** perfection; but Romeo proceeds to exploit two other
meanings: (1) flower (2) punches in an ornamental design    **63
pump** shoe;    **well-flowered** ornamented with pinking (with
pun on *floored*)    **67 solely singular** (1) single-soled (i.e., weak)
(2) uniquely remarkable (literally, "uniquely unique")    **72 Swits**
switches    **72–73 cry a match** claim a victory    **74–75 wild-goose
chase** cross-country game of "follow the leader" on horseback
**77 goose** end of the chase (i.e., end of the punning match)
**79 goose** prostitute    **81 good . . . not** proverbial for "Spare
me!"    **82 bitter sweeting** tart kind of apple    **84–85 sweet
goose** tender goose (here probably referring to Mercutio; but
the expression "Sour sauce for sweet meat" was proverbial)
**86 cheveril** kid leather, easily stretched    **87 ell broad** forty-
five inches wide    **89 broad** indecent (?)

for love? Now art thou sociable, now art thou
Romeo; now art thou what thou art, by art as well as
by nature. For this driveling love is like a great
natural° that runs lolling° up and down to hide his 95
bauble° in a hole.

BENVOLIO   Stop there, stop there!

MERCUTIO   Thou desirest me to stop in my tale
against the hair.°

BENVOLIO   Thou wouldst else have made thy tale 100
large.°

MERCUTIO   O, thou art deceived! I would have made
it short; for I was come to the whole depth of my
tale, and meant indeed to occupy the argument° no
longer.                                                    105

ROMEO   Here's goodly gear!°

*Enter* NURSE *and her man* [PETER].

A sail, a sail!

MERCUTIO   Two, two! A shirt and a smock.°

NURSE   Peter!

PETER   Anon.                                              110

NURSE   My fan, Peter.

MERCUTIO   Good Peter, to hide her face; for her fan's
the fairer face.

NURSE   God ye good morrow, gentlemen.

MERCUTIO   God ye good-den,° fair gentlewoman.    115

NURSE   Is it good-den?

MERCUTIO   'Tis no less, I tell ye; for the bawdy hand
of the dial is now upon the prick° of noon.

NURSE   Out upon you! What a man are you!

ROMEO   One, gentlewoman, that God hath made, 120
himself to mar.

NURSE   By my troth, it is well said. "For himself to
mar," quoth 'a?° Gentlemen, can any of you tell me
where I may find the young Romeo?

ROMEO   I can tell you; but young Romeo will be 125
older when you have found him than he was when you
sought him. I am the youngest of that name, for fault
of a worse.°

NURSE   You say well.

MERCUTIO   Yea, is the worst well? Very well took,° 130
i' faith! Wisely, wisely.

NURSE   If you be he, sir, I desire some confidence° with
you.

BENVOLIO   She will endite° him to some supper.

MERCUTIO   A bawd, a bawd, a bawd! So ho!°       135

ROMEO   What hast thou found?

MERCUTIO   No hare,° sir; unless a hare, sir, in a
lenten pie,° that is something stale and hoar° ere it be
spent.

[*He walks by them and sings.*]

An old hare hoar,                                    140
And an old hare hoar,
Is very good meat in Lent;
But a hare that is hoar
Is too much for a score
When it hoars ere it be spent.                       145

Romeo, will you come to your father's? We'll to
dinner thither.

ROMEO   I will follow you.

MERCUTIO   Farewell, ancient lady. Farewell, [*singing*]
"Lady, lady, lady."° *Exeunt* [MERCUTIO, BENVOLIO].  150

NURSE   I pray you, sir, what saucy merchant was this
that was so full of his ropery?°

ROMEO   A gentleman, nurse, that loves to hear himself talk and will speak more in a minute than he will
stand to in a month.                                      155

NURSE   And 'a speak anything against me, I'll take
him down, and 'a were lustier than he is, and twenty
such Jacks; and if I cannot, I'll find those that shall.
Scurvy knave! I am none of his flirt-gills;° I am none
of his skainsmates.° And thou must stand by too, and 160
suffer every knave to use me at his pleasure!

PETER   I saw no man use you at his pleasure. If I had,
my weapon should quickly have been out, I warrant
you. I dare draw as soon as another man, if I see
occasion in a good quarrel, and the law on my side.  165

NURSE   Now, afore God, I am so vexed that every part
about me quivers. Scurvy knave! Pray you, sir, a
word; and, as I told you, my young lady bid me
inquire you out. What she bid me say, I will keep
to myself; but first let me tell ye, if ye should lead 170
her in a fool's paradise,° as they say, it were a very
gross kind of behavior, as they say; for the gentlewoman is young; and therefore, if you should deal
double with her, truly it were an ill thing to be off'red
to any gentlewoman, and very weak° dealing.        175

ROMEO   Nurse, commend me to thy lady and mistress.
I protest unto thee—

NURSE   Good heart, and i' faith I will tell her as much.
Lord, Lord, she will be a joyful woman.

ROMEO   What wilt thou tell her, nurse? Thou dost not 180
mark me.

NURSE   I will tell her, sir, that you do protest, which,
as I take it, is a gentlemanlike offer.

ROMEO
Bid her devise
Some means to come to shrift this afternoon;         185
And there she shall at Friar Lawrence' cell
Be shrived and married. Here is for thy pains.

NURSE   No, truly, sir; not a penny.

ROMEO   Go to! I say you shall.

NURSE   This afternoon, sir? Well, she shall be there.  190

ROMEO
And stay, good nurse, behind the abbey wall.
Within this hour my man shall be with thee
And bring thee cords made like a tackled stair,°

---

95 **natural** idiot; **lolling** with tongue hanging out   96 **bauble**
trinket (with ribald innuendo)   99 **against the hair** against
my inclination   101 **large** indecent   104 **occupy the argument** discuss the matter   106 **gear** stuff   108 **shirt . . .
smock** a man and a woman   115 **good-den** good evening
(i.e., afternoon)   118 **prick** point on the dial of a clock (with
bawdy innuendo)   123 **quoth 'a** indeed (literally, "said he")
127–28 **for . . . worse** mock-modestly parodying "for want
of a better"   130 **took** understood   132 **confidence** conference
(possibly a malapropism)   134 **endite** invite (Benvolio's
intentional malapropism?)   135 **So ho** cry on sighting a quarry
137 **hare** prostitute   138 **lenten pie** rabbit pie (eaten sparingly
and hence stale); **hoar** grayhaired, moldy (wordplay on *hare*
and *whore*)

150 **Lady, lady, lady** ballad refrain from "Chaste Susanna"
152 **ropery** rascally talk   159 **flirt-gills** flirting wenches
160 **skainsmates** harlots (?) daggers' mates (i.e., outlaws'
mates)   171 **fool's paradise** seduction   175 **weak** unmanly,
unscrupulous   193 **tackled stair** rope ladder

Which to the high topgallant° of my joy
Must be my convoy° in the secret night.          195
Farewell. Be trusty, and I'll quit° thy pains.
Farewell. Commend me to thy mistress.

NURSE
Now God in heaven bless thee! Hark you, sir.

ROMEO
What say'st thou, my dear nurse?

NURSE
Is your man secret? Did you ne'er hear say,          200
Two may keep counsel, putting one away?

ROMEO
Warrant thee my man's as true as steel.

NURSE   Well, sir, my mistress is the sweetest lady.
Lord, Lord! When 'twas a little prating thing—O,
there is a nobleman in town, one Paris, that would fain          205
lay knife aboard;° but she, good soul, had as lieve° see
a toad, a very toad, as see him. I anger her sometimes,
and tell her that Paris is the properer man; but I'll
warrant you, when I say so, she looks as pale as any
clout° in the versal world.° Doth not rosemary and          210
Romeo begin both with a letter?

ROMEO   Ay, nurse; what of that? Both with an R.

NURSE   Ah, mocker! That's the dog's name.° R is for
the—no; I know it begins with some other letter; and
she hath the prettiest sententious° of it, of you and          215
rosemary, that it would do you good to hear it.

ROMEO   Commend me to thy lady.

NURSE   Ay, a thousand times. [*Exit* ROMEO.] Peter!

PETER   Anon.

NURSE   Before, and apace.          *Exit* [*after* PETER]. 220

[Scene V. *Capulet's orchard.*]

*Enter* JULIET.

JULIET
The clock struck nine when I did send the nurse;
In half an hour she promised to return.
Perchance she cannot meet him. That's not so.
O, she is lame! Love's heralds should be thoughts,
Which ten times faster glides than the sun's beams          5
Driving back shadows over low'ring hills.
Therefore do nimble-pinioned doves° draw Love,
And therefore hath the wind-swift Cupid wings.
Now is the sun upon the highmost hill
Of this day's journey, and from nine till twelve          10
Is three long hours; yet she is not come.
Had she affections and warm youthful blood,
She would be as swift in motion as a ball;
My words would bandy her° to my sweet love,
And his to me.          15
But old folks, many feign as they were dead°—
Unwieldy, slow, heavy, and pale as lead.

*Enter* NURSE [*and* PETER].

O God, she comes! O honey nurse, what news?
Hast thou met with him? Send thy man away.

NURSE
Peter, stay at the gate.          [*Exit* PETER.] 20

JULIET
Now, good sweet nurse—O Lord, why lookest thou
   sad?
Though news be sad, yet tell them merrily;
If good, thou shamest the music of sweet news
By playing it to me with so sour a face.

NURSE
I am aweary, give me leave awhile.          25
Fie, how my bones ache! What a jaunce° have I!

JULIET
I would thou hadst my bones, and I thy news.
Nay, come, I pray thee speak. Good, good nurse,
   speak.

NURSE
Jesu, what haste! Can you not stay° awhile?
Do you not see that I am out of breath?          30

JULIET
How art thou out of breath when thou hast breath
To say to me that thou art out of breath?
The excuse that thou dost make in this delay
Is longer than the tale thou dost excuse.
Is thy news good or bad? Answer to that.          35
Say either, and I'll stay the circumstance.°
Let me be satisfied, is't good or bad?

NURSE   Well, you have made a simple° choice; you
know not how to choose a man. Romeo? No, not
he. Though his face be better than any man's, yet          40
his leg excels all men's; and for a hand and a foot,
and a body, though they be not to be talked on,
yet they are past compare. He is not the flower of
courtesy, but, I'll warrant him, as gentle as a lamb.
Go thy ways, wench; serve God. What, have you          45
dined at home?

JULIET
No, no. But all this did I know before.
What says he of our marriage? What of that?

NURSE
Lord, how my head aches! What a head have I!
It beats as it would fall in twenty pieces.          50
My back a° t' other side—ah, my back, my back!
Beshrew° your heart for sending me about
To catch my death with jauncing up and down!

JULIET
I' faith, I am sorry that thou art not well.
Sweet, sweet, sweet nurse, tell me, what says my
   love?          55

NURSE   Your love says, like an honest gentleman, and
a courteous, and a kind, and a handsome, and, I
warrant, a virtuous—where is your mother?

JULIET
Where is my mother? Why, she is within.
Where should she be? How oddly thou repliest!          60
"Your love says, like an honest gentleman,
'Where is your mother?'"

NURSE                    O God's Lady dear!

---

194 **topgallant** summit (mast above the topmast)   195
**convoy** conveyance   196 **quit** reward   206 **lay knife aboard**
take a slice; **had as lieve** would rather   210 **clout** cloth;
**versal world** universe   213 **dog's name** the R sound suggests
a dog's growl   215 **sententious** sentences, pithy sayings
**II.v.7 nimble-pinioned doves** swift-winged doves (sacred to
Venus)   14 **bandy her** speed her   16 **old . . . dead** many old
people move about as if they were almost dead

26 **jaunce** jaunt, fatiguing walk   29 **stay** wait   36 **stay the
circumstance** wait for the details   38 **simple** foolish   51 **a** on
52 **Beshrew** curse (in the sense of "shame on")

Are you so hot?° Marry come up, I trow.°
Is this the poultice for my aching bones?
Henceforward do your messages yourself.     65

JULIET
Here's such a coil!° Come, what says Romeo?

NURSE
Have you got leave to go to shrift today?

JULIET
I have.

NURSE
Then hie you hence to Friar Lawrence' cell;
There stays a husband to make you a wife.     70
Now comes the wanton blood up in your cheeks:
They'll be in scarlet straight° at any news.
Hie you to church; I must another way,
To fetch a ladder, by the which your love
Must climb a bird's nest soon when it is dark.     75
I am the drudge, and toil in your delight;
But you shall bear the burden soon at night.
Go; I'll to dinner; hie you to the cell.

JULIET
Hie to high fortune! Honest nurse, farewell.    *Exeunt.*

[Scene VI. *Friar Lawrence's cell.*]

*Enter* FRIAR [*Lawrence*] *and* ROMEO.

FRIAR
So smile the heavens upon this holy act
That afterhours with sorrow chide us not!

ROMEO
Amen, amen! But come what sorrow can,
It cannot countervail° the exchange of joy
That one short minute gives me in her sight.     5
Do thou but close our hands with holy words,
Then love-devouring death do what he dare—
It is enough I may but call her mine.

FRIAR
These violent delights have violent ends
And in their triumph die, like fire and powder,     10
Which, as they kiss, consume. The sweetest honey
Is loathsome in his own deliciousness
And in the taste confounds° the appetite.
Therefore love moderately: long love doth so;
Too swift arrives as tardy as too slow.     15

*Enter* JULIET.

Here comes the lady. O, so light a foot
Will ne'er wear out the everlasting flint.°
A lover may bestride the gossamers°
That idles in the wanton° summer air,
And yet not fall; so light is vanity.°     20

JULIET
Good even to my ghostly confessor.

FRIAR
Romeo shall thank thee, daughter, for us both.

JULIET
As much to him,° else is his thanks too much.

ROMEO
Ah, Juliet, if the measure of thy joy
Be heaped like mine, and that thy skill be more     25
To blazon it,° then sweeten with thy breath
This neighbor air, and let rich music's tongue
Unfold the imagined happiness that both
Receive in either by this dear encounter.

JULIET
Conceit, more rich in matter than in words,     30
Brags of his substance, not of ornament.°
They are but beggars that can count their worth;
But my true love is grown to such excess
I cannot sum up sum of half my wealth.

FRIAR
Come, come with me, and we will make short work;    35
For, by your leaves, you shall not stay alone
Till holy church incorporate two in one.     [*Exeunt.*]

# [ACT III]

### [Scene I. *A public place.*]

*Enter* MERCUTIO, BENVOLIO, *and* MEN.

BENVOLIO
I pray thee, good Mercutio, let's retire.
The day is hot, the Capels are abroad,
And, if we meet, we shall not 'scape a brawl,
For now, these hot days, is the mad blood stirring.

MERCUTIO   Thou art like one of these fellows that,    5
when he enters the confines of a tavern, claps me his
sword upon the table and says, "God send me no
need of thee!" and by the operation of the second cup
draws him on the drawer,° when indeed there is no
need.     10

BENVOLIO   Am I like such a fellow?

MERCUTIO   Come, come, thou art as hot a Jack in thy
mood as any in Italy; and as soon moved to be moody,°
and as soon moody to be moved.°

BENVOLIO   And what to?     15

MERCUTIO   Nay, and there were two such, we should
have none shortly, for one would kill the other.
Thou! Why, thou wilt quarrel with a man that hath
a hair more or a hair less in his beard than thou hast.
Thou wilt quarrel with a man for cracking nuts,    20
having no other reason but because thou hast hazel
eyes. What eye but such an eye would spy out such
a quarrel? Thy head is as full of quarrels as an egg is
full of meat; and yet thy head hath been beaten as
addle as an egg for quarreling. Thou hast quarreled    25
with a man for coughing in the street, because he hath
wakened thy dog that hath lain asleep in the sun.

---

**63 hot** angry; **Marry . . . trow** Indeed, come now, by the
Virgin   **66 coil** disturbance   **72 straight** straightway
**II.vi.4 countervail** equal   **13 confounds** destroys   **17 Will
. . . flint** Juliet's feet are lighter than waterdrops, which are
proverbially said to wear away stones   **18 gossamers** spiders'
webs   **19 wanton** capricious   **20 vanity** a transitory thing (an
earthly lover and his love)

**23 As . . . him** the same greeting to Romeo   **25–26 thy . . .
it** you are better able to set it forth   **30–31 Conceit . . .
ornament** True understanding is its own proud manifestation
and does not need words
**III.i.9 draws . . . drawer** draws his sword on the waiter   **13
moody** angry   **14 moody . . . moved** quick-tempered

Didst thou not fall out with a tailor for wearing his
new doublet° before Easter? With another for tying
his new shoes with old riband?° And yet thou wilt 30
tutor me from quarreling!

BENVOLIO  And I were so apt to quarrel as thou art,
any man should buy the fee simple° of my life for an
hour and a quarter.°

MERCUTIO  The fee simple? O simple!° 35

*Enter* TYBALT, PETRUCHIO,° *and others.*

BENVOLIO  By my head, here comes the Capulets.

MERCUTIO  By my heel, I care not.

TYBALT
Follow me close, for I will speak to them.
Gentlemen, good-den.° A word with one of you.

MERCUTIO
And but one word with one of us? 40
Couple it with something; make it a word and a blow.

TYBALT  You shall find me apt enough to that, sir,
and you will give me occasion.

MERCUTIO  Could you not take some occasion without giving? 45

TYBALT  Mercutio, thou consortest with Romeo.

MERCUTIO  Consort?° What, dost thou make us
minstrels? And thou make minstrels of us, look to hear
nothing but discords. Here's my fiddlestick;° here's
that shall make you dance. Zounds,° consort! 50

BENVOLIO
We talk here in the public haunt of men.
Either withdraw unto some private place,
Or reason coldly of your grievances,
Or else depart. Here all eyes gaze on us.

MERCUTIO
Men's eyes were made to look, and let them gaze. 55
I will not budge for no man's pleasure, I.

*Enter* ROMEO.

TYBALT
Well, peace be with you, sir. Here comes my man.°

MERCUTIO
But I'll be hanged, sir, if he wear your livery.°
Marry, go before to field,° he'll be your follower!
Your worship in that sense may call him man. 60

TYBALT
Romeo, the love I bear thee can afford
No better term than this: thou art a villain.°

ROMEO
Tybalt, the reason that I have to love thee
Doth much excuse the appertaining° rage
To such a greeting. Villain am I none. 65
Therefore farewell. I see thou knowest me not.

TYBALT
Boy, this shall not excuse the injuries
That thou hast done me; therefore turn and draw.

ROMEO
I do protest I never injured thee,
But love thee better than thou canst devise° 70
Till thou shalt know the reason of my love;
And so, good Capulet, which name I tender°
As dearly as mine own, be satisfied.

MERCUTIO
O calm, dishonorable, vile submission!
Alla stoccata° carries it away. 75

[*Draws.*]

Tybalt, you ratcatcher, will you walk?°

TYBALT
What wouldst thou have with me?

MERCUTIO  Good King of Cats, nothing but one of
your nine lives. That I mean to make bold withal,°
and, as you shall use me hereafter, dry-beat° the rest of 80
the eight. Will you pluck your sword out of his
pilcher° by the ears? Make haste, lest mine be about
your ears ere it be out.

TYBALT  I am for you.

[*Draws.*]

ROMEO
Gentle Mercutio, put thy rapier up. 85

MERCUTIO  Come, sir, your passado!°

[*They fight.*]

ROMEO
Draw, Benvolio; beat down their weapons.
Gentlemen, for shame! Forbear this outrage!
Tybalt, Mercutio, the prince expressly hath
Forbid this bandying° in Verona streets. 90
Hold, Tybalt! Good Mercutio!

[TYBALT *under Romeo's arm thrusts*
MERCUTIO *in, and flies.*]

MERCUTIO                    I am hurt.
A plague a° both houses! I am sped.°
Is he gone and hath nothing?

BENVOLIO                    What, art thou hurt?

MERCUTIO
Ay, ay, a scratch, a scratch. Marry, 'tis enough.
Where is my page? Go, villain, fetch a surgeon. 95

[*Exit* PAGE.]

ROMEO
Courage, man. The hurt cannot be much.

MERCUTIO  No, 'tis not so deep as a well, nor so wide
as a church door; but 'tis enough, 'twill serve. Ask
for me tomorrow, and you shall find me a grave°
man. I am peppered,° I warrant, for this world. A 100
plague a both your houses! Zounds, a dog, a rat, a
mouse, a cat, to scratch a man to death! A braggart,
a rogue, a villain, that fights by the book of arithmetic!°
Why the devil came you between us? I was hurt
under your arm. 105

---

29 **doublet** jacket  30 **riband** ribbon  33 **fee simple** absolute
possession  33–34 **for . . . quarter** i.e., the life expectancy of
one with Mercutio's penchant for quarreling  35 **O simple**
O stupid  35 **s.d. Petruchio** in I.v he is one of Capulet's guests,
but has no lines  39 **good-den** good evening (i.e., afternoon)
47 **Consort** (1) to keep company with (2) company of musicians
49 **fiddlestick** sword  50 **Zounds** by God's wounds  57 **man**
Mercutio takes this to mean "manservant"  58 **livery** servant's
uniform  59 **field** dueling field  62 **villain** low fellow  64
**appertaining** appropriate

70 **devise** imagine  72 **tender** value  75 **Alla stoccata** a
term in fencing ("at the thrust") which Mercutio uses contemptuously as a nickname for Tybalt  76 **walk** step aside
79 **make bold withal** make bold with; take  80 **dry-beat**
thrash  82 **pilcher** scabbard  86 **passado** lunge  90 **bandying** brawling  92 **a** on; **sped** wounded  99 **grave** (1) extremely
serious (2) ready for the grave  100 **am peppered** have been
given a deathblow  103 **by . . . arithmetic** by formal rules

ROMEO
I thought all for the best.
MERCUTIO
Help me into some house, Benvolio,
Or I shall faint. A plague a both your houses!
They have made worms' meat of me. I have it,°
And soundly too. Your houses!                                    110
                    *Exit* [MERCUTIO *and* BENVOLIO].
ROMEO
This gentleman, the prince's near ally,°
My very° friend, hath got this mortal hurt
In my behalf—my reputation stained
With Tybalt's slander—Tybalt, that an hour
Hath been my cousin. O sweet Juliet,                             115
Thy beauty hath made me effeminate
And in my temper soft'ned valor's steel!°

*Enter* BENVOLIO.

BENVOLIO
O Romeo, Romeo, brave Mercutio is dead!
That gallant spirit hath aspired° the clouds,
Which too untimely here did scorn the earth.                     120
ROMEO
This day's black fate on moe° days doth depend;°
This but begins the woe others must end.

[*Enter* TYBALT.]

BENVOLIO
Here comes the furious Tybalt back again.
ROMEO
Alive in triumph, and Mercutio slain?
Away to heaven respective lenity,°                               125
And fire-eyed fury be my conduct° now!
Now, Tybalt, take the "villain" back again
That late thou gavest me; for Mercutio's soul
Is but a little way above our heads,
Staying for thine to keep him company.                           130
Either thou or I, or both, must go with him.
TYBALT
Thou, wretched boy, that didst consort him here,
Shalt with him hence.
ROMEO                          This shall determine that.

*They fight.* TYBALT *falls.*

BENVOLIO
Romeo, away, be gone!
The citizens are up, and Tybalt slain.                           135
Stand not amazed. The prince will doom thee death
If thou art taken. Hence, be gone, away!
ROMEO
O, I am fortune's fool!°
BENVOLIO                    Why dost thou stay?
                                        *Exit* ROMEO.

*Enter* CITIZENS.

CITIZEN
Which way ran he that killed Mercutio?
Tybalt, that murderer, which way ran he?                          140

BENVOLIO
There lies that Tybalt.
CITIZEN                    Up, sir, go with me.
I charge thee in the prince's name obey.

*Enter* PRINCE, *old* MONTAGUE, CAPULET, *their*
WIVES, *and all.*

PRINCE
Where are the vile beginners of this fray?
BENVOLIO
O noble prince, I can discover° all
The unlucky manage° of this fatal brawl.                          145
There lies the man, slain by young Romeo,
That slew thy kinsman, brave Mercutio.
LADY CAPULET
Tybalt, my cousin! O my brother's child!
O prince! O cousin! Husband! O, the blood is spilled
Of my dear kinsman! Prince, as thou art true,                    150
For blood of ours shed blood of Montague.
O cousin, cousin!
PRINCE
Benvolio, who began this bloody fray?
BENVOLIO
Tybalt, here slain, whom Romeo's hand did slay.
Romeo, that spoke him fair, bid him bethink                       155
How nice° the quarrel was, and urged° withal
Your high displeasure. All this—utterèd
With gentle breath, calm look, knees humbly bowed—
Could not take truce with the unruly spleen°
Of Tybalt deaf to peace, but that he tilts°                       160
With piercing steel at bold Mercutio's breast;
Who, all as hot, turns deadly point to point,
And, with a martial scorn, with one hand beats
Cold death aside and with the other sends
It back to Tybalt, whose dexterity                                165
Retorts it. Romeo he cries aloud,
"Hold, friends! Friends, part!" and swifter than his
    tongue,
His agile arm beats down their fatal points,
And 'twixt them rushes; underneath whose arm
An envious° thrust from Tybalt hit the life                       170
Of stout Mercutio, and then Tybalt fled;
But by and by comes back to Romeo,
Who had but newly entertained° revenge,
And to't they go like lightning; for, ere I
Could draw to part them, was stout Tybalt slain;                  175
And, as he fell, did Romeo turn and fly.
This is the truth, or let Benvolio die.
LADY CAPULET
He is a kinsman to the Montague;
Affection makes him false, he speaks not true.
Some twenty of them fought in this black strife,                  180
And all those twenty could but kill one life.
I beg for justice, which thou, prince, must give.
Romeo slew Tybalt; Romeo must not live.
PRINCE
Romeo slew him; he slew Mercutio.
Who now the price of his dear blood doth owe?                     185
CAPULET
Not Romeo, prince; he was Mercutio's friend;

109 **I have it** I have received my deathblow    111 **ally** relative
112 **very** true    117 **in . . . steel** softened the valorous part
of my character    119 **aspired** climbed to    121 **moe** more;
**depend** hang over    125 **respective lenity** discriminating
mercifulness    126 **conduct** guide    138 **fool** plaything, dupe

144 **discover** reveal    145 **manage** course    156 **nice** trivial;
**urged** mentioned    159 **spleen** ill nature    160 **tilts** thrusts    170
**envious** full of enmity    173 **entertained** contemplated

His fault concludes but what the law should end,
The life of Tybalt.
PRINCE                    And for that offense
Immediately we do exile him hence.
I have an interest in your hate's proceeding,                    190
My blood° for your rude brawls doth lie a-bleeding;
But I'll amerce° you with so strong a fine
That you shall all repent the loss of mine.
I will be deaf to pleading and excuses;
Nor tears nor prayers shall purchase out abuses.                    195
Therefore use none. Let Romeo hence in haste,
Else, when he is found, that hour is his last.
Bear hence this body and attend our will.°
Mercy but murders, pardoning those that kill.
                                    *Exit [with others].*

[Scene II. *Capulet's orchard.*]

*Enter* JULIET *alone.*

JULIET
Gallop apace, you fiery-footed steeds,°
Towards Phoebus' lodging!° Such a wagoner
As Phaëthon° would whip you to the west
And bring in cloudy night immediately.
Spread thy close curtain, love-performing night,                    5
That runaways'° eyes may wink,° and Romeo
Leap to these arms untalked of and unseen.
Lovers can see to do their amorous rites,
And by their own beauties; or, if love be blind,
It best agrees with night. Come, civil night,                    10
Thou sober-suited matron all in black,
And learn me how to lose a winning match,
Played for a pair of stainless maidenhoods.
Hood° my unmanned° blood, bating° in my cheeks,
With thy black mantle till strange° love grow bold,                    15
Think true love acted simple modesty.
Come, night; come, Romeo; come, thou day in
    night;
For thou wilt lie upon the wings of night
Whiter than new snow upon a raven's back.
Come, gentle night; come, loving, black-browed
    night;                    20
Give me my Romeo; and, when he shall die,
Take him and cut him out in little stars,
And he will make the face of heaven so fine
That all the world will be in love with night
And pay no worship to the garish sun.                    25
O, I have bought the mansion of a love,
But not possessed it; and though I am sold,
Not yet enjoyed. So tedious is this day
As is the night before some festival
To an impatient child that hath new robes                    30
And may not wear them. O, here comes my nurse,

*Enter* NURSE, *with cords.*

And she brings news; and every tongue that speaks
But Romeo's name speaks heavenly eloquence.
Now, nurse, what news? What hast thou there, the
    cords
That Romeo bid thee fetch?
NURSE                    Ay, ay, the cords.                    35
JULIET
Ay me! What news? Why dost thou wring thy
    hands?
NURSE
Ah, weraday!° He's dead, he's dead, he's dead!
We are undone, lady, we are undone!
Alack the day! He's gone, he's killed, he's dead!
JULIET
Can heaven be so envious?
NURSE                    Romeo can,                    40
Though heaven cannot. O Romeo, Romeo!
Who ever would have thought it? Romeo!
JULIET
What devil art thou that dost torment me thus?
This torture should be roared in dismal hell.
Hath Romeo slain himself? Say thou but "Ay,"                    45
And that bare vowel "I" shall poison more
Than the death-darting eye of cockatrice.°
I am not I, if there be such an "Ay,"°
Or those eyes' shot° that makes thee answer "Ay."
If he be slain, say "Ay"; or if not, "No."                    50
Brief sounds determine of my weal or woe.
NURSE
I saw the wound, I saw it with mine eyes,
(God save the mark!°) here on his manly breast.
A piteous corse,° a bloody piteous corse;
Pale, pale as ashes, all bedaubed in blood,                    55
All in gore-blood. I sounded° at the sight.
JULIET
O, break, my heart! Poor bankrout,° break at once!
To prison, eyes, ne'er look on liberty!
Vile earth,° to earth resign;° end motion here,
And thou and Romeo press one heavy bier!                    60
NURSE
O Tybalt, Tybalt, the best friend I had!
O courteous Tybalt! Honest gentleman!
That ever I should live to see thee dead!
JULIET
What storm is this that blows so contrary?
Is Romeo slaught'red, and is Tybalt dead?                    65
My dearest cousin, and my dearer lord?
Then, dreadful trumpet, sound the general doom!°
For who is living, if those two are gone?
NURSE
Tybalt is gone, and Romeo banishèd;
Romeo that killed him, he is banishèd.                    70
JULIET
O God! Did Romeo's hand shed Tybalt's blood?
NURSE
It did, it did! Alas the day, it did!

191 **My blood** Mercutio was the Prince's relative    192 **amerce** punish by fine    198 **attend our will** respect my decision
**III.ii.1 fiery-footed steeds** horses of the sun god, Phoebus    2 **Towards Phoebus' lodging** beneath the horizon    3 **Phaëthon** Phoebus' son, who mismanaged the horses and let them run away    6 **runaways'** of the horses (?); **wink** shut    14 **Hood** cover with a hood, as in falconry; **unmanned** (1) untamed (2) unmated; **bating** fluttering    15 **strange** unfamiliar

37 **weraday** welladay, alas    47 **cockatrice** basilisk (a serpent fabled to have a killing glance)    48 **Ay** (1) I (2) eye    49 **eyes' shot** the Nurse's glance    53 **God . . . mark** God avert the bad omen    54 **corse** corpse    56 **sounded** swooned    57 **bankrout** bankrupt    59 **Vile earth** referring to her own body; **resign** return    67 **dreadful . . . doom** sound the trumpet of doomsday

JULIET

O serpent heart, hid with a flow'ring face!
Did ever dragon keep so fair a cave?
Beautiful tyrant! Fiend angelical!                                     75
Dove-feathered raven! Wolvish-ravening lamb!
Despisèd substance of divinest show!
Just opposite to what thou justly seem'st—
A damnèd saint, an honorable villain!
O nature, what hadst thou to do in hell                                80
When thou didst bower the spirit of a fiend
In mortal paradise of such sweet flesh?
Was ever book containing such vile matter
So fairly bound? O, that deceit should dwell
In such a gorgeous palace!

NURSE                                   There's no trust,             85
No faith, no honesty in men; all perjured,
All forsworn, all naught, all dissemblers.
Ah, where's my man? Give me some aqua vitae.°
These griefs, these woes, these sorrows make me old.
Shame come to Romeo!

JULIET                             Blistered be thy tongue            90
For such a wish! He was not born to shame.
Upon his brow shame is ashamed to sit;
For 'tis a throne where honor may be crowned
Sole monarch of the universal earth.
O, what a beast was I to chide at him!                                 95

NURSE

Will you speak well of him that killed your cousin?

JULIET

Shall I speak ill of him that is my husband?
Ah, poor my lord, what tongue shall smooth thy
    name
When I, thy three-hours wife, have mangled it?
But wherefore, villain, didst thou kill my cousin?                    100
That villain cousin would have killed my husband.
Back, foolish tears, back to your native spring!
Your tributary° drops belong to woe,
Which you, mistaking, offer up to joy.
My husband lives, that Tybalt would have slain;                       105
And Tybalt's dead, that would have slain my husband.
All this is comfort; wherefore weep I then?
Some word there was, worser than Tybalt's death,
That murd'red me. I would forget it fain;
But O, it presses to my memory                                        110
Like damnèd guilty deeds to sinners' minds!
"Tybalt is dead, and Romeo—banishèd."
That "banishèd," that one word "banishèd,"
Hath slain ten thousand Tybalts. Tybalt's death
Was woe enough, if it had ended there;                                115
Or, if sour woe delights in fellowship
And needly will be ranked with° other griefs,
Why followed not, when she said "Tybalt's dead,"
Thy father, or thy mother, nay, or both,
Which modern° lamentation might have moved?                           120
But with a rearward° following Tybalt's death,
"Romeo is banishèd"—to speak that word
Is father, mother, Tybalt, Romeo, Juliet,
All slain, all dead. "Romeo is banishèd"—
There is no end, no limit, measure, bound,                            125

In that word's death; no words can that woe sound.
Where is my father and my mother, nurse?

NURSE

Weeping and wailing over Tybalt's corse.
Will you go to them? I will bring you thither.

JULIET

Wash they his wounds with tears? Mine shall be spent,  130
When theirs are dry, for Romeo's banishment.
Take up those cords. Poor ropes, you are beguiled,
Both you and I, for Romeo is exiled.
He made you for a highway to my bed;
But I, a maid, die maiden-widowèd.                                    135
Come, cords; come, nurse. I'll to my wedding bed;
And death, not Romeo, take my maidenhead!

NURSE

Hie to your chamber. I'll find Romeo
To comfort you. I wot° well where he is.
Hark ye, your Romeo will be here at night.                            140
I'll to him; he is hid at Lawrence' cell.

JULIET

O, find him! Give this ring to my true knight
And bid him come to take his last farewell.
                                        *Exit* [*with* NURSE].


[Scene III. *Friar Lawrence's cell.*]

*Enter* FRIAR [*Lawrence*].

FRIAR

Romeo, come forth; come forth, thou fearful° man.
Affliction is enamored of thy parts,°
And thou art wedded to calamity.

[*Enter* ROMEO.]

ROMEO

Father, what news? What is the prince's doom?°
What sorrow craves acquaintance at my hand             5
That I yet know not?

FRIAR                          Too familiar
Is my dear son with such sour company.
I bring thee tidings of the prince's doom.

ROMEO

What less than doomsday° is the prince's doom?

FRIAR

A gentler judgment vanished° from his lips—           10
Not body's death, but body's banishment.

ROMEO

Ha, banishment? Be merciful, say "death";
For exile hath more terror in his look,
Much more than death. Do not say "banishment."

FRIAR

Here from Verona art thou banishèd.                    15
Be patient, for the world is broad and wide.

ROMEO

There is no world without Verona walls,
But purgatory, torture, hell itself.
Hence banishèd is banished from the world,
And world's exile is death. Then "banishèd"           20
Is death mistermed. Calling death "banishèd,"

---

**88 aqua vitae** spirits   **103 tributary** contributed   **117 needly
. . . with** must be accompanied by   **120 modern** ordinary
**21 rearward** rear guard

**139 wot** know
**III.iii.1 fearful** frightened   **2 Affliction . . . parts** affliction
is in love with your attractive qualities   **4 doom** final decision
**9 doomsday** my death   **10 vanished** escaped

Thou cut'st my head off with a golden ax
And smilest upon the stroke that murders me.

FRIAR
O deadly sin! O rude unthankfulness!
Thy fault our law calls death; but the kind prince,    25
Taking thy part, hath rushed° aside the law,
And turned that black word "death" to "banishment."
This is dear mercy, and thou see'st it not.

ROMEO
'Tis torture, and not mercy. Heaven is here,
Where Juliet lives; and every cat and dog    30
And little mouse, every unworthy thing,
Live here in heaven and may look on her;
But Romeo may not. More validity,°
More honorable state, more courtship° lives
In carrion flies than Romeo. They may seize    35
On the white wonder of dear Juliet's hand
And steal immortal blessing from her lips,
Who, even in pure and vestal° modesty,
Still blush, as thinking their own kisses sin;°
But Romeo may not, he is banishèd.    40
Flies may do this but I from this must fly;
They are freemen, but I am banishèd.
And sayest thou yet that exile is not death?
Hadst thou no poison mixed, no sharp-ground knife,
No sudden mean of death, though ne'er so mean,°    45
But "banishèd" to kill me—"banishèd"?
O friar, the damnèd use that word in hell;
Howling attends it! How hast thou the heart,
Being a divine, a ghostly confessor,
A sin-absolver, and my friend professed,    50
To mangle me with that word "banishèd"?

FRIAR
Thou fond° mad man, hear me a little speak.

ROMEO
O, thou wilt speak again of banishment.

FRIAR
I'll give thee armor to keep off that word;
Adversity's sweet milk, philosophy,    55
To comfort thee, though thou art banishèd.

ROMEO
Yet° "banishèd"? Hang up philosophy!
Unless philosophy can make a Juliet,
Displant a town, reverse a prince's doom,
It helps not, it prevails not. Talk no more.    60

FRIAR
O, then I see that madmen have no ears.

ROMEO
How should they, when that wise men have no eyes?

FRIAR
Let me dispute° with thee of thy estate.°

ROMEO
Thou canst not speak of that thou dost not feel.
Wert thou as young as I, Juliet thy love,    65
An hour but married, Tybalt murderèd,
Doting like me, and like me banishèd,
Then mightst thou speak, then mightst thou tear thy
   hair,

And fall upon the ground, as I do now,
Taking the measure° of an unmade grave.    70

*Enter* NURSE *and knock.*

FRIAR
Arise, one knocks. Good Romeo, hide thyself.

ROMEO
Not I; unless the breath of heartsick groans
Mistlike infold me from the search of eyes.

[*Knock.*]

FRIAR
Hark, how they knock! Who's there? Romeo, arise;
Thou wilt be taken.—Stay awhile!—Stand up;    75

[*Knock.*]

Run to my study.—By and by!°—God's will,
What simpleness° is this.—I come, I come!

*Knock.*

Who knocks so hard? Whence come you? What's
   your will?

*Enter* NURSE.

NURSE
Let me come in, and you shall know my errand.
I come from Lady Juliet.

FRIAR            Welcome then.    80

NURSE
O holy friar, O, tell me, holy friar,
Where is my lady's lord, where's Romeo?

FRIAR
There on the ground, with his own tears made drunk.

NURSE
O, he is even in my mistress' case,°
Just in her case! O woeful sympathy!    85
Piteous predicament! Even so lies she,
Blubb'ring and weeping, weeping and blubb'ring.
Stand up, stand up! Stand, and you be a man.
For Juliet's sake, for her sake, rise and stand!
Why should you fall into so deep an O?°    90

ROMEO [*Rises.*]    Nurse—

NURSE
Ah sir, ah sir! Death's the end of all.

ROMEO
Spakest thou of Juliet? How is it with her?
Doth not she think me an old murderer,
Now I have stained the childhood of our joy    95
With blood removed but little from her own?
Where is she? And how doth she! And what says
My concealed lady to our canceled° love?

NURSE
O, she says nothing, sir, but weeps and weeps;
And now falls on her bed, and then starts up,    100
And Tybalt calls; and then on Romeo cries,
And then down falls again.

ROMEO          As if that name,

---

26 **rushed** pushed   33 **validity** value   34 **courtship** opportunity for courting   38 **vestal** virgin   39 **their . . . sin** sin, when they touch each other   45 **mean . . . mean** method . . . lowly   52 **fond** foolish   57 **Yet** still   63 **dispute** discuss; **estate** situation

70 **Taking the measure** measuring by my outstretched body   76 **By and by** in a moment (said to the person knocking)   77 **simpleness** silly behavior (Romeo refuses to rise)   84 **case** with bawdy innuendo complementing "stand," "rise," etc., in lines 85–90; but the Nurse is unaware of this possible interpretation   90 **so . . . O** such a fit of moaning   98 **canceled** invalidated

Shot from the deadly level° of a gun,
Did murder her; as that name's cursèd hand
Murdered her kinsman. O, tell me, friar, tell me,        105
In what vile part of this anatomy
Doth my name lodge? Tell me, that I may sack°
The hateful mansion.

[*He offers to stab himself, and* NURSE *snatches the dagger away.*]

FRIAR                    Hold thy desperate hand.
Art thou a man? Thy form cries out thou art;
Thy tears are womanish, thy wild acts denote        110
The unreasonable° fury of a beast.
Unseemly° woman in a seeming man!
And ill-beseeming beast in seeming both!°
Thou hast amazed me. By my holy order,
I thought thy disposition better tempered.        115
Hast thou slain Tybalt? Wilt thou slay thyself?
And slay thy lady that in thy life lives,
By doing damnèd hate upon thyself?
Why railest thou on thy birth, the heaven, and earth?
Since birth and heaven and earth,° all three do meet        120
In thee at once; which thou at once wouldst lose.°
Fie, fie, thou shamest thy shape, thy love, thy wit,°
Which,° like a usurer, abound'st in all,
And usest none in that true use indeed
Which should bedeck° thy shape, thy love, thy wit.        125
Thy noble shape is but a form of wax,
Digressing from the valor of a man;°
Thy dear love sworn but hollow perjury,
Killing that love which thou hast vowed to cherish;
Thy wit, that ornament to shape and love,        130
Misshapen in the conduct° of them both,
Like powder in a skilless soldier's flask,°
Is set afire by thine own ignorance,
And thou dismemb'red with thine own defense.°
What, rouse thee, man! Thy Juliet is alive,        135
For whose dear sake thou wast but lately dead.°
There art thou happy.° Tybalt would kill thee,
But thou slewest Tybalt. There art thou happy.
The law, that threat'ned death, becomes thy friend
And turns it to exile. There art thou happy.        140
A pack of blessings light upon thy back;
Happiness courts thee in her best array;
But, like a misbehaved and sullen wench,
Thou puts up thy fortune and thy love.
Take heed, take heed, for such die miserable.        145
Go get thee to thy love, as was decreed,
Ascend her chamber, hence and comfort her.
But look thou stay not till the watch be set,
For then thou canst not pass to Mantua,
Where thou shalt live till we can find a time        150
To blaze° your marriage, reconcile your friends,

Beg pardon of the prince, and call thee back
With twenty hundred thousand times more joy
Than thou went'st forth in lamentation.
Go before, nurse. Commend me to thy lady,        155
And bid her hasten all the house to bed,
Which heavy sorrow makes them apt unto.
Romeo is coming.
NURSE
O Lord, I could have stayed here all the night
To hear good counsel. O, what learning is!        160
My lord, I'll tell my lady you will come.
ROMEO
Do so, and bid my sweet prepare to chide.

[NURSE *offers to go in and turns again.*]

NURSE
Here, sir, a ring she bid me give you, sir.
Hie you, make haste, for it grows very late.        [*Exit.*]
ROMEO
How well my comfort is revived by this!        165
FRIAR
Go hence; good night; and here stands all your state:°
Either be gone before the watch be set,
Or by the break of day disguised from hence.
Sojourn in Mantua. I'll find out your man,
And he shall signify from time to time        170
Every good hap to you that chances here.
Give me thy hand. 'Tis late. Farewell; good night.
ROMEO
But that a joy past joy calls out on me,
It were a grief so brief to part with thee.
Farewell.                    *Exeunt.*        175

[Scene IV. *A room in Capulet's house.*]

*Enter old* CAPULET, *his wife* [LADY CAPULET], *and*
PARIS.

CAPULET
Things have fall'n out, sir, so unluckily
That we have had no time to move° our daughter.
Look you, she loved her kinsman Tybalt dearly,
And so did I. Well, we were born to die.
'Tis very late; she'll not come down tonight.        5
I promise° you, but for your company,
I would have been abed an hour ago.
PARIS
These times of woe afford no times to woo.
Madam, good night. Commend me to your daughter.
LADY [CAPULET]
I will, and know her mind early tomorrow;        10
Tonight she's mewed up to her heaviness.°
CAPULET
Sir Paris, I will make a desperate tender°
Of my child's love. I think she will be ruled
In all respects by me; nay more, I doubt it not.
Wife, go you to her ere you go to bed;        15
Acquaint her here of my son Paris' love

103 **level** aim    107 **sack** plunder    111 **unreasonable** irrational
112 **Unseemly** indecorous    113 **ill-beseeming . . . both**
inappropriate even to a beast in being both man and woman
120 **birth . . . earth** family origin, soul, and body    121 **lose**
abandon    122 **wit** intellect    123 **Which** who    125 **bedeck**
do honor to    127 **valor . . . man** his manly qualities    131
**conduct** management    132 **flask** powder flask    134 **dismemb'red . . . defense** your intellect, properly the defender
of shape and love, is set off independently and destroys all    136
**dead** declaring yourself dead    137 **happy** fortunate    151 **blaze**
announce publicly

166 **here . . . state** this is your situation
**III.iv.2 move** discuss the matter with    6 **promise** assure    11
**mewed . . . heaviness** shut up with her grief    12 **make . . .
tender** risk an offer

And bid her (mark you me?) on Wednesday next—
But soft! What day is this?

PARIS                   Monday, my lord.

CAPULET
Monday! Ha, ha! Well, Wednesday is too soon.
A° Thursday let it be—a Thursday, tell her,      20
She shall be married to this noble earl.
Will you be ready? Do you like this haste?
We'll keep no great ado—a friend or two;
For hark you, Tybalt being slain so late,
It may be thought we held him carelessly,      25
Being our kinsman, if we revel much.
Therefore we'll have some half a dozen friends,
And there an end. But what say you to Thursday?

PARIS
My lord, I would that Thursday were tomorrow.

CAPULET
Well, get you gone. A Thursday be it then.      30
Go you to Juliet ere you go to bed;
Prepare her, wife, against° this wedding day.
Farewell, my lord.—Light to my chamber, ho!
Afore me,° it is so very late
That we may call it early by and by.°      35
Good night.                   *Exeunt.*

[Scene V. *Capulet's orchard.*]

*Enter* ROMEO *and* JULIET *aloft.*

JULIET
Wilt thou be gone? It is not yet near day.
It was the nightingale, and not the lark,
That pierced the fearful° hollow of thine ear.
Nightly she sings on yond pomegranate tree.
Believe me, love, it was the nightingale.      5

ROMEO
It was the lark, the herald of the morn;
No nightingale. Look, love, what envious streaks
Do lace the severing clouds in yonder east.
Night's candles are burnt out, and jocund day
Stands tiptoe on the misty mountaintops.      10
I must be gone and live, or stay and die.

JULIET
Yond light is not daylight; I know it, I.
It is some meteor that the sun exhales°
To be to thee this night a torchbearer
And light thee on thy way to Mantua.      15
Therefore stay yet; thou need'st not to be gone.

ROMEO
Let me be ta'en, let me be put to death.
I am content, so thou wilt have it so.
I'll say yon gray is not the morning's eye,
'Tis but the pale reflex of Cynthia's brow;°      20
Nor that is not the lark whose notes do beat
The vaulty heaven so high above our heads.
I have more care to stay than will to go.
Come, death, and welcome! Juliet wills it so.
How is't, my soul? Let's talk; it is not day.      25

JULIET
It is, it is! Hie hence, be gone, away!
It is the lark that sings so out of tune,
Straining harsh discords and unpleasing sharps.
Some say the lark makes sweet division;°
This doth not so, for she divideth us.      30
Some say the lark and loathèd toad change eyes;
O, now I would they had changed voices too,
Since arm from arm that voice doth us affray,°
Hunting thee hence with hunt's-up° to the day.
O, now be gone! More light and light it grows.      35

ROMEO
More light and light—more dark and dark our woes.

*Enter* NURSE.

NURSE    Madam!

JULIET    Nurse?

NURSE
Your lady mother is coming to your chamber.
The day is broke; be wary, look about.      [*Exit.*]   40

JULIET
Then, window, let day in, and let life out.

ROMEO
Farewell, farewell! One kiss, and I'll descend.

[*He goeth down.*]

JULIET
Art thou gone so, love-lord, ay husband-friend?°
I must hear from thee every day in the hour,
For in a minute there are many days.      45
O, for this count I shall be much in years°
Ere I again behold my Romeo!

ROMEO
Farewell!
I will omit no opportunity
That may convey my greetings, love, to thee.      50

JULIET
O, think'st thou we shall ever meet again?

ROMEO
I doubt it not; and all these woes shall serve
For sweet discourses in our times to come.

JULIET
O God, I have an ill-divining° soul!
Methinks I see thee, now thou art so low,      55
As one dead in the bottom of a tomb.
Either my eyesight fails, or thou lookest pale.

ROMEO
And trust me, love, in my eye so do you.
Dry° sorrow drinks our blood. Adieu, adieu!      *Exit.*

JULIET
O Fortune, Fortune! All men call thee fickle.      60
If thou art fickle, what dost thou° with him
That is renowned for faith? Be fickle, Fortune,
For then I hope thou wilt not keep him long
But send him back.

*Enter mother* [LADY CAPULET].

20 **A** on   32 **against** in preparation for   34 **Afore me** indeed
(a light oath)   35 **by and by** soon
III.v.3 **fearful** fearing   13 **exhales** gives out   20 **reflex** . . .
**brow** reflection of the edge of the moon

29 **division** melody (i.e., a division of notes)   33 **affray**
frighten   34 **hunt's-up** morning song (for hunters)   43
**husband-friend** husband-lover   46 **much in years** much
older   54 **ill-divining** foreseeing evil   59 **Dry** thirsty (as grief
was thought to be)   61 **what dost thou** what business have
you

LADY CAPULET
Ho, daughter! Are you                                              65

JULIET
Who is't that calls? It is my lady mother.
Is she not down so late,° or up so early?
What unaccustomed cause procures her hither?

LADY CAPULET
Why, how now, Juliet?

JULIET                    Madam, I am not well.

LADY CAPULET
Evermore weeping for your cousin's death?           70
What, wilt thou wash him from his grave with tears?
And if thou couldst, thou couldst not make him live.
Therefore have done. Some grief shows much of love;
But much of grief shows still some want of wit.

JULIET
Yet let me weep for such a feeling loss.°            75

LADY CAPULET
So shall you feel the loss, but not the friend
Which you weep for.

JULIET                    Feeling so the loss,
I cannot choose but ever weep the friend.

LADY CAPULET
Well, girl, thou weep'st not so much for his death
As that the villain lives which slaughtered him.     80

JULIET
What villain, madam?

LADY CAPULET          That same villain Romeo.

JULIET [*Aside.*]
Villain and he be many miles asunder—
God pardon him! I do, with all my heart;
And yet no man like he doth grieve my heart.

LADY CAPULET
That is because the traitor murderer lives.          85

JULIET
Ay, madam, from the reach of these my hands.
Would none but I might venge my cousin's death!

LADY CAPULET
We will have vengeance for it, fear thou not.
Then weep no more. I'll send to one in Mantua,
Where that same banished runagate° doth live,       90
Shall give him such an unaccustomed dram
That he shall soon keep Tybalt company;
And then I hope thou wilt be satisfied.

JULIET
Indeed I never shall be satisfied
With Romeo till I behold him—dead°—                 95
Is my poor heart so for a kinsman vexed.
Madam, if you could find out but a man
To bear a poison, I would temper° it;
That Romeo should, upon receipt thereof,
Soon sleep in quiet. O, how my heart abhors        100
To hear him named and cannot come to him,
To wreak° the love I bore my cousin
Upon his body that hath slaughtered him!

LADY CAPULET
Find thou the means, and I'll find such a man.
But now I'll tell thee joyful tidings, girl.        105

JULIET
And joy comes well in such a needy time.
What are they, beseech your ladyship?

LADY CAPULET
Well, well, thou hast a careful° father, child;
One who, to put thee from thy heaviness,
Hath sorted out° a sudden day of joy               110
That thou expects not nor I looked not for.

JULIET
Madam, in happy time!° What day is that?

LADY CAPULET
Marry, my child, early next Thursday morn
The gallant, young, and noble gentleman,
The County Paris, at Saint Peter's Church,         115
Shall happily make thee there a joyful bride.

JULIET
Now by Saint Peter's Church, and Peter too,
He shall not make me there a joyful bride!
I wonder at this haste, that I must wed
Ere he that should be husband comes to woo.        120
I pray you tell my lord and father, madam,
I will not marry yet; and when I do, I swear
It shall be Romeo, whom you know I hate,
Rather than Paris. These are news indeed!

LADY CAPULET
Here comes your father. Tell him so yourself,      125
And see how he will take it at your hands.

*Enter* CAPULET *and* NURSE.

CAPULET
When the sun sets the earth doth drizzle dew,
But for the sunset of my brother's son
It rains downright.
How now? A conduit,° girl? What, still in tears?   130
Evermore show'ring? In one little body
Thou counterfeits a bark, a sea, a wind:
For still thy eyes, which I may call the sea,
Do ebb and flow with tears; the bark thy body is,
Sailing in this salt flood; the winds, thy sighs,  135
Who, raging with thy tears and they with them,
Without a sudden° calm will overset
Thy tempest-tossèd body. How now, wife?
Have you delivered to her our decree?

LADY CAPULET
Ay, sir; but she will none, she gives you thanks.°  140
I would the fool were married to her grave!

CAPULET
Soft! Take me with you,° take me with you, wife.
How? Will she none? Doth she not give us thanks?
Is she not proud? Doth she not count her blest,
Unworthy as she is, that we have wrought°          145
So worthy a gentleman to be her bride?

JULIET
Not proud° you have, but thankful that you have.
Proud can I never be of what I hate,
But thankful even for hate that is meant love.

CAPULET
How, how, how, how, chopped-logic?° What is this?  150

---

67 not . . . late so late getting to bed   75 feeling loss loss to be felt   90 runagate renegade   95 dead Lady Capulet takes this to refer to "him"; Juliet takes it to refer to "heart"   98 temper (1) mix (2) weaken   102 wreak (1) avenge (2) give expression to

108 careful solicitous   110 sorted out selected   112 in happy time most opportunely   130 conduit water pipe   137 sudden unanticipated, immediate   140 she . . . thanks she'll have none of it, thank you   142 Soft . . . you Wait! Help me to understand you   145 wrought arranged   147 proud highly pleased   150 chopped-logic chop logic, sophistry

"Proud"—and "I thank you"—and "I thank you
   not"—
And yet "not proud"? Mistress minion° you,
Thank me no thankings, nor proud me no prouds,
But fettle° your fine joints 'gainst Thursday next
To go with Paris to Saint Peter's Church,      155
Or I will drag thee on a hurdle° thither.
Out, you greensickness° carrion! Out, you baggage!°
You tallow-face!

LADY CAPULET   Fie, fie! What, are you mad?

JULIET
Good father, I beseech you on my knees,
Hear me with patience but to speak a word.     160

CAPULET
Hang thee, young baggage! Disobedient wretch!
I tell thee what—get thee to church a Thursday
Or never after look me in the face.
Speak not, reply not, do not answer me!
My fingers itch. Wife, we scarce thought us blest   165
That God had lent us but this only child;
But now I see this one is one too much,
And that we have a curse in having her.
Out on her, hilding!°

NURSE          God in heaven bless her!
You are to blame, my lord, to rate° her so.     170

CAPULET
And why, my Lady Wisdom? Hold your tongue,
Good Prudence. Smatter with your gossips,° go!

NURSE
I speak no treason.

CAPULET       O, God-i-god-en!°

NURSE
May not one speak?

CAPULET        Peace, you mumbling fool!
Utter your gravity o'er a gossip's bowl,     175
For here we need it not.

LADY CAPULET       You are too hot.

CAPULET
God's bread!° It makes me mad.
Day, night; hour, tide, time; work, play;
Alone, in company; still my care hath been
To have her matched; and having now provided   180
A gentleman of noble parentage,
Of fair demesnes,° youthful, and nobly trained,
Stuffed, as they say, with honorable parts,
Proportioned as one's thought would wish a man—
And then to have a wretched puling° fool,     185
A whining mammet,° in her fortune's tender,°
To answer "I'll not wed, I cannot love;
I am too young, I pray you pardon me"!
But, and you will not wed, I'll pardon you!°
Graze where you will, you shall not house with me.   190
Look to't, think on't; I do not use to jest.°

Thursday is near; lay hand on heart, advise:°
And you be mine, I'll give you to my friend;
And you be not, hang, beg, starve, die in the streets,
For, by my soul, I'll ne'er acknowledge thee,    195
Nor what is mine shall never do thee good.
Trust to't. Bethink you. I'll not be forsworn.    *Exit.*

JULIET
Is there no pity sitting in the clouds
That sees into the bottom of my grief?
O sweet my mother, cast me not away!     200
Delay this marriage for a month, a week;
Or if you do not, make the bridal bed
In that dim monument where Tybalt lies.

LADY CAPULET
Talk not to me, for I'll not speak a word.
Do as thou wilt, for I have done with thee.    *Exit.* 205

JULIET
O God!—O nurse, how shall this be prevented?
My husband is on earth, my faith in heaven.°
How shall that faith return again to earth
Unless that husband send it me from heaven
By leaving earth?° Comfort me, counsel me.    210
Alack, alack, that heaven should practice stratagems
Upon so soft a subject as myself!
What say'st thou? Hast thou not a word of joy?
Some comfort, nurse.

NURSE         Faith, here it is.
Romeo is banished; and all the world to nothing°  215
That he dares ne'er come back to challenge you;
Or if he do, it needs must be by stealth.
Then, since the case so stands as now it doth,
I think it best you married with the county.
O, he's a lovely gentleman!     220
Romeo's a dishclout° to him. An eagle, madam,
Hath not so green, so quick, so fair an eye
As Paris hath. Beshrew° my very heart,
I think you are happy in this second match,
For it excels your first; or if it did not,    225
Your first is dead—or 'twere as good he were
As living here and you no use of him.

JULIET
Speak'st thou from thy heart?

NURSE
And from my soul too; else beshrew them both.

JULIET  Amen!     230

NURSE  What?

JULIET
Well, thou hast comforted me marvelous much.
Go in; and tell my lady I am gone,
Having displeased my father, to Lawrence' cell,
To make confession and to be absolved.    235

NURSE
Marry, I will; and this is wisely done.    [*Exit.*]

JULIET
Ancient damnation!° O most wicked fiend!
Is it more sin to wish me thus forsworn,°

---

152 minion minx   154 fettle make ready   156 hurdle sledge on which traitors were taken to execution   157 greensickness anemic, after the fashion of young girls; baggage strumpet 169 hilding worthless person   170 rate scold   172 Smatter . . . gossips save your chatter for your cronies   173 God-i-god-en God give you good even! (here equivalent to "Get on with you!")   177 God's bread By the sacred host!   182 demesnes domains   185 puling whining   186 mammet puppet; in . . . tender (1) on good fortune's offer (2) subject to fortuitous circumstance (?)   189 I'll pardon you i.e., in a way you don't expect   191 do . . . jest am not in the habit of joking

Or to dispraise my lord with that same tongue
Which she hath praised him with above compare          240
So many thousand times? Go, counselor!
Thou and my bosom henceforth shall be twain.°
I'll to the friar to know his remedy.
If all else fail, myself have power to die.          *Exit.*


# [ ACT IV ]

### [Scene I. *Friar Lawrence's cell.*]

*Enter* FRIAR [*Lawrence*] *and County* PARIS.

FRIAR
On Thursday, sir? The time is very short.
PARIS
My father Capulet will have it so,
And I am nothing slow to slack his haste.°
FRIAR
You say you do not know the lady's mind.
Uneven° is the course; I like it not.          5
PARIS
Immoderately she weeps for Tybalt's death,
And therefore have I little talked of love;
For Venus smiles not in a house of tears.
Now, sir, her father counts it dangerous
That she do give her sorrow so much sway,          10
And in his wisdom hastes our marriage
To stop the inundation of her tears,
Which, too much minded° by herself alone,°
May be put from her by society.
Now do you know the reason of this haste.          15
FRIAR [*Aside.*]
I would I knew not why it should be slowed,—
Look, sir, here comes the lady toward my cell.

*Enter* JULIET.

PARIS
Happily met, my lady and my wife!
JULIET
That may be, sir, when I may be a wife.
PARIS
That "may be" must be, love, on Thursday next.          20
JULIET
What must be shall be.
FRIAR                    That's a certain text.
PARIS
Come you to make confession to this father?
JULIET
To answer that, I should confess to you.
PARIS
Do not deny to him that you love me.
JULIET
I will confess to you that I love him.          25
PARIS
So will ye, I am sure, that you love me.

JULIET
If I do so, it will be of more price,
Being spoke behind your back, than to your face.
PARIS
Poor soul, thy face is much abused with tears.
JULIET
The tears have got small victory by that,          30
For it was bad enough before their spite.°
PARIS
Thou wrong'st it more than tears with that report.
JULIET
That is no slander, sir, which is a truth;
And what I spake, I spake it to my face.
PARIS
Thy face is mine, and thou hast sland'red it.          35
JULIET
It may be so, for it is not mine own.
Are you at leisure, holy father, now,
Or shall I come to you at evening mass?°
FRIAR
My leisure serves me, pensive daughter, now.
My lord, we must entreat the time alone.°          40
PARIS
God shield° I should disturb devotion!
Juliet, on Thursday early will I rouse ye.
Till then, adieu, and keep this holy kiss.          *Exit.*
JULIET
O, shut the door, and when thou hast done so,
Come weep with me—past hope, past care, past help!          45
FRIAR
O Juliet, I already know thy grief;
It strains me past the compass of my wits.
I hear thou must, and nothing may prorogue° it,
On Thursday next be married to this county.
JULIET
Tell me not, friar, that thou hearest of this,          50
Unless thou tell me how I may prevent it.
If in thy wisdom thou canst give no help,
Do thou but call my resolution wise
And with this knife I'll help it presently.°
God joined my heart and Romeo's, thou our hands;          55
And ere this hand, by thee to Romeo's sealed,
Shall be the label° to another deed,°
Or my true heart with treacherous revolt
Turn to another, this shall slay them both.
Therefore, out of thy long-experienced time,          60
Give me some present counsel; or, behold,
'Twixt my extremes and me this bloody knife
Shall play the umpire, arbitrating that
Which the commission° of thy years and art
Could to no issue of true honor bring.          65
Be not so long to speak. I long to die
If what thou speak'st speak not of remedy.
FRIAR
Hold, daughter. I do spy a kind of hope,
Which craves as desperate an execution
As that is desperate which we would prevent.          70

242 **Thou . . . twain** You shall henceforth be separated from
my trust
**IV.i.3 I . . . haste** I shall not check his haste by being slow
myself   **5 Uneven** irregular   **13 minded** thought about; **by
herself alone** when she is alone

**31 before their spite** before they marred it   **38 evening mass**
evening mass was still said occasionally in Shakespeare's time
**40 entreat . . . alone** ask to have this time to ourselves
**41 God shield** God forbid   **48 prorogue** delay   **54 presently**
at once   **57 label** bearer of the seal; **deed** (1) act (2) legal
document   **64 commission** authority

If, rather than to marry County Paris,
Thou hast the strength of will to slay thyself,
Then is it likely thou wilt undertake
A thing like death to chide away this shame,
That cop'st° with death himself to scape from it;     75
And, if thou darest, I'll give thee remedy.

JULIET
O, bid me leap, rather than marry Paris,
From off the battlements of any tower,
Or walk in thievish° ways, or bid me lurk
Where serpents are; chain me with roaring bears,     80
Or hide me nightly in a charnel house,°
O'ercovered quite with dead men's rattling bones,
With reeky° shanks and yellow chapless° skulls;
Or bid me go into a new-made grave
And hide me with a dead man in his shroud—     85
Things that, to hear them told, have made me
    tremble—
And I will do it without fear or doubt,
To live an unstained wife to my sweet love.

FRIAR
Hold, then. Go home, be merry, give consent
To marry Paris. Wednesday is tomorrow.     90
Tomorrow night look that thou lie alone;
Let not the nurse lie with thee in thy chamber.
Take thou this vial, being then in bed,
And this distilling° liquor drink thou off;
When presently through all thy veins shall run     95
A cold and drowsy humor;° for no pulse
Shall keep his native° progress, but surcease;°
No warmth, no breath, shall testify thou livest;
The roses in thy lips and cheeks shall fade
To wanny° ashes, thy eyes' windows° fall     100
Like death when he shuts up the day of life;
Each part, deprived of supple government,°
Shall, stiff and stark and cold, appear like death;
And in this borrowed likeness of shrunk death
Thou shalt continue two-and-forty hours,     105
And then awake as from a pleasant sleep.
Now, when the bridegroom in the morning comes
To rouse thee from thy bed, there art thou dead.
Then, as the manner of our country is,
In thy best robes uncovered on the bier     110
Thou shalt be borne to that same ancient vault
Where all the kindred of the Capulets lie.
In the meantime, against° thou shalt awake,
Shall Romeo by my letters know our drift;°
And hither shall he come; and he and I     115
Will watch thy waking, and that very night
Shall Romeo bear thee hence to Mantua.
And this shall free thee from this present shame,
If no inconstant toy° nor womanish fear
Abate thy valor in the acting it.     120

JULIET
Give me, give me! O, tell not me of fear!

FRIAR
Hold! Get you gone, be strong and prosperous

75 cop'st negotiates   79 thievish infested with thieves   81
charnel house vault for old bones   83 reeky damp; chapless
jawless   94 distilling infusing   96 humor fluid   97 native
natural; surcease stop   100 wanny pale; windows lids   102
supple government faculty for maintaining motion   113
against before   114 drift purpose   119 inconstant toy
whim

In this resolve. I'll send a friar with speed
To Mantua, with my letters to thy lord.

JULIET
Love give me strength, and strength shall help afford.     125
Farewell, dear father.         *Exit [with* FRIAR].

[Scene II. *Hall in Capulet's house.*]

*Enter father* CAPULET, *mother* [LADY CAPULET],
NURSE, *and* SERVINGMEN, *two or three.*

CAPULET
So many guests invite as here are writ.
                [*Exit a* SERVINGMAN.]
Sirrah, go hire me twenty cunning° cooks.

SERVINGMAN You shall have none ill, sir; for I'll try°
if they can lick their fingers.

CAPULET
How canst thou try them so?     5

SERVINGMAN Marry, sir, 'tis an ill cook that cannot
lick his own fingers.° Therefore he that cannot lick
his fingers goes not with me.

CAPULET Go, begone.         [*Exit* SERVINGMAN.]
We shall be much unfurnished° for this time.     10
What, is my daughter gone to Friar Lawrence?

NURSE Ay, forsooth.

CAPULET
Well, he may chance to do some good on her.
A peevish self-willed harlotry it is.°

*Enter* JULIET.

NURSE
See where she comes from shrift with merry look.     15

CAPULET
How now, my headstrong? Where have you been
    gadding?

JULIET
Where I have learnt me to repent the sin
Of disobedient opposition
To you and your behests, and am enjoined
By holy Lawrence to fall prostrate here     20
To beg your pardon. Pardon, I beseech you!
Henceforward I am ever ruled by you.

CAPULET
Send for the county. Go tell him of this.
I'll have this knot knit up tomorrow morning.

JULIET
I met the youthful lord at Lawrence' cell     25
And gave him what becomèd° love I might,
Not stepping o'er the bounds of modesty.

CAPULET
Why, I am glad on't. This is well. Stand up.
This is as't should be. Let me see the county.
Ay, marry, go, I say, and fetch him hither.     30
Now, afore God, this reverend holy friar,
All our whole city is much bound to him.

JULIET
Nurse, will you go with me into my closet°

IV.ii.2 cunning skillful   3 try test   6–7 cannot . . . fingers
cannot taste his own cooking   10 unfurnished unprovisioned
14 A . . . is She's a silly good-for-nothing   26 becomèd
proper   33 closet private chamber

To help me sort such needful ornaments
As you think fit to furnish me tomorrow?                    35

LADY CAPULET
No, not till Thursday. There is time enough.

CAPULET
Go, nurse, go with her. We'll to church tomorrow.
                              *Exeunt* [JULIET *and* NURSE].

LADY CAPULET
We shall be short in our provision.
'Tis now near night.

CAPULET                    Tush, I will stir about,
And all things shall be well, I warrant thee, wife.           40
Go thou to Juliet, help to deck up her.
I'll not to bed tonight; let me alone.
I'll play the housewife for this once. What, ho!
They are all forth; well, I will walk myself
To County Paris, to prepare up him                          45
Against° tomorrow. My heart is wondrous light,
Since this same wayward girl is so reclaimed.
                              *Exit* [*with* LADY CAPULET].


[Scene III. *Juliet's chamber.*]

*Enter* JULIET *and* NURSE.

JULIET
Ay, those attires are best; but, gentle nurse,
I pray thee leave me to myself tonight;
For I have need of many orisons°
To move the heavens to smile upon my state,°
Which, well thou knowest, is cross° and full of sin.         5

*Enter mother* [LADY CAPULET].

LADY CAPULET
What, are you busy, ho? Need you my help?

JULIET
No, madam; we have culled such necessaries
As are behoveful° for our state° tomorrow.
So please you, let me now be left alone,
And let the nurse this night sit up with you;               10
For I am sure you have your hands full all
In this so sudden business.

LADY CAPULET                    Good night.
Get thee to bed, and rest; for thou hast need.
                              *Exeunt* [LADY CAPULET *and* NURSE].

JULIET
Farewell! God knows when we shall meet again.
I have a faint° cold fear thrills through my veins          15
That almost freezes up the heat of life.
I'll call them back again to comfort me.
Nurse!—What should she do here?
My dismal scene I needs must act alone.
Come, vial.                                                 20
What if this mixture do not work at all?
Shall I be married then tomorrow morning?
No, no! This shall forbid it. Lie thou there.

[*Lays down a dagger.*]

What if it be a poison which the friar
Subtly hath minist'red° to have me dead,                    25

Lest in this marriage he should be dishonored
Because he married me before to Romeo?
I fear it is; and yet methinks it should not,
For he hath still° been tried° a holy man.
How if, when I am laid into the tomb,                       30
I wake before the time that Romeo
Come to redeem me? There's a fearful point!
Shall I not then be stifled in the vault,
To whose foul mouth no healthsome air breathes in,
And there die strangled ere my Romeo comes?                 35
Or, if I live, is it not very like
The horrible conceit° of death and night,
Together with the terror of the place—
As in a vault, an ancient receptacle
Where for this many hundred years the bones                 40
Of all my buried ancestors are packed;
Where bloody Tybalt, yet but green in earth,°
Lies fest'ring in his shroud; where, as they say,
At some hours in the night spirits resort—
Alack, alack, is it not like that I,                        45
So early waking—what with loathsome smells,
And shrieks like mandrakes° torn out of the earth,
That living mortals, hearing them, run mad—
I, if I wake, shall I not be distraught,°
Environèd with all these hideous fears,                     50
And madly play with my forefathers' joints,
And pluck the mangled Tybalt from his shroud,
And, in this rage, with some great kinsman's bone
As with a club dash out my desp'rate brains?
O, look! Methinks I see my cousin's ghost                   55
Seeking out Romeo, that did spit his body
Upon a rapier's point. Stay, Tybalt, stay!
Romeo, Romeo, Romeo, I drink to thee.

[*She falls upon her bed within the curtains.*]


[Scene IV. *Hall in Capulet's house.*]

*Enter lady of the house* [LADY CAPULET] *and* NURSE.

LADY CAPULET
Hold, take these keys and fetch more spices, nurse.

NURSE
They call for dates and quinces in the pastry.°

*Enter old* CAPULET.

CAPULET
Come, stir, stir, stir! The second cock hath crowed,
The curfew bell hath rung, 'tis three o'clock.
Look to the baked meats,° good Angelica;°                    5
Spare not for cost.

NURSE                    Go, you cotquean,° go,
Get you to bed! Faith, you'll be sick tomorrow
For this night's watching.°

CAPULET
No, not a whit. What, I have watched ere now
All night for lesser cause, and ne'er been sick.            10

**29 still** always; **tried** proved   **37 conceit** thought   **42 green
in earth** newly entombed   **47 mandrakes** plant with forked
root, resembling the human body (supposed to shriek when
uprooted and drive the hearer mad)   **49 distraught** driven mad
**IV.iv.2 pastry** pastrycook's room   **5 baked meats** meat pies;
**Angelica** the Nurse's name   **6 cotquean** man who does
woman's work   **8 watching** staying awake

**46 Against** in anticipation of
**IV.iii.3 orisons** prayers   **4 state** condition   **5 cross** perverse
**8 behoveful** expedient; **state** pomp   **15 faint** causing faintness   **25 minist'red** provided

LADY CAPULET
Ay, you have been a mouse hunt° in your time;
But I will watch you from such watching now.
               *Exit* LADY CAPULET *and* NURSE.

CAPULET
A jealous hood,° a jealous hood!

*Enter three or four* [FELLOWS] *with spits and logs and baskets.*

                       Now, fellow,
What is there?
FIRST FELLOW
Things for the cook, sir; but I know not what.     15
CAPULET
Make haste, make haste. [*Exit* FIRST FELLOW.]
   Sirrah, fetch drier logs.
Call Peter; he will show thee where they are.
SECOND FELLOW
I have a head, sir, that will find out logs°
And never trouble Peter for the matter.
CAPULET
Mass,° and well said; a merry whoreson,° ha!     20
Thou shalt be loggerhead.°
          [*Exit* SECOND FELLOW, *with the others.*]
               Good faith, 'tis day.
The county will be here with music straight,
For so he said he would.    *Play music.*
               I hear him near.
Nurse! Wife! What, ho! What, nurse, I say!

*Enter* NURSE.

Go waken Juliet; go and trim her up.     25
I'll go and chat with Paris. Hie, make haste,
Make haste! The bridegroom he is come already:
Make haste, I say.               [*Exit.*]


        [Scene V. *Juliet's chamber.*]

NURSE°
Mistress! What, mistress! Juliet! Fast,° I warrant her,
   she.
Why, lamb! Why, lady! Fie, you slugabed.°
Why, love, I say! Madam; sweetheart! Why, bride!
What, not a word? You take your pennyworths° now;
Sleep for a week; for the next night, I warrant,     5
The County Paris hath set up his rest°
That you shall rest but little. God forgive me!
Marry, and amen. How sound is she asleep!
I needs must wake her. Madam, madam, madam!
Ay, let the county take you in your bed;     10
He'll fright you up, i' faith. Will it not be?

[*Draws aside the curtains.*]

11 **mouse hunt** night prowler, woman chaser   **13 A jealous hood** you wear the cap of a jealous person   **18 will . . . logs** has an affinity for logs (i.e., is wooden also)   **20 Mass** by the Mass; **whoreson** rascal   **21 loggerhead** blockhead   **IV.v.1 Nurse** at the conclusion of the last scene the Nurse presumably did not go off stage but remained on the forestage, and after Capulet's departure she now walks to the rear to open the curtains, revealing Juliet; **Fast** fast asleep   **2 slugabed** sleepyhead   **4 pennyworths** small portions (i.e., short naps)   **6 set . . . rest** firmly resolved (with bawdy suggestion of having a lance in readiness)

What, dressed, and in your clothes, and down° again?
I must needs wake you. Lady! Lady! Lady!
Alas, alas! Help, help! My lady's dead!
O weraday° that ever I was born!     15
Some aqua vitae,° ho! My lord! My lady!

[*Enter* LADY CAPULET.]

LADY CAPULET
What noise is here?
NURSE             O lamentable day!
LADY CAPULET
What is the matter?
NURSE             Look, look! O heavy day!
LADY CAPULET
O me, O me! My child, my only life!
Revive, look up, or I will die with thee!     20
Help, help! Call help.

*Enter father* [CAPULET].

CAPULET
For shame, bring Juliet forth; her lord is come.
NURSE
She's dead, deceased; she's dead, alack the day!
LADY CAPULET
Alack the day, she's dead, she's dead, she's dead!
CAPULET
Ha! Let me see her. Out alas! She's cold,     25
Her blood is settled, and her joints are stiff;
Life and these lips have long been separated.
Death lies on her like an untimely frost
Upon the sweetest flower of all the field.
NURSE
O lamentable day!
LADY CAPULET    O woeful time!     30
CAPULET
Death, that hath ta'en her hence to make me wail,
Ties up my tongue and will not let me speak.

*Enter* FRIAR [*Lawrence*] *and the County* [PARIS, *with* MUSICIANS].

FRIAR
Come, is the bride ready to go to church?
CAPULET
Ready to go, but never to return.
O son, the night before thy wedding day     35
Hath Death lain with thy wife. There she lies,
Flower as she was, deflowerèd by him.
Death is my son-in-law, Death is my heir;
My daughter he hath wedded. I will die
And leave him all. Life, living, all is Death's.     40
PARIS
Have I thought, love, to see this morning's face,
And doth it give me such a sight as this?
LADY CAPULET
Accursed, unhappy, wretched, hateful day!
Most miserable hour that e'er time saw
In lasting labor of his pilgrimage!     45
But one, poor one, one poor and loving child,
But one thing to rejoice and solace in,
And cruel Death hath catched it from my sight.
NURSE
O woe! O woeful, woeful, woeful day!

**12 down** gone back to bed   **15 weraday** welladay, alas   **16 aqua vitae** spirits

Most lamentable day, most woeful day
That ever ever I did yet behold!
O day, O day, O day! O hateful day!
Never was seen so black a day as this.
O woeful day! O woeful day!  50

PARIS
Beguiled, divorcèd, wrongèd, spited, slain!  55
Most detestable Death, by thee beguiled,
By cruel, cruel thee quite overthrown.
O love! O life!—not life, but love in death!

CAPULET
Despised, distressèd, hated, martyred, killed!
Uncomfortable° time, why cam'st thou now  60
To murder, murder our solemnity?
O child, O child! My soul, and not my child!
Dead art thou—alack, my child is dead,
And with my child my joys are buried!

FRIAR
Peace, ho, for shame! Confusion's cure lives not  65
In these confusions. Heaven and yourself
Had part in this fair maid—now heaven hath all,
And all the better is it for the maid.
Your part in her you could not keep from death,
But heaven keeps his part in eternal life.  70
The most you sought was her promotion,
For 'twas your heaven she should be advanced;
And weep ye now, seeing she is advanced
Above the clouds, as high as heaven itself?
O, in this love, you love your child so ill  75
That you run mad, seeing that she is well.°
She's not well married that lives married long,
But she's best married that dies married young.
Dry up your tears and stick your rosemary°
On this fair corse, and, as the custom is,  80
And in her best array bear her to church;
For though fond nature° bids us all lament,
Yet nature's tears are reason's merriment.

CAPULET
All things that we ordainèd festival
Turn from their office to black funeral—  85
Our instruments to melancholy bells,
Our wedding cheer to a sad burial feast;
Our solemn hymns to sullen dirges change;
Our bridal flowers serve for a buried corse;
And all things change them to the contrary.  90

FRIAR
Sir, go you in; and, madam, go with him;
And go, Sir Paris. Everyone prepare
To follow this fair corse unto her grave.
The heavens do low'r° upon you for some ill;
Move them no more by crossing their high will.  95
*Exeunt [casting rosemary on her and shutting the
curtains]. Manet° [the NURSE and MUSICIANS].*

FIRST MUSICIAN
Faith, we may put up our pipes and be gone.

NURSE
Honest good fellows, ah, put up, put up!
For well you know this is a pitiful case.°  *[Exit.]*

FIRST MUSICIAN
Ay, by my troth, the case may be amended.

*Enter [PETER].*

PETER  Musicians, O, musicians, "Heart's ease,"  100
"Heart's ease"! O, and you will have me live, play
"Heart's ease."
FIRST MUSICIAN  Why "Heart's ease"?
PETER  O, musicians, because my heart itself plays
"My heart is full." O, play me some merry dump° to  105
comfort me.
FIRST MUSICIAN  Not a dump we! 'Tis no time to
play now.
PETER  You will not then?
FIRST MUSICIAN  No.  110
PETER  I will then give it you soundly.
FIRST MUSICIAN  What will you give us?
PETER  No money, on my faith, but the gleek.° I will
give you° the minstrel.
FIRST MUSICIAN  Then will I give you the serving-  15
creature.
PETER  Then will I lay the serving-creature's dagger
on your pate. I will carry° no crotchets.° I'll re you,
I'll fa° you. Do you note° me?
FIRST MUSICIAN  And you re us and fa us, you note  120
us.°
SECOND MUSICIAN  Pray you put up your dagger,
and put out° your wit. Then have at you with my wit!
PETER  I will dry-beat you with an iron wit, and put
up my iron dagger. Answer me like men.  125
    "When griping grief the heart doth wound,
        And doleful dumps the mind oppress,
    Then music with her silver sound"°—
Why "silver sound"? Why "music with her silver
sound"? What say you, Simon Catling?°  130
FIRST MUSICIAN  Marry, sir, because silver hath a
sweet sound.
PETER  Pretty! What say you, Hugh Rebeck?°
SECOND MUSICIAN  I say "silver sound" because
musicians sound for silver.  135
PETER  Pretty too! What say you, James Soundpost?°
THIRD MUSICIAN  Faith, I know not what to say.
PETER  O, I cry you mercy,° you are the singer. I will
say for you. It is "music with her silver sound" because
musicians have no gold for sounding.  140
    "Then music with her silver sound
        With speedy help doth lend redress."  *Exit.*
FIRST MUSICIAN  What a pestilent knave is this
same!
SECOND MUSICIAN  Hang him, Jack! Come, we'll  145
in here, tarry for the mourners, and stay dinner.
    *Exit [with others].*

---

60 **Uncomfortable** discomforting  76 **well** in blessed condition, in heaven  79 **rosemary** an evergreen, signifying remembrance  82 **fond nature** foolish human nature  94 **low'r** frown  95 **s.d. Manet** remains (Latin)  98 **case** (1) situation (2) instrument case

105 **dump** sad tune  113 **gleek** gibe  114 **give you** call you  118 **carry** endure; **crotchets** (1) whims (2) quarter notes  118–19 **re . . . fa** musical notes, but used perhaps with puns on *ray*, or *bewray* = befoul, and *fay* = polish (see H. Kökeritz, *Shakespeare's Pronunciation*, pp. 105–06)  119 **note** understand  120–21 **note us** set us to music  123 **put out** set out, display  126–28 **When . . . sound** the song is from Richard Edwards' "In Commendation of Music," in *The Paradise of Dainty Devices* (1576)  130 **Catling** catgut, a lute string  133 **Rebeck** a three-stringed fiddle  136 **Soundpost** peg that gives internal support to a violin  138 **cry you mercy** beg your pardon

# [ ACT V ]

### [Scene I. *Mantua. A street.*]

*Enter* ROMEO.

ROMEO
If I may trust the flattering° truth of sleep,
My dreams presage some joyful news at hand.
My bosom's lord° sits lightly in his throne,
And all this day an unaccustomed spirit
Lifts me above the ground with cheerful thoughts.　5
I dreamt my lady came and found me dead
(Strange dream that gives a dead man leave to think!)
And breathed such life with kisses in my lips
That I revived and was an emperor.
Ah me! How sweet is love itself possessed,　　10
When but love's shadows° are so rich in joy!

*Enter Romeo's* MAN [*Balthasar, booted*].

News from Verona! How now, Balthasar?
Dost thou not bring me letters from the friar?
How doth my lady? Is my father well?
How fares my Juliet? That I ask again,　　15
For nothing can be ill if she be well.
MAN
Then she is well, and nothing can be ill.
Her body sleeps in Capel's monument,°
And her immortal part with angels lives.
I saw her laid low in her kindred's vault　　20
And presently took post° to tell it you.
O, pardon me for bringing these ill news,
Since you did leave it for my office,° sir.
ROMEO
Is it e'en so? Then I defy you, stars!
Thou knowest my lodging. Get me ink and paper　25
And hire post horses. I will hence tonight.
MAN
I do beseech you, sir, have patience.
Your looks are pale and wild and do import°
Some misadventure.
ROMEO　　　　　　　　Tush, thou art deceived.
Leave me and do the thing I bid thee do.　　30
Hast thou no letters to me from the friar?
MAN
No, my good lord.
ROMEO　　　　　　No matter. Get thee gone.
And hire those horses. I'll be with thee straight.
*Exit* [MAN].
Well, Juliet, I will lie with thee tonight.
Let's see for means. O mischief, thou art swift　35
To enter in the thoughts of desperate men!
I do remember an apothecary,
And hereabouts 'a dwells, which late I noted
In tatt'red weeds,° with overwhelming° brows,
Culling of simples.° Meager were his looks,　　40
Sharp misery had worn him to the bones;
And in his needy shop a tortoise hung,
An alligator stuffed, and other skins

Of ill-shaped fishes; and about his shelves
A beggarly account° of empty boxes,　　　45
Green earthen pots, bladders, and musty seeds,
Remnants of packthread, and old cakes of roses°
Were thinly scattered, to make up a show.
Noting this penury, to myself I said,
"And if a man did need a poison now　　　50
Whose sale is present death in Mantua,
Here lives a caitiff° wretch would sell it him."
O, this same thought did but forerun my need,
And this same needy man must sell it me.
As I remember, this should be the house.　　55
Being holiday, the beggar's shop is shut.
What, ho! Apothecary!

[*Enter* APOTHECARY.]

APOTHECARY　　　　　　Who calls so loud?
ROMEO
Come hither, man. I see that thou art poor.
Hold, there is forty ducats. Let me have
A dram of poison, such soon-speeding gear°　　60
As will disperse itself through all the veins
That the life-weary taker may fall dead,
And that the trunk° may be discharged of breath
As violently as hasty powder fired
Doth hurry from the fatal cannon's womb.　　65
APOTHECARY
Such mortal drugs I have; but Mantua's law
Is death to any he that utters° them.
ROMEO
Art thou so bare and full of wretchedness
And fearest to die? Famine is in thy cheeks,
Need and oppression starveth° in thy eyes,　　70
Contempt and beggary hangs upon thy back:
The world is not thy friend, nor the world's law;
The world affords no law to make thee rich;
Then be not poor, but break it and take this.
APOTHECARY
My poverty but not my will consents.　　　75
ROMEO
I pay thy poverty and not thy will.
APOTHECARY
Put this in any liquid thing you will
And drink it off, and if you had the strength
Of twenty men, it would dispatch you straight.
ROMEO
There is thy gold—worse poison to men's souls,　80
Doing more murder in this loathsome world,
Than these poor compounds that thou mayst not sell.
I sell thee poison; thou hast sold me none.
Farewell. Buy food and get thyself in flesh.
Come, cordial° and not poison, go with me　　85
To Juliet's grave; for there must I use thee.　*Exeunt.*

### [Scene II. *Friar Lawrence's cell.*]

*Enter Friar* JOHN *to Friar* LAWRENCE.

JOHN
Holy Franciscan friar, brother, ho!

---

**V.i.1 flattering** illusory　**3 bosom's lord** heart　**11 shadows**
dreams　**18 monument** tomb　**21 post** post horses　**23 office**
duty　**28 import** suggest　**39 weeds** clothes; **overwhelming**
overhanging　**40 Culling of simples** collecting medicinal
herbs

**45 account** number　**47 cakes of roses** pressed rose petals
(for perfume)　**52 caitiff** miserable　**60 soon-speeding gear**
fast-working stuff　**63 trunk** body　**67 utters** dispenses　**70
starveth** stand starving　**85 cordial** restorative

*Enter [Friar]* LAWRENCE.

LAWRENCE
This same should be the voice of Friar John.
Welcome from Mantua. What says Romeo?
Or, if his mind be writ, give me his letter.

JOHN
Going to find a barefoot brother out,       5
One of our order, to associate° me
Here in this city visiting the sick,
And finding him, the searchers° of the town,
Suspecting that we both were in a house
Where the infectious pestilence did reign,      10
Sealed up the doors, and would not let us forth,
So that my speed to Mantua there was stayed.

LAWRENCE
Who bare my letter, then, to Romeo?

JOHN
I could not send it—here it is again—
Nor get a messenger to bring it thee,       15
So fearful were they of infection.

LAWRENCE
Unhappy fortune! By my brotherhood,°
The letter was not nice,° but full of charge,°
Of dear import; and the neglecting it
May do much danger. Friar John, go hence,    20
Get me an iron crow° and bring it straight
Unto my cell.

JOHN          Brother, I'll go and bring it thee. *Exit.*

LAWRENCE
Now must I to the monument alone.
Within this three hours will fair Juliet wake.
She will beshrew° me much that Romeo     25
Hath had no notice of these accidents;°
But I will write again to Mantua,
And keep her at my cell till Romeo come—
Poor living corse, closed in a dead man's tomb! *Exit.*

[Scene III. *A churchyard; in it a monument
belonging to the Capulets.*]

*Enter* PARIS *and his* PAGE [*with flowers and sweet water*].

PARIS
Give me thy torch, boy. Hence, and stand aloof.
Yet put it out, for I would not be seen.
Under yond yew trees lay thee all along,°
Holding thy ear close to the hollow ground.
So shall no foot upon the churchyard tread    5
(Being loose, unfirm, with digging up of graves)
But thou shalt hear it. Whistle then to me,
As signal that thou hearest something approach.
Give me those flowers. Do as I bid thee, go.

PAGE [*Aside.*]
I am almost afraid to stand alone       10
Here in the churchyard; yet I will adventure.°
                       [*Retires.*]

PARIS
Sweet flower, with flowers thy bridal bed I strew
   (O woe! thy canopy is dust and stones)
Which with sweet° water nightly I will dew;
   Or, wanting that, with tears distilled by moans.    15
The obsequies that I for thee will keep
Nightly shall be to strew thy grave and weep.

*Whistle* BOY.

The boy gives warning something doth approach.
What cursèd foot wanders this way tonight
To cross° my obsequies and true love's rite?    20
What, with a torch? Muffle° me, night, awhile.
                       [*Retires.*]

*Enter* ROMEO [*and* BALTHASAR *with a torch, a mattock,
and a crow of iron*].

ROMEO
Give me that mattock and the wrenching iron.
Hold, take this letter. Early in the morning
See thou deliver it to my lord and father.
Give me the light. Upon thy life I charge thee,    25
Whate'er thou hearest or see'st, stand all aloof
And do not interrupt me in my course.
Why I descend into this bed of death
Is partly to behold my lady's face,
But chiefly to take thence from her dead finger   30
A precious ring—a ring that I must use
In dear employment.° Therefore hence, be gone.
But if thou, jealous,° dost return to pry
In what I farther shall intend to do,
By heaven, I will tear thee joint by joint      35
And strew this hungry churchyard with thy limbs.
The time and my intents are savage-wild,
More fierce and more inexorable far
Than empty tigers or the roaring sea.

BALTHASAR
I will be gone, sir, and not trouble ye.       40

ROMEO
So shalt thou show me friendship. Take thou that.
Live, and be prosperous; and farewell, good fellow.

BALTHASAR [*Aside.*]
For all this same, I'll hide me hereabout.
His looks I fear, and his intents I doubt.°    [*Retires.*]

ROMEO
Thou detestable maw,° thou womb of death,    45
Gorged with the dearest morsel of the earth,
Thus I enforce thy rotten jaws to open,
And in despite° I'll cram thee with more food.

[ROMEO *opens the tomb.*]

PARIS
This is that banished haughty Montague
That murd'red my love's cousin—with which grief   50
It is supposed the fair creature died—
And here is come to do some villainous shame
To the dead bodies. I will apprehend him.
Stop thy unhallowèd toil, vile Montague!
Can vengeance be pursued further than death?    55

---

V.ii.6 **associate** accompany   8 **searchers** health officers
17 **brotherhood** religious order   18 **nice** trivial; **charge**
importance   21 **crow** crowbar   25 **beshrew** blame   26
**accidents** happenings
V.iii.3 **lay . . . along** lie at full length   11 **adventure** risk it

14 **sweet** perfumed   20 **cross** interrupt   21 **Muffle** hide   32
**dear employment** important business   33 **jealous** curious
44 **doubt** suspect   45 **maw** stomach   48 **in despite** to spite
you

Condemnèd villain, I do apprehend thee.
Obey, and go with me; for thou must die.

ROMEO
I must indeed; and therefore came I hither.
Good gentle youth, tempt not a desp'rate man.
Fly hence and leave me. Think upon these gone;     60
Let them affright thee. I beseech thee, youth,
Put not another sin upon my head
By urging me to fury. O, be gone!
By heaven, I love thee better than myself,
For I come hither armed against myself.     65
Stay not, be gone. Live, and hereafter say
A madman's mercy bid thee run away.

PARIS
I do defy thy conjurations.°
And apprehend thee for a felon here.

ROMEO
Wilt thou provoke me? Then have at thee, boy!     70

[They fight.]

PAGE
O Lord, they fight! I will go call the watch.
                             [Exit. PARIS falls.]

PARIS
O, I am slain! If thou be merciful,
Open the tomb, lay me with Juliet.            [Dies.]

ROMEO
In faith, I will. Let me peruse this face.
Mercutio's kinsman, noble County Paris!     75
What said my man when my betossèd soul
Did not attend° him as we rode? I think
He told me Paris should have married Juliet.
Said he not so, or did I dream it so?
Or am I mad, hearing him talk of Juliet,     80
To think it was so? O, give me thy hand,
One writ with me in sour misfortune's book!
I'll bury thee in a triumphant grave.
A grave? O, no, a lanthorn,° slaught'red youth,
For here lies Juliet, and her beauty makes     85
This vault a feasting presence° full of light.
Death, lie thou there, by a dead man interred.

[Lays him in the tomb.]

How oft when men are at the point of death
Have they been merry! Which their keepers° call
A lightning before death. O, how may I     90
Call this a lightning? O my love, my wife!
Death, that hath sucked the honey of thy breath,
Hath had no power yet upon thy beauty.
Thou art not conquered. Beauty's ensign° yet
Is crimson in thy lips and in thy cheeks,     95
And death's pale flag is not advancèd there.
Tybalt, liest thou there in thy bloody sheet?
O, what more favor can I do to thee
Than with that hand that cut thy youth in twain
To sunder his that was thine enemy?     100
Forgive me, cousin! Ah, dear Juliet,
Why art thou yet so fair? Shall I believe
That unsubstantial Death is amorous,

And that the lean abhorrèd monster keeps
Thee here in dark to be his paramour?     105
For fear of that I still will stay with thee
And never from this pallet of dim night
Depart again. Here, here will I remain
With worms that are thy chambermaids. O, here
Will I set up my everlasting rest     110
And shake the yoke of inauspicious stars
From this world-wearied flesh. Eyes, look your last!
Arms, take your last embrace! And, lips, O you
The doors of breath, seal with a righteous kiss
A dateless° bargain to engrossing° death!     115
Come, bitter conduct;° come, unsavory guide!
Thou desperate pilot,° now at once run on
The dashing rocks thy seasick weary bark!
Here's to my love! [Drinks.] O true apothecary!
Thy drugs are quick. Thus with a kiss I die.     120

[Falls.]

Enter FRIAR [Lawrence], with lanthorn, crow, and spade.

FRIAR
Saint Francis be my speed!° How oft tonight
Have my old feet stumbled° at graves! Who's there?

BALTHASAR
Here's one, a friend, and one that knows you well.

FRIAR
Bliss be upon you! Tell me, good my friend,
What torch is yond that vainly lends his light     125
To grubs and eyeless skulls? As I discern,
It burneth in the Capels' monument.

BALTHASAR
It doth so, holy sir; and there's my master,
One that you love.

FRIAR               Who is it?

BALTHASAR                  Romeo.

FRIAR
How long hath he been there?

BALTHASAR                 Full half an hour.     130

FRIAR
Go with me to the vault.

BALTHASAR               I dare not, sir.
My master knows not but I am gone hence,
And fearfully did menace me with death
If I did stay to look on his intents.

FRIAR
Stay then; I'll go alone. Fear comes upon me.     135
O, much I fear some ill unthrifty° thing.

BALTHASAR
As I did sleep under this yew tree here,
I dreamt my master and another fought,
And that my master slew him.

FRIAR                   Romeo!
Alack, alack, what blood is this which stains     140
The stony entrance of this sepulcher?
What mean these masterless and gory swords
To lie discolored by this place of peace?

[Enters the tomb.]

Romeo! O, pale! Who else? What, Paris too?

68 conjurations solemn charges    77 attend give attention to
84 lanthorn lantern (a windowed erection on the top of a
dome or room to admit light)    86 feasting presence festive
presence chamber    89 keepers jailers    94 ensign banner

115 dateless eternal; engrossing all-buying, all-encompassing
116 conduct guide    117 desperate pilot himself    121 speed
help    122 stumbled a bad omen    136 unthrifty unlucky

And steeped in blood? Ah, what an unkind° hour    145
Is guilty of this lamentable chance!
The lady stirs.

[JULIET *rises*.]

JULIET
O comfortable° friar! Where is my lord?
I do remember well where I should be,
And there I am. Where is my Romeo?    150
FRIAR
I hear some noise. Lady, come from that nest
Of death, contagion, and unnatural sleep.
A greater power than we can contradict
Hath thwarted our intents. Come, come away.
Thy husband in thy bosom there lies dead;    155
And Paris too. Come, I'll dispose of thee
Among a sisterhood of holy nuns.
Stay not to question, for the watch is coming.
Come, go, good Juliet. I dare no longer stay.
JULIET
Go, get thee hence, for I will not away. *Exit* [FRIAR].    160
What's here? A cup, closed in my truelove's hand?
Poison, I see, hath been his timeless° end.
O churl!° Drunk all, and left no friendly drop
To help me after? I will kiss thy lips.
Haply some poison yet doth hang on them    165
To make me die with a restorative.

[*Kisses him*.]

Thy lips are warm!
CHIEF WATCHMAN [*Within*.] Lead, boy. Which
way?
JULIET
Yea, noise? Then I'll be brief. O happy° dagger!    170

[*Snatches Romeo's dagger*.]

This is thy sheath; there rust, and let me die.

[*She stabs herself and falls*.]

*Enter* [*Paris'*] BOY *and* WATCH.

BOY
This is the place. There, where the torch doth burn.
CHIEF WATCHMAN
The ground is bloody. Search about the churchyard.
Go, some of you; whoe'er you find attach.
                    [*Exeunt some of the* WATCH.]
Pitiful sight! Here lies the county slain;    175
And Juliet bleeding, warm, and newly dead,
Who here hath lain this two days burièd.
Go, tell the prince; run to the Capulets;
Raise up the Montagues; some others search.
                    [*Exeunt others of the* WATCH.]
We see the ground whereon these woes do lie,    180
But the true ground° of all these piteous woes
We cannot without circumstance° descry.

*Enter* [*some of the* WATCH, *with*] *Romeo's man*
[BALTHASAR].

SECOND WATCHMAN
Here's Romeo's man. We found him in the church-
yard.
CHIEF WATCHMAN
Hold him in safety till the prince come hither.

*Enter* FRIAR [*Lawrence*] *and another* WATCHMAN.

THIRD WATCHMAN
Here is a friar that trembles, sighs, and weeps.    185
We took this mattock and this spade from him
As he was coming from this churchyard's side.
CHIEF WATCHMAN
A great suspicion! Stay the friar too.

*Enter the* PRINCE [*and* ATTENDANTS].

PRINCE
What misadventure is so early up,
That calls our person from our morning rest?    190

*Enter* CAPULET *and his wife* [LADY CAPULET, *with
others*].

CAPULET
What should it be, that is so shrieked abroad?
LADY CAPULET
O, the people in the street cry "Romeo,"
Some "Juliet," and some "Paris"; and all run
With open outcry toward our monument.
PRINCE
What fear is this which startles in your ears?    195
CHIEF WATCHMAN
Sovereign, here lies the County Paris slain;
And Romeo dead; and Juliet, dead before,
Warm and new killed.
PRINCE
Search, seek, and know how this foul murder comes.
CHIEF WATCHMAN
Here is a friar, and slaughtered Romeo's man,    200
With instruments upon them fit to open
These dead men's tombs.
CAPULET
O heavens! O wife, look how our daughter bleeds!
This dagger hath mista'en, for, lo, his house°
Is empty on the back of Montague,    205
And it missheathèd in my daughter's bosom!
LADY CAPULET
O me, this sight of death is as a bell
That warns my old age to a sepulcher.

*Enter* MONTAGUE [*and others*].

PRINCE
Come, Montague; for thou art early up
To see thy son and heir more early down.    210
MONTAGUE
Alas, my liege, my wife is dead tonight!
Grief of my son's exile hath stopped her breath.
What further woe conspires against mine age?
PRINCE
Look, and thou shalt see.
MONTAGUE
O thou untaught! What manners is in this,    215
To press before thy father to a grave?

---

145 **unkind** unnatural   148 **comfortable** comforting   162
**timeless** untimely   163 **churl** rude fellow   170 **happy**
opportune   181 **ground** cause   182 **circumstance** details

204 **his house** its sheath

PRINCE

Seal up the mouth of outrage° for a while,
Till we can clear these ambiguities
And know their spring, their head, their true descent;
And then will I be general of your woes°      220
And lead you even to death. Meantime forbear,
And let mischance be slave to patience.
Bring forth the parties of suspicion.

FRIAR

I am the greatest, able to do least,
Yet most suspected, as the time and place      225
Doth make against me, of this direful murder;
And here I stand, both to impeach and purge°
Myself condemnèd and myself excused.

PRINCE

Then say at once what thou dost know in this.

FRIAR

I will be brief, for my short date of breath°      230
Is not so long as is a tedious tale.
Romeo, there dead, was husband to that Juliet;
And she, there dead, that's Romeo's faithful wife.
I married them; and their stol'n marriage day
Was Tybalt's doomsday, whose untimely death      235
Banished the new-made bridegroom from this city;
For whom, and not for Tybalt, Juliet pined.
You, to remove that siege of grief from her,
Betrothed and would have married her perforce
To County Paris. Then comes she to me      240
And with wild looks bid me devise some mean
To rid her from this second marriage,
Or in my cell there would she kill herself.
Then gave I her (so tutored by my art)
A sleeping potion; which so took effect      245
As I intended, for it wrought on her
The form of death. Meantime I writ to Romeo
That he should hither come as° this dire night
To help to take her from her borrowed grave,
Being the time the potion's force should cease.      250
But he which bore my letter, Friar John,
Was stayed by accident, and yesternight
Returned my letter back. Then all alone
At the prefixèd hour of her waking
Came I to take her from her kindred's vault;      255
Meaning to keep her closely° at my cell
Till I conveniently could send to Romeo.
But when I came, some minute ere the time
Of her awakening, here untimely lay
The noble Paris and true Romeo dead.      260
She wakes; and I entreated her come forth
And bear this work of heaven with patience;
But then a noise did scare me from the tomb,
And she, too desperate, would not go with me,
But, as it seems, did violence on herself.      265
All this I know, and to the marriage

Her nurse is privy;° and if aught in this
Miscarried by my fault, let my old life
Be sacrificed some hour before his time
Unto the rigor of severest law.      270

PRINCE

We still° have known thee for a holy man.
Where's Romeo's man? What can he say to this?

BALTHASAR

I brought my master news of Juliet's death;
And then in post he came from Mantua
To this same place, to this same monument.      275
This letter he early bid me give his father,
And threat'ned me with death, going in the vault,
If I departed not and left him there.

PRINCE

Give me the letter. I will look on it.
Where is the county's page that raised the watch?      280
Sirrah, what made your master° in this place?

BOY

He came with flowers to strew his lady's grave;
And bid me stand aloof, and so I did.
Anon comes one with light to ope the tomb;
And by and by° my master drew on him;      285
And then I ran away to call the watch.

PRINCE

This letter doth make good the friar's words,
Their course of love, the tidings of her death;
And here he writes that he did buy a poison
Of a poor pothecary and therewithal°      290
Came to this vault to die and lie with Juliet.
Where be these enemies? Capulet, Montague,
See what a scourge is laid upon your hate,
That heaven finds means to kill your joys with love.
And I, for winking at° your discords too,      295
Have lost a brace° of kinsmen. All are punished.

CAPULET

O brother Montague, give me thy hand.
This is my daughter's jointure,° for no more
Can I demand.

MONTAGUE      But I can give thee more;
For I will raise her statue in pure gold,      300
That whiles Verona by that name is known,
There shall no figure at such rate° be set
As that of true and faithful Juliet.

CAPULET

As rich shall Romeo's by his lady's lie—
Poor sacrifices of our enmity!      305

PRINCE

A glooming° peace this morning with it brings.
     The sun for sorrow will not show his head.
Go hence, to have more talk of these sad things;
     Some shall be pardoned, and some punishèd;
For never was a story of more woe      310
Than this of Juliet and her Romeo.      [*Exeunt omnes.*]

---

217 **the . . . outrage** these violent cries   **220 general . . . woes** leader in your sorrowing   **227 impeach and purge** make charges and exonerate   **230 date of breath** term of life   **248 as** on   **256 closely** hidden     **267 privy** accessory   **271 still** always   **281 made your master** was your master doing   **285 by and by** soon   **290 therewithal** therewith   **295 winking at** closing eyes to   **296 brace** pair (i.e., Mercutio and Paris)   **298 jointure** marriage settlement   **302 rate** value   **306 glooming** cloudy

# A MIDSUMMER NIGHT'S DREAM

EDITED BY WOLFGANG CLEMEN

## Introduction

A study of Shakespeare's development as a dramatic artist shows that one of his supreme achievements during his "middle period" consists in combining heterogeneous elements in a single play. The dramas of Shakespeare's predecessors all exist on a smaller scale, mostly adhering to one particular type and keeping within more limited resources of style and subject matter. However, even in his very first comedies, *The Two Gentlemen of Verona*, *The Comedy of Errors*, and *Love's Labor's Lost*, we see Shakespeare widening the scope of the dramatic genre to which these plays belong and introducing new elements taken over from other sections of the literary tradition of the past. *A Midsummer Night's Dream*, then, which must have been written about 1595, combines for the first time totally disparate worlds into one unified whole; the sharp contrasts brought together there would have destroyed the play's balance in the hands of any lesser playwright. For, indeed, it required Shakespeare's genius to bring together Bottom and Puck, the crude realism of the artisans and the exquisite delicacy of the fairy world, the stylized and pointed repartee of the Athenian lovers and the dignified manner of Theseus and Hippolyta. What we find are contrasts on many levels, exemplified by diversified means. Yet Shakespeare strikes an equilibrium between these contrasts, reconciling and fusing the discordant factors within the organic body of his comedy. *A Midsummer Night's Dream*, therefore, not only exhibits bold contrasts and divergent elements of plot, atmosphere, and character; it also illustrates the unifying power of the spirit of comedy and the poetic imagination. We further find that the play's unity is reinforced by a subtle technique of counterpoint and juxtaposition, a skillful contrasting of different strands of plot, and the creation of an atmosphere full of illusion, wonder, and strangeness, all of which facilitate the many transitions occurring during the course of the play.

Some facts about its origin and title may help us better to understand the particular nature of the play. *A Midsummer Night's Dream* is clearly related to the practices of midsummer night, the night before June 24, which was the date of Saint John the Baptist's festival and hence connected with merrymaking, various superstitions and folk customs, dances, pageants, and revels. More than any other night in the year, midsummer night suggested enchantment and witchcraft, something which Shakespeare has superbly embodied in his fairy world. To an Elizabethan audience, moreover, the play's title would have immediately called to mind the so-called midsummer madness, which was a state of mind marked by a heightened readiness to believe in the delusions of the imagination that were thought to befall the minds of men after days of great summer heat. Thus, by means of his highly suggestive title, Shakespeare has firmly planted the dreamlike action of his drama in the popular beliefs and customs of his time. Furthermore the title gives theatergoers and readers a clue as to how the work should be understood—namely, as an unrealistic creation of the imagination, a series of dream images containing all the contradictions and inconsistencies that dreams normally possess, but containing too their symbolic content. Indeed, the dreamlike character of what takes place is repeatedly alluded to. In Puck's Epilogue, for instance, the audience themselves are explicitly addressed:

> And this weak and idle theme,
> No more yielding but a dream,
> Gentles, do not reprehend. (V.i.426–28)

In short, the play's title makes significant allusion to the nature and meaning of the work, though it makes no reference to the period of time during which the events of the drama occur. In fact, the action takes place between April 29 and May 1, the latter date, being that of May Day, demanding of course particular celebrations, and for that reason it is perhaps a suitable day for the marriage of Theseus and Hippolyta.

Now the wedding of the princely pair is not only the destination of the action; it is also the occasion for which the play itself was written. *A Midsummer Night's Dream* was undoubtedly intended as a dramatic epithalamium to celebrate the marriage of some aristocratic couple. (The attempts made to fix on a definite historical marriage, however, must remain conjectural.) Plays written for such festive occasions addressed themselves to an aristocratic audience. They were mostly performed on private stages rather than in public theaters and revealed an entirely different style of performance from the popular dramas. The relationship of *A Midsummer Night's Dream* to the court masque—something which V.i.40 draws attention to —also comes in here. The masques formed a central part of the entertainments that were always given at court celebrations, and several noticeable features in *A Midsummer Night's Dream* clearly relate to the genre of the court masque. The music and dances, the appearance of fairylike creatures possessed of supernatural qualities, the employment of motifs involving magic and metamorphosis, and the vigorous stylization and symmetrical structure of some parts do indeed remind one of the court masque. Finally, the scenes with Bottom, Quince, and company may be compared to the antimasque, which formed the burlesque and realistic counterpart performed together with the masque itself.

In referring to the masque, one is only pointing out a single aspect of *A Midsummer Night's Dream*. We must also remember that Shakespeare has similarly taken over stylistic and formal elements from his own early comedies, popular drama, the romantic play, and the mythological dream plays of John Lyly. Shakespeare has tapped many sources, but he has nevertheless been able to create an original and independent form of drama that includes skillful organization of plot—involving the manipulation of three subplots that run parallel to one another—as well as a rich suffusion of the whole by both the atmosphere of nature and that of magic. Between a descriptive and retrospective kind of dramatic method and one that makes us see the process of things in action Shakespeare has struck a perfect sense of balance.

A study of the interrelation of the four plots reveals how their contrasts, juxtapositions, and dovetailing help to disclose the meaning of the drama. The play begins with a scene between Theseus and Hippolyta, who do not appear again until Act IV. In Act V their wedding is celebrated. The plot involving Theseus and Hippolyta can therefore be styled an "enveloping action" that provides the play with a definite framework and a firmly established temporal scaffolding; it stands outside the world of dream, enchantment, and love entanglements, suggesting the sphere of everyday reality out of which the events of the drama first develop and to which they then ultimately return. The section in I.i with Egeus, Hermia, Lysander, and Demetrius relates the Theseus-Hippolyta plot to that of the lovers, for Theseus himself appears as arbitrator in the love dispute and it will be on his wedding day that the harsh verdict he passes on Hermia is to take effect, should she not have changed her mind by that date. This verdict is the cause of Hermia and Lysander's decision to flee into the wood near Athens, so that with this the events of the second and third acts have already been determined. The comic subplot, moreover, beginning in I.ii with the gathering of the artisans to prepare themselves for rehearsal, is also announced in I.i, insofar as we learn of the entertainments to be presented on Theseus' wedding day. Theseus' promise to woo Hippolyta "With pomp, with triumph, and with reveling" can also be understood as an allusion to the dramatic entertainments that are to come later. From the very beginning, then, our expectations are raised in connection with the wedding day, which is to bring with it the artisans' play, the decision regarding the love

dispute between the Athenian couples, and the festive marriage of Theseus and Hippolyta.

If this were all that Shakespeare had given us, we would have had a comedy little different from his early ones. The plot connected with the fairies, however, with Oberon and Titania at its center, not only brings considerable complications into the course of the above-mentioned matters, but also adds to the whole drama a new feature that Shakespeare had never employed before. For the supernatural, which intervenes in the activities of the characters, turns their intentions upside down, and directs their actions. It is the fairies who are responsible for the confusion, and also for the final reconciliation, thus substituting enchantment and arbitrariness for the lovers' own responsibility and power of will. Yet these influences also have repercussions on the fairies themselves, because Titania thereby falls in love with the ass-headed Bottom. Thus the world of the fairies is linked with that of the artisans, and we get those incomparably comic situations that are themselves the outcome of the fairies' intervention. Finally, a link between the plots dealing with the fairies and Theseus emerges in the conversation between Oberon and Titania in which the fairy rulers' earlier connections with Theseus and Hippolyta are recalled; and this is a moment that accelerates the pair's mutual jealousy and estrangement.

Since the fairies remain always invisible to the other members of the dramatis personae (only Bottom is ironically allowed the privilege of seeing Titania), and their deeds are accomplished without the knowledge of the other characters, Shakespeare has been able to achieve a highly dramatic effect of "double awareness." We as audience are aware of Puck's magic juice and therefore look forward with pleasure to what might develop. We know even more than the usually omniscient Oberon, who does not realize till some time later the confusion that Puck has caused by mistake. This error on Puck's part bears deeper significance, for it shows that even the fairies can err and that the influences they exert as supernatural agents in the play do not in the least answer to anything providential, but rather contain filaments of arbitrariness, self-deception, and folly.

An insight into the peculiar nature of the fairy world in *A Midsummer Night's Dream* helps us to understand the entire play, for although the fairies certainly possess supernatural qualities, they are nevertheless closely linked to the world of mankind and have their share of human frailties. Their origin in the realm of the elemental and their partly instinctive, partly playful nature, together with their capriciousness and irrationality, indicate which forces and qualities Shakespeare wanted us to see as conditioning and influencing human love relationships; for the haphazard and arbitrary game that love plays with the two Athenian couples appears as a projection of the irrationality, irresponsibility, and playfulness characterizing the nature of the fairies themselves. However, the fairies not only make other people behave in a way that corresponds, as it were, to their own fairy natures; they also strengthen and reinforce people's latent tendencies. Previous to the fairies' intervention, we learn from Demetrius that he has loved Helena before bestowing his affections on Hermia (I.i.106-07, 242-43); it is not for nothing that he is termed "spotted and inconstant man" (I.i.110).

Shakespeare has interspersed his text with numerous illuminating hints referring to the fairies' peculiar traits of character and sphere of existence, so that we are able to get a vivid picture of the type of creatures they are. Although the world of the fairies exhibits several characteristics common to popular belief and folklore tradition, it is to a considerable extent a new creation of Shakespeare's own. This is particularly true when we think of Puck, whose descent from Robin Goodfellow or Hobgoblin, as he is called by one of the fairies when he first appears (II.i.34, 40), only accounts for one aspect of his being. If one examines the numerous statements that Puck utters about himself and that the other characters utter about him, one immediately realizes that Shakespeare has created a complex dramatic figure to whom is assigned a key position within the fabric of the play. Not only is Puck the comically rough and earthbound goblin with his mischievous pranks, blunt speech, and intervention in day-to-day affairs; he is also a spirit closely linked with the elements, having command over supernatural powers and capable of moving at incredible speed. As "Oberon's jester" he is close to the fools of Shakespeare's later comedies, enjoying his own jests and possessing the gift of sharp, critical observation. Keeping this last point in mind, we see that Shakespeare has assigned him the role of spectator several times during the course of the play, and as such he comments on the action and aptly characterizes the people taking part. Hence it is he who, in view of the confusion he has caused among the lovers, cries out:

Shall we their fond pageant see?
Lord, what fools these mortals be!     (III.ii.114-15)

Thus Puck becomes the interpreter of the play's dramatic situations and intermediary between stage and audience as he places himself at a distance from events that have depended on and been influenced by him, and to which in the Epilogue, significantly spoken by him, he is able to look back, as from a higher vantage point. Indeed, it is remarkable how many motives determining the play's action derive from Puck, how many invisible wires he holds in his hand. Yet his interventions in the development of the plot are as much the result of a casual mood or mischievous whim as they are the result of premeditated instructions from his master, Oberon. This is shown, for instance, in the case of Bottom's transformation in the first scene of Act III. It is a paradox of the dramatic action that Oberon's well-meaning intention is turned into its opposite through Puck's mistake (Lysander, instead of Demetrius, is anointed with the magic herb), so that the activity of the supernatural forces seems to be largely conditioned by error and coincidence. Still, it is precisely this fickleness and inconstancy of fate that Puck acknowledges in his laconic answer to Oberon when the latter reproves him for the mistake: "Then fate o'errules. . . ." With these words Puck gives utterance to a basic motif in the drama.

It has often been stressed that in *A Midsummer Night's Dream* Shakespeare wanted to portray the irrational nature of love, the shifting and unstable "fancy" that continually falls prey to illusion, regards itself as being playful and short-lived, and is accompanied by a certain irresponsibility; whereas in *Romeo and Juliet*, written during the same period, love appears in quite a different shape, as a fateful and all-consuming force making claims to absolute authority and demanding that the whole of the self be yielded up to it.

But Shakespeare makes clear to us in several ways that the love between the Athenian couples is not rooted in actuality. Puck's magic juice, operating as a supernatural medium, is of course only one of the means by which Shakespeare places the relationships of the four Athenian lovers outside of reality. The love entanglements occur during a night full of dreams and enchantment, of which only an imprecise picture afterward remains in the memory of those concerned. Furthermore, it is undoubtedly the poet's deliberate intention (contrary to his practice in other plays of the same period) that the lovers should be so weakly characterized that it is impossible for us to retain them in our memory as real and differentiated human beings. We may likewise take it for granted that their symmetrical grouping and their appearance in pairs is the result of conscious stylization on Shakespeare's part. And if the style of their dialogues, together with the handling of the verse, often seems to be flat, trite, and frankly silly, this neither signifies Shakespeare's lack of skill nor justifies the contention that passages have been left in from an earlier version of the same play. Rather it gives evidence that Shakespeare intended the four lovers to be just what they are, puppets and not fully realized characters. Even the spectator to those scenes of confusion in the wood soon has no idea where he is or who precisely is in love with whom.

Above all, however, the dreamlike atmosphere of such scenes accentuates our feeling that the four lovers appear to be quite removed from any criteria applicable to reality. "The willing suspension of disbelief" that Coleridge designated as one of the poet's chief aims Shakespeare achieves by creating a world of illusion that manifests itself from the first scene onward. Dream world and reality merge imperceptibly, so that the persons concerned are not sure themselves in which sphere they move, nor whether what they have experienced has been imagination or truth. The idea that what has happened has been a dream, illusion, or "vision" is often expressed from various standpoints by the characters themselves. *Dream* is a key word in the drama, and the idea that everything is based on imagination is given frequent and subtle variation. The art with which Shakespeare shifts from the dream world to reality is unique. This is evident in the first scene of Act IV, where both the lovers and Bottom are depicted as awaking out of their dreams—a scene in which all four plots are brought together for the first time, whereby the mind of the spectator is made to see the boundaries separating them as being simultaneously nonexistent and yet firmly fixed. Finally, as if in a series of flashbacks, the incidents that have occurred during the night of dreams are lit up once again from a distance by means of Theseus' famous speech describing "the lunatic, the lover, and the poet" as being "of imagination all compact." These words refer once more to that faculty which lies behind not only dreams, but the poet's own creations as well and under whose spell we, as spectators, have been kept during the whole course of the play; for we too have been enchanted, responding eagerly to the call of the poetry and accepting the play as an organism that conforms to its own rules, a world where strange and real things mingle in a curious way.

The illusion of a dream sequence scurrying past is also enhanced by a sense of the forward surge of time. Not only is the passing of night into morning given expression through the shifting movement of light and dark within a series of superb images and subtle allusions: the impatience and longing with which the different characters look forward to the future are perceptible from the very start, thus making time flow in an anticipatory way. Again, the language of the play is rich in images and expressions indicating quick movement, lightness, and transitoriness, thereby contributing to the overall atmospheric impression. How delicately and accurately the play's particular atmosphere, together with its theme and leitmotifs, is rendered from the very beginning, an examination of the first scene of the play alone would show, although we can permit ourselves only a few observations here.

The very first exchange between Theseus and Hippolyta conveys to us a twofold awareness of time, from the standpoint of which we contemplate a time span that culminates in the wedding day, the date of which is fixed immediately at the outset. This emerges when Hippolyta's "Four days will quickly steep themselves in night;/Four nights will quickly dream away the time" (I.i.7–8) is contrasted with Theseus' "but, O, methinks, how slow/This old moon wanes!" (I.i.3–4). During this initial dialogue Shakespeare skillfully puts us in tune with the moonlit scenes that follow by means of Theseus' comparison of the "old moon" with "a stepdame, or a dowager,/Long withering out a young man's revenue" (I.i.5–6). In this scene alone "moon" and "night" each occur five times, "dream" three times. The lines just quoted also suggest the aristocratic world of the court, where a part of the action is to take place. A further element is introduced when, immediately following, we read these instructions to Philostrate:

Stir up the Athenian youth to merriments,
Awake the pert and nimble spirit of mirth.　　(I.i.12–13)

Yet the entry of Egeus immediately afterward, leading in his daughter Hermia and, "full of vexation," bringing accusations against Lysander because the latter "hath bewitched the bosom of [his] child," ushers in the radically contrasting note of discord, deception, and trickery, something that is never missing in any Shakespearean comedy and is always present as an undercurrent in *A Midsummer Night's Dream;* for the final state of harmony reached at the end of the play both in the world of the fairies and that of the court turns out to be a resolution of previously opposed forces, a reconciliation attained after former estrangement, and "the concord of this discord" (V.i.60).

The main theme of the drama—namely, the transitoriness and inconstancy of love—is also anticipated in this first scene when Lysander describes love as

　　　　momentany as a sound,
Swift as a shadow, short as any dream,
Brief as the lightning in the collied night,
That, in a spleen, unfolds both heaven and earth,
And ere a man hath power to say, "Behold!"
The jaws of darkness do devour it up:
So quick bright things come to confusion.　　(I.i.143–49)

This passage is illuminating because it shows how Shakespeare not only bodies forth the themes and motifs of his drama in terms of action, but also gives them expression through imagery. In no other play by Shakespeare's middle period do we find so much poetry and verse melody, or indeed nature imagery, with its references to plants, animals, and other natural phenomena; nature itself even enters the drama as a participating agent alongside the characters. *A Midsummer Night's Dream* should therefore be apprehended as poetry and music, and not only be absorbed and endorsed by the eye and intellect as a connected series of actions. For the play's language, by means of its images, its subtle allusions and suggestions, its verbal repetitions and rhythmic patterns, has built up a complex and finely varied tissue of ideas, impressions, and associations that constantly act on our powers of imagination and stimulate them to participate. The great range and delicacy of impact that poetic drama possesses, as opposed to prose drama, can be perfectly witnessed in *A Midsummer Night's Dream.*

The degree to which the language, with its proliferation of allusions, ironies, and ambiguities, creates the overall dramatic effect is made clear by those prose scenes with the artisans, where the lyrical and poetic are completely lacking. Apart from suggesting a wealth of gestures, the language used by Bottom and company is rich in implications and evokes delightful misunderstandings; it gives expression to the artisans' ludicrous ambition for higher things as well as to their rustic limitations. All this gives rise to that constant incongruity which is the prerequisite for great comedy—the incongruity existing between the basic natures of the characters and their pretensions. The scenes with Bottom, Quince, and company provide a comic and realistic contrast to the poetry of the fairies and the artificial and stylized love scenes of the Athenians. Thus the delicacy, polished bearing, and lightness inherent in all other sections of the play are counterbalanced by the uncouthness, the heavy solidity of everyday life, and a naive roughness that the artisans bring into the magical fairy world of the moonlit scenes. Puck, the shrewd onlooker, at one stage justly calls them "hempen homespuns." But Shakespeare has made far more out of this antimasque than a merely amusing subplot filled with clownlike figures; during the course of the play one of them has come to be the most unforgettable character in the entire drama. For the lack of vitality and pronounced individuality noticeable in the other personages we are fully recompensed in Bottom, who has justly been described as the greatest comic creation in the dramatist's early work. Abundantly endowed with remarkable qualities, Bottom is continually putting himself in a comic light. There are no features of his character that at one point or another do not lead to some ridiculous situation, some unforgettable moment of contrast or unintentionally provoked comparison. Bottom's supreme satisfaction with himself and his sense of ease remain with him even in his transformed state, while his stage ambitions (he wants to play the part of the lion as well as that of Pyramus, Thisby, and the tyrant) parody the profession of acting and yet at the same time form a characteristic trait that fits him remarkably well. That his ambitions are fulfilled even before the Pyramus and Thisby drama takes place, insofar as Bottom has to play the parts of both ass and lover, is significant, just as is the marked irony that Bottom alone, out of all the persons in the play, is permitted to come into contact with the fairies—though this encounter does not impress him in the least or signify for him any unusual experience. In Titania's presence he discards nothing at all of his own personality; the ass's head, which with other people would have resulted in monstrous caricature, in his case is something that illuminates for us his real nature.

If the story of the craftsmen forms a satirical counterbalance to the plot of the lovers, then it is also true to say that the drama of Pyramus and Thisby initiates a twofold, even threefold kind of awareness. For what we get in this parody of the love tragedy is an exaggerated depiction of the four lovers' sentimentality, their high-flown protestations of love, and their pseudo-solemnity—a depiction in the form of a flashback that they themselves are now able to contemplate as spectators, serenely calm and reconciled with one another. The lovers' own relationships have likewise been a play that the fairies have found highly amusing, and these entanglements parallel the quarrel between Oberon and Titania, the quarrel from which the confusion among the lovers originated.

The play-within-the-play, superbly worked out by Shakespeare, makes us particularly aware that the entire drama has indeed been a "play," summoned into life by the dramatist's magic wand and just as easily made to vanish. When Puck refers in the first line of his Epilogue ("If we shadows have offended") not merely to the fairies, previously termed "shadows," but also to all the actors who have taken part, we realize that Shakespeare is once more making it clear to us that we have been watching a "magic-lantern show," something where appearance, not reality, is the operative factor.

It is peculiarly ironic that Bottom, Quince, and company perform the tragedy of Pyramus and Thisby as an auspicious offering on behalf of the newly established love union, thereby, one might say, presenting the material of *Romeo and Juliet* in a comic and grotesque manner. Thus an exaggerated form of tragedy is employed so that the preceding scenes may be parodied as comedy. The play of Pyramus and Thisby parodies not only the torments of love, which the Athenian lovers can now look back on with serene calmness, but also the Senecan style of Elizabethan tragedy with its melodrama and ponderous conventions. Shakespeare parodies these conventions here by means of exaggeration or clumsy and grotesque usage—the too explicit Prologue, for instance; the verbose self-explanation and commentaries; the stereotyped phrases for expressing grief; and the excessive use of such rhetorical devices as apostrophe, alliteration, hyperbole, and rhetorical question.

Even the elements of comedy and parody in the Pyramus and Thisby performance appear in a twofold light. Though they themselves are being mocked, the lovers smile at these awkward efforts on the part of the craftsmen, and Theseus even adds a highly suggestive commentary.

In the craftsmen's play, Shakespeare is also parodying the whole life of the theater. He calmly takes the shortcomings of all theatrical production and acting, drives them to absurd lengths, and holds them up for inspection. The lantern, which is supposed to represent the moon, makes us conscious of how equally inadequate Pyramus and Thisby are in their roles and suggests that such in-

adequacy may time and again have made its appearance on the Elizabethan stage. For those Elizabethan playgoers who viewed a play superficially, without using their own powers of imagination, much in Shakespearean drama must have remained completely unintelligible. It is at such narrow-minded theatergoers as these that Shakespeare is indirectly poking fun. And he enables us to see the limitations of his own stage, which had to portray a large world and create atmosphere without the elaborate scenery and technical equipment that we have today.

But the very inadequacy of the artisans' production gives emphasis to the true art of dramatic illusion and magic, as we have witnessed it in the preceding scenes, in which the evocative power of Shakespeare's language, assisted by our imagination, enables us to experience moonlight and nighttime in the woods. Theseus himself makes this point when, in answer to Hippolyta's remark, "This is the silliest stuff that ever I heard," he says: "The best in this kind are but shadows; and the worst are no worse, if imagination amend them" (V.i.211–13).[1]

## A NOTE ON THE SOURCE

*A Midsummer Night's Dream* is, together with *Love's Labor's Lost* and *The Tempest*, one of those few plays for which no specific source appears to exist. The plot, with its skillful interplay of four different actions, is of Shakespeare's own making, although single incidents and motives as well as some names and details come from widely different origins.

Thus, the enveloping action of Theseus and Hippolyta derives in part from Chaucer's *The Knight's Tale*. This tale begins, as our play does, with Theseus' victorious return from war with Hippolyta and also ends with a celebration at court. Moreover, the story of Palamon and Arcite in *The Knight's Tale* is linked with the Theseus story in a similar way and also illustrates how friendship is broken by love. But Shakespeare has modified this motif in a characteristic way, replacing the two men by two young women and adding a fourth lover, thereby not only establishing symmetry but also providing for those multiple combinations and varying relationships between Lysander, Hermia, Demetrius, and Helena that constitute the *comedy of errors* of the night in the forest. Shakespeare's portrait of Theseus may have been further influenced by the figure of Theseus in Plutarch's *Lives*, which Shakespeare read in Sir Thomas North's translation. Theseus' function as a wise judge as well as his tolerance and benevolence toward the craftsmen are features that find a parallel in Plutarch.

Oberon as the fairy king with a kingdom in the East had been made familiar through the French romance *Huon of Bordeaux*, while the name of Titania for the fairy queen in *A Midsummer Night's Dream* may have been suggested by the epithet given to Diana in Ovid's *Metamorphoses* (III.173). Diana, however, occurs as the "lady of the fairies" in Reginald Scot's *The Discoverie of Witchcraft* (1584), which supplied Shakespeare with much information about witches, fairies, and transformations

---

[1] The editor wishes to express his thanks to Dr. Dieter Mehl for assistance in the compilation of the notes.

and contends at the same time that belief in Robin Good-fellow was declining, and that all those stories about fairies were untrue. Bottom's "assification" may also have been suggested by Scot's account of the spells exercised by the witches but has another parallel in Apuleius' *The Golden Ass*, which had been translated in 1566. For the magic juice, several analogues have been pointed out, the closest being in Montemayor's prose pastoral *Diana Enamorada* (1542).

The story of Pyramus and Thisby existed in Elizabethan times in many poetical versions, some of them exhibiting those sentimental and melodramatic exaggerations that must have prompted Shakespeare to his subtle and complex parody. It is significant that George Pettie in his *Petite Pallace of Pettie his Pleasure* (1576) sees in this story a parallel with the account of *Romeo and Juliet*. Shakespeare in his play-within-the-play obviously creates an ironic and comic parallel to his own tragedy—no matter whether *Romeo and Juliet* was already in existence then or soon to appear. Geoffrey Bullough, in the second volume of his *Narrative and Dramatic Sources of Shakespeare*, reprints eleven pieces from which Shakespeare may have drawn.

The most interesting of our play's sources are, however, the unwritten ones. For the fairy world that is presented by so many graphic details and concrete features owes much to folklore and the living tradition of the Warwickshire countryside. Shakespeare must have been intensely alive to the mass of popular superstition, legend, and folk custom still to be found in his own times. He took what he could use from these sources, adding, however, many details of his own invention and modifying several traditional traits. The fairy world which thus emerges is—if we consider its dramatic function—a new creation of Shakespeare's own poetic imagination, which has at each stage transmuted the source material "into something rich and strange."

## A NOTE ON THE TEXT

The chief authority for the text of *A Midsummer Night's Dream* is the first quarto of 1600 (Q1), possibly printed from Shakespeare's own manuscript. The second quarto of 1619 (Q2), fraudulently dated 1600, and the First Folio of 1623 (F) correct a few obvious mistakes of Q1 and add some new ones. The Folio introduces division into acts. The present text follows Q1 as closely as possible, but modernizes punctuation and spelling (and prints "and" as "an" when it means "if"), occasionally alters the lineation (for example, prints as prose some lines that were mistakenly set as verse), expands and regularizes the speech prefixes, slightly alters the position of stage directions where necessary, and corrects obvious typographical errors. Other departures from Q1 are listed below, the adopted reading first in boldface, and then Q1's reading in roman. If the adopted reading is derived from Q2 or from F, the fact is noted in a bracket following the reading.

I.i.4 **wanes** [Q2] waues  10 **New-bent** Now bent  19 **s.d. Lysander** [F] Lysander and Helena  24 **Stand forth, Demetrius** [printed as s.d. in Q1 Q2, F]  26 **Stand forth, Lysander** [printed as s.d. in Q1, Q2, F]  102 **Demetrius'** Demetrius  136 **low** loue  187 **Yours would** Your words  191 **I'd** ile  216 **sweet** sweld  219 **stranger companies** strange companions

II.i.69 **steep** [Q2] steppe  79 **Aegles** Eagles  109 **thin** chinne  158 **the west** [F] west  190 **slay . . . slayeth** stay . . . stayeth  201 **not nor** [F] not not

II.ii.9, 13, 24 [speech prefixes added by editor]  39 **Be't** Bet it  47 **is** [Q2] it

III.i.12 **By'r lakin** Berlakin  28–29 **yourselves** [F] your selfe  55 **Bottom** [Q2] Cet  68 **and let** or let  82 **Odors, odors** [F] odours, odorous  87 **Puck** [F] Quin  162–63 **Peaseblossom . . . All** [Q1, Q2, and F print as a single speech, attributed to "Fairies"]  175–78 **Peaseblossom . . . Mustardseed. Hail** [Q1, Q2, and F print thus: 1 Fai. Haile mortall, haile./2 Fai. Haile./3. Fai. Haile]  195 **you of** you

III.ii.19 **mimic** [F] Minnick  80 **part I so** part I  85 **sleep** slippe  213 **first, like** first life  220 **passionate words** [F] words  250 **prayers** praise  299 **gentlemen** [Q2] gentleman  323 **she's** [Q2] she is  406 **Speak! In some bush?** Speake in some bush  426 **shalt** [Q2] shat  451 **To your eye** your eye

IV.i.74 **o'er** or  83 **sleep of all these five** sleepe: of all these, fine  118 **Seemed** seeme  129 **this is my** [Q2] this my  173 **saw** see  200 **let us** [Q2] lets  208 **to expound** [Q2] expound  210 **a patched** [F] patcht a

IV.ii.3 **Starveling** [F] Flute

V.i.34 **our** [F] or  156 **Snout** [F] Flute  191 **up in thee** [F] now againe  272 **gleams** beams  317 **mote** moth  350 **Bottom** [F] Lion  370 **lion** Lyons  371 **behowls** beholds  418–19 **And the owner . . . rest** [these two lines are transposed in Q1, Q2, and F]

# A MIDSUMMER NIGHT'S DREAM

[Dramatis Personae

THESEUS *Duke of Athens*
EGEUS *father to Hermia*
LYSANDER ⎱ *in love with Hermia*
DEMETRIUS ⎰
PHILOSTRATE *Master of the Revels to Theseus*
PETER QUINCE *a carpenter; Prologue in the play*
SNUG *a joiner; Lion in the play*
NICK BOTTOM *a weaver; Pyramus in the play*
FRANCIS FLUTE *a bellows mender; Thisby in the play*
TOM SNOUT *a tinker; Wall in the play*
ROBIN STARVELING *a tailor; Moonshine in the play*

HIPPOLYTA *Queen of the Amazons, betrothed to Theseus*
HERMIA *daughter to Egeus, in love with Lysander*
HELENA *in love with Demetrius*
OBERON *King of the Fairies*
TITANIA *Queen of the Fairies*
PUCK *or Robin Goodfellow*
PEASEBLOSSOM ⎫
COBWEB ⎬ *fairies*
MOTH ⎪
MUSTARDSEED ⎭
OTHER FAIRIES *attending their king and queen*
ATTENDANTS *on Theseus and Hippolyta*

*Scene:* Athens, and a wood near it]

## ACT I

[Scene I. *The palace of Theseus.*]

*Enter* THESEUS, HIPPOLYTA, [PHILOSTRATE,] *with others.*

THESEUS
Now, fair Hippolyta, our nuptial hour
Draws on apace. Four happy days bring in
Another moon; but, O, methinks, how slow
This old moon wanes! She lingers° my desires,
Like a stepdame, or a dowager,                           5
Long withering out a young man's revenue.°
HIPPOLYTA
Four days will quickly steep themselves in night;

Four nights will quickly dream away the time;
And then the moon, like to a silver bow
New-bent in heaven, shall behold the night          10
Of our solemnities.
THESEUS                    Go, Philostrate,
Stir up the Athenian youth to merriments,
Awake the pert° and nimble spirit of mirth,
Turn melancholy forth to funerals;
The pale companion° is not for our pomp.°           15
                            [*Exit* PHILOSTRATE.]
Hippolyta, I wooed thee with my sword,°
And won thy love, doing thee injuries;
But I will wed thee in another key,
With pomp, with triumph, and with reveling.

*Enter* EGEUS *and his daughter* HERMIA, *and* LYSANDER, *and* DEMETRIUS.

*The decorative border above appeared on the title page of the second quarto edition of* A Midsummer Night's Dream, *1619.*

**I.i.4 lingers** makes to linger, delays   **6 Long . . . revenue** diminishing the young man's money (because she must be supported by him)

**13 pert** lively   **15 companion** fellow (contemptuous); **pomp** festive procession   **16 I . . . sword** Theseus had captured Hippolyta when he conquered the Amazons

EGEUS

Happy be Theseus, our renownèd duke!     20

THESEUS

Thanks, good Egeus.° What's the news with thee?

EGEUS

Full of vexation come I, with complaint
Against my child, my daughter Hermia.
Stand forth, Demetrius. My noble lord,
This man hath my consent to marry her.     25
Stand forth, Lysander. And, my gracious duke,
This man hath bewitched the bosom of my child.
Thou, thou, Lysander, thou hast given her rhymes,
And interchanged love tokens with my child.
Thou hast by moonlight at her window sung,     30
With feigning voice, verses of feigning love,
And stol'n the impression of her fantasy°
With bracelets of thy hair, rings, gauds, conceits,
Knacks,° trifles, nosegays, sweetmeats, messengers
Of strong prevailment in unhardened youth.     35
With cunning hast thou filched my daughter's heart,
Turned her obedience, which is due to me,
To stubborn harshness. And, my gracious duke,
Be it so she will not here before your grace
Consent to marry with Demetrius,     40
I beg the ancient privilege of Athens:
As she is mine, I may dispose of her,
Which shall be either to this gentleman
Or to her death, according to our law
Immediately° provided in that case.     45

THESEUS

What say you, Hermia? Be advised, fair maid.
To you your father should be as a god,
One that composed your beauties; yea, and one
To whom you are but as a form in wax
By him imprinted and within his power     50
To leave the figure or disfigure it.
Demetrius is a worthy gentleman.

HERMIA

So is Lysander.

THESEUS     In himself he is;
But in this kind, wanting your father's voice,°
The other must be held the worthier.     55

HERMIA

I would my father looked but with my eyes.

THESEUS

Rather your eyes must with his judgment look.

HERMIA

I do entreat your grace to pardon me.
I know not by what power I am made bold,
Nor how it may concern my modesty,     60
In such a presence here to plead my thoughts;
But I beseech your grace that I may know
The worst that may befall me in this case,
If I refuse to wed Demetrius.

THESEUS

Either to die the death, or to abjure     65
Forever the society of men.

Therefore, fair Hermia, question your desires;
Know of° your youth, examine well your blood,°
Whether, if you yield not to your father's choice,
You can endure the livery of a nun,     70
For aye to be in shady cloister mewed,°
To live a barren sister all your life,
Chanting faint hymns to the cold fruitless moon.°
Thrice-blessèd they that master so their blood,
To undergo such maiden pilgrimage;     75
But earthlier happy is the rose distilled,°
Than that which, withering on the virgin thorn,
Grows, lives, and dies in single blessedness.

HERMIA

So will I grow, so live, so die, my lord,
Ere I will yield my virgin patent° up     80
Unto his lordship, whose unwished yoke
My soul consents not to give sovereignty.

THESEUS

Take time to pause; and, by the next new moon—
The sealing day betwixt my love and me,
For everlasting bond of fellowship—     85
Upon that day either prepare to die
For disobedience to your father's will,
Or else to wed Demetrius, as he would,
Or on Diana's altar to protest
For aye austerity and single life.     90

DEMETRIUS

Relent, sweet Hermia: and, Lysander, yield
Thy crazèd title° to my certain right.

LYSANDER

You have her father's love, Demetrius;
Let me have Hermia's: do you marry him.

EGEUS

Scornful Lysander! True, he hath my love,     95
And what is mine my love shall render him.
And she is mine, and all my right of her
I do estate unto° Demetrius.

LYSANDER

I am, my lord, as well derived as he,
As well possessed;° my love is more than his;     100
My fortunes every way as fairly ranked
(If not with vantage°) as Demetrius';
And, which is more than all these boasts can be,
I am beloved of beauteous Hermia.
Why should not I then prosecute my right?     105
Demetrius, I'll avouch it to his head,°
Made love to Nedar's daughter, Helena,
And won her soul; and she, sweet lady, dotes,
Devoutly dotes, dotes in idolatry,
Upon this spotted° and inconstant man.     110

THESEUS

I must confess that I have heard so much,
And with Demetrius thought to have spoke thereof;
But, being overfull of self-affairs,
My mind did lose it. But, Demetrius, come;
And come, Egeus. You shall go with me;     115
I have some private schooling for you both.

---

**21 Egeus** pronounced "E-gé-us"    **32 stol'n . . . fantasy** fraudulently impressed your image upon her imagination    **33-34 gauds, conceits, Knacks** trinkets, cleverly devised tokens, knickknacks    **45 Immediately** expressly    **54 But . . . voice** but in this particular respect, lacking your father's approval

**68 Know of** ascertain from; **blood** passions    **71 mewed** caged    **73 moon** Diana, goddess of chastity    **76 distilled** made into perfumes    **80 patent** privilege    **92 crazèd title** flawed claim    **98 estate unto** settle upon    **100 As well possessed** as rich    **102 If . . . vantage** if not better    **106 to his head** in his teeth    **110 spotted** morally stained

For you, fair Hermia, look you arm yourself
To fit your fancies to your father's will;
Or else the law of Athens yields you up—
Which by no means we may extenuate—                    120
To death, or to a vow of single life.
Come, my Hippolyta. What cheer, my love?
Demetrius and Egeus, go along.
I must employ you in some business
Against° our nuptial, and confer with you               125
Of something nearly° that concerns yourselves.

EGEUS
With duty and desire we follow you.
                *Exeunt [all but* LYSANDER *and* HERMIA].

LYSANDER
How now, my love! Why is your cheek so pale?
How chance° the roses there do fade so fast?

HERMIA
Belike° for want of rain, which I could well            130
Beteem° them from the tempest of my eyes.

LYSANDER
Ay me! For aught that I could ever read,
Could ever hear by tale or history,
The course of true love never did run smooth;
But, either it was different in blood—                   135

HERMIA
O cross! Too high to be enthralled to low!

LYSANDER
Or else misgraffèd° in respect of years—

HERMIA
O spite! Too old to be engaged to young!

LYSANDER
Or else it stood upon the choice of friends—

HERMIA
O hell! To choose love by another's eyes!               140

LYSANDER
Or, if there were a sympathy in choice,
War, death, or sickness did lay siege to it,
Making it momentany° as a sound,
Swift as a shadow, short as any dream,
Brief as the lightning in the collied° night,           145
That, in a spleen,° unfolds both heaven and earth,
And ere a man hath power to say, "Behold!"
The jaws of darkness do devour it up:
So quick bright things come to confusion.

HERMIA
If then true lovers have been ever crossed,             150
It stands as an edict in destiny:
Then let us teach our trial patience,°
Because it is a customary cross,
As due to love as thoughts and dreams and sighs,
Wishes and tears, poor Fancy's° followers.              155

LYSANDER
A good persuasion.° Therefore, hear me, Hermia.
I have a widow aunt, a dowager
Of great revenue, and she hath no child.
From Athens is her house remote seven leagues,

And she respects me as her only son.                    160
There, gentle Hermia, may I marry thee,
And to that place the sharp Athenian law
Cannot pursue us. If thou lovest me, then,
Steal forth thy father's house tomorrow night;
And in the wood, a league without the town,             165
Where I did meet thee once with Helena,
To do observance to a morn of May,
There will I stay for thee.

HERMIA                              My good Lysander!
I swear to thee, by Cupid's strongest bow,
By his best arrow with the golden head,°                170
By the simplicity of Venus' doves,
By that which knitteth souls and prospers loves,
And by that fire which burned the Carthage queen,°
When the false Troyan under sail was seen,
By all the vows that ever men have broke,               175
In number more than ever women spoke,
In that same place thou hast appointed me,
Tomorrow truly will I meet with thee.

LYSANDER
Keep promise, love. Look, here comes Helena.

*Enter* HELENA.

HERMIA
God speed fair Helena! Whither away?                    180

HELENA
Call you me fair? That fair again unsay.
Demetrius loves your fair.° O happy fair!
Your eyes are lodestars,° and your tongue's sweet air°
More tunable than lark to shepherd's ear,
When wheat is green, when hawthorn buds appear.         185
Sickness is catching. O, were favor° so,
Yours would I catch, fair Hermia, ere I go;
My ear should catch your voice, my eye your eye,
My tongue should catch your tongue's sweet melody.
Were the world mine, Demetrius being bated,°            190
The rest I'd give to be to you translated.°
O, teach me how you look, and with what art
You sway the motion of Demetrius' heart!

HERMIA
I frown upon him, yet he loves me still.

HELENA
O that your frowns would teach my smiles such skill!    195

HERMIA
I give him curses, yet he gives me love.

HELENA
O that my prayers could such affection move!

HERMIA
The more I hate, the more he follows me.

HELENA
The more I love, the more he hateth me.

HERMIA
His folly, Helena, is no fault of mine.                 200

HELENA
None, but your beauty: would that fault were
    mine!

---

125 **Against** in preparation for   126 **nearly** closely   129
**How chance** how does it come that   130 **Belike** perhaps
131 **Beteem** allow, afford   137 **misgraffèd** ill matched,
misgrafted   143 **momentany** momentary, passing   145 **collied**
blackened   146 **spleen** sudden fit of passion   152 **teach . . .
patience** teach ourselves to be patient   155 **Fancy's** Love's
156 **persuasion** principle

170 **arrow . . . head** Cupid's gold-headed arrows caused love,
the leaden ones dislike   173 **Carthage queen** Dido (who
burned herself on a funeral pyre when the Trojan Aeneas left
her)   182 **fair** beauty   183 **lodestars** guiding stars; **air** music
186 **favor** looks   190 **bated** excepted   191 **translated**
transformed

HERMIA
Take comfort. He no more shall see my face;
Lysander and myself will fly this place.
Before the time I did Lysander see,
Seemed Athens as a paradise to me.                                    205
O, then, what graces in my love do dwell,
That he hath turned a heaven unto a hell!

LYSANDER
Helen, to you our minds we will unfold.
Tomorrow night, when Phoebe° doth behold
Her silver visage in the wat'ry glass,                                210
Decking with liquid pearl the bladed grass,
A time that lovers' flights doth still° conceal,
Through Athens' gates have we devised to steal.

HERMIA
And in the wood, where often you and I
Upon faint primrose beds were wont to lie,                            215
Emptying our bosoms of their counsel sweet,
There my Lysander and myself shall meet,
And thence from Athens turn away our eyes,
To seek new friends and stranger companies.°
Farewell, sweet playfellow. Pray thou for us;                        220
And good luck grant thee thy Demetrius!
Keep word, Lysander. We must starve our sight
From lovers' food till tomorrow deep midnight.

LYSANDER
I will, my Hermia. *Exit* HERMIA. Helena, adieu.
As you on him, Demetrius dote on you!                                 225
                                        *Exit* LYSANDER.

HELENA
How happy some o'er other some° can be!
Through Athens I am thought as fair as she.
But what of that? Demetrius thinks not so;
He will not know what all but he do know.
And as he errs, doting on Hermia's eyes,                              230
So I, admiring of his qualities.
Things base and vile, holding no quantity,°
Love can transpose to form and dignity.
Love looks not with the eyes, but with the mind,
And therefore is winged Cupid painted blind.                         235
Nor hath Love's mind of any judgment taste;
Wings, and no eyes, figure° unheedy haste:
And therefore is Love said to be a child,
Because in choice he is so oft beguiled.
As waggish boys in game themselves forswear,                         240
So the boy Love is perjured everywhere.
For ere Demetrius looked on Hermia's eyne,°
He hailed down oaths that he was only mine;
And when this hail some heat from Hermia felt,
So he dissolved, and show'rs of oaths did melt.                      245
I will go tell him of fair Hermia's flight.
Then to the wood will he tomorrow night
Pursue her; and for this intelligence°
If I have thanks, it is a dear expense:°
But herein mean I to enrich my pain,                                 250
To have his sight thither and back again.          *Exit.*

---

**209 Phoebe** the moon   **212 still** always   **219 stranger companies** the company of strangers   **226 some . . . some** some in comparison with others   **232 holding no quantity** having no proportion (therefore unattractive)   **237 figure** symbolize   **242 eyne** eyes   **248 intelligence** piece of news   **249 dear expense** (1) expense gladly incurred (2) heavy cost (in Demetrius' opinion)

---

[Scene II. *Quince's house.*]

*Enter* QUINCE *the carpenter, and* SNUG *the joiner, and*
BOTTOM *the weaver, and* FLUTE *the bellows mender,*
*and* SNOUT *the tinker, and* STARVELING *the tailor.*°

QUINCE  Is all our company here?
BOTTOM  You were best to call them generally,° man
by man, according to the scrip.
QUINCE  Here is the scroll of every man's name,
which is thought fit, through all Athens, to play in  5
our interlude° before the duke and the duchess, on
his wedding day at night.
BOTTOM  First, good Peter Quince, say what the play
treats on; then read the names of the actors; and so
grow to a point.                                           10
QUINCE  Marry,° our play is, "The most lamentable
comedy, and most cruel death of Pyramus and
Thisby."
BOTTOM  A very good piece of work, I assure you,
and a merry. Now, good Peter Quince, call forth  15
your actors by the scroll. Masters, spread yourselves.
QUINCE  Answer as I call you. Nick Bottom, the
weaver.
BOTTOM  Ready. Name what part I am for, and
proceed.                                                   20
QUINCE  You, Nick Bottom, are set down for
Pyramus.
BOTTOM  What is Pyramus? A lover, or a tyrant?
QUINCE  A lover that kills himself, most gallant, for
love.                                                      25
BOTTOM  That will ask some tears in the true performing of it: if I do it, let the audience look to their
eyes. I will move storms, I will condole° in some
measure. To the rest: yet my chief humor° is for a
tyrant. I could play Ercles° rarely, or a part to tear a  30
cat in,° to make all split.

          The raging rocks
          And shivering shocks
          Shall break the locks
             Of prison gates;                               35
          And Phibbus' car°
          Shall shine from far,
          And make and mar
             The foolish Fates.

This was lofty! Now name the rest of the players.  40
This is Ercles' vein, a tyrant's vein. A lover is more
condoling.
QUINCE  Francis Flute, the bellows mender.
FLUTE  Here, Peter Quince.
QUINCE  Flute, you must take Thisby on you.           45
FLUTE  What is Thisby? A wand'ring knight?
QUINCE  It is the lady that Pyramus must love.

---

**I.ii.s.d.** the names of the clowns suggest their trades: *Bottom* object on which the yarn is wound; *Quince* quines, blocks of wood used for building; *Snug* close-fitting; *Flute* suggesting fluted bellows (for church organs); *Snout* spout of a kettle; *Starveling* an allusion to the proverbial thinness of tailors   **2 generally** Bottom means *individually*   **6 interlude** dramatic entertainment   **11 Marry** an interjection (originally an oath, "By the Virgin Mary")   **28 condole** lament   **29 humor** disposition   **30 Ercles** Hercules (a part notorious for ranting)   **30-31 part . . . in** railing part   **36 Phibbus' car** mispronunciation for *Phoebus' car*, or chariot (i.e., the sun)

FLUTE  Nay, faith, let not me play a woman. I have a beard coming.

QUINCE  That's all one.° You shall play it in a mask, 50 and you may speak as small° as you will.

BOTTOM  An° I may hide my face, let me play Thisby too. I'll speak in a monstrous little voice, "Thisne,° Thisne!" "Ah Pyramus, my lover dear! Thy Thisby dear, and lady dear!" 55

QUINCE  No, no; you must play Pyramus: and, Flute, you Thisby.

BOTTOM  Well, proceed.

QUINCE  Robin Starveling, the tailor.

STARVELING  Here, Peter Quince. 60

QUINCE  Robin Starveling, you must play Thisby's mother. Tom Snout, the tinker.

SNOUT  Here, Peter Quince.

QUINCE  You, Pyramus' father: myself, Thisby's father: Snug, the joiner; you, the lion's part. And I 65 hope here is a play fitted.

SNUG  Have you the lion's part written? Pray you, if it be, give it me, for I am slow to study.

QUINCE  You may do it extempore, for it is nothing but roaring. 70

BOTTOM  Let me play the lion too. I will roar that° I will do any man's heart good to hear me. I will roar, that I will make the duke say, "Let him roar again, let him roar again."

QUINCE  An you should do it too terribly, you would 75 fright the duchess and the ladies, that they would shriek; and that were enough to hang us all.

ALL  That would hang us, every mother's son.

BOTTOM  I grant you, friends, if you should fright the ladies out of their wits, they would have no more 80 discretion but to hang us: but I will aggravate° my voice so that I will roar you as gently as any sucking dove; I will roar you an 'twere° any nightingale.

QUINCE  You can play no part but Pyramus; for Pyramus is a sweet-faced man; a proper° man as one 85 shall see in a summer's day; a most lovely, gentleman-like man: therefore you must needs play Pyramus.

BOTTOM  Well, I will undertake it. What beard were I best to play it in?

QUINCE  Why, what you will. 90

BOTTOM  I will discharge it in either your straw-color beard, your orange-tawny beard, your purple-in-grain° beard, or your French-crown-color° beard, your perfit° yellow.

QUINCE  Some of your French crowns° have no hair 95 at all, and then you will play barefaced.° But, masters, here are your parts; and I am to entreat you, request you, and desire you, to con° them by tomorrow night; and meet me in the palace wood, a mile with-out the town, by moonlight. There will we rehearse, 100 for if we meet in the city, we shall be dogged with company, and our devices° known. In the meantime

I will draw a bill of properties,° such as our play wants. I pray you, fail me not.

BOTTOM  We will meet; and there we may rehearse 105 most obscenely° and courageously. Take pains; be perfit: adieu.

QUINCE  At the Duke's Oak we meet.

BOTTOM  Enough; hold or cut bowstrings.°    Exeunt.

# [ A C T   I I ]

[Scene I. *A wood near Athens.*]

*Enter a* FAIRY *at one door, and Robin Goodfellow* [PUCK] *at another.*

PUCK
How now, spirit! Wither wander you?

FAIRY
Over hill, over dale,
   Thorough bush, thorough brier,
Over park, over pale,°
   Thorough flood, thorough fire, 5
I do wander everywhere,
Swifter than the moon's sphere;°
And I serve the Fairy Queen,
To dew her orbs° upon the green.
The cowslips tall her pensioners° be: 10
In their gold coats spots you see;
Those be rubies, fairy favors,°
In those freckles live their savors.°
I must go seek some dewdrops here,
And hang a pearl in every cowslip's ear. 15
Farewell, thou lob° of spirits; I'll be gone.
Our queen and all her elves come here anon.

PUCK
The king doth keep his revels here tonight.
Take heed the queen come not within his sight.
For Oberon is passing fell and wrath,° 20
Because that she as her attendant hath
A lovely boy, stolen from an Indian king;
She never had so sweet a changeling.°
And jealous Oberon would have the child
Knight of his train, to trace° the forests wild. 25
But she perforce withholds the lovèd boy,
Crowns him with flowers, and makes him all her joy.
And now they never meet in grove or green,
By fountain clear, or spangled starlight sheen,°
But they do square,° that all their elves for fear 30
Creep into acorn cups and hide them there.

103 **bill of properties** list of stage furnishings  106 **obscenely** Bottom means *seemly*  109 **hold . . . bowstrings** keep your word or give it up (?)
II.i.4 **pale** enclosed land, park  7 **moon's sphere** according to the Ptolemaic system, the moon was fixed in a hollow sphere that surrounded and revolved about the earth  9 **orbs** fairy rings (i.e., circles of darker grass)  10 **pensioners** bodyguards (referring to Elizabeth I's bodyguard of fifty splendid young noblemen)  12 **favors** gifts  13 **savors** perfumes  16 **lob** lubber, clumsy fellow  20 **passing . . . wrath** very fierce and angry  23 **changeling** usually a child left behind by fairies in exchange for one stolen, but here applied to the stolen child  25 **trace** traverse  29 **starlight sheen** brightly shining starlight  30 **square** clash, quarrel

50 **That's all one** It makes no difference  51 **small** softly  52 **An** if  53 **Thisne** perhaps Shakespeare wrote "thisne," meaning "in this manner"  71 **that** so that  81 **aggravate** Bottom means *moderate*  83 **an 'twere** as if it were  85 **proper** handsome  92–93 **purple-in-grain** dyed with a fast purple  93 **French-crown-color** color of French gold coin  94 **perfit** perfect  95 **crowns** (1) gold coins (2) heads bald from the French disease (syphilis)  96 **barefaced** (1) bald (2) brazen  98 **con** study  102 **devices** plans

FAIRY
Either I mistake your shape and making quite,
Or else you are that shrewd and knavish sprite
Called Robin Goodfellow. Are not you he
That frights the maidens of the villagery,°          35
Skim milk, and sometimes labor in the quern,°
And bootless° make the breathless housewife churn,
And sometime make the drink to bear no barm,°
Mislead night wanderers, laughing at their harm?
Those that Hobgoblin call you, and sweet Puck,     40
You do their work, and they shall have good luck.
Are not you he?
PUCK                  Thou speakest aright;
I am that merry wanderer of the night.
I jest to Oberon, and make him smile,
When I a fat and bean-fed horse beguile,          45
Neighing in likeness of a filly foal:
And sometime lurk I in a gossip's° bowl,
In very likeness of a roasted crab;°
And when she drinks, against her lips I bob
And on her withered dewlap° pour the ale.         50
The wisest aunt, telling the saddest° tale,
Sometime for three-foot stool mistaketh me;
Then slip I from her bum, down topples she,
And "tailor"° cries, and falls into a cough;
And then the whole quire° hold their hips and laugh, 55
And waxen° in their mirth, and neeze,° and swear
A merrier hour was never wasted° there.
But, room, fairy! Here comes Oberon.
FAIRY
And here my mistress. Would that he were gone!

*Enter [OBERON,] the King of Fairies, at one door, with
his TRAIN; and [TITANIA,] the Queen, at another, with
hers.*

OBERON
Ill met by moonlight, proud Titania.             60
TITANIA
What, jealous Oberon! Fairy, skip hence.
I have forsworn his bed and company.
OBERON
Tarry, rash wanton;° am not I thy lord?
TITANIA
Then I must be thy lady: but I know
When thou hast stolen away from fairy land       65
And in the shape of Corin° sat all day,
Playing on pipes of corn,° and versing love
To amorous Phillida. Why art thou here,
Come from the farthest steep of India?
But that, forsooth, the bouncing° Amazon,        70
Your buskined° mistress and your warrior love,
To Theseus must be wedded, and you come
To give their bed joy and prosperity.

OBERON
How canst thou thus for shame, Titania,
Glance at my credit with Hippolyta,              75
Knowing I know thy love to Theseus?
Didst not thou lead him through the glimmering
     night
From Perigenia, whom he ravishèd?
And make him with fair Aegles break his faith,
With Ariadne and Antiopa?°                        80
TITANIA
These are the forgeries of jealousy:
And never, since the middle summer's spring,°
Met we on hill, in dale, forest, or mead,
By pavèd° fountain or by rushy brook,
Or in the beachèd margent° of the sea,           85
To dance our ringlets to the whistling wind,
But with thy brawls thou hast disturbed our sport.
Therefore the winds, piping to us in vain,
As in revenge, have sucked up from the sea
Contagious° fogs; which, falling in the land,    90
Hath every pelting° river made so proud,
That they have overborne their continents.°
The ox hath therefore stretched his yoke in vain,
The plowman lost his sweat, and the green corn°
Hath rotted ere his youth attained a beard;      95
The fold stands empty in the drownèd field,
And crows are fatted with the murrion flock;°
The nine men's morris° is filled up with mud;
And the quaint mazes° in the wanton green,°
For lack of tread, are undistinguishable.       100
The human mortals want their winter here;
No night is now with hymn or carol blest.
Therefore the moon, the governess of floods,
Pale in her anger, washes all the air,
That rheumatic diseases do abound.              105
And thorough this distemperature° we see
The seasons alter: hoary-headed frosts
Fall in the fresh lap of the crimson rose,
And on old Hiems'° thin and icy crown
An odorous chaplet° of sweet summer buds        110
Is, as in mockery, set. The spring, the summer,
The childing° autumn, angry winter, change
Their wonted liveries;° and the mazèd° world,
By their increase, now knows not which is which.
And this same progeny of evils comes            115
From our debate,° from our dissension;
We are their parents and original.
OBERON
Do you amend it, then; it lies in you:
Why should Titania cross her Oberon?

---

35 villagery villagers  36 quern hand mill for grinding
grain  37 bootless in vain  38 barm yeast, froth  47
gossip's old woman's  48 crab crabapple  50 dewlap fold
of skin on the throat  51 saddest most serious  54 tailor
suggesting the posture of a tailor squatting; or a term of abuse
(Middle English *taillard* = thief)  55 quire company, choir
56 waxen increase; neeze sneeze  57 wasted passed  63 rash
wanton hasty willful creature  66 Corin like "Phillida,"
line 68, a traditional name for a lover in pastoral poetry  67
pipes of corn musical instruments made of grain stalks  70
bouncing swaggering  71 buskined wearing a hunter's
boot (buskin)

78–80 Perigenia . . . Antiopa girls Theseus loved and
deserted  82 middle summer's spring beginning of midsummer  84 pavèd with pebbly bottom  85 margent margin,
shore  90 Contagious generating pestilence  91 pelting
petty  92 continents containers (i.e., banks)  94 corn grain
97 murrion flock flock dead of cattle disease (murrain)
98 nine men's morris square cut in the turf (for a game in
which each player has nine counters, or "men")  99 quaint
mazes intricate meandering paths on the grass (kept fresh by
running along them); wanton green grass growing without
check  106 distemperature disturbance in nature  109 old
Hiems' the winter's  110 chaplet wreath  112 childing
breeding, fruitful  113 wonted liveries accustomed apparel;
mazèd bewildered  116 debate quarrel

I do but beg a little changeling boy,                                     120
To be my henchman.°

TITANIA                    Set your heart at rest.
The fairy land buys not° the child of me.
His mother was a vot'ress° of my order,
And, in the spicèd Indian air, by night,
Full often hath she gossiped by my side,                                  125
And sat with me on Neptune's yellow sands,
Marking th' embarkèd traders on the flood;
When we have laughed to see the sails conceive
And grow big-bellied with the wanton wind;
Which she, with pretty and with swimming gait                             130
Following—her womb then rich with my young
    squire—
Would imitate, and sail upon the land,
To fetch me trifles, and return again,
As from a voyage, rich with merchandise.
But she, being mortal, of that boy did die;                               135
And for her sake do I rear up her boy,
And for her sake I will not part with him.

OBERON
How long within this wood intend you stay?

TITANIA
Perchance till after Theseus' wedding day.
If you will patiently dance in our round,°                                140
And see our moonlight revels, go with us.
If not, shun me, and I will spare° your haunts.

OBERON
Give me that boy, and I will go with thee.

TITANIA
Not for thy fairy kingdom. Fairies, away!
We shall chide downright, if I longer stay.                               145
        Exeunt [TITANIA and her TRAIN].

OBERON
Well, go thy way. Thou shalt not from this grove
Till I torment thee for this injury.
My gentle Puck, come hither. Thou rememb'rest
Since° once I sat upon a promontory,
And heard a mermaid, on a dolphin's back,                                 150
Uttering such dulcet and harmonious breath,
That the rude sea grew civil° at her song,
And certain stars shot madly from their spheres,
To hear the sea maid's music.

PUCK                          I remember.

OBERON
That very time I saw, but thou couldst not,                               155
Flying between the cold moon and the earth,
Cupid all armed. A certain aim he took
At a fair vestal° thronèd by the west,
And loosed his love shaft smartly from his bow,
As it should° pierce a hundred thousand hearts.                          160
But I might° see young Cupid's fiery shaft
Quenched in the chaste beams of the wat'ry moon,
And the imperial vot'ress passèd on,
In maiden meditation, fancy-free.°
Yet marked I where the bolt of Cupid fell.                                165

It fell upon a little western flower,
Before milk-white, now purple with love's wound,
And maidens call it love-in-idleness.°
Fetch me that flow'r; the herb I showed thee once:
The juice of it on sleeping eyelids laid                                  170
Will make or man or woman° madly dote
Upon the next live creature that it sees.
Fetch me this herb, and be thou here again
Ere the leviathan° can swim a league.

PUCK
I'll put a girdle round about the earth                                   175
In forty minutes.                         [Exit.]

OBERON                    Having once this juice,
I'll watch Titania when she is asleep,
And drop the liquor of it in her eyes.
The next thing then she waking looks upon,
Be it on lion, bear, or wolf, or bull,                                    180
On meddling monkey, or on busy° ape,
She shall pursue it with the soul of love.
And ere I take this charm from off her sight,
As I can take it with another herb,
I'll make her render up her page to me.                                   185
But who comes here? I am invisible,
And I will overhear their conference.

*Enter* DEMETRIUS, HELENA *following him.*

DEMETRIUS
I love thee not, therefore pursue me not.
Where is Lysander and fair Hermia?
The one I'll slay, the other slayeth me.                                  190
Thou told'st me they were stol'n unto this wood;
And here am I, and wood° within this wood,
Because I cannot meet my Hermia.
Hence, get thee gone, and follow me no more!

HELENA
You draw me, you hardhearted adamant;°                                    195
But yet you draw not iron, for my heart
Is true as steel. Leave you your power to draw,
And I shall have no power to follow you.

DEMETRIUS
Do I entice you? Do I speak you fair?°
Or, rather, do I not in plainest truth                                    200
Tell you, I do not nor I cannot love you?

HELENA
And even for that do I love you the more.
I am your spaniel; and, Demetrius,
The more you beat me, I will fawn on you.
Use me but as your spaniel, spurn me, strike me,                          205
Neglect me, lose me; only give me leave,
Unworthy as I am, to follow you.
What worser place can I beg in your love—
And yet a place of high respect with me—
Than to be usèd as you use your dog?                                      210

DEMETRIUS
Tempt not too much the hatred of my spirit,
For I am sick when I do look on thee.

HELENA
And I am sick when I look not on you.

121 **henchman** page  122 **The . . . not** even your whole
domain could not buy  123 **vot'ress** woman who has taken
a vow  140 **round** circular dance  142 **spare** keep away
from  149 **Since** when  152 **civil** well behaved  158 **vestal**
virgin (possibly an allusion to Elizabeth, the Virgin Queen)
160 **As it should** as if it would  161 **might** could  164
**fancy-free** free from the power of love

168 **love-in-idleness** pansy  171 **or man or woman** either
man or woman  174 **leviathan** sea monster, whale  181
**busy** meddlesome  192 **wood** out of my mind (with perhaps
an additional pun on *wooed*)  195 **adamant** (1) very hard gem
(2) lodestone; magnet  199 **speak you fair** speak kindly to you

DEMETRIUS

You do impeach° your modesty too much,
To leave the city, and commit yourself          215
Into the hands of one that loves you not,
To trust the opportunity of night
And the ill counsel of a desert° place
With the rich worth of your virginity.

HELENA

Your virtue is my privilege.° For that          220
It is not night when I do see your face,
Therefore I think I am not in the night;
Nor doth this wood lack worlds of company,
For you in my respect° are all the world.
Then how can it be said I am alone,          225
When all the world is here to look on me?

DEMETRIUS

I'll run from thee and hide me in the brakes,°
And leave thee to the mercy of wild beasts.

HELENA

The wildest hath not such a heart as you.
Run when you will, the story shall be changed:          230
Apollo flies, and Daphne° holds the chase;
The dove pursues the griffin;° the mild hind°
Makes speed to catch the tiger; bootless speed,
When cowardice pursues, and valor flies.

DEMETRIUS

I will not stay° thy questions. Let me go!          235
O, if thou follow me, do not believe
But I shall do thee mischief in the wood.

HELENA

Ay, in the temple, in the town, the field,
You do me mischief. Fie, Demetrius!
Your wrongs do set a scandal on my sex.          240
We cannot fight for love, as men may do;
We should be wooed, and were not made to woo.
          [Exit DEMETRIUS.]
I'll follow thee, and make a heaven of hell,
To die upon° the hand I love so well.          [Exit.]

OBERON

Fare thee well, nymph: ere he do leave this grove,          245
Thou shalt fly him, and he shall seek thy love.

Enter PUCK.

Hast thou the flower there? Welcome, wanderer.

PUCK

Ay, there it is.

OBERON          I pray thee, give it me.
I know a bank where the wild thyme blows,
Where oxlips and the nodding violet grows,          250
Quite overcanopied with luscious woodbine,
With sweet musk roses, and with eglantine.
There sleeps Titania sometime of the night,
Lulled in these flowers with dances and delight;
And there the snake throws° her enameled skin,          255
Weed° wide enough to wrap a fairy in.
And with the juice of this I'll streak her eyes,

And make her full of hateful fantasies.
Take thou some of it, and seek through this grove.
A sweet Athenian lady is in love          260
With a disdainful youth. Anoint his eyes;
But do it when the next thing he espies
May be the lady. Thou shalt know the man
By the Athenian garments he hath on.
Effect it with some care that he may prove          265
More fond on her° than she upon her love:
And look thou meet me ere the first cock crow.

PUCK

Fear not, my lord, your servant shall do so.          Exeunt.

[Scene II. Another part of the wood.]

Enter TITANIA, Queen of Fairies, with her TRAIN.

TITANIA

Come, now a roundel° and a fairy song;
Then, for the third part of a minute, hence;
Some to kill cankers in the musk-rose buds,
Some war with reremice° for their leathern wings
To make my small elves coats, and some keep back          5
The clamorous owl, that nightly hoots and wonders
At our quaint° spirits Sing me now asleep.
Then to your offices, and let me rest.

FAIRIES sing.

FIRST FAIRY

You spotted snakes with double tongue,
          Thorny hedgehogs, be not seen;          10
Newts and blindworms,° do no wrong,
          Come not near our Fairy Queen.

CHORUS

Philomele,° with melody
          Sing in our sweet lullaby;
Lulla, lulla, lullaby, lulla, lulla, lullaby:          15
          Never harm
          Nor spell nor charm,
Come our lovely lady nigh;
          So, good night, with lullaby.

FIRST FAIRY

Weaving spiders, come not here;          20
          Hence, you long-legged spinners, hence!
Beetles black, approach not near;
          Worm nor snail, do no offense.

CHORUS

Philomele, with melody, &c.

SECOND FAIRY

Hence, away! Now all is well.          25
          One aloof stand sentinel.
          [Exeunt FAIRIES. TITANIA sleeps.]

Enter OBERON [and squeezes the flower on Titania's eyelids].

OBERON

What thou see'st when thou dost wake,
Do it for thy truelove take;
Love and languish for his sake.

214 **impeach** expose to reproach 218 **desert** deserted, uninhabited 220 **Your . . . privilege** Your inherent power is my warrant 224 **in my respect** in my opinion 227 **brakes** thickets 231 **Daphne** a nymph who fled from Apollo (at her prayer she was changed into a laurel tree) 232 **griffin** fabulous monster with an eagle's head and a lion's body; **hind** doe 235 **stay** wait for 244 **To die upon** dying by 255 **throws** casts off 256 **Weed** garment

266 **fond on her** foolishly in love with her
**II.ii.1 roundel** dance in a ring 4 **reremice** bats 7 **quaint** dainty 11 **blindworms** small snakes 13 **Philomele** nightingale

Be it ounce,° or cat, or bear,                    30
Pard,° or boar with bristled hair,
In thy eye that shall appear
When thou wak'st, it is thy dear.
Wake when some vile thing is near.        [*Exit.*]

*Enter* LYSANDER *and* HERMIA.

LYSANDER
Fair love, you faint with wand'ring in the wood;  35
And to speak troth,° I have forgot our way.
We'll rest us, Hermia, if you think it good,
And tarry for the comfort of the day.

HERMIA
Be't so, Lysander. Find you out a bed;
For I upon this bank will rest my head.          40

LYSANDER
One turf shall serve as pillow for us both,
One heart, one bed, two bosoms, and one troth.

HERMIA
Nay, good Lysander. For my sake, my dear,
Lie further off yet, do not lie so near.

LYSANDER
O, take the sense,° sweet, of my innocence!      45
Love takes the meaning° in love's conference.
I mean, that my heart unto yours is knit,
So that but one heart we can make of it:
Two bosoms interchainèd with an oath;
So then two bosoms and a single troth.°          50
Then by your side no bed-room me deny,
For lying so, Hermia, I do not lie.°

HERMIA
Lysander riddles very prettily.
Now much beshrew° my manners and my pride,
If Hermia meant to say Lysander lied.            55
But, gentle friend, for love and courtesy
Lie further off, in human modesty.
Such separation as may well be said
Becomes a virtuous bachelor and a maid,
So far be distant; and, good night, sweet friend.  60
Thy love ne'er alter till thy sweet life end!

LYSANDER
Amen, amen, to that fair prayer, say I,
And then end life when I end loyalty!
Here is my bed. Sleep give thee all his rest!

HERMIA
With half that wish the wisher's eyes be pressed!  65

[*They sleep.*]

*Enter* PUCK.

PUCK
Through the forest have I gone,
But Athenian found I none,
On whose eyes I might approve°
This flower's force in stirring love.
Night and silence.—Who is here?                  70
Weeds° of Athens he doth wear:
This is he, my master said,

Despisèd the Athenian maid;
And here the maiden, sleeping sound,
On the dank and dirty ground.                    75
Pretty soul! She durst not lie
Near this lack-love, this kill-courtesy.
Churl,° upon thy eyes I throw
All the power this charm doth owe.°
When thou wak'st, let love forbid               80
Sleep his seat on thy eyelid.
So awake when I am gone,
For I must now to Oberon.           *Exit.*

*Enter* DEMETRIUS *and* HELENA, *running.*

HELENA
Stay, though thou kill me, sweet Demetrius.

DEMETRIUS
I charge thee, hence, and do not haunt me thus.   85

HELENA
O, wilt thou darkling° leave me? Do not so.

DEMETRIUS
Stay, on thy peril! I alone will go.       [*Exit.*]

HELENA
O, I am out of breath in this fond° chase!
The more my prayer, the lesser is my grace.
Happy is Hermia, wheresoe'er she lies,           90
For she hath blessèd and attractive eyes.
How came her eyes so bright? Not with salt tears.
If so, my eyes are oft'ner washed than hers.
No, no, I am as ugly as a bear,
For beasts that meet me run away for fear.       95
Therefore no marvel though Demetrius
Do, as a monster, fly my presence thus.
What wicked and dissembling glass of mine
Made me compare with Hermia's sphery eyne?°
But who is here? Lysander! On the ground!        100
Dead? Or asleep? I see no blood, no wound.
Lysander, if you live, good sir, awake.

LYSANDER [*Awaking.*]
And run through fire I will for thy sweet sake.
Transparent° Helena! Nature shows art,
That through thy bosom makes me see thy heart.   105
Where is Demetrius? O, how fit a word
Is that vile name to perish on my sword!

HELENA
Do not say so, Lysander, say not so.
What though he love your Hermia? Lord, what
   though?
Yet Hermia still loves you. Then be content.     110

LYSANDER
Content with Hermia! No; I do repent
The tedious minutes I with her have spent.
Not Hermia but Helena I love:
Who will not change a raven for a dove?
The will° of man is by his reason swayed         115
And reason says you are the worthier maid.
Things growing are not ripe until their season:
So I, being young, till now ripe not° to reason.
And touching now the point of human skill,°

30 ounce lynx  31 Pard leopard  36 troth truth  45 take
the sense understand the true meaning  46 Love . . . meaning lovers understand the true meaning of what they say to each
other  50 troth faithful love  52 lie be untrue  54 beshrew
curse (but commonly, as here, in a light sense)  68 approve
try  71 Weeds garments

78 Churl boorish fellow  79 owe possess  86 darkling in
the dark  88 fond (1) doting (2) foolish  99 sphery eyne
starry eyes  104 Transparent bright  115 will desire  118
ripe not have not ripened  119 touching . . . skill now
reaching the fullness of human reason

Reason becomes the marshal to my will, 120
And leads me to your eyes, where I o'erlook
Love's stories, written in love's richest book.

HELENA
Wherefore was I to this keen mockery born?
When at your hands did I deserve this scorn?
Is't not enough, is't not enough, young man, 125
That I did never, no, nor never can,
Deserve a sweet look from Demetrius' eye,
But you must flout° my insufficiency?
Good troth,° you do me wrong, good sooth, you do,
In such disdainful manner me to woo. 130
But fare you well. Perforce I must confess
I thought you lord of more true gentleness.°
O, that a lady, of one man refused,
Should of another therefore be abused!     *Exit.*

LYSANDER
She sees not Hermia. Hermia, sleep thou there, 135
And never mayst thou come Lysander near!
For as a surfeit of the sweetest things
The deepest loathing to the stomach brings,
Or as the heresies that men do leave
Are hated most of those they did deceive, 140
So thou, my surfeit and my heresy,
Of all be hated, but the most of me!
And, all my powers, address° your love and might
To honor Helen and to be her knight!     *Exit.*

HERMIA [*Awaking.*]
Help me, Lysander, help me! Do thy best 145
To pluck this crawling serpent from my breast!
Ay me, for pity! What a dream was here!
Lysander, look how I do quake with fear.
Methought a serpent eat° my heart away,
And you sat smiling at his cruel prey.° 150
Lysander! What, removed? Lysander! Lord!
What, out of hearing? Gone? No sound, no word?
Alack, where are you? Speak, an if° you hear;
Speak, of° all loves! I swoon almost with fear.
No? Then I well perceive you are not nigh. 155
Either death or you I'll find immediately.     *Exit.*

# [ A C T   I I I ]

[Scene I. *The wood.* TITANIA *lying asleep.*]

*Enter the clowns* [QUINCE, SNUG, BOTTOM, FLUTE,
SNOUT, *and* STARVELING].

BOTTOM  Are we all met?
QUINCE  Pat,° pat; and here's a marvail's° convenient
place for our rehearsal. This green plot shall be our
stage, this hawthorn brake° our tiring house,° and we
will do it in action as we will do it before the duke. 5
BOTTOM  Peter Quince?

QUINCE  What sayest thou, bully° Bottom?
BOTTOM  There are things in this comedy of Pyramus
and Thisby that will never please. First, Pyramus must
draw a sword to kill himself; which the ladies cannot 10
abide. How answer you that?
SNOUT  By'r lakin,° a parlous° fear.
STARVELING  I believe we must leave the killing out,
when all is done.
BOTTOM  Not a whit. I have a device to make all well. 15
Write me a prologue and let the prologue seem to
say, we will do no harm with our swords, and that
Pyramus is not killed indeed; and, for the more
better assurance, tell them that I Pyramus am not
Pyramus, but Bottom the weaver. This will put 20
them out of fear.
QUINCE  Well, we will have such a prologue, and it
shall be written in eight and six.°
BOTTOM  No, make it two more; let it be written in
eight and eight. 25
SNOUT  Will not the ladies be afeard of the lion?
STARVELING  I fear it, I promise you.
BOTTOM  Masters, you ought to consider with yourselves. To bring in—God shield us!—a lion among
ladies, is a most dreadful thing. For there is not a 30
more fearful wild fowl than your lion living; and
we ought to look to't.
SNOUT  Therefore another prologue must tell he is
not a lion.
BOTTOM  Nay, you must name his name, and half his 35
face must be seen through the lion's neck, and he
himself must speak through, saying thus, or to the
same defect—"Ladies"—or, "Fair ladies—I would
wish you"—or, "I would request you"—or, "I
would entreat you—not to fear, not to tremble: my 40
life for yours. If you think I come hither as a lion,
it were pity of my life.° No, I am no such thing. I am
a man as other men are." And there indeed let him
name his name, and tell them plainly, he is Snug the
joiner. 45
QUINCE  Well, it shall be so. But there is two hard
things; that is, to bring the moonlight into a chamber;
for, you know, Pyramus and Thisby meet by moonlight.
SNOUT  Doth the moon shine that night we play our 50
play?
BOTTOM  A calendar, a calendar! Look in the almanac;
find out moonshine, find out moonshine.
QUINCE  Yes, it doth shine that night.
BOTTOM  Why, then may you leave a casement of the 55
great chamber window, where we play, open, and
the moon may shine in at the casement.
QUINCE  Ay; or else one must come in with a bush of
thorns° and a lantern, and say he comes to disfigure,°
or to present, the person of Moonshine. Then, there 60
is another thing, we must have a wall in the great
chamber; for Pyramus and Thisby, says the story, did
talk through the chink of a wall.

---

128 **flout** jeer at  129 **Good troth** indeed (an expletive, like
"Good sooth")  132 **gentleness** noble character  143 **address**
apply  149 **eat** ate (pronounced "et")  150 **prey** act of preying
153 **an if** if  154 **of** for the sake of
III.i.2 **Pat** exactly, on the dot; **marvail's** Quince means *mar-*
*velous*  4 **brake** thicket; **tiring house** attiring house, dressing
room

7 **bully** good fellow  12 **By'r lakin** by Our Lady (ladykin
= little lady); **parlous** perilous, terrible  23 **in . . . six** in
alternate lines of eight and six syllables (ballad stanza)  42 **pity**
**. . . life** a bad thing for me  58–59 **bush of thorns** legend
held that the man in the moon had been placed there for
gathering firewood on Sunday  59 **disfigure** Quince means
*figure,* "represent"

SNOUT You can never bring in a wall. What say you, Bottom? 65

BOTTOM Some man or other must present Wall: and let him have some plaster, or some loam, or some roughcast° about him, to signify Wall; and let him hold his fingers thus, and through that cranny shall Pyramus and Thisby whisper. 70

QUINCE If that may be, then all is well. Come, sit down, every mother's son, and rehearse your parts. Pyramus, you begin. When you have spoken your speech, enter into that brake; and so everyone according to his cue. 75

*Enter Robin [PUCK].*

PUCK
What hempen homespuns° have we swagg'ring here, So near the cradle of the Fairy Queen? What, a play toward!° I'll be an auditor; An actor too perhaps, if I see cause.

QUINCE Speak, Pyramus. Thisby, stand forth. 80

PYRAMUS [BOTTOM]
Thisby, the flowers of odious savors sweet—

QUINCE Odors, odors.

PYRAMUS —odors savors sweet:
So hath thy breath, my dearest Thisby dear. But hark, a voice! Stay thou but here awhile, 85 And by and by° I will to thee appear. *Exit.*

PUCK
A stranger Pyramus than e'er played here! [*Exit.*]

THISBY [FLUTE] Must I speak now?

QUINCE Ay, marry, must you. For you must understand he goes but to see a noise that he heard, and is to 90 come again.

THISBY
Most radiant Pyramus, most lily-white of hue, Of color like the red rose on triumphant brier, Most brisky juvenal,° and eke° most lovely Jew,° As true as truest horse, that yet would never tire, 95 I'll meet thee, Pyramus, at Ninny's° tomb.

QUINCE "Ninus' tomb," man. Why, you must not speak that yet. That you answer to Pyramus. You speak all your part at once, cues and all. Pyramus, enter. Your cue is past; it is "never tire." 100

THISBY
O—as true as truest horse, that yet would never tire.

[*Re-enter PUCK, and BOTTOM with an ass's head.*]

PYRAMUS
If I were fair, Thisby, I were only thine.

QUINCE O monstrous! O strange! We are haunted. Pray, masters! Fly, masters! Help!

[*Exeunt all the CLOWNS but BOTTOM.*]

PUCK
I'll follow you, I'll lead you about a round,° 105 Through bog, through bush, through brake, through brier.

Sometime a horse I'll be, sometime a hound, A hog, a headless bear, sometime a fire; And neigh, and bark, and grunt, and roar, and burn, Like horse, hound, hog, bear, fire, at every turn. *Exit.* 110

BOTTOM Why do they run away? This is a knavery of them to make me afeard.

*Enter SNOUT.*

SNOUT O Bottom, thou art changed! What do I see on thee?

BOTTOM What do you see? You see an ass head of 115 your own, do you? [*Exit SNOUT.*]

*Enter QUINCE.*

QUINCE Bless thee, Bottom! Bless thee! Thou art translated.° *Exit.*

BOTTOM I see their knavery. This is to make an ass of me; to fright me, if they could. But I will not stir 120 from this place, do what they can. I will walk up and down here, and will sing, that they shall hear I am not afraid.

[*Sings.*]
The woosel° cock so black of hue, With orange-tawny bill, 125 The throstle with his note so true, The wren with little quill—°

TITANIA [*Awaking.*]
What angel wakes me from my flow'ry bed?

BOTTOM [*Sings.*]
The finch, the sparrow, and the lark, The plain-song cuckoo° gray, 130 Whose note full many a man doth mark, And dares not answer nay— for, indeed, who would set his wit° to so foolish a bird? Who would give a bird the lie,° though he cry "cuckoo" never so?° 135

TITANIA
I pray thee, gentle mortal, sing again: Mine ear is much enamored of thy note; So is mine eye enthrallèd to thy shape; And thy fair virtue's force perforce doth move me On the first view to say, to swear, I love thee. 140

BOTTOM Methinks, mistress, you should have little reason for that. And yet, to say the truth, reason and love keep little company together nowadays; the more the pity, that some honest neighbors will not make them friends. Nay, I can gleek° upon 145 occasion.

TITANIA
Thou art as wise as thou art beautiful.

BOTTOM Not so, neither; but if I had wit enough to get out of this wood, I have enough to serve mine own turn. 150

TITANIA
Out of this wood do not desire to go.

---

68 **roughcast** lime mixed with gravel to plaster outside walls 76 **hempen homespuns** coarse fellows (clad in homespun cloth of hemp) 78 **toward** in preparation 86 **by and by** shortly 94 **juvenal** youth; **eke** also; **Jew** probably added for its jingle with "juvenal" 96 **Ninny's** blunder for *Ninus'* (Ninus was the legendary founder of Nineveh) 105 **about a round** roundabout

118 **translated** transformed 124 **woosel** ouzel, blackbird 127 **quill** literally, "reed pipe"; here, "piping voice" 130 **the plain-song cuckoo** the cuckoo, who sings a simple song 133 **set his wit** use his intelligence to answer 134 **give . . . lie** contradict a bird (the cuckoo's song supposedly tells a man he is a cuckold) 135 **never so** ever so often 145 **gleek** make a satirical jest

Thou shalt remain here, whether thou wilt or no.
I am a spirit of no common rate.°
The summer still doth tend° upon my state;
And I do love thee. Therefore, go with me.          155
I'll give thee fairies to attend on thee,
And they shall fetch thee jewels from the deep,
And sing, while thou on pressèd flowers dost sleep:
And I will purge thy mortal grossness so,
That thou shalt like an airy spirit go.          160
Peaseblossom! Cobweb! Moth!° And Mustardseed!

*Enter four fairies* [PEASEBLOSSOM, COBWEB, MOTH,
*and* MUSTARDSEED].

PEASEBLOSSOM   Ready.
COBWEB
And I.
MOTH   And I.
MUSTARDSEED   And I.
ALL                          Where shall we go?
TITANIA
Be kind and courteous to this gentleman;
Hop in his walks, and gambol in his eyes;          165
Feed him with apricocks and dewberries,°
With purple grapes, green figs, and mulberries;
The honey bags steal from the humblebees,°
And for night tapers crop their waxen thighs,
And light them at the fiery glowworm's eyes,          170
To have my love to bed and to arise;
And pluck the wings from painted butterflies,
To fan the moonbeams from his sleeping eyes.
Nod to him, elves, and do him courtesies.
PEASEBLOSSOM   Hail, mortal!          175
COBWEB   Hail!
MOTH   Hail!
MUSTARDSEED   Hail!
BOTTOM   I cry your worships mercy,° heartily: I
beseech your worship's name.          180
COBWEB   Cobweb.
BOTTOM   I shall desire you of more acquaintance,°
good Master Cobweb: if I cut my finger,° I shall make
bold with you. Your name, honest gentleman?
PEASEBLOSSOM   Peaseblossom.          185
BOTTOM   I pray you, commend me to Mistress Squash,°
your mother, and to Master Peascod,° your father.
Good Master Peaseblossom, I shall desire you of more
acquaintance too. Your name, I beseech you, sir?
MUSTARDSEED   Mustardseed.          190
BOTTOM   Good Master Mustardseed, I know your
patience well. That same cowardly, giantlike ox-beef
hath devoured° many a gentleman of your house. I
promise you your kindred hath made my eyes water
ere now. I desire you of more acquaintance, good          195
Master Mustardseed.

TITANIA
Come, wait upon him; lead him to my bower.
The moon methinks looks with a wat'ry eye;
And when she weeps, weeps every little flower,
Lamenting some enforcèd° chastity.          200
Tie up my lover's tongue, bring him silently.
*Exit* [TITANIA, *with* BOTTOM *and* FAIRIES].

[*Scene II. Another part of the wood.*]

*Enter* [OBERON,] *King of Fairies, and Robin Goodfellow*
[PUCK].

OBERON
I wonder if Titania be awaked;
Then, what it was that next came in her eye,
Which she must dote on in extremity.°
Here comes my messenger. How now, mad spirit!
What night-rule° now about this haunted grove?          5
PUCK
My mistress with a monster is in love.
Near to her close° and consecrated bower,
While she was in her dull and sleeping hour,
A crew of patches,° rude mechanicals,°
That work for bread upon Athenian stalls,          10
Were met together to rehearse a play,
Intended for great Theseus' nuptial day.
The shallowest thickskin of that barren sort,°
Who Pyramus presented in their sport,
Forsook his scene, and entered in a brake.          15
When I did him at this advantage take,
An ass's nole° I fixèd on his head.
Anon° his Thisby must be answerèd,
And forth my mimic comes. When they him spy,
As wild geese that the creeping fowler eye,          20
Or russet-pated choughs, many in sort,°
Rising and cawing at the gun's report,
Sever themselves and madly sweep the sky,
So, at his sight, away his fellows fly;
And, at our stamp, here o'er and o'er one falls;          25
He murder cries, and help from Athens calls.
Their sense thus weak, lost with their fears thus strong,
Made senseless things begin to do them wrong;
For briers and thorns at their apparel snatch,
Some sleeves, some hats, from yielders all things catch.          30
I led them on in this distracted fear,
And left sweet Pyramus translated there:
When in that moment, so it came to pass,
Titania waked, and straightway loved an ass.
OBERON
This falls out better than I could devise.          35
But hast thou yet latched° the Athenian's eyes
With the love juice, as I did bid thee do?
PUCK
I took him sleeping—that is finished too—

---

153 **rate** rank   154 **still doth tend** always waits upon   161
**Moth** pronounced "mote," and probably a speck rather than
an insect is denoted   166 **apricocks and dewberries** apricots
and blackberries   168 **humblebees** bumblebees   179 **I . . .
mercy** I beg pardon of your honors   182 **I . . . acquaintance**
I shall want to be better acquainted with you   183 **if . . .
finger** cobweb was used for stanching blood   186 **Squash**
unripe peapod   187 **Peascod** contrary to squash, a ripe
peapod   193 **devoured** because beef is often eaten with
mustard

200 **enforcèd** violated
**III.ii.3 in extremity** to the extreme   5 **night-rule** happenings during the night   7 **close** private, secret   9 **patches** fools,
clowns; **rude mechanicals** uneducated workingmen   13
**barren sort** stupid group   17 **nole** "noodle," head   18 **Anon**
presently   21 **russet-pated . . . sort** gray-headed jackdaws,
many in a flock   36 **latched** fastened (or possibly "moistened")

And the Athenian woman by his side;
That, when he waked, of force° she must be eyed.    40

*Enter* DEMETRIUS *and* HERMIA.

OBERON
Stand close:° this is the same Athenian.

PUCK
This is the woman, but not this the man.

DEMETRIUS
O, why rebuke you him that loves you so?
Lay breath so bitter on your bitter foe.

HERMIA
Now I but chide; but I should use thee worse,    45
For thou, I fear, hast given me cause to curse.
If thou hast slain Lysander in his sleep,
Being o'er shoes in blood, plunge in the deep,
And kill me too.
The sun was not so true unto the day    50
As he to me. Would he have stolen away
From sleeping Hermia? I'll believe as soon
This whole° earth may be bored, and that the moon
May through the center creep, and so displease
Her brother's° noontide with th' Antipodes.°    55
It cannot be but thou hast murd'red him.
So should a murderer look, so dead,° so grim.

DEMETRIUS
So should the murdered look; and so should I,
Pierced through the heart with your stern cruelty.
Yet you, the murderer, look as bright, as clear,    60
As yonder Venus in her glimmering sphere.

HERMIA
What's this to my Lysander? Where is he?
Ah, good Demetrius, wilt thou give him me?

DEMETRIUS
I had rather give his carcass to my hounds.

HERMIA
Out, dog! Out, cur! Thou driv'st me past the bounds    65
Of maiden's patience. Hast thou slain him, then?
Henceforth be never numb'red among men!
O, once tell true! Tell true, even for my sake!
Durst thou have looked upon him being awake?
And hast thou killed him sleeping? O brave touch!°    70
Could not a worm, an adder, do so much?
An adder did it; for with doubler tongue
Than thine, thou serpent, never adder stung.

DEMETRIUS
You spend your passion on a misprised mood:°
I am not guilty of Lysander's blood;    75
Nor is he dead, for aught that I can tell.

HERMIA
I pray thee, tell me then that he is well.

DEMETRIUS
An if I could, what should I get therefore?°

HERMIA
A privilege, never to see me more.
And from thy hated presence part I so.    80
See me no more, whether he be dead or no.    *Exit.*

DEMETRIUS
There is no following her in this fierce vein.
Here therefore for a while I will remain.
So sorrow's heaviness doth heavier grow
For debt that bankrout sleep doth sorrow owe;°    85
Which now in some slight measure it will pay,
If for his tender° here I make some stay.

*Lie down [and sleep].*

OBERON
What hast thou done? Thou hast mistaken quite,
And laid the love juice on some truelove's sight.
Of thy misprision° must perforce ensue    90
Some true love turned, and not a false turned true.

PUCK
Then fate o'errules, that, one man holding troth,
A million fail, confounding oath on oath.°

OBERON
About the wood go swifter than the wind,
And Helena of Athens look thou find.    95
All fancy-sick° she is and pale of cheer,°
With sighs of love, that costs the fresh blood
    dear:
By some illusion see thou bring her here.
I'll charm his eyes against she do appear.°

PUCK
I go, I go; look how I go,    100
Swifter than arrow from the Tartar's bow.    *[Exit.]*

OBERON
            Flower of this purple dye,
            Hit with Cupid's archery,
            Sink in apple of his eye.
            When his love he doth espy,    105
            Let her shine as gloriously
            As the Venus of the sky.
            When thou wak'st, if she be by,
            Beg of her for remedy.

*Enter* PUCK.

PUCK
            Captain of our fairyband,    110
            Helena is here at hand;
            And the youth, mistook by me,
            Pleading for a lover's fee.
            Shall we their fond pageant° see?
            Lord, what fools these mortals be!    115

OBERON
Stand aside. The noise they make
Will cause Demetrius to awake.

PUCK
            Then will two at once woo one;
            That must needs be sport alone;°
            And those things do best please me    120
            That befall prepost'rously.

*Enter* LYSANDER *and* HERMIA.

---

40 **of force** by necessity    41 **close** concealed    53 **whole** solid
55 **Her brother's** the sun's; **Antipodes** the inhabitants of the
other side of the earth    57 **dead** deadly pale    70 **brave touch**
splendid exploit (ironic)    74 **misprised mood** mistaken anger
78 **therefore** in return

85 **For . . . owe** because of the debt that bankrupt sleep owes
to sorrow    87 **tender** offer    90 **misprision** mistake    93
**confounding . . . oath** breaking oath after oath    96 **fancy-
sick** lovesick; **cheer** face    99 **against . . . appear** in preparation for her appearance    114 **fond pageant** foolish exhibition
119 **alone** unique, supreme

LYSANDER

Why should you think that I should woo in scorn?
   Scorn and derision never come in tears:
Look, when I vow, I weep; and vows so born,
   In their nativity all truth appears.     125
How can these things in me seem scorn to you,
Bearing the badge of faith,° to prove them true?

HELENA

You do advance° your cunning more and more.
   When truth kills truth, O devilish-holy fray!
These vows are Hermia's: will you give her o'er?     130
   Weigh oath with oath, and you will nothing
     weigh.
Your vows to her and me, put in two scales,
Will even weigh; and both as light as tales.

LYSANDER

I had no judgment when to her I swore.

HELENA

Nor none, in my mind, now you give her o'er.     135

LYSANDER

Demetrius loves her, and he loves not you.

DEMETRIUS [*Awaking.*]

O Helen, goddess, nymph, perfect, divine!
To what, my love, shall I compare thine eyne?
Crystal is muddy. O, how ripe in show°
Thy lips, those kissing cherries, tempting grow!     140
That pure congealèd white, high Taurus'° snow,
Fanned with the eastern wind, turns to a crow
When thou hold'st up thy hand: O, let me kiss
This princess of pure white, this seal of bliss!

HELENA

O spite! O hell! I see you all are bent     145
To set against me for your merriment:
If you were civil° and knew courtesy,
You would not do me thus much injury.
Can you not hate me, as I know you do,
But you must join in souls to mock me too?     150
If you were men, as men you are in show,
You would not use a gentle° lady so;
To vow, and swear, and superpraise my parts,°
When I am sure you hate me with your hearts.
You both are rivals, and love Hermia;     155
And now both rivals to mock Helena:
A trim° exploit, a manly enterprise,
To conjure tears up in a poor maid's eyes
With your derision! None of noble sort
Would so offend a virgin, and extort°     160
A poor soul's patience, all to make you sport.

LYSANDER

You are unkind, Demetrius. Be not so;
For you love Hermia; this you know I know.
And here, with all good will, with all my heart,
In Hermia's love I yield you up my part;     165
And yours of Helena to me bequeath,
Whom I do love, and will do till my death.

HELENA

Never did mockers waste more idle° breath.

DEMETRIUS

Lysander, keep thy Hermia; I will none.
If e'er I loved her, all that love is gone.     170
My heart to her but as guestwise sojourned,
And now to Helen is it home returned,
There to remain.

LYSANDER        Helen, it is not so.

DEMETRIUS

Disparage not the faith thou dost not know,
Lest, to thy peril, thou aby it dear.°     175
Look, where thy love comes; yonder is thy dear.

*Enter* HERMIA.

HERMIA

Dark night, that from the eye his° function takes,
The ear more quick of apprehension makes;
Wherein it doth impair the seeing sense,
It pays the hearing double recompense.     180
Thou art not by mine eye, Lysander, found;
Mine ear, I thank it, brought me to thy sound.
But why unkindly didst thou leave me so?

LYSANDER

Why should he stay, whom love doth press to go?

HERMIA

What love could press Lysander from my side?     185

LYSANDER

Lysander's love, that would not let him bide,
Fair Helena, who more engilds the night
Than all yon fiery oes° and eyes of light.
Why seek'st thou me? Could not this make thee know,
The hate I bare thee made me leave thee so?     190

HERMIA

You speak not as you think: it cannot be.

HELENA

Lo, she is one of this confederacy!
Now I perceive they have conjoined all three
To fashion this false sport, in spite of me.
Injurious° Hermia! Most ungrateful maid!     195
Have you conspired, have you with these contrived
To bait° me with this foul derision?
Is all the counsel that we two have shared,
The sister's vows, the hours that we have spent,
When we have chid the hasty-footed time     200
For parting us—O, is all forgot?
All school days friendship, childhood innocence?
We, Hermia, like two artificial° gods,
Have with our needles created both one flower,
Both on one sampler,° sitting on one cushion,     205
Both warbling of one song, both in one key;
As if our hands, our sides, voices, and minds,
Had been incorporate.° So we grew together,
Like to a double cherry, seeming parted,
But yet an union in partition;     210
Two lovely berries molded on one stem;
So, with two seeming bodies, but one heart;
Two of the first, like coats in heraldry,
Due but to one, and crownèd with one crest.°

---

127 **badge of faith** Lysander means his tears   128 **advance** exhibit, display   139 **show** appearance   141 **Taurus'** of the Taurus Mountains (in Turkey)   147 **civil** civilized   152 **gentle** well-born   153 **parts** qualities   157 **trim** splendid (ironical)   160 **extort** wear out by torturing   168 **idle** vain, futile

175 **aby it dear** pay dearly for it   177 **his** its (the eye's)   188 **oes** orbs   195 **Injurious** insulting   196–97 **contrived To bait** plotted to assail   203 **artificial** skilled in art   205 **sampler** work of embroidery   208 **incorporate** one body   213–14 **Two . . . crest** Helena apparently envisages a shield on which the coat of arms appears twice but which has a single crest; Helena and Hermia have two bodies but a single heart

And will you rent° our ancient love asunder,          215
To join with men in scorning your poor
   friend?
It is not friendly, 'tis not maidenly.
Our sex, as well as I, may chide you for it,
Though I alone do feel the injury.

HERMIA
I am amazèd at your passionate words.          220
I scorn you not. It seems that you scorn me.

HELENA
Have you not set Lysander, as in scorn,
To follow me and praise my eyes and face?
And made your other love, Demetrius
(Who even but now did spurn me with his
   foot),          225
To call me goddess, nymph, divine and rare,
Precious, celestial? Wherefore speaks he this
To her he hates? And wherefore doth Lysander
Deny your love,° so rich within his soul,
And tender me (forsooth) affection,          230
But by your setting on, by your consent?
What though I be not so in grace° as you,
So hung upon with love, so fortunate,
But miserable most, to love unloved?
This you should pity rather than despise.          235

HERMIA
I understand not what you mean by this.

HELENA
Ay, do! Persever,° counterfeit sad° looks,
Make mouths° upon me when I turn my back;
Wink each at other; hold the sweet jest up.
This sport, well carried, shall be chronicled.          240
If you have any pity, grace, or manners,
You would not make me such an argument.°
But fare ye well. 'Tis partly my own fault,
Which death or absence soon shall remedy.

LYSANDER
Stay, gentle Helena; hear my excuse:          245
My love, my life, my soul, fair Helena!

HELENA
O excellent!

HERMIA          Sweet, do not scorn her so.

DEMETRIUS
If she cannot entreat,° I can compel.

LYSANDER
Thou canst compel no more than she entreat.
Thy threats have no more strength than her weak
   prayers.          250
Helen, I love thee; by my life, I do!
I swear by that which I will lose for thee,
To prove him false that says I love thee not.

DEMETRIUS
I say I love thee more than he can do.

LYSANDER
If thou say so, withdraw and prove it too.          255

DEMETRIUS
Quick, come!

HERMIA          Lysander, whereto tends all this?

LYSANDER
Away, you Ethiope!°

DEMETRIUS          No, no; he'll
Seem to break loose; take on as° you would follow,
But yet come not: you are a tame man, go!

LYSANDER
Hang off, thou cat, thou burr! Vile thing, let loose,          260
Or I will shake thee from me like a serpent!

HERMIA
Why are you grown so rude! What change is this,
Sweet love?

LYSANDER   Thy love! Out, tawny Tartar, out!
Out, loathèd med'cine! O hated potion, hence!

HERMIA
Do you not jest?

HELENA          Yes, sooth;° and so do you.          265

LYSANDER
Demetrius, I will keep my word° with thee.

DEMETRIUS
I would I had your bond, for I perceive
A weak bond holds you. I'll not trust your word.

LYSANDER
What, should I hurt her, strike her, kill her dead?
Although I hate her, I'll not harm her so.          270

HERMIA
What, can you do me greater harm than hate?
Hate me! Wherefore? O me! What news, my love!
Am not I Hermia? Are not you Lysander?
I am as fair now as I was erewhile.°
Since night° you loved me; yet since night you left me.          275
Why, then you left me—O, the gods forbid!—
In earnest, shall I say?

LYSANDER          Ay, by my life!
And never did desire to see thee more.
Therefore be out of hope, of question, of doubt;
Be certain, nothing truer. 'Tis no jest          280
That I do hate thee, and love Helena.

HERMIA
O me! You juggler! You canker blossom!°
You thief of love! What, have you come by night
And stol'n my love's heart from him?

HELENA          Fine, i' faith!
Have you no modesty, no maiden shame,          285
No touch of bashfulness? What, will you tear
Impatient answers from my gentle tongue?
Fie, fie! You counterfeit, you puppet, you!

HERMIA
Puppet? Why so? Ay, that way goes the game.
Now I perceive that she hath made compare°          290
Between our statures; she hath urged her height,
And with her personage, her tall personage,
Her height, forsooth, she hath prevailed with him.
And are you grown so high in his esteem,
Because I am so dwarfish and so low?          295
How low am I, thou painted maypole? Speak!
How low am I? I am not yet so low
But that my nails can reach unto thine eyes.

215 rent rend, tear   229 your love his love for you   232 in
grace in favor   237 Persever persevere (but accented on
second syllable); sad grave   238 Make mouths make mocking
faces   242 argument subject (of scorn)   248 entreat prevail
by entreating

257 Ethiope blackamoor (brunette)   258 take on as make a
fuss as if   265 sooth truly   266 my word my promise to fight
with you   274 erewhile a little while ago   275 Since night
since the beginning of this night   282 canker blossom dog
rose (or possibly worm that cankers the blossom)   290 compare comparison

**HELENA**

I pray you, though you mock me, gentlemen,
Let her not hurt me. I was never curst;° 300
I have no gift at all in shrewishness;
I am a right maid° for my cowardice.
Let her not strike me. You perhaps may think,
Because she is something lower than myself,
That I can match her.

**HERMIA**                    Lower! Hark, again! 305

**HELENA**

Good Hermia, do not be so bitter with me.
I evermore did love you, Hermia,
Did ever keep your counsels, never wronged
    you;
Save that, in love unto Demetrius,
I told him of your stealth unto this wood. 310
He followed you; for love I followed him.
But he hath chid me hence, and threatened me
To strike me, spurn me, nay, to kill me too.
And now, so you will let me quiet go,
To Athens will I bear my folly back, 315
And follow you no further. Let me go.
You see how simple and how fond° I am.

**HERMIA**

Why, get you gone. Who is't that hinders you?

**HELENA**

A foolish heart, that I leave here behind.

**HERMIA**

What, with Lysander?

**HELENA**                    With Demetrius. 320

**LYSANDER**

Be not afraid. She shall not harm thee, Helena.

**DEMETRIUS**

No, sir, she shall not, though you take her part.

**HELENA**

O, when she's angry, she is keen and shrewd!°
She was a vixen when she went to school;
And though she be but little, she is fierce. 325

**HERMIA**

"Little" again! Nothing but "low" and "little"!
Why will you suffer her to flout me thus?
Let me come to her.

**LYSANDER**                    Get you gone, you dwarf;
You minimus,° of hind'ring knotgrass° made;
You bead, you acorn!

**DEMETRIUS**                    You are too officious 330
In her behalf that scorns your services.
Let her alone. Speak not of Helena;
Take not her part; for, if thou dost intend°
Never so little show of love to her,
Thou shalt aby° it.

**LYSANDER**                    Now she holds me not. 335
Now follow, if thou dar'st, to try whose right,
Of thine or mine, is most in Helena.

**DEMETRIUS**

Follow! Nay, I'll go with thee, cheek by jowl.

[*Exeunt* LYSANDER *and* DEMETRIUS.]

**HERMIA**

You, mistress, all this coil is 'long of you:°
Nay, go not back

**HELENA**                    I will not trust you, I, 340
Nor longer stay in your curst company.
Your hands than mine are quicker for a fray,
My legs are longer though, to run away.

**HERMIA**

I am amazed,° and know not what to say.

*Exeunt* [HELENA *and* HERMIA].

**OBERON**

This is thy negligence. Still thou mistak'st, 345
Or else committ'st thy knaveries willfully.

**PUCK**

Believe me, king of shadows, I mistook.
Did not you tell me I should know the man
By the Athenian garments he had on?
And so far blameless proves my enterprise, 350
That I have 'nointed an Athenian's eyes;
And so far am I glad it so did sort,°
As this their jangling I esteem a sport.

**OBERON**

Thou see'st these lovers seek a place to fight.
Hie therefore, Robin, overcast the night. 355
The starry welkin° cover thou anon
With drooping fog, as black as Acheron;°
And lead these testy° rivals so astray,
As° one come not within another's way.
Like to Lysander sometime frame thy tongue, 360
Then stir Demetrius up with bitter wrong;°
And sometime rail thou like Demetrius.
And from each other look thou lead them thus,
Till o'er their brows death-counterfeiting sleep
With leaden legs and batty° wings doth creep. 365
Then crush this herb into Lysander's eye,
Whose liquor hath this virtuous° property,
To take from thence all error with his might,
And make his eyeballs roll with wonted sight.
When they next wake, all this derision° 370
Shall seem a dream and fruitless vision,
And back to Athens shall the lovers wend,
With league whose date° till death shall never end.
Whiles I in this affair do thee employ,
I'll to my queen and beg her Indian boy; 375
And then I will her charmèd eye release
From monster's view, and all things shall be peace.

**PUCK**

My fairy lord, this must be done with haste,
For night's swift dragons cut the clouds full fast,
And yonder shines Aurora's harbinger;° 380
At whose approach, ghosts, wand'ring here and there,
Troop home to churchyards: damnèd spirits all,
That in crossways and floods have burial,
Already to their wormy beds are gone.
For fear lest day should look their shames upon, 385
They willfully themselves exile from light,
And must for aye consort with black-browed night.

---

**339 all . . . you** all this turmoil is brought about by you   **344
amazed** in confusion   **352 sort** turn out   **356 welkin** sky
**357 Acheron** one of the rivers of the underworld   **358 testy**
excited, angry   **359 As** that   **361 wrong** insult   **365 batty**
bat-like   **367 virtuous** potent   **370 derision** ludicrous delusion   **373 With . . . date** in union whose term   **380
Aurora's harbinger** dawn's herald (i.e., the morning star)

---

**300 curst** quarrelsome   **302 right maid** true young woman
**317 fond** foolish   **323 keen and shrewd** sharp-tongued and
shrewish   **329 minimus** smallest thing; **knotgrass** a weed
that allegedly stunted one's growth   **333 intend** give sign,
direct (or possibly "pretend")   **335 aby** pay for

OBERON
But we are spirits of another sort.
I with the morning's love° have oft made sport;
And, like a forester, the groves may tread,                              390
Even till the eastern gate, all fiery-red,
Opening on Neptune with fair blessèd beams,
Turns into yellow gold his salt green streams.
But, notwithstanding, haste; make no delay.
We may effect this business yet ere day.            [*Exit.*] 395

PUCK
             Up and down, up and down,
             I will lead them up and down:
             I am feared in field and town:
             Goblin,° lead them up and down.
Here comes one.                                                       400

*Enter* LYSANDER.

LYSANDER
Where art thou, proud Demetrius? Speak thou now.

PUCK
Here, villain; drawn° and ready. Where art thou?

LYSANDER
I will be with thee straight.

PUCK                        Follow me, then,
To plainer° ground.                    [*Exit* LYSANDER.]

*Enter* DEMETRIUS.

DEMETRIUS          Lysander! Speak again!
Thou runaway, thou coward, art thou fled?            405
Speak! In some bush? Where dost thou hide thy head?

PUCK
Thou coward, art thou bragging to the stars,
Telling the bushes that thou look'st for wars,
And wilt not come? Come, recreant! Come, thou
   child!
I'll whip thee with a rod. He is defiled              410
That draws a sword on thee.

DEMETRIUS               Yea, art thou there?

PUCK
Follow my voice. We'll try no manhood° here.
                                          *Exeunt.*

[*Enter* LYSANDER.]

LYSANDER
He goes before me and still dares me on:
When I come where he calls, then he is gone.
The villain is much lighter-heeled than I.            415
I followed fast, but faster he did fly,
That fallen am I in dark uneven way,
And here will rest me. [*Lies down.*] Come, thou gentle
   day!
For if but once thou show me thy gray light,
I'll find Demetrius, and revenge this spite.          420

[*Sleeps.*]

[*Enter*] *Robin* [PUCK] *and* DEMETRIUS.

PUCK
Ho, ho, ho! Coward, why com'st thou not?

DEMETRIUS
Abide me,° if thou dar'st; for well I wot°
Thou runn'st before me, shifting every place,
And dar'st not stand, nor look me in the face.
Where art thou now?

PUCK                   Come hither. I am here.   425

DEMETRIUS
Nay, then, thou mock'st me. Thou shalt buy this dear,°
If ever I thy face by daylight see.
Now, go thy way. Faintness constraineth me
To measure out my length on this cold bed.
By day's approach look to be visited.°               430

[*Lies down and sleeps.*]

*Enter* HELENA.

HELENA
O weary night, O long and tedious night,
   Abate° thy hours! Shine comforts from the east,
That I may back to Athens by daylight,
   From these that my poor company detest:
And sleep, that sometimes shuts up sorrow's eye,      435
Steal me awhile from mine own company.

*Sleep.*

PUCK
             Yet but three? Come one more.
             Two of both kinds makes up four.
             Here she comes, curst° and sad:
             Cupid is a knavish lad,                  440
             Thus to make poor females mad.

[*Enter* HERMIA.]

HERMIA
Never so weary, never so in woe;
   Bedabbled with the dew and torn with briers,
I can no further crawl, no further go;
   My legs can keep no pace with my desires.          445
Here will I rest me till the break of day.
Heavens shield Lysander, if they mean a fray!

[*Lies down and sleeps.*]

PUCK
             On the ground
             Sleep sound:
             I'll apply                               450
             To your eye,
             Gentle lover, remedy.

[*Squeezing the juice on Lysander's eye.*]

             When thou wak'st,
             Thou tak'st
             True delight                             455
             In the sight
             Of thy former lady's eye:
             And the country proverb known,
             That every man should take his own,
             In your waking shall be shown.           460
                Jack shall have Jill;
                Nought shall go ill;
             The man shall have his mare again,
                and all shall be well.        [*Exit.*]

---

389 **the morning's love** Aurora (or possibly her lover
Cephalus)  399 **Goblin** Hobgoblin (one of Puck's names)
402 **drawn** with drawn sword  404 **plainer** more level
412 **try no manhood** have no test of valor

422 **Abide me** wait for me; **wot** know  426 **buy this dear**
pay dearly for this  430 **look . . . visited** be sure to be sought
out  432 **Abate** make shorter  439 **curst** cross

# [ACT IV]

[Scene I. *The wood.* LYSANDER, DEMETRIUS, HELENA, *and* HERMIA, *lying asleep.*]

*Enter* [TITANIA,] *Queen of Fairies, and* [BOTTOM *the*] *clown, and* FAIRIES; *and* [OBERON,] *the King, behind them.*

TITANIA
Come, sit thee down upon this flow'ry bed,
  While I thy amiable cheeks do coy,°
And stick musk roses in thy sleek smooth head,
  And kiss thy fair large ears, my gentle joy.
BOTTOM  Where's Peaseblossom?                              5
PEASEBLOSSOM  Ready.
BOTTOM  Scratch my head, Peaseblossom. Where's
Mounsieur Cobweb?
COBWEB  Ready.
BOTTOM  Mounsieur Cobweb, good mounsieur, get  10
you your weapons in your hand, and kill me a red-
hipped humblebee on the top of a thistle; and, good
mounsieur, bring me the honey bag. Do not fret
yourself too much in the action, mounsieur; and,
good mounsieur, have a care the honey bag break  15
not; I would be loath to have you overflown with
a honey bag, signior. Where's Mounsieur Mustard-
seed?
MUSTARDSEED  Ready.
BOTTOM  Give me your neaf,° Mounsieur Mustard-  20
seed. Pray you, leave your curtsy,° good mounsieur.
MUSTARDSEED  What's your will?
BOTTOM  Nothing, good mounsieur, but to help
Cavalery° Cobweb to scratch. I must to the barber's,
mounsieur; for methinks I am marvail's° hairy about  25
the face; and I am such a tender ass, if my hair do but
tickle me, I must scratch.
TITANIA
What, wilt thou hear some music, my sweet love?
BOTTOM  I have a reasonable good ear in music. Let's
have the tongs and the bones.°                            30
TITANIA
Or say, sweet love, what thou desirest to eat.
BOTTOM  Truly, a peck of provender. I could munch
your good dry oats. Methinks I have a great desire
to a bottle° of hay. Good hay, sweet hay, hath no
fellow.°                                                  35
TITANIA
I have a venturous fairy that shall seek
The squirrel's hoard, and fetch thee new nuts.
BOTTOM  I had rather have a handful or two of dried
peas. But, I pray you, let none of your people stir me:
I have an exposition of° sleep come upon me.             40
TITANIA
Sleep thou, and I will wind thee in my arms.
Fairies, be gone, and be all ways° away.
                                        [*Exeunt* FAIRIES.]

IV.i.2 **While . . . coy** while I caress your lovely cheeks **20 neaf** fist, hand  **21 leave your curtsy** stop bowing, leave your hat on (a curtsy was any gesture of respect) **24 Cavalery** Cavalier **25 marvail's** Bottom means *marvelous* **30 tongs . . . bones** rustic music, made by tongs struck with metal and by bone clappers held between the fingers **34 bottle** bundle **35 fellow** equal **40 exposition of** Bottom means *disposition for* **42 all ways** in every direction

So doth the woodbine the sweet honeysuckle
Gently entwist; the female ivy° so
Enrings the barky fingers of the elm.                     45
O, how I love thee! How I dote on thee!
[*They sleep.*]
*Enter Robin Goodfellow* [PUCK].
OBERON [*Advancing.*]
Welcome, good Robin. See'st thou this sweet sight?
Her dotage now I do begin to pity:
For, meeting her of late behind the wood,
Seeking sweet favors° for this hateful fool,             50
I did upbraid her, and fall out with her.
For she his hairy temples then had rounded
With coronet of fresh and fragrant flowers;
And that same dew, which sometime° on the buds
Was wont° to swell, like round and orient° pearls,       55
Stood now within the pretty flouriets'° eyes,
Like tears, that did their own disgrace bewail.
When I had at my pleasure taunted her,
And she in mild terms begged my patience,
I then did ask of her her changeling child;              60
Which straight she gave me, and her fairy sent
To bear him to my bower in fairy land.
And now I have the boy, I will undo
This hateful imperfection of her eyes:
And, gentle Puck, take this transformèd scalp            65
From off the head of this Athenian swain,
That, he awaking when the other° do,
May all to Athens back again repair,
And think no more of this night's accidents,°
But as the fierce vexation of a dream.                   70
But first I will release the Fairy Queen.
    Be as thou wast wont to be;
    See as thou wast wont to see.
    Dian's bud o'er Cupid's flower
    Hath such force and blessèd power.                    75
Now, my Titania, wake you, my sweet queen.
TITANIA
My Oberon, what visions have I seen!
Methought I was enamored of an ass.
OBERON
There lies your love.
TITANIA                        How came these things to pass?
O, how mine eyes do loathe his visage now!               80
OBERON
Silence awhile. Robin, take off this head.
Titania, music call; and strike more dead
Than common sleep of all these five the sense.
TITANIA
Music, ho, music! Such as charmeth sleep!
PUCK
Now, when thou wak'st, with thine own fool's eyes
  peep.                                                   85
OBERON
Sound, music! [*Music.*] Come, my queen, take hands
  with me,
And rock the ground whereon these sleepers be.
[*Dance.*]

**44 female ivy** called female because it clings to the elm and is supported by it  **50 favors** love tokens (probably flowers) **54 sometime** formerly  **55 Was wont** used to; **orient** lustrous  **56 flouriets'** flowerets'  **67 other** others  **69 accidents** happenings

Now thou and I are new in amity,
And will tomorrow midnight solemnly°
Dance in Duke Theseus' house triumphantly,°          90
And bless it to all fair prosperity.
There shall the pairs of faithful lovers be
Wedded, with Theseus, all in jollity.

PUCK
        Fairy King, attend, and mark:
        I do hear the morning lark.                95

OBERON
        Then, my queen, in silence sad,°
        Trip we after night's shade.
        We the globe can compass soon,
        Swifter than the wand'ring moon.

TITANIA
        Come, my lord; and in our flight,          100
        Tell me how it came this night,
        That I sleeping here was found
        With these mortals on the ground.  *Exeunt.*

*Wind horn. Enter* THESEUS, *and all his* TRAIN;
[HIPPOLYTA, EGEUS].

THESEUS
Go, one of you, find out the forester,
For now our observation° is performed;          105
And since we have the vaward° of the day,
My love shall hear the music of my hounds.
Uncouple in the western valley; let them go.
Dispatch, I say, and find the forester.
                [*Exit an* ATTENDANT.]
We will, fair queen, up to the mountain's top,          110
And mark the musical confusion
Of hounds and echo in conjunction.

HIPPOLYTA
I was with Hercules and Cadmus once,
When in a wood of Crete they bayed° the bear
With hounds of Sparta. Never did I hear          115
Such gallant chiding; for, besides the groves,
The skies, the fountains, every region near
Seemed all one mutual cry. I never heard
So musical a discord, such sweet thunder.

THESEUS
My hounds are bred out of the Spartan kind,          120
So flewed, so sanded;° and their heads are hung
With ears that sweep away the morning dew;
Crook-kneed, and dew-lapped like Thessalian bulls;
Slow in pursuit, but matched in mouth like bells,
Each under each.° A cry° more tunable          125
Was never holloed to, nor cheered with horn,
In Crete, in Sparta, nor in Thessaly.
Judge when you hear. But, soft!° What nymphs are
    these?

EGEUS
My lord, this is my daughter here asleep;
And this, Lysander; this Demetrius is;          130
This Helena, old Nedar's Helena:
I wonder of their being here together.

THESEUS
No doubt they rose up early to observe
The rite of May; and, hearing our intent,
Came here in grace of our solemnity.°          135
But speak, Egeus. Is not this the day
That Hermia should give answer of her choice?

EGEUS
It is, my lord.

THESEUS
Go, bid the huntsmen wake them with their
    horns.

*Shout within. They all start up. Wind horns.*

Good morrow, friends. Saint Valentine is past:          140
Begin these wood birds but to couple now?°

LYSANDER
Pardon, my lord.

THESEUS        I pray you all, stand up.
I know you two are rival enemies.
How comes this gentle concord in the world,
That hatred is so far from jealousy,°          145
To sleep by hate, and fear no enmity?

LYSANDER
My lord, I shall reply amazedly,°
Half sleep, half waking: but as yet, I swear,
I cannot truly say how I came here.
But, as I think—for truly would I speak,          150
And now I do bethink me, so it is—
I came with Hermia hither. Our intent
Was to be gone from Athens, where we might,
Without° the peril of the Athenian law—

EGEUS
Enough, enough, my lord; you have enough.          155
I beg the law, the law, upon his head.
They would have stol'n away; they would, Demetrius,
Thereby to have defeated° you and me,
You of your wife and me of my consent,
Of my consent that she should be your wife.          160

DEMETRIUS
My lord, fair Helen told me of their stealth,°
Of this their purpose hither to this wood,
And I in fury hither followed them,
Fair Helena in fancy° following me.
But, my good lord, I wot not by what power—          165
But by some power it is—my love to Hermia,
Melted as the snow, seems to me now
As the remembrance of an idle gaud,°
Which in my childhood I did dote upon;
And all the faith, the virtue° of my heart,          170
The object and the pleasure of mine eye,
Is only Helena. To her, my lord,
Was I betrothed ere I saw Hermia:
But, like a sickness,° did I loathe this food;
But, as in health, come to my natural taste,          175
Now I do wish it, love it, long for it,
And will for evermore be true to it.

89 **solemnly** ceremoniously  90 **triumphantly** in festive procession  96 **sad** serious, solemn  105 **observation** observance of the rite of May (cf. I.i.167)  106 **vaward** vanguard (i.e., morning)  114 **bayed** brought to bay  121 **So . . . sanded** like Spartan hounds, with hanging cheeks and of sandy color  125 **Each under each** of different tone (like the chime of bells); **cry** pack of hounds  128 **soft** stop  135 **in . . . solemnity** in honor of our festival  141 **Begin . . . now** it was supposed that birds began to mate on February 14, Saint Valentine's Day  145 **jealousy** suspicion  147 **amazedly** confusedly  154 **Without** outside of  158 **defeated** deprived by fraud  161 **stealth** stealthy flight  164 **in fancy** in love, doting  168 **idle gaud** worthless trinket  170 **virtue** power  174 **like a sickness** like one who is sick

THESEUS
Fair lovers, you are fortunately met.
Of this discourse we more will hear anon.
Egeus, I will overbear your will, 180
For in the temple, by and by,° with us
These couples shall eternally be knit;
And, for the morning now is something worn,°
Our purposed hunting shall be set aside.
Away with us to Athens! Three and three, 185
We'll hold a feast in great solemnity.
Come, Hippolyta. [Exeunt THESEUS, HIPPOLYTA,
EGEUS, and TRAIN.]

DEMETRIUS
These things seem small and undistinguishable,
Like far-off mountains turnèd into clouds.

HERMIA
Methinks I see these things with parted eye,° 190
When everything seems double.

HELENA 　　　　　　　　So methinks:
And I have found Demetrius like a jewel,
Mine own, and not mine own.

DEMETRIUS 　　　　　　　　　Are you sure
That we are awake? It seems to me
That yet we sleep, we dream. Do not you think 195
The duke was here, and bid us follow him?

HERMIA
Yea, and my father.

HELENA 　　　　　　　And Hippolyta.

LYSANDER
And he did bid us follow to the temple.

DEMETRIUS
Why, then, we are awake. Let's follow him,
And by the way let us recount our dreams. [Exeunt.] 200

BOTTOM [Awaking.] When my cue comes, call me,
and I will answer. My next is, "Most fair Pyramus."
Heigh-ho! Peter Quince? Flute, the bellows mender?
Snout, the tinker? Starveling? God's my life,° stol'n
hence, and left me asleep? I have had a most rare
vision. I have had a dream, past the wit of man to say
what dream it was. Man is but an ass, if he go about°
to expound this dream. Methought I was—there is no
man can tell what. Methought I was—and methought
I had—but man is but a patched° fool if he will offer 210
to say what methought I had. The eye of man hath
not heard, the ear of man hath not seen, man's hand is
not able to taste, his tongue to conceive, nor his heart
to report,° what my dream was. I will get Peter
Quince to write a ballet° of this dream. It shall be 215
called "Bottom's Dream," because it hath no bottom;
and I will sing it in the latter end of a play, before the
duke. Peradventure to make it the more gracious, I
shall sing it at her death.° 　　　　　　　[Exit.]

[Scene II. Athens. Quince's house.]

Enter QUINCE, FLUTE,° THISBY, and the rabble
[SNOUT, STARVELING].

QUINCE Have you sent to Bottom's house? Is he
come home yet?

STARVELING He cannot be heard of. Out of doubt he
is transported.°

FLUTE If he come not, then the play is marred. It 5
goes not forward, doth it?

QUINCE It is not possible. You have not a man in all
Athens able to discharge° Pyramus but he.

FLUTE No, he hath simply the best wit of any handi-
craft man in Athens. 10

QUINCE Yea, and the best person too; and he is a very
paramour for a sweet voice.

FLUTE You must say "paragon." A paramour is, God
bless us, a thing of nought.°

Enter SNUG the joiner.

SNUG Masters, the duke is coming from the temple, 15
and there is two or three lords and ladies more married.
If our sport had gone forward, we had all been made
men.°

FLUTE O sweet bully Bottom! Thus hath he lost
sixpence a day° during his life. He could not have 20
scaped sixpence a day. An the duke had not given him
sixpence a day for playing Pyramus, I'll be hanged.
He would have deserved it. Sixpence a day in Pyramus,
or nothing.

Enter BOTTOM.

BOTTOM Where are these lads? Where are these 25
hearts?

QUINCE Bottom! O most courageous° day! O most
happy hour!

BOTTOM Masters, I am to discourse wonders: but ask
me not what; for if I tell you, I am not true Athenian. 30
I will tell you everything, right as it fell out.

QUINCE Let us hear, sweet Bottom.

BOTTOM Not a word of me.° All that I will tell you
is, that the duke hath dined. Get your apparel together,
good strings to your beards, new ribbons to your 35
pumps; meet presently° at the palace; every man look
o'er his part; for the short and the long is, our play is
preferred.° In any case, let Thisby have clean linen;
and let not him that plays the lion pare his nails, for
they shall hang out for the lion's claws. And, most 40
dear actors, eat no onions nor garlic, for we are to utter
sweet breath,° and I do not doubt but to hear them say
it is a sweet comedy. No more words. Away! Go,
away! 　　　　　　　　　　　　　　　[Exeunt.]

---

181 by and by shortly　183 something worn somewhat spent
190 with parted eye with the eyes out of focus　204 God's
my life an oath (possibly from "God bless my life")
207 go about endeavor　210 patched referring to the patch-
work dress of jesters　211–14 The . . . report compare
I Corinthians, 2:9 ff.: "Eye hath not seen, nor ear heard,
neither have entered into the heart of man the things which
God hath prepared for them that love Him"　215 ballet
ballad　219 her death Thisby's death in the play

IV.ii.s.d. Flute Shakespeare seems to have forgotten that Flute
and Thisby are the same person　4 transported carried off (by
the fairies)　8 discharge play　14 thing of nought wicked
thing　17–18 made men men whose fortunes are made
20 sixpence a day a pension　27 courageous brave, splendid
33 of me from me　36 presently immediately　38 preferred
put forward, recommended　42 breath (1) exhalation (2)
words

# [ACT V]

[Scene I. *Athens. The palace of Theseus.*]

*Enter* THESEUS, HIPPOLYTA, *and* PHILOSTRATE,
[LORDS, *and* ATTENDANTS].

HIPPOLYTA
'Tis strange, my Theseus, that these lovers speak of.
THESEUS
More strange than true. I never may believe
These antique° fables, nor these fairy toys.°
Lovers and madmen have such seething brains,
Such shaping fantasies,° that apprehend　　　　　　5
More than cool reason ever comprehends.
The lunatic, the lover, and the poet
Are of imagination all compact.°
One sees more devils than vast hell can hold,
That is the madman. The lover, all as frantic,　　10
Sees Helen's beauty in a brow of Egypt.°
The poet's eye, in a fine frenzy rolling,
Doth glance from heaven to earth, from earth to
　　heaven;
And as imagination bodies forth
The forms of things unknown, the poet's pen　　15
Turns them to shapes, and gives to airy nothing
A local habitation and a name.
Such tricks hath strong imagination,
That, if it would but apprehend some joy,
It comprehends some bringer of that joy;°　　　20
Or in the night, imagining some fear,°
How easy is a bush supposed a bear!
HIPPOLYTA
But all the story of the night told over,
And all their minds transfigured so together,
More witnesseth than fancy's images,　　　　　25
And grows to something of great constancy;°
But, howsoever, strange and admirable.°

*Enter lovers:* LYSANDER, DEMETRIUS, HERMIA, *and*
HELENA.

THESEUS
Here come the lovers, full of joy and mirth.
Joy, gentle friends! Joy and fresh days of love
Accompany your hearts!
LYSANDER　　　　　　More than to us　　30
Wait in your royal walks, your board, your bed!
THESEUS
Come now, what masques,° what dances shall we
　　have,
To wear away this long age of three hours
Between our aftersupper° and bedtime?
Where is our usual manager of mirth?　　　　35
What revels are in hand? Is there no play,
To ease the anguish of a torturing hour?
Call Philostrate.
PHILOSTRATE　　Here, mighty Theseus.

THESEUS
Say, what abridgment° have you for this evening?
What masque? What music? How shall we beguile　　40
The lazy time, if not with some delight?
PHILOSTRATE
There is a brief° how many sports are ripe:°
Make choice of which your highness will see first.

[*Giving a paper.*]

THESEUS
"The battle with the centaurs, to be sung
By an Athenian eunuch to the harp."　　　　　45
We'll none of that. That have I told my love,
In glory of my kinsman Hercules.
"The riot of the tipsy Bacchanals,
Tearing the Thracian singer° in their rage."
That is an old device;° and it was played　　　50
When I from Thebes came last a conqueror.
"The thrice three Muses mourning for the death
Of learning, late deceased in beggary."
That is some satire, keen and critical,
Not sorting with° a nuptial ceremony.　　　　55
"A tedious brief scene of young Pyramus
And his love Thisby; very tragical mirth."
Merry and tragical? Tedious and brief?
That is, hot ice and wondrous strange snow.
How shall we find the concord of this discord?　　60
PHILOSTRATE
A play there is, my lord, some ten words long,
Which is as brief as I have known a play;
But by ten words, my lord, it is too long,
Which makes it tedious. For in all the play
There is not one word apt, one player fitted.　　65
And tragical, my noble lord, it is,
For Pyramus therein doth kill himself.
Which, when I saw rehearsed, I must confess,
Made mine eyes water; but more merry tears
The passion° of loud laughter never shed.　　70
THESEUS
What are they that do play it?
PHILOSTRATE
Hard-handed men, that work in Athens here,
Which never labored in their minds till now;
And now have toiled their unbreathed° memories
With this same play, against° your nuptial.　　75
THESEUS
And we will hear it.
PHILOSTRATE　　　　No, my noble lord;
It is not for you. I have heard it over,
And it is nothing, nothing in the world;
Unless you can find sport in their intents,
Extremely stretched and conned with cruel pain,　　80
To do you service.
THESEUS　　　　I will hear that play;
For never anything can be amiss,
When simpleness and duty tender it.
Go, bring them in: and take your places, ladies.
[*Exit* PHILOSTRATE.]

V.i.3 **antique** (1) ancient (2) grotesque (antic); **fairy toys**
trifles about fairies　**5 fantasies** imagination　**8 compact**
composed　**11 brow of Egypt** face of a gypsy　**20 It . . .
joy** it includes an imagined bringer of the joy　**21 fear** object
of fear　**26 constancy** consistency (and reality)　**27 admirable**
wonderful　**32 masques** courtly entertainments with masked
dancers　**34 aftersupper** refreshment served after early supper

**39 abridgment** entertainment (to abridge or shorten the time)
**42 brief** written list; **ripe** ready to be presented　**49 Thracian
singer** Orpheus　**50 device** show　**55 sorting with** suited to
**70 passion** strong emotion　**74 unbreathed** unexercised　**75
against** in preparation for

**HIPPOLYTA**
I love not to see wretchedness o'ercharged,°   85
And duty in his service perishing.

**THESEUS**
Why, gentle sweet, you shall see no such thing.

**HIPPOLYTA**
He says they can do nothing in this kind.°

**THESEUS**
The kinder we, to give them thanks for nothing.
Our sport shall be to take what they mistake:   90
And what poor duty cannot do, noble respect
Takes it in might,° not merit.
Where I have come, great clerks° have purposèd
To greet me with premeditated welcomes;
Where I have seen them shiver and look pale,   95
Make periods in the midst of sentences,
Throttle their practiced accent in their fears,
And, in conclusion, dumbly have broke off,
Not paying me a welcome. Trust me, sweet,
Out of this silence yet I picked a welcome;   100
And in the modesty of fearful duty
I read as much as from the rattling tongue
Of saucy and audacious eloquence.
Love, therefore, and tongue-tied simplicity
In least speak most, to my capacity.°   105

*[Enter* PHILOSTRATE.*]*

**PHILOSTRATE**
So please your grace, the Prologue is addressed.°

**THESEUS**
Let him approach.

*[Flourish trumpets.] Enter the* PROLOGUE *[Quince].*

**PROLOGUE**
If we offend, it is with our good will.
 That you should think, we come not to offend,
But with good will. To show our simple skill,   110
 That is the true beginning of our end.°
Consider, then, we come but in despite.
 We do not come, as minding to content you,
Our true intent is. All for your delight,
 We are not here. That you should here repent you,  115
The actors are at hand; and, by their show,°
You shall know all, that you are like to know.

**THESEUS** This fellow doth not stand upon points.°

**LYSANDER** He hath rid his prologue like a rough colt;
he knows not the stop.° A good moral, my lord: it is  120
not enough to speak, but to speak true.

**HIPPOLYTA** Indeed he hath played on this prologue
like a child on a recorder;° a sound, but not in government.°

**THESEUS** His speech was like a tangled chain; nothing  125
impaired, but all disordered. Who is next?

*Enter* PYRAMUS *and* THISBY *and* WALL *and* MOON-
SHINE *and* LION *[as in dumb show].*

**PROLOGUE**
Gentles, perchance you wonder at this show;
 But wonder on, till truth make all things plain.
This man is Pyramus, if you would know;
 This beauteous lady Thisby is certain.   130
This man, with lime and roughcast, doth present
 Wall, that vile Wall which did these lovers sunder;
And through Wall's chink, poor souls, they are content
 To whisper. At the which let no man wonder.
This man, with lantern, dog, and bush of thorn,  135
 Presenteth Moonshine; for, if you will know,
By moonshine did these lovers think no scorn
 To meet at Ninus' tomb, there, there to woo.
This grisly beast, which Lion hight° by name,
 The trusty Thisby, coming first by night,  140
Did scare away, or rather did affright;
 And, as she fled, her mantle she did fall,°
 Which Lion vile with bloody mouth did stain.
Anon comes Pyramus, sweet youth and tall,°
 And finds his trusty Thisby's mantle slain:  145
Whereat, with blade, with bloody blameful blade,
 He bravely broached° his boiling bloody breast;
And Thisby, tarrying in mulberry shade,
 His dagger drew, and died. For all the rest,
Let Lion, Moonshine, Wall, and lovers twain  150
 At large° discourse, while here they do remain.

**THESEUS** I wonder if the lion be to speak.

**DEMETRIUS** No wonder, my lord. One lion may,
when many asses do.

   *Exit* LION, THISBY, *and* MOONSHINE.

**WALL**
In this same interlude it doth befall  155
That I, one Snout by name, present a wall;
And such a wall, as I would have you think,
That had in it a crannied hole or chink,
Through which the lovers, Pyramus and Thisby,
Did whisper often very secretly.  160
This loam, this roughcast, and this stone, doth show
That I am that same wall; the truth is so;
And this the cranny is, right and sinister,°
Through which the fearful lovers are to whisper.

**THESEUS** Would you desire lime and hair to speak  165
better?

**DEMETRIUS** It is the wittiest partition° that ever I
heard discourse, my lord.

**THESEUS** Pyramus draws near the wall. Silence!

**PYRAMUS**
O grim-looked night! O night with hue so black!  170
 O night, which ever art when day is not!
O night, O night! Alack, alack, alack,
 I fear my Thisby's promise is forgot!
And thou, O wall, O sweet, O lovely wall,
That stand'st between her father's ground and mine!  175

---

**85 wretchedness o'ercharged** lowly people overburdened **88 in this kind** in this kind of thing (i.e., acting) **92 Takes . . . might** considers the ability and the effort made **93 clerks** scholars **105 to my capacity** according to my understanding **106 addressed** ready **111 end** aim **116 show** probably referring to a kind of pantomime—"dumb show"—that was to follow, in which the action of the play was acted without words while the Prologue gave his account **118 stand upon points** (1) care about punctuation (2) worry about niceties **120 stop** (1) technical term for the checking of a horse (2) mark of punctuation **123 recorder** flutelike instrument **123-24 government** control

**139 hight** is called **142 fall** let fall **144 tall** brave **147 bravely broached** gallantly stabbed **151 At large** at length **163 right and sinister** running right and left, horizontal **167 wittiest partition** most intelligent wall (with a pun on *partition*, a section of a book or of an oration)

Thou wall, O wall, O sweet and lovely wall,
  Show me thy chink, to blink through with mine
    eyne!

[WALL *holds up his fingers.*]

Thanks, courteous wall. Jove shield thee well for this!
  But what see I? No Thisby do I see.
O wicked wall, through whom I see no bliss!   180
  Cursed be thy stones for thus deceiving me!
THESEUS   The wall, methinks, being sensible,° should
curse again.°
PYRAMUS   No, in truth, sir, he should not. "Deceiving
me" is Thisby's cue. She is to enter now, and I am to   185
spy her through the wall. You shall see it will fall pat°
as I told you. Yonder she comes.

*Enter* THISBY.

THISBY
O wall, full often hast thou heard my moans,
  For parting my fair Pyramus and me!
My cherry lips have often kissed thy stones,   190
  Thy stones with lime and hair knit up in thee.
PYRAMUS
I see a voice: now will I to the chink,
  To spy an I can hear my Thisby's face.
Thisby!
THISBY   My love thou art, my love I think.
PYRAMUS
Think what thou wilt, I am thy lover's grace;°   195
And, like Limander,° am I trusty still.
THISBY
And I like Helen,° till the Fates me kill.
PYRAMUS
Not Shafalus to Procrus° was so true.
THISBY
As Shafalus to Procrus, I to you.
PYRAMUS
O kiss me through the hole of this vile wall!   200
THISBY
I kiss the wall's hole, not your lips at all.
PYRAMUS
Wilt thou at Ninny's tomb meet me straightway?
THISBY
'Tide life, 'tide death,° I come without delay.
              [*Exeunt* PYRAMUS *and* THISBY.]
WALL
Thus have I, Wall, my part dischargèd so;
And, being done, thus wall away doth go.   [*Exit.*]   205
THESEUS   Now is the moon used° between the two
neighbors.
DEMETRIUS   No remedy, my lord, when walls are so
willful to hear without warning.°
HIPPOLYTA   This is the silliest stuff that ever I heard.   210

THESEUS   The best in this kind° are but shadows; and
the worst are no worse, if imagination amend them.
HIPPOLYTA   It must be your imagination then, and
not theirs.
THESEUS   If we imagine no worse of them than they   215
of themselves, they may pass for excellent men. Here
come two noble beasts in, a man and a lion.

*Enter* LION *and* MOONSHINE.

LION
You, ladies, you, whose gentle hearts do fear
  The smallest monstrous mouse that creeps on floor,
May now perchance both quake and tremble here,   220
  When lion rough in wildest rage doth roar.
Then know that I, as Snug the joiner, am
A lion fell,° nor else no lion's dam;
For, if I should as lion come in strife
Into this place, 'twere pity on my life.°   225
THESEUS   A very gentle° beast, and of a good con-
science.
DEMETRIUS   The very best at a beast, my lord, that
e'er I saw.
LYSANDER   This lion is a very fox for his valor.   230
THESEUS   True; and a goose for his discretion.
DEMETRIUS   Not so, my lord; for his valor cannot
carry° his discretion, and the fox carries the goose.
THESEUS   His discretion, I am sure, cannot carry his
valor; for the goose carries not the fox. It is well.   235
Leave it to his discretion, and let us listen to the moon.
MOONSHINE
This lanthorn° doth the hornèd moon present—
DEMETRIUS   He should have worn the horns on his
head.°
THESEUS   He is no crescent, and his horns are invisible   240
within the circumference.
MOONSHINE
This lanthorn doth the hornèd moon present,
Myself the man i' th' moon do seem to be.
THESEUS   This is the greatest error of all the rest. The
man should be put into the lanthorn. How is it else   245
the man i' th' moon?
DEMETRIUS   He dares not come there for the candle;
for, you see, it is already in snuff.°
HIPPOLYTA   I am aweary of this moon. Would he
would change!   250
THESEUS   It appears, by his small light of discretion,
that he is in the wane; but yet, in courtesy, in all
reason, we must stay the time.
LYSANDER   Proceed, Moon.
MOONSHINE   All that I have to say is to tell you that   255
the lanthorn is the moon; I, the man i' th' moon; this
thorn bush, my thorn bush; and this dog, my dog.
DEMETRIUS   Why, all these should be in the lanthorn;
for all these are in the moon. But, silence! Here
comes Thisby.   260

*Enter* THISBY.

182 sensible conscious   183 again in return   186 pat exactly
195 thy lover's grace thy gracious lover   196 Limander
Bottom means Leander, but blends him with Alexander   197
Helen Hero, beloved of Leander, is probably meant   198
Shafalus to Procrus Cephalus and Procris are meant, legendary
lovers   203 'Tide . . . death come (betide) life or death   206
moon used the quartos read thus, the Folio reads *morall
downe;* among suggested emendations are "mural down" and
"moon to see"   208–09 when . . . warning when walls are
so eager to listen without warning the parents (?)

211 in this kind of this sort, i.e., plays (or players?)   223 lion
fell fierce lion (perhaps with a pun on *fell* = skin)   225
pity . . . life a dangerous thing for me   226 gentle
gentlemanly, courteous   233 carry carry away   237 lanthorn so spelled, and perhaps pronounced "lant-horn," because
lanterns were commonly made of horn   238–39 horns . . .
head cuckolds were said to have horns   248 in snuff (1) in
need of snuffing (2) resentful

THISBY
This is old Ninny's tomb. Where is my love?
LION   Oh—

[*The* LION *roars.* THISBY *runs off.*]

DEMETRIUS   Well roared, Lion.
THESEUS   Well run, Thisby.
HIPPOLYTA   Well shone, Moon. Truly, the moon 265
shines with a good grace.

[*The* LION *shakes Thisby's mantle, and exit.*]

THESEUS   Well moused,° Lion.
DEMETRIUS   And then came Pyramus.
LYSANDER   And so the lion vanished.

*Enter* PYRAMUS.

PYRAMUS
Sweet Moon, I thank thee for thy sunny beams;        270
    I thank thee, Moon, for shining now so bright;
For, by thy gracious, golden, glittering gleams,
    I trust to take of truest Thisby sight.
            But stay, O spite!°
            But mark, poor knight,        275
    What dreadful dole° is here!
            Eyes, do you see?
            How can it be?
    O dainty duck! O dear!
            Thy mantle good,        280
            What, stained with blood!
    Approach, ye Furies fell!°
            O Fates, come, come,
            Cut thread and thrum;°
    Quail,° crush, conclude, and quell!°        285
THESEUS   This passion, and the death of a dear friend,
would go near to make a man look sad.
HIPPOLYTA   Beshrew° my heart, but I pity the man.
PYRAMUS
O wherefore, nature, didst thou lions frame?
Since lion vile hath here deflow'red my dear:        290
Which is—no, no—which was the fairest dame
    That lived, that loved, that liked, that looked with
        cheer.°
            Come, tears, confound;
            Out, sword, and wound
    The pap of Pyramus;        295
            Ay, that left pap,
            Where heart doth hop.

[*Stabs himself.*]

            Thus die I, thus, thus, thus.
            Now am I dead,
            Now am I fled;        300
    My soul is in the sky.
            Tongue, lose thy light;
            Moon, take thy flight.

                    [*Exit* MOONSHINE.]

    Now die, die, die, die, die.        [*Dies.*]

DEMETRIUS   No die, but an ace,° for him; for he is 305
but one.
LYSANDER   Less than an ace, man; for he is dead, he is
nothing.
THESEUS   With the help of a surgeon he might yet
recover, and yet prove an ass.        310
HIPPOLYTA   How chance° Moonshine is gone before
Thisby comes back and finds her lover?
THESEUS   She will find him by starlight. Here she
comes; and her passion° ends the play.

[*Enter* THISBY.]

HIPPOLYTA   Methinks she should not use a long one 315
for such a Pyramus. I hope she will be brief.
DEMETRIUS   A mote will turn the balance, which
Pyramus, which Thisby, is the better; he for a man,
God warr'nt us; she for a woman, God bless us!
LYSANDER   She hath spied him already with those 320
sweet eyes.
DEMETRIUS   And thus she means,° videlicet:
THISBY
        Asleep, my love?
            What, dead, my dove?
        O Pyramus, arise!        325
            Speak, speak. Quite dumb?
            Dead, dead? A tomb
        Must cover thy sweet eyes.
            These lily lips,
            This cherry nose,        330
        These yellow cowslip cheeks,
            Are gone, are gone.
            Lovers, make moan.
        His eyes were green as leeks.
            O Sisters Three,°        335
            Come, come to me,
        With hands as pale as milk;
            Lay them in gore,
            Since you have shore°
        With shears his thread of silk.        340
            Tongue, not a word.
            Come, trusty sword,
        Come, blade, my breast imbrue!°

[*Stabs herself.*]

            And, farewell, friends.
            Thus Thisby ends.        345
            Adieu, adieu, adieu.        [*Dies.*]
THESEUS   Moonshine and Lion are left to bury the
dead.
DEMETRIUS   Ay, and Wall too.
BOTTOM   [*Starting up.*]   No, I assure you; the wall is 350
down that parted their fathers. Will it please you to
see the epilogue, or to hear a Bergomask dance°
between two of our company?
THESEUS   No epilogue, I pray you; for your play
needs no excuse. Never excuse, for when the players 355
are all dead, there need none to be blamed. Marry, if

---

**267 moused** shaken (like a mouse)   **274 spite** vexation   **276 dole** sorrowful thing   **282 fell** fierce   **284 thread and thrum** i.e., everything ("thrum" = the end of the warp thread)   **285 Quail** destroy; **quell** kill   **288 Beshrew** curse (but a mild word)   **292 cheer** countenance

**305 No . . . ace** not a die (singular of *dice*), but a one-spot on a die   **311 How chance** how does it come that   **314 passion** passionate speech   **322 means** laments   **335 Sisters Three** the three Fates   **339 shore** shorn   **343 imbrue** stain with blood   **352 Bergomask dance** rustic dance

he that writ it had played Pyramus and hanged himself in Thisby's garter, it would have been a fine
tragedy: and so it is, truly; and very notably discharged. But, come, your Bergomask. Let your 360
epilogue alone.

[*A dance.*]

The iron tongue of midnight hath told° twelve.
Lovers, to bed; 'tis almost fairy time.
I fear we shall outsleep the coming morn,
As much as we this night have overwatched.                    365
This palpable-gross° play hath well beguiled
The heavy gait of night. Sweet friends, to bed.
A fortnight hold we this solemnity,
In nightly revels and new jollity.              *Exeunt.*

*Enter* PUCK [*with a broom*].

PUCK
    Now the hungry lion roars,                           370
      And the wolf behowls the moon;
    Whilst the heavy plowman snores,
      All with weary task fordone.°
    Now the wasted° brands do glow,
      Whilst the screech owl, screeching loud,       375
    Puts the wretch that lies in woe
      In remembrance of a shroud.
    Now it is the time of night,
      That the graves, all gaping wide,
    Every one lets forth his sprite,                    380
      In the churchway paths to glide:
    And we fairies, that do run
      By the triple Hecate's team,°
    From the presence of the sun,
      Following darkness like a dream,               385
    Now are frolic.° Not a mouse
    Shall disturb this hallowed house:
    I am sent, with broom, before,
    To sweep the dust behind the door.°

*Enter* [OBERON *and* TITANIA,] *King and Queen of*
*Fairies, with all their* TRAIN.

OBERON
    Through the house give glimmering light,            390
      By the dead and drowsy fire:
    Every elf and fairy sprite
      Hop as light as bird from brier;
    And this ditty, after me,
    Sing, and dance it trippingly.                      395

TITANIA
    First, rehearse your song by rote,
    To each word a warbling note:
    Hand in hand, with fairy grace,
    Will we sing, and bless this place.

[*Song and dance.*]

OBERON
    Now, until the break of day,                         400
    Through this house each fairy stray.
    To the best bride-bed will we,
    Which by us shall blessèd be;
    And the issue there create°
    Ever shall be fortunate.                             405
    So shall all the couples three
    Ever true in loving be;
    And the blots of nature's hand
    Shall not in their issue stand.
    Never mole, harelip, nor scar,                       410
    Nor mark prodigious,° such as are
    Despisèd in nativity,
    Shall upon their children be.
    With this field-dew consecrate,
    Every fairy take his gait,°                          415
    And each several° chamber bless,
    Through this palace, with sweet peace,
    And the owner of it blest
    Ever shall in safety rest.
    Trip away; make no stay;                             420
    Meet me all by break of day.
              *Exeunt* [*all but* PUCK].

PUCK
    If we shadows have offended,
    Think but this, and all is mended:
    That you have but slumb'red here,
    While these visions did appear.                      425
    And this weak and idle° theme,
    No more yielding but° a dream,
    Gentles, do not reprehend:
    If you pardon, we will mend.
    And, as I am an honest Puck,                         430
    If we have unearnèd luck
    Now to scape the serpent's tongue,°
    We will make amends ere long;
    Else the Puck a liar call:
    So, good night unto you all.                         435
    Give me your hands,° if we be friends,
    And Robin shall restore amends.°       [*Exit.*]

**362 told** counted, tolled  **366 palpable-gross** obviously
grotesque  **373 fordone** worn out  **374 wasted** used-up
**383 triple Hecate's team** i.e., because she had three names:
Phoebe in heaven, Diana on earth, Hecate in Hades (like her
chariot—drawn by black horses or dragons—the elves were
abroad only at night; but III.ii.388–93 says differently)  **386
frolic** frolicsome  **389 behind the door** from behind the door
(Puck traditionally helped with household chores)

**404 create** created  **411 mark prodigious** ominous birthmark
**415 take his gait** proceed  **416 several** individual  **426 idle**
foolish  **427 No . . . but** yielding no more than  **432 to
. . . tongue** to escape hisses from the audience  **436 Give
. . . hands** applaud  **437 restore amends** make amends

# THE LIFE AND DEATH OF
# KING JOHN

EDITED BY WILLIAM H. MATCHETT

## Introduction[1]

*The Life and Death of King John* was probably not Shakespeare's title. The editors of the 1623 Folio harmonized the plays they grouped as "Histories" by giving them titles as nearly alike as possible. *Richard II*, for example, is also "The Life and Death of . . ." in the Folio, though prior to 1623 it had appeared as "The Tragedy of . . . ." The Folio titles are designed to fit the plays into a general pattern.

This point is worth attention only because so many readers assume, on the basis of the title, that John must be the hero of the play. He is not. He is no more the hero of the play bearing his name than Henry IV is the hero of either of the plays bearing his name or, for that matter, Julius Caesar of the play bearing his. Each of Shakespeare's plays is best considered an individual experiment in dramatic structure; too often they are distorted for the sake of fitting them into some generic theory, understood in terms designed to make them conform to a definition. In the plays based on English history, Shakespeare is less involved with the exploits of kings, or indeed with the actual history of the period, than he is with exploring situations that test moral or political theory against complex psychological reality. Only in *Richard III* does the king dominate the stage: *Richard II* balances its verbose king against the silent Bolingbroke as the wronger becomes the wronged, the wronged the wronger; and the primary balance of moral positions in *Henry IV, Part One*, is triple —Hal played off against Hotspur and Falstaff, each in his own way both attractive and reprehensible. *King John* is also built upon a triple balance. To attain it, Shakespeare has mingled freely reordered historical material with pure fiction; just as he invented Falstaff and took years from Hotspur for the sake of that dramatic structure, so he invented the Bastard and took years from Arthur for the sake of this. His is a drama of ideas and not just a chronicle history.

A second stumbling block to appreciating Shakespeare's accomplishment in *King John* has been the general assumption that his play is based on another, *The Troublesome Reign of John, King of England*, which can thus be used to

"explain" Shakespeare's departures from history (the Bastard, the ignoring of the Magna Carta, and so on). We are told that we may not blame these on—or credit them to—Shakespeare, who "merely took them over from his source." The Note on the Sources (p. 561) gives a brief account of my reasons for thinking that *King John* is not dependent on *The Troublesome Reign* but that the dependence is the other way around. (Indeed, *The Troublesome Reign of King John* is more likely to have been Shakespeare's original title, taken over by the imitation, than is the title given it by the editors of the Folio.) It is sufficient here to say that, even if I were wrong, even if Shakespeare *had* based his play on the other, we would still have to consider the result as a finished play deserving independent judgment. John is the rightful king at the beginning of *The Troublesome Reign;* the Bastard is but a shadow of Shakespeare's character.

The King John of history came to the throne legitimately, the heir named by his dying brother, Richard I. True, their nephew Arthur was the son of a brother older than John, and some supported his claim, but John's was in fact the better. Primogeniture was not the only legal route to a crown. John enters Shakespeare's play, however, as an acknowledged usurper. Unlike his mother, he offers no objection to Chatillion's reference to his "borrowed majesty" (I.i.4), and even Queen Elinor's objection is a political gesture, not an assertion of principle, as is clear as soon as Chatillion has left the stage. By thus transforming history, Shakespeare is able to play John's "possession" against Arthur's "right," the *de facto* king against the king *de jure*, and by that means to pose a political and moral question. By adding the Bastard to this balance, he further divides the claims to the throne and makes the questions more significant. Richard's illegitimate son, with neither possession of, nor right to, the crown, has yet inherited his father's personal qualities—"The very spirit of Plantagenet!" (I.i.167)—which would make him a better king than either John or Arthur. It is this division of qualifications that the playwright both invents and explores.

The memory of Richard *Coeur de Lion* haunts this play as the mythically heightened image of a good and heroic

---

[1] Portions of this introduction have been recast from passages of my article "Richard's Divided Heritage in *King John*," *Essays in Criticism*, XII (1962), 231–53, by permission of the editors.

king. He triumphantly combined the royal right, possession, and character which the first act distinguishes as having been divided among his nephew, the child Arthur, his brother, the man John, and his son, the youthful Bastard. The division is an imbalance demanding resolution: which—right, possession, or character—is the essential ingredient for a king? As we are introduced to the abstract issues in the early lines of the play, we are prone to the easy assumption that the throne obviously *ought* to go to Arthur, to whom by right it belongs. This point, so clear in the first act before we have seen Arthur, becomes more ambiguous in the second; we meet Arthur in circumstances which overshadow his right. While his immaturity and weakness attract some personal sympathy, sympathy for his cause is dissipated as we observe the company he keeps. King Richard's rightful heir is first seen agreeing to "Embrace . . . love . . . welcome" and "forgive" (II.i.11–12) Austria, the man who killed King Richard. He is a pawn moved by an ambitious mother and surrounded by an unscrupulous, self-seeking, foreign league. Were he to gain his right and become king, the results would presumably be disastrous for England.

With the death of Arthur, the failure and eventual collapse of John, and, through the course of the play, the Bastard's increasing perception of the distinction between self-interest and true honor, it would appear that the Bastard is being groomed to take over as king, as the most deserving of that position. And, indeed, so he is. In order to lead our expectations more firmly in that direction, Shakespeare has let us think the Bastard will be the only one left, withholding the historical fact of the existence of another heir; only in the final scenes of his play does he first mention John's son, Prince Henry. Bringing him in defeats these expectations, but it does not subvert the issue; it shifts the emphasis from the original questions to a deeper consideration of the requirements of honor. The very qualities that constitute the Bastard's fitness for the throne lead to his repudiation of personal ambition and his kneeling to Prince Henry. True honor, a matter not of prestige and power but of duty, is decided on the basis of what is best for England. The Bastard, in kneeling, renounces his recently established claim to the throne and thus prevents further civil war. True honor makes the Bastard the best of subjects in a unified England, and this, in the logic of the play, is more important than the character of the king.

Insofar as the play has a hero, then, it is the Bastard, and, indeed, a large part of the first act is devoted to introducing him to us. He repeats the national situation on a domestic scale. He also is in possession of an estate to which another, his half brother Robert, is the rightful heir. Our sympathies, like John's, are of course with the "good blunt fellow" (I.i.71); under the influence of those sympathies, however, both "right" and "honor" begin to twist in our hands. Robert's assumed moral right to his inheritance is denied by John in the name of another right, the legal fiction of the Bastard's legitimacy. Everyone knows that Robert, for lack of sufficient proof, like Arthur, for lack of sufficient power, is being "legally" cheated.

But the Bastard, unlike John, is not permitted to enjoy his dishonorably held possessions. To save him for his later role in the play, he is presented with a choice between "honor" and possessions. He chooses "honor" (here merely

"reputation"), and his ambitious choice immediately pays off, for John knights him. There is in his response an impetuous decisiveness, uncalculating, heedless of consequences, a little naive. He is not one to ask, like John, "What follows if we disallow of this?" (I.i.16), but says at once, "I'll take my chance" (I.i.151).

Many have been bothered by the contradiction between the self-sufficient character of the Bastard and his pursuit here of an honor that is merely reputation. They try to explain it away, just as they tell us he "does not really mean what he says" in his "commodity" speech at the end of II.i. The contradiction exists. The Bastard's discovery and handling of it is a primary development in the play. But the reputation he chooses in Act I is one to which he has, in fact, a right; gambling on future "chance," he trades his spurious respectability for an honest reputation as a royal bastard. He makes the right choice for the wrong reason; he has yet to add insight to the character which is intrinsic—"I am I, howe'er I was begot" (I.i.175). It is safe to say that the first act leaves the audience more interested in what will happen to him than in the immediate challenge to John.

The second act, however, is concerned almost entirely with the dynastic struggle, and the Bastard, though he attempts once, unsuccessfully, to control the action, serves primarily as an observant commentator. His presence as an observer needs to be stressed since, in the shade of his lively comments, one might overlook its importance: his political education is beginning and he has much to learn. By the end of the act the once naive young man has found the proper name for the political motivation he observes.

Tracing this view of the main structure of the play unfortunately involves slighting many of its subsidiary felicities, as well as some of its weaknesses. John, Elinor, and Pandulph would each repay closer attention than can be given them here, but earlier generations would be particularly incensed at such neglect of Constance, whose laments for her son in this act made her, for actresses and audiences alike, the most attractive character in the play. This is a view I cannot share, though she is indeed forceful in her claims for sympathy. I find it noteworthy that many actresses, in creating their conception of her suffering motherhood, found it necessary to omit some of her more violent speeches, especially in her screeching exchanges with Elinor. Constance *is* a suffering mother, there is no doubt, but she is also an ambitious one, a strident, domineering tigress. No one would think of applying to her Lear's praise of Cordelia's voice, "ever soft,/Gentle and low—an excellent thing in woman" (V.iii.274–75). Friend and enemy alike fail in their continuous attempts to silence her. John is brutal—"Bedlam, have done" (II.i.183)—while Austria (line 134) and King Philip (line 195) are merely trying to reconcile her to the etiquette of political duplicity, but even Arthur joins the chorus—"Good my mother, peace!" (line 163)—to no avail. She is equally uncontrollable in her appearances in the next act and is ultimately reported to have died "in a frenzy" (IV.ii.122). She is wronged, indeed, but she is one of the reasons that Arthur would be such a disastrous king for England.

In direct contrast with Arthur, the Bastard shows an immediate antipathy to Austria, motivated of course by the lionskin Richard's killer is wearing. (Shakespeare is already thinking in terms of total dramatic effect on a stage, not just in terms of lines.) Whatever the moral masquerades of the political schemers, the Bastard, as Richard's son, has a personal loyalty which he will not deny. If this personal warmth is in contrast with the calculated zeal of the other opponents, it is in even greater contrast with the dispassionately calculated neutrality of Hubert.

Given the opposed armies at his gates, Hubert's position has all the appearance of eminent sense: "we are the King of England's subjects . . . he that proves the king,/To him will we prove loyal" (II.i.267–71). But, however appealing the arguments on the virtues of neutrality, Hubert's position is unacceptable in *King John*. This is not the moral superiority of "A plague a both your houses!" with which Mercutio, "the prince's near ally," rejects the parochial quarrel that has caused his death (*Romeo and Juliet*, III.i.108–10); this is the willingness of common citizens to accept either of two contradictory national loyalties. It has the sound sense of self-preservation—and perhaps today that seems enough—but it is meant to have little else: as comes increasingly clear in Hubert's progressive responses, it is not a moral position at all, but a refusal to face the issue. (That the issue is not resolvable in the terms in which it has been set does not, apparently, excuse a man from involvement.)

Hubert's response sounds fine until probed: "he that proves the king,/To him will we prove loyal." What kind of loyalty is this? Like "honor" in the first act, it is not the real article, but a calculated substitute; what ought to be the warm and total response of a committed man is here the small change of a self-indulgent apathy. What "proves the king"—the issue itself—is precisely what Hubert avoids, and his restatements, the "worthiest" or "greatest" (II.i.281, 332), are equally hollow, assuming only that might makes right. Hubert abdicates the citizen's duty to act according to his best moral lights and, selfishly holding himself aloof, leaves the decision to naked force.

Though superior to Hubert here in his loyalty and his freedom from selfish calculation, the Bastard is not himself facing any moral issues. His response is warm and total, but it is not yet what one would call perceptive. He, no less than Hubert, leaves the decision to naked force; the difference is his willingness to involve himself on the side to which he is loyal. This involvement leads to his first venture in political strategy, his "wild" (II.i.395) suggestion that the kings join forces against Angiers before turning back to their own quarrel. His "Smacks it not something of the policy?" (II.i.396) shows his naive pride in what he is pleased to consider his approach to political wisdom, but what is the rash response of naive loyalty in the Bastard becomes insane ruthlessness when it is accepted and given royal sanction by John.

It is from Blanch, however, that the Bastard learns the most. Though her role in the play is brief, it is crucial. Hubert's suggestion that she be married to the Dauphin disgusts the Bastard, but both kings see in the suggestion a way of saving face while abandoning their sterile enmity. Lewis, too, plays the game with a will, and his ability to switch rapidly from enemy to lover, patently insincere, gilding his political opportunism with the language of a sonneteer, is in sharp contrast not only with the Bastard's disgusted and less flexible sincerity, but with the honesty of his bride-to-be. Blanch is as much a political pawn as Arthur, but, without loss of dignity or feminine propriety,

she is hardly less plain-spoken—when called upon to speak—than the Bastard: "Further I will not flatter you, my lord,/That all I see in you is worthy love . . ." (II.i.516–17). When John asks for her formal assent, she pronounces herself "bound in honor still to do/What you in wisdom still vouchsafe to say" (II.i.522–23). This is the only use of the word "honor" in the second act (it had been used—misused—eight times before) and its first appearance in the play as a high-minded sense of personal obligation, a trait of character rather than a mere claim for public approval. Blanch is controlled by her honor, whatever the personal consequences. The Bastard is silent, but his education has now truly begun, as comes clear when he is left alone at the end of the scene.

In his well-known soliloquy—"Mad world! Mad kings! Mad composition!" (II.i.561)—with new insight he gives the name, missing so far in the play, to the primary motivating force behind what we have seen: "commodity," the unprincipled self-interest which perverts "all indifferency, . . . direction, purpose, course, intent" (lines 579–80), and brings the noblest-sounding resolutions to the most ignominious results. Having named it, he formally adopts it, for the Bastard's final words are "Gain, be my lord, for I will worship thee!" (line 598). Many of the difficulties commentators have with this speech arise from their attempts to make of it a summation of the Bastard's character, a final position rather than a stage in his development. He is not static, and it is enough in the second act that he has begun to consider where he is. What was blind loyalty now sees madness on both sides. For the first time he is critical of John. Though he is wrong in his estimate of King Philip's original motive, accepting the public declaration for the fact, the important point is that he is beginning to judge for himself and no longer just following chance. The word "honorable" in the Bastard's mouth now, though we may demur from "honorable war" (line 585), is not what it was in the first act, but what he has learned from Blanch.

After this insight into the kings, there is surely a hesitation (between lines 586 and 587) when, in his honesty, the Bastard recognizes the application to himself: "And why rail I on this commodity?/But for because he hath not wooed me yet" (lines 587–88). Must we demand conversion at the very incipience of self-knowledge? The Bastard, realizing that he has been living in the same spirit he has condemned in the kings, concludes most humanly by reversing his complaint and turning their conduct into a rationalization for his own. But he has found a name for such conduct; he has seen commodity and its opposite. Never again can he remain unconscious in following chance. It is enough for now. It is a place to end a scene but not a play.

The Bastard is not the only one who is educated during the course of this play. Hubert, the man who thought he could hold himself aloof from commitment, is caught between the claims of political allegiance and those of simple compassion. The warmth of John's fawning—"O my gentle Hubert,/We owe thee much!" (III.ii.29–30)— has a multiple motivation. John is not merely flattering Hubert in order to bring him to murder Arthur, but indeed owes Hubert much, just as he says: he may owe him the very capture of Arthur, as the entry would seem to imply, and he presumably owes him Angiers, Hubert apparently having made his choice after France broke the league. John is promising a reward already due and hinting for just one further service. Whatever the circumstances that determined him, Hubert is no longer in a position to maintain his neutrality; he has made, or has been forced to make, his choice, and the loyalty once so coldly promised to the stronger must now be delivered. After a number of false starts, John finally manages the most pointed of commissions, as though his will were less tainted for showing naked so briefly:

KING JOHN
Death.
HUBERT   My lord.
KING JOHN          A grave.
HUBERT                    He shall not live.
KING JOHN                              Enough.
(III.ii.76)

John leaves the promised reward unspecified, but the more significant ambiguity lies in the sinister irony of his final statement to Arthur that Hubert will attend on him "With all true duty" (III.ii.83). True to whom? to what? in what sense? The nature of "true duty"—whether Hubert's, John's, the Bastard's, Blanch's, King Philip's, Pandulph's, Lady Faulconbridge's, Robert Faulconbridge's, the English nobles', or Melun's—is precisely what is at issue in this play, whether we call it that, or "loyalty," or "honor."

However unexpected, and even illogical, the shift in intent from murder to blinding—or, more likely, to murder as an "accident" during blinding—the resultant stage business is an image of the moral situation, an image that is echoed and re-echoed in the lines. It is Hubert's "duty" that is iron; human sympathy is the living eye that he must put out. Hubert, with his hot irons and concealed accomplices, is brute power; the child Arthur is powerless innocence, wronged right. In the difficulty of putting innocent goodness on the stage, Shakespeare makes of Arthur, as he does of Blanch at the end of III.i, a formal image of victimized virtue—Arthur the image of suffering innocence, Blanch of suffering integrity. Perhaps the ultimate horror in the viciousness of "this iron age" (IV.i.60) is the recognition by innocence that its own appearance must be suspect: "Nay, you may think my love was crafty love,/And call it cunning" (IV.i.53–54).

The choice between theory and humanity forced upon Hubert is rather like the choice facing the Duke of York in the final act of *Richard II*, but that old man, pursuing an abstraction (as he does with consistently high-minded inefficacy throughout the play), becomes ridiculous in his prosecution of his son, while Hubert, choosing humane mercy over political theory, grows toward probity. His decision to spare Arthur, his choice of a higher duty over a lower, creates no moral millennium, however; only the most naive faith would expect such a result. He is immediately involved in duplicity—he must lie to John—and in "Much danger" (IV.i.133).

Hubert and the Bastard discover each other, as it were, over the body of Arthur. The Bastard is sent to England in III.ii, so that he is off the stage when John gives his charge to Hubert, which, for the sake of later developments, Shakespeare could not permit him to witness. The Bastard and Hubert are also kept apart from each other during IV.ii, sharing the stage only as the Bastard reports on his travels "through the land" (line 143) and on the prophecy of Peter of Pomfret. Thus the Bastard observes neither the effect of Hubert's false announcement of Arthur's death nor John's later struggle to shift the responsibility and Hubert's revelation of his disobedient innocence. Hubert, in turn, has little chance to recognize the new maturity of the Bastard: he hears the Bastard's annoyance with John—"But if you be afeard to hear the worst,/Then let the worst unheard fall on your head" (IV.ii.135–36)—but not the Bastard's invitation for the denial which John does not make—"I met [the English lords]/. . . going to seek the grave/Of Arthur, whom they say is killed tonight/On your suggestion" (IV.ii.162–66). The Bastard is no less open, no less loyal, but he approaches decisions more slowly, suspending judgment without concealing his suspicion.

The scene in which these two, the Bastard and Hubert, recognize each other's worth is superbly constructed. Arthur's body lies unfound while the English lords reveal that they have already been in treasonable correspondence with Pandulph; their claim to outraged principles has been but an act, a pretext for saving their skins during the expected French invasion. In contrast, though he shares their suspicions that John has killed Arthur, the Bastard puts his duty to England first. Discovery of Arthur's body should confirm all suspicions, and the audience waits in suspense for the Bastard's response while the lords indulge in self-justifying superlatives of horror. "Sir Richard, what think you?" Salisbury asks (IV.iii.41), but he and Pembroke both favor the Bastard with their own I-told-you-so's before—following surely a lengthy pause—he answers simply and directly: "It is a damnèd and a bloody work,/The graceless action of a heavy hand,/If that it be the work of any hand" (IV.iii.57–59). His conditional conclusion, which can only strike the eager lords as pusillanimous, is a sign of his increasing wisdom, undergirded for the audience by our knowledge that the death was in fact accidental.

Hubert's untimely message that Arthur lives can hardly be expected to convince anyone, and the Bastard is forced to defend him from the lords' wrath, though his "If" is still unresolved. Shown Arthur's body, Hubert weeps, which the hypocrites naturally take for hypocrisy but, held off by the Bastard, they cannot attack him, and they leave to join the Dauphin. Though willing to defend Hubert from attack while the facts are unclear, the Bastard has not abandoned his own strong suspicions. Hubert, in spite of his choice of a higher duty, is entangled in circumstantial evidence. The Bastard demands a direct answer ("Knew you of this fair work?" [IV.iii.116]), and indicates both his stand if the answer is *yes* ("There is not yet so ugly a fiend of hell/As thou shalt be, if thou didst kill this child" [lines 123–24]) and his honest opinion ("I do suspect thee very grievously" [line 134]). This is the new, more thoughtful, less hotheaded but no less forthright man that the Bastard has grown to be, a far cry from the unthinking enthusiast he was in the first act. And he need only listen to the quality of Hubert's brief denial to accept it without further question. In a world of commodity, the two who have abandoned it look into each other's hearts and recognize what they have found.

Having accepted Hubert's innocence, however, the

Bastard is left with his suspicions of John. The issues surrounding Arthur's death are more complex, more muddled and human than many have been willing to allow. The moral responsibility naturally depends on whether one emphasizes the accident or the justified fear of John which forced Arthur to take the chance. What John wanted was Arthur's death without the responsibility for it. The consequences of the alleged death have no sooner forced him to welcome the news that Arthur is still alive than fate gives him exactly what he had wanted. But it is too late, and the thing he wanted becomes its own opposite: though, as it turned out, he lacked the power, he is left with the responsibility—or at least the apparent responsibility, which does equal harm. The Bastard knows less of this than we, and his response is the appropriate one for any conscientious man: "I am amazed, methinks, and lose my way/Among the thorns and dangers of this world" (IV. iii.140–41). The moral life is rarely, for a perceptive man, a simple choice between well-marked paths, but life in a maze. The ambiguity of the Bastard's ensuing soliloquy reflects the ambiguity of the issues themselves, and his conclusion the necessity to act in spite of it. He recognizes both Arthur's right to the throne and the fact that the very question is no longer relevant; that "England," the rightful king, is dead, but that England, the country, remains to suffer, "and vast confusion waits,/As doth a raven on a sick-fall'n beast,/The imminent decay of wrested pomp" (lines 152–54). This is what commodity has cost. Though he recognizes now that John's pomp was wrested, the Bastard sees no honorable choice for one who would serve England but continuing loyalty: "I'll to the king" (line 157).

Arriving with his bad news, he is again closely observing John and controlling his disgust only with difficulty. The conclusion of his report—"And wild amazement hurries up and down/The little number of your doubtful friends" (V.i.35–36)—is not only general but pointedly personal ("I am amazed"); though others may be "doubtful friends" because they are both fearful and untrusting, he is a trustworthy and fearless friend tormented by doubt. John's assumption that Arthur yet lives sounds to the Bastard like the sheerest evasion and almost leads to a break. Given the Bastard's suspicions, "some damned hand" (line 41) is dangerously blunt, backing down not at all from the firm position already taken when Arthur's body was found. There is a crescendo of excitement when John, in horror and guilt, attempts again to place the blame on Hubert, and the Bastard, convinced of Hubert's innocence, responds with a direct insinuation of John's responsibility for murder:

KING JOHN
That villain Hubert told me he did live.
BASTARD
So, on my soul, he did, for aught he knew.   (V.i.42–43)

The final pronoun, clearing Hubert, accuses John. This exchange, in which tempers have risen on both sides, must be followed by a long, electric silence, while John cringes and the Bastard cools to consider what he is doing. England must again be uppermost in his thoughts, for he stops his attack in midstream and turns to rallying John's spirits for the battle with the invaders. This self-control, this ability to quell his passionate outrage in order to undertake what is required by a higher loyalty, demonstrates the maturity the Bastard has reached. His moral superiority to John is obvious; it is one of his glorious moments and prepares us to accept what follows.

Though the Bastard has, technically, misjudged the details of Arthur's death, he has not in fact misjudged John. He pleads now only that the man act with the outer semblance of a king in order to inspire his followers. But John has just abandoned his authority to Pandulph and, pleased merely to have retained his throne, considers it a "happy peace" (V.i.63). Such peace with an invading army horrifies the Bastard—"O inglorious league!" (line 65)—and leads to so overwhelming a remonstrance that John, having yielded to Pandulph, yields his authority again, this time to the Bastard: "Have thou the ordering of this present time" (line 77). John, though a vigorous usurper, and swift to defend Angiers in the first act, has not been able to maintain his grasp. Once he has given way to the temptation to order Arthur's death, his fortunes decline: his nobles abandon him; the French invade England; his mother dies; he capitulates to Pandulph. He has proven a king incapable of kingship and now is finally replaced in action by the man most capable of it.

The Bastard has in fact become the king. Though he speaks to Pandulph and Lewis of "the scope/And warrant limited unto my tongue" (V.ii.122–23), we know that his warrant has not in fact been limited. Such a pose is but a way of keeping his own counsel, of postponing decision until he learns how things stand; once he knows the situation, he assumes full authority: "Now hear our English king,/For thus his royalty doth speak in me" (lines 128–29). The king of and for whom he speaks—who "is prepared" (line 130), who "doth smile" (line 134) at the invasion, "the gallant monarch" (line 148), "warlike John" (line 176)—is of course not the man John but a verbal image of the king England needs. The image is not a fiction, however, for it is personified in the Bastard himself. As though to ensure this distinction between the image and the fact, the brief third scene shows us, in direct contrast to "warlike John," the utter impotence of the man beneath the public image. Ill with fever, he is ordered from the field by the Bastard, lest he confuse and dishearten the soldiers. The kingly role has been entirely transferred. Richard's son has become "Richard" (V.iii.12); "That misbegotten devil, Faulconbridge,/In spite of spite, alone upholds the day" (V.iv.4–5).

It is against the quality of this man that Shakespeare displays the formalizations of allegiance, the hollow rites which political practice substitutes for such living loyalty: Arthur's "embracing" of Austria; Lewis' marriage to Blanch and the treaty it attests; the "king's oath" (II.ii.10) which Constance has from Philip; the casuistry of Pandulph's "falsehood falsehood cures" (III.i.203); John's second coronation, enforcing new oaths of allegiance after excommunication has freed his followers from their former oaths; excommunication itself, not here a spiritual issue but merely the weapon of another power politician; the show of outrage with which the nobles cover their desertion; John's yielding his crown to, and accepting it back from, Pandulph, again with no religious significance but simply as a political bargain—"Now keep your holy word: go meet the French" (V.i.5). The fourth scene of Act V twists the ironic complications of meaningless oaths and meaningful loyalty about as far as they can be wrung. The dying Melun, breaking an oath (his to the Dauphin) which broke an oath (the Dauphin's and his to the English nobles) which broke an oath (the nobles' to John), reveals to the nobles that the Dauphin intends to execute them as soon as his battle is won. Abandoning their "holy vow" (IV.iii.67), they hasten to return to John. Who is to disentangle true honor from such a web as this? But Melun, saving their lives, says that he does so for the love of "one Hubert" (V.iv.40–41), and because he himself had an English grandfather. This personal loyalty stands out above the meaningless oaths as a return to sanity and honor. The men thus saved by his love for Hubert are, however, the very men who most misjudged and misused Hubert for their selfish ends. They are saved by love for the man they scorned, a cutting of the web which carries distinct overtones of Christian forgiveness.

The two who have lifted themselves above commodity come together in another key scene when Hubert brings the Bastard the news that John is dying. No time is wasted in the play on the mechanics of John's death—poisoning by a monk is supplied by history as Shakespeare knew it; his attention, however, is not on John but on the effect of the approaching death on the Bastard. As they meet in the night, Hubert's "Who art thou?" (V.vi.9) is precisely the question that remains to be settled, and the Bastard's "Who thou wilt" in answer, coupled with the reminder of his Plantagenet blood, stresses the possibility toward which the play has apparently been aiming. We have seen Hubert grow from his attempt at a coldly rational avoidance of the problem of choice between loyalties to a realization that a man is forced to commit himself and can only try to do so honorably. We have seen the Bastard grow from a naive enthusiast following chance to a man of mature insight and ability. What Hubert brings the Bastard now is, in effect, an invitation to take the throne, to assume the role he has in fact been filling and for which the character he inherited from his father has proven so eminently fitted. Arthur is dead; John is dying; he is the obvious successor. It is all understated, but the implications are clear: "I left him almost speechless, and broke out/To acquaint you with this evil, that you might/The better arm you to the sudden time" (V.vi.24–26). Hubert foresees a struggle, and he wants the Bastard to have the throne—as do we. A struggle with whom? "The lords are all come back" (line 33). Clearly they must not gain control. But then the surprising new complication is introduced: "And brought Prince Henry in their company" (line 34). This is the first mention in the play that John has a son and heir; dramatically it is startling news.

Nor is the structure of the play affected by whether or not the audience "knows all the time" that John must, historically, be followed on the throne by his son Henry. The "structure of expectation" may be affected—Henry's arrival could, in fact, fulfill a historical expectation—but an audience expecting Henry should still see his arrival as cutting across the prior course of the action, upsetting a suggested balance. For, whether or not the audience is surprised by the conclusion, the fact remains that the play, in its original division of claimants to the throne and its eventual elimination of two of them, appears to be moving toward the coronation of the third claimant, and

only alters that appearance at the last minute by introducing the hitherto unmentioned heir. Not only has Henry been unmentioned, but Shakespeare has not even acknowledged that John had a wife (two, in fact). Suppressing Isabell, as he suppressed Constance's third husband, allows him to develop the relationship between John and his mother without dramatic confusion; it also serves to keep Henry better hidden.

Prince Henry is apparently, like Arthur, a young successor surrounded by a self-seeking league. The Bastard is in the situation that faced John upon the death of Richard, and the question is, will he, like John, usurp the throne? However self-seeking such a move might appear, it could well be considered, given the Bastard's kingly character and Prince Henry's companions, the best hope for England. The Bastard's immediate response is a prayer, as much for England as for himself: "Withhold thine indignation, mighty God,/And tempt us not to bear above our power!" (V.vi.37–38). It is not a decision, but it is surely an aspiration to withstand the temptations of commodity. He is, in fact, not even willing at the moment to entertain the possibility of usurpation. His immediate revelation that he has lost "half my power this night" (line 39) has been taken to mean that he is forced to his dynastic decision only by his inability to muster sufficient strength to seize the throne from the combined forces of the returning noblemen. It is rather the explanation to Hubert of his prayer that God withhold His indignation. His worry is, as always, for England, facing the invaders now with decimated forces. The invasion, not the succession, is his business at the moment. And the question is doubly untimely, for John is still "the king" (line 43).

But we know, as the Bastard does not, that Lewis has also suffered grievous losses. Structurally, it remains only for John to die and the Bastard to reach his decision. Shakespeare first shows us Prince Henry, however, though the lines give no clue as to how the author may have advised his fellow actor to play the part. The prince's few speeches leave him sounding a sensitive enough young man facing the death of his father, but it would be equally possible to play him as a weakling reminiscent of Arthur or as a young man of promising strength of character, reminiscent of the Bastard. And the effect he creates will naturally cast its light on the Bastard's decision. If he is Arthur all over again, surrounded by the returning nobles, the Bastard's kneeling to him will flood the end of the play with a dreadful irony; if he has a suggestion of the royal character as well as the royal right, the Bastard's homage, acknowledging his possession of the throne, will create a triumphant rejoining of the qualifications divided at the beginning of the play.

The director and the actor, I would suggest, are called upon to attempt a compromise: Henry must be kept young enough to underline the similarity between the Bastard's choice and that which originally faced John; at the same time, he must show vitality and promise, for a suggestion of his complete dominance by the former traitors would be out of key with the generally hopeful conclusion of the play. This ambiguity in the prince's role is in part indicative of the fact that our attention no longer remains solely on the question of what qualifies a king, but has shifted over to that of how, given this situation, the Bastard ought to act.

John, who commenced the play as a successful usurper, dies miserably as he listens to the Bastard's news of England's losses. Even as John lies dying, his faithful follower pays him the compliment of not tempering the truth. And, though "God He knows how we shall answer" Lewis (V.vii.60), John is no sooner dead than the Bastard turns to rallying the defense. But defense is not necessary, for the others know that Lewis has already sued for peace. There remains then but the single question, and it is quickly settled: the Bastard turns and kneels to Prince Henry. Whether the prince combines the true kingly character with the possession and the right here acknowledged, the lines give us little chance of knowing. It is going to be up to the director. That, however, is no longer the main point. The very strength of character which made the Bastard the most worthy of Richard's heirs leads him to relinquish any divisive personal ambitions and to acknowledge a true duty to support the new king. This is the heir who alone remains of those who were established in the first act as having a share in Richard's heritage; this is the young man who once said, "Gain, be my lord, for I will worship thee!"; this is the efficient commander who, as John failed, has actually been wielding the royal power, filling the role of England's king. In spite of all these indications of a contrary denouement, he kneels to Prince Henry, acknowledging him King Henry. In a world of self-seekers, his conception of honor has grown until he is capable of this self-denying loyalty to England. It is, of course, one of the tragic ironies of politics that a man may be cut off from authority by the very act which best demonstrates his worthiness to wield it.

Though it has taken a paragraph to sketch the implications of the Bastard's kneeling—and more could be said—he is not to be seen as one who has thought it all through. He is as impulsive at the close as he was at the beginning, but his impulses are those of one whose original promise has come to maturity. His closing speech, with its ringing final couplet, has sometimes been dismissed as a platitudinous set piece, as "Armada rhetoric." But Armada rhetoric can be moving if one has just survived the threat of the Armada, and the Bastard's speech is platitudinous only when lifted out of its historical and textual context, only when we fail to see that the play has demonstrated most effectively the moral complexity of the problem of loyalty, while the Bastard has shown us (as, in his lesser role, has Hubert) the self-denying acceptance of a higher duty which true loyalty demands from the man of honor.

## A NOTE ON THE SOURCES

In 1591, one Sampson Clarke published in London an anonymous two-part play, the lengthy title of which begins *The Troublesome Reign of John, King of England . . .*; many, indeed most, editors and scholars assume this to be the source of Shakespeare's play.[2] The plots are in fact so similar that, in spite of continual, line-by-line differences,[3] there are only three logically possible relationships between them: either *King John* (*KJ*) is based on *The Troublesome Reign* (*TR*), or *TR* is based on *KJ*, or each is based on some third play, now missing. Missing sources are tantalizing but rarely of any use; though always logically possible, no such third play need be posited to explain the similarities between the two we have. It is sufficient to assume that one is based upon the other.

But which upon which? *TR* is a play of little verbal distinction with a firm anti-Roman-Catholic bias. It is commonly said that Shakespeare improved the verse and cut down on the anti-Catholicism. At the same time he is said to have been careless with his handling of the plot, so that one must read *TR* to understand *KJ*. For example, the Bastard's annoyance at the marriage of Blanch and Lewis is said to be understandable only when we know that in *TR* Elinor had already promised Blanch to the Bastard. One may, however, reverse such an argument and say that, based upon *KJ*, *TR* supplies the crudest of (misleading) motivation for what is more meaningful thematically in Shakespeare's play. In *KJ*, the Bastard's annoyance is with the blatant political expediency of the marriage; to reduce this to personal jealousy is to confuse the issue and cheapen the play. (It is noteworthy that Elinor's promise is first, and last, mentioned only when the political marriage has been suggested [*TR*, I.828–30]; the author of *TR* may well be scraping up a motive for something he has failed to understand.) What is taken as "better plotting" in *TR* can be consistently explained as an expansion and cheapening of Shakespeare's implications.[4]

One may, in addition, indicate many scenes in which *TR* muddles issues, or reproduces the outline of an action while missing the thematic point. The following are examples:

1. Blanch asks Lewis not to forsake his bride on his wedding day, but says nothing of her divided loyalty.
2. Pandulph and Lewis have their private conference after the departure of King Philip and Constance, but little reason for it remains. Pandulph's Machiavellian exposition of the complex political necessities (*KJ*, III.iii.107–83) is reduced to two lines in an eleven-line

[3] Two lines alone appear unchanged in both plays (*King John*, II.i.528 and V.iv.42 are identical with *The Troublesome Reign*, I.862 and II.793), but there are other lines which are within a word or phrase of exact repetition—for example, *King John*: "With them a bastard of the king's deceased" (II.i.65); *The Troublesome Reign*: "Next them a bastard of the king's (deceased)" (I.512). Though divided into two parts, each with its own title page, *The Troublesome Reign* is in fact only a few hundred lines longer than *King John*.

[4] Major examples would of course be the *TR* scene (written largely in Skeltonics and thus unlike anything else in the play) during which the Bastard, raiding the monasteries, finds a nun hidden in the abbot's chest and a friar in the nun's, and the attention paid to the monk who poisons John, which diverts attention from the Bastard's choice. This scene of the monk and the abbot (supplying a motivation not taken from Holinshed) takes the place, in fact, of the night meeting of Hubert and the Bastard, which does not occur in *TR*. Similarly, though some find *TR* "more effective" because the Bastard chases Austria and captures Richard's lionskin, here again *TR* may simply bring into the lines what is implied in *KJ*: if the Bastard enters wearing the lionskin as well as carrying Austria's head, the point is visual and requires no speeches. His complaint of the heat as he enters is a thoroughly effective reference to what he is wearing. To say more is to detract.

scene: "Arthur is safe, let John alone with him!/Thy title next is fair'st to England's crown" (*TR*, I.1232–33).

3. The Bastard comes on stage, bringing Peter of Pomfret to John, *before*—and remains on stage during—John's decision, openly announced to the nobles, to kill Arthur, which announcement itself precedes Hubert's entry with the (mis)information that Arthur is dead. The Bastard is still on stage when Hubert tells John that Arthur is in fact alive. This removes from the Bastard any necessity of making up his mind about either John or Hubert and thus drains most of its meaning from the scene in which he is tested by the finding of Arthur's body.

4. In that scene, the nobles find Arthur's body the moment they come on stage, which—along with their having heard John's announcement—supplies them with a sufficient motive for a treachery which in *KJ* is based upon a tangled skein of suspicion and hypocritical self-seeking, rendering doubly ironic Salisbury's reference to "our pure honors" (*KJ*, IV.iii.25). *TR* is elementary; *KJ* is morally complex and interesting.

5. The Bastard himself boasts that "King Richard's fortune hangs/Upon the plume of warlike Philip's [that is, his own] helm" (II.759–60), but John and the Bastard fight alongside each other against Lewis, without John's structurally important conferring of royal power upon the Bastard ("Have thou the ordering of this present time" [*KJ*, V.i.77]).

6. The dying Melun has two reasons for revealing Lewis' plot to the English nobles, but only one is common to both plays ("For that my grandsire was an Englishman"—the second of the two identical lines). In *TR*, the other reason is his dramatically trite (however relevant) desire to save his soul, "to leave this mansion free of guilt" (II.791); in *KJ* it is the thematic and ironic complexity of "Commend me to one Hubert, with your king:/The love of him . . ./Awakes my conscience to confess all this (V.iv.40–43). Thus *TR* lacks the entire irony of the nobles' being saved for love of the man they have most scorned.

7. John, at his death, asks for "the frozen Alps,/To tumble on, and cool this inward heat" (II.1089–90), without any of the development which, throughout *KJ*, ties heat and cold, fever and cool zeal, blood and eyes into a web of thematic images.

At each of these points, and many others, it is possible to argue that Shakespeare has improved on a *TR* source; but it is equally possible to argue that *TR* has missed the point of the *KJ* scene upon which it is based. It is possible that Shakespeare omitted scenes from *TR* and developed others; it would seem more likely that the author of *TR*, working not from the text of *KJ* but from his memory of performances, invented material to fill out what he considered opportunities too inviting to be missed, and reproduced some actions and stage groupings of which the meaning in *KJ* had quite escaped him. Apart from *KJ*, it is difficult to see why some of these incidents occur in *TR*; drained of their dramatic meaning, they are fragments, implying, like fossils, that they are remnants of a living organism, not that they are random protoplasm which might be blown into future viability.

And yet, if the author of *TR* was remembering performances of *KJ*—if, however he may have misunderstood it, he is reproducing the action as well as he is—how is it possible that he remembered so few of its words, and those few so flat, so peripheral? Why are there no traces of the metaphors or of the forceful lines which strike us as the most obviously Shakespearean element in *KJ*? The absence of all trace of Shakespeare's characteristic language is surely the strongest of arguments against *TR*'s having been based upon *KJ*. To counter it, one is forced to invent a man with no ear for poetry, no memory for lines, who has at the same time a surprisingly good memory for the scene-by-scene progress of the plot. It is possible to conceive such a man, working perhaps some weeks later from a plot outline made immediately after a performance, but he is an unlikely combination, and it is on the basis of this difficulty that one must say that the source question remains open.

For, in terms of plot development, the evidence seems, to me at least, to go strongly the other way. Consider one final relationship in which *TR* is clearer than *KJ*: the question of John's orders to Hubert. The situation is definitely confusing in Shakespeare's play: John hints to Hubert, first obliquely and then directly, to kill Arthur (III.ii.69–77). We therefore assume, when we see Hubert preparing instruments with the help of an unspecified number of brutes (labeled, indeed, *Executioners* by the entries and the speech-headings), that he is about to carry out John's wish. However, it turns out that he is going to blind Arthur instead, and he shows the boy written orders to that effect (IV.i.33–39). This is the first surprise; the second comes when, having reported Arthur dead, Hubert is defending himself against John's unjustified anger. Nothing is said of blinding in this scene, and Hubert's "Here is your hand and seal for what I did" (IV.ii.215) apparently refers to written orders to kill Arthur. Whether we are to assume two differing written orders, or a confusion about the contents of one order, is not clear.

This is another situation in which we are told that we must go to *TR* if we are to understand what is happening. There, John puts Arthur into Hubert's custody, saying:

> Hubert, keep him safe,
> For on his life doth hang thy sovereign's crown,
> But in his death consists thy sovereign's bliss.
> Then, Hubert, as thou shortly hear'st from me,
> So use the prisoner I have given in charge.          (I.1176–80)

John clearly has conflicting motives, but he gives no such direct hint as we have in Shakespeare. We cannot be sure what the further orders will be. The scene between Hubert and Arthur keeps us in suspense. (The entry calls for "*Hubert de Burgh with three men*," and the single speech-heading labels them *Attendants*.) Hubert is about to commit some form of violence against Arthur, and we expect that he may be going to kill him, but this is first denied in favor of something worse (I.1425–29), and then Hubert reads the words of the order—"put out the eyes of Arthur Plantagenet" (line 1443). This settles our doubts, and the scene proceeds to Hubert's ultimate decision not to carry out the order. When Hubert returns to John, the king has just informed the nobles that "The brat shall die" (line 1737), but this is presumably a new decision, and Hubert brings the (false) news that "According to your Highness' strict command/Young Arthur's eyes are blinded and extinct" (lines 1744–45), adding that he died of the "extreme pain" (line 1747). This twist is in accordance with Hubert's plan (lines 1520–21) and is presumably a way of covering his failure to obey orders. Whether he is intending to help Arthur escape or merely to keep him hidden, is not mentioned. Finally, however, when John curses Hubert—"Furies haunt thee still/For killing him whom all the world laments" (lines 1797–98)—Hubert's reply, "Why here's—my lord—your Highness' hand and seal,/Charging on life's regard to do the deed!" (lines 1799–1800), would seem, as in *KJ*, to refer to an order for Arthur's death and not to the document shown to Arthur at the time. Here is the same confusion; without comparing the scene with *KJ*, however, one might be willing to take "the deed" as blinding.

At any rate, apart from this final detail, the development is logical in *TR*, while it is confused in its major outline in *KJ*, and the argument goes that this is further evidence that *TR* was the original. If so, we have the curious Shakespeare of certain textual scholars, the man who grew toward mastery of his craft through carelessness in handling a perfectly clear source. That Shakespeare was sometimes careless—that he was careless here—there is no doubt; but his carelessness is of a differing kind if he is not following a source which has already solved the problem he then creates. Which is more likely: that an author finding confusion in his source would attempt to straighten it out? or that an author finding clarity would muddle it? It would appear, *prima facie*, more likely that *TR* followed *KJ* than that *KJ* followed *TR*. *TR*'s improvement at this point is of a piece with its supplying of motivation for the Bastard's resentment of Blanch's marriage, its supplying of a scene in the monastery and a scene dealing with John's poisoner; the author of *TR* was developing what appeared to him faulty or insufficient. The difference is that in the orders to Hubert there was a genuine confusion which, indeed, he only partially resolved.

How then, if I am arguing for the general superiority of Shakespeare's text and the superficiality of *TR*'s "improvements," how then do I account for the confusion of Shakespeare's handling of these scenes? First, it must be clear that any "inferiority" is in the single matter of inconsistent orders; the scenes are vastly superior in every other respect. Only the presence of the inconsistency needs explanation.

It would be difficult to account for the inconsistency if *KJ* were in fact based upon *TR*. However, the contradiction comes right out of Holinshed:

> True it is that great suit was made to have Arthur set at liberty, as well by the French king as by William de Riches, a valiant baron of Poictou, and divers other noblemen of Brittany, who, when they could not prevail in their suit, banded themselves together and, joining in confederacy with Robert, Earl of Alençon, the Viscount Beaumont, William de Fulgiers, and others, they began to levy sharp wars against King John in divers places, insomuch (as it was thought) that so long as Arthur lived there would be no quiet in those parts; whereupon it was reported that King John, through persuasion of his

counselors, appointed certain persons to go to Falais, where Arthur was kept in prison, under the charge of Hubert de Burgh, and there to put out the young gentleman's eyes.

The point is that the move from "so long as Arthur lived" to the order to "put out the young gentleman's eyes" is not logical in Holinshed, which thus provides a basis for the lack of logic in *KJ*. Furthermore, it is clear that Shakespeare's attention has been caught less by the illogicality, which he reproduces, than by the dramatic possibilities, especially the possibilities for thematic development of both stage and verse imagery in the attack by the "hot irons" of brute power upon the helpless eyes of suffering innocence. Shakespeare would not then be seen as a playwright who carelessly muddled a structure that was clear, as a botcher of someone else's play, but as an artist creating drama from the raw material of the chronicle. The structure he gave *KJ*, the structure indicated in my introduction, is his own; it is not in Holinshed, and it is mangled by *TR*. If he has taken over this one illogicality from his source, it is because his attention at that point was focused so firmly on the poetic possibilities. He was attempting to write a new kind of play, a play with a dramatic structure, not just a chronicle history; the man who tried to reproduce it in *TR* quite missed Shakespeare's point. He thought he was dealing with another play like one of the parts of *Henry VI*, and indeed the same man may have been responsible for all three quartos.

For *TR* may be seen as having the same relationship to *KJ* as *The First part of the Contention betwixt the two famous Houses of Yorke and Lancaster* and *The True Tragedie of Richard Duke of Yorke* have to *2* and *3 Henry VI*. Long considered to have been the sources of Shakespeare's plays, these are now generally acknowledged to have been "bad quartos," versions of Shakespeare's plays concocted on the basis of some familiarity with performances of them. *TR* may well be a bad quarto of similar origin; it need not be Shakespeare's source.

That Holinshed is Shakespeare's source, or one of his sources, is further attested (to give one or two of a multitude of examples) by the page in the chronicle at which we last looked. The succeeding paragraph concludes:

> Howbeit, to satisfy his mind for the time and to stay the rage of the Britains [men of Brittany], he [Hubert de Burgh] caused it to be bruited abroad through the country that the King's commandment was fulfilled, and that Arthur also, through sorrow and grief, was departed out of this life. For the space of fifteen days this rumor incessantly ran through both the realms of England and France, and there was ringing for him through the towns and villages as [though] it had been for his funeral.

Two pages earlier in Holinshed is the account of the spectacle of the five moons, but it is given no interpretation. Shakespeare brings these two items together in Hubert's report:

KING JOHN
Five moons?

HUBERT   Old men and beldams in the streets
Do prophesy upon it dangerously;
Young Arthur's death is common in their mouths.
(IV.ii.185–87)

And the Bastard has already reported: "I find the people strangely fantasied,/Possessed with rumors . . ." (IV.ii. 144–45). There is nothing of these rumors in *TR*; had that been Shakespeare's source, he would still have to be seen as having gone also to Holinshed. Similarly, Holinshed probably accounts for Shakespeare's use of the word "commodity." The Bastard has no commodity soliloquy in *TR*. Just after Holinshed's mention of the fall of Angiers, however, we find:

The French king all this while conceiving another exploit in his head, more commodious to him than as yet to attempt war against the Englishmen upon so light an occasion, dissembled the matter. . . .

It is in this coupling of "commodious" with dissembling that I would see the origin of Shakespeare's use of "commodity." Again, if he were using *TR*, he would still have to be seen as going to Holinshed. That is the position to which some scholars have in fact now arrived. If Shakespeare used Holinshed, however, he had no need of *TR*, while *TR* is difficult to explain on the basis of Holinshed without *KJ*—though its author did refer to some chronicle or other for a few details that Shakespeare had not used (the full name Hubert de Burgh, Chester and Beauchamp as the names of additional barons, and so on). Though neither case has yet been proved, I join Professors Alexander and Honigmann in thinking that the conflicting evidence tends to converge upon Holinshed as Shakespeare's major source and *TR* as a bad quarto.

Here for once we do not need to decide between Holinshed's chronicle and Hall's, for Hall does not deal with the reign of John. However, in inventing the character of the Bastard, based on a brief mention in Holinshed, it is clear that Shakespeare recalled an incident in Hall which he already knew in connection with his writing of *1 Henry VI*. He may have associated the name Faulconbridge with a bastard on the basis of another passage in Hall which he had used in *3 Henry VI*. There he has Margaret say, "Stern Faulconbridge commands the Narrow Seas" (I.i.239); in Hall, this man is identified as "one Thomas Nevel, bastard son to Thomas, Lord Faulconbridge, the valiant captain, a man of no less courage than audacity (who for [in spite of] his evil conditions was such an apt person that a more meet could not be chosen to set all the world in a broil, and to put the estate of the realm on an ill hazard), had of new begun a great commotion. This bastard was before this time appointed by the Earl of Warwick to be Vice-Admiral of the sea. . . ." Hall describes a foolhardy rebel against Edward IV; in Margaret's speech he is, of course, a faithful partisan of Henry VI. Since we know Shakespeare to have been working with this chronicle material for his preceding plays, we have here additional weight for the argument that he is the one who invented the Bastard of *KJ* as the blunt and dauntless Englishman. (This association in turn probably accounts for his giving the name Faulconbridge to Portia's English suitor, "a proper man's picture" but untaught in other languages, in *The Merchant of Venice*, I.ii. Shakespeare used the name elsewhere but with no strikingly obvious reason for the choice. Longaville's Maria is "an heir of Faulconbridge" in *Love's Labor's Lost* [II.i.205]. In the quarto text of *2 Henry IV* there is an entry for "Fauconbridge" among the

rebels [I.iii]; since he has no speeches, most editors drop him.) Though there are possibly other sources from which Shakespeare picked up a detail or two (Bullough reproduces several, as well as *TR*, in *Narrative and Dramatic Sources of Shakespeare*, IV), they are not central to the play.

Though the source question remains unsettled, and a serious investigator must naturally study *TR* also, I consider Holinshed's *Chronicles* to have been the point of departure for Shakespeare's creative imagination in *KJ*. These are now most conveniently studied in *Shakespeare's Holinshed*, a selection edited by Richard Hosley (1968). In comparing the play with the chronicles, as in comparing any of his plays with their literary sources—as in comparing the earlier history plays or the later *Macbeth* with other portions of the same chronicles—the point is in seeing not simply the source itself as a literary curiosity but what Shakespeare used, omitted, modified, or invented. It is in understanding his selective approach to a source that we can perhaps come closest to understanding how that creative imagination quickened raw substance into a work of art.

## A NOTE ON THE TEXT

Though mentioned by Francis Meres in 1598, *King John* was not printed until 1623, in the Folio. It has usually been thought that it must have been written between 1591, the publication date of *The Troublesome Reign of King John*, upon which many consider Shakespeare's play to have been based, and 1598, when Meres mentioned it. Since, as the Note on the Sources indicates, I am convinced that it preceded *The Troublesome Reign*, I naturally date Shakespeare's play before 1591, somewhere, probably, between 1588 and 1590. I would think that the writing of *1, 2, and 3 Henry VI*, certainly, and of *Richard III*, probably, preceded it, and thus I would differ on the dates of composition for all of these plays from those given in the table in the General Introduction (p. 5). *King John* should be seen as belonging with these early plays but, in its conception, a long step forward from them.

To see *The Troublesome Reign* as based upon Shakespeare's play is not to make it a trustworthy quarto. Its author imitates Shakespeare's plot but has little memory for his lines. The Folio remains the only substantive text.

Such inconsistencies as the Folio text contains suggest that the play was printed from author's manuscript and not from a theatrical promptbook. The chief of these inconsistencies is the Act II entry of "*a Citizen upon the walls*" of Angiers, followed by the speech-heading *Cit.* for his first four speeches, after which, in midscene, he becomes *Hubert* for one speech, and then *Hub.* Presumably this change represents the author's decision, while writing, to develop the anonymous Citizen into a character of importance to the plot, and such confusion of speech-heading would have been removed from the promptbook. To the detriment of the play, most editors have carried the unnamed Citizen through the act, thus introducing Hubert as a new character in III.ii. Hubert's development as a man forced to take a stand is only clear when we recognize his attempt to avoid involvement during Act II.

The errors in act and scene headings were presumably made by the compositor. His repetition of *Actus Quartus* where he needed *Actus Quintus* may have been carried over from his copy, but a less obvious confusion would seem most simply explained on the basis of his having misunderstood what he found. *Actus Primus, Scaena Prima* is followed by a *Scaena Secunda* covering more than four double-column pages, to be followed in turn by an *Actus Secundus* covering little more than half of one page, which makes for a total first act of more than seven pages, and a second act of less than one. Editors, following Theobald, have generally turned the *Scaena Secunda* into Act II, and *Actus Secundus* into III.i, which necessitates considering the Folio's *Actus Tertius, Scaena Prima* a further error. Since Constance throws herself to the ground at the conclusion of *Actus Secundus* and is apparently still there at the opening of *Actus Tertius* (in spite of her being listed as entering with the others), editors have felt justified in making those scenes continuous in spite of the indicated division.

It is much more likely, as Honigmann suggests in the Arden edition, that the compositor mistook a simple manuscript *two* (or *2*, or *II*), meaning Act II, as indicating Scene II, reversing the process when he came to the next *two* (or *2*, or *II*) and labeling an intended second scene of Act II as though it were the whole act. This edition therefore follows Honigmann and differs from other editors by including a II.ii and thus beginning III.i in accordance with the Folio. Given the continuous action of an Elizabethan production, the presence of Constance seated on stage from one act to the next is not a serious challenge to following the Folio at that point.

Several scholars have noted that, at III.i.81, the Folio prints "heaven" where the context clearly demands the word "God," and they have suggested that censorship intervened at some point between the original manuscript and the Folio. But editors have not considered the implications of this argument.

In only one other history play, *Henry VIII*, does "heaven" appear more frequently than "God" ("heaven" 44 times, "God" 21); in *1 Henry VI* and *3 Henry VI* they appear an equal number of times (16 times each in the first, 20 times each in the second); in the other five history plays "heaven" appears 115 times to "God's" 270, with the greatest discrepancy in *Richard III* (29 to 79). In all these plays, the lowest frequency of appearance of the word "God" is the 16 times it appears in *1 Henry VI*, and the highest frequency of the word "heaven" is the 44 times in *Henry VIII*. Compare with these figures the fact that "heaven" appears 51 times in the Folio text of *King John*, while "God" appears only 5 times, and the suggestion of censorship is greatly strengthened.

Such being likely, each appearance of the word "heaven" in this play becomes suspect. V.vii.60 is, as clearly as III.i.81, an instance in which "God" was the original

word. In phrases like "heaven and earth" (II.i.173), "clouds of heaven" (II.i.252), or "heaven or hell" (II.i.407), it is obvious that no change should be made. But this leaves a large group of doubtful instances. On the basis of context (verbal, rhythmic, and dramatic) I have made the change from "heaven" to "God" eight times where it seems thoroughly justified, as noted below. Eleven places where I would also prefer to make the change but, in line with the conservative textual policy of this edition, have not done so are I.i.83, 84, 256; II.i.373; III.i.162, 168, 192 (twice); IV.i.55; IV.iii.82; and V.i.29. Eighteen other places where the change would be possible but where, for contextual reasons (with which others might disagree), I would not make it are I.i.70; II.i.35, 86, 170, 171; III.i.22, 33, 34, 62; III.ii.37, 68; III.iii.48; IV.i.23, 91, 109; and IV.iii.10, 145, 159. (In addition to the three instances mentioned previously, I consider "heaven" obviously correct in II.i.174; III.ii.44; III.iii.77, 87, 158; IV.ii.15, 216; V.ii.52; V.v.1; and V.vii.72.)

Speech-headings in this edition are regularized by spelling them out in full. Spelling and punctuation have been modernized (conservatively), and obvious typographical errors have been corrected. I have changed to "*Dauphin*" and "*Melun*" in stage directions, but have left the old spellings, "*Dolphin*" and "*Meloone*," in the speeches for the sake of pronunciation. Other than these changes, departures from the Folio text are listed below, the adopted reading first, in boldface, followed by the original, in roman.

**I.i.1 s.d. with Chatillion** with the Chattylion **43 God** heauen **62 God** heauen **147 I would** It would **203 Pyrenean** Perennean **208 smack** smoake **237 Could he get me** Could get me **II.i. ACT II** Scaena Secunda **s.d. King Philip . . . Austria and his Attendants** Philip King of France, Lewis, Daulphin, Austria, Constance, Arthur **1 King Philip** Lewis [the text several times confuses the French king's name] **18 Ah, noble boy** A noble boy **63 Ate** Ace **127 Than thou and John in manners, being as like** Then thou and Iohn, in manners being as like **149 Philip** Lewis **150 King Philip** Lew. **152 Anjou** Angiers **201 s.d. Hubert** a Citizen [not identified as Hubert until the speech-heading at line 325] **215 Confronts your** Comfort yours **259 roundure** rounder **368 Hubert** Fra[nce]. **487 Anjou** Angiers [the error—see also II.i.152—is probably not the author's, for Angiers is the city excepted in line 489; cf. also line 528, where Folio has "Aniow"] **II.ii. Scene II** Actus Secundus **III.i.36 day** daies **74 task** tast **81 God** heauen **238 God** heauen **III.iii.64 friends** fends **IV.i.77 God's** heauen **91 mote** moth **IV.ii.1 again crowned** against crowned **42 when** then **73 Does** Do **IV.iii.33 man** mans **V. ACT V** Actus Quartus **V.ii.26 Were** Was **43 hast thou fought** hast fought **66 God** heauen **133 unhaired** vn-heard **V.v.3 measured** measure **V.vi.37 God** heauen **V.vii.17 mind** winde **21 cygnet** Symet **42 strait** straight **60 God** heauen

# THE LIFE AND DEATH OF
# KING JOHN

[Dramatis Personae

KING JOHN
PRINCE HENRY *son to the king*
ARTHUR *Duke of Brittany, nephew to the king*
BIGOT
ESSEX
PEMBROKE } *English lords*
SALISBURY
ROBERT FAULCONBRIDGE *son to Sir Robert
 Faulconbridge*
PHILIP THE BASTARD *his half brother*
HUBERT *a citizen of Angiers*
JAMES GURNEY *servant to Lady Faulconbridge*
PETER OF POMFRET *a prophet*
PHILIP *King of France*

LEWIS *the Dauphin* (*Dolphin*)
LYMOGES *Duke of Austria*
CARDINAL PANDULPH *the pope's legate*
COUNT MELUN (*Meloone*) *a French lord*
CHATILLION *ambassador from France*
QUEEN ELINOR *mother to King John*
CONSTANCE *mother to Arthur*
BLANCH OF SPAIN *niece to King John*
LADY FAULCONBRIDGE *widow to Sir Robert
 Faulconbridge*
LORDS SHERIFF HERALDS OFFICERS
 SOLDIERS EXECUTIONERS MESSENGERS
 OTHER ATTENDANTS

*Scene:* England and France]

## ACT I

Scene I. [*England. King John's court.*]

*Enter* KING JOHN, *Queen* ELINOR, PEMBROKE,
ESSEX, *and* SALISBURY, *with* CHATILLION *of France.*

KING JOHN
Now say, Chatillion, what would France with us?
CHATILLION
Thus, after greeting, speaks the King of France
In my behavior° to the majesty,
The borrowed° majesty, of England here.
ELINOR
A strange beginning: "borrowed majesty"!            5
KING JOHN
Silence, good mother; hear the embassy.

CHATILLION
Philip of France, in right and true behalf
Of thy deceasèd brother Geoffrey's son,
Arthur Plantagenet, lays most lawful claim
To this fair island and the territories:            10
To Ireland, Poictiers, Anjou, Touraine, Maine,
Desiring thee to lay aside the sword
Which sways usurpingly these several titles,
And put the same into young Arthur's hand,
Thy nephew and right royal sovereign.               15
KING JOHN
What follows if we disallow of° this?
CHATILLION
The proud control° of fierce and bloody war,
To enforce these rights so forcibly withheld.
KING JOHN
Here have we war for war and blood for blood,
Controlment° for controlment: so answer France.    20

*The decorative border shown above appeared on the first page of*
King John *in the First Folio edition of Shakespeare's plays, 1623.*
**I.i.3 In my behavior** through me   **4 borrowed** usurped

**16 disallow of** deny   **17 proud control** resolute compulsion
**20 Controlment** compulsion

**CHATILLION**
Then take my king's defiance from my mouth,
The farthest limit of° my embassy.

**KING JOHN**
Bear mine to him, and so depart in peace.
Be thou as lightning in the eyes of France,
For, ere thou canst report,° I will be there:    25
The thunder of my cannon shall be heard.
So, hence! Be thou the trumpet° of our wrath
And sullen presage of your own decay.°
An honorable conduct° let him have:
Pembroke, look to't. Farewell, Chatillion.    30

*Exit* CHATILLION *and* PEMBROKE.

**ELINOR**
What now, my son! Have I not ever said
How that ambitious Constance would not cease
Till she had kindled France and all the world
Upon the right and party of her son?
This might have been prevented and made whole    35
With very easy arguments of love,°
Which now the manage° of two kingdoms must
With fearful bloody issue arbitrate.

**KING JOHN**
Our strong possession and our right for us.

**ELINOR**
Your strong possession much more than your right,    40
Or else it must go wrong with you and me;
So much my conscience whispers in your ear,
Which none but God, and you, and I, shall hear.

*Enter a* SHERIFF.

**ESSEX**
My liege, here is the strangest controversy,
Come from the country to be judged by you,    45
That e'er I heard. Shall I produce the men?

**KING JOHN**
Let them approach.
Our abbeys and our priories shall pay
This expeditious charge.°

*Enter* ROBERT *Faulconbridge, and Philip [his* BASTARD
*brother].*

What men° are you?

**BASTARD**
Your faithful subject, I, a gentleman,    50
Born in Northamptonshire, and eldest son,
As I suppose, to Robert Faulconbridge,
A soldier, by the honor-giving hand
Of Cordelion° knighted in the field.

**KING JOHN**
What art thou?    55

**ROBERT**
The son and heir to that same Faulconbridge.

**KING JOHN**
Is that the elder, and art thou the heir?
You came not of one mother then, it seems.

**BASTARD**
Most certain of one mother, mighty king;
That is well known; and, as I think, one father:    60
But for the certain knowledge of that truth
I put you o'er° to God and to my mother;
Of that I doubt, as all men's children may.

**ELINOR**
Out on thee, rude man! Thou dost shame thy mother,
And wound her honor with this diffidence.°    65

**BASTARD**
I, madam? No, I have no reason for it;
That is my brother's plea and none of mine;
The which if he can prove, 'a° pops me out
At least from fair five hundred pound a year.
Heaven guard my mother's honor and my land!    70

**KING JOHN**
A good blunt fellow. Why, being younger born,
Doth he lay claim to thine inheritance?

**BASTARD**
I know not why, except to get the land.
But once he slandered me with bastardy.
But whe'r° I be as true begot or no,    75
That still I lay upon my mother's head;°
But that I am as well begot, my liege—
Fair fall° the bones that took the pains for me—
Compare our faces and be judge yourself.
If old Sir Robert did beget us both,    80
And were our father, and this son like him,
O old Sir Robert, father, on my knee
I give heaven thanks I was not like to thee!

**KING JOHN**
Why, what a madcap hath heaven lent us here!

**ELINOR**
He hath a trick° of Cordelion's face;    85
The accent of his tongue affecteth° him:
Do you not read some tokens of my son
In the large composition° of this man?

**KING JOHN**
Mine eye hath well examinèd his parts,
And finds them perfect Richard. Sirrah, speak,    90
What doth move you° to claim your brother's land?

**BASTARD**
Because he hath a half-face° like my father!
With half that face° would he have all my land—
A half-faced groat° five hundred pound a year!

**ROBERT**
My gracious liege, when that my father lived,    95
Your brother did employ my father much—

**BASTARD**
Well sir, by this you cannot get my land:
Your tale must be how he employed my mother.

**ROBERT**
And once dispatched° him in an embassy

**22 farthest limit of** most extreme measure permitted by
**25 report** (1) give an account (2) make a noise like a gun (cf.
"thunder," line 26) **27 trumpet** herald **28 sullen presage
. . . decay** gloomy foreteller of your own destruction **29
conduct** escort **36 arguments of love** (1) expressions of
love (2) friendly discussions (?) **37 manage** government(s)
**49 expeditious charge** (1) sudden expense (2) speedy attack;
**What men** who (of what name) **54 Cordelion** *Coeur de
Lion* (Lionhearted), i.e., King Richard I, John's older brother

**62 put you o'er** refer you **65 diffidence** mistrust **68 'a** he
**75 whe'r** whether **76 lay . . . head** leave up to my mother
**78 Fair fall** may good befall **85 trick** distinctive trait **86
affecteth** tends toward, resembles **88 large composition**
(1) large size (2) general features **91 you** Robert (John shows
his partiality for the Bastard by the shift of pronoun—cf. line
55—and by his use of the slightly contemptuous "Sirrah")
**92 half-face** (1) profile (2) imperfect or emaciated face **93
With . . . face** (1) with a face like that (2) with such impudence
**94 half-faced groat** (1) small silver coin with a profile stamped
on it (2) imperfect or clipped coin **99 dispatched** (1) sent
(2) disposed of

To Germany, there with the emperor                                100
To treat of high affairs touching that time.
Th' advantage of his absence took the king,
And in the meantime sojourned at my father's,
Where how he did prevail I shame to speak—
But truth is truth: large lengths of seas and shores        105
Between my father and my mother lay,
As I have heard my father speak himself,
When this same lusty° gentleman was got.°
Upon his deathbed he by will bequeathed
His lands to me, and took it on his death°            110
That this my mother's son was none of his;
And if° he were, he came into the world
Full fourteen weeks before the course of time.
Then, good my liege, let me have what is mine,
My father's land, as was my father's will.            115

KING JOHN
Sirrah, your brother is legitimate.
Your father's wife did after wedlock bear him;
And if she did play false, the fault was hers;
Which fault lies on° the hazards of all husbands
That marry wives. Tell me, how if my brother,    120
Who, as you say, took pains to get this son,
Had of your father claimed this son for his?
In sooth, good friend, your father might have kept
This calf, bred from his cow, from all the world.
In sooth he might; then, if he were my brother's,    125
My brother might not claim him, nor your father,
Being none of his, refuse him: this concludes.°
My mother's son did get your father's heir;
Your father's heir must have your father's land.

ROBERT
Shall then my father's will be of no force          130
To dispossess that child which is not his?

BASTARD
Of no more force to dispossess me, sir,
Than was his will to get me, as I think.

ELINOR
Whether hadst thou° rather be, a Faulconbridge,
And like thy brother,° to enjoy thy land,          135
Or the reputed son of Cordelion,
Lord of thy presence° and no land beside?

BASTARD
Madam, and if my brother had my shape
And I had his, Sir Robert's his,° like him,
And if my legs were two such riding-rods,°          140
My arms such eelskins stuffed, my face so thin
That in mine ear I durst not stick a rose
Lest men should say, "Look, where three-farthings°
    goes!"
And, to° his shape, were heir to all this land,
Would I might never stir from off this place,      145

I would give it every foot to have this face:
I would not be Sir Nob° in any case.°

ELINOR
I like thee well: wilt thou forsake thy fortune,
Bequeath° thy land to him, and follow me?
I am a soldier and now bound to France.            150

BASTARD
Brother, take you my land, I'll take my chance.
Your face hath got five hundred pound a year,
Yet sell your face for fivepence and 'tis dear.
Madam, I'll follow you unto the death.

ELINOR
Nay, I would have you go before me thither.        155

BASTARD
Our country manners give our betters way.

KING JOHN
What is thy name?

BASTARD
Philip, my liege, so is my name begun—
Philip, good old Sir Robert's wife's eldest son.

KING JOHN
From henceforth bear his name whose form thou
    bearest:                                                    160
Kneel thou down Philip, but rise more great,
Arise Sir Richard, and Plantagenet.°

BASTARD
Brother by th' mother's side, give me your hand:
My father gave me honor, yours gave land.
Now blessèd be the hour,° by night or day,        165
When I was got, Sir Robert was away!

ELINOR
The very spirit of Plantagenet!
I am thy grandam, Richard; call me so.

BASTARD
Madam, by chance but not by truth;° what though?
Something about,° a little from the right,          170
In at the window, or else o'er the hatch:
Who dares not stir by day must walk by night,
And have is have, however men do catch.
Near or far off, well won is still well shot,°
And I am I, howe'er I was begot.                      175

KING JOHN
Go, Faulconbridge. Now hast thou thy desire:
A landless knight makes° thee a landed squire.
Come, madam, and come, Richard, we must speed
For France, for France, for it is more than need.

BASTARD
Brother, adieu: good fortune come to thee!          180
For thou wast got i' th' way of honesty.
                              *Exeunt all but* BASTARD.
A foot of honor better than I was,
But many a many foot of land the worse.
Well, now can I make any Joan° a lady.

---

**108 lusty** merry; **got** conceived   **110 took . . . death** swore at the peril of his soul   **112 And if** if (a frequent Elizabethan usage)   **119 lies on** is among   **127 concludes** is decisive   **134 Whether hadst thou** which would you   **135 like thy brother** resembling Robert (in physique and character)   **137 Lord . . . presence** master of your own physique and character   **139 Sir Robert's his** Sir Robert's (a double genitive)   **140 riding-rods** switches for horses   **143 three-farthings** the smallest of a number of coins which were distinguished from coins of similar sizes by the presence of a rose behind the ear in Queen Elizabeth's portrait   **144 to** in addition to

**147 Nob** nickname for Robert (?)—perhaps with puns on *head* and *knob*, continuing mockery of his brother's appearance; **in any case** (1) under any circumstances (2) in any covering (clothing, body)   **149 Bequeath** legally transfer (immediately; his death is not implied)   **162 Plantagenet** surname of the royal family   **165 hour** (1) hour (2) whore (then identically pronounced)   **169 truth** virtue   **170 Something about** a bit off course   **171–74 In . . . shot** all proverbial expressions   **177 A landless knight makes** (1) the Bastard makes (2) making the Bastard landless makes   **184 Joan** common girl

"Good den, Sir Richard!"—"God-amercy,° fel-
low"°—                     185
And if his name be George, I'll call him Peter,
For new-made honor doth forget men's names:
'Tis too respective and too sociable
For your conversion.° Now your traveler,
He and his toothpick° at my worship's mess,°     190
And when my knightly stomach is sufficed,
Why then I suck my teeth° and catechize
My pickèd° man of countries: "My dear sir"—
Thus, leaning on mine elbow, I begin—
"I shall beseech you"—that is Question now;     195
And then comes Answer like an Absey-book:°
"O, sir," says Answer, "at your best command,
At your employment, at your service, sir";
"No, sir," says Question, "I, sweet sir, at yours";
And so, ere Answer knows what Question would,    200
Saving in dialogue of compliment,
And talking of the Alps and Apennines,
The Pyrenean and the river Po,
It draws toward supper in conclusion so.
But this is worshipful society,               205
And fits the mounting spirit like myself;
For he is but a bastard to the time°
That doth not smack of observation.°
And so am I, whether I smack or no:
And not alone in habit and device,°           210
Exterior form, outward accoutrement,
But from the inward motion° to deliver
Sweet, sweet, sweet poison° for the age's tooth,
Which, though I will not practice to deceive,
Yet, to avoid deceit,° I mean to learn;          215
For it shall strew the footsteps of my rising.°
But who comes in such haste in riding-robes?
What woman-post° is this? Hath she no husband
That will take pains to blow a horn before her?°

*Enter* LADY FAULCONBRIDGE *and James* GURNEY.

O me! 'Tis my mother. How now, good lady!    220
What brings you here to court so hastily?
LADY FAULCONBRIDGE
Where is that slave, thy brother? Where is he,
That holds in chase° mine honor up and down?

BASTARD
My brother Robert? Old Sir Robert's son?
Colbrand the giant,° that same mighty man?    225
Is it Sir Robert's son that you seek so?
LADY FAULCONBRIDGE
Sir Robert's son? Aye, thou unreverend boy,
Sir Robert's son! Why scorn'st thou at Sir Robert?
He is Sir Robert's son, and so art thou.
BASTARD
James Gurney, wilt thou give us leave awhile?    230
GURNEY
Good leave,° good Philip.
BASTARD                  Philip, sparrow!° James,
There's toys° abroad: anon I'll tell thee more.
                      *Exit James* [GURNEY].
Madam, I was not old Sir Robert's son.
Sir Robert might have eat his part in me
Upon Good Friday and ne'er broke his fast:    235
Sir Robert could do well—marry, to confess°—
Could he get me! Sir Robert could not do it.
We know his handiwork: therefore, good mother,
To whom am I beholding for these limbs?
Sir Robert never holp° to make this leg.°     240
LADY FAULCONBRIDGE
Hast thou conspirèd with thy brother too,
That for thine own gain shouldst defend mine honor?
What means this scorn, thou most untoward° knave?
BASTARD
Knight, knight, good mother, Basilisco-like.°
What! I am dubbed; I have it on my shoulder.    245
But, mother, I am not Sir Robert's son;
I have disclaimed Sir Robert and my land;
Legitimation, name, and all is gone.
Then, good my mother, let me know my father;
Some proper° man I hope: who was it, mother?    250
LADY FAULCONBRIDGE
Hast thou denied thyself a Faulconbridge?
BASTARD
As faithfully as I deny the devil.
LADY FAULCONBRIDGE
King Richard Cordelion was thy father.
By long and vehement suit I was seduced
To make room for him in my husband's bed.    255
Heaven lay not my transgression to my charge,
That art° the issue of my dear offense,
Which was so strongly urged past my defense.
BASTARD
Now, by this light, were I to get° again,
Madam, I would not wish a better father.     260
Some sins do bear their privilege° on earth,
And so doth yours: your fault was not your folly.

185 Good den . . . God-amercy usual greetings (elisions of "God give you good evening" and "God have mercy on you"); fellow used for one of lower rank   188–89 'Tis . . . conversion It (remembering names) is too respectful and too amiable for my change in rank ("your" is general and vague: any conversion)   190 toothpick an un-English affectation; mess dinner table   192 suck my teeth scorning a toothpick   193 pickèd (1) affected (2) with his teeth picked   196 Abseybook ABC book, a child's question-and-answer primer   207 but . . . time not a true child of his time   208 observation (1) paying attention (2) obsequiousness   210 habit and device dress and emblem (the heraldic symbol on his shield will be crossed by a black band, the "bar sinister" denoting a bastard)   212 motion incitement, intention   213 sweet poison flattery   215 deceit deception (i.e., being deceived)   216 it . . . rising flattery will be thrown before me as I rise just as flowers are thrown to welcome a great man   218 woman-post female messenger   219 blow . . . her (1) clear the way for her (as a herald announced an important arrival, or as the speeding post blew his post horn) (2) announce her adultery (the cuckold was said to wear horns)   223 holds in chase pursues (as a huntsman)

225 Colbrand the giant Guy of Warwick's final opponent in the popular old romances   231 Good leave willingly; Philip, sparrow Philip, a common name for a pet sparrow, is too paltry for the newly knighted Bastard   232 toys trifling gifts (i.e., knighthoods) or rumors (?)   236 marry, to confess indeed, to speak the truth   240 holp helped; to . . . leg (1) to form a leg like mine (2) to give me courtly manners like this (to make a leg = to bow; the Bastard must bow, perhaps ironically, as he requests her answer)   243 untoward perverse, ill-mannered   244 Basilisco-like Basilisco was a bragging knight in an earlier play, Soliman and Perseda   250 proper handsome, respectable   257 That art thou that art   259 get be conceived   261 bear their privilege carry their immunity (because of their good results?)

Needs must you lay your heart at his dispose,
Subjected tribute° to commanding love,
Against whose fury and unmatchèd force                    265
The aweless lion could not wage the fight,
Nor keep his princely heart from Richard's hand.°
He that perforce robs lions of their hearts
May easily win a woman's. Ay, my mother,
With all my heart I thank thee for my father!°           270
Who lives and dares but say thou didst not well
When I was got, I'll send his soul to hell.
Come, lady, I will show thee to my kin,
And they shall say, when Richard me begot,
If thou hadst said him nay, it had been sin.             275
Who says it was, he lies; I say 'twas not!°   Exeunt.


# ACT II

## [Scene I. France.]

*Enter before [the gate of] Angiers, KING PHILIP of France,
LEWIS the Dauphin, CONSTANCE, ARTHUR, and their
ATTENDANTS and, from the other side, AUSTRIA and his
ATTENDANTS.*

KING PHILIP
Before Angiers well met, brave Austria.
Arthur, that great forerunner of thy blood,°
Richard, that robbed the lion of his heart
And fought the holy wars in Palestine,
By this brave duke° came early to his grave;            5
And for amends to his posterity,
At our importance° hither is he come
To spread his colors,° boy, in thy behalf,
And to rebuke the usurpation
Of thy unnatural uncle, English John:                   10
Embrace him, love him, give him welcome hither.
ARTHUR
God shall forgive you Cordelion's death
The rather that you give his offspring life,
Shadowing° their right under your wings of war.
I give you welcome with a powerless hand,               15
But with a heart full of unstainèd love:
Welcome before the gates of Angiers, duke.
LEWIS
Ah, noble boy, who would not do thee right?
AUSTRIA
Upon thy cheek lay I this zealous kiss,
As seal to this indenture° of my love:                  20
That to my home I will no more return
Till Angiers, and the right thou hast in France,

Together with that pale, that white-faced shore,°
Whose foot spurns back the ocean's roaring tides
And coops° from other lands her islanders,              25
Even till that England, hedged in with the main,
That water-wallèd bulwark, still° secure
And confident from foreign purposes,
Even till that utmost corner of the west
Salute thee for her king; till then, fair boy,          30
Will I not think of home, but follow arms.
CONSTANCE
O take his mother's thanks, a widow's thanks,
Till your strong hand shall help to give him strength
To make a more requital to° your love.
AUSTRIA
The peace of heaven is theirs that lift their swords    35
In such a just and charitable war.
KING PHILIP
Well then, to work: our cannon shall be bent°
Against the brows of this resisting town.
Call for our chiefest men of discipline,°
To cull the plots of best advantages.°                  40
We'll lay before this town our royal bones,
Wade to the marketplace in Frenchmen's blood:
But we will make it subject to this boy.
CONSTANCE
Stay for an answer to your embassy,
Lest unadvised you stain your swords with blood.        45
My Lord Chatillion may from England bring
That right in peace which here we urge in war,
And then we shall repent each drop of blood
That hot rash haste so indirectly° shed.

*Enter CHATILLION.*

KING PHILIP
A wonder, lady! Lo, upon thy wish,                       50
Our messenger Chatillion is arrived!
What England says, say briefly, gentle lord;
We coldly pause for thee; Chatillion, speak.
CHATILLION
Then turn your forces from this paltry siege
And stir them up against a mightier task:               55
England, impatient of your just demands,
Hath put himself in arms; the adverse winds,
Whose leisure I have stayed, have given him time
To land his legions all as soon as I;
His marches are expedient° to this town,                60
His forces strong, his soldiers confident.
With him along is come the mother-queen,
An Ate,° stirring him to blood and strife;
With her her niece, the Lady Blanch of Spain;
With them a bastard of the king's deceased;°            65
And all th' unsettled humors° of the land,
Rash, inconsiderate, fiery voluntaries,°

---

264 **Subjected tribute** tribute required of a vassal  266–67 **The . . . hand** the legend was that Richard's epithet came from his having eaten the heart he tore out by reaching, barehanded, down the throat of a living lion  270 **for my father** (1) on behalf of my father (2) for the father you have given me  276 **not** (1) not (2) naught, i.e., nothing (3) naught, i.e., wickedness (sexual immorality; cf. *Richard III*, I.i.97–100)  **II.i.2 forerunner . . . blood** predecessor in your line (Arthur was Richard's nephew)  5 **this brave duke** Austria (that Austria killed Richard is not historical, but see note to III.i.40)  7 **importance** importunity  8 **spread his colors** unfurl his battle flags  14 **Shadowing** sheltering  20 **indenture** sealed agreement

23 **that pale, that white-faced shore** reference to the chalk cliffs on England's southern coast (a pale is also a limited territory)  25 **coops** encloses for protection  27 **still** always  34 **more requital to** larger recompense for  37 **bent** aimed (as is a bow)  39 **discipline** military training  40 **To . . . advantages** to choose the best location (for the cannons)  49 **indirectly** wrongly  60 **expedient** speedy  63 **Ate** goddess of vengeance  65 **of . . . deceased** of the deceased king  66 **unsettled humors** unsteady rabble (humors were bodily fluids, the balance of which supposedly determined a man's disposition)  67 **voluntaries** volunteers

With ladies' faces and fierce dragons' spleens,°
Have sold their fortunes at their native homes,
Bearing their birthrights proudly on their backs,°    70
To make a hazard of° new fortunes here.
In brief, a braver choice of dauntless spirits
Than now the English bottoms° have waft o'er
Did never float upon the swelling tide,
To do offense and scathe in Christendom.    75

*Drum beats.*

The interruption of their churlish drums
Cuts off more circumstance:° they are at hand,
To parley or to fight; therefore prepare.

KING PHILIP
How much unlooked for is this expedition!°

AUSTRIA
By how much unexpected, by so much    80
We must awake endeavor for defense,
For courage mounteth with occasion:
Let them be welcome then; we are prepared.

*Enter* KING [JOHN] *of England,* BASTARD, *Queen*
[ELINOR], BLANCH, PEMBROKE, *and others.*

KING JOHN
Peace be to France, if France in peace permit
Our just and lineal° entrance to our own;    85
If not, bleed France, and peace ascend to heaven,
Whiles we, God's wrathful agent, do correct°
Their proud contempt that beats His peace to heaven.

KING PHILIP
Peace be to England, if that war return
From France to England, there to live in peace.    90
England we love, and for that England's sake
With burden of our armor here we sweat.
This toil of ours should be a work of thine,
But thou from loving England art so far
That thou hast underwrought° his lawful king,    95
Cut off the sequence of posterity,
Outfacèd infant state,° and done a rape
Upon the maiden virtue of the crown.
Look here upon thy brother Geoffrey's face:
These eyes, these brows, were molded out of his;    100
This little abstract° doth contain that large
Which died in Geoffrey, and the hand of time
Shall draw this brief into as huge a volume.
That Geoffrey was thy elder brother born,
And this his son; England was Geoffrey's right    105
And this° is Geoffrey's in the name of God.
How comes it then that thou art called a king,
When living blood doth in these temples beat,
Which owe° the crown that thou o'ermasterest?

KING JOHN
From whom hast thou this great commission, France,    110
To draw my answer from thy articles?°

KING PHILIP
From that supernal judge that stirs good thoughts
In any beast of strong authority
To look into the blots and stains of right;
That judge hath made me guardian to this boy,    115
Under whose warrant I impeach thy wrong
And by whose help I mean to chastise it.

KING JOHN
Alack, thou dost usurp authority.

KING PHILIP
Excuse it is to beat usurping down.

ELINOR
Who is it thou dost call usurper, France?    120

CONSTANCE
Let me make answer: thy usurping son.

ELINOR
Out, insolent! Thy bastard shall be king
That thou mayst be a queen° and check the world!

CONSTANCE
My bed was ever to thy son as true
As thine was to thy husband, and this boy    125
Liker in feature to his father Geoffrey
Than thou and John in manners, being as like
As rain to water, or devil to his dam.
My boy a bastard! By my soul I think
His father never was so true begot:    130
It cannot be and if thou wert his mother.

ELINOR
There's a good mother, boy, that blots thy father.

CONSTANCE
There's a good grandam, boy, that would blot thee.

AUSTRIA
Peace!

BASTARD    Hear the crier.°

AUSTRIA               What the devil art thou?

BASTARD
One that will play the devil, sir, with you,    135
And 'a° may catch your hide° and you alone:
You are the hare of whom the proverb goes,
Whose valor plucks dead lions by the beard.
I'll smoke° your skin-coat, and I catch you right;
Sirrah, look to't; i' faith, I will, i' faith.    140

BLANCH
O well did he become that lion's robe,
That did disrobe the lion of that robe!

BASTARD
It lies as sightly° on the back of him
As great Alcides' shoes upon an ass.°
But, ass, I'll take that burden from your back,    145
Or lay on that shall make your shoulders crack.

AUSTRIA
What cracker° is this same that deafs our ears
With this abundance of superfluous breath?
King Philip, determine what we shall do straight.

---

68 **spleens** the spleen was considered the location of the emotions   70 **Bearing . . . backs** having invested their patrimonies in armor   71 **make . . . of** take a chance on winning   73 **bottoms** ships   77 **circumstance** detailed information   79 **expedition** speed   85 **lineal** inherited   87 **correct** chastise   95 **underwrought** undermined   97 **Outfacèd infant state** arrogantly defied the child king   101 **abstract** summary, abridgment (cf. "brief" and "volume" in line 103)   106 **this** possibly the English crown, which John is wearing, the city of Angiers, or Arthur himself   109 **owe** own   111 **To . . . articles** to compel me to answer your accusations

123 **queen** (1) queen (2) *quean* = whore (3) queen in chess (cf. "check" later in line)   134 **crier** law-court official who called for silence   136 **And 'a** if he; **hide** Richard's lionskin, which Austria is wearing   139 **smoke** (1) disinfect (2) beat   143 **sightly** handsomely   144 **Alcides' . . . ass** (1) Hercules' shoes (proverbial) on an ass (2) Hercules appears (Folio's "shoces" may also mean shows) mounted on an ass (3) Hercules' lionskin (he wore the skin of the Nemean lion which he had killed) appears on an ass   147 **cracker** (1) braggart (2) firecracker

KING PHILIP
Women and fools, break off your conference.            150
King John, this is the very sum of all:
England and Ireland, Anjou, Touraine, Maine,
In right of Arthur do I claim of thee:
Wilt thou resign them and lay down thy arms?

KING JOHN
My life as soon! I do defy thee, France.               155
Arthur of Britain,° yield thee to my hand,
And out of my dear love I'll give thee more
Than e'er the coward hand of France can win;
Submit thee, boy.

ELINOR                    Come to thy grandam, child.

CONSTANCE
Do, child, go to it grandam, child;                    160
Give grandam kingdom, and it grandam will
Give it a plum, a cherry, and a fig;
There's a good grandam.°

ARTHUR                    Good my mother, peace!
I would that I were low laid in my grave.
I am not worth this coil° that's made for me.          165

ELINOR
His mother shames him so, poor boy, he weeps.

CONSTANCE
Now shame upon you, whe'r she does or no!
His grandam's wrongs, and not his mother's shames,
Draws° those heaven-moving pearls from his poor eyes,
Which heaven shall take in nature of° a fee:           170
Ay, with these crystal beads heaven shall be bribed°
To do him justice and revenge on you.

ELINOR
Thou monstrous slanderer of heaven and earth!

CONSTANCE
Thou monstrous injurer of heaven and earth!
Call not me slanderer; thou and thine usurp           175
The dominations,° royalties, and rights
Of this oppressèd boy: this is thy eldest son's son,°
Infortunate in nothing but in thee:
Thy sins are visited° in this poor child;
The canon of the law° is laid on him,                 180
Being but the second generation
Removèd from thy sin-conceiving womb.

KING JOHN
Bedlam,° have done.

CONSTANCE                    I have but this to say,
That he is not only plaguèd for her sin,
But God hath made her sin° and her the plague°        185
On this removèd issue,° plagued for her
And with her plague; her sin his injury,
Her injury the beadle° to her sin,
All punished in the person of this child,
And all for her; a plague upon her!                   190

156 **Britain** Brittany  160–63 **Do . . . grandam** baby talk
165 **coil** fuss  169 **Draws** draw (it is not unusual for a plural
subject to have a verb in -s)  170 **in nature of** in place of, as
though it were  171 **with . . . bribed** these crystal beads—
pearls, tears—will bribe heaven both as precious gems and as
prayer beads  176 **dominations** dominions  177 **eldest son's
son** oldest grandson (*not* oldest-son's son)  179 **visited** punished
180 **canon . . . law** Exodus 20:5  183 **Bedlam** lunatic  185
**her sin** John (?); **the plague** the great plagues were commonly explained as punishment for a sinful nation—Elinor is
both the cause of Arthur's punishment and that punishment
itself  186 **this removèd issue** this remote descendant (i.e.,
Arthur)  188 **beadle** parish official who whipped sinners

ELINOR
Thou unadvisèd scold, I can produce
A will° that bars the title of thy son.

CONSTANCE
Aye, who doubts that? A will! A wicked will;
A woman's will;° a cankered grandam's will!

KING PHILIP
Peace, lady! Pause, or be more temperate:             195
It ill beseems this presence° to cry aim
To° these ill-tunèd repetitions.
Some trumpet summon hither to the walls
These men of Angiers. Let us hear them speak
Whose title they admit, Arthur's or John's.           200

*Trumpet sounds.*

*Enter* HUBERT *upon the walls.*

HUBERT
Who is it that hath warned° us to the walls?

KING PHILIP
'Tis France, for England.

KING JOHN                    England for itself.
You men of Angiers, and my loving subjects—

KING PHILIP
You loving men of Angiers, Arthur's subjects,
Our trumpet called you to this gentle parle°—         205

KING JOHN
For our advantage; therefore hear us first:
These flags of France, that are advancèd° here
Before the eye and prospect of your town,
Have hither marched to your endamagement.
The cannons have their bowels full of wrath,          210
And ready mounted are they to spit forth
Their iron indignation 'gainst your walls.
All preparation for a bloody siege
And merciless proceeding by these French
Confronts your city's eyes, your winking° gates,      215
And but for our approach those sleeping stones,
That as a waist° doth girdle you about,
By the compulsion of their ordinance°
By this time from their fixèd beds of lime
Had been dishabited,° and wide havoc made             220
For bloody power to rush upon your peace.
But on the sight of us your lawful king,
Who painfully with much expedient march
Have brought a countercheck before your gates,
To save unscratched your city's threatened cheeks,    225
Behold, the French, amazed, vouchsafe a parle;
And now, instead of bullets wrapped in fire,
To make a shaking fever in your walls,
They shoot but calm words folded up in smoke,
To make a faithless error° in your ears;              230
Which trust accordingly, kind citizens,
And let us in, your king, whose labored° spirits,
Forwearied° in this action of swift speed,
Craves harborage within your city walls.

192 **A will** Richard's will named John his heir; Shakespeare
plays this down to present John as a usurper  194 **A woman's
will** Constance suggests that Elinor wrote the will, and
women's wills were not legal  196 **presence** royal assembly
196–97 **cry aim To** encourage  201 **warned** summoned  205
**parle** parley  207 **advancèd** raised  215 **winking** able to
open and shut (the gates are like eyelids)  217 **waist** belt or
sash  218 **ordinance** cannons  220 **dishabited** disinhabited,
dislodged  230 **faithless error** treacherous lie  232 **labored**
overworked  233 **Forwearied** tired out

KING PHILIP
When I have said,° make answer to us both.                    235
Lo, in this right hand, whose protection
Is most divinely vowed upon the right
Of him it holds, stands young Plantagenet,
Son to the elder brother of this man,
And king o'er him and all that he enjoys:                    240
For this downtrodden equity° we tread
In warlike march these greens before your town,
Being no further enemy to you
Than the constraint of hospitable zeal°
In the relief of this oppressèd child                    245
Religiously provokes. Be pleasèd then
To pay that duty which you truly owe
To him that owes° it, namely this young prince;
And then our arms, like to a muzzled bear,
Save in aspect, hath° all offense sealed up:                    250
Our cannons' malice vainly shall be spent
Against th' invulnerable clouds of heaven,
And with a blessèd and unvexed retire,°
With unhacked swords and helmets all unbruised,
We will bear home that lusty blood again                    255
Which here we came to spout against your town,
And leave your children, wives, and you in peace.
But if you fondly pass° our proffered offer,
'Tis not the roundure° of your old-faced walls°
Can hide you from our messengers of war,                    260
Though all these English and their discipline
Were harbored in their rude circumference.
Then tell us, shall your city call us° lord,
In that behalf which° we have challenged it?
Or shall we give the signal to our rage                    265
And stalk in blood to our possession?
HUBERT
In brief, we are the King of England's subjects:
For him, and in his right, we hold this town.
KING JOHN
Acknowledge then the king, and let me in.
HUBERT
That can we not; but he that proves° the king,                    270
To him will we prove loyal: till that time
Have we rammed up° our gates against the world.
KING JOHN
Doth not the crown of England prove the king?
And if not that, I bring you witnesses,
Twice fifteen thousand hearts of England's breed—                    275
BASTARD
Bastards, and else.°
KING JOHN
To verify our title with their lives.
KING PHILIP
As many and as wellborn bloods° as those—
BASTARD
Some bastards, too.

KING PHILIP
Stand in his face to contradict his claim.                    280
HUBERT
Till you compound° whose right is worthiest,
We for the worthiest hold the right from both.
KING JOHN
Then God forgive the sin of all those souls
That to their everlasting residence,
Before the dew of evening fall, shall fleet,°                    285
In dreadful trial of our kingdom's king!
KING PHILIP
Amen, amen! Mount, chevaliers! To arms!
BASTARD
Saint George, that swinged° the dragon, and e'er since
Sits on's horseback at mine hostess' door,°
Teach us some fence!° [To AUSTRIA.] Sirrah, were I                    290
    at home
At your den, sirrah, with your lioness,
I would set an ox head to your lion's hide,
And make a monster° of you.
AUSTRIA                                   Peace! No more.
BASTARD
O tremble, for you hear the lion roar.
KING JOHN
Up higher to the plain, where we'll set forth                    295
In best appointment all our regiments.
BASTARD
Speed then, to take advantage of the field.
KING PHILIP
It shall be so; and at the other hill
Command the rest to stand. God, and our right!
                                        *Exeunt.*

*Here, after excursions,° enter the* HERALD OF FRANCE
*with trumpets, to the gates.*

FRENCH HERALD
You men of Angiers, open wide your gates,                    300
And let young Arthur, Duke of Britain, in,
Who by the hand of France this day hath made
Much work for tears in many an English mother,
Whose sons lie scattered on the bleeding ground:
Many a widow's husband groveling lies,                    305
Coldly embracing the discolored earth,
And victory with little loss doth play
Upon the dancing banners of the French,
Who are at hand, triumphantly displayed,°
To enter conquerors and to proclaim                    310
Arthur of Britain England's king, and yours.

*Enter* ENGLISH HERALD, *with trumpet.*

ENGLISH HERALD
Rejoice, you men of Angiers, ring your bells:
King John, your king and England's, doth approach,
Commander of this hot malicious day.
Their armors, that marched hence so silver-bright,                    315
Hither return all gilt° with Frenchmen's blood;

235 said finished speaking  241 equity right  244 the . . . zeal
the obligations of generous resolution  248 owes owns  250
hath will have  253 unvexed retire orderly departure  258
fondly pass foolishly disregard  259 roundure roundness;
old-faced walls walls so well built they had not required
refacing  263 us King Philip (England, with Arthur as king,
would be subordinate to France)  264 In . . . which on behalf of him for whom  270 proves proves to be  272 rammed up barricaded  276 else others  278 bloods (1) men of
courage (2) men of good family

281 compound settle  285 fleet pass away, fly  288
swinged beat  289 Sits . . . door painted on an inn sign
290 fence skill with the sword  293 monster (1) ox-headed
lion (2) cuckold  299 s.d. excursions sallies, raids (in the
theater, stage-crossings and clashes to represent a battle)  309
displayed spread out (for a parade, not for a battle)  316 gilt
gilded, i.e., reddened (gold was considered red as in "his
golden blood," *Macbeth,* II.iii.114)

There stuck no plume in any English crest
That is removèd by a staff° of France.
Our colors do return in those same hands
That did display them when we first marched forth,   320
And, like a jolly troop of huntsmen, come
Our lusty English, all with purpled hands,
Dyed in the dying slaughter° of their foes.
Open your gates and give the victors way.

HUBERT
Heralds, from off our tow'rs we might behold,   325
From first to last, the onset and retire°
Of both your armies, whose equality
By our best eyes cannot be censured.°
Blood hath bought blood, and blows have answered
   blows,
Strength matched with strength, and power confronted
   power.   330
Both are alike, and both alike we like:
One must prove greatest. While they weigh so even,
We hold our town for neither, yet for both.

*Enter the two* KINGS, *with their* POWERS, *at several°
doors.*

KING JOHN
France, hast thou yet more blood to cast away?
Say, shall the current of our right roam on?   335
Whose passage, vexed with thy impediment,
Shall leave his native channel and o'erswell,
With course disturbed, even thy confining shores,
Unless thou let his silver water keep
A peaceful progress to the ocean.   340

KING PHILIP
England, thou hast not saved one drop of blood
In this hot trial more than we of France;
Rather, lost more. And by this hand I swear,
That sways the earth this climate overlooks,
Before we will lay down our just-borne arms,   345
We'll put thee down, 'gainst whom these arms we
   bear,
Or add a royal number° to the dead,
Gracing the scroll that tells of this war's loss
With slaughter coupled to the name of kings.°

BASTARD
Ha, majesty! How high thy glory tow'rs°   350
When the rich blood of kings is set on fire!
O now doth Death line his dead chaps° with steel;
The swords of soldiers are his teeth, his fangs;
And now he feasts, mousing° the flesh of men
In undetermined differences° of kings.   355
Why stand these royal fronts° amazèd thus?
Cry "Havoc!"° kings; back to the stainèd field,
You equal potents,° fiery kindled spirits!
Then let confusion° of one part° confirm
The other's peace; till then, blows, blood, and death!   360

KING JOHN
Whose party do the townsmen yet° admit?

KING PHILIP
Speak, citizens, for England: who's your king?

HUBERT
The King of England, when we know the king.

KING PHILIP
Know him in us, that here hold up his right.

KING JOHN
In us, that are our own great deputy,   365
And bear possession of our person° here,
Lord of our presence,° Angiers, and of you.

HUBERT
A greater pow'r than we denies all this,
And, till it be undoubted, we do lock
Our former scruple in our strong-barred gates,   370
Kings of our fear,° until our fears, resolved,
Be by some certain king purged and deposed.

BASTARD
By heaven, these scroyles° of Angiers flout you, kings,
And stand securely on their battlements
As in a theater, whence they gape and point   375
At your industrious scenes and acts of death.
Your royal presences be ruled by me:
Do like the mutines° of Jerusalem,
Be friends awhile and both conjointly bend
Your sharpest deeds of malice on this town.   380
By east and west let France and England mount
Their battering cannon chargèd to the mouths,
Till their soul-fearing° clamors have brawled down°
The flinty ribs of this contemptuous city.
I'd play incessantly upon° these jades,°   385
Even till unfencèd° desolation
Leave them as naked as the vulgar° air.
That done, dissever your united strengths,
And part your mingled colors once again;
Turn face to face and bloody point to point.   390
Then, in a moment, Fortune shall cull° forth
Out of one side her happy minion,°
To whom in favor she shall give the day,
And kiss him with a glorious victory.
How like you this wild counsel, mighty states?°   395
Smacks it not something of the policy?°

KING JOHN
Now, by the sky that hangs above our heads,
I like it well. France, shall we knit our pow'rs
And lay this Angiers even with the ground,
Then after fight who shall be king of it?   400

BASTARD
And if thou hast the mettle of a king,
Being wronged as we are by this peevish town,

---

318 **staff** spear, lance   323 **Dyed . . . slaughter** hunters
customarily dipped their hands in the deer's blood (cf. *Julius
Caesar,* III.i.106 ff.)   326 **retire** withdrawal   328 **censurèd**
judged   333 **s.d. several** separate   347 **royal number** king's
name as one item in the list   349 **With . . . kings** with a
king slaughtered as well as slaughtering   350 **tow'rs** soars
(hawking jargon)   352 **chaps** jaws   354 **mousing** tearing,
biting   355 **undetermined differences** unsettled disputes
356 **fronts** foreheads   357 **Havoc** the call for general
slaughter with no taking of prisoners   358 **potents** potentates,
powers   359 **confusion** defeat; **part** party

361 **yet** now   366 **bear . . . person** owe no allegiance to anyone
else (unlike Arthur, who has apparently done homage to Philip
—cf. line 263)   367 **presence** person   371 **Kings . . . fear**
kings as a result of our fear (forced by our fears to be our own
kings)   373 **scroyles** scoundrels   378 **mutines** mutineers (factions fighting each other in Jerusalem in 70 A.D. united to fight the
Romans)   383 **soul-fearing** causing the soul to fear; **brawled
down** noisily laid waste   385 **play . . . upon** (1) play guns
upon (2) make sport of; **jades** wretches (a jade is a worn-out
horse or a wanton woman)   386 **unfencèd** unfortified   387
**vulgar** common   391 **cull** (1) choose (2) fondle, hug   392
**minion** darling, favorite   395 **states** kings   396 **the policy**
political skill, perhaps specifically Machiavellian political
cunning

Turn thou the mouth of thy artillery,
As we will ours, against these saucy walls;
And when that we have dashed them to the ground, 405
Why then defy each other, and, pell-mell,°
Make work° upon ourselves, for heaven or hell.°

KING PHILIP
Let it be so. Say, where will you assault?

KING JOHN
We from the west will send destruction
Into this city's bosom. 410

AUSTRIA
I from the north.

KING PHILIP          Our thunder° from the south
Shall rain their drift° of bullets on this town.

BASTARD [Aside.]
O prudent discipline! From north to south
Austria and France shoot in each other's mouth.
I'll stir them to it: come, away, away! 415

HUBERT
Hear us, great kings: vouchsafe a while to stay
And I shall show you peace and fair-faced league,
Win you this city without stroke or wound,
Rescue those breathing lives to die in beds,
That here come sacrifices for the field. 420
Persever not, but hear me, mighty kings.

KING JOHN
Speak on with favor; we are bent° to hear.

HUBERT
That daughter there of Spain, the Lady Blanch,
Is near to England:° look upon the years
Of Lewis the Dolphin° and that lovely maid. 425
If lusty love should go in quest of beauty,
Where should he find it fairer than in Blanch?
If zealous° love should go in search of virtue,
Where should he find it purer than in Blanch?
If love, ambitious, sought a match of birth, 430
Whose veins bound° richer blood than Lady Blanch?
Such as she is, in beauty, virtue, birth,
Is the young Dolphin every way complete;°
If not complete of,° say he is not she,
And she again wants° nothing, to name want,° 435
If want it be not° that she is not he.
He is the half part of a blessèd man,
Left to be finishèd by such as she,
And she a fair divided excellence,
Whose fullness of perfection lies in him. 440
O, two such silver currents when they join
Do glorify the banks that bound them in;
And two such shores, to two such streams made one,
Two such controlling bounds shall you be, kings,
To these two princes, if you marry them. 445
This union shall do more than battery can
To our fast-closèd gates: for at this match,°

With swifter spleen° than powder can enforce,
The mouth of passage shall we fling wide ope,
And give you entrance. But without this match, 450
The sea enragèd is not half so deaf,
Lions more confident, mountains and rocks
More free from motion, no, not Death himself
In mortal fury half so peremptory,°
As we to keep this city.

BASTARD          Here's a stay° 455
That shakes the rotten carcass of old Death
Out of his rags! Here's a large mouth, indeed,
That spits forth death and mountains, rocks and seas,
Talks as familiarly of roaring lions
As maids of thirteen do of puppy dogs. 460
What cannoneer begot this lusty blood?
He speaks plain cannon fire, and smoke, and bounce;°
He gives the bastinado° with his tongue:
Our ears are cudgeled; not a word of his
But buffets better than a fist of France. 465
Zounds!° I was never so bethumped with words
Since I first called my brother's father dad.

ELINOR
Son, list to this conjunction,° make this match;
Give with our niece a dowry large enough,
For by this knot thou shalt so surely tie 470
Thy now unsured assurance° to the crown
That yon green boy shall have no sun to ripe
The bloom that promiseth a mighty fruit.
I see a yielding in the looks of France:
Mark how they whisper. Urge them while their souls 475
Are capable of this ambition,°
Lest zeal,° now melted by the windy breath
Of soft petitions, pity, and remorse,
Cool and congeal again to what it was.

HUBERT
Why answer not the double majesties 480
This friendly treaty° of our threatened town?

KING PHILIP
Speak England first, that hath been forward first
To speak unto this city: what say you?

KING JOHN
If that the Dolphin there, thy princely son,
Can in this book of beauty read "I love," 485
Her dowry shall weigh equal with a queen:
For Anjou and fair Touraine, Maine, Poictiers,
And all that we upon this side the sea°—
Except this city now by us besieged—
Find liable° to our crown and dignity, 490
Shall gild her bridal bed and make her rich
In titles, honors, and promotions,
As she in beauty, education, blood,
Holds hand with° any princess of the world.

KING PHILIP
What say'st thou, boy? Look in the lady's face. 495

406 pell-mell headlong, tumultuously  407 Make work work havoc; for . . . hell to the death  411 thunder cannons  412 drift shower  422 bent determined  424 near to England closely related to King John (she was the daughter of John's sister and of the King of Castile)  425 Dolphin Dauphin  428 zealous sanctified  431 bound hold  433 complete fully endowed  434 of therein  435 wants lacks; to name want to speak of defects  436 If . . . be not if it is not a deficiency (the verbal quibbling of these lines is more to the Elizabethan taste than to ours, but it marks also the impersonal formality of Hubert's proposal)  445 if . . . them i.e., to each other  447 match (1) marriage (2) wick for igniting powder

448 spleen impetuosity  454 peremptory resolute  455 stay check, hindrance  462 bounce explosive noise  463 bastinado cudgeling  466 Zounds By God's wounds!  468 list . . . conjunction listen to (accept) this union  471 unsured assurance uncertain title  476 capable . . . ambition ready to accept this desire for alliance  477 zeal King Philip's eagerness to support Arthur  481 treaty proposal  488 sea the English Channel  490 liable subject  494 Holds hand with is the equal of

LEWIS
I do, my lord, and in her eye I find
A wonder, or a wondrous miracle,
The shadow° of myself formed in her eye,
Which, being but the shadow of your son,
Becomes a sun, and makes your son a shadow:      500
I do protest I never loved myself
Till now infixèd I beheld myself,
Drawn in the flattering table° of her eye.

*Whispers with* BLANCH.

BASTARD
Drawn° in the flattering table of her eye!
Hanged in the frowning wrinkle of her brow!      505
And quartered° in her heart! He doth espy
Himself love's traitor; this is pity now,
That, hanged and drawn and quartered, there should
        be
In such a love so vile a lout as he.

BLANCH [*To* LEWIS.]
My uncle's will in this respect is mine:      510
If he see aught in you that makes him like,
That anything he sees which moves his liking,
I can with ease translate it to my will;°
Or, if you will, to speak more properly,
I will enforce it eas'ly to my love.      515
Further I will not flatter you, my lord,
That all I see in you is worthy love,
Than this: that nothing do I see in you,
Though churlish thoughts themselves should be your
        judge,
That I can find should merit any hate.      520

KING JOHN
What say these young ones? What say you, my niece?

BLANCH
That she is bound in honor still° to do
What you in wisdom still vouchsafe to say.

KING JOHN
Speak then, Prince Dolphin: can you love this lady?

LEWIS
Nay, ask me if I can refrain from love,      525
For I do love her most unfeignèdly.

KING JOHN
Then do I give Volquessen, Touraine, Maine,
Poictiers, and Anjou, these five provinces,
With her to thee; and this addition more,
Full thirty thousand marks of English coin.      530
Philip of France, if thou be pleased withal,
Command thy son and daughter to join hands.

KING PHILIP
It likes us° well. Young princes, close your hands.

AUSTRIA
And your lips too, for I am well assured
That I did so when I was first assured.°      535

KING PHILIP
Now, citizens of Angiers, ope your gates;
Let in that amity which you have made,
For at Saint Mary's Chapel presently
The rites of marriage shall be solemnized.
Is not the Lady Constance in this troop?      540
I know she is not, for this match made up
Her presence would have interrupted much.
Where is she and her son? Tell me, who knows.

LEWIS
She is sad and passionate° at your highness' tent.

KING PHILIP
And, by my faith, this league that we have made      545
Will give her sadness very little cure.
Brother of England, how may we content
This widow lady? In her right we came,
Which we, God knows, have turned another way,
To our own vantage.

KING JOHN                  We will heal up all,      550
For we'll create young Arthur Duke of Britain
And Earl of Richmond, and this rich fair town
We make him lord of. Call the Lady Constance.
Some speedy messenger bid her repair
To our solemnity.° I trust we shall,      555
If not fill up the measure of her will,
Yet in some measure satisfy her so
That we shall stop her exclamation.°
Go we, as well as haste will suffer us,
To this unlooked for, unprepared pomp.°      560
              *Exeunt [all but the* BASTARD].

BASTARD
Mad world! Mad kings! Mad composition!°
John, to stop Arthur's title in the whole,
Hath willingly departed with° a part,
And France, whose armor conscience buckled on,
Whom zeal and charity brought to the field      565
As God's own soldier, rounded in the ear
With° that same purpose-changer, that sly devil,
That broker° that still breaks the pate of faith,
That daily break-vow, he that wins of all,
Of kings, of beggars, old men, young men, maids,      570
Who,° having no external thing to lose
But the word "maid," cheats the poor maid of that,
That smooth-faced° gentleman, tickling° commodity,°
Commodity, the bias° of the world,
The world, who of itself is peisèd° well,      575
Made to run even upon even ground,
Till this advantage, this vile drawing° bias,
This sway° of motion,° this commodity,

498 **shadow** image   503 **Drawn . . . table** portrayed on the flattering surface (the whole of the Dauphin's speech—"eye," "sun," "son," "shadow"—is conventional; he simply says what is expected of him)   504 **Drawn** (1) portrayed (2) disemboweled   506 **quartered** (1) lodged (2) cut or torn in four parts (traitors were hanged, drawn and quartered)   513 **translate . . . will** I can bend my will to my uncle's desires (Blanch is much less conventional, and much more honest, than Lewis)   522 **still** always   533 **It likes us** we like it   535 **assured** engaged to be married

544 **passionate** enraged   555 **solemnity** ceremony (the wedding and the granting of titles to Arthur)   558 **stop her exclamation** silence her complaining   560 **pomp** ceremony   561 **composition** compromise   563 **departed with** given away   566–67 **rounded . . . With** whispered to by   568 **broker** pander   571 **Who** elliptical; begins by referring to "maids," ends, as the subject of "cheats," by referring to "commodity," the subject of this whole series of appositions   573 **smooth-faced** ingratiating, deceitful; **tickling** (1) teasing—the maids (2) flattering—anyone; **commodity** self-interest   574 **bias** oblique course (in bowling, the bowl went on an oblique course because of the weight built into one side; *bias* was the word for either the course or the weight itself)   575 **peisèd** weighted   577 **vile drawing** two adjectives, but also "vile-drawing," drawing to evil   578 **sway** that which sways; diverter, corrupter; **motion** (1) movement (2) intention

Makes it take head° from all indifferency,°
From all direction, purpose, course, intent.            580
And this same bias, this commodity,
This bawd, this broker, this all-changing word,
Clapped on the outward eye° of fickle France,
Hath drawn him from his own determined aid,
From a resolved° and honorable war,                     585
To a most base and vile-concluded peace.
And why rail I on this commodity?
But for because° he hath not wooed me yet:
Not that I have the power to clutch my hand,°
When his fair angels° would salute my palm,             590
But for my hand, as unattempted° yet,
Like a poor beggar, raileth on the rich.
Well, whiles I am a beggar, I will rail
And say there is no sin but to be rich;
And being rich, my virtue then shall be               595
To say there is no vice but beggary.
Since kings break faith upon° commodity,
Gain, be my lord, for I will worship thee!      *Exit.*

Scene II. [*King Philip's tent.*]

*Enter* CONSTANCE, ARTHUR, *and* SALISBURY.

CONSTANCE
Gone to be married! Gone to swear a peace!
False blood to false blood joined! Gone to be friends!
Shall Lewis have Blanch, and Blanch those provinces?
It is not so; thou hast misspoke, misheard;
Be well advised, tell o'er thy tale again.              5
It cannot be; thou dost but say 'tis so.
I trust I may not trust thee, for thy word
Is but the vain breath of a common man;
Believe me, I do not believe thee, man:
I have a king's oath to the contrary.                   10
Thou shalt be punished for thus frighting me,
For I am sick and capable of fears,
Oppressed with wrongs, and therefore full of fears,
A widow, husbandless,° subject to fears,
A woman naturally born to fears;                        15
And though thou now confess thou didst but jest,
With my vexed spirits I cannot take a truce,°
But they will quake and tremble all this day.
What dost thou mean by shaking of thy head?
Why dost thou look so sadly on my son?                  20
What means that hand upon that breast of thine?
Why holds thine eye that lamentable rheum,°
Like a proud river peering o'er° his bounds?

Be these sad signs confirmers of thy words?
Then speak again, not all thy former tale,              25
But this one word, whether thy tale be true.
SALISBURY
As true as I believe you think them false
That give you cause to prove my saying true.
CONSTANCE
O if thou teach me to believe this sorrow,
Teach thou this sorrow how to make me die!              30
And let belief and life encounter so
As doth the fury of two desperate men
Which in the very meeting fall and die.
Lewis marry Blanch! O boy, then where art thou?
France friend with England, what becomes of me?        35
Fellow, be gone! I cannot brook thy sight.
This news hath made thee a most ugly man.
SALISBURY
What other harm have I, good lady, done,
But spoke the harm that is by others done?
CONSTANCE
Which harm within itself so heinous is                  40
As it makes harmful all that speak of it.
ARTHUR
I do beseech you, madam, be content.°
CONSTANCE
If thou, that bid'st me be content, wert grim,
Ugly and sland'rous° to thy mother's womb,
Full of unpleasing blots° and sightless° stains,       45
Lame, foolish, crooked, swart, prodigious,°
Patched with foul moles and eye-offending marks,
I would not care, I then would be content,
For then I should not love thee: no, nor thou
Become thy great birth, nor deserve a crown.           50
But thou art fair, and at thy birth, dear boy,
Nature and Fortune joined to make thee great.
Of Nature's gifts thou mayst with lilies boast
And with the half-blown° rose. But Fortune, O,
She is corrupted, changed, and won from thee;          55
Sh' adulterates hourly° with thine uncle John,
And with her golden hand° hath plucked on° France
To tread down fair respect of sovereignty,
And made his majesty the bawd to theirs.
France is a bawd to Fortune and King John,             60
That strumpet Fortune, that usurping John!
Tell me, thou fellow, is not France forsworn?
Envenom° him with words, or get thee gone
And leave those woes alone which I alone
Am bound to underbear.°
SALISBURY                    Pardon me, madam,          65
I may not go without you to the kings.
CONSTANCE
Thou mayst; thou shalt: I will not go with thee.
I will instruct my sorrows to be proud,°
For grief is proud° and makes his owner stoop.°

579 **take head** run; **indifferency** impartiality, disinterestedness
583 **outward eye** (1) physical vision, as opposed to moral
vision or conscience (2) in bowling, the bowl had an "eye"
which received the weight, the bias    585 **resolved** the decision
to undertake it having been made    588 **But for because** only
because    589 **clutch my hand** refuse the bribe    590 **angels**
(1) commodity's agents, the fallen angels (2) gold coins called
angels because they carried a picture of the archangel Michael
killing a dragon    591 **unattempted** untested, untempted    597
**upon** as a result of
**II.ii.14 A widow, husbandless** not necessarily a tautology:
the historical Constance, though Geoffrey's widow, was at this
time married to her third husband; his presence would, however, be a dramatic confusion, and Shakespeare simplifies to
increase her isolation    17 **take a truce** make peace    22 **that
lamentable rheum** those sorrowful tears    23 **peering o'er**
overflowing

42 **content** calm, satisfied    44 **sland'rous** a disgrace, giving
cause for slander    45 **blots** spots, disfigurements; **sightless**
unsightly    46 **prodigious** deformed, hence a prodigy or bad
omen    54 **half-blown** half-opened    56 **hourly** (1) every
hour (2) like a whore (cf. I.i.165)    57 **golden hand** hand
which dispenses gold; **plucked on** drawn along    63 **Envenom**
(1) poison (2) curse    65 **underbear** endure, suffer    68, 69
**proud** (1) proud (2) prou'd = proved = tested    69 **stoop**
bow down (Constance is made to bow down under her grief,
but she will also make the kings bow down to it)

To me and to the state° of my great grief                     70
Let kings assemble, for my grief's so great
That no supporter but the huge firm earth
Can hold it up: here I and sorrows sit;
Here is my throne; bid kings come bow to it.

> [Seats herself on the ground. Exeunt
> SALISBURY and ARTHUR.°]

# ACT III

### Scene I. [King Philip's tent.]

*Enter* KING JOHN, [KING PHILIP *of*] France, [LEWIS
*the*] *Dauphin*, BLANCH, ELINOR, *Philip* [*the* BASTARD],
AUSTRIA, [*and* ATTENDANTS, *to*] CONSTANCE,
[*seated on the ground*°].

KING PHILIP
'Tis true, fair daughter, and this blessèd day
Ever in France shall be kept festival:°
To solemnize this day the glorious sun
Stays in his course and plays the alchemist,
Turning with splendor of his precious eye             5
The meager cloddy earth to glittering gold.
The yearly course that brings this day about
Shall never see it but a holy day.
CONSTANCE [*Rising.*]
A wicked day, and not a holy day!
What hath this day deserved? What hath it done      10
That it in golden letters should be set
Among the high tides° in the calendar?
Nay, rather turn this day out of the week,
This day of shame, oppression, perjury.
Or, if it must stand still,° let wives with child    15
Pray that their burdens may not fall this day,
Lest that their hopes prodigiously be crossed:°
But° on this day let seamen fear no wrack;°
No bargains° break that are not this day made;
This day all things begun come to ill end,           20
Yea, faith itself to hollow falsehood change!
KING PHILIP
By heaven, lady, you shall have no cause
To curse the fair proceedings of this day:
Have I not pawned to you my majesty?°
CONSTANCE
You have beguiled me with a counterfeit°             25
Resembling majesty, which, being touched and tried,°
Proves valueless: you are forsworn, forsworn!

You came in arms° to spill mine enemies' blood,
But now, in arms,° you strengthen it with yours.
The grappling vigor and rough frown of war          30
Is cold in amity and painted peace,°
And our oppression° hath made up this league.
Arm, arm, you heavens, against these perjured kings!
A widow cries; be husband to me, heavens!
Let not the hours of this ungodly day               35
Wear out° the day in peace; but, ere sunset,
Set armèd discord 'twixt these perjured kings!
Hear me! O, hear me!
AUSTRIA                          Lady Constance, peace!
CONSTANCE
War! War! No peace! Peace is to me a war.
O, Lymoges!° O, Austria! Thou dost shame            40
That bloody spoil:° thou slave, thou wretch, thou
      coward!
Thou little valiant, great in villainy!
Thou ever strong upon the stronger side!
Thou Fortune's champion, that dost never fight
But when her humorous° ladyship is by               45
To teach thee safety! Thou art perjured too,
And sooth'st up° greatness. What a fool art thou,
A ramping° fool, to brag and stamp and swear
Upon my party!° Thou cold-blooded slave,
Hast thou not spoke like thunder on my side?        50
Been sworn my soldier, bidding me depend
Upon thy stars, thy fortune, and thy strength,
And dost thou now fall over° to my foes?
Thou wear a lion's hide! Doff it for shame,
And hang a calfskin° on those recreant° limbs.      55
AUSTRIA
O that a man should speak those words to me!
BASTARD
And hang a calfskin on those recreant limbs.
AUSTRIA
Thou dar'st not say so, villain, for thy life!
BASTARD
And hang a calfskin on those recreant limbs.
KING JOHN
We like not this; thou dost forget thyself.         60

*Enter* PANDULPH.

KING PHILIP
Here comes the holy legate of the pope.
PANDULPH
Hail, you anointed deputies of heaven!
To thee, King John, my holy errand is.
I Pandulph, of fair Milan cardinal,
And from Pope Innocent the legate here,             65
Do in his name religiously demand

---

70 **state** (1) condition (2) high rank (3) government (4) throne
74 **s.d. Exeunt . . . Arthur** it is not clear whether Salisbury
should lead Arthur off or they should go in opposite directions;
it is only clear that they are not present during the next scene
and that Arthur next appears, in III.ii, as John's prisoner
**III.i.s.d. seated . . . ground** the action is of course continuous
from the end of the second act  **2 festival** as a holiday  **12
high tides** principal anniversaries  **15 stand still** always remain
**17 prodigiously be crossed** be denied by the birth of a deformed child  **18 But** except; **wrack** disaster (here, of
course, shipwreck)  **19 bargains** agreements  **24 pawned
. . . majesty** pledged you my word as a king  **25 counterfeit** false coin  **26 touched and tried** its gold tested on a
touchstone

28–29 **in arms . . . in arms** armed . . . embracing  **31 Is
. . . peace** lies dead in your friendship and false peace  **32 our
oppression** your oppression of us  **36 Wear out** last through
**40 Lymoges** Limoges and Austria were, historically, two men,
but are here combined; Richard *Coeur de Lion* was actually
killed, not by Austria, but while besieging Limoges  **41
bloody spoil** the lionskin  **45 humorous** full of humors,
capricious  **47 sooth'st up** flatterest  **48 ramping** (1) raging
(2) threatening—chiefly said of lions (3) standing on the hind
legs, like a heraldic lion  **49 Upon my party** as one of my
supporters  **53 fall over** go over  **55 calfskin** (1) indicating
a calf, or meek, cowardly fellow, in sharpest contrast with a
lion (2) traditional coat (?) for a household fool or idiot kept
for amusement; **recreant** cowardly

Why thou against the church, our holy mother,
So willfully dost spurn;° and force perforce°
Keep Stephen Langton, chosen Archbishop
Of Canterbury, from that holy see:                                 70
This, in our foresaid holy father's name,
Pope Innocent, I do demand of thee.

KING JOHN
What earthy name to interrogatories°
Can task the free breath of a sacred king?°
Thou canst not, cardinal, devise a name                            75
So slight, unworthy, and ridiculous,
To charge me to an answer,° as the pope.
Tell him this tale, and from the mouth of England
Add thus much more, that no Italian priest
Shall tithe or toll° in our dominions;                             80
But as we, under God, are supreme head,
So under Him that great supremacy
Where we do reign, we will alone uphold
Without th' assistance of a mortal hand:
So tell the pope, all reverence set apart                          85
To him and his usurped authority.

KING PHILIP
Brother of England, you blaspheme in this.

KING JOHN
Though you and all the kings of Christendom
Are led so grossly° by this meddling priest,°
Dreading the curse that money may buy out,°                        90
And by the merit of vile gold, dross, dust,
Purchase corrupted pardon of a man,
Who in that sale sells pardon from himself:°
Though you and all the rest, so grossly led,
This juggling witchcraft with revenue cherish,°                    95
Yet I alone, alone do me oppose
Against the pope, and count his friends my foes.

PANDULPH
Then, by the lawful power that I have,
Thou shalt stand curst and excommunicate:
And blessèd shall he be that doth revolt                          100
From his allegiance to an heretic;
And meritorious shall that hand be called,
Canonized and worshiped as a saint,
That takes away by any secret course
Thy hateful life.

CONSTANCE          O lawful let it be                             105
That I have room with Rome° to curse awhile!
Good father cardinal, cry thou "Amen"
To my keen curses, for without my wrong
There is no tongue hath power to curse him right.

PANDULPH
There's law and warrant, lady, for my curse.                      110

CONSTANCE
And for mine too: when law can do no right,

Let it be lawful that law bar no wrong!
Law cannot give my child his kingdom here,
For he that holds his kingdom holds the law;
Therefore, since law itself is perfect wrong,                     115
How can the law forbid my tongue to curse?

PANDULPH
Philip of France, on peril of a curse,
Let go the hand of that arch-heretic,
And raise the power of France upon his head,°
Unless he do submit himself to Rome.                              120

ELINOR
Look'st thou pale, France? Do not let go thy hand.

CONSTANCE
Look to that, Devil, lest that France repent,
And by disjoining hands, hell lose a soul.

AUSTRIA
King Philip, listen to the cardinal.

BASTARD
And hang a calfskin on his recreant limbs.                        125

AUSTRIA
Well, ruffian, I must pocket up these wrongs,
Because—

BASTARD Your breeches best may carry them.

KING JOHN
Philip, what say'st thou to the cardinal?

CONSTANCE
What should he say, but as the cardinal?

LEWIS
Bethink you, father, for the difference                           130
Is purchase of a heavy curse from Rome,
Or the light loss of England for a friend:
Forgo the easier.°

BLANCH                      That's the curse of Rome.

CONSTANCE
O Lewis, stand fast! The devil tempts thee here
In likeness of a new untrimmed° bride.                            135

BLANCH
The Lady Constance speaks not from her faith,
But from her need."

CONSTANCE                     O, if thou grant my need,
Which only lives but by the death of faith,
That need must needs infer° this principle,
That faith would live again by death of need.                     140
O then tread down my need, and faith mounts up;
Keep my need up, and faith is trodden down!

KING JOHN
The king is moved, and answers not to this.

CONSTANCE
O be removed from him, and answer well!

AUSTRIA
Do so, King Philip; hang no more in doubt.                        145

BASTARD
Hang nothing but a calfskin, most sweet lout.

KING PHILIP
I am perplexed, and know not what to say.

PANDULPH
What canst thou say but will perplex thee more,
If thou stand excommunicate and cursed?

---

68 **spurn** kick contemptuously; **force perforce** by violent means  73 **interrogatories** questions asked formally in a law court  73–74 **What . . . king** What mortal can force a king to answer charges?  77 **charge . . . answer** command an answer from me  80 **tithe or toll** collect church revenues  89 **grossly** (1) stupidly (2) materially—as opposed to spiritually; **this meddling priest** the pope  90 **buy out** remove  93 **sells . . . himself** (1) i.e., not from God (2) loses his own pardon through the transaction  95 **This . . . cherish** cling to, and nourish financially, this deceptive wickedness  106 **room with Rome** the words were presumably homonyms

119 **upon his head** against him  133 **the easier** the lighter, the less oppressive  135 **untrimmèd** still possessing her maidenhead  136–37 **speaks . . . need** is interested not in truth but in advancing her cause  139 **infer** imply

KING PHILIP

Good reverend father, make my person yours,°      150
And tell me how you would bestow yourself.
This royal hand and mine are newly knit,
And the conjunction of our inward souls
Married in league, coupled and linked together
With all religious strength of sacred vows;      155
The latest breath that gave the sound of words
Was deep-sworn faith, peace, amity, true love
Between our kingdoms and our royal selves;
And even before this truce, but new° before,
No longer than we well could wash our hands      160
To clap this royal bargain up of peace,°
Heaven knows, they were besmeared and overstained
With slaughter's pencil,° where revenge did paint
The fearful difference° of incensèd kings:
And shall all these hands, so lately purged of blood,      165
So newly joined in love, so strong in both,°
Unyoke this seizure and this kind regreet?°
Play fast and loose° with faith? so jest with heaven,
Make such unconstant children of ourselves
As now again to snatch our palm from palm,°      170
Unswear faith sworn, and on the marriage bed
Of smiling peace to march a bloody host,
And make a riot on the gentle brow
Of true sincerity? O holy sir,
My reverend father, let it not be so!      175
Out of your grace, devise, ordain, impose
Some gentle order, and then we shall be blessed
To do your pleasure and continue friends.

PANDULPH

All form is formless, order orderless,
Save what is opposite to England's love.      180
Therefore to arms! Be champion of our church,
Or let the church, our mother, breathe her curse,
A mother's curse, on her revolting son.
France, thou mayst hold a serpent by the tongue,
A casèd° lion by the mortal° paw,      185
A fasting tiger safer by the tooth,
Than keep in peace that hand which thou dost hold.

KING PHILIP

I may disjoin my hand, but not my faith.

PANDULPH

So mak'st thou faith an enemy to faith,°
And like a civil war set'st oath to oath,      190
Thy tongue against thy tongue. O, let thy vow,
First made to heaven, first be to heaven performed,
That is, to be the champion of our church.
What since thou swor'st° is sworn against thyself
And may not be performèd by thyself,      195
For that which thou hast sworn to do amiss

Is not amiss when it is truly done;°
And being not done, where doing tends to ill,
The truth is then most done not doing it.
The better act of purposes mistook      200
Is to mistake again; though indirect,
Yet indirection thereby grows direct,
And falsehood falsehood cures, as fire cools fire
Within the scorchèd veins of one new burned.
It is religion that doth make vows kept,      205
But thou hast sworn against religion
(By what thou swear'st against the thing thou swear'st°)
And mak'st an oath the surety for thy truth
(Against an oath the truth°); thou art unsure
To swear°—swears only not to be forsworn,°      210
Else what a mockery should it be to swear!
But thou dost swear only to be forsworn,
And most forsworn, to keep° what thou dost swear;
Therefore thy later vows against thy first
Is in thyself rebellion to thyself:      215
And better conquest never canst thou make
Than arm° thy constant and thy nobler parts
Against these giddy loose suggestions;°
Upon which better part° our prayers come in,
If thou vouchsafe° them. But if not, then know      220
The peril of our curses light on thee
So heavy as thou shalt not shake them off,
But in despair die under their black weight.

AUSTRIA

Rebellion, flat rebellion!

BASTARD                        Will't not be?°
Will not a calfskin stop that mouth of thine?      225

LEWIS

Father, to arms!

BLANCH                  Upon thy wedding day?
Against the blood that thou hast married?
What, shall our feast be kept with slaughtered
    men?
Shall braying trumpets and loud churlish drums,
Clamors of hell, be measures° to our pomp?      230
O husband, hear me! Ay, alack, how new
Is "husband" in my mouth! Even for that name,
Which till this time my tongue did ne'er pronounce,
Upon my knee I beg, go not to arms
Against mine uncle.

CONSTANCE                 O, upon my knee,      235
Made hard with kneeling, I do pray to thee,

---

**150 make . . . yours** put yourself in my place   **159 new** just
**161 clap . . . peace** shake hands on this agreement, this royal
peace treaty   **163 pencil** paintbrush   **164 difference** dissension   **166 so . . . both** (1) hands so strong in both blood and
love (2) love so strong in both kings (?)   **167 Unyoke . . .
regreet** release their clasp and friendly counterclasp   **168 Play
. . . loose** cheat   **170 palm** (1) hand (2) symbol of peace
**185 casèd** caged (?) wearing its own hide (i.e., living) (?);
**mortal** deadly   **189 So . . . faith** thus you make your
loyalty to your oath to John an enemy to your loyalty to the
true faith, the church   **194 What . . . swor'st** what you have
sworn at any time after your original vow to the church

**197 truly done** done as it ought to be done, rather than done
in accordance with your unsound oath (this argument for swearing one thing and doing another is the so-called doctrine of
equivocation for which Elizabethan Protestants particularly
hated and feared the Jesuits)   **207 By . . . swear'st** by your
oath to John against your religion   **209 Against . . . truth**
the truth itself (religion) stands against the oath (to John)
which you make the basis of your loyalty   **209–10 thou . . .
swear** you are untrustworthy in your oaths   **210 swears . . .
forsworn** one swears in the first place to ensure that one will
not later swear the opposite (the complex, parenthetical style
of Pandulph's argument creates a dramatic effect of quibbling
ingenuity as opposed to an effect of plain-spoken truth)   **213
And . . . keep** and you would be most forsworn if you were
to keep   **217 arm** to arm   **218 giddy loose suggestions**
inconstant, unrestrained temptations   **219 Upon . . . part** in
behalf of which preferable party or faction   **220 vouchsafe**
permit   **224 Will't not be** Will this not cease?   **230 measures**
melodies

Thou virtuous Dolphin, alter not the doom
Forethought by God!°

BLANCH
Now shall I see thy love: what motive may
Be stronger with thee than the name of wife?    240

CONSTANCE
That which upholdeth him that thee upholds,
His honor: O thine honor, Lewis, thine honor!

LEWIS
I muse your majesty doth seem so cold,
When such profound respects° do pull you on!

PANDULPH
I will denounce° a curse upon his head.    245

KING PHILIP
Thou shalt not need. England, I will fall from° thee.

CONSTANCE
O fair return of banished majesty!

ELINOR
O foul revolt of French inconstancy!

KING JOHN
France, thou shalt rue this hour within this hour.

BASTARD
Old Time the clock-setter, that bald sexton° Time,    250
Is it as he will?° Well then, France shall rue.

BLANCH
The sun's o'ercast with blood: fair day, adieu!
Which is the side that I must go withal?
I am with both: each army hath a hand,
And in their rage, I having hold of both,
They whirl asunder and dismember me.    255
Husband, I cannot pray that thou mayst win;
Uncle, I needs must pray that thou mayst lose;
Father,° I may not wish the fortune thine;
Grandam, I will not wish thy wishes thrive:    260
Whoever wins, on that side shall I lose;
Assurèd loss before the match be played.

LEWIS
Lady, with me, with me thy fortune lies.

BLANCH
There where my fortune lives, there my life dies.

KING JOHN
Cousin,° go draw our puissance° together.    265
                [Exit BASTARD.]
France, I am burned up with inflaming wrath,
A rage whose heat hath this condition,°
That nothing can allay, nothing but blood,
The blood, and dearest-valued blood, of France.

KING PHILIP
Thy rage shall burn thee up, and thou shalt turn    270
To ashes, ere our blood shall quench that fire!
Look to thyself, thou art in jeopardy.

KING JOHN
No more than he that threats. To arms let's hie!
                    Exeunt.

Scene II. [Battlefield near Angiers.]

Alarums,° excursions. Enter BASTARD, with Austria's
head.°

BASTARD
Now, by my life, this day° grows wondrous hot.
Some airy devil hovers in the sky
And pours down mischief.° Austria's head lie there,

Enter [KING] JOHN, ARTHUR, HUBERT.

While Philip breathes.°

KING JOHN
Hubert, keep this boy. Philip, make up:°    5
My mother is assailèd in our tent,
And ta'en, I fear.

BASTARD        My lord, I rescued her;°
Her highness is in safety, fear you not:
But on, my liege, for very little pains
Will bring this labor to an happy end.      Exit [all].°   10

Alarums, excursions, retreat. [Re-]enter [KING] JOHN,
ELINOR, ARTHUR, BASTARD, HUBERT, [and]
LORDS.

KING JOHN [To ELINOR.]
So shall it be: your grace shall stay behind
So strongly guarded. [To ARTHUR.] Cousin, look not
    sad;
Thy grandam loves thee, and thy uncle will
As dear be to thee as thy father was.

ARTHUR
O this will make my mother die with grief!    15

KING JOHN [To the BASTARD.]
Cousin, away for England! Haste before,°
And, ere our coming, see thou shake the bags°
Of hoarding abbots; imprisoned angels°
Set at liberty: the fat ribs of peace
Must by the hungry now be fed upon!    20
Use our commission in his° utmost force.

BASTARD
Bell, book, and candle° shall not drive me back
When gold and silver becks° me to come on.
I leave your highness. Grandam, I will pray
(If ever I remember to be holy)    25
For your fair safety; so I kiss your hand.

ELINOR
Farewell, gentle cousin.

KING JOHN         Coz,° farewell.
                   [Exit BASTARD.]

---

237-38 alter . . . God don't interfere with divine intervention
244 respects inducements 245 denounce pronounce 246
fall from desert 250 sexton gravedigger and bell-ringer
251 Is . . . will is that the way he wants it 259 Father
father-in-law (King Philip) 265 Cousin kinsman (commonly, as here, nephew); puissance army 267 condition
characteristic

III.ii.s.d. Alarums trumpets, battle cries; with Austria's
head though there is no mention of the lionskin, the Bastard
should presumably wear it in this scene and perhaps from now
on; his complaint of the heat may be in part a comic reference
to this addition to his costume 1 this day (1) the day itself
(2) the battle 2-3 Some . . . mischief some invisible devil
has made the day so hot, or the battle so fierce 4 breathes
catches his breath 5 make up advance, press on 7 I rescued
her Shakespeare gives the Bastard credit for a rescue historically
effected by John 10 s.d. Exit [all] because the stage is cleared,
many editors begin a new scene here 16 before ahead of us
17 shake the bags empty the moneybags ("Shak[e]bag" is a
"desperate ruffi[a]n" in Arden of Feversham, 1592) 18 angels
coins (cf. II.i.590) 21 his its 22 Bell . . . candle excommunication 23 becks beckons 27 Coz cousin, kinsman

ELINOR
Come hither, little kinsman. Hark, a word.

[*She takes* ARTHUR *aside.*]

KING JOHN
Come hither, Hubert. O my gentle Hubert,
We owe thee much!° Within this wall of flesh          30
There is a soul counts thee her creditor,
And with advantage° means to pay° thy love;
And, my good friend, thy voluntary oath
Lives in this bosom, dearly cherishèd.
Give me thy hand. I had a thing to say,          35
But I will fit it with some better tune.°
By heaven, Hubert, I am almost ashamed
To say what good respect° I have of thee.
HUBERT
I am much bounden° to your majesty.
KING JOHN
Good friend, thou hast no cause to say so yet,          40
But thou shalt have; and creep time ne'er so slow,
Yet it shall come for me to do thee good.
I had a thing to say, but let it go.
The sun is in the heaven, and the proud day,
Attended with the pleasures of the world,          45
Is all too wanton and too full of gauds
To give me audience.° If the midnight bell
Did, with his iron tongue and brazen mouth,
Sound on into the drowsy race° of night;
If this same were a churchyard where we stand,          50
And thou possessèd with a thousand wrongs;
Or if that surly spirit, melancholy,
Had baked thy blood and made it heavy, thick,
Which else runs tickling up and down the veins,
Making that idiot, laughter, keep° men's eyes          55
And strain° their cheeks to idle merriment,
A passion hateful to my purposes;
Or if that thou couldst see me without eyes,
Hear me without thine ears, and make reply
Without a tongue, using conceit° alone,          60
Without eyes, ears, and harmful sound of words;
Then, in despite of brooded° watchful day,
I would into thy bosom pour my thoughts:
But, ah, I will not; yet I love thee well,
And, by my troth, I think thou lov'st me well.          65
HUBERT
So well, that what you bid me undertake,
Though that my death were adjunct to° my act,
By heaven, I would do it.
KING JOHN                  Do not I know thou wouldst?

Good Hubert, Hubert, Hubert, throw thine eye
On yon young boy; I'll tell thee what, my friend,          70
He is a very serpent in my way,
And wheresoe'er this foot of mine doth tread
He lies before me: dost thou understand me?
Thou art his keeper.
HUBERT                  And I'll keep him so
That he shall not offend your majesty.          75
KING JOHN
Death.
HUBERT  My lord.
KING JOHN          A grave.
HUBERT                  He shall not live.
KING JOHN                          Enough.
I could be merry now. Hubert, I love thee.
Well, I'll not say what I intend for thee:
Remember. Madam, fare you well.
I'll send those powers o'er to your majesty.          80
ELINOR
My blessing go with thee!
KING JOHN                  For England, cousin, go.
Hubert shall be your man,° attend on you
With all true duty. On toward Calais,° ho!     *Exeunt.*

Scene III. [*King Philip's tent.*]

*Enter* [KING PHILIP *of*] *France,* [LEWIS *the*] *Dauphin,*
PANDULPH, ATTENDANTS.

KING PHILIP
So, by a roaring tempest on the flood,°
A whole armado° of convicted° sail
Is scattered and disjoined from fellowship.
PANDULPH
Courage and comfort! All shall yet go well.
KING PHILIP
What can go well, when we have run° so ill?          5
Are we not beaten? Is not Angiers lost?
Arthur ta'en prisoner? divers° dear friends slain?
And bloody England into England gone,
O'erbearing interruption, spite of° France?
LEWIS
What he hath won, that hath he fortified.          10
So hot a speed with such advice disposed,°
Such temperate order in so fierce a cause,
Doth want example:° who hath read or heard
Of any kindred action like to this?
KING PHILIP
Well could I bear that England had this praise,          15
So° we could find some pattern° of our shame.

*Enter* CONSTANCE.

Look, who comes here! a grave unto a soul,
Holding th' eternal spirit, against her will,

---

**30 We . . . much** perhaps the entry after line 3 indicates
that Hubert is responsible for the capture of Arthur; at
any rate, Hubert is now clearly loyal to John, not to France
**32 advantage** interest; **pay** recompense, repay **36 fit . . .
tune** (1) set it to more appropriate music (2) render it
in a better style (i.e., reward you with more than words)
**38 good respect** high regard  **39 bounden** bound, indebted
**46–47 too full . . . audience** (1) the mind of the day is too
full of trinkets to listen to me (2) the day is too full of florid
beauties for you to pay proper attention to my harsh meaning
**49 race** course, progress (many editors substitute "ear" for
"race," but this destroys the oxymoron "drowsy race") **55
keep** employ for its own purposes  **56 strain** constrain, limit
**60 conceit** imagination, understanding  **62 brooded** brooding
**67 adjunct to** an essential constituent of

**82 man** servant  **83 Calais** pronounced to rhyme with *palace*
**III.iii.1 flood** sea  **2 armado** armada, fleet of armed ships;
**convicted** doomed  **5 run** (1) proceeded (2) run away  **7
divers** various  **9 spite of** in spite of  **11 with . . . disposed**
carried out with such determination  **13 Doth want example**
is without parallel  **16 So** if; **pattern** example, parallel

In the vile prison of afflicted breath.°
I prithee, lady, go away with me.                               20

CONSTANCE
Lo, now! now see the issue of your peace!

KING PHILIP
Patience, good lady! Comfort, gentle Constance!

CONSTANCE
No, I defy° all counsel, all redress,
But that which ends all counsel, true redress:
Death, Death, O, amiable, lovely Death!                         25
Thou odoriferous stench! sound rottenness!
Arise forth from the couch of lasting night,°
Thou hate and terror to prosperity,
And I will kiss thy detestable bones,
And put my eyeballs in thy vaulty° brows,                       30
And ring these fingers with thy household worms,
And stop this gap of breath° with fulsome° dust,
And be a carrion monster like thyself:
Come, grin on me, and I will think thou smil'st
And buss° thee as thy wife! Misery's love,                      35
O, come to me!

KING PHILIP          O fair affliction,° peace!

CONSTANCE
No, no, I will not, having breath to cry!
O that my tongue were in the thunder's mouth!
Then with a passion would I shake the world,
And rouse from sleep that fell anatomy°                         40
Which cannot hear a lady's feeble voice,
Which scorns a modern invocation.°

PANDULPH
Lady, you utter madness, and not sorrow.

CONSTANCE
Thou art holy to belie me so!°
I am not mad: this hair I tear is mine;                         45
My name is Constance; I was Geoffrey's wife;
Young Arthur is my son, and he is lost!
I am not mad: I would to heaven I were,
For then 'tis like° I should forget myself!
O, if I could, what grief should I forget!                      50
Preach some philosophy to make me mad,
And thou shalt be canonized, cardinal.
For, being not mad but sensible of° grief,
My reasonable part produces reason
How° I may be delivered of° these woes,                         55
And teaches me to kill or hang myself:
If I were mad, I should forget my son,
Or madly think a babe of clouts° were he.
I am not mad: too well, too well I feel
The different plague of each calamity.                          60

KING PHILIP
Bind up those tresses! O, what love I note
In the fair multitude of those her hairs!

Where but by chance a silver drop° hath fall'n,
Even to that drop ten thousand wiry friends°
Do glue° themselves in sociable grief,                          65
Like true, inseparable, faithful loves,
Sticking together in calamity.

CONSTANCE
To England, if you will.°

KING PHILIP                    Bind up your hairs.

CONSTANCE
Yes, that I will; and wherefore will I do it?
I tore them from their bonds and cried aloud,                   70
"O that these hands could so redeem my son,
As they have given these hairs their liberty!"
But now I envy at° their liberty,
And will again commit them to their bonds,
Because my poor child is a prisoner.                            75
And, father cardinal, I have heard you say
That we shall see and know our friends in heaven:
If that be true, I shall see my boy again,
For since the birth of Cain, the first male child,
To him that did but yesterday suspire,                          80
There was not such a gracious° creature born.
But now will canker-sorrow° eat my bud
And chase the native beauty from his cheek,
And he will look as hollow as a ghost,
As dim and meager as an ague's fit,                             85
And so he'll die; and rising so again,
When I shall meet him in the court of heaven
I shall not know him: therefore never, never
Must I° behold my pretty Arthur more.

PANDULPH
You hold too heinous a respect° of grief.                       90

CONSTANCE
He talks to me that never had a son.

KING PHILIP
You are as fond of° grief as of your child.

CONSTANCE
Grief fills the room up of my absent child,
Lies in his bed, walks up and down with me,
Puts on his pretty looks, repeats his words,                    95
Remembers° me of all his gracious parts,
Stuffs out his vacant garments with his form;
Then have I reason to be fond of grief!
Fare you well: had you such a loss as I,
I could give better comfort than you do.                        100
I will not keep this form° upon my head,
When there is such disorder in my wit!°
O Lord! My boy, my Arthur, my fair son!
My life, my joy, my food, my all the world!
My widow-comfort, and my sorrows' cure!      *Exit.* 105

KING PHILIP
I fear some outrage, and I'll follow her.          *Exit.*

---

**19 afflicted breath** tormented life   **23 defy** reject   **27 couch . . . night** lair of eternal night (i.e., hell)   **30 vaulty** (1) arched (2) tomblike   **32 stop . . . breath** stop up this mouth; **fulsome** loathsome   **35 buss** kiss   **36 affliction** (1) afflicted one (2) one who now afflicts us   **40 fell anatomy** cruel skeleton (i.e. Death)   **42 modern invocation** common or ordinary entreaty   **44 Thou . . . so** as it stands, the line must be sarcastic; it is short a syllable, and many editors follow the fourth edition of the Folio (1685) in supplying "not" before "holy"   **49 like** likely   **53 sensible of** capable of feeling   **54–55 reason How** the idea of a way in which   **55 be delivered of** (1) give birth to (2) be delivered from   **58 babe of clouts** rag doll

**63 drop** tear   **64 wiry friends** hairs ("wiry" was a common, and not pejorative, epithet for hair)   **65 glue** sympathetically attach   **68 To . . . will** Constance here responds to King Philip's invitation at line 20; the separation is often taken as evidence that her "mad scene" is an interpolation, though the leap back to an earlier subject may simply be another symptom of her agitation   **73 envy at** am envious of   **81 gracious** (1) attractive, pleasing (2) holy, expressing and meriting divine grace   **82 canker-sorrow** sorrow as a canker-worm   **89 Must I** can I   **90 heinous a respect** atrocious a conception   **92 fond of** foolishly enamored with   **96 Remembers** reminds   **101 form** order (she had bound up her hair at lines 69–75, and now unbinds it again)   **102 wit** mind

LEWIS

There's nothing in this world can make me joy;
Life is as tedious as a twice-told tale,
Vexing the dull ear of a drowsy man,
And bitter shame hath spoiled the sweet words' taste,° 110
That it yields nought but shame and bitterness.

PANDULPH

Before the curing of a strong disease,
Even in the instant of repair° and health,
The fit is strongest: evils that take leave,
On their departure most of all show evil.° 115
What have you lost by losing of this day?°

LEWIS

All days of glory, joy, and happiness.

PANDULPH

If you had won it, certainly you had.
No, no; when Fortune means to men most good,
She looks upon them with a threat'ning eye: 120
'Tis strange to think how much King John hath lost
In this which he accounts so clearly won—
Are not you grieved that Arthur is his prisoner?

LEWIS

As heartily as he is glad he hath him.

PANDULPH

Your mind is all as youthful as your blood. 125
Now hear me speak with a prophetic spirit,
For even the breath of what I mean to speak
Shall blow each dust,° each straw, each little rub,°
Out of the path which shall directly lead
Thy foot to England's throne. And therefore mark: 130
John hath seized Arthur, and it cannot be
That, whiles warm life plays in that infant's veins,
The misplaced° John should entertain an hour,
One minute, nay, one quiet breath of rest.
A scepter snatched with an unruly hand 135
Must be as boisterously° maintained as gained,
And he that stands upon a slipp'ry place
Makes nice of no vile hold to stay him up:°
That John may stand, then Arthur needs must fall;
So be it, for it cannot be but so. 140

LEWIS

But what shall I gain by young Arthur's fall?

PANDULPH

You, in the right of Lady Blanch your wife,
May then make all the claim that Arthur did.

LEWIS

And lose it, life and all, as Arthur did.

PANDULPH

How green you are and fresh in this old world! 145
John lays you plots;° the times conspire with you,
For he that steeps his safety in true blood°

Shall find but bloody safety and untrue.
This act so evilly borne° shall cool the hearts
Of all his people, and freeze up their zeal, 150
That none so small advantage° shall step forth
To check his reign, but they will cherish it;
No natural exhalation° in the sky,
No scope of nature,° no distempered° day,
No common wind, no customèd event, 155
But they will pluck away his° natural cause
And call them meteors,° prodigies, and signs,
Abortives,° presages, and tongues of heaven,
Plainly denouncing vengeance upon John.

LEWIS

May be he will not touch young Arthur's life, 160
But hold himself safe in his prisonment.

PANDULPH

O sir, when he shall hear of your approach,
If that young Arthur be not gone already,
Even at that news he dies; and then the hearts
Of all his people shall revolt from him 165
And kiss the lips of unacquainted change,°
And pick strong matter° of revolt and wrath
Out of the bloody fingers' ends of John.
Methinks I see this hurly° all on foot;°
And, O, what better matter breeds° for you 170
Than I have named! The bastard Faulconbridge
Is now in England ransacking the church,
Offending charity:° if but a dozen French
Were there in arms, they would be as a call°
To train° ten thousand English to their side, 175
Or as a little snow, tumbled about,
Anon° becomes a mountain. O noble Dolphin,
Go with me to the king: 'tis wonderful
What may be wrought out of their discontent,
Now that their souls are topful of offense.° 180
For England go; I will whet on° the king.

LEWIS

Strong reasons makes° strange actions! Let us go:
If you say aye, the king will not say no.        *Exeunt.*

# A C T   I V

Scene I. [*England. A room in a castle.*]

*Enter* HUBERT *and* EXECUTIONERS.

HUBERT

Heat me these irons hot, and look thou stand
Within the arras.° When I strike my foot

110 **sweet words' taste** the words of the tale, sweet on first telling, are bitter on second telling; many editors follow Pope in emending the Folio's "words" to "world's"   113 **repair** recovery   116 **losing . . . day** losing today's battle   128 **dust** particle of dust; **rub** obstacle (from bowling, a roughness in the path of the bowl)   133 **misplaced** out of his proper place (i.e., usurping)   136 **boisterously** violently   138 **Makes . . . up** is not fastidious about his means of holding himself up   146 **lays you plots** prepares the course for you to follow   147 **steeps . . . blood** saturates his own security in loyal, or legitimate, blood (the specific aim of Pandulph's generalization is, of course, John's inevitable need to murder the true king, Arthur)

149 **borne** (1) born (2) carried out   151 **none . . . advantage** no opportunity, however small   153 **exhalation** meteor   154 **scope of nature** event at the limit of natural possibility; **distempered** stormy   156 **his** its   157 **meteors** supernatural omens (opposed to the "natural exhalation" of line 153)   158 **Abortives** misshaped creations (also considered omens)   166 **kiss . . . change** amorously welcome any alteration   167 **matter** (1) reason, cause (2) corrupt matter, pus   169 **hurly** turmoil; **on foot** under way   170 **breeds** is being prepared   173 **charity** right feeling among Christians   174 **call** decoy   175 **train** entice   177 **Anon** at once   180 **topful of offense** (1) filled to the brim with John's offenses (2) thoroughly offended   181 **whet on** urge   182 **makes** make (the verb form may imply "having strong reasons")   **IV.i.2 Within the arras** behind the curtain

Upon the bosom of the ground, rush forth
And bind the boy which you shall find with me
Fast to the chair. Be heedful. Hence, and watch.    5

EXECUTIONER
I hope your warrant will bear out° the deed.

HUBERT
Uncleanly° scruples! Fear not you! Look to't.
                   [EXECUTIONERS *hide*.]
Young lad, come forth; I have to say with° you.

*Enter* ARTHUR.

ARTHUR
Good morrow, Hubert.

HUBERT             Good morrow, little prince.

ARTHUR
As little prince, having so great a title      10
To be more prince, as may be.° You are sad.

HUBERT
Indeed, I have been merrier.

ARTHUR              Mercy on me!
Methinks nobody should be sad but I:
Yet I remember, when I was in France,
Young gentlemen would be as sad as night,      15
Only for wantonness.° By my Christendom,°
So° I were out of prison, and kept sheep,
I should be as merry as the day is long;
And so I would be here, but that I doubt°
My uncle practices° more harm to me.      20
He is afraid of me, and I of him:
Is it my fault that I was Geoffrey's son?
No, indeed, is't not; and I would to heaven
I were your son, so you would love me, Hubert.

HUBERT [*Aside*.]
If I talk to him, with his innocent prate°      25
He will awake my mercy, which lies dead:
Therefore I will be sudden and dispatch.°

ARTHUR
Are you sick, Hubert? You look pale today.
In sooth, I would you were a little sick,
That I might sit all night and watch with you.      30
I warrant I love you more than you do me.

HUBERT [*Aside*.]
His words do take possession of my bosom.

[*To* ARTHUR.]

Read here, young Arthur. [*Showing a paper*.]
            [*Aside*.] How now, foolish rheum!°
Turning dispiteous torture° out of door!
I must be brief, lest resolution drop      35
Out at mine eyes in tender womanish tears.

[*To* ARTHUR.]

Can you not read it? Is it not fair writ?°

ARTHUR
Too fairly, Hubert, for so foul effect:°
Must you with hot irons burn out both mine eyes?

HUBERT
Young boy, I must.

ARTHUR             And will you?

HUBERT                 And I will.      40

ARTHUR
Have you the heart? When your head did but ache,
I knit my handkercher about your brows
(The best I had, a princess wrought it me°—
And I did never ask it you° again)
And with my hand at midnight held your head,      45
And like the watchful minutes to the hour,°
Still and anon° cheered up the heavy time,
Saying, "What lack you?" and "Where lies your
    grief?"
Or "What good love° may I perform for you?"
Many a poor man's son would have lien° still,      50
And ne'er have spoke a loving word to you;
But you at your sick service had° a prince.
Nay, you may think my love was crafty° love,
And call it cunning. Do and if you will.
If heaven be pleased that you must use me ill,      55
Why then you must. Will you put out mine eyes?
These eyes that never did nor never shall
So much as frown on you?

HUBERT             I have sworn to do it,
And with hot irons must I burn them out.

ARTHUR
Ah, none but in this iron age would do it!      60
The iron of itself, though heat° red-hot,
Approaching near these eyes, would drink my tears
And quench this fiery indignation
Even in the matter° of mine innocence!
Nay, after that, consume away in rust,      65
But for° containing fire to harm mine eye!
Are you more stubborn-hard than hammered iron?
And if an angel should have come to me
And told me Hubert should put out mine eyes,
I would not have believed him—no tongue but      70
    Hubert's.

HUBERT [*Stamps*.]
Come forth.

[EXECUTIONERS *come forth with a cord, irons, etc*.]

            Do as I bid you do.

ARTHUR
O save me, Hubert, save me! My eyes are out
Even with the fierce looks of these bloody men.

HUBERT
Give me the iron, I say, and bind him here.

ARTHUR
Alas, what need you be so boist'rous rough?      75
I will not struggle; I will stand stone still!
For God's sake, Hubert, let me not be bound!

---

**6 bear out** vindicate, give authority for   **7 Uncleanly** improper   **8 to say with** something to say to   **10–11 As . . . may be** considering my title (king) to be even greater, I am presently as little prince as may be   **16 wantonness** whim; **By my Christendom** as I am a Christian (perhaps literally "by my baptism")   **17 So** if only   **19 doubt** fear   **20 practices** schemes   **25 prate** prattle   **27 dispatch** finish the job quickly   **33 rheum** (1) tears (2) room (in his bosom, Arthur's words threatening to displace the torture there)   **34 dispiteous torture** merciless torture (1) threatened to Arthur (2) now tormenting Hubert   **37 fair writ** written clearly

**38 effect** purpose   **43 wrought it me** worked (embroidered) it for me   **44 ask it you** ask you for it   **46 like . . . hour** as frequently as there are observable minutes in an hour (?)   **47 Still and anon** continually   **49 love** labor of love   **50 lien** (disyllabic) lain   **52 you . . . had** you, sick, had at your service   **53 crafty** feigned   **61 heat** heated   **64 matter** substance (i.e., tears)   **66 But for** merely as a result of

Nay, hear me, Hubert! Drive these men away,
And I will sit as quiet as a lamb.
I will not stir, nor winch,° nor speak a word,                    80
Nor look upon the iron angerly:
Thrust but these men away, and I'll forgive you,
Whatever torment you do put me to.

**HUBERT**
Go, stand within; let me alone with him.

**EXECUTIONER**
I am best pleased to be from° such a deed.                    85

[*Exeunt* EXECUTIONERS.]

**ARTHUR**
Alas, I then have chid away my friend!
He hath a stern look, but a gentle heart:
Let him come back, that his compassion may
Give life to yours.

**HUBERT**                    Come, boy, prepare yourself.

**ARTHUR**
Is there no remedy?

**HUBERT**                    None, but to lose your eyes.                    90

**ARTHUR**
O heaven, that there were but a mote in yours,
A grain, a dust, a gnat, a wandering hair,
Any annoyance in that precious sense:
Then feeling what small things are boisterous° there,
Your vile intent must needs seem horrible.                    95

**HUBERT**
Is this your promise? Go to,° hold your tongue.

**ARTHUR**
Hubert, the utterance of a brace° of tongues
Must needs want° pleading for a pair of eyes:
Let me not hold my tongue! let me not,° Hubert!
Or, Hubert, if you will, cut out my tongue,                    100
So° I may keep mine eyes. O, spare mine eyes,
Though to no use but still to look on you!
Lo, by my troth, the instrument is cold
And would not° harm me.

**HUBERT**                    I can heat it, boy.

**ARTHUR**
No, in good sooth; the fire is dead with grief,                    105
Being create° for comfort, to be used°
In undeserved extremes.° See else° yourself.
There is no malice in this burning coal.
The breath of heaven hath blown his spirit out
And strewed repentant ashes on his head.                    110

**HUBERT**
But with my breath I can revive it, boy.

**ARTHUR**
And if you do, you will but make it blush
And glow with shame of your proceedings, Hubert:
Nay, it perchance will sparkle in° your eyes,
And, like a dog that is compelled to fight,                    115
Snatch at his master that doth tarre him on.°
All things that you should use to do me wrong

Deny their office:° only you do lack
That mercy which fierce fire and iron extends,°
Creatures of note for mercy-lacking uses.°                    120

**HUBERT**
Well, see to live: I will not touch thine eye
For all the treasure that thine uncle owes;°
Yet am I sworn and I did purpose, boy,
With this same very iron to burn them out.

**ARTHUR**
O, now you look like Hubert! All this while                    125
You were disguisèd.

**HUBERT**                    Peace! No more. Adieu.
Your uncle must not know but° you are dead.
I'll fill these doggèd° spies with false reports;
And, pretty child, sleep doubtless and secure°
That Hubert, for the wealth of all the world,                    130
Will not offend thee.

**ARTHUR**                    O heaven! I thank you, Hubert.

**HUBERT**
Silence! No more! Go closely° in with me.
Much danger do I undergo for thee.                    *Exeunt.*

Scene II. [*King John's court.*]

*Enter* [KING] JOHN, PEMBROKE, SALISBURY, *and*
*other* LORDS.

**KING JOHN**
Here once again we sit, once again crowned,°
And looked upon, I hope, with cheerful eyes.

**PEMBROKE**
This "once again," but that your highness pleased,
Was once superfluous:° you were crowned before,
And that high royalty was ne'er plucked off,                    5
The faiths of men ne'er stainèd with revolt;
Fresh expectation° troubled not the land
With any longed-for change or better state.°

**SALISBURY**
Therefore, to be possessed with double pomp,°
To guard° a title that was rich before,                    10
To gild refinèd gold, to paint the lily,
To throw a perfume on the violet,
To smooth the ice, or add another hue
Unto the rainbow, or with taper-light
To seek the beauteous eye of heaven to garnish,°                    15
Is wasteful and ridiculous excess.°

**PEMBROKE**
But that your royal pleasure must be done,

---

80 **winch** wince    85 **from** away from    94 **boisterous** painful
96 **Go to** disapproving exclamation, equivalent, perhaps, to
"come, come"    97 **brace** pair    98 **want** be insufficient    99
**let me not** (1) repeating the previous plea (2) hinder me not
101 **So** if thereby    104 **would not** (1) would not be able
to (2) does not wish to    106 **create** created; **to be used** at
the prospect of being used    107 **In undeserved extremes**
for undeserved cruelties (with pun on Latin *in extremis*, in the
final agonies of dying); **else** further    114 **sparkle in** throw
sparks into    116 **tarre him on** incite him

118 **Deny their office** contradict their customary functions
119 **extends** extend, grant    120 **Creatures . . . uses** creatures
(i.e., fire and iron) famous for cruel uses    122 **owes** owns
127 **but** anything but that    128 **doggèd** surly    129 **doubtless**
**and secure** certain and assured    132 **closely** secretly
**IV.ii.1 once again crowned** John has just had a second
coronation, enforcing new oaths of allegiance to counteract the
excommunication, which freed his followers from their original
oaths (see III.i.100–01)    4 **once superfluous** one time more
than necessary    7 **Fresh expectation** (1) eager anticipation
(2) anticipation of something new    8 **state** (1) government
(2) condition    9 **pomp** ceremony (i.e., coronation)    10 **guard**
(1) ornament (2) defend    14–15 **with . . . garnish** to seek to
embellish the sun's beauty with a candle    16 **excess** extravagance ("excess" may also refer to usury—see *Merchant of
Venice*, I.iii.59—and may here connote Salisbury's sense that
John is extorting too much money from his subjects)

This act is as an ancient tale new told,
And, in the last repeating, troublesome,
Being urgèd at a time unseasonable.    20

SALISBURY
In this the antique and well-noted° face
Of plain old form° is much disfigurèd,
And like a shifted wind unto a sail,
It makes the course of thoughts to fetch about,°
Startles and frights consideration,°    25
Makes sound opinion sick and truth suspected,
For putting on so new a fashioned robe.°

PEMBROKE
When workmen strive to do better than well,
They do confound° their skill in covetousness,°
And oftentimes excusing of a fault    30
Doth make the fault the worse by th' excuse,
As patches set upon a little breach°
Discredit more in hiding of the fault
Than did the fault before it was so patched.

SALISBURY
To this effect, before you were new crowned,    35
We breathed° our counsel: but it pleased your highness
To overbear it, and we are all well pleased,°
Since all and every part of what we would°
Doth make a stand at° what your highness will.°

KING JOHN
Some reasons of this double coronation    40
I have possessed you with,° and think them strong;
And more, more strong, when lesser is my fear,
I shall indue° you with. Meantime but ask
What you would have reformed that is not well,
And well shall you perceive how willingly    45
I will both hear and grant you your requests.

PEMBROKE
Then I, as one that am the tongue of these
To sound the purposes° of all their hearts,
Both for myself and them—but, chief of all,
Your safety, for the which, myself and them°    50
Bend their best studies°—heartily request
Th' enfranchisement of Arthur, whose restraint
Doth move the murmuring lips of discontent
To break into this dangerous argument:
If what in rest° you have, in right you hold,    55
Why then° your fears, which, as they say, attend
The steps of wrong, should move you to mew up
Your tender kinsman, and to choke his days
With barbarous ignorance, and deny his youth
The rich advantage of good exercise?°    60

That the time's enemies° may not have this
To grace occasions.° let it be our suit,
That you have bid us ask his liberty,°
Which for our goods° we do no further ask
Than whereupon our weal,° on you depending,    65
Counts it your weal he have his liberty.

*Enter* HUBERT.

KING JOHN
Let it be so:° I do commit his youth
To your direction. Hubert, what news with you?

[*Takes him aside.*]

PEMBROKE
This is the man should do the bloody deed:
He showed his warrant to a friend of mine.    70
The image of a wicked heinous fault
Lives in his eye; that close aspect° of his
Does show the mood of a much troubled breast,
And I do fearfully believe 'tis done,
What we so feared he had a charge to do.    75

SALISBURY
The color of the king doth come and go
Between his purpose and his conscience,
Like heralds 'twixt two dreadful battles° set:
His passion is so ripe, it needs must break.

PEMBROKE
And when it breaks, I fear will issue thence    80
The foul corruption° of a sweet child's death.

KING JOHN
We cannot hold° mortality's strong hand.
Good lords, although my will to give is living,
The suit which you demand is gone and dead.
He tells us Arthur is deceased tonight.    85

SALISBURY
Indeed we feared his sickness was past cure.

PEMBROKE
Indeed we heard how near his death he was,
Before the child himself felt he was sick:
This must be answered either here or hence.°

KING JOHN
Why do you bend such solemn brows° on me?    90
Think you I bear the shears of destiny?°
Have I commandment on the pulse of life?

SALISBURY
It is apparent foul play, and 'tis shame

---

21 **well-noted** well-known   22 **old form** customary methods   24 **fetch about** (nautical) take a new tack   25 **frights consideration** frightens contemplation (raising the whole question of his right to the crown)   27 **so . . . robe** (1) a robe so newly made, as opposed to John's original coronation robe (2) a robe of such new style (as opposed to "plain old form," line 22)   29 **confound** disrupt, destroy; **covetousness** (1) desire to do better (2) greed   32 **breach** tear in a garment, perhaps with a pun on the garment itself   36 **breathed** uttered quietly or hesitantly   37 **we . . . pleased** it is becoming increasingly clear that they are not in the least pleased   38 **would** would do, wish   39 **Doth . . . at** stops at (the limits of); **will** wishes to do   41 **possessed you with** given you   43 **indue** endow, supply   48 **sound the purposes** give sound to the intentions   50 **them** they (themselves?)   51 **Bend . . . studies** exert their (our?) hardest efforts   55 **rest** peace   56 **Why then** why, then, is it that   60 **exercise** education in those qualities befitting a gentleman

61 **the time's enemies** those opposed to present arrangements   62 **grace occasions** embellish their excuses or opportunities (for rebellion)   63 **That . . . liberty** as punctuated here—and in the Folio—Pembroke asks that it be given out that John encouraged them to ask for Arthur's liberty; many editors, following Rowe, place a comma after "ask" to mean "let his liberty be the suit you have offered to grant us"   64 **our goods** our own good   65 **whereupon our weal** in so far as our own well-being   67 **Let . . . so** John, seeing Hubert, grants their request on the supposition that Arthur is already dead; many editors, following Dr. Johnson, have destroyed this detail by moving the entry to the middle of line 68   72 **close aspect** severe appearance, guarded look   78 **battles** armies drawn up for battle   81 **corruption** pus   82 **hold** restrain   89 **This . . . hence** amends must be made for this either in this world or the next   90 **bend . . . brows** scowl   91 **shears of destiny** with which Atropos, one of the three Fates, cuts the thread of life

That greatness should so grossly offer it:°
So thrive it in your game!° and so, farewell.          95
PEMBROKE
Stay yet, Lord Salisbury. I'll go with thee
And find th' inheritance of this poor child,
His little kingdom of a forcèd° grave.
That blood which owed° the breadth of all this isle,
Three foot of it doth hold: bad world the while!°     100
This must not be thus borne; this will break out
To all our sorrows, and ere long, I doubt.°
                          *Exeunt* [LORDS].
KING JOHN
They burn in indignation. I repent.

*Enter* MESSENGER.

There is no sure foundation set on blood,
No certain life achieved by others' death.            105
A fearful eye thou hast. Where is that blood
That I have seen inhabit in those cheeks?
So foul a sky clears not without a storm;
Pour down thy weather: how goes all in France?
MESSENGER
From France to England; never such a pow'r           110
For any foreign preparation°
Was levied in the body of a land.
The copy of your speed is learned by them:°
For when you should be told they do prepare,
The tidings comes that they are all arrived.          115
KING JOHN
O, where hath our intelligence° been drunk?
Where hath it slept? Where is my mother's care,
That such an army could be drawn in France
And she not hear of it?
MESSENGER                My liege, her ear
Is stopped with dust: the first of April died         120
Your noble mother; and, as I hear, my lord,
The Lady Constance in a frenzy died
Three days° before—but this from rumor's tongue
I idly° heard; if true or false I know not.
KING JOHN
Withhold thy speed, dreadful occasion!°               125
O, make a league with me, till I have pleased
My discontented peers. What! Mother dead!
How wildly then walks my estate in France!
Under whose conduct came those pow'rs of France
That thou for truth giv'st out are landed here?       130
MESSENGER
Under the Dolphin.

*Enter* BASTARD *and* PETER *of Pomfret.*

KING JOHN              Thou hast made me giddy
With these ill tidings. [*To* BASTARD.] Now, what says
    the world

To your proceedings? Do not seek to stuff
My head with more ill news, for it is full.
BASTARD
But if you be afeard to hear the worst,               135
Then let the worst unheard fall on your head.
KING JOHN
Bear with me, cousin, for I was amazed°
Under the tide; but now I breathe again
Aloft° the flood, and can give audience
To any tongue, speak it of what it will.              140
BASTARD
How I have sped° among the clergymen,
The sums I have collected shall express.
But as I travailed° hither through the land,
I find the people strangely fantasied,°
Possessed with rumors, full of idle dreams,           145
Not knowing what they fear, but full of fear.
And here's a prophet that I brought with me
From forth the streets of Pomfret,° whom I found
With many hundreds treading on his heels,
To whom he sung, in rude harsh-sounding rhymes,       150
That ere the next Ascension Day at noon,
Your highness should deliver up your crown.
KING JOHN
Thou idle dreamer, wherefore didst thou so?
PETER
Foreknowing that the truth will fall out so.
KING JOHN
Hubert, away with him: imprison him,                  155
And on that day at noon, whereon he says
I shall yield up my crown, let him be hanged.
Deliver him to safety° and return,
For I must use thee.    [*Exit* HUBERT, *with* PETER.]
                   O my gentle° cousin,
Hear'st thou the news abroad, who are arrived?        160
BASTARD
The French, my lord; men's mouths are full of it—
Besides, I met Lord Bigot and Lord Salisbury,
With eyes as red as new-enkindled fire,
And others more, going to seek the grave
Of Arthur, whom they say is killed tonight            165
On your suggestion.
KING JOHN              Gentle kinsman, go,
And thrust thyself into their companies.
I have a way to win their loves again;
Bring them before me.
BASTARD                I will seek them out.
KING JOHN
Nay, but make haste: the better foot before!°         170
O, let me have no subject enemies,
When adverse foreigners affright my towns
With dreadful pomp of stout invasion.
Be Mercury,° set feathers to thy heels,
And fly, like thought, from them to me again.         175
BASTARD
The spirit of the time shall teach me speed.    *Exit.*

94 **so grossly offer it** present (such foul play) so flagrantly
95 **So . . . game** May your schemes come to the same end!
98 **forcèd** enforced, violently brought about  99 **blood which owed** life which owned  100 **the while** during the time this can be true  102 **doubt** fear  111 **foreign preparation** force for foreign invasion  113 **The . . . them** they have learned to copy your speed  116 **intelligence** spy service  123 **Three days** Shakespeare compresses three years to three days  124 **idly** carelessly, without paying attention  125 **occasion** course of events

137 **amazed** in a maze, bewildered  139 **Aloft** on top of  141 **sped** fared  143 **travailed** (1) labored (2) traveled (the words had not yet been separated)  144 **strangely fantasied** filled with strange fancies  148 **Pomfret** Pontefract, in the West Riding of Yorkshire  158 **safety** close custody  159 **gentle** noble, wellborn  170 **better foot before** as fast as you can  174 **Mercury** messenger of the gods, who wore winged sandals

**KING JOHN**
Spoke like a sprightful° noble gentleman.
Go after him, for he perhaps shall need
Some messenger betwixt me and the peers,
And be thou he.

**MESSENGER** With all my heart, my liege. [*Exit.*] 180

**KING JOHN**
My mother dead!

*Enter* HUBERT.

**HUBERT**
My lord, they say five moons were seen tonight:
Four fixèd, and the fifth did whirl about
The other four in wondrous motion.

**KING JOHN**
Five moons?

**HUBERT** Old men and beldams° in the streets 185
Do prophesy upon it° dangerously;
Young Arthur's death is common in their mouths,
And, when they talk of him, they shake their heads
And whisper one another in the ear,
And he that speaks doth gripe the hearer's wrist, 190
Whilst he that hears makes fearful action,
With wrinkled brows, with nods, with rolling eyes.
I saw a smith stand with his hammer, thus,
The whilst his iron did on the anvil cool,
With open mouth swallowing a tailor's news, 195
Who, with his shears and measure in his hand,
Standing on slippers, which his nimble haste
Had falsely thrust upon contrary feet,
Told of a many thousand warlike French,
That were embattailèd° and ranked in Kent. 200
Another lean unwashed artificer
Cuts off his tale and talks of Arthur's death.

**KING JOHN**
Why seek'st thou to possess me with these fears?
Why urgest thou so oft young Arthur's death?
Thy hand hath murdered him: I had a mighty cause 205
To wish him dead, but thou hadst none to kill him.

**HUBERT**
No had,° my lord? Why, did you not provoke° me?

**KING JOHN**
It is the curse of kings to be attended
By slaves that take their humors° for a warrant
To break within the bloody house of life, 210
And on the winking of authority
To understand a law,° to know the meaning
Of dangerous majesty, when perchance it frowns
More upon humor than advised respect.°

**HUBERT**
Here is your hand and seal for what I did. 215

**KING JOHN**
O, when the last accompt° twixt heaven and earth
Is to be made, then shall this hand and seal
Witness against us to damnation!
How oft the sight of means to do ill deeds

Make deeds ill done!° Hadst not thou been by, 220
A fellow by the hand of nature marked,
Quoted° and signed° to do a deed of shame,
This murder had not come into my mind;
But taking note of thy abhorred aspect,
Finding thee fit for bloody villainy, 225
Apt, liable° to be employed in danger,
I faintly broke with thee of° Arthur's death;
And thou, to be endearèd to a king,
Made it no conscience to destroy° a prince.

**HUBERT**
My lord— 230

**KING JOHN**
Hadst thou but shook thy head or made a pause
When I spake darkly° what I purposèd,
Or turned an eye of doubt upon my face,
As° bid me tell my tale in express words,
Deep shame had struck me dumb, made me break off, 235
And those thy fears might have wrought fears in me.
But thou didst understand me by my signs
And didst in signs again parley with sin;°
Yea, without stop,° didst let thy heart consent,
And consequently thy rude hand to act 240
The deed, which both our tongues held vile to name.
Out of my sight, and never see me more!
My nobles leave me, and my state is braved,°
Even at my gates, with ranks of foreign pow'rs;
Nay, in the body of this fleshly land,° 245
This kingdom, this confine° of blood and breath,
Hostility and civil tumult reigns
Between my conscience and my cousin's death.

**HUBERT**
Arm you against your other enemies:
I'll make a peace between your soul and you. 250
Young Arthur is alive! This hand of mine
Is yet a maiden and an innocent hand,
Not painted with the crimson spots of blood.
Within this bosom never entered yet
The dreadful motion° of a murderous thought, 255
And you have slandered nature in my form,°
Which, howsoever rude exteriorly,
Is yet the cover of a fairer mind
Than to be butcher of an innocent child.

**KING JOHN**
Doth Arthur live? O, haste thee to the peers! 260
Throw this report on their incensèd rage,
And make them tame to their obedience.°
Forgive the comment that my passion made
Upon thy feature, for my rage was blind,
And foul imaginary eyes of blood° 265
Presented thee more hideous than thou art.

177 **sprightful** full of spirit 185 **beldams** grandmothers 186 **prophesy upon it** expound its meaning 200 **embattailed** marshaled for battle 207 **No had** had I not; **provoke** urge; order (?) 209 **humors** moods, whims 211-12 **on . . . law** take as law the mere hints (or oversights) of one in authority 214 **advised respect** deliberate consideration 216 **accompt** account

220 **deeds ill done** (1) evil deeds done (2) deeds done badly 222 **Quoted** (1) marked, as with a line in the margin of a book (2) noted, recorded; **signed** (1) marked with some distinguishing characteristic, such as the sign of Cain (2) assigned, appointed 226 **liable** suitable 227 **broke . . . of** disclosed to thee my desire for 229 **Made . . . destroy** had no scruples about destroying 232 **darkly** obscurely 234 **As** as to 238 **sin** (1) sin (2) sign 239 **stop** hesitation 243 **braved** challenged 245 **the . . . land** my own body (conceived as a microcosm) 246 **confine** limited territory 255 **motion** impulse, inclination 256 **form** features 262 **tame . . . obedience** subject to their oaths 265 **imaginary . . . blood** (1) John's eyes, imagining bloodshed (2) Hubert's eyes, imagined bloodthirsty (3) Arthur's eyes, imagined as empty sockets

O, answer not, but to my closet° bring
The angry lords with all expedient haste.
I conjure° thee but slowly: run more fast.     *Exeunt.*

Scene III. [*Before a castle.*]

*Enter* ARTHUR, *on the walls.*

ARTHUR
The wall is high, and yet will I leap down.
Good ground, be pitiful and hurt me not!
There's few or none do know me; if they did,
This ship-boy's semblance hath disguised me quite.
I am afraid, and yet I'll venture it.     5
If I get down, and do not break my limbs,
I'll find a thousand shifts° to get away.
As good to die and go, as die and stay.

[*Leaps down.*]

O me! my uncle's spirit is in these stones!
Heaven take my soul, and England keep my bones!    10
                        *Dies.*

*Enter* PEMBROKE, SALISBURY, *and* BIGOT.

SALISBURY
Lords, I will meet him at Saint Edmundsbury.°
It is our safety, and we must embrace
This gentle offer of the perilous time.
PEMBROKE
Who brought that letter from the cardinal?
SALISBURY
The Count Meloone, a noble lord of France,    15
Whose private with° me of the Dolphin's love
Is much more general° than these lines import.
BIGOT
Tomorrow morning let us meet him then.
SALISBURY
Or rather then set forward, for 'twill be
Two long days' journey, lords, or ere° we meet.    20

*Enter* BASTARD.

BASTARD
Once more today well met, distempered° lords!
The king by me requests your presence straight.°
SALISBURY
The king hath dispossessed himself of us;
We will not line his thin bestainèd cloak
With our pure honors, nor attend the foot    25
That leaves the print of blood where'er it walks.
Return and tell him so: we know the worst.
BASTARD
Whate'er you think, good words, I think, were best.
SALISBURY
Our griefs, and not our manners, reason° now.
BASTARD
But there is little reason in your grief!    30
Therefore 'twere reason you had manners now.
PEMBROKE
Sir, sir, impatience hath his privilege.

BASTARD
'Tis true, to hurt his master, no man else.
SALISBURY
This is the prison. [*Sees* ARTHUR.] What is he lies here?
PEMBROKE
O Death, made proud with pure and princely beauty!    35
The earth had not a hole to hide this deed.
SALISBURY
Murder, as hating what himself hath done,
Doth lay it open to urge on revenge.
BIGOT
Or when he doomed this beauty to a grave,
Found it too precious princely for a grave.°    40
SALISBURY
Sir Richard, what think you? You have beheld:
Or have you° read or heard, or could you think,
Or do you almost think, although you see,
That° you do see? Could thought, without this object,
Form such another? This is the very top,    45
The height, the crest, or crest unto the crest,
Of murder's arms:° this is the bloodiest shame,
The wildest savagery, the vilest stroke,
That ever walleyed° wrath or staring rage°
Presented to the tears of soft remorse.°    50
PEMBROKE
All murders past do stand excused in this:
And this, so sole and so unmatchable,
Shall give a holiness, a purity,
To the yet unbegotten sin of times,°
And prove a deadly bloodshed but a jest,    55
Exampled by° this heinous spectacle.
BASTARD
It is a damnèd and a bloody work,
The graceless° action of a heavy° hand,
If that it be the work of any hand.
SALISBURY
If that it be the work of any hand!    60
We had a kind of light° what would ensue:
It is the shameful work of Hubert's hand,
The practice° and the purpose of the king—
From whose obedience I forbid my soul,
Kneeling before this ruin of sweet life,    65
And breathing to his breathless excellence
The incense of a vow, a holy vow,
Never to taste the pleasures of the world,
Never to be infected with delight,°
Nor conversant with ease and idleness,    70
Till I have set a glory to this hand,
By giving it the worship of revenge.°

267 **closet** private council-chamber   269 **conjure** entreat
**IV.iii.**7 **shifts** tricks   11 **Saint Edmundsbury** Bury Saint
Edmunds, in Suffolk   16 **private with** private message to
17 **general** comprehensive   20 **or ere** before   21 **distempered**
peevish   22 **straight** immediately   29 **reason** control our
conduct

40 **too . . . grave** the bodies of royalty were not buried but
placed in monuments   42 **Or have you** have you either   44
**That** that which   47 **arms** (1) heraldic insignia (2) power
49 **walleyed** glaring; **rage** insanity   50 **remorse** pity   54
**times** future times   56 **Exampled by** in comparison with
58 **graceless** lacking divine sanction, damned; **heavy** oppressive, evil   61 **light** intimation (perhaps with the sarcastic connotation of "divinely inspired," following the
Bastard's "damnèd" and "graceless")   63 **practice** plot   69
**infected with delight** given these circumstances, delight
would be unhealthy   71–72 **set . . . revenge** put a halo
around Arthur's hand (as opposed to Hubert's, in line 62) by
showing my veneration through revenge (he will make Arthur
a saint by worshiping him as one); some editors would read
"this hand" as Salisbury's own, but that causes difficulties with
the religious imagery

PEMBROKE, BIGOT
Our souls religiously confirm thy words.

*Enter* HUBERT.

HUBERT
Lords, I am hot with haste in seeking you:
Arthur doth live; the king hath sent for you.          75
SALISBURY
O, he is bold and blushes not at death.
Avaunt, thou hateful villain, get thee gone!
HUBERT
I am no villain.
SALISBURY [*Drawing his sword.*]   Must I rob the law?
BASTARD
Your sword is bright, sir; put it up again.
SALISBURY
Not till I sheathe it in a murderer's skin.            80
HUBERT
Stand back, Lord Salisbury, stand back, I say!
By heaven, I think my sword's as sharp as yours.
I would not have you, lord, forget yourself,
Nor tempt° the danger of my true defense,
Lest I, by marking of° your rage, forget                85
Your worth, your greatness, and nobility.
BIGOT
Out, dunghill! dar'st thou brave° a nobleman?
HUBERT
Not for my life: but yet I dare defend
My innocent life against an emperor.
SALISBURY
Thou art a murderer.
HUBERT                   Do not prove me so:°           90
Yet° I am none. Whose tongue soe'er speaks false,
Not truly speaks; who speaks not truly, lies.
PEMBROKE
Cut him to pieces!°
BASTARD              Keep the peace, I say.
SALISBURY
Stand by,° or I shall gall° you, Faulconbridge.
BASTARD
Thou wert better gall the devil, Salisbury.            95
If thou but frown on me, or stir thy foot,
Or teach thy hasty spleen° to do me shame,°
I'll strike thee dead. Put up thy sword betime,°
Or I'll so maul you and your toasting-iron
That you shall think the devil is come from hell.      100
BIGOT
What wilt thou do, renownèd Faulconbridge?
Second a villain and a murderer?
HUBERT
Lord Bigot, I am none.
BIGOT                    Who killed this prince?
HUBERT
'Tis not an hour since I left him well:

I honored him, I loved him, and will weep              105
My date° of life out for his sweet life's loss.
SALISBURY
Trust not those cunning waters of his eyes,
For villainy is not without such rheum,
And he, long traded° in it, makes it seem
Like rivers of remorse and innocency.                  110
Away with me, all you whose souls abhor
Th' uncleanly savors of a slaughterhouse,
For I am stifled with this smell of sin.
BIGOT
Away toward Bury, to the Dolphin there!
PEMBROKE
There tell the king he may inquire us out.             115
                              *Exeunt* LORDS.
BASTARD
Here's a good world! Knew you of this fair work?
Beyond the infinite and boundless reach
Of mercy, if thou didst this deed of death,
Art thou damned, Hubert.
HUBERT
Do but hear me, sir—
BASTARD               Ha! I'll tell thee what:          120
Thou'rt damned as black—nay, nothing is so black—
Thou art more deep damned than Prince Lucifer:
There is not yet so ugly a fiend of hell
As thou shalt be, if thou didst kill this child.
HUBERT
Upon my soul—
BASTARD          If thou didst but consent              125
To this most cruel act, do but despair,°
And if thou want'st a cord, the smallest thread
That ever spider twisted from her womb
Will serve to strangle thee! A rush will be a beam
To hang thee on. Or wouldst thou drown thyself,        130
Put but a little water in a spoon
And it shall be as all the ocean,
Enough to stifle such a villain° up.
I do suspect thee very grievously.
HUBERT
If I in act, consent, or sin of thought,               135
Be guilty of the stealing that sweet breath
Which was embounded in this beauteous clay,
Let hell want pains enough to torture me!
I left him well.
BASTARD          Go, bear him in thine arms.
I am amazed,° methinks, and lose my way                140
Among the thorns and dangers of this world.
How easy dost thou take all England° up!
From forth this morsel of dead royalty,
The life, the right and truth of all this realm
Is fled to heaven, and England now is left             145
To tug and scamble° and to part by th' teeth°
The unowed interest° of proud swelling state.

---

**84 tempt** test   **85 marking of** (1) observing (2) striking at
**87 brave** challenge   **90 Do . . . so** by forcing me to kill you
**91 Yet** up to now   **93 Cut . . . pieces** Hubert, as a mere
citizen, is not considered worthy of the dueling code; the lords'
honor demands that they kill him for calling them liars, but
they will not bother to kill him as a gentleman   **94 by** aside;
**gall** wound   **97 spleen** ill temper; **do me shame** treat me
contemptuously (as you have Hubert)   **98 betime** soon,
before it is too late

**106 date** period   **109 traded** practiced   **126 do but despair**
do nothing other than commit suicide (you are damned already; it is your only choice)   **133 such a villain** apparently,
the greater the villain, the easier suicide   **140 amazed** in a
maze, bewildered   **142 all England** in calling Arthur "England," the Bastard acknowledges his right to the throne   **146
scamble** scramble; **part . . . teeth** tear apart as would a
pack of dogs or wolves   **147 unowed interest** (1) unowned
title (2) the interest (duty, obedience) not owed to any king

Now for the bare-picked bone of majesty
Doth doggèd° war bristle his angry crest
And snarleth in the gentle eyes of peace:                          150
Now powers from home and discontents at home
Meet in one line,° and vast confusion waits,
As doth a raven on a sick-fall'n beast,
The imminent decay of wrested pomp.°
Now happy he whose cloak and center° can                          155
Hold out this tempest. Bear away that child,
And follow me with speed: I'll to the king.
A thousand businesses are brief in hand,°
And heaven itself doth frown upon the land.

                                        *Exit [both].*


# ACT V

### Scene I. [*King John's court.*]

*Enter* KING JOHN *and* PANDULPH [*with*] ATTEN-
DANTS.

[KING JOHN *gives* PANDULPH *his crown.*]

KING JOHN
Thus have I yielded up into your hand
The circle of my glory.

PANDULPH [*Returning him the crown.*]    Take again
From this my hand, as holding of° the pope,
Your sovereign greatness and authority.

KING JOHN
Now keep your holy word: go meet the French,                      5
And from his holiness use all your power
To stop their marches 'fore we are enflamed.
Our discontented counties° do revolt;
Our people quarrel with obedience,
Swearing allegiance and the love of soul°                         10
To stranger blood, to foreign royalty.
This inundation of mistempered humor
Rests by you only to be qualified.°
Then pause not, for the present time's so sick
That present med'cine must be ministered,                         15
Or overthrow incurable ensues.

PANDULPH
It was my breath that blew this tempest up,
Upon° your stubborn usage of the pope,

But since you are a gentle convertite,°
My tongue shall hush again this storm of war                      20
And make fair weather in your blust'ring land.
On this Ascension Day, remember well,
Upon your oath of service to the pope,
Go I to make the French lay down their arms.    *Exit.*

KING JOHN
Is this Ascension Day? Did not the prophet                        25
Say that before Ascension Day at noon
My crown I should give off?° Even so I have!
I did suppose it should be on constraint,
But, heaven be thanked, it is but voluntary.

*Enter* BASTARD.

BASTARD
All Kent hath yielded—nothing there holds out                     30
But Dover Castle—London hath received,
Like a kind host, the Dolphin and his powers.
Your nobles will not hear you, but are gone
To offer service to your enemy;
And wild amazement° hurries up and down                           35
The little number of your doubtful° friends.°

KING JOHN
Would not my lords return to me again
After they heard young Arthur was alive?

BASTARD
They found him dead and cast into the streets,
An empty casket, where the jewel of life                          40
By some damned hand was robbed and ta'en away.

KING JOHN
That villain Hubert told me he did live.

BASTARD
So, on my soul, he did, for aught he knew.
But wherefore do you droop? Why look you sad?
Be great in act, as you have been in thought;                     45
Let not the world see fear and sad distrust°
Govern the motion of a kingly eye;
Be stirring° as the time; be fire with fire.
Threaten the threat'ner, and outface° the brow
Of bragging° horror: so shall inferior eyes,                      50
That borrow their behaviors from the great,
Grow great by your example and put on
The dauntless spirit of resolution.
Away, and glister like the god of war
When he intendeth to become° the field:                           55
Show boldness and aspiring confidence!
What, shall they seek the lion in his den,
And fright him there? and make him tremble there?
O, let it not be said! Forage,° and run
To meet displeasure farther from the doors,                       60
And grapple with him ere he come so nigh.

KING JOHN
The legate of the pope hath been with me,
And I have made a happy° peace with him,

---

149 **doggèd** cruel   151–52 **powers . . . line** a confusing image: it may mean either that English deserters fight face to face with English defenders who are themselves discontented, or that foreign invaders—powers away from their homes—are allied in a single army with English rebels; both senses are apt, and the complexity is an appropriate preparation for the "vast confusion" which impends   154 **wrested pomp** (1) the royal magnificence John usurped from Arthur (2) the position which his enemies threaten to wrest from John   155 **center** cincture, belt   158 **brief in hand** immediately demanded ("brief," used here in some apparently unique adjectival sense, is perhaps related to the noun meaning "a royal mandate" or "a summary statement")
**V.i.3 as holding of** as a leasehold from   8 **counties** shires; nobles (?)   10 **love of soul** soul's love, loyalty   12–13 **This . . . qualified** Only you can moderate this flooding of the body (of the state) with turbulent humor (in medieval physiology, health and disposition were considered dependent upon the balance maintained among four bodily fluids, called humors)   18 **Upon** as a result of

19 **convertite** convert   27 **give off** relinquish   35 **amazement** confusion, uncertainty   36 **doubtful** (1) fearful (2) untrustworthy   35–36 **hurries . . . friends** either "hurries them up and down" or "hurries among them"   46 **sad distrust** sorrowful lack of self-confidence   48 **stirring** energetic   49 **outface** defy, stare down   50 **bragging** threatening   55 **become** grace   59 **Forage** sally forth   63 **happy** blessed, favorable

And he hath promised to dismiss the powers
Led by the Dolphin.

BASTARD               O inglorious league!      65
Shall we, upon the footing of our land,°
Send fair-play orders° and make compromise,
Insinuation,° parley, and base truce
To arms invasive? Shall a beardless boy,
A cockered° silken wanton,° brave° our fields      70
And flesh° his spirit in a warlike soil,
Mocking the air with colors idly° spread,
And find no check? Let us, my liege, to arms!
Perchance the cardinal cannot make your peace;
Or if he do, let it at least be said      75
They saw we had a purpose of defense.

KING JOHN
Have thou the ordering of this present time.

BASTARD
Away then, with good courage! Yet, I know,
Our party may well meet a prouder° foe.     *Exeunt.*


Scene II. [*Bury Saint Edmunds. The Dauphin's camp.*]

*Enter, in arms,* [LEWIS *the*] *Dauphin,* SALISBURY,
MELUN, PEMBROKE, BIGOT, [*and*] SOLDIERS.

LEWIS
My Lord Meloone, let this be copied out,
And keep it safe for our remembrance;
Return the precedent° to those lords again,
That, having our fair order° written down,
Both they and we, perusing o'er these notes,      5
May know wherefore we took the sacrament,
And keep our faiths firm and inviolable.

SALISBURY
Upon our sides it never shall be broken.
And, noble Dolphin, albeit we swear
A voluntary zeal and an unurged faith      10
To your proceedings, yet believe me, prince,
I am not glad that such a sore of time
Should seek a plaster° by contemned° revolt,
And heal the inveterate canker° of one wound
By making many. O, it grieves my soul      15
That I must draw this metal° from my side
To be a widow-maker! O, and there
Where honorable rescue° and defense
Cries out upon° the name of Salisbury!
But such is the infection of the time      20
That, for the health and physic° of our right,
We cannot deal° but with the very hand
Of stern injustice and confusèd wrong.
And is't not pity, O my grievèd friends,

That we, the sons and children of this isle,      25
Were born to see so sad an hour as this
Wherein we step after a stranger, march
Upon her gentle bosom, and fill up
Her enemies' ranks—I must withdraw and weep
Upon the spot° of this enforcèd cause—      30
To grace° the gentry of a land remote,
And follow unacquainted colors° here?
What, here? O nation, that thou couldst remove!°
That Neptune's arms, who clippeth° thee about,
Would bear° thee from the knowledge of thyself,      35
And cripple° thee unto a pagan shore
Where these two Christian armies might combine
The blood of malice in a vein° of league,
And not to spend it so unneighborly!°

LEWIS
A noble temper dost thou show in this,      40
And great affections° wrestling in thy bosom
Doth make an earthquake of nobility.
O, what a noble combat hast thou fought
Between compulsion and a brave respect!°
Let me wipe off this honorable dew,      45
That silverly doth progress° on thy cheeks:
My heart hath melted at a lady's tears,
Being an ordinary inundation,
But this effusion of such manly drops,
This show'r, blown up by tempest of the soul,      50
Startles mine eyes, and makes me more amazed
Than had I seen the vaulty top of heaven
Figured quite o'er with° burning meteors.
Lift up thy brow, renownèd Salisbury,
And with a great heart heave away this storm.      55
Commend° these waters to those baby eyes
That never saw the giant-world° enraged,
Nor met with fortune, other than at feasts,
Full warm of blood,° of mirth, of gossiping.
Come, come; for thou shalt thrust thy hand as deep      60
Into the purse of rich prosperity
As Lewis himself: so, nobles, shall you all,
That knit your sinews to the strength of mine.

*Enter* PANDULPH.

And even there, methinks, an angel° spake.

---

66 **upon . . . land** based upon our native land   67 **fair-play orders** challenges and injunctions following the rules of chivalry   68 **Insinuation** ingratiating actions   70 **cockered** pampered; **wanton** spoiled child; **brave** (1) defy (2) display his splendid outfit in   71 **flesh** initiate   72 **idly** (1) carelessly (2) uselessly (if they meet no defense)   79 **prouder** (1) more powerful (2) more splendid (a last scoff at the Dauphin)

**V.ii.3 precedent** original (the "this" of line 1)   4 **fair order** reasonable terms of agreement   13 **plaster** medical dressing; **contemned** despised   14 **inveterate canker** persistent ulcer   16 **metal** (1) sword (2) mettle, courage   18 **Where honorable rescue** England, where (the need for) honorable rescue (or, where noblemen needing rescue)   19 **Cries out upon** appeal to   21 **physic** medical treatment   22 **deal** contend

30 **Upon the spot** (1) on the location (2) because of the disgrace   31 **grace** (1) embellish (2) be gracious to, welcome, honor   32 **unacquainted colors** foreign flags   33 **remove** go somewhere else   34 **clippeth** embraces   35 **bear** (1) carry (2) bare, strip   36 **cripple** disable (playing upon the sound-echo of "clippeth" in line 34)   38 **vein** (1) blood vessel (2) inclination   39 **unneighborly** meiosis, or understatement for rhetorical effect—Salisbury has created the image of a brutal rape by Neptune which would be preferable to the present "unneighborly" prospect   41 **affections** passions (perhaps "affection's" to make "wrestling" the subject of "Doth")   44 **Between . . . respect** between what you were compelled to do and a courageous (or ostentatious?) consideration (or carefulness)   46 **progress** make a ceremonious journey   53 **Figured . . . with** with a complete pattern of   56 **Commend** entrust, deliver to the keeping of   57 **giant-world** (1) the baby's world of giants (2) the large world beyond the baby's perception   59 **Full . . . blood** fully warmed with human feeling   64 **angel** various possibilities: (1) Lewis himself, punning on *angel* as a coin (following "purse" and "nobles" in lines 61 and 62, a noble also being a coin) and attesting his sincerity (2) Pandulph, who has just arrived with, Lewis thinks, heavenly assistance (3) a trumpet, which has just announced Pandulph's arrival

Look where the holy legate comes apace,                          65
To give us warrant from the hand of God,
And on our actions set° the name of right
With holy breath.
PANDULPH            Hail, noble prince of France!
The next is this: King John hath reconciled
Himself to Rome; his spirit is come in,°                         70
That so stood out against the holy church,
The great metropolis and see of Rome.
Therefore thy threat'ning colors now wind up,
And tame the savage spirit of wild war,
That, like a lion fostered up at hand,                           75
It may lie gently at the foot of peace,
And be no further harmful than in show.
LEWIS
Your grace shall° pardon me, I will not back:°
I am too high-born to be propertied,°
To be a secondary at control,°                                   80
Or useful servingman and instrument
To any sovereign state throughout the world.
Your breath first kindled the dead coal of wars
Between this chastised kingdom and myself,
And brought in matter° that should feed this fire;              85
And now 'tis far too huge to be blown out
With that same weak wind which enkindled it!
You taught me how to know the face of right,
Acquainted me with interest° to this land,
Yea, thrust this enterprise into my heart;                       90
And come ye now to tell me John hath made
His peace with Rome? What is that peace to me?
I, by the honor of my marriage bed,
After young Arthur, claim this land for mine,
And, now it is half-conquered, must I back                       95
Because that John hath made his peace with Rome?
Am I Rome's slave? What penny hath Rome borne?
What men provided? what munition sent,
To underprop this action? Is't not I
That undergo this charge?° Who else but I,                      100
And such as to my claim are liable,°
Sweat in this business and maintain this war?
Have I not heard these islanders shout out,
"Vive le roi!" as I have banked° their towns?
Have I not here the best cards for the game                     105
To win this easy match played for a crown?
And shall I now give o'er the yielded set?°
No, no, on my soul, it never shall be said.
PANDULPH
You look but on the outside of this work.
LEWIS
Outside or inside, I will not return                            110
Till my attempt so much be glorified
As to my ample hope was promisèd
Before I drew this gallant head of war,°
And culled° these fiery spirits from the world,

To outlook° conquest and to win renown                          115
Even in the jaws of danger and of death.

[*Trumpet sounds.*]

What lusty trumpet thus doth summon us?

*Enter* BASTARD.

BASTARD
According to the fair-play° of the world,
Let me have audience; I am sent to speak:
My holy Lord of Milan, from the king                            120
I come, to learn how you have dealt for him,
And, as you answer, I do know the scope
And warrant limited unto my tongue.°
PANDULPH
The Dolphin is too willful-opposite,°
And will not temporize° with my entreaties:                     125
He flatly says he'll not lay down his arms.
BASTARD
By all the blood that ever fury breathed,
The youth says well. Now hear our English king,
For thus his royalty doth speak in me:
He is prepared, and reason to he should°—                       130
This apish and unmannerly approach,
This harnessed masque and unadvisèd revel,°
This unhaired° sauciness and boyish troops,
The king doth smile at, and is well prepared
To whip this dwarfish war, this° pigmy arms,                    135
From out the circle of his territories.
That hand which had the strength, even at your door,
To cudgel you and make you take the hatch,°
To dive like buckets in concealèd wells,
To crouch in litter° of your stable planks,                     140
To lie like pawns,° locked up in chests and trunks,
To hug with swine, to seek sweet safety out
In vaults and prisons, and to thrill and shake
Even at the crying of your nation's crow,°
Thinking this voice an armèd Englishman—                        145
Shall that victorious hand be feebled here
That in your chambers gave you chastisement?
No! Know the gallant monarch is in arms
And, like an eagle, o'er his aerie tow'rs,°
To souse° annoyance° that comes near his nest.                  150
And you degenerate, you ingrate revolts,°
You bloody Neroes,° ripping up the womb
Of your dear mother England, blush for shame:
For your own ladies and pale-visaged maids,

115 **outlook** stare down  118 **fair-play** accepted rules for
battle  122–23 **as . . . tongue** depending upon your answer,
I know what I am authorized to say  124 **willful-opposite**
obstinately quarrelsome  125 **temporize** make terms  130
**reason . . . should** there is reason also (too) that he should
be prepared (?) reason to be prepared he indeed has (?) he should
also debate, or give his reasons (?)  132 **harnessed . . . revel**
masque performed in armor and misguided entertainment
133 **unhaired** beardless  135 **this** these  138 **take the hatch**
jump over the bottom of a half-door without pausing to open
it (cf. I.i.171)  140 **litter** bedding  141 **pawns** articles pawned
144 **crow** cock (the Frenchmen were frightened, so the Bastard
claims, by the crowing of the very Gallic cock which symbolizes
France)  149 **tow'rs** (hawking term) mounts up, soars  150
**souse** (i) dive, swoop down on (2) beat severely; **annoyance**
any threat  151 **ingrate revolts** ungrateful rebels  152 **Neroes**
among his other crimes, Nero, the Roman emperor, was said
not only to have murdered his mother but to have torn open
her womb

67 **set** place, as an official seal  70 **is come in** has submitted
78 **shall** must; **back** go back  79 **propertied** treated as a
property, made a means to some other end  80 **secondary at
control** subordinate under the control of another  85 **matter**
(1) fuel (2) arguments  89 **interest** title  100 **charge** burden,
expense  101 **liable** subject  104 **banked** coasted past (?) built
military embankments around (?) (with *Vive le roi* this is also
part of the card-playing metaphor)  107 **set** contest  113 **drew
. . . war** assembled this gallant army  114 **culled** selected

Like Amazons, come tripping after drums, 155
Their thimbles into armèd gauntlets change,
Their needles° to lances, and their gentle hearts
To fierce and bloody inclination.

LEWIS
There end thy brave,° and turn thy face in peace.
We grant thou canst outscold us: fare thee well; 160
We hold our time too precious to be spent
With such a brabbler.°

PANDULPH                    Give me leave to speak.

BASTARD
No, I will speak.

LEWIS                    We will attend to neither.
Strike up the drums, and let the tongue of war
Plead for our interest and our being here. 165

BASTARD
Indeed, your drums, being beaten, will cry out;
And so shall you, being beaten: do but start
An echo with the clamor of thy drum,
And, even at hand, a drum is ready braced°
That shall reverberate° all, as loud as thine. 170
Sound but another, and another shall,
As loud as thine, rattle the welkin's ear
And mock the deep-mouthed thunder: for at hand—
Not trusting to this halting° legate here,
Whom he hath used rather for sport than need— 175
Is warlike John; and in his forehead sits
A bare-ribbed Death, whose office is this day
To feast upon whole thousands of the French.

LEWIS
Strike up our drums to find this danger out.

BASTARD
And thou shalt find it, Dolphin, do not doubt. 180
                                        Exeunt.

Scene III. [A battlefield.]

Alarums. Enter [KING] JOHN and HUBERT.

KING JOHN
How goes the day with us? O, tell me, Hubert.

HUBERT
Badly, I fear. How fares your majesty?

KING JOHN
This fever, that hath troubled me so long,
Lies heavy on me: O, my heart is sick!

Enter a MESSENGER.

MESSENGER
My lord, your valiant kinsman, Faulconbridge, 5
Desires your majesty to leave the field
And send him word by me which way you go.

KING JOHN
Tell him, toward Swinstead,° to the abbey there.

MESSENGER
Be of good comfort, for the great supply°
That was expected by the Dolphin here, 10

Are wracked three nights ago on Goodwin sands.°
This news was brought to Richard but even now:
The French fight coldly and retire themselves.

KING JOHN
Ay me! this tyrant fever burns me up,
And will not let me welcome this good news. 15
Set on toward Swinstead; to my litter straight:
Weakness possesseth me, and I am faint.    Exeunt.

Scene IV. [Elsewhere on the field.]

Enter SALISBURY, PEMBROKE, and BIGOT.

SALISBURY
I did not think the king so stored with friends.

PEMBROKE
Up once again: put spirit in the French;
If they miscarry, we miscarry too.

SALISBURY
That misbegotten devil, Faulconbridge,
In spite of spite,° alone upholds the day. 5

PEMBROKE
They say King John, sore sick, hath left the field.

Enter MELUN wounded.

MELUN
Lead me to the revolts of England here.

SALISBURY
When we were happy, we had other names.

PEMBROKE
It is the Count Meloone.

SALISBURY                    Wounded to death.

MELUN
Fly, noble English, you are bought and sold;° 10
Unthread the rude eye of rebellion,°
And welcome home again discarded° faith.
Seek out King John and fall before his feet:
For if the French be lords of this loud day,
He° means to recompense the pains you take 15
By cutting off your heads! Thus hath he sworn,
And I with him, and many moe° with me,
Upon the altar at Saint Edmundsbury,
Even on that altar where we swore to you
Dear amity and everlasting love. 20

SALISBURY
May this be possible? May this be true?

MELUN
Have I not hideous death within my view,
Retaining but a quantity° of life,
Which bleeds away, even as a form of wax°
Resolveth from his figure° 'gainst the fire? 25
What in the world should make me now deceive,
Since I must lose the use° of all deceit?
Why should I then be false, since it is true

11 **Goodwin sands** shoals in the Straits of Dover
**V.iv.5 In spite of spite** despite any opposition  **10 bought and sold** duped  **11 Unthread . . . rebellion** rebellion as a needle into which they have threaded themselves  **12 discarded** (1) cast off (2) badly carded (their faith as ill-made thread)  **15 He** Lewis  **17 moe** more  **23 quantity** fragment  **24 form of wax** wax image (such, perhaps, as might be used by a witch to represent her victim)  **25 Resolveth . . . figure** relaxes its form, melts  **27 use** advantage

157 **needles** monosyllabic, pronounced "neels"  **159 brave** bravado, defiant boasting  **162 brabbler** brawler  **169 braced** stretched taut (the drumhead)  **170 reverberate** drive back (both the army and the echo)  **174 halting** imperfect, shifting  **V.iii.8 Swinstead** a mistake, historically, for Swineshead Abbey in Lincolnshire  **9 supply** of men

That I must die here, and live hence, by Truth?°
I say again, if Lewis do win the day, 30
He is forsworn° if e'er those eyes of yours
Behold another day break in the east:
But even this night, whose black contagious breath
Already smokes° about the burning crest
Of the old, feeble, and day-wearièd sun, 35
Even this ill night, your breathing shall expire,
Paying the fine° of rated° treachery
Even with a treacherous fine of all your lives,
If Lewis by your assistance win the day.
Commend me to one Hubert, with your king: 40
The love of him, and this respect° besides,
For that° my grandsire was an Englishman,
Awakes my conscience to confess all this.
In lieu whereof,° I pray you bear me hence
From forth the noise and rumor° of the field, 45
Where I may think the remnant of my thoughts
In peace, and part this body and my soul
With contemplation and devout desires.

SALISBURY
We do believe thee, and beshrew° my soul
But I do° love the favor and the form° 50
Of this most fair occasion, by the which
We will untread° the steps of damnèd flight,
And like a bated° and retirèd flood,
Leaving our rankness° and irregular course,
Stoop low within those bounds we have o'erlooked,° 55
And calmly run on in obedience
Even to our ocean, to our great King John.
My arm shall give thee help to bear thee hence,
For I do see the cruel pangs of death
Right° in thine eye. Away, my friends! New flight, 60
And happy newness,° that intends old right.
*Exeunt [assisting* MELUN].

Scene V. [*The Dauphin's camp.*]

*Enter* [ LEWIS *the*] *Dauphin, and his* TRAIN.

LEWIS
The sun of heaven methought was loath to set,
But stayed and made the western welkin blush,
When English measured backward their own ground
In faint retire!° O, bravely came we off,°
When with a volley of our needless shot, 5
After such bloody toil, we bid good night
And wound our tott'ring colors clearly up,°

---

**29 die . . . Truth** only if he dies undissembling and
serving God can he hope for eternal life in heaven **31 is
forsworn** will be perjured **34 smokes** spreads like smoke
**37 fine** penalty (but in the next line "fine" = end); **rated**
(1) evaluated (2) chided **41 respect** consideration **42 For
that** because **44 lieu whereof** exchange for which **45
rumor** tumult **49 beshrew** a curse upon **50 But I do**
if I do not; **favor . . . form** appearance **52 untread**
retrace **53 bated** subsided **54 rankness** (1) excessive
size (2) impetuous violence (3) offensive odor **55 Stoop . . .
o'erlooked** (1) contract within those banks we have overflowed (2) kneel to accept those obligations we have disregarded **60 Right** clearly **61 happy newness** appropriate
and favorable change
**V.v.4 faint retire** cowardly retreat; **bravely . . . off** (1) fear-
lessly and (2) worthily we left the field **7 wound . . . up**
rolled up our (1) tattered (2) flapping banners without interference

---

Last in the field, and almost lords of it!

*Enter a* MESSENGER.

MESSENGER
Where is my prince, the Dolphin?
LEWIS                                   Here. What news?
MESSENGER
The Count Meloone is slain; the English lords
By his persuasion are again fall'n off,
And your supply, which you have wished so long, 10
Are cast away and sunk on Goodwin sands.
LEWIS
Ah, foul, shrewd° news! Beshrew thy very heart!
I did not think to be so sad tonight 15
As this hath made me. Who was he that said
King John did fly an hour or two before
The stumbling° night did part our weary pow'rs?
MESSENGER
Whoever spoke it, it is true, my lord.
LEWIS
Well!° keep good quarter and good care tonight: 20
The day shall not be up so soon as I
To try the fair adventure of tomorrow. *Exeunt.*

Scene VI. [*Near Swinstead.*]

*Enter* BASTARD *and* HUBERT, *severally.*°

HUBERT
Who's there? Speak, ho! speak quickly, or I shoot.
BASTARD
A friend. What art thou?
HUBERT                              Of the part° of England.
BASTARD
Whither dost thou go?
HUBERT
What's that to thee? Why may not I demand
Of thine affairs as well as thou of mine? 5
BASTARD
Hubert, I think?
HUBERT              Thou hast a perfect° thought.
I will upon all hazards well believe
Thou art my friend, that know'st my tongue so well.
Who art thou?°
BASTARD              Who thou wilt: and if thou please,
Thou mayst befriend me so much as to think 10
I come one way of the Plantagenets.
HUBERT
Unkind remembrance!° thou and endless night
Have done me shame.° Brave soldier, pardon me,
That any accent breaking from thy tongue
Should scape the true acquaintance of mine ear. 15
BASTARD
Come, come! sans compliment,° what news abroad?

---

**14 shrewd** grievous, cursed **18 stumbling** stumbling-causing
**20 Well** Good!
**V.vi.s.d. severally** from opposite sides **2 Of the part** on
the side **6 perfect** correct **9 Who art thou** given John's
weakness and Arthur's death, this is now a key question **12
remembrance** (1) reminder (2) memory **12–13 thou . . .
shame** the Bastard, by recognizing Hubert's voice though
Hubert did not recognize his; the night, by concealing his
features **16 sans compliment** without courtly flattery

HUBERT
  Why, here walk I, in the black brow° of night,
  To find you out.
BASTARD          Brief, then; and what's the news?
HUBERT
  O, my sweet sir, news fitting to the night,
  Black, fearful, comfortless, and horrible.        20
BASTARD
  Show me the very wound of this ill news:
  I am no woman; I'll not swound° at it.
HUBERT
  The king, I fear, is poisoned by a monk:
  I left him almost speechless, and broke out°
  To acquaint you with this evil, that you might        25
  The better arm you to the sudden time°
  Than if you had at leisure° known of this.
BASTARD
  How did he take it? Who did taste to° him?
HUBERT
  A monk, I tell you, a resolvèd° villain
  Whose bowels suddenly burst out.° The king        30
  Yet speaks, and peradventure° may recover.
BASTARD
  Who didst thou leave to tend his majesty?
HUBERT
  Why, know you not? The lords are all come back,
  And brought Prince Henry° in their company,
  At whose request the king hath pardoned them,        35
  And they are all about his majesty.
BASTARD
  Withhold thine indignation, mighty God,
  And tempt us not to bear above our power!°
  I'll tell thee, Hubert, half my power° this night,
  Passing these flats,° are taken by the tide;        40
  These Lincoln Washes have devourèd them;
  Myself, well mounted, hardly have escaped.
  Away before! Conduct me to the king;
  I doubt° he will be dead or ere° I come.        *Exeunt.*

Scene VII. [*An orchard at Swinstead Abbey.*]

*Enter* PRINCE HENRY, SALISBURY, *and* BIGOT.

PRINCE HENRY
  It is too late: the life of all his blood
  Is touched corruptibly,° and his pure° brain,
  Which some suppose the soul's frail dwelling house,
  Doth, by the idle° comments that it makes,

  Foretell the ending of mortality.        5

*Enter* PEMBROKE.

PEMBROKE
  His highness yet doth speak, and holds belief
  That, being brought into the open air,
  It would allay the burning quality
  Of that fell° poison which assaileth him.
PRINCE HENRY
  Let him be brought into the orchard here.        10
  Doth he still rage?°
PEMBROKE        He is more patient
  Than when you left him; even now he sung.
           [*Exit* PEMBROKE.]
PRINCE HENRY
  O, vanity of sickness! fierce extremes
  In their continuance will not feel themselves.°
  Death, having preyed upon the outward parts,        15
  Leaves them invisible,° and his siege is now
  Against the mind, the which he pricks and wounds
  With many legions of strange fantasies,
  Which, in their throng and press to that last hold,°
  Confound themselves.° 'Tis strange that death should
       sing!        20
  I am the cygnet to this pale faint swan,
  Who chants a doleful hymn to his own death,°
  And from the organ-pipe of frailty sings
  His soul and body to their lasting rest.
SALISBURY
  Be of good comfort, prince, for you are born        25
  To set a form upon that indigest°
  Which he hath left so shapeless and so rude.

[KING] JOHN *brought in.*

KING JOHN
  Ay, marry, now my soul hath elbowroom,
  It would not out at windows, nor at doors;°
  There is so hot a summer in my bosom        30
  That all my bowels crumble up to dust!
  I am a scribbled form, drawn with a pen
  Upon a parchment, and against this fire
  Do I shrink up.
PRINCE HENRY    How fares your majesty?
KING JOHN
  Poisoned—ill fare!° dead, forsook, cast off,        35
  And none of you will bid the winter come
  To thrust his icy fingers in my maw,
  Nor let my kingdom's rivers take their course
  Through my burned bosom, nor entreat the north
  To make his bleak winds kiss my parchèd lips        40
  And comfort me with cold. I do not ask you much—

**17 in . . . brow** under the threatening countenance    **22
swound** faint    **24 broke out** left abruptly    **26 arm . . .
time** prepare yourself (both psychologically and materially)
for the crisis    **27 at leisure** without haste    **28 taste to**
act as taster for (the taster sampled each dish to detect
possible poison)    **29 resolvèd** resolute (he poisoned himself,
by tasting, in order to poison the king)    **30 Whose . . . out**
cf. the death of Judas (Acts 1:18)    **31 peradventure** perhaps
**34 Prince Henry** John's son (this is the first mention of him in
the play)    **38 tempt . . . power** (1) do not tempt us to undertake more than we can accomplish (2) do not test us by imposing
more suffering than we can endure    **39 power** army    **40
these flats** the tidal flats at the mouth of the River Welland in
The Wash, a large inlet between Lincolnshire and Norfolk
**44 doubt** fear; **or ere** before
**V.vii.2 touched corruptibly** infected to the point of decom-
position; **pure** lucid    **4 idle** irrational

**9 fell** cruel    **11 rage** rave    **13–14 fierce . . . themselves** as
the sufferings of a dying man continue he loses awareness
of them    **16 invisible** modifies "Death" but suggests also,
as modifying "outward parts," John's present disregard of his
pains    **19 hold** stronghold    **20 Confound themselves**
defeat or destroy one another (the fantasies seeking to capture
John's mind so get in each other's way that no one of them
succeeds)    **22 Who . . . death** the swan was fabled to sing
only as it died    **26 indigest** shapeless confusion    **28–29 now
. . . doors** either now my soul has room to escape me,
which it did not have inside the abbey, or now that my soul
has room, it still refuses to leave my body    **35 ill fare** (1) ill
fortune (2) bad food

I beg cold comfort—and you are so strait,°
And so ingrateful, you deny me that.

PRINCE HENRY

O, that there were some virtue° in my tears
That might relieve you!

KING JOHN                 The salt in them is hot.          45
Within me is a hell, and there the poison
Is as a fiend confined to tyrannize
On unreprievable condemnèd blood.

*Enter* BASTARD.

BASTARD

O, I am scalded° with my violent motion
And spleen° of speed to see your majesty!          50

KING JOHN

O cousin, thou art come to set mine eye!°
The tackle of my heart is cracked and burnt,
And all the shrouds° wherewith my life should sail
Are turnèd to one thread, one little hair:
My heart hath one poor string to stay it by,          55
Which holds but till thy news be utterèd,
And then all this thou see'st is but a clod
And module° of confounded° royalty.

BASTARD

The Dolphin is preparing hitherward,
Where God He knows° how we shall answer him,          60
For in a night the best part of my pow'r,
As I upon advantage did remove,°
Were in the Washes all unwarily°
Devourèd by the unexpected flood.   [*The* KING *dies*.]

SALISBURY

You breathe these dead news° in as dead an ear.          65
My liege! my lord!—but now a king, now thus!

PRINCE HENRY

Even so must I run on, and even so stop.
What surety° of the world, what hope, what stay,°
When this was now a king, and now is clay?

BASTARD

Art thou gone so? I do but stay behind          70
To do the office for thee of revenge,
And then my soul shall wait on thee to heaven,
As it on earth hath been thy servant still.°
Now, now, you stars that move in your right spheres,°
Where be your pow'rs?° Show now your mended
    faiths,          75
And instantly return with me again,
To push destruction and perpetual shame

Out of the weak door of our fainting land:
Straight° let us seek, or straight we shall be sought.
The Dolphin rages at our very heels.          80

SALISBURY

It seems you know not, then, so much as we:
The Cardinal Pandulph is within at rest,
Who half an hour since came from the Dolphin
And brings from him such offers of our peace
As we with honor and respect may take,          85
With purpose presently to leave this war.

BASTARD

He will the rather do it when he sees
Ourselves well sinewèd to our defense.

SALISBURY

Nay, 'tis in a manner done already,
For many carriages° he hath dispatched          90
To the seaside, and put his cause and quarrel
To the disposing of the cardinal,
With whom yourself, myself, and other lords,
If you think meet, this afternoon will post°
To consummate this business happily.          95

BASTARD

Let it be so; and you, my noble prince,
With other princes that may best be spared,
Shall wait upon° your father's funeral.

PRINCE HENRY

At Worcester must his body be interred,
For so he willed it.

BASTARD                 Thither shall it then.          100
And happily° may your sweet self put on
The lineal state° and glory of the land!
To whom, with all submission, on my knee,
I do bequeath my faithful services
And true subjection everlastingly.          105

SALISBURY

And the like tender° of our love we make,
To rest without a spot° for evermore.

PRINCE HENRY

I have a kind soul that would give thanks,
And knows not how to do it but with tears.

BASTARD

O, let us pay the time but needful woe,          110
Since it hath been beforehand with our griefs.°
This England never did, nor never shall,
Lie at the proud foot of a conqueror
But when it first did help to wound itself.
Now these her princes are come home again,          115
Come the three corners° of the world in arms,
And we shall shock them!° Naught shall make us rue
If England to itself do rest but true!          *Exeunt.*

---

42 **strait** narrow, severe, stingy   44 **virtue** healing power
49 **scalded** overheated, covered with hot liquid (perspiration)
50 **spleen** impetuous violence, eagerness   51 **set mine eye**
close my eyes after I die   53 **shrouds** (1) ropes holding a
mast in place; with a contextually, but not syntactically,
appropriate reminder of (2) winding sheets   58 **module**
image; **confounded** defeated, destroyed   60 **God He knows**
God only knows   62 **upon . . . remove** seizing the chance
changed my location   63 **unwarily** without warning   65 **dead
news** (1) deadly news (2) news of death   68 **surety** guarantee, certainty; **stay** (1) support (2) continuance   73 **still** constantly   74 **stars . . . spheres** noblemen who have returned
to your proper positions   75 **pow'rs** (1) armed troops (2)
astral influences

79 **Straight** immediately   90 **carriages** wagons   94 **post**
hasten   98 **wait upon** escort ceremonially   101 **happily**
fittingly   102 **lineal state** directly inherited rank (as king), or
the crown, etc., denoting that rank   106 **tender** offer   107
**spot** stain (of disloyalty)   110–11 **let . . . griefs** let us weep
no more than necessary since time has anticipated our griefs
(providing compensation: the French abandonment of the
invasion offsetting the English losses; Henry replacing John)
116 **the three corners** presumably England is the fourth
117 **shock them** (1) meet them in battle (2) throw them into
confusion (3) tie them in bundles like sheaves (?)

# THE MERCHANT OF VENICE

### EDITED BY KENNETH MYRICK

## Introduction

*The Merchant of Venice* is the earliest of three superb comedies in which Shakespeare has set a generous and clear-sighted woman in sharp contrast to a no less unusual, but markedly unsocial man. From beginning to end, Portia and Shylock—like Rosalind and Jaques in *As You Like It* and Viola and Malvolio in *Twelfth Night*—remain poles apart. It is significant that Portia in her greatest scene, and the two other heroines in nearly all of their scenes, are disguised as men. Only the audience and one confidante share their secret. Knowing it, the spectators naturally tend to center their interest in them and to view the play through their eyes. Portia, Rosalind, and Viola tend to overshadow their lovers, not because, as is often asserted, the men are not worthy of them, but because of their fascinating double roles.

Their respective opponents—Shylock, Jaques, and Malvolio—are all vivid, but strange and isolated figures. None is an actual villain, but each has been accurately called an *antihero*.

On the Elizabethan stage, it was probably easier for Portia to take the leading role than it is in the modern theater. In Shakespeare's company there was a better balance than in modern times, when the star actor tends to overshadow all the others. The lady's handicap is especially formidable when the star is, like Sir Henry Irving, both the manager of the theater and even the director of the troupe. Ellen Terry was at her best, she said, when she played against Irving, but she could not be the central figure of the play that Portia is meant to be. At times in the nineteenth century, Shylock so overshadowed everyone else that the beautiful final act was omitted entirely.

It is pretty clear today that when Jaques or Malvolio is allowed to usurp the leading role, the entire play is thrown out of balance. In *The Merchant of Venice* the problem is complicated by other factors. The late E. E. Stoll, in a justly famous essay, argued that Shylock was always an unsympathetic figure to the Elizabethans because he is a miser, a usurer, and a Jew. The attitude of the civilized world has changed toward all three. We have hardly ever known a miser. The usurer seems only a man who lends money at interest. And prejudice against Jews is hateful to all fair-minded people. How then can any decent person appreciate this comedy in the spirit in which Stoll thought it was written? How valid is his view?

The strength of Stoll's interpretation lies in his strong common sense, massive erudition, and insights into dramatic method. He stressed the great importance of the common beliefs, prejudices, and superstitions that distinguish Shakespeare's time from our own era. He emphasized the significance of our vivid first impressions, of the contrasts of character with character and plot with subplot, and the necessity of approaching a play as a play and not as a book. He saw that as readers we tend to respond as individuals, but as spectators we tend to catch the contagion of the crowd and respond like everyone else. With all his gifts as an interpreter of Shakespeare, however, Stoll appears sometimes to have been strangely insensitive to the humanizing ideals of Shakespeare's age and the poetic atmosphere of his plays.

"*The Merchant of Venice* is a fairy tale," declared that wise man of the theater, Harley Granville-Barker. We may think he made too much of this point, but he reminded us forcibly that the play is set in the realm of high romance. We cannot understand it in terms of modern realism. Strange and wonderful are the stories of the caskets, the pound of flesh, and the beautiful girl disguised as a wise young judge—not to mention the miser's daughter who blossoms into a delightful and virtuous lady, filled with the joy of life. We begin to sense this poetic atmosphere in the very first scene.

### ACT I

*Antonio and Bassanio.* Antonio is not in the least the stodgy, smug, intolerant businessman that he is often supposed to be. A great merchant prince of the fabulous city of Venice, he sends out his splendid ships as far as Mexico and the Indies and shares his wealth with the needy and oppressed. In his quiet way, he—like Bassanio and Portia, Lorenzo and Jessica—is a figure of romance. His friends see poetry in his commercial ventures:

Your argosies with portly sail—
Like signiors and rich burghers on the flood,
Or as it were the pageants of the sea—
Do overpeer the petty traffickers
That cursy to them, do them reverence,
As they fly by them with their woven wings.    (I.i.9–14)

His friends see also a great and ever-present danger. The modern merchant is often depicted as a type enjoying comfortable security. Salerio and Solanio, like people today when they think of the astronauts, are fascinated and appalled by the risks that Antonio takes. Yet he faces these constant dangers with a quiet mind. Shakespeare, like the medieval poets, could find romance in the old themes of love and battle; but with a poet's insight into men and affairs, he discovered it also in the merchant-adventurer's commerce, in which, as in knightly times, danger went hand in hand with beauty and high achievement.

Antonio is admired and beloved for his good deeds. Yet the poet has wisely given him a relatively passive role. If we felt his emotions too keenly, the scene of his trial would be too painful for comedy. His "sadness" contributes to this passiveness. One guess about the cause of his melancholy is that he fears Bassanio's approaching marriage will separate him from his friend. Another is that he is just in a strange mood. Antonio, however, is too generous to regret his friend's happy marriage, and the emphasis given to his mood suggests an important meaning.

We can find it in one of the common ideas of the Elizabethan age, the belief in presentiments. Shakespeare uses it in many plays to foreshadow future events, especially dangers and misfortunes. It is somewhat analogous to the faith in extrasensory perception, which (though not shared by the present editor) is held by some of our very intelligent contemporaries. A striking parallel to Antonio's sadness is in *Richard II*, which was probably written just before *The Merchant of Venice*. In one scene Queen Isabel's attendants are troubled about her sadness, a much more violent melancholy than Antonio's. Suddenly, after only a few moments, she hears the shocking news of Bolingbroke's rebellion, which is to bring about the dethronement and murder of her husband. She instantly recognizes the meaning of her presentiment.

Antonio's unaccountable sadness is a less violent experience than Queen Isabel's, apparently because the danger is more remote and because in the end he escapes it. But in kind, though not in degree, the two presentiments are alike.

Few moderns have such faith in extrasensory perception as many intelligent Elizabethans had in presentiments. Therefore, we go astray if we invent rationalistic explanations for Antonio's sadness which neither the poet nor his audience had in mind—just as we do when we explain Banquo's ghost, or King Hamlet's, as a figment of the imagination. These are cases that require the "willing suspension of disbelief."

Antonio's presentiment has an important dramatic function. It suggests to the audience some great danger of which he and his friends are totally unconscious. Thus it creates dramatic irony, quickens suspense, and awakens a warm concern for this modest and generous merchant

prince, who is so much admired and beloved. In his next scene it also heightens our concern for him when he readily agrees to Shylock's apparently jovial suggestion that Antonio forfeit a pound of flesh if the three thousand ducats are not paid back on time.

Bassanio has sometimes been misunderstood even more seriously than Antonio—as a contemptible man of fashion who puts his friend's life in danger so that he can gamble on winning an heiress. His best qualities, as Professor Bernard Grebanier has remarked, have become increasingly rare in the last century and a half. He speaks with "an elegance which is innate and unconscious. . . . The miraculous thing is that . . . this patrician quality of the mind is united . . . with a manliness, an unaggressive virility of a kind to which the twentieth century is becoming totally a stranger." His first words about Portia—"In Belmont is a lady richly left" (I.i.161)—do not mean that he wants to marry her for money, but that "there is good reason to promise the return of the loan" he is asking of his friend. His eloquent words about Portia herself assure us that his love for her is genuine.

As the play develops, we find Bassanio's friend, Gratiano, asking to go with him to Belmont. A loud extrovert, Gratiano "speaks an infinite deal of nothing," and is the last person Bassanio would choose to accompany him on a delicate mission. But with a few very frank words of caution, he generously accedes to his friend's surprising request, without the slightest trace of irritation. At Belmont we see Bassanio not only as a delightful gentleman, but as a man of thought and insight as he meditates on which casket to choose. When he has won Portia, we like him for his overwhelming joy, his modesty, and his entire devotion to her.

The world of Bassanio and Antonio is not ours. Its values are chiefly those of a governing class—courage, justice, a high sense of honor, courtesy, learning, a love of beauty, compassion, and humility. Lord Bassanio has the highest rank of anyone in the play except the Duke, yet he never shows even a trace of arrogance. Like Sir Philip Sidney, the most admired and beloved young Englishman of Shakespeare's time, Bassanio has lived beyond his means because of the position he occupies. For him, as for Sidney and Castiglione, life is at once an earnest task, an adventure, and a fine art. To Sidney, Shakespeare, and their contemporaries, the marriage of so fine a nobleman as Bassanio with a virtuous, gifted, humanely educated, and wholly delightful lady of wealth would be altogether fitting.

*Portia.* As for Portia, even most of Shylock's warmest partisans commonly find her irresistible in her early scenes, however they may dislike her way of defeating him in the court scene. Some, of course, grumble at her deft satire of her egregious parcel of wooers, and one critic can declare solemnly, "Portia herself, for some reason, is the least lovable of Shakespeare's comedy heroines." Harley Granville-Barker, who saw nearly all the characters with remarkable clarity, observed that the poet reveals Portia's character "to us mainly in little things, and lets us feel its whole happy virtue in the melody of her speech." Granville-Barker also points out that, hedged about as she is by her father's will in the early scenes, there is very little for her to do. However this may be, the strangeness of her situation captures our attention, and the naturalness of her thoughts and feelings leads us to identify ourselves at once with her cause and to sense the irony of her situation. Although her father did not trust her to choose a husband for herself, yet, as her shrewd comments on her suitors reveal, few women ever had a keener insight into men's characters than she. Nevertheless, she does not really rebel against her father's will, and when she learns it has driven away six unwelcome suitors, she is amazed and delighted at the old man's foresight. Her filial piety meant more to the Elizabethans than to us, but her quick feelings, her sense of responsibility, her wit and keen perception of the ridiculous belong to every age and make her one of the most magnetic of heroines.

*Shylock and Antonio.*

SHYLOCK   Three thousand ducats—well.
BASSANIO   Ay, sir, for three months.
SHYLOCK   For three months—well.          (I.iii.1–3)

Shylock comes before us abruptly, with no previous hint that he exists. Antonio and Portia, in their first speeches, confide their thoughts and feelings to their friends. Bassanio, alone with Antonio, pours out his heart. But Shylock, from the first words he utters, is a strangely isolated figure, secretive and calculating. We begin to discover his real thoughts only when he utters them aside as Antonio enters. The hatred that he expresses so vehemently and his efforts later in the scene to appear as Antonio's cordial friend are in glaring contradiction.

Defenders of Shylock often argue that at first his offer of friendship is sincere, and that he never meant the forfeit of a pound of Antonio's flesh as anything but "a merry jest," until Jessica deserted him to elope with one of Antonio's Christian friends. This interpretation ignores the basic principle that every essential point must be clear to the simplest groundling. When a character in Shakespeare speaks aside to the audience, he always speaks his real thoughts. When Shylock says, as Antonio enters,

If I can catch him once upon the hip,
I will feed fat the ancient grudge I bear him   (I.iii.43–44)

we have no choice but to believe him.

E. E. Stoll's famous, though one-sided, interpretation of Shylock is indispensable for an understanding of Shylock's real character. Stoll demonstrates that the issue between the Jewish money lender and the Christian merchant is not simply the taking of interest. It is the usurer's merciless exploitation of his victims. He is no mere "banker," as H. B. Charlton called him, but a crafty and ruthless loan shark. The Tudor laws against usury stated an ideal and then compromised with the practical facts of trade. They outlawed any interest on any loan but imposed no penalty if the rate did not exceed ten percent (nearly twice the rate commonly charged today for a mortgage loan). The typical usurer, however, found devious ways of exacting far more than the law allowed. His special victims were the inexperienced and the very needy—widows and orphans, and young gentlemen not yet possessed of their inheritance. For an original loan of a hundred pounds, the clever usurer might gain in a few years real estate worth five hundred or a thousand pounds, bringing his wretched debtor to beggary or death. The Elizabethan hatred of usury was sanctioned by Aristotle's theory that money cannot breed money; but far more important were the enormous interest rates and fraudulent contracts of clever scoundrels. Recognizing Shylock as a usurer, the Elizabethans must have been hostile to him, especially when they saw him plotting against Antonio's life.

Why does he hate this generous merchant? Antonio has denounced Shylock in public. He has loaned money to the usurer's victims, has charged them no interest at all and thus enabled many of them to escape total ruin. Although he has never till now either charged interest on a loan, or paid it, Antonio is ready to "break a custom" rather than have his best friend risk losing Portia. For this, many critics, supposing the issue to involve one of Antonio's absolute principles, charge him with hypocrisy. But Antonio, as a man of affairs, is less interested in theory than in results. The charge would be valid only if he were exacting interest from a debtor. To rescue the usurer's victims, he has loaned them money at no interest. To enable Bassanio to win Portia, he will himself pay interest on a loan, rather than let his best friend lose his dearest hopes. In each case his concern is to bring generous aid to those in need.

While discussing the loan with Antonio, Shylock suddenly digresses and pours out one of his most eloquent and moving speeches. In the Rialto, he declares, in full view of crowds of merchants, Antonio has publicly disgraced him. He has called him dog, kicked him, and spat upon him. Some very intelligent readers have refused to believe these charges, but Antonio himself confirms them.

I am as like to call thee so again,
To spet on thee again, to spurn thee too.   (I.iii.127–28)

It is a strange and shameful fact that for many centuries Christians held it to be proper to spit in a Jew's face on certain occasions. The idea goes back to the Crucifixion, when the Jews mocked Christ and spat upon him. Similarly, the horrible idea that the Jews had become a race accursed by God arose from their refusal to accept Jesus as the Messiah. In spite of these bitter prejudices, however, it is hard to believe that Shakespeare approved Antonio's way of publicly denouncing the usurer. The words he gives Shylock seem designed to show us how it feels to be an outcast in a Christian society.

It is hard to know the exact meaning of a gesture common four centuries ago. Just what did it mean in the social context of Elizabethan England? The great queen herself once "spat upon a courtier's cloak that displeased her." The act of thumbing the nose was originally an obscene insult, but we have seen friends use it as a bit of light teasing.

As a compassionate man, outraged by the usurer's inhumanity to his victims, Antonio is capable of hot indignation, as we see in his answer to Shylock's charge. Today he might expose a dangerous public enemy in a newspaper or television interview, or by presenting the facts to the prosecuting attorney. In Shakespeare's Venice, where the practice of usury seems to have been as inhuman as anywhere else, Antonio takes the kind of direct action that decent Americans sometimes took against an unscrupulous man in pioneer days on the frontier. Antonio deliberately insults the usurer, literally kicks him out of his place of business, does all he can to turn public opinion against him, and spends his own money to rescue Shylock's victims. Christ himself, though he preached the gospel of love, denounced the oppressors and hypocrites in public and whipped the money changers out of the temple. Antonio's just indignation is natural and understandable, and so is Shylock's bitter resentment. We begin to see Shylock as his own worst enemy, poisoned by greed and hate.

## ACTS II AND III

From the harsh but strangely compelling figure of the antihero, we turn immediately to Portia. In her scenes with Morocco and Aragon, she is a marvel of self-control and courtesy, although some of her speeches to them are edged with an irony that they never catch. Her whole future happiness is at stake, for neither Morocco nor Aragon can appreciate the best qualities of a Renaissance lady. Morocco is a warmhearted man of honor and courage, who has the grace to think he may not deserve her. But there is something naive, almost barbaric, in his desire that his fate be decided by having his rivals and himself cut their flesh to see whose blood is reddest. His mind is very simple; hers is highly endowed by nature and has acquired the best culture of a remarkable age and country. We wish Morocco well, but he is no mate for Portia. As for Aragon, he has the presumptuous pride that the Elizabethans disliked in the Spaniards. He has also the naiveté to suppose that a man could actually deserve such a woman as Portia, and that he is that man. Most of Shakespeare's genuine lovers are, like Portia and Bassanio, humbled by their love.

One key to the meaning of a Shakespeare play is the way he directs our sympathies. In many of his masterpieces there is one person, or more, through whose eyes we are particularly invited to see the other characters and the events. In *Henry IV* it is chiefly Prince Hal, in *Hamlet* it is Horatio and Hamlet, in *Twelfth Night* it is Viola. Who is it in *The Merchant of Venice*?

In the opening scene, in which Antonio is the center of attention but at first does little, we see him as four of his friends do. In Shylock's first scene, many modern readers see him as he sees himself, but those who realize what a usurer actually was will look at him as Bassanio and Antonio do. Stoll, in a long analysis, argued that whenever we begin to sympathize with Shylock, his greed and hatred are emphasized. He accuses Antonio of disgracing him and then plots to kill him. He speaks of Launcelot as a kind patch, but adds that he is "a huge feeder." He speaks kindly to his daughter as "Jessica, my girl," and instantly remembers his dream of moneybags. In one of his greatest scenes, he pours out a passionate defense of the Jewish people and a challenge to Christians to practice the mercy and humility that they profess; but he ends the speech on the note of revenge, arranging with Tubal to meet him at the synagogue to plan the legalized murder of a generous Christian merchant.

Stoll makes an important point. But we can turn it around and show, on his own evidence, that in each of Shylock's scenes, except the briefest, he wins the sympathy of the audience for at least a few moments. When do we ever see the least touch of kindly feeling in Iago or Goneril?

Shylock differs, too, from other Shakespearean villains—from Angelo in *Measure for Measure*, with whom he is often compared, and from Hamlet's uncle, King Claudius—in that these men are entirely conscious of their villainy. At the trial, Shylock can ask, apparently in all sincerity, "What judgment shall I dread, doing no wrong?" The unique thing about Shylock is this strange sincerity. He can nurse the most diabolical passions and imagine he does no wrong.

Doubtless the Elizabethans laughed with Solanio and Salerio when they baited Shylock, for as Stoll has emphasized, a general audience in the theater will respond to the mood of the characters on stage. Yet we must never suppose that these two friends of Antonio express more than a very small part of Shakespeare's attitude toward the Jew. These characters can scarcely be distinguished from one another, and we do not go to such people to find Shakespeare's whole meaning. Their function is chiefly to release the feelings of the audience or to tell us news. In the court scene, the jeers and imprecations of Gratiano provide a similar release. But "Gratiano speaks an infinite deal of nothing, more than any man in all Venice." The shallow comments of this excited extrovert contrast with the wisdom of Portia and the considered judgment of Antonio.

Throughout the play, Shakespeare has invited us to look at the other characters and the action through Portia's eyes, and to share her sympathies. One way he does this is in the skillful arrangement of contrasting scenes. He places Shylock's first scene between Portia's first and second, and her third just after Jessica's flight. Beginning with Portia's fourth scene (II.ix), he alternates her scenes with Shylock's with almost exact regularity until their encounter in the courtroom. In this way the poet silently draws ever more sharply the contrast between the usurer and the wise Renaissance lady, before either has any idea of the other's existence.

Our sympathies are never so strongly with Portia, or with Bassanio, as in the beautiful scene where he wins her, particularly in the tense moments while she watches him meditating on which casket to choose, and in the climax that brings them a happiness they can hardly express. When the sudden news comes of Antonio's catastrophic losses, Portia instantly offers her entire fortune to save her husband's friend of whom until now she has never heard. Like Bassanio and Antonio, she knows how to "give and hazard all she hath." In this scene of love and generous friendship, we see Portia at her best.

In the next scene we find Shylock at his worst, raging madly at Antonio and promising to take his life. It is his one scene in the play in which we can have no spark of sympathy for him. Is destiny on his side, or on Portia's?

## SHYLOCK AND JUDAISM

As we approach the court scene, we must face the question of Shakespeare's attitude toward the Jews. Stoll and some others believed he shared the hateful prejudice that had disgraced Christianity for over fifteen centuries. In 1935, Professor John W. Draper sharply challenged this view. "Shylock the Jew was merely exotic local color," he declared. "Shylock the usurer was a commentary on London life." The second statement is certainly true; there were many usurers in the great city, and their cruelty was notorious. The first statement is partly true. Dr. J. L. Cardozo seems to have proved that—contrary to common opinion—there were no Jews, or almost none, dwelling anywhere in Shakespeare's London, unless we except the small band of a few hundred Portuguese who had converted from Judaism to Christianity. Shylock must have been an exotic figure to the Elizabethans.

His Judaism, however, is emphasized again and again. In Shylock the great virtues of the ancient Hebrews have often been corrupted into the nearest vices. Reverence for law has degenerated into legalism, loyalty to his own people into a vehement antipathy to Christians, practical sagacity into the love of money, a noble love of justice into a fanatical thirst for a revenge that excludes every thought of mercy. Yet until the climax of the court scene, Shylock is blindly unconscious of doing anything wrong. Here is no mere comic butt, no mere hypocrite and villain, but a warped and dangerous fanatic—sometimes comic, sometimes hateful—impervious to any normal appeal to common sense or natural kindness, but always strangely human. Something has poisoned this man, and apparently a whole people, originally splendidly endowed by nature.

Most modern readers find the source of the poison in Christian persecution. Shakespeare touches on this idea, especially in Shylock's great defense of the humanity of the Jews. But his emphasis lies elsewhere. Shylock is fiercely conscious of his "sacred nation." He defends the iniquitous practice of usury by citing the Old Testament. As Christians had always said of the Jews from the days of Saint Paul, he insists on the bare letter of the law and ignores the spirit. He goes to the synagogue to plan Antonio's death. In the court scene he declares solemnly he has "an oath in heaven" that he will cut the pound of flesh from Antonio. Earlier we see momentarily a better side of his Judaism, in his memory of his wife's first gift. It is obvious, nevertheless, that Shakespeare has many times connected Shylock's worst qualities with the Hebrew religion.

So hateful is this idea to us that we must be very certain just what it meant to Shakespeare. The prejudice is not at all the Nazi's hatred of the Jew's blood and supposed race, for Jessica is "a daughter to his blood" but not to "his manners," that is, his moral values and actions. The hostility is directed against Shylock's code of ethics and the religion that is assumed to be its source.

How could the humane and clear-sighted Shakespeare ever have taken such a view of one of the world's great religions? Perhaps we can most easily understand his view if we remember the attitude toward Puritans that is held today by some humane but not well-informed people. Without examining the facts with an open mind, they see the Puritans as narrow zealots or even hypocrites, who—like Shylock—despised beauty and merrymaking, loved money, and looked down with contempt on their less sanctified neighbors. Although these people think of themselves as enlightened and tolerant, they regard the Puritan religion as a fanaticism—a perverted view of life which warped a man's mind, chilled his sympathies, and poisoned his relations with all who did not share the special outlook of the chosen few. There is some truth in this picture, but impartial historians know it to be, on the whole, distorted and unjust.

The analogy with Judaism is very close, for the Puritans' emphasis on the Old Testament made them the most Hebraic of Christian groups. In Elizabeth's reign, even men of large minds and generous sympathies could regard the Jewish faith very much as many of our contemporaries regard Puritanism. For centuries Christians had been taught almost universally that the ancient religion of Israel had degenerated into a narrow fanaticism, teaching a pedantic adherence to the mere letter of the law and ignoring the spirit. "The letter killeth but the spirit giveth life," wrote Saint Paul. As a Christian scholar of our time, James Parkes, wrote: "The inadequacy of the law . . . was [the church fathers'] continual accusation against the Jews." Parkes also observed that our English word *law* is no adequate equivalent for the original word *Torah* in the Hebrew text:

> The written law was . . . the basis of *Torah*, but *Torah* itself was the complete revelation of the holy community or nation through which the individual in every act could fulfill the purpose of God in his creation.

Between this lofty Hebrew concept and the Christian idea of the divine mercy which at once fulfills and transcends the law, there is no irreconcilable conflict. Shakespeare and the members of his audience, however, could not know what scholars so wise as Richard Hooker (1554?–1600) had not discovered.

The modern parallel to Shylock is not the Jews. It is the Nazi persecutors of the Jews.

## THE TRIAL

The scene of Antonio's trial surpasses almost anything Shakespeare had ever written previously in both range and power. The sustained clash of wills, the battle of ideas, the variety of characterization, the prolonged suspense (relieved now and then by touches of comedy), the deepening irony, and the stunning reversal of fortune when Portia finally turns Shylock's own weapon against himself—all these reveal the hand of a great craftsman and the inspiration of a master poet.

Often in the nineteenth century, and sometimes in the twentieth, this scene has been interpreted as "The Tragedy of Shylock." Stoll interpreted it as harsh comedy. After the reversal of fortune, he says, "The Jew's very words are echoed by Portia and Gratiano as they jeer, and at every turn that justice takes . . . there are now peals and shouts of laughter." Neither interpretation does justice to Shakespeare's sane and compassionate view.

In the first place, though everyone else is appalled at Shylock's cruelty, he himself is here a figure of real dignity. The mad fierceness of his last two scenes is gone. As he addresses the Duke, his language is eloquent, and his strange reasoning is cogent. Confident in the justice of his cause, he regards Gratiano's bitter curse with amused indifference. To the Duke and Portia he shows a courteous respect. Up to the sudden reversal of his fortunes, he treats her with admiration and genuine friendliness. In one sense, we see him at his best in this scene. With some exceptions, his bearing in more than half the scene is that of a civilized man of affairs. The contrast between his manner and his fanatical purpose heightens the effect. He is a shrewd and persuasive advocate in his astounding case. When the Duke makes a powerful appeal that he show "human gentleness and love," Shylock defends with powerful logic his right to take Antonio's life.

DUKE
How shalt thou hope for mercy, rend'ring none?
SHYLOCK
What judgment shall I dread, doing no wrong?

(IV.i.88–89)

The tension of the scene mounts steadily, but Shakespeare skillfully breaks it now and then. Just before Bellario's messenger (Nerissa) comes in, we are deeply moved by the selfless friendship of Bassanio and Antonio, as each insists that he should die for the other. Then the sight of Nerissa trying, without quite perfect success, to act the part of an experienced law clerk brings a hint of comedy. As spectators we need not laugh, but all will feel a slight lessening of tension. When Shylock takes the occasion to whet his knife on his sole, the grotesque act brings us still nearer to comedy.

Portia enters dressed as a judge and gets quickly down to business. Shylock's procedure cannot be attacked under the law.

Then must the Jew be merciful.
On what compulsion must I?                (IV.i.181–82)

The question reveals how tightly his moral code is bound to the letter of the law. What it forbids he will never do. But he can neither give nor forgive. Portia, in a speech that almost sums up the meaning of the play, explains that mercy must be an entirely free gift. It blesses the giver and the receiver alike. To show mercy is the privilege of kings, of God himself. But if Shylock insists on the letter of the law, sentence must be given against the merchant. Then comes Portia's quiet masterstroke.

Tarry a little; there is something else.
This bond doth give thee here no jot of blood.

(IV.i.304–05)

Stunned as he is, Shylock tries to accept the previous offer of thrice the bond. But having refused it, he now has no claim on it or even on the bare principal. The law has yet another hold on him. He, an alien, has plotted against a citizen's life. All his vast wealth is forfeit, half to Antonio, half to the state, and his life lies "in the mercy of the Duke only."

Portia has appealed in vain to reason, to charity, and to self-interest. Now she has turned the letter of the law against Shylock. He has been guilty of the mad presumption that the Greeks called *hubris*. For him this sudden blow is a profound psychological shock. No longer can he boast he does no wrong. *By his own code*, the letter of the law, he knows he is guilty of a deadly crime. Stunned and broken, he kneels before the Duke.

The strict court of Venice understands mercy as well as justice. Justice demands that the offender be punished, be forced to make amends to the injured party, and be restrained from doing further harm. Mercy draws a distinction between a crime willed and a crime enacted. As the

prince of Christian humanists, Erasmus, says of charity, mercy requires that the Christian "be an enemy only to vice. Let him kill the Turk, but save the man." Let Portia and the Duke kill his fanaticism, but save the man.

Can we honestly say that he receives mercy? By the mere letter of the law he receives it abundantly. He now owns not a penny's worth of property, and his life is forfeit. The Duke instantly pardons him his life, but Shylock is ready to die. It is now Antonio's opportunity to show mercy. Under the law, one half of Shylock's wealth is now Antonio's, the other half the state's. Following a hint of the Duke's, the merchant proposes, first, that the half which is the state's be restored conditionally to Shylock. Second, he offers to use his own half as a permanent loan without interest, and at the Jew's death to give it outright to Jessica and Lorenzo. He imposes two conditions: first, that the young couple shall receive all Shylock's property at his death; second, that he immediately become a Christian.

In view of Shylock's own cruelty to his luckless debtors, these terms would seem to us both just and merciful, were it not for the forced conversion. This we are bound to resent if we think of the Hebrew faith only as it really is. But if we see it as it had been misunderstood by Christians for over fifteen centuries, we can describe it in the words of Edmund Burke (written with no reference to Judaism) as "an uncouth, pernicious, and degrading superstition." As we painfully rediscovered in Hitler's Germany, the perversion of the instincts of religion and human loyalty can be one of the most dangerous forces in the world. The fanatical Nazis had to be reeducated before they could ever be trusted; so Shylock, too, must give up his fanatical adherence to the letter of the law. It is noteworthy that Antonio, the Duke, and Portia never show any hatred of Shylock. In their view he is being saved from himself. Shakespeare's information about a great religious faith was defective and largely mistaken, but his own values are universal.

FULFILLMENT

The final scene at Portia's estate will seem irrelevant and bitterly ironical to those who still regard Shylock as a victim of Christian bigotry. To others it will be something very different. A good man has been saved from death. A dangerous but greatly gifted man has begun to see life in an altogether new way. Now, in the peace and the magical beauty of the evening, Lorenzo and Jessica are recalling famous lovers of the past. Their earnest mood, broken by playful teasing, Lorenzo's poetic nature as revealed in his words about the music of the spheres, the entrance of Portia and Nerissa, happy in a work of redemption fully achieved—all this suggests powerfully the happy harmony of life at its best. Gratiano's sudden quarrel with Nerissa and the women's harmless teasing of the men about the rings they gave away bring us back to ordinary life and to the mood of comedy. Portia's news that three of Antonio's argosies "Are richly come to harbor suddenly" (V.i.277) and her good news also for Jessica and Lorenzo give promise of long happiness for them. Gratiano's final speech brings a laugh from the audience.

To those who can see Shylock as neither an entire villain nor a hero, but a gifted man whose fanatical hatred makes him his own worst enemy until he is saved from himself, *The Merchant of Venice* is no tragedy. To those who can view the play from the point of view of the wise, realistic, and compassionate heroine, it is one of Shakespeare's most beautiful and most significant comedies.

## A NOTE ON THE SOURCES

Some of Shakespeare's plays are close to their sources, and it is useful and often illuminating to see how he departs from Plutarch or Holinshed, Greene or Lodge. But no known work can be the only source for *The Merchant of Venice*. Apparently Shakespeare combined a number of sources, all of which repay careful study.

If he drew chiefly on a single source, it may have been a play called *The Jew*, which Stephen Gosson mentioned favorably in 1579, in his *School of Abuse*, and which he said showed "the greediness of worldly choosers" and the "bloody minds of usurers." Some scholars believe that the term "worldly choosers" shows that the casket story (in which worldly-minded suitors are discomfited by choosing the gold or silver casket) has been combined with the story of the usurer and the pound of flesh. Yet "greediness" seems less appropriate to suitors than to usurers. In any case, *The Jew* is not extant, and speculation about Shakespeare's debt to it is idle.

Of extant works, *Il Pecorone* (*The Dunce*), an Italian collection of prose tales by an author who calls himself Ser Giovanni Fiorentino, is the most relevant. The first tale of the fourth day concerns the Lady of Belmonte, a widow who demands that each traveler seek to possess her; if he does, she will wed him, but if he fails, all his goods are forfeit. Giannetto voyages to Belmonte twice; twice he is drugged and therefore fails and loses his goods. His god-father then borrows from a Jewish usurer and furnishes him for a third voyage. (Giannetto has lied, telling his godfather that the goods were lost in shipwrecks.) This time Giannetto—warned by the lady's maid—is successful. There follows the usurer's demand for the overdue money, the cleverness of the lawyer, the lady in disguise (as in Shakespeare), and the business of the ring.

There is no indubitable proof that Shakespeare borrowed directly from *Il Pecorone*. He could have found the tale of the pound of flesh in other works, such as Alexander Silvayne's *The Orator* and Anthony Munday's *Zelauto*. It seems more than possible, however, that Shakespeare read *Il Pecorone* either in a translation or in Italian—a language which, with his good knowledge of Latin, he might very easily have acquired.

If he read it in one language or another, probably his most notable changes are the alteration of the indecent test imposed on the wooer, the addition of the usurer's daughter, and the omission of the wooer's incredibly long forgetfulness of his benefactor's danger, together with the ennoblement of all the leading characters.

The story of the caskets comes ultimately from Oriental folklore. Shakespeare's immediate source is believed to be an English version of the *Gesta Romanorum*, a collection of medieval Latin tales, translated into English in 1577 and "bettered" by the same translator in 1595. Possibly the author of the old play *The Jew* is responsible for joining the casket plot to the bond plot, but we know little about

the play; Shakespeare may have been the first to combine the two stories.

Finally, it should be mentioned that Shakespeare's play about Christians and a Jew must owe something to Marlowe's *The Jew of Malta*, and also to the trial, in 1594, of Dr. Roderigo Lopez, the converted Portuguese Jew who, though very probably innocent, was convicted and executed on the charge of plotting to poison Queen Elizabeth I. In *The Jew of Malta*, Shakespeare would have found a Jew who is a scoundrel but is, at certain moments, a really human figure wronged by the Christians around him. Shylock's daughter Jessica may owe something to Marlowe's Abigail, who loves a Christian, but both Abigail and her beloved are killed, whereas Jessica escapes into a happy marriage with Lorenzo. In the Lopez trial, Shakespeare would have found the usual depiction of the murderous Jew.

Geoffrey Bullough, in the first volume of his *Narrative and Dramatic Sources of Shakespeare*, has brought together selections from Silvayne's *The Orator*, Anthony Munday's *Zelauto*, and *Il Pecorone*. To anyone who browses through this material, it is clear enough that Shakespeare did not invent the chief episodes of his play. It is no less clear that the remarkable characterizations, the moral tone, the poetry, and probably the deft interweaving of the various strands of the plot are the work of a great dramatic poet.

## A NOTE ON THE TEXT

The exact date of the play's composition is uncertain, but the play was in existence in 1598, when Francis Meres mentioned it in *Palladis Tamia*, and it may have been written as early as 1596, if the reference to the ship *Andrew* in I.i.27 is indebted—as has been conjectured—to news of the capture of the Spanish ship *Saint Andrew* in the Cádiz expedition. In 1598 and in 1600 the play was entered in the Stationers' Register. It was first published in a quarto (Q1) in 1600. The interesting part of the title page runs thus: "The most excellent/Historie of the Merchant/o/ Venice./With the extreame crueltie of Shylocke the Iewe/ towards the sayd Merchant, in cutting a iust pound/of his flesh: and the obtayning of Portia/by the choyse of three/ chests./As it hath beene diuers times acted by the Lord/ Chamberlaine his Seruants./Written by William Shake-speare." The absence of some necessary stage directions (for example, entrances of some characters who later speak) suggests that the copy for this quarto could not have been a promptbook. Conversely, there are some bits of evidence that suggest the copy was very close to Shakespeare's manuscript; for example, such a stage direction as "*Enter Portia for Balthazar*" seems to reflect an author's conception of his action. But plays that are commonly thought to be printed from Shakespeare's manuscript usually have some confusions in them, the result of a somewhat illegible manuscript, and *The Merchant of Venice* lacks such confusions. Probably, then, the printer's copy for the first quarto was a scribe's careful and clean copy of the manuscript—but, of course, it is unwise to be dogmatic about such matters.

In 1619 a second quarto (Q2) appeared, falsely dated 1600. Q2 was based on Q1, and though it corrects some palpable errors in Q1, Q2 has no independent authority.

In 1623 the play was again reprinted, in the First Folio, again from Q1. And again, of course, there are some slight departures from Q1, ranging from misprints to the addition of some interesting stage directions that doubtless reflect playhouse practice. The most notable are directions calling for the flourishing of cornets.

Q1, then, the only authoritative text, and the source of all others, serves as the basis for the present edition, but some changes have been made. Solanio, Salarino, and Salerio have, as in most modern editions, been reduced to Solanio and Salerio. (Possibly Shakespeare began with three such characters in mind, but as he worked he apparently found he could make do with two, and Salarino disappeared. The name Salarino—which in Q1 occurs in stage directions at I.i; II.iv, vi, viii; III.i—in this edition is replaced by Salerio. Salarino is a diminutive of Salerio, and it is possible that Shakespeare did not intend them to be distinct. In any case, the name Salerio must stay, because it appears in the dialogue as well as in the stage directions.) Spelling and punctuation have been modernized, and speech prefixes have been regularized (for example, we give "Shylock," though Q1 varies between "Shylock," "Shy.," and "Iew"). Act divisions, first introduced in the Folio, are given, and for ease of reference, the scene divisions established by the Globe edition are given. These additions, like necessary stage directions that are not found in Q1, are enclosed in brackets. A superfluous stage direction ("*Enter Tubal*," at III.i.75) has been deleted, the positions of a few stage directions are slightly altered, and obvious typographical errors have been corrected. Other departures from Q1 are listed below, the adopted reading given first, in boldface type, the rejected reading in roman type. If the adopted reading comes from Q2 or F, that fact is indicated.

**I.i.27 docked** docks  **113 Is** It is
**I.ii.59 throstle** Trassell
**II.i.s.d. Morocco** Morochus  **35 page** rage
**II.ii.98 last** [Q2] lost
**II.vii.69 tombs** timber
**II.viii.39 Slubber** [Q2, F] slumber
**III.i.103 Heard** heere
**III.ii.67 eyes** [F] eye  **81 vice** voyce
**III.iii.s.d. Solanio** Salerio
**III.iv.49 Padua** Mantua  **50 cousin's** [Q2, F] cosin  **81 my** [Q2, F] my my
**III.v.22 e'en** [Q2, F] in  **28 comes.** come?  **77 merit it** meane it, it  **84 a wife** [F] wife
**IV.i.30 his state** [Q2, F] this states  **31 flint** [Q2] flints  **51 Master** Maisters  **74 bleat** [F] bleake  **75 mountain** [F] mountaine of  **100 is mine** as mine  **229 No, not** [Q2] Not not  **397 Gratiano** [Q2, F] Shy [lock]
**V.i.41–42 Master Lorenzo and Mistress Lorenzo?** M. Lorenzo, & M. Lorenzo  **49 Sweet soul** [concludes Launcelot's speech]  **51 Stephano** [Q2] Stephen  **87 Erebus** [F] Terebus  **152 it you** [Q2, F] you

# THE MERCHANT OF VENICE

[Dramatis Personae

DUKE OF VENICE
PRINCE OF MOROCCO }
PRINCE OF ARAGON } *suitors to Portia*
ANTONIO *a merchant of Venice*
BASSANIO *his friend, suitor to Portia*
GRATIANO }
SALERIO } *friends to Antonio and Bassanio*
SOLANIO }
LORENZO *in love with Jessica*
SHYLOCK *a Jew*
TUBAL *a Jew, his friend*

LAUNCELOT GOBBO *a clown, servant to Shylock*
OLD GOBBO *father to Launcelot*
LEONARDO *servant to Bassanio*
BALTHASAR }
STEPHANO } *servants to Portia*
PORTIA *an heiress*
NERISSA *her waiting woman*
JESSICA *daughter to Shylock*
MAGNIFICOES *of Venice* OFFICERS *of the*
*court of justice* JAILER SERVANTS OTHER
ATTENDANTS

*Scene:* Venice and Belmont]

## [ ACT I ]

[Scene I. *Venice. A street.*]

*Enter* ANTONIO, SALERIO, *and* SOLANIO.

ANTONIO
In sooth I know not why I am so sad.°
It wearies me, you say it wearies you;
But how I caught it, found it, or came by it,
What stuff 'tis made of, whereof it is born,
I am to learn;°                                         5
And such a want-wit° sadness° makes of me
That I have much ado to know myself.
SALERIO
Your mind is tossing on the ocean,°
There where your argosies° with portly° sail—

*The decorative border shown above is a repeated ornament which
appeared on the title page of the first quarto edition of* The Merchant
of Venice, *1600.*

**I.i.1 sad** sober, depressed   **5 am to learn** need to learn,
cannot guess (the incomplete line indicates a short pause)
**6 want-wit** dull fellow; **sadness** depression   **8 ocean**
pronounced "ó-ce-an"   **9 argosies** great merchant ships;
**portly** stately

Like signiors and rich burghers on the flood,       10
Or as it were the pageants° of the sea—
Do overpeer the petty traffickers
That cursy° to them, do them reverence,
As they fly by them with their woven wings.
SOLANIO
Believe me, sir, had I such venture° forth,          15
The better part of my affections would
Be with my hopes abroad. I should be still°
Plucking the grass to know where sits the wind,
Peering in maps for ports and piers and roads;°
And every object that might make me fear             20
Misfortune to my ventures, out of doubt
Would make me sad.
SALERIO                My wind cooling my broth
Would blow me to an ague° when I thought
What harm a wind too great might do at sea.
I should not see the sandy hourglass run             25
But I should think of shallows and of flats,

**11 pageants** floats, splendidly decorated wagons in the shape
of castles, dragons, etc.   **13 cursy** curtsy, bow   **15 venture**
unpredictable enterprise   **17 still** always   **19 roads** harbors
**23 ague** trembling fit

And see my wealthy *Andrew*° docked in sand,
Vailing° her high top lower than her ribs
To kiss her burial. Should I go to church
And see the holy edifice of stone                                    30
And not bethink me straight of dangerous rocks,
Which touching but my gentle° vessel's side
Would scatter all her spices on the stream,
Enrobe the roaring waters with my silks—
And in a word, but even now worth this,°                              35
And now worth nothing?° Shall I have the thought
To think on this, and shall I lack the thought
That such a thing bechanced° would make me sad?
But tell not me! I know Antonio
Is sad to think upon his merchandise.                                40

ANTONIO
Believe me, no. I thank my fortune for it,
My ventures are not in one bottom° trusted,
Nor to one place; nor is my whole estate
Upon the fortune of this present year.
Therefore my merchandise makes me not sad.                           45

SOLANIO
Why then you are in love.

ANTONIO                                     Fie, fie!

SOLANIO
Not in love neither? Then let us say you are sad
Because you are not merry; and 'twere as easy
For you to laugh and leap, and say you are merry
Because you are not sad. Now by two-headed Janus,°                   50
Nature hath framed strange° fellows in her time:
Some that will evermore peep through their eyes
And laugh like parrots at a bagpiper,
And other of such vinegar aspect
That they'll not show their teeth in way of smile                    55
Though Nestor° swear the jest be laughable.

*Enter* BASSANIO, LORENZO, *and* GRATIANO.

Here comes Bassanio, your most noble kinsman,
Gratiano, and Lorenzo. Fare ye well;
We leave you now with better company.

SALERIO
I would have stayed till I had made you merry,                       60
If worthier friends had not prevented° me.

ANTONIO
Your worth is very dear in my regard.
I take it your own business calls on you,
And you embrace th' occasion to depart.

SALERIO
Good morrow, my good lords.                                           65

BASSANIO
Good signiors both, when shall we laugh? Say, when?
You grow exceeding strange;° must it be so?

SALERIO
We'll make our leisures to attend on yours.
                    *Exeunt* SALERIO *and* SOLANIO.

LORENZO
My Lord Bassanio, since you have found Antonio,
We two will leave you; but at dinner time                            70
I pray you have in mind where we must meet.

BASSANIO
I will not fail you.

GRATIANO
You look not well, Signior Antonio.
You have too much respect upon° the world;
They lose it that do buy it with much care.                          75
Believe me, you are marvelously changed.

ANTONIO
I hold the world but as the world, Gratiano—
A stage, where every man must play a part,
And mine a sad one.

GRATIANO                    Let me play the fool!
With mirth and laughter let old wrinkles come,                       80
And let my liver° rather heat with wine
Than my heart cool with mortifying groans.°
Why should a man whose blood is warm within
Sit like his grandsire, cut in alabaster?
Sleep when he wakes? And creep into the jaundice°                    85
By being peevish? I tell thee what, Antonio—
I love thee, and 'tis my love that speaks—
There are a sort of men whose visages
Do cream and mantle° like a standing pond,
And do a willful stillness entertain°                                90
With purpose to be dressed in an opinion°
Of wisdom, gravity, profound conceit,°
As who should say, "I am Sir Oracle,°
And when I ope my lips, let no dog bark!"
O my Antonio, I do know of these                                     95
That therefore only are reputed wise
For saying nothing; when I am very sure
If they should speak, would almost dam° those ears,
Which hearing them would call their brothers
  fools.
I'll tell thee more of this another time.                            100
But fish not with this melancholy bait
For this fool gudgeon,° this opinion.
Come, good Lorenzo. Fare ye well awhile;
I'll end my exhortation after dinner.

LORENZO
Well, we will leave you then till dinner time.                       105
I must be one of these same dumb wise men,
For Gratiano never lets me speak.

---

27 **Andrew** the name of a ship   28 **Vailing** lowering, in recognition of a superior   32 **gentle** noble and gentle; hence, splendid and frail   35, 36 **this, nothing** spoken with an emphatic gesture   38 **bechanced** should it happen   42 **bottom** ship   50 **two-headed Janus** Roman god of entrances and hence of all beginnings; depicted with two faces, one cheerful, one sad, symbolizing the uncertainty of the future (Solanio suggests that Antonio is as strange a figure as Janus)   51 **strange** marvelously queer   56 **Nestor** the oldest and most venerable Greek leader in the Trojan War; a type of gravity and wisdom   61 **prevented** forestalled   67 **strange** distant

74 **respect upon** regard for   81 **liver** one of the supposed seats of the passions   82 **mortifying groans** groans supposed to deaden vitality (by drawing blood from the heart)   85 **jaundice** disease thought to be caused by peevishness   89 **cream and mantle** become impassive like thick cream on a bowl of milk, or a mantle of scum on a pond   90 **entertain** assume   91 **opinion** reputation (as in line 102)   92 **profound conceit** power of forming profound conceptions   93 **I . . . Oracle** I am as wise as a Greek oracle (inspired by the gods)   98 **dam** often emended to "damn," and probably a pun: if these silent and reputedly wise men ever did speak, the abundance of their foolish words would not only dam up the ears of the listeners, but also make the listeners call the formerly silent men fools, and thus bring on the listeners the penalty of damnation which is pronounced on all who apply this term to a brother man (see Matthew 5:22)   101–02 **But . . . gudgeon** don't cultivate melancholy to gain a reputation for silent wisdom, for the judgment of the multitude is stupid (a gudgeon was proverbially a foolish fish)

**GRATIANO**
Well, keep me company but two years moe,°
Thou shalt not know the sound of thine own tongue.

**ANTONIO**
Fare you well; I'll grow a talker for this gear.° 110

**GRATIANO**
Thanks i' faith; for silence is only commendable
In a neat's tongue° dried and a maid not vendible.°
        *Exeunt* [GRATIANO *and* LORENZO].

**ANTONIO** Is that anything now?

**BASSANIO** Gratiano speaks an infinite deal of nothing, more than any man in all Venice. His reasons are 115
as two grains of wheat hid in two bushels of chaff: you
shall seek all day ere you find them, and when you
have them they are not worth the search.

**ANTONIO**
Well, tell me now, what lady is the same
To whom you swore a secret pilgrimage 120
That you today promised to tell me of?

**BASSANIO**
'Tis not unknown to you, Antonio,
How much I have disabled mine estate,
By something° showing a more swelling port°
Than my faint means would grant continuance.° 125
Nor do I now make moan to be abridged°
From such a noble rate;° but my chief care
Is to come fairly off from the great debts
Wherein my time, something too prodigal,°
Hath left me gaged.° To you, Antonio, 130
I owe the most in money and in love,
And from your love I have a warranty
To unburden all my plots and purposes
How to get clear of all the debts I owe.

**ANTONIO**
I pray you, good Bassanio, let me know it, 135
And if it stand as you yourself still° do,
Within the eye of honor, be assured
My purse, my person, my extremest means
Lie all unlocked to your occasions.°

**BASSANIO**
In my schooldays, when I had lost one shaft° 140
I shot his fellow° of the selfsame flight°
The selfsame way, with more advisèd° watch,
To find the other forth; and by adventuring both
I oft found both. I urge this childhood proof°
Because what follows is pure innocence.° 145
I owe you much, and like a willful youth°
That which I owe is lost; but if you please
To shoot another arrow that self way
Which you did shoot the first, I do not doubt,

As I will watch the aim, or° to find both, 150
Or bring your latter hazard° back again
And thankfully rest debtor for the first.

**ANTONIO**
You know me well, and herein spend but time
To wind about my love with circumstance;°
And out of doubt you do me now more wrong 155
In making question of my uttermost
Than if you had made waste of all I have.
Then do but say to me what I should do
That in your knowledge may by me be done,
And I am prest unto it.° Therefore speak. 160

**BASSANIO**
In Belmont is a lady richly left;°
And she is fair and, fairer than that word,
Of wondrous virtues.° Sometimes from her eyes
I did receive fair speechless messages.
Her name is Portia, nothing undervalued 165
To° Cato's daughter, Brutus' Portia;°
Nor is the wide world ignorant of her worth,
For the four winds blow in from every coast
Renownèd suitors, and her sunny locks
Hang on her temples like a golden fleece, 170
Which makes her seat° of Belmont Colchos' strond,°
And many Jasons come in quest of her.
O my Antonio, had I but the means
To hold a rival place with one of them,
I have a mind presages me° such thrift° 175
That I should questionless be fortunate!

**ANTONIO**
Thou know'st that all my fortunes are at sea;
Neither have I money, nor commodity°
To raise a present sum. Therefore go forth;
Try what my credit can in Venice do. 180
That shall be racked° even to the uttermost
To furnish thee to Belmont, to fair Portia.
Go presently° inquire, and so will I,
Where money is; and I no question make
To have it of my trust or for my sake.° *Exeunt.* 185

[Scene II. *Belmont. Portia's house.*]

*Enter* PORTIA *with her waiting woman,* NERISSA.

**PORTIA** By my troth,° Nerissa, my little body is
aweary of this great world.

**NERISSA** You would be, sweet madam, if your
miseries were in the same abundance as your good
fortunes are; and yet for aught I see, they are as sick 5
that surfeit° with too much as they that starve with

---

**108 moe** more (*moe* is the old positive form of which *more* was the comparative) **110 gear** stuff (a mild jest, showing that Gratiano has cheered Antonio for a moment) **112 neat's tongue** beef tongue; **vendible** salable (i.e., marriageable) **124 something** somewhat; **swelling port** impressive style of living **125 grant continuance** allow me to continue **126 abridged** cut down **127 rate** scale **129 my . . . prodigal** the lavish way I spent my time **130 gaged** pledged **136 still** always **139 occasions** needs **140 shaft** arrow **141 fellow** duplicate; **selfsame flight** identical in size and in the feathers **142 advisèd** considered **144 proof** experience **145 pure innocence** childlike sincerity **146 like . . . youth** like one who neglected sound advice and learned by making mistakes

**150 or** either **151 hazard** thing risked **154 To . . . circumstance** to approach my love circuitously with elaborate talk **160 prest unto it** ready to aid you in it (from Latin *praesto* = at hand, ready) **161 richly left** left rich **163 virtues** powers and gifts (a more inclusive word than today) **165–66 nothing undervalued To** of no less value than **166 Brutus' Portia** famed for her intellectual gifts, her resolution, and her wifely devotion (see *Julius Caesar*, II.i.234–309) **171 seat** estate; **Colchos' strond** the shore east of the Black Sea where Jason won the Golden Fleece **175 mind presages me** presentiment that foretells me; **thrift** thriving, success **178 commodity** merchandise **181 racked** stretched to the point of torture (as on the rack) **183 presently** instantly **185 of . . . sake** on my credit or on the basis of friendship **I.ii.1 troth** faith **6 surfeit** are overfed, glutted

nothing. It is no mean° happiness, therefore, to be
seated in the mean;° superfluity comes sooner by°
white hairs, but competency° lives longer.

PORTIA  Good sentences,° and well pronounced.     10

NERISSA  They would be better if well followed.

PORTIA  If to do were as easy as to know what were
good to do, chapels had been° churches, and poor
men's cottages princes' palaces. It is a good divine that
follows his own instructions; I can easier teach twenty 15
what were good to be done, than to be one of the
twenty to follow mine own teaching. The brain may
devise laws for the blood,° but a hot temper° leaps o'er
a cold decree;° such a hare is madness the youth to skip
o'er the meshes° of good counsel the cripple. But this 20
reasoning is not in the fashion° to choose me a husband.
O me, the word "choose"! I may neither choose who
I would nor refuse who I dislike, so is the will of a
living daughter curbed by the will° of a dead father.
Is it not hard, Nerissa, that I cannot choose one, nor 25
refuse none?°

NERISSA  Your father was ever virtuous, and holy men
at their death have good inspirations. Therefore the
lott'ry that he hath devised in these three chests of
gold, silver, and lead, whereof who chooses his mean- 30
ing chooses you, will no doubt never be chosen by any
rightly but one who you shall rightly love. But what
warmth is there in your affection towards any of these
princely suitors that are already come?

PORTIA  I pray thee overname them; and as thou 35
namest them I will describe them, and according to my
description level at my affection.

NERISSA  First, there is the Neapolitan prince.

PORTIA  Ay, that's a colt indeed, for he doth nothing
but talk of his horse, and he makes it a great appropri- 40
ation of his own good parts° that he can shoe him
himself. I am much afeard my lady his mother played
false with a smith.

NERISSA  Then is there the County° Palatine.

PORTIA  He doth nothing but frown—as who should 45
say, "And° you will not have me, choose!" He hears
merry tales and smiles not; I fear he will prove the
weeping philosopher° when he grows old, being so
full of unmannerly sadness° in his youth. I had rather
be married to a death's-head with a bone in his mouth 50
than to either of these. God defend me from these two!

NERISSA  How say you by the French lord, Monsieur
Le Bon?

PORTIA  God made him, and therefore let him pass
for a man. In truth, I know it is a sin to be a mocker, 55
but he! Why, he hath a horse better than the Neapolitan's, a better bad habit of frowning than the
Count Palatine; he is every man in no man. If a

throstle° sing, he falls straight a-cap'ring; he will fence
with his own shadow. If I should° marry him, I 60
should° marry twenty husbands. If he would despise
me, I would forgive him; for if he love me to madness,
I shall never requite him.

NERISSA  What say you then to Falconbridge, the
young baron of England? 65

PORTIA  You know I say nothing to him, for he
understands not me, nor I him. He hath neither Latin,
French, nor Italian; and you will come into the court
and swear that I have a poor pennyworth in the
English. He is a proper° man's picture, but alas, who 70
can converse with a dumbshow? How oddly he is
suited! I think he bought his doublet° in Italy, his
round hose° in France, his bonnet in Germany, and
his behavior everywhere.

NERISSA  What think you of the Scottish lord, his 75
neighbor?

PORTIA  That he hath a neighborly charity in him,
for he borrowed a box of the ear of the Englishman
and swore he would pay him again when he was able.
I think the Frenchman° became his surety and sealed 80
under for another.

NERISSA  How like you the young German,° the
Duke of Saxony's nephew?

PORTIA  Very vilely in the morning when he is sober,
and most vilely in the afternoon when he is drunk. 85
When he is best he is a little worse than a man, and
when he is worst he is little better than a beast.° And
the worst fall that ever fell, I hope I shall make shift°
to go without him.

NERISSA  If he should offer to choose, and choose the 90
right casket, you should refuse to perform your
father's will if you should refuse to accept him.

PORTIA  Therefore, for fear of the worst, I pray thee
set a deep glass of Rhenish wine on the contrary
casket, for if the devil be within and that temptation 95
without, I know he will choose it. I will do anything,
Nerissa, ere I will be married to a sponge.

NERISSA  You need not fear, lady, the having any of
these lords. They have acquainted me with their deter-
minations; which is indeed to return to their home, and 100
to trouble you with no more suit, unless you may be
won by some other sort° than your father's imposition,° depending on the caskets.

PORTIA  If I live to be as old as Sibylla,° I will die as
chaste as Diana unless I be obtained by the manner of 105
my father's will. I am glad this parcel of wooers are so
reasonable, for there is not one among them but I dote
on his very absence; and I pray God grant them a fair
departure.

---

**7, 8 mean** (1) slight (2) golden mean  **8 comes sooner by**
acquires sooner  **9 competency** a modest but comfortable
fortune  **10 sentences** sententious maxims  **13 had been**
would have been  **18 blood** passion; **hot temper** ardent
temperament  **18–19 cold decree** decision made in cold judgment  **20 meshes** nets for catching small creatures  **21 in the
fashion** of the sort  **23–24 will . . . will** wish . . . last will
and testament  **26 refuse none** refuse any  **40–41 appropria-
tion . . . parts** personal accomplishment added to his talents
**44 County** Count  **46 And** if  **47–48 the weeping philosopher** another Heraclitus  **49 unmannerly sadness** unbecoming seriousness

**59 throstle** song thrush  **60–61 should . . . should** were to . . .
would be obliged to  **70 proper** handsome  **72 doublet**
upper garment, corresponding to the modern coat  **73
round hose** lower garment, combining the functions of
breeches and stockings  **75–80 Scottish . . . Frenchman**
an allusion to the French promises of aid to the Scots against
the English, promises that were often broken  **82 German**
Germans were proverbially heavy drinkers  **86–87 best . . .
beast** a pun, "beast" being pronounced almost like "best"
(such quibbles were not necessarily comic, but were considered clever and interesting)  **88 make shift** find a way
**102 sort** manner  **102–03 imposition** command  **104
Sibylla** the Cumean Sibyl (Apollo promised her as many years
of life as were the grains of sand she was holding in her hand)

NERISSA  Do you not remember, lady, in your father's 110
time, a Venetian, a scholar and a soldier, that came
hither in company of the Marquis of Montferrat?
PORTIA  Yes, yes, it was Bassanio!—as I think, so was
he called.
NERISSA  True, madam. He, of all the men that ever 115
my foolish eyes looked upon, was the best deserving
a fair lady.
PORTIA  I remember him well, and I remember him
worthy of thy praise.

*Enter a* SERVINGMAN.

How now? What news?                                    120
SERVINGMAN  The four strangers° seek for you,
madam, to take their leave; and there is a forerunner
come from a fifth, the Prince of Morocco, who brings
word the prince his master will be here tonight.
PORTIA  If I could bid the fifth welcome with so good 125
heart as I can bid the other four farewell, I should be
glad of his approach. If he have the condition of a saint
and the complexion of a devil, I had rather he should
shrive me than wive me. Come, Nerissa. Sirrah,° go
before. Whiles we shut the gate upon one wooer, 130
another knocks at the door.                   *Exeunt.*

[Scene III. *Venice. A public place.*]

*Enter* BASSANIO *with* SHYLOCK *the Jew.*

SHYLOCK  Three thousand ducats—well.
BASSANIO  Ay, sir, for three months.
SHYLOCK  For three months—well.
BASSANIO  For the which, as I told you, Antonio shall
be bound.°                                              5
SHYLOCK  Antonio shall become bound—well.
BASSANIO  May° you stead° me? Will you pleasure
me? Shall I know your answer?
SHYLOCK  Three thousand ducats for three months,
and Antonio bound.                                     10
BASSANIO  Your answer to that.
SHYLOCK  Antonio is a good man.°
BASSANIO  Have you heard any imputation to the
contrary?
SHYLOCK  Ho no, no, no, no! My meaning in saying 15
he is a good man. is to have you understand me that he
is sufficient.° Yet his means are in supposition:° he hath
an argosy bound to Tripolis, another to the Indies; I
understand, moreover, upon the Rialto,° he hath a
third at Mexico, a fourth for England—and other 20
ventures he hath, squand'red abroad. But ships are but
boards, sailors but men; there be land rats and water
rats, water thieves and land thieves—I mean pirates°—

and then there is the peril of waters, winds, and rocks.
The man is, notwithstanding, sufficient. Three 25
thousand ducats—I think I may take his bond.
BASSANIO  Be assured you may.
SHYLOCK  I will be assured I may. And that I may be
assured, I will bethink me. May I speak with Antonio?
BASSANIO  If it please you to dine with us.            30
SHYLOCK  Yes, to smell pork, to eat of the habitation
which your prophet the Nazarite° conjured the devil
into! I will buy with you, sell with you, talk with you,
walk with you, and so following; but I will not eat
with you, drink with you, nor pray with you. What 35
news on the Rialto? Who is he comes here?

*Enter* ANTONIO.

BASSANIO
This is Signior Antonio.
SHYLOCK [*Aside.*]
How like a fawning publican° he looks.
I hate him for° he is a Christian;
But more, for that in low simplicity                   40
He lends out money gratis, and brings down
The rate of usance° here with us in Venice.
If I can catch him once upon the hip,°
I will feed fat the ancient grudge I bear him.
He hates our sacred nation, and he rails,               45
Even there where merchants most do congregate,
On me, my bargains, and my well-won thrift,°
Which he calls interest. Cursèd be my tribe
If I forgive him.
BASSANIO              Shylock, do you hear?
SHYLOCK
I am debating of my present store,°                     50
And by the near guess of my memory
I cannot instantly raise up the gross°
Of full three thousand ducats. What of that?
Tubal, a wealthy Hebrew of my tribe,
Will furnish me. But soft,° how many months            55
Do you desire? [*To* ANTONIO.] Rest you fair, good
    signior!
Your worship was the last man in our mouths.
ANTONIO
Shylock, albeit I neither lend nor borrow
By taking nor by giving of excess,
Yet to supply the ripe wants of my friend,             60
I'll break a custom. [*To* BASSANIO.] Is he yet pos-
    sessed°
How much ye would?°
SHYLOCK              Ay, ay, three thousand ducats.
ANTONIO
And for three months.
SHYLOCK
I had forgot—three months, you told me so.
Well then, your bond. And let me see—but hear you: 65

121 **four strangers** apparently Shakespeare originally described
four suitors, then added two more, and forgot to change
"four" to "six"  129 **Sirrah** a regular form of address to a
social inferior; Portia speaks to the servant
**I.iii.5 bound** under legal obligation as cosigner of the bond
7 **May** can; **stead** be of service to  12 **good man** good
business risk (Bassanio takes the word as referring to moral
character)  17 **sufficient** adequate, responsible; **in supposition**
doubtful  19 **Rialto** famous bridge in Venice, the center of
commercial activity  23 **pirates** pronounced "pi-rats," with
quibble on *rats*

32 **the Nazarite** Christ (the allusion is to the episode in Mark
5:1–13, Luke 8:26–33)  38 **publican** sometimes glossed as a
Roman tax gatherer, as in Matthew 11:17 and 31:30 ff., and
sometimes as an Elizabethan innkeeper; perhaps Shylock uses
it as an inexact but bitter term of reproach  39 **for** because
42 **usance** interest  43 **upon the hip** at a disadvantage (a
term in wrestling)  47 **thrift** prosperity  50 **present store**
stock of ready money  52 **gross** whole amount  55 **soft**
hold, stay  61 **possessed** apprised  62 **would** desire

Methoughts° you said you neither lend nor borrow
Upon advantage.°
ANTONIO            I do never use it.
SHYLOCK
When Jacob° grazed his uncle Laban's sheep—
This Jacob from our holy Abram was,
As his wise mother wrought in his behalf,            70
The third possessor; ay, he was the third—
ANTONIO
And what of him? Did he take interest?
SHYLOCK
No, not take interest—not as you would say
Directly int'rest. Mark what Jacob did:
When Laban and himself were compremised°            75
That all the eanlings which were streaked and pied
Should fall as Jacob's hire, and ewes being rank
In end of autumn turnèd to the rams;
And when the work of generation was
Between these woolly breeders in the act,            80
The skillful shepherd pilled° me° certain wands,
And in the doing of the deed of kind°
He stuck them up before the fulsome ewes,
Who then conceiving, did in eaning° time
Fall parti-colored lambs, and those were Jacob's.            85
This was a way to thrive, and he was blest;
And thrift is blessing if men steal it not.
ANTONIO
This was a venture,° sir, that Jacob served for,
A thing not in his power to bring to pass,
But swayed and fashioned by the hand of heaven.            90
Was this inserted to make interest good?
Or is your gold and silver ewes and rams?
SHYLOCK
I cannot tell; I make it breed as fast.
But note me, signior—
ANTONIO            Mark you this, Bassanio,
The devil can cite Scripture for his purpose.            95
An evil soul producing holy witness
Is like a villain with a smiling cheek,
A goodly° apple rotten at the heart.
O what a goodly outside falsehood hath!
SHYLOCK
Three thousand ducats—'tis a good round sum.            100
Three months from twelve—then let me see, the rate—
ANTONIO
Well, Shylock, shall we be beholding° to you?
SHYLOCK
Signior Antonio, many a time and oft
In the Rialto you have rated° me
About my moneys and my usances.            105
Still° have I borne it with a patient shrug,
For suff'rance° is the badge of all our tribe.
You call me misbeliever, cutthroat dog,
And spet upon my Jewish gaberdine,°
And all for use of that which is mine own.            110
Well then, it now appears you need my help.

Go to, then.° You come to me and you say,
"Shylock, we would have moneys"—you say so,
You that did void your rheum° upon my beard
And foot me as you spurn a stranger cur            115
Over your threshold! Moneys is your suit.
What should I say to you? Should I not say,
"Hath a dog money? Is it possible
A cur can lend three thousand ducats?" Or
Shall I bend low, and in a bondman's key,            120
With bated breath, and whisp'ring humbleness,
Say this:
"Fair sir, you spet on me on Wednesday last,
You spurned me such a day, another time
You called me dog; and for these courtesies            125
I'll lend you thus much moneys"?
ANTONIO
I am as like to call thee so again,
To spet on thee again, to spurn thee too.
If thou wilt lend this money, lend it not
As to thy friends—for when did friendship take            130
A breed for barren metal° of his friend?—
But lend it rather to thine enemy,
Who if he break,° thou mayst with better face
Exact the penalty.
SHYLOCK            Why look you, how you storm!
I would be friends with you, and have your love,            135
Forget the shames that you have stained me with,
Supply your present wants, and take no doit°
Of usance for my moneys; and you'll not hear me.
This is kind° I offer.
BASSANIO
This were kindness.
SHYLOCK            This kindness will I show:
Go with me to a notary; seal me there
Your single° bond, and, in a merry sport,
If you repay me not on such a day,
In such a place, such sum or sums as are
Expressed in the condition, let the forfeit            145
Be nominated for an equal pound
Of your fair flesh, to be cut off and taken
In what part of your body pleaseth me.
ANTONIO
Content, in faith. I'll seal to such a bond,
And say there is much kindness° in the Jew.            150
BASSANIO
You shall not seal to such a bond for me!
I'll rather dwell in my necessity.
ANTONIO
Why fear not, man; I will not forfeit it.
Within these two months—that's a month before
This bond expires—I do expect return            155
Of thrice three times the value of this bond.
SHYLOCK
O father Abram, what these Christians are,
Whose own hard dealings teaches them suspect
The thoughts of others! Pray you tell me this:

66 Methoughts it seemed to me  67 advantage interest
68 Jacob see Genesis 30:25–43, 31:1–13  75 were compre-
mised had reached an agreement  81 pilled stripped; me the
ethical dative  82 kind nature  84 eaning lambing  88
venture unpredictable enterprise  98 goodly fine-appearing
102 beholding beholden, obligated  104 rated berated, reviled
106 Still always  107 suff'rance long-suffering  109 gaberdine the distinctive gown or mantle of the Jews

112 Go to, then an exclamation suggesting annoyance  114
rheum spittle  131 breed . . . metal interest (Aristotelian
doctrine held that money, unlike living things, cannot reproduce)  133 break become insolvent  137 doit tiny Dutch
coin, valued at one eighth of an English penny  139 kind
kind and natural (in contrast to usurious dealings)  142 single
without further security  150 kindness natural friendliness

If he should break his day,° what should I gain    160
By the exaction of the forfeiture?
A pound of man's flesh taken from a man
Is not so estimable, profitable neither,
As flesh of muttons, beefs, or goats. I say
To buy his favor I extend this friendship.    165
If he will take it, so; if not, adieu.°
And for my love I pray you wrong me not.°

ANTONIO
Yes, Shylock, I will seal unto this bond.

SHYLOCK
Then meet me forthwith at the notary's;
Give him direction for this merry bond,    170
And I will go and purse the ducats straight,
See to my house, left in the fearful° guard
Of an unthrifty knave,° and presently°
I'll be with you.                *Exit.*

ANTONIO       Hie thee, gentle Jew.°
The Hebrew will turn Christian; he grows kind.    175

BASSANIO
I like not fair terms and a villain's mind.

ANTONIO
Come on. In this there can be no dismay;
My ships come home a month before the day.
                         *Exeunt.*

# [ A C T   I I ]

[Scene I. *Belmont. Portia's house.*]

[*Flourish of cornets.*] *Enter* [*the Prince of*] MOROCCO, *a tawny Moor all in white, and three or four* FOLLOWERS *accordingly, with* PORTIA, NERISSA, *and their* TRAIN.

MOROCCO
Mislike me not for my complexion,
The shadowed° livery° of the burnished sun,
To whom I am a neighbor and near bred.
Bring me the fairest creature northward born,
Where Phoebus'° fire scarce thaws the icicles,    5
And let us make incision° for your love
To prove whose blood is reddest, his or mine.
I tell thee, lady, this aspect° of mine
Hath feared the valiant.° By my love I swear,
The best-regarded virgins of our clime    10
Have loved it too. I would not change this hue,
Except to steal your thoughts, my gentle queen.

PORTIA
In terms of choice° I am not solely led
By nice° direction of a maiden's eyes.
Besides, the lott'ry of my destiny    15

Bars me the right of voluntary choosing.
But if my father had not scanted° me,
And hedged me by his wit° to yield myself
His wife who wins me by that means I told you,
Yourself, renownèd prince, then stood as fair    20
As any comer I have looked on yet
For my affection.

MOROCCO           Even for that I thank you.
Therefore I pray you lead me to the caskets
To try my fortune. By this scimitar,
That slew the Sophy,° and a Persian prince    25
That won three fields of Sultan Solyman,
I would o'erstare° the sternest eyes that look,
Outbrave the heart most daring on the earth,
Pluck the young sucking cubs from the she-bear,
Yea, mock the lion when 'a° roars for prey,    30
To win thee, lady. But alas the while,
If Hercules and Lichas° play at dice
Which is the better man, the greater throw
May turn by fortune from the weaker hand.
So is Alcides° beaten by his page,    35
And so may I, blind fortune leading me,
Miss that which one unworthier may attain,
And die with grieving.

PORTIA           You must take your chance,
And either not attempt to choose at all,
Or swear before you choose, if you choose wrong    40
Never to speak to lady afterward
In way of marriage. Therefore be advised.°

MOROCCO
Nor will not.° Come, bring me unto my chance.

PORTIA
First, forward to the temple; after dinner
Your hazard shall be made.

MOROCCO           Good fortune then,    45
To make me blest or cursèd'st among men!
          [*Flourish of cornets.*] *Exeunt.*

[Scene II. *Venice. A street.*]

*Enter* [LAUNCELOT *Gobbo*] *the clown, alone.*

LAUNCELOT   Certainly my conscience will serve me to run from this Jew my master. The fiend is at mine elbow and tempts me, saying to me, "Gobbo, Launcelot Gobbo, good Launcelot," or "good Gobbo," or "good Launcelot Gobbo—use your legs, take the start, run away." My conscience says, "No. Take heed, honest Launcelot; take heed, honest Gobbo," or as aforesaid, "honest Launcelot Gobbo, do not run; scorn running with thy heels."° Well, the most courageous fiend bids me pack. "Fia!"° says the fiend; "away!" says the fiend. "For the heavens,° rouse up a brave mind," says the fiend, "and run." Well, my conscience hanging about the neck of my heart says

---

160 **break his day** break his promise to pay on the due date   166 **adieu** probably the word has the original meaning "I commend you to God"   167 **And . . . not** And for the friendship I have shown you, please don't misjudge me in the future   172 **fearful** hazardous   173 **unthrifty knave** careless youngster; **presently** instantly   174 **gentle Jew** courteous Jew (with a pun on *gentile*)
**II.i.2 shadowed** dark; **livery** uniform for a king's or nobleman's retainers   5 **Phoebus'** the sun-god's   6 **make incision** cut our flesh   8 **aspect** pronounced "a-spèct"   9 **feared the valiant** caused the valiant to fear   13 **In . . . choice** with respect to my choice   14 **nice** fastidious

17 **scanted** limited   18 **hedged . . . wit** fenced me in by his clever intellect   25 **Sophy** Shah of Persia   27 **o'erstare** outstare   30 **'a** he   32 **Lichas** Hercules' page   35 **Alcides** Hercules   42 **be advised** consider well   43 **Nor will not** nor will I (ever woo another for my wife)
**II.ii.9 scorn . . . heels** (1) scorn to run away with your feet (2) scorn utterly to run   10 **Fia** from Italian *via* = away   11 **For the heavens** by heaven, or for heaven's sake (in either case a grotesque thing for the fiend to say)

very wisely to me, "My honest friend Launcelot, being
an honest man's son"—or rather an honest woman's 15
son, for indeed my father did something smack,
something grow to, he had a kind of taste°—Well, my
conscience says, "Launcelot, budge not." "Budge,"
says the fiend. "Budge not," says my conscience.
"Conscience," say I, "you counsel well." "Fiend," say 20
I, "you counsel well." To be ruled by my conscience,
I should stay with the Jew my master who (God bless
the mark!°) is a kind of devil; and to run away from
the Jew, I should be ruled by the fiend who, saving
your reverence, is the devil himself. Certainly the Jew 25
is the very devil incarnation;° and in my conscience,
my conscience is but a kind of hard conscience to offer
to counsel me to stay with the Jew. The fiend gives the
more friendly counsel. I will run, fiend; my heels are
at your commandment, I will run. 30

*Enter old* GOBBO *with a basket.*

GOBBO  Master young man, you, I pray you, which is
the way to Master Jew's?
LAUNCELOT [*Aside.*] O heavens, this is my true-
begotten father who, being more than sand-blind,°
high-gravel-blind,° knows me not. I will try confusions 35
with him.
GOBBO  Master young gentleman, I pray you which is
the way to Master Jew's?
LAUNCELOT  Turn up on your right hand at the next
turning, but at the next turning of all, on your left; 40
marry,° at the very next turning turn of no hand, but
turn down indirectly to the Jew's house.
GOBBO  Be God's sonties,° 'twill be a hard way to hit!
Can you tell me whether one Launcelot that dwells
with him, dwell with him or no? 45
LAUNCELOT  Talk you of young Master Launcelot?
[*Aside.*] Mark me now! Now will I raise the waters.°—
Talk you of young Master Launcelot?
GOBBO  No master,° sir, but a poor man's son. His
father, though I say't, is an honest exceeding poor man 50
and, God be thanked, well to live.°
LAUNCELOT  Well, let his father be what 'a will, we
talk of young Master Launcelot.
GOBBO  Your worship's friend,° and Launcelot, sir.
LAUNCELOT  But I pray you, ergo° old man, ergo I 55
beseech you, talk you of young Master Launcelot?
GOBBO  Of Launcelot, an't° please your mastership.
LAUNCELOT  Ergo, Master Launcelot. Talk not of
Master Launcelot, father, for the young gentleman,
according to Fates and Destinies and such odd sayings, 60
the Sisters Three and such branches of learning, is
indeed deceased, or as you would say in plain terms,
gone to heaven.

GOBBO  Marry, God forbid! The boy was the very
staff of my age, my very prop. 65
LAUNCELOT [*Aside.*]  Do I look like a cudgel or a
hovel-post, a staff, or a prop?° Do you know me,
father?°
GOBBO  Alack the day, I know you not, young gentleman, but I pray you tell me, is my boy—God rest his 70
soul—alive or dead?
LAUNCELOT  Do you not know me, father?°
GOBBO  Alack, sir, I am sand-blind! I know you not.
LAUNCELOT  Nay, indeed if you had your eyes you
might fail of the knowing me. It is a wise father that 75
knows his own child. Well, old man, I will tell you
news of your son. [*Kneels, with his back to his father.*]
Give me your blessing. Truth will come to light;
murder cannot be hid long—a man's son may, but in
the end truth will out. 80
GOBBO  Pray you, sir, stand up. I am sure you are not
Launcelot, my boy.
LAUNCELOT  Pray you let's have no more fooling
about it, but give me your blessing. I am Launcelot—
your boy that was, your son that is, your child that 85
shall be.
GOBBO  I cannot think you are my son.
LAUNCELOT  I know not what I shall think of that;
but I am Launcelot, the Jew's man, and I am sure
Margery your wife is my mother. 90
GOBBO  Her name is Margery indeed! I'll be sworn, if
thou be Launcelot thou art mine own flesh and blood.
Lord worshipped might He be, what a beard° hast thou
got! Thou hast got more hair on thy chin than Dobbin
my fill-horse° has on his tail. 95
LAUNCELOT [*Rises.*]  It should seem then that Dobbin's
tail grows backward. I am sure he had more hair of his
tail than I have of my face when I last saw him.
GOBBO  Lord, how art thou changed! How dost thou
and thy master agree? I have brought him a present. 100
How 'gree you now?
LAUNCELOT  Well, well; but for mine own part, as I
have set up my rest° to run away, so I will not rest till I
have run some ground. My master's a very Jew. Give
him a present? Give him a halter!° I am famished in 105
his service; you may tell° every finger I have with my
ribs. Father, I am glad you are come. Give me your
present to one Master Bassanio, who indeed gives rare
new liveries. If I serve not him I will run as far as God
has any ground. O rare fortune, here comes the man. 110
To him, father, for I am a Jew if I serve the Jew any
longer.

*Enter* BASSANIO, *with* [LEONARDO *and*] *a* FOLLOWER
*or two.*

BASSANIO  You may do so, but let it be so hasted that
supper be ready at the farthest by five of the clock.

16–17 did something smack . . . had a kind of taste both
phrases indicate a tendency to vice  22–23 God . . . mark
used, like "saving your reverence" in lines 24–25, to avert a
bad omen  26 incarnation blunder for *incarnate*  34 sand-
blind dull of sight  35 high-gravel-blind Launcelot's comic
superlative for "sand-blind" earlier  41 marry a mild interjection (originally an oath, "By the Virgin Mary")  43 Be
God's sonties by God's little saints  47 raise the waters
rouse a storm of emotion (a nautical metaphor?)  49 No
master as a servant, Launcelot has no claim to the title of
master  50–51 exceeding . . . live poverty-stricken and
well-to-do  54 Your worship's friend he politely insists on
his son's humble status  55 ergo therefore  57 an't if it

66–67 Do . . . prop spoken directly to the audience  68, 72
father a term of courtesy often used by the young to the old,
without implying blood relationship  93 beard the sand-blind
father places his hand on his son's head, and mistakes
Launcelot's fashionable long hair for a huge beard  95 fill-
horse cart horse  103 set . . . rest wagered all (with word
play on "rest" and "run")  105 halter hangman's noose  106
tell count

See these letters delivered, put the liveries to making, 115
and desire Gratiano to come anon° to my lodging.
                                              [*Exit one of his* MEN.]
LAUNCELOT   To him, father!
GOBBO   God bless your worship!
BASSANIO   Gramercy.° Wouldst thou aught with me?
GOBBO   Here's my son, sir, a poor boy—                         120
LAUNCELOT   Not a poor boy, sir, but the rich Jew's
man, that would, sir, as my father shall specify—
GOBBO   He hath a great infection,° sir, as one would
say, to serve—
LAUNCELOT   Indeed, the short and the long is, I serve   125
the Jew, and have a desire, as my father shall specify—
GOBBO   His master and he, saving your worship's
reverence, are scarce cater-cousins.°
LAUNCELOT   To be brief, the very truth is that the
Jew, having done me wrong, doth cause me, as my   130
father, being I hope an old man, shall frutify° unto
you—
GOBBO   I have here a dish of doves that I would bestow
upon your worship, and my suit is—
LAUNCELOT   In very brief, the suit is impertinent° to   135
myself, as your worship shall know by this honest old
man, and though I say it, though old man, yet poor
man, my father.
BASSANIO   One speak for both. What would you?
LAUNCELOT   Serve you, sir.                                      140
GOBBO   That is the very defect° of the matter, sir.
BASSANIO
I know thee well; thou hast obtained thy suit.
Shylock thy master spoke with me this day,
And hath preferred° thee, if it be preferment
To leave a rich Jew's service to become                         145
The follower of so poor a gentleman.
LAUNCELOT   The old proverb° is very well parted
between my master Shylock and you, sir. You have
the grace of God, sir, and he hath enough.
BASSANIO
Thou speak'st it well. Go, father, with thy son;               150
Take leave of thy old master and inquire
My lodging out. [*To a* SERVANT.] Give him a livery
More guarded° than his fellows'. See it done.
LAUNCELOT   Father, in. I cannot get a service; no! I
have ne'er a tongue in my head! Well! [*Studies his*   155
*palm*.] If any man in Italy have a fairer table° which
doth offer to swear upon a book—I shall have good
fortune! Go to, here's a simple line of life. Here's a
small trifle of wives. Alas, fifteen wives is nothing;
eleven widows and nine maids is a simple coming-in   160
for one man. And then to scape drowning thrice, and
to be in peril of my life with the edge of a feather bed!
Here are simple scapes.° Well, if Fortune be a woman,
she's a good wench for this gear.° Father, come. I'll
take my leave of the Jew in the twinkling.                      165
                   *Exit clown* [LAUNCELOT, *with old* GOBBO].

BASSANIO
I pray thee, good Leonardo, think on this:
These things being bought and orderly bestowed,
Return in haste, for I do feast tonight
My best-esteemed acquaintance. Hie thee, go.
LEONARDO
My best endeavors shall be done herein.                        170

*Enter* GRATIANO.

GRATIANO
Where's your master?
LEONARDO                        Yonder, sir, he walks.
                                              *Exit* LEONARDO.
GRATIANO
Signior Bassanio!
BASSANIO                   Gratiano!
GRATIANO
I have suit to you.
BASSANIO                   You have obtained it!
GRATIANO
You must not deny me. I must go with you to
   Belmont.
BASSANIO
Why then you must. But hear thee, Gratiano:                    175
Thou art too wild, too rude, and bold of voice—
Parts that become thee happily enough
And in such eyes as ours appear not faults;
But where thou art not known—why, there they show
Something too liberal.° Pray thee take pain                    180
To allay with some cold drops of modesty
Thy skipping spirit, lest through thy wild behavior
I be misconst'red° in the place I go to,
And lose my hopes.
GRATIANO                  Signior Bassanio, hear me:
If I do not put on a sober habit,°                             185
Talk with respect, and swear but now and then,
Wear prayer books in my pocket, look demurely—
Nay more, while grace is saying hood mine eyes
Thus with my hat, and sigh and say amen,
Use all the observance of civility°                            190
Like one well studied in a sad ostent°
To please his grandam, never trust me more.
BASSANIO
Well, we shall see your bearing.
GRATIANO
Nay, but I bar tonight. You shall not gauge me
By what we do tonight.
BASSANIO                   No, that were pity.                 195
I would entreat you rather to put on
Your boldest suit of mirth, for we have friends
That purpose merriment. But fare you well;
I have some business.
GRATIANO
And I must to Lorenzo and the rest,                            200
But we will visit you at supper time.          *Exeunt.*

---

**116 anon** straightway   **119 Gramercy** many thanks (French
*grand merci*)   **123 infection** Gobbo's mistake for *affection*
(i.e., liking)   **128 cater-cousins** great friends   **131 frutify**
for *fructify*, a blunder for a word like *signify*   **135 impertinent**
for *pertinent*   **141 defect** for *effect*   **144 preferred** recommended
for a higher position   **147 proverb** such as, "He that hath
the grace of God hath enough"   **153 guarded** ornamented
**156 table** palm   **163 scapes** escapes   **164 gear** business (i.e.,
the good fortune that he pretends to read in his palm)

**180 liberal** free (a kind word to describe Gratiano!)   **183
misconst'red** misconstrued   **185 habit** (1) bearing (2) garment
**190 civility** civilized behavior   **191 sad ostent** sober and
earnest appearance

[Scene III. *Venice. Shylock's house.*]

*Enter* JESSICA *and* [LAUNCELOT] *the clown.*

JESSICA
I am sorry thou wilt leave my father so;
Our house is hell, and thou a merry devil
Didst rob it of some taste of tediousness.
But fare thee well; there is a ducat for thee.
And, Launcelot, soon at supper shalt thou see          5
Lorenzo, who is thy new master's guest.
Give him this letter; do it secretly.
And so farewell. I would not have my father
See me in talk with thee.
LAUNCELOT    Adieu!° Tears exhibit° my tongue. Most    10
beautiful pagan, most sweet Jew, if a Christian do not
play the knave and get thee, I am much deceived.°
But adieu! These foolish drops do something drown
my manly spirit. Adieu!
JESSICA
Farewell, good Launcelot.          [*Exit* LAUNCELOT.]    15
Alack, what heinous sin is it in me
To be ashamed to be my father's child!
But though I am a daughter to his blood,
I am not to his manners. O Lorenzo,
If thou keep promise, I shall end this strife,          20
Become a Christian and thy loving wife!          *Exit.*

[Scene IV. *Venice. A street.*]

*Enter* GRATIANO, LORENZO, SALERIO, *and*
SOLANIO.

LORENZO
Nay, we will slink away in supper time,
Disguise us at my lodging, and return
All in an hour.
GRATIANO
We have not made good preparation.
SALERIO
We have not spoke us yet of torchbearers.°          5
SOLANIO
'Tis vile, unless it may be quaintly ordered,°
And better in my mind not undertook.
LORENZO
'Tis now but four of clock. We have two hours
To furnish us.

*Enter* LAUNCELOT [*with a letter*].

                    Friend Launcelot, what's the news?
LAUNCELOT    And it shall please you to break up° this,    10
it shall seem to signify.
LORENZO
I know the hand. In faith, 'tis a fair hand,

And whiter than the paper it° writ on
Is the fair hand that writ.
GRATIANO                    Love-news, in faith!
LAUNCELOT    By your leave, sir.          15
LORENZO    Whither goest thou?
LAUNCELOT    Marry, sir, to bid° my old master the
Jew to sup tonight with my new master the Christian.
LORENZO
Hold here, take this. [*Gives money.*] Tell gentle° Jessica
I will not fail her. Speak it privately.          20
                    *Exit clown* [LAUNCELOT].
Go, gentlemen;
Will you prepare you for this masque tonight?
I am provided of a torchbearer.
SALERIO
Ay marry, I'll be gone about it straight.
SOLANIO
And so will I.
LORENZO          Meet me and Gratiano          25
At Gratiano's lodging some hour hence.
SALERIO
'Tis good we do so.          *Exit* [*with* SOLANIO].
GRATIANO
Was not that letter from fair Jessica?
LORENZO
I must needs tell thee all. She hath directed
How I shall take her from her father's house,          30
What gold and jewels she is furnished with,
What page's suit she hath in readiness.
If e'er the Jew her father come to heaven,
It will be for his gentle° daughter's sake;
And never dare misfortune cross her foot,°          35
Unless she do it under this excuse,
That she is issue to a faithless° Jew.
Come, go with me; peruse this as thou goest.
Fair Jessica shall be my torchbearer.°
                    *Exit* [*with* GRATIANO].

[Scene V. *Venice. Before Shylock's house.*]

*Enter* [SHYLOCK *the*] *Jew and* [LAUNCELOT,] *his man
that was the clown.*

SHYLOCK
Well, thou shalt see, thy eyes shall be thy judge,
The difference of old Shylock and Bassanio.—
What,° Jessica!—Thou shalt not gormandize
As thou hast done with me.—What, Jessica!—
And sleep, and snore, and rend apparel out.—          5
Why, Jessica, I say!
LAUNCELOT          Why, Jessica!
SHYLOCK
Who bids thee call? I do not bid thee call.
LAUNCELOT    Your worship was wont to tell me I
could do nothing without bidding.

*Enter* JESSICA.

II.iii.10 **Adieu** perhaps not merely "good-by," but "I commend you to God"; **exhibit** for *inhibit*    11–12 **if . . . deceived** perhaps Launcelot is giving a hint of what happens
in II.v, but perhaps "do" should be emended to "did," and
"get" should be understood in the sense of "beget"
II.iv.5 **spoke . . . torchbearers** talked about getting torchbearers (who were regularly used in this sort of street festivity)
6 **quaintly ordered** artfully arranged    10 **break up** open

13 **it** the hand    17 **bid** ask    19, 34 **gentle** charming and
possessed of all attributes of a lady (with a pun on *gentile*, as
elsewhere)    35 **cross her foot** cross her path    37 **faithless**
lacking the Christian faith    39 **torchbearer** i.e., disguised as
a page
II.v.3 **What** exclamation of impatience, like "Why" in line 6

JESSICA   Call you? What is your will?     10

SHYLOCK
I am bid forth to supper, Jessica.
There are my keys. But wherefore should I go?
I am not bid for love—they flatter me.
But yet I'll go in hate, to feed upon
The prodigal Christian. Jessica my girl,     15
Look to my house. I am right loath to go.
There is some ill a-brewing towards my rest,
For I did dream of moneybags tonight.°

LAUNCELOT   I beseech you, sir, go. My young master
doth expect your reproach.°     20

SHYLOCK   So do I his.

LAUNCELOT   And they have conspired together. I will
not say you shall see a masque, but if you do, then it
was not for nothing that my nose fell a-bleeding on
Black Monday° last at six o'clock i' th' morning,    25
falling out that year on Ash Wednesday was four year
in th' afternoon.°

SHYLOCK
What, are there masques? Hear you me, Jessica:
Lock up my doors; and when you hear the drum
And the vile squealing of the wry-necked fife,°     30
Clamber not you up to the casements then,
Nor thrust your head into the public street
To gaze on Christian fools with varnished faces;°
But stop my house's ears—I mean my casements;
Let not the sound of shallow fopp'ry enter     35
My sober house. By Jacob's staff I swear
I have no mind of feasting forth tonight;
But I will go. Go you before me, sirrah.
Say I will come.

LAUNCELOT      I will go before, sir.
Mistress, look out at window for all this:     40
        There will come a Christian by
        Will be worth a Jewess' eye.    [Exit.]

SHYLOCK
What says that fool of Hagar's offspring,° ha?

JESSICA
His words were "Farewell, mistress"—nothing else.

SHYLOCK
The patch° is kind enough, but a huge feeder,     45
Snail-slow in profit,° and he sleeps by day
More than the wildcat. Drones hive not with me;
Therefore I part with him, and part with him
To one that I would have him help to waste
His borrowed purse. Well, Jessica, go in;     50
Perhaps I will return immediately.
Do as I bid you, shut doors after you.

---

**18 tonight** last night (the premonition is serious for Shylock,
comic for the audience)   **20 reproach** Launcelot's word for
*approach*   **25 Black Monday** Easter Monday   **26–27 falling
. . . afternoon** apparently Launcelot means "four years ago
on Ash Wednesday," but he may be intentionally talking
nonsense   **30 wry-necked fife** fife-player with neck twisted
to one side (the mouthpiece of the Elizabethan fife was set at
an angle, and these words are therefore sometimes taken to
mean the instrument; but Shylock would be less scornful of
the instrument than of the gay fool with his neck at a crazy
angle)   **33 varnished faces** painted masks (Shylock no
doubt puns on *varnished* in the sense of "insincere")   **43
Hagar's offspring** Ishmael, son of Abraham by the servant
Hagar (mother and son were cast out by Abraham after
Isaac's birth)   **45 patch** fool   **46 in profit** in any profitable
activity

Fast bind, fast find,
A proverb never stale in thrifty mind.     *Exit.*

JESSICA
Farewell; and if my fortune be not crost,     55
I have a father, you a daughter, lost.     *Exit.*

[Scene VI. *Venice. Before Shylock's house.*]

*Enter the masquers* GRATIANO *and* SALERIO.

GRATIANO
This is the penthouse° under which Lorenzo
Desired us to make stand.

SALERIO           His hour is almost past.

GRATIANO
And it is marvel he outdwells his hour,
For lovers ever run before the clock.

SALERIO
O ten times faster Venus' pigeons° fly     5
To seal love's bonds new-made, than they are wont
To keep obligèd faith° unforfeited!

GRATIANO
That ever holds. Who riseth from a feast
With that keen appetite that he sits down?
Where is the horse that doth untread again     10
His tedious measures° with the unbated fire
That he did pace them first? All things that are
Are with more spirit chasèd than enjoyed.
How like a younger° or a prodigal
The scarfèd° bark puts from her native bay,     15
Hugged and embracèd by the strumpet wind!
How like the prodigal doth she return,
With overweathered° ribs and ragged sails,
Lean, rent, and beggared by the strumpet wind!

*Enter* LORENZO.

SALERIO
Here comes Lorenzo: more of this hereafter.     20

LORENZO
Sweet friends, your patience for my long abode.°
Not I but my affairs have made you wait.
When you shall please to play the thieves for wives,
I'll watch as long for you then. Approach;
Here dwells my father Jew. Ho, who's within?     25

[*Enter*] JESSICA *above* [*in boy's clothes*].

JESSICA
Who are you? Tell me for more certainty,
Albeit I'll swear that I do know your tongue.

LORENZO
Lorenzo, and thy love.

JESSICA
Lorenzo certain, and my love indeed,
For who love I so much? And now who knows     30
But you, Lorenzo, whether I am yours?

LORENZO
Heaven and thy thoughts are witness that thou art.

---

**II.vi.1 penthouse** shelter formed by a projecting roof   **5
Venus' pigeons** they drew her chariot   **7 obligèd faith**
faith pledged (in marriage)   **11 measures** paces   **14 younger**
younger son   **15 scarfèd** decorated with scarfs (i.e., flags
and streamers)   **18 overweathered** long exposed to stormy
weather   **21 abode** delay

JESSICA
Here, catch this casket; it is worth the pains.
I am glad 'tis night, you° do not look on me,
For I am much ashamed of my exchange.° 35
But love is blind, and lovers cannot see
The pretty follies that themselves commit;
For if they could, Cupid himself would blush
To see me thus transformèd to a boy.

LORENZO
Descend, for you must be my torchbearer. 40

JESSICA
What, must I hold a candle to my shames?
They in themselves, good sooth, are too too light.°
Why, 'tis an office of discovery,° love,
And I should be obscured.

LORENZO              So are you, sweet,
Even in the lovely garnish° of a boy. 45
But come at once;
For the close° night doth play the runaway,
And we are stayed for at Bassanio's feast.

JESSICA
I will make fast the doors and gild myself
With some moe° ducats, and be with you straight. 50
                      [*Exit above.*]

GRATIANO
Now by my hood, a gentle° and no Jew!

LORENZO
Beshrow° me but I love her heartily!
For she is wise, if I can judge of her,
And fair she is, if that mine eyes be true,
And true she is, as she hath proved herself; 55
And therefore, like herself, wise, fair, and true,
Shall she be placèd in my constant soul.

*Enter* JESSICA [*below*].

What, art thou come? On, gentlemen, away!
Our masquing mates by this time for us stay.
              *Exit* [*with* JESSICA *and* SALERIO].

*Enter* ANTONIO.

ANTONIO  Who's there? 60
GRATIANO  Signior Antonio?
ANTONIO
Fie, fie, Gratiano, where are all the rest?
'Tis nine o'clock, our friends all stay for you.
No masque tonight. The wind is come about;
Bassanio presently° will go aboard. 65
I have sent twenty out to seek for you.

GRATIANO
I am glad on't. I desire no more delight
Than to be under sail and gone tonight.    *Exeunt.*

[Scene VII. *Belmont. Portia's house.*]

[*Flourish of cornets.*] *Enter* PORTIA, *with* MOROCCO
*and both their* TRAINS.

PORTIA
Go, draw aside the curtains and discover°
The several caskets to this noble prince.
Now make your choice.

MOROCCO
This first, of gold, who this inscription bears,
"Who chooseth me shall gain what many men desire." 5
The second, silver, which this promise carries,
"Who chooseth me shall get as much as he deserves."
This third, dull lead, with warning all as blunt,°
"Who chooseth me must give and hazard all he hath."
How shall I know if I do choose the right? 10

PORTIA
The one of them contains my picture, prince.
If you choose that, then I am yours withal.

MOROCCO
Some god direct my judgment! Let me see—
I will survey th' inscriptions back again.
What says this leaden casket? 15
"Who chooseth me must give and hazard all he hath."
Must give—for what? For lead! Hazard for lead?
This casket threatens; men that hazard all
Do it in hope of fair advantages.
A golden mind stoops not to shows of dross; 20
I'll then nor give nor hazard aught for lead.
What says the silver with her virgin hue?
"Who chooseth me shall get as much as he deserves."
As much as he deserves? Pause here, Morocco,
And weigh thy value with an even hand: 25
If thou be'st rated by thy estimation,°
Thou dost deserve enough, and yet enough
May not extend so far as to the lady;
And yet to be afeard of my deserving
Were but a weak disabling° of myself. 30
As much as I deserve? Why that's the lady!
I do in birth deserve her, and in fortunes,
In graces, and in qualities of breeding;
But more than these, in love I do deserve.
What if I strayed no farther, but chose here? 35
Let's see once more this saying graved in gold:
"Who chooseth me shall gain what many men desire."
Why that's the lady! All the world desires her;
From the four corners of the earth they come
To kiss this shrine, this mortal breathing saint. 40
The Hyrcanian deserts° and the vasty wilds
Of wide Arabia are as throughfares now
For princes to come view fair Portia.
The watery kingdom, whose ambitious head
Spets in the face of heaven, is no bar 45
To stop the foreign spirits, but they come
As o'er a brook to see fair Portia.
One of these three contains her heavenly picture.
Is't like that lead contains her? 'Twere damnation
To think so base a thought; it were too gross° 50
To rib her cerecloth° in the obscure° grave.

**34 'tis night, you** an ellipsis, "and" being understood  **35 exchange** of clothes  **42 light** immodest (with a pun)  **43 office of discovery** task in which my disguise will be revealed  **45 garnish** pleasing attire  **47 close** secret  **50 moe** more  **51 gentle** refined lady (with the usual pun on *gentile*)  **52 Beshrow** a light word for *curse*  **65 presently** at this present moment

**II.vii.1 discover** reveal  **8 as blunt** as blunt as the lead is dull (with quibbles on *blunt* in the senses of "abrupt in speech and manner" and "not sharp," and on *dull* in the senses of "not sharp" and "not shining")  **26 estimation** reputation  **30 disabling** undervaluing  **41 Hyrcanian deserts** Persian deserts (famous for savage beasts)  **50 it . . . gross** lead would be too coarse (bodies of wealthy persons were often encased in lead)  **51 cerecloth** waxed embalming cloth; **obscure** accent on first syllable

Or shall I think in silver she's immured,
Being ten times undervalued to tried gold?
O sinful thought! Never so rich a gem
Was set in worse than gold. They have in England          55
A coin that bears the figure of an angel
Stampèd in gold—but that's insculped° upon;
But here an angel° in a golden bed
Lies all within. Deliver me the key.
Here do I choose, and thrive I as I may!          60

PORTIA
There, take it, prince; and if my form lie there,
Then I am yours.          [*He opens the golden casket.*]

MOROCCO          O hell! What have we here?
A carrion death,° within whose empty eye
There is a written scroll! I'll read the writing.
     "All that glisters is not gold;°          65
     Often have you heard that told.
     Many a man his life hath sold
     But my outside to behold;
     Gilded tombs do worms infold.
     Had you been as wise as bold,          70
     Young in limbs, in judgment old,
     Your answer had not been inscrolled.°
     Fare you well, your suit is cold."
Cold indeed, and labor lost.
Then farewell heat, and welcome frost!          75
Portia, adieu. I have too grieved a heart
To take a tedious leave. Thus losers part.
          *Exit* [*with his* TRAIN. *Flourish of cornets*].

PORTIA
A gentle° riddance. Draw the curtains, go.
Let all of his complexion° choose me so.          *Exeunt.*


[Scene VIII. *Venice. A street.*]

*Enter* SALERIO *and* SOLANIO.

SALERIO
Why, man, I saw Bassanio under sail;
With him is Gratiano gone along,
And in their ship I am sure Lorenzo is not.

SOLANIO
The villain° Jew with outcries raised the duke,
Who went with him to search Bassanio's ship.          5

SALERIO
He came too late, the ship was under sail.
But there the duke was given to understand
That in a gondola were seen together
Lorenzo and his amorous Jessica.
Besides, Antonio certified the duke          10
They were not with Bassanio in his ship.

SOLANIO
I never heard a passion° so confused,
So strange, outrageous, and so variable
As the dog Jew did utter in the streets:
"My daughter! O my ducats! O my daughter!          15
Fled with a Christian! O my Christian ducats!

Justice! The law! My ducats and my daughter!
A sealèd bag, two sealèd bags of ducats,
Of double ducats, stol'n from me by my daughter!
And jewels—two stones, two rich and precious stones,          20
Stol'n by my daughter! Justice! Find the girl!
She hath the stones upon her, and the ducats!"

SALERIO
Why, all the boys in Venice follow him,
Crying his stones, his daughter, and his ducats.

SOLANIO
Let good Antonio look he keep his day,°          25
Or he shall pay for this.

SALERIO                    Marry, well rememb'red.
I reasoned° with a Frenchman yesterday,
Who told me, in the narrow seas° that part
The French and English there miscarrièd
A vessel of our country richly fraught.°          30
I thought upon Antonio when he told me,
And wished in silence that it were not his.

SOLANIO
You were best to tell Antonio what you hear.
Yet do not suddenly, for it may grieve him.

SALERIO
A kinder gentleman treads not the earth.          35
I saw Bassanio and Antonio part.
Bassanio told him he would make some speed
Of his return; he answered, "Do not so.
Slubber° not business for my sake, Bassanio,
But stay the very riping of the time;          40
And for the Jew's bond which he hath of me,
Let it not enter in your mind of love.°
Be merry, and employ your chiefest thoughts
To courtship and such fair ostents° of love
As shall conveniently become you there."          45
And even there, his eye being big with tears,
Turning his face, he put his hand behind him,
And with affection wondrous sensible°
He wrung Bassanio's hand; and so they parted.

SOLANIO
I think he only loves the world for him.          50
I pray thee let us go and find him out,
And quicken his embracèd heaviness°
With some delight or other.

SALERIO                    Do we so.          *Exeunt.*


[Scene IX. *Belmont. Portia's house.*]

*Enter* NERISSA *and a* SERVITOR.

NERISSA
Quick, quick I pray thee, draw the curtain straight.°
The Prince of Aragon hath ta'en his oath,
And comes to his election° presently.°

**57 insculped** sculptured  **58 angel** Portia's picture  **63 death** death's head  **65 All . . . gold** proverbial  **72 inscrolled** written on the scroll  **78 gentle** well-bred  **79 complexion** temperament (not merely coloring)
**II.viii.4 villain** low-bred fellow (not scoundrel; a vaguer term than today)  **12 passion** emotional outburst

**25 keep his day** pay on the exact day appointed  **27 reasoned** talked  **28 narrow seas** English Channel  **30 fraught** freighted  **39 Slubber** hurry over in a slovenly way  **42 mind of love** loving thoughts (probably about both Antonio and Portia)  **44 ostents** shows, expressions  **48 affection wondrous sensible** wonderfully strong emotion  **52 quicken . . . heaviness** lighten the gloom which he has embraced
**II.ix.1 straight** at once  **3 election** choice; **presently** at this present moment, instantly

*[Flourish of cornets.] Enter* ARAGON, *his* TRAIN, *and*
PORTIA.

PORTIA
Behold, there stand the caskets, noble prince.
If you choose that wherein I am contained,                          5
Straight shall our nuptial rites be solemnized;
But if you fail, without more speech, my lord,
You must be gone from hence immediately.

ARAGON
I am enjoined by oath to observe three things:
First, never to unfold to any one                                   10
Which casket 'twas I chose; next, if I fail
Of the right casket, never in my life
To woo a maid in way of marriage;
Lastly, if I do fail in fortune of my choice,
Immediately to leave you and be gone.                               15

PORTIA
To these injunctions everyone doth swear
That comes to hazard for my worthless self.

ARAGON
And so° have I addressed me.° Fortune now
To my heart's hope! Gold, silver, and base lead.
"Who chooseth me must give and hazard all he hath."                 20
You shall look fairer ere I give or hazard.
What says the golden chest? Ha, let me see!
"Who chooseth me shall gain what many men desire."
What many men desire—that "many" may be meant
By° the fool multitude that choose by show,                         25
Not learning more than the fond° eye doth teach,
Which pries not to th' interior, but like the martlet°
Builds in the weather on the outward wall,
Even in the force and road of casualty.°
I will not choose what many men desire,                             30
Because I will not jump with° common spirits
And rank me with the barbarous multitudes.
Why then, to thee, thou silver treasure house!
Tell me once more what title thou dost bear.
"Who chooseth me shall get as much as he deserves."                 35
And well said too, for who shall go about
To cozen° fortune, and be honorable
Without the stamp of merit? Let none presume
To wear an undeservèd dignity.
O that estates, degrees,° and offices°                              40
Were not derived corruptly, and that clear honor
Were purchased by the merit of the wearer!
How many then should cover° that stand bare!
How many be commanded that command;
How much low peasantry would then be gleanèd°                       45
From the true seed of honor!° And how much honor
Picked from the chaff and ruin of the times
To be new varnished.° Well, but to my choice.
"Who chooseth me shall get as much as he deserves."
I will assume desert. Give me a key for this,                       50
And instantly unlock my fortunes here.

*[He opens the silver casket.]*

PORTIA
Too long a pause for that which you find there.°

ARAGON
What's here? The portrait of a blinking idiot
Presenting me a schedule!° I will read it.
How much unlike art thou to Portia!                                 55
How much unlike my hopes and my deservings!
"Who chooseth me shall have as much as he deserves."
Did I deserve no more than a fool's head?
Is that my prize? Are my deserts no better?

PORTIA
To offend and judge are distinct offices,                           60
And of opposèd natures.°

ARAGON                          What is here?
"The fire° seven times tried this;°
Seven times tried that judgment is
That did never choose amiss.
Some there be that shadows kiss;                                    65
Such have but a shadow's bliss.
There be fools alive iwis,°
Silvered o'er,° and so was this.
Take what wife you will to bed,
I° will ever be your head.                                          70
So be gone; you are sped."°
Still more fool I shall appear
By the time I linger here.
With one fool's head I came to woo,
But I go away with two.                                             75
Sweet, adieu. I'll keep my oath,
Patiently to bear my wroath.° *[Exit, with his* TRAIN.]

PORTIA
Thus hath the candle singed the moth.
O these deliberate fools! When they do choose,
They have the wisdom by their wit° to lose.                         80

NERISSA
The ancient saying is no heresy:
Hanging and wiving goes by destiny.

PORTIA
Come draw the curtain, Nerissa.

*Enter* MESSENGER.

MESSENGER
Where is my lady?

PORTIA                          Here. What would my lord?°

MESSENGER
Madam, there is alighted at your gate                               85
A young Venetian, one that comes before
To signify th' approaching of his lord,
From whom he bringeth sensible regreets,°
To wit, besides commends and courteous breath,
Gifts of rich value. Yet I have not seen°                           90
So likely° an ambassador of love.

18 **so** on these terms; **have . . . me** I have addressed myself
(to this affair) 25 **By** with regard to 26 **fond** foolish 27
**martlet** martin, a bird 29 **in . . . casualty** exposed to the
tyrannic force of mischance and lying in the open road 31
**jump with** accord with 37 **cozen** cheat 40 **degrees** ranks;
**offices** official positions 43 **cover** wear hats, in sign of
authority 45 **gleanèd** picked out, as in gleaning grain (cf.
line 47, "Picked from the chaff") 46 **seed of honor** descendants of ancient nobility 48 **To . . . varnished** to have the
luster of their family restored

52 **Too . . . there** probably an aside 54 **schedule** scroll
60–61 **To . . . natures** The offender is not to judge himself
62 **fire** pronounced fí-er; **this** the silver of the casket 67 **iwis**
certainly 68 **Silvered o'er** with the gray hair usually associated
with wisdom 70 **I** the "blinking idiot" of line 53 71 **you are
sped** you have achieved your fortune 77 **wroath** heavy lot (?)
80 **wit** cleverness 84 **What . . . lord** a gay, jesting retort
to the Messenger's "my lady" 88 **sensible regreets** a
quibble: greetings (1) expressing strong feeling, and (2)
conveying tangible gifts 90 **Yet . . . seen** not yet have I
seen 91 **likely** promising

A day in April never came so sweet
To show how costly° summer was at hand,
As this forespurrer° comes before his lord.

PORTIA
No more, I pray thee. I am half afeard      95
Thou wilt say anon he is some kin to thee,
Thou spend'st such high-day wit° in praising him.
Come, come, Nerissa, for I long to see
Quick Cupid's post° that comes so mannerly.

NERISSA
Bassanio, Lord Love,° if thy will it be!      *Exeunt.* 100

# [ACT III]

## [Scene I. *Venice. A street.*]

[*Enter*] SOLANIO *and* SALERIO.

SOLANIO Now what news on the Rialto?
SALERIO Why, yet it lives there unchecked° that
Antonio hath a ship of rich lading wracked on the
narrow seas°—the Goodwins° I think they call the place
—a very dangerous flat, and fatal, where the carcasses 5
of many a tall ship lie buried as they say, if my gossip°
Report be an honest woman of her word.
SOLANIO I would she were as lying a gossip in that, as
ever knapped° ginger or made her neighbors believe
she wept for the death of a third husband. But it is 10
true, without any slips of prolixity° or crossing the
plain highway of talk,° that the good Antonio, the
honest Antonio—O that I had a title good enough to
keep his name company!—
SALERIO Come, the full stop.°      15
SOLANIO Ha, what sayest thou? Why the end is, he
hath lost a ship.
SALERIO I would it might prove the end of his losses.
SOLANIO Let me say amen betimes,° lest the devil
cross my prayer, for here he comes in the likeness of a 20
Jew.

*Enter* SHYLOCK.

How now, Shylock? What news among the merchants?
SHYLOCK You knew, none so well, none so well as
you, of my daughter's flight.
SALERIO That's certain. I for my part knew the tailor 25
that made the wings she flew withal.
SOLANIO And Shylock for his own part knew the
bird was fledge,° and then it is the complexion° of
them all to leave the dam.
SHYLOCK She is damned for it.      30
SALERIO That's certain, if the devil may be her judge.

SHYLOCK My own flesh and blood to rebel!
SOLANIO Out upon it, old carrion! Rebels it° at these
years?
SHYLOCK I say my daughter is my flesh and my 35
blood.
SALERIO There is more difference between thy flesh
and hers than between jet and ivory, more between
your bloods than there is between red wine and
Rhenish. But tell us, do you hear whether Antonio 40
have had any loss at sea or no?
SHYLOCK There I have another bad match! A bankrout,° a prodigal, who dare scarce show his head on
the Rialto, a beggar that was used to come so smug°
upon the mart! Let him look to his bond. He was wont 45
to call me usurer. Let him look to his bond. He was
wont to lend money for a Christian cursy.° Let him
look to his bond.
SALERIO Why, I am sure if he forfeit thou wilt not
take his flesh. What's that good for?      50
SHYLOCK To bait fish withal. If it will feed nothing
else, it will feed my revenge. He hath disgraced me, and
hind'red me half a million, laughed at my losses,
mocked at my gains, scorned my nation, thwarted my
bargains, cooled my friends, heated mine enemies— 55
and what's his reason? I am a Jew. Hath not a Jew
eyes? Hath not a Jew hands, organs, dimensions,°
senses, affections,° passions?—fed with the same food,
hurt with the same weapons, subject to the same
diseases, healed by the same means, warmed and 60
cooled by the same winter and summer as a Christian
is? If you prick us, do we not bleed? If you tickle us,
do we not laugh? If you poison us, do we not die?
And if you wrong us, shall we not revenge? If we are
like you in the rest, we will resemble you in that. If a 65
Jew wrong a Christian, what is his humility?° Revenge!
If a Christian wrong a Jew, what should his sufferance
be by Christian example? Why revenge! The villainy
you teach me I will execute, and it shall go hard but I
will better the instruction.      70

*Enter a* MAN *from Antonio.*

[MAN] Gentlemen, my master Antonio is at his house,
and desires to speak with you both.
SALERIO We have been up and down to seek him.

*Enter* TUBAL.

SOLANIO Here comes another of the tribe. A third
cannot be matched, unless the devil himself turn Jew. 75
     *Exeunt gentlemen* [SOLANIO, SALERIO, *and* MAN].
SHYLOCK How now, Tubal! What news from Genoa?
Hast thou found my daughter?
TUBAL I often came where I did hear of her, but cannot
find her.
SHYLOCK Why there, there, there, there! A diamond 80
gone cost me two thousand ducats in Frankford! The
curse never fell upon our nation till now; I never felt
it till now. Two thousand ducats in that, and other
precious, precious jewels. I would my daughter were

---

93 **costly** rich, plenteous   94 **forespurrer** advance messenger
(one who spurs his horse ahead of his party)   97 **high-day wit**
imagination befitting a festive occasion   99 **post** messenger
100 **Lord Love** god of love
III.i.2 **it . . . unchecked** it is reported without dispute   4
**narrow seas** English Channel;   **Goodwins** Goodwin
Sands, a shoal   6 **gossip** talkative comrade   9 **knapped**
snapped, bit   11 **slips of prolixity** long-winded lies   11–12
**crossing . . . talk** going counter to honest speech   15 **Come
. . . stop** Come to the end of your sentence   19 **betimes**
promptly   28 **fledge** feathered, able to fly;   **complexion**
natural disposition

33 **Rebels it** a contemptuous pun on "flesh and blood" in line
32 in the sense of fleshly desire   42–43 **bankrout** bankrupt
44 **smug** well-groomed   47 **cursy** courtesy   57 **dimensions**
limbs, features, etc.   58 **affections** feelings   66 **what . . .
humility** what does his Christian humility amount to

dead at my foot, and the jewels in her ear! Would she 85
were hearsed at my foot, and the ducats in her coffin!
No news of them? Why, so! And I know not what's
spent in the search. Why thou loss upon loss—the
thief gone with so much, and so much to find the
thief!—and no satisfaction, no revenge, nor no ill luck 90
stirring but what lights o' my shoulders, no sighs but
o' my breathing, no tears but o' my shedding.

TUBAL  Yes, other men have ill luck too. Antonio, as I
heard in Genoa—

SHYLOCK  What, what, what? Ill luck, ill luck?  95

TUBAL  Hath an argosy cast away coming from
Tripolis.

SHYLOCK  I thank God, I thank God! Is it true, is it
true?

TUBAL  I spoke with some of the sailors that escaped the 100
wrack.

SHYLOCK  I thank thee, good Tubal. Good news,
good news! Ha, ha! Heard in Genoa?

TUBAL  Your daughter spent in Genoa, as I heard, one
night fourscore ducats.  105

SHYLOCK  Thou stick'st a dagger in me. I shall never
see my gold again. Fourscore ducats at a sitting, fourscore ducats!

TUBAL  There came divers of Antonio's creditors in my
company to Venice that swear he cannot choose but 110
break.°

SHYLOCK  I am very glad of it. I'll plague him; I'll
torture him. I am glad of it.

TUBAL  One of them showed me a ring that he had of
your daughter for a monkey.  115

SHYLOCK  Out upon her! Thou torturest me, Tubal.
It was my turquoise; I had it of Leah° when I was a
bachelor. I would not have given it for a wilderness of
monkeys.

TUBAL  But Antonio is certainly undone.  120

SHYLOCK  Nay, that's true, that's very true. Go,
Tubal, fee me an officer;° bespeak° him a fortnight
before. I will have the heart of him if he forfeit, for
were he out of Venice I can make what merchandise° I
will. Go, Tubal, and meet me at our synagogue; go, 125
good Tubal; at our synagogue, Tubal.  *Exeunt.*

[Scene II. *Belmont. Portia's house.*]

*Enter* BASSANIO, PORTIA, GRATIANO, [NERISSA,]
*and all their* TRAINS.

PORTIA
I pray you tarry; pause a day or two
Before you hazard, for in choosing wrong
I lose your company. Therefore forbear awhile.
There's something tells me (but it is not love)
I would not lose you; and you know yourself  5
Hate counsels not in such a quality.°
But lest you should not understand me well—
And yet a maiden hath no tongue but thought—
I would detain you here some month or two
Before you venture for me. I could teach you  10

How to choose right, but then I am forsworn.
So will I never be. So may you miss me.
But if you do, you'll make me wish a sin—
That I had been forsworn. Beshrow° your eyes!
They have o'erlooked° me and divided me;  15
One half of me is yours, the other half yours—
Mine own I would say; but if mine then yours,
And so all yours! O these naughty° times
Puts bars between the owners and their rights!
And so, though yours, not yours. Prove it so,°  20
Let fortune go to hell for it, not I.
I speak too long, but 'tis to peize° the time,
To eche° it and to draw it out in length,
To stay you from election.
BASSANIO                     Let me choose,
For as I am, I live upon the rack.°  25
PORTIA
Upon the rack, Bassanio? Then confess
What treason there is mingled with your love.°
BASSANIO
None but that ugly treason of mistrust,
Which makes me fear th' enjoying of my love.
There may as well be amity and life  30
'Tween snow and fire, as treason and my love.
PORTIA
Ay, but I fear you speak upon the rack,
Where men enforcèd° do speak anything.
BASSANIO
Promise me life, and I'll confess the truth.
PORTIA
Well then, confess and live.
BASSANIO                        Confess and love  35
Had been the very sum of my confession!
O happy torment, when my torturer
Doth teach me answers for deliverance.°
But let me to my fortune and the caskets.
PORTIA
Away then! I am locked in one of them;  40
If you do love me, you will find me out.
Nerissa and the rest, stand all aloof.
Let music sound while he doth make his choice;
Then if he lose he makes a swanlike end,°
Fading in music. That the comparison  45
May stand more proper, my eye shall be the stream
And wat'ry deathbed for him. He may win;
And what is music then? Then music is
Even as the flourish° when true subjects bow
To a new-crownèd monarch. Such it is  50
As are those dulcet sounds in break of day,
That creep into the dreaming bridegroom's ear
And summon him to marriage. Now he goes,
With no less presence,° but with much more love,

111 **break** go bankrupt  117 **Leah** Shylock's wife  122 **officer**
to arrest Antonio; **bespeak** engage  124 **merchandise** wealth
III.ii.6 **in . . . quality** in such a manner of speech as I am
using to you

14 **Beshrow** curse (but a playful word)  15 **o'erlooked**
bewitched  18 **naughty** wicked  20 **Prove it so** if it should
prove so  22 **peize** weigh down, hence retard  23 **eche** eke
out (i.e., lengthen)  25 **rack** instrument of torture, on which
the body was pulled with great force, often breaking the
joints; used to force confessions, especially in trials for treason
27 **What . . . love** spoken playfully  33 **enforcèd** compelled
(by torture)  38 **answers for deliverance** answers to free
me from torture  44 **swanlike end** an end like the swan's
(who was supposed never to sing until it sang enchantingly
at its death)  49 **flourish** fanfare of trumpets  54 **presence**
noble bearing

Than young Alcides,° when he did redeem 55
The virgin tribute° paid by howling Troy
To the sea monster. I stand for sacrifice;
The rest aloof are the Dardanian wives,
With bleared visages come forth to view
The issue of th' exploit. Go, Hercules! 60
Live thou,° I live. With much, much more dismay°
I view the fight than thou that mak'st the fray.°

*A song the whilst* BASSANIO *comments on the caskets to himself.*

     Tell me where is fancy° bred,
     Or in the heart, or in the head?
     How begot, how nourishèd? 65
      Reply, reply.
     It is engend'red in the eyes,
     With gazing fed, and fancy dies
     In the cradle where it lies.
     Let us all ring fancy's knell. 70
     I'll begin it—Ding, dong, bell.
ALL      Ding, dong, bell.

BASSANIO
So° may the outward shows be least themselves;°
The world is still° deceived with ornament.
In law, what plea so tainted and corrupt, 75
But being seasoned with a gracious voice,
Obscures the show of evil? In religion,
What damnèd error but some sober brow
Will bless it, and approve it with a text,°
Hiding the grossness with fair ornament? 80
There is no vice so simple but assumes
Some mark of virtue on his outward parts.
How many cowards whose hearts are all as false
As stairs of sand, wear yet upon their chins
The beards of Hercules and frowning Mars, 85
Who inward searched, have livers white as milk!°
And these assume but valor's excrement°
To render them redoubted.° Look on beauty,
And you shall see 'tis purchased by the weight,
Which therein works a miracle in nature, 90
Making them lightest° that wear most of it:
So are those crispèd° snaky golden locks,
Which maketh such wanton° gambols with the wind
Upon supposèd fairness, often known
To be the dowry° of a second head, 95
The skull that bred them in the sepulcher.
Thus ornament is but the guilèd° shore
To a most dangerous sea, the beauteous scarf
Veiling an Indian° beauty; in a word,
The seeming truth which cunning times put on 100
To entrap the wisest. Therefore then, thou gaudy gold,
Hard food for Midas, I will none of thee;

Nor none of thee, thou pale and common drudge°
'Tween man and man. But thou, thou meager° lead
Which rather threaten'st than dost promise aught, 105
Thy paleness moves me more than eloquence;
And here choose I. Joy be the consequence!
PORTIA [*Aside.*]
How all the other passions fleet to air,
As doubtful thoughts, and rash-embraced despair,
And shudd'ring fear, and green-eyed jealousy. 110
O love, be moderate, allay thy ecstasy,
In measure rain thy joy, scant° this excess!
I feel too much thy blessing. Make it less
For fear I surfeit.°
BASSANIO [*Opening the leaden casket.*]
       What find I here?
Fair Portia's counterfeit!° What demigod° 115
Hath come so near creation? Move these eyes?
Or whether, riding on the balls of mine,°
Seem they in motion? Here are severed lips
Parted with sugar breath; so sweet a bar°
Should sunder such sweet friends.° Here in her hairs 120
The painter plays the spider, and hath woven
A golden mesh t' entrap the hearts of men
Faster° than gnats in cobwebs. But her eyes—
How could he see to do them? Having made one,
Methinks it should have power to steal both his 125
And leave itself unfurnished.° Yet look how far
The substance° of my praise doth wrong this shadow°
In underprizing it, so far this shadow°
Doth limp behind the substance.° Here's the scroll,
The continent and summary° of my fortune. 130
     "You that choose not by the view
     Chance as fair,° and choose as true.
     Since this fortune falls to you,
     Be content and seek no new.
     If you be well pleased with this 135
     And hold your fortune for your bliss,
     Turn you where your lady is,
     And claim her with a loving kiss."
A gentle° scroll. Fair lady, by your leave.

[*Kisses her.*]

I come by note,° to give and to receive. 140
Like one of two contending in a prize,°
That thinks he hath done well in people's eyes,
Hearing applause and universal shout,
Giddy in spirit, still gazing in a doubt
Whether those peals of praise be his° or no— 145
So, thrice-fair lady, stand I even so,
As doubtful whether what I see be true,
Until confirmed, signed, ratified by you.

**55 Alcides** Hercules   **56 virgin tribute** Hesione, Priam's sister, who was offered as a divine sacrifice to be devoured by a sea monster; Hercules slew the monster and saved her   **61 Live thou** if thou live; **dismay** alarm and terror   **62 fray** combat   **63 fancy** love based only on the senses, especially the sight   **73 So** thus; **least themselves** least what they really are   **74 still** continually   **79 approve . . . text** prove it by a biblical text   **86 livers . . . milk** a pale liver supposedly caused cowardice   **87 excrement** excrescence, outer appearance   **88 redoubted** dreaded   **91 lightest** a pun on *light* in the sense of "unchaste"   **92 crispèd** curled   **93 wanton** playful   **95 dowry** gift of property (i.e., hair from a dead person's head)   **97 guilèd** full of guile, treacherous   **99 Indian** East Indian. hence dusky

**103 pale . . . drudge** pale hack worker (i.e., silver)   **104 meager** poverty-stricken, of slight value   **112 scant** lessen   **114 surfeit** grow sick with too much (i.e., too much joy)   **115 counterfeit** image; **demigod** half-divine painter   **117 balls of mine** my eyeballs   **119 so . . . bar** Portia's breath   **120 sweet friends** her lips   **123 Faster** tighter   **126 unfurnished** not provided with its mate (since the picture of the first eye has taken away both of the painter's eyes)   **127, 129 The substance** Portia herself   **127, 128 this shadow** her picture   **130 continent and summary** that which contains and sums up   **132 Chance as fair** have as fair fortune   **139 gentle** courteous, well-bred   **140 by note** according to instructions (in lines 137–38)   **141 prize** contest for a prize, as in a tournament   **145 his** intended for him

PORTIA
You see me, Lord Bassanio, where I stand,
Such as I am. Though for myself alone                    150
I would not be ambitious in my wish
To wish myself much better, yet for you
I would be trebled twenty times myself,
A thousand times more fair, ten thousand times more
  rich,
That only to stand high in your account,°                155
I might in virtues, beauties, livings,° friends,
Exceed account.° But the full sum of me
Is sum of something—which, to term in gross,°
Is an unlessoned girl, unschooled, unpracticed;
Happy in this, she is not yet so old                     160
But she may learn; happier than this,
She is not bred so dull but she can learn;
Happiest of all, is that her gentle spirit
Commits itself to yours to be directed,
As from her lord, her governor, her king.                165
Myself, and what is mine, to you and yours
Is now converted.° But now° I was the lord
Of this fair mansion, master of my servants,
Queen o'er myself; and even now, but now,
This house, these servants, and this same myself         170
Are yours, my lord's. I give them with this ring,
Which when you part from, lose, or give away,
Let it presage° the ruin of your love
And be my vantage to exclaim on° you.
BASSANIO
Madam, you have bereft me of all words.                  175
Only my blood speaks to you in my veins,
And there is such confusion in my powers
As, after some oration fairly spoke
By a belovèd prince,° there doth appear
Among the buzzing pleasèd multitude;                     180
Where every something being blent together
Turns to a wild of nothing, save of joy
Expressed and not expressed. But when this ring
Parts from this finger, then parts life from hence!
O then be bold to say Bassanio's dead!                   185
NERISSA
My lord and lady, it is now our time,
That have stood by and seen our wishes prosper,
To cry "good joy." Good joy, my lord and lady!
GRATIANO
My Lord Bassanio, and my gentle lady,
I wish you all the joy that you can wish—                190
For I am sure you can wish none from° me;
And when your honors mean to solemnize
The bargain of your faith, I do beseech you
Even at that time I may be married too.
BASSANIO
With all my heart, so° thou canst get a wife.            195
GRATIANO
I thank your lordship, you have got me one.
My eyes, my lord, can look as swift as yours:

You saw the mistress, I beheld the maid.
You loved, I loved; for intermission°
No more pertains to me, my lord, than you.               200
Your fortune stood upon the caskets there,
And so did mine too, as the matter falls;
For wooing here until I sweat again,°
And swearing till my very roof° was dry
With oaths of love, at last—if promise last°—            205
I got a promise of this fair one here
To have her love, provided that your fortune
Achieved her mistress.
PORTIA                          Is this true, Nerissa?
NERISSA
Madam, it is, so you stand pleased withal.
BASSANIO
And do you, Gratiano, mean good faith?                   210
GRATIANO    Yes, faith, my lord.
BASSANIO
Our feast shall be much honored in your marriage.
GRATIANO    We'll play with them the first boy for a
thousand ducats.
NERISSA    What, and stake down?°                        215
GRATIANO    No, we shall ne'er win at that sport, and
stake down.
But who comes here? Lorenzo and his infidel!°
What, and my old Venetian friend Salerio!

*Enter* LORENZO, JESSICA, *and* SALERIO, *a messenger
from Venice.*

BASSANIO
Lorenzo and Salerio, welcome hither,                     220
If that the youth of my new int'rest° here
Have power to bid you welcome. By your leave,
I bid my very friends and countrymen,
Sweet Portia, welcome.
PORTIA                    So do I, my lord.
They are entirely welcome.                               225
LORENZO
I thank your honor. For my part, my lord,
My purpose was not to have seen you here,
But meeting with Salerio by the way,
He did entreat me past all saying nay
To come with him along.
SALERIO                        I did, my lord,           230
And I have reason for it. Signior Antonio
Commends him to you.° [*Gives* BASSANIO *a letter.*]
BASSANIO                    Ere I ope his letter,
I pray you tell me how my good friend doth.
SALERIO
Not sick, my lord, unless it be in mind,
Nor well, unless in mind. His letter there               235
Will show you his estate.°

*Open the letter.*

GRATIANO
Nerissa, cheer yond stranger; bid her welcome.
Your hand, Salerio. What's the news from Venice?

---

155 **account** esteem, regard    156 **livings** possessions    157
**account** computation    158 **term in gross** describe in
broad terms    167 **converted** changed (i.e., made yours); **But
now** only now    173 **presage** foretell    174 **vantage . . . on**
opportunity to cry out against (lines 173–74 are spoken playfully)    179 **prince** a feminine as well as a masculine noun;
hence suitably applied to Portia    191 **from** away from    195
**so** provided

199 **intermission** pausing    203 **again** again and again    204
**roof** roof of the mouth    205 **if promise last** if her promise
holds    215 **stake down** a betting term (with an off-color pun)
218 **infidel** one who lacks the true faith (Gratiano applies the
term playfully to Jessica; cf. II.vi.51)    221 **int'rest** claim
232 **Commends . . . you** sends you his best wishes    236
**estate** state, condition

How doth that royal merchant,° good Antonio?
I know he will be glad of our success;                                    240
We are the Jasons, we have won the Fleece.

SALERIO
I would you had won the fleece° that he hath lost!

PORTIA
There are some shrowd° contents in yond same paper
That steals the color from Bassanio's cheek:
Some dear friend dead, else nothing in the world    245
Could turn so much the constitution
Of any constant man. What, worse and worse?
With leave, Bassanio—I am half yourself,
And I must freely have the half of anything
That this same paper brings you.

BASSANIO                          O sweet Portia,     250
Here are a few of the unpleasant'st words
That ever blotted paper! Gentle lady,
When I did first impart my love to you,
I freely told you all the wealth I had
Ran in my veins—I was a gentleman.                  255
And then I told you true; and yet, dear lady,
Rating myself at nothing, you shall see
How much I was a braggart. When I told you
My state° was nothing, I should then have told you
That I was worse than nothing; for indeed           260
I have engaged° myself to a dear friend,
Engaged my friend to his mere° enemy
To feed my means. Here is a letter, lady,
The paper as the body of my friend,
And every word in it a gaping wound                 265
Issuing lifeblood. But is it true, Salerio?
Hath all his ventures failed? What, not one hit?
From Tripolis, from Mexico and England,
From Lisbon, Barbary, and India,
And not one vessel scape the dreadful touch         270
Of merchant-marring rocks?

SALERIO                          Not one, my lord.
Besides, it should appear that if he had
The present° money to discharge° the Jew,
He would not take it. Never did I know
A creature that did bear the shape of man           275
So keen and greedy to confound° a man.
He plies the duke at morning and at night,
And doth impeach the freedom of the state°
If they deny him justice. Twenty merchants,
The duke himself, and the magnificoes              280
Of greatest port° have all persuaded with him,
But none can drive him from the envious° plea
Of forfeiture, of justice, and his bond.

JESSICA
When I was with him, I have heard him swear
To Tubal and to Chus, his countrymen,              285
That he would rather have Antonio's flesh
Than twenty times the value of the sum
That he did owe him; and I know, my lord,
If law, authority, and power deny not,
It will go hard with poor Antonio.                 290

PORTIA
Is it your dear friend that is thus in trouble?

BASSANIO
The dearest friend to me, the kindest man,
The best-conditioned° and unwearied spirit
In doing courtesies, and one in whom
The ancient Roman honor more appears               295
Than any that draws breath in Italy.

PORTIA
What sum owes he the Jew?

BASSANIO
For me, three thousand ducats.

PORTIA                          What, no more?
Pay him six thousand, and deface° the bond.
Double six thousand and then treble that,          300
Before a friend of this description
Shall lose a hair through Bassanio's fault.
First go with me to church and call me wife,
And then away to Venice to your friend!
For never shall you lie by Portia's side            305
With an unquiet soul. You shall have gold
To pay the petty debt twenty times over;
When it is paid, bring your true friend along.
My maid Nerissa and myself meantime
Will live as maids and widows. Come away!           310
For you shall hence° upon your wedding day.
Bid your friends welcome, show a merry cheer;
Since you are dear bought, I will love you dear.
But let me hear the letter of your friend.

[BASSANIO (Reads.)] "Sweet Bassanio, my ships have  315
all miscarried, my creditors grow cruel, my estate is
very low, my bond to the Jew is forfeit. And since in
paying it, it is impossible I should live, all debts are
cleared between you and I if I might but see you at my
death. Notwithstanding, use your pleasure. If your     320
love do not persuade you to come, let not my letter."

PORTIA
O love, dispatch all business and be gone!

BASSANIO
Since I have your good leave to go away,
I will make haste; but till I come again
No bed shall e'er be guilty of my stay,             325
Nor rest be interposer 'twixt us twain.      Exeunt.


[Scene III. Venice. A street.]

Enter [SHYLOCK] the Jew and SOLANIO and ANTONIO
and the JAILER.

SHYLOCK
Jailer, look to him. Tell not me of mercy.
This is the fool that lent out money gratis.
Jailer, look to him.

ANTONIO                          Hear me yet, good Shylock.

SHYLOCK
I'll have my bond! Speak not against my bond!
I have sworn an oath that I will have my bond.       5
Thou call'dst me dog before thou hadst a cause,
But since I am a dog, beware my fangs.
The duke shall grant me justice. I do wonder,

239 **royal merchant** merchant prince  242 **fleece** pun on
*fleets*  243 **shrowd** evil, grievous; literally, "cursed"  259
**state** estate, fortune  261 **engaged** pledged  262 **mere**
absolute  273 **present** ready; **discharge** pay  276 **confound**
ruin, destroy  278 **impeach . . . state** charge that Venice is
no free state  280–81 **magnificoes . . . port** nobles of
highest dignity  282 **envious** malignant

293 **The best-conditioned** of the best disposition  299
**deface** destroy  311 **shall hence** must go hence

Thou naughty° jailer, that thou art so fond°
To come abroad with him at his request.                    10

ANTONIO
I pray thee hear me speak.

SHYLOCK
I'll have my bond. I will not hear thee speak.
I'll have my bond, and therefore speak no more.
I'll not be made a soft and dull-eyed fool,
To shake the head, relent, and sigh, and yield          15
To Christian intercessors. Follow not.
I'll have no speaking; I will have my bond.
                    *Exit* [SHYLOCK *the*] *Jew.*

SOLANIO
It is the most impenetrable cur
That ever kept° with men.

ANTONIO                         Let him alone;
I'll follow him no more with bootless° prayers.          20
He seeks my life. His reason well I know:
I oft delivered from his forfeitures°
Many that have at times made moan to me.
Therefore he hates me.

SOLANIO                         I am sure the duke
Will never grant this forfeiture to hold.                 25

ANTONIO
The duke cannot deny the course of law;
For the commodity° that strangers° have
With us in Venice, if it be denied,
Will much impeach the justice of the state,
Since that the trade and profit of the city               30
Consisteth of all nations. Therefore go.
These griefs° and losses have so bated° me
That I shall hardly spare a pound of flesh
Tomorrow to my bloody creditor.
Well, jailer, on. Pray God Bassanio come            35
To see me pay his debt, and then I care not!  *Exeunt.*


[Scene IV. *Belmont. Portia's house.*]

*Enter* PORTIA, NERISSA, LORENZO, JESSICA, *and*
[BALTHASAR,] *a man of Portia's.*

LORENZO
Madam, although I speak it in your presence,
You have a noble and a true conceit°
Of godlike amity,° which appears most strongly
In bearing thus the absence of your lord.
But if you knew to whom you show this honor,        5
How true a gentleman you send relief,
How dear a lover° of my lord your husband,
I know you would be prouder of the work
Than customary bounty can enforce you.°

PORTIA
I never did repent for doing good,                        10
Nor shall not now; for in companions
That do converse and waste° the time together,

Whose souls do bear an egal° yoke of love,
There must be needs a like proportion
Of lineaments, of manners, and of spirit;                15
Which makes me think that this Antonio,
Being the bosom lover of my lord,
Must needs be like my lord. If it be so,
How little is the cost I have bestowed
In purchasing° the semblance° of my soul            20
From out the state of hellish cruelty!
This comes too near the praising of myself;
Therefore no more of it. Hear other things:
Lorenzo, I commit into your hands
The husbandry° and manage of my house,            25
Until my lord's return. For mine own part,
I have toward heaven breathed a secret vow
To live in prayer and contemplation,
Only attended by Nerissa here,
Until her husband and my lord's return.                30
There is a monast'ry two miles off,
And there we will abide. I do desire you
Not to deny this imposition,°
The which my love and some necessity
Now lays upon you.

LORENZO                         Madam, with all my heart;  35
I shall obey you in all fair commands.

PORTIA
My people do already know my mind,
And will acknowledge you and Jessica
In place of Lord Bassanio and myself.
So fare you well till we shall meet again.               40

LORENZO
Fair thoughts and happy hours attend on you!

JESSICA
I wish your ladyship all heart's content.

PORTIA
I thank you for your wish, and am well pleased
To wish it back on you. Fare you well, Jessica.
                    *Exeunt* [JESSICA *and* LORENZO].
Now, Balthasar,                                            45
As I have ever found thee honest-true,
So let me find thee still. Take this same letter,
And use thou all th' endeavor of a man
In speed to Padua. See thou render this
Into my cousin's hands, Doctor Bellario;               50
And look what° notes and garments he doth give thee
Bring them, I pray thee, with imagined speed°
Unto the tranect,° to the common ferry
Which trades to Venice. Waste no time in words
But get thee gone. I shall be there before thee.       55

BALTHASAR
Madam, I go with all convenient speed.°       [*Exit.*]

PORTIA
Come on, Nerissa; I have work in hand
That you yet know not of. We'll see our husbands
Before they think of us.

NERISSA                         Shall they see us?

III.iii.9 **naughty** wicked; **fond** foolish **19 kept** dwelt
**20 bootless** unavailing **22 forfeitures** penalties that he could
have legally exacted   **27 commodity** commercial advantage;
**strangers** foreigners   **32 griefs** pains; **bated** reduced
III.iv.2 **conceit** idea, conception **3 amity** friendship **7
lover** friend **8–9 prouder . . . you** prouder of this action
than even your habitual kindness can make you   **12 converse
and waste** associate and spend

**13 egal** equal   **20 purchasing** gaining; **semblance** likeness
(Portia refers to the old idea that a genuine friend or lover is
a second self; Antonio is like Bassanio, and therefore like Portia)
**25 husbandry** care   **33 imposition** task that I impose   **51
look what** whatever   **52 imagined speed** speed of imagination   **53 tranect** ferry   **56 convenient speed** speed suited
(to this emergency)

PORTIA
They shall, Nerissa, but in such a habit°      60
That they shall think we are accomplishèd°
With that we lack. I'll hold thee any wager,
When we are both accoutered like young men,
I'll prove the prettier° fellow of the two,
And wear my dagger with the braver grace,°      65
And speak between the change of man and boy
With a reed° voice, and turn two mincing steps
Into a manly stride, and speak of frays
Like a fine bragging youth; and tell quaint° lies,
How honorable ladies sought my love,      70
Which I denying, they fell sick and died—
I could not do withal!° Then I'll repent,
And wish, for all that,° that I had not killed them.
And twenty of these puny lies I'll tell,
That men shall swear I have discontinued school      75
Above a twelvemonth. I have within my mind
A thousand raw tricks of these bragging Jacks,°
Which I will practice.
NERISSA      Why, shall we turn to° men?
PORTIA
Fie, what a question's that,
If thou wert near a lewd° interpreter!      80
But come, I'll tell thee all my whole device
When I am in my coach, which stays for us
At the park gate; and therefore haste away,
For we must measure twenty miles today.      *Exeunt.*

[Scene V. *Belmont. A garden.*]

*Enter* [LAUNCELOT *the*] *clown and* JESSICA.

LAUNCELOT      Yes truly; for look you, the sins of the
father are to be laid upon the children.° Therefore, I
promise you I fear you.° I was always plain with you,
and so now I speak my agitation° of the matter.
Therefore be o' good cheer, for truly I think you are      5
damned. There is but one hope in it that can do you
any good, and that is but a kind of bastard hope
neither.
JESSICA      And what hope is that, I pray thee?
LAUNCELOT      Marry, you may partly hope that your      10
father got you not—that you are not the Jew's
daughter.
JESSICA      That were a kind of bastard hope indeed!
So° the sins of my mother should be visited upon me.
LAUNCELOT      Truly then, I fear you are damned both      15
by father and mother. Thus when I shun Scylla your
father, I fall into Charybdis your mother. Well, you
are gone both ways.
JESSICA      I shall be saved by my husband.° He hath
made me a Christian.      20

LAUNCELOT      Truly, the more to blame he! We were
Christians enow° before,° e'en as many as could well
live one by another.° This making of Christians will
raise the price of hogs; if we grow all to be pork-
eaters, we shall not shortly have a rasher° on the coals      25
for money.

*Enter* LORENZO.

JESSICA      I'll tell my husband, Launcelot, what you
say. Here he comes.
LORENZO      I shall grow jealious° of you shortly,
Launcelot, if you thus get my wife into corners.      30
JESSICA      Nay, you need not fear us, Lorenzo. Launcelot
and I are out.° He tells me flatly there's no mercy for
me in heaven because I am a Jew's daughter; and he
says you are no good member of the commonwealth,
for in converting Jews to Christians you raise the price      35
of pork.
LORENZO      [*To* LAUNCELOT.] I shall answer that
better to the commonwealth than you can the getting
up of the Negro's belly. The Moor° is with child by
you, Launcelot!      40
LAUNCELOT      It is much that the Moor should be more
than reason; but if she be less than an honest° woman,
she is indeed more than I took her for.
LORENZO      How every fool can play upon the word! I
think the best grace° of wit will shortly turn into      45
silence, and discourse grow commendable in none
only but parrots. Go in, sirrah; bid them prepare for
dinner.
LAUNCELOT      That is done, sir. They have all stomachs.
LORENZO      Goodly Lord, what a wit-snapper are you!      50
Then bid them prepare dinner.
LAUNCELOT      That is done too, sir. Only "cover"° is
the word.
LORENZO      Will you cover then, sir?
LAUNCELOT      Not so, sir, neither! I know my duty.      55
LORENZO      Yet more quarreling with occasion!° Wilt
thou show the whole wealth of thy wit in an instant?
I pray thee understand a plain man in his plain mean-
ing: go to thy fellows, bid them cover the table, serve
in the meat, and we will come in to dinner.      60
LAUNCELOT      For the table,° sir, it shall be served in;
for the meat, sir, it shall be covered;° for your coming
in to dinner, sir, why let it be as humors and conceits°
shall govern.      *Exit clown* [LAUNCELOT].
LORENZO
O dear discretion,° how his words are suited!°      65
The fool hath planted in his memory
An army of good words; and I do know
A many° fools that stand in better place,
Garnished° like him, that for a tricksy word

---

60 **habit** garment (i.e., men's clothes)   61 **accomplishèd**
provided   64 **prettier** more dashing   65 **braver grace** finer
masculine grace   67 **reed** high or squeaky, like the sound of a
reed pipe   69 **quaint** clever and elaborate   72 **I . . . withal**
I could not help it   73 **for all that** in spite of that   77 **Jacks**
fellows   78 **turn to** turn into (with an off-color pun; cf. I.iii.
78)   80 **lewd** bad
III.v.1–2 **sins . . . children** see Exodus 20:5   3 **fear you**
fear for you   4 **agitation** blunder for *cogitation*   14 **So** thus
19 **saved . . . husband** see I Corinthians 7:14

22 **enow** enough; **before** before you turned Christian   23 **one
by another** one off another   25 **rasher** slice of bacon   29
**jealious** jealous   32 **out** at odds   39 **Moor** pronounced
"more"; hence Launcelot quibbles on *much, more,* and *Moor*
42 **honest** chaste   45 **grace** virtue   52 **cover** cover the table
(Launcelot proceeds to quibble on *cover* in the sense of "wear
a hat")   56 **quarreling with occasion** caviling at every
opportunity   61 **table** (1) the piece of furniture (2) the meal
62 **covered** i.e., to be kept hot   63 **humors and conceits**
fancies and notions   65 **dear discretion** precious common
sense; **suited** fitted together (?) dressed up (?)   68 **A many**
an old idiom for a large number   69 **Garnished** decked out

Defy the matter.° How cheer'st thou,° Jessica?                    70
And now, good sweet, say thy opinion—
How dost thou like the Lord Bassanio's wife?

JESSICA
Past all expressing. It is very meet
The Lord Bassanio live an upright life,
For having such a blessing in his lady,                          75
He finds the joys of heaven here on earth;
And if on earth he do not merit it,
In reason he should never come to heaven.
Why, if two gods should play some heavenly match
And on the wager lay° two earthly women,                         80
And Portia one, there must be something else°
Pawned with the other, for the poor rude world
Hath not her fellow.

LORENZO                      Even such a husband
Hast thou of me as she is for a wife.

JESSICA
Nay, but ask my opinion too of that!                             85

LORENZO
I will anon. First let us go to dinner.

JESSICA
Nay, let me praise you while I have a stomach.°

LORENZO
No, pray thee, let it serve for table-talk;
Then howsome'er° thou speak'st, 'mong other things
I shall digest it.

JESSICA                      Well, I'll set you forth.°          90
                                        Exit [with LORENZO].


# [ A C T   I V ]

[Scene I. Venice. A court of justice.]

*Enter the* DUKE, *the* MAGNIFICOES, ANTONIO,
BASSANIO, [SALERIO,] *and* GRATIANO [*with others*].

DUKE   What,° is Antonio here?

ANTONIO   Ready, so please your grace.

DUKE
I am sorry for thee. Thou art come to answer
A stony adversary, an inhuman wretch,
Uncapable of pity, void and empty
From any dram° of mercy.                                          5

ANTONIO                      I have heard
Your grace hath ta'en great pains to qualify°
His rigorous course; but since he stands obdurate,
And that no lawful means can carry me
Out of his envy's reach,° I do oppose                            10
My patience to his fury, and am armed
To suffer with a quietness of spirit
The very tyranny and rage° of his.

DUKE
Go one, and call the Jew into the court.

SALERIO
He is ready at the door; he comes, my lord.                      15

*Enter* SHYLOCK.

DUKE
Make room, and let him stand before our° face.
Shylock, the world thinks, and I think so too,
That thou but leadest this fashion of thy malice
To the last hour of act; and then 'tis thought
Thou'lt show thy mercy and remorse° more strange°               20
Than is thy strange° apparent cruelty;
And where thou now exacts the penalty,
Which is a pound of this poor merchant's flesh,
Thou wilt not only loose° the forfeiture,
But touched with human gentleness and love,                      25
Forgive a moiety° of the principal,
Glancing an eye of pity on his losses,
That have of late so huddled on his back—
Enow° to press a royal merchant° down
And pluck commiseration of his state                             30
From brassy bosoms and rough hearts of flint,
From stubborn Turks and Tartars never trained
To offices of tender courtesy.
We all expect° a gentle° answer, Jew.

SHYLOCK
I have possessed° your grace of what I purpose,                  35
And by our holy Sabbath have I sworn
To have the due and forfeit of my bond.
If you deny it, let the danger light
Upon your charter and your city's freedom!°
You'll ask me why I rather choose to have                        40
A weight of carrion flesh than to receive
Three thousand ducats. I'll not answer that,
But say it is my humor. Is it answered?
What if my house be troubled with a rat,
And I be pleased to give ten thousand ducats                     45
To have it baned?° What, are you answered yet?
Some men there are love not a gaping pig,°
Some that are mad if they behold a cat,
And others, when the bagpipe sings i' th' nose,
Cannot contain their urine; for affection,°                      50
Master of passion,° sways it to the mood
Of what it likes or loathes. Now for your answer:
As there is no firm reason to be rend'red
Why he cannot abide a gaping pig,
Why he a harmless necessary cat,                                 55
Why he° a woolen bagpipe, but of force°

---

70 **the matter** good sense; **How cheer'st thou** How
is it with thee? (the implication is that he kisses her)  80
**lay** stake   81 **something else** i.e., to make the wager
fair   87 **stomach** a pun on the senses of "desire" (to praise
you) and an "appetite" for dinner   89 **howsome'er** however
90 **I'll . . . forth** I'll give a fine account of you
IV.i.1 **What** why (interjection)   6 **dram** mite, drop (literally
an eighth of an ounce)   7 **qualify** moderate   10 **his envy's
reach** the reach of his malignant hate   13 **tyranny and rage**
savagery and passion

16 **our** the royal "we," appropriate in giving an order, but in
the next line the duke uses "I," the informal singular, suited for
a personal appeal to Shylock's feelings   20 **remorse** compassion; **strange** wonderful   21 **strange** astonishing   24 **loose**
release   26 **moiety** portion   29 **Enow** enough; **royal
merchant** merchant prince   34 **expect** await; **gentle** befitting
a gentleman   35 **possessed** informed   38–39 **danger . . .
freedom** cf. III.iii.27–31   46 **baned** poisoned   47 **gaping
pig** young roast pig, often served with fruit in its open mouth
(Shylock invokes the old theory of natural antipathy to
explain his hatred of Antonio, thus concealing the real cause;
cf. I.iii.39–42)   50 **affection** natural sympathy or antipathy
51 **passion** powerful emotion   54–56 **he . . . he . . . he**
pronounced with heavy emphasis: this man . . . that man . . .
another   56 **of force** of necessity, against his will

Must yield to such inevitable shame°
As to offend, himself being offended;
So can I give no reason, nor I will not,
More than a lodged° hate and a certain° loathing     60
I bear Antonio, that I follow thus
A losing suit against him. Are you answered?

BASSANIO
This is no answer, thou unfeeling man,
To excuse the current of thy cruelty!

SHYLOCK
I am not bound° to please thee with my answers.     65

BASSANIO
Do all men kill the things they do not love?

SHYLOCK
Hates any man the thing he would not kill?

BASSANIO
Every offense is not a hate at first.

SHYLOCK
What, wouldst thou have a serpent sting thee twice?

ANTONIO
I pray you think you question° with the Jew.     70
You may as well go stand upon the beach
And bid the main flood bate his° usual height;
You may as well use question with the wolf,
Why he hath made the ewe bleat for the lamb;
You may as well forbid the mountain pines     75
To wag their high tops and to make no noise
When they are fretten° with the gusts of heaven;
You may as well do anything most hard
As seek to soften that—than which what's harder?—
His Jewish heart. Therefore I do beseech you     80
Make no moe offers, use no farther means,
But with all brief and plain conveniency°
Let me have judgment, and the Jew his will.

BASSANIO
For thy three thousand ducats here is six.

SHYLOCK
If every ducat in six thousand ducats     85
Were in six parts, and every part a ducat,
I would not draw° them. I would have my bond.

DUKE
How shalt thou hope for mercy, rend'ring none?

SHYLOCK
What judgment shall I dread, doing no wrong?
You have among you many a purchased slave,     90
Which like your asses and your dogs and mules
You use in abject and in slavish parts,°
Because you bought them. Shall I say to you,
"Let them be free! Marry them to your heirs!
Why sweat they under burdens? Let their beds     95
Be made as soft as yours, and let their palates
Be seasoned with such viands"? You will answer,
"The slaves are ours." So do I answer you:
The pound of flesh which I demand of him
Is dearly bought, is mine, and I will have it.     100
If you deny me, fie upon your law!
There is no force in the decrees of Venice.
I stand for judgment. Answer; shall I have it?

DUKE
Upon my power I may dismiss this court
Unless Bellario, a learned doctor     105
Whom I have sent for to determine this,
Come here today.

SALERIO          My lord, here stays without
A messenger with letters from the doctor,
New come from Padua.

DUKE
Bring us the letters. Call the messenger.     110

BASSANIO
Good cheer, Antonio! What, man, courage yet!
The Jew shall have my flesh, blood, bones, and all,
Ere thou shalt lose for me one drop of blood.

ANTONIO
I am a tainted wether° of the flock,
Meetest° for death. The weakest kind of fruit     115
Drops earliest to the ground, and so let me.
You cannot better be employed, Bassanio,
Than to live still, and write mine epitaph.

*Enter* NERISSA [*dressed like a lawyer's clerk*].

DUKE
Came you from Padua, from Bellario?

NERISSA
From both, my lord. Bellario greets your grace.     120

[*Presents a letter.*]

BASSANIO
Why dost thou whet thy knife so earnestly?

SHYLOCK
To cut the forfeiture from that bankrout there.

GRATIANO
Not on thy sole, but on thy soul, harsh Jew,
Thou mak'st thy knife keen; but no metal can—
No, not the hangman's° ax—bear° half the keenness     125
Of thy sharp envy.° Can no prayers pierce thee?

SHYLOCK
No, none that thou hast wit enough to make.

GRATIANO
O be thou damned, inexecrable° dog,
And for thy life let justice be accused!°
Thou almost mak'st me waver in my faith,     130
To hold opinion with Pythagoras°
That souls of animals infuse themselves
Into the trunks of men. Thy currish spirit
Governed a wolf who, hanged for human slaughter,°
Even from the gallows did his fell° soul fleet,     135
And whilst thou layest in thy unhallowed dam,°
Infused itself in thee; for thy desires
Are wolvish, bloody, starved, and ravenous.

SHYLOCK
Till thou canst rail the seal from off my bond,

**57 shame** as in line 50, above  **60 lodged** fixed; **certain** assured, steadfast  **65 bound** bound by law  **70 think you question** remember you argue  **72 main . . . his** ocean at high tide reduce its  **77 fretten** fretted  **82 brief . . . conveniency** suitable brevity and directness  **87 draw** take  **92 parts** duties

**114 tainted wether** infected ram  **115 Meetest** fittest  **125 hangman's** executioner's; **bear** have  **126 envy** malignant hate  **128 inexecrable** most execrable, detestable  **129 And . . . accused** a much-debated line; probably "Let justice be accused because you have been allowed to live so long"  **131 Pythagoras** Greek philosopher of the sixth century B.C. who taught the doctrine of the transmigration of souls  **134 hanged . . . slaughter** wolves, dogs, and other animals were sometimes hanged for killing or attacking people; hence the phrase *hangdog look*  **135 fell** fierce  **136 dam** mother of an animal, here a shewolf

Thou but offend'st thy lungs to speak so loud.
Repair thy wit, good youth, or it will fall
To cureless ruin.° I stand here for law.

DUKE
This letter from Bellario doth commend
A young and learned doctor to our court.
Where is he?

NERISSA    He attendeth here hard by    145
To know your answer whether you'll admit him.

DUKE
With all my heart. Some three or four of you
Go give him courteous conduct to this place.
Meantime the court shall hear Bellario's letter.

[CLERK (*Reads.*)]  "Your grace shall understand that at 150
the receipt of your letter I am very sick; but in the
instant that your messenger came, in loving visitation
was with me a young doctor of Rome. His name is
Balthasar. I acquainted him with the cause in controversy between the Jew and Antonio the merchant. 155
We turned o'er many books together. He is furnished
with my opinion which, bettered with his own
learning, the greatness whereof I cannot enough
commend, comes with him at my importunity to fill
up° your grace's request in my stead. I beseech you 160
let his lack of years be no impediment to let° him lack
a reverend estimation, for I never knew so young a
body with so old a head. I leave him to your gracious
acceptance, whose trial° shall better publish his commendation."    165

*Enter* PORTIA *for Balthasar,* [*dressed like a doctor of laws*].

DUKE
You hear the learned Bellario, what he writes;
And here, I take it, is the doctor come.
Give me your hand. Come you from old Bellario?

PORTIA
I did, my lord.

DUKE            You are welcome; take your place.
Are you acquainted with the difference°    170
That holds this present question° in the court?

PORTIA
I am informèd throughly° of the cause.°
Which is the merchant here? And which the Jew?

DUKE
Antonio and old Shylock, both stand forth.

PORTIA
Is your name Shylock?

SHYLOCK            Shylock is my name.    175

PORTIA
Of a strange° nature is the suit you follow,
Yet in such rule that° the Venetian law
Cannot impugn you as you do proceed.

[*To* ANTONIO.]
You stand within his danger,° do you not?

ANTONIO
Ay, so he says.

PORTIA            Do you confess the bond?    180

ANTONIO
I do.

PORTIA    Then must the Jew be merciful.

SHYLOCK
On what compulsion must I? Tell me that.

PORTIA
The quality of mercy is not strained;°
It droppeth as the gentle rain from heaven
Upon the place beneath. It is twice blest;    185
It blesseth him that gives and him that takes.
'Tis mightiest in the mightiest; it becomes
The thronèd monarch better than his crown.
His scepter shows the force of temporal power,
The attribute to awe and majesty,    190
Wherein doth sit the dread and fear of kings;
But mercy is above this scept'red sway;
It is enthronèd in the hearts of kings,
It is an attribute to God Himself,
And earthly power doth then show likest God's    195
When mercy seasons justice. Therefore, Jew,
Though justice be thy plea, consider this:
That, in the course of justice, none of us
Should see salvation.° We do pray for mercy,
And that same prayer doth teach us all to render    200
The deeds of mercy. I have spoke thus much
To mitigate the justice of thy plea;
Which if thou follow, this strict court of Venice
Must needs give sentence 'gainst the merchant there.

SHYLOCK
My deeds upon my head! I crave the law,    205
The penalty and forfeit of my bond.

PORTIA
Is he not able to discharge the money?

BASSANIO
Yes, here I tender it for him in the court,
Yea, twice° the sum. If that will not suffice,
I will be bound to pay it ten times o'er    210
On forfeit of my hands, my head, my heart.
If this will not suffice, it must appear
That malice bears down truth. And I beseech you,
Wrest once the law to your authority.°
To do a great right, do a little wrong,    215
And curb this cruel devil of his will.

PORTIA
It must not be. There is no power in Venice
Can alter a decree establishèd.
'Twill be recorded for a precedent,
And many an error by the same example    220
Will rush into the state. It cannot be.

SHYLOCK
A Daniel come to judgment!° Yea, a Daniel!
O wise young judge, how I do honor thee!

---

**183 strained** constrained, compelled **198–99 That . . .
salvation** referring to the doctrine that God can justly condemn every man, since none is free of sin **209 twice** in lines
226 and 233 "thrice" the money has been offered, and most
editors therefore emend "twice" to "thrice," on the assumption
that here the compositor misread the manuscript; but in line
84 the offered amount is indeed double—six thousand ducats
for three thousand—and therefore emendation to "thrice" still
leaves an inconsistency, unless the point is that as Bassanio's fears
for Antonio grow, he raises the offer **214 Wrest . . . authority**
For once twist the law a little and subject it to your authority
**222 Daniel . . . judgment** the young biblical hero who
secured justice for Susannah (see Apocrypha, Susannah 42–64)

---

141–42 **fall . . . ruin** i.e., like a house too long out of repair
159–60 **fill up** satisfy    161 **to let** to cause    164 **trial** conduct
when brought to the test    170 **difference** dispute    171 **question** case under judicial examination    172 **throughly**
thoroughly; **cause** case    176 **strange** astonishing    177 **in . . .
that** within the rule so that    179 **danger** power to harm

**PORTIA**
I pray you let me look upon the bond.

**SHYLOCK**
Here 'tis, most reverend doctor, here it is.  225

**PORTIA**
Shylock, there's thrice thy money off'red thee.

**SHYLOCK**
An oath, an oath! I have an oath in heaven;
Shall I lay perjury upon my soul?
No, not for Venice!

**PORTIA**                    Why, this bond is forfeit;
And lawfully by this the Jew can claim  230
A pound of flesh, to be by him cut off
Nearest the merchant's heart. Be merciful.
Take thrice thy money; bid me tear the bond.

**SHYLOCK**
When it is paid, according to the tenure.°
It doth appear you are a worthy judge;  235
You know the law, your exposition
Hath been most sound. I charge you by the law,
Whereof you are a well-deserving pillar,
Proceed to judgment. By my soul I swear
There is no power in the tongue of man  240
To alter me. I stay° here on my bond.

**ANTONIO**
Most heartily I do beseech the court
To give the judgment.

**PORTIA**                    Why then, thus it is:
You must prepare your bosom for his knife—

**SHYLOCK**
O noble judge! O excellent young man!  245

**PORTIA**
For the intent and purpose of the law
Hath full relation to° the penalty,
Which here appeareth due upon the bond.

**SHYLOCK**
'Tis very true. O wise and upright judge!
How much more elder art thou than thy looks!  250

**PORTIA**
Therefore lay bare your bosom.

**SHYLOCK**                    Ay, his breast—
So says the bond, doth it not, noble judge?
"Nearest his heart"; those are the very words.

**PORTIA**
It is so. Are there balance° here to weigh
The flesh?

**SHYLOCK**  I have them ready.  255

**PORTIA**
Have by some surgeon, Shylock, on your charge,°
To stop his wounds, lest he do bleed to death.

**SHYLOCK**
Is it so nominated in the bond?

**PORTIA**
It is not so expressed, but what of that?
'Twere good you do so much for charity.  260

**SHYLOCK**
I cannot find it; 'tis not in the bond.

**PORTIA**
You, merchant, have you anything to say?

**ANTONIO**
But little. I am armed and well prepared.
Give me your hand, Bassanio; fare you well.
Grieve not that I am fall'n to this for you,  265
For herein Fortune shows herself more kind
Than is her custom: it is still her use°
To let the wretched man outlive his wealth,
To view with hollow eye and wrinkled brow
An age of poverty; from which ling'ring penance  270
Of such misery doth she cut me off.
Commend me to your honorable wife.
Tell her the process° of Antonio's end,
Say how I loved you, speak me fair in death;
And when the tale is told, bid her be judge  275
Whether Bassanio had not once a love.°
Repent but you° that you shall lose your friend,
And he repents not° that he pays your debt;
For if the Jew do cut but deep enough,
I'll pay it instantly with all my heart.°  280

**BASSANIO**
Antonio, I am married to a wife
Which is as dear to me as life itself;
But life itself, my wife, and all the world
Are not with me esteemed above thy life.
I would lose all, ay sacrifice them all  285
Here to this devil, to deliver you.

**PORTIA**
Your wife would give you little thanks for that
If she were by to hear you make the offer.

**GRATIANO**
I have a wife who I protest I love.
I would she were in heaven, so she could  290
Entreat some power to change this currish Jew.

**NERISSA**
'Tis well you offer it behind her back;
The wish would make else an unquiet house.

**SHYLOCK**
These be the Christian husbands! I have a daughter;
Would any of the stock of Barabbas°  295
Had been her husband, rather than a Christian!
We trifle time. I pray thee pursue sentence.

**PORTIA**
A pound of that same merchant's flesh is thine.
The court awards it and the law doth give it—

**SHYLOCK**
Most rightful judge!  300

**PORTIA**
And you must cut this flesh from off his breast.
The law allows it, and the court awards it.

**SHYLOCK**
Most learned judge! A sentence! Come, prepare!

**PORTIA**
Tarry a little; there is something else.
This bond doth give thee here no jot of blood;  305
The words expressly are "a pound of flesh."
Take then thy bond, take thou thy pound of flesh;

---

234 **tenure** conditions  241 **stay** take my stand  247 **Hath**
. . . **to** is related inseparably to  254 **balance** plural: scales
256 **on your charge** at your expense

267 **still her use** ever her custom  273 **process** whole story
276 **love** friend (with a quibble on *love* in the sense of "lover")
277 **Repent but you** if you but feel sorrow  278 **And . . .
not** then he regrets not  280 **with . . . heart** a quibble on
*heart* in the senses of "soul" and of the physical organ  295
**Barabbas** (1) the thief freed by Pilate when the people
demanded that Christ be crucified (2) the name of the
villainous hero in Marlowe's *The Jew of Malta*

But in the cutting it, if thou dost shed
One drop of Christian blood, thy lands and goods
Are by the laws of Venice confiscate                          310
Unto the state of Venice.

GRATIANO
O upright judge! Mark, Jew. O learned judge!

SHYLOCK
Is that the law?

PORTIA                Thyself shalt see the act;
For, as thou urgest justice, be assured
Thou shalt have justice more than thou desir'st.             315

GRATIANO
O learned judge! Mark, Jew. A learned judge!

SHYLOCK
I take this offer then. Pay the bond thrice
And let the Christian go.

BASSANIO                            Here is the money.

PORTIA
Soft!
The Jew shall have all justice. Soft, no haste;              320
He shall have nothing but the penalty.

GRATIANO
O Jew! An upright judge, a learnèd judge!

PORTIA
Therefore prepare thee to cut off the flesh.
Shed thou no blood, nor cut thou less nor more
But just a pound of flesh. If thou tak'st more              325
Or less than a just° pound, be it but so much
As makes it light or heavy in the substance°
Or the division° of the twentieth part
Of one poor scruple°—nay, if the scale do turn
But in the estimation° of a hair—                           330
Thou diest, and all thy goods are confiscate.

GRATIANO
A second Daniel! A Daniel, Jew!
Now, infidel, I have you on the hip!

PORTIA
Why doth the Jew pause? Take thy forfeiture.

SHYLOCK
Give me my principal, and let me go.                        335

BASSANIO
I have it ready for thee; here it is.

PORTIA
He hath refused it in the open court.
He shall have merely justice and his bond.

GRATIANO
A Daniel still say I, a second Daniel!
I thank thee, Jew, for teaching me that word.               340

SHYLOCK
Shall I not have barely my principal?

PORTIA
Thou shalt have nothing but the forfeiture,
To be so taken at thy peril, Jew.

SHYLOCK
Why, then the devil give him good of it!
I'll stay no longer question.°

PORTIA                            Tarry, Jew!               345
The law hath yet another hold on you.
It is enacted in the laws of Venice,
If it be proved against an alien

That by direct or indirect attempts
He seek the life of any citizen,                            350
The party 'gainst the which he doth contrive
Shall seize° one half his goods; the other half
Comes to the privy coffer° of the state;
And the offender's life lies in the mercy
Of the duke only, 'gainst all other voice.                  355
In which predicament° I say thou stand'st,
For it appears by manifest proceeding
That indirectly, and directly too,
Thou hast contrived against the very life
Of the defendant, and thou hast incurred                    360
The danger formerly by me rehearsed.°
Down therefore, and beg mercy of the duke.

GRATIANO
Beg that thou mayst have leave to hang thyself!
And yet, thy wealth being forfeit to the state,
Thou hast not left the value of a cord;                     365
Therefore thou must be hanged at the state's charge.

DUKE
That thou shalt see the difference of our spirit,
I pardon thee thy life before thou ask it.
For° half thy wealth, it is Antonio's;
The other half comes to the general state,                  370
Which humbleness may drive unto a fine.°

PORTIA
Ay, for the state, not for Antonio.

SHYLOCK
Nay, take my life and all! Pardon not that!
You take my house, when you do take the prop
That doth sustain my house. You take my life                375
When you do take the means whereby I live.

PORTIA
What mercy can you render him, Antonio?

GRATIANO
A halter gratis! Nothing else, for God's sake!

ANTONIO
So please my lord the duke and all the court
To quit° the fine for one half of his goods,                380
I am content; so° he will let me have
The other half in use,° to render it
Upon his death unto the gentleman
That lately stole his daughter.
Two things provided more: that for this favor               385
He presently° become a Christian;
The other, that he do record a gift
Here in the court of all he dies possessed
Unto his son Lorenzo and his daughter.

DUKE
He shall do this, or else I do recant°                      390
The pardon that I late pronouncèd here.

PORTIA
Art thou contented, Jew? What dost thou say?

SHYLOCK
I am content.

PORTIA                Clerk, draw a deed of gift.

352 seize take possession of   353 privy coffer equivalent to
British privy purse, money provided for the monarch's own
use   356 predicament situation   361 rehearsed cited   369 For
as for   371 may . . . fine may persuade me to reduce to a
fine   380 quit remit   381 so provided   382 in use in trust,
to use in his business   386 presently instantly   390 recant
retract

326 just exact   327 substance amount   328 division portion
328–29 twentieth . . . scruple one grain   330 estimation
value   345 stay . . . question remain for no more talk

SHYLOCK
I pray you give me leave to go from hence.
I am not well. Send the deed after me,                    395
And I will sign it.
DUKE                    Get thee gone, but do it.
GRATIANO
In christ'ning shalt thou have two godfathers.
Had I been judge, thou shouldst have had ten more°—
To bring thee to the gallows, not to the font.
                              *Exit* [SHYLOCK].
DUKE
Sir, I entreat you home with me to dinner.              400
PORTIA
I humbly do desire your grace of pardon.
I must away this night toward Padua,
And it is meet I presently set forth.
DUKE
I am sorry that your leisure serves you not.°
Antonio, gratify° this gentleman,                       405
For in my mind you are much bound to him.
                    *Exit* DUKE *and his* TRAIN.
BASSANIO
Most worthy gentleman, I and my friend
Have by your wisdom been this day acquitted
Of grievous penalties, in lieu whereof,°
Three thousand ducats due unto the Jew                   410
We freely cope° your courteous pains withal.
ANTONIO
And stand indebted, over and above,
In love and service to you evermore.
PORTIA
He is well paid that is well satisfied,
And I, delivering you, am satisfied,                     415
And therein do account myself well paid;
My mind was never yet more mercenary.
I pray you know me when we meet again.
I wish you well, and so I take my leave.
BASSANIO
Dear sir, of force I must attempt you further.          420
Take some remembrance of us as a tribute,
Not as fee. Grant me two things, I pray you—
Not to deny me, and to pardon me.
PORTIA
You press me far, and therefore I will yield.
Give me your gloves; I'll wear them for your sake.      425

[BASSANIO *takes off his gloves*.]

And for your love I'll take this ring from you.
Do not draw back your hand; I'll take no more,
And you in love° shall not deny me this.
BASSANIO
This ring, good sir, alas, it is a trifle!
I will not shame myself to give you this.              430
PORTIA
I will have nothing else but only this,
And now methinks I have a mind to it.
BASSANIO
There's more depends on this than on the value.°

The dearest ring in Venice will I give you,
And find it out by proclamation.                        435
Only for this, I pray you pardon me.°
PORTIA
I see, sir, you are liberal in offers.
You taught me first to beg, and now methinks
You teach me how a beggar should be answered.
BASSANIO
Good sir, this ring was given me by my wife,           440
And when she put it on she made me vow
That I should neither sell nor give nor lose it.
PORTIA
That 'scuse serves many men to save their gifts.
And if your wife be not a madwoman,
And know how well I have deserved this ring,           445
She would not hold out enemy forever
For giving it to me. Well, peace be with you!
                    *Exeunt* [PORTIA *and* NERISSA].
ANTONIO
My Lord Bassanio, let him have the ring.
Let his deservings, and my love withal,
Be valued 'gainst your wife's commandement.°           450
BASSANIO
Go, Gratiano, run and overtake him;
Give him the ring, and bring him if thou canst
Unto Antonio's house. Away, make haste!
                              *Exit* GRATIANO.
Come, you and I will thither presently,
And in the morning early will we both                   455
Fly toward Belmont. Come, Antonio.          *Exeunt*.


[Scene II. *Venice. A street*.]

*Enter* [PORTIA *and*] NERISSA, [*disguised as before*].

PORTIA
Inquire the Jew's house out, give him this deed,°
And let him sign it. We'll away tonight
And be a day before our husbands home.
This deed will be well welcome to Lorenzo.

*Enter* GRATIANO.

GRATIANO
Fair sir, you are well o'erta'en.                         5
My Lord Bassanio upon more advice°
Hath sent you here this ring, and doth entreat
Your company at dinner.
PORTIA                    That cannot be.
His ring I do accept most thankfully,
And so I pray you tell him. Furthermore,                 10
I pray you show my youth old Shylock's house.
GRATIANO
That will I do.
NERISSA          Sir, I would speak with you.

[*Aside to* PORTIA.]

I'll see if I can get my husband's ring,
Which I did make him swear to keep forever.

---

398 **ten more** to make a jury of twelve  404 **serves you not** is not sufficient for you  405 **gratify** show your gratitude to  409 **in lieu whereof** in return for which  411 **We freely cope** of our own free will we require  428 **in love** in your good will to me  433 **the value** the ring's value

436 **Only . . . me** Only as for this ring, I beg you to excuse me  450 **commandement** four syllables
IV.ii.1 **this deed** the deed of gift for Lorenzo and Jessica
6 **upon more advice** on further consideration

PORTIA [*Aside to* NERISSA.]
Thou mayst, I warrant. We shall have old swearing° 15
That they did give the rings away to men;
But we'll outface them, and outswear them too.
Away, make haste! Thou know'st where I will tarry.

NERISSA
Come, good sir, will you show me to this house?

[*Exeunt.*]

# [ A C T   V ]

[*Scene I. Belmont. A garden before Portia's house.*]

*Enter* LORENZO *and* JESSICA.

LORENZO
The moon shines bright. In such a night as this,
When the sweet wind did gently kiss the trees
And they did make no noise, in such a night
Troilus° methinks mounted the Troyan walls,
And sighed his soul toward the Grecian tents 5
Where Cressid° lay that night.

JESSICA                                    In such a night
Did Thisbe° fearfully o'ertrip the dew,
And saw the lion's shadow ere himself,
And ran dismayed away.

LORENZO                        In such a night
Stood Dido° with a willow° in her hand 10
Upon the wild sea banks, and waft° her love
To come again to Carthage.

JESSICA                                    In such a night
Medea° gathered the enchanted herbs
That did renew old Aeson.°

LORENZO                        In such a night
Did Jessica steal° from the wealthy Jew, 15
And with an unthrift love° did run from Venice
As far as Belmont.

JESSICA                  In such a night
Did young Lorenzo swear he loved her well,
Stealing her soul with many vows of faith,
And ne'er a true one.

LORENZO                        In such a night 20
Did pretty Jessica, like a little shrow,°
Slander her love, and he forgave it her.

JESSICA
I would out-night you, did nobody come;
But hark, I hear the footing of a man.

*Enter* [Stephano,] *a* MESSENGER.

LORENZO
Who comes so fast in silence of the night? 25

MESSENGER   A friend.

LORENZO
A friend? What friend? Your name I pray you, friend.

MESSENGER
Stephano is my name, and I bring word
My mistress will before the break of day
Be here at Belmont. She doth stray about 30
By holy crosses° where she kneels and prays
For happy wedlock hours.

LORENZO                                 Who comes with her?

MESSENGER
None but a holy hermit and her maid.
I pray you, is my master yet returned?

LORENZO
He is not, nor we have not heard from him. 35
But go we in, I pray thee, Jessica,
And ceremoniously let us prepare
Some welcome for the mistress of the house.

*Enter* [LAUNCELOT *the*] *clown.*

LAUNCELOT   Sola,° sola! Wo ha! Ho sola, sola!

LORENZO   Who calls? 40

LAUNCELOT   Sola! Did you see Master Lorenzo and
Mistress Lorenzo? sola, sola!

LORENZO   Leave holloaing, man! Here.

LAUNCELOT   Sola! Where? Where?

LORENZO   Here! 45

LAUNCELOT   Tell him there's a post come from my
master, with his horn full of good news.° My master
will be here ere morning.          [*Exit.*]

LORENZO
Sweet soul, let's in, and there expect° their coming.
And yet no matter; why should we go in? 50
My friend Stephano, signify, I pray you,
Within the house, your mistress is at hand,
And bring your music forth into the air.

[*Exit* MESSENGER.]

How sweet the moonlight sleeps upon this bank!
Here will we sit and let the sounds of music 55
Creep in our ears; soft stillness and the night
Become° the touches° of sweet harmony.
Sit, Jessica. Look how the floor of heaven
Is thick inlaid with patens° of bright gold.
There's not the smallest orb which thou behold'st 60
But in his motion like an angel sings,
Still quiring° to the young-eyed cherubins;
Such harmony is in immortal souls,
But whilst this muddy vesture of decay°
Doth grossly close it in, we cannot hear it. 65

[*Enter* MUSICIANS.]

**15 old swearing** a lot of hard swearing
**V.i.1–22** the lovers' playful contest in verse-making belongs to a type of poetic dialogue as old as Virgil's *Eclogues*   **4 Troilus** hero of Chaucer's *Troilus and Cressida* and of Shakespeare's play of the same title; a type of the faithful lover   **6 Cressid** Cressida, a type of the faithless woman   **7 Thisbe** heroine of the tragic tale of *Pyramus and Thisbe* in Ovid's *Metamorphoses*   **10 Dido** Queen of Carthage whom Aeneas loved but abandoned at the call of duty;   **willow** proverbially associated with forsaken love   **11 waft** waved (with the willow branch)   **13 Medea** princess and sorceress who helped Jason to obtain the Golden Fleece, and later was deserted by him   **14 Aeson** father of Jason, restored to youth by Medea   **15 steal** a pun: steal money, steal away   **16 unthrift love** a pun: a love which disregards wealth, and a lover without wealth   **21 shrow** shrew

**31 holy crosses** a common sight in Renaissance Italy, used to mark shrines on hilltops, beside roads, etc.   **39 Sola** Launcelot imitates a courier's horn   **47 horn full of good news** Launcelot puns on the cornucopia, "the horn of plenty"   **49 expect** await   **57 Become** befit   **57, 67 touches** notes produced by touching the strings or stops of a musical instrument   **59 patens** tiles   **62 quiring** making music (a reference to the music of the spheres; it was thought that the harmonious movement of the spheres, in Ptolemaic astronomy, produced a heavenly music inaudible to human ears)   **64 muddy . . . decay** earthy garment subject to decay (i.e., the body)

Come ho, and wake Diana° with a hymn!
With sweetest touches° pierce your mistress' ear
And draw her home with music.

*Play music.*

JESSICA
I am never merry when I hear sweet music.
LORENZO
The reason is, your spirits are attentive. 70
For do but note a wild and wanton° herd
Or race of youthful and unhandled colts
Fetching mad bounds, bellowing and neighing loud,
Which is the hot condition° of their blood:
If they but hear perchance a trumpet sound, 75
Or any air of music touch their ears,
You shall perceive them make a mutual stand,°
Their savage eyes turned to a modest gaze
By the sweet power of music. Therefore the poet
Did feign that Orpheus° drew trees, stones, and floods; 80
Since naught so stockish,° hard, and full of rage°
But music for the time doth change his nature.
The man that hath no music in himself,
Nor is not moved with concord of sweet sounds,
Is fit for treasons, stratagems, and spoils;° 85
The motions° of his spirit are dull as night,
And his affections° dark as Erebus.°
Let no such man be trusted. Mark the music.

*Enter* PORTIA *and* NERISSA.

PORTIA
That light we see is burning in my hall;
How far that little candle throws his beams! 90
So shines a good deed in a naughty° world.
NERISSA
When the moon shone we did not see the candle.
PORTIA
So doth the greater glory dim the less.
A substitute° shines brightly as a king
Until a king be by, and then his state 95
Empties itself,° as doth an inland brook
Into the main of waters.° Music, hark!
NERISSA
It is your music, madam, of the house.
PORTIA
Nothing is good, I see, without respect;°
Methinks it sounds much sweeter than by day. 100
NERISSA
Silence bestows that virtue on it, madam.
PORTIA
The crow doth sing as sweetly as the lark
When neither is attended;° and I think
The nightingale, if she should sing by day
When every goose is cackling, would be thought 105

No better a musician than the wren.
How many things by season, seasoned are
To their right praise and true perfection!°
Peace! [*Music ceases.*] How the° moon sleeps with
   Endymion,°
And would not be awaked.°
LORENZO                    That is the voice, 110
Or I am much deceived, of Portia.
PORTIA
He knows me as the blind man knows the cuckoo,
By the bad voice.
LORENZO          Dear lady, welcome home.
PORTIA
We have been praying for our husbands' welfare,
Which speed we hope the better for our words. 115
Are they returned?
LORENZO          Madam, they are not yet,
But there is come a messenger before
To signify their coming.
PORTIA                    Go in, Nerissa.
Give order to my servants that they take
No note at all of our being absent hence— 120
Nor you, Lorenzo—Jessica, nor you.

[*A tucket° sounds.*]

LORENZO
Your husband is at hand; I hear his trumpet.
We are no telltales, madam; fear you not.
PORTIA
This night methinks is but the daylight sick;
It looks a little paler. 'Tis a day 125
Such as the day is when the sun is hid.

*Enter* BASSANIO, ANTONIO, GRATIANO, *and their*
FOLLOWERS.

BASSANIO
We should hold day with the Antipodes,°
If you would walk in absence of the sun.
PORTIA
Let me give light,° but let me not be light,
For a light wife doth make a heavy° husband, 130
And never be Bassanio so for me.
But God sort all!° You are welcome home, my lord.
BASSANIO
I thank you, madam. Give welcome to my friend.
This is the man, this is Antonio,
To whom I am so infinitely bound. 135
PORTIA
You should in all sense° be much bound to him,
For, as I hear, he was much bound for you.

66 **Diana** goddess of the moon and of chastity **71 wanton**
frolicsome, untrained **74 hot condition** impetuous nature
**77 make . . . stand** stand still by common consent **80**
**Orpheus** famous legendary Greek poet and musician **81**
**stockish** blockish, dull; **rage** passion **85 spoils** plundering
**86 motions** inward promptings **87 affections** emotions;
**Erebus** the dark underworld of the Greeks **91 naughty** evil
**94 substitute** deputy **95–96 his . . . itself** his own glory
merges into the king's **97 main of waters** ocean **99**
**without respect** without reference to circumstances **103**
**attended** heeded

**107–08 by . . . perfection** by the right occasion are made
ready to receive their fitting praise and attain their full
perfection **109 Peace! How the** the quarto reads "Peace,
how the"; editors often emend to "Peace, ho! The";
**Endymion** a handsome shepherd, beloved of Diana **109–10**
**Peace . . . awaked** addressed to the musicians **121 s.d.**
**tucket** trumpet call (Bassanio, like every nobleman,
had his individual tucket) **127 Antipodes** dwellers on the
opposite side of the earth **129, 130 light, heavy** Portia
quibbles on *light* in the senses of radiance, unchaste, and of
little weight, and on *heavy* in the senses of weighty and despondent, weighed down with trouble **132 God sort all**
let God ordain all according to his wisdom **136 in all sense**
(1) in all reason (2) in all senses

ANTONIO
No more than I am well acquitted of.°

PORTIA
Sir, you are very welcome to our house.
It must appear in other ways than words;                    140
Therefore I scant this breathing courtesy.°

GRATIANO [*To* NERISSA.]
By yonder moon I swear you do me wrong!
In faith, I gave it to the judge's clerk.
Would he were gelt° that had it, for my part,°
Since you do take it, love, so much at heart.              145

PORTIA
A quarrel, ho, already! What's the matter?

GRATIANO
About a hoop of gold, a paltry ring
That she did give me, whose posy° was
For all the world like cutler's poetry
Upon a knife, "Love me, and leave me not."               150

NERISSA
What° talk you of the posy or the value?
You swore to me when I did give it you
That you would wear it till your hour of death,
And that it should lie with you in your grave.
Though not for me,° yet for your vehement oaths,          155
You should have been respective° and have kept it.
Gave it a judge's clerk! No, God's my judge,
The clerk will ne'er wear hair on's face that had it!

GRATIANO
He will, and if he live to be a man.

NERISSA
Ay, if a woman live to be a man.                           160

GRATIANO
Now by this hand, I gave it to a youth,
A kind of boy, a little scrubbèd° boy
No higher than thyself, the judge's clerk,
A prating boy that begged it as a fee.
I could not for my heart deny it him.                     165

PORTIA
You were to blame—I must be plain with you—
To part so slightly with your wife's first gift,
A thing stuck on with oaths upon your finger,
And so riveted with faith unto your flesh.
I gave my love a ring, and made him swear                 170
Never to part with it; and here he stands.
I dare be sworn for him he would not leave it°
Nor pluck it from his finger, for the wealth
That the world masters.° Now in faith, Gratiano,
You give your wife too unkind° a cause of grief.          175
And, 'twere to me, I should be mad° at it.

BASSANIO [*Aside*.]
Why, I were best to cut my left hand off
And swear I lost the ring defending it.

GRATIANO
My Lord Bassanio gave his ring away
Unto the judge that begged it, and indeed                 180

Deserved it too; and then the boy, his clerk
That took some pains in writing, he begged mine;
And neither man nor master would take aught
But the two rings.

PORTIA                    What ring gave you, my lord?
Not that, I hope, which you received of me.               185

BASSANIO
If I could add a lie unto a fault,°
I would deny it; but you see my finger
Hath not the ring upon it—it is gone.

PORTIA
Even so void is your false heart of truth.
By heaven, I will ne'er come in your bed                  190
Until I see the ring!

NERISSA                    Nor I in yours
Till I again see mine!

BASSANIO                    Sweet Portia,
If you did know to whom I gave the ring,
If you did know for whom I gave the ring,
And would conceive for what° I gave the ring,            195
And how unwillingly I left the ring
When naught would be accepted but the ring,
You would abate the strength of your displeasure.

PORTIA
If you had known the virtue of the ring,
Or half her worthiness that gave the ring,                200
Or your own honor to contain° the ring,
You would not then have parted with the ring.
What man is there so much unreasonable,
If you had pleased to have defended it
With any terms of zeal,° wanted the modesty               205
To urge the thing held as a ceremony?°
Nerissa teaches me what to believe;
I'll die for't but some woman had the ring!

BASSANIO
No, by my honor, madam! By my soul
No woman had it, but a civil doctor,°                     210
Which did refuse three thousand ducats of me
And begged the ring, the which I did deny him,
And suffered him to go displeased away,
Even he that had held up the very life
Of my dear friend. What should I say, sweet lady?        215
I was enforced to send it after him.
I was beset with shame and courtesy.°
My honor would not let ingratitude
So much besmear it. Pardon me, good lady!
For by these blessèd candles of the night,                220
Had you been there, I think you would have begged
The ring of me to give the worthy doctor.

PORTIA
Let not that doctor e'er come near my house.
Since he hath got the jewel that I loved,
And that which you did swear to keep for me,              225
I will become as liberal° as you;
I'll not deny him anything I have,

---

**138 acquitted of** freed from  **141 breathing courtesy**
courtesy that is only breath (i.e., words)  **144 gelt** castrated;
**for my part** so far as I care  **148 posy** a contraction of *poesy*
(i.e., *poetry*); motto (inscribed on a ring)  **151 What** why
**155 Though . . . me** if not for my sake  **156 respective**
regardful, heedful  **162 scrubbèd** stunted  **172 leave it** let it
go  **174 masters** possesses  **175 unkind** unnaturally cruel
**176 mad** in a frenzy

**186 fault** faulty act  **195 conceive for what** form a conception of why  **201 honor to contain** honorable duty to
retain  **205 terms of zeal** ardent language  **205–06 wanted
. . . ceremony** would have been so lacking in modesty as to
urge a claim on the thing you were keeping as a hallowed
symbol  **210 civil doctor** doctor of civil law  **217 beset . . .
courtesy** assailed by feelings of shame and the obligations of
courtesy  **226 liberal** (1) licentious (2) generous

No, not my body nor my husband's bed.
Know him I shall, I am well sure of it.
Lie not a night from home. Watch me like Argus.° 230
If you do not, if I be left alone—
Now by mine honor which is yet mine own,
I'll have that doctor for mine bedfellow.

NERISSA
And I his clerk. Therefore be well advised°
How you do leave me to mine own protection. 235

GRATIANO
Well, do you so. Let not me take° him then!
For if I do, I'll mar the young clerk's pen.°

ANTONIO
I am th' unhappy subject of these quarrels.

PORTIA
Sir, grieve not you; you are welcome not with-
standing.

BASSANIO
Portia, forgive me this enforcèd wrong,° 240
And in the hearing of these many friends
I swear to thee, even by thine own fair eyes,
Wherein I see myself—

PORTIA                    Mark you but that!
In both my eyes he doubly sees himself,
In each eye one. Swear by your double self,° 245
And there's an oath of credit.°

BASSANIO                    Nay, but hear me.
Pardon this fault, and by my soul I swear
I never more will break an oath with thee.

ANTONIO
I once did lend my body for his wealth,°
Which but for him that had your husband's ring 250
Had quite miscarried. I dare be bound again,
My soul upon the forfeit, that your lord
Will never more break faith advisedly.°

PORTIA
Then you shall be his surety. Give him this,
And bid him keep it better than the other. 255

ANTONIO
Here, Lord Bassanio. Swear to keep this ring.

BASSANIO
By heaven, it is the same I gave the doctor!

PORTIA
I had it of him. Pardon me, Bassanio,
For by this ring the doctor lay with me.

NERISSA
And pardon me, my gentle Gratiano, 260
For that same scrubbèd boy, the doctor's clerk,
In lieu of° this, last night did lie with me.

GRATIANO
Why, this is like the mending of highways
In summer, where the ways are fair enough.
What, are we cuckolds° ere we have deserved it? 265

PORTIA
Speak not so grossly. You are all amazed.°
Here is a letter; read it at your leisure.
It comes from Padua from Bellario.
There you shall find that Portia was the doctor,
Nerissa there her clerk. Lorenzo here 270
Shall witness I set forth as soon as you,
And even but now returned. I have not yet
Entered my house. Antonio, you are welcome,
And I have better news in store for you
Than you expect. Unseal this letter soon; 275
There you shall find three of your argosies
Are richly come to harbor suddenly.
You shall not know by what strange° accident
I chancèd on this letter.

ANTONIO                    I am dumb!

BASSANIO
Were you the doctor, and I knew you not? 280

GRATIANO
Were you the clerk that is to make me cuckold?

NERISSA
Ay, but the clerk that never means to do it,
Unless he live until he be a man.

BASSANIO
Sweet doctor, you shall be my bedfellow.
When I am absent, then lie with my wife. 285

ANTONIO
Sweet lady, you have given me life and living!
For here I read for certain that my ships
Are safely come to road.°

PORTIA                    How now, Lorenzo?
My clerk hath some good comforts too for you.

NERISSA
Ay, and I'll give them him without a fee. 290
There do I give to you and Jessica
From the rich Jew, a special deed of gift,
After his death, of all he dies possessed of.

LORENZO
Fair ladies, you drop manna in the way
Of starvèd people.°

PORTIA                    It is almost morning, 295
And yet I am sure you are not satisfied
Of these events at full.° Let us go in,
And charge us there upon° inter'gatories,°
And we will answer all things faithfully.

GRATIANO
Let it be so. The first inter'gatory 300
That my Nerissa shall be sworn on° is,
Whether till the next night she had rather stay,
Or go to bed now, being two hours to day.
But were the day come, I should wish it dark
Till I were couching with the doctor's clerk. 305
Well, while I live I'll fear no other thing
So sore, as keeping safe Nerissa's ring. *Exeunt.*

---

230 **Argus** a monstrous giant of Greek myth, with a hundred eyes; a type of never-failing watchfulness 234 **be well advised** be very careful 236 **take** get hold of 237 **pen** double entendre 240 **this enforcèd wrong** this wrong I was forced to commit 245 **double self** a quibble (1) two-fold image (2) double-dealing character 246 **oath of credit** oath to be believed (spoken in irony) 249 **wealth** welfare 253 **advisedly** deliberately 262 **In lieu of** in return for 265 **cuckolds** husbands of faithless wives

266 **amazed** utterly bewildered; literally, "entangled in a maze (or labyrinth)" 278 **strange** astonishing 288 **road** anchorage 295 **starvèd people** Lorenzo, though of good social position, was, like Bassanio, far from rich 296–97 **not . . . full** not fully satisfied how these events came to pass 298 **charge . . . upon** load us with questions; **inter'gatories** interrogatories (i.e., questions formally drawn up to be put to a defendant or witness and answered under oath) 301 **sworn on** sworn to under oath

# THE HISTORY OF
# HENRY THE FOURTH
## [PART ONE]

### EDITED BY MAYNARD MACK

## Introduction

Readers who come to *Henry IV [Part One]* from *Richard II* (and they are well advised who do so) find themselves in a changed world. The new king's second word is "shaken"—"So shaken as we are, so wan with care" (I.i.1). His realm's peace, "frighted," pants to catch her breath. The English earth, invoked in vain by Richard in the earlier play for aid against Henry's invading power (III.ii.4 ff.), like a perverted mother has been sucking "her own children's blood." Englishmen have met Englishmen "in the . . . furious close of civil butchery." The "edge" of war's knife has cut his master.

Though the new king assigns these troubles to the past, we are speedily assured they will not stay there. Present news is equally bloody. In the West, a thousand of Mortimer's men have been "butchered," and afterward mutilated. In the North, ten thousand Scottish corpses were seen by Sir Walter Blunt "balked in their own blood." Throughout the play we shall hear continually of this sort of thing: of "guns and drums and wounds" (I.iii.55) and "many a good tall fellow" destroyed (I.iii.61); of "bloody noses and cracked crowns" (II.iii.92); wearing "a garment all of blood" (III.ii.135); noblemen offered up "hot and bleeding" to "the fire-eyed maid of smoky war" (IV.i.113–14); ragamuffins tossed dead into a pit— "Tut, tut, good enough to toss; food for powder. . . ." (IV.ii.65–66)—or consigned, maimed, to the town's end, "to beg during life" (V.iii.38). Richard returned from wars in Ireland in the earlier play, and the present king, then Henry Hereford, known as Bolingbroke, invaded England; but we never heard of doings like these. This is indeed a changed world: the world of outrage that is anticipated in the next-to-last scene of *Richard II* by the brutal murder of the king and, earlier, in the deposition scene, by the warning of the Bishop of Carlisle:

What subject can give sentence on his king?
And who sits here that is not Richard's subject?

    .        .        .

My Lord of Hereford here, whom you call king,
Is a foul traitor to proud Hereford's king;
And if you crown him, let me prophesy
The blood of England shall manure the ground,

And future ages groan for this foul act;
Peace shall go sleep with Turks and infidels,
And, in this seat of peace, tumultuous wars
Shall kin with kin, and kind with kind, confound;
Disorder, horror, fear, and mutiny
Shall here inhabit, and this land be called
The field of Golgotha and dead men's skulls.
O, if you raise this house against this house,
It will the woefullest division prove
That ever fell upon this cursèd earth!
Prevent it, resist it, let it not be so,
Lest child, child's children, cry against you woe.

             (IV.i.121–22, 134–49)

The violence predicted by Carlisle takes over immediately in *1 Henry IV*, as we have seen. But the bishop's enunciation of what is sometimes called "the Tudor myth" —the thesis that an ever-watchful Providence brings retribution on peoples who displace their lawful sovereigns, and, specifically, that England's sufferings between the murder of Richard in 1399 and the accession of the first Tudor monarch in 1485 were a divinely appointed punishment for the assault on Richard—the enunciation of this doctrine better suits Shakespeare's earlier treatment of these disorders in the Henry VI plays and *Richard III* than the Henry IV plays. The world that produces Henry is changed in this respect, too. The old scheme of celestial superintendence hangs loosely over it, to be glanced at in moments of introspection and anxiety; but to all dramatic intents and purposes, Henry's world, like Henry himself, is secular. One reason may be that Shakespeare saw in secularism the necessary condition of a usurper's success. A more compelling reason, doubtless, is that his attention had increasingly shifted from the interpretive moral and theological scheme with which his sources provided him toward the complexities and crosscurrents of human beings as they act and react on one another: in Yeats's words, toward "the fury and the mire of human veins."

The best anticipation of the mood of our play, from this point of view, is Richard's own warning, addressed to the man whose betrayal of him enabled Henry to seize the throne:

> Northumberland, thou ladder wherewithal
> The mounting Bolingbroke ascends my throne,
> The time shall not be many hours of age
> More than it is, ere foul sin, gathering head,
> Shall break into corruption. Thou shalt think,
> Though he divide the realm and give thee half,
> It is too little, helping him to all;
> He shall think that thou which knowest the way
> To plant unrightful kings, wilt know again,
> Being ne'er so little urged another way,
> To pluck him headlong from the usurped throne.
> The love of wicked men converts to fear,
> That fear to hate, and hate turns one or both
> To worthy danger and deservèd death.       (V.i.55–68)

These lines pay tribute to the overall theological scheme ("foul sin, gathering head"), but this fact should not blind us to the principles of *realpolitik* which they put forward as the mode of action that will govern in the hearts of Henry and his associates.

The irony of the new king's position, we soon learn, springs from these principles. As a successful usurper with the blood of a predecessor on his conscience, he is himself a principle of the disorder on which, as Shakespeare's Macbeth will learn at length, no lasting order can be built. Lawlessness springs up about him as if like Jason he had sown the dragon's teeth. It comes not only in the form of the Percys' rebellion and the behavior of his son, but in the knavery of Falstaff and the murky atmosphere of the inn at Rochester (to some extent an image of England), where all order is in decay and no man trusts another. All these are reflections cast by Henry in the mirror of the body politic. If there are highwaymen on the public road and other highwaymen at Glendower's plotting to snatch the crown, these circumstances cannot be separated from the circumstance that one who has acted like a highwayman is king.

Thus the Tudor theme of the harsh wages of usurpation by no means vanishes from the play. Minimizing it as doctrine, Shakespeare makes it part of the poetic and dramatic texture, while he qualifies and complicates it by presenting to us in Henry a capable and even admirable king—one who, though never granted the security and peace he longs for, maintains his crown by a combination of strength, sagacity, severity, and lenience, and passes it on to an eventually deserving son. The ambivalence of his position is brought out by continual questioning of his title. The rebels question it on many occasions verbally (I.iii. 10 ff., 143 ff.; IV.iii.52 ff.; V.i.30 ff.) and, subsequently, by force of arms. The king himself seems to cast a doubt on it when he dresses others "in his coats" to confuse the enemy at Shrewsbury, as if royalty were a costume or blazon to be laid on at will. When Falstaff "acts" the king in the tavern, this doubt assumes a compelling visual shape, as does a further doubt whether "that father ruffian," as Hal calls Falstaff when he himself assumes the king's part, is more a ruffian in some respects than the deposer and murderer of Richard. Meantime, in the language of the play, this subject is teased at incessantly: we hear of the "grace" that Hal will or will not have when he is king; of

the "*true*[1] prince" knowable by instinct; of the "heir *apparent*"[1]— with a lurking pun in the second term; of false or cracked coins (bearing the king's image) to be passed current; of "nobles" appreciated to "royals"; and of many forms of "counterfeiting." Perhaps the ambiguities surrounding Henry's claim are expressed most succinctly in two remarks made by the Scottish Douglas during the battle. Douglas is engaged in killing all who wear the king's coats as fast as he can find them. "I fear thou art another counterfeit," he says as he sees Henry approach in the same garb. "And yet, in faith, thou bearest thee like a king." The first sentence suggests the emptiness of Henry's title in that he is not the rightful king; the second suggests the justness of his title in that he is a man who knows how to rule. We notice, however, that the king's life is saved neither by the stratagem of the coats nor by kingly "bearing," but by the chivalry of his son.

*Henry IV* [*Part One*] was published in 1598; it was probably written and acted in 1596–97. There are some topical allusions in the play to these years, notably the Second Carrier's reference to the high cost of oats that killed Robin Ostler (II.i.12). Topical in a more important sense, during the whole of the 1590's, was the play's general subject matter. Though contemporary concern about succession to the throne need not (though it may) have influenced Shakespeare's choice of materials for his English histories, it inevitably gave them an extra dimension. Elizabeth was now in her sixties, and there was no assured heir, only a multiplicity of candidates, including her sometimes favorite, the Earl of Essex. Many recalled anxiously the chaos in times past when the center of power in the monarchical system had ceased to be sharply defined and clearly visible. This had occurred to an extent after Henry VIII's death, and earlier after Henry V's, and still earlier after the murder of Richard II.

If Shakespeare was at all influenced by these anxieties, his rendering of them is on the whole buoyant and optimistic in his second English tetralogy and especially so in *1 Henry IV*. True, the England seen in this play and its immediate successor is far from reassuring. It has even been described as

> an England, on the one side, of bawdy house and thieves'-kitchen, of waylaid merchants, badgered and bewildered Justices, and a peasantry wretched, betrayed, and recruited for the wars; an England, on the other side, of the chivalrous wolf pack of Hotspur and Douglas, and of state-sponsored treachery in the person of Prince John—the whole presided over by a sick King, hagridden by conscience, dreaming of a Crusade to the Holy Land as M. Remorse [Falstaff] thinks of slimming and repentance.[2]

But this is only half the picture. Beside it, for the first Henry IV play, we must place the warmth, wit, and high spirits of the tavern scenes, the impetuous charm of Hotspur, the amusing domesticities of Kate and Glendower's daughter, the touching loyalty of Francis, the affections that (along with sponging) bind Falstaff to Hal, and Hal's own magnanimity and self-command. For both the

---

[1] The italics are, of course, the editor's.
[2] J. F. Danby, *Shakespeare's Doctrine of Nature: A Study of King Lear* (1949), pp. 97–98.

first and second plays, we must weigh heavily into the account the character of the story told. This, the greatest of monarchical success stories in English popular history, traces the evolution of an engaging scapegrace into one of the most admired of English kings. Chicanery and appetite in the first play, apathy and corruption in the second, form an effective theatrical background against which the oncoming sunbright majesty of the future Henry V may shine more brightly—as we are assured precisely that it will do on our first meeting with him (I.ii).

When Shakespeare turned to this subject in 1596–97, he found in his historical sources, mainly Holinshed's *Chronicles*, two dominant motifs. One was the moral and theological interpretation of the troubles attending Henry IV's reign in consequence of his usurpation. This we have already discussed. The other was the legend of the madcap youth of Henry's son and heir—a legend already exploited in an anonymous play of which we have today only a debased and possibly abbreviated text: *The Famous Victories of Henry the Fifth*. The *Famous Victories* contributes to *1 Henry IV* the germ of the robbery incident (though the Prince's involvement in a thieving episode is found in the chronicles as well); the germ of the tavern high jinks and parodying of authority; the germ of the expectation of Hal's reign as a golden age of rascals; and the germ of the reconciliation scene between the prince and his father. The extent to which these hints are fleshed out and transfigured by Shakespeare's imagination may be seen in the character of Mistress Quickly. Her entire original in the *Famous Victories* is a sentence spoken by the prince, favoring a rendezvous at "the old tavern in Eastcheap" because "there is a pretty wench that can talk well."

From the *Famous Victories* come also the names Gad's Hill (for the arranger of the robbery), Ned (our Ned Poins), and Jockey Oldcastle. The last was Shakespeare's name for Falstaff when the play was first performed, as references throughout the early seventeenth century show; Hal's addressing him as "my old lad of the castle" in the play as we have it (I.ii.42) is a survival from this. By the time the play was printed, the name had been altered to Falstaff for reasons that can now only be guessed at. Possibly there had been a protest by Oldcastle's descendants, one of whom was Lord Chamberlain during part of 1596–97. How the historical Oldcastle (d. 1417), a man of character who was made High Sheriff of Herefordshire and eventually Lord Cobham, came to be metamorphosed into the roisterer of the *Famous Victories* is also an unsolved mystery, though no more mysterious than the dramatic imagination that exalted this dull stage roisterer, lacking eloquence, wit, mendacity, thirst, and fat, into the Falstaff we know.

On Holinshed and minor sources like Samuel Daniel's epic *The First Four Books of the Civil Wars between the Two Houses of Lancaster and York* (1595), Shakespeare based his treatment of the Percy rebellion, recasting the materials to give them an inner coherence. The Hotspur of history, for example, was twenty-three years older than Hal and two years older than the king himself, who at the date of the battle of Shrewsbury was only thirty-seven, his eldest son being then sixteen, and Prince John thirteen. Shakespeare followed the lead of Daniel and made Hotspur a youth, in order to establish dramatic rivalry between him and Hal. He then aged Henry rapidly so that by the

time of the battle the king can speak of crushing his "old limbs in ungentle steel" and be the more appropriately rescued (this episode is also derived from Daniel) by his vigorous heir. For the same dramatic purpose, he assigned to Hal the triumph over Hotspur—though the inspiration for this may have come from misreading an ambiguous sentence in Holinshed. The reconciliation of prince and king, touched on in the chronicles and dramatized briefly in the *Famous Victories* as occurring in Henry's latter years, he moved forward to a position before Shrewsbury, in order to enhance the human drama of father and son and further sharpen our anticipation of Hal's meeting with Hotspur. Hotspur's blunt, uncourtly humor, the conception of Glendower as scholar and poet fired by a Celtic imagination, the entertaining clash of temperament and mood that this makes possible at Glendower's house, not only between Welshman and Englishman, but between romantic lovers and seasoned man and wife—all this again is Shakespeare's invention. His transformation of Holinshed, like his transformation of the *Famous Victories*, may best be indicated by a specific example. All of Hotspur's deliciously impetuous speech about the popinjay lord who came to Holmedon to demand his prisoners, not to mention the wonderfully ebullient scene in which it occurs, has behind it in Holinshed only seventeen words: "the King demanded of the Earl and his son such Scottish prisoners as were taken at Homeldon. . . ."

Hal's triumphant journey from tippling in taverns to glory on the field of battle derives from one other "source," more influential than any yet mentioned here. This is the *psychomachia* of the morality plays—that is, the struggle of virtues and vices for possession of a man's soul, a theme acted again and again in the plays of the early sixteenth century, which the drama of Marlowe and Shakespeare superseded. In these plays, youthful virtue is beset by temptations and misleaders but customarily sees the true light at last and is saved. In the same general manner, Prince Hal "has to choose, Morality-fashion, between Sloth or Vanity, to which he is drawn by his bad companions, and Chivalry, to which he is drawn by his father and brother. And he chooses Chivalry."[3]

The play that Shakespeare built from these miscellaneous materials is simple in its large outlines. It brings before us three contrasting environments at once, each with a commanding personality. The court is Henry's domain; the tavern is Falstaff's; the feudal countryside is Hotspur's. What essentially takes place during the first three acts is the progress of Hal, the one unattached player, from Falstaff's environment to Henry's. Hal then returns in the last scene of Act III to mobilize the tavern world for war, after which Falstaff's environment dissolves. We then have two environments, both military and political in nature, one of them dominated by Hotspur, the other (beginning with Act IV) increasingly by Hal. Falstaff, now in his turn the unattached man, makes appropriate comments on each.

Within this simple framework, Shakespeare accomplishes an articulation of complementary images, cross-references, and ironic contrasts that is without parallel in the history of English stage comedy. The highway robbery comments on the Percys' plot and also on the king's usurpation, as we saw a few moments ago. Gadshill, boasting of the

---

[3] E. M. W. Tillyard, *Shakespeare's History Plays* (1944), p. 265.

quality of his confederates (II.i), anticipates Hotspur's misplaced confidence in the fidelity of his fellow rebels (II.iii). Falstaff bawling for his horse (II.ii) has satirical affinities with Hotspur chattering to the same purpose (II.iii). Hal describes Hotspur talking to his wife (II.iv) as if he had been an eavesdropper in the scene preceding, and points our attention to a tavern monomania in Francis which is perhaps reminiscent of Hotspur's monomania for "palisadoes, frontiers, parapets." Hotspur describes a presumed but perhaps wholly imaginary fight between Glendower and Mortimer in epic terms (I.iii); Falstaff does the same for a definitely imaginary contest with eleven men in buckram (II.iv). Falstaff keeps telling us he is about to reform; Hal actually does so. Hal's interview with his father (III.ii) is broadened and deepened for us in advance by the burlesque of it (II.iv) and by the failure of Hotspur to achieve a similar self-discipline (III.i). Glendower and Hotspur mirror each other in egoism, contrast vividly in the pedantic refinements of the one, the countrified heartiness of the other. Falstaff's remarks on honor, as everyone knows, complement those we have heard earlier from Hotspur; the comic account of Falstaff's conscripted derelicts corrects and supplements the description of Hal's army by a general who loves parades (IV.i.97 ff.) and the anticipation of destroying it by a general who loves carnage (IV.i.113 ff.); Falstaff's cynical "They'll fill a pit as well as better" hangs over the ensuing battle, enveloping especially those who are to fill a pit simply because the king has dressed them in his coats; and so on. This list of cross-references could be extended almost indefinitely.

Only through such qualifying optics as these does Shakespeare allow us to view the simple morality "choice" described by Professor Tillyard. Hotspur is one term in that choice—at first glance, a wholly negative term. He misjudges Henry, seeing only the king's duplicity. He misjudges Hal, seeing only the truant, overlooking Hal's sagacity and versatility. Magnanimity is also beyond his reach. His manners are rude, not courtly. His reaction to Glendower is both impolitic and provincial. Yet the play shows us there is much to be said on behalf of this misguided and hotheaded young man. In many respects, he is set apart from, and above, the company he keeps. In being free of scheming policy, he is differentiated from his uncle Worcester and the king. In fighting (for a time) the nation's battles, he has in the past surpassed Hal. He can be counted on when needed and is thereby distinguished from Glendower, Mortimer, and his father. His valor in battle is total. In this he is unlike Douglas, who makes a fine display of fearlessness but in the pinch flees. And he is naively frank-hearted. Hotspur, Worcester knows, would be moved to meet what seems the king's generous offer of amnesty with equal generosity, and the battle would probably not be fought.

Falstaff, the other term of the choice, is similarly complex. First of all, he is endowed by Shakespeare with a comic imagination that enables him (as Antony will later be enabled by the imagination of Cleopatra) to show his back above the element he lives in. His shattering of official clichés and stained-glass attitudes throughout the play is a measure of his penetration as well as, sometimes, his irresponsibility: "Why, Hal, 'tis my vocation, Hal. 'Tis no sin for a man to labor in his vocation" (I.ii.105-06); "A plague of sighing and grief, it blows a man up like a bladder" (II.iv.334-36); "Thou knowest in the state of innocency Adam fell, and what should poor Jack Falstaff do in the days of villainy? Thou see'st I have more flesh than another man, and therefore more frailty" (III.iii. 172-76); "Rebellion lay in his way, and he found it" (V.i.28). These show the same gift of comic insight that enables him to multiply images of himself as a shotten herring or a poulterer's hare, to raise the stock role of *miles gloriosus*, or braggart soldier, into the most rapturous flight of mendacity the comic stage has ever seen (II.iv), and to fling into the tense silence before the robbery one of those searching questions about the nature of man and his societies that a wide-eyed child will sometimes propound: "Zounds, will they not rob *us*?" (II.ii.64). (In *2 Henry IV*, appealing to "law of nature" to account for the way of a pike with a dace, he will make this Hobbesian question a proposition.)

Falstaff is also set apart by his genuine affections, his joy in his friends: "Gallants, lads, boys, hearts of gold, all the titles of good fellowship come to you!" (II.iv.280-81). He is even set apart by a certain kind of honesty. He will lie to others inexhaustibly, but that life is sweeter to him than honor, sack than killing, money in the pocket more gratifying than a fine squad of soldiers, he never seeks to hide from himself. Yet it would be folly to ignore that his honesty makes him no less a rascal, his affection no less a parasite, his perspicacity about some matters no less willful-blind about the rest. Falstaff is much more than —but he also is—a glutton, drunkard, liar, coward, and thief.

Hotspur and Falstaff are extremes, and we see the gulf that separates them when Hotspur goes down fighting while Falstaff plays dead to save his skin. But extremes (so runs the familiar saying) meet, and we see them meet when Falstaff, having taken Hotspur's body on his back, assures Hal he is "not a double man." The phrase reminds us that he and Hotspur are in some respects outsized versions of the same thing. Both are chivalric figures, Falstaff being, however backslidden, a knight; both exemplify ways in which chivalry may go to seed. "A harebrained Hotspur, governed by a spleen," as his uncle Worcester describes him, can sacrifice to spleen a true knight's fealty and stain the honor he so prizes by making it the ground his egoism walks on. As for Falstaff, that "huge bombard of sack," that "roast Manningtree ox with the pudding in his belly": in his knight's bosom, "there's no room for faith, truth, nor honesty; . . . it is all filled up with guts and midriff."

Falstaff and Hotspur help us see that Hal's course is a mean between extremes. King Henry helps us see that Hal's mean is not a path of least resistance but a creative will that points toward a new kind of world. A master of appearances, as his description of his behavior in King Richard's time informs us (III.ii), Henry is at the same time their victim. If he seriously imagines that he would ever actually go on that crusade whose "dear expedience" occupies his council at the opening of the play (I.i), he is obviously self-deceived; if he does not intend to go, it is a calculated charade. The sketches of Hotspur and his son which he draws for us in the same scene are unmistakably sincere; but we soon discover they are wrong—mere stereotypes of martial prowess and libertinism. Henry does not really understand either his son or Hotspur. When he holds up Hotspur for a model in the reconciliation scene (III.ii), when he exhibits his delusion that what he was to King Richard, Hotspur is now to Hal, when he speaks of Hal's "barren pleasures" to us who have just seen the tavern bulge with an energy and feeling never to be matched at Henry's court, we understand how far he has become prisoner of a royalism that is less imaginative than his son's. And when the battle comes, we understand more clearly against this background the meaning of the contrasts there: the king "has many marching in his coats"; the prince offers to decide the issue by taking the danger on himself alone; the king, thinking in political terms, sends his enemies to execution and within these terms is perfectly right to do so; the prince thinks in larger terms and spares Douglas, not for political reasons (though doubtless he is aware of these), but because, as in his praise of Hotspur, he can cherish "high deeds/Even in the bosom of our adversaries." Even Falstaff at his most ignominious, wounding Hotspur's corpse and claiming credit for having killed him, the prince can bring himself to excuse; he will gild his lie "with the happiest terms I have."

Thus by the play's end, Hal casts an inclusive shadow. He has met the claims of Hotspur's world, of Falstaff's, and of Henry's, without narrowing himself to any one. He has practiced mercy as well as justice, politics as well as friendship, shown himself capable of mockery as well as reverence, detachment as well as commitment, and brought into a practicable balance court, field, and tavern. He is on the way to becoming the luminous figure toward whom, in *Henry V*, Welshman, Irishman, Scot, and Englishman will alike be drawn. In this figure, combining valor, courtliness, hard sense, and humor in an ideal image of the potentialities of the English character, Shakespeare seems to have discerned grounds for that optimism about the future of his country which permeates his historical vision in the plays from *Richard II* to *Henry V*. We ourselves may find in it, if not so local and particular an image, glimpses of an ideal form that remains relevant to us— such a form as Socrates and Glaucon, in the ninth book of the *Republic*, allude to in their discussion of the perfect city. Glaucon, the doubter, says: "But the city whose foundation we have been describing has its being only in words; there is no spot on earth where it exists." And Socrates replies: "No; but it is laid up in heaven as a pattern for him who wills to see, and seeing, to found that city in himself. Whether it exists anywhere, or ever will exist, is no matter."

### A NOTE ON THE SOURCES

So far as we know, the sources on which Shakespeare chiefly drew in writing *Henry IV [Part One]* were the following: (1) the pages on Henry's reign in Volume III of Raphael Holinshed's compilation of British history, *Chronicles of England, Scotland, and Ireland*, first published in 1577 but later reissued (1586–87) in an enlarged edition, which seems to have been the text actually consulted by Shakespeare; (2) the relevant stanzas in Book III of Samuel Daniel's long poem, *The First Four Books of the Civil Wars between the Two Houses of Lancaster and York* (1595); and (3) *The Famous Victories of Henry the Fifth, Containing the Honorable Battle of Agincourt*—an anonymous play of uncertain date, first printed in 1598, today extant in only

one known copy. For a brief account of the playwright's management of his sources in the completed play, see the Introduction, p. 640.

### A NOTE ON THE TEXT

The text for the present edition as a whole is the first quarto of 1598. This is generally believed to have been set from an earlier edition of the same year (Q0), of which today only four leaves are known—containing the text of the play from I.iii.199 to II.ii.112. Q0, so far as we have it, shows characteristics which relate it closely to an authorial manuscript, probably a corrected working manuscript rather than a fair copy. Q1 may therefore be regarded as still reasonably faithful to what Shakespeare wrote. The later quartos (Q2, 1599; Q3, 1604; Q4, 1608; Q5, 1613), each set from the one preceding, and the Folio (1623), set from Q5, have increasingly less authority.

Apart from spelling and punctuation, which are modernized in this edition, and regularization of speech prefixes, I have followed Q1, and, where it exists, Q0. With one exception (IV.i.12–13), I preserve the lineation of these editions, printing therefore as prose a number of passages so printed in Q1 but now almost invariably divided into lines of verse. It is possible, even probable, that some of these passages were intended to be verse; but the wide differences exhibited by editors in lineating them persuade me to reserve this entertainment for readers who wish to engage in it. I have usually indicated in the footnotes one or more of the traditional patterns of lineation for each passage.

The table below records departures from Q0–Q1. The first reading (boldface) is that which I have adopted in the text; the second is that of Q1. Almost all of the emendations were made in the quartos or in the First Folio, indicating that in Shakespeare's own day the passages in question were suspect; but because these early texts have no authority, they are not cited as sources.

Division into acts and scenes is here that of the Folio, save that I follow Capell and most other editors (including those of the Globe edition) in dividing the Folio's V.ii into V.ii and V.iii and renumbering the subsequent scenes. In the quartos there is no indication of acts or scenes.

**I.i.62 a dear** deere  **69 blood did** bloud. Did  **76 In faith it is** [the quartos and folios give to the king]
**I.ii.80 similes** smiles  **161 Bardolph, Peto** Haruey, Rossill [these are names that Shakespeare evidently meant originally to assign to Falstaff's associates: see below, II.iv.174–77, 181–82]
**I.iii.199–206** [Q0–Q4 do not assign to Hotspur, but give as part of Northumberland's speech]
**II.ii.16 two and twenty** xxii
**II.iii.4 respect** the respect  **70 A roan** Roane
**II.iv.34 precedent** present  **37** [assigned to prince]  **174–77** [assigned to Gadshill, Ross (= Russell: see above, I.ii.161), Falstaff, Ross]  **181–82** [assigned to Ross]  **246 eelskin** elsskin  **343 Owen** O  **398 tristful** trustfull
**III.i.99 cantle** scantle  **128 on** an
**III.ii.115 Enlargèd** Enlargd
**III.iii.37 that's** that  **61 tithe** tight  **92 s.d. them** him  **180 guests** ghesse  **208 o'** of
**IV.i.20 I, my lord** I my mind  **54 is** tis  **107 dropped** drop  **125 cannot** can  **126 yet** it
**IV.iii.21 horse** horses  **28 ours** our  **82 country's** Countrey
**V.i.138 will it** wil
**V.ii.3 undone** vnder one  **25 s.d. Hotspur** Percy
**V.iii.22 A** Ah
**V.iv.66 Nor** Now  **74 s.d. who** he  **157 ours** our

# THE HISTORY OF

# HENRY THE FOURTH

# [PART ONE]

[Dramatis Personae

KING HENRY THE FOURTH
HENRY *Prince of Wales* } *the king's*
PRINCE JOHN OF LANCASTER } *sons*
EARL OF WESTMORELAND
SIR WALTER BLUNT
THOMAS PERCY *Earl of Worcester*
HENRY PERCY *Earl of Northumberland*
HENRY PERCY ("HOTSPUR") *his son*
EDMUND MORTIMER *Earl of March*
RICHARD SCROOP *Archbishop of York*
ARCHIBALD *Earl of Douglas*
OWEN GLENDOWER
SIR RICHARD VERNON
SIR JOHN FALSTAFF

SIR MICHAEL *a friend of the Archbishop of York*
POINS
GADSHILL
PETO
BARDOLPH
FRANCIS *a waiter*
LADY PERCY *Hotspur's wife and Mortimer's sister*
LADY MORTIMER *Glendower's daughter and Mortimer's wife*
MISTRESS QUICKLY *hostess of the tavern*
SHERIFF VINTNER CHAMBERLAIN TWO
  CARRIERS OSTLER MESSENGERS
  TRAVELERS ATTENDANTS

*Scene:* England and Wales]

## [ ACT I ]

[Scene I. *London. The palace.*]

*Enter the* KING, *Lord* JOHN *of Lancaster, Earl of* WEST-
MORELAND, [*Sir Walter* BLUNT,] *with others.*

KING
So shaken as we are, so wan with care,
Find we a time for frighted peace to pant°
And breathe short-winded accents of new broils
To be commenced in stronds° afar remote.
No more the thirsty entrance of this soil           5
Shall daub her lips with her own children's blood,
No more shall trenching° war channel her fields,
Nor bruise her flow'rets with the armèd hoofs
Of hostile paces. Those opposèd eyes

Which, like the meteors° of a troubled heaven,     10
All of one nature, of one substance bred,°
Did lately meet in the intestine° shock
And furious close° of civil butchery,
Shall now in mutual well-beseeming° ranks
March all one way and be no more opposed           15
Against acquaintance, kindred, and allies.
The edge of war, like an ill-sheathèd knife,
No more shall cut his master. Therefore, friends,
As far as to the sepulcher of Christ°—
Whose soldier now, under whose blessèd cross       20
We are impressèd and engaged° to fight—
Forthwith a power° of English shall we levy,
Whose arms were molded in their mother's womb
To chase these pagans in those holy fields

*The decorative border shown above appeared on the first page of the fifth quarto edition of* The History of Henry the Fourth [Part One], *1613.*

**I.i.2 pant** catch (her) breath  **4 stronds** shores  **7 trenching** (1) cutting (2) encroaching

**10 meteors** atmospheric disturbances  **11 All . . . bred** i.e., because believed to originate from vapors  **12 intestine** internal  **13 close** grappling  **14 mutual well-beseeming** interdependent well-ordered  **19 As . . . Christ** to Jerusalem  **21 impressèd and engaged** conscripted and pledged (by Henry's vow after the murder of Richard: cf. *Richard II*, V.vi.45–50)  **22 power** army

Over whose acres walked those blessèd feet          25
Which fourteen hundred years ago were nailed
For our advantage on the bitter cross.
But this our purpose now is twelvemonth old,
And bootless° 'tis to tell you we will go.
Therefor we meet not now.° Then let me hear          30
Of you, my gentle cousin° Westmoreland,
What yesternight our council did decree
In forwarding this dear expedience.°

WESTMORELAND
My liege, this haste was hot in question°
And many limits of the charge° set down          35
But yesternight; when all athwart° there came
A post° from Wales, loaden with heavy news,
Whose worst was that the noble Mortimer,
Leading the men of Herefordshire to fight
Against the irregular and wild° Glendower,          40
Was by the rude hands of that Welshman taken,
A thousand of his people butcherèd;
Upon whose dead corpse there was such misuse,
Such beastly shameless transformation
By those Welshwomen done, as may not be          45
Without much shame retold or spoken of.°

KING
It seems then that the tidings of this broil
Brake off our business for the Holy Land.

WESTMORELAND
This, matched with other, did, my gracious lord;
For more uneven° and unwelcome news          50
Came from the north, and thus it did import:
On Holy-rood Day° the gallant Hotspur there,
Young Harry Percy, and brave Archibald,
That ever-valiant and approvèd Scot,
At Holmedon° met, where they did spend          55
A sad and bloody hour;
As by discharge of their artillery
And shape of likelihood° the news was told;
For he that brought them,° in the very heat
And pride of their contention° did take horse,          60
Uncertain of the issue° any way.

KING
Here is a dear, a true industrious° friend,
Sir Walter Blunt, new lighted from his horse,
Stained with the variation of each soil
Betwixt that Holmedon and this seat° of ours,          65
And he hath brought us smooth and welcome news.
The Earl of Douglas is discomfited;
Ten thousand bold Scots, two and twenty knights,
Balked° in their own blood did Sir Walter see
On Holmedon's plains. Of prisoners, Hotspur took          70

Mordake, Earl of Fife and eldest son
To beaten Douglas, and the Earl of Athol,
Of Murray, Angus, and Menteith.
And is not this an honorable spoil?
A gallant prize? Ha, cousin, is it not?          75

WESTMORELAND
In faith it is. A conquest for a prince to boast of

KING
Yea, there thou mak'st me sad, and mak'st me sin
In envy that my Lord Northumberland
Should be the father to so blest a son:
A son who is the theme of honor's tongue,          80
Amongst a grove the very straightest plant;
Who is sweet fortune's minion° and her pride;
Whilst I, by looking on the praise of him,
See riot and dishonor stain the brow
Of my young Harry. O that it could be proved          85
That some night-tripping fairy° had exchanged
In cradle clothes our children where they lay,
And called mine Percy, his Plantagenet!°
Then would I have his Harry, and he mine.
But let him from my thoughts. What think you, coz,°          90
Of this young Percy's pride? The prisoners
Which he in this adventure hath surprised°
To his own use he keeps, and sends me word
I shall have none but Mordake, Earl of Fife.

WESTMORELAND
This is his uncle's teaching, this is Worcester,          95
Malevolent to you in all aspects,°
Which makes him prune° himself and bristle up
The crest of youth against your dignity.

KING
But I have sent for him to answer this;
And for this cause awhile we must neglect          100
Our holy purpose to Jerusalem.
Cousin, on Wednesday next our council we
Will hold at Windsor, so inform the lords:
But come yourself with speed to us again,
For more is to be said and to be done          105
Than out of anger can be utterèd.°

WESTMORELAND
I will, my liege.                              Exeunt.


[Scene II. London. The prince's lodging.]

Enter PRINCE of Wales and Sir John FALSTAFF.

FALSTAFF  Now, Hal, what time of day is it, lad?
PRINCE  Thou art so fat-witted with drinking of old
sack,° and unbuttoning thee after supper, and sleeping
upon benches after noon, that thou hast forgotten to
demand that truly which thou wouldest truly know.          5
What a devil hast thou to do with the time of the day?
Unless hours were cups of sack, and minutes capons,

---

29 **bootless** useless   30 **Therefor . . . now** That is not the
reason we now meet   31 **gentle cousin** noble kinsman   33
**dear expedience** urgent enterprise   34 **hot in question**
undergoing hot discussion   35 **limits . . . charge** apportion-
ings of tasks and costs   36 **athwart** crosswise, i.e., interfering
37 **post** messenger   40 **irregular and wild** i.e., as border-
raider and guerrilla   43–46 **such . . . of** the phrasing in
Holinshed, Shakespeare's source, suggests that the dead
English were castrated   50 **uneven** cf. "smooth" in line 66
52 **Holy-rood Day** September 14   55 **Holmedon** Humbleton
in Northumberland   58 **shape of likelihood** probability
59 **them** the news   59–60 **heat . . . contention** peak of
battle   61 **issue** outcome   62 **true industrious** loyally zealous
65 **seat** dwelling, i.e., the palace   69 **Balked** (1) heaped (2)
thwarted

82 **minion** darling   86 **fairy** fairies were thought sometimes
to steal a beautiful infant, leaving an ugly "changeling" in its
place   88 **Plantagenet** family name of Henry IV   90 **coz**
kinsman (short for *cousin*)   92 **surprised** taken   96 **Malevolent
. . . aspects** an astrological expression comparing Worcester
to a planet whose influence obstructs Henry's designs   97
**prune** preen his feathers for action (like a hawk)   106 **utterèd**
transacted in public
**I.ii.3 sack** Spanish white wine

and clocks the tongues of bawds, and dials° the signs
of leaping houses,° and the blessed sun himself a fair hot
wench in flame-colored taffeta, I see no reason why    10
thou shouldst be so superfluous to° demand the time
of the day.

FALSTAFF    Indeed you come near me° now, Hal; for
we that take purses go by° the moon and the seven
stars,° and not by Phoebus,° he, that wand'ring knight    15
so fair.° And I prithee, sweet wag, when thou art a
king, as, God save thy grace°—majesty I should say,
for grace thou wilt have none—

PRINCE    What, none?

FALSTAFF    No, by my troth; not so much as will serve    20
to be prologue to an egg and butter.

PRINCE    Well, how then? Come, roundly, roundly.°

FALSTAFF    Marry,° then, sweet wag, when thou art
king, let not us that are squires of the night's body be
called thieves of the day's beauty.° Let us be Diana's°    25
foresters, gentlemen of the shade, minions° of the
moon; and let men say we be men of good government,° being governed, as the sea is, by our noble and
chaste mistress the moon, under whose countenance
we steal.    30

PRINCE    Thou sayest well, and it holds well° too; for
the fortune of us that are the moon's men doth ebb
and flow like the sea, being governed as the sea is by
the moon. As, for proof now: a purse of gold most
resolutely snatched on Monday night and most    35
dissolutely spent on Tuesday morning; got with
swearing "Lay by," and spent with crying "Bring
in";° now in as low an ebb as the foot of the ladder,° and
by and by in as high a flow as the ridge of the gallows.

FALSTAFF    By the Lord, thou say'st true, lad—and is    40
not my hostess of the tavern a most sweet wench?

PRINCE    As the honey of Hybla,° my old lad of the castle°
—and is not a buff jerkin° a most sweet robe of durance?

FALSTAFF    How now, how now, mad wag? What, in
thy quips and thy quiddities?° What a plague have I to    45
do with a buff jerkin?

PRINCE    Why, what a pox° have I to do with my
hostess of the tavern?

FALSTAFF    Well, thou hast called her to a reckoning°
many a time and oft.    50

PRINCE    Did I ever call for thee to pay thy part?

FALSTAFF    No; I'll give thee thy due, thou hast paid all
there.

PRINCE    Yea, and elsewhere, so far as my coin would
stretch; and where it would not, I have used my credit.    55

FALSTAFF    Yea, and so used it that, were it not here
apparent that thou art heir apparent—But I prithee,
sweet wag, shall there be gallows standing in England
when thou art king? And resolution thus fubbed° as
it is with the rusty curb of old father Antic° the law?    60
Do not thou, when thou art king, hang a thief.

PRINCE    No; thou shalt.

FALSTAFF    Shall I? O rare! By the Lord, I'll be a brave°
judge.

PRINCE    Thou judgest false already. I mean, thou shalt    65
have the hanging of the thieves and so become a rare
hangman.

FALSTAFF    Well, Hal, well; and in some sort it jumps
with my humor° as well as waiting in the court, I can
tell you.    70

PRINCE    For obtaining of suits?°

FALSTAFF    Yea, for obtaining of suits, whereof the
hangman hath no lean wardrobe. 'Sblood,° I am as
melancholy as a gib-cat° or a lugged° bear.

PRINCE    Or an old lion, or a lover's lute.    75

FALSTAFF    Yea, or the drone° of a Lincolnshire bagpipe.

PRINCE    What sayest thou to a hare,° or the melancholy of Moorditch?°

FALSTAFF    Thou hast the most unsavory similes, and    80
art indeed the most comparative,° rascalliest, sweet
young prince. But, Hal, I prithee trouble me no more
with vanity.° I would to God thou and I knew where
a commodity° of good names were to be bought. An
old lord of the council rated° me the other day in the    85
street about you, sir, but I marked him not; and yet he
talked very wisely, but I regarded him not; and yet he
talked wisely, and in the street too.

---

**8 dials** sundial  **9 leaping houses** brothels  **11 so superfluous to** so irrelevant as to  **13 near me** close to understanding me (as if Hal were shooting at a mark)  **14 go
by** (1) walk under (2) tell time by (3) regulate our lives by
**14–15 seven stars** constellation Pleiades  **15 Phoebus** the
sun  **15–16 he . . . fair** Falstaff possibly quotes here, or sings, a line
of a lost ballad; the sun was readily thought of as an eternal
wanderer or "knight-errant"  **17 grace** Falstaff puns on "your
grace" a title which Hal as king will exchange for "your majesty"
—and spiritual grace and, in lines 20–21, on grace before eating
**22 roundly** i.e., get to the point (but possibly with a glance at
Falstaff's girth)  **23 Marry** a mild oath, from "By the Virgin
Mary"  **24–25 squires . . . beauty** Falstaff's puns on *night/
knight*—knights were often attended by body-squires—and
probably on *body/beauty/booty*; the "day's beauty" in one of its
senses here is the sun and balances "the night's body," which in
one sense is the moon  **25 Diana** goddess of the moon and the
hunt (by identifying the hunt with hunting for "booty"—
and "beauty"—Falstaff presents himself and his crew as
Diana's companion foresters, her titled "gentlemen of the
shade," her "minions," who "steal"—i.e., [1] move silently
[2] take purses under her "countenance"—i.e., under [1] her face
[2] her protection)  **26 minions** servants and favorites  **27–28
of good government** (1) well-behaved (2) ruled by a good ruler
**31 it holds well** it's a good comparison  **37–38 Lay by . . .
Bring in** the highwayman's commands: the first to his victims,
the second to the waiter in the tavern where he spends his
gains  **38 ladder** leading up to the gallows  **42 Hybla** Sicilian
source of fine honey; **old . . . castle** rowdy (with pun on
*Oldcastle*, Falstaff's original name, and probably on *The Castle*,
a well-known London brothel)  **43 buff jerkin** tan (leather)
jacket (a "robe of durance" because both durable and suggesting
imprisonment [durance] because worn by the sheriff's officers)

**44–45 What . . . quiddities** So you're in a witty mood,
are you?  **47 pox** the Prince turns Falstaff's "plague" (line
45) into a disease more characteristic of tavern hostesses
**49 called . . . reckoning** (1) called her to a showdown
(2) asked her for the bill  **59 resolution thus fubbed**
courage (i.e., in the highwayman) thus cheated of its
reward  **60 old father Antic** "that old screwball"  **63
brave** (1) excellent (2) handsomely decked out  **68–69 jumps
. . . humor** agrees with my frame of mind  **71 suits**
petitions for court favor (but Falstaff takes it in the sense of
the victim's garments, which were forfeit to the executioner)
**73 'Sblood** by God's (i.e., Christ's) blood  **74 gib-cat**
tomcat; **lugged** tied to a stake and baited by dogs, as entertainment  **76 drone** single note of a bagpipe's bass pipe
**78 hare** proverbially melancholy  **79 Moorditch** foul London
drainage ditch  **81 comparative** full of (insulting) comparisons  **83 vanity** worldly considerations (Falstaff here takes
up one of his favorite humorous roles, assuming for the next
several lines the sanctimonious attitudes and vocabulary of
Elizabethan Puritanism)  **84 commodity** supply  **85 rated**
scolded

PRINCE  Thou didst well, for wisdom cries out in the streets, and no man regards it.°    90

FALSTAFF  O, thou hast damnable iteration,° and art indeed able to corrupt a saint. Thou hast done much harm upon me, Hal—God forgive thee for it! Before I knew thee, Hal, I knew nothing; and now am I, if a man should speak truly, little better than one of the wicked.° I must give over this life, and I will give it over! By the Lord, and° I do not, I am a villain! I'll be damned for never a king's son in Christendom.    95

PRINCE  Where shall we take a purse tomorrow, Jack?    100

FALSTAFF  Zounds,° where thou wilt, lad! I'll make one. An° I do not, call me villain and baffle° me.

PRINCE  I see a good amendment of life in thee—from praying to purse-taking.

FALSTAFF  Why, Hal, 'tis my vocation,° Hal. 'Tis no sin for a man to labor in his vocation.    105

*Enter* POINS.

Poins! Now shall we know if Gadshill have set a match.° O, if men were to be saved by merit,° what hole in hell were hot enough for him? This is the most omnipotent villain that ever cried "Stand!" to a true° man.    110

PRINCE  Good morrow, Ned.

POINS  Good morrow, sweet Hal. What says Monsieur Remorse? What says Sir John Sack and Sugar?° Jack, how agrees the devil and thee about thy soul, that thou soldest him on Good Friday last for a cup of Madeira and a cold capon's leg?    115

PRINCE  Sir John stands to his word, the devil shall have his bargain; for he was never yet a breaker of proverbs. He will give the devil his due.    120

POINS  Then art thou damned for keeping thy word with the devil.

PRINCE  Else he had been damned for cozening° the devil.

POINS  But, my lads, my lads, tomorrow morning, by four o'clock early, at Gad's Hill!° There are pilgrims going to Canterbury with rich offerings,° and traders riding to London with fat purses. I have vizards° for you all; you have horses for yourselves. Gadshill lies tonight in Rochester. I have bespoke supper tomorrow night at Eastcheap.° We may do it as secure as sleep.    125    130

If you will go, I will stuff your purses full of crowns; if you will not, tarry at home and be hanged!

FALSTAFF  Hear ye, Yedward:° if I tarry at home and go not, I'll hang you for going.    135

POINS  You will, chops?°

FALSTAFF  Hal, wilt thou make one?

PRINCE  Who, I rob? I a thief? Not I, by my faith.

FALSTAFF  There's neither honesty, manhood, nor good fellowship in thee, nor thou cam'st not of the blood royal° if thou darest not stand for° ten shillings.    140

PRINCE  Well then, once in my days I'll be a madcap.

FALSTAFF  Why, that's well said.

PRINCE  Well, come what will, I'll tarry at home.

FALSTAFF  By the Lord, I'll be a traitor then, when thou art king.    145

PRINCE  I care not.

POINS  Sir John, I prithee, leave the prince and me alone. I will lay him down such reasons for this adventure that he shall go.    150

FALSTAFF  Well, God give thee the spirit of persuasion and him the ears of profiting, that what thou speakest may move° and what he hears may be believed, that the true prince may (for recreation sake) prove a false thief; for the poor abuses of the time want countenance.° Farewell; you shall find me in Eastcheap.    155

PRINCE  Farewell, the° latter spring! Farewell, All-hallown summer!°    [*Exit* FALSTAFF.]

POINS  Now, my good sweet honey lord, ride with us tomorrow. I have a jest to execute that I cannot manage alone. Falstaff, Bardolph, Peto, and Gadshill shall rob those men that we have already waylaid;° yourself and I will not be there; and when they have the booty, if you and I do not rob them, cut this head off from my shoulders.    160    165

PRINCE  How shall we part with them in setting forth?

POINS  Why, we will set forth before or after them and appoint them a place of meeting, wherein it is at our pleasure to fail; and then will they adventure upon the exploit themselves, which they shall have no sooner achieved, but we'll set upon them.    170

PRINCE  Yea, but 'tis like that they will know us by our horses, by our habits,° and by every other appointment,° to be ourselves.

POINS  Tut! Our horses they shall not see—I'll tie them in the wood; our vizards we will change after we leave them; and, sirrah,° I have cases of buckram for the nonce,° to immask our noted outward garments.    175

PRINCE  Yea, but I doubt° they will be too hard for us.

POINS  Well, for two of them, I know them to be as true-bred cowards as ever turned back; and for the    180

---

**89–90 Thou . . . it** Hal quotes Proverbs 1:20–24: "Wisdom crieth without, and putteth forth her voice in the streets . . . saying . . . 'I have stretched out my hand, and no man regarded' "  **91 damnable iteration** a sinful way of repeating and (mis)applying holy texts  **95–96 the wicked** Puritan idiom for those who were not Puritans; cf. "saint" in line 92, which glances at the Puritans' way of referring collectively to themselves  **97 and** if  **101 Zounds** by God's (i.e., Christ's) wounds  **102 An** if; **baffle** hang upside down (a punishment allotted perjured knights)  **105 vocation** calling (with reference to the Puritan stress on a man's being "called" by God to his work)  **107–08 set a match** arranged a robbery  **108 merit** good works (in Puritan doctrine wholly insufficient for salvation)  **110 true** honest  **114 Sack and Sugar** sack sweetened with sugar was particularly the drink of the elderly, but there may be a pun, in this context, on sackcloth, symbol of penance  **123 cozening** cheating  **126 Gad's Hill** a place notorious for holdups on the road from Rochester to London  **127 offerings** for the shrine of Saint Thomas à Becket  **128 vizards** masks  **131 Eastcheap** London street and district

**134 Yedward** dialect form of Edward  **136 chops** "fat-face"  **141 royal** pun on *royal*, a ten-shilling coin; **stand for** (1) pass for (as a coin) (2) contest for (in a robbery)  **151–53 God . . . move** mimicry again of the Puritans, who claimed to act only when the spirit moved in them  **155–56 want countenance** lack protection (royal and aristocratic)  **157 the** sometimes used in the sixteenth century for *thou* and *you*  **157–58 All-hallown summer** Poins compares Falstaff's youthfulness in old age to the belated summer that occurs around All Hallows Day  **162 waylaid** set our trap for  **173 habits** dress  **173–74 appointment** piece of equipment  **177 sirrah** term of address showing great familiarity  **177–78 cases . . . nonce** outer coverings of coarse linen for the purpose  **179 doubt** fear

third, if he fight longer than he sees reason, I'll forswear arms. The virtue of this jest will be the incom-
prehensible° lies that this same fat rogue will tell us
when we meet at supper: how thirty, at least, he fought     185
with; what wards,° what blows, what extremities he
endured; and in the reproof° of this lives the jest.

PRINCE   Well, I'll go with thee. Provide us all things
necessary and meet me tomorrow night° in Eastcheap.
There I'll sup. Farewell.                                   190

POINS   Farewell, my lord.                          *Exit.*

PRINCE
I know you all, and will awhile uphold
The unyoked humor° of your idleness.
Yet herein will I imitate the sun,°
Who doth permit the base contagious° clouds             195
To smother up his beauty from the world,
That, when he please again to be himself,
Being wanted,° he may be more wond'red at
By breaking through the foul and ugly mists
Of vapors that did seem to strangle him.                200
If all the year were playing holidays,
To sport would be as tedious as to work;
But when they seldom come, they wished-for come,
And nothing pleaseth but rare accidents.°
So when this loose behavior I throw off                 205
And pay the debt I never promisèd,
By how much better than my word I am,
By so much shall I falsify men's hopes;°
And, like bright metal on a sullen° ground,
My reformation, glitt'ring o'er my fault,               210
Shall show more goodly and attract more eyes
Than that which hath no foil° to set it off.
I'll so offend to make offense a skill,
Redeeming time° when men think least I will.   *Exit.*


[Scene III. *Windsor. The council chamber.*]


*Enter the* KING, NORTHUMBERLAND, WORCESTER,
HOTSPUR, *Sir Walter* BLUNT, *with others.*

KING
My blood hath been too cold and temperate,
Unapt to stir at these indignities,
And you have found me,° for accordingly
You tread upon my patience; but be sure
I will from henceforth rather be myself,°                5
Mighty and to be feared, than my condition,°

Which hath been smooth as oil, soft as young down,
And therefore lost that title of respect
Which the proud soul ne'er pays but to the proud.

WORCESTER
Our house, my sovereign liege, little deserves          10
The scourge of greatness to be used on it—
And that same greatness too which our own hands
Have holp° to make so portly.°

NORTHUMBERLAND                        My lord—

KING
Worcester, get thee gone, for I do see
Danger and disobedience in thine eye.                   15
O, sir, your presence is too bold and peremptory,
And majesty might never yet endure
The moody frontier° of a servant brow.
You have good leave to leave us: when we need
Your use and counsel, we shall send for you.            20
                         *Exit* WORCESTER.
You were about to speak.

NORTHUMBERLAND        Yea, my good lord.
Those prisoners in your highness' name demanded
Which Harry Percy here at Holmedon took,
Were, as he says, not with such strength denied
As is deliverèd to your majesty.                        25
Either envy,° therefore, or misprision°
Is guilty of this fault, and not my son.

HOTSPUR
My liege, I did deny no prisoners.
But I remember, when the fight was done,
When I was dry with rage and extreme toil,              30
Breathless and faint, leaning upon my sword,
Came there a certain lord, neat and trimly dressed,
Fresh as a bridegroom, and his chin new reaped°
Showed like a stubble land at harvest home.
He was perfumèd like a milliner,                        35
And 'twixt his finger and his thumb he held
A pouncet box,° which ever and anon
He gave his nose, and took't away again;
Who° therewith angry, when it next came there,
Took it in snuff;° and still he smiled and talked;      40
And as the soldiers bore dead bodies by,
He called them untaught knaves, unmannerly,
To bring a slovenly unhandsome corse°
Betwixt the wind and his nobility.
With many holiday and lady° terms                       45
He questioned° me, amongst the rest demanded
My prisoners in your majesty's behalf.
I then, all smarting with my wounds being cold,
To be so pest'red with a popingay,°
Out of my grief° and my impatience                      50
Answered neglectingly, I know not what—
He should, or he should not; for he made me mad
To see him shine so brisk, and smell so sweet,
And talk so like a waiting gentlewoman

183–84 **incomprehensible** unlimited   186 **wards** strategies
of defense (in swordsmanship)   187 **reproof** disproof   189
**tomorrow night** they will meet for the robbery tomorrow
morning, but Hal is thinking ahead to the jest on Falstaff
that night   193 **unyoked humor** undisciplined inclinations
194 **sun** royalty's traditional symbol   195 **contagious clouds**
were thought to breed pestilence   198 **wanted** lacked, missed
204 **rare accidents** unexpected or uncommon events   208
**hopes** expectations   209 **sullen** dull   212 **foil** contrasting
background   214 **Redeeming time** making amends (Hal
alludes to Ephesians 5:7 ff., which bears in a general way on
much that has been said in this scene: "Be not ye therefore
partakers with them, for ye were sometimes darkness, but
now are ye light in the Lord: walk as children of light. . . .
See then that ye walk circumspectly, not as fools, but as wise;
redeeming the time, because the days are evil.")
**I.iii.3 found me** found me out   **5 myself** what I am as king
**6 my condition** what I am by nature

13 **holp** helped; **portly** stately   18 **frontier** rampart (as
if Worcester were an enemy fortress)   26 **envy** malice;
**misprision** misapprehension   33 **reaped** i.e., with the
closely clipped beard of a man of fashion   37 **pouncet
box** perfume box   39 **Who** his nose   40 **Took . . . snuff**
proverbial, meaning "took offense," but here with pun on
"snuffing" the perfume   43 **corse** corpse   45 **holiday and
lady** fastidious and effeminate   46 **questioned** talked to
49 **popingay** parrot (here, one who is gaudy in dress and
chatters emptily)   50 **grief** pain

Of guns and drums and wounds—God save the
  mark!°—                                                    55
And telling me the sovereignest° thing on earth
Was parmacity° for an inward bruise,
And that it was great pity, so it was,
This villainous saltpeter should be digged
Out of the bowels of the harmless earth,            60
Which many a good tall° fellow had destroyed
So cowardly, and but for these vile guns,
He would himself have been a soldier.
This bald unjointed chat of his, my lord,
I answered indirectly,° as I said,                      65
And I beseech you, let not his report
Come current° for an accusation
Betwixt my love and your high majesty.

BLUNT
The circumstance considerèd, good my lord,
Whate'er Lord Harry Percy then had said       70
To such a person, and in such a place,
At such a time, with all the rest retold,
May reasonably die, and never rise
To do him wrong,° or any way impeach
What then he said, so° he unsay it now.           75

KING
Why, yet he doth deny his prisoners,
But with proviso and exception,
That we at our own charge shall ransom straight
His brother-in-law, the foolish Mortimer;
Who, on my soul, hath willfully betrayed       80
The lives of those that he did lead to fight
Against that great magician, damned Glendower—
Whose daughter, as we hear, that Earl of March
Hath lately married. Shall our coffers, then,
Be emptied to redeem a traitor home?             85
Shall we buy treason, and indent° with fears°
When they have lost and forfeited themselves?
No, on the barren mountains let him starve!
For I shall never hold that man my friend
Whose tongue shall ask me for one penny cost    90
To ransom home revolted Mortimer.

HOTSPUR
Revolted Mortimer?
He never did fall off, my sovereign liege,
But by the chance of war. To prove that true
Needs no more but one tongue for all those wounds,  95
Those mouthèd wounds,° which valiantly he took
When on the gentle Severn's sedgy bank,
In single opposition hand to hand,
He did confound° the best part of an hour
In changing hardiment° with great Glendower.   100
Three times they breathed,° and three times did they
  drink,

Upon agreement, of swift Severn's flood;
Who° then affrighted with their bloody looks
Ran fearfully among the trembling reeds
And hid his crisp° head in the hollow bank,      105
Bloodstainèd with these valiant combatants.
Never did bare and rotten policy°
Color° her working with such deadly wounds;
Nor never could the noble Mortimer
Receive so many, and all willingly.                   110
Then let not him be slanderèd with revolt.°

KING
Thou dost belie° him, Percy, thou dost belie him!
He never did encounter with Glendower.
I tell thee, he durst as well have met the devil alone
As Owen Glendower for an enemy.               115
Art thou not ashamed? But, sirrah,° henceforth
Let me not hear you speak of Mortimer.
Send me your prisoners with the speediest means,
Or you shall hear in such a kind from me
As will displease you. My Lord Northumberland,  120
We license your departure with your son.
Send us your prisoners, or you will hear of it.
        *Exit* KING [*with* BLUNT *and* TRAIN].

HOTSPUR
And if° the devil come and roar for them,
I will not send them. I will after straight
And tell him so, for I will ease my heart,         125
Albeit I make a hazard of° my head.

NORTHUMBERLAND
What, drunk with choler?° Stay, and pause awhile.
Here comes your uncle.

    *Enter* WORCESTER.

HOTSPUR                           Speak of Mortimer?
Zounds, I will speak of him, and let my soul
Want mercy if I do not join with him!             130
Yea, on his part I'll empty all these veins,
And shed my dear blood drop by drop in the dust,
But I will lift the downtrod Mortimer
As high in the air as this unthankful king,
As this ingrate and cank'red° Bolingbroke.°     135

NORTHUMBERLAND
Brother, the king hath made your nephew mad.

WORCESTER
Who struck this heat up after I was gone?

HOTSPUR
He will forsooth have all my prisoners;
And when I urged the ransom once again
Of my wife's brother, then his cheek looked pale,  140
And on my face he turned an eye of death,
Trembling even at the name of Mortimer.

WORCESTER
I cannot blame him. Was not he proclaimed
By Richard that dead is, the next of blood?°

NORTHUMBERLAND
He was, I heard the proclamation:                    145

---

55 **God . . . mark** a ritual phrase originally used to invoke a
blessing, but here expressing scorn  56 **sovereignest** best
57 **parmacity** spermaceti (medicinal substance found in sperm
whales)  61 **tall** stalwart  65 **indirectly** absently  67 **Come
current** (1) be accepted (as of true coin) (2) intrude  74 **To . . .
wrong** to be held against him  75 **so** provided  86 **indent**
bargain; **fears** (1) cowards (2) traitors, i.e., those who by
"fear" have yielded to the enemy and so become traitors
"to be feared"  96 **mouthèd wounds** wounds that speak for
him (based on the likeness of a bloody flesh wound to a mouth)
99 **confound** spend  100 **changing hardiment** battling
101 **breathed** paused for breath

103 **Who** the river  105 **crisp** used punningly to mean
both "curled" (of a man's head) and "rippling" (of a river);
"head" also refers punningly to a river's force  107 **policy**
cunning  108 **Color** (1) disguise (2) redden (i.e., with blood)
111 **revolt** treason  112 **belie** misrepresent  116 **sirrah** term
of address to an inferior, here insulting  123 **And if** if  126
**make . . . of** risk  127 **choler** anger  135 **cank'red** infected;
**Bolingbroke** the king  144 **next of blood** heir to the throne

And then it was when the unhappy king
(Whose wrongs in us° God pardon!) did set forth
Upon his Irish expedition;
From whence he intercepted° did return
To be deposed, and shortly murderèd. 150

WORCESTER
And for whose death we in the world's wide mouth
Live scandalized and foully spoken of.

HOTSPUR
But soft, I pray you, did King Richard then
Proclaim my brother Edmund Mortimer
Heir to the crown?

NORTHUMBERLAND    He did, myself did hear it. 155

HOTSPUR
Nay, then I cannot blame his cousin king,
That wished him on the barren mountains starve.
But shall it be that you, that set the crown
Upon the head of this forgetful man,
And for his sake wear the detested blot 160
Of murderous subornation°—shall it be
That you a world of curses undergo,
Being the agents or base second means,
The cords, the ladder, or the hangman rather?
O, pardon me that I descend so low 165
To show the line° and the predicament°
Wherein you range under this subtle king!
Shall it for shame be spoken in these days,
Or fill up chronicles in time to come,
That men of your nobility and power 170
Did gage° them both in an unjust behalf
(As both of you, God pardon it, have done)
To put down Richard, that sweet lovely rose,
And plant this thorn, this canker° Bolingbroke?
And shall it in more shame be further spoken 175
That you are fooled, discarded, and shook off
By him for whom these shames ye underwent?
No, yet time serves wherein you may redeem
Your banished honors and restore yourselves
Into the good thoughts of the world again; 180
Revenge the jeering and disdained contempt
Of this proud king, who studies day and night
To answer all the debt he owes to you
Even with the bloody payment of your deaths.
Therefore I say—

WORCESTER      Peace, cousin, say no more; 185
And now I will unclasp a secret book,
And to your quick-conceiving° discontents
I'll read you matter deep and dangerous,
As full of peril and adventurous spirit
As to o'erwalk a current roaring loud 190
On the unsteadfast footing of a spear.

HOTSPUR
If he fall in, good night, or sink, or swim!°
Send danger from the east unto the west,
So honor cross it from the north to south,

And let them grapple. O, the blood more stirs 195
To rouse a lion than to start a hare!

NORTHUMBERLAND
Imagination of some great exploit
Drives him beyond the bounds of patience.

HOTSPUR
By heaven, methinks it were an easy leap
To pluck bright honor from the palefaced moon, 200
Or dive into the bottom of the deep,
Where fathom line could never touch the ground,
And pluck up drownèd honor by the locks,
So° he that doth redeem her thence might wear
Without corrival° all her dignities; 205
But out upon this half-faced fellowship!°

WORCESTER
He apprehends a world of figures° here,
But not the form of what he should attend.
Good cousin, give me audience for a while.

HOTSPUR
I cry you mercy.° 210

WORCESTER
Those same noble Scots that are your prisoners—

HOTSPUR
I'll keep them all.
By God, he shall not have a Scot of them!
No, if a Scot° would save his soul, he shall not.
I'll keep them, by this hand!

WORCESTER      You start away 215
And lend no ear unto my purposes.
Those prisoners you shall keep.

HOTSPUR      Nay, I will! That's flat!
He said he would not ransom Mortimer,
Forbade my tongue to speak of Mortimer,
But I will find him when he lies asleep, 220
And in his ear I'll hollo "Mortimer."
Nay, I'll have a starling shall be taught to speak
Nothing but "Mortimer," and give it him
To keep his anger still in motion.

WORCESTER
Hear you, cousin, a word. 225

HOTSPUR
All studies° here I solemnly defy°
Save how to gall and pinch this Bolingbroke;
And that same sword-and-buckler° Prince of Wales,
But that I think his father loves him not
And would be glad he met with some mischance, 230
I would have him poisonèd with a pot of ale.°

WORCESTER
Farewell, kinsman: I'll talk to you
When you are better tempered to attend.

NORTHUMBERLAND
Why, what a wasp-stung and impatient fool
Art thou to break into this woman's mood, 235
Tying thine ear to no tongue but thine own!

---

**147 in us** at our hands   **149 intercepted** interrupted   **161 murderous subornation** confederacy in murder   **166 line** degree, station (but also "hangman's rope" [cf. line 164] and "tether" [cf. line 167]);   **predicament** category (but also "perilous position")   **171 gage** pledge   **174 canker** dog-rose (an inferior rose, but with suggestions of "cankerworm" and "ulcer")   **187 quick-conceiving** eagerly responsive   **192 good . . . swim** the man is doomed whether he sinks at once or is swept away by the current

**204 So** provided   **205 corrival** partner   **206 out . . . fellowship** down with this half-and-half sharing (of honors)   **207 figures** (1) figures of speech (2) airy fancies (as opposed to substantial "form" line 208)   **210 cry you mercy** beg your pardon   **214 Scot** pun on *scot*, meaning "small payment"   **226 studies** interest;   **defy** reject   **228 sword-and-buckler** "low-down" (sword and shield were arms of the lower classes)   **231 ale** a further glance at Hal's presumed low tastes, gentlemen's drink being wine

HOTSPUR
Why, look you, I am whipped and scourged with rods,
Nettled, and stung with pismires,° when I hear
Of this vile politician, Bolingbroke.
In Richard's time—what do you call the place?          240
A plague upon it! It is in Gloucestershire;
'Twas where the madcap duke his uncle kept,°
His uncle York—where I first bowed my knee
Unto this king of smiles, this Bolingbroke—
'Sblood!—when you and he came back from Ravens-
    purgh°—                                           245
NORTHUMBERLAND
At Berkeley Castle.
HOTSPUR
You say true.
Why, what a candy deal° of courtesy
This fawning greyhound then did proffer me!
"Look when his infant fortune came to age,"         250
And "gentle Harry Percy," and "kind cousin"—
O, the devil take such cozeners!°—God forgive me!
Good uncle, tell your tale; I have done.
WORCESTER
Nay, if you have not, to it again.
We will stay your leisure.
HOTSPUR                          I have done, i' faith.   255
WORCESTER
Then once more to your Scottish prisoners:
Deliver them up without their ransom straight,
And make the Douglas' son your only mean
For powers in Scotland—which, for divers reasons
Which I shall send you written, be assured           260
Will easily be granted. [*To* NORTHUMBERLAND.]
    You, my lord,
Your son in Scotland being thus employed,
Shall secretly into the bosom creep
Of that same noble prelate well-beloved,
The Archbishop.
HOTSPUR                 Of York, is it not?            265
WORCESTER
True; who bears hard°
His brother's death at Bristow,° the Lord Scroop.
I speak not this in estimation,°
As what I think might be, but what I know
Is ruminated, plotted, and set down,                 270
And only stays but to behold the face
Of that occasion that shall bring it on.
HOTSPUR
I smell it.° Upon my life, it will do well.
NORTHUMBERLAND
Before the game is afoot thou still let'st slip.°
HOTSPUR
Why, it cannot choose but be a noble plot.           275
And then the power of Scotland and of York
To join with Mortimer, ha?
WORCESTER                     And so they shall.

HOTSPUR
In faith, it is exceedingly well aimed.
WORCESTER
And 'tis no little reason bids us speed
To save our heads by raising of a head;°            280
For, bear ourselves as even as we can,
The king will always think him in our debt,
And think we think ourselves unsatisfied,
Till he hath found a time to pay us home.°
And see already how he doth begin                    285
To make us strangers to his looks of love.
HOTSPUR
He does, he does! We'll be revenged on him.
WORCESTER
Cousin, farewell. No further go in this
Than I by letters shall direct your course.
When time is ripe, which will be suddenly,°          290
I'll steal to Glendower and Lord Mortimer,
Where you and Douglas, and our pow'rs at once,
As I will fashion it, shall happily meet,
To bear our fortunes in our own strong arms,
Which now we hold at much uncertainty.               295
NORTHUMBERLAND
Farewell, good brother. We shall thrive, I trust.
HOTSPUR
Uncle, adieu. O, let the hours be short
Till fields and blows and groans applaud our sport!
                                        *Exeunt.*

# [ A C T  I I ]

[Scene I. *Rochester. An inn yard.*]

*Enter a* CARRIER *with a lantern in his hand.*

FIRST CARRIER  Heigh-ho! An it be not four by the
day,° I'll be hanged. Charles' wain° is over the new
chimney, and yet our horse not packed. What, ostler!
OSTLER [*Within.*]  Anon, anon.
FIRST CARRIER  I prithee, Tom, beat° Cut's saddle,    5
put a few flocks in the point;° poor jade is wrung in
the withers° out of all cess.°

*Enter another* CARRIER.

SECOND CARRIER  Peas and beans are as dank here as
a dog, and that is the next° way to give poor jades the
bots.° This house is turned upside down since Robin   10
Ostler died.
FIRST CARRIER  Poor fellow never joyed since the
price of oats rose; it was the death of him.
SECOND CARRIER  I think this be the most villainous
house in all London road for fleas, I am stung like a   15
tench.°

**238 pismires** ants  **242 kept** dwelt  **245 Ravenspurgh**
harbor in Yorkshire (where Hotspur's father had gone to
take sides with Bolingbroke—who was returning from exile
on the Continent—against the absent King Richard II)  **248
candy deal** sugared bit  **252 cozeners** cheats (with pun on
"cousin" of previous line)  **266 bears hard** because his brother
had been executed by Henry  **267 Bristow** Bristol  **268 in
estimation** as a guess  **273 smell it** i.e., like a hound catching
the scent  **274 let'st slip** let loose (the dogs)

**280 head** army  **284 home** with a "home" thrust  **290
suddenly** speedily
**II.i.1–2 by the day** in the morning  **2 Charles' wain** the
Great Bear  **5 beat** i.e., to soften it  **6 a few . . . point** a
little padding in the pommel  **6–7 wrung . . . withers**
rubbed raw at the shoulders  **7 out . . . cess** to excess  **9 next**
nearest  **10 bots** worms  **16 tench** fish with red spots (as if
flea-bitten)

FIRST CARRIER  Like a tench? By the mass, there is ne'er a king christen could be better bit than I have been° since the first cock.°

SECOND CARRIER  Why, they will allow us ne'er a 20 jordan,° and then we leak in your chimney,° and your chamber-lye° breeds fleas like a loach.°

FIRST CARRIER  What, ostler! Come away and be hanged! Come away!

SECOND CARRIER  I have a gammon° of bacon and 25 two razes° of ginger, to be delivered as far as Charing Cross.

FIRST CARRIER  God's body! The turkeys in my pannier° are quite starved. What, ostler! A plague on thee, hast thou never an eye in thy head? Canst not 30 hear? And 'twere not as good deed as drink to break the pate on thee, I am a very villain. Come, and be hanged! Hast no faith in thee?

*Enter* GADSHILL.

GADSHILL  Good morrow, carriers, what's o'clock?

FIRST CARRIER  I think it be two o'clock.                    35

GADSHILL  I prithee lend me thy lantern to see my gelding in the stable.

FIRST CARRIER  Nay, by God, soft!° I know a trick worth two of that, i' faith.

GADSHILL  I pray thee lend me thine.                         40

SECOND CARRIER  Ay, when? Canst tell?° Lend me thy lantern, quoth he? Marry, I'll see thee hanged first!

GADSHILL  Sirrah carrier, what time do you mean to come to London?

SECOND CARRIER  Time enough to go to bed with a 45 candle,° I warrant thee. Come, neighbor Mugs, we'll call up the gentlemen, they will along with company, for they have great charge.°      *Exeunt* [CARRIERS].

GADSHILL  What, ho! Chamberlain!

*Enter* CHAMBERLAIN.

CHAMBERLAIN  "At hand,° quoth pickpurse."       50

GADSHILL  That's even as fair as "at hand, quoth the chamberlain"; for thou variest no more from picking of purses than giving direction doth from laboring: thou layest the plot how.

CHAMBERLAIN  Good morrow, Master Gadshill. It 55 holds current° that I told you yesternight: there's a franklin° in the Wild of Kent° hath brought three hundred marks° with him in gold, I heard him tell it to one of his company last night at supper—a kind of auditor,° one that hath abundance of charge too, God 60 knows what. They are up already and call for eggs and butter, they will away presently.

GADSHILL  Sirrah, if they meet not with Saint Nicholas' clerks,° I'll give thee this neck.

CHAMBERLAIN  No, I'll none of it; I pray thee keep 65 that for the hangman; for I know thou worshippest Saint Nicholas as truly as a man of falsehood may.

GADSHILL  What talkest thou to me of the hangman? If I hang, I'll make a fat pair of gallows; for if I hang, old Sir John hangs with me, and thou knowest he is no 70 starveling. Tut! There are other Troyans° that thou dream'st not of, the which for sport sake are content to do the profession some grace; that would (if matters should be looked into) for their own credit sake make all whole. I am joined with no foot-landrakers,° no 75 long-staff sixpenny strikers,° none of these mad mustachio purple-hued maltworms;° but with nobility and tranquillity,° burgomasters and great oneyers,° such as can hold in,° such as will strike sooner than speak,° and speak sooner than drink, and drink sooner 80 than pray—and yet, zounds, I lie, for they pray continually to their saint, the commonwealth, or rather, not pray to her, but prey on her, for they ride up and down on her and make her their boots.°

CHAMBERLAIN  What, the commonwealth their 85 boots? Will she hold out water in foul way?°

GADSHILL  She will, she will! Justice hath liquored° her. We steal as in a castle, cocksure. We have the receipt of fernseed,° we walk invisible.

CHAMBERLAIN  Nay, by my faith, I think you are 90 more beholding to the night than to fernseed for your walking invisible.

GADSHILL  Give me thy hand. Thou shalt have a share in our purchase,° as I am a true man.

CHAMBERLAIN  Nay, rather let me have it, as you are 95 a false thief.

GADSHILL  Go to; 'homo' is a common name to all men.° Bid the ostler bring my gelding out of the stable. Farewell, you muddy knave.      [*Exeunt.*]

[Scene II. *The highway, near Gad's Hill.*]

*Enter* PRINCE, POINS, *and* PETO, *etc.*

POINS  Come, shelter, shelter! I have removed Falstaff's horse, and he frets° like a gummed velvet.

PRINCE  Stand close.

[*They step aside.*]

*Enter* FALSTAFF.

**63–64 Saint Nicholas' clerks** highwaymen (Saint Nicholas was reckoned the patron of all travelers, including traveling thieves) **71 Troyans** good fellows **75 foot-landrakers** footloose vagabonds **76 long-staff . . . strikers** men who would pull you from your horse with long staves even to steal sixpence **77 mustachio . . . maltworms** big-mustached purple-faced drunkards **78 tranquillity** Gadshill's witty coinage, on the analogy of "nobility": people who don't have to scrounge their living; **oneyers** ones (?) **79 hold in** keep confidence **80 speak** say "hands up" **84 boots** with pun on *boots/booty* **86 in foul way** on muddy roads **87 liquored** (1) greased (as with boots) (2) made her drunk **89 receipt of fernseed** recipe of fernseed (popularly supposed to render one invisible) **94 purchase** euphemism for loot **97–98 homo . . . men** the Latin for man, *homo* is a term that covers all men, true (i.e., honest) or false
**II.ii.2 frets** chafes (with pun on the fretting or fraying of velvet as the gum used to stiffen it wore away)

**17–19 there . . . been** not even a Christian king (though kings get the best of everything) could have surpassed my record in fleabites **19 the first cock** midnight **21 jordan** chamberpot; **chimney** fireplace **22 chamber-lye** urine; **loach** fish that breeds often **25 gammon** haunch **26 razes** roots **29 pannier** basket **38 soft** "listen to him!" **41 Ay . . . tell** standard retort to an inopportune request **45–46 Time . . . candle** evasively spoken, the carriers being suspicious of Gadshill **48 charge** luggage **50 At hand** a popular tag meaning "Ready, sir!" but relevant here to the Chamberlain's filching way of life, as Gadshill points out **56 current** true **57 franklin** rich farmer; **Wild of Kent** name of a room at the inn (*wild = weald*, open country) **57–58 three hundred marks** £200 (Elizabethan value) **60 auditor** revenue officer

FALSTAFF  Poins! Poins, and be hanged! Poins!

PRINCE  [*Comes forward.*]  Peace, ye fat-kidneyed 5
rascal! What a brawling dost thou keep!

FALSTAFF  Where's Poins, Hal?

PRINCE  He is walked up to the top of the hill; I'll go
seek him.

[*Steps aside.*]

FALSTAFF  I am accursed to rob in that thief's company. 10
The rascal hath removed my horse and tied him I
know not where. If I travel but four foot by the
squire° further afoot, I shall break my wind. Well, I
doubt not but to die a fair death for all this, if I scape
hanging for killing that rogue. I have forsworn his 15
company hourly any time this two and twenty years,
and yet I am bewitched with the rogue's company. If
the rascal have not given me medicines to make me
love him, I'll be hanged. It could not be else: I have
drunk medicines. Poins! Hal! A plague upon you 20
both! Bardolph! Peto! I'll starve° ere I'll rob a foot
further. And 'twere not as good a deed as drink to
turn true man and to leave these rogues, I am the
veriest varlet that ever chewed with a tooth. Eight
yards of uneven ground is threescore and ten miles 25
afoot with me, and the stony-hearted villains know it
well enough. A plague upon it when thieves cannot be
true one to another! (*They whistle.*) Whew! A plague
upon you all! Give me my horse, you rogues! Give
me my horse and be hanged! 30

PRINCE [*Comes forward.*]  Peace, ye fat-guts! Lie down,
lay thine ear close to the ground, and list if thou canst
hear the tread of travelers.

FALSTAFF  Have you any levers to lift me up again,
being down? 'Sblood, I'll not bear mine own flesh so 35
far afoot again for all the coin in thy father's exchequer.
What a plague mean ye to colt° me thus?

PRINCE  Thou liest, thou art not colted, thou art
uncolted.°

FALSTAFF  I prithee, good Prince Hal, help me to my 40
horse, good king's son.

PRINCE  Out, ye rogue! Shall I be your ostler?

FALSTAFF  Hang thyself in thine own heir-apparent
garters!° If I be ta'en, I'll peach° for this. And I have
not ballads made on you all, and sung to filthy tunes, 45
let a cup of sack be my poison. When a jest is so
forward—and afoot too—I hate it.

*Enter* GADSHILL [*and* BARDOLPH].

GADSHILL  Stand!

FALSTAFF  So I do, against my will.

POINS  O, 'tis our setter;° I know his voice. [*Comes* 50
*forward.*] Bardolph, what news?

BARDOLPH  Case ye, case ye! On with your vizards!
There's money of the king's coming down the hill;
'tis going to the king's exchequer.

FALSTAFF  You lie, ye rogue! 'Tis going to the king's 55
tavern.

GADSHILL  There's enough to make us all—

FALSTAFF  To be hanged.

PRINCE  Sirs, you four shall front them in the narrow
lane; Ned Poins and I will walk lower; if they scape 60
from your encounter, then they light on us.

PETO  How many be there of them?

GADSHILL  Some eight or ten.

FALSTAFF  Zounds, will they not rob us?

PRINCE  What, a coward, Sir John Paunch? 65

FALSTAFF  Indeed, I am not John of Gaunt° your
grandfather, but yet no coward, Hal.

PRINCE  Well, we leave that to the proof.°

POINS  Sirrah Jack, thy horse stands behind the hedge.
When thou need'st him, there thou shalt find him. 70
Farewell and stand fast.

FALSTAFF  Now cannot I strike him, if I should be
hanged.

PRINCE [*Aside to* POINS.]  Ned, where are our disguises? 75

POINS [*Aside to* PRINCE.]  Here, hard by. Stand close.
[*Exeunt* PRINCE *and* POINS.]

FALSTAFF  Now, my masters, happy man be his dole,°
say I. Every man to his business.

*Enter the* TRAVELERS.

TRAVELER  Come, neighbor. The boy shall lead our
horses down the hill; we'll walk afoot awhile and ease 80
our legs.

THIEVES  Stand!

TRAVELER  Jesus bless us!

FALSTAFF  Strike! Down with them! Cut the villains'
throats! Ah, whoreson caterpillars!° Bacon-fed 85
knaves! They hate us youth. Down with them!
Fleece them!

TRAVELER  O, we are undone, both we and ours
forever!

FALSTAFF  Hang ye, gorbellied° knaves, are ye 90
undone? No, ye fat chuffs;° I would your store° were
here! On, bacons, on! What, ye knaves, young men
must live. You are grandjurors,° are ye? We'll jure ye,
faith!       *Here they rob them and bind them. Exeunt.*

*Enter the* PRINCE *and* POINS [*disguised*].

PRINCE  The thieves have bound the true men. Now 95
could thou and I rob the thieves and go merrily to
London, it would be argument° for a week, laughter
for a month, and a good jest forever.

POINS  Stand close! I hear them coming.

[*They stand aside.*]

*Enter the thieves again.*

FALSTAFF  Come, my masters, let us share, and then to 100
horse before day. And the prince and Poins be not
two arrant° cowards, there's no equity stirring.°
There's no more valor in that Poins than in a wild
duck.

13 **squire** rule  21 **starve** die  37 **colt** trick  39 **uncolted**
unhorsed  43–44 **heir-apparent garters** Falstaff adapts a proverbial phrase to fit a crown prince  44 **peach** inform on you
50 **setter** one who makes arrangements for a robbery

66 **John of Gaunt** Hal's grandfather (but in reply to "Sir John
Paunch" Falstaff puns on *gaunt/thin* which Hal evidently is [cf.
II.iv.226–50])  68 **proof** test  77 **happy . . . dole** may happiness be our lot  85 **whoreson caterpillars** miserable parasites
90 **gorbellied** great-bellied  91 **chuffs** misers; **store** total
wealth  93 **grandjurors** men of substance (as required for
service on a grand jury)  97 **be argument** make conversation  102 **arrant** thorough; **no equity stirring** no justice left
alive

*As they are sharing, the Prince and Poins set upon them. They all run away, and Falstaff, after a blow or two, runs away too, leaving the booty behind them.*

PRINCE   Your money!    105
POINS   Villains!

PRINCE   Got with much ease. Now merrily to horse. The thieves are all scattered, and possessed with fear so strongly that they dare not meet each other: each takes his fellow for an officer. Away, good Ned. 110 Falstaff sweats to death and lards the lean earth as he walks along. Were't not for laughing, I should pity him.°

POINS   How the fat rogue roared!      *Exeunt.*

---

[Scene III. *Northumberland. Warkworth Castle.*]

*Enter* HOTSPUR *solus,° reading a letter.*

HOTSPUR   "But, for mine own part, my lord, I could be well contented to be there, in respect of the love I bear your house."° He could be contented—why is he not then? In respect of the love he bears our house! He shows in this he loves his own barn better than he 5 loves our house. Let me see some more. "The purpose you undertake is dangerous"—why, that's certain! 'Tis dangerous to take a cold, to sleep, to drink; but I tell you, my lord fool, out of this nettle, danger, we pluck this flower, safety. "The purpose you undertake 10 is dangerous, the friends you have named uncertain, the time itself unsorted,° and your whole plot too light for the counterpoise of so great an opposition." Say you so, say you so? I say unto you again, you are a shallow, cowardly hind,° and you lie. What a lack- 15 brain is this! By the Lord, our plot is a good plot as ever was laid; our friends true and constant: a good plot, good friends, and full of expectation; an excellent plot, very good friends. What a frosty-spirited rogue is this! Why, my Lord of York° commends the plot 20 and the general course of the action. Zounds, and I were now by this rascal, I could brain him with his lady's fan. Is there not my father, my uncle, and myself; Lord Edmund Mortimer, my Lord of York, and Owen Glendower? Is there not, besides, the Douglas? 25 Have I not all their letters to meet me in arms by the ninth of the next month, and are they not some of them set forward already? What a pagan° rascal is this, an infidel! Ha! you shall see now, in very sincerity of fear and cold heart will he to the king and lay open 30 all our proceedings. O, I could divide myself and go to buffets° for moving such a dish of skim milk with so honorable an action! Hang him, let him tell the king! We are prepared. I will set forward tonight.

*Enter his* LADY.

How now, Kate? I must leave you within these two 35 hours.

LADY   O my good lord, why are you thus alone? For what offense have I this fortnight been A banished woman from my Harry's bed? Tell me, sweet lord, what is't that takes from thee 40 Thy stomach,° pleasure, and thy golden sleep? Why dost thou bend thine eyes upon the earth, And start so often when thou sit'st alone? Why hast thou lost the fresh blood in thy cheeks And given my treasures and my rights of thee 45 To thick-eyed musing and cursed° melancholy? In thy faint slumbers I by thee have watched,° And heard thee murmur tales of iron wars, Speak terms of manage to thy bounding steed, Cry "Courage! To the field!" And thou hast talked 50 Of sallies and retires, of trenches, tents, Of palisadoes,° frontiers,° parapets, Of basilisks,° of cannon, culverin,° Of prisoners' ransom, and of soldiers slain, And all the currents° of a heady° fight. 55 Thy spirit within thee hath been so at war, And thus hath so bestirred thee in thy sleep, That beads of sweat have stood upon thy brow Like bubbles in a late-disturbèd stream, And in thy face strange motions have appeared, 60 Such as we see when men restrain their breath On some great sudden hest.° O, what portents are these? Some heavy business hath my lord in hand, And I must know it, else he loves me not.

HOTSPUR   What, ho!

[*Enter a* SERVANT.]

Is Gilliams with the packet gone? 65
SERVANT   He is, my lord, an hour ago.
HOTSPUR   Hath Butler brought those horses from the sheriff?
SERVANT   One horse, my lord, he brought even now.
HOTSPUR   What horse? A roan, a crop-ear, is it not? 70
SERVANT   It is, my lord.
HOTSPUR   That roan shall be my throne. Well, I will back him straight. O Esperance!° Bid Butler lead him forth into the park.°      [*Exit* SERVANT.]
LADY   But hear you, my lord. 75
HOTSPUR   What say'st thou, my lady?
LADY   What is it carries you away?°
HOTSPUR   Why, my horse, my love—my horse!
LADY   Out, you mad-headed ape! A weasel hath not such a deal of spleen° as you are tossed with. In faith, 80 I'll know your business, Harry, that I will! I fear my brother Mortimer doth stir about his title and hath sent for you to line° his enterprise; but if you go°—

---

41 **stomach** appetite   46 **cursed** peevish   47 **watched** lain awake   52 **palisadoes** defenses made of stakes; **frontiers** fortifications   53 **basilisks, culverin** sizes and types of cannon   55 **currents** occurrences; **heady** violent   62 **hest** (1) command (?) (2) resolution (?)   73 **Esperance** hope (part of the Percy motto)   72-74 **That . . . park** Pope and many later editors print as verse, with line breaks after "throne/Esperance/park"   77 **away** (1) from home (2) from your usual self   80 **spleen** caprice   83 **line** strengthen   79-83 **Out . . . go** printed by Pope and many later editors as verse, but with a variety of lineations

107-13 **Got . . . him** printed as verse by Pope and many later editors, with line breaks after "horse/fear/other/officer/death/along/him"
**II.iii.s.d. solus** alone (Latin)   3 **house** family   12 **unsorted** unsuitable   15 **hind** menial   20 **Lord of York** Archbishop of York (cf. I.iii.264 ff.)   28 **pagan** faithless   31-32 **divide . . . buffets** split myself into two, and set the halves fighting

HOTSPUR   So far afoot, I shall be weary, love.

LADY   Come, come, you paraquito,° answer me   85
directly unto this question that I ask. In faith, I'll break
thy little finger, Harry, and if thou wilt not tell me all
things true.°

HOTSPUR
Away, away, you trifler! Love? I love thee not;
I care not for thee, Kate. This is no world   90
To play with mammets° and to tilt° with lips.
We must have bloody noses and cracked crowns,°
And pass them current too. Gods me,° my horse!
What say'st thou, Kate? What wouldst thou have
    with me?

LADY
Do you not love me? Do you not indeed?   95
Well, do not then; for since you love me not,
I will not love myself. Do you not love me?
Nay, tell me if you speak in jest or no.

HOTSPUR
Come, wilt thou see me ride?
And when I am a-horseback, I will swear   100
I love thee infinitely. But hark you, Kate:
I must not have you henceforth question me
Whither I go, nor reason whereabout.
Whither I must, I must, and—to conclude,
This evening must I leave you, gentle Kate.   105
I know you wise—but yet no farther wise
Than Harry Percy's wife; constant you are—
But yet a woman; and for secrecy,
No lady closer—for I well believe
Thou wilt not utter what thou dost not know,   110
And so far will I trust thee, gentle Kate—

LADY   How? So far?

HOTSPUR
Not an inch further. But hark you, Kate:
Whither I go, thither shall you go too;
Today will I set forth, tomorrow you.   115
Will this content you, Kate?

LADY                         It must of force.°

                                            *Exeunt.*

[Scene IV. *Eastcheap. The tavern.°*]

*Enter* PRINCE *and* POINS.

PRINCE   Ned, prithee come out of that fat° room and
lend me thy hand to laugh a little.

POINS   Where hast been, Hal?

PRINCE   With three or four loggerheads° amongst
three or fourscore hogsheads. I have sounded the very   5
bass-string of humility. Sirrah, I am sworn brother to
a leash° of drawers° and can call them all by their

christen names, as Tom, Dick, and Francis. They
take it already upon their salvation° that, though I
be but Prince of Wales, yet I am the king of courtesy,   10
and tell me flatly I am no proud Jack° like Falstaff,
but a Corinthian,° a lad of mettle, a good boy (by the
Lord, so they call me!), and when I am King of
England I shall command all the good lads in Eastcheap. They call drinking deep, dyeing scarlet;° and   15
when you breathe in your watering,° they cry "hem!"
and bid you play it off.° To conclude, I am so good
a proficient in one quarter of an hour that I can drink
with any tinker in his own language during my life.
I tell thee, Ned, thou hast lost much honor that thou   20
wert not with me in this action. But, sweet Ned—
to sweeten which name of Ned, I give thee this
pennyworth of sugar,° clapped even now into my
hand by an under-skinker,° one that never spake
other English in his life than "Eight shillings and   25
sixpence," and "You are welcome," with this shrill
addition, "Anon,° anon, sir! Score° a pint of bastard°
in the Half-moon,"° or so—but, Ned, to drive away
the time till Falstaff come, I prithee do thou stand in
some by-room while I question my puny drawer to   30
what end he gave me the sugar; and do thou never
leave calling "Francis!" that his tale to me may be
nothing but "Anon!" Step aside, and I'll show thee a
precedent.°

POINS   Francis!   35

PRINCE   Thou art perfect.

POINS   Francis!

[POINS *steps aside.*]

*Enter* [FRANCIS, *a*] *drawer.*

FRANCIS   Anon, anon, sir. Look down into the
Pomgarnet,° Ralph.

PRINCE   Come hither, Francis.   40

FRANCIS   My lord?

PRINCE   How long hast thou to serve,° Francis?

FRANCIS   Forsooth, five years, and as much as to—

POINS [*Within.*]   Francis!

FRANCIS   Anon, anon, sir.   45

PRINCE   Five year! By'r Lady,° a long lease for the
clinking of pewter. But, Francis, darest thou be so
valiant as to play the coward with thy indenture° and
show it a fair pair of heels and run from it?

FRANCIS   O Lord, sir, I'll be sworn upon all the books   50
in England I could find in my heart—

POINS [*Within.*]   Francis!

FRANCIS   Anon, sir.

PRINCE   How old art thou, Francis?

FRANCIS   Let me see: about Michaelmas° next I shall   55
be—

POINS [*Within.*]   Francis!

---

85 **paraquito** parrot   85–88 **Come . . . true** printed by
Pope and many later editors as verse, with line breaks after
"me/ask/Harry/true"   91 **mammets** dolls; **tilt** duel   92
**crowns** (1) heads (2) coins—which when "cracked" were hard
to "pass current" (possibly there is an allusion to the "crown"
of kingship, which, though not genuine when usurped,
may be passed current by force)   93 **Gods me** God save me
116 **of force** of necessity
**II.iv.s.d. tavern** the tavern is said to be in Eastcheap, but it is
never explicitly named; references to a boar in *2 Henry IV*
suggest it is the Boar's Head   1 **fat** hot   4 **loggerheads**
blockheads   7 **leash** trio; **drawers** tapsters

9 **take . . . salvation** pledge their salvation   11 **Jack** fellow   12
**Corinthian** gay blade   15 **dyeing scarlet** i.e., from the complexion it gives a man   16 **breathe . . . watering** pause for
breath while drinking   17 **play it off** down it   23 **sugar**
for sweetening wine (cf. I.ii.114)   24 **under-skinker** under-
tapster   27 **Anon** (I'm coming) at once; **Score** charge;
**bastard** Spanish wine   28 **Half-moon** one of the inn's
rooms   34 **precedent** example   39 **Pomgarnet** Pomegranate
(another of the inn's rooms)   42 **serve** as an apprentice
(apprenticeship ran for seven years)   46 **By'r Lady** by Our
Lady (mild oath)   48 **indenture** contract   55 **Michaelmas**
September 29

FRANCIS   Anon, sir. Pray stay a little, my lord.

PRINCE   Nay, but hark you, Francis. For the sugar thou gavest me—'twas a pennyworth, was't not?    60

FRANCIS   O Lord! I would it had been two!

PRINCE   I will give thee for it a thousand pound. Ask me when thou wilt, and thou shalt have it.

POINS [*Within.*]   Francis!

FRANCIS   Anon, anon.    65

PRINCE   Anon, Francis?° No, Francis; but tomorrow, Francis; or, Francis, a Thursday; or indeed, Francis, when thou wilt. But, Francis—

FRANCIS   My lord?

PRINCE   Wilt thou rob this leathern-jerkin, crystal- 70 button, not-pated, agate-ring, puke-stocking, caddis-garter, smooth-tongue, Spanish-pouch?°

FRANCIS   O Lord, sir, who do you mean?

PRINCE   Why then, your brown bastard is your only drink; for look you, Francis, your white canvas 75 doublet will sully. In Barbary, sir, it cannot come to so much.°

FRANCIS   What, sir?

POINS [*Within.*]   Francis!

PRINCE   Away, you rogue! Dost thou not hear them 80 call?

*Here they both call him. The drawer stands amazed, not knowing which way to go.*

*Enter* VINTNER.°

VINTNER   What, stand'st thou still, and hear'st such a calling? Look to the guests within.   [*Exit* FRANCIS.] My lord, old Sir John, with half a dozen more, are at the door. Shall I let them in?    85

PRINCE   Let them alone awhile, and then open the door. [*Exit* VINTNER.] Poins!

POINS [*Within.*]   Anon, anon, sir.

*Enter* POINS.

PRINCE   Sirrah, Falstaff and the rest of the thieves are at the door. Shall we be merry?    90

POINS   As merry as crickets, my lad. But hark ye; what cunning match have you made with this jest of the drawer? Come, what's the issue?°

PRINCE   I am now of all humors that have showed themselves humors since the old days of goodman 95 Adam to the pupil age of this present twelve o'clock at midnight.°

[*Enter* FRANCIS.]

What's o'clock, Francis?

FRANCIS   Anon, anon, sir.          [*Exit.*]

PRINCE   That ever this fellow should have fewer 100

words than a parrot, and yet the son of a woman! His industry is upstairs and downstairs, his eloquence the parcel of a reckoning.° I am not yet of Percy's mind, the Hotspur of the North: he that kills me some six or seven dozen of Scots at a breakfast, washes his hands, 105 and says to his wife, "Fie upon this quiet life! I want work." "O my sweet Harry," says she, "how many hast thou killed today?" "Give my roan horse a drench,"° says he, and answers "Some fourteen," an hour after, "a trifle, a trifle." I prithee call in Falstaff. 110 I'll play Percy, and that damned brawn° shall play Dame Mortimer his wife. "Rivo!"° says the drunkard. Call in Ribs, call in Tallow.

*Enter* FALSTAFF, [GADSHILL, BARDOLPH, *and* PETO; FRANCIS *follows with wine*].

POINS   Welcome, Jack. Where hast thou been?

FALSTAFF   A plague of° all cowards, I say, and a 115 vengeance too! Marry and amen! Give me a cup of sack, boy. Ere I lead this life long, I'll sew netherstocks,° and mend them and foot them too. A plague of all cowards! Give me a cup of sack, rogue. Is there no virtue extant?    120

*He drinketh.*

PRINCE   Didst thou never see Titan° kiss a dish of butter (pitiful-hearted Titan!) that melted at the sweet tale of the sun's? If thou didst, then behold that compound.

FALSTAFF   You rogue, here's lime° in this sack too! 125 There is nothing but roguery to be found in villainous man. Yet a coward is worse than a cup of sack with lime in it—a villainous coward! Go thy ways, old Jack, die when thou wilt; if manhood, good manhood, be not forgot upon the face of the earth, then am I a 130 shotten herring.° There lives not three good men unhanged in England; and one of them is fat, and grows old. God help the while! A bad world, I say. I would I were a weaver; I could sing psalms° or anything. A plague of all cowards, I say still!    135

PRINCE   How now, woolsack? What mutter you?

FALSTAFF   A king's son! If I do not beat thee out of thy kingdom with a dagger of lath° and drive all thy subjects afore thee like a flock of wild geese, I'll never wear hair on my face more. You Prince of Wales?    140

PRINCE   Why, you whoreson round man, what's the matter?

FALSTAFF   Are not you a coward? Answer me to that —and Poins there?

---

**66 Anon, Francis** Hal pretends to take Francis' "anon"— at once—to Poins as meaning he wants the thousand pounds at once   **70–72 this . . . Spanish-pouch** the innkeeper, whose middle-class appearance Hal details: leather jacket with crystal buttons, short hair, agate ring, wool stockings, plain worsted (not fancy) garters, ingratiating (and probably unctuous) speech, money pouch of Spanish leather   **74–77 Why . . . much** semi-nonsense; but the implication seems clear that Francis must stick to his trade   **81 s.d. Vintner** the innkeeper   **93 issue** outcome, point (of the jest)   **94–97 I . . . midnight** I am ready for every kind of gaiety that men have invented since the beginning of the world

**101–03 His industry . . . reckoning** his whole activity is running up and down stairs, his whole conversation the totaling of bills   **109 drench** dose of medicine   **111 brawn** fat boar   **112 Rivo** drinking cry of uncertain meaning   **115 of** on   **117 netherstocks** stockings   **121 Titan** the sun (of which Hal is possibly reminded by Falstaff's broad face, and his melting effect on the sack)   **125 lime** added to make poor wine seem dry and clear   **131 shotten herring** herring that has cast its roe (and is therefore long and lean)   **133–34 God . . . psalms** Falstaff reassumes his role of comic Puritan: English weavers were often psalm-singing Protestants who had fled from the Roman Catholic Continent   **138 dagger of lath** wooden dagger (by this phrase Falstaff associates himself with a character called "the Vice" in the old religious plays, who drove the devil offstage by beating him with a wooden dagger)

POINS    Zounds, ye fat paunch, and ye call me coward, 145
by the Lord, I'll stab thee.

FALSTAFF    I call thee coward? I'll see thee damned ere I
call thee coward, but I would give a thousand pound
I could run as fast as thou canst. You are straight
enough in the shoulders; you care not who sees your 150
back. Call you that backing of your friends? A plague
upon such backing, give me them that will face me.
Give me a cup of sack. I am a rogue if I drunk today.

PRINCE    O villain, thy lips are scarce wiped since thou
drunk'st last.    155

FALSTAFF    All is one for that. (*He drinketh.*) A plague
of all cowards, still say I.

PRINCE    What's the matter?

FALSTAFF    What's the matter? There be four of us
here have ta'en a thousand pound this day morning.    160

PRINCE    Where is it, Jack, where is it?

FALSTAFF    Where is it? Taken from us it is. A hundred
upon poor four of us!

PRINCE    What, a hundred, man?

FALSTAFF    I am a rogue if I were not at half-sword° 165
with a dozen of them two hours together. I have
scaped by miracle. I am eight times thrust through the
doublet,° four through the hose;° my buckler cut
through and through; my sword hacked like a handsaw—ecce signum!° I never dealt° better since I was a 170
man. All would not do. A plague of all cowards! Let
them speak. If they speak more or less than truth, they
are villains and the sons of darkness.°

PRINCE    Speak, sirs. How was it?

GADSHILL    We four set upon some dozen—    175

FALSTAFF    Sixteen at least, my lord.

GADSHILL    And bound them.

PETO    No, no, they were not bound.

FALSTAFF    You rogue, they were bound, every man of
them, or I am a Jew else—an Ebrew Jew.    180

GADSHILL    As we were sharing, some six or seven
fresh men set upon us—

FALSTAFF    And unbound the rest, and then come in the
other.°

PRINCE    What, fought you with them all?    185

FALSTAFF    All? I know not what you call all, but if I
fought not with fifty of them, I am a bunch of radish!°
If there were not two or three and fifty° upon poor
old Jack, then am I no two-legged creature.

PRINCE    Pray God you have not murd'red some of 190
them.

FALSTAFF    Nay, that's past praying for. I have peppered two of them. Two I am sure I have paid,° two
rogues in buckram suits. I tell thee what, Hal—if I tell
thee a lie, spit in my face, call me horse. Thou knowest 195
my old ward:° here I lay, and thus I bore my point.
Four rogues in buckram let drive at me.

PRINCE    What, four? Thou said'st but two even now.

FALSTAFF    Four, Hal. I told thee four.

POINS    Ay, ay, he said four.    200

FALSTAFF    These four came all afront and mainly°
thrust at me. I made me no more ado but took all their
seven points in my target, thus.

PRINCE    Seven? Why, there were but four even now.

FALSTAFF    In buckram?    205

POINS    Ay, four, in buckram suits.

FALSTAFF    Seven, by these hilts, or I am a villain else.

PRINCE [*Aside to* POINS.]    Prithee let him alone. We
shall have more anon.

FALSTAFF    Dost thou hear me, Hal?    210

PRINCE    Ay, and mark° thee too, Jack.

FALSTAFF    Do so, for it is worth the list'ning to. These
nine in buckram that I told thee of—

PRINCE    So, two more already.

FALSTAFF    Their points being broken—    215

POINS    Down fell their hose.°

FALSTAFF    Began to give me ground; but I followed
me close, came in, foot and hand, and with a thought°
seven of the eleven I paid.

PRINCE    O monstrous! Eleven buckram men grown 220
out of two!

FALSTAFF    But, as the devil would have it, three misbegotten knaves in Kendal green came at my back and
let drive at me; for it was so dark, Hal, that thou
couldest not see thy hand.    225

PRINCE    These lies are like their father that begets them
—gross as a mountain, open, palpable. Why, thou
clay-brained guts, thou knotty-pated° fool, thou
whoreson obscene greasy tallow-catch°—

FALSTAFF    What, art thou mad? Art thou mad? Is not 230
the truth the truth?

PRINCE    Why, how couldst thou know these men in
Kendal green when it was so dark thou couldst not see
thy hand? Come, tell us your reason. What sayest thou
to this?    235

POINS    Come, your reason, Jack, your reason.

FALSTAFF    What, upon compulsion? Zounds, and I
were at the strappado° or all the racks in the world, I
would not tell you on compulsion. Give you a reason
on compulsion? If reasons° were as plentiful as 240
blackberries, I would give no man a reason upon
compulsion, I.

PRINCE    I'll be no longer guilty of this sin; this
sanguine° coward, this bed-presser, this horseback-
breaker, this huge hill of flesh—    245

FALSTAFF    'Sblood, you starveling, you eelskin, you
dried neat's-tongue,° you bull's pizzle,° you stockfish°
—O for breath to utter what is like thee!—you tailor's
yard, you sheath, you bowcase, you vile standing
tuck!°    250

---

165 at half-sword infighting at close quarters  168 doublet
Elizabethan upper garment; hose Elizabethan breeches  170
ecce signum behold the evidence (Latin; spoken as he shows
his sword); dealt dealt blows  173 sons of darkness i.e.,
damned (but cf. also I.ii.24)  184 other others  187 bunch
of radish again an object long and lean  188 three and
fifty fifty-three was the number of Spanish ships popularly
reputed to have opposed Sir Richard Grenville at the battle
of the Azores in 1591; Falstaff thus humorously claims for
his fight the status of a national epic  193 paid settled with
196 ward fencing posture

201 mainly mightily  211 mark pay close attention to  216
Down . . . hose Poins wittily takes "points" in the sense of
laces holding the breeches to the doublet  218 with a thought
quick as a thought  228 knotty-pated blockheaded  229
tallow-catch (1) pan to catch drippings under roasting meat
(?) (2) tallow-keech, roll of fat for making candles (?)  238
strappado instrument of torture  240 reasons pronounced
like "raisins," and hence comparable to blackberries  244
sanguine ruddy (and hence valorous-seeming)  247 neat's
tongue ox-tongue; pizzle penis; stockfish dried codfish
249–50 standing tuck upright rapier

PRINCE   Well, breathe awhile, and then to it again; and when thou hast tired thyself in base comparisons, hear me speak but this.

POINS   Mark, Jack.

PRINCE   We two saw you four set on four, and bound 255 them and were masters of their wealth. Mark now how a plain tale shall put you down. Then did we two set on you four and, with a word,° outfaced you from your prize, and have it; yea, and can show it you here in the house. And, Falstaff, you carried your 260 guts away as nimbly, with as quick dexterity, and roared for mercy, and still run and roared, as ever I heard bullcalf. What a slave art thou to hack thy sword as thou hast done, and then say it was in fight! What trick, what device, what starting hole° canst 265 thou now find out to hide thee from this open and apparent shame?

POINS   Come, let's hear, Jack. What trick hast thou now?

FALSTAFF   By the Lord, I knew ye as well as he that 270 made ye. Why, hear you, my masters. Was it for me to kill the heir apparent? Should I turn upon the true prince? Why, thou knowest I am as valiant as Hercules, but beware instinct. The lion will not touch the true prince.° Instinct is a great matter. I was now a coward 275 on instinct. I shall think the better of myself, and thee, during my life—I for a valiant lion, and thou for a true prince. But, by the Lord, lads, I am glad you have the money. Hostess, clap to the doors. Watch tonight, pray tomorrow.° Gallants, lads, boys, hearts of gold, 280 all the titles of good fellowship come to you! What, shall we be merry? Shall we have a play extempore?

PRINCE   Content—and the argument° shall be thy running away.

FALSTAFF   Ah, no more of that, Hal, and thou lovest 285 me!

*Enter* HOSTESS.

HOSTESS   O Jesu, my lord the prince!

PRINCE   How now, my lady the hostess? What say'st thou to me?

HOSTESS   Marry, my lord, there is a nobleman of the 290 court at door would speak with you. He says he comes from your father.

PRINCE   Give him as much as will make him a royal man,° and send him back again to my mother.

FALSTAFF   What manner of man is he?                          295

HOSTESS   An old man.

FALSTAFF   What doth gravity° out of his bed at midnight? Shall I give him his answer?

PRINCE   Prithee do, Jack.

FALSTAFF   Faith, and I'll send him packing.        *Exit.* 300

PRINCE   Now, sirs. By'r Lady, you fought fair; so did you, Peto; so did you, Bardolph. You are lions too,

you ran away upon instinct, you will not touch the true prince; no—fie!

BARDOLPH   Faith, I ran when I saw others run.        305

PRINCE   Faith, tell me now in earnest, how came Falstaff's sword so hacked?

PETO   Why, he hacked it with his dagger, and said he would swear truth out of England but he would make you believe it was done in fight, and persuaded us to 310 do the like.

BARDOLPH   Yea, and to tickle our noses with speargrass to make them bleed, and then to beslubber our garments with it and swear it was the blood of true men. I did that° I did not this seven year before—I 315 blushed to hear his monstrous devices.

PRINCE   O villain Thou stolest a cup of sack eighteen years ago and wert taken with the manner,° and ever since thou hast blushed extempore. Thou hadst fire° and sword on thy side, and yet thou ran'st away. 320 What instinct hadst thou for it?

BARDOLPH   My lord, do you see these meteors?° Do you behold these exhalations?°

PRINCE   I do.

BARDOLPH   What think you they portend?              325

PRINCE   Hot livers and cold purses.°

BARDOLPH   Choler,° my lord, if rightly taken.

PRINCE   No, if rightly taken, halter.

*Enter* FALSTAFF.

Here comes lean Jack; here comes bare-bone. How now, my sweet creature of bombast?° How long is't 330 ago, Jack, since thou sawest thine own knee?

FALSTAFF   My own knee? When I was about thy years, Hal, I was not an eagle's talent° in the waist; I could have crept into any alderman's thumb-ring. A plague of sighing and grief, it blows a man up like a 335 bladder. There's villainous news abroad. Here was Sir John Bracy from your father: you must to the court in the morning. That same mad fellow of the north, Percy, and he of Wales that gave Amamon the bastinado, and made Lucifer cuckold, and swore the 340 devil his true liegeman upon the cross of a Welsh hook°—what a plague call you him?

POINS   Owen Glendower.

FALSTAFF   Owen, Owen—the same; and his son-in-law Mortimer, and old Northumberland, and that 345 sprightly Scot of Scots, Douglas, that runs a-horseback up a hill perpendicular—

PRINCE   He that rides at high speed and with his pistol kills a sparrow flying.

FALSTAFF   You have hit it.                               350

PRINCE   So did he never the sparrow.

---

**315 that** what    **318 taken . . . manner** caught with the goods **319 fire** the alcoholic hue of Bardolph's face    **322, 323 meteors, exhalations** the pimples and other features of Bardolph's face, spoken of as if they were meteorological portents    **326 Hot . . . purses** the two notable results of excessive drink **327 Choler** anger (Bardolph implies that he is choleric, and therefore no coward; Hal proceeds to understand "choler" as "collar," which in Bardolph's case will be—"if rightly taken"—the hangman's noose)    **330 bombast** cotton stuffing **333 talent** talon    **339-42 he . . . hook** Falstaff alludes to Glendower's supposed magical powers: he has cudgeled a devil named Amamon, made horns grow on Lucifer, and forced the devil to swear allegiance to him on the cross of a weapon that has no cross

---

**258 with a word** (1) in brief (?) (2) with a mere shout to scare you (?)    **265 starting hole** hiding place    **274-75 lion . . . prince** a traditional belief about lions    **279-80 Watch . . . tomorrow** cf. Matthew 26:41, "Watch and pray, that ye enter not into temptation"; Falstaff puns on *watch*, which means "carouse" as well as "keep vigil"    **283 argument** subject **293-94 royal man** cf. "noble" in the previous speech, but with a pun on *royal*, a coin worth ten shillings, which was of greater value than the *noble*, worth six shillings eight pence **297 gravity** sober age

**FALSTAFF**  Well, that rascal hath good metal° in him;
he will not run.

**PRINCE**  Why, what a rascal art thou then, to praise
him so for running!                                                                          355

**FALSTAFF**  A-horseback, ye cuckoo! But afoot he will
not budge a foot.

**PRINCE**  Yes, Jack, upon instinct.

**FALSTAFF**  I grant ye, upon instinct. Well, he is there
too, and one Mordake, and a thousand bluecaps° more.    360
Worcester is stol'n away tonight; thy father's beard is
turned white with the news; you may buy land now as
cheap as stinking mack'rel.

**PRINCE**  Why then, it is like, if there come a hot June,
and this civil buffeting hold, we shall buy maidenheads    365
as they buy hobnails, by the hundreds.°

**FALSTAFF**  By the mass, lad, thou sayest true; it is like
we shall have good trading that way. But tell me, Hal,
art not thou horrible afeard? Thou being heir apparent,
could the world pick thee out three such enemies again    370
as that fiend Douglas, that spirit Percy, and that devil
Glendower? Art thou not horribly afraid? Doth not
thy blood thrill° at it?

**PRINCE**  Not a whit, i' faith. I lack some of thy instinct.

**FALSTAFF**  Well, thou wilt be horribly chid tomorrow    375
when thou comest to thy father. If thou love me,
practice an answer.

**PRINCE**  Do thou stand for my father and examine me
upon the particulars of my life.

**FALSTAFF**  Shall I? Content. This chair shall be my    380
state,° this dagger my scepter, and this cushion my
crown.

**PRINCE**  Thy state is taken for° a joined-stool, thy
golden scepter for a leaden dagger, and thy precious
rich crown for a pitiful bald crown.                                          385

**FALSTAFF**  Well, and the fire of grace be not quite out
of thee, now shalt thou be moved. Give me a cup of
sack to make my eyes look red, that it may be thought
I have wept; for I must speak in passion, and I will do
it in King Cambyses' vein.°                                                         390

**PRINCE**  Well, here is my leg.

**FALSTAFF**  And here is my speech. Stand aside,
nobility.°

**HOSTESS**  O Jesu, this is excellent sport, i' faith!

**FALSTAFF**
Weep not, sweet queen,° for trickling tears are vain.    395

**HOSTESS**  O, the Father, how he holds his countenance!°

**FALSTAFF**
For God's sake, lords, convey my tristful° queen!
For tears do stop the floodgates of her eyes.

**HOSTESS**  O Jesu, he doth it as like one of these    400
harlotry° players as ever I see!

**FALSTAFF**  Peace, good pintpot. Peace, good tickle-
brain. Harry, I do not only marvel where thou spendest
thy time, but also how thou art accompanied. For
though the camomile,° the more it is trodden on, the    405
faster it grows, so° youth, the more it is wasted, the
sooner it wears. That thou art my son I have partly
thy mother's word, partly my own opinion, but
chiefly a villainous trick° of thine eye and a foolish
hanging of thy nether lip that doth warrant me. If    410
then thou be son to me, here lies the point: why,
being son to me, art thou so pointed at? Shall the
blessed sun of heaven prove a micher and eat blackberries?° A question not to be asked. Shall the son°
of England prove a thief and take purses? A question    415
to be asked. There is a thing, Harry, which thou hast
often heard of, and it is known to many in our land by
the name of pitch. This pitch (as ancient writers do
report) doth defile; so doth the company thou keepest.
For, Harry, now I do not speak to thee in drink, but in    420
tears; not in pleasure, but in passion; not in words only,
but in woes also: and yet there is a virtuous man whom
I have often noted in thy company, but I know not his
name.

**PRINCE**  What manner of man, and it like your    425
majesty?

**FALSTAFF**  A goodly portly° man, i' faith, and a corpulent;° of a cheerful look, a pleasing eye, and a most
noble carriage; and, as I think, his age some fifty, or,
by'r Lady, inclining to threescore; and now I re-    430
member me, his name is Falstaff. If that man should
be lewdly given,° he deceiveth me; for, Harry, I see
virtue in his looks. If then the tree may be known by
the fruit,° as the fruit by the tree, then, peremptorily°
I speak it, there is virtue in that Falstaff. Him keep    435
with, the rest banish. And tell me now, thou naughty
varlet, tell me where hast thou been this month?

**PRINCE**  Dost thou speak like a king? Do thou stand
for me, and I'll play my father.

**FALSTAFF**  Depose me? If thou dost it half so gravely,    440
so majestically, both in word and matter, hang me up
by the heels for a rabbit-sucker° or a poulter's hare.

**PRINCE**  Well, here I am set.

**FALSTAFF**  And here I stand. Judge, my masters.

**PRINCE**  Now, Harry, whence come you?                              445

**FALSTAFF**  My noble lord, from Eastcheap.

**PRINCE**  The complaints I hear of thee are grievous.

**FALSTAFF**  'Sblood, my lord, they are false! Nay, I'll
tickle ye for a young prince,° i' faith.

---

**352 good metal** with pun on *mettle* (spirit, courage)  **360
bluecaps** Scots  **364–66 if . . . hundreds** the prince applies
the analogy of selling cheap what won't keep to the reactions of virgins as they see all the men going off to war
**373 thrill** shiver (with fear)  **381 state** chair of state  **383
taken for** either "seen to be merely," or, alternatively, this is a
meditative comment, possibly an aside, in the detached vein
of I.ii.192 and II.iv.486, with "thy" referring to the king
**390 King Cambyses' vein** the old ranting style of Preston's
*King Cambyses* (1569)  **393 nobility** addressed to his motley
ragamuffins  **395 queen** addressed to the Hostess, who is
evidently tearful with laughter; probably with a standard pun
on *quean* = tart, prostitute  **396–97 holds his countenance**
keep a straight face  **398 tristful** sad

**401 harlotry** rascally  **405 camomile** aromatic herb (Falstaff
proceeds to satirize the highflown style of the court by using
a manner of speech called euphuism—from John Lyly's
fictional narrative, *Euphues* [1578], which introduced it—
based on similes drawn from natural history, intricate balance,
antithesis, and repetition of sounds, words, and ideas)  **406 so**
some editors emend to "yet," but the imperfect logical correspondence of "though . . . so" may be part of Falstaff's
mockery  **409 trick** mannerism (possibly a twitch)  **413–14
prove . . . blackberries** be a truant from duty and go
blackberrying  **414 son** with pun on *sun*, the royal symbol
**427 portly** stately  **427–28 corpulent** well filled out  **432
lewdly given** inclined to evildoing  **433–34 If . . . fruit**
cf. Matthew 12:33, "The tree is known by his fruit"  **434
peremptorily** decisively  **442 rabbit-sucker** suckling rabbit
**448–49 I'll . . . prince** I'll act a prince that will amuse you

PRINCE   Swearest thou, ungracious boy? Henceforth 450
ne'er look on me. Thou art violently carried away
from grace. There is a devil haunts thee in the likeness
of an old fat man; a tun° of man is thy companion.
Why dost thou converse with that trunk of humors,°
that bolting-hutch° of beastliness, that swoll'n parcel 455
of dropsies,° that huge bombard° of sack, that stuffed
cloakbag of guts, that roasted Manningtree° ox with
the pudding in his belly, that reverend vice,° that gray
iniquity,° that father ruffian,° that vanity° in years?
Wherein is he good, but to taste sack and drink it? 460
Wherein neat and cleanly, but to carve a capon and
eat it? Wherein cunning, but in craft?° Wherein
crafty, but in villainy? Wherein villainous, but in all
things? Wherein worthy, but in nothing?

FALSTAFF   I would your grace would take me with 465
you.° Whom means your grace?

PRINCE   That villainous abominable misleader of
youth, Falstaff, that old white-bearded Satan.

FALSTAFF   My lord, the man I know.

PRINCE   I know thou dost. 470

FALSTAFF   But to say I know more harm in him than
in myself were to say more than I know. That he is
old, the more the pity, his white hairs do witness it;
but that he is, saving your reverence, a whoremaster,
that I utterly deny. If sack and sugar be a fault, God 475
help the wicked! If to be old and merry be a sin, then
many an old host that I know is damned. If to be fat
be to be hated, then Pharaoh's lean kine° are to be
loved. No, my good lord: banish Peto, banish
Bardolph, banish Poins; but for sweet Jack Falstaff, 480
kind Jack Falstaff, true Jack Falstaff, valiant Jack Falstaff,
and therefore more valiant being, as he is, old Jack
Falstaff, banish not him thy Harry's company, banish
not him thy Harry's company, banish plump Jack, and
banish all the world! 485

PRINCE   I do, I will.      [*A knocking heard. Exeunt*
HOSTESS, FRANCIS, *and* BARDOLPH.]

*Enter* BARDOLPH, *running.*

BARDOLPH   O, my lord, my lord! The sheriff with a
most monstrous watch° is at the door.

FALSTAFF   Out, ye rogue! Play out the play, I have
much to say in the behalf of that Falstaff. 490

*Enter the* HOSTESS.

HOSTESS   O Jesu, my lord, my lord!

PRINCE   Heigh, heigh, the devil rides upon a fiddlestick! What's the matter?

HOSTESS   The sheriff and all the watch are at the door.
They are come to search the house. Shall I let them in? 495

453 **tun** hogshead   454 **trunk of humors** receptacle of body
fluids (with allusion to the diseases that were thought to be the
product of these fluids)   455 **bolting-hutch** sifting-bin (where
impurities collect)   456 **dropsies** internal fluids; **bombard**
leather wine vessel   457 **Manningtree** town in Essex (where at
annual fairs plays were acted and, evidently, great oxen were
stuffed and barbecued)   458–59 **vice . . . iniquity . . .
ruffian . . . vanity** names intended to associate Falstaff with
characters of the old morality plays, all of whom were corrupters
of virtue; but unlike Falstaff, who ought to know better, *they*
were young   462 **Wherein . . . craft** wherein skillful
but in underhanded skills   465–66 **take . . . you** let me
follow your meaning   478 **kine** cows (cf. Genesis 41:19–21)
488 **watch** group of constables

FALSTAFF   Dost thou hear, Hal? Never call a true
piece of gold a counterfeit. Thou art essentially made
without seeming so.°

PRINCE   And thou a natural coward without instinct.

FALSTAFF   I deny your major.° If you will deny the 500
sheriff, so; if not, let him enter. If I become not a cart°
as well as another man, a plague on my bringing up!
I hope I shall as soon be strangled with a halter as
another.

PRINCE   Go hide thee behind the arras.° The rest walk 505
up above. Now, my masters, for a true face and good
conscience.

FALSTAFF   Both which I have had; but their date is
out, and therefore I'll hide me.       *Exit.*

PRINCE   Call in the sheriff. 510
         [*Exeunt all but the* PRINCE *and* PETO.]

*Enter* SHERIFF *and the* CARRIER.

Now, master sheriff, what is your will with me?

SHERIFF
First, pardon me, my lord. A hue and cry
Hath followed certain men unto this house.

PRINCE   What men?

SHERIFF
One of them is well known, my gracious lord— 515
A gross fat man

CARRIER          As fat as butter.

PRINCE
The man, I do assure you, is not here,
For I myself at this time have employed him.°
And, sheriff, I will engage my word to thee
That I will by tomorrow dinner time 520
Send him to answer thee, or any man,
For anything he shall be charged withal;
And so let me entreat you leave the house.

SHERIFF
I will, my lord. There are two gentlemen
Have in this robbery lost three hundred marks. 525

PRINCE
It may be so. If he have robbed these men,
He shall be answerable; and so farewell.

SHERIFF
Good night, my noble lord.

PRINCE
I think it is good morrow, is it not?

SHERIFF
Indeed, my lord, I think it be two o'clock. 530
         *Exit* [*with* CARRIER].

PRINCE   This oily rascal is known as well as Paul's. Go
call him forth.

PETO   Falstaff! Fast asleep behind the arras, and snort-
ing° like a horse.

PRINCE   Hark how hard he fetches breath. Search his 535
pockets.

*He searcheth his pocket and findeth certain papers.*

496–98 **Never . . . so** a difficult passage, perhaps meaning
that Falstaff, as a true piece of gold despite appearances,
should not be turned over to the sheriff by a royal friend who
is also true gold despite appearances   500 **major** major
premise, with pun on *mayor*   501 **cart** hangman's cart   505
**arras** wall-hanging   517–18 **The . . . him** Hal's reply is
equivocal: Falstaff is not "here," in the heir-apparent's
presence, but "employed" behind the arras   533–34 **snorting**
snoring

What hast thou found?

PETO   Nothing but papers, my lord.

PRINCE   Let's see what they be. Read them.

[PETO *reads*.]

"Item, A capon   .   .   .   .   .   . 2s. 2d.   540
Item, Sauce   .   .   .   .   . 4d.
Item, Sack two gallons.   .   .   . 5s. 8d.
Item, Anchovies and sack after supper   . 2s. 6d.
Item, Bread   .   .   .   .   . ob."°

PRINCE   O monstrous! But one halfpennyworth of 545
bread to this intolerable deal° of sack! What there is
else, keep close; we'll read it at more advantage. There
let him sleep till day. I'll to the court in the morning.
We must all to the wars, and thy place shall be honorable. I'll procure this fat rogue a charge of foot,° and 550
I know his death will be a march of twelve score.°
The money shall be paid back again with advantage.°
Be with me betimes° in the morning, and so good
morrow, Peto.

PETO   Good morrow, good my lord.          *Exeunt.* 555


# [ A C T   I I I ]

[Scene I. *Wales. A room.*]

*Enter* HOTSPUR, WORCESTER, *Lord* MORTIMER,
*Owen* GLENDOWER.

MORTIMER
These promises are fair, the parties sure,
And our induction° full of prosperous hope.

HOTSPUR   Lord Mortimer, and cousin Glendower,
will you sit down? And uncle Worcester. A plague
upon it! I have forgot the map.                            5

GLENDOWER   No, here it is. Sit, cousin Percy, sit,
good cousin Hotspur, for by that name as oft as
Lancaster doth speak of you, his cheek looks pale, and
with a rising sigh he wisheth you in heaven.

HOTSPUR   And you in hell, as oft as he hears Owen 10
Glendower spoke of.°

GLENDOWER
I cannot blame him. At my nativity
The front of heaven was full of fiery shapes
Of burning cressets,° and at my birth
The frame and huge foundation of the earth          15
Shakèd like a coward.

HOTSPUR   Why, so it would have done at the same
season if your mother's cat had but kittened, though
yourself had never been born.

GLENDOWER
I say the earth did shake when I was born.           20

HOTSPUR
And I say the earth was not of my mind,
If you suppose as fearing you it shook.

GLENDOWER
The heavens were all on fire, the earth did tremble.

HOTSPUR
O, then the earth shook to see the heavens on fire,
And not in fear of your nativity.                      25
Diseasèd nature oftentimes breaks forth
In strange eruptions; oft the teeming earth
Is with a kind of colic pinched and vexed
By the imprisoning of unruly wind
Within her womb, which, for enlargement striving,   30
Shakes the old beldame° earth and topples down
Steeples and mossgrown towers. At your birth
Our grandam earth, having this distemp'rature,°
In passion° shook.

GLENDOWER          Cousin, of many men
I do not bear these crossings. Give me leave          35
To tell you once again that at my birth
The front of heaven was full of fiery shapes,
The goats ran from the mountains, and the herds
Were strangely clamorous to the frighted fields.
These signs have marked me extraordinary,             40
And all the courses of my life do show
I am not in the roll of common men.
Where is he living, clipped in with° the sea
That chides the banks of England, Scotland, Wales,
Which calls me pupil or hath read to° me?             45
And bring him out that is but woman's son
Can trace° me in the tedious ways of art°
And hold me pace in deep experiments.

HOTSPUR   I think there's no man speaks better Welsh.°
I'll to dinner.                                        50

MORTIMER
Peace, cousin Percy; you will make him mad.

GLENDOWER
I can call spirits from the vasty deep.

HOTSPUR
Why, so can I, or so can any man;
But will they come when you do call for them?

GLENDOWER   Why, I can teach you, cousin, to com-  55
mand the devil.

HOTSPUR
And I can teach thee, coz, to shame the devil—
By telling truth. Tell truth and shame the devil.
If thou have power to raise him, bring him hither,
And I'll be sworn I have power to shame him hence.    60
O, while you live, tell truth and shame the devil!

MORTIMER
Come, come, no more of this unprofitable chat.

GLENDOWER
Three times hath Henry Bolingbroke made head
Against my power; thrice from the banks of Wye
And sandy-bottomed Severn have I sent him             65
Bootéless° home and weather-beaten back.

---

544 **ob.** obolus, halfpenny   546 **deal** lot   550 **charge of
foot** company of infantry   551 **twelve score** twelvescore
paces   552 **advantage** interest   553 **betimes** early
**III.i.2 induction** beginning   3–11 **Lord . . . of** many
editors revise to read as verse, with line breaks after "down/it/
is/Hotspur/you/sigh/hell/of"; or, leaving Hotspur's lines as
prose, revise Glendower's speech to read as verse with breaks
after "Percy/name/you/sigh/heaven"   14 **cressets** beacons

31 **beldame** grandmother (cf. "grandam" in line 33)   33
**distemp'rature** physical disorder   34 **passion** pain   43
**clipped in with** embraced by   45 **read to** tutored   47 **trace**
follow; **art** magic   49 **speaks better Welsh** (1) brags better
(2) talks more unintelligibly   66 **Bootéless** profitless (probably
trisyllabic)

HOTSPUR
Home without boots, and in foul weather too?
How scapes he agues,° in the devil's name?

GLENDOWER
Come, here is the map. Shall we divide our right°
According to our threefold order ta'en?    70

MORTIMER
The archdeacon hath divided it
Into three limits° very equally.
England, from Trent and Severn hitherto,
By south and east is to my part assigned;
All westward, Wales beyond the Severn shore,    75
And all the fertile land within that bound,
To Owen Glendower; and, dear coz, to you
The remnant northward lying off from Trent.
And our indentures tripartite° are drawn,
Which being sealèd interchangeably°    80
(A business that this night may execute),
Tomorrow, cousin Percy, you and I
And my good Lord of Worcester will set forth
To meet your father and the Scottish power,
As is appointed us, at Shrewsbury.    85
My father Glendower is not ready yet,
Nor shall we need his help these fourteen days.

[*To* GLENDOWER.]

Within that space you may have drawn together
Your tenants, friends, and neighboring gentlemen.

GLENDOWER
A shorter time shall send me to you, lords;    90
And in my conduct shall your ladies come,
From whom you now must steal and take no leave,
For there will be a world of water shed
Upon the parting of your wives and you.

HOTSPUR
Methinks my moiety,° north from Burton here,    95
In quantity equals not one of yours.
See how this river comes me cranking° in
And cuts me from the best of all my land
A huge half-moon, a monstrous cantle° out.
I'll have the current in this place dammed up,    100
And here the smug° and silver Trent shall run
In a new channel fair and evenly.
It shall not wind with such a deep indent
To rob me of so rich a bottom° here.

GLENDOWER
Not wind? It shall, it must! You see it doth.    105

MORTIMER   Yea, but mark how he bears his course,
and runs me up with like advantage° on the other side,
gelding the opposèd continent° as much as on the
other side it takes from you.°

WORCESTER
Yea, but a little charge° will trench° him here    110

And on this north side win this cape of land;
And then he runs straight and even.

HOTSPUR
I'll have it so, a little charge will do it.

GLENDOWER
I'll not have it alt'red.

HOTSPUR          Will not you?

GLENDOWER
No, nor you shall not.

HOTSPUR          Who shall say me nay?    115

GLENDOWER
Why, that will I.

HOTSPUR
Let me not understand you then; speak it in Welsh.

GLENDOWER
I can speak English, lord, as well as you;
For I was trained up in the English court,
Where, being but young, I framèd to the harp    120
Many an English ditty lovely well,
And gave the tongue a helpful ornament°—
A virtue that was never seen in you.

HOTSPUR
Marry, and I am glad of it with all my heart!
I had rather be a kitten and cry mew    125
Than one of these same meter ballad-mongers.°
I had rather hear a brazen canstick turned°
Or a dry wheel grate on the axletree,
And that would set my teeth nothing on edge,
Nothing so much as mincing° poetry.    130
'Tis like the forced gait of a shuffling nag.

GLENDOWER
Come, you shall have Trent turned.

HOTSPUR
I do not care. I'll give thrice so much land
To any well-deserving friend;
But in the way of bargain, mark ye me,    135
I'll cavil on the ninth part of a hair.
Are the indentures drawn? Shall we be gone?

GLENDOWER
The moon shines fair; you may away by night.
I'll haste the writer, and withal
Break with° your wives of your departure hence.    140
I am afraid my daughter will run mad,
So much she doteth on her Mortimer.      *Exit.*

MORTIMER
Fie, cousin Percy, how you cross my father!

HOTSPUR
I cannot choose. Sometime he angers me
With telling me of the moldwarp° and the ant,    145
Of the dreamer Merlin and his prophecies,
And of a dragon and a finless fish,
A clip-winged grifin and a moulten raven,
A couching° lion and a ramping° cat,

---

68 **agues** i.e., catching cold   69 **our right** the kingdom they hope to win   72 **limits** regions   79 **indentures tripartite** three-way agreements   80 **interchangeably** i.e., by all three parties   95 **moiety** share   97 **cranking** winding   99 **cantle** piece   101 **smug** smooth   104 **bottom** valley   107 **advantage** disadvantage   108 **gelding . . . continent** cutting out of the opposite bank   106–09 **Yea . . . you** revised by most editors to four or five lines of verse, with little agreement about lineation   110 **charge** cost; **trench** make a new course for

122 **gave . . . ornament** (1) ornamented the words with music (?) (2) benefited the English language by my poems (?) 126 **meter ballad-mongers** singers of doggerel ballads   127 **canstick turned** candlestick in process of being burnished (and therefore raucously scraped)   130 **mincing** affected 140 **Break with** inform   145 **moldwarp** mole, i.e., Henry   149 **couching, ramping** Hotspur ridicules heraldic crouching and rearing beasts; evidently Glendower talked of ancient prophecies which held that the kingdom of the mole should be divided by the lion, dragon and wolf, which were the crests of Percy, Glendower, and Mortimer

And such a deal of skimble-skamble° stuff 150
As puts me from my faith. I tell you what—
He held me last night at least nine hours
In reckoning up the several devils' names
That were his lackeys. I cried "hum," and "Well,
   go to!"
But marked him not a word. O, he is as tedious 155
As a tired horse, a railing wife;
Worse than a smoky house. I had rather live
With cheese and garlic in a windmill far
Than feed on cates° and have him talk to me
In any summer house in Christendom. 160

MORTIMER
In faith, he is a worthy gentleman,
Exceedingly well read and profited
In strange concealments,° valiant as a lion,
And wondrous affable, and as bountiful
As mines of India. Shall I tell you, cousin? 165
He holds your temper in a high respect
And curbs himself even of his natural scope°
When you come 'cross his humor.° Faith, he does.
I warrant you that man is not alive
Might so have tempted him as you have done 170
Without the taste of danger and reproof.
But do not use it oft, let me entreat you.

WORCESTER
In faith, my lord, you are too willful-blame,°
And since your coming hither have done enough
To put him quite besides his patience. 175
You must needs learn, lord, to amend this fault.
Though sometimes it show greatness, courage,
   blood°—
And that's the dearest grace it renders you—
Yet oftentimes it doth present° harsh rage,
Defect of manners, want of government,° 180
Pride, haughtiness, opinion,° and disdain;
The least of which haunting a nobleman
Loseth men's hearts, and leaves behind a stain
Upon the beauty of all parts besides,
Beguiling them of commendation. 185

HOTSPUR
Well, I am schooled. Good manners be your speed!°
Here come our wives, and let us take our leave.

*Enter* GLENDOWER *with the* LADIES.

MORTIMER
This is the deadly spite° that angers me—
My wife can speak no English, I no Welsh.

GLENDOWER
My daughter weeps; she'll not part with you, 190
She'll be a soldier too, she'll to the wars.

MORTIMER
Good father, tell her that she and my aunt Percy
Shall follow in your conduct speedily.

GLENDOWER *speaks to her in Welsh, and she answers
him in the same.*

GLENDOWER
She is desperate here.
A peevish self-willed harlotry,° one that no persuasion 195
can do good upon.

*The* LADY *speaks in Welsh.*

MORTIMER
I understand thy looks. That pretty Welsh°
Which thou pourest down from these swelling
   heavens°
I am too perfect in; and, but for shame,
In such a parley° should I answer thee. 200

*The* LADY *again in Welsh.*

I understand thy kisses, and thou mine,
And that's a feeling disputation.°
But I will never be a truant, love,
Till I have learnt thy language; for thy tongue
Makes Welsh as sweet as ditties highly penned,° 205
Sung by a fair queen in a summer's bow'r,
With ravishing division,° to her lute.

GLENDOWER
Nay, if you melt, then will she run mad.

*The* LADY *speaks again in Welsh.*

MORTIMER
O, I am ignorance itself in this!

GLENDOWER
She bids you on the wanton° rushes lay you down 210
And rest your gentle head upon her lap,
And she will sing the song that pleaseth you
And on your eyelids crown the god of sleep,°
Charming your blood with pleasing heaviness,
Making such difference 'twixt wake and sleep 215
As is the difference betwixt day and night
The hour before the heavenly-harnessed team°
Begins his golden progress in the east.

MORTIMER
With all my heart I'll sit and hear her sing.
By that time will our book,° I think, be drawn. 220

GLENDOWER
Do so, and those musicians that shall play to you
Hang in the air a thousand leagues from hence,
And straight they shall be here: sit, and attend.

HOTSPUR    Come, Kate, thou art perfect in lying down.
Come, quick, quick, that I may lay my head in thy lap. 225

LADY PERCY    Go, ye giddy goose.

*The music plays.*

HOTSPUR
Now I perceive the devil understands Welsh,
And 'tis no marvel he is so humorous,°
By'r Lady, he is a good musician.

LADY PERCY
Then should you be nothing but musical,
For you are altogether governed by humors. 230
Lie still, ye thief, and hear the lady sing in Welsh.

---

150 **skimble-skamble** meaningless   159 **cates** delicacies
162–63 **profited . . . concealments** expert in secret arts   167
**scope** tendencies   168 **come . . . humor** clash with his
temperament   173 **too willful-blame** blamable for too
much willfulness   177 **blood** spirit   179 **present** indicate
180 **government** self-control   181 **opinion** arrogance
186 **be your speed** bring you success   188 **spite** misfortune

195 **harlotry** ninny, fool   197 **That pretty Welsh** her tears
198 **heavens** her eyes   200 **parley** meeting (of tears)   202
**feeling disputation** dialogue by (1) touching (2) the feelings
205 **highly penned** lofty   207 **division** musical variation
210 **wanton** luxurious   213 **crown . . . sleep** give sleep
sovereignty   217 **the heavenly-harnessed team** the horses of
the sun   220 **book** agreement   228 **humorous** capricious

HOTSPUR   I had rather hear Lady, my brach,° howl in Irish.

LADY PERCY   Wouldst thou have thy head broken?   235

HOTSPUR   No.

LADY PERCY   Then be still.

HOTSPUR   Neither! 'Tis a woman's fault.

LADY PERCY   Now God help thee!

HOTSPUR   To the Welsh lady's bed.   240

LADY PERCY   What's that?

HOTSPUR   Peace! She sings.

*Here the* LADY *sings a Welsh song.*

Come, Kate, I'll have your song too.

LADY PERCY   Not mine, in good sooth.°

HOTSPUR   Not yours, in good sooth? Heart, you   245
swear like a comfit-maker's° wife. "Not you, in good
sooth!" and "as true as I live!" and "as God shall mend
me!" and "as sure as day!"
And givest such sarcenet surety° for thy oaths
As if thou never walk'st further than Finsbury.°   250
Swear me, Kate, like a lady as thou art,
A good mouth-filling oath, and leave "in sooth"
And such protest of pepper gingerbread°
To velvet guards° and Sunday citizens.
    Come, sing.

LADY PERCY   I will not sing.   255

HOTSPUR   'Tis the next way to turn tailor° or be
red-breast-teacher.° And the indentures be drawn, I'll
away within these two hours; and so come in when
ye will.            *Exit.*

GLENDOWER

Come, come, Lord Mortimer. You are as slow   260
As hot Lord Percy is on fire to go.
By this our book is drawn; we'll but seal,
And then to horse immediately.

MORTIMER             With all my heart.
                       *Exeunt.*

[Scene II. *London. The palace.*]

*Enter the* KING, PRINCE *of Wales, and others.*

KING

Lords, give us leave: the Prince of Wales and I
Must have some private conference; but be near at
    hand,
For we shall presently have need of you.
                   *Exeunt* LORDS.
I know not whether God will have it so
For some displeasing service I have done,   5
That, in his secret doom,° out of my blood°
He'll breed revengement and a scourge for me;
But thou dost in thy passages° of life

Make me believe that thou art only marked
For the hot vengeance and the rod of heaven   10
To punish my mistreadings.° Tell me else,
Could such inordinate° and low desires,
Such poor, such bare, such lewd, such mean attempts,
Such barren pleasures, rude society,
As thou art matched withal° and grafted to,   15
Accompany the greatness of thy blood
And hold their level with thy princely heart?

PRINCE

So please your majesty, I would I could
Quit° all offenses with as clear excuse
As well° as I am doubtless I can purge   20
Myself of many I am charged withal.
Yet such extenuation let me beg
As, in reproof of many tales devised,
Which oft the ear of greatness needs must hear
By smiling pickthanks and base newsmongers,   25
I may, for some things true wherein my youth
Hath faulty wand'red and irregular,
Find pardon on my true submission.°

KING

God pardon thee! Yet let me wonder, Harry,
At thy affections,° which do hold a wing   30
Quite from the flight of all thy ancestors.
Thy place in council thou hast rudely lost,
Which by thy younger brother is supplied,
And art almost an alien to the hearts
Of all the court and princes of my blood.   35
The hope and expectation of thy time°
Is ruined, and the soul of every man
Prophetically do forethink thy fall.
Had I so lavish of my presence been,
So common-hackneyed in the eyes of men,   40
So stale and cheap to vulgar company,
Opinion,° that did help me to the crown,
Had still kept loyal to possession°
And left me in reputeless banishment,
A fellow of no mark nor likelihood.   45
By being seldom seen, I could not stir
But, like a comet, I was wond'red at;
That men would tell their children, "This is he!"
Others would say, "Where? Which is Bolingbroke?"
And then I stole all courtesy from heaven,°   50
And dressed myself in such humility
That I did pluck allegiance from men's hearts,
Loud shouts and salutations from their mouths
Even in the presence of the crownèd king.
This did I keep my person fresh and new,   55
My presence, like a robe pontifical,
Ne'er seen but wond'red at; and so my state,
Seldom but sumptuous, showed like a feast

---

233 **brach** bitch-hound   244 **sooth** truth   246 **comfit-maker's** confectioner's   249 **sarcenet surety** flimsy security ("sarcenet" = a thin silk)   250 **Finsbury** favorite resort near London (frequented by the middle-class groups whom Hotspur satirizes)   253 **pepper gingerbread** i.e., insubstantial, crumbling in the mouth   254 **velvet guards** shopkeepers, who favored velvet trimmings for Sunday wear   256 **tailor** like weavers, tailors were famed for singing at their work   257 **red-breast-teacher** singing master to songbirds
**III.ii.6 doom** judgment; **blood** heirs   8 **passages** courses

9–11 **thou . . . mistreadings** (1) heaven is punishing me through you (2) heaven will punish you to punish me   12 **inordinate** out of order (for one of your rank)   15 **withal** with   19 **Quit** clear myself of   20 **As well** and as well   22–28 **Yet . . . submission** Yet let me beg such extenuation that when I have confuted many manufactured charges (which the ear of greatness is bound to hear from informers and tattletales) I may be pardoned for some true faults of which my youth has been guilty   30 **affections** tastes   36 **time** reign   42 **Opinion** public opinion   43 **possession** i.e., Richard II   50 **I . . . heaven** I took a godlike graciousness on myself

And won by rareness such solemnity.
The skipping king, he ambled up and down                    60
With shallow jesters and rash bavin° wits,
Soon kindled and soon burnt; carded° his state;
Mingled his royalty with cap'ring fools;
Had his great name profanèd with their scorns
And gave his countenance, against his name,°              65
To laugh at gibing boys and stand the push°
Of every beardless vain comparative;°
Grew a companion to the common streets,
Enfeoffed himself to popularity;°
That, being daily swallowed by men's eyes,                 70
They surfeited with honey and began
To loathe the taste of sweetness, whereof a little
More than a little is by much too much.
So, when he had occasion to be seen,
He was but as the cuckoo is in June,                       75
Heard, not regarded—seen, but with such eyes
As, sick and blunted with community,°
Afford no extraordinary gaze,
Such as is bent on sunlike majesty
When it shines seldom in admiring eyes;                    80
But rather drowsed and hung their eyelids down,
Slept in his face, and rend'red such aspect
As cloudy° men use to their adversaries,
Being with his presence glutted, gorged, and full.
And in that very line, Harry, standest thou;              85
For thou hast lost thy princely privilege
With vile participation.° Not an eye
But is aweary of thy common sight,
Save mine, which hath desired to see thee more;
Which now doth that I would not have it do—                90
Make blind itself with foolish tenderness.°

PRINCE
I shall hereafter, my thrice-gracious lord,
Be more myself.

KING                    For all the world,
As thou art to this hour was Richard then
When I from France set foot at Ravenspurgh;               95
And even as I was then is Percy now.
Now, by my scepter, and my soul to boot,
He hath more worthy interest° to the state
Than thou the shadow of succession;
For of no right, nor color° like to right,                100
He doth fill fields with harness° in the realm,
Turns head against the lion's armèd jaws,
And, being no more in debt to years than thou,
Leads ancient lords and reverend bishops on
To bloody battles and to bruising arms.                   105
What never-dying honor hath he got
Against renownèd Douglas! whose high deeds,
Whose hot incursions and great name in arms
Holds from all soldiers chief majority°

And military title capital°                               110
Through all the kingdoms that acknowledge Christ.
Thrice hath this Hotspur, Mars in swathling clothes,
This infant warrior, in his enterprises
Discomfited great Douglas; ta'en him once,
Enlargèd him, and made a friend of him,                   115
To fill the mouth of deep defiance up°
And shake the peace and safety of our throne.
And what say you to this? Percy, Northumberland,
The Archbishop's grace of York, Douglas, Mortimer
Capitulate° against us and are up.°                       120
But wherefore do I tell these news to thee?
Why, Harry, do I tell thee of my foes,
Which art my nearest and dearest° enemy?
Thou that art like enough, through vassal fear,
Base inclination, and the start of spleen,                125
To fight against me under Percy's pay,
To dog his heels and curtsy at his frowns,
To show how much thou art degenerate.

PRINCE
Do not think so, you shall not find it so.
And God forgive them that so much have swayed             130
Your majesty's good thoughts away from me.
I will redeem all this on Percy's head
And, in the closing of some glorious day,
Be bold to tell you that I am your son,
When I will wear a garment all of blood,                  135
And stain my favors° in a bloody mask,
Which, washed away, shall scour my shame with it.
And that shall be the day, whene'er it lights,
That this same child of honor and renown,
This gallant Hotspur, this all-praisèd knight,            140
And your unthought-of Harry chance to meet.
For every honor sitting on his helm,
Would they were multitudes, and on my head
My shames redoubled! For the time will come
That I shall make this northern youth exchange            145
His glorious deeds for my indignities.
Percy is but my factor,° good my lord,
To engross° up glorious deeds on my behalf;
And I will call him to so strict account
That he shall render every glory up,                      150
Yea, even the slightest worship of his time,°
Or I will tear the reckoning from his heart.
This in the name of God I promise here;
The which if he be pleased I shall perform,
I do beseech your majesty may salve                       155
The long-grown wounds of my intemperance.
If not, the end of life cancels all bands,°
And I will die a hundred thousand deaths
Ere break the smallest parcel° of this vow.

KING
A hundred thousand rebels die in this!                    160
Thou shalt have charge and sovereign trust herein.

*Enter* BLUNT.

How now, good Blunt? Thy looks are full of speed.

---

**61 bavin** brushwood (which flares and burns out)  **62 carded** debased  **65 his name** (1) his kingly title (2) his kingly authority  **66 stand the push** put up with the impudence  **67 comparative** deviser of insulting comparisons  **69 Enfeoffed . . . popularity** bound himself to low company  **77 with community** by familiarity (with the king)  **83 cloudy** sullen (but also with reference to "clouds" obscuring the royal "sun")  **87 participation** companionship  **91 tenderness** tears  **98 worthy interest** claim based on worth (as compared with a "shadow" claim by inheritance)  **100 color** pretense  **101 harness** armor  **109 majority** preeminence

**110 capital** topmost  **116 fill . . . up** deepen the noise of defiance  **120 Capitulate** (1) make a "head" or armed force (?) (2) draw up "heads" of an argument (?); **up** in arms  **123 dearest** (1) most loved (2) costliest  **136 favors** features  **147 factor** agent  **148 engross** hoard  **151 worship . . . time** honor he has gained in his lifetime  **157 bands** bonds, promises  **159 parcel** item

BLUNT
So hath the business° that I come to speak of.
Lord Mortimer of Scotland hath sent word
That Douglas and the English rebels met                    165
The eleventh of this month at Shrewsbury.
A mighty and a fearful head they are,
If promises be kept on every hand,
As ever off'red foul play in a state.

KING
The Earl of Westmoreland set forth today;                  170
With him my son, Lord John of Lancaster:
For this advertisement is five days old.
On Wednesday next, Harry, you shall set forward;
On Thursday we ourselves will march. Our meeting
Is Bridgenorth; and, Harry, you shall march              175
Through Gloucestershire; by which account,
Our business valuèd,° some twelve days hence
Our general forces at Bridgenorth shall meet.
Our hands are full of business. Let's away:
Advantage feeds him° fat while men delay.    *Exeunt.*  180

[Scene III. *Eastcheap. The tavern.*]

*Enter* FALSTAFF *and* BARDOLPH.

FALSTAFF  Bardolph, am I not fall'n away vilely since
this last action? Do I not bate?° Do I not dwindle?
Why, my skin hangs about me like an old lady's loose
gown! I am withered like an old apple-john.° Well,
I'll repent, and that suddenly, while I am in some lik-  5
ing.° I shall be out of heart° shortly, and then I shall
have no strength to repent. And I have not forgotten
what the inside of a church is made of, I am a
peppercorn,° a brewer's horse.° The inside of a church!
Company, villainous company, hath been the spoil of  10
me.
BARDOLPH  Sir John, you are so fretful you cannot
live long.
FALSTAFF  Why, there is it! Come, sing me a bawdy
song, make me merry. I was as virtuously given as a  15
gentleman need to be, virtuous enough: swore little,
diced not above seven times a week, went to a bawdy
house not above once in a quarter of an hour, paid money
that I borrowed three or four times,° lived well, and
in good compass;° and now I live out of all order, out  20
of all compass.
BARDOLPH  Why, you are so fat, Sir John, that you
must needs be out of all compass—out of all reasonable
compass, Sir John.
FALSTAFF  Do thou amend thy face, and I'll amend my  25
life. Thou art our admiral,° thou bearest the lantern

in the poop—but 'tis in the nose of thee: thou art the
Knight of the Burning Lamp.
BARDOLPH  Why, Sir John, my face does you no
harm.                                                      30
FALSTAFF  No, I'll be sworn. I make as good use of it
as many a man doth of a death's-head° or a memento
mori.° I never see thy face but I think upon hellfire
and Dives° that lived in purple; for there he is in his
robes, burning, burning. If thou wert any way given  35
to virtue, I would swear by thy face; my oath should
be "By this fire, that's God's angel."° But thou art
altogether given over, and wert indeed, but for the
light in thy face, the son of utter darkness. When
thou ran'st up Gad's Hill in the night to catch my  40
horse, if I did not think thou hadst been an ignis
fatuus° or a ball of wildfire,° there's no purchase in
money. O, thou art a perpetual triumph,° an everlasting bonfire-light! Thou hast saved me a thousand
marks in links° and torches, walking with thee in the  45
night betwixt tavern and tavern; but the sack that
thou hast drunk me would have bought me lights as
good cheap° at the dearest chandler's° in Europe.
I have maintained that salamander° of yours with
fire any time this two and thirty years. God reward  50
me for it!
BARDOLPH  'Sblood, I would my face were in your
belly!°
FALSTAFF  God-amercy! So should I be sure to be
heart-burned.                                             55

*Enter* HOSTESS.

How now, Dame Partlet° the hen? Have you enquired
yet who picked my pocket?
HOSTESS  Why, Sir John, what do you think, Sir
John? Do you think I keep thieves in my house? I have
searched, I have enquired, so has my husband, man by  60
man, boy by boy, servant by servant. The tithe° of a
hair was never lost in my house before.
FALSTAFF  Ye lie, hostess. Bardolph was shaved and
lost many a hair, and I'll be sworn my pocket was
picked. Go to, you are a woman, go!                        65
HOSTESS  Who, I? No;° I defy thee! God's light, I was
never called so in mine own house before!
FALSTAFF  Go to, I know you well enough.
HOSTESS  No, Sir John; you do not know me, Sir
John. I know you, Sir John. You owe me money, Sir  70
John, and now you pick a quarrel to beguile me of it.
I bought you a dozen of shirts to your back.

163 **So . . . business** the business too has speed (must be
dealt with speedily)  177 **Our business valuèd** having sized
up what we have to do  180 **him** itself
**III.iii.2 bate** lose weight  4 **old apple-john** apple with
shriveled skin  5–6 **am . . . liking** (1) am in the mood (2)
still have some flesh left  6 **out of heart** (1) out of the mood
(2) out of shape  9 **peppercorn, brewer's horse** Falstaff this
time picks objects *not* long and thin, but dry, withered,
decrepit  17–19 **diced . . . times** probably spoken with
significant pauses after "diced not," "once," "borrowed"
20 **compass** order (but Bardolph takes it in the sense of "size")
26 **admiral** flagship (recognizable by its lantern)

32 **death's-head** ring with a skull  32–33 **memento mori**
reminder of death  34 **Dives** uncharitable rich man who
burns in hell (Luke 16:19–31)  37 **angel** alluding to the
Scriptural accounts of angels manifesting themselves as fire, or
possibly to the seraphs, highest order of angels, who were fire
41–42 **ignis fatuus** will-o'-the-wisp  42 **ball of wildfire**
firework  43 **triumph** i.e., of the Roman kind, with torches
45 **links** flares  48 **good cheap** cheaply; **chandler's** candle
maker's  49 **salamander** lizard supposed to live in fire
52–53 **I . . . belly** proverbial retort, to which Falstaff's reply
gives new life  56 **Dame Partlet** traditional name for a hen,
and well suited to the clucking hostess  61 **tithe** tenth part
66 **No** the Hostess suspects that any word or phrase of Falstaff's
may contain hidden innuendoes about her moral character;
she sometimes retorts with comments containing amusing
innuendoes about herself that she is too ignorant to understand

FALSTAFF  Dowlas,° filthy dowlas! I have given them away to bakers' wives; they have made bolters° of them. 75

HOSTESS  Now, as I am a true woman, holland° of eight shillings an ell.° You owe money here besides, Sir John, for your diet and by-drinkings,° and money lent you, four and twenty pound.

FALSTAFF  He had his part of it; let him pay. 80

HOSTESS  He? Alas, he is poor; he hath nothing.

FALSTAFF  How? Poor? Look upon his face. What call you rich?° Let them coin his nose, let them coin his cheeks. I'll not pay a denier.° What, will you make a younker° of me? Shall I not take mine ease in mine 85 inn but I shall have my pocket picked? I have lost a seal ring of my grandfather's worth forty mark.

HOSTESS  O Jesu, I have heard the prince tell him, I know not how oft, that that ring was copper!

FALSTAFF  How? The prince is a Jack,° a sneak-up.° 90 'Sblood, and he were here, I would cudgel him like a dog if he would say so.

*Enter the* PRINCE *[and* POINS*], marching, and* FALSTAFF *meets them, playing upon his truncheon° like a fife.*

How now, lad? Is the wind in that door,° i' faith? Must we all march?

BARDOLPH  Yea, two and two,° Newgate fashion. 95

HOSTESS  My lord, I pray you hear me.

PRINCE  What say'st thou, Mistress Quickly? How doth thy husband? I love him well, he is an honest man.

HOSTESS  Good my lord, hear me. 100

FALSTAFF  Prithee let her alone and list to me.

PRINCE  What say'st thou, Jack?

FALSTAFF  The other night I fell asleep here behind the arras and had my pocket picked. This house is turned bawdy house; they pick pockets. 105

PRINCE  What didst thou lose, Jack?

FALSTAFF  Wilt thou believe me, Hal, three or four bonds of forty pound apiece and a seal ring of my grandfather's.

PRINCE  A trifle, some eightpenny matter. 110

HOSTESS  So I told him, my lord, and I said I heard your grace say so; and, my lord, he speaks most vilely of you, like a foulmouthed man as he is, and said he would cudgel you.

PRINCE  What! He did not? 115

HOSTESS  There's neither faith, truth, nor womanhood in me else.

FALSTAFF  There's no more faith in thee than in a stewed prune,° nor no more truth in thee than in a drawn° fox; and for womanhood, Maid Marian may 120 be the deputy's wife of the ward to thee.° Go, you thing, go!

73 Dowlas coarse linen 74 bolters sieves 76 holland fine linen 77 ell one and a quarter yards 78 by-drinkings drinks between meals 83 rich referring to its red-gold and copper hues 84 denier tenth of a penny 85 younker greenhorn 90 Jack rascal; sneak-up sneak 92 s.d. truncheon cudgel 93 Is . . . door is that how things are going 95 two and two bound in pairs like prisoners on the way to (Newgate) prison 119 stewed prune evidently chosen by Falstaff because stewed prunes were associated with bawdy houses 120 drawn drawn from his lair and trying every trick to get back to it 120–21 Maid . . . thee a disreputable female in country May games is chaste as the wife of the ward's most respectable citizen in comparison with you

HOSTESS  Say, what thing, what thing?

FALSTAFF  What thing? Why, a thing to thank God on.

HOSTESS  I am no thing to thank God on, I would thou 125 shouldst know it! I am an honest man's wife, and, setting thy knighthood aside, thou art a knave to call me so.

FALSTAFF  Setting thy womanhood aside, thou art a beast to say otherwise. 130

HOSTESS  Say, what beast, thou knave, thou?

FALSTAFF  What beast? Why, an otter.

PRINCE  An otter, Sir John? Why an otter?

FALSTAFF  Why, she's neither fish nor flesh; a man knows not where to have her. 135

HOSTESS  Thou art an unjust man in saying so. Thou or any man knows where to have me, thou knave, thou!

PRINCE  Thou say'st true, hostess, and he slanders thee most grossly. 140

HOSTESS  So he doth you, my lord, and said this other day you ought° him a thousand pound.

PRINCE  Sirrah, do I owe you a thousand pound?

FALSTAFF  A thousand pound, Hal? A million! Thy love is worth a million, thou owest me thy love. 145

HOSTESS  Nay, my lord, he called you Jack and said he would cudgel you.

FALSTAFF  Did I, Bardolph?

BARDOLPH  Indeed, Sir John, you said so.

FALSTAFF  Yea, if he said my ring was copper. 150

PRINCE  I say 'tis copper. Darest thou be as good as thy word now?

FALSTAFF  Why, Hal, thou knowest, as thou art but man, I dare; but as thou art prince, I fear thee as I fear the roaring of the lion's whelp. 155

PRINCE  And why not as the lion?

FALSTAFF  The king himself is to be feared as the lion. Dost thou think I'll fear thee as I fear thy father? Nay, and I do, I pray God my girdle break.

PRINCE  O, if it should, how would thy guts fall about 160 thy knees! But, sirrah, there's no room for faith, truth, nor honesty in this bosom of thine. It is all filled up with guts and midriff. Charge an honest woman with picking thy pocket? Why, thou whoreson, impudent, embossed° rascal,° if there were anything 165 in thy pocket but tavern reckonings, memorandums of bawdy houses, and one poor pennyworth of sugar candy to make thee long-winded—if thy pocket were enriched with any other injuries° but these, I am a villain. And yet you will stand to it; you will not 170 pocket up wrong. Art thou not ashamed?

FALSTAFF  Dost thou hear, Hal? Thou knowest in the state of innocency Adam fell, and what should poor Jack Falstaff do in the days of villainy? Thou see'st I have more flesh than another man, and therefore more 175 frailty. You confess then, you picked my pocket?

PRINCE  It appears so by the story.

FALSTAFF  Hostess, I forgive thee, go make ready breakfast, love thy husband, look to thy servants, cherish thy guests. Thou shalt find me tractable to any 180 honest reason. Thou see'st I am pacified still. Nay, prithee be gone.          *Exit* HOSTESS.

142 ought owed   165 embossed (1) swollen (2) foaming at the mouth (of a deer); rascal (1) rogue (2) lean young deer 169 injuries things whose loss you call injuries

Now, Hal, to the news at court. For the robbery, lad
—how is that answered?
PRINCE  O my sweet beef, I must still be good angel 185
to thee. The money is paid back again.
FALSTAFF  O, I do not like that paying back! 'Tis a
double labor.
PRINCE  I am good friends with my father, and may
do anything. 190
FALSTAFF  Rob me the exchequer the first thing thou
doest, and do it with unwashed hands° too.
BARDOLPH  Do, my lord.
PRINCE  I have procured thee, Jack, a charge of foot.
FALSTAFF  I would it had been of horse. Where shall I 195
find one that can steal well? O for a fine thief° of the
age of two and twenty or thereabouts! I am heinously
unprovided. Well, God be thanked for these rebels,
they offend none but the virtuous: I laud them, I
praise them. 200
PRINCE  Bardolph!
BARDOLPH  My lord?
PRINCE
Go bear this letter to Lord John of Lancaster,
To my brother John; this to my Lord of Westmore-
land.         [*Exit* BARDOLPH.]
Go, Peto, to horse, to horse; for thou and I 205
Have thirty miles to ride yet ere dinner time.
        [*Exit* PETO.]
Jack, meet me tomorrow in the Temple Hall
At two o'clock in the afternoon.
There shalt thou know thy charge, and there receive
Money and order for their furniture.° 210
The land is burning, Percy stands on high,
And either we or they must lower lie.    [*Exit.*]
FALSTAFF
Rare words! Brave world! Hostess, my breakfast,
come.
O, I could wish this tavern were my drum!°   [*Exit.*]


# [ ACT IV ]

[Scene I. *The rebel camp, near Shrewsbury*.]

[*Enter* HOTSPUR, WORCESTER, *and* DOUGLAS.]

HOTSPUR
Well said, my noble Scot. If speaking truth
In this fine age were not thought flattery,
Such attribution° should the Douglas have
As not a soldier of this season's stamp
Should go so general current° through the world. 5
By God, I cannot flatter, I do defy°
The tongues of soothers!° But a braver place
In my heart's love hath no man than yourself.
Nay, task me° to my word; approve me, lord

DOUGLAS
Thou art the king of honor. 10
No man so potent breathes upon the ground
But I will beard° him.

*Enter one with letters.*

HOTSPUR        Do so, and 'tis well.—
What letters hast thou there?—I can but thank you.
MESSENGER
These letters come from your father.
HOTSPUR
Letters from him? Why comes he not himself? 15
MESSENGER
He cannot come, my lord, he is grievous sick.
HOTSPUR
Zounds! How has he the leisure to be sick
In such a justling° time? Who leads his power?
Under whose government° come they along?
MESSENGER
His letters bears° his mind, not I, my lord. 20
WORCESTER
I prithee tell me, doth he keep his bed?
MESSENGER
He did, my lord, four days ere I set forth,
And at the time of my departure thence
He was much feared° by his physicians.
WORCESTER
I would the state of time had first been whole 25
Ere he by sickness had been visited.
His health was never better worth than now.
HOTSPUR
Sick now? Droop now? This sickness doth infect
The very lifeblood of our enterprise.
'Tis catching hither, even to our camp. 30
He writes me here that inward sickness—
And that his friends by deputation°
Could not so soon be drawn; nor did he think it meet
To lay so dangerous and dear a trust
On any soul removed but on his own. 35
Yet doth he give us bold advertisement,
That with our small conjunction° we should on,
To see how fortune is disposed to us;
For, as he writes, there is no quailing now,
Because the king is certainly possessed° 40
Of all our purposes. What say you to it?
WORCESTER
Your father's sickness is a maim to us.
HOTSPUR
A perilous gash, a very limb lopped off.
And yet, in faith, it is not! His present want
Seems more than we shall find it. Were it good 45
To set° the exact wealth of all our states
All at one cast? To set so rich a main°
On the nice° hazard of one doubtful hour?
It were not good; for therein should we read
The very bottom and the soul° of hope, 50

---

**192 with unwashed hands** with no delay  **196 thief** i.e., to
steal a horse  **210 furniture** equipment  **214 drum** recruiting
center
**IV.i.3 attribution** recognition  **5 go . . . current** be as
widely accepted (the image is of a coin of recent mintage:
"this season's stamp")  **6 defy** despise  **7 soothers** flatterers
**9 task me** try me, test me

**12 beard** oppose  **18 justling** jostling, unquiet  **19 government** command  **20 bears** a singular verb with plural subject is
not uncommon in Elizabethan English  **24 feared** feared for
**32 deputation** a deputy  **37 conjunction** combination of
forces  **40 possessed** informed  **46 set** risk  **47 main** (1) stake
(in gambling) (2) army  **48 nice** precarious  **50 soul** (1)
essence (2) sole (cf. "bottom")

The very list,° the very utmost bound
Of all our fortunes.
DOUGLAS                Faith, and so we should.
Where now remains a sweet reversion,°
We may boldly spend upon the hope of what is to
     come in.
A comfort of retirement° lives in this.                    55
HOTSPUR
A rendezvous, a home to fly unto,
If that the devil and mischance look big°
Upon the maidenhead of our affairs.
WORCESTER
But yet I would your father had been here.
The quality and hair° of our attempt                       60
Brooks° no division. It will be thought
By some that know not why he is away,
That wisdom, loyalty, and mere dislike
Of our proceedings kept the earl from hence.
And think how such an apprehension                          65
May turn the tide of fearful° faction
And breed a kind of question in our cause.
For well you know we of the off'ring side°
Must keep aloof from strict arbitrament,°
And stop all sight-holes, every loop° from whence          70
The eye of reason may pry in upon us.
This absence of your father's draws° a curtain
That shows the ignorant a kind of fear
Before not dreamt of.
HOTSPUR                You strain too far.
I rather of his absence make this use:                      75
It lends a luster and more great opinion,°
A larger dare to our great enterprise,
Than if the earl were here; for men must think,
If we, without his help, can make a head°
To push against a kingdom, with his help                    80
We shall o'erturn it topsy-turvy down.
Yet all goes well; yet all our joints are whole.
DOUGLAS
As heart can think. There is not such a word
Spoke of in Scotland as this term of fear.

*Enter Sir Richard* VERNON.

HOTSPUR
My cousin Vernon, welcome, by my soul.                      85
VERNON
Pray God my news be worth a welcome, lord.
The Earl of Westmoreland, seven thousand strong,
Is marching hitherwards; with him Prince John.
HOTSPUR
No harm. What more?
VERNON                And further, I have learned
The king himself in person is set forth,                    90
Or hitherwards intended speedily,
With strong and mighty preparation.
HOTSPUR
He shall be welcome too. Where is his son,
The nimble-footed madcap Prince of Wales,

And his comrades, that daffed° the world aside             95
And bid it pass?
VERNON                All furnished, all in arms;
All plumed like estridges° that with the wind
Bated° like eagles having lately bathed;
Glittering in golden coats like images;
As full of spirit as the month of May                      100
And gorgeous as the sun at midsummer;
Wanton° as youthful goats, wild as young bulls.
I saw young Harry with his beaver° on,
His cushes° on his thighs, gallantly armed,
Rise from the ground like feathered Mercury,               105
And vaulted with such ease into his seat
As if an angel dropped down from the clouds
To turn and wind° a fiery Pegasus
And witch the world with noble horsemanship.
HOTSPUR
No more, no more! Worse than the sun in March,             110
This praise doth nourish agues.° Let them come.
They come like sacrifices in their trim,
And to the fire-eyed maid° of smoky war
All hot and bleeding will we offer them.
The mailèd Mars shall on his altars sit                    115
Up to the ears in blood. I am on fire
To hear this rich reprisal° is so nigh,
And yet not ours. Come, let me taste my horse,
Who is to bear me like a thunderbolt
Against the bosom of the Prince of Wales.                  120
Harry to Harry shall, hot horse to horse,
Meet, and ne'er part till one drop down a corse.
O that Glendower were come!
VERNON                          There is more news.
I learned in Worcester, as I rode along,
He cannot draw his power this fourteen days.               125
DOUGLAS
That's the worst tidings that I hear of yet.
WORCESTER
Ay, by my faith, that bears a frosty sound.
HOTSPUR
What may the king's whole battle° reach unto?
VERNON
To thirty thousand.
HOTSPUR                Forty let it be.
My father and Glendower being both away,                   130
The powers of us may serve so great a day.
Come, let us take a muster speedily.
Doomsday is near. Die all, die merrily.
DOUGLAS
Talk not of dying. I am out of fear
Of death or death's hand for this one half year.           135
                                        *Exeunt.*

[Scene II. *A road near Coventry.*]

*Enter* FALSTAFF [*and*] BARDOLPH.

FALSTAFF  Bardolph, get thee before to Coventry;

51 **list** limit  53 **reversion** inheritance still to be received  55 **comfort of retirement** security to fall back on  57 **big** menacingly  60 **hair** nature  61 **Brooks** allows of  66 **fearful** timid  68 **we . . . side** we who take the offensive  69 **arbitrament** evaluation  70 **loop** loophole  72 **draws** draws aside  76 **opinion** prestige  79 **a head** (1) an army (2) headway

95 **daffed** thrust  97 **estridges** ostriches (ostrich plumes are the emblem of the Prince of Wales)  98 **Bated** shook their wings  102 **Wanton** exuberant  103 **beaver** helmet  104 **cushes** thigh armor  108 **wind** wheel about  111 **agues** chills and fever (the spring sun was believed to set them going)  113 **maid** Bellona, goddess of war  117 **reprisal** prize  128 **battle** army

fill me a bottle of sack. Our soldiers shall march
through. We'll to Sutton Co'fil' tonight.

BARDOLPH   Will you give me money, captain?

FALSTAFF   Lay out,° lay out.                              5

BARDOLPH   This bottle makes an angel.°

FALSTAFF   And if it do, take it for thy labor; and if it
make twenty, take them all; I'll answer the coinage.
Bid my lieutenant Peto meet me at town's end.

BARDOLPH   I will, captain. Farewell.          *Exit.* 10

FALSTAFF   If I be not ashamed of my soldiers, I am a
soused gurnet.° I have misused the king's press°
damnably. I have got, in exchange of a hundred and
fifty soldiers, three hundred and odd pounds. I press
me none but good householders, yeomen's sons;° 15
inquire me out contracted bachelors, such as had been
asked twice on the banes°—such a commodity of
warm° slaves as had as lief hear the devil as a drum,
such as fear the report of a caliver° worse than a
struck fowl or a hurt wild duck. I pressed me none 20
but such toasts-and-butter, with hearts in their bellies
no bigger than pins' heads, and they have bought
out their services; and now my whole charge consists
of ancients,° corporals, lieutenants, gentlemen of
companies°—slaves as ragged as Lazarus° in the 25
painted cloth,° where the glutton's dogs licked his
sores; and such as indeed were never soldiers, but
discarded unjust° servingmen, younger sons to
younger brothers, revolted° tapsters, and ostlers
trade-fall'n;° the cankers° of a calm world and a long 30
peace; ten times more dishonorable ragged than an
old fazed ancient;° and such have I to fill up the
rooms of them as have bought out their services that
you would think that I had a hundred and fifty tattered
prodigals lately come from swine-keeping, from eating 35
draff° and husks. A mad fellow met me on the way,
and told me I had unloaded all the gibbets and pressed
the dead bodies. No eye hath seen such scarecrows.
I'll not march through Coventry with them, that's
flat. Nay, and the villains march wide betwixt the 40
legs, as if they had gyves° on, for indeed I had the
most of them out of prison. There's not a shirt and a
half in all my company, and the half-shirt is two
napkins tacked together and thrown over the shoulders
like a herald's coat without sleeves; and the shirt, to 45
say the truth, stol'n from my host at Saint Albans, or
the red-nose innkeeper at Daventry. But that's all
one; they'll find linen enough on every hedge.°

*Enter the* PRINCE *[and the] Lord of* WESTMORELAND.

PRINCE   How now, blown° Jack?° How now, quilt?

FALSTAFF   What, Hal? How now, mad wag? What a 50
devil dost thou in Warwickshire? My good Lord of
Westmoreland, I cry you mercy. I thought your honor
had already been at Shrewsbury.

WESTMORELAND   Faith, Sir John, 'tis more than time
that I were there, and you too, but my powers are 55
there already. The king, I can tell you, looks for us all,
we must away all night.

FALSTAFF   Tut, never fear me: I am as vigilant as a cat
to steal cream.

PRINCE   I think, to steal cream indeed, for thy theft 60
hath already made thee butter. But tell me, Jack, whose
fellows are these that come after?

FALSTAFF   Mine, Hal, mine.

PRINCE   I did never see such pitiful rascals.

FALSTAFF   Tut, tut, good enough to toss;° food for 65
powder, food for powder, they'll fill a pit as well as
better. Tush, man, mortal men, mortal men.

WESTMORELAND   Ay, but, Sir John, methinks they
are exceeding poor and bare, too beggarly.

FALSTAFF   Faith, for their poverty, I know not where 70
they had that, and for their bareness, I am sure they
never learned that of me.

PRINCE   No, I'll be sworn, unless you call three
fingers° in the ribs bare. But, sirrah, make haste. Percy
is already in the field.          *Exit.* 75

FALSTAFF   What, is the king encamped?

WESTMORELAND   He is, Sir John. I fear we shall stay
too long.

FALSTAFF   Well, to the latter end of a fray and the
beginning of a feast fits a dull fighter and a keen 80
guest.          *Exeunt.*°

[Scene III. *The rebel camp, near Shrewsbury.*]

*Enter* HOTSPUR, WORCESTER, DOUGLAS, VERNON.

HOTSPUR
We'll fight with him tonight.

WORCESTER                        It may not be.

DOUGLAS
You give him then advantage.

VERNON                        Not a whit.

HOTSPUR
Why say you so? Looks he not for supply?°

VERNON
So do we.

HOTSPUR   His is certain, ours is doubtful.

WORCESTER
Good cousin, be advised; stir not tonight.          5

IV.ii.5 **Lay out** pay out of your own pocket   6 **angel** coin
worth, at various times, six shillings eightpence to ten shillings
(Bardolph means that Falstaff now owes him an angel, but
Falstaff jokingly takes "make" in the literal sense—as if the
bottle were minting angels; he tells Bardolph to take them all
and he will guarantee they are not counterfeit)   12 **soused
gurnet** pickled fish; **press** power of conscription   15 **good
. . . sons** men of some means who could pay to be let off
17 **asked . . . banes** on the verge of marriage (banns [banes]
were announcements of intent to marry, published usually
three times at weekly intervals)   18 **warm** comfortable   19
**caliver** musket   24 **ancients** ensigns   24–25 **gentlemen of
companies** lesser officers   25 **Lazarus** the beggar in the
Dives parable (Luke 16:19–31)   26 **painted cloth** painted
wall-hanging   28 **unjust** dishonest   29 **revolted** runaway
30 **trade-fall'n** unemployed   32 **fazed**
**ancient** tattered flag   36 **draff** pig-swill (the prodigal son,
in Luke 15:15–16, was so hungry he longed for draff)   41
**gyves** fetters

48 **hedge** where linen was put out to dry   49 **blown** (1)
swelled (2) short of wind; **Jack** (1) Falstaff's name (2) soldier's
quilted jacket   65 **toss** i.e., on the end of a pike   73–74 **three
fingers** i.e., of fat   81 **s.d. Exeunt** the quarto's "Exeunt,"
implying that Westmoreland goes off with Falstaff, may be
wrong. Falstaff's last speech sounds as if Westmoreland had
departed, and Falstaff winks at the audience
**IV.iii.3 supply** reinforcement

VERNON
Do not, my lord.

DOUGLAS You do not counsel well.
You speak it out of fear and cold heart.

VERNON
Do me no slander, Douglas. By my life—
And I dare well maintain it with my life—
If well-respected° honor bid me on,                    10
I hold as little counsel with weak fear
As you, my lord, or any Scot that this day lives.
Let it be seen tomorrow in the battle
Which of us fears.

DOUGLAS Yea, or tonight.

VERNON Content.

HOTSPUR
Tonight, say I.                                        15

VERNON
Come, come, it may not be.
I wonder much, being men of such great leading° as
  you are,
That you foresee not what impediments
Drag back our expedition.° Certain horse
Of my cousin Vernon's are not yet come up.             20
Your uncle Worcester's horse came but today;
And now their pride and mettle is asleep,
Their courage with hard labor tame and dull,
That not a horse is half the half of himself.

HOTSPUR
So are the horses of the enemy                         25
In general journey-bated° and brought low.
The better part of ours are full of rest.

WORCESTER
The number of the king exceedeth ours.
For God's sake, cousin, stay till all come in.

*The trumpet sounds a parley. Enter Sir Walter* BLUNT.

BLUNT
I come with gracious offers from the king,             30
If you vouchsafe me hearing and respect.

HOTSPUR
Welcome, Sir Walter Blunt, and would to God
You were of our determination.°
Some of us love you well; and even those some
Envy your great deservings and good name,             35
Because you are not of our quality,°
But stand against us like an enemy.

BLUNT
And God defend° but still I should stand so,
So long as out of limit° and true rule
You stand against anointed majesty.                    40
But to my charge.° The king hath sent to know
The nature of your griefs, and whereupon
You conjure from the breast of civil peace
Such bold hostility, teaching his duteous land
Audacious cruelty. If that the king                    45
Have any way your good deserts forgot,
Which he confesseth to be manifold,
He bids you name your griefs, and with all speed

You shall have your desires with interest,
And pardon absolute for yourself and these             50
Herein misled by your suggestion.°

HOTSPUR
The king is kind, and well we know the king
Knows at what time to promise, when to pay.
My father and my uncle and myself
Did give him that same royalty he wears;               55
And when he was not six and twenty strong,
Sick in the world's regard, wretched and low,
A poor unminded outlaw sneaking home,
My father gave him welcome to the shore;
And then he heard him swear and vow to God             60
He came but to be Duke of Lancaster,
To sue his livery and beg his peace,°
With tears of innocency and terms of zeal,
My father, in kind heart and pity moved,
Swore him assistance, and performed it too.            65
Now when the lords and barons of the realm
Perceived Northumberland did lean to him,
The more and less came in with cap and knee;°
Met him in boroughs, cities, villages,
Attended him on bridges, stood in lanes,°              70
Laid gifts before him, proffered him their oaths,
Gave him their heirs as pages, followed him
Even at the heels in golden multitudes.
He presently, as greatness knows itself,°
Steps me a little higher than his vow                  75
Made to my father, while his blood was poor,
Upon the naked shore at Ravenspurgh;
And now, forsooth, takes on him to reform
Some certain edicts and some strait° decrees
That lie too heavy on the commonwealth;                80
Cries out upon abuses, seems to weep
Over his country's wrongs; and by this face,
This seeming brow of justice, did he win
The hearts of all that he did angle for;
Proceeded further—cut me off the heads                 85
Of all the favorites that the absent king
In deputation° left behind him here
When he was personal° in the Irish war.

BLUNT
Tut! I came not to hear this.

HOTSPUR Then to the point.
In short time after, he deposed the king;              90
Soon after that deprived him of his life;
And in the neck of that° tasked° the whole state;
To make that worse, suff'red his kinsman March
(Who is, if every owner were well placed,
Indeed his king) to be engaged in Wales,               95
There without ransom to lie forfeited;
Disgraced me in my happy victories,
Sought to entrap me by intelligence;°
Rated° mine uncle from the council board;
In rage dismissed my father from the court;           100

**51 suggestion** instigation **62 sue . . . peace** sue for the delivery of his lands (which Richard II had arrogated to the crown) and make his peace with the king **68 with . . . knee** with cap off and bended knee (in token of allegiance) **70 lanes** facing rows **74 as . . . itself** as greatness begins to feel its strength **79 strait** strict **87 In deputation** as deputies **88 personal** personally engaged **92 in . . . that** next; **tasked** taxed **98 intelligence** spies **99 Rated** scolded (cf. I.iii.14–20)

**10 well-respected** well-considered **17 leading** generalship **19 expedition** hastening into battle **26 journey-bated** travel-weakened **33 determination** party **36 quality** company **38 defend** forbid **39 limit** a subject's proper imits **41 charge** message

Broke oath on oath, committed wrong on wrong;
And in conclusion drove us to seek out
This head° of safety, and withal to pry
Into his title, the which we find
Too indirect° for long continuance.      105

**BLUNT**

Shall I return this answer to the king?

**HOTSPUR**

Not so, Sir Walter. We'll withdraw awhile.
Go to the king; and let there be impawned
Some surety for a safe return again,
And in the morning early shall mine uncle      110
Bring him our purposes; and so farewell.

**BLUNT**

I would you would accept of grace and love.

**HOTSPUR**

And may be so we shall.

**BLUNT**      Pray God you do.   [*Exeunt.*]


[Scene IV. *York. The Archbishop's palace.*]

*Enter* [*the*] ARCHBISHOP *of York* [*and*] SIR MICHAEL.

**ARCHBISHOP**

Hie, good Sir Michael; bear this sealèd brief°
With wingèd haste to the Lord Marshal;
This to my cousin Scroop; and all the rest
To whom they are directed. If you knew
How much they do import, you would make haste.      5

**SIR MICHAEL**

My good lord, I guess their tenor.

**ARCHBISHOP**

Like enough you do.
Tomorrow, good Sir Michael, is a day
Wherein the fortune of ten thousand men
Must bide the touch;° for, sir, at Shrewsbury,      10
As I am truly given to understand,
The king with mighty and quick-raisèd power
Meets with Lord Harry; and I fear, Sir Michael,
What with the sickness of Northumberland,
Whose power was in the first proportion,°      15
And what with Owen Glendower's absence thence,
Who with them was a rated sinew° too
And comes not in, overruled by prophecies—
I fear the power of Percy is too weak
To wage an instant trial with the king.      20

**SIR MICHAEL**

Why, my good lord, you need not fear;
There is Douglas and Lord Mortimer.

**ARCHBISHOP**

No, Mortimer is not there.

**SIR MICHAEL**

But there is Mordake, Vernon, Lord Harry Percy,
And there is my Lord of Worcester, and a head      25
Of gallant warriors, noble gentlemen.

**ARCHBISHOP**

And so there is; but yet the king hath drawn

---

The special head° of all the land together—
The Prince of Wales, Lord John of Lancaster,
The noble Westmoreland and warlike Blunt,      30
And many moe corrivals° and dear° men
Of estimation and command in arms.

**SIR MICHAEL**

Doubt not, my lord, they shall be well opposed.

**ARCHBISHOP**

I hope no less, yet needful 'tis to fear;
And, to prevent the worst, Sir Michael, speed.      35
For if Lord Percy thrive not, ere the king
Dismiss his power, he means to visit us,
For he hath heard of our confederacy,
And 'tis but wisdom to make strong against him.
Therefore make haste. I must go write again      40
To other friends; and so farewell, Sir Michael.

*Exeunt.*


# [ ACT V ]

[Scene I. *The king's camp, near Shrewsbury.*]

*Enter the* KING, PRINCE *of Wales, Lord* JOHN *of Lancaster, Earl of* WESTMORELAND,° *Sir Walter* BLUNT, FALSTAFF.

**KING**

How bloodily the sun begins to peer
Above yon bulky hill! The day looks pale
At his distemp'rature.°

**PRINCE**      The southern wind
Doth play the trumpet° to his° purposes
And by his hollow whistling in the leaves      5
Foretells a tempest and a blust'ring day.

**KING**

Then with the losers let it sympathize,
For nothing can seem foul to those that win.

*The trumpet sounds. Enter* WORCESTER [*and* VERNON].

How now, my Lord of Worcester? 'Tis not well
That you and I should meet upon such terms      10
As now we meet. You have deceived our trust
And made us doff our easy robes of peace
To crush our old limbs in ungentle steel.
This is not well, my lord; this is not well.
What say you to it? Will you again unknit      15
This churlish knot of all-abhorrèd war,
And move in that obedient orb° again
Where you did give a fair and natural light,
And be no more an exhaled meteor,°     
A prodigy of fear, and a portent      20
Of broachèd° mischief to the unborn times?

---

**28 head** army    **31 moe corrivals** more associates; **dear** important
**V.i.s.d. Earl of Westmoreland** in V.ii.28 we learn that Westmoreland has been held as the "surety" of IV.iii.109, but at this point Shakespeare apparently had not decided who was the hostage    **3 his distemp'rature** the sun's apparent ailment    **4 play the trumpet** (1) act the announcer (2) blow as if playing a trumpet; **his** the sun's    **17 obedient orb** orbit of obedience    **19 exhaled meteor** wandering body (not subject to orbit, and thought an omen or "prodigy")    **21 broachèd** opened

**103 head** army    **105 indirect** (1) not in the direct line (from Richard) (2) morally oblique
**IV.iv.1 brief** message    **10 bide the touch** stand the test (as metal is tested by the touchstone to know if it is gold)    **15 proportion** magnitude    **17 rated sinew** highly valued strength

**WORCESTER**
Hear me, my liege.
For mine own part, I could be well content
To entertain the lag-end of my life
With quiet hours, for I protest                                    25
I have not sought the day of this dislike.

**KING**
You have not sought it! How comes it then?

**FALSTAFF**
Rebellion lay in his way, and he found it.

**PRINCE**
Peace, chewet,° peace!

**WORCESTER**
It pleased your majesty to turn your looks             30
Of favor from myself and all our house;
And yet I must remember° you, my lord,
We were the first and dearest of your friends.
For you my staff of office did I break
In Richard's time, and posted day and night          35
To meet you on the way and kiss your hand
When yet you were in place and in account
Nothing so strong and fortunate as I.
It was myself, my brother, and his son
That brought you home and boldly did outdare     40
The dangers of the time. You swore to us,
And you did swear that oath at Doncaster,
That you did nothing purpose 'gainst the state,
Nor claim no further than your new-fall'n° right,
The seat° of Gaunt, dukedom of Lancaster.          45
To this we swore our aid. But in short space
It rained down fortune show'ring on your head,
And such a flood of greatness fell on you—
What with our help, what with the absent king,
What with the injuries of a wanton time,               50
The seeming sufferances that you had borne,
And the contrarious winds that held the king
So long in his unlucky Irish wars
That all in England did repute him dead—
And from this swarm of fair advantages                 55
You took occasion to be quickly wooed
To gripe° the general sway into your hand;
Forgot your oath to us at Doncaster;
And, being fed by us, you used us so
As that ungentle gull,° the cuckoo's bird,°            60
Useth the sparrow—did oppress our nest,
Grew by our feeding to so great a bulk
That even our love durst not come near your sight
For fear of swallowing; but with nimble wing
We were enforced for safety sake to fly                 65
Out of your sight and raise this present head;
Whereby we stand opposèd by such means
As you yourself have forged against yourself
By unkind usage, dangerous° countenance,
And violation of all faith and troth                          70
Sworn to us in your younger enterprise.

**KING**
These things, indeed, you have articulate,°

Proclaimed at market crosses, read in churches,
To face° the garment of rebellion
With some fine color° that may please the eye      75
Of fickle changelings and poor discontents,
Which gape and rub the elbow° at the news
Of hurlyburly innovation.°
And never yet did insurrection want
Such water colors to impaint his cause,                 80
Nor moody beggars, starving for a time
Of pell-mell havoc and confusion.

**PRINCE**
In both your armies there is many a soul
Shall pay full dearly for this encounter,
If once they join in trial. Tell your nephew           85
The Prince of Wales doth join with all the world
In praise of Henry Percy. By my hopes,
This present enterprise set off his head,°
I do not think a braver gentleman,
More active-valiant or more valiant-young,          90
More daring or more bold, is now alive
To grace this latter age with noble deeds.
For my part, I may speak it to my shame,
I have a truant been to chivalry;
And so I hear he doth account me too.                   95
Yet this before° my father's majesty—
I am content that he shall take the odds
Of his great name and estimation,
And will, to save the blood on either side,
Try fortune with him in a single fight.                  100

**KING**
And, Prince of Wales, so dare we venture thee;
Albeit,° considerations infinite
Do make against it. No, good Worcester, no!
We love our people well; even those we love
That are misled upon your cousin's part;             105
And, will they take the offer of our grace,°
Both he, and they, and you, yea, every man
Shall be my friend again, and I'll be his.
So tell your cousin, and bring me word
What he will do. But if he will not yield,               110
Rebuke and dread correction wait on us,°
And they shall do their office.° So be gone.
We will not now be troubled with reply.
We offer fair; take it advisedly.
                    *Exit* WORCESTER [*with* VERNON].

**PRINCE**
It will not be accepted, on my life.                        115
The Douglas and the Hotspur both together
Are confident against the world in arms.

**KING**
Hence, therefore, every leader to his charge;
For, on their answer, will we set on them,
And God befriend us as our cause is just!            120
          *Exeunt. Manent*° PRINCE [*and*] FALSTAFF.

**FALSTAFF**   Hal, if thou see me down in the battle and
bestride me, so!° 'Tis a point of friendship.

---

**29 chewet** (1) jackdaw, i.e., chatterer (2) meat pie **32 remember** remind   **44 new-fall'n** by the death of his father, John of Gaunt   **57 gripe** grab   **60 gull, bird** nestling (the cuckoo lays its eggs in other birds' nests, and the young cuckoos when hatched speedily destroy the other nestlings)   **69 dangerous** menacing   **72 articulate** spelled out

**74 face** trim   **75 color** (1) hue (2) rhetorical coloring (hence, pretext)   **77 rub the elbow** hug themselves with delight   **78 innovation** revolution   **88 set . . . head** removed from his record   **96 this before** let me say this in the presence of   **102 Albeit** on the other hand   **106 grace** pardon   **111 wait on us** are in our service   **112 office** duty   **120 s.d. Manent** remain (Latin)   **122 so** I shan't object

PRINCE  Nothing but a colossus can do thee that
friendship. Say thy prayers, and farewell.
FALSTAFF  I would 'twere bedtime, Hal, and all well. 125
PRINCE  Why, thou owest God a death.°          [Exit.]
FALSTAFF  'Tis not due yet: I would be loath to pay
him before his day. What need I be so forward with
him that calls not on me? Well, 'tis no matter; honor
pricks° me on. Yea, but how if honor prick° me off 130
when I come on? How then? Can honor set to a leg?
No. Or an arm? No. Or take away the grief of a
wound? No. Honor hath no skill in surgery then? No.
What is honor? A word. What is in that word honor?
What is that honor? Air—a trim° reckoning! Who 135
hath it? He that died a Wednesday. Doth he feel it?
No. Doth he hear it? No. 'Tis insensible then? Yea,
to the dead. But will it not live with the living? No.
Why? Detraction° will not suffer it. Therefore I'll
none of it. Honor is a mere scutcheon°—and so ends 140
my catechism.                                    Exit.

[Scene II.  The rebel camp, near Shrewsbury.]

Enter WORCESTER [and] Sir Richard VERNON.

WORCESTER
O no, my nephew must not know, Sir Richard,
The liberal and kind offer of the king.
VERNON
'Twere best he did.
WORCESTER               Then are we all undone.
It is not possible, it cannot be,
The king should keep his word in loving us.          5
He will suspect us still and find a time
To punish this offense in other faults.
Supposition all our lives shall be stuck full of eyes;°
For treason is but trusted like the fox,
Who, never so tame, so cherished and locked up,     10
Will have a wild trick° of his ancestors.
Look how we can, or sad or° merrily,
Interpretation will misquote our looks,
And we shall feed like oxen at a stall,
The better cherished still the nearer death.         15
My nephew's trespass may be well forgot;
It hath the excuse of youth and heat of blood,
And an adopted name of privilege°—
A harebrained Hotspur, governed by a spleen.
All his offenses live upon my head                   20
And on his father's. We did train° him on;
And, his corruption being ta'en° from us,
We, as the spring of all, shall pay for all.
Therefore, good cousin, let not Harry know,
In any case, the offer of the king.                  25

Enter HOTSPUR [and DOUGLAS].

VERNON
Deliver° what you will, I'll say 'tis so.
Here comes your cousin.
HOTSPUR                     My uncle is returned.
Deliver up my Lord of Westmoreland.°
Uncle, what news?
WORCESTER
The king will bid you battle presently.             30
DOUGLAS
Defy him by the Lord of Westmoreland.
HOTSPUR
Lord Douglas, go you and tell him so.
DOUGLAS
Marry, and shall, and very willingly.        Exit.
WORCESTER
There is no seeming mercy in the king.
HOTSPUR
Did you beg any? God forbid!                         35
WORCESTER
I told him gently of our grievances,
Of his oath-breaking, which he mended thus,
By now forswearing that he is forsworn.
He calls us rebels, traitors, and will scourge
With haughty arms this hateful name in us.           40

Enter DOUGLAS.

DOUGLAS
Arm, gentlemen, to arms, for I have thrown
A brave defiance in King Henry's teeth,
And Westmoreland, that was engaged,° did bear it;
Which cannot choose but bring him quickly on.
WORCESTER
The Prince of Wales stepped forth before the king   45
And, nephew, challenged you to single fight.
HOTSPUR
O, would the quarrel lay upon our heads,
And that no man might draw short breath today
But I and Harry Monmouth! Tell me, tell me,
How showed his tasking?° Seemed it in contempt?     50
VERNON
No, by my soul. I never in my life
Did hear a challenge urged more modestly,
Unless a brother should a brother dare
To gentle exercise and proof of arms.
He gave you all the duties of a man;°               55
Trimmed up your praises with a princely tongue;
Spoke your deservings like a chronicle;°
Making you ever better than his praise
By still dispraising praise valued with you;°
And, which became him like a prince indeed,          60
He made a blushing cital of° himself,
And chid his truant youth with such a grace
As if he mast'red there a double spirit
Of teaching and of learning instantly.°
There did he pause; but let me tell the world,       65
If he outlive the envy of this day,

126 death pronounced like debt, in which sense Falstaff takes it
130 pricks spurs; prick check (as a casualty)   135 trim fine
(spoken ironically)   139 Detraction slander   140 scutcheon
painted shield with coat of arms identifying a dead nobleman
V.ii.8 Supposition . . . eyes suspicion will always be spying
on us   11 trick (1) trait (2) wile   12 or sad or either sad or
18 an . . . privilege a nickname which carries a privilege (to
be impulsive) with it   21 train (1) draw (2) aim   22 ta'en
taken (like an infection)

26 Deliver report   28 Westmoreland who has been hostage
for the safe return of Worcester and Vernon   43 engaged
held as hostage   50 tasking challenging   55 duties . . . man
duties that one man can owe another   57 like a chronicle
with the itemized detail characteristic of a chronicle history
59 dispraising . . . you i.e., because it must fall so far short
of your deservings   61 cital of reference to   64 instantly
simultaneously

England did never owe° so sweet a hope,
So much misconstrued in° his wantonness.

HOTSPUR
Cousin, I think thou art enamorèd
On his follies. Never did I hear                                    70
Of any prince so wild a liberty.°
But be he as he will, yet once ere night
I will embrace him with a soldier's arm,
That° he shall shrink under my courtesy.
Arm, arm with speed! And, fellows, soldiers, friends,   75
Better consider what you have to do
Than I, that have not well the gift of tongue,
Can lift your blood up with persuasion.

*Enter a* MESSENGER.

MESSENGER
My lord, here are letters for you.

HOTSPUR
I cannot read them now.—                                           80
O gentlemen, the time of life is short!
To spend that shortness basely were too long
If life did ride upon a dial's point,
Still ending at the arrival of an hour.°
And if we live, we live to tread on kings;                         85
If die, brave death, when princes die with us!
Now for our consciences, the arms are fair,
When the intent of bearing them is just.

*Enter another* [MESSENGER].

MESSENGER
My lord, prepare. The king comes on apace.

HOTSPUR
I thank him that he cuts me from my tale,                          90
For I profess not talking: only this—
Let each man do his best; and here draw I
A sword whose temper I intend to stain
With the best blood that I can meet withal
In the adventure of this perilous day.                             95
Now, Esperance! Percy! and set on.
Sound all the lofty instruments of war,
And by that music let us all embrace;
For, heaven to earth,° some of us never shall
A second time do such a courtesy.                                 100
          *Here they embrace. The trumpets sound.* [*Exeunt.*]


[*Scene III. Shrewsbury. The battlefield.*]

*The* KING *enters with his power. Alarum to the battle.*
[*Exeunt.*] *Then enter* DOUGLAS, *and Sir Walter* BLUNT
[*disguised as the king*].

BLUNT
What is thy name, that in battle thus thou crossest me?
What honor dost thou seek upon my head?

DOUGLAS
Know then my name is Douglas,
And I do haunt thee in the battle thus
Because some tell me that thou art a king.                          5

BLUNT
They tell thee true.

DOUGLAS
The Lord of Stafford dear today hath bought
Thy likeness, for instead of thee, King Harry,
This sword hath ended him: so shall it thee,
Unless thou yield thee as my prisoner.                             10

BLUNT
I was not born a yielder, thou proud Scot;
And thou shalt find a king that will revenge
Lord Stafford's death.

*They fight.* DOUGLAS *kills* BLUNT. *Then enter*
HOTSPUR.

HOTSPUR
O Douglas, hadst thou fought at Holmedon thus,
I never had triumphed upon a Scot.                                 15

DOUGLAS
All's done, all's won: here breathless lies the king.

HOTSPUR   Where?

DOUGLAS   Here.

HOTSPUR
This, Douglas? No. I know this face full well.
A gallant knight he was, his name was Blunt;                       20
Semblably° furnished like the king himself.

DOUGLAS
A fool° go with thy soul, whither it goes!
A borrowed title hast thou bought too dear:
Why didst thou tell me that thou wert a king?

HOTSPUR
The king hath many marching in his coats.                          25

DOUGLAS
Now, by my sword, I will kill all his coats;
I'll murder all his wardrobe, piece by piece,
Until I meet the king.

HOTSPUR                    Up and away!
Our soldiers stand full fairly for the day.      [*Exeunt.*]

*Alarum. Enter* FALSTAFF *solus.*

FALSTAFF   Though I could scape shot-free° at London,   30
I fear the shot here. Here's no scoring° but upon the
pate. Soft! Who are you? Sir Walter Blunt. There's
honor for you! Here's no vanity!° I am as hot as
molten lead, and as heavy too. God keep lead out of
me. I need no more weight than mine own bowels.    35
I have led my rag-of-muffins where they are peppered.°
There's not three of my hundred and fifty left alive,
and they are for the town's end, to beg during life.
But who comes here?

*Enter the* PRINCE.

PRINCE
What, stands thou idle here? Lend me thy sword.    40
Many a nobleman lies stark and stiff
Under the hoofs of vaunting enemies,
Whose deaths are yet unrevenged. I prithee
Lend me thy sword.

**V.iii.21 Semblably** similarly **22 fool** the title "fool"
**30 shot-free** without paying the bill **31 scoring** (1) billing
(2) striking **33 Here's no vanity** spoken ironically: i.e.,
here *is* "vanity"—futility, foolishness; but vanity also implies
lightness, which is then set against the "heaviness" of life: cf.
"lead," "heavy," "weight" **36 I . . . peppered** a common practice of officers, who drew the dead soldiers' pay

**67 owe** own **68 in** with respect to **71 liberty** reckless
freedom **74 That** so that **82–84 To . . . hour** If life were
measured by a clock's hand, closing after a single hour, it
would still be too long if basely spent **99 heaven to earth**
the odds are as great as heaven to earth

FALSTAFF  O Hal, I prithee give me leave to breathe 45
awhile. Turk Gregory° never did such deeds in arms
as I have done this day. I have paid° Percy, I have
made him sure.

PRINCE
He is indeed, and living to kill thee.
I prithee lend me thy sword. 50

FALSTAFF  Nay, before God, Hal, if Percy be alive,
thou gets not my sword; but take my pistol if thou
wilt.

PRINCE  Give it me. What, is it in the case?

FALSTAFF  Ay, Hal. 'Tis hot, 'tis hot.° There's that 55
will sack a city.

*The* PRINCE *draws it out and finds it to be a bottle of sack.*

PRINCE
What, is it a time to jest and dally now?
　　　　　　　　　*He throws the bottle at him. Exit.*

FALSTAFF  Well, if Percy be alive, I'll pierce° him. If
he do come in my way, so; if he do not, if I come in
his willingly, let him make a carbonado° of me. I like 60
not such grinning honor as Sir Walter hath. Give me
life; which if I can save, so; if not, honor comes
unlooked for, and there's an end.　　　　　*[Exit.]*

[Scene IV. *Shrewsbury. The battlefield.*]

*Alarum. Excursions.° Enter the* KING, *the* PRINCE, *Lord*
JOHN *of Lancaster, Earl of* WESTMORELAND.

KING
I prithee, Harry, withdraw thyself, thou bleedest too
　much.
Lord John of Lancaster, go you with him.

JOHN
Not I, my lord, unless I did bleed too.

PRINCE
I beseech your majesty make up,°
Lest your retirement do amaze° your friends. 5

KING
I will do so. My Lord of Westmoreland, lead him to
　his tent.

WESTMORELAND
Come, my lord, I'll lead you to your tent.

PRINCE
Lead me, my lord? I do not need your help;
And God forbid a shallow scratch should drive
The Prince of Wales from such a field as this, 10
Where stained nobility lies trodden on,
And rebels' arms triumph in massacres!

JOHN
We breathe° too long. Come, cousin Westmoreland,
Our duty this way lies. For God's sake, come.
　　　[*Exeunt* JOHN *of Lancaster and* WESTMORELAND.]

**46 Turk Gregory** in Shakespeare's time, "Turk" was a byword for any ruthless man; "Gregory" may refer to the
irascible Pope Gregory VII, or to Elizabeth's enemy, Pope
Gregory XIII; Pope and Turk were regarded as the two great
enemies of Protestant Christendom　**47 paid** killed　**55 hot** he
has fired it so often he has had to put it away to cool　**58 pierce**
pronounced "perse"　**60 carbonado** meat slashed open for
broiling
**V.iv.s.d. Excursions** sorties　**4 make up** move forward　**5
amaze** dismay　**13 breathe** pause

PRINCE
By God, thou hast deceived me, Lancaster! 15
I did not think thee lord of such a spirit.
Before, I loved thee as a brother, John,
But now I do respect thee as my soul.

KING
I saw him hold Lord Percy at the point
With lustier maintenance than I did look for 20
Of such an ungrown warrior.

PRINCE
O, this boy lends mettle to us all!　　　*Exit.*

[*Enter* DOUGLAS.]

DOUGLAS
Another king? They grow like Hydra's° heads.
I am the Douglas, fatal to all those
That wear those colors on them. What art thou 25
That counterfeit'st the person of a king?

KING
The king himself, who, Douglas, grieves at heart
So many of his shadows thou hast met,
And not the very king. I have two boys
Seek Percy and thyself about the field; 30
But, seeing thou fall'st on me so luckily,
I will assay thee; so defend thyself.

DOUGLAS
I fear thou art another counterfeit;
And yet, in faith, thou bearest thee like a king.
But mine I am sure thou art, whoe'er thou be, 35
And thus I win thee.

*They fight, the* KING *being in danger. Enter* PRINCE *of*
*Wales.*

PRINCE
Hold up thy head, vile Scot, or thou art like
Never to hold it up again. The spirits
Of valiant Shirley, Stafford, Blunt° are in my arms.
It is the Prince of Wales that threatens thee, 40
Who never promiseth but he means to pay.

　　　　　　　　　*They fight.* DOUGLAS *flieth.*
Cheerly, my lord. How fares your grace?
Sir Nicholas Gawsey hath for succor sent,
And so hath Clifton. I'll to Clifton straight.

KING
Stay and breathe awhile. 45
Thou hast redeemed thy lost opinion,°
And showed thou mak'st some tender° of my life,
In this fair rescue thou hast brought to me.

PRINCE
O God, they did me too much injury
That ever said I heark'ned for your death. 50
If it were so, I might have let alone
The insulting hand of Douglas over you,
Which would have been as speedy in your end
As all the poisonous potions in the world,
And saved the treacherous labor of your son. 55

KING
Make up to Clifton; I'll to Sir Nicholas Gawsey.
　　　　　　　　　　　　　　　　　*Exit.*

*Enter* HOTSPUR.

**23 Hydra** a many-headed monster which grew two heads
for each one destroyed　**39 Shirley, Stafford, Blunt** those
whom Douglas has killed wearing the king's coats　**46 opinion**
reputation　**47 tender** value

HOTSPUR
If I mistake not, thou art Harry Monmouth.
PRINCE
Thou speak'st as if I would deny my name.
HOTSPUR
My name is Harry Percy.
PRINCE
Why, then I see a very valiant rebel of the name.    60
I am the Prince of Wales, and think not, Percy,
To share with me in glory any more.
Two stars keep not their motion in one sphere,°
Nor can one England brook° a double reign
Of Harry Percy and the Prince of Wales.    65
HOTSPUR
Nor shall it, Harry, for the hour is come
To end the one of us; and would to God
Thy name in arms were now as great as mine!
PRINCE
I'll make it greater ere I part from thee,
And all the budding honors on thy crest    70
I'll crop to make a garland for my head.
HOTSPUR
I can no longer brook thy vanities.

*They fight.*

*Enter* FALSTAFF.

FALSTAFF   Well said, Hal! To it, Hal! Nay, you shall
find no boy's play here, I can tell you.

*Enter* DOUGLAS. *He fighteth with* FALSTAFF, [*who*]
*falls down as if he were dead.* [*Exit* DOUGLAS.] *The*
PRINCE *killeth* PERCY.

HOTSPUR
O Harry, thou hast robbed me of my youth!    75
I better brook the loss of brittle life
Than those proud titles thou hast won of me.
They wound my thoughts worse than thy sword my
    flesh.
But thoughts, the slaves of life, and life, time's fool,°
And time, that takes survey of all the world,    80
Must have a stop. O, I could prophesy,
But that the earthy and cold hand of death
Lies on my tongue. No, Percy, thou art dust,
And food for—                                    [*Dies.*]
PRINCE
For worms, brave Percy. Fare thee well, great heart.    85
Ill-weaved ambition, how much art thou shrunk!
When that this body did contain a spirit,
A kingdom for it was too small a bound;
But now two paces of the vilest earth
Is room enough. This earth that bears thee dead    90
Bears not alive so stout° a gentleman.
If thou wert sensible of courtesy,
I should not make so dear° a show of zeal.
But let my favors° hide thy mangled face;
And, even in thy behalf, I'll thank myself    95
For doing these fair rites of tenderness.
Adieu, and take thy praise with thee to heaven.

Thy ignominy sleep with thee in the grave,
But not rememb'red in thy epitaph.

*He spieth* FALSTAFF *on the ground.*

What, old acquaintance? Could not all this flesh    100
Keep in a little life? Poor Jack, farewell!
I could have better spared a better man.
O, I should have a heavy miss° of thee
If I were much in love with vanity.°
Death hath not struck so fat a deer° today,    105
Though many dearer,° in this bloody fray.
Emboweled° will I see thee by-and-by;
Till then in blood by noble Percy lie.    *Exit.*

FALSTAFF *riseth up.*

FALSTAFF   Emboweled? If thou embowel me today,
I'll give you leave to powder° me and eat me too    110
tomorrow. 'Sblood, 'twas time to counterfeit, or that
hot termagant° Scot had paid me scot and lot° too.
Counterfeit? I lie; I am no counterfeit. To die is to be
a counterfeit, for he is but the counterfeit of a man who
hath not the life of a man; but to counterfeit dying    115
when a man thereby liveth, is to be no counterfeit,
but the true and perfect image of life indeed. The
better part of valor is discretion,° in the which better
part I have saved my life. Zounds, I am afraid of this
gunpowder Percy, though he be dead. How if he    120
should counterfeit too, and rise? By my faith, I am
afraid he would prove the better counterfeit. Therefore
I'll make him sure; yea, and I'll swear I killed him.
Why may not he rise as well as I? Nothing confutes
me but eyes, and nobody sees me. Therefore, sirrah    125
[*stabs him*], with a new wound in your thigh, come
you along with me.

*He takes up* HOTSPUR *on his back. Enter* PRINCE [*and*]
JOHN *of Lancaster.*

PRINCE
Come, brother John; full bravely hast thou fleshed
Thy maiden sword.
JOHN                        But, soft! whom have we here?
Did you not tell me this fat man was dead?    130
PRINCE
I did; I saw him dead,
Breathless and bleeding on the ground. Art thou alive,
Or is it fantasy that plays upon our eyesight?
I prithee speak. We will not trust our eyes
Without our ears. Thou art not what thou seem'st.    135
FALSTAFF   No, that's certain, I am not a double man;°
but if I be not Jack Falstaff, then am I a Jack.° There is
Percy. If your father will do me any honor, so; if not,
let him kill the next Percy himself. I look to be either
earl or duke, I can assure you.    140
PRINCE   Why, Percy I killed myself, and saw thee
dead!

---

**63 sphere** orbit   **64 brook** put up with   **79 slaves . . . fool**
i.e., because thoughts are dependent on life and because life is
subservient to time   **91 stout** valiant   **93 dear** heartfelt   **94
favors** probably Hal's ostrich plumes, his emblem as Prince of
Wales

**103 heavy miss** "heavy" loss (in two senses)   **104 vanity**
frivolity (and lightness)   **105 deer** with pun on *dear*   **106
dearer** nobler, more valuable   **107 Emboweled** disemboweled (for embalming)   **110 powder** salt   **112 termagant**
bloodthirsty; **paid . . . lot** killed me (literally, "paid me in
full"; "scot" and "lot" were parish taxes)   **117–18 The . . .
discretion** Falstaff willfully misinterprets the maxim that valor
is the better for being accompanied by discretion   **136 double
man** (1) wraith (2) twofold man   **137 Jack** rascal

FALSTAFF  Didst thou? Lord, Lord, how this world is
given to lying. I grant you I was down, and out of
breath, and so was he; but we rose both at an instant 145
and fought a long hour by Shrewsbury clock. If I
may be believed, so; if not, let them that should
reward valor bear the sin upon their own heads. I'll
take it upon my death, I gave him this wound in
the thigh. If the man were alive and would deny it, 150
zounds! I would make him eat a piece of my sword.

JOHN
This is the strangest tale that ever I heard.

PRINCE
This is the strangest fellow, brother John.
Come, bring your luggage nobly on your back.
For my part, if a lie may do thee grace,                 155
I'll gild it with the happiest terms I have.

*A retreat is sounded.*

The trumpet sounds retreat; the day is ours.
Come, brother, let us to the highest of the field,
To see what friends are living, who are dead.
          *Exeunt* [PRINCE *Henry and Prince* JOHN].

FALSTAFF  I'll follow,° as they say, for reward. He that 160
rewards me, God reward him. If I do grow great, I'll
grow less; for I'll purge,° and leave sack, and live
cleanly, as a nobleman should do.
                    *Exit* [*bearing off the body*].

[Scene V. *Shrewsbury. The battlefield.*]

*The trumpets sound. Enter the* KING, PRINCE *of Wales,*
*Lord* JOHN *of Lancaster, Earl of* WESTMORELAND, *with*
WORCESTER *and* VERNON *prisoners.*

KING
Thus ever did rebellion find rebuke.
Ill-spirited Worcester, did not we send grace,
Pardon, and terms of love to all of you?
And wouldst thou turn our offers contrary?
Misuse the tenor of thy kinsman's trust?                 5
Three knights upon our party slain today,
A noble earl, and many a creature else
Had been alive this hour,

160 **follow** i.e., as hounds do when the quarry is killed, to
receive their reward   162 **purge** repent

If like a Christian thou hadst truly borne
Betwixt our armies true intelligence.°                   10

WORCESTER
What I have done my safety urged me to;
And I embrace this fortune patiently,
Since not to be avoided it falls on me.

KING
Bear Worcester to the death, and Vernon too;
Other offenders we will pause upon.                      15
          [*Exeunt* WORCESTER *and* VERNON, *guarded.*]
How goes the field?

PRINCE
The noble Scot, Lord Douglas, when he saw
The fortune of the day quite turned from him,
The noble Percy slain, and all his men
Upon the foot of fear, fled with the rest;               20
And falling from a hill, he was so bruised
That the pursuers took him. At my tent
The Douglas is, and I beseech your grace
I may dispose of him.

KING                        With all my heart.

PRINCE
Then, brother John of Lancaster, to you              25
This honorable bounty shall belong.
Go to the Douglas and deliver him
Up to his pleasure, ransomless and free.
His valors shown upon our crests today
Have taught us how to cherish such high deeds,          30
Even in the bosom of our adversaries.

JOHN
I thank your grace for this high courtesy,
Which I shall give away immediately.

KING
Then this remains, that we divide our power.
You, son John, and my cousin Westmoreland,              35
Towards York shall bend you with your dearest speed
To meet Northumberland and the prelate Scroop,
Who, as we hear, are busily in arms.
Myself and you, son Harry, will towards Wales
To fight with Glendower and the Earl of March.          40
Rebellion in this land shall lose his sway,
Meeting the check of such another day;
And since this business° so fair is done,
Let us not leave till all our own be won.      *Exeunt.*

**V.v.10 intelligence** information   **43 business** (trisyllabic)

# THE SECOND PART OF
# HENRY THE FOURTH

EDITED BY NORMAN N. HOLLAND, JR.

## Introduction

Betrayal, someone has said, is the quintessential Shakespearean theme. Certainly, it would seem to be in *Henry IV, Part Two*, for this play hinges on two betrayals. Prince John promises the rebels in a battlefield parley their "griefs shall be with speed redressed. Upon my soul, they shall." Then, once the rebels' troops are discharged, he tells them he will indeed redress their grievances "with a most Christian care"—but executes them as rebels. "God, and not we, hath safely fought today." (Some outraged critics have called the line blasphemous.) Then, at the end of the play, after the death of Henry IV, Falstaff expects to be "one of the greatest men in this realm" in something other than size. He cheers his newly crowned Hal only to be answered by one of the most magnificent and brutal lines in all literature: "I know thee not, old man. Fall to thy prayers." Dismissed, banished, he dies in *Henry V* because "The king has killed his heart."

The ethical rightness or wrongness of these actions[1] constitutes one of the two bones of contention this play has cast among critics. The other is the relation of this play to *Henry IV, Part One*: are Parts One and Two[2] separate plays or one long ten-act play? The answers to both (like all questions we ask of Shakespeare) must come from a recognition of the significant wholeness of the work of art he has created, for these two seeming betrayals, morally ambiguous as they may appear, make only two among a host of other such incidents in the play.

For example, in an episode that Shakespeare carefully retained from his sources, the old king, believing a prophecy he is to die "in Jerusalem," expects to die on a crusade. Instead, he finds himself dying, not in the city Jerusalem but in a room in Westminster called "Jerusalem." Once Henry IV is dead, the Lord Chief Justice (who had clapped Hal in prison) thinks himself a man doomed, but

instead, the new king creates him Chief Justice anew, "a father to my youth," and puts him in charge of Falstaff. Bringing these and many other such reversals to a fullness and completion is, of course, the reformation of Hal himself from the madcap prince to what he will be in *Henry V*, "the mirror of all Christian kings." "Let the end try the man," he had warned earlier; and at the end he acts

> To mock the expectation of the world,
> To frustrate prophecies, and to raze out
> Rotten opinion, who hath writ me down
> After my seeming.           (V.ii.126–29)

"Expectation mocked" is the key, a theme that pervades and informs the comic scenes as well as the serious ones. To the Lord Chief Justice's amused outrage, Falstaff, who illustrates "all the characters of age," has the gall to set down his name "in the scroll of youth" and—even—call the Justice old. He manages to elude the legal powers of the Lord Chief Justice (roughly equivalent to the Chief Justice of the U. S. Supreme Court), and then he has the effrontery to try to borrow a thousand pounds from him. Mistress Quickly believes Falstaff will marry her (perhaps the silliest of all expectations in a play of silly expectations), and thus Falstaff manages to turn her lawsuit into a cozy dinner party. Old Justice Shallow, in one of the most exquisite moments of the play, turns away from that death that hovers over all the characters to a startling image of vitality and (in Elizabethan English) virility:

> SHALLOW  Jesu, Jesu, the mad days that I have spent!
> And to see how many of my old acquaintance are dead!
> SILENCE  We shall all follow, cousin.
> SHALLOW  Certain, 'tis certain, very sure, very sure. Death, as the psalmist saith, is certain to all, all shall die. How [much for] a good yoke of bullocks at Stamford Fair?           (III.ii.34–40)

Shallow, the classic portrait of the old grad, makes much of "the wildness of his youth," but we find that his talk is all an old man's lying. Young Shallow was thin, puny, "ever in the rearward of the fashion," and yet, notes

---

[1] Mr. Stanley McKenzie, in an unpublished paper, very skillfully analyzes the ethical problem of the two "betrayals" in terms of the structure and imagery of the play. I am indebted to him for a number of the ideas which follow.

[2] "Part Two" in the title of an Elizabethan history play simply means that the play deals with events later in the reign of the king named in the title than those the Part One play deals with. It does not imply that the play in question is an integral part of a series, like a chapter in a novel.

Falstaff ruefully, "Now has he lands and beeves." Everywhere expectation is overturned. Falstaff picks (from Shallow's point of view) precisely the wrong men for his recruits. Yet even so, Francis Feeble of valorous name turns out to have that stoical acceptance of destiny that constitutes (as we shall see) the essential ethic the play puts forward.

The same sense of expectation mocked permeates the language and imagery of the play. What should give hope or security does not. Armor "worn in heat of day . . . scald'st with safety," while, conversely, "In poison there is physic." Hopes, like ships, "touch ground and dash themselves to pieces," while even houses are "giddy and unsure." The very buds,

> which to prove fruit,
> Hope gives not so much warrant as despair
> That frosts will bite them. (I.iii.39–41)

Fathers who care for their sons, like bees that gather honey, "are murdered for [their] pains." Sleep, in the king's lovely apostrophe, comes to the least likely, the shipboy suffering a storm in the crows' nest:

> Canst thou, O partial sleep, give thy repose
> To the wet sea-son in an hour so rude,
> And in the calmest and most stillest night,
> With all appliances and means to boot,
> Deny it to a king? Then happy low, lie down!
> Uneasy lies the head that wears a crown. (III.i.26–31)

The least fortunate are most fortunate—one cannot predict, for premonitions themselves run by opposites:

> Against ill chances men are ever merry,
> But heaviness foreruns the good event. (IV.ii.81–82)

Even the mere dramaturgic context of 2 Henry IV mocks expectation. The madcap prince of Part Two reverses the reformation we have already seen in Part One. The odd Epilogue treats the plays as the unsuccessful payment of a debt—an expectation—and goes on to contract a further debt: "Our humble author will continue the story, with Sir John in it." But Falstaff does not appear in Henry V, and further, he is not to be confused with the character you expected him to be; "Oldcastle died martyr, and this is not the man" (see p. 723n.).

Even odder than the Epilogue is the Induction with Rumor as the presenter. Shakespeare, as always, sets up the internal logic of his work from the very opening lines: Rumor, whatever else he may be, is the creator and defeater of expectations par excellence, bringer of "smooth comforts false, worse than true wrongs." Here, he announces falsely a rebel victory at Shrewsbury and the death of Prince Hal under the sword of Northumberland's son Hotspur. Then, almost the entire first scene of the play deals with expectations created and defeated (even down to the opening lines in which a porter says that Northumberland will be found in the orchard, but then the Earl himself unexpectedly appears). And, of course, no one expected the madcap prince to overcome "the never-daunted Percy." Learning of his son's death, Northumberland says,

> these news,
> Having been well, that would have made me sick,
> Being sick, have in some measure made me well. (I.i.137–39)

Much later in the play, another old man, King Henry IV, will echo his paradox: "Wherefore should these good news make me sick?" In either case, news—words—seem to have an effect opposite to what one would expect.

The first scene shifts to the second, from one diseased old man to another:

FALSTAFF Sirrah . . . what says the doctor to my water [urine]?
PAGE He said, sir, the water itself was a good healthy water; but, for the party that [owned] it, he might have [more] diseases than he knew for. (I.ii.1–5)

The Page's response, itself a mockery of what we might expect from a doctor, continues from the previous scene the tension between words and body.

As we might expect from Falstaff's "throng of words" or, indeed, the figure of Rumor, "painted full of tongues," words—"prophecies," "seeming," "rotten opinion," "news"—all play a key role in 2 Henry IV in creating expectations that deeds and persons then defeat in fact, as

> chances, mocks,
> And changes fill the cup of alteration
> With divers liquors. (III.i.51–53)

Most notably, Prince John tricks the rebels with his "princely word": "I give it you, and will maintain my word"—though the letter, not the spirit. But there are others whose words create false expectations: Mistress Quickly's malapropisms and Pistol's ranting in garbled quotations make us expect to hear one thing; then, when we hear their blunder, our expectation is mocked. And the rebels, too, create false hopes with words:

> We fortify in paper and in figures,
> Using the names of men instead of men,
> Like one that draws the model of an house
> Beyond his power to build it. (I.iii.56–59)

As Lord Bardolph's words hint, this play uses (unusually often for Shakespeare) names that tag their bearers in a manner almost Dickensian: Pistol, Shallow, Shadow, and Moldy; Doll Tearsheet and Jane Nightwork of amorous name; the sheriff's men, Fang and Snare; Mistress Quickly, whose name, in Elizabethan pronunciation, conceals a ribald pun; Goodman Puff, fat as Falstaff, and hungry Francis Pickbone; Travers, who, in the opening scene, denies ("traverses") Lord Bardolph's report. Yet, as one would expect in a play of expectations mocked, the actual, physical characters often belie their tags; Sampson Stockfish is a fruiterer, Bullcalf a coward, and Feeble brave.

We would be wrong, though, to conclude that words always build up false expectations, that 2 Henry IV envisions no larger plan that one can trust—such a skepticism would be utterly foreign to Shakespeare and the Elizabethans' sense of cosmic order. There is, as the king says, a plan, though a bitter one, "the book of fate" that lists the defeats of our expectations:

O, if this were seen,
The happiest youth, viewing his progress through,
What perils past, what crosses to ensue,
Would shut the book, and sit him down and die.
                                        (III.i.53–56)

And Warwick goes on to make an important statement of the Elizabethans' anecdotal or symbolistic view of history:

There is a history in all men's lives,
Figuring the nature of the times deceased,
The which observed, a man may prophesy,
With a near aim, of the main chance of things
As yet not come to life.               (III.i.80–84)

There is, then, a larger order, and some of the characters find their place in it. Others, notably Falstaff and the rebels who are "betrayed," do not. What is the essential difference between those who find a place and those who are "betrayed"?

As so often in Shakespeare, a peripheral episode tells us, a scene superfluous to the main plot but one which Shakespeare spent some pains to improve from his sources. Hal, thinking his father dead, takes his crown into another room. His father revives and accuses him of wishing parricide. It is, of course, one more episode of expectations mocked, but the king's words tell us more: he accuses Hal of being "hasty," unable to "stay," of wishing his father's death: "What! Canst thou not forbear me half an hour?" Slowly, Hal answers. He did not "affect," that is, crave, desire, the crown. Rather, he took is as an enemy: it "hath fed upon the body of my father." Its gold is no medicine, but rather "hast eat thy bearer up." The king is pleased with his son's "pleading so wisely." Wherein does the wisdom lie?

The king explains in his next speech, "the very latest counsel that ever I shall breathe," presumably, therefore, the most important. He recalls the way he took the crown from Richard in *Richard II*,

How troublesome it sat upon my head.
To thee it shall descend with better quiet.  (IV.v.186–87)

                    It seemed in me
But as an honor snatched with boisterous hand.
                                        (IV.v.190–91)

                    And now my death
Changes the mood, for what in me was purchased
Falls upon thee in a more fairer sort,
So thou the garland wear'st successively.  (IV.v.198–201)

The word "purchased" is important: a legal term, it refers to the acquiring of land other than by inherited succession ("successively"). The word reflects, as the whole play does, the feudal and Renaissance prejudice against those who violate the natural order of things by taking for themselves against the ordained patterns of birth and inheritance. Henry sinned when he "snatched" the crown, but Hal will wear it free of such sin, for he inherits it. The king's accusations tell us Hal's wrong in taking the crown from his sleeping father lay in his inability to "forbear," to "stay," in his "wish," his being "hasty."

Thou hast stol'n that which after some few hours
Were thine without offense.          (IV.v.101–02)

Hal's answer is wise in that he says he did not crave the crown, but rather recognized that the crown is an enemy that feeds on its bearer, eats its bearer up.

Appetite is both the sin and the danger, that appetite which, as the prince had jokingly confessed earlier, "was not princely got." To be truly a prince, one must not crave and try to take, but rather forbear, wait, trust, put oneself in that larger order: God's, nature's, his father's. Appetite governs the common man, not the prince, and, indeed, it was the common people's appetite that let Henry take the crown from Richard, though, says the archbishop,

The commonwealth is sick of their own choice;
Their overgreedy love hath surfeited.    (I.iii.87–88)

Thou, beastly feeder, art so full of [Henry]
That thou provok'st thyself to cast him up.
So, so, thou common dog, didst thou disgorge
Thy glutton bosom of the royal Richard;
And now thou wouldst eat thy dead vomit up,
And howl'st to find it. What trust is in these times?
                                        (I.iii.95–100)

The wise monarch provides for his people's appetites. Henry's last counsel—for his expectation was again foiled, his statement of Hal's rightful title was not his "latest counsel"—Henry's last advice is to "busy giddy minds with foreign quarrels," to turn appetite elsewhere, for Henry knows all too well the rebel and vain spirit is one that seeks to take for itself rather than accept the natural order of monarchy.

That larger order is not wholly beneficent, for it includes, as Shallow reminds us, death. "Death, as the psalmist saith, is certain to all, all shall die," all: Northumberland, the king, Shallow, Silence, Falstaff, the Lord Chief Justice—all the old men in this play of old men are dying. Some try to put it aside, like Falstaff: "Peace, good Doll! Do not speak like a death's head. Do not bid me remember my end." But death cannot be put aside. In Sir Thomas Browne's beautiful sentence, "This world is not an inn but an hospital," not a place to feed but a place to die in. One may consult the doctor as Falstaff does; or, as the archbishop's rebellion tries to do,

          diet rank minds sick of happiness
And purge th' obstructions which begin to stop
Our very veins of life.              (IV.i.64–66)

But purges and potions, be they the medicinable gold that the crown so distinctly is not or the sherris-sack whose virtues Falstaff so eloquently proclaims, are of no real use, for death is certain. Though it may be unexpected, in a chamber named Jerusalem instead of the city, death itself is certain.

The play's images of medicines represent one kind of defense against the acceptance of a larger, cosmic order that includes disease and death; words represent another. Thus, the rebels project and plan, emitting words, "publish[ing] the occasion of our arms." They "fortify with the names of men." The archbishop, so "deep within the books of God," turns himself into "an iron man talking." In general, the rebels emit words and then take them for things, as their predecessor Hotspur did,

> who lined himself with hope
> Eating the air and promise of supply. (I.iii.27–28)

They forget their physical selves and ask only for their "articles," "this schedule," their "conditions" in a "true substantial form." And verbal form is all John gives them.

Falstaff, too, emits a "throng of words" that wrench the "true cause the false way." Contrasted with them, taking language in,

> The prince but studies his companions
> Like a strange tongue, wherein, to gain the language,
> 'Tis needful that the most immodest word
> Be looked upon and learned, (IV.iv.68–71)

but once learned, he will no longer speak, emit, such words, but rather take them "as a pattern or a measure" with which to judge the lives of others.

In other words, the prince will not thrust up a merely verbal reality against the larger order. Rather, he will make himself and his language a part of that larger order, as Prince John does: "God, and not we, hath safely fought today." Pathetically, the rebels themselves try to become part of some larger order: "We are time's subjects."

> We see which way the stream of time doth run,
> And are enforced from our most quiet there
> By the rough torrent of occasion. (IV.i.70–72)

But "occasion" is a transitory thing, a creature of time, and time itself is a great betrayer. The king's party fits into a firmer order: "Construe the times to their necessities." When Warwick states the Elizabethan view of history, he speaks of it as a "necessary form." When King Henry disclaims any intent on his part of seizing Richard's crown, he says,

> necessity so bowed the state
> That I and greatness were compelled to kiss. (III.i.73–74)

And he accepts the rebel threat—

> Are these things then necessities?
> Then let us meet them like necessities. (III.i.92–93)

The rebels, however, are responding, not to "necessities," but their "most just and right desires," the "demands" they seek to "enjoy." Appetite is their failure, and John's strategy simply traps them as animals are baited and trapped by their appetites. They drink as token of their wishes granted, but the drink also symbolizes their failure and defeat through appetite. (Indeed, the archbishop after drinking finds himself "passing light in spirit.")

The real drinker, though, the very essence of appetite, is, of course, Falstaff. "He hath eaten me out of house and home," Mistress Quickly complains. "The old boar" (earlier he had been a sow) doth "feed in the old frank," monetarily, emotionally, and gastrically. At Shallow's, "We shall do nothing but eat, and make good cheer."

Falstaff feeds on Shallow, too, taking a thousand pounds from him, promising to turn him into verbal jokes just as he himself ("the cause that wit is in other men") turns himself to words. Hal's succession provokes him into a riot of appetite: "Let us take any man's horses; the laws of England are at my commandment."

Thus, it is supremely appropriate that Hal reject him ("the feeder of my riots") in terms of food, as, earlier, he had taken leave of a Falstaff richly symbolized as a withered apple. In the coronation scene, Falstaff calls out, "My King! My Jove!" (thus identifying himself with Saturn, the Titan who devoured his own children). Hal replies:

> I know thee not, old man. Fall to thy prayers.
> How ill white hairs becomes a fool and jester!
> I have long dreamt of such a kind of man,
> So surfeit-swelled, so old, and so profane,
> But, being awaked, I do despise my dream.
> Make less thy body hence, and more thy grace.
> Leave gormandizing. Know the grave doth gape
> For thee thrice wider than for other men.
> Reply not to me with a fool-born jest. (V.v.47–55)

Not only does Hal put aside appetite—he fends off Falstaff's wordmongering (even as he himself lapses into two jokes—though he immediately counters, "Presume not that I am the thing I was"). Saddest of all, most brutal but most necessary, he reminds Falstaff of his role as an old man and of the grave's mouth that gapes so widely for him.

The mouth, food and medicine going into it, words coming out, these images dominating a play of appetites and expectations mocked—Shakespeare here harks back to a truth of infancy, to a time when life was a life of the mouth. Psychologists such as Erik Erikson have been stressing in recent years the crucial importance of that time when we must discover our own identities; when we learn, taught by our own appetites, that we must await, trust, expect another to feed us. It is this ability to trust in another that enables the infant to experience that other as an existence separate from his own desires, to experience, therefore, his own separateness, his identity. The paradox continues into later life: it is the ability to give up one's own desires, to trust, even to merge and identify with the "necessity" represented by others, even, in a sense, to tolerate being engulfed by or devoured by it (as King Henry's crown, emblem of the larger order, has eaten its bearer up), that enables us to reemerge, as we did in earliest infancy, into a new sense of identity, a new role. In a paradox almost biblical, we must lose ourselves to find ourselves.

So with Falstaff: to grow into the new role he should assume now that Hal is king, he must curb his appetites ("Leave gormandizing") and learn to depend on another (the "competence of life" his new king allows him). He must live with the certainty that the grave gapes for him, that he will himself be devoured. As for the rebels, they do not let themselves be merged into the larger necessity represented by the monarch; instead, they try to create roles for themselves out of their own words (or mouths). Necessarily, they fail.

Prince Hal, too, must give up an identity based on his own appetites, that of the madcap prince, and accept an identity set out for him, that of the hero-king. As Ernst

Kris points out in a psychoanalytic study of this play, Hal, until his father's death, refuses to fall back into the role his father has planned for him. Rather, he puts aside his father, stained and imperfect as a curber of appetites because he himself "snatched" the crown "with boisterous hand," and he takes an identity from Falstaff, a father-substitute. Once his real father is dead, however, he can put aside Falstaff (ultimately rendering him as dead as his true father) and be taken into the role his father wished for him. Indeed, he can even accept a proper father-substitute in the person of the Lord Chief Justice.

Food is our earliest experience of trust; justice is a later one. Again, we must learn to wait rather than try to grab—we must trust in the largre necessity of law. *2 Henry IV* gives us a pair of justices: a true one in the Lord Chief Justice, a false one in Shallow, who succumbs to his servant's entreaty to "bear out a knave against an honest man." Shallow lets himself merge into a larger order, but one of his servants' making, so that, as Falstaff points out, they become like foolish justices, he a justicelike servingman. The Lord Chief Justice, however, speaks to Hal with "the person of your father"; "the image of his power lay then in me." He justifies his earlier action of imprisoning the prince by reminding the new young king that he, now, has a new identity—"As you are a king, speak in your state." And Hal responds by assuming his kingly role, merging himself in his father's identity so that "I live to speak my father's words." To the Lord Chief Justice,

> You shall be as a father to my youth.
> My voice shall sound as you do prompt mine ear.
> And I will stoop and humble my intents
> To your well-practiced wise directions.          (V.ii.118–21)

> .          .          .

> My father is gone wild into his grave,
> For in his tomb lie my [appetites],
> And with his spirits sadly I survive,
> To mock the expectation of the world.          (V.ii.123–26)

Thus, Hal merges into his father and contrasts with the archbishop, who rebelled though he was "the imagined voice of God himself"; he did

> misuse the reverence of [his] place,
> Employ the countenance and grace of heaven,
> As a false favorite doth his prince's name,
> In deeds dishonorable.          (IV.ii.23–26)

The right people of the play merge into a larger order; the wrong people resist or misuse that larger order. Shallow's very name tells us something about their failure: as Prince John says to the rebels,

> You are too shallow, Hastings, much too shallow,
> To sound the bottom of the after-times.          (IV.ii.50–51)

The image is of a river, and the archbishop had earlier compared himself and the other rebels to a river in flood, saying that, if their demands are granted, "We come within our awful banks again." Henry IV, too, is linked to a flooding river: in a detail Shakespeare retained from his sources, Henry (who was himself a rebel) dies as the Thames thrice floods without ebb. As for Hal,

> The tide of blood in me
> Hath proudly flowed in vanity till now.
> Now doth it turn and ebb back to the sea,
> Where it shall mingle with the state of floods
> And flow henceforth in formal majesty.          (V.ii.129–33)

He has put aside flooding and merged himself into the identity ordained for him by that larger order, vast as the sea. The play can end now, as it began, with a rumor. But now a true rumor, for a bird sings the music of true expectation, the king's will merged into the nation's destiny.

In short, the theme of betrayal permeates and informs the language, incidents, and characters of *2 Henry IV*, but it is betrayal in a special sense: "expectations mocked." That is, the play begins with a sense of hunger or appetite:

> Open your ears, for which of you will stop
> The vent of hearing when loud Rumor speaks? (Ind.1–2)

Then, against selfish or foolish appetite, the play poises a larger, parental plan of justice or monarchy or necessity that threatens to swallow up the characters by danger, disease, or death. And yet this larger necessity offers the paradoxical and unexpected possibility of a new identity, a kind of rebirth into a new self for those who can merge themselves into it. True princeliness calls for this ability to trust in the larger order, to achieve identity by the very act of curbing the self and its appetites and being merged into the greater plan. True rebellion means—in its most primitive sense—feeding oneself, resisting trust in that larger order by substituting one's own medicines, words, appetite, food, plans: "eating the air." And thus, the play itself answers the critics who have been troubled by Prince John's trick on the political rebels and Prince Hal's rejection of the appetitive rebel, Falstaff. These two "betrayals" become necessary and inevitable if we take the play on its own emotional and intellectual terms: the original failure of trust was the rebels' own inability to merge (without wordy conditions) into the larger order of nature.

Again, if we take the play on its own terms, we can see the answer to the second critical issue: the relation of *2 Henry IV* to *1 Henry IV*. The external evidence from Elizabethan stage-practice that the two plays must have been separate and self-sufficient entities is clear enough. The internal evidence is clear, too. *1* and *2 Henry IV* are quite different in their essential dramatic ideas, but they make a matched pair.

We can see the difference in the Falstaffs of the two parts. Twinned in avoirdupois, soldiering, and appetites, they nevertheless differ in some important ways. In both parts, Falstaff is a creature who defeats expectation, not only in the action, but also in our response (as Freud notes). From the point of view of the literary historian, as Bernard Spivack has shown, this mocking of our expectations places him in the tradition of the deceptive Vice of the morality plays or the tricky Ambidexter of a

*Cambises*. But in *1 Henry IV*, Falstaff seems more triumphant: the Chaplinesque clown who, by his ability to play many parts, triumphs even over death, as (in the final battle) he feigns a death-and-rebirth. In *2 Henry IV*, Falstaff resists, but succumbs to, the preordained role pointed out by Philip Williams and C. L. Barber. He becomes the slain god, the Lord of Misrule who must be banished to restore health to the land. Hal is absorbed into the role of the hero-king, while Falstaff is engulfed by a mythic significance that demands his rejection and death.

Miss Caroline Spurgeon noted some years ago that the Falstaff of *1 Henry IV* uses many images from books and the Bible, while the Falstaff of *2 Henry IV* speaks in grotesque, rough, coarse similes drawn from body functions and appetites. We can add that Falstaff One uses a very distinctive figure of speech, the enthymeme: "If I travel but four foot by the squire further afoot, I shall break my wind." "If the rascal have not given me medicines to make me love him, I'll be hanged." "And 'twere not as good a deed as drink to turn true man and to leave these rogues, I am the veriest varlet that ever chewed with a tooth." (These all occur within ten lines in *1 Henry IV*, suggesting the frequency of the figure.) Falstaff Two almost entirely lacks this figure of speech; instead, he has become something of a monologist. He takes in a character, then turns him into a satirical portrait: we see Falstaff Two do this with himself, his page, his tailor, Pistol, Prince Hal, Poins, Bardolph, Shallow, Prince John, and, of course, sherris-sack, in monologues quite different in style from his catechism of honor in *1 Henry IV* (which tests a role). Falstaff Two may be responding to the same taste that led Jonson to put such incidental character sketches into *Every Man Out of His Humor* and *Cynthia's Revels* or that accounts for the popularity of the character-books of Hall, Overbury, and others in the early seventeenth century, but, in any case, he has shifted from acting out different roles (often taken from books and the Bible) to a more passive taking in of what he sees, then spewing it out in words (the image of vomit occurs several times in *2 Henry IV*). Falstaff One's big comic scene is the play-within-the-play in the tavern, when he tries on the roles of King Henry and Prince Hal. Falstaff Two's big comic scene is the recruiting, when he looks at the prospective draftees and coins them into a mint of witty remarks. In short, he becomes the walking embodiment of everything the play rejects: appetite, wordmongering, resistance to one's proper role. He becomes, like Iago in the tragedies, or Autolycus and Caliban in the last plays, Shakespeare's *homo repudiandus*, the character who focuses in himself everything to be rejected. This, then, is the essential difference between the Falstaffs of *1 and 2 Henry IV*: the earlier Falstaff actively tries on different roles; the later and more passive Falstaff finds himself forced into a pattern laid down for him by his context.

And so does Hal. In *1 Henry IV*, he actively chooses the role of hero; in *2 Henry IV*, he lapses into kingship. The rest of the characters show the same passivity. *1 Henry IV* gave us an active, scrappy group of rebels; *2 Henry IV* represents rebellion by talkers and bargainers. *1 Henry IV* sharply opposed characters as good son—bad son; good father—bad father; hot spur and false staff; and Hal forged a role for himself between such extremes. *2 Henry IV*

makes only one such sharp pairing: the good justice, who merges into his master's voice, as against the bad justice, who merges into his servant's. Mostly, *2 Henry IV* bunches fairly nondescript characters into the roles they must assume—and so the Folio text lists them, in bracketed groups as "Opposites against King Henrie the Fourth," "Of the Kings Partie," "Country Soldiers," "Irregular Humorists," and the women. In the same way, *2 Henry IV* abounds in references to parts of the body, parts of a house, parts of a kingdom—the later play constantly stresses a sense of role within a larger plan.

These different ways of dealing with role are what make *1 and 2 Henry IV* quite separate but nevertheless a matched pair. In both, the problem is to bring Hal to the role laid down for him by his father, his king, his God. *1 Henry IV* offers the active solution; *2 Henry IV*, the passive. In the first play, Hal takes from the takers, robs Hotspur and Falstaff of the honors or money they had robbed from others. In the second, Hal is the taker taken: he learns to put down his cravings and appetites and be taken up into the larger plan. *1 Henry IV* is the sunnier version—my pun is intentional—for it looks at the problem of Hal's achieving at-oneness with his father from the point of view of the son who actively battles the rebel within and without. *2 Henry IV* sees the theme with the eyes of a dying father, in terms of passive expectation, trust, and acceptance of necessity. It is this atmosphere of passivity that keeps the magnificent fighter-Hal of *1 Henry IV* out of the action—what action there is—in *2 Henry IV*. Finally, in *Henry V*, these active and passive solutions fuse. Hal's active battling fulfills the role he must passively accept. He brings the drives and appetites of others and their roles as Scot, Irishman, Welshman, or French princess into the service of his kingly function:

> Upon the king! Let us our lives, our souls,
> Our debts, our careful wives,
> Our children, and our sins, lay on the king!
>
> (*Henry V*, IV.i.230–32)

The king must bear all—all but a few traitors and "irregular humorists" who insist on keeping separate. They must die.

Betrayal is the quintessential Shakespearean theme—provided we recognize the special tone that Shakespeare gives it. All his works deal with the taming of shrewishness: the masking over or mastery of hate by love. Betrayal, for Shakespeare, seems to mean a situation in which one can expect love, but in which love falls away and reveals an unsuspected or unmastered hate beneath. Iago is the obvious example, but we can look at all the tragedies as situations in which the love between a man and a woman, love either new or preexisting or expectable, fails to master hate. When love succeeds, the issue is comic, as in *Measure for Measure* and *The Merchant of Venice*, which temper hard justice with feminine mercy. All's well that ends well—that ends in love as Henry V's wars in France will.

So understood, *2 Henry IV*, written near the end of 1597 or early in 1598, occupies a pivotal point in the Shakespearean canon. In the early comedies, romantic love overcomes feuds and hatreds, while in the early histories and tragedies, family or romantic love fails to control political and social aggressions. In the plays of

1598–1601, Shakespeare seems to play with the thought that passivity best counters aggression or romantic assertiveness. Claudio in *Much Ado About Nothing* lets his prince do his wooing for him. In *Twelfth Night*, the woman takes the role of wooer, as she does in *As You Like It*. *2 Henry IV* also looks forward to the tragedies, the uncurbed and parricidal drives of Brutus and Cassius, and even more, to that character who, more than any other in Shakespeare, resists the role his father had set up for him, putting up instead his own smokescreen of words—Hamlet. In many ways, but notably in the special, paternal way love controls rebellion and aggression, *2 Henry IV* seems closer to the tragedies and "problem plays" than to the earlier histories.

The passivity of *2 Henry IV* may also explain why it has become less popular than the other histories. It was apparently as popular as *1 Henry IV* in the eighteenth century, but, then, eighteenth-century audiences were still committed to a larger, hierarchical plan in society. The nineteenth and twentieth centuries prize precisely the acquisitive, assertive behavior that resists inherited patterns and plans, and this particular history play, which so sharply rejects such social individualism, has fallen in popularity. But *2 Henry IV* can look for better days with newer approaches to Shakespeare. Nineteenth-century audiences concentrated on the events represented by the plays rather than on the plays as themselves events and, therefore, they wanted to see in the histories one long epic glorifying England's history—to them, *2 Henry IV* marked a sordid low. Today, however, we recognize that Shakespeare's histories embody Elizabethan political views, not nineteenth-century Whiggery, and we are better at accepting Shakespeare's plays on their own terms, as things-in-themselves. When we do so accept *2 Henry IV*, we find it offers moments as fine as any in the Shakespearean canon: the brilliant and pathetic portrait of Shallow; the grotesquery of Pistol; the prince's reconciliation with his father; the king's apostrophe to sleep; the rejection of Falstaff. More important, when we accept the play itself as an event, our experience of the play becomes our own act of trust.

## A NOTE ON THE SOURCES

As was his custom in the histories, Shakespeare developed *Henry IV, Part Two* from several sources. Chiefly, he used his favorite, Raphael Holinshed's *Chronicles of England, Scotland, and Ireland* (probably the 1587 edition), and an old, anonymous play, *The Famous Victories of Henry V* (performed before 1588, but the earliest extant printing is of 1598). Almost certainly, he drew a few details from Samuel Daniel's long narrative poem, *The First Four Books of the Civil Wars between the Two Houses of Lancaster and York* (1595). He may also have looked at Edward Hall's earlier chronicle, more moralistic than Holinshed's, *The Union of the Two Noble and Illustre Fameliese of Lancastre and Yorke* (1548) or John Stow's *The Chronicles of England* (1580). The story of the prince's giving the Lord Chief Justice a box on the ear and being sent to prison for it was first printed in Sir Thomas Elyot's *Boke Named the Governour* (1531), though the story was widely retold and much stressed in the *Famous Victories*.

Shakespeare took from the *Famous Victories* the broad outlines of the comic sections of *1 and 2 Henry IV* and the battles of *Henry V*. The old play was strong on Hal's roistering and his swaggering companions, and, though it has neither Pistol nor Mistress Quickly, it does offer a crude prototype of Falstaff in "Jockey" or "Sir John Oldcastle" (see p. 723n.), though he is no more than a tadpole compared to Shakespeare's full-blown conception. Holinshed, Daniel, and the other sources were used for the portrait of Henry IV as a king sick in body and soul and also for facts about the various rebellions and battles.

Shakespeare saved from his chronicle sources even small details if they fitted his theme, the failure to fit into a larger order because of a selfish appetite for food, drink, words, or power. Thus, he dutifully recounted from Holinshed the drinking between the armies, the archbishop's preoccupation with his articles, and the floods that mark Henry IV's death. At the same time, he altered large patterns of history where it suited his purpose. Of these changes, one stands out particularly. Shakespeare attributes the "betrayal" of the rebels to Prince John as well as to Westmoreland, though Holinshed had painted Westmoreland as the sole author of the strategy. Obviously, to understand the play fully, we must be able to account for such a marked and faintly discrediting change.

If you can obtain copies of the sources, you can see in still other details how Shakespeare's style of thought differs from his contemporaries', for example by examining three episodes from Shakespeare's play in which he does follow his sources fairly closely. They are rich moments in the Shakespearean world: the scene of the king's death with Hal's precipitate taking of the crown; the coronation scene with the rejection of Falstaff; the forgiving of the Lord Chief Justice. Holinshed sees the first with the eye of a political reporter, interested in events and statecraft, while Daniel sees the king's death in terms of the psychology of the noble classes, and the anonymous author of the *Famous Victories* pleased his broader public with the almost folkloric regeneration of a prodigal son. Reading *2 Henry IV*, IV.v, V.v, and V.ii against these parts of the sources, one experiences not only Shakespeare's fusing of popular and courtly traditions but also that special transmuting touch which was his alone.

## A NOTE ON THE TEXT

*Henry IV, Part Two* comes to us in two—or really, three—texts: the Folio of 1623 and the quarto of 1600; the quarto, however, occurs in two forms, the second (Qb) a modification of the first, evidently to admit a scene (III.i) omitted in Qa. The researches of a number of scholars[3] have now converged to give us a history of these three texts.

Shakespeare wrote the play in late 1597 or early 1598, and from his manuscript (called "foul papers") the Chamberlain's Men had a transcript made to serve as the promptbook for performances. In 1600, possibly to forestall pirating, the company sold the publication rights to *Much Ado About Nothing* and *2 Henry IV*, which were then entered in the Stationers' Register on August 23. The foul papers were sent to the printshop of Valentine

---

[3] Notably J. Dover Wilson, Matthias Shaaber, James McManaway, and John H. Smith.

Simmes for publication in quarto form. While there, perhaps while the copy was being cast off into page-length units for the compositors, the sheets containing Act III.i were misplaced (perhaps mixed into the sheets of *Much Ado About Nothing*, which were in the same handwriting). At this point, the deputy of the Bishop of London, whose task it was to censor the play, read the manuscript and ordered the deletion of eight short passages that might conceivably compare Elizabeth to Richard II or otherwise tend to rebellion. He did not, however, see and censor the longer and more important references to Richard in III.i, for the sheets containing that scene had been mislaid. In due course, Simmes and his men finished and issued the first quarto version of *2 Henry IV*, Qa, and turned to work on *Much Ado About Nothing*. But then someone discovered a scene was missing, and Simmes had to put aside *Much Ado About Nothing* and, at some cost to himself, correct his error by resetting two leaves as four to accommodate the omitted scene. Simmes then issued this second version of the quarto, Qb.

Shakespeare's acting company, meanwhile, was using a transcript of the foul papers for their prompt copy and altering it to indicate their stage-practices: removing profanity, omitting mute characters, revising stage business, and so on. There is, of course, no way to tell whether Shakespeare agreed to these changes or whether they simply accumulated over the years. Further, at some point, the prompt copy itself may have been recopied—perhaps for a collector of plays, perhaps preparatory to printing the Folio; if so, the copyist was probably someone used to working with play texts, who systematically took out colloquial and vulgar expressions, improved the punctuation, and rewrote the stage directions. The Folio text of the play was then set up either directly from the altered prompt copy or indirectly through a transcript of it.

Thus, Qa (supplemented by III.i from Qb) comes closest to Shakespeare's original words and imagined staging—though often in the form of "bunched" stage directions (simply an initial listing at the beginning of a scene of the characters who will appear in it). The Folio suggests alterations in staging that Shakespeare may (or may not) have participated in, and it supplies eight passages the censor removed, but for the most part the Folio is authoritative only to correct obvious blunders or otherwise help in deciphering the oddly punctuated quarto text. Accordingly, I have modernized spelling and punctuation, regularized the speech-tags and the printing of prose and verse, and supplied the Globe act and scene divisions used in standard reference books, but otherwise I have followed the quartos closely, with a few exceptions.

The eight passages I have supplied from the Folio that do not appear in Qa or Qb are: I.i.166–79, *You cast . . . to be?* I.i.189–209, *The gentle . . . follow him.* I.iii.21–24, *Till we . . . admitted.* I.iii.36–55, *Yes, if . . . Or else.* I.iii.85–108, *Let us . . . worst.* II.iii.23–45, *He had . . . grave.* IV.i.55–79, *And with . . . wrong.* IV.i.101–37, *O, my . . . the king.* The Folio also includes many small expansions, some of a word or two, others of whole sentences or phrases. I have included the longer ones, but not those so short as likely to be mere compositors' expansions. Finally, the list of characters appearing at the end of the Folio text I have here reproduced at the beginning.

Occasionally I have adopted certain readings that do not appear in the quartos; these readings are listed in the following, with the accepted reading first in boldface, the rejected reading second in roman. Since, in almost all these cases, I have used the Folio reading instead of the quartos', unless otherwise indicated, the accepted reading is from the Folio (F), the rejected from quarto Qa.

**Ind.36 Where** When **40 s.d. Rumor** [ed.] Rumours **I.i.96 say so** [Q omits] **161 Lord Bardolph** Vmfr[evile] **162 Morton** Bard. [Mour. at line 163] **164 Lean on your** Leaue on you **166–79** [Q omits; F, with editorial *brought* from "bring" at line 178] **189–209** [Q omits] **I.ii.38 smooth** smoothy **49 Where's Bardolph** [after "through it" in Q] **50 into** in **93 hath** haue **99 an age** [ed.] an ague [Q] age [F] **174–75 this age shapes them, are** his age shapes the one **205–06 and Prince Harry** [Q omits] **I.iii.s.d.** [Q includes a mute character, Fauconbridge] **21–24** [Q omits] **26 case** [ed.] cause [F, Q] **36–55** Q omits] **71 Are** And **79 He . . . Welsh** French and Welch he leaues his/back vnarmde, they **85–108** [Q omits] **109 Mowbray** Bish. **II.i.14 and** that [Q omits] **21 vice** view **25 continuantly** continually **43 Sir John** [Q omits] **147 tapestries** tapestrie **171 Basingstoke** Billingsgate **II.ii.s.d. Poins, with** [ed.] Poynes, sir Iohn Russel, with **15 viz.** with **16 ones** once **21 thy the 22 made a shift to** [Q omits] **77 e'en now** [ed.] enow [Q] euen now [F] **83 rabbit** rabble **125–33** [Q and F give to Poins] **132 familiars** family **II.iii.11 endeared** endeere **23–45** [Q omits] **II.iv.12 s.d.** [occurs after line 18, Q; F omits] **13 Will** Dra[wer] [Q; F omits] **177 Die men** Men **225 A** Ah **272 master's** master **285 so to III.i.26 thy** them [Qb] **81 nature of** natures or [Qb] **III.ii.1 come on.** [Qa] come on sir [Qb] **113 Falstaff. Prick him.** Iohn prickes him. [as stage direction, Q] **146 his** [Q omits] **291 would** [ed.] will [F] wooll [Q] **303 Exeunt** [ed.] exit **304–37** [Q assigns this speech to Shallow] **318 invisible** [ed.] inuincible [Q, F] **320 ever** ouer **IV.i.s.d. Mowbray, Hastings** Mowbray, Bardolfe, Hastings **12 could** ["would" in some copies of Q] **30 Then, my lord** [omitted in some copies of Q] **36 appeared** [ed.] appeare **45 figure** ["figures" in some copies of Q] **55–79** [Q omits] After line 92, line omitted: And consecrate commotions bitter edge. [appears in some copies of Q] After line 93, line omitted: To brother borne an houshold cruelty [appears in some copies of Q, but it seems probable that Shakespeare had marked on his ms. that both these lines were to be deleted] **101–37** [Q omits] **114 force** [ed.] forc'd [F] **178 And** [ed.] At [Q, F] **183 not that. If** [ed.] not, that if [F, Q] **IV.ii.1** [notice that there should be no scene division, the action being continuous, and the stage not having emptied. The stage direction at IV.i.224 follows Q] **8 Than** That **19 imagined** [ed.] imagine [Q, F] **24 Employ** Imply **48 this** his **67–71** [as in F; Q assigns 67–68 to bishop, 69–71 to prince] **117 and such acts as yours** [Q omits] **122 these traitors** this traitour **IV.iii.1** [as at IV.ii.1, there should be no scene division] **IV.iv.33 he's** he is **52 Canst thou tell that?** [Q omits] **77 others** other **104 write** wet; **letters** termes **120 and will break out** [Q omits] **132 Softly, pray** [Q omits] **IV.v.1** [as at IV.ii.1, there should be no scene division] **13 altered** vttred [Q, some copies] **49 How fares your grace?** [Q omits] **60–61** [one line in Q] **74 culling** toling **75–79** [text follows F] Our thigh, packt with waxe our mouthes with hony,/We bring it to the hiue: and like the bees,/Are murdred for our paines, this bitter taste/Yeelds his engrossements to the ending father [Q] **79 s.d.** at line 81 in Q **81 hath** hands **107 Which** Whom **160 worst of** worse then **161 is** [Q omits] **177 O my son** [Q omits] **178 it** [Q omits] **204 my** [ed.] thy [Q, F] **220 My gracious liege** [Q omits] **V.i.25 the other day** [Q omits]; **Hinckley** Hunkly **50 but a very** [Q omits] **V.ii.s.d. Enter the Earl of Warwick and the Lord Chief Justice.** Enter Warwike, duke Humphrey, L. chiefe Iustice, Thomas Clarence Prince, Iohn Westmerland **46 mix** mixt **V.iii.5–6 a, a** [Q omits] **35 wag** wags **131 knighthood** Knight **V.iv.s.d. Beadle** Sinckclo [Q, and so in the Q speech-tags for this scene; Sinckclo was a small-part actor in Shakespeare's company] **V.v.25 Falstaff** [Q omits] **30 all** [Q omits]

# THE SECOND PART OF
# HENRY THE FOURTH

The Actors' Names

RUMOR *the Presenter*
KING HENRY THE FOURTH
PRINCE HENRY *afterwards crowned King Henry
    the Fifth*
PRINCE JOHN OF
    LANCASTER
HUMPHREY OF          } *sons to Henry IV and
GLOUCESTER*              *brethren of Henry V*
THOMAS OF CLARENCE
[EARL OF] NORTHUMBERLAND
[RICHARD SCROOP] *the Arch-
    bishop of York*
[LORD] MOWBRAY       } *opposites
[LORD] HASTINGS        against
LORD BARDOLPH          King
TRAVERS                Henry IV*
MORTON
[SIR JOHN] COLEVILLE
[EARL OF] WARWICK
[EARL OF] WESTMORELAND
[EARL OF] SURREY     } *of the king's
[SIR JOHN BLUNT]       party*
GOWER
HARCOURT
LORD CHIEF JUSTICE

POINS
[SIR JOHN] FALSTAFF
BARDOLPH             } *irregular humorists*
PISTOL
PETO [*Falstaff's*] PAGE
[ROBERT] SHALLOW     } *both country justices*
SILENCE
DAVY *servant to Shallow*
FANG AND SNARE *two sergeants*
[RALPH] MOLDY
[SIMON] SHADOW
[THOMAS] WART        } *country soldiers*
[FRANCIS] FEEBLE
[PETER] BULLCALF
NORTHUMBERLAND'S WIFE
PERCY'S WIDOW [*Lady Percy*]
HOSTESS QUICKLY
DOLL TEARSHEET
[*A Dancer as*] EPILOGUE
DRAWERS BEADLES GROOMS
[PORTER MESSENGER SOLDIERS
LORDS ATTENDANTS

*Scene:* England]

686

# [ INDUCTION ]

*Enter* RUMOR, *painted full of tongues.*

[RUMOR]
Open your ears, for which of you will stop
The vent of hearing when loud Rumor speaks?
I, from the orient to the drooping west,
Making the wind my post horse, still unfold
The acts commencèd on this ball of earth. 5
Upon my tongues continual slanders ride,
The which in every language I pronounce,
Stuffing the ears of men with false reports.
I speak of peace while covert enmity
Under the smile of safety wounds the world. 10
And who but Rumor, who but only I,
Make fearful musters and prepared defense
Whiles the big year, swoln with some other grief,
Is thought with child by the stern tyrant, war,
And no such matter? Rumor is a pipe° 15
Blown by surmises, jealousies, conjectures,
And of so easy and so plain a stop
That the blunt° monster with uncounted heads,
The still-discordant wav'ring multitude,
Can play upon it. But what need I thus 20
My well-known body to anatomize
Among my household?° Why is Rumor here?
I run before King Harry's victory,
Who in a bloody field by Shrewsbury
Hath beaten down young Hotspur° and his troops, 25
Quenching the flame of bold rebellion
Even with the rebels' blood. But what mean I
To speak so true at first? My office is
To noise abroad that Harry Monmouth° fell
Under the wrath of noble Hotspur's sword, 30
And that the king before the Douglas' rage
Stooped his anointed head as low as death.
This have I rumored through the peasant towns
Between that royal field of Shrewsbury
And this worm-eaten hole of ragged° stone, 35
Where Hotspur's father, old Northumberland,
Lies crafty-sick.° The posts come tiring° on,
And not a man of them brings other news
Than they have learned of me. From Rumor's tongues
They bring smooth comforts false, worse than true
wrongs. *Exit* RUMOR. 40

# [ ACT I ]

[Scene I. *Northumberland's castle.*]

*Enter the* LORD BARDOLPH *at one door.*

LORD BARDOLPH
Who keeps the gate here, ho? Where is the earl?

PORTER [*Within.*]
What shall I say you are?
LORD BARDOLPH　　　　　Tell thou the earl
That the Lord Bardolph doth attend him here.
PORTER
His lordship is walked forth into the orchard.
Please it your honor, knock but at the gate, 5
And he himself will answer.

*Enter the Earl* [*of*] NORTHUMBERLAND.

LORD BARDOLPH　　　　　Here comes the earl.
NORTHUMBERLAND
What news, Lord Bardolph? Every minute now
Should be the father of some stratagem.
The times are wild. Contention, like a horse
Full of high feeding, madly hath broke loose
And bears down all before him. 10
LORD BARDOLPH　　　　　Noble earl,
I bring you certain news from Shrewsbury.
NORTHUMBERLAND
Good, and° God will!
LORD BARDOLPH　　　As good as heart can wish.
The king is almost wounded to the death;
And, in the fortune of my lord your son, 15
Prince Harry slain outright; and both the Blunts
Killed by the hand of Douglas; young Prince John
And Westmoreland and Stafford fled the field;
And Harry Monmouth's brawn,° the hulk Sir John,
Is prisoner to your son. O, such a day, 20
So fought, so followed, and so fairly won,
Came not till now to dignify the times
Since Caesar's fortunes!
NORTHUMBERLAND　　　How is this derived?
Saw you the field? Came you from Shrewsbury?
LORD BARDOLPH
I spake with one, my lord, that came from thence, 25

*Enter* TRAVERS.

A gentleman well bred and of good name,
That freely rend'red me these news for true.
NORTHUMBERLAND
Here comes my servant Travers,° who I sent
On Tuesday last to listen after news.
LORD BARDOLPH
My lord, I overrode° him on the way, 30
And he is furnished with no certainties
More than he haply° may retail from me.
NORTHUMBERLAND
Now, Travers, what good tidings comes with you?
TRAVERS
My lord, Sir John Umfrevile turned me back
With joyful tidings, and, being better horsed, 35
Outrode me. After him came spurring hard
A gentleman, almost forspent° with speed,
That stopped by me to breathe his bloodied horse.
He asked the way to Chester, and of him
I did demand what news from Shrewsbury. 40
He told me that rebellion had bad luck,
And that young Harry Percy's spur was cold.
With that, he gave his able horse the head,

*The decorative border shown on page 686 appeared on the first page of the fifth quarto edition of* The History of Henry the Fourth [Part One], *1613.*

**Ind.15 pipe** wind instrument **18 blunt** dull **22 my household** the audience **25 Hotspur** Harry Percy, the Earl of Northumberland's son, a rebel against King Henry IV, killed by the Prince of Wales **29 Harry Monmouth** the Prince of Wales, Prince Hal **35 ragged** rough-edged **37 crafty-sick** feigning sickness; **tiring** exhausting themselves

**I.i.13 and** if **19 brawn** fattened boar **28 Travers** to "traverse" is to deny **30 overrode** outrode **32 haply** perhaps **37 forspent** totally used up

And bending forward struck his armèd heels
Against the panting sides of his poor jade°          45
Up to the rowel-head, and starting so
He seemed in running to devour the way,
Staying no longer question.

NORTHUMBERLAND          Ha? Again.
Said he young Harry Percy's spur was cold?
Of Hotspur Coldspur? That rebellion          50
Had met ill luck?

LORD BARDOLPH   My lord, I'll tell you what.
If my young lord your son have not the day,
Upon mine honor, for a silken point°
I'll give my barony. Never talk of it.

NORTHUMBERLAND
Why should that gentleman that rode by Travers          55
Give then such instances of loss?

LORD BARDOLPH          Who, he?
He was some hilding° fellow that had stol'n
The horse he rode on, and, upon my life,
Spoke at a venture. Look, here comes more news.

*Enter* MORTON.

NORTHUMBERLAND
Yea, this man's brow, like to a title-leaf,          60
Foretells the nature of a tragic volume.
So looks the strond° whereon the imperious flood
Hath left a witnessed° usurpation.
Say, Morton, didst thou come from Shrewsbury?

MORTON
I ran from Shrewsbury, my noble lord,          65
Where hateful death put on his ugliest mask
To fright our party.

NORTHUMBERLAND   How doth my son and brother?
Thou tremblest, and the whiteness in thy cheek
Is apter than thy tongue to tell thy errand.
Even such a man, so faint, so spiritless,          70
So dull, so dead in look, so woebegone,
Drew Priam's curtain in the dead of night,
And would have told him half his Troy was burnt.
But Priam found the fire ere he his tongue
And I my Percy's death ere thou report'st it.          75
This thou wouldst say, "Your son did thus and thus;
Your brother thus. So fought the noble Douglas,"
Stopping my greedy ear with their bold deeds.
But in the end, to stop my ear indeed,
Thou hast a sigh to blow away this praise,          80
Ending with "Brother, son, and all are dead."

MORTON
Douglas is living, and your brother—yet;
But, for my lord your son—

NORTHUMBERLAND          Why, he is dead!
See what a ready tongue suspicion hath!
He that but fears the thing he would not know          85
Hath by instinct knowledge from others' eyes
That what he feared is chanced. Yet speak, Morton.
Tell thou an earl his divination lies,
And I will take it as a sweet disgrace
And make thee rich for doing me such wrong.          90

MORTON
You are too great to be by me gainsaid.
Your spirit is too true, your fears too certain.

NORTHUMBERLAND
Yet, for all this, say not that Percy's dead.
I see a strange confession in thine eye.
Thou shak'st thy head and hold'st it fear, or sin,          95
To speak a truth. If he be slain, say so.
The tongue offends not that reports his death;
And he doth sin that doth belie the dead,
Not he which says the dead is not alive.
Yet the first bringer of unwelcome news          100
Hath but a losing office, and his tongue
Sounds ever after as a sullen bell,
Rememb'red tolling a departing friend.

LORD BARDOLPH
I cannot think, my lord, your son is dead.

MORTON
I am sorry I should force you to believe          105
That which I would to God I had not seen.
But these mine eyes saw him in bloody state,
Rend'ring faint quittance,° wearied and out-breathed,
To Harry Monmouth, whose swift wrath beat down
The never-daunted Percy to the earth,          110
From whence with life he never more sprung up.
In few,° his death, whose spirit lent a fire
Even to the dullest peasant in his camp,
Being bruited° once, took fire and heat away
From the best-tempered courage in his troops.          115
For from his mettle was his party steeled,
Which once in him abated, all the rest
Turned on themselves, like dull and heavy lead.
And as the thing that's heavy in itself,
Upon enforcement flies with greatest speed,          120
So did our men, heavy in Hotspur's loss,
Lend to this weight such lightness with their fear
That arrows fled not swifter toward their aim
Than did our soldiers, aiming at their safety,
Fly from the field. Then was that noble Worcester          125
So soon ta'en prisoner. And that furious Scot,
The bloody Douglas, whose well-laboring sword
Had three times slain th' appearance of the king,°
'Gan vail his stomach° and did grace° the shame
Of those that turned their backs, and in his flight,          130
Stumbling in fear, was took. The sum of all
Is that the king hath won, and hath sent out
A speedy power to encounter you, my lord,
Under the conduct of young Lancaster
And Westmoreland. This is the news at full.          135

NORTHUMBERLAND
For this I shall have time enough to mourn.
In poison there is physic;° and these news,
Having been well, that° would have made me sick,
Being sick, have in some measure made me well.
And, as the wretch whose fever-weak'ned joints,          140
Like strengthless hinges, buckle under life,
Impatient of his fit, breaks like a fire
Out of his keeper's arms, even so my limbs,
Weak'ned with grief, being now enraged with grief,°
Are thrice themselves. Hence, therefore, thou nice°
          crutch!          145

---

108 **quittance** repaying (of blows)   112 **few** few words   114
**bruited** noised about   128 **th' appearance of the king**
noblemen disguised as the king   129 **'Gan . . . stomach**
began to abate his courage; **grace** favor   137 **physic** medicine
138 **Having . . . that** that, had they been well   144 **grief
. . . grief** sickness . . . sorrow   145 **nice** delicate

45 **jade** nag   53 **point** lace (used to tie breeches up)   57
**hilding** base   62 **strond** shore   63 **a witnessed** evidence of

A scaly gauntlet now with joints of steel
Must glove this hand. And hence, thou sickly quoif!°
Thou art a guard too wanton° for the head
Which princes, fleshed with° conquest, aim to hit.
Now bid my brows with iron, and approach    150
The ragged'st° hour that time and spite dare bring
To frown upon th' enraged Northumberland!
Let heaven kiss earth! Now let not nature's hand
Keep the wild flood confined! Let order die!
And let this world no longer be a stage    155
To feed contention in a ling'ring act!°
But let one spirit of the first-born Cain
Reign in all bosoms, that, each heart being set
On bloody courses, the rude scene may end,
And darkness be the burier of the dead!    160

LORD BARDOLPH
This strainèd passion doth you wrong, my lord.

MORTON
Sweet earl, divorce not wisdom from your honor.
The lives of all your loving complices
Lean on your health, the which, if you give o'er
To stormy passion, must perforce decay.    165
You cast th' event° of war, my noble lord,
And summed the account of chance, before you said,
"Let us make head."° It was your presurmise
That, in the dole° of blows, your son might drop.
You knew he walked o'er perils, on an edge,    170
More likely to fall in than to get o'er.
You were advised his flesh was capable
Of wounds and scars and that his forward spirit
Would lift him where most trade of danger ranged.
Yet did you say, "Go forth." And none of this,    175
Though strongly apprehended, could restrain
The stiff-borne° action. What hath then befall'n,
Or what hath this bold enterprise brought forth,
More than that being which was like to be?

LORD BARDOLPH
We all that are engagèd° to this loss    180
Knew that we ventured on such dangerous seas
That if we wrought out life 'twas ten to one.
And yet we ventured, for the gain proposed
Choked the respect° of likely peril feared.
And since we are o'erset,° venture again.    185
Come, we will all put forth,° body and goods.

MORTON
'Tis more than time. And, my most noble lord,
I hear for certain, and dare speak the truth:
The gentle Archbishop of York is up
With well-appointed pow'rs.° He is a man    190
Who with a double° surety binds his followers.
My lord your son had only but the corpse,
But shadows and the shows of men, to fight.
For that same word "rebellion" did divide
The action of their bodies from their souls,    195
And they did fight with queasiness, constrained,

As men drink potions, that their weapons only
Seemed on our side. But for their spirits and souls,
This word "rebellion," it had froze them up
As fish are in a pond. But now the bishop    200
Turns insurrection to religion.
Supposed sincere and holy in his thoughts,
He's followed both with body and with mind,
And doth enlarge his rising with the blood
Of fair King Richard, scraped from Pomfret° stones;    205
Derives from heaven his quarrel and his cause;
Tells them he doth bestride a bleeding land,
Gasping for life under great Bolingbroke;°
And more and less° do flock to follow him.

NORTHUMBERLAND
I knew of this before; but, to speak truth,    210
This present grief had wiped it from my mind.
Go in with me, and counsel every man
The aptest way for safety and revenge.
Get° posts and letters, and make° friends with speed.
Never so few, and never yet more need.    *Exeunt.*   215

[Scene II. *London.*]

*Enter Sir John [FALSTAFF] alone, with his PAGE bearing his sword and buckler.*

FALSTAFF   Sirrah, you giant,° what says the doctor to
my water?°

PAGE   He said, sir, the water itself was a good healthy
water; but, for the party that owed° it, he might have
moe° diseases than he knew for.    5

FALSTAFF   Men of all sorts take a pride to gird° at me.
The brain of this foolish compounded clay, man,° is
not able to invent anything that intends to laughter
more than I invent or is invented on me. I am not only
witty in myself, but the cause that wit is in other men.    10
I do here walk before thee like a sow that hath overwhelmed all her litter but one. If the prince put thee
into my service for any other reason than to set me off,
why then I have no judgment. Thou whoreson mandrake,° thou art fitter to be worn in my cap than to    15
wait at my heels. I was never manned with an agate°
till now, but I will inset you neither in gold nor silver,
but in vile apparel, and send you back again to your
master, for a jewel—the juvenal,° the prince your
master, whose chin is not yet fledge.° I will sooner    20
have a beard grow in the palm of my hand than he
shall get one off his cheek, and yet he will not stick to
say his face is a face-royal.° God may finish it when he
will, 'tis not a hair amiss yet. He may keep it still at a
face-royal,° for a barber shall never earn sixpence out    25
of it; and yet he'll be crowing as if he had writ° man

---

**205 Pomfret** Pomfret castle (where Richard II was murdered)
**208 Bolingbroke** King Henry IV   **209 more and less** high
and low   **214 Get** beget; **make** collect
**I.ii.1 giant** the Page was played by an unusually small boy, who
probably mimicked Falstaff   **2 water** urine   **4 owed** owned
**5 moe** more   **6 gird** mock   **7 compounded clay, man** man,
compounded of clay   **14–15 mandrake** man-shaped root   **16
manned . . . agate** attended by a servingman small as a
figure carved in a jewel   **19 juvenal** juvenile (echoing jewel)
**20 fledge** feathered   **23, 25 face-royal** the king's face on a
ten-shilling coin (the royal), which presumably would not
need the attention of a barber   **26 writ** styled himself

**147 quoif** nightcap   **148 wanton** light   **149 fleshed with**
having savored   **151 ragged'st** roughest   **156 act** (1) deed
(2) section of a play   **166 cast th' event** estimated the outcome
**168 make head** raise an army   **169 dole** dealing out   **177
stiff-borne** determinedly carried on   **180 engagèd** bound
by contract   **184 respect** consideration   **185 o'erset** (1) upset,
capsized (2) outwagered   **186 put forth** wager   **190 well-
appointed pow'rs** well-equipped armies   **191 double** i.e., of
body and soul

ever since his father was a bachelor. He may keep his own grace,° but he's almost out of mine, I can assure him. What said Master Dummelton about the satin for·my short cloak and my slops?°                                    30

PAGE  He said, sir, you should procure him better assurance° than Bardolph. He would not take his band° and yours; he liked not the security.

FALSTAFF  Let him be damned, like the glutton!° Pray God his tongue be hotter! A whoreson Achito-  35 phel!° A rascal, yea-forsooth knave!° To bear a gentle-man in hand, and then stand upon security! The whoreson smooth-pates° do now wear nothing but high shoes,° and bunches of keys° at their girdles; and if a man is through with them in honest taking up,  40 then they must stand upon security.° I had as lief they would put ratsbane in my mouth as offer to stop it with "security." I looked 'a° should have sent me two-and-twenty yards of satin, as I am a true knight, and he sends me "security." Well, he may sleep in  45 security, for he hath the horn° of abundance, and the lightness° of his wife shines through it. And yet cannot he see, though he have his own lanthorn° to light him. Where's Bardolph?

PAGE  He's gone into Smithfield° to buy your worship  50 a horse.

FALSTAFF  I bought him in Paul's,° and he'll buy me a horse in Smithfield. And I could get me but a wife in the stews,° I were manned, horsed, and wived.°

*Enter Lord* CHIEF JUSTICE [*and* SERVANT].

PAGE  Sir, here comes the nobleman that committed°  55 the prince for striking him about Bardolph.

FALSTAFF  Wait close—I will not see him.

CHIEF JUSTICE  What's he that goes there?

SERVANT  Falstaff, and't please your lordship.

CHIEF JUSTICE  He that was in question° for the  60 robb'ry?

SERVANT  He, my lord. But he hath since done good service at Shrewsbury, and, as I hear, is now going with some charge° to the Lord John of Lancaster.

CHIEF JUSTICE  What, to York? Call him back again.  65

SERVANT  Sir John Falstaff!

FALSTAFF  Boy, tell him I am deaf.

PAGE  You must speak louder; my master is deaf.

CHIEF JUSTICE  I am sure he is—to the hearing of anything good. Go, pluck him by the elbow. I must  70 speak with him.

SERVANT  Sir John!

FALSTAFF  What! A young knave, and begging! Is there not wars? Is there not employment? Doth not the king lack subjects? Do not the rebels need soldiers?  75 Though it be a shame to be on any side but one, it is worse shame to beg than to be on the worst side, were it worse than the name of rebellion can tell how to make it.

SERVANT  You mistake me, sir.                                80

FALSTAFF  Why, sir, did I say you were an honest man? Setting my knighthood and my soldiership aside,° I had lied in my throat if I had said so.

SERVANT  I pray you, sir, then set your knighthood and your soldiership aside and give me leave to tell you  85 you lie in your throat if you say I am any other than an honest man.

FALSTAFF  I give thee leave to tell me so! I lay aside that which grows to me! If thou get'st any leave of me, hang me. If thou tak'st leave, thou wert better be  90 hanged. You hunt counter.° Hence! Avaunt!

SERVANT  Sir, my lord would speak with you.

CHIEF JUSTICE  Sir John Falstaff, a word with you.

FALSTAFF  My good lord! God give your lordship good time of day. I am glad to see your lordship abroad.  95 I heard say your lordship was sick. I hope your lordship goes abroad by advice.° Your lordship, though not clean past your youth, hath yet some smack of an age° in you, some relish of the saltness of time in you; and I most humbly beseech your lordship  100 to have a reverent care of your health.

CHIEF JUSTICE  Sir John, I sent for you before your expedition to Shrewsbury.

FALSTAFF  And't please your lordship, I hear his majesty is returned with some discomfort from Wales.  105

CHIEF JUSTICE  I talk not of his majesty. You would not come when I sent for you.

FALSTAFF  And I hear, moreover, his highness is fall'n into this same whoreson apoplexy.

CHIEF JUSTICE  Well, God mend him! I pray you, let  110 me speak with you.

FALSTAFF  This apoplexy, as I take it, is a kind of lethargy, and't please your lordship, a kind of sleeping in the blood, a whoreson tingling.

CHIEF JUSTICE  What, tell you me of it? Be it as it is.  115

FALSTAFF  It hath it original° from much grief, from study and perturbation of the brain. I have read the cause of his effects in Galen.° It is a kind of deafness.

CHIEF JUSTICE  I think you are fall'n into the disease, for you hear not what I say to you.                    120

FALSTAFF  Very well, my lord, very well. Rather, and't please you, it is the disease of not listening, the malady of not marking, that I am troubled withal.

CHIEF JUSTICE  To punish you by the heels° would

---

28 **grace** (1) title, "your grace" (2) favor  30 **slops** wide breeches  32 **assurance** security (Bardolph is not Lord Bardolph, but one of Falstaff's cronies)  33 **band** bond  34 **glutton** Dives (who in Luke 16:24 asked for water to cool his tongue)  35–36 **Achitophel** the counselor who betrayed Absalom (II Samuel 15–17)  36 **yea-forsooth knave** one who swears sissy oaths like "yea, forsooth"  38 **smooth-pates** tradesmen (who wore their hair short, not like a nobleman's)  39 **high shoes** sign of pride; **keys** sign of possessions  40–41 **if . . . security** after a man completes a bargain on credit with them, they suddenly demand security  43 **'a** he  46 **horn** (1) cornucopia (2) cuckold's horn  47 **lightness** unchastity  48 **lanthorn** lantern (in which a light shines through horn panels)  50 **Smithfield** the horse market  52 **Paul's** unemployed men loitered in Saint Paul's cathedral seeking service  54 **stews** brothels; **manned . . . wived** a proverb: "Who goes to Westminster for a wife, to Paul's for a man, or to Smithfield for a horse, may meet with a whore, a knave, and a jade"  55 **committed** i.e., to prison (notice that the audience needed only this brief allusion to the story about Hal striking the Lord Chief Justice)  60 **in question** suspected  64 **charge** commission for soldiers

82–83 **Setting . . . aside** i.e., because knights and soldiers ought not to lie  91 **counter** in the wrong direction  97 **advice** a physician's advice  99 **age** pun on *ague*; cf. IV.i.34  116 **it original** its origin  118 **Galen** Greek physician (A.D. 129–99) whose writings dominated Renaissance medical practice  124 **punish . . . heels** put you in fetters or the stocks

amend the attention of your ears, and I care not if I do 125
become your physician.

FALSTAFF  I am as poor as Job, my lord, but not so
patient. Your lordship may minister the potion of
imprisonment to me in respect of poverty; but how
I should be your patient to follow your prescriptions, 130
the wise may make some dram° of a scruple,° or indeed
a scruple itself.

CHIEF JUSTICE  I sent for you, when there were
matters against you for your life, to come speak with
me. 135

FALSTAFF  As I was then advised by my learned counsel
in the laws of this land-service,° I did not come.

CHIEF JUSTICE  Well, the truth is, Sir John, you live
in great infamy.

FALSTAFF  He that buckles himself in my belt cannot 140
live in less.

CHIEF JUSTICE  Your means are very slender and
your waste is great.

FALSTAFF  I would it were otherwise. I would my
means were greater and my waist slender. 145

CHIEF JUSTICE  You have misled the youthful prince.

FALSTAFF  The young prince hath misled me. I am the
fellow with the great belly,° and he my dog.

CHIEF JUSTICE  Well, I am loath to gall a new-healed
wound. Your day's service at Shrewsbury hath a little 150
gilded over your night's exploit° on Gad's Hill. You
may thank th' unquiet time for your quiet o'erposting°
that action.

FALSTAFF  My lord?

CHIEF JUSTICE  But since all is well, keep it so. Wake 155
not a sleeping wolf.

FALSTAFF  To wake a wolf is as bad as smell a fox.°

CHIEF JUSTICE  What! You are as a candle, the better
part burnt out.

FALSTAFF  A wassail candle,° my lord, all tallow. If I 160
did say of wax,° my growth would approve the truth.

CHIEF JUSTICE  There is not a white hair in your face
but should have his effect of gravity.

FALSTAFF  His effect of gravy,° gravy, gravy.

CHIEF JUSTICE  You follow the young prince up and 165
down like his ill angel.

FALSTAFF  Not so, my lord. Your ill angel° is light,°
but I hope he that looks upon me will take me without
weighing. And yet, in some respects, I grant, I cannot
go.° I cannot tell. Virtue is of so little regard in these 170
costermongers'° times that true valor is turned berod.°
Pregnancy° is made a tapster, and hath his quick wit
wasted in giving reckonings.° All the other gifts
appertinent to man, as the malice of this age shapes

them, are not worth a gooseberry. You that are old 175
consider not the capacities of us that are young. You
do measure the heat of our livers with the bitterness of
your galls. And we that are in the vaward° of our
youth, I must confess, are wags too.

CHIEF JUSTICE  Do you set down your name in the 180
scroll of youth, that are written down old with all the
characters of age? Have you not a moist eye, a dry hand,
a yellow cheek, a white beard, a decreasing leg, an
increasing belly? Is not your voice broken, your wind
short, your chin double, your wit single,° and every 185
part about you blasted with antiquity, and will you
yet call yourself young? Fie, fie, fie, Sir John!

FALSTAFF  My lord, I was born about three of the
clock in the afternoon, with a white head and something a round belly. For my voice, I have lost it with 190
hallowing° and singing of anthems. To approve° my
youth further, I will not. The truth is, I am only old
in judgment and understanding; and he that will
caper° with me for a thousand marks, let him lend me
the money, and have at him! For the box of the ear 195
that the prince gave you, he gave it like a rude prince,
and you took it like a sensible lord. I have checked°
him for it, and the young lion repents, marry, not
in ashes and sackcloth, but in new silk and old
sack.° 200

CHIEF JUSTICE  Well, God send the prince a better
companion!

FALSTAFF  God send the companion a better prince!
I cannot rid my hands of him.

CHIEF JUSTICE  Well, the king hath severed you and 205
Prince Harry. I hear you are going with Lord John of
Lancaster against the archbishop and the Earl of
Northumberland.

FALSTAFF  Yea, I thank your pretty sweet wit for it.
But look you° pray, all you that kiss my lady peace 210
at home, that our armies join not in a hot day, for, by
the Lord, I take but two shirts out with me, and I
mean not to swear extraordinarily. If it be a hot day,
and I brandish anything but a bottle, I would I might
never spit white° again. There is not a dangerous action 215
can peep out his head but I am thrust upon it. Well, I
cannot last ever. But it was alway yet the trick of our
English nation, if they have a good thing, to make it
too common. If ye will needs say I am an old man,
you should give me rest. I would to God my name were 220
not so terrible to the enemy as it is. I were better to be
eaten to death with a rust than to be scoured to nothing
with perpetual motion.

CHIEF JUSTICE  Well, be honest, be honest, and God
bless your expedition! 225

FALSTAFF  Will your lordship lend me a thousand
pound to furnish me forth?

CHIEF JUSTICE  Not a penny, not a penny. You are
too impatient to bear crosses.° Fare you well. Commend me to my cousin Westmoreland. 230

[*Exeunt* CHIEF JUSTICE *and* SERVANT.]

131 **dram, scruple** apothecaries' small weights   137 **land-service** a play on military service—in which Falstaff's sword would be his "learned counsel"—as against the service of a legal summons   148 **belly** so large he cannot see where he is going and therefore needs a dog to lead him (?); a reference to some well-known beggar (?)   151 **exploit** the robbery in *1 Henry IV*, II.ii. and II.iv   152 **quiet o'erposting** quietly getting past   157 **smell a fox** be suspicious   160 **wassail candle** large candle designed to last a whole night, as at a feast   161 **wax** a play on (1) beeswax (2) grow   164 **gravy** with pun on the sense "fatty sweat"   167 **ill angel** clipped coin; **light** (1) not due weight (2) wanton   170 **go** (1) pass for currency (2) copulate (?)   171 **costermongers'** hucksters'; **berod** bear-herd, one who leads tame bears   172 **Pregnancy** quickness of wit   173 **reckonings** tavern bills

178 **vaward** vanguard   185 **single** weak   191 **hallowing** (1) sanctifying (2) "halloing," shouting to hounds; **approve** prove   194 **caper** compete at dancing   197 **checked** reproved   200 **sack** sherry   210 **look you** make sure you   215 **spit white** (1) suffer a dry mouth from carousing (2) emit semen (?)   229 **crosses** (1) afflictions (2) coins marked with a cross

FALSTAFF  If I do, fillip° me with a three-man beetle.°
A man can no more separate age and covetousness
than 'a can part young limbs and lechery. But the
gout galls the one and the pox pinches the other, and
so both the degrees° prevent° my curses. Boy!          235

PAGE  Sir?

FALSTAFF  What money is in my purse?

PAGE  Seven groats° and twopence.

FALSTAFF  I can get no remedy against this consumption of the purse. Borrowing only lingers and lingers  240
it out, but the disease is incurable. Go bear this letter
to my Lord of Lancaster, this to the prince, this to the
Earl of Westmoreland, and this to old Mistress Ursula,
whom I have weekly sworn to marry since I perceived
the first white hair of my chin. About it. You know   245
where to find me. [Exit PAGE.] A pox of this gout!
Or a gout of this pox! For the one or the other plays
the rogue with my great toe. 'Tis no matter if I do
halt°—I have the wars for my color,° and my pension
shall seem the more reasonable. A good wit will make  250
use of anything. I will turn diseases to commodity.°
                                                    [Exit.]

[Scene III. The rebels' meeting place.]

Enter th' ARCHBISHOP, Thomas MOWBRAY (Earl
Marshall), the Lord HASTINGS and [LORD] BARDOLPH.

ARCHBISHOP
Thus have you heard our cause and known our means;
And, my most noble friends, I pray you all,
Speak plainly your opinions of our hopes.
And first, Lord Marshall, what say you to it?

MOWBRAY
I well allow the occasion° of our arms,                 5
But gladly would be better satisfied
How in our means we should advance ourselves
To look with forehead bold and big enough
Upon the power and puissance° of the king.

HASTINGS
Our present musters grow upon the file°               10
To five-and-twenty thousand men of choice;
And our supplies° live largely in the hope
Of great Northumberland, whose bosom burns
With an incensèd fire of injuries.

LORD BARDOLPH
The question then, Lord Hastings, standeth thus:      15
Whether our present five-and-twenty thousand
May hold up head without Northumberland?

HASTINGS
With him, we may.

LORD BARDOLPH          Yea, marry,° there's the point.
But if without him we be thought too feeble,
My judgment is, we should not step too far            20

Till we had his assistance by the hand.
For in a theme so bloody-faced as this,
Conjecture, expectation, and surmise
Of aids incertain should not be admitted.

ARCHBISHOP
'Tis very true, Lord Bardolph, for indeed             25
It was young Hotspur's case at Shrewsbury.

LORD BARDOLPH
It was, my lord, who lined° himself with hope,
Eating the air and promise of supply,
Flatt'ring himself in project of a power
Much smaller than° the smallest of his thoughts,      30
And so, with great imagination
Proper to madmen, led his powers to death
And, winking,° leaped into destruction.

HASTINGS
But, by your leave, it never yet did hurt
To lay down likelihoods and forms of hope.            35

LORD BARDOLPH
Yes, if this present quality of war.°
Indeed the instant action, a cause on foot,
Lives so in hope as in an early spring
We see th' appearing buds, which to prove fruit,
Hope gives not so much warrant as despair°            40
That frosts will bite them. When we mean to build,
We first survey the plot, then draw the model.°
And when we see the figure° of the house,
Then must we rate the cost of the erection,
Which if we find outweighs ability,                   45
What do we then but draw anew the model
In fewer offices,° or at least° desist
To build at all? Much more, in this great work,
Which is almost to pluck a kingdom down
And set another up, should we survey                  50
The plot of situation and the model,
Consent° upon a sure foundation,
Question surveyors, know our own estate,
How able such a work to undergo,
To weigh against his opposite.° Or else               55
We fortify in paper and in figures,
Using the names of men instead of men,
Like one that draws the model of an house
Beyond his power to build it, who, half through,
Gives o'er and leaves his part-created cost°          60
A naked subject to the weeping clouds
And waste for churlish winter's tyranny.

HASTINGS
Grant that our hopes, yet likely of fair birth,
Should be stillborn, and that we now possessed
The utmost man of expectation,                        65
I think we are so, body strong enough
Even as we are, to equal with the king.

LORD BARDOLPH
What, is the king but five-and-twenty thousand?

231 fillip flip; three-man beetle a battering-ram carried by three men (what it would take to "fillip" Falstaff) 235 degrees stations in life; prevent act before 238 groats fourpenny coins 249 halt limp; color (1) pretense (2) battle flag 251 commodity something to sell
I.iii.5 allow the occasion approve the cause 9 puissance strength 10 file catalog 12 supplies reinforcements 18 marry a mild oath, "By the Virgin Mary"

27 lined reinforced (as in tailoring) 29-30 in . . . than in planning on the basis of an army that in fact was much smaller than 33 winking shutting his eyes 36 Yes . . . war a famous obscurity, perhaps saying: Yes, it does do hurt to plan if this planning present (i.e., represent, substitute for) quality (i.e., true substance, strength) of war 40 despair (supply: "gives warrant") 42 model plan 43 figure design 47 offices rooms for service; least worst 52 Consent agree 55 his opposite its opposition 60 part-created cost half-realized expenditure

**HASTINGS**
To us no more, nay, not so much, Lord Bardolph.
For his divisions, as the times do brawl,     70
Are in three heads: one power against the French,
And one against Glendower, perforce a third
Must take up us. So is the unfirm king
In three divided, and his coffers sound
With hollow poverty and emptiness.     75

**ARCHBISHOP**
That he should draw his several° strengths together
And come against us in full puissance°
Need not to be dreaded.

**HASTINGS**         If he should do so,
He leaves his back unarmed, the French and Welsh
Baying him at the heels. Never fear that.     80

**LORD BARDOLPH**
Who is it like° should lead his forces hither?

**HASTINGS**
The Duke of Lancaster and Westmoreland.
Against the Welsh, himself and Harry Monmouth.
But who is substituted against the French,
I have no certain notice.

**ARCHBISHOP**       Let us on,     85
And publish the occasion of our arms.
The commonwealth is sick of their own choice;
Their overgreedy love hath surfeited.
An habitation giddy and unsure
Hath he that buildeth on the vulgar heart.     90
O thou fond many,° with what loud applause
Didst thou beat° heaven with blessing Bolingbroke,
Before he was what thou wouldst have him be!
And being now trimmed° in thine own desires,
Thou, beastly feeder, art so full of him     95
That thou provok'st thyself to cast him up.
So, so, thou common dog, didst thou disgorge
Thy glutton bosom of the royal Richard;
And now thou° wouldst eat thy dead vomit up,
And howl'st to find it. What trust is in these times?     100
They that when Richard lived would have him die
Are now become enamored on his grave.
Thou° that threw'st dust upon his goodly head
When through proud London he came sighing on
After th' admired heels of Bolingbroke     105
Criest now, "O earth, yield us that king again,
And take thou this!" O thoughts of men accursed!
"Past and to come seems best, things present worst."°

**MOWBRAY**
Shall we go draw our numbers° and set on?

**HASTINGS**
We are time's subjects, and time bids be gone.     110

*Exeunt.*

---

76 **several** separate   77 **puissance** power   81 **like** likely   91 **fond many** foolish multitude   92 **beat** assault (with noise or prayer)   94 **trimmed** dressed   99 **thou** the multitude (compared to a dog, as described in Proverbs 16:11)   103 **Thou** the multitude   108 **Past . . . worst** proverbial   109 **draw our numbers** assemble our troops

# [ACT II]

### [Scene I. London.]

*Enter* HOSTESS *of the Tavern and an* OFFICER *or two* [FANG *and another, followed by* SNARE].

**HOSTESS** Master Fang, have you ent'red the action?°

**FANG** It is ent'red.

**HOSTESS** Where's your yeoman?° Is't a lusty yeoman? Will 'a stand to't?°

**FANG** Sirrah—where's Snare?°     5

**HOSTESS** O Lord, ay! Good Master Snare!

**SNARE** Here, here.

**FANG** Snare, we must arrest Sir John Falstaff.

**HOSTESS** Yea, good Master Snare, I have ent'red him and all.     10

**SNARE** It may chance cost some of us our lives, for he will stab.

**HOSTESS** Alas the day! Take heed of him. He stabbed me in mine own house, and that most beastly. In good faith, 'a cares not what mischief he does, if his weapon     15 be out. He will foin° like any devil; he will spare neither man, woman, nor child.

**FANG** If I can close with him, I care not for his thrust.

**HOSTESS** No, nor I neither. I'll be at your elbow.

**FANG** And I but fist him once, and 'a come but within     20 my vice°—

**HOSTESS** I am undone by his going. I warrant you, he's an infinitive° thing upon my score.° Good Master Fang, hold him sure. Good Master Snare, let him not 'scape. 'A comes continuantly° to Pie Corner°—     25 saving° your manhoods—to buy a saddle; and he is indited° to dinner to the Lubber's Head° in Lumbert° Street, to Master Smooth's the silkman. I pray you, since my exion° is ent'red and my case so openly known to the world, let him be brought in to his     30 answer. A hundred mark is a long one for a poor lone woman to bear, and I have borne,° and borne, and borne, and have been fubbed off,° and fubbed off, and fubbed off, from this day to that day, that it is a shame to be thought on. There is no honesty in such dealing,     35 unless a woman should be made an ass and a beast, to bear every knave's wrong. Yonder he comes, and that arrant malmsey-nose° knave, Bardolph, with him. Do your offices, do your offices. Master Fang and Master Snare, do me, do me, do me your offices.     40

*Enter Sir John* [FALSTAFF] *and* BARDOLPH, *and the boy* [PAGE].

**FALSTAFF** How now! Whose mare's dead?° What's the matter?

---

**II.i.1 ent'red the action** filed the lawsuit (with a ribald second meaning)   3 **yeoman** assistant (i.e., constable)   4 **stand to't** not collapse in the face of danger (with a ribald second meaning)   5 **Snare** evidently hanging back   16 **foin** thrust (with, again, a second meaning)   21 **vice** grip   23 **infinitive** infinite; **score** account at the tavern   25 **continuantly** a mix-up of *continually* and *incontinently* (Mistress Quickly speaks in a stream of malapropisms, many with indecent second meanings); **Pie Corner** the cook's quarter (with an indecent pun)   26 **saving** no offense meant to   27 **indited** invited; **Lubber's Head** Libbard's (i.e., Leopard's) Head; **Lumbert** Lombard   29 **exion** action   32 **borne** endured (with a second, ribald sense)   33 **fubbed off** put off   33 **malmsey-nose** nose reddened from winebibbing   41 **Whose mare's dead** What's all the commotion?

FANG  Sir John, I arrest you at the suit of Mistress Quickly.

FALSTAFF  Away, varlets! Draw, Bardolph! Cut me 45 off the villain's head. Throw the quean° in the channel.°

HOSTESS  Throw me in the channel! I'll throw thee in the channel. Wilt thou? Wilt thou? Thou bastardly° rogue! Murder, murder! Ah, thou honeysuckle° villain! Wilt thou kill God's officers and the king's? 50 Ah, thou honeyseed° rogue! Thou art a honeyseed, a man-queller,° and a woman-queller.

FALSTAFF  Keep them off, Bardolph.

FANG  A rescue!° A rescue!

HOSTESS  Good people, bring a rescue or two. Thou 55 wo't, wo't thou? Thou wo't, wo't ta? Do, do, thou rogue! Do, thou hempseed!°

PAGE  Away, you scullion!° You rampallian!° You fustilarian!° I'll tickle your catastrophe.°

*Enter Lord* CHIEF JUSTICE *and his* MEN.

CHIEF JUSTICE  What is the matter? Keep the peace 60 here, ho!

HOSTESS  Good my lord, be good to me. I beseech you, stand to me.°

CHIEF JUSTICE
How now, Sir John! What are you brawling here?
Doth this become your place, your time and business? 65
You should have been well on your way to York.
Stand from him, fellow. Wherefore hang'st thou upon him?

HOSTESS  O my most worshipful lord, and't please your grace, I am a poor widow of Eastcheap, and he is arrested at my suit. 70

CHIEF JUSTICE  For what sum?

HOSTESS  It is more than for some, my lord, it is for all I have. He hath eaten me out of house and home; he hath put all my substance into that fat belly of his. But I will have some of it out again, or I will ride thee 75 o' nights like the mare.°

FALSTAFF  I think I am as like to ride the mare,° if I have any vantage of ground° to get up.

CHIEF JUSTICE  How comes this, Sir John? What man of good temper would endure this tempest of 80 exclamation? Are you not ashamed to enforce a poor widow to so rough a course to come by her own?

FALSTAFF  What is the gross sum that I owe thee?

HOSTESS  Marry, if thou wert an honest man, thyself and the money too. Thou didst swear to me upon a 85 parcel-gilt° goblet, sitting in my Dolphin° chamber, at the round table, by a sea-coal fire, upon Wednesday in Wheeson° week, when the prince broke thy head for liking° his father to a singing-man of Windsor, thou

didst swear to me then, as I was washing thy wound, 90 to marry me and make me my lady thy wife. Canst thou deny it? Did not goodwife Keech, the butcher's wife, come in then and call me gossip° Quickly? Coming in to borrow a mess of vinegar, telling us she had a good dish of prawns,° whereby thou didst 95 desire to eat some, whereby I told thee they were ill for a green° wound? And didst thou not, when she was gone downstairs, desire me to be no more so familiarity with such poor people, saying that ere long they should call me "madam"? And didst thou not kiss me 100 and bid me fetch thee thirty shillings? I put thee now to thy book-oath. Deny it, if thou canst.

FALSTAFF  My lord, this is a poor mad soul, and she says up and down the town that her eldest son is like you. She hath been in good case,° and the truth is, 105 poverty hath distracted her.° But for these foolish officers, I beseech you I may have redress against them.

CHIEF JUSTICE  Sir John, Sir John, I am well acquainted with your manner of wrenching the true cause the false way. It is not a confident brow, nor the 110 throng of words that come with such more than impudent sauciness from you, can thrust me from a level° consideration. You have, as it appears to me, practiced upon° the easy-yielding spirit of this woman, and made her serve your uses both in purse and in 115 person.

HOSTESS  Yea, in truth, my lord.

CHIEF JUSTICE  Pray thee, peace. Pay her the debt you owe her and unpay the villainy you have done with her. The one you may do with sterling money, 120 and the other with current° repentance.

FALSTAFF  My lord, I will not undergo this sneap° without reply. You call honorable boldness impudent sauciness. If a man will make curtsy and say nothing, he is virtuous. No, my lord, my humble duty re- 125 memb'red, I will not be your suitor. I say to you, I do desire deliverance from these officers, being upon hasty employment in the king's affairs.

CHIEF JUSTICE  You speak as having power to do wrong. But answer in th' effect of° your reputation, 130 and satisfy the poor woman.

FALSTAFF  Come hither, hostess.

*Enter a messenger* [GOWER].

CHIEF JUSTICE  Now, Master Gower, what news?

GOWER
The king, my lord, and Harry Prince of Wales
Are near at hand. The rest the paper tells. 135

[*They draw aside.*]

FALSTAFF [*To* HOSTESS.]  As I am a gentleman!

HOSTESS  Faith, you said so before.

FALSTAFF  As I am a gentleman, come, no more words of it.

HOSTESS  By this heavenly ground I tread on, I must 140 be fain° to pawn both my plate and the tapestry of my dining chambers.

**46 quean** scold; **channel** gutter  **48 bastardly** mixing *dastardly* and *bastard* (1) illegitimate (2) a sweetened wine  **49 honeysuckle** homicidal  **51 honeyseed** homicide  **52 man-queller** man-killer  **54 rescue** forcible taking of persons out of legal custody  **57 hempseed** a child destined for the gallows (but also homicide, as in line 51—Mistress Quickly is referring to the Page)  **58 scullion** kitchen wench; **rampallian** rampant whore  **59 fustilarian** derived from *fustilugs*, a frowsy, fat woman; **catastrophe** ending  **63 stand to me** be firm for me (with a second sense)  **76 mare** female (but also the "two-legged mare," i.e., the gallows)  **78 vantage of ground** advantage of higher ground  **86 parcel-gilt** partly gilded; **Dolphin** the sign marking the room  **88 Wheeson** Whitsun  **89 liking** likening

**93 gossip** friend (a common form of address)  **95 prawns** shrimp  **97 green** new  **105 case** situation, i.e., well-to-do  **106 distracted her** driven her mad  **113 level** straight  **114 practiced upon** deceived  **121 current** (1) progressive (2) opposite of counterfeit  **122 sneap** snub  **130 in . . . of** so as to fulfill  **141 fain** obliged

FALSTAFF  Glasses, glasses, is the only drinking.° And
for thy walls, a pretty slight drollery,° or the story of
the Prodigal, or the German hunting° in waterwork,° 145
is worth a thousand of these bed-hangers° and these
fly-bitten tapestries. Let it be ten pound, if thou canst.
Come, and 'twere not for thy humors,° there's not a
better wench in England. Go, wash thy face, and
draw° the action. Come, thou must not be in this 150
humor with me. Dost not know me? Come, come, I
know thou wast set on to this.

HOSTESS  Pray thee, Sir John, let it be but twenty
nobles.° I' faith, I am loath to pawn my plate, so God
save me, la! 155

FALSTAFF  Let it alone; I'll make other shift. You'll be
a fool still.°

HOSTESS  Well, you shall have it, though I pawn my
gown. I hope you'll come to supper. You'll pay me all
together? 160

FALSTAFF  Will I live? [*To* BARDOLPH]. Go, with
her, with her. Hook on,° hook on!

HOSTESS  Will you have Doll Tearsheet meet you at
supper?

FALSTAFF  No more words. Let's have her. 165

*Exit* HOSTESS *and sergeant* [FANG,
BARDOLPH *and others*].

CHIEF JUSTICE  [*To* GOWER.]  I have heard better
news.

FALSTAFF  What's the news, my lord?

CHIEF JUSTICE [*Ignoring* FALSTAFF.]  Where lay the
king tonight?° 170

GOWER  At Basingstoke, my lord.

FALSTAFF  I hope, my lord, all's well. What is the
news, my lord?

CHIEF JUSTICE  Come all his forces back?

GOWER
No. Fifteen hundred foot, five hundred horse, 175
Are marched up to my Lord of Lancaster,
Against Northumberland and the archbishop.

FALSTAFF
Comes the king back from Wales, my noble lord?

CHIEF JUSTICE [*To his men.*]
You shall have letters of me presently.
Come, go along with me, good Master Gower. 180

FALSTAFF  My lord!

CHIEF JUSTICE  What's the matter?

FALSTAFF  Master Gower, shall I entreat you with me
to dinner?

GOWER  I must wait upon my good lord here, I thank 185
you, good Sir John.

CHIEF JUSTICE  Sir John, you loiter here too long,
being you are to take soldiers up° in counties as you go.

FALSTAFF  Will you sup with me, Master Gower?

CHIEF JUSTICE  What foolish master taught you these 190
manners, Sir John?

FALSTAFF  Master Gower, if they become me not, he

was a fool that taught them me. This is the right°
fencing grace, my lord—tap for tap, and so part fair.

CHIEF JUSTICE  Now the Lord lighten° thee! Thou 195
art a great fool. [*Exeunt.*]

[Scene II. *The prince's house.*]

*Enter the* PRINCE [*Henry*], POINS, *with others.*

PRINCE  Before God, I am exceeding weary.°

POINS  Is't come to that? I had thought weariness durst
not have attached° one of so high blood.

PRINCE  Faith, it does me, though it discolors the
complexion° of my greatness to acknowledge it. Doth 5
it not show vilely in me to desire small beer?

POINS  Why, a prince should not be so loosely studied°
as to remember so weak a composition.°

PRINCE  Belike, then, my appetite was not princely
got,° for, by my troth, I do now remember the poor 10
creature, small beer. But indeed these humble considerations make me out of love with my greatness.
What a disgrace is it to me to remember thy name!°
Or to know thy face tomorrow! Or to take note how
many pair of silk stockings thou hast, viz. these, and 15
those that were thy peach-colored ones! Or to bear
the inventory of thy shirts, as: one for superfluity and
another for use! But that the tennis-court-keeper
knows better than I; for it is a low ebb of linen with
thee when thou keepest not racket there,° as thou 20
hast not done a great while, because the rest of thy low
countries° have made a shift° to eat up thy holland.°
And God knows whether those that bawl out the
ruins of thy linen shall inherit His kingdom. But the
midwives say the children are not in the fault,° 25
whereupon the world increases, and kindreds° are
mightily strengthened.

POINS  How ill it follows, after you have labored so
hard, you should talk so idly! Tell me, how many good
young princes would do so, their fathers being so sick 30
as yours at this time is?

PRINCE  Shall I tell thee one thing, Poins?

POINS  Yes, faith, and let it be an excellent good thing.

PRINCE  It shall serve among wits of no higher breeding than thine. 35

POINS  Go to. I stand the push° of your one thing that
you will tell.

PRINCE  Marry, I tell thee, it is not meet° that I should
be sad, now my father is sick. Albeit I could tell to
thee, as to one it pleases me, for fault of a better, to call 40
my friend, I could be sad, and sad indeed, too.

---

193 **right** correct   195 **lighten** (1) enlighten (2) make [you]
weigh less
**II.ii.1 weary** having just ridden from Wales   **3 attached**
arrested   **4–5 discolors the complexion** causes a blush   **7
loosely studied** carelessly or wantonly applied   **8 so . . .
composition** so unstable and trivial a compound (as small
beer)   **10 got** begotten   **13 disgrace . . . name** i.e., unlike
"graceful" courtiers who affect to forget the names of their
inferiors   **19–20 it . . . there** if you have as many as two
shirts, one to play in, a second to change into, you frequent the
tennis courts   **21–22 low countries** Netherlands (with an
obscene pun)   **22 shift** (1) contrivance (2) shirt; **holland** linen
made in Holland   **25 in the fault** share the sin (of their
illegitimacy, with a pun on French, *foutre* = to copulate)
**26 kindreds** clans   **36 push** thrust   **38 meet** fitting

---

143 **glasses, is . . . drinking** glasses are in fashion now, not
metal tankards   144 **drollery** comic picture   145 **German
hunting** hunting the boar; **waterwork** imitation tapestry
146 **bed-hangers** bed-curtains   148 **humors** (1) whims (2)
general character   150 **draw** withdraw   154 **nobles** coins
worth six shillings eightpence   156–57 **be . . . still** always
lose your chance   162 **Hook on** stick to her   170 **tonight** last
night   188 **take soldiers up** recruit men

POINS  Very hardly° upon such a subject.

PRINCE  By this hand, thou thinkest me as far in the devil's book as thou and Falstaff for obduracy and persistency. Let the end° try the man. But I tell thee, 45 my heart bleeds inwardly that my father is so sick. And keeping such vile company as thou art hath in reason taken from me all ostentation° of sorrow.

POINS  The reason?

PRINCE  What wouldst thou think of me if I should 50 weep?

POINS  I would think thee a most princely hypocrite.

PRINCE  It would be every man's thought, and thou art a blessed fellow to think as every man thinks. Never a man's thought in the world keeps the roadway 55 better than thine. Every man would think me an hypocrite indeed. And what accites° your most worshipful thought to think so?

POINS  Why, because you have been so lewd and so much engraffed° to Falstaff. 60

PRINCE  And to thee.

POINS  By this light, I am well spoke on; I can hear it with mine own ears. The worst that they can say of me is that I am a second brother° and that I am a proper fellow of my hands,° and those two things I 65 confess I cannot help. By the mass, here comes Bardolph.

*Enter* BARDOLPH *and boy* [PAGE].

PRINCE  And the boy that I gave Falstaff. 'A had him from me Christian, and look if the fat villain have not transformed him ape.° 70

BARDOLPH  God save your grace.

PRINCE  And yours, most noble Bardolph.

POINS  Come, you virtuous ass, you bashful fool, must you be blushing?° Wherefore blush you now? What a maidenly man-at-arms are you become! Is't such a 75 matter to get a pottle-pot's° maidenhead?

PAGE  'A calls me e'en now, my lord, through a red lattice,° and I could discern no part of his face from the window. At last I spied his eyes, and methought he had made two holes in the alewife's petticoat and so 80 peeped through.

PRINCE  Has not the boy profited?°

BARDOLPH  Away, you whoreson upright rabbit, away!

PAGE  Away, you rascally Althaea's dream,° away! 85

PRINCE  Instruct us, boy. What dream, boy?

PAGE  Marry, my lord, Althaea dreamed she was delivered of a firebrand, and therefore I call him her dream.

PRINCE  A crown's worth of good interpretation. 90 There 'tis, boy. [*Tips him.*]

POINS  O, that this blossom could be kept from cankers!° Well, there is sixpence to preserve° thee.

BARDOLPH  And you do not make him hanged among you, the gallows shall have wrong. 95

PRINCE  And how doth thy master, Bardolph?

BARDOLPH  Well, my lord. He heard of your grace's coming to town. There's a letter for you.

POINS  Delivered with good respect. And how doth the martlemas,° your master? 100

BARDOLPH  In bodily health, sir.

POINS  Marry, the immortal part needs a physician, but that moves not him. Though that be sick, it dies not.

PRINCE  I do allow this wen° to be as familiar with me 105 as my dog, and he holds his place, for look you how he writes.

POINS  [*Reads.*]  "John Falstaff, knight"—every man must know that, as oft as he has occasion to name himself. Even like those that are kin to the king, for 110 they never prick their finger but they say, "There's some of the king's blood spilt." "How comes that?" says he that takes upon him not to conceive. The answer is as ready as a borrowed cap,° "I am the king's poor cousin, sir." 115

PRINCE  Nay, they will be kin to us, or they will fetch it from Japhet.° But the letter. [*Reads.*] "Sir John Falstaff, knight, to the son of the king nearest his father, Harry Prince of Wales, greeting."

POINS  Why, this is a certificate.° 120

PRINCE  Peace! [*Reads.*] "I will imitate the honorable Romans in brevity."

POINS  He sure means brevity in breath, shortwinded.

[PRINCE *reads.*]  "I commend me to thee, I commend 125 thee, and I leave thee. Be not too familiar with Poins, for he misuses thy favors so much that he swears thou art to marry his sister Nell. Repent at idle times as thou mayst, and so farewell.

"Thine, by yea and no, which is as much as to say, 130 as thou usest him, JACK FALSTAFF with my familiars, JOHN with my brothers and sisters, and SIR JOHN with all Europe."

POINS  My lord, I'll steep this letter in sack and make him eat it. 135

PRINCE  That's to make him eat twenty of his words. But do you use me thus, Ned? Must I marry your sister?

POINS  God send the wench no worse fortune! But I never said so. 140

PRINCE  Well, thus we play the fools with the time, and the spirits of the wise sit in the clouds and mock us. Is your master here in London?

BARDOLPH  Yea, my lord.

PRINCE  Where sups he? Doth the old boar feed in the 145 old frank?°

---

42 **Very hardly** with great difficulty  45 **end** outcome  48 **ostentation** show  57 **accites** summons (a judicial term)  60 **engraffed** grafted (like a plant)  64 **a second brother** one who inherits nothing  65 **proper . . . hands** skillful with my hands as a fighter (or as a thief?)  70 **transformed him ape** dressed him fantastically  74 **blushing** redfaced (from drinking)  76 **pottle-pot** two-quart tankard  77–78 **red lattice** such a window was the sign of an alehouse  82 **profited** i.e., from his association with Falstaff  85 **Althaea's dream** the dream he describes in lines 87–89 was actually Hecuba's; the Fates told Althaea her son would live only as long as a log on the fire remained unconsumed; perhaps the boy has not "profited" as much as the prince thought

93 **cankers** plant-destroying worms; **preserve** i.e., because Elizabethan coins bore crosses  100 **martlemas** a beef fattened for slaughter before winter on Martinmas Day (November 11)  105 **wen** swelling  114 **borrowed cap** which the borrower promptly tips  116–17 **fetch . . . Japhet** fetch their ancestry from that one of Noah's sons whose offspring peopled Europe  120 **certificate** patent (in formal style)  146 **frank** sty (presumably a glance at the famous Boar's Head tavern)

BARDOLPH  At the old place, my lord, in Eastcheap.
PRINCE  What company?
PAGE  Ephesians,° my lord, of the old church.°
PRINCE  Sup any women with him?                            150
PAGE  None, my lord, but old Mistress Quickly and
Mistress Doll Tearsheet.
PRINCE  What pagan° may that be?
PAGE  A proper gentlewoman, sir, and a kinswoman of
my master's.                                               155
PRINCE  Even such kin as the parish heifers are to the
town bull. Shall we steal upon them, Ned, at supper?
POINS  I am your shadow, my lord; I'll follow you.
PRINCE  Sirrah,° you boy, and Bardolph, no word to
your master that I am yet come to town. There's for 160
your silence. [*Tips them.*]
BARDOLPH  I have no tongue, sir.
PAGE  And for mine, sir, I will govern it.
PRINCE  Fare you well; go. [*Exeunt* BARDOLPH *and*
PAGE.] This Doll Tearsheet should be some road.°    165
POINS  I warrant you, as common as the way between
Saint Alban's and London.
PRINCE  How might we see Falstaff bestow himself to-
night in his true colors, and not ourselves be seen?
POINS  Put on two leathern jerkins° and aprons, and 170
wait upon him at his table as drawers.°
PRINCE  From a god to a bull? A heavy descension!
It was Jove's case.° From a prince to a prentice? A
low transformation! That shall be mine, for in every-
thing the purpose must weigh with° the folly. Follow 175
me, Ned.                                          *Exeunt.*

[*Scene III. Northumberland's castle.*]

*Enter* NORTHUMBERLAND, *his wife* [LADY NORTH-
UMBERLAND], *and the wife to Harry Percy* [LADY
PERCY].

NORTHUMBERLAND
I pray thee, loving wife, and gentle daughter,°
Give even way° unto my rough affairs.
Put not you on the visage of the times
And be like them to Percy° troublesome.
LADY NORTHUMBERLAND
I have given over; I will speak no more.                   5
Do what you will, your wisdom be your guide.
NORTHUMBERLAND
Alas, sweet wife, my honor is at pawn,
And, but° my going, nothing can redeem it.
LADY PERCY
O yet, for God's sake, go not to these wars!
The time was, father, that you broke your word,          10
When you were more endeared to it than now,
When your own Percy, when my heart's dear Harry,

Threw many a northward look to see his father
Bring up his powers, but he did long in vain.
Who then persuaded you to stay at home?                   15
There were two honors lost, yours and your son's.
For yours, the God of heaven brighten it!
For his, it stuck upon him as the sun
In the gray vault of heaven, and by his light
Did all the chivalry of England move                      20
To do brave acts. He was indeed the glass°
Wherein the noble youth did dress themselves.
He° had no legs that practiced not his° gait;
And speaking thick,° which nature made his blemish,
Became the accents of the valiant,                        25
For those that could speak low and tardily
Would turn their own perfection to abuse,
To seem like him. So that in speech, in gait,
In diet, in affections of delight,°
In military rules, humors of blood,°                      30
He was the mark and glass, copy and book,
That fashioned others. And him! O wondrous! Him!
O miracle of men! Him did you leave,
Second to none, unseconded by you,
To look upon the hideous god of war                       35
In disadvantage, to abide a field°
Where nothing but the sound of Hotspur's name
Did seem defensible. So you left him.
Never, O never, do his ghost the wrong
To hold your honor more precise and nice°                 40
With others than with him! Let them alone.
The marshal and the archbishop are strong.
Had my sweet Harry had but half their numbers,
Today might I, hanging on Hotspur's neck,
Have talked of Monmouth's° grave.
NORTHUMBERLAND                      Beshrew° your
                                              heart, 45
Fair daughter, you do draw my spirits from me
With new lamenting ancient oversights.
But I must go and meet with danger there,
Or it will seek me in another place
And find me worse provided.
LADY NORTHUMBERLAND  O, fly to Scotland,°          50
Till that the nobles and the arm'd commons
Have of their puissance° made a little taste.
LADY PERCY
If they get ground and vantage of the king,
Then join you with them, like a rib of steel,
To make strength stronger. But, for all our loves,       55
First let them try themselves. So did your son;
He was so suff'red.° So came I a widow,
And never shall have length of life enough
To rain° upon remembrance with mine eyes,
That it may grow and sprout as high as heaven,           60
For recordation° to my noble husband.
NORTHUMBERLAND
Come, come, go in with me. 'Tis with my mind
As with the tide swelled up unto his height,

**149 Ephesians . . . church** libertines (who had to be corrected
by Saint Paul—Ephesians 5:3–8)  **153 pagan** prostitute (love-
worshiper)  **159 Sirrah** form of address to an inferior  **165
road** prostitute (one to be ridden, open to all)  **170 jerkins**
jackets  **171 drawers** tavern waiters  **173 Jove's case** he
transformed himself into a bull to seduce Europa  **175 weigh
with** match
**II.iii.1 daughter** daughter-in-law  **2 Give even way** allow
free passage  **4 Percy** Northumberland, "the Percy"  **8 but**
except for

**21 glass** looking glass  **23 He** any man; **his** Harry Percy's
**24 thick** fast (crowding the words)  **29 affections of delight**
preferences in pleasure  **30 humors of blood** disposition  **36
abide a field** endure on a battlefield  **40 nice** punctilious  **45
Monmouth's** Prince Hal's; **Beshrew** cursed be  **50 Scotland**
i.e., far from the battle  **52 puissance** strength  **57 suff'red**
allowed (to fight alone)  **59 rain** crop tears  **61 recordation**
memorial

That makes a still-stand, running neither way.
Fain would I go to meet the archbishop, 65
But many thousand reasons hold me back.
I will resolve for Scotland. There am I,
Till time and vantage° crave my company.   *Exeunt.*

[Scene IV. *Mistress Quickly's tavern.*]

*Enter a* DRAWER *or two* [FRANCIS *and another*].

FRANCIS  What the devil hast thou brought there?
Apple-johns?° Thou knowest Sir John cannot endure
an apple-john.
DRAWER  Mass, thou say'st true. The prince once set
a dish of apple-johns before him, and told him there 5
were five more Sir Johns, and, putting off his hat, said,
"I will now take my leave of these six dry, round, old
withered knights." It ang'red him to the heart. But he
hath forgot that.
FRANCIS  Why, then, cover,° and set them down. 10
And see if thou canst find out Sneak's noise.° Mistress
Tearsheet would fain hear some music.

*Enter* WILL [*a third drawer*].

WILL  Dispatch! The room where they supped is too
hot. They'll come in straight.
FRANCIS  Sirrah, here will be the prince and Master 15
Poins anon, and they will put on two of our jerkins
and aprons, and Sir John must not know of it. Bardolph
hath brought word.
DRAWER  By the mass, here will be old Utis.° It will
be an excellent stratagem. 20
FRANCIS  I'll see if I can find out Sneak.   *Exit.*

*Enter Mistress Quickly* [*the* HOSTESS] *and* DOLL
*Tearsheet.*

HOSTESS  I' faith, sweetheart, methinks now you are in
an excellent good temperality.° Your pulsidge° beats
as extraordinarily as heart would desire, and your
color, I warrant you, is as red as any rose, in good 25
truth, la! But, i' faith, you have drunk too much
canaries,° and that's a marvelous searching wine, and
it perfumes the blood ere one can say, "What's this?"
How do you now?
DOLL  Better than I was. Hem! 30
HOSTESS  Why, that's well said. A good heart's worth
gold. Lo, here comes Sir John.

*Enter Sir John* [FALSTAFF].

FALSTAFF [*Sings.*]  "When Arthur first in court"°—
Empty the jordan!°—"And was a worthy king."—
How now, Mistress Doll! 35
HOSTESS  Sick of a calm,° yea, good faith.
FALSTAFF  So is all her sect.° And they be once in a
calm, they are sick.

DOLL  A pox damn you, you muddy° rascal, is that all
the comfort you give me? 40
FALSTAFF  You make fat rascals,° Mistress Doll.
DOLL  I make them? Gluttony and diseases make, I
make them not.
FALSTAFF  If the cook help to make the gluttony, you
help to make the diseases, Doll. We catch of you, 45
Doll, we catch of you. Grant that, my poor virtue,
grant that.
DOLL  Yea, joy, our chains and our jewels.
FALSTAFF  "Your brooches, pearls, and ouches."° For
to serve bravely is to come halting off, you know. To 50
come off the breach with his pike bent bravely, and to
surgery bravely; to venture upon the charged cham-
bers° bravely—
DOLL  Hang yourself, you muddy conger,° hang
yourself! 55
HOSTESS  By my troth, this is the old fashion. You
two never meet but you fall to some discord. You are
both, i' good truth, as rheumatic° as two dry toasts.°
You cannot one bear with another's confirmities.°
What the goodyear!° One must bear,° and that must 60
be you [*to* DOLL]. You are the weaker vessel, as they
say, the emptier vessel.
DOLL  Can a weak empty vessel bear such a huge full
hogshead? There's a whole merchant's venture of
Bordeaux stuff° in him. You have not seen a hulk 65
better stuffed in the hold. Come, I'll be friends with
thee, Jack. Thou art going to the wars, and whether
I shall ever see thee again or no, there is nobody cares.

*Enter* DRAWER.

DRAWER  Sir, Ancient° Pistol's below and would
speak with you. 70
DOLL  Hang him, swaggering° rascal! Let him not
come hither. It is the foul-mouthed'st rogue in
England.
HOSTESS  If he swagger, let him not come here. No,
by my faith. I must live among my neighbors. I'll no 75
swaggerers. I am in good name and fame with the
very best. Shut the door, there comes no swaggerers
here. I have not lived all this while to have swaggering
now. Shut the door, I pray you.
FALSTAFF  Dost thou hear, hostess? 80
HOSTESS  Pray ye, pacify yourself, Sir John. There
comes no swaggerers here.
FALSTAFF  Dost thou hear? It is mine ancient.
HOSTESS  Tilly-fally, Sir John, ne'er tell me. And your
ancient swagg'rer comes not in my doors. I was 85
before Master Tisick,° the debuty, t' other day,
and, as he said to me, 'twas no longer ago than
Wednesday last, "I' good faith, neighbor Quickly,"

---

68 **vantage** profitable opportunity
**II.iv.2 Apple-johns** apples ripened on Saint John's Day,
midsummer, but eaten two years later when withered—
perhaps they remind Sir John of age or impotency  10
**cover** spread the tablecloth  11 **noise** band of musicians
19 **old Utis** grand festival (*utaves* was the eighth day or "octave"
of a feast)  23 **temperality** temper or temperance; **pulsidge**
pulse  27 **canaries** Canary wine  33 **When . . . court** first
line of a ballad  34 **jordan** chamber pot  36 **calm** qualm  37
**sect** prostitutes (love-worshippers)

39 **muddy** filthy  41 **You . . . rascals** a rascal was a lean
deer—you say or cause the lean to fat, i.e., become bloated or
to sweat as a cure for the pox  49 **Your . . . ouches** another
scrap of ballad; "ouches" are both brooches and scabs  52–53
**charged chambers** loaded cannon (used, like other words in
this speech, with a bawdy second meaning)  54 **conger** eel
58 **rheumatic** she means *splenetic* or *choleric*, the hot and dry
humor—like toast; **dry toasts** that would scratch one another
59 **confirmities** infirmities  60 **What the goodyear** What
the plague!; **bear** (1) endure (2) support  64–65 **merchant's
. . . stuff** shipload of wine  69 **Ancient** ensign, standard-
bearer  71 **swaggering** blustering  86 **Tisick** phthisic,
consumption (?)

says he—Master Dumbe, our minister, was by then
—"neighbor Quickly," says he, "receive those that 90
are civil, for," said he, "you are in an ill name."
Now 'a said so, I can tell whereupon. "For," says
he, "you are an honest woman, and well thought on;
therefore take heed what guests you receive. Receive,"
says he, "no swaggering companions."° There comes 95
none here. You would bless you to hear what he said.
No, I'll no swagg'rers.

FALSTAFF He's no swagg'rer, hostess, a tame cheater,°
i' faith. You may stroke him as gently as a puppy
greyhound. He'll not swagger with a Barbary hen,° 100
if her feathers turn back in any show of resistance.
Call him up, drawer.      [Exit DRAWER.]

HOSTESS Cheater, call you him? I will bar no honest
man my house, nor no cheater. But I do not love
swaggering, by my troth. I am the worse when one 105
says "swagger." Feel, masters, how I shake, look you,
I warrant you.

DOLL So you do, hostess.

HOSTESS Do I? Yea, in very truth, do I, and 'twere
an aspen leaf. I cannot abide swagg'rers.      110

*Enter Ancient* PISTOL, [BARDOLPH], *and Bardolph's
boy* [PAGE].

PISTOL God save you, Sir John!

FALSTAFF Welcome, Ancient Pistol.° Here, Pistol, I
charge° you with a cup of sack. Do you discharge°
upon mine hostess.

PISTOL I will discharge upon her, Sir John, with two 115
bullets.°

FALSTAFF She is pistol-proof, sir; you shall not
hardily° offend her.

HOSTESS Come, I'll drink no proofs nor no bullets.
I'll drink no more than will do me good, for no man's 120
pleasure, I.

PISTOL Then to you, Mistress Dorothy; I will charge
you.

DOLL Charge me! I scorn you, scurvy companion.
What! You poor, base, rascally, cheating, lack-linen 125
mate! Away, you moldy rogue, away! I am meat°
for your master.

PISTOL I know you, Mistress Dorothy.

DOLL Away, you cut-purse rascal! You filthy bung,°
away! By this wine, I'll thrust my knife in your 130
moldy chaps,° and you play the saucy cuttle° with
me. Away, you bottle-ale° rascal! You basket-hilt
stale juggler,° you! Since when, I pray you, sir?
God's light, with two points° on your shoulder?
Much!      135

PISTOL God let me not live but I will murder your
ruff° for this.

FALSTAFF No more, Pistol; I would not have you go
off here. Discharge yourself of our company, Pistol.

HOSTESS No, good Captain Pistol, not here, sweet 140
captain.

DOLL Captain! Thou abominable damned cheater,
art thou not ashamed to be called captain? And
captains were of my mind, they would truncheon°
you out for taking their names upon you before you 145
have earned them. You a captain! You slave, for
what? For tearing a poor whore's ruff in a bawdy
house? He a captain! Hang him, rogue! He lives
upon moldy stewed prunes° and dried cakes. A
captain! God's light, these villains will make the 150
word as odious as the word "occupy,"° which was
an excellent good word before it was ill sorted.°
Therefore captains° had need look to't.

BARDOLPH Pray thee, go down, good ancient.

FALSTAFF Hark thee hither, Mistress Doll.      155

PISTOL Not I! I tell thee what, Corporal Bardolph, I
could tear her! I'll be revenged of her!

PAGE Pray thee, go down.

PISTOL I'll see her damned first, to Pluto's damnèd
lake,° by this hand, to th' infernal deep, with Erebus 160
and tortures vile also.° Hold hook and line,° say I.
Down, down, dogs! Down, faitors!° Have we not
Hiren° here?

HOSTESS Good Captain Pizzle, be quiet. 'Tis very
late, i' faith. I beseek you now, aggravate° your choler. 165

PISTOL
These be good humors, indeed! Shall packhorses
And hollow pampered jades° of Asia,
Which cannot go but thirty mile a day,
Compare with Caesars, and with Cannibals,°
And Trojan Greeks? Nay, rather damn them with      170
King Cerberus,° and let the welkin° roar.
Shall we fall foul for toys?°

HOSTESS By my troth, captain, these are very bitter
words.

BARDOLPH Be gone, good ancient. This will grow 175
to a brawl anon.

PISTOL Die men like dogs! Give crowns like pins!
Have we not Hiren here?

HOSTESS O' my word, captain, there's none such here.
What the goodyear! Do you think I would deny 180
her?° For God's sake, be quiet.

PISTOL
Then feed, and be fat, my fair Calipolis.
Come, give's some sack.
"Si fortune me tormente, sperato me contento."°

144 **truncheon** cudgel    149 **stewed prunes** put in the
windows of brothels, "stews," as a sign    151 **occupy** had
acquired the sense of "fornicate"    152 **ill sorted** put in bad
company    153 **captains** Falstaff is a captain    160 **lake** he
means the river Styx; **Erebus** passageway to Hades    161
**and . . . also** Pistol begins to rave in his characteristic way,
spewing out garbled scraps from old declamatory plays—
or, indeed, any line that comes to his mind; **Hold . . .
line** a fisherman's cry    162 **faitors** fates (?)    163 **Hiren**
Pistol applies this name (Irene) from a play to his sword,
punning on *iron*    165 **aggravate** she means *moderate*    167 **jades**
nags    169 **Cannibals** he means *Hannibals*    171 **Cerberus**
three-headed dog that guarded Hades; **welkin** sky    172 **toys**
trivia (like Doll)    180-81 **deny her** the Hostess evidently
thinks Pistol is calling for a special girl    184 **Si . . . contento**
a garbled proverb—"If fortune torments me, hope contents me"

95 **companions** fellows    98 **cheater** cardsharper's decoy
100 **Barbary hen** guinea hen (whose feathers are already
ruffled; also, a prostitute)    112 **Pistol** pronounced almost like
*pizzle* (= penis) hence leading to this series of obscene puns
113 **charge** (1) toast (2) load (a pistol); **discharge** go off (i.e.,
sound a return toast, explode like a pistol—or sexually    116
**bullets** an indecency    117-18 **not hardily** by no means    126
**meat** flesh    129 **bung** pickpocket    131 **chaps** cheeks; **cuttle**
(1) cutthroat (2) cuttlefish (that spews out a fluid used for sauce)
132 **bottle-ale** cheap (?)    132-33 **basket-hilt stale juggler**
doer of sword-tricks with an old-fashioned sword with hilt
shaped like a basket    134 **points** laces for tying on armor
136-37 **murder your ruff** tear your collar

Fear we broadsides? No, let the fiend give fire.                    185
Give me some sack. And, sweetheart, lie thou there.

[*Lays down his sword.*]

Come we to full points° here, and are etceteras° no
things?°

FALSTAFF   Pistol, I would be quiet.

PISTOL   Sweet knight, I kiss thy neaf.° What! We
have seen the seven stars.°                                         190

DOLL   For God's sake, thrust him downstairs. I cannot
endure such a fustian° rascal.

PISTOL   Thrust him downstairs! Know we not
Galloway nags?°

FALSTAFF   Quoit° him down, Bardolph, like a shove-    195
groat shilling.° Nay, and 'a do nothing but speak
nothing, 'a shall be nothing here.

BARDOLPH   Come, get you downstairs.

PISTOL

What! Shall we have incision? Shall we imbrue?°

[*Snatches up his sword.*]

Then death rock me asleep, abridge my doleful days!    200
Why, then, let grievous, ghastly, gaping wounds
Untwined the Sisters Three!° Come, Atropos, I say!

HOSTESS   Here's goodly stuff toward!

FALSTAFF   Give me my rapier, boy.

DOLL   I pray thee, Jack, I pray thee, do not draw.       205

FALSTAFF   Get you downstairs!

[*Draws, and threatens* PISTOL.]

HOSTESS   Here's a goodly tumult! I'll forswear
keeping house afore I'll be in these tirrits° and frights.
So, murder, I warrant now. Alas, alas! Put up your
naked weapons, put up your naked weapons.            210

    [FALSTAFF *drives* PISTOL *out,* BARDOLPH *following.*]

DOLL   I pray thee, Jack, be quiet. The rascal's gone.
Ah, you whoreson little valiant villain, you!

HOSTESS   Are you not hurt i' th' groin? Methought 'a
made a shrewd thrust at your belly.

[*Enter* BARDOLPH.]

FALSTAFF   Have you turned him out o' doors?            215

BARDOLPH   Yea, sir. The rascal's drunk. You have
hurt him, sir, i' th' shoulder.

FALSTAFF   A rascal! To brave° me!

DOLL   Ah, you sweet little rogue, you! Alas, poor ape,
how thou sweat'st! Come, let me wipe thy face.          220
Come on, you whoreson chops.° Ah, rogue! I' faith,
I love thee. Thou art as valorous as Hector of Troy,
worth five of Agamemnon, and ten times better than
the Nine Worthies.° Ah, villain!

FALSTAFF   A rascally slave! I will toss the rogue in a    225
blanket.

DOLL   Do, and thou dar'st for thy heart. And thou
dost, I'll canvas° thee between a pair of sheets.

[*Enter* MUSICIANS.]

PAGE   The music is come, sir.

FALSTAFF   Let them play. Play, sirs. Sit on my knee,     230
Doll. A rascal bragging slave! The rogue fled from me
like quicksilver.

DOLL   I' faith [*aside*] and thou followedst him like a
church. Thou whoreson little tidy Bartholomew
boar-pig,° when wilt thou leave fighting o' days and    235
foining° o' nights, and begin to patch up thine old body
for heaven?

*Enter* PRINCE *and* POINS [*disguised*].

FALSTAFF   Peace, good Doll! Do not speak like a
death's-head.° Do not bid me remember mine end.°

DOLL   Sirrah, what humor's the prince° of?              240

FALSTAFF   A good shallow young fellow. 'A would
have made a good pantler,° 'a would ha' chipped°
bread well.

DOLL   They say Poins has a good wit.

FALSTAFF   He a good wit? Hang him, baboon! His    245
wit's as thick as Tewksbury mustard.° There's no more
conceit° in him than is in a mallet.°

DOLL   Why does the prince love him so, then?

FALSTAFF   Because their legs are both of a bigness, and
'a plays at quoits well, and eats conger and fennel,°     250
and drinks off candles' ends for flap-dragons,° and
rides the wild-mare° with the boys, and jumps upon
joined-stools,° and swears with a good grace, and
wears his boots very smooth, like unto the Sign of
the Leg,° and breeds no bate° with telling of discreet    255
stories; and such other gambol° faculties 'a has, that
show a weak mind and an able body, for the which
the prince admits him. For the prince himself is such
another; the weight of a hair will turn scales between
their avoirdupois.                                             260

PRINCE   Would not this nave° of a wheel have his
ears cut off?

POINS   Let's beat him before his whore.

PRINCE   Look, whe'r° the withered elder° hath not his
poll° clawed° like a parrot.                                  265

POINS   Is it not strange that desire should so many
years outlive performance?

187 **full points** stops, periods (closed sentences); **etceteras**
open-ended statements—with an obscene sense); **no things**
with a second meaning: women who are "naughty"; the line
as a whole means: Aren't we going to do anything more here?
189 **kiss thy neaf** kiss thy fist (a chivalric gesture)   190 **seven
stars** the Pleiades (we have made a night of it)   192 **fustian**
cheap cloth or talk   194 **Galloway nags** small Irish horses (bad
to ride)   195 **Quoit** pitch (with a pun on *quiet*)   195–96
**shove-groat shilling** coin used in a game like shuffleboard
("shove-ha'penny")   199 **imbrue** shed blood   202 **Sisters
Three** the Fates who spun the thread of life, cut by the
third, Atropos   208 **tirrits** a blending of *terrors* and *fits* (?)
218 **brave** defy   221 **chops** fat-cheeked man   224 **Nine
Worthies** Hector, Alexander, Julius Caesar, Joshua, David,
Judas Maccabaeus, King Arthur, Charlemagne, Godfrey of
Bouillon

228 **canvas** toss (as in a canvas)   234–35 **Bartholomew boar-
pig** young male pig fattened as a special delicacy for the Bartholomew Fair on August 24 at West Smithfield   236 **foining**
thrusting (as a sword)   239 **death's-head** figure of a skull
used to remind one of mortality; **end** double sense   240
**prince** Doll may have spied Hal and Poins   242 **pantler**
pantryworker; **chipped** chopped   246 **Tewksbury mustard**
Tewksbury was famed for good mustard   247 **conceit** conception; **mallet** i.e., a blockhead   250 **conger and fennel** eel
(the eating of which was thought to make one stupid) dressed
or flattered by fennel sauce   251 **flap-dragons** flaming raisins
were floated on spirit and the players tried to snap them up,
or drink the liquor; here candle ends are used to fool Poins
252 **wild-mare** seesaw   253 **joined-stools** carefully carpen-
tered stools   254–55 **Sign of the Leg** sign over a bootmaker's
255 **bate** debate, quarrel   256 **gambol** playful   261 **nave**
(1) fat hub on a cart wheel (2) pun on *knave*   264 **whe'r**
whether; **elder** (1) old man (2) sapless tree   265 **poll** hair;
**clawed** by Doll

FALSTAFF  Kiss me, Doll.

PRINCE  Saturn and Venus this year in conjunction!
What says th' almanac to that?                         270

POINS  And look whether the fiery Trigon,° his man,
be not lisping to his master's old tables,° his notebook,
his counsel-keeper.

FALSTAFF  Thou dost give me flattering busses.°

DOLL  By my troth, I kiss thee with a most constant  275
heart.

FALSTAFF  I am old, I am old.

DOLL  I love thee better than I love e'er a scurvy young
boy of them all.

FALSTAFF  What stuff wilt have a kirtle° of? I shall  280
receive money o' Thursday. Shalt have a cap tomorrow.
A merry song, come. 'A grows late; we'll to bed.
Thou'lt forget me when I am gone.

DOLL  By my troth, thou'lt set me a-weeping, and
thou say'st so. Prove that ever I dress myself handsome  285
till thy return. Well, hearken o' th' end.°

FALSTAFF  Some sack, Francis.

PRINCE, POINS  Anon, anon, sir.

*[Coming forward.]*

FALSTAFF  Ha! A bastard son of the king's? And art
not thou Poins his brother?                            290

PRINCE  Why, thou globe of sinful continents,° what
a life doth thou lead!

FALSTAFF  A better than thou. I am a gentleman, thou
art a drawer.

PRINCE  Very true, sir, and I come to draw you out  295
by the ears.

HOSTESS  O, the Lord preserve thy grace! By my
troth, welcome to London. Now, the Lord bless that
sweet face of thine! O Jesu, are you come from Wales?

FALSTAFF  Thou whoreson mad compound° of  300
majesty, by this light° flesh and corrupt blood, thou
art welcome.

DOLL  How, you fat fool! I scorn you.

POINS  My lord, he will drive you out of your revenge
and turn all to a merriment, if you take not the heat.  305

PRINCE  You whoreson candle-mine° you, how vilely
did you speak of me now before this honest, virtuous,
civil gentlewoman!

HOSTESS  God's blessing of your good heart! And so
she is, by my troth.                                   310

FALSTAFF  Didst thou hear me?

PRINCE  Yea, and you knew me, as you did when you
ran away by Gad's Hill.° You knew I was at your
back, and spoke it on purpose to try my patience.

FALSTAFF  No, no, no, not so. I did not think thou  315
wast within hearing.

PRINCE  I shall drive you then to confess the willful
abuse, and then I know how to handle you.

FALSTAFF  No abuse, Hal, o' mine honor, no abuse.

PRINCE  Not to dispraise me and call me pantler and  320
bread-chipper and I know not what?

FALSTAFF  No abuse, Hal.

POINS  No abuse?

FALSTAFF  No abuse, Ned, i' the' world. Honest Ned,
none. I dispraised him before the wicked, that the  325
wicked might not fall in love with thee. In which
doing, I have done the part of a careful friend and a
true subject, and thy father is to give me thanks for
it. No abuse, Hal. None, Ned, none. No, faith, boys,
none.                                                  330

PRINCE  See now, whether pure fear and entire
cowardice doth not make thee wrong this virtuous
gentlewoman to close° with us. Is she of the wicked?
Is thine hostess here of the wicked? Or is thy boy of
the wicked? Or honest Bardolph, whose zeal burns in  335
his nose, of the wicked?

POINS  Answer, thou dead elm, answer.

FALSTAFF  The fiend hath pricked down° Bardolph
irrecoverable, and his face is Lucifer's privy-kitchen,
where he doth nothing but roast malt-worms.° For  340
the boy, there is a good angel about him, but the
devil blinds him too.

PRINCE  For the women?

FALSTAFF  For one of them, she's in hell already, and
burns° poor souls. For th' other, I owe her money,  345
and whether she be damned for that, I know not.

HOSTESS  No, I warrant you.

FALSTAFF  No, I think thou art not. I think thou art
quit for that.° Marry, there is another indictment upon
thee, for suffering flesh° to be eaten in thy house,  350
contrary to the law, for the which I think thou wilt
howl.

HOSTESS  All victuallers do so. What's a joint of
mutton° or two in a whole Lent?

PRINCE  You, gentlewoman—                              355

DOLL  What says your grace?

FALSTAFF  His grace says that which his flesh rebels
against.°

PETO *knocks at door.*

HOSTESS  Who knocks so loud at door? Look to th'
door there, Francis.                                   360

*[Enter PETO.]*

PRINCE
Peto, how now! What news?

PETO
The king your father is at Westminster,
And there are twenty weak and wearied posts°
Come from the north. And as I came along
I met and overtook a dozen captains,                   365
Bareheaded, sweating, knocking at the taverns,
And asking everyone for Sir John Falstaff.

PRINCE
By heaven, Poins, I feel me much to blame,

271 **fiery Trigon** the conjunction of the three fiery signs of the
Zodiac: Aries, Leo, and Sagittarius (in Bardolph's face)  272
**tables** tablet or engagement book (i.e., bawd, Mistress Quickly)
274 **busses** kisses  280 **kirtle** skirt  286 **hearken . . . end**
see how it turns out  291 **continents** (1) vast land surfaces
(2) contents (3) pun on *continence*  300 **compound** mixture
301 **light** unchaste (he is referring to Doll)  306 **candle-mine**
reservoir of tallow  312–13 **as . . . Hill** the robbery of the
robbers in *1 Henry IV*, II.ii. and II.iv

333 **close** make peace  338 **pricked down** checked off  340
**malt-worms** (1) weevils in beer (2) drunkards (3) the white
material in Bardolph's pimples  345 **burns** gives burning
diseases to  349 **quit for that** paid off for that  350 **flesh**
(1) meat (2) womanflesh  354 **mutton** also meant a prostitute
357–58 **His grace . . . against** his grace calls her a gentlewoman, but his animal flesh rises up at the idea  363 **posts**
messengers

So idly to profane the precious time,
When tempest of commotion,° like the south°    370
Borne with black vapor,° doth begin to melt
And drop upon our bare unarmèd heads.
Give me my sword and cloak. Falstaff, good night.
    *Exeunt* PRINCE *and* POINS, [PETO, *and* BARDOLPH].
FALSTAFF   Now comes in the sweetest morsel of the
night, and we must hence and leave it unpicked. 375
[*Sound of knocking.*] More knocking at the door?
[*Enter* BARDOLPH.] How now! What's the matter?
BARDOLPH
You must away to court, sir, presently.°
A dozen captains stay at door for you.
FALSTAFF [*To the* PAGE.]   Pay the musicians, sirrah. 380
Farewell, hostess. Farewell, Doll. You see, my good
wenches, how men of merit are sought after. The
undeserver may sleep when the man of action is called
on. Farewell, good wenches. If I be not sent away
post,° I will see you again ere I go.     385
DOLL   I cannot speak. If my heart be not ready to
burst—well, sweet Jack, have a care of thyself.
FALSTAFF   Farewell, farewell. *Exit* [*with* BARDOLPH].
HOSTESS   Well, fare thee well. I have known thee
these twenty-nine years, come peascod-time,° but an 390
honester and truer-hearted man—well, fare thee well.
BARDOLPH [*Within.*]   Mistress Tearsheet!
HOSTESS   What's the matter?
BARDOLPH [*Within.*]   Bid Mistress Tearsheet come to
my master.     395
HOSTESS   O, run, Doll, run, run, good Doll. Come.
[*To* BARDOLPH *within.*] She comes blubbered.° Yea,
will you come, Doll?       *Exeunt.*


# [ A C T   I I I ]

[Scene I. *The palace.*]

*Enter the* KING *in his nightgown,*° *alone.*

KING [*To a* PAGE, *within.*]
Go, call the Earls of Surrey and of Warwick.
But, ere they come, bid them o'erread these letters
And well consider of them. Make good speed!
How many thousand of my poorest subjects
Are at this hour asleep! O sleep, O gentle sleep,    5
Nature's soft nurse, how have I frighted thee,
That thou no more wilt weigh my eyelids down
And steep my senses in forgetfulness?
Why rather, sleep, liest thou in smoky cribs,°
Upon uneasy pallets° stretching thee     10
And hushed with buzzing night-flies° to thy slumber,
Than in the perfumed° chambers of the great,

Under the canopies of costly state,°
And lulled with sound of sweetest melody?
O thou dull god, why li'st thou with the vile    15
In loathsome beds, and leavest the kindly couch
A watchcase° or a common 'larum-bell?°
Wilt thou upon the high and giddy mast
Seal up the ship-boy's eyes, and rock his brains
In cradle of the rude imperious surge     20
And in the visitation of the winds,
Who take the ruffian billows by the top,
Curling their monstrous heads and hanging them
With deafing° clamor in the slippery clouds,
That, with the hurly,° death itself awakes?    25
Canst thou, O partial° sleep, give thy repose
To the wet sea-son in an hour so rude,
And in the calmest and most stillest night,
With all appliances and means to boot,°
Deny it to a king? Then happy low,° lie down!    30
Uneasy lies the head that wears a crown.

*Enter* WARWICK, SURREY, *and Sir John* BLUNT.

WARWICK
Many good morrows to your majesty!
KING
Is it good morrow, lords?
WARWICK
'Tis one o'clock, and past.
KING
Why, then, good morrow to you all, my lords.    35
Have you read o'er the letter that I sent you?
WARWICK
We have, my liege.
KING
Then you perceive the body of our kingdom
How foul it is, what rank° diseases grow,
And with what danger, near the heart of it.     40
WARWICK
It is but as a body yet distempered,°
Which to his former strength may be restored
With good advice and little medicine.
My Lord Northumberland will soon be cooled.
KING
O God, that one might read the book of fate,    45
And see the revolution of the times
Make mountains level, and the continent,°
Weary of solid firmness, melt itself
Into the sea! And other times to see
The beachy girdle of the ocean     50
Too wide for Neptune's hips. How chances, mocks,
And changes fill the cup of alteration
With divers liquors! O, if this were seen,
The happiest youth, viewing his progress through,
What perils past, what crosses° to ensue,    55
Would shut the book, and sit him down and die.
'Tis not ten years gone
Since Richard and Northumberland, great friends,

---

**370 commotion** rebellion; **south** south wind   **371 Borne
. . . vapor** laden with black clouds   **378 presently** at present,
at once   **385 post** posthaste   **390 peascod-time** early summer
(but there is evidently a ribald sense, too)   **397 blubbered**
disfigured with weeping
**III.i.s.d. nightgown** dressing gown (the customary indoor
garment)   **9 smoky cribs** chimneyless hovels   **10 uneasy
pallets** comfortless straw beds   **11 night-flies** nocturnal insects
**12 perfumed** Elizabethans who could afford perfume tried to
keep out fresh air

**13 canopies . . . state** bed-curtains of those in a wealthy state
**17 watchcase** (1) sentry box (2) case of a constantly ticking
watch; **'larum-bell** alarm-bell (hence, constantly watchful)
**24 deafing** deafening   **25 hurly** hurly-burly   **26 partial** not
impartial   **29 means to boot** measures to further (sleep)
**30 low** lowborn   **39 rank** swelling   **41 yet distempered**
as yet but sickened   **47 continent** land surface   **55 crosses**
punishments

Did feast together,° and in two years after
Were they at wars. It is but eight years since    60
This Percy was the man nearest my soul,
Who like a brother toiled in my affairs
And laid his love and life under my foot,°
Yea, for my sake, even to the eyes of Richard
Gave him defiance. But which of you was by—    65
[*To* WARWICK.] You, cousin Nevil,° as I may
   remember—
When Richard, with his eye brimful of tears,
Then checked° and rated° by Northumberland,
Did speak these words, now proved a prophecy:
"Northumberland, thou ladder by the which    70
My cousin Bolingbroke ascends my throne"—
Though then, God knows, I had no such intent,
But that necessity so bowed the state
That I and greatness were compelled to kiss—
"The time shall come," thus did he follow it,    75
"The time will come that foul sin, gathering head,°
Shall break into corruption."° So went on,
Foretelling this same time's condition
And the division of our amity.

WARWICK
There is a history in all men's lives,    80
Figuring° the nature of the times deceased,
The which observed, a man may prophesy,
With a near aim, of the main chance of things
As yet not come to life, who in their seeds
And weak beginning lie intreasurèd.    85
Such things become the hatch and brood of time,
And by the necessary form of this°
King Richard might create a perfect guess
That great Northumberland, then false to him,
Would of that seed grow to a greater falseness,    90
Which should not find a ground to root upon,
Unless on you.

KING          Are these things then necessities?
Then let us meet them like necessities.
And that same word even now cries out on us.
They say the bishop and Northumberland    95
Are fifty thousand strong.

WARWICK         It cannot be, my lord.
Rumor doth double, like the voice and echo,
The numbers of the feared. Please it your grace
To go to bed. Upon my soul, my lord,
The powers that you already have sent forth    100
Shall bring this prize in very easily.
To comfort you the more, I have received
A certain instance° that Glendower is dead.
Your majesty hath been this fortnight ill,
And these unseasoned° hours perforce must add    105
Unto your sickness.

KING          I will take your counsel.
And were these inward° wars once out of hand,°
We would, dear lords, unto the Holy Land. *Exeunt.*

[Scene II. *Outside Justice Shallow's house.*]

*Enter Justice* SHALLOW *and Justice* SILENCE [*with*
MOLDY, SHADOW, WART, FEEBLE, BULLCALF].

SHALLOW   Come on, come on, come on. Give me
your hand, sir, give me your hand, sir; an early stirrer,
by the rood!° And how doth my good cousin Silence?
SILENCE   Good morrow, good cousin Shallow.
SHALLOW   And how doth my cousin, your bedfellow?   5
And your fairest daughter and mine, my goddaughter
Ellen?
SILENCE   Alas, a black ousel,° cousin Shallow!
SHALLOW   By yea and no,° sir, I dare say my cousin
William is become a good scholar. He is at Oxford   10
still, is he not?
SILENCE   Indeed, sir, to my cost.
SHALLOW   'A must, then, to the Inns o' Court°
shortly. I was once of Clement's Inn,° where I think
they will talk of mad Shallow yet.   15
SILENCE   You were called "lusty Shallow" then,
cousin.
SHALLOW   By the mass, I was called anything. And I
would have done anything indeed too, and roundly°
too. There was I, and little John Doit of Staffordshire,   20
and black George Barnes, and Francis Pickbone, and
Will Squele,° a Cotswold° man; you had not four
such swinge-bucklers° in all the Inns o' Court again.
And I may say to you we knew where the bona-robas°
were and had the best of them all at commandment.   25
Then was Jack Falstaff, now Sir John, a boy, and page
to Thomas Mowbray, Duke of Norfolk.
SILENCE   This Sir John, cousin, that comes hither anon
about soldiers?
SHALLOW   The same Sir John, the very same. I see   30
him break Scoggin's° head at the court-gate, when 'a
was a crack° not thus high. And the very same day
did I fight with one Sampson Stockfish,° a fruiterer,
behind Gray's Inn.° Jesu, Jesu, the mad days that I
have spent! And to see how many of my old acquain-   35
tance are dead!
SILENCE   We shall all follow, cousin.
SHALLOW   Certain, 'tis certain, very sure, very sure.
Death, as the psalmist saith, is certain to all, all shall
die. How° a good yoke of bullocks at Stamford Fair?   40
SILENCE   By my troth, I was not there.
SHALLOW   Death is certain. Is old Double° of your
town living yet?
SILENCE   Dead, sir.
SHALLOW   Jesu, Jesu, dead! 'A drew a good bow, and   45
dead! 'A shot a fine shoot. John a Gaunt° loved him

---

**59 Did feast together** Shakespeare here alters history for
dramatic purposes; this appears neither in Holinshed nor in
his own *Richard II*   **63 under my foot** in subservience to
me   **66 Nevil** historical error for *Beauchamps*   **68 checked,
rated** rebuked   **76 gathering head** (1) coming to a head
(2) collecting an army   **70–77 Northumberland . . . corruption** paraphrased from *Richard II*, V.i.55 ff.   **81 Figuring**
symbolizing   **87 necessary . . . this** inevitable operation of
this principle of analogy   **103 instance** proof   **105 unseasoned**
unusual   **107 inward** internal; **out of hand** finished

**III.ii.3 rood** cross   **8 ousel** blackbird   **9 By . . . no** a
puritan's oath   **13 Inns o' Court** law schools (which functioned
as universities for the gentry)   **14 Clement's Inn** one of
the Inns of Chancery, admitting students unable to get into the
Inns of Court   **19 roundly** fully   **20–22 Doit . . . Barnes
. . . Pickbone . . . Squele** the names are suggestive of in-
significance, a doit being a half-farthing; country wealth
(barns); stinginess; squealing cowardice   **22 Cotswold** a range
of hills in Gloucestershire   **23 swinge-bucklers** shield-beaters
i.e., blusterers   **24 bona-robas** high-class whores (Italian *buon-
aroba* = good material)   **31 Scoggin's** the name means a
coarse joker   **32 crack** perky boy   **33 Stockfish** a dried fish
(suggestive of an impotent man)   **34 Gray's Inn** another Inn of
Court   **40 How** how much for   **42 Double** suggests one
doubled over with age   **46 John a Gaunt** Henry IV's father

well and betted much money on his head. Dead! 'A
would have clapped i' th' clout at twelve score, and
carried you a forehand shaft a fourteen and fourteen
and a half,° that it would have done a man's heart 50
good to see. How a score of ewes now?

SILENCE   Thereafter as they be.° A score of good ewes
may be worth ten pounds.

SHALLOW   And is old Double dead?

SILENCE   Here come two of Sir John Falstaff's men, as 55
I think.

*Enter* BARDOLPH *and one with him.*

Good morrow, honest gentlemen.

BARDOLPH   I beseech you, which is Justice Shallow?

SHALLOW   I am Robert Shallow, sir, a poor esquire°
of this county, and one of the king's justices of the 60
peace. What is your good pleasure with me?

BARDOLPH   My captain, sir, commends him to you,
my captain, Sir John Falstaff, a tall° gentleman, by
heaven, and a most gallant leader.

SHALLOW   He greets me well, sir. I knew him a good 65
backsword° man. How doth the good knight? May I
ask how my lady his wife doth?

BARDOLPH   Sir, pardon, a soldier is better accommo-
dated° than with a wife.

SHALLOW   It is well said, in faith, sir, and it is well said 70
indeed too. "Better accommodated"! It is good, yea,
indeed, is it. Good phrases are surely, and ever were,
very commendable. "Accommodated"! It comes of
"accommodo." Very good, a good phrase.

BARDOLPH   Pardon, sir. I have heard the word. 75
"Phrase" call you it? By this good day, I know not
the phrase, but I will maintain the word with my
sword to be a soldierlike word, and a word of exceeding good command, by heaven. "Accommodated," that is, when a man is, as they say, 80
accommodated; or when a man is, being, whereby 'a
may be thought to be accommodated, which is an
excellent thing.

*Enter* FALSTAFF.

SHALLOW   It is very just.° Look, here comes good Sir
John. Give me your good hand, give me your wor- 85
ship's good hand. By my troth, you like° well and bear
your years very well. Welcome, good Sir John.

FALSTAFF   I am glad to see you well, good Master
Robert Shallow. Master Surecard,° as I think?

SHALLOW   No, Sir John, it is my cousin Silence, in 90
commission° with me.

FALSTAFF   Good Master Silence, it well befits you
should be of the peace.

SILENCE   Your good worship is welcome.

FALSTAFF   Fie! This is hot weather, gentlemen. Have 95
you provided me here half a dozen sufficient men?

SHALLOW   Marry, have we, sir. Will you sit?

FALSTAFF   Let me see them, I beseech you.

SHALLOW   Where's the roll? Where's the roll?
Where's the roll? Let me see, let me see, let me see. So, 100
so, so, so so, so—so. Yea, marry, sir. Rafe Moldy! Let
them appear as I call, let them do so, let them do so.
Let me see, where is Moldy?

MOLDY   Here, and't please you.

SHALLOW   What think you, Sir John? A good-limbed 105
fellow, young, strong, and of good friends.

FALSTAFF   Is thy name Moldy?

MOLDY   Yea, and't please you.

FALSTAFF   'Tis the more time thou wert used.

SHALLOW   Ha, ha, ha! Most excellent, i' faith! Things 110
that are moldy lack use. Very singular good! In faith,
well said, Sir John, very well said.

FALSTAFF   Prick him.°

MOLDY   I was pricked° well enough before, and you
could have let me alone. My old dame° will be undone 115
now for one to do her husbandry and her drudgery.
You need not to have pricked me. There are other
men fitter to go out than I.

FALSTAFF   Go to. Peace, Moldy, you shall go. Moldy,
it is time you were spent. 120

MOLDY   Spent?

SHALLOW   Peace, fellow, peace. Stand aside. Know
you where you are? For th' other, Sir John, let me see.
Simon Shadow!°

FALSTAFF   Yea, marry, let me have him to sit under. 125
He's like to be a cold soldier.

SHALLOW   Where's Shadow?

SHADOW   Here, sir.

FALSTAFF   Shadow, whose son art thou?

SHADOW   My mother's son, sir. 130

FALSTAFF   Thy mother's son! Like enough, and thy
father's shadow. So the son° of the female is the
shadow of the male. It is often so, indeed, but much°
of the father's substance!

SHALLOW   Do you like him, Sir John? 135

FALSTAFF   Shadow will serve for summer. Prick him,
for we have a number of shadows fill up the muster-
book.

SHALLOW   Thomas Wart!

FALSTAFF   Where's he? 140

WART   Here, sir.

FALSTAFF   Is thy name Wart?

WART   Yea, sir.

FALSTAFF   Thou art a very ragged° wart.

SHALLOW   Shall I prick him, Sir John? 145

FALSTAFF   It were superfluous,° for his apparel is built
upon his back and the whole frame stands upon pins.
Prick him no more.

SHALLOW   Ha, ha, ha! You can do it,° sir! You can
do it! I commend you well. Francis Feeble! 150

FEEBLE   Here, sir.

---

48–50 clapped . . . half hit the bull's-eye at 240 yards, and
shot a heavy arrow (for point-blank shooting) 280 or 290
yards   52 Thereafter . . . be according to their condition
59 esquire gentleman (ranking just below a knight)   63 tall
brave   66 backsword stick with a hilt used by apprentices in
fencing   68–69 accommodated provided (a "perfumed
term," according to Ben Jonson)   84 just exact   86 like get
on   89 Surecard absolute winner (at cards)   90–91 in commission commissioned as justice of the peace

113 Prick him check him off   114 pricked (1) chosen (2)
worried (and a ribald third meaning)   115 dame old wife (or
mother)   124 Shadow (1) likeness (2) shade (3) fictitious
name in the muster roll for which an officer collected pay
(Falstaff jokes on all three meanings)   132 son he is punning on
sun   133 much little (sarcastic)   144 ragged having rough
projections (referring to his pinned-together clothes)   146
superfluous i.e., to "prick him," pin his clothes together
149 you . . . it you know how to joke

SHALLOW  What trade art thou, Feeble?

FEEBLE  A woman's tailor, sir.

SHALLOW  Shall I prick him, sir?

FALSTAFF  You may. But if he had been a man's 155
tailor, he'd a' pricked you. Wilt thou make as many
holes in an enemy's battle° as thou hast done in a
woman's petticoat?

FEEBLE  I will do my good will, sir. You can have no
more.                                                    160

FALSTAFF  Well said, good woman's tailor! Well said,
courageous Feeble! Thou wilt be as valiant as the
wrathful dove or most magnanimous° mouse. Prick
the woman's tailor well,° Master Shallow, deep,°
Master Shallow.                                          165

FEEBLE  I would Wart might have gone, sir.

FALSTAFF  I would thou wert a man's tailor, that thou
mightst mend him and make him fit to go. I cannot
put him to° a private soldier that is the leader of so
many thousands.° Let that suffice, most forcible 170
Feeble.

FEEBLE  It shall suffice, sir.

FALSTAFF  I am bound to thee, reverend Feeble. Who
is next?

SHALLOW  Peter Bullcalf o' th' green!                   175

FALSTAFF  Yea, marry, let's see Bullcalf.

BULLCALF  Here, sir.

FALSTAFF  'Fore God, a likely fellow! Come, prick°
Bullcalf till he roar again.

BULLCALF  O Lord, good my lord captain—               180

FALSTAFF  What, dost thou roar before thou art
pricked?

BULLCALF  O Lord, sir, I am a diseased man.

FALSTAFF  What disease hast thou?

BULLCALF  A whoreson cold, sir, a cough, sir, which I 185
caught with ringing in° the king's affairs upon his
coronation day, sir.

FALSTAFF  Come, thou shalt go to the wars in a gown.°
We will have away thy cold, and I will take such
order that thy friends shall ring for thee.° Is here all? 190

SHALLOW  Here is two more called than your number.
You must have but four° here, sir. And so, I pray you
go in with me to dinner.

FALSTAFF  Come, I will go drink with you, but I
cannot tarry dinner. I am glad to see you, by my troth, 195
Master Shallow.

SHALLOW  O, Sir John, do you remember since we
lay all night in the Windmill° in Saint George's Field?

FALSTAFF  No more of that, Master Shallow.

SHALLOW  Ha! 'Twas a merry night, And is Jane 200
Nightwork alive?

FALSTAFF  She lives, Master Shallow.

SHALLOW  She never could away with° me.

FALSTAFF  Never, never, she would always say she
could not abide Master Shallow.                         205

SHALLOW  By the mass, I could anger° her to th'

heart. She was then a bona-roba. Doth she hold her
own well?

FALSTAFF  Old, old, Master Shallow.

SHALLOW  Nay, she must be old. She cannot choose 210
but be old. Certain she's old, and had Robin Nightwork by old Nightwork before I came to Clement's
Inn.

SILENCE  That's fifty-five year ago.

SHALLOW  Ha, cousin Silence, that thou hadst seen 215
that that this knight and I have seen! Ha, Sir John,
said I well?

FALSTAFF  We have heard the chimes at midnight,
Master Shallow.

SHALLOW  That we have, that we have, that we have, 220
in faith, Sir John, we have. Our watchword was
"Hem,° boys!" Come, let's to dinner, come, let's to
dinner. Jesus, the days that we have seen! Come,
come.          Exeunt [FALSTAFF and the JUSTICES].

BULLCALF  Good Master Corporate° Bardolph, stand 225
my friend, and here's four Harry ten shillings in French
crowns° for you. In very truth, sir, I had as lief be
hanged, sir, as go. And yet for mine own part, sir, I
do not care, but rather, because I am unwilling, and,
for mine own part, have a desire to stay with my 230
friends. Else, sir, I did not care, for mine own part, so
much.

BARDOLPH  Go to, stand aside.

MOLDY  And, good Master Corporal Captain, for my
dame's sake, stand my friend. She has nobody to do 235
anything about her when I am gone, and she is old
and cannot help herself. You shall have forty,° sir.

BARDOLPH  Go to, stand aside.

FEEBLE  By my troth, I care not. A man can die but
once. We owe God a death.° I'll ne'er bear a base 240
mind. And't be my destiny, so. And't be not, so. No
man's too good to serve's prince. And let it go which
way it will, he that dies this year is quit° for the next.

BARDOLPH  Well said. Th' art a good fellow.

FEEBLE  Faith, I'll bear no base mind.                  245

*Enter* FALSTAFF *and the* JUSTICES.

FALSTAFF  Come, sir, which men shall I have?

SHALLOW  Four of which you please.

BARDOLPH  Sir, a word with you. [*Aside.*] I have three
pound to free Moldy and Bullcalf.

FALSTAFF  Go to, well.

SHALLOW  Come, Sir John, which four will you 250
have?

FALSTAFF  Do you choose for me.

SHALLOW  Marry, then, Moldy, Bullcalf, Feeble, and
Shadow.                                                 255

FALSTAFF  Moldy and Bullcalf. For you, Moldy, stay
at home till you are past service.° And for your part,
Bullcalf, grow till you come unto it. I will none of you.

SHALLOW  Sir John, Sir John, do not yourself wrong.

---

157 **battle** battle line   163 **magnanimous** big-spirited   164
**well, deep** quibbles on Shallow's name   169 **put him to** set
him to the occupation of   170 **thousands** of lice   178 **prick**
here the word refers to the sticking of a bull with a goad
in bullbaiting   186 **ringing in** ringing the church bells to
celebrate   188 **gown** dressing gown   190 **ring for thee** toll
your funeral   192 **four** he settles for three   198 **Windmill**
evidently a brothel   203 **away with** put up with   206 **anger**
inflame

222 **Hem** the equivalent of "Bottoms up!"   225 **Corporate**
blunder for *corporal*   226–27 **four . . . crowns** a country
way of counting out £1: the amount of four pieces, formerly
of ten shillings' value but currently five, rendered in five four-
shilling pieces, "French crowns"; Bullcalf is offering around
$200 in today's values   237 **forty** forty shillings (about $400
today)   240 **death** pronounced like *debt*, hence a pun   243 **is
quit** owes nothing   257 **service** (1) military (2) domestic
(3) bull's

They are your likeliest men, and I would have you 260
served with the best.

FALSTAFF  Will you tell me, Master Shallow, how to
choose a man? Care I for the limb, the thews,° the
stature, bulk, and big assemblance° of a man? Give me
the spirit, Master Shallow! Here's Wart. You see what 265
a ragged appearance it is. 'A shall charge you and discharge you with the motion of a pewterer's hammer,°
come off and on swifter than he that gibbets on the
brewer's bucket.° And this same half-faced fellow,
Shadow. Give me this man. He presents no mark to 270
the enemy: the foeman may with as great aim level
at the edge of a penknife. And for a retreat, how
swiftly will this Feeble the woman's tailor run off!
O, give me the spare men, and spare me the great
ones. Put me a caliver° into Wart's hand, Bardolph. 275

BARDOLPH  Hold, Wart, traverse.° Thus, thus, thus.

FALSTAFF  Come, manage me your caliver. So. Very
well. Go to. Very good, exceeding good. O, give me
always a little, lean, old, chopped,° bald shot.° Well
said, i' faith. Wart. Th'art a good scab.° Hold, there's 280
a tester° for thee.

SHALLOW  He is not his craft's master, he doth not do
it right. I remember at Mile-End Green, when I lay at
Clement's Inn—I was then Sir Dagonet in Arthur's
show°—there was a little quiver° fellow, and 'a would 285
manage you his piece thus, and 'a would about and
about, and come you in and come you in. "Rah, tah,
tah," would 'a say, "Bounce," would 'a say, and away
again would 'a go, and again would 'a come. I shall
ne'er see such a fellow. 290

FALSTAFF  These fellows would do well, Master
Shallow. God keep you, Master Silence. I will not use
many words with you. Fare you well, gentlemen both.
I thank you. I must a dozen mile tonight. Bardolph,
give the soldiers coats. 295

SHALLOW  Sir John, the Lord bless you! God prosper
your affairs! God send us peace! At your return visit
our house, let our old acquaintance be renewed.
Peradventure I will with ye to the court.

FALSTAFF  'Fore God, would you would. 300

SHALLOW  Go to, I have spoke at a word.° God keep
you.

FALSTAFF  Fare you well, gentle gentlemen [*Exeunt*
JUSTICES.] On, Bardolph, lead the men away.
[*Exeunt all but* FALSTAFF.] As I return, I will fetch 305
off° these justices. I do see the bottom of Justice
Shallow. Lord, Lord, how subject we old men are
to this vice of lying! This same starved justice hath
done nothing but prate to me of the wildness of his
youth and the feats he hath done about Turnbull 310
Street,° and every third word a lie, duer° paid to

the hearer than the Turk's tribute.° I do remember
him at Clement's Inn like a man made after supper
of a cheese-paring. When 'a was naked, he was, for
all the world, like a forked radish, with a head fan- 315
tastically carved upon it with a knife. 'A was so
forlorn that his dimensions to any thick° sight were
invisible. 'A was the very genius° of famine, yet
lecherous as a monkey, and the whores called him
mandrake.° 'A came ever in the rearward of the 320
fashion, and sung those tunes to the overscutched
huswives° that he heard the carmen whistle, and
sware they were his fancies or his goodnights.° And
now is this Vice's dagger° become a squire, and talks
as familiarly of John a Gaunt as if he had been sworn 325
brother to him, and I'll be sworn 'a ne'er saw him but
once in the Tilt-yard, and then he° burst his head for
crowding among the marshal's men. I saw it, and told
John a Gaunt he beat his own name, for you might
have thrust him and all his apparel into an eelskin— 330
the case of a treble hautboy° was a mansion for him,
a court. And now has he land and beeves. Well, I'll
be acquainted with him, if I return, and't shall go hard
but I'll make him a philosopher's two stones° to me.
If the young dace° be a bait for the old pike, I see no 335
reason in the law of nature but I may snap at him. Let
time shape, and there an end.  [*Exit.*]

## [ ACT IV ]

[*Scene I. With the rebel army.*]

*Enter the* ARCHBISHOP [*of York*], MOWBRAY,
HASTINGS [*and others*], *within the Forest of Gaultree.*

ARCHBISHOP
What is this forest called?

HASTINGS
'Tis Gaultree Forest, and't shall please your grace.

ARCHBISHOP
Here stand, my lords, and send discoverers° forth
To know the numbers of our enemies.

HASTINGS
We have sent forth already.

ARCHBISHOP                        'Tis well done. 5
My friends and brethren in these great affairs,
I must acquaint you that I have received
New-dated letters from Northumberland,
Their cold intent, tenor, and substance, thus:
Here doth he wish his person, with such powers° 10
As might hold sortance with his quality,°

---

263 **thews** bodily forces  264 **assemblance** appearance  267
**motion . . . hammer** a rapid tap-tap  268–69 **gibbets . . .
bucket** hoists with the beam ("bucket") of a brewer's crane
275 **caliver** light musket  276 **traverse** cross over  279
**chopped** chapped; **shot** shooter (musketeers had to run nimbly
behind the pikemen or spearmen to reload)  280 **scab** wart
281 **tester** sixpence  284–85 **Arthur's show** an annual archery
show at Mile-End Green in which the contestants took the
names of knights of the Round Table; Sir Dagonet was
Arthur's fool  285 **quiver** nimble  301 **at a word** on an
impulse  305–06 **fetch off** trick  310–11 **Turnbull Street**
a red-light district  311 **duer** more duly, regularly

312 **than . . . tribute** than tribute is paid to the Turk  317
**thick** imperfect  318 **genius** spirit  320 **mandrake** forked
root, shaped like the lower half of a man  321–22 **overscutched huswives** often-whipped whores  323 **his . . .
his goodnights** goodnight songs or his own musical improvisa-
tions  324 **Vice's dagger** thin wooden dagger carried by the
Vice, clown in the old morality plays  327 **he** John of Gaunt
331 **treble hautboy** smallest oboe  334 **philosopher's
two stones** twice as profitable as one philosopher's stone
which would transmute base metals to gold—and a ribald
second sense  335 **dace** thin, small fish
IV.i.3 **discoverers** spies  10 **powers** armies  11 **hold . . .
quality** accord with his rank

The which he could not levy. Whereupon
He is retired, to ripe° his growing fortunes,
To Scotland, and concludes in hearty prayers
That your attempts may overlive° the hazard     15
And fearful meeting of° their opposite.

MOWBRAY

Thus do the hopes we have in him touch ground°
And dash themselves to pieces.

*Enter* MESSENGER.

HASTINGS                 Now, what news?
MESSENGER

West of this forest, scarcely off a mile,
In goodly form comes on the enemy,
And, by the ground they hide, I judge their number     20
Upon or near the rate of thirty thousand.

MOWBRAY

The just proportion that we gave them out.°
Let us sway° on and face them in the field.

ARCHBISHOP

What well-appointed° leader fronts° us here?     25

*Enter* WESTMORELAND.

MOWBRAY

I think it is my Lord of Westmoreland.

WESTMORELAND

Health and fair greeting from our general,
The prince, Lord John and Duke of Lancaster.

ARCHBISHOP

Say on, my Lord of Westmoreland, in peace.
What doth concern your coming?

WESTMORELAND          Then, my lord,     30
Unto your grace do I in chief° address
The substance of my speech. If that rebellion
Came like itself, in base and abject routs,°
Led on by bloody youth, guarded with rage,°
And countenanced° by boys and beggary,°     35
I say, if damned commotion° so appeared,
In his true, native and most proper shape,
You, reverend father, and these noble lords
Had not been here, to dress the ugly form
Of base and bloody insurrection     40
With your fair honors. You, Lord Archbishop,
Whose see° is by a civil peace maintained,
Whose beard the silver hand of peace hath touched,
Whose learning and good letters° peace hath tutored,
Whose white investments figure° innocence,     45
The dove and very blessèd spirit of peace,
Wherefore do you so ill translate° yourself
Out of the speech of peace that bears such grace,
Into the harsh and boisterous tongue of war,
Turning your books to graves, your ink to blood,     50

Your pens to lances, and your tongue divine
To a loud trumpet and a point of war?°

ARCHBISHOP

Wherefore do I this? So the question stands.
Briefly to this end: we are all diseased,
And with our surfeiting and wanton° hours     55
Have brought ourselves into a burning fever,
And we must bleed° for it. Of which disease
Our late king, Richard, being infected, died.
But, my most noble Lord of Westmoreland,
I take not on me here as a physician,°     60
Nor do I as an enemy to peace
Troop in the throngs of military men,
But rather show awhile like fearful war,
To diet rank° minds sick of happiness
And purge th' obstructions which begin to stop     65
Our very veins of life. Hear me more plainly.
I have in equal° balance justly weighed
What wrongs our arms may do, what wrongs we
    suffer,
And find our griefs° heavier than our offenses.
We see which way the stream of time doth run,     70
And are enforced from our most quiet there
By the rough torrent of occasion,
And have the summary of all our griefs,
When time shall serve, to show in articles;°
Which long ere this we offered to the king,     75
And might by no suit gain our audience.
When we are wronged and would unfold our griefs,
We are denied access unto his person
Even by those men that most have done us wrong.
The dangers of the days but newly gone,     80
Whose memory is written on the earth
With yet-appearing blood, and the examples
Of every minute's instance,° present now,
Hath put us in these ill-beseeming arms,
Not to break peace or any branch of it,     85
But to establish here a peace indeed,
Concurring both in name and quality.°

WESTMORELAND

When ever yet was your appeal denied?
Wherein have you been gallèd° by the king?
What peer hath been suborned to grate on° you,     90
That you should seal this lawless bloody book
Of forged rebellion with a seal divine?°

ARCHBISHOP

My brother general,° the commonwealth,
I make my quarrel in particular.

WESTMORELAND

There is no need of any such redress,     95
Or if there were, it not belongs to you.

MOWBRAY

Why not to him in part, and to us all

---

13 **ripe** ripen   15 **overlive** survive   15-16 **hazard . . . of** the fearful risk of meeting   17 **touch ground** like a ship   23 **just . . . out** exact number we allowed for   24 **sway** move   25 **well-appointed** well-furnished; **fronts** confronts   31 **in chief** chiefly   33 **routs** mobs   34 **guarded with rage** trimmed with false bluster (and pun on *rag*)   35 **countenanced** faced out, added to; **beggary** beggars   36 **commotion** rebellion   42 **see** seat, throne, hence diocese   44 **good letters** humane scholarship   45 **investments figure** vestments symbolize   47 **translate** transform (but note the extended metaphor of language in lines 48-52)

52 **point of war** bugle call   55 **wanton** self-indulgent   57 **bleed** be bled (as a purgative)   60 **I . . . physician** I do not presume to act as the doctor (to do the bleeding; I will but "show"—line 63)   64 **rank** swollen   67 **equal** unbiased   69 **griefs** grievances   74 **articles** formal listing   83 **Of . . . instance** proof in every minute   87 **quality** substance   89 **gallèd** irritated   90 **suborned . . . on** set on to vex   92 **divine** see A Note on the Text, p. 685   93 **brother general** brother in a general sense as opposed to my brother by birth; Henry IV had executed the archbishop's brother—*1 Henry IV*, I.iii; see A Note on the Text, p. 685

That feel the bruises of the days before,
And suffer the condition of these times
To lay a heavy and unequal° hand                                    100
Upon our honors?
WESTMORELAND  O, my good Lord Mowbray,
Construe the times to their necessities,°
And you shall say indeed, it is the time,
And not the king, that doth you injuries.
Yet for your part, it not appears to me                             105
Either from the king or in the present time
That you should have an inch of any ground
To build a grief on. Were you not restored
To all the Duke of Norfolk's signories,°
Your noble and right well-rememb'red father's?                      110
MOWBRAY
What thing, in honor, had my father lost,
That need to be revived and breathed in me?
The king that loved him, as the state stood then,
Was force perforce° compelled to banish him.
And then that Henry Bolingbroke and he,                             115
Being mounted and both rousèd in their seats,°
Their neighing coursers daring of° the spur,
Their armèd staves in charge, their beavers° down,
Their eyes of fire sparkling through sights of steel,
And the loud trumpet blowing them together,                         120
Then, then, when there was nothing could have
    stayed
My father from the breast of Bolingbroke—
O, when the king did throw his warder° down
His own life hung upon the staff he threw.
Then threw he down himself and all their lives                      125
That by indictment and by dint° of sword
Have since miscarried° under Bolingbroke.
WESTMORELAND
You speak, Lord Mowbray, now you know not
    what.
The Earl of Hereford was reputed then
In England the most valiant gentleman.                              130
Who knows on whom Fortune would then have
    smiled?
But if your father had been victor there,
He ne'er had borne it° out of Coventry.°
For all the country in a general voice
Cried hate upon him, and all their prayers and love                 135
Were set on Hereford, whom they doted on
And blessed and graced—and did more than° the
    king.
But this is mere digression from my purpose.
Here come I from our princely general
To know your griefs, to tell you from his grace                     140
That he will give you audience, and wherein
It shall appear that your demands are just,
You shall enjoy them, everything set off°
That might so much as think you enemies.

MOWBRAY
But he hath forced us to compel this offer,                         145
And it proceeds from policy,° not love.
WESTMORELAND
Mowbray, you overween° to take it so.
This offer comes from mercy, not from fear.
For, lo, within a ken° our army lies,
Upon mine honor, all too confident                                  150
To give admittance to a thought of fear.
Our battle° is more full of names° than yours,
Our men more perfect in the use of arms,
Our armor all as strong, our cause the best.
Then reason will° our hearts should be as good.                     155
Say you not then our offer is compelled.
MOWBRAY
Well, by my will we shall admit no parley.
WESTMORELAND
That argues but the shame of your offense.
A rotten° case abides no handling.
HASTINGS
Hath the Prince John a full commission,                             160
In very ample virtue° of his father,
To hear and absolutely to determine
Of what conditions we shall stand upon?
WESTMORELAND
That is intended in the general's name.°
I muse° you make so slight a question.                              165
ARCHBISHOP
Then take, my Lord of Westmoreland, this schedule,
For this contains our general grievances.
Each several article herein redressed,°
All members of our cause, both here and hence°
That are insinewed° to this action,                                 170
Acquitted by a true substantial form°
And present execution of our wills
To us and our purposes confined,°
We° come within our awful banks° again
And knit our powers to the arm of peace.                            175
WESTMORELAND
This will I show the general. Please you, lords,
In sight of both our battles we may meet,
And either end in peace—which God so frame—
Or to the place of diff'rence° call the swords
Which must decide it.
ARCHBISHOP            My lord, we will do so.                        180
                                *Exit* WESTMORELAND.
MOWBRAY
There is a thing within my bosom tells me
That no conditions° of our peace can stand.
HASTINGS
Fear you not that. If we can make our peace
Upon such large terms and so absolute

---

100 **unequal** not impartial  102 **Construe . . . necessities**
interpret the present state of things according to the forces that
inevitably make them the way they are  109 **signories** lands
114 **force perforce** willy-nilly (for the trial by battle described
in lines 115–37, see *Richard II*, I.iii  116 **seats** saddles  117
**daring of** ready for  118 **armèd . . . beavers** lances at the
ready, their helmet-visors  123 **warder** ceremonial baton
126 **dint** force  127 **miscarried** perished  133 **it** the prize;
**Coventry** the scene of this trial by battle  137 **did more**
**than** did so more than for  143 **set off** put aside, ignored

146 **policy** statecraft  147 **overween** calculate too much  149
**ken** look  152 **battle** battle line; **names** men with warlike
reputations  155 **reason will** it will be reasonable that
159 **rotten** fragile (proverbial statement)  161 **In . . . virtue**
with exactly the ample power  164 **intended . . . name**
implicit in the king's making his son the general  165 **muse** am
puzzled  168 **Each . . . redressed** if each . . . is redressed,
etc.  169 **hence** elsewhere  170 **insinewed** bound by strong
sinews  171 **substantial form** firm formal agreement  172–
73 **wills . . . confined** demands restricted (in scope) to us
and our grievances  174 **We** then we; **banks** i.e., they will
subside like a stream that had been in flood  179 **diff'rence**
conflict  182 **conditions** provisions in the contract

As our conditions shall consist upon,    185
Our peace shall stand as firm as rocky mountains.

MOWBRAY
Yea, but our valuation° shall be such
That every slight and false-derivèd cause,
Yea, every idle, nice, and wanton° reason
Shall to the king taste of this action,    190
That, were our royal faiths martyrs in love,°
We shall be winnowed with so rough a wind
That even our corn shall seem as light as chaff
And good from bad find no partition.°

ARCHBISHOP
No, no, my lord. Note this. The king is weary    195
Of dainty° and such picking° grievances.
For he hath found to end one doubt by death
Revives two greater in the heirs of life,°
And therefore will he wipe his tables° clean
And keep no telltale to his memory    200
That may repeat and history his loss
To new remembrance. For full well he knows
He cannot so precisely° weed this land
As his misdoubts° present occasion.
His foes are so enrooted with his friends    205
That, plucking to unfix an enemy,
He doth unfasten so and shake a friend.
So that this land, like an offensive wife
That hath enraged him on to offer strokes,
As he is striking, holds his infant up    210
And hangs resolved correction° in the arm
That was upreared to execution.

HASTINGS
Besides, the king hath wasted all his rods
On late offenders, that he now doth lack
The very instruments of chastisement.    215
So that his power, like to a fangless lion,
May offer,° but not hold.

ARCHBISHOP            'Tis very true.
And therefore be assured, my good Lord Marshal,
If we do now make our atonement° well,
Our peace will, like a broken limb united,    220
Grow stronger for the breaking.

MOWBRAY            Be it so.
Here is returned my Lord of Westmoreland.

*Enter* WESTMORELAND.

WESTMORELAND
The prince is here at hand. Pleaseth your lordship
To meet his grace just distance° 'tween our armies.

*Enter Prince John [of* LANCASTER] *and his* ARMY.

MOWBRAY
Your Grace of York, in God's name then, set forward.    225

ARCHBISHOP
Before, and greet his grace, my lord; we come.

[Scene II. *The same.*]°

LANCASTER
You are well encount'red here, my cousin Mowbray.
Good day to you, gentle Lord Archbishop.
And so to you, Lord Hastings, and to all.
My Lord of York, it better showed with you
When that your flock, assembled by the bell,    5
Encircled you to hear with reverence
Your exposition on the holy text
Than now to see you here an iron° man talking,
Cheering a rout of rebels with your drum,
Turning the word to sword and life to death.    10
That man that sits within a monarch's heart
And ripens in the sunshine of his favor,
Would he abuse the countenance of the king,
Alack, what mischiefs might he set abroach°
In shadow of such greatness! With you, Lord Bishop,    15
It is even so. Who hath not heard it spoken
How deep you were within the books of God?
To us the speaker in His parliament,
To us th' imagined voice of God himself,
The very opener and intelligencer°    20
Between the grace, the sanctities of heaven
And our dull workings.° O, who shall believe
But you misuse the reverence of your place,
Employ the countenance and grace of heaven,
As a false favorite doth his prince's name,    25
In deeds dishonorable? You have ta'en up,°
Under the counterfeited zeal° of God,
The subjects of His substitute,° my father,
And both against the peace of heaven and him
Have here upswarmed° them.

ARCHBISHOP      Good my Lord of Lancaster,    30
I am not here against your father's peace,
But, as I told my Lord of Westmoreland,
The time misord'red doth, in common sense,°
Crowd us and crush us to this monstrous° form,
To hold our safety up. I sent your grace    35
The parcels° and particulars of our grief,
The which hath been with scorn shoved from the
    court,
Whereon this Hydra° son of war is born,
Whose dangerous eyes may well be charmed asleep
With grant of our most just and right desires,    40
And true obedience, of this madness cured,
Stoop tamely to the foot of majesty.

MOWBRAY
If not, we ready are to try our fortunes
To the last man.

HASTINGS      And though we here fall down,
We have supplies to second° our attempt.    45
If they miscarry, theirs° shall second them,

---

**187 valuation** i.e., in the king's eyes   **189 nice, and wanton** petty and frivolous   **191 were . . . love** even if we were as faithful in love to his royal self as martyrs   **194 partition** dividing   **196 dainty, picking** finicky   **197–98 to end . . . life** to rid himself of one doubtful subject by executing him creates two even more treacherous foes in those who live on after the dead man   **199 tables** notebook   **203 precisely** thoroughly   **204 misdoubts** suspicions   **211 resolved correction** a check on his resolution   **217 offer** threaten   **219 atonement** becoming at one   **224 just distance** halfway

**IV.ii.s.d.** notice there should be no scene division, the action being continuous and the stage not having emptied   **8 iron** (1) armored (2) merciless   **14 abroach** open (like a cask)   **20 opener and intelligencer** interpreter and informant   **22 workings** mental operations   **26 ta'en up** enlisted   **27 zeal** with a pun on *seal*   **28 substitute** deputy   **30 upswarmed** made (them) swarm up   **33 in common sense** to anybody's senses   **34 monstrous** unnatural   **36 parcels** small parts   **38 Hydra** many-headed monster   **45 supplies to second** reinforcements to back up   **46 theirs** their supplies

And so success° of mischief shall be born
And heir from heir shall hold this quarrel up
Whiles England shall have generation.°

LANCASTER
You are too shallow, Hastings, much too shallow,    50
To sound° the bottom of the after-times.

WESTMORELAND
Pleaseth your grace to answer them directly
How far forth you do like their articles.

LANCASTER
I like them all, and do allow them well,
And swear here, by the honor of my blood,    55
My father's purposes have been mistook,
And some about him have too lavishly°
Wrested° his meaning and authority.
My lord, these griefs shall be with speed redressed.
Upon my soul, they shall. If this may please you,    60
Discharge your powers unto their several counties,
As we will ours. And here between the armies
Let's drink together friendly and embrace,
That all their eyes may bear those tokens home
Of our restorèd love and amity.    65

ARCHBISHOP
I take your princely word for these redresses.

LANCASTER
I give it you, and will maintain my word.
And thereupon I drink unto your grace.

[He drinks.]

HASTINGS
Go, captain, and deliver to the army
This news of peace. Let them have pay, and part.°    70
I know it will well please them. Hie thee, captain.
[Exit OFFICER.]

ARCHBISHOP
To you, my noble Lord of Westmoreland.

[He drinks.]

WESTMORELAND
I pledge your grace, and, if you knew what pains
I have bestowed to breed this present peace,
You would drink freely. But my love to ye    75
Shall show itself more openly hereafter.

ARCHBISHOP
I do not doubt you.

WESTMORELAND    I am glad of it.
Health to my lord and gentle cousin, Mowbray.

MOWBRAY
You wish me health in very happy season,
For I am, on the sudden, something° ill.    80

ARCHBISHOP
Against° ill chances men are ever merry,
But heaviness foreruns the good event.

WESTMORELAND
Therefore be merry, coz, since sudden sorrow
Serves to say thus, "Some good thing comes to-
morrow."

ARCHBISHOP
Believe me, I am passing° light in spirit.    85

MOWBRAY
So much the worse, if your own rule be true.

Shout [within].

LANCASTER
The word of peace is rend'red. Hark, how they shout!

MOWBRAY
This had been cheerful after victory.

ARCHBISHOP
A peace is of the nature of a conquest,
For then both parties nobly are subdued,    90
And neither party loser.

LANCASTER                Go, my lord,
And let our army be dischargèd too.
[Exit WESTMORELAND.]
And, good my lord, so please you, let our trains°
March by us, that we may peruse the men
We should have coped withal.°

ARCHBISHOP                Go, good Lord Hastings,    95
And, ere they be dismissed, let them march by.
[Exit HASTINGS.]

LANCASTER
I trust, lords, we shall lie tonight together.

Enter WESTMORELAND.

Now cousin, wherefore stands our army still?

WESTMORELAND
The leaders, having charge from you to stand,
Will not go off until they hear you speak.    100

LANCASTER
They know their duties.

Enter HASTINGS.

HASTINGS
My lord, our army is dispersed already.
Like youthful steers unyoked, they take their courses
East, west, north, south, or, like a school broke up,    105
Each hurries toward his home and sporting-place.°

WESTMORELAND
Good tidings, my Lord Hastings, for the which
I do arrest thee, traitor, of high treason.
And you, Lord Archbishop, and you, Lord Mowbray,
Of capital° treason I attach° you both.

MOWBRAY    110
Is this proceeding just and honorable?

WESTMORELAND
Is your assembly so?

ARCHBISHOP [To LANCASTER.]
Will you thus break your faith?

LANCASTER                I pawned° thee none.
I promised you redress of these same grievances
Whereof you did complain, which, by mine honor,    115
I will perform with a most Christian care.
But for you, rebels, look to taste the due
Meet for rebellion and such acts as yours.
Most shallowly did you these arms commence,
Fondly° brought here and foolishly sent hence.    120
Strike up our drums, pursue the scatt'red stray.

---

47 **success** succession  49 **generation** offspring  51 **sound**
measure the depth of  57 **lavishly** loosely  58 **Wrested**
twisted  70 **part** depart  80 **something** somewhat  81 **Against**
expecting  85 **passing** surpassingly

93 **our trains** those who follow us  95 **coped withal** been
matched with  105 **sporting-place** playground  109 **capital**
punishable by death; **attach** arrest  112 **pawned** pledged  119
**Fondly** foolishly

God, and not we, hath safely fought today.
Some guard these traitors to the block of death,
Treason's true bed and yielder up of breath. [*Exeunt.*]


[Scene III. *The same.*]°

*Alarum. Enter* FALSTAFF [*and* COLEVILLE, *meeting*].
*Excursions.*°

FALSTAFF   What's your name, sir? Of what condition°
are you, and of what place?

COLEVILLE   I am a knight, sir, and my name is
Coleville of the Dale.°

FALSTAFF   Well, then, Coleville is your name, a knight   5
is your degree, and your place the Dale. Coleville
shall be still your name, a traitor your degree, and the
dungeon your place, a place deep enough. So shall
you be still Coleville of the Dale.

COLEVILLE   Are not you Sir John Falstaff?     10

FALSTAFF   As good a man as he, sir, whoe'er I am. Do
ye yield, sir, or shall I sweat for you? If I do sweat,
they are the drops of thy lovers,° and they weep for
thy death. Therefore rouse up fear and trembling,
and do observance to my mercy.     15

COLEVILLE   I think you are Sir John Falstaff, and in
that thought yield me.

FALSTAFF   I have a whole school° of tongues in this
belly of mine, and not a tongue of them all speaks
any other word but my name. And I had but a belly   20
of any indifferency,° I were simply the most active
fellow in Europe. My womb,° my womb, my womb
undoes° me. Here comes our general.

*Enter* [*Prince*] *John* [*of* LANCASTER], WESTMORE-
LAND, [BLUNT,] *and the rest. Retreat* [*sounded*].

LANCASTER
The heat° is past, follow no further now.
Call in the powers, good cousin Westmoreland.     25
             [*Exit* WESTMORELAND.]
Now, Falstaff, where have you been all this while?
When everything is ended, then you come.
These tardy tricks of yours will, on my life,
One time or other break some gallows' back.

FALSTAFF   I would be sorry, my lord, but it should be   30
thus. I never knew yet but rebuke and check was the
reward of valor. Do you think me a swallow, an arrow,
or a bullet? Have I, in my poor and old motion, the
expedition of thought? I have speeded hither with the
very extremest inch of possibility. I have found'red°   35
nine score and odd posts,° and here, travel-tainted as
I am, have, in my pure and immaculate valor, taken
Sir John Coleville of the Dale, a most furious knight
and valorous enemy. But what of that? He saw me,
and yielded, that I may justly say, with the hook-nosed   40

fellow of Rome, "There, cousin,° I came, saw, and
overcame."

LANCASTER   It was more of his courtesy than your
deserving.

FALSTAFF   I know not. Here he is, and here I yield   45
him. And I beseech your grace, let it be booked with
the rest of this day's deeds, or, by the Lord, I will have
it in a particular ballad else,° with mine own picture
on the top on't, Coleville kissing my foot. To the
which course if I be enforced, if you do not all show   50
like gilt twopences° to° me, and I in the clear sky of
fame o'ershine you as much as the full moon doth the
cinders of the element,° which show like pins' heads
to her, believe not the word of the noble. Therefore
let me have right, and let desert mount.     55

LANCASTER   Thine's too heavy to mount.

FALSTAFF   Let it shine, then.

LANCASTER   Thine's too thick to shine.

FALSTAFF   Let it do something, my good lord, that
may do me good, and call it what you will.     60

LANCASTER   Is thy name Coleville?

COLEVILLE   It is, my lord.

LANCASTER   A famous rebel art thou, Coleville.

FALSTAFF   And a famous true subject took him.

COLEVILLE
I am, my lord, but as my betters are     65
That led me hither. Had they been ruled by me,
You should have won them dearer than you have.

FALSTAFF   I know not how they sold themselves. But
thou, like a kind fellow, gavest thyself away gratis,
and I thank thee for thee.     70

*Enter* WESTMORELAND.

LANCASTER
Now, have you left pursuit?

WESTMORELAND
Retreat is made° and execution stayed.°

LANCASTER
Send Coleville with his confederates
To York, to present° execution.
Blunt, lead him hence, and see you guard him sure.   75
       [*Exeunt* BLUNT *and others with* COLEVILLE.]
And now dispatch° we toward the court, my lords.
I hear the king my father is sore sick.
Our news shall go before us to his majesty,
Which, cousin, you shall bear to comfort him,
And we with sober speed will follow you.     80

FALSTAFF
My lord, I beseech you give me leave to go
Through Gloucestershire. And when you come to court,
Stand° my good lord in your good report.

LANCASTER
Fare you well, Falstaff. I, in my condition,°
Shall better speak of you than you deserve.     85
       [*Exeunt all but* FALSTAFF.]

---

**IV.iii.s.d.** again, there should be no scene division; see
A Note on the Text, p. 685; **Excursions** brief combats   1
**condition** rank   **4 Dale** deep place   **13 drops . . . lovers**
teardrops of those who love you   **18 school** multitude (he is
saying "my belly proclaims my identity as loudly as a multitude")   **21 indifferency** undistinguished quality   **22 womb**
belly   **23 undoes** unmans   **24 heat** hot fighting   **35 found'red**
lamed   **36 posts** post horses (Falstaff is, after all, heavy)

**41 There, cousin** a gross familiarity to Prince John; the
Folio reads "their Caesar"   **48 particular ballad else**
special broadside ballad otherwise   **51 gilt twopences** silver
twopenny pieces, if gilded, could pass for gold half crowns;
**to** in comparison to   **53 cinders . . . element** stars   **72
Retreat is made** the order for retreat has been given;
**stayed** halted   **74 present** immediate   **76 dispatch** hurry
**83 Stand** act as   **84 condition** present state of mind (but Falstaff takes his meaning as "rank")

FALSTAFF  I would you had the wit. 'Twere better than your dukedom. Good faith, this same young sober-blooded boy doth not love me, nor a man cannot make him laugh. But that's no marvel, he drinks no wine. There's never none of these demure 90 boys come to any proof,° for thin drink doth so over-cool their blood, and making many fish-meals, that they fall into a kind of male greensickness,° and then, when they marry, they get° wenches. They are generally fools and cowards, which some of us should 95 be too, but for inflammation.° A good sherris-sack° hath a twofold operation in it. It ascends me into the brain, dries me there all the foolish and dull and cruddy° vapors which environ it, makes it apprehensive,° quick, forgetive,° full of nimble, fiery, and 100 delectable shapes, which, delivered o'er to the voice, the tongue, which is the birth, becomes excellent wit.° The second property of your excellent sherris is the warming of the blood, which, before cold and settled, left the liver° white and pale, which is the badge of 105 pusillanimity and cowardice. But the sherris warms it and makes it course from the inwards to the parts extremes. It illumineth the face, which as a beacon gives warning to all the rest of this little kingdom, man, to arm, and then the vital commoners and inland 110 petty spirits° muster me all to their captain, the heart, who, great and puffed up with this retinue, doth any deed of courage, and this valor comes of sherris. So that skill in the weapon is nothing without sack, for that sets it a-work, and learning a mere 115 hoard of gold kept by a devil, till sack commences it° and sets it in act and use. Hereof comes it that Prince Harry is valiant, for the cold blood he did naturally inherit of his father, he hath, like lean, sterile, and bare land, manured,° husbanded, and tilled 120 with excellent endeavor of drinking good and good store of fertile sherris, that he is become very hot and valiant. If I had a thousand sons, the first humane principle I would teach them should be to forswear thin potations and to addict themselves to sack. 125

*Enter* BARDOLPH.

How now, Bardolph?
BARDOLPH  The army is discharged all and gone.
FALSTAFF  Let them go. I'll through Gloucestershire, and there will I visit Master Robert Shallow, Esquire. I have him already temp'ring° between my finger 130 and my thumb, and shortly will I seal° with him. Come away.                    [*Exeunt.*]

---

[Scene IV. *Westminster.*]

*Enter the* KING, WARWICK, KENT, *Thomas Duke of* CLARENCE, *Humphrey* [*Duke*] *of* GLOUCESTER, [*and others*].

KING
Now, lords, if God doth give successful end
To this debate that bleedeth at our doors,
We will our youth lead on to higher fields
And draw no swords but what are sanctified.°
Our navy is addressed,° our power° collected,     5
Our substitutes in absence well invested,°
And everything lies level° to our wish.
Only, we want° a little personal strength
And pause us, till these rebels, now afoot,
Come underneath the yoke of government.          10
WARWICK
Both which we doubt not but your majesty
Shall soon enjoy.
KING                 Humphrey, my son of Gloucester,
Where is the prince your brother?
GLOUCESTER
I think he's gone to hunt, my lord, at Windsor.
KING
And how accompanied?
GLOUCESTER            I do not know, my lord.  15
KING
Is not his brother, Thomas of Clarence, with him?
GLOUCESTER
No, my good lord, he is in presence° here.
CLARENCE
What would my lord and father?
KING
Nothing but well to thee, Thomas of Clarence.
How chance thou art not with the prince thy brother? 20
He loves thee, and thou dost neglect him Thomas;
Thou hast a better place in his affection
Than all thy brothers. Cherish it, my boy,
And noble offices thou mayst effect
Of mediation, after I am dead,                   25
Between his greatness and thy other brethren.
Therefore omit him not, blunt not his love,
Nor lose the good advantage of his grace
By seeming cold or careless of his will.
For he is gracious,° if he be observed.°         30
He hath a tear for pity and a hand
Open as day for meeting charity.
Yet notwithstanding, being incensed, he's flint,
As humorous° as winter and as sudden
As flaws congealèd° in the spring of day.        35
His temper, therefore, must be well observed.
Chide him for faults, and do it reverently,
When you perceive his blood inclined to mirth,
But, being moody, give him time and scope,
Till that his passions, like a whale on ground,  40
Confound° themselves with working.° Learn this,
  Thomas,

---

91 come . . . proof stand much testing  93 greensickness anemia common to young girls  94 get beget  96 inflammation i.e., of the spirits with liquor; sherris-sack sherry (wine from the Jerez district in Spain; "sack" is from the French, *sec* = dry)  99 cruddy curded  99–100 apprehensive quick to take in  100 forgetive begetting, procreative  102 wit intelligence  105 liver seat of the passions, including courage  110–11 vital . . . spirits fluids within the body that give it life and motion  116–17 commences it gives it a university degree (licensing it to act)  120 manured tilled by hand  130 temp'ring softening (like sealing wax)  131 seal (1) squeeze (2) close the deal

IV.iv.4 sanctified i.e., in a crusade  5 addressed at the ready; power army  6 invested clothed (with authority)  7 level according  8 want lack  17 presence the royal presence  30 gracious full of royal grace; observed respected  34 humorous given to whims  35 flaws congealèd snowstorms turned to sleet  41 Confound defeat; working acting out

And thou shalt prove a shelter to thy friends,
A hoop of gold to bind thy brothers in,
That the united vessel of their blood,
Mingled with venom of suggestion°— 45
As, force perforce,° the age will pour it in—
Shall never leak, though it do work as strong
As aconitum° or rash gunpowder.

CLARENCE
I shall observe him with all care and love.

KING
Why art thou not at Windsor with him, Thomas? 50

CLARENCE
He is not there today. He dines in London.

KING
And how accompanied? Canst thou tell that?

CLARENCE
With Poins and other his continual followers.

KING
Most subject is the fattest° soil to weeds,
And he, the noble image of my youth, 55
Is overspread with them. Therefore my grief
Stretches itself beyond the hour of death.
The blood weeps from my heart when I do shape
In forms imaginary th' unguided days
And rotten times that you shall look upon 60
When I am sleeping with my ancestors.
For when his headstrong riot hath no curb,
When rage° and hot blood are his counselors,
When means and lavish manners° meet together,
O, with what wings shall his affections° fly 65
Towards fronting° peril and opposed decay!

WARWICK
My gracious lord, you look beyond° him quite.
The prince but studies his companions
Like a strange tongue, wherein, to gain the language,
'Tis needful that the most immodest word 70
Be looked upon and learned, which once attained,
Your highness knows, comes to no further use
But to be known and hated. So, like gross terms,
The prince will in the perfectness of time
Cast off his followers, and their memory 75
Shall as a pattern or a measure live,
By which his grace must mete° the lives of others,
Turning past evils to advantages.

KING
'Tis seldom when the bee doth leave her comb
In the dead carrion.° Who's here? Westmoreland? 80

Enter WESTMORELAND.

WESTMORELAND
Health to my sovereign, and new happiness
Added to that that I am to deliver.
Prince John your son doth kiss your grace's hand.
Mowbray, the Bishop Scroop, Hastings and all
Are brought to the correction of your law. 85
There is not now a rebel's sword unsheathed,

But peace puts forth her olive everywhere.
The manner how this action hath been borne
Here at more leisure may your highness read,
With every course° of his particular. 90

KING
O Westmoreland, thou art a summer bird,
Which ever in the haunch° of winter sings
The lifting up of day.

Enter HARCOURT.

                        Look, here's more news.

HARCOURT
From enemies, heavens keep your majesty,
And, when they stand against you, may they fall 95
As those that I am come to tell you of!
The Earl Northumberland and the Lord Bardolph,
With a great power of English and of Scots,
Are by the shrieve° of Yorkshire overthrown.
The manner and true order of the fight 100
This packet, please it you, contains at large.

KING
And wherefore should these good news make me sick?
Will Fortune never come with both hands full,
But write her fair words still° in foulest letters?
She either gives a stomach° and no food— 105
Such are the poor, in health—or else a feast
And takes away the stomach—such are the rich
That have abundance and enjoy it not.
I should rejoice now at this happy news,
And now my sight fails, and my brain is giddy. 110
O me! Come near me. Now I am much ill.

GLOUCESTER
Comfort, your majesty!

CLARENCE                        O my royal father!

WESTMORELAND
My sovereign lord, cheer up yourself, look up.

WARWICK
Be patient, princes. You do know these fits
Are with his highness very ordinary. 115
Stand from him, give him air, he'll straight° be well.

CLARENCE
No, no, he cannot long hold out these pangs.
Th' incessant care and labor of his mind
Hath wrought the mure° that should confine it in
So thin that life looks through and will break out. 120

GLOUCESTER
The people fear me,° for they do observe
Unfathered° heirs and loathly° births off nature.
The seasons change their manners, as° the year
Had found some months asleep and leaped them over.

CLARENCE
The river° hath thrice flowed,° no ebb between, 125
And the old folk, time's doting chronicles,
Say it did so a little time before
That our great-grandsire, Edward,° sicked and died.

WARWICK
Speak lower, princes, for the king recovers.

45 suggestion insinuations 46 force perforce willy-nilly 48 aconitum wolfsbane (a poison) 54 fattest richest 63 rage passion 64 lavish manners loose behavior 65 affections desires 66 fronting confronting 67 look beyond misjudge, i.e., you look further into the future than the evidence warrants 77 mete measure, judge 79–80 'Tis . . . carrion The bee who has created sweetness in rottenness rarely abandons it

90 course occurrence 92 haunch back portion 99 shrieve sheriff 104 still ever 105 stomach appetite 116 straight straightway 119 wrought the mure worked the wall 121 fear me make me fear 122 Unfathered supernaturally begotten; loathly monstrous 123 as as if 125 river Thames; flowed flooded 128 Edward Edward III

GLOUCESTER
This apoplexy will certain be his end.                    130
KING
I pray you, take me up, and bear me hence
Into some other chamber. Softly, pray.

[*They bear him to another part of the stage.*]


[Scene V. *The same.*]°

[KING]
Let there be no noise made, my gentle friends,
Unless some dull and favorable° hand
Will whisper music to my weary spirit.
WARWICK
Call for the music in the other room.
KING
Set me the crown upon my pillow here.                     5
CLARENCE
His eye is hollow, and he changes° much.
WARWICK
Less noise, less noise!

*Enter* [PRINCE] *Harry.*

PRINCE                       Who saw the Duke of Clarence?
CLARENCE
I am here, brother, full of heaviness.
PRINCE
How now! Rain° within doors, and none abroad!
How doth the king?                                        10
GLOUCESTER
Exceeding ill.
PRINCE          Heard he the good news yet?
Tell it him.
GLOUCESTER
He altered much upon the hearing it.
PRINCE
If he be sick with joy, he'll recover without physic.
WARWICK
Not so much noise, my lords. Sweet prince, speak low.   15
The king your father is disposed to sleep.
CLARENCE
Let us withdraw into the other room.
WARWICK
Will't please your grace to go along with us?
PRINCE
No, I will sit and watch here by the king.
                          [*Exeunt all but* PRINCE *Hal.*]
Why doth the crown lie there upon his pillow,            20
Being so troublesome a bedfellow?
O polished perturbation! Golden care!
That keep'st the ports° of slumber open wide
To many a watchful night! Sleep with it now!
Yet not so sound and half so deeply sweet                25
As he whose brow with homely biggen° bound

Snores out the watch of night. O majesty!
When thou dost pinch thy bearer, thou dost sit
Like a rich armor worn in heat of day,
That scald'st with safety.° By his gates of breath°      30
There lies a downy feather which stirs not.
Did he suspire,° that light and weightless down
Perforce must move. My gracious lord, my father!
This sleep is sound indeed. This is a sleep
That from this golden rigol° hath divorced              35
So many English kings. Thy due from me
Is tears and heavy sorrows of the blood,
Which nature, love, and filial tenderness
Shall, O dear father, pay thee plenteously.
My due from thee is this imperial crown,                40
Which, as immediate from° thy place and blood,
Derives° itself to me. [*Puts on the crown.*] Lo, where it
    sits,
Which God shall guard. And put the world's whole
    strength
Into one giant arm, it shall not force
This lineal° honor from me. This from thee               45
Will I to mine leave, as 'tis left to me.         *Exit.*
KING [*Waking.*]
Warwick! Gloucester! Clarence!

*Enter* WARWICK, GLOUCESTER, CLARENCE.

CLARENCE
Doth the king call?
WARWICK
What would your majesty? How fares your grace?
KING
Why did you leave me here alone, my lords?               50
CLARENCE
We left the prince my brother here, my liege,
Who undertook to sit and watch by you.
KING
The Prince of Wales! Where is he? Let me see him.
He is not here.
WARWICK
This door is open. He is gone this way.                  55
GLOUCESTER
He came not through the chamber where we stayed.
KING
Where is the crown? Who took it from my pillow?
WARWICK
When we withdrew, my liege, we left it here.
KING
The prince hath ta'en it hence. Go, seek him out.
Is he so hasty that he doth suppose                      60
My sleep my death?
Find him, my Lord of Warwick, chide him hither.
                                    [*Exit* WARWICK.]
This part° of his conjoins with my disease
And helps to end me. See, sons, what things you are!
How quickly nature falls into revolt                     65
When gold becomes her object!
For this the foolish overcareful fathers
Have broke their sleep with thoughts,
Their brains with care, their bones with industry.

---

IV.v.s.d. the stage is not emptied, the king being lifted onto a
bed and moved to the inner stage or another part of the outer
stage, and the quarto and the Folio indicate no scene division;
the conventional nineteenth-century scene division is superfluous  **2 dull and favorable** drowsy and kindly  **6 changes**
changes color  **9 Rain** tears  **23 ports** city gates (as the eyes
are to the mind)  **26 biggen** nightcap

**30 scald'st with safety** scorches while it protects; **gates of
breath** lips  **32 suspire** breathe  **35 rigol** circle  **41 as
immediate from** as nothing is between me and  **42 Derives**
flows down  **45 lineal** inherited (as against taken)  **63 part** act

For this they have engrossèd° and piled up                              70
The cank'red° heaps of strange-achievèd° gold;
For this they have been thoughtful° to invest
Their sons with arts° and martial exercises.
When, like the bee, culling from every flower
The virtuous sweets, our thighs packed with wax,                        75
Our mouths with honey, we bring it to the hive,
And, like the bees, are murdered for our pains.
This bitter taste yields his engrossments°
To the ending father.

*Enter* WARWICK.

Now, where is he that will not stay so long                             80
Till his friend sickness hath determined° me?

KING

WARWICK
My lord, I found the prince in the next room,
Washing with kindly° tears his gentle cheeks,
With such a deep demeanor° in great sorrow
That tyranny, which never quaffed but blood,                            85
Would, by beholding him, have washed his knife
With gentle eye-drops. He is coming hither.

KING
But wherefore did he take away the crown?

*Enter* [PRINCE] *Harry.*

Lo, where he comes. Come hither to me, Harry.
Depart the chamber, leave us here alone.                                90
                    *Exeunt* [WARWICK *and the others*].

PRINCE
I never thought to hear you speak again.

KING
Thy wish was father, Harry, to that thought.
I stay too long by thee,° I weary thee.
Dost thou so hunger for mine empty chair
That thou wilt needs invest thee with my honors                         95
Before thy hour be ripe? O foolish youth!
Thou seek'st the greatness that will overwhelm thee.
Stay but a little, for my cloud of dignity
Is held from falling with so weak a wind°
That it will quickly drop. My day is dim.                               100
Thou hast stol'n that which after some few hours
Were thine without offense, and at my death
Thou hast sealed up° my expectation.
Thy life did manifest thou lov'dst me not,
And thou wilt have me die assured of it.                                105
Thou hid'st a thousand daggers in thy thoughts,
Which thou hast whetted on thy stony heart,
To stab at half an hour of my life.
What! Canst thou not forbear me half an hour?
Then get thee gone and dig my grave thyself,                            110
And bid the merry bells ring to thine ear
That thou art crownèd, not that I am dead.
Let all the tears that should bedew my hearse
Be drops of balm° to sanctify thy head.
Only compound° me with forgotten dust.                                  115
Give that which gave thee life unto the worms.

Pluck down my officers, break my decrees,
For now a time is come to mock at form.°
Harry the Fifth is crowned. Up, vanity!
Down, royal state! All you sage counselors, hence!                      120
And to the English court assemble now,
From every region, apes of idleness!
Now, neighbor confines,° purge you of your scum.
Have you a ruffian that will swear, drink, dance,
Revel the night, rob, murder, and commit                                125
The oldest sins the newest kind of ways?
Be happy, he will trouble you no more.
England shall double gild his treble guilt,
England shall give him office, honor, might,
For the fifth Harry from curbed license plucks                          130
The muzzle of restraint, and the wild dog
Shall flesh° his tooth on every innocent.
O my poor kingdom, sick with civil blows!
When that my care could not withhold thy riots,
What wilt thou do when riot is thy care?                                135
O, thou wilt be a wilderness again,
Peopled with wolves, thy old inhabitants.

PRINCE
O, pardon me, my liege! But for my tears,
The moist impediments unto my speech,
I had forestalled this dear° and deep rebuke                            140
Ere you with grief had spoke and I had heard
The course of it so far. There is your crown,
And He that wears the crown immortally
Long guard it yours. If I affect° it more
Than as your honor and as your renown,                                  145
Let me no more from this obedience° rise,
Which my most inward true and duteous spirit
Teacheth, this prostrate and exterior bending.
God witness with me, when I here came in,
And found no course° of breath within your majesty,                     150
How cold it struck my heart. If I do feign,
O, let me in my present wildness die
And never live to show th' incredulous world
The noble change that I have purposèd.
Coming to look on you, thinking you dead,                               155
And dead almost, my liege, to think you were,
I spake unto this crown as having sense,
And thus upbraided it: "The care on thee depending
Hath fed upon the body of my father.
Therefore, thou best of gold art worst of gold.                         160
Other, less fine in carat,° is more precious,
Preserving life in medicine potable,°
But thou, most fine, most honored, most renowned,
Hast eat thy bearer up." Thus, my most royal liege,
Accusing it, I put it on my head,                                       165
To try with it, as with an enemy
That had before my face murdered my father,
The quarrel of a true inheritor.
But if it did infect my blood with joy,
Or swell my thoughts to any strain° of pride,                           170
If any rebel or vain spirit of mine
Did with the least affection of a welcome

---

70 **engrossèd** bought up   71 **cank'red** (1) rusting (2) malignant;
**strange-achievèd** hard-won   72 **thoughtful** careful   73 **arts**
liberal arts   78 **yields his engrossments** his accumulations
yield   81 **determined** ended   83 **kindly** natural   84 **deep
demeanor** intense manner   93 **by thee** (1) with thee (2) in thy
opinion   99 **wind** breath   103 **sealed up** confirmed   114
**balm** coronation oil   115 **Only compound** just mix

118 **form** order   123 **neighbor confines** nearby regions
132 **flesh** sink in flesh   140 **dear** heartfelt   144 **affect** desire
146 **obedience** low curtsy   150 **course** occurrence   161 **carat**
with pun on *charact*, character   162 **medicine potable** gold
in solution (prescribed as medicine)   170 **strain** musical theme
(i.e., feeling)

Give entertainment to the might of it,
Let God forever keep it from my head
And make me as the poorest vassal is                    175
That doth with awe and terror kneel to it.

KING
O my son,
God put it in thy mind to take it hence,
That thou mightst win the more thy father's love,
Pleading so wisely in excuse of it!                     180
Come hither, Harry, sit thou by my bed,
And hear, I think, the very latest° counsel
That ever I shall breathe. God knows, my son,
By what bypaths and indirect crooked ways
I met° this crown, and I myself know well              185
How troublesome it sat upon my head.
To thee it shall descend with better quiet,
Better opinion, better confirmation,
For all the soil° of the achievement goes
With me into the earth. It seemed in me                 190
But as an honor snatched with boisterous° hand,
And I had many living to upbraid
My gain of it by their assistances,
Which daily grew to quarrel and to bloodshed
Wounding supposèd peace. All these bold fears°         195
Thou see'st with peril I have answered,
For all my reign hath been but as a scene
Acting that argument.° And now my death
Changes the mood,° for what in me was purchased°
Falls upon thee in a more fairer sort,                  200
So thou the garland wear'st successively.°
Yet, though thou stand'st more sure than I could do,
Thou art not firm enough, since griefs are green.°
And all my friends, which thou must make thy friends,
Have but their stings and teeth newly ta'en out,        205
By whose fell° working I was first advanced
And by whose power I well might lodge a fear
To be again displaced. Which to avoid,
I cut them off, and had a purpose now
To lead out many to the Holy Land,                      210
Lest rest and lying still might make them look
Too near° unto my state. Therefore, my Harry,
Be it thy course to busy giddy minds
With foreign quarrels, that action, hence borne out,°
May waste the memory of the former days.                215
More would I, but my lungs are wasted so
That strength of speech is utterly denied me.
How I came by the crown, O God forgive,
And grant it may with thee in true peace live!

PRINCE
My gracious liege,                                      220
You won it, wore it, kept it, gave it me.
Then plain and right must my possession be,
Which I with more than with a common pain°
'Gainst all the world will rightfully maintain.

*Enter [Prince John of]* LANCASTER *[and* WARWICK*].*

KING
Look, look, here comes my John of Lancaster.            225
LANCASTER
Health, peace, and happiness to my royal father!
KING
Thou bring'st me happiness and peace, son John,
But health, alack, with youthful wings is flown
From this bare, withered trunk. Upon thy sight
My worldly business makes a period.                     230
Where is my Lord of Warwick?
PRINCE                           My Lord of Warwick!
KING
Doth any name particular belong
Unto the lodging where I first did swoon?
WARWICK
'Tis called "Jerusalem,"° my noble lord.
KING
Laud° be to God! Even there my life must end.           235
It hath been prophesied to me many years
I should not die but "in Jerusalem,"
Which vainly I supposed the Holy Land.
But bear me to that chamber; there I'll lie.
In that "Jerusalem" shall Harry die.    *[Exeunt.]*     240


# [ACT V]

## [Scene I. *Justice Shallow's home.*]

*Enter* SHALLOW, FALSTAFF, *and* BARDOLPH *[and* PAGE*].*

SHALLOW  By cock and pie,° sir, you shall not away tonight. What, Davy, I say!
FALSTAFF  You must excuse me, Master Robert Shallow.
SHALLOW  I will not excuse you. You shall not be    5
excused. Excuses shall not be admitted. There is no excuse shall serve. You shall not be excused. Why, Davy!

*[Enter* DAVY.*]*

DAVY  Here, sir.
SHALLOW  Davy, Davy, Davy, Davy, let me see,        10
Davy. Let me see, Davy, let me see. Yea, marry, William cook, bid him come hither. Sir John, you shall not be excused.
DAVY  Marry, sir, thus, those precepts° cannot be served. And, again, sir, shall we sow the headland°  15
with wheat?
SHALLOW  With red wheat,° Davy. But for William cook—are there no young pigeons?
DAVY  Yes, sir. Here is now the smith's note° for shoeing and plow-irons.                              20

---

**182 latest** last   **185 met** i.e., as one meets one's fate   **189 soil** dirt   **191 boisterous** rough   **195 fears** things causing fear   **198 argument** plot (in a play)   **199 mood** punning on *mode;* **purchased** a legal term: acquired by deed rather than inheritance   **201 successively** by hereditary succession   **203 green** fresh and growing   **206 fell** fierce   **211–12 look Too near** (1) examine (2) aspire too closely   **214 hence borne out** carried on elsewhere   **223 pain** effort (and note the formal rhymes)

**234 Jerusalem** Holinshed states correctly that the "Jerusalem chamber" is in Westminster Abbey, not Westminster Palace; Shakespeare leaves the setting of IV.iv and IV.v ambiguous until this line—see the stage direction at IV.iv.1   **235 Laud** praise
**V.i.1 By ... pie** a mild oath   **14 precepts** orders   **15 headland** unploughed strip between two ploughed fields   **17 red wheat** sown in late August   **19 note** bill

SHALLOW   Let it be cast° and paid. Sir John, you shall
not be excused.

DAVY   Now, sir, a new link to the bucket° must needs
be had. And, sir, do you mean to stop any of William's
wages, about the sack he lost the other day at Hinckley 25
Fair?°

SHALLOW   'A shall answer it. Some pigeons, Davy, a
couple of short-legged hens, a joint of mutton, and
any pretty little tiny kickshaws,° tell William cook.

DAVY   Doth the man of war stay all night, sir?     30

SHALLOW   Yea, Davy. I will use him well. A friend i'
th' court is better than a penny in purse. Use his men
well, Davy, for they are arrant knaves and will
backbite.

DAVY   No worse than they are backbitten,° sir, for 35
they have marvelous foul linen.

SHALLOW   Well conceited,° Davy. About thy business,
Davy.

DAVY   I beseech you, sir, to countenance° William
Visor of Woncot against Clement Perkes o' th' hill. 40

SHALLOW   There is many complaints, Davy, against
that Visor. That Visor is an arrant knave, on my
knowledge.

DAVY   I grant your worship that he is a knave, sir,
but yet, God forbid, sir, but a knave should have some 45
countenance at his friend's request. An honest man,
sir, is able to speak for himself, when a knave is not.
I have served your worship truly, sir, this eight years
—and I cannot once or twice in a quarter bear out° a
knave against an honest man, I have but a very little 50
credit with your worship. The knave is mine honest
friend, sir. Therefore, I beseech you, let him be
countenanced.

SHALLOW   Go to, I say he shall have no wrong. Look
about,° Davy! [Exit DAVY.] Where are you, Sir 55
John? Come, come, come, off with your boots. Give
me your hand, Master Bardolph.

BARDOLPH   I am glad to see your worship.

SHALLOW   I thank thee with my heart, kind Master
Bardolph. [To the PAGE.] And welcome, my tall 60
fellow. Come, Sir John.

FALSTAFF   I'll follow you, good Master Robert
Shallow. [Exit SHALLOW.] Bardolph, look to our
horses. [Exeunt BARDOLPH and PAGE.] If I were
sawed into quantities,° I should make four dozen of such 65
bearded hermits' staves as Master Shallow. It is a
wonderful thing to see the semblable coherence° of
his men's spirits and his. They, by observing him,
do bear themselves like foolish justices. He, by conversing with them, is turned into a justicelike serving- 70
man. Their spirits are so married in conjunction with
the participation of society° that they flock together
in consent,° like so many wild geese. If I had a suit to
Master Shallow, I would humor his men with the
imputation of being near their master. If to his men, 75
I would curry° with Master Shallow that no man

could better command his servants. It is certain that
either wise bearing° or ignorant carriage is caught, as
men take diseases, one of another. Therefore let men
take heed of their company.° I will devise matter 80
enough out of this Shallow to keep Prince Harry in
continual laughter the wearing out of six fashions,
which is four terms,° or two actions,° and 'a shall laugh
without intervallums.° O, it is much that a lie with a
slight oath and a jest with a sad brow will do with a 85
fellow that never had the ache in his shoulders! O,
you shall see him laugh till his face be like a wet cloak
ill laid up!°

SHALLOW [Within.]   Sir John!

FALSTAFF   I come, Master Shallow. I come, Master 90
Shallow.                [Exit.]

[Scene II. London.]

Enter the Earl of WARWICK and the Lord CHIEF JUSTICE
[meeting].

WARWICK
How now, my Lord Chief Justice! Whither away?

CHIEF JUSTICE
How doth the king?

WARWICK
Exceeding well. His cares are now all ended.

CHIEF JUSTICE
I hope, not dead.

WARWICK         He's walked the way of nature,
And to our° purposes he lives no more.          5

CHIEF JUSTICE
I would his majesty had called me with him.
The service that I truly° did his life
Hath left me open to all injuries.

WARWICK
Indeed I think the young king loves you not.

CHIEF JUSTICE
I know he doth not, and do arm myself        10
To welcome the condition of the time,
Which cannot look more hideously upon me
Than I have drawn it in my fantasy.

Enter [Prince] John [of LANCASTER], Thomas [of
CLARENCE], and Humphrey [of GLOUCESTER].

WARWICK
Here come the heavy issue° of dead Harry.
O that the living Harry had the temper°        15
Of he,° the worst of these three gentlemen!
How many nobles then should hold their places
That must strike° sail to spirits of vile sort!

CHIEF JUSTICE
O God, I fear all will be overturned!

LANCASTER
Good morrow, cousin Warwick, good morrow.    20

---

21 cast checked   23 link . . . bucket chain link for the yoke
25–26 Hinckley Fair held on August 26, thirty miles northeast
of Stratford   29 kickshaws fancy things (French, quelque
chose)   35 backbitten i.e., with lice   37 conceited conceived
39 countenance show favor to    49 bear out help out   54–55
Look about look sharp!   65 quantities lengths   67 semblable coherence visible similarity   72 society association   73
in consent unanimously   76 curry curry favor

78 bearing behavior   80 take . . . company ironical, coming
from Falstaff   83 terms court sessions (four in the year);
actions lawsuits   84 intervallums intersessions   88 ill laid
up put away wrinkled
V.ii.5 our living men's as contrasted to God's   7 truly faithfully
14 heavy issue grieving sons   15 temper temperament
16 he whoever is   18 strike lower (i.e., submit to pirates)

GLOUCESTER, CLARENCE
Good morrow, cousin.

LANCASTER
We meet like men that had forgot to speak.

WARWICK
We do remember, but our argument°
Is all too heavy to admit much talk.

LANCASTER
Well, peace be with him that hath made us heavy.  25

CHIEF JUSTICE
Peace be with us, lest we be heavier.

GLOUCESTER
O, good my lord, you have lost a friend indeed,
And I dare swear you borrow not that face
Of seeming sorrow—it is sure your own.

LANCASTER
Though no man be assured what grace to find,  30
You stand in coldest expectation.
I am the sorrier. Would 'twere otherwise.

CLARENCE
Well, you must now speak Sir John Falstaff fair,
Which swims against your stream of quality.°

CHIEF JUSTICE
Sweet princes, what I did, I did in honor,  35
Led by th' impartial conduct of my soul,
And never shall you see that I will beg
A ragged and forestalled remission.°
If truth and upright innocency fail me,
I'll to the king my master that is dead,  40
And tell him who hath sent me after him.

WARWICK
Here comes the prince.

*Enter the prince [as* KING *Henry the Fifth] and* BLUNT.

CHIEF JUSTICE
Good morrow, and God save your majesty!

KING
This new and gorgeous garment, majesty,
Sits not so easy on me as you think.  45
Brothers, you mix your sadness with some fear.
This is the English, not the Turkish court.
Not Amurath° an Amurath succeeds,
But Harry Harry. Yet be sad, good brothers,
For, by my faith, it very well becomes you.  50
Sorrow so royally in you appears°
That I will deeply° put the fashion on
And wear it in my heart. Why then, be sad,
But entertain no more of it, good brothers,
Than a joint burden paid upon us all.  55
For me, by heaven, I bid you be assured,
I'll be your father and your brother too.
Let me but bear your love, I'll bear your cares.
Yet weep that Harry's dead, and so will I,
But Harry lives, that shall convert those tears  60
By number into hours of happiness.

BROTHERS
We hope no otherwise from your majesty.

KING
You all look strangely on me. [*To the* CHIEF JUSTICE.]
And you most.
You are, I think, assured I love you not.

CHIEF JUSTICE
I am assured, if I be measured rightly,  65
Your majesty hath no just cause to hate me.

KING
No?
How might a prince of my great hopes forget
So great indignities you laid upon me?
What! Rate,° rebuke, and roughly send to prison  70
Th' immediate heir of England! Was this easy?°
May this be washed in Lethe,° and forgotten?

CHIEF JUSTICE
I then did use the person° of your father.
The image of his power lay then in me.
And, in th' administration of his law,  75
Whiles I was busy for the commonwealth,
Your highness pleasèd to forget my place,
The majesty and power of law and justice,
The image of the king whom I presented,
And struck me in my very seat of judgment.  80
Whereon, as an offender to your father,
I gave bold way to my authority
And did commit° you. If the deed were ill,
Be you contented, wearing now the garland,
To have a son set your decrees at nought?  85
To pluck down justice from your awful° bench?
To trip the course of law and blunt the sword
That guards the peace and safety of your person?
Nay, more, to spurn at your most royal image
And mock your workings in a second body?°  90
Question your royal thoughts. Make the case yours.
Be now the father and propose° a son:
Hear your own dignity so much profaned,
See your most dreadful laws so loosely slighted,
Behold yourself so by a son disdained,  95
And then imagine me taking your part
And in your power soft silencing your son.
After this cold consideration,° sentence me,
And, as you are a king, speak in your state°
What I have done that misbecame my place,  100
My person, or my liege's sovereignty.

KING
You are right, Justice, and you weigh this well.
Therefore still bear the balance and the sword.
And I do wish your honors may increase,
Till you do live to see a son of mine  105
Offend you—and obey you—as I did.
So shall I live to speak my father's words:
"Happy am I, that have a man so bold
That dares do justice on my proper° son,
And not less happy, having such a son  110
That would deliver up his greatness so
Into the hands of justice." You did commit me.

---

23 **argument** situation  34 **swims . . . quality** goes against the current of your disposition and rank  38 **ragged . . . remission** beggarly and already prevented pardon  48 **Amurath** Amurath IV of Turkey strangled his brothers on his accession in 1574  51 **appears** they are wearing black, he royal red  52 **deeply** (1) solemnly (2) within  70 **Rate** berate  71 **easy** unimportant (the legend was well known; see above, note to I.ii.55–56)  72 **Lethe** the river of forgetfulness in Hades  73 **use the person** act in the character  83 **commit** send to prison  86 **awful** causing awe  90 **in . . . body** i.e., one who uses your person (see line 73)  92 **propose** put the case of (legal term)  98 **cold considerance** cool consideration  99 **state** station  109 **proper** own

For, which, I do commit into your hand
Th' unstainèd sword that you have used to bear,
With this remembrance,° that you use the same    115
With the like bold, just, and impartial spirit
As you have done 'gainst me. There is my hand.
You shall be as a father to my youth.
My voice shall sound as you do prompt mine ear,
And I will stoop and humble my intents    120
To your well-practiced wise directions.
And, princes all, believe me, I beseech you,
My father is gone wild° into his grave,
For in his tomb lie my affections,°
And with his spirits° sadly I survive,    125
To mock the expectation of the world,
To frustrate prophecies, and to raze° out
Rotten opinion, who hath writ me down
After my seeming.° The tide of blood in me
Hath proudly flowed in vanity till now.    130
Now doth it turn and ebb back to the sea,
Where it shall mingle with the state of floods°
And flow henceforth in formal majesty.
Now call we our high court of parliament.
And let us choose such limbs of noble counsel    135
That the great body of our state may go
In equal rank with the best-governed nation;
That war, or peace, or both at once, may be
As things acquainted and familiar to us,
In which you, father, shall have foremost hand.    140
Our coronation done, we will accite,°
As I before rememb'red,° all our state,°
And, God consigning° to my good intents,
No prince nor peer shall have just cause to say,
God shorten Harry's happy life one day!    145
                     *Exit [with the rest].*

[Scene III. *Justice Shallow's home.*]

*Enter Sir John* [FALSTAFF], SHALLOW, SILENCE,
DAVY, BARDOLPH, PAGE.

SHALLOW   Nay, you shall see my orchard, where, in
an arbor, we will eat a last year's pippin° of mine own
graffing,° with a dish of caraways,° and so forth.
Come, cousin Silence. And then to bed.
FALSTAFF   'Fore God, you have here a goodly dwelling   5
and a rich.
SHALLOW   Barren, barren, barren. Beggars all, beggars
all, Sir John. Marry, good air. Spread, Davy, spread,
Davy. Well said, Davy.
FALSTAFF   This Davy serves you for good uses. He is   10
your servingman and your husband.°
SHALLOW   A good varlet,° a good varlet, a very good
varlet, Sir John. By the mass, I have drunk too much

sack at supper. A good varlet. Now sit down, now sit
down. Come, cousin.    15
SILENCE   Ah, sirrah, quoth-a,° we shall

[*Sings.*]

     Do nothing but eat, and make good cheer,
     And praise God for the merry year,
     When flesh° is cheap and females dear,
     And lusty lads roam here and there    20
         So merrily,
     And ever among so merrily.

FALSTAFF   There's a merry heart! Good Master
Silence, I'll give you a health for that anon.
SHALLOW   Give Master Bardolph some wine, Davy.   25
DAVY   Sweet sir, sit, I'll be with you anon. Most sweet
sir, sit. Master page, good master page, sit. [*Makes
them sit down, at another table.*] Proface!° What you
want° in meat, we'll have in drink. But you must
bear,° the heart's all.                [*Exit.*]   30
SHALLOW   Be merry, Master Bardolph, and, my little
soldier there, be merry.
SILENCE [*Sings.*]
     Be merry, be merry, my wife has all,
     For women are shrews, both short and tall.
     'Tis merry in hall when beards wag all,    35
       And welcome merry Shrovetide.°
     Be merry, be merry.
FALSTAFF   I did not think Master Silence had been a
man of this mettle.
SILENCE   Who, I? I have been merry° twice and once   40
ere now.

*Enter* DAVY.

DAVY [*To* BARDOLPH.]   There's a dish of leather-
coats° for you.
SHALLOW   Davy!
DAVY   Your worship! [*To* BARDOLPH.] I'll be with   45
you straight.—A cup of wine, sir?
SILENCE [*Sings.*]
     A cup of wine that's brisk and fine,
     And drink unto the leman° mine,
     And a merry heart lives long-a.
FALSTAFF   Well said, Master Silence.    50
SILENCE [*Sings.*]   And we shall be merry, now comes
in the sweet o' the night.
FALSTAFF   Health and long life to you, Master
Silence.
SILENCE [*Sings.*]
     Fill the cup, and let it come,    55
     I'll pledge you a mile° to th' bottom.
SHALLOW   Honest Bardolph, welcome. If thou
want'st anything, and wilt not call, beshrew° thy
heart. [*To the* PAGE.] Welcome, my little tiny thief,
and welcome indeed too. I'll drink to Master Bardolph,   60
and to all the cabileros° about London.
DAVY   I hope to see London once ere I die.

---

**115 remembrance** entry in the records (legal term) **123
wild** uncivilized **124 affections** appetites **125 spirits**
character (based on his humors) **127 raze** erase **129 my
seeming** the way I seem outwardly **132 state of floods**
majesty of the ocean **141 accite** summon **142 rememb'red**
noted (cf. line 115); **state** great men of the land **143 con-
signing** signing ratification (legal term; notice Hal's knowledge of different "languages")
**V.iii.2 pippin** type of apple **3 graffing** grafting; **caraways**
caraway seeds **11 husband** housemanager **12 varlet** servant

**16 quoth-a** said he **19 flesh** meat (with a ribald second sense)
**28 Proface** a dinner welcome **29 want** lack **30 bear** endure
**36 Shrovetide** period of feasting just before Lent **40 merry**
tipsy (?) **42–43 leather-coats** russet apples **48 leman** sweetheart **56 pledge . . . mile** drink in one draught though it
were a mile deep **58 beshrew** cursed be **61 cabileros**
cavaliers

BARDOLPH  And I might see you there, Davy—

SHALLOW  By the mass, you'll crack° a quart together, ha! Will you not, Master Bardolph?    65

BARDOLPH  Yea, sir, in a pottle-pot.°

SHALLOW  By God's liggens,° I thank thee. The knave will stick by thee, I can assure thee that. 'A will not out,° 'a. 'Tis true bred.

BARDOLPH  And I'll stick by him, sir.    70

*One knocks at door.*

SHALLOW  Why, there spoke a king. Lack nothing. Be merry. Look who's at door there, ho! Who knocks?                          [*Exit* DAVY.]

FALSTAFF [*To* SILENCE, *seeing him drinking.*] Why, now you have done me right.°    75

SILENCE [*Kneels, drinks and sings.*]
          Do me right,
          And dub me knight.°
          Samingo.°
Is't not so?

FALSTAFF  'Tis so.    80

SILENCE  Is't so? Why then, say an old man can do somewhat.

[*Enter* DAVY.]

DAVY  And't please your worship, there's one Pistol come from the court with news.

FALSTAFF  From the court! Let him come in.    85

*Enter* PISTOL.

How now, Pistol!

PISTOL  Sir John, God save you!

FALSTAFF  What wind blew you hither, Pistol?

PISTOL  Not the ill wind which blows no man to good. Sweet knight, thou art now one of the greatest 90 men in this realm.

SILENCE  By'r lady, I think 'a be, but goodman Puff° of Barson.

PISTOL  Puff!°
Puff i' thy teeth, most recreant coward base!    95
Sir John, I am thy Pistol and thy friend,
And helter-skelter have I rode to thee,
And tidings do I bring and lucky joys
And golden times and happy news of price.

FALSTAFF  I pray thee now, deliver them like a man of 100 this world.°

PISTOL
A foutra° for the world and worldlings base!
I speak of Africa° and golden joys.

FALSTAFF
O base Assyrian° knight, what is thy news?
Let King Cophetua° know the truth thereof.    105

SILENCE [*Sings.*]
"And Robin Hood, Scarlet, and John."

PISTOL
Shall dunghill curs confront the Helicons?°
And shall good news be baffled?°
Then, Pistol, lay thy head in Furies' lap.

SHALLOW  Honest gentleman, I know not your 110 breeding.

PISTOL  Why then, lament therefore.°

SHALLOW  Give me pardon, sir. If, sir, you come with news from the court, I take it there's but two ways, either to utter them, or conceal them. I am, sir, 115 under the king, in some authority.

PISTOL
Under which king, Besonian?° Speak, or die.

SHALLOW
Under King Harry.

PISTOL              Harry the Fourth, or Fifth?

SHALLOW
Harry the Fourth.

PISTOL                A foutra for thine office!°
Sir John, thy tender lambkin now is king.    120
Harry the fifth's the man. I speak the truth.
When Pistol lies, do this,° and fig me, like
The bragging Spaniard.

FALSTAFF
What, is the old king dead?

PISTOL
As nail in door. The things I speak are just.    125

FALSTAFF  Away, Bardolph! Saddle my horse. Master Robert Shallow, choose what office thou wilt in the land, 'tis thine. Pistol, I will double-charge° thee with dignities.

BARDOLPH
O joyful day!    130
I would not take a knighthood for my fortune.

PISTOL
What! I do bring good news.°

FALSTAFF  Carry Master Silence to bed. Master Shallow, my Lord Shallow—be what thou wilt, I am fortune's steward! Get on thy boots! We'll ride all 135 night! O sweet Pistol! Away, Bardolph! [*Exit* BARDOLPH.] Come, Pistol, utter more to me, and withal devise something to do thyself good. Boot, boot, Master Shallow. I know the young king is sick for me. Let us take any man's horses;° the laws of 140 England are at my commandment. Blessed are they that have been my friends, and woe to my Lord Chief Justice!

PISTOL
Let vultures vile seize on his lungs also!
"Where is the life that late I led?"° say they.    145
Why, here it is. Welcome these pleasant days!
                              *Exit* [*with the rest*].

64 **crack** split, share  66 **pottle-pot** two-quart tankard  67 **By God's liggens** an oath of unknown meaning, possibly because Shallow is tipsy  69 **out** pass out  75 **done me right** pledged to my pledge  77 **knight** drinking a deep draught while kneeling entitled one to be called "knight"  78 **Samingo** Monsieur Mingo, the hero of the song  92 **but goodman Puff** except for yeoman Puff (whose name suggests a shape and size as "great" as Falstaff's)  94 **Puff** swaggerer  100–01 **man . . . world** ordinary man  102 **foutra** French, *foutre*, accompanied by an indecent gesture  103 **Africa** where the gold comes from  104 **Assyrian** pun on *ass* (?) (Falstaff adopts Pistol's style in hopes of communicating with him)  105 **Cophetua** African king in a famous ballad

107 **Helicons** poets (?)  108 **baffled** treated shamefully  112 **therefore** for that  117 **Besonian** beggarly recruit  119 **thine office** the king's death terminated Shallow's appointment  122 **do this** make an insulting gesture, the "fig," by putting the thumb between the index and third fingers  128 **double-charge** twice-load (a pistol)  132 **What! . . . news** a knighthood is evidently not enough for Pistol or perhaps he is responding to Silence's sudden collapse  140 **take . . . horses** "press" them (for they are on the king's service)  145 **Where . . . led** scrap of an old song

[Scene IV. *London.*]

*Enter* BEADLE° *and three or four* OFFICERS [*with* HOSTESS *Quickly and* DOLL *Tearsheet*].

HOSTESS  No, thou arrant knave, I would to God that I might die, that I might have thee hanged.° Thou hast drawn my shoulder out of joint.
BEADLE  The constables have delivered her over to me, and she shall have whipping-cheer,° I warrant 5 her. There hath been a man or two killed about° her.
DOLL  Nut-hook,° nut-hook, you lie. Come on, I'll tell thee what, thou damned tripe-visaged° rascal, and the child I go with do miscarry, thou wert better thou hadst struck thy mother, thou paper-faced° villain. 10
HOSTESS  O the Lord, that Sir John were come! I would make this a bloody day to somebody. But I pray God the fruit of her womb miscarry!°
BEADLE  If it do, you shall have a dozen of cushions again. You have but eleven° now. Come, I charge 15 you both go with me, for the man is dead that you and Pistol beat amongst you.
DOLL  I'll tell you what, you thin man in a censer,° I will have you as soundly swinged° for this—you blue-bottle° rogue, you filthy famished correctioner, if you 20 be not swinged, I'll forswear half-kirtles.°
BEADLE  Come, come, you she-knight-errant, come.
HOSTESS  O God, that right should thus overcome might!° Well, of sufferance° comes ease.
DOLL  Come, you rogue, come. Bring me to a justice. 25
HOSTESS  Ay, come, you starved bloodhound.
DOLL  Goodman death, goodman bones!
HOSTESS  Thou atomy,° thou!
DOLL  Come, you thin thing! Come, you rascal!°
BEADLE  Very well.      [*Exeunt.*] 30

[Scene V. *London.*]

*Enter* STREWERS *of rushes.*

FIRST STREWER  More rushes, more rushes!°
SECOND STREWER  The trumpets have sounded twice.
THIRD STREWER  'Twill be two o'clock ere they come from the coronation. Dispatch, dispatch. 5
     [*Exeunt.*]

*Trumpets sound, and the* KING *and his* TRAIN *pass over the stage. After them enter* FALSTAFF, SHALLOW, PISTOL, BARDOLPH, *and the boy* [PAGE].

FALSTAFF  Stand here by me, Master Shallow. I will make the king do you grace.° I will leer° upon him as 'a comes by, and do but mark the countenance that he will give me.
PISTOL  God bless thy lungs, good knight. 10
FALSTAFF  Come here, Pistol, stand behind me. [*To* SHALLOW.] O, if I had had time to have made new liveries,° I would have bestowed the thousand pound I borrowed of you. But 'tis no matter; this poor show doth better. This doth infer° the zeal I had to see him. 15
PISTOL  It doth so.
FALSTAFF  It shows my earnestness of affection—
PISTOL  It doth so.
FALSTAFF  My devotion—
PISTOL  It doth, it doth, it doth. 20
FALSTAFF  As it were, to ride day and night, and not to deliberate, not to remember, not to have patience to shift me°—
SHALLOW  It is best, certain.
FALSTAFF  But to stand stained with travel, and 25 sweating with desire to see him, thinking of nothing else, putting all affairs else in oblivion, as if there were nothing else to be done but to see him.
PISTOL  'Tis "semper idem,"° for "obsque hoc nihil est."° 'Tis all in every part.° 30
SHALLOW  'Tis so, indeed.
PISTOL
My knight, I will inflame thy noble liver,°
And make thee rage.
Thy Doll, and Helen of thy noble thoughts,
Is in base durance and contagious° prison, 35
Haled thither by most mechanical° and dirty hand.
Rouse up revenge from ebon° den with fell Alecto's° snake,
For Doll is in. Pistol speaks nought but truth.
FALSTAFF
I will deliver her.
PISTOL
There roared the sea, and trumpet clangor sounds. 40

[*Trumpets sound.*] *Enter the* KING *and his* TRAIN [*including the Lord* CHIEF JUSTICE].

FALSTAFF
God save thy grace, King Hal, my royal Hal!
PISTOL
The heavens thee guard and keep, most royal imp° of fame!
FALSTAFF
God save thee, my sweet boy!
KING
My Lord Chief Justice, speak to that vain man.
CHIEF JUSTICE
Have you your wits? Know you what 'tis you speak? 45

V.iv.s.d. **Beadle** parish officer (who punished petty offenders) **2 hanged** for murdering me **5 whipping-cheer** hospitality of the whip **6 about** (1) because of, or (2) in the presence of **7 Nut-hook** slang for the "catchpole" carried by beadles **8 tripe-visaged** pock-marked **10 paper-faced** thin and pale **13 miscarry** she goes along with Doll's threat **15 eleven** Doll having used one to simulate pregnancy **18 thin . . . censer** figure of a man stamped on the lid of a pan for burning incense (?) **19 swinged** beaten **19–20 blue-bottle** beadles, like modern policemen, wore blue coats **21 half-kirtles** skirts **23–24 O . . . might** a typical Quickly blunder **24 of sufferance** out of suffering (but "sufferance" means tolerance) **28 atomy** atom (does she mean *anatomy* = cadaver?) **29 rascal** lean dear
V.v.1 **rushes** the usual floor covering; here, strewn in the streets

**7 do you grace** show you favor; **leer** glance slyly (instead of reverently bowing his head) **13 liveries** servants' uniforms **15 infer** imply **23 shift me** change my clothes **29 semper idem** ever the same **29–30 obsque . . . est** without this, nothing (both phrases are mottoes, the second garbled **30 all . . . part** absolute (another motto) **32 liver** seat of the passions (love as well as rage) **35 contagious** pestilential **36 mechanical** working-class **37 ebon** black; **Alecto** one of the Furies **42 imp** (1) scion (2) graft (in falconry or gardening —that which adds to)

FALSTAFF
My king! My Jove! I speak to thee, my heart!

KING
I know thee not,° old man. Fall to thy prayers.
How ill white hairs becomes a fool and jester!
I have long dreamt of such a kind of man,
So surfeit-swelled, so old, and so profane,                          50
But, being awaked, I do despise my dream.
Make less thy body hence,° and more thy grace.
Leave gormandizing. Know the grave doth gape
For thee thrice wider than for other men.
Reply not to me with a fool-born° jest.                              55
Presume not that I am the thing I was,
For God doth know, so shall the world perceive,
That I have turned away my former self.
So will I those that kept me company.
When thou dost hear I am as I have been,                             60
Approach me, and thou shalt be as thou wast,
The tutor and the feeder of my riots.
Till then, I banish thee, on pain of death,
As I have done the rest of my misleaders,
Not to come near our person by ten mile.                             65
For competence of life° I will allow you,
That lack of means enforce you not to evils.
And, as we hear you do reform yourselves,
We will, according to your strengths and qualities,
Give you advancement. Be it your charge, my lord,                    70
To see performed the tenor of my word.
Set on.                    [*Exeunt the* KING *and his* TRAIN.]

FALSTAFF    Master Shallow, I owe you a thousand
pound.

SHALLOW    Yea, marry, Sir John, which I beseech you           75
to let me have home with me.

FALSTAFF    That can hardly be, Master Shallow. Do
not you grieve at this. I shall be sent for in private to
him. Look you, he must seem thus to the world. Fear
not your advancements; I will be the man yet that       80
shall make you great.

SHALLOW    I cannot perceive how, unless you give me
your doublet and stuff me out with straw. I beseech
you, good Sir John, let me have five hundred of my
thousand.                                                       85

FALSTAFF    Sir, I will be as good as my word. This
that you heard was but a color.°

SHALLOW    A color° that I fear you will die° in, Sir
John.

FALSTAFF    Fear no colors.° Go with me to dinner.       90
Come, Lieutenant° Pistol. Come, Bardolph. I shall be
sent for soon at night.°

*Enter* [*Lord* CHIEF] JUSTICE *and Prince John* [*of*
LANCASTER, *and* OFFICERS].

CHIEF JUSTICE
Go, carry Sir John Falstaff to the Fleet.°
Take all his company along with him.

FALSTAFF
My lord, my lord—                                               95

CHIEF JUSTICE
I cannot now speak. I will hear you soon.
Take them away.

PISTOL
"Si fortuna me tormenta, spero contenta."°
            *Exeunt* [*all but Prince John of* LANCASTER
                              *and the* CHIEF JUSTICE].

LANCASTER
I like this fair proceeding of the king's.
He hath intent his wonted° followers                            100
Shall all be very well provided for,
But all are banished till their conversations
Appear more wise and modest to the world.

CHIEF JUSTICE
And so they are.

LANCASTER
The king hath called his parliament, my lord.                   105

CHIEF JUSTICE
He hath.

LANCASTER
I will lay odds that, ere this year expire,
We bear our civil swords° and native fire
As far as France. I heard a bird so sing,
Whose music, to my thinking, pleased the king.                  110
Come, will you hence?                                [*Exeunt.*]


# EPILOGUE°

[*Spoken by a* DANCER.]

First my fear,° then my curtsy, last my speech. My
fear is your displeasure; my curtsy my duty; and my
speech to beg your pardons. If you look for a good
speech now, you undo° me, for what I have to say is
of mine own making, and what indeed I should say          5
will, I doubt,° prove mine own marring. But to the
purpose, and so to the venture. Be it known to you,
as it is very well, I was lately here in the end of a
displeasing play,° to pray your patience for it and to
promise you a better. I meant indeed to pay you with     10
this, which, if like an ill venture° it come unluckily
home, I break,° and you, my gentle creditors, lose.
Here I promised you I would be and here I commit
my body to your mercies. Bate me some° and I will
pay you some and, as most debtors do, promise you        15
infinitely, and so I kneel down before you, but, indeed,
to pray for the queen.

   If my tongue cannot entreat you to acquit me, will
you command me to use my legs? And yet that were

47 I . . . not see Matthew 25:10–12   52 hence henceforth
55 fool-born note the pun   66 competence of life allowance for necessaries   87 color pretense   88 color punning on
*choler,* and *collar,* i.e., noose);   die punning on *dye*   90 colors
enemy flags (a proverb)   91 Lieutenant note the promotion
92 soon at night at early evening   93 Fleet prison for
distinguished prisoners temporarily detained for inquiry ("I
will hear you soon"—line 96)

98 Si . . . contenta if fortune torments me, hope contents me
100 wonted customary   108 civil swords swords presently
used in civil war
Epilogue evidently, as in *A Midsummer Night's Dream,* a mingling of epilogues: the first paragraph is for one occasion, the
second and third for another, and epilogues for any occasion
could be built up out of separate parts   1 fear stage fright
(pretended)   4 undo ruin   6 doubt fear   9 displeasing play
unidentified   11 venture business venture   12 break (1) break
my promise (2) go bankrupt   14 Bate me some forgive part
of my debt

but light payment, to dance out of your debt. But a 20 good conscience will make any possible satisfaction, and so would I. All the gentlewomen here have forgiven me.° If the gentlemen will not, then the gentlemen do not agree with the gentlewomen, which was never seen in such an assembly. 25

One word more, I beseech you. If you be not too much cloyed with fat meat, our humble author will continue the story, with Sir John in it,° and make you merry with fair Katharine of France. Where, for anything I know, Falstaff shall die of a sweat, unless 30 already 'a be killed with your hard opinions, for

**22–23 have forgiven me** perhaps the Epilogue was spoken by the Page   **28 Sir . . . it** but Falstaff does not appear in *Henry V*

Oldcastle° died martyr, and this is not the man. My tongue is weary. When my legs are too, I will bid you good night.

[*End with a dance.*]

**32 Oldcastle** Sir John Oldcastle was the name of the prince's boon companion in the source play, *The Famous Victories of Henry V*, and, evidently, in Shakespeare's first versions of the Henry IV plays. *Old.* appears as a speech tag at quarto *2 Henry IV*, I.ii.125. (See also *1 Henry IV*, I.ii.42.) In this Epilogue, Shakespeare is saying his Falstaff is not the historical Oldcastle, executed in 1417 and honored by Protestant chroniclers as a Lollard martyr (though Catholic chroniclers said he was a drunkard and a robber). The name was probably removed from Shakespeare's plays at the behest of Oldcastle's descendant, Lord Cobham—who was promptly nicknamed by the Essex faction Sir John Falstaff.

# MUCH ADO ABOUT NOTHING

### EDITED BY DAVID L. STEVENSON

## Introduction

*Much Ado About Nothing* presents an editor with no significant problems as to when it was written, the correctness of the text, the kind of source material that it reanimates and makes into a play. It was published in quarto in 1600, when Shakespeare was thirty-six, with his name on the title page, and was further identified as having been "publicly acted" by the acting company for which he wrote and of which he was a member. The evidence is quite clear that it had been written within a year or a year and a half of its publication (that is, at about mid-point in Shakespeare's career as a dramatist). The text itself is an excellent one, the basis of the posthumous Folio text of 1623, with only a few minor difficulties as to the assignment of lines and as to the intent, here and there, of the original punctuation. The Hero–Claudio–Don John plot, with its lady's maid, caught with her lover, being mistaken for the lady herself, has been traced back to a Greek source of about the year 400. The sixteenth-century Italian collector of tales, Bandello, used the plot in Story XXII of his *Novelle* (1554), as did Ariosto somewhat earlier in Book V of his *Orlando Furioso*,[1] and as did Spenser in Book II, Canto 4, of *The Faerie Queene* (1590). Beatrice and Benedick, if one wishes to abstract them from the play to view them in historical context, are part of a battle of the sexes with deep roots in the culture and in the literature of the Western world (as I have tried to demonstrate in *The Love-Game Comedy*, 1946). Dogberry and Verges have self-evident origins in that which they parody.

*Much Ado About Nothing*, moreover, has never provoked elaborate critical appraisal, perhaps because it has always seemed serenely self-contained, a comedy that does its work so well when seen on a stage, or when read, that it does not particularly invite extended comment. Its brilliance as a comedy, then (to justify the admirable quietness of its critics), can be briefly verbalized in two interrelated ways. We can describe the dramatic strategies employed in the play, which create its idiosyncratic "tone" as a comedy. We can also try to define the unique identity of *Much Ado* by an exploration of its substance, the special

aspect of existence blocked out for dramatization in the play.

The primary identifying fact about *Much Ado*, I think, is that it is the most realistic of Shakespeare's love comedies written during the reign of Elizabeth. And it is realistic despite the basic improbability (or conventionality) of Claudio's deception by Don John. It abandons completely the romantic landscape, the romantic disguisings, the romantic dialogue of Portia's and Bassanio's Belmont, of Rosalind's and Orlando's Forest of Arden, of Viola's and Duke Orsino's Illyria. In *Much Ado* we enter a dramatic world created in very close imitation of the habitable one we know outside the theater.

From its very beginning, the play forces this real world upon us. Its characters are a small group of aristocrats who have all known each other a long time and who are introduced to us, in I.i, talking about each other on the basis of old familiarity. Hero, for example, recognizes at once Beatrice's oblique reference to Benedick as "Signior Mountanto." Beatrice, we are to understand, has taunted Benedick's valor sometime before the immediate moments of the play and remembers that she has promised "to eat all of his killing" in the wars that have just concluded. She has also previously ridiculed his pretensions as a lover. She recalls: "He set up his bills here in Messina and challenged Cupid at the flight." Leonato refers easily to the long-standing "merry war betwixt Signior Benedick" and Beatrice. Claudio confesses to earlier amorous thoughts about Hero before he went off to the "rougher task" of the wars. Even Don John (I.iii) has already been sufficiently irritated by the "exquisite" Claudio to abhor the elegance of this "very forward March-chick," this "start-up," and to be "sick in displeasure to him" (II.ii).

Our sense of the close approximation of *Much Ado* to an actual social world is further enhanced by a certain casualness and easiness in the confrontations of one character with another. In this respect, and scene by scene, *Much Ado* is more like *Hamlet*, for example, than it is like *As You Like It* or *Twelfth Night*. The first and the last scene in the play are perhaps the most brilliant illustrations of this casualness, this incredible ease with which characters react to each other. But it is an ease that is completely

---

[1] The famous Elizabethan translation (1591) was by Sir John Harington, the favorite of the queen.

sustained as "tone" or manner throughout the play. One finds it in Don Pedro's teasing of Balthasar (and in Benedick's teasing of him as he is hidden in the arbor), for example, for his reluctance to sing in front of them (II.iii). It is the element which gives credibility to Borachio's rambling discourse to Conrade on fashion (III.iii). It is what makes Benedick's sudden playing the role of schoolteacher and grammarian ("How now? Interjections?") in the church scene (IV.i) so believable and so desperately ironic. It is what makes so devastating the unexpected and embarrassed encounter that Don Pedro and Claudio have with Leonato and Antonio after the disgracing of Hero (V.i).

Another aspect of the sustained, mimetic realism of *Much Ado* has to do with the kind of language that makes up the complex, closely interwoven dialogue of the play. The language used to carry the interchanges between Rosalind and Orlando, or between Viola and Duke Orsino, is romantically stylized and tempts us to immerse ourselves in some ideal, golden world of love. The language used for the interchanges between characters in *Much Ado* constantly reminds us of the flow of clever discourse in the best moments of the actual world we all inhabit. And the potency of this language of *Much Ado* is such that it seems capable of generating the natural, this-worldly atmosphere of the play just in itself. It is not the formalized repartee, the carefully contrived and balanced give and take of wit in Restoration comedy. Rather, its special quality is its air of the spontaneous. In *Much Ado* it is as if the characters themselves were inventing in front of us their quick ironic retorts and their exultant gaiety at the accomplishment.

The characters in this play take their dramatic world to be so much alive that they are constantly remembering what they have said to each other earlier in the action. The most striking example of this sort of realism is the acid repetition to Benedick by Don Pedro and by Claudio (V.i and V.iv) of Benedick's extravagant description (I.i) of what may be done to him if he ever falls in love. But Beatrice, who turns the word "stuffed" inside out in her ridicule of Benedick (I.i), later tempts Margaret to use it against her (III.iv): "A maid, and stuffed!" Don Pedro, with Claudio by (V.i), catches his anger at Leonato's importunate language in the deftly sardonic phrase, "we will not wake your patience." Claudio, moments later in the same scene (after he learns that he has been grossly fooled), expresses his genuine contrition to Leonato by slightly varying the same phrase: "I know not how to pray your patience." Even the two members of the watch, who are worried about "one Deformed" in III.iii, find Dogberry carefully remembering in V.i to have Borachio examined "upon that point."

The sustained, conversational quality of the dialogue of *Much Ado*, which accompanies and gives body to the nonchalant casualness of the character confrontations in the play, is perhaps the ultimate essence of the play's mimetic richness. The characters may individualize what they say, but they all speak essentially the same sophisticated-realistic language of their group. In its imagery it is much concerned with the act of sex and with the expected cuckoldry of their society ("he that is less than a man, I am not for him"; "Tush, fear not, man! We'll tip thy horns with gold"). It is also full of the kind of literary reference that would be known to a person of such a

society. Hercules, Ate, Europa and Jove, Baucis and Philemon are tossed into the stream of discourse; Kyd's *Spanish Tragedy* and *A Handful of Pleasant Delights* are quoted; Beatrice makes use of current attitudes already exploited in Davies' poem *Orchestra* in her description of marriage as a dance. But beyond all this sort of identifying conversational style is an "aliveness" in what the characters say to one another. It is this extravagant "aliveness," in combination with the play's other dramatic devices, that gives to *Much Ado* its separate identity of discourse. In no other of Shakespeare's comedies could one of its characters call another, with such eloquent understatement, "my Lady Tongue."

The substance of *Much Ado* is that of the romantic comedies, sex, love, and marriage. But this play's differentiated way of regarding this substance, its sophisticated realism, is certainly intentionally suggested by its title. Within the play itself there are two views of this substance. One view is that assumed by Claudio, Don Pedro, Leonato, and Hero. Claudio is the central, dominating voice of this group as he acts out its social assumptions. He is presented as a conventional young man, one who regards love and marriage as the making of a sensible match with a virtuous and attractive young girl who brings a good dowry and the approval of her father and of his friends. Although a young man today, a member of a similar social group, might put his feelings in somewhat more romantic terms, if he were of a "good" family in any city of the Western world, he might essentially agree with Claudio's view.

Claudio is certainly no passionate Romeo, and there is no indication in the play that he has done more than regard Hero as an attractive member of the aristocratic society to which they both belong. He is (perhaps somewhat in the position of Paris, in *Romeo and Juliet*) a young man capable of an easy romanticizing of sexual attraction, as his comment on Hero to Don Pedro fully reveals:

> now I am returned and that war-thoughts
> Have left their places vacant, in their rooms
> Come thronging soft and delicate desires,
> All prompting me how fair young Hero is,
> Saying I liked her ere I went to wars. (I.i.294-98)

Claudio, again like Paris, is the young man bent on doing "the right thing" in his society. He is attractive as a man, as his worst enemy, Don John, lets us know by his envy. But Claudio is also, as people aware only of the right thing to do tend to be, terrifyingly naive (and terrifyingly obtuse). As Benedick puts it, Claudio reacts like a hurt bird when he thinks Don Pedro has taken Hero from him ("Alas, poor hurt fowl! Now will he creep into sedges," II.i.196-97). And Benedick places Claudio's romantic inclinations toward Hero at the level of the feelings of a small child by comparing Claudio to a "schoolboy who, being overjoyed with finding a bird's nest, shows it his companion, and he [Don Pedro] steals it" (II.i.214-16). Claudio's politeness, his sense of the socially appropriate, even leads him to suggest that he abandon his bride immediately after his marriage and accompany his sponsor, Don Pedro, from Messina to Aragon. Don Pedro again identifies for us the childlike quality of Claudio's feelings for Hero when he replies: "that would be as great a soil in the new gloss of your marriage as to show a child his new coat and forbid him to wear it" (III.ii.5–7).

In the church scene, Claudio's turning on Hero for her supposed assignation on the eve of her marriage is wholly in keeping with the nature of his feelings for her and with the codes of his group. He moves toward his denunciation in the sententiously arrogant, teasing manner of the overly conventional person who has been fooled about something rather important and who will now take great pleasure in a measured retaliation. Claudio, the exquisite, reacts appropriately like a child cheated over a toy promised to him. And the absolute "rightness" of his attitude in the play is made quite clear by the fact that Hero's father and Don Pedro instantly agree with it. Leonato, who was as concerned as Claudio and Don Pedro with a "good" marriage, reacts, indeed, much as Capulet (also a socially conventional man) had reacted when Juliet had refused to marry Paris:

> Why had I one?
> Why ever wast thou lovely in my eyes?
>
> .            .            .
>
> And mine that I was proud on, mine so much
> That I myself was to myself not mine,
> Valuing of her—why she, O, she is fall'n
> Into a pit of ink.            (IV.i.128–29, 136–39)

Beatrice and Benedick, wholly unchildlike, present another view of the essential stuff of this play, a view that cuts across the conventional one, and insinuates doubts lurking in sophisticated minds as to its necessary validity. They are everywhere presented as completely aware of the fact that they are playing roles with and for each other— Beatrice as shrew, Benedick as misogynist—and enjoying the playing. The subject matter of their game is a distaste for institutionalized romantic love leading to marriage, the precise kind of "love" that Claudio and Hero accept easily and without thought. The only obstacle to Claudio's pursuit would be the sort of thing he thinks has happened, a lack of sexual virtue on the part of the girl who has caught his fancy. The subtle obstacle to the union of Benedick and Beatrice is that neither is ever sure of what he or she would be like if they agreed to quit playing their respective roles. Indeed, part of the dramatic (and psychological) excitement at the play's end is that neither one of this pair is yet certain of what emotions really lie below the level of the role-playing.

The love game of Beatrice and Benedick is an intricate one in *Much Ado*, because both of them are teasing something more complicated than just conventional romantic love. They are dramatized as testing the antiromantic roles they are actually playing against their sense of what it would be like to be a Hero or a Claudio, to fall into the words and phrases and stances of institutionalized romance. Moreover, in their dueling in the self-accepted roles of the man and the woman too knowing to wear the yoke of marriage and to "sigh away Sundays," it is always made dramatically obvious that both characters are aware that with any slipping either or both could easily *become* a Hero or a Claudio and turn husband and wife. Benedick's first direct comment on Beatrice, early in the play (I.i. 186–88), is, it seems to me, self-evident acknowledgment

of this fact: "and she were not possessed with a fury, [Beatrice] exceeds [Hero] as much in beauty as the first of May doth the last of December."

It is this ambivalent element of their love game, I think, that made Beatrice and Benedick so fascinating to their own age, and now also to us. And the basis of the fascination is that in their own probing of their reactions to ritualized romantic love, they invite us to probe the usually inaccessible areas of our own knowing, our own awareness in such matters. More important, if we think, at the play's end, that Beatrice and Benedick merely exist for five acts to be tricked into admitting that they are fundamentally as conventionally involved in sex, love, and marriage as Hero and Claudio, we have missed the essential purport of the play.

Beatrice is the more open of the two in her acknowledgment of the ambiguity of her role-playing. Her acid remarks in the first scene of Act I concerning Benedick's challenge to Cupid, and her uncle's fool's response (that is, Beatrice herself?), carry the suggestion, never made overt in the play, either that Beatrice had never been sure of her role as Lady Tongue or that she had once tried out a romantic role with Benedick himself. She is presented as openly uneasy (II.i) over the fact that Hero has got herself a husband ("I may sit in a corner and cry 'Heigh-ho for a husband!' "). And she once darkly hints an earlier involvement with Benedick when she tells Don Pedro that Benedick lent his heart to her for a while, "and I gave him use for it, a double heart for his single one. Marry, once before he won it of me with false dice" (II.i.268–70).

The ambiguousness in Benedick's role as misogynic bachelor is perhaps best suggested by the extravagant language he always uses to defend his role:

> Prove that ever I lose more blood with love than I will get
> again with drinking, pick out mine eyes with a ballad
> maker's pen and hang me up at the door of a brothel
> house for the sign of blind Cupid.            (I.i.243–47)

His taunt to Claudio concerning Hero ("Would you buy her, that you inquire after her?" I.i.175–76), and his headlong flight from Beatrice (II.i) with the bitter comment that "while she is here" he could live as quietly in hell, are but further illustrations of this extravagance. Dramatically, to be sure, such soaring flights of words prepare us for the irony of his surrender to love of a sort. Psychologically, they tempt us to wonder that a man could hate so vehemently what he professes to have no interest in.

The marriage of Hero and Claudio turns on the simple problem as to whether Hero is a virgin or not, that is, as to whether she is socially and therefore personally acceptable to Claudio in his aristocratic world of arranged marriages. The marriage of Beatrice and Benedick turns on the ability of their peers to trick them out of their self-conscious role-playing. It is of interest to note that the latter pair's willingness to surrender to love and marriage takes place while Hero's virtue is still under a cloud as far as Claudio is concerned, and therefore at a moment when their previous bantering would be inappropriate. It is equally important to note that both Beatrice and Benedick, if somewhat subdued, actually bring alive again, at the play's end, something of the ambiguity toward love that they had had from the beginning of the play.

Beatrice's final words are not those of a Rosalind or a Viola:

I yield upon great persuasion, and partly to save your life, for I was told you were in a consumption. (V.iv.95–96)

Benedick's penultimate comments are addressed not to Beatrice, but rather to Don Pedro. And Benedick insists upon being as ambiguous about his feelings, now that he has agreed to conform to marriage, as he had been earlier, when he could only exclaim against it. He insists to Don Pedro that "since I do purpose to marry, I will think nothing to any purpose that the world can say against it" (V.iv.104–06). He concludes that Don Pedro himself had better marry in order that he too may join the gay company of cuckolds-to-be:

get thee a wife, get thee a wife! There is no staff more reverend than one tipped with horn. (V.iv.122–24)

In *Romeo and Juliet*, written about four years before *Much Ado*, Shakespeare had dramatized the lyric, fragile love of very young people not yet wise enough to yield to the social realities—and therefore broken by them. He had presented their love as a highly perishable commodity, one as subject to accident as to time. It is not only Romeo and Juliet, but we, as audience, who acquiesce in their deaths because we are fully aware that in "reality" there can only be either slow dilution or abrupt extinction of such flowerlike love. In *Twelfth Night*, written probably a year or so later than *Much Ado*, we are kept within the elegant, golden confines of courtly, aristocratic romance —a place full of music and of bodily forms (to borrow from Yeats) "of hammered gold and gold enameling," set singing to keep some "drowsy Emperor awake."

The kind of love encompassed by the dialogue of *Much Ado*, and by its two sets of lovers, is love in the social world. This comedy, indeed, is a highly novel one for Shakespeare to have written. The play ends with its characters and the audience accepting the two marriages that have been in the making from its beginning. But the power of the comedy lies not in our accepting the fragility of youthful passion or in our surrender to idyllic romance. Rather, *Much Ado*, by all its strategies of language and characterization, moves so close to reality that it cannot reach a denouement in which the simply understood mood or attitude of *Romeo and Juliet* or of *Twelfth Night* reaches final focus.

The essential uniqueness of *Much Ado* as a comedy, and its fascination, lies in the fact that it invokes our awareness of the complicated relationship between the indeterminate nature of private feeling and the simplicities of the decorous behavior which is supposed to embody such feeling. That is to say, *Much Ado* dramatizes sex, love, and marriage in close imitation of their complexity in actuality. This play, of course, is far too stylized to be "real," and it keeps us comically insulated from too deep involvement with its characters and its substance. The play's final moment of balance, of standing still, then, is necessarily somewhat different from that of the Shakespearean romances where a long ritual of wooing comes to a ritualized conclusion. In *Much Ado* we are given, in its last scene, the dramatic illusion that the pair of marriages has been created by the volition of the characters themselves. They seem to be marrying out of their own desire to find, if only momentarily, a way of being at peace with themselves and with each other.

## A NOTE ON THE SOURCE

*Much Ado About Nothing* combines two plots, the Hero-Claudio tragicomic one and the Beatrice-Benedick comic one. Shakespeare himself seems to have hit on the idea of joining the two, though if he knew of an earlier work in which they had already been combined, he surely would not have scrupled to follow suit.

The gist of the Hero-Claudio plot—a girl is said to be false and her fiancé is so deceived that he denounces her, though later they are reconciled—is ancient. It is also the basis of a series of stories popular in the sixteenth century. It can scarcely be doubted that Shakespeare knew it in the versions of Ariosto (*Orlando Furioso* was translated by Sir John Harington and plundered by Edmund Spenser) and Bandello (the *Novelle* were translated into French by Belleforest). Quite possibly Shakespeare was acquainted with a number of other versions. Shakespeare's own addition of Dogberry and Verges, for which at best he had only bare hints, gives this Hero-Claudio plot most of its vitality.

The comic intrigue of Beatrice and Benedick is scarcely a plot, and it would be foolish to attempt to isolate a source for it. Sixteenth-century literature offers numerous ladies and gentlemen who wittily scorn each other. In the English drama before Shakespeare, John Lyly had made something of a specialty of such combats. There are, moreover, nondramatic works (Lyly is again relevant) that may also have given Shakespeare hints. Possibly a paragraph in Castiglione's *Il Cortegiano* (translated by Sir Thomas Hoby) sparked his imagination:

I have also seen a most fervent love spring in the heart of a woman toward one that seemed at first not to bear him the least affection in the world, only for that they heard say that the opinion of many was that they loved together.

It should be remembered, too, that Beatrice and Benedick are not Shakespeare's first witty, bickering lovers. In *Love's Labor's Lost*, Biron ("not a word with him but a jest") and Rosaline ("a wightly wanton") anticipate Beatrice and Benedick.

Passages from several books that probably influenced *Much Ado* are given in the second volume of Geoffrey Bullough's *Narrative and Dramatic Sources of Shakespeare*, but when one has read *Much Ado* each source seems like Charles Lamb's poor relation: "the most irrelevant thing in nature—a piece of impertinent correspondency."

## A NOTE ON THE TEXT

The present text of *Much Ado About Nothing* is based upon the quarto edition of the play, published in 1600. The Folio text of 1623 is a slightly edited version of this quarto.

In I.ii Antonio is designated "Old" in the quarto, meaning old man. In II.i Antonio's speeches are assigned to "Brother." In IV.ii "Kemp" and "Cowley," the actors intended for the roles, are assigned the speeches for Dogberry and Verges. The present edition regularizes all speech prefixes. All act and scene divisions are bracketed, since (like indications of locale) these are not in the quarto. Spelling and punctuation have been modernized, and obvious typographical errors have been corrected. The positions of a few stage directions have been slightly altered; necessary directions that are not given in the quarto are added in brackets. Other substantial departures from the quarto are listed below, the adopted reading first, in boldface, and then the quarto's reading in roman type.

If the adopted reading comes from the Folio, the fact is indicated by [F] following it.

**I.i.s.d.** [Q has "Innogen his wife," i.e., Leonato's wife, before "Hero"; she does not appear in the play] **1 Don Pedro** Don Peter **9 Don Pedro** Don Peter **197 s.d. Enter Don Pedro** Enter don Pedro, Iohn the bastard
**II.i.s.d. Hero** his wife, Hero; **niece** neece, and a kinsman **80 s.d. Don John** or dumb Iohn **203 s.d.** [Q adds "Iohn and Borachio, and Conrade"]
**II.iii.137 us of** [F] of vs
**III.ii.51 Don Pedro** [F] Bene
**IV.ii.s.d.** [Q places "Borachio" immediately after "Constables"
**V.iii.10 dumb** [F] dead **22 Claudio** Lo[rd]
**V.iv.54 Antonio** Leo **97 Benedick** Leon

# MUCH ADO ABOUT NOTHING

[Dramatis Personae

DON PEDRO *Prince of Aragon*
DON JOHN *his bastard brother*
CLAUDIO *a young lord of Florence*
BENEDICK *a young lord of Padua*
LEONATO *Governor of Messina*
ANTONIO *an old man, his brother*
BALTHASAR *attendant on Don Pedro*
BORACHIO ⎫
CONRADE ⎬ *followers of Don John*
FRIAR FRANCIS

DOGBERRY *a constable*
VERGES *a headborough*
A SEXTON
A BOY
HERO *daughter to Leonato*
BEATRICE *niece to Leonato*
MARGARET ⎫
URSULA ⎬ *gentlewomen attending on Hero*
MESSENGERS WATCH ATTENDANTS ETC.

*Scene:* Messina]

## [ ACT I ]

[Scene I. *Before Leonato's house.*]

*Enter* LEONATO, *Governor of Messina,* HERO *his daughter, and* BEATRICE *his niece, with a* MESSENGER.

LEONATO  I learn in this letter that Don Pedro of Aragon comes this night to Messina.

MESSENGER  He is very near by this. He was not three leagues off when I left him.

LEONATO  How many gentlemen° have you lost in 5 this action?

MESSENGER  But few of any sort,° and none of name.°

LEONATO  A victory is twice itself when the achiever brings home full numbers. I find here that Don Pedro hath bestowed much honor on a young Florentine 10 called Claudio.

MESSENGER  Much deserved on his part, and equally rememb'red by Don Pedro. He hath borne himself beyond the promise of his age, doing, in the figure of a lamb, the feats of a lion. He hath indeed better 15 bett'red expectation° than you must expect of me to tell you how.

LEONATO  He hath an uncle° here in Messina will be very much glad of it.

MESSENGER  I have already delivered him letters, and 20 there appears much joy in him; even so much that joy could not show itself modest enough without a badge° of bitterness.

LEONATO  Did he break out into tears?

MESSENGER  In great measure. 25

LEONATO  A kind overflow of kindness.° There are no faces truer than those that are so washed. How much better is it to weep at joy than to joy at weeping!

BEATRICE  I pray you, is Signior Mountanto° returned from the wars or no? 30

MESSENGER  I know none of that name, lady. There was none such in the army of any sort.

LEONATO  What is he that you ask for, niece?

HERO  My cousin means Signior Benedick of Padua.

*The decorative border shown above appeared on the title page of the quarto edition of* Much Ado About Nothing, *1600.*

**I.i.5 gentlemen** men of upper class  **7 sort** rank; **name** distinguished family

**15–16 better bett'red expectation** greatly exceeded anticipated valor  **18 uncle** does not appear in the play  **23 badge** emblem  **26 kind . . . kindness** natural overflow of tenderness  **29 Mountanto** a fencing thrust

MESSENGER   O, he's returned, and as pleasant° as ever 35
he was.

BEATRICE   He set up his bills° here in Messina and
challenged Cupid at the flight;° and my uncle's fool,
reading the challenge, subscribed° for Cupid and
challenged him at the burbolt.° I pray you, how 40
many hath he killed and eaten in these wars? But how
many hath he killed? For indeed, I promised to eat all
of his killing.

LEONATO   Faith, niece, you tax° Signior Benedick too
much; but he'll be meet° with you, I doubt it not.    45

MESSENGER   He hath done good service, lady, in
these wars.

BEATRICE   You had musty victual, and he hath holp
to eat it. He is a very valiant trencherman;° he hath an
excellent stomach.    50

MESSENGER   And a good soldier too, lady.

BEATRICE   And a good soldier to° a lady. But what is
he to a lord?

MESSENGER   A lord to a lord, a man to a man; stuffed
with all honorable virtues.    55

BEATRICE   It is so, indeed; he is no less than a stuffed
man.° But for the stuffing—well, we are all mortal.

LEONATO   You must not, sir, mistake my niece.
There is a kind of merry war betwixt Signior Benedick
and her. They never meet but there's a skirmish of wit 60
between them.

BEATRICE   Alas, he gets nothing by that! In our last
conflict four of his five wits° went halting° off, and
now is the whole man governed with one; so that if he
have wit enough to keep himself warm, let him bear 65
it for a difference between himself and his horse. For
it is all the wealth that he hath left to be known a
reasonable creature. Who is his companion now? He
hath every month a new sworn brother.

MESSENGER   Is't possible?    70

BEATRICE   Very easily possible. He wears his faith but
as the fashion of his hat; it ever changes with the next
block.°

MESSENGER   I see, lady, the gentleman is not in your
books.°    75

BEATRICE   No. And° he were, I would burn my study.
But I pray you, who is his companion? Is there no
young squarer° now that will make a voyage with
him to the devil?

MESSENGER   He is most in the company of the right 80
noble Claudio.

BEATRICE   O Lord, he will hang upon him like a
disease. He is sooner caught than the pestilence, and
the taker runs presently° mad. God help the noble
Claudio if he have caught the Benedict;° it will cost 85
him a thousand pound ere 'a° be cured.

MESSENGER   I will hold friends with you, lady.

35 **pleasant** lively   37 **bills** advertising placards   38 **flight**
shooting contest (i.e., he thought himself a lady-killer)   39
**subscribed** signed up   40 **burbolt** blunt arrow   44 **tax** i.e.,
tease too hard   45 **meet** even   49 **trencherman** eater
52 **to** in comparison with   56–57 **stuffed man** dummy
63 **five wits** common sense, imagination, fancy, estimation,
memory;   **halting** limping   72–73 **next block** most recent
shape   75 **books** favor   76 **And** if   78 **squarer** brawler   84
**presently** immediately (the usual sense in Shakespeare)   85
**Benedict** the change in spelling suggests a disease based on
Benedick's name   86 **'a** he

BEATRICE   Do, good friend.

LEONATO   You will never run mad,° niece.

BEATRICE   No, not till a hot January.    90

MESSENGER   Don Pedro is approached.

*Enter* DON PEDRO, CLAUDIO, BENEDICK, BAL-
THASAR, *and* [DON] JOHN *the bastard.*

DON PEDRO   Good Signior Leonato, are you come to
meet your trouble? The fashion of the world is to
avoid cost, and you encounter it.

LEONATO   Never came trouble to my house in the 95
likeness of your grace; for trouble being gone,
comfort should remain. But when you depart from
me, sorrow abides, and happiness takes his leave.

DON PEDRO   You embrace your charge° too willingly.
I think this is your daughter.    100

LEONATO   Her mother hath many times told me so.

BENEDICK   Were you in doubt, sir, that you asked
her?

LEONATO   Signior Benedick, no; for then were you a
child.    105

DON PEDRO   You have it full, Benedick. We may
guess by this what you are, being a man. Truly the
lady fathers herself.° Be happy, lady, for you are like
an honorable father.

BENEDICK   If Signior Leonato be her father, she would 110
not have his head° on her shoulders for all Messina, as
like him as she is.

BEATRICE   I wonder that you will still° be talking,
Signior Benedick; nobody marks you.

BENEDICK   What, my dear Lady Disdain! Are you 115
yet living?

BEATRICE   Is it possible Disdain should die while she
hath such meet food to feed it as Signior Benedick?
Courtesy itself must convert to Disdain if you come
in her presence.    120

BENEDICK   Then is courtesy a turncoat. But it is
certain I am loved of all ladies,° only you excepted;
and I would I could find in my heart that I had not a
hard heart; for truly I love none.

BEATRICE   A dear happiness to women! They would 125
else have been troubled with a pernicious suitor. I
thank God and my cold blood, I am of your humor for
that.° I had rather hear my dog bark at a crow than
a man swear he loves me.

BENEDICK   God keep your ladyship still in that mind, 130
so some gentleman or other shall scape a predestinate
scratched face.

BEATRICE   Scratching could not make it worse and
'twere such a face as yours were.

BENEDICK   Well, you are a rare parrot-teacher.°    135

BEATRICE   A bird of my tongue is better than a beast
of yours.

BENEDICK   I would my horse had the speed of your
tongue, and so good a continuer.° But keep your way,
a God's name! I have done.    140

89 **run mad** catch the Benedict   99 **charge** burden (of my visit)
108 **fathers herself** shows who her father is by resembling him
111 **his head** white-haired and bearded (?)   113 **still** always
(the usual sense in Shakespeare)   122 **loved . . . ladies**
he had "challenged Cupid"   127–28 **of . . . that** in agreement on that   135 **parrot-teacher** monotonous speaker of
nonsense   139 **continuer** staying power

BEATRICE   You always end with a jade's trick.° I know you of old.

DON PEDRO   That is the sum of all,° Leonato. Signior Claudio and Signior Benedick, my dear friend Leonato hath invited you all. I tell him we shall stay here, at the 145 least a month, and he heartily prays some occasion may detain us longer. I dare swear he is no hypocrite, but prays from his heart.

LEONATO   If you swear, my lord, you shall not be forsworn. [*To* DON JOHN.] Let me bid you welcome, 150 my lord; being reconciled to the prince your brother, I owe you all duty.

DON JOHN   I thank you. I am not of many words, but I thank you.

LEONATO   Please it your grace lead on?      155

DON PEDRO   Your hand, Leonato. We will go together.

    *Exeunt. Manent*° BENEDICK *and* CLAUDIO.

CLAUDIO   Benedick, didst thou note the daughter of Signior Leonato?

BENEDICK   I noted° her not, but I looked on her.    160

CLAUDIO   Is she not a modest young lady?

BENEDICK   Do you question me as an honest man should do, for my simple true judgment? Or would you have me speak after my custom, as being a professed tyrant to their sex?      165

CLAUDIO   No, I pray thee speak in sober judgment.

BENEDICK   Why, i' faith, methinks she's too low for a high praise, too brown for a fair praise, and too little for a great praise. Only this commendation I can afford her, that were she other than she is, she were 170 unhandsome, and being no other but as she is, I do not like her.

CLAUDIO   Thou thinkest I am in sport. I pray thee tell me truly how thou lik'st her.

BENEDICK   Would you buy her, that you inquire 175 after her?

CLAUDIO   Can the world buy such a jewel?

BENEDICK   Yea, and a case to put it into. But speak you this with a sad brow?° Or do you play the flouting Jack, to tell us Cupid is a good hare-finder and 180 Vulcan a rare carpenter?° Come, in what key shall a man take you to go in the song?

CLAUDIO   In mine eye she is the sweetest lady that ever I looked on.

BENEDICK   I can see yet without spectacles, and I see 185 no such matter. There's her cousin, and she were not possessed with a fury, exceeds her as much in beauty as the first of May doth the last of December. But I hope you have no intent to turn husband, have you?

CLAUDIO   I would scarce trust myself, though I had 190 sworn the contrary, if Hero would be my wife.

BENEDICK   Is't come to this? In faith, hath not the world one man but he will wear his cap with suspicion?° Shall I never see a bachelor of threescore

again? Go to, i' faith! And thou wilt needs thrust thy 195 neck into a yoke, wear the print of it and sigh away Sundays.° Look! Don Pedro is returned to seek you.

*Enter* DON PEDRO.

DON PEDRO   What secret hath held you here, that you followed not to Leonato's?

BENEDICK   I would your grace would constrain me 200 to tell.

DON PEDRO   I charge thee on thy allegiance.°

BENEDICK   You hear, Count Claudio; I can be secret as a dumb man. I would have you think so. But, on my allegiance—mark you this—on my allegiance! He is 205 in love. With who? Now that is your grace's part. Mark how short his answer is—with Hero, Leonato's short daughter.

CLAUDIO   If this were so, so were it utt'red.

BENEDICK   Like the old tale, my lord: "It is not so, 210 nor 'twas not so, but indeed, God forbid it should be so!"

CLAUDIO   If my passion change not shortly, God forbid it should be otherwise.

DON PEDRO   Amen, if you love her, for the lady is 215 very well worthy.

CLAUDIO   You speak this to fetch me in, my lord.

DON PEDRO   By my troth, I speak my thought.

CLAUDIO   And, in faith, my lord, I spoke mine.

BENEDICK   And, by my two faiths and troths, my 220 lord, I spoke mine.

CLAUDIO   That I love her, I feel.

DON PEDRO   That she is worthy, I know.

BENEDICK   That I neither feel how she should be loved, nor know how she should be worthy, is the 225 opinion that fire cannot melt out of me. I will die in it at the stake.

DON PEDRO   Thou wast ever an obstinate heretic in the despite of° beauty.

CLAUDIO   And never could maintain his part but in 230 the force of his will.°

BENEDICK   That a woman conceived me, I thank her; that she brought me up, I likewise give her most humble thanks. But that I will have a rechate° winded in my forehead, or hang my bugle in an invisible 235 baldrick,° all women shall pardon me. Because I will not do them the wrong to mistrust any, I will do myself the right to trust none; and the fine° is (for the which I may go the finer), I will live a bachelor.

DON PEDRO   I shall see thee, ere I die, look pale with 240 love.

BENEDICK   With anger, with sickness, or with hunger, my lord, not with love. Prove that ever I lose more blood with love than I will get again with drinking, pick out mine eyes with a ballad maker's pen and 245 hang me up at the door of a brothel house for the sign of blind Cupid.

DON PEDRO   Well, if ever thou dost fall from this faith, thou wilt prove a notable argument.°

---

141 **jade's trick** trick of a vicious horse (i.e., a sudden stop?) 143 **sum of all** end of the sparring match 157 **s.d. Manent** remain (Latin) 160 **noted** (1) scrutinized (2) set to music (3) stigmatized 179 **with . . . brow** seriously 180–81 **to . . . carpenter** to mock us with nonsense (Cupid was blind, Vulcan was a blacksmith) 193–94 **but . . . suspicion** who (because he is unmarried) will not fear that he has a cuckold's horns

195–97 **thrust . . . Sundays** enjoy the tiresome bondage of marriage 202 **allegiance** solemn obligation to a prince 228–29 **in . . . of** in contempt of 231 **will** sexual appetite 234 **rechate** recheate, notes on a hunting horn 236 **baldrick** belt, sling (the reference here, and in "rechate," is to the horns of a cuckold) 238 **fine** finis, result 249 **notable argument** famous example

BENEDICK   If I do, hang me in a bottle° like a cat and 250
shoot at me; and he that hits me, let him be clapped
on the shoulder and called Adam.°

DON PEDRO   Well, as time shall try:
"In time the savage bull doth bear the yoke."

BENEDICK   The savage bull may, but if ever the sensible 255
Benedick bear it, pluck off the bull's horns and set
them in my forehead, and let me be vilely painted,
and in such great letters as they write "Here is good
horse to hire," let them signify under my sign "Here
you may see Benedick the married man." 260

CLAUDIO   If this should ever happen, thou wouldst be
horn-mad.°

DON PEDRO   Nay, if Cupid have not spent all his
quiver in Venice,° thou wilt quake for this shortly.

BENEDICK   I look for an earthquake too then. 265

DON PEDRO   Well, you will temporize with the
hours.° In the meantime, good Signior Benedick,
repair to Leonato's. Commend me to him and tell him
I will not fail him at supper; for indeed he hath made
great preparation. 270

BENEDICK   I have almost matter° enough in me for
such an embassage, and so I commit you—

CLAUDIO   To the tuition° of God. From my house, if
I had it—

DON PEDRO   The sixth of July. Your loving friend, 275
Benedick.

BENEDICK   Nay, mock not, mock not. The body of
your discourse is sometime guarded° with fragments,
and the guards are but slightly basted on neither.
Ere you flout old ends° any further, examine your 280
conscience. And so I leave you.                    *Exit.*

CLAUDIO   My liege, your highness now may do me
good.

DON PEDRO
My love is thine to teach. Teach it but how,
And thou shalt see how apt it is to learn 285
Any hard lesson that may do thee good.

CLAUDIO
Hath Leonato any son, my lord?

DON PEDRO
No child but Hero; she's his only heir.
Dost thou affect° her, Claudio?

CLAUDIO                              O my lord,
When you went onward on this ended action,° 290
I looked upon her with a soldier's eye,
That liked, but had a rougher task in hand
Than to drive liking to the name of love.
But now I am returned and that° war-thoughts
Have left their places vacant, in their rooms 295
Come thronging soft and delicate desires,
All prompting me how fair young Hero is,
Saying I liked her ere I went to wars.

DON PEDRO
Thou wilt be like a lover presently

And tire the hearer with a book of words. 300
If thou dost love fair Hero, cherish it,
And I will break° with her and with her father,
And thou shalt have her. Was't not to this end
That thou began'st to twist so fine a story?

CLAUDIO
How sweetly you do minister to love, 305
That know love's grief by his complexion!°
But lest my liking might too sudden seem,
I would have salved it with a longer treatise.

DON PEDRO
What need the bridge much broader than the flood?
The fairest grant is the necessity.° 310
Look, what will serve is fit. 'Tis once,° thou lovest,
And I will fit thee with the remedy.
I know we shall have reveling tonight.
I will assume thy part in some disguise
And tell fair Hero I am Claudio, 315
And in her bosom I'll unclasp my heart
And take her hearing prisoner with the force
And strong encounter of my amorous tale;
Then after to her father will I break,
And the conclusion is, she shall be thine. 320
In practice let us put it presently.         *Exeunt.*

[Scene II. *Leonato's house.*]

*Enter* LEONATO *and an old man* [ANTONIO], *brother to
Leonato.*

LEONATO   How now, brother? Where is my cousin°
your son? Hath he provided this music?

ANTONIO   He is very busy about it. But, brother, I
can tell you strange news that you yet dreamt not of.

LEONATO   Are they° good? 5

ANTONIO   As the events stamps them.° But they have
a good cover, they show well outward. The prince
and Count Claudio, walking in a thick-pleached alley
in mine orchard,° were thus much overheard by a man
of mine. The prince discovered° to Claudio that he 10
loved my niece your daughter and meant to acknowledge it this night in a dance, and if he found her
accordant,° he meant to take the present time by the
top° and instantly break with you of it.

LEONATO   Hath the fellow any wit that told you this? 15

ANTONIO   A good sharp fellow. I will send for him,
and question him yourself.

LEONATO   No, no. We will hold it as a dream till it
appear itself. But I will acquaint my daughter withal,
that she may be the better prepared for an answer, if 20
peradventure this be true. Go you and tell her of it.

[*Enter* ATTENDANTS.]

Cousin, you know what you have to do. O, I cry you
mercy,° friend. Go you with me, and I will use your
skill. Good cousin, have a care this busy time.    *Exeunt.*

250 bottle basket   252 Adam Adam Bell, one of the three
superlative archers in the ballad "Adam Bell"   262 horn-mad
mad with jealousy (perhaps also "sexually insatiable")   264
Venice famous for sexual license   266–67 temporize . . .
hours change temper or attitude with time   271 matter sense
273 tuition custody   278 guarded trimmed (used of clothing)
280 flout old ends i.e., indulge in derision at my expense
289 affect love   290 ended action war just concluded   294
that because

302 break open negotiations   306 complexion appearance
310 The . . . necessity The most attractive giving is when the
receiver really needs something   311 'Tis once in short
I.ii.1 cousin kinsman   5 they the news (plural in the sixteenth
century)   6 As . . . them as the outcome proves them to be
(a plural noun, especially when felt to be singular, often has
a verb ending in –s)   8–9 thick-pleached . . . orchard
walk or arbor fenced by interwoven branches in my garden
10 discovered disclosed   13 accordant agreeing   14 top
forelock   22–23 cry you mercy beg your pardon

[Scene III. *Leonato's house*.]

*Enter Sir* [DON] JOHN *the bastard and* CONRADE, *his companion*.

CONRADE  What the goodyear,° my lord! Why are you thus out of measure sad?°

DON JOHN  There is no measure in the occasion that breeds; therefore the sadness is without limit.

CONRADE  You should hear reason.                                5

DON JOHN  And when I have heard it, what blessing brings it?

CONRADE  If not a present remedy, at least a patient sufferance.

DON JOHN  I wonder that thou, being (as thou say'st  10 thou art) born under Saturn,° goest about to apply a moral medicine to a mortifying mischief.° I cannot hide what I am. I must be sad when I have cause, and smile at no man's jests; eat when I have stomach, and wait for no man's leisure; sleep when I am drowsy,  15 and tend on no man's business; laugh when I am merry, and claw no man in his humor.°

CONRADE  Yea, but you must not make the full show of this till you may do it without controlment. You have of late stood out against your brother, and he  20 hath ta'en you newly into his grace, where it is impossible you should take true root but by the fair weather that you make yourself. It is needful that you frame° the season for your own harvest.

DON JOHN  I had rather be a canker° in a hedge than  25 a rose in his grace, and it better fits my blood to be disdained of all than to fashion a carriage° to rob love from any. In this, though I cannot be said to be a flattering honest man, it must not be denied but I am a plain-dealing villain. I am trusted with a muzzle and  30 enfranchised with a clog; therefore I have decreed not to sing in my cage. If I had my mouth, I would bite; if I had my liberty, I would do my liking. In the meantime let me be that I am, and seek not to alter me.

CONRADE  Can you make no use of your discontent?  35

DON JOHN  I make all use of it, for I use it only. Who comes here?

*Enter* BORACHIO.

What news, Borachio?

BORACHIO  I came yonder from a great supper. The prince your brother is royally entertained by Leonato,  40 and I can give you intelligence° of an intended marriage.

DON JOHN  Will it serve for any model to build mischief on? What is he for a fool that betroths himself to unquietness?                                        45

BORACHIO  Marry,° it is your brother's right hand.

DON JOHN  Who? The most exquisite Claudio?

BORACHIO  Even he.

DON JOHN  A proper squire!° And who? And who? Which way looks he?                                    50

BORACHIO  Marry, one Hero, the daughter and heir of Leonato.

DON JOHN  A very forward March-chick!° How came you to this?

BORACHIO  Being entertained for° a perfumer, as I  55 was smoking° a musty room, comes me the prince and Claudio, hand in hand in sad° conference. I whipped me behind the arras and there heard it agreed upon that the prince should woo Hero for himself, and having obtained her, give her to Count Claudio.  60

DON JOHN  Come, come, let us thither. This may prove food to my displeasure. That young start-up hath all the glory of my overthrow. If I can cross him any way, I bless myself every way. You are both sure,° and will assist me?                                65

CONRADE  To the death, my lord.

DON JOHN  Let us to the great supper. Their cheer is the greater that I am subdued. Would the cook were o' my mind! Shall we go prove° what's to be done?

BORACHIO  We'll wait upon your lordship.          70

*Exit* [*with others*].

# [ ACT II ]

[Scene I. *Leonato's house*.]

*Enter* LEONATO, *his brother* [ANTONIO], HERO *his daughter, and* BEATRICE *his niece,* [*also* MARGARET *and* URSULA].

LEONATO  Was not Count John here at supper?

ANTONIO  I saw him not.

BEATRICE  How tartly that gentleman looks! I never can see him but I am heartburned an hour after.

HERO  He is of a very melancholy° disposition.      5

BEATRICE  He were an excellent man that were made just in the midway between him and Benedick. The one is too like an image and says nothing, and the other too like my lady's eldest son,° evermore tattling.

LEONATO  Then half Signior Benedick's tongue in  10 Count John's mouth, and half Count John's melancholy in Signior Benedick's face—

BEATRICE  With a good leg and a good foot,° uncle, and money enough in his purse, such a man would win any woman in the world, if 'a could get her good  15 will.

LEONATO  By my troth, niece, thou wilt never get thee a husband if thou be so shrewd° of thy tongue.

ANTONIO  In faith, she's too curst.°

BEATRICE  Too curst is more than curst. I shall lessen  20 God's sending that way, for it is said, "God sends a curst cow short horns"; but to a cow too curst he sends none.

---

**I.iii.1 What the goodyear** an expletive  **2 out . . . sad** unduly morose  **11 under Saturn** i.e., naturally sullen  **12 mortifying mischief** killing calamity  **17 claw . . . humor** flatter no man ("claw" = pat or scratch on the back; "humor" = whim)  **24 frame** bring about  **25 canker** wild rose  **27 fashion a carriage** contrive a behavior  **41 intelligence** information  **46 Marry** an expletive, from "By the Virgin Mary"

**49 proper squire** fine young fellow  **53 forward March-chick** precocious fellow (i.e., born in early spring)  **55 entertained for** employed as  **56 smoking** fumigating (or possibly merely perfuming)  **57 sad** serious  **65 sure** reliable  **69 prove** try  **II.i.5 melancholy** ill-tempered  **9 eldest son** i.e., overly confident (as heir presumptive)  **13 foot** perhaps with a pun on French *foutre* = to copulate—i.e., a good lover  **18 shrewd** sharp  **19 curst** shrewish

LEONATO  So, by being too curst, God will send you no horns.°

BEATRICE  Just,° if he send me no husband; for the 25 which blessing I am at him upon my knees every morning and evening. Lord, I could not endure a husband with a beard on his face. I had rather lie in the woolen!°

LEONATO  You may light on a husband that hath no 30 beard.

BEATRICE  What should I do with him? Dress him in my apparel and make him my waiting gentlewoman? He that hath a beard is more than a youth, and he that hath no beard is less than a man; and he that is more 35 than a youth is not for me; and he that is less than a man, I am not for him. Therefore I will even take sixpence in earnest° of the berrord° and lead his apes into hell.°

LEONATO  Well then, go you into hell? 40

BEATRICE  No; but to the gate, and there will the devil meet me like an old cuckold with horns on his head, and say, "Get you to heaven, Beatrice, get you to heaven. Here's no place for you maids." So deliver I up my apes, and away to Saint Peter. For the heavens, 45 he shows me where the bachelors° sit, and there live we as merry as the day is long.

ANTONIO [To HERO.]  Well, niece, I trust you will be ruled by your father.

BEATRICE  Yes, faith. It is my cousin's duty to make 50 cursy° and say, "Father, as it please you." But yet for all that, cousin, let him be a handsome fellow, or else make another cursy, and say, "Father, as it please me."

LEONATO [To BEATRICE.]  Well, niece, I hope to see you one day fitted° with a husband. 55

BEATRICE  Not till God make men of some other metal° than earth. Would it not grieve a woman to be overmastered with a piece of valiant dust? To make an account of her life to a clod of wayward marl?° No, 60 uncle, I'll none. Adam's sons are my brethren, and truly I hold it a sin to match in my kindred.

LEONATO  Daughter, remember what I told you. If the prince do solicit you in that kind, you know your answer.

BEATRICE  The fault will be in the music, cousin, if 65 you be not wooed in good time. If the prince be too important,° tell him there is measure° in everything, and so dance out the answer. For, hear me, Hero: wooing, wedding, and repenting is as a Scotch jig, a measure, and a cinquepace.° The first suit is hot and 70 hasty like a Scotch jig (and full as fantastical); the wedding, mannerly modest, as a measure, full of state and ancientry; and then comes Repentance and with

his bad legs falls into the cinquepace faster and faster till he sink into his grave. 75

LEONATO  Cousin, you apprehend passing shewdly.

BEATRICE  I have a good eye, uncle; I can see a church by daylight.

LEONATO  The revelers are ent'ring, brother. Make good room. 80

[All put on their masks.]

Enter Prince [DON] PEDRO, CLAUDIO, and BENE-DICK, and BALTHASAR [masked; and without masks BORACHIO and] DON JOHN.

DON PEDRO  Lady, will you walk about with your friend?°

HERO  So you walk softly and look sweetly and say nothing, I am yours for the walk; and especially when I walk away. 85

DON PEDRO  With me in your company?

HERO  I may say so when I please.

DON PEDRO  And when please you to say so?

HERO  When I like your favor,° for God defend° the lute should be like the case!° 90

DON PEDRO  My visor° is Philemon's° roof; within the house is Jove.

HERO  Why then, your visor should be thatched.

DON PEDRO  Speak low if you speak love.

[Draws her aside.]

BENEDICK°  Well, I would you did like me. 95

MARGARET  So would not I for your own sake, for I have many ill qualities.

BENEDICK  Which is one?

MARGARET  I say my prayers aloud.

BENEDICK  I love you the better. The hearers may cry 100 amen.

MARGARET  God match me with a good dancer!

BALTHASAR [Interposing.]  Amen.

MARGARET  And God keep him out of my sight when the dance is done! Answer, clerk. 105

BALTHASAR  No more words. The clerk is answered.

URSULA  I know you well enough. You are Signior Antonio.

ANTONIO  At a word, I am not.

URSULA  I know you by the waggling° of your head. 110

ANTONIO  To tell you true, I counterfeit him.

URSULA  You could never do him so ill-well unless you were the very man. Here's his dry° hand up and down. You are he, you are he!

ANTONIO  At a word I am not. 115

URSULA  Come, come, do you think I do not know you by your excellent wit? Can virtue hide itself? Go to, mum, you are he. Graces will appear, and there's an end.

BEATRICE  Will you not tell me who told you so? 120

BENEDICK  No, you shall pardon me.

BEATRICE  Nor will you not tell me who you are?

BENEDICK  Not now.

---

24 **no horns** horn used as phallic symbol, as Beatrice's next remark makes plain   25 **Just** exactly   28–29 **in the woolen** between scratchy blankets   38 **in earnest** (1) advance payment (2) in all seriousness; **berrord** bearward, animal keeper   38–39 **lead . . . hell** traditional punishment for dying unwed   46 **bachelors** unwed persons (female as well as male)   51 **cursy** curtsy   55 **fitted** continues playful sexual innuendo of the scene   57 **metal** substance   59 **marl** earth   67 **important** importunate; **measure** (1) discernible time sequence (2) moderation (the entire speech is a light parody of Sir John Davies' *Orchestra, A Poem of Dancing* [1596]; cf. stanza 23: "Time the measure of all moving is/And dancing is a moving all in measure")   70 **cinquepace** lively dance

82 **friend** lover   89 **favor** face; **defend** forbid   89–90 **the lute . . . case** your face be as ugly as your mask   91 **visor** mask; **Philemon** peasant who entertained Jove in his house   95 **Benedick** many editors emend the quarto, and give this and Benedick's two subsequent speeches to Balthasar; but in V.ii Benedick and Margaret spar, and they may well do so here   110 **waggling** palsy   113 **dry** dried-up (with age)

BEATRICE   That I was disdainful, and that I had my good wit out of the "Hundred Merry Tales."° Well, 125 this was Signior Benedick that said so.

BENEDICK   What's he?

BEATRICE   I am sure you know him well enough.

BENEDICK   Not I, believe me.

BEATRICE   Did he never make you laugh? 130

BENEDICK   I pray you, what is he?

BEATRICE   Why, he is the prince's jester, a very dull fool. Only his° gift is in devising impossible slanders. None but libertines delight in him, and the commendation is not in his wit, but in his villainy; for he both 135 pleases men and angers them, and then they laugh at him and beat him. I am sure he is in the fleet;° I would he had boarded me.

BENEDICK   When I know the gentleman, I'll tell him what you say. 140

BEATRICE   Do, do. He'll but break a comparison or two on me; which peradventure (not marked or not laughed at), strikes him into melancholy, and then there's a partridge wing saved, for the fool will eat no supper that night. [Music.] We must follow the 145 leaders.

BENEDICK   In every good thing.

BEATRICE   Nay, if they lead to any ill, I will leave them at the next turning.

*Dance.*

*Exeunt [all except* DON JOHN, BORACHIO *and* CLAUDIO].

DON JOHN   Sure my brother is amorous on Hero and 150 hath withdrawn her father to break with him about it. The ladies follow her and but one visor remains.

BORACHIO   And that is Claudio. I know him by his bearing.

DON JOHN   Are not you Signior Benedick? 155

CLAUDIO   You know me well. I am he.

DON JOHN   Signior, you are very near my brother in his love. He is enamored on Hero. I pray you dissuade him from her; she is no equal for his birth. You may do the part of an honest man in it. 160

CLAUDIO   How know you he loves her?

DON JOHN   I heard him swear his affection.

BORACHIO   So did I too, and he swore he would marry her tonight.

DON JOHN   Come, let us to the banquet.° 165

*Exeunt. Manet* CLAUDIO.

CLAUDIO
Thus answer I in name of Benedick
But hear these ill news with the ears of Claudio.
'Tis certain so. The prince woos for himself.
Friendship is constant in all other things
Save in the office° and affairs of love. 170
Therefore all hearts in love use their own tongues;
Let every eye negotiate for itself
And trust no agent; for beauty is a witch
Against whose charms faith melteth into blood.°

This is an accident of hourly proof,° 175
Which I mistrusted not. Farewell therefore Hero!

*Enter* BENEDICK.

BENEDICK   Count Claudio?

CLAUDIO   Yea, the same.

BENEDICK   Come, will you go with me?

CLAUDIO   Whither? 180

BENEDICK   Even to the next° willow,° about your own business, county.° What fashion will you wear the garland of? About your neck, like an usurer's chain? Or under your arm, like a lieutenant's scarf? You must wear it one way, for the prince hath got your 185 Hero.

CLAUDIO   I wish him joy of her.

BENEDICK   Why, that's spoken like an honest drovier.° So they sell bullocks. But did you think the prince would have served you thus? 190

CLAUDIO   I pray you leave me.

BENEDICK   Ho! Now you strike like the blind man! 'Twas the boy that stole your meat, and you'll beat the post.°

CLAUDIO   If it will not be, I'll leave you.    *Exit.* 195

BENEDICK   Alas, poor hurt fowl! Now will he creep into sedges. But, that my Lady Beatrice should know me, and not know me! The prince's fool! Ha! It may be I go under that title because I am merry. Yea, but so I am apt to do myself wrong. I am not so reputed. 200 It is the base (though bitter) disposition of Beatrice that puts the world into her person and so gives me out.° Well, I'll be revenged as I may.

*Enter the prince* [DON PEDRO], HERO, LEONATO.

DON PEDRO   Now, signior, where's the count? Did you see him? 205

BENEDICK   Troth, my lord, I have played the part of Lady Fame.° I found him here as melancholy as a lodge in a warren.° I told him, and I think I told him true, that your grace had got the good will of this young lady, and I off'red him my company to a willow 210 tree, either to make him a garland, as being forsaken, or to bind him up a rod, as being worthy to be whipped.

DON PEDRO   To be whipped? What's his fault?

BENEDICK   The flat transgression of a schoolboy who, being overjoyed with finding a bird's nest, shows it his 215 companion, and he steals it.

DON PEDRO   Wilt thou make a trust a transgression? The transgression is in the stealer.

BENEDICK   Yet it had not been amiss the rod had been made, and the garland too; for the garland he might 220 have worn himself, and the rod he might have bestowed on you, who (as I take it) have stol'n his bird's nest.

DON PEDRO   I will but teach them to sing and restore them to the owner. 225

BENEDICK   If their singing answer your saying, by my faith you say honestly.

125 **Hundred Merry Tales** a popular collection of amusing, coarse anecdotes  133 **only his** his only  137 **fleet** group (the related meaning, group of ships, leads to "boarded me," but perhaps too there is an allusion to Fleet Prison)  165 **banquet** light meal, or course, of fruit, wine, and dessert  170 **office** business  174 **blood** passion, desire  175 **accident . . . proof** common happening  181 **next** nearest; **willow** symbol of unrequited love  182 **county** count  188 **drovier** cattle dealer  193–94 **beat the post** strike out blindly  201–03 **It . . . out** It is the low and harsh disposition of Beatrice to assume her opinion of me is the world's opinion of me  207 **Lady Fame** goddess of rumor  208 **in a warren** in a lonely place

DON PEDRO   The Lady Beatrice hath a quarrel to you. The gentleman that danced with her told her she is much wronged by you.   230

BENEDICK   O, she misused me past the endurance of a block! An oak but with one green leaf on it would have answered her; my very visor began to assume life and scold with her. She told me, not thinking I had been myself, that I was the prince's jester, that I   235 was duller than a great thaw; huddling jest upon jest with such impossible conveyance° upon me that I stood like a man at a mark,° with a whole army shooting at me. She speaks poniards, and every word stabs. If her breath were as terrible as her terminations,°   240 there were no living near her; she would infect to the North Star. I would not marry her though she were endowed with all that Adam had left him before he transgressed. She would have made Hercules have turned spit, yea, and have cleft his club to make the fire   245 too. Come, talk not of her. You shall find her the infernal Ate° in good apparel. I would to God some scholar would conjure her,° for certainly, while she is here, a man may live as quiet in hell as in a sanctuary; and people sin upon purpose, because they would go   250 thither; so indeed all disquiet, horror, and perturbation follows her.

*Enter* CLAUDIO *and* BEATRICE.

DON PEDRO   Look, here she comes.

BENEDICK   Will your grace command me any service to the world's end? I will go on the slightest errand   255 now to the Antipodes that you can devise to send me on; I will fetch you a toothpicker now from the furthest inch of Asia; bring you the length of Prester John's° foot; fetch you a hair off the great Cham's° beard; do you any embassage to the Pygmies—rather   260 than hold three words' conference with this harpy. You have no employment for me?

DON PEDRO   None, but to desire your good company.

BENEDICK   O God, sir, here's a dish I love not! I cannot endure my Lady Tongue.   *Exit.*   265

DON PEDRO   Come, lady, come; you have lost the heart of Signior Benedick.

BEATRICE   Indeed, my lord, he lent it me awhile, and I gave him use° for it, a double heart for his single one. Marry, once before he won it of me with false dice;   270 therefore your grace may well say I have lost it.

DON PEDRO   You have put him down, lady; you have put him down.

BEATRICE   So I would not he should do me, my lord, lest I should prove the mother of fools.° I have brought   275 Count Claudio, whom you sent me to seek.

DON PEDRO   Why, how now, count? Wherefore are you sad?

CLAUDIO   Not sad, my lord.

DON PEDRO   How then? Sick?   280

CLAUDIO   Neither, my lord.

BEATRICE   The count is neither sad, nor sick, nor merry, nor well; but civil count, civil° as an orange, and something of that jealous complexion.°

DON PEDRO   I' faith, lady, I think your blazon° to be   285 true; though I'll be sworn, if he be so, his conceit° is false. Here, Claudio. I have wooed in thy name, and fair Hero is won. I have broke with her father, and his good will obtained. Name the day of marriage, and God give thee joy!   290

LEONATO   Count, take of me my daughter, and with her my fortunes. His grace hath made the match, and all grace say amen to it!

BEATRICE   Speak, count, 'tis your cue.

CLAUDIO   Silence is the perfectest herald of joy. I were   295 but little happy if I could say how much. Lady, as you are mine, I am yours. I give away myself for you and dote upon the exchange.

BEATRICE   Speak, cousin; or (if you cannot) stop his mouth with a kiss and let not him speak neither.   300

DON PEDRO   In faith, lady, you have a merry heart.

BEATRICE   Yea, my lord; I thank it, poor fool, it keeps on the windy° side of care. My cousin tells him in his ear that he is in her heart.

CLAUDIO   And so she doth, cousin.   305

BEATRICE   Good Lord, for alliance! Thus goes everyone to the world but I, and I am sunburnt.° I may sit in a corner and cry "Heigh-ho for a husband!"

DON PEDRO   Lady Beatrice, I will get you one.

BEATRICE   I would rather have one of your father's   310 getting.° Hath your grace ne'er a brother like you? Your father got excellent husbands, if a maid could come by them.

DON PEDRO   Will you have me, lady?

BEATRICE   No, my lord, unless I might have another   315 for working days; your grace is too costly to wear every day. But I beseech your grace pardon me. I was born to speak all mirth and no matter.

DON PEDRO   Your silence most offends me, and to be merry best becomes you, for out o' question you were   320 born in a merry hour.

BEATRICE   No, sure, my lord, my mother cried; but then there was a star danced, and under that was I born. Cousins, God give you joy!

LEONATO   Niece, will you look to those things I told   325 you of?

BEATRICE   I cry you mercy,° uncle. By your grace's pardon.   *Exit* BEATRICE.

DON PEDRO   By my troth, a pleasant-spirited lady.

LEONATO   There's little of the melancholy element in   330 her, my lord. She is never sad but when she sleeps, and not ever° sad then; for I have heard my daughter say she hath often dreamt of unhappiness and waked herself with laughing.

DON PEDRO   She cannot endure to hear tell of a   335 husband.

LEONATO   O, by no means! She mocks all her wooers out of suit.

DON PEDRO   She were an excellent wife for Benedick.

LEONATO   O Lord, my lord! If they were but a week 340
married, they would talk themselves mad.

DON PEDRO   County Claudio, when mean you to go
to church?

CLAUDIO   Tomorrow, my lord. Time goes on
crutches till Love have all his rites. 345

LEONATO   Not till Monday, my dear son, which is
hence a just sevennight; and a time too brief too, to
have all things answer my mind.

DON PEDRO   Come, you shake the head at so long a
breathing; but I warrant thee, Claudio, the time shall 350
not go dully by us. I will in the interim undertake one
of Hercules' labors, which is, to bring Signior Benedick
and the Lady Beatrice into a mountain of affection th'
one with th' other. I would fain have it a match, and
I doubt not but to fashion it if you three will but 355
minister such assistance as I shall give you direction.

LEONATO   My lord, I am for you, though it cost me
ten nights' watchings.°

CLAUDIO   And I, my lord.

DON PEDRO   And you too, gentle Hero? 360

HERO   I will do any modest office, my lord, to help my
cousin to a good husband.

DON PEDRO   And Benedick is not the unhopefullest
husband that I know. Thus far can I praise him: he is
of a noble strain, of approved° valor and confirmed 365
honesty. I will teach you how to humor your cousin,
that she shall fall in love with Benedick; and I [to
LEONATO and CLAUDIO], with your two helps, will
so practice on° Benedick that, in despite of his quick
wit and his queasy stomach, he shall fall in love with 370
Beatrice. If we can do this, Cupid is no longer an
archer; his glory shall be ours, for we are the only
love-gods. Go in with me, and I will tell you my drift.
*Exit [with the others].*

[Scene II. *Leonato's house.*]

*Enter [DON] JOHN and BORACHIO.*

DON JOHN   It is so. The Count Claudio shall marry
the daughter of Leonato.

BORACHIO   Yea, my lord; but I can cross it.

DON JOHN   Any bar, any cross, any impediment will
be medicinable to me. I am sick in displeasure to him, 5
and whatsoever comes athwart his affection ranges
evenly° with mine. How canst thou cross this marriage?

BORACHIO   Not honestly, my lord; but so covertly
that no dishonesty shall appear in me.

DON JOHN   Show me briefly how. 10

BORACHIO   I think I told your lordship, a year since,
how much I am in the favor of Margaret, the waiting
gentlewoman to Hero.

DON JOHN   I remember.

BORACHIO   I can, at any unseasonable instant of the 15
night, appoint her to look out at her lady's chamber
window.

DON JOHN   What life is in that to be the death of this
marriage?

BORACHIO   The poison of that lies in you to temper. 20
Go you to the prince your brother; spare not to tell
him that he hath wronged his honor in marrying the
renowned Claudio (whose estimation do you mightily
hold up) to a contaminated stale,° such a one as Hero.

DON JOHN   What proof shall I make of that? 25

BORACHIO   Proof enough to misuse the prince, to vex
Claudio, to undo Hero, and kill Leonato. Look you
for any other issue?

DON JOHN   Only to despite them I will endeavor
anything. 30

BORACHIO   Go then; find me a meet hour° to draw
Don Pedro and the Count Claudio alone; tell them
that you know that Hero loves me; intend° a kind of
zeal both to the prince and Claudio (as in love of your
brother's honor, who hath made this match, and his 35
friend's reputation, who is thus like to be cozened°
with the semblance of a maid) that you have discovered
thus. They will scarcely believe this without trial.
Offer them instances;° which shall bear no less likelihood than to see me at her chamber window, hear me 40
call Margaret Hero, hear Margaret term me Claudio;
and bring them to see this the very night before the
intended wedding. For in the meantime I will so
fashion the matter that Hero shall be absent; and there
shall appear such seeming truth of Hero's disloyalty 45
that jealousy° shall be called assurance and all the
preparation overthrown.

DON JOHN   Grow this to what adverse issue it can, I
will put it in practice. Be cunning in the working this,
and thy fee is a thousand ducats. 50

BORACHIO   Be you constant in the accusation, and my
cunning shall not shame me.

DON JOHN   I will presently go learn their day of
marriage.   *Exit [with BORACHIO].*

[Scene III. *Leonato's garden.*]

*Enter BENEDICK alone.*

BENEDICK   Boy!

[*Enter BOY.*]

BOY   Signior?

BENEDICK   In my chamber window lies a book. Bring
it hither to me in the orchard.°

BOY   I am here already, sir. 5

BENEDICK   I know that, but I would have made thee
hence and here again. (*Exit [BOY].*) I do much wonder
that one man, seeing how much another man is a fool
when he dedicates his behaviors to love, will, after he
hath laughed at such shallow follies in others, become 10
the argument° of his own scorn by falling in love; and
such a man is Claudio. I have known when there was
no music with him but the drum and the fife; and
now had he rather hear the tabor and the pipe.° I have

358 **ten nights' watchings** ten nights awake   365 **approved**
tested   369 **practice on** deceive
II.ii.6–7 **ranges evenly** goes in a straight line (i.e., suits me
exactly)

24 **stale** prostitute   31 **meet hour** suitable time   33 **intend**
pretend   36 **cozened** cheated   39 **instances** proofs   46
**jealousy** mistrust
II.iii.4 **orchard** garden   11 **argument** subject matter   14
**tabor . . . pipe** music of an unmartial sort

known when he would have walked ten mile afoot to 15
see a good armor; and now will he lie ten nights awake
carving the fashion° of a new doublet. He was wont to
speak plain and to the purpose, like an honest man and
a soldier; and now is he turned orthography;° his
words are a very fantastical banquet—just so many 20
strange dishes. May I be so converted and see with
these eyes? I cannot tell; I think not. I will not be
sworn but love may transform me to an oyster; but
I'll take my oath on it, till he have made an oyster of
me he shall never make me such a fool. One woman 25
is fair, yet I am well; another is wise, yet I am well;
another virtuous, yet I am well. But till all graces be
in one woman, one woman shall not come in my
grace. Rich she shall be, that's certain; wise, or I'll
none; virtuous, or I'll never cheapen° her; fair, or I'll 30
never look on her; mild, or come not near me; noble,
or not I for an angel;° of good discourse,° an excellent
musician, and her hair shall be of what color it please
God. Ha, the prince and Monsieur Love! [*Retiring.*] I
will hide me in the arbor. 35

*Enter Prince* [DON PEDRO], LEONATO, CLAUDIO, [*to
the sound of*] *music.*

DON PEDRO
Come, shall we hear this music?
CLAUDIO
Yea, my good lord. How still the evening is,
As hushed on purpose to grace harmony!
DON PEDRO
See you where Benedick hath hid himself?
CLAUDIO
O, very well, my lord. The music ended, 40
We'll fit the kid fox with a pennyworth.°

*Enter* BALTHASAR *with music.*

DON PEDRO
Come, Balthasar, we'll hear that song again.
BALTHASAR
O, good my lord, tax not so bad a voice
To slander music any more than once.
DON PEDRO
It is the witness still of excellency 45
To put a strange face on his own perfection.
I pray thee sing, and let me woo no more.
BALTHASAR
Because you talk of wooing, I will sing,
Since many a wooer doth commence his suit
To her he thinks not worthy, yet he woos, 50
Yet will he swear he loves.
DON PEDRO              Nay, pray thee come;
Or if thou wilt hold longer argument,
Do it in notes.
BALTHASAR      Note this before my notes:
There's not a note of mine that's worth the noting.

DON PEDRO
Why, these are very crotchets° that he speaks! 55
Note notes, forsooth, and nothing!°

[*Music.*]

BENEDICK [*Aside.*]   Now divine air! Now is his soul
ravished! Is it not strange that sheep's guts should hale
souls out of men's bodies? Well, a horn for my money,
when all's done. 60

[BALTHASAR *sings.*]

          *The Song.*
    Sigh no more, ladies, sigh no more,
        Men were deceivers ever,
    One foot in sea, and one on shore,
        To one thing constant never.
            Then sigh not so, 65
            But let them go,
        And be you blithe and bonny,
    Converting all your sounds of woe
        Into hey nonny, nonny.

    Sing no more ditties, sing no moe, 70
        Of dumps° so dull and heavy;
    The fraud of men was ever so,
        Since summer first was leavy.
        Then sigh not so, &c.

DON PEDRO   By my troth, a good song. 75
BALTHASAR   And an ill singer, my lord.
DON PEDRO   Ha, no, no, faith! Thou sing'st well
enough for a shift.°
BENEDICK [*Aside.*]   And he had been a dog that should
have howled thus, they would have hanged him; and 80
I pray God his bad voice bode no mischief. I had as
live° have heard the night raven, come what plague
could have come after it.
DON PEDRO   Yea, marry. Dost thou hear, Balthasar? I
pray thee get us some excellent music; for tomorrow 85
night we would have it at the Lady Hero's chamber
window.
BALTHASAR   The best I can, my lord.
DON PEDRO   Do so. Farewell.
                    *Exit* BALTHASAR [*with* MUSICIANS].
Come hither, Leonato. What was it you told me of 90
today? That your niece Beatrice was in love with
Signior Benedick?
CLAUDIO   O, ay! [*In a low voice to* DON PEDRO.]
Stalk on, stalk on; the fowl sits. [*In full voice.*] I did
never think that lady would have loved any man. 95
LEONATO   No, nor I neither; but most wonderful that
she should so dote on Signior Benedick, whom she
hath in all outward behaviors seemed ever to abhor.
BENEDICK [*Aside.*]   Is't possible? Sits the wind in that
corner? 100
LEONATO   By my troth, my lord, I cannot tell what to
think of it, but that she loves him with an enraged
affection, it is past the infinite of thought.
DON PEDRO   May be she doth but counterfeit.
CLAUDIO   Faith, like enough. 105
LEONATO   O God, counterfeit? There was never

---

17 **carving the fashion** considering the design   19 **orthography** i.e., into a pedant (?)   30 **cheapen** bargain for
31–32 **noble . . . angel** puns: both words are Elizabethan
coins   32 **discourse** conversation   41 **We'll . . . pennyworth** We'll give Benedick a little something (perhaps "kid
fox" means "young fox," perhaps "known fox")

55 **crotchets** (1) whims (2) musical notes   56 **nothing**
pronounced "noting," hence a pun   71 **dumps** sad songs   78
**shift** makeshift   82 **live** lief

counterfeit of passion came so near the life of passion as she discovers° it.

DON PEDRO  Why, what effects of passion shows she?

CLAUDIO [*In a low voice.*]  Bait the hook well! This fish will bite. 110

LEONATO  What effects, my lord? She will sit you, you heard my daughter tell you how.

CLAUDIO  She did indeed.

DON PEDRO  How, how, I pray you? You amaze me! I would have thought her spirit had been invincible against all assaults of affection. 115

LEONATO  I would have sworn it had, my lord— especially against Benedick.

BENEDICK [*Aside.*]  I should think this a gull° but that the white-bearded fellow speaks it. Knavery cannot, sure, hide himself in such reverence. 120

CLAUDIO [*In a low voice.*]  He hath ta'en th' infection; hold° it up.

DON PEDRO  Hath she made her affection known to Benedick? 125

LEONATO  No, and swears she never will. That's her torment.

CLAUDIO  'Tis true indeed. So your daughter says. "Shall I," says she, "that have so oft encount'red him with scorn, write to him that I love him?" 130

LEONATO  This says she now when she is beginning to write to him; for she'll be up twenty times a night, and there will she sit in her smock till she have writ a sheet of paper. My daughter tells us all. 135

CLAUDIO  Now you talk of a sheet of paper, I remember a pretty jest your daughter told us of.

LEONATO  O, when she had writ it, and was reading it over, she found "Benedick" and "Beatrice" between the sheet? 140

CLAUDIO  That.

LEONATO  O, she tore the letter into a thousand halfpence,° railed at herself that she should be so immodest to write to one that she knew would flout her. "I measure him," says she, "by my own spirit; for I should flout him if he writ to me. Yea, though I love him, I should." 145

CLAUDIO  Then down upon her knees she falls, weeps, sobs, bears her heart, tears her hair, prays, curses—"O sweet Benedick! God give me patience!" 150

LEONATO  She doth indeed; my daughter say so; and the ecstasy° hath so much overborne her that my daughter is sometime afeard she will do a desperate outrage to herself. It is very true.

DON PEDRO  It were good that Benedick knew of it by some other, if she will not discover it. 155

CLAUDIO  To what end? He would make but a sport of it and torment the poor lady worse.

DON PEDRO  And he should, it were an alms° to hang him! She's an excellent sweet lady, and, out of all suspicion, she is virtuous. 160

CLAUDIO  And she is exceeding wise.

DON PEDRO  In everything but in loving Benedick.

LEONATO  O, my lord, wisdom and blood° combating in so tender a body, we have ten proofs to one that 165

blood hath the victory. I am sorry for her, as I have just cause, being her uncle and her guardian.

DON PEDRO  I would she had bestowed this dotage on me; I would have daffed all other respects° and made her half myself. I pray you tell Benedick of it and hear what 'a will say. 170

LEONATO  Were it good, think you?

CLAUDIO  Hero thinks surely she will die; for she says she will die if he love her not, and she will die ere she make her love known, and she will die, if he woo her, rather than she bate° one breath of her accustomed crossness. 175

DON PEDRO  She doth well. If she should make tender° of her love, 'tis very possible he'll scorn it; for the man, as you know all, hath a contemptible° spirit. 180

CLAUDIO  He is a very proper° man.

DON PEDRO  He hath indeed a good outward happiness.

CLAUDIO  Before God, and in my mind, very wise.

DON PEDRO  He doth indeed show some sparks that are like wit.° 185

CLAUDIO  And I take him to be valiant.

DON PEDRO  As Hector, I assure you. And in the managing of quarrels you may say he is wise, for either he avoids them with great discretion, or undertakes them with a most Christianlike fear. 190

LEONATO  If he do fear God, 'a must necessarily keep peace. If he break the peace, he ought to enter into a quarrel with fear and trembling.

DON PEDRO  And so will he do; for the man doth fear God, howsoever it seems not in him by some large jests° he will make. Well, I am sorry for your niece. Shall we go seek Benedick and tell him of her love? 195

CLAUDIO  Never tell him, my lord; let her wear it out with good counsel. 200

LEONATO  Nay, that's impossible; she may wear her heart out first.

DON PEDRO  Well, we will hear further of it by your daughter. Let it cool the while. I love Benedick well, and I could wish he would modestly examine himself to see how much he is unworthy so good a lady. 205

LEONATO  My lord, will you walk? Dinner is ready.

[*They walk away.*]

CLAUDIO  If he do not dote on her upon this, I will never trust my expectation.

DON PEDRO  Let there be the same net spread for her, and that must your daughter and her gentlewomen carry.° The sport will be, when they hold one an opinion of another's dotage, and no such matter. That's the scene that I would see, which will be merely a dumb show.° Let us send her to call him in to dinner. 210 215

[*Exeunt* DON PEDRO, CLAUDIO, *and* LEONATO.]

BENEDICK [*Advancing.*]  This can be no trick; the conference was sadly° borne. They have the truth of this from Hero. They seem to pity the lady; it seems her affections have their full bent.° Love me? Why, it

108 **discovers** reveals, betrays  120 **gull** trick  124 **hold** keep 142–43 **halfpence** i.e., small pieces  152 **ecstasy** madness 159 **an alms** a charity  164 **blood** passion

169 **daffed . . . respects** put aside all other considerations (i.e., of disparity in rank)  176 **bate** abate, give up  178 **tender** offer  180 **contemptible** disdainful  181 **proper** handsome  186 **wit** intelligence  196–97 **large jests** broad jokes 212 **carry** manage  215 **dumb show** pantomime (because of embarrassment)  217 **sadly** seriously  219 **affections . . . bent** emotions are tightly stretched (like a bent bow)

must be requited. I hear how I am censured. They say 220
I will bear myself proudly if I perceive the love come
from her. They say too that she will rather die than
give any sign of affection. I did never think to marry;
I must not seem proud. Happy are they that hear their
detractions and can put them to mending. They say 225
the lady is fair—'tis a truth, I can bear them witness;
and virtuous—'tis so, I cannot reprove it; and wise, but
for loving me; by my troth, it is no addition to her
wit, nor no great argument of her folly; for I will be
horribly in love with her. I may chance have some 230
odd quirks and remnants of wit broken on me because
I have railed so long against marriage; but doth not
the appetite alter? A man loves the meat in his youth
that he cannot endure in his age. Shall quips and sen-
tences° and these paper bullets of the brain awe a man 235
from the career° of his humor? No, the world must be
peopled. When I said I would die a bachelor, I did not
think I should live till I were married. Here comes
Beatrice. By this day, she's a fair lady. I do spy some
marks of love in her. 240

*Enter* BEATRICE.

BEATRICE  Against my will I am sent to bid you come
in to dinner.
BENEDICK  Fair Beatrice, I thank you for your pains.
BEATRICE  I took no more pains for those thanks than
you take pains to thank me. If it had been painful, I 245
would not have come.
BENEDICK  You take pleasure then in the message?
BEATRICE  Yea, just so much as you may take upon a
knife's point, and choke a daw withal.° You have no
stomach,° signior? Fare you well.                    *Exit.* 250
BENEDICK  Ha! "Against my will I am sent to bid you
come in to dinner." There's a double meaning in that.
'I took no more pains for those thanks than you took
pains to thank me." That's as much as to say, "Any
pains that I take for you is as easy as thanks." If I do 255
not take pity of her, I am a villain; if I do not love her,
I am a Jew. I will go get her picture.               *Exit.*

# [ ACT III ]

[Scene I. *Leonato's garden.*]

*Enter* HERO *and two gentlewomen,* MARGARET *and*
URSULA.

HERO
Good Margaret, run thee to the parlor.
There shalt thou find my cousin Beatrice
Proposing with° the prince and Claudio.
Whisper her ear and tell her, I and Ursley
Walk in the orchard, and our whole discourse       5
Is all of her. Say that thou overheard'st us;
And bid her steal into the pleachèd bower,

Where honeysuckles, ripened by the sun,
Forbid the sun to enter—like favorites,
Made proud by princes, that advance their pride    10
Against that power that bred it.° There will she hide
    her
To listen our propose. This is thy office;°
Bear thee well in it and leave us alone.
MARGARET
I'll make her come, I warrant you, presently.  [*Exit.*]
HERO
Now, Ursula, when Beatrice doth come,              15
As we do trace° this alley up and down,
Our talk must only be of Benedick.
When I do name him, let it be thy part
To praise him more than ever man did merit.
My talk to thee must be how Benedick              20
Is sick in love with Beatrice. Of this matter
Is little Cupid's crafty° arrow made,
That only° wounds by hearsay.

*Enter* BEATRICE.

                              Now begin;
For look where Beatrice like a lapwing runs
Close by the ground, to hear our conference.       25
URSULA
The pleasant'st angling is to see the fish
Cut with her golden oars the silver stream
And greedily devour the treacherous bait;
So angle we for Beatrice, who even now
Is couched in the woodbine coverture.°             30
Fear you not my part of the dialogue.
HERO
Then go we near her, that her ear lose nothing
Of the false sweet bait that we lay for it.

[*They approach the bower.*]

No, truly, Ursula, she is too disdainful.
I know her spirits are as coy° and wild           35
As haggards° of the rock.
URSULA                     But are you sure
That Benedick loves Beatrice so entirely?
HERO
So says the prince, and my new-trothèd lord.
URSULA
And did they bid you tell her of it, madam?
HERO
They did entreat me to acquaint her of it;        40
But I persuaded them, if they loved Benedick,
To wish him wrestle with affection
And never to let Beatrice know of it.
URSULA
Why did you so? Doth not the gentleman
Deserve as full as fortunate a bed                45
As ever Beatrice shall couch upon?
HERO
O god of love! I know he doth deserve
As much as may be yielded to a man;
But Nature never framed a woman's heart

---

234–35 **sentences** maxims  236 **career** course  249 **withal**
with  249–50 **no stomach** no wish to argue (as well as "no
appetite")
**III.i.3 Proposing with** talking to

10–11 **Made . . . it** an Elizabethan audience of c. 1600
would be reminded of the Earl of Essex  12 **office** duty  16
**trace** walk  22 **crafty** skillfully wrought  23 **only** solely  30
**woodbine coverture** honeysuckle thicket  35 **coy** disdainful
36 **haggards** wild and intractable hawks

Of prouder stuff than that of Beatrice.    50
Disdain and Scorn ride sparkling in her eyes,
Misprizing° what they look on; and her wit
Values itself so highly that to her
All matter else seems weak. She cannot love,
Nor take no shape nor project° of affection,    55
She is so self-endeared.

URSULA           Sure I think so;
And therefore certainly it were not good
She knew his love, lest she'll make sport of it.

HERO
Why, you speak truth. I never yet saw man,
How wise, how noble, young, how rarely featured,    60
But she would spell him backward. If fair-faced,
She would swear the gentleman should be her sister;
If black,° why, Nature, drawing of an antic,°
Made a foul blot; if tall, a lance ill-headed;
If low, an agate very vilely cut;°    65
If speaking, why, a vane blown with all winds;
If silent, why, a block movèd with none.
So turns she every man the wrong side out
And never gives to truth and virtue that
Which simpleness and merit purchaseth.    70

URSULA
Sure, sure, such carping is not commendable.

HERO
No, not to be so odd, and from all fashions,°
As Beatrice is, cannot be commendable.
But who dare tell her so? If I should speak,
She would mock me into air; O, she would laugh me   75
Out of myself, press me to death with wit!
Therefore let Benedick, like covered fire,
Consume away in sighs, waste inwardly.
It were a better death than die with mocks,
Which is as bad as die with tickling.    80

URSULA
Yet tell her of it. Hear what she will say.

HERO
No; rather I will go to Benedick
And counsel him to fight against his passion.
And truly, I'll devise some honest° slanders
To stain my cousin with. One doth not know    85
How much an ill word may empoison liking.

URSULA
O, do not do your cousin such a wrong!
She cannot be so much without true judgment
(Having so swift and excellent a wit
As she is prized to have) as to refuse    90
So rare a gentleman as Signior Benedick.

HERO
He is the only man of Italy,
Always excepted my dear Claudio.

URSULA
I pray you be not angry with me, madam,
Speaking my fancy. Signior Benedick,    95
For shape, for bearing, argument, and valor,
Goes foremost in report through Italy.

HERO
Indeed he hath an excellent good name.

URSULA
His excellence did earn it ere he had it.
When are you married, madam?    100

HERO
Why, everyday tomorrow!° Come, go in.
I'll show thee some attires, and have thy counsel
Which is the best to furnish° me tomorrow.

[*They walk away.*]

URSULA
She's limed,° I warrant you! We have caught her,
madam.

HERO
If it prove so, then loving goes by haps;°    105
Some Cupid kills with arrows, some with traps.

[*Exeunt* HERO *and* URSULA.]

BEATRICE [*Coming forward.*]
What fire is in mine ears? Can this be true?
Stand I condemned for pride and scorn so much?
Contempt, farewell! And maiden pride, adieu!
No glory lives behind the back of such.    110
And, Benedick, love on; I will requite thee,
Taming my wild heart to thy loving hand.
If thou dost love, my kindness shall incite thee
To bind our loves up in a holy band;
For others say thou dost deserve, and I    115
Believe it better than reportingly.°        *Exit.*

[Scene II. *Leonato's house.*]

*Enter prince* [DON PEDRO], CLAUDIO, BENEDICK,
*and* LEONATO.

DON PEDRO   I do but stay till your marriage be consummate, and then go I toward Aragon.

CLAUDIO   I'll bring you thither, my lord, if you'll
vouchsafe° me.

DON PEDRO   Nay, that would be as great a soil in the   5
new gloss of your marriage as to show a child his new
coat and forbid him to wear it. I will only be bold with
Benedick for his company; for, from the crown of his
head to the sole of his foot, he is all mirth. He hath
twice or thrice cut Cupid's bowstring,° and the little   10
hangman dare not shoot at him. He hath a heart as
sound as a bell; and his tongue is the clapper, for what
his heart thinks, his tongue speaks.

BENEDICK   Gallants, I am not as I have been.

LEONATO   So say I. Methinks you are sadder.°    15

CLAUDIO   I hope he be in love.

DON PEDRO   Hang him truant?° There's no true drop
of blood in him to be truly touched with love. If he be
sad, he wants money.

BENEDICK   I have the toothache.    20

DON PEDRO   Draw it.°

---

52 **Misprizing** despising   55 **project** notion   63 **black**
dark-complexioned; **antic** grotesque figure   65 **agate . . .**
**cut** poorly done miniature   72 **from all fashions** contrary
84 **honest** appropriate

101 **everyday tomorrow** tomorrow I shall be married forever
103 **furnish** dress   104 **limed** caught (as a bird is caught in
birdlime, a sticky substance smeared on branches)   105 **haps**
chance   116 **reportingly** mere hearsay
III.ii.4 **vouchsafe** permit   10 **cut Cupid's bowstring**
avoided falling in love   15 **sadder** graver   17 **truant** i.e., as
unfaithful to his anti-romantic stance   21 **Draw it** Extract
it (but "draw" also means eviscerate; traitors were hanged,
drawn, and quartered. "Draw it" thus leads to the exclamation "Hang it")

BENEDICK  Hang it!

CLAUDIO  You must hang it first and draw it afterwards.

DON PEDRO  What? Sigh for the toothache?  25

LEONATO  Where is but a humor or a worm.°

BENEDICK  Well, everyone cannot master a grief but he that has it.°

CLAUDIO  Yet say I he is in love.

DON PEDRO  There is no appearance of fancy° in him,  30 unless it be a fancy that he hath to strange disguises; as to be a Dutchman today, a Frenchman tomorrow; or in the shape of two countries at once, as a German from the waist downward, all slops,° and a Spaniard from the hip upward, no doublet.° Unless he have a  35 fancy to this foolery, as it appears he hath, he is no fool for fancy, as you would have it appear he is.

CLAUDIO  If he be not in love with some woman, there is no believing old signs; 'a brushes his hat o' mornings. What should that bode?  40

DON PEDRO  Hath any man seen him at the barber's?

CLAUDIO  No, but the barber's man hath been seen with him, and the old ornament of his cheek hath already stuffed tennis balls.°

LEONATO  Indeed he looks younger than he did, by  45 the loss of a beard.

DON PEDRO  Nay, 'a rubs himself with civet.° Can you smell him out by that?

CLAUDIO  That's as much as to say, the sweet youth's in love.  50

DON PEDRO  The greatest note of it is his melancholy.

CLAUDIO  And when was he wont to wash his face?

DON PEDRO  Yea, or to paint himself?° For the which I hear what they say of him.

CLAUDIO  Nay, but his jesting spirit, which is now  55 crept into a lutestring, and now governed by stops.°

DON PEDRO  Indeed that tells a heavy tale for him. Conclude, conclude, he is in love.

CLAUDIO  Nay, but I know who loves him.

DON PEDRO  That would I know too. I warrant, one  60 that knows him not.

CLAUDIO  Yes, and his ill conditions;° and in despite of all,° dies° for him.

DON PEDRO  She shall be buried with her face upwards.°  65

BENEDICK  Yet is this no charm for the toothache. Old signior, walk aside with me; I have studied eight or nine wise words to speak to you, which these hobbyhorses° must not hear.

[*Exeunt* BENEDICK *and* LEONATO.]

DON PEDRO  For my life, to break with him about  70 Beatrice!

26 humor . . . worm supposed causes of tooth decay; "humor = secretion  27–28 Well . . . it A man has to have a grief first before he can master it (Benedick does not admit that he has a grief; but some editors emend "cannot" to "can")  30 fancy love  34 slops loose breeches  35 doublet close-fitting jacket  43–44 the . . . balls cf. Beatrice's remark, II.i.27–28, "I could not endure a husband with a beard on his face"  47 civet perfume  53 to paint himself to use cosmetics  56 stops frets (on the lute)  62 conditions qualities  62–63 in . . . all notwithstanding  63 dies (1) pines away (2) is willing to "die" in the act of sex  64–65 She . . . upwards continues sexual innuendo  68–69 hobbyhorses jokers (originally an imitation horse fastened around the waist of a morris dancer)

CLAUDIO  'Tis even so. Hero and Margaret have by this played their parts with Beatrice, and then the two bears will not bite one another when they meet.

*Enter* [DON] JOHN *the bastard.*

DON JOHN  My lord and brother, God save you.  75

DON PEDRO  Good den,° brother.

DON JOHN  If your leisure served, I would speak with you.

DON PEDRO  In private?

DON JOHN  If it please you. Yet Count Claudio may  80 hear, for what I would speak of concerns him.

DON PEDRO  What's the matter?

DON JOHN  [*To* CLAUDIO.]  Means your lordship to be married tomorrow?

DON PEDRO  You know he does.  85

DON JOHN  I know not that, when he knows what I know.

CLAUDIO  If there be any impediment, I pray you discover it.

DON JOHN  You may think I love you not; let that  90 appear hereafter, and aim better at me° by that° I now will manifest. For my brother (I think he holds you well, and in dearness of heart) hath holp to effect your ensuing marriage—surely suit ill spent and labor ill bestowed!  95

DON PEDRO  Why, what's the matter?

DON JOHN  I came hither to tell you, and, circumstances short'ned (for she has been too long a-talking of), the lady is disloyal.

CLAUDIO  Who? Hero?  100

DON JOHN  Even she—Leonato's Hero, your Hero, every man's Hero.

CLAUDIO  Disloyal?

DON JOHN  The word is too good to paint out her wickedness. I could say she were worse. Think you of  105 a worse title, and I will fit her to it. Wonder not till further warrant. Go but with me tonight, you shall see her chamber window ent'red, even the night before her wedding day. If you love her then, tomorrow wed her. But it would better fit your honor to change your  110 mind.

CLAUDIO  May this be so?

DON PEDRO  I will not think it.

DON JOHN  If you dare not trust that you see, confess not that you know. If you will follow me, I will show  115 you enough; and when you have seen more and heard more, proceed accordingly.

CLAUDIO  If I see anything tonight why I should not marry her tomorrow, in the congregation where I should wed, there will I shame her.  120

DON PEDRO  And, as I wooed for thee to obtain her, I will join with thee to disgrace her.

DON JOHN  I will disparage her no farther till you are my witnesses. Bear it coldly° but till midnight, and let the issue show itself.  125

DON PEDRO  O day untowardly turned!

CLAUDIO  O mischief strangely thwarting!

DON JOHN  O plague right well prevented! So will you say when you have seen the sequel.  [*Exeunt.*]

76 Good den good evening  91 aim . . . me judge better of me; that that which  124 coldly calmly

[Scene III. A street.]

*Enter* DOGBERRY *and his compartner* [VERGES,] *with the* WATCH.

DOGBERRY  Are you good men and true?

VERGES  Yea, or else it were pity but they should suffer salvation,° body and soul.

DOGBERRY  Nay, that were a punishment too good for them if they should have any allegiance in them, being chosen for the prince's watch. 5

VERGES  Well, give them their charge,° neighbor Dogberry.

DOGBERRY  First, who think you the most desartless man to be constable? 10

FIRST WATCH  High Oatcake, sir, or George Seacole, for they can write and read.

DOGBERRY  Come hither, neighbor Seacole. God hath blessed you with a good name. To be a well-favored° man is the gift of fortune, but to write and read comes 15 by nature.

SECOND WATCH  Both which, Master Constable—

DOGBERRY  You have; I knew it would be your answer. Well, for your favor, sir, why, give God thanks and make no boast of it; and for your writing 20 and reading, let that appear when there is no need of such vanity. You are thought here to be the most senseless and fit man for the constable of the watch. Therefore bear you the lanthorn. This is your charge: you shall comprehend all vagrom° men; you are to 25 bid any man stand,° in the prince's name.

SECOND WATCH  How if 'a will not stand?

DOGBERRY  Why then, take no note of him, but let him go, and presently call the rest of the watch together and thank God you are rid of a knave. 30

VERGES  If he will not stand when he is bidden, he is none of the prince's subjects.

DOGBERRY  True, and they are to meddle with none but the prince's subjects. You shall also make no noise in the streets; for, for the watch to babble and to talk 35 is most tolerable, and not to be endured.

WATCH°  We will rather sleep than talk; we know what belongs to a watch.

DOGBERRY  Why, you speak like an ancient and most quiet watchman, for I cannot see how sleeping should 40 offend. Only, have a care that your bills° be not stol'n. Well, you are to call at all the alehouses and bid those that are drunk get them to bed.

WATCH  How if they will not?

DOGBERRY  Why then, let them alone till they are 45 sober. If they make you not then the better answer, you may say they are not the men you took them for.

WATCH  Well, sir.

DOGBERRY  If you meet a thief, you may suspect him, by virtue of your office, to be no true man; and for 50 such kind of man, the less you meddle or make with them, why, the more is for your honesty.

WATCH  If we know him to be a thief, shall we not lay hands on him?

DOGBERRY  Truly, by your office you may; but I 55 think they that touch pitch will be defiled. The most peaceable way for you, if you do take a thief, is to let him show himself what he is, and steal out of your company.

VERGES  You have been always called a merciful man, 60 partner.

DOGBERRY  Truly, I would not hang a dog by my will, much more a man who hath any honesty in him.

VERGES  If you hear a child cry in the night, you must call to the nurse and bid her still it. 65

WATCH  How if the nurse be asleep and will not hear us?

DOGBERRY  Why then, depart in peace and let the child wake her with crying; for the ewe that will not hear her lamb when it baes will never answer a calf 70 when he bleats.

VERGES  'Tis very true.

DOGBERRY  This is the end of the charge: you, constable, are to present the prince's own person. If you meet the prince in the night, you may stay him. 75

VERGES  Nay, by'r Lady, that I think 'a cannot.

DOGBERRY  Five shillings to one on't, with any man that knows the statutes, he may stay him! Marry, not without the prince be willing; for indeed the watch ought to offend no man, and it is an offense to stay a 80 man against his will.

VERGES  By'r Lady, I think it be so.

DOGBERRY  Ha, ah, ha! Well, masters, good night. And there be any matter of weight chances, call up me. Keep your fellows' counsels and your own, and good 85 night. Come, neighbor.

WATCH  Well, masters, we hear our charge. Let us go sit here upon the church bench till two, and then all to bed.

DOGBERRY  One word more, honest neighbors. I 90 pray you watch about Signior Leonato's door; for the wedding being there tomorrow, there is a great coil° tonight. Adieu. Be vigitant, I beseech you.

*Exeunt* [DOGBERRY *and* VERGES].

*Enter* BORACHIO *and* CONRADE.

BORACHIO  What, Conrade!

WATCH [*Aside.*]  Peace! Stir not. 95

BORACHIO  Conrade, I say!

CONRADE  Here, man. I am at thy elbow.

BORACHIO  Mass,° and my elbow itched; I thought there would a scab° follow.

CONRADE  I will owe thee an answer for that; and now 100 forward with thy tale.

BORACHIO  Stand thee close then under this penthouse,° for it drizzles rain, and I will, like a true drunkard,° utter all to thee.

WATCH [*Aside.*]  Some treason, masters; yet stand 105 close.

BORACHIO  Therefore know I have earned of Don John a thousand ducats.

**III.iii.3 salvation** damnation (the beginning of the mala-propisms basic to the comedy of Dogberry and Verges)  **7 charge** instructions  **14 well-favored** handsome  **25 comprehend all vagrom** apprehend all vagrant  **26 stand** halt, stop  **37 Watch** neither the quarto nor the Folio differentiates again between First Watch and Second Watch until the end of this scene  **41 bills** constables' pikes

**92 coil** to-do, turmoil  **98 Mass** an interjection, from "By the Mass"  **99 scab** (1) crust over a wound (2) contemptible person  **102–03 penthouse** shed, lean-to  **104 drunkard** his name is based on the Spanish *borracho* = drunkard

CONRADE   It is possible that any villainy should be so dear?   110

BORACHIO   Thou shouldst rather ask if it were possible any villainy should be so rich; for when rich villains have need of poor ones, poor ones may make what price they will.

CONRADE   I wonder at it.   115

BORACHIO   That shows thou art unconfirmed.° Thou knowest that the fashion of a doublet, or a hat, or a cloak, is nothing to a man.°

CONRADE   Yes, it is apparel.

BORACHIO   I mean the fashion.   120

CONRADE   Yes, the fashion is the fashion.

BORACHIO   Tush! I may as well say the fool's the fool. But see'st thou not what a deformed thief this fashion is?

WATCH [Aside.]   I know that Deformed; 'a has been a   125
vile thief this seven year; 'a goes up and down like a gentleman. I remember his name.

BORACHIO   Didst thou not hear somebody?

CONRADE   No; 'twas the vane on the house.

BORACHIO   See'st thou not, I say, what a deformed   130
thief this fashion is? How giddily 'a turns about all the hotbloods between fourteen and five-and-thirty? Sometimes fashioning them like Pharaoh's soldiers in the reechy° painting, sometime like god Bel's priests° in the old church window, sometime like the shaven   135
Hercules in the smirched worm-eaten tapestry, where his codpiece° seems as massy as his club?

CONRADE   All this I see; and I see that the fashion wears out more apparel than the man. But art not thou thyself giddy with the fashion too, that thou   140
hast shifted out of thy tale into telling me of the fashion?

BORACHIO   Not so neither. But know that I have tonight wooed Margaret, the Lady Hero's gentlewoman, by the name of Hero. She leans me out at her   145
mistress' chamber window, bids me a thousand times good night. I tell this tale vilely—I should first tell thee how the prince, Claudio, and my master, planted and placed and possessed° by my master Don John, saw afar off in the orchard this amiable encounter.   150

CONRADE   And thought they Margaret was Hero?

BORACHIO   Two of them did, the prince and Claudio; but the devil my master knew she was Margaret; and partly by his oaths, which first possessed them, partly by the dark night, which did deceive them, but   155
chiefly by my villainy, which did confirm any slander that Don John had made, away went Claudio enraged; swore he would meet her, as he was appointed, next morning at the temple, and there, before the whole congregation, shame her with what he saw o'ernight   160
and send her home again without a husband.

FIRST WATCH   We charge you in the prince's name stand!

SECOND WATCH   Call up the right Master Constable. We have here recovered the most dangerous piece of   165
lechery that ever was known in the commonwealth.

FIRST WATCH   And one Deformed is one of them; I know him; 'a wears a lock.°

CONRADE   Masters, masters—

SECOND WATCH   You'll be made bring Deformed   170
forth, I warrant you.

CONRADE   Masters, never speak; we charge you let us obey you to go with us.°

BORACHIO   We are like to prove a goodly commodity, being taken up of these men's bills.°   175

CONRADE   A commodity in question,° I warrant you. Come, we'll obey you.   *Exeunt.*

[Scene IV. *Leonato's house.*]

*Enter* HERO, *and* MARGARET, *and* URSULA.

HERO   Good Ursula, wake my cousin Beatrice and desire her to rise.

URSULA   I will, lady.

HERO   And bid her come hither.

URSULA   Well.   [*Exit.*]   5

MARGARET   Troth, I think your other rabato° were better.

HERO   No, pray thee, good Meg, I'll wear this.

MARGARET   By my troth, 'snot so good, and I warrant your cousin will say so.   10

HERO   My cousin's a fool, and thou art another. I'll wear none but this.

MARGARET   I like the new tire° within° excellently, if the hair were a thought browner; and your gown's a most rare fashion, i' faith. I saw the Duchess of Milan's   15
gown that they praise so.

HERO   O, that exceeds, they say.

MARGARET   By my troth, 'sbut a nightgown° in respect of yours—cloth o' gold and cuts,° and laced with silver, set with pearls, down sleeves, side-sleeves,° and skirts,   20
round underborne with a bluish tinsel. But for a fine, quaint,° graceful, and excellent fashion, yours is worth ten on't.

HERO   God give me joy to wear it, for my heart is exceeding heavy.   25

MARGARET   'Twill be heavier soon by the weight of a man.

HERO   Fie upon thee! Art not ashamed?

MARGARET   Of what, lady? Of speaking honorably? Is not marriage honorable in a beggar? Is not your   30
lord honorable without marriage? I think you would have me say, "saving your reverence, a husband." And bad thinking do not wrest true speaking, I'll offend nobody. Is there any harm in "the heavier for a husband"? None, I think, and it be the right   35

---

**168 lock** lovelock, curl of hair hanging by the ear   **172–73 Masters . . . us** Conrade is mocking the language of the Second Watch; he means, "Say no more, we will go along with you"   **174–75 We . . . bills** Borachio continues the mockery with a series of puns: "commodity" = (1) merchandise (2) profit; "taken up" = (1) arrested (2) bought on credit; "bills" = (1) pikes (2) bonds or sureties   **176 in question** (1) subject to judicial examination (2) of doubtful value
**III.iv.6 rabato** ruff   **13 tire** headdress; **within** in the next room   **18 nightgown** dressing gown   **19 cuts** slashes to show rich fabric underneath   **20 down sleeves, side-sleeves** long sleeves covering the arms, open sleeves hanging from the shoulder   **22 quaint** pretty, dainty

**116 unconfirmed** innocent   **118 is . . . man** fails to reveal his actual character   **134 reechy** grimy, filthy; **god Bel's priests** from the Apocrypha   **137 codpiece** decorative pouch at the fly on a sixteenth-century man's breeches   **149 possessed** informed, deluded

husband and the right wife; otherwise 'tis light,° and
not heavy. Ask my Lady Beatrice else. Here she comes.

*Enter* BEATRICE.

HERO   Good morrow, coz.

BEATRICE   Good morrow, sweet Hero.

HERO   Why, how now? Do you speak in the sick 40
tune?

BEATRICE   I am out of all other tune, methinks.

MARGARET   Clap's into° "Light o' love." That goes
without a burden.° Do you sing it, and I'll dance it.

BEATRICE   Ye light o' love with your heels!° Then, if 45
your husband have stables enough, you'll see he shall
lack no barns.°

MARGARET   O illegitimate construction! I scorn that
with my heels.

BEATRICE   'Tis almost five o'clock, cousin; 'tis time 50
you were ready. By my troth, I am exceeding ill.
Heigh-ho!

MARGARET   For a hawk, a horse, or a husband?

BEATRICE   For the letter that begins them all, H.°

MARGARET   Well, and you be not turned Turk,° 55
there's no more sailing by the star.

BEATRICE   What means the fool, trow?°

MARGARET   Nothing I; but God send everyone their
heart's desire!

HERO   These gloves the count sent me, they are an 60
excellent perfume.

BEATRICE   I am stuffed,° cousin; I cannot smell.

MARGARET   A maid, and stuffed!° There's goodly
catching of cold.

BEATRICE   O, God help me! God help me! How long 65
have you professed apprehension?°

MARGARET   Ever since you left it. Doth not my wit
become me rarely?

BEATRICE   It is not seen enough. You should wear it
in your cap. By my troth, I am sick. 70

MARGARET   Get you some of this distilled Carduus
Benedictus° and lay it to your heart. It is the only
thing for a qualm.°

HERO   There thou prick'st her with a thistle.

BEATRICE   Benedictus? Why Benedictus? You have 75
some moral° in this Benedictus.

MARGARET   Moral? No, by my troth, I have no moral
meaning. I meant plain holy thistle. You may think
perchance that I think you are in love. Nay, by'r lady,
I am not such a fool to think what I list;° nor I list not 80
to think what I can; nor indeed I cannot think, if I
would think my heart out of thinking, that you are in
love, or that you will be in love, or that you can be in
love. Yet Benedick was such another, and now is he
become a man. He swore he would never marry; and 85
yet now in despite of his heart he eats his meat without
grudging.° And how you may be converted I know

not; but methinks you look with your eyes as other
women do.

BEATRICE   What pace is this that thy tongue keeps? 90

MARGARET   Not a false gallop.

*Enter* URSULA.

URSULA   Madam, withdraw. The prince, the count,
Signior Benedick, Don John, and all the gallants of the
town are come to fetch you to church.

HERO   Help to dress me, good coz, good Meg, good 95
Ursula.                                              [*Exeunt.*]

[Scene V. *Another room in Leonato's house.*]

*Enter* LEONATO *and the Constable* [DOGBERRY], *and the*
*Headborough* [VERGES].

LEONATO   What would you with me, honest neighbor?

DOGBERRY   Marry, sir, I would have some confidence
with you that decerns you nearly.

LEONATO   Brief, I pray you, for you see it is a busy 5
time with me.

DOGBERRY   Marry, this it is, sir.

VERGES   Yes, in truth it is, sir.

LEONATO   What is it, my good friends?

DOGBERRY   Goodman Verges, sir, speaks a little off 10
the matter—an old man, sir, and his wits are not so
blunt as, God help, I would desire they were; but, in
faith, honest as the skin between his brows.

VERGES   Yes, I thank God I am as honest as any man
living that is an old man and no honester than I. 15

DOGBERRY   Comparisons are odorous; palabras,°
neighbor Verges.

LEONATO   Neighbors, you are tedious.

DOGBERRY   It pleases your worship to say so, but we
are the poor duke's officers; but truly, for mine own 20
part, if I were as tedious as a king, I could find in my
heart to bestow it all of your worship.

LEONATO   All thy tediousness on me, ah?

DOGBERRY   Yea, and 'twere a thousand pound more
than 'tis; for I hear as good exclamation on your 25
worship as of any man in the city, and though I be but
a poor man, I am glad to hear it.

VERGES   And so am I.

LEONATO   I would fain know what you have to say.

VERGES   Marry, sir, our watch tonight, excepting 30
your worship's presence, ha' ta'en a couple of as arrant
knaves as any in Messina.

DOGBERRY   A good old man, sir; he will be talking.
As they say, "When the age is in, the wit is out." God
help us! It is a world to see! Well said, i' faith, neighbor 35
Verges. Well, God's a good man. And two men ride of
a horse, one must ride behind. An honest soul, i' faith,
sir, by my troth he is, as ever broke bread; but God is
to be worshiped; all men are not alike, alas, good
neighbor! 40

LEONATO   Indeed, neighbor, he comes too short of
you.

DOGBERRY   Gifts that God gives.

LEONATO   I must leave you.

---

**36 light** pun on *wanton*   **43 Clap's into** let us sing   **44**
**burden** bass part (with pun on "the heavier for a husband")
**45 Ye . . . heels** sexual innuendo   **47 barns** pun on *bairns*,
children   **54 H** *ache* was pronounced "aitch"   **55 turned**
**Turk** completely changed   **57 trow** I wonder   **62 I am**
**stuffed** I have a head cold   **63 stuffed** filled (as with a child)
**66 apprehension** wit   **71–72 Carduus Benedictus** blessed
thistle, a medicinal herb   **73 qualm** sensation of sickness   **76**
**moral** special meaning   **80 list** please   **86–87 he . . .**
**grudging** he finds that he can still eat

**III.v.16 palabras** for Spanish *pocas palabras* = few words

DOGBERRY  One word, sir. Our watch, sir, have in-  45
deed comprehended two aspicious persons, and we
would have them this morning examined before your
worship.

LEONATO  Take their examination yourself and bring
it me; I am now in great haste, as it may appear unto  50
you.

DOGBERRY  It shall be suffigance.

LEONATO  Drink some wine ere you go. Fare you
well.

*[Enter a MESSENGER.]*

MESSENGER  My lord, they stay for you to give your  55
daughter to her husband.

LEONATO  I'll wait upon them. I am ready.
                    *Exit* [LEONATO, *with* MESSENGER].

DOGBERRY  Go, good partner, go get you to Francis
Seacole; bid him bring his pen and inkhorn to the jail.
We are now to examination these men.  60

VERGES  And we must do it wisely.

DOGBERRY  We will spare for no wit, I warrant you;
here's that shall drive some of them to a non-come.°
Only get the learned writer to set down our excommunication, and meet me at the jail.        *[Exeunt.]*  65


# [ A C T   I V ]

## [Scene I. *A church.*]

*Enter prince* [DON PEDRO], [DON JOHN *the*] *bastard,*
LEONATO, FRIAR [*Francis*], CLAUDIO, BENEDICK,
HERO, *and* BEATRICE [*and* ATTENDANTS].

LEONATO  Come, Friar Francis, be brief. Only to the
plain form of marriage, and you shall recount their
particular° duties afterwards.

FRIAR  You come hither, my lord, to marry this lady?

CLAUDIO  No.  5

LEONATO  To be married to her; friar, you come to
marry her.

FRIAR  Lady, you come hither to be married to this
count?

HERO  I do.  10

FRIAR  If either of you know any inward impediment
why you should not be conjoined, I charge you on your
souls to utter it.

CLAUDIO  Know you any, Hero?

HERO  None, my lord.  15

FRIAR  Know you any, count?

LEONATO  I dare make his answer, none.

CLAUDIO  O, what men dare do! What men may do!
What men daily do, not knowing what they do!

BENEDICK  How now? Interjections? Why then, some  20
be of° laughing, as, ah, ha, he!°

CLAUDIO
Stand thee by,° friar. Father, by your leave,
Will you with free and unconstrainèd soul
Give me this maid your daughter?

LEONATO
As freely, son, as God did give her me.  25

CLAUDIO
And what have I to give you back whose worth
May counterpoise this rich and precious gift?

DON PEDRO
Nothing, unless you render her again.

CLAUDIO
Sweet prince, you learn me noble thankfulness.
There, Leonato, take her back again.  30
Give not this rotten orange to your friend.
She's but the sign and semblance of her honor.
Behold how like a maid she blushes here!
O, what authority and show of truth
Can cunning sin cover itself withal!  35
Comes not that blood, as modest evidence,
To witness simple virtue? Would you not swear,
All you that see her, that she were a maid,
By these exterior shows? But she is none.
She knows the heat of a luxurious° bed;  40
Her blush is guiltiness, not modesty.

LEONATO
What do you mean, my lord?

CLAUDIO                    Not to be married,
Not to knit my soul to an approvèd° wanton.

LEONATO
Dear my lord, if you, in your own proof,°
Have vanquished the resistance of her youth  45
And made defeat of her virginity—

CLAUDIO
I know what you would say: if I have known° her,
You will say she did embrace me as a husband,
And so extenuate the 'forehand sin.  50
No, Leonato,
I never tempted her with word too large,
But, as a brother to his sister, showed
Bashful sincerity and comely love.

HERO
And seemed I ever otherwise to you?

CLAUDIO
Out on thee, seeming! I will write against it.  55
You seem to me as Dian in her orb,
As chaste as is the bud ere it be blown;°
But you are more intemperate in your blood°
Than Venus, or those pamp'red animals
That rage in savage sensuality.  60

HERO
Is my lord well that he doth speak so wide?°

LEONATO
Sweet prince, why speak not you?

DON PEDRO                    What should I
                                        speak?
I stand dishonored that have gone about
To link my dear friend to a common stale.°

LEONATO
Are these things spoken, or do I but dream?  65

DON JOHN
Sir, they are spoken, and these things are true.

---

63 **non-come** *non compos mentis*
**IV.i.3 particular** personal  **20–21 some be of** some are con-
cerned with  **21 ah, ha, he** examples of interjections  **22
Stand thee by** stand aside

**40 luxurious** lustful  **43 approvèd** tested  **44 proof** experience
**47 known** had intercourse with  **57 blown** blossomed  **58
blood** sexual desire  **61 so wide** so far from the truth  **64
stale** prostitute

**BENEDICK**
This looks not like a nuptial.

**HERO**                                    "True," O God!

**CLAUDIO**
Leonato, stand I here?
Is this the prince? Is this the prince's brother?
Is this face Hero's? Are our eyes our own?                         70

**LEONATO**
All this is so. But what of this, my lord?

**CLAUDIO**
Let me but move one question to your daughter;
And by that fatherly and kindly° power
That you have in her, bid her answer truly.

**LEONATO**
I charge thee do so, as thou art my child.                         75

**HERO**
O, God defend me! How am I beset!
What kind of catechizing call you this?

**CLAUDIO**
To make you answer truly to your name.

**HERO**
Is it not Hero? Who can blot that name
With any just reproach?

**CLAUDIO**                    Marry, that can Hero!                 80
Hero itself can blot out Hero's virtue.
What man was he talked with you yesternight,
Out at your window betwixt twelve and one?
Now, if you are a maid, answer to this.

**HERO**
I talked with no man at that hour, my lord.                        85

**DON PEDRO**
Why, then are you no maiden, Leonato,
I am sorry you must hear. Upon mine honor
Myself, my brother, and this grievèd count
Did see her, hear her, at that hour last night
Talk with a ruffian at her chamber window                          90
Who hath indeed, most like a liberal° villain,
Confessed the vile encounters they have had
A thousand times in secret.

**DON JOHN**
Fie, fie! They are not to be named, my lord—
Not to be spoke of;                                                95
There is not chastity enough in language
Without offense to utter them. Thus, pretty lady,
I am sorry for thy much misgovernment.

**CLAUDIO**
O Hero! What a Hero hadst thou been
If half thy outward graces had been placed                        100
About thy thoughts and counsels of thy heart!
But fare thee well, most foul, most fair, farewell;
Thou pure impiety and impious purity,
For thee I'll lock up all the gates of love,
And on my eyelids shall conjecture° hang,                         105
To turn all beauty into thoughts of harm,
And never shall it more be gracious.

**LEONATO**
Hath no man's dagger here a point for me?

[HERO *swoons*.]

**BEATRICE**
Why, how now, cousin? Wherefore sink you down?

**DON JOHN**
Come, let us go. These things, come thus to light,         110
Smother her spirits up.

[*Exeunt* DON PEDRO, DON JOHN, *and* CLAUDIO.]

**BENEDICK**
How doth the lady?

**BEATRICE**                    Dead, I think. Help, uncle!
Hero! Why, Hero! Uncle! Signior Benedick!
Friar!

**LEONATO**
O fate, take not away thy heavy hand!
Death is the fairest cover for her shame                    115
That may be wished for.

**BEATRICE**                    How now, cousin Hero?

**FRIAR**
Have comfort, lady.

**LEONATO**
Dost thou look up?

**FRIAR**                    Yea, wherefore should she not?

**LEONATO**
Wherefore? Why, doth not every earthly thing
Cry shame upon her? Could she here deny                     120
The story that is printed in her blood?°
Do not live, Hero; do not ope thine eyes;
For, did I think thou wouldst not quickly die,
Thought I thy spirits were stronger than thy shames,
Myself would on the rearward of reproaches                  125
Strike at thy life. Grieved I, I had but one?
Chid I for that at frugal nature's frame?°
O, one too much by thee! Why had I one?
Why ever wast thou lovely in my eyes?
Why had I not with charitable hand                          130
Took up a beggar's issue at my gates,
Who smirchèd thus and mired with infamy,
I might have said, "No part of it is mine;
This shames derives itself from unknown loins"?
But mine, and mine I loved, and mine I praised,             135
And mine that I was proud on, mine so much
That I myself was to myself not mine,
Valuing of her—why she, O, she is fall'n
Into a pit of ink, that the wide sea
Hath drops too few to wash her clean again,                 140
And salt too little which may season give°
To her foul tainted flesh!

**BENEDICK**                    Sir, sir, be patient.
For my part, I am so attired in wonder,
I know not what to say.

**BEATRICE**
O, on my soul, my cousin is belied!                         145

**BENEDICK**
Lady, were you her bedfellow last night?

**BEATRICE**
No, truly, not; although, until last night,
I have this twelvemonth been her bedfellow.

**LEONATO**
Confirmed, confirmed! O, that is stronger made
Which was before barred up with ribs of iron!              150
Would the two princes lie, and Claudio lie,
Who loved her so that, speaking of her foulness,
Washed it with tears? Hence from her! Let her die.

---

**73 kindly** natural  **91 liberal** licentious  **105 conjecture** suspicion  **121 printed . . . blood** written in her blushes  **127 frame** plan  **141 season give** act as a preservative

FRIAR
Hear me a little;
For I have only been silent so long,                                      155
And given way unto this course of fortune,
By noting of the lady. I have marked
A thousand blushing apparitions
To start into her face, a thousand innocent shames
In angel whiteness beat away those blushes,                                160
And in her eye there hath appeared a fire
To burn the errors that these princes hold
Against her maiden truth. Call me a fool;
Trust not my reading nor my observations,
Which with experimental seal° doth warrant                                 165
The tenor° of my book; trust not my age,
My reverence, calling, nor divinity,
If this sweet lady lie not guiltless here
Under some biting error.
LEONATO                         Friar, it cannot be.
Thou see'st that all the grace that she hath left                          170
Is that she will not add to her damnation
A sin of perjury; she not denies it.
Why seek'st thou then to cover with excuse
That which appears in proper nakedness?
FRIAR
Lady, what man is he you are accused of?                                   175
HERO
They know that do accuse me; I know none.
If I know more of any man alive
Than that which maiden modesty doth warrant,
Let all my sins lack mercy! O my father,
Prove you that any man with me conversed                                   180
At hours unmeet, or that I yesternight
Maintained the change° of words with any creature,
Refuse me, hate me, torture me to death!
FRIAR
There is some strange misprision° in the princes.
BENEDICK
Two of them have the very bent° of honor;                                  185
And if their wisdoms be misled in this,
The practice° of it lives in John the bastard,
Whose spirits toil in frame of villainies.
LEONATO
I know not. If they speak but truth of her,
These hands shall tear her. If they wrong her honor,       190
The proudest of them shall well hear of it.
Time hath not yet so dried this blood of mine,
Nor age so eat up my invention,°
Nor fortune made such havoc of my means,
Nor my bad life reft me so much of friends,                                195
But they shall find awaked in such a kind
Both strength of limb and policy of mind,
Ability in means, and choice of friends,
To quit° me of them throughly.
FRIAR                              Pause awhile
And let my counsel sway you in this case.                                  200
Your daughter here the princes left for dead.
Let her awhile be secretly kept in,
And publish it that she is dead indeed;

Maintain a mourning ostentation,°
And on your family's old monument                                          205
Hang mournful epitaphs, and do all rites
That appertain unto a burial.
LEONATO
What shall become of this? What will this do?
FRIAR
Marry, this well carried shall on her behalf
Change slander to remorse; that is some good.              210
But not for that dream I on this strange course,
But on this travail look for greater birth.
She dying, as it must be so maintained,
Upon the instant that she was accused,
Shall be lamented, pitied, and excused                                     215
Of every hearer. For it so falls out
That what we have we prize not to the worth
Whiles we enjoy it; but being lacked and lost,
Why, then we rack° the value, then we find
The virtue that possession would not show us                              220
Whiles it was ours. So will it fare with Claudio.
When he shall hear she died upon his words,
Th' idea of her life shall sweetly creep
Into his study of imagination,°
And every lovely organ° of her life                                       225
Shall come appareled in more precious habit,°
More moving, delicate, and full of life,
Into the eye and prospect of his soul
Than when she lived indeed. Then shall he mourn,
If ever love had interest in his liver,°                                  230
And wish he had not so accusèd her,
No, though he thought his accusation true.
Let this be so, and doubt not but success°
Will fashion the event° in better shape
Than I can lay it down in likelihood.                                     235
But if all aim, but this, be leveled false,°
The supposition of the lady's death
Will quench the wonder of her infamy;
And if it sort° not well, you may conceal her,
As best befits her wounded reputation,                                    240
In some reclusive and religious life,
Out of all eyes, tongues, minds, and injuries.
BENEDICK
Signior Leonato, let the friar advise you;
And though you know my inwardness° and love
Is very much unto the prince and Claudio,                                 245
Yet, by mine honor, I will deal in this
As secretly and justly as your soul
Should with your body.
LEONATO                       Being that I flow in grief,
The smallest twine may lead me.
FRIAR
'Tis well consented. Presently away;                                      250
For to strange sores strangely they strain the cure.
Come, lady, die to live. This wedding day
Perhaps is but prolonged. Have patience and endure.
            *Exit* [*with all but* BEATRICE *and* BENEDICK].

165 **experimental seal** seal of experience  166 **tenor** purport  182 **maintained the change** held exchange  184 **misprision** mistaking  185 **bent** shape (or perhaps "inclination")  187 **practice** scheming  193 **invention** inventiveness  199 **quit** revenge

204 **Maintain . . . ostentation** perform the outward show of mourning  219 **rack** stretch  224 **study of imagination** meditation, musing  225 **organ** physical feature  226 **habit** dress  230 **liver** supposed seat of love  233 **success** what follows  234 **event** outcome  236 **But . . . false** but if all conjecture, except this (i.e., the mere supposition of Hero's death), be aimed ("leveled") falsely  239 **sort** turn out  244 **inwardness** most intimate feelings

BENEDICK   Lady Beatrice, have you wept all this while?    255

BEATRICE   Yea, and I will weep a while longer.

BENEDICK   I will not desire that.

BEATRICE   You have no reason. I do it freely.

BENEDICK   Surely I do believe your fair cousin is wronged.    260

BEATRICE   Ah, how much might the man deserve of me that would right her!

BENEDICK   Is there any way to show such friendship?

BEATRICE   A very even° way, but no such friend.

BENEDICK   May a man do it?    265

BEATRICE   It is a man's office, but not yours.

BENEDICK   I do love nothing in the world so well as you. Is not that strange?

BEATRICE   As strange as the thing I know not. It were as possible for me to say I loved nothing so well as you.    270 But believe me not; and yet I lie not. I confess nothing, nor I deny nothing. I am sorry for my cousin.

BENEDICK   By my sword, Beatrice, thou lovest me.

BEATRICE   Do not swear and eat it.

BENEDICK   I will swear by it that you love me, and I    275 will make him eat it that says I love not you.

BEATRICE   Will you not eat your word?

BENEDICK   With no sauce that can be devised to it. I protest° I love thee.

BEATRICE   Why then, God forgive me!    280

BENEDICK   What offense, sweet Beatrice?

BEATRICE   You have stayed me in a happy hour.° I was about to protest I loved you.

BENEDICK   And do it with all thy heart.

BEATRICE   I love you with so much of my heart that    285 none is left to protest.

BENEDICK   Come, bid me do anything for thee.

BEATRICE   Kill Claudio.

BENEDICK   Ha! Not for the wide world!

BEATRICE   You kill me to deny it. Farewell.    290

BENEDICK   Tarry, sweet Beatrice.

*[He holds her.]*

BEATRICE   I am gone, though I am here; there is no love in you. Nay, I pray you let me go!

BENEDICK   Beatrice—

BEATRICE   In faith, I will go!    295

BENEDICK   We'll be friends first.

*[He lets her go.]*

BEATRICE   You dare easier be friends with me than fight with mine enemy.

BENEDICK   Is Claudio thine enemy?

BEATRICE   Is 'a not approved in the height a villain,    300 that hath slandered, scorned, dishonored my kinswoman? O that I were a man! What, bear her in hand° until they come to take hands; and then, with public accusation, uncovered slander, unmitigated rancor— O God, that I were a man! I would eat his heart in the    305 market place!

BENEDICK   Hear me, Beatrice—

BEATRICE   Talk with a man out at a window! A proper saying!

BENEDICK   Nay, but Beatrice—    310

BEATRICE   Sweet Hero, she is wronged, she is sland'red, she is undone.

BENEDICK   Beat—

BEATRICE   Princes and counties! Surely, a princely testimony, a goodly count, Count Comfect;° a sweet    315 gallant surely! O that I were a man for his sake! Or that I had any friend would be a man for my sake! But manhood is melted into cursies,° valor into compliment, and men are only turned into tongue, and trim ones too. He is now as valiant as Hercules that only tells a    320 lie, and swears it. I cannot be a man with wishing; therefore I will die a woman with grieving.

BENEDICK   Tarry, good Beatrice. By this hand, I love thee.

BEATRICE   Use it for my love some other way than    325 swearing by it.

BENEDICK   Think you in your soul the Count Claudio hath wronged Hero?

BEATRICE   Yea, as sure as I have a thought or a soul.

BENEDICK   Enough, I am engaged. I will challenge    330 him. I will kiss your hand, and so I leave you. By this hand, Claudio shall render me a dear account. As you hear of me, so think of me. Go comfort your cousin. I must say she is dead. And so farewell.    *[Exeunt.]*

## [Scene II. *A prison.*]

*Enter the constables* [DOGBERRY *and* VERGES] *and the town clerk* [SEXTON] *in gowns,* BORACHIO, [CONRADE, *and* WATCH].

DOGBERRY   Is our whole dissembly appeared?

VERGES   O, a stool and a cushion for the sexton.

SEXTON   Which be the malefactors?

DOGBERRY   Marry, that am I and my partner.

VERGES   Nay, that's certain. We have the exhibition    5 to examine.

SEXTON   But which are the offenders that are to be examined? Let them come before Master Constable.

DOGBERRY   Yea, marry, let them come before me. What is your name, friend?    10

BORACHIO   Borachio.

DOGBERRY   Pray write down Borachio. Yours, sirrah?°

CONRADE   I am a gentleman, sir, and my name is Conrade.    15

DOGBERRY   Write down Master Gentleman Conrade. Masters, do you serve God?

BOTH   Yea, sir, we hope.

DOGBERRY   Write down that they hope they serve God; and write God first, for God defend but God    20 should go before such villains! Masters, it is proved already that you are little better than false knaves, and it will go near to be thought so shortly. How answer you for yourselves?

CONRADE   Marry, sir, we say we are none.    25

DOGBERRY   A marvelous witty fellow, I assure you; but I will go about with him.° Come you hither, sirrah;

---

**264 even** direct    **279 protest** avow    **282 in . . . hour** just in time    **302 bear . . . hand** fool her

**315 Comfect** sugar candy    **318 cursies** curtsies
**IV.ii.13 sirrah** term of address used to an inferior    **27 go . . . him** get the better of him

a word in your ear. Sir, I say to you, it is thought you
are false knaves.

BORACHIO   Sir, I say to you we are none.°    30

DOGBERRY   Well, stand aside. 'Fore God, they are
both of a tale.° Have you writ down that they are
none?

SEXTON   Master Constable, you go not the way to
examine. You must call forth the watch that are their    35
accusers.

DOGBERRY   Yea, marry, that's the eftest° way. Let the
watch come forth. Masters, I charge you in the prince's
name, accuse these men.

FIRST WATCH   This man said, sir, that Don John the    40
prince's brother was a villain.

DOGBERRY   Write down Prince John a villain. Why,
this is flat perjury, to call a prince's brother villain.

BORACHIO   Master Constable!

DOGBERRY   Pray thee, fellow, peace. I do not like thy    45
look, I promise thee.

SEXTON   What heard you him say else?

SECOND WATCH   Marry, that he had received a
thousand ducats of Don John for accusing the Lady
Hero wrongfully.    50

DOGBERRY   Flat burglary as ever was committed.

VERGES   Yea, by mass, that it is.

SEXTON   What else, fellow?

FIRST WATCH   And that Count Claudio did mean,
upon his words, to disgrace Hero before the whole    55
assembly, and not marry her.

DOGBERRY   O villain! Thou wilt be condemned into
everlasting redemption for this.

SEXTON   What else?

WATCH   This is all.    60

SEXTON   And this is more, masters, than you can deny.
Prince John is this morning secretly stol'n away. Hero
was in this manner accused, in this very manner
refused, and upon the grief of this suddenly died.
Master Constable, let these men be bound and brought    65
to Leonato's. I will go before and show him their
examination.    [Exit.]

DOGBERRY [To the WATCH.]   Come, let them be
opinioned.°

VERGES   Let them be in the hands of Coxcomb.°    70

DOGBERRY   God's my life, where's the sexton? Let
him write down the prince's officer Coxcomb. Come,
bind them. Thou naughty° varlet!

CONRADE   Away! You are an ass, you are an ass.

DOGBERRY   Dost thou not suspect my place? Dost    75
thou not suspect my years? O that he were here to
write me down an ass! But, masters, remember that I
am an ass. Though it be not written down, yet forget
not that I am an ass. No, thou villain, thou art full of
piety, as shall be proved upon thee by good witness. I    80
am a wise fellow; and which is more, an officer; and
which is more, a householder; and which is more, as
pretty a piece of flesh as any is in Messina, and one that
knows the law, go to! And a rich fellow enough, go
to! And a fellow that hath had losses; and one that    85
hath two gowns and everything handsome about him.
Bring him away. O that I had been writ down an ass!

*Exit* [with the others.]

# [ A C T   V ]

[Scene I. *Before Leonato's house.*]

*Enter* LEONATO *and his brother* [ANTONIO].

ANTONIO
If you go on thus, you will kill yourself,
And 'tis not wisdom thus to second° grief
Against yourself.

LEONATO            I pray thee cease thy counsel,
Which falls into mine ears as profitless
As water in a sieve. Give not me counsel,    5
Nor let no comforter delight mine ear
But such a one whose wrongs do suit with° mine.
Bring me a father that so loved his child,
Whose joy of her is overwhelmed like mine,
And bid him speak of patience.    10
Measure his woe the length and breadth of mine,
And let it answer every strain° for strain,
As thus for thus, and such a grief for such,
In every lineament, branch, shape, and form.
If such a one will smile and stroke his beard,    15
And sorrow wag,° cry "hem" when he should groan;
Patch grief with proverbs, make misfortune drunk
With candle-wasters;° bring him yet° to me,
And I of him will gather patience.
But there is no such man. For, brother, men    20
Can counsel and speak comfort to that grief
Which they themselves not feel; but, tasting it,
Their counsel turns to passion, which before
Would give preceptial medicine° to rage,
Fetter strong madness in a silken thread,    25
Charm ache with air and agony with words.
No, no! 'Tis all men's office to speak patience
To those that wring under the load of sorrow,
But no man's virtue nor sufficiency
To be so moral° when he shall endure    30
The like himself. Therefore give me no counsel;
My griefs cry louder than advertisement.°

ANTONIO
Therein do men from children nothing differ.

LEONATO
I pray thee peace. I will be flesh and blood;
For there was never yet philosopher    35
That could endure the toothache patiently,
However they have writ the style of gods
And made a push at chance and sufferance.°

30 **none** apparently pronounced the same as *known*, and so
taken by Dogberry in his next speech   **31–32 they . . . tale**
their stories agree   **37 eftest** quickest   **69 opinioned** he means
*pinioned*   **70 Coxcomb** apparently Verges thinks this is an
elegant name for one of the Watch; editors commonly emend
"of Coxcomb" to "off, coxcomb," and give to Conrade   **73
naughty** wicked

**V.i.2 second** assist   **7 suit with** accord with   **12 strain**
quality, trait   **16 wag** wave away   **18 candle-wasters**
revelers (?) philosophers (?); **yet** then   **24 preceptial medicine**
medicine of precepts (cf. line 17, "Patch grief with proverbs")
**30 moral** moralizing   **32 advertisement** counsel   **38 made
. . . sufferance** defied mischance and suffering

ANTONIO
Yet bend not all the harm upon yourself.
Make those that do offend you suffer too.                    40

LEONATO
There thou speak'st reason. Nay, I will do so.
My soul doth tell me Hero is belied;
And that shall Claudio know; so shall the prince,
And all of them that thus dishonor her.

*Enter prince* [DON PEDRO] *and* CLAUDIO.

ANTONIO
Here comes the prince and Claudio hastily.                    45

DON PEDRO
Good den, good den.

CLAUDIO                    Good day to both of you.

LEONATO
Hear you, my lords—

DON PEDRO                    We have some haste, Leonato.

LEONATO
Some haste, my lord! Well, fare you well, my lord.
Are you so hasty now? Well, all is one.

DON PEDRO
Nay, do not quarrel with us, good old man.                    50

ANTONIO
If he could right himself with quarreling,
Some of us would lie low.

CLAUDIO                    Who wrongs him?

LEONATO
Marry, thou dost wrong me, thou dissembler, thou!
Nay, never lay thy hand upon thy sword;
I fear thee not.

CLAUDIO          Marry, beshrew° my hand                    55
If it should give your age such cause of fear.
In faith, my hand meant nothing to my sword.

LEONATO
Tush, tush, man! Never fleer° and jest at me.
I speak not like a dotard nor a fool,
As under privilege of age to brag                    60
What I have done being young, or what would do,
Were I not old. Know, Claudio, to thy head,°
Thou hast so wronged mine innocent child and me
That I am forced to lay my reverence by
And, with gray hairs and bruise of many days,                    65
Do challenge thee to trial of a man.°
I say thou hast belied mine innocent child.
Thy slander hath gone through and through her heart,
And she lies buried with her ancestors;
O, in a tomb where never scandal slept,                    70
Save this of hers, framed° by thy villainy!

CLAUDIO
My villainy?

LEONATO          Thine, Claudio; thine I say.

DON PEDRO
You say not right, old man.

LEONATO                    My lord, my lord,
I'll prove it on his body if he dare,
Despite his nice fence° and his active practice,                    75
His May of youth and bloom of lustihood.

CLAUDIO
Away! I will not have to do with you.

LEONATO
Canst thou so daff° me? Thou hast killed my child.
If thou kill'st me, boy, thou shalt kill a man.

ANTONIO
He shall kill two of us, and men indeed.                    80
But that's no matter; let him kill one first.
Win me and wear me! Let him answer me.
Come, follow me, boy; come, sir boy; come, follow me.
Sir boy, I'll whip you from your foining° fence!
Nay, as I am a gentleman, I will.                    85

LEONATO    Brother—

ANTONIO
Content yourself. God knows I loved my niece;
And she is dead, slandered to death by villains,
That dare as well answer a man indeed
As I dare take a serpent by the tongue.                    90
Boys, apes, braggarts, Jacks,° milksops!

LEONATO                    Brother
                                        Anthony—

ANTONIO
Hold you content. What, man! I know them, yea,
And what they weigh, even to the utmost scruple;°
Scambling,° outfacing, fashionmonging° boys,
That lie and cog° and flout, deprave and slander,                    95
Go anticly,° and show outward hideousness,
And speak off half a dozen dang'rous words,
How they might hurt their enemies, if they durst;
And this is all.

LEONATO
But, brother Anthony—

ANTONIO                    Come, 'tis no matter.                    100
Do not you meddle; let me deal in this.

DON PEDRO
Gentlemen both, we will not wake your patience.°
My heart is sorry for your daughter's death.
But, on my honor, she was charged with nothing
But what was true, and very full of proof.                    105

LEONATO
My lord, my lord!

DON PEDRO
I will not hear you.

LEONATO
No? Come, brother, away! I will be heard!

ANTONIO
And shall, or some of us will smart for it.
                    *Exeunt ambo°* [LEONATO *and* ANTONIO].

*Enter* BENEDICK.

DON PEDRO    See, see! Here comes the man we went    110
to seek.

CLAUDIO    Now, signior, what news?

BENEDICK    Good day, my lord.

DON PEDRO    Welcome, signior. You are almost come
to part almost a fray.                    115

CLAUDIO    We had liked to have had our two noses
snapped off with two old men without teeth.

---

55 **beshrew** curse (but not a strong word)    58 **fleer** sneer
62 **head** face    66 **trial . . . man** manly test, i.e., a duel    71
**framed** made    75 **nice fence** elegant fencing

78 **daff** put off    84 **foining** thrusting    91 **Jacks** a contemptuous term of no precise meaning    93 **scruple** smallest unit    94 **Scambling** brawling; **fashionmonging** fashionfollowing    95 **cog** cheat    96 **anticly** grotesquely dressed    102 **wake your patience** arouse your indulgence (heavily ironic)    109 **s.d. ambo** both (Latin)

DON PEDRO    Leonato and his brother. What think'st thou? Had we fought, I doubt° we should have been too young for them.    120

BENEDICK    In a false quarrel there is no true valor. I came to seek you both.

CLAUDIO    We have been up and down to seek thee; for we are high-proof° melancholy, and would fain have it beaten away. Wilt thou use thy wit?    125

BENEDICK    It is in my scabbard. Shall I draw it?

DON PEDRO    Dost thou wear thy wit by thy side?

CLAUDIO    Never any did so, though very many have been beside their wit. I will bid thee draw, as we do the minstrels: draw° to pleasure us.    130

DON PEDRO    As I am an honest man, he looks pale. Art thou sick, or angry?

CLAUDIO    What, courage, man! What though care killed a cat, thou hast mettle enough in thee to kill care.

BENEDICK    Sir, I shall meet your wit in the career° 135 and you charge° it against me. I pray you choose another subject.

CLAUDIO    Nay then, give him another staff. This last was broke cross.°

DON PEDRO    By this light, he changes more and more. 140 I think he be angry indeed.

CLAUDIO    If he be, he knows how to turn his girdle.°

BENEDICK    Shall I speak a word in your ear?

CLAUDIO    God bless me from a challenge!

BENEDICK    [Aside to CLAUDIO.] You are a villain; I 145 jest not; I will make it good how you dare, with what you dare, and when you dare. Do me right, or I will protest° your cowardice. You have killed a sweet lady, and her death shall fall heavy on you. Let me hear from you.    150

CLAUDIO    Well, I will meet you, so I may have good cheer.

DON PEDRO    What, a feast, a feast?

CLAUDIO    I' faith, I thank him; he hath bid me to a calf's head and a capon; the which if I do not carve 155 most curiously,° say my knife's naught. Shall I not find a woodcock° too?

BENEDICK    Sir, your wit ambles well; it goes easily.

DON PEDRO    I'll tell thee how Beatrice praised thy wit the other day. I said thou hadst a fine wit. "True," said 160 she, "a fine little one." "No," said I, "a great wit." "Right," says she, "a great gross one." "Nay," said I, "a good wit." "Just," said she, "it hurts nobody." "Nay," said I, "the gentleman is wise." "Certain," said she, "a wise gentleman." "Nay," said I, "he hath 165 the tongues."° "That I believe," said she, "for he swore a thing to me on Monday night which he forswore on Tuesday morning; there's a double tongue; there's two tongues." Thus did she an hour together transshape° thy particular virtues. Yet at last she 170

concluded with a sigh, thou wast the prop'rest° man in Italy.

CLAUDIO    For the which she wept heartily and said she cared not.

DON PEDRO    Yea, that she did; but yet, for all that, 175 and if she did not hate him deadly, she would love him dearly. The old man's daughter told us all.

CLAUDIO    All, all! And moreover, God saw him when he was hid in the garden.

DON PEDRO    But when shall we set the savage bull's 180 horns on the sensible Benedick's head?

CLAUDIO    Yea, and text underneath, "Here dwells Benedick, the married man"?

BENEDICK    Fare you well, boy; you know my mind. I will leave you now to your gossiplike humor; you 185 break jests as braggards do their blades, which God be thanked hurt not. [To DON PEDRO.] My lord, for your many courtesies I thank you. I must discontinue your company. Your brother the bastard is fled from Messina. You have among you killed a sweet and 190 innocent lady. For my Lord Lackbeard there, he and I shall meet; and till then peace be with him.    [Exit.]

DON PEDRO    He is in earnest.

CLAUDIO    In most profound earnest; and, I'll warrant you, for the love of Beatrice.    195

DON PEDRO    And hath challenged thee?

CLAUDIO    Most sincerely.

DON PEDRO    What a pretty thing man is when he goes in his doublet and hose and leaves off his wit!

*Enter constables* [DOGBERRY, VERGES, *and the* WATCH, *with*] CONRADE *and* BORACHIO.

CLAUDIO    He is then a giant to an ape; but then is an 200 ape a doctor to such a man.°

DON PEDRO    But, soft you, let me be! Pluck up, my heart, and be sad. Did he not say my brother was fled?

DOGBERRY    Come you, sir. If justice cannot tame you, she shall ne'er weigh more reasons in her balance. Nay, 205 and you be a cursing hypocrite once, you must be looked to.

DON PEDRO    How now? Two of my brother's men bound? Borachio one.

CLAUDIO    Hearken after° their offense, my lord.    210

DON PEDRO    Officers, what offense have these men done?

DOGBERRY    Marry, sir, they have committed false report; moreover, they have spoken untruths; secondarily, they are slanders; sixth and lastly, they have 215 belied a lady; thirdly, they have verified unjust things; and to conclude, they are lying knaves.

DON PEDRO    First, I ask thee what they have done; thirdly, I ask thee what's their offense; sixth and lastly, why they are committed; and to conclude, what you 220 lay to their charge.

CLAUDIO    Rightly reasoned, and in his own division; and, by my troth, there's one meaning well suited.°

DON PEDRO    Who have you offended, masters, that you are thus bound° to your answer? This learned 225

119 **doubt** suspect    124 **high-proof** in the highest degree    130 **draw** draw not a sword but a fiddle bow    135 **in the career** headlong    136 **charge** i.e., as in tilting with staves or lances    139 **broke cross** ineptly broken (by crossing the opponent's shield instead of striking it headlong)    142 **turn his girdle** challenge me (by reaching for his dagger?)    148 **protest** proclaim    156 **curiously** skillfully    157 **woodcock** stupid bird (Claudio reduces the duel to a carving up of symbols of stupidity—a calf's head, a capon, and a woodcock) **165–66 hath the tongues** knows foreign languages    170 **transshape** distort

171 **prop'rest** most handsome    200–01 **He . . . man** An ape would consider him important, but an ape is actually a scholar ("doctor") compared to such a fool    210 **Hearken after** inquire into    223 **well suited** well dressed out    225 **bound** arraigned

constable is too cunning° to be understood. What's
your offense?

BORACHIO  Sweet prince, let me go no farther to mine
answer. Do you hear me, and let this count kill me.
I have deceived even your very eyes. What your 230
wisdoms could not discover, these shallow fools have
brought to light, who in the night overheard me
confessing to this man, how Don John your brother
incensed me to slander the Lady Hero; how you were
brought into the orchard and saw me court Margaret 235
in Hero's garments; how you disgraced her when you
should marry her. My villainy they have upon record,
which I had rather seal with my death than repeat over
to my shame. The lady is dead upon mine and my
master's false accusation; and briefly, I desire nothing 240
but the reward of a villain.

DON PEDRO  Runs not this speech like iron through
your blood?

CLAUDIO  I have drunk poison whiles he uttered it.

DON PEDRO  But did my brother set thee on to this? 245

BORACHIO  Yea, and paid me richly for the practice
of it.

DON PEDRO  He is composed and framed of treachery,
And fled he is upon this villainy.

CLAUDIO  Sweet Hero, now the image doth appear 250
In the rare semblance that I loved it first.

DOGBERRY  Come, bring away the plaintiffs. By this
time our sexton hath reformed Signior Leonato of the
matter. And, masters, do not forget to specify, when
time and place shall serve, that I am an ass. 255

VERGES  Here, here comes Master Signior Leonato,
and the sexton too.

*Enter* LEONATO, *his brother* [ANTONIO], *and the*
SEXTON.

LEONATO
Which is the villain? Let me see his eyes,
That, when I note another man like him,
I may avoid him. Which of these is he? 260

BORACHIO
If you would know your wronger, look on me.

LEONATO
Art thou the slave that with thy breath hast killed
Mine innocent child?

BORACHIO                     Yea, even I alone.

LEONATO
No, not so, villain! Thou beliest thyself.
Here stand a pair of honorable men; 265
A third is fled, that had a hand in it.
I thank you, princes, for my daughter's death.
Record it with your high and worthy deeds.
'Twas bravely done, if you bethink you of it.

CLAUDIO
I know not how to pray your patience;° 270
Yet I must speak. Choose your revenge yourself;
Impose me to what penance your invention°
Can lay upon my sin. Yet sinned I not
But in mistaking.

DON PEDRO               By my soul, nor I;
And yet, to satisfy this good old man, 275

I would bend under any heavy weight
That he'll enjoin me to.

LEONATO
I cannot bid you bid my daughter live;
That were impossible; but I pray you both,
Possess° the people in Messina here 280
How innocent she died; and if your love
Can labor aught in sad invention,
Hang her an epitaph upon her tomb,
And sing it to her bones, sing it tonight.
Tomorrow morning come you to my house; 285
And since you could not be my son-in-law,
Be yet my nephew. My brother hath a daughter,
Almost the copy of my child that's dead,
And she alone is heir to both of us.
Give her the right° you should have giv'n her cousin, 290
And so dies my revenge.

CLAUDIO                     O noble sir!
Your overkindness doth wring tears from me.
I do embrace your offer; and dispose
For henceforth of poor Claudio.

LEONATO
Tomorrow then I will expect your coming; 295
Tonight I take my leave. This naughty man
Shall face to face be brought to Margaret,
Who I believe was packed° in all this wrong,
Hired to it by your brother.

BORACHIO                     No, by my soul, she was not;
Nor knew not what she did when she spoke to me; 300
But always hath been just and virtuous
In anything that I do know by her.

DOGBERRY  Moreover, sir, which indeed is not under
white and black,° this plaintiff here, the offender, did
call me ass. I beseech you let it be rememb'red in his 305
punishment. And also the watch heard them talk of one
Deformed; they say he wears a key° in his ear, and a
lock hanging by it, and borrows money in God's
name, the which he hath used so long and never paid
that now men grow hardhearted and will lend nothing 310
for God's sake. Pray you examine him upon that point.

LEONATO  I thank thee for thy care and honest pains.

DOGBERRY  Your worship speaks like a most thankful
and reverent youth, and I praise God for you.

LEONATO  There's for thy pains. 315

[*Gives money.*]

DOGBERRY  God save the foundation!°

LEONATO  Go. I discharge° thee of thy prisoner, and I
thank thee.

DOGBERRY  I leave an arrant knave with your worship,
which I beseech your worship to correct yourself, for 320
the example of others. God keep your worship! I
wish your worship well. God restore you to health!
I humbly give you leave to depart; and if a merry
meeting may be wished, God prohibit it! Come,
neighbor.          [*Exeunt* DOGBERRY *and* VERGES.] 325

---

226 **cunning** intelligent  270 **pray your patience** ask your
forgiveness  272 **invention** imagination

280 **Possess** inform  290 **right** Hero had a right to claim
Claudio as her husband; probably there is also a pun on *rite*
298 **packed** combined, i.e., an accomplice  303–04 **not . . .
black** not in the official record  307 **key** ring (but perhaps
Dogberry merely assumes that if a man wears a lock in his
hair he must wear a key too)  316 **the foundation** as if
Leonato were a charitable institution  317 **discharge** relieve

LEONATO
Until tomorrow morning, lords, farewell.

ANTONIO
Farewell, my lords. We look for you tomorrow.

DON PEDRO
We will not fail.

CLAUDIO    Tonight I'll mourn with Hero.
[*Exeunt* DON PEDRO *and* CLAUDIO.]

LEONATO [*To the* WATCH.]
Bring you these fellows on.
We'll talk with Margaret,    330
How her acquaintance grew with this lewd° fellow.
*Exeunt* [*separately*].

[Scene II. *Leonato's garden.*]

*Enter* BENEDICK *and* MARGARET [*meeting*].

BENEDICK    Pray thee, sweet Mistress Margaret, deserve well at my hands by helping me to the speech of Beatrice.

MARGARET    Will you then write me a sonnet in praise of my beauty?    5

BENEDICK    In so high a style,° Margaret, that no man living shall come over it; for in most comely truth thou deservest it.

MARGARET    To have no man come over me!° Why, shall I always keep belowstairs?°    10

BENEDICK    Thy wit is as quick as the greyhound's mouth; it catches.

MARGARET    And yours as blunt as the fencer's foils, which hit but hurt not.

BENEDICK    A most manly wit, Margaret; it will not    15
hurt a woman. And so, I pray thee call Beatrice. I give thee the bucklers.°

MARGARET    Give us the swords; we have bucklers of our own.

BENEDICK    If you use them, Margaret, you must put    20
in the pikes° with a vice;° and they are dangerous weapons for maids.

MARGARET    Well, I will call Beatrice to you, who I think hath legs.    *Exit* MARGARET.

BENEDICK    And therefore will come.    25
[*Sings.*]    The god of love,
That sits above
And knows me, and knows me,
How pitiful I deserve—

I mean in singing; but in loving, Leander the good    30
swimmer, Troilus° the first employer of panders, and a whole book full of these quondam carpetmongers,° whose names yet run smoothly in the even road of a blank verse—why, they were never so truly turned over and over as my poor self in love. Marry, I cannot    35
show it in rhyme. I have tried. I can find out no rhyme

to "lady" but "baby," an innocent rhyme; for "scorn," "horn," a hard rhyme; for "school," "fool," a babbling rhyme. Very ominous endings. No, I was not born under a rhyming planet, nor I cannot woo in    40
festival terms.

*Enter* BEATRICE.

Sweet Beatrice, wouldst thou come when I called thee?

BEATRICE    Yea, signior, and depart when you bid me.

BENEDICK    O, stay but till then!    45

BEATRICE    "Then" is spoken. Fare you well now. And yet, ere I go, let me go with that I came, which is, with knowing what hath passed between you and Claudio.

BENEDICK    Only foul words; and thereupon I will    50
kiss thee.

BEATRICE    Foul words is but foul wind, and foul wind is but foul breath, and foul breath is noisome. Therefore I will depart unkissed.

BENEDICK    Thou hast frighted the word out of his    55
right sense, so forcible is thy wit. But I must tell thee plainly, Claudio undergoes my challenge; and either I must shortly hear from him or I will subscribe him° a coward. And I pray thee now tell me, for which of my bad parts didst thou first fall in love with me?    60

BEATRICE    For them all together, which maintained so politic a state° of evil that they will not admit any good part to intermingle with them. But for which of my good parts did you first suffer love for me?

BENEDICK    Suffer love! A good epithet. I do suffer    65
love indeed, for I love thee against my will.

BEATRICE    In spite of your heart, I think. Alas, poor heart! If you spite it for my sake, I will spite it for yours, for I will never love that which my friend hates.    70

BENEDICK    Thou and I are too wise to woo peaceably.

BEATRICE    It appears not in this confession. There's not one wise man among twenty that will praise himself.

BENEDICK    An old, an old instance,° Beatrice, that    75
lived in the time of good neighbors. If a man do not erect in this age his own tomb ere he dies, he shall live no longer in monument than the bell rings and the widow weeps.

BEATRICE    And how long is that, think you?    80

BENEDICK    Question: why, an hour in clamor and a quarter in rheum;° therefore is it most expedient for the wise, if Don Worm, his conscience, find no impediment to the contrary, to be the trumpet of his own virtues, as I am to myself. So much for praising    85
myself, who, I myself will bear witness, is praiseworthy. And now tell me, how doth your cousin?

BEATRICE    Very ill.

BENEDICK    And how do you?

BEATRICE    Very ill too.    90

BENEDICK    Serve God, love me, and mend. There will I leave you too, for here comes one in haste.

*Enter* URSULA.

URSULA    Madam, you must come to your uncle.

331 lewd low
V.ii.6 style pun on *stile*, a set of steps for passing over a fence   9 come over me the beginning of an interchange of sexual innuendoes   10 keep belowstairs dwell in the servants' quarters   16–17 I give . . . bucklers I yield   21 pikes spikes in the center of bucklers; vice screw   30–31 Leander . . . Troilus legendary lovers; Leander nightly swam the Hellespont to visit Hero, Troilus was aided in his love for Cressida by Pandarus   32 quondam carpetmongers ancient boudoir knights

58 subscribe him write him down   62 politic a state wellordered a community   75 instance example   82 rheum tears

Yonder's old coil° at home. It is proved my Lady Hero
hath been falsely accused, the prince and Claudio 95
mightily abused, and Don John is the author of all,
who is fled and gone. Will you come presently?

BEATRICE   Will you go hear this news, signior?

BENEDICK   I will live in thy heart, die in thy lap, and
be buried in thy eyes; and moreover, I will go with 100
thee to thy uncle's.

        *Exit* [*with* BEATRICE *and* URSULA].


#### [Scene III. *A church.*]

*Enter* CLAUDIO, *prince* [DON PEDRO, LORD,] *and*
*three or four with tapers* [ *followed by* MUSICIANS].

CLAUDIO   Is this the monument of Leonato?

LORD   It is, my lord.

CLAUDIO [*Reads from a scroll.*]


        *Epitaph.*

  Done to death by slanderous tongues
    Was the Hero that here lies;
  Death, in guerdon° of her wrongs,                    5
    Gives her fame which never dies.
  So the life that died with shame
  Lives in death with glorious fame.

[*Hangs up the scroll.*]

  Hang thou there upon the tomb,
  Praising her when I am dumb.                    10

CLAUDIO
Now, music, sound, and sing your solemn hymn.


        *Song.*

  Pardon, goddess of the night,°
  Those that slew thy virgin knight;
  For the which, with songs of woe,
  Round about her tomb they go.                    15
  Midnight, assist our moan;
  Help us to sigh and groan,
    Heavily, heavily.
  Graves, yawn and yield your dead,
  Till death be utterèd,                    20
    Heavily, heavily.

CLAUDIO
Now unto thy bones good night!
Yearly will I do this rite.

DON PEDRO
Good morrow, masters; put your torches out.
  The wolves have preyed, and look, the gentle day, 25
Before the wheels of Phoebus,° round about
  Dapples the drowsy east with spots of gray.
Thanks to you all, and leave us. Fare you well.

CLAUDIO
Good morrow, masters; each his several way.

DON PEDRO
Come, let us hence and put on other weeds,°          30
And then to Leonato's we will go.

CLAUDIO
And Hymen° now with luckier issue speeds°
Than this for whom we rend'red up this woe. *Exeunt.*


#### [Scene IV. *Leonato's house.*]

*Enter* LEONATO, BENEDICK, [BEATRICE,] MAR-
GARET, URSULA, *old man* [ANTONIO], FRIAR
[*Francis*], HERO.

FRIAR
Did I not tell you she was innocent?

LEONATO
So are the prince and Claudio, who accused her
Upon the error that you heard debated.
But Margaret was in some fault for this,
Although against her will, as it appears                    5
In the true course of all the question.°

ANTONIO
Well, I am glad that all things sorts° so well.

BENEDICK
And so am I, being else by faith enforced
To call young Claudio to a reckoning for it.

LEONATO
Well, daughter, and you gentlewomen all,          10
Withdraw into a chamber by yourselves,
And when I send for you, come hither masked.
The prince and Claudio promised by this hour
To visit me. You know your office, brother;
You must be father to your brother's daughter,          15
And give her to young Claudio.          *Exeunt* LADIES.

ANTONIO
Which I will do with confirmed° countenance.

BENEDICK
Friar, I must entreat your pains, I think.

FRIAR
To do what, signior?

BENEDICK
To bind me, or undo me—one of them.          20
Signior Leonato, truth it is, good signior,
Your niece regards me with an eye of favor.

LEONATO
That eye my daughter lent her; 'tis most true.

BENEDICK
And I do with an eye of love requite her.

LEONATO
The sight whereof I think you had from me,          25
From Claudio, and the prince. But what's your will?

BENEDICK
Your answer, sir, is enigmatical.
But, for my will, my will is, your good will
May stand with ours, this day to be conjoined
In the state of honorable marriage;          30
In which, good friar, I shall desire your help.

LEONATO
My heart is with your liking.

FRIAR                                        And my help.
Here comes the prince and Claudio.

*Enter prince* [DON PEDRO] *and* CLAUDIO *and two or*
*three other.*


---

94 **old coil** plenty of confusion
**V.iii.5 guerdon** reward   **12 goddess . . . night** Diana,
goddess of the moon and of chastity   **26 wheels of Phoebus**
wheels of the sun god's chariot   **30 weeds** apparel

**32 Hymen** god of marriage; **speeds** succeeds
**V.iv.6 question** investigation   **7 sorts** turn out   **17 con-**
**firmed** steady

DON PEDRO
Good morrow to this fair assembly.
LEONATO
Good morrow, prince; good morrow, Claudio.    35
We here attend you. Are you yet determined
Today to marry with my brother's daughter?
CLAUDIO
I'll hold my mind, were she an Ethiope.
LEONATO
Call her forth, brother. Here's the friar ready.
                              [*Exit* ANTONIO.]
DON PEDRO
Good morrow, Benedick. Why, what's the matter    40
That you have such a February face,
So full of frost, of storm, and cloudiness?
CLAUDIO
I think he thinks upon the savage bull.°
Tush, fear not, man! We'll tip thy horns with gold,°
And all Europa° shall rejoice at thee,    45
As once Europa did at lusty Jove
When he would play the noble beast in love.
BENEDICK
Bull Jove, sir, had an amiable low,
And some such strange bull leaped your father's cow
And got a calf in that same noble feat    50
Much like to you, for you have just his bleat.

*Enter* [*Leonato's*] *brother* [ANTONIO], HERO, BEATRICE,
MARGARET, URSULA, [*the ladies wearing masks*].

CLAUDIO
For this I owe you.° Here comes other reck'nings.
Which is the lady I must seize upon?
ANTONIO
This same is she, and I do give you her.
CLAUDIO
Why then, she's mine. Sweet, let me see your face.    55
LEONATO
No, that you shall not till you take her hand
Before this friar and swear to marry her.
CLAUDIO
Give me your hand; before this holy friar
I am your husband if you like of me.
HERO
And when I lived I was your other wife; [*unmasking*]    60
And when you loved you were my other husband.
CLAUDIO
Another Hero!
HERO                Nothing certainer.
One Hero died defiled; but I do live,
And surely as I live, I am a maid.
DON PEDRO
The former Hero! Hero that is dead!    65
LEONATO
She died, my lord, but whiles° her slander lived.
FRIAR
All this amazement can I qualify,°
When, after that the holy rites are ended,

I'll tell you largely° of fair Hero's death.
Meantime let wonder seem familiar,    70
And to the chapel let us presently.
BENEDICK
Soft and fair, friar. Which is Beatrice?
BEATRICE [*Unmasking.*]
I answer to that name. What is your will?
BENEDICK
Do not you love me?
BEATRICE                Why, no; no more than reason.
BENEDICK
Why, then your uncle, and the prince, and Claudio    75
Have been deceived—they swore you did.
BEATRICE
Do not you love me?
BENEDICK                Troth, no; no more than reason.
BEATRICE
Why, then my cousin, Margaret, and Ursula
Are much deceived; for they did swear you did.
BENEDICK
They swore that you were almost sick for me.    80
BEATRICE
They swore that you were well-nigh dead for me.
BENEDICK
'Tis no such matter. Then you do not love me?
BEATRICE
No, truly, but in friendly recompense.
LEONATO
Come, cousin, I am sure you love the gentleman.
CLAUDIO
And I'll be sworn upon't that he loves her;    85
For here's a paper written in his hand,
A halting° sonnet of his own pure brain,
Fashioned to Beatrice.
HERO                And here's another,
Writ in my cousin's hand, stol'n from her pocket,
Containing her affection unto Benedick.    90
BENEDICK  A miracle! Here's our own hands against
  our hearts. Come, I will have thee; but, by this light, I
  take thee for pity.
BEATRICE  I would not deny you; but, by this good
  day, I yield upon great persuasion, and partly to save    95
  your life, for I was told you were in a consumption.
BENEDICK°  Peace! I will stop your mouth.

[*Kisses her.*]

DON PEDRO  How dost thou, Benedick, the married
  man?
BENEDICK  I'll tell thee what, prince: a college of    100
  witcrackers cannot flout me out of my humor. Dost
  thou think I care for a satire or an epigram? No. If a
  man will be beaten with brains, 'a shall wear nothing
  handsome about him. In brief, since I do purpose to
  marry, I will think nothing to any purpose that the    105
  world can say against it; and therefore never flout at
  me for what I have said against it; for man is a giddy
  thing, and this is my conclusion. For thy part, Claudio,
  I did think to have beaten thee; but in that thou art

43 savage bull refers to I.i.254    44 tip . . . gold make your
cuckolding something to be proud of    45 Europa Europe
(though in the next line the word designates the girl that
Jupiter wooed in the guise of a bull)    52 I owe you I will pay
you back (for calling me a calf and a bastard)    66 but whiles
only while    67 qualify abate

69 largely in detail    87 halting limping    97 Benedick
both quarto and Folio assign this line to Leonato; possibly
the original reading is correct, and Leonato forces Benedick
to kiss Beatrice

like to be my kinsman, live unbruised, and love my 110
cousin.

CLAUDIO  I had well hoped thou wouldst have denied
Beatrice, that I might have cudgeled thee out of thy
single life, to make thee a double-dealer,° which out
of question thou wilt be if my cousin do not look 115
exceeding narrowly to thee.

BENEDICK  Come, come, we are friends. Let's have a
dance ere we are married, that we may lighten our
own hearts and our wives' heels.

LEONATO  We'll have dancing afterward.                    120

BENEDICK  First, of my word; therefore play, music.

Prince, thou art sad; get thee a wife, get thee a wife!
There is no staff more reverend than one tipped with
horn.°

*Enter* MESSENGER.

MESSENGER
My lord, your brother John is ta'en in flight,            125
And brought with armèd men back to Messina.

BENEDICK  Think not on him till tomorrow. I'll
devise thee brave punishments for him. Strike up,
pipers!

*Dance.*                                        [*Exeunt.*]

114 **double-dealer** (1) married man (2) unfaithful husband

123–24 **with horn** final reference to the horns of a cuckold

# THE LIFE OF
# HENRY THE FIFTH

### EDITED BY JOHN RUSSELL BROWN

## Introduction

In the theater *The Life of Henry the Fifth* is renowned for pageantry, battles, and crowd scenes, its varied collection of minor characters, and the unquestioned dominance of its hero. After Shakespeare's day it first became popular as the theaters began to use ambitious stage settings and more elaborate stage management. Shakespeare's play was embellished in 1761 by a coronation scene, and in 1839 with a moving "diorama"—an extensive panoramic view which moved across the back of the stage—that depicted the journey from Southampton to Harfleur. In recent years it has been performed in battle-dress against film sequences showing twentieth-century warfare or, as at Stratford-upon-Avon in 1964, with painstaking realism of gunsmoke and bloody shattered bodies. (Sir Laurence Olivier made it the subject of a film.) For actors the play has always been hard work, with many changes of costume as pageantry is displaced by mobilization and then by warfare and hardship; and then there is another switch back to pageantry. But rewards are there, too, in the great number of parts that Shakespeare has individually realized for two or three episodes, or even a single scene: Mistress Quickly, Bardolph, Nym, the boy; William and Bates—or even a strangely effective gentleness in the one-line part of Court; Jamy, Gower, MacMorris; the dauphin, Princess Katherine, the King of France, Montjoy, Burgundy. Press criticisms show that *Henry V* is the minor actor's opportunity; a boy or Mistress Quickly, a princess or Burgundy can steal a large part of the notice.

Yet it also has an undoubted hero. For other history plays, the leading actor in a company might play the Bastard rather than King John, Falstaff or Hotspur rather than Prince Hal or Henry IV—even Bolingbroke in preference to Richard II. But here Fluellen and Pistol are the most considerable rivals to the hero, and neither is effectively present in more than six or seven scenes, or has more than incidental contact with the king.

Written in 1599, a year or so before *Hamlet*, *Henry V* was Shakespeare's last history play for ten years or more, and he appears to have taken no risks. Despite its crowd scenes and wide range of characters, it has a simple plot of wars, a battle, and a peace, centered on its undoubted hero. A Chorus, before each act, encourages the audience's warmest responses, and invites its imagination to see two mighty monarchies and to follow Harry as a type of virtue, "the mirror of all Christian kings" (II.Cho.6). For most of the play, the king appears publicly, in ceremonial consultation or address, or as leader of his army; his words are well-ordered, and clearly and fully understood. When he surprises the French ambassador with defiance or the three traitors with a knowledge of their crimes, the audience has been prepared in advance so that its understanding suffers no shock. The minor characters are all dependent on Harry and yet make only occasional appearances in unconsecutive scenes, usually without the hero, so that the independent plot-interest they awaken is both small and quickly answered. Except for the French royal house, none already established has a place in the last long scene; but two entirely new characters are then introduced to eminence, Isabel and the Duke of Burgundy. The play's structure is firmly centered; its setting splendid, varied, broad. In its sweeping, general impression, and usually in performance, *Henry V* is a popular pageant play of the "star of England," and incidentally of his people and his victories.

But this view of Shakespeare's achievement will not satisfy many critics and scholars who have studied the play and resisted the confident tone of the Chorus. They can see it as a routine and unwieldy continuation of other histories, without the imaginative argumentation or consistency of earlier plays. Or, especially if they concentrate attention on the words of the hero, they can read it as a careful investigation of the human failings of a politician. (E. M. W. Tillyard's *Shakespeare's History Plays* and Honor Matthews' treatment of the play in her *Character and Symbol in Shakespeare's Plays* are eloquent spokesmen for these opposing views.) In the theater, too, the play can seem merely routine, especially in association with Shakespeare's other histories. When acted at Stratford-upon-Avon in 1951, as the fourth of a continuous series of plays, from *Richard II* and the two parts of *Henry IV*, it seemed something of an appendix. The stage designer was led to elaborate the single setting that had served for the other three plays with flags, drapes, and properties. The official book on the season speaks of the play in these terms:

By the time we reach *Henry V* the particular interest of the "presentation in cycle" is all but over.

When *Henry V* was performed at the same theater in 1964 in a longer series after the two parts of *Henry IV* and before *Richard III* and the three parts of *Henry VI*, its Harry ("the mirror of all Christian kings") was hailed as a plain man's king, a pacifist warrior, or, fashionably, a self-questioning antihero. Shakespeare's ground plan for the hero-centered pageant narrative can sustain very different edifices.

Indeed, in many small details of the play's structure Shakespeare seems to be guarding against too broad or relaxed a reception of the play. The comedy is carefully restricted, its incidents being short-lived and its characters severely limited in sensibility—that is, in vocabulary and ideas. And on the other hand, Shakespeare used contrasts between consecutive scenes to sharpen the audience's appreciation: so Harry's "Once more unto the breach, dear friends . . .," confident that there is none "so mean and base" that has not a "noble luster" in his eyes (III.i.1 ff.), is followed by Bardolph's mimicry and by thoughts of "a pot of ale, and safety" (III.ii.1–13); such "friends" have to be driven to the breach by Fluellen calling them "dogs" and "cullions." The broad expanse of the stage-picture has no dark shadows in which attention can dwell and no individual issues on which it can concentrate; but, cunningly, its lines are kept sharp and agile. In particular Shakespeare has ensured by small details that the central figure can arouse the keenest perceptions. The duologue of two bishops that prepares the audience for Harry's first appearance presents two differing qualities in the man without suggesting conflict: his "grace," or "celestial spirits," and his "policy" that makes even God's ministers circumspect toward him. His own early speeches easily command the responses he wishes from those presented with him, thus suggesting a superior awareness not fully explicit in his words; and for all their verbal control, they are fired by a wide range of ideas, thus hinting at a varied awareness stretching beyond the immediate context. His reply to the French ambassador (I.ii.259 ff.), for instance, gives jest for jest, mentions his "wilder days" with equal firmness as his present "majesty," and moves lightly from his own will ("I will keep my state . . . When I do rouse me . . . But I will rise there . . . I will dazzle") to the will of God ("But this lies all within the will of God . . . in whose name . . ."). These last transitions may also cause some of the audience to see Harry as a limited figure, apparently unaware of the size of the assumptions he makes; and so may the manner in which he speaks of widows, curses, and tears with no slackened pace or tender epithet. Yet these incipient inquiries are never made a dramatic issue by presenting alternative courses, or by criticism of Harry on stage, or by a hint of his private thoughts, such as Shakespeare had already achieved for Prince Hal or Henry IV and was to develop so fully in *Julius Caesar* and *Hamlet*, written one or two years later. The Chorus is at hand to keep the picture fully animated and expectation forward, with:

Now all the youth of England are on fire,
And silken dalliance in the wardrobe lies. (II.Cho.1–2)

So the predominant focus is maintained, a wide view of a pageant narrative.

But even the first act is not superficial. Because Shakespeare has not sharpened the focus by his usual devices as he could so effectively have done, this needs to be especially noticed. The audience's appreciation is quickened without bringing the hero closely and intimately to its attention; there is no soliloquy, no aside, no self-conscious or nervous speech, no sudden, unprepared exit or utterance or transition of mood. The audience's view is centered on Harry and its perception is acute, but Harry is always the central figure of a group, and the audience knows him in the same kind of terms as it knows the other characters.

The second act, like the first, gives no occasion for an intense focus on Harry, but Shakespeare has ensured still greater clarity, and more deeply questioning responses. Among the noisy quarrels of Pistol and his fellows comes news that Falstaff is sick and broken in heart after Harry has banished him; and this, in turn, is followed by the contrasting affirmation, "The king is a good king . . . it must be as it may. . . . lambkins, we will live"; here the audience cannot give one simple emotional response. Then Harry in public discloses the treachery of three friends, elaborating formally on the evil hearts under their apparent goodness:

thy fall hath left a kind of blot
To mark the full-fraught man and best indued
With some suspicion. (II.ii.138–40)

The audience is being made aware that the wide scene can be viewed in more than one way. Harry himself may be moved, for before pronouncing judgment he speaks a short sentence:

I will weep for thee;
For this revolt of thine, methinks, is like
Another fall of man. (II.ii.140–42)

This is not a clear intensification of the focus in a deeply revealing soliloquy, for the words are spoken formally for all to hear; but it makes sure that any questioning aroused by this incident may touch Harry as well as others. Then he concludes the scene securely, with a final conciseness that is habitual to him:

Let us deliver
Our puissance into the hand of God,
Putting it straight in expedition.
Cheerly to sea; the signs of war advance:
No king of England, if not King of France! (II.ii.189–93)

But now even this does not remain simple: Harry's confident committal into the "hand of God" is followed by the Hostess' reflective account of Falstaff fumbling with the sheets and playing with flowers, and crying out, "God, God, God." three or four times:

Now I, to comfort him, bid him 'a should not think of God; I hoped there was no need to trouble himself with any such thoughts yet. So 'a bade me lay more clothes on his feet. (II.iii.19–23)

Harry went to France asserting that he went hand in hand with God; Falstaff is said to have gone "away and it had been any christom child"; and then Pistol leaves to follow the king:

> Let us to France, like horse-leeches, my boys,
> To suck, to suck, the very blood to suck! (II.iii.55-56)

Contrasts sharpen the wide view; and some of the audience, if they stopped to consider, would think they knew more of the overall issues than any one of the dramatis personae.

Bickering at the French court, differences among Harry's soldiers, the charm, absurdity and prim bawdiness of the French Princess learning English, all may cause the audience to question, in a general way, the motives and comprehension of the characters. And Harry's invocation of the "fleshed soldier, rough and hard of heart . . . With conscience wide as hell" as a threat to Harfleur (III.iii.1–43), may heighten its sense of what is involved and cause it to question Harry's attitude to the brutality he is prepared to encourage. Then, as the battle of Agincourt approaches, his reply to Montjoy, the French herald, shows all his earlier resource—vaunting wit, pride, modest self-blame, confidence in God, unhesitating threat of carnage, concise utterance. Expectation for the crisis of the action is heightened and wide, but in a new manner "objective" or watchful. The audience has seen more aspects of each figure in the picture than those figures seem to have seen themselves.

Yet the battle is prepared for in leisurely manner. The Chorus describes its setting with careful artistry, as in the multiple epithets of "cripple tardy-gaited night," or the Spenserian prettiness of "paly flames." Then Harry, disguised in a great cloak, wanders alone, meeting his various soldiers. He is no longer attended as a king, and speaking as a man in isolation he comes closer to the audience. Two very brief soliloquies are his first in the play. Then, talking to Williams, a tendentious, "ordinary" soldier, he considers the responsibility for life and death and deeds in a new vein:

> some (peradventure) have on them the guilt of premed-
> itated and contrived murder; some, of beguiling virgins
> . . .; some, making the wars their bulwark, that have
> before gored the gentle bosom of peace with pillage and
> robbery. Now, if these men have defeated the law and
> outrun native punishment, though they can outstrip men,
> they have no wings to fly from God. (IV.i.161–68)

This is the voice of Hamlet:

> That skull had a tongue in it, and could sing once. How
> the knave jowls it to the ground, as if 'twere Cain's jaw-
> bone, that did the first murder! This might be the pate of
> a politician, which this ass now o'erreaches, one that would
> circumvent God, might it not? (V.i.75–80)

These thoughts were to stay in Shakespeare's mind as he wrote *Macbeth*, five or six years later:

> Faith, here's an equivocator, that could swear in both the
> scales against either scale; who committed treason enough
> for God's sake, yet could not equivocate to heaven.
> (II.iii.8–11)

Despite its length, Harry's meditative, elaborating prose has the conviction to keep Williams silent until its conclusion, when his only comment is simple agreement. For the audience, the unusual lack of concision, meter, and pace gives Harry a new voice, helping to realize the new range of his thought and feeling which may well embody some of their own incipient comments on the action. As the soldiers move off and Harry is alone, the dramatic focus will be, for the first time, potentially intense and deep. There follows a questioning, yet formal consideration of the cares of kingship, and a lyrical, yet still formal, consideration of a peasant's laboring life. This is yet another aspect of Harry's response, but he seems to shape his thoughts consciously and concludes as if presenting another concise summing-up in public. When Erpingham enters to call him to battle, the widest view seems about to be reestablished. But this valued messenger is sent away and Harry falls on his knees and prays: "O God of battles, steel my soldiers' hearts" (IV.i.289). He knows their weakness:

> Possess them not with fear! Take from them now
> The sense of reck'ning, or th' opposèd numbers
> Pluck their hearts from them. (IV.i.290–92)

Then he speaks of himself, urgently, repetitively, impulsively. He mentions precisely a fear which hitherto has not been made an issue anywhere on the surface of the drama:

>                         Not today, O Lord,
> O, not today, think not upon the fault
> My father made in compassing the crown!
> I Richard's body have interrèd new,
> And on it have bestowed more contrite tears
> Than from it issued forcèd drops of blood.
> Five hundred poor I have in yearly pay. (IV.i.292–98)

The expression of purpose—"to pardon blood"—is emphasized by word order and by meter, and twice the lines break before their end, to give urgency and weight to a new idea:

> Five hundred poor I have in yearly pay,
> Who twice a day their withered hands hold up
> Toward heaven, to pardon blood;
> And I have built two chantries,
> Where the sad and solemn priests sing still
> For Richard's soul. More will I do:
> Though all that I can do is nothing worth;
> Since that my penitence comes after all,
> Imploring pardon. (IV.i.298–306)

There is a half-line pause, then Gloucester enters and Harry is once more the leader, assured and ready:

> GLOUCESTER  My liege!
> KING
>   My brother Gloucester's voice? Ay.
>   I know thy errand; I will go with thee.
>   The day, my friends, and all things stay for me.
> (IV.i.307–10)

This sequence has shown Harry as king, son, and man, conscious of his responsibility and that of other men in war as in peace, and acknowledging a fear within himself, an awareness that, though he may outstrip the judgment of men, he has "no wings to fly from God." As he prepares for battle a short moment of intense focus has revealed his inmost secrets, and his knowledge that no human help can redress the past.

It is possible to read Harry's prayer as another calculated maneuver—to judge, with Una Ellis-Fermor in her *Frontiers of Drama*, that:

> when he prays, . . . he is more than ever in the council chamber driving an astute bargain, a piece of shrewd diplomacy, between one king and another.

But this is to disregard the newly urgent style of utterance, and the considerable preparation for this moment. Harry had perhaps wept for the traitors as they reminded him that a "full-fraught" man may be suspected. He had earnestly commanded the archbishop to justify his title to the French crown with

> conscience washed
> As pure as sin with baptism.          (I.ii.31–32)

Moreover, the need for an honest heart and Harry's equal responsibility with all men are taken up in the following scenes in ways which can betray to the audience's intensified interest his deep concern with these issues.

His address to the soldiers before battle is not a spurring on of others, in the vein of "Once more unto the breach, dear friends, once more." Compared with that conjuring up of the blood before Harfleur, it is thoughtful:

> if it be a sin to covet honor,
> I am the most offending soul alive.          (IV.iii.28–29)

Because it is their feast day, he remembers the two noble brothers, Crispin and Crispian, who during the Roman persecution served as shoemakers yet were still martyred for their obvious Christianity; and they become an image for his men in battle:

> We few, we happy few, we band of brothers;
> For he today that sheds his blood with me
> Shall be my brother; be he ne'er so vile,
> This day shall gentle his condition.          (IV.iii.60–63)

Harry covets honor in his heart and would have his soldiers do so with him; and this is his battle cry. In fight he is still valiant, gay almost with hardiness, angry, ruthless, efficient. He is again the Harry of the first three acts, ready in anger to kill all his prisoners. But afterward there are further reminders of his inward knowledge and need. Perhaps the repeated insistence with which he gives all credit to God is one. Certainly when Fluellen, the robustly confident Welshman, claims brotherhood—

> I am your majesty's countryman, I care not who know it!
> . . . I need not to be ashamed of your majesty, praised be God, so long as your majesty is an honest man—
>                                              (IV.vii.110–13)

Harry answers directly and simply, "God keep me so" —that is, an "honest man"—and only then turns to public, urgent matters. Later, when Williams excuses his quarrel, his words must strike the monarch more deeply than the puzzled soldier could guess:

> All offenses, my lord, come from the heart: never came any from mine that might offend your majesty.
>                                              (IV.viii.46–48)

Some of the audience, at least, will remember that this king has recognized an "offending" heart within himself. (As Shakespeare directed Harry to listen to Williams after battle, the seed for the Epilogue to *The Tempest* may have been in his mind: "As you from crimes would pardoned be,/Let your indulgence set me free.")

In that *Henry V* has a central scene of intense focus that shows the king acknowledging his guilt, it is obviously indebted to *2 Henry IV*. But Shakespeare has modified his purpose and his technique. Harry does not win peace like his father, only a recognition of the need for pardon; moreover, he remains a figure in the center of others. In this play, the predominantly wide view is reestablished and the audience's inward knowledge of Harry's personal crisis is used to deepen the view of the whole scene, and of the many other characters to whom, unlike Henry IV, this king is dramatically related. Williams, Fluellen, Montjoy, and the soldiers are only the first to reenter the picture; the whole fifth act sustains and develops this experience.

It begins with the ludicrous unmasking of the braggart, Pistol, who is forced to eat Fluellen's leek. This is more than a comic counterpart to heroism, for he is left alone onstage and in a direct and immediate soliloquy he may briefly provoke empathetic sympathy:

> Old I do wax, and from my weary limbs
> Honor is cudgeled.          (V.i.85–86)

The moment is passed as he gathers confidence and decides to return to England to cheat and steal. And the audience's view is fully extended as the kings of France and England and their nobility fill the stage for the final scene in quiet and formal meeting. In a long, deliberate speech, the peace-maker, the Duke of Burgundy, describes France ravaged by war and a generation of her sons growing

> like savages—as soldiers will,
> That nothing do but meditate on blood.          (V.ii.59–60)

The whole play, its action and consequences, passes in general review, seen this time with French eyes—or rather with a timeless concern with the arts and sciences of peace, and with natural affections. This new perspective is generalized, but as the two parties leave the stage to debate the terms of peace, Harry remains with Katherine, Princess of France, and her maid: here the dramatic interest is as narrow as before Agincourt. As Harry woos his bride, he speaks sometimes as if in soliloquy, for she cannot understand all he says. It is a complex scene: clearly this is to be a political, but also a personally felt, marriage; clearly Harry offers himself as a simple man, but he does so with wit and eloquence; clearly he is confident and a conqueror, but he is also suitor. And as he warms to his theme he speaks again, directly and with immediacy, of a "good heart":

> a good leg will fall, a straight back will stoop, a black beard will turn white, a curled pate will grow bald, a fair face will wither, a full eye will wax hollow: but a good heart, Kate, is the sun and the moon, or rather, the sun, and not the moon, for it shines bright and never changes, but keeps his course truly. (V.ii.161–67)

Katherine questions, "Is it possible dat I sould love de ennemie of France?" And he can answer only with a riddle:

> No, it is not possible . . . but in loving me you should love the friend of France: for I love France so well, that I will not part with a village of it—I will have it all mine. And, Kate, when France is mine and I am yours, then yours is France, and you are mine. (V.ii.173–78)

He gets the deserved response: "I cannot tell wat is dat," and the plain soldier is forced to attempt "false French." Yet now they speak more freely, and as Harry's blood "begins to flatter" him that he is loved, he speaks lightly of his father's ambition, which had held him in prayer before battle:

> Now beshrew my father's ambition! He was thinking of civil wars when he got me, therefore was I created with a stubborn outside, with an aspect of iron, that when I come to woo ladies, I fright them. (V.ii.227–30)

Too much should not be made of this reference; it shows a relaxation of mind, not a conscious change of attitude. Soon, against the "custom" of France, they kiss, and are silent together. And then, gently and with an intimate, relaxing jest, Harry acknowledges what has been given and taken, and understood without words:

> You have witchcraft in your lips, Kate: there is more eloquence in a sugar touch of them than in the tongues of the French council . . . . (V.ii.279–81)

The stage fills again, the relaxed mood being sustained by Burgundy's heavy teasing of the bridegroom. The latter still insists on receiving the cities of the bride's dowry and the title of Inheritor of France, but with a general "Amen," the contesting sides stand solemnly side by side in agreement. As the focus thus widens fully again, and steadies, there is another silence as Harry kisses Kate before them all, as his "sovereign queen." But the view is also acute and questioning. Shakespeare has not attempted to show a love match, or a union in which the audience may be easily confident; and now the bride's mother reminds them frankly of

> fell jealousy,
> Which troubles oft the bed of blessed marriage.
> (V.ii.363–64)

The long wooing scene—far more elaborate than at first seems to be required by the dramatic context—serves to show afresh and with an intermittent intensity the need for an honest heart, and the danger and embarrassment of relying on words alone; and, in the kiss, it suggests an inward understanding, peace, affection, unity, that is a greater solvent, a more powerful reorganizing power,

than words or battles: the silence of the kiss is a shared silence in which the audience instinctively participates.

Representatives of two societies take up, with remembrances of past action and hopes and prayers for the future, their final positions of concord; and Harry, speaking formally within the wide picture, closes the play with a further pointer to the heart of all matters:

> we'll take your oath,
> And all the peers', for surety of our leagues.
> Then shall I swear to Kate, and you to me,
> *And may our oaths well kept and prosp'rous be!*[1]
> (V.ii.371–74)

Shakespeare has finished his long series of history plays by presenting a group of people standing together: behind appearances and oaths there is need for an "honest heart"; within the wide range, the audience is invited to search for signs of inward peace, good faith, affection, trust, of that which "never changes, but keeps his course truly." When the stage empties and the Chorus announces the end of the action, he also speaks of later times when all France was lost and England bled again. If this play has received its intended "acceptance," it will not be destructive or irrelevant to remind the audience that the final, peaceful grouping was neither fully honest nor fully permanent.

*Henry V* is a hero-centered historical pageant that presents a clear narrative and varied characters. In that respect it differs from Shakespeare's earlier histories, with their concern with political necessity or "commodity," with rebellion, power, and conscience, and with God's providence. But it was not an easy, or routine, declension from a more serious drama. The play tries to relate the personal, instinctive, and affectionate truth of human relationships, exemplified in the acceptance of Kate and Harry, with warfare, politics, and national rivalries; and it has effected this in the wide range of characters that is such an important aid to the full acceptance of this play. Mistress Quickly's account of Falstaff's death, Fluellen's incongruous loyalty and familiarity with his king, Williams' defense of his honest heart, Pistol's recognition of the end of his campaign, and Kate and Harry's kiss, all represent the necessary element of human understanding, as eloquent as Burgundy's general evocation of the virtues of peace. The audience's involvement in these moments is of a different nature from its involvement in the narrative of war and politics, and is of pervasive, because unthinking, importance in the reception of the play as a whole.

## A NOTE ON THE SOURCES

Shakespeare's main source for this play was Holinshed's *Chronicles.* He simplified the king's continual wars in France by concentrating on the siege of Harfleur, the battle of Agincourt, and the Treaty of Troyes; in his play the successful negotiations for peace immediately follow victory, without the abortive discussions and further years of fighting recounted by Holinshed. Shakespeare also omitted all but one early reference to the Scots and every incident concerned with the dissenting Lollards in England and the execution of Sir John Oldcastle.

---

[1] Editor's italics.

In this source Shakespeare found no doubt expressed about the greatness of Henry V: the character sketch included in the account of his death speaks, in terms similar to the Chorus of the play, of "a pattern in princehood, a lodestar in honor, and mirror of magnificence," and marginal notes highlight his various wise decisions and valiant acts. Yet at the same time the terrible effects of Henry's wars are considered by Holinshed with sympathy for their victims, and something of Shakespeare's complexity of view may have been suggested by the chronicler; accounts of the sieges of Harfleur and Rouen and comments on the killing of prisoners are particularly relevant here. The Duke of Burgundy's affecting introduction to the peace talks at the beginning of V.ii may owe something to Holinshed's account of French opinion after Agincourt. Henry's prayer for pardon, which details his penance for his father's "fault . . . in compassing the crown" (IV.i.293 ff.), obviously owes something to Holinshed's description of Richard II's burial at the beginning of the reign and possibly to his comment on the Earl of Cambridge; Holinshed, like Shakespeare, recognized the weakness of Henry's claim to the English throne while showing that he claimed the French in the name of justice and right.

A further source for the play was the anonymous history play, *The Famous Victories of Henry the Fifth*, published in 1598. Some resemblances may well be accidental, but the handling of the English claims to the French crown, the tennis ball challenge, the Treaty of Troyes, and the royal wooing suggests a direct indebtedness. Some of Pistol's episodes may derive from low comedy scenes in *The Famous Victories*.

Even while following Holinshed in story and occasionally in words, Shakespeare also referred to Hall's *The Union of the Noble and Illustre Famelies of Lancastre and York* (1542). This earlier version of the chronicle seems to have influenced the first act especially, and perhaps Exeter's speech on the calamities of war in II.iv and the French view of the English in III.v and III.vii.

For various small details in the narrative and for discussions of military discipline and the rights of war and government, Shakespeare echoed numerous Elizabethan books. Among these are John Lyly's *Euphues and his England* (1580) for the archbishop's account of the kingdom of the bees in I.ii, Tacitus' *Annals* (translated 1598) for Henry's talk with the common soldiers before battle, and *A Brief Discourse of War* (1590) written by the Welsh knight Sir Roger Williams for some parts of Fluellen's disquisitions.

### A NOTE ON THE TEXT

The first edition of *Henry V* was a quarto published in 1600 with a title page reading:

THE
CRONICLE
History of Henry the fift,
With his battell fought at *Agin Court* in
*France*. Togither with *Auntient
Pistoll*.

*As it hath bene sundry times playd by the Right honorable the Lord Chamberlaine his seruants.*

This was a shortened version and a "bad" text; probably some actors had pieced together their own text, which was subsequently cut and rearranged a little for the convenience of a touring company.

Two more quarto editions followed in 1602 and 1619 (its title page, however, being dated 1608); both were reprints from the first edition.

The first, and only, authoritative edition appeared in the collected folio of Shakespeare's *Comedies, Histories, and Tragedies* that was published in 1623. Spellings, punctuation, variations in nomenclature, and the nature of some of the stage directions and of some of the errors all suggest that this was printed either from Shakespeare's autograph working-manuscript (or "foul papers" as bibliographers usually term this, despite its general clarity and uniformity), or else from a good copy of Shakespeare's manuscript. A few directions for noises and a duplicate entry suggest that the manuscript may have been annotated lightly by a bookkeeper (or stage manager).

This Folio text is divided into five unequal acts by the occurrence of entries for the Chorus to speak appropriate prologues, but another division, running the first two acts together and dividing Act IV into two after its sixth scene, is marked with act headings. Both arrangements involve difficulties: that of the printed headings disregards the Chorus' prologues that clearly belong to the original composition of the play; that of the Chorus suggests that the play was partly rewritten at some stage of composition. This rewriting must have involved the early Pistol and Mrs. Quickly episodes: the Chorus before Act II announces that the scene

Is now transported, gentles, to Southampton.
There is the playhouse now, there must you sit,
And thence to France . . . . (II.Cho.35–37)

but in II.i the scene is still London, in Eastcheap, and then, after one scene at Southampton, II.iii is again London for the account of Falstaff's death. These confusions are partly covered up by the concluding lines to II.Cho.:

But, till the king come forth, and not till then,
Unto Southampton do we shift our scene.

Probably II.i and II.iii were both invented and inserted after the composition of the first two acts had been completed, or nearly completed, in a form that is now lost. If so, it seems likely that Shakespeare began the play intending to fulfill his promise in the Epilogue to *2 Henry IV*, and take Falstaff to France—and that he then decided to omit Falstaff and so had to effect some cutting, rewriting, and patching. Such a decision may have affected later parts of the play as well: some editors believe that Pistol has inherited some of the business originally designed for Falstaff (but not his idiom); others that Henry's talk with Pistol and the soldiers before Agincourt is a late addition. There can, of course, be no certain knowledge of such processes of composition; what is undoubted is that the Folio text is a good, authoritative version of the play as Shakespeare wrote or rewrote it.

Obviously the Folio must be the basis for any modern text. This edition reproduces it wherever possible, modernizing spelling, and altering punctuation and verse lineations where the editor's sense of literary and dramatic fitness dictated. Abbreviations have been expanded and speech prefixes regularized. Stage directions have been amplified where necessary, such additions being printed within brackets. Obvious typographical errors have been corrected and eccentric spellings regularized where appropriate without notice, but all significant emendations are noted below. In this list the adopted reading is given in boldface type and is followed by the rejected Folio reading in roman or a note of the Folio's omission within brackets. If the adopted reading occurs in the first quarto edition it is followed by "Q" within brackets.

**I.ii.74 heir** [Q] th'Heire  **131 blood** Bloods  **163 her** their  **197 majesty** [Q] Maiesties  **212 End** [Q] And
**II.i.24 mare** name  **43, 44 Iceland** Island  **74 thee defy** [Q] defie thee  **81 enough** [Q] enough to  **106–07 Nym. I shall . . . betting?** [Q; F omits]  **117 that's** that  **119 Ah** A
**II.ii.87 him with** with  **107 a** an  **139 mark the** make thee  **147 Henry** [Q] Thomas  **159 I** in  **176 have sought** [Q] sought  **181 s.d. Exeunt** Exit
**II.iii.17 'a babbled** a Table  **25 so upward** [Q] so vp-peer'd  **49 word** [Q] world
**II.iv.107 pining** [Q] priuy
**III.Cho.4 Hampton** Douer  **6 fanning** fayning
**III.i.7 conjure** commune  **17 noble** Noblish  **24 men** me  **32 Straining** Straying
**III.iii.32 heady** headly  **35 Defile** Desire
**III.iv.1 été** este  **1–2 parles bien** bien parlas  **8–13 Et les doigts . . . écolier** [F assigns "Et les doigts" to Alice, lines 9–11 to Katherine, and "La main . . . écolier" (in lines 12–13) to Alice]  **10

**souviendrai** souemeray  **16 Nous** [F omits]  **41 pas déjà** y desia  **43 Non** Nome  **47 Sauf** Sans
**III.v.11 Dieu** du  **45 Foix** Loys  **46 knights** Kings
**III.vi.31 her** [Q] his  **103 o' fire** a fire  **112 lenity** [Q] Leuitie
**III.vii.12 pasterns** postures  **13 Ça, ha!** ch' ha:  **61 lief** liue  **67 et la truie** est la leuye
**IV.Cho.27 Presenteth** Presented
**IV.i.3 Good** God  **35 Qui va là?** Che vous la?  **94 Thomas** Iohn  **179 mote** Moth  **229 s.d. Exeunt Soldiers** Exit Souldiers [after line 229]  **245 What** What?;  **adoration** Odoration  **291 or** of  **310 friends** [Q] friend
**IV.ii.2 Montez à** Monte;  **Varlet** Verlot  **5 eaux et la terre** ewes & terre  **6 le feu** feu  **7 Ciel** Cein  **26 'gainst** against  **50 gimmaled** Iymold
**IV.iii.13–14 Exeter. And yet . . . valor** [F gives after lines 11 and 12, spoken by Bedford]  **26 earns** yernes  **48 And say . . . Crispin's day.** [Q; F omits]  **105 grazing** crazing
**IV.iv.15 Or** for  **36 à cette heure** asture  **37 couper** couppes  **54 l'avez promis** layt a promets  **57 remercîments** remercious  **57–58 suis tombé** intombe  **59 distingué** distinie  **67 Suivez** Saaue
**IV.v.2–3 perdu . . . perdu** perdia . . . perdie  **4 Mort** Mor  **13 in honor** in  **17 by a** [Q] a base
**IV.vi.34 mistful** mixtfull
**IV.vii.16 great** grear  **77 their** with  **109 countryman** [Q] countrymen  **114 God** [Q] Good
**IV.viii.44 martial** Marshall  **112 we** me
**V.i.72 begun** began  **83 Of** of a  **90 swear** swore
**V.ii.12 England** Ireland  **50 all** withall  **72 tenors** Tenures  **77 cursitory** curselarie  **93 Haply** Happily  **118 pleines** plein  **191 est meilleur** & melieus  **256 abaissiez** abbaisse  **257 d'une de votre** d'une nostre  **262 baisées** baisee;  **coutume** costume  **266 baiser** buisse  **324 never ent'red** entred  **365 paction** Pation

# THE LIFE OF

# HENRY THE FIFTH

[Dramatis Personae

CHORUS
KING HENRY THE FIFTH
DUKES OF GLOUCESTER AND BEDFORD *brothers of the king*
DUKE OF EXETER *uncle of the king*
DUKE OF YORK *cousin of the king*
EARLS OF SALISBURY, WESTMORELAND, WARWICK, AND CAMBRIDGE
ARCHBISHOP OF CANTERBURY
BISHOP OF ELY
LORD SCROOP
SIR THOMAS GREY
SIR THOMAS ERPINGHAM
GOWER, FLUELLEN, MACMORRIS, JAMY *officers in the English army*
JOHN BATES, ALEXANDER COURT, MICHAEL WILLIAMS *soldiers in the English army*
PISTOL, NYM, BARDOLPH

BOY
AN ENGLISH HERALD
CHARLES THE SIXTH *King of France*
LEWIS *the dauphin*
DUKES OF BURGUNDY, ORLEANS, BOURBON, BERRI, AND BRETAGNE
CONSTABLE OF FRANCE
RAMBURES AND GRANDPRÉ *French lords*
GOVERNOR OF HARFLEUR
MONTJOY *a French herald*
AMBASSADORS *to King Henry*
ISABEL *Queen of France*
KATHERINE *daughter of the French king and queen*
ALICE *an attendant to Katherine*
HOSTESS QUICKLY *of an Eastcheap tavern, married to Pistol*
LORDS LADIES OFFICERS SOLDIERS CITIZENS MESSENGERS ATTENDANTS

*Scene:* England; France]

*Enter* PROLOGUE.

O for a Muse of fire,° that would ascend
The brightest heaven of invention:°
A kingdom for a stage, princes to act,
And monarchs to behold the swelling° scene!
Then should the warlike Harry, like himself,°  5
Assume the port of Mars,° and at his heels
(Leashed in, like hounds) should famine, sword, and fire
Crouch for employment. But pardon, gentles° all,
The flat unraisèd spirits° that hath dared
On this unworthy scaffold° to bring forth  10
So great an object. Can this cockpit hold
The vasty fields of France? Or may we cram
Within this wooden O° the very casques°
That did affright the air at Agincourt?
O, pardon—since a crooked figure° may  15
Attest in little place a million;
And let us, ciphers° to this great accompt,°

*The decorative border shown above appeared on the title page of the quarto edition of Henry V, 1608.*

**I.Pro.1 fire** (1) most airy (sublime) of the four elements (2) warlike nature (cf. line 6 below and II.Cho.1)  **2 invention** imaginative creation  **4 swelling** stately  **5 like himself** (1) incomparable (2) worthy of himself  **6 port of Mars** bearing of the god of war

**8 gentles** gentlefolk  **9 flat unraisèd spirits** i.e., dull, uninspired actors and playwright  **10 scaffold** stage (technical term)  **13 wooden O** small wooden circle; i.e., the theater of the King's Men (at the first performance, this was probably the curtain); **very casques** helmets, even without the men who wore them  **15 crooked figure** a nought, that could change 100,000 into 1,000,000  **17 ciphers** nothings; **accompt** (1) sum total (2) story

On your imaginary° forces work.
Suppose within the girdle of these walls
Are now confined two mighty monarchies,                              20
Whose high, uprearèd and abutting fronts°
The perilous narrow ocean parts asunder.°
Piece out our imperfections with your thoughts:
Into a thousand parts divide one man
And make imaginary puissance.°                                       25
Think, when we talk of horses, that you see them
Printing their proud° hoofs i' th' receiving earth;
For 'tis your thoughts that now must deck our kings,
Carry them° here and there, jumping o'er times,
Turning th' accomplishment of many years                            30
Into an hourglass; for the which supply,°
Admit me Chorus to this history;
Who, Prologue-like, your humble patience pray,
Gently to hear, kindly to judge our play.        *Exit.*

# ACT I

Scene I. [*London. An antechamber in the king's palace.*]

*Enter the two bishops* [*the Archbishop*] *of* CANTERBURY
*and* [*the Bishop of*] ELY.

CANTERBURY
My lord, I'll tell you, that self° bill is urged
Which in th' eleventh year of the last king's reign°
Was like,° and had indeed against us passed
But that the scambling° and unquiet time
Did push it out of farther question.                                 5
ELY
But how, my lord, shall we resist it now?
CANTERBURY
It must be thought on. If it pass against us,
We lose the better half of our possession;
For all the temporal° lands which men devout
By testament have given to the Church                               10
Would they strip from us; being valued thus—
As much as would maintain, to the king's honor,
Full fifteen earls and fifteen hundred knights,
Six thousand and two hundred good esquires,
And to relief of lazars,° and weak age                              15
Of indigent faint souls, past corporal toil,
A hundred almshouses right well supplied;
And to the coffers of the king beside,
A thousand pounds by th' year. Thus runs the bill.
ELY
This would drink deep.
CANTERBURY             'Twould drink the cup and all.                20
ELY
But what prevention?
CANTERBURY
The king is full of grace and fair regard.°

ELY
And a true lover of the holy Church.
CANTERBURY
The courses of his youth promised it not.
The breath no sooner left his father's body                         25
But that his wildness, mortified° in him,
Seemed to die too; yea, at that very moment
Consideration° like an angel came
And whipped th' offending Adam° out of him,
Leaving his body as a paradise                                      30
T' envelop and contain celestial spirits.
Never was such a sudden scholar made;
Never came reformation in a flood
With such a heady currance° scouring faults;
Nor never Hydra-headed° willfulness                                 35
So soon did lose his seat°—and all at once—
As in this king.
ELY                    We are blessèd in the change.
CANTERBURY
Hear him but reason° in divinity,
And, all-admiring, with an inward wish
You would desire the king were made a prelate;                      40
Hear him debate of commonwealth affairs,
You would say it hath been all in all° his study;
List° his discourse of war, and you shall hear
A fearful battle rend'red you in music;°
Turn him to any cause of policy,°                                   45
The Gordian knot° of it he will unloose,
Familiar as his garter; that when he speaks,
The air, a chartered libertine,° is still,
And the mute wonder° lurketh in men's ears
To steal his sweet and honeyed sentences;°                          50
So that the art and practic part of life
Must be the mistress to this theoric;°
Which is a wonder how his grace° should glean it,
Since his addiction was to courses vain,
His companies° unlettered, rude, and shallow,                       55
His hours filled up with riots, banquets, sports;
And never noted in him any study,
Any retirement, any sequestration
From open haunts and popularity.°
ELY
The strawberry grows underneath the nettle,                         60
And wholesome berries thrive and ripen best
Neighbored by fruit of baser quality;
And so the prince obscured his contemplation°
Under the veil of wildness, which (no doubt)
Grew like the summer grass, fastest by night,                       65
Unseen, yet crescive in his faculty.°

---

18 **imaginary** imaginative   21 **fronts** frontiers   21–22 **high . . . asunder** i.e., the cliffs of Dover and Calais, on opposite sides of the English Channel   25 **puissance** (trisyllabic) armed force   27 **proud** spirited   29 **them** i.e., thoughts (?) kings (?)   31 **for . . . supply** to help you in which
I.i.1 **self** same   2 **eleventh . . . reign** 1410   3 **like** likely (to be passed)   4 **scambling** scuffling, disordered   9 **temporal** secular (as opposed to sacred)   15 **lazars** lepers   22 **regard** repute

26 **mortified** dead (a religious usage)   28 **Consideration** meditation   29 **whipped . . . Adam** drove original sin   34 **heady currance** headlong current   35 **Hydra-headed** Hydra was a mythological beast with nine heads, growing two more for every one cut off   36 **seat** throne   38 **reason** debate   42 **all in all** all things in all respects   43 **List** listen to   44 **rend'red . . . music** recounted with harmonious and stirring eloquence   45 **cause of policy** political problem   46 **Gordian knot** tied by Gordius when chosen King of Gordium; the oracle declared that whoever loosened it would rule Asia; Alexander the Great cut through it with his own sword   48 **chartered libertine** one licensed to go his own way   49 **wonder** wonderer   50 **sentences** sayings   51–52 **art . . . theoric** practice and experience must have taught him theory   53 **grace** majesty (a formal title)   55 **companies** companions   59 **open . . . popularity** public places and familiarity   63 **contemplation** study of life   66 **crescive . . . faculty** growing because that is its nature

CANTERBURY
It must be so, for miracles are ceased;°
And therefore we must needs admit the means°
How things are perfected.

ELY                                    But, my good lord,
How now for mitigation of this bill                            70
Urged by the commons?° Doth his majesty
Incline to it, or no?

CANTERBURY            He seems indifferent;°
Or rather swaying more upon our part
Than cherishing th' exhibiters° against us;
For I have made an offer to his majesty—                       75
Upon our spiritual convocation,°
And in regard of causes° now in hand,
Which I have opened° to his grace at large,
As touching France—to give a greater sum
Than ever at one time the clergy yet                           80
Did to his predecessors part withal.

ELY
How did this offer seem received, my lord?

CANTERBURY
With good acceptance of his majesty;
Save that there was not time enough to hear,
As I perceived his grace would fain have done,                 85
The severals and unhidden passages°
Of his true titles to some certain dukedoms,
And generally to the crown and seat of France,
Derived from Edward, his great-grandfather.

ELY
What was th' impediment that broke this off?                   90

CANTERBURY
The French ambassador upon that instant
Craved audience; and the hour I think is come
To give him hearing. Is it four o'clock?

ELY   It is.

CANTERBURY
Then go we in to know his embassy;                             95
Which I could with a ready guess declare
Before the Frenchman speak a word of it.

ELY
I'll wait upon you, and I long to hear it.        *Exeunt.*


[Scene II. *The presence chamber in the palace.*]

*Enter the* KING, *Humphrey* [*Duke of* GLOUCESTER],
BEDFORD, CLARENCE, WARWICK, WESTMORE-
LAND, *and* EXETER, [*with* ATTENDANTS].

KING
Where is my gracious Lord of Canterbury?

EXETER
Not here in presence.

KING                         Send for him, good uncle.

WESTMORELAND
Shall we call in th' ambassador, my liege?

KING
Not yet, my cousin.° We would be resolved,°
Before we hear him, of some things of weight                    5
That task° our thoughts concerning us and France.

*Enter two bishops* [*the Archbishop of* CANTERBURY *and
the Bishop of* ELY].

CANTERBURY
God and his angels guard your sacred throne,
And make you long become it!

KING                         Sure we thank you.
My learnèd lord, we pray you to proceed,
And justly and religiously unfold                              10
Why the Law Salique, that they have in France,
Or should or° should not bar us in our claim.
And God forbid, my dear and faithful lord,
That you should fashion, wrest, or bow your reading,°
Or nicely charge your understanding soul                       15
With opening titles miscreate,° whose right°
Suits not in native colors with the truth;°
For God doth know how many now in health
Shall drop their blood in approbation°
Of what your reverence shall incite us to.                     20
Therefore take heed how you impawn° our person,
How you awake our sleeping sword of war.
We charge you in the name of God, take heed;
For never two such kingdoms did contend
Without much fall of blood, whose guiltless drops              25
Are every one a woe, a sore complaint
'Gainst him whose wrongs° gives edge unto the swords
That makes such waste in brief mortality.
Under this conjuration, speak, my lord:
For we will hear, note, and believe in heart                   30
That what you speak is in your conscience washed
As pure as sin with baptism.

CANTERBURY
Then hear me, gracious sovereign, and you peers,
That owe yourselves, your lives, and services
To this imperial throne. There is no bar                       35
To make° against your highness' claim to France
But this which they produce from Pharamond:°
"In terram Salicam mulieres ne succedant";
"No woman shall succeed in Salique land."
Which Salique land the French unjustly gloze°                  40
To be the realm of France, and Pharamond
The founder of this law and female bar.
Yet their own authors faithfully affirm
That the land Salique is in Germany,
Between the floods of Sala and of Elbe;                        45
Where Charles the Great having subdued the Saxons,
There left behind and settled certain French;
Who, holding in disdain the German women
For some dishonest manners° of their life,
Established then this law: to wit, no female                   50

---

**67 miracles are ceased** Protestants believed miracles ceased to
occur after the revelation of Christ   **68 means** i.e., natural cause
**71 commons** House of Commons in the parliament of England
**72 indifferent** impartial   **74 exhibiters** presenters of the bill
**76 convocation** formal meeting of the clergy   **77 causes**
affairs   **78 opened** revealed   **86 severals . . . passages**
details and clear (obvious) lines of descent

**I.ii.4 cousin** kinsman;  **be resolved** have doubts removed
**6 task** burden   **12 Or . . . or** either . . . or   **14 reading**
interpretation   **15-16 nicely . . . miscreate** by subtle
reasoning lay to the charge of your soul—which knows right
and wrong—the fault of advancing illegitimate claims   **16
right** claim   **17 Suits . . . truth** plainly told would not be
taken as true   **19 approbation** support   **21 impawn** pledge,
hazard   **27 wrongs** wrongdoings   **36 make** i.e., be made
**37 Pharamond** legendary king of Salian Franks   **40 gloze**
interpret   **49 dishonest manners** unchaste conduct

Should be inheritrix in Salique land;
Which Salique (as I said) 'twixt Elbe and Sala
Is at this day in Germany, called Meisen.
Then doth it well appear the Salique Law
Was not devisèd for the realm of France;                             55
Nor did the French possess the Salique land
Until four hundred one and twenty years
After defunction° of King Pharamond,
Idly supposed the founder of this law,
Who died within the year of our redemption                           60
Four hundred twenty-six; and Charles the Great
Subdued the Saxons, and did seat the French
Beyond the river Sala, in the year
Eight hundred five. Besides, their writers say,
King Pepin,° which deposèd Childeric,                                65
Did, as heir general,° being descended
Of Blithild, which was daughter to King Clothair,
Make claim and title to the crown of France.
Hugh Capet also—who usurped the crown
Of Charles the Duke of Lorraine, sole heir male                      70
Of the true line and stock of Charles the Great—
To find° his title with some shows of truth,
Though in pure truth it was corrupt and naught,
Conveyed° himself as heir to th' Lady Lingard,
Daughter to Charlemain,° who was the son                             75
To Lewis the Emperor, and Lewis the son
Of Charles the Great. Also King Lewis the Tenth,°
Who was sole heir to the usurper Capet,
Could not keep quiet in his conscience,
Wearing the crown of France, till satisfied                          80
That fair Queen Isabel, his grandmother,
Was lineal° of the Lady Ermengard,
Daughter to Charles the foresaid Duke of Lorraine;
By the which marriage the line of Charles the
    Great
Was reunited to the crown of France.                                 85
So that, as clear as is the summer's sun,
King Pepin's title and Hugh Capet's claim,
King Lewis his satisfaction,° all appear
To hold in right and title of the female:
So do the kings of France unto this day.                             90
Howbeit they would hold up this Salique Law
To bar your highness claiming from the female,
And rather choose to hide them in a net
Than amply to imbar their crooked titles°
Usurped from you and your progenitors.                               95

KING
May I with right and conscience make this claim?

CANTERBURY
The sin upon my head, dread sovereign!
For in the Book of Numbers is it writ:
When the man dies, let the inheritance
Descend unto the daughter. Gracious lord,                           100
Stand for your own, unwind your bloody flag,
Look back into your mighty ancestors;

Go, my dread lord, to your great-grandsire's° tomb,
From whom you claim; invoke his warlike spirit,
And your great-uncle's, Edward the Black Prince,                    105
Who on the French ground played a tragedy,°
Making defeat on the full power° of France,
Whiles his most mighty father on a hill
Stood smiling, to behold his lion's whelp
Forage in blood of French nobility.                                 110
O noble English, that could entertain
With half their forces° the full pride of France,
And let another half stand laughing by,
All out of work, and cold for° action!

ELY
Awake remembrance of these valiant dead                             115
And with your puissant arm renew their feats.
You are their heir; you sit upon their throne;
The blood and courage that renownèd them
Runs in your veins: and my thrice-puissant° liege
Is in the very May-morn of his youth                                120
Ripe for exploits and mighty enterprises.

EXETER
Your brother kings and monarchs of the earth
Do all expect that you should rouse yourself,
As did the former lions of your blood.

WESTMORELAND
They know your grace hath° cause and means and
    might;                                                          125
So hath your highness. Never king of England
Had nobles richer and more loyal subjects,
Whose hearts have left their bodies here in England
And lie pavilioned in the fields of France.

CANTERBURY
O, let their bodies follow, my dear liege,                          130
With blood, and sword and fire, to win your right!
In aid whereof we of the spirituality
Will raise your highness such a mighty sum
As never did the clergy at one time
Bring in to any of your ancestors.                                  135

KING
We must not only arm t' invade the French,
But lay down our proportions° to defend
Against the Scot, who will make road° upon us
With all advantages.°

CANTERBURY
They of those marches,° gracious sovereign,                         140
Shall be a wall sufficient to defend
Our inland° from the pilfering borderers.

KING
We do not mean the coursing° snatchers only;
But fear the main intendment° of the Scot,
Who hath been still° a giddy neighbor to us;                        145
For you shall read that my great-grandfather
Never went with his forces into France

---

**98 defunction** discharge, death  **65 Pepin** King of Franks  **56 general** through male or female line of descent  **72 find** provide  **74 Conveyed** passed on  **75 Charlemain** Holinshed's error for Charles the Bold  **77 Tenth** Holinshed's error for Ninth  **82 lineal** lineally descended  **88 his satisfaction** see line 80  **93–94 to hide . . . titles** to take refuge in a tangle of sophistical arguments than make the most of (bar in, secure) their own false claims (by admitting female succession)

**103 great-grandsire's** Edward III's (whose mother, Isabella, was daughter of Philip IV of France)  **106 a tragedy** the battle of Crécy (1346)  **107 power** army  **112 half their forces** one third was held in reserve with the king  **114 for** for lack of  **119 thrice-puissant** i.e., for the three reasons just stated  **125 hath** accented  **137 lay . . . proportions** estimate the size of our forces  **138 road** raid  **139 With all advantages** at every favorable opportunity, with everything in their favor  **140 marches** border country  **142 inland** heart of the country  **143 coursing** marauding  **144 main intendment** general purpose  **145 still** always

But that the Scot on his unfurnished° kingdom
Came pouring like the tide into a breach,
With ample and brim fullness of his force,     150
Galling the gleanèd° land with hot assays,
Girding with grievous siege castles and towns;
That England, being empty of defense,
Hath shook and trembled at th' ill neighborhood.°

CANTERBURY
She hath been then more feared° than harmed, my
    liege;     155
For hear her but exampled° by herself:
When all her chivalry hath been in France,
And she a mourning widow of her nobles,
She hath herself not only well defended
But taken and impounded as a stray°     160
The King of Scots;° whom she did send to France
To fill King Edward's fame with prisoner kings,
And make her chronicle as rich with praise
As is the ooze and bottom° of the sea
With sunken wrack° and sumless treasuries.     165

ELY
But there's a saying very old and true—
      "If that you will France win,
      Then with Scotland first begin."
For once the eagle (England) being in prey,°
To her unguarded nest the weasel (Scot)     170
Comes sneaking, and so sucks her princely eggs
(Playing the mouse in absence of the cat)
To tame° and havoc more than she can eat.

EXETER
It follows then, the cat must stay at home;
Yet that is but a crushed° necessity,     175
Since we have locks to safeguard necessaries
And pretty traps to catch the petty thieves.
While that the armèd hand doth fight abroad,
Th' advisèd° head defends itself at home;
For government, though high, and low, and lower,     180
Put into parts,° doth keep in one consent,°
Congreeing° in a full and natural close,°
Like music.

CANTERBURY   Therefore doth heaven divide
The state° of man in divers functions,
Setting endeavor in continual motion;°     185
To which is fixèd, as an aim or butt,
Obedience; for so work the honeybees,
Creatures that by a rule in nature° teach
The act° of order to a peopled kingdom.
They have a king, and officers of sorts,°     190
Where some like magistrates correct° at home,
Others like merchants venture trade abroad,

Others like soldiers armèd in their stings
Make boot upon° the summer's velvet buds,
Which pillage they with merry march bring home     195
To the tent-royal of their emperor—
Who, busied in his majesty, surveys
The singing masons building roofs of gold,
The civil citizens kneading up the honey,
The poor mechanic° porters crowding in     200
Their heavy burdens at his narrow gate,
The sad-eyed justice, with his surly° hum,
Delivering o'er to executors° pale
The lazy yawning drone. I this infer,°
That many things, having full reference°     205
To one consent, may work contrariously;
As many arrows loosèd several ways°
Come to one mark, as many ways meet in one town,
As many fresh streams meet in one salt sea,
As many lines close in the dial's center,     210
So may a thousand actions, once afoot,
End in one purpose, and be all well borne°
Without defeat. Therefore to France, my liege!
Divide your happy England into four,
Whereof take you one quarter into France,     215
And you withal shall make all Gallia shake.
If we, with thrice such powers left at home,
Cannot defend our own doors from the dog,
Let us be worried, and our nation lose
The name of hardiness and policy.°     220

KING
Call in the messengers sent from the dauphin.
      [Exeunt some ATTENDANTS.]
Now are we well resolved,° and by God's help
And yours, the noble sinews of our power,
France being ours,° we'll bend it to our awe,°
Or break it all to pieces. Or there we'll sit,     225
Ruling in large and ample empery°
O'er France and all her (almost) kingly dukedoms,
Or lay these bones in an unworthy urn,°
Tombless, with no remembrance° over them.
Either our history shall with full mouth     230
Speak freely of our acts, or else our grave,
Like Turkish mute,° shall have a tongueless mouth,
Not worshipped° with a waxen° epitaph.

*Enter* AMBASSADORS *of France* [*and* ATTENDANTS].

Now are we well prepared to know the pleasure
Of our fair cousin dauphin; for we hear     235
Your greeting is from him, not from the king.

AMBASSADOR
May't please your majesty to give us leave
Freely to render what we have in charge;
Or shall we sparingly° show you far off
The dauphin's meaning, and our embassy?     240

148 unfurnished undefended 151 gleanèd i.e., stripped of defenders 154 neighborhood neighborliness 155 feared alarmed 156 exampled furnished with a precedent 160 stray animal found wandering out of bounds 161 King of Scots David II 164 ooze and bottom oozy bottom 165 wrack wreck 169 in prey engaged in preying 173 tame broach (as a weasel breaks into eggs to suck their meat) 175 crushed strained, needless 179 advisèd prudent 181 parts (1) members of the body politic (2) melodies of the various instruments in concerted music; consent (1) agreement (2) harmony 182 Congreeing agreeing; close (1) union (2) conclusion of a piece of music 184 state estate, kingdom 185 Setting . . . motion giving a perpetual stimulus to effort 188 in nature instinctive 189 act operation 190 sorts various kinds 191 correct administer justice

194 Make boot upon plunder 200 mechanic engaged in manual labor 202 surly stern 203 executors executioners 204 infer adduce 205 reference relation 207 loosèd several ways shot from various places 212 borne carried out 220 policy statesmanship 222 resolved (1) convinced (2) determined 224 ours i.e., by right of inheritance; bend . . . awe subdue it to our authority 226 empery dominion 228 urn grave 229 remembrance memorial inscription 232 Turkish mute certain slaves in the Turkish royal household had their tongues cut out to ensure secrecy 233 worshipped honored; waxen easily effaced 239 sparingly with reserve, discreetly

KING
We are no tyrant, but a Christian king,
Unto whose grace° our passion is as subject
As is our wretches fett'red in our prisons;
Therefore with frank and with uncurbèd plainness,
Tell us the dauphin's mind.

AMBASSADOR                    Thus then, in few:°                245
Your highness, lately sending into France,
Did claim some certain dukedoms, in the right
Of your great predecessor, King Edward the Third.
In answer of which claim, the prince our master
Says that you savor too much of your youth,              250
And bids you be advised:° There's naught in France
That can be with a nimble galliard° won;
You cannot revel into dukedoms there.
He therefore sends you, meeter for your spirit,
This tun° of treasure; and in lieu of this,              255
Desires you let the dukedoms that you claim
Hear no more of you. This the dauphin speaks.

KING
What treasure, uncle?

EXETER                    Tennis balls, my liege.

KING
We are glad the dauphin is so pleasant° with us—
His present, and your pains, we thank you for.           260
When we have matched our rackets to these balls,
We will in France° (by God's grace) play a set
Shall strike his father's crown° into the hazard.°
Tell him he hath made a match with such a wrangler°
That all the courts° of France will be disturbed         265
With chases.° And we understand him well,
How he comes o'er us with° our wilder days,
Not measuring what use we made of them.
We never valued this poor seat° of England,
And therefore, living hence,° did give ourself           270
To barbarous license; as 'tis ever common
That men are merriest when they are from home.
But tell the dauphin I will keep my state,°
Be like a king, and show my sail of greatness,°
When I do rouse me in my throne of France.               275
For that I have laid by my majesty,
And plodded like a man for working days;°
But I will rise there with so full a glory
That I will dazzle all the eyes of France,
Yea, strike the dauphin blind to look on us.°            280
And tell the pleasant prince this mock of his
Hath turned his balls to gunstones,° and his soul
Shall stand sore chargèd for the wasteful vengeance

That shall fly with them; for many a thousand widows
Shall this his mock mock out of their dear husbands,     285
Mock mothers from their sons, mock castles down;
And some are yet ungotten and unborn
That shall have cause to curse the dauphin's scorn.°
But this lies all within° the will of God,
To whom I do appeal, and in whose name,                  290
Tell you the dauphin, I am coming on
To venge me as I may, and to put forth
My rightful hand in a well-hallowed cause.
So get you hence in peace. And tell the dauphin
His jest will savor but of shallow wit,                  295
When thousands weep more than did laugh at it.
Convey them with safe conduct. Fare you well.
            *Exeunt* AMBASSADORS [*and* ATTENDANTS].

EXETER
This was a merry message.

KING
We hope to make the sender blush at it.
Therefore, my lords, omit no happy hour°                 300
That may give furth'rance to our expedition;°
For we have now no thought in us but France,
Save those to God, that run before° our business.
Therefore let our proportions° for these wars
Be soon collected, and all things thought upon           305
That may with reasonable swiftness add
More feathers to our wings; for, God before,°
We'll chide this dauphin at his father's door.
Therefore let every man now task his thought
That this fair action may on foot° be brought.           310
                                        *Exeunt.*


# [ A C T   I I ]

*Flourish.° Enter* CHORUS.

Now all the youth of England are on fire,
And silken dalliance in the wardrobe lies;°
Now thrive the armorers, and honor's thought
Reigns solely° in the breast of every man.
They sell the pasture now, to buy the horse;             5
Following the mirror° of all Christian kings
With wingèd heels, as English Mercuries.°
For now sits Expectation in the air
And hides a sword, from hilts° unto the point,
With crowns imperial, crowns and coronets                10
Promised to Harry and his followers.
The French, advised by good intelligence°
Of this most dreadful preparation,
Shake in their fear, and with pale policy°

---

242 **grace** gracious disposition  245 **few** few words  251 **be advised** take care  252 **galliard** lively dance  255 **tun** cask  259 **pleasant** jocular, merry  262 **France** (1) tennis court (2) the country  263 **crown** (1) coin (stake money) (2) throne and power; **hazard** (1) opening in the walls of an old-fashioned tennis court; the ball entering it became "dead" and a point was scored (2) peril, jeopardy  264 **wrangler** (1) adversary (2) disputant  265 **courts** (1) tennis courts (2) courts of princes  266 **chases** (1) bouncings twice of tennis ball (scoring points) (2) pursuits  267 **comes . . . with** affects superiority over us by reason of  269 **seat** throne (lines 269–72 are ironical)  270 **hence** i.e., away from the court  273 **state** position of power  274 **show . . . greatness** demean myself proudly  276–77 **For . . . days** To be able to achieve this I have divested myself of greatness and learned what it is to live as a laboring man  278–80 **But . . . us** cf. *1 Henry IV*, I.ii.192–214  282 **gunstones** stones used for cannonballs

288 **scorn** taunt  289 **lies all within** depends wholly upon  300 **omit . . . hour** lose no favorable occasion  301 **expedition** enterprise  303 **run before** i.e., as prayers precede  304 **proportions** forces and supplies  307 **God before** God leading us  310 **on foot** in active operation
**II.Cho.s.d. Flourish** trumpet fanfare  2 **silken . . . lies** pastimes and luxuries are laid aside like clothes  4 **solely** alone  6 **mirror** model  7 **Mercuries** in classical mythology Mercury, or Hermes, was the gods' messenger; he was pictured as wearing winged helmet and sandals  9 **hilts** hilt (plural for singular, as frequently)  12 **advised . . . intelligence** informed by efficient espionage  14 **pale policy** contrivance inspired by fear

Seek to divert the English purposes. 15
O England, model° to thy inward greatness,
Like little body with a mighty heart,
What mightst thou do, that honor would thee do,
Were all thy children kind and natural!°
But see, thy fault° France° hath in thee found out— 20
A nest of hollow° bosoms—which he fills
With treacherous crowns;° and three corrupted men—
One, Richard Earl of Cambridge, and the second,
Henry Lord Scroop of Masham, and the third,
Sir Thomas Grey, knight, of Northumberland— 25
Have, for the gilt° of France (O guilt indeed!),
Confirmed conspiracy with fearful France,
And by their hands this grace° of kings must die,
If hell and treason hold their promises,
Ere he take ship for France, and in Southampton. 30
Linger your patience on, and we'll digest
Th' abuse of distance;° force° a play:—
The sum is paid; the traitors are agreed;
The king is set from London; and the scene
Is now transported, gentles, to Southampton. 35
There is the playhouse now, there must you sit,
And thence to France shall we convey you safe
And bring you back, charming the narrow seas°
To give you gentle pass;° for, if we may,
We'll not offend one stomach° with our play. 40
But, till the king come forth, and not till then,
Unto Southampton do we shift our scene.     *Exit.*

[Scene I. *London. A street.*]

*Enter Corporal* NYM *and Lieutenant* BARDOLPH.

BARDOLPH   Well met, Corporal Nym.
NYM   Good morrow, Lieutenant° Bardolph.
BARDOLPH   What, are Ancient° Pistol and you friends
yet?
NYM   For my part, I care not; I say little; but when 5
time shall serve,° there shall be smiles—but that shall
be as it may. I dare not fight; but I will wink° and
hold out mine iron.° It is a simple one; but what
though? It will toast cheese, and it will endure cold,°
as another man's sword will—and there's an end.° 10
BARDOLPH   I will bestow° a breakfast to make you
friends, and we'll be all three sworn brothers° to
France. Let't be so, good Corporal Nym.
NYM   Faith, I will live so long as I may, that's the

certain of it; and when I cannot live any longer, I will 15
do as I may.° That is my rest,° that is the rendezvous°
of it.
BARDOLPH   It is certain, corporal, that he is married
to Nell Quickly, and certainly she did you wrong,
for you were troth-plight° to her. 20
NYM   I cannot tell. Things must be as they may; men
may sleep, and they may have their throats about
them at that time, and some say knives have edges.
It must be as it may; though patience be a tired mare,
yet she will plod;° there must be conclusions. Well, 25
I cannot tell.

*Enter* PISTOL *and* [HOSTESS] *Quickly.*

BARDOLPH   Here comes Ancient Pistol and his wife.
Good corporal, be patient here. How now, mine host
Pistol?
PISTOL
Base tyke, call'st thou me host? 30
Now by this hand I swear I scorn the term;
Nor shall my Nell keep lodgers!
HOSTESS   No, by my troth, not long; for we cannot
lodge and board a dozen or fourteen gentlewomen
that live honestly° by the prick of their needles, but 35
it will be thought we keep a bawdy house straight.
[NYM *draws his sword.*] O well-a-day, Lady, if he be
not hewn now! We shall see willful adultery and
murder committed.

[PISTOL *draws.*]

BARDOLPH   Good lieutenant—good corporal—offer 40
nothing here.
NYM   Pish!
PISTOL   Pish for thee, Iceland dog;° thou prick-eared
cur of Iceland!
HOSTESS   Good Corporal Nym, show thy valor, and 45
put up your sword.°
NYM   Will you shog off?° I would have you solus.°
PISTOL
"Solus," egregious° dog? O viper vile!
The "solus" in thy most marvelous face!
The "solus" in thy teeth, and in thy throat, 50
And in thy hateful lungs, yea, in thy maw,° perdy!°
And, which is worse, within thy nasty mouth!
I do retort the "solus" in thy bowels;
For I can take,° and Pistol's cock is up,°
And flashing fire will follow. 55

---

**16 model** form   **19 kind and natural** loving and naturally
affectionate   **20 fault** imperfection; **France** the King of France
**21 hollow** (1) false (2) empty   **22 crowns** coins   **26 gilt**
i.e., golden crowns   **28 grace** ornament   **31–32 digest . . .
distance** dispose of the wrong done to fact in moving from
place to place in the play's action   **32 force** cram full   **38
charming . . . seas** laying spells on the English Channel   **39
pass** passage   **40 offend one stomach** (1) displease anyone (2)
make anyone seasick
**II.i.2 Lieutenant** Bardolph was a corporal in *2 Henry IV* and
Nym calls him so again at III.ii.3, below   **3 Ancient** ensign,
standard bearer   **6 serve** be opportune   **7 wink** (1) shut my
eyes (2) give a meaningful look   **8 iron** sword   **9 will
endure cold** does not mind being naked   **10 there's an end**
that's all there is to it   **11 bestow** treat you to   **12 sworn
brothers** comrades pledged to share each other's fortunes
(cf. III.ii.44–45)

**15–16 I will . . . may** cf. the proverb, "He that cannot do as
he would must do as he may"   **16 rest** what I stand to win or
lose (the stakes in a game of primero, the loss of which brings
about the end of the game); **rendezvous** last resort
**20 troth-plight** betrothed (more binding than a modern
engagement)   **24–25 patience . . . plod** patience is wearisome, yet it achieves its purpose in the end   **35 honestly** (1)
decently (2) chastely ("prick" of the same line sustains the
bawdy allusion)   **43 Iceland dog** white sharp-eared dog, so
shaggy that neither its face nor body can be seen (a favorite
lapdog)   **45–46 show . . . sword** unintentionally apposite,
for Nym had so little valor that he could not fight   **47
shog off** move off (slang); **solus** alone (Pistol takes it to
mean single, i.e., unmarried; or, ignorant of Latin, some great
insult)   **48 egregious** outsized   **51 maw** stomach; **perdy**
by God   **54 take** (1) cause harm to befall (by his elaborate
exorcism or curse) (2) strike (3) take fire; **cock is up** is cocked for
firing (punning on his name)

NYM   I am not Barbason;° you cannot conjure° me;
I have an humor to knock you indifferently° well. If
you grow foul with me, Pistol, I will scour you with
my rapier,° as I may, in fair terms.° If you would walk
off, I would prick your guts a little in good terms,° as 60
I may, and that's the humor° of it.

PISTOL
O braggard vile, and damnèd furious wight,°
The grave doth gape,° and doting° death is near;
Therefore exhale!°

BARDOLPH   Hear me, hear me what I say! He that 65
strikes the first stroke, I'll run him up to the hilts,° as
I am a soldier.

[*Draws.*]

PISTOL
An oath of mickle° might, and fury shall abate.

[PISTOL *and* NYM *sheathe their swords.*]

Give me thy fist, thy forefoot° to me give.
Thy spirits are most tall.°                                      70

NYM   I will cut thy throat one time or other in fair
terms, that is the humor of it.

PISTOL
Couple a gorge!°
That is the word. I thee defy° again.
O hound of Crete,° think'st thou my spouse to get?   75
No; to the spital° go,
And from the powd'ring tub° of infamy
Fetch forth the lazar kite of Cressid's kind,°
Doll Tearsheet,° she by name, and her espouse.
I have, and I will hold, the quondam° Quickly         80
For the only she;° ar d—pauca,° there's enough.
Go to!

*Enter the* BOY.

BOY   Mine host Pistol, you must come to my master°—
and your hostess. He is very sick and would to bed.
Good Bardolph, put thy face° between his sheets, 85
and do the office of a warming pan. Faith, he's very ill.

BARDOLPH   Away, you rogue!

HOSTESS   By my troth, he'll yield the crow a pudding°

56 **Barbason** name of a fiend; **conjure** exorcise   57 **indifferently** fairly   57–59 **If . . . rapier** a pistol was said to be "foul" after firing, and was normally cleaned with a ramrod or scouring rod   59 **in fair terms** fairly (a fashionable cliché)   60 **in good terms** on a good footing (another fashionable cliché)   61 **humor** fancy, inclination (yet another cliché)   62 **wight** person   63 **gape** (1) open (2) greedily desire; **doting** loving, fond   64 **exhale** draw forth   66 **run . . . hilts** drive the whole sword blade into him   68 **mickle** great (already, in Shakespeare's day, archaistic)   69 **forefoot** paw   70 **tall** courageous   73 **Couple a gorge** cut the throat (a comic version of the French *couper la gorge*, appropriate to the coming campaign)   74 **defy** challenge   75 **hound of Crete** another shaggy dog; cf. note to line 43   76 **spital** hospital   77 **powd'ring tub** pickling vat (frequently applied to the sweating tub used for curing veneral disease)   78 **lazar . . . kind** leprous whore (a stock phrase; a kite is a bird of prey)   79 **Doll Tearsheet** cf. *2 Henry IV*, II.ii.165–67 and V.iv   80 **quondam** former   81 **only she** one woman in the world; **pauca** few words (Latin *pauca verba*)   83 **my master** Falstaff (the boy is the page given to Falstaff by Prince Hal, *2 Henry IV*, I.ii)   85 **thy face** Bardolph's was red, like fire   88 **he'll . . . pudding** i.e., the boy will make food (*pudding* = stuffed intestines) for crows on the gallows (proverbial)

one of these days. The king has killed his heart.° Good
husband, come home presently.°                    *Exit.* 90

BARDOLPH   Come, shall I make you two friends? We
must to France together: why the devil should we
keep knives to cut one another's throats?

PISTOL
Let floods o'erswell, and fiends for food howl on!°

NYM   You'll pay me the eight shillings I won of you 95
at betting?

PISTOL
Base is the slave that pays.°

NYM   That now I will have; that's the humor of it.

PISTOL
As manhood shall compound.° Push° home.

[*They*] *draw.*

BARDOLPH   By this sword, he that makes the first 100
thrust, I'll kill him! By this sword, I will.

[*Draws.*]

PISTOL
"Sword" is an oath, and oaths must have their course.

[*Sheathes his sword.*]

BARDOLPH   Corporal Nym, and° thou wilt be friends,
be friends; and thou wilt not, why then be enemies
with me too. Prithee put up.°                              105

NYM   I shall have my eight shillings I won of you at
betting?

PISTOL
A noble° shalt thou have, and present° pay;
And liquor likewise will I give to thee,
And friendship shall combine, and brotherhood.    110
I'll live by Nym, and Nym shall live by me.
Is not this just? For I shall sutler° be
Unto the camp, and profits will accrue.
Give me thy hand.

[NYM *sheathes his sword.*]

NYM   I shall have my noble?                              115

PISTOL
In cash, most justly paid.

NYM   Well then, that's the humor of 't.

*Enter* HOSTESS.

HOSTESS   As ever you come of women, come in
quickly to Sir John. Ah, poor heart! he is so shaked
of a burning quotidian tertian° that it is most lament- 120
able to behold. Sweet men, come to him.

NYM   The king hath run bad humors° on the knight;
that's the even° of it.

89 **king . . . heart** by rejecting Falstaff; cf. *2 Henry IV*, V.v.47–72   90 **presently** immediately   94 **Let . . . on** Let riot thrive and the devils be deprived of their prey   97 **Base . . . pays** a corruption of the proverb, "The poor man always pays"   99 **manhood shall compound** valor decides; **Push** thrust (of a sword)   103 **and if**   105 **put up** sheathe   108 **noble** coin worth six shillings and eight pence; **present** immediate   112 **sutler** seller of provisions to a camp or garrison   120 **quotidian tertian** two kinds of intermittent fevers, the first recurring daily, the second every third day (a nonsensical phrase)   122 **run bad humors** vented his ill humor   123 **even** truth

**PISTOL**
Nym, thou hast spoke the right;
His heart is fracted and corroborate.°     125

**NYM**   The king is a good king, but it must be as it may:
he passes some humors, and careers.°

**PISTOL**
Let us condole the knight; for, lambkins, we will live.
*[Exeunt.]*

[*Scene II. Southampton.*]

*Enter* EXETER, BEDFORD, *and* WESTMORELAND.

**BEDFORD**
'Fore God, his grace is bold to trust these traitors.

**EXETER**
They shall be apprehended by and by.°

**WESTMORELAND**
How smooth and even° they do bear themselves,
As if allegiance in their bosoms sat,
Crowned with faith and constant loyalty!     5

**BEDFORD**
The king hath note° of all that they intend,
By interception which they dream not of.

**EXETER**
Nay, but the man that was his bedfellow,°
Whom he hath dulled and cloyed° with gracious
    favors—
That he should, for a foreign purse, so sell     10
His sovereign's life to death and treachery!

*Sound trumpets. Enter the* KING, SCROOP, CAMBRIDGE,
*and* GREY, [LORDS, *and* ATTENDANTS].

**KING**
Now sits the wind fair, and we will aboard.
My Lord of Cambridge, and my kind Lord of
    Masham,
And you, my gentle knight, give me your thoughts:
Think you not that the pow'rs we bear with us     15
Will cut their passage through the force of France,
Doing the execution and the act
For which we have in head° assembled them?

**SCROOP**
No doubt, my liege, if each man do his best.

**KING**
I doubt not that, since we are well persuaded     20
We carry not a heart with us from hence
That grows° not in a fair consent° with ours,
Nor leave not one behind that doth not wish
Success and conquest to attend on us.

**CAMBRIDGE**
Never was monarch better feared and loved     25
Than is your majesty. There's not, I think, a subject
That sits in heart-grief and uneasiness
Under the sweet shade° of your government.

**GREY**
True. Those that were your father's enemies

Have steeped their galls° in honey, and do serve you     30
With hearts create° of duty, and of zeal.

**KING**
We therefore have great cause of thankfulness,
And shall forget the office° of our hand
Sooner than quittance° of desert and merit
According to the weight and worthiness.     35

**SCROOP**
So service shall with steelèd sinews toil,
And labor shall refresh itself with hope,
To do your grace incessant services.

**KING**
We judge no less. Uncle of Exeter,
Enlarge° the man committed yesterday     40
That railed against our person. We consider
It was excess of wine that set him on,
And on his more advice,° we pardon him.

**SCROOP**
That's mercy, but too much security:°
Let him be punished, sovereign, lest example     45
Breed (by his sufferance°) more of such a kind.

**KING**
O, let us yet° be merciful!

**CAMBRIDGE**
So may your highness, and yet punish too.

**GREY**
Sir,
You show great mercy if you give him life     50
After the taste° of much correction.

**KING**
Alas, your too much love and care of me
Are heavy orisons° 'gainst this poor wretch!
If little faults proceeding on distemper°
Shall not be winked° at, how shall we stretch° our eye     55
When capital° crimes, chewed, swallowed, and
    digested,
Appear before us? We'll yet enlarge that man,
Though Cambridge, Scroop, and Grey, in their dear°
    care
And tender preservation of our person,
Would have him punished. And now to our French
    causes.°     60
Who are the late° commissioners?

**CAMBRIDGE**
I one, my lord.
Your highness bade me ask for it° today.

**SCROOP**
So did you me, my liege.

**GREY**
And I, my royal sovereign.     65

**KING**
Then, Richard Earl of Cambridge, there is yours;
There yours, Lord Scroop of Masham; and, sir knight,
Grey of Northumberland, this same is yours:

---

125 **fracted and corroborate** broken and joined together (?)
127 **passes . . . careers** indulges some whims and liveliness
**II.ii.2 apprehended by and by** arrested soon   3 **even**
unruffled   6 **note** knowledge   8 **bedfellow** Scroop   9 **dulled
and cloyed** bored and overindulged   18 **in head** as an
organized force   22 **grows** lives; **consent** agreement   28
**shade** protection

30 **galls** bitterness   31 **create** created   33 **office** proper function   34 **quittance** requital   40 **Enlarge** set at liberty   43
**on . . . advice** on maturer reflection   44 **security** want of
caution   46 **by his sufferance** by not checking him   47 **yet**
now as always   51 **taste** experience   53 **heavy orisons**
weighty pleas   54 **proceeding on distemper** i.e., committed when drunk   55 **winked** connived; **stretch** open wide
56 **capital** punishable by death   58 **dear** (1) deeply felt (2)
dire   60 **causes** affairs   61 **late** recently appointed   63 **it**
the written commission

Read them, and know I know your worthiness.
My Lord of Westmoreland, and uncle Exeter,　　70
We will aboard tonight.—Why, how now, gentle-
　men?
What see you in those papers that you lose
So much complexion?°—Look ye, how they change!
Their cheeks are paper.—Why, what read you there
That have so cowarded and chased your blood　　75
Out of appearance?°

CAMBRIDGE　　　　　I do confess my fault,
And do submit me to your highness' mercy.

GREY, SCROOP

To which we all appeal.

KING

The mercy that was quick in us but late,
By your own counsel is suppressed and killed.　　80
You must not dare (for shame) to talk of mercy,
For your own reasons turn into your bosoms,
As dogs upon their masters, worrying you.
See you, my princes and my noble peers,
These English monsters! My Lord of Cambridge
　here—　　85
You know how apt our love was to accord°
To furnish him with all appertinents
Belonging to his honor; and this man
Hath, for a few light° crowns, lightly° conspired
And sworn unto the practices° of France　　90
To kill us here in Hampton; to the which
This knight, no less for bounty bound to us
Than Cambridge is, hath likewise sworn. But O,
What shall I say to thee, Lord Scroop, thou cruel,
Ingrateful, savage, and inhuman creature?　　95
Thou that didst bear the key of all my counsels,
That knew'st the very bottom of my soul,
That (almost) mightst have coined me into gold,
Wouldst thou have practiced on me for thy use?°
May it be possible that foreign hire　　100
Could out of thee extract one spark of evil
That might annoy my finger? 'Tis so strange
That, though the truth of it stands off as gross°
As black and white, my eye will scarcely see it.
Treason and murder ever kept together,　　105
As two yoke-devils° sworn to either's purpose,
Working so grossly in a natural cause
That admiration did not hoop at them;°
But thou ('gainst all proportion°) didst bring in
Wonder to wait on treason and on murder;　　110
And whatsoever cunning fiend it was
That wrought upon thee so preposterously°
Hath got the voice° in hell for excellence;
And other devils that suggest° by treasons
Do botch and bungle up damnation　　115
With patches, colors, and with forms being fetched
From glist'ring semblances of piety;°

But he that tempered° thee bade thee stand up,°
Gave thee no instance why thou shouldst do treason,
Unless to dub° thee with the name of traitor.　　120
If that same demon that hath gulled thee thus
Should with his lion gait° walk the whole world,
He might return to vasty Tartar° back
And tell the legions,° "I can never win
A soul so easy as that Englishman's."　　125
O, how hast thou with jealousy infected°
The sweetness of affiance!° Show° men dutiful?
Why, so didst thou. Seem they grave and learned?
Why, so didst thou. Come they of noble family?
Why, so didst thou. Seem they religious?　　130
Why, so didst thou. Or are they spare in diet,
Free from gross passion, or of mirth or anger,
Constant in spirit, not swerving with the blood,°
Garnished and decked in modest complement,°
Not working with the eye without the ear,°　　135
And but in purgèd judgment trusting neither?
Such and so finely bolted° didst thou seem;
And thus thy fall hath left a kind of blot
To mark the full-fraught° man and best indued°
With some suspicion. I will weep for thee;　　140
For this revolt of thine, methinks, is like
Another fall of man. Their faults are open.°
Arrest them to the answer° of the law;
And God acquit° them of their practices!

EXETER　 I arrest thee of high treason by the name of　　145
Richard Earl of Cambridge.
　　I arrest thee of high treason by the name of Henry
Lord Scroop of Masham.
　　I arrest thee of high treason by the name of Thomas
Grey, knight, of Northumberland.　　150

SCROOP

Our purposes God justly hath discovered,
And I repent my fault more than my death—
Which I beseech your highness to forgive,
Although my body pay the price of it.

CAMBRIDGE

For me, the gold of France did not seduce,　　155
Although I did admit it as a motive
The sooner to effect what I intended.
But God be thankèd for prevention,°
Which I in sufferance° heartily will rejoice,°
Beseeching God, and you, to pardon me.　　160

GREY

Never did faithful subject more rejoice
At the discovery of most dangerous treason
Than I do at this hour joy o'er myself,
Prevented from a damnèd enterprise.
My fault, but not my body, pardon, sovereign.　　165

---

73 **complexion** color　76 **appearance** sight　86 **accord** agree　89 **light** trivial; **lightly** readily　90 **practices** intrigues　99 **practiced . . . use** plotted against me for your own profit　103 **off as gross** out as plain　106 **yoke-devils** fellow-devils　107–08 **so . . . them** so obviously in a matter natural to them that no one cried out in wonder　109 **proportion** propriety　112 **preposterously** unnaturally　113 **voice** vote　114 **suggest** tempt　115–17 **Do . . . piety** disguise the fact of damnation with folly, false pretexts, and behavior borrowed from bright outward manifestations of piety

118 **tempered** worked upon; **stand up** make a stand straightforwardly　120 **dub** invest (with a title)　122 **lion gait** cf. I Peter 5:8, "Your adversary, the devil, as a roaring lion, walketh about, seeking whom he may devour"　123 **Tartar** Tartarus, hell　124 **legions** i.e., of devils　126 **jealousy infected** suspicion tainted　127 **affiance** confidence; **Show** seem　133 **swerving . . . blood** erring after the flesh　134 **modest complement** unostentatious demeanor　135 **Not . . . ear** i.e., listening as well as seeing　137 **bolted** sifted (as flour)　139 **full-fraught** completely gifted; **indued** endowed　142 **open** patent　143 **answer** punishment　144 **acquit** requite　158 **prevention** four syllables　159 **sufferance** suffering the penalty; **rejoice** i.e., rejoice at

KING
God quit° you in His mercy! Hear your sentence.
You have conspired against our royal person,
Joined with an enemy proclaimed, and from his coffers
Received the golden earnest° of our death;
Wherein you would have sold your king to slaughter, 170
His princes and his peers to servitude,
His subjects to oppression and contempt,
And his whole kingdom into desolation.
Touching our person, seek we no revenge,
But we our kingdom's safety must so tender,° 175
Whose ruin you have sought, that to her laws
We do deliver you. Get you therefore hence
(Poor miserable wretches) to your death;
The taste° whereof God of His mercy give
You patience to endure, and true repentance 180
Of all your dear° offenses! Bear them hence.
    *Exeunt* [CAMBRIDGE, SCROOP, *and* GREY, *guarded*].
Now, lords, for France; the enterprise whereof
Shall be to you as us, like° glorious.
We doubt not of a fair and lucky war,
Since God so graciously hath brought to light 185
This dangerous treason, lurking in our way
To hinder our beginnings. We doubt not now
But every rub° is smoothèd on our way.
Then, forth, dear countrymen. Let us deliver
Our puissance° into the hand of God, 190
Putting it straight in expedition.°
Cheerly to sea; the signs of war advance:°
No king of England, if not King of France!
                 *Flourish.* [*Exeunt.*]

[Scene III. *London. Before a tavern.*]

*Enter* PISTOL, NYM, BARDOLPH, BOY, *and* HOSTESS.

HOSTESS   Prithee, honey-sweet husband, let me bring
thee to Staines.°
PISTOL
No; for my manly heart doth earn.°
Bardolph, be blithe; Nym, rouse thy vaunting veins;°
Boy, bristle thy courage up; for Falstaff he is dead, 5
And we must earn therefore.
BARDOLPH   Would I were with him, wheresome'er
he is, either in heaven or in hell!
HOSTESS   Nay sure, he's not in hell! He's in Arthur's
bosom,° if ever man went to Arthur's bosom. 'A° 10
made a finer end,° and went away and° it had been
any christom child.° 'A parted ev'n just between
twelve and one, ev'n at the turning o' th' tide.° For
after I saw him fumble with the sheets, and play with
flowers, and smile upon his finger's end, I knew there 15
was but one way; for his nose was as sharp as a pen,°

and 'a babbled° of green fields. "How now, Sir John?"
quoth I. "What, man? Be o' good cheer." So 'a cried
out, "God, God, God!" three or four times. Now I,
to comfort him, bid him 'a should not think of God; 20
I hoped there was no need to trouble himself with any
such thoughts yet. So 'a bade me lay more clothes on
his feet. I put my hand into the bed, and felt them,
and they were as cold as any stone. Then I felt to his
knees, and so upward, and upward, and all was as cold 25
as any stone.
NYM   They say he cried out of° sack.
HOSTESS   Ah, that 'a did.
BARDOLPH   And of women.
HOSTESS   Nay, that 'a did not. 30
BOY   Yes, that 'a did, and said they were devils
incarnate.°
HOSTESS   'A could never abide carnation;° 'twas a
color he never liked.
BOY   'A said once, the devil would have him about 35
women.
HOSTESS   'A did in some sort, indeed, handle° women;
but then he was rheumatic,° and talked of the Whore
of Babylon.°
BOY   Do you not remember 'a saw a flea stick upon 40
Bardolph's nose, and 'a said it was a black soul burning
in hell?
BARDOLPH   Well, the fuel° is gone that maintained
that fire: that's all the riches I got in his service.
NYM   Shall we shog?° The king will be gone from 45
Southampton.
PISTOL
Come, let's away. My love, give me thy lips.
Look to my chattels and my movables.
Let senses rule. The word is "Pitch and pay."°
Trust none; 50
For oaths are straws, men's faiths are wafer-cakes,°
And Hold-fast is the only dog,° my duck.
Therefore Caveto° be thy counselor.
Go, clear thy crystals.° Yokefellows in arms,
Let us to France, like horse-leeches, my boys, 55
To suck, to suck, the very blood to suck!
BOY   And that's but unwholesome food, they say.

---

**17 'a babbled** the Folio has "a Table," which seems meaningless
to most readers. Lewis Theobald's conjecture, in 1726, that a
compositor misread the copy's "a babld" has been widely
accepted. One might argue that the compositor misread "a
talkd," but "babbled" is more appropriate than "talked" to
the childishness—referred to earlier in the speech—of an old
man's last moments. Recently the Folio reading has been
defended, though not convincingly. One student, for example,
takes "Table" in the sense of "picture" or "tableau," and
paraphrases thus: Falstaff's nose was sharp as the pointed stakes
of a pinfold, in a picture of green fields. Various interpretations
are usefully surveyed in E. G. Fogel, *Shakespeare Quarterly*,
IX [1958], 485–92; but Theobald's conjecture seems better
sense and better Shakespeare   **27 cried out of** complained
loudly of   **32 incarnate** in human shape   **33 carnation** flesh
color   **37 handle** speak of   **38 rheumatic** perhaps a mistake
for *lunatic;* probably pronounced "rome-atic"; see next note
**38–39 Whore of Babylon** (1) the "scarlet woman" of
Revelation 17:4–5 (2) the Church of Rome   **43 fuel** liquor
provided by Falstaff   **45 shog** move off   **49 Let . . . pay**
Keep your wits about you. The motto is "Cash down"   **51
wafer-cakes** i.e., easily broken   **52 Hold-fast . . . dog**
cf. the proverb, "Brag is a good dog, but Hold-fast is a better"
**53 Caveto** take care   **54 clear thy crystals** wipe your eyes

**166 quit** absolve   **169 golden earnest** advance payment
**175 tender** care for   **179 taste** experience   **181 dear** dire
**183 like** equally   **188 rub** obstacle   **190 puissance** armed
force   **191 expedition** motion   **192 signs . . . advance**
raise up the banners
**II.iii.2 Staines** on the road to Southampton   **3 earn** grieve
**4 vaunting veins** rising spirits   **9–10 Arthur's bosom** a
mistake for *Abraham's bosom*   **10 'A** he   **11 finer end** i.e., than
going to hell; **and** as if   **12 christom child** infant in christening robe (the proper form was "chrisom"), innocent babe
**13 at . . . tide** according to popular belief, persons near
the sea died at the turn of the tide   **14–16 fumble . . . pen**
traditionally accepted signs of the imminence of death

PISTOL
Touch her soft mouth, and march.
BARDOLPH    Farewell, hostess.

[*Kisses her.*]

NYM    I cannot kiss, that is the humor of it; but adieu! 60
PISTOL
Let housewifery° appear; keep close,° I thee command.
HOSTESS    Farewell! Adieu!                    *Exeunt.*

[*Scene IV. France. The French king's palace.*]

*Flourish. Enter the French* KING, *the* DAUPHIN, *the Dukes of* BERRI *and* BRETAGNE, [*the* CONSTABLE, *and others*].

KING
Thus comes the English with full power upon us,
And more than carefully it us concerns
To answer royally in our defenses.
Therefore the Dukes of Berri and of Bretagne,
Of Brabant and of Orleans, shall make forth,                    5
And you, Prince Dauphin, with all swift dispatch
To line° and new repair our towns of war
With men of courage, and with means defendant;
For England his approaches makes as fierce
As waters to the sucking of a gulf.°                    10
It fits us then to be as provident
As fear may teach us out of late examples°
Left by the fatal and neglected° English
Upon our fields.
DAUPHIN                    My most redoubted father,
It is most meet we arm us 'gainst the foe;                    15
For peace itself should not so dull a kingdom
(Though war nor no known quarrel were in question)
But that defenses, musters, preparations
Should be maintained, assembled, and collected,°
As were a war in expectation.                    20
Therefore I say, 'tis meet we all go forth
To view the sick and feeble parts of France;
And let us do it with no show of fear—
No, with no more than if we heard that England
Were busied with a Whitsun morris dance;°                    25
For, my good liege, she is so idly kinged,
Her scepter so fantastically borne,°
By a vain, giddy, shallow, humorous° youth,
That fear attends° her not.
CONSTABLE                    O peace, Prince Dauphin!
You are too much mistaken in this king.                    30
Question your grace the late ambassadors,
With what great state he heard their embassy,
How well supplied with noble counselors,
How modest in exception,° and withal
How terrible in constant resolution;                    35
And you shall find his vanities forespent°

Were but the outside of the Roman Brutus,°
Covering discretion with a coat of folly;
As gardeners do with ordure hide those roots
That shall first spring and be most delicate.                    40
DAUPHIN
Well, 'tis not so, my Lord High Constable!
But though we think it so, it is no matter;
In cases of defense, 'tis best to weigh
The enemy more mighty than he seems;
So the proportions of defense are filled,                    45
Which of a weak and niggardly projection°
Doth, like a miser, spoil his coat with scanting°
A little cloth.
KING                    Think we King Harry strong;
And, princes, look you strongly arm to meet him.
The kindred of him hath been fleshed° upon us;                    50
And he is bred out of that bloody strain°
That haunted° us in our familiar paths;
Witness our too much memorable shame
When Crécy battle fatally was struck,
And all our princes captived, by the hand                    55
Of that black name, Edward, Black Prince of Wales;
Whiles that his mountain sire°—on mountain standing,
Up in the air, crowned with the golden sun—
Saw his heroical seed,° and smiled to see him
Mangle the work of nature, and deface                    60
The patterns° that by God and by French fathers
Had twenty years been made. This is a stem
Of that victorious stock; and let us fear
The native mightiness and fate° of him.

*Enter a* MESSENGER.

MESSENGER
Ambassadors from Harry, King of England,                    65
Do crave admittance to your majesty.
KING
We'll give them present° audience. Go, and bring
them.          [*Exeunt* MESSENGER *and certain* LORDS.]
You see this chase is hotly followed, friends.
DAUPHIN
Turn head,° and stop pursuit; for coward dogs
Most spend their mouths° when what they seem to
threaten                    70
Runs far before them. Good my sovereign,
Take up the English short, and let them know
Of what a monarchy you are the head.
Self-love,° my liege, is not so vile a sin
As self-neglecting.

*Enter* [LORDS, *with*] EXETER [*and* TRAIN].

KING                    From our brother of England?                    75
EXETER
From him, and thus he greets your majesty:

61 **housewifery** good housekeeping; **keep close** stay at home
**II.iv.7 line** fortify    10 **gulf** whirlpool    12 **late examples**
i.e., battles of Crécy (1346) and Poitiers (1356)    13 **fatal
and neglected** fatally underestimated    19 **maintained . . .
collected** these verbs refer singly to the nouns of the
previous line, in order    25 **Whitsun morris dance** folk dance
celebrating the coming of summer    27 **Her . . . borne** her
royal powers so freakishly exercised    28 **humorous** capricious
29 **attends** accompanies    34 **exception** expressing disapproval
36 **forespent** already used up

37 **Brutus** Lucius Junius Brutus feigned stupidity in order to
escape repressive action when planning to free Rome from the
Tarquin tyranny    45–46 **So . . . projection** in this way the
defending forces are fully mustered which if on a weak and
sparing scheme    47 **scanting** stinting    50 **fleshed** (1) encouraged by a foretaste of success (2) initiated to bloodshed    51
**strain** stock    52 **haunted** pursued    57 **mountain sire** father
of more than human proportions    59 **seed** issue, son    61
**patterns** examples of Frenchmen    64 **fate** what he is destined
to achieve    67 **present** immediate    69 **Turn head** stand at
bay (like stags)    70 **spend their mouths** give cry    74 **Self-
love** i.e., in praising oneself

He wills you, in the name of God Almighty,
That you divest yourself, and lay apart
The borrowed glories that by gift of heaven,
By law of nature and of nations, 'longs      80
To him and to his heirs—namely, the crown
And all wide-stretchèd honors that pertain
By custom, and the ordinance of times,°
Unto the crown of France. That you may know
'Tis no sinister nor no awkward° claim,      85
Picked from the wormholes° of long-vanished days,
Nor from the dust of old oblivion raked,
He sends you this most memorable line,°

*[giving a paper]*

In every branch truly demonstrative;
Willing you overlook° this pedigree;      90
And when you find him evenly° derived
From his most famed of famous ancestors,
Edward the Third, he bids you then resign
Your crown and kingdom, indirectly° held
From him, the native° and true challenger.      95

KING
Or else what follows?

EXETER
Bloody constraint; for if you hide the crown
Even in your hearts, there will he rake for it.
Therefore in fierce tempest is he coming,
In thunder and in earthquake, like a Jove;
That if requiring° fail, he will compel;      100
And bids you, in the bowels of the Lord,°
Deliver up the crown, and to take mercy
On the poor souls for whom this hungry war
Opens his vasty jaws; and on your head      105
Turning the widows' tears, the orphans' cries,
The dead men's blood, the pining maidens' groans,
For husbands, fathers, and betrothèd lovers
That shall be swallowed in this controversy.
This is his claim, his threat'ning, and my message;      110
Unless the dauphin be in presence here,
To whom expressly I bring greeting too.

KING
For us, we will consider of this further.
Tomorrow shall you bear our full intent
Back to our brother of England.

DAUPHIN                 For the dauphin,      115
I stand here for him: what to him from England?

EXETER
Scorn and defiance, slight regard, contempt,
And anything that may not misbecome
The mighty sender, doth he prize you at.
Thus says my king: and if your father's highness      120
Do not, in grant of all demands at large,
Sweeten the bitter mock you sent his majesty,
He'll call you to so hot an answer of it
That caves and womby vaultages° of France

Shall chide your trespass, and return your mock      125
In second accent of his ordinance.°

DAUPHIN
Say: if my father render fair return,
It is against my will; for I desire
Nothing but odds with England. To that end,
As matching to his youth and vanity,      130
I did present him with the Paris balls.°

EXETER
He'll make your Paris Louvre shake for it,
Were it the mistress° court of mighty Europe;
And be assured, you'll find a difference,
As we his subjects have in wonder found,      135
Between the promise of his greener° days
And these he masters now. Now he weighs° time
Even to the utmost grain: that you shall read
In your own losses, if he stay in France.

KING
Tomorrow shall you know our mind at full.      140

*Flourish.*

EXETER
Dispatch us with all speed, lest that our king
Come here himself to question our delay;
For he is footed in this land already.

KING
You shall be soon dispatched, with fair conditions.
A night is but small breath and little pause      145
To answer matters of this consequence.      *Exeunt.*

# A C T   [ I I I ]

*Flourish. Enter* CHORUS.

Thus with imagined° wing our swift scene flies,
In motion of no less celerity
Than that of thought. Suppose that you have seen
The well-appointed king at Hampton pier
Embark his royalty; and his brave° fleet      5
With silken streamers the young Phoebus fanning.°
Play with your fancies, and in them behold
Upon the hempen tackle shipboys climbing;
Hear the shrill whistle° which doth order give
To sounds confused; behold the threaden sails,      10
Borne with th' invisible and creeping wind,
Draw the huge bottoms° through the furrowed sea,
Breasting the lofty surge. O, do but think
You stand upon the rivage,° and behold
A city on th' inconstant billows dancing;      15
For so appears this fleet majestical,
Holding due course to Harfleur. Follow, follow!
Grapple your minds to sternage of° this navy,
And leave your England, as dead midnight, still,
Guarded with grandsires, babies, and old women,      20

**83 ordinance of times** established usage   **85 no sinister . . . awkward** neither irregular nor illegitimate   **86 Picked . . . wormholes** ingeniously derived from neglected (wormeaten) books   **88 memorable line** noteworthy pedigree **90 Willing you overlook** desiring you to peruse   **91 evenly** directly   **94 indirectly** wrongfully   **95 native** rightful   **101 requiring** demand   **102 in . . . Lord** a phrase found in Holinshed, and derived from Philippians 1:8   **124 womby vaultages** hollow caverns

**126 second . . . ordinance** echo of his cannon   **131 Paris balls** tennis balls   **133 mistress** chief   **136 greener** more inexperienced   **137 weighs** values
**III.Cho.1 imagined** of imagination   **5 brave** splendid   **6 young Phoebus fanning** seen fluttering against the rising sun **9 whistle** blown by the master of a ship   **12 bottoms** ships **14 rivage** shore   **18 to sternage of** astern

Either past or not arrived to pith° and puissance;
For who is he whose chin is but enriched
With one appearing hair that will not follow
These culled and choice-drawn° cavaliers to France?
Work, work your thoughts, and therein see a siege:     25
Behold the ordinance° on their carriages,
With fatal mouths gaping on girded° Harfleur.
Suppose th' ambassador from the French comes back;
Tells Harry that the king doth offer him
Katherine his daughter, and with her to dowry     30
Some petty and unprofitable dukedoms.
The offer likes not; and the nimble gunner
With linstock° now the devilish cannon touches,°

*Alarum, and chambers° go off.*

And down goes all before them. Still be kind,
And eke out our performance with your mind.   *Exit.*  35

### [Scene I. *France. Harfleur.*]

*Enter the* KING, EXETER, BEDFORD, *and*
GLOUCESTER. *Alarum. [Enter* SOLDIERS *carrying]*
*scaling ladders at Harfleur.*

KING
Once more unto the breach, dear friends, once more;
Or close the wall up with our English dead!
In peace there's nothing so becomes a man
As modest stillness° and humility;
But when the blast of war blows in our ears,     5
Then imitate the action of the tiger:
Stiffen the sinews, conjure up the blood,
Disguise fair nature with hard-favored rage;
Then lend the eye a terrible aspect;
Let it pry through the portage° of the head     10
Like the brass cannon; let the brow o'erwhelm it
As fearfully as doth a gallèd° rock
O'erhang and jutty his confounded° base,
Swilled° with the wild and wasteful ocean.
Now set the teeth, and stretch the nostril wide,     15
Hold hard the breath, and bend up° every spirit
To his full height! On, on, you noble English,
Whose blood is fet° from fathers of war-proof;°
Fathers that like so many Alexanders°
Have in these parts from morn till even fought     20
And sheathed their swords for lack of argument.°
Dishonor° not your mothers; now attest
That those whom you called fathers did beget you!
Be copy now to men of grosser blood
And teach them how to war! And you, good yeomen,     25
Whose limbs were made in England, show us here
The mettle of your pasture.° Let us swear
That you are worth your breeding; which I doubt not,

For there is none of you so mean and base
That hath not noble luster in your eyes.     30
I see you stand like greyhounds in the slips,°
Straining upon the start. The game's afoot!
Follow your spirit; and upon this charge,°
Cry, "God for Harry, England, and Saint George!"
          *[Exeunt.] Alarum, and chambers go off.*

### [Scene II. *Harfleur.*]

*Enter* NYM, BARDOLPH, PISTOL, *and* BOY.

BARDOLPH   On, on, on, on, on, to the breach, to the
breach!
NYM   Pray thee, corporal, stay; the knocks are too
hot; and, for mine own part, I have not a case° of lives.
The humor of it is too hot; that is the very plain-song°  5
of it.
PISTOL
The plain-song is most just; for humors do abound.
Knocks go and come; God's vassals drop and die;
          And sword and shield
               In bloody field     10
               Doth win immortal fame.
BOY   Would I were in an alehouse in London! I would
give all my fame for a pot of ale, and safety.
PISTOL
And I:
          If wishes would prevail with me,     15
          My purpose should not fail with me,
               But thither would I hie.
BOY          As duly, but not as truly,°
               As bird doth sing on bough.

*Enter* FLUELLEN.

FLUELLEN   Up to the breach, you dogs! Avaunt, you     20
cullions!°
PISTOL
Be merciful, great duke, to men of mold!°
Abate thy rage, abate thy manly rage,
Abate thy rage, great duke!
Good bawcock, bate thy rage! Use lenity, sweet
     chuck!°     25
NYM   These be good° humors. Your honor wins bad
humors.°          *Exit, [with all but* BOY].
BOY   As young as I am, I have observed these three
swashers. I am boy to them all three; but all they three,
though they would serve me, could not be man to     30
me; for indeed three such antics° do not amount to a
man. For Bardolph, he is white-livered° and redfaced; by the means whereof 'a faces it out, but fights
not. For Pistol, he hath a killing tongue and a quiet
sword; by the means whereof 'a breaks words,° and     35
keeps whole weapons. For Nym, he hath heard that
men of few words are the best men, and therefore he

---

**21 pith** strength   **24 choice-drawn** chosen with special care
**26 ordinance** ordnance, cannon   **27 girded** besieged   **33
linstock** staff holding lighted match; **touches** touches off,
fires   **33 s.d. chambers** small pieces of ordnance (usually for
ceremonial purposes)
**III.i.4 stillness** silence, staidness (?)   **10 portage** portholes
**12 gallèd** sea-beaten   **13 confounded** demolished   **14
Swilled** greedily swallowed   **16 bend up** strain   **18 fet**
fetched; **war-proof** proved in war   **19 Alexanders** i.e.,
sighing for more worlds to conquer   **21 argument** i.e.,
opponents   **22 Dishonor** i.e., by throwing doubts on your
paternity   **27 mettle . . . pasture** fine quality of your rearing

**31 slips** leashes   **33 upon this charge** as you charge
**III.ii.4 case** set   **5 plain-song** simple air without variations,
i.e., simple truth   **18 truly** (1) honorably (2) in tune   **21
cullions** base fellows   **22 mold** clay   **25 bawcock . . . chuck**
ingratiating familiarities   **26 good** ironical   **26–27 Your . . .
humors** Valor is dangerous (so he runs off)   **31 antics** buffoons
**32 white-livered** cowardly   **35 breaks words** (1) breaks
promises (2) exchanges words

scorns to say his prayers, lest 'a should be thought a coward; but his few bad words are matched with as few good deeds, for 'a never broke any man's head 40 but his own, and that was against a post when he was drunk. They will steal anything, and call it purchase.° Bardolph stole a lute-case, bore it twelve leagues, and sold it for three halfpence. Nym and Bardolph are sworn brothers in filching; and in Calais they stole a 45 fire-shovel. I knew by that piece of service the men would carry coals.° They would have me as familiar with men's pockets as their gloves or their hand-kerchers; which makes much against my manhood, if I should take from another's pocket to put into mine; 50 for it is plain pocketing up of wrongs.° I must leave them, and seek some better service. Their villainy goes against my weak stomach,° and therefore I must cast it up.°                                                      *Exit.*

*Enter* GOWER [*and* FLUELLEN].

GOWER  Captain Fluellen, you must come presently° 55 to the mines; the Duke of Gloucester would speak with you.

FLUELLEN  To the mines? Tell you the duke, it is not so good to come to the mines; for look you, the mines is not according to the disciplines of the war.° The 60 concavities of it is not sufficient; for look you, th' athversary, you may discuss° unto the duke, look you, is digt himself four yard under the countermines.° By Cheshu, I think 'a will plow° up all, if there is not better directions.                                         65

GOWER  The Duke of Gloucester, to whom the order of the siege is given, is altogether directed by an Irishman, a very valiant gentleman, i'faith.

FLUELLEN  It is Captain Macmorris, is it not?

GOWER  I think it be.                                          70

FLUELLEN  By Cheshu, he is an ass, as in the world! I will verify as much in his beard.° He has no more directions in the true disciplines of the wars, look you, of the Roman disciplines, than is a puppy-dog.

*Enter* MACMORRIS *and Captain* JAMY.

GOWER  Here 'a comes, and the Scots captain, Captain 75 Jamy, with him.

FLUELLEN  Captain Jamy is a marvelous falorous gentleman, that is certain, and of great expedition° and knowledge in th' aunchient wars, upon my particular° knowledge of his directions. By Cheshu, he will main- 80 tain his argument as well as any military man in the world in the disciplines of the pristine wars of the Romans.

JAMY  I say gud day, Captain Fluellen.

FLUELLEN  God-den to your worship, good Captain 85 James.

GOWER  How now, Captain Macmorris? Have you quit the mines? Have the pioners° given o'er?

MACMORRIS  By Chrish, law, tish ill done! The work ish give over, the trompet sound the retreat. By my 90 hand I swear, and my father's soul, the work ish ill done! It ish give over. I would have blowed up the town, so Chrish save me, law, in an hour. O, tish ill done, tish ill done! By my hand, tish ill done!

FLUELLEN  Captain Macmorris, I beseech you now, 95 will you voutsafe me, look you, a few disputations with you, as partly touching or concerning the disci-plines of the war, the Roman wars?—in the way of argument, look you, and friendly communication; partly to satisfy my opinion, and partly for the satis- 100 faction, look you, of my mind—as touching the direction of the military discipline, that is the point.

JAMY  It sall be vary gud, gud feith, gud captens bath, and I sall quit° you with gud leve, as I may pick occasion. That sall I, mary.°                                105

MACMORRIS  It is no time to discourse, so Chrish save me! The day is hot, and the weather, and the wars, and the king, and the dukes; it is no time to discourse; the town is beseeched,° and the trumpet call us to the breach, and we talk, and, be Chrish, do nothing; 'tis 110 shame for us all, so God sa' me, 'tis shame to stand still, it is shame, by my hand! And there is throats to be cut, and works to be done, and there ish nothing done, so Chrish sa' me, law!

JAMY  By the mess, ere theise eyes of mine take them- 115 selves to slomber, I'll do gud service, or I'll lig i' th' grund for it! Ay or go to death! And I'll pay't as valorously as I may, that sall I suerly do, that is the breff and the long. Mary, I wad full fain heard some question 'tween you tway.                                120

FLUELLEN  Captain Macmorris, I think, look you, under your correction, there is not many of your nation—

MACMORRIS  Of my nation? What ish my nation? Ish a villain, and a basterd, and a knave, and a rascal. 125 What ish my nation? Who talks of my nation?

FLUELLEN  Look you, if you take the matter otherwise than is meant, Captain Macmorris, peradventure I shall think you do not use me with that affability as in discretion you ought to use me, look you, being as 130 good a man as yourself, both in the disciplines of war, and in the derivation of my birth, and in other particu-larities.

MACMORRIS  I do not know you so good a man as myself; so Chrish save me, I will cut off your head! 135

GOWER  Gentlemen both, you will° mistake each other.

JAMY  Ah, that's a foul fault!

*A parley* [*sounded*].

GOWER  The town sounds a parley.

FLUELLEN  Captain Macmorris when there is more 140 better opportunity to be required,° look you, I will be so bold as to tell you I know the disciplines of war; and there is an end.                          *Exit* [*with others*].

42 **purchase** booty (thieves' slang)  47 **carry coals** (1) do dirty work (2) submit to insult  51 **pocketing . . . wrongs** (1) receiving stolen goods (2) submitting to insult  52–53 **goes . . . stomach** (1) is against my disposition (2) makes me sick  53–54 **cast it up** (1) run from their service (2) be sick  55 **presently** immediately  60 **disciplines . . . war** military experience  62 **discuss** declare  63 **four . . . countermines** countermines four yards under the mines  64 **plow** the first of Fluellen's dialect substitutions of *p* for *b*  72 **verify . . . beard** prove it to his face  78 **expedition** readiness in disputation (rhetorical term)  79 **particular** personal

88 **pioners** pioneers, miners  104 **quit** answer  105 **mary** Jamy's pronunciation of "marry," a mild oath, from "By the Virgin Mary"  109 **beseeched** for *besieged*  136 **will** are determined to  141 **to be required** serves

[Scene III. *Before the gates of Harfleur.*]

*Enter the* KING [*Henry*] *and all his* TRAIN *before the gates.*

KING
How yet resolves the governor of the town?
This is the latest parle we will admit:
Therefore to our best mercy give yourselves,
Or, like to men proud of destruction,°
Defy us to our worst; for, as I am a soldier,          5
A name that in my thoughts becomes me best,
If I begin the batt'ry once again,
I will not leave the half-achieved Harfleur
Till in her ashes she lie buried.
The gates of mercy shall be all shut up,          10
And the fleshed° soldier, rough and hard of heart,
In liberty of bloody hand shall range
With conscience wide as hell, mowing like grass
Your fresh fair virgins and your flow'ring infants.
What is it then to me if impious war,          15
Arrayed in flames like to the prince of fiends,
Do with his smirched complexion all fell° feats
Enlinked to waste and desolation?
What is't to me, when you yourselves are cause,
If your pure maidens fall into the hand          20
Of hot and forcing violation?
What rein can hold licentious wickedness
When down the hill he holds his fierce career?°
We may as bootless spend our vain command
Upon th' enragèd soldiers in their spoil°          25
As send precepts° to the leviathan°
To come ashore. Therefore, you men of Harfleur,
Take pity of your town and of your people
Whiles yet my soldiers are in my command,
Whiles yet the cool and temperate wind of grace          30
O'erblows the filthy and contagious clouds
Of heady murder, spoil, and villainy.
If not—why, in a moment look to see
The blind° and bloody soldier with foul hand
Defile the locks of your shrill-shrieking daughters;          35
Your fathers taken by the silver beards,
And their most reverend heads dashed to the walls;
Your naked infants spitted upon pikes,
Whiles the mad mothers with their howls confused
Do break the clouds, as did the wives of Jewry          40
At Herod's bloody-hunting slaughtermen.
What say you? Will you yield, and this avoid?
Or, guilty in defense,° be thus destroyed?

*Enter* GOVERNOR [*on the wall*].

GOVERNOR
Our expectation hath this day an end;
The dauphin, whom of succors we entreated,          45
Returns us that his powers are yet not ready
To raise so great a siege. Therefore, great king,
We yield our town and lives to thy soft mercy.
Enter our gates, dispose of us and ours,
For we no longer are defensible.°          50

III.iii.4 **proud of destruction** glorying in death  11 **fleshed**
initiated in slaughter  17 **fell** savage  23 **career** gallop  25
**spoil** plundering  26 **precepts** written instructions; **leviathan**
legendary aquatic animal of enormous size (common in
Hebrew poetry)  34 **blind** reckless  43 **guilty in defense** to
blame for holding out  50 **defensible** able to make a defense

KING
Open your gates. Come, uncle Exeter,
Go you and enter Harfleur; there remain
And fortify it strongly 'gainst the French.
Use mercy to them all. For us, dear uncle,
The winter coming on, and sickness growing          55
Upon our soldiers, we will retire to Calais.
Tonight in Harfleur will we be your guest;
Tomorrow for the march are we addrest.°
          *Flourish, and enter the town.*

[Scene IV. *Rouen. A room in the palace.*]

*Enter* KATHERINE *and* [ALICE,] *an old gentlewoman.*

KATHERINE  Alice, tu as été en Angleterre, et tu parles
bien le langage.
ALICE  Un peu, madame.
KATHERINE  Je te prie m'enseignez; il faut que
j'apprenne à parler. Comment appelez-vous la main  5
en anglais?
ALICE  La main? Elle est appelée de hand.
KATHERINE  De hand. Et les doigts?
ALICE  Les doigts? Ma foi, j'oublie les doigts; mais je
me souviendrai. Les doigts? Je pense qu'ils sont          10
appelés de fingres; oui, de fingres.
KATHERINE  La main, de hand; les doigts, le fingres.
Je pense que je suis le bon écolier; j'ai gagné deux mots
d'anglais vitement. Comment appelez-vous les
ongles?          15
ALICE  Les ongles? Nous les appelons de nails.
KATHERINE  De nails. Ecoutez; dites-moi si je parle
bien: de hand, de fingres, et de nails.
ALICE  C'est bien dit, madame; il est fort bon anglais.
KATHERINE  Dites-moi l'anglais pour le bras.          20
ALICE  De arm, madame.
KATHERINE  Et le coude.
ALICE  D' elbow.
KATHERINE  D' elbow. Je m'en fais la répétition de
tous les mots que vous m'avez appris dès à présent.          25
ALICE  Il est trop difficile, madame, comme je pense.

58 **addrest** prepared
**III.iv** (translated)
KATHERINE  Alice, you have been in England and speak the
   language well.
ALICE  A little, my lady.
KATHERINE  I pray you, teach me; I have to learn to speak it.
   What do you call *la main* in English?
ALICE  *La main?* It is called de hand.
KATHERINE  De hand. And *les doigts?*
ALICE  *Les doigts?* Oh dear, I forget *les doigts;* but I shall
   remember. *Les doigts?* I think that they are called de fingres;
   yes, de fingres.
KATHERINE  *Le main,* de hand; *les doigts, le* fingres. I think that
   I am an apt scholar; I have learned two words of English
   quickly. What do you call *les ongles?*
ALICE  *Les ongles?* We call them de nails.
KATHERINE  De nails. Listen; tell me if I speak correctly:
   de hand, de fingres, and de nails.
ALICE  Well said, my lady; it is very good English.
KATHERINE  Tell me the English for *le bras.*
ALICE  De arm, my lady.
KATHERINE  And *le coude.*
ALICE  D' elbow.
KATHERINE  D' elbow. I shall repeat all the words you have
   taught me so far.
ALICE  It is too hard, my lady, I think.

KATHERINE  Excusez-moi, Alice; écoutez: d' hand, de fingre, de nails, d' arma, de bilbow.

ALICE  D' elbow, madame.

KATHERINE  O Seigneur Dieu, je m'en oublie! D' elbow. Comment appelez-vous le col? 30

ALICE  De nick, madame.

KATHERINE  De nick. Et le menton?

ALICE  De chin.

KATHERINE  De sin. Le col, de nick; le menton, de sin. 35

ALICE  Oui. Sauf votre honneur, en vérité, vous prononcez les mots aussi droit que les natifs d'Angleterre.

KATHERINE  Je ne doute point d'apprendre, par la grace de Dieu, et en peu de temps. 40

ALICE  N'avez-vous pas déjà oublié ce que je vous ai enseigné?

KATHERINE  Non, je réciterai à vous promptement: d' hand, de fingre, de mails—

ALICE  De nails, madame. 45

KATHERINE  De nails, de arm, de ilbow—

ALICE  Sauf votre honneur, d' elbow.

KATHERINE  Ainsi dis-je; d' elbow, de nick, et de sin. Comment appelez-vous le pied et la robe?

ALICE  Le foot, madame; et le count. 50

KATHERINE  Le foot et le count! O Seigneur Dieu! Ils sont les mots de son mauvais, corruptible, gros, et impudique, et non pour les dames d'honneur d'user: je ne voudrais prononcer ces mots devant les seigneurs de France pour tout le monde. Foh, le foot et le count! 55 Néanmoins, je réciterai une autre fois ma leçon ensemble: d' hand, de fingre, de nails, d' arm, d' elbow, de nick, de sin, de foot, le count.

ALICE  Excellent, madame!

KATHERINE  C'est assez pour une fois: allons-nous à 60 diner. *Exit, [with ALICE].*

KATHERINE  Pardon me, Alice; listen: d' hand, de fingre, de nails, d' arma, de bilbow.

ALICE  D' elbow, my lady.

KATHERINE  O dear Lord, I forget. D' elbow. What do you call *le col?*

ALICE  De nick, my lady.

KATHERINE  De nick. And *le menton?*

ALICE  De chin.

KATHERINE  De sin. *Le col*, de nick; *le menton*, de sin.

ALICE  Yes. By your leave, indeed you pronounce the words just like a native of England.

KATHERINE  I have no doubt that I shall learn, with God's help, and in little time.

ALICE  Have you not already forgotten what I have taught you?

KATHERINE  No, I shall recite to you now: d' hand, de fingre, de mails—

ALICE  De nails, my lady.

KATHERINE  De nails, de arm, de ilbow—

ALICE  By your leave, d' elbow.

KATHERINE  That's what I said: d' elbow, de nick, and de sin. What do you call *le pied* and *la robe?*

ALICE  The foot, my lady; and the count. [editor's note: these words are similar in sound to the French equivalents of the English "four-letter" words; "count" is an attempt at "gown"]

KATHERINE  The foot and the count! O dear Lord! Those are bad words, wicked, vulgar, and indecent, and respectable ladies don't use them. I wouldn't utter those words before French gentlemen for the whole world. Fie, the foot and the count! Still, I shall recite once more my whole lesson: d' hand, de fingre, de nails, d' arm, d' elbow, de sin, de foot, the count.

ALICE  Excellent, my lady.

KATHERINE  That's enough for one session; let's go to dinner.

[Scene V. *Rouen. A room in the palace.*]

*Enter the* KING *of France, the* DAUPHIN, [BRETAGNE,] *the* CONSTABLE *of France, and others.*

KING
'Tis certain he hath passed the river Somme.

CONSTABLE
And if he be not fought withal, my lord,
Let us not live in France; let us quit all
And give our vineyards to a barbarous people.

DAUPHIN
O Dieu vivant! Shall a few sprays of us,° 5
The emptying° of our father's luxury,
Our scions, put in wild and savage stock,°
Spirt° up so suddenly into the clouds
And overlook their grafters?

BRETAGNE
Normans, but bastard Normans, Norman bastards! 10
Mort Dieu! Ma vie! if they march along
Unfought withal, but I will sell my dukedom
To buy a slobb'ry° and a dirty farm
In that nook-shotten° isle of Albion.°

CONSTABLE
Dieu de batailles! where have they this mettle? 15
Is not their climate foggy, raw, and dull,
On whom, as in despite, the sun looks pale,
Killing their fruit with frowns? Can sodden° water,
A drench for sur-reined jades, their barley broth,°
Decoct° their cold blood to such valiant heat? 20
And shall our quick blood, spirited with wine,
Seem frosty? O, for honor of our land,
Let us not hang like roping° icicles
Upon our houses' thatch, whiles a more frosty people
Sweat drops of gallant youth in our rich fields— 25
"Poor" we call them° in their native lords!

DAUPHIN
By faith and honor,
Our madams mock at us and plainly say
Our mettle is bred out,° and they will give
Their bodies to the lust of English youth, 30
To new-store France with bastard warriors.

BRETAGNE
They bid us to the English dancing schools
And teach lavoltas° high, and swift corantos,°
Saying our grace° is only in our heels,°
And that we are most lofty° runaways. 35

KING
Where is Montjoy, the herald? Speed him hence;
Let him greet England with our sharp defiance.
Up, princes, and with spirit of honor edged
More sharper than your swords, hie to the field.

**III.v.5 sprays of us** offshoots, bastards  **6 emptying** expenditure  **7 scions . . . stock** i.e., Norman French mating with Anglo-Saxon (scions are shoots, for grafting)  **8 Spirt** sprout, shoot  **13 slobb'ry** waterlogged  **14 nook-shotten** full of odd angles, shapeless; **Albion** an ancient poetical name for Britain, alluding to the white cliffs visible from France  **18 sodden** boiled  **19 drench . . . broth** medicinal draught (or mash) given to overridden nags, (which is much the same as) their beer  **20 Decoct** warm up  **23 roping** hanging down together like rope  **26 them** i.e., the "rich fields" of France  **29 bred out** exhausted, degenerate  **33 lavoltas** dances with high leaps; **corantos** dances with a running step  **34 grace** virtue, saving grace (?); **our heels** (1) dancing (2) running away  **35 lofty** stately, pompous

Charles Delabreth, High Constable of France,                    40
You Dukes of Orleans, Bourbon, and of Berri,
Alençon, Brabant, Bar, and Burgundy;
Jacques Chatillon, Rambures, Vaudemont,
Beaumont, Grandpré, Roussi, and Faulconbridge,
Foix, Lestrale, Bouciqualt, and Charolois,                      45
High dukes, great princes, barons, lords, and knights,
For your great seats° now quit you of great shames:
Bar Harry England, that sweeps through our land
With pennons painted in the blood of Harfleur;
Rush on his host, as doth the melted snow                       50
Upon the valleys whose low vassal seat
The Alps doth spit and void his° rheum upon.
Go down upon him—you have power enough—
And in a captive chariot into Rouen
Bring him our prisoner.
CONSTABLE                    This becomes the great.         55
Sorry am I his numbers are so few,
His soldiers sick, and famished in their march;
For I am sure, when he shall see our army,
He'll drop his heart into the sink° of fear
And, for achievement,° offer us his ransom.                     60
KING
Therefore, Lord Constable, haste on Montjoy,
And let him say to England that we send
To know what willing ransom he will give.
Prince Dauphin, you shall stay with us in Rouen.
DAUPHIN
Not so, I do beseech your majesty.                              65
KING
Be patient, for you shall remain with us.
Now forth, Lord Constable, and princes all,
And quickly bring us word of England's fall.   *Exeunt.*

[Scene VI. *France. The English camp in Picardy.*]

*Enter captains, English and Welsh:* GOWER *and*
FLUELLEN.

GOWER   How now, Captain Fluellen, come you from
the bridge?°
FLUELLEN   I assure you, there is very excellent
services° committed at the bridge.
GOWER   Is the Duke of Exeter safe?                             5
FLUELLEN   The Duke of Exeter is as magnanimous as
Agamemnon, and a man that I love and honor with
my soul, and my heart, and my duty, and my live,
and my living, and my uttermost power. He is not—
God be praised and blessed!—any hurt in the world,             10
but keeps the bridge most valiantly, with excellent
discipline. There is an aunchient lieutenant° there at
the pridge, I think in my very conscience he is as
valiant a man as Mark Anthony, and he is a man of no
estimation in the world, but I did see him do as gallant       15
service.
GOWER   What do you call him?
FLUELLEN   He is called Aunchient Pistol.
GOWER   I know him not.

*Enter* PISTOL.

FLUELLEN   Here is the man.                                     20
PISTOL
Captain, I thee beseech to do me favors;
The Duke of Exeter doth love thee well.
FLUELLEN   Ay, I praise God; and I have merited some
love at his hands.
PISTOL
Bardolph, a soldier firm and sound of heart,                    25
And of buxom° valor, hath by cruel fate,
And giddy Fortune's furious fickle wheel—
That goddess blind,
That stands upon the rolling restless stone—
FLUELLEN   By your patience, Aunchient Pistol.              30
Fortune is painted blind, with a muffler afore her eyes,
to signify to you that Fortune is blind; and she is
painted also with a wheel, to signify to you, which is
the moral of it, that she is turning and inconstant, and
mutability, and variation; and her foot, look you, is           35
fixed upon a spherical stone, which rolls, and rolls, and
rolls. In good truth, the poet makes a most excellent
description of it; Fortune is an excellent moral.°
PISTOL
Fortune is Bardolph's foe, and frowns on him;
For he hath stol'n a pax,° and hangèd must 'a be—           40
A damnèd death!
Let gallows gape for dog; let man go free,
And let not hemp his windpipe suffocate.
But Exeter hath given the doom° of death
For pax of little price.                                        45
Therefore, go speak—the duke will hear thy voice;
And let not Bardolph's vital thread be cut
With edge of penny cord, and vile reproach.
Speak, captain, for his life, and I will thee requite.
FLUELLEN   Aunchient Pistol, I do partly understand          50
your meaning.
PISTOL
Why then, rejoice therefore!
FLUELLEN   Certainly, aunchient, it is not a thing to
rejoice at; for if, look you, he were my brother, I
would desire the duke to use his good pleasure, and            55
put him to execution; for discipline ought to be used.
PISTOL
Die and be damned! and figo° for thy friendship!
FLUELLEN   It is well.
PISTOL
The fig of Spain!°                                   *Exit.*
FLUELLEN   Very good.                                           60
GOWER   Why, this is an arrant° counterfeit rascal! I
remember him now—a bawd, a cutpurse.
FLUELLEN   I'll assure you, 'a utt'red as prave words at
the pridge, as you shall see in a summer's day. But it
is very well. What he has spoke to me, that is well, I         65
warrant you, when time is serve.
GOWER   Why, 'tis a gull,° a fool, a rogue, that now
and then goes to the wars, to grace himself at his

47 **seats** estates   52 **his** the Alps'   59 **sink** pit   60 **achieve-**
**ment** acquisition (i.e., for France)
III.vi.2 **the bridge** over the Ternoise, captured on October
23, 1415, two days before the battle of Agincourt   4 **services**
exploits   12 **aunchient lieutenant** sublieutenant

26 **buxom** lively   38 **moral** symbolical figure   40 **pax**
tablet depicting the Crucifixion, kissed by priest and then
communicants at Mass   44 **doom** sentence   57 **figo** Spanish
for *fig* (see next note)   59 **fig of Spain** contemptuous and
obscene gesture made by thrusting the thumb between the
fingers or into the mouth   61 **arrant** out-and-out   67 **gull**
simpleton

return into London, under the form of a soldier. And such fellows are perfect in the great commanders' 70 names, and they will learn you by rote where services° were done: at such and such a sconce,° at such a breach, at such a convoy; who came off° bravely, who was shot, who disgraced, what terms the enemy stood on;° and this they con° perfectly in the phrase of war, which 75 they trick up with new-tuned oaths;° and what a beard of the general's cut° and a horrid suit of the camp will do among foaming bottles and ale-washed wits is wonderful to be thought on. But you must learn to know such slanders of the age, or else you may 80 be marvelously mistook.

FLUELLEN  I tell you what, Captain Gower: I do perceive he is not the man that he would gladly make show to the world he is. If I find a hole in his coat,° I will tell him my mind. [*Drum within.*] Hark you, the 85 king is coming, and I must speak with him from the pridge.

*Drum and colors. Enter the* KING *and his poor* SOLDIERS [*and* GLOUCESTER].

God pless your majesty!

KING
How now, Fluellen, cam'st thou from the bridge?

FLUELLEN  Ay, so please your majesty: the Duke of 90 Exeter has very gallantly maintained the pridge; the French is gone off, look you, and there is gallant and most prave passages.° Marry, th' athversary was have possession of the pridge, but he is enforced to retire, and the Duke of Exeter is master of the pridge. I can 95 tell your majesty, the duke is a prave man.

KING  What men have you lost, Fluellen?

FLUELLEN  The perdition of th' athversary hath been very great, reasonable great: marry, for my part, I think the duke hath lost never a man, but one that is 100 like to be executed for robbing a church—one Bardolph, if your majesty know the man. His face is all bubukles and whelks,° and knobs, and flames o' fire, and his lips blows at his nose, and it is like a coal of fire, sometimes plue and sometimes red; but his nose is 105 executed,° and his° fire's out.

KING  We would have all such offenders so cut off;° and we give express charge that in our marches through the country there be nothing compelled from the villages, nothing taken but paid for; none of 110 the French upbraided or abused in disdainful language; for when lenity and cruelty play for a kingdom, the gentler gamester is the soonest winner.

*Tucket.° Enter* MONTJOY.

MONTJOY  You know me by my habit.°

KING  Well then, I know thee. What shall I know of 115 thee?

MONTJOY  My master's mind.

KING  Unfold it.

MONTJOY  Thus says my king: Say thou to Harry of England, though we seemed dead, we did but sleep. 120 Advantage° is a better soldier than rashness. Tell him, we could have rebuked him at Harfleur, but that we thought not good to bruise an injury° till it were full ripe. Now we speak upon our cue, and our voice is imperial: England shall repent his folly, see his weak- 125 ness, and admire our sufferance.° Bid him therefore consider of his ransom, which must proportion the losses we have borne, the subjects we have lost, the disgrace we have digested; which in weight to re-answer, his pettiness would bow under.° For our 130 losses, his exchequer is too poor; for th' effusion of our blood, the muster of his kingdom too faint a number; and for our disgrace, his own person kneeling at our feet but a weak and worthless satisfaction. To this add defiance; and tell him for conclusion, he hath 135 betrayed his followers, whose condemnation is pronounced. So far my king and master; so much my office.

KING
What is thy name? I know thy quality.

MONTJOY  Montjoy.°                                                     140

KING
Thou dost thy office fairly. Turn thee back,
And tell thy king, I do not seek him now,
But could be willing to march on to Calais
Without impeachment;° for, to say the sooth,
Though 'tis no wisdom to confess so much               145
Unto an enemy of craft and vantage,°
My people are with sickness much enfeebled,
My numbers lessened; and those few I have
Almost no better than so many French,
Who when they were in health, I tell thee, herald,    150
I thought upon one pair of English legs
Did march three Frenchmen. Yet forgive me, God,
That I do brag thus! This your air of France
Hath blown that vice in me. I must repent.
Go therefore tell thy master, here I am;              155
My ransom is this frail and worthless trunk;
My army but a weak and sickly guard;
Yet, God before, tell him we will come on,
Though France himself and such another neighbor
Stand in our way. There's for thy labor, Montjoy.     160

[*Gives a purse.*]

Go bid thy master well advise himself:
If we may pass, we will; if we be hind'red,
We shall your tawny ground with your red blood
Discolor; and so, Montjoy, fare you well.
The sum of all our answer is but this:                165
We would not seek a battle as we are,
Nor, as we are, we say we will not shun it.
So tell your master.

**71 services** exploits  **72 sconce** small fort or earthwork  **73 came off** got clear  **74 what . . . on** what the position of the enemy depended on  **75 con** learn  **76 trick . . . oaths** adorn with newly phrased oaths  **77 of . . . cut** shaped in the same fashion as the general's  **84 hole . . . coat** some fault in him  **93 passages** i.e., of arms  **103 bubukles and whelks** abscesses-and-carbuncles (a confusion of two words) and pimples  **106 executed** i.e., slit (as he stood in the pillory before being hanged); **his** its  **107 cut off** put to death  **113 s.d. Tucket** a personal trumpet call  **114 habit** i.e., the herald's tabard

**121 Advantage** favorable opportunity  **123 bruise an injury** squeeze out a festering wound  **126 admire our sufferance** wonder at our patience  **129–30 in . . . under** to compensate in full would be too much for his small resources  **140 Montjoy** title of chief herald of France, not his name  **144 impeachment** hindrance  **146 craft and vantage** cunning and superiority

MONTJOY
I shall deliver so. Thanks to your highness.          [*Exit.*]
GLOUCESTER
I hope they will not come upon us now.          170
KING
We are in God's hand, brother, not in theirs.
March to the bridge, it now draws toward night;
Beyond the river we'll encamp ourselves,
And on tomorrow bid them march away.          *Exeunt.*

[Scene VII. *France. The French camp, near Agincourt.*]

*Enter the* CONSTABLE *of France, the Lords* RAMBURES,
ORLEANS, DAUPHIN, *with others.*

CONSTABLE   Tut! I have the best armor of the world.
Would it were day!
ORLEANS   You have an excellent armor; but let my
horse have his due.
CONSTABLE   It is the best horse of Europe.          5
ORLEANS   Will it never be morning?
DAUPHIN   My Lord of Orleans, and my Lord High
Constable, you talk of horse and armor?
ORLEANS   You are as well provided of both as any
prince in the world.          10
DAUPHIN   What a long night is this! I will not change
my horse with any that treads but on four pasterns.
Ça, ha! He bounds from the earth, as if his entrails
were hairs;° le cheval volant, the Pegasus, chez les
narines de feu!° When I bestride him, I soar, I am a          15
hawk; he trots the air; the earth sings when he touches
it. The basest horn of his hoof is more musical than the
pipe of Hermes.°
ORLEANS   He's of the color of the nutmeg.
DAUPHIN   And of the heat of the ginger. It is a beast          20
for Perseus:° he is pure air and fire; and the dull
elements of earth and water never appear in him, but
only in patient stillness while his rider mounts him.
He is indeed a horse, and all other jades° you may call
beasts.          25
CONSTABLE   Indeed, my lord, it is a most absolute and
excellent horse.
DAUPHIN   It is the prince of palfreys;° his neigh is like
the bidding of a monarch, and his countenance
enforces homage.          30
ORLEANS   No more, cousin.
DAUPHIN   Nay, the man hath no wit that cannot, from
the rising of the lark to the lodging of the lamb, vary°
deservèd praise on my palfrey; it is a theme as fluent
as the sea. Turn the sands into eloquent tongues, and          35
my horse is argument° for them all. 'Tis a subject for
a sovereign to reason° on, and for a sovereign's
sovereign to ride on; and for the world, familiar to us

and unknown, to lay apart their particular functions,
and wonder at him. I once writ a sonnet in his          40
praise and began thus, "Wonder of nature!"
ORLEANS   I have heard a sonnet begin so to one's
mistress.
DAUPHIN   Then did they imitate that which I composed to my courser, for my horse is my mistress.          45
ORLEANS   Your mistress bears well.°
DAUPHIN   Me well, which is the prescript° praise and
perfection of a good and particular° mistress.
CONSTABLE   Nay, for methought yesterday your
mistress shrewdly° shook your back.          50
DAUPHIN   So perhaps did yours.
CONSTABLE   Mine was not bridled.°
DAUPHIN   O, then belike she was old and gentle, and
you rode like a kern° of Ireland, your French hose°
off, and in your strait strossers.°          55
CONSTABLE   You have good judgment in horseman-
ship.°
DAUPHIN   Be warned by me then: they that ride so,
and ride not warily, fall into foul bogs. I had rather
have my horse to my mistress.          60
CONSTABLE   I had as lief have my mistress a jade.°
DAUPHIN   I tell thee, constable, my mistress wears his
own hair.°
CONSTABLE   I could make as true a boast as that, if I
had a sow to my mistress.          65
DAUPHIN   "Le chien est retourné à son propre vomis-
sement, et la truie lavée au bourbier."° Thou mak'st
use of anything.
CONSTABLE   Yet do I not use my horse for my mis-
tress, or any such proverb so little kin to the purpose.          70
RAMBURES   My Lord Constable, the armor that I saw
in your tent tonight—are those stars or suns upon it?
CONSTABLE   Stars, my lord.
DAUPHIN   Some of them will fall tomorrow, I hope.
CONSTABLE   And yet my sky shall not want.          75
DAUPHIN   That may be, for you bear a many super-
fluously, and 'twere more honor some were away.
CONSTABLE   Ev'n as your horse bears your praises,
who would trot as well, were some of your brags
dismounted.          80
DAUPHIN   Would I were able to load him with his
desert! Will it never be day? I will trot tomorrow a
mile, and my way shall be paved with English faces.
CONSTABLE   I will not say so, for fear I should be faced
out of my way;° but I would it were morning, for I          85
would fain be about the ears of the English.
RAMBURES   Who will go to hazard° with me for
twenty prisoners?
CONSTABLE   You must first go yourself to hazard, ere
you have them.          90

III.vii.13–14 as if . . . hairs i.e., as if he were a tennis ball (or perhaps "hairs" = hares)   14–15 cheval . . . feu the flying horse, Pegasus, with fiery nostrils   17–18 The basest . . . Hermes the winged horse, Pegasus, struck Mount Helicon with his hoof and the fountain of the Muses sprang forth; Hermes, alias Mercury, invented the pipe and charmed to sleep Argus of the hundred eyes   21 Perseus Pegasus sprang from the blood of the gorgon, Medusa, when Perseus cut off her head   24 jades nags   28 palfreys saddle horses (too light for use in battle)   33 vary express in different ways   36 argument subject   37 reason discourse

46 bears well carries her rider well   47 prescript prescribed   48 particular private   50 shrewdly (1) severely (2) shrewishly (cf. line 52)   52 bridled as (1) a horse (2) a shrew compelled to wear a bridle   54 kern lightly armed Irish foot soldier; French hose loose, wide breeches   55 strait strossers tight trousers (i.e., bare-legged)   56–57 horsemanship with a pun on whores-manship   61 jade (1) poor horse (2) loose woman   62–63 wears . . . hair i.e., doesn't need a (fashionable) wig   66–67 Le chien . . . bourbier cf. II Peter 2:22, "The dog is turned to his own vomit again, and the sow that was washed to her wallowing in the mire"   84–85 faced . . . way (1) put out of countenance (2) driven off   87 go to hazard take a wager

DAUPHIN 'Tis midnight; I'll go arm myself.    *Exit.*

ORLEANS The dauphin longs for morning.

RAMBURES He longs to eat the English.

CONSTABLE I think he will eat all he kills.

ORLEANS By the white hand of my lady, he's a 95 gallant prince.

CONSTABLE Swear by her foot, that she may tread out° the oath.

ORLEANS He is simply the most active gentleman of France. 100

CONSTABLE Doing is activity, and he will still be doing.°

ORLEANS He never did harm, that I heard of.

CONSTABLE Nor will do none tomorrow; he will keep that good name still. 105

ORLEANS I know him to be valiant.

CONSTABLE I was told that, by one that knows him better than you.

ORLEANS What's he?

CONSTABLE Marry, he told me so himself, and he said 110 he cared not who knew it.

ORLEANS He needs not; it is no hidden virtue in him.

CONSTABLE By my faith, sir, but it is! Never anybody saw it but his lackey;° 'tis a hooded valor, and when it appears, it will bate.° 115

ORLEANS Ill will never said well.

CONSTABLE I will cap that proverb with, "There is flattery in friendship."

ORLEANS And I will take up that with, "Give the devil his due." 120

CONSTABLE Well placed! There stands your friend for the devil. Have at the very eye of that proverb with, "A pox of the devil!"

ORLEANS You are the better at proverbs, by how much "a fool's bolt is soon shot." 125

CONSTABLE You have shot over.°

ORLEANS 'Tis not the first time you were overshot.°

*Enter a* MESSENGER.

MESSENGER My Lord High Constable, the English lie within fifteen hundred paces of your tents.

CONSTABLE Who hath measured the ground? 130

MESSENGER The Lord Grandpré.

CONSTABLE A valiant and most expert gentleman. Would it were day! Alas, poor Harry of England! He longs not for the dawning, as we do.

ORLEANS What a wretched and peevish° fellow is 135 this King of England, to mope with his fat-brained followers so far out of his knowledge!

CONSTABLE If the English had any apprehension,° they would run away.

ORLEANS That they lack; for if their heads had any 140 intellectual armor, they could never wear such heavy headpieces.

RAMBURES That island of England breeds very valiant creatures: their mastiffs are of unmatchable courage.

ORLEANS Foolish curs, that run winking° into the 145 mouth of a Russian bear, and have their heads crushed like rotten apples! You may as well say, that's a valiant flea, that dare eat his breakfast on the lip of a lion.

CONSTABLE Just, just! And the men do sympathize with the mastiffs in robustious and rough coming on, 150 leaving their wits with their wives: and then give them great meals of beef, and iron and steel; they will eat like wolves and fight like devils.

ORLEANS Ay, but these English are shrewdly° out of beef. 155

CONSTABLE Then shall we find tomorrow they have only stomachs° to eat, and none to fight. Now is it time to arm; come, shall we about it?

ORLEANS
It is now two o'clock; but let me see—by ten
We shall have each a hundred Englishmen.    *Exeunt.* 160

# A C T [ I V ]

*[Enter]* CHORUS.

Now entertain conjecture of a time
When creeping murmur and the poring° dark
Fills the wide vessel of the universe.
From camp to camp, through the foul womb of night,
The hum of either army stilly° sounds;      5
That the fixed sentinels almost receive
The secret whispers of each other's watch.
Fire answers fire, and through their paly° flames
Each battle° sees the other's umbered° face.
Steed threatens steed, in high and boastful neighs    10
Piercing the night's dull ear; and from the tents
The armorers accomplishing° the knights,
With busy hammers closing rivets up,
Give dreadful note° of preparation.
The country cocks do crow, the clocks do toll;    15
And the third hour of drowsy morning named.
Proud of their numbers, and secure° in soul,
The confident and over-lusty° French
Do the low-rated English play° at dice;
And chide the cripple tardy-gaited night      20
Who like a foul and ugly witch doth limp
So tediously away. The poor condemnèd English,
Like sacrifices, by their watchful° fires
Sit patiently, and inly ruminate
The morning's danger; and their gesture° sad,    25
Investing° lank-lean cheeks and war-worn coats,
Presenteth them unto the gazing moon
So many horrid ghosts. O, now, who will behold
The royal captain of this ruined band
Walking from watch to watch, from tent to tent,    30
Let him cry, "Praise and glory on his head!"
For forth he goes and visits all his host,

97–98 **tread out** (1) obliterate (2) treat with contempt   102 **doing** having sexual intercourse   114 **but his lackey** i.e., he has beaten no one but his footboy   114–15 **hooded . . . bate** valor like a hawk hooded before action, which flatters and beats its wings when its hood is removed   115 **bate** (1) beat its wings (2) become dejected   126 **over** beyond the mark   127 **overshot** (1) wide of the mark (2) beaten in shooting   135 **peevish** senseless   138 **apprehension** understanding, grasp of mind

145 **winking** with eyes shut   154 **shrewdly** very much   157 **stomachs** disposition   IV.Cho.2 **poring** eye-straining   5 **stilly** softly   8 **paly** pale (poetic)   9 **battle** army; **umbered** shadowed   12 **accomplishing** equipping   14 **note** indication   17 **secure** confident   18 **over-lusty** too lively   19 **play** play for   23 **watchful** used for keeping watch   25 **gesture** bearing   26 **Investing** accompanying

Bids them good morrow with a modest smile,
And calls them brothers, friends, and countrymen.
Upon his royal face there is no note                                35
How dread an army hath enrounded him;
Nor doth he dedicate one jot of color
Unto° the weary and all-watchèd° night;
Bur freshly looks, and overbears attaint°
With cheerful semblance and sweet majesty;             40
That every wretch, pining and pale before,
Beholding him, plucks comfort from his looks.
A largess universal, like the sun,
His liberal eye doth give to everyone,
Thawing cold fear, that mean and gentle all            45
Behold, as may unworthiness define,°
A little touch of Harry in the night.
And so our scene must to the battle fly;
Where (O for pity!) we shall much disgrace,
With four or five most vile and ragged foils°          50
Right ill-disposed in brawl ridiculous,
The name of Agincourt. Yet sit and see,
Minding true things by what their mock'ries° be.

*Exit.*

[Scene I. *France. The English camp at Agincourt.*]

*Enter the* KING, BEDFORD, *and* GLOUCESTER.

KING
Gloucester, 'tis true that we are in great danger;
The greater therefore should our courage be.
Good morrow, brother Bedford. God Almighty!
There is some soul of goodness in things evil,
Would men observingly distill it out;                          5
For our bad neighbor makes us early stirrers,
Which is both healthful, and good husbandry.°
Besides, they are our outward° consciences,
And preachers to us all, admonishing
That we should dress us° fairly for our end.            10
Thus may we gather honey from the weed
And make a moral° of the devil himself.

*Enter* ERPINGHAM.

Good morrow, old Sir Thomas Erpingham:
A good soft pillow for that good white head
Were better than a churlish turf of France.            15

ERPINGHAM
Not so, my liege. This lodging likes me better,
Since I may say, "Now lie I like a king."

KING
'Tis good for men to love their present pains
Upon° example: so the spirit is eased;
And when the mind is quick'ned, out of doubt          20
The organs,° though defunct° and dead before,
Break up their drowsy grave, and newly° move
With casted slough and fresh legerity.°

Lend me thy cloak, Sir Thomas. Brothers both,
Commend me to the princes in our camp;                25
Do my good morrow to them, and anon
Desire them all to my pavilion.

GLOUCESTER
We shall, my liege.

ERPINGHAM
Shall I attend your grace?

KING                                   No, my good knight.
Go with my brothers to my lords of England.           30
I and my bosom must debate awhile,
And then I would no other company.

ERPINGHAM
The Lord in heaven bless thee, noble Harry!

*Exeunt [all but the* KING].

KING
God-a-mercy, old heart! thou speak'st cheerfully.

*Enter* PISTOL.

PISTOL   Qui va là?°                                      35
KING   A friend.
PISTOL
Discuss° unto me; art thou officer,
Or art thou base, common, and popular?°
KING   I am a gentleman of a company.
PISTOL
Trail'st thou the puissant pike?°                        40
KING   Even so. What are you?
PISTOL
As good a gentleman as the emperor.
KING   Then you are a better than the king.
PISTOL
The king's a bawcock,° and a heart of gold,
A lad of life, an imp° of fame,                          45
Of parents good, of fist most valiant.
I kiss his dirty shoe, and from heartstring
I love the lovely bully.° What is thy name?
KING   Harry le Roy.
PISTOL
Le Roy? A Cornish name. Art thou of Cornish crew?  50
KING   No, I am a Welshman.
PISTOL
Know'st thou Fluellen?
KING   Yes.
PISTOL
Tell him I'll knock his leek about his pate
Upon Saint Davy's day.°                                  55
KING   Do not you wear your dagger in your cap that
day, lest he knock that about yours.
PISTOL
Art thou his friend?
KING   And his kinsman too.
PISTOL
The figo° for thee then!                                 60
KING   I thank you. God be with you!
PISTOL
My name is Pistol called.                       *Exit.*

37–38 **dedicate . . . Unto** look pale on account of   **38**
**all-watchèd** entirely spent in watches   **39 overbears attaint**
overcomes any sign of exhaustion   **46 as . . . define** as far as
our unworthy selves can present it   **50 foils** light fencing
weapons   **53 mock'ries** imitations
**IV.i.7 husbandry** careful management   **8 outward** i.e., not
our own inner   **10 dress us** prepare ourselves   **12 moral**
improving lesson   **19 Upon** in pursuance of   **21 organs** parts
of the body; **defunct** out of use   **22 newly** a snake is torpid
before casting its slough   **23 legerity** nimbleness

35 **Qui va là** Who goes there?   37 **Discuss** declare   38
**popular** vulgar   40 **Trail'st . . . pike** i.e., Are you an
infantryman? (a pike was held below its head, the butt trailing
behind on the ground)   44 **bawcock** fine fellow (familiar
term)   45 **imp** child   48 **bully** fine fellow (familiar, endearing
term)   55 **Saint Davy's day** March 1   60 **figo** fig (Spanish),
contemptuous and obscene gesture

KING   It sorts° well with your fierceness.

                *Manet° KING [aside].*

*Enter* FLUELLEN *and* GOWER.

GOWER   Captain Fluellen!

FLUELLEN   So! in the name of Jesu Christ, speak 65
fewer.° It is the greatest admiration in the universal
world, when the true and aunchient prerogatifes and
laws of the wars is not kept. If you would take the
pains but to examine the wars of Pompey the Great,
you shall find, I warrant you, that there is no tiddle 70
taddle nor pibble babble in Pompey's camp; I warrant
you, you shall find the ceremonies of the wars, and
the cares of it, and the forms of it, and the sobriety of
it, and the modesty° of it, to be otherwise.

GOWER   Why, the enemy is loud; you hear him all 75
night.

FLUELLEN   If the enemy is an ass and a fool and a
prating coxcomb, is it meet, think you, that we should
also, look you, be an ass and a fool and a prating
coxcomb, in your own conscience now?         80

GOWER   I will speak lower.

FLUELLEN   I pray you, and beseech you that you will.

                *Exit, [with GOWER].*

KING
Though it appear a little out of fashion,°
There is much care and valor in this Welshman.

*Enter three soldiers: John* BATES, *Alexander* COURT,
*and Michael* WILLIAMS.

COURT   Brother John Bates, is not that the morning 85
which breaks yonder?

BATES   I think it be; but we have no great cause to
desire the approach of day.

WILLIAMS   We see yonder the beginning of the day,
but I think we shall never see the end of it. Who goes 90
there?

KING   A friend.

WILLIAMS   Under what captain serve you?

KING   Under Sir Thomas Erpingham.

WILLIAMS   A good old commander, and a most kind 95
gentleman. I pray you, what thinks he of our estate?°

KING   Even as men wracked upon a sand, that look to
be washed off the next tide.

BATES   He hath not told his thought to the king?

KING   No; nor it is not meet he should. For though I 100
speak it to you, I think the king is but a man, as I am:
the violet smells to him, as it doth to me; the element
shows° to him, as it doth to me; all his senses have but
human conditions.° His ceremonies° laid by, in his
nakedness he appears but a man; and though his 105
affections are higher mounted than ours, yet when they
stoop,° they stoop with the like wing: therefore,
when he sees reason of° fears, as we do, his fears, out
of doubt, be of the same relish as ours are. Yet, in
reason, no man should possess him with any appearance 110

of fear, lest he, by showing it, should dishearten his
army.

BATES   He may show what outward courage he will;
but I believe, as cold a night as 'tis, he could wish
himself in Thames up to the neck; and so I would he 115
were, and I by him, at all adventures,° so we were quit
here.°

KING   By my troth, I will speak my conscience° of the
king: I think he would not wish himself anywhere but
where he is.         120

BATES   Then I would he were here alone; so should
he be sure to be ransomed, and a many poor men's
lives saved.

KING   I dare say you love him not so ill to wish him
here alone; howsoever you speak this to feel other 125
men's minds. Methinks I could not die anywhere so
contented as in the king's company, his cause being
just and his quarrel honorable.

WILLIAMS   That's more than we know.

BATES   Ay, or more than we should seek after; for we 130
know enough if we know we are the king's subjects:
if his cause be wrong, our obedience to the king wipes
the crime of it out of us.

WILLIAMS   But if the cause be not good, the king
himself hath a heavy reckoning to make, when all 135
those legs and arms and heads, chopped off in a battle,
shall join together at the latter day and cry all, "We
died at such a place," some swearing, some crying for
a surgeon, some upon their wives left poor behind
them, some upon the debts they owe, some upon their 140
children rawly° left. I am afeard there are few die well°
that die in a battle; for how can they charitably dispose
of anything when blood is their argument? Now, if
these men do not die well, it will be a black matter for
the king that led them to it; who to disobey, were 145
against all proportion of subjection.°

KING   So, if a son that is by his father sent about
merchandise do sinfully miscarry° upon the sea, the
imputation of his wickedness, by your rule, should be
imposed upon his father that sent him; or if a servant, 150
under his master's command transporting a sum of
money, be assailed by robbers and die in many
irreconciled° iniquities, you may call the business of
the master the author of the servant's damnation. But
this is not so. The king is not bound to answer° the 155
particular endings of his soldiers, the father of his son,
nor the master of his servant; for they purpose not
their death when they purpose their services. Besides,
there is no king, be his cause never so spotless, if it
come to the arbitrament of swords, can try it out with 160
all unspotted soldiers: some (peradventure) have on
them the guilt of premeditated and contrived murder;
some, of beguiling virgins with the broken seals° of
perjury; some, making the wars their bulwark,° that
have before gored the gentle bosom of peace with 165
pillage and robbery. Now, if these men have defeated

---

63 **sorts** suits (the Elizabethan pistol was notably noisy and
ineffective)   63 **s.d. Manet** remains (Latin)   66 **fewer** less   74
**modesty** moderation   83 **out of fashion** odd   96 **estate**
state, condition   102–03 **element shows** sky appears   104
**conditions** characteristics; **ceremonies** accompaniments of
royalty   107 **stoop** used of a hawk swooping down on its prey
108 **of** for

116 **at all adventures** whatever the consequences   116–17
**quit here** done with this job   118 **conscience** inmost thought
141 **rawly** (1) unprepared (2) at immature age; **well** i.e., a
Christian death   146 **proportion of subjection** due
relation of subject to monarch   148 **sinfully miscarry** perish
in his sins   153 **irreconciled** not atoned for   155 **answer**
render account for   163 **seals** sealed covenants   164 **bulwark**
defense (against pursuing justice)

the law and outrun native° punishment, though they can outstrip men, they have no wings to fly from God. War is his beadle,° war is his vengeance; so that here men are punished for before-breach° of the king's laws 170 in now the king's quarrel. Where they feared the death, they have borne life away; and where they would be safe, they perish. Then if they die unprovided,° no more is the king guilty of their damnation that he was before guilty of those impieties for the 175 which they are now visited.° Every subject's duty is the king's, but every subject's soul is his own. Therefore should every soldier in the wars do as every sick man in his bed—wash every mote out of his conscience; and dying so, death is to him advantage; or not dying, 180 the time was blessedly lost wherein such preparation was gained; and in him that escapes, it were not sin to think that, making God so free° an offer, He let him outlive that day, to see His greatness, and to teach others how they should prepare.                          185

WILLIAMS   'Tis certain, every man that dies ill, the ill upon his own head; the king is not to answer it.

BATES   I do not desire he should answer for me, and yet I determine to fight lustily for him.

KING   I myself heard the king say he would not be 190 ransomed.

WILLIAMS   Ay, he said so, to make us fight cheerfully; but when our throats are cut, he may be ransomed, and we ne'er the wiser.

KING   If I live to see it, I will never trust his word after. 195

WILLIAMS   You pay him° then! That's a perilous shot out of an elder-gun,° that a poor and a private° displeasure can do against a monarch! You may as well go about to turn the sun to ice with fanning in his face with a peacock's feather. You'll never trust his word 200 after! Come, 'tis a foolish saying.

KING   Your reproof is something too round;° I should be angry with you, if the time were convenient.

WILLIAMS   Let it be a quarrel between us, if you live.

KING   I embrace it.                                         205

WILLIAMS   How shall I know thee again?

KING   Give me any gage° of thine, and I will wear it in my bonnet. Then, if ever thou dar'st acknowledge it, I will make it my quarrel.

WILLIAMS   Here's my glove. Give me another of 210 thine.

KING   There.

WILLIAMS   This will I also wear in my cap. If ever thou come to me and say, after tomorrow, "This is my glove," by this hand, I will take° thee a box on the 215 ear.

KING   If ever I live to see it, I will challenge it.

WILLIAMS   Thou dar'st as well be hanged.

KING   Well, I will do it, though I take thee in the king's company.                                          220

WILLIAMS   Keep thy word. Fare thee well.

BATES   Be friends, you English fools, be friends! We

have French quarrels enow, if you could tell how to reckon.

KING   Indeed the French may lay twenty French 225 crowns° to one they will beat us, for they bear them on their shoulders;° but it is no English treason° to cut French crowns, and tomorrow the king himself will be a clipper.                              *Exeunt* SOLDIERS.

"Upon the king! Let us our lives, our souls,         230
Our debts, our careful° wives,
Our children, and our sins, lay on the king!"
We must bear all. O hard condition,
Twin-born with greatness, subject to the breath°
Of every fool, whose sense no more can feel         235
But his own wringing!° What infinite heart's-ease
Must kings neglect that private men enjoy!
And what have kings that privates have not too,
Save ceremony, save general ceremony?
And what art thou, thou idol Ceremony?               240
What kind of god art thou, that suffer'st more
Of mortal griefs than do thy worshippers?
What are thy rents? What are thy comings-in?
O Ceremony, show me but thy worth!
What is thy soul of adoration?°                       245
Art thou aught else but place, degree, and form,°
Creating awe and fear in other men?
Wherein thou art less happy, being feared,
Than they in fearing.
What drink'st thou oft, instead of homage sweet,     250
But poisoned flattery? O, be sick, great greatness,
And bid thy ceremony give thee cure!
Thinks thou the fiery fever will go out
With titles blown° from adulation?
Will it give place to flexure° and low bending?      255
Canst thou, when thou command'st the beggar's knee,
Command the health of it? No, thou proud dream,
That play'st so subtlely with a king's repose.
I am a king that find° thee; and I know
'Tis not the balm, the scepter, and the ball,°       260
The sword, the mace, the crown imperial,
The intertissued robe of gold and pearl,
The farcèd° title running 'fore the king,
The throne he sits on, nor the tide of pomp
That beats upon the high shore° of this world—       265
No, not all these, thrice-gorgeous ceremony,
Not all these, laid in bed majestical,
Can sleep so soundly as the wretched slave,
Who, with a body filled, and vacant mind,
Gets him to rest, crammed with distressful° bread;   270
Never sees horrid night, the child of hell;
But like a lackey,° from the rise to set,
Sweats in the eye of Phoebus,° and all night

---

167 **native** rightful   169 **beadle** parish officer for punishing petty offenders   170 **before-breach** previous breach   173–74 **unprovided** unprepared   176 **visited** punished   183 **free** complete, wholehearted   196 **pay him** pay him out   197 **elder-gun** popgun (child's toy); **private** single and common man's   202 **round** plainspoken   207 **gage** pledge   215 **take** strike

226 **crowns** (1) coins, worth about six shillings each (2) heads 226–27 **for . . . shoulders** i.e., the French can lay such bets because (1) they so outnumber the English (2) they are still alive   227 **treason** it was a treasonable offense to debase the coinage by "clipping," or paring the edges of coins, to take their gold   231 **careful** anxious   234 **breath** speech 236 **wringing** stomach ache   245 **thy . . . adoration** the real nature of thy worship   246 **form** good order   254 **blown** inflated   255 **flexure** obsequious bowing   259 **find** discover the true character of   260 **ball** orb   263 **farcèd** stuffed out with pompous phrases   265 **high shore** exalted places   270 **distressful** gained by hard toil   272 **lackey** footman who ran by the coach of his master   273 **Phoebus** sun-god

Sleeps in Elysium;° next day after dawn,
Doth rise and help Hyperion° to his horse;     275
And follows so the ever-running year
With profitable labor to his grave;
And but for ceremony, such a wretch,
Winding up° days with toil and nights with sleep,
Had the forehand° and vantage of a king.     280
The slave, a member of° the country's peace,
Enjoys it; but in gross° brain little wots
What watch the king keeps to maintain the peace,
Whose hours the peasant best advantages.°

*Enter* ERPINGHAM.

ERPINGHAM
My lord, your nobles, jealous° of your absence,     285
Seek through your camp to find you.
KING                       Good old knight,
Collect them all together at my tent.
I'll be before thee.
ERPINGHAM      I shall do't, my lord.        *Exit.*
KING
O God of battles, steel my soldiers' hearts,
Possess them not with fear! Take from them now     290
The sense of reck'ning, or th' opposèd numbers
Pluck their hearts from them. Not today, O Lord,
O, not today, think not upon the fault°
My father made in compassing the crown!
I Richard's body have interrèd new,     295
And on it have bestowed more contrite tears
Than from it issued forcèd drops of blood.
Five hundred poor I have in yearly pay,
Who twice a day their withered hands hold up
Toward heaven, to pardon blood;     300
And I have built two chantries,
Where the sad and solemn priests sing still
For Richard's soul. More will I do:
Though all that I can do is nothing worth;
Since that my penitence comes after all,     305
Imploring pardon.

*Enter* GLOUCESTER.

GLOUCESTER    My liege!
KING
My brother Gloucester's voice? Ay.
I know thy errand; I will go with thee.
The day, my friends, and all things stay for me.     310
                      *Exeunt.*

[Scene II. *France. The French camp.*]

*Enter the* DAUPHIN, ORLEANS, RAMBURES, *and*
BEAUMONT.

ORLEANS
The sun doth gild our armor. Up, my lords!
DAUPHIN   Montez à cheval!° My horse! Varlet,
lacquais! Ha!

ORLEANS   O brave spirit!
DAUPHIN   Via! les eaux et la terre°—     5
ORLEANS   Rien puis? L'air et le feu.
DAUPHIN   Ciel, cousin Orleans.

*Enter* CONSTABLE.

Now, my Lord Constable?
CONSTABLE
Hark how our steeds for present service neigh!
DAUPHIN
Mount them, and make incision in their hides,     10
That their hot blood may spin° in English eyes
And dout them with superfluous courage,° ha!
RAMBURES
What, will you have them weep our horses' blood?
How shall we then behold their natural tears?

*Enter* MESSENGER.

MESSENGER
The English are embattailed, you French peers.     15
CONSTABLE
To horse, you gallant princes! straight to horse!
Do but behold yond poor and starvèd band,
And your fair show° shall suck away their souls,
Leaving them but the shales° and husks of men.
There is not work enough for all our hands,     20
Scarce blood enough in all their sickly veins
To give each naked curtle ax° a stain
That our French gallants shall today draw out
And sheathe for lack of sport. Let us but blow on them,
The vapor of our valor will o'erturn them.     25
'Tis positive 'gainst all exceptions,° lords,
That our superfluous lackeys and our peasants,
Who in unnecessary action swarm
About our squares of battle, were enow
To purge this field of such a hilding° foe,     30
Though we upon this mountain's basis by
Took stand for idle speculation:°
But that our honors must not. What's to say?
A very little little let us do,
And all is done. Then let the trumpets sound     35
The tucket sonance° and the note to mount;
For our approach shall so much dare° the field
That England shall couch° down in fear and yield.

*Enter* GRANDPRÉ.

GRANDPRÉ
Why do you stay so long, my lords of France?
Yond island carrions,° desperate° of their bones,     40
Ill-favoredly become the morning field.
Their ragged curtains° poorly are let loose,
And our air shakes them passing° scornfully.
Big Mars seems bankrout° in their beggared host,

---

274 **Elysium** in mythology, the abode of the blessed after death  275 **Hyperion** sun-god (more correctly, his father) 279 **Winding up** passing  280 **forehand** upper hand  281 **member of** sharer in  282 **gross** stupid  284 **peasant best advantages** most benefit the peasant  285 **jealous** anxious 293 **the fault** i.e., the deposition of Richard II, and the suggestion for his subsequent murder
**IV.ii.2 Montez à cheval** To horse!

**5 Via . . . terre** Begone, water and earth (the dauphin is still thinking of his horse; Orleans asks if he does not wish to ride further, to "air and fire"; the dauphin replies, "Heaven") **11 spin** gush forth  **12 dout . . . courage** extinguish them with overflowing blood (the supposed source of courage) **18 fair show** spectacular appearance  **19 shales** shells  **22 curtle ax** cutlass (broad-cutting sword)  **26 exceptions** objections  **30 hilding** worthless  **32 speculation** looking on **36 sonance** sound  **37 dare** dazzle  **38 couch** crouch  **40 carrions** skeletons; **desperate** careless, without hope of saving **42 curtains** banner  **43 passing** extremely  **44 bankrout** bankrupt

And faintly through a rusty beaver° peeps.                    45
The horsemen sit like fixèd candlesticks
With torch-staves in their hand; and their poor jades
Lob° down their heads, dropping the hides and hips,
The gum down roping° from their pale-dead eyes,
And in their pale dull mouths the gimmaled° bit          50
Lies foul with chawed grass, still and motionless;
And their executors, the knavish crows,
Fly o'er them all, impatient for their hour.
Description cannot suit itself in words
To demonstrate the life of° such a battle                    55
In life so lifeless as it shows itself.

CONSTABLE
They have said their prayers, and they stay for death.

DAUPHIN
Shall we go send them dinners, and fresh suits,
And give their fasting horses provender,
And after fight with them?                                          60

CONSTABLE
I stay but for my guard. On to the field!
I will the banner from a trumpet° take
And use it for my haste. Come, come away!
The sun is high, and we outwear the day.        *Exeunt.*


[Scene III. *France. The English camp.*]

*Enter* GLOUCESTER, BEDFORD, EXETER, ERPING-
HAM *with all his* HOST, SALISBURY, *and* WESTMORE-
LAND.

GLOUCESTER
Where is the king?

BEDFORD
The king himself is rode to view their battle.°

WESTMORELAND
Of fighting men they have full three-score thousand.

EXETER
There's five to one; besides they all are fresh.

SALISBURY
God's arm strike with us! 'Tis a fearful odds.          5
God bye° you, princes all; I'll to my charge.
If we no more meet, till we meet in heaven,
Then joyfully, my noble Lord of Bedford,
My dear Lord Gloucester, and my good Lord Exeter,
And my kind kinsman, warriors all, adieu!              10

BEDFORD
Farewell, good Salisbury, and good luck go with thee!

EXETER
Farewell, kind lord. Fight valiantly today;
And yet I do thee wrong to mind thee of it,
For thou art framed of the firm truth of valor.
                                        [*Exit* SALISBURY.]

BEDFORD
He is as full of valor as of kindness,                        15
Princely in both.

*Enter the* KING.

WESTMORELAND   O that we now had here

But one ten thousand of those men in England
That do no work today!

KING                                     What's he that wishes so?
My cousin Westmoreland? No, my fair cousin.
If we are marked to die, we are enow                        20
To do our country loss; and if to live,
The fewer men, the greater share of honor.
God's will! I pray thee wish not one man more.
By Jove, I am not covetous for gold,
Nor care I who doth feed upon my cost;                   25
It earns° me not if men my garments wear;
Such outward things dwell not in my desires:
But if it be a sin to covet honor,
I am the most offending soul alive.
No, faith, my coz, wish not a man from England.    30
God's peace! I would not lose so great an honor
As one man more methinks would share from me
For the best hope I have. O, do not wish one more!
Rather proclaim it, Westmoreland, through my host,
That he which hath no stomach° to this fight,        35
Let him depart; his passport shall be made,
And crowns for convoy put into his purse;
We would not die in that man's company
That fears his fellowship° to die with us.
This day is called the Feast of Crispian:°              40
He that outlives this day, and comes safe home,
Will stand a-tiptoe when this day is named,
And rouse him at the name of Crispian.
He that shall see this day, and live old age,
Will yearly on the vigil feast his neighbors          45
And say, "Tomorrow is Saint Crispian."
Then will he strip his sleeve and show his scars,
And say, "These wounds I had on Crispin's day."
Old men forget; yet all shall be forgot,
But he'll remember, with advantages,°                  50
What feats he did that day. Then shall our names,
Familiar in his mouth as household words—
Harry the King, Bedford and Exeter,
Warwick and Talbot, Salisbury and Gloucester—
Be in their flowing cups freshly rememb'red.       55
This story shall the good man teach his son;
And Crispin Crispian shall ne'er go by,
From this day to the ending of the world,
But we in it shall be rememberèd—
We few, we happy few, we band of brothers;        60
For he today that sheds his blood with me
Shall be my brother;° be he ne'er so vile,°
This day shall gentle his condition.°
And gentlemen in England, now abed,
Shall think themselves accursed they were not here;  65
And hold their manhoods cheap whiles any speaks
That fought with us upon Saint Crispin's day.

*Enter* SALISBURY.

SALISBURY
My sovereign lord, bestow yourself with speed:

**26 earns** grieves   **35 stomach** inclination   **39 fellowship**
participation   **40 Crispian** the brothers Crispin and Crispian
(cf. line 57) fled from Rome during the persecutions of Dio-
cletian and supported and hid themselves as humble shoemakers; they were martyred A.D. 286   **50 advantages** added
luster   **60-62 brothers . . . brother** like the brother martyrs;
see note to line 40   **62 vile** low of birth   **63 gentle his condition** ennoble his rank

**45 beaver** face guard of a helmet   **48 Lob** droop   **49 roping**
hanging like rope   **50 gimmaled** jointed   **55 the life of**
to the life   **62 trumpet** trumpeter
**IV.iii.2 battle** battle array   **6 bye** be with

The French are bravely° in their battles set
And will with all expedience° charge on us.    70

**KING**
All things are ready, if our minds be so.

**WESTMORELAND**
Perish the man whose mind is backward now!

**KING**
Thou dost not wish more help from England, coz?

**WESTMORELAND**
God's will, my liege! would you and I alone,
Without more help, could fight this royal battle!    75

**KING**
Why, now thou hast unwished five thousand men!
Which likes me better than to wish us one.
You know your places: God be with you all!

*Tucket. Enter* MONTJOY.

**MONTJOY**
Once more I come to know of thee, King Harry,
If for thy ransom thou wilt now compound,°    80
Before thy most assurèd overthrow;
For certainly thou art so near the gulf
Thou needs must be englutted.° Besides, in mercy,
The constable desires thee thou wilt mind°
Thy followers of repentance, that their souls    85
May make a peaceful and a sweet retire°
From off these fields, where (wretches!) their poor
    bodies
Must lie and fester.

**KING**            Who hath sent thee now?

**MONTJOY**
The Constable of France.

**KING**
I pray thee bear my former answer back:    90
Bid them achieve° me, and then sell my bones.
Good God, why should they mock poor fellows thus?
The man that once did sell the lion's skin
While the beast lived, was killed with hunting him.
A many of our bodies shall no doubt    95
Find native graves; upon the which, I trust,
Shall witness live in brass of this day's work.
And those that leave their valiant bones in France,
Dying like men, though buried in your dunghills,
They shall be famed; for there the sun shall greet them    100
And draw their honors reeking° up to heaven,
Leaving their earthly parts to choke your clime,
The smell whereof shall breed a plague in France.
Mark then abounding valor in our English:
That, being dead, like to the bullet's grazing,    105
Break out into a second course of mischief,
Killing in relapse of mortality.°
Let me speak proudly. Tell the constable,
We are but warriors for the working day:°
Our gayness and our gilt are all besmirched    110
With rainy marching in the painful° field.
There's not a piece of feather in our host—
Good argument, I hope, we will not fly—

And time hath worn us into slovenry.
But, by the mass, our hearts are in the trim;°    115
And my poor soldiers tell me, yet ere night
They'll be in fresher robes,° or they will pluck
The gay new coats o'er the French soldiers' heads
And turn them° out of service. If they do this
(As, if God please, they shall), my ransom then    120
Will soon be levied. Herald, save thou thy labor.
Come thou no more for ransom, gentle herald;
They shall have none, I swear, but these my joints;
Which if they have as I will leave 'em them,
Shall yield them little, tell the constable.    125

**MONTJOY**
I shall, King Harry. And so fare thee well:
Thou never shalt hear herald any more.        *Exit.*

**KING**
I fear thou wilt once more come again for a ransom.°

*Enter* YORK.

**YORK**
My lord, most humbly on my knee I beg
The leading of the vaward.°    130

**KING**
Take it, brave York. Now, soldiers, march away;
And how thou pleasest, God, dispose the day! *Exeunt.*

[*Scene IV. France. The field of battle.*]

*Alarum. Excursions. Enter* PISTOL, FRENCH SOLDIER,
BOY.

**PISTOL** Yield, cur!

**FRENCH SOLDIER** Je pense que vous êtes le gentilhomme de bonne qualité.°

**PISTOL** Qualtitie calmie custure me!° Art thou a
gentleman? What is thy name? Discuss.    5

**FRENCH SOLDIER** O Seigneur Dieu!

**PISTOL**
O Signieur Dew should be a gentleman.
Perpend° my words, O Signieur Dew, and mark:
O Signieur Dew, thou diest on point of fox,°
Except, O signieur, thou do give to me    10
Egregious° ransom.

**FRENCH SOLDIER** O, prenez miséricorde, ayez pitié
de moi!°

**PISTOL**
Moy° shall not serve; I will have forty moys,
Or I will fetch thy rim° out at thy throat    15
In drops of crimson blood.

**FRENCH SOLDIER** Est-il impossible d'échapper la
force de ton bras?°

**PISTOL** Brass, cur?

69 **bravely** finely arrayed   70 **expedience** expedition, speed
80 **compound** make terms   83 **englutted** swallowed   84
**mind** remind   86 **retire** retreat (sarcastic)   91 **achieve** kill
101 **reeking** exhaling, rising   107 **relapse of mortality** (1)
renewed deadliness (2) with a deadly rebound (?)   109 **for
. . . day** i.e., (1) who mean business (2) who are not dressed in
finery   111 **painful** arduous

115 **in the trim** (1) in fine fettle (2) fashionably attired   117
**in fresher robes** i.e., in heavenly robes   119 **them** the
soldiers   128 **I . . . ransom** (ironic)   130 **vaward** vanguard
**IV.iv.2-3 Je . . . qualité** I think you are a gentleman of
high rank   4 **Qualtitie . . . me** possibly a corruption of an
Irish refrain to a popular song: "Calen o custure me," for "the
girl from the (river) Suir"   8 **Perpend** consider   9 **fox** kind of
sword   11 **Egregious** huge   12-13 **O . . . moi** O, have
mercy, take pity on me!   14 **Moy** no coin so called existed;
possibly a reference to the measure, about a bushel   15 **rim**
lining of the stomach   17-18 **Est-il . . . bras** Is there no
way to escape the strength of your arm? (in Shakespeare's time
the *s* in *bras* was still sounded before a pause)

Thou damnèd and luxurious mountain goat,°        20
Offer'st me brass?

FRENCH SOLDIER  O, pardonnez-moi!

PISTOL
Say'st thou me so? Is that a ton of moys?
Come hither, boy; ask me this slave in French
What is his name.        25

BOY  Ecoutez: comment êtes-vous appelé?

FRENCH SOLDIER  Monsieur le Fer.

BOY  He says his name is Master Fer.

PISTOL  Master Fer? I'll fer him, and firk° him, and
ferret° him! Discuss the same in French unto him.        30

BOY  I do not know the French for "fer," and "ferret,"
and "firk."

PISTOL  Bid him prepare, for I will cut his throat.

FRENCH SOLDIER  Que dit-il, monsieur?

BOY  Il me commande de vous dire que vous faites        35
vous prêt; car ce soldat ici est disposé tout à cette heure
de couper votre gorge.°

PISTOL
Owy, cuppele gorge, permafoy!
Peasant, unless thou give me crowns, brave crowns;
Or mangled shalt thou be by this my sword.        40

FRENCH SOLDIER  O, je vous supplie, pour l'amour
de Dieu, me pardonner! Je suis gentilhomme de
bonne maison. Gardez ma vie, et je vous donnerai
deux cents écus.°

PISTOL
What are his words?        45

BOY  He prays you to save his life; he is a gentleman
of a good house, and for his ransom he will give you
two hundred crowns.

PISTOL
Tell him my fury shall abate, and I
The crowns will take.        50

FRENCH SOLDIER  Petit monsieur, que dit-il?

BOY  Encore qu'il est contre son jurement de pardonner aucun prisonnier; néanmoins, pour les écus
que vous l'avez promis, il est content de vous donner
la liberté, le franchisement.        55

FRENCH SOLDIER  Sur mes genoux je vous donne
mille remercîments; et je m'estime heureux que je suis
tombé entre les mains d'un chevalier, je pense, le plus
brave, vaillant, et très distingué seigneur d'Angleterre.°

PISTOL
Expound unto me, boy.        60

BOY  He gives you, upon his knees, a thousand thanks,
and he esteems himself happy that he hath fall'n into
the hands of one (as he thinks) the most brave, valorous,
and thrice-worthy signieur of England.

PISTOL
As I suck blood, I will some mercy show!        65
Follow me.

BOY  Suivez-vous le grand capitaine. [*Exeunt* PISTOL
*and* FRENCH SOLDIER.] I did never know so full a
voice issue from so empty° a heart; but the saying is
true, "The empty vessel makes the greatest sound."        70
Bardolph and Nym had ten times more valor than
this roaring devil i' th' old play that everyone may pare
his nails° with a wooden dagger;° and they are both
hanged; and so would this be, if he durst steal anything
adventurously. I must stay with the lackeys with the        75
luggage of our camp—the French might have a good
prey of us, if he knew of it, for there is none to guard
it but boys.        *Exit.*

[Scene V. *France. Another part of the field.*]

*Enter* CONSTABLE, ORLEANS, BOURBON, DAUPHIN,
*and* RAMBURES.

CONSTABLE  O diable!

ORLEANS  O Seigneur! le jour est perdu, tout est
perdu!°

DAUPHIN
Mort Dieu, ma vie! all is confounded, all!
Reproach and everlasting shame        5
Sits mocking in our plumes.

*A short alarum.*

O méchante° fortune! Do not run away.

CONSTABLE
Why, all our ranks are broke.

DAUPHIN
O perdurable° shame! Let's stab ourselves.
Be these the wretches that we played at dice for?        10

ORLEANS
Is this the king we sent to for his ransom?

BOURBON
Shame, and eternal shame, nothing but shame!
Let us die in honor. Once more back again!
And he that will not follow Bourbon now,
Let him go hence, and with his cap in hand        15
Like a base pander hold the chamber door
Whilst by a slave, no gentler° than my dog,
His fairest daughter is contaminated.

CONSTABLE
Disorder, that hath spoiled° us, friend us now!
Let us on° heaps go offer up our lives.        20

ORLEANS
We are enow yet living in the field
To smother up the English in our throngs,
If any order might be thought upon.

BOURBON
The devil take order now! I'll to the throng;
Let life be short, else shame will be too long.        25
*Exit [with others.]*

20 **luxurious mountain goat** lustful wild lecher  29 **firk**
a euphemistic pronunciation of the common four-letter
obscenity  30 **ferret** go for, search out  34–37 **Que . . .
gorge** What does he say, sir?  *Boy*  He bids me tell you that
you must prepare yourself, for this soldier intends to cut your
throat immediately  41–44 **O . . . écus** O, I pray you, for
the love of God, to pardon me. I am a gentleman of good
house. Preserve my life, and I will give you two hundred écus
52–59 **Encore . . . d'Angleterre** I say again that it is against
his oath to spare any prisoner; nevertheless, because of the
écus you have promised him, he is willing to give you liberty,
freedom. *French Soldier* On my knees I give you a thousand
thanks; and I count myself happy that I have fallen into the
hands of a knight, as I think, the bravest, most valiant, and
eminent gentleman in England

69 **empty** cowardly  72–73 **pare his nails** clip his wings (a
proverbial phrase)  73 **wooden dagger** weapon of the Vice
in early Elizabethan plays
IV.v.2–3 **O . . . perdu** O sir, the day is lost, all is lost
7 **méchante** evil, spiteful  9 **perdurable** lasting  17 **gentler**
(1) more noble (2) less rough  19 **spoiled** ruined  20 **on** in

[Scene VI. *France. Another part of the field.*]

*Alarum. Enter the* KING *and his* TRAIN, [EXETER, *and others,*] *with* PRISONERS.

KING
Well have we done, thrice-valiant countrymen,
But all's not done; yet keep the French the field.

EXETER
The Duke of York commends him to your majesty.

KING
Lives he, good uncle? Thrice within this hour
I saw him down; thrice up again and fighting.          5
From helmet to the spur all blood he was.

EXETER
In which array, brave soldier, doth he lie,
Larding° the plain; and by his bloody side,
Yoke-fellow to his honor-owing° wounds,
The noble Earl of Suffolk also lies.                   10
Suffolk first died; and York, all haggled° over,
Comes to him, where in gore he lay insteeped,
And takes him by the beard, kisses the gashes
That bloodily did yawn upon his face.
He cries aloud, "Tarry, my cousin Suffolk!             15
My soul shall thine keep company to heaven.
Tarry, sweet soul, for mine, then fly abreast;
As in this glorious and well-foughten field
We kept together in our chivalry!"
Upon these words I came, and cheered him up;           20
He smiled me in the face, raught° me his hand,
And, with a feeble gripe, says, "Dear my lord,
Commend my service to my sovereign."
So did he turn, and over Suffolk's neck
He threw his wounded arm, and kissed his lips;         25
And so, espoused to death, with blood he sealed
A testament of noble-ending love.
The pretty° and sweet manner of it forced
Those waters from me which I would have stopped;
But I had not so much of man in me,                    30
And all my mother° came into mine eyes
And gave me up to tears.

KING                              I blame you not;
For, hearing this, I must perforce compound°
With mistful eyes, or they will issue too.

*Alarum.*

But hark, what new alarum is this same?                35
The French have reinforced their scattered men.
Then every soldier kill his prisoners!
Give the word through.               *Exit,* [*with others*].


[Scene VII. *France. Another part of the field.*]

*Enter* FLUELLEN *and* GOWER.

FLUELLEN  Kill the poys and the luggage? 'Tis expressly against the law of arms; 'tis as arrant a piece of knavery, mark you now, as can be offert—in your conscience, now, is it not?

GOWER  'Tis certain there's not a boy left alive, and   5
the cowardly rascals that ran from the battle ha' done
this slaughter; besides, they have burned and carried
away all that was in the king's tent; wherefore the
king most worthily hath caused every soldier to cut
his prisoner's throat. O, 'tis a gallant king!         10

FLUELLEN  Ay, he was porn at Monmouth, Captain
Gower. What call you the town's name where
Alexander the Pig was born?

GOWER  Alexander the Great.

FLUELLEN  Why, I pray you, is not "pig" great? The    15
pig, or the great, or the mighty, or the huge, or the
magnanimous, are all one reckonings, save the phrase
is a little variations.°

GOWER  I think Alexander the Great was born in
Macedon; his father was called Philip of Macedon, as  20
I take it.

FLUELLEN  I think it is in Macedon where Alexander
is porn. I tell you, Captain, if you look in the maps of
the 'orld, I warrant you sall find, in the comparisons
between Macedon and Monmouth, that the situations,    25
look you, is both alike. There is a river in Macedon,
and there is also moreover a river at Monmouth. It is
called Wye at Monmouth; but it is out of my prains
what is the name of the other river. But 'tis all one;
'tis alike as my fingers is to my fingers, and there is  30
salmons in both. If you mark Alexander's life well,
Harry of Monmouth's life is come after it indifferent
well, for there is figures° in all things. Alexander, God
knows, and you know, in his rages, and his furies,
and his wraths, and his cholers, and his moods, and    35
his displeasures, and his indignations, and also being a
little intoxicates in his prains, did, in his ales and his
angers, look you, kill his best friend, Cleitus.

GOWER  Our king is not like him in that; he never
killed any of his friends.                             40

FLUELLEN  It is not well done, mark you now, to take
the tales out of my mouth, ere it is made and finished.
I speak but in the figures and comparisons of it: as
Alexander killed his friend Cleitus, being in his ales
and his cups, so also Harry Monmouth, being in his    45
right wits and his good judgments, turned away the
fat knight with the great-belly° doublet—he was full
of jests, and gipes, and knaveries, and mocks; I have
forgot his name.

GOWER  Sir John Falstaff.                              50

FLUELLEN  That is he: I'll tell you there is good men
porn at Monmouth.

GOWER  Here comes his majesty.

*Alarum. Enter* KING *Harry and* BOURBON, [WARWICK,
GLOUCESTER, EXETER, *and others,*] *with* PRISONERS.
*Flourish.*

KING
I was not angry since I came to France
Until this instant. Take a trumpet,° herald,           55
Ride thou unto the horsemen on yond hill:
If they will fight with us, bid them come down,
Or void the field: they do offend our sight.
If they'll do neither, we will come to them,

IV.vi.8 Larding enriching  9 owing owning  11 haggled
mangled  21 raught reached  28 pretty lovely  31 mother
inherited womanly feelings  33 compound come to terms

IV.vii.18 variations for *varied*  33 figures parallels  47
great-belly (1) styled with stuffed lining (2) large-sized
(appropriate to Falstaff's girth)  55 trumpet trumpeter

And make them skirr° away, as swift as stones          60
Enforcèd from the old Assyrian slings.
Besides, we'll cut the throats of those we have,
And not a man of them that we shall take
Shall taste our mercy. Go and tell them so.

*Enter* MONTJOY.

EXETER
Here comes the herald of the French, my liege.          65
GLOUCESTER
His eyes are humbler than they used to be.
KING
How now? What means this, herald? Know'st thou
    not
That I have fined° these bones of mine for ransom?
Com'st thou again for ransom?
HERALD                                    No, great king.
I come to thee for charitable license,          70
That we may wander o'er this bloody field
To book° our dead, and then to bury them;
To sort our nobles from our common men.
For many of our princes (woe the while!)
Lie drowned and soaked in mercenary blood;          75
So do our vulgar drench their peasant limbs
In blood of princes, and their wounded steeds
Fret fetlock-deep in gore, and with wild rage
Yerk° out their armèd heels at their dead masters,
Killing them twice. O, give us leave, great king,          80
To view the field in safety, and dispose
Of their dead bodies!
KING                                    I tell thee truly, herald,
I know not if the day be ours or no,
For yet a many of your horsemen peer°
And gallop o'er the field.
HERALD                          The day is yours.          85
KING
Praised be God, and not our strength for it!
What is this castle called that stands hard by?
HERALD
They call it Agincourt.
KING
Then call we this the field of Agincourt,
Fought on the day of Crispin Crispianus.          90
FLUELLEN   Your grandfather° of famous memory,
an't please your majesty, and your great-uncle Edward
the Plack Prince of Wales, as I have read in the
chronicles, fought a most prave pattle here in France.
KING   They did, Fluellen.          95
FLUELLEN   Your majesty says very true. If your
majesties is rememb'red of it, the Welshmen did good
service in a garden where leeks did grow, wearing
leeks in their Monmouth caps; which your majesty
know to this hour is an honorable badge of the service;°          100
and I do believe your majesty takes no scorn to wear
the leek upon Saint Tavy's day.
KING
I wear it for a memorable honor;
For I am Welsh, you know, good countryman.

FLUELLEN   All the water in Wye cannot wash your          105
Majesty's Welsh plood out of your pody, I can tell you
that: God pless it, and preserve it, as long as it pleases
his grace, and his majesty too!
KING   Thanks, good my countryman.
FLUELLEN   By Jeshu, I am your majesty's countryman,          110
I care not who know it! I will confess it to all the 'orld;
I need not to be ashamed of your majesty, praised be
God, so long as your majesty is an honest man.
KING
God keep me so!

*Enter* WILLIAMS.

                    Our heralds go with him;
Bring me just notice of the numbers dead          115
On both our parts.
          [*Exeunt* HERALDS, MONTJOY, *and others,*
                              *including* GOWER.]
                    Call yonder fellow hither.
EXETER   Soldier, you must come to the king.
KING   Soldier, why wear'st thou that glove in thy cap?
WILLIAMS   And't please your majesty, 'tis the gage of
one that I should fight withal, if he be alive.          120
KING   An Englishman?
WILLIAMS   And't please your majesty, a rascal that
swaggered with me last night; who, if alive, and ever
dare to challenge this glove, I have sworn to take° him
a box o' th' ear; or if I can see my glove in his cap,          125
which he swore, as he was a soldier, he would wear
(if alive), I will strike it out soundly.
KING   What think you, Captain Fluellen, is it fit this
soldier keep his oath?
FLUELLEN   He is a craven and a villain else, and't          130
please your majesty, in my conscience.
KING   It may be his enemy is a gentleman of great
sort,° quite from the answer of his degree.°
FLUELLEN   Though he be as good a gentleman as the
devil is, as Lucifer and Belzebub himself, it is necessary,          135
look your grace, that he keep his vow and his oath.
If he be perjured, see you now, his reputation is as
arrant a villain and a Jack-sauce° as ever his black shoe
trod upon God's ground and his earth, in my con-
science, law!          140
KING   Then keep thy vow, sirrah,° when thou meet'st
the fellow.
WILLIAMS   So I will, my liege, as I live.
KING   Who serv'st thou under?
WILLIAMS   Under Captain Gower, my liege.          145
FLUELLEN   Gower is a good captain, and is good
knowledge and literatured in the wars.
KING   Call him hither to me, soldier.
WILLIAMS   I will, my liege.                    *Exit.*
KING   Here, Fluellen, wear thou this favor for me,          150
and stick it in thy cap; when Alençon and myself were
down together, I plucked this glove from his helm. 
If any man challenge this, he is a friend to Alençon
and an enemy to our person. If thou encounter any
such, apprehend him, and° thou dost me love.          155
FLUELLEN   Your grace doo's me as great honors as
can be desired in the hearts of his subjects. I would fain

60 skirr scurry   68 fined paid as a fine (he staked his bones,
and having won he now has every right to them)   72 book
record   79 Yerk kick   84 peer are in sight   91 grandfather
in fact Edward III was Henry V's great-grandfather   97–100
Welshmen . . . the service the custom is usually said to
commemorate a British victory over the Saxons, A.D. 540

124 take strike   133 sort rank; from . . . degree above that
corresponding to his own rank   138 Jack-sauce saucy Jack
141 sirrah term of address to an inferior   155 and if

see the man, that has but two legs, that shall find him-
self aggriefed at this glove; that is all. But I would fain
see it once, and please God of his grace that I might see. 160
KING  Know'st thou Gower?
FLUELLEN  He is my dear friend, and please you.
KING  Pray thee go seek him, and bring him to my
tent.
FLUELLEN  I will fetch him.                    Exit. 165
KING
My Lord of Warwick, and my brother Gloucester,
Follow Fluellen closely at the heels.
The glove which I have given him for a favor
May haply purchase him a box o' th' ear;
It is the soldier's. I by bargain should          170
Wear it myself. Follow, good cousin Warwick:
If that the soldier strike him—as I judge
By his blunt bearing, he will keep his word—
Some sudden mischief may arise of it;
For I do know Fluellen valiant,                    175
And, touched° with choler, hot as gunpowder,
And quickly will return an injury.
Follow, and see there be no harm between them.
Go you with me, uncle of Exeter.         Exeunt.

[Scene VIII. France. Another part of the field.]

Enter GOWER and WILLIAMS.

WILLIAMS  I warrant it is to knight you, Captain.

Enter FLUELLEN.

FLUELLEN  God's will and his pleasure, Captain, I
beseech you now, come apace to the king. There is
more good toward you peradventure than is in your
knowledge to dream of.                              5
WILLIAMS  Sir, know you this glove?
FLUELLEN  Know the glove? I know the glove is a
glove.
WILLIAMS  I know this, and thus I challenge it.

Strikes him.

FLUELLEN  'Sblood, an arrant traitor as any's in the 10
universal world, or in France, or in England!
GOWER  How now, sir? You villain!
WILLIAMS  Do you think I'll be forsworn?
FLUELLEN  Stand away, Captain Gower. I will give
treason his payment into plows, I warrant you.      15
WILLIAMS  I am no traitor.
FLUELLEN  That's a lie in thy throat. I charge you in
his majesty's name apprehend him: he's a friend of the
Duke Alençon's.

Enter WARWICK and GLOUCESTER.

WARWICK  How now, how now? What's the matter? 20
FLUELLEN  My Lord of Warwick, here is (praised be
God for it!) a most contagious treason come to light,
look you, as you shall desire in a summer's day. Here
is his majesty.

Enter KING and EXETER.

KING  How now? What's the matter?                  25
FLUELLEN  My liege, here is a villain and a traitor that,

look your grace, has struck the glove which your
majesty is take out of the helmet of Alençon.
WILLIAMS  My liege, this was my glove, here is the
fellow of it; and he that I gave it to in change promised 30
to wear it in his cap. I promised to strike him if he did.
I met this man with my glove in his cap, and I have
been as good as my word.
FLUELLEN  Your majesty hear now, saving your
majesty's manhood, what an arrant, rascally, beggarly, 35
lousy knave it is! I hope your majesty is pear me
testimony and witness, and will avouchment,° that
this is the glove of Alençon that your majesty is give
me, in your conscience, now.
KING
Give me thy glove, soldier. Look, here is the fellow of
it.                                                 40
'Twas I indeed thou promisèd'st to strike;
And thou hast given me most bitter terms.
FLUELLEN  And please your majesty, let his neck
answer for it, if there is any martial law in the world.
KING  How canst thou make me satisfaction?         45
WILLIAMS  All offenses, my lord, come from the
heart: never came any from mine that might offend
your majesty.
KING  It was ourself thou didst abuse.
WILLIAMS  Your majesty came not like yourself: you 50
appeared to me but as a common man; witness the
night, your garments, your lowliness. And what your
highness suffered under that shape, I beseech you take
it for your own fault, and not mine; for had you been
as I took you for, I made no offense. Therefore I 55
beseech your highness pardon me.
KING
Here, uncle Exeter, fill this glove with crowns,
And give it to this fellow. Keep it, fellow,
And wear it for an honor in thy cap,
Till I do challenge it. Give him the crowns;        60
And, captain, you must needs be friends with him.
FLUELLEN  By this day and this light, the fellow has
mettle enough in his belly. Hold, there is twelve pence
for you; and I pray you to serve God, and keep you
out of prawls and prabbles, and quarrels and dissen- 65
sions, and, I warrant you, it is the better for you.
WILLIAMS  I will none of your money.
FLUELLEN  It is with a good will, I can tell you; it will
serve you to mend your shoes. Come, wherefore
should you be so pashful? Your shoes is not so good. 70
'Tis a good silling, I warrant you, or I will change it.

Enter [an English] HERALD.

KING
Now, herald, are the dead numb'red?
HERALD
Here is the number of the slaught'red French.

[Gives a paper.]

KING
What prisoners of good sort° are taken, uncle?
EXETER
Charles Duke of Orleans, nephew to the king;      75
John Duke of Bourbon and Lord Bouciqualt:

Of other lords and barons, knights and squires,
Full fifteen hundred, besides common men.

KING
This note doth tell me of ten thousand French
That in the field lie slain. Of princes, in this number,   80
And nobles bearing banners,° there lie dead
One hundred twenty-six; added to these,
Of knights, esquires, and gallant gentlemen,
Eight thousand and four hundred; of the which,
Five hundred were but yesterday dubbed knights.   85
So that in these ten thousand they have lost
There are but sixteen hundred mercenaries;
The rest are princes, barons, lords, knights, squires,
And gentlemen of blood and quality.
The names of those their nobles that lie dead:   90
Charles Delabreth, High Constable of France;
Jacques of Chatillon, Admiral of France;
The master of the crossbows, Lord Rambures;
Great Master of France, the brave Sir Guichard
   Dauphin;
John Duke of Alençon; Anthony Duke of Brabant,   95
The brother to the Duke of Burgundy;
And Edward Duke of Bar; of lusty earls,
Grandpré and Roussi, Faulconbridge and Foix,
Beaumont and Marle, Vaudemont and Lestrale.
Here was a royal fellowship of death!   100
Where is the number of our English dead?

[HERALD *gives another paper.*]

Edward the Duke of York, the Earl of Suffolk,
Sir Richard Ketly, Davy Gam, esquire;
None else of name; and of all other men
But five-and-twenty. O God, thy arm was here!   105
And not to us, but to thy arm alone,
Ascribe we all! When, without stratagem,
But in plain shock and even play of battle,
Was ever known so great and little loss
On one part and on th' other? Take it, God,   110
For it is none but thine!

EXETER                     'Tis wonderful!

KING
Come, go we in procession to the village;
And be it death proclaimèd through our host
To boast of this, or take that praise from God
Which is His only.   115

FLUELLEN   Is it not lawful, and please your majesty,
to tell how many is killed?

KING
Yes, Captain; but with this acknowledgment,
That God fought for us.

FLUELLEN   Yes, my conscience, he did us great good.   120

KING
Do we all holy rites:
Let there be sung "Non nobis" and "Te Deum,"
The dead with charity° enclosed in clay,
And then to Calais; and to England then;
Where ne'er from France arrived more happy men.   125
                                             *Exeunt.*

81 **bearing banners** i.e., with coats of arms   123 **charity** pious
concern

# ACT V

*Enter* CHORUS.

Vouchsafe to those that have not read the story
That I may prompt them; and of such as have,
I humbly pray them to admit th' excuse°
Of time, of numbers, and due course of things
Which cannot in their huge and proper life   5
Be here presented. Now we bear the king
Toward Calais. Grant him there. There seen,
Heave him away upon your wingèd thoughts
Athwart the sea. Behold the English beach
Pales in° the flood, with men, wives, and boys,   10
Whose shouts and claps outvoice the deep-mouthed sea,
Which, like a mighty whiffler° fore the king,
Seems to prepare his way. So let him land,
And solemnly see him set on to London.
So swift a pace hath thought that even now   15
You may imagine him upon Blackheath;
Where that his lords desire him to have borne
His bruisèd helmet and his bended sword
Before him through the city. He forbids it,
Being free from vainness and self-glorious pride;   20
Giving full trophy, signal, and ostent°
Quite from himself, to God. But now behold,
In the quick forge and working house of thought,
How London doth pour out her citizens!
The mayor and all his brethren in best sort°—   25
Like to the senators of th' antique Rome,
With the plebeians swarming at their heels—
Go forth and fetch their conqu'ring Caesar in;
As, by a lower but by loving° likelihood,
Were now the general° of our gracious empress   30
(As in good time he may) from Ireland coming,
Bringing rebellion broachèd° on his sword,
How many would the peaceful city quit
To welcome him! Much more, and much more cause,
Did they this Harry. Now in London place him;   35
As yet the lamentation of the French
Invites° the King of England's stay at home;
The emperor's coming° in behalf of France
To order peace between them; and omit
All the occurrences, whatever chanced,   40
Till Harry's back-return again to France.
There must we bring him; and myself have played°
The interim, by rememb'ring you 'tis past.
Then brook° abridgment; and your eyes advance,
After your thoughts, straight back again to France.   45
                                             *Exit.*

**V.Cho.3 th' excuse** i.e., the reasons why the actors rely on
the Chorus rather than full stage enactment   **10 Pales in**
encloses   **12 whiffler** officer who clears the way for a procession   **21 trophy . . . ostent** token, sign, and show (of victory)
**25 sort** array   **29 loving** lovingly anticipated   **30 general**
i.e., the Earl of Essex, who left to suppress rebellion in Ireland
on March 27, 1599 (by the end of June 1599 Essex's failure became obvious)   **32 broachèd** impaled   **37 Invites** i.e., gives
excuse and safety for   **38 emperor's coming** the Holy Roman
Emperor came to England, May 1, 1416   **42 played** filled up,
represented   **44 brook** tolerate

[*Scene I. France. The English camp.*]

*Enter* FLUELLEN *and* GOWER.

GOWER   Nay, that's right. But why wear you your leek today? Saint Davy's day is past.

FLUELLEN   There is occasions and causes why and wherefore in all things. I will tell you ass my friend, Captain Gower: the rascally, scauld,° beggarly, lousy, 5 pragging knave, Pistol—which you and yourself, and all the world, know to be no petter than a fellow, look you now, of no merits—he is come to me, and prings me pread and salt yesterday, look you, and bid me eat my leek. It was in a place where I could not breed no 10 contention with him; but I will be so bold as to wear it in my cap till I see him once again, and then I will tell him a little piece of my desires.

*Enter* PISTOL.

GOWER   Why, here he comes, swelling like a turkey cock. 15

FLUELLEN   'Tis no matter for his swellings nor his turkey cocks. God pless you, Aunchient Pistol! You scurvy, lousy knave, God pless you!

PISTOL
Ha, art thou bedlam?° Dost thou thirst, base Trojan,°
To have me fold up Parca's° fatal web? 20
Hence! I am qualmish at the smell of leek.

FLUELLEN   I peseech you heartily, scurvy, lousy knave, at my desires, and my requests, and my petitions, to eat, look you, this leek. Because, look you, you do not love it, nor your affections, and your appetites and 25 your disgestions doo's not agree with it, I would desire you to eat it.

PISTOL
Not for Cadwallader° and all his goats.°

FLUELLEN   There is one goat for you. (*Strikes him.*) Will you be so good, scauld knave, as eat it? 30

PISTOL
Base Trojan, thou shalt die!

FLUELLEN   You say very true, scauld knave, when God's will is. I will desire you to live in the meantime, and eat your victuals. Come, there is sauce for it. [*Strikes him.*] You called me yesterday mountain- 35 squire;° but I will make you today a squire of low degree.° I pray you fall to; if you can mock a leek, you can eat a leek.

GOWER   Enough, captain, you have astonished° him.

FLUELLEN   I say I will make him eat some part of my 40 leek, or I will peat his pate four days.—Bite, I pray you; it is good for your green° wound, and your ploody coxcomb.°

PISTOL   Must I bite?

FLUELLEN   Yes, certainly, and out of doubt, and out 45 of question too, and ambiguities.

PISTOL   By this leek, I will most horribly revenge—I eat and eat—I swear°—

FLUELLEN   Eat, I pray you. Will you have some more sauce to your leek? There is not enough leek to swear 50 by.

PISTOL   Quiet thy cudgel, thou dost see I eat.

FLUELLEN   Much good do° you, scauld knave, heartily. Nay, pray you throw none away, the skin is good for your broken coxcomb. When you take 55 occasions to see leeks hereafter, I pray you mock at 'em; that is all.

PISTOL   Good.

FLUELLEN   Ay, leeks is good. Hold you, there is a groat to heal your pate. 60

PISTOL   Me a groat?

FLUELLEN   Yes verily, and in truth you shall take it, or I have another leek in my pocket which you shall eat.

PISTOL
I take thy groat in earnest° of revenge. 65

FLUELLEN   If I owe you anything, I will pay you in cudgels; you shall be a woodmonger, and buy nothing of me but cudgels. God bye° you, and keep you, and heal your pate.      *Exit.*

PISTOL
All hell shall stir for this! 70

GOWER   Go, go; you are a counterfeit cowardly knave. Will you mock at an ancient tradition, begun upon an honorable respect,° and worn as a memorable trophy of predeceased valor, and dare not avouch in your deeds any of your words? I have seen you gleeking and 75 galling° at this gentleman twice or thrice. You thought, because he could not speak English in the native garb, he could not therefore handle an English cudgel. You find it otherwise, and henceforth let a Welsh correction teach you a good English condition. Fare ye well. *Exit.* 80

PISTOL
Doth Fortune play the huswife° with me now?
News have I, that my Doll° is dead i' th' spital
Of malady of France;°
And there my rendezvous° is quite cut off.
Old I do wax, and from my weary limbs 85
Honor is cudgeled. Well, bawd I'll turn,
And something lean to° cutpurse of quick hand.
To England will I steal, and there I'll steal;
And patches will I get unto these cudgeled scars,
And swear I got them in the Gallia wars.      *Exit.* 90

47–48 **By . . . swear** Pistol changes his tune as his view of the situation changes; Fluellen probably cudgels him on "revenge" and "swear" and is placated while he is actually eating   53 **do** i.e., may it do you   65 **in earnest** as a token   68 **bye** be with   73 **respect** regard, consideration   75–76 **gleeking and galling** gibing and annoying   81 **huswife** hussy   82 **my Doll** Doll Tearsheet (said to be in the spital—i.e., hospital—in II.i.76–79; a change or confusion in Shakespeare's mind must have been involved here, for Pistol's wife was Nell Quickly; or, perhaps, for "Doll" the text should read "Nell"—other proper names are confused in the Folio)   83 **malady of France** venereal disease   84 **rendezvous** refuge, retreat   87 **something lean to** have a leaning toward the profession of

**V.i.5 scauld** scurvy   **19 bedlam** mad; **Trojan** boon companion, dissolute adventurer (slang)   **20 Parca** i.e., Parcae, the three Fates, said to spin the web of man's destiny (they cut the thread when the pattern was completed, so ending a life)   **28 Cadwallader** the last British king; **goats** inhabitants of the Welsh mountains and, hence, used contemptuously of Welshmen   **35–36 mountain-squire** owner of worthless land (term of contempt)   **36–37 squire . . . degree** reference to the title of a medieval metrical romance; also a quibble on "low," as opposed to "mountain," line 35   **39 astonished** stunned, dismayed   **42 green** raw   **43 coxcomb** (1) cap worn by a fool (2) head (ludicrously)

[Scene II. *France. An apartment in the French king's palace.*]

*Enter, at one door,* KING HENRY, EXETER, BEDFORD,
[GLOUCESTER,] WARWICK, [WESTMORELAND,] *and
other lords; at another,* QUEEN *Isabel, the King* [*of*
FRANCE], *the Duke of* BURGUNDY, [*the Princess*
KATHERINE, ALICE,] *and other* FRENCH.

KING HENRY

Peace to this meeting, wherefore we are met!°
Unto our brother France and to our sister
Health and fair time of day; joy and good wishes
To our most fair and princely cousin Katherine;
And as a branch and member of this royalty,          5
By whom this great assembly is contrived,
We do salute you, Duke of Burgundy;
And, princes French, and peers, health to you all!

FRANCE

Right joyous are we to behold your face,
Most worthy brother England; fairly met;            10
So are you, princes English, every one.

QUEEN

So happy be the issue, brother England,
Of this good day and of this gracious meeting
As we are now glad to behold your eyes—
Your eyes which hitherto have borne in them,        15
Against the French that met them in their bent,°
The fatal balls of murdering basilisks.°
The venom of such looks, we fairly hope,
Have lost their quality, and that this day
Shall change all griefs and quarrels into love.     20

KING HENRY

To cry amen to that, thus we appear.

QUEEN

You English princes all, I do salute you.

BURGUNDY

My duty to you both, on° equal love,
Great Kings of France and England! That I have
    labored
With all my wits, my pains, and strong endeavors    25
To bring your most imperial majesties
Unto this bar° and royal interview,
Your mightiness on both parts best can witness.
Since, then, my office hath so far prevailed
That, face to face and royal eye to eye,            30
You have congreeted,° let it not disgrace me
If I demand before this royal view,
What rub,° or what impediment there is
Why that the naked, poor, and mangled Peace,
Dear nurse of arts, plenties, and joyful births,    35
Should not, in this best garden of the world,
Our fertile France, put up her lovely visage.
Alas, she hath from France too long been chased!
And all her husbandry doth lie on heaps,°
Corrupting in it° own fertility.                     40
Her vine, the merry cheerer of the heart,
Unprunèd dies; her hedges even-pleached,°

Like prisoners wildly overgrown with hair,
Put forth disordered twigs; her fallow leas°
The darnel,° hemlock, and rank fumitory             45
Doth root upon, while that the coulter° rusts
That should deracinate° such savagery;
The even mead, that erst brought sweetly forth
The freckled cowslip, burnet, and green clover,
Wanting the scythe, all uncorrected, rank,          50
Conceives by idleness,° and nothing teems°
But hateful docks, rough thistles, kecksies,° burrs,
Losing both beauty and utility.
And all our vineyards, fallows, meads, and hedges,
Defective in their natures, grow to wildness,       55
Even so our houses, and ourselves, and children,
Have lost, or do not learn for want of time,
The sciences that should become our country;
But grow like savages—as soldiers will,
That nothing do but meditate on blood—              60
To swearing, and stern looks, diffused° attire,
And everything that seems unnatural.
Which to reduce° into our former favor°
You are assembled; and my speech entreats
That I may know the let° why gentle Peace           65
Should not expel these inconveniences,
And bless us with her former qualities.

KING HENRY

If, Duke of Burgundy, you would° the peace,
Whose want gives growth to th' imperfections
Which you have cited, you must buy that peace       70
With full accord to all our just demands;
Whose tenors and particular effects
You have, enscheduled briefly, in your hands.

BURGUNDY

The king hath heard them; to the which as yet
There is no answer made.

KING HENRY                     Well then, the peace,   75
Which you before so urged, lies in his answer.

FRANCE

I have but with a cursitory° eye
O'erglanced the articles. Pleaseth your grace
To appoint some of your council presently
To sit with us once more, with better heed          80
To resurvey them, we will suddenly
Pass our accept and peremptory answer.°

KING HENRY

Brother, we shall. Go, uncle Exeter,
And brother Clarence, and you, brother Gloucester,
Warwick, and Huntingdon—go with the king,           85
And take with you free power to ratify,
Augment, or alter, as your wisdoms best
Shall see advantageable for our dignity,
Anything in or out of our demands,
And we'll consign° thereto. Will you, fair sister,  90
Go with the princes or stay here with us?

---

**V.ii.1 Peace . . . met** Peace, for which we are here met, be
to this meeting **16 bent** direction **17 basilisks** (1) fabulous
reptiles, said to kill with their breath and look (2) large cannon
**23 on** of **27 bar** place of judgment **31 congreeted** exchanged
greetings **33 rub** obstacle **39 on heaps** fallen in ruin **40 it**
its **42 even-pleached** neatly interwoven and trimmed

**44 fallow leas** unsown arable land **45 darnel** ryegrass
(injurious to growing grain) **46 coulter** knife that precedes
the ploughshare **47 deracinate** root up **51 Conceives by
idleness** cf. the proverb, "Idleness is the mother of vice";
**teems** is brought forth **52 kecksies** umbelliferous plants
(e.g., cow parsley) **61 diffused** disorderly **63 reduce** restore;
**favor** appearance **65 let** hindrance **68 would** desire **77
cursitory** cursory **81–82 suddenly . . . answer** in very
short time deliver our accepted and conclusive answer **90
consign** agree

QUEEN
Our gracious brother, I will go with them;
Haply a woman's voice may do some good
When articles too nicely° urged be stood° on.

KING HENRY
Yet leave our cousin Katherine here with us.          95
She is our capital demand, comprised
Within the fore-rank of our articles.

QUEEN
She hath good leave.

     *Exeunt omnes. Manet*° KING [HENRY] *and*
     KATHERINE, [*with the gentlewoman* ALICE].

KING HENRY       Fair Katherine, and most fair!
Will you vouchsafe to teach a soldier terms
Such as will enter at a lady's ear,                   100
And plead his love suit to her gentle heart?

KATHERINE  Your majesty shall mock at me; I cannot
speak your England.

KING HENRY  O fair Katherine, if you will love me
soundly with your French heart, I will be glad to hear 105
you confess it brokenly with your English tongue. Do
you like me, Kate?

KATHERINE  Pardonnez-moi, I cannot tell wat is "like
me."

KING HENRY  An angel is like you, Kate, and you are    110
like an angel.

KATHERINE  Que dit-il? Que je suis semblable à les
anges?

ALICE  Oui, vraiment, sauf votre grace, ainsi dit-il.°

KING HENRY  I said so, dear Katherine, and I must not  115
blush to affirm it.

KATHERINE  O bon Dieu! les langues des hommes
sont pleines de tromperies.

KING HENRY  What says she, fair one? That the
tongues of men are full of deceits?                   120

ALICE  Oui, dat de tongues of de mans is be full of
deceits:—dat is de princesse.°

KING HENRY  The princess is the better Englishwoman.° I' faith, Kate, my wooing is fit for thy
understanding; I am glad thou canst speak no better  125
English, for if thou couldst, thou wouldst find me
such a plain king that thou wouldst think I had sold
my farm to buy my crown. I know no ways to mince
it° in love, but directly to say, "I love you." Then, if
you urge me farther than to say, "Do you in faith?"  130
I wear out my suit.° Give me your answer, i' faith, do;
and so clap hands,° and a bargain. How say you,
lady?

KATHERINE  Sauf votre honneur, me understand well.

KING HENRY  Marry, if you would put me to verses,   135
or to dance for your sake, Kate, why, you undid me.
For the one I have neither words nor measure;° and
for the other, I have no strength in measure,° yet a
reasonable measure in strength. If I could win a lady at
leapfrog, or by vaulting into my saddle with my armor  140
on my back, under the correction of bragging be it
spoken, I should quickly leap into a wife.° Or if I might
buffet for my love, or bound my horse for her favors,
I could lay on like a butcher, and sit like a jackanapes,°
never off. But, before God, Kate, I cannot look        145
greenly,° nor gasp out my eloquence, nor I have no
cunning in protestation: only downright oaths, which
I never use till urged, nor never break for urging. If
thou canst love a fellow of this temper, Kate, whose
face is not worth sunburning,° that never looks in his   150
glass for love of anything he sees there, let thine eye be
thy cook.° I speak to thee plain soldier: if thou canst
love me for this, take me; if not, to say to thee that I
shall die, is true—but for thy love, by the Lord, no;
yet I love thee too. And while thou liv'st, dear Kate,    155
take a fellow of plain and uncoined° constancy, for he
perforce must do thee right, because he hath not the
gift to woo in other places; for these fellows of infinite
tongue, that can rhyme themselves into ladies' favors,
they do always reason themselves out again. What! A     160
speaker is but a prater; a rhyme is but a ballad;° a good
leg will fall, a straight back will stoop, a black beard
will turn white, a curled pate will grow bald, a fair
face will wither, a full eye will wax hollow: but a good
heart, Kate, is the sun and the moon, or rather, the sun,  165
and not the moon, for it shines bright and never
changes, but keeps his course truly. If thou would
have such a one, take me; and take me, take a soldier;
take a soldier, take a king. And what say'st thou then
to my love? Speak, my fair—and fairly, I pray thee.    170

KATHERINE  Is it possible dat I sould love de ennemie
of France?

KING HENRY  No, it is not possible you should love
the enemy of France, Kate; but in loving me you
should love the friend of France: for I love France so    175
well, that I will not part with a village of it—I will
have it all mine. And, Kate, when France is mine and
I am yours, then yours is France, and you are mine.

KATHERINE  I cannot tell wat is dat.

KING HENRY  No, Kate? I will tell thee in French,     180
which I am sure will hang upon my tongue like a
new-married wife about her husband's neck, hardly to
be shook off. Je quand sur le possession de France, et
quand vous avez le possession de moi (let me see, what
then? Saint Denis° be my speed!), donc votre est       185
France, et vous êtes mienne.° It is as easy for me, Kate,
to conquer the kingdom as to speak so much more
French; I shall never move thee in French, unless it be
to laugh at me.

KATHERINE  Sauf votre honneur, le français que vous    190
parlez, il est meilleur que l'anglais lequel je parle.°

---

**94 nicely** minutely, scrupulously; **stood** insisted  **98 s.d.
Manet** remains (in Elizabethan stage directions the Latin third
person singular commonly occurs with a plural subject)
**112–14 Que . . . dit-il** What does he say? That I am like the
angels? *Alice* Yes, truly, save your grace, he says so  **122
dat . . . princesse** that is what the princess says  **123–24 is
. . . Englishwoman** because she sees through flattery  **128–29
mince it** make it prettily  **131 wear . . . suit** spend all my
courtship  **132 clap hands** shake hands (in token of a bargain)
**137 measure** meter  **138 strength in measure** ability for
dancing  **139–42 win . . . wife** to "leap" and "vault" were common
in bawdy senses, and clearly used so by Shakespeare
in other plays  **144 jackanapes** ape  **146 greenly** foolishly,
sheepishly  **150 not worth sunburning** so ugly that the sun
cannot make it more so  **151–52 thine . . . cook** your eye
present me more attractively than I would be without its help
**156 uncoined** (1) not yet current (2) unalloyed  **161 ballad**
the most popular and unsophisticated verse form  **185 Saint
Denis** patron saint of France  **183–86 Je . . . mienne**
When I have possession of France, and when you have
possession of me . . . then France is yours, and you are mine
**190–91 Sauf . . . parle** Save your honor, the French that you
speak is better than the English that I speak

KING HENRY  No, faith, is't not, Kate. But thy speaking of my tongue, and I thine, most truly-falsely,° must needs be granted to be much at one.° But, Kate, dost thou understand thus much English? Canst thou 195 love me?

KATHERINE  I cannot tell.°

KING HENRY  Can any of your neighbors tell, Kate? I'll ask them. Come, I know thou lovest me; and at night, when you come into your closet,° you'll 200 question this gentlewoman about me; and I know, Kate, you will to her dispraise those parts in me that you love with your heart; but, good Kate, mock me mercifully, the rather, gentle princess, because I love thee cruelly. If ever thou beest mine, Kate—as I have a 205 saving faith within me tells me thou shalt—I get thee with scambling,° and thou must therefore needs prove a good soldier-breeder. Shall not thou and I, between Saint Denis and Saint George, compound a boy, half French, half English, that shall go to Constantinople,° 210 and take the Turk by the beard? Shall we not? What say'st thou, my fair flower-de-luce?

KATHERINE  I do not know dat.

KING HENRY  No; 'tis hereafter to know, but now to promise. Do but now promise, Kate, you will endeavor 215 for your French part of such a boy; and for my English moiety take the word of a king, and a bachelor. How answer you, la plus belle Katherine du monde, mon très cher et devin déesse?°

KATHERINE  Your majestee ave fausse French enough 220 to deceive de most sage demoiselle dat is en France.

KING HENRY  Now, fie upon my false French! By mine honor in true English, I love thee, Kate; by which honor I dare not swear thou lovest me, yet my blood begins to flatter me that thou dost, notwith- 225 standing the poor and untempering° effect of my visage. Now beshrew my father's ambition! He was thinking of civil wars when he got me, therefore was I created with a stubborn outside, with an aspect of iron, that when I come to woo ladies, I fright them. 230 But in faith, Kate, the elder I wax the better I shall appear. My comfort is that old age, that ill layer-up° of beauty, can do no more spoil upon my face. Thou hast me, if thou hast me, at the worst; and thou shalt wear me, if thou wear me,° better and better; and 235 therefore tell me, most fair Katherine, will you have me? Put off your maiden blushes; avouch the thoughts of your heart with the looks of an empress; take me by the hand, and say, "Harry of England, I am thine!" which word thou shalt no sooner bless mine ear withal, 240 but I will tell thee aloud, "England is thine, Ireland is thine, France is thine, and Henry Plantagenet is thine"; who, though I speak it before his face, if he be not fellow with the best king, thou shalt find the best king of good fellows. Come, your answer in broken° music; 245

for thy voice is music, and thy English broken; therefore, queen of all, Katherine, break thy mind to me in broken English: Wilt thou have me?

KATHERINE  Dat is as it sall please de roi mon père.

KING HENRY  Nay, it will please him well, Kate; it 250 shall please him, Kate.

KATHERINE  Den it sall also content me.

KING HENRY  Upon that I kiss your hand, and I call you my queen.

KATHERINE  Laissez, mon seigneur, laissez, laissez! Ma 255 foi, je ne veux point que vous abaissiez votre grandeur en baisant la main d'une de votre seigneurie indigne serviteur. Excusez-moi, je vous supplie, mon très puissant seigneur.°

KING HENRY  Then I will kiss your lips, Kate. 260

KATHERINE  Les dames et demoiselles pour être baisées devant leur noces, il n'est pas la coutume de France.°

KING HENRY  Madame my interpreter, what says she?

ALICE  Dat it is not be de fashon pour le ladies of 265 France—I cannot tell wat is "baiser" en Anglish.

KING HENRY  To kiss.

ALICE  Your majestee entendre bettre que moi.

KING HENRY  It is not a fashion for the maids in France to kiss before they are married, would she say? 270

ALICE  Oui, vraiment.

KING HENRY  O Kate, nice° customs cursy° to great kings. Dear Kate, you and I cannot be confined within the weak list° of a country's fashion: we are the makers of manners, Kate; and the liberty that follows 275 our places° stops the mouth of all find-faults, as I will do yours for upholding the nice fashion of your country in denying me a kiss. Therefore patiently, and yielding. [Kisses her.] You have witchcraft in your lips, Kate: there is more eloquence in a sugar touch of them 280 than in the tongues of the French council; and they should sooner persuade Harry of England than a general petition of monarchs. Here comes your father.

*Enter the French* POWER *and the English* LORDS.

BURGUNDY  God save your majesty! My royal cousin, teach you our princess English? 285

KING HENRY  I would have her learn, my fair cousin, how perfectly I love her, and that is good English.

BURGUNDY  Is she not apt?

KING HENRY  Our tongue is rough, coz, and my con-dition° is not smooth; so that, having neither the voice 290 nor the heart of flattery about me, I cannot so conjure up the spirit of love in her that he will appear in his true likeness.

BURGUNDY  Pardon the frankness of my mirth if I answer you for that. If you would conjure in her, you 295 must make a circle; if conjure up love in her in his true likeness, he must appear naked and blind. Can you blame her then, being a maid yet rosed over with the virgin crimson of modesty, if she deny the appearance

193 truly-falsely in good faith but bad French and English 194 at one (1) alike (2) in sympathy  197 I cannot tell (1) I don't know (2) I cannot speak  200 closet private chamber 207 scambling scrimmaging  210 Constantinople taken by the Turks in 1453, thirty-one years after Henry's death; throughout the sixteenth century Christian princes aspired to crusade against the Turks  218–19 la . . . déesse the fairest Katherine in the world, my dearest and divine goddess 226 untempering without softening influence  232 ill layer-up ill preserver, wrinkler  235 if . . . me if you possess me 245 broken arranged for parts

255–59 Laissez . . . seigneur Stop, my lord, stop, stop! Indeed, I do not wish to lower your greatness by kissing the hand of your unworthy servant. Excuse me, I beg you, my most powerful lord  261–63 Les . . . France It is not cus-tomary in France for ladies and young girls to be kissed before their marriage  272 nice fastidious; cursy curtsy, bow  274 list limit, bound  275–76 follows our places is the consequence of our royal status  289–90 condition temperament

of a naked blind boy in her naked° seeing self? It were, 300
my lord, a hard condition° for a maid to consign° to.

KING HENRY  Yet they do wink° and yield, as love is
blind and enforces.

BURGUNDY  They are then excused, my lord, when
they see not what they do. 305

KING HENRY  Then, good my lord, teach your cousin
to consent winking.

BURGUNDY  I will wink° on her to consent, my lord,
if you will teach her to know my meaning; for maids
well summered, and warm kept, are like flies at 310
Bartholomew-tide,° blind, though they have their
eyes; and then they will endure handling which before
would not abide looking on.

KING HENRY  This moral ties me over° to time and a
hot summer; and so I shall catch the fly, your cousin, 315
in the latter end, and she must be blind too.

BURGUNDY  As love is, my lord, before it loves.

KING HENRY  It is so; and you may, some of you,
thank love for my blindness, who cannot see many a
fair French city for one fair French maid that stands 320
in my way.

FRANCE  Yes, my lord, you see them perspectively,°
the cities turned into a maid; for they are all girdled
with maiden walls that war hath never ent'red.

KING HENRY  Shall Kate be my wife? 325

FRANCE  So please you.

KING HENRY  I am content, so the maiden cities you
talk of may wait on her; so the maid that stood in the
way for my wish shall show me the way to my will.°

FRANCE
We have consented to all terms of reason. 330

KING HENRY
Is't so, my lords of England?

WESTMORELAND
The king hath granted every article:
His daughter first; and in sequel, all,
According to their firm proposèd natures.

EXETER  Only he hath not yet subscribed this: Where 335
your majesty demands that the King of France, having
any occasion to write for matter of grant,° shall name
your highness in this form, and with this addition, in
French, "Notre très cher fils Henri, Roi d'Angleterre,
Héritier de France"; and thus in Latin, "Praeclarissimus 340
filius noster Henricus, Rex Angliae, et Haeres
Franciae."

FRANCE
Nor this I have not, brother, so denied
But your request shall make me let it pass.

KING HENRY
I pray you then, in love and dear alliance, 345
Let that one article rank with the rest,
And thereupon give me your daughter.

FRANCE
Take her, fair son, and from her blood raise up
Issue to me, that the contending kingdoms

Of France and England, whose very shores look pale° 350
With envy of each other's happiness,
May cease their hatred, and this dear° conjunction
Plant neighborhood° and Christian-like accord
In their sweet bosoms; that never war advance
His bleeding sword 'twixt England and fair France. 355

LORDS  Amen!

KING HENRY
Now, welcome, Kate; and bear me witness all,
That here I kiss her as my sovereign queen.

*Flourish.*

QUEEN
God, the best maker of all marriages,
Combine your hearts in one, your realms in one! 360
As man and wife, being two, are one in love,
So be there 'twixt your kingdoms such a spousal
That never may ill office,° or fell jealousy,
Which troubles oft the bed of blessed marriage,
Thrust in between the paction° of these kingdoms 365
To make divorce of their incorporate° league;
That English may as French, French Englishmen,
Receive each other! God speak this Amen!

ALL  Amen!

KING HENRY
Prepare we for our marriage; on which day, 370
My Lord of Burgundy, we'll take your oath,
And all the peers', for surety of our leagues.
Then shall I swear to Kate, and you to me,
And may our oaths well kept and prosp'rous be!

*Sennet.° Exeunt.*

# [ E P I L O G U E ]

*Enter* CHORUS.

Thus far with rough, and all-unable pen,
   Our bending° author hath pursued the story,
In little room confining mighty men,
   Mangling by starts° the full course of their glory.
Small time: but in that small, most greatly lived 5
   This star of England. Fortune made his sword;
By which, the world's best garden° he achieved;
   And of it left his son imperial lord.
Henry the Sixth, in infant bands crowned king
   Of France and England, did this king succeed; 10
Whose state so many had the managing,
   That they lost France, and made his England bleed:
Which oft our stage hath shown;° and for their sake,
   In your fair minds let this acceptance take.°

350 **pale** an allusion to the white cliffs bordering the English Channel   352 **dear** (1) significant (2) loving (3) dearly bought (?)   353 **neighborhood** neighborliness   363 **office** performance of a function or duty   365 **paction** compact   366 **incorporate** united in one body (appropriate to both marriage and peace settlement)   374 **s.d. Sennet** trumpet call for the departure of a procession
**Epi.2 bending** (1) bending under the weight of his task (2) "stooping to your clemency" (*Hamlet*, III.ii.153)   **4 starts** fits and starts   **7 world's best garden** i.e., France (cf. V.ii.36)   **13 oft . . . shown** a reference to *1, 2, and 3 Henry VI*   **14 this acceptance take** this play find favor

300 **naked** unprotected   301 **condition** (1) stipulation (2) state of being; **consign** agree   302 **wink** shut their eyes   308 **wink** give a significant look   311 **Bartholomew-tide** Saint Bartholomew's day is August 24; by this time flies have become torpid   314 **ties me over** restricts me   322 **perspectively** as through an optical glass giving strange, displaced or broken images   329 **will** (1) desire (2) sexual desire   337 **grant** granting lands or titles

# THE TRAGEDY OF
# JULIUS CAESAR

EDITED BY WILLIAM AND BARBARA ROSEN

## Introduction

Thomas Platter, a Swiss traveler to England, recorded his visit of September 21, 1599, to a London theater: at about two o'clock, after lunch, he and his party crossed the river, and in a house with a thatched roof saw an excellent performance of the tragedy of the first Emperor Julius Caesar. (Platter was mistaken in giving to Caesar the title of "Emperor," either because he was weak in history or because he was impressed by the imperious portrayal of the title role.) He went on to note that there was a cast of about fifteen, and that after the play, according to custom, there was a most elegant and curious dance, two participants being dressed in men's clothes, and two in women's.

The dance that Platter saw was the jig, and the play was undoubtedly Shakespeare's *The Tragedy of Julius Casear*, performed at the newly constructed Globe Theatre. It is quite probable that Shakespeare wrote the play early in 1599, and it marks an important stage in his development. His previous work, *Henry V* (1599), was the last of a long series of English history plays; and while attention shifts to Roman times in *Julius Caesar*, Shakespeare incorporates those ideas of history that grew through the English plays. Starting as a chronicle of wars and bloody events, the histories progressively move toward a recognition of tragedy through historical process. As the histories unfold, Shakespeare's horror of civil war becomes increasingly apparent; and as the focus narrows to individual rulers, we see the development of his intense belief in the divine quality of kingship as the only possible safeguard against civil dissension.

In *Julius Caesar* Shakespeare continues to explore the drama of power politics and personal conscience; only now, as if to gain perspective on the great issues of the histories, he moves the setting to a more distant time. The shift to ancient history would have sharpened rather than blunted the play's contemporary relevance because of the acknowledged Elizabethan habit of viewing history as a series of object lessons for present conduct.

We must not forget how widespread was the longing for unshakable rule and how overwhelming was the dread of civil war at the time *Julius Caesar* was first performed. Elizabeth I had come to the throne in 1558 when the country was in such a state of rebellion and confusion that it seemed likely to slip back into the horrors of the Wars of the Roses. Elizabeth had given her subjects peace, and the nation had prospered; for many years she had been a strong ruler, despite the repeated Catholic claims that she was illegitimate and therefore not a true successor. Attempts at assassination had been many. By 1599 she was old and visibly failing. She had no direct heir; there was no one whose claim to the throne after her was beyond dispute. Childless like Caesar, she could pass on the office only by naming an heir, and this she refused to do, perhaps in order to prevent the growth of factions. The shadow of war and dissension grew ominous. In such circumstances, we see first among the issues of *Julius Caesar* the very topical and concrete problem of a disputed succession, and the more abstract problem of killing—and replacing—the ruler.

Even without Machiavelli many Elizabethans knew that the moral problems of government are not necessarily the same as the moral problems of men. It was precisely because Elizabeth had compromised her personal beliefs whenever the public interest demanded it that she had been so successful a ruler; indeed, in many cases it is still impossible to know what she as a private person believed. Mary Tudor, who had tried to rule in accordance with religious principles, had brought about years of bloodshed. The theory of divine grace accorded to the public actions of a duly appointed ruler was not childish authoritarianism but a philosophical way of resolving the well-perceived gap between what the man might believe and what the ruler must do.

When we view *Julius Caesar* in the light of the political considerations of its own time, many of the difficulties of the play can be seen in perspective. Caesar *is* proud, and destined for the punishment of *hubris*; he is, nonetheless, "the ruler" by ability as well as power, as Plutarch himself suggests in *The Life of Julius Caesar*, a primary source for Shakespeare's work:

. . . the Romans, inclining to Caesar's prosperity and taking the bit in the mouth, supposing that to be ruled by one man alone, it would be a good mean for them to take breath a little, after so many troubles and miseries as they had abidden in these civil wars, they chose him perpetual Dictator. . . . And now for himself, after he had ended

100-50 BC

his civil wars, he did so honorably behave himself, that there was no fault to be found in him. . . .

Plutarch goes on to list Caesar's achievements and enterprises, and suggests that his only failing is a desire to be *called* king. However, Caesar's personal faults have no bearing upon his public abilities.

Brutus is high-minded and disinterested, even though his love of political liberty leads him to transgress the rules of allegiance to a ruler and gratitude to a benefactor. His personal virtues, however, have no bearing upon his public abilities. He is naive enough to believe that a republic needs no power structure, that the removal of Caesar will simply allow power to flow back to the officers of the republic. But of course events prove otherwise, and he and Cassius are forced in their turn to assume power against those who would "destroy the revolution." Neither Brutus nor Cassius has the ability—or the right—to rule, and both are defeated. Yet the man who ultimately replaces them is not the man who roused the public against them, but the one whose impersonal manner from the beginning marks him as the next possessor of the power to rule—Octavius Caesar.

Brutus, Octavius, and Antony all become guilty as men. Brutus kills his friend; Octavius joins the others of the triumvirate in condemning innocent men to death; Antony deliberately rouses a mob and turns it loose to do what mischief it will. What they do, however, does not matter in considering the fitness of each to rule. Personal innocence or guilt is not in question, and we are not asked to feel that one man or another is "right." We are asked to see that while a just man in private life is to be praised, a just man in public life may very well bring about catastrophe. The wicked—or, like Caesar, the conceited and superstitious— may be the genius as a ruler. Man's worth as a private individual does not necessarily ensure his value as a public ruler. Less sentimental than many of his critics, Shakespeare sees that a morally repulsive act may at times be a politically desirable one; that a man who acts from the highest of motives may be too busy keeping his conscience clean to lead well; that a man who once does evil in the expectation that good will be the final result may be forced more deeply into self-deception and impotence than a man who acts simply from expediency. But he also sees that the pursuit of expediency and lack of scruple do not in themselves guarantee ability to govern—else why not, ultimately, an Antony in command?

There is a natural inclination to desire unequivocal answers and absolute judgments, to simplify events until they can be seen as black or white; and we are naturally bewildered when forced into a position that requires us to judge but forbids us the use of simple terms of reference. It is not surprising, therefore, that we may be confounded by *Julius Caesar*, for often we confront situations in which personalities and actions are neither wholly right nor wholly wrong. We cannot feel unreserved hate or love for any character; each seems to call for a different response as he reacts to the seemingly irreconcilable demands of public and private life. Caesar is deaf, aging, subject to epileptic fits, inclined to superstition, warmhearted to his friends in private yet inflexible in public. But if we can believe Antony at all, Caesar has a genuine love of his country. His fault is a kind of ecstasy that the exercise of his office brings upon him. As a private individual he shows many weaknesses;

as a public institution he sees himself superior to all ordinary dangers, and believes that his office is a power that must not be opposed. Indeed, Caesar constantly uses his name to speak of his alter ego, the dictator, and in an early speech to Antony, in which he reveals his distrust of Cassius, he sums up the two views of himself as he unwittingly contrasts two attitudes: the public office that is perfect, and the private individual who is defective. It is as though his public self is quite dissociated from his personal weaknesses:

> I rather tell thee what is to be feared
> Than what I fear; for always I am Caesar.
> Come on my right hand, for this ear is deaf,
> And tell me truly what thou think'st of him. (I.ii.211–14)

Caesar may have a number of weaknesses, but none of the personal defects impair the spirit of Caesar—the capacity to rule. The play vividly demonstrates that there is more stability, freedom, and justice in Rome with Caesar alive than with Caesar dead.

We may be far more sympathetic to the personality of Brutus; yet we must admit that neither he nor Cassius has any specific charges that would warrant the killing of Caesar. Cassius derides Caesar's weaknesses. His attacks are the result of personal envy—why should the fact that Caesar failed in a swimming contest, or suffered from fever, make him contemptible as a ruler? And Brutus admits that he has no immediate cause for indicting his friend. His soliloquy at the beginning of Act II is an agonized attempt to reconcile the idea of tyranny with the personal Caesar he knows. He begins his analysis of the situation with the conclusion—"It must be by his death"—and then, unable to find anything concrete for which Caesar deserves death, he has to resort to possibilities and probabilities: "He would be crowned./How that might change his nature, there's the question." In the end he convinces himself of the necessity of murder by thinking not of what is but what might be, by imagining the future abuse of power, and finally, by employing false analogy:

> And therefore think him as a serpent's egg
> Which hatched, would as his kind grow mischievous,
> And kill him in the shell. (II.i.32–34)

But Caesar is a man, not a serpent's egg; and Brutus is no less mistaken when he tries to kill the spirit of Caesar by doing away with the man. He only succeeds in killing the man, not his spirit—and this is forcefully dramatized when, after the assassination, the people are eager to transfer their allegiance to Brutus, just as they had abandoned Pompey for Caesar:

> THIRD PLEBEIAN
> Let him be Caesar.
> FOURTH PLEBEIAN Caesar's better parts
> Shall be crowned in Brutus. (III.ii.51–52)

It is not only Brutus' misfortune but his fault that his achievements turn out, ironically, to be the reverse of his best intentions. He brings to Rome anarchy and the horrors of civil war, not "Peace, freedom, and liberty."

In dramatizing the complex issues of power politics,

*Julius Caesar* offers no easy solution to problems that are no less baffling to our own age. Many will find that this work is one of Shakespeare's most perplexing, for it is disconcerting when a play—or history itself—appeals to man's earnest desire to judge actions in terms of simple, personal standards of right and wrong and then betrays and mocks his deepest convictions by suggesting that Power is better than Virtue, that efficiency may be preferable to goodness, or that conscience may be dangerously inadequate in determining political action.

An individual's scrupulous concern for morality may, indeed, be disastrously impolitic. Cassius leads Brutus to an abhorrent deed, but when the consequences involve Brutus in the exercise of power, Brutus continues to think and act in accordance with private morality. His scruples about killing Antony or about unjustly raising money hinder the success of the conspiracy. His wish to fight a pitched battle, to decide the matter once and for all, instead of following stratagems and winning by attrition, is also the decision of a man who refuses to take on the role of politician. It is noteworthy that Cassius, after his initial victory, consistently defers to Brutus' moral scruples; knowing him to be wrong in his strategy, he is still swayed by the very image of nobility for which Brutus was chosen as the figurehead of the conspiracy. The irony is unmistakable: the politic man sets up an image of virtue, dissociated from politics, to serve his own purposes, to endear him to the populace; but once that image is established, his freedom to act without it is curbed, and he is hampered in the achievement of his political ends by the very image he has fostered.

The spirit of Caesar that dominates the play is to be associated, finally, with the exercise of supreme power. When Caesar dies, power is without a master, and as such, indiscriminately destructive. Each man in his turn tries to grasp the lightning that has been set free, and is fearfully transformed, until finally it comes to rest upon the man who alone, by gift of personality and legitimate succession, may wield it unscathed.

Shakespeare fully delineates the intriguing pattern of shifting power as an old Caesar is succeeded by a young one. The politic Cassius gives in to an impolitic Brutus and both fail as a result. Antony, Octavius, and Lepidus begin with complete ruthlessness; however, this does not guarantee them power or even win the battle for them—their opponents defeat themselves through mistakes. Lepidus, the "straw man," is first burdened with responsibility, then eliminated; and afterward, effortlessly, Antony, the ruthless and emotional partner, is displaced by the man without a temperament, the personification of impersonal rule.

The transfer of power from Antony to Octavius is subtly and swiftly dramatized in V.i, when Octavius suddenly opposes Antony's command and leads his troops in his own way—"I do not cross you," he tells Antony, "but I will do so." From this point Antony refers to his partner as "Caesar," whereas until that moment he had called him only "Octavius." Even when Octavius asks for advice immediately after he has asserted his independence (V.i.23), Antony calls him "Caesar" before bidding him "Make forth." And soon afterward Octavius is seen as the one who is beginning to prevail; it is he who gives directions: "Come, Antony; away!" In the last scene of the play

Octavius is in total charge of the action, while Antony is returned to his first prominent role, that of funeral orator. Antony may deliver the wonderful eulogy for Brutus, but Octavius, in businesslike fashion, gives the orders for burial, and without consulting or mentioning Antony, says to his former adversaries: "All that served Brutus, I will entertain them," as if he were in sole command. Finally, Octavius renders the play's concluding speech, which is conventionally given by the person of highest rank, whose task is to restore order to the state.

In portraying Octavius and describing his rise to power, Shakespeare departs from his primary source, Plutarch's *Lives*, and his changes are important for our understanding of the play. Plutarch's Octavius is not an exceptional soldier but an outwardly pleasant person of charm and wit, the very opposite of Shakespeare's characterization. And whereas Shakespeare's Octavius gains stature at the battle of Philippi, in Plutarch's *The Life of Marcus Antonius* he is sick at this time, and Antony "had the chiefest glory of all this victory." In Plutarch's *Life of Marcus Brutus* it is further reported that Octavius was absent from the battle; he had himself carried from his camp because of a friend's ominous dream, "and no man could tell what became of Octavius Caesar after he was carried out of his camp."

Shakespeare's independent treatment of Octavius reveals his conception of the kind of man who can wield power in the spirit of Caesar. Brutus, Cassius, and Antony grasp at power and are unable to retain it, perhaps because in exercising it they are more swayed by personal passions than Caesar. Octavius had no part in the murder; he is the only person in the play as free of the passions of love or hate as Caesar claimed to be. In his speech at the beginning of Act V he identifies himself with the spirit of Caesar, makes himself spiritually his heir, and assumes the duty of revenge:

> Look,
> I draw a sword against conspirators.
> When think you that the sword goes up again?
> Never, till Caesar's three and thirty wounds
> Be well avenged; or till another Caesar
> Have added slaughter to the sword of traitors.
>
> (V.i.50–55)

At the close of the play we are meant to feel that the exercise of power necessary for these times has once more been placed in adequate hands. The spirit of Caesar, for good or ill, has not been put to rest.

### A NOTE ON THE SOURCE

Shakespeare's main source for *Julius Caesar* was Sir Thomas North's *Lives of the Noble Grecians and Romans*, printed in 1579 and again in 1595, an English translation of Jacques Amyot's French version of Plutarch's Greek. A number of other sources have been suggested for this play, and discussions of these may be found in Geoffrey Bullough's *Narrative and Dramatic Sources of Shakespeare* (Vol. V), in the introduction to the New Arden edition of *Julius Caesar*, edited by T. S. Dorsch, and in Kenneth Muir's book, *Shakespeare's Sources* (Vol. I). None of the problematic sources has more than peripheral importance, whereas Shakespeare's use of Plutarch throughout the play is detailed, literal, and incontrovertible.

Sometimes Shakespeare seems to versify directly from the *Lives*; at other times he selects, cuts, compresses, and amalgamates events from the full range of Plutarch's material dealing with the history of Julius Caesar. One comes to a full understanding of Shakespeare's dramatic skills only by reading through Plutarch's comparisons of Demetrius with Antony, of Dion with Brutus, and the chapters on Julius Caesar, Brutus, and Antony, where we sometimes find three variant accounts of the same event, from each of which Shakespeare has taken some details to construct his own version.

The most puzzling aspect of *Julius Caesar* is its ambivalent attitude toward the main characters. The play is not wholly sympathetic to Caesar, the conspirators, Antony, or Octavius. Caesar is killed at the beginning of the third act, and the audience's involvement is so divided among the other characters that the play seems to have no single "hero." Shakespeare's dramatic construction here and in the other Roman plays may well be a reflection of Plutarch's method in the *Comparisons*, where he strives for an objective view of his subjects by alternating favorable and unfavorable assessments without giving final approval to either.

### A NOTE ON THE TEXT

The First Folio of 1623 provides us with the text for *Julius Caesar*; there are no early quarto editions. In setting this play for the press, the printer's compositors probably worked from the playhouse promptbook, for the Folio text contains remarkably few misprints, serious errors in punctuation, or misattribution of speeches. The stage directions, unusually numerous and detailed, also suggest a stage manager's prompt copy; stage directions like "*Alarum still*" and "*Enter boy with wine and tapers*" are obviously closely connected with actual performance.

In the present edition, the names of characters have been normalized so that *Marullus* appears for the Folio Murellus (and Murrellus), *Casca* for Caska, *Lucilius* for Lucillius. Occasionally the Folio uses the forms "Antonio" (I.ii.3, 4, 6, 190; I.iii.37), "Claudio" (IV.iii.239, 241, 241 s.d., 286), "Flavio," "Labio" (V.iii.108), "Octavio" (III.i.275 s.d., V.ii.4), "Varrus" (IV.iii.241, 241 s.d., 286); these are standardized, appearing as *Antonius, Claudius, Flavius, Labeo, Octavius*, and *Varro*. The present edition modernizes spelling and punctuation, corrects a few obvious misprints, translates the act divisions from Latin into English, expands the speech prefixes, and alters the lineation of a few passages. The only other substantial departures from the Folio are listed below, the present reading in boldface type and then the Folio's reading in roman.

**I.iii.129 In favor's** Is Fauors
**II.i.40 ides** first   **213 eighth** eight
**II.ii.19 fought** fight   **23 did neigh** do neigh   **46 are** heare
**III.i.39 law** lane   **113 states** State   **115 lies** lye   **283 for** from
**III.ii.105 art** are
**IV.iii.247 not** it not
**V.i.41 teeth** teethes
**V.iii.104 Thasos** Tharsus
**V.iv.7 Lucilius** [F omits, and prints "Lucilius" as the prefix to line 9]

# THE TRAGEDY OF
# JULIUS CAESAR

[Dramatis Personae

| | |
|---|---|
| JULIUS CAESAR | |
| OCTAVIUS CAESAR | |
| MARCUS ANTONIUS | *triumvirs after the death* |
| M. AEMILIUS LEPIDUS | *of Julius Caesar* |
| CICERO | |
| PUBLIUS | *senators* |
| POPILIUS LENA | |
| MARCUS BRUTUS | |
| CASSIUS | |
| CASCA | |
| TREBONIUS | *conspirators against Julius* |
| LIGARIUS | *Caesar* |
| DECIUS BRUTUS | |
| METELLUS CIMBER | |
| CINNA | |
| FLAVIUS | *tribunes* |
| MARULLUS | |
| ARTEMIDORUS OF CNIDOS *a teacher of rhetoric* | |
| A SOOTHSAYER | |

| | |
|---|---|
| CINNA *a poet* | |
| ANOTHER POET | |
| LUCILIUS | |
| TITINIUS | |
| MESSALA | *friends to Brutus and Cassius* |
| YOUNG CATO | |
| VOLUMNIUS | |
| VARRO | |
| CLITUS | |
| CLAUDIUS | |
| STRATO | *servants to Brutus* |
| LUCIUS | |
| DARDANIUS | |
| PINDARUS *servant to Cassius* | |
| CALPHURNIA *wife to Caesar* | |
| PORTIA *wife to Brutus* | |
| SENATORS CITIZENS GUARDS | |
| ATTENDANTS ETC. | |

*Scene:* During most of the play, at Rome; afterward near Sardis, and near Philippi]

## ACT I

### Scene I. [*Rome. A street.*]

*Enter* FLAVIUS, MARULLUS, *and certain* COMMONERS *over the stage.*

FLAVIUS
Hence! Home, you idle creatures, get you home!
Is this a holiday? What, know you not,
Being mechanical,° you ought not walk
Upon a laboring day without the sign
Of your profession?° Speak, what trade art thou?     5

CARPENTER  Why, sir, a carpenter.
MARULLUS
Where is thy leather apron and thy rule?
What dost thou with thy best apparel on?
You, sir, what trade are you?
COBBLER  Truly, sir, in respect of a fine° workman, I     10
am but, as you would say, a cobbler.°
MARULLUS
But what trade art thou? Answer me directly.°
COBBLER  A trade, sir, that, I hope, I may use with a
safe conscience, which is indeed, sir, a mender of bad
soles.°     15

*The decorative border shown above appeared on the first page of* Julius Caesar *in the First Folio edition of Shakespeare's plays, 1623.*

**I.i.3 mechanical** of the working class  **4–5 sign . . . profession** mark of your trade, i.e., working clothes

**10 in . . . fine** in comparison with a skilled  **11 cobbler** (1) shoemaker (2) bungler  **12 directly** straightforwardly  **15 soles** pun on *souls*

FLAVIUS
  What trade, thou knave? Thou naughty° knave, what
  trade?
COBBLER   Nay, I beseech you, sir, be not out° with
  me: yet, if you be out,° sir, I can mend you.°
MARULLUS
  What mean'st thou by that? Mend me, thou saucy
  fellow?
COBBLER   Why, sir, cobble you.     20
FLAVIUS
  Thou art a cobbler, art thou?
COBBLER   Truly, sir, all that I live by is with the awl:
  I meddle with no tradesman's matters, nor women's
  matters; but withal,° I am indeed, sir, a surgeon to old
  shoes: when they are in great danger, I recover° them. 25
  As proper men as ever trod upon neat's leather° have
  gone upon my handiwork.
FLAVIUS
  But wherefore art not in thy shop today?
  Why dost thou lead these men about the streets?
COBBLER   Truly, sir, to wear out their shoes, to get 30
  myself into more work. But indeed, sir, we make
  holiday to see Caesar and to rejoice in his triumph.°
MARULLUS
  Wherefore rejoice? What conquest brings he home?
  What tributaries° follow him to Rome,
  To grace in captive bonds his chariot wheels?     35
  You blocks, you stones, you worse than senseless things!
  O you hard hearts, you cruel men of Rome,
  Knew you not Pompey?° Many a time and oft
  Have you climbed up to walls and battlements,
  To tow'rs and windows, yea, to chimney tops,     40
  Your infants in your arms, and there have sat
  The livelong day, with patient expectation,
  To see great Pompey pass the streets of Rome.
  And when you saw his chariot but appear,
  Have you not made an universal shout,     45
  That Tiber trembled underneath her banks
  To hear the replication° of your sounds
  Made in her concave shores?°
  And do you now put on your best attire?
  And do you now cull out a holiday?     50
  And do you now strew flowers in his way
  That comes in triumph over Pompey's blood?°
  Be gone!
  Run to your houses, fall upon your knees,
  Pray to the gods to intermit° the plague     55
  That needs must light on this ingratitude.
FLAVIUS
  Go, go, good countrymen, and, for this fault,
  Assemble all the poor men of your sort;
  Draw them to Tiber banks and weep your tears
  Into the channel, till the lowest stream     60
  Do kiss the most exalted shores of all.°
                    *Exeunt all the* COMMONERS.

See, whe'r° their basest mettle° be not moved;
They vanish tongue-tied in their guiltiness.
Go you down that way towards the Capitol;
This way will I. Disrobe the images,     65
If you do find them decked with ceremonies.°
MARULLUS
  May we do so?
  You know it is the feast of Lupercal.°
FLAVIUS
  It is not matter; let no images
  Be hung with Caesar's trophies. I'll about     70
  And drive away the vulgar° from the streets;
  So do you too, where you perceive them thick.
  These growing feathers plucked from Caesar's wing
  Will make him fly an ordinary pitch,°
  Who else would soar above the view of men     75
  And keep us all in servile fearfulness.      *Exeunt.*


[Scene II. *A public place.*]

*Enter* CAESAR, ANTONY (*for the course*), CALPHURNIA,
PORTIA, DECIUS, CICERO, BRUTUS, CASSIUS,
CASCA, *a* SOOTHSAYER; *after them,* MARULLUS *and*
FLAVIUS.

CAESAR
  Calphurnia!
CASCA       Peace, ho! Caesar speaks.
CAESAR                      Calphurnia!
CALPHURNIA   Here, my lord.
CAESAR
  Stand you directly in Antonius' way
  When he doth run his course. Antonius!
ANTONY
  Caesar, my lord?     5
CAESAR
  Forget not in your speed, Antonius,
  To touch Calphurnia; for our elders say
  The barren, touchèd in this holy chase,
  Shake off their sterile curse.
ANTONY            I shall remember:
  When Caesar says "Do this," it is performed.     10
CAESAR
  Set on, and leave no ceremony out.
SOOTHSAYER   Caesar!
CAESAR   Ha! Who calls?
CASCA
  Bid every noise be still; peace yet again!
CAESAR
  Who is it in the press° that calls on me?     15
  I hear a tongue, shriller than all the music,
  Cry "Caesar." Speak; Caesar is turned to hear.
SOOTHSAYER
  Beware the ides of March.°
CAESAR            What man is that?

**16 naughty** worthless   **17 out** angry   **18 be out** have worn-
out shoes; **mend you** (1) mend your shoes (2) improve
your character   **24 withal** (1) nevertheless (2) with awl (3)
with all   **25 recover** (1) resole (2) cure   **26 neat's leather**
cattle's hide   **32 triumph** triumphal celebration   **34 tributaries** captives   **38 Pompey** defeated by Caesar in 48 B.C.,
later murdered   **47 replication** echo   **48 concave shores**
hollowed-out banks   **52 in . . . blood** as the conqueror of
Pompey's sons   **55 intermit** hold back   **61 most . . . all**
highest water mark

**62 whe'r** whether; **mettle** (1) substance (2) disposition   **66
ceremonies** robes (or ornaments)   **68 Lupercal** fertility
festival held on February 15; Caesar's triumph really took
place in the previous October, but Shakespeare combines
events and shortens time spans for dramatic effect   **71 vulgar**
common people   **74 pitch** height
**I.ii.15 press** crowd   **18 ides of March** March 15

**BRUTUS**
A soothsayer bids you beware the ides of March.

**CAESAR**
Set him before me; let me see his face.                                20

**CASSIUS**
Fellow, come from the throng; look upon Caesar.

**CAESAR**
What say'st thou to me now? Speak once again.

**SOOTHSAYER**
Beware the ides of March.

**CAESAR**
He is a dreamer, let us leave him. Pass.
    *Sennet.° Exeunt. Mane[n]t° BRUTUS and CASSIUS.*

**CASSIUS**
Will you go see the order of the course?°                              25

**BRUTUS**   Not I.

**CASSIUS**   I pray you do.

**BRUTUS**
I am not gamesome:° I do lack some part
Of that quick spirit° that is in Antony.
Let me not hinder, Cassius, your desires;                              30
I'll leave you.

**CASSIUS**
Brutus, I do observe you now of late;
I have not from your eyes that gentleness
And show of love as I was wont° to have;
You bear too stubborn and too strange a hand°                          35
Over your friend that loves you.

**BRUTUS**                            Cassius,
Be not deceived: if I have veiled my look,
I turn the trouble of my countenance
Merely upon myself.° Vexèd I am
Of late with passions of some difference,°                             40
Conceptions only proper to myself,°
Which give some soil,° perhaps, to my behaviors;
But let not therefore my good friends be grieved
(Among which number, Cassius, be you one)
Nor construe° any further my neglect                                   45
Than that poor Brutus, with himself at war,
Forgets the shows° of love to other men.

**CASSIUS**
Then, Brutus, I have much mistook your passion;°
By means whereof° this breast of mine hath buried
Thoughts of great value, worthy cogitations.                           50
Tell me, good Brutus, can you see your face?

**BRUTUS**
No, Cassius; for the eye sees not itself
But by reflection, by some other things.

**CASSIUS**
'Tis just:°
And it is very much lamented, Brutus,                                  55

That you have no such mirrors as will turn
Your hidden worthiness into your eye,
That you might see your shadow.° I have heard
Where many of the best respect° in Rome
(Except immortal Caesar), speaking of Brutus,                          60
And groaning underneath this age's yoke,
Have wished that noble Brutus had his eyes.

**BRUTUS**
Into what dangers would you lead me, Cassius,
That you would have me seek into myself
For that which is not in me?                                           65

**CASSIUS**
Therefore, good Brutus, be prepared to hear;
And since you know you cannot see yourself
So well as by reflection, I, your glass,°
Will modestly discover to yourself
That of yourself which you yet know not of.                            70
And be not jealous on° me, gentle Brutus:
Were I a common laughter,° or did use
To stale with ordinary oaths my love
To every new protester;° if you know
That I do fawn on men and hug them hard,                               75
And after scandal° them; or if you know
That I profess myself° in banqueting
To all the rout,° then hold me dangerous.

*Flourish° and shout.*

**BRUTUS**
What means this shouting? I do fear the people
Choose Caesar for their king.

**CASSIUS**                            Ay, do you fear it?            80
Then must I think you would not have it so.

**BRUTUS**
I would not, Cassius, yet I love him well.
But wherefore do you hold me here so long?
What is it that you would impart to me?
If it be aught toward the general good,°                               85
Set honor in one eye and death i' th' other,
And I will look on both indifferently;°
For let the gods so speed me,° as I love
The name of honor more than I fear death.

**CASSIUS**
I know that virtue to be in you, Brutus,                               90
As well as I do know your outward favor.°
Well, honor is the subject of my story.
I cannot tell what you and other men
Think of this life, but for my single self,
I had as lief not be,° as live to be                                   95
In awe of such a thing as I myself.°
I was born free as Caesar; so were you:
We both have fed as well, and we can both
Endure the winter's cold as well as he:
For once, upon a raw and gusty day,                                    100

---

24 **s.d. Sennet** flourish of trumpets marking ceremonial entrance or exit; **Mane[n]t** (they) remain  25 **order . . . course** progress of the race  28 **gamesome** (1) fond of sport (2) merry  29 **quick spirit** (1) lively nature (2) prompt obedience  34 **wont** accustomed  35 **bear . . . hand** treat too haughtily and distantly, keep at arm's length (the metaphor is from horsemanship)  37–39 **if . . . myself** If I have seemed withdrawn, it is because I am displeased with myself and no one else ("Merely" = wholly)  40 **passions . . . difference** conflicting emotions  41 **Conceptions . . . myself** ideas concerning me only  42 **soil** blemish  45 **construe** interpret  47 **shows** manifestations  48 **passion** feelings  49 **By means whereof** as a consequence of which  54 **just** true

58 **shadow** reflection, i.e., yourself as others see you  59 **best respect** highest reputation  68 **glass** mirror  71 **jealous on** suspicious of  72 **laughter** object of mockery  72–74 **did . . . protester** were accustomed to make cheap with glib and frequent avowals to every new promiser of friendship ("ordinary" = [1] tavern [2] everyday)  76 **scandal** slander  77 **profess myself** declare my friendship  78 **rout** vulgar crowd  78 **s.d. Flourish** ceremonial sounding of trumpets  85 **general good** public welfare  87 **indifferently** impartially  88 **speed me** make me prosper  91 **favor** appearance  95 **as . . . be** just as soon not exist  96 **such . . . myself** i.e., another human being (Caesar)

The troubled Tiber chafing with° her shores,
Caesar said to me "Dar'st thou, Cassius, now
Leap in with me into this angry flood,
And swim to yonder point?" Upon the word,
Accout'red° as I was, I plungèd in                              105
And bade him follow: so indeed he did.
The torrent roared, and we did buffet it
With lusty sinews, throwing it aside
And stemming it with hearts of controversy.°
But ere we could arrive the point proposed,          110
Caesar cried "Help me, Cassius, or I sink!"
I, as Aeneas,° our great ancestor,
Did from the flames of Troy upon his shoulder
The old Anchises bear, so from the waves of Tiber
Did I the tired Caesar. And this man                       115
Is now become a god, and Cassius is
A wretched creature, and must bend his body
If Caesar carelessly but nod on him.
He had a fever when he was in Spain,
And when the fit was on him, I did mark             120
How he did shake; 'tis true, this god did shake.
His coward lips did from their color fly;°
And that same eye whose bend° doth awe the world
Did lose his° luster; I did hear him groan;
Ay, and that tongue of his, that bade the Romans    125
Mark him and write his speeches in their books,
Alas, it cried, "Give me some drink, Titinius,"
As a sick girl. Ye gods! It doth amaze me,
A man of such a feeble temper° should
So get the start of° the majestic world,                  130
And bear the palm° alone.

*Shout. Flourish.*

BRUTUS
Another general shout?
I do believe that these applauses are
For some new honors that are heaped on Caesar.

CASSIUS
Why, man, he doth bestride the narrow world         135
Like a Colossus,° and we petty men
Walk under his huge legs and peep about
To find ourselves dishonorable° graves.
Men at some time are masters of their fates:
The fault, dear Brutus, is not in our stars,°          140
But in ourselves, that we are underlings.
Brutus and Caesar: what should be in that "Caesar"?
Why should that name be sounded° more than yours?
Write them together, yours is as fair a name;
Sound them, it doth become the mouth as well;      145

Weigh them, it is as heavy; conjure with 'em,
"Brutus" will start° a spirit as soon as "Caesar."
Now, in the names of all the gods at once,
Upon what meat doth this our Caesar feed,
That he is grown so great? Age, thou art shamed!    150
Rome, thou hast lost the breed of noble bloods!
When went there by an age, since the great flood,°
But it was famed with° more than with one man?
When could they say (till now) that talked of Rome,
That her wide walks encompassed but one man?      155
Now is it Rome indeed, and room° enough,
When there is in it but one only man.
O, you and I have heard our fathers say,
There was a Brutus° once that would have brooked°
Th' eternal devil to keep his state in Rome            160
As easily as a king.

BRUTUS
That you do love me, I am nothing jealous;°
What you would work me to,° I have some aim;°
How I have thought of this, and of these times,
I shall recount hereafter. For this present,           165
I would not so (with love I might entreat you)
Be any further moved. What you have said
I will consider; what you have to say
I will with patience hear, and find a time
Both meet° to hear and answer such high things.    170
Till then, my noble friend, chew° upon this:
Brutus had rather be a villager
Than to repute himself a son of Rome
Under these hard conditions as this time
Is like to lay upon us.

CASSIUS                          I am glad             175
That my weak words have struck but thus much show
Of fire from Brutus.

*Enter* CAESAR *and his* TRAIN.°

BRUTUS
The games are done, and Caesar is returning.

CASSIUS
As they pass by, pluck Casca by the sleeve,
And he will (after his sour fashion) tell you         180
What hath proceeded worthy note today.

BRUTUS
I will do so. But look you, Cassius,
The angry spot doth glow on Caesar's brow,
And all the rest look like a chidden train:
Calphurnia's cheek is pale, and Cicero                185
Looks with such ferret° and such fiery eyes
As we have seen him in the Capitol,
Being crossed in conference° by some senators.

CASSIUS
Casca will tell us what the matter is.

CAESAR Antonius.                                            190
ANTONY Caesar?

---

101 **chafing with** raging against   105 **Accout'red** fully
armed   109 **stemming . . . controversy** moving forward
against it (1) aggressively (2) in rivalry   112 **Aeneas** legendary
founder of the Roman state, and hero of Virgil's *Aeneid;*
Anchises was his feeble father   122 **His . . . fly** the color fled
from his lips like a deserter fleeing from his banner in battle
("color" = [1] hue [2] banner)   123 **bend** glance   124 **his** its
129 **feeble temper** weak constitution   130 **get . . . of**
outdistance   131 **bear the palm** carry off the victor's prize
136 **Colossus** an immense statue of Apollo, said to straddle
the entrance to the harbor of Rhodes so that ships sailed under
its legs   138 **dishonorable** because we are dominated by
Caesar   140 **stars** destinies (in Shakespeare's day one's temperament, and therefore one's actions and course of life, were
thought to be largely determined by the position of the planets
at one's birth   143 **sounded** (1) spoken (2) proclaimed by
trumpet

147 **start** raise   152 **great flood** classical story told of the
drowning of all mankind except Deucalion and his wife
Pyrrha, spared by Zeus because of their virtue   153 **But . . .
with** without the age being made famous by   156 **Rome . . .
room** homonyms, hence a pun   159 **a Brutus** Lucius Junius
Brutus helped expel the Tarquins and found the Republic in
509 B.C.; **brooked** tolerated   162 **nothing jealous** not at all
doubtful   163 **work me to** persuade me of; **aim** idea
170 **meet** suitable   171 **chew** reflect   177 **s.d. Train** retinue
186 **ferret** ferretlike (a ferret is a vicious, weasellike animal with
red eyes)   188 **conference** debate

CAESAR
Let me have men about me that are fat,
Sleek-headed men, and such as sleep a-nights.
Yond Cassius has a lean and hungry look;
He thinks too much: such men are dangerous.  195
ANTONY
Fear him not, Caesar, he's not dangerous;
He is a noble Roman, and well given.°
CAESAR
Would he were fatter! But I fear him not.
Yet if my name were liable to fear,°
I do not know the man I should avoid  200
So soon as that spare Cassius. He reads much,
He is a great observer, and he looks
Quite through the deeds° of men. He loves no plays,
As thou dost, Antony; he hears no music;°
Seldom he smiles, and smiles in such a sort°  205
As if he mocked himself, and scorned his spirit
That could be moved to smile at anything.
Such men as he be never at heart's ease
Whiles they behold a greater than themselves,
And therefore are they very dangerous.  210
I rather tell thee what is to be feared
Than what I fear; for always I am Caesar.
Come on my right hand, for this ear is deaf,
And tell me truly what thou think'st of him.
                    *Sennet. Exeunt* CAESAR *and his* TRAIN.
CASCA
You pulled me by the cloak; would you speak with
        me?  215
BRUTUS
Ay, Casca; tell us what hath chanced today,
That Caesar looks so sad.°
CASCA
Why, you were with him, were you not?
BRUTUS
I should not then ask Casca what had chanced.
CASCA  Why, there was a crown offered him; and  220
being offered him, he put it by° with the back of his
hand, thus; and then the people fell a-shouting.
BRUTUS  What was the second noise for?
CASCA  Why, for that too.
CASSIUS
They shouted thrice; what was the last cry for?  225
CASCA  Why, for that too.
BRUTUS  Was the crown offered him thrice?
CASCA  Ay, marry,° was't, and he put it by thrice,
every time gentler than other; and at every putting-by
mine honest neighbors shouted.  230
CASSIUS
Who offered him the crown?
CASCA                    Why, Antony.
BRUTUS
Tell us the manner of it, gentle Casca.
CASCA  I can as well be hanged as tell the manner of it:
it was mere foolery; I did not mark it. I saw Mark

Antony offer him a crown—yet 'twas not a crown  235
neither, 'twas one of these coronets°—and, as I told
you, he put it by once; but for all that, to my thinking,
he would fain° have had it. Then he offered it to him
again; then he put it by again; but to my thinking, he
was very loath to lay his fingers off it. And then he  240
offered it the third time. He put it the third time by;
and still° as he refused it, the rabblement hooted, and
clapped their chopt° hands, and threw up their sweaty
nightcaps,° and uttered such a deal of stinking breath
because Caesar refused the crown, that it had, almost,  245
choked Caesar; for he swounded° and fell down at it.
And for mine own part, I durst not laugh, for fear of
opening my lips and receiving the bad air.
CASSIUS
But, soft,° I pray you; what, did Caesar swound?
CASCA  He fell down in the market place, and foamed  250
at mouth, and was speechless.
BRUTUS
'Tis very like he hath the falling-sickness.°
CASSIUS
No, Caesar hath it not; but you, and I,
And honest Casca, we have the falling-sickness.°
CASCA  I know not what you mean by that, but I am  255
sure Caesar fell down. If the tag-rag people° did not
clap him and hiss him, according as he pleased and
displeased them, as they use° to do the players in the
theater, I am no true man.
BRUTUS
What said he when he came unto himself?  260
CASCA  Marry, before he fell down, when he perceived
the common herd was glad he refused the crown, he
plucked me ope his doublet° and offered them his
throat to cut. An I had been a man of any occupation,°
if I would not have taken him at a word, I would I  265
might go to hell among the rogues. And so he fell.
When he came to himself again, he said, if he had done
or said anything amiss, he desired their worships to
think it was his infirmity. Three or four wenches,
where I stood, cried "Alas, good soul!" and forgave  270
him with all their hearts; but there's no heed to be
taken of them; if Caesar had stabbed their mothers,
they would have done no less.
BRUTUS
And after that, he came thus sad away?
CASCA  Ay.  275
CASSIUS
Did Cicero say anything?
CASCA  Ay, he spoke Greek.
CASSIUS  To what effect?
CASCA  Nay, an I tell you that, I'll ne'er look you i' th'
face again. But those that understood him smiled at  280
one another and shook their heads; but for mine own
part, it was Greek to me. I could tell you more news

197 **given** disposed  199 **if . . . fear** if the idea of fear could
ever be associated with me  203 **through the deeds** to the
hidden motives of actions  204 **hears no music** cf. *Merchant
of Venice*, V.i.83 ff.: "The man that hath no music in himself,
Nor is not moved with concord of sweet sounds, Is fit for
treasons . . . Let no such man be trusted"  205 **sort** manner
217 **sad** serious  221 **put it by** pushed it aside  228 **marry**
truly (originally an oath, "By the Virgin Mary")

236 **coronets** small crowns  238 **fain** gladly  242 **still**
every time  243 **chopt** rough, chapped  244 **nightcaps**
contemptuous term for workingmen's caps  246 **swounded**
fainted  249 **soft** slowly, "wait a minute"  252 **falling-sickness** epilepsy  254 **we . . . falling-sickness** we are
becoming powerless and are declining under Caesar's rule
256 **tag-rag people** ragged mob  258 **use** are accustomed
263 **ope his doublet** open his jacket  264 **man . . .
occupation** (1) workingman, i.e., one of those to whom
Caesar's speech was addressed (2) "man of action"

too: Marullus and Flavius, for pulling scarfs off
Caesar's images, are put to silence.° Fare you well.
There was more foolery yet, if I could remember it. 285

CASSIUS  Will you sup with me tonight, Casca?

CASCA  No, I am promised forth.°

CASSIUS  Will you dine with me tomorrow?

CASCA  Ay, if I be alive, and your mind hold,° and
your dinner worth the eating. 290

CASSIUS  Good; I will expect you.

CASCA  Do so. Farewell, both.                    *Exit.*

BRUTUS
What a blunt fellow is this grown to be!
He was quick mettle° when he went to school.

CASSIUS
So is he now in execution 295
Of any bold or noble enterprise,
However he puts on this tardy form.°
This rudeness is a sauce to his good wit,°
Which gives men stomach° to disgest° his words
With better appetite. 300

BRUTUS
And so it is. For this time I will leave you.
Tomorrow, if you please to speak with me,
I will come home to you; or if you will,
Come home to me, and I will wait for you.

CASSIUS
I will do so. Till then, think of the world.° 305
                                       *Exit* BRUTUS.
Well, Brutus, thou art noble; yet I see
Thy honorable mettle° may be wrought
From that it is disposed;° therefore it is meet°
That noble minds keep ever with their likes;
For who so firm that cannot be seduced? 310
Caesar doth bear me hard,° but he loves Brutus.
If I were Brutus now, and he were Cassius,
He should not humor° me. I will this night,
In several hands,° in at his windows throw,
As if they came from several citizens, 315
Writings, all tending to° the great opinion
That Rome holds of his name; wherein obscurely
Caesar's ambition shall be glancèd at.°
And after this, let Caesar seat him sure;°
For we will shake him, or worse days endure. *Exit.* 320

[Scene III. *A street.*]

*Thunder and lightning. Enter [ from opposite sides]* CASCA
*and* CICERO.

CICERO
Good even, Casca; brought you Caesar home?
Why are you breathless? And why stare you so?

CASCA
Are not you moved, when all the sway of earth°
Shakes like a thing unfirm? O Cicero,
I have seen tempests, when the scolding winds 5
Have rived° the knotty oaks, and I have seen
Th' ambitious ocean swell and rage and foam,
To be exalted with° the threat'ning clouds;
But never till tonight, never till now,
Did I go through a tempest dropping fire. 10
Either there is a civil strife in heaven,
Or else the world, too saucy° with the gods,
Incenses them to send destruction.

CICERO
Why, saw you anything more wonderful?

CASCA
A common slave—you know him well by sight— 15
Held up his left hand, which did flame and burn
Like twenty torches joined, and yet his hand,
Not sensible of° fire, remained unscorched.
Besides—I ha' not since put up my sword—
Against° the Capitol I met a lion, 20
Who glazed° upon me and went surly by
Without annoying me. And there were drawn
Upon a heap° a hundred ghastly° women,
Transformèd with their fear, who swore they saw
Men, all in fire, walk up and down the streets. 25
And yesterday the bird of night° did sit
Even at noonday upon the market place,
Hooting and shrieking. When these prodigies°
Do so conjointly meet,° let not men say,
"These are their reasons, they are natural," 30
For I believe they are portentous things
Unto the climate° that they point upon.

CICERO
Indeed, it is a strange-disposèd° time:
But men may construe things after their fashion,°
Clean from the purpose° of the things themselves. 35
Comes Caesar to the Capitol tomorrow?

CASCA
He doth; for he did bid Antonius
Send word to you he would be there tomorrow.

CICERO
Good night then, Casca; this disturbèd sky
Is not to walk in.

CASCA                    Farewell, Cicero.    *Exit* CICERO. 40

*Enter* CASSIUS.

CASSIUS
Who's there?

CASCA                    A Roman.

CASSIUS                                        Casca, by your voice.

CASCA
Your ear is good. Cassius, what night is this?

---

**284 put to silence** silenced (by being stripped of their tribune-ships, and perhaps exiled or executed)  **287 am promised forth** have a previous engagement  **289 hold** does not change  **294 quick mettle** of a lively disposition  **297 tardy form** sluggish appearance  **298 wit** intelligence  **299 stomach** appetite; **disgest** digest  **305 the world** the current state of affairs  **307 mettle** (1) disposition (2) metal  **307–08 wrought . . . disposed** shaped (like iron) contrary to its natural form  **308 meet** fitting  **311 bear me hard** hold a grudge against me  **313 humor** cajole, influence by flattery  **314 several hands** different handwritings  **316 tending to** bearing on  **318 glancèd at** indirectly touched upon  **319 seat him sure** make his position secure

**I.iii.3 all . . . earth** the whole scheme of things ("sway" = ruling principle)  **6 rived** split  **8 exalted with** elevated to  **12 saucy** presumptuous  **13 sensible of** sensitive to  **20 Against** directly opposite (?) near (?)  **21 glazed** stared  **22–23 drawn . . . heap** huddled together  **23 ghastly** white as ghosts  **26 bird of night** owl (a bird of ill omen)  **28 prodigies** unnatural events  **29 conjointly meet** coincide  **32 climate** region  **33 strange-disposèd** abnormal  **34 after their fashion** in their own way  **35 Clean . . . purpose** quite contrary to the real meaning

**CASSIUS**

A very pleasing night to honest men.

**CASCA**

Who ever knew the heavens menace so?

**CASSIUS**

Those that have known the earth so full of faults.    45
For my part, I have walked about the streets,
Submitting me unto the perilous night,
And thus unbracèd,° Casca, as you see,
Have bared my bosom to the thunder-stone;°
And when the cross° blue lightning seemed to open    50
The breast of heaven, I did present myself
Even in the aim and very flash of it.

**CASCA**

But wherefore did you so much tempt the heavens?
It is the part° of men to fear and tremble
When the most mighty gods by tokens° send    55
Such dreadful heralds to astonish° us.

**CASSIUS**

You are dull, Casca, and those sparks of life
That should be in a Roman you do want,°
Or else you use not. You look pale, and gaze,
And put on° fear, and cast yourself in wonder,°    60
To see the strange impatience of the heavens;
But if you would consider the true cause
Why all these fires, why all these gliding ghosts,
Why birds and beasts from quality and kind,°
Why old men,° fools, and children calculate,°    65
Why all these things change from their ordinance,°
Their natures and preformèd faculties,°
To monstrous quality,° why, you shall find
That heaven hath infused them with these spirits°
To make them instruments of fear and warning    70
Unto some monstrous state.°
Now could I, Casca, name to thee a man
Most like this dreadful night,
That thunders, lightens, opens graves, and roars
As doth the lion in the Capitol;    75
A man no mightier than thyself, or me,
In personal action, yet prodigious° grown
And fearful,° as these strange eruptions° are.

**CASCA**

'Tis Caesar that you mean, is it not, Cassius?

**CASSIUS**

Let it be who it is; for Romans now    80
Have thews° and limbs like to their ancestors;
But, woe the while!° Our fathers' minds are dead,
And we are governed with our mothers' spirits;
Our yoke and sufferance° show us womanish.

**CASCA**

Indeed, they say the senators tomorrow    85

Mean to establish Caesar as a king;
And he shall wear his crown by sea and land,
In every place save here in Italy.

**CASSIUS**

I know where I will wear this dagger then;
Cassius from bondage will deliver Cassius.    90
Therein,° ye gods, you make the weak most strong;
Therein, ye gods, you tyrants do defeat.
Nor stony tower, nor walls of beaten brass,
Nor airess dungeon, nor strong links of iron,
Can be retentive to° the strength of spirit;    95
But life, being weary of these worldly bars,
Never lacks power to dismiss itself.
If I know this, know all the world besides,
That part of tyranny that I do bear
I can shake off at pleasure. *Thunder still.*

**CASCA**                    So can I;    100
So every bondman in his own hand bears
The power to cancel his captivity.

**CASSIUS**

And why should Caesar be a tyrant then?
Poor man, I know he would not be a wolf
But that he sees the Romans are but sheep;    105
He were no lion, were not Romans hinds.°
Those that with haste will make a mighty fire
Begin it with weak straws. What trash is Rome,
What rubbish and what offal, when it serves
For the base matter to illuminate    110
So vile a thing as Caesar! But, O grief,
Where hast thou led me? I, perhaps, speak this
Before a willing bondman; then I know
My answer must be made.° But I am armed,
And dangers are to me indifferent.°    115

**CASCA**

You speak to Casca, and to such a man
That is no fleering° tell-tale. Hold, my hand.
Be factious° for redress of all these griefs,
And I will set this foot of mine as far
As who goes farthest. [*They clasp hands.*]

**CASSIUS**                There's a bargain made.    120
Now know you, Casca, I have moved already
Some certain of the noblest-minded Romans
To undergo° with me an enterprise
Of honorable dangerous consequence;
And I do know, by this° they stay for me    125
In Pompey's porch;° for now, this fearful night,
There is no stir or walking in the streets,
And the complexion of the element°
In favor's like° the work we have in hand,
Most bloody, fiery, and most terrible.    130

*Enter* CINNA.

**CASCA**

Stand close° awhile, for here comes one in haste.

**48 unbracèd** with doublet unfastened **49 thunder-stone** lightning bolt **50 cross** jagged **54 part** role **55 tokens** prophetic signs **56 astonish** stun **58 want** lack **60 put on** display; **cast . . . wonder** are amazed **64 from . . . kind** (act) against their natures **65 old men** the senile, in second childhood; **calculate** make predictions (cf. proverb, "Fools and children often do prophesy") **66 ordinance** natural order of behavior **67 preformèd faculties** innate qualities **68 monstrous quality** unnatural condition **69 spirits** supernatural powers **71 monstrous state** abnormal state of affairs **77 prodigious** ominous **78 fearful** causing fear; **eruptions** disturbances of nature **81 thews** sinews **82 woe the while** alas for the times **84 yoke and sufferance** servitude and the meek endurance of it

**91 Therein** i.e., in suicide **95 be retentive to** hold in **106 hinds** (1) female deer (2) peasants (3) servants **114 My . . . made** I shall have to answer for my words **115 indifferent** unimportant **117 fleering** flattering **118 factious** active in forming a political party **123 undergo** undertake **125 by this** by this time **126 Pompey's porch** portico of Pompey's Theater **128 complexion . . . element** condition of the sky **129 In favor's like** in appearance is like **131 close** hidden

CASSIUS
'Tis Cinna; I do know him by his gait;
He is a friend. Cinna, where haste you so?

CINNA
To find out you. Who's that? Metellus Cimber?

CASSIUS
No, it is Casca, one incorporate                               135
To° our attempts. Am I not stayed° for, Cinna?

CINNA
I am glad on't.° What a fearful night is this!
There's two or three of us have seen strange sights.

CASSIUS
Am I not stayed for? Tell me.

CINNA                                            Yes, you are.
O Cassius, if you could                                       140
But win the noble Brutus to our party—

CASSIUS
Be you content. Good Cinna, take this paper,
And look you lay it in the praetor's chair,°
Where Brutus may but find it;° and throw this
In at his window; set this up with wax                        145
Upon old Brutus'° statue. All this done,
Repair° to Pompey's porch, where you shall find us.
Is Decius° Brutus and Trebonius there?

CINNA
All but Metellus Cimber, and he's gone
To seek you at your house. Well, I will hie,°                 150
And so bestow these papers as you bade me.

CASSIUS
That done, repair to Pompey's Theater. *Exit* CINNA.
Come, Casca, you and I will yet ere day
See Brutus at his house; three parts of him
Is ours already, and the man entire                           155
Upon the next encounter yields him ours.

CASCA
O, he sits high in all the people's hearts;
And that which would appear offense in us,
His countenance,° like richest alchemy,°
Will change to virtue and to worthiness.                      160

CASSIUS
Him, and his worth, and our great need of him,
You have right well conceited.° Let us go,
For it is after midnight, and ere day
We will awake him and be sure of him.          *Exeunt.*

# A C T   I I

## [Scene I. *Rome.*]

*Enter* BRUTUS *in his orchard.*°

135–36 **incorporate To** intimately bound up with   136
**stayed** waited   137 **on't** of it (i.e., that Casca has joined the
conspiracy)   143 **praetor's chair** official chair in which Brutus
would sit as chief magistrate, an office next in rank to consul
144 **Where . . . it** where only Brutus may find it   146 **old
Brutus'** Lucius Junius Brutus, founder of the Roman Republic
147 **Repair** go   148 **Decius** actually Decimus, a kinsman of
Marcus Brutus; the error is found in North's Plutarch   150
**hie** hurry   159 **countenance** support; **alchemy** the "science"
by which many experimenters tried to turn base metals into
gold   162 **conceited** (1) understood (2) described in an
elaborate simile
**II.i.s.d. orchard** garden

BRUTUS
What, Lucius, ho!
I cannot, by the progress of the stars,
Give guess how near to day. Lucius, I say!
I would it were my fault to sleep so soundly.
When, Lucius, when? Awake, I say! What, Lucius!     5

*Enter* LUCIUS.

LUCIUS   Called you, my lord?
BRUTUS
Get me a taper° in my study, Lucius.
When it is lighted, come and call me here.

LUCIUS   I will, my lord.                          *Exit.*
BRUTUS
It must be by his death; and for my part,            10
I know no personal cause to spurn at° him,
But for the general.° He would be crowned.
How that might change his nature, there's the question.
It is the bright day that brings forth the adder,
And that craves° wary walking. Crown him that,      15
And then I grant we put a sting in him
That at his will he may do danger° with.
Th' abuse of greatness is when it disjoins
Remorse° from power; and, to speak truth of Caesar,
I have not known when his affections swayed°        20
More than his reason. But 'tis a common proof°
That lowliness° is young ambition's ladder,
Whereto the climber upward turns his face;
But when he once attains the upmost round,°
He then unto the ladder turns his back,             25
Looks in the clouds, scorning the base degrees°
By which he did ascend. So Caesar may;
Then lest he may, prevent.° And, since the quarrel°
Will bear no color° for the thing he is,
Fashion it° thus: that what he is, augmented,        30
Would run to these and these extremities;°
And therefore think him as a serpent's egg
Which hatched, would as his kind° grow mischievous,
And kill him in the shell.

*Enter* LUCIUS.

LUCIUS
The taper burneth in your closet,° sir.             35
Searching the window for a flint, I found
This paper thus sealed up, and I am sure
It did not lie there when I went to bed.

*Gives him the letter.*

BRUTUS
Get you to bed again; it is not day.
Is not tomorrow, boy, the ides of March?            40
LUCIUS   I know not, sir.

7 **taper** candle   11 **spurn at** rebel (literally, "kick") against
12 **general** public welfare   15 **craves** demands   17
**danger** harm   18–19 **disjoins Remorse** separates mercy
20 **affections swayed** emotions ruled   21 **common proof**
matter of common experience   22 **lowliness** humility   24
**round** rung   26 **base degrees** (1) low steps of the ladder
(2) less important grades of office (3) common people   28
**prevent** take action to forestall; **quarrel** cause of complaint
29 **bear no color** have no excuse   30 **Fashion it** construct
the case   31 **these . . . extremities** such and such extremes
(of tyranny)   33 **as his kind** according to its nature   35
**closet** study

**BRUTUS**
Look in the calendar and bring me word.

**LUCIUS**    I will, sir.    *Exit.*

**BRUTUS**
The exhalations° whizzing in the air
Give so much light that I may read by them.    45

*Opens the letter and reads.*

"Brutus, thou sleep'st; awake, and see thyself.
Shall Rome, &c.° Speak, strike, redress.
Brutus, thou sleep'st; awake."
Such instigations have been often dropped
Where I have took them up.    50
"Shall Rome, &c." Thus must I piece it out:°
Shall Rome stand under one man's awe?° What,
Rome?
My ancestors did from the streets of Rome
The Tarquin drive, when he was called a king.
"Speak, strike, redress." Am I entreated    55
To speak and strike? O Rome, I make thee promise,
If the redress will follow, thou receivest
Thy full petition at the hand of° Brutus!

*Enter* LUCIUS.

**LUCIUS**
Sir, March is wasted fifteen days.

*Knock within.*

**BRUTUS**
'Tis good. Go to the gate; somebody knocks.    60
[*Exit* LUCIUS.]
Since Cassius first did whet° me against Caesar,
I have not slept.
Between the acting of a dreadful thing
And the first motion,° all the interim is
Like a phantasma,° or a hideous dream.    65
The genius° and the mortal instruments°
Are then in council, and the state of a man,
Like to a little kingdom, suffers then
The nature of an insurrection.°

*Enter* LUCIUS.

**LUCIUS**
Sir, 'tis your brother° Cassius at the door,    70
Who doth desire to see you.

**BRUTUS**                Is he alone?

**LUCIUS**
No, sir, there are moe° with him.

**BRUTUS**                Do you know them?

**LUCIUS**
No, sir; their hats are plucked about their ears,
And half their faces buried in their cloaks,
That by no means I may discover° them    75
By any mark of favor.°

**BRUTUS**        Let 'em enter. [*Exit* LUCIUS.]

They are the faction. O conspiracy,
Sham'st thou to show thy dang'rous brow by night,
When evils are most free?° O, then by day
Where wilt thou find a cavern dark enough    80
To mask thy monstrous visage? Seek none, conspiracy;
Hide it in smiles and affability:
For if thou path,° thy native semblance° on,
Not Erebus° itself were dim enough
To hide thee from prevention.°    85

*Enter the conspirators,* CASSIUS, CASCA, DECIUS,
CINNA, METELLUS [*Cimber*], *and* TREBONIUS.

**CASSIUS**
I think we are too bold upon° your rest.
Good morrow, Brutus; do we trouble you?

**BRUTUS**
I have been up this hour, awake all night.
Know I these men that come along with you?

**CASSIUS**
Yes every man of them; and no man here    90
But honors you; and every one doth wish
You had but that opinion of yourself
Which every noble Roman bears of you.
This is Trebonius.

**BRUTUS**                He is welcome hither.

**CASSIUS**
This, Decius Brutus.

**BRUTUS**                He is welcome too.    95

**CASSIUS**
This, Casca; this, Cinna; and this, Metellus Cimber.

**BRUTUS**
They are all welcome.
What watchful cares° do interpose themselves
Betwixt your eyes and night?

**CASSIUS**
Shall I entreat a word?

*They whisper.*    100

**DECIUS**
Here lies the east; doth not the day break here?

**CASCA**    No.

**CINNA**
O, pardon, sir, it doth; and yon gray lines
That fret° the clouds are messengers of day.

**CASCA**
You shall confess that you are both deceived.    105
Here, as I point my sword, the sun arises,
Which is a great way growing on° the south,
Weighing° the youthful season of the year.
Some two months hence, up higher toward the north
He first presents his fire; and the high° east    110
Stands as the Capitol, directly here.

**BRUTUS**
Give me your hands all over, one by one.

**CASSIUS**
And let us swear our resolution.

44 **exhalations** meteors   47, 51 **&c.** read "et cetera"   51
**piece it out** develop the meaning   52 **under . . . awe** in
awe of one man   58 **Thy . . . of** all you ask from   61 **whet**
incite   64 **motion** prompting   65 **phantasma** hallucination
66 **genius** guardian spirit (?) reasoning spirit (?); **mortal
instruments** the emotions and physical powers (which should
be ruled and guided by reason)   69 **nature . . . insurrection**
a kind of insurrection   70 **brother** brother-in-law (Cassius
was married to Brutus' sister)   72 **moe** more   75 **discover**
recognize   76 **favor** appearance

79 **evils . . . free** evil things roam most freely   83 **path**
walk (verb); **native semblance** true appearance   84 **Erebus**
dark region between earth and Hades   85 **from prevention**
from being forestalled and hindered   86 **upon** in intruding on
98 **watchful cares** cares that keep you awake   104 **fret**
pattern, interlace   107 **growing on** tending toward   108
**Weighing** considering   110 **high** due

BRUTUS
No, not an oath. If not the face of men,°
The sufferance° of our souls, the time's abuse°—  115
If these be motives weak, break off betimes,°
And every man hence to his idle bed.
So let high-sighted° tyranny range° on
Till each man drop by lottery.° But if these
(As I am sure they do) bear fire enough  120
To kindle cowards and to steel with valor
The melting spirits of women, then, countrymen,
What need we any spur but our own cause
To prick° us to redress? What other bond
Than secret Romans° that have spoke the word,  125
And will not palter?° And what other oath
Than honesty° to honesty engaged°
That this shall be, or we will fall for it?
Swear° priests and cowards and men cautelous,°
Old feeble carrions° and such suffering souls  130
That welcome wrongs; unto bad causes swear
Such creatures as men doubt; but do not stain
The even° virtue of our enterprise,
Nor th' insuppressive mettle° of our spirits,
To think that or our cause or° our performance  135
Did need an oath; when every drop of blood
That every Roman bears, and nobly bears,
Is guilty of a several bastardy°
If he do break the smallest particle
Of any promise that hath passed from him.  140

CASSIUS
But what of Cicero? Shall we sound him?
I think he will stand very strong with us.

CASCA
Let us not leave him out.

CINNA                    No, by no means.

METELLUS
O, let us have him, for his silver hairs
Will purchase us a good opinion,°  145
And buy men's voices to commend our deeds.
It shall be said his judgment ruled our hands;
Our youths and wildness shall no whit° appear,
But all be buried in his gravity.°

BRUTUS
O, name him not! Let us not break with him;°  150
For he will never follow anything
That other men begin.

CASSIUS              Then leave him out.

CASCA
Indeed, he is not fit.

DECIUS
Shall no man else be touched but only Caesar?

CASSIUS
Decius, well urged.° I think it is not meet  155
Mark Antony, so well beloved of Caesar,
Should outlive Caesar; we shall find of° him
A shrewd contriver;° and you know, his means,
If he improve° them, may well stretch so far
As to annoy° us all; which to prevent,°  160
Let Antony and Caesar fall together.

BRUTUS
Our course will seem too bloody, Caius Cassius,
To cut the head off and then hack the limbs,
Like wrath in death and envy° afterwards;
For Antony is but a limb of Caesar.  165
Let's be sacrificers, but not butchers, Caius.
We all stand up against the spirit of Caesar,°
And in the spirit of men there is no blood.
O, that we then could come by° Caesar's spirit,
And not dismember Caesar! But, alas,  170
Caesar must bleed for it. And, gentle° friends,
Let's kill him boldly, but not wrathfully;
Let's carve him as a dish fit for the gods,
Not hew him as a carcass fit for hounds.
And let our hearts, as subtle masters do,  175
Stir up their servants° to an act of rage,
And after seem to chide 'em. This shall make
Our purpose necessary, and not envious;°
Which so appearing to the common eyes,
We shall be called purgers,° not murderers.  180
And for Mark Antony, think not of him;
For he can do no more than Caesar's arm
When Caesar's head is off.

CASSIUS                        Yet I fear him;
For in the ingrafted° love he bears to Caesar—

BRUTUS
Alas, good Cassius, do not think of him.  185
If he love Caesar, all that he can do
Is to himself—take thought° and die for Caesar.
And that were much he should,° for he is given
To sports, to wildness, and much company.

TREBONIUS
There is no fear° in him; let him not die,  190
For he will live and laugh at this hereafter.

*Clock strikes.*

BRUTUS
Peace! Count the clock.

CASSIUS                    The clock hath stricken three.

TREBONIUS
'Tis time to part.

CASSIUS            But it is doubtful yet
Whether Caesar will come forth today or no;

114 **face of men** sincere and resolute appearance of the conspirators, which should not be distrusted  115 **sufferance** patient endurance; **time's abuse** corruption of the age (i.e., Caesar's assumption of unconstitutional powers)  116 **betimes** immediately  118 **high-sighted** arrogant (viewing widely from on high, like a falcon ready to swoop on prey); **range** rove or fly in search of prey  119 **by lottery** by chance, i.e., at the tyrant's whim  124 **prick** urge  125 **secret Romans** the fact that we are Romans capable of maintaining secrecy  126 **palter** equivocate  127 **honesty** personal honor; **engaged** pledged  129 **Swear** bind by oath; **cautelous** deceitful  130 **carrions** wretches almost dead and rotting  133 **even** unblemished, perfect  134 **insuppressive mettle** indomitable temper  135 **or ... or** either ... or  138 **guilty ... bastardy** guilty of an act not truly Roman  145 **opinion** reputation  148 **no whit** not in the slightest  149 **gravity** sobriety and stability (Latin *gravitas*)  150 **break with him** divulge our plan to him

155 **urged** suggested  157 **of** in  158 **shrewd contriver** cunning and malicious plotter  159 **improve** make good use of  160 **annoy** harm; **prevent** forestall  164 **envy** malice, i.e., as though we were killing Caesar for personal spite and hatred  167 **spirit of Caesar** principles (of tyranny) for which Caesar stands  169 **come by** get possession of  171 **gentle** noble  176 **servants** (1) the hands (2) the passions  178 **envious** malicious  180 **purgers** healers  184 **ingrafted** firmly rooted  187 **take thought** grow melancholy with brooding  188 **that ... should** that would be too much to expect of him  190 **no fear** nothing to fear

For he is superstitious grown of late,                                    195
Quite from the main° opinion he held once
Of fantasy, of dreams, and ceremonies.°
It may be these apparent prodigies,°
The unaccustomed terror of this night,
And the persuasion of his augurers°                                       200
May hold him from the Capitol today.

DECIUS
Never fear that. If he be so resolved,
I can o'ersway him;° for he loves to hear
That unicorns may be betrayed with trees,°
And bears with glasses,° elephants with holes,°                           205
Lions with toils,° and men with flatterers;
But when I tell him he hates flatterers,
He says he does, being then most flatterèd.
Let me work;
For I can give his humor° the true bent,°                                 210
And I will bring him to the Capitol.

CASSIUS
Nay, we will all of us be there to fetch him.

BRUTUS
By the eighth hour; is that the uttermost?°

CINNA
Be that the uttermost, and fail not then.

METELLUS
Caius Ligarius doth bear Caesar hard,°                                    215
Who rated° him for speaking well of Pompey.
I wonder none of you have thought of him.

BRUTUS
Now, good Metellus, go along by him.°
He loves me well, and I have given him reasons;
Send him but hither, and I'll fashion° him.                              220

CASSIUS
The morning comes upon's; we'll leave you, Brutus.
And, friends, disperse yourselves; but all remember
What you have said, and show yourselves true
    Romans.

BRUTUS
Good gentlemen, look fresh and merrily.
Let not our looks put on° our purposes,                                   225
But bear it° as our Roman actors do,
With untired spirits and formal constancy.°
And so good morrow to you every one.
                        *Exeunt. Manet*° BRUTUS.
Boy! Lucius! Fast asleep? It is no matter;
Enjoy the honey-heavy dew° of slumber.                                    230
Thou hast no figures nor no fantasies°
Which busy care draws in the brains of men;
Therefore thou sleep'st so sound.

*Enter* PORTIA.

PORTIA                                          Brutus, my lord.
BRUTUS
Portia, what mean you? Wherefore rise you now?
It is not for your health thus to commit                                  235
Your weak condition to the raw cold morning.
PORTIA
Nor for yours neither. Y'have ungently,° Brutus,
Stole from my bed; and yesternight at supper
You suddenly arose and walked about,
Musing and sighing, with your arms across;°                               240
And when I asked you what the matter was,
You stared upon me with ungentle looks.
I urged you further; then you scratched your head,
And too impatiently stamped with your foot.
Yet I insisted, yet you answered not,                                     245
But with an angry wafter° of your hand
Gave sign for me to leave you. So I did,
Fearing to strengthen that impatience
Which seemed too much enkindled, and withal°
Hoping it was but an effect of humor,°                                    250
Which sometime hath his° hour with every man.
It will not let you eat, nor talk, nor sleep,
And could it work so much upon your shape
As it hath much prevailed on your condition,°
I should not know you° Brutus. Dear my lord,                             255
Make me acquainted with your cause of grief.
BRUTUS
I am not well in health, and that is all.
PORTIA
Brutus is wise and, were he not in health,
He would embrace the means to come by it.
BRUTUS
Why, so I do. Good Portia, go to bed.                                     260
PORTIA
Is Brutus sick, and is it physical°
To walk unbracèd° and suck up the humors°
Of the dank morning? What, is Brutus sick,
And will he steal out of his wholesome bed,
To dare the vile contagion of the night,°                                 265
And tempt the rheumy and unpurgèd air°
To add unto his sickness? No, my Brutus;
You have some sick offense° within your mind,
Which by the right and virtue of my place°
I ought to know of; and upon my knees                                     270
I charm° you, by my once commended beauty,
By all your vows of love, and that great vow
Which did incorporate° and make us one,
That you unfold to me, your self, your half,
Why you are heavy,° and what men tonight                                  275
Have had resort to you; for here have been
Some six or seven, who did hide their faces
Even from darkness.
BRUTUS                          Kneel not, gentle Portia.

196 Quite . . . main at variance with the strong  197 ceremonies omens  198 apparent prodigies obvious signs of
disaster  200 augurers augurs (priests who foretold, from
omens, the future)  203 o'ersway him persuade him to change
his mind  204 betrayed with trees tricked into running at a
tree (at the last moment its prey steps aside so that the horn is
deeply embedded and the unicorn is helpless)  205 glasses
mirrors; holes pitfalls  206 toils nets, snares  210 humor
temperament; bent direction  213 uttermost latest  215
bear Caesar hard has a grudge against Caesar  216 rated
berated  218 him his house  220 fashion shape (to our
designs)  225 put on display  226 bear it play our parts  227
formal constancy consistent decorum  228 s.d. Manet
remains  230 dew refreshment  231 figures . . . fantasies
both words specify figments of the imagination

237 ungently discourteously  240 across folded (a sign of
melancholy)  246 wafter waving  249 withal also  250
effect of humor sign of a temporary mood  251 his its
254 condition disposition  255 know you recognize you as
261 physical healthy  262 unbracèd with doublet unfastened;
humors dampness, mist  265 night night air was thought to
be harmful, even poisonous  266 tempt . . . air risk the
damp and unpurified (by the sun) air  268 sick offense
sickness that harms  269 place situation (as wife)  271
charm entreat  273 incorporate make us one flesh (cf.
Matthew 19:5, "They twain shall be one flesh")  275 heavy
dejected

PORTIA

I should not need, if you were gentle Brutus.
Within the bond of marriage, tell me, Brutus,     280
Is it excepted° I should know no secrets
That appertain to you? Am I your self
But, as it were, in sort or limitation,°
To keep with you at meals, comfort your bed,
And talk to you sometimes? Dwell I but in the suburbs°   285
Of your good pleasure? If it be no more,
Portia is Brutus' harlot, not his wife.

BRUTUS

You are my true and honorable wife,
As dear to me as are the ruddy drops
That visit my sad heart.     290

PORTIA

If this were true, then should I know this secret.
I grant I am a woman; but withal°
A woman that Lord Brutus took to wife.
I grant I am a woman; but withal
A woman well reputed, Cato's daughter.°     295
Think you I am no stronger than my sex,
Being so fathered and so husbanded?
Tell me your counsels,° I will not disclose 'em.
I have made strong proof of my constancy,°
Giving myself a voluntary wound     300
Here in the thigh; can I bear that with patience,
And not my husband's secrets?

BRUTUS           O ye gods,
Render me worthy of this noble wife!

*Knock.*

Hark, hark! One knocks. Portia, go in a while,
And by and by thy bosom shall partake     305
The secrets of my heart.
All my engagements° I will construe° to thee,
All the charactery of° my sad brows.
Leave me with haste.           *Exit* PORTIA.

*Enter* LUCIUS *and* [CAIUS] *Ligarius.*

          Lucius, who's that knocks?

LUCIUS

Here is a sick man that would speak with you.     310

BRUTUS

Caius Ligarius, that Metellus spake of.
Boy, stand aside. Caius Ligarius! How?°

CAIUS

Vouchsafe° good morrow from a feeble tongue.

BRUTUS

O, what a time have you chose out, brave° Caius,
To wear a kerchief!° Would you were not sick!     315

CAIUS

I am not sick, if Brutus have in hand
Any exploit worthy the name of honor.

BRUTUS

Such an exploit have I in hand, Ligarius,
Had you a healthful ear to hear of it.

CAIUS

By all the gods that Romans bow before,     320
I here discard my sickness! Soul of Rome,
Brave son, derived from honorable loins,°
Thou, like an exorcist,° hast conjured up
My mortifièd° spirit. Now bid me run,
And I will strive with things impossible,     325
Yea, get the better of them. What's to do?

BRUTUS

A piece of work that will make sick men whole.°

CAIUS

But are not some whole that we must make sick?

BRUTUS

That must we also. What it is, my Caius,
I shall unfold to thee, as we are going     330
To whom° it must be done.

CAIUS           Set on° your foot,
And with a heart new-fired I follow you,
To do I know not what; but it sufficeth
That Brutus leads me on.     *Thunder.*

BRUTUS           Follow me, then.     *Exeunt.*

---

[Scene II. *Caesar's house.*]

*Thunder and lightning. Enter Julius* CAESAR *in his nightgown.°*

CAESAR

Nor heaven nor earth have been at peace tonight:
Thrice hath Calphurnia in her sleep cried out,
"Help, ho! They murder Caesar!" Who's within?

*Enter a* SERVANT.

SERVANT   My lord?

CAESAR

Go bid the priests do present° sacrifice,     5
And bring me their opinions of success.°

SERVANT   I will, my lord.           *Exit.*

*Enter* CALPHURNIA.

CALPHURNIA

What mean you, Caesar? Think you to walk forth?
You shall not stir out of your house today.

CAESAR

Caesar shall forth. The things that threatened me     10
Ne'er looked but on my back; when they shall see
The face of Caesar, they are vanishèd.

CALPHURNIA

Caesar, I never stood on ceremonies,°
Yet now they fright me. There is one within,

---

281 **excepted** made an exception that   283 **in . . . limitation** after a fashion or within a certain restriction (legal terms)   285 **suburbs** outlying districts (where the brothels and least respectable taverns were found)   292 **withal** at the same time   295 **Cato's daughter** Marcus Porcius Cato was famous for his integrity; he joined Pompey against Caesar and killed himself at Utica in 46 B.C. to avoid capture; he was Brutus' uncle as well as father-in-law   298 **counsels** secrets   299 **proof . . . constancy** trial of my resolution   307 **engagements** commitments; **construe** explain   308 **charactery of** writing upon, i.e., wrinkles of grief and worry   312 **How** How are you?   313 **Vouchsafe** please accept   314 **brave** noble   315 **To . . . kerchief** as a protection against drafts, i.e., to be sick

322 **from honorable loins** i.e., descent from Lucius Junius Brutus, founder of the Roman Republic   323 **exorcist** conjurer   324 **mortifièd** deadened   327 **whole** healthy   331 **To whom** to the house of him to whom; **Set on** advance   II.ii.s.d. **nightgown** dressing gown   5 **present** immediate   6 **opinions of success** judgment as to the future course of events   13 **stood on ceremonies** paid attention to omens

Besides the things that we have heard and seen,                    15
Recounts most horrid sights seen by the watch.°
A lioness hath whelpèd in the streets,
And graves have yawned, and yielded up their dead;
Fierce fiery warriors fought upon the clouds
In ranks and squadrons and right form° of war,                     20
Which drizzled blood upon the Capitol;
The noise of battle hurtled° in the air,
Horses did neigh and dying men did groan,
And ghosts did shriek and squeal about the streets.
O Caesar, these things are beyond all use,°                         25
And I do fear them.

CAESAR                          What can be avoided
Whose end is purposed by the mighty gods?
Yet Caesar shall go forth; for these predictions
Are to° the world in general as to Caesar.

CALPHURNIA
When beggars die, there are no comets seen;                        30
The heavens themselves blaze forth° the death of
  princes.

CAESAR
Cowards die many times before their deaths;
The valiant never taste of death but once.
Of all the wonders that I yet have heard,
It seems to me most strange that men should fear,                  35
Seeing that death, a necessary end,
Will come when it will come.

*Enter a* SERVANT.

                          What say the augurers?

SERVANT
They would not have you to stir forth today.
Plucking the entrails of an offering forth,
They could not find a heart within the beast.                      40

CAESAR
The gods do this in shame of cowardice:
Caesar should° be a beast without a heart°
If he should stay at home today for fear.
No, Caesar shall not. Danger knows full well
That Caesar is more dangerous than he.                             45
We are two lions littered in one day,
And I the elder and more terrible,
And Caesar shall go forth.

CALPHURNIA                      Alas, my lord,
Your wisdom is consumed in confidence.°
Do not go forth today. Call it my fear                             50
That keeps you in the house and not your own.
We'll send Mark Antony to the Senate House,
And he shall say you are not well today.
Let me, upon my knee, prevail in this.

CAESAR
Mark Antony shall say I am not well,                               55
And for thy humor,° I will stay at home.

*Enter* DECIUS.

Here's Decius Brutus, he shall tell them so.

DECIUS
Caesar, all hail! Good morrow, worthy Caesar;
I come to fetch° you to the Senate House.

CAESAR
And you are come in very happy time°                              60
To bear my greeting to the senators,
And tell them that I will not come today.
Cannot, is false; and that I dare not, falser:
I will not come today. Tell them so, Decius.

CALPHURNIA
Say he is sick.

CAESAR          Shall Caesar send a lie?                          65
Have I in conquest stretched mine arm so far
To be afeard to tell graybeards the truth?
Decius, go tell them Caesar will not come.

DECIUS
Most mighty Caesar, let me know some cause,
Lest I be laughed at when I tell them so.                         70

CAESAR
The cause is in my will: I will not come.
That is enough to satisfy the Senate.
But for your private satisfaction,
Because I love you, I will let you know.
Calphurnia here, my wife, stays° me at home.                      75
She dreamt tonight° she saw my statue,°
Which, like a fountain with an hundred spouts,
Did run pure blood, and many lusty Romans
Came smiling and did bathe their hands in it.
And these does she apply for° warnings and
  portents°                                                        80
And evils imminent, and on her knee
Hath begged that I will stay at home today.

DECIUS
This dream is all amiss interpreted;
It was a vision fair and fortunate:
Your statue spouting blood in many pipes,                         85
In which so many smiling Romans bathed,
Signifies that from you great Rome shall suck
Reviving blood, and that great men shall press
For tinctures, stains, relics, and cognizance.°
This by Calphurnia's dream is signified.                          90

CAESAR
And this way have you well expounded it.

DECIUS
I have, when you have heard what I can say;
And know it now, the Senate have concluded
To give this day a crown to mighty Caesar.
If you shall send them word you will not come,                    95
Their minds may change. Besides, it were a mock
Apt to be rendered,° for someone to say,
"Break up the Senate till another time,
When Caesar's wife shall meet with better dreams."
If Caesar hide himself, shall they not whisper,                  100
"Lo, Caesar is afraid"?
Pardon me, Caesar, for my dear dear love

---

**16 watch** night watchmen   **20 right form** proper military
formation  **22 hurtled** clashed  **25 use** normal experience
**29 Are to** apply to  **31 blaze forth** proclaim (by comets
and meteors)  **42 should** would; **heart** the organ of courage
**49 consumed in confidence** destroyed by too much confidence
**56 humor** whim   **59 fetch** escort

**60 happy time** favorable time (i.e., just at the right moment)
**75 stays** keeps  **76 tonight** last night; **statue** trisyllabic;
pronounced "stat-u-a"  **80 apply for** explain as; **portents**
accent on last syllable  **89 tinctures . . . cognizance** Samuel
Johnson paraphrases the line: "The Romans, says Decius, all
come to you, as to a saint, for relics; as to a prince, for honors";
**tinctures** (1) alchemical elixirs (2) colors, metals, etc. used in
heraldry; **stains** colors in a coat of arms; **relics** venerated
property of a martyr; **cognizance** mark of identification
worn by a nobleman's followers  **96-97 mock . . . rendered**
jeering remark likely to be made

To your proceeding° bids me tell you this,
And reason to my love is liable.°

CAESAR
How foolish do your fears seem now, Calphurnia!    105
I am ashamèd I did yield to them.
Give me my robe,° for I will go.

*Enter* BRUTUS, LIGARIUS, METELLUS [*Cimber*],
CASCA, TREBONIUS, CINNA, *and* PUBLIUS.

And look where Publius is come to fetch me.

PUBLIUS
Good morrow, Caesar.

CAESAR              Welcome, Publius.
What, Brutus, are you stirred so early too?    110
Good morrow, Casca. Caius Ligarius,
Caesar was ne'er so much your enemy°
As that same ague which hath made you lean.
What is't o'clock?

BRUTUS           Caesar, 'tis strucken eight.

CAESAR
I thank you for your pains and courtesy.    115

*Enter* ANTONY.

See! Antony, that revels long a-nights,
Is notwithstanding up. Good morrow, Antony.

ANTONY
So to most noble Caesar.

CAESAR           Bid them prepare° within.
I am to blame to be thus waited for.
Now, Cinna; now, Metellus; what, Trebonius,    120
I have an hour's talk in store for you;
Remember that you call on me today;
Be near me, that I may remember you.

TREBONIUS
Caesar, I will [*aside*] and so near will I be,
That your best friends shall wish I had been further.    125

CAESAR
Good friends, go in and taste some wine with me,
And we (like friends) will straightway go together.

BRUTUS [*Aside*.]
That every like is not the same,° O Caesar,
The heart of Brutus earns° to think upon.      *Exeunt.*

[*Scene* III. *A street near the Capitol, close to Brutus' house.*]

*Enter* ARTEMIDORUS [*reading a paper*].

[ARTEMIDORUS] "Caesar, beware of Brutus; take
heed of Cassius; come not near Casca; have an eye to
Cinna; trust not Trebonius; mark well Metellus Cimber; Decius Brutus loves thee not; thou hast wronged
Caius Ligarius. There is but one mind in all these men,   5
and it is bent° against Caesar. If thou beest not immortal, look about you: security gives way to conspiracy.°

The mighty gods defend thee!
                 Thy lover,° *Artemidorus.*"
Here will I stand till Caesar pass along,      10
And as a suitor° will I give him this.
My heart laments that virtue cannot live
Out of the teeth of emulation.°
If thou read this, O Caesar, thou mayest live;
If not, the Fates with traitors do contrive.°      *Exit.*   15

[*Scene* IV. *Another part of the street.*]

*Enter* PORTIA *and* LUCIUS.

PORTIA
I prithee, boy, run to the Senate House;
Stay not to answer me, but get thee gone.
Why dost thou stay?

LUCIUS         To know my errand, madam.

PORTIA
I would have had thee there and here again
Ere I can tell thee what thou shouldst do there.    5
O constancy,° be strong upon my side;
Set a huge mountain 'tween my heart and tongue!
I have a man's mind, but a woman's might.°
How hard it is for women to keep counsel!°
Art thou here yet?

LUCIUS       Madam, what should I do?    10
Run to the Capitol, and nothing else?
And so return to you, and nothing else?

PORTIA
Yes, bring me word, boy, if thy lord look well,
For he went sickly forth; and take good note
What Caesar doth, what suitors press to him.    15
Hark, boy, what noise is that?

LUCIUS    I hear none, madam.

PORTIA             Prithee, listen well.
I heard a bustling rumor like a fray,°
And the wind brings it from the Capitol.

LUCIUS
Sooth,° madam, I hear nothing.             20

*Enter the* SOOTHSAYER.

PORTIA
Come hither, fellow. Which way hast thou been?

SOOTHSAYER
At mine own house, good lady.

PORTIA
What is't o'clock?

SOOTHSAYER      About the ninth hour, lady.

PORTIA
Is Caesar yet gone to the Capitol?

SOOTHSAYER
Madame, not yet; I go to take my stand,    25
To see him pass on to the Capitol.

---

**103 proceeding** advancement   **104 reason . . . liable** my
affection proves stronger than my judgment (of impropriety)
in telling you this ("liable" = subordinate)   **107 robe** toga
**112 enemy** Ligarius had supported Pompey against Caesar in
the Civil War and had recently been pardoned by Caesar
**118 prepare** set out the wine mentioned in line 126   **128 That
. . . same** what a pity that those who appear like friends may
actually be enemies   **129 earns** grieves
**II.iii.6 bent** directed   **7 security . . . conspiracy** overconfidence gives conspiracy its opportunity

**9 lover** devoted friend   **11 as a suitor** like a petitioner   **13
Out . . . emulation** beyond the reach of envious rivalry   **15
contrive** conspire
**II.iv.6 constancy** resolution   **8 might** physical strength
**9 counsel** secret (Brutus has obviously told her of the conspiracy, though "stage time" has allowed no opportunity for
this; the inconsistency is not noticeable during a performance)
**18 bustling . . . fray** confused noise as of battle   **20 Sooth**
truly

PORTIA
Thou hast some suit to Caesar, hast thou not?
SOOTHSAYER
That I have, lady; if it will please Caesar
To be so good to Caesar as to hear me,
I shall beseech him to befriend himself.                    30
PORTIA
Why, know'st thou any harm's intended towards him?
SOOTHSAYER
None that I know will be, much that I fear may
    chance.°
Good morrow to you. Here the street is narrow;
The throng that follows Caesar at the heels,
Of senators, of praetors, common suitors,                    35
Will crowd a feeble man almost to death.
I'll get me to a place more void,° and there
Speak to great Caesar as he comes along.         Exit.
PORTIA
I must go in. Ay me, how weak a thing
The heart of woman is! O Brutus,                             40
The heavens speed° thee in thine enterprise!
Sure, the boy heard me—Brutus hath a suit
That Caesar will not grant—O, I grow faint.
Run, Lucius, and commend me° to my lord;
Say I am merry;° come to me again,                           45
And bring me word what he doth say to thee.
                                    Exeunt [severally].


# A C T   I I I

[Scene I. *Rome. Before the Capitol.*]

*Flourish. Enter* CAESAR, BRUTUS, CASSIUS, CASCA,
DECIUS, METELLUS [*Cimber*], TREBONIUS, CINNA,
ANTONY, LEPIDUS, ARTEMIDORUS, PUBLIUS,
[POPILIUS,] *and the* SOOTHSAYER.

CAESAR
The ides of March are come.
SOOTHSAYER
Ay, Caesar, but not gone.
ARTEMIDORUS
Hail, Caesar! Read this schedule.°
DECIUS
Trebonius doth desire you to o'er-read,
At your best leisure, this his humble suit.                   5
ARTEMIDORUS
O Caesar, read mine first; for mine's a suit
That touches° Caesar nearer. Read it, great Caesar.
CAESAR
What touches us ourself shall be last served.
ARTEMIDORUS
Delay not, Caesar; read it instantly.
CAESAR
What, is the fellow mad?
PUBLIUS                    Sirrah, give place.°        10

CASSIUS
What, urge you your petitions in the street?
Come to the Capitol.

[CAESAR *goes to the Capitol, the rest following.*]

POPILIUS
I wish your enterprise today may thrive.
CASSIUS
What enterprise, Popilius?
POPILIUS                    Fare you well.

[*Advances to* CAESAR.]

BRUTUS
What said Popilius Lena?                                      15
CASSIUS
He wished today our enterprise might thrive.
I fear our purpose is discoverèd.
BRUTUS
Look how he makes to° Caesar; mark him.
CASSIUS
Casca, be sudden,° for we fear prevention.°
Brutus, what shall be done? If this be known,                20
Cassius or Caesar never shall turn back,°
For I will slay myself.
BRUTUS                    Cassius, be constant.°
Popilius Lena speaks not of our purposes;
For look, he smiles, and Caesar doth not change.°
CASSIUS
Trebonius knows his time; for look you, Brutus,              25
He marks Mark Antony out of the way.
                    [*Exeunt* ANTONY *and* TREBONIUS.]
DECIUS
Where is Metellus Cimber? Let him go
And presently prefer° his suit to Caesar.
BRUTUS
He is addressed.° Press near and second him.
CINNA
Casca, you are the first that rears your hand.              30
CAESAR
Are we all ready? What is now amiss
That Caesar and his Senate must redress?
METELLUS
Most high, most mighty, and most puissant° Caesar,
Metellus Cimber throws before thy seat
An humble heart. [*Kneeling.*]
CAESAR                    I must prevent thee, Cimber.     35
These couchings° and these lowly courtesies°
Might fire the blood of ordinary men,
And turn preordinance and first decree°
Into the law of children. Be not fond°
To think that Caesar bears such rebel blood°                40
That will be thawed from the true quality°
With that° which melteth fools—I mean sweet words,
Low-crookèd curtsies, and base spaniel° fawning.

32 **chance** happen   37 **more void** more empty (less crowded)
41 **speed** prosper   44 **commend me** give my love   45
**merry** cheerful
**III.i.3 schedule** scroll   7 **touches** concerns   10 **Sirrah, give
place** Fellow, get out of the way

18 **makes to** heads for   19 **sudden** swift; **prevention** being
forestalled   21 **turn back** return alive   22 **constant** calm   24
**change** change his expression   28 **presently prefer** immediately present   29 **addressed** ready   33 **puissant** powerful
36 **couchings** low bowings; **lowly courtesies** humble
obeisances   38 **preordinance . . . decree** customs and laws
established from antiquity   39 **fond** so foolish as   40 **bears
. . . blood** has such uncontrolled emotions   41 **true quality**
proper quality (i.e., firmness)   42 **With that** by those things
43 **spaniel** doglike, cringing

Thy brother by decree is banishèd.
If thou dost bend and pray and fawn for him,                    45
I spurn thee like a cur out of my way.
Know, Caesar doth not wrong, nor without cause
Will he be satisfied.

METELLUS
Is there no voice more worthy than my own,
To sound more sweetly in great Caesar's ear                     50
For the repealing° of my banished brother?

BRUTUS
I kiss thy hand, but not in flattery, Caesar,
Desiring thee that Publius Cimber may
Have an immediate freedom of repeal.°

CAESAR
What, Brutus?

CASSIUS          Pardon, Caesar; Caesar, pardon!              55
As low as to thy foot doth Cassius fall
To beg enfranchisement° for Publius Cimber.

CAESAR
I could be well moved, if I were as you;
If I could pray to move,° prayers would move me;
But I am constant as the Northern Star,°                        60
Of whose true-fixed and resting° quality
There is no fellow° in the firmament.
The skies are painted with unnumb'red° sparks,
They are all fire and every one doth shine;
But there's but one in all doth hold° his place.                65
So in the world; 'tis furnished well with men,
And men are flesh and blood, and apprehensive;°
Yet in the number I do know but one
That unassailable holds on his rank,°
Unshaked of motion;° and that I am he,                          70
Let me a little show it, even in this—
That I was constant° Cimber should be banished,
And constant do remain to keep him so.

CINNA
O Caesar—

CAESAR          Hence! Wilt thou lift up Olympus?°

DECIUS
Great Caesar—

CAESAR          Doth not Brutus bootless° kneel?              75

CASCA   Speak hands for me!

*They stab* CAESAR.

CAESAR
Et tu, Brutè?° Then fall Caesar.                    *Dies.*

CINNA
Liberty! Freedom! Tyranny is dead!
Run hence, proclaim, cry it about the streets.

CASSIUS
Some to the common pulpits,° and cry out                        80
"Liberty, freedom, and enfranchisement!"

BRUTUS
People, and senators, be not affrighted.
Fly not; stand still; ambition's debt is paid.°

CASCA
Go to the pulpit, Brutus.

DECIUS                          And Cassius too.

BRUTUS
Where's Publius?°                                               85

CINNA
Here, quite confounded with this mutiny.°

METELLUS
Stand fast together, lest some friend of Caesar's
Should chance—

BRUTUS
Talk not of standing.° Publius, good cheer;
There is no harm intended to your person,                       90
Nor to no Roman else. So tell them, Publius.

CASSIUS
And leave us, Publius, lest that the people
Rushing on us should do your age some mischief.

BRUTUS
Do so; and let no man abide° this deed
But we the doers.                                               95

*Enter* TREBONIUS.

CASSIUS
Where is Antony?

TREBONIUS          Fled to his house amazed.°
Men, wives, and children stare, cry out and run,
As° it were doomsday.

BRUTUS                    Fates, we will know your pleasures.
That we shall die, we know; 'tis but the time,
And drawing days out, that men stand upon.°                    100

CASCA
Why, he that cuts off twenty years of life
Cuts off so many years of fearing death.

BRUTUS
Grant that, and then is death a benefit.
So are we Caesar's friends, that have abridged
His time of fearing death. Stoop, Romans, stoop,              105
And let us bathe our hands in Caesar's blood
Up to the elbows, and besmear our swords.
Then walk we forth, even to the market place,°
And waving our red weapons o'er our heads,
Let's all cry, "Peace, freedom, and liberty!"                 110

CASSIUS
Stoop then, and wash. How many ages hence
Shall this our lofty scene be acted over
In states unborn and accents yet unknown!

BRUTUS
How many times shall Caesar bleed in sport,°

---

51 **repealing** recalling  54 **freedom of repeal** permission to
be recalled from exile  57 **enfranchisement** recall, freedom
59 **pray to move** beg others to change their minds  60 **constant
. . . Star** unchanging as the polestar  61 **resting** changeless
62 **fellow** equal  63 **unnumb'red** innumerable  65 **hold**
keep  67 **apprehensive** capable of reason  69 **holds . . .
rank** maintains his position  70 **Unshaked of motion**
unmoved by internal or external forces  72 **constant** firmly
determined  74 **Olympus** a mountain in Greece where the
gods lived and held court  75 **bootless** in vain  77 **Et tu,
Brutè** And you (too), Brutus?  80 **pulpits** platforms for
public speakers

83 **ambition's . . . paid** ambition has received what was due to
it  85 **Publius** an old senator, too infirm to flee  86 **confounded
. . . mutiny** overwhelmed by this uproar  89 **Talk . . .
standing** Don't worry about making a stand, organizing
resistance  94 **abide** bear the consequences of  96 **amazed**
utterly confused  98 **As** as if  100 **drawing . . . upon**
(hope of) prolonging life, that men are concerned about  108
**the market place** the Roman Forum, center of business and
public affairs  114 **in sport** for entertainment, i.e., as part
of a play

That now on Pompey's basis° lies along°                    115
No worthier than the dust!
CASSIUS                              So oft as that shall be,
So often shall the knot° of us be called
The men that gave their country liberty.
DECIUS
What, shall we forth?
CASSIUS                          Ay, every man away.
Brutus shall lead, and we will grace° his heels         120
With the most boldest and best hearts of Rome.

*Enter a* SERVANT.

BRUTUS
Soft,° who comes here? A friend of Antony's.
SERVANT
Thus, Brutus, did my master bid me kneel;
Thus did Mark Antony bid me fall down;
And, being prostrate, thus he bade me say:            125
Brutus is noble, wise, valiant, and honest;°
Caesar was mighty, bold, royal,° and loving.
Say I love Brutus and I honor him;
Say I feared Caesar, honored him, and loved him.
If Brutus will vouchsafe that Antony                     130
May safely come to him and be resolved°
How Caesar hath deserved to lie in death,
Mark Antony shall not love Caesar dead
So well as Brutus living; but will follow
The fortunes and affairs of noble Brutus                135
Thorough° the hazards of this untrod state°
With all true faith. So says my master Antony.
BRUTUS
Thy master is a wise and valiant Roman;
I never thought him worse.
Tell him, so° please him come unto this place,        140
He shall be satisfied and, by my honor,
Depart untouched.
SERVANT              I'll fetch him presently.°
                                        *Exit* SERVANT.
BRUTUS
I know that we shall have him well to friend.°
CASSIUS
I wish we may. But yet have I a mind
That fears him much; and my misgiving still           145
Falls shrewdly to the purpose.°

*Enter* ANTONY.

BRUTUS
But here comes Antony. Welcome, Mark Antony.
ANTONY
O mighty Caesar! Dost thou lie so low?
Are all thy conquests, glories, triumphs, spoils,
Shrunk to this little measure? Fare thee well.         150
I know not, gentlemen, what you intend,

Who else must be let blood,° who else is rank.°
If I myself, there is no hour so fit
As Caesar's death's hour, nor no instrument
Of half that worth as those your swords, made rich      155
With the most noble blood of all this world.
I do beseech ye, if you bear me hard,°
Now, whilst your purpled° hands do reek and smoke,°
Fulfill your pleasure. Live° a thousand years,
I shall not find myself so apt° to die;                 160
No place will please me so, no mean° of death,
As here by Caesar, and by you cut off,
The choice and master spirits of this age.
BRUTUS
O Antony, beg not your death of us!
Though now we must appear bloody and cruel,            165
As by our hands and this our present act
You see we do, yet see you but our hands
And this the bleeding business they have done.
Our hearts you see not; they are pitiful;°
And pity to the general wrong of Rome—                 170
As fire drives out fire, so pity pity°—
Hath done this deed on Caesar. For your part,
To you our swords have leaden° points, Mark Antony:
Our arms in strength of malice, and our hearts
Of brothers' temper,° do receive you in               175
With all kind love, good thoughts, and reverence.
CASSIUS
Your voice° shall be as strong as any man's
In the disposing of new dignities.°
BRUTUS
Only be patient till we have appeased
The multitude, beside themselves with fear,           180
And then we will deliver° you the cause
Why I, that did love Caesar when I struck him,
Have thus proceeded.
ANTONY              I doubt not of your wisdom.
Let each man render me his bloody hand.
First, Marcus Brutus, will I shake with you;          185
Next, Caius Cassius, do I take your hand;
Now, Decius Brutus, yours; now yours, Metellus;
Yours, Cinna; and, my valiant Casca, yours;
Though last, not least in love, yours, good Trebonius.
Gentlemen all—alas, what shall I say?                  190
My credit° now stands on such slippery ground
That one of two bad ways you must conceit° me,
Either a coward or a flatterer.
That I did love thee, Caesar, O, 'tis true!
If then thy spirit look upon us now,                   195
Shall it not grieve thee dearer° than thy death
To see thy Antony making his peace,
Shaking the bloody fingers of thy foes,

---

115 **basis** pedestal of statue; **along** stretched out   117 **knot** closely bound group   120 **grace** do honor to   122 **Soft** wait a moment   126 **honest** honorable   127 **royal** of princely generosity   131 **be resolved** have it explained to his satisfaction   136 **Thorough** through; **untrod state** new and uncertain state of affairs   140 **so** if it should   142 **presently** immediately   143 **well to friend** as a good friend   145–46 **my . . . purpose** my forebodings always turn out to be justified

152 **let blood** (1) bled, purged (common Elizabethan practice of drawing blood to cure those swollen with disease) (2) put to death; **rank** (1) swollen with disease (2) overgrown, i.e., too powerful   157 **bear me hard** have a grudge against me   158 **purpled** (1) made scarlet (with blood) (2) made royal (?); **reek and smoke** steam (with freshly shed warm blood)   159 **Live** though I live   160 **apt** prepared   161 **mean** manner   169 **pitiful** full of pity   171 **pity pity** pity for Rome's subjection drove out pity for Caesar   173 **leaden** blunt   174–75 **Our arms . . . temper** our arms, strong with the might inspired by enmity, and our hearts, full of brotherly feeling   177 **voice** vote   178 **dignities** offices   181 **deliver** communicate to   191 **credit** reputation   192 **conceit** judge   196 **dearer** more deeply

Most noble, in the presence of thy corse?°
Had I as many eyes as thou hast wounds,                    200
Weeping as fast as they stream forth thy blood,
It would become me better than to close°
In terms of friendship with thine enemies.
Pardon me, Julius! Here wast thou bayed,° brave hart;°
Here didst thou fall, and here thy hunters stand,         205
Signed in thy spoil° and crimsoned in thy lethe.°
O world, thou wast the forest to this hart;
And this indeed, O world, the heart of thee.
How like a deer, stroken° by many princes,
Dost thou here lie!                                        210

CASSIUS
Mark Antony—

ANTONY                    Pardon me, Caius Cassius.
The enemies of Caesar shall say this;
Then, in a friend, it is cold modesty.°

CASSIUS
I blame you not for praising Caesar so;
But what compact mean you to have with us?                215
Will you be pricked in number° of our friends,
Or shall we on,° and not depend on you?

ANTONY
Therefore I took your hands, but was indeed
Swayed from the point by looking down on Caesar.
Friends am I with you all, and love you all,              220
Upon this hope, that you shall give me reasons
Why, and wherein, Caesar was dangerous.

BRUTUS
Or else were this a savage spectacle.
Our reasons are so full of good regard°
That were you, Antony, the son of Caesar,                 225
You should be satisfied.

ANTONY                    That's all I seek;
And am moreover suitor that I may
Produce° his body to the market place,
And in the pulpit, as becomes a friend,
Speak in the order° of his funeral.                       230

BRUTUS
You shall, Mark Antony.

CASSIUS                    Brutus, a word with you.

[Aside to BRUTUS.]

You know not what you do; do not consent
That Antony speak in his funeral.
Know you how much the people may be moved
By that which he will utter?

BRUTUS                    By your pardon:                  235
I will myself into the pulpit first,
And show the reason of our Caesar's death.
What Antony shall speak, I will protest°
He speaks by leave and by permission,
And that we are contented Caesar shall                    240

Have all true° rites and lawful ceremonies.
It shall advantage° more than do us wrong.°

CASSIUS
I know not what may fall;° I like it not.

BRUTUS
Mark Antony, here, take you Caesar's body.
You shall not in your funeral speech blame us,           245
But speak all good you can devise of Caesar,
And say you do't by our permission;
Else shall you not have any hand at all
About his funeral. And you shall speak
In the same pulpit whereto I am going,                    250
After my speech is ended.

ANTONY                    Be it so;
I do desire no more.

BRUTUS
Prepare the body then, and follow us.

                    Exeunt. Manet ANTONY.

ANTONY
O pardon me, thou bleeding piece of earth,
That I am meek and gentle with these butchers!          255
Thou art the ruins of the noblest man
That ever lived in the tide of times.°
Woe to the hand that shed this costly blood!
Over thy wounds now do I prophesy
(Which like dumb mouths do ope their ruby lips          260
To beg the voice and utterance of my tongue),
A curse shall light upon the limbs of men;
Domestic fury and fierce civil strife
Shall cumber° all the parts of Italy;
Blood and destruction shall be so in use,°              265
And dreadful objects so familiar,
That mothers shall but smile when they behold
Their infants quartered with the hands of war,
All pity choked with custom of fell deeds;°
And Caesar's spirit, ranging° for revenge,              270
With Atè° by his side come hot from hell,
Shall in these confines° with a monarch's voice
Cry "Havoc,"° and let slip° the dogs of war,
That this foul deed shall smell above the earth
With carrion men, groaning for burial.                  275

Enter Octavius' SERVANT.

You serve Octavius Caesar, do you not?

SERVANT
I do, Mark Antony.

ANTONY
Caesar did write for him to come to Rome.

SERVANT
He did receive his letters and is coming,
And bid me say to you by word of mouth—                 280
O Caesar!

[Seeing the body.]

ANTONY
Thy heart is big;° get thee apart and weep.

---

199 **corse** corpse  202 **close** make an agreement  204 **bayed**
brought to bay; **hart** (1) deer (2) heart  206 **Signed . . . spoil**
marked with the signs of your slaughter; **lethe** dissyllabic; the
river of oblivion from which the dead drank in Hades; here, by
extension, "stream of death," of "lifeblood"  209 **stroken** struck
down  213 **modesty** moderation  216 **pricked in number**
marked down (the modern "ticks off names"; the Roman
made small holes in his wax-covered tablets)  217 **on** proceed
224 **good regard** sound considerations  228 **Produce** bring
forth  230 **order** course of ceremonies  238 **protest** declare

241 **true** proper  242 **advantage** benefit; **wrong** harm  243
**fall** happen  257 **tide of times** course (ebb and flow) of history
264 **cumber** burden, oppress  265 **in use** customary  269
**custom . . . deeds** habituation to cruel acts  270 **ranging**
roving widely in search of prey  271 **Atè** Greek goddess
of discord and vengeance  272 **confines** boundaries, regions
273 **Cry "Havoc"** give the signal for unrestricted slaughter
and looting; **let slip** unleash  275 **carrion** dead and rotting
282 **big** swollen (with grief)

Passion,° I see, is catching, for mine eyes,
Seeing those beads of sorrow stand in thine,
Began to water. Is thy master coming?                              285
SERVANT
He lies tonight within seven leagues of Rome.
ANTONY
Post° back with speed, and tell him what hath chanced.°
Here is a mourning Rome, a dangerous Rome,
No Rome° of safety for Octavius yet.
Hie° hence and tell him so. Yet stay awhile;                       290
Thou shalt not back till I have borne this corse
Into the market place; there shall I try°
In my oration how the people take
The cruel issue° of these bloody men;
According to the which, thou shalt discourse                       295
To young Octavius of the state of things.
Lend me your hand.                                    *Exeunt.*

[Scene II. *The Forum.*]

*Enter* BRUTUS *and goes into the pulpit, and* CASSIUS,
*with the* PLEBEIANS.

PLEBEIANS
We will be satisfied!° Let us be satisfied!
BRUTUS
Then follow me, and give me audience, friends.
Cassius, go you into the other street
And part the numbers.°
Those that will hear me speak, let 'em stay here;                   5
Those that will follow Cassius, go with him;
And public reasons shall be renderèd
Of Caesar's death.
FIRST PLEBEIAN    I will hear Brutus speak.
SECOND PLEBEIAN
I will hear Cassius, and compare their reasons,
When severally° we hear them renderèd.                             10
        [*Exit* CASSIUS, *with some of the* PLEBEIANS.]
THIRD PLEBEIAN
The noble Brutus is ascended. Silence!
BRUTUS    Be patient till the last.°
Romans, countrymen, and lovers,° hear me for my
cause, and be silent, that you may hear. Believe me for
mine honor, and have respect° to mine honor, that you   15
may believe. Censure° me in your wisdom, and awake
your senses,° that you may the better judge. If there
be any in this assembly, any dear friend of Caesar's, to
him I say that Brutus' love to Caesar was no less than
his. If then that friend demand why Brutus rose against  20
Caesar, this is my answer: Not that I loved Caesar
less, but that I loved Rome more. Had you rather
Caesar were living, and die all slaves, than that Caesar
were dead, to live all free men? As Caesar loved me, I
weep for him; as he was fortunate, I rejoice at it; as he   25

was valiant, I honor him; but, as he was ambitious, I
slew him. There is tears, for his love; joy, for his
fortune; honor, for his valor; and death, for his
ambition. Who is here so base, that would be a bondman?° If any, speak; for him have I offended. Who is   30
here so rude,° that would not be a Roman? If any,
speak; for him have I offended. Who is here so vile,
that will not love his country? If any, speak; for him
have I offended. I pause for a reply.
ALL    None, Brutus, none!                                          35
BRUTUS    Then none have I offended. I have done no
more to Caesar than you shall do° to Brutus. The
question of his death is enrolled° in the Capitol; his
glory not extenuated,° wherein he was worthy, nor
his offenses enforced,° for which he suffered death.    40

*Enter Mark* ANTONY, *with Caesar's body.*

Here comes his body, mourned by Mark Antony,
who, though he had no hand in his death, shall receive
the benefit of his dying, a place° in the common-
wealth, as which of you shall not? With this I depart,
that, as I slew my best lover° for the good of Rome,    45
I have the same dagger for myself, when it shall please
my country to need my death.
ALL    Live, Brutus! Live, live!
FIRST PLEBEIAN
Bring him with triumph home unto his house.
SECOND PLEBEIAN
Give him a statue with his ancestors.                               50
THIRD PLEBEIAN
Let him be Caesar.
FOURTH PLEBEIAN    Caesar's better parts°
Shall be crowned in Brutus.
FIRST PLEBEIAN
We'll bring him to his house with shouts and clamors.
BRUTUS
My countrymen—
SECOND PLEBEIAN    Peace! Silence! Brutus speaks.
FIRST PLEBEIAN    Peace, ho!                                        55
BRUTUS
Good countrymen, let me depart alone,
And, for my sake, stay here with Antony.
Do grace to Caesar's corpse, and grace his speech°
Tending° to Caesar's glories, which Mark Antony,
By our permission, is allowed to make.                              60
I do entreat you, not a man depart,
Save I alone, till Antony have spoke.         *Exit.*
FIRST PLEBEIAN
Stay, ho! And let us hear Mark Antony.
THIRD PLEBEIAN
Let him go up into the public chair;°
We'll hear him. Noble Antony, go up.                                65
ANTONY
For Brutus' sake, I am beholding° to you.

---

283 **Passion** intense emotion, grief    287 **Post** ride post (with
relays of horses), hasten; **chanced** happened    289 **Rome**
another play on the pronunciation "room"; cf. I.ii.156    290
**Hie** hurry    292 **try** test    294 **cruel issue** outcome of the
cruelty
III.ii.1 **will be satisfied** want a full explanation    4 **part
the numbers** divide the crowd    10 **severally** separately    12
**last** conclusion (of my speech)    13 **lovers** dear friends    15
**respect** regard    16 **Censure** judge    17 **senses** powers of
understanding, reason

29–30 **bondman** slave    31 **rude** barbarous    37 **shall do** i.e., if
I should become equally tyrannical    37–38 **The question . . .
enrolled** the considerations that made necessary his death are
recorded    39 **extenuated** depreciated    40 **enforced** exaggerated    43 **place** i.e., as a free citizen    45 **lover** friend
51 **parts** qualities    58 **Do . . . speech** show respect to dead
Caesar and listen respectfully to Antony's speech    59 **Tending**
relating    64 **public chair** pulpit, rostrum    66 **beholding**
beholden, indebted

FOURTH PLEBEIAN
What does he say of Brutus?

THIRD PLEBEIAN            He says, for Brutus' sake,
He finds himself beholding to us all.

FOURTH PLEBEIAN
'Twere best he speak no harm of Brutus here!

FIRST PLEBEIAN
This Caesar was a tyrant.

THIRD PLEBEIAN            Nay, that's certain.    70
We are blest that Rome is rid of him.

SECOND PLEBEIAN
Peace! Let us hear what Antony can say.

ANTONY
You gentle Romans—

ALL                        Peace, ho! Let us hear him.

ANTONY
Friends, Romans, countrymen, lend me your ears;
I come to bury Caesar, not to praise him.    75
The evil that men do lives after them,
The good is oft interrèd with their bones;
So let it be with Caesar. The noble Brutus
Hath told you Caesar was ambitious.
If it were so, it was a grievous fault,    80
And grievously hath Caesar answered° it.
Here, under leave of Brutus and the rest
(For Brutus is an honorable man,
So are they all, all honorable men),
Come I to speak in Caesar's funeral.    85
He was my friend, faithful and just to me;
But Brutus says he was ambitious,
And Brutus is an honorable man.
He hath brought many captives home to Rome,
Whose ransoms did the general coffers° fill;    90
Did this in Caesar seem ambitious?
When that the poor have cried, Caesar hath wept;
Ambition should be made of sterner stuff.
Yet Brutus says he was ambitious;
And Brutus is an honorable man.    95
You all did see that on the Lupercal
I thrice presented him a kingly crown,
Which he did thrice refuse. Was this ambition?
Yet Brutus says he was ambitious;
And sure he is an honorable man.    100
I speak not to disprove what Brutus spoke,
But here I am to speak what I do know.
You all did love him once, not without cause;
What cause withholds you then to mourn for him?
O judgment, thou art fled to brutish beasts,    105
And men have lost their reason! Bear with me;
My heart is in the coffin there with Caesar,
And I must pause till it come back to me.

FIRST PLEBEIAN
Methinks there is much reason in his sayings.

SECOND PLEBEIAN
If thou consider rightly of the matter,    110
Caesar has had great wrong.

THIRD PLEBEIAN            Has he, masters?
I fear there will a worse come in his place.

FOURTH PLEBEIAN
Marked ye his words? He would not take the crown,
Therefore 'tis certain he was not ambitious.

FIRST PLEBEIAN
If it be found so, some will dear abide it.°    115

SECOND PLEBEIAN
Poor soul, his eyes are red as fire with weeping.

THIRD PLEBEIAN
There's not a nobler man in Rome than Antony.

FOURTH PLEBEIAN
Now mark him, he begins again to speak.

ANTONY
But yesterday the word of Caesar might
Have stood against the world; now lies he there,    120
And none so poor to° do him reverence.
O masters! If I were disposed to stir
Your hearts and minds to mutiny and rage,
I should do Brutus wrong and Cassius wrong,
Who, you all know, are honorable men.    125
I will not do them wrong; I rather choose
To wrong the dead, to wrong myself and you,
Than I will wrong such honorable men.
But here's a parchment with the seal of Caesar;
I found it in his closet;° 'tis his will.    130
Let but the commons° hear this testament,
Which, pardon me, I do not mean to read,
And they would go and kiss dead Caesar's wounds,
And dip their napkins° in his sacred blood;
Yea, beg a hair of him for memory,    135
And dying, mention it within their wills,
Bequeathing it as a rich legacy
Unto their issue.°

FOURTH PLEBEIAN
We'll hear the will; read it, Mark Antony.

ALL
The will, the will! We will hear Caesar's will!    140

ANTONY
Have patience, gentle friends, I must not read it.
It is not meet° you know how Caesar loved you.
You are not wood, you are not stones, but men;
And being men, hearing the will of Caesar,
It will inflame you, it will make you mad.    145
'Tis good you know not that you are his heirs;
For if you should, O, what would come of it?

FOURTH PLEBEIAN
Read the will! We'll hear it, Antony!
You shall read us the will, Caesar's will!

ANTONY
Will you be patient? Will you stay° awhile?    150
I have o'ershot myself° to tell you of it.
I fear I wrong the honorable men
Whose daggers have stabbed Caesar; I do fear it.

FOURTH PLEBEIAN
They were traitors. Honorable men!

ALL
The will! The testament!

SECOND PLEBEIAN            They were villains,    155
Murderers! The will! Read the will!

ANTONY
You will compel me then to read the will?
Then make a ring about the corpse of Caesar,

---

**115 dear abide it** pay dearly for it    **121 so poor to** so low in rank as to    **130 closet** study (?) desk (?)    **131 commons** plebeians    **134 napkins** handkerchiefs    **138 issue** heirs    **142 meet** fitting    **150 stay** wait    **151 o'ershot myself** gone further than I intended

**81 answered** paid the penalty for    **90 general coffers** public treasury

And let me show you him that made the will.
Shall I descend? And will you give me leave?    160
ALL   Come down.
SECOND PLEBEIAN   Descend.

[ANTONY *comes down.*]

THIRD PLEBEIAN   You shall have leave.
FOURTH PLEBEIAN   A ring! Stand round.
FIRST PLEBEIAN
Stand from the hearse, stand from the body!    165
SECOND PLEBEIAN
Room for Antony, most noble Antony!
ANTONY
Nay, press not so upon me; stand far° off.
ALL   Stand back! Room! Bear back.
ANTONY
If you have tears, prepare to shed them now.
You all do know this mantle:° I remember    170
The first time ever Caesar put it on:
'Twas on a summer's evening, in his tent,
That day he overcame the Nervii.°
Look, in this place ran Cassius' dagger through;
See what a rent the envious° Casca made;    175
Through this the well-belovèd Brutus stabbed,
And as he plucked his cursèd steel away,
Mark how the blood of Caesar followed it,
As° rushing out of doors, to be resolved°
If Brutus so unkindly° knocked, or no;    180
For Brutus, as you know, was Caesar's angel.°
Judge, O you gods, how dearly Caesar loved him!
This was the most unkindest° cut of all;
For when the noble Caesar saw him stab,
Ingratitude, more strong than traitors' arms,    185
Quite vanquished him. Then burst his mighty heart;
And, in his mantle muffling up his face,
Even at the base° of Pompey's statue°
(Which all the while ran blood) great Caesar fell.
O, what a fall was there, my countrymen!    190
Then I, and you, and all of us fell down,
Whilst bloody treason flourished° over us.
O, now you weep, and I perceive you feel
The dint° of pity; these are gracious drops.
Kind souls, what° weep you when you but behold    195
Our Caesar's vesture° wounded? Look you here,
Here is himself, marred° as you see with° traitors.
FIRST PLEBEIAN   O piteous spectacle!
SECOND PLEBEIAN   O noble Caesar!
THIRD PLEBEIAN   O woeful day!    200
FOURTH PLEBEIAN   O traitors, villains!
FIRST PLEBEIAN   O most bloody sight!
SECOND PLEBEIAN   We will be revenged.
[ALL]   Revenge! About!° Seek! Burn! Fire! Kill!
Slay! Let not a traitor live!    205
ANTONY   Stay, countrymen.

FIRST PLEBEIAN   Peace there! Hear the noble Antony.
SECOND PLEBEIAN   We'll hear him, we'll follow him,
we'll die with him!
ANTONY
Good friends, sweet friends, let me not stir you up    210
To such a sudden flood of mutiny.
They that have done this deed are honorable.
What private griefs° they have, alas, I know not,
That made them do it. They are wise and honorable,
And will, no doubt, with reasons answer you.    215
I come not, friends, to steal away your hearts;
I am no orator, as Brutus is;
But (as you know me all) a plain blunt man
That love my friend, and that they know full well
That gave me public leave to speak° of him.    220
For I have neither writ, nor words, nor worth,
Action, nor utterance,° nor the power of speech
To stir men's blood; I only speak right on.°
I tell you that which you yourselves do know,
Show you sweet Caesar's wounds, poor poor dumb    225
mouths,
And bid them speak for me. But were I Brutus,
And Brutus Antony, there were an Antony
Would ruffle up° your spirits, and put a tongue
In every wound of Caesar that should move
The stones of Rome to rise and mutiny.    230
ALL
We'll mutiny.
FIRST PLEBEIAN   We'll burn the house of Brutus.
THIRD PLEBEIAN
Away, then! Come, seek the conspirators.
ANTONY
Yet hear me, countrymen. Yet hear me speak.
ALL
Peace, ho! Hear Antony, most noble Antony!
ANTONY
Why, friends, you go to do you know not what:    235
Wherein hath Caesar thus deserved your loves?
Alas, you know not; I must tell you then:
You have forgot the will I told you of.
ALL
Most true, the will! Let's stay and hear the will.
ANTONY
Here is the will, and under Caesar's seal.    240
To every Roman citizen he gives,
To every several° man, seventy-five drachmas.
SECOND PLEBEIAN
Most noble Caesar! We'll revenge his death!
THIRD PLEBEIAN   O royal° Caesar!
ANTONY   Hear me with patience.    245
ALL   Peace, ho!
ANTONY
Moreover, he hath left you all his walks,°
His private arbors, and new-planted orchards,°
On this side Tiber; he hath left them you,

167 far farther   170 mantle cloak (here, the toga)   173 Nervii a fierce tribe decisively conquered by Caesar in 57 B.C.   175 envious spiteful   179 As as though; to be resolved to learn for certain   180 unkindly (1) cruelly (2) unnaturally   181 angel favorite (i.e., considered incapable of evil)   183 most unkindest most cruel and unnatural   188 base pedestal; statue pronounced "stat-u-a"   192 flourished (1) swaggered (2) brandished a sword in triumph   194 dint stroke   195 what why   196 vesture clothing   197 marred mangled; with by   204 About Let's go!

213 private griefs personal grievances   220 public . . . speak permission to speak in public   221–22 neither . . . utterance neither a written speech, nor fluency, nor reputation, nor (an orator's) gestures, nor good delivery (perhaps "writ" should be emended to "wit," meaning "intellectual cleverness")   223 right on directly, without premeditation   228 ruffle up incite to rage   242 several individual   244 royal nobly generous   247 walks parks   248 orchards gardens

And to your heirs forever: common pleasures,° 250
To walk abroad and recreate yourselves.
Here was a Caesar! When comes such another?

FIRST PLEBEIAN
Never, never! Come, away, away!
We'll burn his body in the holy place,
And with the brands fire the traitors' houses. 255
Take up the body.

SECOND PLEBEIAN　Go fetch fire.

THIRD PLEBEIAN　Pluck down benches.

FOURTH PLEBEIAN　Pluck down forms, windows,°
anything!　　　　Exeunt PLEBEIANS [with the body]. 260

ANTONY
Now let it work:° Mischief, thou art afoot,
Take thou what course thou wilt.

Enter SERVANT.

　　　　　　　　　　　How now, fellow?

SERVANT
Sir, Octavius is already come to Rome.

ANTONY　Where is he?

SERVANT
He and Lepidus are at Caesar's house. 265

ANTONY
And thither will I straight° to visit him;
He comes upon a wish.° Fortune is merry,
And in this mood will give us anything.

SERVANT
I heard him say, Brutus and Cassius
Are rid° like madmen through the gates of Rome. 270

ANTONY
Belike° they had some notice of° the people,
How I had moved them. Bring me to Octavius.
　　　　　　　　　　　　　　Exeunt.

[Scene III. A street.]

Enter CINNA the poet, and after him the PLEBEIANS.

CINNA
I dreamt tonight° that I did feast with Caesar,
And things unluckily charge my fantasy.°
I have no will to wander forth° of doors,
Yet something leads me forth.

FIRST PLEBEIAN　What is your name? 5

SECOND PLEBEIAN　Whither are you going?

THIRD PLEBEIAN　Where do you dwell?

FOURTH PLEBEIAN　Are you a married man or a
bachelor?

SECOND PLEBEIAN　Answer every man directly.° 10

FIRST PLEBEIAN　Ay, and briefly.

FOURTH PLEBEIAN　Ay, and wisely.

THIRD PLEBEIAN　Ay, and truly, you were best.

CINNA　What is my name? Whither am I going?

Where do I dwell? Am I a married man or a bachelor? 15
Then, to answer every man directly and briefly, wisely
and truly: wisely I say, I am a bachelor.

SECOND PLEBEIAN　That's as much as to say, they are
fools that marry; you'll bear me a bang° for that, I fear.
Proceed directly. 20

CINNA　Directly, I am going to Caesar's funeral.

FIRST PLEBEIAN　As a friend or an enemy?

CINNA　As a friend.

SECOND PLEBEIAN　That matter is answered directly.

FOURTH PLEBEIAN　For your dwelling, briefly. 25

CINNA　Briefly, I dwell by the Capitol.

THIRD PLEBEIAN　Your name, sir, truly.

CINNA　Truly, my name is Cinna.

FIRST PLEBEIAN　Tear him to pieces! He's a conspirator. 30

CINNA　I am Cinna the poet! I am Cinna the poet!

FOURTH PLEBEIAN　Tear him for his bad verses! Tear
him for his bad verses!

CINNA　I am not Cinna the conspirator.

FOURTH PLEBEIAN　It is no matter, his name's Cinna; 35
pluck but his name out of his heart, and turn him
going.°

THIRD PLEBEIAN　Tear him, tear him! [They attack
him.] Come, brands, ho! Firebrands! To Brutus', to
Cassius'! Burn all! Some to Decius' house, and some 40
to Casca's; some to Ligarius'! Away, go!
　　　Exeunt all the PLEBEIANS, [with CINNA].

# ACT IV

[Scene I. A house in Rome.]

Enter ANTONY, OCTAVIUS, and LEPIDUS.

ANTONY
These many then shall die; their names are pricked.°

OCTAVIUS
Your brother too must die; consent you, Lepidus?

LEPIDUS
I do consent—

OCTAVIUS　　　Prick him down, Antony.

LEPIDUS
Upon condition Publius shall not live,
Who is your sister's son, Mark Antony. 5

ANTONY
He shall not live; look, with a spot I damn him.°
But, Lepidus, go you to Caesar's house;
Fetch the will hither, and we shall determine
How to cut off some charge° in legacies.

LEPIDUS
What, shall I find you here? 10

OCTAVIUS
Or° here or at the Capitol.　　Exit LEPIDUS.

250 common pleasures public places of recreation 259
forms, windows long benches (and) shutters 261 work (1)
ferment (as yeast) (2) work itself out 266 will I straight
will I (go) at once 267 upon a wish just as I wished 270
Are rid have ridden 271 Belike probably; notice of news
about
III.iii.1 tonight last night 2 things . . . fantasy events
give ominous weight to my imaginings 3 forth out 10
directly straightforwardly

19 bear . . . bang get a blow from me 36–37 turn him
going dispatch him
IV.i.1 pricked ticked off, marked on the list 6 with . . . him
with a dot (on the wax tablet) I condemn him 9 cut . . .
charge reduce expenses (by altering the amount left in bequests) 11 Or either

ANTONY

This is a slight unmeritable° man,
Meet° to be sent on errands; is it fit,
The threefold world° divided, he should stand
One of the three to share it?

OCTAVIUS                    So you thought him,    15
And took his voice° who should be pricked to die
In our black sentence° and proscription.°

ANTONY

Octavius, I have seen more days° than you;
And though we lay these honors on this man,
To ease ourselves of divers sland'rous loads,°    20
He shall but bear them as the ass bears gold,
To groan and sweat under the business,°
Either led or driven, as we point the way;
And having brought our treasure where we will,
Then take we down his load, and turn him off,°    25
(Like to the empty° ass) to shake his ears
And graze in commons.°

OCTAVIUS                    You may do your will;
But he's a tried and valiant soldier.°

ANTONY

So is my horse, Octavius, and for that
I do appoint him store° of provender.    30
It is a creature that I teach to fight,
To wind,° to stop, to run directly on,
His corporal° motion governed by my spirit.°
And, in some taste,° is Lepidus but so.°
He must be taught, and trained, and bid go forth.    35
A barren-spirited° fellow; one that feeds
On objects, arts, and imitations,°
Which, out of use and staled° by other men,
Begin his fashion.° Do not talk of him
But as a property.° And now, Octavius,    40
Listen great things. Brutus and Cassius
Are levying powers;° we must straight make head.°
Therefore let our alliance be combined,
Our best friends made,° our means stretched;°
And let us presently° go sit in council    45
How covert matters may be best disclosed,
And open perils surest answerèd.°

OCTAVIUS

Let us do so; for we are at the stake,°

12 **slight unmeritable** insignificant and undeserving 13
**Meet** fit   14 **threefold world** three areas of the Roman
empire, Europe, Asia, and Africa   16 **voice** vote   17 **black
sentence** sentence of death; **proscription** condemnation to
death or exile   18 **have . . . days** am older (and more
experienced)   20 **divers sland'rous loads** blame which will
be laid upon us for our various actions   22 **business** hard labor
25 **turn him off** drive him away   26 **empty** unburdened
27 **in commons** on public pasture   28 **soldier** trisyllabic
30 **appoint him store** allot him a supply   32 **wind** turn
33 **corporal** physical; **spirit** mind   34 **taste** measure; **so** the
same   36 **barren-spirited** lacking initiative or ideas of his own
37 **objects . . . imitations** curiosities, artifices, and fashions
(or styles)   38 **staled** made common   39 **Begin his fashion**
i.e., he is always far behind the times   40 **property** mere tool
(a thing rather than a person)   42 **powers** armed forces;
**straight make head** immediately gather troops   44 **Our
. . . made** let our closest allies be selected; **stretched** be used
to the fullest advantage   45 **presently** immediately   46–47
**How . . . answerèd** to decide how hidden dangers may best
be discovered and open dangers most safely encountered
48 **at the stake** metaphor derived from Elizabethan sport of
bearbaiting: like a bear tied to a stake and set upon by many
dogs

And bayed about with many enemies;
And some that smile have in their hearts, I fear,    50
Millions of mischiefs.°                    *Exeunt.*

[Scene II. *Camp near Sardis.*]

*Drum. Enter* BRUTUS, LUCILIUS, [LUCIUS,] *and the*
ARMY. TITINIUS *and* PINDARUS *meet them.*

BRUTUS    Stand ho!
LUCILIUS    Give the word, ho! and stand.
BRUTUS

What now, Lucilius, is Cassius near?

LUCILIUS

He is at hand, and Pindarus is come
To do you salutation from his master.    5

BRUTUS

He greets me well.° Your master, Pindarus,
In his own change, or by ill officers,°
Hath given me some worthy° cause to wish
Things done undone; but if he be at hand,
I shall be satisfied.°

PINDARUS                    I do not doubt    10
But that my noble master will appear
Such as he is, full of regard° and honor.

BRUTUS

He is not doubted. A word, Lucilius,
How he received you; let me be resolved.°

LUCILIUS

With courtesy and with respect enough,    15
But not with such familiar instances,°
Nor with such free and friendly conference°
As he hath used of old.

BRUTUS                    Thou hast described
A hot friend cooling. Ever note, Lucilius,
When love begins to sicken and decay    20
It useth an enforcèd ceremony.°
There are no tricks in plain and simple faith;
But hollow° men, like horses hot at hand,°
Make gallant show and promise of their mettle;°

*Low march within.*

But when they should endure the bloody spur,    25
They fall their crests,° and like deceitful jades°
Sink in the trial.° Comes his army on?

LUCILIUS

They mean this night in Sardis to be quartered;
The greater part, the horse in general,°
Are come with Cassius.

*Enter* CASSIUS *and his* POWERS.

BRUTUS                    Hark! He is arrived.    30
March gently° on to meet him.

51 **mischiefs** plans to injure us
**IV.ii.6 He . . . well** he sends greetings by a very good man
7 **In . . . officers** either from a change in his feelings toward
me or through the actions of bad subordinates   8 **worthy**
substantial   10 **be satisfied** receive a satisfactory explanation
12 **full of regard** worthy of respect   14 **resolved** fully
informed   16 **familiar instances** marks of friendship   17
**conference** conversation   21 **enforcèd ceremony** strained
formality   23 **hollow** insincere; **hot at hand** overspirited at
the start   24 **mettle** quality, courage   26 **fall their crests**
let fall the ridges of their necks; **jades** nags   27 **Sink . . .
trial** fail when put to the test   29 **the horse in general** all
the cavalry   31 **gently** slowly

CASSIUS   Stand, ho!

BRUTUS   Stand, ho! Speak the word along.

[FIRST SOLDIER]   Stand!

[SECOND SOLDIER]   Stand!       35

[THIRD SOLDIER]   Stand!

CASSIUS

Most noble brother, you have done me wrong.

BRUTUS

Judge me, you gods! Wrong I mine enemies?

And if not so, how should I wrong a brother.

CASSIUS

Brutus, this sober form° of yours hides wrongs;       40

And when you do them—

BRUTUS              Cassius, be content.°

Speak your griefs° softly; I do know you well.

Before the eyes of both our armies here

(Which should perceive nothing but love from us)

Let us not wrangle. Bid them move away;       45

Then in my tent, Cassius, enlarge° your griefs,

And I will give you audience.

CASSIUS              Pindarus,

Bid our commanders lead their charges° off

A little from this ground.

BRUTUS

Lucilius, do you the like, and let no man       50

Come to our tent till we have done our conference.

Let Lucius and Titinius guard our door.

        *Exeunt. Mane[n]t* BRUTUS *and* CASSIUS.

[Scene III. *Brutus' tent.*]

CASSIUS

That you have wronged me doth appear in this:

You have condemned and noted° Lucius Pella

For taking bribes here of the Sardians;

Wherein my letters, praying on his side,°

Because I knew the man, was slighted off.°       5

BRUTUS

You wronged yourself to write in such a case.

CASSIUS

In such a time as this it is not meet

That every nice offense should bear this comment.°

BRUTUS

Let me tell you, Cassius, you yourself

Are much condemned to have an itching palm,°       10

To sell and mart° your offices for gold

To undeservers.

CASSIUS       I an itching palm?

You know that you are Brutus that speaks this,

Or, by the gods, this speech were else your last.

BRUTUS

The name of Cassius honors° this corruption,       15

And chastisement doth therefore hide his head.

CASSIUS   Chastisement!

BRUTUS

Remember March, the ides of March remember.

Did not great Julius bleed for justice' sake?

What villain touched his body, that did stab,       20

And not° for justice? What, shall one of us,

That struck the foremost man of all this world

But for supporting robbers,° shall we now

Contaminate our fingers with base bribes,

And sell the mighty space of our large honors°       25

For so much trash° as may be graspèd thus?°

I had rather be a dog, and bay° the moon,

Than such a Roman.

CASSIUS            Brutus, bait° not me;

I'll not endure it. You forget yourself

To hedge me in.° I am a soldier, I,       30

Older in practice, abler than yourself

To make conditions.°

BRUTUS           Go to! You are not, Cassius.

CASSIUS   I am.

BRUTUS   I say you are not.

CASSIUS

Urge° me no more. I shall forget myself;       35

Have mind upon your health;° tempt° me no farther.

BRUTUS   Away, slight° man!

CASSIUS

Is't possible?

BRUTUS       Hear me, for I will speak.

Must I give way and room to your rash choler?°

Shall I be frighted when a madman stares?°       40

CASSIUS

O ye gods, ye gods! Must I endure all this?

BRUTUS

All this? Ay, more: fret till your proud heart break.

Go show your slaves how choleric you are,

And make your bondmen tremble. Must I budge?°

Must I observe° you? Must I stand and crouch°       45

Under your testy humor?° By the gods,

You shall digest the venom° of your spleen,°

Though it do split you; for, from this day forth,

I'll use you for my mirth, yea, for my laughter,

When you are waspish.

CASSIUS           Is it come to this?       50

BRUTUS

You say you are a better soldier:

Let it appear so; make your vaunting° true,

---

**40 sober form** staid manner   **41 be content** keep calm
**42 griefs** grievances   **46 enlarge** freely express   **48 charges**
troops
**IV.iii.2 noted** publicly disgraced   **4 praying . . . side**
appealing on his behalf   **5 was slighted off** was contemptuously disregarded ("letters" takes a singular verb because of
its singular meaning)   **8 nice . . . comment** trivial fault
should receive criticism ("his" = its)   **10 condemned . . .
palm** accused of being mercenary   **11 mart** traffic in   **15
honors** lends an air of respectability

**21 And not** except   **23 supporting robbers** protecting
dishonest officials (a point made by Plutarch but mentioned
only now by Shakespeare)   **25 mighty . . . honors** vast
capacity to be honorable and magnanimous (with suggestion
of potentiality for making other men free, and honorable
in office)   **26 trash** rubbish, i.e., money; **graspèd thus** the
small confined area of the closed fist contrasts with the
"mighty space" gained by their honorable deeds in abolishing
injustice and corruption   **27 bay** howl at   **28 bait** harass and
worry (as a bear tied to a stake is baited by dogs)   **30 hedge
me in** limit my freedom of action   **32 make conditions**
manage practical matters   **35 Urge** drive, bully   **36 health**
safety; **tempt** provoke   **37 slight** insignificant   **39 give
. . . choler** let your hasty temper have free vent and run
its course unchecked   **40 stares** glares   **44 budge** defer to it
**45 observe** wait on; **crouch** bow   **46 testy humor** irritability
**47 digest the venom** swallow the poison; **spleen** considered
the source of sudden passion: i.e., fiery temper   **52 vaunting**
boasting

And it shall please me well. For mine own part,
I shall be glad to learn of° noble men.

CASSIUS
You wrong me every way; you wrong me, Brutus;    55
I said, an elder soldier, not a better.
Did I say, better?

BRUTUS                    If you did, I care not.

CASSIUS
When Caesar lived, he durst not thus have moved°
  me.

BRUTUS
Peace, peace, you durst not so have tempted° him.

CASSIUS    I durst not?    60

BRUTUS    No.

CASSIUS
What? Durst not tempt him?

BRUTUS                    For your life you durst not.

CASSIUS
Do not presume too much upon my love;
I may do that I shall be sorry for.

BRUTUS
You have done that you should be sorry for.    65
There is no terror, Cassius, in your threats;
For I am armed so strong in honesty°
That they pass by me as the idle wind,
Which I respect° not. I did send to you
For certain sums of gold, which you denied me;    70
For I can raise no money by vile means.
By heaven, I had rather coin my heart
And drop my blood for drachmas than to wring
From the hard hands of peasants their vile trash
By any indirection.° I did send    75
To you for gold to pay my legions,
Which you denied me. Was that done like Cassius?
Should I have answered Caius Cassius so?
When Marcus Brutus grows so covetous
To lock such rascal counters° from his friends,    80
Be ready, gods, with all your thunderbolts,
Dash him to pieces!

CASSIUS                    I denied you not.

BRUTUS
You did.

CASSIUS    I did not. He was but a fool
That brought my answer back. Brutus hath rived° my
  heart.
A friend should bear his friend's infirmities;    85
But Brutus makes mine greater than they are.

BRUTUS
I do not, till you practice them on me.

CASSIUS
You love me not.

BRUTUS                    I do not like your faults.

CASSIUS
A friendly eye could never see such faults.

BRUTUS
A flatterer's would not, though they do appear    90
As huge as high Olympus.

CASSIUS
Come, Antony, and young Octavius, come,
Revenge yourselves alone° on Cassius,
For Cassius is aweary of the world:
Hated by one he loves; braved° by his brother;    95
Checked° like a bondman; all his faults observed,
Set in a notebook, learned and conned by rote°
To cast into my teeth.° O, I could weep
My spirit from mine eyes! There is my dagger,
And here my naked breast; within, a heart    100
Dearer than Pluto's mine,° richer than gold;
If that thou be'st a Roman, take it forth.
I, that denied thee gold, will give my heart.
Strike as thou didst at Caesar; for I know,
When thou didst hate him worst, thou lovedst him
  better    105
Than ever thou lovedst Cassius.

BRUTUS                    Sheathe your dagger.
Be angry when you will, it shall have scope.°
Do what you will, dishonor shall be humor.°
O Cassius, you are yokèd with a lamb
That carries anger as the flint bears fire,    110
Who, much enforced,° shows a hasty spark,
And straight° is cold again.

CASSIUS                    Hath Cassius lived
To be but mirth and laughter to his Brutus
When grief and blood ill-tempered° vexeth him?

BRUTUS
When I spoke that, I was ill-tempered too.    115

CASSIUS
Do you confess so much? Give me your hand.

BRUTUS    And my heart too.

CASSIUS                    O Brutus!

BRUTUS                    What's the matter?

CASSIUS
Have not you love enough to bear with me
When that rash humor° which my mother gave me
Makes me forgetful?

BRUTUS                    Yes, Cassius, and from henceforth,    120
When you are over-earnest with your Brutus,
He'll think your mother° chides, and leave you
  so.°

*Enter a* POET, [*followed by* LUCILIUS, TITINIUS, *and*
LUCIUS].

POET
Let me go in to see the generals;
There is some grudge° between 'em; 'tis not meet
They be alone.

LUCILIUS    You shall not come to them.    125

54 **learn of** (1) hear about the exploits of (2) take lessons
from  58 **moved** exasperated  59 **tempted** provoked  67
**honesty** integrity  69 **respect** heed  75 **indirection** irregular
methods  80 **rascal counters** base (and worthless) coins  84
**rived** broken

93 **alone** only  95 **braved** defied  96 **Checked** rebuked
97 **conned by rote** learned by heart  98 **cast . . . teeth**
throw in my face  101 **Dearer . . . mine** more precious than
all the riches in the earth (Pluto, god of the underworld, and
Plutus, god of riches, were frequently confused)  107 **shall
have scope** (your anger) shall have free play  108 **dishonor
. . . humor** insults shall be regarded as quirks of temperament
111 **much enforcèd** greatly provoked  112 **straight**
immediately  114 **blood ill-tempered** a "black mood"  119
**rash humor** hasty temperament  122 **your mother** i.e.,
your inherited temperament; **leave you so** leave it at that
124 **grudge** bad feeling

POET
  Nothing but death shall stay me.
CASSIUS                    How now. What's the matter?
POET
  For shame, you generals! What do you mean?
  Love, and be friends, as two such men should be;
  For I have seen more years, I'm sure, than ye.
CASSIUS
  Ha, ha! How vilely doth this cynic° rhyme!          130
BRUTUS
  Get you hence, sirrah! Saucy° fellow, hence!
CASSIUS
  Bear with him, Brutus, 'tis his fashion.
BRUTUS
  I'll know his humor when he knows his time.°
  What should the wars do with these jigging° fools?
  Companion,° hence!
CASSIUS                   Away, away, be gone!          135
                              *Exit* POET.

BRUTUS
  Lucilius and Titinius, bid the commanders
  Prepare to lodge their companies tonight.
CASSIUS
  And come yourselves, and bring Messala with you
  Immediately to us.  [*Exeunt* LUCILIUS *and* TITINIUS.]
BRUTUS                 Lucius, a bowl of wine.
                              [*Exit* LUCIUS.]
CASSIUS
  I did not think you could have been so angry.       140
BRUTUS
  O Cassius, I am sick of many griefs.
CASSIUS
  Of your philosophy you make no use,
  If you give place° to accidental evils.°
BRUTUS
  No man bears sorrow better. Portia is dead.
CASSIUS   Ha? Portia?                                  145
BRUTUS   She is dead.
CASSIUS
  How scaped I killing when I crossed° you so?
  O insupportable and touching° loss!
  Upon° what sickness?
BRUTUS                 Impatient of° my absence,
  And grief that young Octavius with Mark Antony      150
  Have made themselves so strong—for with her death
  That tidings came°—with this she fell distract,°
  And (her attendants absent) swallowed fire.°
CASSIUS
  And died so?
BRUTUS       Even so.
CASSIUS             O ye immortal gods!

---

**130 cynic** rude fellow  **131 Saucy** impertinent  **133 I'll . . .
time** I'll accept his eccentricity when he can judge the suitable
time for it  **134 jigging** doggerel-writing, rhyming  **135
Companion** base fellow  **143 place** way; **accidental evils**
misfortunes brought on by chance (Brutus seems not to be
behaving as a Stoic philosopher should)  **147 crossed** contradicted  **148 touching** wounding, grievous  **149 Upon** as
a result of; **Impatient of** unable to endure  **151–52 for . . .
came** news of her death came at the same time as news of
their strength  **152 fell distract** became distraught  **153
swallowed fire** (according to Plutarch she choked herself by
putting hot coals into her mouth)

---

*Enter boy* [LUCIUS] *with wine and tapers.*

BRUTUS
  Speak no more of her. Give me a bowl of wine.       155
  In this I bury all unkindness, Cassius.

*Drinks.*

CASSIUS
  My heart is thirsty for that noble pledge.
  Fill, Lucius, till the wine o'erswell the cup;
  I cannot drink too much of Brutus' love.
                      [*Drinks. Exit* LUCIUS.]

*Enter* TITINIUS *and* MESSALA.

BRUTUS
  Come in, Titinius! Welcome, good Messala.           160
  Now sit we close about this taper here,
  And call in question° our necessities.
CASSIUS
  Portia, art thou gone?
BRUTUS                 No more, I pray you.
  Messala, I have here received letters
  That young Octavius and Mark Antony                  165
  Come down upon us with a mighty power,°
  Bending their expedition° toward Philippi.
MESSALA
  Myself have letters of the selfsame tenure.°
BRUTUS
  With what addition?
MESSALA
  That by proscription° and bills of outlawry°        170
  Octavius, Antony, and Lepidus
  Have put to death an hundred senators.
BRUTUS
  Therein our letters do not well agree.
  Mine speak of seventy senators that died
  By their proscriptions, Cicero being one.           175
CASSIUS
  Cicero one?
MESSALA     Cicero is dead,
  And by that order of proscription.
  Had you your letters from your wife, my lord?
BRUTUS   No, Messala.
MESSALA
  Nor nothing in your letters writ of her?            180
BRUTUS
  Nothing, Messala.
MESSALA            That methinks is strange.
BRUTUS
  Why ask you? Hear you aught of her in yours?
MESSALA   No, my lord.
BRUTUS
  Now as you are a Roman, tell me true.
MESSALA
  Then like a Roman bear the truth I tell,            185
  For certain she is dead, and by strange manner.
BRUTUS
  Why, farewell, Portia. We must die, Messala.

---

**162 call in question** consider  **166 power** army  **167 Bending their expedition** directing their rapid march  **168
tenure** tenor, general meaning  **170 proscription** proclamation of the death sentence; **bills of outlawry** lists of those
proscribed

With meditating that she must die once,°
I have the patience to endure it now.
MESSALA
Even so great men great losses should endure.    190
CASSIUS
I have as much of this in art° as you,
But yet my nature could not bear it so.°
BRUTUS
Well, to our work alive.° What do you think
Of marching to Philippi presently?°
CASSIUS
I do not think it good.
BRUTUS                    Your reason?
CASSIUS                              This it is:    195
'Tis better that the enemy seek us;
So shall he waste his means, weary his soldiers,
Doing himself offense,° whilst we, lying still,
Are full of rest, defense, and nimbleness.
BRUTUS
Good reasons must of force° give place to better.    200
The people 'twixt Philippi and this ground
Do stand but in a forced affection;°
For they have grudged us contribution.
The enemy, marching along by them,
By them shall make a fuller number up,    205
Come on refreshed, new-added° and encouraged;
From which advantage shall we cut him off
If at Philippi we do face him there,
These people at our back.
CASSIUS              Hear me, good brother.
BRUTUS
Under your pardon.° You must note beside    210
That we have tried the utmost of our friends,
Our legions are brimful, our cause is ripe.
The enemy increaseth every day;
We, at the height, are ready to decline.
There is a tide in the affairs of men    215
Which, taken at the flood, leads on to fortune;
Omitted,° all the voyage of their life
Is bound in° shallows and in miseries.
On such a full sea are we now afloat,
And we must take the current when it serves,    220
Or lose our ventures.°
CASSIUS              Then, with your will,° go on;
We'll along ourselves and meet them at Philippi.
BRUTUS
The deep of night is crept upon our talk,
And nature must obey necessity,
Which we will niggard with a little rest.°    225
There is no more to say?

CASSIUS                    No more. Good night.
Early tomorrow will we rise and hence.°

*Enter* LUCIUS.

BRUTUS
Lucius, my gown.°                    *Exit* LUCIUS.
                  Farewell, good Messala.
Good night, Titinius. Noble, noble Cassius,
Good night, and good repose.
CASSIUS              O my dear brother,    230
This was an ill beginning of the night
Never come° such division 'tween our souls!
Let it not, Brutus.

*Enter* LUCIUS *with the gown.*

BRUTUS              Everything is well.
CASSIUS
Good night, my lord.
BRUTUS              Good night, good brother.
TITINIUS, MESSALA
Good night, Lord Brutus.
BRUTUS              Farewell, every one. *Exeunt.*    235
Give me the gown. Where is thy instrument?°
LUCIUS
Here in the tent.
BRUTUS        What, thou speak'st drowsily?
Poor knave,° I blame thee not; thou art o'erwatched.°
Call Claudius and some other of my men;
I'll have them sleep on cushions in my tent.    240
LUCIUS  Varro and Claudius!

*Enter* VARRO *and* CLAUDIUS.

VARRO  Calls my lord?
BRUTUS
I pray you, sirs, lie in my tent and sleep.
It may be I shall raise° you by and by
On business to my brother Cassius.    245
VARRO
So please you, we will stand and watch your pleasure.°
BRUTUS
I will not have it so; lie down, good sirs;
It may be I shall otherwise bethink me.°

[VARRO *and* CLAUDIUS *lie down.*]

Look, Lucius, here's the book I sought for so;
I put it in the pocket of my gown.    250
LUCIUS
I was sure your lordship did not give it me.
BRUTUS
Bear with me, good boy, I am much forgetful.
Canst thou hold up thy heavy eyes awhile,
And touch° thy instrument a strain° or two?
LUCIUS
Ay, my lord, an't° please you.
BRUTUS              It does, my boy.    255
I trouble thee too much, but thou art willing.

188 once at some time  191 this in art i.e., this Stoicism in theory  178–92 Had . . . so some editors suggest that this was the original version of Shakespeare's account of Portia's death and that he later deleted this and wrote in lines 140–54, preferring to demonstrate Brutus' humanity rather than his Stoicism; the Folio printer then set up both versions by mistake; line 155 would follow 139—as 193 would follow 177—neatly enough to make this an attractive theory  193 alive as men still living  194 presently immediately  198 offense harm  200 force necessity  202 Do . . . affection support us only under compulsion  206 new-added reinforced  210 Under your pardon excuse me  217 Omitted neglected  218 bound in limited to  221 ventures shipping trade, i.e., risks; with your will as you wish  225 niggard . . . rest put off with the shortest possible sleep

227 hence leave this place  228 gown dressing gown  232 Never come may there never again come  236 instrument probably a lute  238 knave boy; o'erwatched tired out from lack of sleep  244 raise rouse  246 watch your pleasure be on the watch for your command  248 otherwise bethink me change my mind  254 touch play on; strain tune  255 an't if it

LUCIUS   It is my duty, sir.

BRUTUS
I should not urge thy duty past thy might;
I know young bloods° look for a time of rest.

LUCIUS   I have slept, my lord, already.      260

BRUTUS
It was well done, and thou shalt sleep again;
I will not hold thee long. If I do live,
I will be good to thee.

*Music, and a song.*

This is a sleepy tune. O murd'rous° slumber!
Layest thou thy leaden° mace° upon my boy,      265
That plays thee music? Gentle knave, good night;
I will not do thee so much wrong to wake thee.
If thou dost nod, thou break'st thy instrument;
I'll take it from thee; and, good boy, good night.
Let me see, let me see; is not the leaf turned down    270
Where I left reading? Here it is, I think.

*Enter the GHOST of Caesar.*

How ill this taper burns.° Ha! Who comes here?
I think it is the weakness of mine eyes
That shapes this monstrous apparition.
It comes upon° me. Art thou anything?      275
Art thou some god, some angel, or some devil,
That mak'st my blood cold, and my hair to stare?°
Speak to me what thou art.

GHOST
Thy evil spirit, Brutus.

BRUTUS                Why com'st thou?

GHOST
To tell thee thou shalt see me at Philippi.      280

BRUTUS   Well; then I shall see thee again?

GHOST   Ay, at Philippi.

BRUTUS
Why, I will see thee at Philippi then.    [*Exit GHOST.*]
Now I have taken heart thou vanishest.
Ill spirit, I would hold more talk with thee.      285
Boy! Lucius! Varro! Claudius! Sirs, awake!
Claudius!

LUCIUS   The strings, my lord, are false.°

BRUTUS
He thinks he still is at his instrument.
Lucius, awake!

LUCIUS   My lord?      290

BRUTUS
Didst thou dream, Lucius, that thou so criedst out?

LUCIUS
My lord, I do not know that I did cry.

BRUTUS
Yes, that thou didst. Didst thou see anything?

LUCIUS   Nothing, my lord.

BRUTUS
Sleep again, Lucius. Sirrah Claudius!      295

[*To VARRO.*]

Fellow thou, awake!

VARRO   My lord?

CLAUDIUS   My lord?

BRUTUS
Why did you so cry out, sirs, in your sleep?

BOTH
Did we, my lord?

BRUTUS            Ay. Saw you anything?      300

VARRO
No, my lord, I saw nothing.

CLAUDIUS            Nor I, my lord.

BRUTUS
Go and commend me° to my brother Cassius;
Bid him set on his pow'rs betimes before,°
And we will follow.

BOTH            It shall be done, my lord. *Exeunt.*

# ACT V

## [Scene I. *The plains of Philippi.*]

*Enter OCTAVIUS, ANTONY, and their ARMY.*

OCTAVIUS
Now, Antony, our hopes are answerèd;
You said the enemy would not come down,
But keep the hills and upper regions.
It proves not so; their battles° are at hand;
They mean to warn° us at Philippi here,      5
Answering before we do demand° of them.

ANTONY
Tut, I am in their bosoms,° and I know
Wherefore they do it. They could be content
To visit other places,° and come down
With fearful° bravery,° thinking by this face°      10
To fasten in our thoughts° that they have courage;
But 'tis not so.

*Enter a MESSENGER.*

MESSENGER   Prepare you, generals,
The enemy comes on in gallant show;
Their bloody sign° of battle is hung out,
And something to be done immediately.      15

ANTONY
Octavius, lead your battle softly° on
Upon the left hand of the even° field.

OCTAVIUS
Upon the right hand I; keep thou the left.

ANTONY
Why do you cross° me in this exigent?°

OCTAVIUS
I do not cross you; but I will do so.      20

302 **commend me** give my greetings   303 **set . . . before**
advance his forces early in the morning before me
V.i.4 **battles** armies   5 **warn** challenge   6 **Answering . . .
demand** appearing in opposition before we force a meeting
7 **I . . . bosoms** I understand their inmost thoughts   8–9
**They . . . places** they would prefer to be somewhere else
10 **fearful**(1) frightened (2) awe-inspiring; **bravery** bravado
(and show of splendor); **face** appearance   11 **fasten . . .
thoughts** persuade us   14 **bloody sign** red flag   16 **battle
softly** army slowly   17 **even** level   19 **cross** oppose,
contradict   19 **exigent** crisis

259 **young bloods** youthful constitutions   264 **murd'rous**
deathlike   265 **leaden** heavy (association also with death, for
lead was used in coffinmaking); **mace** staff of office (with
which a man was touched on the shoulder when arrested)
272 **How . . . burns** lights allegedly burned dimly or blue in
the presence of a supernatural being   275 **upon** toward   277
**stare** stand on end   288 **false** out of tune

*March. Drum. Enter* BRUTUS, CASSIUS, *and their* ARMY; [LUCILIUS, TITINIUS, MESSALA, *and others*].

BRUTUS
They stand, and would have parley.

CASSIUS
Stand fast, Titinius, we must out and talk.

OCTAVIUS
Mark Antony, shall we give sign of battle?

ANTONY
No, Caesar, we will answer on their charge.°
Make forth;° the generals would have some words.    25

OCTAVIUS
Stir not until the signal.

BRUTUS
Words before blows; is it so, countrymen?

OCTAVIUS
Not that we love words better, as you do.

BRUTUS
Good words are better than bad strokes, Octavius.

ANTONY
In your bad strokes, Brutus, you give good words;    30
Witness the hole you made in Caesar's heart,
Crying "Long live! Hail, Caesar!"

CASSIUS                                    Antony,
The posture° of your blows are yet unknown;
But for your words, they rob the Hybla° bees,
And leave them honeyless.

ANTONY                          Not stingless too.    35

BRUTUS
O, yes, and soundless too;
For you have stol'n their buzzing, Antony,
And very wisely threat before you sting.

ANTONY
Villains! You did not so, when your vile daggers
Hacked one another in the sides of Caesar.    40
You showed your teeth° like apes, and fawned like
    hounds,
And bowed like bondmen, kissing Caesar's feet;
Whilst damnèd Casca, like a cur, behind
Struck Caesar on the neck. O you flatterers!

CASSIUS
Flatterers! Now, Brutus, thank yourself;    45
This tongue had not offended so today,
If Cassius might have ruled.°

OCTAVIUS
Come, come, the cause.° If arguing make us sweat,
The proof° of it will turn to redder drops.
Look,    50
I draw a sword against conspirators.
When think you that the sword goes up° again?
Never, till Caesar's three and thirty wounds
Be well avenged; or till another Caesar°
Have added slaughter to° the sword of traitors.    55

BRUTUS
Caesar, thou canst not die by traitors' hands,
Unless thou bring'st them with thee.

OCTAVIUS                                    So I hope.
I was not born to die on Brutus' sword.

BRUTUS
O, if thou wert the noblest of thy strain,°
Young man, thou couldst not die more honorable.    60

CASSIUS
A peevish° schoolboy, worthless° of such honor,
Joined with a masker and a reveler.°

ANTONY
Old Cassius still!

OCTAVIUS          Come, Antony; away!
Defiance, traitors, hurl we in your teeth.
If you dare fight today, come to the field;    65
If not, when you have stomachs.°
                    *Exit* OCTAVIUS, ANTONY, *and* ARMY.

CASSIUS
Why, now blow wind, swell billow, and swim bark!
The storm is up, and all is on the hazard.°

BRUTUS
Ho, Lucilius, hark, a word with you.

LUCILIUS *and* MESSALA *stand forth.*

LUCILIUS                                    My lord?

[BRUTUS *and* LUCILIUS *converse apart.*]

CASSIUS
Messala.

MESSALA    What says my general?

CASSIUS                          Messala,    70
This is my birthday; as this very day
Was Cassius born. Give me thy hand, Messala:
Be thou my witness that against my will
(As Pompey was)° am I compelled to set°
Upon one battle all our liberties.    75
You know that I held Epicurus strong,°
And his opinion; now I change my mind,
And partly credit things that do presage.°
Coming from Sardis, on our former° ensign
Two mighty eagles fell,° and there they perched,    80
Gorging and feeding from our soldiers' hands,
Who to Philippi here consorted° us.
This morning are they fled away and gone,
And in their steads do ravens, crows, and kites°
Fly o'er our heads and downward look on us    85
As we were sickly° prey; their shadows seem
A canopy most fatal,° under which
Our army lies, ready to give up the ghost.

MESSALA
Believe not so.

CASSIUS          I but believe it partly,

59 **strain** family, line of descent    61 **peevish** childish (Octavius was 21); **worthless** unworthy    62 **masker . . . reveler** i.e., that dissipated Antony, who loved participating in masques and wild parties (cf. I.ii.203–04, II.i.188–89, II.ii.116)    66 **stomachs** inclination, appetite    68 **on the hazard** at stake    74 **As Pompey was** at Pharsalus where, having been persuaded to give battle against his will, he was decisively defeated and later murdered; **set** stake    76 **held Epicurus strong** believed strongly in the philosophy of Epicurus (a materialist who believed that because the gods were not interested in human affairs omens were to be discounted)    78 **presage** foretell the future    79 **former** foremost    80 **fell** swooped down    82 **consorted** accompanied    84 **ravens . . . kites** scavengers; traditionally, they know when a battle is pending and accompany the armies    86 **sickly** ready for death    87 **fatal** presaging death

24 **answer . . . charge** meet them when they attack    25 **Make forth** go forward    33 **posture** nature, quality    34 **Hybla** a Sicilian town famous for its sweet honey    41 **showed your teeth** grinned    47 **ruled** had his way (i.e., in urging that Antony be slain)    48 **cause** business at hand    49 **proof** test    52 **up** into the sheath    54 **another Caesar** i.e., Octavius himself    55 **Have . . . to** has also been killed by

For I am fresh of spirit and resolved                    90
To meet all perils very constantly.°
BRUTUS
Even so, Lucilius.
CASSIUS                    Now, most noble Brutus,
The gods today stand friendly, that we may,
Lovers° in peace, lead on our days to age!
But since the affairs of men rests still incertain,°    95
Let's reason with the worst that may befall.°
If we do lose this battle, then is this
The very last time we shall speak together.
What are you then determinèd to do?
BRUTUS
Even by the rule of that philosophy°                    100
By which I did blame Cato for the death
Which he did give himself; I know not how,
But I do find it cowardly and vile,
For fear of what might fall,° so to prevent°
The time° of life, arming myself with patience       105
To stay the providence° of some high powers
That govern us below.
CASSIUS                    Then, if we lose this battle,
You are contented to be led in triumph°
Thorough the streets of Rome?
BRUTUS
No, Cassius, no; think not, thou noble Roman,          110
That ever Brutus will go bound to Rome;
He bears too great a mind. But this same day
Must end that work the ides of March begun;
And whether we shall meet again I know not.
Therefore our everlasting farewell take.               115
Forever, and forever, farewell, Cassius!
If we do meet again, why, we shall smile;
If not, why then this parting was well made.
CASSIUS
Forever, and forever, farewell, Brutus!
If we do meet again, we'll smile indeed;               120
If not, 'tis true this parting was well made.
BRUTUS
Why then, lead on. O, that a man might know
The end of this day's business ere it come!
But it sufficeth that the day will end,
And then the end is known. Come, ho! Away!            125
                                        *Exeunt.*

[Scene II. *The field of battle.*]

*Alarum.° Enter* BRUTUS *and* MESSALA.

BRUTUS
Ride, ride, Messala, ride, and give these bills°
Unto the legions on the other side.°

*Loud alarum.*

Let them set on at once; for I perceive

But cold demeanor° in Octavius' wing,
And sudden push° gives them the overthrow.             5
Ride, ride, Messala! Let them all come down. *Exeunt.*

[Scene III. *The field of battle.*]

*Alarums. Enter* CASSIUS *and* TITINIUS.

CASSIUS
O, look, Titinius, look, the villains° fly!
Myself have to mine own° turned enemy.
This ensign° here of mine was turning back;
I slew the coward, and did take it° from him.
TITINIUS
O Cassius, Brutus gave the word too early,             5
Who, having some advantage on Octavius,
Took it too eagerly; his soldiers fell to spoil,°
Whilst we by Antony are all enclosed.

*Enter* PINDARUS.

PINDARUS
Fly further off, my lord, fly further off!
Mark Antony is in your tents, my lord.                 10
Fly, therefore, noble Cassius, fly far° off!
CASSIUS
This hill is far enough. Look, look, Titinius!
Are those my tents where I perceive the fire?
TITINIUS
They are, my lord.
CASSIUS                    Titinius, if thou lovest me,
Mount thou my horse and hide thy spurs in him         15
Till he have brought thee up to yonder troops
And here again, that I may rest assured
Whether yond troops are friend or enemy.
TITINIUS
I will be here again even with a thought.°       *Exit.*
CASSIUS
Go, Pindarus, get higher on that hill;                 20
My sight was ever thick.° Regard Titinius,
And tell me what thou not'st about the field.
                              [*Exit* PINDARUS.]
This day I breathèd first. Time is come round,
And where I did begin, there shall I end.
My life is run his compass.° Sirrah, what news?       25
PINDARUS (*Above.*)° O my lord!
CASSIUS    What news?
PINDARUS [*Above.*]
Titinius is enclosèd round about
With horsemen that make to him on the spur;°
Yet he spurs on. Now they are almost on him.          30
Now, Titinius! Now some light.° O, he lights too!
He's ta'en!° (*Shout.*) And, hark! They shout for joy.
CASSIUS
Come down; behold no more.

4 **But cold demeanor** marked lack of spirit in fighting   5
**push** attack
V.iii.1 **villains** cowardly soldiers of his own side   2 **mine own**
my own men   3 **ensign** standard-bearer   4 **it** the standard
7 **spoil** looting   11 **far** farther   19 **even . . . thought** as
quickly as thought   21 **My . . . thick** I have always been
nearsighted   25 **is . . . compass** has completed its circuit
26 **s.d. Above** on the upper stage   29 **make . . . spur** ride
toward him at top speed   31 **light** dismount   32 **ta'en**
taken, captured

91 **constantly** resolutely   94 **Lovers** devoted friends   95 **rests**
**still incertain** always stand in doubt   96 **reason . . . befall**
consider what must be done if the worst happens   100 **that**
**philosophy** Stoicism   104 **fall** befall; **prevent** anticipate   105
**time** term, natural end   106 **stay the providence** await the
ordained fate   108 **in triumph** (as a captive) in the victor's
procession
V.ii. s.d. **Alarum** call to arms (drums or trumpets)   1 **bills**
written orders   2 **side** wing (commanded by Cassius)

O, coward that I am, to live so long,
To see my best friend ta'en before my face!    35

*Enter* PINDARUS.

Come hither, sirrah.
In Parthia did I take thee prisoner;
And then I swore thee, saving of° thy life,
That whatsoever I did bid thee do,
Thou shouldst attempt it. Come now, keep thine
  oath.    40
Now be a freeman, and with this good sword,
That ran through Caesar's bowels, search° this bosom.
Stand° not to answer. Here, take thou the hilts,
And when my face is covered, as 'tis now,
Guide thou the sword—Caesar, thou art revenged,    45
Even with the sword that killed thee.    [*Dies.*]

PINDARUS
So, I am free; yet would not so have been,
Durst I have done my will. O Cassius!
Far from this country Pindarus shall run,
Where never Roman shall take note of him.    [*Exit.*]  50

*Enter* TITINIUS *and* MESSALA.

MESSALA
It is but change,° Titinius; for Octavius
Is overthrown by noble Brutus' power,
As Cassius' legions are by Antony.

TITINIUS
These tidings will well comfort Cassius.

MESSALA
Where did you leave him?

TITINIUS                                    All disconsolate,    55
With Pindarus his bondman, on this hill.

MESSALA
Is not that he that lies upon the ground?

TITINIUS
He lies not like the living. O my heart!

MESSALA
Is not that he?

TITINIUS            No, this was he, Messala,
But Cassius is no more. O setting sun,    60
As in thy red rays thou dost sink to night,
So in his red blood Cassius' day is set.
The sun of Rome is set. Our day is gone;
Clouds, dews,° and dangers come; our deeds are
  done!
Mistrust of° my success hath done this deed.    65

MESSALA
Mistrust of good success hath done this deed.
O hateful Error, Melancholy's child,°
Why dost thou show to the apt° thoughts of men
The things that are not? O Error, soon conceived,
Thou never com'st unto a happy birth,    70
But kill'st the mother° that engend'red thee!

TITINIUS
What, Pindarus! Where art thou, Pindarus?

MESSALA
Seek him, Titinius, whilst I go to meet
The noble Brutus, thrusting this report
Into his ears. I may say "thrusting" it;    75
For piercing steel and darts envenomèd
Shall be as welcome to the ears of Brutus
As tidings of this sight.

TITINIUS                        Hie° you, Messala,
And I will seek for Pindarus the while.

                                    [*Exit* MESSALA.]

Why didst thou send me forth, brave° Cassius?    80
Did I not meet thy friends, and did not they
Put on my brows this wreath of victory,
And bid me give it thee? Didst thou not hear their
  shouts?
Alas, thou hast misconstrued everything!
But hold thee,° take this garland on thy brow;    85
Thy Brutus bid me give it thee, and I
Will do his bidding. Brutus, come apace,°
And see how I regarded° Caius Cassius.
By your leave,° gods. This is a Roman's part:°
Come, Cassius' sword, and find Titinius' heart. *Dies.*  90

*Alarum. Enter* BRUTUS, MESSALA, *young* CATO,
STRATO, VOLUMNIUS, *and* LUCILIUS.

BRUTUS
Where, where, Messala, doth his body lie?

MESSALA
Lo, yonder, and Titinius mourning it.

BRUTUS
Titinius' face is upward.

CATO                        He is slain.

BRUTUS
O Julius Caesar, thou art mighty yet!
Thy spirit walks abroad, and turns our swords    95
In our own proper° entrails. *Low alarums.*

CATO                        Brave° Titinius!
Look, whe'r° he have not crowned dead Cassius.

BRUTUS
Are yet two Romans living such as these?
The last of all the Romans, fare thee well!
It is impossible that ever Rome    100
Should breed thy fellow.° Friends, I owe moe° tears
To this dead man than you shall see me pay.
I shall find time, Cassius; I shall find time.
Come, therefore, and to Thasos° send his body;
His funerals shall not be in our camp,    105
Lest it discomfort us.° Lucilius, come,
And come, young Cato; let us to the field.
Labeo and Flavius set our battles° on.
'Tis three o'clock; and, Romans, yet ere night
We shall try fortune in a second fight.    *Exeunt.*  110

38 **swore . . . of** made you swear, when I spared    42 **search**
penetrate    43 **Stand** delay    51 **change** exchange (of fortune)
64 **dews** considered unwholesome    65 **Mistrust of** lack
of confidence in    67 **Melancholy's child** i.e., those of
despondent temperament are likely to be introspective and
full of imaginary fears    68 **apt** easily impressed    71 **mother**
the melancholy person, Cassius, who conceived the error

78 **Hie** hasten    80 **brave** noble    85 **hold thee** wait a moment
87 **apace** quickly    88 **regarded** honored    89 **By your leave**
with your permission (because he is ending his life before the
time appointed by the gods); **part** role, duty    96 **own
proper** (emphatic) very own; **Brave** noble    97 **whe'r**
whether    101 **fellow** equal; **moe** more    104 **Thasos** an
island near Philippi    106 **discomfort us** dishearten our troops
108 **battles** armies

[Scene IV. *The field of battle.*]

*Alarum. Enter* BRUTUS, MESSALA, [*young*] CATO,
LUCILIUS, *and* FLAVIUS.

BRUTUS
Yet, countrymen, O, yet hold up your heads!
                          [*Exit, with* FOLLOWERS.]

CATO
What bastard° doth not? Who will go with me?
I will proclaim my name about the field.
I am the son of Marcus Cato,° ho!
A foe to tyrants, and my country's friend.       5
I am the son of Marcus Cato, ho!

*Enter* SOLDIERS *and fight.*

[LUCILIUS]°
And I am Brutus, Marcus Brutus, I;
Brutus, my country's friend; know me for Brutus!
                       [*Young* CATO *falls.*]
O young and noble Cato, art thou down?
Why, now thou diest as bravely as Titinius,    10
And mayst be honored, being Cato's son.
[FIRST] SOLDIER
Yield, or thou diest.
LUCILIUS         Only I yield to die.°
There is so much° that thou wilt kill me straight;°
Kill Brutus, and be honored in his death.
[FIRST] SOLDIER
We must not. A noble prisoner!    15

*Enter* ANTONY.

SECOND SOLDIER
Room, ho! Tell Antony, Brutus is ta'en.
FIRST SOLDIER
I'll tell the news. Here comes the general.
Brutus is ta'en, Brutus is ta'en, my lord.
ANTONY   Where is he?
LUCILIUS
Safe, Antony; Brutus is safe enough.    20
I dare assure thee that no enemy
Shall ever take alive the noble Brutus.
The gods defend him from so great a shame!
When you do find him, or alive or dead,
He will be found like Brutus, like himself.°    25
ANTONY
This is not Brutus, friend, but, I assure you,
A prize no less in worth. Keep this man safe;
Give him all kindness. I had rather have
Such men my friends than enemies. Go on,
And see whe'r Brutus be alive or dead,    30
And bring us word unto Octavius' tent
How everything is chanced.°         *Exeunt.*

[Scene V. *The field of battle.*]

*Enter* BRUTUS, DARDANIUS, CLITUS, STRATO, *and*
VOLUMNIUS.

BRUTUS
Come, poor remains° of friends, rest on this rock.
CLITUS
Statilius showed the torchlight,° but, my lord,
He came not back; he is or ta'en or slain.
BRUTUS
Sit thee down, Clitus. Slaying is the word;
It is a deed in fashion. Hark thee, Clitus.    5

[*Whispers.*]

CLITUS
What, I, my lord? No, not for all the world!
BRUTUS
Peace then, no words.
CLITUS              I'll rather kill myself.
BRUTUS
Hark thee, Dardanius. [*Whispers.*]
DARDANIUS          Shall I do such a deed?
CLITUS  O Dardanius!
DARDANIUS   O Clitus!    10
CLITUS
What ill request did Brutus make to thee?
DARDANIUS
To kill him, Clitus. Look, he meditates.
CLITUS
Now is that noble vessel° full of grief,
That it runs over even at his eyes.
BRUTUS
Come hither, good Volumnius; list° a word.    15
VOLUMNIUS
What says my lord?
BRUTUS           Why, this, Volumnius:
The ghost of Caesar hath appeared to me
Two several° times by night; at Sardis once,
And this last night here in Philippi fields.
I know my hour is come.
VOLUMNIUS          Not so, my lord.    20
BRUTUS
Nay, I am sure it is, Volumnius.
Thou see'st the world, Volumnius, how it goes;
Our enemies have beat us to the pit.°

*Low alarums.*

It is more worthy to leap in ourselves
Than tarry till they push us. Good Volumnius,    25
Thou know'st that we two went to school together;
Even for that our love of old, I prithee
Hold thou my sword-hilts whilst I run on it.
VOLUMNIUS
That's not an office for a friend, my lord.

*Alarum still.*°

**V.iv.2 What bastard** who is such a low fellow that he **4
son . . . Cato** son of Cato of Utica, hence, brother of
Brutus' wife **7 Lucilius** the Folio fails to provide a speech
prefix for lines 7–8, but because it is clear from Plutarch and
from line 14 that Lucilius impersonates Brutus it is plausible
to attribute 7–8 to Lucilius **12 Only . . . die** I yield only to
die **13 so much** so great an inducement. i.e., gaining great
honor by killing Brutus (?), so much to be blamed for (?), a
sum of money (offered to the soldier) (?); **straight** immediately
**25 like himself** behaving in accordance with his noble nature
**32 is chanced** has turned out

**V.v.1 poor remains** wretched survivors **2 showed the
torchlight** Statilius had volunteered to see if Cassius' camp was
occupied by the enemy; he signaled on arrival there but was
obviously captured thereafter **13 vessel** figurative for
"human being"; also an allusion to the small jars of tears
offered to the dead **15 list** hear **18 several** separate **23 pit**
(1) trap for capturing wild animals (2) grave **29 s.d. still**
continuing

**CLITUS**
Fly, fly, my lord, there is no tarrying here.                    30
**BRUTUS**
Farewell to you; and you; and you, Volumnius.
Strato, thou hast been all this while asleep;
Farewell to thee too, Strato. Countrymen,
My heart doth joy that yet in all my life
I found no man but he was true to me.                    35
I shall have glory by this losing day
More than Octavius and Mark Antony
By this vile conquest° shall attain unto.
So far you well at once,° for Brutus' tongue
Hath almost ended his life's history.                    40
Night hangs upon mine eyes; my bones would rest,
That have but labored to attain this hour.°

*Alarum. Cry within,* "Fly, fly, fly!"

**CLITUS**    Fly, my lord, fly!
**BRUTUS**                    Hence! I will follow.
    [*Exeunt* CLITUS, DARDANIUS, *and* VOLUMNIUS.]
I prithee, Strato, stay thou by thy lord,
Thou art a fellow of a good respect.°                    45
Thy life hath had some smatch° of honor in it;
Hold then my sword, and turn away thy face,
While I do run upon it. Wilt thou, Strato?
**STRATO**
Give me your hand first. Fare you well, my lord.
**BRUTUS**
Farewell, good Strato—Caesar, now be still;                    50
I killed not thee with half so good a will.    *Dies.*

*Alarum.    Retreat.    Enter* ANTONY,    OCTAVIUS,
MESSALA, LUCILIUS, *and the* ARMY.

**OCTAVIUS**
What man is that?
**MESSALA**
My master's man.° Strato, where is thy master?
**STRATO**
Free from the bondage you are in, Messala;
The conquerors can but make a fire of him.                    55

For Brutus only overcame himself,°
And no man else hath honor by his death.
**LUCILIUS**
So Brutus should be found. I thank thee, Brutus,
That thou hast proved Lucilius' saying° true.
**OCTAVIUS**
All that served Brutus, I will entertain° them.                    60
Fellow, wilt thou bestow° thy time with me?
**STRATO**
Ay, if Messala will prefer° me to you.
**OCTAVIUS**
Do so, good Messala.
**MESSALA**
How died my master, Strato?
**STRATO**
I held the sword, and he did run on it.                    65
**MESSALA**
Octavius, then take him to follow thee,
That did the latest° service to my master.
**ANTONY**
This was the noblest Roman of them all.
All the conspirators save only he
Did that they did in envy of great Caesar;                    70
He, only in a general honest thought
And common good to all, made one of them.°
His life was gentle,° and the elements°
So mixed° in him that Nature might stand up
And say to all the world, "This was a man!"                    75
**OCTAVIUS**
According to his virtue,° let us use° him
With all respect and rites of burial.
Within my tent his bones tonight shall lie,
Most like a soldier ordered honorably.°
So call the field° to rest, and let's away                    80
To part° the glories of this happy day.    *Exeunt omnes.*

56 **Brutus . . . himself** only Brutus overcame Brutus
59 **saying** see V.iv.21–25    60 **entertain** take into service
61 **bestow** spend    62 **prefer** recommend    67 **latest** last
71–72 **He . . . them** he, moved only by impersonal
motives directed to the good of the community, joined
the conspirators    73 **gentle** noble; **elements** the four
opposed elements, of which all nature was thought to be
composed, were represented in the human body by the four
liquids, bile, phlegm, blood, and choler; the dominance of
these determined a man's temperament—melancholic, phlegmatic, sanguine, or choleric)    74 **So mixed** so well-balanced
76 **virtue** excellence; **use** treat    79 **ordered honorably**
arrayed (and treated) with all honor    80 **field** army    81 **part**
divide

38 **vile conquest** overthrow of the revolution against
tyranny    39 **at once** without further delay    42 **but . . . hour**
worked hard only to reach this goal of death (which brings, for
a Stoic, rest from life's trials)    45 **respect** reputation    46
**smatch** smack, taste    53 **man** servant

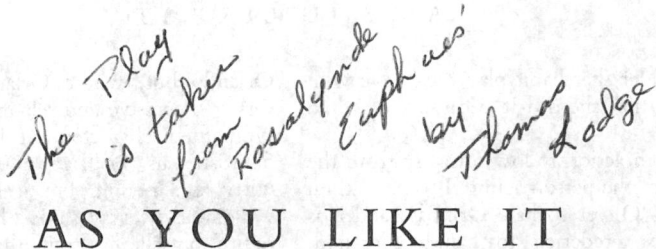

# AS YOU LIKE IT

EDITED BY ALBERT GILMAN

## Introduction

Samuel Johnson found the story of *As You Like It* "wild and pleasing," the dialogue "sprightly," but regretted Shakespeare's "hastening to the end of his work," especially because it meant suppressing the "dialogue between the usurper and the hermit" and thereby losing "an opportunity of exhibiting a moral lesson." From the eighteenth century on, critics have often said that Shakespeare's craftsmanship in *As You Like It* is poor. G. B. Shaw, perhaps with tongue in cheek, in *The Dark Lady of the Sonnets* has Will Shakespear say to Queen Elizabeth: "I have also stole from a book of idle wanton tales two of the most damnable foolishnesses in the world, in the one of which a woman goeth in man's attire and maketh impudent love to her swain, who pleaseth the groundlings by overthrowing a wrestler. . . . I have writ these to save my friends from penury, yet shewing my scorn for such follies and for them that praise them by calling the one As You Like It, meaning that it is not as *I* like it."

Some critics have complained of inconsistencies in the plotting. From several speeches in the play, it would appear that Duke Senior has been banished to the Forest of Arden for a long time, but other speeches suggest that his banishment is recent. In the first scene of the play Shakespeare gives the name Jaques to the middle son of Sir Rowland de Boys, but this Jaques does not appear until the close of the play and his speeches are simply marked "Second Brother." In the meantime we have heard much from another Jaques, the melancholy Jaques, who is one of Duke Senior's retainers. Two characters called by the same name can make for some confusion. These bits of carelessness, if that is what they are, are not unusual in Shakespeare and not peculiar to this play. What is unusual is the extraordinary dispatch with which the plot unfolds. Almost everything that is to happen, happens in the first act; murders are attempted, ribs are cracked, and several major characters are packed off to the Forest of Arden. In the ensuing acts Shakespeare scarcely concerns himself with the troubles that were introduced in the first act. Except for three short scenes we are always in Arden, where the dangers we are chiefly aware of are falling in love or being worsted in a discussion. So that the audience may go home, the two villains are reported to have been converted and four pairs of lovers are lined up to be wed.

Shakespeare has certainly handled the narrative expeditiously. It is very much as if he were eager to be in Arden to "fleet the time carelessly as they did in the golden world." We cannot regret that he missed the "opportunity of exhibiting a moral lesson." Nor can we regret that he gave himself a holiday from the intricate plotting that marks what seems to be the comedy anterior to *As You Like It*, *Much Ado About Nothing*. Who has not looked at his watch during the last act of a well-made plot and sighed to think of the knots still to be untied? We had rather be in Arden where the wicked are converted by fiat and lovers marry in half-dozen lots.

The plot moves swiftly in the beginning of *As You Like It* (and then stands almost still until the fifth act) because the interest of the play is not intended to arise out of the action or situation. And, as William Hazlitt has remarked, it does not. The play is chiefly concerned with two enduring human illusions—the pastoral ideal, or the dream of a simple life, and the ideal of romantic love. These are given an extremely complex representation through dialogue and contrasting relationships. The plot creates the conditions for this representation. The characters are given reason to wander in the woodland, the proper setting in which to develop the theme of pastoralism. Four diverse pairs are caused to fall in love and their contrasting romances will exemplify the varieties of love. Rosalind, given a double identity, can spoof love and yet be a lover. The plot does very well what it is designed to do.

The motives of the chief characters in *As You Like It* are as simple and abrupt as the action of the play, and they could surely be put in evidence by those who think the play a piece of indifferent craftsmanship. Oliver would see an end to his brother Orlando. Why? "For my soul, yet I know not why, hates nothing more than he." Duke Frederick, the usurper who has banished Duke Senior, would now banish Rosalind. The reason? "Grounded upon no other argument/But that the people praise her for her virtues." In her scenes with Orlando, Rosalind is in no danger; thus her original reason for pretending to be a man does not apply. Yet she does pretend, and it is only her disguise that prevents their immediate marriage. How is so crucial a decision motivated? "I will speak to him like

839

a saucy lackey, and under that habit play the knave with him." Which is to say that she did it because she would do it.

In *As You Like It* each action follows directly from the uncomplicated nature of the person acting. It is his natural wickedness that impels Oliver to hate Orlando, and it is wickedness that causes Frederick to banish Rosalind. Antonio, in Shakespeare's *The Tempest*, is another younger brother who banishes his elder brother (Prospero) and usurps the dukedom. But Antonio's case is more complex than Frederick's, since, while the usurpation is not justified, there is the excuse that Prospero had neglected his duties as a ruler, and Antonio, Prospero's delegate, through the exercise of ducal power, came to believe (as a liar may come to believe his lie) that he was in fact the duke. But neither Rosalind nor Duke Senior is culpable, and Duke Frederick's usurpation is not said to result from any such interesting state of mind as Antonio's. Duke Frederick's crimes derive from his nature alone. In *As You Like It* a good nature is as unfailingly manifest as a bad one. Because their hearts are blithe, Celia and Rosalind are able to go into exile saying: "Now go in we content/To liberty, and not to banishment." Because his nature is noble, Duke Senior can say "Sweet are the uses of adversity" and can find "good in everything." The good in this play will be good whatever the occasion seems to warrant and the evil, at first, will be evil. Of Shakespeare's comedies only *The Comedy of Errors* makes so simple a connection between temperament and action. *The Comedy of Errors* is a farce, but *As You Like It* is not.

Englishmen in the Renaissance liked to construe life as an interaction of Fortune and Nature, and in *As You Like It* there is some talk of these two goddesses. Rosalind, for instance, instructs Celia: "Fortune reigns in gifts of the world, not in the lineaments of Nature." The only tension in the plot of *As You Like It*, set up in the first act, derives from Fortune's unjust distribution of the gifts of the world. The nobler natures, Duke Senior, Rosalind, Celia, and Orlando, are made to suffer by Fortune while the wicked, Oliver and Duke Frederick, thrive. This imbalance between Fortune and Nature requires resolution. The resolution provided is exceptionally good-humored, far more so than in either *Much Ado About Nothing* or *Twelfth Night*, the two plays with which *As You Like It* is conventionally grouped. The wicked are not punished or left rancorous but are converted and, now as virtuous men, Frederick and Oliver bring the fortunes of Duke Senior, Rosalind, and Orlando into harmony with their natures. Frederick's conversion is accomplished by contact with an old religious man, Oliver's by Orlando's generosity in saving his life. Fortunes are adjusted and dark natures are brightened by the simple impact of virtue. All of this makes a tidy package if Fortune and Nature are conceived as the major forces in life and if these forces are thought to work toward human happiness. Shakespeare's world view was ordinarily more complex.

It is, after all, a kind of innocence to believe that evil is certain men and that goodness is certain other men. And it is the sunniest optimism to believe that the evil are converted by contact with the good. In other plays of Shakespeare, even in the other comedies, temperaments are not so consistently agreeable or disagreeable and resolutions are not so sweet. Orsino, in *Twelfth Night*, is as romantic as Orlando but, where Orlando is vigorous and sensible, Orsino is passive and self-indulgent. Orsino is a generally sympathetic character, but there is something in him which dissatisfies us. Beatrice, in *Much Ado About Nothing*, is as witty as Rosalind but lacks her self-knowledge and is sometimes near to shrewishness. Beatrice is an attractive figure, but she has traits that threaten her happiness. The unsympathetic Malvolio, in *Twelfth Night*, is not transformed by contact with goodness; his last line is: "I'll be revenged on the whole pack of you." Shakespeare's characters ordinarily mix good with evil. His dramatic tension often derives from irreconcilable desires within each nature rather than from an easily corrected malallocation of Fortune's gifts. The exercise of virtue in some of his plays only stimulates the wicked to further wickedness. Why are these darker principles suspended in *As You Like It*?

The play is intended to suggest that human life can be harmoniously lived; that good sense, love, humor, and a generous disposition will produce happiness. Such a view requires not suppression of, but inattention to, those aspects of motivation and of human relationship that, in life, continually postpone a general harmony. A world that includes irreconcilable personal conflict and unrepenting evil can achieve justice, but not universal happiness.

*As You Like It* causes us to entertain seriously an illusion —a view of life in which a human wish plays a greater role than reality. Yet the play is far from being continuously idyllic. It is filled with sharp comment and disillusioning fact, particularly in connection with its chief subjects—the simple life and romantic love. These subjects are themselves illusions, conventional illusions, sentimental and foolish. Shakespeare laughs at their conventional treatment, threatens them with contrary views and conflicting facts, but in the end preserves them. The play reconciles the ideal with the actual. But not all of the actual. Shakespeare has looked away from the uglier facts, the ultimate ironies that cannot be integrated into a vision of harmony and happiness. Perhaps it is only *The Tempest* and *The Winter's Tale*, plays written after the great tragedies, that make happiness seem to be generally possible and yet also offer powerful representations of evil and suffering.

If *As You Like It* offered a completely one-sided presentation of harmony, we might be armed against it. But it does not. It presents numerous contrary arguments, and the tension they bring to the debate in Arden lends credence to the resolution. For as long as the play lasts we do not notice that the case against the ideal has not been as strong as it could be; that matters that cannot be reconciled with the ideal have been passed over. It is an illusion that *As You Like It* creates, but an illusion that admits so much of life as to seem possible.

What is the nature of the contrarieties that are reconciled with the pastoral ideal and the ideal of romantic love? Arrived in Arden, Touchstone is asked how he likes the shepherd's life and he replies:

> In respect that it is solitary, I like it very well; but in respect
> that it is private, it is a very vile life. Now in respect it is in
> the fields, it pleaseth me well; but in respect it is not in the
> court, it is tedious. As it is a spare life, look you, it fits my
> humor well; but as there is no more plenty in it, it goes
> much against my stomach.             (III.ii.15–21)

The expression of one idea stimulates Touchstone to the expression of its contrary. But the ideas are not contraries of objective fact. To be solitary is to be private; to be in the fields is to be not in the court; to lead a spare life is to lead a life that has no more plenty in it. The objective facts are the same and the opposition is one of sentiment. A life spent apart from others can be agreeable or it can be disagreeable. When it is agreeable Touchstone would call it solitary and when it is disagreeable he would call it private. What can cause the same objective condition to change its nature?

Rosalind, who stands in the center of all things in this play, answers our question, but with reference to time rather than life in the forest. "Time," she says, "travels in divers paces with divers persons." She goes on to particularize. For a young maid "between the contract of her marriage and the day it is solemnized" time trots too slowly. For a rich man who "hath not the gout" time ambles most agreeably. For a thief on his way to the gallows time goes too swiftly. To generalize Rosalind's remarks: time and life in the forest are apprehended differently by different persons and differently by one person according to his condition of life and state of appetite. Life in the forest and romantic love are ideal in their season but they are not for all seasons. Like a holiday, the greenwood and true love offer refreshment and regeneration. Prolonged beyond their season they become absurd and distasteful.

Touchstone concludes the speech quoted above by asking Corin: "Hast any philosophy in thee, shepherd?" Corin's response begins: "No more, but that I know the more one sickens, the worse at ease he is." At first this reply seems a simple extension of Touchstone's list of on-the-one-hand-this, but-on-the-other-hand-that. Then one realizes that the contrast between Corin's two terms, "the more one sickens" and "the worse at ease," does not follow Touchstone's principle. Corin's terms are objective synonyms as are Touchstone's, but Corin's are also subjective synonyms; to be sick and to be ill at ease are both disagreeable. It seems then that simple Corin has missed the point. Except that sickness is one of the things in life that is not psychologically relative; we never have an appetite for it. It is an absolute evil. Without knowing just how much philosophy the old shepherd had in him, we can take his line as the text for another proposition about *As You Like It*. The relativism of the play's discourse is bounded by a set of moral absolutes that cannot be taken as you like it.

Touchstone's speech concerns the pastoral life and this is a major subject of the conversations in Arden through III.ii. Pastoralism is a place and time apart. It is the restorative greenwood, where men live in the simplicity of nature. It is a remote Golden Age of harmony and innocence. The modern time and the corrupt court are its antithesis.

Duke Senior realizes the pastoral dream in Arden, finding "books in the running brooks" and "sermons in stones." Amiens sings sweetly of pastoralism in "Under the Greenwood Tree." But Jaques, who is of another humor, adds a jaundiced verse calling that man a fool who leaves wealth and ease for the wilderness. In course of time it develops that the winds are cold in Arden and the ground is hard, that the deer, "native burghers of this desert city," can be as indifferent to the misery of one of their kind as human beings can be, and that at least one lion and one snake are among the animal life. Life in the forest is not a fixed reality. It is able to produce happiness and able to produce misery. Love has potentialities that are more complex.

Love is revealed directly in the romance of Rosalind and Orlando and, by contrast, in the matching of Silvius with Phebe, and the mating of Audrey with Touchstone. The former pair disenchants us with certain aspects of both pastoralism and love. Silvius at first appears as the lovelorn shepherd of pastoral romance and Phebe as his pouting shepherdess. The sighing and spurning that are so graceful in the classical picture are distasteful when we see a little more of them. Silvius is an abject figure with his "Sweet Phebe, pity me." He shows what love can descend to when it is not combined with good sense. Phebe shows the response such love will inspire in a petulant nature:

> But since that thou canst talk of love so well,
> Thy company, which erst was irksome to me,
> I will endure; and I'll employ thee too.
> But do not look for further recompense
> Than thine own gladness that thou art employed.
>
> (III.v.94–98)

We delight in Rosalind's pungent advice to Phebe: "Sell when you can, you are not for all markets."

For Touchstone love is a ubiquitous human need that seeks an object; it is very like a need that in animals is seasonal. Audrey, falling within his tolerance limits, is taken as an object. Romantic love does not have an object; it has an incomparable inspiration. Orlando, with Rosalind for inspiration, hangs love poems on trees and cries her name throughout the forest. Rosalind, hearing that Celia has seen Orlando, excitedly asks: "What did he when thou saw'st him? What said he? How looked he? Wherein went he? What makes he here?"

The several aspects of love are revealed by the three unlike love affairs. They are revealed also in the running discourse in Arden. There is no scene in which the nature of love is debated. No one keeps to the subject for long; Rosalind ends her catechism of love, in which Orlando and Phebe echo Silvius' exalted sentiments, with: "Pity you, no more of this; 'tis like the howling of Irish wolves against the moon." The discourse is composed of an ironic remark from Touchstone in one scene, something extravagantly amorous from Orlando in another, a joke from Celia in still another. The touches of color, the shading, the points of light, are distributed in time, but they come together to make a rather complex representation.

The disillusioned remarks on love, as on pastoralism, come chiefly from Jaques and Touchstone. Jaques is a man who has traveled and come back a weary malcontent; he stands somewhat detached from life. He is a variation on a familiar kind of stage figure in Shakespeare's day, a type first found in the snarling verse satires written by John Marston and Joseph Hall in the 1590's. After 1599 the type appears in the drama: the bitter critic who defends his railing and abusive language by saying that such attacks as his are the only way to purge the world of its vices. In II.vii, Duke Senior attacks Jaques as if he were a perfect instance of this type, and Jaques responds with the critic's familiar defense. In fact, however, Shakespeare has departed from the type.

Jaques ridicules human ideals, but his attacks are not

corrosive and they are entertainingly expressed. Seeing Touchstone and Audrey press in among the country copulatives, Jaques remarks: "There is, sure, another flood toward, and these couples are coming to the ark." That he enjoys hearing Amiens sing argues a certain sweetness of nature, sweeter at any rate than the nature of Shylock, to whom music is the "vile squeaking of the wry-necked fife." The other characters appear to enjoy the company of Jaques as they would not the company of so vicious a satirist as Thersites in *Troilus and Cressida*. Duke Senior loves to be with him in his "sullen fits," for then Jaques is "full of matter," and at the end the duke urges Jaques to return with him to the court.

The darker potentialities of Jaques are hinted at, but on the whole he is an entertaining fellow and much that he says about love is true—when one is not in love. However, those who are most in love do not envy Jaques' detachment and knowledge of life. Rosalind gives her opinion that those who are either too sad or too merry are "abominable fellows," but between the two she would rather "have a fool to make me merry than experience to make me sad."

In Touchstone we have the fool Rosalind asks for. He sees as little in life to make one sad as Jaques sees to make one merry. Jaques is perhaps a disappointed idealist; but Touchstone is a realist who believes that happiness derives from the satisfactions of the body and from a wit that is quick to see the absurdity and folly in life. As Miss Gardner and Professor Goldsmith point out, Touchstone is the great parodist of the play (see, for instance, his love poem to Rosalind following those of Orlando). Touchstone's marriage to Audrey, the simple-minded shepherdess, who in fact is a goatherd, is itself a parody, but one of Shakespeare's making rather than Touchstone's. It is a parody on romance and pastoralism; but it is also the author's comment on the limitations of Touchstone's view of life.

Touchstone and Jaques are alike in their rejection of the ideal and alike therefore in their incompleteness. They show us the ideal as absurdity and sentimentality. Orlando and Rosalind show us romantic love as the best part of life so long as it is understood to be only a part, something that is here and now and should be enjoyed in its time. The play as a whole presents this view, but it is fully articulated by Rosalind alone.

Many romantic lines come from Orlando and Rosalind, and if they were to follow one upon another it would be "to have honey a sauce to sugar." Between sweets, however, there is always something sharp to taste. Sometimes it is provided by Jaques or Touchstone or Celia but most often perhaps by Rosalind as Ganymede. The contrast preserves the flavor. When Orlando swears that he will die of love if he cannot have Rosalind, she gives him her answer: "Men have died from time to time, and worms have eaten them, but not for love."

To speak of contrast is to suggest that one aspect is subordinate to the others; in the extreme case, that it exists only to set off the others. This is not the case with Rosalind's statements about love. Rosalind's line is comically matter-of-fact, very flat, but, after all, true. It checks Orlando just as he is about to move into absurdity. He loves her and it seems to him now that he cannot live without her, but if, in fact, he could not have her he would find reason to live.

Romantic love strains toward eternity. Memory and observation and the foresight they give are its enemies.

When Orlando swears that he will love forever and a day, Rosalind responds: "Say 'a day' without the 'ever.' No, no, Orlando. Men are April when they woo, December when they wed. Maids are May when they are maids, but the sky changes when they are wives."

On another occasion Rosalind as Ganymede teases Orlando by insisting that he has not the look of the distracted lover. "You are rather point-device in your accouterments, as loving yourself than seeming the lover of any other." Here again she is ridiculing the extremities of romantic love. At times she makes jokes that are bawdy and so reveal a facet of love. Orlando brings his destiny with him, she says. "What's that?" he asks. "Why horns; which such as you are fain to be beholding to your wives for." And when Orlando asks if she will love him—"Ay, and twenty such."

Yet Rosalind is unquestionably in love. To Celia she confides "that thou didst know how many fathom deep I am in love. But it cannot be sounded. My affection hath an unknown bottom, like the Bay of Portugal." Rosalind's disguise as Ganymede and her game with Orlando in which she is supposed to try to cure him of love provide an excuse for the expression of her many unromantic sentiments. But they are not to be understood as ideas invented for Ganymede with no validity for Rosalind. While in love she is able to realize what love may become in time and how it can appear to those who are not in love. She sees all around her subject, combining perspectives in the manner of certain Picasso portraits. In Rosalind's conversation we see love's two eyes and also its profile and the back of its neck.

Rosalind integrates the ideal and the workaday world; love is a good time of life, it is youth and springtime. It is not everything, but in its season it would be folly not to enjoy it. "Come, woo me, woo me," she says, "for now I am in a holiday humor and like enough to consent." Rosalind, whose nature unites ardor and intelligence, synthesizes the ideas of the play.

When so much has been said about cuckoldry and about April turning to December, it may be a little difficult to accept the four marriages of the last scene as a happy ending. But the jokes and the irony and the mockery have been directed primarily at love, not at marriage. Marriage belongs to the institutions of a stable society, and these are never questioned in the play. The responsibility of an elder brother for a younger is the institutional frame that immediately establishes Oliver's villainy. The respect a younger brother owes an elder is the standard that marks Frederick a scoundrel. And the last words about love, the words that assign it to its proper place in an orderly society and prepare for the festive dance at the end, are delivered by Hymen:

> Wedding is great Juno's crown,
>   O blessed bond of board and bed!
> 'Tis Hymen peoples every town;
>   High wedlock then be honorèd.          (V.iv.141–44)

*A note on the date:*

On August 4, 1600, the Lord Chamberlain's Men entered *As You Like It* and three other plays in the Stationers' Register "to be staied" as a way of preventing their unauthorized publication. This entry sets the later limit for the date of *As You Like It*. An earlier limit is set by its absence from the list of Shakespeare's plays given by Francis Meres in *Palladis Tamia* (1598). In one of her speeches Celia says: "Since the little wit that fools have was silenced, the little foolery that wise men have makes a great show" (I.ii). This remark may be a reference to an official order of June 1, 1599, whereby the published writings of a number of satirists were burnt and the future printing of satires prohibited. In view of this possibility and the two limiting dates, the best supposition is that the play was written in the latter half of 1599 or early in 1600.

## A NOTE ON THE SOURCE

Shakespeare's source for *As You Like It* is Thomas Lodge's pastoral romance, *Rosalynde or Euphues' Golden Legacy*, printed in 1590. This romance in turn is based in part on a short narrative poem of the fourteenth century, "The Tale of Gamelyn," telling of the unjust treatment of Gamelyn by his older brother, the bloody fights between them, Gamelyn's flight to the greenwood, where he becomes the leader of a happy band of outlaws, and the eventual recovery of his land after his brother has been hanged. The only reference to love comes in the last lines, where we are told that Gamelyn took a "wyf bothe good and feyr."

To this rapid and brutally humorous narrative, Lodge added the story of a banished king, Gerismond, and three love stories: one of these concerns Rosader (Gamelyn of the early poem and Shakespeare's Orlando) and Rosalynde; the others, Alinda and Saladyne (Shakespeare's Celia and Oliver) and Phoebe and Montanus (Shakespeare's Phebe and Silvius). Interspersed throughout *Rosalynde* are elegant love poems. The whole, a medley of folk tale, pastoral love eclogue, and pastoral romance, is predominantly written in the highly mannered style known as euphuism, a style made popular by John Lyly in the 1570's, but it is enlivened by homely phrases and proverbs.

Although there is no evidence that Shakespeare drew directly upon any work other than Lodge's, it is possible that three plays were in Shakespeare's mind when he came to write *As You Like It*. Two Robin Hood plays performed in 1598 by the Admiral's Company, *The Downfall of Robert Earl of Huntingdon* and *The Death of Robert Earl of Huntingdon*, may have inspired Shakespeare's treatment of the singing outlaws, and *Sir Clyomon and Clamydes* (printed in 1599) may have suggested the rustics, Audrey and William. (In *Sir Clyomon* a princess disguised as a man meets a crude but amusing shepherd named Corin who describes in plain language the love-making of real shepherds and country girls.)

To return from conjecture to fact: *As You Like It* owes a great deal to *Rosalynde*. Shakespeare follows the outline of Lodge's plot closely and develops many of its situations, such as the enmity of two sets of characters, the wrestling match, the flight to the forest, Orlando's desperate demand for food, the momentary hesitation of Orlando to save his brother from the lioness, the wooing of Rosalind disguised as Ganymede, the marriage of Celia and Oliver, the disdain of Phebe and her use of Silvius as messenger, and the return to the court. The title too may come from Lodge, who in a note to his "gentlemen readers," says, "If you like it, so."

It is not only in plot and situation that Shakespeare is indebted to Lodge. Lodge's two princesses possess in embryo almost all the characteristics of their counterparts, but compared to Shakespeare's heroine Lodge's Rosalynde is wooden. She does not master events as does Rosalind, and as a woman in love she is scarcely differentiated from Alinda (Shakespeare's Celia) or, at some points, from Phoebe.

The differences are as striking as the resemblances. Some of the changes were required by the genre. For example, Shakespeare omits an internal debate of Rosader's on whether to save his brother, condensing the gist of a passage of over five hundred words into two and a half lines. Separate events are combined and compressed. Shakespeare omits two reconciliations between Rosader and Saladyne and in place of a sequence where Rosader is chained as a lunatic by Saladyne and then set free by Adam with whose help he kills some of his brother's guests, Shakespeare has the brief third scene of the second act. Some material is rearranged so that major plot lines are not long lost to sight. Whereas in Lodge the Rosader-Saladyne plot is dropped for about fifteen pages when Alinda and Rosalynde appear in the forest, in Shakespeare Orlando flees to the forest at about the same time as the two girls. Lodge develops his three love affairs consecutively; one is virtually completed before the next is begun, and each is developed at almost equal length. Shakespeare quickly disposes of the Celia-Oliver romance and has Phebe fall in love with Ganymede much earlier than does Lodge. He is thus able to develop the love affairs concurrently, including the added one of Audrey and Touchstone, and to play them off one against the other.

Shakespeare retains little of the brutality of the novel. Orlando is far gentler than Rosader, the wrestler and his young opponents are injured rather than killed, and Saladyne's rescue of the ladies from a band of robbers is omitted. For Lodge's final battle in which Torismond, the usurper, dies, Shakespeare substitutes the miraculous conversion of Duke Frederick. The diminution of action and violence is in harmony with the spirit of the play and allows Shakespeare to develop contrasting emotions, values, and attitudes. Even when Shakespeare adheres to the general outline of a conversation in Lodge, he so alters the details that what is stilted in the novel becomes vivid, natural, engaging.

A few of Shakespeare's smaller changes can be mentioned here. Shakespeare gives far greater emphasis to Adam's age and long, faithful service. He links the two groups of court characters by making the two dukes brothers and the dead Sir Rowland de Boys an enemy of Duke Frederick. In Lodge, Rosalynde and Alinda see Rosader-Orlando in the forest at the same time; in Shakespeare, Celia sees him first, and her report to Rosalind allows us to see Rosalind's impulsive reaction and to hear some witty byplay.

Perhaps the most significant change is the addition of Jaques and Touchstone (Audrey, William, Mar-text, and Le Beau are far less important additions). Jaques and Touchstone have little effect on the development of the plot, but the Forest of Arden would be a duller and less realistic place without their presence. They help transform a piece of prose fiction, which is charming and often skillfully narrated but intellectually thin and sometimes tedious, into a play as rich in wisdom and knowledge as it is in laughter.

## A NOTE ON THE TEXT

*As You Like It* did not appear in print until the First Folio of 1623. The text is a good one and may represent a carefully prepared promptbook. Act and scene division is intelligent; exits and entrances are for the most part correctly indicated; and the stage directions are brief but generally adequate. The present edition follows the Folio text closely, admitting only those emendations that seem clearly necessary. A few directions not in the Folio but helpful in clarifying the action are placed in brackets. Spelling and punctuation are modernized, speech prefixes are extended from abbreviations, obvious typographical errors and mislineation are corrected, and the Latin divisions into act and scene are translated. Other significant departures from the Folio (F) are listed below, the present reading in boldface type followed by F's reading in roman.

**I.i.107 she** hee   **158 Oliver** [F omits]
**I.ii.3 yet I were** yet were   **51 goddesses and hath** goddesses, hath   **82 Celia** Ros   **90 Le Beau** the Beu   **285 Rosalind** Rosaline [from here on, F uses either form]

**I.iii.77 her patience** per patience
**II.i.49 much** must   **59 of the country** of Countrie
**II.iii.10 some** seeme   **16 Orlando** [F omits]   **29 Orlando** Ad[am]   **71 seventeen** seauentie
**II.iv.1 weary** merry   **42 thy wound** they would   **67 you, friend** your friend
**II.v.1 Amiens** [F omits]   **41–42 no enemy . . . weather** &c   **46 Jaques** Amy [i.e., Amiens]
**II.vii.55 Not to seem** Seeme   **87 comes** come   **173 Amiens** [F omits]   **181 Then** the
**III.ii.125 this a desert** this Desert   **145 her** his   **155 pulpiter** Iupiter   **258 b' wi'** buy   **361 deifying** defying
**III.iv.29 of a lover** of Louer
**III.v.127–28 yet I have** yet Haue
**IV.i.1 me be better** me better   **18 my** by   **29 b' wi'** buy   **208 in, it** in, in
**IV.ii.7 Another Lord** Lord
**IV.iii.5 s.d. Enter Silvius** [F places after "brain"]   **8 Phebe bid** Phebe, did bid   **141 In** I   **154 his blood** this bloud
**V.ii.7 nor her sudden** nor sodaine
**V.iii.18 In springtime** In the spring time   **15–32** [the fourth stanza here appears as the second in F]   **39 b' wi'** buy
**V.iv.34 s.d. Enter . . . Audrey** [F prints after line 33]   **81 so to the** so ro   **114 her hand** his hand   **164 them** him   **197 we will** wee'l

# AS YOU LIKE IT

[Dramatis Personae

DUKE SENIOR *in banishment in the Forest of Arden*
DUKE FREDERICK *his brother, usurper of the dukedom*
AMIENS ⎱
JAQUES ⎰ *lords attending on Duke Senior*
LE BEAU *a courtier*
CHARLES *a wrestler*
OLIVER ⎱
JAQUES ⎰ *sons of Sir Rowland de Boys*
ORLANDO ⎰
ADAM ⎱ *servants to Oliver*
DENNIS ⎰

TOUCHSTONE *a clown*
SIR OLIVER MAR-TEXT *a vicar*
CORIN ⎱ *shepherds*
SILVIUS ⎰
WILLIAM *a country fellow*
HYMEN
ROSALIND *daughter to Duke Senior*
CELIA *daughter to Duke Frederick*
PHEBE *a shepherdess*
AUDREY *a country girl*
LORDS    PAGES   FORESTERS   ATTENDANTS

*Scene:* Oliver's house; the court; the Forest of Arden]

## ACT I

Scene I. [*Orchard of Oliver's house.*]

*Enter* ORLANDO *and* ADAM.

ORLANDO  As I remember, Adam, it was upon this fashion bequeathed me by will but poor a° thousand crowns, and, as thou say'st, charged my brother on his blessing to breed me well; and there begins my sadness. My brother Jaques he keeps at school, and report 5 speaks goldenly of his profit.° For my part, he keeps me rustically° at home or, to speak more properly, stays me here at home unkept;° for call you that keeping for a gentleman of my birth that differs not from the stalling of an ox? His horses are bred better, 10 for, besides that they are fair° with their feeding, they are taught their manage,° and to that end riders dearly

*The decorative border shown above appeared on the first page of* As You Like It *in the First Folio edition of Shakespeare's plays, 1623.*

**I.i.2 poor a** a mere  **6 goldenly . . . profit** glowingly of his progress  **6–7 keeps me rustically** supports me like a peasant  **8 unkept** uncared for  **11 fair** handsome  **12 manage** paces

hired; but I, his brother, gain nothing under him but growth, for the which his animals on his dunghills are as much bound to him as I. Besides this nothing 15 that he so plentifully gives me, the something that nature gave me his countenance° seems to take from me. He lets me feed with his hinds,° bars me the place of a brother, and, as much as in him lies, mines my gentility° with my education. This is it, Adam, that 20 grieves me; and the spirit of my father, which I think is within me, begins to mutiny against this servitude. I will no longer endure it, though yet I know no wise remedy how to avoid it.

*Enter* OLIVER.

ADAM  Yonder comes my master, your brother. 25
ORLANDO  Go apart, Adam, and thou shalt hear how he will shake me up.°
OLIVER  Now, sir, what make you° here?

**17 countenance** behavior  **18 hinds** farm hands  **19–20 mines my gentility** undermines my good birth  **27 shake me up** berate me  **28 make you** are you doing (in the next line Orlando pretends to take the phrase to mean "accomplish")

ORLANDO  Nothing. I am not taught to make any- 30
thing.

OLIVER  What mar you then, sir?

ORLANDO  Marry,° sir, I am helping you to mar that
which God made, a poor unworthy brother of yours,
with idleness.

OLIVER  Marry, sir, be better employed, and be naught 35
awhile.°

ORLANDO  Shall I keep your hogs and eat husks with
them? What prodigal portion have I spent° that I
should come to such penury?

OLIVER  Know you where° you are, sir? 40

ORLANDO  O, sir, very well. Here in your orchard.

OLIVER  Know you before whom, sir?

ORLANDO  Ay, better than him I am before knows
me. I know you are my eldest brother, and in the
gentle condition of blood° you should so know me. 45
The courtesy of nations° allows you my better in that
you are the first born, but the same tradition takes not
away my blood were there twenty brothers betwixt us.
I have as much of my father in me as you, albeit I
confess your coming before me is nearer to his 50
reverence.°

OLIVER  What, boy!

[Strikes him.]

ORLANDO  Come, come, elder brother, you are too
young in this.

[Seizes him.]

OLIVER  Wilt thou lay hands on me, villain?° 55

ORLANDO  I am no villain. I am the youngest son of
Sir Rowland de Boys; he was my father, and he is
thrice a villain that says such a father begot villains.
Wert thou not my brother, I would not take this hand
from thy throat till this other had pulled out thy 60
tongue for saying so. Thou hast railed on thyself.

ADAM  Sweet masters, be patient. For your father's
remembrance, be at accord.

OLIVER  Let me go, I say.

ORLANDO  I will not till I please. You shall hear me. My 65
father charged you in his will to give me good education. You have trained me like a peasant, obscuring
and hiding from me all gentlemanlike qualities.° The
spirit of my father grows strong in me, and I will no
longer endure it. Therefore allow me such exercises° 70
as may become a gentleman, or give me the poor
allottery° my father left me by testament; with that I
will go buy my fortunes.

OLIVER  And what wilt thou do? Beg when that is
spent? Well, sir, get you in. I will not long be troubled 75
with you. You shall have some part of your will. I
pray you leave me.

ORLANDO  I will no further offend you than becomes
me for my good.

OLIVER  Get you with him, you old dog. 80

ADAM  Is "old dog" my reward? Most true, I have lost
my teeth in your service. God be with my old master;
he would not have spoke such a word.

                    Exeunt ORLANDO, ADAM.

OLIVER  Is it even so? Begin you to grow upon me?° I
will physic your rankness° and yet give no thousand 85
crowns neither. Holla, Dennis!

Enter DENNIS.

DENNIS  Calls your worship?

OLIVER  Was not Charles, the duke's wrestler, here to
speak with me?

DENNIS  So please you, he is here at the door and 90
importunes access to you.

OLIVER  Call him in. [Exit DENNIS.] 'Twill be a good
way; and tomorrow the wrestling is.

Enter CHARLES.

CHARLES  Good morrow to your worship.

OLIVER  Good Monsieur Charles, what's the new 95
news at the new court?

CHARLES  There's no news at the court, sir, but the old
news. That is, the old duke° is banished by his younger
brother the new duke, and three or four loving lords
have put themselves into voluntary exile with him, 100
whose lands and revenues enrich the new duke;
therefore he gives them good leave to wander.

OLIVER  Can you tell if Rosalind, the duke's daughter,
be banished with her father?

CHARLES  O, no; for the duke's daughter, her cousin, 105
so loves her, being ever from their cradles bred together, that she would have followed her exile, or
have died to stay behind her. She is at the court, and
no less beloved of her uncle than his own daughter,
and never two ladies loved as they do. 110

OLIVER  Where will the old duke live?

CHARLES  They say he is already in the Forest of
Arden,° and a many merry men with him; and there
they live like the old Robin Hood of England. They
say many young gentlemen flock to him every day, 115
and fleet the time carelessly° as they did in the golden
world.°

OLIVER  What, you wrestle tomorrow before the new
duke?

CHARLES  Marry, do I, sir; and I came to acquaint you 120
with a matter. I am given, sir, secretly to understand
that your younger brother, Orlando, hath a disposition
to come in disguised against me to try a fall.° Tomorrow, sir, I wrestle for my credit, and he that
escapes me without some broken limb shall acquit 125
him well. Your brother is but young and tender, and
for your love I would be loath to foil° him, as I must
for my own honor if he come in. Therefore, out of

32 Marry an expletive, from "By the Virigin Mary"   35–36
be naught awhile don't bother me   37–38 Shall . . . spent
an allusion to the story of the Prodigal Son. See Luke 15:11–32
40 where in whose presence (Orlando pretends to take it
literally)   44–45 in . . . blood of the same good blood   46
courtesy of nations sanctioned custom of primogeniture
50–51 your . . . reverence as the eldest son you are head
of the family and therefore entitled to respect   55 villain
Oliver uses it in the sense of "wicked person," but Orlando
plays on its other meaning, "low-born person"   68 qualities
accomplishments   70 exercises occupations   72 allottery
share

84 grow upon me usurp my place   85 physic your rankness
purge your overgrowth   98 old duke Duke Senior   112–13
Forest of Arden Ardennes (in France; though Shakespeare
may also have had in mind the Forest of Arden near his
birthplace)   116 fleet . . . carelessly pass the time at ease
116–17 golden world the Golden Age of classical mythology,
when men were free of sin, want, and care   123 fall bout   127
foil throw, defeat

my love to you, I came hither to acquaint you withal,
that either you might stay him from his intendment, 130
or brook° such disgrace well as he shall run into, in
that it is a thing of his own search and altogether
against my will.

OLIVER   Charles, I thank thee for thy love to me, which
thou shalt find I will most kindly requite. I had myself 135
notice of my brother's purpose herein and have by
underhand means° labored to dissuade him from it;
but he is resolute. I'll tell thee, Charles, it is the stub-
bornest young fellow of France; full of ambition, an
envious emulator° of every man's good parts,° a 140
secret and villainous contriver against me his natural°
brother. Therefore use thy discretion. I had as lief°
thou didst break his neck as his finger. And thou wert
best look to't; for if thou dost him any slight disgrace,
or if he do not mightily grace himself on thee,° he will 145
practice° against thee by poison, entrap thee by some
treacherous device, and never leave thee till he hath
ta'en thy life by some indirect means or other; for, I
assure thee, and almost with tears I speak it, there is
not one so young and so villainous this day living. I 150
speak but brotherly of him, but should I anatomize°
him to thee as he is, I must blush and weep, and thou
must look pale and wonder.

CHARLES   I am heartily glad I came hither to you. If he
come tomorrow, I'll give him his payment. If ever he 155
go alone° again, I'll never wrestle for prize more. And
so God keep your worship.            *Exit.*

OLIVER   Farewell, good Charles. Now will I stir this
gamester.° I hope I shall see an end of him; for my
soul, yet I know not why, hates nothing more than 160
he. Yet he's gentle,° never schooled and yet learned,
full of noble device,° of all sorts° enchantingly beloved;
and indeed so much in the heart of the world, and
especially of my own people, who best know him, that
I am altogether misprized.° But it shall not be so long; 165
this wrestler shall clear all.° Nothing remains but that
I kindle the boy thither, which now I'll go about.
                               *Exit.*

Scene II. [*The duke's palace.*]

*Enter* ROSALIND *and* CELIA.

CELIA   I pray thee, Rosalind, sweet my coz,° be merry.

ROSALIND   Dear Celia, I show more mirth than I am
mistress of, and would you yet I were merrier? Unless
you could teach me to forget a banished father, you
must not learn° me how to remember any extra- 5
ordinary pleasure.

CELIA   Herein I see thou lov'st me not with the full
weight that I love thee. If my uncle, thy banished
father, had banished thy uncle, the duke my father,

so° thou hadst been still with me, I could have taught 10
my love to take thy father for mine. So wouldst thou,
if the truth of thy love to me were so righteously
tempered° as mine is to thee.

ROSALIND   Well, I will forget the condition of my
estate° to rejoice in yours. 15

CELIA   You know my father hath no child but I, nor
none is like to have; and truly, when he dies, thou
shalt be his heir; for what he hath taken away from
thy father perforce,° I will render thee again in affection. By mine honor, I will, and when I break that 20
oath, let me turn monster. Therefore, my sweet Rose,
my dear Rose, be merry.

ROSALIND   From henceforth I will, coz, and devise
sports. Let me see, what think you of falling in love?

CELIA   Marry, I prithee, do, to make sport withal; but 25
love no man in good earnest, nor no further in sport
neither than with safety of a pure° blush thou mayst
in honor come off° again.

ROSALIND   What shall be our sport then?

CELIA   Let us sit and mock the good housewife° 30
Fortune from her wheel,° that her gifts may henceforth
be bestowed equally.

ROSALIND   I would we could do so, for her benefits
are mightily misplaced, and the bountiful blind
woman doth most mistake in her gifts to women. 35

CELIA   'Tis true, for those that she makes fair,° she
scarce makes honest,° and those that she makes honest,
she makes very ill-favoredly.°

ROSALIND   Nay, now thou goest from Fortune's
office° to Nature's. Fortune reigns in gifts of the world,° 40
not in the lineaments of Nature.°

*Enter* [TOUCHSTONE *the*] *clown.*

CELIA   No; when Nature hath made a fair creature,
may she not by Fortune fall into the fire? Though
Nature hath given us wit to flout at Fortune, hath not
Fortune sent in this fool to cut off the argument? 45

ROSALIND   Indeed, there is Fortune too hard for
Nature when Fortune makes Nature's natural° the
cutter-off of Nature's wit.

CELIA   Peradventure° this is not Fortune's work
neither, but Nature's, who perceiveth our natural wits 50
too dull to reason of such goddesses and hath sent this
natural for our whetstone. For always the dullness of
the fool is the whetstone of the wits. How now, wit;
whither wander you?

TOUCHSTONE   Mistress, you must come away to your 55
father.

CELIA   Were you made the messenger?

TOUCHSTONE   No, by mine honor, but I was bid to
come for you.

ROSALIND   Where learned you that oath, fool? 60

---

131 **brook** endure   136–37 **by underhand means** indirectly
140 **envious emulator** malicious rival; **parts** abilities   141
**natural** blood   142 **lief** soon   145 **grace . . . thee** gain
credit at your expense   146 **practice** plot   151 **anatomize**
fully describe   156 **go alone** walk without crutches   159
**gamester** athlete, sportsman   161 **gentle** endowed with the
qualities of a gentleman   162 **noble device** gentlemanlike
purposes; **all sorts** all kinds of people   165 **misprized** scorned
166 **clear all** settle matters
**I.ii.1 sweet my coz** my sweet cousin   5 **learn** teach

10 **so** provided that   12–13 **righteously tempered** perfectly composed   15 **estate** fortune   19 **perforce** forcibly
27 **pure** mere   28 **come off** get away   30 **housewife** (1)
woman of the house (with a spinning wheel) (2) inconstant
hussy   31 **wheel** the wheel turned by Fortune, blind goddess
who distributed her favors at random, elevated some men and
hurled others down   36 **fair** beautiful   37 **honest** chaste
38 **ill-favoredly** ugly   40 **office** function; **gifts . . .
world** e.g., wealth, power   41 **lineaments of Nature** e.g.,
virtue, intelligence   47 **natural** born fool, halfwit   49
**Peradventure** perhaps

TOUCHSTONE  Of a certain knight that swore by his honor they were good pancakes, and swore by his honor the mustard was naught.° Now I'll stand to it,° the pancakes were naught, and the mustard was good, and yet was not the knight forsworn.°   65

CELIA  How prove you that in the great heap of your knowledge?

ROSALIND  Ay, marry, now unmuzzle your wisdom.

TOUCHSTONE  Stand you both forth now. Stroke your chins, and swear by your beards that I am a  70 knave.

CELIA  By our beards, if we had them, thou art.

TOUCHSTONE  By my knavery, if I had it, then I were; but if you swear by that that is not, you are not forsworn; no more was this knight, swearing by his  75 honor, for he never had any; or if he had, he had sworn it away before ever he saw those pancakes or that mustard.

CELIA  Prithee, who is't that thou mean'st?

TOUCHSTONE  One that old Frederick, your father,  80 loves.

CELIA  My father's love is enough to honor him enough. Speak no more of him; you'll be whipped for taxation° one of these days.

TOUCHSTONE  The more pity that fools may not  85 speak wisely what wise men do foolishly.

CELIA  By my troth,° thou sayest true, for since the little wit that fools have was silenced, the little foolery that wise men have makes a great show. Here comes Monsieur Le Beau.   90

*Enter LE BEAU.*

ROSALIND  With his mouth full of news.

CELIA  Which he will put° on us as pigeons feed their young.

ROSALIND  Then shall we be news-crammed.

CELIA  All the better; we shall be the more marketable.  95 Bon jour, Monsieur Le Beau, what's the news?

LE BEAU  Fair princess, you have lost much good sport.

CELIA  Sport? Of what color?°

LE BEAU  What color, madam? How shall I answer  100 you?

ROSALIND  As wit and fortune° will.

TOUCHSTONE  Or as the Destinies decrees.°

CELIA  Well said; that was laid on with a trowel.

TOUCHSTONE  Nay, if I keep not my rank—   105

ROSALIND  Thou losest thy old smell.

LE BEAU  You amaze° me, ladies. I would have told you of good wrestling, which you have lost the sight of.°

ROSALIND  Yet tell us the manner of the wrestling.   110

LE BEAU  I will tell you the beginning; and if it please your ladyships, you may see the end, for the best is yet to do,° and here, where you are, they are coming to perform it.

CELIA  Well, the beginning that is dead and buried.   115

LE BEAU  There comes an old man and his three sons—

CELIA  I could match this beginning with an old tale.°

LE BEAU  Three proper° young men, of excellent growth and presence.

ROSALIND  With bills° on their necks "Be it known  120 unto all men by these presents."°

LE BEAU  The eldest of the three wrestled with Charles, the duke's wrestler; which Charles in a moment threw him and broke three of his ribs, that there is little hope of life in him. So he served the second, and  125 so the third. Yonder they lie, the poor old man, their father, making such pitiful dole° over them that all the beholders take his part with weeping.

ROSALIND  Alas!

TOUCHSTONE  But what is the sport, monsieurs that  130 the ladies have lost?

LE BEAU  Why, this that I speak of.

TOUCHSTONE  Thus men may grow wiser every day. It is the first time that ever I heard breaking of ribs was sport for ladies.   135

CELIA  Or I, I promise thee.

ROSALIND  But is there any° else longs to see this broken music° in his sides? Is there yet another dotes upon rib-breaking? Shall we see this wrestling, cousin?

LE BEAU  You must, if you stay here, for here is the  140 place appointed for the wrestling, and they are ready to perform it.

CELIA  Yonder sure they are coming. Let us now stay and see it.

*Flourish.° Enter* DUKE [FREDERICK], LORDS, ORLANDO, CHARLES, *and* ATTENDANTS.

DUKE FREDERICK  Come on. Since the youth will not  145 be entreated, his own peril on his forwardness.

ROSALIND  Is yonder the man?

LE BEAU  Even he, madam.

CELIA  Alas, he is too young; yet he looks successfully.°

DUKE FREDERICK  How now, daughter and cousin;  150 are you crept hither to see the wrestling?

ROSALIND  Ay, my liege, so please you give us leave.

DUKE FREDERICK  Your will take little delight in it, I can tell you, there is such odds in the man.° In pity of the challenger's youth I would fain° dissuade him, but  155 he will not be entreated. Speak to him, ladies; see if you can move him.

CELIA  Call him hither, good Monsieur Le Beau.

DUKE FREDERICK  Do so. I'll not be by.

LE BEAU  Monsieur the challenger, the princess calls  160 for you.

ORLANDO  I attend them with all respect and duty.

ROSALIND  Young man, have you challenged Charles the wrestler?

ORLANDO  No, fair princess. He is the general chal-  165 lenger; I come but in as others do, to try with him the strength of my youth.

CELIA  Young gentleman, your spirits are too bold for

---

63 **naught** worthless; **stand to it** swear  65 **forsworn** perjured  84 **taxation** slander  87 **troth** faith  92 **put** force  99 **color** sort  102 **fortune** good luck  103 **decrees** the ending *-s* was a common variant in the third person plural  107 **amaze** confuse  108–09 **lost . . . of** missed  113 **do** be done  117 **old tale** Le Beau's story has a "Once upon a time" beginning  118 **proper** fine  120 **bills** notices  121 **by these presents** part of the opening formula of many legal documents; Rosalind puns on Le Beau's use of "presence," meaning "bearing"  127 **dole** lamentation  137 **any** anyone  138 **broken music** music arranged in parts for different instruments  144 **s.d. Flourish** trumpet fanfare  149 **successfully** able to succeed  154 **such . . . man** the odds are all in Charles' favor  155 **fain** like to

your years. You have seen cruel proof of this man's
strength; if you saw yourself with your eyes or knew 170
yourself with your judgment, the fear of your adventure would counsel you to a more equal enterprise.
We pray you for your own sake to embrace your own
safety and give over this attempt.

ROSALIND  Do, young sir. Your reputation shall not 175
therefore be misprized;° we will make it our suit to the
duke that the wrestling might not go forward.

ORLANDO  I beseech you, punish me not with your
hard thoughts, wherein I confess me much guilty to
deny so fair and excellent ladies anything. But let your 180
fair eyes and gentle wishes go with me to my trial;
wherein if I be foiled,° there is but one shamed that
was never gracious;° if killed, but one dead that is
willing to be so. I shall do my friends no wrong, for I
have none to lament me; the world no injury, for in 185
it I have nothing. Only in the world I° fill up a place,
which may be better supplied when I have made it
empty.

ROSALIND  The little strength that I have, I would it
were with you. 190

CELIA  And mine to eke° out hers.

ROSALIND  Fare you well. Pray heaven I be deceived
in you!°

CELIA  Your heart's desires be with you!

CHARLES  Come, where is this young gallant that is so 195
desirous to lie with his mother earth?

ORLANDO  Ready, sir; but his will hath in it a more
modest working.°

DUKE FREDERICK  You shall try but one fall.

CHARLES  No, I warrant your grace you shall not 200
entreat him to a second that have so mightily persuaded
him from a first.

ORLANDO  You mean to mock me after. You should
not have mocked me before. But come your ways.°

ROSALIND  Now Hercules be thy speed,° young man! 205

CELIA  I would I were invisible, to catch the strong
fellow by the leg.

*Wrestle.*

ROSALIND  O excellent young man!

CELIA  If I had a thunderbolt in mine eye, I can tell
who should down. 210

[CHARLES *is thrown.] Shout.*

DUKE FREDERICK  No more, no more.

ORLANDO  Yes, I beseech your grace; I am not yet
well breathed.°

DUKE FREDERICK  How dost thou, Charles?

LE BEAU  He cannot speak, my lord. 215

DUKE FREDERICK  Bear him away. What is thy name,
young man?

ORLANDO  Orlando, my liege, the youngest son of
Sir Rowland de Boys.

DUKE FREDERICK
I would thou hadst been son to some man else. 220

The world esteemed thy father honorable,
But I did find him still mine enemy.
Thou shouldst have better pleased me with this deed
Hadst thou descended from another house.
But fare thee well; thou art a gallant youth; 225
I would thou hadst told me of another father.
                    *Exit* DUKE [FREDERICK, *with* TRAIN].

CELIA
Were I my father, coz, would I do this?

ORLANDO
I am more proud to be Sir Rowland's son,
His youngest son, and would not change that calling°
To be adopted heir to Frederick. 230

ROSALIND
My father loved Sir Rowland as his soul,
And all the world was of my father's mind.
Had I before known this young man his son,
I should have given him tears unto° entreaties
Ere he should thus have ventured.

CELIA                    Gentle cousin, 235
Let us go thank him and encourage him.
My father's rough and envious disposition
Sticks° me at heart. Sir, you have well deserved;
If you do keep your promises in love
But justly° as you have exceeded all promise, 240
Your mistress shall be happy.

ROSALIND                    Gentleman, [*gives chain*]
Wear this for me, one out of suits° with Fortune,
That could° give more but that her hand lacks means.
Shall we go, coz?

CELIA                    Ay. Fare you well, fair gentleman.

ORLANDO
Can I not say, "I thank you"? My better parts° 245
Are all thrown down, and that which here stands up
Is but a quintain,° a mere lifeless block.

ROSALIND
He calls us back. My pride fell with my fortunes;
I'll ask him what he would. Did you call, sir?
Sir, you have wrestled well, and overthrown 250
More than your enemies.

CELIA                    Will you go, coz?

ROSALIND
Have with you.° Fare you well.    *Exit,* [*with* CELIA].

ORLANDO
What passion° hangs these weights upon my tongue?
I cannot speak to her, yet she urged conference.°

*Enter* LE BEAU.

O poor Orlando, thou art overthrown! 255
Or Charles or something weaker masters thee.

LE BEAU
Good sir, I do in friendship counsel you
To leave this place. Albeit you have deserved
High commendation, true applause, and love,
Yet such is now the duke's condition 260
That he misconsters° all that you have done.

176 misprized despised  182 foiled thrown  183 gracious
graced by Fortune  186 Only . . . I in the world I only
191 eke stretch  192–193 deceived in you wrong in my
estimation of your strength  198 modest working humble
aim  204 come your ways let's get started  205 Hercules
. . . speed may Hercules help you  213 well breathed
fully warmed up

222 still always  229 calling name  234 unto as well as
238 Sticks pains  240 justly exactly  242 out of suits in
disfavor  243 could would  245 parts qualities  247 quintain
wooden post (used for tilting practice)  252 Have with you
I'm coming  253 passion strong feeling  254 conference
conversation  261 misconsters misinterprets

The duke is humorous.° What he is, indeed,
More suits you to conceive° than I to speak of.
ORLANDO
I thank you, sir; and pray you, tell me this:
Which of the two was daughter of the duke,    265
That here was at the wrestling?
LE BEAU
Neither his daughter, if we judge by manners,
But yet indeed the taller° is his daughter,
The other is daughter to the banished duke,
And here detained by her usurping uncle    270
To keep his daughter company, whose loves
Are dearer than the natural bond of sisters.
But I can tell you that of late this duke
Hath ta'en displeasure 'gainst his gentle niece,
Grounded upon no other argument°    275
But that the people praise her for her virtues
And pity her for her good father's sake;
And, on my life, his malice 'gainst the lady
Will suddenly break forth. Sir, fare you well.
Hereafter, in a better world° than this,    280
I shall desire more love and knowledge of you.
ORLANDO
I rest much bounden° to you. Fare you well.

                    [*Exit* LE BEAU.]

Thus must I from the smoke into the smother,°
From tyrant duke unto a tyrant brother.
But heavenly Rosalind!    *Exit.* 285


Scene III. [*The palace.*]

*Enter* CELIA *and* ROSALIND.

CELIA  Why, cousin, why, Rosalind! Cupid have
mercy, not a word?
ROSALIND  Not one to throw at a dog.
CELIA  No, thy words are too precious to be cast away
upon curs; throw some of them at me; come, lame    5
me with reasons.
ROSALIND  Then there were two cousins laid up,
when the one should be lamed with reasons and the
other mad° without any.
CELIA  But is all this for your father?    10
ROSALIND  No, some of it is for my child's father.° O,
how full of briers is this working-day world!
CELIA  They are but burrs, cousin, thrown upon thee
in holiday foolery; if we walk not in the trodden
paths, our very petticoats will catch them.    15
ROSALIND  I could shake them off my coat; these
burrs are in my heart.
CELIA  Hem° them away.
ROSALIND  I would try, if I could cry "hem,"° and
have him.    20
CELIA  Come, come, wrestle with thy affections.°

ROSALIND  O, they take the part of a better wrestler
than myself!
CELIA  O, a good wish upon you! You will try° in
time, in despite of a fall. But turning these jests out of    25
service,° let us talk in good earnest. Is it possible on
such a sudden you should fall into so strong a liking
with old Sir Rowland's youngest son?
ROSALIND  The duke my father loved his father
dearly.    30
CELIA  Doth it therefore ensue that you should love
his son dearly? By this kind of chase,° I should hate
him, for my father hated his father dearly; yet I hate
not Orlando.
ROSALIND  No, faith, hate him not, for my sake.    35
CELIA  Why should I not? Doth he not deserve well?°

*Enter* DUKE [FREDERICK], *with* LORDS.

ROSALIND  Let me love him for that,° and do you love
him because I do. Look, here comes the duke.
CELIA  With his eyes full of anger.
DUKE FREDERICK
Mistress, dispatch you with your safest haste    40
And get you from our court.
ROSALIND                            Me, uncle?
DUKE FREDERICK                            You, cousin.°
Within these ten days if that thou beest found
So near our public court as twenty miles,
Thou diest for it.
ROSALIND          I do beseech your grace
Let me the knowledge of my fault bear with me.    45
If with myself I hold intelligence°
Or have acquaintance with mine own desires,
If that I do not dream or be not frantic,°
As I do trust I am not; then, dear uncle,
Never so much as in a thought unborn    50
Did I offend your highness.
DUKE FREDERICK          Thus do all traitors.
If their purgation° did consist in words,
They are as innocent as grace° itself.
Let it suffice thee that I trust thee not.
ROSALIND
Yet your mistrust cannot make me a traitor.    55
Tell me whereon the likelihoods° depends.
DUKE FREDERICK
Thou art thy father's daughter, there's enough.
ROSALIND
So was I when your highness took his dukedom;
So was I when your highness banished him.
Treason is not inherited, my lord,    60
Or if we did derive it from our friends,°
What's that to me? My father was no traitor.
Then, good my liege, mistake me not so much
To think my poverty is treacherous.
CELIA
Dear sovereign, hear me speak.    65

262 **humorous** moody  263 **conceive** understand  268
**taller** unless "taller" is a printer's slip for "smaller," Shakespeare
here erred; Rosalind is later said to be taller  275 **argument**
basis  280 **a better world** better times  282 **bounden** indebted  283 **smother** smothering smoke (the idea is: "Out of
the frying pan into the fire")
**I.iii.9 mad** melancholy  11 **child's father** future husband,
Orlando  18 **Hem** (1) cough (2) tuck  19 **cry "hem"** clear
my throat (with a pun on *him*)  21 **affections** feelings

24 **try** chance a bout  25–26 **turning . . . service** to stop
joking  32 **chase** pursuit (of the argument)  36 **deserve well**
deserve to be hated (if Rosalind's reasoning is valid, it follows
that Celia should hate Orlando)  37 **for that** for his virtues
(Rosalind takes "deserve well" in its usual sense)  41 **cousin**
kinsman  46 **hold intelligence** communicate  48 **frantic**
insane  52 **purgation** clearance  53 **grace** virtue  56 **likelihoods** possibilities  61 **friends** relatives

**DUKE FREDERICK**
Ay, Celia. We stayed° her for your sake,
Else had she with her father ranged° along.

**CELIA**
I did not then entreat to have her stay;
It was your pleasure and your own remorse.°
I was too young that time to value her, 70
But now I know her. If she be a traitor,
Why, so am I. We still° have slept together,
Rose at an instant, learned, played, eat° together;
And wheresoe'er we went, like Juno's swans,
Still we went coupled and inseparable. 75

**DUKE FREDERICK**
She is too subtile° for thee; and her smoothness,
Her very silence and her patience,
Speak to the people, and they pity her.
Thou art a fool. She robs thee of thy name,
And thou wilt show more bright and seem more
   virtuous° 80
When she is gone. Then open not thy lips.
Firm and irrevocable is my doom°
Which I have passed upon her; she is banished.

**CELIA**
Pronounce that sentence then on me, my liege;
I cannot live out of her company. 85

**DUKE FREDERICK**
You are a fool. You, niece, provide yourself;
If you outstay the time, upon mine honor,
And in the greatness° of my word, you die.

                 *Exit* DUKE [FREDERICK], *&c.*

**CELIA**
O my poor Rosalind, whither wilt thou go?
Wilt thou change fathers? I will give thee mine. 90
I charge thee be not thou more grieved than I am.

**ROSALIND**
I have more cause.

**CELIA**           Thou hast not, cousin.
Prithee be cheerful. Know'st thou not the duke
Hath banished me, his daughter?

**ROSALIND**           That he hath not.

**CELIA**
No? Hath not? Rosalind lacks then the love 95
Which teacheth thee that thou and I am one.
Shall we be sund'red, shall we part, sweet girl?
No, let my father seek another heir.
Therefore devise with me how we may fly,
Whither to go, and what to bear with us; 100
And do not seek to take your change° upon you,
To bear your griefs yourself and leave me out;
For, by this heaven, now at our sorrows pale,°
Say what thou canst, I'll go along with thee.

**ROSALIND**
Why, whither shall we go? 105

**CELIA**
To seek my uncle in the Forest of Arden.

**ROSALIND**
Alas, what danger will it be to us,

Maids as we are, to travel forth so far!
Beauty provoketh thieves sooner than gold.

**CELIA**
I'll put myself in poor and mean° attire 110
And with a kind of umber° smirch my face;
The like do you; so shall we pass along
And never stir assailants.

**ROSALIND**           Were it not better,
Because that I am more than common° tall,
That I did suit me all points° like a man? 115
A gallant curtle-ax° upon my thigh,
A boar-spear in my hand; and, in my heart
Lie there what hidden woman's fear there will,
We'll have a swashing° and a martial outside,
As many other mannish cowards have 120
That do outface° it with their semblances.°

**CELIA**
What shall I call thee when thou art a man?

**ROSALIND**
I'll have no worse a name than Jove's own page,
And therefore look you call me Ganymede.
But what will you be called? 125

**CELIA**
Something that hath a reference to my state:
No longer Celia, but Aliena.°

**ROSALIND**
But, cousin, what if we assayed° to steal
The clownish fool out of your father's court;
Would he not be a comfort to our travel? 130

**CELIA**
He'll go along o'er the wide world with me;
Leave me alone to woo° him. Let's away
And get our jewels and our wealth together,
Devise the fittest time and safest way
To hide us from pursuit that will be made 135
After my flight. Now go in we content
To liberty, and not to banishment.      *Exeunt.*

# ACT II

### Scene I. [*The Forest of Arden.*]

*Enter* DUKE SENIOR, AMIENS, *and two or three* LORDS,
*like foresters.*

**DUKE SENIOR**
Now, my co-mates and brothers in exile,°
Hath not old custom made this life more sweet
Than that of painted pomp? Are not these woods
More free from peril than the envious court?
Here feel we not° the penalty of Adam;° 5
The seasons' difference, as° the icy fang
And churlish° chiding of the winter's wind,

---

66 **stayed** kept   67 **ranged** wandered   69 **remorse** pity
72 **still** always   73 **eat** eaten   76 **subtile** crafty   80 **virtuous**
full of good qualities   82 **doom** sentence   88 **greatness**
power   101 **change** change of fortune   103 **now . . . pale**
now pale at our sorrows

110 **mean** lowly   111 **umber** reddish-brown color   114
**common** usually   115 **suit . . . points** dress myself entirely
116 **curtle-ax** cutlass   119 **swashing** blustering   121 **outface** bluff; **semblances** appearances (of bravery)   127 **Aliena**
Latin = the estranged one   128 **assayed** attempted   132 **woo**
coax
**II.i.1 exile** accent on second syllable   5 **feel we not** we do not
feel (some editors emend "not" to "but"); **penalty of Adam**
loss of Eden   6 **as** for example   7 **churlish** harsh

Which, when it bites and blows upon my body
Even till I shrink with cold, I smile and say,
"This is no flattery; these are counselors 10
That feelingly° persuade me what I am."
Sweet are the uses of adversity,
Which, like the toad, ugly and venomous,
Wears yet a precious jewel° in his head;
And this our life, exempt from public haunt,° 15
Finds tongues in trees, books in the running brooks,
Sermons in stones, and good in everything.

AMIENS
I would not change it; happy is your grace
That can translate the stubbornness° of fortune
Into so quiet and so sweet a style. 20

DUKE SENIOR
Come, shall we go and kill us venison?
And yet it irks me the poor dappled fools,°
Being native burghers° of this desert° city,
Should, in their own confines, with forkèd heads°
Have their round haunches gored.

FIRST LORD                    Indeed, my lord, 25
The melancholy Jaques° grieves at that,
And in that kind° swears you do more usurp
Than doth your brother that hath banished you.
Today my Lord of Amiens and myself
Did steal behind him as he lay along° 30
Under an oak, whose antique root peeps out
Upon the brook that brawls° along this wood,
To the which place a poor sequest'red° stag
That from the hunter's aim had ta'en a hurt
Did come to languish; and indeed, my lord, 35
The wretched animal heaved forth such groans
That their discharge did stretch his leathern coat
Almost to bursting, and the big round tears
Coursed one another down his innocent nose
In piteous chase; and thus the hairy fool, 40
Much markèd of° the melancholy Jaques,
Stood on th' extremest verge of the swift brook,
Augmenting it with tears.

DUKE SENIOR                    But what said Jaques?
Did he not moralize° this spectacle?

FIRST LORD
O, yes, into a thousand similes. 45
First, for his weeping into the needless° stream:
"Poor deer," quoth he, "thou mak'st a testament
As worldlings do, giving thy sum of more
To that which had too much." Then, being there
    alone,
Left and abandoned of his velvet° friend: 50
"'Tis right," quoth he, "thus misery doth part
The flux° of company." Anon a careless° herd,
Full of the pasture, jumps along by him
And never stays to greet him; "Ay," quoth Jaques,

"Sweep on, you fat and greasy citizens, 55
'Tis just the fashion; wherefore do you look°
Upon that poor and broken bankrupt there?"
Thus most invectively he pierceth through
The body of the country, city, court,
Yea, and of this our life, swearing that we 60
Are mere usurpers, tyrants, and what's worse,
To fright the animals and to kill them up
In their assigned° and native dwelling place.

DUKE SENIOR
And did you leave him in this contemplation?

SECOND LORD
We did, my lord, weeping and commenting 65
Upon the sobbing deer.

DUKE SENIOR                    Show me the place.
I love to cope° him in these sullen fits,
For then he's full of matter.

FIRST LORD
I'll bring you to him straight.°                    Exeunt.


Scene II. [The palace.]

Enter DUKE [FREDERICK], with LORDS.

DUKE FREDERICK
Can it be possible that no man saw them?
It cannot be; some villains of my court
Are of consent and sufferance° in this.

FIRST LORD
I cannot hear of any that did see her.
The ladies, her attendants of her chamber, 5
Saw her abed, and in the morning early
They found the bed untreasured of their mistress.

SECOND LORD
My lord, the roynish° clown at whom so oft
Your grace was wont to laugh is also missing.
Hisperia, the princess' gentlewoman, 10
Confesses that she secretly o'erheard
Your daughter and her cousin much commend
The parts and graces° of the wrestler
That did but lately foil the sinewy Charles,
And she believes, wherever they are gone, 15
That youth is surely in their company.

DUKE FREDERICK
Send to his brother, fetch that gallant hither;
If he be absent, bring his brother to me;
I'll make him find him. Do this suddenly,°
And let not search and inquisition quail° 20
To bring again these foolish runaways.          Exeunt.


Scene III. [Oliver's house.]

Enter ORLANDO and ADAM.

ORLANDO  Who's there?

ADAM
What, my young master, O my gentle master,

11 feelingly (1) through the senses (2) with intensity   14 a
precious jewel the fabled toadstone   15 public haunt society
19 stubbornness hardness   22 fools simple creatures   23
burghers citizens; desert deserted   24 forkèd heads arrows
26 Jaques dissyllabic, pronounced "Jā′ kis"   27 kind way
30 along stretched out   32 brawls makes noise   33 sequest'-
red separated   41 markèd of noted by   44 moralize sermon-
ize   46 needless needing no more water   50 velvet i.e.,
courtierlike (the furry skin on the antlers, or the sleek hide,
makes the deer resemble a velvet-clad courtier)   52 flux
stream; Anon a careless soon an untroubled

56 wherefore . . . look why should you bother looking
63 assigned allotted (by nature)   67 cope encounter   69
straight at once
II.ii.3 Are . . . sufferance approved and helped   8 roynish
scurvy   13 parts and graces good qualities and manner
19 suddenly immediately   20 quail fail

O my sweet master, O you memory
Of old Sir Rowland, why, what make you° here?
Why are you virtuous? Why do people love you?                    5
And wherefore are you gentle, strong, and valiant?
Why would you be so fond° to overcome
The bonny prizer° of the humorous° duke?
Your praise is come too swiftly home before you.
Know you not, master, to some kind of men                        10
Their graces serve them but as enemies?
No more° do yours. Your virtues, gentle master,
Are sanctified and holy traitors to you.°
O, what a world is this, when what is comely
Envenoms him that bears it!                                      15

ORLANDO
Why, what's the matter?

ADAM                              O unhappy youth,
Come not within these doors; within this roof
The enemy of all your graces lives.
Your brother—no, no brother, yet the son—
Yet not the son, I will not call him son,                        20
Of him I was about to call his father—
Hath heard your praises, and this night he means
To burn the lodging where you use° to lie
And you within it. If he fail of that,
He will have other means to cut you off.                         25
I overheard him, and his practices;°
This is no place, this house is but a butchery;°
Abhor it, fear it, do not enter it!

ORLANDO
Why, whither, Adam, wouldst thou have me go?

ADAM
No matter whither, so you come not here.                         30

ORLANDO
What, wouldst thou have me go and beg my food,
Or with a base and boist'rous° sword enforce
A thievish living on the common road?°
This I must do, or know not what to do;
Yet this I will not do, do how I can.                            35
I rather will subject me to the malice
Of a diverted° blood and bloody brother.

ADAM
But do not so. I have five hundred crowns,
The thrifty hire I saved° under your father,
Which I did store to be my foster nurse                          40
When service should in my old limbs lie lame
And unregarded age in corners thrown.
Take that, and he that doth the ravens feed,
Yea, providently caters for the sparrow,°
Be comfort to my age. Here is the gold;                          45
All this I give you. Let me be your servant;
Though I look old, yet I am strong and lusty,
For in my youth I never did apply
Hot and rebellious° liquors in my blood,
Nor did not with unbashful forehead° woo                         50

The means of weakness and debility;
Therefore my age is as a lusty winter,
Frosty, but kindly. Let me go with you;
I'll do the service of a younger man
In all your business and necessities.                            55

ORLANDO
O good old man, how well in thee appears
The constant° service of the antique world,°
When service sweat for duty, not for meed!°
Thou art not for the fashion of these times,
Where none will sweat but for promotion,                         60
And having that, do choke their service up
Even with the having; it is not so with thee.
But, poor old man, thou prun'st a rotten tree
That cannot so much as a blossom yield
In lieu of° all thy pains and husbandry.                         65
But come thy ways, we'll go along together,
And ere we have thy youthful wages spent,
We'll light upon some settled low content.°

ADAM
Master, go on, and I will follow thee
To the last gasp with truth and loyalty.                         70
From seventeen years till now almost fourscore
Here lived I, but now live here no more;
At seventeen years many their fortunes seek,
But at fourscore it is too late a week;°
Yet fortune cannot recompense be better                          75
Than to die well and not my master's debtor. *Exeunt.*

Scene IV. [*The Forest of Arden.*]

*Enter* ROSALIND *for Ganymede,* CELIA *for Aliena, and
clown, alias* TOUCHSTONE.

ROSALIND   O Jupiter, how weary are my spirits!

TOUCHSTONE   I care not for my spirits if my legs were
not weary.

ROSALIND   I could find in my heart to disgrace my
man's apparel and to cry like a woman; but I must   5
comfort the weaker vessel, as doublet and hose° ought
to show itself courageous to petticoat. Therefore,
courage, good Aliena!

CELIA   I pray you bear with me; I cannot go no further.

TOUCHSTONE   For my part, I had rather bear with   10
you than bear you; yet I should bear no cross° if I did
bear you, for I think you have no money in your
purse.

ROSALIND   Well, this is the Forest of Arden.

TOUCHSTONE   Ay, now am I in Arden, the more fool   15
I. When I was at home, I was in a better place, but
travelers must be content.

*Enter* CORIN *and* SILVIUS.

ROSALIND
Ay, be so, good Touchstone. Look you, who comes
here,
A young man and an old in solemn talk.

II.iii.4 make you are you doing   7 fond foolish   8 bonny
prizer stout fighter; humorous moody, temperamental   12 No
more no better   12–13 Your . . . you Orlando's blessed
virtues have worked against him   23 use are accustomed
26 practices plots   27 butchery slaughterhouse   32 base and
boist'rous low and swaggering   33 common road highway
37 diverted estranged   39 thrifty . . . saved wages I
carefully saved   43–44 he . . . sparrow see Psalms 147:9,
Luke 12:6   49 rebellious causing the flesh to rebel   50
unbashful forehead bold face

57 constant faithful; the antique world the past   58 meed
reward   65 In lieu of in return for   68 low content humble
way of life   74 week time
II.iv.6 doublet and hose jacket and breeches   11 cross (1)
trouble (2) coin stamped with a cross

**CORIN**
That is the way to make her scorn you still.    20

**SILVIUS**
O Corin, that thou knew'st how I do love her!

**CORIN**
I partly guess, for I have loved ere now.

**SILVIUS**
No, Corin, being old, thou canst not guess,
Though in thy youth thou wast as true a lover
As ever sighed upon a midnight pillow.    25
But if thy love were ever like to mine,
As sure I think did never man love so,
How many actions most ridiculous
Hast thou been drawn to by thy fantasy?°

**CORIN**
Into a thousand that I have forgotten.    30

**SILVIUS**
O, thou didst then never love so heartily!
If thou rememb'rest not the slightest folly
That ever love did make thee run into,
Thou hast not loved.
Or if thou hast not sat as I do now,    35
Wearing° thy hearer in thy mistress' praise,
Thou hast not loved.
Or if thou hast not broke from company
Abruptly, as my passion now makes me,
Thou hast not loved.    40
O Phebe, Phebe, Phebe!        *Exit.*

**ROSALIND**
Alas, poor shepherd! Searching of° thy wound,
I have by hard adventure° found mine own.

**TOUCHSTONE** And I mine. I remember, when I was
in love I broke my sword upon a stone and bid him 45
take that for coming a-night to Jane Smile; and I
remember the kissing of her batler,° and the cow's
dugs that her pretty chopt° hands had milked; and I
remember the wooing of a peascod° instead of her,
from whom I took two cods, and giving her them 50
again, said with weeping tears, "Wear these for my
sake." We that are true lovers run into strange capers;
but as all is mortal in nature, so is all nature in love
mortal in folly.°

**ROSALIND** Thou speak'st wiser than thou art ware° of. 55

**TOUCHSTONE** Nay, I shall ne'er be ware of mine own
wit° till I break my shins against it.

**ROSALIND**
Jove, Jove! This shepherd's passion
Is much upon my fashion.

**TOUCHSTONE** And mine, but it grows something 60
stale with me.

**CELIA**
I pray you, one of you question yond man
If he for gold will give us any food.
I faint almost to death.

**TOUCHSTONE**        Holla, you clown!°

**ROSALIND**
Peace, fool! He's not thy kinsman.    65

**CORIN**
Who calls?

**TOUCHSTONE** Your betters, sir.

**CORIN**                 Else are they very wretched.

**ROSALIND**
Peace, I say! Good even to you, friend.

**CORIN**
And to you, gentle sir, and to you all.

**ROSALIND**
I prithee, shepherd, if that love or gold
Can in this desert place buy entertainment,°    70
Bring us where we may rest ourselves and feed.
Here's a young maid with travel much oppressed,
And faints for succor.

**CORIN**           Fair sir, I pity her
And wish, for her sake more than for mine own,
My fortunes were more able to relieve her;    75
But I am shepherd to another man
And do not shear the fleeces that I graze.
My master is of churlish° disposition
And little recks° to find the way to heaven
By doing deeds of hospitality.    80
Besides, his cote,° his flocks, and bounds of feed°
Are now on sale, and at our sheepcote now,
By reason of his absence, there is nothing
That you will feed on; but what is, come see,
And in my voice° most welcome shall you be.    85

**ROSALIND**
What is he that shall buy his flock and pasture?

**CORIN**
That young swain that you saw here but erewhile,°
That little cares for buying anything.

**ROSALIND**
I pray thee, if it stand° with honesty,
Buy thou the cottage, pasture, and the flock,    90
And thou shalt have° to pay for it of us.

**CELIA**
And we will mend° thy wages. I like this place
And willingly could waste° my time in it.

**CORIN**
Assuredly the thing is to be sold.
Go with me; if you like upon report    95
The soil, the profit, and this kind of life,
I will your very faithful feeder° be
And buy it with your gold right suddenly.        *Exeunt.*

Scene V. [*The forest.*]

*Enter* AMIENS, JAQUES, *and others.*

*Song.*

**AMIENS**
     Under the greenwood tree
       Who loves to lie with me,
     And turn° his merry note

---

**29 fantasy** love (and all its fancies)   **36 Wearing** exhausting
**42 Searching of** probing   **43 hard adventure** bad luck
**47 batler** wooden paddle (used in washing clothes)   **48 chopt**
chapped   **49 peascod** peapod   **52–54 as . . . folly** just as
everything that lives must die, so all who love inevitably do
foolish things   **55 art ware** know   **57 wit** wisdom   **64 clown**
(1) rustic (2) fool

**70 entertainment** food and shelter   **78 churlish** miserly
**79 recks** thinks   **81 cote** cottage; **bounds of feed** pastures
**85 in my voice** as far as my position allows   **87 erewhile** a
short while ago   **89 stand** be consistent   **91 have** have the
money   **92 mend** improve   **93 waste** spend   **97 feeder**
servant
**II.v.3 turn** attune, adapt

Unto the sweet bird's throat,
Come hither, come hither, come hither.                    5
Here shall he see no enemy
But winter and rough weather.

JAQUES  More, more, I prithee more!

AMIENS  It will make you melancholy, Monsieur
Jaques.                                                   10

JAQUES  I thank it. More, I prithee more! I can suck
melancholy out of a song as a weasel sucks eggs. More,
I prithee more!

AMIENS  My voice is ragged. I know I cannot please
you.                                                      15

JAQUES  I do not desire you to please me; I do desire
you to sing. Come, more, another stanzo! Call you
'em stanzos?

AMIENS  What you will, Monsieur Jaques.

JAQUES  Nay, I care not for their names; they owe me    20
nothing.° Will you sing?

AMIENS  More at your request than to please myself.

JAQUES  Well then, if ever I thank any man, I'll thank
you. But that they call compliment° is like th' encounter of two dog-apes,° and when a man thanks me    25
heartily, methinks I have given him a penny and he
renders me the beggarly thanks.° Come, sing; and you
that will not, hold your tongues.

AMIENS  Well, I'll end the song. Sirs, cover the while;°
the duke will drink under this tree. He hath been all   30
this day to look you.

JAQUES  And I have been all this day to avoid him. He
is too disputable for my company. I think of as many
matters as he, but I give heaven thanks and make no
boast of them. Come, warble, come.                      35

Song.
All together here.

Who doth ambition shun
And loves to live i' th' sun,
Seeking the food he eats,
And pleased with what he gets,
Come hither, come hither, come hither.                  40
Here shall he see no enemy
But winter and rough weather.

JAQUES  I'll give you a verse to this note° that I made
yesterday in despite of my invention.°

AMIENS  And I'll sing it.                                45

JAQUES  Thus it goes.

If it do come to pass
That any man turn ass,
Leaving his wealth and ease
A stubborn will to please,                              50
Ducdame,° ducdame, ducdame.
Here shall he see gross fools as he,
An if° he will come to me.

AMIENS  What's that "ducdame"?

JAQUES  'Tis a Greek° invocation to call fools into a    55
circle. I'll go sleep, if I can; if I cannot, I'll rail against all
the first-born of Egypt.°

AMIENS  And I'll go seek the duke. His banquet° is
prepared.                                      Exeunt.

## Scene VI. [*The forest.*]

*Enter* ORLANDO *and* ADAM.

ADAM  Dear master, I can go no further. O, I die for
food. Here lie I down and measure out my grave.
Farewell, kind master.

ORLANDO  Why, how now, Adam? No greater heart
in thee? Live a little, comfort° a little, cheer thyself a   5
little. If this uncouth° forest yield anything savage, I
will either be food for it or bring it for food to thee.
Thy conceit° is nearer death than thy powers. For my
sake be comfortable; hold death awhile at the arm's
end. I will here be with thee presently,° and if I bring   10
thee not something to eat, I will give thee leave to die;
but if thou diest before I come, thou art a mocker of
my labor. Well said; thou look'st cheerly, and I'll be
with thee quickly. Yet thou liest in the bleak air.
Come, I will bear thee to some shelter, and thou shalt   15
not die for lack of a dinner if there live anything in this
desert. Cheerly, good Adam.                    Exeunt.

## Scene VII. [*The forest.*]

*Enter* DUKE SENIOR, *and* LORDS, *like outlaws.*

DUKE SENIOR
I think he be transformed into a beast,
For I can nowhere find him like a man.

FIRST LORD
My lord, he is but even now gone hence;
Here was he merry, hearing of a song.

DUKE SENIOR
If he, compact of jars,° grow musical,                   5
We shall have shortly discord in the spheres.°
Go seek him; tell him I would speak with him.

*Enter* JAQUES.

FIRST LORD
He saves my labor by his own approach.

DUKE SENIOR
Why, how now, monsieur, what a life is this,
That your poor friends must woo your company?          10
What, you look merrily.

JAQUES
A fool, a fool! I met a fool i' th' forest,

---

20–21 names . . . nothing Jaques plays on the word *name*, a
term for the borrower's signature on a loan  24 compliment
politeness  25 dog-apes baboons  25–27 and when . . .
thanks the hearty thanks of polite society are no more sincere
than the extravagant gratitude of a beggar given a small coin
29 cover the while lay the table in the meantime  43 note
tune  44 in . . . invention without using my imagination
51 Ducdame various derivations have been suggested:
Romany *dukrā mē* ("I tell fortunes"); Welsh *de vch 'da mi*
("come with me"); Latin *duc ad me* ("bring [him] to me");
Italian *Duc' da mè* ("duke by myself" or "duke without a
dukedom"); probably the word is nonsense  53 An if if only

55 Greek unintelligible  57 first-born of Egypt perhaps
"persons of high rank," but perhaps an allusion to life in the
Forest of Arden: Exodus 11,12 reports that when the first-born
of Egypt died, the Israelites were sent into the wilderness  58
banquet light meal
II.vi.5 comfort take comfort  6 uncouth wild  8 conceit
thought  10 presently at once
II.vii.5 compact of jars made up of discord  6 discord . . .
spheres Ptolemaic astronomy taught that the planetary spheres
produced a ravishing harmony as they revolved

A motley° fool! A miserable world!
As I do live by food, I met a fool
Who laid him down and basked him in the sun          15
And railed on Lady Fortune in good terms,
In good set terms,° and yet a motley fool.
"Good morrow, fool," quoth I. "No, sir," quoth he,
"Call me not fool till heaven hath sent me fortune."°
And then he drew a dial from his poke,°              20
And looking on it with lack-luster eye,
Says very wisely, "It is ten o'clock.
Thus we may see," quoth he, "how the world wags.°
'Tis but an hour ago since it was nine,
And after one hour more 'twill be eleven;            25
And so, from hour to hour,° we ripe and ripe,
And then, from hour to hour, we rot and rot;
And thereby hangs a tale." When I did hear
The motley fool thus moral° on the time,
My lungs began to crow like chanticleer°            30
That fools should be so deep contemplative;
And I did laugh sans intermission°
An hour by his dial. O noble fool,
A worthy fool! Motley's the only wear.

DUKE SENIOR
What fool is this?                                   35

JAQUES
O worthy fool! One that hath been a courtier,
And says, if ladies be but young and fair,
They have the gift to know it. And in his brain,
Which is as dry as the remainder biscuit°
After a voyage, he hath strange places crammed      40
With observation, the which he vents°
In mangled forms. O that I were a fool!
I am ambitious for a motley coat.

DUKE SENIOR
Thou shalt have one.

JAQUES                    It is my only suit,°
Provided that you weed your better judgments         45
Of all opinion that grows rank° in them
That I am wise. I must have liberty
Withal, as large a charter° as the wind,
To blow on whom I please, for so fools have.
And they that are most gallèd° with my folly,        50
They most must laugh. And why, sir, must they so?
The why is plain as way to parish church:
He that a fool doth very wisely hit
Doth very foolishly, although he smart,
Not to seem senseless of the bob.° If not,           55
The wise man's folly is anatomized°
Even by the squand'ring glances° of the fool.
Invest° me in my motley, give me leave
To speak my mind, and I will through and through

Cleanse the foul body of th' infected world,         60
If they will patiently receive my medicine.

DUKE SENIOR
Fie on thee! I can tell what thou wouldst do.

JAQUES
What, for a counter,° would I do but good?

DUKE SENIOR
Most mischievous foul sin, in chiding sin.
For thou thyself hast been a libertine,              65
As sensual as the brutish sting° itself;
And all th' embossèd° sores and headed evils
That thou with license of free foot° hast caught,
Wouldst thou disgorge into the general world.

JAQUES
Why, who cries out on pride                          70
That can therein tax any private party?°
Doth it not flow as hugely as the sea
Till that the weary very means do ebb?°
What woman in the city do I name
When that I say the city woman bears                 75
The cost° of princes on unworthy shoulders?
Who can come in and say that I mean her,
When such a one as she, such is her neighbor?
Or what is he of basest function°
That says his bravery is not on my cost,°            80
Thinking that I mean him, but therein suits
His folly to the mettle of my speech?°
There then, how then, what then? Let me see wherein
My tongue hath wronged him. If it do him right,
Then he hath wronged himself. If he be free,°        85
Why, then my taxing like a wild goose flies
Unclaimed of any man. But who comes here?

*Enter* ORLANDO [*with his sword drawn*].

ORLANDO
Forbear, and eat no more!

JAQUES                    Why, I have eat none yet.

ORLANDO
Nor shalt not, till necessity be served.

JAQUES
Of what kind° should this cock come of?              90

DUKE SENIOR
Art thou thus boldened, man, by thy distress,
Or else a rude despiser of good manners,
That in civility thou seem'st so empty?

ORLANDO
You touched my vein at first.° The thorny point
Of bare distress hath ta'en from me the show        95
Of smooth civility; yet am I inland bred°
And know some nurture.° But forbear, I say!
He dies that touches any of this fruit
Till I and my affairs are answerèd.°

13 **motley** garbed in the multicolored costume of the court fool (a motley costume is commonly thought to be checkered or patched; Leslie Hotson, in *Shakespeare's Motley*, argues it was of varicolored threads but drab, like a tweed)  17 **set terms** precise phrases  19 **Call . . . fortune** fortune proverbially favors fools  20 **dial . . . poke** sundial from his pocket  23 **wags** goes  26 **hour to hour** perhaps with a pun on *whore*  29 **moral** moralize  30 **chanticleer** traditional name for a rooster  32 **sans intermission** without stop  39 **remainder biscuit** leftover hardtack  41 **vents** gives forth  44 **suit** (1) garment (2) petition  46 **rank** luxuriant  48 **large a charter** liberal license  50 **gallèd** chafed  55 **senseless . . . bob** unaware of the hit  56 **anatomized** revealed  57 **squand'ring glances** chance hits  58 **Invest** clothe

63 **counter** worthless coin  66 **the brutish sting** lust  67 **embossèd** swollen  68 **license . . . foot** complete freedom  71 **tax . . . party** criticize any particular person  73 **weary . . . ebb** perhaps: "ostentation eventually exhausts the wealth that makes it possible"; some editors emend "weary" to "wearer's"  76 **cost** wealth  79 **function** position  80 **his . . . cost** his fine dress is not paid for by me (and therefore is not my business)  81–82 **suits . . . speech** matches his folly to the substance of my words  85 **free** innocent  90 **kind** breed  94 **You . . . first** the duke's first supposition is correct  96 **inland bred** brought up in civilized society  97 **nurture** good breeding  99 **answerèd** provided for

JAQUES
An° you will not be answered with reason,° I must die. 100
DUKE SENIOR
What would you have? Your gentleness shall force
More than your force move us to gentleness.
ORLANDO
I almost die for food, and let me have it!
DUKE SENIOR
Sit down and feed, and welcome to our table.
ORLANDO
Speak you so gently? Pardon me, I pray you.            105
I thought that all things had been savage here,
And therefore put I on the countenance
Of stern commandment. But whate'er you are
That in this desert inaccessible,
Under the shade of melancholy boughs,                 110
Lose and neglect the creeping hours of time;
If ever you have looked on better days,
If ever been where bells have knolled° to church,
If ever sat at any good man's feast,
If ever from your eyelids wiped a tear                115
And know what 'tis to pity and be pitied,
Let gentleness my strong enforcement° be;
In the which hope I blush, and hide my sword.
DUKE SENIOR
True is it that we have seen better days,
And have with holy bell been knolled to church,       120
And sat at good men's feasts, and wiped our eyes
Of drops that sacred pity hath engend'red;
And therefore sit you down in gentleness,
And take upon command° what help we have
That to your wanting° may be minist'red.              125
ORLANDO
Then but forbear your food a little while,
Whiles, like a doe, I go to find my fawn
And give it food. There is an old poor man
Who after me hath many a weary step
Limped in pure love. Till he be first sufficed,       130
Oppressed with two weak evils,° age and hunger,
I will not touch a bit.
DUKE SENIOR                      Go find him out,
And we will nothing waste° till you return.
ORLANDO
I thank ye, and be blest for your good comfort!
                                        [Exit.]
DUKE SENIOR
Thou see'st we are not all alone unhappy:             135
This wide and universal theater
Presents more woeful pageants° than the scene
Wherein we play in.
JAQUES                   All the world's a stage,
And all the men and women merely players;
They have their exits and their entrances,            140
And one man in his time plays many parts,
His acts being seven ages.° At first, the infant,

Mewling° and puking in the nurse's arms.
Then the whining schoolboy, with his satchel
And shining morning face, creeping like snail         145
Unwillingly to school. And then the lover,
Sighing like furnace, with a woeful ballad
Made to his mistress' eyebrow. Then a soldier,
Full of strange oaths and bearded like the pard,°
Jealous° in honor, sudden° and quick in quarrel,      150
Seeking the bubble reputation
Even in the cannon's mouth. And then the justice,
In fair round belly with good capon lined,°
With eyes severe and beard of formal cut,
Full of wise saws° and modern instances;°             155
And so he plays his part. The sixth age shifts
Into the lean and slippered pantaloon,°
With spectacles on nose and pouch on side;
His youthful hose° well saved, a world too wide
For his shrunk shank, and his big manly voice,        160
Turning again toward childish treble, pipes
And whistles in his° sound. Last scene of all,
That ends this strange eventful history,
Is second childishness and mere° oblivion,
Sans teeth, sans eyes, sans taste, sans everything.   165

*Enter* ORLANDO, *with* ADAM.

DUKE SENIOR
Welcome. Set down your venerable burden
And let him feed.
ORLANDO
I thank you most for him.
ADAM                                    So had you need.
I scarce can speak to thank you for myself.
DUKE SENIOR
Welcome, fall to. I will not trouble you              170
As yet to question you about your fortunes.
Give us some music; and, good cousin, sing.
                         *Song.*
AMIENS
   Blow, blow, thou winter wind,
   Thou art not so unkind°
      As man's ingratitude:                           175
   Thy tooth is not so keen,
   Because thou art not seen,
      Although thy breath be rude.
Heigh-ho, sing heigh-ho, unto the green holly.
Most friendship is faining,° most loving mere folly:  180
   Then, heigh-ho, the holly.
   This life is most jolly.

   Freeze, freeze, thou bitter sky
   That dost not bite so nigh
      As benefits forgot:                             185
   Though thou the waters warp,°
   Thy sting is not so sharp
      As friend rememb'red not.
Heigh-ho, sing, &c.

100 **An** if; **reason** perhaps Jaques puns, eating a raisin (grape) 113 **knolled** rung 117 **enforcement** support 124 **upon command** as you wish 125 **wanting** need 131 **weak evils** evils causing weakness 133 **waste** consume 137 **pageants** scenes 142 **seven ages** for a survey in art and literature of the image of man's life divided into ages, see Samuel C. Chew, " 'This Strange Eventful History,' " in *Joseph Quincy Memorial Studies*, ed. James G. McManaway et al.

143 **Mewling** bawling 149 **pard** leopard 150 **Jealous** touchy; **sudden** rash 153 **capon lined** perhaps an allusion to the practice of bribing a judge with a capon 155 **saws** sayings; **modern instances** commonplace examples 157 **pantaloon** ridiculous old man (from Pantalone, a stock figure in Italian comedy) 159 **hose** breeches 162 **his** its 164 **mere** utter 174 **unkind** unnatural 180 **faining** longing (perhaps with a pun on *feigning*, pretending) 186 **warp** turn (into ice)

DUKE SENIOR
If that you were the good Sir Rowland's son,                    190
As you have whispered faithfully you were,
And as mine eye doth his effigies° witness
Most truly limned° and living in your face,
Be truly welcome hither. I am the duke
That loved your father. The residue of your fortune    195
Go to my cave and tell me. Good old man,
Thou art right welcome, as thy master is.
Support him by the arm. Give me your hand,
And let me all your fortunes understand.          *Exeunt.*

# ACT III

## Scene I. [*The palace.*]

*Enter* DUKE [FREDERICK], LORDS, *and* OLIVER.

DUKE FREDERICK
Not see him since? Sir, sir, that cannot be.
But were I not the better part made mercy,°
I should not seek an absent argument°
Of my revenge, thou present. But look to it:
Find out thy brother, wheresoe'er he is;                    5
Seek him with candle; bring him dead or living
Within this twelvemonth, or turn° thou no more
To seek a living in our territory.
Thy lands, and all things that thou dost call thine
Worth seizure, do we seize into our hands              10
Till thou canst quit° thee by thy brother's mouth°
Of what we think against thee.

OLIVER
O that your highness knew my heart in this!
I never loved my brother in my life.

DUKE FREDERICK
More villain thou. Well, push him out of doors,       15
And let my officers of such a nature°
Make an extent upon° his house and lands.
Do this expediently° and turn him going.       *Exeunt.*

## Scene II. [*The forest.*]

*Enter* ORLANDO [*with a paper*].

ORLANDO
Hang there, my verse, in witness of my love;
    And thou, thrice-crownèd Queen of Night,° survey
With thy chaste eye, from thy pale sphere above,
    Thy huntress' name° that my full life doth sway.
O Rosalind! These trees shall be my books,              5
    And in their barks my thoughts I'll character,°
That every eye which in this forest looks
    Shall see thy virtue witnessed° everywhere.

Run, run, Orlando, carve on every tree
The fair, the chaste, and unexpressive she.°      *Exit.*  10

*Enter* CORIN *and* [TOUCHSTONE *the*] *clown.*

CORIN   And how like you this shepherd's life, Master
Touchstone?
TOUCHSTONE   Truly, shepherd, in respect of itself, it
is a good life; but in respect that it is a shepherd's life, it
is naught.° In respect that it is solitary, I like it very   15
well; but in respect that it is private,° it is a very vile
life. Now in respect it is in the fields, it pleaseth me
well; but in respect it is not in the court, it is tedious.
As it is a spare° life, look you, it fits my humor° well;
but as there is no more plenty in it, it goes much    20
against my stomach. Hast any philosophy° in thee,
shepherd?
CORIN   No more, but that I know the more one
sickens, the worse at ease he is; and that he that wants°
money, means, and content is without three good      25
friends; that the property of rain is to wet and fire to
burn; that good pasture makes fat sheep, and that a
great cause of the night is lack of the sun; that he that
hath learned no wit by nature nor art° may complain°
of good breeding, or comes of a very dull kindred.     30
TOUCHSTONE   Such a one is a natural philosopher.°
Wast ever in court, shepherd?
CORIN   No, truly.
TOUCHSTONE   Then thou art damned.
CORIN   Nay, I hope.                                        35
TOUCHSTONE   Truly thou art damned, like an ill-
roasted egg, all on one side.
CORIN   For not being at court? Your reason.
TOUCHSTONE   Why, if thou never wast at court, thou
never saw'st good manners;° if thou never saw'st good   40
manners, then thy manners must be wicked; and
wickedness is sin, and sin is damnation. Thou art in a
parlous° stage, shepherd.
CORIN   Not a whit, Touchstone. Those that are good
manners at the court are as ridiculous in the country   45
as the behavior of the country is most mockable at the
court. You told me you salute not at the court but you
kiss° your hands. That courtesy would be uncleanly if
courtiers were shepherds.
TOUCHSTONE   Instance,° briefly. Come, instance.        50
CORIN   Why, we are still° handling our ewes, and their
fells° you know are greasy.
TOUCHSTONE   Why, do not your courtier's hands
sweat? And is not the grease of a mutton as wholesome
as the sweat of a man? Shallow, shallow. A better    55
instance, I say. Come.
CORIN   Besides, our hands are hard.
TOUCHSTONE   Your lips will feel them the sooner.
Shallow again. A more sounder instance, come.
CORIN   And they are often tarred over with the surgery°  60

---

**192 effigies** likeness (accent on second syllable)   **193 limned**
depicted
**III.i.2 the . . . mercy** so merciful   **3 argument** object (i.e.,
Orlando)   **7 turn** return   **11 quit** acquit; **mouth** testimony
**16 of . . . nature** appropriate   **17 Make . . . upon** seize by
writ   **18 expediently** speedily
**III.ii.2 thrice-crownèd . . . Night** Diana (goddess of the
moon, the hunt, and chastity)   **4 Thy huntress' name**
Rosalind, who, because she is chaste, serves Diana   **6 character**
write   **8 virtue witnessed** power attested to

**10 unexpressive she** woman beyond description   **15 naught**
worthless   **16 private** lonely   **19 spare** frugal; **humor** disposition   **21 philosophy** learning   **24 wants** lacks   **29 by . . .
art** by birth or education; **complain** cry the lack   **31 a
natural philosopher** (1) wise by nature (2) a wise idiot   **40
manners** (1) behavior (2) morals   **43 parlous** dangerous
**47–48 but you kiss** without kissing   **50 Instance** proof
**51 still** always   **52 fells** fleeces   **60–61 tarred . . . surgery**
shepherds used tar as an ointment   ·

of our sheep, and would you have us kiss tar? The courtier's hands are perfumed with civet.°

TOUCHSTONE Most shallow man! Thou worms' meat° in respect of° a good piece of flesh indeed! Learn of the wise, and perpend.° Civet is of a baser 65 birth than tar, the very uncleanly flux° of a cat. Mend the instance,° shepherd.

CORIN You have too courtly a wit for me; I'll rest.

TOUCHSTONE Wilt thou rest damned? God help thee, shallow man! God make incision in thee!° Thou 70 art raw.°

CORIN Sir, I am a true laborer; I earn that° I eat, get that I wear, owe no man hate, envy no man's happiness, glad of other men's good, content with my harm;° and the greatest of my pride is to see my ewes graze 75 and my lambs suck.

TOUCHSTONE That is another simple sin in you; to bring the ewes and the rams together and to offer to get your living by the copulation of cattle, to be bawd to a bell-wether° and to betray a she-lamb of a twelve- 80 month to a crookèd-pated° old cuckoldly° ram, out of all reasonable match. If thou beest not damned for this, the devil himself will have no shepherds; I cannot see else how thou shouldst 'scape.

CORIN Here comes young Master Ganymede, my 85 new mistress' brother.

*Enter* ROSALIND, [*reading a paper*].

ROSALIND
    "From the east to western Ind,
    No jewel is like Rosalind.
    Her worth, being mounted on the wind,
    Through all the world bears Rosalind.
    All the pictures fairest lined°           90
    Are but black to Rosalind.
    Let no face be kept in mind
    But the fair° of Rosalind."

TOUCHSTONE I'll rhyme you so eight years together, 95 dinners and suppers and sleeping hours excepted. It is the right butterwomen's rank to market.°

ROSALIND Out, fool!

TOUCHSTONE For a taste:
    If a hart do lack a hind,            100
    Let him seek out Rosalind.
    If the cat will after kind,°
    So be sure will Rosalind.
    Wintred° garments must be lined,°
    So must slender Rosalind.           105
    They that reap must sheaf and bind,
    Then to cart° with Rosalind.

    Sweetest nut hath sourest rind,
    Such a nut is Rosalind.
    He that sweetest rose will find      110
    Must find love's prick, and Rosalind.
This is the very false gallop of verses. Why do you infect yourself with them?

ROSALIND Peace, you dull fool! I found them on a tree.           115

TOUCHSTONE Truly the tree yields bad fruit.

ROSALIND I'll graff° it with you and then I shall graff it with a medlar.° Then it will be the earliest fruit i' th' country; for you'll be rotten ere you be half ripe, and that's the right virtue° of the medlar.          120

TOUCHSTONE You have said; but whether wisely or no, let the forest judge.

*Enter* CELIA *with a writing.*

ROSALIND Peace! Here comes my sister reading; stand aside.

CELIA
    "Why should this a desert be?       125
    For° it is unpeopled? No.
    Tongues I'll hang on every tree
    That shall civil sayings° show:
    Some, how brief the life of man
    Runs his erring pilgrimage,        130
    That the stretching of a span°
    Buckles in° his sum of age;
    Some, of violated vows
    'Twixt the souls of friend and friend;
    But upon the fairest boughs,       135
    Or at every sentence end,
    Will I 'Rosalinda' write,
    Teaching all that read to know
    The quintessence of every sprite°
    Heaven would in little° show.       140
    Therefore heaven Nature charged
    That one body should be filled
    With all graces wide-enlarged.
    Nature presently° distilled
    Helen's cheek, but not her heart,°    145
    Cleopatra's majesty,
    Atalanta's better part,°
    Sad° Lucretia's° modesty.
    Thus Rosalind of many parts
    By heavenly synod° was devised,    150
    Of many faces, eyes, and hearts,
    To have the touches° dearest prized.
    Heaven would that she these gifts should have,
    And I to live and die her slave."

ROSALIND O most gentle pulpiter, what tedious 155 homily of love have you wearied your parishioners withal, and never cried, "Have patience, good people"!

---

62 **civet** perfume obtained from the civet cat   **63–64 worms' meat** food for worms   **64 respect of** comparison with   **65 perpend** consider   **66 flux** secretion   **66–67 Mend the instance** give a better example   **70 make . . . thee** let your blood (a common cure, here for folly)   **71 raw** (1) inexperienced (2) sore   **72 that** what   **74 content . . . harm** bear with my troubles   **80 bell-wether** the leading sheep of a flock carries a bell   **81 crookèd-pated** with crooked horns; **cuckoldy** because horned   **91 lined** drawn   **94 fair** lovely face   **97 right . . . market** the verses jog along exactly like a procession of women riding to market   **102 kind** its own kind   **104 Wintred** prepared for winter; **lined** stuffed   **107 to cart** perhaps an allusion not only to the harvest but to the custom of transporting prostitutes to jail in a cart

**117 graff** graft   **118 medlar** (1) an applelike fruit, not ready to eat until it is almost rotten (2) interferer   **120 right virtue** true quality   **126 For** because   **128 civil sayings** civilized maxims   **131 stretching . . . span** span of an open hand   **132 Buckles in** limits   **139 sprite** soul   **140 in little** in miniature (i.e., the microcosm)   **144 presently** thereupon   **145 cheek . . . heart** Helen's beauty but not her false heart   **147 Atalanta's better part** Rosalind has the gracefulness but not the cruelty of Atalanta, a huntress famed in Greek mythology for her fleetness   **148 Sad** dignified; **Lucretia** a Roman matron who killed herself rather than live dishonored   **150 synod** council   **152 touches** features

CELIA   How now? Back, friends. Shepherd, go off a little. Go with him, sirrah.

TOUCHSTONE   Come, shepherd, let us make an 160 honorable retreat; though not with bag and baggage, yet with scrip and scrippage.°        *Exit, [with* CORIN].

CELIA   Didst thou hear these verses?

ROSALIND   O, yes, I heard them all, and more too; for some of them had in them more feet° than the verses 165 would bear.

CELIA   That's no matter. The feet might bear the verses.

ROSALIND   Ay, but the feet were lame, and could not bear themselves without the verse, and therefore stood 170 lamely in the verse.

CELIA   But didst thou hear without wondering how thy name should be hanged and carved upon these trees?

ROSALIND   I was seven of the nine days° out of the 175 wonder before you came; for look here what I found on a palm tree. I was never so berhymed since Pythagoras'° time that° I was an Irish rat,° which I can hardly remember.

CELIA   Trow° you who hath done this?        180

ROSALIND   Is it a man?

CELIA   And a chain that you once wore, about his neck. Change you color?

ROSALIND   I prithee who?

CELIA   O Lord, Lord, it is a hard matter for friends to 185 meet; but mountains may be removed with earthquakes, and so encounter.

ROSALIND   Nay, but who is it?

CELIA   Is it possible?

ROSALIND   Nay, I prithee now with most petitionary 190 vehemence,° tell me who it is.

CELIA   O wonderful, wonderful, and most wonderful wonderful, and yet again wonderful, and after that, out of all hooping!°

ROSALIND   Good my complexion!° Dost thou think, 195 though I am caparisoned° like a man, I have a doublet and hose in my disposition? One inch of delay more is a South Sea of discovery.° I prithee tell me who is it quickly, and speak apace.° I would thou couldst stammer, that thou mightst pour this concealed man 200 out of thy mouth as wine comes out of a narrow-mouthed bottle; either too much at once, or none at all. I prithee take the cork out of thy mouth, that I may drink thy tidings.

CELIA   So you may put a man in your belly.        205

ROSALIND   Is he of God's making? What manner of man? Is his head worth a hat? Or his chin worth a beard?

CELIA   Nay, he hath but a little beard.

ROSALIND   Why, God will send more, if the man will 210

be thankful. Let me stay° the growth of his beard, if thou delay me not the knowledge of his chin.

CELIA   It is young Orlando, that tripped up the wrestler's heels and your heart both in an instant.

ROSALIND   Nay, but the devil take mocking! Speak 215 sad brow and true maid.°

CELIA   I' faith, coz, 'tis he.

ROSALIND   Orlando?

CELIA   Orlando.

ROSALIND   Alas the day! What shall I do with my 220 doublet and hose? What did he when thou saw'st him? What said he? How looked he? Wherein went he?° What makes he here? Did he ask for me? Where remains he? How parted he with thee? And when shalt thou see him again? Answer me in one word. 225

CELIA   You must borrow me Gargantua's° mouth first; 'tis a word too great for any mouth of this age's size. To say "ay" and "no" to these particulars is more than to answer in a catechism.

ROSALIND   But doth he know that I am in this forest, 230 and in man's apparel? Looks he as freshly° as he did the day he wrestled?

CELIA   It is as easy to count atomies° as to resolve the propositions° of a lover; but take a taste of my finding him, and relish it with good observance.° I found him 235 under a tree, like a dropped acorn.

ROSALIND   It may well be called Jove's tree° when it drops forth fruit.

CELIA   Give me audience,° good madam.

ROSALIND   Proceed.        240

CELIA   There lay he stretched along like a wounded knight.

ROSALIND   Though it be pity to see such a sight, it well becomes the ground.

CELIA   Cry "holla"° to the tongue, I prithee; it curvets° 245 unseasonably. He was furnished° like a hunter.

ROSALIND   O, ominous! He comes to kill my heart.°

CELIA   I would sing my song without a burden.° Thou bring'st me out of tune.

ROSALIND   Do you not know I am a woman? When 250 I think, I must speak. Sweet, say on.

*Enter* ORLANDO *and* JAQUES.

CELIA   You bring me out. Soft. Comes he not here?

ROSALIND   'Tis he! Slink by, and note him.

JAQUES   I thank you for your company; but, good faith, I had as lief have been myself alone.        255

ORLANDO   And so 'had I; but yet for fashion sake I thank you too for your society.

JAQUES   God b' wi' you; let's meet as little as we can.

ORLANDO   I do desire we may be better strangers.

JAQUES   I pray you mar no more trees with writing 260 love songs in their barks.

ORLANDO   I pray you mar no moe° of my verses with reading them ill-favoredly.°

162 **scrip and scrippage** shepherd's pouch and its contents   165 **feet** metrical units   175 **seven . . . days** cf. the phrase *nine days's wonder*   178 **Pythagoras** Greek philosopher who taught the doctrine of the transmigration of souls; **that** when; **Irish rat** it was believed that Irish sorcerers could kill rats with rhymed spells   180 **Trow** know   190–91 **with . . . vehemence** i.e., I beg you   194 **out . . . hooping** beyond all measure   195 **Good my complexion** a mild expletive   196 **caparisoned** dressed   197–98 **One . . . discovery** Another minute more will seem as long as it takes to voyage to the South Seas   199 **apace** quickly

211 **stay** wait for   216 **sad . . . maid** seriously and truthfully   222–23 **Wherein went he** How was he dressed?   226 **Gargantua** a giant in Rabelais and other writers   231 **freshly** handsome   233 **atomies** motes   233–34 **resolve the propositions** answer the questions   235 **good observance** close attention   237 **Jove's tree** the oak, sacred to Jove   239 **Give me audience** listen   245 **holla** whoa; **curvets** frolics   246 **furnished** dressed   247 **heart** pun on *hart*   248 **burden** refrain   262 **moe** more   263 **ill-favoredly** badly

JAQUES  Rosalind is your love's name?

ORLANDO  Yes, just.  265

JAQUES  I do not like her name.

ORLANDO  There was no thought of pleasing you when she was christened.

JAQUES  What stature is she of?

ORLANDO  Just as high as my heart.  270

JAQUES  You are full of pretty answers. Have you not been acquainted with goldsmiths' wives, and conned them out of rings?°

ORLANDO  Not so; but I answer you right painted cloth,° from whence you have studied your questions.  275

JAQUES  You have a nimble wit; I think 'twas made of Atalanta's heels.° Will you sit down with me, and we two will rail against our mistress the world and all our misery.

ORLANDO  I will chide no breather° in the world but myself, against whom I know most faults.  280

JAQUES  The worst fault you have is to be in love.

ORLANDO  'Tis a fault I will not change for your best virtue. I am weary of you.

JAQUES  By my troth, I was seeking for a fool when I found you.  285

ORLANDO  He is drowned in the brook. Look but in and you shall see him.

JAQUES  There I shall see mine own figure.

ORLANDO  Which I take to be either a fool or a cipher.°  290

JAQUES  I'll tarry no longer with you. Farewell, good Signior Love.

ORLANDO  I am glad of your departure. Adieu, good Monsieur Melancholy.  [Exit JAQUES.]  295

ROSALIND  I will speak to him like a saucy lackey, and under that habit° play the knave with him. Do you hear, forester?

ORLANDO  Very well. What would you?

ROSALIND  I pray you, what is't o'clock?  300

ORLANDO  You should ask me, what time o' day. There's no clock in the forest.

ROSALIND  Then there is no true lover in the forest, else sighing every minute and groaning every hour would detect° the lazy foot of Time as well as a clock.  305

ORLANDO  And why not the swift foot of Time? Had not that been as proper?

ROSALIND  By no means, sir. Time travels in divers paces with divers persons. I'll tell you who Time ambles withal, who Time trots withal, who Time gallops withal, and who he stands still withal.  310

ORLANDO  I prithee, who doth he trot withal?

ROSALIND  Marry, he trots hard with a young maid between the contract of her marriage° and the day it is solemnized. If the interim be but a se'nnight,° Time's pace is so hard that it seems the length of seven year.  315

ORLANDO  Who ambles Time withal?

ROSALIND  With a priest that lacks Latin and a rich man that hath not the gout; for the one sleeps easily because he cannot study, and the other lives merrily because he feels no pain; the one lacking the burden of lean and wasteful° learning, the other knowing no burden of heavy tedious penury. These Time ambles withal.  320 325

ORLANDO  Who doth he gallop withal?

ROSALIND  With a thief to the gallows; for though he go as softly° as foot can fall, he thinks himself too soon there.

ORLANDO  Who says it still withal?  330

ROSALIND  With lawyers in the vacation; for they sleep between term° and term, and then they perceive not how time moves.

ORLANDO  Where dwell you, pretty youth?

ROSALIND  With this shepherdess, my sister; here in the skirts of the forest, like fringe upon a petticoat.  335

ORLANDO  Are you native of this place?

ROSALIND  As the cony° that you see dwell where she is kindled.°

ORLANDO  Your accent is something finer than you could purchase° in so removed° a dwelling.  340

ROSALIND  I have been told so of many. But indeed an old religious° uncle of mine taught me to speak, who was in his youth an inland° man; one that knew courtship° too well, for there he fell in love. I have heard him read many lectures against it; and I thank God I am not a woman, to be touched° with so many giddy° offenses as he hath generally taxed their whole sex withal.  345

ORLANDO  Can you remember any of the principal evils that he laid to the charge of women?  350

ROSALIND  There were none principal. They were all like one another as halfpence are, every one fault seeming monstrous till his fellow fault came to match it.  355

ORLANDO  I prithee recount some of them.

ROSALIND  No, I will not cast away my physic but on those that are sick. There is a man haunts the forest that abuses our young plants with carving "Rosalind" on their barks, hangs odes upon hawthorns, and elegies on brambles; all, forsooth, deifying the name of Rosalind. If I could meet that fancy-monger,° I would give him some good counsel, for he seems to have the quotidian° of love upon him.  360

ORLANDO  I am he that is so love-shaked. I pray you tell me your remedy.  365

ROSALIND  There is none of my uncle's marks upon you. He taught me how to know a man in love; in which cage of rushes° I am sure you are not prisoner.

ORLANDO  What were his marks?  370

ROSALIND  A lean cheek, which you have not; a blue eye° and sunken, which you have not; an unquestionable° spirit, which you have not; a beard neglected, which you have not—but I pardon you for that, for

272–73 conned . . . rings memorized the sentimental sayings inscribed in rings  274–75 painted cloth cheap substitute for tapestry, on which were painted pictures with trite sayings  277 Atalanta's heels Atalanta was a symbol of speed  280 breather creature  291 cipher zero  297 habit guise  305 detect show  314 contract . . . marriage betrothal  315 a se'nnight seven days, a week

323 wasteful causing one to waste away  328 softly slowly  332 term court session  338 cony rabbit  339 kindled born  341 purchase acquire; removed remote  343 religious a member of a religious order  344 inland city  345 courtship (1) court manners (2) wooing  347 touched tainted  348 giddy frivolous  362 fancy-monger dealer in love  364 quotidian daily fever  369 cage of rushes prison easy to escape from  371–72 a blue eye dark circles under the eyes  372–73 unquestionable averse to conversation

simply your having° in beard is a younger brother's 375
revenue.° Then your hose should be ungartered, your
bonnet unbanded, your sleeve unbuttoned, your shoe
untied, and everything about you demonstrating a
careless desolation.° But you are no such man: you are
rather point-device in your accouterments,° as loving 380
yourself than seeming the lover of any other.

ORLANDO   Fair youth, I would I could make thee
believe I love.

ROSALIND   Me believe it? You may as soon make her
that you love believe it, which I warrant she is apter 385
to do than to confess she does; that is one of the points
in the which women still give the lie to their consciences. But in good sooth, are you he that hangs the
verses on the trees wherein Rosalind is so admired?

ORLANDO   I swear to thee, youth, by the white hand 390
of Rosalind, I am that he, that unfortunate he.

ROSALIND   But are you so much in love as your
rhymes speak?

ORLANDO   Neither rhyme nor reason can express how
much. 395

ROSALIND   Love is merely° a madness, and, I tell you,
deserves as well a dark house and a whip° as madmen
do; and the reason why they are not so punished and
cured is that the lunacy is so ordinary that the whippers
are in love too. Yet I profess curing it by counsel. 400

ORLANDO   Did you ever cure any so?

ROSALIND   Yes, one, and in this manner. He was to
imagine me his love, his mistress; and I set him every
day to woo me. At which time would I, being but a
moonish° youth, grieve, be effeminate, changeable, 405
longing and liking, proud, fantastical,° apish, shallow,
inconstant, full of tears, full of smiles; for every
passion something and for no passion truly anything,
as boys and women are for the most part cattle of this
color; would now like him, now loathe him; then 410
entertain him, then forswear him; now weep for him,
then spit at him; that I drave my suitor from his mad
humor° of love to a living° humor of madness, which
was, to forswear the full stream of the world and to
live in a nook merely monastic. And thus I cured him; 415
and this way will I take upon me to wash your liver°
as clean as a sound sheep's heart, that there shall not be
one spot of love in't.

ORLANDO   I would not be cured, youth.

ROSALIND   I would cure you, if you would but call 420
me Rosalind and come every day to my cote and
woo me.

ORLANDO   Now, by the faith of my love, I will. Tell
me where it is.

ROSALIND   Go with me to it, and I'll show it you; 425
and by° the way you shall tell me where in the forest
you live. Will you go?

ORLANDO   With all my heart, good youth.

ROSALIND   Nay, you must call me Rosalind. Come,
sister, will you go?                              *Exeunt.* 430

---

**Scene III.** [*The forest.*]

*Enter* [TOUCHSTONE *the*] *clown,* AUDREY; *and*
JAQUES [*apart*].

TOUCHSTONE   Come apace,° good Audrey. I will
fetch up your goats, Audrey. And how, Audrey, am I
the man yet? Doth my simple feature° content you?

AUDREY   Your features, Lord warrant° us! What
features? 5

TOUCHSTONE   I am here with thee and thy goats, as
the most capricious poet, honest Ovid, was among the
Goths.°

JAQUES [*Aside.*]   O knowledge ill-inhabited,° worse
than Jove in a thatched house! 10

TOUCHSTONE   When a man's verses cannot be understood, nor a man's good wit seconded with° the forward child, understanding, it strikes a man more dead
than a great reckoning in a little room.° Truly, I
would the gods had made thee poetical. 15

AUDREY   I do not know what poetical is. Is it honest
in deed and word? Is it a true thing?

TOUCHSTONE   No, truly; for the truest poetry is the
most feigning, and lovers are given to poetry, and
what they swear in poetry may be said as lovers they 20
do feign.°

AUDREY   Do you wish then that the gods had made
me poetical?

TOUCHSTONE   I do truly; for thou swear'st to me
thou art honest. Now, if thou wert a poet, I might 25
have some hope thou didst feign.

AUDREY   Would you not have me honest?

TOUCHSTONE   No, truly, unless thou wert hard-
favored;° for honesty coupled to beauty is to have
honey a sauce to sugar. 30

JAQUES [*Aside.*]   A material° fool.

AUDREY   Well, I am not fair, and therefore I pray the
gods make me honest.

TOUCHSTONE   Truly, and to cast away honesty upon
a foul slut were to put good meat into an unclean dish. 35

AUDREY   I am not a slut, though I thank the gods I am
foul.

TOUCHSTONE   Well, praised be the gods for thy
foulness! Sluttishness may come hereafter. But be it as
it may be, I will marry thee; and to that end I have 40
been with Sir° Oliver Mar-text, the vicar of the next
village, who hath promised to meet me in this place of
the forest and to couple us.

JAQUES [*Aside.*]   I would fain see this meeting.

AUDREY   Well, the gods give us joy! 45

TOUCHSTONE   Amen. A man may, if he were of a
fearful heart, stagger° in this attempt; for here we have
no temple but the wood, no assembly but horn-
beasts.° But what though? Courage! As horns are

---

**375 simply your having** truthfully what you have   **375–76
younger brother's revenue** small portion   **378–79 a careless
desolation** indifferent despondency   **380 point-device . . .
accouterments** precise in your dress   **396 merely** completely   **397 a dark . . . whip** the usual treatment of the
insane in Shakespeare's day   **405 moonish** changeable   **406
fantastical** capricious   **413 humor** condition; **living** real
**416 liver** thought to be the seat of love   **426 by** along

**III.iii.1 apace** swiftly   **3 feature** appearance   **4 warrant**
save   **7–8 capricious . . . Goths** the Roman poet Ovid
was exiled among the Goths—pronounced in Elizabethan
England the same as "goats"—for the immorality of his
verses: Touchstone plays on the words "honest" (chaste)
and "capricious" (derived from Latin *caper* = male goat)
**9 ill-inhabited** ill-housed   **12 with** by   **14 great . . . room**
large bill for poor accommodations   **21 feign** (1) pretend
(2) desire (a pun on *fain*)   **28–29 hard-favored** ugly   **31
material** full of good matter   **41 Sir** an old form of address
for a priest   **47 stagger** tremble   **48–49 horn-beasts** (1) horned
animals (2) cuckolds

odious, they are necessary.° It is said, "Many a man 50 knows no end of his goods." Right! Many a man has good horns and knows no end of them. Well, that is the dowry of his wife; 'tis none of his own getting. Horns! Even so, poor men alone. No, no; the noblest deer hath them as huge as the rascal.° Is the single man 55 therefore blessed? No; as a walled town is more worthier than a village, so is the forehead of a married man more honorable than the bare brow of a bachelor; and by how much defense° is better than no skill, by so much is a horn more precious than to want.° 60

*Enter Sir* OLIVER MAR-TEXT.

Here comes Sir Oliver. Sir Oliver Mar-text, you are well met. Will you dispatch us° here under this tree, or shall we go with you to your chapel?

OLIVER MAR-TEXT   Is there none here to give the woman? 65

TOUCHSTONE   I will not take her on gift of any man.

OLIVER MAR-TEXT   Truly, she must be given, or the marriage is not lawful.

JAQUES [*Comes forward.*]   Proceed, proceed; I'll give 70 her.

TOUCHSTONE   Good even, good Master What-ye-call't.° How do you, sir? You are very well met. God 'ield you for your last company;° I am very glad to see you. Even a toy° in hand here, sir. Nay, pray be 75 covered.°

JAQUES   Will you be married, motley?

TOUCHSTONE   As the ox hath his bow,° sir, the horse his curb, and the falcon her bells, so man hath his desires; and as pigeons bill, so wedlock would be 80 nibbling.

JAQUES   And will you, being a man of your breeding, be married under a bush like a beggar? Get you to church, and have a good priest that can tell you what marriage is. This fellow will but join you together as 85 they join wainscot;° then one of you will prove a shrunk panel, and like green timber warp, warp.

TOUCHSTONE [*Aside.*]   I am not in the mind but° I were better to be married of him than of another; for he is not like to marry me well; and not being well 90 married,° it will be a good excuse for me hereafter to leave my wife.

JAQUES   Go thou with me and let me counsel thee.

TOUCHSTONE
Come, sweet Audrey.
We must be married, or we must live in bawdry. 95
Farewell, good Master Oliver: not
      O sweet Oliver,
      O brave Oliver,
      Leave me not behind thee;

but 100
      Wind° away,
      Be gone, I say;
      I will not to wedding with thee.

OLIVER MAR-TEXT   'Tis no matter. Ne'er a fantastical° knave of them all shall flout me out of my 105 calling.            *Exeunt.*

Scene IV. [*The forest.*]

*Enter* ROSALIND *and* CELIA.

ROSALIND   Never talk to me; I will weep. 1

CELIA   Do, I prithee; but yet have the grace to consider that tears do not become a man.

ROSALIND   But have I not cause to weep?

CELIA   As good cause as one would desire; therefore 5 weep.

ROSALIND   His very hair is of the dissembling color.°

CELIA   Something browner than Judas'. Marry, his kisses are Judas' own children.

ROSALIND   I' faith, his hair is of a good color. 10

CELIA   An excellent color. Your chestnut was ever the only color.

ROSALIND   And his kissing is as full of sanctity as the touch of holy bread.°

CELIA   He hath bought a pair of cast° lips of Diana.° A 15 nun of winter's sisterhood° kisses not more religiously; the very ice of chastity is in them.

ROSALIND   But why did he swear he would come this morning, and comes not?

CELIA   Nay, certainly there is no truth in him. 20

ROSALIND   Do you think so?

CELIA   Yes; I think he is not a pickpurse nor a horse-stealer, but for his verity in love, I do think him as concave° as a covered goblet or a worm-eaten nut.

ROSALIND   Not true in love? 25

CELIA   Yes, when he is in, but I think he is not in.

ROSALIND   You have heard him swear downright he was.

CELIA   "Was" is not "is." Besides, the oath of a lover is no stronger than the word of a tapster;° they are 30 both the confirmer of false reckonings. He attends here in the forest on the duke your father.

ROSALIND   I met the duke yesterday and had much question° with him. He asked me of what parentage I was. I told him, of as good as he; so he laughed and 35 let me go. But what talk we of fathers when there is such a man as Orlando?

CELIA   O, that's a brave° man; he writes brave verses, speaks brave words, swears brave oaths, and breaks them bravely, quite traverse,° athwart the heart of 40 his lover, as a puisny° tilter, that spurs his horse but on one side, breaks his staff like a noble goose. But all's

50 necessary inevitable   55 rascal inferior deer   59 defense the art of defense   60 want lack horns   62 dispatch us finish our business   72–73 Master What-ye-call't Touchstone delicately avoids the name "Jaques," which could be pronounced "jakes," a privy   73–74 God . . . company God reward you for the last time we met   75 toy trifle 75–76 pray be covered Jaques has removed his hat   78 bow yoke   86 wainscot wood paneling   88 I . . . but I am not sure but that   90–91 well married (1) legally married (2) happily married (3) married into wealth

101 Wind turn   104–05 fantastical odd
III.iv.7 dissembling color red, like the hair of Judas   14 holy bread not the sacramental wafer, but bread brought to church to be blessed and then distributed to the poor   15 cast (1) molded (2) castoff; Diana goddess of chastity   16 winter's sisterhood the most rigorous chastity   24 concave hollow 30 tapster waiter in a tavern   34 question talk   38 brave fine   40 traverse at an angle (instead of head-on)   41 puisny inexperienced

brave that youth mounts and folly guides. Who
comes here?

*Enter* CORIN.

CORIN
Mistress and master, you have oft enquired          45
After the shepherd that complained° of love,
Who you saw sitting by me on the turf,
Praising the proud disdainful shepherdess
That was his mistress.
CELIA                     Well, and what of him?
CORIN
If you will see a pageant° truly played              50
Between the pale complexion of true love
And the red glow of scorn and proud disdain,
Go hence a little, and I shall conduct you,
If you will mark it.
ROSALIND                O, come, let us remove:
The sight of lovers feedeth those in love.           55
Bring us to this sight, and you shall say
I'll prove a busy actor in their play.          *Exeunt.*


Scene V. [*The forest.*]

*Enter* SILVIUS *and* PHEBE.

SILVIUS
Sweet Phebe, do not scorn me; do not, Phebe!
Say that you love me not, but say not so
In bitterness. The common executioner,
Whose heart th' accustomed sight of death makes hard,
Falls° not the ax upon the humbled neck              5
But first begs pardon. Will you sterner be
Than he that dies and lives° by bloody drops?

*Enter [apart]* ROSALIND, CELIA, *and* CORIN.

PHEBE
I would not be thy executioner.
I fly thee, for I would not injure thee.
Thou tell'st me there is murder in mine eye:         10
'Tis pretty, sure, and very probable
That eyes, that are the frail'st and softest things,
Who shut their coward gates on atomies,°
Should be called tyrants, butchers, murderers.
Now I do frown on thee with all my heart,            15
And if mine eyes can wound, now let them kill thee.
Now counterfeit to swound;° why, now fall down;
Or if thou canst not, O, for shame, for shame,
Lie not, to say mine eyes are murderers.
Now show the wound mine eye hath made in thee;       20
Scratch thee but with a pin, and there remains
Some scar of it; lean upon a rush,
The cicatrice and capable impressure°
Thy palm some moment keeps; but now mine eyes,
Which I have darted at thee, hurt thee not,          25
Nor I am sure there is no force in eyes
That can do hurt.
SILVIUS            O dear Phebe,

If ever, as that ever may be near,°
You meet in some fresh cheek the power of fancy,°
Then shall you know the wounds invisible             30
That love's keen arrows make.
PHEBE                         But till that time
Come thou not near me; and when that time comes,
Afflict me with thy mocks, pity me not,
As till that time I shall not pity thee.
ROSALIND
And why, I pray you? Who might be your mother,       35
That you insult, exult, and all at once,
Over the wretched? What though you have no beauty
(As, by my faith, I see no more in you
Than without candle may go dark to bed°)
Must you be therefore proud and pitiless?            40
Why, what means this? Why do you look on me?
I see no more in you than in the ordinary
Of nature's sale-work.° 'Od's° my little life,
I think she means to tangle my eyes too!
No, faith, proud mistress, hope not after it;        45
'Tis not your inky brows, your black silk hair,
Your bugle° eyeballs, nor your cheek of cream
That can entame my spirits to your worship.
You foolish shepherd, wherefore do you follow her,
Like foggy south,° puffing with wind and rain?       50
You are a thousand times a properer° man
Than she a woman. 'Tis such fools as you
That makes the world full of ill-favored children.
'Tis not her glass,° but you, that flatters her,
And out of you she sees herself more proper          55
Than any of her lineaments can show her.
But mistress, know yourself. Down on your knees,
And thank heaven, fasting, for a good man's love;
For I must tell you friendly in your ear,
Sell when you can, you are not for all markets.      60
Cry the man mercy,° love him, take his offer;
Foul° is most foul, being foul to be a scoffer;
So take her to thee, shepherd. Fare you well.
PHEBE
Sweet youth, I pray you chide a year together;
I had rather hear you chide than this man woo.       65
ROSALIND [*Aside.*]   He's fall'n in love with your foul-
ness, and she'll fall in love with my anger. If it be so, as
fast as she answers thee with frowning looks, I'll
sauce her with bitter words. [*To* PHEBE.] Why look
you so upon me?                                      70
PHEBE
For no ill will I bear you.
ROSALIND
I pray you do not fall in love with me,
For I am falser than vows made in wine.
Besides, I like you not. If you will know my house,
'Tis at the tuft of olives, here hard° by.           75
Will you go, sister? Shepherd, ply her hard.
Come, sister. Shepherdess, look on him better
And be not proud. Though all the world could see,

46 complained lamented   50 pageant scene, show
III.v.5 Falls lets fall   7 dies and lives earns his living   13
atomies motes   17 counterfeit to swound pretend to swoon
23 cicatrice . . . impressure mark and visible impression

28 as . . . near and may the time be soon   29 fancy love
39 Than . . . bed your beauty is not so dazzling as to light up
the room   42–43 ordinary . . . sale-work usual product of
nature's manufacture   43 'Od's God save   47 bugle black and
glassy   50 south south wind   51 properer more handsome
54 glass mirror   61 Cry . . . mercy ask the man's forgiveness
62 Foul (1) ugliness (2) wickedness   75 hard near

None could be so abused° in sight as he.
Come, to our flock.      *Exit, [with* CELIA *and* CORIN]. 8o

PHEBE
Dead shepherd, now I find thy saw° of might,
"Who ever loved that loved not at first sight?"°

SILVIUS
Sweet Phebe.

PHEBE          Ha! What say'st thou, Silvius?

SILVIUS
Sweet Phebe, pity me.

PHEBE
Why, I am sorry for thee, gentle Silvius.          85

SILVIUS
Wherever sorrow is, relief would be.
If you do sorrow at my grief in love,
By giving love your sorrow and my grief
Were both extermined.°

PHEBE
Thou hast my love. Is not that neighborly?°          90

SILVIUS
I would have you.

PHEBE                    Why, that were covetousness.
Silvius, the time was that I hated thee;
And yet it is not that I bear thee love,
But since that thou canst talk of love so well,
Thy company, which erst° was irksome to me,          95
I will endure; and I'll employ thee too;
But do not look for further recompense
Than thine own gladness that thou art employed.

SILVIUS
So holy and so perfect is my love,
And I in such a poverty of grace,°          100
That I shall think it a most plenteous crop
To glean the broken ears after the man
That the main harvest reaps. Loose now and then
A scatt'red° smile, and that I'll live upon.

PHEBE
Know'st thou the youth that spoke to me erewhile?° 105

SILVIUS
Not very well, but I have met him oft,
And he hath bought the cottage and the bounds
That the old carlot° once was master of.

PHEBE
Think not I love him, though I ask for him;
'Tis but a peevish boy; yet he talks well.          110
But what care I for words? Yet words do well
When he that speaks them pleases those that hear.
It is a pretty youth. Not very pretty.
But sure he's proud. And yet his pride becomes him.
He'll make a proper man. The best thing in him          115
Is his complexion. And faster than his tongue
Did make offense, his eye did heal it up.
He is not very tall. Yet for his years he's tall.
His leg is but so so. And yet 'tis well.
There was a pretty redness in his lip,          120
A little riper and more lusty red

Than that mixed in his cheek. 'Twas just the difference
Betwixt the constant° red and mingled damask.°
There be some women, Silvius, had they marked him
In parcels° as I did, would have gone near          125
To fall in love with him; but, for my part,
I love him not nor hate him not. And yet
I have more cause to hate him than to love him;
For what had he to do to chide at me?
He said mine eyes were black and my hair black;          130
And, now I am rememb'red,° scorned at me.
I marvel why I answered not again.
But that's all one: omittance is no quittance.°
I'll write to him a very taunting letter,
And thou shalt bear it. Wilt thou, Silvius?          135

SILVIUS
Phebe, with all my heart.

PHEBE                    I'll write it straight;°
The matter's in my head and in my heart;
I will be bitter with him and passing short.°
Go with me, Silvius.                    *Exeunt.*

# ACT IV

## Scene I. [*The forest.*]

*Enter* ROSALIND *and* CELIA *and* JAQUES.

JAQUES  I prithee, pretty youth, let me be better
acquainted with thee.

ROSALIND  They say you are a melancholy fellow.

JAQUES  I am so; I do love it better than laughing.

ROSALIND  Those that are in extremity of° either are  5
abominable fellows, and betray themselves to every
modern censure° worse than drunkards.

JAQUES  Why, 'tis good to be sad and say nothing.

ROSALIND  Why then, 'tis good to be a post.

JAQUES  I have neither the scholar's melancholy,  10
which is emulation;° nor the musician's, which is
fantastical; nor the courtier's, which is proud; nor the
soldier's, which is ambitious; not the lawyer's, which is
politic;° nor the lady's, which is nice;° nor the lover's,
which is all these: but it is a melancholy of mine own,  15
compounded of many simples,° extracted from many
objects, and indeed the sundry contemplation of my
travels, in which my often rumination° wraps me in a
most humorous sadness.

ROSALIND  A traveler! By my faith, you have great  20
reason to be sad. I fear you have sold your own lands
to see other men's. Then to have seen much and to
have nothing is to have rich eyes and poor hands.

JAQUES  Yes, I have gained my experience.

*Enter* ORLANDO.

---

79 **abused** deceived  81 **saw** saying  82 **Who . . . sight**
a line from Christopher Marlowe's poem *Hero and Leander*,
published in 1598; the "dead shepherd" is Marlowe, who
died in 1593  89 **extermined** ended  90 **neighborly**
friendly (perhaps alluding to the commandment to love one's
neighbor)  95 **erst** formerly  100 **a poverty of grace** small
favor  104 **scatt'red** stray  105 **erewhile** a short time ago
108 **carlot** countryman

123 **constant** uniform; **mingled damask** pink and white
125 **In parcels** piece by piece  131 **remember'd** reminded
133 **omittance . . . quittance** the fact that I did not reply
does not mean I will not do so later  136 **straight** at once
138 **passing short** very curt
IV.i.5 **are . . . of** go to extremes in  6–7 **every modern
censure** the average man's disapproval  11 **emulation** envy
14 **politic** i.e., put on to seem grave; **nice** fastidious  16
**simples** ingredients  18 **often rumination** constant reflection

ROSALIND  And your experience makes you sad. I had 25
rather have a fool to make me merry than experience
to make me sad—and to travel° for it too.

ORLANDO  Good day and happiness, dear Rosalind.

JAQUES  Nay then, God b' wi' you, an° you talk in
blank verse.                                [Exit.] 30

ROSALIND  Farewell, Monsieur Traveler. Look you
lisp° and wear strange suits, disable° all the benefits of
your own country, be out of love with your nativity,°
and almost chide God for making you that countenance you are; or I will scarce think you have swam 35
in a gundello.° Why, how now, Orlando, where have
you been all this while? You a lover? An you serve me
such another trick, never come in my sight more.

ORLANDO  My fair Rosalind, I come within an hour
of my promise.                                      40

ROSALIND  Break an hour's promise in love? He that
will divide a minute into a thousand parts and break
but a part of the thousand part of a minute in the
affairs of love, it may be said of him that Cupid hath
clapped° him o' th' shoulder, but I'll warrant him 45
heart-whole.

ORLANDO  Pardon me, dear Rosalind.

ROSALIND  Nay, an you be so tardy, come no more in
my sight. I had as lief be wooed of a snail.

ORLANDO  Of a snail?                                50

ROSALIND  Ay, of a snail; for though he comes slowly,
he carries his house on his head; a better jointure,° I
think, than you make a woman. Besides, he brings his
destiny with him.

ORLANDO  What's that?                               55

ROSALIND  Why, horns; which such as you are fain
to be beholding to your wives for; but he comes
armed° in his fortune and prevents° the slander of his
wife.

ORLANDO  Virtue is no horn-maker, and my Rosalind 60
is virtuous.

ROSALIND  And I am your Rosalind.

CELIA  It pleases him to call you so; but he hath a
Rosalind of a better leer° than you.

ROSALIND  Come, woo me, woo me; for now I am 65
in a holiday humor and like enough to consent. What
would you say to me now, an I were your very very
Rosalind?

ORLANDO  I would kiss before I spoke.

ROSALIND  Nay, you were better speak first, and when 70
you were graveled for lack of matter,° you might take
occasion to kiss. Very good orators, when they are
out,° they will spit; and for lovers, lacking—God
warn° us!—matter, the cleanliest shift is to kiss.

ORLANDO  How if the kiss be denied?                 75

ROSALIND  Then she puts you to entreaty, and there
begins new matter.

ORLANDO  Who could be out, being before his
beloved mistress?

ROSALIND  Marry, that should you, if I were your 80

mistress, or I should think my honesty ranker° than my
wit.

ORLANDO  What, of my suit?

ROSALIND  Not out of your apparel, and yet out of
your suit.° Am not I your Rosalind?                 85

ORLANDO  I take some joy to say you are, because I
would be talking of her.

ROSALIND  Well, in her person, I say I will not have
you.

ORLANDO  Then, in mine own person, I die.          90

ROSALIND  No, faith, die by attorney.° The poor
world is almost six thousand years old, and in all this
time there was not any man died in his own person,°
videlicet,° in a love cause. Troilus° had his brains
dashed out with a Grecian club; yet he did what he 95
could to die before, and he is one of the patterns of
love. Leander,° he would have lived many a fair year
though Hero had turned nun, if it had not been for
a hot midsummer night; for, good youth, he went
but forth to wash him in the Hellespont, and being 100
taken with the cramp, was drowned; and the foolish
chroniclers of that age found° it was "Hero of Sestos."
But these are all lies. Men have died from time to
time, and worms have eaten them, but not for love.

ORLANDO  I would not have my right Rosalind of this 105
mind, for I protest her frown might kill me.

ROSALIND  By this hand, it will not kill a fly. But
come, now I will be your Rosalind in a more coming-
on disposition; and ask me what you will, I will
grant it.                                           110

ORLANDO  Then love me, Rosalind.

ROSALIND  Yes, faith, will I, Fridays and Saturdays
and all.

ORLANDO  And wilt thou have me?

ROSALIND  Ay, and twenty such.                      115

ORLANDO  What sayest thou?

ROSALIND  Are you not good?

ORLANDO  I hope so.

ROSALIND  Why then, can one desire too much of a
good thing? Come, sister, you shall be the priest and 120
marry us. Give me your hand, Orlando. What do you
say, sister?

ORLANDO  Pray thee marry us.

CELIA  I cannot say the words.

ROSALIND  You must begin, "Will you, Orlando—" 125

CELIA  Go to.° Will you, Orlando, have to wife this
Rosalind?

ORLANDO  I will.

ROSALIND  Ay, but when?

ORLANDO  Why now, as fast as she can marry us. 130

ROSALIND  Then you must say, "I take thee, Rosalind,
for wife."

ORLANDO  I take thee, Rosalind, for wife.

ROSALIND  I might ask you for your commission;° but
I do take thee, Orlando, for my husband. There's a 135

---

27 **travel** pun on *travail*  29 **an** if  32 **lisp** speak affectedly;
**disable** disparage  33 **nativity** birthplace  36 **gundello**
gondola  45 **clapped** touched  52 **jointure** marriage settlement  58 **armed** i.e., with horns; **prevents** (1) forestalls (2)
anticipates (?)  64 **leer** face  71 **graveled . . . matter** hard
put for something to say  73 **out** out of material  74 **warn**
protect (warrant)

81 **honesty ranker** virtue fouler  85 **suit** (1) apparel (2)
entreaty  91 **attorney** proxy  93 **in . . . person** in real life
(as opposed to fiction)  94 **videlicet** that is to say;  **Troilus**
Priam's son, betrayed in love by Cressida and killed by the
spear of Achilles; "as true as Troilus" became a proverbial
expression  97 **Leander** a prototype of dedicated love, who
swam the Hellespont nightly to see his mistress, Hero of
Sestos  102 **found** gave the verdict  126 **Go to** that's enough
134 **commission** license

girl goes before° the priest, and certainly a woman's thought runs before her actions.

ORLANDO   So do all thoughts; they are winged.

ROSALIND   Now tell me how long you would have her after you have possessed her.                    140

ORLANDO   For ever and a day.

ROSALIND   Say "a day," without the "ever." No, no, Orlando. Men are April when they woo, December when they wed. Maids are May when they are maids, but the sky changes when they are wives. I will be 145 more jealous of thee than a Barbary cock-pigeon° over his hen, more clamorous than a parrot against° rain, more newfangled° than an ape, more giddy° in my desires than a monkey. I will weep for nothing, like Diana in the fountain,° and I will do that when 150 you are disposed to be merry; I will laugh like a hyen, and that when thou art inclined to sleep.

ORLANDO   But will my Rosalind do so?

ROSALIND   By my life, she will do as I do.

ORLANDO   O, but she is wise.                    155

ROSALIND   Or else she could not have the wit to do this; the wiser, the waywarder. Make° the doors upon a woman's wit, and it will out at the casement; shut that, and 'twill out at the keyhole; stop that, 'twill fly with the smoke out at the chimney.                    160

ORLANDO   A man that had a wife with such a wit, he might say, "Wit, whither wilt?"°

ROSALIND   Nay, you might keep that check° for it till you met your wife's wit going to your neighbor's bed.                    165

ORLANDO   And what wit could wit have to excuse that?

ROSALIND   Marry, to say she came to seek you there. You shall never take her without her answer unless you take her without her tongue. O, that woman that 170 cannot make her fault her husband's occasion,° let her never nurse her child herself, for she will breed it like a fool.

ORLANDO   For these two hours, Rosalind, I will leave thee.                    175

ROSALIND   Alas, dear love, I cannot lack thee two hours!

ORLANDO   I must attend the duke at dinner. By two o'clock I will be with thee again.

ROSALIND   Ay, go your ways, go your ways; I knew 180 what you would prove. My friends told me as much, and I thought no less. That flattering tongue of yours won me. 'Tis but one cast away,° and so, come death! Two o'clock is your hour?

ORLANDO   Ay, sweet Rosalind.                    185

ROSALIND   By my troth, and in good earnest, and so God mend me, and by all pretty oaths that are not dangerous, if you break one jot of your promise or come one minute behind your hour, I will think you

the most pathetical° break-promise, and the most 190 hollow lover, and the most unworthy of her you call Rosalind, that may be chosen out of the gross° band of the unfaithful. Therefore beware my censure and keep your promise.

ORLANDO   With no less religion° than if thou wert 195 indeed my Rosalind. So adieu.

ROSALIND   Well, Time is the old justice that examines all such offenders, and let Time try. Adieu.

                    *Exit* [ORLANDO].

CELIA   You have simply misused° our sex in your love-prate. We must have your doublet and hose 200 plucked over your head, and show the world what the bird hath done to her own nest.

ROSALIND   O coz, coz, coz, my pretty little coz, that thou didst know how many fathom deep I am in love! But it cannot be sounded. My affection hath an un- 205 known bottom, like the Bay of Portugal.

CELIA   Or rather, bottomless, that as fast as you pour affection in, it runs out.

ROSALIND   No, that same wicked bastard of Venus° that was begot of thought,° conceived of spleen,° and 210 born of madness, that blind rascally boy that abuses every one's eyes because his own are out, let him be judge how deep I am in love. I'll tell thee, Aliena, I cannot be out of the sight of Orlando. I'll go find a shadow, and sigh till he come.                    215

CELIA   And I'll sleep.                    *Exeunt.*


Scene II. [*The forest.*]

*Enter* JAQUES; *and* LORDS, [*like*] *foresters.*

JAQUES   Which is he that killed the deer?

LORD   Sir, it was I.

JAQUES   Let's present him to the duke like a Roman conqueror; and it would do well to set the deer's horns upon his head for a branch of victory. Have you 5 no song, forester, for this purpose?

ANOTHER LORD   Yes, sir.

JAQUES   Sing it. 'Tis no matter how it be in tune, so it make noise enough.

*Music.*

                    *Song.*

What shall he have that killed the deer?                    10
His leather skin and horns to wear:
    Then sing him home. The rest shall bear
    This burden.°

Take thou no scorn° to wear the horn,
It was a crest ere thou wast born,                    15

---

136 **goes before** runs ahead (Rosalind has not waited for Celia to say, "Will you, Rosalind, have to husband") 146 **Barbary cock-pigeon** Barb pigeon ("Barbary" suggests jealousy) 147 **against** before 148 **newfangled** given to novelty; **giddy** changeable 150 **like . . . fountain** i.e., steadily (Diana was a popular subject for fountain statuary) 157 **Make** shut 162 **Wit, whither wilt** where are your senses 163 **check** rebuke 171 **make . . . occasion** turn defense of her own actions into an accusation of her husband's 183 **one cast away** one girl deserted

190 **pathetical** (1) pitiful (2) passionate (?) 192 **gross** large 195 **religion** faith 199 **simply misused** completely abused 209 **bastard of Venus** Cupid 210 **thought** despondency; **spleen** sheer impulse
IV.ii.12–13 **The rest . . . burden** i.e., not only the forester who killed the deer but all men will wear the horns of cuckoldry (many editors read the line as a stage direction: the other foresters ["the rest"] are to join in the refrain ["burden"] after one forester has sung the first three lines of the song; if the Folio version—here followed—is correct, it is likely that all sing the song from the beginning) 14 **Take . . . scorn** do not be ashamed

Thy father's father wore it,
And thy father bore it.
The horn, the horn, the lusty horn,
Is not a thing to laugh to scorn.°    *Exeunt.*

Scene III. [*The forest.*]

*Enter* ROSALIND *and* CELIA.

ROSALIND  How say you now, is it not past two
o'clock? And here much° Orlando!
CELIA  I warrant you, with pure love and troubled
brain, he hath ta'en his bow and arrows and is gone
forth to sleep.                                               5

*Enter* SILVIUS.

Look who comes here.
SILVIUS
My errand is to you, fair youth.
My gentle Phebe bid me give you this.
I know not the contents, but, as I guess
By the stern brow and waspish action                          10
Which she did use as she was writing of it,
It bears an angry tenor. Pardon me;
I am but as a guiltless messenger.
ROSALIND
Patience herself would startle at this letter
And play the swaggerer. Bear this, bear all!                  15
She says I am not fair, that I lack manners;
She calls me proud, and that she could not love me,
Were man as rare as phoenix.° 'Od's my will!
Her love is not the hare that I do hunt.
Why writes she so to me? Well, shepherd, well,              20
This is a letter of your own device.
SILVIUS
No, I protest, I know not the contents.
Phebe did write it.
ROSALIND              Come, come, you are a fool,
And turned into the extremity° of love.
I saw her hand. She has a leathern hand,                     25
A freestone-colored° hand. I verily did think
That her old gloves were on, but 'twas her hands.
She has a housewife's hand; but that's no matter:
I say she never did invent° this letter;
This is a man's invention and his hand.                     30
SILVIUS
Sure it is hers.
ROSALIND
Why, 'tis a boisterous and a cruel style,
A style for challengers. Why, she defies me
Like Turk to Christian. Woman's gentle brain
Could not drop forth such giant-rude° invention,            35
Such Ethiop words, blacker in their effect
Than in their countenance. Will you hear the letter?
SILVIUS
So please you, for I never heard it yet;
Yet heard too much of Phebe's cruelty.

ROSALIND
She Phebes me.° Mark how the tyrant writes. (*Read.*)  40
    "Art thou god, to shepherd turned,
        That a maiden's heart hath burned?"
Can a woman rail thus?
SILVIUS                        Call you this railing?
ROSALIND (*Read.*)
    "Why, thy godhead laid apart,°
        Warr'st thou with a woman's heart?"                   45
Did you ever hear such railing?
    "Whiles the eye of man did woo me,
        That could do no vengeance° to me."
Meaning me a beast.
    "If the scorn of your bright eyne°                        50
    Have power to raise such love in mine,
    Alack, in me what strange effect
    Would they work in mild aspect!°
    Whiles you chid me, I did love;
    How then might your prayers move!                         55
    He that brings this love to thee
    Little knows this love in me;
    And by him seal up thy mind,°
    Whether that thy youth and kind°
    Will the faithful offer take                              60
    Of me and all that I can make,°
    Or else by him my love deny,
    And then I'll study how to die."
SILVIUS
Call you this chiding?
CELIA                      Alas, poor shepherd!
ROSALIND  Do you pity him? No, he deserves no pity.  65
Wilt thou love such a woman? What, to make thee an
instrument,° and play false strains upon thee? Not to
be endured! Well, go your way to her, for I see love
hath made thee a tame snake,° and say this to her: that
if she love me, I charge her to love thee; if she will not,  70
I will never have her unless thou entreat for her. If you
be a true lover, hence, and not a word; for here comes
more company.                          *Exit* SILVIUS.

*Enter* OLIVER.

OLIVER
Good morrow, fair ones. Pray you, if you know,
Where in the purlieus° of this forest stands                 75
A sheepcote, fenced about with olive trees?
CELIA
West of this place, down in the neighbor bottom.°
The rank of osiers° by the murmuring stream
Left on your right hand brings you to the place.
But at this hour the house doth keep itself;                 80
There's none within.
OLIVER
If that an eye may profit by a tongue,
Then should I know you by description,
Such garments and such years: "The boy is fair,

---

19 **laugh to scorn** ridicule
IV.iii.2 **much** i.e., not much  18 **phoenix** a legendary
bird, of which there was only one in the world at any time
24 **turned . . . extremity** became the very essence  26
**freestone-colored** yellowish-brown  29 **invent** compose
35 **giant-rude** incredibly rude

40 **She Phebes me** She writes with her customary disdain
44 **thy . . . apart** having assumed human form  48 **vengeance** harm  50 **eyne** eyes  53 **aspect** (1) look (2) planetary
influence  58 **seal . . . mind** tell your feelings in a letter
59 **youth and kind** youthful nature  61 **make** give
66–67 **make . . . instrument** use you  69 **tame snake** poor
worm  75 **purlieus** borders  77 **neighbor bottom** nearby
valley  78 **rank of osiers** row of willows

Of female favor,° and bestows° himself     85
Like a ripe sister;° the woman low,°
And browner than her brother." Are not you
The owner of the house I did enquire for?

CELIA
It is no boast, being asked, to say we are.

OLIVER
Orlando doth commend him to you both,     90
And to that you he calls his Rosalind
He sends this bloody napkin.° Are you he?

ROSALIND
I am. What must we understand by this?

OLIVER
Some of my shame, if you will know of me
What man I am, and how and why and where     95
This handkercher was stained.

CELIA             I pray you tell it.

OLIVER
When last the young Orlando parted from you,
He left a promise to return again
Within an hour; and pacing through the forest,
Chewing the food of sweet and bitter fancy,°     100
Lo, what befell. He threw his eye aside,
And mark what object did present itself:
Under an old oak, whose boughs were mossed with age
And high top bald with dry antiquity,
A wretched ragged man, o'ergrown with hair,     105
Lay sleeping on his back; about his neck
A green and gilded snake had wreathed itself,
Who with her head, nimble in threats, approached
The opening of his mouth; but suddenly,
Seeing Orlando, it unlinked itself     110
And with indented° glides did slip away
Into a bush, under which bush's shade
A lioness, with udders all drawn dry,
Lay couching,° head on ground, with catlike watch
When that the sleeping man should stir; for 'tis     115
The royal disposition of that beast
To prey on nothing that doth seem as dead.
This seen, Orlando did approach the man
And found it was his brother, his elder brother.

CELIA
O, I have heard him speak of that same brother,     120
And he did render° him the most unnatural
That lived amongst men.

OLIVER            And well he might so do,
For well I know he was unnatural.

ROSALIND
But, to Orlando: did he leave him there,
Food to the sucked and hungry lioness?     125

OLIVER
Twice did he turn his back and purposed so;
But kindness,° nobler ever than revenge,
And nature, stronger than his just occasion,°
Made him give battle to the lioness,
Who quickly fell before him; in which hurtling     130
From miserable slumber I awaked.

CELIA
Are you his brother?

ROSALIND          Was't you he rescued?

CELIA
Was't you that did so oft contrive° to kill him?

OLIVER
'Twas I. But 'tis not I. I do not shame
To tell you what I was, since my conversion     135
So sweetly tastes, being the thing I am.

ROSALIND
But, for the bloody napkin?

OLIVER           By and by.°
When from the first to last, betwixt us two,
Tears our recountments° had most kindly bathed,
As how I came into that desert place:     140
In brief, he led me to the gentle duke,
Who gave me fresh array and entertainment,°
Committing me unto my brother's love,
Who led me instantly unto his cave,
There stripped himself, and here upon his arm     145
The lioness had torn some flesh away,
Which all this while had bled; and now he fainted,
And cried, in fainting, upon Rosalind.
Brief, I recovered° him, bound up his wound;
And after some small space, being strong at heart,     150
He sent me hither, stranger as I am,
To tell this story, that you might excuse
His broken promise, and to give this napkin,
Dyed in his blood, unto the shepherd youth
That he in sport doth call his Rosalind.     155

[ROSALIND *swoons*.]

CELIA
Why, how now, Ganymede, sweet Ganymede!

OLIVER
Many will swoon when they do look on blood.

CELIA
There is more in it. Cousin Ganymede!

OLIVER
Look, he recovers.

ROSALIND
I would I were at home.

CELIA          We'll lead you thither.     160
I pray you, will you take him by the arm?

OLIVER Be of good cheer, youth. You a man! You
lack a man's heart.

ROSALIND I do so, I confess it. Ah, sirrah, a body
would think this was well counterfeited.° I pray you     165
tell your brother how well I counterfeited. Heigh-ho!

OLIVER This was not counterfeit. There is too great
testimony in your complexion that it was a passion of
earnest.°

ROSALIND Counterfeit, I assure you.     170

OLIVER Well then, take a good heart and counterfeit
to be a man.

ROSALIND So I do; but, i' faith, I should have been a
woman by right.

CELIA Come, you look paler and paler. Pray you     175
draw homewards. Good sir, go with us.

---

85 **favor** features; **bestows** carries   86 **ripe sister** grownup woman (some editors emend "sister" to "forester"); **low** short   92 **napkin** handkerchief   100 **fancy** love   111 **indented** serpentine   114 **couching** crouching   121 **render** describe   127 **kindness** familial affection   128 **occasion** opportunity

133 **contrive** plot   137 **By and by** soon   139 **recountments** recital (of our adventures since we last met)   142 **entertainment** hospitality   149 **recovered** revived   165 **counterfeited** pretended   168–69 **passion of earnest** real emotion

OLIVER
That will I, for I must bear answer back
How you excuse my brother, Rosalind.
ROSALIND   I shall devise something. But I pray you
commend my counterfeiting to him. Will you go?   180
                                        *Exeunt.*

# ACT V

### Scene I. [*The forest.*]

*Enter* [TOUCHSTONE *the*] *clown and* AUDREY.

TOUCHSTONE   We shall find a time, Audrey. Patience,
gentle Audrey.
AUDREY   Faith, the priest was good enough, for all the
old gentleman's saying.
TOUCHSTONE   A most wicked Sir Oliver, Audrey, a   5
most vile Mar-text. But, Audrey, there is a youth here
in the forest lays claim to you.
AUDREY   Ay, I know who 'tis. He hath no interest in
me in the world. Here comes the man you mean.

*Enter* WILLIAM.

TOUCHSTONE   It is meat and drink to me to see a   10
clown;° by my troth, we that have good wits have
much to answer for. We shall be flouting;° we cannot
hold.°
WILLIAM   Good ev'n, Audrey.
AUDREY   God ye° good ev'n, William.   15
WILLIAM   And good ev'n to you, sir.
TOUCHSTONE   Good ev'n, gentle friend. Cover thy
head,° cover thy head. Nay, prithee be covered. How
old are you, friend?
WILLIAM   Five-and-twenty, sir.   20
TOUCHSTONE   A ripe° age. Is thy name William?
WILLIAM   William, sir.
TOUCHSTONE   A fair name. Wast born i' th' forest
here?
WILLIAM   Ay, sir, I thank God.   25
TOUCHSTONE   "Thank God." A good answer. Art
rich?
WILLIAM   Faith, sir, so so.
TOUCHSTONE   "So so" is good, very good, very
excellent good; and yet it is not, it is but so so. Art   30
thou wise?
WILLIAM   Ay, sir, I have a pretty wit.
TOUCHSTONE   Why, thou say'st well. I do now
remember a saying, "The fool doth think he is wise,
but the wise man knows himself to be a fool." The   35
heathen philosopher, when he had a desire to eat a
grape, would open his lips when he put it into his
mouth, meaning thereby that grapes were made to
eat and lips to open. You do love this maid?
WILLIAM   I do, sir.   40
TOUCHSTONE   Give me your hand. Art thou learned?
WILLIAM   No, sir.
TOUCHSTONE   Then learn this of me: to have is to

have; for it is a figure° in rhetoric that drink, being
poured out of a cup into a glass, by filling the one doth   45
empty the other; for all your writers do consent that
ipse° is he. Now, you are not ipse, for I am he.
WILLIAM   Which he, sir?
TOUCHSTONE   He, sir, that must marry this woman.
Therefore, you clown, abandon—which is in the   50
vulgar, leave—the society—which in the boorish is,
company—of this female—which in the common is,
woman. Which together is, abandon the society of this
female, or, clown, thou perishest; or, to thy better
understanding, diest; or to wit, I kill thee, make thee   55
away, translate thy life into death, thy liberty into
bondage. I will deal in poison with thee, or in bastinado,° or in steel; I will bandy with thee in faction;° I
will o'errun thee with policy;° I will kill thee a
hundred and fifty ways. Therefore tremble and depart.   60
AUDREY   Do, good William.
WILLIAM   God rest you merry, sir.   *Exit.*

*Enter* CORIN.

CORIN   Our master and mistress seeks you. Come
away, away!
TOUCHSTONE   Trip, Audrey, trip, Audrey. I attend,°   65
I attend.   *Exeunt.*

### Scene II. [*The forest.*]

*Enter* ORLANDO *and* OLIVER.

ORLANDO   Is't possible that on so little acquaintance
you should like her? That but seeing, you should love
her? And loving, woo? And wooing, she should grant?
And will you persever to enjoy her?
OLIVER   Neither call the giddiness° of it in question,   5
the poverty of her, the small acquaintance, my sudden
wooing, nor her sudden consenting; but say with me,
I love Aliena; say with her that she loves me; consent
with both that we may enjoy each other. It shall be to
your good; for my father's house, and all the revenue   10
that was old Sir Rowland's, will I estate° upon you,
and here live and die a shepherd.

*Enter* ROSALIND.

ORLANDO   You have my consent. Let your wedding
be tomorrow: thither will I invite the duke and all's
contented followers. Go you and prepare Aliena; for   15
look you, here comes my Rosalind.
ROSALIND   God save you, brother.
OLIVER   And you, fair sister.   [*Exit.*]
ROSALIND   O my dear Orlando, how it grieves me to
see thee wear thy heart in a scarf!°   20
ORLANDO   It is my arm.
ROSALIND   I thought thy heart had been wounded
with the claws of a lion.
ORLANDO   Wounded it is, but with the eyes of a lady.
ROSALIND   Did your brother tell you how I   25

V.i.11 clown yokel   12 flouting mocking   13 hold keep
from mocking   15 God ye God give you   17–18 Cover thy
head William has removed his hat   21 ripe fine
V.ii.5 giddiness suddenness   11 estate settle   20 scarf sling

44 figure figure of speech   47 ipse he himself (Latin)
57–58 bastinado cudgeling   58 bandy . . . faction argue
with you as do politicians   59 o'errun . . . policy overwhelm you with craft   65 attend come

counterfeited to sound° when he showed me your handkercher?

ORLANDO  Ay, and greater wonders than that.

ROSALIND  O, I know where you are! Nay, 'tis true. There was never anything so sudden but the fight of 30 two rams and Caesar's thrasonical° brag of "I came, saw, and overcame"; for your brother and my sister no sooner met but they looked; no sooner looked but they loved; no sooner loved but they sighed; no sooner sighed but they asked one another the reason; 35 no sooner knew the reason but they sought the remedy: and in these degrees° have they made a pair of stairs to marriage, which they will climb incontinent, or else be incontinent° before marriage: they are in the very wrath of love, and they will together; clubs 40 cannot part them.

ORLANDO  They shall be married tomorrow, and I will bid the duke to the nuptial. But, O, how bitter a thing it is to look into happiness through another man's eyes! By so much the more shall I tomorrow be 45 at the height of heart-heaviness, by how much I shall think my brother happy in having what he wishes for.

ROSALIND  Why then, tomorrow I cannot serve your turn for Rosalind?

ORLANDO  I can live no longer by thinking.  50

ROSALIND  I will weary you then no longer with idle talking. Know of me then, for now I speak to some purpose, that I know you are a gentleman of good conceit.° I speak not this that you should bear a good opinion of my knowledge, insomuch I say I know 55 you are; neither do I labor for a greater esteem than may in some little measure draw a belief from you, to do yourself good, and not to grace me.° Believe then, if you please, that I can do strange things. I have, since I was three year old, conversed° with a magician, 60 most profound in his art and yet not damnable.° If you do love Rosalind so near the heart as your gesture° cries it out, when your brother marries Aliena shall you marry her. I know into what straits of fortune she is driven; and it is not impossible to me, 65 if it appear not inconvenient° to you, to set her before your eyes tomorrow, human as she is,° and without any danger.

ORLANDO  Speak'st thou in sober meanings?

ROSALIND  By my life, I do, which I tender dearly,° 70 though I say I am a magician.° Therefore put you in your best array, bid your friends; for if you will be married tomorrow, you shall; and to Rosalind, if you will.

*Enter* SILVIUS *and* PHEBE.

Look, here comes a lover of mine and a lover of hers. 75

PHEBE  
Youth, you have done me much ungentleness  
To show the letter that I writ to you.

ROSALIND  
I care not if I have. It is my study°  
To seem despiteful° and ungentle to you.  
You are there followed by a faithful shepherd:      80  
Look upon him, love him; he worships you.

PHEBE  
Good shepherd, tell this youth what 'tis to love.

SILVIUS  
It is to be all made of sighs and tears;  
And so am I for Phebe.

PHEBE  
And I for Ganymede.      85

ORLANDO  
And I for Rosalind.

ROSALIND  
And I for no woman.

SILVIUS  
It is to be all made of faith and service;  
And so am I for Phebe.

PHEBE  
And I for Ganymede.      90

ORLANDO  
And I for Rosalind.

ROSALIND  
And I for no woman.

SILVIUS  
It is to be all made of fantasy,°  
All made of passion, and all made of wishes,  
All adoration, duty, and observance,°      95  
All humbleness, all patience, and impatience,  
All purity, all trial, all observance;°  
And so am I for Phebe.

PHEBE  
And so am I for Ganymede.

ORLANDO  
And so am I for Rosalind.      100

ROSALIND  
And so am I for no woman.

PHEBE  
If this be so, why blame you me to love you?

SILVIUS  
If this be so, why blame you me to love you?

ORLANDO  
If this be so, why blame you me to love you?

ROSALIND  Why do you speak too,° "Why blame 105 you me to love you?"

ORLANDO  
To her that is not here, nor doth not hear.

ROSALIND  Pray you, no more of this; 'tis like the howling of Irish wolves against the moon. [*To* SILVIUS.] I will help you if I can. [*To* PHEBE.] I 110 would love you if I could. Tomorrow meet me all together. [*To* PHEBE.] I will marry you if ever I marry woman, and I'll be married tomorrow. [*To* ORLANDO.] I will satisfy you if ever I satisfied man, and you shall be married tomorrow. [*To* SILVIUS.] I will content 115 you if what pleases you contents you, and you shall be married tomorrow. [*To* ORLANDO.] As you love Rosalind, meet. [*To* SILVIUS.] As you love Phebe,

**26 sound** swoon  **31 thrasonical** boastful (after the braggart soldier Thraso in Terence's comedy *Eunuchus*)  **37 degrees** a pun on the literal meaning, "steps"  **38–39 incontinent . . . incontinent** with all haste . . . unchaste  **54 conceit** understanding  **58 to grace me** to do credit to myself  **60 conversed** spent time  **61 not damnable** because he practices white, not black, magic  **63 gesture** conduct  **66 inconvenient** unfitting  **67 human . . . is** Rosalind herself, not a spirit  **70 tender dearly** hold precious  **71 though . . . magician** a magician could be punished with death

**78 study** intention  **79 despiteful** scornful  **93 fantasy** fancy  **95 observance** devoted attention  **97 observance** some editors emend to "obedience"  **105 Why . . . too** some editors emend to "Who do you speak to"

meet. And as I love no woman, I'll meet. So fare you
well. I have left you commands.                              120
SILVIUS  I'll not fail if I live.
PHEBE  Nor I.
ORLANDO  Nor I.                              *Exeunt.*

### Scene III. [*The forest.*]

*Enter* [TOUCHSTONE *the*] *clown and* AUDREY.

TOUCHSTONE  Tomorrow is the joyful day, Audrey;
tomorrow will we be married.
AUDREY  I do desire it with all my heart; and I hope it
is no dishonest desire to desire to be a woman of the
world.° Here come two of the banished duke's pages.   5

*Enter two* PAGES.

FIRST PAGE  Well met, honest° gentleman.
TOUCHSTONE  By my troth, well met. Come, sit,
sit, and a song!
SECOND PAGE  We are for you. Sit i' th' middle.
FIRST PAGE  Shall we clap into't roundly,° without   10
hawking or spitting or saying we are hoarse, which
are the only° prologues to a bad voice?
SECOND PAGE  I' faith, i' faith! and both in a tune,°
like two gypsies on a horse.

*Song.*

It was a lover and his lass,                              15
    With a hey, and a ho, and a hey nonino,
That o'er the green cornfield° did pass
    In springtime, the only pretty ringtime,°
When birds do sing, hey ding a ding, ding.
Sweet lovers love the spring.                            20

Between the acres° of the rye,
    With a hey, and a ho, and a hey nonino,
These pretty country folks would lie
    In springtime, &c.

This carol they began that hour,                         25
    With a hey, and a ho, and a hey nonino,
How that a life was but a flower
    In springtime, &c.

And therefore take° the present time,
    With a hey, and a ho, and a hey nonino,            30
For love is crownèd with the prime°
    In springtime, &c.

TOUCHSTONE  Truly, young gentlemen, though
there was no great matter in the ditty,° yet the note°
was very untuneable.                                     35
FIRST PAGE  You are deceived, sir. We kept time, we
lost not our time.
TOUCHSTONE  By my troth, yes; I count it but time
lost to hear such a foolish song. God b' wi' you, and
God mend your voices. Come, Audrey.    *Exeunt.* 40

V.iii.4–5 a woman . . . world (1) married (2) fashionable
6 honest honorable   10 clap into't roundly begin directly
12 the only merely the   13 in a tune in unison  17
cornfield wheatfield  18 ringtime the time for giving
marriage rings  21 Between the acres in the strips of
unploughed land  29 take seize  31 prime spring  34 ditty
words of the song; note melody

### Scene IV. [*The forest.*]

*Enter* DUKE SENIOR, AMIENS, JAQUES, ORLANDO,
OLIVER, CELIA.

DUKE SENIOR
Dost thou believe, Orlando, that the boy
Can do all this that he hath promisèd?
ORLANDO
I sometimes do believe, and sometimes do not,
As those that fear they hope,° and know they fear.

*Enter* ROSALIND, SILVIUS, *and* PHEBE.

ROSALIND
Patience once more, whiles our compact is urged.°   5
You say, if I bring in your Rosalind,
You will bestow her on Orlando here?
DUKE SENIOR
That would I, had I kingdoms to give with her.
ROSALIND
And you say you will have her when I bring her?
ORLANDO
That would I, were I of all kingdoms king.        10
ROSALIND
You say you'll marry me, if I be willing?
PHEBE
That will I, should I die the hour after.
ROSALIND
But if you do refuse to marry me,
You'll give yourself to this most faithful shepherd?
PHEBE
So is the bargain.                                15
ROSALIND
You say that you'll have Phebe, if she will?
SILVIUS
Though to have her and death were both one thing.
ROSALIND
I have promised to make all this matter even.°
Keep you your word, O duke, to give your daughter;
You yours, Orlando, to receive his daughter;      20
Keep you your word, Phebe, that you'll marry me,
Or else, refusing me, to wed this shepherd;
Keep your word, Silvius, that you'll marry her
If she refuse me; and from hence I go,
To make these doubts all even.                    25
                        *Exit* ROSALIND *and* CELIA.
DUKE SENIOR
I do remember in this shepherd boy
Some lively° touches of my daughter's favor.°
ORLANDO
My lord, the first time that I ever saw him
Methought he was a brother to your daughter.
But, my good lord, this boy is forest-born,       30
And hath been tutored in the rudiments
Of many desperate° studies by his uncle,
Whom he reports to be a great magician,
Obscurèd° in the circle of this forest.

*Enter* [TOUCHSTONE *the*] *clown and* AUDREY.

V.iv.4 hope hope in vain  5 compact is urged agreement is
restated  18 make . . . even straighten out everything  27
lively living; favor features  32 desperate dangerous  34
Obscurèd hidden

JAQUES  There is, sure, another flood toward,° and 35 these couples are coming to the ark.° Here comes a pair of very strange beasts, which in all tongues are called fools.

TOUCHSTONE  Salutation and greeting to you all!

JAQUES  Good my lord, bid him welcome. This is the 40 motley-minded gentleman that I have so often met in the forest. He hath been a courtier, he swears.

TOUCHSTONE  If any man doubt that, let him put me to my purgation.° I have trod a measure;° I have flattered a lady; I have been politic° with my friend, 45 smooth with mine enemy; I have undone° three tailors; I have had four quarrels, and like to have fought one.°

JAQUES  And how was that ta'en up?°

TOUCHSTONE  Faith, we met, and found the quarrel 50 was upon the seventh cause.

JAQUES  How seventh cause? Good my lord, like this fellow.

DUKE SENIOR  I like him very well.

TOUCHSTONE  God 'ield° you, sir; I desire you of the 55 like.° I press in here, sir, amongst the rest of the country copulatives,° to swear and to forswear, according as marriage binds and blood breaks.° A poor virgin, sir, an ill-favored thing, sir, but mine own; a poor humor° of mine, sir, to take that that no man else 60 will. Rich honesty° dwells like a miser, sir, in a poor house, as your pearl in your foul oyster.

DUKE SENIOR  By my faith, he is very swift and sententious.°

TOUCHSTONE  According to the fool's bolt,° sir, and 65 such dulcet diseases.°

JAQUES  But, for the seventh cause. How did you find the quarrel on the seventh cause?

TOUCHSTONE  Upon a lie seven times removed— bear your body more seeming,° Audrey—as thus, sir. 70 I did dislike the cut of a certain courtier's beard. He sent me word, if I said his beard was not cut well, he was in the mind it was: this is called the Retort Courteous. If I sent him word again it was not well cut, he would send me word he cut it to please himself: this is called 75 the Quip Modest.° If again, it was not well cut, he disabled° my judgment: this is called the Reply Churlish. If again, it was not well cut, he would answer I spake not true: this is called the Reproof Valiant. If again, it was not well cut, he would say I lie: this is 80 called the Countercheck° Quarrelsome: and so to the Lie Circumstantial° and the Lie Direct.

JAQUES  And how oft did you say his beard was not well cut?

TOUCHSTONE  I durst go no further than the Lie 85 Circumstantial, nor he durst not give me the Lie Direct; and so we measured swords° and parted.

JAQUES  Can you nominate° in order now the degrees of the lie?

TOUCHSTONE  O sir, we quarrel in print, by the 90 book,° as you have books for good manners. I will name you the degrees. The first, the Retort Courteous; the second, the Quip Modest; the third, the Reply Churlish; the fourth, the Reproof Valiant; the fifth, the Countercheck Quarrelsome; the sixth, the Lie with 95 Circumstance; the seventh, the Lie Direct. All these you may avoid but the Lie Direct, and you may avoid that too, with an If. I knew when seven justices could not take up° a quarrel, but when the parties were met themselves, one of them thought but of an If: as, "If 100 you said so, then I said so"; and they shook hands and swore brothers. Your If is the only peacemaker. Much virtue in If.

JAQUES  Is not this a rare fellow, my lord? He's as good at anything, and yet a fool. 105

DUKE SENIOR  He uses his folly like a stalking horse,° and under the presentation° of that he shoots his wit.

*Enter* HYMEN,° ROSALIND, *and* CELIA. *Still*° *music.*

HYMEN
      Then is there mirth in heaven
      When earthly things made even°
        Atone together.° 110
      Good duke, receive thy daughter;
      Hymen from heaven brought her,
        Yea, brought her hither,
      That thou mightst join her hand with his
      Whose heart within his bosom is. 115

ROSALIND [*To* DUKE.]
To you I give myself, for I am yours.

[*To* ORLANDO.]

To you I give myself, for I am yours.

DUKE SENIOR
If there be truth in sight, you are my daughter.

ORLANDO
If there be truth in sight, you are my Rosalind.

PHEBE
If sight and shape be true, 120
Why then, my love adieu!

ROSALIND [*To* DUKE.]
I'll have no father, if you be not he.

[*To* ORLANDO.]

I'll have no husband, if you be not he.

[*To* PHEBE.]

Nor ne'er wed woman, if you be not she.

HYMEN  Peace ho! I bar confusion: 125
      'Tis I must make conclusion
        Of these most strange events.

**35 toward** approaching  **36 couples . . . ark** cf. Genesis 7:2, "and of beasts that are not clean by two, the male and his female"  **43–44 put . . . purgation** test me  **44 measure** stately dance  **45 politic** crafty  **46 undone** ruined (by not paying his bills)  **47–48 like . . . one** almost fought over one  **49 ta'en up** settled  **55 God 'ield** God reward  **56–57 I . . . like** may I return the compliment  **57 copulatives** couples soon to be wed  **58 blood breaks** sexual interest wanes  **60 humor** whim  **61 honesty** virtue  **63–64 swift and sententious** quick-witted and pithy  **65 According . . . bolt** cf. the proverb "A fool's bolt (arrow) is soon shot"  **66 dulcet diseases** pleasing weaknesses  **70 seeming** becomingly  **76 Modest** moderate  **77 disabled** did not value  **81 Countercheck** contradiction  **82 Circumstantial** indirect

**87 measured swords** swords were measured before a duel  **88 nominate** name  **90–91 by the book** according to the rules  **99 take up** settle  **106 stalking horse** any object under cover of which a hunter pursues his game  **107 presentation** protection  **107 s.d. Hymen** god of marriage; **Still** soft  **109 made even** reconciled  **110 Atone together** are set at one

Here's eight that must take hands
To join in Hymen's bands,
    If truth holds true contents.°    130

[*To* ORLANDO *and* ROSALIND.]

You and you no cross° shall part.

[*To* OLIVER *and* CELIA.]

You and you are heart in heart.

[*To* PHEBE.]

You to his love must accord,°
Or have a woman to your lord.

[*To* TOUCHSTONE *and* AUDREY.]

You and you are sure together°    135
As the winter to foul weather.

[*To all.*]

Whiles a wedlock hymn we sing,
Feed yourselves with questioning,
That reason wonder may diminish
How thus we met, and these things finish.    140
            *Song.*
    Wedding is great Juno's crown,
        O blessed bond of board and bed!
    'Tis Hymen peoples every town;
        High° wedlock then be honorèd.
    Honor, high honor, and renown    145
    To Hymen, god of every town!

DUKE SENIOR
O my dear niece, welcome thou art to me,
Even daughter,° welcome, in no less degree!
PHEBE [*To* SILVIUS.]
I will not eat my word, now thou art mine;
Thy faith my fancy to thee doth combine.°    150

*Enter* SECOND BROTHER [*Jaques de Boys*].

SECOND BROTHER
Let me have audience for a word or two.
I am the second son of old Sir Rowland
That bring these tidings to this fair assembly.
Duke Frederick hearing how that every day
Men of great worth resorted to this forest,    155
Addressed a mighty power,° which were on foot
In his own conduct,° purposely to take
His brother here and put him to the sword;
And to the skirts of this wild wood he came,
Where, meeting with an old religious man,°    160
After some question° with him, was converted
Both from his enterprise and from the world,
His crown bequeathing to his banished brother,
And all their lands restored to them again
That were with him exiled. This to be true    165
I do engage° my life.
DUKE SENIOR            Welcome, young man.
Thou offer'st fairly° to thy brothers' wedding:

To one, his lands withheld; and to the other,
A land itself as large, a potent° dukedom.
First, in this forest let us do those ends°    170
That here were well begun and well begot;
And after, every° of this happy number
That have endured shrewd° days and nights with us
Shall share the good of our returnèd fortune,
According to the measure° of their states.    175
Meantime forget this new-fall'n° dignity
And fall into our rustic revelry.
Play, music, and you brides and bridegrooms all,
With measure heaped in joy, to th' measures° fall.
JAQUES
Sir, by your patience. If I heard you rightly,    180
The duke hath put on a religious life
And thrown into neglect the pompous court.°
SECOND BROTHER    He hath.
JAQUES
To him will I. Out of these convertites°
There is much matter to be heard and learned.    185

[*To* DUKE.]

You to your former honor I bequeath;
Your patience and your virtue well deserves it.

[*To* ORLANDO.]

You to a love that your true faith doth merit;

[*To* OLIVER.]

You to your land and love and great allies;

[*To* SILVIUS.]

You to a long and well-deservèd bed;    190

[*To* TOUCHSTONE.]

And you to wrangling, for thy loving voyage
Is but for two months victualled. So, to your pleasures:
I am for other than for dancing measures.
DUKE SENIOR    Stay, Jaques, stay.
JAQUES
To see no pastime I. What you would have    195
I'll stay to know at your abandoned cave.    *Exit.*
DUKE SENIOR
Proceed, proceed. We will begin these rites,
As we do trust they'll end, in true delights.
            *Exit* [*after the dance*].


# [ E P I L O G U E ]

ROSALIND    It is not the fashion to see the lady the
epilogue, but it is no more unhandsome° than to see
the lord the prologue. If it be true that good wine needs
no bush,° 'tis true that a good play needs no epilogue;
yet to good wine they do use good bushes, and good    5

---

130 If . . . contents if the truth is true    131 cross quarrel
133 accord agree    135 sure together securely bound
144 High solemn    148 Even daughter even as a daughter
150 combine unite    156 Addressed . . . power prepared
a mighty army    157 conduct leadership    160 old religious
man a hermit (?)    161 question talk    166 engage pledge
167 offer'st fairly bring a good gift

169 potent powerful    170 do those ends complete those
purposes    172 every each one    173 shrewd hard    175
measure rank    176 new-fall'n newly acquired    179 measures
dance steps    182 thrown . . . court given up the ceremonious life of the court    184 convertites converts
Epi.2 unhandsome unbecoming    4 no bush no advertisement
(in Shakespeare's time vintners used an ivybush as a sign)

plays prove the better by the help of good epilogues. What a case am I in then, that am neither a good epilogue, nor cannot insinuate with you° in the behalf of a good play! I am not furnished° like a beggar; therefore to beg will not become me. My way is to conjure° you, and I'll begin with the women. I charge you, O women, for the love you bear to men, to like as much of this play as please you; and I charge you, O men, for the love you bear to women—as I perceive by your simpering none of you hates them—that between you and the women the play may please. If I were a woman,° I would kiss as many of you as had beards that pleased me, complexions that liked° me, and breaths that I defied° not; and I am sure, as many as have good beards, or good faces, or sweet breaths, will, for my kind offer, when I make curtsy, bid me farewell.°　　　　　　　　　　　　　　*Exit.*

**8 insinuate with you** slyly get your approval　**9 furnished** dressed　**11 conjure** (1) solemnly entreat (2) charm (by magic)　**16–17 If . . . woman** Rosalind, of course, was played by a boy　**18 liked** pleased　**19 defied** disliked　**21–22 bid me farewell** applaud

# TWELFTH NIGHT,
# OR, WHAT YOU WILL

EDITED BY HERSCHEL BAKER

## Introduction

*Twelfth Night* is such a genial, charming play that for a certain kind of reader its charm is self-defeating. Johnson, for example, admired its elegance and ease and its exquisite humor, and he conceded that it might be diverting on the stage; but because the principal action "wants credibility" and "exhibits no just picture of life," he remarked with disapproval, it cannot be instructive or tell us anything important. In short, it fails the test of relevance.

This great critic's cold opinion of the most profound of Shakespeare's so-called "golden comedies" presents us with a hard decision: either to dismiss *Twelfth Night* as false and fatuous or to accept it as a version of romance—deft and entertaining, to be sure, but remote from our concerns and exempt from any common-sense appraisal. As usual, Johnson, a man not given to unconsidered judgments, seems to argue from the facts. For one thing, what we know or may infer about the circumstances of its first production would indicate that *Twelfth Night* was conceived and written as a kind of bagatelle. If, as many scholars think, it was commissioned for performance by the fledgling lawyers of the Middle Temple at the romp that crowned their Christmas celebration, the play was tailored to an annual frolic when duty and convention were ignored, and when, in a saturnalian Feast of Misrule, mirth became the order of the day. Even the subtitle—*What You Will*—repudiates, or so it seems, the drab and probable for the promise of the unexpected.[1] Life, as most men come to know it, is a frayed and tattered thing of unexpressed desires and disappointed hopes, and its tumults rarely find repose. In the world depicted by *Twelfth Night*, however, it would seem that perturbation leads to calm and all suspensions are resolved, so that by happy if implausible coincidence afflicted virtue is rewarded, folly is exposed, and error yields to knowledge.

The ingredients of this consoling fiction are the staple items of romance: shipwreck, alienation, and wandering in a remote realm where a pair of high-born lovers melodiously indulge a set of attitudes untested by experience, where a maiden in distress by luck and pluck gets everything she wants, and where the pretensions of an "affectioned ass" are demolished by a pack of gay tormentors. The main plot, articulated by the ancient devices of disguise and mistaken identity, presents a love story (or a brace of interlocking love stories) that leads through skillful convolutions to a final recognition scene; and the subplot—a kind of antimasque—involves the "lighter people" in a complicated jest. Finally, all these knotted strands of action are conducted in a language so precise that form and function seem to coincide, with Orsino's artful "fancy" and Viola's deep but muted love as charmingly conveyed as Sir Toby's burly humor and the wit and music of the Clown.

Indeed, this play, which starts and ends with music, and which is studded with so many lovely songs, might be said to approach the condition of that art where form and style are everything, and where there is, or should be, no appeal to values and criteria not inherent in the work itself. In more severely imitative kinds of art, the reverse, of course, is true. Because Holbein's portrait of Sir Thomas More or Richardson's *Clarissa*—which, incidentally, was one of Johnson's favorite books—seek in different, complicated ways to represent contemporary experience with fidelity, at least a part of our response to them is based on what we know of life, and therefore we require that they express some aspect of the truth about the things they represent. On the other hand, a Mozart serenade stands for nothing but itself; it has a logic of its own, and it creates an independent frame of reference that baffles any moral or utilitarian test. *Twelfth Night* is not this kind of

---

[1] Despite Leslie Hotson's interesting attempt in *The First Night of Twelfth Night* (1954) to show that the play was commissioned for performance before the Queen and court at Whitehall on Twelfth Night (January 6) in 1601 to celebrate the splendid visit of Virginio Orsini, Duke of Bracchiano, most scholars still accept an entry of February 2, 1602, in the diary of John Manningham, a barrister of the Middle Temple, as pointing to its first production in the Middle Temple hall on Twelfth Night of that year: "At our feast we had a play called *Twelve Night, or What You Will*, much like the *Comedy of Errors* or *Menechmi* in Plautus, but most like and near to that in Italian called *Inganni*. A good practice in it to make the steward believe his Lady widow was in love with him, by counterfeiting a letter as from his Lady in general terms, telling him what she liked best in him, and prescribing his gesture in smiling, his apparel, etc., and then when he came to practice making him believe they took him to be mad." On Manningham's clever guess about Nicolò Secchi's *Gl'Inganni*, see A Note on the Source, pp. 878–79.

work, of course, but it is such a triumph of artifice and style, and shows such mastery of convention, that some readers might regard it as a self-subsistent artifact, or, at any rate, as a work invulnerable to the expectations and probabilities derived from everyday experience. Beguiled by its mazy plot and music, they would not even dare to ask if it is "true." For them, therefore, Johnson's test of relevance would appear to be irrelevant, and his common-sense, adverse opinion merely an impertinence.

To regard *Twelfth Night* either as escapist folderol or adroit but meaningless romance is, however, to forget its function as a play. But since it is a play, and since a play, as Aristotle said, is the imitation of an action, it must meet the test of relevance. This test can never be evaded in a literary production, because no true work of literature ignores what Johnson means by "life," and no honest writer, however much concerned with form and style, neglects his only proper subject, which is the human situation. It is not that we require an easy calculus of triumph for the good and disaster for the bad, but that a play reveal—or permit us to infer—a necessary connection between what happens to a man and the kind of man he is. When this requirement is evaded, as it seems to be evaded, for example, in the last act of *Measure for Measure*, we are baffled and uneasy because we feel a lack of moral sequence. Conversely, when the conduct of the action, however painful, satisfies our moral expectations, we are forced to yield assent. Thus, although the conclusion of *King Lear* is as harrowing as anything in drama, we accept it, in our anguish, because we recognize its dreadful logic.

We do not look for dreadful logic in *Twelfth Night*, of course, but we do expect to find a real connection between its artful, entertaining fiction and those aspects of experience that it seeks to represent. We expect to find some reference, even if oblique and stylized, to the world which each of us inhabits—a refinement of our own perceptions, an enlargement of our knowledge or compassion, a demonstration of how men and women act, and why. Otherwise art deteriorates to mere technique, and literature becomes gesticulation.

What, then, is there in *Twelfth Night* to save it from this danger? For one thing, there is a shaping theme that enables us to view the conventions of romance as a paradigm of our own behavior; for another, there is, in the subplot, such skillful use of sharp and even topical detail in depicting various kinds of folly that the effect is almost photographic. These two features of the work remove it from the realm of pure romance and attach it to our own experience. They remind us that despite its old-fashioned apparatus, its lyric grace, and what Johnson called its lack of "credibility," *Twelfth Night* should not be thought of as a piece of music or as an empty virtuoso exercise in style, but as a play that we may verify by what we know of life.

*Twelfth Night* meets this test with ease, for it concerns a basic human problem; or, if that sounds too severe for such a gay and sprightly work of art, it records and comments on a mode of human action that all men everywhere exhibit. This might be defined as our native bent for self-deception, or, conversely, as our difficulty in achieving self-awareness. Here the theme is given comic statement and presented as romance, but it has a universal application. Is it possible, *Twelfth Night* makes us wonder, for us to know the truth about ourselves? And even if we gain such

knowledge, Shakespeare asks in other, darker plays, can such knowledge be endured? We see these questions posed when Richard II, stripped of crown and power and even of his misconceptions, sits in Pomfret Castle and explores his final, humbling recognition of himself; when Henry V, on the eve of Agincourt, expounds the wide distinction between the common notion of a king and the kingly burden that he bears; when Othello is compelled to face the horror of the deed he did "in honor"; when Lear tears off his clothing to reveal the "unaccommodated man." Such analogues in plays so different from *Twelfth Night* suggest how often, and in what varied contexts, Shakespeare used the theme. For him—as for Sophocles and Pirandello—to show one's growth toward self-awareness is almost coextensive with the art of drama.

This theme, so massive and protean, receives consummate comic statement in *Twelfth Night*. Here Shakespeare has to trim it not merely to the comic form (which requires a complex plot directed toward a happy ending) but also, presumably, to the interests of a special clientele—the debonair young lawyers at their revels in the Middle Temple. Almost inevitably, therefore, he writes a play of love: not love as the annihilating passion shared by Romeo and Juliet or the febrile lust of Troilus, but as a mode of social intercourse that works its way through opposition to eventual satisfaction. He had done this sort of thing before, of course, in such plays as *The Two Gentlemen of Verona* and *As You Like It*; but in *Twelfth Night* he makes a signal innovation, for here the lovers' triumph is delayed not by the customary impediments of parental disapproval or insolvency or politics, but by their own deceits and self-deceptions. To secure this innovation he manipulates the old conventions of romance—notably the stock devices of disguise and mistaken identity—not merely that they might complicate the action and so provide diversion but that they might serve almost as metaphors or emblems for mental obfuscation. The perplexity of the plot—where, among many other sources of confusion, a girl disguised as a boy loves a man who commissions her to woo a lady whose advances she must check—represents in concrete terms the intellectual and emotional bewilderment that almost every character in the play exhibits. As a consequence, the machinery of romance acquires the novel function of articulating theme. To be sure, the convolutions of the plot provide diversion of a sort, but they also bind the characters in a web of interwoven error, and thus they underscore the meaning of the play: that most men never know, and maybe never have a chance to know, the truth about themselves.

But if, as the knotty and perplexing plot suggests, men are forced by circumstances into compounded misconceptions, they are also trapped by their illusions. Between the errors thrust upon them and those they generate themselves, they are caught as in a vise—victims not merely of deceit but also of their own folly. Orsino, for example, though

> Of great estate, of fresh and stainless youth;
> In voices well divulged, free, learned, and valiant,
> And in dimension and the shape of nature
> A gracious person.                    (I.v.257–60)

is in fact so blinded by his image of himself as an ardent but despairing lover that he is maimed by his obsession.

We see him first as he indulges this obsession with his famous speech on music as the food of love, and this speech, however lovely to the ear, reveals the speaker as a narcissistic fool. Much given to discussions about his complicated states of mind, he, like most self-centered persons, is really very simple. Whereas he tells Viola that

> such as I am all true lovers are,
> Unstaid and skittish in all motions else
> Save in the constant image of the creature
> That is beloved.                    (II.iv.17–20)

the only thing he loves is his romantic notion of the lover that he himself exemplifies, and he finds it so appealing that he never even asks if it is true. He leaves the play as he had entered it, with highfalutin talk about his "fancy," but this "fancy" is no more to be confused with love than his lyric self-descriptions are to be confused with fact. His soft, unmanly pleasure in caressing his emotions, his delight in "old and antic" songs as a solace for his "passion," even his petulant threat of violence against Olivia and "Cesario" for their presumed unfaithfulness reveal the sentimentalist who prefers the comfort of his own illusions to the dangers of candid self-appraisal.

In varying degrees, almost all the other characters in the play are shackled by their inability or refusal to comprehend their own emotions, or even to discern their blunders. Olivia's preoccupation with "a brother's dead love" is so unreal that a single visit from "Cesario" is enough to shatter it—and to provide her with a new obsession that is even more absurd, because it rests upon a yet more rudimentary error. Malvolio, "sick of self-love," is so easily led to self-exposure and humiliation that even as we laugh we pity him: "Alas, poor fool, how have they baffled thee!" Sir Andrew's imposing list of follies, both natural and acquired, makes him everybody's fool; and although Sir Toby has a searching eye for other people's foibles, he is usually much too drunk to recognize his own. Even Viola, who at least is in possession of the facts that save her from Olivia's type of blunder, thinks she must embark upon a program of deceit in order to survive. "Conceal me what I am," she tells the captain,

> and be my aid
> For such disguise as haply shall become
> The form of my intent.                    (I.ii.53–55)

Her finest moment in the play—the speech about the love-lorn girl who never told her love—is charming and pathetic, but it shows a certain pleasure in equivocation. Indeed, her skill and relish for the kind of organized deceit on which the action hangs are appropriate for the heroine of a play in which dissimulation and deception are routine. Only the Clown, it seems, is clear-eyed and wise enough to stand somewhat above the antics of the others and to comment on their follies. Knowing that foolery "does walk about the orb like the sun," he is as quick to puncture Orsino's egomania as to expose Olivia's silly posture of bereavement; and it is he, in the amusing but disturbing interview with the "lunatic" Malvolio, who makes us trace the narrow line between the madman and the sage. The Clown alone is immune to the pandemic error in Illyria—but he must wear a mask against contagion and infection, and he must hide his wisdom as the babble

of a licensed fool. In a world where everyone is slightly mad, his motley is a badge of knowledge.

Finally, the plotting, which Johnson found offensive, is also made to demonstrate the fact that most men live by error and illusion. The three main lines of action—Orsino's languid courtship of Olivia, Olivia's imbroglio with Viola and Sebastian, and Malvolio's disgrace—do not appear as isolated plots that run their parallel and independent courses; they come to us instead as reciprocal and reverberating statements of a single situation, which is the gulling of a fool. Writers from Aristophanes to Shaw have used this situation, in one form or another, to pedagogic purpose, for they have brought the gull through ridicule to exposure and correction. It is significant that although Orsino, Olivia, and Malvolio are all the victims of deception fostered either by themselves or others, they learn nothing from experience. Two of them are unmolested in their folly, and the third, though harshly treated, clings to his absurd illusions. Malvolio's credulity—which is no sillier than that which goes unpunished in his betters—is chastised so severely that he becomes, as Lamb observed, an almost tragic figure; but Orsino and Olivia are never even chided. None of them is changed, however, and none surrenders his obsession. The denouement affords a kind of liberation, to be sure, for the proper pairing off of lovers signifies release from labyrinthine misconception. But the ease with which Orsino shifts his "fancy" from Olivia to Viola matches that with which, earlier, Olivia turns from anchorite to ardent lover and then substitutes Sebastian for "Cesario." Neither of these self-indulgent egoists has been compelled to shake off his illusion, and in a sense, therefore, neither earns the triumph he enjoys. Perhaps, as Johnson thought, Sir Andrew's "natural fatuity" renders him ineligible for comic therapy, but at any rate he stays, as he will always stay, a fool. Sir Toby, too, remains what he had been before—a sot and parasite—and in addition he acquires Maria. As for Malvolio, he not only profits nothing from his hard instruction, but as he takes his angry leave we see his self-love stiffened by his sense of injured merit. "I'll be revenged on the whole pack of you," he snarls as he departs.

Hazlitt thought that Shakespeare was "too good-natured and magnanimous" to treat his comic knaves and fools as they deserve. Perhaps for this reason or perhaps because he makes us recognize ourselves in them, we are glad for these deluded people in Illyria, for they teach us what, alas, we need to know: that since we rarely win our way to truth, we must settle for illusion.

### A NOTE ON THE SOURCE

The plot of *Twelfth Night*—the adventures and misadventures of a pair of identical twins—is so old that its origins are lost in the prehistory of European literature. It had been a commonplace in Greek comedy long before Plautus and Terence imported it to Rome; and when young Shakespeare, at the start of his career, fashionably pillaged Plautus for *The Comedy of Errors*, he was following a distinguished Renaissance tradition of Italian, Spanish, French, and English writers who had worked their artful (and sometimes tedious) changes on the basic situation. One such change was the sexual differentiation of the twins, a refinement affording endless possibilities for intrigue and complication. It may be, as John Manningham suggested in the first known comment on *Twelfth Night* (see p. 876 n.), that for this embellishment he drew on Nicolò Secchi's *Gl'Inganni* (1562), but he could have gone to Secchi's source, which was *Gl'Ingannati* ("The Deceived"), a Plautine comedy, produced at Siena in 1531 and published six years later, that had spawned a dozen translations and adaptations through the later sixteenth century. Despite the formidable scholarship that has been brought to bear upon the question,[2] Shakespeare's knowledge of and obligation to most of this material is still a matter of dispute, but concerning his debt to one late recension of *Gl'Ingannati* there is no dispute whatever. This was Barnabe Rich's "Of Apolonius and Silla," the second of a set of eight prose narratives that was published in 1581 as *Riche his Farewell to Militarie profession: conteinyng verie pleasaunt discourses fit for a peaceable tyme.*

The genealogy of "Of Apolonius and Silla" is an instructive example of the free and easy ways of sixteenth-century writers: Rich found the tale (which he eked out with incidental and unacknowledged pilferings from William Painter's *Palace of Pleasure*, a big collection of stories first published in 1566) in Pierre de Belleforest's *Histoires Tragiques* (1579), which was translated from Matteo Bandello's *Novelle* (1554), which was based on *Gl'Ingannati*. Although Shakespeare could have read, and perhaps did read, these and other cognate versions of the story, his use of the *Farewell* would seem to be established by the fact that he took from it four words—*coistrel, gaskins, pavin,* and *galliard*—that appear in *Twelfth Night* and not elsewhere in his plays. Moreover, the fifth tale in Rich's collection ("Of Two Brethren and Their Wives") supplies an analogue for the scene (IV.ii) in which Malvolio is punished, although the subplot of the arrogant steward was apparently Shakespeare's own creation. He may have drawn on other things for this or that detail—for example, on Emanuel Forde's prose romance, *The Famous History of Parismus* (1598), for the shipwreck and for the names Olivia and Violetta, or on the anonymous play *Sir Clyomon and Clamydes* (1599) for the device (which he himself had used in *The Two Gentlemen of Verona*) of a girl disguised as a man in the service of her lover—but of all the alleged or possible sources, "Of Apolonius and Silla" stands closest to *Twelfth Night*. The bibliographical history of the *Farewell* —a book so popular that it was reprinted in 1583, 1594, and 1606—has been treated by Thomas Mabry Cranfill in his edition of the work (1959), pp. liii–lxxxi.

### A NOTE ON THE TEXT

The text of *Twelfth Night*, for which the sole source is the Folio of 1623, is, if not immaculate, so clean and tidy that it presents almost no problems. Apparently set up from the prompt copy or a transcript of it, the Folio of course contains a few misprints (like *incardinate* for *incardinate* at V.i.180–81), a few presumed or obvious errors in speech-headings (like those at II.v.32, 36, where Sir Toby is perhaps confused with Fabian, or at III.iv.24, where Malvolio is assigned a speech that clearly is not his), and a

few lines (for example, II.ii.12 and III.iii.15) that seem to need some sort of emendation. Moreover, the fact that the Clown is given all the lovely songs that were perhaps originally Viola's (as suggested at I.ii.57–59 and II.iv.42–43) has been cited as a token of revision. In general, however, the text, as all its editors have gratefully conceded, is one of almost unexampled purity.

In the present edition, therefore, it is followed very closely, even in such forms as *studient, jealious, wrack* (for *wreck*), and *vild,* which preserve, we may suppose, not only Shakespeare's spelling but also his pronunciation. But *prethee, divil, murther, Satnan* (for *Satan*), *Anthonio,* and *berd* (which occurs once for *beard*) are given in modern spelling. A few emendations sanctioned by long and universal approbation—like Pope's *Arion* for *Orion* at I.ii.15, Theobald's inspired *curl by* for *coole my* at I.iii.95, and Hanmer's *staniel* for *stallion* at II.v.112—have been admitted here, as have one or two superior readings from the later Folios (for example, *tang* for *langer* at III.iv.74). However, such attractive but unnecessary emendations as Pope's *south* for *sound* at I.i.5 have been rejected, and the few real cruxes have been allowed to stand, so that each reader must struggle all alone with Sir Andrew's *damned-colored stock* at I.iii.130, make what he can of the mysterious Lady of the Strachy at II.v.37–38, and unravel Viola's puzzling pronouncement at II.ii.12 without the aid of emendation.

In this edition the spelling has been modernized (with the exceptions noted above), the Latin act and scene divisions of the Folio translated, the punctuation brought into conformity with modern usage, a few lines that through compositorial error were printed as prose restored to verse (IV.ii.74–75), and a few stage directions (like the one at III.iv.14) shifted to accommodate the text. At the conclusion of the first, second, and fourth acts, the Folio has "*Finis Actus . . . ,*" here omitted. All editorial interpolations such as the list of characters, indications of place, and stage directions implied by the text but not indicated in the Folio are enclosed in square brackets. Other material departures from the copy text (excluding obvious typographical errors) are listed below in boldface type, followed in roman by the Folio reading. It will be apparent that most of them required no agonizing reappraisal.

I.ii.15 **Arion** Orion
I.iii.28 **all, most** almost  50 **Andrew** Ma.  95 **curl by** coole my
97 **me** we  111 **kickshawses** kicke-chawses  130 **set** sit  134 **That's** That
I.iv.28 **nuncio's** Nuntio's
I.v.146 **H'** as Ha's  164 s.d. **Viola** Uiolenta  253 **with fertile tears** fertill teares  259 **county's** countes
II.ii.20 **That sure methought** That me thought  31 **our frailty** O frailtie  32 **of** if
II.iii.25 **leman** Lemon  34 **give a—** giue a  135 **a nayword** an ayword
II.iv.53 **Fly . . . fly** Fye . . . fie  55 **yew** Ew  88 **I** It  103 **know—** know
II.v.12 **metal** Mettle  112 **staniel** stallion  141 **born** become; **achieve** atcheeues  154–56 **thee, The Fortunate Unhappy./ Daylight** thee, tht fortunate vnhappy daylight  173 **dear** deero
III.i.8 **king lies** Kings lyes  69 **wise men** wisemens  84 **gait** gate  93 **all ready** already  114 **here** heare
III.ii.8 **see thee the** see the  68 **renegado** Renegatho
III.iv.24 **Olivia** Mal.  74 **tang** langer  92 **How is't with you, man** [The Folio assigns this speech to Fabian]  119 **Ay, biddy I** biddy  150 **Ay, is't, I, ist?**  178 **You . . . for't** Yon . . . fot't  252 **competent** computent
IV.ii.6 **in** in in  15 **Gorboduc** Gorbodacke  38 **clerestories** cleere stores  72 **sport to the** sport the
V.i.199 **pavin** panyn

[2] This scholarship is knowledgeably surveyed by Kenneth Muir, *Shakespeare's Sources,* Vol. 1, *Comedies and Tragedies* (1957), pp. 66–77; and Geoffrey Bullough (ed.), *Narrative and Dramatic Sources of Shakespeare,* Vol. 2 (1958), pp. 269–85.

# TWELFTH NIGHT,
# OR, WHAT YOU WILL

[Dramatis Personae

ORSINO *Duke of Illyria*
SEBASTIAN *brother of Viola*
ANTONIO *a sea captain, friend to Sebastian*
A SEA CAPTAIN *friend to Viola*
VALENTINE }
CURIO } *gentlemen attending on the duke*
SIR TOBY BELCH *uncle to Olivia*
SIR ANDREW AGUECHEEK

MALVOLIO *steward to Olivia*
FABIAN }
FESTE *a clown* } *servants to Olivia*
OLIVIA *a countess*
VIOLA *sister to Sebastian*
MARIA *Olivia's woman*
LORDS A PRIEST SAILORS OFFICERS
MUSICIANS ATTENDANTS

*Scene:* Illyria]

## ACT I

### Scene I. [*The duke's palace.*]

*Enter* ORSINO, DUKE *of Illyria,* CURIO, *and other*
LORDS [*with* MUSICIANS].

DUKE
If music be the food of love, play on,
Give me excess of it, that, surfeiting,
The appetite° may sicken, and so die.
That strain again! It had a dying fall;°
O, it came o'er my ear like the sweet sound          5
That breathes upon a bank of violets,
Stealing and giving odor. Enough, no more!
'Tis not so sweet now as it was before.
O spirit of love, how quick and fresh° art thou,
That,° notwithstanding thy capacity,          10
Receiveth as the sea. Nought enters there,°
Of what validity and pitch° soe'er,
But falls into abatement and low price°

Even in a minute. So full of shapes° is fancy°
That it alone is high fantastical.°          15
CURIO
Will you go hunt, my lord?
DUKE
What, Curio?
CURIO   The hart.
DUKE
Why, so I do, the noblest that I have.
O, when mine eyes did see Olivia first,          20
Methought she purged the air of pestilence.
That instant was I turned into a hart,
And my desires, like fell° and cruel hounds,
E'er since pursue me.°

*Enter* VALENTINE.

How now? What news from her?
VALENTINE
So please my lord, I might not be admitted;          25

*The decorative border shown above was used in the First Folio
edition of Shakespeare's plays, 1623.*

**I.i.3 appetite** the lover's appetite for music   **4 fall** cadence
**9 quick and fresh** lively and eager   **10 That** in that   **11 there**
in the lover's "capacity"   **12 validity and pitch** value and
superiority (in falconry, pitch is the highest point of a bird's
flight)   **13 price** esteem

**14 shapes** fantasies; **fancy** love   **15 high fantastical** pre-
eminently imaginative   **23 fell** fierce   **22–24 That . . . me**
Orsino's mannered play on *hart/heart*—which exemplifies the
lover's "high fantastical" wit—derives from the story of
Actaeon, a famous hunter who, having seen Diana bathing,
was transformed into a stag and torn to pieces by his hounds

880

But from her handmaid do return this answer:
The element° itself, till seven years' heat,°
Shall not behold her face at ample view;
But like a cloistress she will veilèd walk,
And water once a day her chamber round    30
With eye-offending brine: all this to season°
A brother's dead love, which she would keep fresh
And lasting in her sad remembrance.°

DUKE
O, she that hath a heart of that fine frame
To pay this debt of love but to a brother,    35
How will she love when the rich golden shaft°
Hath killed the flock of all affections else°
That live in her; when liver, brain, and heart,°
These sovereign thrones, are all supplied and filled,
Her sweet perfections,° with one self° king.    40
Away before me to sweet beds of flow'rs;
Love-thoughts lie rich when canopied with bow'rs.
                                   *Exeunt.*

Scene II. [*The seacoast.*]

*Enter* VIOLA, *a* CAPTAIN, *and* SAILORS.

VIOLA
What country, friends, is this?
CAPTAIN
This is Illyria,° lady.
VIOLA
And what should I do in Illyria?
My brother he is in Elysium.°
Perchance he is not drowned. What think you, sailors? 5
CAPTAIN
It is perchance that you yourself were saved.
VIOLA
O my poor brother, and so perchance may he be.
CAPTAIN
True, madam; and, to comfort you with chance,°
Assure yourself, after our ship did split,
When you, and those poor number saved with you,   10
Hung on our driving° boat, I saw your brother,
Most provident in peril, bind himself
(Courage and hope both teaching him the practice°)
To a strong mast that lived° upon the sea;
Where, like Arion° on the dolphin's back,   15
I saw him hold acquaintance with the waves
So long as I could see.

VIOLA
For saying so, there's gold.
Mine own escape unfoldeth to my hope,°
Whereto thy speech serves for authority°   20
The like of him. Know'st thou this country?
CAPTAIN
Ay, madam, well, for I was bred and born
Not three hours' travel from this very place.
VIOLA
Who governs here?
CAPTAIN
A noble duke, in nature as in name.   25
VIOLA
What is his name?
CAPTAIN   Orsino.
VIOLA
Orsino! I have heard my father name him.
He was a bachelor then.
CAPTAIN
And so is now, or was so very late;   30
For but a month ago I went from hence,
And then 'twas fresh in murmur° (as you know
What great ones do, the less will prattle of)
That he did seek the love of fair Olivia.
VIOLA   What's she?   35
CAPTAIN
A virtuous maid, the daughter of a count
That died some twelvemonth since, then leaving her
In the protection of his son, her brother,
Who shortly also died: for whose dear love,
They say, she hath abjured the sight   40
And company of men.
VIOLA                  O that I served that lady,
And might not be delivered° to the world,
Till I had made mine own occasion mellow,
What my estate is.°
CAPTAIN          That were hard to compass,°
Because she will admit no kind of suit,   45
No, not° the duke's.
VIOLA
There is a fair behavior in thee, captain,
And though that° nature with a beauteous wall
Doth oft close in° pollution, yet of thee
I will believe thou hast a mind that suits   50
With this thy fair and outward character.°
I prithee (and I'll pay thee bounteously)
Conceal me what I am, and be my aid
For such disguise as haply shall become
The form of my intent.° I'll serve this duke.   55
Thou shalt present me as an eunuch to him;
It may be worth thy pains. For I can sing,
And speak to him in many sorts of music
That will allow° me very worth his service.
What else may hap, to time I will commit;   60
Only shape thou thy silence to my wit.°

27 **element** sky; **heat** course  31 **season** preserve (by the salt in her tears)  33 **remembrance** pronounced with four syllables, "re-mem-ber-ance"  36 **golden shaft** the shaft, borne by Cupid, that causes love (as distinguished from the leaden shaft, which causes aversion and disdain)  37 **all affections else** all other emotions but love  38 **liver . . . heart** the seats respectively of sexual desire, thought, and feeling  40 **perfections** pronounced with four syllables; **self** sole
**I.ii.2 Illyria** region bordering the east coast of the Adriatic  4 **Elysium** heaven (in classical mythology, the abode of the happy dead)  8 **chance** possibility  11 **driving** drifting  13 **practice** procedure  14 **lived** floated  15 **Arion** in classical mythology, a bard who, having leapt into the sea to escape from murderous sailors, was borne to shore by a dolphin that he charmed by his songs

19 **unfoldeth . . . hope** reinforces my hope for my brother's safety  20 **serves for authority** tends to justify  32 **fresh in murmur** being rumored  42 **delivered** disclosed  43–44 **made . . . is** found an appropriate time to reveal my status  44 **compass** effect  45 **not not even**  48 **though that** even though  49 **close in** conceal  51 **character** appearance and demeanor  54–55 **become . . . intent** suit my purpose  59 **allow** certify  61 **wit** skill in carrying out my plan

CAPTAIN
Be you his eunuch,° and your mute I'll be;
When my tongue blabs, then let mine eyes not see.
VIOLA
I thank thee. Lead me on.                          *Exeunt.*

Scene III. [*Olivia's house.*]

*Enter Sir* TOBY *and* MARIA.

TOBY   What a plague means my niece to take the death
of her brother thus? I am sure care's an enemy to life.
MARIA   By my troth, Sir Toby, you must come in
earlier o' nights. Your cousin,° my lady, takes great
exceptions to your ill hours.                                    5
TOBY   Why, let her except before excepted.°
MARIA   Ay, but you must confine yourself within the
modest limits of order.°
TOBY   Confine? I'll confine° myself no finer than I am.
These clothes are good enough to drink in, and so be   10
these boots too. And° they be not, let them hang
themselves in their own straps.
MARIA   That quaffing and drinking will undo you. I
heard my lady talk of it yesterday; and of a foolish
knight that you brought in one night here to be her   15
wooer.
TOBY   Who? Sir Andrew Aguecheek?
MARIA   Ay, he.
TOBY   He's as tall° a man as any's in Illyria.
MARIA   What's that to th' purpose?                          20
TOBY   Why, he has three thousand ducats a year.
MARIA   Ay, but he'll have but a year in all these ducats.
He's a very fool and a prodigal.
TOBY   Fie that you'll say so! He plays o' th' viol-de-
gamboys,° and speaks three or four languages word   25
for word without book, and hath all the good gifts of
nature.
MARIA   He hath indeed all, most natural;° for, besides
that he's a fool, he's a great quarreler; and but that he
hath the gift of a coward to allay the gust° he hath in   30
quarreling, 'tis thought among the prudent he would
quickly have the gift of a grave.
TOBY   By this hand, they are scoundrels and sub-
stractors° that say so of him. Who are they?
MARIA   They that add, moreover, he's drunk nightly   35
in your company.
TOBY   With drinking healths to my niece. I'll drink to
her as long as there is a passage in my throat and drink
in Illyria. He's a coward and a coistrel° that will not
drink to my niece till his brains turn o' th' toe like a   40

parish top.° What, wench? Castiliano vulgo;° for here
comes Sir Andrew Agueface.

*Enter Sir* ANDREW.

ANDREW   Sir Toby Belch. How now, Sir Toby Belch?
TOBY   Sweet Sir Andrew.
ANDREW   Bless you, fair shrew.                              45
MARIA   And you too, sir.
TOBY   Accost, Sir Andrew, accost.
ANDREW   What's that?
TOBY   My niece's chambermaid.°
ANDREW   Good Mistress Accost, I desire better   50
acquaintance.
MARIA   My name is Mary, sir.
ANDREW   Good Mistress Mary Accost.
TOBY   You mistake, knight. "Accost" is front her,
board her, woo her, assail her.                              55
ANDREW   By my troth, I would not undertake her in
this company. Is that the meaning of "accost"?
MARIA   Fare you well, gentlemen.
TOBY   And thou let part so,° Sir Andrew, would thou
mightst never draw sword again.                              60
ANDREW   And you part so, mistress, I would I might
never draw sword again! Fair lady, do you think you
have fools in hand?°
MARIA   Sir, I have not you by th' hand.
ANDREW   Marry,° but you shall have, and here's my   65
hand.
MARIA   Now, sir, thought is free. I pray you, bring
your hand to th' butt'ry° bar and let it drink.
ANDREW   Wherefore, sweetheart? What's your
metaphor?                                                    70
MARIA   It's dry,° sir.
ANDREW   Why, I think so. I am not such an ass but I
can keep my hand dry. But what's your jest?
MARIA   A dry jest, sir.
ANDREW   Are you full of them?                              75
MARIA   Ay, sir, I have them at my finger's ends.
Marry, now I let go your hand, I am barren.°
                                               *Exit* MARIA.
TOBY   O knight, thou lack'st a cup of canary!° When
did I see thee so put down?
ANDREW   Never in your life, I think, unless you see   80
canary put me down. Methinks sometimes I have no
more wit than a Christian or an ordinary man has.
But I am a great eater of beef, and I believe that does
harm to my wit.

**41 parish top** according to George Steevens, a large top
"formerly kept in every village, to be whipped in frosty
weather, that the peasants might be kept warm by exercise,
and out of mischief while they could not work"; however,
the allusion may be to the communal top-spinning whose
origins are buried in religious ritual; **Castiliano vulgo** a
phrase of uncertain meaning; perhaps Sir Toby is suggesting
that Maria assume a grave and ceremonial manner—like that
of the notoriously formal Castilians—for Sir Andrew's
benefit **48–49 What's . . . chambermaid** Sir Andrew
asks the meaning of the word "accost," but Sir Toby thinks
that he is referring to Maria; actually, she was not Olivia's
chambermaid, but rather her companion, or lady in waiting,
as is made clear at I.v.161 **59 so** i.e., without ceremony **63
have . . . hand** are dealing with fools **65 Marry** indeed (a
mild interjection, originally an oath, "By the Virgin Mary")
**68 butt'ry** buttery, a storeroom for butts or casks of liquor
**71 dry** (1) thirsty (2) indicative of impotence **77 barren** (1)
without more jests (2) dull-witted **78 canary** a sweet wine
from the Canary Islands

**62 Be . . . eunuch** this part of the plan was not carried out
**I.iii.4 cousin** a term indicating various degrees of kinship; here,
niece **6 except before excepted** Sir Toby parodies the legal
jargon *exceptis excipiendis* ("with the exceptions previously
noted") commonly used in leases and contracts **8 modest
. . . order** reasonable limits of good behavior **9 confine
clothe 11 And** if (a common Elizabethan usage) **19 tall**
bold and handsome **24–25 viol-de-gamboys** bass viol **28
natural** like a natural fool or idiot **30 gust** gusto **33–34
substractors** slanderers **39 coistrel** knave (literally, a
groom who takes care of a knight's horse)

TOBY  No question. 85

ANDREW  And I thought that, I'd forswear it. I'll ride home tomorrow, Sir Toby.

TOBY  Pourquoi,° my dear knight?

ANDREW  What is "pourquoi"? Do, or not do? I would I had bestowed that time in the tongues that I 90 have in fencing, dancing, and bearbaiting. O, had I but followed the arts!

TOBY  Then hadst thou had an excellent head of hair.°

ANDREW  Why, would that have mended my hair?

TOBY  Past question, for thou see'st it will not curl by 95 nature.

ANDREW  But it becomes me well enough, does't not?

TOBY  Excellent. It hangs like flax on a distaff;° and I hope to see a huswife° take thee between her legs and spin it off. 100

ANDREW  Faith, I'll home tomorrow, Sir Toby. Your niece will not be seen; or if she be, it's four to one she'll none of me. The count himself here hard by woos her.

TOBY  She'll none o' th' count. She'll not match above 105 her degree, neither in estate,° years, nor wit; I have heard her swear't. Tut, there's life in't,° man.

ANDREW  I'll stay a month longer. I am a fellow o' th' strangest mind i' th' world. I delight in masques and revels sometimes altogether. 110

TOBY  Art thou good at these kickshawses,° knight?

ANDREW  As any man in Illyria, whatsoever he be, under the degree of my betters,° and yet I will not compare with an old° man.

TOBY  What is thy excellence in a galliard,° knight? 115

ANDREW  Faith, I can cut a caper.°

TOBY  And I can cut the mutton to't.

ANDREW  And I think I have the back-trick° simply as strong as any man in Illyria.

TOBY  Wherefore are these things hid? Wherefore 120 have these gifts a curtain before 'em? Are they like to take° dust, like Mistress Mall's picture? Why dost thou not go to church in a galliard and come home in a coranto?° My very walk should be a jig. I would not so much as make water but in a sink-a-pace.° What 125 dost thou mean? Is it a world to hide virtues° in? I did think, by the excellent constitution of thy leg, it was formed under the star of a galliard.°

ANDREW  Ay, 'tis strong, and it does indifferent well in a damned-colored stock.° Shall we set about some 130 revels?

TOBY  What shall we do else? Were we not born under Taurus?°

ANDREW  Taurus? That's sides and heart.

TOBY  No, sir; it is legs and thighs. Let me see thee 135 caper. Ha, higher; ha, ha, excellent!  *Exeunt.*

## Scene IV. [*The duke's palace.*]

*Enter* VALENTINE, *and* VIOLA *in man's attire.*

VALENTINE  If the duke continue these favors towards you, Cesario, you are like to be much advanced. He hath known you but three days and already you are no stranger.

VIOLA  You either fear his humor° or my negligence, 5 that° you call in question the continuance of his love. Is he inconstant, sir, in his favors?

VALENTINE  No, believe me.

*Enter* DUKE, CURIO, *and* ATTENDANTS.

VIOLA  I thank you. Here comes the count.

DUKE  Who saw Cesario, ho? 10

VIOLA  On your attendance, my lord, here.

DUKE
Stand you awhile aloof. Cesario,
Thou know'st no less but all.° I have unclasped
To thee the book even of my secret soul.
Therefore, good youth, address thy gait° unto her; 15
Be not denied access, stand at her doors,
And tell them there thy fixèd foot shall grow
Till thou have audience.

VIOLA                Sure, my noble lord,
If she be so abandoned to her sorrow
As it is spoke, she never will admit me. 20

DUKE
Be clamorous and leap all civil bounds
Rather than make unprofited° return.

VIOLA
Say I do speak with her, my lord, what then?

DUKE
O, then unfold the passion of my love;
Surprise her with discourse of my dear° faith; 25
It shall become thee well to act my woes.
She will attend it better in thy youth
Than in a nuncio's° of more grave aspect.°

VIOLA
I think not so, my lord.

DUKE                Dear lad, believe it;
For they shall yet belie thy happy years 30
That say thou art a man. Diana's lip
Is not more smooth and rubious;° thy small pipe°
Is as the maiden's organ, shrill and sound,°
And all is semblative° a woman's part.

88 **Pourquoi** why (French)  93 **Then . . . hair** perhaps Sir Toby is punning on Sir Andrew's "tongues" (line 90) as "tongs" or curling irons  98 **distaff** stick used in spinning  99 **huswife** housewife  106 **estate** fortune  107 **there's life in't** there's hope for you yet  111 **kickshawses** trifles (French *quelque chose*)  113 **under . . . betters** so long as he is not my social superior  114 **old** experienced (?)  115 **galliard** lively dance in triple time  116 **caper** (1) frisky leap (2) spice used to season mutton (hence Sir Toby's remark in the next line)  118 **back-trick** reverse step in dancing  122 **take** gather  124 **coranto** quick running dance  125 **sink-a-pace** cinque-pace (French *cinque pas*), a kind of galliard of five steps (but there is also a scatological pun here)  126 **virtues** talents, accomplishments  128 **star . . . galliard** a dancing star  130 **damned-colored stock** of the many emendations proposed for this stocking of uncertain color—"damasked-colored," "dun-colored," "dove-colored," "damson-colored," and the like—Rowe's "flame-colored" has been most popular

133 **Taurus** the Bull (one of the twelve signs of the zodiac, each of which was thought to influence a certain part of the human body; most authorities assigned Taurus to neither "sides and heart" nor "legs and thighs," but to neck and throat)  **I.iv.5 humor** changeable disposition  **6 that** in that  **13 no . . . all** everything  **15 address thy gait** direct your steps  **22 unprofited** unsuccessful  **25 dear** intense  **28 nuncio's** messenger's; **aspect** accent on second syllable  **32 rubious** ruby-red; **pipe** voice  **33 shrill and sound** high and clear  **34 semblative** like

I know thy constellation° is right apt°                    35
For this affair. Some four or five attend him,
All, if you will; for I myself am best
When least in company. Prosper well in this,
And thou shalt live as freely as thy lord
To call his fortunes thine.

VIOLA                              I'll do my best        40
To woo your lady. [*Aside*.] Yet a barful° strife!
Whoe'er I woo, myself would be his wife.        *Exeunt.*

Scene V. [*Olivia's house.*]

*Enter* MARIA *and* CLOWN.

MARIA    Nay, either tell me where thou hast been, or I
will not open my lips so wide as a bristle may enter in
way of thy excuse. My lady will hang thee for thy
absence.

CLOWN    Let her hang me. He that is well hanged in    5
this world needs to fear no colors.°

MARIA    Make that good.°

CLOWN    He shall see none to fear.

MARIA    A good lenten° answer. I can tell thee where
that saying was born, of "I fear no colors."           10

CLOWN    Where, good Mistress Mary?

MARIA    In the wars; and that may you be bold to say
in your foolery.

CLOWN    Well, God give them wisdom that have it,
and those that are fools, let them use their talents.°    15

MARIA    Yet you will be hanged for being so long
absent, or to be turned away. Is not that as good as a
hanging to you?

CLOWN    Many a good hanging prevents a bad
marriage, and for turning away, let summer bear it    20
out.°

MARIA    You are resolute then?

CLOWN    Not so, neither; but I am resolved on two
points.°

MARIA    That if one break, the other will hold; or if    25
both break, your gaskins° fall.

CLOWN    Apt, in good faith; very apt. Well, go thy
way! If Sir Toby would leave drinking, thou wert as
witty a piece of Eve's flesh° as any in Illyria.

MARIA    Peace, you rogue; no more o' that. Here    30
comes my lady. Make your excuse wisely, you were
best.°                                                        [*Exit.*]

*Enter Lady* OLIVIA, *with* MALVOLIO [*and other*
ATTENDANTS].

CLOWN    Wit, and't° be thy will, put me into good
fooling. Those wits that think they have thee do very
oft prove fools, and I that am sure I lack thee may pass    35

for a wise man. For what says Quinapalus?° "Better
a witty fool than a foolish wit." God bless thee, lady.

OLIVIA    Take the fool away.

CLOWN    Do you not hear, fellows? Take away the
lady.                                                          40

OLIVIA    Go to,° y' are a dry° fool! I'll no more of you.
Besides, you grow dishonest.°

CLOWN    Two faults, madonna,° that drink and good
counsel will amend. For give the dry° fool drink, then
is the fool not dry. Bid the dishonest man mend      45
himself: if he mend, he is no longer dishonest; if he
cannot, let the botcher° mend him. Anything that's
mended is but patched; virtue that transgresses is but
patched with sin, and sin that amends is but patched
with virtue. If that this simple syllogism will serve, so;  50
if it will not, what remedy? As there is no true cuckold
but calamity,° so beauty's a flower. The lady bade take
away the fool; therefore, I say again, take her away.

OLIVIA    Sir, I bade them take away you.

CLOWN    Misprision in the highest degree.° Lady,    55
cucullus non facit monachum.° That's as much to say
as, I wear not motley in my brain. Good madonna,
give me leave to prove you a fool.

OLIVIA    Can you do it?

CLOWN    Dexteriously,° good madonna.                 60

OLIVIA    Make your proof.

CLOWN    I must catechize you for it, madonna. Good
my mouse of virtue,° answer me.

OLIVIA    Well, sir, for want of other idleness,° I'll bide
your proof.                                                    65

CLOWN    Good madonna, why mourn'st thou?

OLIVIA    Good fool, for my brother's death.

CLOWN    I think his soul is in hell, madonna.

OLIVIA    I know his soul is in heaven, fool.

CLOWN    The more fool, madonna, to mourn for your  70
brother's soul, being in heaven. Take away the fool,
gentlemen.

OLIVIA    What think you of this fool, Malvolio? Doth
he not mend?

MALVOLIO    Yes, and shall do till the pangs of death  75
shake him. Infirmity, that decays the wise, doth ever
make the better fool.

CLOWN    God send you, sir, a speedy infirmity, for the
better increasing your folly. Sir Toby will be sworn
that I am no fox,° but he will not pass his word for   80
twopence that you are no fool.

OLIVIA    How say you to that, Malvolio?

MALVOLIO    I marvel your ladyship takes delight in
such a barren° rascal. I saw him put down the other day
with° an ordinary fool that has no more brain than a   85

35 constellation predetermined qualities; apt suitable   41
barful full of impediments
I.v.6 fear no colors fear nothing (with a pun on *color* meaning
"flag" and *collar* meaning "hangman's noose")   7 Make that
good explain it   9 lenten thin, meager (perhaps an allusion to
the colorless, unbleached linen that replaced the customary
liturgical purple or violet during Lent)   15 talents native
intelligence (with perhaps a pun on *talons* meaning "claws")
20-21 let . . . out let the warm weather make it endurable
24 points counts (but Maria takes it in the sense of tagged laces
serving as suspenders)   26 gaskins loose breeches   28-29 thou
. . . flesh you would make as clever a wife   31-32 you were
best it would be best for you   33 and't if it

36 Quinapalus a sage of the Clown's invention   41 Go to
enough; dry stupid   42 dishonest unreliable   43 madonna
my lady   44 dry thirsty   47 botcher mender of clothes
51-52 there . . . calamity although the Clown's chatter should
not be pressed too hard for significance, Kittredge's paraphrase
of this difficult passage is perhaps the least unsatisfactory:
"Every man is wedded to fortune; hence, when one's fortune
is unfaithful, one may in very truth be called a cuckold—the
husband of an unfaithful wife"   55 Misprision . . . degree
an egregious error in mistaken identity   56 cucullus . . .
monachum a cowl does not make a monk   60 Dexteriously
dexterously   62-63 Good . . . virtue my good virtuous
mouse (a term of playful affection)   64 idleness trifling   80
I . . . fox i.e., sly and dangerous (like you)   84 barren
stupid   84-85 put down . . . with bested . . . by

stone. Look you now, he's out of his guard° already. Unless you laugh and minister occasion° to him, he is gagged. I protest I take these wise men that crow° so at these set° kind of fools no better than the fools' zanies.°

OLIVIA   O, you are sick of self-love, Malvolio, and taste with a distempered appetite. To be generous,° guiltless, and of free disposition, is to take those things for birdbolts° that you deem cannon bullets. There is no slander in an allowed° fool, though he do nothing but rail; nor no railing in a known discreet man, though he do nothing but reprove.

CLOWN   Now Mercury indue thee with leasing,° for thou speak'st well of fools.

*Enter* MARIA.

MARIA   Madam, there is at the gate a young gentleman much desires to speak with you.

OLIVIA   From the Count Orsino, is it?

MARIA   I know not, madam. 'Tis a fair young man and well attended.

OLIVIA   Who of my people hold him in delay?

MARIA   Sir Toby, madam, your kinsman.

OLIVIA   Fetch him off, I pray you. He speaks nothing but madman. Fie on him! [*Exit* MARIA.] Go you, Malvolio. If it be a suit from the Count, I am sick, or not at home. What you will, to dismiss it. (*Exit* MALVOLIO.) Now you see, sir, how your fooling grows old,° and people dislike it.

CLOWN   Thou hast spoke for us, madonna, as if thy eldest son should be a fool; whose skull Jove° cram with brains, for—here he comes—one of thy kin has a most weak pia mater.°

*Enter Sir* TOBY.

OLIVIA   By mine honor, half drunk. What is he at the gate, cousin?

TOBY   A gentleman,

OLIVIA   A gentleman? What gentleman?

TOBY   'Tis a gentleman here. A plague o' these pickle-herring!° How now, sot?°

CLOWN   Good Sir Toby.

OLIVIA   Cousin,° cousin, how have you come so early by this lethargy?

TOBY   Lechery? I defy lechery. There's one at the gate.

OLIVIA   Ay, marry, what is he?

TOBY   Let him be the devil and he will, I care not. Give me faith,° say I. Well, it's all one.      *Exit.*

OLIVIA   What's a drunken man like, fool?

CLOWN   Like a drowned man, a fool, and a madman. One draught above heat° makes him a fool, the second mads him, and a third drowns him.

OLIVIA   Go thou and seek the crowner,° and let him sit o' my coz;° for he's in the third degree of drink— he's drowned. Go look after him.

CLOWN   He is but mad yet, madonna, and the fool shall look to the madman.      [*Exit.*]

*Enter* MALVOLIO.

MALVOLIO   Madam, yond young fellow swears he will speak with you. I told him you were sick; he takes on him to understand so much, and therefore comes to speak with you. I told him you were asleep; he seems to have a foreknowledge of that too, and therefore comes to speak with you. What is to be said to him, lady? He's fortified against any denial.

OLIVIA   Tell him he shall not speak with me.

MALVOLIO   H' as° been told so; and he says he'll stand at your door like a sheriff's post,° and be the supporter to a bench, but° he'll speak with you.

OLIVIA   What kind o' man is he?

MALVOLIO   Why, of mankind.°

OLIVIA   What manner of man?

MALVOLIO   Of very ill manner. He'll speak with you, will you or no.

OLIVIA   Of what personage and years is he?

MALVOLIO   Not yet old enough for a man nor young enough for a boy; as a squash° is before 'tis a peascod, or a codling° when 'tis almost an apple. 'Tis with him in standing water,° between boy and man. He is very well-favored and he speaks very shrewishly.° One would think his mother's milk were scarce out of him.

OLIVIA   Let him approach. Call in my gentlewoman.

MALVOLIO   Gentlewoman, my lady calls.      *Exit.*

*Enter* MARIA.

OLIVIA   Give me my veil; come, throw it o'er my face. We'll once more hear Orsino's embassy.

*Enter* VIOLA.

VIOLA   The honorable lady of the house, which is she?

OLIVIA   Speak to me; I shall answer for her. Your will?

VIOLA   Most radiant, exquisite, and unmatchable beauty—I pray you tell me if this be the lady of the house, for I never saw her. I would be loath to cast away my speech; for, besides that it is excellently well penned, I have taken great pains to con° it. Good beauties, let me sustain no scorn. I am very comptible,° even to the least sinister° usage.

OLIVIA   Whence came you, sir?

VIOLA   I can say little more than I have studied, and that question's out of my part. Good gentle one, give me modest° assurance if you be the lady of the house, that I may proceed in my speech.

86 **out . . . guard** defenseless   87 **minister occasion** afford opportunity (for his fooling)   88 **crow** with laughter 89 **set** artificial; **zanies** inferior buffoons   91 **generous** liberal-minded   93 **birdbolts** blunt arrows   94 **allowed** licensed, privileged   97 **Mercury . . . leasing** may the god of trickery endow you with the gift of deception   111 **old** stale, tedious   113 **Jove** if, as is likely, Shakespeare here and elsewhere wrote "God," the printed text reflects the statute of 1606 that prohibited profane stage allusions to the deity 115 **pia mater** brain   120–21 **pickle-herring** to which the drunken Sir Toby attributes his hiccoughing   121 **sot** fool 123 **Cousin** i.e., uncle (see I.iii.4)   128 **faith** in order to resist the devil   131 **above heat** above what is required to make a man normally warm

133 **crowner** coroner   134 **sit . . . coz** hold an inquest on my kinsman   146 **H' as** he has   147 **sheriff's post** post set up before a sheriff's door for placards, notices, and such 148 **but** except   150 **of mankind** like other men   156 **squash** unripe peascod (peapod)   157 **codling** unripe apple   158 **standing water** at the turning of the tide, between ebb and flood, when it flows neither way   159 **shrewishly** tartly   172 **con** learn   173 **comptible** sensitive   174 **sinister** discourteous   178 **modest** reasonable

OLIVIA  Are you a comedian?°                                    180

VIOLA  No, my profound heart;° and yet (by the very
fangs of malice I swear) I am not that° I play. Are you
the lady of the house?

OLIVIA  If I do not usurp° myself, I am.

VIOLA  Most certain, if you are she, you do usurp   185
yourself; for what° is yours to bestow is not yours to
reserve. But this is from my commission.° I will on
with my speech in your praise and then show you the
heart of my message.

OLIVIA  Come to what is important in't. I forgive   190
you° the praise.

VIOLA  Alas, I took great pains to study it, and 'tis
poetical.

OLIVIA  It is the more like to be feigned; I pray you
keep it in. I heard you were saucy at my gates; and   195
allowed your approach rather to wonder at you than
to hear you. If you be not mad, be gone; if you have
reason, be brief. 'Tis not that time of moon with me to
make one in so skipping a dialogue.°

MARIA  Will you hoist sail, sir? Here lies your way.   200

VIOLA  No, good swabber; I am to hull° here a little
longer. Some mollification for your giant,° sweet lady.
Tell me your mind. I am a messenger.°

OLIVIA  Sure you have some hideous matter to deliver,
when the courtesy of it is so fearful.° Speak your   205
office.°

VIOLA  It alone concerns your ear. I bring no overture
of war, no taxation of° homage. I hold the olive° in my
hand. My words are as full of peace as matter.°

OLIVIA  Yet you began rudely. What are you? What   210
would you?

VIOLA  The rudeness that hath appeared in me have I
learned from my entertainment.° What I am, and
what I would, are as secret as maidenhead:° to your
ears, divinity;° to any other's, profanation.   215

OLIVIA  Give us the place alone; we will hear this
divinity. [Exit MARIA and ATTENDANTS.] Now, sir,
what is your text?

VIOLA  Most sweet lady—

OLIVIA  A comfortable° doctrine, and much may be   220
said of it. Where lies your text?

VIOLA  In Orsino's bosom.

OLIVIA  In his bosom? In what chapter of his bosom?

VIOLA  To answer by the method,° in the first of his
heart.   225

OLIVIA  O, I have read it; it is heresy. Have you no
more to say?

VIOLA  Good madam, let me see your face.

OLIVIA  Have you any commission from your lord to
negotiate with my face? You are now out of your   230
text.° But we will draw the curtain and show you the
picture. [Unveils.] Look you, sir, such a one I was this
present.° Is't not well done?

VIOLA  Excellently done, if God did all.

OLIVIA  'Tis in grain,° sir; 'twill endure wind and   235
weather.

VIOLA
'Tis beauty truly blent, whose red and white
Nature's own sweet and cunning° hand laid on.
Lady, you are the cruel'st she alive
If you will lead these graces to the grave,   240
And leave the world no copy.

OLIVIA  O, sir, I will not be so hard-hearted. I will
give out divers schedules° of my beauty. It shall be
inventoried, and every particle and utensil° labeled to
my will:° as, item,° two lips, indifferent red; item,   245
two gray eyes, with lids to them; item, one neck, one
chin, and so forth. Were you sent hither to praise° me?

VIOLA
I see you what you are; you are too proud;
But if° you were the devil, you are fair.
My lord and master loves you. O, such love   250
Could be but recompensed though you were crowned
The nonpareil of beauty.

OLIVIA                    How does he love me?

VIOLA
With adorations, with fertile° tears,
With groans that thunder love, with sighs of fire.

OLIVIA
Your lord does know my mind; I cannot love him.   255
Yet I suppose him virtuous, know him noble,
Of great estate, of fresh and stainless youth;
In voices well divulged,° free, learned, and valiant,
And in dimension° and the shape of nature
A gracious person. But yet I cannot love him.   260
He might have took his answer long ago.

VIOLA
If I did love you in my master's flame,
With such a suff'ring, such a deadly° life,
In your denial I would find no sense;
I would not understand it.

OLIVIA                    Why, what would you?   265

VIOLA
Make me a willow° cabin at your gate
And call upon my soul° within the house;
Write loyal cantons° of contemnèd° love
And sing them loud even in the dead of night;
Hallo your name to the reverberate° hills   270

---

**180 comedian** actor (because he has had to "con" a "part")
**181 my profound heart** my sagacious lady (a bantering
compliment)  **182 that** that which  **184 usurp** counterfeit
(but Viola takes it in the sense "betray," "wrong")  **186 what**
your hand in marriage  **187 from my commission** beyond
my instructions  **190–91 forgive you** excuse you from repeating  **198–99 'Tis . . . dialogue** I am not in the mood to sustain
such aimless banter  **201 hull** lie adrift  **202 giant** an ironical
reference to Maria's small size  **203 Tell . . . messenger**
many editors have divided these sentences, assigning the first to
Olivia and the second to Viola  **205 when . . . fearful**
since your manner is so truculent  **206 office** business  **208
taxation of** demand for;  **olive** the symbol of peace  **209
matter** significant content  **213 entertainment** reception
**214 maidenhead** maidenhood  **215 divinity** a sacred message
**220 comfortable** comforting  **224 method** in the theological
style suggested by "divinity," "profanation," "text," and
"doctrine"

**230–31 You . . . text** You have shifted from talking
of your master's heart to asking about my face  **232–33
this present** just now (like portrait painters, Olivia gives the
age of the subject of the "picture" she has just revealed
by drawing the "curtain" of a veil from her face)  **235
in grain** fast-dyed, indelible  **238 cunning** skillful  **243
schedules** statements  **244 utensil** article  **244–45 labeled
. . . will** i.e., added as a codicil  **245 item** also  **247 praise**
appraise  **249 if** even if  **253 fertile** copious  **258 well
divulged** of good repute  **259 dimension** physique  **263
deadly** doomed to die  **266 willow** emblem of a disconsolate lover  **267 my soul** Olivia  **268 cantons** songs;
**contemnèd** rejected  **270 reverberate** reverberating

And make the babbling gossip of the air°
Cry out "Olivia!" O, you should not rest
Between the elements of air and earth
But° you should pity me.

OLIVIA
You might do much. What is your parentage?        275

VIOLA
Above my fortunes, yet my state° is well.
I am a gentleman.

OLIVIA                Get you to your lord.
I cannot love him. Let him send no more,
Unless, perchance, you come to me again
To tell me how he takes it. Fare you well.        280
I thank you for your pains. Spend this for me.

VIOLA
I am no fee'd post,° lady; keep your purse;
My master, not myself, lacks recompense.
Love make his heart of flint that you shall love;°
And let your fervor, like my master's, be         285
Placed in contempt. Farewell, fair cruelty.        *Exit.*

OLIVIA
"What is your parentage?"
"Above my fortunes, yet my state is well.
I am a gentleman." I'll be sworn thou art.
Thy tongue, thy face, thy limbs, actions, and spirit   290
Do give thee fivefold blazon.° Not too fast; soft,° soft,
Unless the master were the man. How now?
Even so quickly may one catch the plague?
Methinks I feel this youth's perfections
With an invisible and subtle stealth              295
To creep in at mine eyes. Well, let it be.
What ho, Malvolio!

*Enter* MALVOLIO.

MALVOLIO             Here, madam, at your service.

OLIVIA
Run after that same peevish° messenger,
The county's° man. He left this ring behind him,
Would I or not. Tell him I'll none of it.         300
Desire him not to flatter with° his lord
Nor hold him up with hopes. I am not for him.
If that the youth will come this way tomorrow,
I'll give him reasons for't. Hie thee, Malvolio.

MALVOLIO
Madam, I will.                          *Exit.* 305

OLIVIA
I do I know not what, and fear to find
Mine eye too great a flatterer for my mind.°
Fate, show thy force; ourselves we do not owe.°
What is decreed must be—and be this so!    [*Exit.*]

---

# ACT II

## Scene I. [*The seacoast.*]

*Enter* ANTONIO *and* SEBASTIAN.

ANTONIO  Will you stay no longer? Nor will you not
that I go with you?

SEBASTIAN  By your patience,° no. My stars shine
darkly over me; the malignancy of my fate might
perhaps distemper° yours. Therefore I shall crave of 5
you your leave, that I may bear my evils alone. It were
a bad recompense for your love to lay any of them on
you.

ANTONIO  Let me yet know of you whither you are
bound.                                  10

SEBASTIAN  No, sooth,° sir. My determinate° voyage
is mere extravagancy.° But I perceive in you so
excellent a touch of modesty that you will not extort
from me what I am willing to keep in; therefore it
charges me in manners the rather to express myself.° 15
You must know of me then, Antonio, my name is
Sebastian, which I called Roderigo. My father was
that Sebastian of Messaline whom I know you have
heard of. He left behind him myself and a sister, both
born in an hour.° If the heavens had been pleased,   20
would we had so ended! But you, sir, altered that, for
some hour before you took me from the breach° of
the sea was my sister drowned.

ANTONIO  Alas the day!

SEBASTIAN  A lady, sir, though it was said she much 25
resembled me, was yet of many accounted beautiful.
But though I could not with such estimable wonder°
overfar believe that, yet thus far I will boldly publish°
her: she bore a mind that envy could not but call fair.
She is drowned already, sir, with salt water, though I 30
seem to drown her remembrance again with more.

ANTONIO  Pardon me, sir, your bad entertainment.°

SEBASTIAN  O good Antonio, forgive me your
trouble.°

ANTONIO  If you will not murder me° for my love, 35
let me be your servant.

SEBASTIAN  If you will not undo what you have done,
that is, kill him whom you have recovered,° desire
it not. Fare ye well at once. My bosom is full of
kindness, and I am yet so near the manners of my   40
mother that, upon the least occasion more, mine eyes
will tell tales of me.° I am bound to the Count Orsino's
court. Farewell.                          *Exit.*

ANTONIO
The gentleness of all the gods go with thee.
I have many enemies in Orsino's court,              45
Else would I very shortly see thee there.
But come what may, I do adore thee so
That danger shall seem sport, and I will go.  *Exit.*

---

271 **babbling . . . air** echo  274 **But** but that  276 **state**
status  282 **fee'd post** lackey to be tipped  284 **Love . . .
love** may Love make the heart of him you love like flint
291 **blazon** heraldic insignia; **soft** take it slowly  298 **peevish**
truculent, impertinent  299 **county's** count's  301 **flatter with**
encourage  307 **Mine . . . mind** my eye, so susceptible to
external attractions, will betray my judgment  308 **owe** own

**II.i.3 patience** permission  **5 distemper** disorder  **11 sooth**
truly; **determinate** intended  **12 extravagancy** wandering
**14–15 it . . . myself** civility requires that I give some account
of myself  **20 in an hour** in the same hour  **22 breach**
breakers  **27 with . . . wonder** with so much esteem in
my appraisal  **28 publish** describe  **32 bad entertainment**
poor reception at my hands  **33–34 your trouble** the trouble I
have given you  **35 murder me** by forcing me to part from
you  **38 recovered** saved  **40–42 so . . . me** so overwrought
by my sorrow that, like a woman, I shall weep

## Scene II. [*A street near Olivia's house.*]

*Enter* VIOLA *and* MALVOLIO *at several° doors.*

MALVOLIO   Were not you ev'n now with the Countess Olivia?

VIOLA   Even now, sir. On a moderate pace I have since arrived but hither.

MALVOLIO   She returns this ring to you, sir. You might 5 have saved me my pains, to have taken it away yourself. She adds, moreover, that you should put your lord into a desperate assurance° she will none of him. And one thing more, that you be never so hardy to come again in his affairs, unless it be to report your 10 lord's taking of this. Receive it so.

VIOLA   She took the ring of me.° I'll none of it.

MALVOLIO   Come, sir, you peevishly threw it to her, and her will is, it should be so returned. If it be worth stooping for, there it lies, in your eye;° if not, be it his 15 that finds it.                              *Exit.*

VIOLA

I left no ring with her. What means this lady?
Fortune forbid my outside have not charmed her.
She made good view of me; indeed, so much
That sure methought° her eyes had lost her tongue,°   20
For she did speak in starts distractedly.
She loves me sure; the cunning° of her passion
Invites me in this churlish messenger.
None of my lord's ring? Why, he sent her none.
I am the man.° If it be so, as 'tis,                  25
Poor lady, she were better love a dream.
Disguise, I see thou art a wickedness
Wherein the pregnant enemy° does much.
How easy is it for the proper false°
In women's waxen hearts to set their forms!          30
Alas, our frailty is the cause, not we,
For such as we are made of, such we be.
How will this fadge?° My master loves her dearly;
And I (poor monster°) fond° as much on him;
And she (mistaken) seems to dote on me.              35
What will become of this? As I am man,
My state is desperate° for my master's love.
As I am woman (now alas the day!),
What thriftless° sighs shall poor Olivia breathe?
O Time, thou must untangle this, not I;             40
It is too hard a knot for me t' untie.      [*Exit.*]

## Scene III. [*A room in Olivia's house.*]

*Enter Sir* TOBY *and Sir* ANDREW.

TOBY   Approach, Sir Andrew. Not to be abed after midnight is to be up betimes; and "Deliculo surgere,"° thou know'st.

ANDREW   Nay, by my troth, I know not, but I know to be up late is to be up late.                      5

TOBY   A false conclusion; I hate it as an unfilled can.° To be up after midnight, and to go to bed then, is early; so that to go to bed after midnight is to go to bed betimes. Does not our lives consist of the four elements?°                                        10

ANDREW   Faith, so they say; but I think it rather consists of eating and drinking.

TOBY   Th' art a scholar! Let us therefore eat and drink. Marian I say, a stoup° of wine!

*Enter* CLOWN.

ANDREW   Here comes the fool, i' faith.             15

CLOWN   How now, my hearts? Did you never see the picture of We Three?°

TOBY   Welcome, ass. Now let's have a catch.°

ANDREW   By my troth, the fool has an excellent breast.° I had rather than forty shillings I had such a  20 leg,° and so sweet a breath to sing, as the fool has. In sooth, thou wast in very gracious° fooling last night, when thou spok'st of Pigrogromitus,° of the Vapians° passing the equinoctial of Queubus.° 'Twas very good, i' faith. I sent thee sixpence for thy leman.° Hadst it?  25

CLOWN   I did impeticos thy gratillity,° for Malvolio's nose is no whipstock. My lady has a white hand, and the Myrmidons are no bottle-ale houses.°

ANDREW   Excellent. Why, this is the best fooling, when all is done. Now a song!                       30

TOBY   Come on, there is sixpence for you. Let's have a song.

ANDREW   There's a testril° of me too. If one knight give a—°

CLOWN   Would you have a love song, or a song of   35 good life?°

TOBY   A love song, a love song.

ANDREW   Ay, ay, I care not for good life.

CLOWN *sings.*

O mistress mine, where are you roaming?
O, stay and hear, your true-love's coming,        40
   That can sing both high and low.
Trip no further, pretty sweeting;
Journeys end in lovers meeting,
   Every wise man's son doth know.

**II.ii.s.d. several** separate   **8 desperate assurance** hopeless certainty   **12 She . . . me** of the various emendations proposed for this puzzling line, Malone's "She took no ring of me" is perhaps the most attractive   **15 eye** sight   **20 sure methought** "sure," which repairs the defective meter of this line, has been adopted from the Second Folio; another common emendation is "as methought"; **her . . . tongue** her fixed gaze made her lose the power of speech   **22 cunning** craftiness   **25 I . . . man** i.e., whom she loves   **28 pregnant enemy** crafty fiend (i.e., Satan)   **29 proper false** attractive but deceitful suitors   **33 fadge** turn out   **34 monster** because of her equivocal position as both man and woman; **fond** dote   **37 desperate** hopeless   **39 thriftless** unavailing

**II.iii.2 Deliculo surgere** *Diluculo surgere saluberrimum est,* "It is most healthful to rise early" (a tag from William Lily's Latin grammar, which was widely used in sixteenth-century schools)   **6 can** tankard   **9–10 four elements** air, fire, earth, and water, which were thought to be the basic ingredients of all things   **14 stoup** cup   **17 picture . . . Three** picture of two asses, the spectator making the third   **18 catch** round, a simple polyphonic song for several voices   **20 breast** voice   **21 leg** skill in bowing (?)   **22 gracious** delightful   **23–24 Pigrogromitus, Vapians, Queubus** presumably words invented by the Clown as specimens of his "gracious fooling" in mock learning   **25 leman** sweetheart   **26 impeticos thy gratillity** more of the Clown's fooling, which perhaps means something like "pocket your gratuity"   **26–28 Malvolio's . . . houses** probably mere nonsense   **33 testril** tester, sixpence   **33–34 If . . . a—** some editors have tried to supply what seems to be a missing line here, but it is probable that the Clown breaks in without permitting Sir Andrew to finish his sentence   **35–36 of good life** moral, edifying (?)

ANDREW  Excellent good, i' faith.  45
TOBY  Good, good.

CLOWN [*sings*].

   What is love? 'Tis not hereafter;
   Present mirth hath present laughter;
     What's to come is still° unsure:
   In delay there lies no plenty;  50
   Then come kiss me, sweet, and twenty,°
     Youth's a stuff will not endure.

ANDREW  A mellifluous voice, as I am true knight.
TOBY  A contagious breath.°
ANDREW  Very sweet and contagious, i' faith.  55
TOBY  To hear by the nose, it is dulcet in contagion.° But shall we make the welkin° dance indeed? Shall we rouse the night owl in a catch that will draw three souls out of one weaver?° Shall we do that?
ANDREW  And you love me, let's do't. I am dog° at a  60 catch.
CLOWN  By'r Lady, sir, and some dogs will catch well.
ANDREW  Most certain. Let our catch be "Thou knave."
CLOWN  "Hold thy peace, thou knave,"° knight? I  65 shall be constrained in't to call thee knave, knight.
ANDREW  'Tis not the first time I have constrained one to call me knave. Begin, fool. It begins, "Hold thy peace."
CLOWN  I shall never begin if I hold my peace.  70
ANDREW  Good, i' faith! Come, begin.

*Catch sung. Enter* MARIA.

MARIA  What a caterwauling do you keep here? If my lady have not called up her steward Malvolio and bid him turn you out of doors, never trust me.
TOBY  My lady's a Cataian, we are politicians,°  75 Malvolio's a Peg-a-Ramsey,° and [*sings*] "Three merry men be we."° Am not I consanguineous?° Am I not of her blood? Tilly-vally, lady. [*Sings*.] "There dwelt a man in Babylon, lady, lady."
CLOWN  Beshrew° me, the knight's an admirable  8o fooling.
ANDREW  Ay, he does well enough if he be disposed, and so do I too. He does it with a better grace, but I do it more natural.°
TOBY [*Sings*.]  "O the twelfth day of December."  85

MARIA  For the love o' God, peace!  

*Enter* MALVOLIO.

MALVOLIO  My masters, are you mad? Or what are you? Have you no wit,° manners, nor honesty,° but to gabble like tinkers at this time of night? Do ye make an alehouse of my lady's house, that ye squeak out  90 your coziers'° catches without any mitigation or remorse° of voice? Is there no respect of place, persons, nor time in you?
TOBY  We did keep time, sir, in our catches. Sneck up.°
MALVOLIO  Sir Toby, I must be round° with you. My  95 lady bade me tell you that, though she harbors you as her kinsman, she's nothing allied to your disorders. If you can separate yourself and your misdemeanors, you are welcome to the house. If not, and it would please you to take leave of her, she is very willing to bid you  100 farewell.
TOBY [*Sings*.]  "Farewell, dear heart since I must needs be gone."°
MARIA  Nay, good Sir Toby.
CLOWN [*Sings*.]  "His eyes do show his days are almost  105 done."
MALVOLIO  Is't even so?
TOBY [*Sings*.]  "But I will never die."
CLOWN [*Sings*.]  Sir Toby, there you lie.
MALVOLIO  This is much credit to you.  110
TOBY [*Sings*.]  "Shall I bid him go?"
CLOWN [*Sings*.]  "What and if you do?"
TOBY [*Sings*.]  "Shall I bid him go, and spare not?"
CLOWN [*Sings*.]  "O, no, no, no, no, you dare not!"
TOBY  Out o' tune, sir? Ye lie.° Art any more than a  115 steward? Dost thou think, because thou art virtuous, there shall be no more cakes and ale?
CLOWN  Yes, by Saint Anne, and ginger° shall be hot i' th' mouth too.
TOBY  Th' art i' th' right.—Go, sir, rub your chain  120 with crumbs.° A stoup of wine, Maria!
MALVOLIO  Mistress Mary, if you prized my lady's favor at anything more than contempt, you would not give means for this uncivil rule.° She shall know of it, by this hand.  *Exit.*  125
MARIA  Go shake your ears.°
ANDREW  'Twere as good a deed as to drink when a man's ahungry,° to challenge him the field,° and then to break promise with him and make a fool of him.
TOBY  Do't, knight. I'll write thee a challenge; or I'll  130 deliver thy indignation to him by word of mouth.
MARIA  Sweet Sir Toby, be patient for tonight. Since the youth of the count's was today with my lady, she

**49 still** always  **51 Then . . . twenty** so kiss me, my sweet, and then kiss me twenty times again (some editors, taking "twenty" as an intensive, read the line as "so kiss me then, my very sweet one")  **54 contagious breath** catchy song  **56 To . . . contagion** i.e., If we could hear through the nose, the Clown's "breath" would be sweet and not malodorous, as "contagious" breaths usually are  **57 welkin** sky  **59 weaver** weavers were noted for their singing  **60 dog** clever (but in the next line the Clown puns on *dog* = latch, gripping device)  **65 Hold . . . knave** a line from the round proposed by Sir Andrew  **75 My . . . politicians** because Sir Toby and his companions are "politicians" (i.e., tricksters, intriguers) they recognize Maria's warning of Olivia's anger as the ruse of a "Cataian" (i.e., native of Cathay, cheater); hence "Tilly-vally, lady" (line 78), which means something like "Fiddlesticks, lady"  **76 Peg-a-Ramsey** character in an old song whose name Sir Toby uses apparently as a term of contempt  **76–77 Three . . . we** like Sir Toby's other snatches, a fragment of an old song  **77 consanguineous** related, kin (to Olivia)  **80 Beshrew** curse  **84 natural** with an unintentional pun on "nature" as a term for fool or idiot; see I.iii.28

**88 wit** sense; **honesty** decency  **91 coziers'** cobblers'  **91–92 mitigation or remorse** lowering  **94 Sneck up** go hang  **95 round** blunt  **102–03 Farewell . . . gone** what follows, in crude antiphony between Sir Toby and the Clown, is adapted from a ballad, "Corydon's Farewell to Phyllis"  **115 Out . . . lie** Sir Toby accuses the Clown of being out of tune, it seems, because he had added an extra "no" and thus an extra note in line 114, and of lying because he had questioned his valor in "you dare not"; then he turns to berating Malvolio  **118 ginger** commonly used to spice ale  **120–21 rub . . . crumbs** polish your steward's chain, your badge of office  **124 give . . . rule** provide liquor for this brawl  **126 Go . . . ears** i.e., like the ass you are (?)  **128 ahungry** characteristically, Sir Andrew confuses hunger and thirst and thus perverts the proverbial expression; **the field** i.e., to a duel is much out of quiet. For Monsieur Malvolio, let me alone with him. If I do not gull him into a nayword,° 135 and make him a common recreation, do not think I have wit enough to lie straight in my bed. I know I can do it.

TOBY  Possess° us, possess us. Tell us something of him.

MARIA  Marry, sir, sometimes he is a kind of Puritan.° 140

ANDREW  O, if I thought that, I'd beat him like a dog.

TOBY  What, for being a Puritan? Thy exquisite reason, dear knight.

ANDREW  I have no exquisite reason for't, but I have reason good enough. 145

MARIA  The devil a Puritan that he is, or anything constantly° but a time-pleaser;° an affectioned° ass, that cons state without book° and utters it by great swarths;° the best persuaded of himself;° so crammed, as he thinks, with excellencies that it is his grounds of 150 faith that all that look on him love him; and on that vice in him will my revenge find notable cause to work.

TOBY  What wilt thou do?

MARIA  I will drop in his way some obscure epistles of love, wherein by the color of his beard, the shape of 155 his leg, the manner of his gait, the expressure° of his eye, forehead, and complexion, he shall find himself most feelingly personated.° I can write very like my lady your niece; on a forgotten matter we can hardly make distinction of our hands. 160

TOBY  Excellent. I smell a device.

ANDREW  I have't in my nose too.

TOBY  He shall think by the letters that thou wilt drop that they come from my niece, and that she's in love with him. 165

MARIA  My purpose is indeed a horse of that color.

ANDREW  And your horse now would make him an ass.

MARIA  Ass, I doubt not.

ANDREW  O, 'twill be admirable. 170

MARIA  Sport royal, I warrant you. I know my physic will work with him. I will plant you two, and let the fool make a third,° where he shall find the letter. Observe his construction° of it. For this night, to bed, and dream of the event.° Farewell.          Exit. 175

TOBY  Good night, Penthesilea.°

ANDREW  Before me,° she's a good wench.

TOBY  She's a beagle° true-bred, and one that adores me. What o' that?

ANDREW  I was adored once too. 180

TOBY  Let's to bed, knight. Thou hadst need send for more money.

135 **nayword** byword  139 **Possess** inform  140 **Puritan** a straight-laced, censorious person (in lines 146–47 Maria makes it clear that she is not using the label in a strict ecclesiastical sense, as Sir Andrew [line 141] thinks)  147 **constantly** consistently; **time-pleaser** sycophant; **affectioned** affected  148 **cons . . . book** memorizes stately gestures and turns of phrase  149 **swarths** swaths, quantities; **the . . . himself** who thinks most highly of himself  156 **expressure** expression  158 **personated** represented  172–73 **let . . . third** like the plan to have Viola present herself to Duke Orsino as a eunuch (I.ii.62), this plot device was abandoned; it is Fabian, not the Clown, who makes the third spectator to Malvolio's exposé  174 **construction** interpretation  175 **event** outcome  176 **Penthesilea** in classical mythology, the queen of the Amazons  177 **Before me** I swear, with myself as witness  178 **beagle** one of several allusions to Maria's small stature

ANDREW  If I cannot recover° your niece, I am a foul way out.°

TOBY  Send for money, knight. If thou hast her not i' 185 th' end, call me Cut.°

ANDREW  If I do not, never trust me, take it how you will.

TOBY  Come, come; I'll go burn some sack.° 'Tis too late to go to bed now. Come, knight; come, knight. 190
                                                    Exeunt.

Scene IV. [*The duke's palace.*]

*Enter* DUKE, VIOLA, CURIO, *and others.*

DUKE
Give me some music. Now good morrow, friends.
Now, good Cesario, but that piece of song,
That old and antic° song we heard last night.
Methought it did relieve my passion° much,
More than light airs and recollected terms°       5
Of these most brisk and giddy-pacèd times.
Come, but one verse.

CURIO  He is not here, so please your lordship, that should sing it.

DUKE  Who was it?                                  10

CURIO  Feste the jester, my lord, a fool that the Lady Olivia's father took much delight in. He is about the house.

DUKE
Seek him out, and play the tune the while.
                                          [*Exit* CURIO.]

*Music plays.*

Come hither, boy. If ever thou shalt love,        15
In the sweet pangs of it remember me;
For such as I am all true lovers are,
Unstaid and skittish in all motions° else
Save in the constant image of the creature
That is beloved. How dost thou like this tune?    20

VIOLA
It gives a very echo to the seat°
Where Love is throned.

DUKE                    Thou dost speak masterly.
My life upon't, young though thou art, thine eye
Hath stayed upon some favor° that it loves.
Hath it not, boy?

VIOLA             A little, by your favor.         25

DUKE
What kind of woman is't?

VIOLA                     Of your complexion.°

DUKE
She is not worth thee then. What years, i' faith?

VIOLA
About your years, my lord.

DUKE
Too old, by heaven. Let still° the woman take

183 **recover** win  183–4 **a . . . out** badly out of pocket  186 **Cut** a dock-tailed horse  189 **burn some sack** heat and spice some Spanish wine  II.iv.3 **antic** quaint  4 **passion** suffering (from unrequited love)  5 **recollected terms** studied phrases  18 **motions** emotions  21 **seat** the heart (see I.i.38–39)  24 **favor** face  26 **complexion** temperament  29 **still** always

An elder than herself: so wears she° to him,　　　　　30
So sways she level in her husband's heart;°
For, boy, however we do praise ourselves,
Our fancies° are more giddy and unfirm,
More longing, wavering, sooner lost and worn,°
Than women's are.
VIOLA　　　　　　　I think it well, my lord.　　　35
DUKE
Then let thy love be younger than thyself,
Or thy affection cannot hold the bent;°
For women are as roses, whose fair flow'r,
Being once displayed, doth fall that very hour.
VIOLA
And so they are; alas, that they are so.　　　　40
To die, even when they to perfection grow.

*Enter* CURIO *and* CLOWN.

DUKE
O, fellow, come, the song we had last night.
Mark it, Cesario; it is old and plain.
The spinsters° and the knitters in the sun,
And the free° maids that weave their thread with
　bones,°　　　　　　　　　　　　　　　　45
Do use to chant it. It is silly sooth,°
And dallies° with the innocence of love,
Like the old age.°
CLOWN　Are you ready, sir?
DUKE　I prithee sing.　　　　　　　　　50

*Music.*

*The Song.*
Come away, come away, death,
　And in sad cypress° let me be laid.
Fly away, fly away, breath;
　I am slain by a fair cruel maid.
My shroud of white, stuck all with yew,　　　55
　O, prepare it.
My part of death, no one so true
　Did share it.
Not a flower, not a flower sweet,
　On my black coffin let there be strown;　　60
Not a friend, not a friend greet
　My poor corpse, where my bones shall be thrown.
A thousand thousand sighs to save,
　Lay me, O, where
Sad true lover never find my grave,　　　65
　To weep there.
DUKE　There's for thy pains.
CLOWN　No pains, sir. I take pleasure in singing, sir.
DUKE　I'll pay thy pleasure then.
CLOWN　Truly, sir, and pleasure will be paid one time　70
or another.
DUKE　Give me now leave to leave thee.
CLOWN　Now the melancholy god protect thee, and
the tailor make thy doublet of changeable° taffeta, for

tny mind is a very opal. I would have men of such　75
constancy put to sea, that their business might be
everything, and their intent everywhere; for that's it
that always makes a good voyage of nothing. Farewell.
　　　　　　　　　　　　　　　　*Exit.*
DUKE
Let all the rest give place.°
　　　　　　　　[*Exeunt* CURIO *and* ATTENDANTS.]
　　　　　　　Once more, Cesario,
Get thee to yond same sovereign cruelty.°　　　80
Tell her my love, more noble than the world,
Prizes not quantity of dirty lands;
The parts° that fortune hath bestowed upon her
Tell her I hold as giddily° as fortune,
But 'tis that miracle and queen of gems°　　　85
That nature pranks her in° attracts my soul.
VIOLA
But if she cannot love you, sir?
DUKE
I cannot be so answered.
VIOLA　　　　　　Sooth,° but you must.
Say that some lady, as perhaps there is,
Hath for your love as great a pang of heart　　90
As you have for Olivia. You cannot love her.
You tell her so. Must she not then be answered?
DUKE
There is no woman's sides
Can bide° the beating of so strong a passion
As love doth give my heart; no woman's heart　　95
So big to hold so much; they lack retention.°
Alas, their love may be called appetite,
No motion° of the liver° but the palate,
That suffer surfeit, cloyment, and revolt;°
But mine is all as hungry as the sea　　　100
And can digest as much. Make no compare
Between that love a woman can bear me
And that I owe Olivia.
VIOLA　　　　　　Ay, but I know—
DUKE
What dost thou know?
VIOLA
Too well what love women to men may owe.　　105
In faith, they are as true of heart as we.
My father had a daughter loved a man
As it might be perhaps, were I a woman,
I should your lordship.
DUKE　　　　　　And what's her history?
VIOLA
A blank, my lord. She never told her love,　　110
But let concealment, like a worm i' th' bud,
Feed on her damask° cheek. She pined in thought;°
And, with a green and yellow melancholy,
She sat like Patience on a monument,
Smiling at grief. Was not this love indeed?　　115
We men may say more, swear more; but indeed

---

**30 wears she** she adapts herself　**31 sways . . . heart** she keeps steady in her husband's affections　**33 fancies** loves　**34 worn** many editors have adopted the reading "won" from the Second Folio　**37 hold the bent** maintain its strength and tension (the image is that of a bent bow)　**44 spinsters** spinners　**45 free** carefree; **bones** bone bobbins　**46 silly sooth** simple truth　**47 dallies** deals movingly　**48 the old age** the good old times　**52 cypress** a coffin made of cypress wood　**74 changeable** with shifting lights and colors

**79 give place** withdraw　**80 sovereign cruelty** peerless and disdainful lady　**83 parts** gifts (of wealth and social status)　**84 giddily** indifferently　**85 queen of gems** Olivia's beauty　**86 pranks her in** adorns her with　**88 Sooth** truly　**94 bide** endure　**96 retention** the ability to retain　**98 motion** stirring, prompting; **liver** seat of passion　**99 revolt** revulsion　**112 damask** like a pink and white damask rose; **thought** brooding

Our shows are more than will;° for still we prove
Much in our vows but little in our love.

DUKE
But died thy sister of her love, my boy?

VIOLA
I am all the daughters of my father's house,                    120
And all the brothers too, and yet I know not.°
Sir, shall I to this lady?

DUKE                                Ay, that's the theme.
To her in haste. Give her this jewel. Say
My love can give no place,° bide no denay.°    *Exeunt.*

### Scene V. [*Olivia's garden.*]

*Enter Sir* TOBY, *Sir* ANDREW, *and* FABIAN.

TOBY   Come thy ways, Signior Fabian.

FABIAN   Nay, I'll come. If I lose a scruple° of this
sport, let me be boiled° to death with melancholy.

TOBY   Wouldst thou not be glad to have the niggardly
rascally sheep-biter° come by some notable shame?    5

FABIAN   I would exult, man. You know he brought
me out o' favor with my lady about a bearbaiting here.

TOBY   To anger him we'll have the bear again, and we
will fool him black and blue. Shall we not, Sir Andrew?

ANDREW   And we do not, it is pity of our lives.    10

*Enter* MARIA.

TOBY   Here comes the little villain. How now, my
metal of India?°

MARIA   Get ye all three into the box tree. Malvolio's
coming down this walk. He has been yonder i' the sun
practicing behavior to his own shadow this half hour.    15
Observe him, for the love of mockery; for I know this
letter will make a contemplative° idiot of him. Close,°
in the name of jesting. [*The others hide.*] Lie thou there
[*throws down a letter*]; for here comes the trout that
must be caught with tickling.°    *Exit.* 20

*Enter* MALVOLIO.

MALVOLIO   'Tis but fortune; all is fortune. Maria once
told me she did affect me;° and I have heard herself
come thus near, that, should she fancy,° it should be
one of my complexion. Besides, she uses me with a
more exalted respect than anyone else that follows°    25
her. What should I think on't?

TOBY   Here's an overweening rogue.

FABIAN   O, peace! Contemplation makes a rare turkey
cock of him. How he jets° under his advanced°
plumes!    30

ANDREW   'Slight,° I could so beat the rogue.

TOBY   Peace, I say.°

MALVOLIO   To be Count Malvolio.

TOBY   Ah, rogue!

ANDREW   Pistol him, pistol him.    35

TOBY   Peace, peace.

MALVOLIO   There is example for't. The Lady of the
Strachy° married the yeoman of the wardrobe.

ANDREW   Fie on him, Jezebel.°

FABIAN   O, peace! Now he's deeply in. Look how    40
imagination blows him.°

MALVOLIO   Having been three months married to her,
sitting in my state—

TOBY   O for a stonebow,° to hit him in the eye!

MALVOLIO   Calling my officers about me, in my    45
branched° velvet gown; having come from a daybed,°
where I have left Olivia sleeping—

TOBY   Fire and brimstone!

FABIAN   O, peace, peace!

MALVOLIO   And then to have the humor of state;° and    50
after a demure travel of regard,° telling them I know
my place, as I would they should do theirs, to ask for
my kinsman Toby—

TOBY   Bolts and shackles!

FABIAN   O peace, peace, peace, now, now.    55

MALVOLIO   Seven of my people, with an obedient
start, make out for° him. I frown the while, and perchance wind up my watch, or play with my—some
rich jewel.° Toby approaches; curtsies there to me—

TOBY   Shall this fellow live?    60

FABIAN   Though our silence be drawn from us with
cars, yet peace.

MALVOLIO   I extend my hand to him thus, quenching
my familiar smile with an austere regard of control°—

TOBY   And does not Toby take° you a blow o' the    65
lips then?

MALVOLIO   Saying, "Cousin Toby, my fortunes
having cast me on your niece, give me this prerogative
of speech."

TOBY   What, what?    70

MALVOLIO   "You must amend your drunkenness."

TOBY   Out, scab!

FABIAN   Nay, patience, or we break the sinews of our
plot.

MALVOLIO   "Besides, you waste the treasure of your    75
time with a foolish knight"—

ANDREW   That's me, I warrant you.

MALVOLIO   "One Sir Andrew"—

ANDREW   I knew 'twas I, for many do call me fool.

MALVOLIO   What employment° have we here?    80

[*Takes up the letter.*]

FABIAN   Now is the woodcock° near the gin.°

---

117 **Our . . . will** what we show is greater than the passion
that we feel   121 **I know not** because she thinks that her
brother may be still alive   124 **can . . . place** cannot yield;
**denay** denial
II.v.2 **scruple** smallest part   3 **boiled** pronounced "biled,"
quibbling on *bile,* which was thought to be the cause of melancholy   5 **sheep-biter** sneaky dog   12 **metal of India** golden
girl   17 **contemplative** self-centered; **Close** hide   20 **tickling**
stroking, i.e., flattery   22 **she . . . me** Olivia liked me   23
**fancy** love   25 **follows** serves   29 **jets** struts; **advanced** uplifted   31 **'Slight** by God's light (a mild oath)   32 **Peace, I say**
many editors assign this and line 36 to Fabian on the ground
that it is his function throughout the scene to restrain Sir Toby
and Sir Andrew

37–38 **The Lady . . . Strachy** an unidentified allusion to a
great lady who married beneath her   39 **Jezebel** the proud
and wicked queen of Ahab, King of Israel, whom Sir Andrew,
muddled as usual, regards as Malvolio's prototype in arrogance
41 **blows him** puffs him up   44 **stonebow** crossbow that
shoots stones   46 **branched** embroidered; **daybed** sofa   50
**to . . . state** to assume an imperious manner   51 **after
. . . regard** having glanced gravely over my retainers   57
**make out for** go to fetch   58–59 **play . . . jewel** Malvolio
automatically reaches for his steward's chain and then catches
himself   64 **an . . . control** a stern look of authority
65 **take** give   80 **employment** business   81 **woodcock** a
proverbially stupid bird; **gin** snare

TOBY  O, peace, and the spirit of humors intimate reading aloud to him!

MALVOLIO  By my life, this is my lady's hand. These be her very C's, her U's, and her T's; and thus makes she her great P's. It is, in contempt of° question, her hand. 85

ANDREW  Her C's, her U's, and her T's? Why that?

MALVOLIO  [Reads.] "To the unknown beloved, this, and my good wishes." Her very phrases! By your leave, wax.° Soft,° and the impressure her Lucrece,° with which she uses to seal.° 'Tis my lady. To whom should this be? 90

FABIAN  This wins him, liver and all.

MALVOLIO  [Reads.]
              "Jove knows I love,                     95
              But who?
              Lips, do not move;
              No man must know."
"No man must know." What follows? The numbers altered!° "No man must know." If this should be thee, Malvolio? 100

TOBY  Marry, hang thee, brock!°

MALVOLIO  [Reads.]
      "I may command where I adore,
      But silence, like a Lucrece knife,
      With bloodless stroke my heart doth gore.  105
      M. O. A. I. doth sway my life."

FABIAN  A fustian° riddle.

TOBY  Excellent wench,° say I.

MALVOLIO  "M. O. A. I. doth sway my life." Nay, but first, let me see, let me see, let me see. 110

FABIAN  What dish o' poison has she dressed° him!

TOBY  And with what wing the staniel checks at it!°

MALVOLIO  "I may command where I adore." Why, she may command me: I serve her; she is my lady. Why, this is evident to any formal capacity.° There is no obstruction° in this. And the end; what should that alphabetical position portend? If I could make that resemble something in me! Softly, "M. O. A. I." 115

TOBY  O, ay, make up that. He is now at a cold scent.

FABIAN  Sowter will cry upon't for all this, though it be as rank as a fox.° 120

MALVOLIO  M.—Malvolio. M.—Why, that begins my name.

FABIAN  Did not I say he would work it out? The cur is excellent at faults.° 125

MALVOLIO  M.—But then there is no consonancy in the sequel.° That suffers under probation.° A should follow, but O does.

FABIAN  And O° shall end, I hope.

TOBY  Ay, or I'll cudgel him and make him cry O. 130

MALVOLIO  And then I comes behind.

FABIAN  Ay, and you had any eye behind you, you might see more detraction at your heels than fortunes before you.

MALVOLIO  M, O, A, I. This simulation° is not as the former; and yet, to crush° this a little, it would bow to me, for every one of these letters are in my name. Soft, here follows prose. 135

[Reads.]

"If this fall into thy hand, revolve.° In my stars° I am above thee, but be not afraid of greatness. Some are born great, some achieve greatness, and some have greatness thrust upon 'em. Thy Fates open their hands; let thy blood and spirit embrace them; and to inure° thyself to what thou art like to be, cast thy humble slough° and appear fresh. Be opposite with° a kinsman, surly with servants. Let thy tongue tang arguments of state;° put thyself into the trick of singularity.° She thus advises thee that sighs for thee. Remember who commended thy yellow stockings and wished to see thee ever cross-gartered.° I say, remember. Go to, thou art made, if thou desir'st to be so. If not, let me see thee a steward still, the fellow of servants, and not worthy to touch Fortune's fingers. Farewell. She that would alter services with thee, 140 145 150
                          The Fortunate Unhappy." 155
Daylight and champian° discovers° not more. This is open. I will be proud, I will read politic authors,° I will baffle° Sir Toby, I will wash off gross° acquaintance, I will be point-devise,° the very man. I do not now fool myself, to let imagination jade° me, for every reason excites to this,° that my lady loves me. She did commend my yellow stockings of late, she did praise my leg being cross-gartered; and in this she manifests herself to my love, and with a kind of injunction drives me to these habits of her liking.° I thank my stars, I am happy. I will be strange,° stout,° in yellow stockings, and cross-gartered, even with the swiftness of putting on. Jove and my stars be praised. Here is yet a post-script. 160 165

[Reads.]

"Thou canst not choose but know who I am. If thou entertain'st° my love, let it appear in thy smiling. Thy smiles become thee well. Therefore in my presence still smile, dear my sweet, I prithee." 170
Jove, I thank thee. I will smile; I will do everything that thou wilt have me.                    Exit. 175

86 in contempt of beyond   90–91 By . . . wax Excuse me for breaking the seal   91 Soft take it slowly; the . . . Lucrece the seal depicts Lucrece (noble Roman matron who stabbed herself after she was raped by Tarquin, hence a symbol of chastity)   92 uses to seal customarily seals   99–100 The numbers altered the meter changed (in the stanza that follows)   102 brock badger   107 fustian foolish and pretentious   108 wench Maria   111 dressed prepared for   112 with . . . it with what speed the kestrel (a kind of hawk) turns to snatch at the wrong prey   115 formal capacity normal intelligence   116 obstruction difficulty   120–21 Sowter . . . fox The hound will bay after the false scent even though the deceit is gross and clear   125 faults breaks in the scent   126–27 consonancy . . . sequel consistency in what follows   127 suffers under probation does not stand up under scrutiny   129 O sound of lamentation

135 simulation hidden significance   136 crush force   139 revolve reflect; stars fortune   143 inure accustom   145 slough skin (of a snake)   opposite with hostile to   146–47 tang . . . state resound with topics of statecraft   147 trick of singularity affectation of eccentricity   150 cross-gartered with garters crossed above and below the knee   156 champian champaign, open country; discovers reveals   157 politic authors writers on politics   158 baffle publicly humiliate; gross low   159 be point-devise follow the advice in the letter in every detail   160 jade trick   161 excites to this enforces this conclusion   165 these . . . liking this clothing that she likes   166 strange haughty; stout proud   171 entertain'st accept

FABIAN  I will not give my part of this sport for a pension of thousands to be paid from the sophy.°

TOBY  I could marry this wench for this device.

ANDREW  So could I too.

TOBY  And ask no other dowry with her but such another jest. 180

*Enter* MARIA.

ANDREW  Nor I neither.

FABIAN  Here comes my noble gull-catcher.°

TOBY  Wilt thou set thy foot o' my neck?

ANDREW  Or o' mine either? 185

TOBY  Shall I play° my freedom at tray-trip° and become thy bondslave?

ANDREW  I' faith, or I either?

TOBY  Why, thou hast put him in such a dream that, when the image of it leaves him, he must run mad. 190

MARIA  Nay, but say true, does it work upon him?

TOBY  Like aqua vitae° with a midwife.

MARIA  If you will, then, see the fruits of the sport, mark his first approach before my lady. He will come to her in yellow stockings, and 'tis a color she abhors, 195 and cross-gartered, a fashion she detests; and he will smile upon her which will now be so unsuitable to her disposition, being addicted to a melancholy as she is, that it cannot but turn him into a notable contempt. If you will see it, follow me. 200

TOBY  To the gates of Tartar,° thou most excellent devil of wit.

ANDREW  I'll make one° too.                              *Exeunt.*

# ACT III

### Scene I. [*Olivia's garden.*]

*Enter* VIOLA *and* CLOWN [*with a tabor*].

VIOLA  Save thee,° friend, and thy music. Dost thou live by° thy tabor?°

CLOWN  No, sir, I live by the church.

VIOLA  Art thou a churchman?

CLOWN  No such matter, sir. I do live by the church; 5 for I do live at my house, and my house doth stand by the church.

VIOLA  So thou mayst say, the king lies° by a beggar, if a beggar dwell near him; or, the church stands by° thy tabor, if thy tabor stand by the church. 10

CLOWN  You have said, sir. To see this age! A sentence is but a chev'ril° glove to a good wit. How quickly the wrong side may be turned outward!

VIOLA  Nay, that's certain. They that dally nicely° with words may quickly make them wanton.° 15

CLOWN  I would therefore my sister had had no name, sir.

VIOLA  Why, man?

CLOWN  Why, sir, her name's a word, and to dally with that word might make my sister wanton. But 20 indeed words are very rascals since bonds disgraced them.°

VIOLA  Thy reason, man?

CLOWN  Troth,° sir, I can yield you none without words, and words are grown so false I am loath to 25 prove reason with them.

VIOLA  I warrant thou art a merry fellow and car'st for nothing.

CLOWN  Not so, sir; I do care for something; but in my conscience, sir, I do not care for you. If that be to care 30 for nothing, sir, I would it would make you invisible.

VIOLA  Art not thou the Lady Olivia's fool?

CLOWN  No, indeed, sir. The Lady Olivia has no folly. She will keep no fool, sir, till she be married; and fools are as like husbands as pilchers° are to herrings—the 35 husband's the bigger. I am indeed not her fool, but her corrupter of words.

VIOLA  I saw thee late at the Count Orsino's.

CLOWN  Foolery, sir, does walk about the orb° like the sun; it shines everywhere. I would be sorry, sir, 40 but° the fool should be as oft with your master as with my mistress. I think I saw your wisdom there.

VIOLA  Nay, and thou pass upon me,° I'll no more with thee. Hold, there's expenses for thee.

[*Gives a coin.*]

CLOWN  Now Jove, in his next commodity° of hair, 45 send thee a beard.

VIOLA  By my troth, I'll tell thee, I am almost sick for one, though I would not have it grow on my chin. Is thy lady within?

CLOWN  Would not a pair of these° have bred, sir? 50

VIOLA  Yes, being kept together and put to use.°

CLOWN  I would play Lord Pandarus of Phrygia, sir, to bring a Cressida to this Troilus.°

VIOLA  I understand you, sir. 'Tis well begged.

[*Gives another coin.*]

CLOWN  The matter, I hope, is not great, sir, begging 55 but a beggar: Cressida was a beggar.° My lady is within, sir. I will conster° to them whence you come. Who you are and what you would are out of my welkin;° I might say "element," but the word is overworn.°                              *Exit.* 60

177 **sophy** Shah of Persia (perhaps with reference to Sir Anthony Shirley's visit to the Persian court in 1599, from which he returned laden with gifts and honors)  183 **gull-catcher** fool-catcher  186 **play** gamble; **tray-trip** a dice game  192 **aqua vitae** distilled liquors  201 **Tartar** Tartarus (in classical mythology, the infernal regions)  203 **make one** come  III.i.1 **Save thee** God save you  2 **live by** gain a living from (but the Clown takes it in the sense of "reside near"); **tabor** (1) drum (2) taborn, tavern  8 **lies** sojourns  9 **stands by** (1) stands near (2) upholds  12 **chev'ril** cheveril (soft kid leather)  14 **dally nicely** play subtly  15 **wanton** equivocal in meaning (but the Clown takes it in the sense of "unchaste")

21–22 **since . . . them** since it was required that a man's word be guaranteed by a bond (?)  24 **Troth** by my troth  35 **pilchers** pilchards (a kind of small herring)  39 **orb** earth  41 **but** but that  43 **pass upon me** make me the butt of your witticisms  45 **commodity** lot, consignment  50 **these** coins of the sort that Viola had just given him  51 **put to use** put out at interest  52–53 **I . . . Troilus** in the story of Troilus and Cressida, which supplied both Chaucer and Shakespeare the plot for major works, Pandarus was the go-between in the disastrous love affair  56 **Cressida . . . beggar** in Robert Henryson's *Testament of Cressida*, a kind of sequel to Chaucer's poem, the faithless heroine became a harlot and a beggar  57 **conster** explain  59 **welkin** sky  59–60 **I . . . overworn** perhaps a thrust at Ben Jonson, whose fondness for the word "element" had been ridiculed by other writers

VIOLA
This fellow is wise enough to play the fool,
And to do that well craves° a kind of wit.°
He must observe their mood on whom he jests,
The quality of persons, and the time;
And,° like the haggard,° check at° every feather    65
That comes before his eye. This is a practice°
As full of labor as a wise man's art;
For folly that he wisely shows, is fit;
But wise men, folly-fall'n,° quite taint their wit.°

*Enter Sir* TOBY *and* [*Sir*] ANDREW.

TOBY  Save you, gentleman.    70
VIOLA  And you, sir.
ANDREW  Dieu vous garde, monsieur.
VIOLA  Et vous aussi; votre serviteur.°
ANDREW  I hope, sir, you are, and I am yours.
TOBY  Will you encounter° the house? My niece is  75
desirous you should enter, if your trade be to° her.
VIOLA  I am bound to° your niece, sir; I mean, she is
the list° of my voyage.
TOBY  Taste° your legs, sir; put them to motion.
VIOLA  My legs do better understand° me, sir, than I  80
understand what you mean by bidding me taste my
legs.
TOBY  I mean, to go, sir, to enter.
VIOLA  I will answer you with gait and entrance.° But
we are prevented.°    85

*Enter* OLIVIA *and gentlewoman* [MARIA].

Most excellent accomplished lady, the heavens rain
odors on you.
ANDREW  That youth's a rare courtier. "Rain odors"
—well!°
VIOLA  My matter hath no voice,° lady, but to your  90
own most pregnant and vouchsafed ear.
ANDREW  "Odors," "pregnant," and "vouchsafed"—
I'll get 'em all three all ready.
OLIVIA  Let the garden door be shut, and leave me to
my hearing. [*Exeunt Sir* TOBY, *Sir* ANDREW, *and*  95
MARIA.] Give me your hand, sir.
VIOLA
My duty, madam, and most humble service.
OLIVIA
What is your name?
VIOLA
Cesario is your servant's name, fair princess.
OLIVIA
My servant, sir? 'Twas never merry world    100
Since lowly feigning° was called compliment.
Y' are servant to the Count Orsino, youth.

VIOLA
And he is yours, and his must needs be yours.
Your servant's servant is your servant, madam.
OLIVIA
For° him, I think not on him; for his thoughts,    105
Would they were blanks, rather than filled with me.
VIOLA
Madam, I come to whet your gentle thoughts
On his behalf.
OLIVIA            O, by your leave, I pray you.
I bade you never speak again of him;
But, would you undertake another suit,    110
I had rather hear you to solicit that
Than music from the spheres.°
VIOLA                      Dear lady—
OLIVIA
Give me leave,° beseech you. I did send,
After the last enchantment you did here,
A ring in chase of you. So did I abuse°    115
Myself, my servant, and, I fear me, you.
Under your hard construction° must I sit,
To force that on you in a shameful cunning
Which you knew none of yours. What might you
think?
Have you not set mine honor at the stake    120
And baited it with all th' unmuzzled thoughts°
That tyrannous heart can think? To one of your
receiving°
Enough is shown; a cypress,° not a bosom,
Hides my heart. So, let me hear you speak.
VIOLA
I pity you.
OLIVIA      That's a degree° to love.    125
VIOLA
No, not a grize:° for 'tis a vulgar proof°
That very oft we pity enemies.
OLIVIA
Why then, methinks 'tis time to smile again.
O world, how apt the poor are to be proud.
If one should be a prey, how much the better    130
To fall before the lion than the wolf.

*Clock strikes.*

The clock upbraids me with the waste of time.
Be not afraid, good youth, I will not have you,
And yet, when wit and youth is come to harvest,°
Your wife is like to reap a proper° man.    135
There lies your way, due west.°
VIOLA                      Then westward ho!°
Grace and good disposition° attend your ladyship.
You'll nothing, madam, to my lord by me?

62 craves requires; wit intelligence  65 And many editors, following Johnson, have emended this to "not"; haggard untrained hawk; check at leave the true course and pursue  66 practice skill  69 folly-fall'n having fallen into folly; taint their wit betray their common sense  72–73 Dieu . . . serviteur God protect you, sir. And you also; your servant  75 encounter approach  76 trade be to business be with  77 bound to bound for (carrying on the metaphor in "trade")  78 list destination  79 Taste try  80 understand stand under, support  84 with . . . entrance by going and entering (with a pun on gate)  85 prevented anticipated  89 well well put  90 matter . . . voice business must not be revealed  101 lowly feigning affected humility

105 For as for  112 music . . . spheres the alleged celestial harmony of the revolving stars and planets  113 Give me leave do not interrupt me  115 abuse deceive  117 hard construction harsh interpretation  120–21 set . . . thoughts the metaphor is from the Elizabethan sport of bearbaiting, in which a bear was tied to a stake and harassed by savage dogs  122 receiving perception  123 cypress gauzelike material  125 degree step  126 grize step; vulgar proof common knowledge  134 when . . . harvest when you are mature  135 proper handsome  136 due west Olivia is perhaps implying that the sun of her life—Cesario's love—is about to vanish; westward ho cry of Thames watermen  137 good disposition tranquillity of mind

OLIVIA
Stay.
I prithee tell me what thou think'st of me.  140
VIOLA
That you do think you are not what you are.°
OLIVIA
If I think so, I think the same of you.°
VIOLA
Then think you right. I am not what I am.
OLIVIA
I would you were as I would have you be.
VIOLA
Would it be better, madam, than I am?  145
I wish it might, for now I am your fool.°
OLIVIA
O, what a deal of scorn looks beautiful
In the contempt and anger of his lip.
A murd'rous guilt shows not itself more soon
Than love that would seem hid: love's night is noon.°  150
Cesario, by the roses of the spring,
By maidhood,° honor, truth, and everything,
I love thee so that, maugre° all thy pride,
Nor wit nor reason can my passion hide.
Do not extort thy reasons from this clause,°  155
For that° I woo, thou therefore hast no cause;°
But rather reason thus with reason fetter,
Love sought is good, but given unsought is better.
VIOLA
By innocence I swear, and by my youth,
I have one heart, one bosom, and one truth,  160
And that no woman has; nor never none
Shall mistress be of it, save I alone.
And so adieu, good madam. Never more
Will I my master's tears to you deplore.
OLIVIA
Yet come again; for thou perhaps mayst move  165
That heart which now abhors to like his love. *Exeunt.*

Scene II. [*Olivia's house.*]

*Enter Sir* TOBY, *Sir* ANDREW, *and* FABIAN.

ANDREW  No, faith, I'll not stay a jot longer.
TOBY  Thy reason, dear venom; give thy reason.
FABIAN  You must needs yield° your reason, Sir
Andrew.
ANDREW  Marry, I saw your niece do more favors to  5
the count's servingman than ever she bestowed upon
me. I saw't i' th' orchard.
TOBY  Did she see thee the while, old boy? Tell me
that.
ANDREW  As plain as I see you now.  10
FABIAN  This was a great argument° of love in her
toward you.
ANDREW  'Slight, will you make an ass o' me?

FABIAN  I will prove it legitimate,° sir, upon the oaths
of judgment and reason.  15
TOBY  And they have been grand-jurymen since
before Noah was a sailor.
FABIAN  She did show favor to the youth in your sight
only to exasperate you, to awake your dormouse°
valor, to put fire in your heart and brimstone in your  20
liver. You should then have accosted her, and with
some excellent jests, fire-new from the mint, you
should have banged the youth into dumbness. This
was looked for at your hand, and this was balked.°
The double gilt° of this opportunity you let time wash  25
off, and you are now sailed into the North of my
lady's opinion,° where you will hang like an icicle on a
Dutchman's beard° unless you do redeem it by some
laudable attempt either of valor or policy.°
ANDREW  And't be any way, it must be with valor; for  30
policy I hate. I had as lief be a Brownist° as a politician.°
TOBY  Why then, build me thy fortunes upon the
basis of valor. Challenge me the count's youth to fight
with him; hurt him in eleven places. My niece shall
take note of it, and assure thyself there is no love-  35
broker in the world can° more prevail in man's
commendation with woman than report of valor.
FABIAN  There is no way but this, Sir Andrew.
ANDREW  Will either of you bear me a challenge to
him?  40
TOBY  Go, write it in a martial hand. Be curst° and
brief; it is no matter how witty, so it be eloquent and
full of invention. Taunt him with the license of ink.°
If thou thou'st° him some thrice, it shall not be amiss;
and as many lies as will lie in thy sheet of paper,  45
although the sheet were big enough for the bed of
Ware° in England, set 'em down. Go about it. Let
there be gall enough in thy ink, though thou write
with a goose-pen, no matter. About it!
ANDREW  Where shall I find you?  50
TOBY  We'll call thee at the cubiculo.° Go.
*Exit Sir* ANDREW.
FABIAN  This is a dear manikin° to you, Sir Toby.
TOBY  I have been dear to him,° lad, some two thousand strong or so.
FABIAN  We shall have a rare letter from him, but  55
you'll not deliver't?
TOBY  Never trust me then; and by all means stir on
the youth to an answer. I think oxen and wainropes°
cannot hale them together. For Andrew, if he were
opened, and you find so much blood in his liver as will  60
clog the foot of a flea, I'll eat the rest of th' anatomy.°

141 That . . . are That you think you are in love with
a man, and are not  142 If . . . you Olivia misconstrues
Viola's remark to mean that she is out of her mind  146 I am
. . . fool you are making a fool of me  150 love's . . .
noon love is apparent even when it is hidden  152 maidhood maidenhood  153 maugre despite  155 clause premise
156 For that that because; cause i.e., to accept my love
III.ii.3 yield give  11 great argument strong evidence

14 legitimate valid  19 dormouse i.e., sleepy  24 balked
let slip  25 gilt plating  26–27 the . . . opinion her frosty
disdain  27–28 an . . . beard perhaps an allusion to the
arctic voyage (1596–97) of the Dutchman Willem Barents, an
account of which was registered for publication in 1598  29
policy intrigue, trickery  31 Brownist follower of William
Browne, a reformer who advocated the separation of church
and state; politician schemer  36 can that can  41 curst
petulant  43 license of ink freedom that writing permits
44 thou'st use the familiar *thou* instead of the more formal *you*
46–47 bed of Ware famous bedstead, almost eleven feet square,
formerly in an inn at Ware in Hertfordshire  51 cubiculo
little chamber  52 manikin puppet  53 been . . . him
spent his money  58 wainropes wagon ropes  61 anatomy
cadaver

FABIAN   And his opposite,° the youth, bears in his visage no great presage of cruelty.

*Enter* MARIA.

TOBY   Look where the youngest wren° of mine° comes.    65

MARIA   If you desire the spleen,° and will laugh yourselves into stitches, follow me. Yond gull Malvolio is turned heathen, a very renegado; for there is no Christian that means to be saved by believing rightly can ever believe such impossible passages of grossness.° 70 He's in yellow stockings.

TOBY   And cross-gartered?

MARIA   Most villainously; like a pedant that keeps a school i' th' church. I have dogged him like his murderer. He does obey every point of the letter that 75 I dropped to betray him. He does smile his face into more lines than is in the new map with the augmentation of the Indies.° You have not seen such a thing as 'tis. I can hardly forbear hurling things at him. I know my lady will strike him. If she do, he'll smile, and 80 take't for a great favor.

TOBY   Come bring us, bring us where he is.

*Exeunt omnes.*

## Scene III. [*A street.*]

*Enter* SEBASTIAN *and* ANTONIO.

SEBASTIAN
I would not by my will have troubled you;
But since you make your pleasure of your pains,
I will no further chide you.

ANTONIO
I could not stay behind you. My desire
(More sharp than filèd steel) did spur me forth;    5
And not all love to see you (though so much
As might have drawn one to a longer voyage)
But jealousy° what might befall your travel,
Being skilless in° these parts; which to a stranger,
Unguided and unfriended, often prove    10
Rough and unhospitable. My willing love,
The rather by these arguments of fear,°
Set forth in your pursuit.

SEBASTIAN        My kind Antonio,
I can no other answer make but thanks,
And thanks, and ever oft good turns°    15
Are shuffled off with such uncurrent° pay.
But, were my worth° as is my conscience firm,

You should find better dealing. What's to do?
Shall we go see the relics of this town?

ANTONIO
Tomorrow, sir; best first go see your lodging.    20

SEBASTIAN
I am not weary, and 'tis long to night.
I pray you let us satisfy our eyes
With the memorials and the things of fame
That do renown this city.

ANTONIO       Would you'ld pardon° me.
I do not without danger walk these streets.    25
Once in a sea-fight 'gainst the count his galleys°
I did some service; of such note indeed
That, were I ta'en here, it would scarce be answered.°

SEBASTIAN
Belike you slew great number of his people?

ANTONIO
Th' offense is not of such a bloody nature,    30
Albeit the quality° of the time and quarrel
Might well have given us bloody argument.°
It might have since been answered° in repaying
What we took from them, which for traffic's° sake
Most of our city did. Only myself stood out;    35
For which, if I be lapsèd° in this place,
I shall pay dear.

SEBASTIAN       Do not then walk too open.

ANTONIO
It doth not fit me. Hold, sir, here's my purse.
In the south suburbs at the Elephant°
Is best to lodge. I will bespeak our diet,°    40
Whiles° you beguile the time and feed your knowledge
With viewing of the town. There shall you have° me.

SEBASTIAN
Why I your purse?

ANTONIO
Haply your eye shall light upon some toy°
You have desire to purchase, and your store°    45
I think is not for idle markets,° sir.

SEBASTIAN
I'll be your purse-bearer, and leave you for
An hour.

ANTONIO   To th' Elephant.

SEBASTIAN        I do remember.    *Exeunt.*

## Scene IV. [*Olivia's garden.*]

*Enter* OLIVIA *and* MARIA.

OLIVIA
I have sent after him. He says he'll come:°
How shall I feast him? What bestow of° him?
For youth is bought more oft than begged or borrowed.
I speak too loud. Where's Malvolio? He is sad and
civil,°

---

62 **opposite** adversary   64 **youngest wren** smallest of small birds; **mine** most editors adopt Theobald's emendation "nine" 66 **spleen** a fit of laughter   70 **impossible . . . grossness** improbabilities   77–78 **new . . . Indies** presumably a map, prepared under the supervision of Richard Hakluyt and others and published about 1600, that employed the principles of projection and showed North America and the East Indies in fuller detail than any earlier map; it was conspicuous for the rhumb lines marking the meridians
**III.iii.8 jealousy** anxiety   9 **skilless in** unacquainted with   12 **The . . . fear** reinforced by my solicitude for your safety   15 **And thanks . . . turns** the fact that this line is a foot too short has prompted a wide variety of emendations, the most popular of which has been Theobald's "And thanks, and ever thanks; and oft good turns"; later Folios omit this and the following line altogether   16 **uncurrent** worthless   17 **worth** resources

24 **pardon** excuse   26 **count his galleys** count's warships 28 **answered** defended   31 **quality** circumstances   32 **argument** cause   33 **answered** compensated   34 **traffic's** trade's 36 **lapsèd** surprised and apprehended   39 **Elephant** an inn 40 **bespeak our diet** arrange for our meals   41 **Whiles** while   42 **have** find   44 **toy** trifle   45 **store** wealth   46 **idle markets** unnecessary purchases
**III.iv.1 He . . . come** suppose he says he'll come   2 **of** on 4 **sad and civil** grave and formal

And suits well for a servant with my fortunes.          5
Where is Malvolio?

MARIA   He's coming, madam, but in very strange
manner. He is sure possessed,° madam.

OLIVIA   Why, what's the matter? Does he rave?

MARIA   No, madam, he does nothing but smile. Your   10
ladyship were best to have some guard about you if he
come, for sure the man is tainted in 's wits.

OLIVIA
Go call him hither. I am as mad as he,
If sad and merry madness equal be.

*Enter MALVOLIO.*

How now, Malvolio?                                      15

MALVOLIO   Sweet lady, ho, ho!

OLIVIA   Smil'st thou? I sent for thee upon a sad°
occasion.

MALVOLIO   Sad, lady? I could be sad. This does make
some obstruction in the blood, this cross-gartering;   20
but what of that? If it please the eye of one, it is with
me as the very true sonnet° is, "Please one, and
please all."°

OLIVIA   Why, how dost thou, man? What is the
matter with thee?                                      25

MALVOLIO   Not black in my mind, though yellow in
my legs. It did come to his hands, and commands shall
be executed. I think we do know the sweet Roman
hand.°

OLIVIA   Wilt thou go to bed, Malvolio?                 30

MALVOLIO   To bed? Ay, sweetheart, and I'll come to
thee.

OLIVIA   God comfort thee. Why dost thou smile so,
and kiss thy hand so oft?

MARIA   How do you, Malvolio?                           35

MALVOLIO   At your request? Yes, nightingales answer
daws!°

MARIA   Why appear you with this ridiculous boldness
before my lady?

MALVOLIO   "Be not afraid of greatness." 'Twas well   40
writ.

OLIVIA   What mean'st thou by that, Malvolio?

MALVOLIO   "Some are born great."

OLIVIA   Ha?

MALVOLIO   "Some achieve greatness."                    45

OLIVIA   What say'st thou?

MALVOLIO   "And some have greatness thrust upon
them."

OLIVIA   Heaven restore thee!

MALVOLIO   "Remember who commended thy yellow    50
stockings."

OLIVIA   Thy yellow stockings?

MALVOLIO   "And wished to see thee cross-gartered."

OLIVIA   Cross-gartered?

MALVOLIO   "Go to, thou art made, if thou desir'st to   55
be so."

OLIVIA   Am I made?

MALVOLIO   "If not, let me see thee a servant still."

OLIVIA   Why, this is very midsummer madness.°

*Enter SERVANT.*

SERVANT   Madam, the young gentleman of the Count   60
Orsino's is returned. I could hardly entreat him back.
He attends your ladyship's pleasure.

OLIVIA   I'll come to him. [*Exit* SERVANT.] Good
Maria, let this fellow be looked to. Where's my cousin
Toby? Let some of my people have a special care of   65
him. I would not have him miscarry° for the half of my
dowry.                     *Exit* [OLIVIA, *accompanied by* MARIA].

MALVOLIO   O ho, do you come near me° now? No
worse man than Sir Toby to look to me. This concurs
directly with the letter. She sends him on purpose,   70
that I may appear stubborn° to him; for she incites me
to that in the letter. "Cast thy humble slough," says
she; "be opposite with a kinsman, surly with servants;
let thy tongue tang with arguments of state; put thyself
into the trick of singularity." And consequently sets   75
down the manner how: as, a sad face, a reverend
carriage, a slow tongue, in the habit° of some sir° of
note, and so forth. I have limed° her; but it is Jove's
doing, and Jove make me thankful. And when she
went away now, "Let this fellow° be looked to."         80
"Fellow." Not "Malvolio," nor after my degree,° but
"fellow." Why, everything adheres together, that no
dram° of a scruple,° no scruple of a scruple, no obstacle,
no incredulous or unsafe° circumstance—what can be
said? Nothing that can be can come between me and   85
the full prospect of my hopes. Well, Jove, not I, is the
doer of this, and he is to be thanked.

*Enter* [*Sir*] TOBY, FABIAN, *and* MARIA.

TOBY   Which way is he, in the name of sanctity? If all
the devils of hell be drawn in little,° and Legion°
himself possessed him, yet I'll speak to him.            90

FABIAN   Here he is, here he is! How is't with you, sir?

TOBY   How is't with you, man?°

MALVOLIO   Go off; I discard you. Let me enjoy my
private.° Go off.

MARIA   Lo, how hollow the fiend speaks within him!   95
Did not I tell you? Sir Toby, my lady prays you to
have a care of him.

MALVOLIO   Aha, does she so?

TOBY   Go to, go to; peace, peace; we must deal gently
with him. Let me alone. How do you, Malvolio?          100
How is't with you? What, man, defy the devil?
Consider, he's an enemy to mankind.

8 possessed with a devil, mad   17 sad serious   22 sonnet any
short lyric poem   22–23 Please one . . . all so long as I please
the one I love I do not care about the rest (from "A prettie newe
Ballad, intytuled: The Crow sits vpon the wall, Please one
and please all")   28–29 sweet Roman hand italic writing,
an elegant cursive script more fashionable than the crabbed
"secretary hand" commonly used in Shakespeare's time   36–37
At . . . daws Should I reply to a mere servant like you? Yes,
for sometimes nightingales answer jackdaws

59 midsummer madness extreme folly, Midsummer Eve
(June 23) being traditionally associated with irresponsible and
eccentric behavior   66 miscarry come to harm   68 come
near me begin to understand my importance   71 stubborn
hostile   77 habit clothing; sir personage   78 limed caught
(as birds are caught with sticky birdlime)   80 fellow (1)
menial (2) associate (the sense in which Malvolio takes the word)
81 after my degree according to my status   83 dram (1)
minute part (2) apothecary's measure for one-eighth of an
ounce; scruple (1) doubt (2) apothecary's measure for one-
third of a dram   84 incredulous or unsafe incredible or
doubtful   89 in little in small compass; Legion a group of
devils (see Mark 5:8–9)   92 How . . . man the Folio im-
plausibly assigns this speech to Fabian, but the contemptuous
"man" suggests that the speaker must be Malvolio's social
superior   94 private privacy

MALVOLIO  Do you know what you say?

MARIA  La you, and you speak ill of the devil, how he takes it at heart. Pray God he be not bewitched. 105

FABIAN  Carry his water to th' wise woman.°

MARIA  Marry, and it shall be done tomorrow morning if I live. My lady would not lose him for more than I'll say.

MALVOLIO  How now, mistress? 110

MARIA  O Lord.

TOBY  Prithee hold thy peace. This is not the way. Do you not see you move° him? Let me alone with him.

FABIAN  No way but gentleness; gently, gently. The fiend is rough° and will not be roughly used. 115

TOBY  Why, how now, my bawcock?° How dost thou, chuck?°

MALVOLIO  Sir.

TOBY  Ay, biddy, come with me. What, man, 'tis not for gravity to play at cherry-pit with Satan.° Hang 120 him, foul collier!°

MARIA  Get him to say his prayers; good Sir Toby, get him to pray.

MALVOLIO  My prayers, minx?

MARIA  No, I warrant you, he will not hear of 125 godliness.

MALVOLIO  Go hang yourselves all! You are idle° shallow things; I am not of your element.° You shall know more hereafter. *Exit.*

TOBY  Is't possible? 130

FABIAN  If this were played upon a stage now, I could condemn it as an improbable fiction.

TOBY  His very genius° hath taken the infection of the device, man.

MARIA  Nay, pursue him now, lest the device take air 135 and taint.°

FABIAN  Why, we shall make him mad indeed.

MARIA  The house will be the quieter.

TOBY  Come, we'll have him in a dark room and bound. My niece is already in the belief that he's mad. 140 We may carry it° thus, for our pleasure and his penance, will our very pastime, tired out of breath, prompt us to have mercy on him; at which time we will bring the device to the bar and crown thee for a finder of madmen. But see, but see. 145

*Enter Sir* ANDREW.

FABIAN  More matter for a May morning.°

ANDREW  Here's the challenge; read it. I warrant there's vinegar and pepper in't.

FABIAN  Is't so saucy?°

ANDREW  Ay, is't, I warrant him. Do but read. 150

TOBY  Give me. [*Reads.*] "Youth, whatsoever thou art, thou art but a scurvy fellow."

FABIAN  Good, and valiant.

TOBY  [*Reads.*] "Wonder not nor admire° not in thy mind why I do call thee so, for I will show thee no 155 reason for't."

FABIAN  A good note that keeps you from the blow of the law.

TOBY  [*Reads.*] "Thou com'st to the Lady Olivia, and in my sight she uses thee kindly. But thou liest in thy 160 throat; that is not the matter I challenge thee for."

FABIAN  Very brief, and to exceeding good sense—less.

TOBY  [*Reads.*] "I will waylay thee going home; where if it be thy chance to kill me"— 165

FABIAN  Good.

TOBY  [*Reads.*] "Thou kill'st me like a rogue and a villain."

FABIAN  Still you keep o' th' windy side of the law.° Good. 170

TOBY  [*Reads.*] "Fare thee well, and God have mercy upon one of our souls. He may have mercy upon mine, but my hope is better, and so look to thyself. Thy friend, as thou usest him, and thy sworn enemy,
　　　　　　　　　　　　Andrew Aguecheek." 175
If this letter move him not, his legs cannot. I'll give't him.

MARIA  You may have very fit occasion for't. He is now in some commerce° with my lady and will by and by depart. 180

TOBY  Go, Sir Andrew. Scout me for him at the corner of the orchard like a bum-baily.° So soon as ever thou see'st him, draw; and as thou draw'st, swear horrible; for it comes to pass oft that a terrible oath, with a swaggering accent sharply twanged off, gives man- 185 hood more approbation° than ever proof° itself would have earned him. Away!

ANDREW  Nay, let me alone for swearing.° *Exit.*

TOBY  Now will not I deliver his letter; for the behavior of the young gentleman gives him out to be of 190 good capacity and breeding; his employment between his lord and my niece confirms no less. Therefore this letter, being so excellently ignorant, will breed no terror in the youth. He will find it comes from a clodpoll.° But, sir, I will deliver his challenge by word 195 of mouth, set upon Aguecheek a notable report of valor, and drive the gentleman (as I know his youth will aptly receive it) into a most hideous opinion of his rage, skill, fury, and impetuosity. This will so fright them both that they will kill one another by the look, 200 like cockatrices.°

*Enter* OLIVIA *and* VIOLA.

FABIAN  Here he comes with your niece. Give them way till he take leave, and presently after him.°

TOBY  I will meditate the while upon some horrid message for a challenge. 205
　　　　　[*Exeunt Sir* TOBY, FABIAN, *and* MARIA.]

OLIVIA
I have said too much unto a heart of stone

---

106 **Carry . . . woman** for analysis  113 **move** agitate  115 **rough** violent  116 **bawcock** fine fellow (French *beau coq*)  117 **chuck** chick  119–20 **'tis . . . Satan** it is unsuitable for a man of your dignity to play a children's game with Satan  121 **collier** vendor of coals  127 **idle** trifling  128 **element** sphere  133 **genius** nature, personality  135–36 **take . . . taint** be exposed and spoiled  141 **carry it** go on with the joke  146 **More . . . morning** Another subject for a May Day pageant  149 **saucy** with "vinegar and pepper"  154 **admire** marvel

169 **o' . . . law** safe from prosecution  179 **commerce** conversation  182 **bum-baily** bailiff, sheriff's officer  186 **approbation** attestation; **proof** actual trial  188 **let . . . swearing** do not worry about my ability at swearing  195 **clodpoll** dunce  201 **cockatrices** fabulous serpents that could kill with a glance  202–03 **Give . . . him** Do not interrupt them until he goes, and then follow him at once

And laid mine honor too unchary° on't.
There's something in me that reproves my fault;
But such a headstrong potent fault it is
That it but mocks reproof.                                    210

VIOLA
With the same havior° that your passion bears
Goes on my master's griefs.

OLIVIA
Here, wear this jewel° for me; 'tis my picture.
Refuse it not; it hath no tongue to vex you.
And I beseech you come again tomorrow.                       215
What shall you ask of me that I'll deny,
That honor, saved, may upon asking give?

VIOLA
Nothing but this: your true love for my master.

OLIVIA
How with mine honor may I give him that
Which I have given to you?

VIOLA                              I will acquit you.          220

OLIVIA
Well, come again tomorrow. Fare thee well.
A fiend like thee° might bear my soul to hell.  [Exit.]

*Enter [Sir]* TOBY *and* FABIAN.

TOBY  Gentleman, God save thee.
VIOLA  And you, sir.
TOBY  That defense thou hast, betake thee to't. Of 225
what nature the wrongs are thou hast done him, I
know not; but thy intercepter, full of despite,° bloody
as the hunter,° attends° thee at the orchard end.
Dismount thy tuck,° be yare° in thy preparation, for
thy assailant is quick, skillful, and deadly.              230
VIOLA  You mistake, sir. I am sure no man hath any
quarrel to me. My remembrance is very free and
clear from any image of offense done to any man.
TOBY  You'll find it otherwise, I assure you. Therefore,
if you hold your life at any price, betake you to your 235
guard; for your opposite° hath in him what youth,
strength, skill, and wrath can furnish man withal.°
VIOLA  I pray you, sir, what is he?
TOBY  He is knight, dubbed with unhatched° rapier
and on carpet consideration,° but he is a devil in 240
private brawl. Souls and bodies hath he divorced
three; and his incensement at this moment is so
implacable that satisfaction can be none but by pangs
of death and sepulcher. "Hob, nob"° is his word;
"give't or take't."                                         245
VIOLA  I will return again into the house and desire
some conduct° of the lady. I am no fighter. I have
heard of some kind of men that put quarrels purposely
on others to taste° their valor. Belike this is a man of
that quirk.                                                  250
TOBY  Sir, no. His indignation derives itself out of a
very competent° injury; therefore get you on and

give him his desire. Back you shall not to the house,
unless you undertake that with me which with as
much safety you might answer him. Therefore on, or 255
strip your sword stark naked; for meddle° you must,
that's certain, or forswear to wear iron about you.
VIOLA  This is as uncivil as strange. I beseech you do
me this courteous office, as to know of the knight
what my offense to him is. It is something of my 260
negligence,° nothing of my purpose.
TOBY  I will do so. Signior Fabian, stay you by this
gentleman till my return.              *Exit [Sir]* TOBY.
VIOLA  Pray you, sir, do you know of this matter?
FABIAN  I know the knight is incensed against you, 265
even to a mortal arbitrament;° but nothing of the
circumstance more.
VIOLA  I beseech you, what manner of man is he?
FABIAN  Nothing of that wonderful promise, to read
him by his form, as you are like to find him in the 270
proof of his valor. He is indeed, sir, the most skillful,
bloody, and fatal opposite that you could possibly
have found in any part of Illyria. Will you walk towards him? I will make your peace with him if I can.
VIOLA  I shall be much bound to you for't. I am one 275
that had rather go with sir priest than sir knight. I care
not who knows so much of my mettle.°        *Exeunt.°*

*Enter [Sir]* TOBY *and [Sir]* ANDREW.

TOBY  Why, man, he's a very devil; I have not seen
such a firago.° I had a pass° with him, rapier, scabbard,
and all, and he gives me the stuck-in° with such a 280
mortal motion° that it is inevitable; and on the
answer° he pays you as surely as your feet hits the
ground they step on. They say he has been fencer to
the sophy.°
ANDREW  Pox on't, I'll not meddle with him.               285
TOBY  Ay, but he will not now be pacified. Fabian can
scarce hold him yonder.
ANDREW  Plague on't, and I thought he had been
valiant, and so cunning in fence,° I'd have seen him
damned ere I'd have challenged him. Let him let the 290
matter slip, and I'll give him my horse, gray Capilet.
TOBY  I'll make the motion.° Stand here; make a good
show on't. This shall end without the perdition of
souls.° [*Aside.*] Marry, I'll ride your horse as well as I
ride you.                                                    295

*Enter* FABIAN *and* VIOLA.

I have his horse to take up° the quarrel. I have persuaded him the youth's a devil.
FABIAN  He is as horribly conceited of him,° and pants
and looks pale, as if a bear were at his heels.
TOBY  There's no remedy, sir; he will fight with you 300

207 unchary carelessly  211 havior behavior  213 jewel jeweled locket (?)  222 like thee with your attractions  227 despite defiance  227–28 bloody . . . hunter bloodthirsty as a hunting dog  228 attends awaits  229 Dismount thy tuck unsheathe your rapier; yare quick, prompt  236 opposite adversary  237 withal with  239 unhatched unhacked  240 on carpet consideration not because of his exploits in the field but through connections at court  244 Hob, nob have it, or have it not  247 conduct escort  249 taste test  252 competent sufficient
256 meddle engage him, fight  260–61 of my negligence unintentional  266 mortal arbitrament deadly trial  277 mettle character, disposition  277 s.d. Exeunt this stage direction, which leaves the stage empty, properly marks the ending of the scene, but the new scene that opens with the entrance of Sir Toby and Sir Andrew is not indicated as such in the Folio  279 firago virago (probably a phonetic spelling); pass bout  280 stuck-in stoccado, thrust  281 mortal motion deadly pass  282 answer return  284 sophy shah  289 in fence at fencing  292 motion proposal  293–94 perdition of souls loss of life  296 take up settle  298 He . . . him Cesario has just as terrifying a notion of Sir Andrew

for's oath° sake. Marry, he hath better bethought him
of his quarrel,° and he finds that now scarce to be
worth talking of. Therefore draw for the supportance
of his vow.° He protests he will not hurt you.
VIOLA [*Aside.*] Pray God defend me! A little thing 305
would make me tell them how much I lack of a man.
FABIAN   Give ground if you see him furious.
TOBY   Come, Sir Andrew, there's no remedy. The
gentleman will for his honor's sake have one bout
with you; he cannot by the duello° avoid it; but he 310
has promised me, as he is a gentleman and a soldier,
he will not hurt you. Come on, to't.
ANDREW   Pray God he keep his oath!

[*Draws.*]

*Enter* ANTONIO.

VIOLA
I do assure you 'tis against my will.

[*Draws.*]

ANTONIO
Put up your sword. If this young gentleman 315
Have done offense, I take the fault on me;
If you offend him, I for him defy you.
TOBY   You, sir? Why, what are you?
ANTONIO [*Draws.*]
One, sir, that for his love dares yet do more
Than you have heard him brag to you he will. 320
TOBY   Nay, if you be an undertaker,° I am for you.

[*Draws.*]

*Enter* OFFICERS.

FABIAN   O good Sir Toby, hold. Here come the
officers.
TOBY [*To* ANTONIO.] I'll be with you anon.
VIOLA [*To Sir* ANDREW.] Pray, sir, put your sword 325
up, if you please.
ANDREW   Marry, will I, sir; and for that° I promised
you, I'll be as good as my word. He will bear you
easily, and reins well.
FIRST OFFICER   This is the man; do thy office.° 330
SECOND OFFICER
Antonio, I arrest thee at the suit
Of Count Orsino.
ANTONIO            You do mistake me, sir.
FIRST OFFICER
No, sir, no jot. I know your favor° well,
Though now you have no sea-cap on your head.
Take him away. He knows I know him well. 335
ANTONIO
I must obey. [*To* VIOLA.] This comes with seeking
   you.
But there's no remedy; I shall answer it.°
What will you do, now my necessity
Makes me to ask you for my purse? It grieves me
Much more for what I cannot do for you 340

Than what befalls myself. You stand amazed,
But be of comfort.
SECOND OFFICER   Come, sir, away.
ANTONIO
I must entreat of you some of that money.
VIOLA
What money, sir?
For the fair kindness you have showed me here, 345
And part° being prompted by your present trouble,
Out of my lean and low ability
I'll lend you something. My having is not much.
I'll make division of my present° with you.
Hold, there's half my coffer.°
ANTONIO            Will you deny me now? 350
Is't possible that my deserts to you
Can lack persuasion?° Do not tempt my misery,
Lest that it make me so unsound° a man
As to upbraid you with those kindnesses
That I have done for you.
VIOLA            I know of none, 355
Nor know I you by voice or any feature.
I hate ingratitude more in a man
Than lying, vainness,° babbling, drunkenness,
Or any taint of vice whose strong corruption
Inhabits our frail blood.
ANTONIO            O heavens themselves! 360
SECOND OFFICER
Come, sir, I pray you go.
ANTONIO
Let me speak a little. This youth that you see here
I snatched one half out of the jaws of death;
Relieved him with such sanctity of love,
And to his image, which methought did promise 365
Most venerable° worth, did I devotion.
FIRST OFFICER
What's that to us? The time goes by. Away.
ANTONIO
But, O, how vild° an idol proves this god!
Thou hast, Sebastian, done good feature° shame.
In nature there's no blemish but the mind;° 370
None can be called deformed but the unkind.°
Virtue is beauty; but the beauteous evil
Are empty trunks,° o'erflourished° by the devil.
FIRST OFFICER
The man grows mad; away with him! Come, come,
   sir.
ANTONIO   Lead me on.      *Exit*, [*with* OFFICERS]. 375
VIOLA
Methinks his words do from such passion fly
That he believes himself; so do not I.
Prove true, imagination, O, prove true,
That I, dear brother, be now ta'en for you!
TOBY   Come hither, knight; come hither, Fabian. 380
We'll whisper o'er a couplet or two of most sage
saws.°

301 oath oath's   302 his quarrel the cause of his resentment
303–04 draw . . . vow make a show of valor merely for
the satisfaction of his oath   310 duello duelling code   321
an undertaker one who takes up a challenge for another
(with perhaps a pun on *undertaker* as a government agent, i.e.,
scoundrel)   327 for that as for what (i.e., his horse, "gray
Capilet")   330 office duty   333 favor face   337 answer it
try to defend myself against the accusation

346 part partly   349 present present resources   350 coffer
chest, i.e., money   351–52 deserts . . . persuasion claims
on you can fail to be persuasive   353 unsound weak, unmanly
358 vainness (1) falseness (2) boasting   366 venerable worthy
of veneration   368 vild vile   369 feature shape, external
appearance   370 mind as distinguished from body or "feature"
371 unkind unnatural   373 trunks chests; o'erflourished
decorated with carving and painting   381–82 sage saws wise
maxims

**VIOLA**
He named Sebastian. I my brother know
Yet living in my glass.° Even such and so
In favor was my brother, and he went     385
Still in this fashion, color, ornament,
For him I imitate. O, if it prove,
Tempests are kind, and salt waves fresh in love!

                                                  *[Exit.]*

**TOBY** A very dishonest° paltry boy, and more a
coward than a hare. His dishonesty appears in leaving    390
his friend here in necessity and denying him; and for
his cowardship, ask Fabian.

**FABIAN** A coward, a most devout coward; religious
in it.°

**ANDREW** 'Slid,° I'll after him again and beat him.    395

**TOBY** Do; cuff him soundly, but never draw thy
sword.

**ANDREW** And I do not—            *[Exit.]*

**FABIAN** Come, let's see the event.°

**TOBY** I dare lay any money 'twill be nothing yet.°    400

             *Exit, [with Sir* ANDREW *and* FABIAN*].*

# ACT IV

Scene I. *[Before Olivia's house.]*

*Enter* SEBASTIAN *and* CLOWN.

**CLOWN** Will you make me believe that I am not sent
for you?

**SEBASTIAN** Go to, go to, thou art a foolish fellow.
Let me be clear of thee.

**CLOWN** Well held out,° i' faith! No, I do not know   5
you; nor I am not sent to you by my lady, to bid you
come speak with her; nor your name is not Master
Cesario; nor this is not my nose neither. Nothing that
is so is so.

**SEBASTIAN** I prithee vent thy folly somewhere else.   10
Thou know'st not me.

**CLOWN** Vent my folly! He has heard that word of
some great man, and now applies it to a fool. Vent my
folly! I am afraid this great lubber,° the world, will
prove a cockney.° I prithee now, ungird thy strange-   15
ness,° and tell me what I shall vent° to my lady. Shall
I vent to her that thou art coming?

**SEBASTIAN** I prithee, foolish Greek,° depart from me.
There's money for thee. If you tarry longer, I shall give
worse payment.                              20

**CLOWN** By my troth, thou hast an open hand. These
wise men that give fools money get themselves a good
report—after fourteen years' purchase.°

*Enter [Sir]* ANDREW, *[Sir]* TOBY, *and* FABIAN.

**ANDREW** Now, sir, have I met you again? There's for
you!                                            25

*[Strikes* SEBASTIAN*.]*

**SEBASTIAN** Why, there's for thee, and there, and
there!

*[Strikes Sir* ANDREW*.]*

Are all the people mad?

**TOBY** Hold, sir, or I'll throw your dagger o'er the
house.                                         30

*[Seizes* SEBASTIAN*.]*

**CLOWN** This will I tell my lady straight.° I would not
be in some of your coats for twopence.        *[Exit.]*

**TOBY** Come on, sir; hold.

**ANDREW** Nay, let him alone. I'll go another way to
work with him. I'll have an action of battery against   35
him,° if there be any law in Illyria. Though I stroke°
him first, yet it's no matter for that.

**SEBASTIAN** Let go thy hand.

**TOBY** Come, sir, I will not let you go. Come, my
young soldier, put up your iron. You are well fleshed.°   40
Come on.

**SEBASTIAN**
I will be free from thee. *[Frees himself.]* What wouldst
thou now?
If thou dar'st tempt me further, draw thy sword.

**TOBY** What, what? Nay then, I must have an ounce
or two of this malapert° blood from you.          45

*[Draws.]*

*Enter* OLIVIA.

**OLIVIA**
Hold, Toby! On thy life I charge thee hold!

**TOBY** Madam.

**OLIVIA**
Will it be ever thus? Ungracious wretch,
Fit for the mountains and the barbarous caves,
Where manners ne'er were preached! Out of my sight!   50
Be not offended, dear Cesario.
Rudesby,° begone.
     *[Exeunt Sir* TOBY, *Sir* ANDREW, *and* FABIAN*.]*
                  I prithee gentle friend,
Let thy fair wisdom, not thy passion, sway°
In this uncivil° and unjust extent°
Against thy peace. Go with me to my house,       55
And hear thou there how many fruitless pranks
This ruffian hath botched up,° that thou thereby
Mayst smile at this. Thou shalt not choose but go.
Do not deny. Beshrew° his soul for me.
He started° one poor heart° of mine, in thee.     60

**SEBASTIAN**
What relish is in this?° How runs the stream?
Or° I am mad, or else this is a dream.

---

384 **living . . . glass** staring at me from my mirror   389
**dishonest** dishonorable   393–94 **religious in it** dedicated to
his cowardice (following "devout")   395 **'Slid** by God's
eyelid   399 **event** outcome   400 **yet** after all
**IV.i.5 held out** maintained   14 **lubber** lout   15 **cockney**
affected fop   15–16 **ungird thy strangeness** abandon your
silly pretense (of not recognizing me)   16 **vent** say   18 **Greek**
buffoon   23 **after . . . purchase** after a long delay, at a high
price

31 **straight** straightaway, at once   35–36 **have . . . him**
charge him with assaulting me   36 **stroke** struck   40 **well
fleshed** made eager for fighting by having tasted blood   45
**malapert** saucy   52 **Rudesby** ruffian   53 **sway** rule   54
**uncivil** barbarous; **extent** display   57 **botched up** clumsily
contrived   59 **Beshrew** curse   60 **started** roused; **heart** with
a pun on **hart**   61 **What . . . this** What does this mean?
62 **Or** either

Let fancy still my sense in Lethe° steep;
If it be thus to dream, still let me sleep!

OLIVIA
Nay, come, I prithee. Would thou'dst be ruled by me! 65

SEBASTIAN
Madam, I will.

OLIVIA          O, say so, and so be.        *Exeunt.*

Scene II. [*Olivia's house.*]

*Enter* MARIA *and* CLOWN.

MARIA   Nay, I prithee put on this gown and this
beard; make him believe thou art Sir Topas° the
curate; do it quickly. I'll call Sir Toby the whilst.°
                                   [*Exit.*]

CLOWN   Well, I'll put it on, and I will dissemble°
myself in't, and I would I were the first that ever 5
dissembled in such a gown. I am not tall enough to
become the function° well, nor lean enough to be
thought a good student;° but to be said an honest man
and a good housekeeper° goes as fairly as to say a
careful° man and a great scholar. The competitors° 10
enter.

*Enter* [*Sir*] TOBY [*and* MARIA].

TOBY   Jove bless thee, Master Parson.

CLOWN   Bonos dies,° Sir Toby; for, as the old hermit
of Prague,° that never saw pen and ink, very wittily
said to a niece of King Gorboduc,° "That that is"; 15
so I, being Master Parson, am Master Parson; for
what is "that" but that, and "is" but is?

TOBY   To him, Sir Topas.

CLOWN   What ho, I say. Peace in this prison!

TOBY   The knave counterfeits well; a good knave.° 20

MALVOLIO *within.*

MALVOLIO   Who calls there?

CLOWN   Sir Topas the curate, who comes to visit
Malvolio the lunatic.

MALVOLIO   Sir Topas, Sir Topas, good Sir Topas, go
to my lady. 25

CLOWN   Out, hyperbolical° fiend! How vexest thou
this man! Talkest thou nothing but of ladies?

TOBY   Well said, Master Parson.

MALVOLIO   Sir Topas, never was man thus wronged.
Good Sir Topas, do not think I am mad. They have 30
laid me here in hideous darkness.

CLOWN   Fie, thou dishonest Satan. I call thee by the
most modest° terms, for I am one of those gentle ones
that will use the devil himself with courtesy. Say'st
thou that house° is dark? 35

MALVOLIO   As hell, Sir Topas.

CLOWN   Why, it hath bay windows transparent as
barricadoes,° and the clerestories° toward the south
north are as lustrous as ebony; and yet complainest
thou of obstruction? 40

MALVOLIO   I am not mad, Sir Topas. I say to you this
house is dark.

CLOWN   Madman, thou errest. I say there is no darkness but ignorance, in which thou art more puzzled
than the Egyptians in their fog.° 45

MALVOLIO   I say this house is as dark as ignorance,
though ignorance were as dark as hell; and I say there
was never man thus abused. I am no more mad than
you are. Make the trial of it in any constant question.°

CLOWN   What is the opinion of Pythagoras° concern- 50
ing wild fowl?

MALVOLIO   That the soul of our grandam might
happily° inhabit a bird.

CLOWN   What think'st thou of his opinion?

MALVOLIO   I think nobly of the soul and no way ap- 55
prove his opinion.

CLOWN   Fare thee well. Remain thou still in darkness.
Thou shalt hold th' opinion of Pythagoras ere I will
allow of thy wits,° and fear to kill a woodcock,° lest
thou dispossess the soul of thy grandam. Fare thee 60
well.

MALVOLIO   Sir Topas, Sir Topas!

TOBY   My most exquisite Sir Topas!

CLOWN   Nay, I am for all waters.°

MARIA   Thou mightst have done this without thy 65
beard and gown. He sees thee not.

TOBY   To him in thine own voice, and bring me word
how thou find'st him. [*To* MARIA.] I would we were
well rid of this knavery. If he may be conveniently
delivered,° I would he were; for I am now so far in 70
offense with my niece that I cannot pursue with any
safety this sport to the upshot.° [*To the* CLOWN.] Come
by and by to my chamber.      *Exit* [*with* MARIA].

CLOWN [*Sings.*]
    "Hey, Robin, jolly Robin,
      Tell me how thy lady does."° 75

MALVOLIO   Fool.

CLOWN   "My lady is unkind, perdie."°

MALVOLIO   Fool!

CLOWN   "Alas, why is she so?"

MALVOLIO   Fool, I say. 80

CLOWN   "She loves another." Who calls, ha?

MALVOLIO   Good fool, as ever thou wilt deserve well
at my hand, help me to a candle, and pen, ink, and
paper. As I am a gentleman, I will live to be thankful
to thee for't. 85

CLOWN   Master Malvolio?

MALVOLIO   Ay, good fool.

CLOWN   Alas, sir, how fell you besides your five wits?°

---

63 **Lethe** in classical mythology, the river of oblivion in Hades
**IV.ii.2 Sir Topas** the ridiculous hero of Chaucer's *Rime of Sir
Thopas*, a parody of chivalric romances  **3 the whilst** meanwhile  **4 dissemble** disguise  **7 function** clerical office  **8
student** student  **9 good housekeeper** solid citizen  **10
careful** painstaking;  **competitors** confederates  **13 Bonos
dies** good day  **13–14 old . . . Prague** apparently the
Clown's nonsensical invention  **15 King Gorboduc** a
legendary king of Britain  **20 knave** fellow  **26 hyperbolical**
boisterous (a term from rhetoric meaning "exaggerated in
style")  **33 most modest** mildest  **35 house** madman's cell

**38 barricadoes** barricades; **clerestories** upper windows  **45
Egyptians . . . fog** to plague the Egyptians Moses brought a
"thick darkness" that lasted three days; see Exodus 10:21–23
**49 constant question** consistent topic, normal conversation
**50 Pythagoras** ancient Greek philosopher who expounded the
doctrine of the transmigration of souls  **53 happily** haply,
perhaps  **59 allow . . . wits** acknowledge your sanity;
**woodcock** a proverbially stupid bird  **64 I . . . waters** I can
turn my hand to any trade  **70 delivered** released  **72 upshot**
conclusion  **74–75 Hey . . . does** the Clown sings an old
ballad  **77 perdie** certainly  **88 how . . . wits** how did you
happen to become mad

MALVOLIO Fool, there was never man so notoriously°
abused. I am as well in my wits, fool, as thou art. 90

CLOWN But as well? Then you are mad indeed, if you
be no better in your wits than a fool.

MALVOLIO They have here propertied me;° keep me
in darkness, send ministers to me, asses, and do all they
can to face me out of my wits.° 95

CLOWN Advise you° what you say. The minister is
here.°—Malvolio, Malvolio, thy wits the heavens
restore. Endeavor thyself to sleep and leave thy vain
bibble babble.

MALVOLIO Sir Topas. 100

CLOWN Maintain no words with him, good fellow.
—Who, I, sir? Not I, sir. God buy you,° good Sir
Topas.—Marry, amen.—I will, sir, I will.

MALVOLIO Fool, fool, fool, I say!

CLOWN Alas, sir, be patient. What say you, sir? I am 105
shent° for speaking to you.

MALVOLIO Good fool, help me to some light and
some paper. I tell thee, I am as well in my wits as any
man in Illyria.

CLOWN Well-a-day that you were,° sir. 110

MALVOLIO By this hand, I am. Good fool, some ink,
paper, and light; and convey what I will set down to
my lady. It shall advantage thee more than ever the
bearing of letter did.

CLOWN I will help you to't. But tell me true, are you 115
not mad indeed, or do you but counterfeit?°

MALVOLIO Believe me, I am not. I tell thee true.

CLOWN Nay, I'll ne'er believe a madman till I see his
brains. I will fetch you light and paper and ink.

MALVOLIO Fool, I'll requite it in the highest degree. 120
I prithee be gone.

CLOWN [Sings.]
    I am gone, sir.
    And anon, sir,
  I'll be with you again,
    In a trice, 125
  Like to the old Vice,°
  Your need to sustain.°
  Who with dagger of lath,
  In his rage and his wrath,
    Cries "Ah ha" to the devil. 130
  Like a mad lad,
  "Pare thy nails, dad."
    Adieu, goodman devil.°      Exit.

### Scene III. [Olivia's garden.]

Enter SEBASTIAN.

SEBASTIAN
This is the air; that is the glorious sun;
This pearl she gave me, I do feel't and see't;
And though 'tis wonder that enwraps me thus,
Yet 'tis not madness. Where's Antonio then?
I could not find him at the Elephant; 5
Yet there he was,° and there I found this credit,°
That he did range the town to seek me out.
His counsel now might do me golden service;
For though my soul disputes well with my sense°
That this may be some error, but no madness, 10
Yet doth this accident and flood of fortune
So far exceed all instance,° all discourse,°
That I am ready to distrust mine eyes
And wrangle with my reason that persuades me
To any other trust° but that I am mad, 15
Or else the lady's mad. Yet, if 'twere so,
She could not sway° her house, command her
  followers,
Take and give back affairs and their dispatch°
With such a smooth, discreet, and stable bearing
As I perceive she does. There's something in't 20
That is deceivable.° But here the lady comes.

Enter OLIVIA and PRIEST.

OLIVIA
Blame not this haste of mine. If you mean well,
Now go with me and with this holy man
Into the chantry by.° There, before him,
And underneath that consecrated roof, 25
Plight me the full assurance of your faith,
That my most jealous° and too doubtful soul
May live at peace. He shall conceal it
Whiles° you are willing it shall come to note,°
What time we will our celebration keep° 30
According to my birth. What do you say?

SEBASTIAN
I'll follow this good man and go with you
And having sworn truth, ever will be true.

OLIVIA
Then lead the way, good father, and heavens so shine
That they may fairly note° this act of mine.   Exeunt. 35

# ACT V

### Scene I. [Before Olivia's house.]

Enter CLOWN and FABIAN.

FABIAN Now as thou lov'st me, let me see his° letter.

CLOWN Good Master Fabian, grant me another
request.

FABIAN Anything.

89 notoriously outrageously   93 propertied me used
me as a mere object, not a human being   95 face . . .
wits impudently insist that I am mad   96 Advise you
consider carefully   96–97 The . . . here for the next few
lines the Clown uses two voices, his own and that of Sir Topas
102 God buy you God be with you, i.e., good-bye   106 shent
rebuked   110 Well-a-day . . . were alas, if only you were
116 counterfeit pretend   126 Vice in the morality plays, a
stock mischievous character who usually carried a wooden
dagger   127 Your . . . sustain in order to help you resist
the devil   133 Adieu, goodman devil a much emended
line; "goodman" (Folio "good man"), a title for a yeoman or
any man of substance not of gentle birth, roughly corresponds to our "mister"

IV.iii.6 was had been; credit belief   9 my soul . . . sense
my reason agrees with the evidence of my senses   12 instance
precedent; discourse reason   15 trust belief   17 sway rule
18 Take . . . dispatch assume and discharge the management
of affairs   21 deceivable deceptive   24 chantry by nearby
chapel   27 jealous jealous, anxious   29 Whiles until; come
to note be made public   30 our celebration keep celebrate
our marriage ceremony (as distinguished from the formal
compact of betrothal)   35 fairly note look with favor on
V.i.1 his Malvolio's

CLOWN  Do not desire to see this letter. 5
FABIAN  This is to give a dog, and in recompense desire my dog again.

*Enter* DUKE, VIOLA, CURIO, *and* LORDS.

DUKE  Belong you to the Lady Olivia, friends?
CLOWN  Ay, sir, we are some of her trappings.
DUKE  I know thee well. How dost thou, my good 10 fellow?
CLOWN  Truly, sir, the better for my foes, and the worse for my friends.
DUKE  Just the contrary: the better for thy friends.
CLOWN  No, sir, the worse. 15
DUKE  How can that be?
CLOWN  Marry, sir, they praise me and make an ass of me. Now my foes tell me plainly I am an ass; so that by my foes, sir, I profit in the knowledge of myself, and by my friends I am abused;° so that, conclusions 20 to be as kisses,° if your four negatives° make your two affirmatives,° why then, the worse for my friends, and the better for my foes.
DUKE  Why, this is excellent.
CLOWN  By my troth, sir, no, though it please you to 25 be one of my friends.
DUKE  Thou shalt not be the worse for me. There's gold.
CLOWN  But that it would be double-dealing,° sir, I would you could make it another. 30
DUKE  O, you give me ill counsel.
CLOWN  Put your grace° in your pocket, sir, for this once, and let your flesh and blood obey it.
DUKE  Well, I will be so much a sinner to be a double-dealer. There's another.° 35
CLOWN  Primo, secundo, tertio° is a good play;° and the old saying is "The third pays for all." The triplex,° sir, is a good tripping measure; or the bells of Saint Bennet,° sir, may put you in mind—one, two, three.
DUKE  You can fool no more money out of me at this 40 throw.° If you will let your lady know I am here to speak with her, and bring her along with you, it may awake my bounty further.
CLOWN  Marry, sir, lullaby to your bounty till I come again. I go, sir; but I would not have you to think 45 that my desire of having is the sin of covetousness. But, as you say, sir, let your bounty take a nap; I will awake it anon.                    *Exit.*

*Enter* ANTONIO *and* OFFICERS.

VIOLA
Here comes the man, sir, that did rescue me.
DUKE
That face of his I do remember well; 50
Yet when I saw it last, it was besmeared
As black as Vulcan° in the smoke of war.

A baubling° vessel was he captain of,
For shallow draught and bulk unprizable,°
With which such scathful° grapple did he make 55
With the most noble bottom° of our fleet
That very envy and the tongue of loss°
Cried fame and honor on him. What's the matter?
FIRST OFFICER
Orsino, this is that Antonio
That took the *Phoenix* and her fraught° from Candy;° 60
And this is he that did the *Tiger* board
When your young nephew Titus lost his leg.
Here in the streets, desperate of shame and state,°
In private brabble° did we apprehend him.
VIOLA
He did me kindness, sir; drew on my side;° 65
But in conclusion put strange speech upon me.°
I know not what 'twas but distraction.°
DUKE
Notable° pirate, thou salt-water thief,
What foolish boldness brought thee to their mercies
Whom thou in terms so bloody and so dear° 70
Hast made thine enemies?
ANTONIO                  Orsino, noble sir,
Be pleased that I shake off these names you give me.
Antonio never yet was thief or pirate,
Though I confess, on base and ground enough,
Orsino's enemy. A witchcraft drew me hither. 75
That most ingrateful boy there by your side
From the rude sea's enraged and foamy mouth
Did I redeem. A wrack° past hope he was.
His life I gave him, and did thereto add
My love without retention or restraint, 80
All his in dedication. For his sake
Did I expose myself (pure° for his love)
Into the danger of this adverse° town;
Drew to defend him when he was beset;
Where being apprehended, his false cunning 85
(Not meaning to partake with me in danger)
Taught him to face me out of his acquaintance,°
And grew a twenty years removèd thing
While one would wink; denied me mine own purse,
Which I had recommended° to his use 90
Not half an hour before.
VIOLA                  How can this be?
DUKE
When came he to this town?
ANTONIO
Today, my lord; and for three months before,
No int'rim, not a minute's vacancy,
Both day and night did we keep company. 95

*Enter* OLIVIA *and* ATTENDANTS.

20 abused deceived  20–21 conclusions . . . kisses if conclusions may be compared to kisses (when a coy girl's repeated denials really mean assent)  21 negatives lips (?)  22 affirmatives i.e., mouths (?)  29 double-dealing (1) giving twice (2) duplicity  32 grace (1) title of nobility (2) generosity  35 another i.e., coin  36 Primo, secundo, tertio one, two, three; play child's game (?)  37 triplex triple time in dancing  38–39 Saint Bennet Saint Benedict (a church)  41 throw throw of the dice  52 Vulcan Roman god of fire and patron of blacksmiths

53 baubling insignificant  54 For . . . unprizable virtually worthless on account of its small size  55 scathful destructive  56 bottom ship  57 very . . . loss even enmity and the voice of the losers  60 fraught freight, cargo; Candy Candia, Crete  63 desperate . . . state recklessly disregarding his shameful past behavior and the requirements of public order  64 brabble brawl  65 drew . . . side drew his sword in my defense  66 put . . . me spoke to me oddly  67 distraction madness  58 Notable notorious  70 dear grievous  78 wrack wreck  82 pure purely  83 adverse unfriendly  87 to . . . acquaintance brazenly to deny any knowledge of me  90 recommended given

DUKE
Here comes the countess; now heaven walks on earth.
But for° thee, fellow: fellow, thy words are madness.
Three months this youth hath tended upon me;
But more of that anon. Take him aside.
OLIVIA
What would my lord, but that° he may not have,          100
Wherein Olivia may seem serviceable?
Cesario, you do not keep promise with me.
VIOLA  Madam?
DUKE
Gracious Olivia—
OLIVIA
What do you say, Cesario?—Good my lord°—          105
VIOLA
My lord would speak; my duty hushes me.
OLIVIA
If it be aught to the old tune, my lord,
It is as fat and fulsome° to mine ear
As howling after music.
DUKE                            Still so cruel?
OLIVIA
Still so constant, lord.          110
DUKE
What, to perverseness? You uncivil lady,
To whose ingrate and unauspicious° altars
My soul the faithfull'st off'rings have breathed out
That e'er devotion tendered. What shall I do?
OLIVIA
Even what it please my lord, that shall become him.          115
DUKE
Why should I not, had I the heart to do it,
Like to th' Egyptian thief° at point of death,
Kill what I love?—a savage jealousy
That sometime savors nobly. But hear me this:
Since you to non-regardance° cast my faith,          120
And that° I partly know the instrument
That screws° me from my true place in your favor,
Live you the marble-breasted tyrant still.
But this your minion, whom I know you love,
And whom, by heaven I swear, I tender° dearly,          125
Him will I tear out of that cruel eye
Where he sits crownèd in his master's spite.
Come, boy, with me. My thoughts are ripe in mischief.
I'll sacrifice the lamb that I do love
To spite a raven's heart within a dove.          [Going.] 130
VIOLA
And I, most jocund, apt,° and willingly,
To do you rest° a thousand deaths would die.
                                        [Following.]
OLIVIA
Where goes Cesario?
VIOLA                    After him I love

More than I love these eyes, more than my life,
More, by all mores,° than e'er I shall love wife.          135
If I do feign, you witnesses above
Punish my life for tainting of my love!
OLIVIA
Ay me detested, how am I beguiled!
VIOLA
Who does beguile you? Who does do you wrong?
OLIVIA
Hast thou forgot thyself? Is it so long?          140
Call forth the holy father.     [Exit an ATTENDANT.]
DUKE          [To VIOLA.] Come, away!
OLIVIA
Whither, my lord? Cesario, husband, stay.
DUKE
Husband?
OLIVIA     Ay, husband. Can he that deny?
DUKE
Her husband, sirrah?°
VIOLA                    No, my lord, not I.
OLIVIA
Alas, it is the baseness of thy fear          145
That makes thee strangle thy propriety.°
Fear not, Cesario; take thy fortunes up;
Be that thou know'st thou art, and then thou art
As great as that° thou fear'st.

Enter PRIEST.

                    O, welcome, father!
Father, I charge thee by thy reverence          150
Here to unfold—though lately we intended
To keep in darkness what occasion now
Reveals before 'tis ripe—what thou dost know
Hath newly passed between this youth and me.
PRIEST
A contract° of eternal bond of love,          155
Confirmed by mutual joinder of your hands,
Attested by the holy close of lips,
Strength'ned by interchangement of your rings;
And all the ceremony of this compact°
Sealed in my function,° by my testimony;          160
Since when, my watch hath told me, toward my grave
I have traveled but two hours.
DUKE
O thou dissembling cub, what wilt thou be
When time hath sowed a grizzle on thy case?°
Or will not else thy craft° so quickly grow          165
That thine own trip° shall be thine overthrow?
Farewell, and take her; but direct thy feet
Where thou and I, henceforth, may never meet.
VIOLA
My lord, I do protest.
OLIVIA                    O, do not swear.
Hold little° faith, though thou hast too much fear.          170

Enter Sir ANDREW.

97 But for as for   100 but that except that which (i.e., my love)   105 Good my lord i.e., please be silent (so Cesario may speak)   108 fat and fulsome gross and repulsive   112 ingrate and unauspicious ungrateful and unpropitious   117 th' Egyptian thief in Heliodorus' Ethiopica, a Greek romance translated by Thomas Underdown about 1569, the bandit Thyamis, besieged in a cave, plans to kill the captive princess Charicleia, the object of his hopeless love; but in the darkness he kills another woman instead   120 non-regardance neglect   121 that since   122 screws forces   125 tender hold   131 apt readily   132 do you rest give you peace

135 mores possible comparisons   144 sirrah customary form of address to a menial   146 strangle thy propriety deny your identity   149 that him who (i.e., the duke)   155 contract betrothal   159 compact accent on second syllable   160 Sealed . . . function ratified by me in my priestly office   164 a . . . case gray hairs on your skin   165 craft duplicity   166 trip craftiness   170 little at least a little

ANDREW  For the love of God, a surgeon! Send one
presently° to Sir Toby.

OLIVIA  What's the matter?

ANDREW  H' as° broke my head across, and h' as given
Sir Toby a bloody coxcomb° too. For the love of God, 175
your help! I had rather than forty pound I were at
home.

OLIVIA  Who has done this, Sir Andrew?

ANDREW  The count's gentleman, one Cesario. We
took him for a coward, but he's the very devil in- 180
cardinate.°

DUKE  My gentleman Cesario?

ANDREW  Od's lifelings,° here he is! You broke my
head for nothing; and that that I did, I was set on to
do't by Sir Toby.                                    185

VIOLA
Why do you speak to me? I never hurt you.
You drew your sword upon me without cause,
But I bespake you fair° and hurt you not.

*Enter [Sir]* TOBY *and* CLOWN.

ANDREW  If a bloody coxcomb be a hurt, you have
hurt me. I think you set nothing by a bloody coxcomb. 190
Here comes Sir Toby halting;° you shall hear more.
But if he had not been in drink, he would have
tickled you othergates° than he did.

DUKE  How now, gentleman? How is't with you?

TOBY  That's all one! H' as hurt me, and there's th' 195
end on't. Sot,° didst see Dick Surgeon, sot?

CLOWN  O, he's drunk, Sir Toby, an hour agone. His
eyes were set° at eight i' th' morning.

TOBY  Then he's a rogue and a passy measures pavin.°
I hate a drunken rogue.                              200

OLIVIA  Away with him! Who hath made this havoc
with them?

ANDREW  I'll help you, Sir Toby, because we'll be
dressed° together.

TOBY  Will you help—an ass-head and a coxcomb and 205
a knave, a thin-faced knave, a gull?

OLIVIA  Get him to bed, and let his hurt be looked to.
                              [*Exeunt* CLOWN, FABIAN, *Sir* TOBY
                                       *and Sir* ANDREW.]

*Enter* SEBASTIAN.

SEBASTIAN
I am sorry, madam, I have hurt your kinsman;
But had it been the brother of my blood,
I must have done no less with wit and safety.°      210
You throw a strange regard° upon me, and by that
I do perceive it hath offended you.
Pardon me, sweet one, even for the vows
We made each other but so late ago.

DUKE
One face, one voice, one habit,° and two persons—  215
A natural perspective° that is and is not.

SEBASTIAN
Antonio, O my dear Antonio,
How have the hours racked and tortured me
Since I have lost thee!

ANTONIO
Sebastian are you?

SEBASTIAN             Fear'st thou° that, Antonio?    220

ANTONIO
How have you made division of yourself?
An apple cleft in two is not more twin
Than these two creatures. Which is Sebastian?

OLIVIA
Most wonderful.

SEBASTIAN
Do I stand there? I never had a brother;            225
Nor can there be that deity in my nature
Of here and everywhere.° I had a sister,
Whom the blind waves and surges have devoured.
Of charity,° what kin are you to me?
What countryman? What name? What parentage?         230

VIOLA
Of Messaline; Sebastian was my father;
Such a Sebastian was my brother too;
So went he suited° to his watery tomb.
If spirits can assume both form and suit,°
You come to fright us.

SEBASTIAN              A spirit I am indeed,           235
But am in that dimension grossly clad
Which from the womb I did participate.°
Were you a woman, as the rest goes even,°
I should my tears let fall upon your cheek
And say, "Thrice welcome, drownèd Viola!"           240

VIOLA
My father had a mole upon his brow.

SEBASTIAN
And so had mine.

VIOLA
And died that day when Viola from her birth
Had numb'red thirteen years.

SEBASTIAN
O, that record° is lively in my soul!               245
He finishèd indeed his mortal act
That day that made my sister thirteen years.

VIOLA
If nothing lets° to make us happy both
But this my masculine usurped attire,
Do not embrace me till each circumstance            250
Of place, time, fortune do cohere and jump°
That I am Viola; which to confirm,
I'll bring you to a captain in this town,

172 **presently** immediately  174 **H' as** he has  175 **coxcomb**
pate  180–81 **incardinate** incarnate  183 **Od's lifelings** by
God's life  188 **bespake you fair** addressed you courteously
191 **halting** limping  193 **othergates** otherwise  196 **Sot** fool
198 **set** closed  199 **passy measures pavin** *passamezzo* pavan,
a slow and stately dance of eight bars (hence its relevance to
the surgeon whose eyes had "set at eight")  203–04 **be
dressed** have our wounds dressed  210 **with . . . safety** with
a sensible regard for my safety  211 **strange regard** unfriendly
look

215 **habit** costume  216 **A natural perspective** a natural
optical illusion (like that produced by a stereoscope, which
converts two images into one)  220 **Fear'st thou** do you doubt
226–27 **Nor . . . everywhere** nor can I, like God, be everywhere at once  229 **Of charity** out of simple kindness  233
**suited** clothed  234 **form and suit** body and clothing  236–37
**am . . . participate** clothed in the bodily form that, like other
mortals, I acquired at birth  238 **as . . . even** as other circumstances seem to indicate  245 **record** history (accent on second
syllable)  248 **lets** interferes  251 **cohere and jump** fall
together and agree

Where lie my maiden weeds;° by whose gentle help
I was preserved to serve this noble count.                                255
All the occurrence of my fortune since
Hath been between this lady and this lord.
SEBASTIAN [*To* OLIVIA.]
So comes it, lady, you have been mistook.
But nature to her bias drew° in that.
You would have been contracted to a maid;                          260
Nor are you therein, by my life, deceived:
You are betrothed both to a maid and man.
DUKE
Be not amazed; right noble is his blood.
If this be so, as yet the glass° seems true,
I shall have share in this most happy wrack.                         265

[*To* VIOLA.]

Boy, thou hast said to me a thousand times
Thou never shouldst love woman like to me.
VIOLA
And all those sayings will I over° swear,
And all those swearings keep as true in soul
As doth that orbèd continent° the fire                                   270
That severs day from night.
DUKE                                  Give me thy hand,
And let me see thee in thy woman's weeds.
VIOLA
The captain that did bring me first on shore
Hath my maid's garments. He upon some action
Is now in durance, at Malvolio's suit,°                                   275
A gentleman, and follower of my lady's.
OLIVIA
He shall enlarge° him. Fetch Malvolio hither.
And yet alas, now I remember me,
They say, poor gentleman, he's much distract.

*Enter* CLOWN *with a letter, and* FABIAN.

A most extracting° frenzy of mine own                                   280
From my remembrance clearly banished his.
How does he, sirrah?
CLOWN   Truly, madam, he holds Belzebub at the
stave's end° as well as a man in his case° may do.
H' as here writ a letter to you; I should have given't 285
you today morning. But as a madman's epistles are
no gospels, so it skills° not much when they are
delivered.
OLIVIA   Open't and read it.
CLOWN   Look then to be well edified, when the fool  290
delivers the madman. [*Reads in a loud voice.*] "By the
Lord, madam"—
OLIVIA   How now? Art thou mad?
CLOWN   No, madam, I do but read madness. And your
ladyship will have it as it ought to be, you must allow 295
vox.°
OLIVIA   Prithee read i' thy right wits.

CLOWN   So I do, madonna; but to read his right wits is
to read thus. Therefore perpend,° my princess, and
give ear.                                                                              300
OLIVIA [*To* FABIAN.]   Read it you, sirrah.
FABIAN (*Reads.*)   "By the Lord, madam, you wrong
me, and the world shall know it. Though you have
put me into darkness, and given your drunken cousin
rule over me, yet have I the benefit of my senses as 305
well as your ladyship. I have your own letter that
induced me to the semblance I put on; with the which
I doubt not but to do myself much right, or you much
shame. Think of me as you please. I leave my duty a
little unthought of, and speak out of my injury.       310
                                     The madly used Malvolio."
OLIVIA   Did he write this?
CLOWN   Ay, madam.
DUKE   This savors not much of distraction.
OLIVIA
See him delivered, Fabian; bring him hither.          315
                                                      [*Exit* FABIAN.]
My lord, so please you, these things further thought on,
To think me as well a sister as a wife,
One day shall crown th' alliance on't, so please you,
Here at my house and at my proper° cost.
DUKE
Madam, I am most apt° t' embrace your offer.        320

[*To* VIOLA.]

Your master quits° you; and for your service done
    him,
So much against the mettle of your sex,
So far beneath your soft and tender breeding,
And since you called me master for so long,
Here is my hand; you shall from this time be          325
Your master's mistress.
OLIVIA                            A sister; you are she.

*Enter* [FABIAN, *with*] MALVOLIO.

DUKE
Is this the madman?
OLIVIA                     Ay, my lord, this same.
How now, Malvolio?
MALVOLIO              Madam, you have done me wrong,
Notorious° wrong.
OLIVIA                  Have I, Malvolio? No.
MALVOLIO
Lady, you have. Pray you peruse that letter.          330
You must not now deny it is your hand.
Write from it° if you can, in hand or phrase,
Or say 'tis not your seal, not your invention.°
You can say none of this. Well, grant it then,
And tell me, in the modesty of honor,°                  335
Why you have given me such clear lights of favor,
Bade me come smiling and cross-gartered to you,
To put on yellow stockings, and to frown
Upon Sir Toby and the lighter° people;
And, acting this in an obedient hope,                      340

254 **weeds** clothes   259 **nature . . . drew** nature followed
her normal inclination   264 **glass** the "natural perspective"
of line 216   268 **over** repeatedly   270 **orbèd continent**
in Ptolemaic astronomy, the sphere of the sun   274–75
**He . . . suit** at Malvolio's instigation he is now imprisoned
upon some legal charge   277 **enlarge** release   280 **extracting**
obliterating (in that it draws me from all thoughts of
Malvolio's "frenzy")   283–84 **he . . . end** he keeps the fiend
at a distance   284 **case** condition   287 **skills** matters   296
**vox** an appropriately loud voice

299 **perpend** pay attention   319 **proper** own   320 **apt** ready
321 **quits** releases   329 **Notorious** notable   332 **from
it** differently   333 **invention** composition   335 **in . . .
honor** with a proper regard to your own honor   339
**lighter** lesser

Why have you suffered me to be imprisoned,
Kept in a dark house, visited by the priest,
And made the most notorious geck and gull°
That e'er invention played on? Tell me why.

OLIVIA
Alas, Malvolio, this is not my writing,　　　　　345
Though I confess much like the character;
But, out of° question, 'tis Maria's hand.
And now I do bethink me, it was she
First told me thou wast mad; then cam'st in smiling,
And in such forms which here were presupposed°　350
Upon thee in the letter. Prithee be content.
This practice hath most shrewdly passed° upon thee;
But when we know the grounds and authors of it,
Thou shalt be both the plaintiff and the judge
Of thine own cause.

FABIAN　　　　　　　Good madam, hear me speak,　355
And let no quarrel, nor no brawl to come,
Taint the condition of this present hour,
Which I have wond'red at. In hope it shall not,
Most freely I confess myself and Toby
Set this device against Malvolio here,　　　　　360
Upon some stubborn and uncourteous parts°
We had conceived against him. Maria writ
The letter, at Sir Toby's great importance,°
In recompense whereof he hath married her.
How with a sportful malice it was followed　　365
May rather pluck on° laughter than revenge,
If that° the injuries be justly weighed
That have on both sides passed.

OLIVIA
Alas, poor fool,° how have they baffled° thee!

CLOWN Why, "some are born great, some achieve 370
greatness, and some have greatness thrown upon
them." I was one, sir, in this interlude,° one Sir Topas,
sir; but that's all one. "By the Lord, fool, I am not
mad!" But do you remember, "Madam, why laugh
you at such a barren rascal? And you smile not, he's 375
gagged"? And thus the whirligig of time brings in his
revenges.

MALVOLIO I'll be revenged on the whole pack of
you!　　　　　　　　　　　　　　　　　[Exit]

OLIVIA
He hath been most notoriously abused.　　　　380

DUKE
Pursue him and entreat him to a peace.
He hath not told us of the captain yet.
When that is known, and golden time convents,°
A solemn combination shall be made
Of our dear souls. Meantime, sweet sister,　　385
We will not part from hence. Cesario, come—
For so you shall be while you are a man,
But when in other habits you are seen,
Orsino's mistress and his fancy's° queen.
　　　　　　　　Exeunt [all but the CLOWN].

CLOWN sings.°

When that I was and a° little tiny boy,　　　　390
　With hey, ho, the wind and the rain,
A foolish thing was but a toy,°
　For the rain it raineth every day.

But when I came to man's estate,
　With hey, ho, the wind and the rain,　　　　395
'Gainst knaves and thieves men shut their gate,
　For the rain it raineth every day.

But when I came alas, to wive,
　With hey, ho, the wind and the rain,
By swaggering could I never thrive,　　　　　400
　For the rain it raineth every day.

But when I came unto my beds,
　With hey, ho, the wind and the rain,
With tosspots° still had drunken heads,
　For the rain it raineth every day.　　　　　405

A great while ago the world begun,
　Hey, ho, the wind and the rain;
But that's all one, our play is done,
　And we'll strive to please you every day.
　　　　　　　　　　　　　　　　[Exit.]

343 **geck and gull** fool and dupe　347 **out of** beyond　350
**presupposed** imposed　352 **This . . . passed** this trick has
most mischievously worked　361 **Upon . . . parts** because
of some unyielding and discourteous traits of character　363
**importance** importunity　366 **pluck on** prompt　367 **If
that** if　369 **fool** here, a term of affection and compassion;
**baffled** publicly humiliated　372 **interlude** little play

383 **convents** is suitable (?)　389 **fancy's** love's　389 s.d.
**Clown sings** since no source has been found for the Clown's
song—which certain editors have inexplicably denounced as
doggerel—we may assume that it is Shakespeare's　390 **and
a** a　392 **toy** trifle　404 **tosspots** sots

# THE TRAGEDY OF HAMLET
# PRINCE OF DENMARK

EDITED BY EDWARD HUBLER

## Introduction

Tragedy of the first order is a rare phenomenon. It came into being in Greece in the fifth century B.C., where it flourished for a while, and it did not appear again until some two thousand years later when Shakespeare wrote *Hamlet* in 1600. The second incarnation of the spirit of tragedy differs greatly from the first in form and method. In Shakespeare the comic and the serious are not disassociated. His brightest moments pass quickly into shadow, and laughter often illuminates his darkest scenes. The comic and the tragic stand side by side, giving us a fuller view of the thing observed, neither canceling out the other. A hallmark of Shakespeare's mature work is its simultaneity, the presentation of things and their opposites at the same time. Coleridge called him "myriad-minded." There had been an alternation of the dark and the light in English drama almost from the beginning, but it remained for Shakespeare to make each a part of the other. He was able to do so because he knew that the difference between comedy and tragedy has nothing to do with subject matter. Each is a way of looking at life. Neither gives us a total view of life, nor does Shakespeare in his use of both; but he approaches totality more closely than any other dramatist.

In *Hamlet* we laugh at the affected and superficial Osric (this is a lightening before the storm), and we are amused by the garrulous Polonius, whose inadequate worldly wisdom stands in contrast to the deeper truths the play reveals. But the most central use of comedy is Hamlet's mordant wit. His

Thrift, thrift, Horatio. The funeral baked meats
Did coldly furnish forth the marriage tables   (I.ii.180–81)

emphasizes his revulsion at his mother's hasty remarriage. His near-hysteria after the Ghost makes its revelation underlines the degree to which the revelation has disturbed him. The audience may laugh at things such as these, but the laughter is not merry. And there will be no laughter at all when, at the close of Hamlet's interview with his mother, he drags the body of Polonius to the exit, remarking, "I'll lug the guts into the neighbor room." Then he pauses at the threshold to say, "Good night, Mother." And he says it with all the tenderness he has, for she has looked into

her soul and repented, and in the contest with the king she is now on Hamlet's side. Mother and son are again at one. Bringing this about has been the essential business of the scene, and the dragging of the body (though the body must somehow be removed) is in no way necessary to it. Yet this bit of grotesquerie adds to the multiplicity of the scene's effects without in any way detracting from its deep seriousness.

It was Aristotle's belief that a well-constructed plot should be single in issue, and that if any one action were to be displaced or removed, the whole would be disjointed and disturbed. The action of *Hamlet*, however, is far from single in issue, and the play can be judiciously cut for presentation on the stage without serious disturbance of the whole. Shakespeare's plays were so cut in his own theater. The First Folio version of *Hamlet* is based upon the acting version of the play, and it omits some two hundred lines, chiefly reflective passages, which are found in the second quarto. These lines include the soliloquy beginning "How all occasions do inform against me" (IV.iv.32–66). The scene is richer if the soliloquy is included, but its absence does not significantly change the play as a whole. Another passage omitted from the acting version is Hamlet's discourse (I.iv.17–38) on the heavy drinking done in Denmark and the effect of it on the reputation of the Danes. The speech adds little to the action, but in its movement from the particular to the general it helps give the play extension. This is not to suggest that Shakespeare's plays are not unified, but their unity is clearly not Aristotelian.

In a tragedy the hero normally comes to the realization of a truth of which he had been hitherto unaware. There is, as Aristotle has it, "a change from ignorance to knowledge"; but in Greek tragedy this may be little more than the clearing up of a mistaken identity. Not so with the tragedies of Shakespeare's maturity. In *Hamlet* and *King Lear*, for instance, there is a transformation in the character of the hero. Toward the close of his play Lear is the opposite of what he had been at the beginning. He has been purged of his arrogance and pride, and the pomp and circumstance of kingship, on which he had placed great store, is to him no more than an interesting spectacle. What matters now is the love of the daughter he had rejected in the first scene. When we first meet Hamlet he is in a state of depression. The world to him is "an unweeded garden" from which he would willingly depart. He has found corruption not only in the state but in existence itself. We soon learn that he had not always been so. Ophelia tells us that he had been the ideal Renaissance prince—a soldier, scholar, courtier, "the glass of fashion and the mold of form." And though we catch glimpses of his former self in his conversations with Horatio, his state of depression continues. By the final scene, however, his composure has returned. He no longer appears in slovenly dress; he apologizes to Laertes, and he treats Claudius with courtesy up to the point at which Gertrude's death discloses the king's treachery and compels him to the act of vengeance.

All this is not simply a return to Hamlet's former self. In the course of the action he has grown in stature and wisdom. He is no longer troubled by reasoning doubts, for he knows now that reason is not enough. An overreliance on reason and a belief in untrammeled free will are hallmarks of the Shakespearean villain; the heroes learn better. In the beginning of the final scene Hamlet is still beset from without and within—"thou wouldst not think how ill all's here about my heart; but it is no matter." And it does not matter, because he has now come to put his trust in providence. Earlier in the scene he had said,

> Our indiscretion sometime serves us well
> When our deep plots do pall, and that should learn us
> There's a divinity that shapes our ends,
> Rough-hew them how we will.     (V.ii.8–11)

This is not, as has been said, "a fatalist's surrender of his personal responsibility." It is the realization that man is not a totally free agent. With this realization Hamlet can face the fencing match and the king's intrigues without concern for self. What matters at the end of an important tragedy is not success or failure, but what a man *is*. Tragedy of the first order moves into the realm of the human spirit, and at the close we contemplate the nature of man. In this respect Shakespeare and the Greeks are the same, but they reach the end by widely divergent paths. We may consider the path which Shakespeare took.

Early in his career Shakespeare served an apprenticeship to Christopher Marlowe, but he soon surpassed him, and he took the journey from *Romeo and Juliet* to *Hamlet* on his own. His first so-called tragedy, *Titus Andronicus*, is not a tragedy at all. It is a blood-chilling thriller, and, as a recent production at Stratford-upon-Avon demonstrated, an effective one. The management had to have attendants at the theater to minister to the patrons who fainted as the play's horrors were revealed. A like response to tragedy is impossible. Melodrama such as *Titus* uses horror and grief as entertainment, bringing them as close to the spectator as it can. Tragedy uses them as truth. These, it says, are part of our human heritage, and we must face them. And in the end, partly because they are faced, they lose their terror, and the tragedy passes beyond them. It is not surprising, then, that the greatest tragedies are those involving the greatest horrors, for facing a great horror demands greatness of spirit. This greatness of spirit is what we contemplate at the end of a Shakespearean tragedy. At the close of the tragedy we are not so much concerned with Hamlet or Othello as individuals as with the spirit of man triumphant in defeat.

Shakespeare's next attempt at tragedy brings him to the borders of the tragic realm. There is much macabre action and humor in *Richard III*, but the horrors are moral as well as physical, and there is an approach to self-recognition in the remorse Richard feels on waking from his ghost-haunted sleep. This is no longer, or at least not altogether, horror as entertainment. In this play Shakespeare mastered and improved upon Marlowe's techniques. In *Richard II* there is, no doubt, a general indebtedness to Marlowe's *Edward II*. Both kings are weak men who come to a tragic end. Toward the close of Marlowe's play we sympathize with Edward because he is the underdog and because the people who surround him are worse than he, but toward the end of *Richard II* we sympathize with the king because adversity has moved him to a kind of self-realization. There is an approach to the recognition scenes of the later tragedies. Shakespeare has brought his weak and self-willed king to a recognition, if only for a time, of his mortality and the humanity he shares with others. Later, Shakespeare was to do this profoundly with Lear. Here he shows us both power politics at work and a transformation in Richard, and in his characterization of Richard he shows us how the transfer of power to Bolingbroke was possible without Bolingbroke's being a villain. He eschews comedy and physical action, not, we may be sure, out of any disregard for them, but because other matters came first. At this stage of his career Shakespeare was not able to do at one time all the things that needed to be done. He was later to do so in *Hamlet*. In *Richard II* the primary matters are character and theme. There are impressive tableaux, but there is no action comparable to that of the earlier so-called tragedies.

There is more onstage action in *Romeo and Juliet*, and almost all of it is integral to character and theme. The hero and heroine meet, fall in love, mature through adversity, and find that, for them, love is of more worth than life. Nor is their ordeal in vain. They have their love, and their deaths bring peace to Verona. There is laughter in the play, but it is aroused by comic characters. The principals are serious throughout. But the play's laughter and vulgarities are not by any means comic relief. They contribute to a background of lust and hatred against which the story of the young lovers stands in contrast. Besides, Shakespeare's romance is never pure; it is always rooted in reality. It is never in danger of "falling upward, as it were, into vacuity." There is a notable mingling of the comic and the serious in Mercutio's death scene. It has comedy, pathos, and irony, all at once—a promise of things to come. Shakespeare seems never to have viewed things simply, and as soon as he acquired the skill, he made contraries and varying aspects of the same thing stand side by side, nothing canceling anything else out. And so it is here. Mercutio's flippancy in no way reduces the pathos and irony of his death.

After *Romeo and Juliet* Shakespeare turned to comedy and the completion of the historical tetralogy he had begun with *Richard II*. The last of this series, *Henry V*, is a fine play of action with England as its subject and England's national hero as its hero, yet it seems to have brought Shakespeare to a dead end. He was at the height of his success and popularity, but he seems not to have been satisfied with the play. He apologizes, and directly too, for the inability of his theater to present the panoply of war. He refers to his stage as "this unworthy scaffold," and to his theater as "this cockpit," "this wooden O," and he begs the audience to imagine what cannot be shown them. Yet in his next serious play he uses the oldest of dramatic conventions—a few soldiers on either side of the stage representing contending armies—without apology. For with this play the essential thing is not the action itself but the idea that it embodies. In *Julius Caesar* the essential thing, the dramatic thing, is the spirit of man, and this can be portrayed without pageantry. What is needed now are words. What matters now is not so much what a man *does* but what he *is*.[1] Brutus is the precursor of tragic heroes to come. As he is brooding on the outcome of the Battle of Philippi, he says,

> O, that a man might know
> The end of this day's business ere it come!
> But it sufficeth that the day will end,
> And then the end is known.          (V.i.122–25)

It might be the voice of Hamlet before the fencing match: "If it be now, 'tis not to come. . . ." In *Richard II* there is no comedy; now, in *Julius Caesar*, there are only a few comic puns early in the play. First things first. But although *Julius Caesar* was Shakespeare's most important achievement to date, it has, perhaps, too great a separation of action and idea. What was needed was a fusion of the two, and this he achieved in *Hamlet*.[2]

*Hamlet* has onstage action in God's plenty. A ghost walks the stage; people are killed by stabbing and poisoning; a young woman runs mad, is drowned offstage, and is buried on stage; two skeletons are dug up and scattered over the stage; armies march, and there is a fencing match that ends in a general slaughter. Yet one scarcely thinks of

[1] In this paragraph I am indebted to "From *Henry V* to *Hamlet*," by Harley Granville-Barker, in *Aspects of Shakespeare* (1933).
[2] *Hamlet* was first published in 1603. The play is not mentioned in Francis Meres's *Palladis Tamia* (1598), which includes a list of Shakespeare's works. Since Meres mentions so minor a work as *Titus Andronicus*, he would have hardly omitted *Hamlet* had it existed. And it is almost certain that the *Hamlet* played by Shakespeare's company in 1594 and 1596 was not Shakespeare's, for he probably was not yet capable of writing the *Hamlet* we now know; nor is it likely that he revised the story over the better part of a decade, for he worked fast, writing his entire works in the time it took James Joyce to write *Finnegans Wake*. But there is other evidence to narrow the gap between 1598 and 1603—a definite allusion to Shakespeare's *Hamlet* in a note written by Gabriel Harvey in his copy of Speght's edition of Chaucer, published in 1598. Such a note might have been written any time between the publication of the book and Harvey's death in 1631, but in the same note he refers to the Earl of Essex in the present tense. Since Essex was executed on February 25, 1601, it appears that the note was written while Essex was alive and before he made his mad attempt to seize the person of the queen on February 7, 1601. During the fall of 1598 and the following winter, Essex was busy preparing his ill-fated foray into Ireland. He returned in September of 1599. Harvey's reference was therefore presumably made between the autumn of 1599 and early 1601, and it is during that time that *Hamlet* was written. The best date is 1600, which is confirmed by a consideration of Shakespeare's other activities. In 1599 he had rounded out his cycle of history plays with the writing of *Henry V*. He had recently written *The Merry Wives of Windsor* (to please Queen Elizabeth, as tradition has it), and he had completed *Julius Caesar*. He seems to have been looking for new worlds to conquer. He turned to comedy for a while, producing *As You Like It* and *Twelfth Night*. Then came the most important play he had yet written, *Hamlet*.

*Hamlet* as a play of action. There is some comedy, but it is most often used to intensify the serious matters to which it is germane. There are indecencies that were *not* put into the play to please the groundlings. They are the opposite of those employed at the opening of *Romeo and Juliet* to command attention. Hamlet's remarks to Ophelia early in III.ii (the scene of the play-within-the-play) reveal once more his disillusionment with women, and the indecencies of Ophelia's mad songs complete her characterization. Uninhibited in her madness, in a notable anticipation of modern psychology she sings about sex and the father who had dominated her while he lived. To be sure, the play is sometimes diffuse. Everyone is given to generalizing, even the wretched Rosencrantz and Guildenstern. It is, of course, necessary to generalize on the action, and Shakespeare succeeds in doing so; but in the later tragedies he was to do it more compactly. In *Hamlet* Shakespeare was writing tragedy of the first order for the first time, and perhaps he could not be intellectually aware of how to do it until he had once done it, for he had no models to show him the way. (What little he knew of Greek tragedy was through Roman or other adaptations.) In any case, he knew, in 1600, the heights tragedy could achieve, and he was to achieve them again in the next great tragedies—*Othello*, *King Lear*, and *Macbeth*. There is a saying that Shakespeare never repeats. In most respects it is not true, but it is true that he never repeated his successes. The four great tragedies are as different from each other as plays of the same genre by the same author could be.

In each of the plays the hero is transformed into something he had not been at the beginning of the play. He recognizes that he is other than he was, but in *Hamlet* the recognition scene is not explicit. Hamlet emerges from his state of depression, and if he did not the play would be a study in pathology rather than a tragedy; but we do not see him emerging from it as we see, for instance, the change taking place in Othello's speech beginning with "Behold I have a weapon . . ." (V.ii.259–82) or in Lear's prayer for the poor:

> Poor naked wretches, wheresoe'er you are,
> That bide the pelting of this pitiless storm,
> How shall your houseless heads and unfed sides,
> Your looped and windowed raggedness, defend you
> From seasons such as these? O, I have ta'en
> Too little care of this.          (III.iv.28–33)

In this speech Lear is the opposite of the arrogant, unfeeling man he had been at the opening of the play, and we are told that he is. Shakespeare liked to be explicit when he could be. At the end of his play, Hamlet, too, is very different from the man who had earlier longed for death, and contemplated suicide. There is no more "fighting" in his soul; like Lear on his way to prison, he is at peace.

The movement toward Hamlet's regeneration begins with his reflections on the Player's speech about Hecuba; it advances further in the closet scene, and it reaches its culmination in the gravediggers' scene. Although this scene is crowded with action, it is essentially a meditation on the inevitability of death. It begins lightly enough for such a scene, but it grows steadily more serious, more general, and more personal—more personal to Hamlet, and through its increasing generality more personal to us—until in the end it transcends the macabre. At the opening of the scene it is disclosed that someone presumed a suicide is to be buried. Her name is not mentioned, but we know who she is. After some talk about her right to Christian burial, there is a conundrum: "What is he that builds stronger than either the mason, the shipwright, or the carpenter?" And the answer: "a gravemaker. The houses he makes lasts till doomsday." Hamlet and Horatio enter as the digger breaks into a song about advancing age. In the course of the song he digs up a skull, and Hamlet comments on it: "That skull had a tongue in it, and could sing once. How the knave jowls it to the ground, as if 'twere Cain's jawbone, that did the first murder!" Or it might be "the pate of a politician," or a courtier, or "my Lord Such-a-one. . . . And now my Lady Worm's, chapless, and knocked about the mazzard with a sexton's spade." While Shakespeare is thus generalizing about the fact of death, another skull is dug up. It turns out to be the skull of Yorick, the king's jester, and the generalization becomes personal: "I knew him, Horatio, a fellow of infinite jest, of most excellent fancy. He hath borne me on his back a thousand times. And now how abhorred in my imagination it is! My gorge rises at it." Here the scene passes beyond comedy, and Shakespeare tells us so: "Where be your gibes now? Your gambols, your songs? . . . Now get you to my lady's chamber, and tell her, let her paint an inch thick, to this favor she must come. Make her laugh at that." Hamlet's remarks on the bones are his last comment on the discrepancy between appearance and reality. He is coming to accept reality for what it is. Then as the generalization continues, a funeral procession enters, and Hamlet learns who is to be buried today. He has seen the body of an old friend dug up to make room for the body of the woman he loves. He has looked on death at what is for him its worst. It is after the graveyard scene that the man who had continually brooded on death is able to face it. It seems axiomatic that any horror becomes less horrible once we have looked squarely at it. When we see Hamlet again he can defy augury, for the augurs can foretell only such things as success or failure; but there is nothing, except himself, to prevent a man from facing his own private horror and rising above it. And so it is with Hamlet. When Horatio offers to cancel the fencing match "if your mind dislike anything," he is able to reply, "Not a whit, we defy augury. There is special providence in the fall of a sparrow. If it be now, 'tis not to come; if it be not to come, it will be now; if it be not now, yet it will come. The readiness is all. Since no man of aught he leaves knows, what is't to leave betimes? Let be." "Readiness" here means both submitting to providence and being in a state of preparation. It is not that death does not matter; it matters very much indeed, but readiness matters more. Shakespeare's tragic heroes do not renounce the world. The dying Hamlet is concerned about the welfare of the state and his own worldly reputation. Such values are never denied, but at the end of the tragedies they are no longer primary values. At such moments the central thing is the spirit of man achieving grandeur.

## A NOTE ON THE SOURCES

The story of Hamlet is an ancient one. No doubt it had its origin in one of the family feuds familiar in Northern history and saga. Sailors carried it to Ireland, where it picked up accretions of Celtic folklore and legend, and later returned to Scandinavia to become part of the traditional history of Denmark. It was incorporated into written literature in the second half of the twelfth century when a learned clerk, Saxo Grammaticus, retold it in his *Historia Danica*. His narrative is a story of early and relatively barbaric times. For instance, the dismembered body of the prototype of Polonius is thrown into an open latrine to be devoured by scavenging hogs, and there is no trace of the ideals of chivalry and courtesy that we find in Shakespeare's play. Still, the basic elements of Shakespeare's plot are there: the killing of the Danish ruler by his brother, the marriage of the brother and the widowed queen, the pretended madness and real craft of the dead king's son, the son's evasion of the sanity tests, his voyage to England with letters bearing his death warrant, his alteration of the letters, his return, and the accomplishment of his revenge. Saxo also gives us, under different names, the chief characters of the story as we know it in Shakespeare: Claudius (Feng), Gertrude (Gerutha), Hamlet (Amlethus), unnamed prototypes of Ophelia, Polonius, Rosencrantz, and Guildenstern, and perhaps even of Horatio.

Saxo's narrative circulated widely in manuscript. It was printed in Paris in 1514, reprinted elsewhere, and came in time to the attention of François de Belleforest, who in 1576 told his version of the Hamlet story in the fifth volume of his *Histoires Tragiques*. He made one notable addition to the story. He states that the queen committed adultery with her brother-in-law during her marriage to the king. This remains in Shakespeare in the ghost's epithet for his brother, "adulterate," and in Hamlet's "He that hath killed my king, and whored my mother," and it operates as part of the motivation for the revulsion which Hamlet sometimes feels for womankind. Belleforest's *Histoires* seems to have been a popular book. His version was translated very badly into English under the title *The Hystorie of Hamblet* in 1608, too late to serve as a source for Shakespeare. In all likelihood it was called into being by the popularity of Shakespeare's play.

The next version of the Hamlet story was an English play of the 1580's based on Belleforest. It was never printed, and the manuscript seems to be irretrievably lost. Since the late eighteenth century it has been attributed more or less confidently to Thomas Kyd (1557?-1595?). Kyd was a scrivener and playwright, the author of the well-known *Spanish Tragedy*. His words show some advance over that of his predecessors in the creation of character and, especially, in the manipulation of plot. He could wring from a scene all the melodrama it afforded. Kyd's play on the Hamlet story, if, indeed, it is his, served as the immediate source of Shakespeare's play and is called by scholars the *Ur-Hamlet*. The first reference to it is found in Thomas Nashe's preface to Robert Greene's *Menaphon*, 1589. In it Nashe, an established writer, indulged in an attack on certain "trivial translators" and "shifting companions" who "leave the trade of noverint [scribe, copyist] whereto they were born, and busy themselves with the endeavors of art that could scarcely Latinize their neck verse. . . . Yet English Seneca . . . yields many good sentences . . . and if you entreat him fair in a frosty morning, he will afford you whole *Hamlets*, I should say handfuls of tragical speeches. . . . Seneca, let blood, line by line and page by page, at length must needs die to our stage; which makes his famished followers to imitate the Kid in Aesop . . . and these men to intermeddle with Italian translations." The passage has been much debated, but it seems clear that Nashe, by a pun on Kid, associated the Senecan play of *Hamlet* with Kyd. The play is next mentioned in the diary of Philip Henslowe, the theatrical producer, who records that a play called *Hamlet* was performed at the suburban theater of Newington Butts in June, 1594, by the Admiral's and the Chamberlain's Men. It was apparently Henslowe's custom to indicate a new play with the letters "ne," and since there is no such indication at this entry, we may perhaps assume that the play was old; and since the receipts for this performance were only eight shillings, it is possible that *Hamlet* was no longer popular in the playhouse. It seems likely that this is the play to which Nashe referred.

The play was next referred to by Thomas Lodge in his *Wit's Misery*, 1596. He speaks there of the "ghost which cried so miserably at The Theater, like an oyster wife, 'Hamlet, revenge.'" The scorn of Lodge's statement suggests that the play was an outmoded one, and his mention of The Theater as the playhouse at which the ghost cried out tells us that the Chamberlain's Men, the theatrical company to which Shakespeare belonged, had taken over the drama, for the playhouse at which they were then playing was called The Theater. The play, then, was the property of Shakespeare's company, and he was free to use the story for his own purposes. Scholars have been assiduous in their attempts to reconstruct the *Ur-Hamlet* from references to it and from the versions of the story which preceded and followed it. And they have yet another version of the story at hand. There is a German play on the Hamlet story called *Der bestrafte Brudermord oder Prinz Hamlet aus Daennemark*. It was first printed in 1781 from a manuscript dated 1710. The manuscript has been lost, but the printed version has survived.

We know that a *Hamlet* was played by English actors at Dresden in 1626 and that there was another performance of the play, probably in German, in 1665. The latter is probably the origin of *Der bestrafte Brudermord*, a play which, by the eighteenth century, had grossly deteriorated from its original. Still, its dependence on an English *Hamlet* is certain. We must ask if it derives from an early version by Shakespeare as misrepresented in the first quarto or from the *Ur-Hamlet*, and the scholars give us a divided answer. The name Corambus of the German version recalls Corambis of the first quarto and suggests that as a source. On the other hand, Corambis may well have been the name in the *Ur-Hamlet*. There are other similarities to Shakespeare's quarto, but there are great differences from it. The German play opens with a prologue in which Night calls upon the Furies to spur the revenge against the king. This is Senecan rather than Shakespearean. The ghost tells Hamlet that it was reported that he had died of an apoplexy, whereas in the first quarto it was said that he had died of a snake bite. There is no trace of Hamlet's great soliloquies which exist in the first quarto in mangled form. On the whole it seems more likely that *Der bestrafte Brudermord* derives from the *Ur-Hamlet* than from the first quarto.

What, then, was the immediate source of Shakespeare's *Hamlet* like? In answering this question it must be acknowledged that we are not on firm ground, but an informed surmise is better than nothing, provided we remember that we are being tentative. It was Senecan and, in name at least, a tragedy, though in reality a melodrama. A Senecan play would be gory, with the stage cluttered with corpses in the final scene. It was by Thomas Kyd. Why else should Nashe have associated "Kid" and "noverint" with the play? Kyd had been a scrivener, and unlike Nashe, he was not a university man. He had made translations from both Italian and French, and he had turned dramatist. He was able to read Belleforest in French. He knew Seneca intimately. In the play the ghost calls for revenge, and the revengeful ghost is characteristic of Seneca. In Saxo Grammaticus there is no ghost. There is no need for one; the murderer of the king was known to be his brother, and there was, therefore, nothing for the ghost to reveal. The ghost is one of Kyd's contributions to the story. He had used a ghost effectively in his *Spanish Tragedy*, and he was here repeating one of his successful devices. In the *Ur-Hamlet* the ghost made the revelation and urged upon Hamlet the obligation of revenge. In Saxo, Hamlet feigned madness in self-protection and in order to get at the person of the king. Kyd retained the pretended madness, but we cannot know what uses he made of it. The play ended, of course, with Hamlet's triumph and death in a bloody massacre.

## A NOTE ON THE TEXT

Shakespeare's *Hamlet* comes to us in three versions. The first of them, known as the first quarto, was published in 1603 by N. L. [Nicholas Ling] and John Trundell, who advertised it on the title page as having been played "by his Highness Servants in the City of London, as also in the two universities of Cambridge and Oxford, and elsewhere." This was a pirated edition, published without the consent of the owners, and Shakespeare had nothing to do with it. In the preceding year an attempt had been made to forestall just such a venture. On July 26, 1602, James Roberts, a printer friendly to Shakespeare's company, had entered in the Stationers' Register "A book called The Revenge of Hamlet Prince of Denmark as it was lately acted by the Lord Chamberlain his Servants." This was intended to serve as a kind of copyright. It should be said in passing that "his Highness Servants" were the King's Men and that the Chamberlain's Men became the King's Men on May 19, 1603, when James I took Shakespeare's company under his direct protection.

The copy which Ling and Trundell sent to the printer was an extraordinary hodgepodge, so that the first quarto gives us a very poor notion of Shakespeare's play. How this copy came into being has been the subject of much investigation, but there is little agreement. In general there are three schools of thought: (1) the first quarto is a badly reported version of *Hamlet* as Shakespeare wrote it once and for all; (2) it is a badly reported version of an early draft of Shakespeare's play; and (3) it was expanded from some actor's parts of an early version of the play. This last seems most likely, since some of the lines, notably those of Marcellus, are accurate, other passages are partially correct, and still others are sheer invention. All three levels are to be found in the soliloquy (III.i.56 ff.) beginning "To be or not to be."

> To be or not to be, ay there's the point,
> To die, to sleep, is that all? Ay all:
> No, to sleep, to dream, ay marry there it goes,
> For in that dream of death, when we awake,
> And borne before an everlasting judge,
> From whence no passenger ever returned,
> To undiscovered country, at whose sight
> The happy smile, and the accursed damned.
> But for this, the joyful hope of this,
> Who'd bear the scorns and flattery of the world,
> Scorned by the right rich, the rich cursed of the poor?
> The widow being oppressed, the orphan wronged,
> The taste of hunger, or a tyrant's reign,
> And thousand more calamities besides,
> To grunt and sweat under this weary life,
> When that he may his full quietus make,
> With a bare bodkin, who would this endure,
> But for a hope of something after death?
> Which pulses the brain, and doth confound the sense,
> Which makes us rather bear those veils we have,
> Than fly to others that we know not of.
> Ay that, O this conscience makes cowards of us all,
> Lady in thy orisons, be all my sins rememb'red

It is clear that there is a hand other than Shakespeare's in this. That the first quarto is a debased version of an early version of the play is suggested by, most notably, changes in names. Why should Polonius, for instance, become Corambis if the copy were based on the version Shakespeare wrote once and for all?

It was not considered good business to publish a play while it was still popular in the theater, for it could then be acted in the provinces by other than its owners, reducing the public for the play when Shakespeare's company took it on tour. This being so, the publication of the first quarto had done Shakespeare a double injury: the play was in print, and it misrepresented its author. Shakespeare had some leisure at this time, and theaters being closed because of the plague from March 1603 to April 1604. We may suppose that he decided to revise the play and have it printed. In any case, another edition of *Hamlet* appeared in 1604. The title page seems designed to tell the public that this is the genuine article: "The Tragical History of Hamlet, Prince of Denmark. By William Shakespeare. Newly imprinted and enlarged to almost as much again as it was, according to the true and perfect copy." The statement is literally true. The second quarto is almost twice as long as the first quarto, and although it lacks some passages preserved in the First Folio, the second quarto is the fullest and best version of the play.

The third version of *Hamlet* is to be found in the First Folio, 1623, the collected edition of Shakespeare's plays made by his friends and associates in the theater, John Heminges and Henry Condell. Here the text is based on the acting version of the play. The Folio gives us some ninety lines not found in the second quarto. These include two passages of considerable length, II.ii.243–74 and II.ii.344–69, but the Folio does not give us some two hundred lines found in the second quarto. These are mostly reflective passages, including Hamlet's last soliloquy,

"How all occasions do inform against me." As befits an acting version, the Folio stage directions are more numerous and frequently are fuller. Modern editions are made by collation of the second quarto and the First Folio and are therefore longer than either of them.

Because the second quarto is the longest version, giving us more of the play as Shakespeare conceived it than either of the others, it serves as the basic version for this text. Unfortunately the printers of it often worked carelessly. Words and phrases are omitted, there are plain misreadings of Shakespeare's manuscript, speeches are sometimes wrongly assigned. It was therefore necessary to turn to the First Folio for many readings. Neither the first quarto nor the second quarto is divided into acts or scenes; the Folio indicates only the following: I.i, I.ii, I.iii, II, II.ii. The present edition, to allow for easy reference, follows the traditional divisions of the Globe edition, placing them (as well as indications of locale) in brackets to indicate that they are editorial, not authorial. Punctuation and spelling are modernized (*and* is given as *an* when it means "if"), obvious typographical errors are corrected, abbreviations are expanded, speech prefixes are regularized, and the positions of stage directions are slightly altered where necessary. Other departures from the second quarto are listed below. First is given the adopted reading, in boldface type, and then the second quarto's reading, in roman. The vast majority of these adopted readings are from the Folio; if an adopted reading is not from the Folio, the fact is indicated by a bracketed remark explaining, for example, that it is drawn from the first Quarto [Q1] or the Second Folio [F2] or an editor's conjecture [ed.].

**I.i.16 soldier** souldiers **63 Polacks** [F has "Pollax"] pollax **68 my** mine **73 why** with; **cast** cost **88 those** these **91 returned** returne **94 designed** [F2] design **112 mote** [ed.] moth **121 feared** [ed.] feare **138 you** your **140 at it** it **142 s.d. Exit Ghost** [Q2 omits]
**I.ii.1 s.d. Councilors** [ed.] Counsaile: as **41 s.d. Exit Voltemand and Cornelius** [Q2 omits] **53 He hath** Hath **67 so** so much **77 good** coold **82 shapes** [ed.: F has "shewes"] chapes **96 a mind** or minde **132 self-slaughter** seale slaughter **133 weary** wary **137 to this** thus **143 would** should **149 even she** [Q2 omits] **175 to drink deep** for to drinke **178 to see** to **209 Where, as** [ed.] Whereas **224 Indeed, indeed, sirs** Indeede Sirs **237 Very like, very like** Very like **238 hundred** hundreth **257 foul** fonde
**I.iii.3 convoy is** conuay in **12 bulk** bulkes **18 For he himself is subject to his birth** [Q2 omits] **49 like a** a **68 thine** thy **74 Are** Or **75 be** boy **76 loan** loue **83 invites** inuests **109 Tend'ring** [Q2] Wrong [F has "Roaming"] **115 springes** springs **123 parley** parle **125 tether** tider **131 beguile** beguiling
**I.iv.1 shrewdly** shroudly **2 a nipping** nipping **6 s.d. go** [ed.] goes **19 clepe** [ed.] clip **27 the** [ed.] their **33 Their** [ed.] His **36 evil** [ed.] eale **57 s.d. Ghost beckons Hamlet** Beckins **69 my lord** my **70 summit** [ed.] somnet [F has "sonnet"] **82 artere** [ed.] arture [F has "artire"] **87 imagination** imagion
**I.v.47 what** a what **55 lust** but **56 sate** sort **64 leperous** leaprous **68 posset** possesse **91 s.d. Exit** [Q2 omits] **95 stiffly** swiftly **113 Horatio and Marcellus (Within.)** Enter Horatio and Marcellus [Q2 gives the speech to Horatio] **116 bird** and **122 heaven, my lord** heauen **132 Look you, I'll** I will **170 some'er** [ed.] so mere [F has "so ere"]
**II.i.s.d. Reynaldo** or two **28 Faith, no** Fayth **38 warrant** wit **39 sullies** sallies **40 i' th'** with **52–53 at "friend or so," and "gentleman"** [Q2 omits] **112 quoted** coted
**II.ii.43 Assure you** I assure **57 o'erhasty** hastie **58 s.d. Enter Polonius, Voltemand, and Cornelius** Enter Embassadors **90 since brevity** breuitie **108 s.d. the letter** [Q2 omits, but has "letter" at side of line 116] **126 above** about **137 winking**

working 143 his her 148 watch wath 149 a lightness lightnes 151 'tis this this 167 s.d. Enter Hamlet reading on a book Enter Hamlet 189 far gone, far gone far gone 203 you yourself your selfe 204 should be shall growe 212 sanity sanctity 214–15 and suddenly . . . between him [Q2 omits] 218 will will not 227 excellent extent 231 overhappy euer happy 232 cap lap 240 but that but the 243–74 Let me question . . . dreadfully attended [Q2 omits] 278 even euer 284 Why anything Any thing 311 a piece peece 317 woman women 328 of me on me 331–32 the clown . . . o' th' sere [from F, but F has "tickled a" for "tickle o' "; Q2 omits] 333 blank black 344–69 Hamlet. How comes . . . load too [Q2 omits] 349 berattle [ed.: F has "be-ratled"; Q2 omits] 356 most like [ed.; F has "like most"; Q2 omits] 380 lest my let me 405–06 tragical-historical, tragical-comical-historical-pastoral [Q2 omits] 433 By'r Lady by lady 437 French falconers friendly Fankners 450 affectation affection 453 tale talke 463 heraldry heraldy 481 Then senseless Ilium [Q2 omits] 488 And like Like 502 fellies [ed.] follies 511 Mobled queen is good [F has "Inobled" for "Mobled"; Q2 omits] 521 husband's husband 526 whe'r [ed.] where 546–47 a need neede 547 or sixteen lines lines, or sixteene lines 551 till tell 559 his visage the visage 564 to Hecuba to her 566 the cue that 585 ha' fatted [F has "have fatted"] a fatted 588 O, vengeance [Q2 omits] 590 father [Q4; Q2 and F omit] 606 devil, and the devil deale, and the deale
III.i.32–33 myself (lawful espials) Will myself Wee'le 46 loneliness lowliness 55 Let's withdraw with-draw 83 cowards of us all cowards 85 sicklied sickled 92 well, well, well well 107 your honesty you 121 to a nunnery a Nunry 129 knaves all knaues 138 Go, farewell farewell 145 lisp list 146–47 your ignorance ignorance 153 expectancy expectation 158 that what 160 feature stature 162 [Q2 concludes the line with a stage direction, "Exit"] 189 unwatched vnmatcht
III.ii.1 pronounced pronoun'd 23 own feature feature 27 the which which 29 praise praysd 37 us, sir vs 45 s.d. Exit Players [Q2 omits] 49 s.d. Exit Polonius [Q2 omits] 52 ho [F has "hoa"] howe 89 detecting detected 89 s.d. Rosencrantz . . . Flourish [Q2 omits] 115–16 Hamlet. I mean . . . my lord [Q2 omits] 138 s.d. sound [ed.] sounds; very lovingly [Q2 omits]; She kneels . . . unto him [Q2 omits]; Exeunt [Q2 omits] 140 is miching munching 145 keep counsel keepe 159 ground the ground 167 your our 172 In neither Eyther none, in neither 173 love Lord 194 like the 203 Grief joys Greefe ioy 223 An [ed.] And 227 a I be a 231 s.d. sleeps [Q2 omits] 232 s.d. Exit .Exeunt 260 Confederate Considerat 262 infected inuected 264 s.d. Pours the poison in his ears [Q2 omits] 270 Hamlet. What . . . fire [Q2 omits] 280–81 two Provincial prouinciall 314 start stare 324 my business busines 366 and thumb the vmber 375 the top of my my 379 you can you 394–95 Polonius . . . friends Leaue me friends. I will, say so. By and by is easily said 397 breathes breakes 399 bitter business as the day business as the bitter day 404 daggers dagger
III.iii.19 huge hough 22 ruin raine 23 with a a 50 pardoned pardon 58 shove showe 73 pat but 79 hire and salary base and silly
III.iv.5–6 with him . . . Mother, Mother, Mother [Q2 omits] 7 warrant wait 21 inmost most 23 ho [F has "hoa"] how; ho [F has "hoa"] how 25 s.d. kills Polonius [Q2 omits] 53 That roars . . . index [Q2 gives to Hamlet] 60 heaven-kissing heaue, a kissing 89 panders pardons 90 mine eyes into my very soul my very eyes into my soule 91 grainèd greeued 92 will not will 98 tithe kyth 140 Ecstasy [Q2 omits] 144 And I And 159 live leaue 166 Refrain tonight to refraine night 180 Thus This 187 ravel rouell 216 foolish most foolish 218 s.d. exit Hamlet, tugging in Polonius Exit
IV.i.35 dragged dreg'd
IV.ii.1 s.d. Enter Hamlet Enter Hamlet, Rosencraus, and others 2 Gentlemen. (Within.) Hamlet! Lord Hamlet! [Q2 omits] 4 s.d. Enter Rosencrantz and Guildenstern [Q2 omits] 6

Compounded Compound 19 ape apple 31–32 Hide fox, and all after [Q2 omits]
IV.iii.15 Ho [F has "Hoa"] How 44 With fiery quickness [Q2 omits] 53 and so so 69 were ne'er begun will nere begin
IV.v.16 Queen [Q2 gives line 16 as part of the previous speech] 20 s.d. Enter Ophelia [distracted.] Enter Ophelia [placed after line 16] 39 grave ground 42 God good 52 clothes close 57 Indeed, la Indeede 74 s.d. Exit [Q2 omits] 83 in their in 90 his this 97 Queen. Alack, what noise is this [Q2 omits] 98 are is 107 They The 143 swoopstake [ed.] soopstake 153 s.d. Let her come in [Q2 gives to Laertes] 158 Till Tell 161 an old a poore 162–64 Nature . . . loves [Q2 omits] 166 Hey . . . hey nony [Q2 omits] 182 O, you must you may 187 affliction afflictions 195 All flaxen Flaxen 199 Christian souls, I pray God Christians soules 200 see this this
IV.vi.9 an't a 22 good turn turne 26 bore bord 31 He So 32 give you you
IV.vii.6 proceeded proceede 14 conjunctive concliue 20 Would Worke 22 loud a wind loued Arm'd 24 And But; had haue 36 How now . . . Hamlet [Q2 omits] 42 s.d. Exit Messenger [Q2 omits] 45–46 your pardon you pardon 47 and more strange return returne 48 Hamlet [Q2 omits] 56 shall live liue 62 checking the King 88 my me 115 wick [ed.] weeke 119 changes change 122 spendthrift [ed.] spend thrifts 125 in deed [ed.] indeede 134 on ore 138 pass pace 140 for that for 156 ha't hate 159 prepared prefard 167 hoar horry 171 cold cull-cold
V.i.9 se offendendo so offended 12 Argal or all 34–37 Other. Why . . . without arms [Q2 omits] 43 that frame that 55 s.d. Enter Hamlet and Horatio afar off Enter Hamlet and Horatio [Q2 places after line 64] 60 stoup soope 70 daintier dintier 89 mazzard massene 106–07 Is this . . . recoveries [Q2 omits] 108 his vouchers vouchers 109 double ones doubles 120 O or 121 For such a guest is meet [Q2 omits] 142 a gravemaker Graue-maker 143 all the days the dayes 165 corses nowadays corses 172–73 three and twenty 23 183 Let me see [Q2 omits] 185 borne bore 192 chamber table 208–09 as thus [Q2 omits] 216 winter's waters 217 s.d. Enter . . . attendant Enter K. Q. Laertes and the corse 231 Shards, flints Flints 247 treble double 250 s.d. Leaps in the grave [Q2 omits] 261 and rash rash 277 Dost thou doost 285 thus this 298 shortly thirtie 299 Till Tell
V.ii.5 Methought my thought 6 bilboes bilbo 17 unseal vnfold 19 Ah [ed.; F has "Oh"] A 43 as's [F has "assis"] as sir 52 Subscribed Subscribe 57 Why, man . . . employment [Q2 omits] 68–80 To quit . . . comes here [Q2 omits] 78 court [ed.; F has "count"; Q2 omits] 80 s.d. young Osric [Q2 omits] 81 Osric [Q2 prints "Cour" consistently as the speech prefix] 83 humbly humble 94 Put your your 100 sultry sully 101 for or 103 But, my my 109 gentleman [ed.] gentlemen 111 feelingly [ed.] sellingly 143 his weapon [ed.] this weapon 152 hangers [ed.] hanger 159 carriages carriage 162 might be be 165–66 all impawned as all 181 e'en so so 185 Yours, yours. He Yours 190 did comply did 194 yeasty histy 195 fanned [ed.; F has "fond"] prophane; winnowed trennowed 209 to Laertes [ed.] Laertes 211 lose this wager loose 214 But thou thou 217–18 gaingiving gamgiuing 222 If it be now if it be 224 will come well come 242 Sir, in this audience [Q2 omits] 252 keep my my; till all 256 Come on [Q2 omits] 265 bettered better 267 s.d. Prepare to play [Q2 omits] 274 union Vnice 287 s.d. They play [Q2 omits] 288 A touch, a touch [Q2 omits] 302 s.d. play [Q2 omits] 304 s.d. In scuffling they change rapiers [Q2 omits] 305 ho [F has "hoa"] howe 313 Ho [ed.] how 315 Hamlet. Hamlet Hamlet 318 thy my 324 s.d. Hurts the King [Q2 omits] 327 murd'rous, damnèd damned 328 thy union the Onixe 329 s.d. King dies [Q2 omits] 333 s.d. dies [Q2 omits] 347 live I leaue 360 s.d. Dies [Q2 omits] 363 s.d. with drum, colors, and Attendants [Q2 omits] 381 th' yet yet 385 forced for no 394 on no 401 rite [ed.; F has "rites"] right 405 s.d. marching . . . shot off [Q2 omits]

# THE TRAGEDY OF HAMLET
# PRINCE OF DENMARK

[Dramatis Personae

CLAUDIUS *King of Denmark*
HAMLET *son to the late, and nephew to the present,*
  *king*
POLONIUS *Lord Chamberlain*
HORATIO *friend to Hamlet*
LAERTES *son to Polonius*
VOLTEMAND ⎫
CORNELIUS ⎪
ROSENCRANTZ ⎬ *courtiers*
GUILDENSTERN ⎪
OSRIC ⎪
A GENTLEMAN ⎪
A PRIEST ⎭

MARCELLUS ⎫ *officers*
BARNARDO ⎭
FRANCISCO *a soldier*
REYNALDO *servant to Polonius*
PLAYERS
TWO CLOWNS *gravediggers*
FORTINBRAS *Prince of Norway*
A NORWEGIAN CAPTAIN
ENGLISH AMBASSADORS
GERTRUDE *Queen of Denmark, mother to Hamlet*
OPHELIA *daughter to Polonius*
GHOST *of Hamlet's father*
LORDS  LADIES  OFFICERS  SOLDIERS
  SAILORS  MESSENGERS  ATTENDANTS

*Scene:* Elsinore]

## [ A C T   I ]

[Scene I. *A guard platform of the castle.*]

*Enter* BARNARDO *and* FRANCISCO, *two sentinels.*

BARNARDO  Who's there?
FRANCISCO
  Nay, answer me. Stand and unfold° yourself.
BARNARDO  Long live the king!°
FRANCISCO  Barnardo?
BARNARDO  He.                                                      5
FRANCISCO
  You come most carefully upon your hour.
BARNARDO
  'Tis now struck twelve. Get thee to bed, Francisco.

*The decorative border shown above appeared on the first page of*
Hamlet *in the First Folio edition of Shakespeare's plays, 1623.*
**I.i.2 unfold** disclose   **3 Long . . . king** perhaps a password,
perhaps a greeting

FRANCISCO
  For this relief much thanks. 'Tis bitter cold,
  And I am sick at heart.
BARNARDO
  Have you had a quiet guard?
FRANCISCO                      Not a mouse stirring.      10
BARNARDO
  Well, good night.
  If you do meet Horatio and Marcellus,
  The rivals° of my watch, bid them make haste.

*Enter* HORATIO *and* MARCELLUS.

FRANCISCO
  I think I hear them. Stand, ho! Who is there?
HORATIO
  Friends to this ground.
MARCELLUS           And liegemen to the Dane.°      15

**13 rivals** partners   **15 liegemen . . . Dane** loyal subjects to
the King of Denmark

917

FRANCISCO
Give you° good night.

MARCELLUS                    O, farewell, honest soldier.
Who hath relieved you?

FRANCISCO                    Barnardo hath my place.
Give you good night.                    *Exit* FRANCISCO.

MARCELLUS                    Holla, Barnardo!

BARNARDO                                        Say—
What, is Horatio there?

HORATIO                    A piece of him.

BARNARDO
Welcome, Horatio. Welcome, good Marcellus.    20

MARCELLUS
What, has this thing appeared again tonight?

BARNARDO
I have seen nothing.

MARCELLUS
Horatio says 'tis but our fantasy,
And will not let belief take hold of him
Touching this dreaded sight twice seen of us;    25
Therefore I have entreated him along
With us to watch the minutes of this night,
That, if again this apparition come,
He may approve° our eyes and speak to it.

HORATIO
Tush, tush, 'twill not appear.

BARNARDO                    Sit down awhile,    30
And let us once again assail your ears,
That are so fortified against our story,
What we have two nights seen.

HORATIO                    Well, sit we down,
And let us hear Barnardo speak of this.

BARNARDO
Last night of all,    35
When yond same star that's westward from the pole°
Had made his course t' illume that part of heaven
Where now it burns, Marcellus and myself,
The bell then beating one—

*Enter* GHOST.

MARCELLUS
Peace, break thee off. Look where it comes again.    40

BARNARDO
In the same figure like the king that's dead.

MARCELLUS
Thou art a scholar; speak to it, Horatio.

BARNARDO
Looks 'a not like the king? Mark it, Horatio.

HORATIO
Most like: it harrows me with fear and wonder.

BARNARDO
It would be spoke to.

MARCELLUS                    Speak to it, Horatio.    45

HORATIO
What art thou that usurp'st this time of night,
Together with that fair and warlike form
In which the majesty of buried Denmark°
Did sometimes march? By heaven I charge thee, speak.

MARCELLUS
It is offended.

BARNARDO    See, it stalks away.    50

HORATIO
Stay! Speak, speak. I charge thee, speak. *Exit* GHOST.

MARCELLUS
'Tis gone and will not answer.

BARNARDO
How now, Horatio? You tremble and look pale.
Is not this something more than fantasy?
What think you on't?    55

HORATIO
Before my God, I might not this believe
Without the sensible and true avouch°
Of mine own eyes.

MARCELLUS                    Is it not like the king?

HORATIO
As thou art to thyself.
Such was the very armor he had on    60
When he the ambitious Norway° combated:
So frowned he once, when, in an angry parle,°
He smote the sledded Polacks° on the ice.
'Tis strange.

MARCELLUS
Thus twice before, and jump° at this dead hour,    65
With martial stalk hath he gone by our watch.

HORATIO
In what particular thought to work I know not;
But, in the gross and scope° of my opinion,
This bodes some strange eruption to our state.

MARCELLUS
Good now, sit down, and tell me he that knows,    70
Why this same strict and most observant watch
So nightly toils the subject° of the land,
And why such daily cast of brazen cannon
And foreign mart° for implements of war,
Why such impress° of shipwrights, whose sore task    75
Does not divide the Sunday from the week,
What might be toward° that this sweaty haste
Doth make the night joint-laborer with the day?
Who is't that can inform me?

HORATIO                    That can I.
At least the whisper goes so: our last king,    80
Whose image even but now appeared to us,
Was, as you know, by Fortinbras of Norway,
Thereto pricked on by a most emulate pride,
Dared to the combat; in which our valiant Hamlet
(For so this side of our known world esteemed him)    85
Did slay this Fortinbras, who, by a sealed compact
Well ratified by law and heraldry,°
Did forfeit, with his life, all those his lands
Which he stood seized° of, to the conqueror;
Against the which a moiety competent°    90
Was gagèd° by our king, which had returned
To the inheritance of Fortinbras,
Had he been vanquisher, as, by the same comart°
And carriage of the article designed,°
His fell to Hamlet. Now, sir, young Fortinbras,    95

57 **sensible . . . avouch** sensory and true proof   61 **Norway** King of Norway   62 **parle** parley   63 **sledded Polacks** Poles in sledges   65 **jump** just   68 **gross and scope** general drift   72 **toils the subject** makes the subjects toil   74 **mart** trading   75 **impress** forced service   77 **toward** in preparation   87 **law and heraldry** heraldic law (governing the combat)   89 **seized** possessed   90 **moiety competent** equal portion   91 **gagèd** engaged, pledged   93 **comart** agreement   94 **carriage . . . designed** import of the agreement drawn up

16 **Give you** God give you   29 **approve** confirm   36 **pole** polestar   48 **buried Denmark** the buried King of Denmark

Of unimprovèd° mettle hot and full,
Hath in the skirts° of Norway here and there
Sharked up° a list of lawless resolutes,°
For food and diet, to some enterprise
That hath a stomach in't;° which is no other,　　100
As it doth well appear unto our state,
But to recover of us by strong hand
And terms compulsatory, those foresaid lands
So by his father lost; and this, I take it,
Is the main motive of our preparations,　　105
The source of this our watch, and the chief head°
Of this posthaste and romage° in the land.

BARNARDO
I think it be no other but e'en so;
Well may it sort° that this portentous figure
Comes armèd through our watch so like the king　　110
That was and is the question of these wars.

HORATIO
A mote it is to trouble the mind's eye:
In the most high and palmy state of Rome,
A little ere the mightiest Julius fell,
The graves stood tenantless, and the sheeted dead　　115
Did squeak and gibber in the Roman streets;°
As stars with trains of fire and dews of blood,
Disasters° in the sun; and the moist star,°
Upon whose influence Neptune's empire stands,
Was sick almost to doomsday with eclipse.　　120
And even the like precurse° of feared events,
As harbingers° preceding still° the fates
And prologue to the omen° coming on,
Have heaven and earth together demonstrated
Unto our climatures° and countrymen.　　125

*Enter* GHOST.

But soft, behold, lo where it comes again!
I'll cross it,° though it blast me.—Stay, illusion.

*It spreads his° arms.*

It thou hast any sound or use of voice,
Speak to me.
If there be any good thing to be done　　130
That may to thee do ease and grace to me,
Speak to me.
If thou art privy to thy country's fate,
Which happily° foreknowing may avoid,
O, speak!　　135
Or if thou hast uphoarded in thy life
Extorted° treasure in the womb of earth,
For which, they say, you spirits oft walk in death,

*The cock crows.*

Speak of it. Stay and speak. Stop it, Marcellus.

**96 unimprovèd** untried　**97 skirts** borders　**98 Sharked up**
collected indiscriminately (as a shark gulps its prey); **resolutes**
desperadoes　**100 hath . . . in't** requires courage　**106**
**head** fountainhead, origin　**107 romage** bustle　**109 sort**
befit　**116 Did . . . streets** the break in the sense which
follows this line suggests that a line has dropped out　**118**
**Disasters** threatening signs; **moist star** moon　**121 precurse**
precursor, foreshadowing　**122 harbingers** forerunners; **still**
always　**123 omen** calamity　**125 climatures** regions　**127**
**cross it** (1) cross its path, confront it (2) make the sign of the
cross in front of it　**127 s.d. his** its, the Ghost's (though possibly
what is meant is that Horatio spreads his own arms, making a
cross of himself)　**134 happily** haply, perhaps　**137 Extorted**
ill-won

MARCELLUS
Shall I strike at it with my partisan?°　　140

HORATIO
Do, if it will not stand.

BARNARDO　　　　　　　　　　　'Tis here.

HORATIO　　　　　　　　　　　　　　　'Tis here.

MARCELLUS
'Tis gone.　　　　　　　　　　　*Exit* GHOST.
We do it wrong, being so majestical,
To offer it the show of violence,
For it is as the air, invulnerable,　　145
And our vain blows malicious mockery.

BARNARDO
It was about to speak when the cock crew.

HORATIO
And then it started, like a guilty thing
Upon a fearful summons. I have heard,
The cock, that is the trumpet to the morn,　　150
Doth with his lofty and shrill-sounding throat
Awake the god of day, and at his warning,
Whether in sea or fire, in earth or air,
Th' extravagant and erring° spirit hies
To his confine; and of the truth herein　　155
This present object made probation.°

MARCELLUS
It faded on the crowing of the cock.
Some say that ever 'gainst° that season comes
Wherein our Savior's birth is celebrated,
This bird of dawning singeth all night long,　　160
And then, they say, no spirit dare stir abroad,
The nights are wholesome, then no planets strike,°
No fairy takes,° nor witch hath power to charm:
So hallowed and so gracious is that time.

HORATIO
So have I heard and do in part believe it.　　165
But look, the morn in russet mantle clad
Walks o'er the dew of yon high eastward hill.
Break we our watch up, and by my advice
Let us impart what we have seen tonight
Unto young Hamlet, for upon my life　　170
This spirit, dumb to us, will speak to him.
Do you consent we shall acquaint him with it,
As needful in our loves, fitting our duty?

MARCELLUS
Let's do't, I pray, and I this morning know
Where we shall find him most convenient.　　*Exeunt.*　175

[Scene II. *The castle.*]

*Flourish.° Enter Claudius,* KING *of Denmark, Gertrude
the* QUEEN, COUNCILORS, POLONIUS *and his son*
LAERTES, HAMLET, *cum aliis° [including* VOLTEMAND
*and* CORNELIUS].

KING
Though yet of Hamlet our dear brother's death
The memory be green, and that it us befitted

**140 partisan** pike (a long-handled weapon)　**154 extravagant**
**and erring** out of bounds and wandering　**156 probation**
proof　**158 'gainst** just before　**162 strike** exert an evil
influence　**163 takes** bewitches
**I.ii.s.d. Flourish** fanfare of trumpets; **cum aliis** with others
(Latin)

To bear our hearts in grief, and our whole kingdom
To be contracted in one brow of woe,
Yet so far hath discretion fought with nature          5
That we with wisest sorrow think on him
Together with remembrance of ourselves.
Therefore our sometime sister,° now our queen,
Th' imperial jointress° to this warlike state,
Have we, as 'twere, with a defeated joy,               10
With an auspicious° and a dropping eye,
With mirth in funeral, and with dirge in marriage,
In equal scale weighing delight and dole,
Taken to wife. Nor have we herein barred
Your better wisdoms, which have freely gone            15
With this affair along. For all, our thanks.
Now follows that you know young Fortinbras,
Holding a weak supposal of our worth,
Or thinking by our late dear brother's death
Our state to be disjoint and out of frame,°            20
Colleaguèd with this dream of his advantage,°
He hath not failed to pester us with message,
Importing the surrender of those lands
Lost by his father, with all bands of law,
To our most valiant brother. So much for him.          25
Now for ourself and for this time of meeting.
Thus much the business is: we have here writ
To Norway, uncle of young Fortinbras—
Who, impotent and bedrid, scarcely hears
Of this his nephew's purpose—to suppress              30
His further gait° herein, in that the levies,
The lists, and full proportions° are all made
Out of his subject;° and we here dispatch
You, good Cornelius, and you, Voltemand,
For bearers of this greeting to old Norway,            35
Giving to you no further personal power
To business with the king, more than the scope
Of these delated articles° allow.
Farewell, and let your haste commend your duty.

CORNELIUS, VOLTEMAND
In that, and all things, will we show our duty.        40

KING
We doubt it nothing. Heartily farewell.

*Exit* VOLTEMAND *and* CORNELIUS.
And now, Laertes, what's the news with you?
You told us of some suit. What is't, Laertes?
You cannot speak of reason to the Dane
And lose your voice.° What wouldst thou beg, Laertes,   45
That shall not be my offer, not thy asking?
The head is not more native° to the heart,
The hand more instrumental to the mouth,
Than is the throne of Denmark to thy father.
What wouldst thou have, Laertes?

LAERTES                           My dread lord,        50
Your leave and favor to return to France,
From whence, though willingly I came to Denmark
To show my duty in your coronation,
Yet now I must confess, that duty done,

My thoughts and wishes bend again toward France        55
And bow them to your gracious leave and pardon.

KING
Have you your father's leave? What says Polonius?

POLONIUS
He hath, my lord, wrung from me my slow leave
By laborsome petition, and at last
Upon his will I sealed my hard consent.°               60
I do beseech you give him leave to go.

KING
Take thy fair hour, Laertes. Time be thine,
And thy best graces spend it at thy will.
But now, my cousin° Hamlet, and my son—

HAMLET [*Aside.*]
A little more than kin, and less than kind!°           65

KING
How is it that the clouds still hang on you?

HAMLET
Not so, my lord. I am too much in the sun.°

QUEEN
Good Hamlet, cast thy nighted color off,
And let thine eye look like a friend on Denmark.
Do not forever with thy vailèd° lids                   70
Seek for thy noble father in the dust.
Thou know'st 'tis common; all that lives must die,
Passing through nature to eternity.

HAMLET
Ay, madam, it is common.°

QUEEN                             If it be,
Why seems it so particular with thee?                  75

HAMLET
Seems, madam? Nay, it is. I know not "seems."
'Tis not alone my inky cloak, good mother,
Nor customary suits of solemn black,
Nor windy suspiration° of forced breath,
No, nor the fruitful river in the eye,                 80
Nor the dejected havior of the visage,
Together with all forms, moods, shapes of grief,
That can denote me truly. These indeed seem,
For they are actions that a man might play,
But I have that within which passes show;              85
These but the trappings and the suits of woe.

KING
'Tis sweet and commendable in your nature, Hamlet,
To give these mourning duties to your father,
But you must know your father lost a father,
That father lost, lost his, and the survivor bound     90
In filial obligation for some term
To do obsequious° sorrow. But to persever
In obstinate condolement° is a course
Of impious stubbornness. 'Tis unmanly grief.
It shows a will most incorrect to heaven,              95
A heart unfortified, a mind impatient,
An understanding simple and unschooled.
For what we know must be and is as common

---

8 **our sometime sister** my (the royal "we") former sister-in-law  9 **jointress** joint tenant, partner  11 **auspicious** joyful  20 **frame** order  21 **advantage** superiority  31 **gait** proceeding  32 **proportions** supplies for war  33 **Out . . . subject** out of old Norway's subjects and realm  38 **delated articles** detailed documents  45 **lose your voice** waste your breath  47 **native** related

60 **Upon . . . consent** To his desire I gave my reluctant consent  64 **cousin** kinsman  65 **kind** pun on the meanings "kindly" and "natural"; though doubly related—"more than kin"—Hamlet asserts that he neither resembles Claudius in nature nor feels kindly toward him  67 **sun** sunshine of royal favor (with a pun on *son*)  70 **vailèd** lowered  74 **common** (1) universal (2) vulgar  79 **windy suspiration** heavy sighing  92 **obsequious** suitable to obsequies (funerals)  93 **condolement** mourning

As any the most vulgar° thing to sense,
Why should we in our peevish opposition                    100
Take it to heart? Fie, 'tis a fault to heaven,
A fault against the dead, a fault to nature,
To reason most absurd, whose common theme
Is death of fathers, and who still hath cried,
From the first corse° till he that died today,                    105
"This must be so." We pray you throw to earth
This unprevailing° woe, and think of us
As of a father, for let the world take note
You are the most immediate to our throne,
And with no less nobility of love                    110
Than that which dearest father bears his son
Do I impart toward you. For your intent
In going back to school in Wittenberg,
It is most retrograde° to our desire,
And we beseech you, bend you° to remain                    115
Here in the cheer and comfort of our eye,
Our chiefest courtier, cousin, and our son.

QUEEN
Let not thy mother lose her prayers, Hamlet.
I pray thee stay with us, go not to Wittenberg.

HAMLET
I shall in all my best obey you, madam.                    120

KING
Why, 'tis a loving and a fair reply.
Be as ourself in Denmark. Madam, come.
This gentle and unforced accord of Hamlet
Sits smiling to my heart, in grace whereof
No jocund health that Denmark drinks today,                    125
But the great cannon to the clouds shall tell,
And the king's rouse° the heaven shall bruit° again,
Respeaking earthly thunder. Come away.

*Flourish. Exeunt all but* HAMLET.

HAMLET
O that this too too sullied° flesh would melt,
Thaw, and resolve itself into a dew,                    130
Or that the Everlasting had not fixed
His canon° 'gainst self-slaughter. O God, God,
How weary, stale, flat, and unprofitable
Seem to me all the uses of this world!
Fie on't, ah, fie, 'tis an unweeded garden                    135
That grows to seed. Things rank and gross in
    nature
Possess it merely.° That it should come to this:
But two months dead, nay, not so much, not two,
So excellent a king, that was to this
Hyperion° to a satyr, so loving to my mother                    140
That he might not beteem° the winds of heaven
Visit her face too roughly. Heaven and earth,
Must I remember? Why, she would hang on him
As if increase of appetite had grown
By what it fed on; and yet within a month—                    145
Let me not think on't; frailty, thy name is woman—
A little month, or ere those shoes were old
With which she followed my poor father's body

Like Niobe,° all tears, why she, even she—
O God, a beast that wants discourse of reason°                    150
Would have mourned longer—married with my
    uncle,
My father's brother, but no more like my father
Than I to Hercules. Within a month,
Ere yet the salt of most unrighteous tears
Had left the flushing° in her gallèd eyes,                    155
She married. O, most wicked speed, to post°
With such dexterity to incestuous° sheets!
It is not, nor it cannot come to good.
But break my heart, for I must hold my tongue.

*Enter* HORATIO, MARCELLUS, *and* BARNARDO.

HORATIO
Hail to your lordship!

HAMLET                    I am glad to see you well.                    160
Horatio—or I do forget myself.

HORATIO
The same, my lord, and your poor servant ever.

HAMLET
Sir, my good friend, I'll change° that name with you.
And what make you from Wittenberg, Horatio?
Marcellus.                    165

MARCELLUS  My good lord!

HAMLET
I am very glad to see you. [*To* BARNARDO.] Good
    even, sir.
But what, in faith, make you from Wittenberg?

HORATIO
A truant disposition, good my lord.

HAMLET
I would not hear your enemy say so,                    170
Nor shall you do my ear that violence
To make it truster° of your own report
Against yourself. I know you are no truant.
But what is your affair in Elsinore?
We'll teach you to drink deep ere you depart.                    175

HORATIO
My lord, I came to see your father's funeral.

HAMLET
I prithee do not mock me, fellow student.
I think it was to see my mother's wedding.

HORATIO
Indeed, my lord, it followed hard upon.

HAMLET
Thrift, thrift, Horatio. The funeral baked meats                    180
Did coldly furnish forth the marriage tables.
Would I had met my dearest° foe in heaven
Or ever I had seen that day, Horatio!
My father, methinks I see my father.

HORATIO
Where, my lord?

HAMLET                    In my mind's eye, Horatio.                    185

HORATIO
I saw him once. 'A° was a goodly king.

99 vulgar common  105 corse corpse  107 unprevailing
unavailing  114 retrograde contrary  115 bend you incline
127 rouse deep drink; bruit announce noisily  129 sullied
Q2 has "sallied," here modernized to "sullied," which makes
sense and is therefore given; but the Folio reading "solid,"
which fits better with "melt," is quite possibly correct  132
canon law  137 merely entirely  140 Hyperion the sun
god, a model of beauty  141 beteem allow

149 Niobe a mother who wept profusely at the death of
her children  150 wants . . . reason lacks reasoning power
155 left the flushing stopped reddening  156 post hasten
157 incestuous canon law considered marriage with a deceased
brother's widow to be incestuous  163 change exchange
172 truster believer  182 dearest most intensely felt  186
'A he

HAMLET
'A was a man, take him for all in all,
I shall not look upon his like again.
HORATIO
My lord, I think I saw him yesternight.
HAMLET    Saw? Who?                                                            190
HORATIO
My lord, the king your father.
HAMLET                                The king my father?
HORATIO
Season your admiration° for a while
With an attent ear till I may deliver
Upon the witness of these gentlemen
This marvel to you.
HAMLET                        For God's love let me hear!    195
HORATIO
Two nights together had these gentlemen,
Marcellus and Barnardo, on their watch
In the dead waste and middle of the night
Been thus encountered. A figure like your father,
Armèd at point exactly, cap-a-pe,°                              200
Appears before them, and with solemn march
Goes slow and stately by them. Thrice he walked
By their oppressed and fear-surprisèd eyes,
Within his truncheon's length,° whilst they, distilled°
Almost to jelly with the act° of fear,                           205
Stand dumb and speak not to him. This to me
In dreadful° secrecy impart they did,
And I with them the third night kept the watch,
Where, as they had delivered, both in time,
Form of the thing, each word made true and good,    210
The apparition comes. I knew your father.
These hands are not more like.
HAMLET                                  But where was this?
MARCELLUS
My lord, upon the platform where we watched.
HAMLET
Did you not speak to it?
HORATIO                        My lord, I did;
But answer made it none. Yet once methought    215
It lifted up it° head and did address
Itself to motion like as it would speak:
But even then the morning cock crew loud,
And at the sound its shrunk in haste away
And vanished from our sight.
HAMLET                                'Tis very strange.    220
HORATIO
As I do live, my honored lord, 'tis true,
And we did think it writ down in our duty
To let you know of it.
HAMLET
Indeed, indeed, sirs, but this troubles me.
Hold you the watch tonight?
ALL                                We do, my lord.    225
HAMLET    Armed, say you?
ALL    Armed, my lord.
HAMLET
From top to toe?
ALL                        My lord, from head to foot.

HAMLET
Then saw you not his face.
HORATIO
O, yes, my lord. He wore his beaver° up.    230
HAMLET
What, looked he frowningly?
HORATIO
A countenance more in sorrow than in anger.
HAMLET    Pale or red?
HORATIO
Nay, very pale.
HAMLET                And fixed his eyes upon you?
HORATIO
Most constantly.
HAMLET                I would I had been there.    235
HORATIO
It would have much amazed you.
HAMLET
Very like, very like. Stayed it long?
HORATIO
While one with moderate haste might tell° a hundred.
BOTH    Longer, longer.
HORATIO
Not when I saw't.
HAMLET                His beard was grizzled,° no?    240
HORATIO
It was as I have seen it in his life,
A sable silvered.°
HAMLET                I will watch tonight.
Perchance 'twill walk again.
HORATIO                        I warr'nt it will.
HAMLET
If it assume my noble father's person,
I'll speak to it though hell itself should gape    245
And bid me hold my peace. I pray you all,
If you have hitherto concealed this sight,
Let it be tenable° in your silence still,
And whatsomever else shall hap tonight,
Give it an understanding but no tongue;    250
I will requite your loves. So fare you well.
Upon the platform 'twixt eleven and twelve
I'll visit you.
ALL                Our duty to your honor.
HAMLET
Your loves, as mine to you. Farewell.
                                                    Exeunt [all but HAMLET].
My father's spirit—in arms? All is not well.    255
I doubt° some foul play. Would the night were come!
Till then sit still, my soul. Foul deeds will rise,
Though all the earth o'erwhelm them, to men's eyes.
                                                                        Exit.


[Scene III. A room.]

Enter LAERTES and OPHELIA, his sister.

LAERTES
My necessaries are embarked. Farewell.
And, sister, as the winds give benefit

192 **Season your admiration** control your wonder    200
**cap-a-pe** head to foot    204 **truncheon's length** space of a
short staff; **distilled** reduced    205 **act** action    207 **dreadful**
terrified    216 **it** its

230 **beaver** visor, face guard    238 **tell** count    240 **grizzled**
gray    242 **sable silvered** black mingled with white    248
**tenable** held    256 **doubt** suspect

And convoy° is assistant, do not sleep,
But let me hear from you.
OPHELIA                    Do you doubt that?
LAERTES
For Hamlet, and the trifling of his favor,                                    5
Hold it a fashion and a toy° in blood,
A violet in the youth of primy° nature,
Forward,° not permanent, sweet, not lasting,
The perfume and suppliance° of a minute,
No more.
OPHELIA  No more but so?
LAERTES                    Think it no more.                                   10
For nature crescent° does not grow alone
In thews° and bulk, but as this temple° waxes,
The inward service of the mind and soul
Grows wide withal. Perhaps he loves you now,
And now no soil nor cautel° doth besmirch                                     15
The virtue of his will; but you must fear,
His greatness weighed,° his will is not his own.
For he himself is subject to his birth.
He may not, as unvalued° persons do,
Carve for himself; for on his choice depends                                  20
The safety and health of this whole state;
And therefore must his choice be circumscribed
Unto the voice and yielding of that body
Whereof he is the head. Then if he says he loves you,
It fits your wisdom so far to believe it                                       25
As he in his particular act and place
May give his saying deed, which is no further
Than the main voice of Denmark goes withal.
Then weigh what loss your honor may sustain
If with too credent° ear you list his songs,                                  30
Or lose your heart, or your chaste treasure open
To his unmastered importunity.
Fear it, Ophelia, fear it, my dear sister,
And keep you in the rear of your affection,
Out of the shot and danger of desire.                                         35
The chariest maid is prodigal enough
If she unmask her beauty to the moon.
Virtue itself scapes not calumnious strokes.
The canker° galls the infants of the spring
Too oft before their buttons° be disclosed,                                   40
And in the morn and liquid dew of youth
Contagious blastments are most imminent.
Be wary then; best safety lies in fear;
Youth to itself rebels, though none else near.
OPHELIA
I shall the effect of this good lesson keep                                   45
As watchman to my heart, but, good my brother,
Do not, as some ungracious° pastors do,
Show me the steep and thorny way to heaven,
Whiles, like a puffed and reckless libertine,
Himself the primrose path of dalliance treads                                 50
And recks not his own rede.°

*Enter* POLONIUS.

LAERTES                              O, fear me not.
I stay too long. But here my father comes.
A double blessing is a double grace;
Occasion smiles upon a second leave.
POLONIUS
Yet here, Laertes? Aboard, aboard, for shame!                                 55
The wind sits in the shoulder of your sail,
And you are stayed for. There—my blessing with thee,
And these few precepts in thy memory
Look thou character.° Give thy thoughts no tongue,
Nor any unproportioned° thought his act.                                      60
Be thou familiar, but by no means vulgar.
Those friends thou hast, and their adoption tried,
Grapple them unto thy soul with hoops of steel,
But do not dull thy palm with entertainment
Of each new-hatched, unfledged courage.° Beware                               65
Of entrance to a quarrel; but being in,
Bear't that th' opposèd may beware of thee.
Give every man thine ear, but few thy voice;
Take each man's censure,° but reserve thy judgment.
Costly thy habit as thy purse can buy,                                        70
But not expressed in fancy; rich, not gaudy,
For the apparel oft proclaims the man,
And they in France of the best rank and station
Are of a most select and generous, chief in that.°
Neither a borrower nor a lender be,                                           75
For loan oft loses both itself and friend,
And borrowing dulleth edge of husbandry.°
This above all, to thine own self be true,
And it must follow, as the night the day,
Thou canst not then be false to any man.                                      80
Farewell. My blessing season this° in thee!
LAERTES
Most humbly do I take my leave, my lord.
POLONIUS
The time invites you. Go, your servants tend.°
LAERTES
Farewell, Ophelia, and remember well
What I have said to you.
OPHELIA                    'Tis in my memory locked,                          85
And you yourself shall keep the key of it.
LAERTES  Farewell.                              *Exit* LAERTES.
POLONIUS
What is't, Ophelia, he hath said to you?
OPHELIA
So please you, something touching the Lord Hamlet.
POLONIUS
Marry,° well bethought.                                                       90
'Tis told me he hath very oft of late
Given private time to you, and you yourself
Have of your audience been most free and bounteous.
If it be so—as so 'tis put on me,
And that in way of caution—I must tell you                                    95
You do not understand yourself so clearly
As it behooves my daughter and your honor.
What is between you? Give me up the truth.

---

I.iii.3 **convoy** conveyance  6 **toy** idle fancy  7 **primy**
springlike  8 **Forward** premature  9 **suppliance** diversion
11 **crescent** growing  12 **thews** muscles and sinews; **temple**
the body  15 **cautel** deceit  17 **greatness weighed** high rank
considered  19 **unvalued** of low rank  30 **credent** credulous
39 **canker** cankerworm  40 **buttons** buds  47 **ungracious**
lacking grace  51 **recks . . . rede** does not heed his own
advice

59 **character** inscribe  60 **unproportioned** unbalanced  65
**courage** gallant youth  69 **censure** opinion  74 **Are . . . that**
show their fine taste and their gentlemanly instincts more in
that than in any other point of manners (Kittredge)  77
**husbandry** thrift  81 **season this** make fruitful this (advice)
83 **tend** attend  90 **Marry** a light oath, from "By the
Virgin Mary"

**OPHELIA**
He hath, my lord, of late made many tenders°
Of his affection to me.                                                    100
**POLONIUS**
Affection pooh! You speak like a green girl,
Unsifted° in such perilous circumstance.
Do you believe his tenders, as you call them?
**OPHELIA**
I do not know, my lord, what I should think.
**POLONIUS**
Marry, I will teach you. Think yourself a baby        105
That you have ta'en these tenders for true pay
Which are not sterling. Tender yourself more dearly,
Or (not to crack the wind of the poor phrase)
Tend'ring it thus you'll tender me a fool.°
**OPHELIA**
My lord, he hath importuned me with love             110
In honorable fashion.
**POLONIUS**
Ay, fashion you may call it. Go to, go to.
**OPHELIA**
And hath given countenance to his speech, my lord,
With almost all the holy vows of heaven.
**POLONIUS**
Ay, springes to catch woodcocks.° I do know,         115
When the blood burns, how prodigal the soul
Lends the tongue vows. These blazes, daughter,
Giving more light than heat, extinct in both,
Even in their promise, as it is a-making,
You must not take for fire. From this time             120
Be something scanter of your maiden presence.
Set your entreatments° at a higher rate
Than a command to parley. For Lord Hamlet,
Believe so much in him that he is young,
And with a larger tether may he walk                    125
Than may be given you. In few, Ophelia,
Do not believe his vows, for they are brokers,°
Not of that dye° which their investments° show,
But mere implorators° of unholy suits,
Breathing like sanctified and pious bonds,°           130
The better to beguile. This is for all:
I would not, in plain terms, from this time forth
Have you so slander° any moment leisure
As to give words or talk with the Lord Hamlet.
Look to't, I charge you. Come your ways.            135
**OPHELIA**
I shall obey, my lord.                                    *Exeunt.*

[Scene IV. *A guard platform.*]

*Enter* HAMLET, HORATIO, *and* MARCELLUS.

**HAMLET**
The air bites shrewdly;° it is very cold.

**HORATIO**
It is a nipping and an eager° air.
**HAMLET**
What hour now?
**HORATIO**                    I think it lacks of twelve.
**MARCELLUS**
No, it is struck.
**HORATIO**
Indeed? I heard it not. It then draws near the season     5
Wherein the spirit held his wont to walk.

*A flourish of trumpets, and two pieces go off.*

What does this mean, my lord?
**HAMLET**
The king doth wake° tonight and takes his rouse,°
Keeps wassail, and the swagg'ring upspring° reels,
And as he drains his draughts of Rhenish° down      10
The kettledrum and trumpet thus bray out
The triumph of his pledge.°
**HORATIO**                          Is it a custom?
**HAMLET**
Ay, marry, is't,
But to my mind, though I am native here
And to the manner born, it is a custom                    15
More honored in the breach than the observance.
This heavy-headed revel east and west
Makes us traduced and taxed of° other nations.
They clepe° us drunkards and with swinish phrase
Soil our addition,° and indeed it takes                      20
From our achievements, though performed at height,
The pith and marrow of our attribute.°
So oft it chances in particular men
That for some vicious mole° of nature in them,
As in their birth, wherein they are not guilty,           25
(Since nature cannot choose his origin)
By the o'ergrowth of some complexion,°
Oft breaking down the pales° and forts of reason,
Or by some habit that too much o'erleavens°
The form of plausive° manners, that (these men,      30
Carrying, I say, the stamp of one defect,
Being nature's livery, or fortune's star°)
Their virtues else, be they as pure as grace,
As infinite as man may undergo,
Shall in the general censure° take corruption          35
From that particular fault. The dram of evil
Doth all the noble substance of a doubt,
To his own scandal.°

*Enter* GHOST.

**HORATIO**                    Look, my lord, it comes.
**HAMLET**
Angels and ministers of grace defend us!

**99 tenders** offers (in line 103 it has the same meaning, but in line 106 Polonius speaks of "tenders" in the sense of counters or chips; in line 109 "Tend'ring" means "holding," and "tender" means "give," "present")   **102 Unsifted** untried   **109 tender . . . fool** (1) present me with a fool (2) present me with a baby   **115 springes . . . woodcocks** snares to catch stupid birds   **122 entreatments** interviews   **127 brokers** procurers   **128 dye** i.e., kind; **investments** garments   **129 implorators** solicitors   **130 bonds** pledges   **133 slander** disgrace   **I.iv.1 shrewdly** bitterly

**2 eager** sharp   **8 wake** hold a revel by night; **takes his rouse** carouses   **9 upspring** a dance   **10 Rhenish** Rhine wine   **12 triumph . . . pledge** achievement (of drinking a wine cup in one draught) of his toast   **18 taxed of** blamed by   **19 clepe** call   **20 addition** reputation (literally, "title of honor")   **22 attribute** reputation   **24 mole** blemish   **27 complexion** natural disposition   **28 pales** enclosures   **29 o'erleavens** mixes with, corrupts   **30 plausive** pleasing   **32 nature's . . . star** nature's equipment (i.e., "innate"), or a person's destiny determined by the stars   **35 general censure** popular judgment   **36–38 The dram . . . scandal** though the drift is clear, there is no agreement as to the exact meaning of these lines

Be thou a spirit of health° or goblin damned,    40
Bring with thee airs from heaven or blasts from hell,
Be thy intents wicked or charitable,
Thou com'st in such a questionable° shape
That I will speak to thee. I'll call thee Hamlet,
King, father, royal Dane. O, answer me!    45
Let me not burst in ignorance, but tell
Why thy canonized° bones, hearsèd in death,
Have burst their cerements,° why the sepulcher
Wherein we saw thee quietly interred
Hath oped his ponderous and marble jaws    50
To cast thee up again. What may this mean
That thou, dead corse, again in complete steel,
Revisits thus the glimpses of the moon,
Making night hideous, and we fools of nature
So horridly to shake our disposition°    55
With thoughts beyond the reaches of our souls?
Say, why is this? Wherefore? What should we do?

GHOST *beckons* HAMLET.

HORATIO
It beckons you to go away with it,
As if some impartment° did desire
To you alone.
MARCELLUS  Look with what courteous action    60
It waves you to a more removèd ground.
But do not go with it.
HORATIO             No, by no means.
HAMLET
It will not speak. Then I will follow it.
HORATIO
Do not, my lord.
HAMLET        Why, what should be the fear?
I do not set my life at a pin's fee,    65
And for my soul, what can it do to that,
Being a thing immortal as itself?
It waves me forth again. I'll follow it.
HORATIO
What if it tempt you toward the flood, my lord,
Or to the dreadful summit of the cliff    70
That beetles° o'er his base into the sea,
And there assume some other horrible form,
Which might deprive your sovereignty of reason°
And draw you into madness? Think of it.
The very place puts toys° of desperation,    75
Without more motive, into every brain
That looks so many fathoms to the sea
And hears it roar beneath.
HAMLET        It waves me still.
Go on; I'll follow thee.
MARCELLUS
You shall not go, my lord.
HAMLET        Hold off your hands.    80
HORATIO
Be ruled. You shall not go.
HAMLET        My fate cries out
And makes each petty artere° in this body

As hardy as the Nemean lion's nerve.°
Still am I called! Unhand me, gentlemen.
By heaven, I'll make a ghost of him that lets° me!    85
I say, away! Go on. I'll follow thee.
             *Exit* GHOST, *and* HAMLET.
HORATIO
He waxes desperate with imagination.
MARCELLUS
Let's follow. 'Tis not fit thus to obey him.
HORATIO
Have after! To what issue will this come?
MARCELLUS
Something is rotten in the state of Denmark.    90
HORATIO
Heaven will direct it.
MARCELLUS        Nay, let's follow him.    *Exeunt.*

[Scene V. *The battlements.*]

*Enter* GHOST *and* HAMLET.

HAMLET
Whither wilt thou lead me? Speak; I'll go no further.
GHOST
Mark me.
HAMLET  I will.
GHOST        My hour is almost come,
When I to sulf'rous and tormenting flames
Must render up myself.
HAMLET        Alas, poor ghost.
GHOST
Pity me not, but lend thy serious hearing    5
To what I shall unfold.
HAMLET        Speak. I am bound to hear.
GHOST
So art thou to revenge, when thou shalt hear.
HAMLET  What?
GHOST
I am thy father's spirit,
Doomed for a certain term to walk the night,    10
And for the day confined to fast in fires,
Till the foul crimes° done in my days of nature
Are burnt and purged away. But that I am forbid
To tell the secrets of my prison house,
I could a tale unfold whose lightest word    15
Would harrow up thy soul, freeze thy young blood,
Make thy two eyes like stars start from their spheres,°
Thy knotted and combinèd locks to part,
And each particular hair to stand an° end
Like quills upon the fearful porpentine.°    20
But this eternal blazon° must not be
To ears of flesh and blood. List, list, O, list!
If thou didst ever thy dear father love—
HAMLET  O God!
GHOST
Revenge his foul and most unnatural murder.    25
HAMLET  Murder?

**40 spirit of health** good spirit  **43 questionable** (1) capable
of discourse (2) dubious  **47 canonized** buried according to
the canon or ordinance of the church  **48 cerements** waxed
linen shroud  **55 shake our disposition** disturb us  **59
impartment** communication  **71 beetles** juts out  **73 deprive
. . . reason** destroy the sovereignty of your reason  **75 toys**
whims, fancies  **82 artere** artery

**83 Nemean lion's nerve** sinews of the mythical lion slain by
Hercules  **85 lets** (1) allows (2) hinders
**I.v.12 crimes** sins  **17 spheres** in Ptolemaic astronomy, each
planet was fixed in a hollow transparent shell concentric with
the earth  **19 an** on  **20 fearful porpentine** timid porcupine
**21 eternal blazon** revelation of eternity

**GHOST**
Murder most foul, as in the best it is,
But this most foul, strange, and unnatural.
**HAMLET**
Haste me to know't, that I, with wings as swift
As meditation° or the thoughts of love,                    30
May sweep to my revenge.
**GHOST**                              I find thee apt,
And duller shouldst thou be than the fat weed
That roots itself in ease on Lethe wharf,°
Wouldst thou not stir in this. Now, Hamlet, hear.
'Tis given out that, sleeping in my orchard,                35
A serpent stung me. So the whole ear of Denmark
Is by a forgèd process° of my death
Rankly abused. But know, thou noble youth,
The serpent that did sting thy father's life
Now wears his crown.
**HAMLET**                    O my prophetic soul!          40
My uncle?
**GHOST**
Ay, that incestuous, that adulterate° beast,
With witchcraft of his wits, with traitorous gifts—
O wicked wit and gifts, that have the power
So to seduce!—won to his shameful lust                     45
The will of my most seeming-virtuous queen.
O Hamlet, what a falling-off was there,
From me, whose love was of that dignity
That it went hand in hand even with the vow
I made to her in marriage, and to decline                  50
Upon a wretch whose natural gifts were poor
To those of mine.
But virtue, as it never will be moved,
Though lewdness° court it in a shape of heaven,
So lust, though to a radiant angel linked,                 55
Will sate itself in a celestial bed
And prey on garbage.
But soft, methinks I scent the morning air;
Brief let me be. Sleeping within my orchard,
My custom always of the afternoon,                         60
Upon my secure° hour thy uncle stole
With juice of cursed hebona° in a vial,
And in the porches of my ears did pour
The leperous distillment, whose effect
Holds such an enmity with blood of man                     65
That swift as quicksilver it courses through
The natural gates and alleys of the body,
And with a sudden vigor it doth posset°
And curd, like eager° droppings into milk,
The thin and wholesome blood. So did it mine,             70
And a most instant tetter° barked about
Most lazarlike° with vile and loathsome crust  } Luke 16.
All my smooth body.                                 } 20
Thus was I, sleeping, by a brother's hand
Of life, of crown, of queen at once dispatched,           75
Cut off even in the blossoms of my sin,
Unhouseled, disappointed, unaneled,°

No reck'ning made, but sent to my account
With all my imperfections on my head.
O, horrible! O, horrible! Most horrible!                   80
If thou hast nature in thee, bear it not.
Let not the royal bed of Denmark be
A couch for luxury° and damnèd incest.
But howsomever thou pursues this act,
Taint not thy mind, nor let thy soul contrive             85
Against thy mother aught. Leave her to heaven
And to those thorns that in her bosom lodge
To prick and sting her. Fare thee well at once.
The glowworm shows the matin° to be near
And 'gins to pale his uneffectual fire.                    90
Adieu, adieu, adieu. Remember me.            *Exit.*
**HAMLET**
O all you host of heaven! O earth! What else?
And shall I couple hell? O fi! Hold, hold, my heart,
And you, my sinews, grow not instant old,
But bear me stiffly up. Remember thee?                     95
Ay, thou poor ghost, whiles memory holds a seat
In this distracted globe.° Remember thee?
Yea, from the table° of my memory
I'll wipe away all trivial fond° records,
All saws° of books, all forms, all pressures° past       100
That youth and observation copied there,
And thy commandment all alone shall live
Within the book and volume of my brain,
Unmixed with baser matter. Yes, by heaven!
O most pernicious woman!                                  105
O villain, villain, smiling, damnèd villain!
My tables—meet it is I set it down
That one may smile, and smile, and be a villain.
At least I am sure it may be so in Denmark.

[*Writes.*]

So, uncle, there you are. Now to my word:                110
It is "Adieu, adieu, remember me."
I have sworn't.
**HORATIO** *and* **MARCELLUS** (*Within.*)
My lord, my lord!

*Enter* HORATIO *and* MARCELLUS.

**MARCELLUS**          Lord Hamlet!
**HORATIO**                              Heavens secure him!
**HAMLET**   So be it!
**MARCELLUS**
Illo, ho, ho,° my lord!                                   115
**HAMLET**
Hillo, ho, ho, boy! Come, bird, come.
**MARCELLUS**
How is't, my noble lord?
**HORATIO**                        What news, my lord?
**HAMLET**
O, wonderful!
**HORATIO**
Good my lord, tell it.
**HAMLET**                    No, you will reveal it.

---

30 **meditation** thought   33 **Lethe wharf** bank of the river
of forgetfulness in Hades   37 **forgèd process** false account
42 **adulterate** adulterous   54 **lewdness** lust   61 **secure** un-
suspecting   62 **hebona** a poisonous plant   68 **posset** curdle
69 **eager** acid   71 **tetter** scab   72 **lazarlike** leperlike   77
**Unhouseled, disappointed, unaneled** without the sacrament
of communion, unabsolved, without extreme unction

83 **luxury** lust   89 **matin** morning   97 **globe** i.e., his head
98 **table** tablet, notebook   99 **fond** foolish   100 **saws**
maxims; **pressures** impressions   115 **Illo, ho, ho** falconer's
call to his hawk

HORATIO
Not I, my lord, by heaven.
MARCELLUS              Nor I, my lord.          120
HAMLET
How say you then? Would heart of man once think it?
But you'll be secret?
BOTH              Ay, by heaven, my lord.
HAMLET
There's never a villain dwelling in all Denmark
But he's an arrant knave.
HORATIO
There needs no ghost, my lord, come from the grave   125
To tell us this.
HAMLET          Why, right, you are in the right;
And so, without more circumstance° at all,
I hold it fit that we shake hands and part:
You, as your business and desire shall point you,
For every man hath business and desire              130
Such as it is, and for my own poor part,
Look you, I'll go pray.
HORATIO
These are but wild and whirling words my lord.
HAMLET
I am sorry they offend you, heartily;
Yes, faith, heartily.
HORATIO              There's no offense, my lord.    135
HAMLET
Yes, by Saint Patrick, but there is, Horatio,
And much offense too. Touching this vision here,
It is an honest ghost,° that let me tell you.
For your desire to know what is between us,
O'ermaster't as you may. And now, good friends,    140
As you are friends, scholars, and soldiers,
Give me one poor request.
HORATIO
What is't, my lord? We will.
HAMLET
Never make known what you have seen tonight.
BOTH
My lord, we will not.
HAMLET              Nay, but swear't.
HORATIO                          In faith,          145
My lord, not I.
MARCELLUS    Nor I, my lord—in faith.
HAMLET
Upon my sword.
MARCELLUS        We have sworn, my lord, already.
HAMLET
Indeed, upon my sword, indeed.
GHOST cries under the stage.
GHOST  Swear.
HAMLET
Ha, ha, boy, say'st thou so? Art thou there, truepenny?°  150
Come on. You hear this fellow in the cellarage.
Consent to swear.
HORATIO          Propose the oath, my lord.
HAMLET
Never to speak of this that you have seen.
Swear by my sword.
GHOST [Beneath.]  Swear.                            155

HAMLET
Hic et ubique?° Then we'll shift our ground;
Come hither, gentlemen,
And lay your hands again upon my sword.
Swear by my sword
Never to speak of this that you have heard.         160
GHOST [Beneath.]  Swear by his sword.
HAMLET
Well said, old mole! Canst work i' th' earth so fast?
A worthy pioner!° Once more remove, good friends.
HORATIO
O day and night, but this is wondrous strange!
HAMLET
And therefore as a stranger give it welcome.        165
There are more things in heaven and earth, Horatio,
Than are dreamt of in your philosophy.
But come:
Here as before, never, so help you mercy,
How strange or odd some'er I bear myself            170
(As I perchance hereafter shall think meet
To put an antic disposition° on),
That you, at such times seeing me, never shall
With arms encumb'red° thus, or this headshake,
Or by pronouncing of some doubtful phrase,          175
As "Well, well, we know," or "We could, an if we
would,"
Of "If we list to speak," or "There be, an if they
might,"
Or such ambiguous giving out, to note
That you know aught of me—this do swear,
So grace and mercy at your most need help you.      180
GHOST [Beneath.]  Swear.

[They swear.]

HAMLET
Rest, rest, perturbèd spirit. So, gentlemen,
With all my love I do commend me° to you,
And what so poor a man as Hamlet is
May do t' express his love and friending to you,    185
God willing, shall not lack. Let us go in together,
And still your fingers on your lips, I pray.
The time is out of joint. O cursèd spite,
That ever I was born to set it right!
Nay, come, let's go together.         Exeunt.  190

# [ ACT II ]

## [Scene I. A room.]

*Enter old* POLONIUS, *with his man* REYNALDO.

POLONIUS
Give him this money and these notes, Reynaldo.
REYNALDO  I will, my lord.
POLONIUS
You shall do marvell's° wisely, good Reynaldo,

127 **circumstance** details  138 **honest ghost** not a demon in his father's shape  150 **truepenny** honest fellow

156 **Hic et ubique** here and everywhere (Latin)  163 **pioner** digger of mines  172 **antic disposition** fantastic behavior  174 **encumb'red** folded  183 **commend me** entrust myself  II.i.3 **marvell's** marvelous(ly)

Before you visit him, to make inquire
Of his behavior.

REYNALDO    My lord, I did intend it.    5

POLONIUS
Marry, well said, very well said. Look you sir,
Inquire me first what Danskers° are in Paris,
And how, and who, what means, and where they
    keep,°
What company, at what expense; and finding
By this encompassment° and drift of question    10
That they do know my son, come you more nearer
Than your particular demands° will touch it.
Take you as 'twere some distant knowledge of him,
As thus, "I know his father and his friends,
And in part him." Do you mark this, Reynaldo?    15

REYNALDO    Ay, very well, my lord.

POLONIUS
"And in part him, but," you may say, "not well,
But if 't be he I mean, he's very wild,
Addicted so and so." And there put on him
What forgeries° you please; marry, none so rank    20
As may dishonor him—take heed of that—
But, sir, such wanton, wild, and usual slips
As are companions noted and most known
To youth and liberty.

REYNALDO                As gaming, my lord.

POLONIUS
Ay, or drinking, fencing, swearing, quarreling,    25
Drabbing.° You may go so far.

REYNALDO
My lord, that would dishonor him.

POLONIUS
Faith, no, as you may season it in the charge.
You must not put another scandal on him,
That he is open to incontinency.°    30
That's not my meaning. But breathe his faults so
    quaintly°
That they may seem the taints of liberty,
The flash and outbreak of a fiery mind,
A savageness in unreclaimèd blood,
Of general assault.°

REYNALDO                But, my good lord—    35

POLONIUS
Wherefore should you do this?

REYNALDO                            Ay, my lord,
I would know that.

POLONIUS                Marry, sir, here's my drift,
And I believe it is a fetch of warrant.°
You laying these slight sullies on my son
As 'twere a thing a little soiled i' th' working,    40
Mark you,
Your party in converse, him you would sound,
Having ever seen in the prenominate crimes°
The youth you breathe of guilty, be assured
He closes with you in this consequence:°    45
"Good sir," or so, or "friend," or "gentleman"—

According to the phrase or the addition°
Of man and country—

REYNALDO                Very good, my lord.

POLONIUS
And then, sir, does 'a° this—'a does—
What was I about to say? By the mass, I was about    50
to say something! Where did I leave?

REYNALDO    At "closes in the consequence," at "friend
or so," and "gentleman."

POLONIUS
At "closes in the consequence"—Ay, marry!
He closes thus: "I know the gentleman;    55
I saw him yesterday, or t'other day,
Or then, or then, with such or such, and, as you say,
There was 'a gaming, there o'ertook in's rouse,
There falling out at tennis"; or perchance,
"I saw him enter such a house of sale,"    60
Videlicet,° a brothel, or so forth.
See you now—
Your bait of falsehood take this carp of truth,
And thus do we of wisdom and of reach,°
With windlasses° and with assays of bias,°    65
By indirections find directions out.
So, by my former lecture and advice,
Shall you my son. You have me, have you not?

REYNALDO
My lord, I have.

POLONIUS            God bye ye, fare ye well.

REYNALDO    Good my lord.    70

POLONIUS
Observe his inclination in yourself.°

REYNALDO    I shall, my lord.

POLONIUS
And let him ply his music.

REYNALDO                Well, my lord.

POLONIUS
Farewell.                        *Exit* REYNALDO.

*Enter* OPHELIA.

                How now, Ophelia, what's the matter?

OPHELIA
O my lord, my lord, I have been so affrighted!    75

POLONIUS
With what, i' th' name of God?

OPHELIA
My lord, as I was sewing in my closet,°
Lord Hamlet, with his doublet all unbraced,°
No hat upon his head, his stockings fouled,
Ungartered, and down-gyvèd° to his ankle,    80
Pale as his shirt, his knees knocking each other,
And with a look so piteous in purport,°
As if he had been loosèd out of hell
To speak of horrors—he comes before me.

POLONIUS
Mad for thy love?

OPHELIA                My lord, I do not know,    85
But truly I do fear it.

---

**7 Danskers** Danes **8 keep** dwell **10 encompassment**
circling **12 demands** questions **20 forgeries** inventions **26**
**Drabbing** wenching **30 incontinency** habitual licentiousness **31 quaintly** ingeniously, delicately **35 Of general**
**assault** common to all men **38 fetch of warrant** justifiable
device **43 Having . . . crimes** if he has ever seen in the
aforementioned crimes **45 He . . . consequence** he falls in
with you in this conclusion

**47 addition** title **49 'a** he **61 Videlicet** namely **64 reach**
far-reaching awareness (?) **65 windlasses** circuitous courses;
**assays of bias** indirect attempts (metaphor from bowling;
"bias" = curved course) **71 in yourself** for yourself **77**
**closet** private room **78 doublet all unbraced** jacket
entirely unlaced **80 down-gyvèd** hanging down like fetters
**82 purport** expression

POLONIUS        What said he?

OPHELIA

He took me by the wrist and held me hard;
Then goes he to the length of all his arm,
And with his other hand thus o'er his brow
He falls to such perusal of my face      90
As 'a would draw it. Long stayed he so.
At last, a little shaking of mine arm,
And thrice his head thus waving up and down,
He raised a sigh so piteous and profound
As it did seem to shatter all his bulk      95
And end his being. That done, he lets me go,
And, with his head over his shoulder turned,
He seemed to find his way without his eyes,
For out o' doors he went without their helps,
And to the last bended their light on me.      100

POLONIUS

Come, go with me. I will go seek the king.
This is the very ecstasy° of love,
Whose violent property fordoes° itself
And leads the will to desperate undertakings
As oft as any passions under heaven      105
That does afflict our natures. I am sorry.
What, have you given him any hard words of late?

OPHELIA

No, my good lord; but as you did command,
I did repel his letters and denied
His access to me.

POLONIUS      That hath made him mad.      110
I am sorry that with better heed and judgment
I had not quoted° him. I feared he did but trifle
And meant to wrack thee; but beshrew my jealousy.°
By heaven, it is as proper° to our age
To cast beyond ourselves° in our opinions      115
As it is common for the younger sort
To lack discretion. Come, go we to the king.
This must be known, which, being kept close, might
    move
More grief to hide than hate to utter love.°
Come.                 *Exeunt.*   120

[Scene II. *The castle.*]

*Flourish. Enter* KING *and* QUEEN, ROSENCRANTZ,
*and* GUILDENSTERN, [*with others*].

KING

Welcome, dear Rosencrantz and Guildenstern.
Moreover that° we much did long to see you,
The need we have to use you did provoke
Our hasty sending. Something have you heard
Of Hamlet's transformation: so call it,      5
Sith° nor th' exterior nor the inward man
Resembles that it was. What it should be,
More than his father's death, that thus hath put him
So much from th' understanding of himself,
I cannot dream of. I entreat you both      10

That, being of so° young days brought up with him,
And sith so neighbored to his youth and havior,°
That you vouchsafe your rest° here in our court
Some little time, so by your companies
To draw him on to pleasures, and to gather      15
So much as from occasion you may glean,
Whether aught to us unknown afflicts him thus,
That opened° lies within our remedy.

QUEEN

Good gentlemen, he hath much talked of you,
And sure I am, two men there is not living      20
To whom he more adheres. If it will please you
To show us so much gentry° and good will
As to expend your time with us awhile
For the supply and profit of our hope,
Your visitation shall receive such thanks      25
As fits a king's remembrance.

ROSENCRANTZ      Both your majesties
Might, by the sovereign power you have of us,
Put your dread pleasures more into command
Than to entreaty.

GUILDENSTERN   But we both obey,
And here give up ourselves in the full bent°      30
To lay our service freely at your feet,
To be commanded.

KING

Thanks, Rosencrantz and gentle Guildenstern.

QUEEN

Thanks, Guildenstern and gentle Rosencrantz.
And I beseech you instantly to visit      35
My too much changèd son. Go, some of you,
And bring these gentlemen where Hamlet is.

GUILDENSTERN

Heavens make our presence and our practices
Pleasant and helpful to him!

QUEEN            Ay, amen!
*Exeunt* ROSENCRANTZ *and* GUILDENSTERN
[*with some* ATTENDANTS].

*Enter* POLONIUS.

POLONIUS

Th' ambassadors from Norway, my good lord,      40
Are joyfully returned.

KING

Thou still° hast been the father of good news.

POLONIUS

Have I, my lord? Assure you, my good liege,
I hold my duty, as I hold my soul,
Both to my God and to my gracious king;      45
And I do think, or else this brain of mine
Hunts not the trail of policy so sure°
As it hath used to do, that I have found
The very cause of Hamlet's lunacy.

KING

O, speak of that! That do I long to hear.      50

POLONIUS

Give first admittance to th' ambassadors.
My news shall be the fruit to that great feast.

---

102 **ecstasy** madness   103 **property fordoes** quality destroys
112 **quoted** noted   113 **beshrew my jealousy** curse my
suspicions   114 **proper** natural   115 **To . . . ourselves** to be
overcalculating   117–19 **Come . . . love** the general meaning
is that while telling the king of Hamlet's love may anger the
king, more grief would come from keeping it secret
**II.ii.2 Moreover that** besides the fact that   6 **Sith** since

11 **of so** from such   12 **youth and havior** behavior in his
youth   13 **vouchsafe your rest** consent to remain   18 **opened**
revealed   22 **gentry** courtesy   30 **in . . . bent** entirely (the
figure is of a bow bent to its capacity)   42 **still** always
47 **Hunts . . . sure** does not follow clues of political doings
with such sureness

KING
Thyself do grace to them and bring them in.
                              [*Exit* POLONIUS.]
He tells me, my dear Gertrude, he hath found
The head and source of all your son's distemper.                55
QUEEN
I doubt° it is no other but the main,°
His father's death and our o'erhasty marriage.
KING
Well, we shall sift him.

*Enter* POLONIUS, VOLTEMAND, *and* CORNELIUS.
                    Welcome, my good friends.
Say, Voltemand, what from our brother Norway?
VOLTEMAND
Most fair return of greetings and desires.                       60
Upon our first,° he sent out to suppress
His nephew's levies, which to him appeared
To be a preparation 'gainst the Polack;
But better looked into, he truly found
It was against your highness, whereat grieved,                   65
That so his sickness, age, and impotence
Was falsely borne in hand,° sends out arrests
On Fortinbras; which he, in brief, obeys,
Receives rebuke from Norway, and in fine,°
Makes vow before his uncle never more                            70
To give th' assay° of arms against your majesty.
Whereon old Norway, overcome with joy,
Gives him threescore thousand crowns in annual fee
And his commission to employ those soldiers,
So levied as before, against the Polack,                         75
With an entreaty, herein further shown,

[*Gives a paper.*]

That it might please you to give quiet pass
Through your dominions for this enterprise,
On such regards of safety and allowance°
As therein are set down.
KING                        It likes us well;                    80
And at our more considered time° we'll read,
Answer, and think upon this business.
Meantime, we thank you for your well-took labor.
Go to your rest; at night we'll feast together.
Most welcome home!    *Exeunt ambassadors* [VOLTE-
                        MAND *and* CORNELIUS].
POLONIUS             This business is well ended.                85
My liege and madam, to expostulate°
What majesty should be, what duty is,
Why day is day, night night, and time is time,
Were nothing but to waste night, day, and time.
Therefore, since brevity is the soul of wit,°                    90
And tediousness the limbs and outward flourishes,
I will be brief. Your noble son is mad.
Mad call I it, for, to define true madness,
What is't but to be nothing else but mad?
But let that go.
QUEEN           More matter, with less art.                      95
POLONIUS
Madam, I swear I use no art at all.

56 **doubt** suspect; **main** principal point  61 **first** first audience
67 **borne in hand** deceived  69 **in fine** finally  71 **assay** trial
79 **regards . . . allowance** i.e., conditions  81 **considered
time** time proper for considering  86 **expostulate** discuss
90 **wit** wisdom, understanding

That he's mad, 'tis true: 'tis true 'tis pity,
And pity 'tis 'tis true—a foolish figure.°
But farewell it, for I will use no art.
Mad let us grant him then; and now remains             100
That we find out the cause of this effect,
Or rather say, the cause of this defect,
For this effect defective comes by cause.
Thus it remains, and the remainder thus.
Perpend.°                                              105
I have a daughter: have, while she is mine,
Who in her duty and obedience, mark,
Hath given me this. Now gather, and surmise.

[*Reads*] *the letter.*

"To the celestial, and my soul's idol, the most
beautified Ophelia"—                                   110
That's an ill phrase, a vile phrase; "beautified" is a vile
phrase. But you shall hear. Thus:
"In her excellent white bosom, these, &c."
QUEEN
Came this from Hamlet to her?
POLONIUS
Good madam, stay awhile. I will be faithful.           115
        "Doubt thou the stars are fire,
            Doubt that the sun doth move;
        Doubt° truth to be a liar,
            But never doubt I love.
O dear Ophelia, I am ill at these numbers.° I have not 120
art to reckon my groans; but that I love thee best, O
most best, believe it. Adieu.
        Thine evermore, most dear lady,
            whilst this machine° is to him, Hamlet."
This in obedience hath my daughter shown me,           125
And more above° hath his solicitings,
As they fell out by time, by means, and place,
All given to mine ear.
KING                        But how hath she
Received his love?
POLONIUS           What do you think of me?
KING
As of a man faithful and honorable.                    130
POLONIUS
I would fain prove so. But what might you think,
When I had seen this hot love on the wing
(As I perceived it, I must tell you that,
Before my daughter told me), what might you,
Or my dear majesty your queen here, think,             135
If I had played the desk or table book,°
Or given my heart a winking,° mute and dumb,
Or looked upon this love with idle sight?
What might you think? No, I went round to work
And my young mistress thus I did bespeak:              140
"Lord Hamlet is a prince, out of thy star.°
This must not be." And then I prescripts gave her,
That she should lock herself from his resort,
Admit no messengers, receive no tokens.
Which done, she took the fruits of my advice,          145

98 **figure** figure of rhetoric  105 **Perpend** consider carefully
118 **Doubt** suspect  120 **ill . . . numbers** unskilled in verses
124 **machine** complex device (here, his body)  126 **more
above** in addition  136 **played . . . book** i.e., been a passive
recipient of secrets  137 **winking** closing of the eyes  141 **star**
sphere

And he, repellèd, a short tale to make,
Fell into a sadness, then into a fast,
Thence to a watch,° thence into a weakness,
Thence to a lightness,° and, by this declension,
Into the madness wherein now he raves,          150
And all we mourn for.
KING                    Do you think 'tis this?
QUEEN
It may be, very like.
POLONIUS
Hath there been such a time, I would fain know that,
That I have positively said, "'Tis so,"
When it provèd otherwise?
KING                    Not that I know.          155
POLONIUS [Pointing to his head and shoulder.]
Take this from this, if this be otherwise.
If circumstances lead me, I will find
Where truth is hid, though it were hid indeed
Within the center.°
KING                    How may we try it further?
POLONIUS
You know sometimes he walks four hours together          160
Here in the lobby.
QUEEN                    So he does indeed.
POLONIUS
At such a time I'll loose my daughter to him.
Be you and I behind an arras° then.
Mark the encounter. If he love her not,
And be not from his reason fall'n thereon,          165
Let me be no assistant for a state
But keep a farm and carters.
KING                    We will try it.

*Enter* HAMLET *reading on a book.*

QUEEN
But look where sadly the poor wretch comes reading.
POLONIUS
Away, I do beseech you both, away.
                    *Exit* KING *and* QUEEN.
I'll board him presently.° O, give me leave.          170
How does my good Lord Hamlet?
HAMLET  Well, God-a-mercy.
POLONIUS  Do you know me, my lord?
HAMLET  Excellent well. You are a fishmonger.°
POLONIUS  Not I, my lord.          175
HAMLET  Then I would you were so honest a man.
POLONIUS  Honest, my lord?
HAMLET  Ay, sir. To be honest, as this world goes, is
to be one man picked out of ten thousand.
POLONIUS  That's very true, my lord.          180
HAMLET  For if the sun breed maggots in a dead dog,
being a good kissing carrion°— Have you a daughter?
POLONIUS  I have, my lord.
HAMLET  Let her not walk i' th' sun. Conception° is a
blessing, but as your daughter may conceive, friend,          185
look to't.

148 **watch** wakefulness  149 **lightness** mental derangement
159 **center** center of the earth  163 **arras** tapestry hanging in
front of a wall  170 **board him presently** accost him at once
174 **fishmonger** dealer in fish (slang for a procurer)  182 **a
good . . . carrion** perhaps the meaning is "a good piece of
flesh to kiss," but many editors emend "good" to "god,"
taking the word to refer to the sun  184 **Conception** (1)
understanding (2) becoming pregnant

POLONIUS [Aside.]  How say you by that? Still harping
on my daughter. Yet he knew me not at first. 'A said
I was a fishmonger. 'A is far gone, far gone. And truly
in my youth I suffered much extremity for love, very          190
near this. I'll speak to him again.—What do you read,
my lord?
HAMLET  Words, words, words.
POLONIUS  What is the matter, my lord?
HAMLET  Between who?          195
POLONIUS  I mean the matter° that you read, my lord.
HAMLET  Slanders, sir; for the satirical rogue says here
that old men have gray beards, that their faces are
wrinkled, their eyes purging thick amber and plum-
tree gum, and that they have a plentiful lack of wit,          200
together with most weak hams. All which, sir, though
I most powerfully and potently believe, yet I hold it
not honesty° to have it thus set down: for you yourself,
sir, should be old as I am if, like a crab, you could go
backward.          205
POLONIUS [Aside.]  Though this be madness, yet
there is method in't. Will you walk out of the air, my
lord?
HAMLET  Into my grave.
POLONIUS  Indeed, that's out of the air. [Aside.] How          210
pregnant° sometimes his replies are! A happiness° that
often madness hits on, which reason and sanity could
not so prosperously be delivered of. I will leave him
and suddenly contrive the means of meeting between
him and my daughter.—My lord, I will take my leave          215
of you.
HAMLET  You cannot take from me anything that I
will more willingly part withal—except my life, except
my life, except my life.

*Enter* GUILDENSTERN *and* ROSENCRANTZ.

POLONIUS  Fare you well, my lord.          220
HAMLET  These tedious old fools!
POLONIUS  You go to seek the Lord Hamlet? There
he is.
ROSENCRANTZ [To POLONIUS.]  God save you, sir!
                    [Exit POLONIUS.]
GUILDENSTERN  My honored lord!          225
ROSENCRANTZ  My most dear lord!
HAMLET  My excellent good friends! How dost thou,
Guildenstern? Ah, Rosencrantz! Good lads, how do
you both?
ROSENCRANTZ
As the indifferent° children of the earth.          230
GUILDENSTERN
Happy in that we are not overhappy.
On Fortune's cap we are not the very button.
HAMLET  Nor the soles of her shoe?
ROSENCRANTZ  Neither, my lord.
HAMLET  Then you live about her waist, or in the          235
middle of her favors?
GUILDENSTERN  Faith, her privates° we.
HAMLET  In the secret parts of Fortune? O, most true!
She is a strumpet. What news?

196 **matter** Polonius means "subject matter," but Hamlet
pretends to take the word in the sense of "quarrel"  203
**honesty** decency  211 **pregnant** meaningful; **happiness** apt
turn of phrase  230 **indifferent** ordinary  237 **privates**
ordinary men (with a pun on *private parts*)

ROSENCRANTZ   None, my lord, but that the world's 240 grown honest.

HAMLET   Then is doomsday near. But your news is not true. Let me question more in particular. What have you, my good friends, deserved at the hands of Fortune that she sends you to prison hither? 245

GUILDENSTERN   Prison, my lord?

HAMLET   Denmark's a prison.

ROSENCRANTZ   Then is the world one.

HAMLET   A goodly one, in which there are many confines, wards,° and dungeons, Denmark being one 250 o' th' worst.

ROSENCRANTZ   We think not so, my lord.

HAMLET   Why, then 'tis none to you, for there is nothing either good or bad but thinking makes it so. To me it is a prison. 255

ROSENCRANTZ   Why then your ambition makes it one. 'Tis too narrow for your mind.

HAMLET   O God, I could be bounded in a nutshell and count myself a king of infinite space, were it not that I have bad dreams. 260

GUILDENSTERN   Which dreams indeed are ambition, for the very substance of the ambitious is merely the shadow of a dream.

HAMLET   A dream itself is but a shadow.

ROSENCRANTZ   Truly, and I hold ambition of so airy 265 and light a quality that it is but a shadow's shadow.

HAMLET   Then are our beggars bodies, and our monarchs and outstretched heroes the beggars' shadows.° Shall we to th' court? For, by my fay,° I cannot reason. 270

BOTH   We'll wait upon you.

HAMLET   No such matter. I will not sort you with the rest of my servants, for, to speak to you like an honest man, I am most dreadfully attended. But in the beaten way of friendship, what make you at Elsinore? 275

ROSENCRANTZ   To visit you, my lord; no other occasion.

HAMLET   Beggar that I am, I am even poor in thanks, but I thank you; and sure, dear friends, my thanks are too dear a halfpenny.° Were you not sent for? Is 280 it your own inclining? Is it a free visitation? Come, come, deal justly with me. Come, come; nay, speak.

GUILDENSTERN   What should we say, my lord?

HAMLET   Why anything—but to th' purpose. You were sent for, and there is a kind of confession in your 285 looks, which your modesties have not craft enough to color. I know the good king and queen have sent for you.

ROSENCRANTZ   To what end, my lord?

HAMLET   That you must teach me. But let me conjure 290 you by the rights of your fellowship, by the consonancy of our youth, by the obligation of our ever-preserved love, and by what more dear a better proposer can charge you withal, be even and direct with me, whether you were sent for or no. 295

ROSENCRANTZ   [Aside to GUILDENSTERN.]   What say you?

HAMLET   [Aside.]   Nay then, I have an eye of you.—If you love me, hold not off.

GUILDENSTERN   My lord, we were sent for. 300

HAMLET   I will tell you why; so shall my anticipation prevent your discovery,° and your secrecy to the king and queen molt no feather. I have of late, but wherefore I know not, lost all my mirth, forgone all custom of exercises; and indeed, it goes so heavily with my 305 disposition that this goodly frame, the earth, seems to me a sterile promontory; this most excellent canopy, the air, look you, this brave o'erhanging firmament, this majestical roof fretted° with golden fire: why, it appeareth nothing to me but a foul and pestilent 310 congregation of vapors. What a piece of work is a man, how noble in reason, how infinite in faculties, in form and moving how express° and admirable, in action how like an angel, in apprehension how like a god: the beauty of the world, the paragon of animals; 315 and yet to me, what is this quintessence of dust? Man delights not me; nor woman neither, though by your smiling you seem to say so.

ROSENCRANTZ   My lord, there was no such stuff in my thoughts. 320

HAMLET   Why did ye laugh then, when I said, "Man delights not me"?

ROSENCRANTZ   To think, my lord, if you delight not in man, what lenten° entertainment the players shall receive from you. We coted° them on the way, and 325 hither are they coming to offer you service.

HAMLET   He that plays the king shall be welcome; his majesty shall have tribute of me; the adventurous knight shall use his foil and target;° the lover shall not sigh gratis; the humorous man° shall end his part in 330 peace; the clown shall make those laugh whose lungs are tickle o' th' sere;° and the lady shall say her mind freely, or° the blank verse shall halt° for't. What players are they?

ROSENCRANTZ   Even those you were wont to take 335 such delight in, the tragedians of the city.

HAMLET   How chances it they travel? Their residence, both in reputation and profit, was better both ways.

ROSENCRANTZ   I think their inhibition° comes by the means of the late innovation.° 340

HAMLET   Do they hold the same estimation they did when I was in the city? Are they so followed?

ROSENCRANTZ   No indeed, are they not.

HAMLET   How comes it? Do they grow rusty?

ROSENCRANTZ   Nay, their endeavor keeps in the 345 wonted pace, but there is, sir, an eyrie° of children, little eyases, that cry out on the top of question° and are most tyrannically° clapped for't. These are now the fashion, and so berattle the common stages° (so

---

250 **wards** cells   267–69 **Then . . . shadows** By your logic, beggars (lacking ambition) are substantial, and great men are elongated shadows   269 **fay** faith   280 **too . . . halfpenny** not worth a halfpenny

302 **prevent your discovery** forestall your disclosure   309 **fretted** adorned   313 **express** exact   324 **lenten** meager   325 **coted** overtook   329 **target** shield   330 **humorous man** i.e., eccentric man (among stock characters in dramas were men dominated by a "humor" or odd trait)   332 **tickle . . . sere** on hair trigger ("sere" = part of the gunlock)   333 **or** else; **halt** limp   339 **inhibition** hindrance   340 **innovation** probably an allusion to the companies of child actors that had become popular and were offering serious competition to the adult actors   346 **eyrie** nest   347 **eyases . . . question** unfledged hawks that cry shrilly above others in matters of debate   348 **tyrannically** violently   349 **berattle . . . stages** cry down the public theaters (with the adult acting companies)

they call them) that many wearing rapiers are afraid of 350
goosequills° and dare scarce come thither.

HAMLET  What, are they children? Who maintains
'em? How are they escoted?° Will they pursue the
quality° no longer than they can sing? Will they not
say afterwards, if they should grow themselves to 355
common players (as it is most like, if their means are
no better), their writers do them wrong to make them
exclaim against their own succession?°

ROSENCRANTZ  Faith, there has been much to-do on
both sides, and the nation holds it no sin to tarre° them 360
to controversy. There was, for a while, no money bid
for argument° unless the poet and the player went to
cuffs in the question.

HAMLET  Is't possible?

GUILDENSTERN  O, there has been much throwing 365
about of brains.

HAMLET  Do the boys carry it away?

ROSENCRANTZ  Ay, that they do, my lord—Hercules
and his load° too.

HAMLET  It is not very strange, for my uncle is King of 370
Denmark, and those that would make mouths at him
while my father lived give twenty, forty, fifty, a
hundred ducats apiece for his picture in little. 'Sblood,°
there is something in this more than natural, if philosophy could find it out.                                     375

*A flourish.*

GUILDENSTERN  There are the players.

HAMLET  Gentlemen, you are welcome to Elsinore.
Your hands, come then. Th' appurtenance of welcome
is fashion and ceremony. Let me comply° with you in
this garb,° lest my extent° to the players (which I tell 380
you must show fairly outwards) should more appear
like entertainment than yours. You are welcome. But
my uncle-father and aunt-mother are deceived.

GUILDENSTERN  In what, my dear lord?

HAMLET  I am but mad north-northwest:° when the 385
wind is southerly I know a hawk from a handsaw.°

*Enter* POLONIUS.

POLONIUS  Well be with you, gentlemen.

HAMLET  Hark you, Guildenstern, and you too; at
each ear a hearer. That great baby you see there is not
yet out of his swaddling clouts.                          390

ROSENCRANTZ  Happily° he is the second time come
to them, for they say an old man is twice a child.

HAMLET  I will prophesy he comes to tell me of the
players. Mark it.—You say right, sir; a Monday
morning, 'twas then indeed.                               395

POLONIUS  My lord, I have news to tell you.

HAMLET  My lord, I have news to tell you. When
Roscius° was an actor in Rome—

POLONIUS  The actors are come hither, my lord.

HAMLET  Buzz, buzz.°                                      400

POLONIUS  Upon my honor—

HAMLET  Then came each actor on his ass—

POLONIUS  The best actors in the world, either for
tragedy, comedy, history, pastoral, pastoral-comical,
historical-pastoral, tragical-historical, tragical-comical- 405
historical-pastoral; scene individable,° or poem unlimited.° Seneca cannot be too heavy, nor Plautus°
too light. For the law of writ and the liberty,° these are
the only men.

HAMLET  O Jeptha, judge of Israel,° what a treasure 410
hadst thou!  ← Judges 7-7 (Judges 11, 30-39)

POLONIUS  What a treasure had he, my lord?

HAMLET  Why,
   "One fair daughter, and no more,
      The which he lovèd passing well."                    415

POLONIUS [*Aside.*]  Still on my daughter.

HAMLET  Am I not i' th' right, old Jeptha?

POLONIUS  If you call me Jeptha, my lord, I have a
daughter that I love passing well.

HAMLET  Nay, that follows not.                            420

POLONIUS  What follows then, my lord?

HAMLET  Why,
   "As by lot, God wot,"
and then, you know,
   "It came to pass, as most like it was."                 425
The first row of the pious chanson° will show you
more, for look where my abridgment° comes.

*Enter the* PLAYERS.

You are welcome, masters, welcome, all. I am glad to
see thee well. Welcome, good friends. O, old friend,
why, thy face is valanced° since I saw thee last. Com'st 430
thou to beard me in Denmark? What, my young lady°
and mistress? By'r Lady, your ladyship is nearer to
heaven than when I saw you last by the altitude of a
chopine.° Pray God your voice, like a piece of uncurrent gold, be not cracked within the ring.°— 435
Masters, you are all welcome. We'll e'en to't like
French falconers, fly at anything we see. We'll have a
speech straight. Come, give us a taste of your quality.
Come, a passionate speech.

PLAYER  What speech, my good lord?                        440

HAMLET  I heard thee speak me a speech once, but it
was never acted, or if it was, not above once, for the

---

**398 Roscius** a famous Roman comic actor **400 Buzz,
buzz** an interjection, perhaps indicating that the news is
old  **406 scene individable** plays observing the unities of time,
place, and action  **406–07 poem unlimited** plays not restricted
by the tenets of criticism  **407 Seneca** Roman tragic dramatist;
**Plautus** Roman comic dramatist  **408 For . . . liberty**
perhaps "for sticking to the text and improvising"; perhaps
"for classical plays and for modern loosely written plays"
**410 Jeptha . . . Israel** the title of a ballad on the Hebrew judge
who sacrificed his daughter; see Judges 11  **426 row . . .
chanson** stanza of the scriptural song  **427 abridgment** (1)
i.e., entertainers, who abridge the time (2) interrupters  **430
valanced** fringed (with a beard)  **431 young lady** i.e., boy for
female roles  **434 chopine** thick-soled shoe  **434–35 like . . .
ring** a coin was unfit for legal tender if a crack extended from
the edge through the ring enclosing the monarch's head;
Hamlet, punning on *ring*, refers to the change of voice that the
boy actor will undergo

---

351 goosequills pens (of satirists who ridicule the public
theaters and their audiences)  353 escoted financially supported
354 quality profession of acting  358 succession future  360
tarre incite  362 argument plot of a play  368–69 Hercules
. . . load i.e., the whole world (with a reference to the Globe
Theatre, which had a sign that represented Hercules bearing the
globe)  373 'Sblood by God's blood  379 comply be
courteous  380 garb outward show; extent behavior
385 north-northwest i.e., on one point of the compass only
386 hawk from a handsaw "hawk" can refer not only to a
bird but to a kind of pickax; "handsaw"—a carpenter's tool—
may involve a similar pun on *hernshaw*, a heron)  391 Happily
perhaps

play, I remember, pleased not the million; 'twas caviary to the general,° but it was (as I received it, and others, whose judgments in such matters cried in the top of° 445 mine) an excellent play, well digested in the scenes, set down with as much modesty as cunning.° I remember one said there were no sallets° in the lines to make the matter savory; nor no matter in the phrase that might indict the author of affectation, but called it an honest 450 method, as wholesome as sweet, and by very much more handsome than fine.° One speech in't I chiefly loved. 'Twas Aeneas' tale to Dido, and thereabout of it especially when he speaks of Priam's slaughter. If it live in your memory, begin at this line—let me see, let me 455 see:

"The rugged Pyrrhus, like th' Hyrcanian beast°—"
'Tis not so; it begins with Pyrrhus:

"The rugged Pyrrhus, he whose sable° arms,
Black as his purpose, did the night resemble    460
When he lay couchèd in th' ominous horse,°
Hath now this dread and black complexion smeared
With heraldry more dismal.° Head to foot
Now is he total gules, horridly tricked°
With blood of fathers, mothers, daughters, sons,    465
Baked and impasted° with the parching streets,
That lend a tyrannous and a damnèd light
To their lord's murder. Roasted in wrath and fire,
And thus o'ersizèd° with coagulate gore,
With eyes like carbuncles, the hellish Pyrrhus    470
Old grandsire Priam seeks."

So, proceed you.

POLONIUS    Fore God, my lord, well spoken, with good accent and good discretion.

PLAYER                    "Anon he finds him,    475
Striking too short at Greeks. His antique sword,
Rebellious to his arm, lies where it falls,
Repugnant to command.° Unequal matched,
Pyrrhus at Priam drives, in rage strikes wide,
But with the whiff and wind of his fell sword    480
Th' unnervèd father falls. Then senseless Ilium,°
Seeming to feel this blow, with flaming top
Stoops to his base,° and with a hideous crash
Takes prisoner Pyrrhus' ear. For lo, his sword,
Which was declining on the milky head    485
Of reverend Priam, seemed i' th' air to stick.
So as a painted tyrant° Pyrrhus stood,
And like a neutral to his will and matter°
Did nothing.
But as we often see, against° some storm,    490
A silence in the heavens, the rack° stand still,
The bold winds speechless, and the orb below
As hush as death, anon the dreadful thunder
Doth rend the region, so after Pyrrhus' pause,
A rousèd vengeance sets him new awork,    495

And never did the Cyclops' hammers fall
On Mars's armor, forged for proof eterne,°
With less remorse than Pyrrhus' bleeding sword
Now falls on Priam.
Out, out, thou strumpet Fortune! All you gods,    500
In general synod° take away her power,
Break all the spokes and fellies° from her wheel,
And bowl the round nave° down the hill of heaven,
As low as to the fiends."

POLONIUS    This is too long.    505

HAMLET    It shall to the barber's, with your beard.—
Prithee say on. He's for a jig or a tale of bawdry, or he sleeps. Say on; come to Hecuba.

PLAYER
"But who (ah woe!) had seen the mobled° queen—"

HAMLET    "The mobled queen"?    510

POLONIUS    That's good. "Mobled queen" is good.

PLAYER
"Run barefoot up and down, threat'ning the flames
With bisson rheum;° a clout° upon that head
Where late the diadem stood, and for a robe,
About her lank and all o'erteemèd° loins,    515
A blanket in the alarm of fear caught up—
Who this had seen, with tongue in venom steeped
'Gainst Fortune's state would treason have pronounced.
But if the gods themselves did see her then,
When she saw Pyrrhus make malicious sport    520
In mincing with his sword her husband's limbs,
The instant burst of clamor that she made
(Unless things mortal move them not at all)
Would have much milch° the burning eyes of heaven
And passion in the gods."    525

POLONIUS    Look, whe'r° he has not turned his color, and has tears in's eyes. Prithee no more.

HAMLET    'Tis well. I'll have thee speak out the rest of this soon. Good my lord, will you see the players well bestowed?° Do you hear? Let them be well used, for    530 they are the abstract and brief chronicles of the time. After your death you were better have a bad epitaph than their ill report while you live.

POLONIUS    My lord, I will use them according to their desert.    535

HAMLET    God's bodkin,° man, much better! Use every man after his desert, and who shall scape whipping? Use them after your own honor and dignity. The less they deserve, the more merit is in your bounty. Take them in.    540

POLONIUS    Come, sirs.

HAMLET    Follow him, friends. We'll hear a play tomorrow. [Aside to PLAYER.] Dost thou hear me, old friend? Can you play The Murder of Gonzago?

PLAYER    Ay, my lord.    545

HAMLET    We'll ha't tomorrow night. You could for a need study a speech of some dozen or sixteen lines which I would set down and insert in't, could you not?

PLAYER    Ay, my lord.

HAMLET    Very well. Follow that lord, and look you    550

---

443–44 caviary . . . general i.e., too choice for the multitude 445 in the top of overtopping 447 modesty as cunning restraint as art 448 sallets salads, spicy jests 452 more . . . fine well-proportioned rather than ornamented 457 Hyrcanian beast tiger (Hyrcania was in Asia) 459 sable black 461 ominous horse wooden horse at the siege of Troy 463 dismal ill-omened 464 total . . . tricked all red, horridly adorned 466 impasted encrusted 469 o'ersizèd smeared over 478 Repugnant to command disobedient 481 senseless Ilium insensate Troy 483 Stoops . . . base collapses ("his" = its) 487 painted tyrant tyrant in a picture 488 matter task 490 against just before 491 rack clouds

497 proof eterne eternal endurance 501 synod council 502 fellies rims 503 nave hub 509 mobled muffled 513 bisson rheum blinding tears; clout rag 515 o'erteemèd exhausted with childbearing 524 milch moist (literally "milk-giving") 526 whe'r whether 530 bestowed housed, 536 God's bodkin by God's little body

mock him not. My good friends, I'll leave you till
night. You are welcome to Elsinore.

                *Exeunt* POLONIUS *and* PLAYERS.

ROSENCRANTZ   Good my lord.

         *Exeunt* [ROSENCRANTZ *and* GUILDENSTERN].

HAMLET

Ay, so, God bye to you.—Now I am alone.
O, what a rogue and peasant slave am I!        555
Is it not monstrous that this player here,
But in a fiction, in a dream of passion,°
Could force his soul so to his own conceit°
That from her working all his visage wanned,
Tears in his eyes, distraction in his aspect,     560
A broken voice, and his whole function° suiting
With forms° to his conceit? And all for nothing!
For Hecuba!
What's Hecuba to him, or he to Hecuba,
That he should weep for her? What would he do    565
Had he the motive and the cue for passion
That I have? He would drown the stage with tears
And cleave the general ear with horrid speech,
Make mad the guilty and appall the free,°
Confound the ignorant, and amaze indeed     570
The very faculties of eyes and ears.
Yet I,
A dull and muddy-mettled° rascal, peak
Like John-a-dreams,° unpregnant of° my cause,
And can say nothing. No, not for a king,      575
Upon whose property and most dear life
A damned defeat was made. Am I a coward?
Who calls me villain? Breaks my pate across?
Plucks off my beard and blows it in my face?
Tweaks me by the nose? Gives me the lie i' th' throat   580
As deep as to the lungs? Who does me this?
Ha, 'swounds,° I should take it, for it cannot be
But I am pigeon-livered° and lack gall
To make oppression bitter, or ere this
I should ha' fatted all the region kites°     585
With this slave's offal. Bloody, bawdy villain!
Remorseless, treacherous, lecherous, kindless° villain!
O, vengeance!
Why, what an ass am I! This is most brave,°
That I, the son of a dear father murdered,     590
Prompted to my revenge by heaven and hell,
Must, like a whore, unpack my heart with words
And fall a-cursing like a very drab,°
A stallion!° Fie upon't, foh! About,° my brains.
Hum—                    595
I have heard that guilty creatures sitting at a play
Have by the very cunning of the scene
Been struck so to the soul that presently°
They have proclaimed their malefactions.
For murder, though it have no tongue, will speak    600

With most miraculous organ. I'll have these players
Play something like the murder of my father
Before mine uncle. I'll observe his looks.
I'll tent° him to the quick. If 'a do blench,°
I know my course. The spirit that I have seen     605
May be a devil, and the devil hath power
T' assume a pleasing shape, yea, and perhaps
Out of my weakness and my melancholy,
As he is very potent with such spirits,
Abuses me to damn me. I'll have grounds     610
More relative° than this. The play's the thing
Wherein I'll catch the conscience of the king.    *Exit.*

# [ ACT III ]

## [Scene I. *The castle.*]

*Enter* KING, QUEEN, POLONIUS, OPHELIA, ROSEN-
CRANTZ, GUILDENSTERN, LORDS.

KING

And can you by no drift of conference°
Get from him why he puts on this confusion,
Grating so harshly all his days of quiet
With turbulent and dangerous lunacy?

ROSENCRANTZ

He does confess he feels himself distracted,     5
But from what cause 'a will by no means speak.

GUILDENSTERN

Nor do we find him forward to be sounded,°
But with a crafty madness keeps aloof
When we could bring him on to some confession
Of his true state.

QUEEN             Did he receive you well?     10

ROSENCRANTZ

Most like a gentleman.

GUILDENSTERN

But with much forcing of his disposition.°

ROSENCRANTZ

Niggard of question,° but of our demands
Most free in his reply.

QUEEN            Did you assay° him
To any pastime?                    15

ROSENCRANTZ

Madame, it so fell out that certain players
We o'erraught° on the way; of these we told him,
And there did seem in him a kind of joy
To hear of it. They are here about the court,
And, as I think, they have already order     20
This night to play before him.

POLONIUS                  'Tis most true,
And he beseeched me to entreat your majesties
To hear and see the matter.

KING

With all my heart, and it doth much content me
To hear him so inclined.                 25

---

**557 dream of passion** imaginary emotion   **558 conceit**
imagination   **561 function** action   **562 forms** bodily expressions   **569 appall the free** terrify (make pale?) the guiltless
**573 muddy-mettled** weak-spirited   **573–74 peak Like John-
a-dreams** mope like a dreamer   **574 unpregnant of** un-
quickened by   **582 'swounds** by God's wounds   **583 pigeon-
livered** gentle as a dove   **585 region kites** kites (scavenger
birds) of the sky   **587 kindless** unnatural   **589 brave** fine
**593 drab** prostitute   **594 stallion** male prostitute (perhaps
one should adopt the Folio reading, "scullion" = kitchen
wench); **About** to work   **598 presently** immediately

**604 tent** probe; **blench** flinch   **611 relative** probably
"pertinent," but possibly "able to be related plausibly"
**III.i.1 drift of conference** management of conversation   **7
forward . . . sounded** willing to be questioned   **12 forcing
. . . disposition** effort   **13 Niggard of question** uninclined
to talk   **14 assay** tempt   **17 o'erraught** overtook

Good gentlemen, give him a further edge
And drive his purpose into these delights.

ROSENCRANTZ
We shall, my lord.

      *Exeunt* ROSENCRANTZ *and* GUILDENSTERN.

KING         Sweet Gertrude, leave us too,
For we have closely° sent for Hamlet hither,
That he, as 'twere by accident, may here    30
Affront° Ophelia.
Her father and myself (lawful espials°)
Will so bestow ourselves that, seeing unseen,
We may of their encounter frankly judge
And gather by him, as he is behaved,    35
If 't be th' affliction of his love or no
That thus he suffers for.

QUEEN         I shall obey you.
And for your part, Ophelia, I do wish
That your good beauties be the happy cause
Of Hamlet's wildness. So shall I hope your virtues    40
Will bring him to his wonted way again,
To both your honors.

OPHELIA         Madam, I wish it may.

      [*Exit* QUEEN.]

POLONIUS
Ophelia, walk you here.—Gracious, so please you,
We will bestow ourselves. [*To* OPHELIA.] Read on
  this book,
That show of such an exercise may color°    45
Your loneliness. We are oft to blame in this,
'Tis too much proved, that with devotion's visage
And pious action we do sugar o'er
The devil himself.

KING [*Aside*.]      O, 'tis too true.
How smart a lash that speech doth give my conscience!    50
The harlot's cheek, beautied with plast'ring art,
Is not more ugly to the thing that helps it
Than is my deed to my most painted word.
O heavy burden!

POLONIUS
I hear him coming. Let's withdraw, my lord.    55

      [*Exeunt* KING *and* POLONIUS.]

*Enter* HAMLET.

HAMLET
To be, or not to be: that is the question:
Whether 'tis nobler in the mind to suffer
The slings and arrows of outrageous fortune,
Or to take arms against a sea of troubles,
And by opposing end them. To die, to sleep—    60
No more—and by a sleep to say we end
The heartache, and the thousand natural shocks
That flesh is heir to! 'Tis a consummation
Devoutly to be wished. To die, to sleep—
To sleep—perchance to dream: ay, there's the rub,°    65
For in that sleep of death what dreams may come
When we have shuffled off this mortal coil,°
Must give us pause. There's the respect°

That makes calamity of so long life:°
For who would bear the whips and scorns of time,    70
Th' oppressor's wrong, the proud man's contumely,
The pangs of despised love, the law's delay,
The insolence of office, and the spurns
That patient merit of th' unworthy takes,
When he himself might his quietus° make    75
With a bare bodkin?° Who would fardels° bear,
To grunt and sweat under a weary life,
But that the dread of something after death,
The undiscovered country, from whose bourn°
No traveler returns, puzzles the will,    80
And makes us rather bear those ills we have,
Than fly to others that we know not of?
Thus conscience° does make cowards of us all,
And thus the native hue of resolution
Is sicklied o'er with the pale cast° of thought,    85
And enterprises of great pitch° and moment,
With this regard° their currents turn awry,
And lose the name of action.—Soft you now,
The fair Ophelia!—Nymph, in thy orisons°
Be all my sins remembered.

OPHELIA         Good my lord,    90
How does your honor for this many a day?

HAMLET
I humbly thank you; well, well, well.

OPHELIA
My lord, I have remembrances of yours
That I have longèd long to redeliver.
I pray you now, receive them.

HAMLET         No, not I,    95
I never gave you aught.

OPHELIA
My honored lord, you know right well you did,
And with them words of so sweet breath composed
As made these things more rich. Their perfume lost,
Take these again, for to the noble mind    100
Rich gifts wax poor when givers prove unkind.
There, my lord.

HAMLET  Ha, ha! Are you honest?°

OPHELIA  My lord?

HAMLET  Are you fair?    105

OPHELIA  What means your lordship?

HAMLET  That if you be honest and fair, your honesty
should admit no discourse to your beauty.°

OPHELIA  Could beauty, my lord, have better commerce than with honesty?    110

HAMLET  Ay, truly; for the power of beauty will
sooner transform honesty from what it is to a bawd°
than the force of honesty can translate beauty into his
likeness. This was sometime a paradox, but now the
time gives it proof. I did love you once.    115

OPHELIA  Indeed, my lord, you made me believe so.

HAMLET  You should not have believed me, for virtue

---

29 **closely** secretly  31 **Affront** meet face to face  32 **espials** spies  45 **exercise may color** act of devotion may give a plausible hue to (the book is one of devotion)  65 **rub** impediment (obstruction to a bowler's ball)  67 **coil** (1) turmoil (2) a ring of rope (here the flesh encircling the soul)  68 **respect** consideration

69 **makes . . . life** (1) makes calamity so long-lived (2) makes living so long a calamity  75 **quietus** full discharge (a legal term)  76 **bodkin** dagger; **fardels** burdens  79 **bourn** region  83 **conscience** self-consciousness, introspection  85 **cast** color  86 **pitch** height (a term from falconry)  87 **regard** consideration  89 **orisons** prayers  103 **Are you honest** (1) Are you modest? (2) Are you chaste (3) Have you integrity?  **107-08 your honesty . . . beauty** your modesty should permit no approach to your beauty  112 **bawd** procurer

cannot so inoculate° our old stock but we shall relish
of it.° I loved you not.

OPHELIA    I was the more deceived.                               120

HAMLET    Get thee to a nunnery. Why wouldst thou
be a breeder of sinners? I am myself indifferent honest,°
but yet I could accuse me of such things that it were
better my mother had not borne me: I am very proud,
revengeful, ambitious, with more offenses at my beck°      125
than I have thoughts to put them in, imagination to
give them shape, or time to act them in. What should
such fellows as I do crawling between earth and
heaven? We are arrant knaves all; believe none of us.
Go thy ways to a nunnery. Where's your father?            130

OPHELIA    At home, my lord.

HAMLET    Let the doors be shut upon him, that he may
play the fool nowhere but in's own house. Farewell.

OPHELIA    O help him, you sweet heavens!

HAMLET    If thou dost marry, I'll give thee this plague   135
for thy dowry: be thou as chaste as ice, as pure as snow,
thou shalt not escape calumny. Get thee to a nunnery.
Go, farewell. Or if thou wilt needs marry, marry a
fool, for wise men know well enough what monsters°
you make of them. To a nunnery, go, and quickly too.      140
Farewell.

OPHELIA    Heavenly powers, restore him!

HAMLET    I have heard of your paintings, well enough.
God hath given you one face, and you make yourselves
another. You jig and amble, and you lisp; you nick-        145
name God's creatures and make your wantonness your
ignorance.° Go to, I'll no more on't; it hath made me
mad. I say we will have no moe° marriage. Those that
are married already—all but one—shall live. The rest
shall keep as they are. To a nunnery, go.        Exit.    150

OPHELIA
O what a noble mind is here o'erthrown!
The courtier's, soldier's, scholar's, eye, tongue, sword,
Th' expectancy and rose° of the fair state,
The glass of fashion, and the mold of form,°
Th' observed of all observers, quite, quite down!         155
And I, of ladies most deject and wretched,
That sucked the honey of his musicked vows,
Now see that noble and most sovereign reason
Like sweet bells jangled, out of time and harsh,
That unmatched form and feature of blown° youth          160
Blasted with ecstasy.° O, woe is me
T' have seen what I have seen, see what I see!

*Enter* KING *and* POLONIUS.

KING
Love? His affections° do not that way tend,
Nor what he spake, though it lacked form a little,
Was not like madness. There's something in his soul      165
O'er which his melancholy sits on brood,
And I do doubt° the hatch and the disclose
Will be some danger; which for to prevent,

I have in quick determination
Thus set it down: he shall with speed to England          170
For the demand of our neglected tribute.
Haply the seas, and countries different,
With variable objects, shall expel
This something-settled° matter in his heart,
Whereon his brains still beating puts him thus             175
From fashion of himself. What think you on't?

POLONIUS
It shall do well. But yet do I believe
The origin and commencement of his grief
Sprung from neglected love. How now, Ophelia?
You need not tell us what Lord Hamlet said;               180
We heard it all. My lord, do as you please,
But if you hold it fit, after the play,
Let his queen mother all alone entreat him
To show his grief. Let her be round° with him,
And I'll be placed, so please you, in the ear             185
Of all their conference. If she find him not,°
To England send him, or confine him where
Your wisdom best shall think.

KING                                It shall be so.
Madness in great ones must not unwatched go.

                                                  *Exeunt.*


[*Scene II. The castle.*]

*Enter* HAMLET *and three of the* PLAYERS.

HAMLET    Speak the speech, I pray you, as I pronounced
it to you, trippingly on the tongue. But if you mouth
it, as many of our players do, I had as lief the town
crier spoke my lines. Nor do not saw the air too much
with your hand, thus, but use all gently, for in the very  5
torrent, tempest, and (as I may say) whirlwind of your
passion, you must acquire and beget a temperance that
may give it smoothness. O, it offends me to the soul to
hear a robustious periwig-pated° fellow tear a passion
to tatters, to very rags, to split the ears of the ground-  10
lings,° who for the most part are capable of° nothing
but inexplicable dumb shows° and noise. I would have
such a fellow whipped for o'erdoing Termagant. It
out-herods Herod.° Pray you avoid it.

PLAYER    I warrant your honor.                            15

HAMLET    Be not too tame neither, but let your own
discretion be your tutor. Suit the action to the word,
the word to the action, with this special observance,
that you o'erstep not the modesty of nature. For anything so o'erdone is from° the purpose of playing,         20
whose end, both at the first and now, was and is, to
hold, as 'twere, the mirror up to nature; to show virtue
her own feature, scorn her own image, and the very
age and body of the time his form and pressure.° Now,
this overdone, or come tardy off, though it makes the      25

---

118 **inoculate** graft  118–19 **relish of it** smack of it (our old
sinful nature)  122 **indifferent honest** moderately virtuous
125 **beck** call  139 **monsters** horned beasts, cuckolds  146–47
**make . . . ignorance** excuse your wanton speech by pretending ignorance  148 **moe** more  153 **expectancy and rose**
i.e., fair hope  154 **The glass . . . form** the mirror of fashion,
and the pattern of excellent behavior  160 **blown** blooming
161 **ecstasy** madness  163 **affections** inclinations  167 **doubt**
fear

174 **something-settled** somewhat settled  184 **round** blunt
186 **find him not** does not find him out
III.ii.9 **robustious periwig-pated** boisterous wig-headed
10–11 **groundlings** those who stood in the pit of the theater
(the poorest and presumably most ignorant of the audience)  11
**are capable of** are able to understand  12 **dumb shows** it had
been the fashion for actors to preface plays or parts of plays with
silent mime  13–14 **Termagant . . . Herod** boisterous characters in the old mystery plays  20 **from** contrary to  24
**pressure** image, impress

unskillful laugh, cannot but make the judicious grieve,
the censure of the which one must in your allowance
o'erweigh a whole theater of others. O, there be
players that I have seen play, and heard others praise,
and that highly (not to speak it profanely), that neither 30
having th' accent of Christians, nor the gait of Christian, pagan, nor man, have so strutted and bellowed
that I have thought some of Nature's journeymen°
had made men, and not made them well, they imitated
humanity so abominably.                                35
PLAYER   I hope we have reformed that indifferently°
with us, sir.
HAMLET   O, reform it altogether! And let those that
play your clowns speak no more than is set down for
them, for there be of them that will themselves laugh, 40
to set on some quantity of barren spectators to laugh
too, though in the meantime some necessary question
of the play be then to be considered. That's villainous
and shows a most pitiful ambition in the fool that uses
it. Go make you ready.            Exit PLAYERS. 45

*Enter* POLONIUS, GUILDENSTERN, *and*
ROSENCRANTZ.

How now, my lord? Will the king hear this piece of
work?
POLONIUS   And the queen too, and that presently.
HAMLET   Bid the players make haste.
                              *Exit* POLONIUS.
Will you two help to hasten them?            50
ROSENCRANTZ   Ay, my lord.        *Exeunt they two.*
HAMLET   What, ho, Horatio!

*Enter* HORATIO.

HORATIO   Here, sweet lord, at your service.
HAMLET
Horatio, thou art e'en as just a man
As e'er my conversation coped withal.°        55
HORATIO
O, my dear lord—
HAMLET            Nay, do not think I flatter.
For what advancement° may I hope from thee,
That no revenue hast but thy good spirits
To feed and clothe thee? Why should the poor be
   flattered?
No, let the candied° tongue lick absurd pomp,    60
And crook the pregnant° hinges of the knee
Where thrift° may follow fawning. Dost thou hear?
Since my dear soul was mistress of her choice
And could of men distinguish her election,
S' hath sealed thee° for herself, for thou hast been   65
As one, in suff'ring all, that suffers nothing,
A man that Fortune's buffets and rewards
Hast ta'en with equal thanks; and blest are those
Whose blood° and judgment are so well commeddled°
That they are not a pipe for Fortune's finger     70
To sound what stop she please. Give me that man
That is not passion's slave, and I will wear him

In my heart's core, ay, in my heart of heart,
As I do thee. Something too much of this—
There is a play tonight before the king.        75
One scene of it comes near the circumstance
Which I have told thee, of my father's death.
I prithee, when thou see'st that act afoot,
Even with the very comment° of thy soul
Observe my uncle. If his occulted° guilt        80
Do not itself unkennel in one speech,
It is a damnèd ghost that we have seen,
And my imaginations are as foul
As Vulcan's stithy.° Give him heedful note,
For I mine eyes will rivet to his face,          85
And after we will both our judgments join
In censure of his seeming.°
HORATIO                Well, my lord.
If 'a steal aught the whilst this play is playing,
And scape detecting, I will pay the theft.

*Enter trumpets and kettledrums,* KING, QUEEN, POLO-
NIUS, OPHELIA, ROSENCRANTZ, GUILDENSTERN,
*and other* LORDS *attendant, with his* GUARD *carrying
torches. Danish march. Sound a flourish.*

HAMLET   They are coming to the play: I must be idle;° 90
Get you a place.
KING   How fares our cousin Hamlet?
HAMLET   Excellent, i' faith, of the chameleon's dish;°
I eat the air, promise-crammed; you cannot feed
capons so.                                      95
KING   I have nothing with this answer, Hamlet; these
words are not mine.
HAMLET   No, nor mine now. [*To* POLONIUS.] My
lord, you played once i' th' university, you say?
POLONIUS   That did I, my lord, and was accounted a 100
good actor.
HAMLET   What did you enact?
POLONIUS   I did enact Julius Caesar. I was killed i' th'
Capitol; Brutus killed me.
HAMLET   It was a brute part of him to kill so capital a 105
calf there. Be the players ready?
ROSENCRANTZ   Ay, my lord. They stay upon your
patience.
QUEEN   Come hither, my dear Hamlet, sit by me.
HAMLET   No, good mother. Here's metal more       110
attractive.°
POLONIUS [*To the* KING.]   O ho! Do you mark that?
HAMLET   Lady, shall I lie in your lap?

[*He lies at Ophelia's feet.*]

OPHELIA   No, my lord.
HAMLET   I mean, my head upon your lap?          115
OPHELIA   Ay, my lord.
HAMLET   Do you think I meant country matters?°
OPHELIA   I think nothing, my lord.
HAMLET   That's a fair thought to lie between maids'
legs.                                           120
OPHELIA   What is, my lord?

---

**33 journeymen** workers not yet masters of their craft   **36
indifferently** tolerably   **55 coped withal** met with   **57
advancement** promotion   **60 candied** sugared, flattering   **61
pregnant** (1) pliant (2) full of promise of good fortune   **62
thrift** profit   **65 S' . . . thee** she (the soul) has set a mark
on you   **69 blood** passion; **commeddled** blended

**79 very comment** deepest wisdom   **80 occulted** hidden
**84 stithy** forge, smithy   **87 censure . . . seeming** judgment
on his looks   **90 be idle** play the fool   **93 the chameleon's
dish** air (on which chameleons were thought to live)   **111
attractive** magnetic   **117 country matters** rustic doings
(with a pun on the vulgar word for the pudendum)

HAMLET Nothing.

OPHELIA You are merry, my lord.

HAMLET Who, I?

OPHELIA Ay, my lord. 125

HAMLET O God, your only jig-maker!° What should a man do but be merry? For look you how cheerfully my mother looks, and my father died within's two hours.

OPHELIA Nay, 'tis twice two months, my lord. 130

HAMLET So long? Nay then, let the devil wear black, for I'll have a suit of sables.° O heavens! Die two months ago, and not forgotten yet? Then there's hope a great man's memory may outlive his life half a year. But, by'r Lady, 'a must build churches then, or else 135 shall 'a suffer not thinking on, with the hobbyhorse,° whose epitaph is "For O, for O, the hobbyhorse is forgot!"

*The trumpets sound. Dumb show follows:*

*Enter a* KING *and a* QUEEN *very lovingly, the* QUEEN *embracing him, and he her. She kneels; and makes show of protestation unto him. He takes her up, and declines his head upon her neck. He lies him down upon a bank of flowers. She, seeing him asleep, leaves him. Anon come in another man: takes off his crown, kisses it, pours poison in the sleeper's ears, and leaves him. The* QUEEN *returns, finds the* KING *dead, makes passionate action. The* POISONER, *with some three or four, come in again, seem to condole with her. The dead body is carried away. The* POISONER *woos the* QUEEN *with gifts; she seems harsh awhile, but in the end accepts love.* *Exeunt.*

OPHELIA What means this, my lord?

HAMLET Marry, this is miching mallecho;° it means 140 mischief.

OPHELIA Belike this show imports the argument° of the play.

*Enter* PROLOGUE.

HAMLET We shall know by this fellow. The players cannot keep counsel; they'll tell all. 145

OPHELIA Will 'a tell us what this show meant?

HAMLET Ay, or any show that you will show him. Be not you ashamed to show, he'll not shame to tell you what it means.

OPHELIA You are naught,° you are naught; I'll mark 150 the play.

PROLOGUE

  For us, and for our tragedy,

  Here stooping to your clemency,

  We beg your hearing patiently. [*Exit.*]

HAMLET Is this a prologue, or the posy of a ring?° 155

OPHELIA 'Tis brief, my lord.

HAMLET As woman's love.

*Enter* [*two* PLAYERS *as*] *king and queen.*

PLAYER KING

Full thirty times hath Phoebus' cart° gone round

Neptune's salt wash° and Tellus'° orbèd ground,

And thirty dozen moons with borrowed sheen 160

About the world have times twelve thirties been,

Since love our hearts, and Hymen did our hands,

Unite commutual in most sacred bands.

PLAYER QUEEN

So many journeys may the sun and moon

Make us again count o'er ere love be done! 165

But woe is me, you are so sick of late,

So far from cheer and from your former state,

That I distrust° you. Yet, though I distrust,

Discomfort you, my lord, it nothing must.

For women fear too much, even as they love, 170

And women's fear and love hold quantity,

In neither aught, or in extremity.°

Now what my love is, proof° hath made you know,

And as my love is sized, my fear is so.

Where love is great, the littlest doubts are fear; 175

Where little fears grow great, great love grows there.

PLAYER KING

Faith, I must leave thee, love, and shortly too;

My operant° powers their functions leave to do:

And thou shalt live in this fair world behind,

Honored, beloved, and haply one as kind 180

For husband shalt thou—

PLAYER QUEEN    O, confound the rest!

Such love must needs be treason in my breast.

In second husband let me be accurst!

None wed the second but who killed the first.

HAMLET [*Aside.*] That's wormwood.° 185

PLAYER QUEEN

The instances° that second marriage move°

Are base respects of thrift,° but none of love.

A second time I kill my husband dead

When second husband kisses me in bed.

PLAYER KING

I do believe you think what now you speak, 190

But what we do determine oft we break.

Purpose is but the slave to memory,

Of violent birth, but poor validity,°

Which now like fruit unripe sticks on the tree,

But fall unshaken when they mellow be. 195

Most necessary 'tis that we forget

To pay ourselves what to ourselves is debt.

What to ourselves in passion we propose,

The passion ending, doth the purpose lose.

The violence of either grief or joy 200

Their own enactures° with themselves destroy:

Where joy most revels, grief doth most lament;

Grief joys, joy grieves, on slender accident.

This world is not for aye, nor 'tis not strange

That even our loves should with our fortunes change, 205

For 'tis a question left us yet to prove,

Whether love lead fortune, or else fortune love.

The great man down, you mark his favorite flies;

---

126 **jig-maker** composer of songs and dances (often a fool, who performed them) 132 **sables** pun on the meanings "black" and "luxurious furs" 136 **hobbyhorse** mock horse worn by a performer in the morris dance 140 **miching mallecho** sneaking mischief 142 **argument** plot 150 **naught** wicked, improper 155 **posy . . . ring** motto inscribed in a ring 158 **Phoebus' cart** the sun's chariot

159 **Neptune's salt wash** the sea; **Tellus** Roman goddess of the earth 168 **distrust** am anxious about 171–72 **And . . . extremity** perhaps the idea is that women's anxiety is great or little in proportion to their love; the previous line, unrhymed, may be a false start that Shakespeare neglected to delete 173 **proof** experience 178 **operant** active 185 **wormwood** a bitter herb 186 **instances** motives; **move** induce 187 **respects of thrift** considerations of profit 193 **validity** strength 201 **enactures** acts

The poor advanced makes friends of enemies;
And hitherto doth love on fortune tend,                210
For who not needs shall never lack a friend;
And who in want a hollow friend doth try,
Directly seasons him° his enemy.
But, orderly to end where I begun,
Our wills and fates do so contrary run          215
That our devices still are overthrown;
Our thoughts are ours, their ends none of our own.
So think thou wilt no second husband wed,
But die thy thoughts when thy first lord is dead.

PLAYER QUEEN
Nor earth to me give food, nor heaven light,       220
Sport and repose lock from me day and night,
To desperation turn my trust and hope,
An anchor's° cheer in prison be my scope,
Each opposite that blanks° the face of joy
Meet what I would have well, and it destroy:       225
Both here and hence pursue me lasting strife,
If, once a widow, ever I be wife!

HAMLET   If she should break it now!

PLAYER KING
'Tis deeply sworn. Sweet, leave me here awhile;
My spirits grow dull, and fain I would beguile    230
The tedious day with sleep.

PLAYER QUEEN                      Sleep rock thy brain,

[*He*] *sleeps.*

And never come mischance between us twain!   *Exit.*

HAMLET   Madam, how like you this play?
QUEEN   The lady doth protest too much, methinks.
HAMLET   O, but she'll keep her word.        235
KING   Have you heard the argument?° Is there no
offense in't?
HAMLET   No, no, they do but jest, poison in jest; no
offense i' th' world.
KING   What do you call the play?            240
HAMLET   *The Mousetrap.* Marry, how? Tropically.°
The play is the image of a murder done in Vienna:
Gonzago is the duke's name; his wife, Baptista. You
shall see anon. 'Tis a knavish piece of work, but what
of that? Your majesty, and we that have free° souls, it  245
touches us not. Let the galled jade winch;° our withers
are unwrung.

*Enter* LUCIANUS.

This is one Lucianus, nephew to the king.
OPHELIA   You are as good as a chorus, my lord.
HAMLET   I could interpret° between you and your     250
love, if I could see the puppets dallying.
OPHELIA   You are keen ° my lord, you are keen.
HAMLET   It would cost you a groaning to take off
mine edge.
OPHELIA   Still better, and worse.           255
HAMLET   So you mistake° your husbands.—Begin,
murderer. Leave thy damnable faces and begin. Come,
the croaking raven doth bellow for revenge.

LUCIANUS
Thoughts black, hands apt, drugs fit, and time agreeing,
Confederate season,° else no creature seeing,        260
Thou mixture rank, of midnight weeds collected,
With Hecate's ban° thrice blasted, thrice infected,
Thy natural magic and dire property°
On wholesome life usurps immediately.

*Pours the poison in his ears.*

HAMLET   'A poisons him i' th' garden for his estate.   265
His name's Gonzago. The story is extant, and written
in very choice Italian. You shall see anon how the
murderer gets the love of Gonzago's wife.
OPHELIA   The king rises.
HAMLET   What, frighted with false fire?°        270
QUEEN   How fares my lord?
POLONIUS   Give o'er the play.
KING   Give me some light. Away!
POLONIUS   Lights, lights, lights!
                  *Exeunt all but* HAMLET *and* HORATIO.
HAMLET
Why, let the strucken deer go weep,               275
   The hart ungallèd play:
For some must watch, while some must sleep;
   Thus runs the world away.
Would not this, sir, and a forest of feathers°—if the
rest of my fortunes turn Turk° with me—with two  280
Provincial roses° on my razed° shoes, get me a fellow-
ship in a cry° of players?
HORATIO   Half a share.
HAMLET   A whole one, I.
For thou dost know, O Damon dear,             285
   This realm dismantled was
Of Jove himself; and now reigns here
   A very, very—pajock.°
HORATIO   You might have rhymed.°
HAMLET   O good Horatio, I'll take the ghost's word   290
for a thousand pound. Didst perceive?
HORATIO   Very well, my lord.
HAMLET   Upon the talk of poisoning?
HORATIO   I did very well note him.
HAMLET   Ah ha! Come, some music! Come, the   295
recorders!°
   For if the king like not the comedy,
      Why then, belike he likes it not, perdy.°
Come, some music!

*Enter* ROSENCRANTZ *and* GUILDENSTERN.

GUILDENSTERN   Good my lord, vouchsafe me a word   300
with you.
HAMLET   Sir, a whole history.
GUILDENSTERN   The king, sir—
HAMLET   Ay, sir, what of him?
GUILDENSTERN   Is in his retirement marvelous dis-   305
temp'red.

213 **seasons him** ripens him into   223 **anchor's** anchorite's,
hermit's   224 **opposite that blanks** adverse thing that blanches
236 **argument** plot   241 **Tropically** figuratively (with a pun
on *trap*)   245 **free** innocent   246 **galled jade winch** chafed
horse wince   250 **interpret** like a showman explaining the
action of puppets   252 **keen** (1) sharp (2) sexually aroused
256 **mistake** err in taking

260 **Confederate season** the opportunity allied with me   262
**Hecate's ban** the curse of the goddess of sorcery   263 **property**
nature   270 **false fire** blank discharge of firearms   279 **feathers**
plumes were sometimes part of a costume   280 **turn Turk**
go bad, treat me badly   281 **Provincial roses** rosettes like
the roses of Provence (?); **razed** ornamented with slashes   282
**cry** pack, company   288 **pajock** peacock   289 **You . . .
rhymed** i.e., rhymed "was" with "ass"   296 **recorders**
flutelike instruments   298 **perdy** by God (French *par dieu*)

HAMLET  With drink, sir?

GUILDENSTERN  No, my lord, with choler.°

HAMLET  Your wisdom should show itself more richer
to signify this to the doctor, for for me to put him to 310
his purgation would perhaps plunge him into more
choler.

GUILDENSTERN  Good my lord, put your discourse
into some frame,° and start not so wildly from my
affair. 315

HAMLET  I am tame, sir; pronounce.

GUILDENSTERN  The queen, your mother, in most
great affliction of spirit hath sent me to you.

HAMLET  You are welcome.

GUILDENSTERN  Nay, good my lord, this courtesy is 320
not of the right breed. If it shall please you to make me
a wholesome answer, I will do your mother's commandment: if not, your pardon and my return shall
be the end of my business.

HAMLET  Sir, I cannot. 325

ROSENCRANTZ  What, my lord?

HAMLET  Make you a wholesome° answer; my wit's
diseased. But, sir, such answer as I can make you shall
command, or rather, as you say, my mother. Therefore no more, but to the matter. My mother, you say— 330

ROSENCRANTZ  Then thus she says: your behavior
hath struck her into amazement and admiration.°

HAMLET  O wonderful son, that can so stonish a
mother! But is there no sequel at the heels of this
mother's admiration? Impart. 335

ROSENCRANTZ  She desires to speak with you in her
closet° ere you go to bed.

HAMLET  We shall obey, were she ten times our
mother. Have you any further trade with us?

ROSENCRANTZ  My lord, you once did love me. 340

HAMLET  And do still, by these pickers and stealers.°

ROSENCRANTZ  Good my lord, what is your cause of
distemper? You do surely bar the door upon your
own liberty, if you deny your griefs to your friend.

HAMLET  Sir, I lack advancement.° 345

ROSENCRANTZ  How can that be, when you have the
voice of the king himself for your succession in
Denmark?

*Enter the PLAYERS with recorders.*

HAMLET  Ay, sir, but "while the grass grows"—the
proverb° is something musty. O, the recorders. Let 350
me see one. To withdraw° with you—why do you go
about to recover the wind° of me as if you would
drive me into a toil?°

GUILDENSTERN  O my lord, if my duty be too bold,
my love is too unmannerly.° 355

HAMLET  I do not well understand that. Will you play
upon this pipe?

GUILDENSTERN  My lord, I cannot.

HAMLET  I pray you.

GUILDENSTERN  Believe me, I cannot. 360

HAMLET  I pray you.

GUILDENSTERN  Believe me, I cannot.

HAMLET  I do beseech you.

GUILDENSTERN  I know no touch of it, my lord.

HAMLET  It is as easy as lying. Govern these ventages° 365
with your fingers and thumb, give it breath with your
mouth, and it will discourse most eloquent music.
Look you, these are the stops.

GUILDENSTERN  But these cannot I command to any
utt'rance of harmony; I have not the skill. 370

HAMLET  Why, look you now, how unworthy a thing
you make of me! You would play upon me; you
would seem to know my stops; you would pluck out
the heart of my mystery; you would sound me from
my lowest note to the top of my compass;° and there 375
is much music, excellent voice, in this little organ,° yet
cannot you make it speak. 'Sblood, do you think I am
easier to be played on than a pipe? Call me what
instrument you will, though you can fret° me, you
cannot play upon me. 380

*Enter POLONIUS.*

God bless you, sir!

POLONIUS  My lord, the queen would speak with
you, and presently.

HAMLET  Do you see yonder cloud that's almost in
shape of a camel? 385

POLONIUS  By th' mass and 'tis, like a camel indeed.

HAMLET  Methinks it is like a weasel.

POLONIUS  It is backed like a weasel.

HAMLET  Or like a whale.

POLONIUS  Very like a whale. 390

HAMLET  Then I will come to my mother by and by.
[*Aside.*] They fool me to the top of my bent.°—I will
come by and by.°

POLONIUS  I will say so.                            *Exit.*

HAMLET  "By and by" is easily said. Leave me, friends. 395
                    [*Exeunt all but HAMLET.*]
'Tis now the very witching time of night,
When churchyards yawn, and hell itself breathes out
Contagion to this world. Now could I drink hot blood
And do such bitter business as the day
Would quake to look on. Soft, now to my mother. 400
O heart, lose not thy nature; let not ever
The soul of Nero° enter this firm bosom.
Let me be cruel, not unnatural;
I will speak daggers to her, but use none.
My tongue and soul in this be hypocrites: 405
How in my words somever she be shent,°
To give them seals° never, my soul, consent!  *Exit.*

---

**308 choler** anger (but Hamlet pretends to take the word in its sense of "biliousness")  **314 frame** order, control  **327 wholesome** sane  **332 admiration** wonder  **337 closet** private room  **341 pickers and stealers** i.e., hands (with reference to the prayer, "Keep my hands from picking and stealing")  **345 advancement** promotion  **350 proverb** "While the grass groweth, the horse starveth"  **351 withdraw** speak in private  **352 recover the wind** get on the windward side (as in hunting)  **353 toil** snare  **354-55 if . . . unmannerly** if these questions seem rude, it is because my love for you leads me beyond good manners

**365 ventages** vents, stops on a recorder  **375 compass** range of voice  **376 organ** the recorder  **379 fret** vex (with a pun alluding to the frets, or ridges, that guide the fingering on some instruments)  **392 They . . . bent** They compel me to play the fool to the limit of my capacity  **393 by and by** very soon  **402 Nero** Roman emperor who had his mother murdered  **406 shent** rebuked  **407 give them seals** confirm them with deeds

[Scene III. *The castle*.]

*Enter* KING, ROSENCRANTZ, *and* GUILDENSTERN.

KING
I like him not, nor stands it safe with us
To let his madness range. Therefore prepare you.
I your commission will forthwith dispatch,
And he to England shall along with you.
The terms° of our estate may not endure          5
Hazard so near's° as doth hourly grow
Out of his brows.

GUILDENSTERN   We will ourselves provide.
Most holy and religious fear it is
To keep those many many bodies safe
That live and feed upon your majesty.           10

ROSENCRANTZ
The single and peculiar° life is bound
With all the strength and armor of the mind
To keep itself from noyance,° but much more
That spirit upon whose weal depends and rests
The lives of many. The cess of majesty°         15
Dies not alone, but like a gulf° doth draw
What's near it with it; or it is a massy wheel
Fixed on the summit of the highest mount,
To whose huge spokes ten thousand lesser things
Are mortised and adjoined, which when it falls, 20
Each small annexment, petty consequence,
Attends° the boist'rous ruin. Never alone
Did the king sigh, but with a general groan.

KING
Arm° you, I pray you, to this speedy voyage,
For we will fetters put about this fear,          25
Which now goes too free-footed.

ROSENCRANTZ               We will haste us.
*Exeunt gentlemen* [ROSENCRANTZ *and*
GUILDENSTERN].

*Enter* POLONIUS.

POLONIUS
My lord, he's going to his mother's closet.
Behind the arras I'll convey myself
To hear the process.° I'll warrant she'll tax him home,°
And, as you said, and wisely was it said,         30
'Tis meet that some more audience than a mother,
Since nature makes them partial, should o'erhear
The speech of vantage.° Fare you well, my liege.
I'll call upon you ere you go to bed
And tell you what I know.

KING                    Thanks, dear my lord.   35
*Exit* [POLONIUS].
O, my offense is rank, it smells to heaven;
It hath the primal eldest curse° upon't,
A brother's murder. Pray can I not,
Though inclination be as sharp as will.
My stronger guilt defeats my strong intent,       40
And like a man to double business bound

I stand in pause where I shall first begin,
And both neglect. What if this cursèd hand
Were thicker than itself with brother's blood,
Is there not rain enough in the sweet heavens      45
To wash it white as snow? Whereto serves mercy
But to confront° the visage of offense?
And what's in prayer but this twofold force,
To be forestallèd ere we come to fall,
Or pardoned being down? Then I'll look up.         50
My fault is past. But, O, what form of prayer
Can serve my turn? "Forgive me my foul murder"?
That cannot be, since I am still possessed
Of those effects° for which I did the murder,
My crown, mine own ambition, and my queen.         55
May one be pardoned and retain th' offense?
In the corrupted currents of this world
Offense's gilded hand may shove by justice,
And oft 'tis seen the wicked prize itself
Buys out the law. But 'tis not so above.           60
There is no shuffling;° there the action lies
In his true nature, and we ourselves compelled,
Even to the teeth and forehead of our faults,
To give in evidence. What then? What rests?°
Try what repentance can. What can it not?          65
Yet what can it when one cannot repent?
O wretched state! O bosom black as death!
O limèd° soul, that struggling to be free
Art more engaged!° Help, angels! Make assay.°
Bow, stubborn knees, and, heart with strings of steel, 70
Be soft as sinews of the newborn babe.
All may be well.

[*He kneels.*]

*Enter* HAMLET.

HAMLET
Now might I do it pat, now 'a is a-praying,
And now I'll do't. And so 'a goes to heaven,
And so am I revenged. That would be scanned.°      75
A villain kills my father, and for that
I, his sole son, do this same villain send
To heaven.
Why, this is hire and salary, not revenge.
'A took my father grossly, full of bread,°         80
With all his crimes broad blown,° as flush° as May;
And how his audit° stands, who knows save heaven?
But in our circumstance and course of thought,
'Tis heavy with him; and am I then revenged,
To take him in the purging of his soul,            85
When he is fit and seasoned for his passage?
No.
Up, sword, and know thou a more horrid hent.°
When he is drunk asleep, or in his rage,
Or in th' incestuous pleasure of his bed,          90
At game a-swearing, or about some act
That has no relish° of salvation in't—
Then trip him, that his heels may kick at heaven,

---

III.iii.5 **terms** conditions   6 **near's** near us   11 **peculiar** individual, private   13 **noyance** injury   15 **cess of majesty** cessation (death) of a king   16 **gulf** whirlpool   22 **Attends** waits on, participates in   24 **Arm** prepare   29 **process** proceedings; **tax him home** censure him sharply   33 **of vantage** from an advantageous place   37 **primal eldest curse** curse of Cain, who killed Abel

47 **confront** oppose   54 **effects** things gained   61 **shuffling** trickery   64 **rests** remains   68 **limèd** caught (as with bird lime, a sticky substance spread on boughs to snare birds)   69 **engaged** ensnared; **assay** an attempt   75 **would be scanned** ought to be looked into   80 **bread** i.e., wordly gratification   81 **crimes broad blown** sins in full bloom; **flush** vigorous   82 **audit** account   88 **hent** grasp (here, occasion for seizing)   92 **relish** flavor

And that his soul may be as damned and black
As hell, whereto it goes. My mother stays.     95
This physic° but prolongs thy sickly days.     *Exit.*
KING [*Rises.*]
My words fly up, my thoughts remain below.
Words without thoughts never to heaven go.     *Exit.*

[Scene IV. *The queen's closet.*]

*Enter* [QUEEN] *Gertrude and* POLONIUS.

POLONIUS
'A will come straight. Look you lay home° to him.
Tell him his pranks have been too broad° to bear with,
And that your grace hath screened and stood between
Much heat and him. I'll silence me even here.
Pray you be round with him.     5
HAMLET (*Within.*)    Mother, Mother, Mother!
QUEEN   I'll warrant you; fear me not. Withdraw; I
hear him coming.    [POLONIUS *hides behind the arras.*]

*Enter* HAMLET.

HAMLET
Now, Mother, what's the matter?
QUEEN
Hamlet, thou hast thy father much offended.     10
HAMLET
Mother, you have my father much offended.
QUEEN
Come, come, you answer with an idle° tongue.
HAMLET
Go, go, you question with a wicked tongue.
QUEEN
Why, how now, Hamlet?
HAMLET            What's the matter now?
QUEEN
Have you forgot me?
HAMLET         No, by the rood,° not so!     15
You are the queen, your husband's brother's wife,
And, would it were not so, you are my mother.
QUEEN
Nay, then I'll set those to you that can speak.
HAMLET
Come, come, and sit you down. You shall not budge.
You go not till I set you up a glass°     20
Where you may see the inmost part of you!
QUEEN
What wilt thou do? Thou wilt not murder me?
Help, ho!
POLONIUS [*Behind.*]    What, ho! Help!
HAMLET [*Draws.*]
How now? A rat? Dead for a ducat, dead!     25

[*Makes a pass through the arras and*] *kills* POLONIUS.

POLONIUS [*Behind.*]
O, I am slain!
QUEEN        O me, what hast thou done?
HAMLET
Nay, I know not. Is it the king?

96 **physic** Claudius' purgation by prayer, as Hamlet thinks in
line 85
**III.iv.1 lay home** thrust (rebuke) him sharply   **2 broad** unrestrained   **12 idle** foolish   **15 rood** cross   **20 glass** mirror

QUEEN
O, what a rash and bloody deed is this!
HAMLET
A bloody deed—almost as bad, good Mother,
As kill a king, and marry with his brother.     30
QUEEN
As kill a king?
HAMLET        Ay, lady, it was my word.

[*Lifts up the arras and sees* POLONIUS.]

Thou wretched, rash, intruding fool, farewell!
I took thee for thy better. Take thy fortune.
Thou find'st to be too busy is some danger.—
Leave wringing of your hands. Peace, sit you down     35
And let me wring your heart, for so I shall
If it be made of penetrable stuff,
If damnèd custom have not brazed° it so
That it be proof° and bulwark against sense.°
QUEEN
What have I done that thou dar'st wag thy tongue     40
In noise so rude against me?
HAMLET               Such an act
That blurs the grace and blush of modesty,
Calls virtue hypocrite, takes off the rose
From the fair forehead of an innocent love,
And sets a blister° there, makes marriage vows     45
As false as dicers' oaths. O, such a deed
As from the body of contraction° plucks
The very soul, and sweet religion makes
A rhapsody° of words! Heaven's face does glow
O'er this solidity and compound mass     50
With heated visage, as against the doom
Is thoughtsick at the act.°
QUEEN             Ay me, what act,
That roars so loud and thunders in the index?°
HAMLET
Look here upon this picture, and on this,
The counterfeit presentment° of two brothers.     55
See what a grace was seated on this brow:
Hyperion's curls, the front° of Jove himself,
An eye like Mars, to threaten and command,
A station° like the herald Mercury
New lighted on a heaven-kissing hill—     60
A combination and a form indeed
Where every god did seem to set his seal
To give the world assurance of a man.
This was your husband. Look you now what follows.    (15, 22-24)
Here is your husband, like a mildewed ear    Gen 41    65
Blasting his wholesome brother. Have you eyes?
Could you on this fair mountain leave to feed,
And batten° on this moor? Ha! Have you eyes?
You cannot call it love, for at your age
The heyday° in the blood is tame, it's humble,     70
And waits upon the judgment, and what judgment
Would step from this to this? Sense° sure you have,

38 **brazed** hardened like brass   **39 proof** armor; **sense**
feeling   **45 sets a blister** brands (as a harlot)   **47 contraction**
marriage contract   **49 rhapsody** senseless string   **49–52
Heaven's . . . act** The face of heaven blushes over this
earth (compounded of four elements), the face hot, as if
Judgment Day were near, and it is thoughtsick at the act
**53 index** prologue   **55 counterfeit presentment** represented
image   **57 front** forehead   **59 station** bearing   **68 batten**
feed gluttonously   **70 heyday** excitement   **72 Sense** feeling

Else could you not have motion, but sure that sense
Is apoplexed,° for madness would not err,
Nor sense to ecstasy° was ne'er so thralled                    75
But it reserved some quantity of choice
To serve in such a difference. What devil was't
That thus hath cozened you at hoodman-blind?°
Eyes without feeling, feeling without sight,
Ears without hands or eyes, smelling sans° all,                80
Or but a sickly part of one true sense
Could not so mope.°
O shame, where is thy blush? Rebellious hell,
If thou canst mutine in a matron's bones,
To flaming youth let virtue be as wax                          85
And melt in her own fire. Proclaim no shame
When the compulsive ardor° gives the charge,
Since frost itself as actively doth burn,
And reason panders will.°

QUEEN                            O Hamlet, speak no more.
Thou turn'st mine eyes into my very soul,                      90
And there I see such black and grainèd° spots
As will not leave their tinct.°

HAMLET                           Nay, but to live
In the rank sweat of an enseamèd° bed,
Stewed in corruption, honeying and making love
Over the nasty sty—

QUEEN                  O, speak to me no more.                 95
These words like daggers enter in my ears.
No more, sweet Hamlet.

HAMLET                  A murderer and a villain,
A slave that is not twentieth part the tithe°
Of your precedent lord, a vice° of kings,
A cutpurse of the empire and the rule,                         100
That from a shelf the precious diadem stole
And put it in his pocket—

QUEEN                      No more.

*Enter* GHOST.

HAMLET
A king of shreds and patches—
Save me and hover o'er me with your wings,
You heavenly guards! What would your gracious
    figure?                                                    105

QUEEN
Alas, he's mad.

HAMLET
Do you not come your tardy son to chide,
That, lapsed in time and passion, lets go by
Th' important acting of your dread command?
O, say!                                                        110

GHOST
Do not forget. This visitation
Is but to whet thy almost blunted purpose.
But look, amazement on thy mother sits.
O, step between her and her fighting soul!

Conceit° in weakest bodies strongest works.                    115
Speak to her, Hamlet.

HAMLET                         How is it with you, lady?

QUEEN
Alas, how is't with you,
That you do bend your eye on vacancy,
And with th' incorporal° air do hold discourse?
Forth at your eyes your spirits wildly peep,                   120
And as the sleeping soldiers in th' alarm
Your bedded hair° like life in excrements°
Start up and stand an end.° O gentle son,
Upon the heat and flame of thy distemper
Sprinkle cool patience. Whereon do you look?                   125

HAMLET
On him, on him! Look you, how pale he glares!
His form and cause conjoined, preaching to stones,
Would make them capable.°—Do not look upon me,
Lest with this piteous action you convert
My stern effects.° Then what I have to do                      130
Will want true color; tears perchance for blood.

QUEEN
To whom do you speak this?

HAMLET                        Do you see nothing there?

QUEEN
Nothing at all; yet all that is I see.

HAMLET
Nor did you nothing hear?

QUEEN                      No, nothing but ourselves.

HAMLET
Why, look you there! Look how it steals away!                  135
My father, in his habit° as he lived!
Look where he goes even now out at the portal!
                                              *Exit* GHOST.

QUEEN
This is the very coinage of your brain.
This bodiless creation ecstasy
Is very cunning in.

HAMLET               Ecstasy?                                   140
My pulse as yours doth temperately keep time
And makes as healthful music. It is not madness
That I have uttered. Bring me to the test,
And I the matter will reword, which madness
Would gambol° from. Mother, for love of grace,                 145
Lay not that flattering unction° to your soul,
That not your trespass but my madness speaks.
It will but skin and film the ulcerous place
Whiles rank corruption, mining° all within,
Infects unseen. Confess yourself to heaven,                    150
Repent what's past, avoid what is to come,
And do not spread the compost° on the weeds
To make them ranker. Forgive me this my virtue.
For in the fatness of these pursy° times
Virtue itself of vice must pardon beg,                         155
Yea curb° and woo for leave to do him good.

---

QUEEN
O Hamlet, thou hast cleft my heart in twain.

HAMLET
O, throw away the worser part of it,
And live the purer with the other half.
Good night—but go not to my uncle's bed.    160
Assume a virtue, if you have it not.
That monster custom, who all sense doth eat,
Of habits devil, is angel yet in this,
That to the use° of actions fair and good
He likewise gives a frock or livery°    165
That aptly is put on. Refrain tonight,
And that shall lend a kind of easiness
To the next abstinence; the next more easy;
For use almost can change the stamp of nature,
And either° the devil, or throw him out    170
With wondrous potency. Once more, good night,
And when you are desirous to be blest,
I'll blessing beg of you.—For this same lord,
I do repent; but heaven hath pleased it so,
To punish me with this, and this with me,    175
That I must be their° scourge and minister.
I will bestow° him and will answer well
The death I gave him. So again, good night.
I must be cruel only to be kind.
Thus bad begins, and worse remains behind.    180
One word more, good lady.

QUEEN                                What shall I do?

HAMLET
Not this, by no means, that I bid you do:
Let the bloat king tempt you again to bed,
Pinch wanton on your cheek, call you his mouse,
And let him, for a pair of reechy° kisses,    185
Or paddling in your neck with his damned fingers,
Make you to ravel° all this matter out,
That I essentially am not in madness,
But mad in craft. 'Twere good you let him know,
For who that's but a queen, fair, sober, wise,    190
Would from a paddock,° from a bat, a gib,°
Such dear concernings hide? Who would do so?
No, in despite of sense and secrecy,
Unpeg the basket on the house's top,
Let the birds fly, and like the famous ape,    195
To try conclusions,° in the basket creep
And break your own neck down.

QUEEN
Be thou assured, if words be made of breath,
And breath of life, I have no life to breathe
What thou hast said to me.    200

HAMLET
I must to England; you know that?

QUEEN                                Alack,
I had forgot. 'Tis so concluded on.

HAMLET
There's letters sealed, and my two schoolfellows,
Whom I will trust as I will adders fanged,

They bear the mandate;° they must sweep my way    205
And marshal me to knavery. Let it work;
For 'tis the sport to have the enginer°
Hoist with his own petar,° and't shall go hard
But I will delve one yard below their mines
And blow them at the moon. O, 'tis most sweet    210
When in one line two crafts° directly meet.
This man shall set me packing:
I'll lug the guts into the neighbor room.
Mother, good night. Indeed, this counselor
Is now most still, most secret, and most grave,    215
Who was in life a foolish prating knave.
Come, sir, to draw toward an end with you.
Good night, Mother.
        [*Exit the* QUEEN. *Then*] *exit* HAMLET, *tugging in*
                                                Polonius.

# [ ACT IV ]

## [Scene I. *The castle.*]

*Enter* KING *and* QUEEN, *with* ROSENCRANTZ *and*
GUILDENSTERN.

KING
There's matter in these sighs. These profound heaves
You must translate; 'tis fit we understand them.
Where is your son?

QUEEN
Bestow this place on us a little while.
        [*Exeunt* ROSENCRANTZ *and* GUILDENSTERN.]
Ah, mine own lord, what have I seen tonight!    5

KING
What, Gertrude? How does Hamlet?

QUEEN
Mad as the sea and wind when both contend
Which is the mightier. In his lawless fit,
Behind the arras hearing something stir,
Whips out his rapier, cries, "A rat, a rat!"    10
And in this brainish apprehension° kills
The unseen good old man.

KING                                O heavy deed!
It had been so with us, had we been there.
His liberty is full of threats to all,
To you yourself, to us, to every one.    15
Alas, how shall this bloody deed be answered?
It will be laid to us, whose providence°
Should have kept short, restrained, and out of haunt°
This mad young man. But so much was our love
We would not understand what was most fit,    20
But, like the owner of a foul disease,
To keep it from divulging, let it feed
Even on the pith of life. Where is he gone?

QUEEN
To draw apart the body he hath killed;

---

**164 use** practice    **165 livery** characteristic garment (punning on "habits" in line 163)    **170 either** probably a word is missing after "either"; among suggestions are *master, curb,* and *house;* but possibly "either" is a verb meaning "make easier"    **175 their** the heavens'    **177 bestow** stow, lodge    **185 reechy** foul (literally "smoky")    **187 ravel** unravel, reveal    **191 paddock** toad; **gib** tomcat    **196 To try conclusions** to make experiments

**205 mandate** command    **207 enginer** (1) demolition expert (2) contriver    **208 petar** bomb    **211 crafts** (1) boats (2) acts of guile, crafty schemes
**IV.i.11 brainish apprehension** mad imagination    **17 providence** foresight    **18 out of haunt** away from association with others

O'er whom his very madness, like some ore      25
Among a mineral° of metals base,
Shows itself pure. 'A weeps for what is done.
KING
O Gertrude, come away!
The sun no sooner shall the mountains touch
But we will ship him hence, and this vile deed   30
We must with all our majesty and skill
Both countenance and excuse. Ho, Guildenstern!

*Enter* ROSENCRANTZ *and* GUILDENSTERN.

Friends both, go join you with some further aid:
Hamlet in madness hath Polonius slain,
And from his mother's closet hath he dragged him.   35
Go seek him out; speak fair, and bring the body
Into the chapel. I pray you haste in this.
     [*Exeunt* ROSENCRANTZ *and* GUILDENSTERN.]
Come, Gertrude, we'll call up our wisest friends
And let them know both what we mean to do
And what's untimely done . . .°      40
Whose whisper o'er the world's diameter,
As level as the cannon to his blank°
Transports his poisoned shot, may miss our name
And hit the woundless° air. O, come away!
My soul is full of discord and dismay.      *Exeunt.* 45

[*Scene II. The castle.*]

*Enter* HAMLET.

HAMLET   Safely stowed.
GENTLEMEN (*Within.*)   Hamlet! Lord Hamlet!
HAMLET   But soft, what noise? Who calls on Hamlet?
O, here they come.

*Enter* ROSENCRANTZ *and* GUILDENSTERN.

ROSENCRANTZ   What have you done, my lord, with   5
the dead body?
HAMLET
Compounded it with dust, whereto 'tis kin.
ROSENCRANTZ
Tell us where 'tis, that we may take it thence
And bear it to the chapel.
HAMLET   Do not believe it.      10
ROSENCRANTZ   Believe what?
HAMLET   That I can keep your counsel and not mine
own. Besides, to be demanded of° a sponge, what
replication° should be made by the son of a king?
ROSENCRANTZ   Take you me for a sponge, my lord?   15
HAMLET   Ay, sir, that soaks up the king's counten-
ance,° his rewards, his authorities. But such officers do
the king best service in the end. He keeps them, like an
ape, in the corner of his jaw, first mouthed, to be last
swallowed. When he needs what you have gleaned,   20
it is but squeezing you and, sponge, you shall be dry
again.
ROSENCRANTZ   I understand you not, my lord.

HAMLET   I am glad of it: a knavish speech sleeps in a
foolish ear.      25
ROSENCRANTZ   My lord, you must tell us where the
body is and go with us to the king.
HAMLET   The body is with the king, but the king is
not with the body. The king is a thing—
GUILDENSTERN   A thing, my lord?      30
HAMLET   Of nothing. Bring me to him. Hide fox,
and all after.°      *Exeunt.*

[*Scene III. The castle.*]

*Enter* KING, *and two or three.*

KING
I have sent to seek him and to find the body:
How dangerous is it that this man goes loose!
Yet must not we put the strong law on him:
He's loved of the distracted° multitude,
Who like not in their judgment, but their eyes,      5
And where 'tis so, th' offender's scourge is weighed,
But never the offense. To bear° all smooth and even,
This sudden sending him away must seem
Deliberate pause.° Diseases desperate grown
By desperate appliance are relieved,      10
Or not at all.

*Enter* ROSENCRANTZ, [GUILDENSTERN,] *and all the rest.*

                How now? What hath befall'n?
ROSENCRANTZ
Where the dead body is bestowed, my lord,
We cannot get from him.
KING                But where is he?
ROSENCRANTZ
Without, my lord; guarded, to know your pleasure.
KING
Bring him before us.
ROSENCRANTZ      Ho! Bring in the lord.      15

*They enter.*

KING   Now, Hamlet, where's Polonius?
HAMLET   At supper.
KING   At supper? Where?
HAMLET   Not where he eats, but where 'a is eaten. A
certain convocation of politic° worms are e'en at him.   20
Your worm is your only emperor for diet. We fat all
creatures else to fat us, and we fat ourselves for
maggots. Your fat king and your lean beggar is but
variable service°—two dishes, but to one table. That's
the end.      25
KING   Alas, alas!
HAMLET   A man may fish with the worm that hath
eat of a king, and eat of the fish that hath fed of that
worm.
KING   What does thou mean by this?      30

25–26 ore . . . mineral vein of gold in a mine   40 done
. . . evidently something has dropped out of the text;
Capell's conjecture, "So, haply slander," is usually printed
42 blank white center of a target   44 woundless invulnerable
IV.ii.13 demanded of questioned by   14 replication reply
16–17 countenance favor

31–32 Hide . . . after a cry in a game such as hide-and-seek;
Hamlet runs from the stage
IV.iii.4 distracted bewildered, senseless   7 bear carry out
9 pause planning   20 politic statesmanlike, shrewd   24
variable service different courses

HAMLET   Nothing but to show you how a king may
go to progress° through the guts of a beggar.
KING   Where is Polonius?
HAMLET   In heaven. Send thither to see. If your mes-
senger find him not there, seek him i' th' other place 35
yourself. But if indeed you find him not within this
month, you shall nose him as you go up the stairs into
the lobby.
KING [To ATTENDANTS.]   Go seek him there.
HAMLET   'A will stay till you come.                    40
                    [Exeunt ATTENDANTS.]
KING
Hamlet, this deed, for thine especial safety,
Which we do tender° as we dearly grieve
For that which thou hast done, must send thee hence
With fiery quickness. Therefore prepare thyself.
The bark is ready and the wind at help,          45
Th' associates tend,° and everything is bent
For England.
HAMLET          For England?
KING                          Ay, Hamlet.
HAMLET                                  Good.
KING
So is it, if thou knew'st our purposes.
HAMLET   I see a cherub° that sees them. But come, for
England! Farewell, dear Mother.                  50
KING   Thy loving father, Hamlet.
HAMLET   My mother—father and mother is man and
wife, man and wife is one flesh, and so, my mother.
Come, for England!                          Exit
KING
Follow him at foot;° tempt him with speed aboard.   55
Delay it not; I'll have him hence tonight.
Away! For everything is sealed and done
That else leans° on th' affair. Pray you make haste.
                    [Exeunt all but the KING].
And, England, if my love thou hold'st at aught—
As my great power thereof may give thee sense,   60
Since yet thy cicatrice° looks raw and red
After the Danish sword, and thy free awe°
Pays homage to us—thou mayst not coldly set
Our sovereign process,° which imports at full
By letters conguing to that effect            65
The present° death of Hamlet. Do it, England,
For like the hectic° in my blood he rages,
And thou must cure me. Till I know 'tis done,
Howe'er my haps,° my joys were ne'er begun.   Exit.


[Scene IV. A plain in Denmark.]

Enter FORTINBRAS with his ARMY over the stage.

FORTINBRAS
Go, captain, from me greet the Danish king,
Tell him that by his license Fortinbras
Craves the conveyance of° a promised march
Over his kingdom. You know the rendezvous.

If that his majesty would aught with us,          5
We shall express our duty in his eye;°
And let him know so.
CAPTAIN          I will do't, my lord.
FORTINBRAS   Go softly° on.
                    [Exeunt all but the CAPTAIN.]

Enter HAMLET, ROSENCRANTZ, &c.

HAMLET
Good sir, whose powers° are these?
CAPTAIN
They are of Norway, sir.                         10
HAMLET
How purposed, sir, I pray you?
CAPTAIN
Against some part of Poland.
HAMLET
Who commands them, sir?
CAPTAIN
The nephew to old Norway, Fortinbras.
HAMLET
Goes it against the main° of Poland, sir,        15
Or for some frontier?
CAPTAIN
Truly to speak, and with no addition,°
We go to gain a little patch of ground
That hath in it no profit but the name.
To pay five ducats, five, I would not farm it,   20
Nor will it yield to Norway or the Pole
A ranker° rate, should it be sold in fee.°
HAMLET
Why, then the Polack never will defend it.
CAPTAIN
Yes, it is already garrisoned.
HAMLET
Two thousand souls and twenty thousand ducats   25
Will not debate° the question of this straw.
This is th' imposthume° of much wealth and peace,
That inward breaks, and shows no cause without
Why the man dies. I humbly thank you, sir.
CAPTAIN
God bye you, sir.                          [Exit.]
ROSENCRANTZ   Will't please you go, my lord?   30
HAMLET
I'll be with you straight. Go a little before.
                    [Exeunt all but HAMLET.]
How all occasions do inform against me
And spur my dull revenge! What is a man,
If his chief good and market° of his time
Be but to sleep and feed? A beast, no more.      35
Sure he that made us with such large discourse,°
Looking before and after, gave us not
That capability and godlike reason
To fust° in us unused. Now, whether it be
Bestial oblivion,° or some craven scruple        40
Of thinking too precisely on th' event°—
A thought which, quartered, hath but one part wisdom

32 progress royal journey  42 tender hold dear  46
tend wait  49 cherub angel of knowledge  55 at foot
closely  58 leans depends  61 cicatrice scar  62 free awe
uncompelled submission  63–64 coldly . . . process regard
slightly our royal command  66 present instant  67 hectic
fever  69 haps chances, fortunes
IV.iv.3 conveyance of escort for

6 in his eye before his eyes (i.e., in his presence)  8 softly
slowly  9 powers forces  15 main main part  17 with
no addition plainly  22 ranker higher; in fee outright
26 debate settle  27 imposthume abscess, ulcer  34 market
profit  36 discourse understanding  39 fust grow moldy
40 oblivion forgetfulness  41 event outcome

And ever three parts coward—I do not know
Why yet I live to say, "This thing's to do,"
Sith I have cause, and will, and strength, and means   45
To do't. Examples gross° as earth exhort me.
Witness this army of such mass and charge,°
Led by a delicate and tender prince,
Whose spirit, with divine ambition puffed,
Makes mouths at the invisible event,°   50
Exposing what is mortal and unsure
To all that fortune, death, and danger dare,
Even for an eggshell. Rightly to be great
Is not° to stir without great argument,°
But greatly° to find quarrel in a straw   55
When honor's at the stake. How stand I then,
That have a father killed, a mother stained,
Excitements° of my reason and my blood,
And let all sleep, while to my shame I see
The imminent death of twenty thousand men   60
That for a fantasy and trick of fame°
Go to their graves like beds, fight for a plot
Whereon the numbers cannot try the cause,
Which is not tomb enough and continent°
To hide the slain? O, from this time forth,   65
My thoughts be bloody, or be nothing worth!   *Exit.*

[Scene V. *The castle.*]

*Enter* HORATIO, [QUEEN] *Gertrude, and a* GENTLE-
MAN.

QUEEN
I will not speak with her.
GENTLEMAN
She is importunate, indeed distract.
Her mood will needs be pitied.
QUEEN                              What would she have?
GENTLEMAN
She speaks much of her father, says she hears
There's tricks i' th' world, and hems, and beats her
   heart,   5
Spurns enviously at straws,° speaks things in doubt°
That carry but half sense. Her speech is nothing,
Yet the unshapèd use of it doth move
The hearers to collection;° they yawn° at it,
And botch the words up fit to their own thoughts,   10
Which, as her winks and nods and gestures yield them,
Indeed would make one think there might be thought,
Though nothing sure, yet much unhappily.
HORATIO
'Twere good she were spoken with, for she may strew
Dangerous conjectures in ill-breeding minds.   15
QUEEN
Let her come in.                    [*Exit* GENTLEMAN.]

[*Aside.*]

To my sick soul (as sin's true nature is)
Each toy seems prologue to some great amiss;°
So full of artless jealousy° is guilt
It spills° itself in fearing to be spilt.   20

*Enter* OPHELIA [*distracted.*]

OPHELIA
Where is the beauteous majesty of Denmark?
QUEEN   How now, Ophelia?
OPHELIA (*She sings.*)
      How should I your truelove know
         From another one?
      By his cockle hat° and staff   25
         And his sandal shoon.°
QUEEN
Alas, sweet lady, what imports this song?
OPHELIA   Say you? Nay, pray you mark.
                  (*Song.*)
      He is dead and gone, lady,
         He is dead and gone;   30
      At his head a grass-green turf,
         At his heels a stone.
Oh, ho!
QUEEN   Nay, but Ophelia—
OPHELIA   Pray you mark. [*Sings.*]   35
      White his shroud as the mountain snow—

*Enter* KING.

QUEEN   Alas, look here, my lord.
OPHELIA
                  (*Song.*)
      Larded° all with sweet flowers
      Which bewept to the grave did not go
         With truelove showers.   40
KING   How do you, pretty lady?
OPHELIA   Well, God dild° you! They say the owl
was a baker's daughter.° Lord, we know what we are,
but know not what we may be. God be at your table!
KING   Conceit° upon her father.   45
OPHELIA   Pray let's have no words of this, but when
they ask you what it means, say you this:
                  (*Song.*)
      Tomorrow is Saint Valentine's day.°
         All in the morning betime,
      And I a maid at your window,   50
         To be your Valentine.

      Then up he rose and donned his clothes
         And dupped° the chamber door,
      Let in the maid, that out a maid
         Never departed more.   55
KING   Pretty Ophelia.
OPHELIA   Indeed, la, without an oath, I'll make an end
on't: [*Sings.*]

**46 gross** large obvious   **47 charge** expense   **50 Makes . . .
event** makes scornful faces (is contemptuous of) the unseen
outcome   **54 not** the sense seems to require "not not"; **argument** reason   **55 greatly** nobly   **58 Excitements** incentives
**61 fantasy . . . fame** illusion and trifle of reputation   **64
continent** receptacle, container
**IV.v.6 Spurns . . . straws** objects spitefully to insignificant
matters; **in doubt** uncertainly   **8–9 Yet . . . collection** yet
the formless manner of it moves her listeners to gather up
some sort of meaning   **9 yawn** gape (?)

**18 amiss** misfortune   **19 artless jealousy** crude suspicion
**20 spills** destroys   **25 cockle hat** a cockleshell on the hat was
the sign of a pilgrim who had journeyed to shrines overseas;
the association of lovers and pilgrims was a common one   **26
shoon** shoes   **38 Larded** decorated   **42 dild** yield, i.e.,
reward   **43 baker's daughter** an allusion to a tale of a
baker's daughter who begrudged bread to Christ and was
turned into an owl   **45 Conceit** brooding   **48 Saint
Valentine's day** February 14 (the notion was that a bachelor
would become the truelove of the first girl he saw on this day)
**53 dupped** opened (did up)

By Gis° and by Saint Charity,
    Alack, and fie for shame!       60
Young men will do't if they come to't,
    By Cock,° they are to blame.
Quoth she, "Before you tumbled me,
    You promised me to wed."
He answers:                            65
    "So would I 'a' done, by yonder sun,
    An thou hadst not come to my bed."

KING    How long hath she been thus?

OPHELIA    I hope all will be well. We must be patient,
but I cannot choose but weep to think they would lay 70
him i' th' cold ground. My brother shall know of it;
and so I thank you for your good counsel. Come, my
coach! Good night, ladies, good night. Sweet ladies,
good night, good night.                  *Exit.*

KING
Follow her close; give her good watch, I pray you.   75
                             [*Exit* HORATIO.]
O, this is the poison of deep grief; it springs
All from her father's death—and now behold!
O Gertrude, Gertrude,
When sorrows come, they come not single spies,
But in battalions: first, her father slain;       80
Next, your son gone, and he most violent author
Of his own just remove; the people muddied,°
Thick and unwholesome in their thoughts and whispers
For good Polonius' death, and we have done but
    greenly°
In huggermugger° to inter him; poor Ophelia     85
Divided from herself and her fair judgment,
Without the which we are pictures or mere beasts,
Last, and as much containing as all these,
Her brother is in secret come from France,
Feeds on his wonder,° keeps himself in clouds,    90
And wants not buzzers° to infect his ear
With pestilent speeches of his father's death,
Wherein necessity, of matter beggared,°
Will nothing stick° our person to arraign
In ear and ear. O my dear Gertrude, this,      95
Like to a murd'ring piece,° in many places
Gives me superfluous death. *A noise within.*

*Enter a* MESSENGER.

QUEEN                  Alack, what noise is this?

KING
Attend, where are my Switzers?° Let them guard the
    door.
What is the matter?

MESSENGER         Save yourself, my lord.
The ocean, overpeering of his list,°        100
Eats not the flats with more impiteous haste
Than young Laertes, in a riotous head,°
O'erbears your officers. The rabble call him lord,
And, as the world were now but to begin,
Antiquity forgot, customs not known,       105

The ratifiers and props of every word,
They cry, "Choose we! Laertes shall be king!"
Caps, hands, and tongues applaud it to the clouds,
"Laertes shall be king! Laertes king!"

*A noise within.*

QUEEN
How cheerfully on the false trail they cry!     110
O, this is counter,° you false Danish dogs!

*Enter* LAERTES, *with others.*

KING
The doors are broke.

LAERTES
Where is this king?—Sirs, stand you all without.

ALL
No, let's come in.

LAERTES           I pray you give me leave.

ALL
We will, we will.                        115

LAERTES
I thank you. Keep the door. [*Exeunt his* FOLLOWERS.]
    O thou vile king,
Give me my father.

QUEEN             Calmly, good Laertes.

LAERTES
That drop of blood that's calm proclaims me bastard,
Cries cuckold° to my father, brands the harlot
Even here between the chaste unsmirchèd brow   120
Of my true mother.

KING             What is the cause, Laertes,
That thy rebellion looks so giantlike?
Let him go, Gertrude. Do not fear° our person.
There's such divinity doth hedge a king
That treason can but peep to° what it would,    125
Acts little of his will. Tell me, Laertes,
Why thou art thus incensed. Let him go, Gertrude.
Speak, man.

LAERTES
Where is my father?

KING             Dead.

QUEEN                  But not by him.

KING
Let him demand his fill.               130

LAERTES
How came he dead? I'll not be juggled with.
To hell allegiance, vows to the blackest devil,
Conscience and grace to the profoundest pit!
I dare damnation. To this point I stand,
That both the worlds I give to negligence,°    135
Let come what comes, only I'll be revenged
Most throughly for my father.

KING             Who shall stay you?

LAERTES
My will, not all the world's.
And for my means, I'll husband them° so well
They shall go far with little.

KING                Good Laertes,     140

---

59 **Gis** (contraction of *Jesus*)   62 **Cock** (1) God (2) phallus
82 **muddied** muddled   84 **greenly** foolishly   85 **hugger-
mugger** secret haste   90 **wonder** suspicion   91 **wants not
buzzers** does not lack talebearers   93 **of matter beggared**
unprovided with facts   94 **Will nothing stick** will not hesitate
96 **murd'ring piece** a cannon that shot a kind of shrapnel
98 **Switzers** Swiss guards   100 **list** shore   102 **in . . . head**
with a rebellious force

111 **counter** a hound runs counter when he follows the scent
backward from the prey   119 **cuckold** man whose wife is
unfaithful   123 **fear** fear for   125 **peep to** i.e., look at from
a distance   135 **That . . . negligence** i.e., I care not what
may happen (to me) in this world or the next   139 **husband
them** use them economically

If you desire to know the certainty
Of your dear father, is't writ in your revenge
That swoopstake° you will draw both friend and foe,
Winner and loser?

LAERTES
None but his enemies.

KING                          Will you know them then?   145

LAERTES
To his good friends thus wide I'll ope my arms
And like the kind life-rend'ring pelican°
Repast° them with my blood.

KING                          Why, now you speak
Like a good child and a true gentleman.
That I am guiltless of your father's death,   150
And am most sensibly° in grief for it,
It shall as level to your judgment 'pear
As day does to your eye.

*A noise within:* "Let her come in."

LAERTES
How now? What noise is that?

*Enter* OPHELIA.

O heat, dry up my brains; tears seven times salt   155
Burn out the sense and virtue° of mine eye!
By heaven, thy madness shall be paid with weight
Till our scale turn the beam.° O rose of May,
Dear maid, kind sister, sweet Ophelia!
O heavens, is't possible a young maid's wits   160
Should be as mortal as an old man's life?
Nature is fine° in love, and where 'tis fine,
It sends some precious instance° of itself
After the thing it loves.

OPHELIA                          *(Song.)*
They bore him barefaced on the bier   165
    Hey non nony, nony, hey nony
    And in his grave rained many a tear—
Fare you well, my dove!

LAERTES
Hadst thou thy wits, and didst persuade revenge,
It could not move thus.   170

OPHELIA   You must sing "A-down a-down, and you
call him a-down-a." O, how the wheel° becomes it!
It is the false steward, that stole his master's daughter.

LAERTES   This nothing's more than matter.°

OPHELIA   There's rosemary, that's for remembrance.   175
Pray you, love, remember. And there is pansies, that's
for thoughts.

LAERTES   A document° in madness, thoughts and remembrance fitted.

OPHELIA   There's fennel° for you, and columbines.   180

---

**143 swoopstake** in a clean sweep   **147 pelican** thought to
feed its young with its own blood   **148 Repast** feed   **151
sensibly** acutely   **156 virtue** power   **158 turn the beam**
weigh down the bar (of the balance)   **162 fine** refined, delicate
**163 instance** sample   **172 wheel** of uncertain meaning, but
probably a tum or dance of Ophelia's, rather than Fortune's
wheel   **174 This . . . matter** This nonsense has more meaning than matters of consequence   **178 document** lesson   **180
fennel** the distribution of flowers in the ensuing lines has
symbolic meaning, but the meaning is disputed; perhaps
"fennel" = flattery, "columbines" = cuckoldry, "rue" =
sorrow for Ophelia and repentance for the queen, "daisy" =
dissembling, "violets" = faithfulness; for other interpretations,
see J. W. Lever in *Review of English Studies*, New Series 3
[1952], pp. 1h3–29

---

There's rue for you, and here's some for me. We
may call it herb of grace o' Sundays. O, you must
wear your rue with a difference. There's a daisy. I
would give you some violets, but they withered all
when my father died. They say 'a made a good end.   185
*[Sings.]*
    For bonny sweet Robin is all my joy.

LAERTES
Thought and affliction, passion, hell itself,
She turns to favor° and to prettiness.

OPHELIA                          *(Song.)*
    And will 'a not come again?
    And will 'a not come again?   190
        No, no, he is dead,
        Go to thy deathbed,
    He never will come again.

    His beard was as white as snow,
    All flaxen was his poll.°   195
        He is gone, he is gone,
        And we cast away moan.
    God 'a' mercy on his soul!
And of all Christian souls, I pray God. God bye you.
*[Exit.]*

LAERTES
Do you see this, O God?   200

KING
Laertes, I must commune with your grief,
Or you deny me right. Go but apart,
Make choice of whom your wisest friends you will,
And they shall hear and judge 'twixt you and me.
If by direct or by collateral° hand   205
They find us touched,° we will our kingdom, give
Our crown, our life, and all that we call ours,
To you in satisfaction; but if not,
Be you content to lend your patience to us,
And we shall jointly labor with your soul   210
To give it due content.

LAERTES                          Let this be so.
His means of death, his obscure funeral—
No trophy, sword, nor hatchment° o'er his bones,
No noble rite nor formal ostentation°—
Cry to be heard, as 'twere from heaven to earth,   215
That I must call't in question.

KING                          So you shall;
And where th' offense is, let the great ax fall.
I pray you go with me.                          *Exeunt.*

---

[Scene VI. *The castle.*]

*Enter* HORATIO *and others.*

HORATIO   What are they that would speak with me?

GENTLEMAN   Seafaring men, sir. They say they have
letters for you.

HORATIO   Let them come in.   *[Exit* GENTLEMAN.*]*
I do not know from what part of the world   5
I should be greeted, if not from Lord Hamlet.

*Enter* SAILORS.

---

**188 favor** charm, beauty   **195 All . . . poll** white as flax was
his head   **205 collateral** indirect   **206 touched** implicated
**213 hatchment** tablet bearing the coat of arms of the dead
**214 ostentation** ceremony

SAILOR  God bless you, sir.

HORATIO  Let Him bless thee too.

SAILOR  'A shall, sir, an't please Him. There's a letter for you, sir—it came from th' ambassador that was 10 bound for England—if your name be Horatio, as I am let to know it is.

HORATIO  [*Reads the letter.*] "Horatio, when thou shalt have overlooked° this, give these fellows some means to the king. They have letters for him. Ere we 15 were two days old at sea, a pirate of very warlike appointment° gave us chase. Finding ourselves too slow of sail, we put on a compelled valor, and in the grapple I boarded them. On the instant they got clear of our ship; so I alone became their prisoner. They 20 have dealt with me like thieves of mercy, but they knew what they did: I am to do a good turn for them. Let the king have the letters I have sent, and repair thou to me with as much speed as thou wouldest fly death. I have words to speak in thine ear will make 25 thee dumb; yet are they much too light for the bore° of the matter. These good fellows will bring thee where I am. Rosencrantz and Guildenstern hold their course for England. Of them I have much to tell thee. Farewell. 30

He that thou knowest thine, Hamlet."

Come, I will give you way for these your letters,
And do't the speedier that you may direct me
To him from whom you brought them.    *Exeunt.*

[Scene VII. *The castle.*]

*Enter* KING *and* LAERTES.

KING
Now must your conscience my acquittance seal,
And you must put me in your heart for friend,
Sith you have heard, and with a knowing ear,
That he which hath your noble father slain
Pursued my life.

LAERTES      It well appears. But tell me   5
Why you proceeded not against these feats
So criminal and so capital° in nature,
As by your safety, greatness, wisdom, all things else,
You mainly° were stirred up.

KING          O, for two special reasons,
Which may to you perhaps seem much unsinewed,°   10
But yet to me they're strong. The queen his mother
Lives almost by his looks, and for myself—
My virtue or my plague, be it either which—
She is so conjunctive° to my life and soul,
That, as the star moves not but in his sphere,   15
I could not but by her. The other motive
Why to a public count° I might not go
Is the great love the general gender° bear him,
Who, dipping all his faults in their affection,
Would, like the spring that turneth wood to stone,°   20

Convert his gyves° to graces; so that my arrows,
Too slightly timbered° for so loud a wind,
Would have reverted to my bow again,
And not where I had aimed them.

LAERTES
And so have I a noble father lost,   25
A sister driven into desp'rate terms,°
Whose worth, if praises may go back again,°
Stood challenger on mount of all the age
For her perfections. But my revenge will come.

KING
Break not your sleeps for that. You must think   30
That we are made of stuff so flat and dull
That we can let our beard be shook with danger,
And think it pastime. You shortly shall hear more.
I loved your father, and we love ourself,
And that, I hope, will teach you to imagine—   35

*Enter a* MESSENGER *with letters.*

How now? What news?

MESSENGER        Letters, my lord, from Hamlet:
These to your majesty; this to the queen.

KING
From Hamlet? Who brought them?

MESSENGER
Sailors, my lord, they say; I saw them not.
They were given me by Claudio; he received them   40
Of him that brought them.

KING        Laertes, you shall hear them.—
Leave us.            *Exit* MESSENGER.
[*Reads.*] "High and mighty, you shall know I am set
naked° on your kingdom. Tomorrow shall I beg leave
to see your kingly eyes; when I shall (first asking your 45
pardon thereunto) recount the occasion of my sudden
and more strange return.

Hamlet."

What should this mean? Are all the rest come back?
Or is it some abuse,° and no such thing?   50

LAERTES
Know you the hand?

KING        'Tis Hamlet's character.° "Naked"!
And in a postscript here, he says "alone."
Can you devise° me?

LAERTES
I am lost in it, my lord. But let him come.
It warms the very sickness in my heart   55
That I shall live and tell him to his teeth,
"Thus didst thou."

KING        If it be so, Laertes
(As how should it be so? How otherwise?),
Will you be ruled by me?

LAERTES        Ay, my lord,
So you will not o'errule me to a peace.   60

KING
To thine own peace. If he be now returned,
As checking at° his voyage, and that he means

---

IV.vi.14 **overlooked** surveyed  **17 appointment** equipment  **26 bore** caliber (here, "importance")
IV.vii.**7 capital** deserving death  **9 mainly** powerfully  10 **unsinewed** weak  **14 conjunctive** closely united  **17 count** reckoning  **18 general gender** common people  **20 spring . . . stone** a spring in Shakespeare's county was so charged with lime that it would petrify wood placed in it

**21 gyves** fetters  **22 timbered** shafted  **26 terms** conditions  **27 go back again** revert to what is past  **44 naked** destitute  **50 abuse** deception  **51 character** handwriting  **53 devise** advise  **62 checking at** turning away from (a term in falconry)

No more to undertake it, I will work him
To an exploit now ripe in my device,
Under the which he shall not choose but fall;                    65
And for his death no wind of blame shall breathe,
But even his mother shall uncharge the practice°
And call it accident.

LAERTES                    My lord, I will be ruled;
The rather if you could devise it so
That I might be the organ.

KING                         It falls right.                     70
You have been talked of since your travel much,
And that in Hamlet's hearing, for a quality
Wherein they say you shine. Your sum of parts
Did not together pluck such envy from him
As did that one, and that, in my regard,                        75
Of the unworthiest siege.°

LAERTES                    What part is that, my lord?

KING
A very riband in the cap of youth,
Yet needful too, for youth no less becomes
The light and careless livery that it wears
Than settled age his sables and his weeds,°                     80
Importing health and graveness. Two months since
Here was a gentleman of Normandy.
I have seen myself, and served against, the French,
And they can° well on horseback, but this gallant
Had witchcraft in't. He grew unto his seat,                     85
And to such wondrous doing brought his horse
As had he been incorpsed and deminatured
With the brave beast. So far he topped my thought
That I, in forgery° of shapes and tricks,
Come short of what he did.

LAERTES                    A Norman was't?                       90

KING  A Norman.

LAERTES
Upon my life, Lamord.

KING                     The very same.

LAERTES
I know him well. He is the brooch° indeed
And gem of all the nation.

KING
He made confession° of you,                                      95
And gave you such a masterly report,
For art and exercise in your defense,
And for your rapier most especial,
That he cried out 'twould be a sight indeed
If one could match you. The scrimers° of their nation   100
He swore had neither motion, guard, nor eye,
If you opposed them. Sir, this report of his
Did Hamlet so envenom with his envy
That he could nothing do but wish and beg
Your sudden coming o'er to play with you.                       105
Now, out of this—

LAERTES                    What out of this, my lord?

KING
Laertes, was your father dear to you?
Or are you like the painting of a sorrow,
A face without a heart?

LAERTES                    Why ask you this?

KING
Not that I think you did not love your father,                 110
But that I know love is begun by time,
And that I see, in passages of proof,°
Time qualifies° the spark and fire of it.
There lives within the very flame of love
A kind of wick or snuff° that will abate it,                    115
And nothing is at a like goodness still,°
For goodness, growing to a plurisy,°
Dies in his own too-much. That we would do
We should do when we would, for this "would"
  changes,
And hath abatements and delays as many                          120
As there are tongues, are hands, are accidents,
And then this "should" is like a spendthrift sigh,°
That hurts by easing. But to the quick° of th' ulcer—
Hamlet comes back; what would you undertake
To show yourself in deed your father's son                     125
More than in words?

LAERTES                    To cut his throat i' th' church!

KING
No place indeed should murder sanctuarize;°
Revenge should have no bounds. But, good Laertes,
Will you do this? Keep close within your chamber.
Hamlet returned shall know you are come home.                  130
We'll put on those° shall praise your excellence
And set a double varnish on the fame
The Frenchman gave you, bring you in fine° together
And wager on your heads. He, being remiss,
Most generous, and free from all contriving,                   135
Will not peruse the foils, so that with ease,
Or with a little shuffling, you may choose
A sword unbated,° and, in a pass of practice,°
Requite him for your father.

LAERTES                    I will do't,
And for that purpose I'll anoint my sword.                     140
I bought an unction of a mountebank,°
So mortal that, but dip a knife in it,
Where it draws blood, no cataplasm° so rare,
Collected from all simples° that have virtue°
Under the moon, can save the thing from death                  145
That is but scratched withal. I'll touch my point
With this contagion, that, if I gall him slightly,
It may be death.

KING                 Let's further think of this,
Weigh what convenience both of time and means
May fit us to our shape.° If this should fail,                 150
And that our drift look through° our bad performance,
'Twere better not assayed. Therefore this project
Should have a black or second, that might hold
If this did blast in proof.° Soft, let me see.
We'll make a solemn wager on your cunnings—                    155
I ha't!

67 uncharge the practice not charge the device with treachery
76 siege rank   80 sables . . . weeds i.e., sober attire
84 can do   89 forgery invention   93 brooch ornament   95
confession report   100 scrimers fencers

112 passages of proof proved cases   113 qualifies diminishes
115 snuff residue of burnt wick (which dims the light)   116
still always   117 plurisy fullness, excess   122 spendthrift
sigh sighing provides ease, but because it was thought to thin
the blood and so shorten life it was spendthrift   123 quick
sensitive flesh   127 sanctuarize protect   131 We'll . . .
those we'll incite persons who   133 in fine finally   138
unbated not blunted; pass of practice treacherous thrust
141 mountebank quack   143 cataplasm poultice   144 simples medicinal herbs; virtue power (to heal)   150 shape role
151 drift look through purpose show through   154 blast in
proof burst (fail) in performance

When in your motion you are hot and dry—
As make your bouts more violent to that end—
And that he calls for drink, I'll have prepared him
A chalice for the nonce,° whereon but sipping,          160
If he by chance escape your venomed stuck,°
Our purpose may hold there.—But stay, what noise?

*Enter* QUEEN.

QUEEN
One woe doth tread upon another's heel,
So fast they follow. Your sister's drowned, Laertes.

LAERTES  Drowned! O, where?          165

QUEEN
There is a willow grows askant° the brook,
That shows his hoar° leaves in the glassy stream:
Therewith° fantastic garlands did she make
Of crowflowers, nettles, daisies, and long purples,
That liberal° shepherds give a grosser name,          170
But our cold maids do dead men's fingers call them.
There on the pendent boughs her crownet° weeds
Clamb'ring to hang, an envious sliver° broke,
When down her weedy trophies and herself
Fell in the weeping brook. Her clothes spread wide,          175
And mermaidlike awhile they bore her up,
Which time she chanted snatches of old lauds,°
As one incapable° of her own distress,
Or like a creature native and indued°
Unto that element. But long it could not be          180
Till that her garments, heavy with their drink,
Pulled the poor wretch from her melodious lay
To muddy death.

LAERTES          Alas, then she is drowned?

QUEEN  Drowned, drowned.

LAERTES
Too much of water hast thou, poor Ophelia,          185
And therefore I forbid my tears; but yet
It is our trick;° nature her custom holds,
Let shame say what it will: when these are gone,
The woman° will be out. Adieu, my lord.
I have a speech o' fire, that fain would blaze,          190
But that this folly drowns it.          *Exit.*

KING          Let's follow, Gertrude.
How much I had to do to calm his rage!
Now fear I this will give it start again;
Therefore let's follow.          *Exeunt.*

# [ A C T   V ]

[*Scene I. A churchyard.*]

*Enter two* CLOWNS.°

CLOWN  Is she to be buried in Christian burial when
she willfully seeks her own salvation?

OTHER  I tell thee she is. Therefore make her grave
straight.° The crowner° hath sate on her, and finds it
Christian burial.          5

CLOWN  How can that be, unless she drowned herself
in her own defense?

OTHER  Why, 'tis found so.

CLOWN  It must be se offendendo;° it cannot be else.
For here lies the point: if I drown myself wittingly,          10
it argues an act, and an act hath three branches—it is to
act, to do, to perform. Argal,° she drowned herself
wittingly.

OTHER  Nay, but hear you, Goodman Delver.

CLOWN  Give me leave. Here lies the water—good.          15
Here stands the man—good. If the man go to this
water and drown himself, it is, will he nill he,° he goes;
mark you that. But if the water come to him and
drown him, he drowns not himself. Argal, he that is
not guilty of his own death, shortens not his own life.          20

OTHER  But is this law?

CLOWN  Ay marry, is't—crowner's quest° law.

OTHER  Will you ha' the truth on't? If this had not
been a gentlewoman, she should have been buried out
o' Christian burial.          25

CLOWN  Why, there thou say'st. And the more pity ⎤  $Gen\ III$
that great folk should have count'nance° in this world ⎥  $23$
to drown or hang themselves more than their even- ⎬
Christen.° Come, my spade. There is no ancient ⎥
gentlemen but gard'ners, ditchers, and gravemakers. ⎦          30
They hold up° Adam's profession.

OTHER  Was he a gentleman?

CLOWN  'A was the first that ever bore arms.°

OTHER  Why, he had none.

CLOWN  What, art a heathen? How doest thou under-          35
stand the Scripture? The Scripture says Adam digged.
Could he dig without arms? I'll put another question
to thee. If thou answerest me not to the purpose,
confess thyself—

OTHER  Go to.          40

CLOWN  What is he that builds stronger then either
the mason, the shipwright, or the carpenter?

OTHER  The gallowsmaker, for that frame outlives a
thousand tenants.

CLOWN  I like thy wit well, in good faith. The gallows          45
does well. But how does it well? It does well to those
that do ill. Now thou dost ill to say the gallows is
built stronger than the church. Argal, the gallows may
do well to thee. To't again, come.

OTHER  Who builds stronger than a mason, a ship-          50
wright, or a carpenter?

CLOWN  Ay, tell me that, and unyoke.°

OTHER  Marry, now I can tell.

CLOWN  To't.

OTHER  Mass,° I cannot tell.          55

*Enter* HAMLET *and* HORATIO *afar off.*

160 **nonce** occasion  161 **stuck** thrust  166 **askant** aslant
167 **hoar** silver-gray  168 **Therewith** i.e., with willow twigs
170 **liberal** free-spoken, coarse-mouthed  172 **crownet**
coronet  173 **envious sliver** malicious branch  177 **lauds**
hymns  178 **incapable** unaware  179 **indued** in harmony
with  187 **trick** trait, way  189 **woman** i.e., womanly part of
me
**V.i.s.d. clowns** rustics

4 **straight** straightway; **crowner** coroner  9 **se offendendo**
blunder for *se defendendo*, a legal term meaning "in self-
defense"  12 **Argal** blunder for Latin *ergo*, "therefore"  17
**will he . . . he** he will he or will he not (whether he will or
will not)  22 **quest** inquest  27 **count'nance** privilege  28–29
**even-Christen** fellow Christian  31 **hold up** keep up  33
**bore arms** had a coat of arms (the sign of a gentleman)  52
**unyoke** i.e., stop work for the day  55 **Mass** by the mass

CLOWN   Cudgel thy brains no more about it, for your dull ass will not mend his pace with beating. And when you are asked this question next, say "a grave-maker." The houses he makes lasts till doomsday. Go, get thee in, and fetch me a stoup° of liquor.          60

[*Exit* OTHER CLOWN.]

(*Song.*)

In youth when I did love, did love,
    Methought it was very sweet
To contract—O—the time for—a—my behove,°
    O, methought there—a—was nothing—a—meet.

HAMLET   Has this fellow no feeling of his business? 'A    65
sings in gravemaking.

HORATIO   Custom hath made it in him a property of easiness.°

HAMLET   'Tis e'en so. The hand of little employment hath the daintier sense.°          70

CLOWN                    (*Song.*)

But age with his stealing steps
    Hath clawed me in his clutch,
And hath shipped me into the land,
    As if I had never been such.

[*Throws up a skull.*]

HAMLET   That skull had a tongue in it, and could sing    75
once. How the knave jowls° it to the ground, as if
'twere Cain's jawbone, that did the first murder! This
might be the pate of a politician, which this ass now
o'erreaches,° one that would circumvent God, might
it not?          80

HORATIO   It might, my lord.

HAMLET   Or of a courtier, which could say "Good morrow, sweet lord! How dost thou, sweet lord?" This might be my Lord Such-a-one, that praised my Lord Such-a-one's horse when 'a went to beg it, might    85
it not?

HORATIO   Ay, my lord.

HAMLET   Why, e'en so, and now my Lady Worm's, chapless,° and knocked about the mazzard° with a sexton's spade. Here's fine revolution, an we had the    90
trick to see't. Did these bones cost no more the breeding but to play at loggets° with them? Mine ache to think on't.

CLOWN                    (*Song.*)

A pickax and a spade, a spade,
    For and a shrouding sheet;          95
O, a pit of clay for to be made
    For such a guest is meet.

[*Throws up another skull.*]

HAMLET   There's another. Why may not that be the skull of a lawyer? Where be his quiddities° now, his quillities,° his cases, his tenures,° and his tricks? Why    100
does he suffer this mad knave now to knock him about the sconce° with a dirty shovel, and will not tell him

of his action of battery? Hum! This fellow might be in's time a great buyer of land, with his statutes, his recognizances, his fines,° his double vouchers, his    105
recoveries. Is this the fine° of his fines, and the recovery of his recoveries, to have his fine pate full of fine dirt? Will his vouchers vouch him no more of his purchases, and double ones too, than the length and breadth of a pair of indentures?° The very conveyances° of his lands    110
will scarcely lie in this box, and must th' inheritor himself have no more, ha?

HORATIO   Not a jot more, my lord.

HAMLET   Is not parchment made of sheepskins?

HORATIO   Ay, my lord, and of calveskins too.          115

HAMLET   They are sheep and calves which seek out assurance° in that. I will speak to this fellow. Whose grave's this, sirrah?

CLOWN   Mine, sir. [*Sings.*]

        O, a pit of clay for to be made          120
            For such a guest is meet.

HAMLET   I think it be thine indeed, for thou liest in't.

CLOWN   You lie out on't, sir, and therefore 'tis not yours. For my part, I do not lie in't, yet it is mine.

HAMLET   Thou dost lie in't, to be in't and say it is    125
thine. 'Tis for the dead, not for the quick;° therefore thou liest.

CLOWN   'Tis a quick lie, sir; 'twill away again from me to you.

HAMLET   What man dost thou dig it for?          130

CLOWN   For no man, sir.

HAMLET   What woman then?

CLOWN   For none neither.

HAMLET   Who is to be buried in't?

CLOWN   One that was a woman, sir; but, rest her soul,    135
she's dead.

HAMLET   How absolute° the knave is! We must speak by the card,° or equivocation° will undo us. By the Lord, Horatio, this three years I have took note of it, the age is grown so picked° that the toe of the peasant    140
comes so near the heel of the courtier he galls his kibe.° How long hast thou been a gravemaker?

CLOWN   Of all the days i' th' year, I came to't that day that our last king Hamlet overcame Fortinbras.

HAMLET   How long is that since?          145

CLOWN   Cannot you tell that? Every fool can tell that. It was that very day that young Hamlet was born—he that is mad, and sent into England.

HAMLET   Ay, marry, why was he sent into England?

CLOWN   Why, because 'a was mad. 'A shall recover his    150
wits there; or, if 'a do not, 'tis no great matter there.

HAMLET   Why?

CLOWN   'Twill not be seen in him there. There the men are as mad as he.

HAMLET   How came he mad?          155

CLOWN   Very strangely, they say.

HAMLET   How strangely?

60 **stoup** tankard   63 **behove** advantage   67–68 **in . . . easiness** easy for him   70 **hath . . . sense** is more sensitive (because it is not calloused)   76 **jowls** hurls   79 **o'erreaches** (1) reaches over (2) has the advantage over   89 **chapless** lacking the lower jaw; **mazzard** head   92 **loggets** a game in which small pieces of wood were thrown at an object   99 **quiddities** subtle arguments (from Latin *quidditas* = whatness)   100 **quillities** fine distinctions; **tenures** legal means of holding land   102 **sconce** head

105 **his statutes . . . fines** his documents giving a creditor control of a debtor's land, his bonds of surety, his documents changing an entailed estate into fee simple (unrestricted ownership)   106 **fine** end   110 **indentures** contracts; **conveyances** legal documents for the transference of land   117 **assurance** safety   126 **quick** living   137 **absolute** positive, decided   138 **by the card** by the compass card, i.e., exactly; **equivocation** ambiguity   140 **picked** refined   141 **kibe** sore on the back of the heel

CLOWN   Faith, e'en with losing his wits.

HAMLET   Upon what ground?

CLOWN   Why, here in Denmark. I have been sexton 160 here, man and boy, thirty years.

HAMLET   How long will a man lie i' th' earth ere he rot?

CLOWN   Faith, if 'a be not rotten before 'a die (as we have many pocky corses° nowadays that will scarce 165 hold the laying in), 'a will last you some eight year or nine year. A tanner will last you nine year.

HAMLET   Why he, more than another?

CLOWN   Why, sir, his hide is so tanned with his trade that 'a will keep out water a great while, and your 170 water is a sore decayer of your whoreson dead body. Here's a skull now hath lien you i' th' earth three and twenty years.

HAMLET   Whose was it?

CLOWN   A whoreson mad fellow's it was. Whose do 175 you think it was?

HAMLET   Nay, I know not.

CLOWN   A pestilence on him for a mad rogue! 'A poured a flagon of Rhenish on my head once. This same skull, sir, was, sir, Yorick's skull, the king's jester. 180

HAMLET   This?

CLOWN   E'en that.

HAMLET   Let me see. [Takes the skull.] Alas, poor Yorick! I knew him, Horatio, a fellow of infinite jest, of most excellent fancy. He hath borne me on his back 185 a thousand times. And now how abhorred in my imagination it is! My gorge rises at it. Here hung those lips that I have kissed I know not how oft. Where be your gibes now? Your gambols, your songs, your flashes of merriment that were wont to set the table 190 on a roar? Not one now to mock your own grinning? Quite chapfall'n°? Now get you to my lady's chamber, and tell her, let her paint an inch thick, to this favor° she must come. Make her laugh at that. Prithee, Horatio, tell me one thing. 195

HORATIO   What's that, my lord?

HAMLET   Dost thou think Alexander looked o' this fashion i' th' earth?

HORATIO   E'en so.

HAMLET   And smelt so? Pah! 200

[Puts down the skull.[

HORATIO   E'en so, my lord.

HAMLET   To what base uses we may return, Horatio! Why may not imagination trace the noble dust of Alexander till 'a find it stopping a bunghole?

HORATIO   'Twere to consider too curiously,° to con- 205 sider so.

HAMLET   No, faith, not a jot, but to follow him thither with modesty enough,° and likelihood to lead it; as thus: Alexander died, Alexander was buried, Alexander returneth to dust; the dust is earth; of earth we 210 make loam; and why of that loam whereto he was converted might they not stop a beer barrel? Imperious Caesar, dead and turned to clay, Might stop a hole to keep the wind away.

O, that that earth which kept the world in awe 215
Should patch a wall t' expel the winter's flaw!°
But soft, but soft awhile! Here comes the king.

*Enter* KING, QUEEN, LAERTES, *and a coffin, with*
LORDS *attendant [and a* DOCTOR *of Divinity].*

The queen, the courtiers. Who is this they follow?
And with such maimèd° rites? This doth betoken
The corse they follow did with desp'rate hand 220
Fordo it° own life. 'Twas of some estate.°
Couch° we awhile, and mark. [*Retires with* HORATIO.]

LAERTES
What ceremony else?

HAMLET                     That is Laertes,
A very noble youth. Mark.

LAERTES
What ceremony else? 225

DOCTOR
Her obsequies have been as far enlarged
As we have warranty. Her death was doubtful,°
And, but that great command o'ersways the order,
She should in ground unsanctified been lodged
Till the last trumpet. For charitable prayers, 230
Shards,° flints, and pebbles should be thrown on her.
Yet here she is allowed her virgin crants,°
Her maiden strewments,° and the bringing home
Of bell and burial.

LAERTES
Must there no more be done?

DOCTOR                     No more be done. 235
We should profane the service of the dead
To sing a requiem and such rest to her
As to peace-parted souls.

LAERTES                     Lay her i' th' earth,
And from her fair and unpolluted flesh
May violets spring! I tell thee, churlish priest, 240
A minist'ring angel shall my sister be
When thou liest howling!

HAMLET                     What, the fair Ophelia?

QUEEN
Sweets to the sweet! Farewell.

[*Scatters flowers.*]

I hoped thou shouldst have been my Hamlet's wife.
I thought thy bride bed to have decked, sweet maid, 245
And not have strewed thy grave.

LAERTES                     O, treble woe
Fall ten times treble on that cursèd head
Whose wicked deed thy most ingenious sense°
Deprived thee of! Hold off the earth awhile,
Till I have caught her once more in mine arms. 250

*Leaps in the grave.*

Now pile your dust upon the quick and dead
Till of this flat a mountain you have made
T' o'ertop old Pelion° or the skyish head
Of blue Olympus.

---

165 **pocky corses** bodies of persons who had been infected with the pox (syphilis)   192 **chapfall'n** (1) down in the mouth (2) jawless   194 **favor** facial appearance   205 **curiously** minutely   208 **with modesty enough** without exaggeration

216 **flaw** gust   219 **maimèd** incomplete   221 **Fordo it** destroy its; **estate** high rank   222 **Couch** hide   227 **doubtful** suspicious   231 **Shards** broken pieces of pottery   232 **crants** garlands   233 **strewments** i.e., of flowers   248 **most ingenious sense** finely endowed mind   253 **Pelion** according to classical legend, giants in their fight with the gods sought to reach heaven by piling Mount Pelion and Mount Ossa on Mount Olympus

HAMLET   [*Coming forward.*] What is he whose grief
Bears such an emphasis, whose phrase of sorrow      255
Conjures the wand'ring stars,° and makes them stand
Like wonder-wounded hearers? This is I,
Hamlet the Dane.

LAERTES            The devil take thy soul!

[*Grapples with him.*]°

HAMLET
Thou pray'st not well.
I prithee take thy fingers from my throat,      260
For, though I am not splenitive° and rash,
Yet have I in me something dangerous,
Which let thy wisdom fear. Hold off thy hand.

KING
Pluck them asunder.

QUEEN            Hamlet, Hamlet!

ALL
Gentlemen!

HORATIO   Good my lord, be quiet.      265

[ATTENDANTS *part them.*]

HAMLET
Why, I will fight with him upon this theme
Until my eyelids will no longer wag.

QUEEN
O my son, what theme?

HAMLET
I loved Ophelia. Forty thousand brothers
Could not with all their quantity of love      270
Make up my sum. What wilt thou do for her?

KING
O, he is mad, Laertes.

QUEEN
For love of God forbear him.

HAMLET
'Swounds, show me what thou't do.
Woo't weep? Woo't fight? Woo't fast? Woo't tear
    thyself?      275
Woo't drink up eisel?° Eat a crocodile?
I'll do't. Dost thou come here to whine?
To outface me with leaping in her grave?
Be buried quick with her, and so will I.
And if thou prate of mountains, let them throw      280
Millions of acres on us, till our ground,
Singeing his pate against the burning zone,°
Make Ossa like a wart! Nay, an thou'lt mouth,
I'll rant as well as thou.

QUEEN            This is mere madness;
And thus a while the fit will work on him.      285
Anon, as patient as the female dove
When that her golden couplets are disclosed,°
His silence will sit drooping.

HAMLET            Hear you, sir.

What is the reason that you use me thus?
I loved you ever. But it is no matter.      290
Let Hercules himself do what he may,
The cat will mew, and dog will have his day.

KING
I pray thee, good Horatio, wait upon him.
                            *Exit* HAMLET *and* HORATIO.

[*To* LAERTES.]
Strengthen your patience in our last night's speech.
We'll put the matter to the present push.°      295
Good Gertrude, set some watch over your son.
This grave shall have a living° monument.
An hour of quiet shortly shall we see;
Till then in patience our proceeding be.      *Exeunt.*


[Scene II. *The castle.*]

*Enter* HAMLET *and* HORATIO.

HAMLET
So much for this, sir; now shall you see the other.
You do remember all the circumstance?

HORATIO
Remember it, my lord!

HAMLET
Sir, in my heart there was a kind of fighting
That would not let me sleep. Methought I lay      5
Worse than the mutines in the bilboes.° Rashly
(And praised be rashness for it) let us know,
Our indiscretion sometime serves us well
When our deep plots do pall,° and that should learn us
There's a divinity that shapes our ends,      10
Rough-hew them how we will.

HORATIO            That is most certain.

HAMLET
Up from my cabin,
My sea gown scarfed about me, in the dark
Groped I to find out them, had my desire,
Fingered° their packet, and in fine° withdrew      15
To mine own room again, making so bold,
My fears forgetting manners, to unseal
Their grand commission; where I found, Horatio—
Ah, royal knavery!—an exact command,
Larded° with many several sorts of reasons,      20
Importing Denmark's health, and England's too,
With, ho, such bugs and goblins in my life,°
That on the supervise,° no leisure bated,°
No, not to stay the grinding of the ax,
My head should be struck off.

HORATIO            Is't possible?      25

HAMLET
Here's the commission; read it at more leisure.
But wilt thou hear now how I did proceed?

HORATIO   I beseech you.

HAMLET
Being thus benetted round with villains,

---

256 **wand'ring stars** planets   258 **s.d. Grapples with him**
Q1, a bad quarto, presumably reporting a version that toured,
has a previous direction saying "Hamlet leaps in after Laertes";
possibly he does so, somewhat hysterically, but such a direction
—absent from the two good texts, Q2 and F—makes Hamlet
the aggressor, somewhat contradicting his next speech; perhaps
Laertes leaps out of the grave to attack Hamlet   261 **splenitive**
fiery (the spleen was thought to be the seat of anger)   276 **eisel**
vinegar   282 **burning zone** sun's orbit   287 **golden . . . disclosed** the dove lays two eggs, and the newly hatched
("disclosed") young are covered with golden down

295 **present push** immediate test   297 **living** lasting (with
perhaps also a reference to the plot against Hamlet's life)
V.ii.6 **mutines . . . bilboes** mutineers in fetters   9 **pall** fail
15 **Fingered** stole; **in fine** finally   20 **Larded** enriched   22
**such . . . life** such bugbears and imagined terrors if I were
allowed to live   23 **supervise** reading; **leisure bated** delay
allowed

Or° I could make a prologue to my brains, 30
They had begun the play. I sat me down,
Devised a new commission, wrote it fair.
I once did hold it, as our statists° do,
A baseness to write fair,° and labored much
How to forget that learning, but, sir, now 35
It did me yeoman's service. Wilt thou know
Th' effect° of what I wrote?

HORATIO                    Ay, good my lord.

HAMLET
An earnest conjuration from the king,
As England was his faithful tributary,
As love between them like the palm might flourish, 40
As peace should still her wheaten garland wear
And stand a comma° 'tween their amities,
And many suchlike as's of great charge,°
That on the view and knowing of these contents,
Without debatement further, more or less, 45
He should those bearers put to sudden death,
Not shriving° time allowed.

HORATIO                    How was this sealed?

HAMLET
Why, even in that was heaven ordinant.°
I had my father's signet in my purse,
Which was the model° of that Danish seal, 50
Folded the writ up in the form of th' other,
Subscribed it, gave't th' impression, placed it safely,
The changeling never known. Now, the next day
Was our sea fight, and what to this was sequent
Thou knowest already. 55

HORATIO
So Guildenstern and Rosencrantz go to't.

HAMLET
Why, man, they did make love to this employment.
They are not near my conscience; their defeat
Does by their own insinuation° grow.
'Tis dangerous when the baser nature comes 60
Between the pass° and fell° incensèd points
Of mighty opposites.

HORATIO                    Why, what a king is this!

HAMLET
Does it not, think thee, stand me now upon°—
He that hath killed my king, and whored my mother,
Popped in between th' election° and my hopes, 65
Thrown out his angle° for my proper life,°
And with such coz'nage°—is't not perfect conscience
To quit° him with this arm? And is't not to be damned
To let this canker of our nature come
In further evil? 70

HORATIO
It must be shortly known to him from England
What is the issue of the business there.

HAMLET
It will be short; the interim's mine,
And a man's life's no more than to say "one."

But I am very sorry, good Horatio, 75
That to Laertes I forgot myself,
For by the image of my cause I see
The portraiture of his. I'll court his favors.
But sure the bravery° of his grief did put me
Into a tow'ring passion.

HORATIO                    Peace, who comes here? 80

*Enter young* OSRIC, *a courtier.*

OSRIC  Your lordship is right welcome back to Denmark.

HAMLET  I humbly thank you, sir. [*Aside to* HORATIO.]
Dost know this waterfly?

HORATIO [*Aside to* HAMLET.]  No, my good lord. 85

HAMLET [*Aside to* HORATIO.]  Thy state is the more
gracious, for 'tis a vice to know him. He hath much
land, and fertile. Let a beast be lord of beasts, and his
crib shall stand at the king's mess.° 'Tis a chough,° but,
as I say, spacious° in the possession of dirt. 90

OSRIC  Sweet lord, if your lordship were at leisure, I
should impart a thing to you from his majesty.

HAMLET  I will receive it, sir, with all diligence of
spirit. Put your bonnet to his right use. 'Tis for the
head. 95

OSRIC  I thank your lordship, it is very hot.

HAMLET  No, believe me, 'tis very cold; the wind is
northerly.

OSRIC  It is indifferent cold, my lord, indeed.

HAMLET  But yet methinks it is very sultry and hot 100
for my complexion.°

OSRIC  Exceedingly, my lord; it is very sultry, as
'twere—I cannot tell how. But, my lord, his majesty
bade me signify to you that 'a has laid a great wager on
your head. Sir, this is the matter— 105

HAMLET  I beseech you remember.

[HAMLET *moves him to put on his hat.*]

OSRIC  Nay, good my lord; for my ease, in good faith.
Sir, here is newly come to court Laertes—believe me,
an absolute gentleman, full of most excellent differences,° of very soft society and great showing. Indeed, 110
to speak feelingly° of him, he is the card° or calendar of
gentry; for you shall find in him the continent° of
what part a gentleman would see.

HAMLET  Sir, his definement° suffers no perdition° in
you, though, I know, to divide him inventorially 115
would dozy° th' arithmetic of memory, and yet but
yaw neither in respect of his quick sail.° But, in the
verity of extolment, I take him to be a soul of great
article,° and his infusion° of such dearth and rareness
as, to make true diction° of him, his semblable° is his 120
mirror, and who else would trace him, his umbrage,°
nothing more.

OSRIC  Your lordship speaks most infallibly of him.

---

30 **Or** ere  33 **statists** statesmen  34 **fair** clearly  37 **effect**
purport  42 **comma** link  43 **great charge** (1) serious exhortation (2) heavy burden (punning on *as's* and *asses*)  47 **shriving**
absolution  48 **ordinant** ruling  50 **model** counterpart
59 **insinuation** meddling  61 **pass** thrust; **fell** cruel  63 **stand
. . . upon** become incumbent upon me  65 **election** the
Danish monarchy was elective  66 **angle** fishing line; **my
proper life** my own life  67 **coz'nage** trickery  68 **quit** pay
back

79 **bravery** bravado  89 **mess** table; **chough** jackdaw (here,
chatterer)  90 **spacious** well off  101 **complexion** temperament  109–10 **differences** distinguishing characteristics  111
**feelingly** justly; **card** chart  112 **continent** summary  114
**definement** description; **perdition** loss  116 **dozy** dizzy
116–17 **and yet . . . sail** and yet only stagger despite all ("yaw
neither") in trying to overtake his virtues  119 **article** literally,
"item," but here perhaps "traits" or "importance"; **infusion**
essential quality  120 **diction** description; **semblable** likeness
121 **umbrage** shadow

HAMLET  The concernancy,° sir? Why do we wrap the gentleman in our more rawer breath?    125

OSRIC  Sir?

HORATIO  Is't not possible to understand in another tongue? You will to't,° sir, really.

HAMLET  What imports the nomination of this gentleman?    130

OSRIC  Of Laertes?

HORATIO  [Aside to HAMLET.]  His purse is empty already. All's golden words are spent.

HAMLET  Of him, sir.

OSRIC  I know you are not ignorant—    135

HAMLET  I would you did, sir; yet, in faith, if you did, it would not much approve° me. Well, sir?

OSRIC  You are not ignorant of what excellence Laertes is—

HAMLET  I dare not confess that, lest I should compare  140  with him in excellence; but to know a man well were to know himself.

OSRIC  I mean, sir, for his weapon; but in the imputation° laid on him by them, in his meed° he's unfellowed.    145

HAMLET  What's his weapon?

OSRIC  Rapier and dagger.

HAMLET  That's two of his weapons—but well.

OSRIC  The king, sir, hath wagered with him six Barbary horses, against the which he has impawned,°  150  as I take it, six French rapiers and poniards, with their assigns,° as girdle, hangers,° and so. Three of the carriages,° in faith, are very dear to fancy, very responsive° to the hilts, most delicate carriages, and of very liberal conceit.°    155

HAMLET  What call you the carriages?

HORATIO  [Aside to HAMLET.]  I knew you must be edified by the margent° ere you had done.

OSRIC  The carriages, sir, are the hangers.

HAMLET  The phrase would be more germane to the  160  matter if we could carry a cannon by our sides. I would it might be hangers till then. But on! Six Barbary horses against six French swords, their assigns, and three liberal-conceited carriages—that's the French bet against the Danish. Why is this all im-  165  pawned, as you call it?

OSRIC  The king, sir, hath laid, sir, that in a dozen passes between yourself and him he shall not exceed you three hits; he hath laid on twelve for nine, and it would come to immediate trial if your lordship  170  would vouchsafe the answer.

HAMLET  How if I answer no?

OSRIC  I mean, my lord, the opposition of your person in trial.

HAMLET  Sir, I will walk here in the hall. If it please  175  his majesty, it is the breathing time of day with me.° Let the foils be brought, the gentleman willing, and the king hold his purpose, I will win for him an I can;

if not, I will gain nothing but my shame and the odd hits.    180

OSRIC  Shall I deliver you e'en so?

HAMLET  To this effect, sir, after what flourish your nature will.

OSRIC  I commend my duty to your lordship.

HAMLET  Yours, yours. [Exit OSRIC.] He does well to  185  commend it himself; there are no tongues else for's turn.

HORATIO  This lapwing° runs away with the shell on his head.

HAMLET  'A did comply, sir, with his dug° before 'a  190  sucked it. Thus has he, and many more of the same breed that I know the drossy age dotes on, only got the tune of the time and, out of an habit of encounter,° a kind of yeasty° collection, which carries them through and through the most fanned and winnowed opinions;  195  and do but blow them to their trial, the bubbles are out.°

*Enter a* LORD.

LORD  My lord, his majesty commended him to you by young Osric, who brings back to him that you attend him in the hall. He sends to know if your  200  pleasure hold to play with Laertes, or that you will take longer time.

HAMLET  I am constant to my purposes; they follow the king's pleasure. If his fitness speaks, mine is ready; now or whensoever, provided I be so able as now.    205

LORD  The king and queen and all are coming down.

HAMLET  In happy time.

LORD  The queen desires you to use some gentle entertainment° to Laertes before you fall to play.

HAMLET  She well instructs me.    [Exit LORD.]    210

HORATIO  You will lose this wager, my lord.

HAMLET  I do not think so. Since he went into France I have been in continual practice. I shall win at the odds. But thou wouldst not think how ill all's here about my heart. But it is no matter.    215

HORATIO  Nay, good my lord—

HAMLET  It is but foolery, but it is such a kind of gaingiving° as would perhaps trouble a woman.

HORATIO  If your mind dislike anything, obey it. I will forestall their repair hither and say you are not fit.    220

HAMLET  Not a whit, we defy augury. There is special providence in the fall of a sparrow.° If it be now, 'tis not to come; if it be not to come, it will be now; if it be not now, yet it will come. The readiness is all. Since no man of aught he leaves knows, what is't to leave  225  betimes?° Let be.

*A table prepared. [Enter]* TRUMPETS, DRUMS, *and* OFFICERS *with cushions;* KING, QUEEN, [OSRIC,] *and all the* STATE, *[with]* foils, daggers, *[and stoups of wine borne in]; and* LAERTES.

124 **concernancy** meaning  128 **will to't** will get there  137 **approve** commend  143–44 **imputation** reputation  144 **meed** merit  150 **impawned** wagered  152 **assigns** accompaniments; **hangers** straps hanging the sword to the belt  153 **carriages** an affected word for hangers  153–54 **responsive** corresponding  155 **liberal conceit** elaborate design  158 **margent** i.e., marginal (explanatory) comment  176 **breathing . . . me** time when I take exercise  188 **lapwing** the new-hatched lapwing was thought to run around with half its shell on its head  190 '**A . . . dug** he was ceremoniously polite to his mother's breast  193 **out . . . encounter** out of his own superficial way of meeting and conversing with people  194 **yeasty** frothy  196–97 **the . . . out** i.e., they are blown away (the reference is to the "yeasty collection")  208–09 **to . . . entertainment** to be courteous  217–18 **gain-giving** misgiving  222 **the . . . sparrow** cf. Matthew 10:29, "Are not two sparrows sold for a farthing? and one of them shall not fall on the ground without your Father"  226 **betimes** early

KING
Come, Hamlet, come, and take this hand from me.

[*The* KING *puts Laertes' hand into Hamlet's.*]

HAMLET
Give me your pardon, sir. I have done you wrong,
But pardon't, as you are a gentleman.
This presence° knows, and you must needs have heard,    230
How I am punished with a sore distraction.
What I have done
That might your nature, honor, and exception°
Roughly awake, I here proclaim was madness.
Was't Hamlet wronged Laertes? Never Hamlet.    235
If Hamlet from himself be ta'en away,
And when he's not himself does wrong Laertes,
Then Hamlet does it not, Hamlet denies it.
Who does it then? His madness. If't be so,
Hamlet is of the faction° that is wronged;    240
His madness is poor Hamlet's enemy.
Sir, in this audience,
Let my disclaiming from a purposed evil
Free me so far in your most generous thoughts
That I have shot my arrow o'er the house    245
And hurt my brother.

LAERTES                    I am satisfied in nature,
Whose motive in this case should stir me most
To my revenge. But in my terms of honor
I stand aloof, and will no reconcilement
Till by some elder masters of known honor    250
I have a voice and precedent° of peace
To keep my name ungored. But till that time
I do receive your offered love like love,
And will not wrong it.

HAMLET                    I embrace it freely,
And will this brother's wager frankly play.    255
Give us the foils. Come on.

LAERTES                    Come, one for me.

HAMLET
I'll be your foil,° Laertes. In mine ignorance
Your skill shall, like a star i' th' darkest night,
Stick fiery off° indeed.

LAERTES                    You mock me, sir.

HAMLET
No, by this hand.    260

KING
Give them the foils, young Osric. Cousin Hamlet,
You know the wager?

HAMLET                    Very well, my lord.
Your grace has laid the odds o' th' weaker side.

KING
I do not fear it, I have seen you both;
But since he is bettered,° we have therefore odds.    265

LAERTES
This is too heavy; let me see another.

HAMLET
This likes me well. These foils have all a length?

*Prepare to play.*

230 **presence** royal assembly    233 **exception** disapproval
240 **faction** party, side    251 **voice and precedent** authoritative opinion justified by precedent    257 **foil** (1) blunt sword
(2) background (of metallic leaf) for a jewel    259 **Stick fiery
off** stand out brilliantly    265 **bettered** has improved (in
France)

OSRIC
Ay, my good lord.

KING
Set me the stoups of wine upon that table.
If Hamlet give the first or second hit,    270
Or quit° in answer of the third exchange,
Let all the battlements their ordnance fire.
The king shall drink to Hamlet's better breath,
And in the cup an union° shall he throw
Richer than that which four successive kings    275
In Denmark's crown have worn. Give me the cups,
And let the kettle° to the trumpet speak,
The trumpet to the cannoneer without,
The cannons to the heavens, the heaven to earth,
"Now the king drinks to Hamlet." Come, begin.    280

*Trumpets the while.*

And you, the judges, bear a wary eye.

HAMLET
Come on, sir.

LAERTES                    Come, my lord. *They play.*

HAMLET                                        One.

LAERTES                                        No.

HAMLET                                        Judgment?

OSRIC
A hit, a very palpable hit.

*Drum, trumpets, and shot. Flourish; a piece goes off.*

LAERTES                    Well, again.

KING
Stay, give me drink. Hamlet, this pearl is thine.
Here's to thy health. Give him the cup.    285

HAMLET
I'll play this bout first; set it by awhile.
Come. [*They play.*] Another hit. What say you?

LAERTES
A touch, a touch; I do confess't.

KING
Our son shall win.

QUEEN                    He's fat,° and scant of breath.
Here, Hamlet, take my napkin, rub thy brows.    290
The queen carouses to thy fortune, Hamlet.

HAMLET
Good madam!

KING                    Gertrude, do not drink.

QUEEN
I will, my lord; I pray you pardon me.

[*Drinks.*]

KING [*Aside.*]
It is the poisoned cup; it is too late.

HAMLET
I dare not drink yet, madam—by and by.    295

QUEEN
Come, let me wipe thy face.

LAERTES
My lord, I'll hit him now.

KING                    I do not think't.

LAERTES [*Aside.*]
And yet it is almost against my conscience.

271 **quit** repay, hit back    274 **union** pearl    277 **kettle** kettledrum    289 **fat** (1) sweaty (2) out of training

HAMLET
Come for the third, Laertes. You do but dally.
I pray you pass with your best violence;                          300
I am sure you make a wanton° of me.
LAERTES
Say you so? Come on.

[*They*] *play.*

OSRIC
Nothing neither way.
LAERTES
Have at your now!

*In scuffling they change rapiers, [and both are wounded].*

KING                          Part them. They are incensed.
HAMLET
Nay, come—again! [*The* QUEEN *falls.*]
OSRIC                          Look to the queen there, ho!      305
HORATIO
They bleed on both sides. How is it, my lord?
OSRIC
How is't, Laertes?
LAERTES
Why, as a woodcock to mine own springe,° Osric.
I am justly killed with mine own treachery.
HAMLET
How does the queen?
KING                          She sounds° to see them bleed.    310
QUEEN
No, no, the drink, the drink! O my dear Hamlet!
The drink, the drink! I am poisoned.          [*Dies.*]
HAMLET
O villainy! Ho! Let the door be locked.
Treachery! Seek it out.

[LAERTES *falls.*]

LAERTES
It is here, Hamlet. Hamlet, thou art slain;                       315
No med'cine in the world can do thee good.
In thee there is not half an hour's life.
The treacherous instrument is in thy hand,
Unbated and envenomed. The foul practice°
Hath turned itself on me. Lo, here I lie,                          320
Never to rise again. Thy mother's poisoned.
I can no more. The king, the king's to blame.
HAMLET
The point envenomed too?
Then, venom, to thy work.

*Hurts the* KING.

ALL   Treason! Treason!                                           325
KING
O, yet defend me, friends. I am but hurt.
HAMLET
Here, thou incestuous, murd'rous, damnèd Dane,
Drink off this potion. Is thy union here?
Follow my mother.                          KING *dies.*
LAERTES                          He is justly served.
It is a poison tempered° by himself.                              330
Exchange forgiveness with me, noble Hamlet.

Mine and my father's death come not upon thee,
Nor thine on me!                          *Dies.*
HAMLET
Heaven make thee free of it! I follow thee.
I am dead, Horatio. Wretched queen, adieu!                        335
You that look pale and tremble at this chance,
That are but mutes° or audience to this act,
Had I but time (as this fell sergeant,° Death,
Is strict in his arrest) O, I could tell you—
But let it be. Horatio, I am dead;                                340
Thou livest; report me and my cause aright
To the unsatisfied.°
HORATIO                          Never believe it.
I am more an antique Roman° than a Dane.
Here's yet some liquor left.
HAMLET                          As th' art a man,
Give me the cup. Let go. By heaven, I'll ha't!                    345
O God, Horatio, what a wounded name,
Things standing thus unknown, shall live behind me!
If thou didst ever hold me in thy heart,
Absent thee from felicity° awhile,
And in this harsh world draw thy breath in pain,                 350
To tell my story.          *A march afar off.* [*Exit* OSRIC.]
                          What warlike noise is this?

*Enter* OSRIC.

OSRIC
Young Fortinbras, with conquest come from Poland,
To th' ambassadors of England gives
This warlike volley.
HAMLET                          O, I die, Horatio!
The potent poison quite o'ercrows° my spirit.                    355
I cannot live to hear the news from England,
But I do prophesy th' election lights
On Fortinbras. He has my dying voice.
So tell him, with th' occurrents,° more and less,
Which have solicited°—the rest is silence.          *Dies.* 360
HORATIO
Now cracks a noble heart. Good night, sweet prince,
And flights of angels sing thee to thy rest.

[*March within.*]

Why does the drum come hither?

*Enter* FORTINBRAS, *with the* AMBASSADORS *with
drum, colors, and* ATTENDANTS.

FORTINBRAS
Where is this sight?
HORATIO                          What is it you would see?
If aught of woe or wonder, cease your search.                    365
FORTINBRAS
This quarry° cries on havoc.° O proud Death,
What feast is toward° in thine eternal cell
That thou so many princes at a shot
So bloodily hast struck?
AMBASSADOR                          The sight is dismal;

337 **mutes** performers who have no words to speak   338 **fell
sergeant** dread sheriff's officer   342 **unsatisfied** uninformed
343 **antique Roman** with reference to the old Roman fashion
of suicide   349 **felicity** i.e., the felicity of death   355 **o'er-
crows** overpowers (as a triumphant cock crows over its weak
opponent)   359 **occurrents** occurrences   360 **solicited** incited
366 **quarry** heap of slain bodies; **cries on havoc** proclaims
general slaughter   367 **toward** in preparation

301 **wanton** spoiled child   308 **springe** snare   310 **sounds**
swoons   319 **practice** deception   330 **tempered** mixed

And our affairs from England come too late. 370
The ears are senseless that should give us hearing
To tell him his commandment is fulfilled,
That Rosencrantz and Guildenstern are dead.
Where should we have our thanks?

HORATIO                                  Not from his° mouth,
Had it th' ability of life to thank you. 375
He never gave commandment for their death.
But since, so jump° upon this bloody question,
You from the Polack wars, and you from England,
Are here arrived, give order that these bodies
High on a stage° be placèd to the view, 380
And let me speak to th' yet unknowing world
How these things came about. So shall you hear
Of carnal, bloody, and unnatural acts,
Of accidental judgments, casual° slaughters,
Of deaths put on by cunning and forced cause, 385
And, in this upshot, purposes mistook
Fall'n on th' inventors' heads. All this can I
Truly deliver.

FORTINBRAS  Let us haste to hear it,

And call the noblest to the audience.
For me, with sorrow I embrace my fortune. 390
I have some rights of memory° in this kingdom,
Which now to claim my vantage doth invite me.

HORATIO
Of that I shall have also cause to speak,
And from his mouth whose voice will draw on° more.
But let this same be presently performed, 395
Even while men's minds are wild, lest more mischance
On° plots and errors happen.

FORTINBRAS                            Let four captains
Bear Hamlet like a soldier to the stage,
For he was likely, had he been put on,°
To have proved most royal; and for his passage° 400
The soldiers' music and the rite of war
Speak loudly for him.
Take up the bodies. Such a sight as this
Becomes the field,° but here shows much amiss.
Go, bid the soldiers shoot. 405

*Exeunt marching; after the which a peal of ordnance
are shot off.*

374 **his** Claudius'  377 **jump** precisely  380 **stage** platform
384 **casual** not humanly planned, chance

391 **rights of memory** remembered claims  394 **voice . . .
on** vote will influence  397 **On** on top of  399 **put on**
advanced (to the throne)  400 **passage** death  404 **field**
battlefield

# THE MERRY WIVES
# OF WINDSOR

EDITED BY WILLIAM GREEN

## Introduction[1]

What a delightful picture of Elizabethan village life Shakespeare presents in *The Merry Wives of Windsor*. He tickles our palates with hot venison pasty and pippins and cheese. He plunges us into a world where hawking and greyhound racing are matters of concern. He walks us through the town, alluding to the nearby Thames, Datchet Mead, Windsor Castle and its chapel. He takes us into the Garter Inn; and, lastly, he leaves us at midnight under Herne's Oak in Windsor Little Park. Yet his intent is not to extol village life for its own sake, for, as always, Shakespeare is interested in people. In this play he gives us a peek into the private lives of his villagers, showing us how love affects as disparate a group of individuals as one would ever expect to encounter in an English village.

There is, of course, the traditional sweet young maiden —Mistress Anne Page, the picture of "pretty virginity." She is in love with a handsome gentleman. He has for his rivals the shy, colorless nephew of a country justice and a choleric French physician who draws his patients from among the gentry and royalty. These are the principals of the subplot. In the main plot we meet a pair of prosperous townsmen—one given to extreme jealousy—whose vivacious wives prove more than a match for a fat, old, lecherous conniver from London. Rounding out this rich gallery of characters are a Welsh parson more adept at giving a Latin lesson than fighting a duel; a bluff, hearty innkeeper whose equanimity can be shattered only by such a major calamity as the theft of his post horses; a country justice of the peace; a goodhearted housekeeper, skilled as a go-between; and some sharpers parasitically attendant on the lecher.

Shakespeare takes these characters and places them in a fast-paced farce. He blends the two plot lines smoothly, and organically integrates his characters. When the play concludes, the audience may leave in a joyous mood, laughing over the fractured English of Evans and Caius, chuckling at the malapropisms of Mistress Quickly, delighted with the farce escapades, content that Jill got her Jack and that middle-class morality has been upheld.

A major Shakespearean work? Hardly. That audiences have not been disturbed by this question of major or minor is apparent from the long production record the play has had (including a performance before James I in November 1604) and from the adaptations it has undergone, first in John Dennis' dramatic version of 1702 (*The Comical Gallant*) and later in various operatic treatments.

Yet this play, so much the delight of theatergoers, has proved a bane to scholars. If "To thyself be enough" could be applied to *The Merry Wives*, there would be no problem. But since Shakespeare was a playwright in whom a continual line of development can be traced, the play must be considered in relation to the canon as a whole. And here a host of problems arises.

When examined in the study instead of on the stage, *The Merry Wives* engenders question after question. Why does a set of characters from the history plays (*Henry IV* and *Henry V*) appear in the script? No biographical links can be established between the six characters—Falstaff, Bardolph, Pistol, Nym, Justice Shallow, Mistress Quickly —and their namesakes in the history plays. Why does Shakespeare take such pains to give a historically accurate portrait of Windsor in the 1590's in this his sole play dealing entirely with contemporary English life? Why even select Windsor as the locale for a play about country life when Shakespeare knew Warwickshire so well? Why at a time when he had already produced masterful poetry in *A Midsummer Night's Dream* and *Romeo and Juliet* does he write a play almost entirely in prose? The little verse that appears must be classified as inferior. Why when engrossed in writing romantic comedy—*A Midsummer Night's Dream* and *The Merchant of Venice* show how far he had come with the genre since *The Two Gentlemen of Verona*—does he suddenly backtrack to the farcical treatment of love that he successfully presented in *The Taming of the Shrew*? And what source did he use for the play? None has been discovered.

A key to the answers to these questions is found in some allusions to Queen Elizabeth and Windsor Castle in V.v:

Cricket, to Windsor chimneys shalt thou leap.
Where fires thou find'st unraked and hearths unswept,

---

[1] Portions of the following are based on concepts developed in extended form in the editor's *Shakespeare's Merry Wives of Windsor*. Princeton: Princeton University Press, 1962. Permission has been granted by the Princeton University Press.

962

There pinch the maids as blue as bilberry.
Our radiant queen hates sluts and sluttery.    (V.v.45–48)

A few lines later the Fairy Queen instructs:

Search Windsor Castle, elves, within and out.
Strew good luck, ouphs, on every sacred room,
That it may stand till the perpetual doom,
In state as wholesome as in state 'tis fit,
Worthy the owner, and the owner it.
The several chairs of Order look you scour
With juice of balm and every precious flow'r.
Each fair instalment, coat, and several crest,
With loyal blazon, evermore be blest.
And nightly, meadow-fairies, look you sing,
Like to the Garter's compass, in a ring.
Th' expressure that it bears, green let it be,
More fertile-fresh than all the field to see;
And "Honi soit qui mal y pense" write
In emerald tufts, flow'rs purple, blue, and white—
Like sapphire, pearl, and rich embroidery,
Buckled below fair knighthood's bending knee—
Fairies use flow'rs for their charactery.    (V.v.58–75)

Two allusions attract attention in this passage: *Honi soit qui mal y pense*—motto of the Order of the Garter—and the instructions to the fairies to scour "the several chairs of Order." So deliberately does Shakespeare draw attention to the Order that we cannot ignore the references. They stand out even more sharply when we realize that earlier in the play (I.iv) Dr. Caius informed us he was hurrying to court for a "grand affair." Also, in II.i, Mistress Quickly noted that the town was filling with courtiers. Something concerning the Order of the Garter was happening in Windsor, and that something could only be an installation of Knights-Elect.

Now the Windsor setting makes sense, for if Shakespeare chose to allude to a Garter installation, what more appropriate place to locate the play than in Windsor, home of the Order of the Garter since the fourteenth century? Moreover, what need to state that the preparation of castle and chapel is for this ceremonial? The Elizabethans knew that the only Garter rite celebrated in Windsor was an installation—this by decree of Elizabeth in 1567. And the Elizabethans—at least those in courtly circles during the late 1590's—further knew what Garter installation Shakespeare was referring to—that of May 1597.

This last statement cannot be verified, but convincing circumstantial evidence has recently been adduced, and generally accepted by scholars, that the sole Garter occasion to which the allusions point is the April 1597 Feast of Saint George and its attendant ceremonials. On this occasion five individuals were named to the Order. Two of them have particular bearing on the genesis of *The Merry Wives*: Frederick, Duke of Württemberg (to whom we shall return), and George Carey, the second Lord Hunsdon.

Hunsdon, a favorite cousin of Queen Elizabeth, was patron of Shakespeare's company at this time. His connection with the company becomes particularly significant in light of an old stage tradition concerning the composition of *The Merry Wives*. According to the tradition, first recorded by John Dennis in 1702, Queen Elizabeth commanded that the play be written and that the task be

completed within fourteen days. Nicholas Rowe, in his 1709 edition of Shakespeare's *Works*, amplified the tradition by stating that the queen "was so well pleas'd with that admirable character of *Falstaff*, in the two Parts of *Henry* the Fourth, that she commanded him to continue it for one Play more, and to show him in Love."

Stage traditions, especially one appearing eighty-six years after Shakespeare's death, must be taken with skepticism. Yet in the face of no counterevidence, this tradition deserves respect. Its foundation is based on the queen's desire to see Falstaff in love, establishing that she had already become familiar with old tunbelly. Although no court play lists are extant, we do know that Shakespeare's company performed before the courtiers six times during the 1596–97 Christmas play season: December 26, 27, 1596; January 1, 6, and February 6, 8, 1597. That *1 Henry IV* was among the works presented is a strong possibility. Recent study of this first Falstaff play points to the autumn of 1596 as the date for its completion—a date slightly earlier than the generalized 1597 traditionally assigned.

Allowing for conjecture, we may assume that the queen expressed her delight with Falstaff in *1 Henry IV*, wondered aloud how the fat knight would fare in a romantic entanglement, had her remarks picked up by Lord Hunsdon and transmitted to Shakespeare with a request to have the play ready for presentation at the April 1597 Saint George's day festivities. Hunsdon had good reason for making such a request, for not only was he to be named a Garter knight on that occasion, but he also was to become Lord Chamberlain of England. Although this latter event occurred on April 17, Hunsdon knew of the appointment several weeks in advance, as he did of his impending Order election. *The Merry Wives* may be considered his "thank you note" to the queen.

Now, we need not take Dennis' remarks about finishing the play in fourteen days literally, especially since Dennis, in one of his letters, later recorded the time span as ten days. Rather, they point to a short period of time for composition. And *The Merry Wives* bears overwhelming marks of hasty composition, perhaps more than any other play of Shakespeare's. The Shallow-Falstaff quarrel of the opening scene is never resolved; the horse-stealing subplot of the fourth act with its references to a German duke is not in any way integrated into the main plot lines of the play; the Caius-Evans revenge scheme dies aborning; anachronisms in time sequences are present; the costume colors in the fairy scene are hopelessly confused; and various other errors appear in the text. Since by 1597 Shakespeare had established a reputation as a skilled dramatist—only a year later Francis Meres was to cite him among the English as "most excellent" in comedy and tragedy—so much slipshod workmanship must be attributed to writing against the clock.

Creating a play to order on short notice, one showing Falstaff in love, was a formidable task. Shakespeare simplified it first by trying to adapt material already at hand and then by revamping some old play. In the spring of 1597, he appears to have been at work on *2 Henry IV*. The opening of *The Merry Wives* with Falstaff, Shallow, Bardolph, and Pistol in a country setting reminds us strongly of the Gloucestershire scenes in the *Henry* play. Shakespeare initially attempts to create a new plot situation for these characters, but after about a hundred lines he gives up. Under the pressure of time, instead of starting over, he leaves the Falstaff-Shallow quarrel unresolved and attempts to fit Falstaff and crew into the plot of an old play.

This work, in both its main plot and its subplot, bears traits of Italian comedy, and was probably rooted in a tale or tales from the Italian novellas that had been translated into English in various collections since the 1560's. The main plot deals with the stock situation of a clever lover who attempts to deceive a husband. By reversing the roles and making the lover the duped one, a farce situation results. To this plot is grafted—either by Shakespeare or the source author—the traditional Italian tale of two young lovers who cannot gain parental permission to marry. The girl in these stories often is involved with three suitors, at least one of whom is a grotesque character. She also has her maid as a go-between.

Into these tales Shakespeare marches Falstaff and company. Falstaff, of course, converts easily into the duped lover; but the other characters, with the exception of Dame Quickly, who becomes the go-between, cannot be matched with existing characters in the source. Thus Shakespeare is forced to let Shallow wander in and out of the play with no real function and to make what use he can of Bardolph, Nym, and Pistol before writing them out of the script.

In making Falstaff the duped lover, Shakespeare not only fulfilled the Queen's request, but went one step further, for he knew esthetically, as Edmund Malone long ago observed, "what the queen, if the story be true, seems not to have known . . . Falstaff could not love, but by ceasing to be Falstaff. He could only counterfeit love, and his professions could be prompted, not by the hope of pleasure, but of money." The Falstaff of *The Merry Wives* must, therefore, be considered a new character with an old name.

At the start of this play the fat knight does bear some resemblances to his counterpart in the *Henry IV* plays in the lusty, blustering manner with which he outfaces Shallow and Slender. And in his soliloquy in IV.v, Shakespeare may have allowed him to reminisce over the old days with the mad Prince of Wales when Falstaff says,

I would all the world might be cozened, for I have been cozened and beaten too. If it should come to the ear of the court how I have been transformed, and how my transformation hath been washed and cudgeled, they would melt me out of my fat drop by drop, and liquor fishermen's boots with me. I warrant they would whip me with their fine wits till I were as crestfall'n as a dried pear.

(IV.v. 90–97)

However, from the beginning of I.iii—when the action proper gets under way—we have a different Falstaff, one who appears to be a reworking of a scholar or pedant from the source story. Thus the Host says to him, "Speak scholarly and wisely"; Ford, in his disguise as Brooke, notes in II.ii, "Sir, I hear you are a scholar" and follows this up several lines later, observing, "You are a gentleman of excellent breeding, admirable discourse, of great admittance, authentic in your place and person, generally allowed for your many warlike, courtlike, and learned preparations." Literary allusions and such phraseology as "Mistress Ford . . . I see you are obsequious in your love, and I profess requital to a hair's breadth," crop up in Falstaff's speech and contrast sharply with the racy, oath-laden utterances we have come to associate with the "fat-kidneyed rascal."

This scholar-cum-knight is now a butt, a dupe. He is the farcical target of two delightful Windsor housewives. We must forget the merry rogue who, caught in a pack of lies in describing the Gadshill robbery, is able to wheedle out of the situation by exclaiming, "If reasons were as plentiful as blackberries, I would give no man a reason upon compulsion, I."

In reworking Falstaff's cronies—Pistol, Nym, and Shallow—as well as in handling the new characters Slender, Caius, and Ford, Shakespeare proved himself more than a mechanical adapter. He fashioned these characters according to the mold of "humors comedy," a genre newly introduced to the stage by George Chapman in 1596. Shakespeare first attempted portrayals of humors, or temperaments, with some of the fringe characters in *2 Henry IV*, the play, we will remember, that he probably had been working on when interrupted by the queen's command; but he did so here on a rather superficial level. Only Pistol of the "irregular humorists" of *2 Henry IV* emerges as a full-fledged humors character.

The Pistol of *The Merry Wives* is basically the same character he is in *2 Henry IV*, a blusterer full of sound and fury. His cohort Nym, as the name indicates (Middle English *nimen*, "to take"), is a filcher; his deeds proclaim it as he joins with Pistol to part Slender from his purse and Mistress Bridget from the handle of her fan. And his overworked phrase "That's my humor" serves further to betray his generic origin. Their fellow traveler from the history plays, Shallow, remains the talkative, empty-headed country justice of *2 Henry IV*.

Slender and Caius, however, receive fuller treatment, their humors portrayal going beyond the mere use of type names. As the second and third wooer to Anne Page, they function integrally in the plot. They are basically the two grotesques frequently found as suitors to the *amorosa* in Italian comedy; Shakespeare has skillfully retained their grotesque function by casting them as humors figures. Caius is presented as a choleric Frenchman. His medical side is never commented on by Shakespeare. And Slender is portrayed as a country gull. No sooner does he arrive in town than he is robbed by Pistol, Nym, and Bardolph. He is completely passive in the suit to Anne Page. Without his Book of Songs and Sonnets he is unable to woo the lady. Slender of body and slender of mind is he indeed.

The most complete humors portrait in *The Merry Wives* is that of Ford. All Windsor knows, as Quickly relates, that "he's a very jealousy man." Ford even talks of it openly with others. And in private he shows that he is so completely consumed by the flames of jealousy that he would "rather trust a Fleming with my butter, Parson Hugh the Welshman with my cheese, an Irishman with my aqua vitae bottle, or a thief to walk my ambling gelding, than my wife with herself. . . . God be praised for my jealousy." So intense is this emotion that Ford becomes despicable enough to hire another man, Falstaff, to seduce his wife. In this action Shakespeare exploits Ford's humor to increase the plot complications. However, at the proper moment he makes Ford see the foolishness of his ways and repent (IV.iv). The entire handling of Ford's character is one-dimensional and makes an interesting contrast with the deeper study of jealousy found in *Othello*.

What is striking about Shakespeare's treatment of *The Merry Wives* as humors comedy is that nowhere do we see the savage bite of the Jonsonian moralist seeking to strip the mask of hypocrisy from humanity. Nor are follies and vices held up to scorn and ridicule. When Shakespeare exposes the weaknesses of Ford or Caius or Slender, he does so with gentleness—and compassion. Even Nym and Pistol do not meet the fate they deserve. That Shakespeare even was able to graft elements of humors comedy onto the basic farce-comedy plot of *The Merry Wives* is a tribute to his artistry, considering the limited amount of time in which he had to work.

Not only in turning to humors comedy was Shakespeare following the latest dramatic trends, but also in bringing on stage foreign character types. In making Caius a French physician (there is no reason for linking him with the founder of the Cambridge college), Shakespeare may have been mocking the predilection of the upper-class Londoners for foreign physicians. But with Hugh Evans, he was surely capitalizing on the interest in stage Welshmen which started about 1593 and continued unabated for several years. Witness Glendower and Fluellen in Shakespeare's other plays.

Thus far we have seen how Shakespeare, by following popular theatrical trends, reworked his Italianate source and created new interest in what might otherwise have been a dull set of stock characters. Still unaccounted for, however, are the Windsor setting, the Order of the Garter allusions, or the horse-stealing subplot. These are not essential to the action line of the play. In fact, the inferior quarto text excises all references to either the court or the Order of the Garter.

The allusions and setting have already been discussed in establishing the date of the play as 1597. Their presence in the script, however, is more than ornamentation, for Shakespeare does combine them into a logical pattern. Aware of the special occasion for which he was to write the play and the select audience that would see it, Shakespeare apparently decided to include material that would reflect on that occasion and on his patron's own election to the Order.

The initial step was to change the locale of the Italianate original to Windsor, easily done since all this original demanded by way of place was a plausible setting for a group of middle-class characters. Immediately with the Windsor switch a Garter association was set up for an Elizabethan audience. This association is carried still further by depicting activity at Windsor Castle—preparation for a ceremonial that by historical evidence could only be an Order of the Garter installation. Shakespeare then clinched the Garter-Windsor link by penning a tribute to the Order. He also added a compliment to the queen, knowing that she would be at the special performance.

This type of structuring is not unique for Shakespeare. He was a master of depicting multiple activities in his plays, making his audiences aware that there are worlds within worlds. Using the terms Harry Levin has given us in *The Overreacher*,[2] the "grand affair" at the castle becomes

the overplot; the Falstaff-in-love story, the main plot; and the Anne Page-Fenton romance, which parallels the variation on the "course of true love" in the main plot, the underplot. There is even one character who moves from plot to plot: Doctor Caius. We must not forget that three times in I.iv he informs us that he is on his way to the "grand affair," that is, the installation.

One problem still remains in this examination of the plot structure: the presence of the horse-stealing subplot of the fourth act. This section is not based on any of the incidents in the story line proper and disappears from the play as mysteriously as it came. The key character in it is a German duke who never appears but whose men make off with three of the Host's post horses. To be understood, this subplot must be seen as an appendage of the Garter overplot, but alas, it is such a weak appendage that it dangles completely unsupported.

The German duke alluded to is most assuredly Frederick, Duke of Württemberg, who, as previously mentioned, was one of the five individuals elected to the Order in 1597. He was, in fact, the only German ruler made a Garter knight between 1579 and 1612. Ever since 1592 when he had made a trip to England while still Count Mompelgard, Frederick had been obsessed with a desire to become a Knight of the Garter. He badgered Elizabeth and her courtiers with letters and with embassages over the next several years in support of this desire. The queen, for various reasons, paid little heed to his wishes. Finally, in 1597, at a time of serious strain in Anglo-German relations stemming from bitter disagreements over trading policies between the English and the Hanse, Elizabeth sanctioned Frederick's election to the Order. That this was done solely out of political expediency to keep the duke as a German ally is virtually a certainty. Since Frederick had not been particularly discreet in his campaign for election, a goodly segment of those in court circles were fully aware of this vain duke's interest in the Garter.

Even after his election Frederick continued to be a topical figure, for now he began his campaign for investiture and installation—the two final ceremonies for full-fledged Garter membership. Elizabeth may have delayed in sending an investiture mission to Württemberg because the costs were so great or she may have wanted to have a hold over Frederick, as a friendly German prince, so that he would actively support her in the Hanse dispute. This dispute had become so serious by the summer of 1597 that Emperor Rudolph II barred the English Merchant Adventurers from the German empire. Whatever the reason behind Elizabeth's stalling, the queen died in 1603 without either an end to the Hanse dispute or investiture for Frederick.

Soon after James I came to the throne, Emperor Rudolph settled the Hanse dispute, and Duke Frederick renewed his pleas for investiture. This time he succeeded, and he received the long-coveted insignia of the Order during the investiture ceremonies in Stuttgart on November 6, 1603. The following April he sent a proxy delegate for installation at Windsor during the annual Feast of Saint George celebration. Clearly Duke Frederick and his lobbying activities were known to a great number of those in court circles, and clearly the twelve years that those activities span would have brought Frederick to the attention of even a wider circle of Londoners. There is, therefore, no

---

[2] Harry Levin, *The Overreacher* (1952).

reason to doubt the recognition of any allusions to Frederick in the play by the audience at the posited initial Garter production or at subsequent performances through 1604.

Moreover, evidence exists in the horse-stealing subplot to link the "duke de Jamany" with Frederick. In the corrupt quarto version of the subplot appears the curious phrase *cosen garmombles*. The Folio text reads *cozen-Iermans* at the same point. In all probability the Q text preserves the original reading. (We may attribute the Folio version to a revision made after the publication of the quarto text in 1602 when the topicality of a direct reference to Frederick was either no longer proper or intelligible.) *Garmombles*, as Leslie Hotson suggests, represents a scrambling of Garter and Mompelgard. That his suggestion is apt can be supported by the observation that Shallow's scrambling of *Custos Rotulorum* for *Custalorum* in the opening scene is similar in technique. The *cosen* of the phrase is a pun on *cosen* or *cozen*, "to cheat," and on the salutatory address used by a ruler at this time when corresponding with another ruler. This oblique identification of Frederick with the German duke of the play is further established by Doctor Caius' information that "dere is no duke dat de court is know to come." This exactly describes the election of Frederick to the Order, for he was elected *in absentia* (a normal procedure with foreign rulers) and not informed of this until October, five months after the installation ceremonies.

Now, neither of the above allusions links Frederick directly with the theft of the Host's post horses, the action of the sketchy subplot. Impetus for this incident comes, probably, from a post-horse scandal that occurred in September 1596, when Le Sieur Aymar de Chastes, Governor of Dieppe, was returning to France from an embassage to England concerning an Anglo-French defense treaty. De Chastes had been hurrying home to prepare Dieppe for the reciprocating English embassage that had as one of its charges the investiture of Henry IV into the Order of the Garter. En route to the coast, de Chastes, probably through misunderstanding the operations of the English posting system, abused the authority of a warrant he had been issued to assist him in procuring post horses, and, with two of his retinue, tried to take by force post horses from an innkeeper in Gravesend. He also got into difficulty with hackneymen from Rochester for attempting to take post horses beyond the stage for which they had been hired. Knowledge of both incidents was widespread.

Only six months later Shakespeare was presumably working on *The Merry Wives* for presentation at the Garter Feast. Intent on reenforcing the Garter overplot to the play, he reworked the de Chastes posting scandal, having recalled that it was connected with a Garter event —the investiture of Henry IV. Since, for diplomatic reasons, he could not lampoon so distinguished a man as de Chastes, Shakespeare turned him into another foreigner, one even more closely bound up with the Order ceremonials and one who could safely be satirized: the Duke of Württemberg. After all, the English court knew precisely why Frederick had been elected to the Order and how obnoxious he had made himself in lobbying for election. Thus, the three Frenchmen become Germans— a deft stroke at a time when the Hanse troubles would have aroused anti-German sentiment among the normally xenophobic Englishmen; the governor becomes a duke; and the locale shifts from Gravesend and Rochester to Windsor.

Allowing for the conjectural nature of the above account, we see that it does explain the disparate elements of the horse-stealing subplot. The problem is not that this subplot is a fragment of a larger unit, now lost, which developed the Evans-Caius revenge scheme—as some scholars, embarrassed to account for the horse-stealing episode, have hypothesized—but rather that having written the material, Shakespeare could not integrate it into the other plot lines of the play. So he left it alone, an isolated entity mutely joining the fragmentary Shallow-Falstaff quarrel as witnesses to the difficulty of writing against the incessant ticking of a clock.

If history has been dwelled on at length, it is because only through history can we understand the tripartite plot structure of the play. If *The Merry Wives* were written for a special occasion, and here we must realize that the evidence is primarily circumstantial, that occasion must be explored for insight into the peculiar characteristics of the play.

Shakespeare's aim in *The Merry Wives* was to entertain, to counterpoint the serious ceremonials of the 1597 Feast of Saint George with mirth. This he does by writing a farce. Thus he tries to make everyone happy: Queen Elizabeth, by fulfilling her wish to see Falstaff in love; Lord Hunsdon, his patron, by prefiguring Hunsdon's own installation at Windsor a month hence; the courtiers at large, by ridiculing the Garter-obsessed Duke of Württemberg; and the general theatrical public, by bringing before them one of the freshest sets of humors characters in Elizabethan comedy as well as upholding on stage the virtue of English women. (Says Mistress Page, "We'll leave a proof by that which we will do,/Wives may be merry, and yet honest too.") A tall order for a short space of time in which to execute it. Surely Shakespeare deserves some forgiveness for the abundance of loose ends in the play.

## A NOTE ON THE SOURCE

*The Merry Wives* belongs to that small group of Shakespeare's plays that have no known source. But Renaissance Italian novellas afford several duped lovers who, like Falstaff, have three assignations with the wife of a jealous husband. Anne Page, the young maiden sought after by three suitors, finds herself in a situation that is a recurring one in conventional Italian comedy. Thus, there is scholarly consensus that whatever the precise source of *The Merry Wives*, that source was a work based on Italian models.

Italian tales had been known in English translation in the sixteenth century through such collections as Painter's *The Palace of Pleasure* (1566) and Pettie's *A Petite Palace of Pettie his Pleasure* (1576). However, in the face of the stage tradition about hurried composition for *The Merry Wives*, scholars generally believe that Shakespeare, rather than directly having dramatized any of these tales, reworked an old play in the repertory of his company. For convenience, we may term this old play the *Ur-Merry Wives*. That Italianate plays should have been available is not startling; the conventions of Italian comedy had filtered into English drama by the 1570's (even earlier if we allow for influences from Plautus and Terence) through performances of the School Plays—academic comedies presented at Oxford and Cambridge. These comedies were written in imitation of or translated from the Italian *commedia erudita*. The *commedia dell' arte* also may have provided material; extant *commedia dell' arte* scenari reveal traces of the situations found in both the main plot and the subplot of *The Merry Wives*. And Italian actors appeared in England in the 1570's in productions from their native repertory.

The dramatic source—if there was one—of *The Merry Wives* is lost, but three tales have been uncovered that contain resemblances to incidents found in Shakespeare's version. That most closely mirroring events of the main plot is a tale published in 1558 in Ser Giovanni Fiorentino's *Il Pecorone* (Day I, Novella 2). It relates how Bucciuolo, upon completing his legal studies in Bologna, goes to his teacher for instruction on the art of falling in love. Following his teacher's advice, he visits a church, where he becomes enamored of a young lady who, unknown to the student, is the wife of the teacher. She encourages Bucciuolo's attentions and soon invites him to visit her. Bucciuolo, as previously requested by the teacher, keeps him apprised of all progress. This teacher, a very jealous man, begins to suspect that his wife is the young woman. When he learns of the meeting, he rushes home at the appointed time. The wife hides Bucciuolo under a pile of newly laundered clothes, and thus he escapes detection. The young man reports the incident to his mentor the next day and adds that he has been invited back for a rendezvous the following night. This time the teacher, in a great rage, follows the student and knocks on the door as soon as Bucciuolo has entered. The lady opens the door and embraces her husband in such a manner that Bucciuolo is able to slip out safely. She then shouts that her husband has gone mad; the neighbors and her brothers arrive, and when the brothers see the teacher pierce the pile of laundry with his sword, they consider him insane. The husband then threatens the brothers, who beat him with cudgels. Word goes through the neighborhood that the teacher indeed has gone mad. Bucciuolo, in sympathy, comes to visit him, discovers that he has been cuckolding his own teacher, tells the wretched man that he grieves for him, and then leaves Bologna.

The tale contains striking similarities with the main plot of *The Merry Wives*. Fiorentino's story revolves around a jealous husband who gets a full report of the assignations between his wife and her lover. The lover is hidden under laundry, which the husband examines on his second attempt to catch the pair. Each time the lover escapes, and at the end he learns the truth of the situation. The duped husband receives a beating after the second visit. Shakespeare's important change is in making the lover rather than the husband the duped male.

Another story of a duped husband that resembles *The Merry Wives* is "The Tale of the Two Lovers of Pisa" from Tarlton's *Newes out of Purgatorie* (1590). The husband, a physician, is a very jealous man who decides to test the virtue of his wife by encouraging a young man to make love to her. The young man, who does not know that the physician and the husband are one, reports daily on the progress of his affair to the physician. Three assignations take place, and each time the young man escapes when the physician arrives to search for him. In the first instance, the young man is concealed in a vat of feathers, in the second he hides between two ceilings, and in the third he is carried from the house in a chest supposedly containing the physician's papers. At the end the lover learns the truth of the situation.

This tale also opens with an account of how the girl came to marry the physician. The details are similar to incidents in the Anne Page story. Margaret, the daughter of a wealthy gentleman, has many suitors, but her father wants her to marry a rich husband. The father finally selects Mutio, a rich but old and jealous physician, and forces Margaret to marry him. It is possible that the germ for the Anne Page subplot lies in this tale. (Or, as Oscar Campbell has theorized, it may come from one of the *commedia erudita*-type plays.)

The third tale with plot parallels is "Of Two Brethren and their Wives" from *Riche his Farewell to Military Profession* (1581) by Barnaby Riche. This tale is of interest because it deals with the intrigues of a married woman who is involved with three suitors. Two of them, the doctor and lawyer, are comic types. Both are duped by the woman. Possibly the author of the *Ur-Merry Wives* switched elements from the main plot to the subplot and vice versa.

What this brief account of possible source materials shows is that all the details of story found in *The Merry Wives* plot lines were known in both narrative and dramatic form by 1590—several years before the composition of *The Merry Wives*. In adapting the to-hand material, Shakespeare added the Falstaff crew from the *Henry* plays and, as discussed in the Introduction, inserted the topical events reflected in the horse-stealing subplot and in the court and Garter allusions.

## A NOTE ON THE TEXT

Two texts of *The Merry Wives of Windsor* exist: that of the 1602 quarto and that of the 1623 Folio. The play had been entered in the Stationers' Register on January 18, 1602, for publication by John Busby, but Busby immediately transferred his rights to Arthur Johnson. Johnson brought out Q1 later that year with Thomas Creede as his printer. In 1619, Thomas Pavier issued a second quarto that basically reprints Q1 and is therefore without textual authority. The last early quarto of the play, that of 1630, except for some changes in spelling and punctuation, was printed from the Folio. Thus Q1 and F stand as the only texts of editorial importance.

There are significant differences between these two texts. Not only is Q1 some twelve hundred lines shorter, but it omits and transposes scenes, cuts speaking parts for William and Robin, excises all references to the court and Order of the Garter, and makes a jumble of many individual passages. In sum, although coherent, the quarto text is inferior to the Folio version. Yet the quarto contains certain passages and readings—notably Brooke as the alias for Ford, and *cosen garmombles* in place of *cozen-germans*—which appear to be genuinely Shakespeare's.

Various theories have been advanced over the years to account for the two versions of the play. Scholarly consensus marks the Folio text as the authentic version. However, according to a strong current theory, F rests upon a

1597 mother text that had undergone minor modifications between the original production and publication of the Folio in 1623.

The quarto version, it is posited, represents an abridgment of that mother text, illegitimately made through memorial reconstruction for a provincial acting company around 1601. The pirate was most certainly a "hired man" who played the Host in the original Lord Chamberlain's Men productions of the play. While making his memorial reconstruction, this traitor actor seems to have restored to the text the "Brooke" reading that had been altered to "Broome" in 1597. This was done to avoid conflict with the family of William Brooke, Lord Cobham, who had taken umbrage at Shakespeare's original name for Falstaff in *1 Henry IV*—Oldcastle, a Brooke family ancestor. At the same time, the pirate-actor, through his playing knowledge of the original script, corrected other anomalies, such as the confusion over the costume colors in the fairy scene, which hasty composition had let creep into the mother text. Thus, while Q1 must be regarded as a corrupt text, it has helped to get us closer to Shakespeare's original version.

Trying to recapture that original version, we are further handicapped by certain peculiarities in the Folio text. The only stage directions indicate entries and exits; character names are massed at the head of each scene; the play is fully divided into acts and scenes; and there are idiosyncrasies in punctuation. These oddities, considered collectively, are now taken as an indication that the Folio *Merry Wives* is a literary transcription of either the author's manuscript or a prompt copy—it is impossible to tell which—made by Ralph Crane, distinguished scrivener of the King's Men. Since *The Merry Wives* shares these scribal characteristics with the three other plays opening the Folio, it appears as if the original plan was to have Crane make a set of literary transcriptions for all the plays in the Folio, but the plan never was completely executed.

The present edition is based on the Folio text. The massed entries have been changed from the scene heads to the appropriate places within the scene. The Latin of the Folio's act and scene divisions has been translated into English. The French of Doctor Caius is modernized, and the Welsh pronunciations of Sir Hugh Evans are indicated a little more consistently than in the Folio. For example, at I.i.243, where the Folio in a single speech gives both "ord" and "ort," the present edition alters the first to agree with the second. Prose passages set as verse in the Folio

appear here as prose. Added stage directions and indications of locale are in brackets. The name "Broome," which appears regularly in F, is here given as "Brooke," speech prefixes and abbreviations are expanded, spelling and punctuation are modernized, and obvious typographical errors are corrected. Other departures from F are listed below, the adopted reading first, in boldface type, followed by the Folio reading in roman. Adopted readings from Q1 are indicated by a bracketed Q. Readings from later quartos, folios, or those by editors appear unbracketed.

**I.i.42 George** Thomas   **54, 57 Shallow** Slender   **120–21 They carried . . . pocket** [Q; F omits]   **239 contempt** content
**I.ii.12 seese** cheese
**I.iii.14 lime** [Q] liue   **48 well** [Q] will   **52 legion** [Q: legians] legend   **60 oeillades** illiads   **69 cheater** Cheaters   **81 o' th'** ith'   **82 humor** honor   **93 Page** [Q] Ford   **94 Ford** [Q] Page   **98 Page** Ford   **100 mind** mine
**I.iv.21 whey face** [Q: whay coloured] wee-face   **43 boitier vert** boyteene verd
**II.i.56 praised** praise   **61 Hundredth Psalm** hundred Psalms   **133 And there's the humor of it** [Q; F omits]   **203 Ford** Shallow   **208 mynheers** An-heires
**II.ii.22, 50, 302 God** [Q] heauen
**II.iii.54 word** [Q; F omits]   **76 Page, Shallow, and Slender** All
**III.i.83 urinals** [Q] Vrinal   **84–85 for missing your meetings and appointments** [Q; F omits]   **100 Give me thy hand, terrestrial; so** [Q; F omits]
**III.iii.3 Robert** Robin   **147–48 who goes here** [Q; F omits]   **159 uncope** uncape   **185 foolish** foolishion
**III.iv.12 Fenton** [F omits]   **57 God** [Q] Heauen   **62 have** hath   **109 s.d. Exit** Exeunt
**III.v.86 By the Lord** [Q] Yes   **145 s.d. Exit** Exeunt
**IV.i.46 hung** hing   **67 lunatics** Lunaties
**IV.ii.20 lunes** lines   **54 Mrs. Page** [F gives the line as part of the previous speech]   **62 Mrs. Page** [Q] Mist. Ford   **94 direct** direct direct   **98 him** [F omits]   **175 not** [F omits]   **187 Jeshu** [Q] yea and no
**IV.iii.1 Germans desire** Germane desires   **7 them** [Q] him   **9 house** [Q] houses
**IV.iv.7 cold** gold   **32 makes** make   **42 Disguised . . . head** [Q, which has "Horne" for "Herne"; F omits]   **60 Mrs. Ford** Ford   **72 tire** time
**IV.v.43 Simple** Fal.   **51 Tyke** [Q] like   **54 Thou art** [Q] thou are   **99–100 to say my prayers** [Q; F omits]
**IV.vi.27 ever** euen   **39 denote** deuote
**V.ii.3 daughter** [F omits]
**V.iii.12 Hugh** Herne
**V.v.s.d. with a buck's head upon him** [Q; F omits]   **2 hot-blooded** hot-bloodied   **38 s.d. Enter . . . of Fairies** [Q] Enter Fairies   **70 More** Mote   **90 s.d. They . . . starts** [Q; F omits]   **104 s.d. Here . . . rises up** [Q, which gives "red" where we give "green," and "greene" where we give "white," and describes Anne as "being in white"]   **198 white** greene   **202, 208 green** white

# THE MERRY WIVES
# OF WINDSOR

[Dramatis Personae

SIR JOHN FALSTAFF
FENTON *a young gentleman*
SHALLOW *a country justice*
SLENDER *nephew to Shallow*
FORD }
PAGE } *two citizens of Windsor*
WILLIAM PAGE *a boy, son to Page*
SIR HUGH EVANS *a Welsh parson*
DOCTOR CAIUS *a French physician*
HOST *of the Garter Inn*

BARDOLPH }
PISTOL } *followers of Falstaff*
NYM }
ROBIN *page to Falstaff*
SIMPLE *servant to Slender*
RUGBY *servant to Doctor Caius*
MISTRESS FORD
MISTRESS PAGE
ANNE PAGE *her daughter*
MISTRESS QUICKLY *servant to Doctor Caius*
SERVANTS *to Page, Ford, &c.*

*Scene:* Windsor and the neighborhood]

## ACT I

### Scene I. [*Before Page's house.*]

*Enter Justice* SHALLOW, SLENDER, [*and*] *Sir Hugh* EVANS.

SHALLOW  Sir° Hugh, persuade me not; I will make a Star-chamber° matter of it. If he were twenty Sir John Falstaffs, he shall not abuse Robert Shallow, Esquire.

SLENDER  In the county of Gloucester, Justice of Peace, and Coram.°   5

SHALLOW  Ay, cousin Slender, and Custalorum.°

SLENDER  Ay, and Ratolorum° too; and a gentleman born, Master Parson, who writes himself Armigero,° in any bill, warrant, quittance, or obligation—Armigero.   10

SHALLOW  Ay, that I do, and have done any time these three hundred years.

SLENDER  All his successors gone before him hath done't; and all his ancestors that come after him may. They may give° the dozen white luces° in their coat.°   15

SHALLOW  It is an old coat.

EVANS  The dozen white louses do become an old coat well. It agrees well, passant;° it is a familiar beast to man, and signifies love.

SHALLOW  The luce is the fresh fish. The salt fish is an old coat.°   20

SLENDER  I may quarter,° coz?°

SHALLOW  You may, by marrying.

*The decorative border shown above is a repeated ornament which appeared on the title page of the first quarto edition of* The Merry Wives of Windsor, *1602.*

**I.i.1 Sir** title used before the first name of ordinary priests  **2 Star-chamber** court having jurisdiction over cases of riot, forgery, and other specific offenses  **5 Coram** Quorum (term for justices with special legal qualifications)  **6 Custalorum** Custos Rotulorum (a chief justice)  **7 Ratolorum** Slender's garbling of *rotulorum*  **8 Armigero** esquire   **15 give** display; **luces** pikes (fish); **coat** coat of arms  **18 passant** walking (heraldic)  **20–21 The luce . . . coat** obscure line probably containing an involved play on the words *salt* and *saltant* (heraldic term for describing a leaping position for small animals or vermin), *luce* and *louse*, *old coat* (as a garment), *coat of arms,* and *cod* (the fish—sometimes pronounced as a homonym of *coat*); also, there may be a reference to the coat of arms of the Fishmongers Company, which is a composite of the arms of the older Saltfishmongers and those of the Freshfishmongers  **22 quarter** add arms to one's family coat; **coz** kinsman

EVANS  It is marring indeed, if he quarter it.

SHALLOW  Not a whit.                                              25

EVANS  Yes, py'r Lady.° If he has a quarter of your
coat, there is but three skirts for yourself, in my simple
conjectures. But that is all one. If Sir John Falstaff have
committed disparagements unto you, I am of the
Church, and will be glad to do my benevolence to      30
make atonements and compromises between you.

SHALLOW  The Council° shall hear it. It is a riot.

EVANS  It is not meet the Council hear a riot. There is
no fear of Got in a riot. The Council, look you, shall
desire to hear the fear of Got, and not to hear a riot.    35
Take your vizaments° in that.

SHALLOW  Ha! O' my life, if I were young again, the
sword should end it.

EVANS  It is petter that friends is the sword, and end it.
And there is also another device in my prain, which    40
peradventure prings goot discretions with it. There is
Anne Page, which is daughter to Master George Page,
which is pretty virginity.

SLENDER  Mistress Anne Page? She has brown hair,
and speaks small° like a woman?                              45

EVANS  It is that fery person for all the 'orld, as just as
you will desire. And seven hundred pounds of moneys,
and gold and silver, is her grandsire, upon his death's-
bed—Got deliver to a joyful resurrections—give,
when she is able to overtake seventeen years old. It      50
were a goot motion if we leave our pribbles and
prabbles,° and desire a marriage between Master
Abraham and Mistress Anne Page.

SHALLOW  Did her grandsire leave her seven hundred
pound?                                                            55

EVANS  Ay, and her father is make her a petter penny.

SHALLOW  I know the young gentlewoman. She has
good gifts.

EVANS  Seven hundred pounds and possibilities° is
goot gifts.                                                       60

SHALLOW  Well, let us see honest Master Page. Is
Falstaff there?

EVANS  Shall I tell you a lie? I do despise a liar as I do
despise one that is false, or as I despise one that is not
true. The knight Sir John is there; and, I beseech you,   65
be ruled by your well-willers. I will peat the door for
Master Page. [Knocks.] What, ho! Got pless your
house here.

PAGE [Within.]  Who's there?

EVANS  Here is Got's plessing, and your friend, and    70
Justice Shallow; and here young Master Slender, that
peradventures shall tell you another tale, if matters
grow to your likings.

[Enter] Master PAGE.

PAGE  I am glad to see your worships well. I thank you
for my venison, Master Shallow.                             75

SHALLOW  Master Page, I am glad to see you. Much
good do it your good heart! I wished your venison
better—it was ill killed.° How doth good Mistress

Page?—and I thank you always with my heart, la,
with my heart.                                                  80

PAGE  Sir, I thank you.

SHALLOW  Sir, I thank you; by yea and no, I do.

PAGE  I am glad to see you, good Master Slender.

SLENDER  How does your fallow° greyhound, sir? I
heard say he was outrun on Cotsall.°                        85

PAGE  It could not be judged, sir.

SLENDER  You'll not confess, you'll not confess.

SHALLOW  That he will not. 'Tis your fault,° 'tis your
fault. 'Tis a good dog.

PAGE  A cur, sir.                                              90

SHALLOW  Sir, he's a good dog, and a fair dog. Can
there be more said? He is good and fair. Is Sir John
Falstaff here?

PAGE  Sir, he is within. And I would I could do a good
office between you.                                           95

EVANS  It is spoke as a Christians ought to speak.

SHALLOW  He hath wronged me, Master Page.

PAGE  Sir, he doth in some sort confess it.

SHALLOW  If it be confessed, it is not redressed. Is not
that so, Master Page? He hath wronged me; indeed, he  100
hath. At a word, he hath, believe me. Robert Shallow,
Esquire, saith he is wronged.

PAGE  Here comes Sir John.

[Enter Sir John] FALSTAFF, BARDOLPH, NYM, [and]
PISTOL.

FALSTAFF  Now, Master Shallow, you'll complain of
me to the king?                                               105

SHALLOW  Knight, you have beaten my men, killed
my deer, and broke open my lodge.

FALSTAFF  But not kissed your keeper's daughter?

SHALLOW  Tut, a pin!° This shall be answered.

FALSTAFF  I will answer it straight. I have done all this.  110
That is now answered.

SHALLOW  The Council shall know this.

FALSTAFF  'Twere better for you if it were known in
counsel.° You'll be laughed at.

EVANS  Pauca verba;° Sir John, goot worts.              115

FALSTAFF  Good worts?° Good cabbage!—Slender, I
broke your head. What matter° have you against me?

SLENDER  Marry, sir, I have matter in my head against
you, and against your cony-catching° rascals, Bardolph,
Nym, and Pistol. They carried me to the tavern and    120
made me drunk, and afterward picked my pocket.

BARDOLPH [Drawing his sword.]  You Banbury
cheese!°

SLENDER  Ay, it is no matter.

PISTOL [Also draws.]  How now, Mephostophilus!°      125

SLENDER  Ay, it is no matter.

NYM [Drawing.]  Slice, I say! Pauca, pauca. Slice!
That's my humor.°

---

**26 py'r Lady** by our Lady (the use of *p* for *b* here is the first
of Evans' Welsh pronunciations)  **32 Council** King's Council
sitting as the Court of Star-chamber  **36 vizaments** advise-
ments  **45 small** gentle  **51–52 pribbles and prabbles** petty
bickerings  **59 possibilities** prospects of inheritance  **78 ill
killed** (1) improperly killed (?) (2) possibly a reference to
Falstaff's doing the killing (see I.i.106–07)

**84 fallow** brownish yellow  **85 Cotsall** the Cotswold hills in
Gloucestershire (locale of the Cotswold Games and center for
coursing)  **88 fault** misfortune  **109 pin** trifle  **113–14 in
counsel** privately  **115 Pauca verba** few words (Latin)  **116
worts** (1) words (2) cabbage-like plant  **117 matter** dispute
(but in the next line it has the senses of "brain matter" and
"cause")  **119 cony-catching** cheating  **122–23 Banbury
cheese** noted for its thinness, a reference to Slender's build
**125 Mephostophilus** devil (from Marlowe's *Dr. Faustus*)
**128 humor** temperament

SLENDER  Where's Simple, my man? Can you tell, cousin?  130
EVANS  Peace, I pray you. Now let us understand. There is three umpires in this matter, as I understand; that is, Master Page, fidelicet,° Master Page; and there is myself, fidelicet, myself; and the three party is, lastly and finally, mine Host of the Garter.°  135
PAGE  We three to hear it and end it between them.
EVANS  Fery goot. I will make a prief of it in my notebook, and we will afterwards 'ork upon the cause with as great discreetly as we can.
FALSTAFF  Pistol!  140
PISTOL  He hears with ears.
EVANS  The tevil and his tam! What phrase is this, "He hears with ear"? Why, it is affectations.
FALSTAFF  Pistol, did you pick Master Slender's purse?  145
SLENDER  Ay, by these gloves, did he—or I would I might never come in mine own great chamber again else—of seven groats° in mill-sixpences,° and two Edward shovel-boards,° that cost me two shilling and two pence apiece of Yed° Miller, by these gloves.  150
FALSTAFF  Is this true, Pistol?
EVANS  No, it is false, if it is a pickpurse.
PISTOL  Ha, thou mountain-foreigner!° Sir John and master mine, I combat challenge of this latten bilbo.° Word of denial in thy labras° here!  155
Word of denial! Froth and scum, thou liest!
SLENDER  By these gloves, then 'twas he.
NYM  Be avised, sir, and pass good humors. I will say "marry trap"° with you, if you run the nuthook's humor° on me. That is the very note of it.  160
SLENDER  By this hat, then he in the red face had it; for though I cannot remember what I did when you made me drunk, yet I am not altogether an ass.
FALSTAFF  What say you, Scarlet and John?°
BARDOLPH  Why, sir, for my part, I say the gentleman  165 had drunk himself out of his five sentences.
EVANS  It is his "five senses." Fie, what the ignorance is!
BARDOLPH  And being fap,° sir, was, as they say, cashiered;° and so conclusions passed the careers.°  170
SLENDER  Ay, you spake in Latin then too. But 'tis no matter. I'll ne'er be drunk whilst I live again, but in honest, civil, godly company, for this trick. If I be drunk, I'll be drunk with those that have the fear of God, and not with drunken knaves.  175
EVANS  So Got 'udge me, that is a virtuous mind.

FALSTAFF  You hear all these matters denied, gentlemen; you hear it.

[Enter] ANNE PAGE [with wine], MISTRESS FORD [and] MISTRESS PAGE [following].

PAGE  Nay, daughter, carry the wine in; we'll drink within.     [Exit ANNE Page.]  180
SLENDER  O heaven! This is Mistress Anne Page.
PAGE  How now, Mistress Ford!
FALSTAFF  Mistress Ford, by my troth, you are very well met. By your leave, good mistress.

[Kisses her.]

PAGE  Wife, bid these gentlemen welcome. Come, we  185 have a hot venison pasty to dinner. Come, gentlemen, I hope we shall drink down all unkindness.
[Exeunt all except SHALLOW, SLENDER, and EVANS.]
SLENDER  I had rather than forty shillings I had my Book of Songs and Sonnets° here.

[Enter] SIMPLE.

How now, Simple, where have you been? I must  190 wait on myself, must I? You have not the Book of Riddles about you, have you?
SIMPLE  Book of Riddles? Why, did you not lend it to Alice Shortcake upon Allhallowmas° last, a fortnight afore Michaelmas?°  195
SHALLOW  Come, coz; come, coz; we stay for you. A word with you, coz. Marry,° this, coz: there is as 'twere a tender,° a kind of tender, made afar off° by Sir Hugh here. Do you understand me?
SLENDER  Ay, sir, you shall find me reasonable. If it be  200 so, I shall do that that is reason.
SHALLOW  Nay, but understand me.
SLENDER  So I do, sir.
EVANS  Give ear to his motions.° Master Slender, I will description the matter to you, if you be capacity of it.  205
SLENDER  Nay, I will do as my cousin Shallow says. I pray you pardon me. He's a Justice of Peace in his country, simple though° I stand here.
EVANS  But that is not the question. The question is concerning your marriage.  210
SHALLOW  Ay, there's the point, sir.
EVANS  Marry, is it, the very point of it—to Mistress Anne Page.
SLENDER  Why, if it be so, I will marry her upon any reasonable demands.  215
EVANS  But can you affection the 'oman? Let us command to know that of your mouth, or of your lips; for divers° philosophers hold that the lips is parcel° of the mouth. Therefore, precisely, can you carry your goot will to the maid?  220
SHALLOW  Cousin Abraham Slender, can you love her?
SLENDER  I hope, sir, I will do as it shall become one that would do reason.

---

133 fidelicet *videlicet* = namely  135 Garter Garter Inn  148 groats coins worth fourpence; mill-sixpences milled coins  149 Edward shovel-boards shillings from the reign of Edward VI used in the game of shovelboard (rare coins by the 1590's)  150 Yed Ed, Edward  153 mountain-foreigner Welshman  154 latten bilbo brass sword  155 labras lips  159 marry trap a term of insult  159-60 run . . . humor think to involve me with the law ("nuthook" = constable)  164 Scarlet and John Robin Hood's companions (alluding to Bardolph's red face)  169 fap drunk  170 cashiered robbed; conclusions . . . careers an obscure line possibly meaning "and that brought the matter to a speedy end" or "he got what he deserved"—from *pass a careire*, a term in horsemanship

189 Book . . . Sonnets an anthology published by Tottel in 1557, commonly called Tottel's *Miscellany*  194 Allhallowmas All Saints' day, November 1  195 Michaelmas Saint Michael's day, September 29  197 Marry a mild oath, from "By the Virgin Mary"  198 tender offer; afar off indirectly  204 motions proposals  208 simple though as sure as  218 divers various  219 parcel part

EVANS  Nay, Got's lords and his ladies! You must 225
speak possitable,° if you can carry her your desires
towards her.

SHALLOW  That you must. Will you, upon good
dowry, marry her?

SLENDER  I will do a greater thing than that, upon your 230
request, cousin, in any reason.

SHALLOW  Nay, conceive me,° conceive me, sweet
coz. What I do is to pleasure you, coz. Can you love
the maid?

SLENDER  I will marry her, sir, at your request; but if 235
there be no great love in the beginning, yet heaven
may decrease it upon better acquaintance when we are
married and have more occasion to know one another.
I hope upon familiarity will grow more contempt.
But if you say, "Marry her," I will marry her; that I 240
am freely dissolved, and dissolutely.

EVANS  It is a fery discretion answer, save the faul'° is
in the 'ort "dissolutely." The 'ort is, according to our
meaning, "resolutely." His meaning is goot.

SHALLOW  Ay, I think my cousin meant well. 245

SLENDER  Ay, or else I would I might be hanged, la.

[Enter ANNE Page.]

SHALLOW  Here comes fair Mistress Anne.—Would I
were young for your sake, Mistress Anne.

ANNE  The dinner is on the table. My father desires
your worships' company. 250

SHALLOW  I will wait on him, fair Mistress Anne.

EVANS  Od's° plessed will! I will not be absence at the
grace.                    [Exeunt SHALLOW and EVANS.]

ANNE  Will't please your worship to come in, sir?

SLENDER  No, I thank you, forsooth, heartily; I am 255
very well.

ANNE  The dinner attends you, sir.

SLENDER  I am not a-hungry, I thank you, forsooth.
[To SIMPLE.] Go, sirrah,° for all you are my man, go
wait upon my cousin Shallow. [Exit SIMPLE.] A 260
justice of peace sometime may be beholding to his
friend for a man. I keep but three men and a boy yet,
till my mother be dead. But what though? Yet I live
like a poor gentleman born.

ANNE  I may not go in without your worship; they 265
will not sit till you come.

SLENDER  I' faith, I'll eat nothing. I thank you as much
as though I did.

ANNE  I pray you, sir, walk in.

SLENDER  I had rather walk here, I thank you. I 270
bruised my shin th' other day with playing at sword
and dagger with a master of fence—three veneys° for a
dish of stewed prunes—and, by my troth, I cannot
abide the smell of hot meat since. Why do your dogs
bark so? Be there bears i' th' town? 275

ANNE  I think there are, sir; I heard them talked of.

SLENDER  I love the sport° well, but I shall as soon
quarrel at it as any man in England. You are afraid if
you see the bear loose, are you not?

ANNE  Ay, indeed, sir. 280

SLENDER  That's meat and drink to me now. I have

seen Sackerson° loose twenty times, and have taken him
by the chain; but, I warrant you, the women have so
cried and shrieked at it, that it passed. But women,
indeed, cannot abide 'em; they are very ill-favored 285
rough things.

[Enter PAGE.]

PAGE  Come, gentle Master Slender, come. We stay
for you.

SLENDER  I'll eat nothing; I thank you, sir.

PAGE  By cock and pie,° you shall not choose, sir! 290
Come, come.

SLENDER  Nay, pray you, lead the way.

PAGE  Come on, sir.

SLENDER  Mistress Anne, yourself shall go first.

ANNE  Not I, sir; pray you keep on. 295

SLENDER  Truly, I will not go first; truly, la! I will
not do you that wrong.

ANNE  I pray you, sir.

SLENDER  I'll rather be unmannerly than troublesome.
You do yourself wrong, indeed, la!          Exeunt. 300

Scene II. [Before Page's house.]

Enter EVANS and SIMPLE.

EVANS  Go your ways, and ask of Doctor Caius'
house, which is the way; and there dwells one Mistress
Quickly, which is in the manner of his nurse, or his
dry nurse,° or his cook, or his laundry, his washer, and
his wringer. 5

SIMPLE  Well, sir.

EVANS  Nay, it is petter yet. Give her this letter, for it
is a 'oman that altogether's acquaintance with Mistress
Anne Page; and the letter is to desire and require her
to solicit your master's desires to Mistress Anne Page. 10
I pray you be gone. I will make an end of my dinner;
there's pippins and seese° to come.          Exeunt.

Scene III. [Falstaff's room in the Garter Inn.]

Enter FALSTAFF, HOST, BARDOLPH, NYM, PISTOL,
[and ROBIN the] page.

FALSTAFF  Mine Host of the Garter!

HOST  What says my bully rook?° Speak scholarly and
wisely.

FALSTAFF  Truly, mine Host, I must turn away some
of my followers. 5

HOST  Discard, bully Hercules, cashier. Let them wag;°
trot, trot.

FALSTAFF  I sit at° ten pounds a week.

HOST  Thou'rt an emperor—Caesar, Keisar,° and
Pheazar.° I will entertain° Bardolph: he shall draw,° 10
he shall tap.° Said I well, bully Hector?

FALSTAFF  Do so, good mine Host.

---

282 **Sackerson** a famous bear    290 **cock and pie** an oath
**I.ii.4 dry nurse** housekeeper    12 **pippins and seese** apples
and cheese
**I.iii.2 bully rook** friendly term of address used by the Host
6 **wag** depart   8 **I sit at** my expenses run   9 **Keisar** Kaiser
10 **Pheazar** vizier; **entertain** employ; **draw** draw liquor
11 **tap** serve as tapster

---

226 **possitable** positively   232 **conceive me** understand me
242 **faul'** fault   252 **Od's** God's   259 **sirrah** term of address
used to inferiors   272 **veneys** bouts   277 **the sport** bearbaiting

HOST  I have spoke; let him follow. [*To* BARDOLPH.] Let me see thee froth and lime.° I am at a word;° follow.      [*Exit.*] 15

FALSTAFF  Bardolph, follow him. A tapster is a good trade. An old cloak makes a new jerkin; a withered servingman, a fresh tapster. Go, adieu.

BARDOLPH  It is a life that I have desired. I will thrive.

PISTOL  O base Hungarian wight!° Wilt thou the 20 spigot wield?      [*Exit* BARDOLPH.]

NYM  He was gotten° in drink. Is not the humor conceited?°

FALSTAFF  I am glad I am so acquit° of this tinderbox. His thefts were too open. His filching was like an 25 unskillful singer: he kept not time.

NYM  The good humor is to steal at a minute's rest.°

PISTOL  "Convey," the wise it call. "Steal"? Foh, a fico° for the phrase!

FALSTAFF  Well, sirs, I am almost out at heels.° 30

PISTOL  Why then, let kibes° ensue.

FALSTAFF  There is no remedy. I must cony-catch, I must shift.°

PISTOL  Young ravens must have food.

FALSTAFF  Which of you know Ford of this town? 35

PISTOL  I ken° the wight. He is of substance good.

FALSTAFF  My honest lads, I will tell you what I am about.

PISTOL  Two yards, and more.

FALSTAFF  No quips now, Pistol. Indeed, I am in the 40 waist two yards about. But I am now about no waste; I am about thrift. Briefly, I do mean to make love to Ford's wife. I spy entertainment in her: she discourses, she carves,° she gives the leer of invitation. I can construe the action of her familiar style; and the 45 hardest voice of her behavior, to be Englished rightly, is, "I am Sir John Falstaff's."

PISTOL  He hath studied her well, and translated her will, out of honesty° into English.°

NYM  The anchor is deep.° Will that humor pass? 50

FALSTAFF  Now, the report goes she has all the rule of her husband's purse. He hath a legion of angels.°

PISTOL  As many devils entertain. And "To her, boy," say I.

NYM  The humor rises; it is good. Humor me the 55 angels.

FALSTAFF  I have writ me here a letter to her; and here another to Page's wife, who even now gave me good eyes too, examined my parts with most judicious oeillades.° Sometimes the beam of her view gilded my 60 foot, sometimes my portly belly.

PISTOL  [*Aside.*]  Then did the sun on dunghill shine.

NYM  [*Aside.*]  I thank thee for that humor.

FALSTAFF  O, she did so course o'er my exteriors with

such a greedy intention that the appetite of her eye 65 did seem to scorch me up like a burning-glass. Here's another letter to her. She bears the purse too. She is a region in Guiana, all gold and bounty. I will be cheater° to them both, and they shall be exchequers to me. They shall be my East and West Indies, and I will 70 trade to them both. [*To* PISTOL.] Go, bear thou this letter to Mistress Page; [*to* NYM] and thou this to Mistress Ford. We will thrive, lads, we will thrive.

PISTOL
Shall I Sir Pandarus° of Troy become,
And by my side wear steel? Then Lucifer take all! 75

NYM  I will run no base humor. Here, take the humor-letter. I will keep the havior of reputation.

FALSTAFF [*To* ROBIN.]
Hold, sirrah, bear you these letters tightly.°
Sail like my pinnace to these golden shores.
Rogues, hence, avaunt! Vanish like hailstones, go! 80
Trudge, plod away o' th' hoof; seek shelter, pack!°
Falstaff will learn the humor of the age:
French thrift,° you rogues—myself and skirted page.
     [*Exeunt* FALSTAFF *and* ROBIN.]

PISTOL
Let vultures gripe thy guts! For gourd and fullam° holds,
And high and low° beguiles the rich and poor. 85
Tester° I'll have in pouch when thou shalt lack,
Base Phrygian Turk!°

NYM  I have operations which be humors of revenge.

PISTOL  Wilt thou revenge?

NYM  By welkin° and her star! 90

PISTOL  With wit or steel?

NYM
With both the humors, I.
I will discuss° the humor of this love to Page.

PISTOL
And I to Ford shall eke unfold
How Falstaff, varlet vile, 95
His dove will prove, his gold will hold,
And his soft couch defile.

NYM  My humor shall not cool. I will incense Page to deal with poison. I will possess him with yellowness,° for the revolt of mind is dangerous. That is my true 100 humor.

PISTOL  Thou art the Mars of malcontents. I second thee; troop on.      *Exeunt.*

Scene IV. [*A room in Doctor Caius' house.*]

*Enter Mistress* QUICKLY [*and*] SIMPLE.

QUICKLY [*Calling.*]  What, John Rugby! ([*Enter*] *John* RUGBY.) I pray thee, go to the casement and see if you can see my master, Master Doctor Caius, coming. If he do, i' faith, and find anybody in the house, here will

---

**14 froth and lime** cheat the customers by putting a big head of foam on the beer or by adulterating wine with lime; **I . . . word** I speak briefly   **20 base Hungarian wight** beggarly fellow   **22 gotten** begotten   **23 conceited** ingenious   **24 acquit** rid   **27 minute's rest** in the shortest possible interval   **29 fico** fig   **30 out at heels** penniless   **31 kibes** chilblains   **33 shift** devise some stratagem   **36 ken** know   **44 carves** shows courtesy   **49 honesty** chastity; **English** probably with a pun on *ingle* = paramour   **50 The . . . deep** an obscure line possibly meaning (1) it is a deeply thought-out scheme or (2) that wine keg (i.e., Falstaff) is a deep thinker (from *anker*, a wine keg)   **52 angels** gold coins worth about ten shillings   **60 oeillades** amorous glances

**69 cheater** (1) escheator, official who looked after the king's escheats (2) one who defrauds   **74 Sir Pandarus** the go-between in Chaucer's *Troilus and Criseyde*, from whose name the word *pander* comes   **78 tightly** well   **81 pack** be off   **83 French thrift** an allusion to the French custom then current to use one page instead of many servingmen   **84 gourd and fullam** kinds of false dice   **85 high and low** numbers on the dice   **86 Tester** sixpence   **87 Base Phrygian Turk** term of insult   **90 welkin** sky   **93 discuss** declare   **99 yellowness** jealousy

be an old° abusing of God's patience and the king's 5
English.

RUGBY  I'll go watch.

QUICKLY  Go, and we'll have a posset° for't soon at
night, in faith, at the latter end of a sea-coal° fire.
[*Exit* RUGBY.] An honest, willing, kind fellow, as ever 10
servant shall come in house withal;° and, I warrant
you, no telltale, nor no breedbate.° His worst fault is
that he is given to prayer; he is something peevish°
that way, but nobody but has his fault. But let that
pass.—Peter Simple you say your name is? 15

SIMPLE  Ay, for fault of a better.

QUICKLY  And Master Slender's your master?

SIMPLE  Ay, forsooth.

QUICKLY  Does he not wear a great round beard like
a glover's paring knife? 20

SIMPLE  No, forsooth. He hath but a little whey° face,
with a little yellow beard—a Cain-colored° beard.

QUICKLY  A softly-sprighted° man, is he not?

SIMPLE  Ay, forsooth. But he is as tall a man of his
hands° as any is between this and his head. He hath 25
fought with a warrener.°

QUICKLY  How say you? O, I should remember him.
Does he not hold up his head, as it were, and strut in
his gait?

SIMPLE  Yes, indeed does he. 30

QUICKLY  Well, heaven send Anne Page no worse
fortune. Tell Master Parson Evans I will do what I can
for your master. Anne is a good girl, and I wish—

[*Enter* RUGBY.]

RUGBY  Out, alas! Here comes my master!

QUICKLY  We shall all be shent.° Run in here, good 35
young man; go into this closet.° He will not stay long.
[*Shuts* SIMPLE *in the chamber.*] What, John Rugby!
John, what, John, I say! Go, John, go inquire for my
master. I doubt° he be not well, that he comes not
home.                                    [*Exit* RUGBY.] 40
[*Sings.*] "And down, down, adown-a," &c.

[*Enter*] Doctor CAIUS.

CAIUS  Vat is you sing? I do not like dese toys.° Pray
you go and vetch me in my closet un boitier vert—
a box, a green-a box. Do intend° vat I speak? A
green-a box. 45

QUICKLY  Ay, forsooth, I'll fetch it you. [*Aside.*] I am
glad he went not in himself. If he had found the
young man, he would have been horn-mad.°   [*Exit.*]

CAIUS  Fe, fe, fe, fe! Ma foi, il fait fort chaud. Je m'en
vais à la cour—la grande affaire.° 50

QUICKLY  [*Returning with the box.*]  Is it this, sir?

CAIUS  Oui; mette le au mon pocket; dépêche,°
quickly. Vere is dat knave Rugby?

**I.iv.5 old** great, plenty of  **8 posset** hot milk curdled with
ale or wine  **9 sea-coal** coal brought by sea  **11 withal**
with  **12 breedbate** mischiefmaker  **13 peevish** silly  **21
whey** pale (the Folio gives "wee," perhaps a dialectal
pronunciation)  **22 Cain-colored** reddish-yellow (traditional
color of Cain's beard in tapestries)  **23 softly-sprighted**
gentle-spirited  **24–25 tall . . . hands** valiant  **26 warrener**
gamekeeper  **35 shent** scolded  **36 closet** private room  **39
doubt** fear  **42 toys** foolish nonsense  **44 intend** hear
(French *entendre*)  **48 horn-mad** enraged  **49–50 Ma . . .
affaire** Faith, it is very hot. I am going to the court—the
grand affair  **52 Oui . . . dépêche** yes; put it in my pocket;
be quick

QUICKLY  What, John Rugby! John!

[*Enter* RUGBY.]

RUGBY  Here, sir. 55

CAIUS  You are John Rugby, and you are Jack Rugby.
Come, take-a your rapier and come after my heel to
de court.

RUGBY  'Tis ready, sir, here in the porch.

CAIUS  By my trot,° I tarry too long. Od's me! Qu'ai 60
j'oublié?° Dere is some simples° in my closet dat I vill
not for de varld I shall leave behind.

[*Crosses to the chamber.*]

QUICKLY  [*Aside.*]  Ay me, he'll find the young man
there, and be mad.

CAIUS  O diable, diable! Vat is in my closet? Villainy! 65
Larron!° [*Pulls* SIMPLE *out.*] Rugby, my rapier!

QUICKLY  Good master, be content.

CAIUS  Verefore shall I be content-a?

QUICKLY  The young man is an honest man.

CAIUS  Vat shall de honest man do in my closet? Dere 70
is no honest man dat shall come in my closet.

QUICKLY  I beseech you, be not so phlegmatic.° Hear
the truth of it. He came of an errand to me from
Parson Hugh.

CAIUS  Vell? 75

SIMPLE  Ay, forsooth, to desire her to—

QUICKLY  Peace, I pray you.

CAIUS  Peace-a your tongue.—Speak-a your tale.

SIMPLE  To desire this honest gentlewoman, your
maid, to speak a good word to Mistress Anne Page for 80
my master in the way of marriage.

QUICKLY  This is all, indeed, la! But I'll ne'er put my
finger in the fire, and need not.

CAIUS  Sir Hugh send-a you?—Rugby, baille° me
some paper. Tarry you a little-a while. 85

[*Writes.*]

QUICKLY  [*Aside to* SIMPLE.]  I am glad he is so quiet.
If he had been throughly moved, you should have
heard him so loud, and so melancholy. But notwithstanding, man, I'll do you your master what good I
can; and the very yea and the no is, the French doctor, 90
my master—I may call him my master, look you, for
I keep his house; and I wash, wring, brew, bake, scour,
dress meat and drink, make the beds, and do all
myself—

SIMPLE  [*Aside to* QUICKLY.]  'Tis a great charge° to 95
come under one body's hand.

QUICKLY  [*Aside to* SIMPLE.]  Are you avised o' that?
You shall find it a great charge. And to be up early and
down late; but notwithstanding—to tell you in your
ear, I would have no words of it—my master himself 100
is in love with Mistress Anne Page. But notwithstanding that, I know Anne's mind. That's neither
here nor there.

CAIUS  You jack'nape,° give-a dis letter to Sir Hugh.
By gar, it is a shallenge. I vill cut his troat in de Park; 105
and I vill teach a scurvy jackanape priest to meddle or

**60 trot** troth  **60–61 Qu'ai j'oublié** What have I forgotten?
**61 simples** medicinal herbs  **66 Larron** thief  **72 phlegmatic** Quickly's error for *choleric*  **84 baille** fetch  **95 charge**
burden  **104 jack'nape** coxcomb

make. You may be gone; it is not good you tarry here. [*Exit* SIMPLE.] By gar, I vill cut all his two stones;° by gar, he shall not have a stone to trow at his dog.

QUICKLY   Alas, he speaks but for his friend.     110

CAIUS   It is no matter-a ver dat. Do not you tell-a me dat I shall have Anne Page for myself? By gar, I vill kill de Jack° priest; and I have appointed mine Host of de Jarteer to measure our weapon.° By gar, I vill myself have Anne Page.     115

QUICKLY   Sir, the maid loves you, and all shall be well. We must give folks leave to prate. What the good-year!°

CAIUS   Rugby, come to the court vit me. [*To* QUICKLY.] By gar, if I have not Anne Page, I shall    120 turn your head out of my door. Follow my heels, Rugby.       [*Exeunt* CAIUS *and* RUGBY.]

QUICKLY [*Calling after* CAIUS.]   You shall have An°— fool's-head of your own. No, I know Anne's mind for that. Never a woman in Windsor knows more of    125 Anne's mind than I do, nor can do more than I do with her, I thank heaven.

FENTON [*Offstage.*]   Who's within there, ho?

QUICKLY   Who's there, I trow?° Come near° the house, I pray you.     130

[*Enter*] FENTON.

FENTON   How now, good woman. How dost thou?

QUICKLY   The better that it pleases your good worship to ask.

FENTON   What news? How does pretty Mistress Anne?

QUICKLY   In truth, sir, and she is pretty, and honest,°    135 and gentle—and one that is your friend. I can tell you that by the way, I praise heaven for it.

FENTON   Shall I do any good, think'st thou? Shall I not lose my suit?

QUICKLY   Troth, sir, all is in His hands above. But    140 notwithstanding, Master Fenton, I'll be sworn on a book she loves you. Have not your worship a wart above your eye?

FENTON   Yes, marry, have I. What of that?

QUICKLY   Well, thereby hangs a tale. Good faith, it is    145 such another Nan;° but, I detest,° an honest maid as ever broke bread. We had an hour's talk of that wart. I shall never laugh but in that maid's company. But, indeed, she is given too much to allicholy° and musing. But for you—well, go to.     150

FENTON   Well, I shall see her today. Hold, there's money for thee; let me have thy voice in my behalf. If thou see'st her before me, commend me—

QUICKLY   Will I? I' faith, that we will. And I will tell your worship more of the wart the next time we have    155 confidence, and of other wooers.

FENTON   Well, farewell. I am in great haste now.

QUICKLY   Farewell to your worship. [*Exit* FENTON.] Truly, an honest gentleman. But Anne loves him not, for I know Anne's mind as well as another does. Out    160 upon't, what have I forgot?       *Exit.*

---

108 **stones** testicles   113 **Jack** term of contempt   114 **measure our weapon** umpire the duel   118 **good-year** a meaningless expletive   123 **An** (1) Anne (2) an   129 **trow** wonder; **Come near** enter   135 **honest** chaste   146 **such another Nan** i.e., charming female; **detest** Quickly's error for *protest*   149 **allicholy** melancholy

# ACT II

## Scene I. [*Before Page's house.*]

*Enter* MISTRESS PAGE [*with a letter*].

MRS. PAGE   What, have 'scaped love letters in the holiday time° of my beauty, and am I now a subject for them? Let me see.

[*Reads.*]

"Ask me no reason why I love you, for though Love use Reason for his precisian,° he admits him not for    5 his counselor. You are not young, no more am I. Go to then, there's sympathy. You are merry, so am I. Ha, ha, then there's more sympathy. You love sack,° and so do I. Would you desire better sympathy? Let it suffice thee, Mistress Page—at the least, if the love    10 of soldier can suffice—that I love thee. I will not say, pity me—'tis not a soldierlike phrase; but I say, love me. By me,

> Thine own true knight,
> By day or night,     15
> Or any kind of light,
> With all his might
> For thee to fight,
>
>           John Falstaff."

What a Herod of Jewry° is this! O wicked, wicked    20 world. One that is well-nigh worn to pieces with age to show himself a young gallant! What an unweighed° behavior hath this Flemish drunkard° picked—with the devil's name!—out of my conversation° that he dares in this manner assay me? Why, he hath not been    25 thrice in my company. What should I say to him? I was then frugal of my mirth—heaven forgive me! Why, I'll exhibit° a bill in the parliament for the putting down° of men. How shall I be revenged on him? For revenged I will be, as sure as his guts are made    30 of puddings.°

[*Enter*] MISTRESS FORD.

MRS. FORD   Mistress Page! Trust me, I was going to your house.

MRS. PAGE   And, trust me, I was coming to you. You look very ill.     35

MRS. FORD   Nay, I'll ne'er believe that. I have to show to the contrary.

MRS. PAGE   Faith, but you do, in my mind.

MRS. FORD   Well, I do then; yet I say I could show you to the contrary. O Mistress Page, give me some    40 counsel.

MRS. PAGE   What's the matter, woman?

MRS. FORD   O woman, if it were not for one trifling respect, I could come to such honor.

MRS. PAGE   Hang the trifle, woman; take the honor.    45 What is it? Dispense with trifles. What is it?

MRS. FORD   If I would but go to hell for an eternal moment or so, I could be knighted.

---

**II.i.1–2 in . . . time** i.e., in my youth   **5 precisian** inflexible spiritual adviser   **8 sack** Spanish white wine   **20 Herod of Jewry** portrayed as a ranting villain in the miracle plays   **22 unweighed** inconsiderate   **23 Flemish drunkard** the Flemish were notorious for heavy drinking   **24 conversation** behavior   **28 exhibit** submit   **29 putting down** suppressing   **31 puddings** sausages

MRS. PAGE   What? Thou liest. Sir Alice Ford? These
knights will hack;° and so thou shouldst not alter the 50
article of thy gentry.°

MRS. FORD   We burn daylight.° [*Giving her a letter.*]
Here, read, read! Perceive how I might be knighted.
I shall think the worse of fat men as long as I have
an eye to make difference of° men's liking.° And yet 55
he would not swear; praised women's modesty; and
gave such orderly and well-behaved reproof to all
uncomeliness° that I would have sworn his disposition
would have gone to the truth of his words.° But they
do no more adhere and keep place together than the 60
Hundredth Psalm to the tune of "Greensleeves."°
What tempest, I trow, threw this whale, with so many
tuns of oil in his belly, ashore at Windsor? How shall
I be revenged on him? I think the best way were to
entertain him with hope till the wicked fire of lust 65
have melted him in his own grease. Did you ever
hear the like?

MRS. PAGE [*Comparing the two letters.*]   Letter for
letter, but that the name of Page and Ford differs.—
To thy great comfort in this mystery of ill opinions,° 70
here's the twin brother of thy letter. But let thine
inherit first, for I protest mine never shall. I warrant
he hath a thousand of these letters, writ with blank
space for different names—sure, more—and these are
of the second edition. He will print them, out of 75
doubt; for he cares not what he puts into the press,
when he would put us two. I had rather be a giantess
and lie under Mount Pelion.° Well, I will find you
twenty lascivious turtles° ere one chaste man.

[*Gives both letters to* MISTRESS FORD.]

MRS. FORD   Why, this is the very same: the very 80
hand, the very words. What doth he think of us?

MRS. PAGE   Nay, I know not. It makes me almost
ready to wrangle with mine own honesty.° I'll entertain myself like one that I am not acquainted withal;
for sure, unless he know some strain in me that I know 85
not myself, he would never have boarded° me in this
fury.

MRS. FORD   "Boarding" call you it? I'll be sure to
keep him above deck.

MRS. PAGE   So will I. If he come under my hatches, 90
I'll never to sea again. Let's be revenged on him.
Let's appoint him a meeting, give him a show of
comfort in his suit, and lead him on with a fine-
baited° delay till he hath pawned his horses to mine
Host of the Garter.   95

MRS. FORD   Nay, I will consent to act any villainy
against him that may not sully the chariness° of our

honesty. O that my husband saw this letter! It would
give eternal food to his jealousy.

MRS. PAGE   Why, look where he comes, and my 100
goodman° too. He's as far from jealousy as I am from
giving him cause. And that, I hope, is an unmeasurable
distance.

MRS. FORD   You are the happier woman.

MRS. PAGE   Let's consult together against this greasy 105
knight. Come hither.   [*They retire.*]

[*Enter*] *Master* PAGE, [*with*] NYM, [*and*] *Master* FORD,
[*with*] PISTOL.

FORD   Well, I hope it be not so.

PISTOL
Hope is a curtal° dog in some affairs.
Sir John affects° thy wife.

FORD   Why, sir, my wife is not young.   110

PISTOL
He woos both high and low, both rich and poor,
Both young and old, one with another, Ford.
He loves the gallimaufry.° Ford, perpend.°

FORD   Love my wife?

PISTOL
With liver° burning hot. Prevent, or go thou,   115
Like Sir Actaeon° he, with Ringwood° at thy heels.
O, odious is the name!°

FORD   What name, sir?

PISTOL
The horn, I say. Farewell.
Take heed, have open eye, for thieves do foot by night. 120
Take heed, ere summer comes or cuckoo birds° do
sing.
Away, Sir Corporal Nym!
Believe it, Page; he speaks sense.   [*Exit.*]

FORD [*Aside.*]   I will be patient; I will find out this.

NYM [*To* PAGE.]   And this is true; I like not the humor 125
of lying. He hath wronged me in some humors. I
should have borne the humored letter to her, but I
have a sword and it shall bite upon my necessity. He
loves your wife. There's the short and the long. My
name is Corporal Nym; I speak, and I avouch 'tis 130
true. My name is Nym, and Falstaff loves your wife.
Adieu. I love not the humor of bread and cheese.°
And there's the humor of it. Adieu.   [*Exit.*]

PAGE   "The humor of it," quoth 'a? Here's a fellow
frights English out of his wits.   135

FORD   I will seek out Falstaff.

PAGE   I never heard such a drawling, affecting° rogue.

FORD   If I do find it—well.

PAGE   I will not believe such a Cataian,° though the
priest o' th' town commended him for a true man.   140

FORD   'Twas a good sensible fellow—well.

---

**50 hack** meaning not clear in this context; a double entendre
on giving indiscriminate blows with a sword is possible
**51 article . . . gentry** character of your rank   **52 burn
daylight** waste time   **55 make difference of** discriminate between; **liking** looks   **58 uncomeliness** improper
behavior   **58–59 his disposition . . . words** i.e., appearances
are deceiving   **61 Greensleeves** popular love ballad   **70 ill
opinions** sullied reputations   **78 Mount Pelion** mountain in
Thessaly noted in mythology for the attempt of the giants to
reach heaven by piling Mount Ossa on Pelion   **79 turtles**
turtledoves (noted for their fidelity to their mates)
**83 honesty** chastity   **86 boarded** made advances to   **93–94
fine-baited** subtly alluring   **97 chariness** scrupulous integrity

**101 goodman** husband   **108 curtal** with a docked tail
**109 affects** loves   **113 gallimaufry** medley; **perpend** consider   **115 liver** supposed seat of love   **116 Sir Actaeon**
accidentally coming upon Diana bathing, Actaeon was turned
into a stag for punishment and then killed by his own
hounds; **Ringwood** common Elizabethan name for a hound
**117 odious . . . name** allusion to Actaeon as a horned beast,
i.e., a cuckold   **121 cuckoo birds** allusion to cuckoldom from
the cuckoo's habit of laying its eggs in the nests of other birds
**132 bread and cheese** possible allusion to the cuckoo-bread
flower, i.e., feeding cuckoldry   **137 affecting** affected   **139
Cataian** Cathaian (i.e., Chinese; not considered trustworthy
by the Elizabethans)

[MISTRESS PAGE and MISTRESS FORD *come forward.*]

PAGE  How now, Meg.

MRS. PAGE  Whither go you, George? Hark you.

[*They speak aside.*]

MRS. FORD  How now, sweet Frank. Why art thou melancholy? 145

FORD  I melancholy? I am not melancholy. Get you home, go.

MRS. FORD  Faith, thou hast some crotchets° in thy head now. Will you go, Mistress Page?

MRS. PAGE  Have with you.°—You'll come to dinner, 150 George?

[*Enter*] Mistress QUICKLY.

[*Aside to* MISTRESS FORD.] Look who comes yonder. She shall be our messenger to this paltry knight.

MRS. FORD [*Aside to* MISTRESS PAGE.]  Trust me, I thought on her. She'll fit it. 155

MRS. PAGE  You are come to see my daughter Anne?

QUICKLY  Ay, forsooth; and, I pray, how does good Mistress Anne?

MRS. PAGE  Go in with us and see. We have an hour's talk with you. 160

[*Exeunt* MISTRESS PAGE, MISTRESS FORD, *and Mistress* QUICKLY.]

PAGE  How now, Master Ford.

FORD  You heard what this knave told me, did you not?

PAGE  Yes, and you heard what the other told me?

FORD  Do you think there is truth in them? 165

PAGE  Hang 'em, slaves! I do not think the knight would offer° it. But these that accuse him in his intent towards our wives are a yoke° of his discarded men— very rogues, now they be out of service.

FORD  Were they his men? 170

PAGE  Marry were they.

FORD  I like it never the better for that. Does he lie at the Garter?

PAGE  Ay, marry does he. If he should intend this voyage toward my wife, I would turn her loose to 175 him; and what he gets more of her than sharp words, let it lie on my head.°

FORD  I do not misdoubt my wife, but I would be loath to turn them together. A man may be too confident. I would have nothing lie on my head. I cannot be thus 180 satisfied.

[*Enter*] HOST.

PAGE  Look where my ranting Host of the Garter comes. There is either liquor in his pate or money in his purse when he looks so merrily.—How now, mine Host. 185

HOST  How now, bully rook, thou'rt a gentleman. [*Calling behind him.*] Cavaliero° Justice, I say!

[*Enter*] SHALLOW.

SHALLOW  I follow, mine Host, I follow. Good even and twenty,° good Master Page. Master Page, will you go with us? We have sport in hand. 190

HOST  Tell him, Cavaliero Justice; tell him, bully rook.

SHALLOW  Sir, there is a fray to be fought between Sir Hugh the Welsh priest and Caius the French doctor.

FORD  Good mine Host o' th' Garter, a word with you.

[*Draws him aside.*]

HOST  What sayest thou, my bully rook? 195

SHALLOW [*To* PAGE.]  Will you go with us to behold it? My merry Host hath had the measuring of their weapons, and, I think, hath appointed them contrary° places; for, believe me, I hear the parson is no jester. Hark, I will tell you what our sport shall be. 200

[*They converse apart.*]

HOST  Hast thou no suit against my knight, my Guest-Cavaliero?

FORD  None, I protest. But I'll give you a pottle° of burnt° sack to give me recourse to him and tell him my name is Brooke—only for a jest. 205

HOST  My hand, bully. Thou shalt have egress and regress—said I well?—and thy name shall be Brooke. It is a merry knight. Will you go, mynheers?°

SHALLOW  Have with you, mine Host.

PAGE  I have heard the Frenchman hath good skill in 210 his rapier.

SHALLOW  Tut, sir, I could have told you more. In these times you stand on distance,° your passes,° stoccadoes,° and I know not what. 'Tis the heart, Master Page; 'tis here, 'tis here. I have seen the time 215 with my long sword I would have made you four tall fellows skip like rats.

HOST  Here, boys, here, here! Shall we wag?°

PAGE  Have with you. I had rather hear them scold than fight.  *Exeunt* [HOST, SHALLOW, *and* PAGE]. 220

FORD  Though Page be a secure fool and stands so firmly on his wife's frailty, yet I cannot put off my opinion so easily. She was in his company at Page's house, and what they made there, I know not. Well, I will look further into't; and I have a disguise to 225 sound Falstaff. If I find her honest, I lose not my labor. If she be otherwise, 'tis labor well bestowed.  [*Exit.*]

Scene II. [*Falstaff's room in the Garter Inn.*]

*Enter* FALSTAFF [*and*] PISTOL.

FALSTAFF  I will not lend thee a penny.

PISTOL
Why, then the world's mine oyster,
Which I with sword will open.

FALSTAFF  Not a penny. I have been content, sir, you should lay my countenance° to pawn. I have grated 5 upon° my good friends for three reprieves for you

148 **crotchets** peculiar notions  150 **Have with you** I'll go along with you  167 **offer** try  168 **yoke** pair  177 **let . . . head** (1) it's my responsibility (2) I would be cuckolded  187 **Cavaliero** Spanish title for a gentleman trained in arms

188–89 **Good . . . twenty** good evening twenty times over (there is an error in time here, for it is morning)  198 **contrary** different  203 **pottle** two-quart tankard  204 **burnt** heated  208 **mynheers** gentlemen  213 **distance** space between fencers; **passes** lunges  214 **stoccadoes** thrusts  218 **wag** go  II.ii.5 **countenance** reputation  5–6 **grated upon** pestered and your coach-fellow Nym; or else you had looked through the grate, like a geminy° of baboons. I am damned in hell for swearing to gentlemen my friends you were good soldiers and tall fellows. And when Mistress Bridget lost the handle of her fan,° I took't° upon mine honor thou hadst it not.

PISTOL  Didst not thou share? Hadst thou not fifteen pence?

FALSTAFF  Reason, you rogue, reason. Think'st thou I'll endanger my soul gratis? At a word, hang no more about me; I am no gibbet for you. Go! A short knife° and a throng!° To your manor of Pickt-hatch,° go! You'll not bear a letter for me, you rogue? You stand upon your honor! Why, thou unconfinable baseness, it is as much as I can do to keep the terms of my honor precise. I, I, I myself sometimes, leaving the fear of God on the left hand and hiding mine honor in my necessity, am fain to shuffle,° to hedge,° and to lurch;° and yet you, rogue, will ensconce your rags, your cat-a-mountain° looks, your red-lattice° phrases, and your bold-beating° oaths, under the shelter of your honor! You will not do it? You!

PISTOL  I do relent. What would thou more of man?

[Enter] ROBIN.

ROBIN  Sir, here's a woman would speak with you.
FALSTAFF  Let her approach.

[Enter Mistress] QUICKLY.

QUICKLY  Give your worship good morrow.
FALSTAFF  Good morrow, good wife.
QUICKLY  Not so, and't please your worship.
FALSTAFF  Good maid then.
QUICKLY  I'll be sworn, as my mother was the first hour I was born.
FALSTAFF  I do believe the swearer. What with me?
QUICKLY  Shall I vouchsafe your worship a word or two?
FALSTAFF  Two thousand, fair woman, and I'll vouchsafe thee the hearing.
QUICKLY  There is one Mistress Ford—[glancing at PISTOL and ROBIN] sir, I pray, come a little nearer this ways. I myself dwell with Master Doctor Caius.
FALSTAFF  Well, on; Mistress Ford, you say—
QUICKLY  Your worship says very true. I pray your worship, come a little nearer this ways.
FALSTAFF  I warrant thee, nobody hears. Mine own people, mine own people.
QUICKLY  Are they so? God bless them and make them His servants!
FALSTAFF  Well, Mistress Ford, what of her?
QUICKLY  Why, sir, she's a good creature. Lord, Lord, your worship's a wanton! Well, heaven forgive you, and all of us, I pray—
FALSTAFF  Mistress Ford—come, Mistress Ford.
QUICKLY  Marry, this is the short and the long of it.

You have brought her into such a° canaries° as 'tis wonderful. The best courtier of them all, when the court lay at Windsor, could never have brought her to such a canary. Yet there has been knights, and lords, and gentlemen, with their coaches. I warrant you, coach after coach, letter after letter, gift after gift; smelling so sweetly—all musk—and so rushling,° I warrant you, in silk and gold; and in such alligant° terms, and in such wine and sugar of the best and the fairest that would have won any woman's heart; and I warrant you, they could never get an eye-wink of her. I had myself twenty angels given me this morning; but I defy all angels—in any such sort, as they say—but in the way of honesty; and I warrant you, they could never get her so much as sip on a cup with the proudest of them all; and yet there has been earls—nay, which is more, pensioners;° but, I warrant you, all is one with her.

FALSTAFF  But what says she to me? Be brief, my good she-Mercury.°

QUICKLY  Marry, she hath received your letter; for the which she thanks you a thousand times; and she gives you to notify that her husband will be absence from his house between ten and eleven.

FALSTAFF  Ten and eleven.

QUICKLY  Ay, forsooth; and then you may come and see the picture, she says, that you wot° of. Master Ford, her husband, will be from home. Alas, the sweet woman leads an ill life with him; he's a very jealousy man; she leads a very frampold° life with him, good heart.

FALSTAFF  Ten and eleven.—Woman, commend me to her; I will not fail her.

QUICKLY  Why, you say well. But I have another messenger to your worship. Mistress Page hath her hearty commendations to you too; and let me tell you in your ear, she's as fartuous° a civil modest wife, and one, I tell you, that will not miss you morning nor evening prayer, as any is in Windsor, whoe'er be the other. And she bade me tell your worship that her husband is seldom from home, but she hopes there will come a time. I never knew a woman so dote upon a man. Surely I think you have charms, la; yes, in truth.

FALSTAFF  Not I, I assure thee. Setting the attraction of my good parts° aside, I have no other charms.

QUICKLY  Blessing on your heart for't!

FALSTAFF  But, I pray thee, tell me this: has Ford's wife and Page's wife acquainted each other how they love me?

QUICKLY  That were a jest indeed! They have not so little grace, I hope; that were a trick indeed! But Mistress Page would desire you to send her your little page, of all loves;° her husband has a marvelous infection° to the little page; and truly, Master Page is an honest man. Never a wife in Windsor leads a better life than she does. Do what she will, say what she will,

8 geminy pair  11 handle . . . fan often made of gold or silver; took't swore  16 short knife for cutting purses  17 throng crowd of victims;  Pickt-hatch a notorious district of London  23 shuffle act underhandedly;  hedge cheat  24 lurch pilfer  25 cat-a-mountain wildcat;  red-lattice i.e., alehouse  26 bold-beating blustering

58 canaries quandaries (?) mentally intoxicated, as with canary wine (?)  64–65 rushling rustling  66 alligant elegant (?) eloquent (?)  74 pensioners members of the royal bodyguard  77 she-Mercury messenger  84 wot know  87 frampold disagreeable  94 fartuous virtuous  102 parts talents  110 of all loves for love's sake  111 infection affection

take all, pay all, go to bed when she list,° rise when she list, all is as she will. And, truly, she deserves it; for if there be a kind woman in Windsor, she is one. You must send her your page; no remedy. 115

FALSTAFF   Why, I will.

QUICKLY   Nay, but do so then; and look you, he may come and go between you both; and in any case have a nay-word,° that you may know one another's mind, and the boy never need to understand anything; for 'tis not good that children should know any wickedness. Old folks, you know, have discretion, as they say, and know the world. 120

FALSTAFF   Fare thee well, commend me to them both. There's my purse; I am yet thy debtor.—Boy, go along with this woman. [Exeunt Mistress QUICKLY and ROBIN.] This news distracts me.

PISTOL [Aside.]
This punk° is one of Cupid's carriers.° 130
Clap on more sails; pursue; up with your fights;°
Give fire! She is my prize, or ocean whelm them all!
[Exit.]

FALSTAFF   Sayest thou so, old Jack? Go thy ways; I'll make more of thy old body than I have done. Will they yet look after thee? Wilt thou, after the expense of so much money, be now a gainer? Good body, I thank thee. Let them say 'tis grossly done; so it be fairly done, no matter. 135

[Enter] BARDOLPH.

BARDOLPH   Sir John, there's one Master Brooke below would fain speak with you, and be acquainted with you; and hath sent your worship a morning's draught of sack. 140

FALSTAFF   Brooke is his name?

BARDOLPH   Ay, sir.

FALSTAFF   Call him in. [Exit BARDOLPH.] Such Brookes are welcome to me, that o'erflows such liquor. Aha! Mistress Ford and Mistress Page, have I encompassed° you? Go to; via!° 145

[Enter BARDOLPH, with] FORD [disguised].

FORD   Bless you, sir.

FALSTAFF   And you, sir; would you speak with me? 150

FORD   I make bold to press with so little preparation upon you.

FALSTAFF   You're welcome. What's your will?— Give us leave, drawer.          [Exit BARDOLPH.]

FORD   Sir, I am a gentleman that have spent much. My name is Brooke. 155

FALSTAFF   Good Master Brooke, I desire more acquaintance of you.

FORD   Good Sir John, I sue for yours, not to charge° you; for I must let you understand I think myself in better plight for a lender than you are, the which hath something embold'ned me to this unseasoned° intrusion; for they say if money go before, all ways do lie open. 160

FALSTAFF   Money is a good soldier, sir, and will on. 165

FORD   Troth, and I have a bag of money here troubles me. If you will help to bear it, Sir John, take all, or half, for easing me of the carriage.

FALSTAFF   Sir, I know not how I may deserve to be your porter. 170

FORD   I will tell you, sir, if you will give me the hearing.

FALSTAFF   Speak, good Master Brooke. I shall be glad to be your servant.

FORD   Sir, I hear you are a scholar—I will be brief with you—and you have been a man long known to me, though I had never so good means as desire to make myself acquainted with you. I shall discover° a thing to you wherein I must very much lay open mine own imperfection; but, good Sir John, as you have one eye upon my follies, as you hear them unfolded, turn another into the register of your own, that I may pass with a reproof the easier, sith° you yourself know how easy it is to be such an offender. 175 180

FALSTAFF   Very well, sir. Proceed. 185

FORD   There is a gentlewoman in this town, her husband's name is Ford.

FALSTAFF   Well, sir.

FORD   I have long loved her, and, I protest to you, bestowed much on her, followed her with a doting observance, engrossed opportunities° to meet her, fee'd° every slight occasion that could but niggardly give me sight of her, not only bought many presents to give her but have given largely to many to know what she would have given. Briefly, I have pursued her as love hath pursued me, which hath been on the wing of all occasions. But whatsoever I have merited —either in my mind or in my means—meed,° I am sure, I have received none, unless experience be a jewel. That I have purchased at an infinite rate, and that hath taught me to say this, 190 195 200
"Love like a shadow flies when substance love pursues;
Pursuing that that flies, and flying what pursues."

FALSTAFF   Have you received no promise of satisfaction at her hands? 205

FORD   Never.

FALSTAFF   Have you importuned her to such a purpose?

FORD   Never.

FALSTAFF   Of what quality was your love then? 210

FORD   Like a fair house built on another man's ground, so that I have lost my edifice by mistaking the place where I erected it.

FALSTAFF   To what purpose have you unfolded this to me? 215

FORD   When I have told you that, I have told you all. Some say that though she appear honest to me, yet in other places she enlargeth her mirth so far that there is shrewd construction made of her.° Now, Sir John, here is the heart of my purpose: you are a gentleman of excellent breeding, admirable discourse, of great admittance,° authentic° in your place and person, 220

114 list pleases   121 nay-word password   130 punk strumpet; carriers messengers   131 fights screens to conceal and protect crews in naval engagements   147–48 encompassed outwitted   148 via go on   159 charge cause expense to   162 unseasoned unseasonable   178 discover reveal   183 sith since   191 engrossed opportunities manufactured as many opportunities as possible   192 fee'd employed   198 meed reward   218–19 she . . . of her she is so free in her merriment that she has a bad reputation   221–22 great admittance high social prestige   222 authentic duly qualified

generally allowed° for your many warlike, courtlike, and learned preparations.°

FALSTAFF  O sir! 225

FORD  Believe it, for you know it. There is money. Spend it, spend it; spend more; spend all I have. Only give me so much of your time in exchange of it as to lay an amiable siege to the honesty of this Ford's wife. Use your art of wooing; win her to consent to you. If 230 any man may, you may as soon as any.

FALSTAFF  Would it apply well to the vehemency of your affection that I should win what you would enjoy? Methinks you prescribe to yourself very preposterously. 235

FORD  O, understand my drift. She dwells so securely on the excellency of her honor that the folly of my soul dares not present itself. She is too bright to be looked against. Now, could I come to her with any detection in my hand, my desires had instance° and 240 argument to commend themselves. I could drive her then from the ward° of her purity, her reputation, her marriage vow, and a thousand other her defenses, which now are too too strongly embattled against me. What say you to't, Sir John? 245

FALSTAFF  Master Brooke, I will first make bold with your money; next, give me your hand; and last, as I am a gentleman, you shall, if you will, enjoy Ford's wife.

FORD  O good sir! 250

FALSTAFF  I say you shall.

FORD  Want no money, Sir John; you shall want none.

FALSTAFF  Want no Mistress Ford, Master Brooke; you shall want none. I shall be with her, I may tell you, 255 by her own appointment. Even as you came in to me, her assistant, or go-between, parted from me. I say I shall be with her between ten and eleven, for at that time the jealous rascally knave her husband will be forth. Come you to me at night; you shall know how 260 I speed.°

FORD  I am blest in your acquaintance. Do you know Ford, sir?

FALSTAFF  Hang him, poor cuckoldly knave! I know him not. Yet I wrong him to call him poor. They say 265 the jealous wittolly° knave hath masses of money, for the which his wife seems to me well-favored.° I will use her as the key of the cuckoldly rogue's coffer, and there's my harvest-home.°

FORD  I would you knew Ford, sir, that you might 270 avoid him if you saw him.

FALSTAFF  Hang him, mechanical° salt-butter° rogue! I will stare him out of his wits. I will awe him with my cudgel; it shall hang like a meteor o'er the cuckold's horns. Master Brooke, thou shalt know I will pre- 275 dominate over the peasant, and thou shalt lie with his wife. Come to me soon at night. Ford's a knave, and I will aggravate his style.° Thou, Master Brooke, shalt

know him for knave and cuckold. Come to me soon at night. [Exit.] 280

FORD  What a damned Epicurean° rascal is this! My heart is ready to crack with impatience. Who says this is improvident jealousy? My wife hath sent to him, the hour is fixed, the match is made. Would any man have thought this? See the hell of having 285 a false woman! My bed shall be abused, my coffers ransacked, my reputation gnawn at; and I shall not only receive this villainous wrong, but stand under the adoption of abominable terms,° and by him that does me this wrong. Terms! Names! Amaimon 290 sounds well; Lucifer, well; Barbason,° well; yet they are devils' additions,° the names of fiends. But Cuckold! Wittol!°—Cuckold! The devil himself hath not such a name. Page is an ass, a secure° ass. He will trust his wife; he will not be jealous. I will 295 rather trust a Fleming with my butter, Parson Hugh the Welshman with my cheese, an Irishman with my aqua vitae° bottle, or a thief to walk my ambling gelding, than my wife with herself. Then she plots, then she ruminates, then she devises. And what they 300 think in their hearts they may effect, they will break their hearts but they will effect. God be praised for my jealousy. Eleven o'clock the hour. I will prevent this, detect my wife, be revenged on Falstaff, and laugh at Page. I will about it; better three hours too soon than 305 a minute too late. Fie, fie, fie! Cuckold! Cuckold! Cuckold!    Exit.

## Scene III. [A field near Windsor.]

*Enter [Doctor]* CAIUS *[and]* RUGBY.

CAIUS  Jack Rugby!

RUGBY  Sir?

CAIUS  Vat is de clock, Jack?

RUGBY  'Tis past the hour, sir, that Sir Hugh promised to meet. 5

CAIUS  By gar, he has save his soul dat he is no come. He has pray his Pible vell dat he is no come. By gar, Jack Rugby, he is dead already if he be come.

RUGBY  He is wise, sir. He knew your worship would kill him if he came. 10

CAIUS  By gar, de herring is no dead so as I vill kill him. Take your rapier, Jack. I vill tell you how I vill kill him.

RUGBY  Alas, sir, I cannot fence.

CAIUS  Villainy, take your rapier. 15

RUGBY  Forbear; here's company.

*[Enter]* PAGE, SHALLOW, SLENDER, *[and]* HOST.

HOST  Bless thee, bully doctor.

SHALLOW  Save you, Master Doctor Caius.

PAGE  Now, good Master Doctor.

SLENDER  Give you good morrow, sir. 20

223 **allowed** approved  224 **preparations** accomplishments
240 **instance** evidence  242 **ward** defense  261 **speed** succeed
266 **wittolly** cuckoldly  267 **well-favored** (1) well chosen (2)
good-looking  269 **harvest-home** reaped profits  272
**mechanical** low, vulgar; **salt-butter** (1) possible derogatory
allusion to Ford as a merchant (2) ill-smelling  278 **aggravate
his style** add to his title

281 **Epicurean** sensual  288–89 **stand . . . terms** submit to
being called horrible names  290–91 **Amaimon . . . Lucifer
. . . Barbason** names of devils  292 **additions** titles  293
**Wittol** contented cuckold  294 **secure** confident  298 **aqua
vitae** spirits (brandy, whiskey, etc.)

CAIUS Vat be all you, one, two, tree, four, come for?

HOST To see thee fight, to see thee foin,° to see thee traverse;° to see thee here, to see thee there; to see thee pass thy punto, thy stock, thy reverse, thy distance, thy montant.° Is he dead, my Ethiopian?° Is he 25 dead, my Francisco?° Ha, bully? What says my Aesculapius?° My Galen?° My heart of elder?° Ha, is he dead, bully stale?° Is he dead?

CAIUS By gar, he is de coward Jack-priest of de vorld. He is not show his face. 30

HOST Thou art a Castilian King-Urinal!° Hector of Greece,° my boy!

CAIUS I pray you bear vitness dat me have stay six or seven, two, tree hours for him, and he is no come.

SHALLOW He is the wiser man, Master Doctor. He is 35 a curer of souls, and you a curer of bodies. If you should fight, you go against the hair of your professions. Is it not true, Master Page?

PAGE Master Shallow, you have yourself been a great fighter, though now a man of peace. 40

SHALLOW Bodykins,° Master Page, though I now be old and of the peace, if I see a sword out, my finger itches to make one.° Though we are justices and doctors and churchmen, Master Page, we have some salt° of our youth in us. We are the sons of women, 45 Master Page.

PAGE 'Tis true, Master Shallow.

SHALLOW It will be found so, Master Page. Master Doctor Caius, I am come to fetch you home. I am sworn of the peace. You have showed yourself a wise 50 physician, and Sir Hugh hath shown himself a wise and patient churchman. You must go with me, Master Doctor.

HOST Pardon, Guest-Justice.—A word, Monsieur Mock-water.° 55

CAIUS Mock-vater? Vat is dat?

HOST Mock-water, in our English tongue, is valor, bully.

CAIUS By gar, den, I have as much mock-vater as de Englishman.—Scurvy jack-dog priest! By gar, me 60 vill cut his ears.

HOST He will clapperclaw° thee tightly, bully.

CAIUS Clapper-de-claw? Vat is dat?

HOST That is, he will make thee amends.

CAIUS By gar, me do look he shall clapper-de-claw 65 me; for, by gar, me vill have it.

HOST And I will provoke him to't, or let him wag.

CAIUS Me tank you for dat.

HOST And moreover, bully—But first, Master Guest,

and Master Page, and eke Cavaliero Slender [aside to 70 them] go you through the town to Frogmore.°

PAGE Sir Hugh is there, is he?

HOST He is there. See what humor he is in. And I will bring the doctor about by the fields. Will it do well?

SHALLOW We will do it. 75

PAGE, SHALLOW, and SLENDER Adieu, good Master Doctor. [Exeunt PAGE, SHALLOW, and SLENDER.]

CAIUS By gar, me vill kill de priest, for he speak for a jackanape to Anne Page.

HOST Let him die. Sheathe thy impatience; throw cold 80 water on thy choler. Go about the fields with me through Frogmore. I will bring thee where Mistress Anne Page is, at a farmhouse a-feasting; and thou shalt woo her. Cried game;° said I well?

CAIUS By gar, me dank you vor dat. By gar, I love 85 you; and I shall procure-a you de good guest: de earl, de knight, de lords, de gentlemen, my patients.

HOST For the which I will be thy adversary toward Anne Page. Said I well?

CAIUS By gar, 'tis good; vell said. 90

HOST Let us wag then.

CAIUS Come at my heels, Jack Rugby.     Exeunt.

# ACT III

## Scene I. [A field near Frogmore.]

Enter EVANS [and] SIMPLE. [EVANS is in doublet and hose and carries a sword. SIMPLE carries Evans' gown and a book.]

EVANS I pray you now, good Master Slender's servingman, and friend Simple by your name, which way have you looked for Master Caius, that calls himself Doctor of Physic?

SIMPLE Marry, sir, the pittie-ward,° the park-ward,° 5 every way; Old Windsor° way, and every way but the town way.

EVANS I most fehemently desire you, you will also look that way.

SIMPLE I will, sir. [Exit.] 10

EVANS Pless my soul, how full of cholers° I am, and trempling of mind. I shall be glad if he have deceived me.—How melancholies I am.—I will knog his urinals° about his knave's costard° when I have goot opportunities for the 'ork. Pless my soul! [Sings.] 15

> To shallow rivers, to whose falls
> Melodious birds sings madrigals;
> There will we make our peds of roses,
> And a thousand fragrant posies.°
> To shallow— 20

II.iii.22 **foin** thrust   23 **traverse** move back and forth   24–25 **pass . . . montant** in fencing: "punto" = to strike a blow with the point of the sword; "stock" = thrust; "reverse" = backhand stroke; "distance" = keeping the proper space between combatants; "montant" = upward thrust   25 **Ethiopian** dark-bearded or dark-complexioned person   26 **Francisco** Frenchman   27 **Aesculapius** god of medicine; **Galen** Greek physician; **heart of elder** having a soft pith, coward   28 **stale** slang term for a physician, from diagnosing through urine analysis   31 **Castilian King-Urinal** king of doctors (derogatory allusion to Philip II of Spain)   31–32 **Hector of Greece** brave warrior   41 **Bodykins** God's little body (an oath)   43 **make one** join in   45 **salt** liveliness   55 **Mock-water** i.e., physician (precise meaning unclear; possible corruption of *muck-water* or *make-water*, with an allusion to urine analysis)   62 **clapperclaw** thrash

71 **Frogmore** village southeast of Windsor; Caius had been waiting on the north side of the town   84 **Cried game** a puzzling expression, possibly from Elizabethan sporting slang, conjecturally meaning the game is under way

III.i.5 **the pittie-ward** toward Windsor Little Park; **the park-ward** toward Windsor Great Park   6 **Old Windsor** a village south of Frogmore   11 **cholers** choler, anger   13–14 **knog his urinals** smash his equipment for analyzing a patient's urine   14 **costard** head (literally, a type of large apple)   16–19 **To shallow . . . posies** garbled lines from Marlowe's "The Passionate Shepherd to His Love"

Mercy on me, I have a great dispositions to cry. [*Sings.*]

> Melodious birds sing madrigals—
> When as I sat in Pabylon°—
> And a thousand vagram° posies.
> To shallow, &c.                                                    25

[*Enter* SIMPLE.]

SIMPLE  Yonder he is coming, this way, Sir Hugh.
EVANS  He's welcome. [*Sings.*]

> To shallow rivers, to whose falls—

Heaven prosper the right! What weapons is he?
SIMPLE  No weapons, sir. There comes my master, 30 Master Shallow, and another gentleman, from Frogmore, over the stile, this way.
EVANS  Pray you, give me my gown—or else keep it in your arms.

[*Takes the book and reads.*]

[*Enter*] PAGE, SHALLOW, [*and*] SLENDER.

SHALLOW  How now, Master Parson. Good morrow, 35 good Sir Hugh. Keep a gamester from the dice, and a good student from his book, and it is wonderful.
SLENDER [*Aside.*]  Ah, sweet Anne Page!
PAGE  Save you, good Sir Hugh.
EVANS  Pless you from His mercy sake, all of you.  40
SHALLOW  What, the sword and the word?° Do you study them both, Master Parson?
PAGE  And youthful still—in your doublet and hose this raw rheumatic day.
EVANS  There is reasons and causes for it.          45
PAGE  We are come to you to do a good office, Master Parson.
EVANS  Fery well; what is it?
PAGE  Yonder is a most reverend gentleman who, belike having received wrong by some person, is at 50 most odds with his own gravity and patience that ever you saw.
SHALLOW  I have lived fourscore years and upward; I never heard a man of his place, gravity, and learning so wide of his own respect.°                        55
EVANS  What is he?
PAGE  I think you know him: Master Doctor Caius, the renowned French physician.
EVANS  Got's will, and his passion of my heart! I had as lief you would tell me of a mess of porridge.  60
PAGE  Why?
EVANS  He has no more knowledge in Hibocrates° and Galen—and he is a knave besides, a cowardly knave as you would desires to be acquainted withal.
PAGE  I warrant you, he's the man should fight with 65 him.
SLENDER [*Aside.*]  O sweet Anne Page!
SHALLOW  It appears so by his weapons.

[*Enter*] HOST, CAIUS, [*and*] RUGBY.

Keep them asunder; here comes Doctor Caius.
PAGE  Nay, good Master Parson, keep in your weapon. 70
SHALLOW  So do you, good Master Doctor.

HOST  Disarm them, and let them question.° Let them keep their limbs whole and hack our English.
CAIUS  I pray you let-a me speak a word with your ear. Verefore vill you not meet-a me?           75
EVANS [*Aside to* CAIUS.]  Pray you, use your patience. [*Aloud.*] In good time.
CAIUS  By gar, you are de coward, de Jack dog, John ape.
EVANS [*Aside to* CAIUS.]  Pray you, let us not be laugh- 80 ing-stogs° to other men's humors. I desire you in friendship, and I will one way or other make you amends. [*Aloud.*] I will knog your urinals about your knave's cogscomb for missing your meetings and appointments.                                         85
CAIUS  Diable! Jack Rugby, mine Host de Jarteer, have I not stay for him to kill him? Have I not, at de place I did appoint?
EVANS  As I am a Christians soul, now look you, this is the place appointed. I'll be judgment by mine Host 90 of the Garter.
HOST  Peace, I say, Gallia and Gaul,° French and Welsh, soul-curer and body-curer.
CAIUS  Ay, dat is very good, excellent.
HOST  Peace, I say. Hear mine Host of the Garter. Am 95 I politic? Am I subtle? Am I a Machiavel?° Shall I lose my doctor? No; he gives me the potions and the motions.° Shall I lose my parson, my priest, my Sir Hugh? No; he gives me the proverbs and the no-verbs. Give me thy hand, terrestrial; so. Give me thy 100 hand, celestial; so. Boys of art,° I have deceived you both; I have directed you to wrong places. Your hearts are mighty, your skins are whole, and let burnt sack be the issue.° Come, lay their swords to pawn. Follow me, lad of peace; follow, follow, follow.    105
SHALLOW  Trust me, a mad Host.—Follow, gentlemen, follow.
SLENDER [*Aside.*]  O sweet Anne Page!

    [*Exeunt* SHALLOW, SLENDER, PAGE, *and* HOST.]

CAIUS  Ha, do I perceive dat? Have you make-a de sot° of us, ha, ha?                                110
EVANS  This is well! He has made us his vlouting-stog.° I desire you that we may be friends, and let us knog our prains together to be revenge on this same scall,° scurvy, cogging companion,° the Host of the Garter.                                            115
CAIUS  By gar, with all my heart. He promise to bring me where is Anne Page. By gar, he deceive me too.
EVANS  Well, I will smite his noddles. Pray you follow.
                                          [*Exeunt.*]

---

Scene II. [*Windsor. A street.*]

[*Enter*] MISTRESS PAGE [*and*] ROBIN.

MRS. PAGE  Nay, keep your way, little gallant. You were wont to be a follower, but now you are a leader.

---

23 **When . . . Pabylon** from Psalm 137   24 **vagram** fragrant   41 **word** the Bible   55 **wide . . . respect** indifferent to his reputation   62 **Hibocrates** Hippocrates (fifth century B.C. Greek physician)

72 **question** dispute verbally   80–81 **laughing-stogs** laughingstocks   92 **Gallia and Gaul** Wales and France   96 **a Machiavel** an intriguer (from Niccolò Machiavelli, regarded by the Elizabethans as the archintriguer)   98 **motions** bowel movements   101 **art** learning   104 **issue** conclusion   110 **sot** fool   111–12 **vlouting-stog** flouting-stock, laughingstock   114 **scall** scald, scurvy; **cogging companion** cheating rascal

Whether° had you rather lead mine eyes, or eye your master's heels?

ROBIN  I had rather, forsooth, go before you like a 5 man than follow him like a dwarf.

MRS. PAGE  O, you are a flattering boy. Now I see you'll be a courtier.

[Enter] FORD.

FORD  Well met, Mistress Page. Whither go you?

MRS. PAGE  Truly, sir, to see your wife. Is she at 10 home?

FORD  Ay, and as idle as she may hang together,° for want of company. I think if your husbands were dead, you two would marry.

MRS. PAGE  Be sure of that—two other husbands.  15

FORD  Where had you this pretty weathercock?°

MRS. PAGE  I cannot tell what the dickens his name is my husband had him of. What do you call your knight's name, sirrah?

ROBIN  Sir John Falstaff.  20

FORD  Sir John Falstaff!

MRS. PAGE  He, he; I can never hit on's name. There is such a league° between my goodman and he. Is your wife at home indeed?

FORD  Indeed she is.  25

MRS. PAGE  By your leave, sir. I am sick till I see her.
[Exeunt MISTRESS PAGE and ROBIN.]

FORD  Has Page any brains? Hath he any eyes? Hath he any thinking? Sure, they sleep; he hath no use of them. Why, this boy will carry a letter twenty mile as easy as a cannon will shoot pointblank twelve score.° 30 He pieces out° his wife's inclination; he gives her folly motion° and advantage. And now she's going to my wife, and Falstaff's boy with her. A man may hear this shower sing in the wind. And Falstaff's boy with her. —Good plots! They are laid, and our revolted wives 35 share damnation together. Well, I will take him, then torture my wife, pluck the borrowed veil of modesty from the so-seeming Mistress Page, divulge Page himself for a secure and willful Actaeon;° and to these violent proceedings all my neighbors shall cry aim.° 40 [Clock strikes.] The clock gives me my cue, and my assurance bids me search. There I shall find Falstaff. I shall be rather praised for this than mocked, for it is as positive as the earth is firm that Falstaff is there. I will go.  45

[Enter] PAGE, SHALLOW, SLENDER, HOST, EVANS, CAIUS, [and RUGBY].

SHALLOW, PAGE, &C.  Well met, Master Ford.

FORD  Trust me, a good knot.° I have good cheer at home, and I pray you all go with me.

SHALLOW  I must excuse myself, Master Ford.

SLENDER  And so must I, sir. We have appointed to 50 dine with Mistress Anne, and I would not break with her for more money than I'll speak of.

SHALLOW  We have lingered about a match between Anne Page and my cousin Slender, and this day we shall have our answer.  55

SLENDER  I hope I have your good will, father Page.

PAGE  You have, Master Slender. I stand wholly for you. But my wife, Master Doctor, is for you altogether.

CAIUS  Ay, be-gar, and de maid is love-a me; my 60 nursh-a Quickly tell me so mush.

HOST  What say you to young Master Fenton? He capers, he dances, he has eyes of youth, he writes verses, he speaks holiday,° he smells April and May. He will carry't,° he will carry't; 'tis in his buttons;° he 65 will carry't.

PAGE  Not by my consent, I promise you. The gentleman is of no having.° He kept company with the wild prince and Poins;° he is of too high a region; he knows too much. No, he shall not knit a knot in his fortunes 70 with the finger of my substance. If he take her, let him take her simply.° The wealth I have waits on my consent, and my consent goes not that way.

FORD  I beseech you heartily, some of you go home with me to dinner. Besides your cheer, you shall have 75 sport. I will show you a monster. Master Doctor, you shall go. So shall you, Master Page, and you, Sir Hugh.

SHALLOW  Well, fare you well. We shall have the freer wooing at Master Page's.
[Exeunt SHALLOW and SLENDER.]

CAIUS  Go home, John Rugby. I come anon.  80
[Exit RUGBY.]

HOST  Farewell, my hearts. I will to my honest knight Falstaff, and drink canary° with him.  [Exit.]

FORD [Aside.]  I think I shall drink in pipe-wine° first with him; I'll make him dance.—Will you go, gentles?  85

ALL  Have with you to see this monster.  Exeunt.

Scene III. [A room in Ford's house.]

Enter MISTRESS FORD [and] MISTRESS PAGE.

MRS. FORD  What, John! What, Robert!

MRS. PAGE  Quickly, quickly. Is the buck basket°—

MRS. FORD  I warrant. What, Robert, I say!

[Enter] SERVANTS [with a basket].

MRS. PAGE  Come, come, come!

MRS. FORD  Here, set it down.  5

MRS. PAGE  Give your men the charge. We must be brief.

MRS. FORD  Marry, as I told you before, John and Robert, be ready here hard by in the brewhouse; and when I suddenly call you, come forth, and without 10 any pause or staggering, take this basket on your shoulders. That done, trudge with it in all haste, and carry it among the whitsters° in Datchet Mead,° and

64 **speaks holiday** uses choice language  65 **carry't** win; **'tis . . . buttons** he has it in him  68 **having** property  68–69 **wild . . . Poins** Prince Hal and Poins, characters from *1 and 2 Henry IV*  72 **simply** by herself without any dowry  82 **canary** a sweet wine  83 **pipe-wine** wine from the cask; involved punning on *pipe* (1) a cask (2) a musical instrument, and on *canary* (1) a type of wine (2) a lively dance  III.iii.2 **buck basket** basket for soiled linen  13 **whitsters** bleachers of linen; **Datchet Mead** meadow between Windsor Little Park and the Thames

III.ii.3 **Whether** I wonder whether  12 **as idle . . . together** as idle as she can be without going to pieces  16 **weathercock** an allusion to Robin's gaudy clothes  23 **league** friendship  30 **twelve score** at twelve score paces  31 **pieces out** assists  32 **motion** prompting  39 **Actaeon** cuckold  40 **cry aim** applaud (from archery)  47 **knot** company

there empty it in the muddy ditch close by the Thames side. 15

MRS. PAGE You will do it?

MRS. FORD I ha' told them over and over; they lack no direction. Begone, and come when you are called. [*Exeunt* SERVANTS.]

[*Enter*] ROBIN.

MRS. PAGE Here comes little Robin. 20

MRS. FORD How now, my eyas-musket.° What news with you?

ROBIN My master, Sir John, is come in at your back door, Mistress Ford, and requests your company.

MRS. PAGE You little Jack-a-Lent,° have you been 25 true to us?

ROBIN Ay, I'll be sworn. My master knows not of your being here, and hath threat'ned to put me into everlasting liberty if I tell you of it; for he swears he'll turn me away. 30

MRS. PAGE Thou'rt a good boy. This secrecy of thine shall be a tailor to thee and shall make thee a new doublet and hose. I'll go hide me.

MRS. FORD Do so. [*To* ROBIN.] Go tell thy master I am alone. [*Exit* ROBIN.] Mistress Page, remember you 35 your cue.

MRS. PAGE I warrant thee; if I do not act it, hiss me. [*Exit.*]

MRS. FORD Go to, then. We'll use this unwholesome humidity, this gross wat'ry pumpion.° We'll teach him to know turtles from jays.° 40

[*Enter*] FALSTAFF.

FALSTAFF "Have I caught thee, my heavenly jewel?"° Why, now let me die, for I have lived long enough. This is the period° of my ambition. O this blessed hour!

MRS. FORD O sweet Sir John! 45

FALSTAFF Mistress Ford, I cannot cog,° I cannot prate, Mistress Ford. Now shall I sin in my wish: I would thy husband were dead. I'll speak it before the best lord; I would make thee my lady.

MRS. FORD I your lady, Sir John? Alas, I should be a 50 pitiful lady.

FALSTAFF Let the court of France show me such another. I see how thine eye would emulate the diamond. Thou hast the right arched beauty of the brow that becomes the ship-tire,° the tire-valiant,° or 55 any tire of Venetian admittance.°

MRS. FORD A plain kerchief, Sir John. My brows become nothing else, nor that well neither.

FALSTAFF Thou art a tyrant to say so. Thou wouldst make an absolute° courtier, and the firm fixture of 60 thy foot would give an excellent motion to thy gait

in a semicircled farthingale.° I see what thou wert if fortune, thy foe, were—not nature—thy friend.° Come, thou canst not hide it.

MRS. FORD Believe me, there's no such thing in me. 65

FALSTAFF What made me love thee? Let that persuade thee there's something extraordinary in thee. Come, I cannot cog and say thou art this and that, like a many of these lisping hawthorn buds° that come like women in men's apparel and smell like Bucklersbury° 70 in simple-time.° I cannot. But I love thee, none but thee; and thou deserv'st it.

MRS. FORD Do not betray me, sir. I fear you love Mistress Page.

FALSTAFF Thou mightst as well say I love to walk by 75 the Counter-gate,° which is as hateful to me as the reek of a limekiln.

MRS. FORD Well, heaven knows how I love you, and you shall one day find it.

FALSTAFF Keep in that mind; I'll deserve it. 80

MRS. FORD Nay, I must tell you, so you do, or else I could not be in that mind.

[*Enter* ROBIN.]

ROBIN Mistress Ford, Mistress Ford! Here's Mistress Page at the door—sweating and blowing and looking wildly, and would needs speak with you presently.° 85

FALSTAFF She shall not see me; I will ensconce me behind the arras.°

MRS. FORD Pray you, do so; she's a very tattling woman. [FALSTAFF *hides.*]

[*Enter* MISTRESS PAGE.]

What's the matter? How now! 90

MRS. PAGE O Mistress Ford, what have you done? You're shamed, y' are overthrown, y' are undone forever!

MRS. FORD What's the matter, good Mistress Page?

MRS. PAGE O well-a-day, Mistress Ford! Having an 95 honest man to your husband, to give him such cause of suspicion!

MRS. FORD What cause of suspicion?

MRS. PAGE What cause of suspicion! Out upon you; how am I mistook in you! 100

MRS. FORD Why, alas, what's the matter?

MRS. PAGE Your husband's coming hither, woman, with all the officers in Windsor, to search for a gentleman that he says is here now in the house—by your consent—to take an ill advantage of his absence. You 105 are undone.

MRS. FORD 'Tis not so, I hope.

MRS. PAGE Pray heaven it be not so that you have such a man here! But 'tis most certain your husband's coming, with half Windsor at his heels, to search for 110 such a one. I come before to tell you. If you know

21 **eyas-musket** young male sparrow hawk; i.e., a sprightly lad   25 **Jack-a-Lent** an allusion to Robin's gaudy clothes, from the decorated puppet used in Lenten games   39 **pumpion** pumpkin   40 **turtles from jays** faithful women from unfaithful ones   41 **Have . . . jewel** from Sir Philip Sidney's collection of sonnets, *Astrophel and Stella*   43 **period** end   46 **cog** fawn   55 **ship-tire** headdress shaped like a ship; **tire-valiant** fanciful headdress   56 **tire . . . admittance** Venetian-style headdress   60 **absolute** perfect

62 **semicircled farthingale** half-hooped petticoat   62–63 **I . . . friend** Since you are already naturally pretty, I can imagine what you would look like dressed for the world of high society if fortune had not made you a member of the bourgeois class ("Fortune Thy Foe" is the title of an Elizabethan popular ballad)   69 **hawthorn buds** dandies   70 **Bucklersbury** a street in London where herbs were sold   71 **simpletime** herb-selling season   76 **Counter-gate** gate of the debtors' prison, known as an area of foul odors   85 **presently** immediately   87 **arras** hanging tapestry used for wall decoration

yourself clear,° why, I am glad of it; but if you have a friend° here, convey, convey him out. Be not amazed; call all your senses to you; defend your reputation, or bid farewell to your good life forever.     115

MRS. FORD   What shall I do? There is a gentleman, my dear friend; and I fear not mine own shame so much as his peril. I had rather than a thousand pound he were out of the house.

MRS. PAGE   For shame! Never stand° "you had 120 rather" and "you had rather." Your husband's here at hand; bethink you of some conveyance. In the house you cannot hide him.—O, how have you deceived me!—Look, here is a basket. If he be of any reasonable stature, he may creep in here; and throw foul linen 125 upon him, as if it were going to bucking.° Or—it is whiting time°—send him by your two men to Datchet Mead.

MRS. FORD   He's too big to go in there. What shall I do?     130

FALSTAFF [Rushing forward.]   Let me see't, let me see't. O let me see't! I'll in, I'll in! Follow your friend's counsel. I'll in!

MRS. PAGE   What, Sir John Falstaff! [Aside to FALSTAFF.] Are these your letters, knight?     135

FALSTAFF [Aside to MISTRESS PAGE.]   I love thee. Help me away.—Let me creep in here. I'll never—

[Climbs into the basket; they cover him with foul linen.]

MRS. PAGE [To ROBIN.]   Help to cover your master, boy. Call your men, Mistress Ford. [Aside to FALSTAFF.] You dissembling knight!     140

MRS. FORD   What, John! Robert! John!

[Exit ROBIN.]

[Enter SERVANTS.]

Go, take up these clothes here quickly. Where's the cowlstaff?° Look how you drumble!° Carry them to the laundress in Datchet Mead. Quickly, come!

[Enter] FORD, PAGE, CAIUS, [and] EVANS.

FORD [To his companions.]   Pray you, come near. If I 145 suspect without cause, why then make sport at me; then let me be your jest; I deserve it. How now, who goes here? Whither bear you this?

SERVANTS   To the laundress, forsooth.

MRS. FORD   Why, what have you to do whither they 150 bear it? You were best meddle with buck-washing!

FORD   Buck? I would I could wash myself of the buck!° Buck, buck, buck! Ay, buck; I warrant you, buck—and of the season° too, it shall appear. [Exeunt SERVANTS with the basket.] Gentlemen, I have dreamed 155 tonight.° I'll tell you my dream. Here, here, here be my keys. Ascend my chambers; search, seek, find out. I'll warrant we'll unkennel° the fox. Let me stop this way first. [Locks the door.] So, now uncope.°

PAGE   Good Master Ford, be contented. You wrong 160 yourself too much.

FORD   True, Master Page. Up, gentlemen; you shall see sport anon. Follow me, gentlemen.     [Exit.]

EVANS   This is fery fantastical humors and jealousies.

CAIUS   By gar, 'tis no de fashion of France; it is not 165 jealous in France.

PAGE   Nay, follow him, gentlemen. See the issue of his search.     [Exeunt PAGE, CAIUS, and EVANS.]

MRS. PAGE   Is there not a double excellency in this?

MRS. FORD   I know not which pleases me better—that 170 my husband is deceived, or Sir John.

MRS. PAGE   What a taking° was he in when your husband asked who was in the basket!

MRS. FORD   I am half afraid he will have need of washing; so throwing him into the water will do him 175 a benefit.

MRS. PAGE   Hang him, dishonest rascal! I would all of the same strain were in the same distress.

MRS. FORD   I think my husband hath some special suspicion of Falstaff's being here, for I never saw him 180 so gross in his jealousy till now.

MRS. PAGE   I will lay a plot to try that, and we will yet have more tricks with Falstaff. His dissolute disease will scarce obey this medicine.

MRS. FORD   Shall we send that foolish carrion° 185 Mistress Quickly to him, and excuse his throwing into the water, and give him another hope to betray him to another punishment?

MRS. PAGE   We will do it. Let him be sent for tomorrow, eight o'clock, to have amends.     190

[Enter FORD, PAGE, CAIUS, and EVANS.]

FORD   I cannot find him. May be the knave bragged of that he could not compass.

MRS. PAGE [Aside to MISTRESS FORD.]   Heard you that?

MRS. FORD   You use me well, Master Ford, do you?    195

FORD   Ay, I do so.

MRS. FORD   Heaven make you better than your thoughts!

FORD   Amen.

MRS. PAGE   You do yourself mighty wrong, Master 200 Ford.

FORD   Ay, ay, I must bear it.

EVANS   If there be any pody in the house, and in the chambers, and in the coffers, and in the presses,° Heaven forgive my sins at the day of judgment!     205

CAIUS   Be-gar, nor I too; dere is nobodies.

PAGE   Fie, fie, Master Ford, are you not ashamed? What spirit, what devil suggests this imagination? I would not ha' your distemper in this kind for the wealth of Windsor Castle.     210

FORD   'Tis my fault,° Master Page. I suffer for it.

EVANS   You suffer for a pad conscience. Your wife is as honest a 'omans as I will desires among five thousand, and five hundred too.

CAIUS   By gar, I see 'tis an honest woman.     215

FORD   Well, I promised you a dinner. Come, come, walk in the Park. I pray you pardon me. I will hereafter make known to you why I have done this.— Come wife; come, Mistress Page—I pray you pardon me. Pray heartily, pardon me.     220

---

112 **clear** innocent   113 **friend** paramour   120 **stand** lose time over   126 **bucking** washing   127 **whiting time** bleaching time   143 **cowlstaff** pole for carrying a basket between two persons; **drumble** dawdle   153 **buck** horned beast, cuckold   154 **of the season** in season   156 **tonight** last night   158 **unkennel** dislodge   159 **uncope** flush him out (hunting)

172 **taking** fright   185 **carrion** body of corrupting flesh   204 **presses** cupboards   211 **fault** weakness

PAGE  Let's go in, gentlemen; but, trust me, we'll mock him. I do invite you tomorrow morning to my house to breakfast. After, we'll a-birding° together. I have a fine hawk for the bush.° Shall it be so?

FORD  Anything.                                              225

EVANS  If there is one, I shall make two in the company.

CAIUS  If dere be one, or two, I shall make-a de turd.

FORD  Pray you, go, Master Page.

EVANS [Aside to CAIUS.]  I pray you now, remem- 230 brance tomorrow on the lousy knave, mine Host.

CAIUS [Aside to EVANS.]  Dat is good, by gar; with all my heart.

EVANS [Aside to CAIUS.]  A lousy knave, to have his gibes and his mockeries!                    Exeunt. 235


Scene IV. [Before Page's house.]

Enter FENTON [and] ANNE Page.

FENTON
I see I cannot get thy father's love;
Therefore no more turn me to him, sweet Nan.

ANNE
Alas, how then?

FENTON                      Why, thou must be thyself.
He doth object I am too great of birth,
And that my state° being galled with my expense,°   5
I seek to heal it only by his wealth.
Besides these, other bars he lays before me:
My riots past, my wild societies;
And tells me 'tis a thing impossible
I should love thee but as a property.               10

ANNE
May be he tells you true.

FENTON
No, heaven so speed° me in my time to come!
Albeit I will confess thy father's wealth
Was the first motive that I wooed thee, Anne.
Yet, wooing thee, I found thee of more value       15
Than stamps° in gold or sums in sealèd bags;
And 'tis the very riches of thyself
That now I aim at.

ANNE                   Gentle Master Fenton,
Yet seek my father's love; still seek it, sir.
If opportunity and humblest suit                    20
Cannot attain it, why, then—

[Enter] SHALLOW, SLENDER, [and Mistress] QUICKLY.
                              Hark you hither.

[Takes FENTON aside.]

SHALLOW  Break their talk, Mistress Quickly. My kinsman shall speak for himself.

SLENDER  I'll make a shaft or a bolt on't.° 'Slid,° 'tis but venturing.                              25

SHALLOW  Be not dismayed.

SLENDER  No, she shall not dismay me. I care not for that, but that I am afeard.

QUICKLY [To ANNE.]  Hark ye, Master Slender would speak a word with you.                        30

ANNE
I come to him. [Aside.] This is my father's choice.
O, what a world of vile ill-favored faults
Looks handsome in three hundred pounds a year.

QUICKLY  And how does good Master Fenton? Pray you, a word with you.                            35

[They converse together.]

SHALLOW  She's coming; to her, coz. O boy, thou hadst a father!

SLENDER  I had a father, Mistress Anne; my uncle can tell you good jests of him. Pray you, uncle, tell Mistress Anne the jest how my father stole two geese 40 out of a pen, good uncle.

SHALLOW  Mistress Anne, my cousin° loves you.

SLENDER  Ay, that I do, as well as I love any woman in Gloucestershire.

SHALLOW  He will maintain you like a gentlewoman. 45

SLENDER  Ay, that I will, come cut and long-tail, under the degree of a squire.°

SHALLOW  He will make you a hundred and fifty pounds jointure.

ANNE  Good Master Shallow, let him woo for himself. 50

SHALLOW  Marry, I thank you for it; I thank you for that good comfort. She calls you, coz. I'll leave you.

ANNE  Now, Master Slender—

SLENDER  Now, good Mistress Anne—

ANNE  What is your will?                           55

SLENDER  My will? 'Od's heartlings,° that's a pretty jest indeed! I ne'er made my will yet, I thank God. I am not such a sickly creature, I give heaven praise.

ANNE  I mean, Master Slender, what would you with me?                                           60

SLENDER  Truly, for mine own part, I would little or nothing with you. Your father and my uncle have made motions.° If it be my luck, so; if not, happy man be his dole.° They can tell you how things go better than I can. You may ask your father; here he comes. 65

[Enter] PAGE [and] MISTRESS PAGE.

PAGE
Now, Master Slender. Love him, daughter Anne.—
Why, how now! What does Master Fenton here?
You wrong me, sir, thus still to haunt my house.
I told you, sir, my daughter is disposed of.

FENTON
Nay, Master Page, be not impatient.               70

MRS. PAGE
Good Master Fenton, come not to my child.

PAGE
She is no match for you.

FENTON
Sir, will you hear me?

PAGE                      No, good Master Fenton.

---

223 a-birding hawking  224 fine . . . bush a hawk especially trained to fly at small birds sheltered in bushes
III.iv.5 state estate; galled . . . expense squandered away
12 speed prosper  16 stamps coins  24 make . . . on't do it one way or another (literally, use a slender arrow or a thick one); 'Slid God's eyelid (mild oath)

42 cousin kinsman  46–47 cut . . . squire all kinds so long as they are not too high-ranking  56 'Od's heartlings God's little heart (an oath)  63 motions suggestions  63–64 happy . . . dole happiness be his portion

Come, Master Shallow; come, son Slender, in.
Knowing my mind, you wrong me, Master Fenton.     75
[PAGE, SHALLOW, *and* SLENDER *enter the house.*]

QUICKLY     Speak to Mistress Page.

FENTON
Good Mistress Page, for that I love your daughter
In such a righteous fashion as I do,
Perforce, against all checks,° rebukes, and manners,
I must advance the colors° of my love     80
And not retire. Let me have your good will.

ANNE     Good mother, do not marry me to yond fool.

MRS. PAGE     I mean it not. I seek you a better husband.

QUICKLY     [*To* ANNE.] That's my master, Master
Doctor.     85

ANNE
Alas, I had rather be set quick° i' th' earth,
And bowled to death with turnips.

MRS. PAGE
Come, trouble not yourself. Good Master Fenton,
I will not be your friend, nor enemy.
My daughter will I question how she loves you,     90
And as I find her, so am I affected.
Till then, farewell, sir. She must needs go in.
Her father will be angry.
[MISTRESS PAGE *and* ANNE *enter the house.*]

FENTON
Farewell, gentle mistress. Farewell, Nan.

QUICKLY     This is my doing now. "Nay," said I, "will     95
you cast away your child on a fool, and a physician?
Look on Master Fenton." This is my doing.

FENTON
I thank thee, and I pray thee, once° tonight
Give my sweet Nan this ring. There's for thy pains.
[*Gives the ring and some money to* QUICKLY
*and then departs.*]

QUICKLY     Now heaven send thee good fortune! A     100
kind heart he hath. A woman would run through fire
and water for such a kind heart. But yet, I would my
master had Mistress Anne; or I would Master Slender
had her; or, in sooth, I would Master Fenton had her.
I will do what I can for them all three, for so I have     105
promised, and I'll be as good as my word—but
speciously° for Master Fenton. Well, I must of another
errand to Sir John Falstaff from my two mistresses.
What a beast am I to slack it!°     *Exit.*

Scene V. [*Falstaff's room in the Garter Inn.*]

*Enter* FALSTAFF.

FALSTAFF     Bardolph, I say!

[*Enter*] BARDOLPH.

BARDOLPH     Here, sir.

FALSTAFF     Go fetch me a quart of sack—put a toast°
in't. [*Exit* BARDOLPH.] Have I lived to be carried in a
basket like a barrow of butcher's offal, and to be     5
thrown in the Thames? Well, if I be served such
another trick, I'll have my brains ta'en out and

buttered, and give them to a dog for a New-Year's
gift. The rogues slighted° me into the river with as
little remorse as they would have drowned a blind     10
bitch's puppies, fifteen i' th' litter. And you may
know by my size that I have a kind of alacrity in
sinking; if the bottom were as deep as hell, I should
down. I had been drowned but that the shore was
shelvy and shallow—a death that I abhor, for the     15
water swells a man; and what a thing should I have
been when I had been swelled. I should have been a
mountain of mummy.°

[*Enter* BARDOLPH *with two cups of wine.*]

BARDOLPH     Here's Mistress Quickly, sir, to speak with
you.     20

FALSTAFF     Come, let me pour in some sack to the
Thames water, for my belly's as cold as if I had
swallowed snowballs for pills to cool the reins.° Call
her in.

BARDOLPH     Come in, woman.     25

[*Enter Mistress*] QUICKLY.

QUICKLY     By your leave; I cry you mercy.° Give your
worship good morrow.

FALSTAFF     Take away these chalices.° Go brew me a
pottle of sack finely.

BARDOLPH     With eggs, sir?     30

FALSTAFF     Simple of itself; I'll no pullet-sperm in my
brewage. [*Exit* BARDOLPH.] How now.

QUICKLY     Marry, sir, I come to your worship from
Mistress Ford.

FALSTAFF     Mistress Ford? I have had ford enough; I     35
was thrown into the ford; I have my belly full of ford.

QUICKLY     Alas the day, good heart, that was not her
fault. She does so take on with her men; they mistook
their erection.°

FALSTAFF     So did I mine, to build upon a foolish     40
woman's promise.

QUICKLY     Well, she laments, sir, for it that it would
yearn° your heart to see it. Her husband goes this
morning a-birding. She desires you once more to
come to her between eight and nine. I must carry her     45
word quickly. She'll make you amends, I warrant
you.

FALSTAFF     Well, I will visit her. Tell her so, and bid
her think what a man is. Let her consider his frailty,
and then judge of my merit.     50

QUICKLY     I will tell her.

FALSTAFF     Do so.—Between nine and ten, sayest thou?

QUICKLY     Eight and nine, sir.

FALSTAFF     Well, begone. I will not miss her.

QUICKLY     Peace be with you, sir.     55
[*Exit, leaving the door open.*]

FALSTAFF     I marvel I hear not of Master Brooke. He
sent me word to stay within. I like his money well.—
O, here he comes.

[*Enter*] FORD.

FORD     Bless you, sir.

---

**79 checks** reproofs   **80 colors** banners   **86 quick** living   **98
once** sometime   **107 speciously** especially   **109 slack it** be
remiss about it
**III.v.3 a toast** a piece of toast

**9 slighted** tossed contemptuously   **18 mummy** dead flesh
**23 reins** kidneys   **26 cry you mercy** beg your pardon   **28
chalices** drinking cups   **39 erection** direction   **43 yearn**
grieve

FALSTAFF   Now, Master Brooke, you come to know 60
what hath passed between me and Ford's wife?

FORD   That, indeed, Sir John, is my business.

FALSTAFF   Master Brooke, I will not lie to you. I was
at her house the hour she appointed me.

FORD   And sped you,° sir? 65

FALSTAFF   Very ill-favoredly, Master Brooke.

FORD   How so, sir? Did she change her determination?

FALSTAFF   No, Master Brooke, but the peaking
cornuto° her husband, Master Brooke, dwelling in a
continual 'larum of jealousy, comes me in the instant 70
of our encounter, after we had embraced, kissed,
protested, and, as it were, spoke the prologue of our
comedy; and at his heels a rabble° of his companions,
thither provoked and instigated by his distemper,°
and, forsooth, to search his house for his wife's love. 75

FORD   What, while you were there?

FALSTAFF   While I was there.

FORD   And did he search for you, and could not find
you?

FALSTAFF   You shall hear. As good luck would have 80
it, comes in one Mistress Page, gives intelligence of
Ford's approach; and in her invention and Ford's
wife's distraction, they conveyed me into a buck
basket.

FORD   A buck basket? 85

FALSTAFF   By the Lord, a buck basket! Rammed me in
with foul shirts and smocks, socks, foul stockings,
greasy napkins, that,° Master Brooke, there was the
rankest compound of villainous smell that ever
offended nostril. 90

FORD   And how long lay you there?

FALSTAFF   Nay, you shall hear, Master Brooke, what
I have suffered to bring this woman to evil for your
good. Being thus crammed in the basket, a couple of
Ford's knaves, his hinds,° were called forth by their 95
mistress to carry me in the name of foul clothes to
Datchet Lane. They took me on their shoulders; met
the jealous knave their master in the door, who asked
them once or twice what they had in their basket. I
quaked for fear lest the lunatic knave would have 100
searched it; but fate, ordaining he should be a cuckold,
held his hand. Well, on went he for a search, and away
went I for foul clothes. But mark the sequel, Master
Brooke. I suffered the pangs of three several deaths:
first, an intolerable fright to be detected with° a jealous 105
rotten bellwether;° next, to be compassed like a good
bilbo° in the circumference of a peck, hilt to point,
heel to head; and then, to be stopped in, like a strong
distillation, with stinking clothes that fretted° in their
own grease. Think of that, a man of my kidney°— 110
think of that—that am as subject to heat as butter; a
man of continual dissolution° and thaw. It was a
miracle to 'scape suffocation. And in the height of this

bath, when I was more than half stewed in grease, like
a Dutch dish, to be thrown into the Thames, and 115
cooled, glowing hot, in that surge, like a horseshoe.
Think of that—hissing hot—think of that, Master
Brooke!

FORD   In good sadness,° sir, I am sorry that for my
sake you have suffered all this. My suit then is desperate. 120
You'll undertake her no more?

FALSTAFF   Master Brooke, I will be thrown into Etna,
as I have been into Thames, ere I will leave her thus.
Her husband is this morning gone a-birding. I have
received from her another embassy° of meeting. 125
'Twixt eight and nine is the hour, Master Brooke.

FORD   'Tis past eight already, sir.

FALSTAFF   Is it? I will then address me° to my appointment. Come to me at your convenient leisure, and
you shall know how I speed; and the conclusion shall 130
be crowned with your enjoying her. Adieu. You
shall have her, Master Brooke; Master Brooke, you
shall cuckold Ford.           [Exit.]

FORD   Hum! Ha! Is this a vision? Is this a dream? Do
I sleep? Master Ford, awake; awake, Master Ford! 135
There's a hole made in your best coat, Master Ford.
This 'tis to be married; this 'tis to have linen and buck
baskets! Well, I will proclaim myself what I am. I
will now take the lecher; he is at my house; he cannot
'scape me; 'tis impossible he should. He cannot creep 140
into a halfpenny purse, nor into a pepperbox. But, lest
the devil that guides him should aid him, I will search
impossible places. Though what I am I cannot avoid,
yet to be what I would not shall not make me tame.
If I have horns to make one mad, let the proverb go 145
with me—I'll be horn-mad.           Exit.

# ACT IV

### Scene I. [A street.]

*Enter* MISTRESS PAGE, [*Mistress*] QUICKLY, [*and*]
WILLIAM.

MRS. PAGE   Is he at Master Ford's already, think'st
thou?

QUICKLY   Sure he is by this, or will be presently. But,
truly, he is very courageous° mad about his throwing
into the water. Mistress Ford desires you to come 5
suddenly.°

MRS. PAGE   I'll be with her by and by.° I'll but bring
my young man here to school. Look where his master
comes; 'tis a playing-day, I see.

[*Enter*] EVANS.

How now, Sir Hugh! No school today? 10

EVANS   No. Master Slender is let the boys leave to play.

QUICKLY   Blessing of his heart.

MRS. PAGE   Sir Hugh, my husband says my son
profits nothing in the world at his book. I pray you,
ask him some questions in his accidence.° 15

65 **sped you** did you succeed   68–69 **peaking cornuto** prying
cuckold (with a pun on *peak* as the tip of the horn)   73 **rabble**
pack   74 **distemper** ill temper   88 **that** so that   95 **hinds**
servants   105 **with** by   106 **bellwether** ram with a bell
around his neck who led the flock (with an implied reference
to a horned beast or cuckold)   106–07 **compassed . . .
bilbo** bent around like a well-tempered sword blade (a test
for ascertaining the quality of a good blade)   109 **fretted**
decayed   110 **kidney** temperament   112 **dissolution** lique-
faction

119 **sadness** seriousness   125 **embassy** message   128 **address
me** go
IV.i.4 **courageous** outrageous   6 **suddenly** immediately   7
**by and by** quickly   15 **accidence** knowledge of grammatical
inflections

EVANS  Come hither, William. Hold up your head; come.

MRS. PAGE  Come on, sirrah; hold up your head; answer your master; be not afraid.

EVANS  William, how many numbers is in nouns?    20

WILLIAM  Two.

QUICKLY  Truly, I thought there had been one number more, because they say, "Od's nouns."°

EVANS  Peace your tattlings. What is "fair," William?

WILLIAM  "Pulcher."    25

QUICKLY  Polecats!° There are fairer things than polecats, sure.

EVANS  You are a very simplicity 'oman. I pray you peace. What is "lapis," William?

WILLIAM  A stone.    30

EVANS  And what is "a stone," William?

WILLIAM  A pebble.

EVANS  No, it is "lapis." I pray you remember in your prain.

WILLIAM  "Lapis."    35

EVANS  That is a good William. What is he, William, that does lend articles?

WILLIAM  Articles are borrowed of the pronoun, and be thus declined: "Singulariter, nominativo, hic, haec, hoc."    40

EVANS  "Nominativo, hig, hag, hog." Pray you, mark: "genitivo, hujus." Well, what is your accusative case?

WILLIAM  "Accusativo, hinc."

EVANS  I pray you, have your remembrance, child: 45 "accusativo, hung, hang, hog."

QUICKLY  "Hang-hog"° is Latin for bacon, I warrant you.

EVANS  Leave your prabbles, 'oman. What is the focative case, William?    50

WILLIAM  O—"vocativo, O."

EVANS  Remember, William; focative is "caret."°

QUICKLY  And that's a good root.

EVANS  'Oman, forbear.

MRS. PAGE  Peace.    55

EVANS  What is your genitive case plural, William?

WILLIAM  Genitive case?

EVANS  Ay.

WILLIAM  Genitive—"horum, harum, horum."

QUICKLY  Vengeance of Jenny's case!° Fie on her! 60 Never name her, child, if she be a whore.

EVANS  For shame, 'oman.

QUICKLY  You do ill to teach the child such words. He teaches him to hick and to hack,° which they'll do fast enough of themselves, and to call "horum." Fie upon 65 you!

EVANS  'Oman, art thou lunatics? Hast thou no understandings for thy cases and the numbers of the genders?

Thou art as foolish Christian creatures as I would desires.    70

MRS. PAGE  Prithee, hold thy peace.

EVANS  Show me now, William, some declensions of your pronouns.

WILLIAM  Forsooth, I have forgot.

EVANS  It is "qui, quae, quod." If you forget your 75 "qui's," your "quae's," and your "quod's,"° you must be preeches.° Go your ways and play; go.

MRS. PAGE  He is a better scholar than I thought he was.

EVANS  He is a good sprag° memory. Farewell, 80 Mistress Page.

MRS. PAGE  Adieu, good Sir Hugh. [Exit EVANS.] Get you home, boy. Come, we stay too long.    Exeunt.

## Scene II. [A room in Ford's house.]

Enter FALSTAFF [and] MISTRESS FORD.

FALSTAFF  Mistress Ford, your sorrow hath eaten up my sufferance.° I see you are obsequious° in your love, and I profess requital to a hair's breadth, not only, Mistress Ford, in the simple office of love, but in all the accoutrement, complement, and ceremony of it. 5 But are you sure of your husband now?

MRS. FORD  He's a-birding, sweet Sir John.

MRS. PAGE [Within.]  What ho, gossip° Ford. What ho!

MRS. FORD  Step into th' chamber, Sir John.    10

[Exit FALSTAFF.]

[Enter] MISTRESS PAGE.

MRS. PAGE  How now, sweetheart! Who's at home besides yourself?

MRS. FORD  Why, none but mine own people.

MRS. PAGE  Indeed?

MRS. FORD  No, certainly. [Aside to her.] Speak 15 louder.

MRS. PAGE  Truly, I am so glad you have nobody here.

MRS. FOED  Why?

MRS. PAGE  Why, woman, your husband is in his old lunes° again. He so takes on yonder with my husband, 20 so rails against all married mankind, so curses all Eve's daughters—of what complexion soever, and so buffets himself on the forehead, crying, "Peer out,° peer out!" that any madness I ever yet beheld seemed but tameness, civility, and patience to this his distemper 25 he is in now. I am glad the fat knight is not here.

MRS. FORD  Why, does he talk of him?

MRS. PAGE  Of none but him; and swears he was carried out, the last time he searched for him, in a basket; protests to my husband he is now here, and 30 hath drawn him and the rest of their company from their sport to make another experiment of his suspicion. But I am glad the knight is not here. Now he shall see his own foolery.

---

23 **Od's nouns** God's wounds (an oath)  26 **Polecats** (1) wildcats (2) prostitutes  47 **Hang-hog** an allusion to a famous story of the jurist Sir Nicholas Bacon, who told a prisoner named Hog, who tried to have his death sentence commuted on grounds of kindred, that "you and I cannot be of kindred unless you are hanged; for Hog is not Bacon till it be well hanged"  52 **caret** is lacking (Latin)  60 **case** pudendum (Mistress Quickly associates Latin *horum* with *whore,* and *harum* with *hare,* a slang term for a prostitute)  64 **to hick . . . hack** hiccup (?) and go wenching (?; precise meaning unknown, but dissoluteness is implied)

76 **qui's, quae's, quod's** Latin *qu* was pronounced *k,* giving rise to bawdy puns on *keys* = penises, *case* = pudendum, *cods* = testicles)  77 **preeches** breeched, flogged  80 **sprag** sprack, alert  **IV.ii.2 sufferance** suffering; **obsequious** devoted  8 **gossip** friend  20 **lunes** lunacies  23 **Peer out** alluding to the cuckold's horns

MRS. FORD  How near is he, Mistress Page?    35

MRS. PAGE  Hard by, at street end; he will be here anon.

MRS. FORD  I am undone! The knight is here.

MRS. PAGE  Why then you are utterly shamed, and he's but a dead man. What a woman are you! Away  40 with him, away with him. Better shame than murder.

MRS. FORD  Which way should he go? How should I bestow him? Shall I put him into the basket again?

[Enter FALSTAFF.]

FALSTAFF  No, I'll come no more i' th' basket. May I not go out ere he come?    45

MRS. PAGE  Alas, three of Master Ford's brothers watch the door with pistols that none shall issue out; otherwise you might slip away ere he came. But what make you here?

FALSTAFF  What shall I do? I'll creep up into the  50 chimney.

MRS. FORD  There they always use to discharge their birding pieces.

MRS. PAGE  Creep into the kilnhole.°

FALSTAFF  Where is it?    55

MRS. FORD  He will seek there, on my word. Neither press, coffer, chest, trunk, well, vault, but he hath an abstract° for the remembrance of such places, and goes to them by his note. There is no hiding you in the house.    60

FALSTAFF  I'll go out then.

MRS. PAGE  If you go out in your own semblance, you die, Sir John. Unless you go out disguised—

MRS. FORD  How might we disguise him?

MRS. PAGE  Alas the day, I know not. There is no  65 woman's gown big enough for him; otherwise, he might put on a hat, a muffler, and a kerchief, and so escape.

FALSTAFF  Good hearts, devise something. Any extremity rather than a mischief.    70

MRS. FORD  My maid's aunt, the fat woman of Brainford,° has a gown above.

MRS. PAGE  On my word, it will serve him; she's as big as he is. And there's her thrummed° hat and her muffler too. Run up, Sir John.    75

MRS. FORD  Go, go, sweet Sir John. Mistress Page and I will look some linen for your head.

MRS. PAGE  Quick, quick! We'll come dress you straight; put on the gown the while. [Exit FALSTAFF.]

MRS. FORD  I would my husband would meet him in  80 this shape. He cannot abide the old woman of Brainford; he swears she's a witch, forbade her my house, and hath threat'ned to beat her.

MRS. PAGE  Heaven guide him to thy husband's cudgel, and the devil guide his cudgel afterwards!    85

MRS. FORD  But is my husband coming?

MRS. PAGE  Ay, in good sadness, is he; and talks of the basket too, howsoever he hath had intelligence.

MRS. FORD  We'll try that; for I'll appoint my men to carry the basket again, to meet him at the door with it,  90 as they did last time.

MRS. PAGE  Nay, but he'll be here presently. Let's go dress him like the witch of Brainford.

MRS. FORD  I'll first direct my men what they shall do with the basket. Go up; I'll bring linen for him  95 straight.    [Exit.]

MRS. PAGE  Hang him, dishonest° varlet, we cannot misuse him enough.
We'll leave a proof by that which we will do,
Wives may be merry, and yet honest too.    100
We do not act that often jest and laugh;
'Tis old but true, "Still swine eats all the draff."°
    [Exit.]

[Enter MISTRESS FORD, with two] SERVANTS.

MRS. FORD  Go, sirs, take the basket again on your shoulders. Your master is hard at door; if he bid you set it down, obey him. Quickly, dispatch.    [Exit.]    105

FIRST SERVANT  Come, come, take it up.

SECOND SERVANT  Pray heaven, it be not full of knight again.

FIRST SERVANT  I hope not; I had lief as bear so much lead.    110

[They lift the basket.]

[Enter] FORD, PAGE, CAIUS, EVANS, [and] SHALLOW.

FORD  Ay, but if it prove true, Master Page, have you any way then to unfool me again? Set down the basket, villain. Somebody call my wife. Youth in a basket!° O you panderly rascals! There's a knot,° a ging,° a pack, a conspiracy against me. Now shall the  115 devil be shamed.° What, wife, I say! Come, come forth! Behold what honest clothes you send forth to bleaching!

PAGE  Why, this passes,° Master Ford! You are not to go loose any longer; you must be pinioned.    120

EVANS  Why, this is lunatics, this is mad as a mad dog.

SHALLOW  Indeed, Master Ford, this is not well, indeed.

FORD  So say I too, sir.

[Enter MISTRESS FORD.]

Come hither, Mistress Ford; Mistress Ford, the honest  125 woman, the modest wife, the virtuous creature that hath the jealous fool to her husband! I suspect without cause, mistress, do I?

MRS. FORD  Heaven be my witness you do, if you suspect me in any dishonesty.    130

FORD  Well said, brazen-face; hold it out.—Come forth, sirrah!

[Pulling clothes out of the basket.]

PAGE  This passes!

MRS. FORD  Are you not ashamed? Let the clothes alone.    135

FORD  I shall find you anon.

EVANS  'Tis unreasonable. Will you take up your wife's clothes? Come away.

FORD  Empty the basket, I say!

---

**54 kilnhole** oven   **58 abstract** list   **71–72 fat . . . Brainford** an actual personage who kept a tavern in Brentford, a town on the Thames twelve miles east of Windsor   **74 thrummed** fringed

**97 dishonest** unchaste   **102 draff** swill   **113–14 Youth . . . basket** a contemporary phrase apparently connoting a "fortunate lover"   **114 knot** band   **115 ging** gang   **115–16 Now . . . shamed** "Speak the truth and shame the devil" (proverbial)   **119 passes** exceeds everything

MRS. FORD   Why, man, why?   140

FORD   Master Page, as I am a man, there was one conveyed out of my house yesterday in this basket. Why may not he be there again? In my house I am sure he is. My intelligence° is true; my jealousy is reasonable. Pluck me out all the linen.   145

[FORD *and* PAGE *pull out more clothes.*]

MRS. FORD   If you find a man there, he shall die a flea's death.

PAGE   Here's no man.

SHALLOW   By my fidelity, this is not well, Master Ford; this wrongs you.   150

EVANS   Master Ford, you must pray, and not follow the imaginations of your own heart. This is jealousies.

FORD   Well, he's not here I seek for.

PAGE   No, nor nowhere else but in your brain.

FORD   Help to search my house this one time. If I find not what I seek, show no color for my extremity.° Let me forever be your table-sport.° Let them say of me, "As jealous as Ford that searched a hollow walnut for his wife's leman."° Satisfy me once more; once more search with me.   160

MRS. FORD   What ho, Mistress Page, come you and the old woman down. My husband will come into the chamber.

FORD   Old woman? What old woman's that?

MRS. FORD   Why, it is my maid's aunt of Brainford.   165

FORD   A witch, a quean,° an old cozening° quean! Have I not forbid her my house? She comes of errands, does she? We are simple men; we do not know what's brought to pass under the profession of fortunetelling. She works by charms, by spells, by th'   170 figure,° and such daubery° as this is, beyond our element; we know nothing. Come down, you witch, you hag, you; come down, I say!

MRS. FORD   Nay, good, sweet husband! Good gentlemen, let him not strike the old woman.   175

[*Enter* FALSTAFF *in woman's clothes, and* MISTRESS PAGE.]

MRS. PAGE   Come, Mother Prat, come, give me your hand.

FORD   I'll "prat"° her. [*Beats him.*] Out of my door, you witch, you rag, you baggage, you polecat, you runnion!° Out, out! I'll conjure you, I'll fortunetell   180 you!                    [*Exit* FALSTAFF, *running.*]

MRS. PAGE   Are you not ashamed? I think you have killed the poor woman.

MRS. FORD   Nay, he will do it. 'Tis a goodly credit for you.   185

FORD   Hang her, witch!

EVANS   By Jeshu, I think the 'oman is a witch indeed. I like not when a 'oman has a great peard; I spy a great peard under his muffler.

FORD   Will you follow, gentlemen? I beseech you,   190

follow. See but the issue of my jealousy. If I cry out thus upon no trail,° never trust me when I open° again.

PAGE   Let's obey his humor a little further. Come, gentlemen.

[*Exeunt* FORD, PAGE, SHALLOW, CAIUS, *and* EVANS.]

MRS. PAGE   Trust me, he beat him most pitifully.   195

MRS. FORD   Nay, by th' mass, that he did not; he beat him most unpitifully, methought.

MRS. PAGE   I'll have the cudgel hallowed and hung o'er the altar; it hath done meritorious service.

MRS. FORD   What think you? May we, with the   200 warrant of womanhood and the witness of a good conscience, pursue him with any further revenge?

MRS. PAGE   The spirit of wantonness is, sure, scared out of him. If the devil have him not in fee-simple,° with fine and recovery,° he will never, I think, in the   205 way of waste,° attempt us again.

MRS. FORD   Shall we tell our husbands how we have served him?

MRS. PAGE   Yes, by all means, if it be but to scrape the figures° out of your husband's brains. If they can   210 find in their hearts the poor unvirtuous fat knight shall be any further afflicted, we two will still be the ministers.°

MRS. FORD   I'll warrant they'll have him publicly shamed, and methinks there would be no period to the   215 jest, should he not be publicly shamed.

MRS. PAGE   Come, to the forge with it; then shape it. I would not have things cool.          *Exeunt.*

### Scene III. [*A room in the Garter Inn.*]

*Enter* HOST *and* BARDOLPH.

BARDOLPH   Sir, the Germans desire to have three of your horses. The duke himself will be tomorrow at court, and they are going to meet him.

HOST   What duke should that be comes so secretly? I hear not of him in the court. Let me speak with the   5 gentlemen. They speak English?

BARDOLPH   Ay, sir; I'll call them to you.

HOST   They shall have my horses, but I'll make them pay; I'll sauce them.° They have had my house a week at command.° I have turned away my other guests.   10 They must come off.° I'll sauce them. Come. *Exeunt.*

### Scene IV. [*A room in Ford's house.*]

*Enter* PAGE, FORD, MISTRESS PAGE, MISTRESS FORD, *and* EVANS.

EVANS   'Tis one of the best discretions of a 'oman° as ever I did look upon.

PAGE   And did he send you both these letters at an instant?

---

144 **intelligence** information   156 **show . . . extremity** suggest no excuse for my extravagance   157 **table-sport** laughingstock   159 **leman** lover   166 **quean** hussy; **cozening** cheating, deceiving   170–71 **by th' figure** by making wax effigies for enchantments   171 **daubery** false show   178 **prat** beat on the buttocks   180 **runnion** abusive term for a woman

192 **upon no trail** where there is no scent; **open** cry out from picking up a scent (used of hounds)   204 **fee-simple** absolute possession   205 **fine and recovery** legal procedure for transferring an entailed estate into a fee-simple   206 **waste** spoliation   210 **figures** phantasms   213 **ministers** agents
IV.iii.9 **sauce them** make them pay dearly   10 **at command** reserved   11 **come off** pay
IV.iv.1 **best . . . 'oman** most discreet woman

MRS. PAGE  Within a quarter of an hour.                          5

FORD
Pardon me, wife. Henceforth do what thou wilt.
I rather will suspect the sun with cold
Than thee with wantonness. Now doth thy honor
    stand,
In him that was of late an heretic,
As firm as faith.

PAGE                'Tis well, 'tis well; no more.               10
Be not as extreme in submission as in offense.
But let our plot go forward. Let our wives
Yet once again, to make us public sport,
Appoint a meeting with this old fat fellow,
Where we may take him and disgrace him for it.               15

FORD
There is no better way than that they spoke of.

PAGE  How? To send him word they'll meet him in
the Park at midnight? Fie, fie, he'll never come.

EVANS  You say he has been thrown in the rivers, and
has been grievously peaten as an old 'oman. Methinks    20
there should be terrors in him that he should not
come. Methinks his flesh is punished; he shall have no
desires.

PAGE  So think I too.

MRS. FORD
Devise but how you'll use him when he comes,                25
And let us two devise to bring him thither.

MRS. PAGE
There is an old tale goes that Herne the Hunter,
Sometime° a keeper here in Windsor Forest,
Doth all the wintertime, at still midnight,
Walk round about an oak, with great ragg'd horns;          30
And there he blasts° the tree, and takes° the cattle,
And makes milch-kine yield blood, and shakes a chain
In a most hideous and dreadful manner.
You have heard of such a spirit, and well you know
The superstitious idle-headed eld°                          35
Received, and did deliver to our age,
This tale of Herne the Hunter for a truth.

PAGE
Why, yet there want not many that do fear
In deep of night to walk by this Herne's Oak.
But what of this?

MRS. FORD        Marry, this is our device:°                  40
That Falstaff at that oak shall meet with us,
Disguised like Herne, with huge horns on his head.

PAGE
Well, let it not be doubted but he'll come,
And in this shape. When you have brought him
    thither,
What shall be done with him? What is your plot?            45

MRS. PAGE
That likewise have we thought upon, and thus:
Nan Page my daughter, and my little son,
And three or four more of their growth, we'll dress
Like urchins,° ouphs,° and fairies, green and white,
With rounds of waxen tapers on their heads,                50
And rattles in their hands. Upon a sudden,
As Falstaff, she, and I are newly met,
Let them from forth a sawpit rush at once

With some diffusèd° song. Upon their sight,
We two in great amazedness will fly.                        55
The let them all encircle him about,
And, fairy-like, to pinch the unclean knight,
And ask him why, that hour of fairy revel,
In their so sacred paths he dares to tread
In shape profane.

MRS. FORD            And till he tell the truth,              60
Let the supposèd fairies pinch him sound°
And burn him with their tapers.

MRS. PAGE                    The truth being known,
We'll all present ourselves, dis-horn the spirit,
And mock him home to Windsor.

FORD                        The children must
Be practiced well to this, or they'll ne'er do't.           65

EVANS  I will teach the children their behaviors; and I
will be like a jackanapes° also, to burn the knight with
my taber.

FORD
That will be excellent. I'll go buy them vizards.°

MRS. PAGE
My Nan shall be the queen of all the fairies,               70
Finely attirèd in a robe of white.

PAGE
That silk will I go buy. [Aside.] And in that tire°
Shall Master Slender steal my Nan away,
And marry her at Eton.°—Go, send to Falstaff straight.

FORD
Nay, I'll to him again in name of Brooke.                    75
He'll tell me all his purpose. Sure, he'll come.

MRS. PAGE
Fear not you that. Go, get us properties°
And tricking° for our fairies.

EVANS  Let us about it. It is admirable pleasures and
fery honest knaveries.                                       80
                        [Exeunt PAGE, FORD, and EVANS.]

MRS. PAGE
Go, Mistress Ford,
Send Quickly to Sir John, to know his mind.
                            [Exit MISTRESS FORD.]
I'll to the doctor. He hath my good will,
And none but he, to marry with Nan Page.
That Slender, though well landed, is an idiot;               85
And he my husband best of all affects.
The doctor is well moneyed, and his friends
Potent at court. He, none but he, shall have her,
Though twenty thousand worthier come to crave
    her.                                    [Exit.]


Scene V. [The room in the Garter Inn.]

Enter HOST [and] SIMPLE.

HOST  What wouldst thou have, boor? What, thickskin? Speak, breathe, discuss; brief, short, quick, snap.

SIMPLE  Marry, sir, I come to speak with Sir John
Falstaff from Master Slender.

HOST  There's his chamber, his house, his castle, his        5

---

28 **Sometime** formerly   31 **blasts** blights; **takes** bewitches
35 **eld** elders   40 **device** plan   49 **urchins** goblins; **ouphs**
elves

54 **diffusèd** cacophonous   61 **sound** soundly   67 **jackanapes**
monkey   69 **vizards** masks   72 **tire** attire   74 **Eton** across
the river from Windsor   77 **properties** stage properties   78
**tricking** adornment, costumes

standing-bed and truckle bed.° 'Tis painted about
with the story of the Prodigal,° fresh and new. Go,
knock and call. He'll speak like an Anthropophagi-
nian° unto thee. Knock, I say.

SIMPLE   There's an old woman, a fat woman, gone up 10
into his chamber. I'll be so bold as stay, sir, till she
come down. I come to speak with her, indeed.

HOST   Ha, a fat woman? The knight may be robbed.
I'll call. Bully knight, bully Sir John! Speak from thy
lungs military. Art thou there? It is thine Host, thine 15
Ephesian,° calls.

FALSTAFF [Above.]   How now, mine Host?

HOST   Here's a Bohemian-Tartar° tarries the coming
down of thy fat woman. Let her descend, bully, let her
descend. My chambers are honorable. Fie, privacy, 20
fie!

[Enter] FALSTAFF.

FALSTAFF   There was, mine Host, an old fat woman
even now with me, but she's gone.

SIMPLE   Pray you, sir, was't not the wise woman of
Brainford? 25

FALSTAFF   Ay, marry, was it, mussel-shell.° What
would you with her?

SIMPLE   My master, sir, my Master Slender, sent to
her, seeing her go thorough the streets, to know, sir,
whether one Nym, sir, that beguiled him of a chain, 30
had the chain or no.

FALSTAFF   I spake with the old woman about it.

SIMPLE   And what says she, I pray, sir?

FALSTAFF   Marry, she says that the very same man that
beguiled Master Slender of his chain cozened him of it. 35

SIMPLE   I would I could have spoken with the woman
herself. I had other things to have spoken with her too
from him.

FALSTAFF   What are they? Let us know.

HOST   Ay, come; quick! 40

SIMPLE   I may not conceal° them, sir.

HOST   Conceal them, or thou diest.

SIMPLE   Why, sir, they were nothing but about
Mistress Anne Page; to know if it were my master's
fortune to have her, or no. 45

FALSTAFF   'Tis, 'tis his fortune.

SIMPLE   What, sir?

FALSTAFF   To have her, or no. Go; say the woman
told me so.

SIMPLE   May I be bold to say so, sir? 50

FALSTAFF   Ay, Sir Tyke;° who more bold?

SIMPLE   I thank your worship: I shall make my master
glad with these tidings.      [Exit.]

HOST   Thou art clerkly, thou art clerkly,° Sir John.
Was there a wise woman with thee? 55

FALSTAFF   Ay, that there was, mine Host: one that
hath taught me more wit than ever I learned before in
my life; and I paid nothing for it neither, but was paid
for my learning.

[Enter] BARDOLPH.

BARDOLPH   Out, alas, sir, cozenage, mere° cozenage! 60

HOST   Where be my horses? Speak well of them,
varletto.°

BARDOLPH   Run away with the cozeners; for so soon
as I came beyond Eton, they threw me off from
behind one of them, in a slough of mire; and set 65
spurs and away, like three German devils, three
Doctor Faustuses.°

HOST   They are gone but to meet the duke, villain.°
Do not say they be fled: Germans are honest men.

[Enter] EVANS.

EVANS   Where is mine Host? 70

HOST   What is the matter, sir?

EVANS   Have a care of your entertainments.° There is
a friend of mine come to town tells me there is three
cozen-germans° that has cozened all the hosts of
Readins,° of Maidenhead, of Colebrook, of horses 75
and money. I tell you for good will, look you. You
are wise and full of gibes and vlouting-stogs, and
'tis not convenient you should be cozened. Fare you
well.      [Exit.]

[Enter] CAIUS.

CAIUS   Vere is mine Host de Jarteer? 80

HOST   Here, Master Doctor, in perplexity and doubt-
ful° dilemma.

CAIUS   I cannot tell vat is dat; but it is tell-a me dat
you make grand preparation for a duke de Jamany.
By my trot, dere is no duke dat de court is know to 85
come. I tell you for good vill. Adieu.      [Exit.]

HOST   Hue and cry, villain, go! [To FALSTAFF.] Assist
me, knight. I am undone. [To BARDOLPH.] Fly, run,
hue and cry, villain! I am undone!

     [Exeunt HOST and BARDOLPH.]

FALSTAFF   I would all the world might be cozened, for 90
I have been cozened and beaten too. If it should
come to the ear of the court how I have been transformed, and how my transformation hath been
washed and cudgeled, they would melt me out of
my fat drop by drop, and liquor° fishermen's boots 95
with me. I warrant they would whip me with their
fine wits till I were as crestfall'n° as a dried pear. I
never prospered since I forswore myself at primero.°
Well, if my wind were but long enough to say my
prayers, I would repent. 100

[Enter Mistress] QUICKLY.

Now, whence come you?

QUICKLY   From the two parties, forsooth.

FALSTAFF   The devil take one party and his dam the
other! And so they shall be both bestowed. I have
suffered more for their sakes, more than the villainous 105
inconstancy of man's disposition is able to bear.

QUICKLY   And have not they suffered? Yes, I warrant
—speciously° one of them. Mistress Ford, good heart,

---

62 **varletto** rascal   67 **Doctor Faustuses** Faustus was a
German scholar who allegedly obtained magical powers by
making a compact with Lucifer; known to the Elizabethans
primarily through Marlowe's play   68 **villain** base fellow
72 **entertainments** total supplies for running an inn   74
**cozen-germans** (1) cousin-germans, relatives (2) cheating
Germans   75 **Readins** Reading   81–82 **doubtful** fearful   95
**liquor** grease   97 **crestfall'n** undistinguished   98 **primero**
a card game   108 **speciously** especially

IV.v.6 **truckle bed** trundle bed   7 **Prodigal** the Prodigal Son
8–9 **Anthropophaginian** cannibal   16 **Ephesian** boon companion   18 **Bohemian-Tartar** wild man   26 **mussel-shell**
one who gapes   41 **conceal** reveal   51 **Sir Tyke** Master Cur
54 **clerkly** scholarly   60 **mere** pure

is beaten black and blue that you cannot see a white
spot about her.                                                                  110

FALSTAFF   What tell'st thou me of black and blue? I
was beaten myself into all the colors of the rainbow;
and I was like to be apprehended for the witch of
Brainford. But that my admirable dexterity of wit,
my counterfeiting the action of an old woman, 115
delivered me, the knave constable had set me i' th'
stocks, i' th' common stocks, for a witch.

QUICKLY   Sir, let me speak with you in your chamber.
You shall hear how things go, and, I warrant, to your
content. Here is a letter will say somewhat. Good 120
hearts, what ado here is to bring you together. Sure,
one of you does not serve heaven well that you are so
crossed.°

FALSTAFF   Come up into my chamber.                 *Exeunt.*

### Scene VI. [*The Garter Inn.*]

*Enter* FENTON [*and*] HOST.

HOST   Master Fenton, talk not to me. My mind is
heavy; I will give over all.

FENTON
Yet hear me speak. Assist me in my purpose,
And, as I am a gentleman, I'll give thee
A hundred pound in gold more than your loss.           5

HOST   I will hear you, Master Fenton, and I will, at the
least, keep your counsel.

FENTON
From time to time I have acquainted you
With the dear love I bear to fair Anne Page,
Who mutually hath answered my affection,                10
(So far forth as herself might be her chooser)
Even to my wish. I have a letter from her
Of such contents as you will wonder at,
The mirth whereof so larded° with my matter°
That neither singly can be manifested                    15
Without the show of both. Fat Falstaff
Hath a great scene. The image° of the jest
I'll show you here at large. [*Takes out a letter.*]
                                      Hark, good mine Host:
Tonight at Herne's Oak, just 'twixt twelve and one,
Must my sweet Nan present° the Fairy Queen—             20
The purpose why, is here—in which disguise,
While other jests are something rank° on foot,
Her father hath commanded her to slip
Away with Slender, and with him at Eton
Immediately to marry. She hath consented.                25
Now, sir,
Her mother (ever strong against that match
And firm for Doctor Caius) hath appointed
That he shall likewise shuffle° her away,
While other sports are tasking of their minds,           30
And at the dean'ry, where a priest attends,
Straight marry her. To this her mother's plot
She, seemingly obedient, likewise hath
Made promise to the doctor. Now, thus it rests:
Her father means she shall be all in white,              35

And in that habit, when Slender sees his time
To take her by the hand and bid her go,
She shall go with him. Her mother hath intended—
The better to denote her to the doctor,
For they must all be masked and vizarded—                40
That quaint° in green she shall be loose enrobed,
With ribands pendent, flaring 'bout her head;
And when the doctor spies his vantage ripe,
To pinch her by the hand, and on that token°
The maid hath given consent to go with him.              45

HOST
Which means she to deceive, father or mother?

FENTON
Both, my good Host, to go along with me.
And here it rests, that you'll procure the vicar
To stay for me at church 'twixt twelve and one,
And, in the lawful name of marrying,                     50
To give our hearts united ceremony.°

HOST
Well, husband your device;° I'll to the vicar.
Bring you the maid, you shall not lack a priest.

FENTON
So shall I evermore be bound to thee;
Besides, I'll make a present recompense.    *Exeunt.*    55

## ACT V

### Scene I. [*The Garter Inn.*]

*Enter* FALSTAFF [*and Mistress*] QUICKLY.

FALSTAFF   Prithee, no more prattling. Go. I'll hold.°
This is the third time; I hope good luck lies in odd
numbers. Away; go. They say there is divinity° in odd
numbers, either in nativity, chance, or death. Away!

QUICKLY   I'll provide you a chain, and I'll do what I     5
can to get you a pair of horns.

FALSTAFF   Away, I say; time wears. Hold up your
head, and mince.°              [*Exit Mistress* QUICKLY.]

[*Enter*] FORD.

How now, Master Brooke. Master Brooke, the matter
will be known tonight, or never. Be you in the Park    10
about midnight, at Herne's Oak, and you shall see
wonders.

FORD   Went you not to her yesterday,° sir, as you told
me you had appointed?

FALSTAFF   I went to her, Master Brooke, as you see,    15
like a poor old man; but I came from her, Master
Brooke, like a poor old woman. That same knave
Ford, her husband, hath the finest mad devil of
jealousy in him, Master Brooke, that ever governed
frenzy. I will tell you: he beat me grievously, in the  20
shape of a woman; for in the shape of man, Master
Brooke, I fear not Goliath with a weaver's beam,°

---

123 **crossed** thwarted
IV.vi.14 **larded** intermixed; **matter** i.e., courtship problems
17 **image** form   20 **present** represent   22 **something rank**
rather abundantly   29 **shuffle** spirit

41 **quaint** elegantly   44 **token** signal   51 **united ceremony**
union through the marriage rite   52 **husband your device**
manage your plan prudently
V.i.1 **hold** keep the engagement   3 **divinity** divination   8
**mince** trip off   13 **yesterday** a slip; should be "this morning"
22 **Goliath . . . beam** an allusion to Goliath's staff from
I Samuel 17:7 and II Samuel 21:19

because I know also life is a shuttle.° I am in haste. Go
along with me; I'll tell you all, Master Brooke. Since
I plucked geese, played truant, and whipped top, I 25
knew not what 'twas to be beaten till lately. Follow me.
I'll tell you strange things of this knave Ford, on
whom tonight I will be revenged, and I will deliver
his wife into your hand. Follow. Strange things in
hand, Master Brooke! Follow.    *Exeunt.* 30

### Scene II. [*Windsor Little Park.*]

*Enter* PAGE, SHALLOW, [*and*] SLENDER.

PAGE  Come, come; we'll couch° i' th' Castle ditch°
till we see the light of our fairies. Remember, son
Slender, my daughter.
SLENDER  Ay, forsooth; I have spoke with her and we
have a nay-word° how to know one another. I come 5
to her in white, and cry, "mum"; she cries, "budget";°
and by that we know one another.
SHALLOW  That's good too. But what needs either
your "mum," or her "budget"? The white will
decipher her well enough.—It hath struck ten o'clock. 10
PAGE  The night is dark; light and spirits will become
it well. Heaven prosper our sport. No man means evil
but the devil, and we shall know him by his horns.
Let's away; follow me.    *Exeunt.*

### Scene III. [*Outside the Park.*]

*Enter* MISTRESS PAGE, MISTRESS FORD, [*and Doctor*]
CAIUS.

MRS. PAGE  Master Doctor, my daughter is in green.
When you see your time, take her by the hand, away
with her to the deanery, and dispatch it quickly. Go
before into the Park. We two must go together.
CAIUS  I know vat I have to do. Adieu.    5
MRS. PAGE  Fare you well, sir. [*Exit* CAIUS.] My
husband will not rejoice so much at the abuse of
Falstaff as he will chafe at the doctor's marrying my
daughter. But 'tis no matter; better a little chiding
than a great deal of heartbreak.    10
MRS. FORD  Where is Nan now and her troop of
fairies, and the Welsh devil, Hugh?
MRS. PAGE  They are all couched in a pit hard by
Herne's Oak, with obscured lights which at the very
instant of Falstaff's and our meeting they will at once 15
display to the night.
MRS. FORD  That cannot choose but amaze° him.
MRS. PAGE  If he be not amazed, he will be mocked;
if he be amazed, he will every way be mocked.
MRS. FORD  We'll betray him finely.    20
MRS. PAGE
Against such lewdsters° and their lechery,
Those that betray them do no treachery.
MRS. FORD  The hour draws on. To the Oak, to the
Oak!    *Exeunt.*

### Scene IV. [*Outside the Park.*]

*Enter* EVANS [*disguised as a satyr*] *and* [*others as*] FAIRIES.

EVANS  Trib,° trib, fairies. Come, and remember your
parts. Be pold, I pray vou. Follow me into the pit, and
when I give the watch-'ords, do as I pid you. Come,
come; trib, trib.    *Exeunt.*

### Scene V. [*Herne's Oak in Windsor Little Park.*]

*Enter* FALSTAFF [*disguised as Herne,*] *with a buck's head
upon him.*

FALSTAFF  The Windsor bell hath struck twelve; the
minute draws on. Now, the hot-blooded gods assist
me! Remember, Jove, thou wast a bull for thy
Europa;° love set on thy horns. O powerful love, that
in some respects makes a beast a man; in some other, 5
a man a beast. You were also, Jupiter, a swan for the
love of Leda.° O omnipotent love, how near the god
drew to the complexion° of a goose! A fault done
first in the form of a beast. O Jove, a beastly fault!
And then another fault in the semblance of a fowl; 10
think on't, Jove; a foul fault! When gods have hot
backs, what shall poor men do? For me, I am here a
Windsor stag: and the fattest, I think, i' th' forest.
Send me a cool rut-time,° Jove, or who can blame me
to piss my tallow?° Who comes here? My doe? 15

[*Enter*] MISTRESS PAGE [*and*] MISTRESS FORD.

MRS. FORD  Sir John? Art thou there, my deer, my
male deer?
FALSTAFF  My doe with the black scut!° Let the sky
rain potatoes;° let it thunder to the tune of "Greensleeves," hail kissing-comfits,° and snow eringoes.° 20
Let there come a tempest of provocation,° I will
shelter me here.

[*Hugs her.*]

MRS. FORD  Mistress Page is come with me, sweetheart.
FALSTAFF  Divide me like a bribed° buck, each a 25
haunch. I will keep my sides to myself, my shoulders
for the fellow of this walk,° and my horns I bequeath
your husbands. Am I a woodman,° ha? Speak I like
Herne the Hunter? Why, now is Cupid a child of
conscience;° he makes restitution. As I am a true 30
spirit, welcome!

[*Noise within.*]

23 **life . . . shuttle** paraphrased from Job 7:6, "My days are
swifter than a weaver's shuttle"
**V.ii.1 couch** hide; **Castle ditch** a ditch running along the east
side of Windsor Castle  **5 nay-word** password  **6 mum
. . . budget** mumbudget, a game in which the player
pretended to be tongue-tied
**V.iii.17 amaze** frighten  **21 lewdsters** lechers

**V.iv.1 Trib** trip
**V.v.3–4 bull . . . Europa** disguise adopted by Jove for his
abduction of Europa  **6–7 swan . . . Leda** another animal
disguise adopted by Jove in an amorous adventure  **8 complexion** temperament  **14 rut-time** annual period of sexual
excitement for the male deer  **15 piss my tallow** during
rut-time the main food for the hart was the red mushroom,
which supposedly brought on urination  **18 scut** (1) tail (2)
pudendum  **19 potatoes** sweet potatoes, formerly considered
aphrodisiacs  **20 kissing-comfits** perfumed sweetmeats;
**eringoes** candied seaholly (considered an aphrodisiac)  **21
provocation** lustful stimulation  **25 bribed** stolen  **27 fellow
. . . walk** forester on this beat  **28 woodman** hunter (here,
of women)  **29–30 of conscience** conscientious

MRS. PAGE   Alas, what noise?

MRS. FORD   Heaven forgive our sins!

FALSTAFF   What should this be?

MRS. FORD, MRS. PAGE   Away, away!    35

[*They run off.*]

FALSTAFF   I think the devil will not have me damned,
lest the oil that's in me should set hell on fire. He
would never else cross me thus.

*Enter Sir Hugh* [EVANS] *like a satyr,* [ANNE Page] *and*
BOYS *dressed like fairies, Mistress* QUICKLY *like the
Queen of Fairies,* [PISTOL *as Hobgoblin. They carry
tapers.*]

QUICKLY
Fairies, black, gray, green, and white,
You moonshine revelers, and shades of night,    40
You orphan° heirs of fixèd destiny,
Attend your office° and your quality.°
Crier Hobgoblin, make the fairy oyes.°

PISTOL
Elves, list your names; silence, you airy toys!
Cricket, to Windsor chimneys shalt thou leap.    45
Where fires thou find'st unraked° and hearths unswept,
There pinch the maids as blue as bilberry.°
Our radiant queen hates sluts° and sluttery.

FALSTAFF
They are fairies; he that speaks to them shall die.
I'll wink° and couch; no man their works must eye.    50

[*Lies down upon his face.*]

EVANS
Where's Bead? Go you, and where you find a maid
That ere she sleep has thrice her prayers said,
Raise up the organs of her fantasy,°
Sleep she as sound as careless infancy.
But those as sleep and think not on their sins,    55
Pinch them, arms, legs, backs, shoulders, sides, and
  shins.

QUICKLY
About, about.
Search Windsor Castle, elves, within and out.
Strew good luck, ouphs,° on every sacred room,
That it may stand till the perpetual doom,°    60
In state as wholesome as in state 'tis fit,
Worthy the owner, and the owner it.
The several chairs of Order° look you scour
With juice of balm and every precious flow'r.
Each fair instalment,° coat,° and several crest,°    65
With loyal blazon,° evermore be blest.
And nightly, meadow-fairies, look you sing,
Like to the Garter's compass,° in a ring.
Th' expressure° that it bears, green let it be,

More fertile-fresh than all the field to see;    70
And "Honi soit qui mal y pense"° write
In emerald tufts, flow'rs purple, blue, and white—
Like sapphire, pearl, and rich embroidery,
Buckled below fair knighthood's bending knee—
Fairies use flow'rs for their charactery.°    75
Away, disperse! But till 'tis one o'clock,
Our dance of custom round about the oak
Of Herne the Hunter, let us not forget.

EVANS
Pray you, lock hand in hand; yourselves in order set;
And twenty glowworms shall our lanterns be,    80
To guide our measure round about the tree.
But, stay—I smell a man of middle earth.°

FALSTAFF   Heavens defend me from that Welsh fairy,
lest he transform me to a piece of cheese!°

PISTOL
Vile worm, thou wast o'erlooked° even in thy birth.    85

QUICKLY
With trial-fire touch me his finger end.
If he be chaste, the flame will back descend
And turn him to no pain; but if he start,
It is the flesh of a corrupted heart.

PISTOL
A trial, come.

EVANS           Come, will this wood take fire?    90

*They put the tapers to his fingers, and he starts.*

FALSTAFF   O, O, O!

QUICKLY
Corrupt, corrupt, and tainted in desire!
About him, fairies, sing a scornful rhyme;
And, as you trip, still pinch him to your time.

*The Song.*

Fie on sinful fantasy!    95
Fie on lust and luxury!°
Lust is but a bloody fire,°
Kindled with unchaste desire,
Fed in heart, whose flames aspire,
As thoughts do blow them, higher and higher.    100
Pinch him, fairies, mutually;°
Pinch him for his villainy;
Pinch him, and burn him, and turn him about,
Till candles and starlight and moonshine be out.

*Here they pinch him, and sing about him, and* [CAIUS] *the
doctor comes one way and steals away a boy in green. And*
SLENDER *another way; he takes a boy in white. And*
FENTON *steals Mistress* ANNE. *And a noise of hunting is
made within, and all the* FAIRIES *run away.* FALSTAFF
*pulls off his buck's head and rises up.*

[*Enter*] PAGE, FORD, [MISTRESS PAGE, MISTRESS
FORD, *and* EVANS°].

**71 Honi . . . pense** Ill be to him who evil thinks (motto of the
Order of the Garter)   **75 charactery** writing (accent on second
syllable)   **82 middle earth** that section of the universe between
heaven and hell, realm of mortals   **83–84 Heavens . . . cheese**
cheese was the favorite food of Welshmen; since Evans smells
Falstaff, the latter fears he will be turned into cheese and then
devoured   **85 o'erlooked** bewitched   **96 luxury** lasciviousness   **97 bloody fire** fire in the blood   **101 mutually** jointly
**104 s.d. Evans** Q1 brings in Evans and Shallow with the others;
Evans presumably left the stage at the previous direction, when
"all the Fairies run away"; he must reenter because he speaks
later; Shallow speaks no lines, but he may well belong to this
group scene

**41 orphan** possible allusion to the folklore belief that fairies
were born spontaneously and thus had no parents   **42 office**
duty; **quality** profession   **43 oyes** hear ye (public crier's call)
**46 unraked** not properly covered with coals   **47 bilberry**
blueberry   **48 sluts** untidy kitchen-maids   **50 wink** close my
eyes   **53 Raise . . . fantasy** cause her to have pleasant dreams
**59 ouphs** elves   **60 perpetual doom** Day of Judgment   **63
chairs of Order** stalls of the knights of the Order of the Garter
in Saint George's Chapel   **65 instalment** stall; **coat** coat of
arms; **crest** helmet (affixed above the stall)   **66 blazon**
armorial bearings   **68 compass** circle   **69 expressure** image,
picture

PAGE

Nay, do not fly. I think we have watched you° now. 105
Will none but Herne the Hunter serve your turn?

MRS. PAGE [*To* PAGE.]

I pray you, come, hold up the jest no higher.°

[*To* FALSTAFF.]

Now, good Sir John, how like you Windsor wives?
See you these, husband? [*Points to Falstaff's horns.*] Do
   not these fair yokes
Become the forest better than the town? 110

FORD  Now sir, who's a cuckold now? Master Brooke,
Falstaff's a knave, a cuckoldly knave; here are his
horns, Master Brooke. And, Master Brooke, he hath
enjoyed nothing of Ford's but his buck basket, his
cudgel, and twenty pounds of money, which must be 115
paid to Master Brooke; his horses are arrested° for it,
Master Brooke.

MRS. FORD  Sir John, we have had ill luck; we could
never meet.° I will never take you for my love again,
but I will always count you my deer. 120

FALSTAFF  I do begin to perceive that I am made an
ass.

FORD  Ay, and an ox° too: both the proofs° are extant.

FALSTAFF  And these are not fairies? I was three or
four times in the thought they were not fairies; and yet 125
the guiltiness of my mind, the sudden surprise of my
powers,° drove the grossness of the foppery° into a
received belief, in despite of the teeth of all rhyme and
reason, that they were fairies. See now how wit may
be made a Jack-a-Lent, when 'tis upon ill employment. 130

EVANS  Sir John Falstaff, serve Got and leave your
desires, and fairies will not pinse you.

FORD  Well said, fairy Hugh.

EVANS [*To* FORD.]  And leave you your jealousies too,
I pray you. 135

FORD  I will never mistrust my wife again, till thou
art able to woo her in good English.

FALSTAFF  Have I laid my brain in the sun and dried
it, that it wants° matter to prevent so gross o'erreaching
as this? Am I ridden with a Welsh goat too? Shall I 140
have a coxcomb of frieze?° 'Tis time I were choked
with a piece of toasted cheese.

EVANS  Seese is not goot to give putter; your belly is
all putter.

FALSTAFF  "Seese" and "putter"? Have I lived to 145
stand at the taunt of one that makes fritters of English?
This is enough to be the decay of lust and late-walking°
through the realm.

MRS. PAGE  Why, Sir John, do you think though we
would have thrust virtue out of our hearts by the 150
head and shoulders, and have given ourselves without
scruple to hell, that ever the devil could have made
you our delight?

FORD  What, a hodge-pudding?° A bag of flax?

MRS. PAGE  A puffed man? 155

PAGE  Old, cold, withered, and of intolerable entrails?

FORD  And one that is as slanderous as Satan?

PAGE  And as poor as Job?

FORD  And as wicked as his wife?

EVANS  And given to fornications, and to taverns, and 160
sack and wine and metheglins,° and to drinkings and
swearings and starings,° pribbles and prabbles?

FALSTAFF  Well, I am your theme. You have the start
of me; I am dejected;° I am not able to answer the
Welsh flannel.° Ignorance itself is a plummet° o'er me. 165
Use me as you will.

FORD  Marry, sir, we'll bring you to Windsor, to one
Master Brooke, that you have cozened of money, to
whom you should have been a pander. Over and
above that you have suffered, I think to repay that 170
money will be a biting affliction.

PAGE  Yet be cheerful, knight. Thou shalt eat a posset
tonight at my house, where I will desire thee to laugh
at my wife that now laughs at thee. Tell her Master
Slender hath married her daughter. 175

MRS. PAGE [*Aside.*]  Doctors doubt that.° If Anne
Page be my daughter, she is, by this, Doctor Caius'
wife.

[*Enter* SLENDER.]

SLENDER  Whoa, ho, ho, father Page!

PAGE  Son, how now; how now, son! Have you 180
dispatched?°

SLENDER  Dispatched? I'll make the best in Gloucestershire know on't; would I were hanged, la, else.

PAGE  Of what, son?

SLENDER  I came yonder at Eton to marry Mistress 185
Anne Page, and she's a great lubberly boy. If it had
not been i' th' church, I would have swinged° him, or
he should have swinged me. If I did not think it had
been Anne Page, would I might never stir—and 'tis a
postmaster's° boy! 190

PAGE  Upon my life, then, you took the wrong.

SLENDER  What need you tell me that? I think so,
when I took a boy for a girl. If I had been married to
him, for all he was in woman's apparel, I would not
have had him. 195

PAGE  Why, this is your own folly. Did not I tell you
how you should know my daughter by her garments?

SLENDER  I went to her in white, and cried, "mum,"
and she cried, "budget," as Anne and I had appointed;
and yet it was not Anne, but a postmaster's boy. 200

MRS. PAGE  Good George, be not angry. I knew of
your purpose; turned my daughter into green; and
indeed she is now with the doctor at the dean'ry, and
there married.

[*Enter Doctor* CAIUS.]

CAIUS  Vere is Mistress Page? By gar, I am cozened! 205
I ha' married un garçon, a boy; un peasant, by gar, a
boy; it is not Anne Page. By gar, I am cozened!

MRS. PAGE  Why? Did you take her in green?

---

105 **watched you** caught you in the act  107 **hold . . .
higher** put an end to the jest  116 **arrested** seized by warrant
119 **meet** possible aural pun on *mate*  123 **ox** fool (from the
expression "to make an ox of someone"); **proofs** i.e., the long
horns  127 **powers** faculties; **foppery** deceit  139 **wants**
lacks  141 **coxcomb of frieze** fool's cap of coarse Welsh
woolen cloth  147 **late-walking** staying out late  154 **hodge-
pudding** large sausage of many ingredients

161 **metheglins** spiced Welsh mead  162 **starings** swaggerings
164 **dejected** cast down  165 **Welsh flannel** teasing name for
a Welshman; **plummet** (1) garment (from *plumbet*, a
woolen fabric) (2) line for sounding  176 **Doctors doubt that**
expression of disbelief  181 **dispatched** settled the business
187 **swinged** beaten  190 **postmaster** master of post horses

CAIUS  Ay, be-gar, and 'tis a boy. Be-gar, I'll raise all
Windsor.                                          [*Exit.*] 210

FORD  This is strange. Who hath got the right Anne?

PAGE  My heart misgives me. Here comes Master
Fenton.

[*Enter* FENTON *and* ANNE *Page.*]

How now, Master Fenton!

ANNE
Pardon, good father! Good my mother, pardon!    215

PAGE  Now, mistress, how chance you went not with
Master Slender?

MRS. PAGE
Why went you not with Master Doctor, maid?

FENTON
You do amaze° her. Hear the truth of it.
You would have married her most shamefully,       220
Where there was no proportion held in love.
The truth is, she and I, long since contracted,°
Are now so sure° that nothing can dissolve us.
Th' offense is holy that she hath committed,
And this deceit loses the name of craft,          225
Of disobedience, or unduteous title,

Since therein she doth evitate° and shun
A thousand irreligious cursèd hours
Which forcèd marriage would have brought upon her.

FORD
Stand not amazed. Here is no remedy.              230
In love the heavens themselves do guide the state;
Money buys lands, and wives are sold by fate.

FALSTAFF  I am glad, though you have ta'en a special
stand° to strike at me, that your arrow hath glanced.

PAGE
Well, what remedy? Fenton, heaven give thee joy!   235
What cannot be eschewed must be embraced.

FALSTAFF
When night dogs run, all sorts of deer are chased.

MRS. PAGE
Well, I will muse° no further. Master Fenton,
Heaven give you many, many merry days!
Good husband, let us every one go home,            240
And laugh this sport o'er by a country fire;
Sir John and all.

FORD                Let it be so. Sir John,
To Master Brooke you yet shall hold your word;
For he tonight shall lie with Mistress Ford.   *Exeunt.*

---

**219 amaze** perplex  **222 contracted** betrothed  **223 sure**
firmly bound in wedlock

**227 evitate** avoid  **234 stand** hunter's place for shooting
**238 muse** grumble

# THE HISTORY OF
# TROILUS AND CRESSIDA

EDITED BY DANIEL SELTZER

## Introduction

The modern student of *Troilus and Cressida*—reader, spectator, or actor—is faced with complex problems of staging, character, and moral ideas. The challenge of the play has been complicated (in many instances, unnecessarily) by a critical history full of dissension. Some of the insolubles connected with *Troilus and Cressida* concern the auspices of its first performances, or, indeed, whether it was acted at all before it was printed. Others stem from a consideration of the nature of the play itself, because critics have always felt that it is strange and untypical, and somehow flawed, expounding an approach to life which Shakespeare found uncongenial even as he set it forth. It may be helpful, therefore, to review some basic facts, to indicate those questions that can never be settled with the documentation at our disposal, and then to move on to an appraisal of the work itself and its place in Shakespeare's career. Ultimately, we should try to see in the play the attempt Shakespeare was making to solve certain ethical questions in dramatic form.

The history of the play's first production is inextricably bound up in its early textual history. Literary critics as well as bibliographical historians have been interested in the latter for some years, perhaps because it seems unlikely that so strange a play should be accompanied only accidentally by a curious textual provenance. Believing that the tastes of its first audience might help explain the problematic nature of the play, critics have wanted to know where and for whom it was first performed. Certain aspects of the textual history of *Troilus and Cressida* seem to offer answers; this has led to great speculation, some of which has tended to obscure the facts.

The facts are these. In February of 1603, the permission of the Stationers' Company was granted to James Roberts to print, "when he hath gotten sufficient aucthority, the booke of Troilus and Cressida, as yt is acted by my Lord Chamberlens men." From whom Roberts had yet to secure "aucthority" is not immediately apparent; presumably it was from the actors themselves, who wanted to block publication for the time being. Nevertheless, the entry clearly documents the existence and performance of *Troilus and Cressida* by Shakespeare's company, probably during the winter of 1602–03. Roberts, for whatever reason, did not print the play. The first edition of *Troilus and Cressida* did not appear until almost six years later, when two newcomers to the printing business, Richard Bonian and Henry Walley, published a quarto of the text in January 1609. While the book was still in the press, Bonian and Walley altered its title page and added an extra leaf, which carried an epistle to the reader. The first title page announced the play: "As it was acted by the Kings Maiesties seruants at the Globe." The new title page of the quarto, the same as the first in other particulars, replaced this acknowledgment with the phrase: "Excellently expressing the beginning of their [Troilus and Cressida's] loues, with the conceited wooing of Pandarus Prince of Licia." Following the altered title page appeared the epistle to the reader, unsigned, claiming that the play was "neuer stal'd with the Stage, neuer clapper-clawd with the palmes of the vulger . . . not . . . sullied, with the smoaky breath of the multitude." Finally, in 1623, *Troilus and Cressida* was printed by Heminges and Condell in their great folio collection of Shakespeare's plays, in a text occasionally fuller than that of the 1609 quarto, but also containing many errors (see the Note on the Text). *Troilus and Cressida* appears in the section of the Folio containing the tragedies, although its position in this section was altered after printing had begun. The alteration used to be grounds for an inference by some critics that even Shakespeare's editors and colleagues were not certain about the type of play with which they were dealing. More recently, however, textual critics have shown that the change was probably due only to the reluctance of Walley, the surviving publisher of the quarto, to give up his rights to the printer of the Folio—the delay meanwhile causing the latter to withdraw *Troilus and Cressida* after three pages of it had been set up in type, and to reinsert it later when permission was granted. Thus, although Heminges and Condell apparently classified *Troilus and Cressida* as a "Tragedy," and although the writer of the 1609 epistle called it a "Comedy," its position in the Folio has nothing to do with the ambiguous nature of the play itself; after all, both title pages of the 1609 quarto call it a "History." Nothing is really proved by this contradictory nomenclature except how casual the Elizabethan and Jacobean vocabulary was when it came to naming genres.

Although unnecessary problems raised by the play's position in the Folio have been removed, the earlier printer's claim that *Troilus and Cressida* had never been applauded "with the palmes of the vulger" has elicited various and conflicting interpretations: the play, indeed, was never acted; it entered rehearsals, proved too difficult, and was withdrawn; it was acted not for the "vulger" at the public theater, but for an audience of sophisticated and cynical wits at the Inns of Court; it was actually produced at the Globe but was a failure with the "multitude," therefore "neuer clapper-clawd." We should note that all these conjectures are possible only because of the altered title page and printer's epistle in the quarto; but neither of these bibliographical facts should obscure the evidence of the original entry in the Stationers' Register (that Shakespeare's company had acted the play by the beginning of 1603), nor that of the first 1609 title page (which tells us specifically that the play "was acted by the Kings Maiesties seruants at the Globe"). Any further suggestions about the theatrical provenance of the play are clearly conjectural. More important, interpretations of characters, mood, and general intention of *Troilus and Cressida* that are based on such conjecture should be considered with great caution.

One such interpretation that has attained considerable currency is that the play was acted by Shakespeare's company for the young lawyers at one of the Inns of Court, and that it was especially written and rehearsed for this occasion. Such circumstances, the theory maintains, would not only be in keeping with the cynical mood and legalistic rhetoric of the drama, but with the claims of the epistle, whose author is careful to state only that the play was never performed for the "vulger," and not that it had never been performed at all. If this is the case, however, it represents the only example during Shakespeare's career of any play actually subsidized for a special production in this manner. To purchase a single performance for a play already in the public repertory was something else entirely —Elizabeth's court did this frequently—but it was very costly to do so. Moreover, although much in the play would delight the ears of a cynic, and although some of the language in it is drawn (very generally) from legal vocabulary, the fact remains that the bitterness of this drama runs deeper than the self-conscious sneer that often accompanies sarcasm. There is metaphor drawn from the law in many other Shakespearean plays, and one should ask, in reading or seeing *Troilus and Cressida*, whether some of its abstractions and overblown circumlocutions may not have a more general purpose than the pleasure of some law students attending a theatrical charade.

To suggest that Shakespeare wrote the play for the students to act themselves is even more unlikely. *Troilus and Cressida* is extremely difficult for amateurs to perform, even if they are very talented and very cynical. Pandarus' allusions to prostitutes and others employed in the "hold-door trade" would have been absurd in a performance for one of the Inns; illogical, indeed, before any audience except that of the public theater. This epilogue is as unsavory and ugly as anything in Thersites' "mastic" harangues, and although we may not like to think so, it, and the action preceding it, must have been spoken in a public theater by actors in Shakespeare's company.

Whether the public audience applauded it is another matter. *Troilus and Cressida* may not have been performed more than once or twice, and it is very possible that Bonian and Walley, as they prepared the first title page for their 1609 quarto, knew only that the play was by an extremely successful dramatist and that it had once been acted at the Globe. Details of failures, even today, are not often remembered after seven or eight years. Whatever made them decide to alter the title page, deleting the acknowledgment to Shakespeare's company and inserting the epistle to the reader, we can never know. We must keep in mind, however, that possibly their correction was itself a mistake. In any case, the inserted phrase about the "conceited wooing of Pandarus Prince of Licia" was an easy line filler for the deleted acknowledgment, and no publisher has ever shrunk from a descriptive phrase that might promote sales of his book. The tone of the epistle indicates that Bonian and Walley knew a good thing when they saw it, and they were delighted to have in their possession a play by Shakespeare which six years earlier his own company apparently had tried to withhold from publication, and which had been in the repertory but was not generally known.

Our only positive evidence dates *Troilus and Cressida* before February 1603, in performance at the Globe Theatre by the King's Men (then the Lord Chamberlain's Men). Although it is probably impossible to solve the riddle of this play's textual history, it is important to keep that mystery separate from the enigma of the play itself. There is no doubt that the peculiar strengths and failings of *Troilus and Cressida* are unique in the Shakespearean canon; even when compared to the other so-called problem plays (*Measure for Measure, All's Well That Ends Well*), it stands by itself. *Troilus and Cressida* contains speeches that illuminate difficult portions of other plays, but seem somehow incongruous in this one; most of its cast of characters were traditionally associated with ideals of romance and chivalry, but even as they describe heroic emotions and speak the old ringing epithets, these figures appear addicted to long-winded gossip, petty projects, morbid preoccupations, and selfishly narrow ambitions. Such incongruities remind us of the intentions and methods of satire, and it has been suggested that *Troilus and Cressida* was Shakespeare's specific attempt to write in the currently popular vein of "comical satire." But human depravity obviously saddened Shakespeare infinitely more than it angered Marston, Jonson, or Chapman, and the satirical elements of the play have ultimately very little to do with the final impression it makes in reading, or with its overall effect in the theater. If the play has a satirical spokesman, it is Thersites, but Thersites' corrosive voice hardly speaks for balance or good sense, and, if the actor is brave enough to play him correctly, no audience smiles upon him except in embarrassment. At first, one may suspect satirical intention behind such incongruous components as Ulysses' eloquent perceptions and the insignificant use made of them, but much of the pathos of the play occurs in just those scenes that would be mercilessly satirical if Shakespeare were being consistent. It has been proposed, with good logic, that in *Troilus and Cressida* Shakespeare consciously imitated or unconsciously assimilated certain elements of cynicism and satire from the plays then being performed by child actors with great success at Blackfriars and Paul's.

Perhaps less than a year before the composition of *Troilus and Cressida*, Shakespeare allowed Hamlet himself to express surprise that these children should "carry it away," even in competition with "Hercules and his load too." Always alert to the economic problems of his profession as well as to the artistic ones, Shakespeare was inevitably influenced by the issues that the war of the theaters expressed, but although this influence surely affected some aspects of *Troilus and Cressida*, it can never be held accountable for the play as a whole.

In the problems that the drama presents for directors, actors, and stage designers, one may find, perhaps, a clue to its mystery, a way to understand why some parts of it are so emotionally and intellectually satisfying, others so flat and ill-conceived. Problems of modern production often reveal with lucidity the answers to many questions that a purely literary approach cannot solve. Although probably no modern production of this play can make it a satisfactory theatrical experience (as much may have been said of the script in 1602), one quality that does emerge in production tells us much about the development of Shakespeare's ideas around the time *Troilus and Cressida* was written. That quality is one of energetic experimentation—experimentation not of the amateur, unsure of his materials, nor of the craftsman temporarily exhausted and therefore forgetting for the moment the almost automatic use of his tools. Rather, *Troilus and Cressida* reminds one of a study by Michelangelo, boldly and completely rendered in some places, lightly blocked in elsewhere—the whole cartoon groping with line and space to build a conception that seems to develop before us, sometimes obscure but never tentative, and that will require ultimately another form, perhaps even a different medium, for its perfect expression.

In producing *Troilus and Cressida* for the stage, this quality of experimentation, of searching for form, comes to the director when he first tries to develop an overall conception of the action and the general style that should guide him when rehearsals begin, but he is likely to discover early in his efforts that this play defies such an attempt. This is why *Troilus and Cressida*, perhaps more frequently than any other play by Shakespeare, succumbs in preparation to that last effort of the desperate director, a striking form of modern dress. The modern theater has seen *Troilus and Cressida* in Edwardian dress, modish evening clothes, Wild West costumes, and the uniforms of the American Civil War; and there is little doubt that such aberrations occur (invariably in the name of originality or "significance to the modern audience") because the director, in forgivable despair, has begun to mistrust the text itself.

A setting for this play usually presents problems. Perhaps the original plan of the director and his designer is to use a three-sided apron stage, approximating the projection of the platform in the Elizabethan public theaters; they have envisioned the dramatic potentials of certain speeches delivered from different parts of this remarkable acting area: the oaths of the two lovers, for example, just before Pandarus packs them off to bed; Ulysses' two great addresses, the first of which seems especially to require the magnificent plenitude of space provided by the apron stage; the great quintet near the end of the play, when Troilus, Ulysses, and Thersites watch and comment upon

the surrender of Cressida to Diomedes; the last chaotic battle exchanges, which require maximum fluidity of movement. If, however, on the basis of such scenes, a setting is provided that utilizes the large, even epic proportions of the open platform, the director and actors will soon discover that in other portions of the play so much space becomes a burden instead of an advantage. Even scenes that begin with the promise of pomp and procession become, within twenty or thirty lines, scenes of intimate discussion. The Trojan princes marching over the stage (I.ii.189–245) are much less important to the progress of the play than the innuendos and small talk of Cressida and Pandarus; nor is there suspense built in anticipation of the entrance of Troilus himself, for we have already seen him, and, having heard Cressida's replies to Pandarus' gossip, we are even prepared for her coy response when he appears. The combat between Hector and Ajax (IV.v.113) is a red herring for the director, because this combat, when it finally happens, is dramatically uninteresting compared to other portions of the scene—Ulysses' enthusiastic praise of Troilus, for example, or Troilus and Ulysses' short exchange, which ends the episode; the combat is especially pale compared to the byplay between Achilles and Hector. If the director plans the moves of his actors to emphasize the apparent climax of the episode, he will find that the real interest of the scene has shifted elsewhere, that the point of the action is not what he thought it was, and that whatever this scene should be, it is not a scene of pageantry.

The actors themselves will face problems of characterization comparable to the vocal difficulties of an operatic baritone who, while studying his role, comes suddenly upon an aria written in the range of a tenor. If, for example, Hector is as sharply intelligent as he appears throughout the debate with Troilus and Paris (II.ii), the actor playing him will have difficulty portraying the hero's flabby and illogical surrender at the end of the scene. It is true that men commit themselves every day to causes in which they do not believe, but this irony does not impregnate Hector's

> I am yours,
> You valiant offspring of great Priamus.
> I have a roisting challenge sent amongst
> The dull and factious nobles of the Greeks
> Will strike amazement to their drowsy spirits.
> I was advertised their great general slept
> Whilst emulation in the army crept;
> This, I presume, will wake him. (II.ii.206–13)

These lines neither satirize Hector nor (as has been suggested) reveal ironically the fate of reason in a situation of uncontrolled passion. Moreover, they do not contain the sort of formalized change of motivation that occurs frequently in Elizabethan plays, and which an actor must cope with as best he can. These lines are simply a manifestation of the history to which Shakespeare was bound and to which his previous development of Hector's intelligence and viewpoint was inimical.

Experimentation with motive and personality that results in inconsistent characterization presents difficulties for actors in other roles. The actress playing Cressida appears on stage only twice after she has been exchanged by the Trojans for Antenor; earlier (III.ii.61–194 and

IV.ii.100–02) she has managed somehow the character's unrealistic anticipation of her own treachery, but, after her tearful leave-taking of Troilus, in which his repeated cry, "Be true," has touched her own fears, Cressida must parade happily among the Grecian generals, who kiss her "in general," and receive Ulysses' coldly perceptive insult. Whatever the actress has made of Cressida earlier, she is now the brassy and degraded slut the Elizabethans had been taught to expect. She appears only once more, to fall to Diomedes, and the actress must decide how to effect this transition of character. Once again, the problem is not so much one of an unfamiliar convention, but of unreconciled strands of development.

Such difficulties of production, and others similar to them, suggest that one of Shakespeare's major problems in composing *Troilus and Cressida* was not only consistency of character in the normal sense, but the nature of constancy itself, whether in politics or in love. Each of the troublesome matters noted above concerns the continuity of some factor pertinent to all parts of the text, whether that factor is stage setting or characterization. In IV.v Hector's dialogue with Achilles assumes more importance than his short fight with Ajax, because it is Achilles and not Ajax who should have entered the lists against the Trojan champion. It would be in keeping with Elizabethan ideas of order and degree for Achilles to maintain the identity of an active hero, and Ulysses wishes to goad him on toward his proper role. But more important, we listen eagerly to the talk between Hector and Achilles because so much in the play concerns sentiments identical to those motivating these men: Hector's faith in the principles that define what is right and good, and Achilles' surrender to the "one touch of nature" that can make all human beings blind and selfish. The confrontation of these men demands full use of the open stage, with the other actors distributed so as to emphasize it, but the machinery of Ajax's exhibition bout still hangs fire, and Shakespeare, almost as though he were working out the problem before our eyes, develops his main line of interest without bothering to erase false starts and unnecessary detail.

There is no need to examine in every character the way in which inconstancy, as a thematic concern, vitiates dramatic consistency. One final example is provided importantly by the heroine of the play. In the first half of the action Cressida is full and varied, yet her later fall from constancy is so baldly unqualified that Shakespeare's interest seems to have been attracted more to the violence of the metamorphosis than to maintaining the credibility of the character. No simple reliance upon the Elizabethan rumor of Cressida's harlotry can explain her sudden and complete degeneration.

The nature of that constancy which can preserve felicity in love and stability in politics had concerned Shakespeare since he began writing plays, and it was to remain a fundamental concern throughout his career. *Troilus and Cressida* is a pivotal play in the canon because it looks forward and backward simultaneously, indicating the ways in which Shakespeare's view of constancy was developing, and the dramatic forms that eventually would have to be employed to render that development effectively. From the beginning, he had found great dramatic potential in the stability that can be maintained only by the king who mirrors in himself an ordered nation, and in the fidelity of love that can overcome laughable folly or dangerous misunderstanding. By far the greater part of his writing had been, consequently, in varying forms of romantic comedy and patriotic chronicle-histories (the latter a theatrical form that may actually have been Shakespeare's own conception). He had also dramatized, though with less frequency, that form of constancy within the individual which forces him to be so energetically true to himself in love or even in crime that he can no longer be tolerated in the world of living men. In the lives of those tortured kings whose stories had added the aspect of tragedy to some of the history plays, Shakespeare had found that the world of politics could serve as background to the story of an individual whose mind demanded isolation from his surroundings, and whose actions would effect a downfall as inevitable as his virtues were magnificent. The two years preceding *Troilus and Cressida* saw Shakespeare's utilization of Roman politics for the scene of Brutus' individual tragedy. The fall of Julius Caesar, finished by the middle of the play, is patterned after the simple downward movement of Fortune's wheel—the pattern of almost all late medieval and early Tudor tragedies. But Shakespeare intended that his exploration of Brutus' constancy should hold the center of the drama; in *Julius Caesar* his refining hand turned attention in upon the mind of the hero himself. Roughly contemporary with this play were the romantic comedies *As You Like It* and *Twelfth Night*, each touched with a pervasive melancholy, each in its own way implying that only the truth of love can survive the vicissitudes of the world, the "rain [that] raineth every day." Perhaps a year before *Troilus and Cressida* came *Hamlet*, in which the public and private responsibilities of the mind are probed with a range and precision that elude comment. It may be helpful to observe, however, that many of the problems that challenge Hamlet's mind are paralleled by those that confuse the Trojan princes and the Greek generals. In both *Hamlet* and *Troilus and Cressida*, the authority of law is opposed by individual desire or private principle; in both, the ultimate canon of morality is set against the honor, real or supposed, of the individual; and in both, the definition of honor, "rightly to be great," is strenuously argued by those who have most at stake.

In *Troilus and Cressida* Shakespeare tried for the first time to combine in dramatic terms a story of love with a story of public affairs. It is worth noting that in the major tragedies that follow, the personal fate of the hero is inextricably bound up in the world of the state, and that in *Troilus and Cressida* Shakespeare made his first real study of the relationship between the pressures of the public world and the survival of love. Hamlet's uncle believed that "within the very flame of love" there lived a power which would destroy it, that, like goodness itself, it could not remain constant, but would grow "to a plurisy" and die in its own excess (*Hamlet*, IV.vii)—a metaphor very similar to Ulysses' description of passion, the "universal wolf" that would "last eat up himself" (I.iii.121, 124). Whatever Claudius' opinion, however, Shakespeare clearly believed that true love, untainted with destructive appetite, would not alter "when it alteration finds. . . . But [bear] it out even to the edge of doom" (Sonnet 116). These two statements articulate extremes that became the foundations for much of Shakespeare's thinking in the second half of his professional career; again and again he concerned himself with those forms of love that would survive all trials or succumb to the snares of the world. Always the process involved a growth of self-knowledge, and in *King Lear*, his most inclusive tragic statement, Shakespeare was able to show that after the greatest suffering might come the greatest achievement—a perception of constancy more powerful than any worldly reward or punishment; and that after such perception, death could come almost as a reward, as the final felicity.

Naturally, the creation of dramatic situations capable of sustaining this sort of action required a gradual revision of forms in which to work, and Shakespeare searched continually for the most appropriate modes of expression. That he moved from romantic comedy and history to tragedy, and from tragedy to romance, indicates a developing view of life and art; this development should not be divided into sharply limited chronological "periods," each one represented by a different kind of play. Nothing could be more misleading, for even in Shakespeare's earliest plays are individual lines and scenes as typical of his mature outlook as anything in the last romances. His metamorphosis of dramatic forms is more like Beethoven's progress toward the last piano sonatas and string quartets—a steady growth, a long series of experiments and finished monuments, none actually exclusive of the others, but attaining finally an absolute correspondence between idea and expression. Coming where it does in Shakespeare's development, *Troilus and Cressida* contains within it all the components of the playwright's most typical tragic pattern, but arranged in such a way as to prohibit the achievement possible in that form.

In 1601, probably about a year before the first performances of *Troilus and Cressida*, Shakespeare's poem *The Phoenix and the Turtle* was published in *Love's Martyr*, a collection of allegorical and emblematic verse. The subject matter of this poem clarifies the nature of Shakespeare's thematic concerns in his play, and it is no accident that in both poem and play one senses the author's effort to shape difficult materials to his purpose. *The Phoenix and the Turtle* describes the remarkable union of the mythical Phoenix and the Turtledove, in which love was so complete that even Reason stands amazed at the sight. In this mating, we are told, "number . . . in love was slain," for two separate lovers became one, and "Property" itself—the defining essence of the individual thing—was "appalled."

> Property was thus appalled,
> That the self was not the same;
> Single nature's double name
> Neither two nor one was called. (37-40)

These two lovers, in themselves all "Beauty, truth, and rarity," do not survive their own union, but are consumed "In a mutual flame," even as each finds absolute perfection in the other. The implication is that such absolute love cannot survive its own assault upon reason; its achievement is set forth as admirable and its inevitable passing as wonderful, but the poem also articulates the great sadness of such an event. It is a funeral dirge in which Reason, personified as the voice of admiration, composes the closing hymn of praise—a hymn, Shakespeare says specifically, "As chorus to their tragic scene."

Claudius' "too-much" of love, drowning itself in a "plurisy," may be equated with the self-cannibalism of appetite, as described by Ulysses; but these are a far cry from the admirable, yet sadly "tragic scene," which Shakespeare paints in *The Phoenix and the Turtle*. Shakespeare articulated in this poem—perhaps for the first time in his career—what was to become his most powerful dramatic irony in plays still to come: that the purity of love in "the marriage of true minds," while stronger than any other human achievement, cannot survive in the material world; and, as he demonstrated about five years after *Troilus and Cressida*, in the glorious conclusion to *Antony and Cleopatra*, such an achievement in love is inimical to that earthly order which must control the reasonable state. In this sense, the coolly efficient Octavius Caesar, in *Antony and Cleopatra*, and the personified Reason, in *The Phoenix and the Turtle*, both observe the same qualities of constancy in the dead lovers before them. The possession of these qualities was a basic criterion for tragedy, as Shakespeare must have understood the form at this time. The pure strains of love of Troilus for Cressida and of Antony for Cleopatra are, speaking quantitatively, the same; but a tragedy is the result of Antony's love, because he is as constant as Cleopatra's beauty is felicitous. However, "Property" in *Troilus and Cressida* cannot be "appalled" by "simple . . . so well compounded"; in this play no miraculous marriage of "Truth and Beauty" deserves the repose of death.

In its structural position in the play, Troilus' sight of Cressida, as she gives in to Diomedes, corresponds to the insight that carries the truly tragic hero toward his death; but what Troilus sees, though the truth, runs counter to his ideal, and to this ideal he is as constant as any genuinely tragic hero. His vocabulary, as he tries to convince both himself and Ulysses that what he has seen cannot actually have taken place, is very similar to that of *The Phoenix and the Turtle*. "If there be rule in unity itself," he cries, "This was not she" (V.ii.139-40)—recalling the paradox in the poem that "number" (that is, that "one" cannot be "two") "was slain," that the lovers merged into one entity, yet preserved their distinct essences. Building upon the conceit that there must be two Cressidas—his own, faithfully waiting in Troy, and this one, who is Diomedes'—he elaborates the most painful truth in the play: that what has seemed glorious and admirable, is not so.

> This she? No, this is Diomed's Cressida.
> If beauty have a soul, this is not she;
> If souls guide vows, if vows be sanctimonies,
> If sanctimony be the gods' delight,
> If there be rule in unity itself,
> This was not she. O madness of discourse,
> That cause sets up with and against itself:
> Bifold authority, where reason can revolt
> Without perdition, and loss assume all reason
> Without revolt. This is, and is not, Cressid.
> (V.ii.135-44)

Shakespeare wanted to show the disruption of constancy in both streams of action in the play—that of the love affair, and that of the famous war. Troilus' view of Cressida in Diomedes' arms does not give him that sublime lucidity of the tragic hero, but tempts him instead toward nihilism;

his prayer, as the play closes, is that Troy's destruction be swift, that the gods show their mercy by sending "brief plagues." Similarly, the great order of government that is Ulysses' ideal, and in which all men must assume their proper degree, is shown to elude the Greek generals. Shakespeare never maligns the ideal itself (it would be absurd to imagine that the author of the English histories would do so!), but he allows Thersites to remark how "that stale old mouse-eaten dry cheese, Nestor, and that same dog-fox, Ulysses" have failed it:

> O' the t'other side, the policy of those crafty swearing rascals . . . is not proved worth a blackberry. They set me up, in policy, that mongrel cur, Ajax, against that dog of as bad a kind, Achilles; and now is the cur Ajax prouder than the cur Achilles, and will not arm today. Whereupon the Grecians begin to proclaim barbarism, and policy grows into an ill opinion.                    (V.iv.9–17)

Many of the difficulties of this play in performance, as we have seen, occur because the dramatic rendering of inconstancy in love and in the state actually forces an inconstancy of character and a jarring sequence of events. To make the metamorphoses of love and political honor as striking as possible, Shakespeare first had to set forth both in their admirable condition. That Troilus' love and Ulysses' ideal polity come to nothing is not the result of satirical intention, but rather the requirement of the particular history Shakespeare chose to render dramatically. He always chose his plots carefully, and must have realized that the story of the lovers and the war contained the potential for tragedy, as he was beginning to understand it, but never achieved it. In *Antony and Cleopatra*, after all, he was to demonstrate how a "marriage of true minds," violently drawn together with physical and spiritual joy, would admit no impediments, even that of the Roman state; in *Troilus and Cressida*, he chose a plot full of impediments which are appallingly effective. The Trojan lover dotes upon his own ideal of faith as much as he dotes upon his faithless woman, and is blinded to a true perception of worth. His ringing question, "What's aught but as 'tis valued?" implies assessment by only one of two parties in love, for whatever price Troilus puts upon Cressida, he has yet to learn that she holds herself cheap. Similarly, that "policy grows into an ill opinion" in the Greek camp shows that its leaders have been insufficient to Ulysses' early description of divine and earthly order; and they, and Ulysses himself, have substituted machination— Thersites' "policy"—for true statecraft. On stage, what begins as divine intelligence ends as a practical joke.

We must not forget that Shakespeare's Elizabethan audiences (public or private) probably would not have found the inconsistencies of *Troilus and Cressida* where we find them. In the retelling of a story so familiar, they would have been surprised, for example, that so much hope is engendered in the first part of the play for Cressida's constancy, and not that she proves unfaithful. Ulysses' "degree" speech, perhaps the *locus classicus* in modern study of the Elizabethan conception of the "Great Chain of Being," is the sort of speech ordinarily suggestive in Shakespeare of a different dramatic decorum; it explicitly defines an ideal that this play never renders in action.

All this Shakespeare must have realized. The incidents of the Troy story chosen for dramatization predicated disappointment in the love plot and a shambles of order in the story of the war; even if he planned to carry forward the story of Troy in the sequel, which many critics infer from Pandarus' epilogue, surely he knew that in this drama the materials he had chosen demanded an ending in which no realization of the ideal was possible. Moreover, he knew that although the sequence of events and partial characterizations of his history were basically appropriate to the "tragic scene," he would be dealing as well with incongruities of folly and affectation suggestive of comic decorum. Since his audience would be familiar with his fable, he could count on their awareness of traditional characters and events; but even though he did not strive for novelty, he must have wondered how the implicit ethical significance of his rendering would be received. Moreover, since the public nature of the state was the background for the action, he would have realized that he was combining, for the first time with equal importance, a romantic story with an historical story. Clearly he desired to indicate a parallel between the betrayal of love that ends the former and the disintegration of heroism that ends the latter. Shakespeare may have anticipated the intractable nature of some of his materials, and it is quite possible that, during its composition, he knew that *Troilus and Cressida* might turn out to be an imperfect play—but the experiment fascinated him, and it was necessary.

The dangers that can prevent the triumph of love— both external to it and within it—occupied his mind henceforth, but his genius as a practical man of the theater did not always prevent this interest from assuming proportions inappropriate to the play at hand. Just as Shylock's monstrous faith in himself had almost swamped the romantic action of *The Merchant of Venice*, Angelo's morbidly distorted concept of law and love in *Measure for Measure* (written three or four years after *Troilus and Cressida*) was disproportionate to the romantic action surrounding it. Ultimately—but not until *Antony and Cleopatra* had shown him the way—Shakespeare discovered the dramatic form in which the persistent faith necessary for tragic achievement could be preserved in the living world, in which the ideal is made part of reality. The dying life in *Troilus and Cressida* is far from the world of romance, but the qualities of humanity and the grace of nature required to revivify men are so violently excluded from the fabric of the play, that these healing powers become more explicit for their absence. The characters of *Troilus and Cressida* are unable to achieve them, but by implication we know what they must be.

Following an earlier formula for tragical action, Shakespeare created, in *Romeo and Juliet,* a hero and heroine whose hopes seem almost mechanically doomed; the truth and beauty of their faith stand no chance against the external accidents of the world, although their love never alters in purity. After *Romeo and Juliet,* Shakespeare slowly shifted his emphasis; the character's inner strength to withstand external impediments became more important than an arbitrary caprice of fate, and the cause of disaster or tragic achievement was shown thereafter to reside within the human personality itself. Such causes were never again only partially articulated. In *Troilus and Cressida* they are frighteningly explicit, and because of the experimental form of the play they appear to us brutal and even cynical.

But Thersites' view of the world was never Shakespeare's. Never again was he to allow his audiences to witness such despair in the ability of men to achieve grace in love or death.

## A NOTE ON THE SOURCES

There is no single source for *Troilus and Cressida*, but there are several works with which we can be certain Shakespeare was familiar, and which he probably used in composing the play. Modern editions of these are listed at the end of this note. Homer's poem, of course, stands behind the story of the war, and Shakespeare's Greek, while less than his small Latin, might have been sufficient to cope with it. He also used the first parts of Chapman's translation of the *Iliad*, published in 1598 (*Seaven Bookes of the Iliades* and *Achilles Shield*); Chapman's later work on Homer appeared too late for Shakespeare's use in this play. Certain details of characterization and action, however, indicate that he either consulted Homer directly or used one of the full Latin or French translations of the sixteenth century; some of these details, such as the characterization of Ulysses and the abuse of Hector's body, could not have resulted from hearsay or pseudo-Homeric versions. Other aspects of the camp scenes, both Greek and Trojan, stem from Lydgate's *Sege of Troye* (c. 1412–20) or Caxton's *Recuyell of the Historyes of Troye* (1475). Both of these are derived ultimately from early pseudo-Homeric narratives, their more immediate source being the *Historia Troiana* (1287) of Guido delle Colonne; Guido had also provided one of the secondary sources for Chaucer's *Troilus and Criseyde*. Shakespeare also knew Arthur Golding's translation of Ovid's *Metamorphoses*, some parts of which touch upon the story of the Trojan War.

Shakespeare's major source for the love story was Chaucer's great narrative poem, *Troilus and Criseyde* (1382–85), although one must qualify immediately the nature of his reliance upon it. The bones of the story, as Shakespeare knew it, and even some details of the action are from Chaucer, but it would be most misleading to assume that Shakespeare's treatment of the tale resembles Chaucer's. The qualities of the story that attracted Shakespeare, and to which he added much more specific action concerning the characters in the camp scenes, were not those emphasized—not perhaps even recognized—by his most important predecessor in English literature. Chaucer's treatment of the story emphasizes the charm of the lovers and, while it lasts, the delight of their union. Pandarus is a warmhearted, benevolent courtier, himself a servant of love, though unsuccessful in his own amours. His humor is invariably genial, and although some of his jests are broad, they are never obscene. His main desire is the happiness of Troilus and Criseyde, and he is shocked into melancholy silence when he hears the news of Criseyde's betrayal. The heroine herself is a young woman of considerable dignity, imagination, and charm, with none of the coquetry or worldliness of Shakespeare's girl. She yields to Troilus only after long persuasion, and, befriended by Hector himself, enjoys a good reputation throughout the city. Chaucer's Troilus, like Shakespeare's, is a faithful and sensitive lover; but the affair is conducted in a vastly different manner in the two narratives. Pandarus, in Shakespeare's play, is glibly obscene, coarsely sentimental, and, frequently, hardly more than a leering *voyeur*, anxious for the lovers' happiness, but deriving from it what appears to be sexual pleasure for himself. In Chaucer's poem, the powers of love ennoble those who serve it, and the union of Troilus and Criseyde is set forth as an event of great beauty and cheer.

In Chaucer, the significance of Criseyde's fall is set against that of the great city itself, and both become part of a larger and more general sadness. Criseyde is shown to be confused and weak, but her lonely position in the Greek camp is also poignantly described. She becomes an instrument in the fortunes of both Troilus and Diomede, and some emphasis is thereby withdrawn from her faithless act itself. Her treachery is lamentable, but it is somehow overshadowed by the tragedy of Troy and the fate of mankind in general. Far from acknowledging in Criseyde an implicit harlotry, Chaucer sets forth, simply and with deep sadness, the tale of her loss. He is as moved by it as Pandarus, and seems to learn, with Troilus, that solace, if it can be found at all, is to be found in something more permanent than the life of this world. It should not be assumed that Chaucer's psychology was less subtle than Shakespeare's; it is derived in this poem, in fact, from the elaborate pattern of behavior defined in the code of courtly love—a code that could effect great beauty and delicacy of human feeling. Although Shakespeare's times —and ours—would describe such behavior pejoratively, as based in an adulterous relationship, no condemnation is implicit in Chaucer's work. It should be noted that his Criseyde is a widow when she first sees Troilus. His characters are capable of great strength and constancy, but Chaucer shows that the capricious movement of Fortune's wheel can crush what is beautiful and cause what is apparently constant to pass. His narrative is tragic in its treatment of the lovers' fall, comic to the extent that its characters are prone to folly and delusion.

By the time Shakespeare decided to write *Troilus and Cressida*, the story of the lovers had been retold many times, and the character of Cressida had been debased to that of a harlot. Chiefly responsible for this metamorphosis was Henryson's *The Testament of Cresseid*, which after 1532, when it was printed as Chaucer's in an edition of his works, was thought to be authentically Chaucerian. Henryson's poem is a sequel to the earlier narrative, beginning after Diomed, tiring of her, dismisses Cresseid. The girl rails against the gods in whom she had placed her trust, particularly Venus and Cupid, and in anger they transform her into a leper; she laments and goes upon her way, and finally dies—but not before Prince Troilus, upon his horse, passes her in the road and, not recognizing her transformed face, gives her alms. Henryson's tale treats the character of Cresseid sympathetically and with great human insight, although she is condemned for her faithlessness and especially for her great pride. Nevertheless, the Elizabethans read the piece entirely in the light of Cresseid's treachery, and it was not long before she became synonymous with all the evil qualities that the character in Shakespeare's play is willing to acknowledge if she prove false: "Yea, let them say, to stick the heart of falsehood,/'As false as Cressid'" (III.ii.193–94).

There had been other dramatic renderings of the story

before Shakespeare's, but all are lost; there is little doubt, however, that Cressida appeared in these versions as a strumpet. A surviving stage direction from the lost play by Chettle and Dekker (1599) reads, "Enter Cressida, with Beggars"—probably the company of lepers among whom, in Henryson's poem, she dies. References to Cressida as a whore abound in Elizabethan literature, and we may be sure that, just as the word for a base procurer stems from her uncle's name, her own became an equally common epithet.

The significance of this transformation should not be underestimated, although we may regret the violence it appears to do Chaucer and even Henryson. Shakespeare, in fact, may have been attracted to the plot, as I have suggested in the Introduction, because of its apparently unqualified statement of inconstancy. In this sense, his use of Homer (and Chapman's Homer), Lydgate, and Caxton is much closer to our normal understanding of the word "source" than is his reliance upon Chaucer. Although most of the details of the story are transformed, those relating to the camp and council scenes stand much closer to the originals than does his treatment of the love story.

*Modern editions of major sources:*

H. Bergen, ed. Lydgate's *Troy Book. Early English Text Society*, No. 97 (1906); Nos. 103, 106 (1908); No. 126 (1935).

Allardyce Nicoll, ed. *Chapman's Homer* (Bollingen Series XLI). 2 vols. New York: Pantheon Books, Inc., 1956.

F. N. Robinson, ed. *Troilus and Criseyde*, in *The Complete Works of Geoffrey Chaucer*. Boston: Houghton Mifflin Company; London: Oxford University Press, 1933. 2nd ed., 1957.

R. K. Root, ed. *The Book of Troilus and Criseyde by Geoffrey Chaucer*. Princeton, N. J.: Princeton University Press, 1945.

H. O. Sommer, ed. Caxton's *The Recuyell of the Historyes of Troye*. 2 vols. London: 1894.

## A NOTE ON THE TEXT

It is now generally believed that the 1609 quarto of *Troilus and Cressida* was printed from a transcript made from Shakespeare's original draft of the play. It omits about forty-five lines, the Prologue, and many stage directions that appear in the Folio, but on the whole contains a text that stands closer to Shakespeare's original than does that of the Folio. Since the compositors of the Folio apparently worked not only from the quarto but from Shakespeare's autograph manuscript, it is surprising that they did not produce the better text; their readings are mainly inferior to those of the quarto.

The relative values of the two texts (both of them, in different ways, stemming from Shakespeare's manuscript, and both of them, therefore, authoritative) depend on the nature of the copy used by the compositors, and the care and intelligence with which they worked. It is possible that the quarto represents the play as it was shortened for performance, but it is more likely that the transcriber of the original manuscript was confused by Shakespeare's own second thoughts and deletions and failed to record some revisions and added speeches. On the other hand, although

the compositors of the Folio probably had for reference and collation not only the quarto but the original manuscript itself, their goal was speed and not always accuracy. While they added many lines omitted in the quarto, they also introduced many mistaken readings; one compositor in particular evidently suited himself in interpreting difficult words and phrases, and made hash of most of them. Other portions of the Folio text were printed with greater care, however, and since the manuscript at hand may have been used in the playhouse, these portions include more complete stage directions and speech heads than appear in the quarto. The Folio, therefore, supplies the fuller text; it should be used occasionally to emend the quarto, but the earlier edition remains the better text. Its readings are frequently superior to those of the Folio, although, naturally, where the Folio prints speeches entirely omitted in the quarto, these must be considered authoritative. Similarly, those readings in the Folio which introduce corrections on the basis of copy that was either Shakespeare's or very close to his should be followed.

The present edition is based on the quarto but adds passages from the Folio. (These additions are recorded in the list of departures printed below.) Act and scene divisions (none are given for this play in quarto or Folio) have been added in square brackets, along with simple indications of locale. Abbreviations have been amplified, spelling and punctuation have been modernized, and "and" is printed "an" when it means "if." The position of a few stage directions has been slightly altered when necessary. Other departures from the quarto are listed below, the adopted reading first in boldface type, and then the original reading in roman. The adopted reading is most often from the Folio; when it is not, it is followed by [ed.] to indicate that it is an editor's conjecture rather than an authoritative reading.

**Dedicatory address** **39 state** [ed.] states **Prologue** [Q omits] **12 barks** [ed.; F has "Barke"] **19 Sperr** [ed.; F has "Stirre"] **I.i.78 she were not** she were **80 what care I** what I **I.ii.17 they** the **36 s.d. Enter Pandarus** [Q omits] **184 Ilium** Ilion **209 man's heart** man heart **245 s.d. Enter Common Soldiers** [Q omits] **288 s.d. Exit Pandarus** [Q omits] **I.iii.s.d. Sennet** [Q omits] **13 every** euer **31 thy** the **36 patient** ancient **54 Returns** [ed.] Retires **61 thy** the **70–74 Agamemnon. Speak . . . oracle** [Q omits] **75 basis** bases **110 meets** melts **159 unsquared** vnsquare **195 and discredit** our discredit **212 s.d. Tucket** [Q omits] **214 s.d. Enter Aeneas** [Q omits] **247 affair** affaires **250 whisper him** whisper with him **252 the attentive** that attentiue **256 loud** alowd **263 rusty** restie **267 That seeks** And feeds **276 compass** couple **294 one** no **298 will tell** tell **302 youth** men **305 first** sir **309 s.d. Exeunt. Manent Ulysses and Nestor** [Q omits] **315 This 'tis** [Q omits] **334 his honor** those honours **354–56 which . . . the limbs** [F emended from "in his" to "his"; Q omits] **390 tarre** arre **II.i.11 s.d. Strikes him** [Q omits] **14 vinewed'st** [F: whinid'st] vnsalted **17 oration** oration without booke **18 a prayer** praier **40–41 Ajax . . . Do, do** [Q assigns to Thersites as one speech] **45 Thou scurvy-valiant** you scuruy valiant **55 s.d. Enter Achilles and Patroclus** [Q omits] **56 do you** do yee **71 I I'll I** **101 if he knock out** and knocke at **105 your grandsires had nails on their toes** [F emended from "their" to "your"] their grandsiers had nailes **116 brach** [ed.] brooch **123 fifth** first **131 s.d. Exit** [Q omits] **II.ii.14–15 surety, Surety** surely Surely **27 father** fathers **33 at reasons** of reasons **47 Let's** Sets **64 shores** shore **75 truce** ttuce **86 he** be **96 s.d. with her hair about her ears** [Q omits] **104 eld** [ed.; F has "old"] elders **210 strike** shrike

**II.iii.21 s.d. Enter Patroclus** [Q omits] **25 wouldst** couldst **31 art** art not **47 thyself** Thersites **55–59 Patroclus. You . . . a fool** [Q omits] **62–63 commanded of Agamemnon** commanded **66 Creator** Prouer **68 Patroclus** Come Patroclus **69 s.d. Exit** [Q omits] **73–74 Now . . . all** [Q omits] **79 shent** [ed.; F has "sent"] sate **80 appertainments** appertainings **89 A word, my lord** [Q omits] **102 s.d. Enter Patroclus** [Q omits] **130 pettish lunes** [F emended from "lines" to "lunes"] course, and time; **as if** and if **131 carriage of this action** streame of his commencement **141 enter you** entertaine **141 s.d. Exit Ulysses** [Q omits] **158 I hate** I do hate **191 stale** [ed.] staule **193 titled** liked **203 pash** push **212 let his humor's** tell his humorous **220 'A would . . . shares** [Q gives to Ajax] **222 He's . . . warm** [ed.; Q and F give to Ajax] **223 praises** praiers **242 beyond, beyond all erudition** beyond all thy erudition **248 bourn** boord **249 Thy** This **263 cull** call

**III.i.s.d. Music . . . Servant** Enter Pandarus **24 friend** [Q omits] **38 that thou** thou **92 your poor disposer's** your disposers **107 lord** lad **114 In . . . so** [Q omits] **117 shaft confounds** shafts confound **149 these** this **157 thee** her

**III.ii.s.d. and Troilus'** Troylus **3 he stays** stayes **3 s.d. Enter Troilus** [Q omits] **8 Like** like to **10 those** these **15 s.d. Exit Pandarus** [Q omits] **27 s.d. Enter Pandarus** [Q omits] **32 s.d. Exit Pandarus** [Q omits] **36 unawares** vnwares **66 fears** [ed.] teares **80 This is** This **91 merit crown it. No perfection** merit louer part no affection **98 s.d. Enter Pandarus** [Q omits] **131 Cunning** [ed.] Comming **158 aye** age **178 Yet, after** After **183 and** or **191 as wolf** or Wolfe **198 pains** paine

**III.iii.s.d. Flourish** [Q omits] **4 come** [ed.] loue **102 giver** giuers **128 abject** obiect **140 on** one **141 shrinking** shriking **155 one** on **158 hedge** turne **160 hindmost** him, most **161–63 Or . . . on** [F emended from "neere" to "rear"; Q omits] **164 past** passe **177 give** [ed.] goe **183 Than** That **197 every grain of Pluto's gold** euery thing **198 th' uncomprehensive deeps** the vncomprehensiue depth **224 a dewdrop** dew drop **251 he** a **266 ambassador to him** Ambassador **274 most valorous** valorous **278 Grecian army** armie; **Agamemnon, et cetera** Agamemnon **293 God b' wi' you** [ed.] God buy you

**IV.i.4 you** your **16 But Lul'd** beleeue **50 s.d. Exit Aeneas** [Q omits] **52 the soul** soule **56 soilure** soyle **76 you** they

**IV.ii.19 s.d. Within** [Q omits] **22 s.d. Enter Pandarus** [F places after line 20; Q omits] **52 'Tis** Its **58 s.d. Enter Troilus** [Q omits] **64 to us; and for him forthwith** to him, and forthwith **73 nature** neighbor Pandar **106 I will** Ile **110 s.d. Exeunt** [Q omits]

**IV.iv.54 the root** my throate **64 there's** there is **77 They're . . . nature** [Q omits] **79 person** portion **139 s.d. Sound trumpet** [Q omits] **144–48 Deiphobus. Let us . . . chivalry** [F, with 144 assigned to Diomedes; Q omits]

**IV.v.94 Ulysses. They . . . already** [Q omits] **95 Agamemnon** Vlises **98 in deeds** deeds **131 Of our rank feud** [Q omits] **132 drop** day **164–69 But that's . . . integrity** [Q omits] **177 that I affect th' untraded oath** thy affect, the vntraded earth **187 thy th'** **192 shraped** [ed.] shruped **205 As they . . . courtesy** [Q omits] **254 stithied** stichied **291 she loved my Lord**

**V.i.14 these** this **15 boy** box **20 catarrhs** [Q omits] **24 and the like** [Q omits] **48 s.d. Exit** [Q omits] **55 brother** be **57 hanging at his brother's leg** at his bare legge **59 forced faced 61 he is** her's **61 dog, a mule** day, a Moyle **62 fitchew** Fichooke **64–65 Ask me not** aske me **70 s.d. Enter Achilles** [Q omits] **72 good** God **78 sewer** [ed.] sure **79 both at once** both

**V.ii.5 s.d. Enter . . . Ulysses** [Q omits] **14 Cressida** Cal **39 Nay** Now **40 distraction** distruction **47 Adieu** [Q omits] **55 these together** together **57 But will** Will **58 la** [ed.] lo **67 Troilus. I . . . will** [Q omits] **68 Cressida** Troy **79 Nay . . . me** [Q, F assign to Diomedes] **83 Cressida** [Q omits] **89 By** And by **104 s.d. Exit** [Q omits] **116 coact** Court **121 had deceptious** were deceptions **132 soil** spoile **155 five** finde **165 Much as** as much

**V.iii.14 Cassandra** Cres **20–22 To hurt . . . charity** [F emended from "would count" to "would," and from "as" to "use"; Q omits] **23–25 It . . . Hector** [Q assigns to Andromache] **29 mean'st** meanest **58 But by my ruin** [Q omits] **85 distraction** destruction **90 s.d. Exit** [Q omits]

**V.iv.4 young knave's** knaues **9 errand** [F has "errant"] arrant; **O' the Ath 16 begin** [ed.] began **17 s.d. Enter Diomedes and Troilus** [Q omits] **26 art thou** art

**V.v.22 scaled** scaling **41 luck** lust

**V.vii.11 double-horned** [ed.] double-hen'd **12 s.d. Exeunt** [ed.] Exit **23 s.d. Exeunt** Exit

**V.viii.16 One Greek** [F has "Gree."] One

**V.ix.1 what shout is that** what is this

**V.x.2 Never . . . night** [Q assigns to Troilus, and places his entrance before the line] **21–22 But march away. Hector is dead** [Q omits] **23 vile** proud **32–34 Pandarus. But . . . name** [in F these lines appear as well after V.iii.112, concluding that scene] **33 Ignominy and** ignominy **37 traders** [ed.] traitors **49 your aching** my aking **50 hold-door** hold-ore

# A Never Writer, to an Ever Reader.
# News.

Eternal reader, you have here a new play, never staled with the stage, never clapperclawed with the palms of the vulgar, and yet passing full of the palm comical; for it is a birth of your brain° that never undertook anything comical vainly. And were but the 5 vain names of comedies changed for the titles of commodities, or of plays for pleas, you should see all those grand censors, that now style them such vanities, flock to them for the main grace of their gravities—especially this author's comedies, that are so framed to the life 10 that they serve for the most common commentaries of all the actions of our lives, showing such a dexterity and power of wit that the most displeased with plays are pleased with his comedies. And all such dull and heavy-witted worldlings as were never capable of the 15 wit of a comedy, coming by report of them to his representations, have found that wit there that they never found in themselves and have parted better witted than they came, feeling an edge of wit set upon them more than ever they dreamed they had brain to grind 20 it on. So much and such savored salt of wit is in his comedies that they seem, for their height of pleasure, to be born in that sea that brought forth Venus.° Amongst all there is none more witty than this; and had I time I would comment upon it, though I know it needs not, 25 for so much as will make you think your testern° well bestowed, but for so much worth as even poor I know to be stuffed in it. It deserves such a labor as well as the best comedy in Terence or Plautus. And believe this, that when he is gone and his comedies out of sale, 30 you will scramble for them and set up a new English Inquisition. Take this for a warning, and at the peril of your pleasure's loss, and judgment's, refuse not, nor like this the less for not being sullied with the smoky breath of the multitude; but thank fortune for the 35 'scape it hath made amongst you, since by the grand possessors'° wills I believe you should have prayed for them rather than been prayed. And so I leave all such to be prayed for, for the state of their wits' healths, that will not praise it. *Vale.* 40

4 **your brain** i.e., Shakespeare's brain

23 **Venus** the Greek goddess Aphrodite, who, according to Hesiod, was born in ocean foam   26 **testern** sixpence (slang)
36–37 **grand possessors** presumably, the actor-sharers of the King's Men, who may have tried to stop publication

# THE HISTORY OF
# TROILUS AND CRESSIDA

[Dramatis Personae

PRIAM *King of Troy*
HECTOR
TROILUS
PARIS } *his sons*
DEIPHOBUS
HELENUS
MARGARELON *a bastard son of Priam*
AENEAS } *Trojan commanders*
ANTENOR
CALCHAS *a Trojan priest, taking part with the Greeks*
PANDARUS *uncle to Cressida*
AGAMEMNON *the Greek general*
MENELAUS *his brother*

ACHILLES
AJAX
ULYSSES
NESTOR } *Greek commanders*
DIOMEDES
PATROCLUS
THERSITES *a deformed and scurrilous Greek*
ALEXANDER *servant to Cressida*
SERVANT TO TROILUS
SERVANT TO PARIS
SERVANT TO DIOMEDES
HELEN *wife to Menelaus*
ANDROMACHE *wife to Hector*
CASSANDRA *daughter to Priam; a prophetess*
CRESSIDA *daughter to Calchas*
TROJAN AND GREEK SOLDIERS AND ATTENDANTS

*Scene:* Troy, and the Greek camp before it]

## THE PROLOGUE

[*Enter the* PROLOGUE, *armed for battle.*]

In Troy there lies the scene. From isles of Greece
The princes orgulous,° their high blood chafed,
Have to the port of Athens sent their ships,
Fraught with the ministers and instruments
Of cruel war. Sixty and nine, that wore          5
Their crownets regal, from th' Athenian bay
Put forth toward Phrygia;° and their vow is made
To ransack Troy, within whose strong immures°
The ravished Helen, Menelaus' queen,
With wanton Paris sleeps—and that's the quarrel.   10
To Tenedos° they come,
And the deep-drawing barks do there disgorge
Their warlike fraughtage.° Now on Dardan° plains
The fresh and yet unbruisèd Greeks do pitch
Their brave pavilions. Priam's six-gated city,    15
Dardan, and Timbria, Helias, Chetas, Troien,
And Antenonidus,° with massy staples
And corresponsive and fulfilling° bolts,
Sperr up° the sons of Troy.
Now expectation, tickling skittish° spirits,      20
On one and other side, Troyan and Greek,

*The decorative border shown above is a repeated ornament which appeared on the title page of the quarto edition of* Troilus and Cressida, *1609.*

**Pro. 2 orgulous** proud  **7 Phrygia** western Asia Minor  **8 immures** walls

**11 Tenedos** the port of Troy  **13 fraughtage** freight, i.e., soldiers; **Dardan** Trojan (after Dardanus, son of Zeus and the Pleiad Electra, and ancestor of Priam)  **16–17 Dardan . . . Antenonidus** names of the gates of Troy  **18 fulfilling** filling tightly  **19 Sperr up** shut up  **20 skittish** nervous

Sets all on hazard. And hither am I come,
A prologue armed,° but not in confidence
Of author's pen or actor's voice, but suited°
In like conditions as our argument,°  25
To tell you, fair beholders, that our play
Leaps o'er the vaunt° and firstlings of those broils,
Beginning in the middle, starting thence away
To what may be digested in a play.
Like or find fault; do as your pleasures are;  30
Now good or bad, 'tis but the chance of war.

# [ A C T   I ]

## [Scene I. *Within Troy.*]

*Enter* PANDARUS *and* TROILUS.

TROILUS
Call here my varlet,° I'll unarm again.
Why should I war without° the walls of Troy
That find such cruel battle here within?
Each Troyan that is master of his heart,
Let him to field; Troilus, alas, hath none.  5
PANDARUS
Will this gear° ne'er be mended?
TROILUS
The Greeks are strong, and skillful to° their strength,
Fierce to their skill, and to their fierceness valiant;
But I am weaker than a woman's tear,
Tamer than sleep, fonder° than ignorance,  10
Less valiant than the virgin in the night,
And skilless° as unpracticed infancy.
PANDARUS  Well, I have told you enough of this.
For my part, I'll not meddle nor make no farther. He
that will have a cake out of the wheat must tarry the  15
grinding.
TROILUS  Have I not tarried?
PANDARUS  Ay, the grinding; but you must tarry the
bolting.°
TROILUS  Have I not tarried?  20
PANDARUS  Ay, the bolting; but you must tarry the
leavening.
TROILUS  Still have I tarried.
PANDARUS  Ay, to the leavening; but here's yet in the
word "hereafter" the kneading, the making of the  25
cake, the heating the oven, and the baking. Nay, you
must stay the cooling too, or ye may chance burn your
lips.
TROILUS
Patience herself, what goddess e'er she be,
Doth lesser blench° at suff'rance than I do.  30
At Priam's royal table do I sit,
And when fair Cressid comes into my thoughts—
So, traitor,° then she comes when she is thence.°

PANDARUS  Well, she looked yesternight fairer than
ever I saw her look, or any woman else.  35
TROILUS
I was about to tell thee, when my heart,
As wedgèd with a sigh, would rive° in twain,
Lest Hector or my father should perceive me—
I have, as when the sun doth light a-scorn,°
Buried this sigh in wrinkle of a smile;  40
But sorrow, that is couched in seeming gladness,
Is like that mirth fate turns to sudden sadness.
PANDARUS  An° her hair were not somewhat darker
than Helen's—well, go to—there were no more
comparison between the women; but, for my part,  45
she is my kinswoman: I would not, as they term it,
praise her, but I would somebody had heard her talk
yesterday, as I did. I will not dispraise your sister
Cassandra's wit, but—
TROILUS
O Pandarus! I tell thee, Pandarus,  50
When I do tell thee, there my hopes lie drowned,
Reply not in how many fathoms deep
They lie indrenched. I tell thee I am mad
In Cressid's love; thou answer'st she is fair,
Pour'st in the open ulcer of my heart  55
Her eyes, her hair, her cheek, her gait, her voice;
Handlest in thy discourse, O, that her hand°
In whose comparison all whites are ink,
Writing their own reproach; to whose soft seizure°
The cygnet's° down is harsh, and spirit° of sense  60
Hard as the palm of plowman. This thou tell'st me,
As true thou tell'st me, when I say I love her;
But, saying thus, instead of oil and balm,
Thou lay'st in every gash that love hath given me
The knife that made it.  65
PANDARUS  I speak no more than truth.
TROILUS  Thou dost not speak so much.
PANDARUS  Faith, I'll not meddle in it; let her be as
she is. If she be fair, 'tis the better for her; and she be
not, she has the mends° in her own hands.  70
TROILUS  Good Pandarus, how now, Pandarus?
PANDARUS  I have had my labor for my travail;° ill
thought on of her, and ill thought of you; gone be-
tween and between, but small thanks for my labor.
TROILUS  What, art thou angry, Pandarus? What,  75
with me?
PANDARUS  Because she's kin to me, therefore she's
not so fair as Helen. An she were not kin to me, she
would be as fair a'° Friday as Helen is on Sunday.°
But what care I? I care not an she were a blackamoor;  80
'tis all one to me.
TROILUS  Say I she is not fair?
PANDARUS  I do not care whether you do or no. She's
a fool to stay behind her father.° Let her to the Greeks,
and so I'll tell her the next time I see her. For my part,  85
I'll meddle nor make no more i' th' matter.

**23 armed** equipped for fight **24 suited** dressed **25 argument** subject **27 vaunt** beginning
**I.i.1 varlet** servant **2 without** outside **6 gear** business **7 to** in addition to, in proportion to **10 fonder** more unsophisticated, simpler **12 skilless** inept, naive **19 bolting** sifting **30 blench** flinch **33 traitor** a self-rebuke, for suggesting that she is sometimes absent; **then . . . thence** she returns immediately whenever she is absent

**37 rive** split **39 a-scorn** mockingly(?) grudgingly(?) **43 An** if **57 that her hand** that hand of hers **59 seizure** grasp **60 cygnet's** young swan's; **spirit** the thin bodily substance believed to transmit sense impressions through the nerves **70 mends** (1) remedies (2) cosmetics **72 travail** punning on *travel* ("gone between and between") **79 a'** on **79 on Sunday** i.e., in her Sunday best **84 father** Calchas, who had deserted to the Greeks

TROILUS   Pandarus—
PANDARUS   Not I.
TROILUS   Sweet Pandarus—
PANDARUS   Pray you, speak no more to me. I will  90
leave all as I found it, and there an end.     *Exit.*

*Sound alarum.*

TROILUS

Peace, you ungracious clamors! Peace, rude sounds!
Fools on both sides! Helen must needs be fair,
When with your blood you daily paint her thus.
I cannot fight upon this argument;°              95
It is too starved a subject for my sword.
But Pandarus—O gods, how do you plague me!
I cannot come to Cressid but by Pandar;
And he's as tetchy° to be wooed to woo
As she is stubborn, chaste, against all suit.     100
Tell me, Apollo, for thy Daphne's° love,
What Cressid is, what Pandar, and what we.
Her bed is India; there she lies, a pearl.
Between our Ilium° and where she resides
Let it be called the wild and wand'ring flood,     105
Ourself the merchant, and this sailing Pandar
Our doubtful hope, our convoy and our bark.

*Alarum. Enter* AENEAS.

AENEAS

How now, Prince Troilus, wherefore not afield?

TROILUS

Because not there. This woman's answer sorts,°
For womanish it is to be from thence.           110
What news, Aeneas, from the field today?

AENEAS

That Paris is returnèd home, and hurt.

TROILUS

By whom, Aeneas?

AENEAS            Troilus, by Menelaus.

TROILUS

Let Paris bleed; 'tis but a scar to scorn:°
Paris is gored with Menelaus' horn.°          115

*Alarum.*

AENEAS

Hark what good sport is out of town today!

TROILUS

Better at home, if "would I might" were "may."
But to the sport abroad; are you bound thither?

AENEAS

In all swift haste.

TROILUS        Come, go we then together. *Exeunt.*

[Scene II. *Within Troy.*]

*Enter* CRESSIDA *and* [*Alexander,*] *her* MAN.

CRESSIDA

Who were those went by?

MAN             Queen Hecuba and Helen.

---

CRESSIDA

And whither go they?

MAN             Up to the eastern tower,
Whose height commands as subject all the vale,
To see the battle. Hector, whose patience
Is as a virtue fixed, today was moved.          5
He chid Andromache, and struck his armorer,
And, like as there were husbandry° in war,
Before the sun rose he was harnessed° light,
And to the field goes he, where every flower
Did, as a prophet, weep what it foresaw         10
In Hector's wrath.

CRESSIDA         What was his cause of anger?

MAN

The noise goes, this: there is among the Greeks
A lord of Troyan blood, nephew to Hector;
They call him Ajax

CRESSIDA         Good; and what of him?

MAN

They say he is a very man per se           15
And stands alone.

CRESSIDA   So do all men unless they are drunk, sick,
or have no legs.

MAN   This man, lady, hath robbed many beasts of
their particular additions.° He is as valiant as the lion,  20
churlish as the bear, slow as the elephant; a man into
whom nature hath so crowded humors° that his valor
is crushed into folly, his folly sauced with discretion.
There is no man hath a virtue that he hath not a
glimpse° of, nor any man an attaint° but he carries  25
some stain of it. He is melancholy without cause and
merry against the hair.° He hath the joints of everything, but everything so out of joint that he is a gouty
Briareus,° many hands and no use, or purblind Argus,°
all eyes and no sight.                                 30

CRESSIDA   But how should this man that makes me
smile make Hector angry?

MAN   They say he yesterday coped° Hector in the
battle and struck him down, the disdain and shame
whereof hath ever since kept Hector fasting and  35
waking.

*Enter* PANDARUS.

CRESSIDA   Who comes here?

MAN   Madam, your uncle Pandarus.

CRESSIDA   Hector's a gallant man.

MAN   As may be in the world, lady.          40

PANDARUS   What's that? What's that?

CRESSIDA   Good morrow, uncle Pandarus.

PANDARUS   Good morrow, cousin° Cressid. What do
you talk of? Good morrow, Alexander. How do you,
cousin? When were you at Ilium?          45

CRESSIDA   This morning, uncle.

PANDARUS   What were you talking of when I came?

---

**95 argument** theme  **99 tetchy** peevish  **101 Daphne** the
nymph who was changed into a bay tree as she ran to escape
Apollo  **104 Ilium** here, Priam's palace; generally, Troy (for
Ilus, founder of the city, Priam's grandfather)  **109 sorts** is
appropriate  **114 but . . . scorn** i.e., considering its source,
the kind of scar to be scorned  **115 horn** of a cuckold

**I.ii.7 husbandry** good management, thrift  **8 harnessed**
armored  **20 additions** distinctive qualities, characteristics
**22 humors** bodily fluids which, in excess, were thought to
cause emotional disorder  **25 glimpse** momentary shining;
**attaint** imputation of dishonor  **27 against the hair** contrary
to natural tendency (cf. *against the grain*)  **29 Briareus** a
hundred-handed giant;  **Argus** a herdsman with eyes
covering his body  **33 coped** engaged, encountered  **43
cousin** a term of familiarity; here, niece

Was Hector armed and gone ere ye came to Ilium?
Helen was not up, was she?

CRESSIDA    Hector was gone, but Helen was not up.    50

PANDARUS    E'en so, Hector was stirring early.

CRESSIDA    That were we talking of, and of his anger.

PANDARUS    Was he angry?

CRESSIDA    So he says here.

PANDARUS    True, he was so; I know the cause too.    55
He'll lay about him today, I can tell them that; and
there's Troilus will not come far behind him. Let them
take heed of Troilus, I can tell them that too.

CRESSIDA    What, is he angry too?

PANDARUS    Who, Troilus? Troilus is the better man    60
of the two.

CRESSIDA    O Jupiter! There's no comparison.

PANDARUS    What, not between Troilus and Hector?
Do you know a man if you see him?

CRESSIDA    Ay, if I ever saw him before and knew him.    65

PANDARUS    Well, I say Troilus is Troilus.

CRESSIDA    Then you say as I say, for I am sure he is
not Hector.

PANDARUS    No, nor Hector is not Troilus in some
degrees.°    70

CRESSIDA    'Tis just to each of them; he is himself.

PANDARUS    Himself? Alas, poor Troilus, I would he
were.°

CRESSIDA    So he is.

PANDARUS    Condition,° I had gone barefoot to India.    75

CRESSIDA    He is not Hector.

PANDARUS    Himself? No, he's not himself. Would 'a°
were himself. Well, the gods are above; time must
friend or end. Well, Troilus, well, I would my heart
were in her body. No, Hector is not a better man than    80
Troilus.

CRESSIDA    Excuse me.

PANDARUS    He is elder.

CRESSIDA    Pardon me, pardon me.

PANDARUS    Th' other's not come to't;° you shall tell    85
me another tale when th' other's come to't. Hector
shall not have his will° this year.

CRESSIDA    He shall not need it if he have his own.

PANDARUS    Nor his qualities.

CRESSIDA    No matter.    90

PANDARUS    Nor his beauty.

CRESSIDA    'Twould not become him. His own's
better.

PANDARUS    You have no judgment, niece. Helen herself swore th' other day that Troilus, for a brown    95
favor°—for so 'tis, I must confess—not brown neither—

CRESSIDA    No, but brown.

PANDARUS    Faith, to say truth, brown and not
brown.

CRESSIDA    To say the truth, true and not true.    100

PANDARUS    She praised his complexion above Paris.

CRESSIDA    Why, Paris hath color enough.

PANDARUS    So he has.

CRESSIDA    Then Troilus should have too much. If she

praised him above, his complexion is higher than his.    105
He having color enough, and the other higher, is too
flaming a praise for a good complexion. I had as lief
Helen's golden tongue had commended Troilus for a
copper nose.

PANDARUS    I swear to you, I think Helen loves him    110
better than Paris.

CRESSIDA    Then she's a merry Greek° indeed.

PANDARUS    Nay, I am sure she does. She came to
him th' other day into the compassed° window—and,
you know, he has not past three or four hairs on his    115
chin—

CRESSIDA    Indeed, a tapster's arithmetic may soon
bring his particulars therein to a total.

PANDARUS    Why, he is very young; and yet will he,
within three pound, lift as much as his brother Hector.    120

CRESSIDA    Is he so young a man, and so old a lifter?°

PANDARUS    But to prove to you that Helen loves
him, she came and puts me her white hand to his
cloven chin—

CRESSIDA    Juno have mercy; how came it cloven?    125

PANDARUS    Why, you know 'tis dimpled; I think his
smiling becomes him better than any man in all
Phrygia.

CRESSIDA    O, he smiles valiantly.

PANDARUS    Does he not?    130

CRESSIDA    O, yes, an 'twere a cloud in autumn.

PANDARUS    Why go to then. But to prove to you
that Helen loves Troilus—

CRESSIDA    Troilus will stand° to the proof if you'll
prove it so.    135

PANDARUS    Troilus? Why, he esteems her no more
than I esteem an addle° egg.

CRESSIDA    If you love an addle egg as well as you love
an idle head, you would eat chickens i' the shell.

PANDARUS    I cannot choose but laugh to think how    140
she tickled his chin. Indeed, she has a marvel's° white
hand, I must needs confess.

CRESSIDA    Without the rack.°

PANDARUS    And she takes upon her to spy a white
hair on his chin.    145

CRESSIDA    Alas poor chin, many a wart is richer.

PANDARUS    But there was such laughing. Queen
Hecuba laughed that her eyes ran o'er.

CRESSIDA    With millstones.

PANDARUS    And Cassandra laughed.    150

CRESSIDA    But there was a more temperate fire under
the pot of her eyes. Did her eyes run o'er too?

PANDARUS    And Hector laughed.

CRESSIDA    At what was all this laughing?

PANDARUS    Marry,° at the white hair that Helen spied    155
on Troilus' chin.

CRESSIDA    An't had been a green hair, I should have
laughed too.

PANDARUS    They laughed not so much at the hair as
at his pretty answer.    160

CRESSIDA    What was his answer?

---

69–70 **in some degrees** by some distance; in some (specific)
ways (?)    72–73 **I . . . were** i.e., I wish he were himself, and
not in love    75 **Condition** i.e., even if to bring that about
77 **'a** he    85 **come to't** reached manhood    87 **will** some
editors emend to "wit," i.e., intelligence    95–96 **brown favor**
dark complexion

112 **a merry Greek** one of frivolous or loose behavior (slang)
114 **compassed** bay    121 **so . . . lifter** so experienced a
thief (cf. *shoplifter*)    134 **stand** a bawdy pun; cf. Sonnet 151
137 **addle** rotten    141 **marvel's** marvelous    143 **rack** torture
155 **Marry** an interjection, from the oath, "By the Virgin
Mary"

PANDARUS  Quoth she, "Here's but two-and-fifty hairs on your chin, and one of them is white."

CRESSIDA  This is her question.

PANDARUS  That's true, make no question of that. "Two-and-fifty hairs," quoth he, "and one white. That white hair is my father, and all the rest are his sons." "Jupiter!" quoth she, "which of these hairs is Paris, my husband?" "The forked° one," quoth he; "pluck't out, and give it him." But there was such laughing, and Helen so blushed, and Paris so chafed, and all the rest so laughed, that it passed. 165

CRESSIDA  So let it now, for it has been a great while going by.

PANDARUS  Well, cousin, I told you a thing yester- 175 day; think on't.

CRESSIDA  So I do.

PANDARUS  I'll be sworn 'tis true; he will weep you, an° 'twere a man born in April.

*Sound a retreat.*

CRESSIDA  And I'll spring up in his tears, an 'twere a 180 nettle against° May.

PANDARUS  Hark, they are coming from the field. Shall we stand up here and see them as they pass to- ward Ilium? Good niece, do; sweet niece, Cressida.

CRESSIDA  At your pleasure. 185

PANDARUS  Here, here, here's an excellent place; here we may see most bravely.° I'll tell you them all by their names as they pass by, but mark Troilus above the rest.

*Enter AENEAS [and passes across the stage].*

CRESSIDA  Speak not so loud. 190

PANDARUS  That's Aeneas. Is not that a brave° man? He's one of the flowers of Troy, I can tell you. But mark Troilus; you shall see anon.

*Enter ANTENOR [and passes across the stage].*

CRESSIDA  Who's that?

PANDARUS  That's Antenor. He has a shrewd wit, I 195 can tell you; and he's man good enough—he's one o' the soundest judgments in Troy whosoever, and a proper° man of person. When comes Troilus? I'll show you Troilus anon. If he see me, you shall see him nod at me. 200

CRESSIDA  Will he give you the nod?°

PANDARUS  You shall see.

CRESSIDA  If he do, the rich shall have more.°

*Enter HECTOR [and passes across the stage].*

PANDARUS  That's Hector, that, that, look you, that; there's a fellow! Go thy way, Hector! There's a brave 205 man, niece. O brave Hector! Look how he looks; there's a countenance! Is't not a brave man?

CRESSIDA  O, a brave man.

PANDARUS  Is 'a not? It does a man's heart good. Look you what hacks are on his helmet. Look you 210 yonder, do you see? Look you there. There's no jest-

ing; there's laying on, take't off who will,° as they say. There be hacks!

CRESSIDA  Be those with swords?

PANDARUS  Swords, anything, he cares not; an the 215 devil come to him, it's all one. By God's lid, it does one's heart good.

*Enter PARIS [and passes across the stage].*

Yonder comes Paris, yonder comes Paris. Look ye yonder, niece. Is't not a gallant° man too, is't not? Why, this is brave now. Who said he came hurt home 220 today? He's not hurt. Why, this will do Helen's heart good now, ha? Would I could see Troilus now. You shall see Troilus anon.

CRESSIDA  Who's that?

*Enter HELENUS [and passes across the stage].*

PANDARUS  That's Helenus. I marvel where Troilus 225 is. That's Helenus. I think he went not forth today. That's Helenus.

CRESSIDA  Can Helenus fight, uncle?

PANDARUS  Helenus? No. Yes, he'll fight indifferent well. I marvel where Troilus is. Hark, do you not 230 hear the people cry "Troilus"? Helenus is a priest.

CRESSIDA  What sneaking fellow comes yonder?

*Enter TROILUS [and passes across the stage].*

PANDARUS  Where? Yonder? That's Deiphobus. 'Tis Troilus! There's a man, niece, hem? Brave Troilus, the prince of chivalry! 235

CRESSIDA  Peace, for shame, peace!

PANDARUS  Mark him, note him. O brave Troilus! Look well upon him, niece. Look you how his sword is bloodied, and his helm more hacked than Hector's— and how he looks, and how he goes. O admirable 240 youth! He never saw three-and-twenty. Go thy way, Troilus, go thy way! Had I a sister were a grace,° or a daughter a goddess, he should take his choice. O admirable man! Paris? Paris is dirt to him; and I warrant Helen, to change, would give an eye to boot. 245

*Enter COMMON SOLDIERS.*

CRESSIDA  Here comes more.

PANDARUS  Asses, fools, dolts; chaff and bran, chaff and bran; porridge after meat. I could live and die in the eyes of Troilus. Ne'er look, ne'er look. The eagles are gone; crows and daws, crows and daws. I had 250 rather be such a man as Troilus than Agamemnon and all Greece.

CRESSIDA  There is amongst the Greeks Achilles, a better man than Troilus.

PANDARUS  Achilles? A drayman,° a porter, a very 255 camel.°

CRESSIDA  Well, well.

PANDARUS  "Well, well"? Why, have you any dis- cretion, have you any eyes, do you know what a man is? Is not birth, beauty, good shape, discourse, man- 260 hood, learning, gentleness, virtue, youth, liberality, and such like, the spice and salt that season a man?

---

169 **forked** resembling a cuckold's horns (?)  179 **an** as if
181 **against** in advance of  187 **bravely** excellently  191
**brave** fine  198 **proper** handsome  201 **nod** play on *noddy*,
simpleton  203 **the . . . more** i.e., the fool shall become
more foolish

212 **take't . . . will** i.e., whoever cares to say otherwise
(so "lay on" and "take off" were common colloquial tags)
219 **gallant** general term of praise, like *brave*  242 **grace**
attendant goddess  255 **drayman** one who draws a cart  256
**camel** i.e., beast of burden

CRESSIDA   Ay, a minced° man; and then to be baked
with no date in the pie, for then the man's date is out.°
PANDARUS   You are such a woman a man knows not 265
at what ward° you lie.
CRESSIDA   Upon my back, to defend my belly; upon
my wit, to defend my wiles; upon my secrecy, to
defend mine honesty;° my mask, to defend my
beauty; and you, to defend all these. And at all these 270
wards I lie, at a thousand watches.°
PANDARUS   Say one of your watches.
CRESSIDA   Nay, I'll watch you for that; and that's one
of the chiefest of them too. If I cannot ward what I
would not have hit, I can watch you for telling° how 275
I took the blow; unless it swell past hiding,° and then
it's past watching.
PANDARUS   You are such another!

*Enter* [*Troilus'*] BOY.

BOY   Sir, my lord would instantly speak with you.
PANDARUS   Where?                                              280
BOY   At your own house. There he unarms him.
PANDARUS   Good boy, tell him I come. [*Exit* BOY.] I
doubt° he be hurt. Fare ye well, good niece.
CRESSIDA   Adieu, uncle.
PANDARUS   I will be with you, niece, by and by.      285
CRESSIDA   To bring,° uncle.
PANDARUS   Ay, a token from Troilus.
CRESSIDA   By the same token, you are a bawd.

*Exit* PANDARUS.

Words, vows, gifts, tears, and love's full sacrifice
He offers in another's enterprise;                            290
But more in Troilus thousandfold I see
Than in the glass of Pandar's praise may be.
Yet hold I off. Women are angels, wooing;°
Things won are done, joy's soul lies in the doing.
That she° beloved knows nought that knows not this: 295
Men prize the thing ungained more than it is;°
That she was never yet, that ever knew
Love got° so sweet as when desire did sue.
Therefore this maxim out of love° I teach:
Achievement is command; ungained, beseech.°      300
Then, though my heart's content firm love doth bear,
Nothing of that shall from mine eyes appear.   *Exit.*

[Scene III. *The Greek camp.*]

*Sennet.° Enter* AGAMEMNON, NESTOR, ULYSSES,
DIOMEDES, MENELAUS, *with others.*

**263 minced** (1) mincing, affected (2) overspiced (3) divided into
parts beyond recognition   **263–64 then to . . . out** dates
were a common ingredient in most pastries; Cressida's pun
implies that Troilus, as Pandarus compounds him, could
contain no substance and be of no interest, out of date
**266 ward** position of defense in swordplay   **269 honesty**
chastity   **271 watches** periods of the night   **275 watch . . .
telling** i.e., to make certain you do not tell   **276 swell past
hiding** Cressida thus completes her ribald play on words   **283
doubt** suspect that, fear that   **286 To bring** an idiomatic
intensifier, now obsolete, meaning roughly, "indeed" or
"with a vengeance"; Cressida says, with mild sarcasm, "yes,
I am sure you will," although Pandarus picks up the word in
its normal verbal sense   **293 wooing** while being wooed   **295
That she** that woman   **296 it is** its value   **298 got** i.e., by
men   **299 out of love** from love's teaching   **300 Achievement . . . beseech** when men achieve love, they command;
while still trying to gain it, they will beg
**I.iii.s.d. Sennet** a trumpet call announcing specific personages
in a procession

AGAMEMNON
Princes,
What grief hath set these jaundies° o'er your cheeks?
The ample proposition that hope makes
In all designs begun on earth below
Fails in the promised largeness. Checks and disasters   5
Grow in the veins of actions highest reared,
As knots, by the conflux° of meeting sap,
Infects the sound pine and diverts his grain
Tortive and errant° from his course of growth.
Nor, princes, is it matter new to us               10
That we come short of our suppose° so far
That after seven years' siege yet Troy walls stand;
Sith every action that hath gone before,
Whereof we have record, trial did draw
Bias and thwart,° not answering the aim         15
And that unbodied figure of the thought
That gave't surmisèd shape. Why then, you princes,
Do you with cheeks abashed° behold our works
And call them shames, which are indeed nought else
But the protractive° trials of great Jove          20
To find persistive constancy in men?
The fineness of which metal is not found
In Fortune's love; for then, the bold and coward,
The wise and fool, the artist° and unread,
The hard and soft, seem all affined° and kin.    25
But, in the wind and tempest of her frown,
Distinction, with a broad and powerful fan,
Puffing at all, winnows the light away,
And what hath mass or matter by itself
Lies rich in virtue and unmingled.°               30
NESTOR
With due observance of thy godlike seat,
Great Agamemnon, Nestor shall apply°
Thy latest words. In the reproof° of chance
Lies the true proof of men. The sea being smooth,
How many shallow bauble boats dare sail         35
Upon her patient breast, making their way
With those of nobler bulk?
But let the ruffian Boreas° once enrage
The gentle Thetis,° and anon behold
The strong-ribbed bark through liquid mountains
  cut,                                             40
Bounding between the two moist elements
Like Perseus' horse,° where's then the saucy boat,
Whose weak untimbered sides but even now
Corrivaled greatness? Either to harbor fled,
Or made a toast° for Neptune. Even so           45
Doth valor's show° and valor's worth divide
In storms of fortune. For in her ray and brightness
The herd hath more annoyance by the breese°
Than by the tiger; but when the splitting wind

**2 jaundies** jaundice (an obsolete plural)   **7 conflux** flowing
together   **9 Tortive and errant** twisted and wandering
**11 suppose** anticipation   **15 Bias and thwart** to one
side and crosswise   **18 cheeks abashed** faces turned aside
in confusion and shame   **20 protractive** extended   **24
artist** scholar   **25 affined** in affinity, related   **30 unmingled**
unmixed with other essences   **32 apply** show examples
of (as in a rhetorical exercise)   **33 reproof** rebuff   **38
Boreas** the north wind   **39 Thetis** a sea maiden, Achilles'
mother, but here personifying the sea   **42 Perseus' horse**
Pegasus, the winged horse   **45 toast** a piece of toast was usually
soaked in wine   **46 show** outward appearance   **48 breese**
gadfly

Makes flexible the knees of knotted oaks,                            50
And flies fled under shade, why then the thing of
    courage,
As roused with rage, with rage doth sympathize,°
And with an accent tuned in selfsame key
Returns° to chiding fortune.
ULYSSES                         Agamemnon,
Thou great commander, nerves° and bone of Greece,   55
Heart of our numbers, soul and only sprite,°
In whom the tempers and the minds of all
Should be shut up,° hear what Ulysses speaks.
Besides th' applause and approbation
The which [to AGAMEMNON], most mighty for thy
    place and sway,                                                  60

[to NESTOR]

And thou most reverend for thy stretched-out life,
I give to both your speeches—which were such
As Agamemnon and the hand of Greece
Should hold up high in brass; and such again
As venerable Nestor, hatched in silver,°                             65
Should with a bond of air, strong as the axletree
On which heaven rides, knit all the Greekish ears
To his experienced tongue—yet let it please both,
Thou great, and wise, to hear Ulysses speak.
AGAMEMNON
Speak, Prince of Ithaca; and be't of less expect     70
That matter needless, of importless burden,
Divide thy lips than we are confident,
When rank Thersites opes his mastic° jaws,
We shall hear music, wit, and oracle.
ULYSSES
Troy, yet upon his basis, had been down,             75
And the great Hector's sword had lacked a master,
But for these instances.°
The specialty of rule° hath been neglected;
And look, how many Grecian tents do stand
Hollow upon this plain, so many hollow factions.    80
When that the general is not like the hive
To whom the foragers shall all repair,
What honey is expected?° Degree being vizarded°
Th' unworthiest shows as fairly in the mask.
The heavens themselves, the planets, and this center  85
Observe degree, priority, and place,
Insisture,° course, proportion, season, form,
Office, and custom, in all line of order.
And therefore is the glorious planet Sol°
In noble eminence enthroned and sphered             90
Amidst the other;° whose med'cinable eye
Corrects the influence° of evil planets,
And posts, like the commandment of a king,

Sans check, to good and bad. But when the planets
In evil mixture° to disorder wander,                95
What plagues, and what portents, what mutiny,
What raging of the sea, shaking of earth,
Commotion in the winds, frights, changes, horrors,
Divert and crack, rend and deracinate°
The unity and married calm of states                100
Quite from their fixure? O, when degree is shaked,
Which is the ladder of all high designs,
The enterprise is sick. How could communities,
Degrees in schools, and brotherhoods in cities,
Peaceful commerce from dividable shores,             105
The primogenity° and due of birth,
Prerogative of age, crowns, scepters, laurels,
But by degree, stand in authentic place?
Take but degree away, untune that string,
And hark what discord follows. Each thing meets      110
In mere oppugnancy.° The bounded waters
Should lift their bosoms higher than the shores
And make a sop° of all this solid globe;
Strength should be lord of imbecility,°
And the rude son should strike his father dead;      115
Force should be right, or rather right and wrong—
Between whose endless jar° justice resides—
Should lose their names, and so should justice too.
Then everything include itself in power,°
Power into will, will into appetite,                 120
And appetite, an universal wolf,
So doubly seconded with will and power,
Must make perforce an universal prey
And last eat up himself. Great Agamemnon,
This chaos, when degree is suffocate,                125
Follows the choking.
And this neglection of degree it is
That by a pace goes backward with a purpose
It hath to climb.° The general's disdained
By him one step below, he by the next,               130
That next by him beneath; so every step,
Exampled by the first pace that is sick
Of his superior, grows to an envious fever
Of pale and bloodless emulation;°
And 'tis this fever that keeps Troy on foot,         135
Not her own sinews. To end a tale of length,
Troy in our weakness stands, not in her strength.
NESTOR
Most wisely hath Ulysses here discovered
The fever whereof all our power is sick.
AGAMEMNON
The nature of the sickness found, Ulysses,           140
What is the remedy?
ULYSSES
The great Achilles, whom opinion crowns
The sinew and the forehand of our host,
Having his ear full of his airy fame,
Grows dainty of° his worth, and in his tent          145

52 **sympathize** becomes similar to   54 **Returns** replies
55 **nerves** sinews   56 **sprite** spirit   58 **shut up** gathered in
65 **hatched in silver** referring to the silver lines in his hair
73 **mastic** abusive, scourging (sometimes emended to "mas-
tiff")   77 **instances** reasons   78 **The . . . rule** the particular
organization of ruling, the distinction of rights in a chain of
authority   81–83 **When . . . expected** When the endeavors
of the general populace are not similar to those of the agent
which rules them, and to which they are responsible, what
profit can be expected? (?) When the ruling general is dissimilar
in kind to the soldiers in his army, what profit, etc. (?)   83
**Degree being vizarded** the hierarchy of authority being
hidden   87 **Insisture** regularity of position   89 **Sol** the sun
91 **other** others   92 **influence** astrological effect

95 **evil mixture** unlucky or malignant relationship (astrological)   99 **deracinate** uproot   106 **primogenity** right of
the eldest son to succeed to his father's estate   111 **mere
oppugnancy** total strife   113 **sop** pulp   114 **imbecility**
weakness   117 **jar** discord   119 **include . . . power** enclose
itself within power, i.e., become power   127–29 **And . . .
climb** this neglect of hierarchy causes a step toward disintegration each time an attempt is made to climb upward   134
**emulation** rivalry   145 **dainty of** finicky about

Lies mocking our designs. With him Patroclus
Upon a lazy bed the livelong day
Breaks scurril jests,
And with ridiculous and silly action
(Which, slanderer, he imitation° calls)                                   150
He pageants° us. Sometimes, great Agamemnon,
Thy topless deputation° he puts on,
And, like a strutting player, whose conceit
Lies in his hamstring,° and doth think it rich
To hear the wooden dialogue° and sound                                    155
'Twixt his stretched footing° and the scaffoldage,°
Such to-be-pitied and o'erwrested seeming°
He acts thy greatness in; and when he speaks,
'Tis like a chime a-mending,° with terms unsquared,°
Which, from the tongue of roaring Typhon° dropped,                        160
Would seem hyperboles. At this fusty° stuff
The large Achilles, on his pressed bed lolling,
From his deep chest laughs out a loud applause,
Cries, "Excellent! 'tis Agamemnon right.
Now play me Nestor; hem, and stroke thy beard,                            165
As he being drest° to some oration."
That's done, as near as the extremest ends
Of parallels, as like as Vulcan and his wife,°
Yet god Achilles still cries, "Excellent!
'Tis Nestor right. Now play him me,° Patroclus,                           170
Arming to answer in a night alarm."
And then, forsooth, the faint defects of age
Must be the scene of mirth; to cough and spit,
And with a palsy fumbling on his gorget,°
Shake in and out the rivet. And at this sport                             175
Sir Valor dies; cries, "O, enough, Patroclus,
Or give me ribs of steel; I shall split all
In pleasure of my spleen!"° And in this fashion
All our abilities, gifts, natures, shapes,
Severals and generals° of grace exact,                                    180
Achievements, plots, orders, preventions,
Excitements to the field or speech for truce,
Success or loss, what is or is not, serves
As stuff for these two to make paradoxes.°

**NESTOR**
And in the imitation of these twain,                                      185
Who, as Ulysses says, opinion crowns
With an imperial voice, many are infect.
Ajax is grown self-willed, and bears his head
In such a rein,° in full as proud a place
As broad Achilles; keeps his tent like him;                              190

Makes factious feasts; rails on our state of war,
Bold as an oracle, and sets Thersites,
A slave whose gall° coins slanders like a mint,
To match us in comparisons with dirt,
To weaken and discredit our exposure,                                     195
How rank° soever rounded in with danger.

**ULYSSES**
They tax° our policy and call it cowardice,
Count wisdom as no member of the war,
Forestall prescience,° and esteem no act
But that of hand. The still and mental parts                              200
That do contrive how many hands shall strike
When fitness° calls them on, and know by measure
Of their observant toil the enemies' weight—
Why, this hath not a finger's dignity.
They call this bed-work, mapp'ry,° closet war;                            205
So that the ram that batters down the wall,
For the great swinge° and rudeness of his poise,
They place before his hand that made the engine,
Or those that with the fineness of their souls
By reason guide his execution.                                            210

**NESTOR**
Let this be granted, and Achilles' horse°
Makes many Thetis' sons.

*Tucket.*°

**AGAMEMNON**
What trumpet? Look, Menelaus.

**MENELAUS**   From Troy.

*Enter* AENEAS.

**AGAMEMNON**
What would you 'fore our tent?                                            215

**AENEAS**
Is this great Agamemnon's tent, I pray you?

**AGAMEMNON**
Even this.

**AENEAS**
May one that is a herald and a prince
Do a fair message to his kingly eyes?°

**AGAMEMNON**
With surety stronger than Achilles' arm                                   220
'Fore all the Greekish heads, which with one voice
Call Agamemnon head and general.

**AENEAS**
Fair leave and large security. How may
A stranger to those most imperial looks
Know them from eyes of other mortals?

**AGAMEMNON**                                     How?                     225

**AENEAS**
Ay.
I ask, that I might waken reverence,
And bid the cheek be ready with a blush
Modest as morning when she coldly eyes
The youthful Phoebus.°                                                    230

---

149–50 silly . . . imitation Ulysses contrasts such charades
with true imitation to the life, presumably the goal of the
excellent actor  151 pageants mimics  152 topless deputation unlimited office  153–54 conceit . . . hamstring imagination lies in the tendon of his leg  155 wooden dialogue the
thumps of heavy footfalls on the wooden stage floor  156
stretched footing absurdly long strides; scaffoldage scaffold,
stage  157 o'erwrested seeming overstrained impersonation
159 chime a-mending (1) chime being repaired (2) dissonant
combination of sounds just following the ringing of many
chimes (?); unsquared inappropriate  160 roaring Typhon a
monster with serpents' heads and a tremendous voice  161 fusty
stale, second-rate  166 drest carefully prepared for, addressed
168 Vulcan . . . wife Vulcan, god of the smithy and forge,
was depicted as sooty, and was lame besides; his "wife" was
Venus, who cuckolded him with Mars  170 me for me  174
gorget throat armor  178 spleen supposed the seat of the
emotions of anger and hilarity  180 Severals and generals
individual and general qualities  184 paradoxes absurdities
189 In . . . rein so high

193 gall the source of bile, which was thought to produce
rancor and abuse  196 rank densely, abundantly  197 tax
criticize  199 Forestall prescience discount foresight  202
fitness readiness  205 mapp'ry map work  207 swinge
impetus, whirling force  211 Achilles' horse either literally,
or collectively, for his soldiers, the Myrmidons  212 s.d.
Tucket trumpet call  219 to . . . eyes in his presence  230
Phoebus Phoebus Apollo (the sun god)

Which is that god in office, guiding men?
Which is the high and mighty Agamemnon?

AGAMEMNON
This Troyan scorns us, or the men of Troy
Are ceremonious courtiers.

AENEAS
Courtiers as free, as debonair, unarmed,    235
As bending° angels; that's their fame in peace.
But when they would seem soldiers, they have galls,
Good arms, strong joints, true swords—and, great
    Jove's accord,°
Nothing so full of heart. But peace, Aeneas;
Peace, Troyan; lay thy finger on thy lips.    240
The worthiness of praise distains° his worth,
If that the praised himself bring the praise forth.
But what the repining enemy commends,
That breath fame blows; that praise, sole pure,
    transcends.

AGAMEMNON
Sir, you of Troy, call you yourself Aeneas?    245

AENEAS
Ay, Greek, that is my name.

AGAMEMNON
What's your affair, I pray you?

AENEAS
Sir, pardon; 'tis for Agamemnon's ears.

AGAMEMNON
He hears nought privately that comes from Troy.

AENEAS
Nor I from Troy come not to whisper him.    250
I bring a trumpet to awake his ear,
To set his seat on the attentive bent,°
And then to speak.

AGAMEMNON      Speak frankly as the wind;
It is not Agamemnon's sleeping hour.
That thou shalt know, Troyan, he is awake,    255
He tells thee so himself.

AENEAS            Trumpet, blow loud,
Send thy brass voice through all these lazy tents;
And every Greek of mettle, let him know,
What Troy means fairly shall be spoke aloud.

*Sound trumpet.*

We have, great Agamemnon, here in Troy    260
A prince called Hector—Priam is his father—
Who in this dull and long-continued truce
Is rusty grown. He bade me take a trumpet,°
And to this purpose speak: kings, princes, lords,
If there be one among the fair'st of Greece    265
That holds his honor higher than his ease,
That seeks his praise more than he fears his peril,
That knows his valor and knows not his fear,
That loves his mistress more than in confession
With truant vows to her own lips he loves,°    270
And dare avow her beauty and her worth
In other arms than hers°—to him this challenge;

Hector, in view of Troyans and of Greeks,
Shall make it good, or do his best to do it;
He hath a lady wiser, fairer, truer,    275
Than ever Greek did compass in his arms;
And will tomorrow with his trumpet call,
Midway between your tents and walls of Troy,
To rouse a Grecian that is true in love.
If any come, Hector shall honor him;    280
If none, he'll say in Troy when he retires,
The Grecian dames are sunburnt° and not worth
The splinter of a lance. Even so much.

AGAMEMNON
This shall be told our lovers, Lord Aeneas;
If none of them have soul in such a kind,    285
We left them all at home. But we are soldiers;
And may that soldier a mere recreant prove,
That means not, hath not, or is not in love!
If then one is, or hath, or means to be,
That one meets Hector; if none else, I am he.    290

NESTOR
Tell him of Nestor, one that was a man
When Hector's grandsire sucked. He is old now,
But if there be not in our Grecian host
A nobleman that hath one spark of fire
To answer for his love, tell him from me,    295
I'll hide my silver beard in a gold beaver,°
And in my vantbrace° put my withered brawns,°
And, meeting him, will tell him that my lady
Was fairer than his grandam, and as chaste
As may be in the world. His youth in flood,    300
I'll prove this truth with my three drops of blood.

AENEAS
Now heavens forfend such scarcity of youth!

ULYSSES   Amen.

[AGAMEMNON]
Fair Lord Aeneas, let me touch your hand;
To our pavilion shall I lead you first.    305
Achilles shall have word of this intent;
So shall each lord of Greece, from tent to tent.
Yourself shall feast with us before you go,
And find the welcome of a noble foe.
            *Exeunt. Manent°* ULYSSES *and* NESTOR.

ULYSSES   Nestor.    310

NESTOR
What says Ulysses?

ULYSSES
I have a young conception in my brain;
Be you my time to bring it to some shape.°

NESTOR   What is't?

ULYSSES
This 'tis:    315
Blunt wedges rive hard knots; the seeded pride
That hath to this maturity blown up
In rank Achilles, must or now be cropped
Or, shedding,° breed a nursery of like evil
To overbulk us all.    320

NESTOR          Well, and how?

---

**236 bending** bowing   **238 Jove's accord** with Jove on their side   **241 distains** sullies   **252 To . . . bent** to make him, and his place of government, pay attention   **263 trumpet** a trumpeter in attendance   **269–70 That . . . loves** one that loves his mistress even more than the false oaths of lip service (?) more than enough to swear false vows that he loves her (?)   **272 In . . . hers** i.e., with weapons

**282 sunburnt** dark (for the Elizabethans, ugly)   **296 beaver** movable face guard of a helmet   **297 vantbrace** armor fitting the forearm; **brawns** arm (or leg) muscles (an obsolete plural)   **309 s.d. Manent** (they) remain   **312–13 I . . . shape** i.e., I have the beginning of an idea; let me develop it as you listen   **319 shedding** i.e., scattering seed

ULYSSES
This challenge that the gallant Hector sends,
However it is spread in general name,
Relates in purpose only to Achilles.

NESTOR
True, the purpose is perspicuous as substance
Whose grossness little characters sum up;°        325
And, in the publication, make no strain°
But that Achilles, were his brain as barren
As banks of Libya—though, Apollo knows,
'Tis dry enough—will with great speed of judgment,
Ay with celerity, find Hector's purpose        330
Pointing on him.

ULYSSES
And wake him to the answer, think you?

NESTOR
Why, 'tis most meet. Who may you else oppose
That can from Hector bring his honor off,
If not Achilles? Though't be a sportful combat,        335
Yet in the trial much opinion° dwells;
For here the Trojans taste our dear'st repute
With their fin'st palate;° and trust to me, Ulysses,
Our imputation shall be oddly poised
In this vild action.° For the success,        340
Although particular, shall give a scantling°
Of good or bad unto the general;°
And in such indexes, although small pricks
To their subsequent volumes,° there is seen
The baby figure of the giant mass        345
Of things to come at large. It is supposed
He that meets Hector issues from our choice;
And choice, being mutual act of all our souls,
Makes merit her election,° and doth boil,
As 'twere from forth us all, a man distilled        350
Out of our virtues—who miscarrying,
What heart receives from hence a conquering part,
To steel a strong opinion to themselves;
Which entertained, limbs are his° instruments,
In no less working than are swords and bows        355
Directive by the limbs.

ULYSSES
Give pardon to my speech. Therefore 'tis meet
Achilles meet not Hector. Let us, like merchants,
First show foul wares, and think perchance they'll sell;
If not, the luster of the better shall exceed        360
By showing the worse first. Do not consent
That ever Hector and Achilles meet;
For both our honor and our shame in this
Are dogged with two strange followers.°

NESTOR
I see them not with my old eyes; what are they?        365

ULYSSES
What glory our Achilles shares from Hector,
Were he not proud, we all should share with him.

But he already is too insolent,
And it were better parch in Afric sun
Than in the pride and salt° scorn of his eyes,        370
Should he 'scape Hector fair. If he were foiled,
Why then we do our main opinion° crush
In taint of° our best man. No, make a lott'ry;
And by device let blockish Ajax draw
The sort° to fight with Hector; among ourselves        375
Give him allowance for the better man,
For that will physic the great Myrmidon°
Who broils° in loud applause, and make him fall
His crest that prouder than blue Iris° bends.
If the dull brainless Ajax comes safe off,        380
We'll dress him up in voices; if he fail,
Yet go we under our opinion still
That we have better men. But, hit or miss,
Our project's life this shape of sense assumes:
Ajax employed plucks down Achilles' plumes.        385

NESTOR
Now, Ulysses, I begin to relish thy advice,
And I will give a taste thereof forthwith
To Agamemnon. Go we to him straight.
Two curs shall tame each other; pride alone
Must tarre° the mastiffs on, as 'twere a bone.    *Exeunt.*  390

# [ A C T   I I ]

### [Scene I. *The Greek camp.*]

*Enter* AJAX *and* THERSITES.

AJAX   Thersites!

THERSITES   Agamemnon, how if he had boils—full,
all over, generally?

AJAX   Thersites!

THERSITES   And those boils did run?—say so—did        5
not the general run then? Were not that a botchy core?°

AJAX   Dog!

THERSITES   Then would come some matter from him.
I see none now.

AJAX   Thou bitch-wolf's son, canst thou not hear?        10
Feel then.

*Strikes him.*

THERSITES   The plague of Greece upon thee, thou
mongrel beef-witted lord!

AJAX   Speak then, thou vinewed'st leaven,° speak. I
will beat thee into handsomeness.        15

THERSITES   I shall sooner rail thee into wit and holiness; but I think thy horse will sooner con° an oration
than thou learn a prayer without book.° Thou canst
strike, canst thou? A red murrain° o' thy jade's° tricks!

---

**325 Whose . . . up** whose large size can be defined by
small figures   **326 make no strain** you may be sure
**336 opinion** reputation   **337–38 taste . . . palate** put our
most valued reputation to the test of their most careful, sensitive observation   **339–40 Our . . . action** Our reputation
shall be unequally balanced in this trivial action   **341 scantling**
sample   **342 general** (1) general view (2) entire army   **343–44
small . . . volumes** small markings compared to the great
significance to follow   **349 election** criteria for choice   **354 his**
i.e., of the strong opinion   **364 followers** consequences

**370 salt** bitter   **372 our main opinion** the mainstay of our
reputation   **373 In taint of** to the loss of, with the shame of
**375 sort** lot   **377 the great Myrmidon** Achilles, whose
father, Peleus, had subjects called Myrmidons   **378 broils**
bakes; i.e., suns himself   **379 Iris** the rainbow   **390 tarre** incite,
provoke
**II.i.6 botchy core** erupted boil   **14 vinewed'st leaven** most
mildewed dough   **17 con** memorize   **18 without book** by
heart   **19 red murrain** form of plague manifested in red
skin eruptions; **jade's** nag's

AJAX  Toadstool, learn me° the proclamation.                    20

THERSITES  Dost thou think I have no sense, thou strikest me thus?

AJAX  The proclamation!

THERSITES  Thou art proclaimed fool, I think.

AJAX  Do not, porpentine,° do not; my fingers itch.    25

THERSITES  I would thou didst itch from head to foot; an I had the scratching of thee, I would make thee the loathsomest scab in Greece. When thou art forth in the incursions,° thou strikest as slow as another.

AJAX  I say, the proclamation!                    30

THERSITES  Thou grumblest and railest every hour on Achilles, and thou art as full of envy at his greatness as Cerberus° is at Proserpina's° beauty, ay, that thou bark'st at him.

AJAX  Mistress Thersites!                    35

THERSITES  Thou shouldst strike him.

AJAX  Cobloaf!°

THERSITES  He would pun° thee into shivers with his fist, as a sailor breaks a biscuit.

AJAX  You whoreson cur!                    40

[*Beating him.*]

THERSITES  Do, do.

AJAX  Thou stool for a witch!

THERSITES  Ay, do, do, thou sodden-witted lord! thou hast no more brain than I have in mine elbows; an asinico° may tutor thee. Thou scurvy-valiant ass,    45 thou art here but to thrash Troyans, and thou art bought and sold° among those of any wit like a barbarian slave. If thou use to beat me, I will begin at thy heel, and tell what thou art by inches, thou thing of no bowels,° thou!                    50

AJAX  You dog!

THERSITES  You scurvy lord!

AJAX  You cur!

[*Beating him.*]

THERSITES  Mars his° idiot! Do, rudeness; do, camel; do, do.                    55

*Enter* ACHILLES *and* PATROCLUS.

ACHILLES  Why, how now, Ajax, wherefore do you thus? How now, Thersites, what's the matter, man?

THERSITES  You see him there? Do you?

ACHILLES  Ay, what's the matter?

THERSITES  Nay, look upon him.                    60

ACHILLES  So I do. What's the matter?

THERSITES  Nay, but regard him well.

ACHILLES  "Well"—why so I do.

THERSITES  But yet you look not well upon him; for, whosomever° you take him to be, he is Ajax.    65

ACHILLES  I know that, fool.

THERSITES  Ay, but that fool° knows not himself.

AJAX  Therefore I beat thee.

THERSITES  Lo, lo, lo, lo, what modicums of wit he utters! His evasions have ears thus long.° I have    70 bobbed his brain more than he has beat my bones. I will buy nine sparrows for a penny, and his pia mater° is not worth the ninth part of a sparrow. This lord, Achilles, Ajax, who wears his wit in his belly and his guts in his head, I'll tell you what I say of him.    75

ACHILLES  What?

THERSITES  I say, this Ajax—

[AJAX *threatens to strike him.*]

ACHILLES  Nay, good Ajax.

THERSITES  Has not so much wit—

[AJAX *threatens again to strike him.*]

ACHILLES  Nay, I must hold you.                    80

THERSITES  As will stop the eye of Helen's needle, for whom he comes to fight.

ACHILLES  Peace, fool!

THERSITES  I would have peace and quietness, but the fool will not—he there, that he. Look you there.    85

AJAX  O thou damned cur, I shall—

ACHILLES  Will you set° your wit to a fool's?

THERSITES  No, I warrant you; the fool's will shame it.

PATROCLUS  Good words, Thersites.

ACHILLES  What's the quarrel?                    90

AJAX  I bade the vile owl go learn me the tenor of the proclamation, and he rails upon me.

THERSITES  I serve thee not.

AJAX  Well, go to, go to.

THERSITES  I serve here voluntary.                    95

ACHILLES  Your last service was suff'rance, 'twas not voluntary; no man is beaten voluntary. Ajax was here the voluntary, and you as under an impress.°

THERSITES  E'en so. A great deal of your wit, too, lies in your sinews, or else there be liars. Hector shall have    100 a great catch if he knock out either of your brains. 'A were as good crack a fusty nut with no kernel.

ACHILLES  What, with me too, Thersites?

THERSITES  There's Ulysses and old Nestor, whose wit was moldy ere your grandsires had nails on their    105 toes, yoke you like draft oxen and make you plow up the wars.

ACHILLES  What, what?

THERSITES  Yes, good sooth. To, Achilles! To, Ajax! To—°                    110

AJAX  I shall cut out your tongue.

THERSITES  'Tis no matter, I shall speak as much as thou afterwards.

PATROCLUS  No more words, Thersites; peace!

THERSITES  I will hold my peace when Achilles'    115 brach° bids me, shall I?

ACHILLES  There's for you, Patroclus.

THERSITES  I will see you hanged like clotpoles,° ere I come any more to your tents. I will keep where there is wit stirring and leave the faction of fools.    *Exit.*    120

PATROCLUS  A good riddance.

---

**20 learn me** find out for me  **25 porpentine** porcupine  **29 incursions** battle raids, attacks  **33 Cerberus** the monstrous watchdog of Hades;  **Proserpina** a beautiful goddess carried off by Pluto to the underworld  **37 Cobloaf** a badly baked, crusty loaf of bread  **38 pun** pound  **45 asinico** ass, simpleton  **47 bought and sold** made fun of  **50 bowels** mercy (the bowels were thought to be the source of compassion)  **54 Mars his** Mars's  **65 whosomever** whomsoever  **67 that fool** as though Achilles had said, "I know that fool"

**70 thus long** as long as those of an ass  **72 pia mater** brain (literally, the membrane covering the brain)  **87 set** match  **98 impress** pun on impressment, compulsory military service  **109–10 To, Achilles . . . To** imitation of the shouts of a driver, urging on his horses  **116 brach** bitch  **118 clotpoles** blockheads

ACHILLES
Marry, this, sir, is proclaimed through all our host:
That Hector, by the fifth hour° of the sun,
Will, with a trumpet, 'twixt our tents and Troy
Tomorrow morning call some knight to arms    125
That hath a stomach,° and such a one that dare
Maintain—I know not what; 'tis trash. Farewell.

AJAX
Farewell? Who shall answer him?

ACHILLES
I know not. 'Tis put to lott'ry. Otherwise,
He knew his man.    130
                    [*Exeunt* ACHILLES *and* PATROCLUS.]

AJAX
O, meaning you? I will go learn more of it.    *Exit.*


[Scene II. *Troy; Priam's palace.*]

*Enter* PRIAM, HECTOR, TROILUS, PARIS, *and*
HELENUS.

PRIAM
After so many hours, lives, speeches spent,
Thus once again says Nestor from the Greeks:
"Deliver Helen, and all damage else,
As honor, loss of time, travail, expense,
Wounds, friends, and what else dear that is consumed  5
In hot digestion of this cormorant° war,
Shall be struck off." Hector, what say you to't?

HECTOR
Though no man lesser fears the Greeks than I,
As far as toucheth my particular,°
Yet, dread Priam,    10
There is no lady of more softer bowels,°
More spongy to suck in the sense of fear,
More ready to cry out, "Who knows what follows?"
Than Hector is. The wound of peace is surety,°
Surety secure; but modest doubt is called    15
The beacon of the wise, the tent° that searches
To the bottom of the worst. Let Helen go.
Since the first sword was drawn about this question,
Every tithe soul, 'mongst many thousand dismes,°
Hath been as dear as Helen. I mean, of ours.    20
If we have lost so many tenths of ours
To guard a thing not ours nor worth to us,
Had it our name, the value of one ten,°
What merit's in that reason which denies
The yielding of her up?

TROILUS    Fie, fie, my brother!    25
Weigh you the worth and honor of a king
So great as our dread father in a scale
Of common ounces? Will you with counters° sum
The past proportion of his infinite,°

And buckle in a waist most fathomless°    30
With spans° and inches so diminutive
As fears and reasons? Fie, for godly shame!

HELENUS
No marvel, though you bite so sharp at reasons,
You are so empty of them. Should not our father
Bear the great sway of his affairs with reason,    35
Because your speech hath none that tell him so?

TROILUS
You are for dreams and slumbers, brother priest;
You fur your gloves with reason.° Here are your
    reasons:
You know an enemy intends you harm;
You know a sword employed is perilous,    40
And reason flies the object° of all harm.
Who marvels then, when Helenus beholds
A Grecian and his sword, if he do set
The very wings of reason to his heels
And fly like chidden Mercury from Jove,    45
Or like a star disorbed?° Nay, if we talk of reason,
Let's shut our gates and sleep! Manhood and honor
Should have hare-hearts, would they but fat their
    thoughts
With this crammed° reason. Reason and respect
Make livers° pale and lustihood deject.    50

HECTOR
Brother, she is not worth what she doth cost
The keeping.

TROILUS    What's aught but as 'tis valued?

HECTOR
But value dwells not in particular will.°
It holds his° estimate and dignity°
As well wherein 'tis precious of itself    55
As in the prizer.° 'Tis mad idolatry
To make the service greater than the god;
And the will dotes that is attributive°
To what infectiously itself affects,
Without some image of th' affected merit.°    60

TROILUS
I take today a wife, and my election
Is led on in the conduct of my will—°
My will enkindled by mine eyes and ears,
Two traded° pilots 'twixt the dangerous shores
Of will·and judgment. How may I avoid,    65
Although my will distaste what it elected,
The wife I chose? There can be no evasion
To blench° from this and to stand firm by honor.
We turn not back the silks upon the merchant
When we have soiled them, nor the remainder
    viands    70

123 **fifth hour** eleven in the morning  126 **stomach** temperament or relish (here, for chivalric achievement)
II.ii.6 **cormorant** ravenous, rapacious  9 **my particular** me, personally  11 **of . . . bowels** more averse to violence  14 **The . . . surety** peace is endangered by a sense of safety  16 **tent** roll of absorbent material, for cleaning or probing wounds  19 **Every . . . dismes** every tenth soul, among many thousand tens (?) every soul taken by war as its tenth among many thousand such tenths (?)  23 **one ten** one in ten  28 **counters** pieces of worthless metal used for computation  29 **The . . . infinite** his infinite greatness which is past all measurement

30 **fathomless** immeasurable  31 **spans** units of measure averaging nine inches  38 **You . . . reason** You use reason as a comfortable word with which to decorate your speech, much as fur lines gloves  41 **object** here, presentation, sight  46 **disorbed** thrown from its sphere  49 **crammed** filled to excess, doughy  50 **livers** thought to be the seats of passions  53 **particular will** the individual's inclination  54 **his** its; **dignity** value  56 **prizer** appraiser  58 **attributive** dependent, subservient  59–60 **To . . . merit** to what it, to its own infection, desires, with no objective perception of the worth of the thing desired  61–62 **I . . . will** Troilus is setting forth, rhetorically, an example to prove his point; whatever he may be thinking, he is not announcing, of course, his approaching liaison with Cressida  64 **traded** experienced  68 **blench** shrink

We do not throw in unrespective sieve°
Because we now are full. It was thought meet
Paris should do some vengeance on the Greeks.
Your breath with full consent bellied his sails;
The seas and winds, old wranglers, took a truce        75
And did him service; he touched the ports desired,
And for an old aunt° whom the Greeks held captive
He brought a Grecian queen, whose youth and fresh-
    ness
Wrinkles Apollo's and makes pale the morning.
Why keep we her? The Grecians keep our aunt.        80
Is she worth keeping? Why, she is a pearl
Whose price hath launched above a thousand ships
And turned crowned kings to merchants.
If you'll avouch 'twas wisdom Paris went—
As you must needs, for you all cried, "Go, go"—        85
If you'll confess he brought home worthy prize—
As you must needs, for you all clapped your hands
And cried, "Inestimable!"—why do you now
The issue of your proper wisdoms rate,°
And do a deed that never Fortune did:        90
Beggar the estimation° which you prized
Richer than sea and land? O theft most base,
That we have stol'n what we do fear to keep!
But thieves unworthy of a thing so stol'n,
That in their country did them that disgrace°        95
We fear to warrant° in our native place.

*Enter* CASSANDRA *raving, with her hair about her ears.*

CASSANDRA
    Cry, Troyans, cry!
PRIAM                What noise? What shriek is this?
TROILUS
    'Tis our mad sister.° I do know her voice.
CASSANDRA    Cry, Troyans!
HECTOR    It is Cassandra.        100
CASSANDRA
    Cry, Troyans, cry! Lend me ten thousand eyes,
    And I will fill them with prophetic tears.
HECTOR
    Peace, sister, peace!
CASSANDRA
    Virgins and boys, mid-age and wrinkled eld,
    Soft infancy, that nothing canst but cry,        105
    Add to my clamors! Let us pay betimes
    A moiety° of that mass of moan to come.
    Cry, Troyans, cry! Practice your eyes with tears!
    Troy must not be, nor goodly Ilion stand;
    Our firebrand° brother, Paris, burns us all.        110
    Cry, Troyans, cry! A Helen and a woe!
    Cry, cry! Troy burns, or else let Helen go.    *Exit.*
HECTOR
    Now, youthful Troilus, do not these high strains
    Of divination in our sister work

Some touches of remorse? Or is your blood        115
So madly hot that no discourse of reason,
Nor fear of bad success in a bad cause,
Can qualify° the same?
TROILUS                Why, brother Hector,
We may not think the justness of each act
Such and no other than event° doth form it,        120
Nor once deject the courage of our minds
Because Cassandra's mad. Her brainsick raptures°
Cannot distaste° the goodness of a quarrel
Which hath our several honors all engaged
To make it gracious. For my private part,        125
I am no more touched than all Priam's sons;
And Jove forbid there should be done amongst us
Such things as might offend the weakest spleen°
To fight for and maintain.
PARIS
Else might the world convince° of levity        130
As well my undertakings as your counsels;
But I attest the gods, your full consent
Gave wings to my propension° and cut off
All fears attending on so dire a project.
For what, alas, can these my single arms?        135
What propugnation° is in one man's valor
To stand the push and enmity of those
This quarrel would excite? Yet, I protest,
Were I alone to pass° the difficulties,
And had as ample power as I have will,        140
Paris should ne'er retract what he hath done
Nor faint in the pursuit.
PRIAM                Paris, you speak
Like one besotted on your sweet delights.
You have the honey still, but these the gall;
So to be valiant is no praise at all.        145
PARIS
Sir, I propose not merely to myself
The pleasure such a beauty brings with it;
But I would have the soil of her fair rape°
Wiped off in honorable keeping her.
What treason were it to the ransacked° queen,        150
Disgrace to your great worths, and shame to me,
Now to deliver her possession up
On terms of base compulsion! Can it be
That so degenerate a strain as this
Should once set footing in your generous° bosoms?        155
There's not the meanest spirit on our party
Without a heart to dare or sword to draw
When Helen is defended, nor none so noble
Whose life were ill bestowed or death unfamed
Where Helen is the subject. Then, I say,        160
Well may we fight for her whom we know well
The world's large spaces cannot parallel.
HECTOR
Paris and Troilus, you have both said well,
And on the cause and question now in hand
Have glozed°—but superficially: not much        165

---

71 **unrespective sieve** common receptacle   77 **aunt** Hesione, Priam's sister and Ajax's mother, married to Telamon; another son was Teucer, greatest archer among the Greeks   89 **The . . . rate** condemn the result of your own judgments   91 **estimation** thing esteemed   95 **disgrace** i.e., the abduction of Helen   96 **warrant** justify by defense   98 **our mad sister** when Cassandra refused Apollo's love, he destroyed his earlier gift to her of prophecy by causing her never to be believed   107 **moiety** part   110 **firebrand** Hecuba dreamed she was delivered of a firebrand when Paris was born

118 **qualify** moderate   120 **event** outcome   122 **brainsick raptures** fits of prophecy   123 **distaste** make distasteful   128 **spleen** temper, temperament   130 **convince** convict   133 **propension** inclination   136 **propugnation** defense   139 **pass** suffer, undergo   148 **rape** carrying off   150 **ransacked** carried off   155 **generous** nobly born (therefore magnanimous)   165 **glozed** commented, glossed

Unlike young men, whom Aristotle thought
Unfit to hear moral° philosophy.
The reasons you allege do more conduce
To the hot passion of distempered blood
Than to make up a free determination                    170
'Twixt right and wrong; for pleasure and revenge
Have ears more deaf than adders° to the voice
Of any true decision. Nature craves
All dues be rendered to their owners. Now,
What nearer debt in all humanity                        175
Than wife is to the husband? If this law
Of nature be corrupted through affection,°
And that great minds, of partial° indulgence
To their benumbèd° wills, resist the same,
There is a law in each well-ordered nation              180
To curb those raging appetites that are
Most disobedient and refractory.
If Helen, then, be wife to Sparta's king,
As it is known she is, these moral laws
Of nature and of nations speak aloud                    185
To have her back returned. Thus to persist
In doing wrong extenuates° not wrong,
But makes it much more heavy. Hector's opinion
Is this in way of truth. Yet ne'ertheless,
My spritely° brethren, I propend° to you                190
In resolution to keep Helen still;
For 'tis a cause that hath no mean dependence
Upon our joint and several° dignities.

TROILUS
Why, there you touched the life of our design!
Were it not glory that we more affected                 195
Than the performance of our heaving spleens,°
I would not wish a drop of Troyan blood
Spent more in her defense. But, worthy Hector,
She is a theme of honor and renown,
A spur to valiant and magnanimous deeds,                200
Whose present courage may beat down our foes
And fame in time to come canonize us;
For I presume brave Hector would not lose
So rich advantage of a promised glory
As smiles upon the forehead of this action             205
For the wide world's revenue.

HECTOR                            I am yours,
You valiant offspring of great Priamus.
I have a roisting° challenge sent amongst
The dull and factious nobles of the Greeks
Will strike amazement to their drowsy spirits.          210
I was advertisèd° their great general slept
Whilst emulation° in the army crept;
This, I presume, will wake him.            *Exeunt.*

[Scene III. *The Greek camp; near Achilles' tent.*]

*Enter* THERSITES *solus.*

THERSITES  How now, Thersites? What, lost in the
labyrinth of thy fury? Shall the elephant Ajax carry it°
thus? He beats me, and I rail at him. O worthy satisfaction! Would it were otherwise—that I could beat
him, whilst he railed at me. 'Sfoot,° I'll learn to conjure  5
and raise devils, but I'll see° some issue of my spiteful
execrations. Then there's Achilles, a rare enginer.° If
Troy be not taken till these two undermine it, the
walls will stand till they fall of themselves. O thou
great thunder-darter of Olympus, forget that thou art  10
Jove, the king of gods; and, Mercury, lose all the
serpentine craft of thy caduceus,° if ye take not that
little, little, less than little wit from them that they
have; which short-armed ignorance itself knows is so
abundant scarce it will not in circumvention deliver a  15
fly from a spider, without drawing their massy irons
and cutting the web. After this, the vengeance on the
whole camp! Or, rather, the Neapolitan bone-ache,°
for that, methinks, is the curse depending on those that
war for a placket.° I have said my prayers, and devil   20
Envy say "Amen." What ho, my Lord Achilles!

*Enter* PATROCLUS.

PATROCLUS  Who's there? Thersites? Good Thersites,
come in and rail.
THERSITES  If I could 'a' rememb'red a gilt counterfeit, thou wouldst not have slipped° out of my con-    25
templation. But it is no matter; thyself upon thyself!
The common curse of mankind, folly and ignorance,
be thine in great revenue. Heaven bless° thee from a
tutor, and discipline come not near thee. Let thy
blood° be thy direction till thy death. Then, if she that  30
lays thee out says thou art a fair corse,° I'll be sworn
and sworn upon't she never shrouded any but lazars.°
Amen. Where's Achilles?
PATROCLUS  What, art thou devout? Wast thou in
prayer?                                                 35
THERSITES  Ay, the heavens hear me!
PATROCLUS  Amen.

*Enter* ACHILLES.

ACHILLES  Who's there?
PATROCLUS  Thersites, my lord.
ACHILLES  Where? Where? O, where? Art thou    40
come? Why, my cheese, my digestion,° why hast thou
not served thyself in to my table so many meals? Come,
what's Agamemnon?
THERSITES  Thy commander, Achilles. Then tell me,
Patroclus, what's Achilles?                             45

---

167 **moral** Aristotle wrote "political" (*Nicomachean Ethics*, I.3),
but the use of "moral" here is paralleled in Erasmus, Bacon,
and many other contemporary translations and commentaries;
the two words were roughly interchangeable in sixteenth-
century terminology 172 **more . . . adders** cf. Psalm 58:4–5
177 **affection** appetite 178 **partial** biased, favoring 179
**benumbèd** paralyzed (by affection and appetite) 187
**extenuates** lessens 190 **spritely** spirited; **propend** incline
193 **joint and several** collective and individual 196 **heaving
spleens** angry passions 208 **roisting** noisy, clamorous 211
**advertised** informed 212 **emulation** envious rivalry (see
I.iii.134)

II.iii.2 **carry it** carry it off, come out on top 5 **'Sfoot**
an oath; "God's foot" 6 **but I'll see** rather than not see 7
**enginer** a soldier in a company used for ditch digging, tun-
neling, and otherwise undermining the battlements of an
enemy camp 12 **caduceus** Mercury's staff, twined with
serpents 18 **Neapolitan bone-ache** syphilis 20 **placket**
opening in a petticoat (used obscenely, with anatomical suggestion) 25 **slipped** pun on *slip*, a counterfeit coin of brass,
covered with silver or gold 28 **bless** i.e., save 30 **blood**
passion 31 **corse** corpse 32 **lazars** lepers (with decayed
bodies) 41 **my . . . digestion** cheese served as the final
course of a meal was thought to aid digestion

PATROCLUS  Thy lord, Thersites. Then tell me, I pray thee, what's thyself?

THERSITES  Thy knower, Patroclus. Then tell me, Patroclus, what art thou?

PATROCLUS  Thou must tell that knowest.                    50

ACHILLES  O tell, tell.

THERSITES  I'll decline° the whole question. Agamemnon commands Achilles, Achilles is my lord, I am Patroclus' knower, and Patroclus is a fool.

PATROCLUS  You rascal!                                     55

THERSITES  Peace, fool! I have not done.

ACHILLES  He is a privileged man.° Proceed, Thersites.

THERSITES  Agamemnon is a fool, Achilles is a fool, Thersites is a fool, and, as aforesaid, Patroclus is a fool.

ACHILLES  Derive this; come.                               60

THERSITES  Agamemnon is a fool to offer° to command Achilles, Achilles is a fool to be commanded of Agamemnon, Thersites is a fool to serve such a fool, and this Patroclus is a fool positive.

PATROCLUS  Why am I a fool?                                65

THERSITES  Make that demand of the Creator; it suffices me thou art. Look you, who comes here?

*Enter* AGAMEMNON, ULYSSES, NESTOR, DIOMEDES, AJAX, *and* CALCHAS.

ACHILLES  Patroclus, I'll speak with nobody. Come in with me, Thersites.                          *Exit.*

THERSITES  Here is such patchery,° such juggling, and  70
such knavery. All the argument is a whore and a cuckold, a good quarrel to draw emulous° factions and bleed to death upon. Now, the dry serpigo° on the subject, and war and lechery confound all!     [*Exit.*]

AGAMEMNON  Where is Achilles?                              75

PATROCLUS  Within his tent, but ill-disposed, my lord.

AGAMEMNON
Let it be known to him that we are here.
He shent° our messengers, and we lay by
Our appertainments,° visiting of him.                      80
Let him be told so, lest perchance he think
We dare not move° the question of our place
Or know not what we are.

PATROCLUS                    I shall so say to him.
                                          [*Exit.*]

ULYSSES  We saw him at the opening of his tent. He is
not sick.                                                  85

AJAX  Yes, lion-sick, sick of proud heart. You may call it melancholy if you will favor the man; but, by my head, 'tis pride. But why, why? Let him show us a cause. A word, my lord. [*Takes* AGAMEMNON *aside.*]

NESTOR  What moves Ajax thus to bay at him?               90

ULYSSES  Achilles hath inveigled his fool from him.

NESTOR  Who, Thersites?

ULYSSES  He.

NESTOR  Then will Ajax lack matter, if he have lost his argument.°                                          95

ULYSSES  No, you see, he is his argument that has his argument, Achilles.

NESTOR  All the better. Their fraction° is more our wish than their faction.° But it was a strong composure° a fool could disunite.                         100

ULYSSES  The amity that wisdom knits not, folly may easily untie.

*Enter* PATROCLUS.

Here comes Patroclus.

NESTOR  No Achilles with him?

ULYSSES
The elephant hath joints, but none for courtesy.          105
His legs are legs for necessity, not for flexure.°

PATROCLUS
Achilles bids me say he is much sorry
If anything more than your sport and pleasure
Did move your greatness and this noble state°
To call upon him. He hopes it is no other                  110
But, for your health and your digestion sake,
An after-dinner's breath.°

AGAMEMNON                    Hear you, Patroclus.
We are too well acquainted with these answers;
But his evasion, winged thus swift with scorn,
Cannot outfly our apprehensions.°                          115
Much attribute he hath, and much the reason
Why we ascribe it to him; yet all his virtues,
Not virtuously on his own part beheld,°
Do in our eyes begin to lose their gloss—
Yea, like fair fruit in an unwholesome dish,               120
Are like to rot untasted. Go and tell him
We come to speak with him; and you shall not sin
If you do say we think him overproud
And underhonest,° in self-assumption greater
Than in the note of judgment,° and worthier than
    himself                                                125
Here tend the savage strangeness° he puts on,
Disguise the holy strength of their command,
And underwrite in an observing kind
His humorous predominance;° yea, watch
His pettish lunes,° his ebbs and flows, as if             130
The passage and whole carriage of this action
Rode on his tide. Go tell him this; and add
That, if he overhold° his price so much,
We'll none of him; but let him, like an engine°
Not portable, lie under this report:                       135
"Bring action hither, this cannot go to war."
A stirring dwarf we do allowance° give
Before a sleeping giant. Tell him so.

PATROCLUS
I shall, and bring his answer presently.      [*Exit.*]

**98 fraction** fracture, break  **99 faction** union  **99–100 composure** union  **106 flexure** bending  **109 noble state** assemblage of noblemen  **112 breath** exercise  **115 apprehensions** perceptions  **118 Not . . . beheld** not carried with modesty  **124 underhonest** calculating, not open  **125 note of judgment** opinion of men of judgment  **126 tend . . . strangeness** wait upon the rude aloofness  **127–29 Disguise . . . predominance** allow to be hidden the divine authority of their command, and, in a form of acquiescence, subscribe to his eccentric notion of superiority  **130 pettish lunes** capricious variations (like the changes of the moon)  **133 overhold** overvalue  **134 engine** mechanical contrivance (here, military)  **137 allowance** praise

**52 decline** run through (in the grammatical sense, as to decline a noun)  **57 He . . . man** in the sense that the railing of a professional jester or fool was "allowed"  **61 offer** attempt  **70 patchery** roguery  **72 emulous** jealous  **73 serpigo** a quickly spreading skin disease, with eruptions  **79 shent** rebuked  **80 appertainments** rights of rank  **82 move** raise  **95 argument** subject matter

AGAMEMNON
In second voice we'll not be satisfied;                    140
We come to speak with him. Ulysses, enter you.
                                        *Exit* ULYSSES.
AJAX   What is he more than another?
AGAMEMNON   No more than what he thinks he is.
AJAX   Is he so much? Do you not think he thinks
himself a better man than I am?                            145
AGAMEMNON   No question.
AJAX   Will you subscribe his thought, and say he is?
AGAMEMNON   No, noble Ajax; you are as strong, as
valiant, as wise, no less noble, much more gentle, and
altogether more tractable.                                 150
AJAX   Why should a man be proud? How doth pride
grow? I know not what pride is.
AGAMEMNON   Your mind is the clearer and your virtues the fairer. He that is proud eats up himself. Pride
is his own glass,° his own trumpet, his own chronicle;    155
and whatever praises itself but in the deed, devours the
deed in the praise.

*Enter* ULYSSES.

AJAX   I do hate a proud man as I hate the engend'ring
of toads.
NESTOR [*Aside.*]   And yet he loves himself. Is't not    160
strange?
ULYSSES
Achilles will not to the field tomorrow.
AGAMEMNON
What's his excuse?
ULYSSES                        He doth rely on none,
But carries on the stream of his dispose°
Without observance or respect of any,                      165
In will peculiar and in self-admission.°
AGAMEMNON
Why will he not upon our fair request
Untent his person and share th' air with us?
ULYSSES
Things small as nothing, for request's sake only,°
He makes important. Possessed he is with greatness,       170
And he speaks not to himself but with a pride
That quarrels at self-breath.° Imagined worth
Holds in his blood such swoln and hot discourse
That 'twixt his mental and his active parts
Kingdomed° Achilles in commotion rages                    175
And batters down himself. What should I say?
He is so plaguy proud that the death-tokens° of it
Cry "No recovery."
AGAMEMNON              Let Ajax go to him.
Dear lord, go you and greet him in his tent;
'Tis said he holds you well, and will be led             180
At your request a little from himself.
ULYSSES
O Agamemnon, let it not be so!
We'll consecrate the steps that Ajax makes
When they go from Achilles. Shall the proud lord
That bastes his arrogance with his own seam°             185

And never suffers matter of the world
Enter his thoughts, save such as doth revolve
And ruminate himself—shall he be worshiped
Of that we hold an idol more than he?
No, this thrice-worthy and right valiant lord            190
Shall not so stale his palm,° nobly acquired,
Nor, by my will, assubjugate° his merit,
As amply titled as Achilles' is,
By going to Achilles.
That were to enlard his fat-already pride,               195
And add more coals to Cancer° when he burns
With entertaining great Hyperion.°
This lord go to him! Jupiter forbid,
And say in thunder, "Achilles, go to him."
NESTOR [*Aside.*]
O, this is well. He rubs the vein° of him.               200
DIOMEDES [*Aside.*]
And how his silence drinks up his applause!
AJAX
If I go to him, with my armèd fist
I'll pash° him o'er the face.
AGAMEMNON
O, no! You shall not go.
AJAX
An he be proud with me, I'll pheese° his pride.          205
Let me go to him.
ULYSSES
Not for the worth that hangs upon our quarrel.
AJAX   A paltry, insolent fellow!
NESTOR [*Aside.*]   How he describes himself!
AJAX   Can he not be sociable?                            210
ULYSSES [*Aside.*]   The raven chides blackness.
AJAX   I'll let his humor's blood.°
AGAMEMNON [*Aside.*]   He will be the physician that
should be the patient.
AJAX   An all men were of my mind—                       215
ULYSSES [*Aside.*]   Wit would be out of fashion.
AJAX   'A° should not bear it so, 'a should eat swords
first! Shall pride carry it?
NESTOR [*Aside.*]   An 'twould, you'd carry half.
ULYSSES [*Aside.*]   'A would have ten shares.          220
AJAX   I will knead him; I'll make him supple.
NESTOR [*Aside.*]   He's not yet through° warm. Force°
him with praises; pour in, pour, his ambition is dry.
ULYSSES [*To* AGAMEMNON.]
My lord, you feed too much on this dislike.
NESTOR
Our noble general, do not do so.                         225
DIOMEDES
You must prepare to fight without Achilles.
ULYSSES
Why, 'tis this naming of him does him harm.
Here is a man—but 'tis before his face;
I will be silent.
NESTOR              Wherefore should you so?
He is not emulous,° as Achilles is.                      230

155 **glass** mirror  164 **dispose** inclination  166 **In . . . self-admission** with will exclusively his own and with self-approval  169 **for . . . only** only because requested  172 **That . . . self-breath** that quarrels with speech itself  175 **Kingdomed** i.e., as though Achilles were himself a kingdom engaged in civil strife  177 **death-tokens** external symptoms of the plague preceding death  185 **seam** grease, fat

191 **stale his palm** detract from his glory  192 **assubjugate** debase  196 **Cancer** i.e., summer, which begins under this sign of the zodiac  197 **Hyperion** the sun  200 **vein** mood  203 **pash** bash  205 **pheese** settle the business of  212 **let . . . blood** cure him by letting blood, thus decreasing the strength of Achilles' humor, his mood of pride  217 **'A** he  222 **through** thoroughly; **Force** stuff  230 **emulous** jealously competitive

ULYSSES
Know the whole world, he is as valiant—
AJAX
A whoreson dog, that shall palter° with us thus!
Would he were a Troyan!
NESTOR    What a vice were it in Ajax now—
ULYSSES    If he were proud—                                                            235
DIOMEDES    Or covetous of praise—
ULYSSES    Ay, or surly borne—
DIOMEDES    Or strange, or self-affected!°
ULYSSES
Thank the heavens, lord, thou art of sweet composure;
Praise him that gat° thee, she that gave thee suck;            240
Famed be thy tutor, and thy parts of nature
Thrice-famed beyond, beyond all erudition;°
But he that disciplined thine arms to fight,
Let Mars divide eternity in twain
And give him half; and, for thy vigor,                              245
Bull-bearing Milo° his addition° yield
To sinewy Ajax. I will not praise thy wisdom,
Which, like a bourn, a pale,° a shore, confines
Thy spacious and dilated parts. Here's Nestor,
Instructed by the antiquary times,°                                 250
He must, he is, he cannot but be wise;
But pardon, father Nestor, were your days
As green as Ajax, and your brain so tempered,
You should not have the eminence of him,
But be as Ajax.
AJAX                        Shall I call you father?                 255
NESTOR
Ay, my good son.
DIOMEDES                  Be ruled by him, Lord Ajax.
ULYSSES
There is no tarrying here; the hart Achilles
Keeps thicket. Please it our great general
To call together all his state° of war;
Fresh kings are come to Troy. Tomorrow,                             260
We must with all our main° of power stand fast.
And here's a lord—come knights from east to west,
And cull their flower, Ajax shall cope the best.
AGAMEMNON
Go we to council. Let Achilles sleep;
Light boats sail swift, though greater hulks draw deep. 265
                                                        *Exeunt.*

# [ ACT III ]

[Scene I. *Troy; Priam's palace.*]

*Music sounds within. Enter* PANDARUS *and a* SERVANT.

PANDARUS    Friend you, pray you a word. Do you not
follow the young Lord Paris?

SERVANT    Ay, sir, when he goes before me.
PANDARUS    You depend° upon him, I mean.
SERVANT    Sir, I do depend upon the Lord.                           5
PANDARUS    You depend upon a notable gentleman;
I must needs praise him.
SERVANT    The Lord be praised!
PANDARUS    You know me, do you not?
SERVANT    Faith, sir, superficially.                                10
PANDARUS    Friend, know me better. I am the Lord
Pandarus.
SERVANT    I hope I shall know your honor better.
PANDARUS    I do desire it.
SERVANT    You are in the state of grace.°                           15
PANDARUS    Grace?° Not so, friend. Honor and lord-
ship are my titles. What music is this?
SERVANT    I do but partly know, sir. It is music in
parts.°
PANDARUS    Know you the musicians?                                  20
SERVANT    Wholly, sir.
PANDARUS    Who play they to?
SERVANT    To the hearers, sir.
PANDARUS    At whose pleasure, friend?
SERVANT    At mine, sir, and theirs that love music.                25
PANDARUS    Command, I mean, friend.
SERVANT    Who shall I command, sir?
PANDARUS    Friend, we understand not one another. I
am too courtly, and thou too cunning. At whose
request do these men play?                                          30
SERVANT    That's to't, indeed, sir. Marry, sir, at the
request of Paris, my lord, who is there in person; with
him the mortal Venus, the heartblood of beauty, love's
invisible soul.
PANDARUS    Who? My cousin Cressida?                                 35
SERVANT    No, sir, Helen. Could not you find out that
by her attributes?
PANDARUS    It should seem, fellow, that thou hast not
seen the Lady Cressid. I come to speak with Paris from
the Prince Troilus. I will make a complimental assault 40
upon him, for my business seethes.°
SERVANT    Sodden business! There's a stewed° phrase,
indeed.

*Enter* PARIS *and* HELEN, [*with* COURTIERS].

PANDARUS    Fair be to you, my lord, and to all this
fair company. Fair desires in all fair measure fairly   45
guide them. Especially to you, fair queen, fair thoughts
be your fair pillow.
HELEN    Dear lord, you are full of fair words.
PANDARUS    You speak your fair pleasure, sweet
queen. Fair prince, here is good broken music.°         50
PARIS    You have broke it, cousin; and, by my life,
you shall make it whole again; you shall piece it out
with a piece of your performance. Nell, he is full of
harmony.

---

**232 palter** play shifty games, dodge   **238 strange, or self-
affected** haughty, or self-centered   **240 gat** begat   **241–42
thy parts . . . erudition** your natural attributes three times
more famous (i.e., than your tutor), even more famous than
all learning itself   **246 Milo** a famous Greek athlete, said to
have carried a bull upon his shoulders for forty yards; **addition** title, i.e., "Bull-bearing"   **248 a bourn, a pale** a
boundary, a fence   **250 Instructed . . . times** i.e., his wisdom
learned from olden times, all the years of his old age   **259
state** noblemen in council   **261 main** might

**III.i.4 depend** i.e., serve, in a position of dependence
**15 You . . . grace** pretending that Pandarus meant that he
desired his own honor to be better; also, perhaps, the servant is
hinting for a gratuity   **16 Grace** the courtly title of a duke,
etc.   **18–19 music in parts** music containing several vocal or
instrumental parts in counterpoint   **41 seethes** boils, i.e.,
demands immediate attention   **42 stewed** (1) boiled (2)
pertaining to stews, or brothels (?)   **50 broken music** music
the parts for which are written for different solo instruments,
or groups of different instruments

PANDARUS Truly, lady, no. 55

HELEN O, sir!

PANDARUS Rude,° in sooth; in good sooth, very rude.

PARIS Well said, my lord. Well, you say so in fits.°

PANDARUS I have business to my lord, dear queen. My lord, will you vouchsafe me a word? 60

HELEN Nay, this shall not hedge us out. We'll hear you sing, certainly.

PANDARUS Well, sweet queen, you are pleasant with me. But, marry, thus, my lord: my dear lord and most esteemed friend, your brother Troilus— 65

HELEN My Lord Pandarus, honey-sweet lord—

PANDARUS Go to, sweet queen, go to—commends himself most affectionately to you.

HELEN You shall not bob° us out of our melody. If you do, our melancholy upon your head! 70

PANDARUS Sweet queen, sweet queen, that's a sweet queen, i' faith.

HELEN And to make a sweet lady sad is a sour offense.

PANDARUS Nay, that shall not serve your turn; that shall it not, in truth, la. Nay, I care not for such words; 75 no, no. And, my lord, he desires you that, if the king call for him at supper, you will make his excuse.

HELEN My Lord Pandarus—

PANDARUS What says my sweet queen, my very, very sweet queen? 80

PARIS What exploit's in hand? Where sups he tonight?

HELEN Nay, but my Lord—

PANDARUS What says my sweet queen? My cousin will fall out with you.° 85

HELEN You must not know where he sups.

PARIS I'll lay my life, with my disposer° Cressida.

PANDARUS No, no; no such matter; you are wide.° Come, your disposer is sick.

PARIS Well, I'll make excuse. 90

PANDARUS Ay, good my lord. Why should you say Cressida? No, your poor disposer's sick.

PARIS I spy.

PANDARUS You spy? What do you spy? Come, give me an instrument now, sweet queen. 95

HELEN Why, this is kindly done.

PANDARUS My niece is horribly in love with a thing you have, sweet queen.°

HELEN She shall have it, my lord, if it be not my Lord Paris. 100

PANDARUS He? No, she'll none of him; they two are twain.°

HELEN Falling in, after falling out, may make them three.°

PANDARUS Come, come, I'll hear no more of this. 105 I'll sing you a song now.

HELEN Ay, ay, prithee. Now by my troth, sweet lord, thou hast a fine forehead.

PANDARUS Ay, you may, you may.° 

HELEN Let thy song be love. This love will undo us 110 all. O Cupid, Cupid, Cupid!

PANDARUS Love! Ay, that it shall, i' faith.

PARIS Ay, good now, "Love, love, nothing but love."

PANDARUS In good troth, it begins so: [Sings.]
Love, love, nothing but love, still love still more! 115
For, O, love's bow shoots buck and doe.
The shaft confounds not that° it wounds,
But tickles still the sore.°
These lovers cry, O ho! they die!
Yet that which seems the wound to kill 120
Doth turn O ho! to Ha, ha, he!
So dying love lives still.
O ho! a while, but Ha, ha, ha!
O ho! groans out for Ha, ha, ha!—Heigh ho!

HELEN In love, i' faith, to the very tip of the nose. 125

PARIS He eats nothing but doves, love, and that breeds hot blood, and hot blood begets hot thoughts, and hot thoughts beget hot deeds, and hot deeds is love.

PANDARUS Is this the generation of love—hot blood, hot thoughts, and hot deeds? Why, they are vipers. Is 130 love a generation of vipers?° Sweet lord, who's a-field today?

PARIS Hector, Deiphobus, Helenus, Antenor, and all the gallantry of Troy. I would fain have armed today, but my Nell would not have it so. How chance my 135 brother Troilus went not?

HELEN He hangs the lip at something. You know all, Lord Pandarus.

PANDARUS Not I, honey-sweet queen. I long to hear how they sped° today. You'll remember your brother's 140 excuse?

PARIS To a hair.°

PANDARUS Farewell, sweet queen.

HELEN Commend me to your niece.

PANDARUS I will, sweet queen. [Exit.] 145

*Sound a retreat.*

PARIS
They're come from the field. Let us to Priam's hall
To greet the warriors. Sweet Helen, I must woo you
To help unarm our Hector. His stubborn buckles,
With these your white enchanting fingers touched,
Shall more obey than to the edge of steel 150
Or force of Greekish sinews. You shall do more
Than all the island kings°—disarm great Hector.

HELEN
'Twill make us proud to be his servant, Paris;
Yea, what he shall receive of us in duty
Gives us more palm in beauty than we have, 155
Yea, overshines ourself.

PARIS
Sweet, above thought I love thee. *Exeunt.*

57 **Rude** unpolished, rough   **58 fits** sections or divisions of a song (perhaps Paris means, "You say so only at times")   **69 bob** cheat   **84–85 My . . . you** Pandarus lightly pretends that Paris, his "cousin," will become jealous if Helen continues to flirt with him, Pandarus   **87 disposer** i.e., she who rules him (Paris jokingly uses an excessively gallant term)   **88 wide** wide of the mark   **97–98 My . . . queen** i.e., Cressida loves, or would love to have, a sexual partner such as Paris is to Helen   **102 twain** at odds, have nothing in common   **103–04 Falling . . . three** Helen's bawdy joke picks up the train of thought begun by Pandarus

**109 you may** i.e., have your joke   **117 confounds not that** does not distress because   **118 sore** wound (perhaps a pun on the term for a buck in his fourth year)   **131 a . . . vipers** cf. Matthew 3:7   **140 how they sped** i.e., the results of their action   **142 To a hair** does Paris jokingly recall Troilus' "pretty answer" about the hairs on his chin (see I.ii.168–70)?   **152 island kings** kings of the Grecian islands

[Scene II. *Within Troy.*]

*Enter* PANDARUS *and Troilus'* MAN.

PANDARUS  How now, where's thy master? At my
cousin Cressida's?
MAN  No, sir; he stays for you to conduct him thither.

*Enter* TROILUS.

PANDARUS  O, here he comes. How now, how now?
TROILUS  Sirrah, walk off.                    [*Exit* MAN.]  5
PANDARUS  Have you seen my cousin?
TROILUS
No, Pandarus. I stalk about her door
Like a strange soul upon the Stygian° banks
Staying for waftage.° O, be thou my Charon,°
And give me swift transportation to those fields  10
Where I may wallow in the lily beds
Proposed° for the deserver. O gentle Pandar,
From Cupid's shoulder pluck his painted wings,
And fly with me to Cressid.
PANDARUS
Walk here i' th' orchard. I'll bring her straight.  15

*Exit* PANDARUS.

TROILUS
I am giddy; expectation whirls me round.
Th' imaginary relish is so sweet
That it enchants my sense. What will it be
When that the wat'ry° palates taste indeed
Love's thrice-repurèd° nectar? Death, I fear me,  20
Sounding° destruction, or some joy too fine,
Too subtle, potent, tuned too sharp in sweetness
For the capacity of my ruder° powers.
I fear it much; and I do fear besides
That I shall lose distinction° in my joys,  25
As doth a battle, when they charge on heaps
The enemy flying.

*Enter* PANDARUS.

PANDARUS  She's making her ready; she'll come
straight; you must be witty° now. She does so blush,
and fetches her wind so short as if she were frayed with  30
a spirit.° I'll fetch her. It is the prettiest villain;° she
fetches her breath as short as a new-ta'en sparrow.

*Exit* PANDARUS.

TROILUS
Even such a passion doth embrace my bosom.
My heart beats thicker than a feverous pulse,
And all my powers do their bestowing° lose,  35
Like vassalage° at unawares encount'ring
The eye of majesty.

*Enter* PANDARUS *and* CRESSIDA.

PANDARUS  Come, come, what need you blush?
Shame's a baby. Here she is now; swear the oaths now

to her that you have sworn to me. What! Are you  40
gone again? You must be watched ere you be made
tame,° must you? Come your ways, come your ways;
an you draw backward, we'll put you i' the fills.° Why
do you not speak to her? Come, draw this curtain,°
and let's see your picture. Alas the day, how loath you  45
are to offend daylight! An 'twere dark, you'd close°
sooner. So, so; rub on, and kiss the mistress.° How
now, a kiss in fee-farm!° Build there, carpenter; the
air is sweet. Nay, you shall fight your hearts out ere I
part you. The falcon as the tercel, for all the ducks i'  50
the river.° Go to, go to.
TROILUS  You have bereft me of all words, lady.
PANDARUS  Words pay no debts, give her deeds; but
she'll bereave you o' the deeds too if she call your
activity in question. What, billing again? Here's "In  55
witness whereof the parties interchangeably"°—Come
in, come in. I'll go get a fire.          [*Exit.*]
CRESSIDA  Will you walk in, my lord?
TROILUS  O Cressid, how often have I wished me
thus!  60
CRESSIDA  Wished, my lord? The gods grant—O my
lord!
TROILUS  What should they grant? What makes this
pretty abruption?° What too curious° dreg espies my
sweet lady in the fountain of our love?  65
CRESSIDA  More dregs than water, if my fears have
eyes.
TROILUS  Fears make devils of cherubins; they never
see truly.
CRESSIDA  Blind fear, that seeing reason leads, finds  70
safer footing than blind reason stumbling without fear.
To fear the worst oft cures the worse.
TROILUS  O, let my lady apprehend no fear; in all
Cupid's pageant there is presented no monster.°
CRESSIDA  Nor nothing monstrous neither?  75
TROILUS  Nothing but our undertakings when we
vow to weep seas, live in fire, eat rocks, tame tigers,
thinking it harder for our mistress to devise imposition
enough than for us to undergo any difficulty imposed.
This is the monstruosity in love, lady, that the will is  80
infinite and the execution confined; that the desire is
boundless and the act a slave to limit.
CRESSIDA  They say all lovers swear more performance than they are able, and yet reserve an ability that
they never perform, vowing more than the perfection  85
of ten and discharging less than the tenth part

---

III.ii.8 **Stygian** from Styx, the principal river of the underworld  9 **waftage** passage across water; **Charon** ferryman of
the dead, across the Styx to Hades  12 **Proposed** promised
19 **wat'ry** watering (cf. mouth "watering" with appetite)
20 **thrice-repurèd** distilled again and again (i.e., to extract the
purest essence)  21 **Sounding** swooning  23 **ruder** physical
25 **distinction** ability to distinguish  29 **be witty** be alert,
have your wits about you  30–31 **frayed . . . spirit** frightened by a ghost  31 **villain** here a term of endearment  35
**bestowing** proper use  36 **vassalage** vassals

41–42 **watched . . . tame** i.e., prodded on until made submissive (a hawk was tamed by "watching" it, i.e., keeping it
constantly awake)  43 **fills** shafts (of a cart)  44 **curtain** her
veil  46 **close** move together  47 **rub . . . mistress** terms
from bowling, where "to rub" was to meet obstacles in
the way of the small object-ball, called the "mistress"; bowls
are still said "to kiss" when they touch gently  48 **a kiss in
fee-farm** i.e., a long kiss (a fee-farm was a grant of lands in
perpetuity)  50–51 **The falcon . . . river** i.e., I will bet on
the falcon (the term applied only to the female of the species)
against the tercel (the male) to bring down any game  55–56
**"In witness . . . interchangeably"** a legal formula, usually
ending with the words "have set their hands and seals"  64
**abruption** breaking off; **too curious** overly cautious, anxious,
or inquisitive  73–74 **apprehend . . . monster** Troilus refers
to some type of dramatic allegory such as Cupid might be
depicted as "presenting," or the emblematic characters, such as
Fear, in pageants or court masques

of one. They that have the voice of lions and the act of hares—are they not monsters?

TROILUS  Are there such? Such are not we. Praise us as we are tasted,° allow us as we prove; our head shall 90 go bare till merit crown it. No perfection in reversion° shall have a praise in present; we will not name desert before his birth, and, being born, his addition shall be humble.° Few words to fair faith. Troilus shall be such to Cressid, as what envy can say worst shall be a 95 mock for his truth, and what truth can speak truest not truer than Troilus.°

CRESSIDA  Will you walk in, my lord?

*Enter* PANDARUS.

PANDARUS  What, blushing still? Have you not done talking yet? 100

CRESSIDA  Well, uncle, what folly I commit, I dedicate to you.

PANDARUS  I thank you for that. If my lord get a boy of you, you'll give him me. Be true to my lord; if he flinch, chide me for it. 105

TROILUS  You know now your hostages: your uncle's word and my firm faith.

PANDARUS  Nay, I'll give my word for her too. Our kindred, though they be long ere they be wooed, they are constant being won. They are burrs, I can tell you; 110 they'll stick where they are thrown.

CRESSIDA
Boldness comes to me now and brings me heart.
Prince Troilus, I have loved you night and day
For many weary months.

TROILUS
Why was my Cressid then so hard to win? 115

CRESSIDA
Hard to seem won; but I was won, my lord,
With the first glance that ever—pardon me;
If I confess much you will play the tyrant.
I love you now, but, till now, not so much
But I might master it. In faith, I lie; 120
My thoughts were like unbridled children grown
Too headstrong for their mother. See, we fools!
Why have I blabbed? Who shall be true to us
When we are so unsecret to ourselves?
But, though I loved you well, I wooed you not; 125
And yet, good faith, I wished myself a man,
Or that we women had men's privilege
Of speaking first. Sweet, bid me hold my tongue,
For in this rapture I shall surely speak
The thing I shall repent. See, see! Your silence, 130
Cunning in dumbness, from my weakness draws
My very soul of counsel.° Stop my mouth.

TROILUS
And shall, albeit sweet music issues thence.

PANDARUS  Pretty, i' faith.

CRESSIDA
My lord, I do beseech you, pardon me; 135
'Twas not my purpose thus to beg a kiss.

I am ashamed. O heavens, what have I done?
For this time will I take my leave, my lord.

TROILUS
Your leave, sweet Cressid?

PANDARUS  Leave! An you take leave till tomorrow 140 morning—

CRESSIDA
Pray you, content you.

TROILUS                     What offends you, lady?

CRESSIDA
Sir, mine own company.

TROILUS
You cannot shun yourself.

CRESSIDA
Let me go and try. 145
I have a kind of self resides with you;
But an unkind self, that itself will leave
To be another's fool.° I would be gone.
Where is my wit? I know not what I speak.

TROILUS
Well know they what they speak that speak so wisely. 150

CRESSIDA
Perchance, my lord, I show more craft than love,
And fell so roundly° to a large° confession
To angle for your thoughts. But you are wise,
Or else you love not, for to be wise and love
Exceeds man's might;° that dwells with gods above. 155

TROILUS
O that I thought it could be in a woman—
As, if it can, I will presume in you—
To feed for aye her lamp and flames of love;
To keep her constancy in plight and youth,°
Outliving beauty's outward,° with a mind 160
That doth renew swifter than blood decays;
Or that persuasion could but thus convince me
That my integrity and truth to you
Might be affronted° with the match and weight
Of such a winnowed° purity in love: 165
How were I then uplifted! But, alas,
I am as true as truth's simplicity,
And simpler than the infancy of truth.

CRESSIDA
In that I'll war with you.

TROILUS                     O virtuous fight,
When right with right wars who shall be most right! 170
True swains in love shall in the world to come
Approve° their truth by Troilus. When their rhymes,
Full of protest, of oath and big compare,
Wants similes, truth tired with iteration,
"As true as steel, as plantage to the moon,° 175
As sun to day, as turtle° to her mate,
As iron to adamant,° as earth to the center,"
Yet, after all comparisons of truth,
As truth's authentic author to be cited,

---

90 **tasted** tested  91 **reversion** right or anticipation of future possession  93–94 **his . . . humble** it shall be given no high or pompous titles  95–97 **as what . . . Troilus** so that the worst malice can do is sneer at his constancy, and even the best truth that truth can speak will not be truer than Troilus  132 **very . . . counsel** inmost thoughts and secrets

148 **fool** dupe  152 **roundly** frankly, openly; **large** unrestrained  153–55 **But . . . might** i.e., you are reasonable, which means you are not in love, for no man can follow reason and love at the same time  159 **in . . . youth** as it was when it was plighted, and as fresh  160 **beauty's outward** external, transitory beauty  164 **affronted** confronted, i.e., equaled  165 **winnowed** i.e., distilled  172 **Approve** attest  175 **plantage . . . moon** the moon was thought to influence plantage, or vegetation  176 **turtle** turtledove (an emblem of eternally faithful love)  177 **adamant** the loadstone (magnetic)

"As true as Troilus" shall crown up the verse    180
And sanctify the numbers.°
CRESSIDA            Prophet may you be!
If I be false or swerve a hair from truth,
When time is old and hath forgot itself,
When waterdrops have worn the stones of Troy,
And blind oblivion swallowed cities up,    185
And mighty states characterless° are grated
To dusty nothing, yet let memory,
From false to false among false maids in love,
Upbraid my falsehood! When they've said, "As false
As air, as water, wind or sandy earth,    190
As fox to lamb, as wolf to heifer's calf,
Pard to the hind,° or stepdame to her son,"
Yea, let them say, to stick the heart of falsehood,
"As false as Cressid."
PANDARUS   Go to, a bargain made. Seal it, seal it; I'll   195
be the witness. Here I hold your hand, here my
cousin's. If ever you prove false one to another, since
I have taken such pains to bring you together, let all
pitiful goers-between be called to the world's end
after my name; call them all Pandars. Let all constant   200
men be Troiluses, all false women Cressids, and all
brokers-between Pandars! Say, "Amen."
TROILUS   Amen.
CRESSIDA   Amen.
PANDARUS   Amen. Whereupon I will show you a   205
chamber which bed,° because° it shall not speak of
your pretty encounters, press it to death. Away!
               *Exeunt* [TROILUS *and* CRESSIDA.]
And Cupid grant all tongue-tied maidens here
Bed, chamber, Pandar to provide this gear!     *Exit.*

[Scene III. *The Greek camp.*]

*Enter* ULYSSES, DIOMEDES, NESTOR, AGAMEMNON,
[MENELAUS, AJAX, *and*] CALCHAS. *Flourish* [*of*
*trumpets.*]

CALCHAS
Now, princes, for the service I have done,
Th' advantage of the time prompts me aloud
To call for recompense. Appear it to mind
That through the sight° I bear in things to come,
I have abandoned Troy, left my possession,    5
Incurred a traitor's name, exposed myself,
From certain and possessed conveniences,
To doubtful fortunes, sequest'ring° from me all
That time, acquaintance, custom, and condition
Made tame° and most familiar to my nature;    10
And here, to do you service, am become
As new into the world, strange, unacquainted.
I do beseech you, as in way of taste,°
To give me now a little benefit
Out of those many registered in promise,    15
Which, you say, live to come in my behalf.
AGAMEMNON
What wouldst thou of us, Troyan? Make demand.

CALCHAS
You have a Troyan prisoner, called Antenor,
Yesterday took; Troy holds him very dear.
Oft have you—often have you thanks therefor—    20
Desired my Cressid in right great exchange,°
Whom Troy hath still° denied; but this Antenor
I know is such a wrest° in their affairs
That their negotiations all must slack,
Wanting his manage; and they will almost    25
Give us a prince of blood, a son of Priam,
In change of him. Let him be sent, great princes,
And he shall buy my daughter; and her presence
Shall quite strike off all service I have done
In most accepted° pain.    
AGAMEMNON        Let Diomedes bear him,    30
And bring us Cressid hither; Calchas shall have
What he requests of us. Good Diomed,
Furnish you fairly, for this interchange.
Withal bring word if Hector will tomorrow
Be answered in his challenge. Ajax is ready.    35
DIOMEDES
This shall I undertake, and 'tis a burden
Which I am proud to bear.      *Exit,* [*with* CALCHAS].

ACHILLES *and* PATROCLUS *stand in their tent.*°

ULYSSES
Achilles stands i' th' entrance of his tent.
Please it our general pass strangely° by him,
As if he were forgot; and, princes all,    40
Lay negligent and loose regard upon him.
I will come last. 'Tis like he'll question me
Why such unplausive° eyes are bent, why turned, on
   him.
If so, I have derision medicinable
To use between your strangeness and his pride,    45
Which his own will shall have desire to drink.
It may do good; pride hath no other glass
To show° itself but pride, for supple knees
Feed arrogance and are the proud man's fees.
AGAMEMNON
We'll execute your purpose, and put on    50
A form of strangeness as we pass along.
So do each lord, and either greet him not
Or else disdainfully, which shall shake him more
Than if not looked on. I will lead the way.
ACHILLES
What comes the general to speak with me?    55
You know my mind; I'll fight no more 'gainst Troy.
AGAMEMNON
What says Achilles? Would he aught with us?
NESTOR
Would you, my lord, aught with the general?
ACHILLES   No.
NESTOR   Nothing, my lord.    60
AGAMEMNON   The better.
ACHILLES   Good day, good day.

---

181 **numbers** metrical verses   186 **characterless** without an identifying mark   192 **Pard . . . hind** leopard to the doe 206 **which bed** the bed in which; **because** (1) for the reason that (normal usage) (2) in order that (?)
**III.iii.4 sight** foresight   8 **sequest'ring** putting aside   10 **tame** familiar, comfortable   13 **taste** foretaste

21 **right great exchange** exchange for someone sufficiently great   22 **still** always   23 **wrest** a key used for tuning stringed instruments (i.e., the influence of harmony in Trojan discussions) 30 **accepted** cheerfully endured   37 **s.d. stand . . . tent** appear and stand in the entrance of their tent   39 **strangely** aloofly   43 **unplausive** disapproving   48 **show** mirror

MENELAUS   How do you? How do you?

ACHILLES   What, does the cuckold scorn me?

AJAX   How now, Patroclus?    65

ACHILLES   Good morrow, Ajax.

AJAX   Ha?

ACHILLES   Good morrow.

AJAX   Ay, and good next day too.       *Exeunt.*

ACHILLES

  What mean these fellows? Know they not Achilles?   70

PATROCLUS

  They pass by strangely. They were used to bend,

  To send their smiles before them to Achilles,

  To come as humbly as they used to creep

  To holy altars.

ACHILLES      What, am I poor of late?

  'Tis certain, greatness, once fall'n out with fortune,   75

  Must fall out with men too. What the declined is

  He shall as soon read in the eyes of others

  As feel in his own fall; for men, like butterflies,

  Show not their mealy° wings but to the summer,

  And not a man, for being simply man,    80

  Hath any honor, but honor for those honors

  That are without° him, as place, riches, and favor,

  Prizes of accident as oft as merit;

  Which when they fall, as being slippery standers,

  The love that leaned on them as slippery too,    85

  Doth one pluck down another, and together

  Die in the fall. But 'tis not so with me;

  Fortune and I are friends. I do enjoy

  At ample point° all that I did possess,

  Save these men's looks—who do, methinks, find out   90

  Something not worth in me such rich beholding

  As they have often given. Here is Ulysses;

  I'll interrupt his reading.

  How now, Ulysses.

ULYSSES      Now, great Thetis' son.

ACHILLES

  What are you reading?

ULYSSES      A strange fellow here    95

  Writes me that man, how dearly ever parted,°

  How much in having, or without or in,°

  Cannot make boast to have that which he hath,

  Nor feels not what he owes but by reflection;°

  As when his virtues aiming upon others    100

  Heat them, and they retort that heat again

  To the first giver.

ACHILLES      This is not strange, Ulysses.

  The beauty that is borne here in the face

  The bearer knows not, but commends itself

  To others' eyes; nor doth the eye itself,    105

  That most pure spirit of sense, behold itself,

  Not going from itself; but eye to eye opposed

  Salutes each other with each other's form;

  For speculation° turns not to itself

  Till it hath traveled and is married there    110

  Where it may see itself. This is not strange at all.

ULYSSES

  I do not strain at the position°—

  It is familiar—but at the author's drift;

  Who in his circumstance° expressly proves

  That no man is the lord of anything—    115

  Though in and of him there be much consisting°—

  Till he communicate his parts to others.

  Nor doth he of himself know them for aught

  Till he behold them formèd in th' applause

  Where they're extended;° who,° like an arch, rever-

    b'rate    120

  The voice again, or, like a gate of steel

  Fronting the sun, receives and renders back

  His figure and his heat. I was much rapt in this,

  And apprehended here immediately

  Th' unknown Ajax.    125

  Heavens, what a man is there! A very horse,

  That has he knows not what. Nature, what things

    there are

  Most abject in regard and dear in use!°

  What things again most dear in the esteem

  And poor in worth! Now shall we see tomorrow,    130

  An act that very chance doth throw upon him:

  Ajax renowned. O heavens, what some men do,

  While some men leave to do!

  How some men creep in° skittish° Fortune's hall,

  Whiles others play the idiots in her eyes!    135

  How one man eats into another's pride,

  While pride is fasting in his wantonness!°

  To see these Grecian lords—why, even already

  They clap the lubber Ajax on the shoulder,

  As if his foot were on brave Hector's breast,    140

  And great Troy shrinking.

ACHILLES

  I do believe it; for they passed by me

  As misers do by beggars, neither gave to me

  Good word nor look. What, are my deeds forgot?

ULYSSES

  Time hath, my lord, a wallet at his back,    145

  Wherein he puts alms for oblivion,

  A great-sized monster of ingratitudes.

  Those scraps are good deeds past, which are devoured

  As fast as they are made, forgot as soon

  As done. Perseverance, dear my lord,    150

  Keeps honor bright. To have done, is to hang

  Quite out of fashion, like a rusty mail°

  In monumental mock'ry. Take the instant° way;

  For honor travels in a strait so narrow

  Where one but goes abreast. Keep, then, the path;    155

  For emulation hath a thousand sons

  That one by one pursue. If you give way,

  Or hedge aside from the direct forthright,°

  Like to an ent'red tide they all rush by

  And leave you hindmost;    160

---

**79 mealy** powdery   **82 without** external to   **89 At ample point** in full measure, in every way   **96 how . . . parted** however excellently endowed by nature   **97 How . . . or in** however much in possession, whether externally or internally   **99 Nor . . . reflection** and understands what he himself possesses ("owes" = owns) only as it is reflected   **109 speculation** power of sight

**112 position** i.e., that of the writer whom Ulysses paraphrases above   **114 circumstance** detailed discussion   **116 Though . . . consisting** although much exists in him and also because of him   **120 Where they're extended** in which his natural attributes are noised abroad; **who** which   **128 Most . . . use** most despised and yet invaluable   **134 in** into; **skittish** unreliable   **137 his wantonness** its own self-satisfaction   **152 mail** piece of armor   **153 instant** most immediate   **158 direct forthright** course of action clearly at hand, the path straight ahead

Or, like a gallant horse fall'n in first rank,
Lie there for pavement to the abject rear,°
O'errun and trampled on. Then what they do in
    present,
Though less than yours in past, must o'ertop yours.
For time is like a fashionable host,                              165
That slightly shakes his parting guest by the hand,
And with his arms outstretched, as he would fly,
Grasps in the comer. The welcome ever smiles,
And farewell goes out sighing. Let not virtue seek
Remuneration for the thing it was. For beauty, wit,              170
High birth, vigor of bone, desert in service,
Love, friendship, charity, are subjects all
To envious and calumniating time.
One touch of nature° makes the whole world kin,
That all with one consent praise newborn gauds,°                175
Though they are made and molded of things past,
And give to dust that is a little gilt
More laud than gilt o'erdusted.°
The present eye praises the present object.
Then marvel not, thou great and complete man,                    180
That all the Greeks begin to worship Ajax;
Since things in motion sooner catch the eye
Than what stirs not. The cry° went once on thee,
And still it might, and yet it may again,
If thou wouldst not entomb thyself alive                         185
And case° thy reputation in thy tent;
Whose glorious deeds, but in these fields of late,
Made emulous missions° 'mongst the gods themselves
And drave great Mars to faction.°

ACHILLES                           Of this my privacy
I have strong reasons.

ULYSSES                    But 'gainst your privacy               190
The reasons are more potent and heroical.
'Tis known, Achilles, that you are in love
With one of Priam's daughters.°

ACHILLES  Ha! Known!

ULYSSES
Is that a wonder?                                                195
The providence° that's in a watchful state
Knows almost every grain of Pluto's° gold
Finds bottom in th' uncomprehensive° deeps,
Keeps place° with thought, and almost, like the gods,
Do thoughts unveil in their dumb cradles.                        200
There is a mystery—with whom relation°
Durst never meddle—in the soul of state,
Which hath an operation more divine
Than breath or pen can give expressure to.
All the commerce that you have had with Troy                     205
As perfectly is ours as yours, my lord;
And better would it fit Achilles much

To throw down Hector than Polyxena.
But it must grieve young Pyrrhus° now at home,
When fame shall in our islands sound her trump,                  210
And all the Greekish girls shall tripping sing,
"Great Hector's sister did Achilles win,
But our great Ajax bravely beat down him."
Farewell, my lord; I as your lover speak;
The fool slides o'er the ice that you should break.              215
                                                    [Exit.]

PATROCLUS
To this effect, Achilles, have I moved you.
A woman impudent and mannish grown
Is not more loathed than an effeminate man
In time of action. I stand condemned for this;
They think my little stomach to the war                          220
And your great love to me restrains you thus.
Sweet, rouse yourself; and the weak wanton Cupid
Shall from your neck unloose his amorous fold
And, like a dewdrop from the lion's mane,
Be shook to air.

ACHILLES           Shall Ajax fight with Hector?                 225

PATROCLUS
Ay, and perhaps receive much honor by him.

ACHILLES
I see my reputation is at stake.
My fame is shrewdly gored.°

PATROCLUS                   O, then, beware!
Those wounds heal ill that men do give themselves.
Omission to do what is necessary                                 230
Seals a commission to a blank of danger;°
And danger, like an ague, subtly taints°
Even then when they sit idly in the sun.

ACHILLES
Go call Thersites hither, sweet Patroclus.
I'll send the fool to Ajax and desire him                        235
T' invite the Troyan lords after the combat
To see us here unarmed. I have a woman's° longing,
An appetite that I am sick withal,
To see great Hector in his weeds° of peace,
To talk with him and to behold his visage,                       240
Even to my full of view.°

*Enter* THERSITES.

                          A labor saved!

THERSITES  A wonder!

ACHILLES  What?

THERSITES  Ajax goes up and down the field, asking
for himself.°                                                    245

ACHILLES  How so?

THERSITES  He must fight singly tomorrow with
Hector, and is so prophetically proud of an heroical
cudgeling that he raves in saying nothing.

ACHILLES  How can that be?                                       250

---

162 **the abject rear** the miserable, degraded members
of the rear (as in a military charge or parade) 174 **One
. . . nature** a natural inclination, common to all men (to
praise according to superficial values) 175 **gauds** toys,
trifles 178 **More . . . o'erdusted** more praise than gold
covered with dust 183 **cry** public opinion 186 **case** encase
188 **emulous missions** competitive and jealous warfare (the
gods took sides in the Trojan War, fighting among themselves)
189 **to faction** to become a partisan 193 **one . . . daughters**
Polyxena 196 **providence** careful and timely understanding
197 **Pluto's** Shakespeare's error for Plutus, god of wealth;
Pluto was god of the underworld 198 **uncomprehensive**
unfathomable 199 **Keeps place** keeps up, runs parallel
201 **relation** open statement

209 **Pyrrhus** Achilles' son, also called Neoptolemus 228
**shrewdly gored** sorely wounded 231 **Seals . . . danger**
binds one to confront unnamed danger (royal officers sometimes carried blank warrants for arrest, already bearing the
commissioning seal of authority, which could be filled in
as necessary) 232 **taints** infects 237 **woman's** i.e., pregnant
woman's (?) 239 **weeds** apparel 240-41 **to behold . . .
view** since in full armor Hector's face would have been hidden
behind the closed beaver of his helmet 244-45 **asking for
himself** here "Ajax" is probably a pun on a *fakes*, a privy

THERSITES  Why, he stalks up and down like a peacock—a stride and a stand; ruminates like an hostess that hath no arithmetic but her brain to set down her reckoning; bites his lip with a politic regard,° as who should say, "There were wit in this head an 'twould 255 out"; and so there is, but it lies as coldly in him as fire in a flint, which will not show without knocking. The man's undone forever, for if Hector break not his neck i' the combat, he'll break't himself in vainglory. He knows not me. I said, "Good morrow, Ajax"; and he 260 replies, "Thanks, Agamemnon." What think you of this man that takes me for the general? He's grown a very land-fish, languageless, a monster. A plague of opinion! A man may wear it on both sides like a leather jerkin.° 265

ACHILLES  Thou must be my ambassador to him, Thersites.

THERSITES  Who, I? Why, he'll answer nobody. He professes not answering. Speaking is for beggars; he wears his tongue in's arms. I will put on° his presence; 270 let Patroclus make demands to me, you shall see the pageant of Ajax.

ACHILLES  To him, Patroclus. Tell him I humbly desire the valiant Ajax to invite the most valorous Hector to come unarmed to my tent, and to procure 275 safe-conduct for his person of the magnanimous and most illustrious, six-or-seven-times-honored captain-general of the Grecian army, Agamemnon, et cetera. Do this.

PATROCLUS  Jove bless great Ajax! 280

THERSITES  Hum.

PATROCLUS  I come from the worthy Achilles—

THERSITES  Ha!

PATROCLUS  Who most humbly desires you to invite Hector to his tent— 285

THERSITES  Hum!

PATROCLUS  And to procure safe-conduct from Agamemnon.

THERSITES  Agamemnon?

PATROCLUS  Ay, my lord. 290

THERSITES  Ha!

PATROCLUS  What say you to't?

THERSITES  God b' wi' you, with all my heart.

PATROCLUS  Your answer, sir.

THERSITES  If tomorrow be a fair day, by eleven of the 295 clock it will go one way or other; howsoever, he shall pay for me ere he has me.

PATROCLUS  Your answer, sir.

THERSITES  Fare ye well, with all my heart,

ACHILLES  Why, but he is not in this tune, is he? 300

THERSITES  No, but out of tune thus. What music will be in him when Hector has knocked out his brains, I know not; but I am sure none, unless the fiddler Apollo get his sinews to make catlings° on.

ACHILLES  Come, thou shalt bear a letter to him 305 straight.

THERSITES  Let me bear another to his horse, for that's the more capable° creature.

ACHILLES  My mind is troubled, like a fountain stirred,

And I myself see not the bottom of it. 310

[*Exeunt* ACHILLES *and* PATROCLUS.]

THERSITES  Would the fountain of your mind were clear again, that I might water an ass at it! I had rather be a tick in a sheep than such a valiant ignorance.

[*Exit.*]

# [ A C T  I V ]

### [Scene I. *Within Troy.*]

*Enter, at one door,* AENEAS [*with a torch;*] *at another,* PARIS, DEIPHOBUS, ANTENOR, DIOMED *the Grecian,* [*and others,*] *with torches.*

PARIS
See, ho! Who is that there?

DEIPHOBUS                    It is the Lord Aeneas.

AENEAS
Is the prince there in person?
Had I so good occasion to lie long
As you, Prince Paris, nothing but heavenly business
Should rob my bedmate of my company. 5

DIOMEDES
That's my mind too. Good morrow, Lord Aeneas.

PARIS
A valiant Greek, Aeneas; take his hand.
Witness the process° of your speech, wherein
You told how Diomed, a whole week by days,°
Did haunt you in the field.

AENEAS                    Health to you, valiant sir, 10
During all question of the gentle truce;°
But when I meet you armed, as black defiance
As heart can think or courage execute.

DIOMEDES
The one and other Diomed embraces.
Our bloods are now in calm, and, so long, health! 15
But when contention and occasion° meet,
By Jove, I'll play the hunter for thy life
With all my force, pursuit, and policy.°

AENEAS
And thou shalt hunt a lion that will fly
With his face backward. In humane gentleness, 20
Welcome to Troy. Now, by Anchises'° life,
Welcome indeed! By Venus' hand° I swear,
No man alive can love in such a sort
The thing he means to kill more excellently.

DIOMEDES
We sympathize.° Jove, let Aeneas live, 25
If to my sword his fate be not the glory,
A thousand complete courses of the sun!
But, in mine emulous honor, let him die
With every joint a wound, and that tomorrow!

AENEAS
We know each other well. 30

---

254 **politic regard** expression of shrewd judgment  265 **jerkin** close-fitting jacket  270 **put on** imitate  304 **catlings** strings of catgut  308 **capable** intelligent

IV.i.8 **process** gist, drift  9 **by days** day by day  11 **question . . . truce** intercourse made possible by the truce  16 **occasion** opportunity  18 **policy** cunning  21 **Anchises** Aeneas' father  22 **Venus' hand** Diomedes was supposed to have wounded Venus, Aeneas' mother, in the hand  25 **sympathize** have the same feeling

DIOMEDES
We do, and long to know each other worse.

PARIS
This is the most despiteful gentle greeting,
The noblest hateful love, that e'er I heard of.
What business, lord, so early?

AENEAS
I was sent for to the king; but why, I know not.     35

PARIS
His purpose meets you; it was to bring this Greek
To Calchas' house, and there to render him,
For the enfreed Antenor, the fair Cressid.
Let's have your company; or, if you please,
Haste there before us. I constantly° do think—     40
Or rather call my thought a certain knowledge—
My brother Troilus lodges there tonight.
Rouse him and give him note of our approach,
With the whole quality° wherefore. I fear
We shall be much unwelcome.

AENEAS                          That I assure you.     45
Troilus had rather Troy were borne to Greece
Than Cressid borne from Troy.

PARIS                          There is no help.
The bitter disposition of the time
Will have it so. On, lord; we'll follow you.

AENEAS
Good morrow, all.          *Exit* AENEAS.     50

PARIS
And tell me, noble Diomed; faith, tell me true,
Even in the soul of sound good-fellowship,
Who, in your thoughts, deserves fair Helen best,
Myself or Menelaus?

DIOMEDES               Both alike.
He merits well to have her that doth seek her,     55
Not making any scruple of her soilure,
With such a hell of pain and world of charge;°
And you as well to keep her that defend her,
Not palating° the taste of her dishonor,
With such a costly loss of wealth and friends.     60
He, like a puling cuckold, would drink up
The lees and dregs of a flat tamèd piece;°
You, like a lecher, out of whorish loins
Are pleased to breed out your inheritors.
Both merits poised,° each weighs nor less nor more;     65
But he as he, the heavier for a whore.°

PARIS
You are too bitter to your countrywoman.

DIOMEDES
She's bitter to her country! Hear me, Paris—
For every false drop in her bawdy veins
A Grecian's life hath sunk; for every scruple°     70
Of her contaminated carrion weight
A Troyan hath been slain. Since she could speak,

She hath not given so many good words breath
As for her Greeks and Troyans suffered death.

PARIS
Fair Diomed, you do as chapmen° do,     75
Dispraise the thing that you desire to buy;
But we in silence hold this virtue well,
We'll not commend what we intend to sell.°
Here lies our way.          *Exeunt.*

[Scene II. *Within Troy; Calchas' house.*]

*Enter* TROILUS *and* CRESSIDA.

TROILUS
Dear, trouble not yourself; the morn is cold.

CRESSIDA
Then, sweet my lord, I'll call mine uncle down;
He shall unbolt the gates.

TROILUS               Trouble him not;
To bed, to bed. Sleep kill° those pretty eyes,
And give as soft attachment° to thy senses     5
As infants' empty of all thought!

CRESSIDA                          Good morrow then.

TROILUS
I prithee now, to bed.

CRESSIDA          Are you aweary of me?

TROILUS
O Cressida! But that the busy day,
Waked by the lark, hath roused the ribald crows,
And dreaming night will hide our joys no longer,     10
I would not from thee.

CRESSIDA               Night hath been too brief.

TROILUS
Beshrew the witch! With venomous wights° she stays
As tediously as hell, but flies the grasps of love
With wings more momentary-swift than thought.
You will catch cold and curse me.

CRESSIDA               Prithee, tarry;     15
You men will never tarry.
O foolish Cressid! I might have still held off,
And then you would have tarried. Hark, there's one up.

PANDARUS (*Within.*)   What's all the doors open here?

TROILUS   It is your uncle.     20

CRESSIDA
A pestilence on him! Now will he be mocking.
I shall have such a life.

*Enter* PANDARUS.

PANDARUS   How now, how now! How go maidenheads? Here, you maid, where's my cousin Cressid?

CRESSIDA
Go hang yourself, you naughty mocking uncle.     25
You bring me to do°—and then you flout me too.

PANDARUS   To do what? To do what? Let her say
what. What have I brought you to do?

---

**40 constantly** firmly   **44 quality** occasion, explanation   **57
charge** cost   **59 Not palating** insensible to   **62 flat tamèd
piece** (1) cask of wine opened so long that the wine has gone
flat (2) woman so promiscuous that she can no longer excite
or be excited sexually   **65 poised** weighed   **66 But . . .
whore** (1) but he, i.e., Menelaus, as heavy as his small merit
may be, plus the weight of the whore who is, after all, his legal
possession (?) (2) but he, whoever wins her, heavier only by
the weight of a whore (to be "light" was to be morally loose) (?)
**70 scruple** the smallest possible unit of weight

**75 chapmen** hawkers of cheap wares   **78 We'll . . . sell**
i.e., we'll not practice the seller's tricks although you practice
the buyer's (Paris does not imply that Helen is for sale)
**IV.ii 4 kill** overpower   **5 attachment** seizure   **12 venomous
wights** malignant witches (or, simply, evil creatures)   **26
do** used sometimes in obscene sense

CRESSIDA
Come come; beshrew your heart! You'll ne'er be
good,
Nor suffer others.                                              30

PANDARUS  Ha, ha! Alas, poor wretch! A poor
capocchia!° Hast not slept tonight? Would he not, a
naughty man, let it sleep? A bugbear° take him!

CRESSIDA
Did not I tell you? Would he were knocked i' the
head!

*One knocks.*

Who's that at door? Good uncle, go and see.          35
My lord, come you again into my chamber.
You smile and mock me, as if I meant naughtily.

TROILUS  Ha, ha!

CRESSIDA
Come, you are deceived, I think of no such thing.

*Knock.*

How earnestly they knock! Pray you, come in.          40
I would not for half Troy have you seen here.
                              *Exeunt* [TROILUS *and* CRESSIDA].

PANDARUS  Who's there? What's the matter? Will
you beat down the door? How now, what's the
matter?

[*Enter* AENEAS.]

AENEAS
Good morrow, lord, good morrow.                        45

PANDARUS  Who's there? My Lord Aeneas! By my
troth, I knew you not. What news with you so early?

AENEAS
Is not Prince Troilus here?

PANDARUS  Here? What should he do here?

AENEAS
Come, he is here, my lord. Do not deny him.          50
It doth import° him much to speak with me.

PANDARUS  Is he here, say you? 'Tis more than I
know, I'll be sworn. For my own part, I came in late.
What should he do here?

AENEAS  Who!° Nay, then. Come, come, you'll do   55
him wrong ere you are ware. You'll be so true to him,
to be false to him. Do not you know of him, but yet
go fetch him hither; go.

*Enter* TROILUS.

TROILUS  How now, what's the matter?

AENEAS
My lord, I scarce have leisure to salute you,          60
My matter is so rash.° There is at hand
Paris your brother, and Deiphobus,
The Grecian Diomed, and our Antenor
Delivered to us; and for him forthwith,
Ere the first sacrifice, within this hour,              65
We must give up to Diomedes' hand
The Lady Cressida.

TROILUS               Is it so concluded?

AENEAS
By Priam, and the general state° of Troy.
They are at hand and ready to effect it.

TROILUS
How my achievements mock me!                          70
I will go meet them. And, my Lord Aeneas,
We met by chance; you did not find me here.

AENEAS
Good, good, my lord; the secrets° of nature
Have not more gift in taciturnity.
                    *Exeunt* [TROILUS *and* AENEAS].

PANDARUS  Is't possible? No sooner got but lost? The   75
devil take Antenor! The young prince will go mad.
A plague upon Antenor! I would they had broke's
neck!

*Enter* CRESSIDA.

CRESSIDA
How now? What's the matter? Who was here?

PANDARUS  Ah, ah!                                      80

CRESSIDA
Why sigh you so profoundly? Where's my lord?
Gone? Tell me, sweet uncle, what's the matter?

PANDARUS  Would I were as deep under the earth as
I am above!

CRESSIDA  O the gods! What's the matter?              85

PANDARUS  Pray thee, get thee in. Would thou hadst
ne'er been born! I knew thou wouldst be his death. O
poor gentleman! A plague upon Antenor!

CRESSIDA  Good uncle, I beseech you on my knees,
what's the matter?                                      90

PANDARUS  Thou must be gone, wench, thou must be
gone; thou art changed° for Antenor. Thou must to
thy father and be gone from Troilus. 'Twill be his
death; 'twill be his bane;° he cannot bear it.

CRESSIDA
O you immortal gods! I will not go.                    95

PANDARUS  Thou must.

CRESSIDA
I will not, uncle. I have forgot my father;
I know no touch of consanguinity°—
No kin, no love, no blood, no soul so near me
As the sweet Troilus. O you gods divine,              100
Make Cressid's name the very crown of falsehood
If ever she leave Troilus! Time, force, and death,
Do to this body what extremes you can;
But the strong base and building of my love
Is as the very center of the earth,                    105
Drawing all things to it. I will go in and weep—

PANDARUS  Do, do.

CRESSIDA
—Tear my bright hair, and scratch my praisèd cheeks,
Crack my clear voice with sobs, and break my heart
With sounding Troilus. I will not go from Troy.        110
                                        *Exeunt.*

[*Scene III. Within Troy; near Calchas' house.*]

*Enter* PARIS, TROILUS, AENEAS, DEIPHOBUS,
ANTENOR, DIOMEDES.

---

**32 capocchia** simpleton **33 bugbear** hobgoblin **51
doth import** is important to **55 Who** an exclamation of
impatience; sometimes as to call "stop!" to a horse **61 rash**
urgent

**68 general state** noblemen in council **73 secrets** most
unknown parts **92 changed** exchanged **94 bane** poison,
destruction **98 no . . . consanguinity** no sense of relationship

PARIS
It is great morning,° and the hour prefixed
For her delivery to this valiant Greek
Comes fast upon. Good my brother Troilus,
Tell you the lady what she is to do,
And haste her to the purpose.

TROILUS             Walk into her house.    5
I'll bring her to the Grecian presently;°
And to his hand when I deliver her,
Think it an altar, and thy brother Troilus
A priest there off'ring to it his own heart.

PARIS
I know what 'tis to love;    10
And would, as I shall pity, I could help.
Please you walk in, my lords.      *Exeunt.*

[Scene IV. *Within Troy; Calchas' house.*]

*Enter* PANDARUS *and* CRESSIDA.

PANDARUS   Be moderate, be moderate.

CRESSIDA
Why tell you me of moderation?
The grief is fine, full, perfect, that I taste,
And violenteth° in a sense as strong
As that which causeth it. How can I moderate it?    5
If I could temporize with my affections,
Or brew it to a weak and colder palate,°
The like allayment could I give my grief.
My love admits no qualifying dross;°
No more my grief, in such a precious loss.    10

*Enter* TROILUS.

PANDARUS   Here, here, here he comes. Ah, sweet
ducks!

CRESSIDA   O Troilus! Troilus!

PANDARUS   What a pair of spectacles° is here! Let me
embrace too. "O heart," as the goodly saying is—    15
    O heart, heavy heart,
      Why sigh'st thou without breaking?
where he answers again,
     Because thou canst not ease thy smart
      By friendship nor by speaking.    20
There was never a truer rhyme. Let us cast away
nothing, for we may live to have need of such a verse.
We see it, we see it. How now, lambs!

TROILUS
Cressid, I love thee in so strained° a purity,
That the blest gods, as angry with my fancy,°    25
More bright in zeal than the devotion which
Cold lips blow to their deities, take thee from me.

CRESSIDA   Have the gods envy?

PANDARUS   Ay, ay, ay, ay, 'tis too plain a case.

CRESSIDA
And is it true that I must go from Troy?    30

TROILUS
A hateful truth.

CRESSIDA        What, and from Troilus too?

TROILUS
From Troy and Troilus.

CRESSIDA        Is't possible?

TROILUS
And suddenly, where injury of chance°
Puts back leave-taking, justles roughly by
All time of pause, rudely beguiles our lips    35
Of all rejoindure,° forcibly prevents
Our locked embrasures, strangles our dear vows
Even in the birth of our own laboring breath.
We two, that with so many thousand sighs
Did buy each other, must poorly sell ourselves    40
With the rude brevity and discharge of one.
Injurious time now with a robber's haste
Crams his rich thievery up, he knows not how;
As many farewells as be stars in heaven,
With distinct breath and consigned kisses to them,°    45
He fumbles° up into a loose adieu,
And scants us with a single famished kiss,
Distasted° with the salt of broken tears.

AENEAS (*Within.*)   My lord, is the lady ready?

TROILUS
Hark! You are called. Some say the Genius°    50
Cries so to him that instantly must die.
Bid them have patience; she shall come anon.

PANDARUS   Where are my tears? Rain, to lay this
wind, or my heart will be blown up by the root! [*Exit.*]

CRESSIDA
I must, then, to the Grecians?

TROILUS          No remedy.    55

CRESSIDA
A woeful Cressid 'mongst the merry Greeks!
When shall we see again?

TROILUS
Hear me, love. Be thou but true of heart—

CRESSIDA
I true! How now! What wicked deem° is this?

TROILUS
Nay, we must use expostulation kindly,    60
For it is parting from us.°
I speak not "be thou true" as fearing thee,
For I will throw my glove° to Death himself
That there's no maculation° in thy heart;
But "be thou true," say I, to fashion in    65
My sequent protestation:° be thou true,
And I will see thee.

CRESSIDA
O, you shall be exposed, my lord, to dangers
As infinite as imminent; but I'll be true.

TROILUS
And I'll grow friend with danger. Wear this sleeve.    70

CRESSIDA
And you this glove. When shall I see you?

TROILUS
I will corrupt the Grecian sentinels,

---

IV.iii.1 **great morning** broad daylight   6 **presently** immediately

IV.iv.4 **violenteth** rages   7 **palate** taste   9 **qualifying dross** moderating impurity   14 **spectacles** a pun   24 **strained** distilled, filtered   25 **fancy** love

33 **injury of chance** injurious accident   36 **rejoindure** reunion   45 **With . . . them** with the words of each farewell and the kisses which ratify each of them   46 **fumbles** wraps clumsily   48 **Distasted** the taste (of the kiss) ruined   50 **Genius** guardian spirit   59 **deem** thought   60–61 **Nay . . . us** we must be gentle in all remonstrance, for we are now saying good-bye   63 **throw my glove** give challenge   64 **maculation** taint, blemish (i.e., disloyalty)   65–66 **to . . . protestation** as introduction for my own promise to follow

To give thee nightly visitation.
But yet, be true.
CRESSIDA          O heavens! "Be true" again!
TROILUS
Hear why I speak it, love.                                      75
The Grecian youths are full of quality;°
They're loving,° well composed with gift of nature,
And swelling o'er with arts and exercise.°
How novelty may move, and parts with person,°
Alas! A kind of godly jealousy—                               80
Which, I beseech you, call a virtuous sin—
Makes me afeared.
CRESSIDA          O heavens, you love me not!
TROILUS
Die I a villain then!
In this I do not call your faith in question
So mainly as my merit. I cannot sing,                         85
Nor heel the high lavolt,° nor sweeten talk,
Nor play at subtle games—fair virtues all,
To which the Grecians are most prompt and pregnant;°
But I can tell that in each grace of these
There lurks a still and dumb-discoursive° devil              90
That tempts most cunningly. But be not tempted.
CRESSIDA  Do you think I will?
TROILUS  No!
But something may be done that we will not;
And sometimes we are devils to ourselves               95
When we will tempt the frailty of our powers,
Presuming on their changeful potency.°
AENEAS (Within.)
Nay, good my lord!
TROILUS          Come, kiss; and let us part.
PARIS (Within.)
Brother Troilus!
TROILUS          Good brother, come you hither;
And bring Aeneas and the Grecian with you.          100
CRESSIDA
My lord, will you be true?
TROILUS
Who? I? Alas, it is my vice, my fault.
Whiles others fish with craft for great opinion,°
I with great truth catch° mere simplicity;
Whilst some with cunning gild their copper crowns,    105
With truth and plainness I do wear mine bare.
Fear not my truth; the moral° of my wit
Is "plain and true"—there's all the reach of it.

[Enter AENEAS, PARIS, ANTENOR, DEIPHOBUS and
DIOMEDES.]

Welcome, Sir Diomed. Here is the lady
Which for Antenor we deliver you.                            110
At the port,° lord, I'll give her to thy hand,
And by the way possess° thee what she is.
Entreat° her fair; and, by my soul, fair Greek,

If e'er thou stand at mercy of my sword,
Name Cressid, and thy life shall be as safe          115
As Priam is in Ilion.
DIOMEDES          Fair Lady Cressid,
So please you, save the thanks this prince expects.
The luster in your eye, heaven in your cheek,
Pleads your fair usage; and to Diomed
You shall be mistress, and command him wholly.     120
TROILUS
Grecian, thou dost not use me courteously,
To shame the seal of my petition° to thee
In praising her. I tell thee, lord of Greece,
She is as far high-soaring o'er thy praises
As thou unworthy to be called her servant.        125
I charge thee use her well, even for my charge;°
For, by the dreadful Pluto, if thou dost not,
Though the great bulk Achilles be thy guard,
I'll cut thy throat.
DIOMEDES          O, be not moved, Prince Troilus.
Let me be privileged by my place and message      130
To be a speaker free. When I am hence,
I'll answer to my lust;° and know you, lord,
I'll nothing do on charge. To her own worth
She shall be prized; but that you say "be't so,"
I speak it in my spirit and honor, "no."           135
TROILUS
Come, to the port. I'll tell thee, Diomed,
This brave° shall oft make thee to hide thy head.
Lady, give me your hand, and, as we walk,
To our own selves bend we our needful talk.

[Exeunt TROILUS, CRESSIDA, and DIOMEDES.]

Sound trumpet.

PARIS
Hark! Hector's trumpet.
AENEAS          How have we spent this morning!  140
The prince must think me tardy and remiss,
That swore to ride before him to the field.
PARIS
'Tis Troilus' fault. Come, come, to field with him.
DEIPHOBUS
Let us make ready straight.
AENEAS
Yea, with a bridegroom's fresh alacrity,           145
Let us address° to tend on Hector's heels.
The glory of our Troy doth this day lie
On his fair worth and single chivalry.        Exeunt.

[Scene V. The Greek camp.]

Enter AJAX, armed; ACHILLES, PATROCLUS,
AGAMEMNON, MENELAUS, ULYSSES, NESTOR,
CALCHAS, &c.

AGAMEMNON
Here art thou in appointment° fresh and fair,
Anticipating time. With starting° courage,

---

76 **quality** qualities  77 **loving** adept in the arts of love  78
**arts and exercise** talents both in theory and in practice  79
**parts with person** specific qualities and talents, combined
with personal charm  86 **high lavolt** the lavolt was a dance
for two persons, requiring many high steps and bounds  88
**pregnant** ready, fully able  90 **dumb-discoursive** articulate
even in silence  97 **changeful potency** power which may
alter to failure  103 **opinion** reputation  104 **catch** achieve;
i.e., achieve a reputation for  107 **moral** maxim  111 **port**
gate (of the city)  112 **possess** inform  113 **Entreat** treat

122 **To . . . petition** to disdain the worth of my charge
and promise  126 **even . . . charge** simply because I say so
132 **answer . . . lust** do as I please  137 **brave** boast  146
**address** prepare
**IV.v.1 appointment** equipment and apparel  **2 starting**
active, prompt

Give with thy trumpet a loud note to Troy,
Thou dreadful Ajax, that the appallèd air
May pierce the head of the great combatant    5
And hale him hither.

AJAX           Thou, trumpet,° there's my purse.
Now crack thy lungs, and split thy brazen pipe.
Blow, villain, till thy spherèd bias° cheek
Outswell the colic of puffed Aquilon!°
Come, stretch thy chest, and let thy eyes spout blood;   10
Thou blow'st for Hector.

*[Trumpet sounds.]*

ULYSSES
No trumpet answers.

ACHILLES        'Tis but early days.°

AGAMEMNON
Is not yond Diomed with Calchas' daughter?

ULYSSES
'Tis he, I ken the manner of his gait;
He rises on the toe. That spirit of his    15
In aspiration lifts him from the earth.

*[Enter* DIOMEDES, *with* CRESSIDA.*]*

AGAMEMNON
Is this the Lady Cressid?

DIOMEDES        Even she.

AGAMEMNON
Most dearly welcome to the Greeks, sweet lady.

NESTOR
Our general doth salute you with a kiss.

ULYSSES
Yet is the kindness but particular.°    20
'Twere better she were kissed in general.°

NESTOR
And very courtly counsel. I'll begin.
So much for Nestor.

ACHILLES
I'll take that winter° from your lips, fair lady.
Achilles bids you welcome.    25

MENELAUS
I had good argument for kissing once.

PATROCLUS
But that's no argument for kissing now;
For thus popped Paris in his hardiment,°
And parted thus you and your argument.°

ULYSSES
O, deadly gall, and theme of all our scorns,    30
For which we lose our heads to gild his horns.

PATROCLUS
The first was Menelaus' kiss; this, mine.
Patroclus kisses you.

MENELAUS      O, this is trim.

PATROCLUS
Paris and I kiss evermore for him.

MENELAUS
I'll have my kiss, sir. Lady, by your leave.    35

CRESSIDA
In kissing, do you render or receive?

PATROCLUS
Both take and give.

CRESSIDA        I'll make my match to live,°
The kiss you take is better than you give;
Therefore no kiss.

MENELAUS
I'll give you boot;° I'll give you three for one.    40

CRESSIDA
You are an odd° man; give even, or give none.

MENELAUS
An odd man, lady? Every man is odd.

CRESSIDA
No, Paris is not, for you know 'tis true
That you are odd and he is even with you.

MENELAUS
You fillip° me o' the head.

CRESSIDA        No, I'll be sworn.    45

ULYSSES
It were no match, your nail against his horn.°
May I, sweet lady, beg a kiss of you?

CRESSIDA
You may.

ULYSSES   I do desire it.

CRESSIDA        Why, beg then.

ULYSSES
Why, then, for Venus' sake, give me a kiss,
When Helen is a maid again, and his.    50

CRESSIDA
I am your debtor; claim it when 'tis due.

ULYSSES
Never's my day, and then a kiss of you.

DIOMEDES
Lady, a word. I'll bring you to your father.

         *[Exeunt* DIOMEDES *and* CRESSIDA.*]*

NESTOR
A woman of quick sense.

ULYSSES        Fie, fie upon her!°
There's language in her eye, her cheek, her lip;    55
Nay, her foot speaks. Her wanton spirits look out
At every joint and motive° of her body.
O, these encounterers, so glib of tongue,
That give a coasting welcome ere it comes,°
And wide unclasp the tables° of their thoughts    60
To every ticklish reader, set them down
For sluttish spoils of opportunity°
And daughters of the game.°

*Flourish. Enter all of Troy* [HECTOR, PARIS, AENEAS,
HELENUS, TROILUS, *and* ATTENDANTS].

ALL
The Troyans' trumpet.°

AGAMEMNON      Yonder comes the troop.

AENEAS
Hail, all the state of Greece. What shall be done    65

---

37 **I'll . . . live** I'll bet my life   40 **boot** odds   41 **odd** i.e.,
single and singular   45 **fillip** tap   46 **It . . . horn** your nail,
in tapping, would be no match for his hard cuckold's horn
54 **Fie . . . her** Ulysses' exclamation does not imply disagreement with Nestor's observation; the following nine lines
elaborate "quick sense"   57 **motive** moving part   59 **a
coasting . . . comes** a sidelong, flirtatious greeting before
being greeted   60 **tables** tablets   62 **sluttish . . . opportunity** harlots who yield at every opportunity   63 **daughters
. . . game** whores   64 **The Troyans' trumpet** in the
theater, this line becomes a pun on *strumpet*

---

6 **trumpet** trumpeter   8 **bias** puffed-out   9 **the colic . . .
Aquilon** the north wind, distended as if by colic   12 **days in
the day**   20 **particular** single   21 **in general** (1) by the general
(2) universally   24 **that winter** i.e., Nestor's kiss (cold from
old age)   28 **hardiment** boldness   29 **argument** i.e., Helen

To him that victory commands? Or do you purpose
A victor shall be known? Will you the knights
Shall to the edge of all extremity
Pursue each other, or shall they be divided°
By any voice or order of the field?                                70
Hector bade ask.

AGAMEMNON    Which way would Hector have it?

AENEAS
He cares not; he'll obey conditions.

ACHILLES
'Tis done like Hector; but securely° done,
A little proudly, and great deal misprising
The knight opposed.

AENEAS                    If not Achilles, sir.             75
What is your name?

ACHILLES                    If not Achilles, nothing.

AENEAS
Therefore Achilles; but, what'er, know this:
In the extremity of great and little,
Valor and pride excel themselves in Hector;
The one almost as infinite as all,                                80
The other blank as nothing. Weigh him well;
And that which looks like pride is courtesy.
This Ajax is half made of Hector's blood,°
In love whereof half Hector stays at home;
Half heart, half hand, half Hector comes to seek       85
This blended knight, half Troyan, and half Greek.

ACHILLES
A maiden° battle, then? O, I perceive you.

[Enter DIOMEDES.]

AGAMEMNON
Here is Sir Diomed. Go, gentle knight,
Stand by our Ajax. As you and Lord Aeneas
Consent upon the order of their fight,                          90
So be it; either to the uttermost,
Or else a breath.° The combatants being kin
Half stints their strife before their strokes begin.

[AJAX and HECTOR enter the lists.]

ULYSSES
They are opposed already.

AGAMEMNON
What Troyan is that same that looks so heavy?°          95

ULYSSES
The youngest son of Priam, a true knight,
Not yet mature, yet matchless; firm of word,
Speaking in deeds and deedless in his tongue,°
Not soon provoked, nor being provoked soon calmed;
His heart and hand both open and both free,°            100
For what he has he gives, what thinks he shows;
Yet gives he not till judgment guide his bounty,
Nor dignifies an impare thought° with breath;
Manly as Hector, but more dangerous;
For Hector, in his blaze of wrath, subscribes            105
To tender objects,° but he in heat of action

Is more vindicative than jealous love.
They call him Troilus, and on him erect
A second hope as fairly built as Hector.
Thus says Aeneas, one that knows the youth            110
Even to his inches,° and with private soul°
Did in great Ilion thus translate him to me.

*Alarum.* [HECTOR *and* AJAX *fight.*]

AGAMEMNON
They are in action.

NESTOR
Now, Ajax, hold thine own!

TROILUS                    Hector, thou sleep'st; awake thee!

AGAMEMNON
His blows are well disposed.° There, Ajax!             115

DIOMEDES
You must no more. *Trumpets cease.*

AENEAS                    Princes, enough, so please you.

AJAX
I am not warm yet; let us fight again.

DIOMEDES
As Hector pleases.

HECTOR                    Why, then will I no more.
Thou art, great lord, my father's sister's son,
A cousin-german to great Priam's seed;                     120
The obligation of our blood forbids
A gory emulation 'twixt us twain.
Were thy commixtion° Greek and Troyan so
That thou couldst say, "This hand is Grecian all,
And this is Troyan; the sinews of this leg                   125
All Greek, and this all Troy; my mother's blood
Runs on the dexter° cheek, and this sinister°
Bounds in my father's," by Jove multipotent,°
Thou shouldst not bear from me a Greekish member
Wherein my sword had not impressure made            130
Of our rank feud. But the just gods gainsay
That any drop thou borrow'dst from thy mother,
My sacred aunt, should by my mortal sword
Be drained! Let me embrace thee, Ajax—
By him that thunders,° thou hast lusty arms;            135
Hector would have them fall upon him thus.°
Cousin, all honor to thee!

AJAX                    I thank thee, Hector;
Thou art too gentle and too free a man.
I came to kill thee, cousin, and bear hence
A great addition earnèd in thy death.                         140

HECTOR
Not Neoptolemus° so mirable,°
On whose bright crest Fame with her loud'st "Oyes"°
Cries, "This is he!" could promise to himself
A thought of added honor torn from Hector.

AENEAS
There is expectance here from both the sides,           145
What further you will do.

69 **divided** separated during the fight    73 **securely** overconfidently    83 **Hector's blood** see note to II.ii.77    87 **maiden** bloodless (as of novices or men in training, who do not intend to kill)    92 **breath** exercise    95 **heavy** heavyhearted    98 **deedless . . . tongue** free of boasts    100 **free** generous    103 **impare thought** (1) ill-considered thought (2) thought unequal to the dignity of his character    105–06 **subscribes . . . objects** grants merciful terms to the defenseless

111 **Even . . . inches** from head to toe; **with private soul** in confidence    115 **well disposed** well aimed, well placed    123 **commixtion** composition    127 **dexter** right; **sinister** left    128 **multipotent** of many powers    135 **him that thunders** Jove (Zeus)    136 **thus** i.e., embracing him    141 **Neoptolemus** this name probably applies here to Achilles himself, and not to his son, Pyrrhus; **mirable** wonderful    142 **Oyes** cries beginning the proclamations of heralds or sessions of a court

HECTOR                                          We'll answer it.
The issue° is embracement. Ajax, farewell.

AJAX
If I might in entreaties find success—
As seld° I have the chance—I would desire
My famous cousin to our Grecian tents.                    150

DIOMEDES
'Tis Agamemnon's wish; and great Achilles
Doth long to see unarmed the valiant Hector.

HECTOR
Aeneas, call my brother Troilus to me,
And signify° this loving interview
To the expecters of our Troyan part.°                    155
Desire them home.° Give me thy hand, my cousin;
I will go eat with thee and see your knights.

[AGAMEMNON *and the rest approach them.*]

AJAX
Great Agamemnon comes to meet us here.

HECTOR
The worthiest of them tell me name by name;
But for Achilles, my own searching eyes                    160
Shall find him by his large and portly size.

AGAMEMNON
Worthy of all arms [*embraces him*], as welcome as to one
That would be rid of such an enemy—
But that's no welcome. Understand more clear,
What's past and what's to come is strewed with husks    165
And formless ruin of oblivion;
But in this extant° moment, faith and troth,
Strained purely from all hollow bias-drawing,°
Bids thee, with most divine integrity,
From heart of very heart, great Hector, welcome.         170

HECTOR
I thank thee, most imperious Agamemnon.

AGAMEMNON [*To* TROILUS.]
My well-famed lord of Troy, no less to you.

MENELAUS
Let me confirm my princely brother's greeting.
You brace of warlike brothers, welcome hither.

HECTOR
Who must we answer?

AENEAS                          The noble Menelaus.       175

HECTOR
O, you, my lord? By Mars his gauntlet, thanks!
Mock not that I affect th' untraded° oath;
Your quondam° wife swears still by Venus' glove.
She's well, but bade me not commend her to you.

MENELAUS
Name her not now, sir; she's a deadly theme.             180

HECTOR
O, pardon! I offend.

NESTOR
I have, thou gallant Troyan, seen thee oft,

Laboring for destiny,° make cruel way
Through ranks of Greekish youth; and I have seen thee,
As hot as Perseus, spur thy Phrygian steed,              185
Despising many forfeits and subduements,°
When thou hast hung° thy advancèd sword i' th' air,
Not letting it decline on the declinèd,
That I have said to some my standers-by,
"Lo, Jupiter is yonder, dealing life!"°                   190
And I have seen thee pause and take thy breath,
When that a ring of Greeks have shraped° thee in,
Like an Olympian wrestling. This have I seen;
But this thy countenance, still° locked in steel,
I never saw till now. I knew thy grandsire,°             195
And once fought with him. He was a soldier good;
But, by great Mars, the captain of us all,
Never like thee. O, let an old man embrace thee;
And, worthy warrior, welcome to our tents.

AENEAS
'Tis the old Nestor.                                     200

HECTOR
Let me embrace thee, good old chronicle,
That hast so long walked hand in hand with time.
Most reverend Nestor, I am glad to clasp thee.

NESTOR
I would my arms could match thee in contention,
As they contend with thee in courtesy.                   205

HECTOR
I would they could.

NESTOR
Ha,
By this white beard, I'd fight with thee tomorrow.
Well, welcome, welcome. I have seen the time—

ULYSSES
I wonder now how yonder city stands,                     210
When we have here her base and pillar by us.

HECTOR
I know your favor,° Lord Ulysses, well.
Ah, sir, there's many a Greek and Troyan dead,
Since first I saw yourself and Diomed
In Ilion, on your Greekish embassy.                      215

ULYSSES
Sir, I foretold you then what would ensue.
My prophecy is but half his journey yet;
For yonder walls, that pertly front your town,
Yon towers, whose wanton tops do buss° the clouds,
Must kiss their own feet.

HECTOR                         I must not believe you.    220
There they stand yet, and modestly I think,
The fall of every Phrygian stone will cost
A drop of Grecian blood. The end crowns all,
And that old common arbitrator, Time,
Will one day end it.

ULYSSES                      So to him we leave it.       225
Most gentle and most valiant Hector, welcome.
After the general, I beseech you next
To feast with me and see me at my tent.

147 **issue** result, outcome    149 **seld** seldom    154 **signify**
expound, explain    155 **expecters . . . part** those on our side,
the Trojans, awaiting news    156 **Desire them home** ask them
to go home    167 **extant** present    168 **all hollow bias-
drawing** all fruitless and tortuous dealings (in the course of the
war, as in the course given by the bias of a bowl in bowling)
177 **untraded** unusual, unfamiliar (Hector, apologizing for
what might appear to be an affected oath, gives his reason for
using it in the following line, in which he completes a satirical
reference to Menelaus and Helen by alluding to the liaison
between Mars and Venus)    178 **quondam** former

183 **Laboring for destiny** working in behalf of destiny, i.e.,
causing destined deaths    186 **Despising . . . subduements**
ignoring or disdaining those already vanquished, whose lives
were forfeit    187 **hung** held suspended    190 **dealing life**
dispensing life (as a god might do by not causing death)
192 **shraped** trapped    194 **still** always    195 **grandsire**
Laomedon, the builder of Troy    212 **favor** face, features    219
**buss** kiss

ACHILLES
I shall forestall thee, Lord Ulysses, thou!
Now, Hector, I have fed mine eyes on thee;                    230
I have with exact view perused thee, Hector,
And quoted° joint by joint.

HECTOR                          Is this Achilles?

ACHILLES
I am Achilles.

HECTOR
Stand fair,° I pray thee; let me look on thee.

ACHILLES
Behold thy fill.

HECTOR                 Nay, I have done already.                235

ACHILLES
Thou art too brief. I will the second time,
As I would buy thee, view thee limb by limb.

HECTOR
O, like a book of sport thou'lt read me o'er;
But there's more in me than thou understand'st.
Why dost thou so oppress me with thine eye?     240

ACHILLES
Tell me, you heavens, in which part of his body
Shall I destroy him, whether there, or there, or there?
That I may give the local wound a name,
And make distinct the very breach whereout
Hector's great spirit flew. Answer me, heavens!     245

HECTOR
It would discredit the blessed gods, proud man,
To answer such a question. Stand again.
Think'st thou to catch my life so pleasantly°
As to prenominate in nice conjecture°
Where thou wilt hit me dead?

ACHILLES                        I tell thee, yea.     250

HECTOR
Wert thou an oracle to tell me so,
I'd not believe thee. Henceforth guard thee well,
For I'll not kill thee there, not there, nor there;
But, by the forge that stithied° Mars his helm,
I'll kill thee everywhere, yea, o'er and o'er.     255
You wisest Grecians, pardon me this brag.
His insolence draws folly from my lips;
But I'll endeavor deeds to match these words,
Or may I never—

AJAX              Do not chafe thee, cousin;
And you, Achilles, let these threats alone,     260
Till accident or purpose bring you to't.
You may have every day enough of Hector,
If you have stomach.° The general state,° I fear,
Can scarce entreat you to be odd° with him.

HECTOR
I pray you, let us see you in the field.     265
We have had pelting° wars since you refused
The Grecians' cause.

ACHILLES            Dost thou entreat° me, Hector?
Tomorrow do I meet thee, fell° as death;
Tonight all friends.

HECTOR               Thy hand upon that match.

AGAMEMNON
First, all you peers of Greece, go to my tent;     270
There in the full convive° we. Afterwards,
As Hector's leisure and your bounties shall
Concur together, severally° entreat him
To taste your bounties. Let the trumpets blow,
That this great soldier may his welcome know.     275
            Exeunt [all except TROILUS and ULYSSES].

TROILUS
My Lord Ulysses, tell me, I beseech you,
In what place of the field doth Calchas keep?°

ULYSSES
At Menelaus' tent, most princely Troilus.
There Diomed doth feast with him tonight—
Who neither looks upon the heaven nor earth,     280
But gives all gaze and bent of amorous view
On the fair Cressid.

TROILUS
Shall I, sweet lord, be bound to you so much,
After we part from Agamemnon's tent,
To bring me thither?

ULYSSES               You shall command me, sir.     285
But gentle tell me, of what honor was
This Cressida in Troy? Had she no lover there
That wails her absence?

TROILUS
O, sir, to such as boasting show their scars
A mock is due. Will you walk on, my lord?     290
She was beloved, she loved; she is, and doth;
But still sweet love is food for fortune's tooth.
                                        Exeunt.

# [ACT V]

[Scene I. *The Greek camp*.]

*Enter* ACHILLES *and* PATROCLUS.

ACHILLES
I'll heat his blood with Greekish wine tonight,
Which with my scimitar I'll cool tomorrow.
Patroclus, let us feast him to the height.

*Enter* THERSITES.

PATROCLUS
Here comes Thersites.

ACHILLES                 How now, thou cur of envy!
Thou crusty batch° of nature, what's the news?     5

THERSITES  Why, thou picture of what thou seemest,°
and idol of idiot-worshipers, here's a letter for thee.

ACHILLES  From whence, fragment?

THERSITES  Why, thou full dish of fool, from Troy.

PATROCLUS  Who keeps the tent now?°     10

THERSITES  The surgeon's box or the patient's
wound.°

232 **quoted** made exact mental note, scrutinized  234 **Stand
fair** stand openly, face me  248 **pleasantly** casually, merrily
249 **prenominate . . . conjecture** name beforehand in detailed conjecture  254 **stithied** forged  263 **stomach** inclination, relish; **general state** commanders in council  264 **odd**
at odds, engaged in combat  266 **pelting** paltry, petty  267
**entreat** invite  268 **fell** fierce

271 **convive** feast  273 **severally** individually  277 **keep**
dwell
V.i.5 **batch** a mass of anything baked together, or baked
without reheating the oven  6 **thou . . . seemest** i.e., who
is nothing more than one glance sufficiently reveals  10 **Who
. . . now** Thersites can no longer taunt Achilles for refusing
to leave his tent  11 **surgeon's . . . wound** from the play
on *tent*, a surgeon's probe for wounds

PATROCLUS  Well said, adversity, and what needs these tricks?

THERSITES  Prithee, be silent, boy; I profit not by thy 15 talk. Thou art said to be Achilles' male varlet.

PATROCLUS  Male varlet, you rogue! What's that?

THERSITES  Why, his masculine whore. Now, the rotten diseases of the south,° the guts-griping ruptures, catarrhs, loads o' gravel in the back, lethargies, cold 20 palsies,° raw eyes, dirt-rotten livers, wheezing lungs, bladders full of imposthume,° sciaticas, lime-kilns° i' the palm, incurable bone-ache, and the riveled° fee-simple of the tetter,° and the like, take and take again such preposterous discoveries!°                           25

PATROCLUS  Why, thou damnable box of envy, thou, what means thou to curse thus?

THERSITES  Do I curse thee?

PATROCLUS  Why, no, you ruinous butt,° you whoreson indistinguishable° cur, no.                              30

THERSITES  No? Why art thou then exasperate, thou idle immaterial skein of sleave silk,° thou green sarcenet° flap for a sore eye, thou tassel of a prodigal's purse, thou? Ah, how the poor world is pestered with such water-flies, diminutives of nature.           35

PATROCLUS  Out, gall!

THERSITES  Finch egg!

ACHILLES
My sweet Patroclus, I am thwarted quite
From my great purpose in tomorrow's battle.
Here is a letter from Queen Hecuba,                    40
A token from her daughter, my fair love,
Both taxing° me and gaging° me to keep
An oath that I have sworn. I will not break it.
Fall Greeks, fail fame, honor or go or° stay,
My major vow lies here; this I'll obey.                  45
Come, come, Thersites, help to trim my tent;
This night in banqueting must all be spent.
Away, Patroclus!            Exit, [with PATROCLUS].

THERSITES  With too much blood and too little brain, these two may run mad; but if with too much brain 50 and too little blood they do, I'll be a curer of madmen. Here's Agamemnon, an honest fellow enough, and one that loves quails,° but he has not so much brain as ear-wax; and the goodly transformation of Jupiter° there, his brother, the bull, the primitive statue and 55 oblique memorial of cuckolds°—a thrifty° shoeing-horn in a chain, hanging at his brother's leg°—to what form but that he is should wit larded with malice and

malice forced° with wit turn him to? To an ass, were nothing; he is both ass and ox. To an ox, were nothing; 60 he is both ox and ass. To be a dog, a mule, a cat, a fitchew,° a toad, a lizard, an owl, a puttock,° or a herring without a roe, I would not care; but to be Menelaus! I would conspire against destiny. Ask me not what I would be, if I were not Thersites, for I care 65 not to be° the louse of a lazar,° so I were not Menelaus. Hey-day, sprites and fires!

*Enter* AGAMEMNON, ULYSSES, NESTOR, [HECTOR, AJAX, TROILUS, MENELAUS,] *and* DIOMEDES, *with lights.*

AGAMEMNON
We go wrong, we go wrong.

AJAX                              No, yonder 'tis;
There, where we see the lights.

HECTOR                              I trouble you.

AJAX
No, not a whit.

ULYSSES            Here comes himself to guide you.      70

*Enter* ACHILLES.

ACHILLES
Welcome, brave Hector; welcome, princes all.

AGAMEMNON
So now, fair prince of Troy, I bid good night.
Ajax commands the guard to tend on you.

HECTOR
Thanks and good night to the Greeks' general.

MENELAUS
Good night, my lord.                                     75

HECTOR
Good night, sweet Lord Menelaus.

THERSITES  Sweet draught!° "Sweet," quoth 'a! Sweet sink, sweet sewer.

ACHILLES
Good night and welcome both at once, to those
That go or tarry.                                        80

AGAMEMNON  Good night.
                    *Exeunt* AGAMEMNON, MENELAUS.

ACHILLES
Old Nestor tarries, and you too, Diomed,
Keep Hector company an hour or two.

DIOMEDES
I cannot, lord; I have important business,
The tide° whereof is now. Good night, great Hector.   85

HECTOR
Give me your hand.

ULYSSES [*Aside to* TROILUS.]
Follow his torch; he goes
To Calchas' tent. I'll keep you company.

TROILUS
Sweet sir, you honor me.

HECTOR                    And so, good night.
      [*Exeunt* DIOMEDES, *then* ULYSSES *and* TROILUS.]

ACHILLES
Come, come, enter my tent.                               90
      *Exeunt* [ACHILLES, HECTOR, AJAX, *and* NESTOR].

19 diseases . . . south i.e., venereal diseases  20–21 gravel . . . palsies kidney stones, apoplectic strokes, paralysis of the limbs  22 imposthume internal abscess; lime-kilns psoriasis (burning red patches covered with scales)  23 riveled wrinkled  23–24 fee-simple . . . tetter chronic ringworm (?) ("fee-simple" implies unlimited possession)  25 discoveries referring generally to—in Thersites' opinion—such absurd monstrosities as Patroclus  29 ruinous butt dilapidated cask  30 indistinguishable shapeless (here suggesting mongrel)  32 sleave silk soft silk floss  33 sarcenet a fine silk taffeta  42 taxing censuring; gaging engaging to a promise  44 or go or either go or  53 quails prostitutes  54 transformation of Jupiter i.e., into a bull, in which shape he seduced Europa  55–56 primitive . . . cuckolds in having horns, the emblem or symbol of cuckoldry, although since Europa was not married, the parallel to Paris' rape of Helen is "oblique"  56 thrifty stingy  57 hanging . . . leg (1) as Agamemnon's tool, appropriately enough a "horn," his pretext for war (2) as being entirely dependent on Agamemnon

59 forced stuffed, intermixed  62 fitchew polecat; puttock kite, a small hawk feeding on carrion  65–66 I care . . . be I wouldn't mind being  66 lazar leper  77 draught privy, cesspool  85 tide time

THERSITES  That same Diomed's a false-hearted rogue, a most unjust knave; I will no more trust him when he leers than I will a serpent when he hisses. He will spend his mouth and promise like Brabbler the hound;° but when he performs, astronomers foretell 95 it. It is prodigious, there will come some change. The sun borrows of the moon when Diomed keeps his word. I will rather leave to see° Hector than not to dog him. They say he keeps a Troyan drab, and uses the traitor Calchas' tent. I'll after—nothing but lechery! 100 All incontinent varlets!                       [Exit.]


[Scene II. The Greek camp.]

Enter DIOMED.

DIOMEDES  What, are you up here, ho? Speak.
CALCHAS [Within.]  Who calls?
DIOMEDES  Diomed. Calchas, I think. Where's your daughter?
CALCHAS [Within.]  She comes to you.              5

Enter TROILUS and ULYSSES; [after them THERSITES.]

ULYSSES
Stand where the torch may not discover us.

Enter CRESSID.

TROILUS
Cressid comes forth to him.
DIOMEDES                          How now, my charge!
CRESSIDA
Now, my sweet guardian! Hark, a word with you.
[Whispers.]

TROILUS  Yea, so familiar!
ULYSSES  She will sing any man at first sight.      10
THERSITES  And any man may sing her, if he can take her cliff;° she's noted.°
DIOMEDES  Will you remember?
CRESSIDA  Remember? Yes.
DIOMEDES  Nay, but do, then;                       15
And let your mind be coupled with your words.
TROILUS  What shall she remember?
ULYSSES  List!
CRESSIDA
Sweet honey Greek, tempt me no more to folly.
THERSITES  Roguery!                               20
DIOMEDES
Nay, then—
CRESSIDA  I'll tell you what—
DIOMEDES
Foh, foh! Come, tell a pin. You are forsworn.
CRESSIDA
In faith, I cannot. What would you have me do?
THERSITES  A juggling trick—to be secretly° open.

DIOMEDES
What did you swear you would bestow on me?      25
CRESSIDA
I prithee, do not hold me to mine oath;
Bid me do anything but that, sweet Greek.
DIOMEDES  Good night.
TROILUS  Hold, patience!
ULYSSES  How now, Troyan?                          30
CRESSIDA  Diomed—
DIOMEDES
No, no, good night; I'll be your fool no more.
TROILUS
Thy better must.
CRESSIDA            Hark, a word in your ear.
TROILUS
O plague and madness!
ULYSSES
You are moved, prince; let us depart, I pray,    35
Lest your displeasure should enlarge itself
To wrathful terms. This place is dangerous;
The time right deadly. I beseech you, go.
TROILUS
Behold, I pray you!
ULYSSES              Nay, good my lord, go off;
You flow to great distraction. Come, my lord.    40
TROILUS
I prithee, stay.
ULYSSES          You have not patience; come.
TROILUS
I pray you, stay! By hell, and all hell's torments,
I will not speak a word!
DIOMEDES                And so, good night.
CRESSIDA
Nay, but you part in anger.
TROILUS                    Doth that grieve thee?
O withered truth!
ULYSSES          How now, my lord!
TROILUS                          By Jove,          45
I will be patient.
CRESSIDA        Guardian! Why, Greek!
DIOMEDES
Foh, foh! Adieu; you palter.
CRESSIDA
In faith, I do not. Come hither once again.
ULYSSES
You shake, my lord, at something. Will you go?
You will break out.
TROILUS            She strokes his cheek!
ULYSSES                              Come, come.  50
TROILUS
Nay, stay; by Jove, I will not speak a word.
There is between my will and all offenses
A guard of patience. Stay a little while.
THERSITES  How the devil Luxury,° with his fat rump and potato° finger, tickles these together. Fry, lechery, 55 fry!
DIOMEDES  But will you, then?
CRESSIDA
In faith, I will, la; never trust me else.
DIOMEDES
Give me some token for the surety of it.

94–95 Brabbler the hound a hunting hound who would "spend his mouth" in barking while not on the scent would be called "babbler" or "brabbler" by his master  98 leave to see miss seeing
V.ii.12 cliff clef (signifying the musical key; with an obscene pun on cleft; noted reputed a loose woman (with a pun on the sense of musical notes)  24 secretly privately, sexually

54 Luxury lechery  55 potato potatoes were thought to be aphrodisiac

CRESSIDA
I'll fetch you one.                              *Exit.* 60
ULYSSES
You have sworn patience.
TROILUS                              Fear me not, my lord;
I will not be myself, nor have cognition
Of what I feel. I am all patience.

*Enter* CRESSIDA.

THERSITES   Now the pledge! Now, now, now!
CRESSIDA   Here, Diomed, keep this sleeve.        65
TROILUS
O beauty, where is thy faith?
ULYSSES                              My lord—
TROILUS
I will be patient; outwardly I will.
CRESSIDA
You look upon that sleeve; behold it well.
He loved me—O false wench! Give't me again.
DIOMEDES
Whose was't?
CRESSIDA         It is no matter, now I have't again.   70
I will not meet with you tomorrow night.
I prithee, Diomed, visit me no more.
THERSITES   Now she sharpens.° Well said, whetstone!
DIOMEDES
I shall have it.
CRESSIDA   What, this?
DIOMEDES                              Ay, that.
CRESSIDA
O, all you gods! O pretty, pretty pledge!        75
Thy master now lies thinking on his bed
Of thee and me, and sighs, and takes my glove,
And gives memorial° dainty kisses to it,
As I kiss thee. Nay, do not snatch it from me;
He that takes that doth take my heart withal.    80
DIOMEDES
I had your heart before; this follows it.
TROILUS
I did swear patience.
CRESSIDA
You shall not have it, Diomed; faith, you shall not;
I'll give you something else.
DIOMEDES
I will have this. Whose was it?
CRESSIDA                              It is no matter.   85
DIOMEDES
Come, tell me whose it was.
CRESSIDA
'Twas one's that loved me better than you will.
But, now you have it, take it.
DIOMEDES                              Whose was it?
CRESSIDA
By all Diana's waiting-women° yond,
And by herself, I will not tell you whose.       90
DIOMEDES
Tomorrow will I wear it on my helm,
And grieve his spirit that dares not challenge it.

TROILUS
Wert thou the devil, and wor'st it on thy horn,
It should be challenged.
CRESSIDA
Well, well, 'tis done, 'tis past. And yet it is not;   95
I will not keep my word.
DIOMEDES                              Why then, farewell;
Thou never shalt mock Diomed again.
CRESSIDA
You shall not go. One cannot speak a word
But it straight starts you.°
DIOMEDES                              I do not like this fooling.
THERSITES   Nor I, by Pluto; but that that likes° not   100
you pleases me best.
DIOMEDES   What, shall I come? The hour?
CRESSIDA                              Ay, come— O Jove!—
Do come—I shall be plagued.°
DIOMEDES                              Farewell till then.
CRESSIDA
Good night. I prithee, come.        *Exit* [DIOMEDES].
Troilus, farewell. One eye yet looks on thee,
But with my heart the other eye doth see.        105
Ah, poor our sex!° This fault in us I find,
The error° of our eye directs our mind.
What error leads must err. O, then conclude,
Minds swayed by eyes are full of turpitude.    *Exit.*
THERSITES                                                       110
A proof of strength° she could not publish more,°
Unless she said, "My mind is now turned whore."
ULYSSES
All's done, my lord.
TROILUS                              It is.
ULYSSES                              What stay we, then?
TROILUS
To make a recordation to my soul
Of every syllable that here was spoke.
But if I tell how these two did coact,            115
Shall I not lie in publishing a truth?
Sith yet there is a credence in my heart,
An esperance° so obstinately strong
That doth invert th' attest° of eyes and ears,
As if those organs had deceptious° functions,   120
Created only to calumniate.
Was Cressid here?
ULYSSES                 I cannot conjure,° Troyan.
TROILUS
She was not, sure.
ULYSSES                 Most sure she was.
TROILUS
Why, my negation° hath no taste of madness.
ULYSSES                                                          125
Nor mine, my lord. Cressid was here but now.
TROILUS
Let it not be believed for° womanhood!
Think we had mothers; do not give advantage

73 **sharpens** i.e., whets Diomedes' desire   78 **memorial** in remembrance   89 **Diana's waiting-women** the stars clustered about the moon

99 **straight starts you** immediately makes you start angrily away   100 **likes** pleases   103 **plagued** punished   107 **poor our sex** our poor sex   108 **error** wandering (here, physically and morally)   111 **proof of strength** strong proof; **publish more** confess more clearly   119 **esperance** hope   120 **attest** testimony   121 **deceptious** deceiving   123 **conjure** raise spirits   125 **negation** denial   127 **for** for the sake of

To stubborn critics, apt, without a theme,
For depravation,° to square the general sex           130
By Cressid's rule.° Rather think this not Cressid.

ULYSSES
What hath she done, prince, that can soil our mothers?

TROILUS
Nothing at all, unless that this were she.

THERSITES
Will 'a swagger himself out on's own eyes?°

TROILUS
This she? No, this is Diomed's Cressida.           135
If beauty have a soul, this is not she;
If souls guide vows, if vows be sanctimonies,
If sanctimony be the gods' delight,
If there be rule in unity itself,°
This was not she. O madness of discourse,°           140
That cause sets up with and against itself:
Bifold authority,° where reason can revolt
Without perdition, and loss assume all reason
Without revolt.° This is, and is not, Cressid.
Within my soul there doth conduce° a fight           145
Of this strange nature that a thing inseparate°
Divides more wider than the sky and earth;
And yet the spacious breadth of this division
Admits no orifex° for a point as subtle°
As Ariachne's broken woof° to enter.           150
Instance,° O instance, strong as Pluto's gates;
Cressid is mine, tied with the bonds of heaven.
Instance, O instance, strong as heaven itself;
The bonds of heaven are slipped, dissolved, and loosed,
And with another knot, five-finger-tied,°           155
The fractions of her faith, orts° of her love,
The fragments, scraps, the bits, and greasy relics
Of her o'ereaten° faith, are given to Diomed.

ULYSSES
May worthy Troilus be half attached°
With that which here his passion doth express?           160

TROILUS
Ay, Greek! And that shall be divulgèd well
In characters as red as Mars his heart
Inflamed with Venus. Never did young man fancy
With so eternal and so fixed a soul.
Hark, Greek. Much as I do Cressid love,           165

So much by weight hate I her Diomed;
That sleeve is mine that he'll bear on his helm;
Were it a casque° composed by Vulcan's skill,
My sword should bite it. Not the dreadful spout
Which shipmen do the hurricano call,           170
Constringed° in mass by the almighty sun,
Shall dizzy with more clamor Neptune's ear
In his descent than shall my prompted° sword
Falling on Diomed.

THERSITES   He'll tickle it for his concupy.°           175

TROILUS
O Cressid! O false Cressid! False, false, false!
Let all untruths stand by thy stainèd name,
And they'll seem glorious.

ULYSSES                                   O, contain yourself;
Your passion draws ears hither.

*Enter* AENEAS.

AENEAS
I have been seeking you this hour, my lord.           180
Hector, by this, is arming him° in Troy;
Ajax, your guard, stays to conduct you home.

TROILUS
Have with you,° prince. My courteous lord, adieu.
Farewell, revolted fair; and Diomed,
Stand fast, and wear a castle on thy head!           185

ULYSSES
I'll bring you to the gates.

TROILUS
Accept distracted thanks.
            *Exeunt* TROILUS, AENEAS, *and* ULYSSES.

THERSITES   Would I could meet that rogue Diomed.
I would croak like a raven; I would bode,° I would
bode. Patroclus will give me anything for the intelli-           190
gence of this whore. The parrot will not do more for
an almond than he for a commodious drab.° Lechery,
lechery; still wars and lechery; nothing else holds
fashion. A burning devil° take them!           *Exit.*

[Scene III. *Troy; Priam's palace.*]

*Enter* HECTOR *and* ANDROMACHE.

ANDROMACHE
When was my lord so much ungently tempered,
To stop his ears against admonishment?
Unarm, unarm, and do not fight today.

HECTOR
You train° me to offend° you; get you in.
By all the everlasting gods, I'll go.           5

ANDROMACHE
My dreams will, sure, prove ominous to the day.°

HECTOR
No more, I say.

*Enter* CASSANDRA.

129–30 apt . . . depravation ready and eager to claim the
depravity of women, but lacking examples   130–31 square
. . . rule take the measure of womankind by Cressida's
standard   134 Will . . . eyes Will he bluff himself out of
trusting his own sight?   139 If . . . itself i.e., if it is a true
principle that one cannot be two (that Cressida may not be
divided into two persons)   140 discourse reasonable sequence
of thought   141–42 That . . . authority that case of principle
wherein divided authority both supports and confutes the question   142–44 where . . . revolt where reason can rebel without
subsequent chaos, and loss of understanding assume the appearance of reason without reason itself objecting   145 conduce
go on   146 thing inseparate that which is indivisible; i.e.,
Cressida   149 orifex opening; subtle finely sharp   150
Ariachne's broken woof Arachne was a Lydian woman who
challenged Athene to a weaving contest, but the goddess,
angered, tore her work to shreds and changed her to a spider
151 Instance example, proof (here, in the sense of "for instance")   155 five-fingered-tied (1) so tied because Cressida's
hand is now Diomedes' (?) (2) i.e., impossible to untie (?)
156 orts scraps, pieces (as of food)   158 o'ereaten eaten
through, picked over (as a dog will eat the best pieces first, the
last scraps left over)   159 half attached i.e., half so much
affected (as it appears)

168 casque helmet   171 Constringed drawn together   173
prompted urged on, as having its own motive   175 He'll
. . . concupy he'll be well tickled for his concupiscence
("it" refers contemptuously to Diomedes)   181 him himself
183 Have with you let's go along   189 bode portend
disaster   192 commodious drab serviceable whore   194
burning devil venereal disease
V.iii.4 train tempt; offend injure, insult   6 ominous . . .
day omens applicable to this day

CASSANDRA          Where is my brother Hector?
ANDROMACHE
Here, sister; armed and bloody in intent.
Consort with me in loud and dear petition;
Pursue we him on knees, for I have dreamed          10
Of bloody turbulence, and this whole night
Hath nothing been but shapes and forms of slaughter.
CASSANDRA
O, 'tis true.
HECTOR          Ho, bid my trumpet sound.
CASSANDRA
No notes of sally, for the heavens, sweet brother.
HECTOR
Be gone, I say; the gods have heard me swear.          15
CASSANDRA
The gods are deaf to hot and peevish° vows.
They are polluted offerings, more abhorred
Than spotted° livers in the sacrifice.
ANDROMACHE
O, be persuaded! Do not count it holy
To hurt by being just. It is as lawful,          20
For° we would give much, to use violent thefts,
And rob in the behalf of charity.
CASSANDRA
It is the purpose that makes strong the vow;
But vows to every purpose must not hold.°
Unarm, sweet Hector.
HECTOR          Hold you still, I say.          25
Mine honor keeps the weather° of my fate.
Life every man holds dear; but the dear° man
Holds honor far more precious-dear than life.

*Enter* TROILUS.

How now, young man; mean'st thou to fight today?
ANDROMACHE
Cassandra, call my father to persuade.          30
                              *Exit* CASSANDRA.
HECTOR
No, faith, young Troilus; doff thy harness, youth.
I am today i' the vein of chivalry.
Let grow thy sinews till their knots be strong,
And tempt not yet the brushes° of the war.
Unarm thee; go, and doubt thou not, brave boy,          35
I'll stand today for thee and me and Troy.
TROILUS
Brother, you have a vice of mercy in you,
Which better fits a lion than a man.
HECTOR
What vice is that? Good Troilus, chide me for it.
TROILUS
When many times the captive Grecian falls,          40
Even in the fan and wind of your fair sword,
You bid them rise and live.
HECTOR
O, 'tis fair play.
TROILUS          Fool's play, by heaven, Hector.
HECTOR
How now? How now?

TROILUS          For the love of all the gods,
Let's leave the hermit pity with our mother,          45
And when we have our armors buckled on,
The venomed vengeance ride upon our swords,
Spur them to ruthful° work, rein them from ruth.°
HECTOR
Fie, savage, fie!
TROILUS          Hector, then 'tis wars.°
HECTOR
Troilus, I would not have you fight today.          50
TROILUS
Who should withhold me?
Not fate, obedience, nor the hand of Mars
Beck'ning with fiery truncheon° my retire;
Not Priamus and Hecuba on knees,
Their eyes o'ergallèd° with recourse° of tears;          55
Nor you, my brother, with your true sword drawn,
Opposed to hinder me, should stop my way,
But by my ruin.

*Enter* PRIAM *and* CASSANDRA.

CASSANDRA
Lay hold upon him, Priam, hold him fast;
He is thy crutch. Now if thou lose thy stay,°          60
Thou on him leaning, and all Troy on thee,
Fall all together.
PRIAM          Come, Hector, come; go back.
Thy wife hath dreamt, thy mother hath had visions,
Cassandra doth foresee, and I myself
Am like a prophet suddenly enrapt          65
To tell thee that this day is ominous.
Therefore, come back.
HECTOR          Aeneas is afield;
And I do stand engaged to many Greeks,
Even in the faith of valor,° to appear
This morning to them.
PRIAM          Ay, but thou shalt not go.          70
HECTOR
I must not break my faith.
You knew me dutiful; therefore, dear sir,
Let me not shame respect,° but give me leave
To take that course by your consent and voice,
Which you do here forbid me, royal Priam.          75
CASSANDRA
O Priam, yield not to him!
ANDROMACHE          Do not, dear father.
HECTOR
Andromache, I am offended with you.
Upon the love you bear me, get you in.
                              *Exit* ANDROMACHE.
TROILUS
This foolish, dreaming, superstitious girl
Makes all these bodements.°
CASSANDRA          O farewell, dear Hector!          80
Look, how thou diest; look, how thy eye turns pale;
Look, how thy wounds do bleed at many vents!

---

16 **peevish** brash, perverse   18 **spotted** i.e., spoiled   21 **For** because   24 **But . . . hold** vows sworn indiscriminately or to unlawful purpose should not bind the swearer   26 **keeps the weather** i.e., maintains the position of advantage   27 **dear** valuable, worthy   34 **brushes** encounters

48 **ruthful** to be pitied, woeful; **ruth** pity   49 **then 'tis wars** that's what war is   53 **truncheon** a kind of baton used by the referee of a combat to signal the end of the fight   55 **o'er-gallèd** inflamed; **recourse** repeated coursing down, constant flowing   60 **stay** support   69 **faith of valor** a brave man's promise   73 **shame respect** disgrace the respect due to a parent   80 **bodements** evil omens

Hark, how Troy roars, how Hecuba cries out,
How poor Andromache shrills her dolors forth!
Behold, distraction, frenzy, and amazement,    85
Like witless antics,° one another meet,
And all cry Hector! Hector's dead! O Hector!

TROILUS
Away! Away!

CASSANDRA
Farewell. Yet, soft; Hector, I take my leave.
Thou dost thyself and all our Troy deceive.    *Exit.* 90

HECTOR
You are amazed, my liege, at her exclaim.
Go in and cheer the town. We'll forth and fight;
Do deeds worth praise and tell you them at night.

PRIAM
Farewell. The gods with safety stand about thee.
          [*Exeunt* PRIAM *and* HECTOR.]

*Alarum.*

TROILUS
They are at it, hark. Proud Diomed, believe,    95
I come to lose my arm, or win my sleeve.

*Enter* PANDAR.

PANDARUS
Do you hear, my lord? Do you hear?

TROILUS
What now?

PANDARUS
Here's a letter come from yond poor girl.

TROILUS
Let me read.    100

PANDARUS   A whoreson tisick,° a whoreson rascally
tisick so troubles me, and the foolish fortune of this
girl; and what one thing, what another, that I shall
leave you one o' th'se days; and I have a rheum in mine
eyes too, and such an ache in my bones that, unless a    105
man were cursed, I cannot tell what to think on't.
What says she there?

TROILUS
Words, words, mere words, no matter from the heart;
Th' effect doth operate another way.

[*Tearing the letter.*]

Go, wind to wind, there turn and change together.    110
My love with words and errors° still she feeds,
But edifies another with her deeds.    *Exeunt.*

[Scene IV. *The battlefield.*]

[*Alarum.*] *Enter* THERSITES. *Excursions.*

THERSITES   Now they are clapperclawing one another; I'll go look on. That dissembling abominable
varlet, Diomed, has got that same scurvy doting
foolish young knave's sleeve of Troy there in his helm.
I would fain see them meet, that that same young    5
Troyan ass, that loves the whore there, might send
that Greekish whoremasterly villain with the sleeve
back to the dissembling luxurious drab, of a sleeveless°

errand. O' the t'other side, the policy of those crafty
swearing° rascals—that stale old mouseeaten dry    10
cheese, Nestor, and that same dog-fox, Ulysses—is not
proved worth a blackberry. They set me up, in policy,
that mongrel cur, Ajax, against that dog of as bad a
kind, Achilles; and now is the cur Ajax prouder than
the cur Achilles, and will not arm today. Whereupon    15
the Grecians begin to proclaim barbarism,° and policy
grows into an ill opinion.

*Enter* DIOMEDES *and* TROILUS.

Soft, here comes sleeve, and t'other.

TROILUS
Fly not; for shouldst thou take the river Styx,
I would swim after.

DIOMEDES          Thou dost miscall retire.    20
I do not fly, but advantageous care
Withdrew me from the odds of multitude.°
Have at thee!

THERSITES
Hold thy whore, Grecian! Now for thy whore,
Troyan! Now the sleeve, now the sleeve!    25
          [*Exeunt* TROILUS *and* DIOMEDES, *fighting.*]

*Enter* HECTOR.

HECTOR
What art thou, Greek? Art thou for Hector's match?
Art thou of blood and honor?

THERSITES   No, no, I am a rascal, a scurvy railing
knave, a very filthy rogue.

HECTOR   I do believe thee; live.    [*Exit.*] 30

THERSITES   God-a-mercy, that thou wilt believe me;
but a plague break thy neck—for frighting me. What's
become of the wenching rogues? I think they have
swallowed one another. I would laugh at that miracle
—yet, in a sort, lechery eats itself. I'll seek them. *Exit.* 35

[Scene V. *The battlefield.*]

*Enter* DIOMED *and* SERVANT.

DIOMEDES
Go, go, my servant, take thou Troilus' horse;
Present the fair steed to my Lady Cressid.
Fellow, commend my service to her beauty;
Tell her I have chastised the amorous Troyan,
And am her knight by proof.

SERVANT          I go, my lord.    [*Exit.*] 5

*Enter* AGAMEMNON.

AGAMEMNON
Renew, renew! The fierce Polydamas
Hath beat down Menon; bastard Margarelon
Hath Doreus prisoner,
And stands colossus-wise, waving his beam,°
Upon the pashèd corses° of the kings    10
Epistrophus and Cedius; Polyxenes is slain,

---

86 antics madmen   101 tisick cough   111 errors meander-
ings, i.e., underhanded tricks (?)
V.iv.8 sleeveless futile, fruitless

9–10 crafty swearing craftily swearing, i.e., crafty to the
extent of perjury   16 proclaim barbarism recognize the
authority of chaos (to replace policy)   21–22 advantageous
. . . multitude care for my own advantage led me to avoid
facing absurdly heavy odds
V.v.9 beam spear   10 pashèd corses battered corpses

Amphimachus and Thoas deadly hurt,
Patroclus ta'en or slain, and Palamedes
Sore hurt and bruised. The dreadful Sagittary°
Appals our numbers. Haste we, Diomed,    15
To reinforcement, or we perish all.

*Enter* NESTOR.

NESTOR
Go, bear Patroclus' body to Achilles,
And bid the snail-paced Ajax arm for shame.
There is a thousand Hectors in the field;
Now here he fights on Galathe his horse,    20
And there lacks work; anon he's there afoot,
And there they fly or die, like scalèd sculls°
Before the belching whale; then is he yonder,
And there the strawy Greeks, ripe for his edge,°
Fall down before him, like a mower's swath.    25
Here, there, and everywhere, he leaves and takes,
Dexterity so obeying appetite
That what he will he does, and does so much
That proof° is called impossibility.

*Enter* ULYSSES.

ULYSSES
O, courage, courage, princes! Great Achilles    30
Is arming, weeping, cursing, vowing vengeance!
Patroclus' wounds have roused his drowsy blood,
Together with his mangled Myrmidons,
That noseless, handless, hacked and chipped, come to
     him,
Crying on Hector. Ajax hath lost a friend,    35
And foams at mouth, and he is armed and at it,
Roaring for Troilus, who hath done today
Mad and fantastic execution,
Engaging and redeeming of himself
With such a careless force and forceless° care    40
As if that luck, in very spite of cunning,
Bade him win all.

*Enter* AJAX.

AJAX
Troilus, thou coward Troilus!        *Exit.*
DIOMEDES        Ay, there, there.
NESTOR
So, so, we draw together.        *Exit.*

*Enter* ACHILLES.

ACHILLES        Where is this Hector?
Come, come, thou boy-queller,° show thy face;    45
Know what it is to meet Achilles angry.
Hector, where's Hector? I will none but Hector.
           *Exit.*

[Scene VI. *The battlefield.*]

*Enter* AJAX.

AJAX
Troilus, thou coward Troilus, show thy head!

*Enter* DIOMEDES.

DIOMEDES
Troilus, I say, where's Troilus?
AJAX        What wouldst thou?
DIOMEDES
I would correct him.
AJAX
Were I the general, thou shouldst have my office
Ere that correction.° Troilus, I say! What, Troilus!    5

*Enter* TROILUS.

TROILUS
O traitor Diomed! Turn thy false face, thou traitor,
And pay thy life thou owest me for my horse.°
DIOMEDES
Ha, art thou there?
AJAX
I'll fight with him alone. Stand, Diomed.
DIOMEDES
He is my prize; I will not look upon.°    10
TROILUS
Come, both you cogging° Greeks; have at you both!
           [*Exeunt, fighting.*]

[*Enter* HECTOR.]

HECTOR
Yea, Troilus? O, well fought, my youngest brother!

*Enter* ACHILLES.

ACHILLES
Now do I see thee, ha! Have at thee, Hector!

[*They fight;* ACHILLES *tires.*]

HECTOR
Pause, if thou wilt.
ACHILLES
I do disdain thy courtesy, proud Troyan;    15
Be happy that my arms are out of use.
My rest and negligence befriends thee now,
But thou anon shalt hear of me again;
Till when, go seek thy fortune.        *Exit.*
HECTOR        Fare thee well;
I would have been much more a fresher man,    20
Had I expected thee.

*Enter* TROILUS.

           How now, my brother!
TROILUS    Ajax hath ta'en° Aeneas! Shall it be?
No, by the flame of yonder glorious heaven,
He shall not carry him;° I'll be ta'en too,
Or bring him off. Fate, hear me what I say!    25
I reck not though thou end my life today.        *Exit.*

*Enter one in armor.*

HECTOR
Stand, stand, thou Greek; thou art a goodly mark.
No? Wilt thou not? I like thy armor well;
I'll frush° it and unlock the rivets all,
But I'll be master of it. Wilt thou not, beast, abide?    30
Why then, fly on, I'll hunt thee for thy hide.
           *Exit* [*in pursuit*].

---

14 **Sagittary** a centaur (half man, half horse), who was a
splendid archer and aided the Trojans   22 **scalèd sculls** scaly
schools of fish   24 **strawy . . . edge** Greeks who are like
straw, ripe for the edge of the scythe   29 **proof** visible fact
40 **forceless** casual, reckless   45 **boy-queller** boy-killer

V.vi.5 **correction** i.e., privilege to correct   7 **horse** with a
pun on *whore*?   10 **look upon** stand by   11 **cogging** deceitful
22 **ta'en** taken captive   24 **carry him** prevail over him   29
**frush** smash

[Scene VII. *The battlefield.*]

*Enter* ACHILLES, *with* MYRMIDONS.

ACHILLES
Come here about me, you my Myrmidons;
Mark what I say. Attend me where I wheel.
Strike not a stroke, but keep yourselves in breath.
And when I have the bloody Hector found,
Empale him° with your weapons round about;          5
In fellest° manner execute° your arms.
Follow me, sirs, and my proceedings eye;
It is decreed Hector the great must die.
                              *Exit,* [*with* MYRMIDONS].

*Enter* THERSITES, MENELAUS, PARIS [*the last two
fighting*].

THERSITES   The cuckold and the cuckold-maker are
at it. Now, bull! Now, dog! 'Loo,° Paris, 'loo! Now,    10
my double-horned Spartan! 'Loo, Paris, 'loo! The
bull has the game;° 'ware horns, ho!
                              *Exeunt* PARIS *and* MENELAUS.

*Enter* BASTARD [*Margarelon*].

BASTARD   Turn, slave, and fight.
THERSITES   What art thou?
BASTARD   A bastard son of Priam's.                    15
THERSITES   I am a bastard too; I love bastards. I am
bastard begot, bastard instructed, bastard in mind,
bastard in valor, in everything illegitimate. One bear
will not bite another, and wherefore should one bastard? Take heed, the quarrel's most ominous to us. If   20
the son of a whore fight for a whore, he tempts judgment. Farewell, bastard.
BASTARD   The devil take thee, coward!     *Exeunt.*

[Scene VIII. *The battlefield.*]

*Enter* HECTOR.

HECTOR
Most putrefièd core, so fair without,
Thy goodly armor thus hath cost thy life.
Now is my day's work done; I'll take my breath.
Rest, sword; thou hast thy fill of blood and death.
[*Puts off his helmet, and hangs his shield behind him.*]

*Enter* ACHILLES *and* MYRMIDONS.

ACHILLES
Look, Hector, how the sun begins to set,                5
How ugly night comes breathing at his heels.
Even with the vail° and dark'ning of the sun,
To close the day up, Hector's life is done.
HECTOR
I am unarmed; forgo this vantage, Greek.
ACHILLES
Strike, fellows, strike. This is the man I seek.       10
                              [HECTOR *falls.*]

V.vii.5 Empale him hem him in   6 fellest cruelest; execute
use   10 Now, bull . . . 'Loo Thersites compares the combat
of Menelaus and Paris to the baiting of a bull by a dog, as it was
done in such arenas as the Paris Garden   12 has the game
wins
V.viii.7 vail sinking, going down

So, Ilion, fall thou next! Come, Troy, sink down!
Here lies thy heart, thy sinews, and thy bone.
On, Myrmidons, and cry you all amain,
"Achilles hath the mighty Hector slain!"

*Retreat.*

Hark, a retire upon our Grecian part.                  15
ONE GREEK
The Troyans' trumpets sound the like, my lord.
ACHILLES
The dragon wing of night o'erspreads the earth.
And, sticklerlike,° the armies separates.
My half-supped sword, that frankly° would have fed,
Pleased with this dainty bait, thus goes to bed.       20
[*Sheathes his sword.*]
Come, tie his body to my horse's tail;
Along the field I will the Troyan trail.     *Exeunt.*

[Scene IX. *The battlefield.*]

*Enter* AGAMEMNON, AJAX, MENELAUS, NESTOR,
DIOMED, *and the rest, marching.* [*Sound retreat. Shout.*]

AGAMEMNON
Hark, hark, what shout is that?
NESTOR                                Peace, drums!
SOLDIERS (*Within.*)                            Achilles!
Achilles! Hector's slain! Achilles!
DIOMEDES
The bruit° is, Hector's slain, and by Achilles.
AJAX
If it be so, yet bragless let it be;
Great Hector was as good a man as he.                  5
AGAMEMNON
March patiently along. Let one be sent
To pray Achilles see us at our tent.
If in his death the gods have us befriended,
Great Troy is ours, and our sharp wars are ended.
                              *Exeunt.*

[Scene X. *The battlefield.*]

*Enter* AENEAS, PARIS, ANTENOR, DEIPHOBUS.

AENEAS
Stand, ho! Yet are we masters of the field.
Never go home; here starve we out the night.

*Enter* TROILUS.

TROILUS
Hector is slain.
ALL                   Hector! The gods forbid!
TROILUS
He's dead and at the murderer's horse's tail,
In beastly sort, dragged through the shameful field.   5
Frown on, you heavens, effect your rage with speed;
Sit, gods, upon your thrones, and smile° at Troy.
I say, at once let your brief plagues be mercy,°
And linger not our sure destructions on.

18 sticklerlike like an umpire separating combatants, and
ordering the field   19 frankly freely, abundantly
V.ix.3 bruit rumor
V.x.7 smile i.e., in derision   8 let . . . mercy be merciful in
letting the plagues you send destroy us quickly

AENEAS
My lord, you do discomfort all the host.                              10

TROILUS
You understand me not that tell me so.
I do not speak of flight, of fear, of death,
But dare all imminence that gods and men
Address their dangers in.° Hector is gone.
Who shall tell Priam so, or Hecuba?                                  15
Let him that will a screech owl° aye be called
Go in to Troy, and say there Hector's dead.
There is a word will Priam turn to stone,
Make wells and Niobes° of the maids and wives,
Cold statues of the youth, and in a word                             20
Scare Troy out of itself. But march away.
Hector is dead; there is no more to say.
Stay yet. You vile abominable tents,
Thus proudly pitched upon our Phrygian plains,
Let Titan° rise as early as he dare,                                 25
I'll through and through you! And, thou great-sized
    coward,°
No space of earth shall sunder our two hates.
I'll haunt thee like a wicked conscience still,
That moldeth goblins swift as frenzy's thoughts.
Strike a free march to Troy. With comfort go;                        30
Hope of revenge shall hide our inward woe.

*Enter PANDARUS.*

PANDARUS
But hear you, hear you!

13–14 But . . . in but instead dare whatever imminent
dangers gods and men may be preparing   16 screech-owl a
bearer of ill omen   19 Niobes Niobe wept for her slain
children until she was turned into a column of stone, from
which tears continued to flow   25 Titan Helios, the sun,
one of the Titans   26 coward Achilles

TROILUS
Hence, broker, lackey! Ignominy and shame
Pursue thy life, and live aye with thy name.
                          *Exeunt all but PANDARUS.*

PANDARUS   A goodly medicine for my aching bones!   35
O world, world! Thus is the poor agent despised. O
traders and bawds, how earnestly are you set awork,
and how ill requited! Why should our endeavor be so
loved, and the performance so loathed? What verse
for it? What instance for it? Let me see.                            40
    Full merrily the humble-bee doth sing,
      Till he hath lost his honey and his sting;
    And being once subdued in armèd tail,
      Sweet honey and sweet notes together fail.
Good traders in the flesh, set this in your painted
    cloths:°                                                         45
"As many as be here of Pandar's hall,
Your eyes, half out, weep out at Pandar's fall;
Or if you cannot weep, yet give some groans,
Though not for me, yet for your aching bones."
Brethren and sisters of the hold-door trade,°                        50
Some two months hence my will shall here be made.
It should be now, but that my fear is this,
Some gallèd goose of Winchester° would hiss.
Till then I'll sweat° and seek about for eases,
And at that time bequeath you my diseases.    [*Exit.*]   55

45 painted cloths painted cloth hangings, used in brothels,
sometimes bearing mottoes   50 hold-door trade prostitution
53 gallèd . . . Winchester angry prostitute (the Bishop of
Winchester had once held jurisdiction over the area of London
called Southwark, where many brothels stood; a prostitute—
and sometimes a venereal disease—was called a "Winchester
goose")   54 sweat a treatment for gout or rheumatism, as well
as for venereal disease

# ALL'S WELL THAT ENDS WELL

EDITED BY SYLVAN BARNET

## Introduction

It has been customary since the late nineteenth century to call *All's Well That Ends Well* a "problem play," or a "dark comedy." The first term relates it to the sort of drama we associate chiefly with Ibsen, a play about a social system in need of repair, a system with, say, faulty attitudes toward female emancipation or toward venereal disease. Because *All's Well* (like much other Elizabethan comedy) includes speeches on the nature of virtue and presents us with a picture of a virtuous but lowborn woman rejected by her snobbish husband, there was enough point in the comparison to give it some life for more than half a century. But what is the problem? Because Shakespeare's Helena seemed to resemble Ibsen's Nora, *All's Well* gained Shaw's approval (as much of Shakespeare did not), but it is not really very like a nineteenth-century *pièce à thèse*. It does not move toward a debate in which some commonly held code is called into doubt; it does not preach the abandonment of humbug; it does not suggest that the world will go well if only people will give up romantic ideas. It does not really anatomize the problem of nobility —Does nobility reside in lineage or in deeds?—because the lowborn heroine is so clearly right and the snobbish aristocrat so clearly wrong that there is no debate.

Abandoning the hunt for this sort of "problem," then, we can turn to a different sort of problem that has vexed students of the play: Where does it fit in Shakespeare's career? Here we confront the term "dark comedy," which associates this play with an alleged period in Shakespeare's life, about 1601–06, when he supposedly lost faith in the golden world he had seen about him (and had dramatized in *A Midsummer Night's Dream*, *As You Like It*, and *Twelfth Night*) and fell into the bitter cynicism that—users of the term commonly say—marks this play as well as *Measure for Measure*, *Troilus and Cressida*, *Hamlet*, *King Lear*, and *Timon of Athens*. The late E. K. Chambers—a great scholar, with whom one may differ only humbly and reluctantly— in *Shakespeare: A Survey* puts it this way: *All's Well*

groups itself undeniably with *Troilus and Cressida* and *Measure for Measure*, as one of the bitter comedies; for it is a comedy from which all laughter has evaporated, save the grim laughter which follows the dubious sallies of

Monsieur Lavache and the contemptuous laughter which presides over the plucking bare of the ineffable Parolles. The spiritual affinities of Helena's story are indeed far less with the radiant humor of *Twelfth Night* and *As You Like It* than with the analytic psychology of the great advance-guard of tragedy, *Julius Caesar* and *Hamlet*, which was almost contemporary with these.

The theory runs that for some reason Shakespeare became unhappy and turned to tragedy and to bitter comedy. Why he did so is variously explained. For some proponents, the sonnets tell a story of the poet's discovery of betrayal; the friend's infidelity, or the Dark Lady's lust, drove Shakespeare to despair, and the despair is manifested in the plays. Or the fall of Essex shattered Shakespeare's world. (Chambers very tentatively inclines to the suggestion that "Shakespeare's world-sickness" may be most plausibly related to the failure of Essex's conspiracy.) Or the death of Shakespeare's father in 1601 was a crushing blow. Or the advent of the unimpressive James I, following the death of Queen Elizabeth in 1603, was enough to cause the poet great unhappiness. But all these speculations are based on the shaky premise that a professional dramatist's works mirror his state of mind, as a romantic lyric poet's are supposed to. He writes tragedies when tragedy has struck home, and he writes comedies when all is going well. Probably an Elizabethan dramatist would have been surprised to learn that he had been writing autobiography when all along he had thought he was writing tragedy, comedy, history, or whatever else his company wanted or was currently in vogue.

The play was first published in the Folio of 1623, seven years after Shakespeare's death. There is no external evidence of the date of *All's Well*—no reference to it by any witness, no quotation from it in a datable work, no detected allusion in it to any current event. Conjectures about its date must be based on theories about Shakespeare's progressive use of certain motifs and the development of Shakespeare's style.

To take the question of motif first: most readers find the bed trick, or the "substitute bride motif" (to use the delicate term that folklorists apply to stories in which a wife substitutes herself for another woman to deceive her would-be adulterous husband), so arresting that the play is felt to closely resemble *Measure for Measure*, in which Angelo beds with Mariana, to whom he was betrothed, rather than with Isabella, whom he thinks he has seduced. In *All's Well*, the caddish Bertram vows he will not live with his wife Helena until she can get a ring from his finger and show him a child she has had by him; Helena, taking advantage of Bertram's illicit interest in the chaste Diana, is at length able to fulfill these seemingly impossible conditions. Shakespeare, however, was a great user and re-user of folk motifs, and there is really not much strength in the argument that because the "substitute bride" is used in *All's Well* the play must be close in date to *Measure for Measure*, given at court in December, 1604. After all, there is a tale of shipwreck at the start of *The Comedy of Errors* and there is an apparent shipwreck at the start of *The Tempest*, but some twenty years separate the two. Similarly, there are outlaws in *The Two Gentlemen of Verona* and in *As You Like It*, but no one would seriously argue that the plays were written in close proximity. On the other hand, *The Comedy of Errors* and *Love's Labor's Lost*—universally agreed to be among Shakespeare's earliest work—share no common motifs; *Love's Labor's Lost* does not even conclude with the unions or reunions that are almost the *sine qua non* of Shakespeare's comedies.

The bed trick in *Measure for Measure* is managed not by the bride but by a duke who advises her how to outwit a would-be seducer. The bed trick in *All's Well* is the bride's idea, and in its clever heroine *All's Well* differs from *Measure for Measure* and resembles the earlier comedies: *The Merchant of Venice* (in which Portia is more resourceful than all the Venetian men), *As You Like It* (in which Rosalind, banished to the woods, manipulates two weddings), and *Twelfth Night* (in which Viola at length weds the man whom she has loved for four and a half acts). Like these comedies, moreover, *All's Well* is a play about love and marriage: the "dark" *Troilus and Cressida*, less about love than about dishonor and disillusion, concludes with the lovers separated; *Measure for Measure* concludes with a strong hint of a marriage, but the play is less about love than it is about lust and justice and mercy.

The subject matter offers no compelling argument to date the play later than the "happy" comedies and along with *Measure for Measure*, but there are abundant passages in a style more mature than the style (or, rather, styles) typical of the earliest plays. Much of the verse in *All's Well* has a complexity, weightiness, and forcefulness that resemble the verse in *Hamlet* and *Measure for Measure*. Here are two examples:

> Why not a mother? When I said "a mother"
> Methought you saw a serpent. What's in "mother"
> That you start at it? I say I am your mother,
> And put you in the catalogue of those
> That were enwombèd mine. 'Tis often seen
> Adoption strives with nature, and choice breeds
> A native slip to us from foreign seeds.
> You ne'er oppressed me with a mother's groan,
> Yet I express to you a mother's care. (I.iii.141–49)

> That thou didst love her, strikes some scores away
> From the great compt; but love that comes too late,

> Like a remorseful pardon slowly carried,
> To the great sender turns a sour offense,
> Crying, "That's good that's gone." Our rash faults
> Make trivial price of serious things we have,
> Not knowing them, until we know their grave. (V.iii.56–62)

But this business of choosing passages is tricky; no play is all of a piece, and in selecting these a fair number in a different style were skipped. There are more than a few passages that are so simple, so jingling, so unsophisticated that they seem like apprentice work:

> If she, my liege, can make me know this clearly,
> I'll love her dearly, ever, ever dearly. (V.iii.315–16)

> Here is my hand; the premises observed,
> Thy will by my performance shall be served;
> So make the choice of thy own time, for I,
> Thy resolved patient, on thee still rely.
> More should I question thee, and more I must,
> Though more to know could not be more to trust. (II.i.204–09)

Various explanations can be offered for the rhymes—that here they add to a sense of ritual, that there they are used for a letter (which must be set off), that they deal with the past, that they make a contrast with a previous speech, that they are vestiges of an old play Shakespeare is revising, and so on—but the fact remains that the style is not sufficiently uniform to allow the easy generalization that it resembles the style of *Measure for Measure*. The most noticeable sign of maturity is the high percentage of run-on lines (giving a flexibility and power lacking in much of the early highly regular verse)—but this percentage is not significantly different from that in *The Merchant of Venice*, published in 1598 and quite possibly written a year or two earlier. It should be mentioned, too, that some of the least slick, the most "weighty" passages in *All's Well* may owe part of their weight to the fact that the printer did not correctly decipher the manuscript; the text is not a particularly good one, and some of the obscurity (often associated with maturity) perhaps has its origin in printing house uncertainties.

"Obscurity" gets us back to the idea of a "dark" play. The bed trick has seemed unpleasant to most readers (though it should be noted that by this trick Helena saves Bertram from committing adultery, and ultimately restores to him the wife who, we have seen, is a loving as well as an enterprising woman), but no one in the play minds it. The virtuous Widow, who would avoid "any staining act," pronounces the plan "lawful," and the king is sufficiently delighted by the outcome to reward the Widow's daughter. The other allegedly "dark" aspect of the play that has attracted a good deal of comment is the beginning, which is weighty with talk of death and disease:

> COUNTESS In delivering my son from me I bury a
> second husband.
> BERTRAM And I in going, madam, weep o'er my
> father's death anew; but I must attend his majesty's
> command. . . .

COUNTESS  What hope is there of his majesty's amendment?

LAFEW  He hath abandoned his physicians.

                                        (I.i.1–5, 12–14)

The play goes on, with talk of "haggish age" that has brought about the king's illness, the death of Bertram's father, and presumably the death of Helena's father. Yet how do Elizabethan comedies usually open if not with some sorrowful problem at hand, whose dissolution will be the matter of the play? The first speech in *The Comedy of Errors* is a couplet spoken by a man who knows he will be sentenced to death (it contains the words "fall," "doom of death," and "woes"); when he is assured that he is indeed sentenced to death, he tells a woeful tale of shipwreck and separation from wife and children. *The Two Gentlemen of Verona* begins with friends separating; *Love's Labor's Lost* begins with a vigorous speech announcing a method of securing eternal fame, but this very speech is full of awareness of "brazen tombs," "disgrace of death," and "cormorant devouring Time." The fact is that the first scene of *All's Well* mingles with its references to sorrow references to renewal, rebirth—the happy ending that characterizes comedy. The countess is losing her son, but she is assured she will find in the king "a husband"; Helena's father has died, but his prescription lives in papers that Helena possesses, and the king will soon be restored to health. Helena seems to be grieving for her dead father, but in fact her mind is on the young man whom she loves, and though her love seems hopeless she wins him as her husband. If *As You Like It* included the bed trick, which is to say if Orlando were a cad, quite possibly the embarrassed and unhappy critics would have found that play, commonly called happy and golden, as dark as *All's Well*. After all, *As You Like It* begins with the bitter complaints of a younger brother, quickly moves to a fight between the brothers and to some churlish words ("old dog") spoken to an aged faithful retainer, and then to news that the rightful duke has been banished by his brother: family treachery, the tragic stuff that makes *King Lear*. Of course Bertram, the young lover in *All's Well*, is far less engaging than Orlando, but several of Shakespeare's lovers are unamiable people (Proteus in *The Two Gentlemen*, Claudio in *Much Ado About Nothing*), yet the comedies are not therefore dark. (It can even be argued that Lysander's delightful transient infidelity in *A Midsummer Night's Dream* has its affinity with Bertram's perverse desire to seduce Diana when he is furnished with Helena, but it must be admitted that the spirit of holiday foolery, dominant in *A Midsummer Night's Dream*, is sparse in *All's Well*.)

An old theory, now rarely held because of the tendency to call it a problem play and to date it about 1602, suggests that *All's Well That Ends Well* is the play Francis Meres called *Love's Labor's Won* when he listed a dozen of Shakespeare's plays in 1598. Meres says that Shakespeare excels both in comedy and tragedy:

For comedy, witness his *Gentlemen of Verona*, his *Errors*, his *Love Labor's Lost*, his *Love Labor's Won*, his *Midsummer's Night Dream*, and his *Merchant of Venice;* for tragedy his *Richard the Second*, *Richard the Third*, *Henry the Fourth*, *King John*, *Titus Andronicus*, and his *Romeo and Juliet*.

Of these, only *Love Labor's Won* has not come down to us, or has not come down to us under that title. If Meres was not mistaken (he seems to know what he is talking about), and Shakespeare had indeed written the play, it is reasonable to assume that it is included in the Folio, but under a different title. (The Folio was prepared by long-standing friends of Shakespeare, who sought to collect his plays as his memorial.) *The Taming of the Shrew* has been the favorite candidate because it is unquestionably early enough for Meres to have known of it in 1598, but the recent discovery of a page from an account book for 1603 lists—among other plays—both *The Taming of the Shrew* and *Love's Labor Won* (sic), and so the two cannot be identical. The plot of *All's Well* makes it an eminently suitable candidate; Helena certainly labors to win her beloved. If the identity of *All's Well* and *Love's Labor's Won* (to combine Meres's spelling and that of the account book) were established, it would prove that *All's Well* had been written by 1598 and published by 1603—but no proof is available. Put it this way: if Meres was correct that Shakespeare wrote *Love's Labor's Won*, quite possibly it survives (presumably with substantial revision) as *All's Well*, and we should alter our conception of Shakespeare's development; but if Meres was mistaken, and the play was by another hand (hence omitted from the Folio), we have been wasting our time.

Although the play dramatizes the triumph of love's labor, Helena engages in activities that have distressed some readers. Her dialogue with Parolles (I.i.) in which she bandies jokes about virginity may seem neither witty nor decorous to us, but we ought to recall that Bassanio's Portia, a paragon, makes off-color jokes, as do several of Shakespeare's other chaste comic heroines. This dialogue, moreover, is not mere irrelevant foolery; Helena insists that she will maintain her chastity awhile, as a virtuous heroine should, and the dialogue concludes with Parolles' advice, "Get thee a good husband, and use him as he uses thee." The play deals with Helena's getting a husband; in one sense she does not use him as he uses her (she returns his scorn with love); in another sense she does, for she deceives him—to a good end—as he deceives her. He accepts her as his wife but fabricates a means of leaving her without consummating the marriage, and she fabricates a means of saving him from adultery and of guiding him into what we must assume will be (as in the world of all comedy) a marriage in which they live happily ever after. That Helena engages in deception is not in itself bad. Deception in Elizabethan drama is commonly used to assist a love affair. No one is upset by the "honest slanders" devised to bring Beatrice and Benedick together in *Much Ado*, and the list of heroines who in one way or another deceive their beloved for a good purpose is a long one. Helena takes advantage of Bertram's pursuit of Diana to substitute herself for Diana:

Why then tonight
Let us assay our plot, which, if it speed,
Is wicked meaning in a lawful deed,
And lawful meaning in a lawful act,
Where both not sin, and yet a sinful fact.    (III.vii.43–47)

Because Bertram intends adultery, for him it will be a "wicked meaning," but it will be a lawful deed because a chaste wife will be in bed with her husband; it will be, for Helena, a "lawful meaning in a lawful act," and though Bertram will think he is sinning, there is no sin because he and his partner are husband and wife. Bertram is an "unseasoned courtier," a foolish young prig whom Helena must bring to a healthy condition (he has "sick desires" for Diana) rather as she must heal the king's disease. Like Shakespeare's better-known heroines, Rosalind, Portia, Beatrice, and Viola, Helena is energetic yet thoroughly womanly. If one thinks she is too inclined to wear the pants, what of Julia, Rosalind, and Viola, all of whom—unlike Helena—literally wear pants in their efforts to bring matters to a happy ending? Helena has something of the earnestness of Brutus' Portia combined with the resourcefulness of Bassanio's Portia; she fears that her "ambitious love" has "offended," and that Bertram is "too good and fair" for her, but no character except Bertram ever speaks ill of her, and it is evident to all readers that Bertram is (until the end, when he accepts Helena) far from "good and fair."

Perhaps our chief dissatisfaction with Helena arises from the fact that we cannot laugh at her—unless we feel that Parolles has the better of the argument on virginity. Rosalind (to give only one example) is engaging partly because we enjoy her discomfort when she learns that her beloved Orlando is in the Forest of Arden:

Alas the day! What shall I do with my doublet and hose? What did he when thou saw'st him? What said he? How looked he? Wherein went he? What makes he here? Did he ask for me? Where remains he? How parted he with thee? And when shalt thou see him again? Answer me in one word. (*As You Like It*, III.ii.220–25)

We get nothing like this, and we miss it. But if we never experience the delightful intimacy of laughing at one with whom we sympathize, it does not follow that we must find Helena an unpleasant man-hunter. She feigns death—but in *Much Ado* and in *A Winter's Tale* similar false reports of death are issued for the good purpose of restoring a man to his loving wife. The women in those two plays do not themselves contrive the report, but no discredit accrues to the contrivers and none ought to accrue to Helena. It is better to say that Helena resourcefully persists in love than that (E. K. Chambers' words) she "passes from dishonor to dishonor."

The offensive person in the play is not Helena, who loves Bertram and brings him to love her, but Bertram, whose folly is abundantly remarked upon. His mother, Lafew, and the king all rebuke him, and though one can sympathize with his plea that in the choice of a wife he might reasonably be allowed the help of his own eyes, it is clear that he is blind—not only to Helena's goodness but to Parolles' folly. Bertram believes that the cowardly braggart Parolles is a soldier simply because he talks and dresses the part. Bertram squares his guesses by shows (to take a line that appears in another context), values the worthless Parolles and (a sort of corollary) scorns the virtuous Helena. Fortunately, he lives in the world of comedy; "comedy is full of purposes mistook, not 'falling on the inventor's head' but luckily misfiring altogether. In comedy, as often happens in life, people are mercifully saved from being as wicked as they meant to be."[1]

It is commonly said that the world of *All's Well*, like that of *Measure for Measure*, is a depraved place, a cynic's vision—again the "dark" realm of an embittered writer. Readers of the essay "*Measure for Measure*"[2] by R. W. Chambers (not to be confused with E. K. Chambers) will not be likely to see *Measure for Measure* as "dark." Nor is the world of *All's Well* wretched. Bertram is a fool, Parolles is close to a scoundrel, but the rest of the characters—including the Clown, whose bawdry is playful enough—are tolerable and tolerant, endowed with no more than the usual faults of men and (if we keep in mind Helena, Lafew, the king, and the countess) with more than the usual virtues. Bertram's failure to value Helena and his failure to see through Parolles are abundantly remarked upon, but when Parolles has been exposed and Helena is reputed dead, and nothing can come of further dwelling on Bertram's past folly, Lafew, the countess, and the king forgive him. Lafew asserts that Bertram was "misled with [i.e., by] a snipped taffeta fellow," the countess (who had spoken sharply to Bertram when sharp-speaking might have been of some use) now urges the king

to make it
Natural rebellion done i' th' blade of youth,
When oil and fire, too strong for reason's force,
O'erbears it and burns on. (V.iii.5–8)

and the king replies that he has "forgiven and forgotten all." Indeed, despite his immaturity Bertram has won repute in battle and now, apparently aware of his opprobrious behavior, he begs pardon for his "high-repented blames." It is recognized that Bertram has done abundant wrong to the king, to his mother, to Helena, and

to himself
The greatest wrong of all. He lost a wife
Whose beauty did astonish the survey
Of richest eyes; whose words all ears took captive;
Whose dear perfection hearts that scorned to serve
Humbly called mistress. (V.iii.14–19)

But this greatest wrong has not in fact been done; love and Providence have contrived that all shall end well. "What things are we!" exclaims the First Lord, and the Second Lord replies:

Merely our own traitors. And as in the common course of all treasons we still see them reveal themselves till they attain to their abhorred ends, so he that in this action contrives against his own nobility, in his proper stream o'erflows himself. (IV.iii.21–25)

In another context this is the stuff of tragedy. Macbeth, for example, urged by his wife, contrives against his own nobility and destroys himself. The violence he does to his king recoils upon him and he finds he has achieved not "honor, love, obedience, troops of friends," but only curses, false friends, and sleepless nights. In *All's Well* men are not angels, but neither are they devils; love and forgiveness are no less evident than folly and youthful lust. The vision is no darker than that radiant moment in *The*

[1] Helen Gardner, "*As You Like It*," in *More Talking of Shakespeare*, ed. John Garret (1959).

[2] In R. W. Chambers, *Man's Unconquerable Mind* (1952).

*Merchant of Venice* when Portia, appealing to Shylock to show mercy toward the man who has indeed forfeited his bond, says:

> Though justice be thy plea, consider this:
> That, in the course of justice, none of us
> Should see salvation. We do pray for mercy,
> And that same prayer doth teach us all to render
> The deeds of mercy.                    (IV.i.197–201)

The world of *The Merchant of Venice* is more lyrical, filled with moonlight and music—when Shylock is not onstage —but the vision of humanity is no higher; lower, indeed, for Shylock is malevolent where Bertram and Parolles are foolish. In Shakespeare's comedies, folly is not something scourged but something enjoyed. For example, in *Love's Labor's Lost*, a delightful spoof on the folly of trying to live as though men were disembodied minds, the King of Navarre, leader of the scheme to form a society of scholars who shall give no audience to women, proudly tells his followers that they "war against affections [passions],/And the huge army of the world's desire." How noble, and yet how foolish. Nor is it cynical to say that this is folly; Berowne aptly points out that "every man with his affects is born,/Not by might mastered, but by special grace," and as though to prove his point a constable brings in a clown who has already broken the vow to forswear women. The affects have their place, no less than reason. Even our faults can serve us. "The web of our life," says a French lord in *All's Well*, "is of a mingled yarn, good and ill together; our virtues would be proud if our faults whipped them not, and our crimes would despair if they were not cherished by our virtues" (IV.iii.71–74). If mortals are fools, Shakespeare seems to cherish them as much for their folly as Puck does, and (notably in *Much Ado*, where the clowns bring about the denouement) he turns their folly to use. The delightful thing about folly is that it insulates a man from despair and fills him with a zest for living. Othello's occupation is gone when Desdemona is (he thinks) unfaithful, but Parolles can easily enough find another livelihood when his military claims are exposed.

> If my heart were great
> 'Twould burst at this. Captain I'll be no more,
> But I will eat and drink and sleep as soft
> As captain shall. Simply the thing I am
> Shall make me live. Who knows himself a braggart,
> Let him fear this; for it will come to pass
> That every braggart shall be found an ass.
> Rust, sword; cool, blushes; and Parolles live
> Safest in shame! Being fooled, by fool'ry thrive!
> There's place and means for every man alive.
> I'll after them.                    *Exit.*
>                    (IV.iii.334–44)

Othello kills himself, "for he was great of heart," but Parolles is protected from Othello's greatness ("*If my heart were great*") and therefore from murdering a Desdemona and from committing suicide. Lafew, who had been the first to detect Parolles, treats him generously enough at last: "Though you are a fool and a knave you shall eat." Parolles, indeed, in the final act becomes an engaging fool; another comic dramatist would have whipped him from the stage, but Shakespeare exposes Parolles not merely for moral reasons but "for the love of laughter" (twice repeated), and finds a place for the braggart-turned-fool in the abundant comic world.

All ends well, partly because most of the people in the play are decent, but chiefly because of a beneficent Providence. By the time the play reaches its end, not only has the king been restored to health, Parolles cured of his pretensions, Diana equipped with a dowry, and Bertram brought to his senses, but Helena is wed in deed as well as name to a loving husband. Now, it is the nature of a play, or any work of art, in contrast to real life, that the doings of the characters are remarkably coherent. In the theater we look attentively for a few hours at a few people and we see the course of a lifetime, or all that presumably is significant in a lifetime, whereas in life things go on for years, mingled with a good deal of irrelevance. Life may or may not be a chaos; art is a pattern. Something like Fate presides in all plays, however vivid and energetic the characters may be. "Hanging and wiving goes by destiny," Nerissa lightly says, providing us with a tag that summarizes tragedy and comedy. "Who can control his fate?" Othello asks. Surely not the tragic heroes—unless we see them as men who get exactly what they deserve. No fewer than five of Euripides' plays include (with one variation) these lines:

> Many indeed the shapes and changes are
> Of heavenly beings. Many things the gods
> Achieve beyond our judgment. What we thought
> Is not confirmed, and what we thought not God
> Contrives. And so it happens in this story.[3]

The comic version of Fate is Fortune or Time or beneficent Providence:

> All other doubts, by Time let them be cleared.
> Fortune brings in some boats that are not steered.
>                    (*Cymbeline*, IV.iii.45–46)

> O Time, thou must untangle this, not I;
> It is too hard a knot for me t' untie.
>                    (*Twelfth Night*, II.ii.40–41)

In *All's Well*, numerous references to Providence make explicit the pattern that underlies all comedy. "The very hand of heaven" cures the king. Later, Helena is providentially brought to the very place and persons that can restore her to Bertram:

>                    Doubt not but heaven
> Hath brought me up to be your daughter's dower,
> As it hath fated her to be my motive [i.e., means]
> And helper to a husband.                    (IV.iv.18–21)

In Shakespeare's source, the heroine "purposed to find means to attain the two things, that thereby she might recover her husband," and she set out for Florence. But in *All's Well*, when Helena sets out on her pilgrimage to Saint Jaques we are not given any reason to believe that she

[3] Translation by Rex Warner, in *Three Great Plays of Euripides*, New York: The New American Library of World Literature, Inc. (Mentor Books), 1958.

is pursuing Bertram. Learning of the seemingly impossible conditions Bertram has imposed, she says almost nothing, allowing the countess and others to censure him. When the countess and lords leave the stage, in a soliloquy she blames herself for driving Bertram to the wars where he may "be the mark/Of smoky muskets."

> Shall I stay here to do't? No, no, although
> The air of paradise did fan the house
> And angels officed all. I will be gone,
> That pitiful rumor may report my flight
> To consolate thine ear. Come night, end day;
> For with the dark, poor thief, I'll steal away.        *Exit.*
>                                                 (III.ii.124-29)

We learn (from a letter) that she has set out on a pilgrimage, and that Bertram may thus return to Rousillon. We next meet Helena in Florence, where by chance she engages in conversation a widow who, as it turns out, is the mother of a young girl whom Bertram is courting. We have no right to assume that Helena lied in her soliloquy (to whom could she be lying?) and that she set out to catch Bertram; we can only assume that the hand of heaven has brought about the encounter in Florence with the Widow, her daughter, and Bertram. It is worth mentioning, too, that in the source the heroine meets a Florentine woman who leads her to the widow, but Shakespeare's Helena happens on the Widow unaided. The effect is to increase the sense of Providence precisely because it is so improbable that Helena would encounter the Widow herself. To say that in *All's Well* there is often a sense of Providence is not, of course, to say that the characters are mindless puppets who undertake nothing for themselves. Helena herself argues (I.i.217-30) to the contrary. Readiness, however, is all:

> But with the word the time will bring on summer.
> When briars shall have leaves as well as thorns,
> And be as sweet as sharp. We must away;
> Our wagon is prepared, and time revives us.
> All's well that ends well; still the fine's the crown
> Whate'er the course, the end is the renown. (IV.iv.31-36)

("The fine's the crown" is an idea Shakespeare stated more than once; in the second part of *Henry VI* we get "La fin couronne les oeuvres," in *Troilus and Cressida* "The end crowns all"; elsewhere there are variations.) The co-operation with time that Helena here urges she urges again at Marseilles, when the Widow despairs that they have come too late.

> WIDOW
> Lord, how we lose our pains!
> HELENA
> All's well that ends well yet,
> Though time seem so adverse and means unfit.
> I do beseech you, whither is he gone?
>
>                    .        .        .
>
>           We must to horse again.        (V.i.24-27, 37)

In V.iii the king forgives Bertram and observes that "The time is fair again":

>                                   All is whole.
> Not one word more of the consumèd time.
> Let's take the instant by the forward top;
> For we are old, and on our quick'st decrees
> Th' inaudible and noiseless foot of Time
> Steals ere we can effect them.        (V.iii.37-42)

But the time (here, with a suggestion of the age, the present state) is not yet "whole," for Helena is still thought dead, hence the appropriateness of the melancholy note introduced by the king's reflections on his old age. The melancholy deepens as thoughts return to the "dead" Helena, whom Bertram now laments. The king repeats his forgiveness:

>                                   Well excused.
> That thou didst love her, strikes some scores away
> From the great compt; but love that comes too late,
> Like a remorseful pardon slowly carried,
> To the great sender turns a sour offense,
> Crying, "That's good that's gone."        (V.iii.55-60)

Reluctantly skipping this near-chance to compare the motif of "That's good that's gone" with its occurrence in the tragedies, notably in *Antony and Cleopatra*, we move on and note that the last lines in the play (excluding the Epilogue) are:

> All yet seems well, and if it end so meet,
> The bitter past, more welcome is the sweet.

The tragic lesson that the Greek dramatists often preached was "Count no man happy until he is dead"; Oedipus *seemed* happy, but because he had killed his father and married his mother he was a contaminated wretch whose *life* was tragic though he did not know it until near the end of the play. His actions (to borrow from Aristotle's ethical theories) were not in accordance with virtue and therefore he was not genuinely happy. Conversely, in *All's Well*, though Helena is dogged by misfortune, and Bertram is for a while a fool, Helena's persistent virtue, in combination with God's grace, saves Bertram from himself and brings happiness to herself and to a variety of lesser characters. "Choose thou thy husband," the delighted king says to Diana, "and I'll pay thy dower." All has ended well, which means that a happy *beginning* is in store for Helena and Bertram, and for Diana and whomever she elects. Correspondingly, the end of the play glances back to the beginning. The king's invitation to Diana to choose a husband echoes his earlier agreement to let Helena choose a husband. Still another link between end and beginning is found in the Epilogue; the king says,

> The king's a beggar now the play is done,

appealing to the audience for applause, but in his sudden loss of power our minds may travel back to the weak king in the first act; and in the full realization that he is a king only insofar as our imagination takes his clothing to be an external symbol of an internal reality, we may recall that Parolles' military garb covered nothing substantial. The story is over, the characters live happily ever after, disembodied from the actors who have presented them and who in the workaday world daily—"with strife"—seek to please the audience. For a moment the audience becomes a benevolent Providence, governing the figures on the stage by bestowing the applause which allows them to depart.

## A NOTE ON THE SOURCE

*All's Well That Ends Well* is derived from the ninth story of the third day of Boccaccio's *Decameron* (written 1348–58), presumably in William Painter's translation in *The Palace of Pleasure* (1566). (Nothing is gained by assuming that Shakespeare used a French translation of Boccaccio.) Boccaccio's story, offered as an illustration of the rewards of diligence, was based on an old and widespread folk motif: a woman must perform a seeming impossibility if she is to win the man she desires. Boccaccio tells his story fairly directly; Shakespeare characteristically complicates it, in part working by indirections. He invents several characters, notably the countess, her Clown, Lafew, and Parolles. The countess and Lafew, by approving of Helena and by disapproving of Bertram, help us to see where our sympathies should lie. Parolles serves partly as a misleader of Bertram, thus forming a contrast to Helena, who is something of Bertram's good angel. Bertram finally moves from fellowship with Parolles to fellowship with Helena, thus reflecting the pattern of the old morality plays in which a representative of fallible mankind at last is redeemed. From Boccaccio, then, Shakespeare got the gist of his story, but he reworked it into a plot of his own, or, rather, into a plot more or less along the lines of one of the native dramatic traditions. The "source" is thus not only Boccaccio's short story, but more generally something like the story revised in the light of a secular interpretation of two centuries of English religious drama; and both of these sources are transformed into something uniquely Shakespearean.

## A NOTE ON THE TEXT

A bookseller's reference in 1603 to "love's labor won" suggests that there was by that date a published version of a play so entitled. No copies survive. Some scholars identify this title with *All's Well*, but whatever the validity of the identification, the only authoritative text for *All's Well* is that of the First Folio (1623). Exactly what sort of text for this play the Folio's editors worked from is not certain, but probably it was either Shakespeare's finished manuscript or a scribe's copy of the manuscript. The play seems complete; it is not, for example, notably short, like *Timon of Athens*, and although it has some loose ends, they do not bulk large, as they do in *Timon*, which must be incomplete. There are, of course, puzzling words and lines, possibly as a result of a scribe's failure to transcribe accurately, and there are signs that a little tidying up remained to be done. For example, there is some inconsistency in the assignment of speeches to the two French lords, and some of their speeches are puzzlingly designated

"G" and "E"—possibly the initials of actors for whom the speeches were written. And in a stage direction at III.v there is given the name "Violenta," yet no such character speaks or is addressed. Possibly Violenta was Shakespeare's first thought of a name for the Widow's daughter, who is later called Diana, or possibly Violenta is a character that Shakespeare at first believed he would use in the scene but (as he worked further into the scene) decided was of no use. In a way, these minor confusions are reassuring; they suggest we have the play as Shakespeare wrote it, rather than a neat stage version that perhaps omits some of his material.

The present text modernizes spelling and punctuation, expands abbreviations, straightens out some confusion in the assignment of lines to the First and Second Lords, regularizes speech prefixes (for example, the Folio's "Mother," "Mo.," "Coun[tess]," "La[dy]," and so on, all are given as "Countess"), and regularly gives in the stage directions "Bertram" (for the Folio's "Count," or "Count Rosse," and so on) and "Helena" (because the Folio's first stage direction and first reference to her in dialogue call her so, though the Folio later calls her "Helen"). The act divisions are translated from Latin into English. The Folio does not divide the play into scenes, giving only "Actus Primus. Scoena Prima," but the conventional and convenient scene divisions of the Globe text have been given here. These additions and others (locales and necessary stage directions not found in the Folio) have been placed in brackets. The position of an authentic stage direction has occasionally been slightly altered when necessary, and some passages that are printed as prose in the Folio are printed as verse here. Other substantial departures from the Folio are listed below, the present reading given first in boldface type, followed by the original reading in roman.

I.i.131 **got** goe   150 **ten** two   160 **wear** were
I.iii.19 **I** w   115 **Diana no queen** Queene   172 **loneliness** louelinesse   178 **t' one to th' other** 'ton tooth to th'other   203 **inteemable** intemible   236 **Haply** Happily
II.i.45 **with his cicatrice, an emblem** his sicatrice, with an Embleme   65 **fee** see   147 **sits** shifts   158 **impostor** Impostrue   195 **heaven** helpe
II.ii.62 **An** And
II.iii.95 **her** heere   126 **when** whence   131 **it is** is is   295 **detested** detected
II.v.26 **End** And   28 **one** on   50 **think not** thinke
III.i.23 **the** th the
III.ii.9 **sold** hold   18 **E'en** In   110 **still-piecing** still-peering
III.v.s.d. **her daughter Diana** her daughter, Violenta   33 **le** la   65 **warrant** write
III.vi.36 **his** this   37 **ore** ours
III.vii.19 **Resolved** Resolue
IV.i.92 **art** are
IV.iii.82–85 **They . . . midnight** [Folio gives to Bertram]   120 **Hush, hush** [Folio gives to Bertram]   141 **All's . . . him** [Folio gives to Parolles]   200 **lordship** Lord
IV.iv.9 **Marseilles** Marcella   16 **you** your
IV.v.39 **name** maine   80 **Marseilles** Marcellus
V.i.6 s.d. **Gentleman, a stranger** gentle Astringer
V.ii.24 **similes** smiles
V.iii.122 **tax** taze   155 **since** sir   157 s.d. **Widow [and] Diana** Widow, Diana, and Parolles   216 **inf'nite cunning** insuite comming
Epi.4 **strife** strift

# ALL'S WELL THAT ENDS WELL

[Dramatis Personae

KING OF FRANCE
DUKE OF FLORENCE
BERTRAM *Count of Rousillon*
LAFEW *an old lord*
PAROLLES *a follower of Bertram*
STEWARD *named Rinaldo*}
CLOWN *named Lavatch* } *servants to the countess*
A PAGE }

TWO FRENCH LORDS *the brothers Dumaine,*
  *serving in the Florentine army*
A GENTLEMAN *a stranger*
COUNTESS OF ROUSILLON *mother to Bertram*
HELENA *an orphan protected by the countess*
A WIDOW *of Florence*
DIANA *daughter to the widow*
MARIANA *neighbor to the widow*
LORDS OFFICERS SOLDIERS ATTENDANTS

*Scene:* Rousillon; Paris; Florence; Marseilles]

## ACT I

Scene I. [*Rousillon.° The count's palace.*]

*Enter young* BERTRAM, *Count of Rousillon, his mother* [*the* COUNTESS], *and* HELENA, *Lord* LAFEW, *all in black.*

COUNTESS  In delivering° my son from me I bury a second husband.

BERTRAM  And I in going, madam, weep o'er my father's death anew; but I must attend his majesty's command, to whom I am now in ward,° evermore in 5 subjection.

LAFEW  You shall find of° the king a husband, madam; you, sir, a father. He that so generally° is at all times good must of necessity hold° his virtue to you, whose

worthiness would stir it up where it wanted,° rather 10 than lack it where there is such abundance.

COUNTESS  What hope is there of his majesty's amendment?

LAFEW  He hath abandoned his physicians, madam, under whose practices he hath persecuted time with 15 hope, and finds no other advantage in the process but only the losing of hope by time.

COUNTESS  This young gentlewoman had a father— O, that "had," how sad a passage° 'tis—whose skill was almost as great as his honesty; had it stretched so 20 far, would have made nature immortal, and death should have play for lack of work. Would for the king's sake he were living! I think it would be the death of the king's disease.

LAFEW  How called you the man you speak of, 25 madam?

COUNTESS  He was famous, sir, in his profession, and it was his great right to be so: Gerard de Narbon.

LAFEW  He was excellent indeed, madam. The king very lately spoke of him admiringly and mourningly; 30 he was skillful enough to have lived still, if knowledge could be set up against mortality.

**I.i.s.d. Rousillon** formerly a province in southern France (usually spelled "Rossillion" in the Folio; the accent is on the second syllable, and *-llion* was probably pronounced *-yun*) **1 delivering** sending away (with pun on the sense "giving birth") **5 to . . . ward** whose ward I now am **7 of** in **8 generally** impartially **9 hold** continue

**10 where it wanted** i.e., even if it (virtue) were lacking **19 passage** (1) incident (2) passing away

BERTRAM What is it, my good lord, the king languishes of?

LAFEW A fistula,° my lord. 35

BERTRAM I heard not of it before.

LAFEW I would it were not notorious. Was this gentlewoman the daughter of Gerard de Narbon?

COUNTESS His sole child, my lord, and bequeathed to my overlooking.° I have those hopes of her good that 40 her education promises; her dispositions she inherits, which makes fair gifts fairer; for where an unclean mind carries virtuous qualities,° there commendations go with pity; they are virtues and traitors too. In her they are the better for their simpleness;° she derives° 45 her honesty and achieves her goodness.

LAFEW Your commendations, madam, get from her tears.

COUNTESS 'Tis the best brine a maiden can season° her praise in. The remembrance of her father never 50 approaches her heart but the tyranny of her sorrows takes all livelihood° from her cheek. No more of this, Helena; go to,° no more, lest it be rather thought you affect° a sorrow than to have—

HELENA I do affect a sorrow indeed, but I have it too. 55

LAFEW Moderate lamentation is the right of the dead, excessive grief the enemy to the living.

COUNTESS If the living be enemy to the grief, the excess makes it soon mortal.

BERTRAM Madam, I desire your holy wishes. 60

LAFEW How understand we that?°

COUNTESS
Be thou blessed, Bertram, and succeed thy father
In manners° as in shape! Thy° blood and virtue
Contend for empire in thee, and thy goodness
Share with thy birthright! Love all, trust a few, 65
Do wrong to none; be able for thine enemy
Rather in power than use,° and keep thy friend
Under thy own life's key. Be checked for silence,
But never taxed° for speech. What heaven more will,
That thee may furnish and my prayers pluck down, 70
Fall on thy head! Farewell. My lord,
'Tis an unseasoned courtier; good my lord,
Advise him.

LAFEW He cannot want° the best
That shall attend his love.

COUNTESS Heaven bless him! Farewell, Bertram. 75
[Exit.]

BERTRAM The best wishes that can be forged in your thoughts be servants to you! [To HELENA.] Be comfortable° to my mother, your mistress, and make much of her.

LAFEW Farewell, pretty lady; you must hold the credit 80 of your father. [Exit, with BERTRAM.]

HELENA
O, were that all! I think not on my father,°
And these great tears grace his remembrance more
Than those I shed for him. What was he like?
I have forgot him; my imagination 85
Carries no favor° in't but Bertram's.
I am undone; there is no living, none,
If Bertram be away; 'twere all one
That I should love a bright particular star,
And think to wed it, he is so above me. 90
In his bright radiance and collateral light
Must I be comforted, not in his sphere.°
Th' ambition in my love thus plagues itself:
The hind that would be mated by the lion
Must die for love. 'Twas pretty, though a plague, 95
To see him every hour, to sit and draw
His archèd brows, his hawking° eye, his curls,
In our heart's table;° heart too capable
Of° every line and trick of his sweet favor.
But now he's gone, and my idolatrous fancy° 100
Must sanctify his relics. Who comes here?

*Enter PAROLLES.°*

One that goes with him. I love him for his sake,
And yet I know him a notorious liar,
Think him a great way fool, solely a coward;
Yet these fixed evils sit so fit in him, 105
That they take place° when virtue's steely bones
Looks bleak i' th' cold wind; withal,° full oft we see
Cold wisdom waiting on superfluous folly.°

PAROLLES Save° you, fair queen!

HELENA And you, monarch! 110

PAROLLES No.

HELENA And no.

PAROLLES Are you meditating on virginity?

HELENA Ay. You have some stain° of soldier in you; let me ask you a question. Man is enemy to virginity; 115 how may we barricado it against him?

PAROLLES Keep him out.

HELENA But he assails; and our virginity, though valiant, in the defense yet is weak. Unfold to us some warlike resistance. 120

PAROLLES There is none. Man, setting down before° you, will undermine you and blow you up.°

HELENA Bless our poor virginity from underminers and blowers-up! Is there no military policy how virgins might blow up men? 125

PAROLLES Virginity being blown down, man will quickly be blown up;° marry,° in blowing him down again, with the breach yourselves made you lose your city. It is not politic in the commonwealth of nature to preserve virginity. Loss of virginity is rational increase, 130

---

**35 fistula** abscess **40 overlooking** guardianship **43 virtuous qualities** skills (not moral qualities) **45 their simpleness** being single, unmixed; **derives** inherits **49 season** preserve **52 livelihood** (1) vitality (2) nourishment **53 go to** a remonstrance, "Stop" **54 affect** feign (Helena enigmatically replies that she both feigns a sorrow—for her father, we later learn—and has one; her use of the word also includes another meaning, "love") **61 Lafew . . . that** perhaps this line is misplaced, and should begin Lafew's previous speech **63 manners** morals; **Thy** may thy **66–67 be able . . . use** let your strength equal your foe's in potentiality, but do not use it **69 taxed** censured **73 want** lack **77–78 comfortable** comforting

**86 favor** (1) face (2) love token **91–92 In his bright . . . sphere** I must content myself with his light, parallel to ("collateral") but above me; I cannot be in his orbit **97 hawking** hawklike, keen **98 table** flat surface on which a picture is drawn **98–99 capable Of** receptive to **100 fancy** lover's fantasy **101 s.d. Parolles** cf. French *paroles* = words, i.e., Talker, Braggart **106 take place** find acceptance (?) **107 withal** besides **108 Cold . . . folly** i.e., a threadbare wise servant attending on a rich fool **109 Save** God save **114 stain** tincture **121 setting down before** laying siege to **122 blow you up** (1) explode you (2) make you pregnant **127 be blown up** be swollen, i.e., reach an orgasm; **marry** a mild oath, "By the Virgin Mary"

and there was never virgin got° till virginity was first
lost. That° you were made of is metal° to make virgins. Virginity by being once lost may be ten times
found; by being ever kept it is ever lost. 'Tis too cold
a companion; away with't!                                    135

HELENA  I will stand for't a little, though therefore I
die a virgin.

PAROLLES  There's little can be said in't; 'tis against
the rule of nature. To speak on the part of virginity, is
to accuse your mothers, which is most infallible dis-       140
obedience. He that hangs himself is a virgin; virginity
murders itself, and should be buried in highways out
of all sanctified limit,° as a desperate offendress against
nature. Virginity breeds mites, much like a cheese,
consumes itself to the very paring, and so dies with       145
feeding his own stomach.° Besides, virginity is peevish,
proud, idle, made of self-love which is the most
inhibited sin in the canon.° Keep° it not; you cannot
choose but lose by't. Out with't! Within ten year it
will make itself ten, which is a goodly increase, and     150
the principal itself not much the worse. Away with't!

HELENA  How might one do, sir, to lose it to her own
liking?

PAROLLES  Let me see. Marry, ill, to like him that
ne'er it likes. 'Tis a commodity will lose the gloss with   155
lying; the longer kept, the less worth. Off with't
while 'tis vendible; answer the time of request. Virginity, like an old courtier, wears her cap out of
fashion, richly suited, but unsuitable,° just like the
brooch and the toothpick, which wear not now.°            160
Your date is better in your pie and your porridge than
in your cheek; and your virginity, your old virginity,
is like one of our French withered pears: it looks ill,
it eats drily; marry, 'tis a withered pear; it was formerly better; marry, yet 'tis a withered pear. Will you   165
anything with it?

HELENA
Not my virginity yet!°
There shall your master have a thousand loves,
A mother, and a mistress, and a friend,
A phoenix,° captain, and an enemy,                           170
A guide, a goddess, and a sovereign,
A counselor, a traitress, and a dear;
His humble ambition, proud humility;
His jarring, concord, and his discord, dulcet;
His faith, his sweet disaster;° with a world                175
Of pretty, fond, adoptious christendoms
That blinking Cupid gossips.° Now shall he—
I know not what he shall. God send him well!
The court's a learning place, and he is one—

PAROLLES
What one, i' faith?

HELENA                    That I wish well. 'Tis pity—     180

PAROLLES
What's pity?

HELENA
That wishing well had not a body in't,
Which might be felt, that we, the poorer born,
Whose baser stars° do shut us up in wishes,
Might with effects of them follow our friends,              185
And show what we alone must think, which never
Returns us thanks.

*Enter* PAGE.

PAGE  Monsieur Parolles, my lord calls for you. [*Exit.*]

PAROLLES  Little Helen, farewell. If I can remember
thee, I will think of thee at court.                         190

HELENA  Monsieur Parolles, you were born under a
charitable star.

PAROLLES  Under Mars, ay.

HELENA  I especially think, under Mars.

PAROLLES  Why under Mars?                                   195

HELENA  The wars hath so kept you under,° that you
must needs be born under Mars.

PAROLLES  When he was predominant.

HELENA  When he was retrograde,° I think rather.

PAROLLES  Why think you so?                                 200

HELENA  You go so much backward when you fight.

PAROLLES  That's for advantage.

HELENA  So is running away, when fear proposes the
safety; but the composition° that your valor and fear
makes in you is a virtue of a good wing, and I like        205
the wear° well.

PAROLLES  I am so full of businesses, I cannot answer
thee acutely. I will return perfect courtier, in the which
my instruction shall serve to naturalize° thee, so thou
wilt be capable of a courtier's counsel, and understand    210
what advice shall thrust upon thee; else thou diest in
thine unthankfulness, and thine ignorance makes thee
away. Farewell. When thou hast leisure, say thy
prayers; when thou hast none, remember thy friends.
Get thee a good husband, and use him as he uses thee.      215
So, farewell.                                      [*Exit.*]

HELENA
Our remedies oft in ourselves do lie,
Which we ascribe to heaven; the fated sky°
Gives us free scope; only doth backward pull
Our slow designs when we ourselves are dull.                220
What power is it which mounts my love so high,
That makes me see, and cannot feed mine eye?
The mightiest space in fortune nature brings
To join like likes, and kiss like native° things.
Impossible be strange attempts to those                     225
That weigh their pains in sense, and do suppose
What hath been cannot be.° Who ever strove
To show her merit that did miss her love?
The king's disease—my project may deceive me,
But my intents are fixed, and will not leave me. *Exit.*    230

131 **got** begotten  132 **That** that which; **metal** (1) substance
(2) coin (3) mettle, spirit  143 **sanctified limit** consecrated
ground  146 **stomach** pride  148 **inhibited . . . canon**
prohibited sin in the Scripture; **Keep** hoard  159 **unsuitable**
unfashionable  160 **wear not now** are not now in fashion
167 **yet** possibly there are missing some ensuing lines in
which Helena comments on Bertram's departure, possibly the
abrupt transition reveals that Helena's thoughts have not been
on Parolles' talk  170 **phoenix** i.e., rarity (literally, a fabulous
bird)  175 **disaster** unfavorable star  176–77 **fond . . .
gossips** foolish, adopted names that blind ("blinking") Cupid
gives as godfather ("gossips")

184 **baser stars** lower destinies  196 **under** in low fortune
199 **retrograde** moving backward (astrological term)  204
**composition** (1) union, mixture (2) truce, surrender  206 **wear**
fashion (if "wing" has referred not only to Parolles' flight but to
a flap on his clothing, "wear" puns—like the modern "fashion"
—on habit and clothing)  209 **naturalize** familiarize  218
**fated sky** sky (heaven) that exerts influence  224 **native** closely
related  225–27 **Impossible . . . cannot be** remarkable deeds
are impossible to persons who cautiously calculate the efforts
and who believe that unusual happenings cannot take place

[Scene II. *Paris. The king's palace.*]

*Flourish° cornets. Enter the* KING *of France with letters, and divers* ATTENDANTS.

KING
The Florentines and Senoys° are by th' ears,°
Have fought with equal fortune, and continue
A braving war.°
FIRST LORD        So 'tis reported, sir.
KING
Nay, 'tis most credible. We here receive it
A certainty, vouched from our cousin° Austria,        5
With caution, that the Florentine will move° us
For speedy aid; wherein our dearest friend
Prejudicates the business, and would seem
To have us make denial.
FIRST LORD        His love and wisdom,
Approved° so to your majesty, may plead        10
For amplest credence.
KING        He hath armed our answer,
And Florence is denied before he comes;
Yet, for our gentlemen that mean to see
The Tuscan service,° freely have they leave
To stand on either part.°
SECOND LORD        It well may serve        15
A nursery° to our gentry, who are sick
For breathing° and exploit.

*Enter* BERTRAM, LAFEW, *and* PAROLLES.

KING        What's he comes here?
FIRST LORD
It is the Count Rousillon, my good lord,
Young Bertram.
KING        Youth, thou bear'st thy father's face.
Frank° nature, rather curious° than in haste,        20
Hath well composed thee. Thy father's moral parts
Mayst thou inherit too! Welcome to Paris.
BERTRAM
My thanks and duty are your majesty's.
KING
I would I had that corporal soundness now,
As when thy father and myself in friendship        25
First tried our soldiership. He did look far
Into the service of the time,° and was
Discipled of the bravest. He lasted long,
But on us both did haggish age steal on,
And wore us out of act.° It much repairs me        30
To talk of your good father; in his youth
He had the wit which I can well observe
Today in our young lords; but they may jest
Till their own scorn return to them unnoted
Ere they can hide their levity in° honor.        35
So like a courtier, contempt nor bitterness
Were in his pride or sharpness; if they were,

His equal had awaked them, and his honor,
Clock to itself, knew the true minute when
Exception° bid him speak, and at this time        40
His tongue obeyed his hand. Who° were below him
He used as creatures of another place,°
And bowed his eminent top to their low ranks,
Making them proud of his humility,
In their poor praise he humbled. Such a man        45
Might be a copy to these younger times;
Which, followed well, would demonstrate them now
But goers backward.
BERTRAM        His good remembrance, sir,
Lies richer in your thoughts than on his tomb;
So in approof lives not his epitaph        50
As in your royal speech.°
KING
Would I were with him! He would always say—
Methinks I hear him now; his plausive° words
He scattered not in ears, but grafted them,
To grow there, and to bear—"Let me not live,"        55
This his good melancholy oft began,
On the catastrophe and heel of pastime,°
When it was out°—"Let me not live," quoth he,
"After my flame lacks oil, to be the snuff°
Of younger spirits, whose apprehensive° senses        60
All but new things disdain; whose judgments are
Mere fathers of their garments; whose constancies
Expire before their fashions." This he wished.
I, after him, do after him° wish too,
Since I nor wax nor honey can bring home,        65
I quickly were dissolvèd from my hive
To give some laborers room.
SECOND LORD        You're loved, sir;
They that least lend it you shall lack you first.
KING
I fill a place, I know't. How long is't, count,
Since the physician at your father's died?        70
He was much famed.
BERTRAM        Some six months since, my lord.
KING
If he were living, I would try him yet.
Lend me an arm. The rest have worn me out
With several applications.° Nature and sickness
Debate it at their leisure. Welcome, count,        75
My son's no dearer.
BERTRAM        Thank your majesty.
        *Exit* [*the* KING, *with the rest*]. *Flourish.*

[Scene III. *Rousillon. The count's palace.*]

*Enter* COUNTESS, STEWARD, *and* CLOWN.

COUNTESS  I will now hear. What say you of this
gentlewoman?

I.ii.s.d. Flourish musical notes heralding an important person
1 Senoys Sienese; by th' ears quarreling 3 braving war
war of challenges 5 cousin fellow sovereign 6 move
petition 10 Approved proven 14 The Tuscan service the
campaign in Tuscany (N. Italy) 15 stand . . . part serve on
either side 16 nursery training school 16–17 sick For
breathing eager for exercise 20 Frank bounteous; curious
careful 26–27 He . . . time he had insight into war (?) he
served long in wars (?) 30 act action 35 hide . . . in i.e.,
join . . . with (?)

40 Exception disapproval 41 Who those who 42 another
place i.e., a higher rank 50–51 So . . . speech the validity
of his epitaph is in no way better confirmed than in your
words 53 plausive laudable 57 On . . . pastime at the
end ("catastrophe," "heel") of pleasure 58 out ended (perhaps punning on the idea "out at heel") 59 snuff burnt wick
that causes the lamp to smell and smolder, preventing the lower
("younger") wick from burning brightly 60 apprehensive
perceptive, apt 64 after him . . . after him later than he
. . . in accordance with him 74 several applications various
treatments

STEWARD  Madam, the care I have had to even° your content I wish might be found in the calendar° of my past endeavors, for then we wound our modesty, and make foul the clearness of our deservings, when of ourselves we publish them.

COUNTESS  What does this knave here? Get you gone, sirrah.° The complaints I have heard of you I do not all believe; 'tis my slowness that I do not, for I know you lack not folly to commit them, and have ability enough to make such knaveries yours.

CLOWN  'Tis not unknown to you, madam, I am a poor fellow.

COUNTESS  Well, sir.

CLOWN  No, madam, 'tis not so well that I am poor, though many of the rich are damned; but, if I may have your ladyship's good will to go to the world,° Isbel the woman and I will do° as we may.

COUNTESS  Wilt thou needs be a beggar?

CLOWN  I do beg your good will in this case.

COUNTESS  In what case?

CLOWN  In Isbel's case° and mine own. Service is no heritage,° and I think I shall never have the blessing of God till I have issue o' my body; for they say barnes° are blessings.

COUNTESS  Tell me thy reason why thou wilt marry.

CLOWN  My poor body, madam, requires it. I am driven on by the flesh, and he must needs go that the devil drives.

COUNTESS  Is this all your worship's reason?

CLOWN  Faith, madam, I have other holy reasons,° such as they are.

COUNTESS  May the world know them?

CLOWN  I have been, madam, a wicked creature, as you and all flesh and blood are, and indeed I do marry that I may repent.

COUNTESS  Thy marriage, sooner than thy wickedness.

CLOWN  I am out o' friends, madam, and I hope to have friends for my wife's sake.

COUNTESS  Such friends are thine enemies, knave.

CLOWN  Y'are shallow, madam, in great friends, for the knaves come to do that for me which I am aweary of. He that ears° my land spares my team, and gives me leave to in° the crop; if I be his cuckold,° he's my drudge. He that comforts my wife is the cherisher of my flesh and blood; he that cherishes my flesh and blood loves my flesh and blood; he that loves my flesh and blood is my friend: ergo, he that kisses my wife is my friend. If men could be contented to be what they are, there were no fear in marriage; for young Charbon the puritan and old Poysam° the papist, howsome'er their hearts are severed in religion, their heads are both

one; they may jowl° horns together like any deer i' th' herd.

COUNTESS  Wilt thou ever be a foul-mouthed and calumnious knave?

CLOWN  A prophet I, madam, and I speak the truth the next° way:

For I the ballad will repeat,
  Which men full true shall find,
Your marriage comes by destiny,
  Your cuckoo sings by kind.°

COUNTESS  Get you gone, sir. I'll talk with you more anon.

STEWARD  May it please you, madam, that he bid Helen come to you. Of her I am to speak.

COUNTESS  Sirrah, tell my gentlewoman I would speak with her—Helen I mean.

CLOWN
Was this fair face the cause, quoth she,
  Why the Grecians sackèd Troy?
Fond° done, done fond,
  Was this King Priam's joy?
With that she sighèd as she stood,
With that she sighèd as she stood,
  And gave this sentence° then:
Among nine bad if one be good,
Among nine bad if one be good,
  There's yet one good in ten.

COUNTESS  What, one good in ten? You corrupt the song, sirrah.

CLOWN  One good woman in ten, madam, which is a purifying o' th' song. Would God would serve the world so all the year! We'd find no fault with the tithe-woman,° if I were the parson. One in ten, quoth 'a!° And° we might have a good woman born but or every blazing star, or° at an earthquake, 'twould mend the lottery well; a man may draw his heart out, ere 'a pluck one.

COUNTESS  You'll be gone, sir knave, and do as I command you!

CLOWN  That man should be at woman's command, and yet no hurt done! Though honesty be no puritan, yet it will do no hurt; it will wear the surplice of humility over the black gown of a big heart.° I am going, forsooth. The business is for Helen to come hither.                                                    Exit.

COUNTESS  Well, now.

STEWARD  I know, madam, you love your gentlewoman entirely.

COUNTESS  Faith, I do. Her father bequeathed her to me, and she herself, without other advantage,° may lawfully make title to as much love as she finds. There is more owing her than is paid, and more shall be paid her than she'll demand.

**I.iii.3 even** make even, satisfy  **4 calendar** record  **9 sirrah** term of address used to an inferior  **18 go . . . world** get married  **19 do** punning on the bawdy meaning "have intercourse"  **23 case** another bawdy pun, "pudendum"  **23–24 Service . . . heritage** i.e., servants acquire no wealth (proverbial)  **25 barnes** bairns, children  **32 holy reasons** probably there is a bawdy pun not only on "holy" but on "reasons," pronounced much like "raisings"  **45 ears** plows  **46 in** bring in; **cuckold** deceived husband (traditionally said to wear horns)  **52–53 Charbon . . . Poysam** Flesh-eater . . . Fish-eater (from French, *chair bonne* = good flesh; *poisson* = fish)

**55 jowl** knock  **60 next** nearest  **64 by kind** according to nature (the cuckoo allegedly sang to men that they were cuckolds)  **73 Fond** foolishly  **77 sentence** wise saying  **86 tithe-woman** tenth woman (sent as part of the tithe, like a tithe-pig)  **86–87 quoth 'a** says he  **87 And if**  **87–88 or . . . or** either . . . or  **95–96 wear . . . heart** i.e., conform outwardly, masking its pride (the Church of England required the wearing of the surplice, but clerics inclined toward Calvinism asserted their independence by wearing beneath the surplice the black Geneva gown)  **103 advantage** interest accruing to a sum of money

STEWARD  Madam, I was very late° more near her than I think she wished me. Alone she was, and did communicate to herself her own words to her own ears. She thought, I dare vow for her, they touched 110 not any stranger sense.° Her matter was, she loved your son. Fortune, she said, was no goddess, that had put such difference betwixt their two estates; Love no god, that would not extend his might only where qualities were level; Diana no queen of virgins, that 115 would suffer her poor knight° surprised without rescue in the first assault or ransom afterward. This she delivered in the most bitter touch of sorrow that e'er I heard virgin exclaim in, which I held my duty speedily to acquaint you withal, sithence° in the loss 120 that may happen it concerns you something to know it.

COUNTESS  You have discharged this honestly; keep it to yourself. Many likelihoods informed me of this before, which hung so tott'ring in the balance that I 125 could neither believe nor misdoubt. Pray you leave me. Stall this° in your bosom, and I thank you for your honest care. I will speak with you further anon.

*Exit* STEWARD.

*Enter* HELENA.

*[Aside.]*

Even so it was with me, when I was young;
If ever we are nature's, these° are ours; this thorn 130
Doth to our rose of youth rightly belong;
Our blood° to us, this to our blood is born.
It is the show and seal of nature's truth,
Where love's strong passion is impressed in youth.
By our remembrances of days foregone, 135
Such were our faults, or then we thought them none.
Her eye is sick on't; I observe her now.

HELENA
What is your pleasure, madam?

COUNTESS  You know, Helen,
I am a mother to you.

HELENA
Mine honorable mistress.

COUNTESS  Nay, a mother. 140
Why not a mother? When I said "a mother"
Methought you saw a serpent. What's in "mother"
That you start at it? I say I am your mother,
And put you in the catalogue of those
That were enwombèd mine. 'Tis often seen 145
Adoption strives with nature, and choice breeds
A native slip to us from foreign seeds.°
You ne'er oppressed me with a mother's groan,
Yet I express to you a mother's care.
God's mercy, maiden, does it curd thy blood 150
To say I am thy mother? What's the matter,
That this distempered° messenger of wet,
The many-colored Iris,° rounds thine eye?
Why, that you are my daughter?

HELENA  That I am not.°
COUNTESS
I say I am your mother.
HELENA  Pardon, madam; 155
The Count Rousillon cannot be my brother.
I am from humble, he from honored name;
No note upon my parents, his all noble.
My master, my dear lord he is, and I
His servant live, and will his vassal die. 160
He must not be my brother.
COUNTESS  Nor I your mother?
HELENA
You are my mother, madam; would you were—
So that my lord, your son, were not my brother—
Indeed my mother! Or were you both our mothers
I care no more for than I do for heaven, 165
So I were not his sister. Can't no other°
But, I your daughter, he must be my brother?
COUNTESS
Yes, Helen, you might be my daughter-in-law.
God shield° you mean it not! "Daughter" and "mother"
So strive upon your pulse! What, pale again? 170
My fear hath catched your fondness!° Now I see
The myst'ry of your loneliness, and find
Your salt tears' head.° Now to all sense 'tis gross:°
You love my son! Invention is ashamed
Against the proclamation of thy passion, 175
To say thou dost not. Therefore tell me true;
But tell me then, 'tis so; for look, thy cheeks
Confess it, t' one to th' other, and thine eyes
See it so grossly shown in thy behaviors,
That in their kind° they speak it; only sin 180
And hellish obstinacy tie thy tongue,
That truth should be suspected. Speak, is't so?
If it be so, you have wound a goodly clew;°
If it be not, forswear't; howe'er, I charge thee,
As heaven shall work in me for thine avail, 185
To tell me truly.
HELENA  Good madam, pardon me!
COUNTESS
Do you love my son?
HELENA  Your pardon, noble mistress!
COUNTESS
Love you my son?
HELENA  Do not you love him, madam?
COUNTESS
Go not about; my love hath in't a bond
Whereof the world takes note. Come, come, disclose 190
The state of your affection, for your passions
Have to the full appeached.°
HELENA  Then I confess,
Here on my knee, before high heaven and you,
That before you, and next unto high heaven,
I love your son. 195
My friends° were poor but honest; so's my love.
Be not offended, for it hurts not him
That he is loved of me; I follow him not

107 **late** lately  110–11 **touched . . . sense** reached no stranger's ear  116 **knight** i.e., chaste follower of Diana  120 **sithence** since  127 **Stall this** keep this enclosed  130 **these** sorrows (?) passions (?)  132 **blood** passion (?) disposition (?)  146–47 **choice . . . seeds** a slip that is chosen for grafting from foreign stock becomes native to us  152 **distempered** disturbed  153 **many-colored Iris** i.e., teardrop (Iris was goddess of the rainbow)

154 **That I am not** Helena plays on the sense "daughter-in-law"  166 **Can't no other** can it not be otherwise  169 **shield** forbid  171 **fondness** foolishness  173 **head** source; **gross** obvious  180 **in their kind** according to their nature, i.e., with tears  183 **clew** ball of string  192 **appeached** accused  196 **friends** relatives

By any token of presumptuous suit,
Not would I have him till I do deserve him;    200
Yet never know how that desert should be.
I know I love in vain, strive against hope;
Yet, in this captious° and inteemable° sieve,
I still pour in the waters of my love,
And lack not to lose still.° Thus, Indian-like,    205
Religious in mine error, I adore
The sun that looks upon his worshipper
But knows of him no more. My dearest madam,
Let not your hate encounter with my love
For loving where you do; but if yourself,    210
Whose agèd honor cites° a virtuous youth,
Did ever, in so true a flame of liking,
Wish chastely, and love dearly that your Dian
Was both herself and Love, O, then give pity
To her whose state is such that cannot choose    215
But lend and give where she is sure to lose;
That seeks not to find that° her search implies,
But, riddle-like, lives° sweetly where she dies.

COUNTESS
Had you not lately an intent—speak truly—
To go to Paris?

HELENA      Madam, I had.

COUNTESS      Wherefore? Tell true.    220

HELENA
I will tell truth, by grace itself, I swear.
You know my father left me some prescriptions
Of rare and proved effects, such as his reading
And manifest experience had collected
For general sovereignty;° and that he willed me    225
In heedfull'st reservation° to bestow them,
As notes whose faculties inclusive were
More than they were in note.° Amongst the rest,
There is a remedy, approved,° set down,
To cure the desperate languishings whereof    230
The king is rendered lost.

COUNTESS      This was your motive
For Paris, was it? Speak.

HELENA
My lord your son made me to think of this;
Else Paris, and the medicine, and the king,
Had from the conversation of my thoughts    235
Haply been absent then.

COUNTESS      But think you, Helen,
If you should tender your supposèd aid,
He would receive it? He and his physicians
Are of a mind; he, that they cannot help him;
They, that they cannot help. How shall they credit    240
A poor unlearnèd virgin, when the schools,
Emboweled of their doctrine,° have left off
The danger to itself?

HELENA      There's something in't

More than my father's skill, which was the great'st
Of his profession, that his good receipt    245
Shall for my legacy be sanctified
By th' luckiest stars in heaven; and would your honor
But give me leave to try success,° I'd venture
The well-lost life of mine on his grace's cure
By such a day, an hour.

COUNTESS      Dost thou believe't?    250

HELENA
Ay, madam, knowingly.

COUNTESS
Why, Helen, thou shalt have my leave and love,
Means and attendants, and my loving greetings
To those of mine in court. I'll stay at home
And pray God's blessing into thy attempt.    255
Be gone tomorrow; and be sure of this,
What I can help thee to, thou shalt not miss.    *Exeunt.*

# ACT II

[Scene I. *Paris. The king's palace.*]

*Enter the* KING, *with divers young* LORDS *taking leave
for the Florentine war;* BERTRAM *and* PAROLLES;
[ATTENDANTS]. *Flourish cornets.*

KING
Farewell, young lords! These warlike principles
Do not throw from you; and you, my lords, farewell!
Share the advice betwixt you; if both gain all,
The gift doth stretch itself as 'tis received,
And is enough for both.

FIRST LORD      'Tis our hope, sir,    5
After well-ent'red soldiers,° to return
And find your grace in health.

KING
No, no, it cannot be; and yet my heart
Will not confess he owes° the malady
That doth my life besiege. Farewell, young lords!    10
Whether I live or die, be you the sons
Of worthy Frenchmen: let higher Italy—
Those bated that inherit but the fall
Of the last monarchy°—see that you come
Not to woo honor, but to wed it, when    15
The bravest questant° shrinks: find what you seek,
That fame may cry you loud. I say, farewell.

FIRST LORD
Health, at your bidding, serve your majesty!

KING
Those girls of Italy, take heed of them.
They say our French lack language to deny    20
If they demand; beware of being captives
Before you serve.

BOTH LORDS      Our hearts receive your warnings.

KING
Farewell. [*To* ATTENDANTS.] Come hither to me.
           [*Exit, with* ATTENDANTS.]

---

203 **captious** (1) capacious (2) deceitful; **inteemable** incapable
of pouring forth (the sieve is capacious enough to accept all
the love poured into it, but is deceptive because it cannot
pour forth love) 205 **lack . . . still** (1) fail not to go on
losing (2) lack not a supply to go on losing 211 **cites**
demonstrates 217 **that** what 218 **lives** i.e., stays in one place
225 **general sovereignty** universal excellence 226 **In heedfull'st reservation** i.e., sparingly 227–28 **notes . . . in note**
i.e., prescriptions ("notes") more powerful in fact than they
were reported ("in note") to be 229 **approved** tested 242
**Emboweled . . . doctrine** emptied of their knowledge

248 **try success** test the outcome
**II.i.6 After well-ent'red soldiers** after becoming experienced
soldiers 9 **owes** owns 13–14 **Those . . . monarchy** except
for those who gain by the fall of the monarchy (?) except
for those who continue in the decadent ways of the past (?) 16
**questant** seeker

FIRST LORD
O my sweet lord, that you will stay behind us!

PAROLLES
'Tis not his fault, the spark.

SECOND LORD                    O, 'tis brave wars!    25

PAROLLES
Most admirable! I have seen those wars.

BERTRAM   I am commanded here,° and kept a coil°
with "Too young," and "The next year," and "'Tis
too early."

PAROLLES   And° thy mind stand to't, boy, steal away 30
bravely.

BERTRAM
I shall stay here the forehorse to a smock,°
Creaking my shoes on the plain masonry,
Till honor be bought up, and no sword worn
But one to dance with! By heaven, I'll steal away.    35

FIRST LORD
There's honor in the theft.

PAROLLES                    Commit it, count.

SECOND LORD
I am your accessary; and so farewell.

BERTRAM   I grow to you, and our parting is a tortured
body.

FIRST LORD   Farewell, captain.    40

SECOND LORD   Sweet Monsieur Parolles!

PAROLLES   Noble heroes, my sword and yours are
kin. Good sparks and lustrous, a word, good metals.°
You shall find in the regiment of the Spinii one
Captain Spurio,° with his cicatrice,° an emblem of 45
war, here on his sinister° cheek; it was this very sword
entrenched it. Say to him I live, and observe his reports
for me.

FIRST LORD   We shall, noble captain.

                              [Exeunt LORDS.]

PAROLLES   Mars dote on you for his novices!° [To 50
BERTRAM.] What will ye do?

BERTRAM   Stay° the king.

PAROLLES   Use a more spacious ceremony to the noble
lords; you have restrained yourself within the list° of
too cold an adieu. Be more expressive to them, for 55
they wear themselves in the cap of the time; there do
muster true gait, eat, speak, and move under the
influence of the most received° star; and though the
devil lead the measure,° such are to be followed. After
them, and take a more dilated° farewell.    60

BERTRAM   And I will do so.

PAROLLES   Worthy fellows, and like to prove most
sinewy sword-men.

                    Exeunt [BERTRAM and PAROLLES].

Enter [the KING and] LAFEW.

LAFEW [Kneeling.]
Pardon, my lord, for me and for my tidings.

KING
I'll fee thee to stand up.°    65

LAFEW [Rising.]
Then here's a man stands that has brought his pardon.
I would you had kneeled, my lord, to ask me mercy,
And that at my bidding you could so stand up.

KING
I would I had, so I had broke thy pate°
And asked thee mercy for't.

LAFEW                    Good faith, across!°    70
But, my good lord, 'tis thus: will you be cured
Of your infirmity?

KING                    No.

LAFEW                    O, will you eat
No grapes, my royal fox?° Yes, but you will
My noble grapes, and if my royal fox
Could reach them. I have seen a medicine    75
That's able to breathe life into a stone,
Quicken° a rock, and make you dance canary°
With sprightly fire and motion, whose simple touch
Is powerful to araise King Pippen,° nay,
To give great Charlemain a pen in's hand,    80
And write to her a love-line.

KING                    What "her" is this?

LAFEW
Why, Doctor She! My lord, there's one arrived,
If you will see her. Now, by my faith and honor,
If seriously I may convey my thoughts
In this my light deliverance,° I have spoke    85
With one that, in her sex, her years, profession,°
Wisdom and constancy, hath amazed me more
Than I dare blame my weakness. Will you see her,
For that is her demand, and know her business?
That done, laugh well at me.

KING                    Now, good Lafew,    90
Bring in the admiration,° that we with thee
May spend our wonder too, or take off thine
By wond'ring how thou took'st it.

LAFEW                    Nay, I'll fit° you,
And not be all day neither.

[Goes to door.]

KING
Thus he his special nothing ever prologues.    95

LAFEW
Nay, come your ways.

Enter HELENA.

KING                    This haste hath wings indeed.

LAFEW
Nay, come your ways!
This is his majesty; say your mind to him.
A traitor you do look like, but such traitors

---

**27 commanded here** ordered to stay here; **kept a coil**
bothered   **30 And** if   **32 the forehorse . . . smock** i.e., in the
service of women ("forehorse" = leader in a team of horses)
**43 metals** with the additional sense of "mettles," spirits   **45
Spurio** from Italian = "false"; **cicatrice** scar   **46 sinister**
left   **50 Mars . . . novices** May the god of war watch over
you as his pupils   **52 Stay** support   **54 list** boundary (literally
the selvage of cloth)   **58 received** fashionable   **59 measure**
dance   **60 dilated** extended

**65 I'll . . . up** i.e., please arise ("fee" = reward)   **69 pate**
head   **70 across** clumsily (an unskilled tilter might break a
lance "across" instead of head-on)   **73 royal fox** alluding to
Aesop's fox who said he did not want grapes, when he could
not reach them; Lafew suggests that the king says he does not
want to be cured because he thinks he cannot be cured   **77
Quicken** endow with life; **canary** a lively dance   **79 Pippen**
Pepin (died 768)   **85 light deliverance** jesting utterance   **86
profession** claims   **91 admiration** wonder   **93 fit** satisfy

His majesty seldom fears. I am Cressid's uncle,° 100
That dare leave two together. Fare you well. *Exit.*

KING

Now, fair one, does your business follow us?

HELENA

Ay, my good lord.
Gerard de Narbon was my father;
In what he did profess, well found.°

KING I knew him. 105

HELENA

The rather will I spare my praises towards him;
Knowing him is enough. On's bed of death
Many receipts he gave me, chiefly one,
Which as the dearest issue of his practice
And of his old experience th' only darling, 110
He bade me store up as a triple° eye,
Safer than mine own two; more dear I have so,
And, hearing your high majesty is touched
With that malignant cause wherein the honor
Of my dear father's gift stands chief in power, 115
I come to tender° it and my appliance,°
With all bound humbleness.

KING We thank you, maiden,
But may not be so credulous of cure,
When our most learnèd doctors leave us, and
The congregated College° have concluded 120
That laboring art° can never ransom nature
From her inaidable estate. I say we must not
So stain our judgment or corrupt our hope,
To prostitute our past-cure malady
To empirics,° or to dissever so 125
Our great self and our credit,° to esteem
A senseless help, when help past sense we deem.

HELENA

My duty then shall pay me for my pains.
I will no more enforce mine office on you,
Humbly entreating from your royal thoughts 130
A modest one to bear me back again.

KING

I cannot give thee less, to be called grateful.
Thou thought'st to help me, and such thanks I give
As one near death to those that wish him live.
But what at full I know, thou know'st no part, 135
I knowing all my peril, thou no art.

HELENA

What I can do can do no hurt to try,
Since you set up your rest° 'gainst remedy:
He that of greatest works is finisher,
Oft does them by the weakest minister. 140
So holy writ in babes hath judgment shown,
When judges have been babes; great floods have flown
From simple sources; and great seas have dried
When miracles have by the great'st° been denied.
Oft expectation fails, and most oft there 145

Where most it promises, and oft it hits
Where hope is coldest and despair most sits.

KING

I must not hear thee; fare thee well, kind maid.
Thy pains not used must by thyself be paid.
Proffers not took reap thanks for their reward. 150

HELENA

Inspirèd merit so by breath° is barred.
It is not so with Him that all things knows,
As 'tis with us that square our guess by shows;°
But most it is presumption in us when
The help of heaven we count the act of men. 155
Dear sir, to my endeavors give consent;
Of heaven, not me, make an experiment.
I am not an impostor, that proclaim
Myself against the level of mine aim,°
But know I think, and think I know most sure, 160
My art is not past power, nor you past cure.

KING

Art thou so confident? Within what space
Hop'st thou my cure?

HELENA The greatest grace lending grace,
Ere twice the horses of the sun shall bring
Their fiery torcher his diurnal ring,° 165
Ere twice in murk and occidental damp°
Moist Hesperus° hath quenched her sleepy lamp,
Or four and twenty times the pilot's glass°
Hath told the thievish minutes how they pass,
What is infirm from your sound parts shall fly, 170
Health shall live free, and sickness freely die.

KING

Upon thy certainty and confidence
What dar'st thou venture?

HELENA Tax° of impudence,
A strumpet's boldness, a divulgèd shame,
Traduced by odious ballads; my maiden's name 175
Seared° otherwise; ne° worse of worst, extended°
With vilest torture, let my life be ended.

KING

Methinks in thee some blessèd spirit doth speak
His powerful sound within an organ weak;
And what impossibility would slay 180
In common sense, sense saves another way.
Thy life is dear, for all that life can rate
Worth name of life in thee hath estimate:°
Youth, beauty, wisdom, courage, all
That happiness and prime° can happy call. 185
Thou this to hazard needs must intimate
Skill infinite or monstrous desperate.
Sweet practicer, thy physic° I will try,
That ministers thine own death if I die.

HELENA

If I break time, or flinch in property° 190

Of what I spoke, unpitied let me die,
And well deserved. Not helping, death's my fee,
But if I help what do you promise me?

KING
Make thy demand.

HELENA                              But will you make it even?°

KING
Ay, by my scepter and my hopes of heaven.          195

HELENA
Then shalt thou give me with thy kingly hand
What husband in thy power I will command:
Exempted be from me the arrogance
To choose from forth the royal blood of France
My low and humble name to propagate          200
With any branch or image of thy state;
But such a one, thy vassal, whom I know
Is free for me to ask, thee to bestow.

KING
Here is my hand; the premises observed,
Thy will by my performance shall be served;          205
So make the choice of thy own time, for I,
Thy resolved patient, on thee still rely.
More should I question thee, and more I must,
Though more to know could not be more to trust;
From whence thou cam'st, how tended on—but rest          210
Unquestioned, welcome, and undoubted blest.
Give me some help here, ho! If thou proceed
As high as word, my deed shall match thy deed.

                    *Flourish. Exit* [KING, *with* HELENA].

[Scene II. *Rousillon. The count's palace.*]

*Enter* COUNTESS *and* CLOWN.

COUNTESS   Come on, sir. I shall now put you to the
height of° your breeding.

CLOWN   I will show myself highly fed and lowly
taught. I know my business is but to the court.

COUNTESS   To the court! Why, what place make you          5
special, when you put off that with such contempt?
"But to the court"!

CLOWN   Truly, madam, if God have lent a man any
manners, he may easily put it off at court. He that
cannot make a leg,° put off's cap, kiss his hand, and say          10
nothing, has neither leg, hands, lip, nor cap; and
indeed such a fellow, to say precisely, were not for the
court. But for me, I have an answer will serve all men.

COUNTESS   Marry, that's a bountiful answer that fits
all questions.          15

CLOWN   It is like a barber's chair that fits all buttocks:
the pin-buttock, the quatch-buttock,° the brawn-
buttock, or any buttock.

COUNTESS   Will your answer serve fit to all questions?          20

CLOWN   As fit as ten groats° is for the hand of an
attorney, as your French crown° for your taffety
punk,° as Tib's rush° for Tom's forefinger, as a pan-

cake for Shrove Tuesday,° a morris° for May Day,
as the nail to his hole, the cuckold to his horn, as a          25
scolding quean° to a wrangling knave, as the nun's lip
to the friar's mouth; nay, as the pudding° to his skin.

COUNTESS   Have you, I say, an answer of such fitness
for all questions?

CLOWN   From below your duke to beneath your          30
constable, it will fit any question.

COUNTESS   It must be an answer of most monstrous
size that must fit all demands.

CLOWN   But a trifle neither,° in good faith, if the
learned should speak truth of it. Here it is, and all that          35
belongs to't. Ask me if I am a courtier; it shall do you
no harm to learn.

COUNTESS   To be young again, if we could, I will be
a fool in question, hoping to be the wiser by your
answer. I pray you, sir, are you a courtier?          40

CLOWN   O Lord, sir!° There's a simple putting off.
More, more, a hundred of them.

COUNTESS   Sir, I am a poor friend of yours, that loves
you.

CLOWN   O Lord, sir! Thick,° thick! Spare not me.          45

COUNTESS   I think, sir, you can eat none of this
homely meat.

CLOWN   O Lord, sir! Nay, put me to't, I warrant you.

COUNTESS   You were lately whipped, sir, as I think.

CLOWN   O Lord, sir! Spare not me.          50

COUNTESS   Do you cry, "O Lord, sir!" at your whipping, and "spare not me"? Indeed, your "O Lord,
sir!" is very sequent to° your whipping; you would
answer very well to a whipping, if you were but
bound to't.°          55

CLOWN   I ne'er had worse luck in my life in my "O
Lord, sir!" I see things may serve long, but not serve
ever.

COUNTESS
I play the noble housewife with the time,
To entertain it so merrily with a fool.          60

CLOWN   O Lord, sir! Why, there't serves well again.

COUNTESS
An end, sir! To your business: give Helen this,
And urge her to a present° answer back.
Commend me to my kinsmen and my son.
This is not much.          65

CLOWN   Not much commendation to them?

COUNTESS   Not much employment for you. You
understand me?

CLOWN   Most fruitfully.° I am there before my legs.

COUNTESS   Haste you again.                    *Exeunt.*          70

[Scene III. *Paris. The king's palace.*]

*Enter* BERTRAM, LAFEW, *and* PAROLLES.

LAFEW   They say miracles are past, and we have our

194 **make it even** fulfill it
II.ii.1–2 **put . . . of** test   10 **make a leg** make obeisance (by
drawing back one leg and bending the other)   17 **quatch-
buttock** fat behind   21 **ten groats** a groat was worth fourpence; ten groats was the usual attorney's fee   22 **French
crown** (1) coin (2) bald or scabby head (caused by syphilis,
"the French disease")   22–23 **taffety punk** finely dressed prostitute   23 **rush** ring made of rush (used in mock weddings)
24 **Shrove Tuesday** day preceding Ash Wednesday, hence a
day of feasting immediately before Lent;   **morris** country
dance   26 **quean** prostitute   27 **pudding** sausage   34
**neither** indeed (negating the Countess' conjecture)   41 **O
Lord, sir** a phrase associated with courtiers   45 **Thick** quickly
53 **is . . . to** i.e., would quickly follow   55 **bound to't** (1)
bound by oath to answer (2) tied to a whipping post   63 **present** immediate   69 **fruitfully** perhaps a bawdy punning
reply, if "understand" means "have intercourse with"

philosophical persons, to make modern° and familiar,
things supernatural and causeless. Hence is it that we
make trifles of terrors, ensconcing° ourselves into
seeming knowledge, when we should submit our- 5
selves to an unknown fear.°

PAROLLES   Why, 'tis the rarest argument of° wonder
that hath shot out in our latter times.

BERTRAM   And so 'tis.

LAFEW   To be relinquished of the artists—°      10

PAROLLES   So I say—both of Galen and Paracelsus.°

LAFEW   Of all the learned and authentic fellows—

PAROLLES   Right; so I say.

LAFEW   That gave him out incurable—

PAROLLES   Why, there 'tis; so say I too.      15

LAFEW   Not to be helped—

PAROLLES   Right, as 'twere a man assured of a—

LAFEW   Uncertain life and sure death.

PAROLLES   Just; you say well. So would I have said.

LAFEW   I may truly say it is a novelty to the world.      20

PAROLLES   It is indeed; if you will have it in showing,
you shall read it in what-do-ye-call there?

LAFEW [Reading.]   "A showing of a heavenly effect in
an earthly actor."

PAROLLES   That's it, I would have said the very same. 25

LAFEW   Why, your dolphin is not lustier;° 'fore me,°
I speak in respect—

PAROLLES   Nay, 'tis strange, 'tis very strange; that is
the brief and the tedious of it, and he's of a most
facinerious° spirit that will not acknowledge it to be 30
the—

LAFEW   Very hand of heaven.

PAROLLES   Ay, so I say.

LAFEW   In a most weak—

PAROLLES   And debile° minister; great power, great 35
transcendence, which should indeed give us a further
use to be made than alone the recov'ry of the king,
as to be—

LAFEW   Generally thankful.

*Enter* KING, HELENA, *and* ATTENDANTS.

PAROLLES   I would have said it. You say well. Here 40
comes the king.

LAFEW   Lustig, as the Dutchman° says. I'll like a maid
the better whilst I have a tooth in my head. Why, he's
able to lead her a coranto.°

PAROLLES   Mor du vinager!° Is not this Helen?      45

LAFEW   'Fore God, I think so.

KING
Go, call before me all the lords in court.
                  [*Exit* ATTENDANT.]
Sit, my preserver, by thy patient's side,
And with this healthful hand, whose banished sense
Thou hast repealed,° a second time receive      50
The confirmation of my promised gift,

Which but attends thy naming.

*Enter three or four* LORDS.

Fair maid, send forth thine eye. This youthful parcel
Of noble bachelors stand at my bestowing,
O'er whom both sovereign power and father's voice    55
I have to use. Thy frank election° make;
Thou hast power to choose, and they none to forsake.

HELENA
To each of you one fair and virtuous mistress
Fall, when Love please! Marry, to each but one!

LAFEW
I'd give bay curtal and his furniture,°      60
My mouth no more were broken° than these boys',
And writ° as little beard.

KING                   Peruse them well:
Not one of those but had a noble father.

HELENA (*She addresses her to a* LORD.)
Gentlemen,
Heaven hath through me restored the king to health.   65

ALL
We understand it, and thank heaven for you.

HELENA
I am a simple maid, and therein wealthiest
That I protest I simply am a maid.
Please it your majesty, I have done already.
The blushes in my cheeks thus whisper me,      70
"We blush that thou shouldst choose; but, be refused,
Let the white death sit on thy cheek forever,
We'll ne'er come there again."

KING                 Make choice and see,
Who shuns thy love shuns all his love in me.

HELENA
Now, Dian, from thy altar do I fly,      75
And to imperial Love, that god most high,
Do my sighs stream. [*To* FIRST LORD.] Sir, will you
     hear my suit?

FIRST LORD
And grant it.

HELENA        Thanks, sir; all the rest is mute.

LAFEW   I had rather be in this choice than throw
ames-ace° for my life.      80

HELENA [*To* SECOND LORD.]
The honor, sir, that flames in your fair eyes,
Before I speak, too threat'ningly replies.
Love make your fortunes twenty times above
Her that so wishes and her humble love!

SECOND LORD
No better, if you please.

HELENA            My wish receive,      85
Which great Love grant; and so, I take my leave.

LAFEW   Do all they deny her?° And they were sons of
mine, I'd have them whipped, or I would send them
to th' Turk to make eunuchs of.

HELENA [*To* THIRD LORD.]
Be not afraid that I your hand should take,      90
I'll never do you wrong, for your own sake.

II.iii.2 **modern** commonplace   **4 ensconcing** fortifying   **6
unknown fear** i.e., inexplicable mystery   **7 argument of**
subject for   **10 artists** physicians   **11 Galen . . . Paracelsus**
renowned physicians; the former was a Greek of the second
century B.C., the latter a German of the sixteenth century   **26
lustier** more vigorous; **'fore me** on my soul   **30 facinerious**
villainous   **35 debile** weak   **42 Dutchman** German   **44
coranto** lively dance   **45 Mor du vinager** death of vinegar
(a meaningless pseudo-French oath)   **50 repealed** recalled from
banishment

**56 frank election** free choice   **60 bay . . . furniture** my
bay horse with the docked tail, and his trappings   **61 broken**
broken to the bit, i.e., tamed (?) missing some teeth (?)   **62
writ** claimed (?)   **80 ames-ace** two aces, the lowest throw in
dicing (the line is ironical, as one might say I would rather be
in this lottery than at death's door)   **87 deny her** Lafew, at
a distance, does not understand that Helena denies the men

Blessing upon your vows, and in your bed
Find fairer fortune if you ever wed!

LAFEW   These boys are boys of ice, they'll none have
her. Sure they are bastards to the English; the French 95
ne'er got° 'em.

HELENA [*To* FOURTH LORD.]
You are too young, too happy, and too good,
To make yourself a son out of my blood.

FOURTH LORD
Fair one, I think not so.

LAFEW   There's one grape yet. I am sure thy father 100
drunk wine.° But if thou be'st not an ass, I am a youth
of fourteen; I have known thee already.

HELENA [*To* BERTRAM.]
I dare not say I take you, but I give
Me and my service, ever whilst I live,
Into your guiding power. This is the man.      105

KING
Why then, young Bertram, take her, she's thy wife.

BERTRAM
My wife, my liege? I shall beseech your highness,
In such a business give me leave to use
The help of mine own eyes.

KING                              Know'st thou not, Bertram,
What she has done for me?

BERTRAM                        Yes, my good lord;      110
But never hope to know why I should marry her.

KING
Thou know'st she has raised me from my sickly bed.

BERTRAM
But follows it, my lord, to bring me down
Must answer for your raising? I know her well;
She had her breeding° at my father's charge:      115
A poor physician's daughter my wife! Disdain
Rather corrupt me ever!°

KING
'Tis only title thou disdain'st in her, the which
I can build up. Strange is it that our bloods,
Of color, weight, and heat, poured all together,      120
Would quite confound distinction, yet stands off
In differences so mighty. If she be
All that is virtuous, save what thou dislik'st—
A poor physician's daughter—thou dislik'st
Of virtue for the name. But do not so:      125
From lowest place when virtuous things proceed,
The place is dignified by th' doer's deed.
Where great additions swell's° and virtue none,
It is a dropsied honor. Good alone
Is good, without a name; vileness is so:      130
The property° by what it is should go,
Not by the title. She is young, wise, fair;
In these to nature she's immediate heir;
And these breed honor. That is honor's scorn
Which challenges itself as honor's born°      135
And is not like the sire. Honors thrive
When rather from our acts we them derive
Than our foregoers. The mere word's a slave,
Deboshed° on every tomb, on every grave

A lying trophy, and as oft is dumb      140
Where dust and damned oblivion is the tomb
Of honored bones indeed. What should be said?
If thou canst like this creature as a maid,
I can create the rest. Virtue and she
Is her own dower; honor and wealth from me.      145

BERTRAM
I cannot love her, nor will strive to do't.

KING
Thou wrong'st thyself, if thou shouldst strive to
choose.

HELENA
That you are well restored, my lord, I'm glad;
Let the rest go.

KING
My honor's at the stake,° which to defeat,      150
I must produce my power. Here, take her hand,
Proud, scornful boy, unworthy this good gift,
That dost in vile misprision° shackle up
My love and her desert; that canst not dream
We, poising us in her defective scale,      155
Shall weigh thee to the beam;° that wilt not know,
It is in us to plant thine honor where
We please to have it grow. Check thy contempt;
Obey our will, which travails in thy good;
Believe not thy disdain, but presently°      160
Do thine own fortunes that obedient right
Which both thy duty owes and our power claims;
Or I will throw thee from my care forever
Into the staggers° and the careless lapse
Of youth and ignorance; both my revenge and hate,      165
Loosing upon thee in the name of justice,
Without all terms of pity. Speak. Thine answer.

BERTRAM
Pardon, my gracious lord; for I submit
My fancy° to your eyes. When I consider
What great creation and what dole° of honor      170
Flies where you bid it, I find that she, which late
Was in my nobler thoughts most base, is now
The praisèd of the king; who, so ennobled,
Is as 'twere born so.

KING                  Take her by the hand,
And tell her she is thine; to whom I promise      175
A counterpoise, if not to thy estate,
A balance more replete.°

BERTRAM                  I take her hand.

KING
Good fortune and the favor of the king
Smile upon this contract; whose ceremony
Shall seem expedient° on the now-born brief,°      180
And be performed tonight. The solemn feast
Shall more attend upon the coming space,
Expecting absent friends.° As thou lov'st her,

96 **got** begot   101 **drunk wine** i.e., was manly   115 **breeding** upbringing   116–17 **Disdain . . . ever** May my disdain of her ruin me forever   128 **additions swell's** titles inflate us   131 **property** quality (here, "good" or "vileness")   135 **challenges . . . born** claims honor by descent   139 **Deboshed** debauched, debased

150 **at the stake** the figure is from bearbaiting; a bear was tied to a stake, and dogs were set upon him   153 **misprision** contempt (with a pun on the sense of "false imprisonment")   155–56 **We . . . beam** i.e., my (royal "we") word added to Helena will outweigh your objection   160 **presently** immediately   164 **staggers** giddiness (disease of animals)   169 **fancy** love   170 **dole** portion   176–77 **A counterpoise . . . replete** a reward that, if it does not equal your estate, will overweigh it (?)   180 **expedient** swift; **brief** royal edict   181–83 **The solemn . . . friends** the ceremonious ("solemn") feast shall await ("attend") until absent friends arrive

Thy love's to me religious; else, does err.

*Exeunt.* PAROLLES *and* LAFEW *stay behind,*
*commenting of this wedding.*

LAFEW  Do you hear, monsieur? A word with you.  185

PAROLLES  Your pleasure, sir?

LAFEW  Your lord and master did well to make his
recantation.

PAROLLES  Recantation! My lord! My master!

LAFEW  Ay; is it not a language I speak?  190

PAROLLES  A most harsh one, and not to be understood without bloody succeeding.° My master!

LAFEW  Are you companion to the Count Rousillon?

PAROLLES  To any count, to all counts; to what is
man.°  195

LAFEW  To what is count's man; count's master is of
another style.

PAROLLES  You are too old, sir; let it satisfy you, you
are too old.

LAFEW  I must tell thee, sirrah, I write man; to which  200
title age cannot bring thee.

PAROLLES  What I dare too well do, I dare not do.

LAFEW  I did think thee, for two ordinaries,° to be a
pretty wise fellow; thou didst make tolerable vent° of
thy travel; it might pass. Yet the scarves° and the  205
bannerets about thee did manifoldly dissuade me from
believing thee a vessel of too great a burden.° I have
now found thee;° when I lose thee again I care not.
Yet art thou good for nothing but taking up, and that
thou'rt scarce worth.  210

PAROLLES  Hadst thou not the privilege of antiquity°
upon thee—

LAFEW  Do not plunge thyself too far in anger, lest
thou hasten thy trial; which if—Lord have mercy on
thee for a hen! So, my good window of lattice, fare  215
thee well; thy casement I need not open, for I look
through thee. Give me thy hand.

PAROLLES  My lord, you give me most egregious
indignity.

LAFEW  Ay, with all my heart, and thou art worthy  220
of it.

PAROLLES  I have not, my lord, deserved it.

LAFEW  Yes, good faith, every dram of it, and I will
not bate thee a scruple.°

PAROLLES  Well, I shall be wiser.  225

LAFEW  Ev'n as soon as thou canst, for thou hast to
pull at a smack o' th' contrary.° If ever thou be'st
bound in thy scarf and beaten, thou shall find what it
is to be proud of thy bondage. I have a desire to hold
my acquaintance with thee, or rather my knowledge,  230
that I may say, in the default,° "He is a man I know."

PAROLLES  My lord, you do me most insupportable
vexation.

LAFEW  I would it were hell-pains for thy sake, and
my poor doing eternal; for doing° I am past, as I will  235

by thee, in what motion age will give me leave. *Exit.*

PAROLLES  Well, thou hast a son shall take this disgrace off me; scurvy, old, filthy, scurvy lord! Well, I
must be patient, there is no fettering of authority. I'll
beat him, by my life, if I can meet him with any con-  240
venience,° and he were double and double a lord. I'll
have no more pity of his age than I would have of—
I'll beat him, and if I could but meet him again.

*Enter* LAFEW.

LAFEW  Sirrah, your lord and master's married; there's
news for you; you have a new mistress.  245

PAROLLES  I most unfeignedly beseech your lordship
to make some reservation of your wrongs. He is my
good lord; whom I serve above is my master.

LAFEW  Who? God?

PAROLLES  Ay, sir.  250

LAFEW  The devil it is that's thy master. Why dost
thou garter up thy arms o' this fashion? Dost make
hose of thy sleeves? Do other servants so? Thou wert
best set thy lower part where thy nose stands. By mine
honor, if I were but two hours younger I'd beat thee.  255
Methink'st thou art a general offense, and every man
should beat thee. I think thou wast created for men to
breathe° themselves upon thee.

PAROLLES  This is hard and undeserved measure, my
lord.  260

LAFEW  Go to, sir. You were beaten in Italy for picking a kernel out of a pom'granate. You are a vagabond
and no true traveler. You are more saucy with lords
and honorable personages than the commission of
your birth and virtue gives you heraldry. You are not  265
worth another word, else I'd call you knave. I leave
you.                                                        *Exit.*

*Enter* BERTRAM.

PAROLLES  Good, very good, it is so then. Good, very
good, let it be concealed awhile.

BERTRAM

Undone and forfeited to cares forever!  270

PAROLLES

What's the matter, sweetheart?

BERTRAM

Although before the solemn priest I have sworn,
I will not bed her.

PAROLLES

What, what, sweetheart?

BERTRAM

O my Parolles, they have married me!  275
I'll to the Tuscan wars and never bed her.

PAROLLES

France is a dog-hole, and it no more merits
The tread of a man's foot; to th' wars!

BERTRAM

There's letters from my mother; what th' import is,
I know not yet.  280

PAROLLES

Ay, that would be known. To th' wars, my boy, to th'
wars!
He wears his honor in a box unseen,

---

**192 succeeding** consequences  **195 man** manly (but Lafew
gives it another sense, "servingman")  **203 ordinaries** tavern
meals  **204 vent** free talk  **205 scarves** military men wore
scarves, usually over the shoulder; cf. the modern *fourragère*
**207 burden** capacity  **208 found thee** found you out  **211
antiquity** old age  **224 bate . . . scruple** i.e., diminish by
one drop what I have said of you  **227 pull . . . contrary**
i.e., take a good taste of your folly  **231 in the default** when
you fail  **235 doing** perhaps with the bawdy meaning,
"copulating"

**240–41 convenience** advantage   **258 breathe** exercise

That hugs his kicky-wicky° here at home,
Spending his manly marrow in her arms,
Which should sustain the bound and high curvet°        285
Of Mars's fiery steed. To other regions!
France is a stable, we that dwell in't jades;°
Therefore to th' war!

BERTRAM
It shall be so. I'll send her to my house,
Acquaint my mother with my hate to her,        290
And wherefore I am fled; write to the king
That which I durst not speak. His present gift
Shall furnish me to those Italian fields
Where noble fellows strike. Wars is no strife
To the dark house and the detested wife.        295

PAROLLES
Will this capriccio° hold in thee, art sure?

BERTRAM
Go with me to my chamber and advise me.
I'll send her straight away. Tomorrow
I'll to the wars, she to her single sorrow.

PAROLLES
Why, these balls bound; there's noise in it. 'Tis hard;        300
A young man married is a man that's marred.
Therefore away, and leave her bravely; go.
The king has done you wrong; but hush 'tis so.
                              *Exit,* [*with* BERTRAM].


[Scene IV. *Paris. The king's palace.*]

*Enter* HELENA *and* CLOWN.

HELENA
My mother greets me kindly. Is she well?°

CLOWN   She is not well, but yet she has her health;
she's very merry, but yet she is not well. But thanks
be given she's very well and wants nothing i' th'
world; but yet she is not well.        5

HELENA   If she be very well what does she ail that
she's not very well?

CLOWN   Truly, she's very well indeed, but for two
things.

HELENA   What two things?        10

CLOWN   One, that she's not in heaven, whither God
send her quickly; the other, that she's in earth, from
whence God send her quickly.

*Enter* PAROLLES.

PAROLLES   Bless you, my fortunate lady!

HELENA   I hope, sir, I have your good will to have        15
mine own good fortune.

PAROLLES   You had my prayers to lead them on, and
to keep them on have them still. O, my knave, how
does my old lady?

CLOWN   So that you had her wrinkles and I her        20
money, I would she did as you say.

PAROLLES   Why, I say nothing.

CLOWN   Marry, you are the wiser man; for many a
man's tongue shakes out his master's undoing. To say
nothing, to do nothing, to know nothing, and to have        25
nothing, is to be a great part of your title°—which is
within a very little of nothing.

PAROLLES   Away, th' art a knave.

CLOWN   You should have said, sir, "Before a knave
th' art a knave"; that's "Before me,° th' art a knave."        30
This had been truth, sir.

PAROLLES   Go to, thou art a witty fool; I have found
thee.

CLOWN   Did you find me in° yourself, sir, or were you
taught to find me? The search, sir, was profitable; and        35
much fool may you find in you, even to the world's
pleasure and the increase of laughter.

PAROLLES
A good knave, i' faith, and well fed.
Madam, my lord will go away tonight,
A very serious business calls on him.        40
The great prerogative and rite of love,
Which as your due time claims, he does acknowledge,
But puts it off to a compelled restraint;
Whose want, and whose delay, is strewed with sweets,
Which they distil now in the curbèd time,°        45
To make the coming hour o'erflow with joy,
And pleasure drown the brim.

HELENA                              What's his will else?

PAROLLES
That you will take your instant leave o' th' king,
And make this haste as your own good proceeding,°
Strength'ned with what apology you think        50
May make it probable need.

HELENA                              What more commands he?

PAROLLES
That, having this obtained, you presently
Attend his further pleasure.

HELENA
In everything I wait upon his will.

PAROLLES
I shall report it so.                              *Exit* PAROLLES.        55

HELENA
I pray you. Come, sirrah.                *Exit,* [*with* CLOWN].


[Scene V. *Paris. The king's palace.*]

*Enter* LAFEW *and* BERTRAM.

LAFEW   But I hope your lordship thinks not him a
soldier.

BERTRAM   Yes, my lord, and of very valiant approof.°

LAFEW   You have it from his own deliverance.°

BERTRAM   And by other warranted testimony.        5

LAFEW   Then my dial goes not true; I took this lark
for a bunting.°

BERTRAM   I do assure you, my lord, he is very great in
knowledge, and accordingly valiant.

LAFEW   I have then sinned against his experience and        10

283 **kicky-wicky** woman (but apparently an obscene term,
perhaps from French *quelque chose* = "something," a euphemism for *pudendum*)   285 **curvet** prancing   287 **jades** nags
296 **capriccio** caprice (an affected Italian word)
**II.iv.1 well** in his reply, the Clown plays on the Elizabethan
euphemism in which the dead are said to be well, i.e., well-off,
being in heaven

26 **title** possession   30 **Before me** punning on the sense "on
my soul"   34 **in** by   45 **curbèd time** delay (?) time spent in
the confining still (?)   49 **as . . . proceeding** as if it originated
from you
**II.v.3 very valiant approof** great proven valor   4 **deliverance** speech   6-7 **took . . . bunting** i.e., underestimated him

transgressed against his valor; and my state that way is dangerous, since I cannot yet find in my heart to repent. Here he comes. I pray you make us friends; I will pursue the amity.

*Enter* PAROLLES.

PAROLLES [*To* BERTRAM.]    These things shall be done, 15 sir.

LAFEW   Pray you, sir, who's his tailor?

PAROLLES   Sir?

LAFEW   O, I know him well. Ay sir, he, sir, 's a good workman, a very good tailor. 20

BERTRAM [*Aside to* PAROLLES.]
Is she gone to the king?

PAROLLES             She is.

BERTRAM
Will she away tonight?

PAROLLES           As you'll have her.

BERTRAM
I have writ my letters, casketed my treasure,
Given order for our horses; and tonight,
When I should take possession of the bride, 25
End ere I do begin.

LAFEW [*Aside.*]   A good traveler is something at the latter end of a dinner, but one that lies three thirds and uses a known truth to pass a thousand nothings with, should be once heard and thrice beaten. [*Aloud.*] 30 God save you, captain.

BERTRAM   Is there any unkindness between my lord and you, monsieur?

PAROLLES   I know not how I have deserved to run into my lord's displeasure. 35

LAFEW   You have made shift° to run into't, boots and spurs and all, like him that leaped into the custard; and out of it you'll run again rather than suffer question for your residence.°

BERTRAM   It may be you have mistaken him, my lord. 40

LAFEW   And shall do so ever, though I took him at's prayers. Fare you well, my lord, and believe this of me, there can be no kernel in this light nut; the soul of this man is his clothes. Trust him not in matter of heavy consequence; I have kept of them tame° and 45 know their natures. Farewell, monsieur; I have spoken better of you than you have or will to deserve at my hand, but we must do good against evil. [*Exit.*]

PAROLLES   An idle° lord, I swear.

BERTRAM   I think not so. 50

PAROLLES   Why, do you not know him?

BERTRAM
Yes, I do know him well, and common speech
Gives him a worthy pass.° Here comes my clog.

*Enter* HELENA.

HELENA
I have, sir, as I was commanded from you,
Spoke with the king, and have procured his leave 55
For present parting; only he desires
Some private speech with you.

BERTRAM          I shall obey his will.

You must not marvel, Helen, at my course,
Which holds not color with the time,° nor does
The ministration and requirèd office 60
On my particular. Prepared I was not
For such a business; therefore am I found
So much unsettled. This drives me to entreat you
That presently you take your way for home,
And rather muse than ask why I entreat you, 65
For my respects° are better than they seem,
And my appointments° have in them a need
Greater than shows itself at the first view
To you that know them not. [*Gives a letter.*] This to
    my mother.
'Twill be two days ere I shall see you, so 70
I leave you to your wisdom.

HELENA          Sir, I can nothing say
But that I am your most obedient servant.

BERTRAM
Come, come; no more of that.

HELENA          And ever shall
With true observance° seek to eke out that
Wherein toward me my homely stars° have failed 75
To equal my great fortune.

BERTRAM          Let that go:
My haste is very great. Farewell; hie home.

HELENA
Pray sir, your pardon.

BERTRAM          Well, what would you say?

HELENA
I am not worthy of the wealth I owe,°
Nor dare I say 'tis mine—and yet it is; 80
But like a timorous thief most fain would steal
What law does vouch mine own.

BERTRAM          What would you have?

HELENA
Something, and scarce so much: nothing, indeed.
I would not tell you what I would, my lord.
Faith, yes— 85
Strangers and foes do sunder and not kiss.

BERTRAM
I pray you, stay not, but in haste to horse.

HELENA
I shall not break your bidding, good my lord.
Where are my other men? Monsieur, farewell.  *Exit.*

BERTRAM
Go thou toward home, where I will never come 90
Whilst I can shake my sword or hear the drum.
Away, and for our flight.

PAROLLES          Bravely, coragio!° [*Exeunt.*]

# ACT III

[Scene I. *Florence. The duke's palace.*]

*Flourish. Enter the* DUKE *of Florence, the two* FRENCH-
MEN, *with a troop of* SOLDIERS.

---

**36 made shift** managed   **38–39 suffer . . . residence** put up with questions on why you are there   **45 kept . . . tame** had some of them as pets   **49 idle** foolish   **53 pass** reputation

**59 holds . . . time** does not match the situation   **66 respects** reasons   **67 appointments** purposes   **74 observance** dutiful service   **75 homely stars** fate of low birth   **79 owe** own   **92 coragio** courage (Italian)

DUKE
So that from point to point now have you heard
The fundamental reasons of this war,
Whose great decision hath much blood let forth,
And more thirsts after.

FIRST LORD                    Holy seems the quarrel
Upon your grace's part; black and fearful                    5
On the opposer.

DUKE
Therefore we marvel much our cousin France
Would in so just a business shut his bosom
Against our borrowing prayers.

SECOND LORD                    Good my lord,
The reasons of our state I cannot yield,°                    10
But like a common and an outward man
That the great figure of a council frames
By self-unable motion;° therefore dare not
Say what I think of it, since I have found
Myself in my incertain grounds to fail                    15
As often as I guessed.

DUKE                    Be it his pleasure.

FIRST LORD
But I am sure the younger of our nature,
That surfeit on° their ease, will day by day
Come here for physic.

DUKE                    Welcome shall they be;
And all the honors that can fly from us                    20
Shall on them settle. You know your places well;
When better fall, for your avails they fell:°
Tomorrow to the field!                    *Flourish; [exeunt].*


[Scene II. *Rousillon. The count's palace.*]

*Enter* COUNTESS *and* CLOWN.

COUNTESS    It hath happened all as I would have had
it, save that he comes not along with her.

CLOWN    By my troth,° I take my young lord to be a
very melancholy man.

COUNTESS    By what observance, I pray you?                    5

CLOWN    Why, he will look upon his boot and sing,
mend the ruff and sing, ask questions and sing, pick
his teeth and sing. I know a man that had his trick of
melancholy sold a goodly manor for a song.

COUNTESS    Let me see what he writes, and when he    10
means to come.

[*Reads a letter.*]

CLOWN    I have no mind to Isbel, since I was at court.
Our old lings° and our Isbels o' th' country are nothing
like your old ling and your Isbels o' th' court. The
brains of my Cupid's knocked out, and I begin to love    15
as an old man loves money, with no stomach.°

COUNTESS    What have we here?

CLOWN    E'en that you have there.                    *Exit.*

COUNTESS [*Reads*] *a letter.* "I have sent you a
daughter-in-law. She hath recovered the king, and    20

undone me. I have wedded her, not bedded her, and
sworn to make the 'not'° eternal. You shall hear
I am run away; know it before the report come. If
there be breadth enough in the world, I will hold a long
distance. My duty to you.                    25
                    Your unfortunate son,
                    Bertram."

This is not well, rash and unbridled boy,
To fly the favors of so good a king,
To pluck his indignation on thy head                    30
By the misprizing° of a maid too virtuous
For the contempt of empire.

*Enter* CLOWN.

CLOWN    O madam, yonder is heavy news within,
between two soldiers and my young lady.

COUNTESS    What is the matter?                    35

CLOWN    Nay, there is some comfort in the news, some
comfort; your son will not be killed so soon as I
thought he would.

COUNTESS    Why should he be killed?

CLOWN    So say I, madam, if he run away, as I hear he    40
does. The danger is in standing to't;° that's the loss of
men, though it be the getting of children. Here they
come will tell you more. For my part, I only hear
your son was run away.

*Enter* HELENA *and two* [*French*] GENTLEMEN.

FIRST LORD    Save you, good madam.                    45

HELENA
Madam, my lord is gone, forever gone.

SECOND LORD    Do not say so.

COUNTESS
Think upon patience. Pray you, gentlemen,
I have felt so many quirks of joy and grief,
That the first face of neither, on the start,                    50
Can woman me° unto't. Where is my son, I pray you?

SECOND LORD
Madam, he's gone to serve the Duke of Florence.
We met him thitherward, for thence we came,
And, after some dispatch in hand at court,
Thither we bend again.                    55

HELENA    Look on his letter, madam, here's my passport.°

[*Reads.*]

"When thou canst get the ring upon my finger, which
never shall come off, and show me a child begotten of
thy body that I am father to, then call me husband; but    60
in such a 'then' I write a 'never.'" This is a dreadful
sentence.

COUNTESS
Brought you this letter, gentlemen?

FIRST LORD                    Ay, madam,
And for the contents' sake are sorry for our pains.

COUNTESS
I prithee, lady, have a better cheer.                    65
If thou engrossest° all the griefs are thine,

---

III.i.10 **yield** produce    13 **self-unable motion** impotent guess
18 **surfeit on** grow sick from    22 **When . . . fell** when
better places fall vacant, for you they will have fallen
III.ii.3 **troth** truth    13 **lings** salt cod (but also with the sense
of "lecherous men")    16 **stomach** appetite

22 **not** with pun on *knot*, the symbol of marriage    31 **misprizing** despising    41 **standing to't** (1) standing one's ground
(2) having sexual intercourse    51 **woman me** make me weep
56–57 **passport** license to wander as a beggar    66 **thou
engrossest** you monopolize

Thou robb'st me of a moiety.° He was my son,
But I do wash his name out of my blood
And thou art all my child. Towards Florence is he?

**SECOND LORD**
Ay, madam.

**COUNTESS** And to be a soldier?     70

**SECOND LORD**
Such is his noble purpose, and, believe 't,
The Duke will lay upon him all the honor
That good convenience° claims.

**COUNTESS**                Return you thither?

**FIRST LORD**
Ay, madam, with the swiftest wing of speed.

**HELENA** [Reads.]
"Till I have no wife, I have nothing in France."     75
'Tis bitter.

**COUNTESS** Find you that there?

**HELENA**                Ay, madam.

**FIRST LORD** 'Tis but the boldness of his hand, haply,°
which his heart was not consenting to.

**COUNTESS**
Nothing in France, until he have no wife!
There's nothing here that is too good for him     80
But only she, and she deserves a lord
That twenty such rude boys might tend upon
And call her, hourly, mistress. Who was with him?

**FIRST LORD**
A servant only, and a gentleman
Which I have sometime known.

**COUNTESS**           Parolles, was it not?     85

**FIRST LORD**
Ay, my good lady, he.

**COUNTESS**
A very tainted fellow, and full of wickedness.
My son corrupts a well-derivèd nature
With his inducement.°

**FIRST LORD**          Indeed, good lady,
The fellow has a deal of that too much,     90
Which holds° him much to have.

**COUNTESS**           Y'are welcome, gentlemen.
I will entreat you, when you see my son,
To tell him that his sword can never win
The honor that he loses; more I'll entreat you
Written to bear along.

**SECOND LORD**       We serve you, madam,     95
In that and all your worthiest affairs.

**COUNTESS**
Not so, but as we change our courtesies.°
Will you draw near?

                Exit, [with LORDS and CLOWN].

**HELENA**
"Till I have no wife, I have nothing in France."
Nothing in France until he has no wife!     100
Thou shalt have none, Rousillon,° none in France;
Then hast thou all again. Poor lord! Is 't I
That chase thee from thy country and expose
Those tender limbs of thine to the event°
Of the none-sparing war? And is it I     105

That drive thee from the sportive court, where thou
Wast shot at with fair eyes, to be the mark
Of smoky muskets? O you leaden messengers,
That ride upon the violent speed of fire,
Fly with false aim, move the still-piecing° air     110
That sings with piercing; do not touch my lord!
Whoever shoots at him, I set him there.
Whoever charges on his forward breast,
I am the caitiff° that do hold him to 't.
And though I kill him not I am the cause     115
His death was so effected. Better 'twere
I met the ravin° lion when he roared
With sharp constraint of hunger; better 'twere
That all the miseries which nature owes°
Were mine at once. No; come thou home, Rousillon,     120
Whence honor but of danger wins a scar,
As oft it loses all.° I will be gone;
My being here it is that holds thee hence.
Shall I stay here to do 't? No, no, although
The air of paradise did fan the house     125
And angels officed° all. I will be gone,
That pitiful rumor may report my flight
To consolate thine ear. Come night, end day;
For with the dark, poor thief, I'll steal away.     Exit.


             [Scene III. Florence.]

*Flourish. Enter the* DUKE *of Florence,* BERTRAM, *drum
and trumpets,* SOLDIERS, PAROLLES.

**DUKE**
The general of our horse thou art, and we,
Great in our hope, lay° our best love and credence
Upon thy promising fortune.

**BERTRAM**             Sir, it is
A charge too heavy for my strength; but yet
We'll strive to bear it for your worthy sake     5
To th' extreme edge of hazard.

**DUKE**               Then go thou forth,
And fortune play upon thy prosperous helm,°
As thy auspicious mistress!

**BERTRAM**            This very day,
Great Mars, I put myself into thy file!
Make me but like my thoughts and I shall prove     10
A lover of thy drum, hater of love.     Exeunt omnes.


       [Scene IV. Rousillon. The count's palace.]

*Enter* COUNTESS *and* STEWARD.

**COUNTESS**
Alas! And would you take the letter of her?
Might you not know she would do as she has done,
By sending me a letter? Read it again.
[STEWARD *reads the*] letter.

---

**67 moiety** share    **73 convenience** propriety    **77 haply**
perhaps    **89 his inducement** i.e., Parolles' influence    **91 holds**
profits    **97 Not . . . courtesies** No, you may serve me only
if I may serve you (a courteous reply)    **101 Rousillon**
Bertram, Count of Rousillon    **104 event** outcome

**110 still-piecing** ever-repairing    **114 caitiff** wretch    **117
ravin** ravenous    **119 owes** owns, has    **121–22 Whence . . .
all** from where honor at best gains from danger a scar, and may
lose everything    **126 officed** served
**III.iii.2 lay** wager    **7 helm** helmet

"I am Saint Jaques' pilgrim,° thither gone.
Ambitious love hath so in me offended                    5
That barefoot plod I the cold ground upon,
With sainted vow my faults to have amended.
Write, write, that from the bloody course of war
My dearest master, your dear son, may hie.°
Bless him at home in peace, whilst I from far          10
His name with zealous fervor sanctify.
His taken° labors bid him me forgive;
I, his despiteful Juno,° sent him forth
From courtly friends with camping foes to live,
Where death and danger dogs the heels of worth.      15
He is too good and fair for death and me,
Whom° I myself embrace to set him° free."
[COUNTESS.]
Ah, what sharp stings are in her mildest words!
Rinaldo, you did never lack advice° so much
As letting her pass so; had I spoke with her,            20
I could have well diverted her intents,
Which thus she hath prevented.
STEWARD                         Pardon me, madam.
If I had given you this at overnight,°
She might have been o'erta'en; and yet she writes,
Pursuit would be but vain.
COUNTESS                    What angel shall           25
Bless this unworthy husband? He cannot thrive,
Unless her prayers, whom heaven delights to hear
And loves to grant, reprieve him from the wrath
Of greatest justice. Write, write, Rinaldo,
To this unworthy husband of his wife;                    30
Let every word weigh heavy of her worth
That he does weigh too light. My greatest grief,
Though little he do feel it, set down sharply.
Dispatch the most convenient messenger.
When haply he shall hear that she is gone,            35
He will return; and hope I may that she,
Hearing so much, will speed her foot again,
Led hither by pure love. Which of them both
Is dearest to me, I have no skill in sense
To make distinction. Provide this messenger.          40
My heart is heavy and mine age is weak;
Grief would have tears, and sorrow bids me speak.
                                        *Exeunt.*


[Scene V. *Outside Florence.*]

*A tucket° afar off. Enter old* WIDOW *of Florence, her
daughter* [DIANA], *and* MARIANA, *with other* CITIZENS.

WIDOW  Nay come, for if they do approach the city,
we shall lose all the sight.
DIANA  They say the French count has done most
honorable service.
WIDOW  It is reported that he has taken their great'st   5
commander, and that with his own hand he slew the

duke's brother. [*Tucket.*] We have lost our labor; they
are gone a contrary way. Hark! You may know by
their trumpets.
MARIANA  Come, let's return again, and suffice our-   10
selves with the report of it. Well, Diana, take heed of
this French earl. The honor of a maid is her name, and
no legacy is so rich as honesty.°
WIDOW  I have told my neighbor how you have been
solicited by a gentleman his companion.                 15
MARIANA  I know that knave, hang him, one Parolles;
a filthy officer he is in those suggestions for the young
earl. Beware of them, Diana: their promises, entice-
ments, oaths, tokens, and all these engines° of lust, are
not the things they go under;° many a maid hath been   20
seduced by them. And the misery is, example, that so
terrible shows in the wrack of maidenhood, cannot for
all that dissuade succession,° but that they are limed°
with the twigs that threatens them. I hope I need not
to advise you further, but I hope your own grace will   25
keep you where you are, though there were no further
danger known but the modesty which is so lost.
DIANA  You shall not need to fear me.

*Enter* HELENA [*disguised as a pilgrim*].

WIDOW  I hope so. Look, here comes a pilgrim. I
know she will lie° at my house; thither they send one   30
another. I'll question her. God save you, pilgrim!
Whither are you bound?
HELENA
To Saint Jaques le Grand.
Where do the palmers° lodge, I do beseech you?
WIDOW
At the Saint Francis here beside the port.°            35
HELENA
Is this the way?
WIDOW
Ay, marry, is't. (*A march afar.*) Hark you! They come
   this way.
If you will tarry, holy pilgrim,
But till the troops come by,
I will conduct you where you shall be lodged;         40
The rather for I think I know your hostess
As ample° as myself.
HELENA                    Is it yourself?
WIDOW
If you shall please so, pilgrim.
HELENA
I thank you, and will stay upon your leisure.°
WIDOW
You came, I think, from France?
HELENA                               I did so.          45
WIDOW
Here you shall see a countryman of yours
That has done worthy service.
HELENA                          His name, I pray you.
DIANA
The Count Rousillon. Know you such a one?

---

HELENA
But by the ear, that hears most nobly of him;
His face I know not.

DIANA            Whatsome'er he is,    50
He's bravely taken° here. He stole from France,
As 'tis reported, for the king had married him
Against his liking. Think you it is so?

HELENA
Ay, surely, mere° the truth. I know his lady.

DIANA
There is a gentleman that serves the count    55
Reports but coarsely of her.

HELENA            What's his name?

DIANA
Monsieur Parolles.

HELENA         O, I believe with him,
In argument of praise, or to the worth
Of the great count himself, she is too mean
To have her name repeated; all her deserving    60
Is a reservèd honesty,° and that
I have not heard examined.

DIANA           Alas, poor lady!
'Tis a hard bondage to become the wife
Of a detesting lord.

WIDOW
I warrant, good creature, wheresoe'er she is,    65
Her heart weighs sadly. This young maid might do her
A shrewd turn,° if she pleased.

HELENA           How do you mean?
Maybe the amorous count solicits her
In the unlawful purpose.

WIDOW          He does indeed,
And brokes° with all that can in such a suit    70
Corrupt the tender honor of a maid;
But she is armed for him, and keeps her guard
In honestest defense.

MARIANA          The gods forbid else!

*Drum and colors. Enter* BERTRAM, PAROLLES, *and the whole* ARMY.

WIDOW
So, now they come.
That is Antonio, the duke's eldest son;    75
That, Escalus.

HELENA         Which is the Frenchman?

DIANA             He—
That with the plume; 'tis a most gallant fellow.
I would he loved his wife. If he were honester
He were much goodlier. Is't not a handsome gentle-
man?

HELENA
I like him well.    80

DIANA
'Tis pity he is not honest. Yond's that same knave
That leads him to these places. Were I his lady
I would poison that vile rascal.

HELENA           Which is he?

DIANA
That jackanapes with scarves. Why is he melancholy?

HELENA
Perchance he's hurt i' th' battle.    85

PAROLLES   Lose our drum! Well.

MARIANA   He's shrewdly° vexed at something. Look,
he has spied us.

WIDOW   Marry, hang you!

MARIANA   And your curtsy, for a ring-carrier!°    90

       *Exit* [BERTRAM, *with* PAROLLES *and the* ARMY].

WIDOW
The troop is past. Come, pilgrim, I will bring you
Where you shall host;° of enjoined° penitents
There's four or five, to great Saint Jaques bound,
Already at my house.

HELENA          I humbly thank you.
Please it this matron and this gentle maid    95
To eat with us tonight, the charge and thanking
Shall be for me; and, to requite you further,
I will bestow some precepts of° this virgin
Worthy the note.

BOTH           We'll take your offer kindly.

              *Exeunt.*

[Scene VI   *The Florentine camp.*]

*Enter* BERTRAM *and the* [*two*] FRENCHMEN, *as at first.*

FIRST LORD   Nay, good my lord, put him to't;° let
him have his way.

SECOND LORD   If your lordship find him not a
hilding,° hold me no more in your respect.

FIRST LORD   On my life, my lord, a bubble.    5

BERTRAM   Do you think I am so far deceived in him?

FIRST LORD   Believe it, my lord, in mine own direct
knowledge, without any malice, but to speak of him
as my kinsman,° he's a most notable coward, an
infinite and endless liar, an hourly promise-breaker,    10
the owner of no one good quality worthy your lordship's entertainment.°

SECOND LORD   It were fit you knew him, lest reposing too far in his virtue which he hath not, he
might at some great and trusty business in a main    15
danger fail you.

BERTRAM   I would I knew in what particular action
to try him.

SECOND LORD   None better than to let him fetch off
his drum,° which you hear him so confidently under-    20
take to do.

FIRST LORD   I, with a troop of Florentines, will suddenly surprise him; such I will have whom I am sure
he knows not from the enemy. We will bind and
hoodwink° him so, that he shall suppose no other but    25
that he carried into the leaguer° of the adversaries
when we bring him to our own tents. Be but your
lordship present at his examination; if he do not for
the promise of his life and in the highest compulsion
of base fear offer to betray you and deliver all the    30

---

51 **bravely taken** well esteemed   54 **mere** absolutely   61
**reservèd honesty** preserved chastity   67 **shrewd turn** nasty
deed (with sexual implication in "turn")   70 **brokes** bargains
  87 **shrewdly** bitterly   90 **ring-carrier** bawd   92 **host** lodge;
**enjoined** bound by oath   98 **of** on
III.vi 1 **put him to't** test him   4 **hilding** worthless fellow
9 **as my kinsman** i.e., impartially   12 **entertainment** maintenance   19–20 **fetch . . . drum** recapture his drum (the loss
of the drum was a military disgrace)   25 **hoodwink** blindfold
26 **leaguer** camp

intelligence° in his power against you, and that with the divine forfeit of his soul upon oath, never trust my judgment in anything.

SECOND LORD　O, for the love of laughter, let him fetch his drum. He says he has a stratagem for't. When 35 your lordship sees the bottom of his success in't, and to what metal this counterfeit lump of ore will be melted, if you give him not John Drum's entertainment° your inclining cannot be removed. Here he comes. 40

*Enter* PAROLLES.

FIRST LORD　O, for the love of laughter, hinder not the honor of his design; let him fetch off his drum in any hand.

BERTRAM　How now, monsieur! This drum sticks sorely in your disposition. 45

SECOND LORD　A pox° on't, let it go, 'tis but a drum.

PAROLLES　"But a drum!" Is't "but a drum"? A drum so lost! There was excellent command: to charge in with our horse upon our own wings, and to rend our own soldiers! 50

SECOND LORD　That was not to be blamed in the command of the service; it was a disaster of war that Caesar himself could not have prevented if he had been there to command.

BERTRAM　Well, we cannot greatly condemn our suc- 55 cess;° some dishonor we had in the loss of that drum, but it is not to be recovered.

PAROLLES　It might have been recovered.

BERTRAM　It might, but it is not now.

PAROLLES　It is to be recovered. But that the merit of 60 service is seldom attributed to the true and exact performer, I would have that drum or another, or hic jacet.°

BERTRAM　Why, if you have a stomach,° to't, monsieur. If you think your mystery° in stratagem can 65 bring this instrument of honor again into his native quarter, be magnanimous in the enterprise, and go on; I will grace the attempt for a worthy exploit. If you speed° well in it, the duke shall both speak of it and extend to you what further becomes his greatness, 70 even to the utmost syllable of your worthiness.

PAROLLES　By the hand of a soldier, I will undertake it.

BERTRAM　But you must not now slumber in it.

PAROLLES　I'll about it this evening, and I will pres- 75 ently pen down my dilemmas,° encourage myself in my certainty, put myself into my mortal preparation;° and by midnight look to hear further from me.

BERTRAM　May I be bold to acquaint his grace you are gone about it? 80

PAROLLES　I know not what the success will be, my lord, but the attempt I vow.

BERTRAM　I know, th'art valiant; and to the possibility° of thy soldiership will subscribe for thee. Farewell.

PAROLLES　I love not many words. *Exit.* 85

FIRST LORD　No more than a fish loves water. Is not this a strange fellow, my lord, that so confidently seems to undertake this business, which he knows is not to be done, damns himself to do, and dares better be damned than to do't. 90

SECOND LORD　You do not know him, my lord, as we do. Certain it is that he will steal himself into a man's favor and for a week escape a great deal of discoveries, but when you find him out you have him ever after. 95

BERTRAM　Why, do you think he will make no deed at all of this that so seriously he does address himself unto?

FIRST LORD　None in the world, but return with an invention, and clap upon you two or three probable 100 lies; but we have almost embossed him.° You shall see his fall tonight, for indeed he is not for your lordship's respect.

SECOND LORD　We'll make you some sport with the fox ere we case° him. He was first smoked° by the old 105 lord Lafew. When his disguise and he is parted, tell me what a sprat° you shall find him; which you shall see this very night.

FIRST LORD　I must go look my twigs; he shall be caught. 110

BERTRAM　Your brother, he shall go along with me.

FIRST LORD　As't please your lordship: I'll leave you. *Exit.*

BERTRAM
Now will I lead you to the house and show you
The lass I spoke of.

SECOND LORD　　　But you say she's honest.

BERTRAM
That's all the fault. I spoke with her but once, 115
And found her wondrous cold, but I sent to her,
By this same coxcomb that we have i' th' wind,°
Tokens and letters which she did re-send,
And this is all I have done. She's a fair creature;
Will you go see her?

SECOND LORD　　　With all my heart, my lord. 120
*Exeunt.*

[Scene VII. *Florence. The Widow's house.*]

*Enter* HELENA *and* WIDOW.

HELENA
If you misdoubt me that I am not she,
I know not how I shall assure your further,
But I shall lose the grounds I work upon.°

WIDOW
Though my estate be fall'n, I was well born,
Nothing acquainted with these businesses, 5
And would not put my reputation now
In any staining act.

HELENA　　　Nor would I wish you.
First give me trust the count he is my husband,

31 **intelligence** information　38–39 **John Drum's entertainment** manhandling　46 **pox** plague (literally, syphilis)　55–56 **success** outcome, fortune (either good or bad)　62–63 **hic jacet** here lies (Latin, beginning an epitaph)　64 **stomach** appetite　65 **mystery** art, skill　69 **speed** prosper　76 **dilemmas** arguments　77 **my mortal preparation** preparation for my death (?) my weapons for killing (?)　83–84 **possibility** capacity

101 **embossed him** exhausted him (hunting term)　105 **case** skin; **smoked** exposed (like a fox smoked out)　107 **sprat** small fish　117 **have . . . wind** are hunting
**III.vii.3 But . . . upon** i.e., unless ("But") I reveal myself to Bertram

And what to your sworn counsel I have spoken°
Is so from word to word; and then you cannot,   10
By the good aid that I of you shall borrow,
Err in bestowing it.
WIDOW              I should believe you,
For you have showed me that which well approves
Y' are great in fortune.
HELENA            Take this purse of gold,
And let me buy your friendly help thus far,   15
Which I will over-pay and pay again
When I have found it. The count he woos your
   daughter,
Lays down his wanton siege before her beauty,
Resolved to carry° her; let her in fine° consent
As we'll direct her how 'tis best to bear it.   20
Now his important° blood will nought deny
That she'll demand; a ring the county° wears,
That downward hath succeeded in his house
From son to son some four or five descents
Since the first father wore it. This ring he holds   25
In most rich choice; yet, in his idle fire,
To buy his will° it would not seem too dear,
Howe'er repented after.
WIDOW             Now I see
The bottom of your purpose.
HELENA
You see it lawful then. It is no more   30
But that your daughter, ere she seems as won,
Desires this ring; appoints him an encounter;
In fine, delivers me to fill the time,
Herself most chastely absent. After,
To marry her° I'll add three thousand crowns   35
To what is passed already.
WIDOW             I have yielded.
Instruct my daughter how she shall persever°
That time and place with this deceit so lawful
May prove coherent.° Every night he comes
With musics of all sorts, and songs composed   40
To her unworthiness. It nothing steads° us
To chide him from our eaves, for he persists
As if his life lay on't.
HELENA           Why then tonight
Let us assay our plot, which, if it speed,°
Is wicked meaning° in a lawful deed,   45
And lawful meaning in a lawful act,
Where both not sin, and yet a sinful fact.
But let's about it.           [Exeunt.]

# ACT IV

### [Scene I. Outside the Florentine camp.]

*Enter one of the Frenchmen,* [FIRST LORD], *with five or six other* SOLDIERS *in ambush.*

FIRST LORD   He can come no other way but by this
hedge-corner. When you sally upon him, speak what
terrible language you will; though you understand it
not yourselves, no matter; for we must not seem to
understand him, unless someone among us whom we   5
must produce for an interpreter.
FIRST SOLDIER   Good captain, let me be th' interpreter.
FIRST LORD   Art not acquainted with him? Knows he
not thy voice?   10
FIRST SOLDIER   No sir, I warrant you.
FIRST LORD   But what linsey-woolsey° hast thou to
speak to us again?
FIRST SOLDIER   E'en such as you speak to me.
FIRST LORD   He must think us some band of stran-   15
gers° i' th' adversary's entertainment. Now he hath a
smack of all neighboring languages; therefore we
must everyone be a man of his own fancy, not to
know what we speak one to another; so we seem to
know is to know straight our purpose; choughs'°   20
language, gabble enough and good enough. As for
you, interpreter, you must seem very politic. But
couch, ho! Here he comes to beguile two hours in a
sleep, and then to return and swear the lies he forges.

*Enter* PAROLLES.

PAROLLES   Ten o'clock. Within these three hours   25
'twill be time enough to go home. What shall I say I
have done? It must be a very plausive° invention that
carries it. They begin to smoke me, and disgraces have
of late knocked too often at my door. I find my tongue
is too foolhardy, but my heart hath the fear of Mars   30
before it and of his creatures, not daring the reports of
my tongue.
FIRST LORD [*Aside.*]   This is the first truth that e'er
thine own tongue was guilty of.
PAROLLES   What the devil should move me to under-   35
take the recovery of this drum, being not ignorant of
the impossibility, and knowing I had no such purpose?
I must give myself some hurts, and say I got them in
exploit. Yet slight ones will not carry it. They will say,
"Came you off with so little?" And great ones I dare   40
not give. Wherefore, what's the instance? Tongue, I
must put you into a butter-woman's° mouth, and buy
myself another of Bajazet's mule° if you prattle me
into these perils.
FIRST LORD [*Aside.*]   Is it possible he should know   45
what he is, and be that he is?
PAROLLES   I would the cutting of my garments would
serve the turn, or the breaking of my Spanish sword.
FIRST LORD [*Aside.*]   We cannot afford you so.°

---

9 to . . . spoken I have confided to you, upon your oath
of secrecy  19 carry conquer; in fine finally  21 important importunate, pressing  22 county count  27 will
lust  35 To marry her i.e., as a dowry to help her marry
37 persever accent on second syllable  39 coherent in
accordance  41 steads helps  44 speed prosper  45 meaning intention (the point of this passage is that Bertram's
intention is wicked, though his deed—copulating with his wife
—will be lawful; Helena's intention and her act will be good,
and the deed will not be a sin though in Bertram's mind he will
be sinning)

IV.i.12 linsey-woolsey nonsense (literally, a coarse fabric of
linen and wool)  15–16 strangers foreigners  20 choughs'
jackdaws  27 plausive plausible  42 butter-woman's i.e.,
shrill-voiced woman's  43 Bajazet's mule mules were
proverbial for muteness, but "Bajazet" is inexplicable  49
afford you so let you off thus

PAROLLES  Or the baring of my beard, and to say it 50
was in stratagem.

FIRST LORD [*Aside.*]  'Twould not do.

PAROLLES  Or to drown my clothes, and say I was
stripped.

FIRST LORD [*Aside.*]  Hardly serve.    55

PAROLLES  Though I swore I leaped from the window
of the citadel—

FIRST LORD [*Aside.*]  How deep?

PAROLLES  Thirty fathom.

FIRST LORD [*Aside.*]  Three great oaths would scarce 60
make that be believed.

PAROLLES  I would I had any drum of the enemy's; I
would swear I recovered it.

FIRST LORD [*Aside.*]  You shall hear one anon.°

PAROLLES  A drum now of the enemy's—    65

*Alarum° within.*

FIRST LORD  Throca movousus, cargo, cargo, cargo.

ALL  Cargo, cargo, cargo, villianda par corbo, cargo.

PAROLLES  O, ransom, ransom! Do not hide mine
eyes.

[*They blindfold him.*]

INTERPRETER  Boskos thromuldo boskos.    70

PAROLLES
I know you are the Muskos' regiment,
And I shall lose my life for want of language.
If there be here German, or Dane, low Dutch,
Italian, or French, let him speak to me,
I'll discover° that which shall undo the Florentine.    75

INTERPRETER  Boskos vauvado. I understand thee,
and can speak thy tongue. Kerelybonto. Sir, betake
thee to thy faith, for seventeen poniards are at thy
bosom.

PAROLLES  O!    80

INTERPRETER  O, pray, pray, pray! Manka revania
dulche.

FIRST LORD  Oscorbidulchos volivorco.

INTERPRETER
The general is content to spare thee yet,
And, hoodwinked as thou art, will lead thee on    85
To gather from thee. Haply thou mayst inform
Something to save thy life.

PAROLLES                    O, let me live!
And all the secrets of our camp I'll show,
Their force, their purposes; nay, I'll speak that
Which you will wonder at.

INTERPRETER                But wilt thou faithfully?    90

PAROLLES
If I do not, damn me.

INTERPRETER            Acordo linta.
Come on, thou art granted space.
                    *Exit,* [*with* PAROLLES *guarded*].

*A short alarum within.°*

FIRST LORD
Go, tell the Count Rousillon and my brother

We have caught the woodcock° and will keep him
muffled
Till we do hear from them.

SOLDIER            Captain, I will.    95

FIRST LORD
'A° will betray us all unto ourselves;
Inform on that.

SOLDIER        So I will, sir.

FIRST LORD
Till then, I'll keep him dark, and safely locked.
                    *Exit,* [*with the others*].

[*Scene II. Florence. The Widow's house.*]

*Enter* BERTRAM *and the maid called* DIANA.

BERTRAM
They told me that your name was Fontibell.

DIANA
No, my good lord, Diana.

BERTRAM                Titled goddess;
And worth it, with addition.° But, fair soul,
In your fine frame hath love no quality?
If the quick fire of youth light not your mind    5
You are no maiden but a monument.
When you are dead you should be such a one
As you are now; for you are cold and stern,
And now you should be as your mother was
When your sweet self was got.    10

DIANA
She then was honest.

BERTRAM            So should you be.

DIANA                        No.
My mother did but duty; such, my lord,
As you owe to your wife.

BERTRAM            No more o' that!
I prithee, do not strive against my vows;
I was compelled to her, but I love thee    15
By love's own sweet constraint, and will forever
Do thee all rights of service.

DIANA                Ay, so you serve us
Till we serve you; but when you have our roses,
You barely leave our thorns to prick ourselves,
And mock us with our bareness.

BERTRAM                How have I sworn!    20

DIANA
'Tis not the many oaths that makes the truth,
But the plain single vow that is vowed true.
What is not holy, that we swear not by,
But take the High'st to witness; then, pray you, tell
me:
If I should swear by Jove's great attributes    25
I loved you dearly, would you believe my oaths
When I did love you ill?° This has no holding,
To swear by Him whom I protest to love
That I will work against Him. Therefore your oaths
Are words and poor conditions but unsealed,°    30
At least in my opinion.

BERTRAM            Change it, change it;
Be not so holy-cruel. Love is holy,

---

64 **anon** soon    65 s.d. **Alarum** call to arms    75 **discover**
reveal    92 s.d. **A . . . within** perhaps Parolles is taken off to
a ruffle of drums

94 **woodcock** stupid bird    96 **'A** he
**IV.ii.3 addition** further distinguished title    27 **ill** not well,
not at all    30 **but unsealed** merely invalid

And my integrity ne'er knew the crafts
That you do charge men with. Stand no more off,
But give thyself unto my sick desires,     35
Who then recovers. Say thou art mine, and ever
My love as it begins shall so persever.

DIANA
I see that men make rope's in such a scarre,°
That we'll forsake ourselves. Give me that ring.

BERTRAM
I'll lend it thee, my dear, but have no power    40
To give it from me.

DIANA            Will you not, my lord?

BERTRAM
It is an honor 'longing to our house,
Bequeathèd down from many ancestors,
Which were the greatest obloquy i' th' world
In me to lose.

DIANA        Mine honor's such a ring;    45
My chastity's the jewel of our house,
Bequeathèd down from many ancestors,
Which were the greatest obloquy i' th' world
In me to lose. Thus your own proper° wisdom
Brings in the champion Honor on my part    50
Against your vain assault.

BERTRAM          Here, take my ring.
My house, mine honor, yea, my life be thine,
And I'll be bid by thee.

DIANA
When midnight comes, knock at my chamber-window:
I'll order take my mother shall not hear.    55
Now will I charge you in the band° of truth,
When you have conquered my yet maiden bed,
Remain there but an hour, nor speak to me.
My reasons are most strong and you shall know them
When back again this ring shall be delivered;    60
And on your finger in the night I'll put
Another ring, that what in time proceeds
May token to the future our past deeds.
Adieu till then; then fail not. You have won
A wife of me, though there my hope be done.    65

BERTRAM
A heaven on earth I have won by wooing thee.
                              [Exit.]

DIANA
For which live long to thank both heaven and me!
You may so in the end.
My mother told me just how he would woo,
As if she sat in's heart. She says all men    70
Have the like oaths. He had sworn to marry me
When his wife's dead; therefore I'll lie with him
When I am buried. Since Frenchmen are so braid,°
Marry that will, I live and die a maid.
Only, in this disguise, I think't no sin    75
To cozen° him that would unjustly win.    Exit.

[Scene III. The Florentine camp.]

Enter the two French CAPTAINS, and some two or three
SOLDIERS.

FIRST LORD    You have not given him his mother's
letter?

SECOND LORD    I have delivered it an hour since.
There is something in't that stings his nature, for on
the reading it he changed almost into another man.    5

FIRST LORD    He has much worthy blame laid upon
him for shaking off so good a wife and so sweet a lady.

SECOND LORD    Especially he hath incurred the everlasting displeasure of the king, who had even tuned
his bounty to sing happiness to him. I will tell you a    10
thing, but you shall let it dwell darkly with you.

FIRST LORD    When you have spoken it, 'tis dead, and
I am the grave of it.

SECOND LORD    He hath perverted a young gentlewoman here in Florence, of a most chaste renown, and    15
this night he fleshes his will in the spoil of her honor;
he hath given her his monumental° ring, and thinks
himself made in the unchaste composition.°

FIRST LORD    Now, God delay our rebellion! As we
are ourselves, what things are we!    20

SECOND LORD    Merely° our own traitors. And as in
the common course of all treasons we still see them
reveal themselves till they attain to their abhorred
ends, so he that in this action contrives against his own
nobility, in his proper° stream o'erflows° himself.    25

FIRST LORD    Is it not meant damnable in us to be
trumpeters of our unlawful intents? We shall not then
have his company tonight?

SECOND LORD    Not till after midnight, for he is
dieted° to his hour.    30

FIRST LORD    That approaches apace. I would gladly
have him see his company anatomized,° that he might
take a measure of his own judgments, wherein so
curiously he had set this counterfeit.°

SECOND LORD    We will not meddle with him till he°    35
come, for his presence must be the whip of the other.

FIRST LORD    In the meantime, what hear you of these
wars?

SECOND LORD    I hear there is an overture of peace.

FIRST LORD    Nay, I assure you, a peace concluded.    40

SECOND LORD    What will Count Rousillon do then?
Will he travel higher, or return again into France?

FIRST LORD    I perceive by this demand you are not
altogether of his council.

SECOND LORD    Let it be forbid, sir; so should I be a    45
great deal of his act.

FIRST LORD    Sir, his wife some two months since fled
from his house. Her pretense° is a pilgrimage to Saint
Jaques le Grand; which holy undertaking with most
austere sanctimony° she accomplished; and, there    50
residing, the tenderness of her nature became as a prey
to her grief; in fine, made a groan of her last breath, and
now she sings in heaven.

SECOND LORD    How is this justified?°

FIRST LORD    The stronger part of it by her own letters,    55
which makes her story true even to the point of her

---

38 I . . . scarre possibly "scarre" means "splice" and thus
"snare," but the text is probably corrupt    49 proper personal
56 band bond    73 braid deceitful (?)    76 cozen deceive

IV.iii.17 monumental serving as a memento    18 composition bargain    21 Merely utterly    25 proper own; o'erflows
(1) betrays in talk (2) drowns    30 dieted restricted    32 company anatomized companion (i.e., Parolles) minutely ana-
lyzed    33–34 wherein . . . counterfeit in which he has so
elaborately set this false jewel    35 him . . . he Parolles . . .
Bertram    48 pretense intention    50 sanctimony holiness
54 justified made certain

death. Her death itself, which could not be her office to say is come, was faithfully confirmed by the rector° of the place.

SECOND LORD  Hath the count all this intelligence?°  60

FIRST LORD  Ay, and the particular confirmations, point from point, to the full arming of the verity.

SECOND LORD  I am heartily sorry that he'll be glad of this.

FIRST LORD  How mightily sometimes we make us  65 comforts of our losses!

SECOND LORD  And how mightily some other times we drown our gain in tears! The great dignity that his valor hath here acquired for him shall at home be encount'red with a shame as ample.  70

FIRST LORD  The web of our life is of a mingled yarn, good and ill together; our virtues would be proud if our faults whipped them not, and our crimes would despair if they were not cherished by our virtues.

*Enter a* MESSENGER.

How now! Where's your master?  75

SERVANT  He met the duke in the street, sir, of whom he hath taken a solemn leave. His lordship will next morning for France. The duke hath offered him letters of commendations to the king.

SECOND LORD  They shall be no more than needful  80 there, if they were more than they can commend.°

FIRST LORD  They cannot be too sweet for the king's tartness.

*Enter* BERTRAM.

Here's his lordship now. How now, my lord? Is't not after midnight?  85

BERTRAM  I have tonight dispatched sixteen businesses, a month's length apiece. By an abstract of success:° I have congied with° the duke, done my adieu with his nearest, buried a wife, mourned for her, writ to my lady mother I am returning, entertained my con-  90 voy,° and between these main parcels of dispatch° effected many nicer° needs; the last was the greatest, but that I have not ended yet.

SECOND LORD  If the business be of any difficulty, and this morning your departure hence, it requires  95 haste of your lordship.

BERTRAM  I mean the business is not ended, as fearing to hear of it hereafter. But shall we have this dialogue between the Fool and the Soldier? Come, bring forth this counterfeit module° has deceived me like a double-  100 meaning prophesier.

SECOND LORD  Bring him forth. [*Exeunt* SOLDIERS.] Has sat i' th' stocks all night, poor gallant° knave.

BERTRAM  No matter, his heels have deserved it, in usurping his spurs so long. How does he carry him-  105 self?

SECOND LORD  I have told your lordship already; the stocks carry him. But to answer you as you would be understood, he weeps like a wench that had shed her milk. He hath confessed himself to Morgan, whom  110 he supposes to be a friar, from the time of his remembrance to this very instant disaster of his setting i' th' stocks. And what think you he hath confessed?

BERTRAM  Nothing of me, has 'a?

SECOND LORD  His confession is taken, and it shall be  115 read to his face. If your lordship be in't, as I believe you are, you must have the patience to hear it.

*Enter* PAROLLES [*guarded*], *with his* INTERPRETER.

BERTRAM  A plague upon him! Muffled!° He can say nothing of me.

FIRST LORD  [*Aside to* BERTRAM.] Hush, hush!  120 Hoodman comes!° [*Aloud.*] Portotartarossa.

INTERPRETER  He calls for the tortures. What will you say without 'em?

PAROLLES  I will confess what I know without con-straint. If ye pinch me like a pasty I can say no more.  125

INTERPRETER  Bosko chimurcho.

FIRST LORD  Boblibindo chicurmurco.

INTERPRETER  You are a merciful general. Our general bids you answer to what I shall ask you out of a note.  130

PAROLLES  And truly, as I hope to live.

INTERPRETER  "First demand of him how many horse the duke is strong." What say you to that?

PAROLLES  Five or six thousand, but very weak and unserviceable. The troops are all scattered and the  135 commanders very poor rogues, upon my reputation and credit, and as I hope to live.

INTERPRETER  Shall I set down your answer so?

PAROLLES  Do. I'll take the sacrament on't, how and which way you will.  140

BERTRAM  [*Aside.*] All's one to him. What a past-saving slave is this!

FIRST LORD  [*Aside to* BERTRAM.] Y' are deceived, my lord; this is Monsieur Parolles, the gallant mili-tarist—that was his own phrase—that had the whole  145 theoric of war in the knot of his scarf, and the practice in the chape° of his dagger.

SECOND LORD  [*Aside.*] I will never trust a man again for keeping his sword clean, nor believe he can have everything in him by wearing his apparel neatly.  150

INTERPRETER  Well, that's set down.

PAROLLES  "Five or six thousand horse," I said—I will say true—"or thereabouts" set down, for I'll speak truth.

FIRST LORD  [*Aside.*] He's very near the truth in this.  155

BERTRAM  [*Aside.*] But I con° him no thanks for't, in the nature he delivers it.

PAROLLES  "Poor rogues," I pray you say.

INTERPRETER  Well, that's set down.

PAROLLES  I humbly thank you, sir; a truth's a truth;  160 the rogues are marvelous poor.

INTERPRETER  "Demand of him of what strength they are a-foot." What say you to that?

---

**58 rector** ruler (?) priest (?)  **60 intelligence** news  **80–81 They shall . . . commend** the recommendations to the king will not be more than needed, even if they commend Bertram excessively (?)  **87 abstract of success** summary of my successes (?) list, in sequence (?)  **88 congied with** taken leave of  **90–91 entertained my convoy** hired my transpor-tation  **91 parcels of dispatch** things to be settled  **92 nicer** (1) more trivial (2) lascivious (alluding to his affair with Diana)  **100 module** image  **103 gallant** finely dressed

**118 Muffled** blindfolded  **121 Hoodman comes** the blind man comes (customary call in the game blindman's buff)  **147 chape** metal plate on a scabbard covering the point  **156 con** give (literally, "learn")

PAROLLES  By my troth, sir, if I were to live this present hour, I will tell true. Let me see: Spurio, a hundred 165
and fifty; Sebastian, so many; Corambus, so many;
Jaques, so many; Guiltian, Cosmo, Lodowick, and
Gratii, two hundred fifty each; mine own company,
Chitopher, Vaumond, Bentii, two hundred fifty each;
so that the muster-file, rotten and sound, upon my life, 170
amounts not to fifteen thousand poll,° half of the
which dare not shake the snow from off their cassocks°
lest they shake themselves to pieces.
BERTRAM [Aside.]  What shall be done to him?
FIRST LORD [To BERTRAM.]  Nothing, but let him 175
have thanks. [To INTERPRETER.]  Demand of him
my condition, and what credit I have with the duke.
INTERPRETER  Well, that's set down. "You shall
demand of him whether one Captain Dumaine be i'
th' camp, a Frenchman; what his reputation is with 180
the duke, what his valor, honesty, and expertness in
wars; or whether he thinks it were not possible with
well-weighing sums of gold to corrupt him to a
revolt." What say you to this? What do you know of
it? 185
PAROLLES  I beseech you, let me answer to the particular of the inter'gatories. Demand them singly.
INTERPRETER  Do you know this Captain Dumaine?
PAROLLES  I know him; 'a was a botcher's° prentice
in Paris, from whence he was whipped for getting the 190
shrieve's fool° with child, a dumb innocent that could
not say him nay.
BERTRAM [Aside to DUMAINE.]  Nay, by your leave,
hold your hands, though I know his brains are forfeit
to the next tile that falls.° 195
INTERPRETER  Well, is this captain in the Duke of
Florence's camp?
PAROLLES  Upon my knowledge he is, and lousy.
FIRST LORD [Aside.]  Nay, look not so upon me; we
shall hear of your lordship anon. 200
INTERPRETER  What is his reputation with the duke?
PAROLLES  The duke knows him for no other but a
poor officer of mine, and writ to me this other day to
turn him out o' th' band. I think I have his letter in
my pocket. 205
INTERPRETER  Marry, we'll search.
PAROLLES  In good sadness,° I do not know; either it
is there or it is upon a file with the duke's other letters
in my tent.
INTERPRETER  Here 'tis; here's a paper; shall I read it 210
to you?
PAROLLES  I do not know if it be it or no.
BERTRAM [Aside.]  Our interpreter does it well.
FIRST LORD [Aside.]  Excellently.
INTERPRETER  "Dian, the count's a fool, and full of 215
gold."
PAROLLES  That is not the duke's letter, sir; that is an
advertisement° to a proper maid in Florence, one
Diana, to take heed of the allurement of one Count
Rousillon, a foolish idle boy, but for all that very 220
ruttish.° I pray you, sir, put it up again.

INTERPRETER  Nay, I'll read it first, by your favor.
PAROLLES  My meaning in't, I protest, was very honest
in the behalf of the maid; for I knew the young count
to be a dangerous and lascivious boy, who is a whale 225
to virginity, and devours up all the fry° it finds.
BERTRAM [Aside.]  Damnable both-sides rogue!
INTERPRETER ([Reads a] letter.)
"When he swears oaths, bid him drop gold, and take
it;
After he scores, he never pays the score.
Half won is match well made; match and well make
it;° 230
He ne'er pays after-debts, take it before.
And say a soldier, Dian, told thee this:
Men are to mell° with, boys are not to kiss:
For count of this, the count's a fool, I know it,
Who pays before, but not when he does owe it. 235
    Thine, as he vowed to thee in thine ear,
                                Parolles."
BERTRAM [Aside.]  He shall be whipped through the
army with this rhyme in's forehead.
SECOND LORD [Aside.]  This is your devoted friend, 240
sir, the manifold linguist, and the armipotent° soldier.
BERTRAM [Aside.]  I could endure anything before but
a cat, and now he's a cat to me.
INTERPRETER  I perceive, sir, by your general's looks,
we shall be fain to hang you. 245
PAROLLES  My life, sir, in any case! Not that I am
afraid to die, but that my offenses being many I would
repent out the remainder of nature. Let me live, sir,
in a dungeon, i' th' stocks, or anywhere, so I may live.
INTERPRETER  We'll see what may be done, so you 250
confess freely. Therefore once more to this Captain
Dumaine: you have answered to his reputation with
the Duke and to his valor: what is his honesty?
PAROLLES  He will steal, sir, an egg out of a cloister;
for rapes and ravishments he parallels Nessus.° He 255
professes not keeping of oaths, in breaking 'em he is
stronger than Hercules. He will lie, sir, with such
volubility that you would think truth were a fool;
drunkenness is his best virtue, for he will be swine-
drunk, and in his sleep he does little harm, save to his 260
bedclothes about him; but they know his conditions°
and lay him in straw. I have but little more to say, sir,
of his honesty—he has everything that an honest man
should not have; what an honest man should have, he
has nothing. 265
FIRST LORD [Aside.]  I begin to love him for this.
BERTRAM [Aside.]  For this description of thine
honesty? A pox upon him for me, he's more and more
a cat.
INTERPRETER  What say you to his expertness in war? 270
PAROLLES  Faith, sir, has led the drum before the
English tragedians°—to belie him I will not—and
more of his soldiership I know not, except in that
country he had the honor to be the officer at a place

171 poll head  172 cassocks soldiers' cloaks  189 botcher's
mender's (e.g., tailor's or cobbler's)  191 shrieve's fool
idiot girl placed under a sheriff's charge  195 tile that falls
i.e., accident  207 sadness seriousness  218 advertisement
advice  221 ruttish lustful

226 fry small fish  230 Half . . . it you are halfway to
success if you bargain well; so bargain well, and you will
prosper (?)  233 mell mingle  241 armipotent mighty
in arms (a huffing word, like "manifold")  255 Nessus
centaur who attempted to rape Deianira, Hercules' wife  261
conditions traits  271–72 led . . . tragedians i.e., been a
low drummer, leading strolling actors rather than soldiers

there called Mile-end,° to instruct for the doubling of 275
files.° I would do the man what honor I can, but of
this I am not certain.
FIRST LORD [*Aside.*]  He hath out-villained villainy
so far that the rarity redeems him.
BERTRAM [*Aside.*]  A pox on him! He's a cat still.  280
INTERPRETER  His qualities being at this poor price, I
need not to ask you if gold will corrupt him to revolt.
PAROLLES  Sir, for a cardecue° he will sell the fee-
simple° of his salvation, the inheritance of it, and cut
th' entail° from all remainders, and a perpetual suc-  285
cession for it perpetually.
INTERPRETER  What's his brother, the other Captain
Dumaine?
SECOND LORD [*Aside.*]  Why does he ask him of me?
INTERPRETER  What's he?  290
PAROLLES  E'en a crow o' th' same nest; not alto-
gether so great as the first in goodness, but greater a
great deal in evil. He excels his brother for a coward,
yet his brother is reputed one of the best that is. In a
retreat he outruns any lackey; marry, in coming on he  295
has a cramp.
INTERPRETER  If your life be saved will you undertake
to betray the Florentine?
PAROLLES  Ay, and the captain of his horse, Count
Rousillon.  300
INTERPRETER  I'll whisper with the general, and know
his pleasure.
PAROLLES [*Aside.*]  I'll no more drumming. A plague
of all drums! Only to seem to deserve well, and to
beguile the supposition of that lascivious young boy,  305
the count, have I run into this danger. Yet who would
have suspected an ambush where I was taken?
INTERPRETER  There is no remedy, sir, but you must
die. The general says you that have so traitorously
discovered the secrets of your army and made such  310
pestiferous reports of men very nobly held, can serve
the world for no honest use; therefore you must die.
Come, headsman, off with his head.
PAROLLES  O Lord, sir, let me live, or let me see my
death!  315
INTERPRETER
That shall you, and take your leave of all your friends.

[*Unmuffles* PAROLLES.]

So, look about you. Know you any here?
BERTRAM  Good morrow, noble captain.
SECOND LORD  God bless you, Captain Parolles.
FIRST LORD  God save you, noble captain.  320
SECOND LORD  Captain, what greeting will you to
my Lord Lafew? I am for France.
FIRST LORD  Good captain, will you give me a copy
of the sonnet you writ to Diana in behalf of the
Count Rousillon? And I were not a very coward I'd  325
compel it of you, but fare you well.
                              *Exeunt* [BERTRAM *and* LORDS].
INTERPRETER  You are undone, captain, all but your
scarf; that has a knot on't yet.

PAROLLES  Who cannot be crushed with a plot?
INTERPRETER  If you could find out a country where  330
but women were that had received so much shame, you
might begin an impudent nation. Fare ye well, sir. I
am for France too; we shall speak of you there.
                              *Exit,* [*with other* SOLDIERS].
PAROLLES
Yet am I thankful. If my heart were great
'Twould burst at this. Captain I'll be no more,  335
But I will eat and drink and sleep as soft
As captain shall. Simply the thing I am
Shall make me live. Who knows himself a braggart,
Let him fear this; for it will come to pass
That every braggart shall be found an ass.  340
Rust, sword; cool, blushes; and Parolles live
Safest in shame! Being fooled, by fool'ry thrive!
There's place and means for every man alive.
I'll after them.                              *Exit.*

[*Scene IV. Florence. The Widow's house.*]

*Enter* HELENA, WIDOW, *and* DIANA.

HELENA
That you may well perceive I have not wronged you,
One of the greatest in the Christian world
Shall be my surety; 'fore whose throne 'tis needful,
Ere I can perfect mine intents, to kneel.
Time was, I did him a desirèd office,  5
Dear almost as his life, which gratitude
Through flinty Tartar's bosom would peep forth,
And answer thanks. I duly am informed
His grace is at Marseilles, to which place
We have convenient convoy.° You must know  10
I am supposèd dead. The army breaking,°
My husband hies him home, where, heaven aiding,
And by the leave of my good lord the king,
We'll be before our welcome.
WIDOW                              Gentle madam,
You never had a servant to whose trust  15
Your business was more welcome.
HELENA                              Nor you, mistress,
Ever a friend whose thoughts more truly labor
To recompense your love. Doubt not but heaven
Hath brought me up to be your daughter's dower,
As it hath fated her to be my motive°  20
And helper to a husband. But, O strange men,
That can such sweet use make of what they hate,
When saucy° trusting of the cozened° thoughts
Defiles the pitchy night! So lust doth play
With what it loathes for that which is away.  25
But more of this hereafter. You, Diana,
Under my poor instructions yet must suffer
Something in my behalf.
DIANA                              Let death and honesty°
Go with your impositions,° I am yours
Upon your will to suffer.
HELENA                              Yet, I pray you;  30
But with the word° the time will bring on summer,

275 **Mile-end** because the citizen militia drilled at Mile-end,
the place was a byname for military incompetence   275–76
**doubling of files** drill maneuver in which pairs of men separate
283 **cardecue** *quart d'écu* (French coin of little value)   283–84
**fee-simple** absolute possession   285 **entail** right of succession

IV.iv.10 **convoy** transportation   11 **breaking** disbanding
20 **motive** means (?)   23 **saucy** lascivious; **cozened** deceived
28 **death and honesty** an honest death   29 **impositions** tasks
imposed on me   31 **with the word** soon (?) as the proverb
says (?)

When briars shall have leaves as well as thorns,
And be as sweet as sharp. We must away;
Our wagon is prepared, and time revives us.
All's well that ends well; still the fine's the crown.° 35
Whate'er the course, the end is the renown.    *Exeunt.*

[*Scene V. Rousillon. The count's palace.*]

*Enter* CLOWN, *old lady* [*the* COUNTESS], *and* LAFEW.

LAFEW   No, no, no, your son was misled with a
snipped taffeta° fellow there, whose villainous saffron°
would have made all the unbaked and doughy youth
of a nation in his color. Your daughter-in-law had
been alive at this hour, and your son here at home, 5
more advanced by the king than by that red-tailed
humble-bee I speak of.

COUNTESS   I would I had not known him; it was the
death of the most virtuous gentlewoman that ever
nature had praise for creating. If she had partaken of 10
my flesh and cost me the dearest groans of a mother,
I could not have owed her a more rooted love.

LAFEW   'Twas a good lady, 'twas a good lady. We
may pick a thousand sallets° ere we light on such
another herb. 15

CLOWN   Indeed, sir, she was the sweet-marjoram of
the sallet, or rather, the herb of grace.°

LAFEW   They are not° herbs, you knave, they are
nose-herbs.

CLOWN   I am no great Nebuchadnezzar, sir; I have 20
not much skill in grace.°

LAFEW   Whether° dost thou profess thyself, a knave or
a fool?

CLOWN   A fool, sir, at a woman's service, and a knave
at a man's. 25

LAFEW   Your distinction?

CLOWN   I would cozen the man of his wife and do his
service.

LAFEW   So you were a knave at his service indeed.

CLOWN   And I would give his wife my bauble,° sir, 30
to do her service.

LAFEW   I will subscribe for thee; thou art both knave
and fool.

CLOWN   At your service.

LAFEW   No, no, no. 35

CLOWN   Why, sir, if I cannot serve you, I can serve
as great a prince as you are.

LAFEW   Who's that? A Frenchman?

CLOWN   Faith, sir, 'a has an English name, but his
fisnomy° is more hotter in France than there. 40

LAFEW   What prince is that?

CLOWN   The Black Prince,° sir, alias the prince of
darkness, alias the devil.

LAFEW   Hold thee, there's my purse. I give thee not
this to suggest thee from° thy master thou talk'st of; 45
serve him still.

CLOWN   I am a woodland fellow, sir, that always
loved a great fire, and the master I speak of ever keeps
a good fire. But sure he is the prince of the world; let
his nobility remain in's court. I am for the house with 50
the narrow gate,° which I take to be too little for pomp
to enter; some that humble themselves may, but the
many will be too chill and tender, and they'll be for
the flow'ry way that leads to the broad gate and the
great fire. 55

LAFEW   Go thy ways; I begin to be aweary of thee,
and I tell thee so before, because I would not fall out
with thee. Go thy ways; let my horses be well looked
to, without any tricks.

CLOWN   If I put any tricks upon 'em, sir, they shall 60
be jades' tricks,° which are their own right by the law
of nature.                        *Exit.*

LAFEW   A shrewd° knave and an unhappy.

COUNTESS   So 'a is. My lord that's gone made himself
much sport out of him; by his authority he remains 65
here, which he thinks is a patent for his sauciness; and
indeed he has no pace, but runs where he will.

LAFEW   I like him well, 'tis not amiss. And I was about
to tell you, since I heard of the good lady's death and
that my lord your son was upon his return home, I 70
moved the king my master to speak in the behalf of
my daughter; which, in the minority of them both,
his majesty out of a self-gracious remembrance did
first propose. His highness hath promised me to do it—
and to stop up the displeasure he hath conceived against 75
your son there is no fitter matter. How does your ladyship like it?

COUNTESS   With very much content, my lord, and I
wish it happily effected.

LAFEW   His highness comes post° from Marseilles, of 80
as able body as when he numbered thirty. 'A will be
here tomorrow, or I am deceived by him that in such
intelligence hath seldom failed.

COUNTESS   It rejoices me that I hope I shall see him
ere I die. I have letters that my son will be here tonight. 85
I shall beseech your lordship to remain with me till
they meet together.

LAFEW   Madam, I was thinking with what manners I
might safely be admitted.

COUNTESS   You need but plead your honorable privi- 90
lege.

LAFEW   Lady, of that I have made a bold charter;° but
I thank my God it holds yet.

*Enter* CLOWN.

CLOWN   O madam, yonder's my lord your son with
a patch of velvet on's face; whether there be a scar 95
under't or not, the velvet knows, but 'tis a goodly
patch of velvet.° His left cheek is a cheek of two pile
and a half, but his right cheek is worn bare.

---

**35 the fine's the crown** the end is the crown (cf. the Latin
proverb, *Finis coronat opus*, "The end crowns the work")
**IV.v.2 snipped taffeta** cloth slashed to show the colors
beneath; **saffron** yellow dye (used to dye starch—for ruffs—
and also dough)   **14 sallets** salads   **17 herb of grace** rue   **18
not** pun on *knot* = flower bed, leading to the contrasting
"nose-herbs" = fragrant but not tasty herbs   **21 grace** pun
on *grass*, following the allusion to the King of Babylon who in
Daniel 4:28-37 is said to have insanely eaten grass   **22
Whether** which   **30 bauble** fool's stick (bawdy innuendo)
**40 fisnomy** physiognomy   **42 Black Prince** (1) son of
Edward III, foe of the French (2) devil

**45 suggest thee from** tempt you away from   **50-51 house
. . . gate** heaven (with bawdy reference to vulva?)   **61
jades' tricks** mischievous doings (like those of undesirable
horses)   **63 shrewd** bitter   **80 post** by rapid relays of horses
**92 charter** claim   **97 patch of velvet** bandage (but it might
cover an honorable scar or dishonorable signs of syphilis)

LAFEW  A scar nobly got, or a noble scar, is a good
liv'ry° of honor; so belike is that.                                    100
CLOWN  But it is your carbonadoed° face.
LAFEW  Let us go see your son, I pray you. I long to
talk with the young noble soldier.
CLOWN  Faith, there's a dozen of 'em with delicate
fine hats and most courteous feathers which bow the   105
head and nod at every man.                          *Exeunt.*

# ACT V

## [Scene I. *Marseilles*.]

*Enter* HELENA, WIDOW, *and* DIANA, *with two*
ATTENDANTS.

HELENA
But this exceeding posting° day and night
Must wear your spirits low; we cannot help it.
But since you have made the days and nights as one,
To wear your gentle limbs in my affairs,
Be bold° you do so grow in my requital°              5
As nothing can unroot you.

*Enter a* GENTLEMAN, *a stranger*.

                               In happy time!°
This man may help me to his majesty's ear,
If he would spend his power. God save you, sir.
GENTLEMAN  And you.
HELENA
Sir, I have seen you in the court of France.          10
GENTLEMAN
I have been sometimes there.
HELENA
I do presume, sir, that you are not fall'n
From the report that goes upon your goodness,
And therefore, goaded with most sharp occasions
Which lay nice manners by, I put you to              15
The use of your own virtues, for the which
I shall continue thankful.
GENTLEMAN                What's your will?
HELENA
That it will please you
To give this poor petition to the king,
And aid me with that store of power you have          20
To come into his presence.
GENTLEMAN
The king's not here.
HELENA                Not here, sir?
GENTLEMAN                         Not indeed.
He hence removed last night, and with more haste
Than is his use.
WIDOW          Lord, how we lose our pains!
HELENA
All's well that ends well yet,                         25
Though time seem so adverse and means unfit.
I do beseech you, whither is he gone?

GENTLEMAN
Marry, as I take it, to Rousillon,
Whither I am going.
HELENA                I do beseech you, sir,
Since you are like to see the king before me,         30
Commend the paper to his gracious hand,
Which I presume shall render you no blame
But rather make you thank your pains for it.
I will come after you with what good speed
Our means will make us means.
GENTLEMAN                This I'll do for you.        35
HELENA
And you shall find yourself to be well thanked,
Whate'er falls° more. We must to horse again.
Go, go, provide.                          [*Exeunt*.]

## [Scene II. *Rousillon. The count's palace*.]

*Enter* CLOWN *and* PAROLLES.

PAROLLES  Good Master Lavatch,° give my Lord
Lafew this letter. I have ere now, sir, been better known
to you, when I have held familiarity with fresher
clothes; but I am now, sir, muddied in Fortune's mood,°
and smell somewhat strong of her strong displeasure.   5
CLOWN  Truly, Fortune's displeasure is but sluttish if
it smell so strongly as thou speak'st of. I will henceforth eat no fish of Fortune's butt'ring. Prithee, allow
the wind.°
PAROLLES  Nay, you need not to stop your nose, sir;   10
I spake but by a metaphor.
CLOWN  Indeed, sir, if your metaphor stink, I will
stop my nose, or against any man's metaphor. Prithee,
get thee further.
PAROLLES  Pray you, sir, deliver me this paper.       15
CLOWN  Foh! Prithee, stand away. A paper from
Fortune's close-stool,° to give to a nobleman! Look,
here he comes himself.

*Enter* LAFEW.

Here is a pur° of Fortune's, sir, or of Fortune's cat,
but not a musk-cat,° that has fall'n into the unclean   20
fishpond of her displeasure, and, as he says, is muddied
withal. Pray you, sir, use the carp as you may, for he
looks like a poor, decayed, ingenious,° foolish, rascally
knave. I do pity his distress in my similes of comfort,
and leave him to your lordship.            [*Exit*.]    25
PAROLLES  My lord, I am a man whom Fortune hath
cruelly scratched.
LAFEW  And what would you have me to do? 'Tis too
late to pare her nails now. Wherein have you played
the knave with Fortune that she should scratch you,   30
who of herself is a good lady and would not have
knaves thrive long under? There's a cardecue° for you.

**37 falls** befalls
**V.ii.1 Lavatch** apparently from French *la vache* = the cow,
or *lavage* = slop  **4 mood** displeasure (with pun on *mud*)
**8–9 allow the wind** let me have the windward side  **17
close-stool** toilet  **19 pur** (1) dung (2) cat's sound (3) knave
in a card game (Lafew picks up this last meaning when he
speaks)  **20 musk-cat** musk deer (which yields perfume)
**23 ingenious** stupid (as though written "un-genius")  **32
cardecue** French coin

**100 liv'ry** badge of noble service  **101 carbonadoed** slashed
(with incisions to drain venereal ulcers)
**V.i.1 exceeding posting** excessive haste  **5 bold** assured;
**requital** debt  **6 In happy time** just at the right moment

Let the justices make you and Fortune friends;° I am
for other business.

PAROLLES  I beseech your honor to hear me one single 35
word.

LAFEW  You beg a single penny more. Come, you
shall ha't; save your word.

PAROLLES  My name, my good lord, is Parolles.

LAFEW  You beg more than "word" then. Cox my 40
passion!° Give me your hand. How does your drum?

PAROLLES  O my good lord, you were the first that
found me.°

LAFEW  Was I, in sooth? And I was the first that lost
thee. 45

PAROLLES  It lies in you, my lord, to bring me in some
grace, for you did bring me out.

LAFEW  Out upon thee, knave! Dost thou put upon
me at once both the office of God and the devil? One
brings thee in grace and the other brings thee out. 50
[*Trumpets sound.*] The king's coming; I know by his
trumpets. Sirrah, inquire further after me. I had talk
of you last night; though you are a fool and a knave
you shall eat. Go to, follow.

PAROLLES  I praise God for you. [*Exeunt.*] 55

[Scene III. *Rousillon. The count's palace.*]

*Flourish. Enter* KING, *old lady* [*the* COUNTESS], LAFEW,
*the two French* LORDS, *with* ATTENDANTS.

KING
We lost a jewel of her, and our esteem°
Was made much poorer by it; but your son,
As mad in folly, lacked the sense to know
Her estimation home.°

COUNTESS                    'Tis past, my liege,
And I beseech your majesty to make it 5
Natural rebellion done i' th' blade° of youth,
When oil and fire, too strong for reason's force,
O'erbears it and burns on.

KING                    My honored lady,
I have forgiven and forgotten all,
Though my revenges were high bent upon him 10
And watched the time to shoot.

LAFEW                    This I must say—
But first I beg my pardon—the young lord
Did to his majesty, his mother, and his lady
Offense of mighty note, but to himself
The greatest wrong of all. He lost a wife 15
Whose beauty did astonish the survey
Of richest eyes; whose words all ears took captive;
Whose dear perfection hearts that scorned to serve
Humbly called mistress.

KING                    Praising what is lost
Makes the remembrance dear. Well, call him hither; 20
We are reconciled, and the first view shall kill
All repetition.° Let him not ask our pardon;

The nature of his great offense is dead,
And deeper than oblivion we do bury
Th' incensing relics° of it. Let him approach, 25
A stranger, no offender; and inform him
So 'tis our will he should.

GENTLEMAN                    I shall, my liege. [*Exit.*]

KING
What says he to your daughter? Have you spoke?

LAFEW
All that he is hath reference° to your highness.

KING
Then shall we have a match. I have letters sent me, 30
That sets him high in fame.

*Enter* BERTRAM.

LAFEW                    He looks well on't.

KING
I am not a day of season,
For thou mayst see a sunshine and a hail
In me at once. But to the brightest beams
Distracted clouds give way; so stand thou forth; 35
The time is fair again.

BERTRAM                    My high-repented blames,°
Dear sovereign pardon to me.

KING                    All is whole.
Not one word more of the consumèd time.
Let's take the instant by the forward top;°
For we are old, and on our quick'st decrees 40
Th' inaudible and noiseless foot of Time
Steals ere we can effect them. You remember
The daughter of this lord?

BERTRAM
Admiringly, my liege. At first
I stuck my choice upon her, ere my heart 45
Durst make too bold a herald of my tongue;
Where, the impression of mine eye infixing,
Contempt his scornful perspective° did lend me,
Which warped the line of every other favor,°
Scorned a fair color or expressed it stol'n, 50
Extended or contracted all proportions
To a most hideous object. Thence it came
That she whom all men praised and whom myself,
Since I have lost, have loved, was in mine eye
The dust that did offend it.

KING                    Well excused. 55
That thou didst love her, strikes some scores away
From the great compt;° but love that comes too late,
Like a remorseful° pardon slowly carried,
To the great sender turns a sour offense,
Crying, "That's good that's gone." Our rash faults 60
Make trivial price of serious things we have,
Not knowing them, until we know their grave.
Oft our displeasures, to ourselves unjust,
Destroy our friends and after weep their dust;
Our own love waking cries to see what's done, 65
While shameful hate sleeps out the afternoon.
Be this sweet Helen's knell, and now forget her.
Send forth your amorous token for fair Maudlin.

33 **Let . . . friends** i.e., appeal to the justices for alms  40–41
**Cox my passion** mild oath, from "God's my passion," i.e., by
God's suffering  43 **found me** found me out
V.iii.1 **esteem** value, i.e., reputation  4 **home** fully  6 **blade**
green shoot (editors distressed by the mixed metaphor produced
by "fire" emend to "blaze")  22 **repetition** i.e., mention
of what is past

25 **incensing relics** reminders that (would) anger  29 **hath
reference** is submitted  36 **blames** blameworthy deeds  39
**take . . . top** seize Time by the forelock  48 **perspective**
optical instrument that distorts (accented on first syllable)  49
**favor** face  57 **compt** account  58 **remorseful** compassionate

The main consents are had, and here we'll stay
To see our widower's second marriage-day,                        70
Which better than the first, O dear heaven, bless!
Or, ere they meet, in me, O nature, cesse!°

LAFEW
Come on, my son, in whom my house's name
Must be digested;° give a favor° from you
To sparkle in the spirits of my daughter,                        75
That she may quickly come. [BERTRAM *gives a ring.*]
    By my old beard,
And ev'ry hair that's on't, Helen that's dead
Was a sweet creature; such a ring as this,
The last that e'er I took her leave at court,
I saw upon her finger.

BERTRAM                        Hers it was not.             80

KING
Now pray you let me see it; for mine eye,
While I was speaking, oft was fastened to't.
This ring was mine, and when I gave it Helen
I bade her, if her fortunes ever stood
Necessitied to help, that by this token                          85
I would relieve her. Had you that craft to reave°
    her
Of what should stead° her most?

BERTRAM                        My gracious sovereign,
Howe'er it pleases you to take it so,
The ring was never hers.

COUNTESS                        Son, on my life,
I have seen her wear it, and she reckoned it                     90
At her life's rate.

LAFEW                        I am sure I saw her wear it.

BERTRAM
You are deceived, my lord; she never saw it.
In Florence was it from a casement thrown me,
Wrapped in a paper which contained the name
Of her that threw it. Noble she was, and thought                 95
I stood ingaged;° but when I had subscribed
To mine own fortune° and informed her fully
I could not answer in that course of honor
As she had made the overture, she ceased
In heavy satisfaction° and would never                           100
Receive the ring again.

KING                        Plutus° himself,
That knows the tinct and multiplying med'cine,°
Hath not in nature's mystery more science°
Than I have in this ring. 'Twas mine, 'twas Helen's,
Whoever gave it you; then if you know                            105
That you are well acquainted with yourself,
Confess 'twas hers, and by what rough enforcement
You got it from her. She called the saints to surety
That she would never put it from her finger
Unless she gave it to yourself in bed,                           110
Where you have never come, or sent it us
Upon her great disaster.

BERTRAM                        She never saw it.

KING
Thou speak'st it falsely, as I love mine honor,
And mak'st conjectural fears to come into me
Which I would fain shut out. If it should prove                  115
That thou art so inhuman—'twill not prove so,
And yet I know not—thou didst hate her deadly,
And she is dead, which nothing but to close
Her eyes myself could win me to believe,
More than to see this ring. Take him away.                       120
My fore-past proofs, howe'er the matter fall,
Shall tax my fears of little vanity,
Having vainly feared too little.° Away with him,
We'll sift this matter further.

BERTRAM                        If you shall prove
This ring was ever hers, you shall as easy                       125
Prove that I husbanded her bed in Florence,
Where yet she never was.                        [*Exit guarded.*]

KING
I am wrapped in dismal thinkings.

*Enter a* GENTLEMAN [*the stranger*].

GENTLEMAN                        Gracious sovereign,
Whether I have been to blame or no, I know not:
Here's a petition from a Florentine                              130
Who hath for four or five removes° come short
To tender it herself. I undertook it,
Vanquished thereto by the fair grace and speech
Of the poor suppliant, who, by this, I know
Is here attending; her business looks in her                     135
With an importing° visage, and she told me,
In a sweet verbal brief, it did concern
Your highness with herself.

[KING *reads*] *a letter.*    "Upon his many protestations to
marry me when his wife was dead, I blush to say it, he           140
won me. Now is the Count Rousillon a widower, his
vows are forfeited to me, and my honor's paid to him.
He stole from Florence, taking no leave, and I follow
him to his country for justice. Grant it me, O king!
In you it best lies; otherwise a seducer flourishes and a        145
poor maid is undone.
                                        Diana Capilet."

LAFEW    I will buy me a son-in-law in a fair, and toll
for° this. I'll none of him.

KING
The heavens have thought well on thee, Lafew,                    150
To bring forth this discov'ry. Seek these suitors.
                                [*Exeunt* ATTENDANTS.]
Go, speedily and bring again the count.
I am afeard the life of Helen, lady,
Was foully snatched.

COUNTESS                        Now, justice on the doers!

*Enter* BERTRAM, [*guarded*].

KING
I wonder, sir, since wives are monsters to you,                  155
And that you fly them as you swear them lordship,

---

72 **cesse** cease    74 **digested** swallowed up (?) assimilated
(?); **favor** token    86 **reave** deprive    87 **stead** help    96
**ingaged** not pledged (to another woman)    96–97 **subscribed . . . fortune** admitted my condition, i.e., that I was
married    100 **heavy satisfaction** sorrowful acceptance    101
**Plutus** god of wealth    102 **tinct . . . med'cine** elixir that
transmutes base metals to gold and multiplies gold    103 **science**
knowledge

121–23 **My fore-past . . . too little** the evidence already
established, however the affair turns out, will rebuke ("tax")
my lightweight ("of little vanity") fears; I have unreasonably
feared too little    131 **removes** stopping places (changes of
residence) on the king's journey    136 **importing** significant
148–49 **toll for** put up for sale

Yet you desire to marry.

*Enter* WIDOW [*and*] DIANA.

What woman's that?

DIANA
I am, my lord, a wretched Florentine,
Derivèd from the ancient Capilet.
My suit, as I do understand, you know, 160
And therefore know how far I may be pitied.

WIDOW
I am her mother, sir, whose age and honor
Both suffer under this complaint we bring,
And both shall cease, without your remedy.°

KING
Come hither, count—do you know these women? 165

BERTRAM
My lord, I neither can nor will deny
But that I know them. Do they charge me further?

DIANA
Why do you look so strange upon your wife?

BERTRAM
She's none of mine, my lord.

DIANA                    If you shall marry,
You give away this hand, and that is mine; 170
You give away heaven's vows, and those are mine;
You give away myself, which is known mine;
For I by vow am so embodied yours
That she which marries you must marry me,
Either both or none. 175

LAFEW Your reputation comes too short for my
daughter; you are no husband for her.

BERTRAM
My lord, this is a fond° and desp'rate creature,
Whom sometime I have laughed with. Let your
    highness
Lay a more noble thought upon mine honor, 180
Than for to think that I would sink it here.

KING
Sir, for my thoughts, you have them ill to friend
Till your deeds gain them; fairer prove your honor
Than in my thought it lies.

DIANA                    Good my lord,
Ask him upon his oath if he does think 185
He had not my virginity.

KING
What say'st thou to her?

BERTRAM            She's impudent, my lord,
And was a common gamester° to the camp.

DIANA
He does me wrong, my lord; if I were so,
He might have bought me at a common price. 190
Do not believe him. O, behold this ring,
Whose high respect and rich validity
Did lack a parallel; yet for all that
He gave it to a commoner o' th' camp,
If I be one.

COUNTESS He blushes, and 'tis hit! 195
Of six preceding ancestors, that gem,
Conferred by testament to th' sequent issue,°

Hath it been owed° and worn. This is his wife,
That ring's a thousand proofs.

KING                    Methought you said
You saw one here in court could witness it. 200

DIANA
I did, my lord, but loath am to produce
So bad an instrument. His name's Parolles.

LAFEW
I saw the man today, if man he be.

KING
Find him and bring him hither.
                                [*Exit an* ATTENDANT.]

BERTRAM                    What of him?
He's quoted for° a most perfidious slave, 205
With all the spots o' th' world taxed and deboshed,°
Whose nature sickens but to speak a truth.
Am I or that or this for what he'll utter,
That will speak anything?

KING                    She hath that ring of yours.

BERTRAM
I think she has. Certain it is I liked her, 210
And boarded her i' th' wanton way of youth.
She knew her distance, and did angle for me,
Madding my eagerness with her restraint,
As all impediments in fancy's° course
Are motives of more fancy; and in fine 215
Her inf'nite cunning with her modern° grace
Subdued me to her rate. She got the ring,
And I had that which any inferior might
At market-price have bought.

DIANA                    I must be patient:
You that have turned off a first so noble wife, 220
May justly diet° me. I pray you yet—
Since you lack virtue I will lose a husband—
Send for your ring, I will return it home,
And give me mine again.

BERTRAM            I have it not.

KING
What ring was yours, I pray you?

DIANA                    Sir, much like 225
The same upon your finger.

KING
Know you this ring? This ring was his of late.

DIANA
And this was it I gave him, being abed.

KING
The story then goes false you threw it him
Out of a casement?

DIANA            I have spoke the truth. 230

*Enter* PAROLLES.

BERTRAM
My lord, I do confess, the ring was hers.

KING
You boggle shrewdly;° every feather starts you.
Is this the man you speak of?

DIANA                    Ay, my lord.

KING
Tell me, sirrah, but tell me true, I charge you,

164 both . . . remedy both my life ("age") and honor will
die unless you give us relief (by having Bertram marry Diana)
178 fond foolish   188 gamester prostitute   197 sequent issue
next heir

198 owed owned   205 quoted for known as   206 taxed
and deboshed censured as debauched   214 fancy's love's
216 modern commonplace   221 diet restrain yourself from
232 boggle shrewdly startle excessively

Not fearing the displeasure of your master,                                      235
Which on your just proceeding I'll keep off—
By him and by this woman here what know you?

PAROLLES   So please your majesty, my master hath
been an honorable gentleman. Tricks he hath had in
him, which gentlemen have.                                                       240

KING   Come, come, to th' purpose: did he love this
woman?

PAROLLES   Faith, sir, he did love her; but how?

KING   How, I pray you?

PAROLLES   He did love her, sir, as a gentleman loves      245
a woman.°

KING   How is that?

PAROLLES   He loved her, sir, and loved her not.°

KING   As thou art a knave and no knave. What an
equivocal companion° is this!                                                    250

PAROLLES   I am a poor man, and at your majesty's
command.

LAFEW   He's a good drum, my lord, but a naughty°
orator.

DIANA   Do you know he promised me marriage?      255

PAROLLES   Faith, I know more than I'll speak.

KING   But wilt thou not speak all thou know'st?

PAROLLES   Yes, so please your majesty. I did go between them as I said; but more than that, he loved her,
for indeed he was mad for her and talked of Satan and      260
of Limbo and of Furies and I know not what; yet I was
in that credit with them at that time that I knew of
their going to bed and of other motions, as promising
her marriage, and things which would derive me ill
will to speak of; therefore I will not speak what I      265
know.

KING   Thou hast spoken all already, unless thou canst
say they are married. But thou art too fine° in thy
evidence; therefore stand aside.
This ring, you say, was yours?

DIANA                                  Ay, my good lord.      270

KING
Where did you buy it? Or who gave it you?

DIANA
It was not given me, nor I did not buy it.

KING
Who lent it you?

DIANA                        It was not lent me neither.

KING
Where did you find it then?

DIANA                                  I found it not.

KING
If it were yours by none of all these ways,      275
How could you give it him?

DIANA                                  I never gave it him.

LAFEW   This woman's an easy glove, my lord; she
goes off and on at pleasure.

KING
This ring was mine; I gave it his first wife.

DIANA
It might be yours or hers for aught I know.      280

KING
Take her away; I do not like her now.
To prison with her. And away with him.
Unless thou tell'st me where thou hadst this ring
Thou diest within this hour.

DIANA                                  I'll never tell you.

KING
Take her away.

DIANA                        I'll put in bail, my liege.      285

KING
I think thee now some common customer.°

DIANA
By Jove, if ever I knew man, 'twas you.

KING
Wherefore hast thou accused him all this while?

DIANA
Because he's guilty and he is not guilty:
He knows I am no maid, and he'll swear to't:      290
I'll swear I am a maid and he knows not.
Great King, I am no strumpet; by my life
I am either maid or else this old man's wife.

KING
She does abuse our ears. To prison with her!

DIANA
Good mother, fetch my bail. [Exit WIDOW.] Stay,
royal sir,      295
The jeweler that owes the ring is sent for
And he shall surety me. But for this lord
Who hath abused me as he knows himself,
Though yet he never harmed me, here I quit° him.
He knows himself my bed he hath defiled,      300
And at that time he got his wife with child.
Dead though she be, she feels her young one kick.
So there's my riddle: one that's dead is quick.°
And now behold the meaning.

Enter HELENA and WIDOW.

KING                                  Is there no exorcist°
Beguiles the truer office of mine eyes?      305
Is't real that I see?

HELENA                        No, my good lord,
'Tis but the shadow of a wife you see,
The name and not the thing.

BERTRAM                        Both, both. O, pardon!

HELENA
O, my good lord, when I was like° this maid,
I found you wondrous kind. There is your ring,      310
And, look you, here's your letter. This it says:
"When from my finger you can get this ring,
And are by me with child," &c. This is done.
Will you be mine, now you are doubly won?

BERTRAM
If she, my liege, can make me know this clearly,      315
I'll love her dearly, ever, ever dearly.

HELENA
If it appear not plain and prove untrue,
Deadly divorce step between me and you!
O, my dear mother, do I see you living?

LAFEW
Mine eyes smell onions, I shall weep anon.      320

---

246 woman in contrast to a highborn lady   248 not perhaps
punning on knot = maidenhead   250 equivocal companion
equivocating fellow ("companion" is contemptuous)   253
naughty (1) worthless, worth naught (2) wicked   268
fine subtle

286 customer prostitute   299 quit acquit   303 quick (1) alive
(2) pregnant   304 exorcist summoner of spirits   309 like i.e..
substitute for

[*To* PAROLLES.]

Good Tom Drum, lend me a handkercher. So, I
thank thee. Wait on me home, I'll make sport with
thee. Let thy curtsies alone, they are scurvy ones.

KING

Let us from point to point this story know,
To make the even truth in pleasure flow.                    325

[*To* DIANA.]

If thou be'st yet a fresh uncroppèd flower,
Choose thou thy husband, and I'll pay thy dower,
For I can guess that by thy honest aid
Thou kept'st a wife herself, thyself a maid.
Of that and all the progress more and less              330
Resolvedly° more leisure shall express.

**331 Resolvedly** so that doubt is removed

All yet seems well, and if it end so meet,
The bitter past, more welcome is the sweet.

*Flourish.*

## [ E P I L O G U E ]

The king's a beggar° now the play is done.
All is well ended if this suit be won,
That you express content; which we will pay
With strife° to please you, day exceeding day.
Ours be your patience then, and yours our parts,°      5
Your gentle hands lend us, and take our hearts.

*Exeunt omnes.*

**Epi.1 beggar** i.e. for applause    **4 strife** striving    **5 Ours
. . . parts** we will silently listen, as you have done, and you are
now the performers

# THE TRAGEDY OF OTHELLO
# THE MOOR OF VENICE

EDITED BY ALVIN KERNAN

## Introduction

When Shakespeare wrote *Othello*, about 1604, his ability to present human nature in all its complexity was at its height. The play offers, even in its minor characters, a number of unusually full and profound studies of humanity: Brabantio, the sophisticated, civilized Venetian senator, unable to comprehend that his delicate daughter could love and marry a Moor, speaking excitedly of black magic and spells to account for what his mind cannot understand; Cassio, the gentleman-soldier, polished in manners and gracious in bearing, wildly drunk and revealing a deeply rooted pride in his ramblings about senior officers being saved before their juniors; Emilia, the sensible waiting woman, making small talk about love and suddenly remarking that though she believes adultery to be wrong, still if the price were high enough she would sell—and so, she believes, would most women. The vision of human nature that the play offers is one of ancient terrors and primal drives—fear of the unknown, pride, greed, lust—underlying smooth, civilized surfaces—the noble senator, the competent and well-mannered lieutenant, the conventional gentlewoman.

The contrast between surface manner and inner nature is even more pronounced in two of the major characters. "Honest Iago" conceals beneath his exterior of the plain soldier and blunt, practical man of the world a diabolism so intense as to defy rational explanation—it must be taken like lust or pride as simply a given part of human nature, an anti-life spirit that seeks the destruction of everything outside the self. Othello appears in the opening acts as the very personification of self-control, of the man with so secure a sense of his own worth that nothing can ruffle the consequent calmness of mind and manner. But the man who has roamed the wild and savage world unmoved by its terrors, who has not changed countenance when the cannon killed his brother standing beside him, this man is still capable of believing his wife a whore on the slightest of evidence and committing murders to revenge himself. In Desdemona alone do the heart and the hand go together: she is what she seems to be. Ironically, she alone is accused of pretending to be what she is not. Her very openness and honesty make her suspect in a world where few men are what they appear, and her chastity is inevitably brought into question in a world where every other major character is in some degree touched with sexual corruption.

Most criticism of *Othello* has concerned itself with exploring the depths of these characters and tracing the intricate, mysterious operations of their minds. I should like, however, to discuss, briefly, what might be called the "gross mechanics" of the play, the larger patterns in which events and characters are arranged. These patterns are the context within which the individual characters are defined, just as the pattern of a sentence is the context that defines the exact meaning of the individual words within it.

*Othello* is probably the most neatly, the most formally constructed of Shakespeare's plays. Every character is, for example, balanced by another similar or contrasting character. Desdemona is balanced by her opposite, Iago; love and concern for others at one end of the scale, hatred and concern for self at the other. The true and loyal soldier Cassio balances the false and traitorous soldier Iago. These balances and contrasts throw into relief the essential qualities of the characters. Desdemona's love, for example, shows up a good deal more clearly in contrast to Iago's hate, and vice versa. The values of contrast are increased and the full range of human nature displayed by extending these simple contrasts into developing series. The essential purity of Desdemona stands in contrast to the more "practical" view of chastity held by Emilia, and her view in turn is illuminated by the workaday view of sensuality held by the courtesan Bianca, who treats love, ordinarily, as a commodity. Or, to take another example, Iago's success in fooling Othello is but the culmination of a series of such betrayals that includes the duping of Roderigo, Brabantio, and Cassio. Each duping is the explanatory image of the other, for in every case Iago's method and end are the same: he plays on and teases to life some hitherto controlled and concealed dark passion in his victim. In each case he seeks in some way the same end, the symbolic murder of Desdemona, the destruction in some form of the life principle of which she is the major embodiment.

These various contrasts and parallelisms ultimately blend into a larger, more general pattern that is the central movement of the play. We can begin to see this pattern in the "symbolic geography" of the play. Every play, or work of art, creates its own particular image of space and time, its own symbolic world. The outer limits of the world of *Othello* are defined by the Turks—the infidels, the unbelievers, the "general enemy" as the play calls them—who, just over the horizon, sail back and forth trying to confuse and trick the Christians in order to invade their dominions and destroy them. Out beyond the horizon, reported but unseen, are also those "anters vast and deserts idle" of which Othello speaks. Out there is a land of "rough quarries, rocks, and hills whose heads touch heaven" inhabited by "cannibals that each other eat" and monstrous forms of men "whose heads grow beneath their shoulders." On the edges of this land is the raging ocean with its "high seas, and howling winds," its "guttered rocks and congregated sands" hidden beneath the waters to "enclog the guiltless keel."

Within the circle formed by barbarism, monstrosity, sterility, and the brute power of nature lie the two Christian strongholds of Venice and Cyprus. Renaissance Venice was known for its wealth acquired by trade, its political cunning, and its courtesans; but Shakespeare, while reminding us of the tradition of the "supersubtle Venetian," makes Venice over into a form of *The City*, the ageless image of government, of reason, of law, and of social concord. Here, when Brabantio's strong passions and irrational fears threaten to create riot and injustice, his grievances are examined by a court of law, judged by reason, and the verdict enforced by civic power. Here, the clear mind of the Senate proves the actions of the Turks, penetrates through their pretenses to their true purposes, makes sense of the frantic and fearful contradictory messages that pour in from the fleet, and arranges the necessary defense. The Senate scene—I.iii—focuses on the magnificent speeches of Othello and Desdemona as they declare their love and explain it, but the lovers are surrounded, guarded, by the assembled, ranked governors of Venice, who control passions that otherwise would have led to a bloody street brawl and being justice out of what otherwise would have been riot. The solemn presence and ordering power of the Senate would be most powerfully realized in a stage production, where the senators would appear in their rich robes, with all their symbols of office, seated in ranks around several excited individuals expressing such primal passions as pride of race, fear of dark powers, and violent love. In a play where so much of the language is magnificent, rich, and of heroic proportions, simpler statements come to seem more forceful; and the meaning of *The City* is perhaps nowhere more completely realized than in Brabantio's brief, secure answer to the first fearful cries of theft and talk of copulating animals that Iago and Roderigo send up from the darkness below his window:

What tell'st thou me of robbing? This is Venice;
My house is not a grange.           (I.i.102–03)

Here then are the major reference points on a map of the world of *Othello*: out at the far edge are the Turks, barbarism, disorder, and amoral destructive powers; closer and more familiar is Venice, *The City*, order, law, and reason. Cyprus, standing on the frontier between barbarism and *The City*, is not the secure fortress of civilization that Venice is. It is rather an outpost, weakly defended and far

out in the raging ocean, close to the "general enemy" and the immediate object of his attack. It is a "town of war yet wild" where the "people's hearts [are] brimful of fear." Here passions are more explosive and closer to the surface than in Venice, and here, instead of the ancient order and established government of *The City*, there is only one man to control violence and defend civilization—the Moor Othello, himself of savage origins and a converted Christian.

The movement of the play is from Venice to Cyprus, from *The City* to the outpost, from organized society to a condition much closer to raw nature, and from collective life to the life of the solitary individual. This movement is a characteristic pattern in Shakespeare's plays, both comedies and tragedies: in *A Midsummer Night's Dream* the lovers and players go from the civilized, daylight world of Athens to the irrational, magical wood outside Athens and the primal powers of life represented by the elves and fairies; Lear moves from his palace and secure identity to the savage world of the heath where all values and all identities come into question; and everyone in *The Tempest* is shipwrecked at some time on Prospero's magic island, where life seen from a new perspective assumes strange and fantastic shapes. At the other end of this journey there is always some kind of return to *The City*, to the palace, and to old relationships, but the nature of this return differs widely in Shakespeare's plays. In *Othello* the movement at the end of the play is back toward Venice, the Turk defeated; but Desdemona, Othello, Emilia, and Roderigo do not return. Their deaths are the price paid for the return.

This passage from Venice to Cyprus to fight the Turk and encounter the forces of barbarism is the geographical form of an action that occurs on the social and psychological levels as well. That is, there are social and mental conditions that correspond to Venice and Cyprus, and there are forces at work in society and in man that correspond to the Turks, the raging seas, and "cannibals that each other eat."

The exposure to danger, the breakdown and the ultimate reestablishment of society—the parallel on the social level to the action on the geographical level—is quickly traced. We have already noted that the Venetian Senate embodies order, reason, justice, and concord, the binding forces that hold *The City* together. In Venice the ancient laws and the established customs of society work to control violent men and violent passions to ensure the safety and well-being of the individual and the group. But there are anarchic forces at work in the city, which threaten traditional social forms and relationships, and all these forces center in Iago. His discontent with his own rank and his determination to displace Cassio endanger the orderly military hierarchy in which the junior serves his senior. He endangers marriage, the traditional form for ordering male and female relationships, by his own unfounded suspicions of his wife and by his efforts to destroy Othello's marriage by fanning to life the darker, anarchic passions of Brabantio and Roderigo. He tries to subvert the operation of law and justice by first stirring up Brabantio to gather his followers and seek revenge in the streets; and then when the two warlike forces are met, Iago begins a quarrel with Roderigo in hopes of starting a brawl. The nature of the antisocial forces that Iago represents are focused in the imagery of his advice to Roderigo on how to call out to her father the news of Desdemona's marriage. Call, he says,

> with like timorous [frightening] accent and dire yell
> As when, by night and negligence, the fire
> Is spied in populous cities. (I.i.72–74)

Fire, panic, darkness, neglect of duty—these are the natural and human forces that destroy great cities and turn their citizens to mobs.

In Venice, Iago's attempts to create civic chaos are frustrated by Othello's calm management of himself and the orderly legal proceedings of the Senate. In Cyprus, however, society is less secure—even as the island is more exposed to the Turks—and Othello alone is responsible for finding truth and maintaining order. Here Iago's poison begins to work, and he succeeds at once in manufacturing the riot that he failed to create in Venice. Seen on stage, the fight on the watch between Cassio and Montano is chaos come again: two drunken officers, charged with the defense of the town, trying to kill each other like savage animals, a bedlam of voices and shouts, broken, disordered furniture, and above all this the discordant clamor of the "dreadful" alarm bell—used to signal attacks and fire. This success is but the prologue for other more serious disruptions of society and of the various human relationships that it fosters. The general is set against his officer, husband against wife, Christian against Christian, servant against master. Justice becomes a travesty of itself as Othello—using legal terms such as "It is the *cause*"—assumes the offices of accuser, judge, jury, and executioner of his wife. Manners disappear as the Moor strikes his wife publicly and treats her maid as a procuress. The brightly lighted Senate chamber is now replaced with a dark Cyprus street where Venetians cut one another down and men are murdered from behind. This anarchy finally gives way in the last scene, when Desdemona's faith is proven, to a restoration of order and an execution of justice on the two major criminals.

What we have followed so far is a movement expressed in geographical and social symbols from Venice to a Cyprus exposed to attack, from *The City* to barbarism, from Christendom to the domain of the Turks, from order to riot, from justice to wild revenge and murder, from truth to falsehood. It now remains to see just what this movement means on the level of the individual in the heart and mind of man. Of the three major characters, Desdemona, Othello, and Iago, the first and the last do not change their natures or their attitudes toward life during the course of the play. These two are polar opposites, the antitheses of each other. To speak in the most general terms, Desdemona expresses in her language and actions an innocent, unselfish love and concern for others. Othello catches her very essence when he speaks of her miraculous love, which transcended their differences in age, color, beauty, and culture:

> She loved me for the dangers I had passed,
> And I loved her that she did pity them. (I.iii.166–67)

This love in its various forms finds expression not only in her absolute commitment of herself to Othello, but in her gentleness, her kindness to others, her innocent trust in all men, her pleas for Cassio's restoration to Othello's favor; and it endures even past death at her husband's hands, for she comes back to life for a moment to answer Emilia's question, "Who hath done this deed?" with the unbelievable words,

> Nobody—I myself. Farewell.
> Commend me to my kind lord. O, farewell!
> (V.ii.124–25)

Iago is her opposite in every way. Where she is open and guileless, he is never what he seems to be; where she thinks the best of everyone, he thinks the worst, usually turning to imagery of animals and physical functions to express his low opinion of human nature; where she seeks to serve and love others, he uses others to further his own dark aims and satisfy his hatred of mankind; where she is emotional and idealistic, he is icily logical and cynical. Desdemona and Iago are much more complicated than this, but perhaps enough has been said to suggest the nature of these two moral poles of the play. One is a life force that strives for order, community, growth, and light. The other is an anti-life force that seeks anarchy, death, and darkness. One is the foundation of all that men have built in the world, including *The City*; the other leads back toward ancient chaos and barbarism.

Othello, like most men, is a combination of the forces of love and hate, which are isolated in impossibly pure states in Desdemona and Iago. His psychic voyage from Venice to Cyprus is a passage of the soul and the will from the values of one of these characters to those of the other. This passage is charted by his acceptance and rejection of one or the other. He begins by refusing to have Iago as his lieutenant, choosing the more "theoretical" though less experienced Cassio. He marries Desdemona. Though he is not aware that he does so, he expresses the full meaning of this choice when he speaks of her in such suggestive terms as "my soul's joy" and refers to her even as he is about to kill her, as "Promethean heat," the vital fire that gives life to the world. Similarly, he comes to know that all that is valuable in life depends on her love, and in the magnificent speech beginning, "O now, forever/Farewell the tranquil mind" (III.iii.344–45), he details the emptiness of all human activity if Desdemona be proved false. But Iago, taking advantage of latent "Iagolike" feelings and thoughts in Othello, persuades him that Desdemona is only common clay. Othello then gives himself over to Iago at the end of III.iii, where they kneel together to plan the revenge, and Othello says, "Now art thou my lieutenant." To which Iago responds with blood-chilling simplicity, "I am your own forever." The full meaning of this choice is expressed, again unconsciously, by Othello when he says to Desdemona,

> Perdition catch my soul
> But I do love thee! and when I love thee not,
> Chaos is come again. (III.iii.90–92)

The murder of Desdemona acts out the final destruction in Othello himself of all the ordering powers of love, of trust, of the bond between human beings.

Desdemona and Iago then represent two states of mind,

OTHELLO, THE MOOR OF VENICE 1093

two understandings of life, and Othello's movement from one to the other is the movement on the level of character and psychology from Venice to Cyprus, from *The City* to anarchy. His return to *The City* and the defeat of the Turk is effected, at the expense of his own life, when he learns *what* he has killed and executes himself as the only fitting judgment on his act. His willingness to speak of what he has done—in contrast to Iago's sullen silence—is a willingness to recognize the meaning of Desdemona's faith and chastity, to acknowledge that innocence and love do exist, and that therefore *The City* can stand, though his life is required to validate the truth and justice on which it is built.

*Othello* offers a variety of interrelated symbols that locate and define in historical, natural, social, moral, and human terms those qualities of being and universal forces that are forever at war in the universe and between which tragic man is always in movement. On one side there are Turks, cannibals, barbarism, monstrous deformities of nature, the brute force of the sea, riot, mobs, darkness, Iago, hatred, lust, concern for the self only, and cynicism. On the other side there are Venice, *The City*, law, senates, amity, hierarchy, Desdemona, love, concern for others, and innocent trust. As the characters of the play act and speak, they bring together, by means of parallelism and metaphor, the various forms of the different ways of life. There is, for example, a meaningful similarity in the underhanded way Iago works and the ruse by which the Turks try to fool the Venetians into thinking they are bound for Rhodes when their object is Cyprus. Or, there is again a flash of identification when we hear that the reefs and shoals that threaten ships are "ensteeped," that is, hidden under the surface of the sea, as Iago is hidden under the surface of his "honesty." But Shakespeare binds the various levels of being more closely together by the use of imagery that compares things on one level of action with things on another. For example, when Iago swears that his low judgment of all female virtue "is true, or else I am a Turk" (II.i.112), logic demands, since one woman, Desdemona, *is* true and chaste, that we account him "a Turk." He is thus identified with the unbelievers, the Ottoman Turks, and that Asiatic power, which for centuries threatened Christendom, is shown to have its social and psychological equivalent in Iago's particular attitude toward life. Similarly, when Othello sees the drunken brawl on the watchtower, he exclaims,

Are we turned Turks, and to ourselves do that
Which heaven hath forbid the Ottomites?   (II.iii.168–69)

At the very time when the historical enemy has been defeated, his fleet providentially routed by the great storm, his characteristics—drunken loss of control, brawling over honor, disorder—begin to conquer the island only so recently and fortuitously saved. The conquest continues, and the defender of the island, Othello, convinced of Desdemona's guilt, compares his determination to revenge himself to "the Pontic Sea,/Whose icy current and compulsive course/Nev'r keeps retiring ebb" (III.iii.450–52). The comparison tells us that in his rage and hatred he has become one with the savage seas and the brute, amoral powers of nature that are displayed in the storm scene at the beginning of Act II. But most important is Othello's

identification of himself at the end of the play as the "base Judean" who "threw a pearl away richer than all his tribe." The more familiar quarto reading is "base Indian," but both words point toward the barbarian who fails to recognize value and beauty when he possesses it—the primitive savage who picks up a pearl and throws it away not knowing its worth; or the Jews (Judas may be specifically meant) who denied and crucified another great figure of love, thinking they were dealing with only a troublesome rabble-rouser. A few lines further on Othello proceeds to the final and absolute identification of himself with the infidel. He speaks of a "malignant and a turbaned Turk" who "beat a Venetian and traduced the state," and he then acknowledges that he is that Turk by stabbing himself, even as he once stabbed the other unbeliever. So he ends as both the Turk and the destroyer of the Turk, the infidel and the defender of the faith.

When Iago's schemes are at last exposed, Othello, finding it impossible for a moment to believe that a *man* could have contrived such evil, stares at Iago's feet and then says sadly, "but that's a fable." What he hopes to find when he looks down are the cloven hoofs of the devil, and had they been there he would have been an actor in a morality play, tempted beyond his strength, like many a man before him, by a supernatural power outside himself. In some ways I have schematized *Othello* as just such a morality play, offering an allegorical journey between heaven and hell on a stage filled with purely symbolic figures. This is the kind of abstraction of art toward which criticism inevitably moves, and in this case the allegorical framework is very solidly there. But Othello does not see the cloven hoofs when he looks down; he sees a pair of human feet at the end of a very human body; and he is forced to realize that far from living in some simplified, "fabulous" world where evil is a metaphysical power raiding human life from without, he dwells where evil is somehow inextricably woven with good into man himself. On his stage the good angel does not return to heaven when defeated, but is murdered, and her body remains on the bed, "cold, cold." He lives where good intentions, past services, psychic weaknesses, and an inability to see through evil cannot excuse an act, as they might in some simpler world where more perfect justice existed. In short, Othello is forced to recognize that he lives in a tragic world, and he pays the price for having been great enough to inhabit it.

Here is the essence of Shakespeare's art, an ability to create immediate, full, and total life as men actually live and experience it; and yet at the same time to arrange this reality so that it gives substance to and derives shape from a formal vision of all life that comprehends and reaches back from man and nature through society and history to cosmic powers that operate through all time and space. His plays are both allegorical and realistic at once; his characters both recognizable men and at the same time devils, demigods, and forces in nature. I have discussed only the more allegorical elements in *Othello*, the skeleton of ideas and formal patterns within which the characters must necessarily be understood. But it is equally true that the exact qualities of the abstract moral values and ideas, their full reality, exist only in the characters. It is necessary to know that Desdemona represents one particular human value, love or charity, in order to avoid making such mistakes as searching for some tragic flaw in her that would justify her death. But at the same time, if we would know what love and charity *are* in all their fullness, then our definition can only be the actions, the language, the emotions of the character Desdemona. She is Shakespeare's word for love. If we wish to know not just the obvious fact that men choose evil over good, but *why* they do so, then we must look both analytically and feelingly at all the evidence that the world offers for believing that Desdemona is false and at all the biases in Othello's mind that predispose him to believe such evidence. Othello's passage from Venice to Cyprus, from absolute love for Desdemona to extinguishing the light in her bedchamber, and to the execution of himself, these are Shakespeare's words for tragic man.

## A NOTE ON THE SOURCE

*Othello* is based on a story in Giraldi Cinthio's *Hecatom-mithi* (III, 7), a collection of a hundred tales printed in Italy in the sixteenth century. So far as is known, there was no English translation of the source story in Shakespeare's time, and while he may have read it in a French translation of Gabriel Chappuys, it seems probable that he read the original Italian. For a discussion of the evidence for this view and a good comparison of the story and the play, see Kenneth Muir, *Shakespeare's Sources* (1957), Vol. I, "Comedies and Tragedies," pp. 122–23.

## A NOTE ON THE TEXT

*Othello* contains some of the most difficult editorial problems of any Shakespearean play. The play was entered in *The Stationer's Register* on October 6, 1621, and printed in a quarto edition, Q1, by Thomas Walkley in 1622, some eighteen or nineteen years after it was first staged. More curiously, at the time that Walkley printed his quarto edition, the plans for printing the folio edition of Shakespeare's collected works were completed and printing was well along. The Folio, F, appeared in late 1623, and the text of *Othello* included in it differs considerably from Q1. A second quarto, Q2, was printed from F in 1630. The chief differences between the two major texts, Q1 and F, are: (1) there are 160 lines in F that are not in Q1; some of these omissions affect the sense in Q1, but others seem to be either intentional cuts in Q1 or additions in F; (2) there are a number of oaths in Q1 that are not in F; this fact can be interpreted in a number of ways, but all arguments go back to the prohibition in 1606 of swearing on stage—but apparently not in printed editions; (3) the stage directions in Q1 are much fuller than in F; (4) there are a large number of variant readings in the two texts, in single words, in phrases, and in lineation; where Q1, for example, reads "toged" (i.e., wearing a toga), F reads "tongued"; where Q1 reads "Worships," F reads "Moorships."

These may seem petty problems, but they present an editor with a series of most difficult questions about what to print at any given point where the two texts are in disagreement. The usual solution in the past has been for the editor to include all material in F and Q1, and where

the two texts are in disagreement to select the reading he prefers. The result is what is known as an eclectic text. But modern bibliographical studies have demonstrated that it is possible to proceed, in some cases at least, in a more precise manner by examining the conflicting texts carefully in order to arrive at something like a reasonable judgment about their relative authority. Shakespearean bibliography has become a most elaborate affair, however, and in most cases it has become necessary to take the word of specialists on these matters. Unfortunately, in the case of *Othello* the experts are not in agreement, and none of their arguments has the ring of certainty. Here is, however, the most general opinion of how the two different texts came into being and how they are related.

After Shakespeare wrote the play, his original draft, usually termed "foul papers," was copied, around 1604, by a scribe and made into what is known as the "prompt-book," the official copy of the play used in the theater as the basis for production. This promptbook was the property of the players' company, the King's Men in this case, and remained in their possession to be used, and perhaps revised, whenever they produced *Othello*. Being a repertory company, they would present a play for a few performances, then drop it for a time, and then present it again when conditions seemed favorable. At some time around 1620, another copy was made of the original foul papers, or some later copy of them, and this served as the basis for the 1622 quarto. Later, when the publishers of the Folio got around to printing *Othello*, they took a copy of Q1 and corrected it by the original promptbook, and this corrected copy was then given to the compositors who were setting type for F. There are genuine objections to this theory, the most telling raised by the most recent editor of the play, M. R. Ridley, in *The Arden Shakespeare* edition of *Othello*; but the theory does explain certain difficult facts, and most bibliographers seem to accept some version of it.

The end of this line of argument is to establish fairly reasonably the authority of the F text as being the closest either to what Shakespeare wrote originally or to the play as he finally left it after playhouse revisions. This agrees with what most scholars find in reading the two texts. Sir Walter Greg puts this common belief in the superiority of F in the strongest terms: "In the great majority of cases there can be no doubt that F has preserved the more Shakespearean reading." (*The Shakespeare First Folio*, 1955, p. 365.) For practical purposes what this means is that where an F reading makes sense, then an editor has no choice but to accept it—even though he "likes" the Q1 reading better and would have used it if he had *written*, instead of only edited, the play. But while an editor may be aided and comforted by the bibliographers' decision that F is more authoritative than Q1, his problems are by no means solved. There are places where F does not make sense but Q1 does, places where F is deficient in some way and Q1 is clear and complete, and places where both fail to make sense or seem to point to a common failure to transcribe correctly their original. When this occurs an editor must try to understand how the trouble occurred and then fall back on his judgment. This will force him to try to reconstruct the original manuscript from which we are told Q1 and F both derive, and he must attempt to deduce the original reading that both scribes mangled or that the typesetters in the different printing houses misread or made a mistake in setting.

This editorial process is endlessly complicated, but the general basis of this edition is as follows: F is taken for the copy text and its readings are preserved wherever they make sense. Oaths and stage directions are, however, taken from Q1, since they were presumably part of the original manuscript, but were deleted by the promptbook transcriber to comply with the prohibition against swearing on stage and because the prompt copy did not require such elaborate stage directions as a reading version—somewhat contrary to common sense, this last, but the bibliographers insist upon it. Where mislineation occurs in F, but Q1 has it correctly, the Q1 lineation is used on the theory that it has a better chance of being the original than any hypothetical reconstruction of my own. Finally, where F and Q1 both produce nonsense, changes, based on the above theory about the transmission of the text and on the work of previous editors, have been made.

Where F is deficient, the reading adopted and printed in this text is given below first in boldface type; unless otherwise stated it is taken from Q1. The original F reading that has been changed follows in roman. Obvious typographical errors in F, expansions of abbreviations, spelling variants ("murder," "murther"), and changes in punctuation and lineation are not noted. The act and scene divisions are translated from Latin, and the division at II.iii is from the Globe edition rather than from F; otherwise the divisions of F and the Globe edition are identical. "The Names of the Actors," here printed at the beginning of the play, in F follows the play.

**I.i.1 Tush, Never** Never  **4 'Sblood, but** But  **26 other** others  **27 Christian** Christen'd  **30 God bless** blesse  **63 full** fall; **thick-lips** Thicks-lips  **83 Zounds, sir** Sir  **105 Zounds, sir** Sir  **110 germans** Germaines  **143 produced** producted  **151 hell-pains** [ed.] hell apines [hells paines Q1]
**I.ii.33 duke** dukes  **37 Even** even  **49 carack** [ed.] Carract [Carrick Q1]  **50 he's made** he' made  **57 Come** Cme  **67 darlings** Deareling  **74 weaken** weakens  **83 Whither** Whether  **86 if I do** if do
**I.iii.53 nor** hor  **74 your** yonr  **99 maimed** main'd  **106 Duke** [F omits]  **107 overt test** oer Test  **110 First Senator** Sen.  **122 till** tell  **138 travel's** trauellours  **140 rocks, and hills** Rocks,

Hills; **heads** head  **142 other** others  **146 thence** hence  **154 intentively** instinctively  **203 preserved** presern'd  **227 couch** [ed.] Coach [Cooch Q1]  **229 alacrity** Alacartie  **259 me** my [F and Q1]  **272 First Senator** Sen.  **286 First Senator** Sen.  **321 balance** braine  **327 scion** [ed.] Seyen [seyen Q1]  **374 snipe** snpe  **377 H' as** She ha's
**II.i.9 mortise** [ed.] morties [morties Q1]  **33 prays** praye  **40 Third Gentleman** Gent.  **53 First Gentleman** Gent.  **56 Second Gentleman** Gent.  **59 Second Gentleman** Gent.  **65 ingener** Ingeniuer  **66 Second Gentleman** Gent.  **93 Second Gentleman** Gent.  **168 gyve** [ed.] giue [catch Q1]  **173 An** and  **175 clyster** cluster  **212 hither** thither  **241 has** he's  **260 mutualities** mutabilities  **298 wife** wist  **306 nightcap** Night-Cape
**II.iii.41 unfortunate** infortunate  **60 to put** put to  **64 God** heauen  **75 God** Heauen  **80 Englishman** Englishmen  **97 thine** thy  **99 'Fore God** Why  **103 God's** heauen's  **112 God forgive** Forgiue  **145 Help . . . within** [F omits; Q1 reads "Helpe, helpe, within"]  **146 Zounds, you** You  **156 God's will** Alas  **160 God's will** Fie, fie  **162 Zounds, I** I  **216 leagued** [ed.] league [F and Q1]  **259 God** Heauen  **273 to** ro  **287 O God** Oh  **340 were't** were to  **359 enmesh** en-mash  **375 By the mass** In troth
**III.i.1 s.d.** [F includes the Clown]  **20 Exit Musicians** Exit Mu.  **25 general's wife** Generall  **30 Cassio** [no speech ascription in F]
**III.ii.6 We'll** Well
**III.iii.74 By'r Lady** Trust me  **94 you** he  **106 By heaven** Alas  **135 free to** free  **136 vile** vild  **139 But some** Wherein  **148 Shape** [ed.] Shapes  **162 By heaven I'll** Ile  **170 fondly** [ed.] soundly [strongly Q1]  **175 God** heauen  **182 exsufflicate** [ed.] exufflicate [F and Q1]; **blown** blowd  **217 my** your  **222 vile** vilde  **248 hold him** him  **258 qualities** Quantities  **259 human** humane  **281 to** too  **335 of** in  **347 makes** make  **372 b' wi'** buy  **392 supervisor** supervision  **437 that was** [Malone's ed.] it was [F and Q1]
**III.iv.77 God** Heauen  **81 Heaven** Blesse  **96 I' faith** In sooth  **169 I' faith** indeed  **185 by my faith** in good troth
**IV.i.21 infected** infectious  **37 Zounds, that's** that's  **78 unsuiting** resulting  **102 conster** conserue  **108 power** dowre  **112 i' faith** indeed  **123 win** winnes  **131 beckons** becomes  **162 Faith, I** I  **216 God save** Save  **246 an obedient** obedient
**IV.ii.16 requite** requit  **30 Nay** May  **48 kinds** kind  **154 in** [Q2]  or  **168 stay** stays
**IV.iii.15 bade** bid  **53 hie** high
**V.i.1 bulk** Barke  **22 hear** heard  **34 hies** highes  **35 Forth** For  **50 heaven's** heauen  **105 out o' th'** o' th'
**V.ii.13 the rose** thy Rose  **35 say so** say  **57 Then Lord** O Heauen  **101 Should** Did  **117 O Lord** Alas  **127 heard** heare  **209 reprobation** Reprobance  **218 O God! O heavenly God** O Heauen! Oh heauenly powres  **219 Zounds** Come

# THE TRAGEDY OF OTHELLO
# THE MOOR OF VENICE

## The Names of the Actors

OTHELLO *the Moor*
BRABANTIO *father to Desdemona*
CASSIO *an honorable lieutenant*
IAGO *a villain*
RODERIGO *a gulled gentleman*
DUKE OF VENICE
SENATORS
MONTANO *Governor of Cyprus*
GENTLEMEN *of Cyprus*

LODOVICO *and* GRATIANO *two noble Venetians*
SAILORS
CLOWN
DESDEMONA *wife to Othello*
EMILIA *wife to Iago*
BIANCA *a courtesan*
[MESSENGER  HERALD  OFFICERS
   GENTLEMEN  MUSICIANS  ATTENDANTS

*Scene:* Venice and Cyprus]

## ACT I

### Scene I. [*Venice. A street.*]

*Enter* RODERIGO *and* IAGO.

RODERIGO
Tush! Never tell me? I take it much unkindly
That thou, Iago, who hast had my purse
As if the strings were thine, shouldst know of this.
IAGO
'Sblood,° but you'll not hear me! If ever I did dream
Of such a matter, abhor me.
RODERIGO                    Thou told'st me          5
Thou didst hold him in thy hate.
IAGO                          Despise me
If I do not. Three great ones of the city,
In personal suit to make me his lieutenant,
Off-capped° to him; and, by the faith of man,
I know my price; I am worth no worse a place.     10
But he, as loving his own pride and purposes,
Evades them with a bombast circumstance,°

Horribly stuffed with epithets of war;
Nonsuits° my mediators. For, "Certes," says he,
"I have already chose my officer." And what was he? 15
Forsooth, a great arithmetician,°
One Michael Cassio, a Florentine,
(A fellow almost damned in a fair wife)°
That never set a squadron in the field,
Nor the division of a battle knows                 20
More than a spinster; unless the bookish theoric,
Wherein the tonguèd° consuls can propose
As masterly as he. Mere prattle without practice
Is all his soldiership. But he, sir, had th' election;
And I, of whom his eyes had seen the proof         25
At Rhodes, at Cyprus, and on other grounds
Christian and heathen, must be belee'd and calmed
By debitor and creditor. This counter-caster,°
He, in good time, must his lieutenant be,
And I—God bless the mark!—his Moorship's ancient.° 30

---

14 **Nonsuits** rejects   16 **arithmetician** theorist (rather than practitioner)   18 **A . . . wife** a much-disputed passage, which is probably best taken as a general sneer at Cassio as a dandy and a ladies' man; but in the story from which Shakespeare took his plot the counterpart of Cassio is married, and it may be that at the beginning of the play Shakespeare had decided to keep him married but later changed his mind   22 **tonguèd** eloquent   28 **counter-caster** i.e., a bookkeeper who "casts" (reckons up) figures on a "counter" (abacus)   30 **ancient** standard-bearer; an underofficer

---

*The decorative border shown above was used in the First Folio edition of Shakespeare's plays, 1623.*
**I.i.4 'Sblood** by God's blood   **9 Off-capped** doffed their caps (as a mark of respect)   **12 bombast circumstance** stuffed, roundabout speech

RODERIGO
By heaven, I rather would have been his hangman.
IAGO
Why, there's no remedy. 'Tis the curse of service:
Preferment goes by letter and affection,°
And not by old gradation,° where each second
Stood heir to th' first. Now, sir, be judge yourself,     35
Whether I in any just term am affined°
To love the Moor.
RODERIGO                    I would not follow him then.
IAGO
O, sir, content you.
I follow him to serve my turn upon him.
We cannot all be masters, nor all masters     40
Cannot be truly followed. You shall mark
Many a duteous and knee-crooking° knave
That, doting on his own obsequious bondage,
Wears out his time, much like his master's ass,
For naught but provender; and when he's old,
     cashiered.     45
Whip me such honest knaves! Others there are
Who, trimmed in forms and visages of duty,
Keep yet their hearts attending on themselves,
And, throwing but shows of service on their lords,
Do well thrive by them, and when they have lined
     their coats,     50
Do themselves homage. These fellows have some soul;
And such a one do I profess myself. For, sir,
It is as sure as you are Roderigo,
Were I the Moor, I would not be Iago.
In following him, I follow but myself.     55
Heaven is my judge, not I for love and duty,
But seeming so, for my peculiar° end;
For when my outward action doth demonstrate
The native° act and figure of my heart
In complement extern,° 'tis not long after     60
But I will wear my heart upon my sleeve
For daws to peck at; I am not what I am.
RODERIGO
What a full fortune does the thick-lips owe°
If he can carry't thus!
IAGO                    Call up her father,
Rouse him. Make after him, poison his delight,     65
Proclaim him in the streets, incense her kinsmen,
And though he in a fertile climate dwell,
Plague him with flies; though that his joy be joy,
Yet throw such chances of vexation on't
As it may lose some color.     70
RODERIGO
Here is her father's house. I'll call aloud.
IAGO
Do, with like timorous° accent and dire yell
As when, by night and negligence, the fire
Is spied in populous cities.
RODERIGO
What, ho, Brabantio! Signior Brabantio, ho!     75
IAGO
Awake! What, ho, Brabantio! Thieves! Thieves!

Look to your house, your daughter, and your bags!
Thieves! Thieves!

BRABANTIO above° [at a window].

BRABANTIO
What is the reason of this terrible summons?
What is the matter there?     80
RODERIGO
Signior, is all your family within?
IAGO
Are your doors locked?
BRABANTIO                    Why, wherefore ask you this?
IAGO
Zounds, sir, y'are robbed! For shame. Put on your
     gown!
Your heart is burst, you have lost half your soul.
Even now, now, very now, an old black ram     85
Is tupping your white ewe. Arise, arise!
Awake the snorting citizens with the bell,
Or else the devil will make a grandsire of you.
Arise, I say.
BRABANTIO     What, have you lost your wits?
RODERIGO
Most reverend signior, do you know my voice?     90
BRABANTIO
Not I. What are you?
RODERIGO
My name is Roderigo.
BRABANTIO                    The worser welcome!
I have charged thee not to haunt about my doors.
In honest plainness thou hast heard me say
My daughter is not for thee; and now, in madness,     95
Being full of supper and distemp'ring draughts,°
Upon malicious knavery dost thou come
To start° my quiet.
RODERIGO
Sir, sir, sir—
BRABANTIO But thou must needs be sure
My spirits and my place° have in their power     100
To make this bitter to thee.
RODERIGO                    Patience, good sir.
BRABANTIO
What tell'st thou me of robbing? This is Venice;
My house is not a grange.°
RODERIGO                    Most grave Brabantio,
In simple and pure soul I come to you.
IAGO Zounds, sir, you are one of those that will not     105
serve God if the devil bid you. Because we come to do
you service and you think we are ruffians, you'll have
your daughter covered with a Barbary° horse, you'll
have your nephews° neigh to you, you'll have coursers
for cousins,° and gennets for germans.°     110
BRABANTIO
What profane wretch art thou?
IAGO I am one, sir, that comes to tell you your

33 **letter and affection** recommendations (from men of power) and personal preference  34 **old gradation** seniority  36 **affined** bound  42 **knee-crooking** bowing  57 **peculiar** personal  59 **native** natural, innate  60 **complement extern** outward appearances  63 **owe** own  72 **timorous** frightening

78 s.d. **above** i.e., on the small upper stage above and to the rear of the main platform stage, which resembled the projecting upper story of an Elizabethan house  96 **distemp'ring draughts** unsettling drinks  98 **start** disrupt  100 **place** rank, i.e., of senator  103 **grange** isolated house  108 **Barbary** Arabian, i.e., Moorish  109 **nephews** i.e., grandsons  110 **cousins** relations; **gennets for germans** Spanish horses for blood relatives

daughter and the Moor are making the beast with two
backs.

BRABANTIO
Thou art a villain.

IAGO　　　　　　　You are—a senator.　　　　　115

BRABANTIO
This thou shalt answer. I know thee, Roderigo.

RODERIGO
Sir, I will answer anything. But I beseech you,
If 't be your pleasure and most wise consent,
As partly I find it is, that your fair daughter,
At this odd-even° and dull watch o' th' night,　　120
Transported, with no worse nor better guard
But with a knave of common hire, a gondolier,
To the gross clasps of a lascivious Moor—
If this be known to you, and your allowance,
We then have done you bold and saucy wrongs;　　125
But if you know not this, my manners tell me
We have your wrong rebuke. Do not believe
That from the sense of all civility°
I thus would play and trifle with your reverence.
Your daughter, if you have not given her leave,　　130
I say again, hath made a gross revolt,
Tying her duty, beauty, wit, and fortunes
In an extravagant° and wheeling stranger
Of here and everywhere. Straight satisfy yourself.
If she be in her chamber, or your house,　　135
Let loose on me the justice of the state
For thus deluding you.

BRABANTIO　　　　　　Strike on the tinder, ho!
Give me a taper! Call up all my people!
This accident° is not unlike my dream.
Belief of it oppresses me already.　　140
Light, I say! Light!　　　　　　Exit [above].

IAGO　　　　　　Farewell, for I must leave you.
It seems not meet, nor wholesome to my place,
To be produced—as, if I stay, I shall—
Against the Moor. For I do know the state,
However this may gall him with some check,°　　145
Cannot with safety cast° him; for he's embarked
With such loud reason to the Cyprus wars,
Which even now stands in act,° that for their souls
Another of his fathom° they have none
To lead their business; in which regard,　　150
Though I do hate him as I do hell-pains,
Yet, for necessity of present life,
I must show out a flag and sign of love,
Which is indeed but sign. That you shall surely find
　him,
Lead to the Sagittary° the raisèd search;　　155
And there will I be with him. So farewell.　　Exit.

Enter BRABANTIO [in his nightgown], with SERVANTS
and torches.

BRABANTIO
It is too true an evil. Gone she is;
And what's to come of my despisèd time

Is naught but bitterness. Now, Roderigo,
Where didst thou see her?—O unhappy girl!—　　160
With the Moor, say'st thou?—Who would be a
　father?—
How didst thou know 'twas she?—O, she deceives me
Past thought!—What said she to you? Get moe°
　tapers!
Raise all my kindred!—Are they married, think you?

RODERIGO
Truly I think they are.　　　　　165

BRABANTIO
O heaven! How got she out? O treason of the blood!
Fathers, from hence trust not your daughters' minds
By what you see them act.° Is there not charms
By which the property° of youth and maidhood
May be abused? Have you not read, Roderigo,　　170
Of some such thing?

RODERIGO　　　　　Yes, sir, I have indeed.

BRABANTIO
Call up my brother.—O, would you had had her!—
Some one way, some another—Do you know
Where we may apprehend her and the Moor?

RODERIGO
I think I can discover him, if you please　　175
To get good guard and go along with me.

BRABANTIO
Pray you lead on. At every house I'll call;
I may command at most.—Get weapons, ho!
And raise some special officers of might.—
On, good Roderigo; I will deserve your pains.°　　180
　　　　　　　　　　　Exeunt.

Scene II. [A street.]

Enter OTHELLO, IAGO, ATTENDANTS with torches.

IAGO
Though in the trade of war I have slain men,
Yet do I hold it very stuff° o' th' conscience
To do no contrived murder. I lack iniquity
Sometime to do me service. Nine or ten times
I had thought t' have yerked° him here, under the ribs. 5

OTHELLO
'Tis better as it is.

IAGO　　　　　　Nay, but he prated,
And spoke such scurvy and provoking terms
Against your honor, that with the little godliness I have
I did full hard forbear him. But I pray you, sir,
Are you fast married? Be assured of this,　　10
That the magnifico° is much beloved,
And hath in his effect a voice potential
As double as the duke's.° He will divorce you,
Or put upon you what restraint or grievance
The law, with all his might to enforce it on,　　15
Will give him cable.°

OTHELLO　　　　　Let him do his spite.
My services which I have done the Signiory°

120 odd-even between night and morning　128 sense . . .
civility feeling of what is proper　133 extravagant vagrant,
wandering (Othello is not Venetian and thus may be considered
a wandering soldier of fortune)　139 accident happening
145 check restraint　146 cast dismiss　148 stands in act takes
place　149 fathom ability　155 Sagittary probably the name
of an inn

163 moe more　168 act do　169 property true nature　180
deserve your pains be worthy of (and reward) your efforts
I.ii.2 stuff essence　5 yerked stabbed　11 magnifico nobleman　12–13 hath . . . duke's i.e., can be as effective as the
duke　16 cable range, scope　17 Signiory the rulers of Venice

Shall out-tongue his complaints. 'Tis yet to know°—
Which when I know that boasting is an honor
I shall promulgate—I fetch my life and being          20
From men of royal siege;° and my demerits°
May speak unbonneted to as proud a fortune
As this that I have reached.° For know, Iago,
But that I love the gentle Desdemona,
I would not my unhousèd° free condition          25
Put into circumscription and confine
For the seas' worth. But look, what lights come
    yond?

*Enter* CASSIO, *with* [OFFICERS *and*] *torches.*

IAGO
Those are the raisèd father and his friends.
You were best go in.
OTHELLO          Not I. I must be found.
My parts, my title, and my perfect soul°          30
Shall manifest me rightly. Is it they?
IAGO
By Janus, I think no.
OTHELLO
The servants of the duke? And my lieutenant?
The goodness of the night upon you, friends.
What is the news?
CASSIO          The duke does greet you, general;          35
And he requires your haste-posthaste appearance
Even on the instant.
OTHELLO          What is the matter, think you?
CASSIO
Something from Cyprus, as I may divine.
It is a business of some heat. The galleys
Have sent a dozen sequent° messengers          40
This very night at one another's heels,
And many of the consuls, raised and met,
Are at the duke's already. You have been hotly called
    for.
When, being not at your lodging to be found,
The Senate hath sent about three several° quests          45
To search you out.
OTHELLO          'Tis well I am found by you.
I will but spend a word here in the house,
And go with you.          [*Exit.*]
CASSIO          Ancient, what makes he here?
IAGO
Faith, he tonight hath boarded a land carack.°
If it prove lawful prize, he's made forever.          50
CASSIO
I do not understand.
IAGO          He's married.
CASSIO          To who?

[*Enter* OTHELLO.]

IAGO
Marry,° to—Come, captain, will you go?
OTHELLO          Have with you.

CASSIO
Here comes another troop to seek for you.

*Enter* BRABANTIO, RODERIGO, *with* OFFICERS *and*
*torches.*

IAGO
It is Brabantio. General, be advised.
He comes to bad intent.
OTHELLO          Holla! Stand there!          55
RODERIGO
Signior, it is the Moor.
BRABANTIO          Down with him, thief!

[*They draw swords.*]

IAGO
You, Roderigo? Come, sir, I am for you.
OTHELLO
Keep up your bright swords, for the dew will rust them.
Good signior, you shall more command with years
Than with your weapons.          60
BRABANTIO
O thou foul thief, where hast thou stowed my
    daughter?
Damned as thou art, thou hast enchanted her!
For I'll refer me to all things of sense,°
If she in chains of magic were not bound,
Whether a maid so tender, fair, and happy,          65
So opposite to marriage that she shunned
The wealthy, curlèd darlings of our nation,
Would ever have, t' incur a general mock,°
Run from her guardage to the sooty bosom
Of such a thing as thou—to fear, not to delight.          70
Judge me the world if 'tis not gross in sense°
That thou hast practiced° on her with foul charms,
Abused her delicate youth with drugs or minerals
That weaken motion.° I'll have't disputed on;
'Tis probable, and palpable to thinking.          75
I therefore apprehend and do attach° thee
For an abuser of the world, a practicer
Of arts inhibited and out of warrant.°
Lay hold upon him. If he do resist,
Subdue him at his peril.
OTHELLO          Hold your hands,          80
Both you of my inclining and the rest.
Were it my cue to fight, I should have known it
Without a prompter. Whither will you that I go
To answer this your charge?
BRABANTIO          To prison, till fit time
Of law and course of direct session          85
Call thee to answer.
OTHELLO          What if I do obey?
How may the duke be therewith satisfied,
Whose messengers are here about my side
Upon some present° business of the state
To bring me to him?
OFFICER          'Tis true, most worthy signior.          90

---

**18 yet to know** unknown as yet  **21 siege** rank; **demerits** deserts  **22–23 May . . . reached** i.e., are the equal of the family I have married into  **25 unhousèd** unconfined  **30 perfect soul** clear, unflawed conscience  **40 sequent** successive  **45 several** separate  **49 carack** treasure ship  **52 Marry** an interjection, from "By the Virgin Mary"

**63 refer . . . sense** base (my argument) on all ordinary understanding of nature  **68 general mock** public shame  **71 gross in sense** obvious  **72 practiced** used tricks  **74 motion** thought, i.e., reason  **76 attach** arrest  **78 inhibited . . . warrant** prohibited and illegal (black magic)  **89 present** immediate

The duke's in council, and your noble self
I am sure is sent for.
BRABANTIO            How? The duke in council?
In this time of the night? Bring him away.
Mine's not an idle cause. The duke himself,
Or any of my brothers° of the state,                              95
Cannot but feel this wrong as 'twere their own;
For if such actions may have passage free,
Bondslaves and pagans shall our statesmen be. *Exeunt.*

Scene III. [*A council chamber.*]

*Enter* DUKE, SENATORS, *and* OFFICERS [*set at a table,
with lights and* ATTENDANTS].

DUKE
There's no composition° in this news
That gives them credit.°
FIRST SENATOR        Indeed, they are disproportioned.
My letters say a hundred and seven galleys.
DUKE
And mine a hundred forty.
SECOND SENATOR            And mine two hundred.         5
But though they jump° not on a just accompt°—
As in these cases where the aim° reports
'Tis oft with difference—yet do they all confirm
A Turkish fleet, and bearing up to Cyprus.
DUKE
Nay, it is possible enough to judgment.°                         10
I do not so secure me in the error,
But the main article I do approve
In fearful sense.°
SAILOR (*Within.*)   What, ho! What, ho! What, ho!

*Enter* SAILOR.

OFFICER
A messenger from the galleys.
DUKE                Now? What's the business?
SAILOR
The Turkish preparation makes for Rhodes.                        15
So was I bid report here to the State
By Signior Angelo.
DUKE
How say you by this change?
FIRST SENATOR                    This cannot be
By no assay of reason. 'Tis a pageant°
To keep us in false gaze.° When we consider                      20
Th' importancy of Cyprus to the Turk,
And let ourselves again but understand
That, as it more concerns the Turk than Rhodes,
So may he with more facile question° bear it,
For that it stands not in such warlike brace,°                   25
But altogether lacks th' abilities

That Rhodes is dressed in. If we make thought of this,
We must not think the Turk is so unskillful
To leave that latest which concerns him first,
Neglecting an attempt of ease and gain
To wake and wage a danger profitless.                            30
DUKE
Nay, in all confidence he's not for Rhodes.
OFFICER
Here is more news.

*Enter a* MESSENGER.

MESSENGER
The Ottomites, reverend and gracious,
Steering with due course toward the isle of Rhodes,
Have there injointed them with an after° fleet.                  35
FIRST SENATOR
Ay, so I thought. How many, as you guess?
MESSENGER
Of thirty sail; and now they do restem
Their backward course, bearing with frank appearance
Their purposes toward Cyprus. Signior Montano,
Your trusty and most valiant servitor,
With his free duty° recommends° you thus,                        40
And prays you to believe him.
DUKE
'Tis certain then for Cyprus.
Marcus Luccicos, is not he in town?
FIRST SENATOR
He's now in Florence.                                            45
DUKE
Write from us to him; post-posthaste dispatch.
FIRST SENATOR
Here comes Brabantio and the valiant Moor.

*Enter* BRABANTIO, OTHELLO, CASSIO, IAGO,
RODERIGO, *and* OFFICERS.

DUKE
Valiant Othello, we must straight° employ you
Against the general° enemy Ottoman.

[*To* BRABANTIO.]

I did not see you. Welcome, gentle signior.                      50
We lacked your counsel and your help tonight.
BRABANTIO
So did I yours. Good your grace, pardon me.
Neither my place, nor aught I heard of business,
Hath raised me from my bed; nor doth the general
    care
Take hold on me; for my particular grief                         55
Is of so floodgate and o'erbearing nature
That it engluts and swallows other sorrows,
And it is still itself.
DUKE                    Why, what's the matter?
BRABANTIO
My daughter! O, my daughter!
SENATORS                        Dead?
BRABANTIO                                Ay, to me.
She is abused, stol'n from me, and corrupted                     60
By spells and medicines bought of mountebanks;
For nature so prepost'rously to err,

---

95 **brothers** i.e., the other senators
**I.iii.1 composition** agreement  **2 gives them credit** makes
them believable  **5 jump** agree; **just accompt** exact counting
**6 aim** approximation  **9 to judgment** when carefully considered  **10–12 I . . . sense** i.e., just because the numbers
disagree in the reports, I do not doubt that the principal information (that the Turkish fleet is out) is fearfully true  **18
pageant** show, pretense  **19 in false gaze** looking the wrong
way  **23 facile question** easy struggle  **24 warlike brace**
"military posture"

35 **after** following  **41 free duty** unlimited respect; **recommends** informs  **48 straight** at once  **49 general** universal

Being not deficient, blind, or lame of sense,
Sans° witchcraft could not.

DUKE

Whoe'er he be that in this foul proceeding    65
Hath thus beguiled your daughter of herself,
And you of her, the bloody book of law
You shall yourself read in the bitter letter
After your own sense; yea, though our proper° son
Stood in your action.°

BRABANTIO          Humbly I thank your grace.    70
Here is the man—this Moor, whom now, it seems,
Your special mandate for the state affairs
Hath hither brought.

ALL          We are very sorry for't.

DUKE [*To* OTHELLO.]
What in your own part can you say to this?

BRABANTIO
Nothing, but this is so.    75

OTHELLO
Most potent, grave, and reverend signiors,
My very noble and approved° good masters,
That I have ta'en away this old man's daughter,
It is most true; true I have married her.
The very head and front° of my offending    80
Hath this extent, no more. Rude am I in my speech,
And little blessed with the soft phrase of peace,
For since these arms of mine had seven years' pith°
Till now some nine moons wasted,° they have used
Their dearest° action in the tented field;    85
And little of this great world can I speak
More than pertains to feats of broils and battle;
And therefore little shall I grace my cause
In speaking for myself. Yet, by your gracious patience,
I will a round° unvarnished tale deliver    90
Of my whole course of love—what drugs, what
     charms,
What conjuration, and what mighty magic,
For such proceeding I am charged withal,
I won his daughter—

BRABANTIO          A maiden never bold,
Of spirit so still and quiet that her motion    95
Blushed at herself;° and she, in spite of nature,
Of years, of country, credit, everything,
To fall in love with what she feared to look on!
It is a judgment maimed and most imperfect
That will confess perfection so could err    100
Against all rules of nature, and must be driven
To find out practices of cunning hell
Why this should be. I therefore vouch again
That with some mixtures pow'rful o'er the blood,
Or with some dram, conjured to this effect,    105
He wrought upon her.

DUKE          To vouch this is no proof,
Without more wider and more overt test
Than these thin habits° and poor likelihoods
Of modern° seeming do prefer against him.

FIRST SENATOR
But, Othello, speak.    110
Did you by indirect and forcèd courses
Subdue and poison this young maid's affections?
Or came it by request, and such fair question°
As soul to soul affordeth?

OTHELLO          I do beseech you,
Send for the lady to the Sagittary    115
And let her speak of me before her father.
If you do find me foul in her report,
The trust, the office, I do hold of you
Not only take away, but let your sentence
Even fall upon my life.

DUKE          Fetch Desdemona hither.    120

OTHELLO
Ancient, conduct them; you best know the place.
     [*Exit* IAGO, *with two or three* ATTENDANTS.]
And till she come, as truly as to heaven
I do confess the vices of my blood,
So justly to your grave ears I'll present
How I did thrive in this fair lady's love,    125
And she in mine.

DUKE          Say it, Othello.

OTHELLO
Her father loved me; oft invited me;
Still° questioned me the story of my life
From year to year, the battle, sieges, fortune
That I have passed.    130
I ran it through, even from my boyish days
To th' very moment that he bade me tell it.
Wherein I spoke of most disastrous chances,
Of moving accidents by flood and field,
Of hairbreadth scapes i' th' imminent° deadly breach,    135
Of being taken by the insolent foe
And sold to slavery, of my redemption thence
And portance° in my travel's history,
Wherein of anters° vast and deserts idle,°
Rough quarries, rocks, and hills whose heads touch
     heaven,    140
It was my hint to speak. Such was my process.
And of the Cannibals that each other eat,
The Anthropophagi,° and men whose heads
Grew beneath their shoulders. These things to hear
Would Desdemona seriously incline;    145
But still the house affairs would draw her thence;
Which ever as she could with haste dispatch,
She'd come again, and with a greedy ear
Devour up my discourse. Which I observing,
Took once a pliant hour, and found good means    150
To draw from her a prayer of earnest heart
That I would all my pilgrimage dilate,°
Whereof by parcels she had something heard,
But not intentively.° I did consent,
And often did beguile her of her tears    155
When I did speak of some distressful stroke
That my youth suffered. My story being done,
She gave me for my pains a world of kisses.
She swore in faith 'twas strange, 'twas passing° strange;

**64 Sans** without **69 proper** own **70 Stood . . . action**
were the accused in your suit **77 approved** tested, proven by
past performance **80 head and front** extreme form ("front"
= forehead) **83 pith** strength **84 wasted** past **85 dearest**
most important **90 round** blunt **95–96 her . . . herself**
she was so modest that she blushed at every thought (and
movement) **108 habits** clothing **109 modern** trivial

**113 question** discussion **128 Still** regularly **135 imminent**
threatening **138 portance** manner of acting **139 anters**
caves; **idle** empty, sterile **143 Anthropophagi** man-eaters
**152 dilate** relate in full **154 intentively** at length and in
sequence **159 passing** surpassing

'Twas pitiful, 'twas wondrous pitiful.    160
She wished she had not heard it; yet she wished
That heaven had made her such a man. She thanked
     me,
And bade me, if I had a friend that loved her,
I should but teach him how to tell my story,
And that would woo her. Upon this hint I spake.    165
She loved me for the dangers I had passed,
And I loved her that she did pity them.
This only is the witchcraft I have used.
Here comes the lady. Let her witness it.

*Enter* DESDEMONA, IAGO, ATTENDANTS.

DUKE
I think this tale would win my daughter too.    170
Good Brabantio, take up this mangled matter at the
     best.°
Men do their broken weapons rather use
Than their bare hands.
BRABANTIO                    I pray you hear her speak.
If she confess that she was half the wooer,
Destruction on my head if my bad blame    175
Light on the man. Come hither, gentle mistress.
Do you perceive in all this noble company
Where most you owe obedience?
DESDEMONA                         My noble father,
I do perceive here a divided duty.
To you I am bound for life and education;    180
My life and education both do learn me
How to respect you. You are the lord of duty,
I am hitherto your daughter. But here's my husband,
And so much duty as my mother showed
To you, preferring you before her father,    185
So much I challenge° that I may profess
Due to the Moor my lord.
BRABANTIO              God be with you. I have done.
Please it your grace, on to the state affairs.
I had rather to adopt a child than get° it.
Come hither, Moor.    190
I here do give thee that with all my heart
Which, but thou hast already, with all my heart
I would keep from thee. For your sake,° jewel,
I am glad at soul I have no other child,
For thy escape would teach me tyranny,    195
To hang clogs on them. I have done, my lord.
DUKE
Let me speak like yourself and lay a sentence°
Which, as a grise° or step, may help these lovers.
When remedies are past, the griefs are ended
By seeing the worst, which late on hopes depended.°    200
To mourn a mischief that is past and gone
Is the next° way to draw new mischief on.
What cannot be preserved when fortune takes,
Patience her injury a mock'ry makes.
The robbed that smiles, steals something from the    205
     thief;
He robs himself that spends a bootless° grief.

BRABANTIO
So let the Turk of Cyprus us beguile:
We lose it not so long as we can smile.
He bears the sentence well that nothing bears
But the free comfort which from thence he hears;    210
But he bears both the sentence and the sorrow
That to pay grief must of poor patience borrow.
These sentences, to sugar, or to gall,
Being strong on both sides, are equivocal.
But words are words. I never yet did hear    215
That the bruisèd heart was piercèd° through the ear.
I humbly beseech you, proceed to th' affairs of state.
DUKE   The Turk with a most mighty preparation
makes for Cyprus. Othello, the fortitude° of the place
is best known to you; and though we have there a    220
substitute° of most allowed sufficiency,° yet opinion,
a more sovereign mistress of effects, throws a more
safer voice on you.° You must therefore be content to
slubber° the gloss of your new fortunes with this more
stubborn and boisterous° expedition.    225
OTHELLO
The tyrant Custom, most grave senators,
Hath made the flinty and steel couch of war
My thrice-driven° bed of down. I do agnize°
A natural and prompt alacrity
I find in hardness and do undertake    230
These present wars against the Ottomites.
Most humbly, therefore, bending to your state,
I crave fit disposition for my wife,
Due reference of place, and exhibition,°
With such accommodation and besort    235
As levels with° her breeding.
DUKE                              Why, at her father's.
BRABANTIO
I will not have it so.
OTHELLO              Nor I.
DESDEMONA              Nor would I there reside,
To put my father in impatient thoughts
By being in his eye. Most gracious duke,
To my unfolding° lend your prosperous° ear,    240
And let me find a charter° in your voice,
T' assist my simpleness.
DUKE                      What would you, Desdemona?
DESDEMONA
That I love the Moor to live with him,
My downright violence, and storm of fortunes,
May trumpet to the world. My heart's subdued    245
Even to the very quality of my lord.°

171 **take . . . best** make the best of this disaster 186 **challenge** claim as right 189 **get** beget 193 **For your sake** because of you 197 **lay a sentence** provide a maxim 198 **grise** step 200 **late . . . depended** was supported by hope (of a better outcome) until lately 202 **next** closest, surest 206 **bootless** valueless

216 **piercèd** some editors emend to "pieced," i.e., "healed"; but "pierced" makes good sense: Brabantio is saying in effect that his heart cannot be further hurt (pierced) by the indignity of the useless, conventional advice the duke offers him; "pierced" can also mean, however, "lanced" in the medical sense, and would then mean "treated" 219 **fortitude** fortification 221 **substitute** viceroy; **most allowed sufficiency** generally acknowledged capability 221–23 **opinion . . . you** the general opinion, which finally controls affairs, is that you would be the best man in this situation 224 **slubber** besmear 225 **stubborn and boisterous** rough and violent 228 **thrice-driven** i.e., softest; **agnize** know in myself 234 **exhibition** grant of funds 236 **levels with** is suitable to 240 **unfolding** explanation; **prosperous** favoring 241 **charter** permission 245–46 **My . . . lord** i.e., I have become one in nature and being with the man I married (therefore, I too would go to the wars like a soldier)

I saw Othello's visage in his mind,
And to his honors and his valiant parts
Did I my soul and fortunes consecrate.
So that, dear lords, if I be left behind,            250
A moth of peace, and he go to the war,
The rites° for why I love him are bereft me,
And I a heavy interim shall support
By his dear absence. Let me go with him.

OTHELLO
Let her have your voice.°                             255
Vouch with me, heaven, I therefore beg it not
To please the palate of my appetite,
Nor to comply with heat°—the young affects°
In me defunct—and proper satisfaction;°
But to be free and bounteous to her mind;           260
And heaven defend° your good souls that you think
I will your serious and great business scant
When she is with me. No, when light-winged toys
Of feathered Cupid seel° with wanton° dullness
My speculative and officed instrument,°             265
That my disports corrupt and taint my business,
Let housewives make a skillet of my helm,
And all indign° and base adversities
Make head° against my estimation!°—

DUKE
Be it as you shall privately determine,             270
Either for her stay or going. Th' affair cries haste,
And speed must answer it.

FIRST SENATOR          You must away tonight.

OTHELLO
With all my heart.

DUKE
At nine i' th' morning here we'll meet again.
Othello, leave some officer behind,                 275
And he shall our commission bring to you,
And such things else of quality and respect
As doth import you.

OTHELLO          So please your grace, my ancient;
A man he is of honesty and trust.
To his conveyance I assign my wife,                 280
With what else needful your good grace shall think
To be sent after me.

DUKE          Let it be so.
Good night to every one. [To BRABANTIO.] And,
    noble signior,
If virtue no delighted° beauty lack,
Your son-in-law is far more fair than black.        285

FIRST SENATOR
Adieu, brave Moor. Use Desdemona well.

BRABANTIO
Look to her, Moor, if thou hast eyes to see:
She has deceived her father, and may thee.
        [Exeunt DUKE, SENATORS, OFFICERS, &c.]

OTHELLO
My life upon her faith! Honest Iago,
My Desdemona must I leave to thee.                  290

I prithee let thy wife attend on her,
And bring them after in the best advantage.°
Come, Desdemona. I have but an hour
Of love, of worldly matter, and direction
To spend with thee. We must obey the time.         295
        Exit [OTHELLO, with DESDEMONA].

RODERIGO  Iago?
IAGO  What say'st thou, noble heart?
RODERIGO  What will I do, think'st thou?
IAGO  Why, go to bed and sleep.
RODERIGO  I will incontinently° drown myself.       300
IAGO  If thou dost, I shall never love thee after. Why,
thou silly gentleman?
RODERIGO  It is silliness to live when to live is torment;
and then have we a prescription to die when death is
our physician.                                      305
IAGO  O villainous! I have looked upon the world for
four times seven years, and since I could distinguish
betwixt a benefit and an injury, I never found man
that knew how to love himself. Ere I would say I
would drown myself for the love of a guinea hen, I   310
would change my humanity with a baboon.
RODERIGO  What should I do? I confess it is my shame
to be so fond, but it is not in my virtue° to amend it.
IAGO  Virtue? A fig! 'Tis in ourselves that we are thus,
or thus. Our bodies are our gardens, to the which our  315
wills are gardeners; so that if we will plant nettles or
sow lettuce, set hyssop and weed up thyme, supply it
with one gender of herbs or distract° it with many—
either to have it sterile with idleness or manured with
industry—why, the power and corrigible° authority   320
of this lies in our wills. If the balance of our lives had
not one scale of reason to poise another of sensuality,
the blood and baseness of our natures would conduct
us to most prepost'rous conclusions.° But we have
reason to cool our raging motions, our carnal stings or  325
unbitted° lusts, whereof I take this that you call love
to be a sect or scion.°
RODERIGO  It cannot be.
IAGO  It is merely a lust of the blood and a permission
of the will. Come, be a man! Drown thyself? Drown   330
cats and blind puppies! I have professed me thy
friend, and I confess me knit to thy deserving with
cables of perdurable toughness. I could never better
stead° thee than now. Put money in thy purse.
Follow thou the wars; defeat thy favor° with an     335
usurped° beard. I say, put money in thy purse. It
cannot be long that Desdemona should continue her
love of the Moor. Put money in thy purse. Nor he
his to her. It was a violent commencement in her and
thou shalt see an answerable° sequestration—put but  340
money in thy purse. These Moors are changeable in
their wills—fill thy purse with money. The food that
to him now is as luscious as locusts° shall be to him
shortly as bitter as coloquintida.° She must change
for youth; when she is sated with his body, she will  345

252 rites may refer either to the marriage rites or to the rites,
formalities, of war  255 voice consent  258 heat lust; affects
passions  259 proper satisfaction i.e. consummation of the
marriage  261 defend forbid  264 seel sew up; wanton
lascivious  265 speculative . . . instrument i.e., sight
(and, by extension, the mind)  268 indign unworthy  269
Make head form an army, i.e., attack; estimation reputation
284 delighted delightful

292 advantage opportunity  300 incontinently at once  313
virtue strength (Roderigo is saying that his nature controls
him)  318 distract vary  320 corrigible corrective  324 conclusions encs  326 unbitted uncontrolled  327 sect or scion
offshoot  334 stead serve  335 defeat thy favor disguise your
face  336 usurped assumed  340 answerable similar  343
locusts a sweet fruit  344 coloquintida a purgative derived
from a bitter apple

find the errors of her choice. Therefore, put money in
thy purse. If thou wilt needs damn thyself, do it a more
delicate way than drowning. Make all the money thou
canst. If sanctimony° and a frail vow betwixt an
erring° barbarian and supersubtle Venetian be not too   350
hard for my wits, and all the tribe of hell, thou shalt
enjoy her. Therefore, make money. A pox of drowning thyself, it is clean out of the way. Seek thou rather
to be hanged in compassing° thy joy than to be
drowned and go without her.   355

RODERIGO   Wilt thou be fast to my hopes, if I depend
on the issue?

IAGO   Thou art sure of me. Go, make money. I have
told thee often, and I retell thee again and again, I
hate the Moor. My cause is hearted;° thine hath no   360
less reason. Let us be conjunctive° in our revenge
against him. If thou canst cuckold him, thou dost
thyself a pleasure, me a sport. There are many events
in the womb of time, which will be delivered.
Traverse, go, provide thy money! We will have more   365
of this tomorrow. Adieu.

RODERIGO   Where shall we meet i' th' morning?

IAGO   At my lodging.

RODERIGO   I'll be with thee betimes.

IAGO   Go to, farewell. Do you hear, Roderigo?   370

RODERIGO   I'll sell all my land.   *Exit.*

IAGO
Thus do I ever make my fool my purse;
For I mine own gained knowledge° should profane
If I would time expend with such snipe
But for my sport and profit. I hate the Moor,   375
And it is thought abroad that 'twixt my sheets
H' as done my office. I know not if 't be true,
But I, for mere suspicion in that kind,
Will do, as if for surety.° He holds me well;
The better shall my purpose work on him.   380
Cassio's a proper° man. Let me see now:
To get his place, and to plume up my will°
In double knavery. How? How? Let's see.
After some time, to abuse Othello's ears
That he is too familiar with his wife.   385
He hath a person and a smooth dispose°
To be suspected—framed° to make women false.
The Moor is of a free and open nature
That thinks men honest that but seem to be so;
And will as tenderly be led by th' nose   390
As asses are.
I have 't! It is engendered! Hell and night
Must bring this monstrous birth to the world's light.
[*Exit.*]

# ACT II

## Scene I. [*Cyprus.*]

*Enter* MONTANO *and two* GENTLEMEN [*one above*].°

MONTANO
What from the cape can you discern at sea?

FIRST GENTLEMAN
Nothing at all, it is a high-wrought flood.
I cannot 'twixt the heaven and the main
Descry a sail.

MONTANO
Methinks the wind hath spoke aloud at land;   5
A fuller blast ne'er shook our battlements.
If it hath ruffianed so upon the sea,
What ribs of oak, when mountains melt on them,
Can hold the mortise? What shall we hear of this?

SECOND GENTLEMAN
A segregation° of the Turkish fleet.   10
For do but stand upon the foaming shore,
The chidden billow seems to pelt the clouds;
The wind-shaked surge, with high and monstrous
main,°
Seems to cast water on the burning Bear
And quench the guards of th' ever-fixèd pole.°   15
I never did like molestation view
On the enchafèd flood.

MONTANO                 If that the Turkish fleet
Be not ensheltered and embayed, they are drowned;
It is impossible to bear it out.

*Enter a* [THIRD] GENTLEMAN.

THIRD GENTLEMAN
News, lads! Our wars are done.   20
The desperate tempest hath so banged the Turks
That their designment halts. A noble ship of Venice
Hath seen a grievous wrack and sufferance°
On most part of their fleet.

MONTANO
How? Is this true?

THIRD GENTLEMAN   The ship is here put in,   25
A Veronesa; Michael Cassio,
Lieutenant to the warlike Moor Othello,
Is come on shore; the Moor himself at sea,
And is in full commission here for Cyprus.

MONTANO
I am glad on 't. 'Tis a worthy governor.   30

THIRD GENTLEMAN
But this same Cassio, though he speak of comfort
Touching the Turkish loss, yet he looks sadly
And prays the Moor be safe, for they were parted
With foul and violent tempest.

MONTANO                 Pray heavens he be;
For I have served him, and the man commands   35
Like a full soldier. Let's to the seaside, ho!
As well to see the vessel that's come in

349 **sanctimony** sacred bond (of marriage)   350 **erring**
wandering   354 **compassing** encompassing, achieving   360
**hearted** deep-seated in the heart   361 **conjunctive** joined
373 **gained knowledge** i.e., practical, worldly wisdom   379
**surety** certainty   381 **proper** handsome   382 **plume . . .
will** many explanations have been offered for this crucial line,
which in Q1 reads "make up my will"; the general sense is
something like "to make more proud and gratify my ego"
386 **dispose** manner   387 **framed** designed

II.i.s.d. the Folio arrangement of this scene requires that the
First Gentleman stand above—on the upper stage—and act as
a lookout, reporting sights that cannot be seen by Montano
standing below on the main stage   10 **segregation** separation
13 **main** both "ocean" and "strength"   14-15 **Seems . . .
pole** the constellation Ursa Minor contains two stars that are
the "guards," or companions, of the "pole," or North Star
23 **sufferance** damage

As to throw out our eyes for brave Othello,
Even till we make the main and th' aerial blue
An indistinct regard.°

THIRD GENTLEMAN  Come, let's do so;                              40
For every minute is expectancy
Of more arrivancie.°

*Enter* CASSIO.

CASSIO
Thanks, you the valiant of the warlike isle,
That so approve° the Moor. O, let the heavens
Give him defense against the elements,                           45
For I have lost him on a dangerous sea.

MONTANO
Is he well shipped?

CASSIO
His bark is stoutly timbered, and his pilot
Of very expert and approved allowance;°
Therefore my hopes, not surfeited to death,°                     50
Stand in bold cure.°
                (*Within.*) "A sail, a sail, a sail!"

CASSIO
What noise?

FIRST GENTLEMAN
The town is empty; on the brow o' th' sea
Stand ranks of people, and they cry, "A sail!"

CASSIO
My hopes do shape him for the governor.                          55

[*A shot.*]

SECOND GENTLEMAN
They do discharge their shot of courtesy:
Our friends at least.

CASSIO                    I pray you, sir, go forth
And give us truth who 'tis that is arrived.

SECOND GENTLEMAN
I shall.                                                 *Exit.*

MONTANO
But, good lieutenant, is your general wived?                     60

CASSIO
Most fortunately. He hath achieved a maid
That paragons° description and wild fame;°
One that excels the quirks of blazoning pens,°
And in th' essential vesture of creation°
Does tire the ingener.°

*Enter* [SECOND] GENTLEMAN.

                How now? Who has put in?             65

SECOND GENTLEMAN
'Tis one Iago, ancient to the general.

CASSIO
H'as had most favorable and happy speed:
Tempests themselves, high seas, and howling winds,

The guttered° rocks and congregated° sands,
Traitors ensteeped° to enclog the guiltless keel,               70
As having sense° of beauty, do omit
Their mortal° natures, letting go safely by
The divine Desdemona.

MONTANO                    What is she?

CASSIO
She that I spake of, our great captain's captain,
Left in the conduct of the bold Iago,                           75
Whose footing° here anticipates our thoughts
A se'nnight's° speed. Great Jove, Othello guard,
And swell his sail with thine own pow'rful breath,
That he may bless this bay with his tall° ship,
Make love's quick pants in Desdemona's arms,                    80
Give renewed fire to our extincted spirits.

*Enter* DESDEMONA, IAGO, RODERIGO, *and* EMILIA.

O, behold! The riches of the ship is come on shore!
You men of Cyprus, let her have your knees.

[*Kneeling.*]

Hail to thee, lady! and the grace of heaven,
Before, behind thee, and on every hand,                         85
Enwheel thee round.

DESDEMONA            I thank you, valiant Cassio.
What tidings can you tell of my lord?

CASSIO
He is not yet arrived, nor know I aught
But that he's well and will be shortly here.

DESDEMONA
O but I fear. How lost you company?

CASSIO
The great contention of sea and skies                           90
Parted our fellowship.

(*Within.*) "A sail, a sail!" [*A shot.*]

                    But hark. A sail!

SECOND GENTLEMAN
They give this greeting to the citadel;
This likewise is a friend.

CASSIO                    See for the news.
                        [*Exit* GENTLEMAN.]
Good ancient, you are welcome. [*To* EMILIA.] Wel-
come, mistress.                                                 95
Let it not gall your patience, good Iago,
That I extend° my manners. 'Tis my breeding°
That gives me this bold show of courtesy.

[*Kisses* EMILIA.]

IAGO
Sir, would she give you so much of her lips
As of her tongue she oft bestows on me,                        100
You would have enough.

DESDEMONA            Alas, she has no speech.

IAGO
In faith, too much.
I find it still when I have leave to sleep.°

39–40 the main . . . regard the sea and sky becomes
indistinguishable  42 arrivancie arrivals  44 approve "honor"
or, perhaps, "are as warlike and valiant as your governor"
49 approved allowance known and tested  50 not . . .
death not so great as to be in danger  51 Stand . . . cure
are likely to be restored  62 paragons exceeds; wild fame
extravagant report  63 quirks . . . pens ingenuities of
praising pens  64 essential . . . creation essential human
nature as given by the Creator  65 tire the ingener a difficult
line, which probably means something like "outdo the human
ability to imagine and picture"

69 guttered jagged; congregated gathered  70 ensteeped
submerged  71 sense awareness  72 mortal deadly  76 footing landing  77 se'nnight's week's  79 tall brave  97 extend
stretch; breeding careful training in manners (Cassio is
considerably more the polished gentleman than Iago, and
aware of it)  103 still . . . sleep even when she allows me
to sleep she continues to scold

Marry, before your ladyship,° I grant,
She puts her tongue a little in her heart          105
And chides with thinking.

EMILIA                        You have little cause to say so.

IAGO
Come on, come on! You are pictures° out of
    door,
Bells in your parlors, wildcats in your kitchens,
Saints in your injuries,° devils being offended,
Players in your housewifery,° and housewives in your
    beds.                                        110

DESDEMONA
O, fie upon thee, slanderer!

IAGO
Nay, it is true, or else I am a Turk:
You rise to play, and go to bed to work.

EMILIA
You shall not write my praise.

IAGO                        No, let me not.

DESDEMONA
What wouldst write of me, if thou shouldst praise
    me?                                          115

IAGO
O gentle lady, do not put me to't,
For I am nothing if not critical.

DESDEMONA
Come on, assay. There's one gone to the harbor?

IAGO
Ay, madam.

DESDEMONA [Aside.]
I am not merry; but I do beguile              120
The thing I am by seeming otherwise.—
Come, how wouldst thou praise me?

IAGO
I am about it; but indeed my invention
Comes from my pate as bird lime° does from
    frieze°—
It plucks out brains and all. But my Muse labors,   125
And thus she is delivered:
If she be fair° and wise: fairness and wit,
The one's for use, the other useth it.

DESDEMONA
Well praised. How if she be black° and witty?

IAGO
If she be black, and thereto have a wit,          130
She'll find a white that shall her blackness fit.

DESDEMONA
Worse and worse!

EMILIA
How if fair and foolish?

IAGO
She never yet was foolish that was fair,
For even her folly helped her to an heir.          135

DESDEMONA  These are old fond° paradoxes to make
fools laugh i' th' alehouse. What miserable praise hast
thou for her that's foul and foolish?

IAGO
There's none so foul, and foolish thereunto,
But does foul pranks which fair and wise ones do.    140

DESDEMONA  O heavy ignorance. Thou praisest the
worst best. But what praise couldst thou bestow on a
deserving woman indeed—one that in the authority
of her merit did justly put on the vouch of very malice
itself?°                                          145

IAGO
She that was ever fair, and never proud;
Had tongue at will, and yet was never loud;
Never lacked gold, and yet went never gay;
Fled from her wish, and yet said "Now I may";
She that being angered, her revenge being nigh,    150
Bade her wrong stay, and her displeasure fly;
She that in wisdom never was so frail
To change the cod's head for the salmon's tail;°
She that could think, and nev'r disclose her mind;
See suitors following, and not look behind:        155
She was a wight° (if ever such wights were)—

DESDEMONA  To do what?

IAGO
To suckle fools and chronicle small beer.°

DESDEMONA  O most lame and impotent conclusion.
Do not learn of him, Emilia, though he be thy husband.  160
How say you, Cassio? Is he not a most profane and
liberal° counselor?

CASSIO  He speaks home,° madam. You may relish
him more in° the soldier than in the scholar. [Takes
Desdemona's hand.]

IAGO [Aside.]  He takes her by the palm. Ay, well said,   165
whisper! With as little a web as this will I ensnare as
great a fly as Cassio. Ay, smile upon her, do! I will
gyve° thee in thine own courtship.—You say true;
'tis so, indeed!—If such tricks as these strip you out of
your lieutenantry, it had been better you had not      170
kissed your three fingers so oft—which now again
you are most apt to play the sir° in. Very good! Well
kissed! An excellent curtsy!° 'Tis so, indeed. Yet
again your fingers to your lips? Would they were
clyster pipes° for your sake! [Trumpets within.] The   175
Moor! I know his trumpet.°

CASSIO  'Tis truly so.

DESDEMONA  Let's meet him and receive him.

CASSIO  Lo, where he comes.

*Enter* OTHELLO *and* ATTENDANTS.

OTHELLO
O my fair warrior!

DESDEMONA            My dear Othello.            180

---

104 **before your ladyship** in your presence  107 **pictures**
models (of virtue)  109 **in your injuries** when you injure
others  110 **housewifery** this word can mean "careful,
economical household management," and Iago would
then be accusing women of only pretending to be good
housekeepers, while in bed they are either (1) economical
of their favors, or more likely (2) serious and dedicated
workers  124 **bird lime** a sticky substance put on branches
to catch birds; **frieze** rough cloth  127 **fair** light-complexioned
129 **black** brunette

136 **fond** foolish  143–45 **one . . . itself** a woman so honest
and deserving that even malice would be forced to approve of
her  153 **To . . . tail** to exchange something valuable for
something useless  156 **wight** person  158 **chronicle small
beer** keep household accounts (the most trivial of occupations,
in Iago's opinion)  162 **liberal** licentious  163 **speaks home**
thrusts deeply with his speech  163–64 **relish . . . in** enjoy
him more as  168 **gyve** bind  172 **the sir** the fashionable
gentleman  173 **curtsy** courtesy, i.e., bow  175 **clyster pipes**
enema tubes  176 **his trumpet** great men had their own
distinctive calls

OTHELLO
It gives me wonder great as my content
To see you here before me. O my soul's joy!
If after every tempest come such calms,
May the winds blow till they have wakened death.
And let the laboring bark climb hills of seas          185
Olympus-high, and duck again as low
As hell's from heaven. If it were now to die,
'Twere now to be most happy; for I fear
My soul hath her content so absolute
That not another comfort like to this          190
Succeeds in unknown fate.
DESDEMONA                    The heavens forbid
But that our loves and comforts should increase
Even as our days do grow.
OTHELLO                    Amen to that, sweet powers!
I cannot speak enough of this content;
It stops me here [touches his heart]; it is too much of joy.          195
And this, and this, the greatest discords be

[They kiss.]

That e'er our hearts shall make!
IAGO [Aside.]                    O, you are well tuned now!
But I'll set down the pegs° that make this music,
As honest as I am.
OTHELLO                    Come, let us to the castle.
News, friends! Our wars are done; the Turks are
    drowned.          200
How does my old acquaintance of this isle?
Honey, you shall be well desired in Cyprus;
I have found great love amongst them. O my sweet,
I prattle out of fashion, and I dote
In mine own comforts. I prithee, good Iago,          205
Go to the bay and disembark my coffers.
Bring thou the master to the citadel;
He is a good one, and his worthiness
Does challenge° much respect. Come, Desdemona,
Once more well met at Cyprus.          210
        Exit OTHELLO and DESDEMONA [and all but
                    IAGO and RODERIGO].
IAGO [To an ATTENDANT.] Do thou meet me pre-
sently at the harbor. [To RODERIGO.] Come hither. If
thou be'st valiant (as they say base men being in love
have then a nobility in their natures more than is
native to them), list me. The lieutenant tonight          215
watches on the court of guard.° First, I must tell thee,
this: Desdemona is directly in love with him.
RODERIGO With him? Why, 'tis not possible.
IAGO Lay thy finger thus [puts his finger to his lips],
and let thy soul be instructed. Mark me with what          220
violence she first loved the Moor but for bragging
and telling her fantastical lies. To love him still for
prating? Let not thy discreet heart think it. Her eye
must be fed. And what delight shall she have to look
on the devil? When the blood is made dull with the          225
act of sport, there should be a game° to inflame it
and to give satiety a fresh appetite, loveliness in
favor,° sympathy in years,° manners, and beauties;

all which the Moor is defective in. Now for want of
these required conveniences,° her delicate tenderness          230
will find itself abused, begin to heave the gorge,°
disrelish and abhor the Moor. Very nature will
instruct her in it and compel her to some second
choice. Now, sir, this granted—as it is a most preg-
nant° and unforced position—who stands so eminent          235
in the degree of this fortune as Cassio does? A knave
very voluble; no further conscionable° than in putting
on the mere form of civil and humane° seeming for
the better compass of his salt° and most hidden loose°
affection. Why, none! Why, none! A slipper° and          240
subtle knave, a finder of occasion, that has an eye can
stamp and counterfeit advantages, though true advantage never present itself. A devilish knave. Besides,
the knave is handsome, young, and hath all those
requisites in him that folly and green minds look after.          245
A pestilent complete knave, and the woman hath
found him already.
RODERIGO I cannot believe that in her; she's full of
most blessed condition.
IAGO Blessed fig's-end! The wine she drinks is made          250
of grapes. If she had been blessed, she would never
have loved the Moor. Blessed pudding! Didst thou
not see her paddle with the palm of his hand? Didst
not mark that?
RODERIGO Yes, that I did; but that was but courtesy.          255
IAGO Lechery, by this hand! [Extends his index finger.]
An index° and obsure prologue to the history of lust
and foul thoughts. They met so near with their lips
that their breaths embraced together. Villainous
thoughts, Roderigo. When these mutualities so          260
marshal the way, hard at hand comes the master and
main exercise, th' incorporate° conclusion: Pish!
But, sir, be you ruled by me. I have brought you
from Venice. Watch you tonight; for the command,
I'll lay't upon you. Cassio knows you not. I'll not be          265
far from you. Do you find some occasion to anger
Cassio, either by speaking too loud, or tainting° his
discipline, or from what other course you please which
the time shall more favorably minister.
RODERIGO Well.          270
IAGO Sir, he's rash and very sudden in choler,° and
haply may strike at you. Provoke him that he may;
for even out of that will I cause these of Cyprus to
mutiny, whose qualification shall come into no true
taste° again but by the displanting of Cassio. So          275
shall you have a shorter journey to your desires by
the means I shall then have to prefer them; and the
impediment most profitably removed without the
which there were no expectation of our prosperity.
RODERIGO I will do this if you can bring it to any          280
opportunity.
IAGO I warrant thee. Meet me by and by at the citadel.
I must fetch his necessaries ashore. Farewell.
RODERIGO Adieu.                    Exit.

230 conveniences advantages  231 heave the gorge vomit
234–35 pregnant likely  237 no further conscionable
having no more conscience  238 humane polite  239 salt
lecherous; loose immoral  240 slipper slippery  257 index
pointer  262 incorporate carnal  267 tainting discrediting
271 choler anger  274–75 qualification . . . taste i.e.,
appeasement will not be brought about (wine was "qualified"
by adding water)

198 set . . . pegs loosen the strings (to produce discord)  209
challenge require, exact  216 court of guard guardhouse
226 game sport (with the added sense of "gamey," "rank")
228 favor countenance, appearance; sympathy in years
sameness of age

IAGO
That Cassio loves her, I do well believe 't;          285
That she loves him, 'tis apt and of great credit.
The Moor, howbeit that I endure him not,
Is of a constant, loving, noble nature,
And I dare think he'll prove to Desdemona
A most dear° husband. Now I do love her too;          290
Not out of absolute° lust, though peradventure°
I stand accountant for as great a sin,
But partly led to diet° my revenge,
For that I do suspect the lusty Moor
Hath leaped into my seat; the thought whereof          295
Doth, like a poisonous mineral, gnaw my inwards;
And nothing can or shall content my soul
Till I am evened with him, wife for wife.
Or failing so, yet that I put the Moor
At least into a jealousy so strong          300
That judgment cannot cure. Which thing to do,
If this poor trash of Venice, whom I trace°
For his quick hunting, stand the putting on,
I'll have our Michael Cassio on the hip,
Abuse him to the Moor in the right garb°          305
(For I fear Cassio with my nightcap too),
Make the Moor thank me, love me, and reward me
For making him egregiously an ass
And practicing upon° his peace and quiet,
Even to madness. 'Tis here, but yet confused:          310
Knavery's plain face is never seen till used.          *Exit.*

Scene II. [*A street.*]

*Enter Othello's* HERALD *with a proclamation.*

HERALD  It is Othello's pleasure, our noble and valiant
general, that upon certain tidings now arrived importing the mere perdition° of the Turkish fleet, every
man put himself into triumph. Some to dance, some
to make bonfires, each man to what sport and revels          5
his addition° leads him. For, besides these beneficial
news, it is the celebration of his nuptial. So much was
his pleasure should be proclaimed. All offices° are
open, and there is full liberty of feasting from this
present hour of five till the bell have told eleven.          10
Bless the isle of Cyprus and out noble general Othello!
          *Exit.*

Scene III. [*The citadel of Cyprus.*]

*Enter* OTHELLO, DESDEMONA, CASSIO, *and*
ATTENDANTS.

OTHELLO
Good Michael, look you to the guard tonight.
Let's teach ourselves that honorable stop,
Not to outsport discretion.

CASSIO
Iago hath direction what to do;
But notwithstanding, with my personal eye          5
Will I look to't.

OTHELLO          Iago is most honest.
Michael, good night. Tomorrow with your earliest
Let me have speech with you. [*To* DESDEMONA.]
     Come, my dear love,
The purchase made, the fruits are to ensue,
That profit's yet to come 'tween me and you.          10
Good night.
          *Exit* [OTHELLO, *with* DESDEMONA
          *and* ATTENDANTS].

*Enter* IAGO.

CASSIO  Welcome, Iago. We must to the watch.
IAGO  Not this hour, lieutenant; 'tis not yet ten o' th'
clock. Our general cast° us thus early for the love of
his Desdemona; who let us not therefore blame. He          15
hath not yet made wanton the night with her, and she
is sport for Jove.
CASSIO  She's a most exquisite lady.
IAGO  And, I'll warrant her, full of game.
CASSIO  Indeed, she's a most fresh and delicate          20
creature.
IAGO  What an eye she has! Methinks it sounds a
parley to provocation.
CASSIO  An inviting eye; and yet methinks right
modest.          25
IAGO  And when she speaks, is it not an alarum° to
love?
CASSIO  She is indeed perfection.
IAGO  Well, happiness to their sheets! Come, lieutenant, I have a stoup° of wine, and here without a          30
brace of Cyprus gallants that would fain have a
measure to the health of black Othello.
CASSIO  Not tonight, good Iago. I have very poor and
unhappy brains for drinking; I could well wish
courtesy would invent some other custom of enter-          35
tainment.
IAGO  O, they are our friends. But one cup! I'll drink
for you.
CASSIO  I have drunk but one cup tonight, and that
was craftily qualified° too; and behold what innovation          40
it makes here. I am unfortunate in the infirmity and
dare not task my weakness with any more.
IAGO  What, man! 'Tis a night of revels, the gallants
desire it.
CASSIO  Where are they?          45
IAGO  Here, at the door. I pray you call them in.
CASSIO  I'll do't, but it dislikes me.          *Exit.*
IAGO
If I can fasten but one cup upon him
With that which he hath drunk tonight already,
He'll be as full of quarrel and offense          50
As my young mistress' dog. Now, my sick fool
     Roderigo,
Whom love hath turned almost the wrong side out,
To Desdemona hath tonight caroused
Potations pottle-deep;° and he's to watch.

---

290 **dear** expensive   291 **out of absolute** absolutely out of;
**peradventure** perchance   293 **diet** feed   302 **trace** most
editors emend to "trash," meaning to hang weights on a dog
to slow his hunting; but "trace" clearly means something like
"put on the trace" or "set on the track"   305 **right garb**
"proper fashion"   309 **practicing upon** scheming to destroy
**II.ii.3 mere perdition** absolute destruction   6 **addition** rank
8 **offices** kitchens and storerooms of food

**II.iii.14 cast** dismissed   26 **alarum** the call to action, "general
quarters"   30 **stoup** two-quart tankard   40 **qualified** diluted
54 **pottle-deep** to the bottom of the cup

Three else° of Cyprus, noble swelling spirits,          55
That hold their honors in a wary distance,°
The very elements of this warlike isle,
Have I tonight flustered with flowing cups,
And they watch too. Now, 'mongst this flock of
    drunkards
Am I to put our Cassio in some action          60
That may offend the isle. But here they come.

*Enter* CASSIO, MONTANO, *and* GENTLEMEN.

If consequence do but approve my dream,
My boat sails freely, both with wind and stream.

CASSIO  'Fore God, they have given me a rouse°
already.          65

MONTANO  Good faith, a little one; not past a pint, as
I am a soldier.

IAGO  Some wine, ho! [*Sings.*]
        And let me the canakin clink, clink;
        And let me the canakin clink.          70
            A soldier's a man;
            O man's life's but a span,
        Why then, let a soldier drink.
Some wine, boys!

CASSIO  'Fore God, an excellent song!          75

IAGO  I learned it in England, where indeed they are
most potent in potting. Your Dane, your German, and
your swag-bellied° Hollander—Drink, ho!—are nothing to your English.

CASSIO  Is your Englishman so exquisite° in his          80
drinking?

IAGO  Why, he drinks you with facility your Dane
dead drunk; he sweats not to overthrow your Almain;
he gives your Hollander a vomit ere the next pottle
can be filled.          85

CASSIO  To the health of our general!

MONTANO  I am for it, lieutenant, and I'll do you
justice.

IAGO  O sweet England! [*Sings.*]
        King Stephen was and a worthy peer;          90
        His breeches cost him but a crown;
        He held them sixpence all too dear,
        With that he called the tailor lown.°
        He was a wight of high renown,
        And thou art but of low degree:          95
        'Tis pride that pulls the country down;
        And take thine auld cloak about thee.
Some wine, ho!

CASSIO  'Fore God, this is a more exquisite song than
the other.          100

IAGO  Will you hear't again?

CASSIO  No, for I hold him to be unworthy of his
place that does those things. Well, God's above all;
and there be souls must be saved, and there be souls
must not be saved.          105

IAGO  It's true, good lieutenant.

CASSIO  For mine own part—no offense to the general,
nor any man of quality—I hope to be saved.

IAGO  And so do I too, lieutenant.

CASSIO  Ay, but, by your leave, not before me. The          110
lieutenant is to be saved before the ancient. Let's have

no more of this; let's to our affairs.—God forgive us
our sins!—Gentlemen, let's look to our business. Do
not think, gentlemen, I am drunk. This is my ancient;
this is my right hand, and this is my left. I am not          115
drunk now. I can stand well enough, and I speak well
enough.

GENTLEMEN  Excellent well!

CASSIO  Why, very well then. You must not think
then that I am drunk.          *Exit.*          120

MONTANO
To th' platform, masters. Come, let's set the watch.

IAGO
You see this fellow that is gone before.
He's a soldier fit to stand by Caesar
And give direction; and do but see his vice.
'Tis to his virtue a just equinox,°          125
The one as long as th' other. 'Tis pity of him.
I fear the trust Othello puts him in,
On some odd time of his infirmity,
Will shake this island.

MONTANO          But is he often thus?

IAGO
'Tis evermore his prologue to his sleep;          130
He'll watch the horologe a double set°
If drink rock not his cradle.

MONTANO          It were well
The general were put in mind of it.
Perhaps he sees it not, or his good nature
Prizes the virtue that appears in Cassio          135
And looks not on his evils. Is not this true?

*Enter* RODERIGO.

IAGO [*Aside.*]
How now, Roderigo?
I pray you after the lieutenant, go!

          [*Exit* RODERIGO.]

MONTANO
And 'tis great pity that the noble Moor
Should hazard such a place as his own second          140
With one of an ingraft° infirmity.
It were an honest action to say so
To the Moor.

IAGO          Not I, for this fair island!
I do love Cassio well and would do much
To cure him of this evil.

("Help! Help!" *Within.*)

          But hark! What noise?          145

*Enter* CASSIO, *pursuing* RODERIGO.

CASSIO
Zounds, you rogue! You rascal!

MONTANO
What's the matter, lieutenant?

CASSIO
A knave teach me my duty? I'll beat the knave into a
    twiggen° bottle.

RODERIGO
Beat me?

---

**55 else** others  **56 hold . . . distance** are scrupulous in maintaining their honor  **64 rouse** drink  **78 swag-bellied** hanging
**80 exquisite** superb  **93 lown** lout

**125 just equinox** exact balance (of dark and light)  **131
watch . . . set** stay awake twice around the clock  **141
ingraft** ingrained  **148 twiggen** wicker-covered

CASSIO
Dost thou prate, rogue?                                        150

[Strikes him.]

MONTANO
Nay, good lieutenant! I pray you, sir, hold your hand.

[Stays him.]

CASSIO
Let me go, sir, or I'll knock you o'er the mazzard.°

MONTANO
Come, come, you're drunk!

CASSIO
Drunk?

[They fight.]

IAGO [Aside to RODERIGO.]
Away, I say! Go out and cry a mutiny!              155
                                        [Exit RODERIGO.]
Nay, good lieutenant. God's will, gentlemen!
Help, ho! Lieutenant. Sir. Montano.
Help, masters! Here's a goodly watch indeed!

[A bell rung.]

Who's that which rings the bell! Diablo, ho!
The town will rise. God's will, lieutenant,            160
You'll be ashamed forever.

Enter OTHELLO and ATTENDANTS.

OTHELLO                    What is the matter here?
MONTANO
Zounds, I bleed still. I am hurt to the death. He dies.

[He and CASSIO fight again.]

OTHELLO
Hold for your lives!

IAGO
Hold, ho! Lieutenant. Sir. Montano. Gentlemen!
Have you forgot all place of sense and duty?       165
Hold! The general speaks to you. Hold, for shame!

OTHELLO
Why, how now, ho? From whence ariseth this?
Are we turned Turks, and to ourselves do that
Which heaven hath forbid the Ottomites?°
For Christian shame put by this barbarous brawl!   170
He that stirs next to carve for his own rage
Holds his soul light;° he dies upon his motion.
Silence that dreadful bell! It frights the isle
From her propriety.° What is the matter, masters?
Honest Iago, that looks dead with grieving,          175
Speak. Who began this? On thy love, I charge thee.

IAGO
I do not know. Friends all, but now, even now,
In quarter° and in terms like bride and groom
Devesting them for bed; and then, but now—
As if some planet had unwitted men—                 180
Swords out, and tilting one at other's breasts
In opposition bloody. I cannot speak
Any beginning to this peevish odds,°

And would in action glorious I had lost
Those legs that brought me to a part of it!          185

OTHELLO
How comes it, Michael, you are thus forgot?

CASSIO
I pray you pardon me; I cannot speak.

OTHELLO
Worthy Montano, you were wont to be civil;
The gravity and stillness of your youth
The world hath noted, and your name is great       190
In mouths of wisest censure.° What's the matter
That you unlace° your reputation thus
And spend your rich opinion° for the name
Of a night-brawler? Give me answer to it.

MONTANO
Worthy Othello, I am hurt to danger.                 195
Your officer, Iago, can inform you,
While I spare speech, which something now offends°
   me,
Of all that I do know; nor know I aught
By me that's said or done amiss this night,
Unless self-charity be sometimes a vice,             200
And to defend ourselves it be a sin
When violence assails us.

OTHELLO                          Now, by heaven,
My blood begins my safer guides to rule,
And passion, having my best judgment collied,°
Assays to lead the way. If I once stir               205
Or do but lift this arm, the best of you
Shall sink in my rebuke. Give me to know
How this foul rout began, who set it on;
And he that is approved in this offense,
Though he had twinned with me, both at a birth,   210
Shall lose me. What? In a town of war
Yet wild, the people's hearts brimful of fear,
To manage° private and domestic quarrel?
In night, and on the court and guard of safety?
'Tis monstrous. Iago, who began't?                   215

MONTANO
If partially affined, or leagued in office,°
Thou dost deliver more or less than truth,
Thou art no soldier.

IAGO                       Touch me not so near.
I had rather have this tongue cut from my mouth
Than it should do offense to Michael Cassio.         220
Yet I persuade myself to speak the truth
Shall nothing wrong him. This it is, general.
Montano and myself being in speech,
There comes a fellow crying out for help,
And Cassio following him with determined sword   225
To execute upon him. Sir, this gentleman
Steps in to Cassio and entreats his pause.
Myself the crying fellow did pursue,
Lest by his clamor—as it so fell out—
The town might fall in fright. He, swift of foot,     230
Outran my purpose; and I returned then rather
For that I heard the clink and fall of swords,

---

152 **mazzard** head   169 **heaven . . . Ottomites** i.e., by
sending the storm which dispersed the Turks   172 **Holds . . .
light** values his soul lightly   174 **propriety** proper order
178 **In quarter** on duty   183 **odds** quarrel

191 **censure** judgment   192 **unlace** undo (the term refers
specifically to the dressing of a wild boar killed in the hunt)
193 **opinion** reputation   197 **offends** harms, hurts   204
**collied** darkened   213 **manage** conduct   216 **If . . . office**
if you are partial because you are related ("affined") or the
brother officer (of Cassio)

And Cassio high in oath; which till tonight
I ne'er might say before. When I came back—
For this was brief—I found them close together          235
At blow and thrust, even as again they were
When you yourself did part them.
More of this matter cannot I report;
But men are men; the best sometimes forget.
Though Cassio did some little wrong to him,              240
As men in rage strike those that wish them best,
Yet surely Cassio I believe received
From him that fled some strange indignity,
Which patience could not pass.°

OTHELLO                                I know, Iago,
Thy honesty and love doth mince° this matter            245
Making it light to Cassio. Cassio, I love thee;
But never more be officer of mine.

*Enter* DESDEMONA, *attended.*

Look if my gentle love be not raised up.
I'll make thee an example.

DESDEMONA                          What is the matter, dear?

OTHELLO
All's well, sweeting; come away to bed.                 250

[*To* MONTANO.]

Sir, for your hurts, myself will be your surgeon.
Lead him off.                        [MONTANO *led off.*]
Iago, look with care about the town
And silence those whom this vile brawl distracted.
Come, Desdemona; 'tis the soldiers' life                255
To have their balmy slumbers waked with strife.
                *Exit,* [*with all but* IAGO *and* CASSIO].

IAGO
What, are you hurt, lieutenant?

CASSIO
Ay, past all surgery.

IAGO
Marry, God forbid!

CASSIO  Reputation, reputation, reputation! O, I have   260
lost my reputation! I have lost the immortal part of
myself, and what remains is bestial. My reputation,
Iago, my reputation.

IAGO  As I am an honest man, I had thought you had
received some bodily wound. There is more sense°       265
in that than in reputation. Reputation is an idle and
most false imposition,° oft got without merit and
lost without deserving. You have lost no reputation
at all unless you repute yourself such a loser. What,
man, there are more ways to recover the general       270
again. You are but now cast in his mood°—a punishment more in policy° than in malice—even so as one
would beat his offenseless dog to affright an imperious
lion. Sue to him again, and he's yours.

CASSIO  I will rather sue to be despised than to deceive  275
so good a commander with so slight, so drunken, and
so indiscreet an officer. Drunk! And speak parrot!°
And squabble! Swagger! Swear! and discourse
fustian° with one's own shadow! O thou invisible

spirit of wine, if thou hast no name to be known by,   280
let us call thee devil!

IAGO  What was he that you followed with your
sword? What had he done to you?

CASSIO  I know not.

IAGO  Is't possible?                                    285

CASSIO  I remember a mass of things, but nothing
distinctly: a quarrel, but nothing wherefore. O God,
that men should put an enemy in their mouths to
steal away their brains! that we should with joy,
pleasance, revel, and applause transform ourselves into  290
beasts!

IAGO  Why, but you are now well enough. How came
you thus recovered?

CASSIO  It hath pleased the devil drunkenness to give
place to the devil wrath. One unperfectness shows me   295
another, to make me frankly despise myself.

IAGO  Come, you are too severe a moraler. As the time,
the place, and the condition of this country stands, I
could heartily wish this had not befall'n; but since it is
as it is, mend it for your own good.                    300

CASSIO  I will ask him for my place again: he shall tell
me I am a drunkard. Had I as many mouths as Hydra,
such an answer would stop them all. To be now a
sensible man, by and by a fool, and presently a beast!
O strange! Every inordinate cup is unblest, and the    305
ingredient is a devil.

IAGO  Come, come, good wine is a good familiar
creature if it be well used. Exclaim no more against it.
And, good lieutenant, I think you think I love you.

CASSIO  I have well approved it, sir. I drunk?          310

IAGO  You or any man living may be drunk at a time,
man. I tell you what you shall do. Our general's wife
is now the general. I may say so in this respect, for
that he hath devoted and given up himself to the
contemplation, mark, and devotement of her parts°      315
and graces. Confess yourself freely to her; importune
her help to put you in your place again. She is of so
free, so kind, so apt, so blessed a disposition she holds
it a vice in her goodness not to do more than she is
requested. This broken joint between you and her       320
husband entreat her to splinter;° and my fortunes
against any lay° worth naming, this crack of your love
shall grow stronger than it was before.

CASSIO  You advise me well.

IAGO  I protest, in the sincerity of love and honest     325
kindness.

CASSIO  I think it freely; and betimes in the morning I
will beseech the virtuous Desdemona to undertake for
me. I am desperate of my fortunes if they check° me.

IAGO  You are in the right. Good night, lieutenant; I    330
must to the watch.

CASSIO  Good night, honest Iago.          *Exit* CASSIO.

IAGO
And what's he then that says I play the villain,
When this advice is free° I give, and honest,
Probal to° thinking, and indeed the course              335
To win the Moor again? For 'tis most easy
Th' inclining° Desdemona to subdue

---

244 **pass** allow to pass   245 **mince** cut up (i.e., tell only part of)
265 **sense** physical feeling   267 **imposition** external thing
271 **cast . . . mood** dismissed because of his anger   272 **in
policy** politically necessary   277 **speak parrot** gabble
without sense   278–79 **discourse fustian** speak nonsense
(fustian was a coarse cotton cloth used for stuffing)

315 **devotement . . . parts** devotion to her qualities
321 **splinter** splint   322 **lay** wager   329 **check** repulse   334
**free** generous and open   335 **Probal to** provable by   337
**inclining** inclined (to be helpful)

In any honest suit; she's framed as fruitful°
As the free elements.° And then for her
To win the Moor—were't to renounce his baptism, 340
All seals and symbols of redeemèd sin—
His soul is so enfettered to her love
That she may make, unmake, do what she list,
Even as her appetite° shall play the god
With his weak function.° How am I then a villain 345
To counsel Cassio to this parallel course,
Directly to his good? Divinity of hell!
When devils will the blackest sins put on,°
They do suggest at first with heavenly shows,°
As I do now. For whiles this honest fool 350
Plies Desdemona to repair his fortune,
And she for him pleads strongly to the Moor,
I'll pour this pestilence into his ear:
That she repeals him° for her body's lust;
And by how much she strives to do him good, 355
She shall undo her credit with the Moor.
So will I turn her virtue into pitch,
And out of her own goodness make the net
That shall enmesh them all. How now, Roderigo?

*Enter* RODERIGO.

RODERIGO  I do follow here in the chase, not like a 360
hound that hunts, but one that fills up the cry.° My
money is almost spent; I have been tonight exceedingly
well cudgeled; and I think the issue will be, I shall have
so much experience for my pains; and so, with no
money at all, and a little more wit, return again to 365
Venice.
IAGO
How poor are they that have not patience!
What wound did ever heal but by degrees?
Thou know'st we work by wit, and not by witchcraft;
And wit depends on dilatory time. 370
Does't not go well? Cassio hath beaten thee,
And thou by that small hurt hath cashiered Cassio.
Though other things grow fair against the sun,
Yet fruits that blossom first will first be ripe.
Content thyself awhile. By the mass, 'tis morning! 375
Pleasure and action make the hours seem short.
Retire thee; go where thou art billeted.
Away, I say! Thou shalt know more hereafter.
Nay, get thee gone!　　　　　　*Exit* RODERIGO.
　　　　　　Two things are to be done:
My wife must move° for Cassio to her mistress; 380
I'll set her on;
Myself awhile° to draw the Moor apart
And bring him jump° when he may Cassio find
Soliciting his wife. Ay, that's the way!
Dull not device by coldness and delay.　　*Exit.* 385

---

# ACT III

## Scene I. [*A street.*]

*Enter* CASSIO [*and*] MUSICIANS.

CASSIO
Masters, play here. I will content your pains.°
Something that's brief; and bid "Good morrow,
　general."
[*They play.*]
[*Enter* CLOWN.°]
CLOWN  Why, masters, have your instruments been in
Naples° that they speak i' th' nose thus?
MUSICIAN  How, sir, how? 5
CLOWN  Are these, I pray you, wind instruments?
MUSICIAN  Ay, marry, are they, sir.
CLOWN  O, thereby hangs a tale.
MUSICIAN  Whereby hangs a tale, sir?
CLOWN  Marry, sir, by many a wind instrument that I 10
know. But, masters, here's money for you; and the
general so likes your music that he desires you, for
love's sake, to make no more noise with it.
MUSICIAN  Well, sir, we will not.
CLOWN  If you have any music that may not be heard, 15
to't again. But, as they say, to hear music the general
does not greatly care.
MUSICIAN  We have none such, sir.
CLOWN  Then put up your pipes in your bag, for I'll
away. Go, vanish into air, away!　*Exit* MUSICIANS. 20
CASSIO  Dost thou hear me, mine honest friend?
CLOWN  No. I hear not your honest friend. I hear you.
CASSIO  Prithee keep up thy quillets.° There's a poor
piece of gold for thee. If the gentlewoman that attends
the general's wife be stirring, tell her there's one 25
Cassio entreats her a little favor of speech. Wilt thou
do this?
CLOWN  She is stirring, sir. If she will stir hither, I shall
seem to notify unto her.°　　　　　*Exit* CLOWN.

*Enter* IAGO.

CASSIO
In happy time, Iago.
IAGO　　　　　　　　You have not been abed then? 30
CASSIO
Why no, the day had broke before we parted.
I have made bold, Iago, to send in to your wife;
My suit to her is that she will to virtuous Desdemona
Procure me some access.
IAGO　　　　　　　　I'll send her to you presently,
And I'll devise a mean to draw the Moor 35
Out of the way, that your converse and business
May be more free.
CASSIO
I humbly thank you for't.　　　　*Exit* [IAGO].
　　　　　　I never knew
A Florentine° more kind and honest.

---

338 **framed as fruitful** made as generous　339 **elements** i.e., basic nature　344 **appetite** liking　345 **function** thought　348 **put on** advance, further　349 **shows** appearances　354 **repeals him** asks for (Cassio's reinstatement)　361 **fills . . . cry** makes up one of the hunting pack, adding to the noise but not actually tracking　380 **move** petition　382 **awhile** at the same time　383 **jump** at the precise moment and place

**III.i.1 content your pains** reward your efforts　2 s.d. **Clown** fool　4 **Naples** this may refer either to the Neapolitan nasal tone, or to syphilis—rife in Naples—which breaks down the nose　23 **quillets** puns　29 **seem . . . her** the Clown is mocking Cassio's overly elegant manner of speaking　39 **Florentine** i.e., Iago is as kind as if he were from Cassio's home town, Florence

*Enter* EMILIA.

EMILIA
Good morrow, good lieutenant. I am sorry                    40
For your displeasure;° but all will sure be well.
The general and his wife are talking of it,
And she speaks for you stoutly. The Moor replies
That he you hurt is of great fame in Cyprus
And great affinity,° and that in wholesome wisdom    45
He might not but refuse you. But he protests he loves
    you,
And needs no other suitor but his likings
To bring you in again.
CASSIO                    Yet I beseech you,
If you think fit, or that it may be done,
Give me advantage of some brief discourse              50
With Desdemona alone.
EMILIA                    Pray you come in.
I will bestow you where you shall have time
To speak your bosom° freely.
CASSIO                    I am much bound to you.
                                                         [*Exeunt.*]


Scene II. [*The citadel.*]

*Enter* OTHELLO, IAGO, *and* GENTLEMEN.

OTHELLO
These letters give, Iago, to the pilot
And by him do my duties to the Senate.
That done, I will be walking on the works;
Repair° there to me.
IAGO                    Well, my good lord, I'll do't.
OTHELLO
This fortification, gentlemen, shall we see't?          5
GENTLEMEN
We'll wait upon your lordship.              *Exeunt.*


Scene III. [*The citadel.*]

*Enter* DESDEMONA, CASSIO, *and* EMILIA.

DESDEMONA
Be thou assured, good Cassio, I will do
All my abilities in thy behalf.
EMILIA
Good madam, do. I warrant it grieves my husband
As if the cause were his.
DESDEMONA
O, that's an honest fellow. Do not doubt, Cassio,      5
But I will have my lord and you again
As friendly as you were.
CASSIO                    Bounteous madam,
Whatever shall become of Michael Cassio,
He's never anything but your true servant.
DESDEMONA
I know't; I thank you. You do love my lord.             10
You have known him long, and be you well assured

He shall in strangeness stand no farther off
Than in a politic distance.°
CASSIO                    Ay, but, lady,
That policy may either last so long,
Or feed upon such nice° and waterish diet,             15
Or breed itself so out of circumstances,°
That, I being absent, and my place supplied,°
My general will forget my love and service.
DESDEMONA
Do not doubt° that; before Emilia here
I give thee warrant of thy place. Assure thee,         20
If I do vow a friendship, I'll perform it
To the last article. My lord shall never rest;
I'll watch him tame° and talk him out of patience;
His bed shall seem a school, his board a shrift;°
I'll intermingle everything he does                     25
With Cassio's suit. Therefore be merry, Cassio,
For thy solicitor shall rather die
Than give thy cause away.

*Enter* OTHELLO *and* IAGO [*at a distance*].

EMILIA
Madam, here comes my lord.
CASSIO
Madam, I'll take my leave.                               30
DESDEMONA
Why, stay, and hear me speak.
CASSIO
Madam, not now. I am very ill at ease,
Unfit for mine own purposes.
DESDEMONA
Well, do your discretion.              *Exit* CASSIO.
IAGO
Ha! I like not that.
OTHELLO              What dost thou say?                 35
IAGO
Nothing, my lord; or if—I know not what.
OTHELLO
Was not that Cassio parted from my wife?
IAGO
Cassio, my lord? No, sure, I cannot think it
That he would steal away so guilty-like,
Seeing you coming.
OTHELLO              I do believe 'twas he.              40
DESDEMONA [*Coming to them.*]
How now, my lord?
I have been talking with a suitor here,
A man that languishes in your displeasure.
OTHELLO
Who is't you mean?
DESDEMONA
Why, your lieutenant, Cassio. Good my lord,            45
If I have any grace or power to move you,
His present° reconciliation take.
For if he be not one that truly loves you,
That errs in ignorance, and not in cunning,

III.iii.12–13 He . . . distance he shall act no more distant to
you than is necessary for political reasons  **15 nice** trivial  **16
Or . . . circumstances** or grow so on the basis of accidental
happenings and political needs  **17 supplied** filled  **19 doubt**
imagine  **23 watch him tame** animals were tamed by being
kept awake  **24 board a shrift** table (seem) a confessional
**47 present** immediate

**41 displeasure** discomforting  **45 affinity** family  **53 bosom**
inmost thoughts
**III.ii.4 Repair** go

I have no judgment in an honest face.                     50
I prithee call him back.

OTHELLO                    Went he hence now?

DESDEMONA
I' sooth so humbled
That he hath left part of his grief with me
To suffer with him. Good love, call him back.

OTHELLO
Not now, sweet Desdemon; some other time.         55

DESDEMONA
But shall't be shortly?

OTHELLO                    The sooner, sweet, for you.

DESDEMONA
Shall't be tonight at supper?

OTHELLO                    No, not tonight.

DESDEMONA
Tomorrow dinner then?

OTHELLO                    I shall not dine at home;
I meet the captains at the citadel.

DESDEMONA
Why then, tomorrow night, on Tuesday morn,        60
On Tuesday noon, or night, on Wednesday morn.
I prithee name the time, but let it not
Exceed three days. In faith, he's penitent;
And yet his trespass, in our common reason
(Save that, they say, the wards must make example  65
Out of her best), is not almost a fault
T' incur a private check.° When shall he come?
Tell me, Othello. I wonder in my soul
What you would ask me that I should deny
Or stand so mamm'ring° on. What? Michael Cassio,  70
That came awooing with you, and so many a time,
When I have spoke of you dispraisingly,
Hath ta'en your part—to have so much to do
To bring him in? By'r Lady, I could do much—

OTHELLO
Prithee no more. Let him come when he will!       75
I will deny thee nothing.

DESDEMONA                    Why, this is not a boon;
'Tis as I should entreat you wear your gloves,
Or feed on nourishing dishes, or keep you warm,
Or sue to you to do a peculiar profit°
To your own person. Nay, when I have a suit        80
Wherein I mean to touch your love indeed,
It shall be full of poise° and difficult weight,
And fearful to be granted.

OTHELLO                    I will deny thee nothing!
Whereon I do beseech thee grant me this,
To leave me but a little to myself.                85

DESDEMONA
Shall I deny you? No. Farewell, my lord.

OTHELLO
Farewell, my Desdemona: I'll come to thee straight.°

DESDEMONA
Emilia, come. Be as your fancies teach you;
Whate'er you be, I am obedient. *Exit, [with* EMILIA].

OTHELLO
Excellent wretch! Perdition catch my soul         90

But I do love thee! And when I love thee not,
Chaos is come again.

IAGO
My noble lord—

OTHELLO                    What dost thou say, Iago?

IAGO
Did Michael Cassio, when you wooed my lady,
Know of your love?                                95

OTHELLO
He did, from first to last. Why dost thou ask?

IAGO
But for a satisfaction of my thought,
No further harm.

OTHELLO                    Why of thy thought, Iago?

IAGO
I did not think he had been acquainted with her.

OTHELLO
O, yes, and went between us° very oft.            100

IAGO
Indeed?

OTHELLO
Indeed? Ay, indeed! Discern'st thou aught in that?
Is he not honest?

IAGO                    Honest, my lord?

OTHELLO                                    Honest? Ay, honest.

IAGO
My lord, for aught I know.

OTHELLO
What dost thou think?

IAGO                    Think, my lord?

OTHELLO                                    Think, my lord?   105
By heaven, thou echoest me,
As if there were some monster in thy thought
Too hideous to be shown. Thou dost mean something.
I heard thee say even now, thou lik'st not that,
When Cassio left my wife. What didst not like?    110
And when I told thee he was of my counsel°
Of my whole course of wooing, thou cried'st, "Indeed?"
And didst contract and purse thy brow together,
As if thou then hadst shut up in thy brain
Some horrible conceit.° If thou dost love me,      115
Show me thy thought.

IAGO
My lord, you know I love you.

OTHELLO                                    I think thou dost;
And, for I know thou'rt full of love and honesty
And weigh'st thy words before thou giv'st them
  breath,
Therefore these stops° of thine fright me the more;  120
For such things in a false disloyal knave
Are tricks of custom;° but in a man that's just
They're close dilations,° working from the heart
That passion cannot rule.

IAGO                    For Michael Cassio,
I dare be sworn, I think that he is honest.        125

OTHELLO
I think so too.

IAGO                    Men should be what they seem;

---

**66–67 is . . . check** is almost not serious enough for a private
rebuke (let alone a public disgrace)   **70 mamm'ring** hesitating
**79 peculiar profit** particularly personal good   **82 poise**
weight   **87 straight** at once

**100 between us** i.e., as messenger   **111 of my counsel** in my
confidence   **115 conceit** thought   **120 stops** interruptions
**122 of custom** customary   **123 close dilations** expressions
of hidden thoughts

Or those that be not, would they might seem none!

OTHELLO
Certain, men should be what they seem.

IAGO
Why then, I think Cassio's an honest man.

OTHELLO
Nay, yet there's more in this?          130
I prithee speak to me as to thy thinkings,
As thou dost ruminate, and give thy worst of thoughts
The worst of words.

IAGO                    Good my lord, pardon me:
Though I am bound to every act of duty,
I am not bound to that all slaves are free to.          135
Utter my thoughts? Why, say they are vile and false,
As where's that palace whereinto foul things
Sometimes intrude not? Who has that breast so pure
But some uncleanly apprehensions
Keep leets and law days,° and in sessions sit          140
With meditations lawful?

OTHELLO
Thou dost conspire against thy friend, Iago,
If thou but think'st him wronged, and mak'st his ear
A stranger to thy thoughts.

IAGO                    I do beseech you—
Though I perchance am vicious in my guess          145
(As I confess it is my nature's plague
To spy into abuses, and of my jealousy
Shape faults that are not), that your wisdom
From one that so imperfectly conceits
Would take no notice, nor build yourself a trouble          150
Out of his scattering and unsure observance.
It were not for your quiet nor your good,
Nor for my manhood, honesty, and wisdom,
To let you know my thoughts.

OTHELLO                    What dost thou mean?

IAGO
Good name in man and woman, dear my lord,          155
Is the immediate jewel of their souls.
Who steals my purse steals trash; 'tis something, nothing;
'Twas mine, 'tis his, and has been slave to thousands;
But he that filches from me my good name
Robs me of that which not enriches him          160
And makes me poor indeed.

OTHELLO
By heaven, I'll know thy thoughts!

IAGO
You cannot, if my heart were in your hand;
Nor shall not whilst 'tis in my custody.

OTHELLO
Ha!

IAGO   O, beware, my lord, of jealousy!          165
It is the green-eyed monster, which doth mock
The meat it feeds on. That cuckold lives in bliss
Who, certain of his fate, loves not his wronger;
But O, what damnèd minutes tells° he o'er
Who dotes, yet doubts—suspects, yet fondly° loves!          170

OTHELLO
O misery.

IAGO
Poor and content is rich, and rich enough;

But riches fineless° is as poor as winter
To him that ever fears he shall be poor.
Good God the souls of all my tribe defend          175
From jealousy!

OTHELLO                    Why? Why is this?
Think'st thou I'd make a life of jealousy,
To follow still° the changes of the moon
With fresh suspicions? No! To be once in doubt
Is to be resolved. Exchange me for a goat          180
When I shall turn the business of my soul
To such exsufflicate and blown° surmises,
Matching thy inference. 'Tis not to make me jealous
To say my wife is fair, feeds well, loves company,
Is free of speech, sings, plays, and dances;          185
Where virtue is, these are more virtuous.
Nor from mine own weak merits will I draw
The smallest fear or doubt of her revolt,
For she had eyes, and chose me. No, Iago;
I'll see before I doubt; when I doubt, prove;          190
And on the proof there is no more but this:
Away at once with love or jealousy!

IAGO
I am glad of this; for now I shall have reason
To show the love and duty that I bear you
With franker spirit. Therefore, as I am bound,          195
Receive it from me. I speak not yet of proof.
Look to your wife; observe her well with Cassio;
Wear your eyes thus: not jealous nor secure.
I would not have your free and noble nature
Out of self-bounty° be abused. Look to't.          200
I know our country disposition well:
In Venice they do let heaven see the pranks
They dare not show their husbands; their best conscience
Is not to leave't undone, but kept unknown.°

OTHELLO
Dost thou say so?          205

IAGO
She did deceive her father, marrying you;
And when she seemed to shake and fear your looks,
She loved them most.

OTHELLO                    And so she did.

IAGO                    Why, go to then!
She that so young could give out such a seeming
To seel° her father's eyes up close as oak°—          210
He thought 'twas witchcraft. But I am much to blame.
I humbly do beseech you of your pardon
For too much loving you.

OTHELLO                    I am bound to thee forever.

IAGO
I see this hath a little dashed your spirits.

OTHELLO
Not a jot, not a jot.

IAGO                    Trust me, I fear it has.          215
I hope you will consider what is spoke
Comes from my love. But I do see y' are moved.
I am to pray you not to strain° my speech

140 leets . . . days meetings of local courts  169 tells counts
170 fondly foolishly

173 fineless infinite  178 To follow still to change always (as the phases of the moon)  182 exsufflicate and blown inflated and flyblown  200 self-bounty innate kindness (which attributes his own motives to others)  203–04 their . . . unknown their morality does not forbid adultery, but it does forbid being found out  210 seel hoodwink; oak a close-grained wood  218 strain enlarge the meaning of

To grosser issues, nor to larger reach°
Than to suspicion.                                              220

OTHELLO
I will not.

IAGO                Should you do so, my lord,
My speech should fall into such vile success
Which my thoughts aimed not. Cassio's my worthy
    friend—
My lord, I see y' are moved.

OTHELLO                          No, not much moved.
I do not think but Desdemona's honest.              225

IAGO
Long live she so. And long live you to think so.

OTHELLO
And yet, how nature erring from itself—

IAGO
Ay, there's the point, as (to be bold with you)
Not to affect many proposèd matches
Of her own clime, complexion, and degree,°      230
Whereto we see in all things nature tends°—
Foh! one may smell in such a will most rank,
Foul disproportions, thoughts unnatural.
But, pardon me, I do not in position°
Distinctly° speak of her; though I may fear      235
Her will, recoiling to her better judgment,
May fall to match° you with her country forms,°
And happily° repent.

OTHELLO                        Farewell, farewell!
If more thou dost perceive, let me know more.
Set on thy wife to observe. Leave me, Iago.      240

IAGO
My lord, I take my leave.

[Going.]

OTHELLO
Why did I marry? This honest creature doubtless
Sees and knows more, much more, than he unfolds.

IAGO [Returns.]
My lord, I would I might entreat your honor
To scan this thing no farther. Leave it to time.  245
Although 'tis fit that Cassio have his place,
For sure he fills it up with great ability,
Yet, if you please to hold him off awhile,
You shall by that perceive him and his means.
Note if your lady strain his entertainment°      250
With any strong or vehement importunity;
Much will be seen in that. In the meantime
Let me be thought too busy in my fears
(As worthy cause I have to fear I am)
And hold her free, I do beseech your honor.       255

OTHELLO
Fear not my government.°

IAGO                          I once more take my leave.
                                                            Exit.

OTHELLO
This fellow's of exceeding honesty,

219 reach meaning  230 degree social station  231 in . . .
tends all things in nature seek out their own kind  234
position general argument  235 Distinctly specifically  237
fall to match happen to compare; country forms i.e.,
the familiar appearances of her countrymen  238 happily by
chance  250 strain his entertainment urge strongly that he
be reinstated  256 government self-control

And knows all qualities,° with a learnèd spirit
Of human dealings. If I do prove her haggard,°
Though that her jesses° were my dear heartstrings,   260
I'd whistle her off and let her down the wind°
To prey at fortune. Haply for° I am black
And have not those soft parts° of conversation
That chamberers° have, or for I am declined
Into the vale of years—yet that's not much—      265
She's gone. I am abused, and my relief
Must be to loathe her. O curse of marriage,
That we can call these delicate creatures ours,
And not their appetites! I had rather be a toad
And live upon the vapor of a dungeon               270
Than keep a corner in the thing I love
For others' uses. Yet 'tis the plague to great ones;
Prerogatived are they less than the base.
'Tis destiny unshunnable, like death.
Even then this forkèd° plague is fated to us      275
When we do quicken.° Look where she comes.

Enter DESDEMONA and EMILIA.

If she be false, heaven mocked itself!
I'll not believe't.

DESDEMONA          How now, my dear Othello?
Your dinner, and the generous islanders
By you invited, do attend° your presence.         280

OTHELLO
I am to blame.

DESDEMONA    Why do you speak so faintly?
Are you not well?

OTHELLO
I have a pain upon my forehead, here.°

DESDEMONA
Why, that's with watching; 'twill away again.
Let me but bind it hard, within this hour         285
It will be well.

OTHELLO          Your napkin° is too little;

[He pushes the handkerchief away, and it falls.]

Let it° alone. Come, I'll go in with you.

DESDEMONA
I am very sorry that you are not well.
                              Exit, [with OTHELLO].

EMILIA
I am glad I have found this napkin;
This was her first remembrance from the Moor.     290
My wayward husband hath a hundred times
Wooed me to steal it; but she so loves the token
(For her conjured her she should ever keep it)
That she reserves it evermore about her
To kiss and talk to. I'll have the work ta'en out°  295
And give't Iago. What he will do with it,

258 qualities natures, types of people  259 haggard a
partly trained hawk which has gone wild again  260
jesses straps which held the hawk's legs to the trainer's
wrist  261 I'd . . . wind I would release her (like an
untamable hawk) and let her fly free  262 Haply for it may
be because  263 soft parts gentle qualities and manners  264
chamberers courtiers—or, perhaps, accomplished seducers
275 forkèd horned (the sign of the cuckold was horns)  276
do quicken are born  280 attend wait  283 here he points
to his imaginary horns  286 napkin elaborately worked
handkerchief  287 it it makes a considerable difference in the
interpretation of later events whether this "it" refers to Othello's
forehead or to the handkerchief; nothing in the text makes the
reference clear  295 work ta'en out needlework copied

Heaven knows, not I; I nothing° but to please his
fantasy.°

*Enter* IAGO.

IAGO
How now? What do you here alone?

EMILIA
Do not you chide; I have a thing for you.

IAGO
You have a thing for me? It is a common thing—          300

EMILIA   Ha?

IAGO
To have a foolish wife.

EMILIA
O, is that all? What will you give me now
For that same handkerchief?

IAGO                              What handkerchief?

EMILIA
What handkerchief!                                        305
Why, that the Moor first gave to Desdemona,
That which so often you did bid me steal.

IAGO
Hast stol'n it from her?

EMILIA
No, but she let it drop by negligence,
And to th' advantage,° I, being here, took't up.          310
Look, here 'tis.

IAGO              A good wench. Give it me.

EMILIA
What will you do with't, that you have been so earnest
To have me filch it?

IAGO                    Why, what is that to you?

*[Takes it.]*

EMILIA
If it be not for some purpose of import,°
Give't me again. Poor lady, she'll run mad               315
When she shall lack° it.

IAGO                      Be not acknown on't.°
I have use for it. Go, leave me.          *Exit* EMILIA.
I will in Cassio's lodging lose this napkin
And let him find it. Trifles light as air
Are to the jealous confirmations strong                   320
As proofs of Holy Writ. This may do something.
The Moor already changes with my poison:
Dangerous conceits are in their natures poisons,
Which at the first are scarce found to distaste,°
But, with a little,° act upon the blood,                  325
Burn like the mines of sulfur. I did say so.

*Enter* OTHELLO.

Look where he comes! Not poppy nor mandragora,°
Nor all the drowsy syrups of the world,
Shall ever medicine thee to that sweet sleep
Which thou owedst° yesterday.

OTHELLO                      Ha! ha! False to me?          330

IAGO
Why, how now, general? No more of that.

OTHELLO
Avaunt! be gone! Thou hast set me on the rack.
I swear 'tis better to be much abused
Than but to know't a little.

IAGO                        How now, my lord?

OTHELLO
What sense had I of her stol'n hours of lust?             335
I saw't not, thought it not, it harmed not me;
I slept the next night well, fed well, was free and merry;
I found not Cassio's kisses on her lips.
He that is robbed, not wanting° what is stol'n,
Let him not know't, and he's not robbed at all.           340

IAGO
I am sorry to hear this.

OTHELLO
I had been happy if the general camp,
Pioners° and all, had tasted her sweet body,
So I had nothing known. O now, forever
Farewell the tranquil mind! Farewell content!             345
Farewell the plumed troops, and the big wars
That makes ambition virtue! O, farewell!
Farewell the neighing steed and the shrill trump,
The spirit-stirring drum, th' ear-piercing fife,
The royal banner; and all quality,                        350
Pride, pomp, and circumstance° of glorious war!
And O you mortal engines° whose rude throats
Th' immortal Jove's dread clamors° counterfeit,
Farewell! Othello's occupation's gone!

IAGO
Is't possible, my lord?                                   355

OTHELLO
Villain, be sure thou prove my love a whore!
Be sure of it; give me the ocular proof;
Or, by the worth of mine eternal soul,
Thou hadst been better have been born a dog
Than answer my waked wrath!

IAGO                        Is't come to this?            360

OTHELLO
Make me to see't; or at the least so prove it
That the probation° bear no hinge nor loop
To hang a doubt on—or woe upon thy life!

IAGO
My noble lord—

OTHELLO
If thou dost slander her and torture me,                  365
Never pray more; abandon all remorse;
On horror's head horrors accumulate;
Do deeds to make heaven weep, all earth amazed;
For nothing canst thou to damnation add
Greater than that.

IAGO                O grace! O heaven forgive me!         370
Are you a man? Have you a soul or sense?
God b' wi' you! Take mine office. O wretched fool,
That lov'st to make thine honesty a vice!
O monstrous world! Take note, take note, O world,
To be direct and honest is not safe.                      375

297 **I nothing** I wish nothing; **fantasy** fancy, whim  310
**to th' advantage** being lucky  314 **import** importance
316 **lack** miss; **Be . . . on't** Forget your ever saw it
324 **are . . . distaste** scarcely can be tasted  325 **with a
little** in a short time  327 **poppy nor mandragora** soporifics
330 **owedst** possessed

339 **wanting** missing  343 **Pioners** the basest manual laborers
in the army, who dug trenches and mines  351 **circumstance**
pageantry  352 **mortal engines** lethal weapons, i.e., cannon
353 **clamors** thunder  362 **probation** proof

I thank you for this profit, and from hence
I'll love no friend, sith° love breeds such offense.

OTHELLO
Nay, stay. Thou shouldst be honest.

IAGO
I should be wise; for honesty's a fool
And loses that it works for.

OTHELLO                           By the world,    380
I think my wife be honest, and think she is not;
I think that thou art just, and think thou art not.
I'll have some proof. My name, that was as fresh
As Dian's° visage, is now begrimed and black
As mine own face. If there be cords, or knives,    385
Poison, or fire, or suffocating streams,
I'll not endure it. Would I were satisfied!

IAGO
I see you are eaten up with passion.
I do repent me that I put it to you.
You would be satisfied?

OTHELLO                    Would? Nay, and I will.    390

IAGO
And may; but how? How satisfied, my lord?
Would you, the supervisor,° grossly gape on?
Behold her topped?

OTHELLO              Death and damnation! O!

IAGO
It were a tedious° difficulty, I think,
To bring them to that prospect.° Damn them then,    395
If ever mortal eyes do see them bolster°
More than their own! What then? How then?
What shall I say? Where's satisfaction?
It is impossible you should see this,
Were they as prime° as goats, as hot as monkeys,    400
As salt° as wolves in pride,° and fools as gross
As ignorance made drunk. But yet, I say,
If imputation and strong circumstances
Which lead directly to the door of truth
Will give you satisfaction, you might have't.    405

OTHELLO
Give me a living reason she's disloyal.

IAGO
I do not like the office.°
But sith I am entered in this cause so far,
Pricked° to't by foolish honesty and love,
I will go on. I lay with Cassio lately,    410
And being troubled with a raging tooth,
I could not sleep.
There are a kind of men so loose of soul
That in their sleeps will mutter their affairs.
One of this kind is Cassio.    415
In sleep I heard him say, "Sweet Desdemona,
Let us be wary, let us hide our loves!"
And then, sir, would he gripe° and wring my hand,
Cry "O sweet creature!" Then kiss me hard,
As if he plucked up kisses by the roots    420
That grew upon my lips; laid his leg o'er my thigh,
And sigh, and kiss, and then cry, "Cursèd fate
That gave thee to the Moor!"

OTHELLO
O monstrous! monstrous!

IAGO                        Nay, this was but his dream.

OTHELLO
But this denoted a foregone conclusion,°    425
'Tis a shrewd doubt,° though it be but a dream.

IAGO
And this may help to thicken other proofs
That do demonstrate° thinly.

OTHELLO                    I'll tear her all to pieces!

IAGO
Nay, yet be wise. Yet we see nothing done;
She may be honest yet. Tell me but this:    430
Have you not sometimes seen a handkerchief
Spotted with strawberries in your wife's hand?

OTHELLO
I gave her such a one; 'twas my first gift.

IAGO
I know not that; but such a handkerchief—
I am sure it was your wife's—did I today    435
See Cassio wipe his beard with.

OTHELLO                        If it be that—

IAGO
If it be that, or any that was hers,
It speaks against her with the other proofs.

OTHELLO
O, that the slave had forty thousand lives!
One is too poor, too weak for my revenge.    440
Now do I see 'tis true. Look here, Iago:
All my fond love thus do I blow to heaven.
'Tis gone.
Arise, black vengeance, from the hollow hell!
Yield up, O Love, thy crown and hearted° throne    445
To tyrannous hate! Swell, bosom, with thy fraught,°
For 'tis of aspics'° tongues.

IAGO                        Yet be content.°

OTHELLO
O, blood, blood, blood!

IAGO
Patience, I say. Your mind may change.

OTHELLO
Never, Iago. Like to the Pontic Sea,°    450
Whose icy current and compulsive course
Nev'r keeps retiring ebb, but keeps due on
To the Propontic and the Hellespont,
Even so my bloody thoughts, with violent pace,
Shall nev'r look back, nev'r ebb to humble love,    455
Till that a capable and wide° revenge
Swallow them up. [He kneels.] Now, by yond marble
   heaven,
In the due reverence of a sacred vow
I here engage my words.

IAGO                    Do not rise yet.

[IAGO kneels.]

Witness, you ever-burning lights above,    460

---

377 **sith** since   384 **Dian's** Diana's (goddess of the moon and
of chastity)   392 **supervisor** onlooker   394 **tedious** hard to
arrange   395 **prospect** sight (where they can be seen)   396
**bolster** go to bed   400–01 **prime, salt** lustful   401 **pride** heat
407 **office** duty   409 **Pricked** spurred   418 **gripe** seize

425 **foregone conclusion** consummated fact   426 **shrewd
doubt** penetrating guess   428 **demonstrate** show, appear
445 **hearted** seated in the heart   446 **fraught** burden   447
**aspics'** asps';   **content** patient, quiet   450 **Pontic Sea** the
Black Sea (famous for the strong and constant current with
which it flows through the Bosporus into the Mediterranean,
where the water level is lower)   456 **capable and wide**
sufficient and far-reaching

You elements that clip° us round about,
Witness that here Iago doth give up
The execution° of his wit, hands, heart
To wronged Othello's service! Let him command,
And to obey shall be in me remorse,°     465
What bloody business ever.° [*They rise.*]

OTHELLO            I greet thy love,
Not with vain thanks but with acceptance bounteous,°
And will upon the instant put thee to't.°
Within these three days let me hear thee say
That Cassio's not alive.     470

IAGO
My friend is dead. 'Tis done at your request.
But let her live.

OTHELLO     Damn her, lewd minx! O, damn her!
Damn her!
Come, go with me apart. I will withdraw
To furnish me with some swift means of death
For the fair devil. Now art thou my lieutenant.     475

IAGO
I am your own forever.            *Exeunt.*

## Scene IV. [*A street.*]

*Enter* DESDEMONA, EMILIA, *and* CLOWN.

DESDEMONA   Do you know, sirrah, where Lieutenant
Cassio lies?°

CLOWN   I dare not say he lies anywhere.

DESDEMONA   Why, man?

CLOWN   He's a soldier, and for me to say a soldier lies, 5
'tis stabbing.

DESDEMONA   Go to. Where lodges he?

CLOWN   To tell you where he lodges is to tell you
where I lie.

DESDEMONA   Can anything be made of this?     10

CLOWN   I know not where he lodges, and for me to
devise a lodging, and say he lies here or he lies there,
were to lie in mine own throat.°

DESDEMONA   Can you enquire him out, and be
edified° by report?     15

CLOWN   I will catechize the world for him; that is,
make questions, and by them answer.

DESDEMONA   Seek him, bid him come hither. Tell
him I have moved° my lord on his behalf and hope all
will be well.     20

CLOWN   To do this is within the compass° of man's
wit, and therefore I will attempt the doing it.
                          *Exit* CLOWN.

DESDEMONA
Where should° I lose the handkerchief, Emilia?

EMILIA
I know not, madam.

DESDEMONA
Believe me, I had rather have lost my purse     25

Full of crusadoes.° And but my noble Moor
Is true of mind, and made of no such baseness
As jealous creatures are, it were enough
To put him to ill thinking.

EMILIA            Is he not jealous?

DESDEMONA
Who? He? I think the sun where he was born     30
Drew all such humors° from him.

EMILIA            Look where he comes.

*Enter* OTHELLO.

DESDEMONA
I will not leave him now till Cassio
Be called to him. How is't with you, my lord?

OTHELLO
Well, my good lady. [*Aside.*] O, hardness to dis-
semble!°—
How do you, Desdemona?

DESDEMONA            Well, my good lord.     35

OTHELLO
Give me your hand. This hand is moist,° my lady.

DESDEMONA
It hath felt no age nor known no sorrow.

OTHELLO
This argues° fruitfulness and liberal° heart,
Hot, hot, and moist. This hand of yours requires
A sequester° from liberty; fasting and prayer;     40
Much castigation; exercise devout;
For here's a young and sweating devil here
That commonly rebels. 'Tis a good hand,
A frank one.

DESDEMONA   You may, indeed, say so;
For 'twas that hand that gave away my heart.     45

OTHELLO
A liberal hand! The hearts of old gave hands,
But our new heraldry° is hands, not hearts.

DESDEMONA
I cannot speak of this. Come now, your promise!

OTHELLO
What promise, chuck?

DESDEMONA
I have sent to bid Cassio come speak with you.     50

OTHELLO
I have a salt and sorry rheum° offends me.
Lend me thy handkerchief.

DESDEMONA            Here, my lord.

OTHELLO   That which I gave you.

DESDEMONA            I have it not about me.

OTHELLO
Not?

DESDEMONA
No, indeed, my lord.

OTHELLO            That's a fault.

---

461 **clip** enfold  463 **execution** workings, action  465 **remorse** pity  466 **ever** soever  467 **bounteous** absolute  468 **to't** i.e., to the work you have said you are prepared to do  **III.iv.2 lies** lodges  13 **lie . . . throat** to lie in the throat is to lie absolutely and completely  15 **edified** enlightened (Desdemona mocks the Clown's overly elaborate diction)  19 **moved** pleaded with  21 **compass** reach  23 **should** might

26 **crusadoes** Portuguese gold coins  31 **humors** characteristics  34 **hardness to dissemble** Othello may refer here either to the difficulty he has in maintaining his appearance of composure, or to what he believes to be Desdemona's hardened hypocrisy  36 **moist** a moist, hot hand was taken as a sign of a lustful nature  38 **argues** suggests; **liberal** free, open (but also with a suggestion of "licentious"; from here on in this scene Othello's words bear a double meaning, seeming to be normal but accusing Desdemona of being unfaithful)  40 **sequester** separation  47 **heraldry** heraldic symbolism  51 **salt . . . rheum** heavy, running head cold

That handkerchief                                                           55
Did an Egyptian to my mother give.
She was a charmer,° and could almost read
The thoughts of people. She told her, while she kept it
'Twould make her amiable° and subdue my father
Entirely to her love; but if she lost it                                    60
Or made a gift of it, my father's eye
Should hold her loathèd, and his spirits should hunt
After new fancies. She, dying, gave it me,
And bid me, when my fate would have me wived,
To give it her. I did so; and take heed on't;                               65
Make it a darling like your precious eye.
To lose't or give't away were such perdition
As nothing else could match.

DESDEMONA                    Is't possible?

OTHELLO
'Tis true. There's magic in the web° of it.
A sibyl that had numbered in the world                                      70
The sun to course two hundred compasses,
In her prophetic fury° sewed the work;
The worms were hallowed that did breed the silk,
And it was dyed in mummy° which the skillful
Conserved of maidens' hearts.

DESDEMONA                    Indeed? Is't true?                             75

OTHELLO
Most veritable. Therefore look to't well.

DESDEMONA
Then would to God that I had never seen't!

OTHELLO    Ha! Wherefore?

DESDEMONA
Why do you speak so startingly and rash?

OTHELLO
Is't lost? Is't gone? Speak, is it out o' th' way?                          80

DESDEMONA    Heaven bless us!

OTHELLO    Say you?

DESDEMONA
It is not lost. But what an if it were?

OTHELLO    How?

DESDEMONA
I say it is not lost.

OTHELLO                    Fetch't, let me see't!                           85

DESDEMONA
Why, so I can; but I will not now.
This is a trick to put me from my suit:
Pray you let Cassio be received again.

OTHELLO
Fetch me the handkerchief! My mind misgives.

DESDEMONA
Come, come!                                                                 90
You'll never meet a more sufficient° man—

OTHELLO
The handkerchief!

DESDEMONA             A man that all his time
Hath founded his good fortunes on your love,
Shared dangers with you—

OTHELLO
The handkerchief!                                                           95

DESDEMONA
I' faith, you are to blame.

OTHELLO    Away!                              Exit OTHELLO.

EMILIA    Is not this man jealous?

DESDEMONA
I nev'r saw this before.
Sure there's some wonder in this handkerchief;                             100
I am most unhappy in the loss of it.

EMILIA
'Tis not a year or two shows us a man.
They are all but stomachs, and we all but food;
They eat us hungerly, and when they are full,
They belch us.

Enter IAGO and CASSIO.

                    Look you, Cassio and my husband.                       105

IAGO
There is no other way; 'tis she must do't.
And lo the happiness! Go and importune her.

DESDEMONA
How now, good Cassio? What's the news with you?

CASSIO
Madam, my former suit. I do beseech you
That by your virtuous means I may again                                    110
Exist, and be a member of his love
Whom I with all the office° of my heart
Entirely honor. I would not be delayed.
If my offense be of such mortal kind
That nor my service past, nor present sorrows,                             115
Nor purposed merit in futurity,
Can ransom me into his love again,
But to know so must be my benefit.°
So shall I clothe me in a forced content,
And shut myself up in some other course                                    120
To fortune's alms.

DESDEMONA             Alas, thrice-gentle Cassio,
My advocation° is not now in tune.
My lord is not my lord; nor should I know him
Were he in favor° as in humor altered.
So help me every spirit sanctified                                         125
As I have spoken for you all my best
And stood within the blank° of his displeasure
For my free speech. You must awhile be patient.
What I can do I will; and more I will
Than for myself I dare. Let that suffice you.                              130

IAGO
Is my lord angry?

EMILIA                    He went hence but now,
And certainly in strange unquietness.

IAGO
Can he be angry? I have seen the cannon
When it hath blown his ranks into the air
And, like the devil, from his very arm                                     135
Puffed his own brother. And is he angry?
Something of moment° then. I will go meet him.
There's matter in't indeed if he be angry.

DESDEMONA
I prithee do so. Exit [IAGO]. Something sure of state,°
Either from Venice or some unhatched practice°                             140
Made demonstrable here in Cyprus to him,
Hath puddled° his clear spirit; and in such cases

---

57 charmer magician   59 amiable desirable   69 web weaving   72 prophetic fury seized by the spirit and able to prophesy   74 mummy liquid drained from embalmed bodies   91 sufficient complete, with all proper qualities

112 office duty   118 benefit good   122 advocation advocacy   124 favor countenance   127 blank bull's-eye of a target   137 moment importance   139 of state state affairs   141 unhatched practice undisclosed plot   142 puddled muddied

Men's natures wrangle with inferior things,
Though great ones are their object. 'Tis even so.
For let our finger ache, and it endues°          145
Our other, healthful members even to a sense
Of pain. Nay, we must think men are not gods,
Nor of them look for such observancy
As fits the bridal. Beshrew me much, Emilia,
I was, unhandsome warrior as I am,          150
Arraigning his unkindness with my soul;
But now I find I had suborned the witness,
And he's indicted falsely.

EMILIA          Pray heaven it be
State matters, as you think, and no conception
Nor no jealous toy° concerning you.          155

DESDEMONA
Alas the day! I never gave him cause.

EMILIA
But jealous souls will not be answered so;
They are not ever jealous for the cause,
But jealous for they're jealous. It is a monster
Begot upon itself, born on itself.          160

DESDEMONA
Heaven keep the monster from Othello's mind!

EMILIA   Lady, amen.

DESDEMONA
I will go seek him. Cassio, walk here about.
If I do find him fit,° I'll move your suit
And seek to effect it to my uttermost.          165

CASSIO
I humbly thank your ladyship.
                    *Exit* [DESDEMONA, *with* EMILIA].

*Enter* BIANCA.

BIANCA
Save you, friend Cassio!

CASSIO          What make you from home?
How is't with you, my most fair Bianca?
I' faith, sweet love, I was coming to your house.

BIANCA
And I was going to your lodging, Cassio.
What, keep a week away? Seven days and nights?          170
Eightscore eight hours? And lovers' absent hours
More tedious than the dial eightscore times?
O weary reck'ning.°

CASSIO          Pardon me, Bianca.
I have this while with leaden thoughts been pressed,          175
But I shall in a more continuate° time
Strike off this score° of absence. Sweet Bianca,

[*Gives her Desdemona's handkerchief.*]

Take me this work out.

BIANCA          O Cassio, whence came this?
This is some token from a newer friend.
To the felt absence now I feel a cause.          180
Is't come to this? Well, well.

CASSIO          Go to, woman!
Throw your vile guesses in the devil's teeth,
From whence you have them. You are jealous now

That this is from some mistress, some remembrance.
No, by my faith, Bianca.

BIANCA          Why, whose is it?          185

CASSIO
I know not neither; I found it in my chamber.
I like the work well; ere it be demanded,°
As like enough it will, I would have it copied.
Take it and do't, and leave me for this time.

BIANCA
Leave you? Wherefore?          190

CASSIO
I do attend here on the general
And think it no addition, nor my wish,
To have him see me womaned.

BIANCA          Why, I pray you?

CASSIO
Not that I love you not.

BIANCA          But that you do not love me!
I pray you bring° me on the way a little,          195
And say if I shall see you soon at night.

CASSIO
'Tis but a little way that I can bring you,
For I attend here; but I'll see you soon.

BIANCA
'Tis very good. I must be circumstanced.°
                    *Exeunt omnes.*

# ACT IV

## Scene I. [*A street.*]

*Enter* OTHELLO *and* IAGO.

IAGO
Will you think so?

OTHELLO          Think so, Iago?

IAGO          What,
To kiss in private?

OTHELLO          An unauthorized° kiss?

IAGO
Or to be naked with her friend in bed
An hour or more, not meaning any harm?

OTHELLO
Naked in bed, Iago, and not mean harm?          5
It is hypocrisy against the devil.
They that mean virtuously, and yet do so,
The devil their virtue tempts, and they tempt heaven.

IAGO
If they do nothing, 'tis a venial slip.
But if I give my wife a handkerchief—          10

OTHELLO   What then?

IAGO
Why, then 'tis hers, my lord; and being hers,
She may, I think, bestow't on any man.

OTHELLO
She is protectress of her honor too.
May she give that?          15

145 endues leads  155 toy trifle  164 fit receptive  174 reck'ning addition  176 continuate uninterrupted  177 Strike . . . score pay this bill (the "score" being the account of drinks kept in a tavern)

187 demanded asked for (by the person who lost it)  195 bring accompany  199 be circumstanced accept things as they are
IV.i.2 unauthorized illicit

IAGO
Her honor is an essence that's not seen;
They have it very oft that have it not.
But for the handkerchief—

OTHELLO
By heaven, I would most gladly have forgot it!
Thou said'st—O, it comes o'er my memory          20
As doth the raven° o'er the infected house,
Boding to all—he had my handkerchief.

IAGO
A y, what of that?

OTHELLO                    That's not so good now.

IAGO
What if I had said I had seen him do you wrong?
Or heard him say—as knaves be such abroad°      25
Who having, by their own importunate suit,
Or voluntary dotage° of some mistress,
Convincèd or supplied° them, cannot choose
But they must blab—

OTHELLO                  Hath he said anything?

IAGO
He hath, my lord; but be you well assured,       30
No more than he'll unswear.

OTHELLO                  What hath he said?

IAGO
Why, that he did—I know not what he did.

OTHELLO  What? what?

IAGO  Lie—

OTHELLO
With her?

IAGO        With her, on her; what you will.    35

OTHELLO  Lie with her? Lie on her?—We say lie on
her when they belie her.—Lie with her! Zounds, that's
fulsome.° — Handkerchief — confessions — handkerchief!—To confess, and be hanged for his labor— first
to be hanged, and then to confess! I tremble at it. 40
Nature would not invest herself in such shadowing
passion without some instruction.° It is not words
that shakes me thus.—Pish! Noses, ears, and lips? Is't
possible?—Confess—Handkerchief?—O devil!

*Falls in a trance.*

IAGO
Work on.                                          45
My med'cine works! Thus credulous fools are caught,
And many worthy and chaste dames even thus,
All guiltless, meet reproach.° What, ho! My Lord!
My lord, I say! Othello!

*Enter* CASSIO.

                    How now, Cassio?

CASSIO
What's the matter?                                50

IAGO
My lord is fall'n into an epilepsy.
This is his second fit; he had one yesterday.

CASSIO
Rub him about the temples.

IAGO
The lethargy° must have his quiet course.
If not, he foams at mouth, and by and by          55
Breaks out to savage madness. Look, he stirs.
Do you withdraw yourself a little while.
He will recover straight. When he is gone,
I would on great occasion° speak with you.
                              [*Exit* CASSIO.]
How is it, general? Have you not hurt your head?  60

OTHELLO
Dost thou mock° me?

IAGO                    I mock you not, by heaven.
Would you would bear your fortune like a man.

OTHELLO
A hornèd man's a monster and a beast.

IAGO
There's many a beast then in a populous city,
And many a civil° monster.                        65

OTHELLO
Did he confess it?

IAGO                Good, sir, be a man.
Think every bearded fellow that's but yoked
May draw° with you. There's millions now alive
That nightly lie in those unproper° beds
Which they dare swear peculiar.° Your case is better. 70
O, 'tis the spite of hell, the fiend's arch-mock,
To lip a wanton in a secure couch,
And to suppose her chaste. No, let me know;
And knowing what I am, I know what she shall be.

OTHELLO
O, thou art wise! 'Tis certain.

IAGO                        Stand you awhile apart;  75
Confine yourself but in a patient list.°
Whilst you were here, o'erwhelmèd with your grief—
A passion most unsuiting such a man—
Cassio came hither. I shifted him away°
And laid good 'scuses upon your ecstasy;°         80
Bade him anon return, and here speak with me;
The which he promised. Do but encave° yourself
And mark the fleers,° the gibes, and notable° scorns
That dwell in every region of his face.
For I will make him tell the tale anew:           85
Where, how how oft, how long ago, and when
He hath, and is again to cope your wife.
I say, but mark his gesture. Marry patience,
Or I shall say you're all in all in spleen,°
And nothing of a man.

OTHELLO            Dost thou hear, Iago?            90
I will be found most cunning in my patience;
But—dost thou hear?—most bloody.

IAGO                        That's not amiss;
But yet keep time in all. Will you withdraw?

---

21 **raven** a harbinger of death   25 **abroad** i.e., in the world
27 **voluntary dotage** weakness of the will   28 **Convincèd or
supplied** persuaded or gratified (the mistress)   38 **fulsome**
foul, repulsive   41–42 **Nature . . . instruction** i.e., my
mind would not become so darkened (with anger) unless there
were something in this (accusation); it should be remembered
that Othello believes in the workings of magic and supernatural forces   48 **reproach** shame

54 **lethargy** coma   59 **great occasion** very important matter
61 **mock** Othello takes Iago's comment as a reference to his
horns—which it is   65 **civil** city-dwelling   68 **draw** i.e., like
the horned ox   69 **unproper** i.e., not exclusively the husband's
70 **peculiar** their own alone   76 **a patient list** the bounds of
patience   79 **shifted him away** got rid of him by a stratagem
80 **ecstasy** trance (the literal meaning, "outside oneself,"
bears on the meaning of the change Othello is undergoing)
82 **encave** hide   83 **fleers** mocking looks or speeches; **notable**
obvious   89 **spleen** passion, particularly anger

[OTHELLO *moves to one side, where his remarks are not audible to* CASSIO *and* IAGO.]

Now will I question Cassio of Bianca,
A huswife° that by selling her desires                             95
Buys herself bread and cloth. It is a creature
That dotes on Cassio, as 'tis the strumpet's plague
To beguile many and be beguiled by one.
He, when he hears of her, cannot restrain
From the excess of laughter. Here he comes.                        100

*Enter* CASSIO.

As he shall smile, Othello shall go mad;
And his unbookish° jealousy must conster°
Poor Cassio's smiles, gestures, and light behaviors
Quite in the wrong. How do you, lieutenant?
CASSIO
The worser that you give me the addition°                          105
Whose want even kills me.
IAGO
Ply Desdemona well, and you are sure on't.
Now, if this suit lay in Bianca's power,
How quickly should you speed!
CASSIO                          Alas, poor caitiff!°
OTHELLO
Look how he laughs already!                                        110
IAGO
I never knew woman love man so.
CASSIO
Alas, poor rogue! I think, i' faith, she loves me.
OTHELLO
Now he denies it faintly, and laughs it out.
IAGO
Do you hear, Cassio?
OTHELLO                          Now he importunes him
To tell it o'er. Go to! Well said, well said!                      115
IAGO
She gives it out that you shall marry her.
Do you intend it?
CASSIO   Ha, ha, ha!
OTHELLO
Do ye triumph, Roman? Do you triumph?
CASSIO   I marry? What, a customer?° Prithee bear                   120
some charity to my wit; do not think it so unwhole-
some. Ha, ha, ha!
OTHELLO   So, so, so, so. They laugh that win.
IAGO
Why, the cry goes that you marry her.
CASSIO   Prithee, say true.                                         125
IAGO   I am a very villain else.
OTHELLO   Have you scored° me? Well.
CASSIO   This is the monkey's own giving out. She is
persuaded I will marry her out of her own love and
flattery, not out of my promise.                                   130
OTHELLO   Iago beckons me; now he begins the story.

[OTHELLO *moves close enough to hear.*]

CASSIO   She was here even now; she haunts me in
every place. I was the other day talking on the sea bank

with certain Venetians, and thither comes the bauble,°
and falls me thus about my neck—                                   135
OTHELLO   Crying "O dear Cassio!" as it were. His
gesture imports it.
CASSIO   So hangs, and lolls, and weeps upon me; so
shakes and pulls me! Ha, ha, ha!
OTHELLO   Now he tells how she plucked him to my                   140
chamber. O, I see that nose of yours, but not that dog
I shall throw it to.
CASSIO   Well, I must leave her company.
IAGO   Before me!° Look where she comes.

*Enter* BIANCA.

CASSIO   'Tis such another fitchew!° Marry a per-                  145
fumed one? What do you mean by this haunting of me?
BIANCA   Let the devil and his dam haunt you! What
did you mean by that same handkerchief you gave me
even now? I was a fine fool to take it. I must take out
the work? A likely piece of work that you should       150
find it in your chamber and know not who left it
there! This is some minx's token, and I must take out
the work? There! [*She throws down the handkerchief.*]
Give it your hobbyhorse.° Wheresoever you had it,
I'll take out no work on't.                                        155
CASSIO   How now, my sweet Bianca? How now?
how now?
OTHELLO   By heaven, that should be my handkerchief!
BIANCA   If you'll come to supper tonight, you may; if
you will not, come when you are next prepared for.°    160
                                                            *Exit.*
IAGO   After her, after her!
CASSIO   Faith, I must; she'll rail in the streets else.
IAGO   Will you sup there?
CASSIO   Yes, I intend so.
IAGO   Well, I may chance to see you, for I would very  165
fain speak with you.
CASSIO   Prithee come. Will you?
IAGO   Go to, say no more.                    [*Exit* CASSIO.]
OTHELLO [*Comes forward.*]   How shall I murder him,
Iago?                                                              170
IAGO   Did you perceive how he laughed at his vice?
OTHELLO   O Iago!
IAGO   And did you see the handkerchief?
OTHELLO   Was that mine?
IAGO   Yours, by this hand! And to see how he prizes   175
the foolish woman your wife! She gave it him, and he
hath giv'n it his whore.
OTHELLO   I would have him nine years a-killing!—A
fine woman, a fair woman, a sweet woman?
IAGO   Nay, you must forget that.                                  180
OTHELLO   Ay, let her rot, and perish, and be damned
tonight; for she shall not live. No, my heart is turned
to stone; I strike it, and it hurts my hand. O, the
world hath not a sweeter creature! She might lie by
an emperor's side and command him tasks.               185
IAGO   Nay, that's not your way.°
OTHELLO   Hang her! I do but say what she is. So
delicate with her needle. An admirable musician. O,

---

95 **huswife** housewife (but with the special meaning here of
"prostitute")   102 **unbookish** ignorant; **conster** construe
105 **addition** title   109 **caitiff** wretch   120 **customer** one
who sells, a merchant (here, a prostitute)   127 **scored** marked,
defaced

134 **bauble** plaything   144 **Before me** an exclamation of
surprise   145 **fitchew** polecat, i.e., strong-smelling creature
154 **hobbyhorse** prostitute   160 **next prepared for** next
expected—i.e., never   186 **way** proper course

she will sing the savageness out of a bear! Of so high
and plenteous wit and invention°—                        190

IAGO   She's the worse for all this.

OTHELLO   O, a thousand, a thousand times. And then,
of so gentle a condition?°

IAGO   Ay, too gentle.

OTHELLO   Nay, that's certain. But yet the pity of it,    195
Iago. O Iago, the pity of it, Iago.

IAGO   If you are so fond over her iniquity, give her
patent to offend; for if it touch° not you, it comes near
nobody.

OTHELLO   I will chop her into messes!° Cuckold me!    200

IAGO   O, 'tis foul in her.

OTHELLO   With mine officer!

IAGO   That's fouler.

OTHELLO   Get me some poison, Iago, this night. I'll
not expostulate with her, lest her body and beauty    205
unprovide my mind° again. This night, Iago!

IAGO   Do it not with poison. Strangle her in her bed,
even the bed she hath contaminated.

OTHELLO   Good, good! The justice of it pleases. Very
good!                                                      210

IAGO   And for Cassio, let me be his undertaker.° You
shall hear more by midnight.

OTHELLO   Excellent good! [A trumpet.]
                    What trumpet is that same?

IAGO
I warrant something from Venice.

*Enter* LODOVICO, DESDEMONA, *and* ATTENDANTS.

                         'Tis Lodovico.
This comes from the duke. See, your wife's with him.    215

LODOVICO
God save you, worthy general.

OTHELLO                         With° all my heart, sir.

LODOVICO
The duke and the senators of Venice greet you.

[*Gives him a letter.*]

OTHELLO
I kiss the instrument of their pleasures.

[*Opens the letter and reads.*]

DESDEMONA
And what's the news, good cousin Lodovico?

IAGO
I am very glad to see you, signior.                      220
Welcome to Cyprus.

LODOVICO
I thank you. How does Lieutenant Cassio?

IAGO                                     Lives, sir.

DESDEMONA
Cousin, there's fall'n between him and my lord
An unkind° breach; but you shall make all well.

OTHELLO   Are you sure of that?                          225

DESDEMONA   My lord?

OTHELLO [*Reads.*]   "This fail you not to do, as you
will—"

LODOVICO
He did not call; he's busy in the paper.
Is there division 'twixt my lord and Cassio?

DESDEMONA
A most unhappy one. I would do much                      230
T' atone° them, for the love I bear to Cassio.

OTHELLO
Fire and brimstone!

DESDEMONA            My lord?

OTHELLO                       Are you wise?

DESDEMONA
What, is he angry?

LODOVICO            May be th' letter moved him;
For, as I think, they do command him home,
Deputing Cassio in his government.°                      235

DESDEMONA
Trust me, I am glad on't.

OTHELLO                    Indeed?

DESDEMONA                          My lord?

OTHELLO
I am glad to see you mad.

DESDEMONA                  Why, sweet Othello—

OTHELLO   Devil!

[*Strikes her.*]

DESDEMONA
I have not deserved this.

LODOVICO
My lord, this would not be believed in Venice,           240
Though I should swear I saw't. 'Tis very much.
Make her amends; she weeps.

OTHELLO                       O devil, devil!
If that the earth could teem° with woman's tears,
Each drop she falls° would prove a crocodile.°
Out of my sight!

DESDEMONA       I will not stay to offend you.           245

[*Going.*]

LODOVICO
Truly, an obedient lady.
I do beseech your lordship call her back.

OTHELLO
Mistress!

DESDEMONA   My lord?

OTHELLO                 What would you with her, sir?

LODOVICO
Who? I, my lord?

OTHELLO
Ay! You did wish that I would make her turn.             250
Sir, she can turn, and turn, and yet go on
And turn again; and she can weep, sir, weep;
And she's obedient; as you say, obedient.
Very obedient. Proceed you in your tears.
Concerning this, sir—O well-painted passion!            255
I am commanded home.—Get you away;
I'll send for you anon.—Sir, I obey the mandate
And will return to Venice.—Hence, avaunt!

[*Exit* DESDEMONA.]

190 **invention** imagination   193 **so . . . condition** (1) so
well born (2) of such a gentle nature   198 **touch** affects
200 **messes** bits   206 **unprovide my mind** undo my resolution   211 **undertaker** not "burier," but "one who undertakes
to do something"   216 **With** i.e., I greet you with   224
**unkind** unnatural

231 **atone** reconcile   235 **government** office   243 **teem**
conceive   244 **falls** drops; **crocodile** the crocodile was supposed to shed false tears to lure its victims

Cassio shall have my place. And sir, tonight
I do entreat that we may sup together.                               260
You are welcome, sir, to Cyprus.—Goats and mon-
keys!                                               *Exit.*

LODOVICO
Is this the noble Moor whom our full Senate
Call all in all sufficient? Is this the nature
Whom passion could not shake? whose solid virtue
The shot of accident nor dart of chance                             265
Could neither graze nor pierce?

IAGO                                    He is much changed.

LODOVICO
Are his wits safe? Is he not light of brain?

IAGO
He's that he is; I may not breathe my censure.
What he might be (if, what he might, he is not)
I would to heaven he were!

LODOVICO                              What, strike his wife?       270

IAGO
Faith, that was not so well; yet would I knew
That stroke would prove the worst.

LODOVICO                                    Is it his use?°
Or did the letters work upon his blood°
And new-create his fault?

IAGO                              Alas, alas!
It is not honesty in me to speak                                    275
What I have seen and known. You shall observe him,
And his own courses° will denote him so
That I may save my speech. Do but go after
And mark how he continues.

LODOVICO
I am sorry that I am deceived in him.          *Exeunt.* 280

### Scene II. [*The citadel.*]

*Enter* OTHELLO *and* EMILIA.

OTHELLO
You have seen nothing then?

EMILIA
Nor ever heard, nor ever did suspect.

OTHELLO
Yes, you have seen Cassio and she together.

EMILIA
But then I saw no harm, and then I heard
Each syllable that breath made up° between them.     5

OTHELLO
What, did they never whisper?

EMILIA                              Never, my lord.

OTHELLO
Nor send you out o' th' way?

EMILIA   Never.

OTHELLO
To fetch her fan, her gloves, her mask, nor nothing?

EMILIA   Never, my lord.                                            10

OTHELLO   That's strange.

EMILIA
I durst, my lord, to wager she is honest,
Lay down my soul at stake° If you think other,
Remove your thought. It doth abuse your bosom.

If any wretch have put this in your head,                           15
Let heaven requite it with the serpent's curse,°
For if she be not honest,° chaste, and true,
There's no man happy. The purest of their wives
Is foul as slander.

OTHELLO                    Bid her come hither. Go.
                                        *Exit* EMILIA.
She says enough; yet she's a simple bawd°                           20
That cannot say as much. This is a subtle whore,
A closet lock and key of villainous secrets,
And yet she'll kneel and pray; I have seen her do't.

*Enter* DESDEMONA *and* EMILIA.

DESDEMONA
My lord, what is your will?

OTHELLO                    Pray you, chuck, come hither.

DESDEMONA
What is your pleasure?

OTHELLO                    Let me see your eyes.                    25
Look in my face.

DESDEMONA          What horrible fancy's this?

OTHELLO [*To* EMILIA.]
Some of your function,° mistress:
Leave procreants alone and shut the door;
Cough or cry hem if anybody come.
Your mystery,° your mystery! Nay, dispatch!                         30
                                        *Exit* EMILIA.

DESDEMONA
Upon my knee, what doth your speech import?
I understand a fury in your words.°

OTHELLO
Why, what art thou?

DESDEMONA          Your wife, my lord; your true
And loyal wife.

OTHELLO          Come, swear it, damn thyself;
Lest, being like one of heaven, the devils themselves                35
Should fear to seize thee. Therefore be double-
damned:
Swear thou art honest.

DESDEMONA          Heaven doth truly know it.

OTHELLO
Heaven truly knows that thou art false as hell.

DESDEMONA
To whom, my lord? With whom? How am I false?

OTHELLO
Ah, Desdemon! Away! Away! Away!                                     40

DESDEMONA
Alas the heavy day! Why do you weep?
Am I the motive° of these tears, my lord?
If haply° you my father do suspect
An instrument of this your calling back,
Lay not your blame on me. If you have lost him,                     45
I have lost him too.

OTHELLO                    Had it pleased heaven
To try me with affliction, had they rained
All kinds of sores and shames on my bare head,
Steeped° me in poverty to the very lips,

---

16 **serpent's curse** God's curse on the serpent after the fall in
Eden   17 **honest** chaste   20 **bawd** procuress   27 **Some . . .
function** do your proper work (as the operator of a brothel)
30 **mystery** trade   32 **words** Q1 adds to this line, "but not
the words"   42 **motive** cause   43 **haply** by chance   49
**Steeped** submerged

272 **use** habit   273 **blood** passion   277 **courses** actions
**IV.ii.5 that . . . up** spoken   13 **at stake** as the wager

Given to captivity me and my utmost hopes,                50
I should have found in some place of my soul
A drop of patience. But, alas, to make me
The fixèd figure for the time of scorn°
To point his slow and moving finger at.
Yet could I bear that too, well, very well.              55
But there where I have garnered up my heart,
Where either I must live or bear no life,
The fountain from the which my current runs
Or else dries up—to be discarded thence,
Or keep it as a cistern for foul toads                   60
To knot and gender° in—turn thy complexion there,
Patience, thou young and rose-lipped cherubin!
I here look grim as hell!°

DESDEMONA
I hope my noble lord esteems me honest.

OTHELLO
O, ay, as summer flies are in the shambles,°             65
That quicken even with blowing.° O thou weed,
Who art so lovely fair, and smell'st so sweet,
That the sense aches at thee, would thou hadst never
    been born!

DESDEMONA
Alas, what ignorant° sin have I committed?

OTHELLO
Was this fair paper, this most goodly book,              70
Made to write "whore" upon? What committed?
Committed? O thou public commoner,°
I should make very forges of my cheeks
That would to cinders burn up modesty,
Did I but speak thy deeds. What committed?               75
Heaven stops the nose at it, and the moon winks;°
The bawdy wind that kisses all it meets
Is hushed within the hollow mine of earth
And will not hear't. What committed?

DESDEMONA
By heaven, you do me wrong!                               80

OTHELLO
Are not you a strumpet?

DESDEMONA                    No, as I am a Christian!
If to preserve this vessel for my lord
From any other foul unlawful touch
Be not to be a strumpet, I am none.

OTHELLO
What, not a whore?

DESDEMONA            No, as I shall be saved!             85

OTHELLO
Is't possible?

DESDEMONA
O, heaven forgive us!

OTHELLO                  I cry you mercy° then.
I took you for that cunning whore of Venice
That married with Othello. [Calling.] You, mistress,

Enter EMILIA.

That have the office opposite to Saint Peter             90
And keep the gate of hell! You, you, ay, you!
We have done our course; there's money for your
    pains.

[Throws her some coins.]

I pray you turn the key and keep our counsel.   Exit.

EMILIA
Alas, what does this gentleman conceive?
How do you, madam? How do you, my good lady?            95

DESDEMONA   Faith, half asleep.

EMILIA
Good madam, what's the matter with my lord?

DESDEMONA   With who?

EMILIA   Why, with my lord, madam.

DESDEMONA
Who is thy lord?

EMILIA              He that is yours, sweet lady.        100

DESDEMONA
I have none. Do not talk to me, Emilia.
I cannot weep, nor answers have I none
But what should go by water.° Prithee tonight
Lay on my bed my wedding sheets, remember;
And call thy husband hither.

EMILIA                    Here's a change indeed!       105
                                            Exit.

DESDEMONA
'Tis meet I should be used so, very meet.
How have I been behaved, that he might stick
The small'st opinion on my least misuse?°

Enter IAGO and EMILIA.

IAGO
What is your pleasure, madam? How is't with you?

DESDEMONA
I cannot tell. Those that do teach young babes          110
Do it with gentle means and easy tasks.
He might have chid me so; for, in good faith,
I am a child to chiding.

IAGO                    What is the matter, lady?

EMILIA
Alas, Iago, my lord hath so bewhored her,
Thrown such despite° and heavy terms upon her          115
That true hearts cannot bear it.

DESDEMONA
Am I that name, Iago?

IAGO                    What name, fair lady?

DESDEMONA
Such as she said my lord did say I was.

EMILIA
He called her whore. A beggar in his drink
Could not have laid such terms upon his callet.°        120

IAGO
Why did he so?

DESDEMONA
I do not know; I am sure I am none such.

IAGO
Do not weep, do not weep. Alas the day.

EMILIA
Hath she forsook so many noble matches,

53 The . . . scorn the very image of scorn in our time
61 knot and gender twist in bunches and procreate  61–63
turn . . . hell the rough sense would seem to be, "even Patience would grow pale ("turn complexion") at Desdemona's
perfidy, but that Othello looks grimly on"  65 shambles
abattoirs  66 quicken . . . blowing become impregnated as
soon as they lay their eggs  69 ignorant unknowing  72
commoner prostitute  76 winks closes its eyes (the moon
was the symbol of chastity)  87 cry you mercy ask your
pardon

103 water tears  107–08 stick . . . misuse base any doubt on
my smallest fault  115 despite abuse  120 callet slut

Her father and her country, and her friends,  125
To be called whore? Would it not make one weep?

DESDEMONA
It is my wretched fortune.

IAGO                    Beshrew° him for't!
How comes this trick upon him?

DESDEMONA                Nay, heaven doth know.

EMILIA
I will be hanged if some eternal villain,
Some busy and insinuating rogue,
Some cogging,° cozening slave, to get some office,  130
Have not devised this slander. I will be hanged else.

IAGO
Fie, there is no such man! It is impossible.

DESDEMONA
If any such there be, heaven pardon him.

EMILIA
A halter pardon him! And hell gnaw his bones!  135
Why should he call her whore? Who keeps her company?
What place? What time? What form? What likelihood?
The Moor's abused by some most villainous knave,
Some base notorious knave, some scurvy fellow.
O heavens, that such companions° thou'dst unfold,°  140
And put in every honest hand a whip
To lash the rascals naked through the world
Even from the east to th' west!

IAGO                    Speak within door.°

EMILIA
O, fie upon them! Some such squire° he was
That turned your wit the seamy side without  145
And made you to suspect me with the Moor.

IAGO
You are a fool. Go to.

DESDEMONA          Alas, Iago,
What shall I do to win my lord again?
Good friend, go to him, for, by this light of heaven,
I know not how I lost him. Here I kneel:  150
If e'er my will did trespass 'gainst his love
Either in discourse of thought° or actual deed,
Or that mine eyes, mine ears, or any sense
Delighted them in any other form;
Or that I do not yet, and ever did,  155
And ever will (though he do shake me off
To beggarly divorcement) love him dearly,
Comfort forswear me. Unkindness may do much,
And his unkindness may defeat° my life,
But never taint my love. I cannot say "whore."  160
It does abhor me now I speak the word;
To do the act that might the addition earn
Not the world's mass of vanity could make me.

IAGO
I pray you be content. 'Tis but his humor.°
The business of the state does him offense.  165

DESDEMONA
If 'twere no other.

IAGO          It is but so, I warrant.

[Trumpets within.]

Hark how these instruments summon to supper.
The messengers of Venice stay the meat.°
Go in, and weep not, All things shall be well.
[Exeunt DESDEMONA and EMILIA.]

Enter RODERIGO.

How now, Roderigo?  170

RODERIGO  I do not find that thou deal'st justly with me.

IAGO  What in the contrary?

RODERIGO  Every day thou daff'st° me with some device,° Iago, and rather, as it seems to me now,  175 keep'st from me all conveniency° than suppliest me with the least advantage of hope. I will indeed no longer endure it; nor am I yet persuaded to put up° in peace what already I have foolishly suffered.

IAGO  Will you hear me, Roderigo?  180

RODERIGO  I have heard too much, and your words and performances are no kin together.

IAGO  You charge me most unjustly.

RODERIGO  With naught but truth. I have wasted myself out of my means. The jewels you have had  185 from me to deliver Desdemona would half have corrupted a votarist.° You have told me she hath received them, and returned me expectations and comforts of sudden respect° and acquaintance; but I find none.  190

IAGO  Well, go to; very well.

RODERIGO  Very well? Go to? I cannot go to, man; nor 'tis not very well. Nay, I think it is scurvy, and begin to find myself fopped° in it.

IAGO  Very well.  195

RODERIGO  I tell you 'tis not very well. I will make myself known to Desdemona. If she will return me my jewels, I will give over my suit and repent my unlawful solicitation. If not, assure yourself I will seek satisfaction of you.  200

IAGO  You have said now?

RODERIGO  Ay, and said nothing but what I protest° intendment of doing.

IAGO  Why, now I see there's mettle° in thee, and even from this instant do build on thee a better opinion than  205 ever before. Give my thy hand, Roderigo. Thou hast taken against me a most just exception;° but yet I protest I have dealt most directly° in thy affair.

RODERIGO  It hath not appeared.

IAGO  I grant indeed it hath not appeared, and your  210 suspicion is not without wit and judgment. But, Roderigo, if thou hast that in thee indeed which I have greater reason to believe now than ever—I mean purpose, courage, and valor—this night show it. If thou the next night following enjoy not Desdemona,  215 take me from this world with treachery and devise engines for° my life.

RODERIGO  Well, what is it? Is it within reason and compass?°

127 Beshrew curse  131 cogging cheating  140 companions fellows, rogues; unfold disclose  143 within door more quietly and moderately  144 squire a term of contempt  152 discourse of thought thinking  159 defeat destroy  164 humor mood

168 stay the meat await the meal  174 daff'st put off  175 device scheme  176 conveniency what is needful  178 put up accept  187 votarist nun  189 sudden respect immediate consideration  194 fopped duped  202 protest aver  204 mettle spirit  207 exception objection  208 directly straightforwardly  217 engines for schemes against

IAGO  Sir, there is especial commission come from
Venice to depute Cassio in Othello's place.    220

RODERIGO  Is that true? Why, then Othello and
Desdemona return again to Venice.

IAGO  O, no; he goes into Mauritania and taketh away
with him the fair Desdemona, unless his abode be    225
lingered here by some accident; wherein none can be
so determinate° as the removing of Cassio.

RODERIGO  How do you mean, removing him?

IAGO  Why, by making him incapable of Othello's
place—knocking out his brains.    230

RODERIGO  And that you would have me to do?

IAGO  Ay, if you dare do yourself a profit and a right.
He sups tonight with a harlotry,° and thither will I go
to him. He knows not yet of his honorable fortune. If
you will watch his going thence, which I will fashion    235
to fall out° between twelve and one, you may take
him at your pleasure. I will be near to second° your
attempt, and he shall fall between us. Come, stand not
amazed at it, but go along with me. I will show you
such a necessity in his death that you shall think    240
yourself bound to put it on him. It is now high supper
time, and the night grows to waste. About it.

RODERIGO  I will hear further reason for this.

IAGO  And you shall be satisfied.    *Exeunt.*


Scene III. [*The citadel.*]

*Enter* OTHELLO, LODOVICO, DESDEMONA, EMILIA,
*and* ATTENDANTS.

LODOVICO
I do beseech you, sir, trouble yourself no further.

OTHELLO
O, pardon me: 'twill do me good to walk.

LODOVICO
Madam, good night. I humbly thank your ladyship.

DESDEMONA
Your honor is most welcome.

OTHELLO
Will you walk, sir? O, Desdemona.    5

DESDEMONA  My lord?

OTHELLO  Get you to bed on th' instant; I will be
returned forthwith. Dismiss your attendant there.
Look 't be done.

DESDEMONA  I will, my lord.    10

*Exit* [OTHELLO, *with* LODOVICO *and* ATTENDANTS].

EMILIA  How goes it now? He looks gentler than he
did.

DESDEMONA
He says he will return incontinent,°
And hath commanded me to go to bed,
And bade me to dismiss you.

EMILIA    Dismiss me?    15

DESDEMONA
It was his bidding; therefore, good Emilia,
Give me my nightly wearing, and adieu.
We must not now displease him.

EMILIA  I would you had never seen him!

DESDEMONA
So would not I. My love doth so approve him    20
That even his stubbornness, his checks,° his frowns—
Prithee unpin me—have grace and favor.

EMILIA  I have laid these sheets you bade me on the
bed.

DESDEMONA
All's one.° Good Father, how foolish are our minds!    25
If I do die before, prithee shroud me
In one of these same sheets.

EMILIA    Come, come! You talk.

DESDEMONA
My mother had a maid called Barbary.
She was in love; and he she loved proved mad
And did forsake her. She had a song of "Willow";    30
An old thing 'twas, but it expressed her fortune,
And she died singing it. That song tonight
Will not go from my mind; I have much to do
But to go hang my head all at one side
And sing it like poor Barbary. Prithee dispatch.    35

EMILIA
Shall I go fetch your nightgown?

DESDEMONA
No, unpin me here.
This Lodovico is a proper man.

EMILIA  A very handsome man.

DESDEMONA  He speaks well.    40

EMILIA  I know a lady in Venice would have walked
barefoot to Palestine for a touch of his nether lip.

DESDEMONA [*Sings.*]
"The poor soul sat singing by a sycamore tree,
    Sing all a green willow;
Her hand on her bosom, her head on her knee,    45
    Sing willow, willow, willow.
The fresh streams ran by her and murmured her moans;
    Sing willow, willow, willow;
Her salt tears fell from her, and soft'ned the stones—
    Sing willow, willow, willow—"    50
Lay by these.

[*Gives* EMILIA *her clothes.*]

    "Willow, Willow"—
Prithee hie° thee; he'll come anon.°
    "Sing all a green willow must be my garland.
    Let nobody blame him; his scorn I approve"—    55
Nay, that's not next. Hark! Who is't that knocks?

EMILIA  It is the wind.

DESDEMONA [*Sings.*]
"I called my love false love; but what said he then?
    Sing willow, willow, willow:
If I court moe° women, you'll couch with moe men."    60
So, get thee gone; good night. Mine eyes do itch.
Doth that bode weeping?

EMILIA    'Tis neither here nor there.

DESDEMONA
I have heard it said so. O, these men, these men.
Dost thou in conscience think, tell me, Emilia,
That there be women do abuse their husbands    65
In such gross kind?

EMILIA    There be some such, no question.

219 compass possibility  227 determinate effective  233
harlotry female  236 fall out occur  237 second support
IV.iii.13 incontinent at once

21 checks rebukes  25 All's one No matter  53 hie hurry;
anon at once  60 moe more

**DESDEMONA**
Wouldst thou do such a deed for all the world?
**EMILIA**
Why, would not you?
**DESDEMONA**            No, by this heavenly light!
**EMILIA**
Nor I neither by this heavenly light.
I might do't as well i' th' dark.     70
**DESDEMONA**
Wouldst thou do such a deed for all the world?
**EMILIA**    The world's a huge thing; it is a great price
for a small vice.
**DESDEMONA**
In troth, I think thou wouldst not.
**EMILIA**    In troth, I think I should; and undo't when I 75
had done. Marry, I would not do such a thing for a
joint-ring,° nor for measures of lawn,° nor for gowns,
petticoats, nor caps, nor any petty exhibition,° but
for all the whole world? Why, who would not make
her husband a cuckold to make him a monarch? I 80
should venture purgatory for't.
**DESDEMONA**
Beshrew me if I would do such a wrong
For the whole world.
**EMILIA**    Why, the wrong is but a wrong i' th' world;
and having the world for your labor, 'tis a wrong in 85
your own world, and you might quickly make it
right.
**DESDEMONA**    I do not think there is any such woman.
**EMILIA**    Yes, a dozen; and as many to th' vantage as
would store° the world they played for. 90
But I do think it is their husbands' faults
If wives do fall. Say that they slack their duties
And pour our treasures into foreign° laps;
Or else break out in peevish jealousies,
Throwing restraint upon us; or say they strike us, 95
Or scant our former having in despite°—
Why, we have galls; and though we have some grace,
Yet have we some revenge. Let husbands know
Their wives have sense like them. They see, and smell,
And have their palates both for sweet and sour, 100
As husbands have. What is it that they do
When they change° us for others? Is it sport?
I think it is. And doth affection° breed it?
I think it doth. Is't frailty that thus errs?
It is so too. And have not we affections? 105
Desires for sport? and frailty? as men have?
Then let them use us well; else let them know,
The ills we do, their ills instruct us so.°
**DESDEMONA**
Good night, good night. Heaven me such uses° send,
Not to pick bad from bad, but by bad mend. *Exeunt.* 110

# ACT V

## Scene I. [*A street.*]

*Enter* IAGO *and* RODERIGO.

**IAGO**
Here, stand behind this bulk;° straight will he come.
Wear thy good rapier bare, and put it home.
Quick, quick! Fear nothing; I'll be at thy elbow.
It makes us, or it mars us, think on that,
And fix most firm thy resolution. 5
**RODERIGO**
Be near at hand; I may miscarry in't.
**IAGO**
Here, at thy hand. Be bold, and take thy stand.

[*Moves to one side.*]

**RODERIGO**
I have no great devotion to the deed,
And yet he hath given me satisfying reasons.
'Tis but a man gone. Forth my sword! He dies! 10
**IAGO**
I have rubbed this young quat° almost to the sense,°
And he grows angry. Now, whether he kill Cassio,
Or Cassio him, or each do kill the other,
Every way makes my gain. Live Roderigo,
He calls me to a restitution large 15
Of gold and jewels that I bobbed° from him
As gifts to Desdemona.
It must not be. If Cassio do remain,
He hath a daily beauty in his life
That makes me ugly; and besides, the Moor 20
May unfold me to him; there stand I in much peril.
No, he must die. But so, I hear him coming.

*Enter* CASSIO.

**RODERIGO**
I know his gait. 'Tis he. Villain, thou diest!

[*Thrusts at* CASSIO.]

**CASSIO**
That thrust had been mine enemy indeed
But that my coat° is better than thou know'st. 25
I will make proof of thine.

[*Fights with* RODERIGO.]

**RODERIGO**           O, I am slain!°
**CASSIO**
I am maimed forever. Help, ho! Murder! Murder!

*Enter* OTHELLO [*to one side*].

**OTHELLO**
The voice of Cassio. Iago keeps his word.

---

77 **joint-ring** a ring with two interlocking halves; **lawn** fine
linen   78 **exhibition** payment   89–90 **to . . . store** in
addition as would fill   93 **foreign** alien, i.e., other than the
wife   96 **scant . . . despite** reduce, in spite, our household
allowance (?)   102 **change** exchange   103 **affection** strong
feeling, desire   108 **instruct us so** teach us to do likewise
109 **uses** practices

**V.i.1 bulk** projecting stall of a shop   11 **quat** pimple; **to the
sense** raw   16 **bobbed** swindled   25 **coat** i.e., a mail shirt
or bulletproof vest   26 **slain** most editors add here a stage
direction which has Iago wounding Cassio in the leg from
behind, but remaining unseen, however, nothing in the text
requires this, and Cassio's wound can be given him in the
fight with Roderigo, for presumably when Cassio attacks
Roderigo the latter would not simply accept the thrust but
would parry, since Iago enters again at line 46, he must exit
at some point after line 22

RODERIGO
O, villain that I am!

OTHELLO                        It is even so.

CASSIO
O help, ho! Light! A surgeon!                        30

OTHELLO
'Tis he. O brave Iago, honest and just,
That hast such noble sense of thy friend's wrong!
Thou teachest me. Minion,° your dear lies dead,
And your unblest° fate hies.° Strumpet, I come.
Forth of my heart those charms, thine eyes, are blotted.   35
Thy bed, lust-stained, shall with lust's blood be
    spotted.                        Exit OTHELLO.

Enter LODOVICO and GRATIANO.

CASSIO
What, ho? No watch? No passage?° Murder! Murder!

GRATIANO
'Tis some mischance. The voice is very direful.

CASSIO   O, help!

LODOVICO   Hark!                        40

RODERIGO   O wretched villain!

LODOVICO
Two or three groan. 'Tis heavy night.
These may be counterfeits. Let's think't unsafe
To come into the cry without more help.

RODERIGO
Nobody come? Then shall I bleed to death.   45

LODOVICO   Hark!

Enter IAGO [with a light].

GRATIANO
Here's one comes in his shirt, with light and weapons.

IAGO
Who's there? Whose noise is this that cries on
    murder?

LODOVICO
We do not know.

IAGO                        Do not you hear a cry?

CASSIO
Here, here! For heaven's sake, help me!

IAGO                        What's the matter?   50

GRATIANO
This is Othello's ancient, as I take it.

LODOVICO
The same indeed, a very valiant fellow.

IAGO
What are you here that cry so grievously?

CASSIO
Iago? O, I am spoiled, undone by villains.
Give me some help.                        55

IAGO
O me, lieutenant! What villains have done this?

CASSIO
I think that one of them is hereabout
And cannot make away.

IAGO                        O treacherous villains!

[To LODOVICO and GRATIANO.]

What are you there? Come in, and give some help.

RODERIGO
O, help me there!                        60

CASSIO
That's one of them.

IAGO                        O murd'rous slave! O villain!

[Stabs RODERIGO.]

RODERIGO
O damned Iago! O inhuman dog!

IAGO
Kill men i' th' dark?—Where be these bloody
    thieves?—
How silent is this town!—Ho! Murder! Murder!—
What may you be? Are you of good or evil?   65

LODOVICO
As you shall prove us, praise us.

IAGO   Signior Lodovico?

LODOVICO   He, sir.

IAGO
I cry you mercy. Here's Cassio hurt by villains.

GRATIANO   Cassio?                        70

IAGO   How is't, brother?

CASSIO
My leg is cut in two.

IAGO                        Marry, heaven forbid!
Light, gentlemen. I'll bind it with my shirt.

Enter BIANCA.

BIANCA
What is the matter, ho? Who is't that cried?

IAGO
Who is't that cried?                        75

BIANCA
O my dear Cassio! My sweet Cassio!
O Cassio, Cassio, Cassio!

IAGO
O notable strumpet!—Cassio, may you suspect
Who they should be that have thus mangled you?

CASSIO   No.                        80

GRATIANO   I am sorry to find you thus. I have been
to seek you.

IAGO
Lend me a garter. So. O for a chair
To bear him easily hence.

BIANCA
Alas, he faints! O Cassio, Cassio, Cassio!   85

IAGO
Gentlemen all, I do suspect this trash
To be a party in this injury.—
Patience awhile, good Cassio.—Come, come.
Lend me a light. Know we this face or no?
Alas, my friend and my dear countryman   90
Roderigo? No.—Yes, sure.—Yes, 'tis Roderigo!

GRATIANO   What, of Venice?

IAGO
Even he, sir. Did you know him?

GRATIANO                        Know him? Ay.

IAGO
Signior Gratiano? I cry your gentle pardon.
These bloody accidents must excuse my manners   95
That so neglected you.

GRATIANO                        I am glad to see you.

IAGO

How do you, Cassio?—O, a chair, a chair!

GRATIANO  Roderigo?

IAGO

He, he, 'tis he! [*A chair brought in.*] O, that's well said;° the chair.

Some good man bear him carefully from hence.                      100

I'll fetch the general's surgeon. [*To* BIANCA.] For you, mistress,

Save you your labor. [*To* CASSIO.] He that lies slain here, Cassio,

Was my dear friend. What malice was between you?

CASSIO

None in the world; nor do I know the man.

IAGO

What, look you pale?—O, bear him out o' th' air.      105

[CASSIO *is carried off.*]

Stay you, good gentlemen.—Look you pale, mistress?

Do you perceive the gastness° of her eye?

Nay, if you stare, we shall hear more anon.

Behold her well; I pray you look upon her.

Do you see, gentlemen? Nay, guiltiness will speak,   110

Though tongues were out of use.°

[*Enter* EMILIA.]

EMILIA

Alas, what is the matter? What is the matter, husband?

IAGO

Cassio hath here been set on in the dark

By Roderigo and fellows that are scaped.

He's almost slain, and Roderigo quite dead.           115

EMILIA

Alas, good gentleman! Alas, good Cassio!

IAGO

This is the fruits of whoring. Prithee, Emilia,

Go know of Cassio where he supped tonight.

[*To* BIANCA.]

What, do you shake at that?

BIANCA

He supped at my house; but I therefore shake not.    120

IAGO

O, did he so? I charge° you go with me.

EMILIA

Oh fie upon thee, strumpet!

BIANCA

I am no strumpet, but of life as honest

As you that thus abuse me.

EMILIA                          As I? Fie upon thee!

IAGO

Kind gentlemen, let's go see poor Cassio dressed.°    125

[*To* BIANCA.]

Come, mistress, you must tell's another tale.

Emilia, run you to the citadel

And tell my lord and lady what hath happed.

[*Exit* EMILIA.]

Will you go on afore? *Exeunt* [*all but* IAGO]. This is the night

That either makes me or fordoes me quite.°    [*Exit.*] 130

Scene II. [*Desdemona's chamber.*]

*Enter* OTHELLO [*with a light*]; *and* DESDEMONA *in her bed.*

OTHELLO

It is the cause, it is the cause, my soul.

Let me not name it to you, you chaste stars.

It is the cause. Yet I'll not shed her blood,

Nor scar that whiter skin of hers than snow,

And smooth as monumental alabaster.                    5

Yet she must die, else she'll betray more men.

Put out the light, and then put out the light.

If I quench thee, thou flaming minister,°

I can again thy former light restore,

Should I repent me; but once put out thy light,        10

Thou cunning'st° pattern of excelling nature,

I know not where is that Promethean heat°

That can thy light relume.° When I have plucked the rose,

I cannot give it vital° growth again;

It needs must wither. I'll smell thee on the tree.      15

[*He kisses her.*]

O balmy breath, that dost almost persuade

Justice to break her sword. One more, one more!

Be thus when thou art dead, and I will kill thee,

And love thee after. One more, and that's the last!

So sweet was ne'er so fatal. I must weep,              20

But they are cruel tears. This sorrow's heavenly;

It strikes where it doth love. She wakes.

DESDEMONA

Who's there? Othello?

OTHELLO                        Ay, Desdemona.

DESDEMONA

Will you come to bed, my lord?

OTHELLO

Have you prayed tonight, Desdemon?

DESDEMONA                              Ay, my lord.    25

OTHELLO

If you bethink yourself of any crime

Unreconciled as yet to heaven and grace,

Solicit for it straight.

DESDEMONA

Alack, my lord, what may you mean by that?

OTHELLO

Well, do it, and be brief; I will walk by.°            30

I would not kill thy unprepared spirit.

No, heavens forfend! I would not kill thy soul.

DESDEMONA

Talk you of killing?

OTHELLO                        Ay, I do.

DESDEMONA                                    Then heaven

Have mercy on me!

OTHELLO                        Amen, with all my heart.

DESDEMONA

If you say so, I hope you will not kill me.            35

OTHELLO  Humh.

---

99 **well said** well done  107 **gastness** terror  111 **tongues . . . use** men no longer spoke  121 **charge** command  125 **dressed** bandaged  130 **fordoes me quite** completely ruins me

**V.ii.8 minister** worker, servant  11 **cunning'st** most intricate and skillfully wrought (by nature excelling itself)  12 **Promethean heat** divine fire (Prometheus is the Titan who stole fire from heaven and gave it to man)  13 **relume** relight  14 **vital** living  30 **by** nearby

DESDEMONA
And yet I fear you; for you're fatal then
When your eyes roll so. Why I should fear I know not,
Since guiltiness I know not; but yet I feel I fear.
OTHELLO
Think on thy sins.
DESDEMONA            They are loves I bear to you.    40
OTHELLO
Ay, and for that thou diest.
DESDEMONA
That death's unnatural that kills for loving.
Alas, why gnaw you so your nether lip?
Some bloody passion shakes your very frame.
These are portents; but yet I hope, I hope,    45
They do not point on me.
OTHELLO                Peace and be still.
DESDEMONA
I will so. What's the matter?
OTHELLO
That handkerchief which I so loved and gave thee,
Thou gav'st to Cassio.
DESDEMONA            No, by my life and soul!
Send for the man and ask him.
OTHELLO                Sweet soul, take heed,    50
Take heed of perjury; thou art on thy deathbed.
DESDEMONA
Ay, but not yet to die.
OTHELLO            Presently.°
Therefore confess thee freely of thy sin,
For to deny each article° with oath
Cannot remove nor choke the strong conception    55
That I do groan withal. Thou art to die.
DESDEMONA
Then Lord have mercy on me.
OTHELLO                I say, amen.
DESDEMONA
And have you mercy too. I never did
Offend you in my life; never loved Cassio
But with such general warranty° of heaven    60
As I might love. I never gave him token.
OTHELLO
By heaven, I saw my handkerchief in's hand!
O perjured woman! thou dost stone° my heart,
And mak'st me call what I intend to do
A murder, which I thought a sacrifice.    65
I saw the handkerchief.
DESDEMONA            He found it then.
I never gave it him. Send for him hither.
Let him confess a truth.
OTHELLO                He hath confessed.
DESDEMONA    What, my lord?
OTHELLO
That he hath used thee.
DESDEMONA            How? Unlawfully?
OTHELLO                Ay.    70
DESDEMONA
He will not say so.
OTHELLO            No, his mouth is stopped.
Honest Iago hath ta'en order for't.°

DESDEMONA
O, my fear interprets. What, is he dead?
OTHELLO
Had all his hairs been lives, my great revenge
Had stomach° for them all.    75
DESDEMONA
Alas, he is betrayed, and I undone!
OTHELLO
Out, strumpet! Weep'st thou for him to my face?
DESDEMONA
O, banish me, my lord, but kill me not!
OTHELLO
Down, strumpet!
DESDEMONA
Kill me tomorrow; let me live tonight!    80
OTHELLO
Nay, if you strive—
DESDEMONA
But half an hour!
OTHELLO            Being done, there is no pause.
DESDEMONA
But while I say one prayer!
OTHELLO                It is too late.

*Smothers her.*

EMILIA *at the door.*

EMILIA [*Calls within.*]
My lord, my lord! What, ho, my lord, my lord!
OTHELLO
What noise is this? Not dead? Not yet quite dead?    85
I that am cruel am yet merciful;
I would not have thee linger in thy pain.
So, so.
EMILIA [*Within.*]
What, ho! My lord, my lord!
OTHELLO                Who's there?
EMILIA [*Within.*]
O, good my lord, I would speak a word with you.    90
OTHELLO
Yes, 'tis Emilia.—By and by.—She's dead.—
'Tis like she comes to speak of Cassio's death.
The noise was high.° Ha! No more moving?
Still as the grave.—Shall she come in? Were't good?—
I think she stirs again. No.—What's best to do?    95
If she come in, she'll sure speak to my wife.
My wife! My wife! What wife? I have no wife.
O, insupportable! O heavy hour!
Methinks it should be now a huge eclipse
Of sun and moon, and that th' affrighted globe    100
Should yawn° at alteration.
EMILIA                [*Within.*] I do beseech you
That I may speak with you, O good my lord!
OTHELLO
I had forgot thee. O, come in, Emilia.
Soft, by and by.—Let me the curtains draw.—

[*Draws the bed hangings and then opens the door.*]

---

**52 Presently** immediately  **54 article** item (of the charge of
adultery, Othello makes heavy use of legal terms in this scene)
**60 warranty** allowance  **63 stone** turn to stone  **72 ta'en
order for't** made sure of it

**75 stomach** appetite  **93 high** loud (Q1 reads "here")
**99–101 Methinks . . . alteration** the Elizabethans believed
that great changes in human affairs were reflected by disorders
in nature  **101 yawn** gape open (as in an earthquake)

Where art thou?

*Enter* EMILIA.

EMILIA                              What's the matter with thee now?   105

O my good lord, yonder's foul murders done!

OTHELLO   What? Now?

EMILIA   But now, my lord.

OTHELLO

It is the very error° of the moon.
She comes more nearer earth than she was wont   110
And makes men mad.

EMILIA

Cassio, my lord, hath killed a young Venetian
Called Roderigo.

OTHELLO                         Roderigo killed?
And Cassio killed?

EMILIA                         No, Cassio is not killed.

OTHELLO

Not Cassio killed? Then murder's out of tune,   115
And sweet revenge grows harsh.

DESDEMONA

O, falsely, falsely murdered!

EMILIA                              O Lord! What cry is that?

OTHELLO   That? What?

EMILIA

Out and alas! that was my lady's voice.
Help! Help, ho! Help! O lady, speak again!   120
Sweet Desdemona! O sweet mistress, speak!

DESDEMONA

A guiltless death I die.

EMILIA

O, who hath done this deed?

DESDEMONA

Nobody—I myself. Farewell.
Commend me to my kind lord. O, farewell!   125
                              [*She dies.*]

OTHELLO

Why, how should she be murd'red?

EMILIA                              Alas, who knows?

OTHELLO

You heard her say herself, it was not I.

EMILIA

She said so. I must needs report the truth.

OTHELLO

She's like a liar gone to burning hell!
'Twas I that killed her.

EMILIA                         O, the more angel she,   130
And you the blacker devil!

OTHELLO

She turned to folly, and she was a whore.

EMILIA

Thou dost belie her, and thou art a devil.

OTHELLO

She was false as water.

EMILIA                         Thou art rash as fire to say
That she was false. O, she was heavenly true!   135

OTHELLO

Cassio did top her. Ask thy husband else.
O, I were damned beneath all depth in hell

But that I did proceed upon just grounds
To this extremity. Thy husband knew it all.

EMILIA   My husband?   140

OTHELLO   Thy husband.

EMILIA

That she was false to wedlock?

OTHELLO

Ay, with Cassio. Had she been true,
If heaven would make me such another world
Of one entire and perfect chrysolite,°   145
I'd not have sold her for it.

EMILIA                              My husband?

OTHELLO

Ay, 'twas he that told me on her first.
An honest man he is, and hates the slime
That sticks on filthy deeds.

EMILIA                              My husband?

OTHELLO

What needs this iterance? Woman, I say thy husband.   150

EMILIA

O mistress, villainy hath made mocks with love!
My husband say she was false?

OTHELLO                         He, woman.
I say, thy husband. Dost understand the word?
My friend, thy husband; honest, honest Iago.

EMILIA

If he say so, may his pernicious soul   155
Rot half a grain a day! He lies to th' heart.
She was too fond of her most filthy bargain.

OTHELLO   Hah?

EMILIA

Do thy worst.
This deed of thine is no more worthy heaven   160
Than thou wast worthy her.

OTHELLO                         Peace, you were best.°

EMILIA

Thou hast not half that pow'r to do me harm
As I have to be hurt. O gull! O dolt!
As ignorant as dirt! Thou hast done a deed—

[OTHELLO *moves to draw his sword.*]

I care not for thy sword; I'll make thee known,   165
Though I lost twenty lives. Help! Help! Ho! Help!
The Moor hath killed my mistress! Murder! murder!

*Enter* MONTANO, GRATIANO, *and* IAGO [*and others*].

MONTANO

What is the matter? How now, general?

EMILIA

O, are you come, Iago? You have done well,
That men must lay their murders on your neck.   170

GRATIANO

What is the matter?

EMILIA

Disprove this villain, if thou be'st a man.
He says thou told'st him that his wife was false.
I know thou didst not; thou'rt not such a villain.
Speak, for my heart is full.   175

IAGO

I told her what I thought, and told no more
Than what he found himself was apt and true.

**109 error** wandering out of regular course (disorders in the
heavens were believed by some to cause disorders on earth,
as well as vice versa)

**145 chrysolite** topaz   **161 Peace . . . best** You had better
be silent

EMILIA
But did you ever tell him she was false?

IAGO  I did.

EMILIA
You told a lie, an odious damnèd lie!          180
Upon my soul, a lie! A wicked lie!
She false with Cassio? Did you say with Cassio?

IAGO
With Cassio, mistress. Go to, charm° your tongue.

EMILIA
I will not charm my tongue; I am bound to speak:
My mistress here lies murdered in her bed.     185

ALL
O heavens forfend!

EMILIA
And your reports have set the murder on.

OTHELLO
Nay, stare not, masters. It is true indeed.

GRATIANO
'Tis a strange truth.

MONTANO
O monstrous act!

EMILIA              Villainy, villainy, villainy!          190
I think upon't—I think I smell't!—O villainy!
I thought so then.—I'll kill myself for grief.—
O villainy, villainy!

IAGO
What, are you mad? I charge you get you home.

EMILIA
Good gentlemen, let me have leave to speak.     195
'Tis proper I obey him, but not now.
Perchance, Iago, I will ne'er go home.

OTHELLO
O! O! O! [Falls on the bed.]

EMILIA         Nay, lay thee down and roar,
For thou hast killed the sweetest innocent
That e'er did lift up eye.

OTHELLO              O, she was foul!          200

[Rises.]

I scarce did know you, uncle. There lies your niece,
Whose breath, indeed, these hands have newly stopped.
I know this act shows horrible and grim.

GRATIANO
Poor Desdemon! I am glad thy father's dead.
Thy match was mortal to him, and pure grief     205
Shore his old thread in twain. Did he live now,
This sight would make him do a desperate turn;
Yea, curse his better angel from his side,
And fall to reprobation.°

OTHELLO
'Tis pitiful; but yet Iago knows               210
That she with Cassio hath the act of shame
A thousand times committed. Cassio confessed it;
And she did gratify his amorous works
With that recognizance and pledge of love,
Which I first gave her. I saw it in his hand.   215
It was a handkerchief, an antique token
My father gave my mother.

EMILIA
O God! O heavenly God!

183 charm control   209 reprobation damnation

IAGO
Zounds, hold your peace!

EMILIA                'Twill out, 'twill out! I peace?
No, I will speak as liberal as the north.°      220
Let heaven and men and devils, let them all,
All, all, cry shame against me, yet I'll speak.

IAGO
Be wise, and get you home.

EMILIA                I will not.

[IAGO draws and threatens EMILIA.]

GRATIANO
Fie! Your sword upon a woman?

EMILIA
O thou dull Moor, that handkerchief thou speak'st of   225
I found by fortune, and did give my husband;
For often with a solemn earnestness—
More than indeed belonged to such a trifle—
He begged of me to steal't.

IAGO                Villainous whore!

EMILIA
She give it Cassio? No, alas, I found it,        230
And I did give't my husband.

IAGO                Filth, thou liest!

EMILIA
By heaven, I do not, I do not, gentlemen.
O murd'rous coxcomb! What should such a fool
Do with so good a wife?

OTHELLO                Are there no stones° in heaven
But what serves for the thunder? Precious villain!   235

[OTHELLO runs at IAGO, but is disarmed by MONTANO.
IAGO kills his wife.]

GRATIANO
The woman falls. Sure he hath killed his wife.

EMILIA
Ay, ay. O, lay me by my mistress' side.  [Exit IAGO.]

GRATIANO
He's gone, but his wife's killed.

MONTANO
'Tis a notorious° villain. Take you this weapon,
Which I have recovered from the Moor.           240
Come, guard the door without. Let him not pass,
But kill him rather. I'll after that same villain,
For 'tis a damnèd slave.
                    Exit, [with all but OTHELLO and EMILIA].

OTHELLO              I am not valiant neither;
But every puny whipster° gets my sword.
But why should honor outlive honesty?           245
Let it go all.

EMILIA         What did thy song bode, lady?
Hark, canst thou hear me? I will play the swan,
And die in music. [Sings.] "Willow, willow, willow."
Moor, she was chaste. She loved thee, cruel Moor,
So come my soul to bliss as I speak true.       250
So speaking as I think, alas, I die.            [She dies.]

OTHELLO
I have another weapon in this chamber;

220 liberal . . . north freely (and bitingly) as the north wind
blows   234 stones thunderbolts   239 notorious out-and-out
244 puny whipster small top-whipping boy (?)

It was a sword of Spain, the ice-brook's temper.
O, here it is.—Uncle, I must come forth.

GRATIANO [*Within.*]
If thou attempt it, it will cost thee dear.                    255
Thou hast no weapon, and perforce must suffer.

OTHELLO
Look in upon me then and speak with me,
Or, naked as I am, I will assault thee.

[*Enter* GRATIANO.]

GRATIANO
What is the matter?

OTHELLO                    Behold, I have a weapon;
A better never did itself sustain                              260
Upon a soldier's thigh. I have seen the day
That with this little arm and this good sword
I have made my way through more impediments
Than twenty times your stop. But O vain boast!
Who can control his fate? 'Tis not so now.                     265
Be not afraid, though you do see me weaponed.
Here is my journey's end, here is my butt,°
And very seamark of my utmost sail.°
Do you go back dismayed? 'Tis a lost fear.
Man but a rush° against Othello's breast,                      270
And he retires. Where should Othello go?
Now, how dost thou look now? O ill-starred wench!
Pale as thy smock! When we shall meet at compt,°
This look of thine will hurl my soul from heaven,
And fiends will snatch at it. Cold, cold, my girl?             275
Even like thy chastity.
O cursèd, cursèd slave! Whip me, ye devils,
From the possession of° this heavenly sight!
Blow me about in winds! roast me in sulfur!
Wash me in steep-down gulfs of liquid fire!                    280
O Desdemon! Dead Desdemon; dead. O! O!

*Enter* LODOVICO, CASSIO, MONTANO, *and* IAGO
[*as prisoner,*] *with* OFFICERS.

LODOVICO
Where is this rash and most unfortunate man?

OTHELLO
That's he that was Othello? Here I am.

LODOVICO
Where is that viper? Bring the villain forth.

OTHELLO
I look down towards his feet°—but that's a fable.             285
If that thou be'st a devil, I cannot kill thee.

[*Wounds* IAGO.]

LODOVICO
Wrench his sword from him. [OTHELLO *is disarmed.*]

IAGO                    I bleed, sir, but not killed.

OTHELLO
I am not sorry neither. I'd have thee live;
For in my sense, 'tis happiness to die.

LODOVICO
O thou Othello that was once so good,                          290

267 butt target, stopping place  268 seamark . . . sail
marker of my farthest journey  270 Man . . . rush attack
with only a reed  273 compt Judgment Day  278 the possession of being possessed by  285 towards his feet i.e., for
his cloven hoofs

Fal'n in the practice° of a cursèd slave,
What shall be said to thee?

OTHELLO                    Why, anything:
An honorable murderer, if you will;
For naught I did in hate, but all in honor.

LODOVICO
This wretch hath part confessed his villainy.                  295
Did you and he consent in Cassio's death?

OTHELLO  Ay.

CASSIO
Dear general, I never gave you cause.

OTHELLO
I do believe it, and I ask your pardon.
Will you, I pray, demand that demi-devil                       300
Why he hath thus ensnared my soul and body?

IAGO
Demand me nothing. What you know, you know.
From this time forth I never will speak word.

LODOVICO
What, not to pray?

GRATIANO                    Torments will ope your lips.

OTHELLO
Well, thou dost best.                                          305

LODOVICO
Sir, you shall understand what hath befall'n,
Which, as I think, you know not. Here is a letter
Found in the pocket of the slain Roderigo;
And here another. The one of them imports
The death of Cassio to be undertook                            310
By Roderigo.

OTHELLO
O villain!

CASSIO    Most heathenish and most gross!

LODOVICO
Now here's another discontented paper
Found in his pocket too; and this, it seems,
Roderigo meant t' have sent this damnèd villain;              315
But that, belike, Iago in the interim
Came in and satisfied him.

OTHELLO                    O thou pernicious caitiff!
How came you, Cassio, by that handkerchief
That was my wife's?

CASSIO                    I found it in my chamber;
And he himself confessed it but even now                       320
That there he dropped it for a special purpose
Which wrought to his desire.

OTHELLO                    O fool! Fool! Fool!

CASSIO
There is besides in Roderigo's letter,
How he upbraids Iago that he made him
Brave me upon the watch; whereon it came                       325
That I was cast; and even but now he spake,
After long seeming dead—Iago hurt him,
Iago set him on.

LODOVICO
You must forsake this room and go with us.
Your power and your command is taken off,                      330
And Cassio rules in Cyprus. For this slave,
If there be any cunning cruelty
That can torment him much and hold him long,
It shall be his. You shall close prisoner rest

291 practice plotting

Till that the nature of your fault be known           335
To the Venetian state. Come, bring away.

OTHELLO
Soft you, a word or two before you go.
I have done the state some service, and they know't.
No more of that. I pray you, in your letters,
When you shall these unlucky deeds relate,           340
Speak of me as I am. Nothing extenuate,
Nor set down aught in malice. Then must you speak
Of one that loved not wisely, but too well;
Of one not easily jealous, but, being wrought,
Perplexed in the extreme; of one whose hand,         345
Like the base Judean,° threw a pearl away
Richer than all his tribe; of one whose subdued eyes,
Albeit unusèd to the melting mood,
Drops tears as fast as the Arabian trees
Their med'cinable gum. Set you down this.            350
And say besides that in Aleppo once,
Where a malignant and a turbaned Turk
Beat a Venetian and traduced the state,
I took by th' throat the circumcisèd dog
And smote him—thus.                                  355

346 **Judean** most editors use the Q1 reading, "Indian," here, but F is clear; both readings point toward the infidel, the unbeliever

[*He stabs himself.*]

LODOVICO
O bloody period!°

GRATIANO           All that is spoke is marred.

OTHELLO
I kissed thee ere I killed thee. No way but this,
Killing myself, to die upon a kiss.

[*He falls over Desdemona and dies.*]

CASSIO
This did I fear, but thought he had no weapon;
For he was great of heart.

LODOVICO   [*To* IAGO.] O Spartan dog,          360
More fell° than anguish, hunger, or the sea!
Look on the tragic loading of this bed.
This is thy work. The object poisons sight;
Let it be hid. [*Bed curtains drawn.*] Gratiano, keep° the house,
And seize upon the fortunes of the Moor,        365
For they succeed on you. To you, lord governor,
Remains the censure of this hellish villain,
The time, the place, the torture. O, enforce it!
Myself will straight aboard, and to the state
This heavy act with heavy heart relate.    *Exeunt.* 370

356 **period** end   361 **fell** cruel   364 **keep** remain in

# MEASURE FOR MEASURE

EDITED BY S. NAGARAJAN

## Introduction

*Measure for Measure* was first published in 1623 in the Folio of Shakespeare's works. It was probably written in 1604, for it is on record that a play called *Mesure for Mesure*, by "Shaxberd" was performed before King James I on December 26 of that year, when it was presumably a new play. It was thus composed just before the writing of the great tragedies in which Shakespeare's powers are seen at their height. It does not seem to have been performed again until 1662, and in fact, until recently, it was not popular on the stage in spite of its theatrical craftsmanship.

For many years it was not popular with the critics either. Coleridge, to whom we owe some of our most penetrating Shakespeare criticism, found it "a hateful work," indeed "the only painful play" that Shakespeare ever wrote. Its comedy disgusted him and its tragedy seemed merely horrible. His sense of justice was revolted by the pardon of Angelo, the corrupt deputy who is virtually guilty of both murder and rape. The heroine, Isabella, was an unamiable character who primly preferred her own chastity to her brother's life. As for that brother, he was a weak, vacillating youth who expected his sister to come to his rescue when he was overtaken by the consequences of his own immorality. The entire play lurched and slithered to an unearned happy ending that was altogether unconvincing. With the notable exception of Walter Pater, who wrote a fine essay on the play in *Appreciations*, most of the nineteenth-century critics of Shakespeare thought the play was a regrettable performance, a dark comedy, full of un-Shakespearean satire and cynicism. The only explanations they could think of were that some personal calamity or disillusionment had befallen the dramatist at the time he wrote the play or that the early sixteenth-century *Zeitgeist* was responsible for the gloom of the play.

In our own day a very different view of the play is favored. Most critics hold that the play should be read not as naturalistic drama in the nineteenth-century mode, but as a dramatic parable, symbolic in character and event, embodying some of the noblest precepts of the Christian faith. (The foremost exponent of this view has been G. Wilson Knight, though it was foreshadowed in the introduction to the play in the American First Folio edition of Charlotte Porter and Helen A. Clarke, 1903-12.) The

new interpretation may occasionally claim a consistency of impression that the play does not quite warrant, but it is more coherent than the old view, which implicitly accused Shakespeare of confusing art with life. While this is the majority view, some modern critics, such as Mary M. Lascelles, feel that the play is uneven, though great at times. They think that Shakespeare's artistic experience has raised questions that cannot properly be answered, sometimes even asked, in the restrictive medium of tragi-comedy. As for the religious significance of the play, they feel that its action and characterization are more intimately inspired by Shakespeare's immediate sources in drama and folklore than by Christianity. The Italian storybook that he probably consulted contains several tales on the theme of a woman forgiving an enemy who has done her an irreparable wrong, and the folklore of Shakespeare's day had popularized the legend of a good monarch who, like the duke in our play, moves among his people in disguise to find out the truth for himself and to protect the good and punish the wicked.

Shakespeare's chief source was almost certainly George Whetstone's *Promos and Cassandra* (1578), an earnest but dull and tedious play in two parts of five acts each. Whetstone made a prose version of the story for his collection of stories called the *Heptameron of Civil Discourses* (1582). In addition to these works, Shakespeare very probably knew the Italian source of Whetstone, the *Hecatommithi* (1565) of Giraldi Cinthio, and Cinthio's dramatized version of the story, *Epitia* (1583). For summaries of these sources, see A Note on the Sources (pp. 1141-42).

When Shakespeare took up Whetstone's tale of Cassandra and Promos, he made certain far-reaching changes. (And let us add here that none of these changes would amount to much but for Shakespeare's poetry, a fact that source-study should not take for granted.) In the first place, Cassandra's enforced acceptance of the loathsome and virtually illusory choice thrust on her by Promos wounds our moral feelings, and her last-minute marriage, by royal fiat, to the violator of her honor merely adds insult to injury. Even in Shakespeare's day Puritan moralists, to mention only one group, held that there were certain wrongs that no marriage could redress. Moreover,

Cassandra's sudden change from hatred to love as soon as she is married to Promos is incredible. Very properly, therefore, Shakespeare made his heroine refuse to yield to Angelo. But since the story required that Angelo's condition somehow be met, he created the character of Mariana and substituted her for Isabella by means of an old folk-tale device that was presumably acceptable to the original audience. The bed trick, as it is usually called, had already been used in what is very likely an earlier play, *All's Well That Ends Well*. The bed trick does not commend itself to modern taste and does not quite agree with the temper of the play, but we must remember that Mariana is deeply in love with Angelo, and the consummation of her love leads to her marriage to him at the end. Our sympathies are so firmly engaged in her behalf that we want her to be happy, and we wink at this otherwise dubious method of securing her happiness.

Shakespeare also altered the significance of the brother's offense. In Whetstone's play, Andrugio is guilty of fornication, committed, as in Shakespeare's play, with the girl's consent. Cassandra attributes her brother's offense partly to the irresistible force of love and partly to his youth. In *Measure for Measure*, however, Claudio explains the reason for his arrest differently:

> From too much liberty, my Lucio, liberty.
> As surfeit is the father of much fast,
> So every scope by the immoderate use
> Turns to restraint. Our natures do pursue,
> Like rats that ravin down their proper bane,
> A thirsty evil, and when we drink, we die. (I.ii.128–33)

In our very nature there is something that drives us into acts of "too much liberty," which we loathe even while we indulge in them. It is the old problem stated by Paul in his Epistle to the Romans:

> For that which I do, I allow not: for what I would, that do I not; but what I hate, that do I. . . . For I know that in me (that is, in my flesh) dwelleth no good thing: for to will is present with me; but how to perform that which is good I find not. For the good that I would, I do not; but the evil which I would not, that I do. . . . I find then a law, that, when I would do good, evil is present with me.

Claudio is angry and disgusted with himself, as we see from the simile that he uses. Self-restraint is essential, but seems impossible. He does not know what to do about his problem. His friend, Lucio, described in the original list of actors as "a fantastic," does not see that there is a problem. His view of the matter is reflected in the imagery of his speech describing Claudio's offense:

> Your brother and his lover have embraced;
> As those that feed grow full, as blossoming time
> That from the seedness the bare fallow brings
> To teeming foison, even so her plenteous womb
> Expresseth his full tilth and husbandry. (I.iv.40–44)

Juliet's "fertility" was realized by Claudio's "tilth." *Not* to do as Claudio did is to be guilty of a lack of "husbandry." Man must be natural in his sexual life, even as nonhuman nature is. Later Lucio implies that sex will stop only when

men give up eating; "one fruitful meal will set me to it." There is enough truth in this view of human sex to make it superficially attractive, but Shakespeare puts us on our guard by showing us its consequences. Corruption boils and bubbles in Vienna. Lucio himself, it transpires, has seduced a girl after promising to marry her, and has abandoned her and the child. (Incidentally, the child has been looked after by a bawd, a fact that should make us distrust theories of Shakespeare's cynicism in *Measure for Measure*.) He has degenerated into a coarse sensualist, bent on his own pleasures and heedless of all the essential obligations of a decent life in society. Even his interest in Claudio's pardon is not altogether unselfish. He tells Claudio that he prays Isabella may persuade Angelo to pardon Claudio "as well for the encouragement of the like, which else would stand under grievous imposition, as for the enjoying of thy life, who I would be sorry should be thus foolishly lost at a game of tick-tack" (I.ii.190–94).

Shakespeare's heroine, Isabella, is a novice of the order of Saint Clare. Why Shakespeare made this change is difficult to explain. It has been argued that he did so in order to make clear to his original audience, brought up, as it were, on heroines who gave up their chastity to save condemned brothers, that *his* heroine was a chip off a much different block, and that she could not yield to the judge because she was going to be a nun. But Shakespeare's young women do not require motivation or cause for chastity. It is an absolute value with them. Her novitiate may be related to the problem raised by her brother: Is self-control possible when the blood prompts? The "prompture of the blood" is one of her own phrases (II.iv.177), and she seems not ignorant of it personally, if we may judge from the accents of her admission to Angelo that women, no less than men, are frail:

> Ay, as the glasses where they view themselves,
> Which are as easy broke as they make forms.
> Women! Help heaven! Men their creation mar
> In profiting by them. Nay, call us ten times frail;
> For we are soft as our complexions are,
> And credulous to false prints. (II.iv.124–29)

And then there is the "singular rigidity of her bearing" when she denounces her brother in the prison for daring to suggest that she yield to Angelo:

>                              O you beast,
> O faithless coward, O dishonest wretch!
> Wilt thou be made a man out of my vice?
> Is't not a kind of incest, to take life
> From thine own sister's shame? What should I think?
> Heaven shield my mother played my father fair,
> For such a warpèd slip of wilderness
> Ne'er issued from his blood. Take my defiance,
> Die, perish! Might but my bending down
> Reprieve thee from thy fate, it should proceed.
> I'll pray a thousand prayers for thy death,
> No word to save thee. (III.i.135–46)

It is not her basic stand, her refusal to yield, that one objects to here—though Sir Arthur Quiller-Couch was moved to declare that there was something rancid in her chastity—but the harsh tone she takes with her poor brother when he is trembling on the brink of the grave. This harshness, I think, reflects her bitterness at being asked to abet the "prompture of the blood." The only rule of the convent that we hear of in the play relates to receiving male visitors, and Isabella desires an even "stricter restraint" upon the votarists of Saint Clare, though that order of nuns has the reputation of being the strictest of the Roman Catholic Church. At the end of the play the duke makes her a proposal which, he says, "much imports her good." It surely cannot be the rank of Duchess of Vienna, because she is not presented in the play as a girl with whom such material considerations would weigh. Presumably she accepts the duke's proposal, for, though the text is silent on that point, the stage action called for when the duke says, "Give me your hand, and say you will be mine" is suggestive. (In Shakespeare's day it was perfectly in order for a novice to go back to secular life.) The novitiate of Isabella, I suggest, is *her* response to the problem of the prompture of the blood, and it is attractive to believe that she finally discovered that the problem could be resolved in the state of marriage also.

She could have learned this from Mariana. The creation of the character, Mariana, it has been noted above, is another change that Shakespeare made in his source. In spite of Angelo's perfidy, which, says the duke, "in all reason should have quenched her love" for him, she continues to cherish him. Nevertheless she hesitates to substitute herself for Isabella in Angelo's bed until she is assured by her spiritual adviser that it is no sin. Hers is a love marked by the depth and not the tumult of the soul; it is a fervent but not ungovernable love. And it is so because it is devoted to the welfare of the beloved's soul. In the last act, when she pleads with the duke to pardon her husband, she claims that "best men are molded out of faults;/And, for the most, become much more the better/For being a little bad" (V.i.441-43). Mariana's love, we may say without undue exaggeration, is a humble human instance of that divine love which, Isabella reminds Angelo in II.ii, found out the remedy when "all the souls that were, were forfeit." We know that Isabella is deeply moved as she listens to the story of Mariana's lovelorn misery, and perhaps Isabella learns from Mariana that a love centered on the soul of the beloved is free from the prompture of the blood.

There is a curious resemblance between Isabella and Angelo. It is intimated, when the duke summons Angelo to take up the reins of office, that he too has lived a life of some seclusion. Lucio tells us that Angelo has tried to "blunt his natural edge/With profits of the mind, study and fast" (I.iv.60-61); the duke admits that Angelo is "precise" and "scarce confesses/That his blood flows" (I.iii.51-52); and Lucio adds irreverently that his "blood/Is very snow-broth" (I.iv.57-58) and "his urine is congealed ice" (III.ii.111-12)! This strictness of conduct is not hypocrisy. Isabella herself allows in V.i that "a due sincerity" governed his official actions until he set eyes on her. But when she appears before him, the prompture of the blood overcomes him. He says, "Never could the strumpet,/With all her double vigor, art and nature,/Once stir my temper" (II.ii.183-85); but the very virtue of Isabella proves his undoing. The truth seems to be that he has identified his virtue wholly with a mode of external conduct. His correct conduct does not represent a trans-

formed will, but is merely a factitious creation. It is not a habit of the soul. He explains to the duke in the last act that he rejected Mariana because he suspected her of levity. It is altogether characteristic of him that he should make this mistake. His ear, coarsened by a strident moralistic code that is throttling the instincts, cannot catch the quiet melody of an ethic that has educated the very rhythm of the blood. So "the natural guiltiness" that Isabella speaks of remains, subverting virtue itself to effect Angelo's downfall. He too is a victim of the problem of "we would, and we would not," as he himself points out (IV.iv.34). And the problem arises, he adds, when we have forgotten our "grace," a word that may have a specific Christian sense in view of Isabella's charge that he is not "new made." The duke's death sentence releases Angelo from an intolerable, meaningless existence, and he welcomes it. We may stretch our belief a bit and take it that he is a new-made man after he is pardoned. To detest him and to quarrel with Shakespeare for letting him off is perhaps natural, for the process of his contrition is not fully presented, but we must try to recognize duly his part in the design of the play.

Angelo's ignorance of the true inwardness of virtue is also the cause of the excessive legalism of his rule. At bottom, the rule of law as Angelo interprets it is ultimately futile. Its severity is aimless, and its achievements are transitory. "There is so great a fever on goodness, that the dissolution of it must cure it," says the disguised duke to Escalus (III.ii 223-24). At best, law can only regulate our outward conduct; it cannot change "the old man" in us. And as long as that change does not take place, sensuality will prevail in Vienna—and elsewhere. The wise old Escalus, the most genial character in the play, tries to deal with the problem in his gentle, humanitarian way, but he discovers that Mistress Overdone is "still forfeit in the same kind" after "double and treble admonition" (III.ii. 194-95). Pompey refuses to change at all. The duke himself, as it happens, intervenes to save Claudio's life precisely when Claudio sues to be rid of it. In dealing with Barnardine, the duke reveals his essentially spiritual approach to the problem of law and justice. Barnardine is a murderer and has "a stubborn soul,/That apprehends no further than this world" (V.i.482-83), and he has lived accordingly. When the duke pardons all Barnardine's earthly faults, he entrusts him to a friar for advice. There seems to be some difference between the duke and Isabella in their attitudes toward dealing with criminals. When Isabella first appears before Angelo, she does not plead, as Cassandra had done before Promos in Whetstone's play, that her brother is willing to marry the girl and that the marriage should be taken as setting right the wrong done. Lucio has told her that what the law seeks is not to enforce marriage between sexual offenders, to regularize irregular sexual unions by means of marriage *ex post facto*, but "to give fear to use and liberty" (I.iv.62). So she pleads simply for mercy. Angelo's reply is that he cannot pardon Claudio because Claudio is a forfeit of the law, not of Angelo. She reminds him that "all the souls that were were forfeit once;/And He that might the vantage best have took/Found out the remedy" (II.ii.74-76). And so would Angelo now, she implies, if he were "new made." Angelo's reply is that he did not make the law, but merely administers it; hence her reference to the remedy is irrelevant. Then she shifts her argument: though many have committed this offense, nobody has *died* for it. Angelo retorts that that is precisely why the law should be enforced now so that intending offenders might take note. She then exclaims: "O, it is excellent/To have a giant's strength; but it is tyrannous/To use it like a giant" (II.ii.108–10). The punishment should be related not to the strength of the punisher, but to the nature of the offense and the capacity of the offender to bear the punishment. If man knew his "glassy essence," he would know in whose image he had been made, and the knowledge would teach him how to exercise his authority. Then she goes on to remind Angelo of the dependence of justice on the social status of the offender. She ends the first day's argument by declaring that none is qualified to judge who himself suffers from "the natural guiltiness." On the second day Angelo opens the argument with the proposition that murder and fornication are equally culpable. When Isabella objects that "'tis set down so in heaven, but not in earth," he invites her to commit fornication to save her brother. She is forced to make a distinction between "lawful mercy" and "foul redemption." Thus the question is raised: What is "lawful mercy"? We have seen the duke's answer: it is "lawful mercy" when the criminal is reformed by means of his spiritual reeducation. The case for lawful mercy to Claudio, his "free pardon," must rest on the fact that Claudio is "new made." How? Once again we must turn to the duke, to what he says and does in the play.

In fact, one of the most significant changes that Shakespeare made from his sources was to enlarge the role of the ruler in the story to make him a disguised spectator of the action of the play, and later an active participant in it, instead of a fifth-act *deus ex machina* solving all the otherwise insoluble problems of the play. Duke Vincentio has been rather slack in his public duties, loving his subjects not wisely but too well, and this is, as he himself rather ruefully confesses, a serious fault in him. But he is a scholar, and his supreme concern has always been to know himself. When he contributes in his indirect way to the debate initiated by Claudio, he implies that self-restraint is both essential and possible. In II.iii he goes to the prison, disguised as a friar, to console "the afflicted spirits" there, and requests the Provost to inform him of the nature of the crimes committed by the condemned prisoners so that he may "minister to them accordingly." With Claudio, the ministration takes the significant form of setting him free from "the deceiving promises of life" and of creating in him a calm resolution to face the approaching end. Sir Thomas More, the Tudor statesman and saint about whom Shakespeare may have helped to write a play, declares in his little treatise, *The Four Last Things*, written to teach the art of "dying well," that nothing can more effectively withdraw the human soul from the wretched affections of the body than a sincere remembrance of death. "The thirsty evil" that Claudio bemoans is the consequence of an excessive attachment to life. The duke succeeds with Claudio to the extent that, after a momentary lapse that shows how strong the hold of life is, Claudio says, "I am so out of love with life, that I will sue to be rid of it" (III.i. 170–71). After this scene Claudio appears very briefly only once more, but the three lines that he speaks (IV.ii.67–69) have a calmness of image and rhythm that is reassuring.

With Angelo the duke seemingly decides on "measure for measure." He also reminds Isabella that the ghost of her brother, whom she supposes to be dead, cries out for vengeance. In condemning Angelo, the duke thus seems to observe the law of the Old Testament—an eye for an eye and a tooth for a tooth. But actually he is testing Isabella's adherence to the New Law, which commands that one's enemy shall be loved as a friend, and that good shall be returned for evil. How superbly she meets the test! She does not plead for Angelo's pardon, for she has seen Mariana's plea for mercy disallowed. With a boldness that takes the breath away, she asserts that Angelo is not guilty at all. There are three charges against him: his "salt imagination" wronged her honor; he violated sacred chastity; and he broke his promise that he would pardon Claudio if the foul ransom was paid. On the first charge, the duke himself has recommended that Angelo be pardoned because that "salt imagination" provided the opportunity for doing a service to Mariana. The second charge is not true, since Mariana was Angelo's wife on "a precontract." As for the "promise-breach," it cannot be denied that Isabella did not in fact lie with Angelo, or that her brother was guilty, after all, of the crime for which he was sentenced. The type of betrothal which Claudio and Juliet had entered upon did not in law give them any marital rights, whereas Mariana's contract with Angelo did, at least in law. Finally, it is true that Angelo intended to violate her, but the intention never became an act, and the law cannot take cognizance of thoughts. "Thoughts are no subjects,/Intents but merely thoughts" (V.i.455–56). Counsel for the defense submits therefore that the accused is not guilty on any count, does not need a pardon, and cannot be punished with "measure for measure." The prosperous art Isabella shows in playing with reason and discourse could hardly go further. These arguments convince the duke not of Angelo's guiltlessness, of course, but of Isabella's adherence to the New Law. When Angelo is pardoned, it is because he, like Claudio earlier, is deeply repentant. We must believe that his evil has quit him.

Such, then, are some of the themes and characters of the play before us. Shakespeare's contemporaries would probably have called it a tragi-comedy, a new genre in those days. Tragi-comedy is not a loose combining of tragedy and comedy, but an independent form of dramatic composition with an aesthetic of its own. As the Italian playwright Giambattista Guarini, who had himself written a tragi-comedy, stated in his *Compendium of Tragi-Comic Poetry* (published in 1601): "He who makes a tragi-comedy does not intend to compose separately either a tragedy or a comedy, but from the two a third thing that will be perfect of its kind, and may take from the others the parts that with most verisimilitude can stand together." From tragedy, said Guarini, tragi-comedy takes the movement but not the disturbance of the feelings, the pleasure and not the sadness, the danger but not the death; from comedy, it takes laughter that is not excessive, modest amusement, feigned difficulty, happy reversal, and, above all, the comic order. Speaking of the style proper to tragi-comedy, Guarini said that the magnificent was its norm, combined not with the grave as in a tragedy, but with the polished. There is something in this description of tragi-comedy that fits *Measure for Measure*. For instance, our awareness of the immanence of the duke, with his declared objective of testing whether power will change purpose effectively, diverts the first part of the play from the tragic course. The intrigue of the fourth act, the "feigned difficulty," does not exist for its own sake, but serves to establish the control of the duke over the action and to lead to a happy conclusion. (The duke has been often compared to Prospero in *The Tempest*, but Prospero's control over what is happening is never in doubt. The same consideration should make us hesitate to accept the extreme conclusion in the Christian interpretation of the play that the duke is Providence; Providence never had such a narrow escape from defeat at human hands.) We have not spoken much of the "modest amusement" of tragi-comedy in *Measure for Measure*, but it is there in plenty, in character, situation, and dialogue; *Measure for Measure* is a funny play, though some of the jokes, admittedly, sail very close to the wind. As for the style, its norm is indeed magnificent, but its range is wide: from the passionate conjurations of Isabella, the tortured self-examinations of Angelo, the exploratory dialectic of Angelo and Isabella in which we see character *developing*, the relentless meditative analysis of the duke, and the surging thrill of terror in Claudio as he gazes into the dark void of the beyond—from all these to the gay, irreverent bawdry of Lucio, which sets up a rival social order and morality, and the petty cunning of Pompey's coiled speech with Escalus. All may not easily agree with F. R. Leavis that *Measure for Measure* is "the most consummate of Shakespeare's achievements," but we must acknowledge with Coleridge that it is Shakespearean throughout.

## A NOTE ON THE SOURCES

The principal sources of *Measure for Measure* are George Whetstone's play of *Promos and Cassandra* (1578) and its prose redaction in the same author's *Heptameron of Civil Discourses* (1582). Whetstone's own source was Giraldi Cinthio's *Hecatommithi* (1565); and Shakespeare almost certainly knew this work, which contains the story of Othello. He may, in addition, have also known Cinthio's posthumously published play of *Epitia* (1583). Brief summaries of these sources are given here for comparison with Shakespeare's treatment of the story.

GIRALDI CINTHIO's *Hecatommithi*, DECADE 8, NOVELLA 5

The Emperor Maximian appoints one of his trusted men, Juriste, to rule over the city of Innsbruck. He charges him particularly to observe justice scrupulously. Juriste, who lacks all self-knowledge, accepts the grave responsibility with alacrity and for a while he is a model ruler.

A young man called Vico is brought before Juriste for violating a virgin, and is condemned to death according to the laws of the city. Vico's sister, Epitia, who is a student of philosophy and has a sweet way of speaking, pleads for her brother: her brother is very young; he was moved by the impulse of love; the ravished maiden is unmarried and Vico is willing to marry her; the law was made so severe only to deter would-be offenders, not really to be enforced. Captivated by Epitia's beauty and eloquence, Juriste promises to reconsider the case. When she meets him again, he proposes that she should lie with him if she wants her brother's sentence to be mitigated. Epitia refuses unless Juriste is willing to marry her afterward. Juriste does not promise to do this, though he hints at the possibility.

When Epitia goes to the prison to prepare her brother for his fate, Vico pleads passionately with her and appeals to her sisterly affection to save him. So Epitia reluctantly consents to Juriste's proposal. Juriste, however, orders the execution of Vico before lying with her.

In the morning Epitia goes home to find that Juriste has indeed kept his promise to release her brother—dead. She thinks of revenge, but instead appeals to the emperor. The emperor sends for Juriste and finds that the complaint is true. He first forces Juriste to marry Epitia, who is quite unwilling, and then he orders that Juriste be put to death. Now that Juriste is her husband, Epitia is in a cruel dilemma. She discourses to the emperor on the superiority of clemency to justice. The emperor is impressed with her forgiving nature and pardons Juriste. Epitia and her husband live happily ever after.

GIRALDI CINTHIO's *Epitia*

The story is much the same as that in the *Hecatommithi*, but there are some new characters and the brother is secretly saved by the captain of the prison. The latter announces this fact at the end of the play, to the astonishment of the other characters and also the reader, who is not given a hint of it in the prefatory "argument."

Principal among the new characters are Angela, Juriste's sister, who conveys an offer of marriage from him to Epitia and testifies against him before the emperor when Juriste breaks his word; a secretary and a podesta who argue respectively for and against forgiving Vico; a messenger who reports how Vico was put to death on special commission from the podesta, who had Juriste's authority to do so; and the captain of the prison, who brings the supposed head of Vico to Epitia.

Epitia refuses to plead for Juriste until she learns that her brother is alive. Believing that Juriste should be punished for evil intent, the emperor is at first unwilling to pardon him even after Vico reappears, but he finally grants Epitia's suit in order that she may have "complete contentment."

WHETSTONE's *Promos and Cassandra* AND *Heptameron*

In the play, Promos is appointed to rule over the city of Julio, and declares his resolve to render justice impartially. Reviving a defunct law, he sentences Andrugio to death for incontinence. The law will not accept marriage as sufficient recompense for the wrong. Andrugio's sister, Cassandra, weeps over the hard fate of her young brother, who appeals to her to plead with Promos. She therefore meets Promos and obtains a postponement of the execution. After she has left, Promos reveals in a soliloquy that he has fallen in love with her but is determined to overcome the temptation. However, having been encouraged by his corrupt servant, Phallax, to believe that Cassandra might be overcome, he is unable to subdue his desire for her. When she meets him again to learn his final decision, he first defends the law and then, when she pleads for mercy, makes his infamous proposal.

Amazed and horrified, Cassandra refuses. Promos promises to make her his wife and gives her two days in which to think it over. She goes to her brother's cell to inform him of Promos' vile condition and to prepare him for death. Andrugio, taken aback that a judge of Promos' supposed integrity has been corrupted by the same lust for which he would condemn another, appeals to his sister to accept the proposed terms and thereby save his life. Brother and sister argue, but finally Cassandra is won over.

After satisfying his desire, Promos decides to break his word, since no one knows of his promise and Cassandra cannot reveal her own shame. He orders that Andrugio should be executed secretly and his head sent to Cassandra. While the girl is eagerly looking forward to welcoming her brother, the jailer brings her the severed head. She conceals her grief, pretending to be quite satisfied. She thinks of suicide, but later decides to appeal to the king. The jailer has in fact brought her the head of an executed criminal and released Andrugio, who goes into hiding. Promos is secretly troubled at what he has done.

In the second part of the play, the king comes to Julio. He hears Cassandra's story and promises to see that justice is done. Upon examination, Promos at once confesses, and the king orders that he first be married to Cassandra and then put to death. Promos pleads for mercy, but in vain. In the meantime, Andrugio, hiding in the woods, comes to know what is happening. Cassandra bewails her hard fate. Duty commands that she should love the husband for whose sentence she has been responsible. She appeals to the king to pardon him, but the ruler is adamant. Andrugio, now in the city under a disguise, sees his sister's unhappiness and resolves to surrender himself to the king at the risk of being put to death. Promos makes a sincere confession of his misdeeds and is led out to execution. Andrugio's boy enters with the news that his master is alive. The king pardons Andrugio, and then pardons Promos for the sake of Cassandra, exhorting Promos always to measure grace with justice. He restores him to the governorship of the city. "The lost sheep found, for joy the feast was made."

Whetstone's play also has a comic underplot, involving a courtesan, unscrupulous officers, informers, and bawds. With the corruption of the magistrates, all the city becomes corrupt.

The version in the *Heptameron* is substantially the same as that of the play. Andrugio is disguised as a hermit, and reveals himself after hearing the king say that Promos might be pardoned if Andrugio were alive. The entire story is narrated by one Isabella.

## Summary

*Measure for Measure* is generally closer to Whetstone's versions than to *Epitia*; but it does show significant correspondences with Cinthio's play at certain points where Whetstone differs markedly. "The relation of *Measure for Measure* to Giraldi's *novella* is ambiguous, since some of the correspondences to that might have come through Whetstone, some through *Epitia*."[1] Among the similarities between *Measure for Measure* and *Epitia* may be mentioned the following: the secretary in *Epitia* protests to the podesta of the harshness of the law and the severity of its enforcement; in a soliloquy he comments on the rigor of those in power (compare Escalus' protests to Angelo in II.i); the criminal whose head is substituted for that of Vico is hopelessly evil (compare Ragozine, described as a notorious pirate); like Isabella, Epitia also distinguishes between act and intention. Some close verbal parallels have been noted by Kenneth Muir.[2]

## A NOTE ON THE TEXT

Our only authority for the text of *Measure for Measure* is the First Folio, whose text is on the whole a good one, probably based on a transcript of Shakespeare's manuscripts made by Ralph Crane, the scrivener of the King's Players. It seems a little disturbed in Act IV; the duke's speech on "place and greatness" in this act would be more appropriate preceding his lines in III.ii, after the exit of Lucio, and Kenneth Muir has made the attractive suggestion that its place should be taken by the duke's soliloquy ending Act III. In the present text the act and scene divisions are translated from Latin and in two places depart from the Folio in order to correspond to the Globe text (the Globe's divisions are used in most books on Shakespeare): Globe I.ii is split in the Folio into a new scene after the exit of Pompey, and Globe III.ii is not marked in the Folio. The present edition corrects obvious typographical errors, modernizes spelling and punctuation, expands and regularizes speech prefixes, adjusts the lineation of a few passages, transfers the indication of locale ("*The Scene:* Vienna") and the *dramatis personae* ("The Names of All the Actors") from the end to the beginning, and slightly alters the position of a few stage directions. Other substantial departures from the Folio are listed below, the present reading in boldface type and then the Folio reading in roman.

**I.iii.27 Becomes more** More   **43 it** in
**I.iv.54 givings-out** giuing-out
**II.i.12 your** our   **39 breaks** brakes
**II.ii.97 new** now   **112 ne'er** neuer
**II.iv.9 sere** feard   **52 or, to** and to   **75 Let me be** Let be   **93 all-binding** all-building
**III.i.31 serpigo** Sapego   **52 Bring me to hear them** Bring them to heare me   **68 Though** Through   **129 penury** periury   **214 by oath** oath
**III.ii.26 eat, array** eate away   **48 extracting it** extracting   **152 dearer** deare   **225 and it** and as it   **276 strings** stings
**IV.i.62 quests** Quest   **64 dreams** dreame
**IV.ii.45–48 if it be too little . . . fits your thief** [F gives to Pompey]
**IV.iii.16 Forthright** Forthlight   **90 yonder** yond
**IV.iv.6 redeliver** reliuer
**V.i.13 me** we   **168 her face** your face   **425 confiscation** confutation   **541 that's** that

---

[1] Madeleine Doran, *Endeavors of Art: A Study of Form in Elizabethan Drama* (1954), pp. 386–87.

[2] *Shakespeare's Sources* (1957), Vol. I, pp. 104–05.

# MEASURE FOR MEASURE

*The Scene:* Vienna

The Names of All the Actors:

VINCENTIO *the Duke*
ANGELO *the Deputy*
ESCALUS *an ancient lord*
CLAUDIO *a young gentleman*
LUCIO *a fantastic*
TWO OTHER LIKE GENTLEMEN
PROVOST
THOMAS⎫ *two friars*
PETER ⎭
[A JUSTICE]
[VARRUS]

ELBOW *a simple constable*
FROTH *a foolish gentleman*
CLOWN [*Pompey, servant to Mistress Overdone*]
ABHORSON *an executioner*
BARNARDINE *a dissolute prisoner*
ISABELLA *sister to Claudio*
MARIANA *betrothed to Angelo*
JULIET *beloved of Claudio*
FRANCISCA *a nun*
MISTRESS OVERDONE *a bawd*
[LORDS OFFICERS CITIZENS BOY
ATTENDANTS]

## ACT I

### Scene I. [*The duke's palace.*]

*Enter* DUKE, ESCALUS, LORDS, [*and* ATTENDANTS].

DUKE  Escalus.
ESCALUS  My lord.
DUKE
Of government the properties° to unfold,
Would seem in me t' affect speech and discourse,
Since I am put to know° that your own science°        5
Exceeds, in that, the lists° of all advice
My strength can give you. Then no more remains.
But that, to your sufficiency as your worth is able,°
And let them work. The nature of our people,
Our city's institutions, and the terms        10

*The decorative border shown above was used in the First Folio
edition of Shakespeare's plays, 1623.*

**1.1.3 properties** characteristics  **5 put to know** given to
understand; **science** knowledge  **6 lists** limits  **8 to . . . able**
perhaps a line is missing after this line

For common justice, y' are as pregnant in°
As art and practice hath enrichèd any
That we remember. There is our commission,
From which we would not have you warp.° Call
   hither,
I say, bid come before us Angelo.        15
                              [*Exit an* ATTENDANT.]
What figure° of us, think you, he will bear?°
For you must know, we have with special soul°
Elected him our absence to supply;
Lent him our terror, dressed him with our love,
And given his deputation all the organs°        20
Of our own pow'r. What think you of it?
ESCALUS
If any in Vienna be of worth
To undergo° such ample grace and honor,
It is Lord Angelo.

*Enter* ANGELO.

DUKE                    Look where he comes.

**11 pregnant in** full of knowledge of  **14 warp** deviate  **16
figure** image; **bear** represent  **17 soul** thought  **20 organs**
means of action  **23 undergo** enjoy

1143

ANGELO
Always obedient to your grace's will,                                    25
I come to know your pleasure.
DUKE                                          Angelo,
There is a kind of character° in thy life,
That to th' observer doth thy history
Fully unfold. Thyself and thy belongings°
Are not thine own so proper° as to waste                                 30
Thyself upon thy virtues, they on thee.
Heaven doth with us as we with torches do,°
Not light them for themselves; for if our virtues
Did not go forth of us, 'twere all alike
As if we had them not. Spirits are not finely touched                    35
But to fine issues,° nor Nature never lends
The smallest scruple° of her excellence
But like a thrifty goddess she determines
Herself the glory of a creditor,
Both thanks and use.° But I do bend° my speech                           40
To one that can my part in him advertise.°
Hold therefore, Angelo°:
In our remove° be thou at full ourself;
Mortality and mercy in Vienna
Live in thy tongue and heart. Old Escalus,                               45
Though first in question,° is thy secondary.°
Take thy commission.
ANGELO                             Now, good my lord,
Let there be some more test made of my mettle°
Before so noble and so great a figure
Be stamped upon it.
DUKE                               No more evasion.                       50
We have with a leavened° and preparèd choice
Proceeded to you; therefore take your honors.
Our haste from hence is of so quick condition
That it prefers itself,° and leaves unquestioned°
Matters of needful value. We shall write to you,                         55
As time and our concernings shall importune,
How it goes with us, and do look to know
What doth befall you here. So fare you well.
To th' hopeful execution do I leave you
Of your commissions.
ANGELO                            Yet give leave, my lord,                60
That we may bring° you something on the way.
DUKE
My haste may not admit it;
Nor need you, on mine honor, have to do
With any scruple; your scope is as mine own,
So to enforce or qualify the laws                                        65
As to your soul seems good. Give me your hand.
I'll privily away; I love the people,
But do not like to stage me to their eyes.
Though it do well, I do not relish well

Their loud applause and aves° vehement.                                  70
Nor do I think the man of safe discretion
That does affect it. Once more, fare you well.
ANGELO
The heavens give safety to your purposes.
ESCALUS
Lead forth and bring you back in happiness.
DUKE
I thank you; fare you well.                        Exit.  75
ESCALUS
I shall desire you, sir, to give me leave
To have free speech with you; and it concerns me
To look into the bottom of my place.°
A pow'r I have, but of what strength and nature,
I am not yet instructed.                                                 80
ANGELO
'Tis so with me. Let us withdraw together,
And we may soon our satisfaction have
Touching that point.
ESCALUS                          I'll wait upon your honor.
                                               Exeunt.


## Scene II. [A street.]

_Enter_ LUCIO _and two other_ GENTLEMEN.

LUCIO   If the duke, with the other dukes, come not to
composition° with the King of Hungary,° why then
all the dukes fall upon the king.
FIRST GENTLEMAN   Heaven grant us its peace, but
not the King of Hungary's!                                               5
SECOND GENTLEMAN   Amen.
LUCIO   Thou conclud'st like the sanctimonious pirate,
that went to sea with the Ten Commandments, but
scraped one out of the table.
SECOND GENTLEMAN   "Thou shalt not steal"?                               10
LUCIO   Ay, that he razed.
FIRST GENTLEMAN   Why, 'twas a commandment to
command the captain and all the rest from their func-
tions: they put forth to steal. There's not a soldier of
us all that, in the thanksgiving before meat, do relish      15
the petition well that prays for peace.
SECOND GENTLEMAN   I never heard any soldier dis-
like it.
LUCIO   I believe thee, for I think thou never wast
where grace was said.                                                    20
SECOND GENTLEMAN   No? A dozen times at least.
FIRST GENTLEMAN   What, in meter?
LUCIO   In any proportion,° or in any language.
FIRST GENTLEMAN   I think, or in any religion.
LUCIO   Ay, why not? Grace is grace, despite of all      25
controversy: as, for example, thou thyself art a
wicked villain, despite of all grace.
FIRST GENTLEMAN   Well, there went but a pair of
shears between us.°
LUCIO   I grant; as there may between the lists° and      30
the velvet. Thou art the list.

27 **character** secret handwriting   29 **belongings** endowments
30 **proper** exclusively   32 **Heaven . . . do** see Luke 11:33,
"No man, when he hath lighted a candle, putteth it in a
secret place, neither under a bushel, but on a candlestick that
they which come in may see the light"; also Matthew 7:16,
"Ye shall know them by their fruits"   35–36 **Spirits . . .
issues** great qualities are bestowed only so that they may
lead to great achievements   37 **scruple** 1/24 oz.   40 **use**
interest; **bend** address   41 **advertise** display prominently
43 **remove** absence   46 **question** consideration; **secondary**
officer just below the chief officer   48 **mettle** pun on _metal_,
i.e., material   51 **leavened** i.e., long-pondered   54 **prefers
itself** takes precedence; **unquestioned** unexamined   61 **bring**
escort

70 **aves** salutations   78 **To look . . . place** to examine
carefully the range of my authority
**I.ii.2 composition** agreement; **Hungary** perhaps a pun on
_hungry_   23 **proportion** length   28–29 **there . . . us** i.e., we
are cut from the same cloth   30 **lists** selvage or border of
a cloth (usually of a different material from the body)

FIRST GENTLEMAN  And thou the velvet. Thou art good velvet; thou'rt a three-piled° piece, I warrant thee. I had as lief be a list of an English kersey,° as be piled, as thou art piled, for a French velvet.° Do I 35 speak feelingly° now?

LUCIO  I think thou dost; and, indeed, with most painful feeling° of thy speech. I will, out of thine own confession, learn to begin thy health; but, whilst I live, forget to drink after thee.° 40

FIRST GENTLEMAN  I think I have done myself wrong, have I not?

SECOND GENTLEMAN  Yes, that thou hast, whether thou art tainted or free.

*Enter bawd* [MISTRESS OVERDONE].

LUCIO  Behold, behold, where Madam Mitigation 45 comes! I have purchased as many diseases under her roof as come to—

SECOND GENTLEMAN  To what, I pray?

LUCIO  Judge.

SECOND GENTLEMAN  To three thousand dolors° a 50 year.

FIRST GENTLEMAN  Ay, and more.

LUCIO  A French crown° more.

FIRST GENTLEMAN  Thou art always figuring diseases in me, but thou art full of error. I am sound. 55

LUCIO  Nay, not as one would say, healthy, but so sound as things that are hollow. Thy bones are hollow; impiety° has made a feast of thee.

FIRST GENTLEMAN  How now! Which of your hips has the most profound sciatica? 60

MISTRESS OVERDONE  Well, well; there's one yonder arrested and carried to prison was worth five thousand of you all.

SECOND GENTLEMAN  Who's that, I pray thee?

MISTRESS OVERDONE  Marry,° sir, that's Claudio, 65 Signior Claudio.

FIRST GENTLEMAN  Claudio to prison? 'Tis not so.

MISTRESS OVERDONE  Nay, but I know 'tis so. I saw him arrested; saw him carried away, and which is more, within these three days his head to be chopped 70 off.

LUCIO  But, after all this fooling, I would not have it so. Art thou sure of this?

MISTRESS OVERDONE  I am too sure of it; and it is for getting Madam Julietta with child. 75

LUCIO  Believe me, this may be. He promised to meet me two hours since, and he was ever precise in promise-keeping.

SECOND GENTLEMAN  Besides, you know, it draws something near to the speech we had to such a purpose. 80

FIRST GENTLEMAN  But, most of all, agreeing with the proclamation.

LUCIO  Away! Let's go learn the truth of it.
*Exit* [LUCIO, *with* GENTLEMEN].

MISTRESS OVERDONE  Thus, what with the war, what with the sweat,° what with the gallows, and 85 what with poverty, I am custom-shrunk.

*Enter clown* [POMPEY].

How now? What's the news with you?

POMPEY  Yonder man is carried to prison.

MISTRESS OVERDONE  Well; what has he done?

POMPEY  A woman. 90

MISTRESS OVERDONE  But what's his offense?

POMPEY  Groping for trouts in a peculiar° river.

MISTRESS OVERDONE  What? Is there a maid with child by him?

POMPEY  No, but there's a woman with maid by him. 95 You have not heard of the proclamation, have you?

MISTRESS OVERDONE  What proclamation, man?

POMPEY  All houses in the suburbs° of Vienna must be plucked down.

MISTRESS OVERDONE  And what shall become of 100 those in the city?

POMPEY  They shall stand for seed: they had gone down too, but that a wise burgher put in for them.

MISTRESS OVERDONE  But shall all our houses of resort in the suburbs be pulled down? 105

POMPEY  To the ground, mistress.

MISTRESS OVERDONE  Why, here's a change indeed in the commonwealth! What shall become of me?

POMPEY  Come, fear not you; good counselors lack no clients. Though you change your place, you need 110 not change your trade; I'll be your tapster° still. Courage, there will be pity taken on you; you that have worn your eyes almost out in the service, you will be considered.

MISTRESS OVERDONE  What's to do here, Thomas 115 Tapster? Let's withdraw.

POMPEY  Here comes Signior Claudio, led by the provost to prison; and there's Madam Juliet. *Exeunt.*

*Enter* PROVOST, CLAUDIO, JULIET, OFFICERS, LUCIO, *and two* GENTLEMEN.

CLAUDIO
Fellow, why dost thou show me thus to th' world?
Bear me to prison, where I am committed. 120

PROVOST
I do it not in evil disposition,
But from Lord Angelo, by special charge.

CLAUDIO
Thus can the demigod Authority
Make us pay down for our offense by weight.
The words of heaven: on whom it will, it will; 125
On whom it will not, so. Yet still 'tis just.°

LUCIO
Why, how now, Claudio! Whence comes this restraint?

33 **three-piled** (1) pile of a treble thickness (2) "piled" (bald) as a result of venereal disease  34 **kersey** coarse cloth (therefore "plain and honest")  35 **French velvet** (1) excellent velvet (2) French prostitute (syphilis was also known as "the French disease")  35–36 **Do . . . feelingly** i.e., Do I touch you there?  38 **feeling** personal experience  39–40 **learn . . . thee** drink to your health but not after you from the same cup (to avoid the infection)  50 **dolors** pun on *dollars*  53 **French crown** (1) *écu* (2) head that has gone bald from venereal disease  58 **impiety** immorality  65 **Marry** a light oath, from "By the Virgin Mary"

85 **sweat** sweating sickness, plague  92 **peculiar** private  98 **suburbs** in Shakespeare's London, the area of the brothels  111 **tapster** bartender, waiter (here, pimp)  125–26 **The words . . . just** see Romans 9:15, 18, "For he saith to Moses, I will have mercy on whom I will have mercy, and I will have compassion on whom I will have compassion. . . . Therefore hath he mercy on whom he will have mercy, and whom he will he hardeneth"

CLAUDIO
From too much liberty, my Lucio, liberty.
As surfeit is the father of much fast,
So every scope by the immoderate use          130
Turns to restraint. Our natures do pursue,
Like rats that ravin down their proper bane,°
A thirsty evil, and when we drink, we die.

LUCIO   If I could speak so wisely under an arrest, I
would send for certain of my creditors. And yet, to 135
say the truth, I had as lief have the foppery° of freedom
as the mortality of imprisonment. What's thy offense,
Claudio?

CLAUDIO
What but to speak of would offend again.

LUCIO   What, is't murder?          140

CLAUDIO   No.

LUCIO   Lechery?

CLAUDIO   Call it so.

PROVOST   Away, sir, you must go.

CLAUDIO
One word, good friend. Lucio, a word with you.   145

LUCIO   A hundred, if they'll do you any good. Is
lechery so looked after?

CLAUDIO
Thus stands it with me: upon a true contract
I got possession of Julietta's bed.
You know the lady, she is fast my wife,          150
Save that we do the denunciation° lack
Of outward order. This we came not to,
Only for propagation° of a dower
Remaining in the coffer of her friends,°
From whom we thought it meet to hide our love  155
Till time had made them for us. But it chances
The stealth of our most mutual entertainment
With character too gross is writ on Juliet.

LUCIO
With child, perhaps?

CLAUDIO                Unhappily, even so.
And the new deputy now for the duke—          160
Whether it be the fault and glimpse of newness,°
Or whether that the body public be
A horse whereon the governor doth ride,
Who, newly in the seat, that it may know
He can command, lets it straight feel the spur;  165
Whether the tyranny be in his place,
Or in his eminence that fills it up,
I stagger in°— but this new governor
Awakes me all the enrollèd° penalties
Which have, like unscoured armor, hung by th' wall 170
So long, that nineteen zodiacs° have gone round,
And none of them been worn; and, for a name,
Now puts the drowsy and neglected act
Freshly on me. 'Tis surely for a name.

LUCIO   I warrant it is, and thy head stands so tickle° 175
on thy shoulders, that a milkmaid, if she be in love,
may sigh it off. Send after the duke, and appeal to him.

CLAUDIO
I have done so, but he's not to be found.
I prithee, Lucio, do me this kind service:
This day my sister should the cloister enter,     180
And there receive her approbation.°
Acquaint her with the danger of my state;
Implore her, in my voice, that she make friends
To the strict deputy; bid herself assay° him.
I have great hope in that; for in her youth       185
There is a prone° and speechless dialect,
Such as move men; beside, she hath prosperous art
When she will play with reason and discourse,
And well she can persuade.

LUCIO   I pray she may; as well for the encouragement 190
of the like, which else would stand under grievous
imposition, as for the enjoying of thy life, who I
would be sorry should be thus foolishly lost at a game
of tick-tack.° I'll to her.

CLAUDIO
I thank you, good friend Lucio.                   195

LUCIO
Within two hours.

CLAUDIO                Come, officer, away!   Exeunt.


Scene III. [A monastery.]

Enter DUKE and FRIAR THOMAS.

DUKE
No, holy father; throw away that thought;
Believe not that the dribbling dart° of love
Can pierce a complete° bosom. Why I desire thee
To give me secret harbor, hath a purpose
More grave and wrinkled° than the aims and ends  5
Of burning youth.

FRIAR THOMAS   May your grace speak of it?

DUKE
My holy sir, none better knows than you
How I have ever loved the life removed,
And held in idle price to haunt assemblies
Where youth and cost, witless bravery° keeps.     10
I have delivered to Lord Angelo,
A man of stricture° and firm abstinence,
My absolute power and place here in Vienna,
And he supposes me traveled to Poland;
For so I have strewed it in the common ear,°      15
And so it is received. Now, pious sir,
You will demand of me why I do this.

FRIAR THOMAS
Gladly, my lord.

DUKE
We have strict statutes and most biting laws,
The needful bits and curbs to headstrong weeds,   20
Which for this fourteen° years we have let slip,
Even like an o'ergrown lion in a cave,

---

132 **ravin . . . bane** greedily devour what is poisonous
to them   136 **foppery** foolishness   151 **denunciation** formal
announcement   153 **propagation** increase   154 **friends** relatives   161 **fault . . . newness** i.e., weakness arising from the
sudden vision of new authority   168 **stagger in** am not sure
169 **enrollèd** inscribed in the rolls of the laws   171 **zodiacs**
i.e., years   175 **tickle** insecure

181 **approbation** novitiate   184 **assay** test, i.e., attempt to
persuade   186 **prone** winning   194 **tick-tack** a game using
a board into which pegs were fitted
**I.iii.2 dribbling dart** arrow feebly shot   3 **complete** protected, independent   5 **wrinkled** mature, aged   10 **witless
bravery** senseless show   12 **stricture** strictness   15 **common
ear** the ear of the people   21 **fourteen** in I.ii.171 the time
was "nineteen" years; doubtless the printer's copy in both lines
had either xiv or xix and in one line was misread

That goes not out to prey. Now, as fond fathers,
Having bound up the threat'ning twigs of birch,
Only to stick it in their children's sight          25
For terror, not to use; in time the rod
Becomes more mocked than feared; so our decrees,
Dead to infliction,° to themselves are dead,
And Liberty° plucks Justice by the nose;
The baby beats the nurse, and quite athwart          30
Goes all decorum.

FRIAR THOMAS     It rested in your grace
To unloose this tied-up Justice when you pleased,
And it in you more dreadful would have seemed
Than in Lord Angelo.

DUKE                    I do fear, too dreadful:
Sith° 'twas my fault to give the people scope,          35
'Twould be my tyranny to strike and gall them
For what I bid them do; for we bid this be done
When evil deeds have their permissive pass,
And not the punishment. Therefore, indeed, my
     father,
I have on Angelo imposed the office,          40
Who may, in th' ambush° of my name, strike home,
And yet my nature never in the fight
To do it slander. And to behold his sway,
I will, as 'twere a brother of your order,
Visit both prince and people. Therefore, I prithee,          45
Supply me with the habit° and instruct me
How I may formally in person bear
Like a true friar. Moe° reasons for this action
At our more leisure shall I render you;
Only, this one: Lord Angelo is precise,°          50
Stands at a guard with envy;° scarce confesses
That his blood flows, or that his appetite
Is more to bread than stone. Hence shall we see,
If power change purpose, what our seemers be.
                              *Exit, [with* FRIAR].

Scene IV. [*A nunnery.*]

*Enter* ISABELLA *and* FRANCISCA, *a nun.*

ISABELLA
And have you nuns no farther privileges?

FRANCISCA
Are not these large enough?

ISABELLA
Yes, truly. I speak not as desiring more,
But rather wishing a more strict restraint
Upon the sisterhood, the votarists of Saint Clare.°          5

LUCIO (*Within.*)
Ho! Peace be in this place!

ISABELLA                    Who's that which calls?

FRANCISCA
It is a man's voice. Gentle Isabella,
Turn you the key, and know his business of him.
You may, I may not: you are yet unsworn.
When you have vowed, you must not speak with men          10
But in the presence of the prioress:

Then, if you speak, you must not show your face,
Or, if you show your face, you must not speak.
He calls again; I pray you, answer him.          [*Exit.*]

ISABELLA
Peace and prosperity! Who is't that calls?          15

[*Enter* LUCIO.]

LUCIO
Hail, virgin—if you be, as those cheek-roses
Proclaim you are no less! Can you so stead° me
As bring me to the sight of Isabella,
A novice of this place and the fair sister
To her unhappy brother, Claudio?          20

ISABELLA
Why "her unhappy brother"? Let me ask,
The rather for I now must make you know
I am that Isabella and his sister.

LUCIO
Gentle and fair, your brother kindly greets you.
Not to be weary with you, he's in prison.          25

ISABELLA
Woe me! For what?

LUCIO
For that which, if myself might be his judge,
He should receive his punishment in thanks:
He hath got his friend with child.

ISABELLA
Sir! Make me not your story.°

LUCIO                    'Tis true.          30
I would not, though 'tis my familiar sin
With maids to seem the lapwing,° and to jest,
Tongue far from heart, play with all virgins so.
I hold you as a thing enskied and sainted,
By your renouncement, an immortal spirit;          35
And to be talked with in sincerity,
As with a saint.

ISABELLA
You do blaspheme the good in mocking me.

LUCIO
Do not believe it. Fewness and truth,° 'tis thus:
Your brother and his lover have embraced;          40
As those that feed grow full, as blossoming time
That from the seedness° the bare fallow brings
To teeming foison,° even so her plenteous womb
Expresseth his full tilth and husbandry.

ISABELLA
Someone with child by him? My cousin Juliet?          45

LUCIO
Is she your cousin?

ISABELLA
Adoptedly, as schoolmaids change their names
By vain, though apt, affection.

LUCIO                    She it is.

ISABELLA
O, let him marry her.

LUCIO                    This is the point:
The duke is very strangely gone from hence;          50
Bore many gentlemen, myself being one,
In hand and hope of action,° but we do learn

---

**28 Dead to infliction** utterly unenforced  **29 Liberty**
license  **35 Sith** since  **41 in th' ambush** under cover  **46
habit** garment  **48 Moe** more  **50 precise** fastidiously strict
**51 Stands . . . envy** defies all malicious criticism
**I.iv.5 Saint Clare** a notably strict order

**17 stead** help  **30 story** subject for mirth  **32 lapwing**
pewit (a bird that runs away from its nest to mislead intruders)
**39 Fewness and truth** briefly and truly  **42 seedness** sowing
**43 foison** harvest  **51–52 Bore . . . action** deluded . . .
with the hope of military action

By those that know the very nerves of state,
His givings-out were of an infinite distance
From his true-meant design. Upon his place, 55
And with full line of his authority,
Governs Lord Angelo, a man whose blood
Is very snow-broth; one who never feels
The wanton stings and motions of the sense,
But doth rebate and blunt his natural edge 60
With profits of the mind, study and fast.
He—to give fear to use and liberty,°
Which have for long run by the hideous law,
As mice by lions—hath picked out an act,
Under whose heavy sense° your brother's life 65
Falls into forfeit; he arrests him on it,
And follows close the rigor of the statute,
To make him an example. All hope is gone,
Unless you have the grace by your fair prayer
To soften Angelo. And that's my pith of business 70
'Twixt you and your poor brother.

ISABELLA
Doth he so? Seek his life?
LUCIO                          Has censured° him
Already, and, as I hear, the provost hath
A warrant for's execution.

ISABELLA
Alas, what poor ability's in me 75
To do him good?
LUCIO                          Assay the pow'r you have.

ISABELLA
My power? Alas, I doubt—
LUCIO                          Our doubts are traitors,
And makes° us lose the good we oft might win,
By fearing to attempt. Go to Lord Angelo,
And let him learn to know, when maidens sue, 80
Men give like gods; but when they weep and kneel,
All their petitions are as freely theirs
As they themselves would owe° them.

ISABELLA
I'll see what I can do.
LUCIO                          But speedily.

ISABELLA
I will about it straight, 85
No longer staying but to give the Mother
Notice of my affair. I humbly thank you;
Commend me to my brother; soon at night
I'll send him certain word of my success.°

LUCIO
I take my leave of you.
ISABELLA                          Good sir, adieu.      Exeunt. 90

# ACT II

## Scene I. [*A room.*]

*Enter* ANGELO, ESCALUS, *and* SERVANTS, JUSTICE.

ANGELO
We must not make a scarecrow of the law,
Setting it up to fear the birds of prey,

And let it keep one shape, till custom make it
Their perch and not their terror.
ESCALUS                          Ay, but yet
Let us be keen, and rather cut a little, 5
Than fall,° and bruise to death. Alas, this gentleman
Whom I would save had a most noble father.
Let but your honor know,
Whom I believe to be most strait° in virtue,
That, in the working of your own affections,° 10
Had time cohered with place or place with wishing,
Or that the resolute acting of your blood
Could have attained th' effect of your own purpose,
Whether you had not sometime in your life
Erred in this point which now you censure him, 15
And pulled the law upon you.

ANGELO
'Tis one thing to be tempted, Escalus,
Another thing to fall. I not deny,
The jury, passing on the prisoner's life,
May in the sworn twelve have a thief or two 20
Guiltier than him they try. What's open made to Justice,
That Justice seizes. What knows the laws
That thieves do pass on thieves? 'Tis very pregnant,°
The jewel that we find, we stoop and take't
Because we see it; but what we do not see 25
We tread upon, and never think of it.
You may not so extenuate his offense
For I have had such faults; but rather tell me,
When I, that censure him, do so offend,
Let mine own judgment pattern out my death, 30
And nothing come in partial. Sir, he must die.
ESCALUS
Be it as your wisdom will.
ANGELO                          Where is the provost?

*Enter* PROVOST.

PROVOST
Here, if it like your honor.
ANGELO                          See that Claudio
Be executed by nine tomorrow morning.
Bring him his confessor, let him be prepared, 35
For that's the utmost of his pilgrimage.
                          [*Exit* PROVOST.]
ESCALUS
Well, heaven forgive him, and forgive us all.
Some rise by sin, and some by virtue fall:
Some run from breaks of ice,° and answer none;
And some condemnèd for a fault° alone. 40

*Enter* ELBOW, FROTH, CLOWN [POMPEY], OFFICERS.

ELBOW  Come, bring them away. If these be good
people in a commonweal that do nothing but use their
abuses in common houses, I know no law. Bring them
away.
ANGELO  How now, sir! What's your name? And 45
what's the matter?
ELBOW  If it please your honor, I am the poor duke's
constable, and my name is Elbow. I do lean upon

---

**62 use and liberty** habitual license   **65 sense** interpretation
**72 censured** pronounced judgment on   **78 makes** a plural
subject sometimes takes a verb ending in –*s*   **83 owe** own
**89 success** outcome

**II.i.6 fall** let fall   **9 strait** strict   **10 affections** passions
**23 pregnant** clear   **39 Some . . . ice** i.e., some escape after
gross violations of chastity   **40 fault** (1) small crack in the ice
(2) act of sex

justice, sir, and do bring in here before your good honor two notorious benefactors. 50

ANGELO  Benefactors? Well, what benefactors are they? Are they not malefactors?

ELBOW  If it please your honor, I know not well what they are, but precise villains they are, that I am sure of, and void of all profanation in the world that good 55 Christians ought to have.

ESCALUS  This comes off well; here's a wise officer.

ANGELO  Go to: what quality° are they of? Elbow is your name? Why dost thou not speak, Elbow?

POMPEY  He cannot, sir; he's out at elbow.° 60

ANGELO  What are you, sir?

ELBOW  He, sir! A tapster, sir, parcel-bawd,° one that serves a bad woman whose house, sir, was, as they say, plucked down in the suburbs, and now she professes a hothouse,° which, I think, is a very ill house too. 65

ESCALUS  How know you that?

ELBOW  My wife, sir, whom I detest° before heaven and your honor—

ESCALUS  How! Thy wife?

ELBOW  Ay, sir—whom, I thank heaven, is an honest° 70 woman—

ESCALUS  Dost thou detest her therefore?

ELBOW  I say, sir, I will detest myself also, as well as she, that this house, if it be not a bawd's house, it is pity of her life, for it is a naughty° house. 75

ESCALUS  How dost thou know that, constable?

ELBOW  Marry, sir, by my wife, who, if she had been a woman cardinally° given, might have been accused in fornication, adultery, and all uncleanliness there.

ESCALUS  By the woman's means? 80

ELBOW  Ay, sir, by Mistress Overdone's means; but as she spit in his face, so she defied him.

POMPEY  Sir, if it please your honor, this is not so.

ELBOW  Prove it before these varlets here, thou honorable man; prove it. 85

ESCALUS  Do you hear how he misplaces?

POMPEY  Sir, she came in great with child; and long-ing, saving your honor's reverence, for stewed prunes.° Sir, we had but two in the house, which at that very distant time stood, as it were, in a fruit dish, a dish of 90 some threepence; your honors have seen such dishes; they are not china dishes, but very good dishes—

ESCALUS  Go to, go to; no matter for the dish, sir.

POMPEY  No, indeed, sir, not of a pin; you are therein in the right; but to the point. As I say, this Mistress 95 Elbow, being, as I say, with child, and being great-bellied, and longing, as I said, for prunes; and having but two in the dish, as I said, Master Froth here, this very man, having eaten the rest, as I said, and, as I say, paying for them very honestly; for, as you know, 100 Master Froth, I could not give you threepence again.

FROTH  No, indeed.

POMPEY  Very well, you being then, if you be remem-b'red, cracking the stones of the foresaid prunes—

FROTH  Ay, so I did indeed. 105

POMPEY  Why, very well; I telling you then, if you

be remem'bred, that such a one and such a one were past cure of the thing you wot° of, unless they kept very good diet, as I told you—

FROTH  All this is true. 110

POMPEY  Why, very well, then—

ESCALUS  Come, you are a tedious fool; to the pur-pose. What was done to Elbow's wife, that he hath cause to complain of? Come me to what was done to her. 115

POMPEY  Sir, your honor cannot come to that yet.°

ESCALUS  No, sir, nor I mean it not.

POMPEY  Sir, but you shall come to it, by your honor's leave. And, I beseech you, look into Master Froth here, sir, a man of fourscore pound a year, 120 whose father died at Hallowmas.° Was't not at Hallow-mas, Master Froth?

FROTH  All-hallond Eve.°

POMPEY  Why, very well; I hope here be truths. He, sir, sitting, as I say, in a lower chair, sir, 'twas in the 125 Bunch of Grapes,° where, indeed, you have a delight to sit, have you not?

FROTH  I have so, because it is an open room, and good for winter.

POMPEY  Why, very well, then; I hope here be truths. 130

ANGELO
This will last out a night in Russia,
When nights are longest there. I'll take my leave,
And leave you to the hearing of the cause,
Hoping you'll find good cause to whip them all.

ESCALUS
I think no less. Good morrow to your lordship. 135
                    *Exit* [ANGELO].
Now, sir, come on: what was done to Elbow's wife, once more?

POMPEY  Once, sir? There was nothing done to her once.

ELBOW  I beseech you, sir, ask him what this man did 140 to my wife.

POMPEY  I beseech your honor, ask me.

ESCALUS  Well, sir; what did this gentleman to her?

POMPEY  I beseech you, sir, look in this gentleman's face. Good Master Froth, look upon his honor; 'tis for 145 a good purpose. Doth your honor mark his face?

ESCALUS  Ay, sir, very well.

POMPEY  Nay, I beseech you, mark it well.

ESCALUS  Well, I do so.

POMPEY  Doth your honor see any harm in his face? 150

ESCALUS  Why, no.

POMPEY  I'll be supposed° upon a book, his face is the worst thing about him. Good, then; if his face be the worst thing about him, how could Master Froth do the constable's wife any harm? I would know that of 155 your honor.

ESCALUS  He's in the right. Constable, what say you to it?

ELBOW  First, and° it like you, the house is a respected° house; next, this is a respected fellow; and his mistress 160 is a respected woman.

---

**58 quality** profession  **60 out at elbow** somewhat seedy  **62 parcel-bawd** partly a bawd  **65 hothouse** bathhouse  **67 detest** he means *protest*  **70 honest** chaste  **75 naughty** immoral  **78 cardinally** he means *carnally*  **88 stewed prunes** a fruit commonly provided in brothels

**108 wot** know  **114–16 Come me . . . yet** the verbs carry a sexual innuendo  **121 Hallowmas** All Saints' day, November 1  **123 All-hallond Eve** October 31  **126 Bunch of Grapes** the name of a room at the tavern  **152 supposed** he means *deposed*  **159 and** if; **respected** he means *suspected*

POMPEY  By this hand, sir, his wife is a more respected person than any of us all.

ELBOW  Varlet, thou liest; thou liest, wicked varlet! The time is yet to come that she was ever respected 165 with man, woman, or child.

POMPEY  Sir, she was respected with him before he married with her.

ESCALUS  Which is the wiser here, Justice or Iniquity?° Is this true? 170

ELBOW  O thou caitiff! O thou varlet! O thou wicked Hannibal!° I respected with her before I was married to her! If ever I was respected with her, or she with me, let not your worship think me the poor duke's officer. Prove this, thou wicked Hannibal, or I'll have 175 mine action of batt'ry on thee.

ESCALUS  If he took you a box o' th' ear, you might have your action of slander too.

ELBOW  Marry, I thank your good worship for it. What is't your worship's pleasure I shall do with this 180 wicked caitiff?

ESCALUS  Truly, officer, because he hath some offenses in him that thou wouldst discover if thou couldst, let him continue in his courses till thou know'st what they are. 185

ELBOW  Marry, I thank your worship for it. Thou see'st, thou wicked varlet, now, what's come upon thee. Thou art to continue now, thou varlet; thou art to continue.

ESCALUS  Where were you born, friend? 190

FROTH  Here in Vienna, sir.

ESCALUS  Are you of fourscore pounds a year?

FROTH  Yes, and't please you, sir.

ESCALUS  So. [To POMPEY.] What trade are you of, sir? 195

POMPEY  A tapster, a poor widow's tapster.

ESCALUS  Your mistress' name?

POMPEY  Mistress Overdone.

ESCALUS  Hath she had any more than one husband?

POMPEY  Nine, sir; Overdone by the last. 200

ESCALUS  Nine! Come hither to me, Master Froth. Master Froth, I would not have you acquainted with tapsters: they will draw you,° Master Froth, and you will hang them. Get you gone, and let me hear no more of you. 205

FROTH  I thank your worship. For mine own part, I never come into any room in a taphouse, but I am drawn in.

ESCALUS  Well, no more of it, Master Froth; farewell. [Exit FROTH.] Come you hither to me, Master 210 Tapster. What's your name, Master Tapster?

POMPEY  Pompey.

ESCALUS  What else?

POMPEY  Bum, sir.

ESCALUS  Troth, and your bum is the greatest thing 215 about you; so that, in the beastliest sense, you are Pompey the Great. Pompey, you are partly a bawd, Pompey, howsoever you color° it in being a tapster, are you not? Come, tell me true; it shall be the better for you. 220

POMPEY  Truly, sir, I am a poor fellow that would live.

ESCALUS  How would you live, Pompey? By being a bawd? What do you think of the trade, Pompey? Is it a lawful trade?

POMPEY  If the law would allow it, sir. 225

ESCALUS  But the law will not allow it, Pompey; nor it shall not be allowed in Vienna.

POMPEY  Does your worship mean to geld and splay all the youth of the city?

ESCALUS  No, Pompey. 230

POMPEY  Truly, sir, in my poor opinion, they will to't, then. If your worship will take order for the drabs and the knaves, you need not to fear the bawds.

ESCALUS  There is pretty orders beginning, I can tell you; it is but heading° and hanging. 235

POMPEY  If you head and hang all that offend that way but for ten year together, you'll be glad to give out a commission for more heads; if this law hold in Vienna ten year, I'll rent the fairest house in it after threepence a bay;° if you live to see this come to pass, 240 say Pompey told you so.

ESCALUS  Thank you, good Pompey; and, in requital of your prophecy, hark you: I advise you, let me not find you before me again upon any complaint whatsoever; no, not for dwelling where you do. If I do, Pompey, 245 I shall beat you to your tent, and prove a shrewd Caesar to you; in plain dealing, Pompey, I shall have you whipped. So, for this time, Pompey, fare you well.

POMPEY  I thank your worship for your good counsel; [aside] but I shall follow it as the flesh and fortune shall 250 better determine.

Whip me? No, no; let carman whip his jade.° The valiant heart's not whipped out of his trade. Exit.

ESCALUS  Come hither to me, Master Elbow; come hither, master constable. How long have you been in 255 this place of constable?

ELBOW  Seven year and a half, sir.

ESCALUS  I thought, by the readiness in the office, you had continued in it some time. You say, seven years together? 260

ELBOW  And a half, sir.

ESCALUS  Alas, it hath been great pains to you. They do you wrong to put you so oft upon't.° Are there not men in your ward sufficient to serve it?

ELBOW  Faith, sir, few of any wit in such matters. As 265 they are chosen, they are glad to choose me for them; I do it for some piece of money, and go through with all.

ESCALUS  Look you bring me in the names of some six or seven, the most sufficient of your parish. 270

ELBOW  To your worship's house, sir?

ESCALUS  To my house. Fare you well. [Exit ELBOW.] What's o'clock, think you?

JUSTICE  Eleven, sir.

ESCALUS  I pray you home to dinner with me. 275

JUSTICE  I humbly thank you.

ESCALUS
It grieves me for the death of Claudio,
But there's no remedy.

---

**169 Justice or Iniquity** personified characters in morality plays  **172 Hannibal** he means *cannibal* = fleshmonger (?)  **203 draw you** (1) draw drinks for you (2) empty you, disembowel you  **218 color** camouflage

**235 heading** beheading  **240 bay** space under a single gable  **252 carman . . . jade** the cartman whipped the whore after carting her through the streets; a "jade" is literally a nag  **263 put . . . upon't** impose on you the task of being constable

JUSTICE
Lord Angelo is severe.
ESCALUS        It is but needful:
Mercy is not itself, that oft looks so;      280
Pardon is still° the nurse of second woe.
But yet—poor Claudio! There is no remedy.
Come, sir.             *Exeunt.*

Scene II. [*A room.*]

*Enter* PROVOST, [*and a*] SERVANT.

SERVANT
He's hearing of a cause; he will come straight:
I'll tell him of you.
PROVOST     Pray you, do. [*Exit* SERVANT.] I'll know
His pleasure; maybe he will relent. Alas,
He hath but as offended in a dream.
All sects,° all ages smack of this vice; and he     5
To die for't!

*Enter* ANGELO.

ANGELO     Now, what's the matter, provost?
PROVOST
Is it your will Claudio shall die tomorrow?
ANGELO
Did not I tell thee yea? Hadst thou not order?
Why dost thou ask again?
PROVOST        Lest I might be too rash.
Under your good correction, I have seen,     10
When, after execution, judgment hath
Repented o'er his doom.
ANGELO        Go to; let that be mine.°
Do you your office, or give up your place,
And you shall well be spared.
PROVOST        I crave your honor's pardon.
What shall be done, sir, with the groaning Juliet?     15
She's very near her hour.
ANGELO        Dispose of her
To some more fitter place, and that with speed.

[*Re-enter* SERVANT.]

SERVANT
Here is the sister of the man condemned
Desires access to you.
ANGELO        Hath he a sister?
PROVOST
Ay, my good lord, a very virtuous maid     20
And to be shortly of a sisterhood,
If not already.
ANGELO     Well, let her be admitted.
            [*Exit* SERVANT.]
See you the fornicatress be removed;
Let her have needful, but not lavish, means;
There shall be order for't.

*Enter* LUCIO *and* ISABELLA.

PROVOST        'Save your honor.     25
ANGELO
Stay a little while. [*To* ISABELLA.] Y' are welcome:
   what's your will?

ISABELLA
I am a woeful suitor to your honor,
Please but your honor hear me.
ANGELO        Well; what's your suit?
ISABELLA
There is a vice that most I do abhor,
And most desire should meet the blow of justice,     30
For which I would not plead, but that I must,
For which I must not plead, but that I am
At war 'twixt will and will not.
ANGELO        Well: the matter?
ISABELLA
I have a brother is condemned to die.
I do beseech you, let it be his fault,°     35
And not my brother.
PROVOST [*Aside.*]     Heaven give thee moving graces.
ANGELO
Condemn the fault, and not the actor of it?
Why, every fault's condemned ere it be done.
Mine were the very cipher of a function,
To fine the faults whose fine stands in record,     40
And let go by the actor.
ISABELLA        O just but severe law!
I had a brother, then. Heaven keep your honor.
LUCIO [*Aside to* ISABELLA.]
Give't not o'er so. To him again, entreat him,
Kneel down before him, hang upon his gown;
You are too cold; if you should need a pin,     45
You could not with more tame a tongue desire it.
To him, I say!
ISABELLA
Must he needs die?
ANGELO        Maiden, no remedy.
ISABELLA
Yes; I do think that you might pardon him,
And neither heaven nor man grieve at the mercy.     50
ANGELO
I will not do't.
ISABELLA        But can you, if you would?
ANGELO
Look what° I will not, that I cannot do.
ISABELLA
But might you do't, and do the world no wrong,
If so your heart were touched with that remorse°
As mine is to him?
ANGELO        He's sentenced; 'tis too late.     55
LUCIO [*Aside to* ISABELLA.]
You are too cold.
ISABELLA
Too late? Why, no: I, that do speak a word,
May call it again. Well, believe this:
No ceremony° that to great ones 'longs,
Not the king's crown, nor the deputed sword,     60
The marshal's truncheon, nor the judge's robe,
Become them with one half so good a grace
As mercy does.
If he had been as you, and you as he,
You would have slipped like him; but he, like you,     65
Would not have been so stern.
ANGELO        Pray you, be gone.

**281 still** always
**II.ii.5 sects** classes    **12 mine** i.e., my responsibility

**35 let . . . fault** condemn his fault, not him    **52 Look what**
whatever    **54 remorse** compassion    **59 ceremony** insignia
of greatness

ISABELLA
I would to heaven I had your potency,
And you were Isabel; should it then be thus?
No; I would tell what 'twere to be a judge,
And what a prisoner.                                         70

LUCIO [*Aside to* ISABELLA.]
Ay, touch him; there's the vein.

ANGELO
Your brother is a forfeit of the law,
And you but waste your words.

ISABELLA                          Alas, alas!
Why, all the souls that were were forfeit once;
And He that might the vantage best have took        75
Found out the remedy. How would you be,
If He, which is the top of judgment, should
But judge you as you are? O, think on that,
And mercy then will breathe within your lips,
Like man new made.

ANGELO               Be you content, fair maid;        80
It is the law, not I, condemn your brother.
Were he my kinsman, brother, or my son,
It should be thus with him; he must die tomorrow.

ISABELLA
Tomorrow! O, that's sudden! Spare him, spare him!
He's not prepared for death. Even for our kitchens    85
We kill the fowl of season:° shall we serve heaven
With less respect than we do minister
To our gross selves? Good, good my lord, bethink you:
Who is it that hath died for this offense?
There's many have committed it.

LUCIO [*Aside to* ISABELLA.]           Ay, well said.   90

ANGELO
The law hath not been dead, though it hath slept.
Those many had not dared to do that evil,
If the first that did th' edict infringe
Had answered for his deed. Now 'tis awake,
Takes note of what is done, and, like a prophet,       95
Looks in a glass,° that shows what future evils,
Either new, or by remissness new conceived,°
And so in progress to be hatched and born,
Are now to have no successive degrees,
But here they live, to end.

ISABELLA                    Yet show some pity.        100

ANGELO
I show it most of all when I show justice,
For then I pity those I do not know,
Which a dismissed° offense would after gall;
And do him right that, answering one foul wrong,
Lives not to act another. Be satisfied;                105
Your brother dies tomorrow; be content.

ISABELLA
So you must be the first that gives this sentence,
And he, that suffers. O, it is excellent
To have a giant's strength; but it is tyrannous
To use it like a giant.

LUCIO [*Aside to* ISABELLA.]   That's well said.       110

ISABELLA
Could great men thunder
As Jove himself does, Jove would ne'er be quiet,

For every pelting,° petty officer
Would use his heaven for thunder.
Nothing but thunder. Merciful heaven,                  115
Thou rather with thy sharp and sulfurous bolt
Splits the unwedgeable and gnarlèd oak
Than the soft myrtle. But man, proud man,
Dressed in a little brief authority,
Most ignorant of what he's most assured,               120
His glassy essence,° like an angry ape,
Plays such fantastic tricks before high heaven
As makes the angels weep; who, with our spleens,°
Would all themselves laugh mortal.

LUCIO [*Aside to* ISABELLA.]
O, to him, to him, wench! He will relent;              125
He's coming; I perceive't.

PROVOST [*Aside.*]            Pray heaven she win him.

ISABELLA
We cannot weigh our brother with ourself:
Great men may jest with saints; 'tis wit in them;
But in the less, foul profanation.

LUCIO
Thou'rt i' th' right, girl; more o' that.              130

ISABELLA
That in the captain's but a choleric word,
Which in the soldier is flat blasphemy.

LUCIO [*Aside to* ISABELLA.]
Art avised° o' that? More on't.

ANGELO
Why do you put these sayings upon me?

ISABELLA
Because authority, though it err like others,          135
Hath yet a kind of medicine in itself,
That skins the vice° o' th' top; go to your bosom,
Knock there, and ask your heart what it doth know
That's like my brother's fault; if it confess
A natural guiltiness such as is his,                   140
Let it not sound a thought upon your tongue
Against my brother's life.

ANGELO [*Aside.*]          She speaks, and 'tis
Such sense, that my sense breeds with it. [*Aloud.*] Fare
you well.

ISABELLA
Gentle my lord, turn back.

ANGELO
I will bethink me; come again tomorrow.                145

ISABELLA
Hark how I'll bribe you; good my lord, turn back.

ANGELO
How? Bribe me?

ISABELLA
Ay, with such gifts that heaven shall share with you.

LUCIO [*Aside to* ISABELLA.]
You had marred all else.

ISABELLA
Not with fond sicles° of the tested gold,              150
Or stones whose rate are either rich or poor
As fancy values them; but with true prayers

86 of season in season   96 glass magic glass   96–97 future
. . . conceived evils that will take place in future, but that
are either now planned or may be planned later ("remissness"
= careless omission of duty)   103 dismissed forgiven

113 pelting paltry   121 glassy essence the rational soul
which reveals to man, as in a mirror, what constitutes him
a human being (?) fragile nature (?)   123 spleens the spleen
was believed the seat of mirth and anger   133 avised
informed   137 skins the vice i.e., covers the sore of vice
with a skin, but does not heal it (or perhaps "skims off the
visible layer of vice")   150 sicles shekels

That shall be up at heaven, and enter there
Ere sunrise, prayers from preservèd souls,
From fasting maids whose minds are dedicate          155
To nothing temporal.

ANGELO                    Well; come to me tomorrow.

LUCIO [*Aside to* ISABELLA.]
Go to; 'tis well; away.

ISABELLA
Heaven keep your honor safe.

ANGELO [*Aside.*]                    Amen:
For I am that way going to temptation,
Where prayers cross.°

ISABELLA                    At what hour tomorrow          160
Shall I attend your lordship?

ANGELO                    At any time 'fore noon.

ISABELLA
'Save your honor.
          [*Exeunt* ISABELLA, LUCIO, *and* PROVOST.]

ANGELO          From thee, even from thy virtue!
What's this? What's this? Is this her fault or mine?
The tempter or the tempted, who sins most?
Ha, not she. Nor doth she tempt; but it is I          165
That, lying by the violet in the sun,
Do as the carrion does, not as the flow'r,
Corrupt with virtuous season.° Can it be
That modesty may more betray our sense
Than woman's lightness? Having waste ground
          enough,                                        170
Shall we desire to raze the sanctuary,
And pitch our evils° there? O fie, fie, fie!
What dost thou, or what art thou, Angelo?
Dost thou desire her foully for those things
That make her good? O, let her brother live:          175
Thieves for their robbery have authority
When judges steal themselves. What, do I love her,
That I desire to hear her speak again,
And feast upon her eyes? What is't I dream on?
O cunning enemy, that, to catch a saint,              180
With saints dost bait thy hook! Most dangerous
Is that temptation that doth goad us on
To sin in loving virtue. Never could the strumpet,
With all her double vigor, art and nature,
Once stir my temper; but this virtuous maid          185
Subdues me quite. Ever till now,
When men were fond,° I smiled, and wond'red how.
                                        *Exit.*


          Scene III. [*The prison.*]

*Enter* DUKE [*disguised as a friar*] *and* PROVOST.

DUKE
Hail to you, provost—so I think you are.

PROVOST
I am the provost. What's your will, good friar?

DUKE
Bound by my charity and my blest order,
I come to visit the afflicted spirits
Here in the prison. Do me the common right          5

To let me see them, and to make me know
The nature of their crimes, that I may minister
To them accordingly.

PROVOST
I would do more than that, if more were needful.

*Enter* JULIET.

Look, here comes one: a gentlewoman of mine,          10
Who, falling in the flaws° of her own youth,
Hath blistered° her report:° she is with child;
And he that got it, sentenced; a young man
More fit to do another such offense
Than die for this.                                      15

DUKE
When must he die?

PROVOST                    As I do think, tomorrow.

[*To* JULIET.]
I have provided for you; stay awhile,
And you shall be conducted.

DUKE
Repent you, fair one, of the sin you carry?

JULIET
I do, and bear the shame most patiently.              20

DUKE
I'll teach you how you shall arraign° your conscience,
And try your penitence, if it be sound
Or hollowly put on.

JULIET                    I'll gladly learn.

DUKE
Love you the man that wronged you?

JULIET
Yes, as I love the woman that wronged him.            25

DUKE
So, then, it seems your most offenseful act
Was mutually committed?

JULIET                    Mutually.

DUKE
Then was your sin of heavier kind than his.

JULIET
I do confess it, and repent it, father.

DUKE
'Tis meet so, daughter. But lest you do repent        30
As that the sin hath brought you to this shame—
Which sorrow is always toward ourselves, not heaven,
Showing we would not spare heaven as we love it,
But as we stand in fear—

JULIET
I do repent me, as it is an evil,                       35
And take the shame with joy.

DUKE                    There rest.
Your partner, as I hear, must die tomorrow,
And I am going with instruction to him.
Grace go with you, Benedicite!°                    *Exit.*

JULIET
Must die tomorrow! O injurious love,                   40
That respites° me a life, whose very comfort
Is still a dying horror.

PROVOST                    'Tis pity of him.          *Exeunt.*

---

**160 cross** are at cross-purposes   **168 Corrupt . . . season**
go bad in the season that blossoms the flower   **172 evils** evil
structures (e.g., perhaps whorehouses or privies)   **187 fond**
infatuated

**II.iii.11 flaws** sudden gusts of wind   **12 blistered** whores
were branded on the forehead; **report** reputation   **21 arraign**
interrogate   **39 Benedicite** bless you   **41 respites** saves

## Scene IV. [*A room.*]

*Enter* ANGELO.

ANGELO
When I would pray and think, I think and pray
To several° subjects: heaven hath my empty words,
Whilst my invention,° hearing not my tongue,
Anchors on Isabel: heaven in my mouth,
As if I did but only chew his name,                                      5
And in my heart the strong and swelling evil
Of my conception.° The state,° whereon I studied,
Is like a good thing, being often read,
Grown sere° and tedious; yea, my gravity,
Wherein, let no man hear me, I take pride,                              10
Could I with boot° change for an idle plume
Which the air beats for vain. O place, O form,
How often dost thou with thy case,° thy habit,°
Wrench awe from fools, and tie the wiser souls
To thy false seeming! Blood, thou art blood.                           15
Let's write "good angel" on the devil's horn,
'Tis not the devil's crest. How now, who's there?

*Enter* SERVANT.

SERVANT
One Isabel, a sister, desires access to you.

ANGELO
Teach her the way. [*Exit* SERVANT.] O heavens,
Why does my blood thus muster to my heart,                             20
Making both it unable for itself,
And dispossessing all my other parts
Of necessary fitness?
So play the foolish throngs with one that swounds,°
Come all to help him, and so stop the air                              25
By which he should revive; and even so
The general,° subject to a well-wished king,
Quit their own part, and in obsequious fondness
Crowd to his presence, where their untaught love
Must needs appear offense.

*Enter* ISABELLA.

                                   How now, fair maid?                 30

ISABELLA
I am come to know your pleasure.

ANGELO
That you might know it, would much better please me
Than to demand what 'tis. Your brother cannot live.

ISABELLA
Even so. Heaven keep your honor.

ANGELO
Yet may he live awhile, and it may be,                                 35
As long as you or I; yet he must die.

ISABELLA
Under your sentence?

ANGELO                  Yea.

ISABELLA
When? I beseech you that in his reprieve,
Longer or shorter, he may be so fitted
That his soul sicken not.                                              40

ANGELO
Ha! Fie, these filthy vices! It were as good

To pardon him that hath from nature stol'n
A man already made, as to remit
Their saucy sweetness° that do coin heaven's image
In stamps that are forbid: 'tis all as easy                            45
Falsely to take away a life true made,
As to put metal in restrainèd° means
To make a false one.

ISABELLA
'Tis set down so in heaven, but not in earth.

ANGELO
Say you so? Then I shall pose° you quickly.                            50
Which had you rather: that the most just law
Now took your brother's life; or, to redeem him,
Give up your body to such sweet uncleanness
As she that he hath stained?

ISABELLA                      Sir, believe this:
I had rather give my body than my soul.                                55

ANGELO
I talk not of your soul; our compelled sins
Stand more for number than for accompt.°

ISABELLA                                    How say you?

ANGELO
Nay, I'll not warrant that; for I can speak
Against the thing I say. Answer to this:
I, now the voice of the recorded law,                                  60
Pronounce a sentence on your brother's life;
Might there not be a charity in sin
To save this brother's life?

ISABELLA                      Please you to do't,
I'll take it as a peril to my soul,
It is no sin at all, but charity.                                      65

ANGELO
Pleased you to do't at peril of your soul,
Were equal poise° of sin and charity.

ISABELLA
That I do beg his life, if it be sin,
Heaven let me bear it. You granting of my suit,
If that be sin, I'll make it my morn prayer                            70
To have it added to the faults of mine,
And nothing of your answer.

ANGELO                       Nay, but hear me.
Your sense pursues not mine; either you are ignorant,
Or seem so, crafty; and that's not good.

ISABELLA
Let me be ignorant, and in nothing good,                               75
But graciously to know I am no better.

ANGELO
Thus wisdom wishes to appear most bright
When it doth tax° itself, as these black masks
Proclaim an enshield° beauty ten times louder
Than beauty could, displayed. But mark me;                             80
To be receivèd plain, I'll speak more gross:
Your brother is to die.

ISABELLA  So.

ANGELO
And his offense is so, as it appears,
Accountant° to the law upon that pain.°                                85

ISABELLA  True.

ANGELO
Admit no other way to save his life—
As I subscribe° not that, nor any other,
But in the loss of question°—that you, his sister,
Finding yourself desired of such a person  90
Whose credit with the judge, or own great place,
Could fetch your brother from the manacles
Of the all-binding law; and that there were
No earthly mean to save him, but that either
You must lay down the treasures of your body  95
To this supposed, or else to let him suffer:
What would you do?

ISABELLA
As much for my poor brother as myself:
That is, were I under the terms of death,
Th' impression of keen whips I'd wear as rubies,  100
And strip myself to death as to a bed
That longing have been sick for, ere I'd yield
My body up to shame.

ANGELO                    Then must your brother die.

ISABELLA
And 'twere the cheaper way.
Better it were a brother died at once  105
Than that a sister, by redeeming him,
Should die forever.

ANGELO
Were not you, then, as cruel as the sentence
That you have slandered so?

ISABELLA
Ignomy in ransom and free pardon  110
Are of two houses; lawful mercy
Is nothing kin to foul redemption.

ANGELO
You seemed of late to make the law a tyrant,
And rather proved the sliding of your brother
A merriment than a vice.  115

ISABELLA
O, pardon me, my lord. It oft falls out,
To have what we would have, we speak not what we
    mean.
I something do excuse the thing I hate
For his advantage that I dearly love.

ANGELO
We are all frail.

ISABELLA                    Else let my brother die,  120
If not a fedary, but only he
Owe and succeed thy weakness.°

ANGELO
Nay, women are frail too.

ISABELLA
Ay, as the glasses where they view themselves,
Which are as easy broke as they make forms.°  125
Women! Help heaven! Men their creation mar
In profiting by them. Nay, call us ten times frail;
For we are soft as our complexions are,
And credulous° to false prints.

ANGELO                    I think it well,

88 **subscribe** assent to  89 **But . . . question** except to
keep alive the argument  121–22 **If . . . weakness** probably
a line has been omitted, but perhaps the meaning is, "Let my
brother die if he is the only inheritor of human frailty instead
of being a mere vassal to it"  125 **forms** images, appearances
129 **credulous** receptive

And from this testimony of your own sex—  130
Since, I suppose, we are made to be no stronger
Than faults may shake our frames—let me be bold:
I do arrest your words.° Be that you are,
That is, a woman; if you be more, you're none;
If you be one, as you are well expressed°  135
By all external warrants, show it now,
By putting on the destined livery.°

ISABELLA
I have no tongue but one; gentle my lord,
Let me entreat you speak the former language.

ANGELO
Plainly conceive, I love you.  140

ISABELLA
My brother did love Juliet,
And you tell me that he shall die for't.

ANGELO
He shall not, Isabel, if you give me love.

ISABELLA
I know your virtue hath a license in't,
Which seems a little fouler than it is,  145
To pluck on° others.

ANGELO                    Believe me, on mine honor,
My words express my purpose.

ISABELLA
Ha! Little honor to be much believed,
And most pernicious purpose. Seeming, seeming!
I will proclaim thee, Angelo; look for't:  150
Sign me a present pardon for my brother,
Or with an outstretched throat I'll tell the world aloud
What man thou art.

ANGELO                    Who will believe thee, Isabel?
My unsoiled name, th' austereness of my life,
My vouch° against you, and my place i' th' state,  155
Will so your accusation overweigh,
That you shall stifle in your own report,
And smell of calumny. I have begun,
And now I give my sensual race the rein.
Fit thy consent to my sharp appetite,  160
Lay by all nicety and prolixious° blushes,
That banish what they sue for; redeem thy brother
By yielding up thy body to my will,°
Or else he must not only die the death,
But thy unkindness° shall his death draw out  165
To ling'ring sufferance.° Answer me tomorrow,
Or, by the affection° that now guides me most,
I'll prove a tyrant to him. As for you,
Say what you can, my false o'erweighs your true.
                                                        *Exit.*

ISABELLA
To whom should I complain? Did I tell this,  170
Who would believe me? O perilous mouths,
That bear in them one and the selfsame tongue,
Either of condemnation or approof;°
Bidding the law make curtsy to their will,
Hooking both right and wrong to th' appetite,  175
To follow as it draws. I'll to my brother.

**133 I . . . words** I take you at your word  **135 expressed**
shown to be  **137 the destined livery** the dress that it is
the destiny of a woman to wear  **146 pluck on** draw on
**155 vouch** testimony  **161 prolixious** tediously drawn-out
**163 will** carnal appetite  **165 unkindness** unnatural behavior
**166 sufferance** torture  **167 affection** passion  **173 approof**
approval

Though he hath fall'n by prompture of the blood,
Yet hath he in him such a mind of honor,
That, had he twenty heads to tender down
On twenty bloody blocks, he'd yield them up,      180
Before his sister should her body stoop
To such abhorred pollution.
Then, Isabel, live chaste, and, brother, die:
"More than our brother is our chastity."
I'll tell him yet of Angelo's request,      185
And fit his mind to death, for his soul's rest.      *Exit.*


# ACT III

## Scene I. [*The prison.*]

*Enter* DUKE [*as a friar*], CLAUDIO, *and* PROVOST.

DUKE
So then, you hope of pardon from Lord Angelo?
CLAUDIO
The miserable have no other medicine
But only hope:
I have hope to live, and am prepared to die.
DUKE
Be absolute° for death; either death or life      5
Shall thereby be the sweeter. Reason thus with life:
If I do lose thee, I do lose a thing
That none but fools would keep; a breath thou art,
Servile to all the skyey influences,°
That dost this habitation, where thou keep'st,°      10
Hourly afflict; merely, thou art death's fool,°
For him thou labor'st by thy flight to shun,
And yet run'st toward him still. Thou art not noble,
For all th' accommodations° that thou bear'st
Are nursed by baseness. Thou'rt by no means valiant,      15
For thou dost fear the soft and tender fork°
Of a poor worm. Thy best of rest is sleep,
And that thou oft provok'st;° yet grossly fear'st
Thy death, which is no more. Thou art not thyself;
For thou exists on many a thousand grains      20
That issue out of dust. Happy thou art not,
For what thou hast not, still thou striv'st to get,
And what thou hast, forget'st. Thou art not certain,°
For thy complexion shifts to strange effects,
After the moon.° If thou art rich, thou'rt poor.      25
For, like an ass whose back with ingots bows,
Thou bear'st thy heavy riches but a journey,
And death unloads thee. Friend hast thou none,
For thine own bowels,° which do call thee sire,
The mere effusion of thy proper loins,°      30
Do curse the gout, serpigo,° and the rheum,°
For ending thee no sooner. Thou hast nor youth nor
      age,

**III.i.5 absolute** unconditionally prepared   **9 skyey influences** influence of the stars   **10 keep'st** dwellest   **11 fool** the professional jester in a nobleman's household, whose job was to keep his master amused   **14 accommodations** necessities **16 fork** forked tongue (of a snake)   **18 provok'st** invokest **23 certain** invariable   **24–25 For . . . moon** your temperament (desire?) moves to numerous things, changeable as (or "influenced by") the moon   **29 bowels** offspring   **30 The mere . . . loins** the very issue of your own loins   **31 serpigo** a skin disease; **rheum** catarrh

But, as it were, an after-dinner's sleep,
Dreaming on both; for all thy blessèd youth
Becomes as agèd, and doth beg the alms      35
Of palsied eld,° and when thou art old and rich,
Thou has neither heat, affection,° limb, nor beauty,
To make thy riches pleasant. What's yet in this
That bears° the name of life? Yet in this life
Lie hid moe thousand deaths; yet death we fear,      40
That makes these odds all even.
CLAUDIO      I humbly thank you.
To sue to live, I find I seek to die,
And seeking death, find life: let it come on.

*Enter* ISABELLA.

ISABELLA
What, ho! Peace here; grace and good company!
PROVOST
Who's there? Come in, the wish deserves a welcome.      45
DUKE
Dear sir, ere long I'll visit you again.
CLAUDIO
Most holy sir, I thank you.
ISABELLA
My business is a word or two with Claudio.
PROVOST
And very welcome. Look, signior, here's your sister.
DUKE
Provost, a word with you.      50
PROVOST
As many as you please.
DUKE
Bring me to hear them speak, where I may be concealed.      [DUKE *and* PROVOST *withdraw.*]
CLAUDIO
Now, sister, what's the comfort?
ISABELLA
Why,
As all comforts are, most good, most good indeed.      55
Lord Angelo, having affairs to heaven,
Intends you for his swift ambassador,
Where you shall be an everlasting leiger:°
Therefore your best appointment° make with speed;
Tomorrow you set on.
CLAUDIO      Is there no remedy?      60
ISABELLA
None, but such remedy as, to save a head,
To cleave a heart in twain.
CLAUDIO      But is there any?
ISABELLA
Yes, brother, you may live;
There is a devilish mercy in the judge,
If you'll implore it, that will free your life,      65
But fetter you till death.
CLAUDIO      Perpetual durance?°
ISABELLA
Ay, just; perpetual durance, a restraint,
Though all the world's vastidity° you had,
To a determined scope.°
CLAUDIO      But in what nature?

**36 eld** old age   **37 affection** feeling   **39 bears** deserves **58 leiger** resident ambassador   **59 appointment** preparation **66 durance** imprisonment   **68 vastidity** vast spaces   **69 determined scope** fixed limit

ISABELLA
In such a one as, you consenting to't,        70
Would bark your honor from that trunk you bear,
And leave you naked.
CLAUDIO            Let me know the point.
ISABELLA
O, I do fear thee, Claudio, and I quake,
Lest thou a feverous life shouldst entertain,
And six or seven winters more respect        75
Than a perpetual honor. Dar'st thou die?
The sense° of death is most in apprehension,°
And the poor beetle that we tread upon
In corporal sufferance finds a pang as great
As when a giant dies.
CLAUDIO           Why give you me this shame?   80
Think you I can a resolution fetch
From flow'ry tenderness? If I must die,
I will encounter darkness as a bride,
And hug it in mine arms.
ISABELLA
There spake my brother, there my father's grave   85
Did utter forth a voice. Yes, thou must die:
Thou art too noble to conserve a life
In base appliances.° This outward-sainted deputy,
Whose settled visage and deliberate word
Nips youth i' th' head, and follies doth enmew°   90
As falcon doth the fowl, is yet a devil;
His filth within being cast,° he would appear
A pond as deep as hell.
CLAUDIO           The prenzie° Angelo!
ISABELLA
O, 'tis the cunning livery of hell,
The damned'st body to invest and cover      95
In prenzie guards.° Dost thou think, Claudio,
If I would yield him my virginity,
Thou mightst be freed?
CLAUDIO           O heavens, it cannot be.
ISABELLA
Yes, he would give't thee, from this rank offense,
So to offend him still. This night's the time    100
That I should do what I abhor to name,
Or else thou diest tomorrow.
CLAUDIO           Thou shalt not do't.
ISABELLA
O, were it but my life,
I'd throw it down for your deliverance
As frankly as a pin.
CLAUDIO           Thanks, dear Isabel.      105
ISABELLA
Be ready, Claudio, for your death tomorrow.
CLAUDIO
Yes. Has he affections° in him,
That thus can make him bite the law by th' nose,
When he would force° it? Sure, it is no sin,
Or of the deadly seven° it is the least.      110
ISABELLA
Which is the least?

CLAUDIO
If it were damnable, he being so wise,
Why would he for the momentary trick
Be perdurably fined?° O Isabel!
ISABELLA
What says my brother?
CLAUDIO           Death is a fearful thing.     115
ISABELLA
And shamèd life a hateful.
CLAUDIO
Ay, but to die, and go we know not where,
To lie in cold obstruction° and to rot,
This sensible° warm motion° to become
A kneaded clod; and the delighted° spirit     120
To bathe in fiery floods, or to reside
In thrilling region of thick-ribbèd ice;
To be imprisoned in the viewless winds,
And blown with restless violence round about
The pendent° world; or to be worse than worst   125
Of those that lawless and incertain thought
Imagine howling—'tis too horrible!
The weariest and most loathèd worldly life
That age, ache, penury, and imprisonment
Can lay on nature is a paradise        130
To what we fear of death.
ISABELLA
Alas, alas.
CLAUDIO Sweet sister, let me live:
What sin you do to save a brother's life,
Nature dispenses with° the deed so far
That it becomes a virtue.
ISABELLA           O you beast,    135
O faithless coward, O dishonest wretch!
Wilt thou be made a man out of my vice?
Is't not a kind of incest, to take life
From thine own sister's shame? What should I think?
Heaven shield my mother played my father fair,   140
For such a warpèd slip of wilderness°
Ne'er issued from his blood. Take my defiance,
Die, perish! Might but my bending down
Reprieve thee from thy fate, it should proceed.
I'll pray a thousand prayers for thy death,     145
No word to save thee.
CLAUDIO
Nay, hear me, Isabel.
ISABELLA           O, fie, fie, fie!
Thy sin's not accidental, but a trade.
Mercy to thee would prove itself a bawd,
'Tis best that thou diest quickly.
CLAUDIO           O, hear me, Isabella!   150

[*The* DUKE *comes forward.*]

DUKE
Vouchsafe a word, young sister, but one word.
ISABELLA What is your will?
DUKE Might you dispense with your leisure, I would
by and by have some speech with you: the satisfaction
I would require is likewise your own benefit.     155

---

**77 sense** feeling; **apprehension** imagination   **88 appliances**
devices   **90 enmew** drive into the water (as a hawk drives a
fowl)   **92 cast** vomited up   **93 prenzie** meaning unknown;
perhaps a slip for *princely*   **96 guards** trimmings   **107 affections** sensual appetites   **109 force** enforce   **110 deadly seven**
pride, envy, wrath, sloth, avarice, gluttony, lechery

**113–14 Why . . . fined** Why for the momentary trifle
(of sexual intercourse) would he be eternally damned?   **118
obstruction** motionlessness   **119 sensible** endowed with
feeling; **motion** organism   **120 delighted** capable of delight
**125 pendent** hanging in space   **134 dispenses with** grants a
dispensation for   **141 wilderness** wild nature without nurture

ISABELLA  I have no superfluous leisure; my stay must be stolen out of other affairs, but I will attend you awhile.

DUKE  [*Aside to* CLAUDIO.]  Son, I have overheard what hath passed between you and your sister. Angelo 160 had never the purpose to corrupt her; only he hath made an assay° of her virtue to practice his judgment with the disposition of natures. She, having the truth of honor in her, hath made him that gracious denial which he is most glad to receive. I am confessor to 165 Angelo, and I know this to be true; therefore prepare yourself to death. Do not satisfy your resolution with hopes that are fallible. Tomorrow you must die; go to your knees, and make ready.

CLAUDIO  Let me ask my sister pardon. I am so out 170 of love with life, that I will sue to be rid of it.

DUKE  Hold you there; farewell. [*Exit* CLAUDIO.] Provost, a word with you.

[*Enter* PROVOST.]

PROVOST  What's your will, father?

DUKE  That now you are come, you will be gone. 175 Leave me awhile with the maid. My mind promises with my habit° no loss shall touch her by my company.

PROVOST  In good time.°             *Exit.*

DUKE  The hand that hath made you fair hath made 180 you good. The goodness that is cheap in beauty makes beauty brief in goodness; but grace, being the soul of your complexion,° shall keep the body of it ever fair. The assault that Angelo hath made to you, fortune hath conveyed to my understanding, and, but that 185 frailty hath examples for his falling, I should wonder at Angelo. How will you do to content this substitute, and to save your brother?

ISABELLA  I am now going to resolve° him. I had rather my brother die by the law than my son should 190 be unlawfully born. But O, how much is the good duke deceived in Angelo! If ever he return and I can speak to him, I will open my lips in vain, or discover his government.°

DUKE  That shall not be much amiss. Yet, as the matter 195 now stands, he will avoid your accusation: he made trial of you only. Therefore fasten your ear on my advisings; to the love I have in doing good a remedy presents itself. I do make myself believe that you may most uprighteously do a poor wronged lady a merited 200 benefit; redeem your brother from the angry law; do no stain to your own gracious person; and much please the absent duke, if peradventure he shall ever return to have hearing of this business.

ISABELLA  Let me hear you speak farther. I have spirit 205 to do anything that appears not foul in the truth of my spirit.

DUKE  Virtue is bold, and goodness never fearful. Have you not heard speak of Mariana, the sister of Frederick, the great soldier who miscarried at sea? 210

ISABELLA  I have heard of the lady, and good words went with her name.

DUKE  She should this Angelo have married; was affianced to her by oath, and the nuptial appointed: between which time of the contract and limit of the 215 solemnity,° her brother Frederick was wracked at sea, having in that perished vessel the dowry of his sister. But mark how heavily this befell to the poor gentlewoman: there she lost a noble and renowned brother, in his love toward her ever most kind and natural; 220 with him, the portion and sinew of her fortune, her marriage dowry; with both, her combinate° husband, this well-seeming Angelo.

ISABELLA  Can this be so? Did Angelo so leave her?

DUKE  Left her in her tears, and dried not one of them 225 with his comfort; swallowed his vows whole, pretending in her discoveries of dishonor: in few, bestowed her on her own lamentation, which she yet wears for his sake; and he, a marble to her tears, is washed with them, but relents not. 230

ISABELLA  What a merit were it in death to take this poor maid from the world! What corruption in this life, that it will let this man live! But how out of this can she avail?°

DUKE  It is a rupture that you may easily heal, and the 235 cure of it not only saves your brother, but keeps you from dishonor in doing it.

ISABELLA  Show me how, good father.

DUKE  This forenamed maid hath yet in her the continuance of her first affection; his unjust unkindness, 240 that in all reason should have quenched her love, hath, like an impediment in the current, made it more violent and unruly. Go you to Angelo; answer his requiring with a plausible obedience; agree with his demands to the point; only refer yourself to this 245 advantage: first, that your stay with him may not be long; that the time may have all shadow and silence in it; and the place answer to convenience. This being granted in course—and now follows all—we shall advise this wronged maid to stead up° your appoint- 250 ment, go in your place. If the encounter° acknowledge itself hereafter, it may compel him to her recompense: and here, by this, is your brother saved, your honor untainted, the poor Mariana advantaged, and the corrupt deputy scaled.° The maid will I frame° and 255 make fit for his attempt. If you think well to carry this, as you may, the doubleness of the benefit defends the deceit from reproof. What think you of it?

ISABELLA  The image of it gives me content already, and I trust it will grow to a most prosperous perfec- 260 tion.

DUKE  It lies much in your holding up. Haste you speedily to Angelo: if for this night he entreat you to his bed, give him promise of satisfaction. I will presently to Saint Luke's; there at the moated grange° 265 resides this dejected Mariana. At that place call upon me, and dispatch with Angelo, that it may be quickly.

ISABELLA  I thank you for this comfort. Fare you well, good father.          *Exit.*

---

162 **assay** test  177 **habit** religious dress  179 **In good time** very well  183 **complexion** character  189 **resolve** answer  193–94 **discover his government** expose his rule  215–16 **limit of the solemnity** date set for the marriage ceremony  222 **combinate** betrothed  234 **avail** benefit  250 **stead up** keep  251 **encounter** i.e., sexual union  255 **scaled** weighed; **frame** prepare  265 **grange** farm

[Scene II. *Before the prison.*]

*Enter, [to the* DUKE,] ELBOW, *clown* [POMPEY, *and*] OFFICERS.

ELBOW  Nay, if there be no remedy for it, but that you will needs buy and sell men and women like beasts, we shall have all the world drink brown and white bastard.°

DUKE  O heavens! What stuff is here?  5

POMPEY  'Twas never merry world since, of two usuries,° the merriest was put down, and the worser allowed by order of law a furred gown to keep him warm; and furred with fox and lamb skins too, to signify that craft, being richer than innocency, stands 10 for the facing.°

ELBOW  Come your way, sir. 'Bless you, good father friar.

DUKE  And you, good brother father. What offense hath this man made you, sir?  15

ELBOW  Marry, sir, he hath offended the law; and, sir, we take him to be a thief too, sir; for we have found upon him, sir, a strange picklock, which we have sent to the deputy.

DUKE
Fie, sirrah, a bawd, a wicked bawd!  20
The evil that thou causest to be done,
That is thy means to live. Do thou but think
What 'tis to cram a maw° or clothe a back
From such a filthy vice; say to thyself,
From their abominable and beastly touches  25
I drink, I eat, array myself, and live.
Canst thou believe thy living is a life,
So stinkingly depending? Go mend, go mend.

POMPEY  Indeed, it does stink in some sort, sir; but yet, sir, I would prove—  30

DUKE
Nay, if the devil have given thee proofs for sin,
Thou wilt prove his. Take him to prison, officer.
Correction and instruction must both work
Ere this rude beast will profit.

ELBOW  He must before the deputy, sir; he has given 35 him warning. The deputy cannot abide a whoremaster; if he be a whoremonger, and comes before him, he were as good go a mile on his errand.°

DUKE
That we were all, as some would seem to be,
From our faults, as faults from seeming, free!  40

*Enter* LUCIO.

ELBOW  His neck will come to your waist—a cord,° sir.

POMPEY  I spy comfort; I cry bail. Here's a gentleman and a friend of mine.

LUCIO  How now, noble Pompey! What, at the wheels of Caesar? Art thou led in triumph? What, is 45 there none of Pygmalion's images,° newly made

woman, to be had now, for putting the hand in the pocket and extracting it clutched? What reply, ha? What say'st thou to this tune, matter and method? Is't not drowned i' th' last rain, ha? What say'st thou, 50 Trot? Is the world as it was, man? Which is the way? Is it sad, and few words? Or how? The trick of it?

DUKE  Still thus, and thus; still worse.

LUCIO  How doth my dear morsel, thy mistress? Procures she still, ha?  55

POMPEY  Troth, sir, she hath eaten up all her beef,° and she is herself in the tub.°

LUCIO  Why, 'tis good. It is the right of it; it must be so: ever your fresh whore and your powdered bawd, an unshunned consequence; it must be so. Art going 60 to prison, Pompey?

POMPEY  Yes, faith, sir.

LUCIO  Why, 'tis not amiss, Pompey. Farewell; go, say I sent thee thither. For debt, Pompey? Or how?

ELBOW  For being a bawd, for being a bawd.  65

LUCIO  Well, then, imprison him. If imprisonment be the due of a bawd, why, 'tis his right. Bawd is he doubtless, and of antiquity too, bawd-born. Farewell, good Pompey. Commend me to the prison, Pompey, you will turn good husband° now, Pompey, you will 70 keep the house.

POMPEY  I hope, sir, your good worship will be my bail.

LUCIO  No, indeed, will I not, Pompey, it is not the wear.° I will pray, Pompey, to increase your bondage. 75 If you take it not patiently, why, your mettle° is the more. Adieu, trusty Pompey. 'Bless you, friar.

DUKE  And you.

LUCIO  Does Bridget paint still, Pompey, ha?

ELBOW  Come your ways, sir, come.  80

POMPEY  You will not bail me then, sir?

LUCIO  Then, Pompey, nor now. What news abroad, friar, what news?

ELBOW  Come your ways, sir, come.

LUCIO  Go to kennel, Pompey, go. [*Exeunt* ELBOW, 85 POMPEY, *and* OFFICERS.] What news, friar, of the duke?

DUKE  I know none. Can you tell me of any?

LUCIO  Some say he is with the Emperor of Russia; other some, he is in Rome: but where is he, think you? 90

DUKE  I know not where; but wheresoever, I wish him well.

LUCIO  It was a mad fantastical trick of him to steal from the state, and usurp the beggary° he was never born to. Lord Angelo dukes it well in his absence; he 95 puts transgression to't.

DUKE  He does well in't.

LUCIO  A little more lenity to lechery would do no harm in him; something too crabbed that way, friar.

DUKE  It is too general a vice, and severity must cure 100 it.

LUCIO  Yes, in good sooth, the vice is of a great

---

**III.ii.4 bastard** sweet Spanish wine   **6–7 two usuries** lechery is a form of usury, since it exacts a high interest   **10–11 stands . . . facing** represents the trimming   **23 maw** belly   **38 he . . . errand** i.e., he has a hard (or fruitless?) journey ahead   **41 His . . . cord** He will be dropped down to your waist (a reference to the cord around a friar's waist)   **46 Pygmalion's images** i.e., prostitutes (Pompey is compared to Pygmalion, sculptor of a female statue that came to life)

**56 beef** prostitutes (who serve as flesh-food)   **57 in the tub** taking the cure for venereal disease (a tub was also used for corning beef, hence the reference to powdering—pickling—in Lucio's next speech)   **70 husband** housekeeper, manager   **75 wear** fashion   **76 mettle** spirit (with pun on *metal*, i.e., of chains)   **94 usurp the beggary** in reference to the duke's voluntary life in vagabondage

kindred, it is well allied; but it is impossible to extirp it quite, friar, till eating and drinking be put down. They say this Angelo was not made by man and woman after this downright way of creation. Is it true, think you? 105

DUKE   How should he be made, then?

LUCIO   Some report a sea maid° spawned him; some, that he was begot between two stockfishes.° But it is certain that when he makes water his urine is congealed ice; that I know to be true. And he is a motion generative;° that's infallible. 110

DUKE   You are pleasant, sir, and speak apace.

LUCIO   Why, what a ruthless thing is this in him, for the rebellion of a codpiece to take away the life of a man! Would the duke that is absent have done this? Ere he would have hanged a man for the getting a hundred bastards, he would have paid for the nursing a thousand. He had some feeling of the sport; he knew the service, and that instructed him to mercy. 115

DUKE   I never heard the absent duke much detected for° women; he was not inclined that way. 120

LUCIO   O, sir, you are deceived.

DUKE   'Tis not possible. 125

LUCIO   Who, not the duke? Yes, your beggar of fifty, and his use was to put a ducat in her clack-dish;° the duke had crotchets° in him. He would be drunk too; that let me inform you.

DUKE   You do him wrong, surely. 130

LUCIO   Sir, I was an inward° of his. A shy fellow was the duke, and I believe I know the cause of his withdrawing.

DUKE   What, I prithee, might be the cause?

LUCIO   No, pardon; 'tis a secret must be locked within the teeth and the lips; but this I can let you understand, the greater file° of the subject held the duke to be wise. 135

DUKE   Wise! Why, no question but he was.

LUCIO   A very superficial, ignorant, unweighing fellow. 140

DUKE   Either this is envy in you, folly, or mistaking. The very stream of his life and the business he hath helmed must, upon a warranted need,° give him a better proclamation. Let him be but testimonied in his own bringings-forth,° and he shall appear to the envious a scholar, a statesman, and a soldier. Therefore you speak unskillfully; or if your knowledge be more, it is much dark'ned in your malice. 145

LUCIO   Sir, I know him, and I love him. 150

DUKE   Love talks with better knowledge, and knowledge with dearer love.

LUCIO   Come, sir, I know what I know.

DUKE   I can hardly believe that, since you know not what you speak. But, if ever the duke return, as our prayers are he may, let me desire you to make your answer before him. If it be honest you have spoke, you have courage to maintain it. I am bound to call upon you, and I pray you, your name? 155

LUCIO   Sir, my name is Lucio, well known to the duke. 160

DUKE   He shall know you better, sir, if I may live to report you.

LUCIO   I fear you not.

DUKE   O, you hope the duke will return no more, or you imagine me too unhurtful an opposite. But, indeed, I can do you little harm; you'll forswear this again. 165

LUCIO   I'll be hanged first; thou art deceived in me, friar. But no more of this. Canst thou tell if Claudio die tomorrow or no? 170

DUKE   Why should he die, sir?

LUCIO   Why? For filling a bottle with a tundish.° I would the duke we talk of were returned again; this ungenitured° agent will unpeople the province with continency; sparrows must not build in his houseeaves, because they are lecherous. The duke yet would have dark deeds darkly answered; he would never bring them to light. Would he were returned! Marry, this Claudio is condemned for untrussing.° Farewell, good friar; I prithee, pray for me. The duke, I say to thee again, would eat mutton on Fridays.° He's now past it, yet, and I say to thee, he would mouth with a beggar, though she smelled brown bread and garlic. Say that I said so. Farewell.          *Exit.* 175 180

DUKE

No might nor greatness in mortality 185
Can censure 'scape; back-wounding calumny
The whitest virtue strikes. What king so strong
Can tie the gall up in the slanderous tongue?
But who comes here?

*Enter* ESCALUS, PROVOST, *and* [OFFICERS, *with*] *bawd* [MISTRESS OVERDONE].

ESCALUS   Go, away with her to prison! 190

MISTRESS OVERDONE   Good my lord, be good to me. Your honor is accounted a merciful man, good my lord.

ESCALUS   Double and treble admonition, and still forfeit in the same kind! This would make mercy swear, and play the tyrant. 195

PROVOST   A bawd of eleven years' continuance, may it please your honor.

MISTRESS OVERDONE   My lord, this is one Lucio's information against me. Mistress Kate Keepdown was with child by him in the duke's time; he promised her marriage; his child is a year and a quarter old, come Philip and Jacob;° I have kept it myself, and see how he goes about to abuse me. 200

ESCALUS   That fellow is a fellow of much license; let him be called before us. Away with her to prison. Go to, no more words. [*Exeunt* OFFICERS, *with* MISTRESS OVERDONE.] Provost, my brother Angelo will not be altered; Claudio must die tomorrow. Let him be furnished with divines, and have all charitable preparation. If my brother wrought by my pity, it should not be so with him. 205 210

---

109 **sea maid** which would explain his fish-like coldness 110 **stockfishes** dried cod   112–13 **motion generative** masculine puppet   122–23 **detected for** accused of   127 **clack-dish** beggar's bowl (metaphorical here)   128 **crotchets** whims   131 **inward** intimate companion   137 **greater file** majority   144 **upon . . . need** if proof be demanded 146 **bringings-forth** public actions

172 **tundish** funnel   174 **ungenitured** sexless   179 **untrussing** undressing   181 **eat . . . Fridays** the duke allegedly ate mutton on a Friday, which was a fast day, and also practiced venery; "mutton" also means "harlot," and Friday is the day of the planet Venus   203 **Philip and Jacob** May 1

PROVOST So please you, this friar hath been with him, and advised him for th' entertainment of death.

ESCALUS Good even, good father. 215

DUKE Bliss and goodness on you!

ESCALUS Of whence are you?

DUKE
Not of this country, though my chance is now
To use it for my time; I am a brother
Of gracious order, late come from the See 220
In special business from his Holiness.

ESCALUS What news abroad i' th' world?

DUKE None, but that there is so great a fever on goodness, that the dissolution of it must cure it,° novelty is only in request,° and it is as dangerous to be aged° in 225 any kind of course as it is virtuous to be constant in any undertaking. There is scarce truth enough alive to make societies secure, but security° enough to make fellowships° accursed. Much upon this riddle runs the wisdom of the world. This news is old enough, yet it 230 is every day's news. I pray you, sir, of what disposition was the duke?

ESCALUS One that, above all other strifes, contended especially to know himself.

DUKE What pleasure was he given to? 235

ESCALUS Rather rejoicing to see another merry, than merry at anything which professed to make him rejoice: a gentleman of all temperance. But leave we him to his events, with a prayer they may prove prosperous, and let me desire to know how you find 240 Claudio prepared. I am made to understand that you have lent him visitation.

DUKE He professes to have received no sinister measure from his judge, but most willingly humbles himself to the determination of justice; yet had he framed 245 to himself, by the instruction of his frailty, many deceiving promises of life; which I, by my good leisure, have discredited to him, and now is he resolved to die.

ESCALUS You have paid the heavens your function, 250 and the prisoner the very debt of your calling. I have labored for the poor gentleman to the extremest shore of my modesty,° but my brother justice have I found so severe, that he hath forced me to tell him he is indeed Justice. 255

DUKE If his own life answer the straitness of his proceeding, it shall become him well; wherein if he chance to fail, he hath sentenced himself.

ESCALUS I am going to visit the prisoner. Fare you well. 260

DUKE Peace be with you!

         [*Exeunt* ESCALUS *and* PROVOST.]
He who the sword of heaven will bear
Should be as holy as severe;
Pattern in himself to know,
Grace to stand, and virtue go;° 265
More nor less to others paying

223–24 **fever . . . cure it** i.e., the dissolution of the fever alone can now restore goodness to its pristine health 224–25 **novelty . . . request** change is urgently needed 225 **aged** old and worn out 228 **security** heedlessness 229 **fellowships** human societies 252–53 **extremest . . . modesty** as far as is proper 264–65 **Pattern . . . go** He should have a model in himself of grace which will stand if virtue elsewhere ebbs

Than by self-offenses weighing.
Shame to him whose cruel striking
Kills for faults of his own liking.
Twice treble shame on Angelo, 270
To weed my° vice and let his grow.
O, what may man within him hide,
Though angel on the outward side!
How may likeness made in crimes,
Making practice on the times, 275
To draw with idle spiders' strings
Most ponderous and substantial things?
Craft against vice I must apply:
With Angelo tonight shall lie
His old betrothèd but despisèd; 280
So disguise shall, by th' disguisèd,
Pay with falsehood false exacting,
And perform an old contracting.      *Exit.*

# ACT IV

Scene I. [*The moated grange.*]

*Enter* MARIANA *and* BOY *singing.*

         *Song.*
     Take, O, take those lips away,
         That so sweetly were forsworn;
     And those eyes, the break of day,
         Lights that do mislead the morn;
     But my kisses bring again, bring again; 5
     Seals of love, but sealed in vain, sealed in vain.

*Enter* DUKE [*disguised as before*].

MARIANA
Break off thy song, and haste thee quick away.
Here comes a man of comfort, whose advice
Hath often stilled my brawling discontent.
             [*Exit* BOY.]
I cry you mercy, sir; and well could wish 10
You had not found me here so musical.
Let me excuse me, and believe me so,
My mirth it much displeased, but pleased my woe.

DUKE
'Tis good; though music oft hath such a charm
To make bad good, and good provoke to harm. 15
I pray you, tell me, hath anybody inquired for me
here today? Much upon this time have I promised here
to meet.

MARIANA You have not been inquired after; I have
sat here all day. 20

*Enter* ISABELLA.

DUKE I do constantly believe you. The time is come
even now. I shall crave your forbearance a little; may
be I will call upon you anon, for some advantage to
yourself.

MARIANA I am always bound to you.      *Exit.* 25

DUKE
Very well met, and well come.
What is the news from this good deputy?

271 **my** used impersonally

**ISABELLA**
He hath a garden circummured° with brick,
Whose western side is with a vineyard backed;
And to that vineyard is a planchèd° gate,    30
That makes his opening with this bigger key.
This other doth command a little door
Which from the vineyard to the garden leads.
There have I made my promise
Upon the heavy middle of the night    35
To call upon him.

**DUKE**
But shall you on your knowledge find this way?

**ISABELLA**
I have ta'en a due and wary note upon't.
With whispering and most guilty diligence,
In action all of precept,° he did show me    40
The way twice o'er.

**DUKE**                    Are there no other tokens
Between you 'greed concerning her observance?°

**ISABELLA**
No, none, but only a repair i' th' dark,
And that I have possessed° him my most stay
Can be but brief; for I have made him know    45
I have a servant comes with me along,
That stays upon° me, whose persuasion° is
I come about my brother.

**DUKE**                    'Tis well borne up.
I have not yet made known to Mariana
A word of this. What, ho, within! Come forth.    50

*Enter* MARIANA.

I pray you, be acquainted with this maid;
She comes to do you good.

**ISABELLA**                    I do desire the like.

**DUKE**
Do you persuade yourself that I respect you?

**MARIANA**
Good friar, I know you do, and have found it.

**DUKE**
Take, then, this your companion by the hand,    55
Who hath a story ready for your ear.
I shall attend your leisure, but make haste;
The vaporous night approaches.

**MARIANA**
Will't please you walk aside?    *Exit,* [*with* ISABELLA].

**DUKE**
O place and greatness, millions of false eyes    60
Are stuck upon thee; volumes of report
Run with these false and most contrarious quests°
Upon thy doings; thousand escapes° of wit
Make thee the father of their idle dreams,
And rack thee in their fancies.

*Enter* MARIANA *and* ISABELLA.

                    Welcome, how agreed?    65

**ISABELLA**
She'll take the enterprise upon her, father,
If you advise it.

**DUKE**                    It is not my consent
But my entreaty too.

**ISABELLA**                    Little have you to say
When you depart from him, but, soft and low,
"Remember now my brother."

**MARIANA**                    Fear me not.    70

**DUKE**
Nor, gentle daughter, fear you not at all.
He is your husband on a precontract;°
To bring you thus together, 'tis no sin,
Sith that the justice of your title to him
Doth flourish the deceit. Come, let us go:    75
Our corn's to reap, for yet our tithe's° to sow.

                    *Exeunt.*

Scene II. [*The prison.*]

*Enter* PROVOST *and clown* [POMPEY].

**PROVOST**  Come hither, sirrah. Can you cut off a
man's head?

**POMPEY**  If the man be a bachelor, sir, I can; but if he
be a married man, he's his wife's head,° and I can never
cut off a woman's head.    5

**PROVOST**  Come, sir, leave me your snatches,° and
yield me a direct answer. Tomorrow morning are to
die Claudio and Barnardine. Here is in our prison a
common executioner, who in his office lacks a helper.
If you will take it on you to assist him, it shall redeem    10
you from your gyves;° if not, you shall have your full
time of imprisonment, and your deliverance with an
unpitied whipping, for you have been a notorious
bawd.

**POMPEY**  Sir, I have been an unlawful bawd time out    15
of mind, but yet I will be content to be a lawful
hangman. I would be glad to receive some instruction
from my fellow partner.

**PROVOST**  What, ho, Abhorson!° Where's Abhorson,
there?    20

*Enter* ABHORSON.

**ABHORSON**  Do you call, sir?

**PROVOST**  Sirrah, here's a fellow will help you tomorrow in your execution. If you think it meet, com-
pound° with him by the year, and let him abide here
with you; if not, use him for the present, and dismiss    25
him. He cannot plead his estimation° with you; he
hath been a bawd.

**ABHORSON**  A bawd, sir? Fie upon him! He will discredit our mystery.°

**PROVOST**  Go to, sir; you weigh equally; a feather    30
will turn the scale.    *Exit.*

**POMPEY**  Pray, sir, by your good favor—for surely,
sir, a good favor° you have, but that you have a
hanging look—do you call, sir, your occupation a
mystery?    35

**ABHORSON**  Ay, sir; a mystery.

**72 precontract** legally binding betrothal agreement **76
tithe** tithe corn
**IV.ii.4 he's . . . head** see Ephesians 5:23, "For the husband
is the head of the wife" **6 snatches** quibbles **11 gyves**
shackles **19 Abhorson** pun on *ab-whore-son*, son from a
whore **23–24 compound** settle **26 estimation** reputation
**29 mystery** craft **33 favor** countenance

**IV.i.28 circummured** walled around   **30 planchèd** planked
**40 In . . . precept** teaching by gestures   **42 her observance**
what she must do   **44 possessed** informed   **47 stays upon**
waits for; **persuasion** conviction   **62 quests** cry of the hound
on the scent   **63 escapes** sallies

POMPEY  Painting, sir, I have heard say, is a mystery;
and your whores, sir, being members of my occupation, using painting, do prove my occupation a
mystery; but what mystery there should be in hanging, 40
if I should be hanged, I cannot imagine.

ABHORSON  Sir, it is a mystery.

POMPEY  Proof?

ABHORSON  Every true man's apparel fits your thief:
if it be too little for your thief, your true man thinks it 45
big enough; if it be too big for your thief, your thief
thinks it little enough: so every true man's apparel fits
your thief.°

*Enter* PROVOST.

PROVOST  Are you agreed?

POMPEY  Sir, I will serve him; for I do find your 50
hangman is a more penitent trade than your bawd; he
doth oft'ner ask forgiveness.°

PROVOST  You, sirrah, provide your block and your
ax tomorrow four o'clock.

ABHORSON  Come on, bawd. I will instruct thee in 55
my trade; follow.

POMPEY  I do desire to learn, sir; and I hope, if you
have occasion to use me for your own turn,° you shall
find me yare;° for, truly, sir, for your kindness I owe
you a good turn. 60

PROVOST
Call hither Barnardine and Claudio.
             *Exit* [POMPEY, *with* ABHORSON].
Th' one has my pity; not a jot the other,
Being a murderer, though he were my brother.

*Enter* CLAUDIO.

Look, here's the warrant, Claudio, for thy death.
'Tis now dead midnight, and by eight tomorrow 65
Thou must be made immortal. Where's Barnardine?

CLAUDIO
As fast locked up in sleep as guiltless labor
When it lies starkly° in the traveler's bones;
He will not wake.

PROVOST           Who can do good on him?
Well, go, prepare yourself. [*Knocking within.*] But,
  hark, what noise?— 70
Heaven give your spirits comfort. [*Exit* CLAUDIO.]
  By and by.
I hope it is some pardon or reprieve
For the most gentle Claudio. Welcome, father.

*Enter* DUKE [*disguised as before*].

DUKE
The best and wholesom'st spirits of the night
Envelop you, good provost! Who called here of late? 75

PROVOST
None since the curfew rung.

DUKE
Not Isabel?

PROVOST  No.

DUKE        They will, then, ere't be long.

PROVOST
What comfort is for Claudio?

DUKE
There's some in hope.

PROVOST
It is a bitter deputy. 80

DUKE
Not so, not so; his life is paralleled
Even with the stroke and line of his great justice.
He doth with holy abstinence subdue
That in himself which he spurs on his pow'r
To qualify° in others; were he mealed° with that 85
Which he corrects, then were he tyrannous;
But this being so, he's just. [*Knocking within.*] Now are
  they come.             [*Exit* PROVOST.]
This is a gentle provost—seldom when
The steelèd jailer is the friend of men.

[*Knocking within.*]

How now, what noise? That spirit's possessed with
  haste 90
That wounds th' unsisting° postern° with these strokes.

[*Enter* PROVOST.]

PROVOST
There he must stay until the officer
Arise to let him in; he is called up.

DUKE
Have you no countermand for Claudio yet,
But he must die tomorrow?

PROVOST          None, sir, none. 95

DUKE
As near the dawning, provost, as it is,
You shall hear more ere morning.

PROVOST          Happily
You something know; yet I believe there comes
No countermand; no such example have we.
Besides, upon the very siege° of justice 100
Lord Angelo hath to the public ear
Professed the contrary.

*Enter a* MESSENGER.

                 This is his lord's man.

DUKE
And here comes Claudio's pardon.

MESSENGER  My lord hath sent you this note, and by
me this further charge, that you swerve not from the 105
smallest article of it, neither in time, matter, or other
circumstance. Good morrow; for, as I take it, it is
almost day.

PROVOST  I shall obey him.      [*Exit* MESSENGER.]

DUKE [*Aside.*]
This is his pardon, purchased by such sin 110
For which the pardoner himself is in.
Hence hath offense his quick celerity,
When it is borne in high authority.
When vice makes mercy, mercy's so extended,
That for the fault's love is th' offender friended. 115
Now, sir, what news?

PROVOST  I told you. Lord Angelo, belike° thinking

---

**44–48 Every . . . thief** interpretation uncertain  **52 ask forgiveness** the executioner always asked the condemned man to forgive him  **58 turn** execution (pun)  **59 yare** ready  **68 starkly** stiffly

**85 qualify** moderate; **mealed** stained  **91 unsisting** perhaps "unassisting," perhaps a printer's slip for "resisting"; **postern** small door  **100 siege** seat  **117 belike** perhaps

me remiss in mine office, awakens me with this unwonted putting-on;° methinks strangely, for he hath
not used it before.                                               120

DUKE  Pray you, let's hear.

PROVOST  [*Reads*] *the letter*. "Whatsoever you may
hear to the contrary, let Claudio be executed by four
of the clock; and in the afternoon Barnardine. For my
better satisfaction, let me have Claudio's head sent  125
me by five. Let this be duly performed with a thought
that more depends on it than we must yet deliver.
Thus fail not to do your office, as you will answer it
at your peril."
What say you to this, sir?                                     130

DUKE  What is that Barnardine who is to be executed
in th' afternoon?

PROVOST  A Bohemian born, but here nursed up and
bred; one that is a prisoner nine years old.

DUKE  How came it that the absent duke had not  135
either delivered him to his liberty or executed him? I
have heard it was ever his manner to do so.

PROVOST  His friends still wrought reprieves for him;
and, indeed, his fact,° till now in the government of
Lord Angelo, came not to an undoubtful proof.          140

DUKE  It is now apparent?

PROVOST  Most manifest, and not denied by himself.

DUKE  Hath he borne himself penitently in prison?
How seems he to be touched?

PROVOST  A man that apprehends death no more  145
dreadfully but as a drunken sleep; careless, reckless, and
fearless of what's past, present, or to come; insensible
of mortality, and desperately mortal.°

DUKE  He wants° advice.

PROVOST  He will hear none. He hath evermore had  150
the liberty of the prison; give him leave to escape
hence, he would not: drunk many times a day, if not
many days entirely drunk. We have very oft awaked
him, as if to carry him to execution, and showed him
a seeming warrant for it; it hath not moved him at all.  155

DUKE  More of him anon. There is written in your
brow, provost, honesty and constancy: if I read it not
truly, my ancient skill beguiles me; but, in the boldness of my cunning,° I will lay myself in hazard.°
Claudio, whom here you have warrant to execute, is  160
no greater forfeit to the law than Angelo who hath
sentenced him. To make you understand this in a
manifested effect,° I crave but four days' respite, for
the which you are to do me both a present° and a
dangerous courtesy.                                            165

PROVOST  Pray, sir, in what?

DUKE  In the delaying death.

PROVOST  Alack, how may I do it, having the hour
limited,° and an express command, under penalty, to
deliver his head in the view of Angelo? I may make  170
my case as Claudio's, to cross this in the smallest.

DUKE  By the vow of mine order I warrant you, if my
instructions may be your guide. Let this Barnardine
be this morning executed, and his head borne to
Angelo.                                                          175

PROVOST  Angelo hath seen them both, and will discover the favor.°

DUKE  O, death's a great disguiser; and you may add
to it. Shave the head, and tie the beard; and say it was
the desire of the penitent to be so bared° before his  180
death; you know the course is common. If anything
fall to you upon this, more than thanks and good
fortune, by the saint whom I profess, I will plead
against it with my life.

PROVOST  Pardon me, good father; it is against my  185
oath.

DUKE  Were you sworn to the duke, or to the
deputy?

PROVOST  To him, and to his substitutes.

DUKE  You will think you have made no offense, if the  190
duke avouch the justice of your dealing?

PROVOST  But what likelihood is in that?

DUKE  Not a resemblance, but a certainty. Yet since
I see you fearful,° that neither my coat, integrity, nor
persuasion can with ease attempt° you, I will go further  195
than I meant, to pluck all fears out of you. Look you,
sir, here is the hand and seal of the duke. You know
the character,° I doubt not, and the signet is not strange
to you.

PROVOST  I know them both.                                  200

DUKE  The contents of this is the return of the duke.
You shall anon overread it at your pleasure, where you
shall find, within these two days he will be here. This
is a thing that Angelo knows not; for he this very day
receives letters of strange tenor, perchance of the  205
duke's death, perchance entering into some monastery,
but by chance nothing of what is writ. Look, th'
unfolding star° calls up the shepherd. Put not yourself
into amazement how these things should be: all
difficulties are but easy when they are known. Call  210
your executioner, and off with Barnardine's head; I
will give him a present shrift,° and advise him for a
better place. Yet you are amazed; but this shall
absolutely resolve° you. Come away; it is almost clear
dawn.                              *Exit*, [*with* PROVOST].  215

### Scene III. [*The prison*.]

*Enter clown* [POMPEY].

POMPEY  I am as well acquainted here as I was in our
house of profession: one would think it were Mistress
Overdone's own house, for here be many of her old
customers. First, here's young Master Rash; he's in
for a commodity° of brown paper and old ginger,  5
ninescore and seventeen pounds, of which he made
five marks,° ready money; marry, then ginger was
not much in request, for the old women were all dead.
Then is there here one Master Caper, at the suit of

119 **putting-on** urging  139 **fact** evil deed  148
**desperately mortal** about to die without hope of
the future  149 **wants** needs  159 **cunning** knowledge;
**lay . . . hazard** take a risk  162–63 **in . . . effect** by open
proof  164 **present** immediate  169 **limited** determined

176–77 **discover the favor** recognize the face  180 **bared** shaved
194 **fearful** full of fear  195 **attempt** move  198 **character**
handwriting  208 **unfolding star** morning star (signaling the
shepherd to lead the sheep from the fold)  212 **shrift** absolution
214 **resolve** convince
**IV.iii.5 commodity** worthless goods whose purchase at a
heavy price was forced on a debtor in dire need by a usurious
creditor, who thus circumvented the contemporary laws
against usury  7 **marks** a mark was about two-thirds of a
pound

Master Three-pile the mercer, for some four suits of 10
peach-colored satin, which now peaches° him a beggar.
Then have we here young Dizzy, and young Master
Deep-vow, and Master Copper-spur,° and Master
Starve-lackey, the rapier and dagger man, and young
Drop-heir that killed lusty Pudding, and Master 15
Forthright the tilter,° and brave Master Shoe-tie° the
great traveler, and wild Half-can° that stabbed Pots,
and, I think, forty more; all great doers in our trade,
and are now "for the Lord's sake."°

*Enter* ABHORSON.

ABHORSON  Sirrah, bring Barnardine hither.          20
POMPEY  Master Barnardine! You must rise and be
hanged, Master Barnardine!
ABHORSON  What, ho, Barnardine!
BARNARDINE (*Within.*)  A pox o' your throats! Who
makes that noise there? What are you?                25
POMPEY  Your friends, sir; the hangman. You must
be so good, sir, to rise and be put to death.
BARNARDINE [*Within.*]  Away, you rogue, away! I
am sleepy.
ABHORSON  Tell him he must awake, and that quickly 30
too.
POMPEY  Pray, Master Barnardine, awake till you are
executed, and sleep afterwards.
ABHORSON  Go into him, and fetch him out.
POMPEY  He is coming, sir, he is coming; I hear his 35
straw rustle.

*Enter* BARNARDINE.

ABHORSON  Is the ax upon the block, sirrah?
POMPEY  Very ready, sir.
BARNARDINE  How now, Abhorson? What's the
news with you?                                      40
ABHORSON  Truly, sir, I would desire you to clap into
your prayers; for, look you, the warrant's come.
BARNARDINE  You rogue, I have been drinking all
night; I am not fitted for't.
POMPEY  O, the better, sir: for he that drinks all 45
night, and is hanged betimes° in the morning, may
sleep the sounder all the next day.

*Enter* DUKE [*disguised as before*].

ABHORSON  Look you, sir; here comes your ghostly°
father. Do we jest now, think you?
DUKE  Sir, induced by my charity, and hearing how 50
hastily you are to depart, I am come to advise you,
comfort you, and pray with you.
BARNARDINE  Friar, not I: I have been drinking hard
all night, and I will have more time to prepare me,
or they shall beat out my brains with billets.° I will 55
not consent to die this day, that's certain.
DUKE
O, sir, you must; and therefore I beseech you
Look forward on the journey you shall go.
BARNARDINE  I swear I will not die today for any
man's persuasion.                                   60

11 **peaches** betrays  13 **Copper-spur** i.e., Master Pretentious
(copper was a bogus substitute for gold)  16 **tilter** fighter;
**Shoe-tie** rosette (worn by gallants)  17 **Half-can** a larger
vessel than a pot  19 **for . . . sake** the cry of prisoners begging
alms from passers-by  46 **betimes** early  48 **ghostly** spiritual
55 **billets** cudgels

DUKE  But hear you—
BARNARDINE  Not a word. If you have anything to
say to me, come to my ward, for thence will not I
today.                                            *Exit.*

*Enter* PROVOST.

DUKE
Unfit to live or die. O gravel heart!             65
After him, fellows; bring him to the block.
                   [*Exeunt* ABHORSON *and* POMPEY.]
PROVOST
Now, sir, how do you find the prisoner?
DUKE
A creature unprepared, unmeet for death;
And to transport him in the mind he is
Were damnable.
PROVOST            Here in the prison, father,       70
There died this morning of a cruel fever
One Ragozine, a most notorious pirate,
A man of Claudio's years, his beard and head
Just of his color. What if we do omit
This reprobate till he were well inclined,            75
And satisfy the deputy with the visage
Of Ragozine, more like to Claudio?
DUKE
O, 'tis an accident that heaven provides.
Dispatch it presently;° the hour draws on
Prefixed° by Angelo. See this be done,               80
And sent according to command, whiles I
Persuade this rude wretch willingly to die.
PROVOST
This shall be done, good father, presently;
But Barnardine must die this afternoon,
And how shall we continue Claudio,                   85
To save me from the danger that might come
If he were known alive?
DUKE                      Let this be done:
Put them in secret holds,° both Barnardine and
  Claudio.
Ere twice the sun hath made his journal° greeting
To yonder generation, you shall find                 90
Your safety manifested.
PROVOST
I am your free dependant.°
DUKE
Quick, dispatch, and send the head to Angelo.
                              *Exit* [PROVOST].
Now will I write letters to Angelo—
The provost, he shall bear them—whose contents 95
Shall witness to him I am near at home,
And that by great injunctions I am bound
To enter publicly. Him I'll desire
To meet me at the consecrated fount,
A league below the city; and from thence,           100
By cold gradation° and well-balanced form,
We shall proceed with Angelo.

*Enter* PROVOST.

PROVOST
Here is the head; I'll carry it myself.

79 **presently** at once  80 **Prefixed** predetermined  88 **holds**
cells  89 **journal** daily  92 **your free dependant** freely at
your service  101 **cold gradation** deliberate steps

DUKE
Convenient is it. Make a swift return,
For I would commune with you of such things    105
That want° no ear but yours.
PROVOST                    I'll make all speed.    *Exit.*
ISABELLA (*Within.*)
Peace, ho, be here!
DUKE
The tongue of Isabel. She's come to know
If yet her brother's pardon be come hither.
But I will keep her ignorant of her good,    110
To make her heavenly comforts of despair
When it is least expected.

*Enter* ISABELLA.

ISABELLA                    Ho, by your leave!
DUKE
Good morning to you, fair and gracious daughter.
ISABELLA
The better, given me by so holy a man.
Hath yet the deputy sent my brother's pardon?    115
DUKE
He hath released him, Isabel, from the world;
His head is off, and sent to Angelo.
ISABELLA
Nay, but it is not so.
DUKE
It is no other. Show your wisdom, daughter,
In your close° patience.    120
ISABELLA
O, I will to him and pluck out his eyes!
DUKE
You shall not be admitted to his sight.
ISABELLA
Unhappy Claudio, wretched Isabel,
Injurious world, most damnèd Angelo!
DUKE
This nor hurts him nor profits you a jot;    125
Forbear it therefore, give your cause to heaven.
Mark what I say, which you shall find
By every syllable a faithful verity.
The duke comes home tomorrow—nay, dry your
      eyes—
One of our covent,° and his confessor,    130
Gives me this instance:° already he hath carried
Notice to Escalus and Angelo,
Who do prepare to meet him at the gates,
There to give up their pow'r. If you can, pace° your
      wisdom
In that good path that I would wish it go,    135
And you shall have your bosom° on this wretch,
Grace of the duke, revenges to your heart,
And general honor.
ISABELLA                    I am directed by you.
DUKE
This letter, then, to Friar Peter give;
'Tis that he sent me of the duke's return.    140
Say, by this token, I desire his company
At Mariana's house tonight. Her cause and yours
I'll perfect him withal, and he shall bring you

Before the duke; and to the head of Angelo
Accuse him home and home. For my poor self,    145
I am combined° by a sacred vow,
And shall be absent. Wend you with this letter;
Command these fretting waters from your eyes
With a light heart; trust not my holy order,
If I pervert your course. Who's here?    150

*Enter* LUCIO.

LUCIO    Good even. Friar, where's the provost?
DUKE    Not within, sir.
LUCIO    O pretty Isabella, I am pale at mine heart to
see thine eyes so red; thou must be patient. I am fain
to dine and sup with water and bran; I dare not for    155
my head fill my belly; one fruitful meal would set me
to't. But they say the duke will be here tomorrow. By
my troth, Isabel, I loved thy brother. If the old
fantastical duke of dark corners had been at home, he
had lived.                    [*Exit* ISABELLA.]    160
DUKE    Sir, the duke is marvelous little beholding to
your reports; but the best is, he lives not in them.
LUCIO    Friar, thou knowest not the duke so well as I
do; he's a better woodman° than thou tak'st him for.
DUKE    Well, you'll answer this one day. Fare ye well.    165
LUCIO    Nay, tarry, I'll go along with thee: I can tell
thee pretty tales of the duke.
DUKE    You have told me too many of him already,
sir, if they be true; if not true, none were enough.
LUCIO    I was once before him for getting a wench    170
with child.
DUKE    Did you such a thing?
LUCIO    Yes, marry, did I; but I was fain to forswear
it: they would else have married me to the rotten
medlar.°    175
DUKE    Sir, your company is fairer than honest. Rest
you well.
LUCIO    By my troth, I'll go with thee to the lane's end.
If bawdy talk offend you, we'll have very little of it.
Nay, friar, I am a kind of burr; I shall stick.    *Exeunt.*    180


Scene IV. [*A room.*]

*Enter* ANGELO *and* ESCALUS.

ESCALUS    Every letter he hath writ hath disvouched
other.
ANGELO    In most uneven and distracted manner. His
actions show much like to madness; pray heaven his
wisdom be not tainted. And why meet him at the    5
gates, and redeliver our authorities there?
ESCALUS    I guess not.
ANGELO    And why should we proclaim it in an hour
before his ent'ring, that if any crave redress of injustice, they should exhibit their petitions in the street?    10
ESCALUS    He shows his reason for that: to have a dispatch of complaints, and to deliver us from devices°
hereafter which shall then have no power to stand
against us.

---

106 **want** need    120 **close** deep, secret    130 **covent** convent
131 **instance** proof    134 **pace** conduct    136 **bosom** desire
146 **combinèd** bound    164 **woodman** hunter (here, of
women)    175 **medlar** applelike fruit edible only when partly
decayed (here, a prostitute)
IV.iv.12 **devices** false complaints

ANGELO
Well, I beseech you, let it be proclaimed.     15
Betimes i' th' morn I'll call you at your house.
Give notice to such men of sort and suit°
As are to meet him.
ESCALUS         I shall, sir. Fare you well.     *Exit.*
ANGELO    Good night.
This deed unshapes me quite, makes me unpregnant,°   20
And dull to all proceedings. A deflow'red maid,
And by an eminent body that enforced
The law against it! But that her tender shame
Will not proclaim against her maiden loss,°
How might she tongue me! Yet reason dares her no;   25
For my authority bears of a credent bulk,°
That no particular scandal once can touch
But it confounds the breather. He should have lived,
Save that his riotous youth, with dangerous sense,°
Might in the times to come have ta'en revenge,     30
By so receiving a dishonored life
With ransom of such shame. Would yet he had lived!
Alack, when once our grace we have forgot,
Nothing goes right; we would, and we would not.
                           *Exit.*

### Scene V. [*Outside the town.*]

*Enter* DUKE [*in his own habit*] *and* FRIAR PETER.

DUKE
These letters at fit time deliver me.°
The provost knows our purpose and our plot.
The matter being afoot, keep your instruction,
And hold you ever to our special drift,
Though sometimes you do blench° from this to that,   5
As cause doth minister. Go call at Flavius' house,
And tell him where I stay; give the like notice
To Valencius, Rowland, and to Crassus,
And bid them bring the trumpets to the gate;
But send me Flavius first.
FRIAR PETER       It shall be speeded well.   10
                             [*Exit.*]

*Enter* VARRIUS.

DUKE
I thank thee, Varrius; thou hast made good haste.
Come, we will walk. There's other of our friends
Will greet us here anon, my gentle Varrius.     *Exeunt.*

### Scene VI. [*Near the city gate.*]

*Enter* ISABELLA *and* MARIANA.

ISABELLA
To speak so indirectly I am loath:
I would say the truth; but to accuse him so,
That is your part. Yet I am advised to do it,
He says, to veil full purpose.
MARIANA         Be ruled by him.
ISABELLA
Besides, he tells me that, if peradventure     5

He speak against me on the adverse side,
I should not think it strange; for 'tis a physic
That's bitter to sweet end.
MARIANA
I would Friar Peter—

*Enter* FRIAR PETER.

ISABELLA           O peace! The friar is come.
FRIAR PETER
Come, I have found you out a stand most fit    10
Where you may have such vantage° on the duke,
He shall not pass you. Twice have the trumpets
    sounded.
The generous° and gravest citizens
Have hent° the gates, and very near upon
The duke is ent'ring: therefore, hence, away! *Exeunt.*   15

## A C T   V

### Scene I. [*The city gate.*]

*Enter* DUKE, VARRIUS, LORDS, ANGELO, ESCALUS,
LUCIO, [PROVOST, OFFICERS, *and*] CITIZENS, *at
several doors.*

DUKE
My very worthy cousin,° fairly met.
Our old and faithful friend, we are glad to see you.
ANGELO, ESCALUS
Happy return be to your royal grace.
DUKE
Many and hearty thankings to you both.
We have made inquiry of you, and we hear     5
Such goodness of your justice, that our soul
Cannot but yield you forth to public thanks,
Forerunning more requital.°
ANGELO          You make my bonds still greater.
DUKE
O, your desert speaks loud, and I should wrong it
To lock it in the wards of covert bosom,°     10
When it deserves, with characters of brass,
A forted residence 'gainst the tooth of time
And razure° of oblivion. Give me your hand,
And let the subject see, to make them know
That outward courtesies would fain proclaim     15
Favors that keep° within. Come, Escalus,
You must walk by us on our other hand—
And good supporters are you.

*Enter* [FRIAR] PETER *and* ISABELLA.

FRIAR PETER
Now is your time: speak loud, and kneel before him.
ISABELLA
Justice, O royal duke! Vail your regard°     20
Upon a wronged—I would fain have said, a maid.

**17 men . . . suit** noblemen   **20 unpregnant** unreceptive
**24 maiden loss** loss of maidenhood   **26 bears . . . bulk**
is derived from trusted material   **29 sense** feeling
**IV.v.1 me** for me   **5 blench** deviate
**IV.vi.11 vantage** advantageous position   **13 generous** high-
born   **14 hent** gathered at
**V.i.1 cousin** a sovereign's address to a nobleman   **8 Forerunning more requital** preceding additional reward   **10
To . . . bosom** to keep it locked hidden in my heart   **13
razure** erasure   **16 keep** dwell   **20 Vail your regard** cast
your attention

O worthy prince, dishonor not your eye
By throwing it on any other object
Till you have heard me in my true complaint,
And given me justice, justice, justice, justice!  25

DUKE
Relate your wrongs. In what? By whom? Be brief.
Here is Lord Angelo shall give you justice;
Reveal yourself to him.

ISABELLA                    O worthy duke,
You bid me seek redemption of the devil.
Hear me yourself, for that which I must speak  30
Must either punish me, not being believed,
Or wring redress from you. Hear me, O hear me, here!

ANGELO
My lord, her wits, I fear me, are not firm.
She hath been a suitor to me for her brother
Cut off by course of justice—

ISABELLA                    By course of justice!  35

ANGELO
And she will speak most bitterly and strange.

ISABELLA
Most strange, but yet most truly, will I speak.
That Angelo's forsworn, is it not strange?
That Angelo's a murderer, is't not strange?
That Angelo is an adulterous thief,  40
An hypocrite, a virgin-violator;
Is it not strange, and strange?

DUKE                    Nay, it is ten times strange.

ISABELLA
It is not truer he is Angelo
Than this is all as true as it is strange.
Nay, it is ten times true, for truth is truth  45
To th' end of reck'ning.

DUKE                    Away with her! Poor soul,
She speaks this in th' infirmity of sense.

ISABELLA
O prince, I conjure thee, as thou believ'st
There is another comfort than this world,
That thou neglect me not, with that opinion  50
That I am touched with madness. Make not impossible
That which but seems unlike. 'Tis not impossible
But one, the wicked'st caitiff° on the ground,
May seem as shy, as grave, as just, as absolute°
As Angelo; even so may Angelo,  55
In all his dressings, caracts,° titles, forms,
Be an arch-villain. Believe it, royal prince;
If he be less, he's nothing; but he's more,
Had I more name for badness.

DUKE                    By mine honesty,
If she be mad, as I believe no other,  60
Her madness hath the oddest frame of sense,
Such a dependency of thing on thing,
As e'er I heard in madness.

ISABELLA                    O gracious duke,
Harp not on that; nor do not banish reason
For inequality,° but let your reason serve  65
To make the truth appear where it seems hid,
And hide the false seems° true.

DUKE                    Many that are not mad
Have, sure, more lack of reason. What would you say?

ISABELLA
I am the sister of one Claudio,
Condemned upon the act of fornication  70
To lose his head, condemned by Angelo.
I, in probation° of a sisterhood,
Was sent to by my brother, one Lucio
As then the messenger—

LUCIO                    That's I, and't like° your grace.
I came to her from Claudio, and desired her  75
To try her gracious fortune with Lord Angelo
For her poor brother's pardon.

ISABELLA                    That's he indeed.

DUKE
You were not bid to speak.

LUCIO                    No, my good lord,
Nor wished to hold my peace.

DUKE                    I wish you now, then;
Pray you, take note of it, and when you have  80
A business for yourself, pray heaven you then
Be perfect.°

LUCIO        I warrant your honor.

DUKE
The warrant's° for yourself; take heed to't.

ISABELLA
This gentleman told somewhat of my tale—

LUCIO  Right.  85

DUKE
It may be right; but you are i' the wrong
To speak before your time. Proceed.

ISABELLA                    I went
To this pernicious caitiff deputy—

DUKE
That's somewhat madly spoken.

ISABELLA                    Pardon it;
The phrase is to the matter.°  90

DUKE
Mended again. The matter: proceed.

ISABELLA
In brief, to set the needless process by,
How I persuaded, how I prayed, and kneeled,
How he refelled° me, and how I replied—
For this was of much length—the vild° conclusion  95
I now begin with grief and shame to utter.
He would not, but by gift of my chaste body
To his concupiscible intemperate lust,
Release my brother; and after much debatement,
My sisterly remorse° confutes mine honor,  100
And I did yield to him; but the next morn betimes,
His purpose surfeiting,° he sends a warrant
For my poor brother's head.

DUKE                    This is most likely!

ISABELLA
O, that it were as like as it is true!

DUKE
By heaven, fond wretch, thou know'st not what thou
        speak'st,  105
Or else thou art suborned against his honor
In hateful practice.° First, his integrity

---

53 **caitiff** wretch  54 **absolute** perfect  56 **caracts** symbols of office  65 **inequality** injustice  67 **seems** which seems

72 **probation** novitiate  74 **and't like** if it please  82 **perfect** thoroughly prepared  83 **warrant** warning  90 **to the matter** appropriate  94 **refelled** refuted  95 **vild** vile  100 **remorse** pity  102 **surfeiting** satiating  107 **practice** plot

Stands without blemish. Next, it imports° no reason
That with such vehemency he should pursue
Faults proper° to himself: if he had so offended,    110
He would have weighed thy brother by himself,
And not have cut him off. Someone hath set you on;
Confess the truth, and say by whose advice
Thou cam'st here to complain.

ISABELLA                 And is this all?
Then, O you blessèd ministers above,    115
Keep me in patience, and with ripened time
Unfold the evil which is here wrapped up
In countenance. Heaven shield your grace from woe,
As I, thus wronged, hence unbelievèd go!

DUKE
I know you'd fain be gone. An officer,    120
To prison with her! Shall we thus permit
A blasting and a scandalous breath to fall
On him so near us? This needs must be a practice.
Who knew of your intent and coming hither?

ISABELLA
One that I would were here, Friar Lodowick.    125

DUKE
A ghostly father, belike. Who knows that Lodowick?

LUCIO
My lord, I know him; 'tis a meddling friar,
I do not like the man. Had he been lay,° my lord,
For certain words he spake against your grace
In your retirement, I had swinged° him soundly.    130

DUKE
Words against me! This's a good friar, belike!
And to set on this wretched woman here
Against our substitute! Let this friar be found.

LUCIO
But yesternight, my lord, she and that friar,
I saw them at the prison; a saucy friar,    135
A very scurvy° fellow.

FRIAR PETER
Blessed be your royal grace!
I have stood by, my lord, and I have heard
Your royal ear abused. First, hath this woman
Most wrongfully accused your substitute,    140
Who is as free from touch or soil with her
As she from one ungot.

DUKE             We did believe no less.
Know you that Friar Lodowick that she speaks of?

FRIAR PETER
I know him for a man divine and holy;
Not scurvy, nor a temporary meddler,°    145
As he's reported by this gentleman;
And, on my trust, a man that never yet
Did, as he vouches, misreport your grace.

LUCIO
My lord, most villainously; believe it.

FRIAR PETER
Well, he in time may come to clear himself,    150
But at this instant he is sick, my lord,
Of a strange fever. Upon his mere request,
Being come to knowledge that there was complaint
Intended 'gainst Lord Angelo, came I hither,
To speak, as from his mouth, what he doth know    155

Is true and false; and what he with his oath
And all probation° will make up full clear,
Whensoever he's convented.° First, for this woman,
To justify this worthy nobleman,
So vulgarly and personally accused,    160
Her shall you hear disprovèd to her eyes,
Till she herself confess it.

DUKE             Good friar, let's hear it.
[ISABELLA *is carried off guarded.*]

*Enter* MARIANA.

Do you not smile at this, Lord Angelo?
O heaven, the vanity of wretched fools!
Give us some seats. Come, cousin Angelo,    165
In this I'll be impartial; be you judge
Of your own cause. Is this the witness, friar?
First, let her show her face, and after speak.

MARIANA
Pardon, my lord; I will not show my face
Until my husband bid me.    170

DUKE    What, are you married?

MARIANA    No, my lord.

DUKE    Are you a maid?

MARIANA    No, my lord.

DUKE    A widow, then?    175

MARIANA    Neither, my lord.

DUKE    Why, you are nothing, then: neither maid,
widow, nor wife?

LUCIO    My lord, she may be a punk;° for many of
them are neither maid, widow, nor wife.    180

DUKE
Silence that fellow. I would he had some cause
To prattle for himself.

LUCIO    Well, my lord.

MARIANA
My lord, I do confess I ne'er was married,
And I confess, besides, I am no maid.    185
I have known° my husband; yet my husband
Knows not that ever he knew me.

LUCIO    He was drunk, then, my lord; it can be no
better.

DUKE    For the benefit of silence, would thou wert so    190
too!

LUCIO    Well, my lord.

DUKE
This is no witness for Lord Angelo.

MARIANA
Now I come to't, my lord:
She that accuses him of fornication,    195
In selfsame manner doth accuse my husband,
And charges him, my lord, with such a time
When I'll depose I had him in mine arms
With all th' effect of love.

ANGELO
Charges she moe than me?

MARIANA           Not that I know.    200

DUKE
No? You say your husband?

MARIANA
Why, just, my lord, and that is Angelo,

---

108 **imports** signifies   110 **proper** belonging   128 **lay** a lay-
man   130 **swinged** thrashed   136 **scurvy** worthless   145
**temporary meddler** meddler in temporal affairs

157 **probation** proof   158 **convented** sent for   179 **punk**
harlot   186 **known** had intercourse with

Who thinks he knows that he ne'er knew my body,
But knows he thinks that he knows Isabel's.

ANGELO
This is a strange abuse. Let's see thy face.          205

MARIANA
My husband bids me; now I will unmask.

[*Unveiling.*]

This is that face, thou cruel Angelo,
Which once thou swor'st was worth the looking on;
This is the hand which, with a vowed contract,
Was fast belocked in thine; this is the body          210
That took away the match° from Isabel,
And did supply thee at thy garden house
In her imagined person.

DUKE                    Know you this woman?

LUCIO
Carnally, she says.

DUKE                    Sirrah, no more!

LUCIO
Enough, my lord.                          215

ANGELO
My lord, I must confess I know this woman:
And five years since there was some speech of marriage
Betwixt myself and her, which was broke off,
Partly for that her promisèd proportions°
Came short of composition,° but in chief,          220
For that her reputation was disvalued
In levity;° since which time of five years
I never spake with her, saw her, nor heard from her,
Upon my faith and honor.

MARIANA                    Noble prince,
As there comes light from heaven and words from
     breath,                          225
As there is sense in truth and truth in virtue,
I am affianced this man's wife as strongly
As words could make up vows; and, my good lord,
But Tuesday night last gone in's garden house
He knew me as a wife. As this is true,          230
Let me in safety raise me from my knees,
Or else forever be confixèd° here,
A marble monument.

ANGELO                    I did but smile till now;
Now, good my lord, give me the scope of justice;
My patience here is touched. I do perceive          235
These poor informal° women are no more
But instruments of some more mightier member
That sets them on. Let me have way, my lord,
To find this practice out.

DUKE                    Ay, with my heart,
And punish them to your height of pleasure.          240
Thou foolish friar and thou pernicious woman,
Compact° with her that's gone, think'st thou thy oaths,
Though they would swear down each particular saint,
Were testimonies against his worth and credit,
That's sealed in approbation?° You, Lord Escalus,          245
Sit with my cousin; lend him your kind pains
To find out this abuse, whence 'tis derived.

There is another friar that set them on;
Let him be sent for.

FRIAR PETER
Would he were here, my lord, for he, indeed,          250
Hath set the women on to this complaint:
Your provost knows the place where he abides,
And he may fetch him.

DUKE                    Go, do it instantly.
                    [*Exit* PROVOST.]
And you, my noble and well-warranted cousin,
Whom it concerns to hear this matter forth,          255
Do with your injuries as seems you best,
In any chastisement. I for a while
Will leave you, but stir not you till you have
Well determined upon these slanderers.

ESCALUS
My lord, we'll do it throughly.          *Exit* [DUKE].  260
Signior Lucio, did not you say you knew that Friar
Lodowick to be a dishonest person?

LUCIO  Cucullus non facit monachum;° honest in
nothing but in his clothes, and one that hath spoke
most villainous speeches of the duke.          265

ESCALUS  We shall entreat you to abide here till he
come, and enforce them against him; we shall find
this friar a notable° fellow.

LUCIO  As any in Vienna, on my word.

ESCALUS  Call that same Isabel here once again; I          270
would speak with her. [*Exit an* ATTENDANT.] Pray
you, my lord, give me leave to question; you shall see
how I'll handle her.

LUCIO  Not better than he, by her own report.

ESCALUS  Say you?          275

LUCIO  Marry, sir, I think, if you handled her privately, she would sooner confess; perchance, publicly,
she'll be ashamed.

*Enter* DUKE [*as a friar*], PROVOST, ISABELLA, [*and*
OFFICERS].

ESCALUS  I will go darkly° to work with her.

LUCIO  That's the way; for women are light at mid-          280
night.

ESCALUS  Come on, mistress, here's a gentlewoman
denies all that you have said.

LUCIO  My lord, here comes the rascal I spoke of—
here with the provost.          285

ESCALUS  In very good time. Speak not you to him
till we call upon you.

LUCIO  Mum.

ESCALUS  Come, sir, did you set these women on to
slander Lord Angelo? They have confessed you did.          290

DUKE  'Tis false.

ESCALUS  How! Know you where you are?

DUKE
Respect to your great place; and let the devil
Be sometime honored for his burning throne.
Where is the duke? 'Tis he should hear me speak.          295

ESCALUS
The duke's in us, and we will hear you speak.
Look you speak justly.

211 **match** meeting  219 **proportions** dowry  220 **composition** previous agreement  221–22 **disvalued In levity** discredited for lightness  232 **confixèd** fixed firmly  236 **informal**
(1) rash (2) informing  242 **Compact** in collusion  245
**approbation** attested integrity

263 **Cucullus . . . monachum** the cowl does not make the
monk (Latin)  268 **notable** notorious  279 **darkly** slyly,
subtly

DUKE
Boldly, at least. But, O poor souls,
Come you to seek the lamb here of the fox?
Good night to your redress. Is the duke gone? 300
Then is your cause gone too. The duke's unjust,
Thus to retort° your manifest° appeal,
And put your trial in the villain's mouth
Which here you come to accuse.

LUCIO
This is the rascal; this is he I spoke of. 305

ESCALUS
Why, thou unreverend and unhallowed friar,
Is't not enough thou hast suborned these women
To accuse this worthy man, but in foul mouth,
And in the witness of his proper° ear,
To call him villain? And then to glance from him 310
To th' duke himself, to tax him with injustice?
Take him hence; to th' rack with him. We'll touse°
    you
Joint by joint, but we will know his purpose.
What, "unjust"!

DUKE        Be not so hot. The duke
Dare no more stretch this finger of mine than he 315
Dare rack his own: his subject am I not,
Nor here provincial.° My business in this state
Made me a looker-on here in Vienna,
Where I have seen corruption boil and bubble
Till it o'errun the stew. Laws for all faults, 320
But faults so countenanced, that the strong statutes
Stand like the forfeits° in a barber's shop,
As much in mock as mark.°

ESCALUS
Slander to th' state! Away with him to prison!

ANGELO
What can you vouch against him, Signior Lucio? 325
Is this the man that you did tell us of?

LUCIO 'Tis he, my lord. Come hither, goodman bald-
pate; do you know me?

DUKE I remember you, sir, by the sound of your
voice. I met you at the prison, in the absence of the 330
duke.

LUCIO O, did you so? And do you remember what
you said of the duke?

DUKE Most notedly, sir.

LUCIO Do you so, sir? And was the duke a flesh- 335
monger, a fool, and a coward, as you then reported
him to be?

DUKE You must, sir, change persons with me, ere you
make that my report. You, indeed, spoke so of him;
and much more, much worse. 340

LUCIO O thou damnable fellow! Did not I pluck thee
by the nose for thy speeches?

DUKE I protest I love the duke as I love myself.

ANGELO Hark, how the villain would close° now,
after his treasonable abuses. 345

ESCALUS Such a fellow is not to be talked withal.
Away with him to prison! Where is the provost?
Away with him to prison, lay bolts enough upon him,

let him speak no more. Away with those giglets° too,
and with the other confederate companion. 350

DUKE [To the PROVOST.] Stay, sir; stay awhile.

ANGELO What, resists he? Help him, Lucio.

LUCIO Come, sir; come, sir; come, sir; foh, sir! Why,
you bald-pated, lying rascal, you must be hooded,
must you? Show your knave's visage, with a pox to 355
you. Show your sheep-biting° face, and be hanged an
hour. Will't not off?

[Pulls off the friar's hood, and discovers the DUKE.]

DUKE
Thou art the first knave that e'er mad'st a duke.
First, provost, let me bail these gentle three.

[To LUCIO.]

Sneak not away, sir; for the friar and you 360
Must have a word anon. Lay hold on him.

LUCIO
This may prove worse than hanging.

DUKE [To ESCALUS.]
What you have spoke I pardon. Sit you down.
We'll borrow place of him. [To ANGELO.] Sir, by
    your leave.
Hast thou or word, or wit, or impudence, 365
That yet can do thee office?° If thou hast,
Rely upon it till my tale be heard,
And hold no longer out.

ANGELO        O my dread lord,
I should be guiltier than my guiltiness,
To think I can be undiscernible, 370
When I perceive your grace, like pow'r divine,
Hath looked upon my passes.° Then, good prince,
No longer session° hold upon my shame,
But let my trial be mine own confession.
Immediate sentence then, and sequent death, 375
Is all the grace I beg.

DUKE        Come hither, Mariana.
Say, wast thou e'er contracted to this woman?

ANGELO
I was, my lord.

DUKE
Go take her hence, and marry her instantly.
Do you the office, friar, which consummate, 380
Return him here again. Go with him, provost.

    Exit [ANGELO, with MARIANA, FRIAR PETER, and
                    PROVOST].

ESCALUS
My lord, I am more amazed at his dishonor
Than at the strangeness of it.

DUKE        Come hither, Isabel.
Your friar is now your prince. As I was then
Advertising and holy° to your business, 385
Not changing heart with habit, I am still
Attorneyed at your service.

ISABELLA        O, give me pardon,
That I, your vassal, have employed and pained
Your unknown sovereignty!

DUKE        You are pardoned, Isabel:
And now, dear maid, be you as free to us. 390

302 retort refer back; manifest clear   309 proper very   312
touse pull   317 provincial belonging to the province or state
322 forfeits extracted teeth (barbers acted as dentists)   323 As
much . . . mark to be mocked at as much as to be seen
344 close come to agreement

349 giglets wanton women   356 sheep-biting currish   366
office service   372 passes trespasses   373 session trial   385
Advertising and holy attentive and devoted

Your brother's death, I know, sits at your heart,
And you may marvel why I obscured myself,
Laboring to save his life, and would not rather
Make rash remonstrance of my hidden pow'r
Than let him so be lost. O most kind maid,          395
It was the swift celerity of his death,
Which I did think with slower foot came on,
That brained my purpose. But, peace be with him.
That life is better life, past fearing death,
Than that which lives to fear. Make it your comfort,     400
So happy is your brother.

*Enter* ANGELO, MARIANA, [FRIAR] PETER, PROVOST.

ISABELLA                I do, my lord.
DUKE
For this new-married man, approaching here,
Whose salt° imagination yet hath wronged
Your well-defended honor, you must pardon
For Mariana's sake. But as he adjudged your brother,     405
Being criminal, in double violation,
Of sacred chastity, and of promise-breach,
Thereon dependent, for your brother's life,
The very mercy of the law cries out
Most audible, even from his proper tongue,              410
"An Angelo for Claudio, death for death!"
Haste still pays haste, and leisure answers leisure;
Like doth quit like, and Measure still for Measure.°
Then, Angelo, thy fault's thus manifested;
Which, though thou wouldst deny, denies thee van-
    tage.                                               415
We do condemn thee to the very block
Where Claudio stooped to death, and with like haste.
Away with him.
MARIANA          O my most gracious lord,
I hope you will not mock me with a husband.
DUKE
It is your husband mocked you with a husband.           420
Consenting to the safeguard of your honor,
I thought your marriage fit; else imputation,°
For that he knew you, might reproach your life,
And choke your good to come. For his possessions,
Although by confiscation they are ours,                 425
We do instate and widow you withal,
To buy you a better husband.
MARIANA                    O my dear lord,
I crave no other, nor no better man.
DUKE
Never crave him; we are definitive.°
MARIANA
Gentle my liege— [*Kneeling.*]
DUKE                You do but lose your labor.         430
Away with him to death! [*To* LUCIO.] Now, sir, to
    you.
MARIANA
O my good lord! Sweet Isabel, take my part,
Lend me your knees, and all my life to come
I'll lend you all my life to do you service.

403 salt lecherous  413 Measure still for Measure see
Matthew 7:1–2, "Judge not, that ye be not judged. For with
what judgment ye judge, ye shall be judged: and with what
measure ye mete, it shall be measured to you again"  422
imputation accusation  429 definitive determined

DUKE
Against all sense you do importune her;                 435
Should she kneel down in mercy of this fact,°
Her brother's ghost his pavèd° bed would break,
And take her hence in horror.
MARIANA                        Isabel,
Sweet Isabel, do yet but kneel by me,
Hold up your hands, say nothing, I'll speak all.        440
They say, best men are molded out of faults;
And, for the most, become much more the better
For being a little bad; so may my husband.
O Isabel, will you not lend a knee?
DUKE
He dies for Claudio's death.
ISABELLA        [*Kneeling.*] Most bounteous sir,      445
Look, if it please you, on this man condemned,
As if my brother lived. I partly think
A due sincerity governèd his deeds,
Till he did look on me. Since it is so,
Let him not die. My brother had but justice,            450
In that he did the thing for which he died.
For Angelo,
His act did not o'ertake his bad intent,
And must be buried but as an intent
That perished by the way. Thoughts are no subjects,°    455
Intents but merely thoughts.
MARIANA                     Merely, my lord.
DUKE
Your suit's unprofitable; stand up, I say.
I have bethought me of another fault.
Provost, how came it Claudio was beheaded
At an unusual hour?
PROVOST        It was commanded so.                     460
DUKE
Had you a special warrant for the deed?
PROVOST
No, my good lord; it was by private message.
DUKE
For which I do discharge you of your office;
Give up your keys.
PROVOST        Pardon me, noble lord.
I thought it was a fault, but knew it not;°             465
Yet did repent me, after more advice;°
For testimony whereof, one in the prison,
That should by private order else have died,
I have reserved alive.
DUKE              What's he?
PROVOST                His name is Barnardine.
DUKE
I would thou hadst done so by Claudio.                  470
Go fetch him hither; let me look upon him.
                            [*Exit* PROVOST.]
ESCALUS
I am sorry, one so learnèd and so wise
As you, Lord Angelo, have still° appeared,
Should slip so grossly, both in the heat of blood,
And lack of tempered judgment afterward.                475
ANGELO
I am sorry that such sorrow I procure,
And so deep sticks it in my penitent heart,

436 fact crime  437 pavèd slab-covered  455 no subjects
i.e., not subject to law  465 knew it not was not sure  466
advice thought  473 still ever

That I crave death more willingly than mercy;
'Tis my deserving, and I do entreat it.

*Enter* BARNARDINE *and* PROVOST, CLAUDIO
[*muffled*], JULIET.

DUKE
Which is that Barnardine?
PROVOST                          This, my lord.           480
DUKE
There was a friar told me of this man.
Sirrah, thou art said to have a stubborn soul,
That apprehends no further than this world,
And squar'st° thy life according. Thou'rt condemned;
But, for those earthly faults, I quit° them all,           485
And pray thee take this mercy to provide
For better times to come. Friar, advise him;
I leave him to your hand. What muffled fellow's that?
PROVOST
This is another prisoner that I saved,
Who should have died when Claudio lost his head;           490
As like almost to Claudio as himself.

[*Unmuffles* CLAUDIO.]

DUKE [*To* ISABELLA.]
If he be like your brother, for his sake
Is he pardoned; and, for your lovely sake,
Give me your hand, and say you will be mine,
He is my brother too; but fitter time for that.           495
By this Lord Angelo perceives he's safe;
Methinks I see a quick'ning° in his eye.
Well, Angelo, your evil quits you well;
Look that you love your wife; her worth, worth yours.
I find an apt remission° in myself,                         500
And yet here's one in place I cannot pardon.

[*To* LUCIO.]

You, sirrah, that knew me for a fool, a coward,
One all of luxury,° an ass, a madman;
Wherein have I so deserved of you,
That you extol me thus?                                    505
LUCIO   'Faith, my lord, I spoke it but according to

the trick.° If you will hang me for it, you may; but I
had rather it would please you I might be whipped.
DUKE
Whipped first, sir, and hanged after.
Proclaim it, provost, round about the city,               510
If any woman wronged by this lewd fellow—
As I have heard him swear himself there's one
Whom he begot with child—let her appear,
And he shall marry her. The nuptial finished,
Let him be whipped and hanged.                            515
LUCIO   I beseech your highness, do not marry me to a
whore. Your highness said even now, I made you a
duke: good my lord, do not recompense me in
making me a cuckold.
DUKE
Upon mine honor, thou shalt marry her.                    520
Thy slanders I forgive; and therewithal
Remit thy other forfeits. Take him to prison,
And see our pleasure herein executed.
LUCIO   Marrying a punk, my lord, is pressing to
death, whipping, and hanging.                             525
DUKE
Slandering a prince deserves it.
                    [*Exeunt* OFFICERS, *with* LUCIO.]
She, Claudio, that you wronged, look you restore.°
Joy to you, Mariana. Love her, Angelo;
I have confessed her, and I know her virtue.
Thanks, good friend Escalus, for thy much goodness;       530
There's more behind° that is more gratulate.°
Thanks, provost, for thy care and secrecy;
We shall employ thee in a worthier place.
Forgive him, Angelo, that brought you home
The head of Ragozine for Claudio's;                       535
Th' offense pardons itself. Dear Isabel,
I have a motion° much imports your good,
Whereto if you'll a willing ear incline,
What's mine is yours, and what is yours is mine.
So, bring us to our palace, where we'll show              540
What's yet behind, that's meet° you all should know.
                                             [*Exeunt.*]

484 squar'st regulate  485 quit pardon  497 quick'ning
animation  500 remission wish to forgive  503 luxury lust
507 trick fashion  527 restore i.e., by marriage  531 behind
to come; gratulate gratifying  537 motion proposal  541
meet fitting

# THE TRAGEDY OF KING LEAR

EDITED BY RUSSELL FRASER

## Introduction

In structure *King Lear* differs significantly from the other tragedies of Shakespeare. It is like them in this: it dramatizes the fall of a hero who, assailed by the rebel passion, gives it sovereign sway and masterdom, and is in consequence destroyed. That is the case of Brutus, Othello, and Macbeth. But the resemblance is more ostensible than real. Ostensibly the play is one long denouement. In fact the declining action, which is the dogging of the hero to death, is complemented by a rising action, which is the hero's regeneration. Yeats' metaphor of the gyres is apposite. As the one wanes to nothing, the other, which lives within it, emerges. This emergent, or renascent, action is a condition of the hero's loss of the world. The play fools us. Its primary story is not the descent of the king into hell, but the ascent of the king as he climbs the mountain of purgatory and is fulfilled. The suspense the play develops is a function of the ascending action, which is not material but spiritual. Battles and thrones are nugatory. What does it profit a man if he gain the whole world and suffer the loss of his soul?

The rising and falling curves, the hero tasting his folly, the hero triumphing over it, intersect in the center of the play, in the fourth scene of Act III. It is on the heath that Lear reaches his nadir. His characteristic utterance is the imperative mood; the wonted reversal follows: he is made less than the slave and sumpter to a detested groom. These are the injuries that he himself has procured. So far the parallel is precise to the action of the other tragedies.

But now the crucial difference. It is also on the heath that Lear is made pregnant to pity. That is another and an unexpected kind of reversal. "In, boy; go first." These words, addressed to the Fool, who stands shivering in the rain before a hovel that is the refuge of a madman, constitute the real, as opposed to the apparent, hinge of the play. They do not signal the decay but the metamorphosis of the king: Lear in a red shirt. The great apostrophe to the poor follows at once. From this point, the action turns upward.

The structure of the subplot duplicates and so of course clarifies and confirms that of the central story. As the king is limed, and by his own folly, so are Gloucester and Edgar: "A credulous father, and a brother noble." The one

is, initially, an unthinking sensualist. The other, the younger, is initially a kind of clown: "and pat he comes like the catastrophe of the old comedy." But the degradation of Gloucester is not ratified. He also undergoes a miraculous transformation. The critical point or pivot at which this transformation is announced is located, like Lear's, in the mathematical center of the play (III.iii), which is also, with a fit symmetry, the metaphysical center. The placatory man, who would have all well between the contending parties, is emboldened suddenly to choose. "If I die for it, as no less is threatened me, the king my old master must be relieved." In that decision is his death, but also his salvation.

The retrieving of Edgar is more spectacular, if not so abruptly achieved. Edgar is conceded the chance to grow and prosper. He seizes his chance; he makes himself over. "Bear free and patient thoughts." The dupe of the opening scenes is the philosopher who dominates in the close of the play.

This is not to pretend that the close is thereby made happy. "All's cheerless, dark, and deadly." Kent's somber valediction is approved. If the kindness of the one daughter hints at the redemption of Nature, it does not deprecate entirely the general curse which twain have brought her to. The implication is uneasy in Edgar's assertion (as of one who is saying "what we ought to say") that man must obey the weight of the time. His flawed heart, on the evidence of the play, is too weak to support it. His nature cannot carry the affliction or the fear.

> What ribs of oak, when mountains melt on them,
> Can hold the mortise?         (*Othello*, II.i.8–9)

Man endures until he expires, dying the pain of death every hour, in a night that pities neither wise man nor fool. What is more unsettling, to be wise is not to be provident. "Man may his fate foresee, but not prevent." And thus Webster's conclusion, in *The White Devil*: " 'Tis better to be fortunate than wise." Man is the natural fool of fortune. That is the title he is born with. It is the stars, and not our own endeavors, that govern. After all we are their tennis balls, struck and bandied which way please them. We do not get our deserts. The optimism is foolishness, to which we are prone.

I would not take this from report: it is,
And my heart breaks at it.                        (IV.vi.141–42)

The wry conjunctions contrived by the playwright—who knows out of what bitterness or whimsy—attest to its fatuity. Edgar, in a sanguine mood, is sure that the worst returns to laughter. He is confronted at once with the bleeding visage of his father.

The worst is not
So long as we can say, "This is the worst."   (IV.i.27–28)

But Shakespeare is not done with him yet. "If ever I return to you again, I'll bring you comfort." That is Edgar's promise to Gloucester before the battle. It is a rash promise, and poor comfort attends on it. A hiatus ensues, filled up with alarums and excursions. Then Edgar reenters and speaks again: "Away, old man. . . . King Lear hath lost."

The optimism of Albany, as it is more eupeptic, is more sternly reproved.

All friends shall taste
The wages of their virtue, and all foes
The cup of their deservings.                     (V.iii.304–06)

In that cheerful saying his philosophy is embodied. But the pentameter line wants its conclusion. Albany, rather cruelly, is made to supply it: "O, see, see!" It is the last agony of Lear to which his attention is directed.

Albany, as he presents the hopeful man who insists, a little too suavely, that God's in His heaven, is Shakespeare's particular butt. It is he who cries, of Cordelia: "The gods defend her!" The stage direction follows, enforcing the most monstrous conjunction in the play: "Enter Lear with Cordelia in his arms." The gods do not defend us. Perhaps they are unable to do so. "The gods reward your kindness," says Kent to Gloucester. That is the reading of the Folio, and surely it is the right reading. But the reading of the quarto provokes speculation: "The gods deserve your kindness." It is as if the gods are weak, and require that man collaborate with them in wielding the world (Shakespeare imitating Will James). Lear, as his ardor for the right grows upon him, shakes the superflux to the wretched. His intent is, as he says, to show the heavens more just. It is at least tenable to interpret: his intent is to justify their feckless ways as he can.

Maybe the heavens are worse than insufficient. What is said of the king,

If Fortune brag of two she loved and hated,
One of them we behold.                           (V.iii.282–83)

suggests not merely a lack of capacity in the ordering of things, but a malevolent purpose, as if the gods had marked us down for their sport. On this reading, Lear's reference to himself and Cordelia as "God's spies" will mean, as Warburton suggested long ago, "spies placed over God Almighty, to watch his motions." Maybe there is need of surveillance, if the human sacrifices on which the gods themselves throw incense are offered up for their delectation; if the brand of fire that parts the pre-destined victims is handed down, and with an antique

malice, from heaven. *Tantaene animis coelestibus irae!* The chill that invades us as, huddled with the others against the roaring wind and rain, we await the advent of unaccommodated man: "What art thou that dost grumble there i' th' straw?" is occasioned by the wild surmise, so much more fearful because it is involuntary, that the fiend is really walking up and down in the earth, and with the sufferance and even the connivance of heaven. In the pitiless conclusion of *King Lear*,

Thou'lt come no more,
Never, never, never, never, never.               (V.iii.309–10)

the dominion of the Prince of Darkness seems confirmed, and his presence a substantial presence as, with his terrible vans, he enshadows and overwhelms the just and the unjust alike.

That is, I daresay, only an apparition, the disnatured child of night thoughts, and as such may be dispelled. But it needs more than to rub one's eyes, or to mutter a pious ejaculation. To such a degree is this true that even critics so tough-minded as Dr. Johnson have averted their eyes rather than acquiesce in the final horror with which the dramatist confronts them. It is too literal, too realistic for "dramatick exhibition." And yet it is remarkable that this play, in which Shakespeare's unremitting fidelity to fact is almost an occasion for scandal, manifests in its beginning a studied and a deliberate indifference to fact. If subsequent scenes are so realistic as hardly to be endured, the opening scenes have not to do with realism but with ritual and ro-mance. Their abiding characteristic is a niggling formality. They do not wear the aspect of life so much as the aspect of art. Kent, lapsing into rude rhyme as he takes his de-parture, catches and communicates that aspect. His lan-guage is gnomic, admonitory, and simple—not naively but consciously simple: "artificial." He is not, for the moment, a real (an eccentric) man who displaces air like Hamlet or Parolles. He is, and by design, a flat character, highly conventionalized, who figures in a mumming or mystery. He would speak a prophecy before he goes.

The language of the other protagonists is of a piece with his. It does not evoke—not yet—the savage business of dragons of the prime (for all that the dragon is portentous in the comminatory speeches of the king), so much as the ceremonious (the otherworldly!) business of proceedings at law and finance. Legal and fiscal metaphors reverberate. Gloucester, treating of his sons, asserts that the elder is no more dear than the younger, in his account. Lear, enacting his intention to abdicate the throne, renounces interest of territory, or possession. In lieu of Kent's insistence that he reserve his state, he stipulates his troop of knights as reservation, explicitly a legalism, in which the action of retaining a privilege is denoted. He would extend his largest bounty where nature challenges merit, or makes title to it. Regan, whose tenders of affection aim at that title, finds that Goneril had anticipated her very deed of love. The king, in whose lexicon love is a commodity, urges his youngest daughter to discover what portion her protesta-tions can draw. But Cordelia loves only according to her bond. Failing to please, her price is fallen. Goneril pleases, in that she is taken as permitting to her father twice the retinue permitted by Regan. Her devotion may therefore be measured. She is precisely twice her sister's love.

Lear is not easily persuaded of his error, that devotion—in his psychology, a ponderable thing—is to be assessed and ought to be requited in ponderable ways. The inadmissible equation is there still, in the crass appeal to Regan when his agony is upon him:

> Thy half o' th' kingdom hast thou not forgot,
> Wherein I thee endowed.                    (II.iv.177–78)

He is appropriately answered, since that respects of fortune are his love: "Good sir, to th' purpose" (II.iv.178).

This patina of the unreal and the ritualistic, overlaying the initial action of the play, is not peculiar to the love test. The characters themselves move in an air of unreality. There is about them a felt sense of disjunction, as between what they are and what they seem to be. Lear is not a king but the show of a king. It is an insubstantial pageant over which he presides, recalling, in its unreality, the specious parade with which an earlier tragedy of Shakespeare's commences, that of Richard II, the mockery king of snows. Kent's acumen is verified when, with a lack of respect that is intended to shock and thereby to quicken perception, he sees and salutes his master, not as a monarch but as an old man.

But if Lear is a simulacrum, so are the wicked daughters. Their essential vacuity, echoing to the touch, announces itself as it issues in their fulsome avowals of love. Kent points to it obliquely in his praise of Cordelia:

> Nor are those empty-hearted whose low sounds
> Reverb no hollowness.                    (I.i.153–54)

Gloucester discerns it, magnified to cosmic proportions, in the disordered state of the macrocosm, riven by machinations, by the hollowness that is hypocrisy. All that glisters is taken for gold. The pretension of the hypocrite, who professes herself

>                     an enemy to all other joys
> Which the most precious square of sense professes
>                                         (I.i.73–74)

weighs more than the practice of the candid and guileless retainer, who professes himself to be no less than he seems. The vizard is everything, and hence what is lifelike and vital is eclipsed. The characters are cut in alabaster. The same metaphor describes the fool and the knave and the paragon of virtue, divesting each of human personality. Gloucester, who seems a good old man, is brazed by self-indulgence, become like hard metal. Regan, in whom nature appears tender-hefted, is hardened to insensibility, made of that self metal as her sister. Cordelia is, conversely, a little-seeming substance. But Cordelia is rendered also in nonhuman terms: her love, a precious metal, is more ponderous than her tongue.

Stylization of language and gesture is notable in such a play as *The Tempest*, and for excellent and obvious reasons. Shakespeare's resort to it in *King Lear* seems, however, gratuitous, and even antipathetic to the spirit of the play. *King Lear* is not masquelike nor, certainly, romantic, in the harrowing story it tells. But observe that *The Tempest* begins, not formally, but realistically, with the faithful depicting of a ship driving on the rocks, a wild and literal

scene in which the blasphemy and execration of real and affrighted persons bass the throbbing of the storm. And then the scene shifts abruptly. The auditor or reader, whose belief is purchased at the outset by a terrific glimpse of the real world, is brought safe to shore: is induced to enter, and willingly, the world of enchantment and romance. The fact of the transition, and the implausibility attendant on it, elude him. The tempest is still dinning in his ears.

In *King Lear* the dramatic problem is exactly reversed. It is to ensure that those whose disenchantment the playwright is already preparing, who are to be compelled to look on the Gorgon features, will not evince incredulity or petrifaction. The problem is resolved by emphasizing at the outset the elements of unreality and romance. The impelling action of *King Lear* is made to resemble a fairy tale, which is, I suppose, its ultimate provenance. The auditor or reader is cozened. Before he is aware, he has become a participant in the fierce and excessively painful dispute between damnation and impassioned clay.

But there is more than craft to Shakespeare's design in thus introducing his drama. He makes his characters unreal initially because he means them, at least in part, to be symbolic. The stylized quality of the beginning, as of a charade, its legalistic and ceremonious nature, the exalting in it of appearance as against reality, all work to the fulfilling of that primary intention. And though *King Lear* is essentially representational drama, though realism very quickly takes precedence over ritual, the element of the symbolic is never dissipated altogether but figures in important ways until the end. Just as in *Twelfth Night*, whose burden is mistaken identity and the hocus-pocus of identical twins, realism intrudes persistently to temper and give substance to romance—

> In nature there's no blemish but the mind;
> None can be called deformed but the unkind.
> Virtue is beauty, but the beauteous evil
> Are empty trunks o'erflourished by the devil
>                                         (III.iv.370–73)

—so in *King Lear*, an antiromantic play in that its burden is a relentless anatomizing of evil, the symbolic declines to yield entirely to the representational. It persists, not to give substance to the real, which is substantial enough—

> Out, vile jelly.
> Where is thy luster now?                    (III.vii.85–86)

—but to order the real and make it meaningful, to avoid a confounding of it with the merely sensational. Not to grasp this ordering function is, necessarily, to run counter, to smell a fault where no fault is. Thus the embarrassment of critics so estimable as Goethe (for whom the action of the play was a tissue of the improbable and absurd), and Coleridge (who saw the first scene as dispensable), and A. C. Bradley (who detected and enumerated in the whole, more and grosser inconsistencies than in any other of the great tragedies).

Misconstruction of the role and character of Cordelia typifies this failure to come to terms with the symbolic. Cordelia is, of old, a deeply disquieting figure. Why does she love, and yet remain silent? The question has engendered a little galaxy of answers. It is a question not to be asked. The first principle of good dramatic manners is to concede to the dramatist his given, so long as he is able to exploit it. Here, the given is the heroine's fatal reserve. It is the lever or prise that starts the play on its progress. As such, it may not be queried, any more than the procedure that governs in chess or in the writing of an Italian sonnet.

But "reserve" is after all the wrong word. It suggests the wrong frame of reference. It leads to the rationalization of conduct, on realistic grounds. To make the horrid point, this judgment of a contemporary critic may be cited, that Cordelia loved her father "less than she loved her own way and hated her sisters." That is a fair sample of the appeal to realism. It is at all costs to be avoided. Cordelia does not betray, what Coleridge thought to perceive, "some little faulty admixture of pride and sullenness." No faintest stain of guilt or responsibility attaches to her. She is not imperious, like the king, not headstrong, not intractable. The appeal to heredity is a variation of the appeal to realism, and is, in this context, equally and altogether inapposite. Shakespeare's characters, unlike Eugene O'Neill's, have no antecedents. It is of no use to say that Cordelia is her father's daughter. The reason she will not speak is because she cannot speak; and she cannot because the heart of a fool is in his mouth but the mouth of the wise is in his heart.

This is to say that the muteness of Cordelia (like the fantastic credulity of Gloucester) is not so much a reflection of character as it is the embodiment of an idea. Less real than symbolic, her affinity is more to a creature of fairy tale like Cinderella than to a heroine of the realistic drama like Blanche DuBois. In delineating her behavior the playwright may be, psychologically, so penetrating and exact as really to catch the manners living as they rise: that is partly a gratuity. More important is his intention, not to portray a veritable woman, but to dramatize the proposition that plainness is more than eloquence, that beauty is to be purchased by the weight, that meager lead, which rather threatens than promises aught, buys more than silver and gold. The agitation of those who worry the details of the love test in an attempt to make it credible, which means to make it conformable to the canons of the realistic theater, is founded on their misapprehension of symbolic action.

When Cordelia is depicted as the last and least, it is not her slightness of stature that the dramatist is glancing at—or not that, decisively. He is preparing an ironic and a pregnant echo, to amplify Kent's assertion, a little later: "Thy youngest daughter does not love thee least" (I.i.152). But more than that, he is invoking the promise of Scripture, unspoken in the play, and yet close to the theme, which is the heart (but not the moral!) of the play: the first shall be last and the last shall be first. When Cordelia herself exclaims, as she prepares to engage the British powers,

> O dear father,
> It is thy business that I go about    (IV.iv.23–24)

it is not altogether the realistic business of an imminent battle to which she is adverting. (Certainly that business does not much preoccupy Shakespeare.) And therefore we are not to wonder why the King of France was, so inopportunely, called back to his kingdom, nor whether

Shakespeare's allegiance or circumspection dictated the victory of the English. We want to catch in what is said an anterior saying, the sentence of the Evangelist, so much more than a literary reminiscence, and estimate accordingly the symbolic role the speaker plays: "Knew ye not that I must go about my father's business." It may be that Cordelia is that quintessence of womanhood celebrated reverentially (and with an appropriate taciturnity as to particulars) by critics like A. W. Schlegel: "Of Cordelia's heavenly beauty of soul, I do not dare to speak." But it is not after all the literal woman to whom Shakespeare is holding up the mirror. Compare Beatrice in *Much Ado About Nothing*, or Rosalind in *As You Like It*.

It is a nice but an indispensable point to adjudicate, just when the dramatist intends that the canons of ordinary realism are to be set aside or, better, transcended. Pretty clearly he wishes to transcend them when, in Act II, Kent is made to sleep in the stocks, and Edgar, unmindful of him, to step forward and tell of his purposed transformation. Bradley is bemused: "One cannot help asking . . . whether Edgar is mad that he should return from his hollow tree . . . to his father's castle in order to soliloquize." But Shakespeare, in juxtaposing the two characters, is not concerned with motivation or, certainly, with locale. No doubt the Bedlam is understood to remain on the heath. But precisely where he is, is not a question that ought to detain us. Neither are we to ask why he fails to perceive that someone else is up there with him on stage, in full view of the audience, and so, presumably, of himself; nor how Kent, for all his travails, can sleep undisturbed through twenty lines of blank verse. In the bringing together of the two good men, each of whom has been driven to the lowest and most dejected point of fortune, a dramatic emblem is achieved, a speaking picture, whose purport is not realistic but symbolic. What Shakespeare is after is this dark collocation, or sequence:

> A good man's fortune may grow out at heels.    (II.ii.160)

> Edgar I nothing am.    (II.iii.21)

In the same way the symbolic overtops the conventionally real when, in the final act, Edgar issues his challenge to Edmund. One is not to belabor the improbability of Edmund's failure to recognize his brother, though, in point of fact, the failure is itself symbolic: the villain is indeed cozened and beguiled, and not for reasons of dramatic exigency but by virtue of his own willful behavior. But what is central to the scene is the intimation one hears, in the blast of the trumpet that announces the combat, of that final trump that vindicates the right and summons the perpetrator of wrong to the Judgment. When—another illustration—Edgar, opposing Oswald, assumes the character of a rustic, the clownish dialect he speaks is, realistically, absurd: what is its occasion? Symbolically, however, it is deeply congruous. The power of truth is attested to, however ludicrous its aspect, and the frailty which is falsehood exposed, in this meeting of the ragged fellow, whose West Country accent gives him out to be a bumpkin, but who intrinsically merits and possesses all honors, and the gilded courtier, whose extrinsic show and sophistication betoken all honors and are as paste and cover to none. "The Prince of Darkness is a gentleman"

(III.iv.141). In Edgar's vanquishing of Oswald, which is the triumph of the lowly and the unprepossessing over the world of robes and furred gowns, Lear's great social speeches are enacted and answered.

A similar intention, to effect on stage a symbolic tableau, dictates the grouping of the protagonists at the end of the play. All are there in the resolution, occupying, I think, the same positions they assumed at first, and not least the wicked sisters, whose dead bodies are brought on, no doubt to exemplify this judgment of the heavens, but more, to direct the attention of the audience back and back, over all the dreadful ground that has been traced, to the opening scene. In their beginning is their ending. Perhaps the great wheel of the play, now come full circle, is impelled in its progress by something more than mechanical law.

What this other law may be is the central question Shakespeare poses and endeavors to answer. Lear, as is fitting, is made to enunciate it: "Who is it that can tell me who I am?" But the question is not peculiar to Lear but is implicit in the utterance and conduct of all those who inhabit the darkness with him. Kent as Caius is interrogated by the king:

> What art thou?
> A man, sir.             (I.iv.9–11)

But what is it, to be a man? What is man to profess? To what law are his services bound? Gloucester interrogates Edgar: "Now, good sir, what are you?" and is answered:

> A most poor man, made tame to fortune's blows;
> Who, by the art of known and feeling sorrows,
> Am pregnant to good pity.      (IV.vi.222–24)

Cornwall, whose disposition will not be rubbed or stopped, does not manifest that pity. It is ascendant, though tardily, in Gloucester, who, if he dies for it, must relieve his master. Why is that? And why had Kent rather break his own heart than the king's? How does one construe that fitness to which Albany appeals, in declining to let his hands obey his blood; or that pleasure, a more intriguing word, which inclines the Old Man to succor the blinded Gloucester, "Come on't what will"? What point inheres in Albany's characterization of Oswald, as Oswald reports it:

> he called me sot,
> And told me I had turned the wrong side out    (IV.ii.8–9)

and in what manner does it comment on the Captain's decision to collaborate in the killing of the king and Cordelia: "If it be man's work, I'll do't" (V.iii.40).

There ought here to ensue a brief though perceptible silence, in token of the irony and expectation with which these laconic words are charged. The dramatist is bidding us essay a definition of the nature of man's work and, concomitantly, of the nature of man. Edmund, with his customary *sang-froid*, addresses himself to the task:

> men
> Are as the time is.           (V.iii.31–32)

Kent speaks to it, describing Oswald: "A tailor made thee" (II.ii.56–57). So in whimsical ways does the Fool, begging pardon of Goneril: "Cry you mercy, I took you for a joint stool" (III.vi.51), and also the king, whose confusion is at once real and assumed: "Your name, fair gentlewoman?" (I.iv.237), and, in sterner ways, the First Servant, drawing his sword against Cornwall: "Nay, then, come on, and take the chance of anger" (III.vii.81). To divine the way in which these lines reticulate is to resolve at least a corner of the mystery which is the play.

## A NOTE ON THE SOURCE

*King Lear* was probably written between 1603 and 1606. The evidence is as follows. Under the date of November 26, 1607, the printers Nathaniel Butter and John Busby entered the play in the Stationers' Register, thereby asserting their right to print it. That right was exercised in the following year, with the appearance of the first quarto of 1608. The title page of that quarto (Q1) announces a performance of the play as having taken place before the king on Saint Stephen's Night (December 26) in the Christmas holidays. The entry in the Stationers' Register (1607), since it refers to the Court performance as occurring on "Christmas Last," fixes the date of that performance as December 26, 1606. This date is therefore the *terminus ad quem* for the composition of the play. The earliest date, that of 1603, is more difficult to establish. Probably it is fixed by the entry in the Stationers' Register, on March 16, 1603, of Samuel Harsnett's *Declaration of Egregious Popishe Impostures*. Harsnett's work, a treatise on diabolism and an attack on the Jesuits, was written in 1602–03. It is utilized by Shakespeare in his play, chiefly for the names of the demons who lurk about Poor Tom. Assume—and it is reasonable to do so—that Shakespeare did not have access to Harsnett's *Declaration* before the date of publication, and 1603 becomes the *terminus a quo* for the writing of *King Lear*.

Astrological reference furnishes another clue. Gloucester, citing as portentous "These late eclipses in the sun and moon" (I.ii.106–07), is commonly thought to be speaking of a contemporary event. There were in fact eclipses in 1601 and, more pertinently, in September (the moon) and October (the sun) of 1605. It has been suggested, moreover, that a publication of 1606, telling of "The Earth's and Moone's late and horrible obscurations," lies directly behind Gloucester's superstitious mutterings. The pamphlet in question, translated from the High Dutch and edited by the almanac writer Edward Gresham, is entitled *Strange fearful & true news which happened at Carlstadt, in the Kingdome of Croatia*. Its preface is dated February 11, 1606.

Finally, there is the reemergence, in the period just before the first recorded performance of Shakespeare's play, of the older dramatic version of his story, *The True Chronicle History of King Leir*. Though this play was probably written about 1590, and was on the boards in 1594, it was published and perhaps acted again in 1605: on May 8, 1605, it is entered in the Stationers' Register. Presumably Shakespeare used the edition appearing in that year, in writing his own play.

The publication, then, of the old chronicle history in 1605, the notable eclipses occurring in the fall of the same year, and the appearance of Gresham's pamphlet early in 1606 seem to point to the winter of 1605–06 as the period in which Shakespeare wrote *King Lear*.

The ultimate source of the play is an ancient folk tale existing in many versions. It first appears as literature in the twelfth-century *Historia Regum Britanniae* (ii, 11–15), by Geoffrey of Monmouth. Throughout the Middle Ages and on into the Renaissance, the Lear story retained its popularity, appearing in some fifty different accounts. Shakespeare was familiar with it from the retelling in what is perhaps his most important source book, the second edition (1587) of *The Chronicles of England, Scotlande, and Irelande* by Raphael Holinshed, first compiled in 1577. From Edmund Spenser, in *The Faerie Queene* (1590), Shakespeare derived the name of Cordelia in its present form, and also the detail of her death by hanging (II.x. 27–32). Other suggestions were furnished by John Higgins, in *A Mirror for Magistrates* (1574), that immensely popular collection of stories of the falls of princes; and of course, by *The True Chronicle History of King Leir and his three daughters*. John Marston, in *The Malcontent* (1604), dramatizes a feigned suicide (4.3) that seems to parallel Gloucester's, at the Cliffs of Dover (IV.vi). The author of *The London Prodigal* (1605), a play once attributed to Shakespeare and performed by his company, anticipates the rustic dialogue affected by Edgar in his combat with Oswald (IV.vi). As previously noted, Harsnett and, possibly, Gresham were also of use to Shakespeare. So, in less tangible ways, was his great French contemporary, Montaigne, whose *Essais* were translated into English by John Florio in 1603. Numerous words and passages in Florio's translation (which Shakespeare may have read in manuscript) are echoed in *King Lear*. More impressive, however, is the impact on Shakespeare of Montaigne's skeptical thought, as expressed particularly in the *Apology for Raymond Sebonde*.

None of these sources of *Lear* includes the analogous story of Gloucester and his two sons. That story Shakespeare adapted from Sir Philip Sidney's account of the unhappy King of Paphlagonia, in his famous romantic narrative *Arcadia* (ii, 10), written early in the 1580's but not published until 1590. The typing of the subplot to the old and sufficiently horrid tale of King Lear and his daughters has, of course, the effect of engrossing the horror, until the audience is almost persuaded that ferocious cruelty is not so much an aberration as the norm. Certainly, if Lear is childed as Edgar is fathered it is no longer possible to see as merely sensational or idiosyncratic the evil that Shakespeare anatomizes in the play. Earlier writers, handling one or the other story, allow of that view. Shakespeare, in fusing the two stories, is at pains to controvert it. What is more, he darkens consistently, in manipulating his sources, whatever dark suggestion is latent in them. In the old *Leir*, in Holinshed, in Spenser, in the *Mirror for Magistrates*, the travails of the king are intermitted at last. Vice is punished and virtue rewarded: Cordelia triumphs over her wicked sisters; her father, restored to the throne, dies at the apogee, and in peace. It is true that, in some sources, Cordelia ends a suicide. But that is an irrelevant epilogue: the chief business of the tale is happily resolved.

It is left to Shakespeare to cancel that happy resolution. He is the first to educe tragedy from what is essentially a melodramatic romance. The madness of Lear is altogether his own contribution. So is the pathetic figure of the Fool. So is the murder of Cordelia, that cruelest stroke of all, which is made to fall just as the good are preparing to taste the wages of their virtue.

## A NOTE ON THE TEXT

The earliest extant version of Shakespeare's *King Lear* is the first quarto of 1608. This premier edition is known as the Pied Bull Quarto, after the sign which hung before the establishment of the printer. The title page reads as follows: "M. William Shak-speare:/HIS/True Chronicle Historie of the life and death of King Lear and his three/Daughters./ *With the vnfortunate life of* Edgar, *sonne*/and heire to the Earle of Gloster, and his/sullen and assumed humor of/Tom of Bedlam:/*As it was played before the Kings Maiestie at Whitehall vpon*/S. Stephans *night in Christmas Hollidayes.*/By his Maiesties seruants playing vsually at the Gloabe/on the Bancke-side./LONDON,/Printed for *Nathaniel Butter*, and are to be sold at his shop in *Pauls*/Church-yard at the signe of the Pide Bull neere/S^t. *Austin's* Gate. 1608." Twelve copies of the first quarto survive. They are, however, in ten different states, because proofreading, and hence correcting, took place as the play was being printed. The instances (167 in all) in which these copies of Q1 differ one from another have been enumerated by contemporary scholarship.[1]

In 1619 the second quarto appeared, known as the N. Butter Quarto, and falsely dated in the same year as the first (the title page reads: "Printed for Nathaniel Butter, 1608"). The source of Q2 was apparently a copy of Q1 in which a number of sheets had been corrected.

Four years later *King Lear* was reprinted once more, this time in the first collection of Shakespeare's works, the First Folio of 1623. The source of the Folio text seems to have been, again, a corrected copy of Q1. The corrections in this copy, however, do not duplicate those in the presumptive source of Q2, but are at once more and less extensive. In some cases the quarto that lies behind the Folio offers corrections not found in the source of Q2. In other cases, corrections incorporated in the course of Q2 are not included in the source of F1. The Folio text, moreover, omits some 300 lines found in the quarto, and thus leads to the supposition that the copy used in preparing the Folio had been collated with the promptbook—a shorter, acting version of the play—in the possession of Shakespeare's company. The Folio text would seem, then, to stand in close relation to Shakespeare's play as it was actually performed. On the other hand, the Folio does include some 100 lines not found in the quarto.

It is now very generally, though not unanimously, agreed that the Folio is superior to the quarto, and ought to serve as the basis of any modern edition. The present text of *King Lear* is based, therefore, on the First Folio of 1623, except when the Folio is guilty of an obvious misprinting, or when it omits pertinent material found in the quarto, or when its version seems to the editor so inferior to the quarto version as to demand precedence for the latter, or when an emendation, even though perhaps

[1] W. W. Greg, *The Variants in the First Quarto of "King Lear,"* London, 1940 (for 1939).

unnecessary (like Edwards' "top th' legitimate"), has been canonized by use and wont.

In the preparation of this text, the spelling of Folio and quarto has been modernized; punctuation and capitalization have been altered, when alteration seemed suitable; character designations have been expanded or clarified (F "Cor." becomes "Cordelia," F "Bastard" and "Steward" become "Edmund" and "Oswald"); contractions not affecting pronunciation have been eliminated (F "banish'd" becomes "banished"); necessary quotation marks (as in the reading of a letter) have been supplied; as have diacritical marks whenever a syllable that is normally unemphasized must be stressed (as in "oppressèd"). Act and scene divisions have been translated from Latin. These changes are not recorded.

All other departures from the Folio appearing in this text are recorded below in boldface type. Unless specifically noted, these departures derive in every case from the first quarto [Q]. If some other source is levied on, such as the second quarto [Q2] or Second Folio [F2] or the conjecture of an editor (for example, [Theobald]), that source is given, within brackets, immediately after the reading. There follows next, in roman type, the Folio reading that has been superseded. If an editor's emendation has been preferred to both Folio and quarto readings, the emendation, with its provenance, is followed by the folio and quarto readings it replaces.

Stage directions are not given lineation. Reference to them in these notes is determined, therefore, by the line of text they follow. If a stage direction occurs at the beginning of a scene, reference is to the line of text it precedes. On occasion, the stage direction in the present text represents a conflation of Folio and quarto. In that case, both Folio and quarto readings are set down in the notes. Stage directions and notations of place, printed within brackets, are, unless otherwise noted, substantially from the Globe edition. The list of dramatis personae, first given by Rowe, is taken also from the Globe edition.

**I.i.5 equalities** qualities **33 s.d. Sound . . . Attendants** Sennet. Enter King Lear, Cornwall, Albany, Gonerill, Regan, Cordelia, and attendants [F] Sound a Sennet, Enter one bearing a Coronet, then Lear, then the Dukes of Albany, and Cornwall, next Gonerill, Regan, Cordelia, with followers [Q] **68 Speak** [F omits] **96 loved me. I** loved me. I loved me **97 Return** I return **104 To love my father all** [F omits] **110 mysteries** [F2] miseries [F] mistress [Q] **155 as a pawn** as pawn **156 nor** nere [i.e., "ne'er"] **163 the** thy **170 sentence** sentences **174 diseases** disasters **188 Gloucester** Cor[delia] **206 on** in **214 best object** object **225 well will 233 Better thou** Better thou hadst **248 respects of fortune** respect and Fortunes **266 s.d. Lear . . . Attendants** [Capell] Exit Lear and Burgundy [Q] **281 shame them derides** with shame derides **289 hath not been** hath been **296 ingrafted** ingraffed **302 let's hit** let us sit
**I.ii.21 top th'** [Edwards] to' th' [F] tooth' [Q] **98-100 Edmund . . . earth** [F omits] **134 Fut** [F omits] **136 Edgar** [F omits] **137 and pat** [Steevens] Pat [F] and out [Q] **147-55 as . . . come** [F omits] **156 Why, the** The **169 brother** [F omits] **176 Go armed** [F omits] **182 s.d. Exit Edgar** Exit
**I.iii.17-21 Not . . . abused** [F omits] **25-26 I would . . . speak** [F omits] **27 Go, prepare** prepare
**I.iv.1 well** will **51 daughter** Daughters **99 Fool** my Boy **114 Lady the Brach** [Steevens] the Lady Brach [F] Ladie oth'e brach [Q] **142-57 That . . . snatching** [F omits] **155 on't** [Q2] [F omits] an't [Q] **156 ladies** [Q corrected] [F omits] lodes [Q uncorrected] **164 crown** Crownes **179 fools** Foole **191 Methinks** [F omits] **217 it had** it's had **220 Come, sir** [F omits] **229 or his** his **233-36 I . . . father** [F omits] **259**

**O . . . come** [F omits] **293 the cause** more of it **306 Yea . . . this** [F omits] **345 You are** [F2] Your are [F] Y'are [Q]. **attasked for** [Q corrected: "attaskt"] at task for [F] alapt [Q uncorrected]
**I.v.1 s.d. Enter . . . Fool** [Q2] Enter Lear, Kent, Gentleman, and Foole **17 Why . . . boy** What can'st tell Boy
**II.i.20 s.d. Enter Edgar** [placed by Theobald] [F prints after line 19] **54 But** And **71 I should** should I **72 ay** [F omits] **79 I . . . him** [F omits] **79 s.d. Tucket within** [placed by Malone] [F prints after line 78] **80 why** wher **88 strange news** strangenesse
**II.ii.23 clamorous** [Q corrected] clamours [F] clamarous [Q uncorrected] **44 s.d. Enter . . . drawn** Enter Bastard, Cornewall, Regan, Gloster, Servants [F] Enter Edmund with his rapier drawne, Gloster the Duke and Dutchesse [Q] **77 too t' 80 Renege** Revenge **81 gale** gall **110 flick'ring** [Pope: "flickering"] flicking [F] flitkering [Q] **125 dread** dead **132 respect** respects **141 s.d. Stocks brought out** [placed by Dyce] [F prints after line 139] [Q omits] **143-47 His . . . with** [F omits] **145 contemnèd'st** [Capell] [F omits] contaned [Q uncorrected] temnest [Q corrected] **153 For . . . legs** [F omits] **154 Come . . . away** [F assigns to Cornwall]; **my good lord** my Lord **154 s.d. Exeunt . . . Kent** Exit [F] [Q omits] **155 duke's** Duke **176 s.d. Sleeps** [F omits]
**II.iii. Scene III** [Steevens] [F, Q omit] **4 unusual** unusall **15 mortified bare arms** mortified Armes **18 sheepcotes** Sheeps-Cotes
**II.iv.1 s.d. Scene IV** [Steevens] [F, Q omit] **2 messenger** Messengers **6 thy** ahy **9 man's** man **18-19 No . . . have** [F omits] **30 panting** painting **33 whose** those **62 the** the the **74 have** hause **85 s.d. Enter . . . Gloucester** [F prints after line 83] **128 mother's** Mother **165 her pride** [F omits] **181 s.d. Enter Oswald** [placed by Dyce] [F and Q print after line 179] **183 fickle** fickly **186 s.d. Enter Goneril** [placed by Johnson] [F and Q print after line 184] **280 s.d. Storm and tempest** [F prints after line 281] [Q omits] **283 s.d. Exeunt . . . Fool** [Q2] Exeunt [F] Exeunt Lear, Leister, Kent, and Foole [Q] **292 s.d. Enter Gloucester** [F and Q print after line 291]
**III.i.7-15 tears . . . all** [F omits] **30-42 But . . . you** [F omits]
**III.ii.3 drowned** drown **71 That** And **78 True . . . boy** True boy
**III.iv.7 skin: so** [Rowe] skinso [F] skin, so [Q] **10 thy** they **27 s.d. Exit** [placed by Johnson] [F prints after line 26] [Q omits] **38 s.d. Enter Fool** [Duthie] Enter Edgar, and Foole [F, which prints after line 36] [Q omits] **44 s.d. Enter Edgar** Enter Edgar, and Foole [F, which prints after line 36] [Q omits] **46 blows . . . wind** blow the windes **47 thy cold bed** thy bed **52 ford** Sword **57 Bless** Blisse **58 Bless** blisse **62 What, has** Ha's **90 deeply deerely** deeply sessa [Malone] Sesey [F] caese [Q] **99 sessa** [Q2] **112 s.d. Enter . . . torch** [F prints after line 108] Enter Gloster [Q, which prints after line 112] **113 foul fiend Flibbertigibbet** foule Flibbertigibbet **114 till . . . cock** at first Cocke **133 hath had** hath
**III.v.13 his** this **26 dearer** deere
**III.vi.5 s.d. Exit** [placed by Capell] [F prints after line 3] **17-55 The . . . 'scape** [F omits] **22 Now** [Q2] [F omits] no [Q] **25 bourn** [Capell] [F omits] broome [Q] **34 cushions** [F omits] cushings [Q] **47 she kicked** [Q2] [F omits] kicked [Q] **53 made on** [Capell] [F omits] made an [Q] **68 lym** [Hanmer] Hym [F] him [Q] **69 tike, or trundle** tight, or Troudle **73 Sessa!** [Malone] sese [F] [Q omits] **84 s.d. Enter Gloucester** [placed by Capell] [F prints after line 80] **96-100 Oppressèd . . . behind** [F omits] **101-14 When . . . lurk** [F omits]
**III.vii.21 s.d. Exit Oswald** [Staunton] [F and Q omit] **23 s.d. Exeunt . . . Edmund** [Staunton] [F (Exit) and Q (Exit Gon. and Bast.) print after line 22] **28 s.d. Enter . . . three** [Q, which prints after "traitor"] Enter Gloucester, and Servants [F, which prints as here after "control"] **60 rash** sticke **65 dearn** sterne **80 s.d. Draw and fight** [F omits] **82 s.d. She . . . him** Killes him [F] Shee . . . behind [Q] **101-09 I'll . . . him** [F omits] **101 Second Servant** [Capell] [F omits] Servant [Q] **102 Third Servant** [Capell] [F omits] 2 Servant [Q] **105 Second Servant** [Capell] [F omits] 1 Ser. [Q] **106 roguish** [Q2] [Q omits] **108 Third Servant** [Capell] [F omits] 2 Ser. [Q] **109 s.d. Exeunt severally** [F omits] Exit [Q]
**IV.i.9 s.d. led by an Old Man** [Q, which prints after line 12] and an Old man [F, which places after line 9, as here] **41 Then,**

prithee, get thee gone Get thee away 59–63 Five . . . master [F omits] 61 Flibbertigibbet [Pope] Stiberdigebit [Q] 62 mopping and mowing [Theobald] Mobing, & Mohinʒ [Q] IV.ii.1 s.d. Enter Goneril and Edmund Enter Gonerill, Bastard, and Steward 2 s.d. [after "way"] Enter Oswald [placed by Theobald] [Q prints after "master," line 2] [F omits] 26 s.d. Exit Edmund [placed by Rowe] Exit [F, which prints after "death"] [Q omits] 29 s.d. Exit [F omits] Exit Stew. [Q] 32–51 I . . . deep [F omits] 33 its ith [Q] 46 benefited [Q corrected] beniflicted [Q uncorrected] 48 these [Jennens; Heath conj.] the [Q uncorrected] this [Q corrected] 50 Humanity [Q corrected] Humanly [Q uncorrected] 54–60 that . . . so [F omits] 57 noiseless [Q corrected] noystles [Q uncorrected] 58 thy state begins to threat [Jennens] thy slayer begin threats [Q uncorrected] thy state begins thereat [Q corrected] thy slaier begins threats [Q2] 59 Whilst [Q corrected] Whil's [Q uncorrected] 63–70 Thou . . . news [F omits] 66 dislocate [Q3] dislecate [Qq. 1, 2] 69 mew [Q corrected] now [Q uncorrected] 69 s.d. Enter a Messenger [F prints after line 62] Enter a Gentleman [Q, which prints after line 70; and Q2, which prints after line 69, as here] 76 thereat enraged threat-enrag'd 80 justicers [Q corrected] Iustices [F, Q] 88 s.d. Exit [F omits]
IV.iii. Scene III Scena Tertia [for Scene IV] 1 s.d. Enter . . . Gentleman [F omits the entire scene] 13 sir [Theobald] say 18 strove [Pope] streme 22 seemed [Pope: "seem'd"] seeme 31 believed [Q2] beleeft 33 moistened [Capell] moystened her 57 Exeunt [Pope] Exit
IV.iv. Scene IV [Pope] Scena Tertia [F] [Q omits] 1 s.d. Cordelia, Doctor, and Soldiers Cordelia, Gentlemen, and Souldiours [F] Cordelia, Doctor and others [Q] 3 femiter Fenitar 6 century Centery 18 distress desires 28 right Rite
IV.v. Scene V [Pope] Scena Quarta [F] [Q omits] 39 meet him meet
IV.vi. Scene VI [Pope] Scena Quinta [Q omits] 17 walk walk'd 34 s.d. He kneels [F omits] 41 s.d. He falls [F omits] 71 whelked wealk'd; enridgèd enraged 83 coining crying 97 had white had the white 164 Through Thorough; small great 165 Plate sin [Theobald] Place sinnes [Q omits] 197 Ay . . . dust [F omits] 198 Good sir [Q2] [F and Q omit] 204 s.d. Exit . . . follow Exit [F] Exit King running [Q] 206 one a 242 I'se [Johnson: "Ise"] ice [F] ile [Q] 244 s.d. They fight [F omits] 252 s.d. He dies [F omits] 271 and . . . venture [Q reads "Venter"] [F omits] [This line, from the First Quarto, is almost universally omitted from editions of the play] 273

indistinguished indinguish'd 286 s.d. Drum afar off [F prints after line 284] A drum a farre off [Q, which prints as here] IV.vii.1 s.d. Enter . . . Gentleman Enter Cordelia, Kent, and Gentleman [F] Enter Cordelia, Kent, and Doctor [Q] 24 doubt not doubt 24–25 Very . . . there [F omits] 32 warring iarring 33–36 To . . . helm [F omits] 79–80 and . . . lost [F omits] 84 s.d. Exeunt . . . Gentleman Exeunt 85–97 Holds . . . fought [F omits]
V.i.11–13 That . . . hers [F omits] 16 Fear me not Feare not 18–19 I . . . me [F omits] 23–28 Where . . . nobly [F omits] 33 I . . . tent [F omits] 36 pray you pray 40 s.d. To those going out [F and Q omit]; To Edgar [F and Q omit]; Exeunt [placed by Cambridge edition] [Q prints after "word," line 39] [F omits] 47 love loues 51 s.d. Exit [placed by Dyce] [F and Q print after line 50]
V.iii.13 hear poor rogues heere (poore Rogues) [reference in F is to Lear and Cordelia] 26 s.d. Exeunt . . . guarded Exit [F] [Q omits] 39–40 I . . . do't [F omits] 40 s.d. Exit Captain [F prints after line 38] [Q omits] 48 and appointed guard [Q corrected, and Q2] [F and Q omit] 55–60 At . . . place [F omits] 56 We [Q corrected, and Q2] mee [Q] 58 sharpness [Q corrected, and Q2] sharpes [Q] 84 attaint arrest 85 sister Sisters 98 he is has 103 Edmund . . . ho, a herald [F omits] 107 s.d. Enter a Herald [placed by Hanmer] [F prints after line 102] [Q omits] 110 Sound, trumpet [F omits] 110 s.d. A trumpet sounds [F prints after line 109] [Q omits] trumpet [F2] Tumpet 116 Sound [F omits] 116 s.d. First trumpet [F prints after line 115] [Q omits] 118 s.d. Enter . . . him Enter Edgar armed [F] Enter Edgar at the third sound, a trumpet before him [Q] 137 illustrious illustrirous 145 some say (some say) 152 s.d. fight Fights [F, which prints after line 153, "him"] [Q omits] 162 Ask . . . know [F gives to Edmund] 162 s.d. Exit [placed here by Q: "Exit. Gonorill"] [F prints after line 161, "for't"] 206–23 This . . . slave [F omits] 215 him [Theobald] me [Q] [F omits] 223 s.d. Enter . . . knife Enter a Gentleman [F] Enter one with a bloudie knife [Q] 234 s.d. Enter Kent [placed by Q2] [F prints after line 231, "Kent"] [Q prints after "allow" in line 235] 240 s.d. The . . . in Gonerill and Regans bodies brought out [F, which prints after line 232] 253 s.d. Exit Messenger [Theobald] [F and Q omit] 259 Howl, howl, howl, howl Howle, howle, howle; you are your are 279 them him 291 You are [Q2] Your are [F] You'r [Q] 296 s.d. Enter a Messenger [F, which prints after "him"] Enter Captaine [Q, placed as here]

# THE TRAGEDY OF KING LEAR

[Dramatis Personae

| | |
|---|---|
| LEAR *King of Britain* | DOCTOR |
| KING OF FRANCE | LEAR'S FOOL |
| DUKE OF BURGUNDY | A CAPTAIN *subordinate to Edmund* |
| DUKE OF CORNWALL *husband to Regan* | GENTLEMEN *attending on Cordelia* |
| DUKE OF ALBANY *husband to Goneril* | A HERALD |
| EARL OF KENT | SERVANTS *to Cornwall* |
| EARL OF GLOUCESTER | GONERIL |
| EDGAR *son to Gloucester* | REGAN } *daughters to Lear* |
| EDMUND *bastard son to Gloucester* | CORDELIA |
| CURAN *a courtier* | KNIGHTS *attending on Lear* OFFICERS |
| OSWALD *steward to Goneril* | MESSENGERS  SOLDIERS  ATTENDANTS |
| OLD MAN *tenant to Gloucester* | |

*Scene:* Britain]

## ACT I

### Scene I. [*King Lear's palace.*]

*Enter* KENT, GLOUCESTER, *and* EDMUND.

KENT  I thought the king had more affected° the Duke of Albany° than Cornwall.

GLOUCESTER  It did always seem so to us; but now, in the division of the kingdom, it appears not which of the dukes he values most, for equalities are so 5 weighed that curiosity in neither can make choice of either's moiety.°

KENT  Is not this your son, my lord?

GLOUCESTER  His breeding,° sir, hath been at my charge. I have so often blushed to acknowledge him 10 that now I am brazed° to't.

KENT  I cannot conceive° you.

GLOUCESTER  Sir, this young fellow's mother could; whereupon she grew round-wombed, and had indeed, sir, a son for her cradle ere she had a husband for her 15 bed. Do you smell a fault?

KENT  I cannot wish the fault undone, the issue° of it being so proper.°

GLOUCESTER  But I have a son, sir, by order of law, some year elder than this, who yet is no dearer in my 20 account:° though this knave° came something saucily° to the world before he was sent for, yet was his mother fair, there was good sport at his making, and the whoreson° must be acknowledged. Do you know this noble gentleman, Edmund? 25

EDMUND  No, my lord.

GLOUCESTER  My Lord of Kent. Remember him hereafter as my honorable friend.

*The decorative border shown above appeared on the first page of* King Lear *in the First Folio edition of Shakespeare's plays, 1623.*

**I.i.1 affected** loved  **2 Albany** Albanacte, whose domain extended "from the river Humber to the point of Caithness" (Holinshed)  **5–7 equalities . . . moiety** shares are so balanced against one another that careful examination by neither can make him wish the other's portion  **9 breeding** upbringing

**11 brazed** made brazen, hardened  **12 conceive** understand (pun follows)  **17 issue** result (child)  **18 proper** handsome  **21 account** estimation; **knave** fellow (without disapproval); **saucily** (1) insolently (2) lasciviously  **24 whoreson** fellow (literally, son of a whore)

EDMUND  My services to your lordship.

KENT  I must love you, and sue° to know you better. 30

EDMUND  Sir, I shall study deserving.

GLOUCESTER  He hath been out° nine years, and away
he shall again. The king is coming.

*Sound a sennet.° Enter one bearing a coronet,° then King*
LEAR, *then the Dukes of* CORNWALL *and* ALBANY, *next*
GONERIL, REGAN, CORDELIA, *and* ATTENDANTS.

LEAR
Attend the lords of France and Burgundy, Gloucester.

GLOUCESTER
I shall, my lord.                              *Exit, [with* EDMUND]. 35

LEAR
Meantime we shall express our darker purpose.°
Give me the map there. Know that we have divided
In three our kingdom; and 'tis our fast° intent
To shake all cares and business from our age,
Conferring them on younger strengths, while we        40
Unburthened crawl toward death. Our son of Corn-
    wall,
And you our no less loving son of Albany,
We have this hour a constant will to publish°
Our daughters' several° dowers, that future strife
May be prevented° now. The princes, France and
    Burgundy,                                          45
Great rivals in our youngest daughter's love,
Long in our court have made their amorous sojourn,
And here are to be answered. Tell me, my daughters
(Since now we will divest us both of rule,
Interest° of territory, cares of state),               50
Which of you shall we say doth love us most,
That we our largest bounty may extend
Where nature doth with merit challenge.° Goneril,
Our eldest-born, speak first.

GONERIL
Sir, I love you more than word can wield° the matter; 55
Dearer than eyesight, space,° and liberty;
Beyond what can be valued, rich or rare;
No less than life, with grace, health, beauty, honor;
As much as child e'er loved, or father found;
A love that makes breath° poor, and speech unable:°  60
Beyond all manner of so much° I love you.

CORDELIA [*Aside.*]
What shall Cordelia speak? Love, and be silent.

LEAR
Of all these bounds, even from this line to this,
With shadowy forests, and with champains riched,°
With plenteous rivers, and wide-skirted meads,°       65
We make thee lady. To thine and Albany's issues°
Be this perpetual.° What says our second daughter,
Our dearest Regan, wife of Cornwall? Speak.

REGAN
I am made of that self mettle° as my sister,
And prize me at her worth.° In my true heart          70
I find she names my very deed of love;°
Only she comes too short, that° I profess
Myself an enemy to all other joys
Which the most precious square of sense professes,°
And find I am alone felicitate°                        75
In your dear highness' love.

CORDELIA [*Aside.*]                    Then poor Cordelia!
And yet not so, since I am sure my love's
More ponderous° than my tongue.

LEAR
To thee and thine hereditary ever
Remain this ample third of our fair kingdom,           80
No less in space, validity,° and pleasure
Than that conferred on Goneril. Now, our joy,
Although our last and least;° to whose young love
The vines of France and milk° of Burgundy
Strive to be interest;° what can you say to draw       85
A third more opulent than your sisters? Speak.

CORDELIA
Nothing, my lord.

LEAR  Nothing?

CORDELIA  Nothing.

LEAR
Nothing will come of nothing. Speak again.             90

CORDELIA
Unhappy that I am, I cannot heave
My heart into my mouth. I love your majesty
According to my bond,° no more nor less.

LEAR
How, how, Cordelia? Mend your speech a little,
Lest you may mar your fortunes.

CORDELIA                         Good my lord,          95
You have begot me, bred me, loved me. I
Return those duties back as are right fit,°
Obey you, love you, and most honor you.
Why have my sisters husbands, if they say
They love you all? Haply,° when I shall wed,           100
That lord whose hand must take my plight° shall
    carry
Half my love with him, half my care and duty.
Sure I shall never marry like my sisters,
To love my father all.

LEAR
But goes thy heart with this?

CORDELIA                         Ay, my good lord.      105

LEAR
So young, and so untender?

CORDELIA
So young, my lord, and true.

LEAR
Let it be so, thy truth then be thy dower!
For, by the sacred radiance of the sun,

---

30 **sue** entreat  32 **out** away, abroad  33 **s.d. sennet** set of
notes played on a trumpet, signaling the entrance or departure
of a procession; **coronet** small crown, intended for Cordelia
36 **darker purpose** hidden intention  38 **fast** fixed  43
**constant . . . publish** fixed intention to proclaim  44
**several** separate  45 **prevented** forestalled  50 **Interest** legal
right  53 **nature . . . challenge** natural affection contends
with desert for (or lays claim to) bounty  55 **wield** handle  56
**space** scope  60 **breath** language; **unable** impotent  61
**Beyond . . . much** beyond all these comparisons  64
**champains riched** enriched plains  65 **wide-skirted meads**
extensive grasslands  66 **issues** descendants  67 **perpetual** in
perpetuity

69 **self mettle** same material or temperament  70 **prize . . .
worth** value me the same (imperative)  71 **my . . . love**
what my love really is (a legalism)  72 **that** in that  74 **Which
. . . professes** which the choicest estimate of sense avows  75
**felicitate** made happy  78 **ponderous** weighty  81 **validity**
value  83 **least** youngest, smallest  84 **milk** i.e., pastures
85 **interest** closely connected, as interested parties  93 **bond**
filial obligation  97 **Return . . . fit** i.e., am correspondingly dutiful  100 **Haply** perhaps  101 **plight** troth plight

The mysteries of Hecate° and the night, 110
By all the operation of the orbs°
From whom we do exist and cease to be,
Here I disclaim all my paternal care,
Propinquity and property of blood,°
And as a stranger to my heart and me 115
Hold thee from this for ever. The barbarous Scythian,°
Or he that makes his generation messes°
To gorge his appetite, shall to my bosom
Be as well neighbored, pitied, and relieved,
As thou my sometime° daughter.

KENT　　　　　　　　　　Good my liege— 120

LEAR
Peace, Kent!
Come not between the dragon° and his wrath.
I loved her most, and thought to set my rest°
On her kind nursery.° Hence and avoid my sight!
So be my grave my peace, as here I give 125
Her father's heart from her! Call France. Who stirs?
Call Burgundy. Cornwall and Albany,
With my two daughters' dowers digest° the third;
Let pride, which she calls plainness, marry her.°
I do invest you jointly with my power, 130
Preeminence, and all the large effects
That troop with majesty.° Ourself,° by monthly
　course,
With reservation° of an hundred knights,
By you to be sustained, shall our abode
Make with you by due turn. Only we shall retain 135
The name, and all th' addition° to a king. The sway,
Revènue, execution of the rest,
Belovèd sons, be yours; which to confirm,
This coronet° part between you.

KENT　　　　　　　　　　Royal Lear,
Whom I have ever honored as my king, 140
Loved as my father, as my master followed,
As my great patron thought on in my prayers—

LEAR
The bow is bent and drawn; make from the shaft.°

KENT
Let it fall° rather, though the fork° invade
The region of my heart. Be Kent unmannerly 145
When Lear is mad. What wouldst thou do, old man?
Thinkst thou that duty shall have dread to speak
When power to flattery bows? To plainness honor's
　bound
When majesty falls to folly. Reserve thy state,°
And in thy best consideration° check 150

110 **mysteries of Hecate** secret rites of Hecate (goddess of
the infernal world, and of witchcraft) 111 **operation** . . .
**orbs** astrological influence 114 **Propinquity . . . blood**
relationship and common blood 116 **Scythian** type of the
savage 117 **makes . . . messes** eats his own offspring 120
**sometime** former 122 **dragon** (1) heraldic device of
Britain (2) emblem of ferocity 123 **set my rest** (1) stake
my all (a term from the card game of primero) (2) find my
rest 124 **nursery** care, nursing 128 **digest** absorb 129
**Let . . . her** Let her pride be her dowry and gain her a
husband 131–32 **effects . . . majesty** accompaniments that
go with kingship 132 **Ourself** the royal "we" 133 **reserva-**
**tion** the action of reserving a privilege (a legalism) 136
**addition** titles and honors 139 **coronet** the crown that was
to have been Cordelia's 143 **make . . . shaft** avoid the
arrow 144 **fall** strike; **fork** forked head of the arrow 149
**Reserve thy state** retain your kingly authority 150 **best**
**consideration** most careful reflection

This hideous rashness. Answer my life my judgment,°
Thy youngest daughter does not love thee least,
Nor are those empty-hearted whose low sounds
Reverb° no hollowness.°

LEAR　　　　　　　　Kent, on thy life, no more!

KENT
My life I never held but as a pawn° 155
To wage° against thine enemies; nor fear to lose it,
Thy safety being motive.°

LEAR　　　　　　　　Out of my sight!

KENT
See better, Lear, and let me still° remain
The true blank° of thine eye.

LEAR
Now by Apollo—

KENT　　　　　　Now by Apollo, king, 160
Thou swear'st thy gods in vain.

LEAR　　　　　　　　O vassal! Miscreant!°

[*Laying his hand on his sword.*]

ALBANY, CORNWALL　Dear sir, forbear!

KENT
Kill thy physician, and the fee bestow
Upon the foul disease. Revoke thy gift,
Or, whilst I can vent clamor° from my throat, 165
I'll tell thee thou dost evil.

LEAR　　　　　　　　Hear me, recreant!°
On thine allegiance,° hear me!
That thou hast sought to make us break our vows,
Which we durst never yet, and with strained° pride
To come betwixt our sentence° and our power, 170
Which nor our nature nor our place can bear,
Our potency made good,° take thy reward.
Five days we do allot thee for provision°
To shield thee from diseases° of the world,
And on the sixth to turn thy hated back 175
Upon our kingdom. If, on the tenth day following,
Thy banished trunk° be found in our dominions,
The moment is thy death. Away! By Jupiter,
This shall not be revoked.

KENT
Fare thee well, king. Sith° thus thou wilt appear, 180
Freedom lives hence, and banishment is here.

[*To* CORDELIA.]

The gods to their dear shelter take thee, maid,
That justly think'st, and hast most rightly said.

[*To* REGAN *and* GONERIL.]

And your large speeches may your deeds approve,°
That good effects° may spring from words of love. 185

151 **Answer . . . judgment** I will stake my life on my
opinion 154 **Reverb** reverberate; **hollowness** (1) emptiness
(2) insincerity 155 **pawn** stake in a wager 156 **wage** (1)
wager (2) carry on war 157 **motive** moving cause 158 **still**
always 159 **blank** the white spot in the center of the target
(at which Lear should aim) 161 **vassal! Miscreant!** base
wretch! Misbeliever 165 **vent clamor** utter a cry 166
**recreant** traitor 167 **On thine allegiance** to forswear, which
is to commit high treason 169 **strained** forced (and so
excessive) 170 **sentence** judgment, decree 172 **Our . . .**
**good** my royal authority being now asserted 173 **for pro-**
**vision** for making preparation 174 **diseases** troubles 177
**trunk** body 180 **Sith** since 184 **approve** prove true 185
**effects** results

Thus Kent, O princes, bids you all adieu;
He'll shape his old course° in a country new.     *Exit.*

*Flourish.° Enter* GLOUCESTER, *with* FRANCE *and*
BURGUNDY; ATTENDANTS.

GLOUCESTER
Here's France and Burgundy, my noble lord.
LEAR
My Lord of Burgundy,
We first address toward you, who with this king    190
Hath rivaled for our daughter. What in the least
Will you require in present° dower with her,
Or cease your quest of love?
BURGUNDY          Most royal majesty,
I crave no more than hath your highness offered,
Nor will you tender° less.
LEAR          Right noble Burgundy,    195
When she was dear° to us, we did hold her so;
But now her price is fallen. Sir, there she stands.
If aught within that little seeming substance,°
Or all of it, with our displeasure pieced,°
And nothing more, may fitly like° your grace,    200
She's there, and she is yours.
BURGUNDY          I know no answer.
LEAR
Will you, with those infirmities she owes,°
Unfriended, new adopted to our hate,
Dow'red with our curse, and strangered° with our
    oath,
Take her, or leave her?
BURGUNDY       Pardon me, royal sir.    205
Election makes not up° on such conditions.
LEAR
Then leave her, sir; for, by the pow'r that made me,
I tell you all her wealth. [*To* FRANCE.] For you, great
    king,
I would not from your love make such a stray
To° match you where I hate; therefore beseech° you   210
T' avert your liking a more worthier way°
Than on a wretch whom nature is ashamed
Almost t' acknowledge hers.
FRANCE          This is most strange,
That she whom even but now was your best object,°
The argument° of your praise, balm of your age,    215
The best, the dearest, should in this trice of time
Commit a thing so monstrous to dismantle°
So many folds of favor. Sure her offense
Must be of such unnatural degree
That monsters it,° or your fore-vouched° affection    220
Fall into taint;° which to believe of her

Must be a faith that reason without miracle
Should never plant in me.°
CORDELIA          I yet beseech your majesty,
If for° I want that glib and oily art
To speak and purpose not,° since what I well intend    225
I'll do't before I speak, that you make known
It is no vicious blot, murder, or foulness,
No unchaste action or dishonored step,
That hath deprived me of your grace and favor;
But even for want of that for which I am richer,    230
A still-soliciting° eye, and such a tongue
That I am glad I have not, though not to have it
Hath lost° me in your liking.
LEAR          Better thou
Hadst not been born than not t' have pleased me better.
FRANCE
Is it but this? A tardiness in nature°    235
Which often leaves the history unspoke°
That it intends to do. My Lord of Burgundy,
What say you° to the lady? Love's not love
When it is mingled with regards° that stands
Aloof from th' entire point.° Will you have her?    240
She is herself a dowry.
BURGUNDY          Royal king,
Give but that portion which yourself proposed,
And here I take Cordelia by the hand,
Duchess of Burgundy.
LEAR
Nothing. I have sworn. I am firm.    245
BURGUNDY
I am sorry then you have so lost a father
That you must lose a husband.
CORDELIA          Peace be with Burgundy.
Since that respects of fortune° are his love,
I shall not be his wife.
FRANCE
Fairest Cordelia, that art most rich being poor,    250
Most choice forsaken, and most loved despised,
Thee and thy virtues here I seize upon.
Be it lawful I take up what's cast away.
Gods, gods! 'Tis strange that from their cold'st
    neglect
My love should kindle to inflamed respect.°    255
Thy dow'rless daughter, king, thrown to my chance,°
Is queen of us, of ours, and our fair France.
Not all the dukes of wat'rish° Burgundy
Can buy this unprized precious° maid of me.
Bid them farewell, Cordelia, though unkind.    260
Thou losest here,° a better where° to find.
LEAR
Thou hast her, France; let her be thine, for we
Have no such daughter, nor shall ever see

187 shape . . . course pursue his customary way 187
s.d. Flourish trumpet fanfare 192 present immediate
195 tender offer 196 dear (1) beloved (2) valued at a high
price 198 little seeming substance person who is (1) incon-
siderable (2) outspoken 199 pieced added to it 200 fitly like
please by its fitness 202 owes possesses 204 strangered
made a stranger 206 Election . . . up no one can choose
209–10 make . . . To stray so far as to 210 beseech I
beseech 211 avert . . . way turn your affections from her
and bestow them on a better person 214 your best object
the one you loved most 215 argument subject 217 dismantle strip off 220 That monsters it as makes it monstrous,
unnatural; fore-vouched previously sworn 221 Fall into
taint must be taken as having been unjustified all along; i.e.,
Cordelia was unworthy of your love from the first

222–23 reason . . . me my reason would have to be supported
by a miracle to make me believe 224 for because 225 purpose not not mean to do what I promise 231 still-soliciting
always begging 233 lost ruined 235 tardiness in nature
natural reticence 236 leaves . . . unspoke does not announce
the action 238 What say you i.e., will you have 239 regards
considerations (the dowry) 239–40 stands . . . point have
nothing to do with the essential question (love) 248
respects of fortune mercenary considerations 255 inflamed respect more ardent affection 256 chance lot
258 wat'rish (1) with many rivers (2) weak, diluted 259
unprized precious unappreciated by others, and yet precious
261 here in this place; where other place

That face of hers again. Therefore be gone,
Without our grace, our love, our benison.°      265
Come, noble Burgundy.

*Flourish. Exeunt* [LEAR, BURGUNDY, CORNWALL,
ALBANY, GLOUCESTER, *and* ATTENDANTS].

FRANCE
Bid farewell to your sisters.

CORDELIA
The jewels of our father,° with washed° eyes
Cordelia leaves you. I know you what you are,
And, like a sister,° am most loath to call      270
Your faults as they are named.° Love well our
father.
To your professèd° bosoms I commit him.
But yet, alas, stood I within his grace,
I would prefer° him to a better place.
So farewell to you both.      275

REGAN
Prescribe not us our duty.

GONERIL                      Let your study
Be to content your lord, who hath received you
At Fortune's alms.° You have obedience scanted,°
And well are worth the want that you have wanted.°

CORDELIA
Time shall unfold what plighted° cunning hides,      280
Who covers faults, at last shame them derides.°
Well may you prosper.

FRANCE                      Come, my fair Cordelia.

*Exit* FRANCE *and* CORDELIA.

GONERIL   Sister, it is not little I have to say of what
most nearly appertains to us both. I think our father
will hence tonight.      285

REGAN   That's most certain, and with you; next
month with us.

GONERIL   You see how full of changes his age is. The
observation we have made of it hath not been little.
He always loved our sister most, and with what poor      290
judgment he hath now cast her off appears too grossly.°

REGAN   'Tis the infirmity of his age; yet he hath ever
but slenderly known himself.

GONERIL   The best and soundest of his time° hath
been but rash; then must we look from his age to      295
receive not alone the imperfections of long-ingrafted°
condition,° but therewithal° the unruly waywardness
that infirm and choleric years bring with them.

REGAN   Such unconstant starts° are we like to have
from him as this of Kent's banishment.      300

GONERIL   There is further compliment° of leave-
taking between France and him. Pray you, let's hit°

together; if our father carry authority with such disposition as he bears,° this last surrender° of his will
but offend° us.      305

REGAN   We shall further think of it.

GONERIL   We must do something, and i' th' heat.°

*Exeunt.*

Scene II. [*The Earl of Gloucester's castle.*]

*Enter* EDMUND [*with a letter*].

EDMUND
Thou, Nature,° art my goddess; to thy law
My services are bound. Wherefore should I
Stand in the plague of custom,° and permit
The curiosity° of nations to deprive me,
For that° I am some twelve or fourteen moonshines°      5
Lag of° a brother? Why bastard? Wherefore base?
When my dimensions are as well compact,°
My mind as generous,° and my shape as true,
As honest° madam's issue? Why brand they us
With base? With baseness? Bastardy? Base? Base?      10
Who, in the lusty stealth of nature, take
More composition° and fierce° quality
Than doth, within a dull, stale, tired bed,
Go to th' creating a whole tribe of fops°
Got° 'tween asleep and wake? Well then,      15
Legitimate Edgar, I must have your land.
Our father's love is to the bastard Edmund
As to th' legitimate. Fine word, "legitimate."
Well, my legitimate, if this letter speed,°
And my invention° thrive, Edmund the base      20
Shall top th' legitimate. I grow, I prosper.
Now, gods, stand up for bastards.

*Enter* GLOUCESTER.

GLOUCESTER
Kent banished thus? and France in choler parted?
And the king gone tonight? prescribed° his pow'r?
Confined to exhibition?° All this done      25
Upon the gad?° Edmund, how now? What news?

EDMUND
So please your lordship, none.

GLOUCESTER
Why so earnestly seek you to put up° that letter?

EDMUND
I know no news, my lord.

GLOUCESTER
What paper were you reading?      30

EDMUND   Nothing, my lord.

GLOUCESTER   No? What needed then that terrible dispatch° of it into your pocket? The quality of nothing hath not such need to hide itself. Let's see. Come, if it be nothing, I shall not need spectacles.    35

EDMUND   I beseech you, sir, pardon me. It is a letter from my brother that I have not all o'er-read; and for so much as I have perused, I find it not fit for your o'erlooking.°

GLOUCESTER   Give me the letter, sir.    40

EDMUND   I shall offend, either to detain or give it. The contents, as in part I understand them, are to blame.°

GLOUCESTER   Let's see, let's see.

EDMUND   I hope, for my brother's justification, he  45 wrote this but as an essay or taste° of my virtue.

GLOUCESTER (*Reads.*)   "This policy and reverence° of age makes the world bitter to the best of our times;° keeps our fortunes from us till our oldness cannot relish° them. I begin to find an idle and fond° bondage  50 in the oppression of aged tyranny, who sways, not as it hath power, but as it is suffered.° Come to me, that of this I may speak more. If our father would sleep till I waked him, you should enjoy half his revenue° for ever, and live the beloved of your brother,    55

                          Edgar."

Hum! Conspiracy? "Sleep till I waked him, you should enjoy half his revenue." My son Edgar! Had he a hand to write this? A heart and brain to breed it in? When came you to this? Who brought it?    60

EDMUND   It was not brought me, my lord; there's the cunning of it. I found it thrown in at the casement of my closet.°

GLOUCESTER   You know the character° to be your brother's?    65

EDMUND   If the matter were good, my lord, I durst swear it were his; but in respect of that,° I would fain° think it were not.

GLOUCESTER   It is his.

EDMUND   It is his hand, my lord; but I hope his  70 heart is not in the contents.

GLOUCESTER   Has he never before sounded° you in this business?

EDMUND   Never, my lord. But I have heard him oft maintain it to be fit that, sons at perfect° age, and  75 fathers declined, the father should be as ward to the son, and the son manage his revenue.

GLOUCESTER   O villain, villain! His very opinion in the letter. Abhorred villain, unnatural, detested,° brutish villain; worse than brutish! Go, sirrah,° seek him.  80 I'll apprehend him. Abominable villain! Where is he?

EDMUND   I do not well know, my lord. If it shall please you to suspend your indignation against my brother till you can derive from him better testimony

of his intent, you should run a certain course;° where,  85 if you violently proceed against him, mistaking his purpose, it would make a great gap° in your own honor and shake in pieces the heart of his obedience. I dare pawn down° my life for him that he hath writ this to feel° my affection to your honor, and to no  90 other pretense of danger.°

GLOUCESTER   Think you so?

EDMUND   If your honor judge it meet,° I will place you where you shall hear us confer of this, and by an auricular assurance° have your satisfaction, and that  95 without any further delay than this very evening.

GLOUCESTER   He cannot be such a monster.

EDMUND   Nor is not, sure.

GLOUCESTER   To his father, that so tenderly and entirely loves him. Heaven and earth! Edmund, seek  100 him out; wind me into him,° I pray you; frame° the business after your own wisdom. I would unstate myself to be in a due resolution.°

EDMUND   I will seek him, sir, presently;° convey° the business as I shall find means, and acquaint you withal.°  105

GLOUCESTER   These late° eclipses in the sun and moon portend no good to us. Though the wisdom of nature° can reason° it thus and thus, yet nature finds itself scourged by the sequent effects.° Love cools, friendship falls off,° brothers divide. In cities, mutinies;°  110 in countries, discord; in palaces, treason; and the bond cracked 'twixt son and father. This villain of mine comes under the prediction,° there's son against father; the king falls from bias of nature,° there's father against child. We have seen the best of our time.° Machina-  115 tions, hollowness,° treachery, and all ruinous disorders follow us disquietly° to our graves. Find out this villain, Edmund; it shall lose thee nothing.° Do it carefully. And the noble and true-hearted Kent banished; his offense, honesty. 'Tis strange.    *Exit.*  120

EDMUND   This is the excellent foppery° of the world, that when we are sick in fortune, often the surfeits of our own behavior,° we make guilty of our disasters the sun, the moon, and stars; as if we were villains on° necessity; fools by heavenly compulsion; knaves,  125 thieves, and treachers by spherical predominance;° drunkards, liars, and adulterers by an enforced obedience of planetary influence;° and all that we are evil in,

---

32–33 **terrible dispatch** hasty putting away   39 **o'erlooking** inspection   42–43 **to blame** blameworthy   46 **essay or taste** test   47 **policy and reverence** policy of reverencing (hendiadys)   48 **best . . . times** best years of our lives (i.e., our youth)   50 **relish** enjoy; **idle and fond** foolish   51–52 **who . . . suffered** which rules, not from its own strength, but from our allowance   54 **revenue** income   62–63 **casement . . . closet** window of my room   64 **character** handwriting   67 **in . . . that** in view of what it is; **fain** prefer to   72 **sounded** sounded you out   75 **perfect** mature   79 **detested** detestable   80 **sirrah** sir (familiar form of address)

85 **run . . . course** proceed safely, know where you are going   87 **gap** breach   89 **pawn down** stake   90 **feel** test   91 **pretense of danger** dangerous purpose   93 **meet** fit   95 **auricular assurance** proof heard with your own ears   101 **wind . . . him** insinuate yourself into his confidence for me; **frame** manage   102–03 **unstate . . . resolution** forfeit my earldom to know the truth   104 **presently** at once; **convey** manage   105 **withal** with it   106 **late** recent   107–08 **wisdom of nature** scientific learning   108 **reason** explain   108–09 **yet . . . effects** nonetheless our world is punished with subsequent disasters   110 **falls off** revolts; **mutinies** riots   112–13 **This . . . prediction** my son's villainous behavior is included in these portents, and bears them out   114 **bias of nature** natural inclination (the metaphor is from the game of bowls)   115 **best . . . time** our best days   116 **hollowness** insincerity   117 **disquietly** unquietly   118 **it . . . nothing** you will not lose by it   121 **foppery** folly   122–23 **often . . . behavior** often caused by our own excesses   124 **on** of   126 **treachers . . . predominance** traitors because of the ascendancy of a particular star at our birth   127–28 **by . . . influence** because we had to submit to the influence of our star

by a divine thrusting on.° An admirable evasion of
whoremaster° man, to lay his goatish° disposition on 130
the charge of a star. My father compounded° with my
mother under the Dragon's Tail,° and my nativity°
was under Ursa Major,° so that it follows I am rough
and lecherous. Fut!° I should have been that° I am,
had the maidenliest star in the firmament twinkled 135
on my bastardizing. Edgar—

*Enter* EDGAR.

and pat he comes, like the catastrophe° of the old
comedy. My cue is villainous melancholy, with a sigh
like Tom o' Bedlam.°—O, these eclipses do portend
these divisions. Fa, sol, la, mi.° 140
EDGAR    How now, brother Edmund; what serious
contemplation are you in?
EDMUND    I am thinking, brother, of a prediction I
read this other day, what should follow these eclipses.
EDGAR    Do you busy yourself with that? 145
EDMUND    I promise you, the effects he writes of suc-
ceed° unhappily: as of unnaturalness° between the
child and the parent, death, dearth, dissolutions of
ancient amities,° divisions in state, menaces and
maledictions against king and nobles, needless diffi- 150
dences,° banishment of friends, dissipation of cohorts,°
nuptial breaches, and I know not what.
EDGAR    How long have you been a sectary astronomical?°
EDMUND    Come, come, when saw you my father last? 155
EDGAR    Why, the night gone by.
EDMUND    Spake you with him?
EDGAR    Ay, two hours together.
EDMUND    Parted you in good terms? Found you no
displeasure in him by word nor countenance?° 160
EDGAR    None at all.
EDMUND    Bethink yourself wherein you may have
offended him; and at my entreaty forbear his presence°
until some little time hath qualified° the heat of his
displeasure, which at this instant so rageth in him that 165
with the mischief of your person it would scarcely
allay.°
EDGAR    Some villain hath done me wrong.
EDMUND    That's my fear, brother. I pray you have a
continent forbearance° till the speed of his rage goes 170
slower; and, as I say, retire with me to my lodging,
from whence I will fitly° bring you to hear my lord

speak. Pray ye, go; there's my key. If you do stir
abroad, go armed.
EDGAR    Armed, brother? 175
EDMUND    Brother, I advise you to the best. Go armed.
I am no honest man if there be any good meaning
toward you. I have told you what I have seen and
heard; but faintly, nothing like the image and horror°
of it. Pray you, away. 180
EDGAR    Shall I hear from you anon?°
EDMUND    I do serve you in this business.
*Exit* EDGAR.
A credulous father, and a brother noble,
Whose nature is so far from doing harms
That he suspects none; on whose foolish honesty 185
My practices° ride easy. I see the business.
Let me, if not by birth, have lands by wit.
All with me's meet° that I can fashion fit.°    *Exit.*

Scene III. [*The Duke of Albany's palace.*]

*Enter* GONERIL, *and* [OSWALD, *her*] *steward.*
GONERIL    Did my father strike my gentleman for
chiding of his Fool?°
OSWALD    Ay, madam.
GONERIL
By day and night he wrongs me. Every hour
He flashes into one gross crime° or other 5
That sets us all at odds. I'll not endure it.
His knights grow riotous,° and himself upbraids us
On every trifle. When he returns from hunting,
I will not speak with him. Say I am sick.
If you come slack of former services,° 10
You shall do well; the fault of it I'll answer.°

[*Horns within.*]

OSWALD    He's coming, madam; I hear him.
GONERIL
Put on what weary negligence you please,
You and your fellows. I'd have it come to question.°
If he distaste° it, let him to my sister, 15
Whose mind and mine I know in that are one,
Not to be overruled. Idle° old man,
That still would manage those authorities
That he hath given away. Now, by my life,
Old fools are babes again, and must be used 20
With checks as flatteries, when they are seen abused.°
Remember what I have said.
OSWALD                        Well, madam.
GONERIL
And let his knights have colder looks among you.
What grows of it, no matter; advise your fellows so.
I would breed from hence occasions, and I shall, 25
That I may speak.° I'll write straight° to my sister
To hold my course. Go, prepare for dinner.    *Exeunt.*

---

129 **divine thrusting on** supernatural compulsion  130
**whoremaster** lecherous; **goatish** lascivious  131 **compounded** (1) made terms (2) formed (a child)  132 **Dragon's
Tail** the constellation Draco; **nativity** birthday  133 **Ursa
Major** the Great Bear  134 **Fut** 'S foot (an impatient oath);
**that** what  137 **catastrophe** conclusion  138–39 **My . . .
Bedlam** I must be doleful, like a lunatic beggar out of
Bethlehem (Bedlam) Hospital, the London madhouse  140 **Fa,
sol, la, mi** Edmund's humming of the musical notes is perhaps
prompted by his use of the word *division*, which describes
a musical variation  146–47 **succeed** follow  147 **unnaturalness** unkindness  149 **amities** friendships  150–51 **diffidences**
distrusts  151 **dissipation of cohorts** falling away of supporters  153–54 **sectary astronomical** believer in astrology
160 **countenance** expression  163 **forbear his presence**
keep away from him  164 **qualified** lessened  166–67 **with
. . . allay** even an injury to you would not appease his anger
169–70 **have . . . forbearance** be restrained and keep
yourself withdrawn  172 **fitly** at a fit time

179 **image and horror** true horrible picture  181 **anon** in a
little while  186 **practices** plots  188 **meet** proper; **fashion
fit** shape to my purpose
I.iii.2 **Fool** court jester  5 **crime** offense  7 **riotous** dissolute
10 **come . . . services** are less serviceable to him than
formerly  11 **answer** answer for  14 **come to question** be
discussed openly  15 **distaste** dislike  17 **Idle** foolish  21
**With . . . abused** with restraints as well as soothing words
when they are misguided  25–26 **breed . . . speak** find in
this opportunities for speaking out  26 **straight** at once

Scene IV. [*A hall in the same.*]

*Enter* KENT [*disguised*].

KENT
If but as well I other accents borrow
That can my speech defuse,° my good intent
May carry through itself to that full issue°
For which I razed my likeness.° Now, banished Kent,
If thou canst serve where thou dost stand condemned,   5
So may it come,° thy master whom thou lov'st
Shall find thee full of labors.

*Horns within.° Enter* LEAR, [KNIGHTS,] *and* ATTEN-
DANTS.

LEAR   Let me not stay° a jot for dinner; go, get it
ready. [*Exit an* ATTENDANT.] How now, what art
thou?   10

KENT   A man, sir.

LEAR   What dost thou profess?° What wouldst thou
with us?

KENT   I do profess° to be no less than I seem, to serve
him truly that will put me in trust, to love him that is   15
honest, to converse with him that is wise and says
little, to fear judgment,° to fight when I cannot
choose, and to eat no fish.°

LEAR   What art thou?

KENT   A very honest-hearted fellow and as poor as   20
the king.

LEAR   If thou be'st as poor for a subject as he's for a
king, thou art poor enough. What wouldst thou?

KENT   Service.

LEAR   Who wouldst thou serve?   25

KENT   You.

LEAR   Dost thou know me, fellow?

KENT   No, sir, but you have that in your countenance°
which I would fain° call master.

LEAR   What's that?   30

KENT   Authority.

LEAR   What services canst thou do?

KENT   I can keep honest counsel,° ride, run, mar a
curious tale in telling it,° and deliver a plain message
bluntly. That which ordinary men are fit for, I am   35
qualified in, and the best of me is diligence.

LEAR   How old art thou?

KENT   Not so young, sir, to love a woman for singing,
nor so old to dote on her for anything. I have years on
my back forty-eight.   40

LEAR   Follow me; thou shalt serve me. If I like thee
no worse after dinner, I will not part from thee yet.
Dinner, ho, dinner! Where's my knave?° my Fool?
Go you and call my Fool hither.

                [*Exit an* ATTENDANT.]

*Enter* OSWALD.

You, you, sirrah, where's my daughter?   45

OSWALD   So please you—           *Exit.*

LEAR   What says the fellow there? Call the clotpoll°
back. [*Exit a* KNIGHT.] Where's my Fool? Ho, I think
the world's asleep.

[*Reenter* KNIGHT.]

How now? Where's that mongrel?   50

KNIGHT   He says, my lord, your daughter is not well.

LEAR   Why came not the slave back to me when I
called him?

KNIGHT   Sir, he answered me in the roundest° manner,
he would not.   55

LEAR   He would not?

KNIGHT   My lord, I know not what the matter is;
but to my judgment your highness is not entertained°
with that ceremonious affection as you were wont.
There's a great abatement of kindness appears as well   60
in the general dependants° as in the duke himself also
and your daughter.

LEAR   Ha? Say'st thou so?

KNIGHT   I beseech you pardon me, my lord, if I be
mistaken; for my duty cannot be silent when I think   65
your highness wronged.

LEAR   Thou but rememb'rest° me of mine own conception.° I have perceived a most faint neglect° of late,
which I have rather blamed as mine own jealous
curiosity° than as a very pretense° and purpose of un-   70
kindness. I will look further into't. But where's my
Fool? I have not seen him this two days.

KNIGHT   Since my young lady's going into France,
sir, the Fool hath much pined away.

LEAR   No more of that; I have noted it well. Go you   75
and tell my daughter I would speak with her. Go you,
call hither my Fool.        [*Exit an* ATTENDANT.]

*Enter* OSWALD.

O, you, sir, you! Come you hither, sir. Who am I,
sir?

OSWALD   My lady's father.   80

LEAR   "My lady's father"? My lord's knave, you
whoreson dog, you slave, you cur!

OSWALD   I am none of these, my lord; I beseech your
pardon.

LEAR   Do you bandy° looks with me, you rascal?   85

[*Striking him.*]

OSWALD   I'll not be strucken,° my lord.

KENT   Nor tripped neither, you base football° player.

[*Tripping up his heels.*]

LEAR   I thank thee, fellow. Thou serv'st me, and I'll
love thee.

KENT   Come, sir, arise, away. I'll teach you differ-   90
ences.° Away, away. If you will measure your lubber's°

---

**I.iv.2 defuse** disguise   **3 full issue** perfect result   **4 razed
my likeness** shaved off, disguised my natural appearance   **6
So . . . come** so may it fall out   **7 s.d. within** offstage   **8
stay** wait   **12 What . . . profess** What do you do?   **14
profess** claim   **17 judgment** by a heavenly or earthly judge
**18 eat no fish** i.e., (1) I am no Catholic, but a loyal Protestant (2) I am no weakling (3) I use no prostitutes   **28
countenance** bearing   **29 fain** like to   **33 honest counsel**
honorable secrets   **33–34 mar . . . it** i.e., I cannot speak like
an affected courtier ("curious" = elaborate, as against plain)
**43 knave** boy

**47 clotpoll** clodpoll, blockhead   **54 roundest** rudest   **58
entertained** treated   **61 dependants** servants   **67 rememb'-
rest** remindest   **67–68 conception** idea   **68 faint neglect**
i.e., "weary negligence" (I.iii.13)   **69–70 mine . . . curiosity**
suspicious concern for my own dignity   **70 very pretense**
actual intention   **85 bandy** exchange insolently (metaphor
from tennis)   **86 strucken** struck   **87 football** a low game
played by idle boys, to the scandal of sensible men   **90–91
differences** of rank   **91 lubber's** lout's

length again, tarry; but away. Go to!° Have you wisdom?° So.°                    [*Pushes* OSWALD *out.*]

LEAR  Now, my friendly knave, I thank thee. There's earnest° of thy service.                                        95

[*Giving* KENT *money.*]

*Enter* FOOL.

FOOL  Let me hire him too. Here's my coxcomb.°

[*Offering* KENT *his cap.*]

LEAR  How now, my pretty knave? How dost thou?
FOOL  Sirrah, you were best° take my coxcomb.
KENT  Why, Fool?
FOOL  Why? For taking one's part that's out of favor. 100 Nay, an° thou canst not smile as the wind sits,° thou'lt catch cold shortly. There, take my coxcomb. Why, this fellow has banished° two on's daughters, and did the third a blessing against his will. If thou follow him, thou must needs wear my coxcomb.—How now, 105 nuncle?° Would I had two coxcombs and two daughters.
LEAR  Why, my boy?
FOOL  If I gave them all my living,° I'd keep my cox-combs myself. There's mine; beg another of thy 110 daughters.
LEAR  Take heed, sirrah—the whip.
FOOL  Truth's a dog must to kennel; he must be whipped out, when Lady the Brach° may stand by th' fire and stink.                                              115
LEAR  A pestilent gall° to me.
FOOL  Sirrah, I'll teach thee a speech.
LEAR  Do.
FOOL  Mark it, nuncle.
    Have more than thou showest,            120
    Speak less than thou knowest,
    Lend less than thou owest,°
    Ride more than thou goest,°
    Learn more than thou trowest,°
    Set less than thou throwest;°            125
    Leave thy drink and thy whore,
    And keep in-a-door,
    And thou shalt have more
    Than two tens to a score.°
KENT  This is nothing, Fool.                          130
FOOL  Then 'tis like the breath of an unfee'd° lawyer —you gave me nothing for't. Can you make no use of nothing, nuncle?
LEAR  Why, no, boy. Nothing can be made out of nothing.                                                135
FOOL [*To* KENT.]  Prithee tell him, so much the rent of his land comes to; he will not believe a fool.

LEAR  A bitter° fool.
FOOL  Dost thou know the difference, my boy, between a bitter fool and a sweet one?                  140
LEAR  No, lad; teach me.
FOOL      That lord that counseled thee
        To give away thy land,
      Come place him here by me,
        Do thou for him stand.        145
    The sweet and bitter fool
        Will presently appear;
      The one in motley° here,
        The other found out° there.°
LEAR  Dost thou call me fool, boy?                    150
FOOL  All thy other titles thou hast given away; that thou wast born with.
KENT  This is not altogether fool, my lord.
FOOL  No, faith; lords and great men will not let me.° If I had a monopoly° out, they would have part on't. 155 And ladies too, they will not let me have all the fool to myself; they'll be snatching. Nuncle, give me an egg, and I'll give thee two crowns.
LEAR  What two crowns shall they be?
FOOL  Why, after I have cut the egg i' th' middle and 160 eat up the meat, the two crowns of the egg. When thou clovest thy crown i' th' middle and gav'st away both parts, thou bor'st thine ass on thy back o'er the dirt.° Thou hadst little wit in thy bald crown when thou gav'st thy golden one away. If I speak like myself° 165 in this, let him be whipped° that first finds it so. [*Singing.*]
    Fools had ne'er less grace in a year,
      For wise men are grown foppish,
    And know not how their wits to wear,
      Their manners are so apish.°        170
LEAR  When were you wont to be so full of songs, sirrah?
FOOL  I have used° it, nuncle, e'er since thou mad'st thy daughters thy mothers; for when thou gav'st them the rod, and put'st down thine own breeches, 175 [*Singing.*]
    Then they for sudden joy did weep,
      And I for sorrow sung,
    That such a king should play bo-peep°
      And go the fools among.
Prithee, nuncle, keep a schoolmaster that can teach 180 thy Fool to lie. I would fain learn to lie.
LEAR  And° you lie, sirrah, we'll have you whipped.
FOOL  I marvel what kin thou and thy daughters are. They'll have me whipped for speaking true; thou'lt have me whipped for lying; and sometimes I am 185

---

92 **Go to** expression of derisive incredulity **92–93 Have you wisdom** i.e., Do you know what's good for you? **93 So** good **95 earnest** money for services rendered **96 coxcomb** professional fool's cap, shaped like a coxcomb **98 you were best** you had better **101 an** if; **smile . . . sits** ingratiate yourself with those in power **103 banished** alienated (by making them independent) **106 nuncle** contraction of "mine uncle" **109 living** property **114 Brach** bitch **116 gall** sore **122 owest** ownest **123 goest** walkest **124 trowest** knowest **125 Set . . . throwest** bet less than you play for (get odds from your opponent) **128–29 have . . . score** i.e., come away with more than you had (two tens, or twenty shillings, make a score, or one pound) **131 unfee'd** unpaid for

138 **bitter** satirical **148 motley** the drab costume of the professional jester **149 found out** revealed; **there** the Fool points at Lear, as a fool in the grain **154 let me** i.e., let me have all the folly to myself **155 monopoly** James I gave great scandal by granting to his "snatching" courtiers royal patents to deal exclusively in some commodity **163 bor'st . . . dirt** like the foolish and unnatural countryman in Aesop's fable **165 like myself** like a fool **166 let . . . whipped** i.e., let the man be whipped for a fool who thinks my true saying to be foolish **167–70 Fools . . . apish** i.e., fools were never in less favor than now, and the reason is that wise men, turning foolish, and not knowing how to use their intelligence, imitate the professional fools and so make them unnecessary **173 used** practiced **178 play bo-peep** (1) act like a child (2) blind himself **182 And** if

whipped for holding my peace. I had rather be any
kind o' thing than a fool, and yet I would not be thee,
nuncle: thou hast pared thy wit o' both sides and left
nothing i' th' middle. Here comes one o' the parings.

*Enter* GONERIL.

LEAR   How now, daughter? What makes that frontlet° 190
on? Methinks you are too much of late i' th' frown.
FOOL   Thou wast a pretty fellow when thou hadst no
need to care for her frowning. Now thou art an O
without a figure.° I am better than thou art now: I am
a fool, thou art nothing. [*To* GONERIL.] Yes, forsooth, 195
I will hold my tongue. So your face bids me, though
you say nothing. Mum, mum,
> He that keeps nor crust nor crum,°
> Weary of all, shall want° some.

[*Pointing to* LEAR.]

That's a shealed peascod.°                 200
GONERIL
Not only, sir, this your all-licensed° Fool,
But other° of your insolent retinue
Do hourly carp and quarrel, breaking forth
In rank° and not-to-be-endurèd riots. Sir,
I had thought by making this well known unto you   205
To have found a safe° redress, but now grow fearful,
By what yourself too late° have spoke and done,
That you protect this course, and put it on
By your allowance;° which if you should, the fault
Would not 'scape censure, nor the redresses sleep,°   210
Which, in the tender of° a wholesome weal,°
Might in their working do you that offense,
Which else were shame, that then necessity
Will call discreet proceeding.°
FOOL   For you know, nuncle,              215
> The hedge-sparrow fed the cuckoo° so long
> That it had it head bit off by it° young.
So out went the candle, and we were left darkling.°
LEAR   Are you our daughter?
GONERIL
Come, sir,                            220
I would you would make use of your good wisdom
Whereof I know you are fraught° and put away
These dispositions° which of late transport you
From what you rightly are.
FOOL   May not an ass know when the cart draws the 225
horse? Whoop, Jug,° I love thee!
LEAR
Does any here know me? This is not Lear.
Does Lear walk thus? Speak thus? Where are his eyes?

Either his notion° weakens, or his discernings°
Are lethargied°—Ha! Waking? 'Tis not so.     230
Who is it that can tell me who I am?
FOOL   Lear's shadow.
LEAR   I would learn that; for, by the marks of sover-
eignty,° knowledge, and reason, I should be false°
persuaded I had daughters.              235
FOOL   Which° they will make an obedient father.
LEAR   Your name, fair gentlewoman?
GONERIL
This admiration,° sir, is much o' th' savor°
Of other your° new pranks. I do beseech you
To understand my purposes aright.         240
As you are old and reverend, should be wise.
Here do you keep a hundred knights and squires,
Men so disordered, so deboshed,° and bold,
That this our court, infected with their manners,
Shows° like a riotous inn. Epicurism° and lust   245
Makes it more like a tavern or a brothel
Than a graced° palace. The shame itself doth speak
For instant remedy. Be then desired°
By her, that else will take the thing she begs,
A little to disquantity your train,°         250
And the remainders° that shall still depend,°
To be such men as may besort° your age,
Which know themselves, and you.
LEAR                    Darkness and devils!
Saddle my horses; call my train together.
Degenerate° bastard, I'll not trouble thee:    255
Yet have I left a daughter.
GONERIL
You strike my people, and your disordered rabble
Make servants of their betters.

*Enter* ALBANY.

LEAR
Woe, that too late repents. O, sir, are you come?
Is it your will? Speak, sir. Prepare my horses.   260
Ingratitude! thou marble-hearted fiend,
More hideous when thou show'st thee in a child
Than the sea-monster.
ALBANY             Pray, sir, be patient.
LEAR
Detested kite,° thou liest.
My train are men of choice and rarest parts,°    265
That all particulars of duty know,
And, in the most exact regard,° support
The worships° of their name. O most small fault,
How ugly didst thou in Cordelia show!
Which, like an engine,° wrenched my frame of nature 270
From the fixed place;° drew from my heart all love,

---

190 **frontlet** frown (literally, ornamental band)   194 **figure**
digit, to give value to the cipher (Lear is a nought)   198 **crum**
soft bread inside the loaf   199 **want** lack   200 **shealed
peascod** empty pea pod   201 **all-licensed** privileged to take
any liberties   202 **other** others   204 **rank** gross   206 **safe**
sure   207 **too late** lately   208–09 **put . . . allowance**
promote it by your approval   209 **allowance** approval   210
**redresses sleep** correction fail to follow   211 **tender of**
desire for; **weal** state   212–14 **Might . . . proceeding** as I
apply it, the correction might humiliate you; but the need to
take action cancels what would otherwise be unfilial conduct in
me   216 **cuckoo** which lays its eggs in the nests of other birds
217 **it** its   218 **darkling** in the dark   222 **fraught** endowed
223 **dispositions** moods   226 **Jug** Joan (a quotation from a
popular song?)

229 **notion** understanding; **discernings** faculties   230
**lethargied** paralyzed   233–34 **marks of sovereignty** i.e.,
tokens that Lear is king, and hence father to his daughters   234
**false** falsely   236 **Which** whom (Lear)   238 **admiration**
(affected) wonderment; **is . . . savor** smacks much   239 **other
your** others of your   243 **deboshed** debauched   245 **Shows**
appears; **Epicurism** riotous living   247 **graced** dignified   248
**desired** requested   250 **disquantity your train** reduce the
number of your dependents   251 **remainders** those who
remain; **depend** attend on you   252 **besort** befit   255
**Degenerate** unnatural   264 **kite** scavenging bird of prey   265
**parts** accomplishments   267 **exact regard** strict attention
to detail   268 **worships** honor   270 **engine** destructive contrivance   270–71 **wrenched . . . place** i.e., disorders my
natural self

And added to the gall.° O Lear, Lear, Lear!
Beat at this gate that let thy folly in

[*Striking his head.*]

And thy dear judgment out. Go, go, my people.
ALBANY
My lord, I am guiltless, as I am ignorant                    275
Of what hath moved you.
LEAR                            It may be so, my lord.
Hear, Nature, hear; dear goddess, hear:
Suspend thy purpose if thou didst intend
To make this creature fruitful.
Into her womb convey sterility,                             280
Dry up in her the organs of increase,°
And from her derogate° body never spring
A babe to honor her. If she must teem,°
Create her child of spleen,° that it may live
And be a thwart disnatured° torment to her.                285
Let it stamp wrinkles in her brow of youth,
With cadent° tears fret° channels in her cheeks,
Turn all her mother's pains and benefits°
To laughter and contempt, that she may feel
How sharper than a serpent's tooth it is                   290
To have a thankless child. Away, away!            *Exit.*
ALBANY
Now, gods that we adore, whereof comes this?
GONERIL
Never afflict yourself to know the cause,
But let his disposition° have that scope
As° dotage gives it.                                        295

*Enter* LEAR.

LEAR
What, fifty of my followers at a clap?°
Within a fortnight?
ALBANY                    What's the matter, sir?
LEAR
I'll tell thee. [*To* GONERIL.] Life and death, I am
    ashamed
That thou hast power to shake my manhood° thus!
That these hot tears, which break from me perforce,°       300
Should make thee worth them. Blasts and fogs upon
    thee!
Th' untented woundings° of a father's curse
Pierce every sense about thee! Old fond° eyes,
Beweep° this cause again, I'll pluck ye out
And cast you, with the waters that you loose,°             305
To temper° clay. Yea, is it come to this?
Ha! Let it be so. I have another daughter,
Who I am sure is kind and comfortable.°
When she shall hear this of thee, with her nails
She'll flay thy wolvish visage. Thou shalt find           310

That I'll resume the shape° which thou dost think
I have cast off for ever.
              *Exit* [LEAR, *with* KENT *and* ATTENDANTS].
GONERIL              Do you mark that?
ALBANY
I cannot be so partial, Goneril,
To the great love I bear you°—
GONERIL
Pray you, content. What, Oswald, ho!                       315

[*To the* FOOL.]

You, sir, more knave than fool, after your master!
FOOL    Nuncle Lear, nuncle Lear, tarry. Take the Fool°
    with thee.
              A fox, when one has caught her,
              And such a daughter,                          320
              Should sure to the slaughter,
              If my cap would buy a halter.°
              So the Fool follows after.°            *Exit.*
GONERIL
This man hath had good counsel. A hundred knights!
'Tis politic° and safe to let him keep                     325
At point° a hundred knights: yes, that on every dream,
Each buzz,° each fancy, each complaint, dislike,
He may enguard° his dotage with their pow'rs
And hold our lives in mercy.° Oswald, I say!
ALBANY
Well, you may fear too far.
GONERIL                    Safer than trust too far.       330
Let me still take away the harms I fear,
Not fear still to be taken.° I know his heart.
What he hath uttered I have writ my sister.
If she sustain him and his hundred knights,
When I have showed th' unfitness—

*Enter* OSWALD.

                            How now, Oswald?               335
What, have you writ that letter to my sister?
OSWALD    Ay, madam.
GONERIL
Take you some company,° and away to horse.
Inform her full of my particular° fear,
And thereto add such reasons of your own                   340
As may compact° it more. Get you gone,
And hasten your return. [*Exit* OSWALD.] No, no, my
    lord,
This milky gentleness and course° of yours,
Though I condemn not,° yet under pardon,
You are much more attasked° for want of wisdom            345
Than praised for harmful mildness.°
ALBANY
How far your eyes may pierce I cannot tell;

---

272 **gall** bitterness  281 **increase** childbearing  282 **derogate**
degraded  283 **teem** conceive  284 **spleen** ill humor  285
**thwart disnatured** perverse unnatural  287 **cadent** falling;
**fret** wear  288 **benefits** the mother's beneficent care of her child
294 **disposition** mood  295 **As** that  296 **at a clap** at one stroke
299 **shake my manhood** i.e., with tears  300 **perforce** involuntarily, against my will  302 **untented woundings**
wounds too deep to be probed with a tent (a roll of lint)  303
**fond** foolish  304 **Beweep** if you weep over  305 **loose** (1)
let loose (2) lose, as of no avail  306 **temper** mix with and
soften  308 **comfortable** ready to comfort

311 **shape** i.e., kingly role  313–14 **I cannot . . . you** i.e.,
even though my love inclines me to you, I must protest  317
**Fool** (1) the Fool himself (2) the epithet or character of "fool"
322–23 **halter, after** pronounced "hauter," "auter"  325
**politic** good policy  326 **At point** armed  327 **buzz** rumor
328 **enguard** protect  329 **in mercy** at his mercy  332 **Not
. . . taken** rather than remain fearful of being overtaken by
them  338 **company** escort  339 **particular** own  341
**compact** strengthen  343 **milky . . . course** mild and gentle
way (hendiadys)  344 **condemn not** condemn it not  345
**attasked** taken to task, blamed  346 **harmful mildness**
dangerous indulgence

Striving to better, oft we mar what's well.
GONERIL   Nay then—
ALBANY   Well, well, th' event.°       *Exeunt.* 350

### Scene V. [*Court before the same.*]

*Enter* LEAR, KENT, *and* FOOL.

LEAR   Go you before to Gloucester with these letters.
Acquaint my daughter no further with anything you
know than comes from her demand out of the letter.°
If your diligence be not speedy, I shall be there afore
you.       5
KENT   I will not sleep, my lord, till I have delivered
your letter.       *Exit.*
FOOL   If a man's brains were in's heels, were't° not in
danger of kibes?°
LEAR   Ay, boy.       10
FOOL   Then I prithee be merry. Thy wit shall not go
slipshod.°
LEAR   Ha, ha, ha.
FOOL   Shalt° see thy other daughter will use thee
kindly;° for though she's as like this as a crab's° like   15
an apple, yet I can tell what I can tell.
LEAR   Why, what canst thou tell, my boy?
FOOL   She will taste as like this as a crab does to a crab.
Thou canst tell why one's nose stands i' th' middle on's°
face?       20
LEAR   No.
FOOL   Why, to keep one's eyes of° either side's nose,
that what a man cannot smell out, he may spy into.
LEAR   I did her wrong.
FOOL   Canst tell how an oyster makes his shell?       25
LEAR   No.
FOOL   Nor I neither; but I can tell why a snail has a
house.
LEAR   Why?
FOOL   Why, to put's head in; not to give it away to   30
his daughters, and leave his horns° without a case.
LEAR   I will forget my nature.° So kind a father! Be
my horses ready?
FOOL   Thy asses are gone about 'em. The reason why
the seven stars° are no moe° than seven is a pretty°   35
reason.
LEAR   Because they are not eight.
FOOL   Yes indeed. Thou wouldst make a good fool.
LEAR   To take't again perforce!° Monster ingratitude!
FOOL   If thou wert my fool, nuncle, I'd have thee   40
beaten for being old before thy time.
LEAR   How's that?
FOOL   Thou shouldst not have been old till thou hadst
been wise.

LEAR
O, let me not be mad, not mad, sweet heaven!       45
Keep me in temper;° I would not be mad!

[*Enter* GENTLEMAN.]

How now, are the horses ready?
GENTLEMAN   Ready, my lord.
LEAR   Come, boy.
FOOL
She that's a maid now, and laughs at my departure,       50
Shall not be a maid long, unless things be cut shorter.°
      *Exeunt.*

# ACT II

### Scene I. [*The Earl of Gloucester's castle.*]

*Enter* EDMUND *and* CURAN, *severally.*°

EDMUND   Save° thee, Curan.
CURAN   And you, sir. I have been with your father,
and given him notice that the Duke of Cornwall and
Regan his duchess will be here with him this night.
EDMUND   How comes that?       5
CURAN   Nay, I know not. You have heard of the
news abroad? I mean the whispered ones, for they are
yet but ear-kissing arguments.°
EDMUND   Not I. Pray you, what are they?
CURAN   Have you heard of no likely° wars toward,°   10
'twixt the Dukes of Cornwall and Albany?
EDMUND   Not a word.
CURAN   You may do, then, in time. Fare you well,
sir.       *Exit.*
EDMUND
The duke be here tonight? The better!° best!       15
This weaves itself perforce° into my business.
My father hath set guard to take my brother,
And I have one thing of a queasy question°
Which I must act. Briefness° and Fortune, work!
Brother, a word; descend. Brother, I say!       20

*Enter* EDGAR.

My father watches. O sir, fly this place.
Intelligence° is given where you are hid.
You have now the good advantage of the night.
Have you not spoken 'gainst the Duke of Cornwall?
He's coming hither, now i' th' night, i' th' haste,°       25
And Regan with him. Have you nothing said
Upon his party° 'gainst the Duke of Albany?
Advise yourself.°
EDGAR       I am sure on't,° not a word.

**350 th' event** i.e., we'll see what happens
**I.v.3. than . . . letter** than her reading of the letter brings
her to ask   **8 were't** i.e., the brains   **9 kibes** chilblains   **11–12
Thy . . . slipshod** Your brains shall not go in slippers (because you have no brains to be protected from chilblains)   **14
Shalt** thou shalt   **15 kindly** (1) affectionately (2) after her kind
or nature; **crab** crab apple   **19 on's** of his   **22** cf **on**   **31
horns** (1) snail's horns (2) cuckold's horns   **32 nature** paternal
instincts   **35 seven stars** the Pleiades; **moe** more; **pretty** apt
**39 To . . . perforce** (1) of Goneril, who has forcibly taken
away Lear's privileges; or (2) of Lear, who meditates a forcible
resumption of authority

**46 in temper** sane   **50–51 She . . . shorter** The maid who
laughs, missing the tragic implications of this quarrel, will not
have sense enough to preserve her virginity ("things" =
penises)
**II.i.s.d. severally** separately (from different entrances
onstage)   **1 Save** God save   **8 ear-kissing arguments**
subjects whispered in the ear   **10 likely** probable; **toward**
impending   **15 The better** So much the better   **16 perforce**
necessarily   **18 of . . . question** that requires delicate
handling (to be "queasy" is to be on the point of vomit-
ing)   **19 Briefness** speed   **22 Intelligence** information   **25
i' th' haste** in great haste   **27 Upon his party** censuring his
enmity   **28 Advise yourself** Reflect; **on't** of it

**EDMUND**
I hear my father coming. Pardon me:
In cunning° I must draw my sword upon you.          30
Draw, seem to defend yourself; now quit you° well.
Yield! Come before my father! Light ho, here!
Fly, brother. Torches, torches!—So farewell.

*Exit* EDGAR.

Some blood drawn on me would beget opinion°

[*Wounds his arm.*]

Of my more fierce endeavor. I have seen drunkards   35
Do more than this in sport. Father, father!
Stop, stop! No help?

*Enter* GLOUCESTER, *and* SERVANTS *with torches.*

**GLOUCESTER**
Now, Edmund, where's the villain?
**EDMUND**
Here stood he in the dark, his sharp sword out,
Mumbling of wicked charms, conjuring the moon       40
To stand auspicious mistress.
**GLOUCESTER**                  But where is he?
**EDMUND**
Look, sir, I bleed.
**GLOUCESTER**       Where is the villain, Edmund?
**EDMUND**
Fled this way, sir, when by no means he could—
**GLOUCESTER**
Pursue him, ho! Go after. [*Exeunt some* SERVANTS.]
   By no means what?
**EDMUND**
Persuade me to the murder of your lordship;          45
But that I told him the revenging gods
'Gainst parricides did all the thunder bend;°
Spoke with how manifold and strong a bond
The child was bound to th' father. Sir, in fine,°
Seeing how loathly opposite° I stood                  50
To his unnatural purpose, in fell° motion°
With his preparèd sword he charges home
My unprovided° body, latched° mine arm;
But when he saw my best alarumed° spirits
Bold in the quarrel's right,° roused to th' encounter, 55
Or whether gasted° by the noise I made,
Full suddenly he fled.
**GLOUCESTER**              Let him fly far.
Not in this land shall he remain uncaught;
And found—dispatch.° The noble duke my master,
My worthy arch° and patron, comes tonight.           60
By his authority I will proclaim it,
That he which finds him shall deserve our thanks,
Bringing the murderous coward to the stake.
He that conceals him, death.°
**EDMUND**
When I dissuaded him from his intent,                65
And found him pight° to do it, with curst° speech

I threatened to discover° him. He replied,
"Thou unpossessing° bastard, dost thou think,
If I would stand against thee, would the reposal°
Of any trust, virtue, or worth in thee               70
Make thy words faithed?° No. What I should deny—
As this I would, ay, though thou didst produce
My very character°—I'd turn it all
To thy suggestion,° plot, and damnèd practice.°
And thou must make a dullard of the world,°          75
If they not thought° the profits of my death
Were very pregnant° and potential spirits°
To make thee seek it."
**GLOUCESTER**            O strange and fastened° villain!
Would he deny his letter, said he? I never got° him.

*Tucket° within.*

Hark, the duke's trumpets. I know not why he comes.  80
All ports° I'll bar; the villain shall not 'scape;
The duke must grant me that. Besides, his picture
I will send far and near, that all the kingdom
May have due note of him; and of my land,
Loyal and natural° boy, I'll work the means          85
To make thee capable.°

*Enter* CORNWALL, REGAN, *and* ATTENDANTS.

**CORNWALL**
How now, my noble friend! Since I came hither,
Which I can call but now, I have heard strange news.
**REGAN**
If it be true, all vengeance comes too short
Which can pursue th' offender. How dost, my lord?    90
**GLOUCESTER**
O madam, my old heart is cracked, it's cracked.
**REGAN**
What, did my father's godson seek your life?
He whom my father named, your Edgar?
**GLOUCESTER**
O lady, lady, shame would have it hid.
**REGAN**
Was he not companion with the riotous knights        95
That tended upon my father?
**GLOUCESTER**
I know not, madam. 'Tis too bad, too bad.
**EDMUND**
Yes, madam, he was of that consort.°
**REGAN**
No marvel then, though he were ill affected.°
'Tis they have put° him on the old man's death,      100
To have th' expense and waste° of his revenues.
I have this present evening from my sister
Been well informed of them, and with such cautions
That, if they come to sojourn at my house,
I'll not be there.
**CORNWALL**         Nor I, assure thee, Regan.       105

30 **In cunning** as a pretense   31 **quit you** acquaint yourself
34 **beget opinion** create the impression   47 **bend** aim   49 **in
fine** finally   50 **loathly opposite** bitterly opposed   51 **fell**
deadly; **motion** thrust (a term from fencing)   53 **unprovided**
unprotected; **latched** wounded (lanced)   54 **best alarumed**
wholly aroused   55 **Bold . . . right** confident in the rightness
of my cause   56 **gasted** struck aghast   59 **dispatch** i.e., he
will be killed   60 **arch** chief   64 **death** the same elliptical
form that characterizes "dispatch," line 59   66 **pight**
determined; **curst** angry

67 **discover** expose   68 **unpossessing** beggarly (landless)   69
**reposal** placing   71 **faithed** believed   73 **character** handwriting   74 **suggestion** instigation; **practice** device   75 **make
. . . world** think everyone stupid   76 **not thought** did not
think   77 **pregnant** teeming with incitement; **potential
spirits** powerful evil spirits   78 **fastened** hardened   79 **got**
begot   79 s.d. **Tucket** Cornwall's special trumpet call   81
**ports** exits, of whatever sort   85 **natural** (1) kind (filial) (2)
illegitimate   86 **capable** able to inherit   98 **consort** company
99 **ill affected** disposed to evil   100 **put** set   101 **expense
and waste** squandering

Edmund, I hear that you have shown your father
A childlike° office.

EDMUND                    It was my duty, sir.

GLOUCESTER
He did bewray his practice,° and received
This hurt you see, striving to apprehend him.

CORNWALL
Is he pursued?

GLOUCESTER  Ay, my good lord.                                    110

CORNWALL
If he be taken, he shall never more
Be feared of doing° harm. Make your own purpose,
How in my strength you please.° For you, Edmund,
Whose virtue and obedience° doth this instant
So much commend itself, you shall be ours.            115
Natures of such deep trust we shall much need;
You we first seize on.

EDMUND                    I shall serve you, sir,
Truly, however else.

GLOUCESTER             For him I thank your grace.

CORNWALL
You know not why we came to visit you?

REGAN
Thus out of season, threading dark-eyed night.       120
Occasions, noble Gloucester, of some prize,°
Wherein we must have use of your advice.
Our father he hath writ, so hath our sister,
Of differences,° which° I best thought it fit
To answer from° our home. The several messengers    125
From hence attend dispatch.° Our good old friend,
Lay comforts to your bosom,° and bestow
Your needful° counsel to our businesses,
Which craves the instant use.°

GLOUCESTER                      I serve you, madam.
Your graces are right welcome.     *Exeunt. Flourish.* 130

Scene II. [*Before Gloucester's castle.*]

*Enter* KENT *and* OSWALD, *severally.*

OSWALD  Good dawning° to thee, friend. Art of this
house?°

KENT  Ay.

OSWALD  Where may we set our horses?

KENT  I' th' mire.                                                5

OSWALD  Prithee, if thou lov'st me, tell me.

KENT  I love thee not.

OSWALD  Why then, I care not for thee.

KENT  If I had thee in Lipsbury Pinfold,° I would make
thee care for me.                                            10

107 **childlike** filial  108 **bewray his practice** disclose his plot
112 **of doing** because he might do  112–13 **Make . . .
please** Use my power freely, in carrying out your plans for his
capture  114 **virtue and obedience** virtuous obedience
121 **prize** importance  124 **differences** quarrels; **which**
referring not to "differences," but to the letter Lear has written
125 **from** away from  126 **attend dispatch** are waiting to be
sent off  127 **Lay . . . bosom** console yourself (about Edgar's
supposed treason)  128 **needful** needed  129 **craves . . .
use** demands immediate transaction
II.ii.1 **dawning** dawn is impending, but not yet arrived  1–2
**Art . . . house** Do you live here?  9 **Lipsbury Pinfold** a
pound or pen in which strayed animals are enclosed ("Lipsbury"
may denote a particular place, or may be slang for "between
my teeth")

OSWALD  Why dost thou use me thus? I know thee
not.

KENT  Fellow, I know thee.

OSWALD  What dost thou know me for?

KENT  A knave, a rascal, an eater of broken meats;°   15
a base, proud, shallow, beggarly, three-suited,°
hundred-pound,° filthy worsted-stocking° knave; a
lily-livered, action-taking,° whoreson, glass-gazing,°
superserviceable,° finical° rogue; one-trunk-inheriting°
slave; one that wouldst be a bawd in way of good   20
service,° and art nothing but the composition° of a
knave, beggar, coward, pander, and the son and heir of
a mongrel bitch; one whom I will beat into clamorous
whining if thou deniest the least syllable of thy
addition.°                                                     25

OSWALD  Why, what a monstrous fellow art thou,
thus to rail on one that is neither known of thee nor
knows thee!

KENT  What a brazen-faced varlet art thou to deny
thou knowest me! Is it two days since I tripped up   30
thy heels and beat thee before the king? [*Drawing his
sword.*] Draw, you rogue, for though it be night, yet
the moon shines. I'll make a sop o' th' moonshine° of
you. You whoreson cullionly barbermonger,° draw!

OSWALD  Away, I have nothing to do with thee.         35

KENT  Draw, you rascal. You come with letters
against the king, and take Vanity the puppet's° part
against the royalty of her father. Draw, you rogue,
or I'll so carbonado° your shanks. Draw, you rascal.
Come your ways!°                                             40

OSWALD  Help, ho! Murder! Help!

KENT  Strike, you slave! Stand, rogue! Stand, you
neat° slave! Strike!

[*Beating him*]

OSWALD  Help, ho! Murder, murder!

*Enter* EDMUND, *with his rapier drawn,* CORNWALL,
REGAN, GLOUCESTER, SERVANTS.

EDMUND  How now? What's the matter? Part!          45

KENT  With you,° goodman boy,° if you please!
Come, I'll flesh° ye, come on, young master.

GLOUCESTER  Weapons? Arms? What's the matter
here?

CORNWALL  Keep peace, upon your lives. He dies   50
that strikes again. What is the matter?

15 **broken meats** scraps of food  16 **three-suited** the
wardrobe permitted to a servant or "knave"  17 **hundred-
pound** the extent of Oswald's wealth, and thus a sneer at his
aspiring to gentility; **worsted-stocking** worn by servants  18
**action-taking** one who refuses a fight and goes to law instead;
**glass-gazing** conceited  19 **superserviceable** sycophantic,
serving without principle; **finical** overfastidious; **one-trunk-
inheriting** possessing only a trunkful of goods  20–21 **bawd
. . . service** pimp, to please his master  21 **composition**
compound  25 **addition** titles  33 **sop . . . moonshine** i.e.,
Oswald will admit the moonlight, and so sop it up, through the
open wounds Kent is preparing to give him  34 **cullionly
barbermonger** base patron of hairdressers (effeminate man)
37 **Vanity the puppet's** Goneril, here identified with one of
the personified characters in the morality plays, which were
sometimes put on as puppet shows  39 **carbonado** cut across,
like a piece of meat before cooking  40 **Come your ways**
Get along!  43 **neat** (1) foppish (2) unmixed, as in "neat wine"
46 **With you** i.e., the quarrel is with you; **goodman boy**
young man (peasants are "goodmen"; "boy" is a term of
contempt)  47 **flesh** introduce to blood (term from hunting)

REGAN    The messengers from our sister and the king.

CORNWALL    What is your difference?° Speak.

OSWALD    I am scarce in breath, my lord.

KENT    No marvel, you have so bestirred° your valor. 55
You cowardly rascal, nature disclaims in thee.° A
tailor made thee.°

CORNWALL    Thou art a strange fellow. A tailor make
a man?

KENT    A tailor, sir. A stonecutter or a painter could 60
not have made him so ill, though they had been but
two years o' th' trade.

CORNWALL
Speak yet, how grew your quarrel?

OSWALD    This ancient ruffian, sir, whose life I have
spared at suit of° his gray beard—                    65

KENT    Thou whoreson zed,° thou unnecessary letter!
My lord, if you will give me leave, I will tread this
unbolted° villain into mortar and daub the wall of a
jakes° with him. Spare my gray beard, you wagtail!°

CORNWALL
Peace, sirrah!                                        70
You beastly° knave, know you no reverence?

KENT
Yes, sir, but anger hath a privilege.

CORNWALL
Why art thou angry?

KENT
That such a slave as this should wear a sword,
Who wears no honesty. Such smiling rogues as these, 75
Like rats, oft bite the holy cords° atwain
Which are too intrince° t' unloose; smooth° every
    passion
That in the natures of their lords rebel,
Being oil to fire, snow to the colder moods;
Renege,° affirm, and turn their halcyon beaks°       80
With every gale and vary° of their masters,
Knowing naught, like dogs, but following.
A plague upon your epileptic° visage!
Smile you° my speeches, as I were a fool?
Goose, if I had you upon Sarum Plain,°               85
I'd drive ye cackling home to Camelot.°

CORNWALL
What, art thou mad, old fellow?

GLOUCESTER
How fell you out? Say that.

KENT
No contraries° hold more antipathy

Than I and such a knave.                              90

CORNWALL
Why dost thou call him knave? What is his fault?

KENT
His countenance likes° me not.

CORNWALL
No more perchance does mine, nor his, nor hers.

KENT
Sir, 'tis my occupation to be plain:
I have seen better faces in my time                   95
Than stands on any shoulder that I see
Before me at this instant.

CORNWALL                      This is some fellow
Who, having been praised for bluntness, doth affect
A saucy roughness, and constrains the garb
Quite from his nature.° He cannot flatter, he;        100
An honest mind and plain, he must speak truth.
And° they will take it, so; if not, he's plain.
These kind of knaves I know, which in this
    plainness
Harbor more craft and more corrupter ends
Than twenty silly-ducking observants°                 105
That stretch their duties nicely.°

KENT
Sir, in good faith, in sincere verity,
Under th' allowance° of your great aspect,°
Whose influence,° like the wreath of radiant fire
On flick'ring Phoebus' front°—

CORNWALL                          What mean'st by this? 110

KENT    To go out of my dialect,° which you discom-
mend so much. I know, sir, I am no flatterer. He° that
beguiled you in a plain accent was a plain knave,
which, for my part, I will not be, though I should
win your displeasure to entreat me to't.°             115

CORNWALL
What was th' offense you gave him?

OSWALD
I never gave him any.
It pleased the king his master very late°
To strike at me, upon his misconstruction;°
When he, compact,° and flattering his displeasure,   120
Tripped me behind; being down, insulted, railed,
And put upon him such a deal of man°
That worthied him,° got praises of the king
For him attempting who was self-subdued;°
And, in the fleshment° of this dread exploit,         125
Drew on me here again.

53 difference quarrel  55 bestirred exercised  56 nature
. . . thee nature renounces any part in you  56–57 A tailor
made thee from the proverb "The tailor makes the man"
65 at suit of out of pity for  66 zed the letter Z, generally omitted in contemporary dictionaries  68 unbolted
unsifted, i.e., altogether a villain  69 jakes privy; wagtail
a bird that bobs its tail up and down, and thus suggests obsequiousness  71 beastly irrational  76 holy cords sacred bonds
of affection (as between husbands and wives, parents and
children)  77 intrince entangled, intricate;  smooth
appease  80 Renege deny; halcyon beaks the halcyon or
kingfisher serves here as a type of the opportunist because,
when hung up by the tail or neck, it was supposed to turn with
the wind, like a weathervane  81 gale and vary varying gale
(hendiadys)  83 epileptic distorted by grinning  84 Smile
you do you smile at  85 Sarum Plain Salisbury Plain  86
Camelot the residence of King Arthur (presumably a
particular point, now lost, is intended here)  89 contraries
opposites

92 likes pleases  99–100 constrains . . . nature forces the
manner of candid speech to be a cloak, not for candor but for
craft  102 And if  105 silly-ducking observants ridiculously
obsequious attendants  106 nicely punctiliously  108 allowance
approval; aspect (1) appearance (2) position of the heavenly
bodies  109 influence astrological power  110 Phoebus' front
forehead of the sun  111 dialect customary manner of
speaking  112 He i.e., the sort of candid-crafty man
Cornwall has been describing  114–15 though . . . to't even
if I were to succeed in bringing your graceless person
("displeasure" personified, and in lieu of the expected form,
"your grace") to beg me to be a plain knave  118 very late
recently  119 misconstruction misunderstanding  120 compact in league with the king  122 put . . . man pretended
such manly behavior  123 worthied him made him seem
heroic  124 For . . . self-subdued for attacking a man
(Oswald) who offered no resistance  125 fleshment the blood-
thirstiness excited by his first success or "fleshing"

KENT                    None of these rogues and cowards
But Ajax is their fool.°
CORNWALL                    Fetch forth the stocks!
You stubborn° ancient knave, you reverent° braggart,
We'll teach you.
KENT                    Sir, I am too old to learn.
Call not your stocks for me, I serve the king,                    130
On whose employment I was sent to you.
You shall do small respect, show too bold malice
Against the grace and person° of my master,
Stocking his messenger.
CORNWALL
Fetch forth the stocks. As I have life and honor,                    135
There shall he sit till noon.
REGAN
Till noon? Till night, my lord, and all night too.
KENT
Why, madam, if I were your father's dog,
You should not use me so.
REGAN                    Sir, being his knave, I will.
CORNWALL
This is a fellow of the selfsame color°                    140
Our sister speaks of. Come, bring away° the stocks.

*Stocks brought out.*

GLOUCESTER
Let me beseech your grace not to do so.
His fault is much, and the good king his master
Will check° him for't. Your purposed° low correction
Is such as basest and contemnèd'st° wretches                    145
For pilf'rings and most common trespasses
Are punished with.
The king his master needs must take it ill
That he, so slightly valued in° his messenger,
Should have him thus restrained.
CORNWALL                    I'll answer° that.                    150
REGAN
My sister may receive it much more worse,
To have her gentleman abused, assaulted,
For following her affairs. Put in his legs.

[KENT *is put in the stocks.*]

Come, my good lord, away!
                    [*Exeunt all but* GLOUCESTER *and* KENT.]
GLOUCESTER
I am sorry for thee, friend. 'Tis the duke's pleasure,                    155
Whose disposition° all the world well knows
Will not be rubbed° nor stopped. I'll entreat for thee.
KENT
Pray do not, sir. I have watched° and traveled hard.
Some time I shall sleep out, the rest I'll whistle.
A good man's fortune may grow out at heels.°                    160

Give° you good morrow.
GLOUCESTER
The duke's to blame in this. 'Twill be ill taken.° *Exit.*
KENT
Good king, that must approve° the common saw,°
Thou out of heaven's benediction com'st
To the warm sun.°                    165
Approach, thou beacon to this under globe,°
That by thy comfortable° beams I may
Peruse this letter. Nothing almost sees miracles
But misery.° I know 'tis from Cordelia,
Who hath most fortunately been informed                    170
Of my obscurèd° course. And shall find time
From this enormous state, seeking to give
Losses their remedies.° All weary and o'erwatched,
Take vantage,° heavy eyes, not to behold
This shameful lodging. Fortune, good night;                    175
Smile once more, turn thy wheel.°

*Sleeps.*

[Scene III. *A wood.*]

*Enter* EDGAR.

EDGAR
I heard myself proclaimed,
And by the happy° hollow of a tree
Escaped the hunt. No port is free, no place
That guard and most unusual vigilance
Does not attend my taking.° Whiles I may 'scape,                    5
I will preserve myself; and am bethought°
To take the basest and most poorest shape
That ever penury, in contempt of man,
Brought near to beast;° my face I'll grime with filth,
Blanket° my loins, elf° all my hairs in knots,                    10
And with presented° nakedness outface°
The winds and persecutions of the sky.
The country gives me proof° and precedent
Of Bedlam° beggars, who, with roaring voices,
Strike° in their numbed and mortified° bare arms                    15
Pins, wooden pricks,° nails, sprigs of rosemary;
And with this horrible object° from low° farms,
Poor pelting° villages, sheepcotes, and mills,
Sometimes with lunatic bans,° sometime with
     prayers,

126–27 None . . . fool i.e., cowardly rogues like Oswald always impose on fools like Cornwall (who is likened to Ajax: [1] the braggart Greek warrior [2] a jakes or privy) 128 stubborn rude; reverent old 133 grace and person i.e., Lear as sovereign and in his personal character 140 color kind 141 away out 144 check correct; purposed intended 145 contemnèd'st most despised 149 slightly valued in little honored in the person of 150 answer answer for 156 disposition inclination 157 rubbed diverted (metaphor from the game of bowls) 158 watched gone without sleep 160 A . . . heels Even a good man may have bad fortune

161 Give God give 162 taken received 163 approve confirm; saw proverb 164–65 Thou . . . sun i.e., Lear goes from better to worse, from heaven's blessing or shelter to lack of shelter 166 beacon . . . globe i.e., the sun, whose rising Kent anticipates comforting 168–69 Nothing . . . misery i.e., True perception belongs only to the wretched 171 obscurèd disguised 171–73 shall . . . remedies a possible reading: Cordelia, away from this monstrous state of things, will find occasion to right the wrongs we suffer 174 vantage advantage (of sleep) 176 turn thy wheel i.e., so that Kent, who is at the bottom, may climb upward II.iii.2 happy lucky 5 attend my taking watch to capture me 6 am bethought have decided 8–9 penury . . . beast poverty, to show how contemptible man is, reduced to the level of a beast 10 Blanket cover only with a blanket; elf tangle (into "elflocks," supposed to be caused by elves) 11 presented the show of; outface brave 13 proof example 14 Bedlam see I.ii.138–39 15 Strike stick; mortified not alive to pain 16 pricks skewers 17 object spectacle; low humble 18 pelting paltry 19 bans curses

Enforce their charity. Poor Turlygod, Poor Tom,°    20
That's something yet: Edgar I nothing am.°    *Exit.*

[*Scene IV. Before Gloucester's castle.* KENT *in the stocks.*]

*Enter* LEAR, FOOL, *and* GENTLEMAN.

LEAR
'Tis strange that they should so depart from home,
And not send back my messenger.
GENTLEMAN            As I learned,
The night before there was no purpose° in them
Of this remove.°
KENT          Hail to thee, noble master.
LEAR   Ha!                          5
Mak'st thou this shame thy pastime?°
KENT             No, my lord.
FOOL   Ha, ha, he wears cruel° garters. Horses are tied
by the heads, dogs and bears by th' neck, monkeys by
th' loins, and men by th' legs. When a man's overlusty
at legs,° then he wears wooden netherstocks.°    10
LEAR
What's he that hath so much thy place mistook
To set thee here?
KENT         It is both he and she,
Your son and daughter.
LEAR   No.
KENT   Yes.                          15
LEAR   No, I say.
KENT   I say yea.
LEAR   No, no, they would not.
KENT   Yes, they have.
LEAR
By Jupiter, I swear no!                20
KENT
By Juno, I swear ay!
LEAR           They durst not do't;
They could not, would not do't. 'Tis worse than
murder
To do upon respect° such violent outrage.
Resolve° me with all modest° haste which way
Thou mightst deserve or they impose this usage,    25
Coming from us.
KENT         My lord, when at their home
I did commend° your highness' letters to them,
Ere I was risen from the place that showed
My duty kneeling, came there a reeking post,°
Stewed° in his haste, half breathless, panting forth    30
From Goneril his mistress salutations,
Delivered letters, spite of intermission,°
Which presently° they read; on° whose contents

They summoned up their meiny,° straight took
horse,
Commanded me to follow and attend    35
The leisure of their answer, gave me cold looks,
And meeting here the other messenger,
Whose welcome I perceived had poisoned mine,
Being the very fellow which of late
Displayed° so saucily against your highness,    40
Having more man than wit° about me, drew;
He raised° the house, with loud and coward cries.
Your son and daughter found this trespass worth°
The shame which here it suffers.
FOOL   Winter's not gone yet, if the wild geese fly that    45
way.°
       Fathers that wear rags
         Do make their children blind,°
       But fathers that bear bags°
         Shall see their children kind.    50
       Fortune, that arrant whore,
         Ne'er turns the key° to th' poor.
But for all this, thou shalt have as many dolors° for
thy daughters as thou canst tell° in a year.
LEAR
O, how this mother° swells up toward my heart!    55
Hysterica passio,° down, thou climbing sorrow,
Thy element's° below. Where is this daughter?
KENT
With the earl, sir, here within.
LEAR                Follow me not;
Stay here.                     *Exit.*
GENTLEMAN
Made you no more offense but what you speak of?    60
KENT   None.
How chance° the king comes with so small a number?
FOOL   And° thou hadst been set i' th' stocks for that
question, thou'dst well deserved it.
KENT   Why, Fool?                    65
FOOL   We'll set thee to school to an ant, to teach thee
there's no laboring i' th' winter.° All that follow their
noses are led by their eyes but blind men, and there's
not a nose among twenty but can smell him that's
stinking.° Let go thy hold when a great wheel runs    70
down a hill, lest it break thy neck with following. But
the great one that goes upward, let him draw thee
after. When a wise man gives thee better counsel, give
me mine again. I would have none but knaves follow
it since a fool gives it.                75

---

20 **Poor . . . Tom** Edgar recites the names a Bedlam beggar
gives himself   21 **That's . . . am** There's a chance for me in
that I am no longer known for myself
**II.iv.3 purpose** intention   4 **remove** removal   6 **Mak'st . . .
pastime** Are you doing this to amuse yourself?   7 **cruel** (1)
painful (2) "crewel," a worsted yarn used in garters   9–10
**overlusty at legs** (1) a vagabond (2) sexually promiscuous (?)
10 **netherstocks** stockings (as opposed to knee breeches, or
upperstocks)   23 **upon respect** (1) on the respect due to the king
(2) deliberately   24 **Resolve** inform; **modest** becoming   27
**commend** deliver   29 **reeking post** sweating messenger   30
**stewed** steaming   32 **spite of intermission** in spite of the
interrupting of my business   33 **presently** at once; **on** on the
strength of

34 **meiny** retinue   40 **Displayed** showed off   41 **more . . .
wit** more manhood than sense   42 **raised** aroused   43 **worth**
deserving   45–46 **Winter's . . . way** More trouble is
to come, since Cornwall and Regan act so ("geese" is
used contemptuously, as in Kent's quarrel with Oswald,
II.ii.85–86)   48 **blind** i.e., indifferent   49 **bags** moneybags
52 **turns the key** i.e., opens the door   53 **dolors** (1)
sorrows (2) dollars (English name for Spanish and
German coins)   54 **tell** (1) tell about (2) count   55–56
**mother . . . Hysterica passio** hysteria, causing suffocation or choking   57 **element** proper place   62 **How
chance** how does it happen that   63 **And** if   66–67 **We'll
. . . winter** in the popular fable the ant, unlike the improvident grasshopper, anticipates the winter when none can labor
by laying up provisions in the summer; Lear, trusting foolishly
to summer days, finds himself unprovided for, and unable to
provide, now that "winter" has come   67–70 **All . . .
stinking** i.e., all can smell out the decay of Lear's fortunes

That sir, which serves and seeks for gain,
    And follows but for form,°
Will pack,° when it begins to rain,
    And leave thee in the storm.
But I will tarry; the Fool will stay,        80
    And let the wise man fly.
The knave turns Fool that runs away,
    The Fool no knave,° perdy.°

KENT  Where learned you this, Fool?

FOOL  Not i' th' stocks, fool.        85

*Enter* LEAR *and* GLOUCESTER.

LEAR
Deny° to speak with me? They are sick, they are
    weary,
They have traveled all the night? Mere fetches,°
The images° of revolt and flying off!°
Fetch me a better answer.

GLOUCESTER          My dear lord,
You know the fiery quality° of the duke,        90
How unremovable and fixed he is
In his own course.

LEAR         Vengeance, plague, death, confusion!
Fiery? What quality? Why, Gloucester, Gloucester,
I'd speak with the Duke of Cornwall and his wife.

GLOUCESTER
Well, my good lord, I have informed them so.    95

LEAR
Informed them? Dost thou understand me, man?

GLOUCESTER
Ay, my good lord.

LEAR
The king would speak with Cornwall. The dear father
Would with his daughter speak, commands—tends°—
    service.
Are they informed of this? My breath and blood!    100
Fiery? The fiery duke, tell the hot duke that—
No, but not yet. May be he is not well.
Infirmity doth still neglect all office
Whereto our health is bound.° We are not ourselves
When nature, being oppressed, commands the mind  105
To suffer with the body. I'll forbear;
And am fallen out° with my more headier will°
To take the indisposed and sickly fit
For the sound man. [*Looking on* KENT.] Death on my
    state!° Wherefore
Should he sit here? This act persuades me    110
That this remotion° of the duke and her
Is practice° only. Give me my servant forth.°
Go tell the duke and's wife I'd speak with them!
Now, presently!° Bid them come forth and hear me,

Or at their chamber door I'll beat the drum    115
Till it cry sleep to death.°

GLOUCESTER
I would have all well betwixt you.        *Exit.*

LEAR
O me, my heart, my rising heart! But down!

FOOL  Cry to it, nuncle, as the cockney° did to the
eels when she put 'em i' th' paste° alive. She knapped°  120
'em o' th' coxcombs° with a stick and cried, "Down,
wantons,° down!" 'Twas her brother that, in pure
kindness to his horse, buttered his hay.°

*Enter* CORNWALL, REGAN, GLOUCESTER, SER-
VANTS.

LEAR
Good morrow to you both.

CORNWALL            Hail to your grace.

KENT *here set at liberty.*

REGAN
I am glad to see your highness.    125

LEAR
Regan, I think you are. I know what reason
I have to think so. If thou shouldst not be glad,
I would divorce me from thy mother's tomb,
Sepulchring an adultress.° [*To* KENT.] O, are you free?
Some other time for that. Beloved Regan,    130
Thy sister's naught.° O Regan, she hath tied
Sharp-toothed unkindness, like a vulture, here.

[*Points to his heart.*]

I can scarce speak to thee. Thou'lt not believe
With how depraved a quality°—O Regan!

REGAN
I pray you, sir, take patience. I have hope .    135
You less know how to value her desert
Than she to scant her duty.°

LEAR         Say? how is that?

REGAN
I cannot think my sister in the least
Would fail her obligation. If, sir, perchance
She have restrained the riots of your followers,    140
'Tis on such ground, and to such wholesome end,
As clears her from all blame.

LEAR
My curses on her!

REGAN         O, sir, you are old,
Nature in you stands on the very verge
Of his confine.° You should be ruled, and led    145

---

**77 form** show  **78 pack** be off  **82–83 The . . . knave** i.e., the faithless man is the true fool, for wisdom requires fidelity; Lear's Fool, who remains faithful, is at least no knave  **83 perdy** by God (French *par Dieu*)  **86 Deny** refuse  **87 fetches** subterfuges, acts of tacking (nautical metaphor)  **88 images** exact likenesses; **flying off** desertion  **90 quality** temperament  **99 tends** attends (i.e., awaits); with, possibly, an ironic second meaning, "tenders," or "offers"  **104 Whereto . . . bound** duties which we are required to perform, when in health  **107 fallen out** angry; **headier will** headlong inclination  **109 state** royal condition  **111 remotion** (1) removal (2) remaining aloof  **112 practice** pretense; **forth** i.e., out of the stocks  **114 presently** at once

**116 cry . . . death** follow sleep, like a cry or pack of hounds, until it kills it  **119 cockney** Londoner (ignorant city dweller)  **120 paste** pastry pie; **knapped** rapped  **121 coxcombs** heads  **122 wantons** i.e., playful things (with a sexual implication)  **123 buttered his hay** i.e., the city dweller does from ignorance what the dishonest ostler does from craft: greases the hay the traveler has paid for, so that the horse will not eat  **128–29 divorce . . . adultress** i.e., repudiate your dead mother as having conceived you by another man  **131 naught** wicked  **134 quality** nature  **135–37 I have . . . duty** despite the double negative, the passage means, "I believe that you fail to give Goneril her due, rather than that she fails to fulfill her duty"  **144–45 Nature . . . confine** i.e., you are nearing the end of your life

By some discretion that discerns your state
Better than you yourself.° Therefore I pray you
That to our sister you do make return,
Say you have wronged her.

LEAR                    Ask her forgiveness?
Do you but mark how this becomes the house:°          150
"Dear daughter, I confess that I am old.

[*Kneeling.*]

Age is unnecessary. On my knees I beg
That you'll vouchsafe me raiment, bed, and food."

REGAN
Good sir, no more. These are unsightly tricks.
Return you to my sister.

LEAR          [*Rising.*] Never, Regan.          155
She hath abated° me of half my train,
Looked black upon me, struck me with her tongue,
Most serpentlike, upon the very heart.
All the stored vengeances of heaven fall
On her ingrateful top!° Strike her young bones,°          160
You taking° airs, with lameness.

CORNWALL               Fie, sir, fie!

LEAR
You nimble lightnings, dart your blinding flames
Into her scornful eyes! Infect her beauty,
You fen-sucked° fogs, drawn by the pow'rful sun,
To fall and blister° her pride.

REGAN               O the blest gods!          165
So will you wish on me when the rash mood is on.

LEAR
No, Regan, thou shalt never have my curse.
Thy tender-hefted° nature shall not give
Thee o'er to harshness. Her eyes are fierce, but
        thine
Do comfort, and not burn. 'Tis not in thee          170
To grudge my pleasures, to cut off my train,
To bandy° hasty words, to scant my sizes,°
And, in conclusion, to oppose the bolt°
Against my coming in. Thou better know'st
The offices of nature, bond of childhood,°          175
Effects° of courtesy, dues of gratitude.
Thy half o' th' kingdom hast thou not forgot,
Wherein I thee endowed.

REGAN               Good sir, to th' purpose.°

*Tucket within.*

LEAR
Who put my man i' th' stocks?

CORNWALL               What trumpet's that?

REGAN
I know't—my sister's. This approves° her letter,          180

That she would soon be here.

*Enter* OSWALD.

                              Is your lady come?

LEAR
This is a slave, whose easy borrowed° pride
Dwells in the fickle grace° of her he follows.
Out, varlet,° from my sight.

CORNWALL               What means your grace?

LEAR
Who stocked my servant? Regan, I have good hope          185
Thou didst not know on't.

*Enter* GONERIL.

                    Who comes here? O heavens!
If you do love old men, if your sweet sway
Allow° obedience, if you yourselves are old,
Make it° your cause. Send down, and take my part.

[*To* GONERIL.]

Art not ashamed to look upon this beard?          190
O Regan, will you take her by the hand?

GONERIL
Why not by th' hand, sir? How have I offended?
All's not offense that indiscretion finds°
And dotage terms so.

LEAR               O sides,° you are too tough!
Will you yet hold? How came my man i' th' stocks?          195

CORNWALL
I set him there, sir; but his own disorders°
Deserved much less advancement.°

LEAR               You? Did you?

REGAN
I pray you, father, being weak, seem so.°
If till the expiration of your month
You will return and sojourn with my sister,          200
Dismissing half your train, come then to me.
I am now from home, and out of that provision
Which shall be needful for your entertainment.°

LEAR
Return to her, and fifty men dismissed?
No, rather I abjure all roofs, and choose          205
To wage° against the enmity o' th' air,
To be a comrade with the wolf and owl,
Necessity's sharp pinch.° Return with her?
Why, the hot-blooded° France, that dowerless took
Our youngest born, I could as well be brought          210
To knee° his throne, and, squirelike,° pension beg
To keep base life afoot. Return with her?
Persuade me rather to be slave and sumpter°
To this detested groom. [*Pointing at* OSWALD.]

GONERIL               At your choice, sir.

LEAR
I prithee, daughter, do not make me mad.          215
I will not trouble thee, my child; farewell.

**146–47 some . . . yourself** some discreet person
who understands your condition more than you do **150
becomes the house** suits my royal and paternal position **156
abated** curtailed **160 top** head; **young bones** the
reference may be to unborn children, rather than to Goneril
herself **161 taking** infecting **164 fen-sucked** drawn up from
swamps by the sun **165 fall and blister** fall upon and raise
blisters **168 tender-hefted** gently framed **172 bandy** volley
( metaphor from tennis); **scant my sizes** reduce my allowances
**173 oppose the bolt** bar the door **175 offices . . . childhood** natural duties, a child's duty to its parent **176 Effects**
manifestations **178 to th' purpose** come to the point **180
approves** confirms

**182 easy borrowed** (1) facile and taken from another (2)
acquired without anything to back it up (like money borrowed
without security) **183 grace** favor **184 varlet** base fellow
**188 Allow** approve of **189 it** my cause **193 finds** judges
**194 sides** breast **196 disorders** misconduct **197 advancement** promotion **198 seem so** act weak **203 entertainment**
maintenance **206 wage** fight **208 Necessity's sharp pinch**
a summing up of the hard choice he has just announced **209
hot-blooded** passionate **211 knee** kneel before; **squirelike**
like a retainer **213 sumpter** pack horse

We'll no more meet, no more see one another.
But yet thou art my flesh, my blood, my daughter,
Or rather a disease that's in my flesh,
Which I must needs call mine. Thou art a boil,          220
A plague-sore, or embossèd carbuncle°
In my corrupted blood. But I'll not chide thee.
Let shame come when it will, I do not call it.
I do not bid the Thunder-bearer° shoot,
Nor tell tales of thee to high-judging° Jove.          225
Mend when thou canst, be better at thy leisure,
I can be patient, I can stay with Regan,
I and my hundred knights.

REGAN                              Not altogether so.
I looked not for you yet, nor am provided
For your fit welcome. Give ear, sir, to my sister,     230
For those that mingle reason with your passion°
Must be content to think you old, and so—
But she knows what she does.

LEAR                               Is this well spoken?

REGAN
I dare avouch° it, sir. What, fifty followers?
Is it not well? What should you need of more?          235
Yea, or so many, sith that° both charge° and danger
Speak 'gainst so great a number? How in one house
Should many people, under two commands,
Hold° amity? 'Tis hard, almost impossible.

GONERIL
Why might not you, my lord, receive attendance        240
From those that she calls servants, or from mine?

REGAN
Why not, my lord? If then they chanced to slack° ye,
We could control them. If you will come to me
(For now I spy a danger), I entreat you
To bring but five-and-twenty. To no more              245
Will I give place or notice.°

LEAR
  I gave you all.

REGAN                  And in good time you gave it.

LEAR
Made you my guardians, my depositaries,°
But kept a reservation° to be followed
With such a number. What, must I come to you          250
With five-and-twenty? Regan, said you so?

REGAN
And speak't again, my lord. No more with me.

LEAR
Those wicked creatures yet do look well-favored°
When others are more wicked; not being the worst
Stands in some rank of praise.° [To GONERIL.] I'll go
  with thee.                                          255
Thy fifty yet doth double five-and-twenty,
And thou art twice her love.°

GONERIL                     Hear me, my lord.
What need you five-and-twenty? ten? or five?

To follow° in a house where twice so many
Have a command to tend you?

REGAN                              What need one?      260

LEAR
O reason° not the need! Our basest beggars
Are in the poorest thing superfluous.°
Allow not nature more than nature needs,°
Man's life is cheap as beast's. Thou art a lady:
If only to go warm were gorgeous,                     265
Why, nature needs not what thou gorgeous wear'st,
Which scarcely keeps thee warm.° But, for true need—
You heavens, give me that patience, patience I need.
You see me here, you gods, a poor old man,
As full of grief as age, wretched in both.            270
If it be you that stirs these daughters' hearts
Against their father, fool° me not so much
To bear° it tamely; touch me with noble anger,
And let not women's weapons, water drops,
Stain my man's cheeks. No, you unnatural hags!        275
I will have such revenges on you both
That all the world shall—I will do such things—
What they are, yet I know not; but they shall be
The terrors of the earth. You think I'll weep.
No, I'll not weep.                                    280

*Storm and tempest.*

I have full cause of weeping, but this heart
Shall break into a hundred thousand flaws°
Or ere° I'll weep. O Fool, I shall go mad!
     *Exeunt* LEAR, GLOUCESTER, KENT, *and* FOOL.

CORNWALL
Let us withdraw, 'twill be a storm.

REGAN
This house is little; the old man and's people        285
Cannot be well bestowed.°

GONERIL
'Tis his own blame; hath° put himself from rest°
And must needs taste his folly.

REGAN
For his particular,° I'll receive him gladly,
But not one follower.

GONERIL              So am I purposed.°               290
Where is my Lord of Gloucester?

CORNWALL
Followed the old man forth.

*Enter* GLOUCESTER.

                              He is returned.

GLOUCESTER
The king is in high rage.

CORNWALL                    Whither is he going?

GLOUCESTER
He calls to horse, but will I know not whither.

---

221 **embossèd carbuncle** swollen boil  224 **Thunder-bearer** Jupiter  225 **high-judging** (1) supreme (2) judging from heaven  231 **mingle . . . passion** i.e., consider your turbulent behavior coolly and reasonably  234 **avouch** swear by  236 **sith that** since;  **charge** expense  239 **Hold** preserve  242 **slack** neglect  246 **notice** recognition  248 **depositaries** trustees  249 **reservation** condition  253 **well-favored** handsome  254–55 **not . . . praise** i.e., that Goneril is not so bad as Regan is one thing in her favor  257 **her love** i.e., as loving as she

259 **follow** attend on you  261 **reason** scrutinize  262 **Are . . . superfluous** have some trifle not absolutely necessary  263 **needs** i.e., to sustain life  265–67 **If . . . warm** If to satisfy the need for warmth were to be gorgeous, you would not need the clothing you wear, which is worn more for beauty than warmth  272 **fool** humiliate  273 **To bear** as to make me bear  282 **flaws** (1) pieces (2) cracks (3) gusts of passion  283 **Or ere** before  286 **bestowed** lodged  287 **hath** he hath;  **rest** (1) place of residence (2) repose of mind  289 **his particular** himself personally  290 **purposed** determined

CORNWALL
'Tis best to give him way, he leads himself.°                     295

GONERIL
My lord, entreat him by no means to stay.

GLOUCESTER
Alack, the night comes on, and the high winds
Do sorely ruffle.° For many miles about
There's scarce a bush.

REGAN                              O, sir, to willful men
The injuries that they themselves procure                         300
Must be their schoolmasters. Shut up your doors.
He is attended with a desperate train,
And what they may incense° him to, being apt
To have his ear abused,° wisdom bids fear.

CORNWALL
Shut up your doors, my lord; 'tis a wild night.                   305
My Regan counsels well. Come out o' th' storm.
                                            *Exeunt.*

# ACT III

Scene I. [*A heath.*]

*Storm still.° Enter* KENT *and a* GENTLEMAN *severally.*

KENT
Who's there besides foul weather?

GENTLEMAN
One minded like the weather most unquietly.°

KENT
I know you. Where's the king?

GENTLEMAN
Contending with the fretful elements;
Bids the wind blow the earth into the sea,                         5
Or swell the curlèd waters 'bove the main,°
That things might change° or cease; tears his white hair,
Which the impetuous blasts, with eyeless° rage,
Catch in their fury, and make nothing of;
Strives in his little world of man° to outscorn                   10
The to-and-fro-conflicting wind and rain.
This night, wherein the cub-drawn° bear would
     couch,°
The lion, and the belly-pinchèd° wolf
Keep their fur dry, unbonneted° he runs,
And bids what will take all.°                                      15

KENT                              But who is with him?

GENTLEMAN
None but the Fool, who labors to outjest
His heart-struck injuries.

KENT                              Sir, I do know you,
And dare upon the warrant of my note°

295 **give . . . himself** let him go; he insists on his
own way 298 **ruffle** rage 303 **incense** incite 303–04
**being . . . abused** he being inclined to harken to bad counsel
III.i.s.d. **still** continually 2 **minded . . . unquietly** disturbed in mind, like the weather 6 **main** land 7 **change** (1)
be destroyed (2) be exchanged (i.e., turned upside down) (3)
change for the better 8 **eyeless** (1) blind (2) invisible 10
**little . . . man** the microcosm, as opposed to the universe or
macrocosm, which it copies in little 12 **cub-drawn** sucked
dry by her cubs, and so ravenously hungry; **couch** take shelter
in its lair 13 **belly-pinchèd** starved 14 **unbonneted** hatless
15 **take all** like the reckless gambler, staking all he has left
18 **warrant . . . note** strength of what I have taken note (of you)

Commend a dear thing° to you. There is division,
Although as yet the face of it is covered                          20
With mutual cunning, 'twixt Albany and Cornwall;
Who have—as who have not, that° their great stars
Throned° and set high?—servants, who seem no less,°
Which are to France the spies and speculations
Intelligent° of our state. What hath been seen,                    25
Either in snuffs and packings° of the dukes,
Or the hard rein which both of them hath borne°
Against the old kind king, or something deeper,
Whereof, perchance, these are but furnishings°—
But, true it is, from France there comes a power°                  30
Into this scattered° kingdom, who already,
Wise in our negligence, have secret feet
In some of our best ports, and are at point°
To show their open banner. Now to you:
If on my credit you dare build° so far                             35
To° make your speed to Dover, you shall find
Some that will thank you, making° just° report
Of how unnatural and bemadding° sorrow
The king hath cause to plain.°
I am a gentleman of blood and breeding,°                           40
And from some knowledge and assurance° offer
This office° to you.

GENTLEMAN
I will talk further with you.

KENT                              No, do not.
For confirmation that I am much more
Than my out-wall,° open this purse and take                        45
What it contains. If you shall see Cordelia,
As fear not but you shall, show her this ring,
And she will tell you who that fellow° is
That yet you do not know. Fie on this storm!
I will go seek the king.                                           50

GENTLEMAN
Give me your hand. Have you no more to say?

KENT
Few words, but, to effect,° more than all yet:
That when we have found the king—in which your
     pain°
That way, I'll this—he that first lights on him,
Holla the other.                          *Exeunt [severally].*     55

Scene II. [*Another part of the heath.*]

*Storm still. Enter* LEAR *and* FOOL.

LEAR
Blow, winds, and crack your cheeks. Rage, blow!
You cataracts and hurricanoes,° spout

19 **Commend . . . thing** entrust important business
22 **that** whom 22–23 **stars Throned** destinies have throned
23 **seem no less** seem to be so 24–25 **speculations Intelligent** giving intelligence 26 **snuffs and packings** quarrels
and plots 27 **hard . . . borne** close and cruel control they
have exercised 29 **furnishings** excuses 30 **power** army
31 **scattered** disunited 33 **at point** ready 35 **If . . . build**
if you can trust me, proceed 36 **To** as to 37 **making** for
making; **just** accurate 38 **bemadding** maddening 39 **plain**
complain of 40 **blood and breeding** noble family
41 **knowledge and assurance** sure and trustworthy information 42 **office** service (i.e., the trip to Dover) 45 **out-wall**
superficial appearance 48 **fellow** companion 52 **to effect**
in their importance 53 **pain** labor
III.ii.2 **hurricanoes** waterspouts

Till you have drenched our steeples, drowned the
  cocks.°
You sulph'rous and thought-executing° fires,
Vaunt-couriers° of oak-cleaving thunderbolts,          5
Singe my white head. And thou, all-shaking
  thunder,
Strike flat the thick rotundity° o' th' world,
Crack Nature's molds,° all germains spill° at once,
That makes ingrateful° man.

FOOL  O nuncle, court holy-water° in a dry house is  10
better than this rain water out o' door. Good nuncle,
in; ask thy daughters blessing. Here's a night pities
neither wise man nor fools.

LEAR
Rumble thy bellyful. Spit, fire. Spout, rain!
Nor rain, wind, thunder, fire are my daughters.       15
I tax° not you, you elements, with unkindness.
I never gave you kingdom, called you children,
You owe me no subscription.° Then let fall
Your horrible pleasure.° Here I stand your slave,
A poor, infirm, weak, and despised old man.           20
But yet I call you servile ministers,°
That will with two pernicious daughters join
Your high-engendered battles° 'gainst a head
So old and white as this. O, ho! 'tis foul.

FOOL  He that has a house to put's head in has a good  25
headpiece.°
      The codpiece° that will house
        Before the head as any,
      The head and he° shall louse:
        So beggars marry many.°                        30
      The man that makes his toe
        What he his heart should make
      Shall of a corn cry woe,
        And turn his sleep to wake.°
For there was never yet fair woman but she made       35
mouths in a glass.°

*Enter* KENT.

LEAR
No, I will be the pattern of all patience,
I will say nothing.
KENT  Who's there?

FOOL  Marry,° here's grace and a codpiece; that's a   40
wise man and a fool.°
KENT
Alas, sir, are you here? Things that love night
Love not such nights as these. The wrathful skies
Gallow° the very wanderers of the dark
And make them keep° their caves. Since I was man,    45
Such sheets of fire, such bursts of horrid° thunder,
Such groans of roaring wind and rain, I never
Remember to have heard. Man's nature cannot carry°
Th' affliction nor the fear.
LEAR                    Let the great gods
That keep this dreadful pudder° o'er our heads        50
Find out their enemies now.° Tremble, thou wretch,
That hast within thee undivulgèd crimes
Unwhipped of justice. Hide thee, thou bloody hand,
Thou perjured,° and thou simular° of virtue
That art incestuous. Caitiff,° to pieces shake,       55
That under covert and convenient seeming
Has practiced on° man's life. Close° pent-up guilts,
Rive° your concealing continents° and cry
These dreadful summoners grace.° I am a man
More sinned against than sinning.
KENT                        Alack, bareheaded?        60
Gracious my lord,° hard by here is a hovel;
Some friendship will it lend you 'gainst the tempest.
Repose you there, while I to this hard house
(More harder than the stones whereof 'tis raised,
Which even but now, demanding after° you,            65
Denied me to come in) return, and force
Their scanted° courtesy.
LEAR                    My wits begin to turn.
Come on, my boy. How dost, my boy? Art cold?
I am cold myself. Where is this straw, my fellow?
The art° of our necessities is strange,              70
That can make vile things precious. Come, your hovel.
Poor Fool and knave, I have one part in my heart
That's sorry yet for thee.
FOOL [*Singing.*]
      He that has and a little tiny wit,
        With heigh-ho, the wind and the rain,        75
      Must make content with his fortunes fit,°
        Though the rain it raineth every day.
LEAR  True, my good boy. Come, bring us to this
hovel.                        *Exit, [with* KENT].
FOOL  This is a brave° night to cool a courtesan. I'll  80
speak a prophecy ere I go:

---

**3 cocks** weathercocks  **4 thought-executing** (1) doing
execution as quick as thought (2) executing or carrying out the thought of him who hurls the lightning
**5 Vaunt-couriers** heralds, scouts who range before the
main body of the army  **7 rotundity** i.e., not only the
sphere of the globe, but the roundness of gestation (Delius)
**8 Nature's molds** the molds or forms in which men are made;
**all germains spill** destroy the basic seeds of life  **9 ingrateful**
ungrateful  **10 court holy-water** flattery  **16 tax** accuse
**18 subscription** allegiance, submission  **19 pleasure** will
**21 ministers** agents  **23 high-engendered battles** armies
formed in the heavens  **26 headpiece** (1) helmet (2) brain
**27 codpiece** penis (literally, padding worn at the crotch of a
man's hose)  **29 he** it  **30 many** i.e., lice  **27–30 The . . .
many** The man who gratifies his sexual appetites before he
has a roof over his head will end up a lousy beggar
**31–34 The . . . wake** The man who, ignoring the fit order of
things, elevates what is base above what is noble, will suffer for
it as Lear has, in banishing Cordelia and enriching her sisters
**35–36 made . . . glass** posed before a mirror (irrelevant
nonsense, except that it calls to mind the general theme of
vanity and folly)

**40 Marry** a mild oath, from "By the Virgin Mary"
**40–41 here's . . . fool** Kent's question is answered: the
king ("grace") is here, as well as the Fool—who customarily wears an exaggerated codpiece; but which is
left ambiguous, since Lear has previously been called a
codpiece  **44 Gallow** frighten  **45 keep** remain inside  **46
horrid** horrible  **48 carry** endure  **50 pudder** turmoil  **51
Find . . . now** i.e., discover sinners by the terror they reveal
**54 perjured** perjurer; **simular** counterfeiter  **55 Caitiff**
wretch  **56 seeming** hypocrisy  **57 practiced on** plotted
against; **Close** hidden  **58 Rive** split open; **continents**
containers  **58–59 cry . . . grace** beg mercy from the vengeful gods (here figured as officers who summoned a man charged
with immorality before the ecclesiastical court)  **61 Gracious
my lord** my gracious lord  **65 demanding after** asking for
**67 scanted** stinted  **70 art** magic powers of the alchemists,
who sought to transmute base metals into precious  **76 Must
. . . fit** must be satisfied with a fortune as tiny as his wit  **80
brave** fine

When priests are more in word than matter;
When brewers mar their malt with water;
When nobles are their tailors' tutors,
No heretics burned, but wenches' suitors;°        85
When every case in law is right,
No squire in debt nor no poor knight;
When slanders do not live in tongues;
Nor cutpurses come not to throngs;
When usurers tell their gold i' th' field,°        90
And bawds and whores do churches build,°
Then shall the realm of Albion°
Come to great confusion.
Then comes the time, who lives to see't,
That going shall be used with feet.°        95
This prophecy Merlin° shall make, for I live before
his time.                                    *Exit.*

### Scene III. [*Gloucester's castle.*]

*Enter* GLOUCESTER *and* EDMUND.

GLOUCESTER  Alack, alack, Edmund, I like not this
unnatural dealing. When I desired their leave that I
might pity° him, they took from me the use of mine
own house, charged me on pain of perpetual displeasure neither to speak of him, entreat for him, or  5
any way sustain° him.

EDMUND  Most savage and unnatural.

GLOUCESTER  Go to; say you nothing. There is
division° between the dukes, and a worse° matter than
that. I have received a letter this night—'tis dangerous  10
to be spoken°—I have locked the letter in my closet.°
These injuries the king now bears will be revenged
home;° there is part of a power° already footed;° we
must incline to° the king. I will look° him and privily°
relieve him. Go you and maintain talk with the duke,  15
that my charity be not of° him perceived. If he ask for
me, I am ill and gone to bed. If I die for it, as no less is
threatened me, the king my old master must be
relieved. There is strange things toward,° Edmund;
pray you be careful.                         *Exit.*  20

EDMUND
This courtesy forbid° thee shall the duke
Instantly know, and of that letter too.
This seems a fair deserving,° and must draw me

---

That which my father loses—no less than all.
The younger rises when the old doth fall.        *Exit.*  25

### Scene IV. [*The heath. Before a hovel.*]

*Enter* LEAR, KENT, *and* FOOL.

KENT
Here is the place, my lord. Good my lord, enter.
The tyranny of the open night's too rough
For nature to endure. *Storm still.*
LEAR                          Let me alone.
KENT
Good my lord, enter here.
LEAR                          Wilt break my heart?°
KENT
I had rather break mine own. Good my lord, enter.  5
LEAR
Thou think'st 'tis much that this contentious storm
Invades us to the skin: so 'tis to thee;
But where the greater malady is fixed,°
The lesser is scarce felt. Thou'dst shun a bear;
But if thy flight lay toward the roaring sea,        10
Thou'dst meet the bear i' th' mouth.° When the
    mind's free,°
The body's delicate. The tempest in my mind
Doth from my senses take all feeling else,
Save what beats there. Filial ingratitude,
Is it not as° this mouth should tear this hand        15
For lifting food to't? But I will punish home.°
No, I will weep no more. In such a night
To shut me out! Pour on, I will endure.
In such a night as this! O Regan, Goneril,
Your old kind father, whose frank° heart gave all—  20
O, that way madness lies; let me shun that.
No more of that.
KENT                          Good my lord, enter here.
LEAR
Prithee go in thyself; seek thine own ease.
This tempest will not give me leave to ponder
On things would hurt me more, but I'll go in.        25

[*To the* FOOL.]

In, boy; go first. You houseless poverty°—
Nay, get thee in. I'll pray, and then I'll sleep.
                                    *Exit* [FOOL].
Poor naked wretches, wheresoe'er you are,
That bide° the pelting of this pitiless storm,
How shall your houseless heads and unfed sides,    30
Your looped and windowed° raggedness, defend you
From seasons such as these? O, I have ta'en
Too little care of this! Take physic, pomp;°
Expose thyself to feel what wretches feel,
That thou mayst shake the superflux° to them,        35
And show the heavens more just.

---

82–85  **When . . . suitors** the first four prophecies
are fulfilled already, and hence "confusion" has come
to England: the priest does not suit his action to his
words; the brewer adulterates his beer; the nobleman is subservient to his tailor (i.e., cares only for fashion); religious
heretics escape, and only those burn (i.e., suffer) who are
afflicted with venereal disease  **90 tell . . . field** count their
money in the open  **86–91 When . . . build** the last six
prophecies, as they are Utopian, are meant ironically; they
will never be fulfilled  **92 Albion** England  **95 going . . .
feet** people will walk on their feet  **96 Merlin** King Arthur's
great magician who, according to Holinshed's *Chronicles*,
lived later than Lear

**III.iii.3 pity** show pity to  **6 sustain** care for  **9 division**
falling out; **worse** more serious (i.e., the French invasion)
**11 spoken** spoken of; **closet** room  **13 home** to the
utmost; **power** army; **footed** landed  **14 incline to** take
the side of; **look** search for; **privily** secretly  **16 of**
by  **19 toward** impending  **21 courtesy forbid** kindness
forbidden (i.e., to Lear)  **23 fair deserving** an action deserving
reward

**III.iv.4 break my heart** i.e., by shutting out the storm which
distracts me from thinking  **8 fixed** lodged (in the mind)  **11
i' th' mouth** in the teeth; **free** i.e., from care  **15 as** as if  **16
home** to the utmost  **20 frank** liberal (magnanimous)  **26
houseless poverty** the unsheltered poor, abstracted  **29 bide**
endure  **31 looped and windowed** full of holes  **33 Take
physic, pomp** Take medicine to cure yourselves, you great
men  **35 superflux** superfluity

EDGAR [*Within.*]   Fathom and half, fathom and half!°
Poor Tom!

*Enter* FOOL.

FOOL   Come not in here, nuncle, here's a spirit. Help
me, help me!                                                    40

KENT
Give me thy hand. Who's there?

FOOL   A spirit, a spirit. He says his name's Poor Tom.

KENT
What art thou that dost grumble there i' th' straw?
Come forth.

*Enter* EDGAR [*disguised as a madman*].

EDGAR   Away! the foul fiend follows me. Through the     45
sharp hawthorn blows the cold wind.° Humh! Go to
thy cold bed, and warm thee.°

LEAR   Didst thou give all to thy daughters? And art
thou come to this?

EDGAR   Who gives anything to Poor Tom? Whom      50
the foul fiend hath led through fire and through flame,
through ford and whirlpool, o'er bog and quagmire;
that hath laid knives under his pillow and halters in
his pew,° set ratsbane° by his porridge,° made him
proud of heart, to ride on a bay trotting horse over   55
four-inched bridges,° to course° his own shadow for° a
traitor. Bless thy five wits,° Tom's a-cold. O, do, de,
do, de, do, de. Bless thee from whirlwinds, star-
blasting,° and taking.° Do Poor Tom some charity,
whom the foul fiend vexes. There could I have him  60
now—and there—and there again—and there.

*Storm still.*

LEAR
What, has his daughters brought him to this pass?°
Couldst thou save nothing? Wouldst thou give 'em
all?

FOOL   Nay, he reserved a blanket,° else we had been
all shamed.                                                     65

LEAR
Now all the plagues that in the pendulous° air
Hang fated o'er° men's faults light on thy daughters!

KENT
He hath no daughters, sir.

LEAR
Death, traitor; nothing could have subdued° nature
To such a lowness but his unkind daughters.           70
Is it the fashion that discarded fathers
Should have thus little mercy on° their flesh?
Judicious punishment—'twas this flesh begot
Those pelican° daughters.

EDGAR   Pillicock sat on Pillicock Hill.° Alow, alow,  75
loo, loo!°

FOOL   This cold night will turn us all to fools and
madmen.

EDGAR   Take heed o' th' foul fiend; obey thy parents;
keep thy word's justice;° swear not; commit not°    80
with man's sworn spouse; set not thy sweet heart on
proud array. Tom's a-cold.

LEAR   What hast thou been?

EDGAR   A servingman, proud in heart and mind; that
curled my hair, wore gloves in my cap;° served the   85
lust of my mistress' heart, and did the act of darkness
with her; swore as many oaths as I spake words, and
broke them in the sweet face of heaven. One that slept
in the contriving of lust, and waked to do it. Wine
loved I deeply, dice dearly; and in woman out-        90
paramoured the Turk.° False of heart, light of ear,°
bloody of hand; hog in sloth, fox in stealth, wolf in
greediness, dog in madness, lion in prey.° Let not the
creaking° of shoes nor the rustling of silks betray thy
poor heart to woman. Keep thy foot out of brothels,  95
thy hand out of plackets,° thy pen from lenders' books,°
and defy the foul fiend. Still through the hawthorn
blows the cold wind; says suum, mun, nonny.°
Dolphin° my boy, boy, sessa!° let him trot by.

*Storm still.*

LEAR   Thou wert better in a grave than to answer°    100
with thy uncovered body this extremity° of the skies.
Is man no more than this? Consider him well. Thou
ow'st° the worm no silk, the beast no hide, the sheep
no wool, the cat° no perfume. Ha! here's three on's°
are sophisticated.° Thou art the thing itself; unaccom-  105
modated° man is no more but such a poor, bare,
forked° animal as thou art. Off, off, you lendings!°
Come, unbutton here.

[*Tearing off his clothes.*]

FOOL   Prithee, nuncle, be contented, 'tis a naughty°
night to swim in. Now a little fire in a wild° field   110
were like an old lecher's heart—a small spark, all the
rest on's° body, cold. Look, here comes a walking fire.

*Enter* GLOUCESTER *with a torch.*

37 **Fathom and half** Edgar, because of the downpour, pretends
to take soundings   45–46 **Through . . . wind** a line from
the ballad of "The Friar of Orders Gray"   46–47 **Go . . .
thee** a reminiscence of *The Taming of the Shrew*, Induction, lines 9–10, which themselves are an echo of a line
in Thomas Kyd's *The Spanish Tragedy*   53–54 **knives
. . . halters . . . ratsbane** the fiend tempts Poor Tom
to suicide   54 **pew** gallery or balcony outside a window;
**porridge** broth   55–56 **ride . . . bridges** i.e., risk his life
56 **course** chase; **for** as   57 **five wits** common wit, imagination, fantasy, estimation, memory   58–59 **star-blasting** the evil
caused by malignant stars   59 **taking** pernicious influences   62
**pass** wretched condition   64 **blanket** i.e., to cover his nakedness   66 **pendulous** overhanging   67 **fated o'er** destined to
punish   69 **subdued** reduced   72 **on** i.e., shown to   74
**pelican** supposed to feed on its parent's blood

75 **Pillicock . . . Hill** probably quoted from a nursery rhyme,
and suggested by "pelican"; "pillicock" is a term of endearment
and the phallus   75–76 **Alow . . . loo** a hunting call, or the
refrain of the song (?)   80 **keep . . . justice** i.e., do not break
thy word; **commit not** i.e., adultery   85 **gloves . . . cap** i.e.,
as a pledge from his mistress   90–91 **out-paramoured the
Turk** had more concubines than the sultan   91 **light
of ear** ready to hear flattery and slander   93 **prey**
preying   94 **creaking** deliberately cultivated, as fashionable
96 **plackets** opening in skirts; **pen . . . books** i.e., do
not enter your name in the moneylender's account book
98 **suum, mun, nonny** the noise of the wind   99
**Dolphin** the French dauphin (identified by the English with
the devil; Poor Tom is presumably quoting from a ballad);
**sessa** an interjection: "Go on!"   100 **answer** confront, bear
the brunt of   101 **extremity** extreme severity   103 **ow'st** have
taken from   104 **cat** civet cat, whose glands yield perfume;
**on's** of us   105 **sophisticated** adulterated, made artificial
105–06 **unaccommodated** uncivilized   107 **forked** i.e., two-
legged; **lendings** borrowed garments   109 **naughty**
wicked   110 **wild** barren   112 **on's** of his

EDGAR  This is the foul fiend Flibbertigibbet.° He
begins at curfew,° and walks till the first cock.° He
gives the web and the pin,° squints° the eye, and makes 115
the harelip; mildews the white° wheat, and hurts the
poor creature of earth.

> Swithold footed thrice the old;°
> He met the nightmare,° and her nine fold;°
> Bid her alight° 120
> And her troth plight,°
> And aroint° thee, witch, aroint thee!

KENT
How fares your grace?

LEAR  What's he?

KENT
Who's there? What is't you seek? 125

GLOUCESTER
What are you there? Your names?

EDGAR  Poor Tom, that eats the swimming frog, the
toad, the todpole, the wall-newt and the water;° that
in the fury of his heart, when the foul fiend rages, eats
cow-dung for sallets,° swallows the old rat and the 130
ditch-dog,° drinks the green mantle° of the standing°
pool; who is whipped from tithing° to tithing, and
stocked, punished, and imprisoned; who hath had
three suits to his back, six shirts to his body,

> Horse to ride, and weapon to wear, 135
> But mice and rats, and such small deer,°
> Have been Tom's food for seven long year.°

Beware my follower!° Peace, Smulkin,° peace, thou
fiend!

GLOUCESTER
What, hath your grace no better company? 140

EDGAR
The Prince of Darkness is a gentleman.
Modo° he's called, and Mahu.°

GLOUCESTER
Our flesh and blood, my lord, is grown so vile
That it doth hate what gets° it.

EDGAR  Poor Tom's a-cold. 145

GLOUCESTER
Go in with me. My duty cannot suffer°
T' obey in all your daughters' hard commands.
Though their injunction be to bar my doors
And let this tyrannous night take hold upon you,
Yet have I ventured to come seek you out 150
And bring you where both fire and food is ready.

LEAR
First let me talk with this philosopher.
What is the cause of thunder?

KENT
Good my lord, take his offer; go into th' house.

LEAR
I'll talk a word with this same learnèd Theban.° 155
What is your study?°

EDGAR
How to prevent° the fiend, and to kill vermin.

LEAR
Let me ask you one word in private.

KENT
Importune him once more to go, my lord.
His wits begin t' unsettle.

GLOUCESTER               Canst thou blame him? 160

*Storm still.*

His daughters seek his death. Ah, that good Kent,
He said it would be thus, poor banished man!
Thou say'st the king grows mad—I'll tell thee, friend,
I am almost mad myself. I had a son,
Now outlawed from my blood;° he sought my life 165
But lately, very late.° I loved him, friend,
No father his son dearer. True to tell thee,
The grief hath crazed my wits. What a night's this!
I do beseech your grace—

LEAR                O, cry you mercy,° sir.
Noble philosopher, your company. 170

EDGAR  Tom's a-cold.

GLOUCESTER
In, fellow, there, into th' hovel; keep thee warm.

LEAR
Come, let's in all.

KENT               This way, my lord.

LEAR                         With him!
I will keep still with my philosopher.

KENT
Good my lord, soothe° him; let him take the fellow. 175

GLOUCESTER
Take him you on.°

KENT
Sirrah, come on; go along with us.

LEAR
Come, good Athenian.°

GLOUCESTER
No words, no words! Hush.

EDGAR
Child Rowland to the dark tower came;° 180
His word was still,° "Fie, foh, and fum,
I smell the blood of a British man."°     *Exeunt.*

Scene V. [*Gloucester's castle.*]

*Enter CORNWALL and EDMUND.*

CORNWALL  I will have my revenge ere I depart his
house.

---

113 **Flibbertigibbet** a figure from Elizabethan demonology  114 **curfew** 9 P.M.; **first cock** midnight  115
**web . . . pin** cataract; **squints** crosses  116 **white** ripening
118 **Swithold . . . old** Withold (an Anglo-Saxon saint who
subdued demons) walked three times across the open country
119 **nightmare** demon; **fold** offspring  120 **alight** i.e., from
the horse she had possessed  121 **her troth plight** pledge her
word  122 **aroint** be gone  128 **todpole . . . water** tadpole,
wall lizard, water newt  130 **sallets** salads  131 **ditch-dog**
dead dog in a ditch; **mantle** scum; **standing** stagnant
132 **tithing** a district comprising ten families  136–37 **But . . .
year** adapted from a popular romance, "Bevis of Hampton"
136 **deer** game  138 **follower** familiar  138–42 **Smulkin
. . . Modo . . . Mahu** Elizabethan devils, from Samuel
Harsnett's *Declaration* of 1603  144 **gets** begets  146 **suffer**
permit me

155 **Theban** i.e., Greek philosopher  156 **study** particular
scientific study  157 **prevent** balk  165 **outlawed . . . blood**
disowned and tainted, like a carbuncle in the corrupted blood
166 **late** recently  169 **cry you mercy** I beg your pardon  175
**soothe** humor  176 **you on** with you  178 **Athenian** i.e.,
philosopher (like "Theban")  180 **Child . . . came** from a lost
ballad (?); "child" = a candidate for knighthood; "Rowland"
was Charlemagne's nephew, the hero of *The Song of Roland*  181
**His . . . still** his motto was always  181–82 **Fie . . . man**
a deliberately absurd linking of the chivalric hero with the
nursery tale of Jack the Giant-Killer

EDMUND  How, my lord, I may be censured,° that nature thus gives way to loyalty, something fears° me to think of. 5

CORNWALL  I now perceive it was not altogether your brother's evil disposition made him seek his death; but a provoking merit, set a-work by a reprovable badness in himself.°

EDMUND  How malicious is my fortune that I must 10 repent to be just! This is the letter which he spoke of, which approves° him an intelligent party° to the advantages° of France. O heavens, that his treason were not! or not I the detector!

CORNWALL  Go with me to the duchess. 15

EDMUND  If the matter of this paper be certain, you have mighty business in hand.

CORNWALL  True or false, it hath made thee Earl of Gloucester. Seek out where thy father is, that he may be ready for our apprehension.° 20

EDMUND  [Aside.]  If I find him comforting° the king, it will stuff his suspicion more fully.—I will persever° in my course of loyalty, though the conflict be sore between that and my blood.°

CORNWALL  I will lay trust upon° thee, and thou shalt 25 find a dearer father in my love.          Exeunt.

Scene VI. [A chamber in a farmhouse adjoining the castle.]

Enter KENT and GLOUCESTER.

GLOUCESTER  Here is better than the open air; take it thankfully. I will piece out the comfort with what addition I can. I will not be long from you.

KENT  All the power of his wits have given way to his impatience.° The gods reward your kindness. 5
                              Exit [GLOUCESTER].

Enter LEAR, EDGAR, and FOOL.

EDGAR  Fraceretto° calls me, and tells me Nero° is an angler in the lake of darkness. Pray, innocent,° and beware the foul fiend.

FOOL  Prithee, nuncle, tell me whether a madman be a gentleman or a yeoman.° 10

LEAR  A king, a king.

FOOL  No, he's a yeoman that has a gentleman to his son; for he's a mad yeoman that sees his son a gentleman before him.

LEAR
To have a thousand with red burning spits 15
Come hizzing° in upon 'em—

EDGAR  The foul fiend bites my back.

FOOL  He's mad that trusts in the tameness of a wolf, a horse's health, a boy's love, or a whore's oath.

LEAR
It shall be done; I will arraign° them straight.° 20

[To EDGAR.]

Come, sit thou here, most learned justice.°

[To the FOOL.]

Thou, sapient° sir, sit here. Now, you she-foxes—

EDGAR  Look, where he° stands and glares. Want'st thou eyes at trial, madam?°
Come o'er the bourn,° Bessy, to me. 25

FOOL
   Her boat hath a leak,
   And she must not speak
Why she dares not come over to thee.°

EDGAR  The foul fiend haunts Poor Tom in the voice of a nightingale.° Hoppedance° cries in Tom's belly 30 for two white herring.° Croak° not, black angel; I have no food for thee.

KENT
How do you, sir? Stand you not so amazed.°
Will you lie down and rest upon the cushions?

LEAR
I'll see their trial first. Bring in their evidence.° 35

[To EDGAR.]

Thou, robèd man of justice, take thy place.

[To the FOOL.]

And thou, his yokefellow of equity,°
Bench° by his side. [To KENT.] You are o' th' commission;°
Sit you too.

EDGAR  Let us deal justly. 40
   Sleepest or wakest thou, jolly shepherd?
      Thy sheep be in the corn;°
   And for one blast of thy minikin° mouth
      Thy sheep shall take no harm.
Purr, the cat is gray.° 45

LEAR  Arraign her first. 'Tis Goneril, I here take my oath before this honorable assembly, she kicked the poor king her father.

FOOL  Come hither, mistress. Is your name Goneril?

LEAR  She cannot deny it. 50

III.v.3 censured judged  4 something fears somewhat frightens  8–9 a provoking . . . himself a stimulating goodness in Edgar, brought into play by a blamable badness in Gloucester  12 approves proves; intelligent party (1) spy (2) well-informed person  12–13 to the advantages on behalf of  20 apprehension arrest  21 comforting supporting (a legalism)  22 persever persevere  24 blood natural feelings  25 lay trust upon (1) trust (2) advance
III.vi.5 impatience raging  6 Fraceretto Elizabethan devil, from Harsnett's Declaration;  Nero who is mentioned by Harsnett, and whose angling is reported by Chaucer in "The Monk's Tale"  7 innocent fool  10 yeoman farmer (just below a gentleman in rank; the Fool asks what class of man has most indulged his children, and thus been driven mad)  16 hizzing hissing

20 arraign bring to trial; straight straightaway  21 justice justicer, judge  22 sapient wise  23 he i.e., a fiend  23–24 Want'st . . . madam (to Goneril) i.e., Do you want eyes to look at you during your trial? The fiend serves that purpose  25 bourn brook (Edgar quotes from a popular ballad)  26–28 Her . . . thee the Fool parodies the ballad  30 nightingale i.e., the Fool's singing; Hoppedance Hoberdidance (another devil from Harsnett's Declaration)  31 white herring unsmoked (as against the black and sulfurous devil?); Croak rumble (because his belly is empty)  33 amazed astonished  35 evidence the evidence of witnesses against them  37 yokefellow of equity partner in justice  38 Bench sit on the bench; commission those commissioned as king's justices  41–44 Sleepest . . . harm probably quoted or adapted from an Elizabethan song  42 corn wheat  43 minikin shrill  45 gray devils were thought to assume the shape of a gray cat

**FOOL**    Cry you mercy, I took you for a joint stool.°

**LEAR**
And here's another, whose warped looks proclaim
What store° her heart is made on. Stop her there!
Arms, arms, sword, fire! Corruption in the place!°
False justicer, why hast thou let her 'scape?                    55

**EDGAR**    Bless thy five wits!

**KENT**
O pity! Sir, where is the patience now
That you so oft have boasted to retain?

**EDGAR** [*Aside.*]
My tears begin to take his part so much
They mar my counterfeiting.°                                      60

**LEAR**
The little dogs and all,
Tray, Blanch, and Sweetheart—see, they bark at me.

**EDGAR**    Tom will throw his head at them. Avaunt,
you curs.
    Be thy mouth or black or° white,                             65
    Tooth that poisons if it bite;
    Mastiff, greyhound, mongrel grim,
    Hound or spaniel, brach° or lym,°
    Or bobtail tike, or trundle-tail°—
    Tom will make him weep and wail;                             70
    For, with throwing° thus my head,
    Dogs leaped the hatch,° and all are fled.
Do, de, de, de. Sessa!° Come, march to wakes° and
fairs and market towns. Poor Tom, thy horn° is dry.

**LEAR**    Then let them anatomize Regan. See what        75
breeds about her heart.° Is there any cause in nature
that make° these hard hearts? [*To* EDGAR.] You, sir, I
entertain° for one of my hundred;° only I do not like
the fashion of your garments. You will say they are
Persian;° but let them be changed.                               80

**KENT**
Now, good my lord, lie here and rest awhile.

**LEAR**
Make no noise, make no noise; draw the curtains.°
So, so. We'll go to supper i' th' morning.

**FOOL**    And I'll go to bed at noon.°

*Enter* GLOUCESTER.

**GLOUCESTER**
Come hither, friend. Where is the king my master?       85

**KENT**
Here, sir, but trouble him not; his wits are gone.

**GLOUCESTER**
Good friend, I prithee take him in thy arms.
I have o'erheard a plot of death upon him.
There is a litter ready; lay him in't
And drive toward Dover, friend, where thou shalt
meet                                                             90
Both welcome and protection. Take up thy master.
If thou shouldst dally half an hour, his life,
With thine and all that offer to defend him,
Stand in assurèd loss. Take up, take up,
And follow me, that will to some provision°                     95
Give thee quick conduct.°

**KENT**                          Oppressèd nature sleeps.
This rest might yet have balmed thy broken sinews,°
Which, if convenience° will not allow,
Stand in hard cure.° [*To the* FOOL.] Come, help to
bear thy master.
Thou must not stay behind.

**GLOUCESTER**                    Come, come, away!              100
                                        *Exeunt [all but* EDGAR].

**EDGAR**
When we our betters see bearing our woes,
We scarcely think our miseries our foes.°
Who alone suffers suffers most i' th' mind,
Leaving free° things and happy shows° behind;
But then the mind much sufferance° doth o'erskip           105
When grief hath mates, and bearing fellowship.°
How light and portable° my pain seems now,
When that which makes me bend makes the king bow.
He childed as I fathered. Tom, away.
Mark the high noises,° and thyself bewray°                     110
When false opinion, whose wrong thoughts° defile
thee,
In thy just proof repeals and reconciles thee.°
What will hap more° tonight, safe 'scape the king!
Lurk,° lurk.                                          [*Exit.*]

## Scene VII. [*Gloucester's castle.*]

*Enter* CORNWALL, REGAN, GONERIL, EDMUND,
*and* SERVANTS.

**CORNWALL** [*To* GONERIL.]    Post speedily to my lord
your husband; show him this letter. The army of
France is landed. [*To* SERVANTS.] Seek out the
traitor Gloucester.    [*Exeunt some of the* SERVANTS.]

**REGAN**    Hang him instantly.                                 5

**GONERIL**    Pluck out his eyes.

**CORNWALL**    Leave him to my displeasure. Edmund,
keep you our sister company. The revenges we are

---

**51 Cry . . . stool** proverbial and deliberately impudent
apology for overlooking a person; a joint stool was a low stool
made by a joiner, perhaps here a stage property to represent
Goneril and, in line 52, Regan, "joint stool" can also suggest
the judicial bench; hence Goneril may be identified by the
Fool, ironically, with those in power, who judge **53 store**
stuff **54 Corruption . . . place** bribery in the court **60
counterfeiting** i.e., feigned madness **65 or . . . or** either
. . . or **68 brach** bitch; **lym** bloodhound (from the liam or
leash with which he was led) **69 bobtail . . . trundle-tail**
short-tailed or long-tailed cur **71 throwing** jerking (as a
hound lifts its head from the ground, the scent having been lost)
**72 leaped the hatch** leaped over the lower half of a divided
door (i.e., left in a hurry) **73 Sessa** Be off!; **wakes** feasts
attending the dedication of a church **74 horn** horn bottle
which the Bedlam used in begging a drink (Edgar is suggesting
that he is unable to play his role any longer) **75–76 Then . . .
heart** i.e., If the Bedlam's horn is dry, let Regan, whose heart
has become as hard as horn, be dissected **77 make** subjunctive
**78 entertain** engage; **hundred** i.e., Lear's hundred knights
**80 Persian** gorgeous (ironically of Edgar's rags) **82 curtains**
Lear imagines himself in bed **84 And . . . noon** the Fool's
last words

**95 provision** maintenance **96 conduct** direction **97
balmed . . . sinews** soothed thy racked nerves **98 convenience** fortunate occasion **99 Stand . . . cure** will be hard to
cure **102 our foes** enemies peculiar to ourselves **104 free**
carefree; **shows** scenes **105 sufferance** suffering **106 bearing fellowship** suffering has company **107 portable** able to
be supported or endured **110 Mark . . . noises** observe
the rumors of strife among those in power; **bewray** reveal
**111 wrong thoughts** misconceptions **112 In . . . thee** on
the manifesting of your innocence recalls you from outlawry
and restores amity between you and your father **113 What
. . . more** whatever else happens **114 Lurk** hide

bound° to take upon your traitorous father are not fit
for your beholding. Advise the duke where you are 10
going, to a most festinate° preparation. We are bound
to the like. Our posts° shall be swift and intelligent°
betwixt us. Farewell, dear sister; farewell, my Lord of
Gloucester.°

*Enter* OSWALD.

How now? Where's the king?                                15

OSWALD
My Lord of Gloucester hath conveyed him hence.
Some five or six and thirty of his knights,
Hot questrists° after him, met him at gate;
Who, with some other of the lords dependants,°
Are gone with him toward Dover, where they boast 20
To have well-armèd friends.

CORNWALL                    Get horses for your mistress.
                              [*Exit* OSWALD.]

GONERIL
Farewell, sweet lord, and sister.

CORNWALL
Edmund, farewell.  [*Exeunt* GONERIL *and* EDMUND.]
              Go seek the traitor Gloucester,
Pinion him like a thief, bring him before us.
                    [*Exeunt other* SERVANTS.]
Though well we may not pass upon° his life    25
Without the form of justice, yet our power
Shall do a court'sy to° our wrath, which men
May blame, but not control.

*Enter* GLOUCESTER, *brought in by two or three.*

                    Who's there, the traitor?

REGAN
Ingrateful fox, 'tis he.

CORNWALL
Bind fast his corky° arms.                    30

GLOUCESTER
What means your graces? Good my friends, consider
You are my guests. Do me no foul play, friends.

CORNWALL
Bind him, I say. [SERVANTS *bind him.*]

REGAN            Hard, hard! O filthy traitor.

GLOUCESTER
Unmerciful lady as you are, I'm none.

CORNWALL
To this chair bind him. Villain, thou shalt find—  35

[REGAN *plucks his beard.*°]

GLOUCESTER
By the kind gods, 'tis most ignobly done
To pluck me by the beard.

REGAN
So white, and such a traitor?

GLOUCESTER                    Naughty° lady
These hairs which thou dost ravish from my chin
Will quicken° and accuse thee. I am your host.   40

With robber's hands my hospitable favors°
You should not ruffle° thus. What will you do?

CORNWALL
Come, sir, what letters had you late° from France?

REGAN
Be simple-answered,° for we know the truth.

CORNWALL
And what confederacy have you with the traitors   45
Late footed in the kingdom?

REGAN
To whose hands you have sent the lunatic king:
Speak.

GLOUCESTER
I have a letter guessingly° set down,
Which came from one that's of a neutral heart,   50
And not from one opposed.

CORNWALL                    Cunning.

REGAN                                And false.

CORNWALL
Where hast thou sent the king?

GLOUCESTER
To Dover.

REGAN
Wherefore to Dover? Wast thou not charged at
      peril°—

CORNWALL
Wherefore to Dover? Let him answer that.        55

GLOUCESTER
I am tied to th' stake, and I must stand the course.°

REGAN
Wherefore to Dover?

GLOUCESTER
Because I would not see thy cruel nails
Pluck out his poor old eyes; nor thy fierce sister
In his anointed° flesh rash° boarish fangs.      60
The sea, with such a storm as his bare head
In hell-black night endured, would have buoyed° up
And quenched the stellèd° fires.
Yet, poor old heart, he holp° the heavens to rain.
If wolves had at thy gate howled that dearn° time, 65
Thou shouldst have said, "Good porter, turn the
      key."°
All cruels else subscribe.° But I shall see
The wingèd° vengeance overtake such children.

CORNWALL
See't shalt thou never. Fellows, hold the chair.
Upon these eyes of thine I'll set my foot.        70

GLOUCESTER
He that will think° to live till he be old,
Give me some help.—O cruel! O you gods!

REGAN
One side will mock° another. Th' other too.

41 **hospitable favors** face of your host  42 **ruffle** tear at
violently  43 **late** recently  44 **simple-answered** straightforward in answering  49 **guessingly** without certain knowledge  54 **charged at peril** ordered under penalty  56 **course**
coursing (in which a relay of dogs baits a bull or bear
tied in the pit)  60 **anointed** holy (because king); **rash** strike
with the tusk, like a boar  62 **buoyed** risen  63 **stellèd** (1)
fixed (as opposed to the planets or wandering stars) (2) starry
64 **holp** helped  65 **dearn** dread  66 **turn the key** i.e.,
unlock the gate  67 **All . . . subscribe** All cruel creatures but
man are compassionate  68 **wingèd** (1) heavenly (2) swift
71 **will think** expects  73 **mock** make ridiculous (because of
the contrast)

III.vii.**9 bound** (1) forced (2) purposing to  **11 festinate**
speedy  **12 posts** messengers; **intelligent** full of information
**13–14 Lord of Gloucester** Edmund, now elevated to the
title  **18 questrists** searchers  **19 lords dependants** attendant
lords (members of Lear's retinue)  **25 pass upon** pass
judgment on  **27 do . . . to** indulge  **30 corky** sapless
(because old)  **35 s.d. plucks his beard** a deadly insult  **38
Naughty** wicked  **40 quicken** come to life

CORNWALL
If you see vengeance—
FIRST SERVANT                    Hold your hand, my lord!
I have served you ever since I was a child; 75
But better service have I never done you
Than now to bid you hold.
REGAN                            How now, you dog?
FIRST SERVANT
If you did wear a beard upon your chin,
I'd shake it° on this quarrel. What do you mean!°
CORNWALL    My villain!°                           80

*Draw and fight.*

FIRST SERVANT
Nay, then, come on, and take the chance of anger.
REGAN
Give me thy sword. A peasant stand up thus?

*She takes a sword and runs at him behind, kills him.*

FIRST SERVANT
O, I am slain! my lord, you have one eye left
To see some mischief° on him. O!
CORNWALL
Lest it see more, prevent it. Out, vile jelly.       85
Where is thy luster now?
GLOUCESTER
All dark and comfortless. Where's my son Edmund?
Edmund, enkindle all the sparks of nature°
To quit° this horrid act.
REGAN                            Out, treacherous villain,
Thou call'st on him that hates thee. It was he    90
That made the overture° of thy treasons to us;
Who is too good to pity thee.
GLOUCESTER
O my follies! Then Edgar was abused.°
Kind gods, forgive me that, and prosper him.
REGAN
Go thrust him out at gates, and let him smell      95
His way to Dover.      *Exit [one], with* GLOUCESTER.
                    How is't, my lord? How look you?°
CORNWALL
I have received a hurt. Follow me, lady.
Turn out that eyeless villain. Throw this slave
Upon the dunghill. Regan, I bleed apace.
Untimely comes this hurt. Give me your arm. *Exeunt.* 100
SECOND SERVANT
I'll never care what wickedness I do,
If this man come to good.
THIRD SERVANT                    If she live long,
And in the end meet the old course of death,°
Women will all turn monsters.
SECOND SERVANT
Let's follow the old earl, and get the Bedlam     105
To lead him where he would. His roguish madness
Allows itself to anything.°

THIRD SERVANT
Go thou. I'll fetch some flax and whites of eggs
To apply to his bleeding face. Now heaven help him.
                              [*Exeunt severally.*]

# ACT IV

Scene I. [*The heath.*]

*Enter* EDGAR.

EDGAR
Yet better thus, and known to be contemned,°
Than still contemned and flattered. To be worst,
The lowest and most dejected° thing of fortune,
Stands still in esperance,° lives not in fear:
The lamentable change is from the best,              5
The worst returns to laughter.° Welcome then,
Thou unsubstantial air that I embrace!
The wretch that thou hast blown unto the worst
Owes° nothing to thy blasts.

*Enter* GLOUCESTER, *led by an* OLD MAN.

                              But who comes here?
My father, poorly led?° World, world, O world!   10
But that thy strange mutations make us hate thee,
Life would not yield to age.°
OLD MAN                          O, my good lord,
I have been your tenant, and your father's tenant,
These fourscore years.
GLOUCESTER
Away, get thee away; good friend, be gone:         15
Thy comforts° can do me no good at all;
Thee they may hurt.°
OLD MAN                    You cannot see your way.
GLOUCESTER
I have no way and therefore want° no eyes;
I stumbled when I saw. Full oft 'tis seen,
Our means secure us, and our mere defects           20
Prove our commodities.° Oh, dear son Edgar,
The food° of thy abusèd° father's wrath!
Might I but live to see thee in° my touch,
I'd say I had eyes again!
OLD MAN                    How now! Who's there?
EDGAR [*Aside.*]
O gods! Who is't can say, "I am at the worst"?      25
I am worse than e'er I was.
OLD MAN                    'Tis poor mad Tom.
EDGAR [*Aside.*]
And worse I may be yet: the worst is not
So long as we can say, "This is the worst."°

---

79 **shake it** an insult comparable to Regan's plucking of
Gloucester's beard; **What . . . mean** i.e., What terrible
thing are you doing?  80 **villain** serf (with a suggestion of the
modern meaning)  84 **mischief** injury  88 **enkindle . . .
nature** fan your natural feeling into flame  89 **quit** requite
91 **overture** disclosure  93 **abused** wronged  96 **How look
you** How are you?  103 **meet . . . death** die the customary
death of old age  106–07 **His . . . anything** his lack of all
self-control leaves him open to any suggestion

IV.i.1 **known . . . contemned** conscious of being despised
3 **dejected** abased  4 **esperance** hope  6 **returns to laughter**
changes for the better  9 **Owes** is in debt for  10 **poorly led**
(1) led like a poor man, with only one attendant (2) led by a
poor man  11–12 **But . . . age** We should not agree to grow
old and hence die, except for the hateful mutability of life
16 **comforts** ministrations  17 **hurt** injure  18 **want** require
20–21 **Our . . . commodities** Our resources make us overconfident, while our afflictions make for our advantage  22
**food** i.e., the object on which Gloucester's anger fed; **abusèd**
deceived  23 **in** i.e., with, by means of  27–28 **the . . .
worst** so long as a man continues to suffer (i.e., is still alive),
even greater suffering may await him

OLD MAN
Fellow, where goest?

GLOUCESTER        Is it a beggar-man?

OLD MAN
Madman and beggar too.        30

GLOUCESTER
He has some reason,° else he could not beg.
I' th' last night's storm I such a fellow saw,
Which made me think a man a worm. My son
Came then into my mind, and yet my mind
Was then scarce friends with him. I have heard more
    since.        35
As flies to wanton° boys, are we to th' gods,
They kill us for their sport.

EDGAR        [Aside.] How should this be?°
Bad is the trade that must play fool to sorrow,
Ang'ring° itself and others. Bless thee, master!

GLOUCESTER
Is that the naked fellow?

OLD MAN        Ay, my lord.        40

GLOUCESTER
Then, prithee, get thee gone: if for my sake
Thou wilt o'ertake us hence a mile or twain
I' th' way toward Dover, do it for ancient° love,
And bring some covering for this naked soul,
Which I'll entreat to lead me.

OLD MAN        Alack, sir, he is mad.        45

GLOUCESTER
'Tis the time's plague,° when madmen lead the blind.
Do as I bid thee, or rather do thy pleasure;°
Above the rest,° be gone.

OLD MAN
I'll bring him the best 'parel° that I have,
Come on't what will.        Exit. 50

GLOUCESTER
Sirrah, naked fellow—

EDGAR
Poor Tom's a-cold. [Aside.] I cannot daub it° further.

GLOUCESTER
Come hither, fellow.

EDGAR [Aside.]
And yet I must.—Bless thy sweet eyes, they bleed.

GLOUCESTER
Know'st thou the way to Dover?        55

EDGAR
Both stile and gate, horse-way and footpath.
Poor Tom hath been scared out of his good wits.
Bless thee, good man's son, from the foul fiend!
Five fiends have been in Poor Tom at once; of lust, as
Obidicut;° Hobbididence, prince of dumbness;° Mahu, 60
of stealing; Modo, of murder; Flibbertigibbet, of
mopping and mowing;° who since possesses chamber-
maids and waiting-women. So, bless thee, master!

31 reason faculty of reasoning   36 wanton (1) playful (2) reckless
37 How . . . be i.e., How can this horror be?   39 Ang'ring
offending   43 ancient (1) the love the Old Man feels, by
virtue of his long tenancy (2) the love that formerly obtained
between master and man   46 time's plague characteristic disorder of this time   47 thy pleasure as you like it   48 the rest
all   49 'parel apparel   52 daub it lay it on (figure from
plastering mortar)   60 Obidicut Hoberdicut, a devil (like the
four that follow, from Harsnett's Declaration);   dumbness
muteness (like the crimes and afflictions in the next lines, the result
of diabolic possession)   62 mopping and mowing grimacing
and making faces

GLOUCESTER
Here, take this purse, thou whom the heavens' plagues
Have humbled to all strokes:° that I am wretched        65
Makes thee the happier. Heavens, deal so still!
Let the superfluous° and lust-dieted° man,
That slaves° your ordinance,° that will not see
Because he does not feel, feel your pow'r quickly;
So distribution should undo excess,°        70
And each man have enough. Dost thou know Dover?

EDGAR   Ay, master.

GLOUCESTER
There is a cliff whose high and bending° head
Looks fearfully° in the confinèd deep:°
Bring me but to the very brim of it,        75
And I'll repair the misery thou dost bear
With something rich about me: from that place
I shall no leading need.

EDGAR        Give me thy arm:
Poor Tom shall lead thee.        Exeunt.

Scene II. [Before the Duke of Albany's palace.]

Enter GONERIL and EDMUND.

GONERIL
Welcome, my lord: I marvel our mild husband
Not met° us on the way.

Enter OSWALD.

       Now, where's your master?

OSWALD
Madam, within; but never man so changed.
I told him of the army that was landed:
He smiled at it. I told him you were coming;        5
His answer was, "The worse." Of Gloucester's
    treachery,
And of the loyal service of his son
When I informed him, then he called me sot,°
And told me I had turned the wrong side out:
What most he should dislike seems pleasant to him;        10
What like,° offensive.

GONERIL [To EDMUND.]
Then shall you go no further.
It is the cowish° terror of his spirit,
That dares not undertake:° he'll not feel wrongs,
Which tie him to an answer.° Our wishes on the way        15
May prove effects.° Back, Edmund, to my brother;
Hasten his musters° and conduct his pow'rs.°
I must change names° at home and give the distaff°

65 humbled . . . strokes brought so low as to bear
anything humbly   67 superfluous possessed of superfluities;
lust-dieted whose lust is gratified (like Gloucester's)   68
slaves (1) tramples, spurns like a slave (2) tears, rends (Old
English slæfan) (?); ordinance law   70 So . . . excess
Then the man with too much wealth would distribute it
among those with too little   73 bending overhanging   74
fearfully occasioning fear; confinèd deep the sea, hemmed in
below
IV.ii.2 Not met did not meet   8 sot fool   11 What like
what he should like   13 cowish cowardly   14 undertake
venture   15 tie . . . answer oblige him to retaliate   15–16
Our . . . effects Our desires (that you might be my husband),
as we journeyed here, may be fulfilled   17 musters collecting
of troops; conduct his pow'rs lead his army   18
change names i.e., exchange the name of "mistress" for
that of "master"; distaff spinning stick (wifely symbol)

Into my husband's hands. This trusty servant
Shall pass between us: ere long you are like to hear, 20
If you dare venture in your own behalf,
A mistress's° command. Wear this; spare speech;

*[Giving a favor.]*

Decline your head.° This kiss, if it durst speak,
Would stretch thy spirits up into the air:
Conceive,° and fare thee well. 25

EDMUND
Yours in the ranks of death.

GONERIL                    My most dear Gloucester!
                              *Exit* [EDMUND].

O, the difference of man and man!
To thee a woman's services are due:
My fool usurps my body.°

OSWALD            Madam, here comes my lord. *Exit.*

*Enter* ALBANY.

GONERIL
I have been worth the whistle.°

ALBANY                    O Goneril! 30
You are not worth the dust which the rude wind
Blows in your face. I fear your disposition:°
That nature which contemns° its origin
Cannot be bordered certain in itself;°
She that herself will sliver and disbranch° 35
From her material sap,° perforce must wither
And come to deadly use.°

GONERIL
No more; the text° is foolish.

ALBANY
Wisdom and goodness to the vile seem vile:
Filths savor but themselves.° What have you done? 40
Tigers, not daughters, what have you performed?
A father, and a gracious agèd man,
Whose reverence even the head-lugged bear° would
     lick,
Most barbarous, most degenerate, have you madded.°
Could my good brother suffer you to do it? 45
A man, a prince, by him so benefited!
If that the heavens do not their visible spirits°
Send quickly down to tame these vile offenses,
It will come,
Humanity must perforce prey on itself,
Like monsters of the deep. 50

GONERIL                    Milk-livered° man!
That bear'st a cheek for blows, a head for wrongs;

Who hast not in thy brows an eye discerning
Thine honor from thy suffering;° that not know'st
Fools do those villains pity who are punished 55
Ere they have done their mischief.° Where's thy drum?
France spreads his banners in our noiseless° land,
With plumèd helm° thy state begins to threat,°
Whilst thou, a moral° fool, sits still and cries,
"Alack, why does he so?"

ALBANY                    See thyself, devil! 60
Proper° deformity seems not in the fiend
So horrid as in woman.

GONERIL                    O vain fool!

ALBANY
Thou changèd and self-covered° thing, for shame,
Be-monster not thy feature.° Were't my fitness°
To let these hands obey my blood,° 65
They are apt enough to dislocate and tear
Thy flesh and bones: howe'er° thou art a fiend,
A woman's shape doth shield thee.

GONERIL
Marry, your manhood mew°—

*Enter a* MESSENGER.

ALBANY  What news? 70

MESSENGER
O, my good lord, the Duke of Cornwall's dead,
Slain by his servant, going to° put out
The other eye of Gloucester.

ALBANY                    Gloucester's eyes!

MESSENGER
A servant that he bred,° thrilled with remorse,°
Opposed against the act, bending his sword 75
To his great master, who thereat enraged
Flew on him, and amongst them felled° him dead,
But not without that harmful stroke which since
Hath plucked him after.°

ALBANY                    This shows you are above,
You justicers,° that these our nether° crimes 80
So speedily can venge.° But, O poor Gloucester!
Lost he his other eye?

MESSENGER            Both, both, my lord.
This letter, madam, craves° a speedy answer;
'Tis from your sister.

GONERIL            [*Aside.*] One way I like this well;

53–54 **discerning . . . suffering** able to distinguish between insults that ought to be resented, and ordinary pain that is to be borne  55–56 **Fools . . . mischief** Only fools are sorry for criminals whose intended criminality is prevented by punishment  57 **noiseless** i.e., the drum, signifying preparation for war, is silent  58 **helm** helmet; **thy . . . threat** France begins to threaten Albany's realm  59 **moral** moralizing; but also with the implication that morality and folly are one  61 **Proper** (1) natural (to a fiend) (2) fair-appearing  63 **changèd and self-covered** i.e., transformed, by the contorting of her woman's face, on which appears the fiendish behavior she has allowed herself (Goneril has disguised nature by wickedness)  64 **Be-monster . . . feature** do not change your appearance into a fiend's; **my fitness** appropriate for me  65 **blood** passion  67 **howe'er** but even if  69 **your manhood mew** (1) coop up or confine (pretended) manhood (2) molt or shed it, if that is what is supposed to "shield" me from you  72 **going to** as he was about to  74 **bred** reared; **thrilled with remorse** pierced by compassion  77 **amongst them felled** others assisting, they felled  79 **plucked him after** i.e., brought Cornwall to death with his servant  80 **justicers** judges; **nether** committed below (on earth)  81 **venge** avenge  83 **craves** demands

22 **mistress's** lover's (and also, Albany having been disposed of, lady's or wife's)  23 **Decline your head** i.e., that Goneril may kiss him  25 **Conceive** understand (with a sexual implication, that includes "stretch thy spirits," line 24; and "death," line 26: "to die," meaning "to experience sexual intercourse")  29 **My . . . body** My husband wrongfully enjoys me  30 **I . . . whistle** i.e., Once you valued me (the proverb is implied, "It is a poor dog that is not worth the whistling")  32 **disposition** nature  33 **contemns** despises  34 **bordered . . . itself** kept within its normal bounds  35 **sliver and disbranch** cut off  36 **material sap** essential and life-giving sustenance  37 **come . . . use** i.e., be as a dead branch for the burning  38 **text** i.e., on which your sermon is based  40 **Filths . . . themselves** the filthy relish only the taste of filth  43 **head-lugged bear** bear-baited by the dogs, and hence enraged  44 **madded** made mad  47 **visible spirits** avenging spirits in material form  51 **Milk-livered** lily-livered (hence cowardly, the liver being regarded as the seat of courage)

But being widow, and my Gloucester with her,      85
May all the building in my fancy pluck
Upon my hateful life.° Another way,°
The news is not so tart.°—I'll read, and answer.   *Exit.*

**ALBANY**
Where was his son when they did take his eyes?

**MESSENGER**
Come with my lady hither.

**ALBANY**                    He is not here.          90

**MESSENGER**
No, my good lord; I met him back° again.

**ALBANY**
Knows he the wickedness?

**MESSENGER**
Ay, my good lord; 'twas he informed against him,
And quit the house on purpose, that their punishment
Might have the freer course.

**ALBANY**                    Gloucester, I live     95
To thank thee for the love thou showed'st the king,
And to revenge thine eyes. Come hither, friend:
Tell me what more thou know'st.        *Exeunt.*

[Scene III. *The French camp near Dover.*]

*Enter* KENT *and a* GENTLEMAN.

**KENT**  Why the King of France is so suddenly gone
back, know you no reason?

**GENTLEMAN**  Something he left imperfect in the
state,° which since his coming forth is thought of,
which imports° to the kingdom so much fear and   5
danger that his personal return was most required and
necessary.

**KENT**
Who hath he left behind him general?

**GENTLEMAN**  The Marshal of France, Monsieur La
Far.                                               10

**KENT**  Did your letters pierce° the queen to any
demonstration of grief?

**GENTLEMAN**
Ay, sir; she took them, read them in my presence,
And now and then an ample tear trilled° down
Her delicate cheek: it seemed she was a queen      15
Over her passion, who most rebel-like
Sought to be king o'er her.

**KENT**                    O, then it moved her.

**GENTLEMAN**
Not to a rage: patience and sorrow strove
Who should express her goodliest.° You have seen
Sunshine and rain at once: her smiles and tears    20
Were like a better way:° those happy smilets°
That played on her ripe lip seemed not to know
What guests were in her eyes, which parted thence
As pearls from diamonds dropped. In brief,

Sorrow would be a rarity most belovèd,             25
If all could so become it.°

**KENT**                    Made she no verbal question?

**GENTLEMAN**
Faith, once or twice she heaved° the name of "father"
Pantingly forth, as if it pressed her heart;
Cried, "Sisters! Sisters! Shame of ladies! Sisters!
Kent! Father! Sisters! What, i' th' storm? i' th' night? 30
Let pity not be believed!"° There she shook
The holy water from her heavenly eyes,
And clamor moistened:° then away she started
To deal with grief alone.

**KENT**                    It is the stars,
The stars above us, govern our conditions;°        35
Else one self mate and make could not beget
Such different issues.° You spoke not with her since?

**GENTLEMAN**  No.

**KENT**
Was this before the king returned?

**GENTLEMAN**                    No, since.

**KENT**
Well, sir, the poor distressèd Lear's i' th' town;   40
Who sometime in his better tune° remembers
What we are come about, and by no means
Will yield to see his daughter.

**GENTLEMAN**                    Why, good sir?

**KENT**
A sovereign° shame so elbows° him: his own unkindness
That stripped her from his benediction, turned her  45
To foreign casualties,° gave her dear rights
To his dog-hearted daughters: these things sting
His mind so venomously that burning shame
Detains him from Cordelia.

**GENTLEMAN**                    Alack, poor gentleman!

**KENT**
Of Albany's and Cornwall's powers you heard not?    50

**GENTLEMAN**
'Tis so;° they are afoot.

**KENT**
Well, sir, I'll bring you to our master Lear,
And leave you to attend him: some dear cause°
Will in concealment wrap me up awhile;
When I am known aright, you shall not grieve        55
Lending me this acquaintance. I pray you, go
Along with me.                    [*Exeunt.*]

[Scene IV. *The same. A tent.*]

*Enter, with drum and colors,* CORDELIA, DOCTOR,
*and* SOLDIERS.

**CORDELIA**
Alack, 'tis he: why, he was met even now
As mad as the vexed sea; singing aloud;

---

**86–87 May . . . life** These things (line 85) may send
my future hopes, my castles in air, crashing upon down
the hateful (married) life I lead now  **87 Another
way** looked at another way  **88 tart** sour  **91 back** going
back
**IV.iii.3–4 imperfect . . . state** unsettled in his own kingdom
**5 imports** portends  **11 pierce** impel  **14 trilled** trickled
**19 Who . . . goodliest** which should give her the most
becoming expression  **21 Were . . . way** i.e., improved on
that spectacle; **smilets** little smiles

**25–26 Sorrow . . . it** sorrow would be a coveted jewel if it
became others as it does her  **27 heaved** expressed with
difficulty  **31 Let . . . believed** Let it not be believed for pity
**33 clamor moistened** moistened clamor, i.e., mixed (and
perhaps assuaged) her outcries with tears  **35 govern our
conditions** determine what we are  **36–37 Else . . . issues**
otherwise the same husband and wife could not produce such
different children  **41 better tune** composed, less jangled
intervals  **44 sovereign** overpowering; **elbows** jogs his elbow
(i.e., reminds him)  **46 casualties** chances  **51 'Tis so** i.e., I
have heard of them  **53 dear cause** important reason

Crowned with rank femiter and furrow-weeds,
With hardocks, hemlock, nettles, cuckoo-flow'rs,
Darnel,° and all the idle weeds that grow                        5
In our sustaining corn.° A century° send forth;
Search every acre in the high-grown field,
And bring him to our eye. [*Exit an* OFFICER.] What
    can man's wisdom°
In the restoring his bereavèd° sense?
He that helps him take all my outward° worth.                    10

DOCTOR
There is means, madam:
Our foster-nurse° of nature is repose,
The which he lacks: that to provoke° in him,
Are many simples operative,° whose power
Will close the eye of anguish.

CORDELIA                              All blest secrets,           15
All you unpublished virtues° of the earth,
Spring with my tears! be aidant and remediate°
In the good man's distress! Seek, seek for him,
Lest his ungoverned rage dissolve the life
That wants the means to lead it.°

*Enter* MESSENGER.

MESSENGER                              News, madam;                20
The British pow'rs are marching hitherward.

CORDELIA
'Tis known before. Our preparation stands
In expectation of them. O dear father,
It is thy business that I go about;
Therefore° great France                                          25
My mourning and importuned° tears hath pitied.
No blown° ambition doth our arms incite,
But love, dear love, and our aged father's right:
Soon may I hear and see him!                  *Exeunt.*

[Scene V. *Gloucester's castle.*]

*Enter* REGAN *and* OSWALD.

REGAN
But are my brother's pow'rs set forth?

OSWALD                                  Ay, madam.

REGAN
Himself in person there?

OSWALD                      Madam, with much ado:°
Your sister is the better soldier.

REGAN
Lord Edmund spake not with your lord at home?

OSWALD
No, madam.                                                        5

REGAN
What might import° my sister's letter to him?

OSWALD
I know not, lady.

REGAN
Faith, he is posted° hence on serious matter.
It was great ignorance,° Gloucester's eyes being out,
To let him live. Where he arrives he moves                       10
All hearts against us: Edmund, I think, is gone,
In pity of his misery, to dispatch
His nighted° life; moreover, to descry
The strength o' th' enemy.

OSWALD
I must needs after him, madam, with my letter.                   15

REGAN
Our troops set forth tomorrow: stay with us;
The ways are dangerous.

OSWALD                          I may not, madam:
My lady charged my duty° in this business.

REGAN
Why should she write to Edmund? Might not you
Transport her purposes° by word? Belike,°                        20
Some things I know not what. I'll love thee much,
Let me unseal the letter.

OSWALD                      Madam, I had rather—

REGAN
I know your lady does not love her husband;
I am sure of that: and at her late° being here
She gave strange eliads° and most speaking looks                 25
To noble Edmund. I know you are of her bosom.°

OSWALD   I, madam?

REGAN
I speak in understanding: y' are; I know't:
Therefore I do advise you, take this note:°
My lord is dead; Edmund and I have talked;                       30
And more convenient° is he for my hand
Than for your lady's: you may gather more.°
If you do find him, pray you, give him this;°
And when your mistress hears thus much from you,
I pray, desire her call° her wisdom to her.                      35
So, fare you well.
If you do chance to hear of that blind traitor,
Preferment° falls on him that cuts him off.

OSWALD
Would I could meet him, madam! I should show
What party I do follow.

REGAN                          Fare thee well.      *Exeunt.* 40

[Scene VI. *Fields near Dover.*]

*Enter* GLOUCESTER *and* EDGAR.

GLOUCESTER
When shall I come to th' top of that same hill?

IV.iv.3–5 **femiter . . . Darnel** *femiter* fumitory, whose
leaves and juice are bitter; *furrow-weeds* weeds that grow in the
furrow, or plowed land; *hardocks* hoar or white docks (?),
burdocks, harlocks; *hemlock* a poison; *nettles* plants that sting
and burn; *cuckoo-flow'rs* identified with a plant employed to
remedy diseases of the brain; *Darnel* tares, noisome weeds  **6
sustaining corn** life-maintaining wheat; **century** sentry (?);
troop of a hundred soldiers  **8 What . . . wisdom** what can
science accomplish  **9 bereavèd** impaired  **10 outward**
material  **12 foster-nurse** fostering nurse  **13 provoke** induce
**14 simples operative** efficacious medicinal herbs  **16
unpublished virtues** i.e., secret remedial herbs  **17
remediate** remedial  **20 wants . . . it** i.e., lacks the reason
to control the rage  **25 Therefore** because of that  **26 importuned** importunate  **27 blown** puffed up
**IV.v.2 ado** bother and persuasion

**6 import** purport, carry as its message  **8 is posted** has ridden
speedily  **9 ignorance** folly  **13 nighted** (1) darkened, because
blinded (2) benighted  **18 charged my duty** ordered me as a
solemn duty  **20 Transport her purposes** convey her
intentions; **Belike** probably  **24 late** recently  **25 eliads**
amorous looks  **26 of her bosom** in her confidence  **29
take this note** take note of this  **31 convenient** fitting  **32
gather more** surmise more yourself  **33 this** this advice  **35
call** recall  **38 Preferment** promotion

EDGAR
You do climb up it now. Look, how we labor.

GLOUCESTER
Methinks the ground is even.

EDGAR          Horrible steep.
Hark, do you hear the sea?

GLOUCESTER          No, truly.

EDGAR
Why then your other senses grow imperfect    5
By your eyes' anguish.°

GLOUCESTER          So may it be indeed.
Methinks thy voice is altered, and thou speak'st
In better phrase and matter than thou didst.

EDGAR
Y' are much deceived: in nothing am I changed
But in my garments.

GLOUCESTER       Methinks y' are better spoken.    10

EDGAR
Come on, sir; here's the place: stand still. How fearful
And dizzy 'tis to cast one's eyes so low!
The crows and choughs° that wing the midway air°
Show scarce so gross° as beetles. Half way down
Hangs one that gathers sampire,° dreadful trade!    15
Methinks he seems no bigger than his head.
The fishermen that walk upon the beach
Appear like mice; and yond tall anchoring° bark
Diminished to her cock;° her cock, a buoy
Almost too small for sight. The murmuring surge    20
That on th' unnumb'red idle pebble° chafes
Cannot be heard so high. I'll look no more,
Lest my brain turn and the deficient sight
Topple° down headlong.

GLOUCESTER          Set me where you stand.

EDGAR
Give me your hand: you are now within a foot    25
Of th' extreme verge: for all beneath the moon
Would I not leap upright.°

GLOUCESTER          Let go my hand.
Here, friend, 's another purse; in it a jewel
Well worth a poor man's taking. Fairies° and gods
Prosper it with thee! Go thou further off;    30
Bid me farewell, and let me hear thee going.

EDGAR
Now fare ye well, good sir.

GLOUCESTER          With all my heart.

EDGAR [Aside.]
Why I do trifle thus with his despair
Is done to cure it.°

GLOUCESTER      O you mighty gods!

He kneels.

This world I do renounce, and in your sights    35
Shake patiently my great affliction off:
If I could bear it longer and not fall

To quarrel with° your great opposeless° wills,
My snuff° and loathèd part of nature should
Burn itself out. If Edgar live, O bless him!    40
Now, fellow, fare thee well. He falls.

EDGAR          Gone, sir, farewell.
And yet I know not how° conceit° may rob
The treasury of life, when life itself
Yields to° the theft. Had he been where he thought,
By this had thought been past. Alive or dead?    45
Ho, you sir! friend! Hear you, sir! speak!
Thus might he pass° indeed: yet he revives.
What are you, sir?

GLOUCESTER       Away, and let me die.

EDGAR
Hadst thou been aught but gossamer, feathers, air,
So many fathom down precipitating,°    50
Thou'dst shivered like an egg: but thou dost breathe;
Hast heavy substance; bleed'st not; speak'st; art sound.
Ten masts at each° make not the altitude
Which thou hast perpendicularly fell:
Thy life's° a miracle. Speak yet again.    55

GLOUCESTER
But have I fall'n, or no?

EDGAR
From the dread summit of this chalky bourn.°
Look up a-height;° the shrill-gorged° lark so far
Cannot be seen or heard: do but look up.

GLOUCESTER
Alack, I have no eyes.    60
Is wretchedness deprived that benefit,
To end itself by death? 'Twas yet some comfort,
When misery could beguile° the tyrant's rage
And frustrate his proud will.

EDGAR          Give me your arm.
Up, so. How is't? Feel you° your legs? You stand.    65

GLOUCESTER
Too well, too well.

EDGAR          This is above all strangeness.
Upon the crown o' th' cliff, what thing was that
Which parted from you?

GLOUCESTER       A poor unfortunate beggar.

EDGAR
As I stood here below, methought his eyes
Were two full moons; he had a thousand noses,    70
Horns whelked° and waved like the enridgèd° sea:
It was some fiend; therefore, thou happy father,°
Think that the clearest° gods, who make them honors
Of men's impossibilities,° have preserved thee.

GLOUCESTER
I do remember now: henceforth I'll bear    75
Affliction till it do cry out itself,
"Enough, enough," and die. That thing you speak of,

IV.vi.6 anguish pain 13 choughs a kind of crow; midway air i.e., halfway down the cliff 14 gross large 15 sampire samphire, an aromatic herb associated with Dover Cliffs 18 anchoring anchored 19 cock cockboat, a small boat usually towed behind the ship 21 unnumb'red idle pebble innumerable pebbles, moved to and fro by the waves to no purpose 23–24 the . . . Topple my failing sight topple me 27 upright i.e., even up in the air, to say nothing of forward, over the cliff 29 Fairies who are supposed to guard and multiply hidden treasure 33–34 Why . . . it I play on his despair in order to cure it

37–38 fall . . . with rebel against 38 opposeless not to be, and not capable of being, opposed 39 snuff the guttering (and stinking) wick of a burnt-out candle 42 how but what; conceit imagination 44 Yields to allows 47 pass die 50 precipitating falling 53 at each one on top of the other 55 life's survival 57 bourn boundary 58 a-height on high; gorged throated, voiced 63 beguile cheat (i.e., by suicide) 65 Feel you have you any feeling in 71 whelked twisted; enridgèd i.e., furrowed into waves 72 happy father fortunate old man 73 clearest purest 73–74 who . . . impossibilities who cause themselves to be honored and revered by performing miracles of which men are incapable

I took it for a man; often 'twould say,
"The fiend, the fiend"—he led me to that place.

EDGAR
Bear free° and patient thoughts.

*Enter* LEAR [*fantastically dressed with wild flowers*].

But who comes here? 80
The safer° sense will ne'er accommodate°
His master thus.

LEAR   No, they cannot touch me for coining;° I am
the king himself.

EDGAR
O thou side-piercing sight! 85

LEAR   Nature's above art in that respect.° There's your
press-money.° That fellow handles his bow like a
crow-keeper;° draw me a clothier's yard.° Look, look,
a mouse! Peace, peace; this piece of toasted cheese will
do't. There's my gauntlet;° I'll prove it on° a giant. 90
Bring up the brown bills.° O, well flown,° bird! i' th'
clout, i' th' clout:° hewgh!° Give the word.°

EDGAR   Sweet marjoram.°

LEAR   Pass.

GLOUCESTER
I know that voice. 95

LEAR   Ha! Goneril, with a white beard! They flattered
me like a dog,° and told me I had white hairs in my
beard ere the black ones were there.° To say "ay" and
"no" to everything that I said! "Ay" and "no" too
was no good divinity.° When the rain came to wet 100
me once and the wind to make me chatter; when the
thunder would not peace at my bidding; there I found
'em, there I smelt 'em out. Go to, they are not men o'
their words: they told me I was everything; 'tis a lie,
I am not ague-proof.° 105

GLOUCESTER
The trick° of that voice I do well remember:
Is't not the king?

LEAR                Ay, every inch a king.
When I do stare, see how the subject quakes.
I pardon that man's life. What was thy cause?°
Adultery? 110

Thou shalt not die: die for adultery! No:
The wren goes to't, and the small gilded fly
Does lecher° in my sight.
Let copulation thrive; for Gloucester's bastard son
Was kinder to his father than my daughters 115
Got° 'tween the lawful sheets.
To't, luxury,° pell-mell! for I lack soldiers.°
Behold yond simp'ring dame,
Whose face between her forks presages snow,°
That minces° virtue and does shake the head 120
To hear of pleasure's name.°
The fitchew,° nor the soilèd° horse, goes to't
With a more riotous appetite.
Down from the waist they are Centaurs,°
Though women all above: 125
But to the girdle° do the gods inherit,°
Beneath is all the fiend's.
There's hell, there's darkness, there is the sulphurous
pit, burning, scalding, stench, consumption; fie, fie, fie!
pah, pah! Give me an ounce of civet;° good apothe- 130
cary, sweeten my imagination: there's money for thee.

GLOUCESTER
O, let me kiss that hand!

LEAR   Let me wipe it first; it smells of mortality.°

GLOUCESTER
O ruined piece of nature! This great world
Shall so wear out to nought.° Dost thou know me? 135

LEAR   I remember thine eyes well enough. Dost thou
squiny° at me? No, do thy worst, blind Cupid;° I'll
not love. Read thou this challenge;° mark but the
penning of it.

GLOUCESTER
Were all thy letters suns, I could not see. 140

EDGAR
I would not take° this from report: it is,
And my heart breaks at it.

LEAR   Read.

GLOUCESTER
What, with the case° of eyes?

LEAR   O, ho, are you there with me?° No eyes in your 145
head, nor no money in your purse? Your eyes are in a
heavy case,° your purse in a light,° yet you see how
this world goes.

GLOUCESTER
I see it feelingly.°

LEAR   What, art mad? A man may see how this world 150
goes with no eyes. Look with thine ears: see how yond

---

**80 free** i.e., emancipated from grief and despair, which fetter the soul   **81 safer** sounder, saner; **accommodate** dress, adorn   **83 touch . . . coining** arrest me for minting coins (the king's prerogative)   **86 Nature's . . . respect** i.e., a born king is superior to legal (and hence artificial) inhibition; there is also a glance here at the popular Renaissance debate concerning the relative importance of nature (inspiration) and art (training)   **87 press-money** paid to conscripted soldiers   **88 crow-keeper** a farmer scaring away crows; **clothier's yard** the standard English arrow was a cloth-yard long; here the injunction is to draw the arrow back, like a powerful archer, a full yard to the ear   **90 gauntlet** armored glove, thrown down as a challenge; **prove it on** maintain my challenge even against   **91 brown bills** halberds varnished to prevent rust (here the reference is to the soldiers who carry them); **well flown** falconer's cry; and perhaps a reference to the flight of the arrow   **92 clout** the target shot at; **hewgh** imitating the whizzing of the arrow (?); **word** password   **93 Sweet marjoram** herb, used as a remedy for brain disease   **97 like a dog** as a dog flatters   **97-98 I . . . there** I was wise before I had even grown a beard   **100 no good divinity** bad theology, because contrary to the biblical saying (II Corinthians 1:18), "Our word toward you was not yea and nay"; see also James 5:12, "But let your yea be yea, and your nay, nay; lest ye fall into condemnation"; and Matthew 5:36-37   **105 ague-proof** secure against fever   **106 trick** intonation   **109 cause** offense

**113 lecher** copulate   **116 Got** begot   **117 luxury** lechery; **for . . . soldiers** i.e., (1) whom copulation will supply (?) (2) and am therefore powerless (?)   **119 Whose . . . snow** whose cold demeanor seems to promise chaste behavior ("forks" = legs)   **120 minces** squeamishly pretends to   **121 pleasure's name** the very name of sexual pleasure   **122 fitchew** polecat (and slang for prostitute); **soilèd** put to pasture, and hence wanton with feeding   **124 Centaurs** lustful creatures, half man and half horse   **126 girdle** waist; **inherit** possess   **130 civet** perfume   **133 mortality** (1) death (2) existence   **134-35 This . . . nought** i.e., The universe (macrocosm) will decay to nothing in the same way as the little world of man (microcosm)   **137 squiny** squint, look sideways, like a prostitute; **blind Cupid** the sign hung before a brothel   **138 challenge** a reminiscence of lines 89-90   **141 take** believe   **144 case** empty sockets   **145 are . . . me** is that what you tell me   **147 heavy case** sad plight (pun on line 144); **light** i.e., empty   **149 feelingly** (1) by touch (2) by feeling pain (3) with emotion

justice rails upon yond simple° thief. Hark, in thine
ear: change places, and, handy-dandy,° which is the
justice, which is the thief? Thou hast seen a farmer's
dog bark at a beggar?        155

GLOUCESTER    Ay, sir.

LEAR    And the creature run from the cur? There thou
mightst behold the great image of authority:° a dog's
obeyed in office.°
Thou rascal beadle,° hold thy bloody hand!        160
Why dost thou lash that whore? Strip thy own back;
Thou hotly lusts to use her in that kind°
For which thou whip'st her. The usurer hangs the
    cozener.°
Through tattered clothes small vices do appear;
Robes and furred gowns° hide all. Plate sin with gold,   165
And the strong lance of justice hurtless° breaks;
Arm it in rags, a pygmy's straw does pierce it.
None does offend, none, I say, none; I'll able° 'em:
Take that° of me, my friend, who have the power
To seal th' accuser's lips. Get thee glass eyes,°        170
And, like a scurvy politician,° seem
To see the things thou dost not. Now, now, now, now.
Pull off my boots: harder, harder: so.

EDGAR
O, matter and impertinency° mixed!
Reason in madness!        175

LEAR
If thou wilt weep my fortunes, take my eyes.
I know thee well enough; thy name is Gloucester:
Thou must be patient; we came crying hither:
Thou know'st, the first time that we smell the air
We wawl and cry. I will preach to thee: mark.     180

GLOUCESTER
Alack, alack the day!

LEAR
When we are born, we cry that we are come
To this great stage of fools. This'° a good block.°
It were a delicate° stratagem, to shoe
A troop of horse with felt: I'll put't in proof;°     185
And when I have stol'n upon these son-in-laws,
Then, kill, kill, kill, kill, kill, kill!

---

**152 simple** common, of low estate   **153 handy-dandy** i.e.,
choose, guess (after the children's game—"Handy-dandy,
prickly prandy"—of choosing the correct hand)   **158 image
of authority** symbol revealing the true meaning of authority
**158–59 a dog's . . . office** i.e., whoever has power is obeyed
**160 beadle** parish constable   **162 kind** i.e., sexual act
**163 The usurer . . . cozener** i.e., The powerful moneylender, in his role as judge, puts to death the petty cheat   **165
Robes . . . gowns** worn by a judge   **166 hurtless** i.e.,
without hurting the sinner   **168 able** vouch for   **169 that**
the immunity just conferred (line 168)   **170 glass eyes** spectacles   **171 scurvy politician** vile politic man   **174 matter
and impertinency** sense and nonsense   **183 This'** this is;
**block** various meanings have been suggested, for example,
the stump of a tree, on which Lear is supposed to climb; a
mounting-block, which suggests "horse" (line 185); a hat
(which Lear or another must be made to wear), from the block
on which a felt hat is molded, and which would suggest a
"felt" (line 185); the proposal here is that "block" be taken to
denote the quintain, whose function is to bear blows, "a mere
lifeless block" (*As You Like It*, I.ii.247), an object shaped like a
man and used for tilting practice; see also *Much Ado About
Nothing*, II.i.231–32, "She misused me past the endurance of a
block!" and, in the same passage, the associated reference, "I
stood like a man at a mark [target]" (lines 237–38)   **184
delicate** subtle   **185 put't in proof** test it

---

*Enter a* GENTLEMAN, [*with* ATTENDANTS].

GENTLEMAN
O, here he is: lay hand upon him. Sir,
Your most dear daughter—

LEAR
No rescue? What, a prisoner? I am even        190
The natural fool° of fortune. Use me well;
You shall have ransom. Let me have surgeons;
I am cut° to th' brains.

GENTLEMAN        You shall have anything.

LEAR
No seconds?° all myself?
Why, this would make a man a man of salt,°       195
To use his eyes for garden water-pots,
Ay, and laying autumn's dust.

GENTLEMAN
Good sir—

LEAR
I will die bravely,° like a smug° bridegroom.° What!
I will be jovial: come, come; I am a king;       200
Masters, know you that?

GENTLEMAN
You are a royal one, and we obey you.

LEAR    Then there's life in't.° Come, and you get it,
you shall get it by running. Sa, sa, sa, sa.°
          *Exit* [*running;* ATTENDANTS *follow*].

GENTLEMAN
A sight most pitiful in the meanest wretch,       205
Past speaking of in a king! Thou hast one daughter
Who redeems Nature from the general curse
Which twain have brought her to.°

EDGAR
Hail, gentle° sir.

GENTLEMAN    Sir, speed° you: what's your will?

EDGAR
Do you hear aught, sir, of a battle toward?°       210

GENTLEMAN
Most sure and vulgar:° every one hears that,
Which can distinguish sound.

EDGAR        But, by your favor,
How near's the other army?

GENTLEMAN
Near and on speedy foot; the main descry
Stands on the hourly thought.°

EDGAR        I thank you, sir: that's all.   215

GENTLEMAN
Though that the queen on special cause is here,
Her army is moved on.

EDGAR        I thank you, sir. *Exit* [GENTLEMAN].

GLOUCESTER
You ever-gentle gods, take my breath from me;

---

**191 natural fool** born sport (with pun on "natural"
= imbecile)   **193 cut** wounded   **194 seconds** supporters
**195 man of salt** i.e., all (salt) tears   **199 bravely** (1)
smartly attired (2) courageously; **smug** spick and span;
**bridegroom** whose "brave" sexual feats are picked up
in the pun on "die"   **203 there's life in't** there's still
hope   **204 Sa . . . sa** hunting and rallying cry; also
an interjection of defiance   **207–08 general . . . to** (1)
universal condemnation which Goneril and Regan have made
for (2) damnation incurred by the original sin of Adam and Eve
**209 gentle** noble; **speed** Godspeed   **210 toward** impending
**211 vulgar** common knowledge   **214–15 the main . . .
thought** we expect to see the main body of the army any hour

Let not my worser spirit° tempt me again
To die before you please.
EDGAR                          Well pray you, father.          220
GLOUCESTER
Now, good sir, what are you?
EDGAR
A most poor man, made tame° to fortune's blows;
Who, by the art of known and feeling sorrows,°
Am pregnant° to good pity. Give me your hand,
I'll lead you to some biding.°
GLOUCESTER                    Hearty thanks;          225
The bounty and the benison° of heaven
To boot, and boot.°

*Enter* OSWALD.

OSWALD                A proclaimed prize!° Most happy!°
That eyeless head of thine was first framed° flesh
To raise my fortunes. Thou old unhappy traitor,
Briefly thyself remember:° the sword is out          230
That must destroy thee.
GLOUCESTER              Now let thy friendly° hand
Put strength enough to't. [EDGAR *interposes*.]
OSWALD                    Wherefore, bold peasant,
Dar'st thou support a published° traitor? Hence!
Lest that th' infection of his fortune take
Like hold on thee. Let go his arm.          235
EDGAR
Chill° not let go, zir, without vurther 'casion.°
OSWALD
Let go, slave, or thou diest!
EDGAR  Good gentleman, go your gait,° and let poor
volk° pass. And chud ha' bin zwaggered° out of my
life, 'twould not ha' bin zo long as 'tis by a vortnight.  240
Nay, come not near th' old man; keep out, che vor'
ye,° or I'se° try whether your costard° or my ballow°
be the harder: chill be plain with you.
OSWALD  Out, dunghill!

*They fight.*

EDGAR  Chill pick your teeth,° zir: come; no matter  245
vor your foins.°

[OSWALD *falls*.]

OSWALD
Slave, thou hast slain me. Villain, take my purse:
If ever thou wilt thrive, bury my body,
And give the letters which thou find'st about° me
To Edmund Earl of Gloucester; seek him out          250
Upon the English party.° O, untimely death!
Death!                                    *He dies.*

EDGAR
I know thee well. A serviceable° villain,
As duteous° to the vices of thy mistress
As badness would desire.
GLOUCESTER            What, is he dead?          255
EDGAR
Sit you down, father; rest you.
Let's see these pockets: the letters that he speaks of
May be my friends. He's dead; I am only sorry
He had no other deathsman.° Let us see:
Leave,° gentle wax;° and, manners, blame us not:          260
To know our enemies' minds, we rip their hearts;
Their papers° is more lawful.

*Reads the letter.*

"Let our reciprocal vows be remembered. You have
many opportunities to cut him off: if your will want
not,° time and place will be fruitfully offered. There is          265
nothing done, if he return the conqueror: then am I
the prisoner, and his bed my jail; from the loathed
warmth whereof deliver me, and supply the place for
your labor.

    "Your—wife, so I would° say—affectionate servant,          270
and for you her own for venture,°
                                        Goneril."

O indistinguished space of woman's will!°
A plot upon her virtuous husband's life;
And the exchange° my brother! Here in the sands          275
Thee I'll rake up,° the post unsanctified°
Of murderous lechers; and in the mature° time,
With this ungracious paper° strike° the sight
Of the death-practiced° duke: for him 'tis well
That of thy death and business I can tell.          280
GLOUCESTER
The king is mad: how stiff° is my vile sense,°
That I stand up, and have ingenious° feeling
Of my huge sorrows! Better I were distract:°
So should my thoughts be severed from my griefs,
And woes by wrong imaginations° lose          285
The knowledge of themselves. *Drum afar off.*
EDGAR                              Give me your hand:
Far off, methinks, I hear the beaten drum.
Come, father, I'll bestow° you with a friend. *Exeunt.*

Scene VII. [*A tent in the French camp.*]

*Enter* CORDELIA, KENT, DOCTOR, *and* GENTLEMAN.
CORDELIA
O thou good Kent, how shall I live and work,

---

**219 worser spirit** bad angel, evil side of my nature  **222 tame**
submissive  **223 art . . . sorrows** instruction of sorrows
painfully experienced  **224 pregnant** disposed  **225 biding**
place of refuge  **226 benison** blessing  **227 To . . .
boot** also, and in the highest degree; **proclaimed prize**
i.e., one with a price on his head; **happy** fortunate
(for Oswald)  **228 framed** created  **230 thyself remember**
i.e., pray, think of your sins  **231 friendly** i.e., because
it offers the death Gloucester covets  **233 published**
proclaimed  **236 Chill** I will (Edgar speaks in rustic
dialect); **vurther 'casion** further occasion  **238 gait** way
**239 volk** folk; **And . . . zwaggered** if I could have
been swaggered  **241–42 che vor' ye** I warrant you  **242 I'se**
I shall; **costard** head (literally, "apple"); **ballow** cudgel
**245 Chill . . . teeth** I will knock your teeth out  **246 foins**
thrusts  **249 about** upon  **251 party** side

**253 serviceable** ready to be used  **254 duteous** obedient
**259 deathsman** executioner  **260 Leave** by your leave;
**wax** with which the letter is sealed  **262 Their papers**
i.e., to rip their papers  **264–65 if . . . not** if your
desire (and lust) be not lacking  **270 would** would like to
**271 and . . . venture** i.e., and one who holds you her own for
venturing (Edmund had earlier been promised union by
Goneril, "If you dare venture in your own behalf," IV.ii.21)
**273 indistinguished . . . will** unlimited range of woman's
lust  **275 exchange** substitute  **276 rake up** cover up, bury;
**post unsanctified** unholy messenger  **277 mature** ripe  **278
ungracious paper** wicked letter; **strike** blast  **279 death-
practiced** whose death is plotted  **281 stiff** unbending; **vile
sense** hateful capacity for feeling  **282 ingenious** conscious
**283 distract** distracted, mad  **285 wrong imaginations**
delusions  **288 bestow** lodge

To match thy goodness? My life will be too short,
And every measure fail me.

**KENT**
To be acknowledged, madam, is o'erpaid.
All my reports go° with the modest truth,      5
Nor more nor clipped,° but so.

**CORDELIA**          Be better suited:°
These weeds° are memories° of those worser hours:
I prithee, put them off.

**KENT**          Pardon, dear madam;
Yet to be known shortens my made intent:°
My boon I make it,° that you know me not      10
Till time and I think meet.°

**CORDELIA**
Then be't so, my good lord. [*To the* DOCTOR.] How
    does the king?

**DOCTOR**
Madam, sleeps still.

**CORDELIA**
O you kind gods!
Cure this great breach in his abusèd° nature.      15
Th' untuned and jarring senses, O, wind up°
Of this child-changèd° father.

**DOCTOR**          So please your majesty
That we may wake the king: he hath slept long.

**CORDELIA**
Be governed by your knowledge, and proceed
I' th' sway of° your own will. Is he arrayed?      20

*Enter* LEAR *in a chair carried by* SERVANTS.

**GENTLEMAN**
Ay, madam; in the heaviness of sleep
We put fresh garments on him.

**DOCTOR**
Be by, good madam, when we do awake him;
I doubt not of his temperance.°

**CORDELIA**          Very well.

**DOCTOR**
Please you, draw near. Louder the music there!      25

**CORDELIA**
O my dear father, restoration hang
Thy medicine on my lips, and let this kiss
Repair those violent harms that my two sisters
Have in thy reverence° made.

**KENT**          Kind and dear princess.

**CORDELIA**
Had you not been their father, these white flakes°      30
Did challenge° pity of them. Was this a face
To be opposed against the warring winds?
To stand against the deep dread-bolted° thunder?
In the most terrible and nimble stroke
Of quick, cross° lightning to watch—poor perdu!°—      35
With this thin helm?° Mine enemy's dog,

Though he had bit me, should have stood that
    night
Against my fire; and wast thou fain,° poor father,
To hovel thee with swine and rogues° forlorn,
In short° and musty straw?° Alack, alack!      40
'Tis wonder that thy life and wits at once
Had not concluded all.° He wakes; speak to him.

**DOCTOR**
Madam, do you; 'tis fittest.

**CORDELIA**
How does my royal lord? How fares your majesty?

**LEAR**
You do me wrong to take me out o' th' grave:      45
Thou art a soul in bliss; but I am bound
Upon a wheel of fire,° that mine own tears
Do scald like molten lead.

**CORDELIA**          Sir, do you know me?

**LEAR**
You are a spirit, I know. Where did you die?

**CORDELIA**
Still, still, far wide.°      50

**DOCTOR**
He's scarce awake: let him alone awhile.

**LEAR**
Where have I been? Where am I? Fair daylight?
I am mightily abused.° I should ev'n die with pity,
To see another thus. I know not what to say.
I will not swear these are my hands: let's see;      55
I feel this pin prick. Would I were assured
Of my condition.

**CORDELIA**          O, look upon me, sir,
And hold your hand in benediction o'er me.
You must not kneel.

**LEAR**          Pray, do not mock me:
I am a very foolish fond° old man,      60
Fourscore and upward, not an hour more nor less;
And, to deal plainly,
I fear I am not in my perfect mind.
Methinks I should know you and know this man,
Yet I am doubtful; for I am mainly° ignorant      65
What place this is, and all the skill I have
Remembers not these garments, nor I know not
Where I did lodge last night. Do not laugh at me,
For, as I am a man, I think this lady
To be my child Cordelia.

**CORDELIA**          And so I am, I am.      70

**LEAR**
Be your tears wet? Yes, faith. I pray, weep not.
If you have poison for me, I will drink it.
I know you do not love me; for your sisters
Have, as I do remember, done me wrong.
You have some cause, they have not.

**CORDELIA**          No cause, no cause.      75

---

**IV.vii.5 go** conform   **6 clipped** curtailed; **suited** attired   **7 weeds** clothes; **memories** reminders   **9 Yet . . . intent** to reveal myself just yet interferes with the plan I have made   **10 My . . . it** I ask this reward   **11 meet** fitting   **15 abusèd** disturbed   **16 wind up** tune   **17 child-changèd** changed, deranged (and also, reduced to a child) by the cruelty of his children   **20 I' . . . of** according to   **24 temperance** sanity   **29 reverence** revered person   **30 flakes** hairs (in long strands)   **31 challenge** claim   **33 deep dread-bolted** deep-voiced and furnished with the dreadful thunderbolt   **35 cross** zigzag; **perdu** (1) sentry in a forlorn position (2) lost one   **36 helm** helmet (his scanty hair)

**38 fain** pleased   **39 rogues** vagabonds   **40 short** when straw is freshly cut, it is long, and suitable for bedding, given its flexibility and crispness; as it is used, it becomes musty, shreds into pieces, is "short"; in contemporary Maine usage, "short manure" refers to dung mixed with straw that has been broken up, "long manure" to dung mixed with coarse new straw   **42 concluded all** come to a complete end   **47 wheel of fire** torment associated by the Middle Ages with hell, where Lear thinks he is   **50 wide** i.e., of the mark (of sanity)   **53 abused** deluded   **60 fond** in dotage   **65 mainly** entirely

LEAR
Am I in France?

KENT            In your own kingdom, sir.

LEAR
Do not abuse° me.

DOCTOR
Be comforted, good madam: the great rage,°
You see, is killed in him: and yet it is danger
To make him even o'er° the time he has lost.          80
Desire him to go in; trouble him no more
Till further settling.°

CORDELIA
Will't please your highness walk?°

LEAR                        You must bear with me.
Pray you now, forget and forgive. I am old and
    foolish. *Exeunt. Mane[n]t°* KENT *and* GENTLEMAN.

GENTLEMAN  Holds it true, sir, that the Duke of 85
Cornwall was so slain?

KENT  Most certain, sir.

GENTLEMAN  Who is conductor of his people?

KENT  As 'tis said, the bastard son of Gloucester.

GENTLEMAN  They say Edgar, his banished son, is 90
with the Earl of Kent in Germany.

KENT  Report is changeable.° 'Tis time to look about;
the powers° of the kingdom approach apace.

GENTLEMAN  The arbitrement° is like to be bloody.
Fare you well, sir.                          *[Exit.]* 95

KENT
My point and period will be throughly wrought,°
Or well or ill, as this day's battle's fought.      *Exit.*

# A C T   V

Scene I. [*The British camp near Dover.*]

*Enter, with drum and colors,* EDMUND, REGAN,
GENTLEMEN, *and* SOLDIERS.

EDMUND
Know° of the duke if his last purpose hold,°
Or whether since he is advised° by aught
To change the course: he's full of alteration
And self-reproving: bring his constant pleasure.°
                *[To a* GENTLEMAN, *who goes out.]*

REGAN
Our sister's man is certainly miscarried.°          5

EDMUND
'Tis to be doubted,° madam.

REGAN                        Now, sweet lord,
You know the goodness I intend upon you:
Tell me, but truly, but then speak the truth,
Do you not love my sister?

EDMUND                    In honored° love.

REGAN
But have you never found my brother's way          10
To the forfended° place?

EDMUND            That thought abuses° you.

REGAN
I am doubtful that you have been conjunct
And bosomed with her, as far as we call hers.°

EDMUND
No, by mine honor, madam.

REGAN
I shall never endure her: dear my lord,            15
Be not familiar with her.

EDMUND            Fear° me not.—
She and the duke her husband!

*Enter, with drum and colors,* ALBANY, GONERIL, [*and*]
SOLDIERS.

GONERIL [*Aside.*]
I had rather lose the battle than that sister
Should loosen° him and me.

ALBANY
Our very loving sister, well be-met.°              20
Sir, this I heard, the king is come to his daughter,
With others whom the rigor of our state°
Forced to cry out. Where I could not be honest,°
I never yet was valiant: for this business,
It touches us, as° France invades our land,        25
Not bolds the king, with others, whom, I fear,
Most just and heavy causes make oppose.°

EDMUND
Sir, you speak nobly.

REGAN              Why is this reasoned?°

GONERIL
Combine together 'gainst the enemy;
For these domestic and particular broils°          30
Are not the question° here.

ALBANY              Let's then determine
With th' ancient of war° on our proceeding.

EDMUND
I shall attend you presently at your tent.

REGAN
Sister, you'll go with us?°

GONERIL  No.                                      35

REGAN
'Tis most convenient;° pray you, go with us.

GONERIL [*Aside.*]
O, ho, I know the riddle.°—I will go.
                *Exeunt both the* ARMIES.

*Enter* EDGAR [*disguised*].

EDGAR
If e'er your grace had speech with man so poor,
Hear me one word.

77 abuse deceive  78 rage frenzy  80 even o'er smooth over by filling in; and hence, "recollect"  82 settling calming  83 walk perhaps in the sense of "withdraw"  84 s.d. Mane[n]t remain  92 Report is changeable rumors are unreliable  93 powers armies  94 arbitrement deciding encounter  96 My . . . wrought the aim and end, the close of my life, will be completely worked out
V.i.1 Know learn; last purpose hold most recent intention (to fight) be maintained  2 advised induced  4 constant pleasure fixed (final) decision  5 miscarried come to grief  6 doubted feared  9 honored honorable
11 forfended forbidden; abuses (1) deceives (2) demeans, is unworthy of  12–13 I . . . hers I fear that you have united with her intimately, in the fullest possible way  16 Fear distrust  19 loosen separate  20 be-met met  22 rigor . . . state tyranny of our government  23 honest honorable  25 touches us, as concerns me, only in that  26–27 Not . . . oppose and not in that France emboldens the king and others, who have been led, by real and serious grievances, to take up arms against us  28 reasoned argued  30 particular broils private quarrels  31 question issue  32 th' ancient of war experienced commanders  34 us me (rather than Edmund)  36 convenient fitting, desirable  37 riddle real reason (for Regan's curious request)

ALBANY [*To those going out.*]
I'll overtake you. [*To* EDGAR.] Speak.                    40
          *Exeunt* [*all but* ALBANY *and* EDGAR].

EDGAR
Before you fight the battle, ope this letter.
If you have victory, let the trumpet sound
For° him that brought it: wretched though I seem,
I can produce a champion that will prove°
What is avouchèd° there. If you miscarry,          45
Your business of° the world hath so an end,
And machination° ceases. Fortune love you.

ALBANY
Stay till I have read the letter.

EDGAR                                I was forbid it.
When time shall serve, let but the herald cry,
And I'll appear again.                                    50

ALBANY
Why, fare thee well: I will o'erlook° thy paper.
                    *Exit* [EDGAR].

*Enter* EDMUND.

EDMUND
The enemy's in view: draw up your powers.
Here is the guess° of their true strength and forces
By diligent discovery;° but your haste
Is now urged on you.

ALBANY                  We will greet° the time.  *Exit.* 55

EDMUND
To both these sisters have I sworn my love;
Each jealous° of the other, as the stung
Are of the adder. Which of them shall I take?
Both? One? Or neither? Neither can be enjoyed,
If both remain alive: to take the widow          60
Exasperates, makes mad her sister Goneril;
And hardly° shall I carry out my side,°
Her husband being alive. Now then, we'll use
His countenance° for the battle; which being done,
Let her who would be rid of him devise          65
His speedy taking off. As for the mercy
Which he intends to Lear and to Cordelia,
The battle done, and they within our power,
Shall never see his pardon; for my state
Stands on me to defend, not to debate.°   *Exit.* 70

Scene II. [*A field between the two camps.*]

*Alarum*° *within. Enter, with drum and colors,* LEAR,
CORDELIA, *and* SOLDIERS, *over the stage; and exeunt.*

*Enter* EDGAR *and* GLOUCESTER.

EDGAR
Here, father,° take the shadow of this tree
For your good host; pray that the right may thrive.

If ever I return to you again,
I'll bring you comfort.

GLOUCESTER              Grace go with you, sir.
                      *Exit* [EDGAR].

*Alarum and retreat*° *within.* [*Re*]*enter* EDGAR.

EDGAR
Away, old man; give me thy hand; away!          5
King Lear hath lost, he and his daughter ta'en:°
Give me thy hand; come on.

GLOUCESTER
No further, sir; a man may rot even here.

EDGAR
What, in ill thoughts again? Men must endure
Their going hence, even as their coming hither:  10
Ripeness° is all. Come on.

GLOUCESTER              And that's true too. *Exeunt.*

Scene III. [*The British camp near Dover.*]

*Enter, in conquest, with drum and colors,* EDMUND;
LEAR *and* CORDELIA, *as prisoners;* SOLDIERS, CAP-
TAIN.

EDMUND
Some officers take them away: good guard,°
Until their greater pleasures° first be known
That are to censure° them.

CORDELIA              We are not the first
Who with best meaning° have incurred the worst.
For thee, oppressèd king, I am cast down;          5
Myself could else out-frown false Fortune's frown.
Shall we not see these daughters and these sisters?

LEAR
No, no, no, no! Come, let's away to prison:
We two alone will sing like birds i' th' cage:
When thou dost ask me blessing, I'll kneel down   10
And ask of thee forgiveness: so we'll live,
And pray, and sing, and tell old tales, and laugh
At gilded butterflies,° and hear poor rogues
Talk of court news; and we'll talk with them too,
Who loses and who wins, who's in, who's out;      15
And take upon's the mystery of things,
As if we were God's spies:° and we'll wear out,°
In a walled prison, packs and sects of great ones
That ebb and flow by th' moon.°

EDMUND                        Take them away.

LEAR
Upon such sacrifices, my Cordelia,                  20
The gods themselves throw incense.° Have I caught
  thee?

---

**42–43 sound For** summon  **44 prove** i.e., by trial of combat
**45 avouchèd** maintained  **46 of** in  **47 machination**
plotting  **51 o'erlook** read over  **53 guess** estimate  **54 By
diligent discovery** obtained by careful reconnoitering
**55 greet** i.e., meet the demands of  **57 jealous** suspicious
**62 hardly** with difficulty; **carry . . . side** (1) satisfy my ambition (2) fulfill my bargain (with Goneril)  **64 countenance**
authority  **69–70 for . . . debate** my position requires me to
act, not to reason about right and wrong
**V.ii.s.d. Alarum** a trumpet call to battle  **1 father** i.e.,
venerable old man (Edgar has not yet revealed his identity)

**4 s.d. retreat** signaled by a trumpet  **6 ta'en** captured  **11
Ripeness** maturity, as of fruit that is ready to fall
**V.iii.1 good guard** let them be well guarded  **2 their greater
pleasures** the will of those in command, the great ones  **3
censure** pass judgment on  **4 meaning** intentions  **13
gilded butterflies** i.e., gorgeously attired courtiers, fluttering after nothing  **16–17 take . . . spies** profess to read the
riddle of existence, as if endowed with divine omniscience  **17
wear out** outlast  **18–19 packs . . . moon** intriguing and
partisan cliques of those in high station, whose fortunes change
every month  **20–21 Upon . . . incense** i.e., the gods
approve our renunciation of the world

He that parts us shall bring a brand from heaven,
And fire us hence like foxes.° Wipe thine eyes;
The good years° shall devour them,° flesh and fell,°
Ere they shall make us weep. We'll see 'em starved
    first.                                                      25
Come.              [*Exeunt* LEAR *and* CORDELIA, *guarded.*]
EDMUND
Come hither, captain; hark.
Take thou this note: go follow them to prison:
One step I have advanced thee; if thou dost
As this instructs thee, thou dost make thy way       30
To noble fortunes: know thou this, that men
Are as the time is:° to be tender-minded
Does not become a sword:° thy great employment
Will not bear question;° either say thou'lt do't,
Or thrive by other means.
CAPTAIN                          I'll do't, my lord.     35
EDMUND
About it; and write happy° when th' hast done.
Mark; I say, instantly, and carry it so°
As I have set it down.
CAPTAIN
I cannot draw a cart, nor eat dried oats;
If it be man's work, I'll do't.           *Exit* CAPTAIN.  40

*Flourish. Enter* ALBANY, GONERIL, REGAN [*another*
CAPTAIN, *and*] SOLDIERS.

ALBANY
Sir, you have showed today your valiant strain,°
And fortune led you well: you have the captives
Who were the opposites of° this day's strife:
I do require them of you, so to use them
As we shall find their merits° and our safety         45
May equally determine.
EDMUND                          Sir, I thought it fit
To send the old and miserable king
To some retention and appointed guard;°
Whose° age had charms in it, whose title more,
To pluck the common bosom on his side,°               50
And turn our impressed lances in our eyes°
Which do command them. With him I sent the queen:
My reason all the same; and they are ready
Tomorrow, or at further space,° t'appear
Where you shall hold your session.° At this time      55
We sweat and bleed: the friend hath lost his friend;
And the best quarrels, in the heat, are cursed
By those that feel their sharpness.°

The question of Cordelia and her father
Requires a fitter place.
ALBANY                     Sir, by your patience,       60
I hold you but a subject of° this war,
Not as a brother.
REGAN                     That's as we list to grace° him.
Methinks our pleasure might have been demanded,
Ere you had spoke so far. He led our powers,
Bore the commission of my place and person;           65
The which immediacy may well stand up
And call itself your brother.°
GONERIL                    Not so hot:
In his own grace he doth exalt himself
More than in your addition.°
REGAN                     In my rights,
By me invested, he compeers° the best.                 70
GONERIL
That were the most,° if he should husband you.°
REGAN
Jesters do oft prove prophets.
GONERIL                    Holla, holla!
That eye that told you so looked but a-squint.°
REGAN
Lady, I am not well; else I should answer
From a full-flowing stomach.° General,                 75
Take thou my soldiers, prisoners, patrimony;°
Dispose of them, of me; the walls is thine:°
Witness the world, that I create thee here
My lord, and master.
GONERIL              Mean you to enjoy him?
ALBANY
The let-alone° lies not in your good will.             80
EDMUND
Nor in thine, lord.
ALBANY               Half-blooded° fellow, yes.
REGAN [*To* EDMUND.]
Let the drum strike, and prove my title thine.°
ALBANY
Stay yet; hear reason. Edmund, I arrest thee
On capital treason; and in thy attaint°
This gilded serpent [*pointing to* GONERIL]. For your
    claim, fair sister,                                     85
I bar it in the interest of my wife.
'Tis she is subcontracted° to this lord,
And I, her husband, contradict your banes.°
If you will marry, make your loves° to me;
My lady is bespoke.°
GONERIL              An interlude!°                    90

**22–23 He . . . foxes** No human agency can separate us, but only divine interposition, as of a heavenly torch parting us like foxes that are driven from their place of refuge by fire and smoke **24 good years** plague and pestilence ("undefined malefic power or agency," *N.E.D.*); **them** the enemies of Lear and Cordelia; **fell** skin **32 as . . . is** i.e., absolutely determined by the exigencies of the moment **33 become a sword** befit a soldier **34 bear question** admit of discussion **36 write happy** style yourself fortunate **37 carry it so** manage the affair in exactly that manner (as if Cordelia had taken her own life) **41 strain** (1) stock (2) character **43 opposites of** opponents in **45 merits** deserts **48 retention . . . guard** confinement under duly appointed guard **49 Whose** i.e., Lear's **50 pluck . . . side** win the sympathy of the people to himself **51 turn . . . eyes** turn our conscripted lancers against us **54 further space** a later time **55 session** trial **57–58 best . . . sharpness** worthiest causes may be judged badly by those who have been affected painfully by them, and whose passion has not yet cooled

**61 subject of** subordinate in **62 list to grace** wish to honor **65–67 Bore . . . brother** was authorized, as my deputy, to take command; his present status, as my immediate representative, entitles him to be considered your equal **69 your addition** honors you have bestowed on him **70 compeers** equals **71 most** most complete investing in your rights; **husband you** become your husband **73 a-squint** cross-eyed **75 From . . . stomach** angrily **76 patrimony** inheritance **77 walls is thine** i.e., Regan's person, which Edmund has stormed and won **80 let-alone** power to prevent **81 Half-blooded** bastard, and so only half noble **82 prove . . . thine** prove by combat your entitlement to my rights **84 in thy attaint** as a sharer in the treason for which you are impeached **87 subcontracted** pledged by a contract which is called into question by the existence of a previous contract (Goneril's marriage) **88 contradict your banes** forbid your announced intention to marry (by citing the precontract) **89 loves** love-suits **90 bespoke** already pledged; **interlude** play

ALBANY
Thou art armed, Gloucester: let the trumpet sound:
If none appear to prove upon thy person
Thy heinous, manifest, and many treasons,
There is my pledge° [*throwing down a glove*]: I'll make°
  it on thy heart,
Ere I taste bread, thou art in nothing less                    95
Than I have here proclaimed thee.
REGAN                              Sick, O, sick!
GONERIL [*Aside.*]
If not, I'll ne'er trust medicine.°
EDMUND [*Throwing down a glove.*]
There's my exchange:° what in the world he is
That names me traitor, villainlike he lies:°
Call by the trumpet:° he that dares approach,          100
On him, on you—who not?—I will maintain
My truth and honor firmly.
ALBANY
A herald, ho!
EDMUND          A herald, ho, a herald!
ALBANY
Trust to thy single virtue;° for thy soldiers,
All levied in my name, have in my name               105
Took their discharge.
REGAN                    My sickness grows upon me.
ALBANY
She is not well; convey her to my tent.
                                [*Exit* REGAN, *led.*]

*Enter a* HERALD.

Come hither, herald. Let the trumpet sound—
And read out this.
CAPTAIN    Sound, trumpet!                            110

*A trumpet sounds.*

HERALD (*Reads.*)  "If any man of quality or degree°
within the lists° of the army will maintain upon Edmund, supposed Earl of Gloucester, that he is a manifold traitor, let him appear by the third sound of the
trumpet: he is bold in his defense."                  115
EDMUND    Sound!

*First trumpet.*

HERALD  Again!

*Second trumpet.*

HERALD  Again!

*Third trumpet.*

*Trumpet answers within. Enter* EDGAR, *at the third
sound, armed, a trumpet before him.°*

ALBANY
Ask him his purposes, why he appears
Upon this call o' th' trumpet.
HERALD                    What are you?            120
Your name, your quality,° and why you answer

This present summons?
EDGAR                    Know, my name is lost;
By treason's tooth bare-gnawn and canker-bit:°
Yet am I noble as the adversary
I come to cope.°
ALBANY              Which is that adversary?        125
EDGAR
What's he that speaks for Edmund, Earl of Gloucester?
EDMUND
Himself: what say'st thou to him?
EDGAR                        Draw thy sword,
That if my speech offend a noble heart,
Thy arm do thee justice: here is mine.
Behold it is my privilege,                            130
The privilege of mine honors,
My oath, and my profession.° I protest,
Maugre° thy strength, place, youth, and eminence,
Despite thy victor sword and fire-new° fortune,
Thy valor and thy heart,° thou art a traitor,        135
False to thy gods, thy brother, and thy father,
Conspirant° 'gainst this high illustrious prince,
And from th' extremest upward° of thy head
To the descent and dust below thy foot,°
A most toad-spotted traitor.° Say thou "No,"          140
This sword, this arm and my best spirits are bent°
To prove upon thy heart, whereto I speak,°
Thou liest.
EDMUND    In wisdom° I should ask thy name,
But since thy outside looks so fair and warlike,
And that thy tongue some say° of breeding breathes,   145
What safe and nicely° I might well delay°
By rule of knighthood, I disdain and spurn:
Back do I toss these treasons° to thy head;
With the hell-hated° lie o'erwhelm thy heart;
Which for they yet glance by and scarcely bruise,     150
This sword of mine shall give them instant way,
Where they shall rest for ever.° Trumpets, speak!

*Alarums. [They] fight.* [EDMUND *falls.*]

ALBANY
Save° him, save him!
GONERIL                This is practice,° Gloucester:
By th' law of war thou wast not bound to answer
An unknown opposite;° thou art not vanquished,        155
But cozened and beguiled.
ALBANY                    Shut your mouth, dame,

123 **canker-bit** eaten by the caterpillar  125 **cope**
encounter  130-32 **it . . . profession** my knighthood
entitles me to challenge you, and to have my challenge
accepted  133 **Maugre** despite  134 **fire-new** fresh from the
forge or mint  135 **heart** courage  137 **Conspirant** conspiring, a conspirator  138 **extremest upward** the very top
139 **the . . . foot** your lowest part (sole) and the dust beneath
it  140 **toad-spotted traitor** spotted with treason (and hence
venomous, as the toad is allegedly marked with spots that
exude venom)  141 **bent** directed  142 **whereto I speak**
Edgar speaks from the heart, and speaks to the heart of Edmund
143 **wisdom** prudence (since he is not obliged to fight with
one of lesser rank)  145 **say** assay (i.e., touch, sign)
146 **safe and nicely** cautiously and punctiliously; **delay**
i.e., avoid  148 **treasons** accusations of treason  149
**hell-hated** hated like hell  150-52 **Which . . . ever**
which accusations of treason, since as yet they do no
harm, even though I have hurled them back, I now thrust upon
you still more forcibly, with my sword, so that they may
remain with you permanently  153 **Save** spare; **practice**
trickery  155 **opposite** opponent

94 **pledge** gage; **make** prove  97 **medicine** poison
98 **exchange** technical term, denoting the glove Edmund
throws down  99 **villainlike he lies** the lie direct, a challenge
to mortal combat  100 **trumpet** trumpeter  104 **single
virtue** unaided valor  111 **quality or degree** rank or
position  112 **lists** rolls  118 **s.d. trumpet before him**
trumpeter preceding him  121 **quality** rank

Or with this paper shall I stop it. Hold, sir;°
Thou° worse than any name, read thine own evil.
No tearing, lady; I perceive you know it.

GONERIL
Say, if I do, the laws are mine, not thine:        160
Who can arraign me for't?

ALBANY                     Most monstrous! O!
Know'st thou this paper?

GONERIL                    Ask me not what I know. *Exit.*

ALBANY
Go after her; she's desperate; govern° her.

EDMUND
What you have charged me with, that have I done;
And more, much more; the time will bring it out.    165
'Tis past, and so am I. But what art thou
That hast this fortune on° me? If thou'rt noble,
I do forgive thee.

EDGAR              Let's exchange charity.°
I am no less in blood° than thou art, Edmund;
If more, the more th' hast wronged me.           170
My name is Edgar, and thy father's son.
The gods are just, and of our pleasant° vices
Make instruments to plague us:
The dark and vicious place° where thee he got°
Cost him his eyes.

EDMUND            Th' hast spoken right, 'tis true;  175
The wheel is come full circle; I am here.°

ALBANY
Methought thy very gait did prophesy°
A royal nobleness: I must embrace thee:
Let sorrow split my heart, if ever I
Did hate thee or thy father!

EDGAR              Worthy° prince, I know't.   180

ALBANY
Where have you hid yourself?
How have you known the miseries of your father?

EDGAR
By nursing them, my lord. List a brief tale;
And when 'tis told, O, that my heart would burst!
The bloody proclamation to escape°               185
That followed me so near—O, our lives' sweetness,
That we the pain of death would hourly die
Rather than die at once!°—taught me to shift
Into a madman's rags, t' assume a semblance
That very dogs disdained: and in this habit°      190
Met I my father with his bleeding rings,°
Their precious stones new lost; became his guide,
Led him, begged for him, saved him from despair;
Never—O fault!—revealed myself unto him,
Until some half-hour past, when I was armed,      195
Not sure, though hoping, of this good success,

I asked his blessing, and from first to last
Told him our pilgrimage.° But his flawed° heart—
Alack, too weak the conflict to support—
'Twixt two extremes of passion, joy and grief,    200
Burst smilingly.

EDMUND          This speech of yours hath moved me,
And shall perchance do good: but speak you on;
You look as you had something more to say.

ALBANY
If there be more, more woeful, hold it in;
For I am almost ready to dissolve,°              205
Hearing of this.

EDGAR          This would have seemed a period°
To such as love not sorrow; but another,
To amplify too much, would make much more,
And top extremity.°
Whilst I was big in clamor,° came there in a man,  210
Who, having seen me in my worst estate,°
Shunned my abhorred° society; but then, finding
Who 'twas that so endured, with his strong arms
He fastened on my neck, and bellowed out
As he'd burst heaven; threw him on my father;     215
Told the most piteous tale of Lear and him
That ever ear received: which in recounting
His grief grew puissant,° and the strings of life
Began to crack: twice then the trumpets sounded,
And there I left him tranced.°

ALBANY                    But who was this?   220

EDGAR
Kent, sir, the banished Kent; who in disguise
Followed his enemy° king, and did him service
Improper for a slave.

*Enter a* GENTLEMAN, *with a bloody knife.*

GENTLEMAN
Help, help, O, help!

EDGAR                What kind of help?

ALBANY                                Speak, man.

EDGAR
What means this bloody knife?

GENTLEMAN                    'Tis hot, it smokes;°  225
It came even from the heart of—O, she's dead!

ALBANY
Who dead? Speak, man.

GENTLEMAN
Your lady, sir, your lady: and her sister
By her is poisoned; she confesses it.

EDMUND
I was contracted° to them both: all three        230
Now marry° in an instant.

EDGAR                    Here comes Kent.

ALBANY
Produce the bodies, be they alive or dead.
                              [*Exit* GENTLEMAN.]

---

**157 Hold, sir** to Edmund: "Just a moment!" **158 Thou** probably Goneril **163 govern** control **167 fortune on** victory over **168 charity** forgiveness and love **169 blood** lineage **170 If more** if I am more noble (since legitimate) **172 of our pleasant** out of our pleasurable **174 place** i.e., the adulterous bed; **got** begot **176 wheel . . . here** i.e., Fortune's wheel, on which Edmund ascended, has now, in its downward turning, deposited him at the bottom, whence he began **177 gait did prophesy** carriage did promise **180 Worthy** honorable **185 to escape** (my wish) to escape the sentence of death **186–88 O . . . once** How sweet is life, that we choose to suffer death every hour rather than make an end at once **190 habit** attire **191 rings** sockets

**198 our pilgrimage** of our (purgatorial) journey; **flawed** cracked **205 dissolve** i.e., into tears **206 period** limit **207–09 but . . . extremity** just one woe more, described too fully, would go beyond the extreme limit **210 big in clamor** loud in lamentation **211 estate** condition **212 abhorred** abhorrent **218 puissant** overmastering **220 tranced** insensible **222 enemy** hostile **225 smokes** steams **230 contracted** betrothed **231 marry** i.e., unite in death

This judgment of the heavens, that makes us tremble,
Touches us not with pity.

*Enter* KENT.

                     O, is this he?
The time will not allow the compliment°    235
Which very manners° urges.

KENT             I am come
To bid my king and master aye° good night:
Is he not here?

ALBANY       Great thing of° us forgot!
Speak, Edmund, where's the king? and where's
     Cordelia?
See'st thou this object,° Kent?    240

*The bodies of Goneril and Regan are brought in.*

KENT
Alack, why thus?

EDMUND      Yet° Edmund was beloved:
The one the other poisoned for my sake,
And after slew herself.

ALBANY
Even so. Cover their faces.

EDMUND
I pant for life:° some good I mean to do,    245
Despite of mine own nature. Quickly send,
Be brief in it, to th' castle; for my writ°
Is on the life of Lear and on Cordelia:
Nay, send in time.

ALBANY       Run, run, O, run!

EDGAR
To who, my lord? Who has the office?° Send    250
Thy token of reprieve.°

EDMUND
Well thought on: take my sword,
Give it the captain.

EDGAR       Haste thee, for thy life.

[*Exit* MESSENGER.]

EDMUND
He hath commission from thy wife and me
To hang Cordelia in the prison, and    255
To lay the blame upon her own despair,
That she fordid° herself.

ALBANY
The gods defend her! Bear him hence awhile.

[EDMUND *is borne off.*]

*Enter* LEAR, *with* CORDELIA *in his arms,* [GENTLEMAN,
*and others following*].

LEAR
How, howl, howl, howl! O, you are men of stones:
Had I your tongues and eyes, I'd use them so    260
That heaven's vault should crack. She's gone for ever.
I know when one is dead and when one lives;
She's dead as earth. Lend me a looking-glass;
If that her breath will mist or stain the stone,°

Why, then she lives.

KENT       Is this the promised end?°    265

EDGAR
Or image° of that horror?

ALBANY       Fall and cease.°

LEAR
This feather stirs; she lives. If it be so,
It is a chance which does redeem° all sorrows
That ever I have felt.

KENT       O my good master.

LEAR
Prithee, away.

EDGAR      'Tis noble Kent, your friend.    270

LEAR
A plague upon you, murderers, traitors all!
I might have saved her; now she's gone for ever.
Cordelia, Cordelia, stay a little. Ha,
What is't thou say'st? Her voice was ever soft,
Gentle and low, an excellent thing in woman.    275
I killed the slave that was a-hanging thee.

GENTLEMAN
'Tis true, my lords, he did.

LEAR       Did I not, fellow?
I have seen the day, with my good biting falchion°
I would have made them skip: I am old now,
And these same crosses° spoil me.° Who are you?    280
Mine eyes are not o' th' best: I'll tell you straight.°

KENT
If Fortune brag of two° she loved and hated,
One of them we behold.

LEAR
This is a dull sight.° Are you not Kent?

KENT       The same,
Your servant Kent. Where is your servant Caius?°    285

LEAR
He's a good fellow, I can tell you that;
He'll strike, and quickly too: he's dead and rotten.

KENT
No, my good lord; I am the very man.

LEAR
I'll see that straight.°

KENT
That from your first of difference and decay°    290
Have followed your sad steps.

LEAR       You are welcome hither.

KENT
Nor no man else:° all's cheerless, dark and deadly.
Your eldest daughters have fordone° themselves,
And desperately° are dead.

LEAR       Ay, so I think.

ALBANY
He knows not what he says, and vain is it    295

235 **compliment** ceremony  236 **very manners** ordinary civility  237 **aye** forever  238 **thing of** matter by  240 **object** sight (the bodies of Goneril and Regan)  241 **Yet** in spite of all  245 **pant for life** gasp for breath  247 **writ** command (ordering the execution)  250 **office** commission  251 **token of reprieve** sign that they are reprieved  257 **fordid** destroyed  264 **stone** i.e., the surface of the crystal looking-glass

265 **promised end** doomsday  266 **image** exact likeness; **Fall and cease** i.e., Let the heavens fall, and all things finish  268 **redeem** make good  278 **falchion** small curved sword  280 **crosses** troubles; **spoil me** i.e., my prowess as a swordsman  281 **tell you straight** recognize you straightaway  282 **two** i.e., Lear, and some hypothetical second, who is also a prime example of Fortune's inconstancy ("loved and hated")  284 **dull sight** (1) melancholy spectacle (2) faulty eyesight (Lear's own, clouded by weeping)  285 **Caius** Kent's name, in disguise  289 **see that straight** attend to that in a moment  290 **your . . . decay** beginning of your decline in fortune  292 **Nor . . . else** no, I am not welcome, nor is anyone else  293 **fordone** destroyed  294 **desperately** in despair

That we present us to him.

EDGAR                              Very bootless.°

*Enter a* MESSENGER.

MESSENGER
Edmund is dead, my lord.

ALBANY                    That's but a trifle here.
You lords and noble friends, know our intent.
What comfort to this great decay may come°
Shall be applied. For us, we° will resign,                    300
During the life of this old majesty,
To him our absolute power: [*to* EDGAR *and* KENT] you,
   to your rights;
With boot,° and such addition° as your honors
Have more than merited. All friends shall taste
The wages of their virtue, and all foes                        305
The cup of their deservings. O, see, see!

LEAR
And my poor fool° is hanged: no, no, no life?
Why should a dog, a horse, a rat, have life,
And thou no breath at all? Thou'lt come no more,
Never, never, never, never, never.                            310
Pray you, undo this button.° Thank you, sir.
Do you see this? Look on her. Look, her lips,
Look there, look there. *He dies.*

EDGAR                    He faints. My lord, my lord!

KENT
Break, heart; I prithee, break.

EDGAR                              Look up, my lord.

KENT
Vex not his ghost:° O, let him pass! He hates him       315
That would upon the rack° of this tough world
Stretch him out longer.°

EDGAR                        He is gone indeed.

KENT
The wonder is he hath endured so long:
He but usurped° his life.

ALBANY
Bear them from hence. Our present business              320
Is general woe. [*To* KENT *and* EDGAR.] Friends of my
   soul, you twain,
Rule in this realm and the gored state sustain.

KENT
I have a journey, sir, shortly to go;
My master calls me, I must not say no.

EDGAR
The weight of this sad time we must obey,°              325
Speak what we feel, not what we ought to say.
The oldest hath borne most: we that are young
Shall never see so much, nor live so long.

                              *Exeunt, with a dead march.*

---

**296 bootless** fruitless   **299 What . . . come** whatever aid
may present itself to this great ruined man   **300 us, we** the
royal "we"   **303 boot** good measure; **addition** additional
titles and rights   **307 fool** Cordelia ("fool" being a term of
endearment; but it is perfectly possible to take the word as
referring also to the Fool)   **311 undo this button** i.e., to
ease the suffocation Lear feels

**315 Vex . . . ghost** do not trouble his departing spirit   **316
rack** instrument of torture, stretching the victim's joints to
dislocation   **317 longer** (1) in time (2) in bodily length   **319
usurped** possessed beyond the allotted term   **325 obey**
submit to

# THE TRAGEDY OF MACBETH

### EDITED BY SYLVAN BARNET

## Introduction

The date of *Macbeth*, like that of many of Shakespeare's plays, is not beyond all dispute, but there are good reasons for believing it was written in 1605–06 and was performed at Hampton Court in 1606 before James I of England and his brother-in-law, Christian of Denmark. The play, indeed, seems to have been written to please James (and perhaps thus to further the fortunes of Shakespeare's theatrical company, which in 1603 had been named the King's Men). The evidence that Shakespeare sought to please James ranges from the highly favorable portrait of Banquo, from whom the Stuarts claimed descent (the pageant in IV.i of Banquo and the eight kings seems to be a polite tribute to James, who was the ninth Stuart monarch), to such a small detail as the omission of a defeat of the Danes —this to avoid embarrassing the visiting Danish king. But for a discussion of all such evidence, the reader must consult Henry N. Paul's *The Royal Play of Macbeth*. Our concern here will not be with the play Shakespeare wrote for the two kings, but with the play he wrote for us.

Although *Macbeth* draws its material from Holinshed's *Chronicles*, a historical compilation that provided Shakespeare with much of the material for the ten plays that in the Folio of 1623 comprise the section labeled "Histories," *Macbeth* was entitled a tragedy and was printed among the tragedies in the Folio. James may have looked on the play as history, but it is not history. (Banquo, for example, was a convenient invention of a Scottish historian who in the early sixteenth century needed to give the Stuart line a proper beginning.) It is something that poets and literary critics customarily consider superior to history: a vision of life that has the concreteness of history and yet the wisdom of philosophy. Of course none of Shakespeare's history plays is satisfactory history; the exclusion of *Macbeth* from the "Histories" does not mean that the editors of the Folio recognized in it any unusual departure from fact. Perhaps *Macbeth* was excluded simply because its dramatis personae are Scottish, not English. But its presence among the "Tragedies" may mean that the editors saw a fundamental difference between *Macbeth* and, say, *Richard III*, which had earlier been published as a tragedy and which is called a tragedy even while it is placed among the "Histories." When one reads or sees *Richard III*, one cannot help

feeling—even despite some familiarity with modern historical accounts that have demonstrated Shakespeare's distortions of fact—that one is experiencing a re-creation or re-presentation of what men did to other men during a segment of English history. When one reads or sees *Macbeth*, one cannot help feeling that one is experiencing a re-creation or re-presentation of what a man is, in the present, even in the timeless.

Suppose we take a definition of tragedy and apply it to *Macbeth*. We may find that the play helps to support the definition, and that when we apply this touchstone we see things in the play that we might otherwise have missed. (But we will also see that the definition shrinks the play, and that after it has served its purpose it must be discarded for another that may further illuminate the play.) Let us take as our first touchstone a line uttered in Cyril Tourneur's *The Revenger's Tragedy*, a play apparently written about the same time as *Macbeth*:

When the bad bleed, then is the tragedy good.

In this view, tragedy shows the punishment of evildoers; at its conclusion (to quote the Duke of Albany, in *King Lear*)

> All friends shall taste
> The wages of their virtue, and all foes
> The cup of their deservings. (V.iii.304–06)

What is there of this in *Macbeth*? If Tourneur's "bad" includes, as it must, a man who knowingly kills his benefactor, and who follows this murder with tyrannical assaults upon the lives of his countrymen (including women and children), then the formula has some relevance to *Macbeth*. For although most discussions of tragedy start from Aristotle's assumption that the best tragedy concerns a man who does a deed of horror in ignorance (Oedipus kills an old man who, unknown to him, is his father; Othello kills Desdemona in the mistaken belief that she is unchaste; Brutus makes errors of judgment that undercut his high-minded aspirations), Macbeth is not confused about the criminal nature of his deed. When he kills the king who is his guest and generous lord, he knows, as Oedipus, Othello, and Brutus do not, that he does a "horrid deed." Even before he does the deed he foresees the outcome, apparently sensing that in the nature of things something rather like Albany's view will come about through the workings of even-handed justice. In his first soliloquy he says:

> we but teach
> Bloody instructions, which, being taught, return
> To plague th' inventor: this even-handed justice
> Commends th' ingredients of our poisoned chalice
> To our own lips.[1] (I.vii.8–12)

Nor does Macbeth lose his moral sense after his first crime. Midway in the play, when he has already suffered violent feelings of guilt, he determines to toughen himself in villainous practice; he has seen the ghost of one of his victims because (he thinks) he is still a fearful novice in crime and he has not yet inured himself by "hard use." A little later, when he fears he is losing his control, he determines that his course must be bloodier:

> From this moment
> The very firstlings of my heart shall be
> The firstlings of my hand. And even now,
> To crown my thoughts with acts, be it thought and done:
> The castle of Macduff I will surprise;
> Seize upon Fife; give to th' edge o' th' sword
> His wife, his babes, and all unfortunate souls
> That trace him in his line. No boasting like a fool;
> This deed I'll do before this purpose cool. (IV.i.146–54)

Another way of seeing something of Macbeth's calculated villainy—something of the quality that puts him in Tourneur's classification of "the bad"—is to see what his opponents are like. Who are they? Chief of them is Malcolm, the heir to the throne—a man chaste, trustworthy, and patriotic—and they include men who are distressed to hear that Macbeth has made "each new morn/New widows howl, new orphans cry." To these enemies of Macbeth, he is a butcher, a tyrant, a hell-kite, a hellhound. Malcolm and his allies, on the other hand, are the instruments of the powers above, and are God's soldiers. The concluding speech sharply contrasts the defeated tyrant (at whose fall, Dr. Johnson says, "every reader rejoices") and the rightful king:

> What's more to do,
> Which would be planted newly with the time—
> As calling home our exiled friends abroad
> That fled the snares of watchful tyranny,
> Producing forth the cruel ministers
> Of this dead butcher and his fiendlike queen,
> Who, as 'tis thought, by self and violent hands
> Took off her life—this, and what needful else
> That calls upon us, by the grace of Grace

[1] By the way, although the idea that an evil act engenders its own punishment is scarcely novel, Shakespeare's use of it here is probably indebted to a passage in Holinshed's *Chronicles*: "For the prick of conscience, as it chanceth ever in tyrants and such as attain to any estate by unrighteous means, caused him ever to fear, lest he should be served of the same cup as he had ministered to his predecessors."

> We will perform in measure, time, and place:
> So thanks to all at once and to each one,
> Whom we invite to see us crowned at Scone.
> (V.viii.64–75)

Macbeth has been allied with witches or fiends, but the rightful ruler will work "by the grace of Grace." Macbeth has been unable to "buckle his distempered cause/Within the belt of rule," but the rightful ruler will perform his actions "in measure, time, and place." Macbeth had heard Duncan say to him "I have begun to plant thee, and will labor/To make thee full of growing," yet he had turned against the source of his growth, killed Duncan, and so made of himself a rootless branch that must become desiccated; the rightful ruler's mind turns to planting newly with the time.

It can be put this way: Macbeth's action is contrary to nature, and he knows it. The mere thought of his deed makes his body function unnaturally. The witches' solicitation, he says,

> doth unfix my hair
> And make my seated heart knock at my ribs,
> Against the use of nature. (I.iii.135–37)

The wounds inflicted on Duncan look like "a breach in nature," and the sun feels the effect of the murder:

> By th' clock 'tis day,
> And yet dark night strangles the traveling lamp:
> Is't night's predominance, or the day's shame,
> That darkness does the face of earth entomb,
> When living light should kiss it? (II.iv.6–10)

To which the Old Man replies: "'Tis unnatural,/Even like the deed that's done."

By turning against the source of his growth, then, Macbeth becomes infected:

> Who then shall blame
> His pestered senses to recoil and start,
> When all that is within him does condemn
> Itself for being there? (V.ii.22–25)

But of course this is not the whole story, and the Macbeth that has been thus far discussed is only a part of Shakespeare's Macbeth. At the outset of the play we meet not Macbeth but the Weird Sisters. The next time they assemble, the third one says, it will be to meet with Macbeth. The incantatory quality of their verse—the power of the rhyme, the alliteration, and the mysterious paradoxes—can be felt even in a single couplet:

> Fair is foul, and foul is fair.
> Hover through the fog and filthy air. (I.i.10–11)

We may insist, on reflection, that Macbeth is a free agent who need not have yielded to the witches' hints; certainly he harbors within him what they present to our eye. Yet can we feel sure that he has not been ensnared: the charm has been wound up, and if he is the tyrant, viewed another way he is the victim of infernal tyranny. "The instruments of darkness tell us truths,/Win us with honest trifles, to betray's/In deepest consequence." The witches can control the winds, and we first see Macbeth on a "blasted heath." The very air he breathes, as it is in part made up of the witches who "melted as breath into the wind," is infected. This second view, of Macbeth as victim, though it must not be pressed (the noble Duncan finds the air sweet—but, in another way, he too is a victim), finds support in Shakespeare's other tragedies and even in his use of the word "tragedy" and its derivatives. He seems never to use it in a context that bears much resemblance to Tourneur's line, "When the bad bleed, then is the tragedy good." Always, or almost always, the word is linked with a violent death that evokes woe or is said to be woeful. Because he does not mention "tragedy" in *Macbeth*, an example must be drawn from another play. One of his earliest uses of the word will suffice. In *1 Henry VI*, Salisbury, an English commander, has been killed by a hidden French gunner. Talbot, Salisbury's cohort, laments the sudden fall:

Accursèd tower! Accursèd fatal hand
That hath contrived this woeful tragedy! (I.iv.76–77)

The reference to the tower, and the word "fatal" ("destined," "fated") are important, for they suggest that tragedy sets its woeful happenings against a mysterious backdrop of inhuman and inscrutable forces.

The Weird Sisters in *Macbeth* are of course part of this inscrutable surrounding. In the Folio their name is spelled "weyard" or "weyward" (perhaps with a glance at "wayward"?) but the stage directions and speech prefixes call them witches. They have the traditional petty malice (and beards) of witches, and they acknowledge "masters," but they also have properties not associated with witches: they vanish like bubbles, and they speak authoritatively. In the fourth act they are closer to the Furies than to mischievous hags. No English play before *Macbeth* has such imposing witches, and if the Weird Sisters resemble witches in their ability to sail in a sieve and in their animal-killing and in their cookery and in their revenge on the sailor's wife, they nevertheless seem also to merit the title Macbeth gives them—"juggling fiends." Their name suggests the Fates (Old English *wyrd*, fate), and Holinshed conjectures that they may be "the goddesses of destiny," though of course Holinshed's view need not be Shakespeare's.

Is it, then, Macbeth's bad luck that the witches wait for him? Or is there something within himself that has attracted them, and that makes him recognize his kinship with them? Are they the dramatist's concrete embodiments of a part of Macbeth? As soon as we ask these questions we realize that debate is futile; we cannot reply by pointing to Elizabethan treatises on demonology; we can only repeat portions of the play; and the play does not provide unequivocal answers.

Equivocation, in fact, is in part what the play is about. The Porter (II.iii) soliloquizes about an equivocator, but we do not have to wait for him to introduce the theme of doubleness or ambiguity. The Weird Sisters, in the first scene, will meet "when the battle's lost and won," and for them "fair is foul, and foul is fair." A few moments later Macbeth will enter, and his first line will be "So foul and fair a day I have not seen" (I.iii.38). One aspect of this pervasive doubleness is in the word-play. The Porter has his quibbles, of course, but so do Macbeth and Lady Macbeth. Second meanings, however, lurk not only under words (for example, *gild/guilt*); there are second meanings under whole speeches and actions. This is not surprising in a play in which the protagonist is advised to "look like th' innocent flower,/But be the serpent under't," and in which we hear "Away, and mock the time with fairest show:/False face must hide what the false heart doth know." Still, it was not inevitable that Shakespeare should so brilliantly follow the innocent Duncan's observation that "There's no art/To find the mind's construction in the face:/He was a gentleman on whom I built/An absolute trust" with a stage direction, "*Enter Macbeth*," that is, enter another whose appearance will deceive Duncan.

It is time that we look more closely at Macbeth's double nature, for if he is the "devilish Macbeth" that Malcolm says he is, he is also something else.

Very early in the play—immediately after the odd ritual of a dozen lines in which the Weird Sisters inform us that they will meet with Macbeth—we get a report of Macbeth's loyalty and courage. He is "brave Macbeth," "valiant cousin! Worthy gentleman," and "noble Macbeth," and by his deeds against rebels and foreign invaders he has earned these words. His first appearance on the stage does not quite confirm this report, but if anything it even more potently engages our sympathetic interest; he starts and seems "to fear/Things that do sound so fair." With hindsight we can say that he starts because he has already harbored criminal impulses that respond to the witches' words, but what is more important is that his apprehensiveness suggests both an apartness from others and a self-division that will make us see in him a good deal more than the blackguard. Twice in this first view of Macbeth we hear him described as "rapt," and his asides—confessing his uncertainties—complicate him and make him more than the hero described in the previous scene. There he had unseamed a rebel from the nave to the chops, had been an eagle, a cannon, and valor's minion. That is, when we first hear of Macbeth we hear of a man of noble and unambiguous action; when we first see Macbeth, we see a man of uncertainty. His first appearance puts him in the company of sympathetic tragic heroes such as Hamlet and Romeo. (Hamlet's first remark is an aside, and his next few speeches reveal he is not at one with his surroundings or himself. When we first see Romeo he is so abstracted that he is unaware of the time of day, and he endures "sad hours.") Conversely, Macbeth is far from the evil Richard III, whose history Shakespeare presented in the tragic shape of a rise and fall. Richard is unambiguously a villain. As early as the thirtieth line of the play he begins

I am determinèd to prove a villain,
And hate the idle pleasures of these days.
Plots have I laid, inductions dangerous,
By drunken prophecies, libels, and dreams,
To set my brother Clarence and the king
In deadly hate, the one against the other.
And if King Edward be as true and just
As I am subtle, false, and treacherous. (I.i.30–37)

This unmitigated villainy is not without its attractions, but contrast it with Macbeth's recoil at his own murderous thoughts:

My thought, whose murder yet is but fantastical,
Shakes so my single state of man that function
Is smothered in surmise, and nothing is
But what is not.                    (I.iii.139–42)

It is not, then, that he commits crimes and at the end
suffers; he suffers even before he commits his first criminal
action, and because he is his own tormentor he scarcely
needs the spectator's punishing eyes. Immediately after
killing Duncan he is afflicted with doubts and has a premonition of the sleeplessness that will ensue. Lady Macbeth
takes a simpler view: "Consider it not so deeply," "These
deeds must not be thought/After these ways; so, it will
make us mad," "A little water clears us of this deed:/How
easy is it then!" (But if she here seems as black as the evil
angel that prompts Mankind to illicit deeds in the old
morality plays, she too reveals inner depths in the sleep-
walking scene, when we see that like her husband she is
troubled with thick-coming fancies that keep her from her
rest.)

Macbeth early recognizes the unnaturalness of his
thoughts, and, as the asides in the first act make clear,
they estrange him from his fellows and even almost from
himself. They

    make my seated heart knock at my ribs,
    Against the use of nature.        (I.iii.136–37)

The soldier who fought along with his countrymen—who
is described as a savior—becomes, by the last act, a man
who knows that he has no friends (enemy troops, rather
than troops of friends, surround him); his soldiers at the
end—those who do not desert him—are mere "constrainèd things/Whose hearts are absent too." His course
in blood has separated him not only from God ("wherefore could I not pronounce 'Amen'?"), and from his
subjects (he cannot banquet at ease with them), but even
from his wife. At the start of the play she is his "dearest
partner of greatness," and his "dearest love." But midway
in the play (though she is "dearest chuck") he keeps from
her the plot against Banquo, and at the end he seems
almost insensible to her death: "She should have died
hereafter." There are many ways of responding to the
news of the death of a beloved one, and in this play
Shakespeare gives us three. It is instructive to compare
Macduff's response (IV.iii) and Old Siward's (V.viii), very
different yet not totally so, and to contrast them to Macbeth's utterly dissimilar response.

What of Macbeth's own death? Its effect on us is complex. When his severed head is brought in, perhaps we
sense a parallel between Macbeth's career and that of the
treacherous Macdonwald, whose head Macbeth had justly
fixed upon the battlements, and a contrast between, first,
Macbeth and the Thane of Cawdor, who confessed his
treasons and yielded up his life "as 'twere a trifle," and,
second, between Macbeth and Young Siward, who died
as "God's soldier"; but perhaps too we feel that there is
something of the soldierly Macbeth in his final contest,
and, equally important, that his death is the release (hence
it is not wholly painful to him) of one who knows he
harvested what he sowed, and who is aweary of the sun.

The speech Macbeth makes before he dies can here be
used to remind us that he holds our interest partly by his

language. It is not a matter of confusing the character
with the author, but simply a matter of recognizing that
one of the things that makes us interested in Macbeth
(and in all the people embodied in the play, or, rather,
the people who embody the play) is memorable speech.
The point might be made by printing the lines he utters
on the nothingness of life just after he learns of Lady
Macbeth's death—lines so potent that although they fit
exactly into their place in the drama they have often
been taken out and held to represent Shakespeare's own
view—yet the role that Macbeth's language plays can be
still better seen by quoting a dying speech that David
Garrick composed for Macbeth in the eighteenth century.
Even the reader who has read only as much of the play
as has been quoted in this introduction must recognize that
every word of Shakespeare's Macbeth will engage him as
Garrick's does not. Garrick's Macbeth says:

        Hell drags me down. I sink,
    I sink. Oh! my soul is lost forever.
    Oh!                              *Dies.*

The final speech of Shakespeare's Macbeth is an almost
indescribable blend of corrupted pride, desperation,
animal fury, and courage; it is not one of the meditative
or descriptive passages that even out of context has a life
of its own, but like all the other lines in the play it holds
us rapt.

### A NOTE ON THE SOURCES

Literature commonly has two sources: it owes something
to the thoughts and activities of the day, and it owes much
to earlier literature. *Macbeth* is no exception.

First, *Macbeth* is indebted to the fact that a Scot had
acceded to the English throne. More specifically, James I
had written a book called *Demonology*, and in it Shakespeare
could have learned, for example, that witches can foretell
the future. If Shakespeare wanted to please or honor James,
who was supposedly descended from Banquo, he would
naturally write a play about Scottish history showing
James' ancestor in a favorable light and making use of
James' interest in witchcraft. (Henry N. Paul's *The Royal
Play of Macbeth* discusses in great detail the connections
between the play and the king.) Yet another, though
smaller, influence of the age is seen in the discussion of
equivocation in II.iii, a topic much in the air after the trial
of the Jesuit Father Garnet (March 1606), who had admitted
that he believed equivocation was justifiable if used for a
good end.

If we turn to books, it is evident that Shakespeare's chief
debt is to Holinshed's *Chronicles of England, Scotland, and
Ireland*. In Holinshed Shakespeare found not only the story
of Macbeth, who killed King Duncan, but another story
of regicide that suited his purposes even better. Holinshed
says that Duncan was "negligent," and that during his
reign "many misruled persons took occasion thereof to
trouble the peace and quiet state of the commonwealth."
According to the *Chronicles*, Macbeth, with Banquo,
openly killed the king; Macbeth's wife is mentioned only
once. Shakespeare, clearly, had to dissociate Banquo from
Macbeth, and perhaps give Macbeth some other ally. He

found a way in Holinshed's story of Donwald, who, urged by his wife, killed his guest, the pious King Duff. But even the story of Donwald and his wife did not contain the sleep-walking scene that Shakespeare invented for Lady Macbeth. A study of the episodes in Holinshed shows that Holinshed actually provided only the broad outline of the story and some hints for particular episodes rather than the characters as we know them or the moral feeling as we sense it.

Other books provided some additional material: possibly Shakespeare browsed through several works on witchcraft and on Scottish history; possibly Seneca's *Agamemnon* helped him (in its portrait of Clytemnestra) to draw Lady Macbeth; certainly *Agamemnon* gave him a few verbal tags, as did the Bible, which also gave him, more important, a conception of the consequences of sin. Finally, it should be mentioned that Shakespeare, like other writers, borrowed from himself. Macbeth owes something to Tarquin in *Lucrece*, who at night performs a deed he knows is repellent and who is aware of his shortsightedness in giving up what Macbeth calls his "eternal jewel":

Who buys a minute's mirth to wail a week?
Or sells eternity to get a toy? (lines 213–14)

## A NOTE ON THE TEXT

*Macbeth*, never printed during Shakespeare's lifetime, was first printed in the Folio of 1623. The play is remarkably short, and it may be that there has been some cutting. That in I.v Lady Macbeth apparently proposes to kill Duncan, and that later in the play Macbeth kills him, is scarcely evidence that a scene had been lost, but the inconsistent stage directions concerning Macbeth's death (one calls for him to be slain on stage, another suggests he is both slain and decapitated offstage) indicate some sort of revision. Nevertheless, when one reads the account of Macbeth in Holinshed (Shakespeare's source), one does not feel that the play as it has come down to us omits anything of significance. If, as seems likely, the play was presented at court, its brevity may well be due to King James' known aversion to long plays. On the other hand, it is generally believed that Hecate is a non-Shakespearean addition to the play (she dominates III.v and has a few lines in IV.i), but the evidence is not conclusive, although the passages (along with IV.i.125–32) sound un-Shakespearean.

The present division into acts and scenes is that of the Folio except for V.viii, a division added by the Globe editors. The present edition silently modernizes spelling and punctuation, regularizes speech prefixes, and translates into English the Folio's Latin designations of act and scene. Other departures from the Folio are listed below. The reading of the present text is given first, in boldface type, and then the reading of the Folio (F) in roman.

**I.i.9 Second Witch . . . Anon** [F attributes to "All," as part of the ensuing speech]
**I.ii.13 gallowglasses** gallowgrosses **14 quarrel** Quarry **26 thunders break** Thunders **33–34 Dismayed . . . Banquo** [one line in F] **33–35 Dismayed . . . lion** [three lines in F, ending: Banquoh, Eagles, Lyon] **42 But . . . faint** [F gives to previous line] **46 So . . . look** [F gives to next line] **59 Sweno . . . king** [F gives to previous line]
**I.iii.5 Give . . . I** [F prints as a separate line] **32 weïrd** weyward [also at I.v.8; II.i.20; "weyard" at III.i.2;

III.iv.133; IV.i 136] **39 Forres** Soris **78 Speak . . . you** [F prints as a separate line] **81–82 Into . . . stayed** [three lines in F, ending: corporall, Winde, stay'd] **98 Came** can **108 why . . . me** [F gives to next line] **111–14 Which . . . not** [five lines in F, ending: loose, Norway, he.pe, labour'd, not] **131 If ill** [F gives to next line] **140–42 Shakes . . . not** [F's lines end: Mar, surmise, not] **143 If . . . crown me** [two lines in F, ending: King, crown me] **149–53 Give . . . time** [seven lines in F, ending: fauour, forgotten, registred, Leafe, them, vpon, time] **156 Till . . . friends** [two lines in F, ending: enough, friends]
**I.iv.1 Are not** Or not [given in F to next line] **2–8 My . . . died** [seven lines in F, ending: back, die, hee, Pardon, Repentance, him, dy'de] **23–27 In . . . honor** [six lines in F, ending: selfe, Duties, State, should, Loue, Honor]
**I.v.22–23 And yet . . . have it** [three lines in F, ending: winne, cryes, haue it]
**I.vi.1 the air** [F gives to next line] **4 martlet** Barlet **9 most must 17–20 Against . . . hermits** [F's lines end: broad, House, Dignities, Ermites]
**I.vii.6 shoal** Schoole [variant spelling] **47 do no 58 as you** [F gives to next line]
**II.i.4 Hold . . . heaven** [two lines in F, ending: Sword, Heauen] **7–9 And . . . repose** [F's endings: sleepe, thoughts, repose] **13–17 He . . . content** [F's endings: Pleasure, Offices, withall, Hostesse, content] **25 when 'tis** [F gives to next line] **55 strides** sides **56 sure** sowre **57 way they** they may
**II.ii.2–6 What . . . possets** [6 lines in F, ending: fire, shriek'd, good-night, open, charge, Possets] **13 s.d. Enter Macbeth** [F places after "die" in line 8] **14 I . . . noise** [two lines in F, ending: deed, noyse] **18–19 Hark . . . chamber** [one line in F] **22–25 There's . . . sleep** [F's endings: sleepe, other, Prayers, sleepe] **32 Stuck . . . throat** [F gives to previous line] **64–65 To wear . . . chamber** [three lines in F, ending: white, entry, Chamber] **68 Hath . . . knocking** [two lines in F, ending: vnattended, knocking] **72–73 To . . . couldst** [four lines in F, ending: deed, my selfe, knocking, could'st. The s.d. "*Knock*" appears after "deed"]
**II.iii.23–25 Faith . . . things** [two lines of verse in F, the second beginning "And"] **42 s.d. Enter Macbeth** [F places after line 42] **51–52 I'll . . . service** [one line of prose in F] **54–61 The night . . . shake** [10 lines in F, ending: vnruly, downe, Ayre, Death, terrible, Euents, time, Night, feuorous, shake] **64 Tongue nor heart** [F gives to next line] **86–87 O . . . murdered** [one line in F] **137–43 What . . . bloody** [nine lines in F, ending: doe, them, Office, easie, England, I, safer, Smiles, bloody]
**II.iv.14 And . . . horses** [F prints as a separate line] **17 make** [F gives to next line] **19 They . . . so** [F prints as a separate line]
**III.i.34–35 Craving . . . with you** [three lines in F, ending: Horse, Night, you] **42–43 The sweeter . . . you** [three lines in F, ending: welcome, alone, you] **72 Who's there** [F prints as a separate line] **75–82 Well . . . might** [ten lines in F, ending: then, speeches, past, fortune, selfe, conference, with you, crost, them, might] **85–91 I . . . ever** [nine lines in F, ending: so, now, meeting, predominant, goe, man, hand, begger'd, euer] **111 I do** [F gives to previous line] **114–15 Both . . . enemy** [one line in F] **128 Your . . . most** [two lines in F, ending: you, most]
**III.ii.16 But . . . suffer** [two lines in F, ending: dis-ioynt, suffer] **22 Duncan . . . grave** [F prints as a separate line] **43 there . . . done** [F gives to next line] **50 and . . . crow** [F gives to next line]
**III.iii.9 The rest** [F gives to next line] **17 O . . . fly, fly, fly** [two lines in F, the first ending: Trecherie] **21 We . . . affair** [two lines in F, ending: lost, Affaire]
**III.iv.20–21 Most . . . perfect** [four lines in F, ending: Sir, scap'd, againe, perfect] **48 Here . . . Highness** [two lines in F, ending: Lord, Highness] **109 broke . . . meeting** [F gives to next line] **121 s.d. Exeunt** Exit **122 blood will have blood** [F prints as a separate line] **144 in deed** indeed
**III.v.36 back again** [F prints as a separate line]
**III.vi.1 My . . . thoughts** [two lines in F, ending: Speeches, Thoughts] **24 son** Sonnes **38 the** their
**IV.i.46–47 Open . . . knocks** [one line in F] **59 germens** Germaine **71 Beware Macduff** [F prints as a separate line] **79 Laugh to scorn** [F prints as a separate line] **86 What is this** [F gives to next line] **93 Dunsinane** Dunsmane **98 Birnam** Byrnan [this F spelling, or with *i* for *y* or with a final *e*, occurs at V.ii.5, 31; V.iii.2, 60; V.iv.3; V.v.34, 44; V.viii.30] **119 eighth** eight **133 Let . . . hour** [F prints as a separate line]

**IV.ii.27 Fathered . . . fatherless** [two lines in F, ending: is, Father-lesse] **34 Poor bird** [F prints as a separate line] **36-44 Why . . . for thee** [ten lines in F, ending: Mother, for, saying, is dead, Father, Husband, Market, againe, wit, thee] **50-51 Every . . . hanged** [two lines of verse in F, ending: Traitor, hang'd] **59-60** [two lines of verse in F, ending: Monkie, Father] **79 What . . . faces** [F prints as a separate line]

**IV.iii.4 down-fall'n** downfall **15 deserve** discerne **25 where**

**. . . doubts** [F prints as a separate line] **102 Fit to govern** [F gives to next line] **107 accursed** accust **133 thy** they **140 I pray you** [F prints as a separate line] **173 O, relation** [F gives to next line] **211-12 Wife . . . found** [one line in F] **212-13 And . . . too** [one line in F]

**V.iii.39 Cure her** Cure **55 senna** Cyme

**V.vi.1 Your . . . down** [F prints as a separate line]

**V.viii.54 behold . . . stands** [F prints as a separate line]

# THE TRAGEDY OF MACBETH

[Dramatis Personae

DUNCAN *King of Scotland*
MALCOLM ⎱ *his sons*
DONALBAIN ⎰
MACBETH
BANQUO
MACDUFF
LENNOX
ROSS ⎱ *noblemen of Scotland*
MENTEITH
ANGUS
CAITHNESS
FLEANCE *son to Banquo*
SIWARD *Earl of Northumberland, general of the English forces*
YOUNG SIWARD *his son*

SEYTON *an officer attending on Macbeth*
SON *to Macduff*
AN ENGLISH DOCTOR
A SCOTTISH DOCTOR
A PORTER
AN OLD MAN
THREE MURDERERS
LADY MACBETH
LADY MACDUFF
A GENTLEWOMAN *attending on Lady Macbeth*
HECATE
WITCHES
APPARITIONS
LORDS OFFICERS SOLDIERS
ATTENDANTS MESSENGERS

*Scene:* Scotland; England]

## ACT I

### Scene I. [*An open place.*]

*Thunder and lightning. Enter three* WITCHES.

FIRST WITCH
When shall we three meet again?
In thunder, lightning, or in rain?
SECOND WITCH
When the hurlyburly's done,
When the battle's lost and won.
THIRD WITCH
That will be ere the set of sun.                    5
FIRST WITCH
Where the place?
SECOND WITCH Upon the heath.
THIRD WITCH
There to meet with Macbeth.
FIRST WITCH
I come, Graymalkin.°

*The decorative border shown above appeared on the first page of* Macbeth *in the First Folio edition of Shakespeare's plays, 1623.*

**I.i.8 Graymalkin** the witch's attendant spirit, a gray cat

SECOND WITCH
Paddock° calls.
THIRD WITCH    Anon!°
ALL
Fair is foul, and foul is fair.                      10
Hover through the fog and filthy air.    *Exeunt.*

### Scene II. [*A camp.*]

*Alarum within.° Enter* KING [*Duncan*], MALCOLM, DONALBAIN, LENNOX, *with* ATTENDANTS, *meeting a bleeding* CAPTAIN.

KING
What bloody man is that? He can report,
As seemeth by his plight, of the revolt
The newest state.
MALCOLM            This is the sergeant°

**9 Paddock** toad; **Anon** at once
**I.ii.s.d. Alarum within** trumpet call offstage   **3 sergeant** i.e., officer (he is called, perhaps with no inconsistency in Shakespeare's day, a captain in the s.d. and speech prefixes; *Sergeant* is trisyllabic)

Who like a good and hardy soldier fought
'Gainst my captivity. Hail, brave friend!                                5
Say to the king the knowledge of the broil°
As thou didst leave it.

CAPTAIN                           Doubtful it stood,
As two spent swimmers, that do cling together
And choke their art.° The merciless Macdonwald—
Worthy to be a rebel for to that                                        10
The multiplying villainies of nature
Do swarm upon him—from the Western Isles°
Of kerns and gallowglasses° is supplied;
And Fortune, on his damnèd quarrel° smiling,
Showed like a rebel's whore:° but all's too weak:                       15
For brave Macbeth—well he deserves that name—
Disdaining Fortune, with his brandished steel,
Which smoked with bloody execution,
Like valor's minion° carved out his passage
Till he faced the slave;                                                20
Which nev'r shook hands, nor bade farewell to him,
Till he unseamed him from the nave to th' chops,°
And fixed his head upon our battlements.

KING
O valiant cousin! Worthy gentleman!

CAPTAIN
As whence the sun 'gins his reflection°                                 25
Shipwracking storms and direful thunders break,
So from that spring whence comfort seemed to come
Discomfort swells. Mark, King of Scotland, mark:
No sooner justice had, with valor armed,
Compelled these skipping kerns to trust their heels                     30
But the Norweyan lord, surveying vantage,°
With furbished arms and new supplies of men,
Began a fresh assault.

KING                              Dismayed not this
Our captains, Macbeth and Banquo?

CAPTAIN                                          Yes;
As sparrows eagles, or the hare the lion.                               35
If I say sooth,° I must report they were
As cannons overcharged with double cracks;°
So they doubly redoubled strokes upon the foe.
Except° they meant to bathe in reeking wounds,
Or memorize another Golgotha,°                                          40
I cannot tell—
But I am faint; my gashes cry for help.

KING
So well thy words become thee as thy wounds;
They smack of honor both. Go get him surgeons.
                                   [*Exit* CAPTAIN, *attended.*]

*Enter* ROSS *and* ANGUS.

Who comes here?
MALCOLM                    The worthy Thane° of Ross.                    45

---

6 **broil** quarrel  9 **choke their art** hamper each other's
doings  12 **Western Isles** Hebrides  13 **Of . . . gallowglasses** with lightly armed Irish foot soldiers and heavily
armed ones  14 **damnèd quarrel** accursed cause  15 **Showed
. . . whore** i.e., falsely appeared to favor Macdonwald  19
**minion** favorite (trisyllabic)  22 **nave . . . chops** navel to
the jaws  25 **reflection** four syllables; the ending *-ion*
here and often elsewhere in the play—is disyllabic
31 **surveying vantage** seeing an opportunity  36 **sooth**
truth  37 **cracks** explosives  39 **Except** unless  40 **memorize another Golgotha** make the place as memorable as
Golgotha, "the place of the skull"  45 **Thane** a Scottish title
of nobility

LENNOX
What a haste looks through his eyes! So should he
   look
That seems to° speak things strange.

ROSS                                    God save the king!

KING
Whence cam'st thou, worthy thane?

ROSS                                    From Fife, great king;
Where the Norweyan banners flout the sky
And fan our people cold.                                                50
Norway° himself, with terrible numbers,
Assisted by that most disloyal traitor
The Thane of Cawdor, began a dismal° conflict;
Till that Bellona's bridegroom, lapped in proof,°
Confronted him with self-comparisons,°                                  55
Point against point, rebellious arm 'gainst arm,
Curbing his lavish° spirit: and, to conclude,
The victory fell on us.

KING                        Great happiness!

ROSS                                    That now
Sweno, the Norway's king, craves composition;°
Nor would we deign him burial of his men                                60
Till he disbursèd, at Saint Colme's Inch,°
Ten thousand dollars° to our general use.

KING
No more that Thane of Cawdor shall deceive
Our bosom interest:° go pronounce his present° death,
And with his former title greet Macbeth.                                65

ROSS
I'll see it done.

KING
What he hath lost, noble Macbeth hath won. *Exeunt.*

Scene III. [*A heath.*]

*Thunder. Enter the three* WITCHES.

FIRST WITCH
Where hast thou been, sister?

SECOND WITCH
Killing swine.

THIRD WITCH
Sister, where thou?

FIRST WITCH
A sailor's wife had chestnuts in her lap,
And mounched, and mounched, and mounched.
   "Give me," quoth I.                                                  5
"Aroint thee,° witch!" the rump-fed ronyon° cries.
Her husband's to Aleppo gone, master o' th' *Tiger:*
But in a sieve I'll thither sail,
And, like a rat without a tail,
I'll do, I'll do, and I'll do.                                          10

SECOND WITCH
I'll give thee a wind.

FIRST WITCH
Th' art kind.

---

47 **seems to** seems about to  51 **Norway** the King
of Norway  53 **dismal** threatening  54 **Bellona's . . .
proof** the mate of the goddess of war, clad in tested
(proved) armor  55 **self-comparisons** counter-movements
57 **lavish** insolent  59 **composition** terms of peace
61 **Inch** island  62 **dollars** Spanish and Dutch currency
64 **Our bosom interest** my (plural of royalty) heart's trust;
**present** immediate
**I.iii.6 Aroint thee** begone; **rump-fed ronyon** fat-rumped
scabby creature

THIRD WITCH
And I another.

FIRST WITCH
I myself have all the other;
And the very ports they blow,°                                    15
All the quarters that they know
I' th' shipman's card.°
I'll drain him dry as hay:
Sleep shall neither night nor day
Hang upon his penthouse lid;°                                    20
He shall live a man forbid:°
Weary sev'nights nine times nine
Shall he dwindle, peak,° and pine:
Though his bark cannot be lost,
Yet it shall be tempest-tossed.°                                 25
Look what I have.

SECOND WITCH
Show me, show me.

FIRST WITCH
Here I have a pilot's thumb,
Wracked as homeward he did come.

*Drum within.*

THIRD WITCH
A drum, a drum!                                                  30
Macbeth doth come.

ALL
The weïrd° sisters, hand in hand,
Posters° of the sea and land,
Thus do go about, about:
Thrice to thine, and thrice to mine,                             35
And thrice again, to make up nine.
Peace! The charm's wound up.

*Enter* MACBETH *and* BANQUO.

MACBETH
So foul and fair a day I have not seen.

BANQUO
How far is't called to Forres? What are these
So withered, and so wild in their attire,                        40
That look not like th' inhabitants o' th' earth,
And yet are on't? Live you, or are you aught
That man may question?° You seem to understand
  me,
By each at once her choppy° fingers laying
Upon her skinny lips. You should be women,                       45
And yet your beards forbid me to interpret
That you are so.

MACBETH      Speak, if you can: what are you?

FIRST WITCH
All hail, Macbeth! Hail to thee, Thane of Glamis!

SECOND WITCH
All hail, Macbeth! Hail to thee, Thane of Cawdor!

THIRD WITCH
All hail, Macbeth, that shalt be king hereafter!                 50

BANQUO
Good sir, why do you start, and seem to fear
Things that do sound so fair? I' th' name of truth,
Are ye fantastical,° or that indeed

Which outwardly ye show? My noble partner
You greet with present grace° and great prediction              55
Of noble having° and of royal hope,
That he seems rapt withal:° to me you speak not.
If you can look into the seeds of time,
And say which grain will grow and which will not,
Speak then to me, who neither beg nor fear                      60
Your favors nor your hate.

FIRST WITCH    Hail!

SECOND WITCH    Hail!

THIRD WITCH    Hail!

FIRST WITCH
Lesser than Macbeth, and greater.                               65

SECOND WITCH
Not so happy,° yet much happier.

THIRD WITCH
Thou shalt get° kings, though thou be none.
So all hail, Macbeth and Banquo!

FIRST WITCH
Banquo and Macbeth, all hail!

MACBETH
Stay, you imperfect° speakers, tell me more:                    70
By Sinel's° death I know I am Thane of Glamis;
But how of Cawdor? The Thane of Cawdor lives,
A prosperous gentleman; and to be king
Stand not within the prospect of belief,
No more than to be Cawdor. Say from whence                      75
You owe° this strange intelligence?° Or why
Upon this blasted heath you stop our way
With such prophetic greeting? Speak, I charge you.

                      WITCHES *vanish.*

BANQUO
The earth hath bubbles as the water has,
And these are of them. Whither are they vanished?              80

MACBETH
Into the air, and what seemed corporal° melted
As breath into the wind. Would they had stayed!

BANQUO
Were such things here as we do speak about?
Or have we eaten on the insane° root
That takes the reason prisoner?                                 85

MACBETH
Your children shall be kings.

BANQUO           You shall be king.

MACBETH
And Thane of Cawdor too. Went it not so?

BANQUO
To th' selfsame tune and words. Who's here?

*Enter* ROSS *and* ANGUS.

ROSS
The king hath happily received, Macbeth,
The news of thy success; and when he reads°                     90
Thy personal venture in the rebels' fight,
His wonders and his praises do contend
Which should be thine or his.° Silenced with that,

---

15 **ports they blow** harbors to which the winds blow (?)
17 **card** compass card   20 **penthouse lid** eyelid (the figure is
of a lean-to)   21 **forbid** cursed   23 **peak** waste away   32 **weird**
destiny-serving (?)   33 **Posters** swift travelers   43 **question**
talk to   44 **choppy** chapped   53 **fantastical** imaginary

55 **grace** honor   56 **having** possession   57 **rapt withal**
entranced by it   66 **happy** fortunate   67 **get** beget   70
**imperfect** incomplete   71 **Sinel** Macbeth's father   76
**owe** own, have; **intelligence** information   81 **corporal**
corporeal   84 **insane** insanity-producing   90 **reads** considers
92–93 **His wonders . . . his** Duncan's speechless admiration, appropriate to him, contends with his desire to praise
you (?)

In viewing o'er the rest o' th' selfsame day,
He finds thee in the stout Norweyan ranks, 95
Nothing afeard of what thyself didst make,
Strange images of death. As thick as tale
Came post with post,° and every one did bear
Thy praises in his kingdom's great defense,
And poured them down before him.

ANGUS                                    We are sent 100
To give thee, from our royal master, thanks;
Only to herald thee into his sight,
Not pay thee.

ROSS
And for an earnest° of a greater honor,
He bade me, from him, call thee Thane of Cawdor; 105
In which addition,° hail, most worthy thane!
For it is thine.

BANQUO        What, can the devil speak true?

MACBETH
The Thane of Cawdor lives: why do you dress me
In borrowed robes?

ANGUS                        Who was the thane lives yet,
But under heavy judgment bears that life 110
Which he deserves to lose. Whether he was combined°
With those of Norway, or did line° the rebel
With hidden help and vantage,° or that with both
He labored in his country's wrack,° I know not;
But treasons capital, confessed and proved, 115
Have overthrown him.

MACBETH        [Aside.] Glamis, and Thane of Cawdor:
The greatest is behind.° [To ROSS and ANGUS.] Thanks
for your pains.

[Aside to BANQUO.]
Do you not hope your children shall be kings,
When those that gave the Thane of Cawdor to me
Promised no less to them?

BANQUO [Aside to MACBETH.] That, trusted home,° 120
Might yet enkindle you unto the crown,
Besides the Thane of Cawdor. But 'tis strange:
And oftentimes, to win us to our harm,
The instruments of darkness tell us truths,
Win us with honest trifles, to betray's 125
In deepest consequence.°
Cousins,° a word, I pray you.

MACBETH                [Aside.] Two truths are told,
As happy prologues to the swelling° act
Of the imperial theme.—I thank you, gentlemen.—

[Aside.]
This supernatural soliciting° 130
Cannot be ill, cannot be good. If ill,
Why hath it given me earnest of success,
Commencing in a truth? I am Thane of Cawdor:
If good, why do I yield to that suggestion
Whose horrid image doth unfix my hair 135
And make my seated° heart knock at my ribs,
Against the use of nature?° Present fears

Are less than horrible imaginings.
My thought, whose murder yet is but fantastical,°
Shakes so my single° state of man that function 140
Is smothered in surmise, and nothing is
But what is not.

BANQUO        Look, how our partner's rapt.

MACBETH [Aside.]
If chance will have me king, why, chance may crown
me,
Without my stir.

BANQUO                New honors come upon him,
Like our strange° garments, cleave not to their mold 145
But with the aid of use.

MACBETH        [Aside.] Come what come may
Time and the hour runs through the roughest day.

BANQUO
Worthy Macbeth, we stay upon your leisure.°

MACBETH
Give me your favor.° My dull brain was wrought
With things forgotten. Kind gentlemen, your pains 150
Are registered where every day I turn
The leaf to read them. Let us toward the king.

[Aside to BANQUO.]
Think upon what hath chanced, and at more time,
The interim having weighed it,° let us speak
Our free hearts° each to other.

BANQUO                Very gladly. 155

MACBETH
Till then, enough. Come, friends.        Exeunt.


Scene IV. [Forres. The palace.]

Flourish.° Enter KING [Duncan], LENNOX, MALCOLM,
DONALBAIN, and ATTENDANTS.

KING
Is execution done on Cawdor? Are not
Those in commission° yet returned?

MALCOLM                        My liege,
They are not yet come back. But I have spoke
With one that saw him die, who did report
That very frankly he confessed his treasons, 5
Implored your highness' pardon and set forth
A deep repentance: nothing in his life
Became him like the leaving it. He died
As one that had been studied° in his death,
To throw away the dearest thing he owed° 10
As 'twere a careless° trifle.

KING                        There's no art
To find the mind's construction in the face:
He was a gentleman on whom I built
An absolute trust.

Enter MACBETH, BANQUO, ROSS, and ANGUS.

                    O worthiest cousin!
The sin of my ingratitude even now 15

97–98 **As thick . . . post** as fast as could be counted came
messenger after messenger  104 **earnest** pledge  106 **addition**
title  111 **combined** allied  112 **line** support  113 **vantage**
opportunity  114 **wrack** ruin  117 **behind** i.e., to follow  120
**home** all the way  126 **In deepest consequence** in the most
significant sequel  127 **Cousins** i.e., fellow noblemen  128
**swelling** stately  130 **soliciting** inviting  136 **seated** fixed
137 **Against . . . nature** contrary to my natural way

139 **fantastical** imaginary  140 **single** unaided, weak (or
"entire"?)  145 **strange** new  148 **stay . . . leisure** await
your convenience  149 **favor** pardon  154 **The . . . it** i.e.,
when we have had time to think  155 **Our free hearts**
our minds freely
**I.iv.s.d. Flourish** fanfare  2 **in commission** i.e., commissioned to oversee the execution  9 **studied** rehearsed  10
**owed** owned  11 **careless** uncared-for

Was heavy on me; thou art so far before,
That swiftest wing of recompense is slow
To overtake thee. Would thou hadst less deserved,
That the proportion° both of thanks and payment
Might have been mine! Only I have left to say,                    20
More is thy due than more than all can pay.

MACBETH
The service and the loyalty I owe,
In doing it, pays itself.° Your highness' part
Is to receive our duties: and our duties
Are to your throne and state children and servants;            25
Which do but what they should, by doing every thing
Safe toward° your love and honor.

KING                                        Welcome hither.
I have begun to plant thee, and will labor
To make thee full of growing. Noble Banquo,
That hast no less deserved, nor must be known                  30
No less to have done so, let me enfold thee
And hold thee to my heart.

BANQUO                            There if I grow,
The harvest is your own.

KING                                My plenteous joys,
Wanton° in fullness, seek to hide themselves
In drops of sorrow. Sons, kinsmen, thanes,                     35
And you whose places are the nearest, know,
We will establish our estate° upon
Our eldest, Malcolm, whom we name hereafter
The Prince of Cumberland: which honor must
Not unaccompanied invest him only,                             40
But signs of nobleness, like stars, shall shine
On all deservers. From hence to Inverness,
And bind us further to you.

MACBETH
The rest is labor, which is not used for you.°
I'll be myself the harbinger, and make joyful                  45
The hearing of my wife with your approach;
So, humbly take my leave.

KING                                My worthy Cawdor!

MACBETH [Aside.]
The Prince of Cumberland! That is a step
On which I must fall down, or else o'erleap,
For in my way it lies. Stars, hide your fires;                 50
Let not light see my black and deep desires:
The eye wink at the hand;° yet let that be
Which the eye fears, when it is done, to see.        Exit.

KING
True, worthy Banquo; he is full so valiant,
And in his commendations° I am fed;                            55
It is a banquet to me. Let's after him,
Whose care is gone before to bid us welcome.
It is a peerless kinsman.            Flourish. Exeunt.


Scene V. [Inverness. Macbeth's castle.]

Enter Macbeth's wife [LADY MACBETH], alone, with a
letter.

LADY MACBETH [Reads.] "They met me in the day

of success; and I have learned by the perfect'st report
they have more in them than mortal knowledge.
When I burned in desire to question them further,
they made themselves air, into which they vanished.    5
Whiles I stood rapt in the wonder of it, came missives°
from the king, who all-hailed me 'Thane of Cawdor';
by which title, before, these weïrd sisters saluted me,
and referred me to the coming on of time, with 'Hail,
king that shalt be!' This have I thought good to      10
deliver thee,° my dearest partner of greatness, that
thou mightst not lose the dues of rejoicing, by being
ignorant of what greatness is promised thee. Lay it to
thy heart, and farewell."

Glamis thou art, and Cawdor, and shalt be             15
What thou art promised. Yet do I fear thy nature;
It is too full o' th' milk of human kindness°
To catch the nearest way. Thou wouldst be great,
Art not without ambition, but without
The illness° should attend it. What thou wouldst
  highly,                                             20
That wouldst thou holily; wouldst not play false,
And yet wouldst wrongly win. Thou'dst have, great
  Glamis,
That which cries, "Thus thou must do" if thou have it;
And that which rather thou dost fear to do
Than wishest should be undone. Hie thee hither,       25
That I may pour my spirits in thine ear,
And chastise with the valor of my tongue
All that impedes thee from the golden round°
Which fate and metaphysical° aid doth seem
To have thee crowned withal.°

Enter MESSENGER.

                                        What is your tidings?    30

MESSENGER
The king comes here tonight.

LADY MACBETH                    Thou'rt mad to say it!
Is not thy master with him, who, were't so,
Would have informed for preparation?

MESSENGER
So please you, it is true. Our thane is coming.
One of my fellows had the speed of him,°              35
Who, almost dead for breath, had scarcely more
Than would make up his message.

LADY MACBETH                        Give him tending;
He brings great news.            Exit MESSENGER.
                        The raven himself is hoarse
That croaks the fatal entrance of Duncan
Under my battlements. Come, you spirits               40
That tend on mortal° thoughts, unsex me here,
And fill me, from the crown to the toe, top-full
Of direst cruelty! Make thick my blood,
Stop up th' access and passage to remorse,°
That no compunctious visitings of nature°            45
Shake my fell° purpose, nor keep peace between
Th' effect° and it! Come to my woman's breasts,
And take my milk for° gall, you murd'ring ministers,°

**19 proportion** preponderance **23 pays itself** is its own
reward **27 Safe toward** safeguarding (?) **34 Wanton**
unrestrained **37 establish our estate** settle the succession
**44 The . . . you** Repose is laborious when not employed for
you **52 wink . . . hand** be blind to the hand's deed **55
his commendations** commendations of him

**I.v.6 missives** messengers **11 deliver thee** report to you
**17 milk . . . kindness** i.e., gentle quality of human nature
**20 illness** wickedness **28 round** crown **29 metaphysical**
supernatural **30 withal** with **35 had . . . him** outdistanced
him **41 mortal** deadly **44 remorse** compassion **45
compunctious . . . nature** natural feelings of compassion
**46 fell** savage **47 effect** fulfillment **48 for** in exchange for;
**ministers** agents

Wherever in your sightless° substances
You wait on° nature's mischief! Come, thick night,  50
And pall° thee in the dunnest° smoke of hell,
That my keen knife see not the wound it makes,
Nor heaven peep through the blanket of the dark,
To cry, "Hold, hold!"

*Enter* MACBETH.

               Great Glamis! Worthy Cawdor!
Greater than both, by the all-hail hereafter!°  55
Thy letters have transported me beyond
This ignorant° present, and I feel now
The future in the instant.°

MACBETH         My dearest love,
Duncan comes here tonight.

LADY MACBETH       And when goes hence?

MACBETH
Tomorrow, as he purposes.

LADY MACBETH      O, never  60
Shall sun that morrow see!
Your face, my thane, is as a book where men
May read strange matters. To beguile the time,°
Look like the time; bear welcome in your eye,
Your hand, your tongue: look like th' innocent
   flower,  65
But be the serpent under't. He that's coming
Must be provided for: and you shall put
This night's great business into my dispatch;°
Which shall to all our nights and days to come
Give solely sovereign sway and masterdom.  70

MACBETH
We will speak further.

LADY MACBETH    Only look up clear.°
To alter favor ever is to fear.°
Leave all the rest to me.       *Exeunt.*

## Scene VI. [*Before Macbeth's castle.*]

*Hautboys*° *and torches. Enter* KING [*Duncan*], MALCOLM,
DONALBAIN, BANQUO, LENNOX, MACDUFF, ROSS,
ANGUS, *and* ATTENDANTS.

KING
This castle hath a pleasant seat;° the air
Nimbly and sweetly recommends itself
Unto our gentle° senses.

BANQUO        This guest of summer,
The temple-haunting martlet,° does approve°
By his loved masionry° that the heaven's breath  5
Smells wooingly here. No jutty,° frieze,
Buttress, nor coign of vantage,° but this bird
Hath made his pendent bed and procreant° cradle.

Where they most breed and haunt,° I have observed
The air is delicate.

*Enter* LADY [MACBETH].

KING        See, see, our honored hostess!  10
The love that follows us sometime is our trouble,
Which still we thank as love.° Herein I teach you
How you shall bid God 'ield° us for your pains
And thank us for your trouble.

LADY MACBETH      All our service
In every point twice done, and then done double,  15
Were poor and single business° to contend
Against those honors deep and broad wherewith
Your majesty loads our house: for those of old,
And the late dignities heaped up to them,
We rest your hermits.°

KING       Where's the Thane of Cawdor?  20
We coursed° him at the heels, and had a purpose
To be his purveyor:° but he rides well,
And his great love, sharp as his spur, hath holp° him
To his home before us. Fair and noble hostess,
We are your guest tonight.

LADY MACBETH      Your servants ever  25
Have theirs, themselves, and what is theirs, in compt,°
To make their audit at your highness' pleasure,
Still° to return your own.

KING         Give me your hand.
Conduct me to mine host: we love him highly,
And shall continue our graces towards him.  30
By your leave, hostess.          *Exeunt.*

## Scene VII. [*Macbeth's castle.*]

*Hautboys. Torches. Enter a* SEWER,° *and diverse* SER-
VANTS *with dishes and service over the stage. Then enter*
MACBETH.

MACBETH
If it were done° when 'tis done, then 'twere well
It were done quickly. If th' assassination
Could trammel up° the consequence, and catch,
With his surcease,° success;° that but this blow
Might be the be-all and the end-all—here,  5
But here, upon this bank and shoal of time,
We'd jump° the life to come. But in these cases
We still° have judgment here; that we but teach
Bloody instructions, which, being taught, return
To plague th' inventor: this even-handed° justice  10
Commends° th' ingredients of our poisoned chalice
To our own lips. He's here in double trust:
First, as I am his kinsman and his subject,
Strong both against the deed; then, as his host,
Who should against his murderer shut the door,  15

---

49 **sightless** invisible  50 **wait on** assist  51 **pall** enshroud;
**dunnest** darkest  55 **all-hail hereafter** the third all-hail (?)
the all-hail of the future (?)  57 **ignorant** unknowing
58 **instant** present  63 **To . . . time** i.e., to deceive
people of the day  68 **dispatch** management  71 **look
up clear** appear undisturbed  72 **To alter . . . fear** To
show a disturbed face is dangerous
I.vi.s.d. **Hautboys** oboes  1 **seat** site  3 **gentle** soothed  4
**temple-haunting martlet** martin (swift) nesting in churches;
**approve** prove  5 **mansionry** nests  6 **jutty** projection  7
**coign of vantage** advantageous corner  8 **procreant** breeding

9 **haunt** visit  11–12 **The love . . . love** The love offered
me sometimes inconveniences me, but still I value it as
love  13 **'ield** reward  16 **single business** feeble service
20 **your hermits** dependents bound to pray for you  21
**coursed** pursued  22 **purveyor** advance-supply officer  23
**holp** helped  26 **Have . . . compt** have their dependents,
themselves, and their possessions in trust  28 **Still** always
I.vii.s.d. **Sewer** chief butler  1 **done** over and done with
3 **trammel up** catch in a net  4 **his surcease** Duncan's death
(?) the consequence's cessation (?); **success** what follows  7
**jump** risk  8 **still** always  10 **even-handed** impartial  11
**Commends** offers

Not bear the knife myself. Besides, this Duncan
Hath borne his faculties° so meek, hath been
So clear° in his great office, that his virtues
Will plead like angels trumpet-tongued against
The deep damnation of his taking-off;                    20
And pity, like a naked newborn babe,
Striding° the blast, or heaven's cherubin horsed
Upon the sightless couriers° of the air,
Shall blow the horrid deed in every eye,
That° tears shall drown the wind. I have no spur    25
To prick the sides of my intent, but only
Vaulting ambition, which o'erleaps itself
And falls on th' other—

*Enter* LADY [MACBETH].

                    How now! What news?
LADY MACBETH
He has almost supped. Why have you left the chamber?
MACBETH
Hath he asked for me?
LADY MACBETH                    Know you not he has?    30
MACBETH
We will proceed no further in this business:
He hath honored me of late, and I have bought°
Golden opinions from all sorts of people,
Which would be worn now in their newest gloss,
Not cast aside so soon.
LADY MACBETH                    Was the hope drunk    35
Wherein you dressed yourself? Hath it slept since?
And wakes it now, to look so green° and pale
At what it did so freely? From this time
Such I account thy love. Art thou afeard
To be the same in thine own act and valor    40
As thou art in desire? Wouldst thou have that
Which thou esteem'st the ornament of life,
And live a coward in thine own esteem,
Letting "I dare not" wait upon° "I would,"
Like the poor cat° i' th' adage?
MACBETH                    Prithee, peace!    45
I dare do all that may become a man;
Who dares do more is none.
LADY MACBETH                    What beast was't then
That made you break° this enterprise to me?
When you durst do it, then you were a man;
And to be more than what you were, you would    50
Be so much more the man. Nor time nor place
Did then adhere,° and yet you would make both.
They have made themselves, and that their° fitness now
Does unmake you. I have given suck, and know
How tender 'tis to love the babe that milks me:    55
I would, while it was smiling in my face,
Have plucked my nipple from his boneless gums,
And dashed the brains out, had I so sworn as you
Have done to this.
MACBETH                    If we should fail?
LADY MACBETH                    We fail?
But° screw your courage to the sticking-place,°    60

And we'll not fail. When Duncan is asleep—
Whereto the rather shall his day's hard journey
Soundly invite him—his two chamberlains
Will I with wine and wassail° so convince,°
That memory, the warder° of the brain,                    65
Shall be a fume, and the receipt of reason
A limbeck only:° when in swinish sleep
Their drenchèd natures lies° as in a death,
What cannot you and I perform upon
Th' unguarded Duncan, what not put upon    70
His spongy° officers, who shall bear the guilt
Of our great quell?°
MACBETH                    Bring forth men-children only;
For thy undaunted mettle° should compose
Nothing but males. Will it not be received,
When we have marked with blood those sleepy two    75
Of his own chamber, and used their very daggers,
That they have done't?
LADY MACBETH                    Who dares receive it other,°
As we shall make our griefs and clamor roar
Upon his death?
MACBETH                    I am settled, and bend up
Each corporal agent to this terrible feat.    80
Away, and mock the time° with fairest show:
False face must hide what the false heart doth know.
                                        *Exeunt.*

# A C T  I I

Scene I. [*Inverness. Court of Macbeth's castle.*]

*Enter* BANQUO, *and* FLEANCE, *with a torch before him.*

BANQUO
How goes the night, boy?
FLEANCE
The moon is down; I have not heard the clock.
BANQUO
And she goes down at twelve.
FLEANCE                    I take't, 'tis later, sir.
BANQUO
Hold, take my sword. There's husbandry° in heaven.
Their candles are all out. Take thee that too.    5
A heavy summons° lies like lead upon me,
And yet I would not sleep. Merciful powers,
Restrain in me the cursèd thoughts that nature
Gives way to in repose!
*Enter* MACBETH, *and a* SERVANT *with a torch.*
                                        Give me my sword!
Who's there?                    10
MACBETH
A friend.
BANQUO
What, sir, not yet at rest? The king's a-bed:
He hath been in unusual pleasure, and

17 **faculties** powers  18 **clear** spotless  22 **Striding** bestriding
23 **sightless couriers** invisible coursers (i.e., the winds)
25 **That** so that  32 **bought** acquired  37 **green** sickly
44 **wait upon** follow  45 **cat** which wants fish but
fears to wet its paws  48 **break** broach  52 **adhere**
suit  53 **that their** their very  60 **But** only; **sticking-place**
notch (holding the bowstring of a taut crossbow)

64 **wassail** carousing; **convince** overpower  65 **warder**
guard  66–67 **receipt . . . only** i.e., the receptacle
("receipt"), which should collect the distillate of thought—
reason—will be a mere vessel ("limbeck") of undistilled liquids
68 **lies** lie  71 **spongy** sodden  72 **quell** killing  73 **mettle**
substance  77 **other** otherwise  81 **mock the time** beguile the
world
**II.i.4 husbandry** frugality  6 **summons** call (to sleep)

Sent forth great largess to your offices:°
This diamond he greets your wife withal,                              15
By the name of most kind hostess; and shut up°
In measureless content.

MACBETH                    Being unprepared,
Our will became the servant to defect,°
Which else should free have wrought.

BANQUO                                        All's well.
I dreamt last night of the three weïrd sisters:                      20
To you they have showed some truth.

MACBETH                          I think not of them.
Yet, when we can entreat an hour to serve,
We would spend it in some words upon that business,
If you would grant the time.

BANQUO                             At your kind'st leisure.

MACBETH
If you shall cleave to my consent, when 'tis,°                        25
It shall make honor for you.

BANQUO                          So° I lose none
In seeking to augment it, but still keep
My bosom franchised° and allegiance clear,°
I shall be counseled.

MACBETH             Good repose the while!

BANQUO
Thanks, sir. The like to you!                                        30

                          Exit BANQUO, [with FLEANCE].

MACBETH
Go bid thy mistress, when my drink is ready,
She strike upon the bell. Get thee to bed.

                                   Exit [SERVANT].

Is this a dagger which I see before me,
The handle toward my hand? Come, let me clutch
  thee.
I have thee not, and yet I see thee still.                           35
Art thou not, fatal vision, sensible°
To feeling as to sight, or art thou but
A dagger of the mind, a false creation,
Proceeding from the heat-oppressèd brain?
I see thee yet, in form as palpable                                  40
As this which now I draw.
Thou marshal'st me the way that I was going;
And such an instrument I was to use.
Mine eyes are made the fools o' th' other senses,
Or else worth all the rest. I see thee still;                        45
And on thy blade and dudgeon° gouts° of blood,
Which was not so before. There's no such thing.
It is the bloody business which informs°
Thus to mine eyes. Now o'er the one half-world
Nature seems dead, and wicked dreams abuse°                          50
The curtained sleep; witchcraft celebrates
Pale Hecate's offerings;° and withered murder,
Alarumed° by his sentinel, the wolf,
Whose howl's his watch, thus with his stealthy pace,
With Tarquin's° ravishing strides, towards his design 55

Moves like a ghost. Thou sure and firm-set earth,
Hear not my steps, which way they walk, for fear
Thy very stones prate of my whereabout,
And take the present horror from the time,
Which now suits with it.° Whiles I threat, he lives:                 60
Words to the heat of deeds too cold breath gives.

*A bell rings.*

I go, and it is done: the bell invites me.
Hear it not, Duncan, for it is a knell
That summons thee to heaven, or to hell.             *Exit.*

        Scene II. [*Macbeth's castle.*]

*Enter* LADY [MACBETH].

LADY MACBETH
That which hath made them drunk hath made me
  bold;
What hath quenched them hath given me fire. Hark!
  Peace!
It was the owl that shrieked, the fatal bellman,
Which gives the stern'st good-night.° He is about it.
The doors are open, and the surfeited grooms          5
Do mock their charge with snores. I have drugged
  their possets,°
That death and nature° do contend about them,
Whether they live or die.

MACBETH          [*Within.*] Who's there? What, ho?

LADY MACBETH
Alack, I am afraid they have awaked
And 'tis not done! Th' attempt and not the deed       10
Confounds° us. Hark! I laid their daggers ready;
He could not miss 'em. Had he not resembled
My father as he slept, I had done't.

*Enter* MACBETH.

                              My husband!

MACBETH
I have done the deed. Didst thou not hear a noise?

LADY MACBETH
I heard the owl scream and the crickets cry.          15
Did not you speak?

MACBETH            When?

LADY MACBETH          Now.

MACBETH                        As I descended?

LADY MACBETH   Ay.

MACBETH   Hark!
Who lies i' th' second chamber?

LADY MACBETH                    Donalbain.

MACBETH   This is a sorry° sight.                     20

LADY MACBETH
A foolish thought, to say a sorry sight.

MACBETH
There's one did laugh in's sleep, and one cried,
  "Murder!"
That they did wake each other. I stood and heard them.

14 **largess . . . offices** gifts to your servants' quarters
16 **shut up** concluded  18 **Our . . . defect** our good
will was hampered by our deficient preparations  25 **cleave
. . . 'tis** join my cause, when the time comes  26 **So**
provided that  28 **franchised** free (from guilt); **clear**
spotless  36 **sensible** perceptible  46 **dudgeon** wooden hilt;
**gouts** large drops  48 **informs** gives shape (?)  50 **abuse**
deceive  52 **Hecate's offerings** offerings to Hecate (goddess
of sorcery)  53 **Alarumed** called to action  55 **Tarquin**
Roman tyrant who ravished Lucrece

59–60 **take . . . it** remove (by noise) the horrible silence
attendant on this moment and suitable to it (?)
**II.ii.3–4 bellman . . . good-night** i.e., the owl's call, portending death, is like the town crier's call to a condemned man
6 **possets** bedtime drinks  7 **nature** natural vitality  11 **Confounds** ruins  20 **sorry** miserable

But they did say their prayers, and addressed them
Again to sleep.
LADY MACBETH    There are two lodged together.    25
MACBETH
One cried, "God bless us!" and "Amen" the other,
As they had seen me with these hangman's° hands:
List'ning their fear, I could not say, "Amen,"
When they did say, "God bless us!"
LADY MACBETH          Consider it not so deeply.
MACBETH
But wherefore could not I pronounce "Amen"?    30
I had most need of blessing, and "Amen"
Stuck in my throat.
LADY MACBETH    These deeds must not be thought
After these ways; so, it will make us mad.
MACBETH
Methought I heard a voice cry "Sleep no more!
Macbeth does murder sleep"—the innocent sleep,    35
Sleep that knits up the raveled sleave° of care,
The death of each day's life, sore labor's bath,
Balm of hurt minds, great nature's second course,°
Chief nourisher in life's feast—
LADY MACBETH          What do you mean?
MACBETH
Still it cried, "Sleep no more!" to all the house:    40
"Glamis hath murdered sleep, and therefore Cawdor
Shall sleep no more: Macbeth shall sleep no more."
LADY MACBETH
Who was it that thus cried? Why, worthy thane,
You do unbend° your noble strength, to think
So brainsickly of things. Go get some water,    45
And wash this filthy witness° from your hand.
Why did you bring these daggers from the place?
They must lie there: go carry them, and smear
The sleepy grooms with blood.
MACBETH                    I'll go no more.
I am afraid to think what I have done;    50
Look on't again I dare not.
LADY MACBETH          Infirm of purpose!
Give me the daggers. The sleeping and the dead
Are but as pictures. 'Tis the eye of childhood
That fears a painted° devil. If he do bleed,
I'll gild° the faces of the grooms withal,    55
For it must seem their guilt.    *Exit. Knock within.*
MACBETH                    Whence is that knocking?
How is't with me, when every noise appalls me?
What hands are here? Ha! They pluck out mine eyes!
Will all great Neptune's ocean wash this blood
Clean from my hand? No; this my hand will rather    60
The multitudinous seas incarnadine,°
Making the green one red.°

*Enter* LADY [MACBETH].

LADY MACBETH
My hands are of your color, but I shame
To wear a heart so white. (*Knock.*) I hear a knocking

At the south entry. Retire we to our chamber.    65
A little water clears us of this deed:
How easy is it then! Your constancy
Hath left you unattended.° (*Knock.*) Hark! more
    knocking.
Get on your nightgown,° lest occasion call us
And show us to be watchers.° Be not lost    70
So poorly° in your thoughts.
MACBETH
To know my deed, 'twere best not know myself.

(*Knock.*)

Wake Duncan with thy knocking! I would thou
    couldst!                              *Exeunt.*

## Scene III. [*Macbeth's castle.*]

*Enter a* PORTER. *Knocking within.*

PORTER    Here's a knocking indeed! If a man were
porter of hell gate, he should have old° turning the key.
(*Knock.*) Knock, knock, knock! Who's there, i' th'
name of Beelzebub? Here's a farmer, that hanged
himself on th' expectation of plenty.° Come in time!    5
Have napkins enow° about you; here you'll sweat for't.
(*Knock.*) Knock, knock! Who's there, in th' other
devil's name? Faith, here an equivocator,° that could
swear in both the scales against either scale; who
committed treason enough for God's sake, yet could    10
not equivocate to heaven. O, come in, equivocator.
(*Knock.*) Knock, knock, knock! Who's there? Faith,
here's an English tailor come hither for stealing out of
a French hose:° come in, tailor. Here you may roast
your goose.° (*Knock.*) Knock, knock; never at quiet!    15
What are you? But this place is too cold for hell. I'll
devil-porter it no further. I had thought to have let in
some of all professions that go the primrose way to th'
everlasting bonfire. (*Knock.*) Anon, anon! [*Opens an
entrance.*] I pray you, remember the porter.    20

*Enter* MACDUFF *and* LENNOX.

MACDUFF
Was it so late, friend, ere you went to bed,
That you do lie so late?
PORTER    Faith, sir, we were carousing till the second
cock:° and drink, sir, is a great provoker of three
things.    25
MACDUFF    What three things does drink especially
provoke?
PORTER    Marry, sir, nose-painting, sleep, and urine.
Lechery, sir, it provokes and unprovokes; it provokes
the desire, but it takes away the performance: therefore    30
much drink may be said to be an equivocator with
lechery: it makes him and it mars him; it sets him on
and it takes him off; it persuades him and disheartens

27 **hangman's** executioner's (i.e., bloody)    36 **knits . . .
sleave** straightens out the tangled skein    38 **second course**
i.e., sleep (the less substantial first course is food)    44 **unbend**
relax    46 **witness** evidence    54 **painted** depicted    55 **gild** paint
61 **incarnadine** redden    62 **the . . . red** perhaps "the green
one" means "the ocean," but perhaps "one" here means
"totally," "uniformly"

67–68 **Your . . . unattended** Your firmness has deserted
you    69 **nightgown** dressing-gown    70 **watchers** i.e., up
late    71 **poorly** weakly
**II.iii.2 should have old** would certainly have plenty of
4–5 **farmer . . . plenty** the farmer hoarded so he could later
sell high, but when it looked as though there would be a crop
surplus he hanged himself    6 **enow** enough    8 **equivocator**
i.e., Jesuit (who allegedly employed deceptive speech to further
God's ends)    14 **French hose** tight-fitting hose    15 **goose**
pressing iron    23–24 **second cock** about 3 A.M.

him; makes him stand to and not stand to; in conclu- 35
sion, equivocates him in a sleep, and giving him the
lie, leaves him.

MACDUFF  I believe drink gave thee the lie° last night.

PORTER  That it did, sir, i' the very throat on me: but
I requited him for his lie, and, I think, being too strong
for him, though he took up my legs sometime, yet I 40
made a shift to cast° him.

MACDUFF  Is thy master stirring?

*Enter* MACBETH.

Our knocking has awaked him; here he comes.

LENNOX
Good morrow, noble sir.

MACBETH                    Good morrow, both.

MACDUFF
Is the king stirring, worthy thane?

MACBETH                    Not yet.                    45

MACDUFF
He did command me to call timely° on him:
I have almost slipped° the hour.

MACBETH                    I'll bring you to him.

MACDUFF
I know this is a joyful trouble to you;
But yet 'tis one.

MACBETH
The labor we delight in physics pain.°                    50
This is the door.

MACDUFF          I'll make so bold to call,
For 'tis my limited service.°          *Exit* MACDUFF.

LENNOX
Goes the king hence today?

MACBETH                    He does: he did appoint so.

LENNOX
The night has been unruly. Where we lay,
Our chimneys were blown down, and, as they say,          55
Lamentings heard i' th' air, strange screams of death,
And prophesying with accents terrible
Of dire combustion° and confused events
New hatched to th' woeful time: the obscure bird°
Clamored the livelong night. Some say, the earth          60
Was feverous and did shake.

MACBETH                    'Twas a rough night.

LENNOX
My young remembrance cannot parallel
A fellow to it.

*Enter* MACDUFF.

MACDUFF
O horror, horror, horror! Tongue nor heart
Cannot conceive nor name thee.

MACBETH AND LENNOX          What's the matter?          65

MACDUFF
Confusion° now hath made his masterpiece.
Most sacrilegious murder hath broke ope
The Lord's anointed temple, and stole thence
The life o' th' building.

MACBETH                    What is't you say? The life?

LENNOX
Mean you his majesty?                    70

MACDUFF
Approach the chamber, and destroy your sight
With a new Gorgon:° do not bid me speak;
See, and then speak yourselves. Awake, awake!
                    *Exeunt* MACBETH *and* LENNOX.
Ring the alarum bell. Murder and treason!
Banquo and Donalbain! Malcolm! Awake!                    75
Shake off this downy sleep, death's counterfeit,°
And look on death itself! Up, up, and see
The great doom's image!° Malcolm! Banquo!
As from your graves rise up, and walk like sprites,°
To countenance° this horror. Ring the bell.                    80

*Bell rings. Enter* LADY [MACBETH].

LADY MACBETH
What's the business,
That such a hideous trumpet calls to parley
The sleepers of the house? Speak, speak!

MACDUFF                    O gentle lady,
'Tis not for you to hear what I can speak:
The repetition,° in a woman's ear,                    85
Would murder as it fell.

*Enter* BANQUO.

                    O Banquo, Banquo!
Our royal master's murdered.

LADY MACBETH                    Woe, alas!
What, in our house?

BANQUO                    Too cruel anywhere.
Dear Duff, I prithee, contradict thyself,
And say it is not so.                    90

*Enter* MACBETH, LENNOX, *and* ROSS.

MACBETH
Had I but died an hour before this chance,
I had lived a blessèd time; for from this instant
There's nothing serious in mortality:°
All is but toys.° Renown and grace is dead,
The wine of life is drawn, and the mere lees°                    95
Is left this vault° to brag of.

*Enter* MALCOLM *and* DONALBAIN.

DONALBAIN
What is amiss?

MACBETH          You are, and do not know't.
The spring, the head, the fountain of your blood
Is stopped; the very source of it is stopped.

MACDUFF
Your royal father's murdered.

MALCOLM                    O, by whom?                    100

LENNOX
Those of his chamber, as it seemed, had done't:
Their hands and faces were all badged° with blood;
So were their daggers, which unwiped we found

---

**37 gave . . . lie** called you a liar (with a pun on the sense of "stretched you out")  **41 cast** with a pun on the sense of "vomit"  **46 timely** early  **47 slipped** let slip  **50 The . . . pain** Labor that gives us pleasure cures discomfort  **52 limited service** appointed duty  **58 combustion** tumult  **59 obscure bird** bird of darkness, i.e., the owl  **66 Confusion** destruction

**72 Gorgon** creature capable of turning beholders to stone  **76 counterfeit** imitation  **78 great doom's image** likeness of Judgment Day  **79 sprites** spirits  **80 countenance** be in keeping with  **85 repetition** report  **93 serious in mortality** worthwhile in mortal life  **94 toys** trifles  **95 lees** dregs  **96 vault** (1) wine vault (2) earth, with the sky as roof (?)  **102 badged** marked

Upon their pillows. They stared, and were distracted.
No man's life was to be trusted with them.                    105
MACBETH
O, yet I do repent me of my fury,
That I did kill them.
MACDUFF                    Wherefore did you so?
MACBETH
Who can be wise, amazed,° temp'rate and furious,
Loyal and neutral, in a moment? No man.
The expedition° of my violent love                    110
Outrun the pauser, reason. Here lay Duncan,
His silver skin laced with his golden blood,
And his gashed stabs looked like a breach in nature
For ruin's wasteful entrance: there, the murderers,
Steeped in the colors of their trade, their daggers    115
Unmannerly breeched with gore.° Who could refrain,°
That had a heart to love, and in that heart
Courage to make's love known?
LADY MACBETH                    Help me hence, ho!
MACDUFF
Look to° the lady.
MALCOLM [Aside to DONALBAIN.]
Why do we hold our tongues,                    120
That most may claim this argument for ours?°
DONALBAIN [Aside to MALCOLM.]
What should be spoken here,
Where our fate, hid in an auger-hole,°
May rush, and seize us? Let's away:
Our tears are not yet brewed.                    125
MALCOLM [Aside to DONALBAIN.]
Nor our strong sorrow
Upon the foot of motion.°
BANQUO                    Look to the lady.
            [LADY MACBETH is carried out.]
And when we have our naked frailties hid,°
That suffer in exposure, let us meet
And question° this most bloody piece of work,    130
To know it further. Fears and scruples° shake us.
In the great hand of God I stand, and thence
Against the undivulged pretense° I fight
Of treasonous malice.
MACDUFF                    And so do I.
ALL                    So all.
MACBETH
Let's briefly° put on manly readiness,                    135
And meet i' th' hall together.
ALL                    Well contented.
            Exeunt [all but MALCOLM and DONALBAIN].
MALCOLM
What will you do? Let's not consort with them.
To show an unfelt sorrow is an office°
Which the false man does easy. I'll to England.
DONALBAIN
To Ireland, I; our separated fortune                    140

Shall keep us both the safer. Where we are
There's daggers in men's smiles; the near in blood,
The nearer bloody.
MALCOLM                    This murderous shaft that's shot
Hath not yet lighted, and our safest way
Is to avoid the aim. Therefore to horse;                    145
And let us not be dainty of° leave-taking,
But shift away. There's warrant° in that theft
Which steals itself° when there's no mercy left.
                    Exeunt.


Scene IV. [Outside Macbeth's castle.]

Enter ROSS with an OLD MAN.

OLD MAN
Threescore and ten I can remember well:
Within the volume of which time I have seen
Hours dreadful and things strange, but this sore° night
Hath trifled former knowings.°
ROSS                    Ha, good father,
Thou see'st the heavens, as troubled with man's act,    5
Threatens his bloody stage. By th' clock 'tis day,
And yet dark night strangles the traveling lamp:°
Is't night's predominance,° or the day's shame,
That darkness does the face of earth entomb,
When living light should kiss it?
OLD MAN                    'Tis unnatural,    10
Even like the deed that's done. On Tuesday last
A falcon, tow'ring in her pride of place,°
Was by a mousing° owl hawked at and killed.
ROSS
And Duncan's horses—a thing most strange and
            certain—
Beauteous and swift, the minions° of their race,    15
Turned wild in nature, broke their stalls, flung out,°
Contending 'gainst obedience, as they would make
War with mankind.
OLD MAN                    'Tis said they eat° each other.
ROSS
They did so, to th' amazement of mine eyes,
That looked upon't.

Enter MACDUFF.

                    Here comes the good Macduff.    20
How goes the world, sir, now?
MACDUFF                    Why, see you not?
ROSS
Is't known who did this more than bloody deed?
MACDUFF
Those that Macbeth hath slain.
ROSS                    Alas, the day!
What good could they pretend?°
MACDUFF                    They were suborned:°
Malcolm and Donalbain, the king's two sons,    25
Are stol'n away and fled, which puts upon them

108 **amazed** bewildered    110 **expedition** haste    116
**Unmannerly . . . gore** covered with unseemly breeches
of blood; **refrain** check oneself    119 **Look to** look after
121 **That . . . ours** who are the most concerned with
this topic    123 **auger-hole** i.e., unsuspected place    125–27
**Our tears . . . motion** i.e., we have not yet had time
for tears nor to express our sorrows in action (?)    128 **naked
frailties hid** poor bodies clothed    130 **question** discuss    131
**scruples** suspicions    133 **undivulged pretense** hidden purpose    135 **briefly** quickly    138 **office** function

146 **dainty of** fussy about    147 **warrant** justification    148
**steals itself** steals oneself away
**II.iv.3 sore** grievous    4 **trifled former knowings** made
trifles of former experiences    7 **traveling lamp** i.e., the sun
8 **predominance** astrological supremacy    12 **tow'ring . . .
place** soaring at her summit    13 **mousing** i.e., normally
mouse-eating    15 **minions** darlings    16 **flung out** lunged
wildly    18 **eat** ate    24 **pretend** hope for; **suborned** bribed

Suspicion of the deed.

ROSS                    'Gainst nature still.
Thriftless° ambition, that will ravin up°
Thine own life's means! Then 'tis most like
The sovereignty will fall upon Macbeth.           30

MACDUFF
He is already named,° and gone to Scone
To be invested.°
ROSS               Where is Duncan's body?

MACDUFF
Carried to Colmekill,
The sacred storehouse of his predecessors
And guardian of their bones.

ROSS                              Will you to Scone?      35

MACDUFF
No, cousin, I'll to Fife.
ROSS                    Well, I will thither.

MACDUFF
Well, may you see things well done there. Adieu,
Lest our old robes sit easier than our new!

ROSS
Farewell, father.

OLD MAN
God's benison° go with you, and with those      40
That would make good of bad, and friends of foes!
                                    *Exeunt omnes.*

# ACT III

## Scene I. [*Forres. The palace.*]

*Enter* BANQUO.

BANQUO
Thou hast it now: king, Cawdor, Glamis, all,
As the weïrd women promised, and I fear
Thou play'dst most foully for't. Yet it was said
It should not stand° in thy posterity,
But that myself should be the root and father      5
Of many kings. If there come truth from them—
As upon thee, Macbeth, their speeches shine—
Why, by the verities on thee made good,
May they not be my oracles as well
And set me up in hope? But hush, no more!           10

*Sennet*° *sounded. Enter* MACBETH *as king,* LADY
[MACBETH], LENNOX, ROSS, LORDS, *and* ATTEN-
DANTS.

MACBETH
Here's our chief guest.
LADY MACBETH        If he had been forgotten,
It had been as a gap in our great feast,
And all-thing° unbecoming.

MACBETH
Tonight we hold a solemn° supper, sir,
And I'll request your presence.

BANQUO                    Let your highness      15

28 **Thriftless** wasteful; **ravin up** greedily devour  31
**named** elected  32 **invested** installed as king  40 **benison**
blessing
**III.i.4 stand** continue  10 s.d. **Sennet** trumpet call  13 **all-
thing** altogether  14 **solemn** ceremonious

Command upon me, to the which my duties
Are with a most indissoluble tie
For ever knit.
MACBETH
Ride you this afternoon?
BANQUO                    Ay, my good lord.
MACBETH
We should have else desired your good advice      20
(Which still° hath been both grave and prosperous°)
In this day's council; but we'll take tomorrow.
Is't far you ride?
BANQUO
As far, my lord, as will fill up the time
'Twixt this and supper. Go not my horse the better,°   25
I must become a borrower of the night
For a dark hour or twain.
MACBETH                    Fail not our feast.
BANQUO
My lord, I will not.
MACBETH
We hear our bloody cousins are bestowed°
In England and in Ireland, not confessing          30
Their cruel parricide, filling their hearers
With strange invention.° But of that tomorrow,
When therewithal we shall have cause of state
Craving us jointly.° Hie you to horse. Adieu,
Till you return at night. Goes Fleance with you?    35
BANQUO
Ay, my good lord: our time does call upon's.
MACBETH
I wish your horses swift and sure of foot,
And so I do commend you to their backs.
Farewell.                            *Exit* BANQUO.
Let every man be master of his time                 40
Till seven at night. To make society
The sweeter welcome, we will keep ourself
Till supper-time alone. While° then, God be with you!
            *Exeunt* LORDS [*and all but* MACBETH
                            *and a* SERVANT].
Sirrah,° a word with you: attend° those men
Our pleasure?
ATTENDANT
They are, my lord, without° the palace gate.
MACBETH
Bring them before us.              *Exit* SERVANT.
To be thus is nothing, but° to be safely thus—
Our fears in° Banquo stick deep,
And in his royalty of nature reigns that            50
Which would° be feared. 'Tis much he dares;
And, to° that dauntless temper° of his mind,
He hath a wisdom that doth guide his valor
To act in safety. There is none but he
Whose being I do fear: and under him                55
My genius is rebuked,° as it is said
Mark Antony's was by Caesar. He chid the sisters,

21 **still** always; **grave and prosperous** weighty and profitable
25 **Go . . . better** unless my horse goes better than I expect
29 **are bestowed** have taken refuge  32 **invention** lies  33–34
**cause . . . jointly** matters of state demanding our joint
attention  43 **While** until  44 **Sirrah** common address to an
inferior; **attend** await  46 **without** outside  48 **but** unless  49
**in** about  51 **would** must  52 **to** added to; **temper** quality
56 **genius is rebuked** guardian spirit is cowed

When first they put the name of king upon me,
And bade them speak to him; then prophetlike
They hailed him father to a line of kings. 60
Upon my head they placed a fruitless crown
And put a barren scepter in my gripe,°
Thence to be wrenched with an unlineal hand,
No son of mine succeeding. If 't be so,
For Banquo's issue have I filed° my mind; 65
For them the gracious Duncan have I murdered;
Put rancors° in the vessel of my peace
Only for them, and mine eternal jewel°
Given to the common enemy of man,°
To make them kings, the seeds of Banquo kings! 70
Rather than so, come, fate, into the list,°
And champion me to th' utterance!° Who's there?

*Enter* SERVANT *and two* MURDERERS.

Now go to the door, and stay there till we call.
                 *Exit* SERVANT.
Was it not yesterday we spoke together?
MURDERERS
It was, so please your highness.
MACBETH           Well then, now 75
Have you considered of my speeches? Know
That it was he in the times past, which held you
So under fortune,° which you thought had been
Our innocent self: this I made good to you
In our last conference; passed in probation° with you, 80
How you were borne in hand,° how crossed;° the
     instruments,°
Who wrought with them, and all things else that
     might
To half a soul° and to a notion° crazed
Say, "Thus did Banquo."
FIRST MURDERER      You made it known to us.
MACBETH
I did so; and went further, which is now 85
Our point of second meeting. Do you find
Your patience so predominant in your nature,
That you can let this go? Are you so gospeled,°
To pray for this good man and for his issue,
Whose heavy hand hath bowed you to the grave 90
And beggared yours for ever?
FIRST MURDERER      We are men, my liege.
MACBETH
Ay, in the catalogue ye go for° men;
As hounds and greyhounds, mongrels, spaniels, curs,
Shoughs, water-rugs° and demi-wolves, are clept°
All by the name of dogs: the valued file° 95
Distinguishes the swift, the slow, the subtle,
The housekeeper,° the hunter, every one
According to the gift which bounteous nature
Hath in him closed,° whereby he does receive

Particular addition, from the bill° 100
That writes them all alike: and so of men.
Now if you have a station in the file,
Not i' th' worst rank of manhood, say 't,
And I will put that business in your bosoms
Whose execution takes your enemy off, 105
Grapples you to the heart and love of us,
Who wear our health but sickly in his life,°
Which in his death were perfect.
SECOND MURDERER      I am one, my liege,
Whom the vile blows and buffets of the world
Hath so incensed that I am reckless what 110
I do to spite the world.
FIRST MURDERER      And I another
So weary with disasters, tugged with fortune,
That I would set° my life on any chance,
To mend it or be rid on 't.
MACBETH      Both of you
Know Banquo was your enemy.
BOTH MURDERERS      True, my lord. 115
MACBETH
So is he mine, and in such bloody distance°
That every minute of his being thrusts
Against my near'st of life:° and though I could
With barefaced power sweep him from my sight
And bid my will avouch° it, yet I must not, 120
For° certain friends that are both his and mine,
Whose loves I may not drop, but wail his fall°
Who I myself struck down: and thence it is
That I to your assistance do make love,
Masking the business from the common eye 125
For sundry weighty reasons.
SECOND MURDERER      We shall, my lord,
Perform what you command us.
FIRST MURDERER      Though our lives—
MACBETH
Your spirits shine through you. Within this hour at
     most
I will advise you where to plant yourselves,
Acquaint you with the perfect spy° o' th' time, 130
The moment on 't;° for 't must be done tonight,
And something° from the palace; always thought°
That I require a clearness:° and with him—
To leave no rubs° nor botches in the work—
Fleance his son, that keeps him company, 135
Whose absence is no less material to me
Than is his father's, must embrace the fate
Of that dark hour. Resolve yourselves apart:°
I'll come to you anon.
MURDERERS      We are resolved, my lord.
MACBETH
I'll call upon you straight.° Abide within. 140

It is concluded: Banquo, thy soul's flight,
If it find heaven, must find it out tonight.    *Exeunt.*

### Scene II. [*The palace.*]

*Enter* [LADY MACBETH] *and a* SERVANT.

LADY MACBETH
Is Banquo gone from court?

SERVANT
Ay, madam, but returns again tonight.

LADY MACBETH
Say to the king, I would attend his leisure
For a few words.

SERVANT                    Madam, I will.                    *Exit.*

LADY MACBETH                    Nought's had, all's spent,
Where our desire is got without content:                    5
'Tis safer to be that which we destroy
Than by destruction dwell in doubtful joy.

*Enter* MACBETH.

How now, my lord! Why do you keep alone,
Of sorriest° fancies your companions making,
Using those thoughts which should indeed have died    10
With them they think on? Things without° all remedy
Should be without regard: what's done is done.

MACBETH
We have scorched° the snake, not killed it:
She'll close° and be herself, whilst our poor malice°
Remains in danger of her former tooth.                    15
But let the frame of things disjoint,° both the worlds°
    suffer,
Ere we will eat our meal in fear, and sleep
In the affliction of these terrible dreams
That shake us nightly: better be with the dead,
Whom we, to gain our peace, have sent to peace,    20
Than on the torture° of the mind to lie
In restless ecstasy.° Duncan is in his grave;
After life's fitful fever he sleeps well.
Treason has done his° worst: nor steel, nor poison,
Malice domestic,° foreign levy, nothing,                    25
Can touch him further.

LADY MACBETH                    Come on.
Gentle my lord, sleek° o'er your rugged° looks;
Be bright and jovial among your guests tonight.

MACBETH
So shall I, love; and so, I pray, be you:
Let your remembrance apply to Banquo;°                    30
Present him eminence,° both with eye and tongue:
Unsafe the while, that we must lave°
Our honors in these flattering streams
And make our faces vizards° to our hearts,
Disguising what they are.

LADY MACBETH                    You must leave this.    35

MACBETH
O, full of scorpions is my mind, dear wife!

Thou know'st that Banquo, and his Fleance, lives.

LADY MACBETH
But in them nature's copy's° not eterne.

MACBETH
There's comfort yet; they are assailable.
Then be thou jocund. Ere the bat hath flown    40
His cloistered flight, ere to black Hecate's summons
The shard-borne° beetle with his drowsy hums
Hath rung night's yawning peal, there shall be done
A deed of dreadful note.

LADY MACBETH                    What's to be done?

MACBETH
Be innocent of the knowledge, dearest chuck,°    45
Till thou applaud the deed. Come, seeling° night,
Scarf up° the tender eye of pitiful day,
And with thy bloody and invisible hand
Cancel and tear to pieces that great bond°
Which keeps me pale! Light thickens, and the crow    50
Makes wing to th' rooky° wood.
Good things of day begin to droop and drowse,
Whiles night's black agents to their preys do rouse.
Thou marvel'st at my words: but hold thee still;
Things bad begun make strong themselves by ill:    55
So, prithee, go with me.                    *Exeunt.*

### Scene III. [*Near the palace.*]

*Enter three* MURDERERS.

FIRST MURDERER
But who did bid thee join with us?

THIRD MURDERER                    Macbeth.

SECOND MURDERER
He needs not our mistrust; since he delivers
Our offices and what we have to do
To the direction just.°

FIRST MURDERER                    Then stand with us.
The west glimmers with some streaks of day.    5
Now spurs the lated° traveler apace
To gain the timely inn, and near approaches
The subject of our watch.

THIRD MURDERER                    Hark! I hear horses.

BANQUO (*Within.*)
Give us a light there, ho!

SECOND MURDERER                    Then 'tis he. The rest
That are within the note of expectation°    10
Already are i' th' court.

FIRST MURDERER                    His horses go about.

THIRD MURDERER
Almost a mile: but he does usually—
So all men do—from hence to th' palace gate
Make it their walk.

*Enter* BANQUO *and* FLEANCE, *with a torch.*

---

III.ii.9 **sorriest** most despicable  11 **without** beyond  13 **scorched** slashed, scored  14 **close** heal; **poor malice** feeble enmity  16 **frame . . . disjoint** universe collapse; **both the worlds** heaven and earth (?)  21 **torture** i.e., rack  22 **ecstasy** frenzy  24 **his** its  25 **Malice domestic** civil war  27 **sleek** smooth; **rugged** furrowed  30 **Let . . . Banquo** focus your thoughts on Banquo  31 **Present him eminence** honor him  32 **Unsafe . . . lave** i.e., you and I are unsafe because we must dip  34 **vizards** masks

38 **nature's copy** nature's lease (?) imitation (i.e., a son) made by nature (?)  42 **shard-borne** borne on scaly wings (?) dung-bred (?)  45 **chuck** chick (a term of endearment)  46 **seeling** eye-closing  47 **Scarf up** blindfold  49 **bond** i.e., between Banquo and fate (?) Banquo's lease on life (?) Macbeth's link to humanity (?)  51 **rooky** full of rooks  III.iii.2–4 **He needs . . . just** We need not mistrust him (the Third Murderer) since he describes our duties according to our exact directions  6 **lated** belated  10 **within . . . expectation** on the list of expected guests

SECOND MURDERER
A light, a light!

THIRD MURDERER    'Tis he.

FIRST MURDERER       Stand to't.      15

BANQUO
It will be rain tonight.

FIRST MURDERER     Let it come down.

[*They set upon* BANQUO.]

BANQUO
O, treachery! Fly, good Fleance, fly, fly, fly!
                           [*Exit* FLEANCE.]
Thou mayst revenge. O slave!      [*Dies.*]

THIRD MURDERER
Who did strike out the light?

FIRST MURDERER       Was't not the way?°

THIRD MURDERER
There's but one down; the son is fled.    20

SECOND MURDERER
We have lost best half of our affair.

FIRST MURDERER
Well, let's away and say how much is done.    *Exeunt.*


Scene IV. [*The palace.*]

*Banquet prepared. Enter* MACBETH, LADY [MACBETH],
ROSS, LENNOX, LORDS, *and* ATTENDANTS.

MACBETH
You know your own degrees;° sit down:
At first and last, the hearty welcome.

LORDS
Thanks to your majesty.

MACBETH
Ourself will mingle with society°
And play the humble host.      5
Our hostess keeps her state,° but in best time
We will require° her welcome.

LADY MACBETH
Pronounce it for me, sir, to all our friends,
For my heart speaks they are welcome.

*Enter* FIRST MURDERER.

MACBETH
See, they encounter° thee with their hearts' thanks.    10
Both sides are even: here I'll sit i' th' midst:
Be large in mirth; anon we'll drink a measure°
The table round. [*Goes to* FIRST MURDERER.] There's
   blood upon thy face.

MURDERER
'Tis Banquo's then.

MACBETH
'Tis better thee without than he within.°    15
Is he dispatched?

MURDERER     My lord, his throat is cut;
That I did for him.

MACBETH       Thou art the best o' th' cutthroats.
Yet he's good that did the like for Fleance;
If thou didst it, thou art the nonpareil.

**19 way** i.e., thing to do
**III.iv.1 degrees** ranks   **4 society** the company   **6 keeps her
state** remains seated in her chair of state   **7 require** request
**10 encounter** meet   **12 measure** goblet   **15 thee . . .
within** outside you than inside him

MURDERER
Most royal sir, Fleance is 'scaped.    20

MACBETH [*Aside.*]
Then comes my fit again: I had else been perfect,
Whole as the marble, founded° as the rock,
As broad and general as the casing° air:
But now I am cabined, cribbed,° confined, bound in
To saucy° doubts and fears.—But Banquo's safe?    25

MURDERER
Ay, my good lord: safe in a ditch he bides,
With twenty trenchèd° gashes on his head,
The least a death to nature.

MACBETH         Thanks for that.

[*Aside.*]
There the grown serpent lies; the worm° that's fled
Hath nature that in time will venom breed,    30
No teeth for th' present. Get thee gone. Tomorrow
We'll hear ourselves° again.   *Exit* [FIRST] MURDERER.

LADY MACBETH      My royal lord,
You do not give the cheer.° The feast is sold
That is not often vouched, while 'tis a-making,
'Tis given with welcome. To feed were best at home;°    35
From thence, the sauce to meat° is ceremony;
Meeting were bare without it.

*Enter the* GHOST *of Banquo, and sits in Macbeth's place.*

MACBETH          Sweet remembrancer!°
Now good digestion wait on appetite,
And health on both!

LENNOX       May't please your highness sit.

MACBETH
Here had we now our country's honor roofed,°    40
Were the graced person of our Banquo present—
Who may I rather challenge for unkindness
Than pity for mischance!°

ROSS       His absence, sir,
Lays blame upon his promise. Please't your highness
To grace us with your royal company?    45

MACBETH
The table's full.

LENNOX     Here is a place reserved, sir.

MACBETH
Where?

LENNOX
Here, my good lord. What is't that moves your highness?

MACBETH
Which of you have done this?

LORDS         What, my good lord?

MACBETH
Thou canst not say I did it. Never shake    50
Thy gory locks at me.

ROSS
Gentlemen, rise, his highness is not well.

**22 founded** firmly based   **23 broad . . . casing** unconfined
as the surrounding   **24 cribbed** penned up   **25 saucy** insolent
**27 trenchèd** trenchlike   **29 worm** serpent   **32 hear ourselves** talk it over   **33 the cheer** a sense of cordiality   **33–35
The feast . . . home** The feast seems sold (not given) during
which the host fails to welcome the guests. Mere eating is best
done at home   **36 meat** food   **37 remembrancer** reminder
**40 our . . . roofed** our nobility under one roof   **42–43 Who
. . . mischance** whom I hope I may reprove because he is
unkind rather than pity because he has encountered an accident

**LADY MACBETH**

Sir, worthy friends. My lord is often thus,
And hath been from his youth. Pray you, keep seat.
The fit is momentary; upon a thought°                      55
He will again be well. If much you note him,
You shall offend him and extend his passion.°
Feed, and regard him not.—Are you a man?

**MACBETH**

Ay, and a bold one, that dare look on that
Which might appall the devil.

**LADY MACBETH** [*Aside to* MACBETH.] O proper stuff!  60
This is the very painting of your fear.
This is the air-drawn dagger which, you said,
Led you to Duncan. O, these flaws° and starts,
Impostors to° true fear, would well become
A woman's story at a winter's fire,                        65
Authorized° by her grandam. Shame itself!
Why do you make such faces? When all's done,
You look but on a stool.

**MACBETH**                          Prithee, see there!
Behold! Look! Lo! How say you?
Why, what care I? If thou canst nod, speak too.           70
If charnel houses° and our graves must send
Those that we bury back, our monuments
Shall be the maws of kites.°              [*Exit* GHOST.]

**LADY MACBETH**      What, quite unmanned in folly?

**MACBETH**

If I stand here, I saw him.

**LADY MACBETH**              Fie, for shame!

**MACBETH**

Blood hath been shed ere now, i' th' olden time,          75
Ere humane statute purged the gentle weal;°
Ay, and since too, murders have been performed
Too terrible for the ear. The times has been
That, when the brains were out, the man would die,
And there an end; but now they rise again,                80
With twenty mortal murders on their crowns,°
And push us from our stools. This is more strange
Than such a murder is.

**LADY MACBETH**              My worthy lord,
Your noble friends do lack you.

**MACBETH**                          I do forget.
Do not muse at me, my most worthy friends;                85
I have a strange infirmity, which is nothing
To those that know me. Come, love and health to all!
Then I'll sit down. Give me some wine, fill full.

*Enter* GHOST.

I drink to th' general joy o' th' whole table,
And to our dear friend Banquo, whom we miss;              90
Would he were here! To all and him we thirst,°
And all to all.°

**LORDS**              Our duties, and the pledge.

**MACBETH**

Avaunt! and quit my sight! Let the earth hide thee!

Thy bones are marrowless, thy blood is cold;
Thou hast no speculation° in those eyes                    95
Which thou dost glare with.

**LADY MACBETH**              Think of this, good peers,
But as a thing of custom; 'tis no other.
Only it spoils the pleasure of the time.

**MACBETH**

What man dare, I dare.
Approach thou like the rugged Russian bear,              100
The armed rhinoceros, or th' Hyrcan° tiger;
Take any shape but that, and my firm nerves°
Shall never tremble. Or be alive again,
And dare me to the desert° with thy sword.
If trembling I inhabit then, protest me                   105
The baby of a girl.° Hence, horrible shadow!
Unreal mock'ry, hence!              [*Exit* GHOST.]
                                    Why, so: being gone,
I am a man again. Pray you, sit still.

**LADY MACBETH**

You have displaced the mirth, broke the good meeting,
With most admired° disorder.

**MACBETH**              Can such things be,  110
And overcome us° like a summer's cloud,
Without our special wonder? You make me strange
Even to the disposition that I owe,°
When now I think you can behold such sights,
And keep the natural ruby of your cheeks,                 115
When mine is blanched with fear.

**ROSS**                          What sights, my lord?

**LADY MACBETH**

I pray you, speak not: he grows worse and worse;
Question enrages him: at once, good night.
Stand not upon the order of your going,°
But go at once.

**LENNOX**              Good night; and better health  120
Attend his majesty!

**LADY MACBETH**      A kind good night to all!
                                    *Exeunt* LORDS.

**MACBETH**

It will have blood, they say: blood will have blood.
Stones have been known to move and trees to speak;
Augures and understood relations° have
By maggot-pies and choughs and rooks brought forth°  125
The secret'st man of blood. What is the night?°

**LADY MACBETH**

Almost at odds° with morning, which is which.

**MACBETH**

How say'st thou, that Macduff denies his person
At our great bidding?

**LADY MACBETH**      Did you send to him, sir?

**MACBETH**

I hear it by the way,° but I will send:                   130
There's not a one of them but in his house

---

55 **upon a thought** as quick as thought  57 **extend his passion** lengthen his fit  63 **flaws** gusts, outbursts  64 **to** compared with  66 **Authorized** vouched for  71 **charnel houses** vaults containing bones  72–73 **our . . . kites** our tombs shall be the bellies of rapacious birds  76 **purged . . . weal** i.e., cleansed the state and made it gentle  81 **mortal . . . crowns** deadly wounds on their heads  91 **thirst** desire to drink  92 **all to all** everything to everybody ?) let everybody drink to everybody (?)

95 **speculation** sight  101 **Hyrcan** of Hyrcania (near the Caspian Sea)  102 **nerves** sinews  104 **the desert** a lonely place  105–06 **If . . . girl** If then I tremble, proclaim me a baby girl  110 **admired** amazing  111 **overcome us** come over us  112–13 **You . . . owe** i.e., You make me wonder what my nature is  119 **Stand . . . going** do not insist on departing in your order of rank  124 **Augures . . . relations** auguries and comprehended reports  125 **By . . . forth** by magpies, choughs, and rooks (telltale birds) revealed  126 **What . . . night** What time of night is it?  127 **at odds** striving  130 **by the way** incidentally

I keep a servant fee'd.° I will tomorrow,
And betimes° I will, to the weïrd sisters:
More shall they speak, for now I am bent° to know
By the worst means the worst. For mine own good    135
All causes° shall give way. I am in blood
Stepped in so far that, should I wade no more,
Returning were as tedious as go o'er.
Strange things I have in head that will to hand,
Which must be acted ere they may be scanned.°    140

LADY MACBETH
You lack the season of all natures,° sleep.

MACBETH
Come, we'll to sleep. My strange and self-abuse°
Is the initiate fear that wants hard use.°
We are yet but young in deed.       *Exeunt.*

Scene V. [*A witches' haunt.*]

*Thunder. Enter the three* WITCHES, *meeting* HECATE.

FIRST WITCH
Why, how now, Hecate! you look angerly.

HECATE
Have I not reason, beldams° as you are,
Saucy and overbold? How did you dare
To trade and traffic with Macbeth
In riddles and affairs of death;       5
And I, the mistress of your charms,
The close contriver° of all harms,
Was never called to bear my part,
Or show the glory of our art?
And, which is worse, all you have done      10
Hath been but for a wayward son,
Spiteful and wrathful; who, as others do,
Loves for his own ends, not for you.
But make amends now: get you gone,
And at the pit of Acheron°         15
Meet me i' th' morning: thither he
Will come to know his destiny.
Your vessels and your spells provide,
Your charms and everything beside.
I am for th' air; this night I'll spend      20
Unto a dismal and a fatal end:
Great business must be wrought ere noon.
Upon the corner of the moon
There hangs a vap'rous drop profound;°
I'll catch it ere it come to ground:       25
And that distilled by magic sleights°
Shall raise such artificial sprites°
As by the strength of their illusion
Shall draw him on to his confusion.°
He shall spurn fate, scorn death, and bear    30
His hopes 'bove wisdom, grace, and fear:

And you all know security°
Is mortals' chiefest enemy.

*Music and a song.*

Hark! I am called; my little spirit, see,
Sits in a foggy cloud and stays for me.    [*Exit.*] 35

*Sing within,* "Come away, come away," &c.

FIRST WITCH
Come, let's make haste; she'll soon be back again.
                      *Exeunt.*

Scene VI. [*The palace.*]

*Enter* LENNOX *and another* LORD.

LENNOX
My former speeches have but hit your thoughts,°
Which can interpret farther. Only I say
Things have been strangely borne.° The gracious
    Duncan
Was pitied of Macbeth: marry, he was dead.
And the right-valiant Banquo walked too late;    5
Whom, you may say, if't please you, Fleance killed,
For Fleance fled. Men must not walk too late.
Who cannot want the thought,° how monstrous
It was for Malcolm and for Donalbain
To kill their gracious father? Damnèd fact!°    10
How it did grieve Macbeth! Did he not straight,
In pious rage, the two delinquents tear,
That were the slaves of drink and thralls° of sleep?
Was not that nobly done? Ay, and wisely too;
For 'twould have angered any heart alive      15
To hear the men deny't. So that I say
He has borne° all things well: and I do think
That, had he Duncan's sons under his key—
As, an't° please heaven, he shall not—they should find
What 'twere to kill a father. So should Fleance.   20
But, peace! for from broad words,° and 'cause he
    failed
His presence at the tyrant's feast, I hear,
Macduff lives in disgrace. Sir, can you tell
Where he bestows himself?

LORD                The son of Duncan,
From whom this tyrant holds the due of birth,°    25
Lives in the English court, and is received
Of the most pious Edward° with such grace
That the malevolence of fortune nothing
Takes from his high respect.° Thither Macduff
Is gone to pray the holy king, upon his aid°    30
To wake Northumberland° and warlike Siward;
That by the help of these, with Him above
To ratify the work, we may again
Give to our tables meat, sleep to our nights,
Free from our feasts and banquets bloody knives,   35

---

132 **fee'd** i.e., paid to spy   133 **betimes** quickly   134 **bent**
determined   136 **causes** considerations   140 **may be scanned**
can be examined   141 **season** . . . **natures** seasoning (preservative) of all living creatures   142 **My** . . . **self-abuse** my
strange delusion   143 **initiate** . . . **use** beginner's fear that
lacks hardening practice
**III.v.2 beldams** hags   7 **close contriver** secret inventor
15 **Acheron** river of Hades   24 **profound** heavy   26
**sleights** arts   27 **artificial sprites** spirits created by magic
arts (?) artful (cunning) spirits (?)   29 **confusion** ruin

32 **security** overconfidence
**III.vi.1 My** . . . **thoughts** My recent words have only coin-
cided with what you have in your mind   3 **borne** managed
8 **cannot** . . . **thought** can fail to think   10 **fact** evil deed
13 **thralls** slaves   17 **borne** managed   19 **an't** if it   21 **for**
. . . **words** because of frank talk   25 **due of birth** birthright
27 **Edward** Edward the Confessor (reigned 1042–66)   28–29
**nothing** . . . **respect** does not diminish the high respect in
which he is held   30 **upon his aid** to aid him (Malcolm)   31
**To wake Northumberland** i.e., to arouse the people in an
English county near Scotland

Do faithful homage and receive free° honors:
All which we pine for now. And this report
Hath so exasperate the king that he
Prepares for some attempt at war.

LENNOX                              Sent he to Macduff?

LORD
He did: and with an absolute "Sir, not I,"          40
The cloudy° messenger turns me his back,
And hums, as who should say, "You'll rue the time
That clogs° me with this answer."

LENNOX                              And that well might
Advise him to a caution, t' hold what distance
His wisdom can provide. Some holy angel             45
Fly to the court of England and unfold
His message ere he come, that a swift blessing
May soon return to this our suffering country
Under a hand accursed!

LORD                              I'll send my prayers with him.
                                                    *Exeunt.*

# ACT IV

## Scene I. [*A witches' haunt.*]

*Thunder. Enter the three* WITCHES.

FIRST WITCH
Thrice the brinded° cat hath mewed.

SECOND WITCH
Thrice and once the hedge-pig° whined.

THIRD WITCH
Harpier° cries. 'Tis time, 'tis time.

FIRST WITCH
Round about the caldron go:
In the poisoned entrails throw.                      5
Toad, that under cold stone
Days and nights has thirty-one
Swelt'red venom sleeping got,°
Boil thou first i' th' charmèd pot.

ALL
Double, double, toil and trouble;                   10
Fire burn and caldron bubble.

SECOND WITCH
Fillet° of a fenny° snake,
In the caldron boil and bake;
Eye of newt and toe of frog,
Wool of bat and tongue of dog,                      15
Adder's fork° and blindworm's° sting,
Lizard's leg and howlet's° wing,
For a charm of pow'rful trouble,
Like a hell-broth boil and bubble.

ALL
Double, double, toil and trouble;                   20
Fire burn and caldron bubble.

THIRD WITCH
Scale of dragon, tooth of wolf,

Witch's mummy,° maw and gulf°
Of the ravined° salt-sea shark,
Root of hemlock digged i' th' dark,                 25
Liver of blaspheming Jew,
Gall of goat, and slips of yew
Slivered in the moon's eclipse,
Nose of Turk and Tartar's lips,
Finger of birth-strangled babe                      30
Ditch-delivered by a drab,°
Make the gruel thick and slab:°
Add thereto a tiger's chaudron,°
For th' ingredience of our caldron.

ALL
Double, double, toil and trouble;                   35
Fire burn and caldron bubble.

SECOND WITCH
Cool it with a baboon's blood,
Then the charm is firm and good.

*Enter* HECATE *and the other three* WITCHES.

HECATE
O, well done! I commend your pains;
And every one shall share i' th' gains:             40
And now about the caldron sing,
Like elves and fairies in a ring,
Enchanting all that you put in.

*Music and a song: "Black spirits," &c.*

[*Exeunt* HECATE *and the other three* WITCHES.]

SECOND WITCH
By the pricking of my thumbs,
Something wicked this way comes:                     45
    Open, locks,
    Whoever knocks!

*Enter* MACBETH.

MACBETH
How now, you secret, black, and midnight hags!
What is't you do?

ALL                              A deed without a name.

MACBETH
I conjure you, by that which you profess,           50
Howe'er you come to know it, answer me:
Though you untie the winds and let them fight
Against the churches; though the yesty° waves
Confound° and swallow navigation up;
Though bladed corn be lodged° and trees blown
    down;                                           55
Though castles topple on their warders' heads;
Though palaces and pyramids do slope°
Their heads to their foundations; though the treasure
Of nature's germens° tumble all together,
Even till destruction sicken,° answer me            60
To what I ask you.

FIRST WITCH                      Speak.

SECOND WITCH                     Demand.

THIRD WITCH                              We'll answer.

---

36 **free** freely granted  41 **cloudy** disturbed  43 **clogs**
burdens
**IV.i.1 brinded** brindled  2 **hedge-pig** hedgehog  3 **Harpier**
an attendant spirit, like Graymalkin and Paddock in I.i  8
**Swelt'red . . . got** venom sweated out while sleeping  12
**Fillet** slice; **fenny** from a swamp  16 **fork** forked tongue;
**blindworm** a legless lizard  17 **howlet** owlet

23 **Witch's mummy** mummified flesh of a witch; **maw and
gulf** stomach and gullet  24 **ravined** ravenous  31 **Ditch-
delivered . . . drab** born in a ditch of a harlot  32 **slab**
viscous  33 **chaudron** entrails  53 **yesty** foamy  54 **Confound** destroy  55 **bladed . . . lodged** grain in the ear be
beaten down  57 **slope** bend  59 **nature's germens** seeds of
all life  60 **sicken** i.e., sicken at its own work

FIRST WITCH
Say, if th' hadst rather hear it from our mouths,
Or from our masters?
MACBETH       Call 'em, let me see 'em.
FIRST WITCH
Pour in sow's blood, that hath eaten
Her nine farrow;° grease that's sweaten°     65
From the murderer's gibbet throw
Into the flame.
ALL       Come, high or low,
Thyself and office° deftly show!

*Thunder.* FIRST APPARITION: *an armed head.*

MACBETH
Tell me, thou unknown power—
FIRST WITCH       He knows thy thought:
Hear his speech, but say thou nought.     70
FIRST APPARITION
Macbeth! Macbeth! Macbeth! Beware Macduff!
Beware the Thane of Fife. Dismiss me: enough.
                         *He descends.*
MACBETH
Whate'er thou art, for thy good caution thanks:
Thou hast harped° my fear aright. But one word
   more—
FIRST WITCH
He will not be commanded. Here's another,     75
More potent than the first.

*Thunder.* SECOND APPARITION: *a bloody child.*

SECOND APPARITION
Macbeth! Macbeth! Macbeth!
MACBETH
Had I three ears, I'd hear thee.
SECOND APPARITION
Be bloody, bold, and resolute! Laugh to scorn
The pow'r of man, for none of woman born    80
Shall harm Macbeth.       *Descends.*
MACBETH
Then live, Macduff: what need I fear of thee?
But yet I'll make assurance double sure,
And take a bond of fate.° Thou shalt not live;
That I may tell pale-hearted fear it lies,     85
And sleep in spite of thunder.

*Thunder.* THIRD APPARITION: *a child crowned, with a
tree in his hand.*

                  What is this,
That rises like the issue° of a king,
And wears upon his baby-brow the round
And top of sovereignty?°
ALL       Listen, but speak not to't.
THIRD APPARITION
Be lion-mettled, proud, and take no care    90
Who chafes, who frets, or where conspirers are:
Macbeth shall never vanquished be until
Great Birnam Wood to high Dunsinane Hill
Shall come against him.       *Descends.*

MACBETH       That will never be.
Who can impress° the forest, bid the tree    95
Unfix his earth-bound root? Sweet bodements,° good!
Rebellious dead,° rise never, till the Wood
Of Birnam rise, and our high-placed Macbeth
Shall live the lease of nature,° pay his breath
To time and mortal custom.° Yet my heart    100
Throbs to know one thing. Tell me, if your art
Can tell so much: shall Banquo's issue ever
Reign in this kingdom?
ALL       Seek to know no more.
MACBETH
I will be satisfied.° Deny me this,
And an eternal curse fall on you! Let me know.    105
Why sinks that caldron? And what noise° is this?

*Hautboys.*

FIRST WITCH   Show!
SECOND WITCH   Show!
THIRD WITCH   Show!
ALL
Show his eyes, and grieve his heart;     110
Come like shadows, so depart!

*A show of eight* KINGS *and* BANQUO, *last* [KING] *with
a glass° in his hand.*

MACBETH
Thou art too like the spirit of Banquo. Down!
Thy crown does sear mine eyelids. And thy hair,
Thou other gold-bound brow, is like the first.
A third is like the former. Filthy hags!    115
Why do you show me this? A fourth! Start,° eyes!
What, will the line stretch out to th' crack of doom?°
Another yet! A seventh! I'll see no more.
And yet the eighth appears, who bears a glass
Which shows me many more; and some I see    120
That twofold balls and treble scepters° carry:
Horrible sight! Now I see 'tis true;
For the blood-boltered° Banquo smiles upon me,
And points at them for his. What, is this so?
FIRST WITCH
Ay, sir, all this is so. But why     125
Stands Macbeth thus amazedly?
Come, sisters, cheer we up his sprites,°
And show the best of our delights:
I'll charm the air to give a sound,
While you perform your antic round,°    130
That this great king may kindly say
Our duties did his welcome pay.

*Music. The* WITCHES *dance, and vanish.*

MACBETH
Where are they? Gone? Let this pernicious hour
Stand aye accursèd in the calendar!
Come in, without there!

---

65 **farrow** young pigs; **sweaten** sweated   68 **office** function
74 **harped** hit upon, struck the note of   84 **take . . . fate** get
a guarantee from fate (i.e., he will kill Macduff and thus will
compel fate to keep its word)   87 **issue** offspring   88–89
**round . . . sovereignty** i.e., crown

95 **impress** conscript   96 **bodements** prophecies   97 **Rebellious dead** perhaps a reference to Banquo, but perhaps a misprint
for "rebellion's head"   99 **lease of nature** natural lifespan   100
**mortal custom** natural death   104 **satisfied** i.e., fully informed
160 **noise** music   111 **s.d. glass** mirror   116 **Start** i.e., from the
sockets   117 **crack of doom** blast (of a trumpet?) at Doomsday
121 **twofold . . . scepters** coronation emblems   123 **bloodboltered** matted with blood   127 **sprites** spirits   130 **antic
round** grotesque circular dance

*Enter* LENNOX.

LENNOX            What's your grace's will?    135

MACBETH
Saw you the weïrd sisters?

LENNOX            No, my lord.

MACBETH
Came they not by you?

LENNOX            No indeed, my lord.

MACBETH
Infected be the air whereon they ride,
And damned all those that trust them! I did hear
The galloping of horse.° Who was't came by?    140

LENNOX
'Tis two or three, my lord, that bring you word
Macduff is fled to England.

MACBETH            Fled to England?

LENNOX
Ay, my good lord.

MACBETH [*Aside.*]
Time, thou anticipat'st° my dread exploits.
The flighty purpose never is o'ertook    145
Unless the deed go with it.° From this moment
The very firstlings of my heart° shall be
The firstlings of my hand. And even now,
To crown my thoughts with acts, be it thought and
    done:
The castle of Macduff I will surprise;°    150
Seize upon Fife; give to th' edge o' th' sword
His wife, his babes, and all unfortunate souls
That trace him in his line.° No boasting like a fool;
This deed I'll do before this purpose cool:
But no more sights!—Where are these gentlemen?    155
Come, bring me where they are.        *Exeunt.*

Scene II. [*Macduff's castle.*]

*Enter Macduff's wife* [LADY MACDUFF], *her* SON, *and*
ROSS.

LADY MACDUFF
What had he done, to make him fly the land?

ROSS
You must have patience, madam.

LADY MACDUFF            He had none:
His flight was madness. When our actions do not,
Our fears do make us traitors.

ROSS            You know not
Whether it was his wisdom or his fear.    5

LADY MACDUFF
Wisdom! To leave his wife, to leave his babes,
His mansion and his titles,° in a place
From whence himself does fly? He loves us not;
He wants the natural touch:° for the poor wren,
The most diminutive of birds, will fight,    10
Her young ones in her nest, against the owl.

All is the fear and nothing is the love;
As little is the wisdom, where the flight
So runs against all reason.

ROSS            My dearest coz,°
I pray you, school° yourself. But, for your husband,    15
He is noble, wise, judicious, and best knows
The fits o' th' season.° I dare not speak much further:
But cruel are the times, when we are traitors
And do not know ourselves; when we hold rumor
From what we fear,° yet know not what we fear,    20
But float upon a wild and violent sea
Each way and move. I take my leave of you.
Shall not be long but I'll be here again.
Things at the worst will cease,° or else climb upward
To what they were before. My pretty cousin,    25
Blessing upon you!

LADY MACDUFF
Fathered he is, and yet he's fatherless.

ROSS
I am so much a fool, should I stay longer,
It would be my disgrace° and your discomfort.
I take my leave at once.        *Exit* ROSS.

LADY MACDUFF            Sirrah,° your father's dead:    30
And what will you do now? How will you live?

SON
As birds do, mother.

LADY MACDUFF            What, with worms and flies?

SON
With what I get, I mean; and so do they.

LADY MACDUFF
Poor bird! thou'dst never fear the net nor lime,°
The pitfall nor the gin.°    35

SON
Why should I, mother? Poor birds they are not set
    for.
My father is not dead, for all your saying.

LADY MACDUFF
Yes, he is dead: how wilt thou do for a father?

SON Nay, how will you do for a husband?

LADY MACDUFF Why, I can buy me twenty at any    40
market.

SON Then you'll buy 'em to sell° again.

LADY MACDUFF
Thou speak'st with all thy wit, and yet, i' faith,
With wit enough for thee.°

SON
Was my father a traitor, mother?    45

LADY MACDUFF Ay, that he was.

SON What is a traitor?

LADY MACDUFF Why, one that swears and lies.°

SON And be all traitors that do so?

LADY MACDUFF Every one that does so is a traitor,    50
and must be hanged.

SON
And must they all be hanged that swear and lie?

LADY MACDUFF Every one.

---

140 **horse** horses (or "horsemen")   144 **anticipat'st** foretold
145–46 **The flighty . . . it** The fleeting plan is never fulfilled
unless an action accompanies it   147 **firstlings . . . heart** i.e.,
first thoughts, impulses   150 **surprise** attack suddenly   153
**trace . . . line** are of his lineage
IV.ii.7 **titles** possessions   9 **wants . . . touch** i.e., lacks
natural affection for his wife and children

14 **coz** cousin   15 **school** control   17 **fits . . . season** disorders
of the time   19–20 **hold . . . fear** believe rumors because we
fear   24 **cease** i.e., cease worsening   29 **It . . . disgrace** i.e., I
would weep   30 **Sirrah** here an affectionate address to a child
34 **lime** bird lime (smeared on branches to catch birds)   35 **gin**
trap   42 **sell** betray   44 **for thee** i.e., for a child   48 **swears
and lies** i.e., takes an oath and breaks it

SON   Who must hang them?

LADY MACDUFF   Why, the honest men.     55

SON   Then the liars and swearers are fools; for there are liars and swearers enow° to beat the honest men and hang up them.

LADY MACDUFF   Now, God help thee, poor monkey! But how wilt thou do for a father?     60

SON   If he were dead, you'd weep for him. If you would not, it were a good sign that I should quickly have a new father.

LADY MACDUFF   Poor prattler, how thou talk'st!

*Enter a* MESSENGER.

MESSENGER
Bless you, fair dame! I am not to you known,     65
Though in your state of honor I am perfect.°
I doubt° some danger does approach you nearly:
If you will take a homely° man's advice,
Be not found here; hence, with your little ones.
To fright you thus, methinks I am too savage;     70
To do worse to you were fell° cruelty,
Which is too nigh your person. Heaven preserve you!
I dare abide no longer.        *Exit* MESSENGER.

LADY MACDUFF        Whither should I fly?
I have done no harm. But I remember now
I am in this earthly world, where to do harm     75
Is often laudable, to do good sometime
Accounted dangerous folly. Why then, alas,
Do I put up that womanly defense,
To say I have done no harm?—What are these faces?

*Enter* MURDERERS.

MURDERER
Where is your husband?

LADY MACDUFF                  80
I hope, in no place so unsanctified
Where such as thou mayst find him.

MURDERER                He's a traitor.

SON
Thou li'st, thou shag-eared° villain!

MURDERER               What, you egg!

[*Stabbing him.*]

Young fry° of treachery!

SON             He has killed me, mother:
Run away, I pray you!             [*Dies.*] 85
       *Exit* [LADY MACDUFF], *crying* "Murder!"
           [*followed by* MURDERERS].

Scene III. [*England. Before the king's palace.*]

*Enter* MALCOLM *and* MACDUFF.

MALCOLM
Let us seek out some desolate shade, and there
Weep our sad bosoms empty.

MACDUFF              Let us rather
Hold fast the mortal° sword, and like good men

Bestride our down-fall'n birthdom.° Each new morn
New widows howl, new orphans cry, new sorrows     5
Strike heaven on the face, that° it resounds
As if it felt with Scotland and yelled out
Like syllable of dolor.°

MALCOLM          What I believe, I'll wail;
What know, believe; and what I can redress,
As I shall find the time to friend,° I will.     10
What you have spoke, it may be so perchance.
This tyrant, whose sole° name blisters our tongues,
Was once thought honest:° you have loved him well;
He hath not touched you yet. I am young; but something
You may deserve of him through me;° and wisdom°     15
To offer up a weak, poor, innocent lamb
T' appease an angry god.

MACDUFF
I am not treacherous.

MALCOLM         But Macbeth is.
A good and virtuous nature may recoil
In° an imperial charge. But I shall crave your pardon;     20
That which you are, my thoughts cannot transpose:°
Angels are bright still, though the brightest° fell:
Though all things foul would wear° the brows of grace,
Yet grace must still look so.°

MACDUFF        I have lost my hopes.

MALCOLM
Perchance even there where I did find my doubts.     25
Why in that rawness° left you wife and child,
Those precious motives, those strong knots of love,
Without leave-taking? I pray you,
Let not my jealousies° be your dishonors,
But mine own safeties. You may be rightly just°     30
Whatever I shall think.

MACDUFF         Bleed, bleed, poor country:
Great tyranny, lay thou thy basis° sure,
For goodness dare not check° thee: wear thou thy wrongs;
The title is affeered.° Fare thee well, lord:
I would not be the villain that thou think'st     35
For the whole space that's in the tyrant's grasp
And the rich East to boot.

MALCOLM         Be not offended:
I speak not as in absolute fear of you.
I think our country sinks beneath the yoke;
It weeps, it bleeds, and each new day a gash     40
Is added to her wounds. I think withal°
There would be hands uplifted in my right;°
And here from gracious England° have I offer
Of goodly thousands: but, for° all this,
When I shall tread upon the tyrant's head,     45
Or wear it on my sword, yet my poor country

**4 Bestride . . . birthdom** protectively stand over our native land  **6 that** so that  **8 Like . . . dolor** similar sound of grief  **10 to friend** friendly, propitious  **12 sole** very  **13 honest** good  **15 deserve . . . me** i.e., earn by betraying me to Macbeth; **wisdom** it may be wise  **19–20 recoil In** give way under  **21 transpose** transform  **22 the brightest** i.e., Lucifer  **23 would wear** desire to wear  **24 so** i.e., like itself  **26 rawness** unprotected condition  **29 jealousies** suspicions  **30 rightly just** perfectly honorable  **32 basis** foundation  **33 check** restrain  **34 affeered** legally confirmed  **41 withal** moreover  **42 in my right** on behalf of my claim  **43 England** i.e., the King of England  **44 for** despite

**57 enow** enough  **66 in . . . perfect** I am fully informed of your honorable rank  **67 doubt** fear  **68 homely** plain  **71 fell** fierce  **83 shag-eared** hairy-eared (?) with shaggy hair hanging over the ears (?)  **84 fry** spawn  **IV.iii.3 mortal** deadly

Shall have more vices than it had before,
More suffer, and more sundry ways than ever,
By him that shall succeed.
MACDUFF                         What should he be?
MALCOLM
It is myself I mean, in whom I know                    50
All the particulars° of vice so grafted°
That, when they shall be opened,° black Macbeth
Will seem as pure as snow, and the poor state
Esteem him as a lamb, being compared
With my confineless harms.°
MACDUFF                         Not in the legions    55
Of horrid hell can come a devil more damned
In evils to top Macbeth.
MALCOLM                         I grant him bloody,
Luxurious,° avaricious, false, deceitful,
Sudden,° malicious, smacking of every sin
That has a name: but there's no bottom, none,       60
In my voluptuousness:° your wives, your daughters,
Your matrons and your maids, could not fill up
The cistern of my lust, and my desire
All continent° impediments would o'erbear,
That did oppose my will. Better Macbeth             65
Than such an one to reign.
MACDUFF                         Boundless intemperance
In nature° is a tyranny; it hath been
Th' untimely emptying of the happy throne,
And fall of many kings. But fear not yet
To take upon you what is yours: you may            70
Convey° your pleasures in a spacious plenty,
And yet seem cold, the time° you may so hoodwink.
We have willing dames enough. There cannot be
That vulture in you, to devour so many
As will to greatness dedicate themselves,           75
Finding it so inclined.
MALCOLM                         With this there grows
In my most ill-composed affection° such
A stanchless° avarice that, were I king,
I should cut off the nobles for their lands,
Desire his jewels and this other's house:           80
And my more-having would be as a sauce
To make me hunger more, that I should forge
Quarrels unjust against the good and loyal,
Destroying them for wealth.
MACDUFF                         This avarice
Sticks deeper, grows with more pernicious root      85
Than summer-seeming° lust, and it hath been
The sword of our slain kings.° Yet do not fear.
Scotland hath foisons to fill up your will
Of your mere own.° All these are portable,°
With other graces weighed.                          90
MALCOLM
But I have none: the king-becoming graces,

As justice, verity, temp'rance, stableness,
Bounty, perseverance, mercy, lowliness,
Devotion, patience, courage, fortitude,
I have no relish of° them, but abound              95
In the division of each several crime,°
Acting in many ways. Nay, had I pow'r, I should
Pour the sweet milk of concord into hell,
Uproar° the universal peace, confound
All unity on earth.
MACDUFF                         O Scotland, Scotland!   100
MALCOLM
If such a one be fit to govern, speak:
I am as I have spoken.
MACDUFF                         Fit to govern!
No, not to live. O nation miserable!
With an untitled tyrant bloody-sceptered,
When shalt thou see thy wholesome days again,      105
Since that the truest issue of thy throne
By his own interdiction° stands accursed,
And does blaspheme his breed?° Thy royal father
Was a most sainted king: the queen that bore thee,
Oft'ner upon her knees than on her feet,           110
Died° every day she lived. Fare thee well!
These evils thou repeat'st upon thyself
Hath banished me from Scotland. O my breast,
Thy hope ends here!
MALCOLM                         Macduff, this noble passion,
Child of integrity, hath from my soul              115
Wiped the black scruples,° reconciled my thoughts
To thy good truth and honor. Devilish Macbeth
By many of these trains° hath sought to win me
Into his power; and modest wisdom° plucks me
From over-credulous haste: but God above           120
Deal between thee and me! For even now
I put myself to° thy direction, and
Unspeak mine own detraction; here abjure
The taints and blames I laid upon myself,
For° strangers to my nature. I am yet              125
Unknown to woman, never was forsworn,
Scarcely have coveted what was mine own,
At no time broke my faith, would not betray
The devil to his fellow, and delight
No less in truth than life. My first false speaking  130
Was this upon myself. What I am truly,
Is thine and my poor country's to command:
Whither indeed, before thy here-approach,
Old Siward, with ten thousand warlike men,
Already at a point,° was setting forth.            135
Now we'll together, and the chance of goodness
Be like our warranted quarrel!° Why are you
  silent?
MACDUFF
Such welcome and unwelcome things at once
'Tis hard to reconcile.

*Enter a DOCTOR.*

51 **particulars** special kinds; **grafted** engrafted  52 **opened** in bloom, i.e., revealed  55 **confineless harms** unbounded evils  58 **Luxurious** lecherous  59 **Sudden** violent  61 **voluptuousness** lust  64 **continent** restraining  67 **In nature** in man's nature  71 **Convey** secretly manage  72 **time** age, i.e., people  77 **ill-composed affection** evilly compounded character  78 **stanchless** never-ending  86 **summer-seeming** befitting summer, i.e., youthful (?) transitory (?)  87 **sword . . . kings** i.e., the cause of death to our kings  88–89 **foisons . . . own** enough abundance of your own to satisfy your covetousness  89 **portable** bearable

95 **relish of** taste for (?) trace of (?)  96 **division . . . crime** variations of each kind of crime  99 **Uproar** put into a tumult  107 **interdiction** curse, exclusion  108 **breed** ancestry  111 **Died** i.e., prepared for heaven  116 **scruples** suspicions  118 **trains** plots  119 **modest wisdom** i.e., prudence  122 **to** under  125 **For** as  135 **at a point** prepared  136–37 **the chance . . . quarrel** May our chance of success equal the justice of our cause

MALCOLM
Well, more anon. Comes the king forth, I pray you? 140

DOCTOR
Ay, sir. There are a crew of wretched souls
That stay° his cure: their malady convinces
The great assay of art;° but at his touch,
Such sanctity hath heaven given his hand,
They presently amend.°

MALCOLM         I thank you, doctor. 145
                         *Exit* [DOCTOR].

MACDUFF
What's the disease he means?

MALCOLM         'Tis called the evil:°
A most miraculous work in this good king,
Which often since my here-remain in England
I have seen him do. How he solicits heaven,
Himself best knows: but strangely visited° people, 150
All swoll'n and ulcerous, pitiful to the eye,
The mere° despair of surgery, he cures,
Hanging a golden stamp° about their necks,
Put on with holy prayers: and 'tis spoken,
To the succeeding royalty he leaves 155
The healing benediction. With this strange virtue°
He hath a heavenly gift of prophecy,
And sundry blessings hang about his throne
That speak° him full of grace.

*Enter* ROSS.

MACDUFF         See, who comes here?

MALCOLM
My countryman; but yet I know him not. 160

MACDUFF
My ever gentle° cousin, welcome hither.

MALCOLM
I know him now: good God, betimes° remove
The means that makes us strangers!

ROSS         Sir, amen.

MACDUFF
Stands Scotland where it did?

ROSS         Alas, poor country!
Almost afraid to know itself! It cannot 165
Be called our mother but our grave, where nothing°
But who knows nothing is once seen to smile;
Where sighs and groans, and shrieks that rent the air,
Are made, not marked;° where violent sorrow seems
A modern ecstasy.° The dead man's knell 170
Is there scarce asked for who, and good men's lives
Expire before the flowers in their caps,
Dying or ere they sicken.

MACDUFF         O, relation
Too nice,° and yet too true!

MALCOLM         What's the newest grief?

ROSS
That of an hour's age doth hiss the speaker;° 175

Each minute teems° a new one.

MACDUFF         How does my wife?

ROSS
Why, well.

MACDUFF    And all my children?

ROSS         Well too.

MACDUFF
The tyrant has not battered at their peace?

ROSS
No; they were well at peace when I did leave 'em.

MACDUFF
Be not a niggard of your speech: how goes't? 180

ROSS
When I came hither to transport the tidings,
Which I have heavily° borne, there ran a rumor
Of many worthy fellows that were out;°
Which was to my belief witnessed° the rather,
For that I saw the tyrant's power° afoot. 185
Now is the time of help. Your eye in Scotland
Would create soldiers, make our women fight,
To doff their dire distresses.

MALCOLM         Be't their comfort
We are coming thither. Gracious England hath
Lent us good Siward and ten thousand men; 190
An older and a better soldier none
That Christendom gives out.°

ROSS         Would I could answer
This comfort with the like! But I have words
That would° be howled out in the desert air,
Where hearing should not latch° them.

MACDUFF         What concern they? 195
The general cause or is it a fee-grief
Due to some single breast?°

ROSS         No mind that's honest
But in it shares some woe, though the main part
Pertains to you alone.

MACDUFF         If it be mine,
Keep it not from me, quickly let me have it. 200

ROSS
Let not your ears despise my tongue for ever,
Which shall possess them with the heaviest sound
That ever yet they heard.

MACDUFF         Humh! I guess at it.

ROSS
Your castle is surprised;° your wife and babes
Savagely slaughtered. To relate the manner, 205
Were, on the quarry° of these murdered deer,
To add the death of you.

MALCOLM         Merciful heaven!
What, man! Ne'er pull your hat upon your brows.
Give sorrow words. The grief that does not speak
Whispers the o'er-fraught heart,° and bids it break. 210

MACDUFF
My children too?

ROSS         Wife, children, servants, all
That could be found.

MACDUFF         And I must be from thence!

---

**142 stay** await **142–43 convinces . . . art** i.e., defies the efforts of medical science **145 presently amend** immediately recover **146 evil** scrofula, called "the king's evil" because it could allegedly be cured by the king's touch **150 strangely visited** oddly afflicted **152 mere** utter **153 stamp** coin **156 virtue** power **159 speak** proclaim **161 gentle** noble **162 betimes** quickly **166 nothing** no one **169 marked** noticed **170 modern ecstasy** i.e., ordinary emotion **173–74 relation Too nice** tale too accurate **175 That . . . speaker** The report of the grief of an hour ago is hissed as stale news

**176 teems** gives birth to **182 heavily** sadly **183 out** i.e., up in arms **184 witnessed** attested **185 power** army **192 gives out** reports **194 would** should **195 latch** catch **196–97 fee-grief . . . breast** i.e., a personal grief belonging to an individual **204 surprised** suddenly attacked **206 quarry** heap of slaughtered game **210 Whispers . . . heart** whispers to the overburdened heart

My wife killed too?

ROSS                               I have said.

MALCOLM                         Be comforted.
Let's make us med'cines of our great revenge,
To cure this deadly grief.                                       215

MACDUFF
He has no children. All my pretty ones?
Did you say all? O hell-kite!° All?
What, all my pretty chickens and their dam
At one fell swoop?

MALCOLM
Dispute° it like a man.

MACDUFF                      I shall do so;          220
But I must also feel it as a man.
I cannot but remember such things were,
That were most precious to me. Did heaven look on,
And would not take their part? Sinful Macduff,
They were all struck for thee! Naught° that I am,   225
Not for their own demerits but for mine
Fell slaughter on their souls. Heaven rest them now!

MALCOLM
Be this the whetstone of your sword. Let grief
Convert to anger; blunt not the heart, enrage it.

MACDUFF
O, I could play the woman with mine eyes,       230
And braggart with my tongue! But, gentle heavens,
Cut short all intermission;° front to front°
Bring thou this fiend of Scotland and myself;
Within my sword's length set him. If he 'scape,
Heaven forgive him too!

MALCOLM                    This time goes manly.   235
Come, go we to the king. Our power is ready;
Our lack is nothing but our leave.° Macbeth
Is ripe for shaking, and the pow'rs above
Put on their instruments.° Receive what cheer you
  may.
The night is long that never finds the day.   *Exeunt.* 240

# ACT V

Scene I. [*Dunsinane. In the castle.*]

*Enter a* DOCTOR *of physic and a waiting-*GENTLE-
WOMAN.

DOCTOR  I have two nights watched with you, but
can perceive no truth in your report. When was it she
last walked?

GENTLEWOMAN  Since his majesty went into the
field, I have seen her rise from her bed, throw her 5
nightgown upon her, unlock her closet,° take forth
paper, fold it, write upon't, read it, afterwards seal it,
and again return to bed; yet all this while in a most
fast sleep.

DOCTOR  A great perturbation in nature, to receive at 10

once the benefit of sleep and do the effects of watching!° In this slumb'ry agitation, besides her walking
and other actual performances,° what, at any time,
have you heard her say?

GENTLEWOMAN  That, sir, which I will not report 15
after her.

DOCTOR  You may to me, and 'tis most meet° you
should.

GENTLEWOMAN  Neither to you nor anyone, having
no witness to confirm my speech.                          20

*Enter* LADY [MACBETH] *with a taper.*

Lo you, here she comes! This is her very guise,° and,
upon my life, fast asleep! Observe her; stand close.°

DOCTOR  How came she by that light?

GENTLEWOMAN  Why, it stood by her. She has light
by her continually. 'Tis her command.                    25

DOCTOR  You see, her eyes are open.

GENTLEWOMAN  Ay, but their sense° are shut.

DOCTOR  What is it she does now? Look, how she rubs
her hands.

GENTLEWOMAN  It is an accustomed action with her, 30
to seem thus washing her hands: I have known her
continue in this a quarter of an hour.

LADY MACBETH  Yet here's a spot.

DOCTOR  Hark! she speaks. I will set down what
comes from her, to satisfy° my remembrance the more 35
strongly.

LADY MACBETH  Out, damned spot! Out, I say!
One: two: why, then 'tis time to do't. Hell is murky.
Fie, my lord, fie! A soldier, and afeard? What need
we fear who knows it, when none can call our pow'r 40
to accompt?° Yet who would have thought the old
man to have had so much blood in him?

DOCTOR  Do you mark that?

LADY MACBETH  The Thane of Fife had a wife.
Where is she now? What, will these hands ne'er be 45
clean? No more o' that, my lord, no more o' that!
You mar all with this starting.

DOCTOR  Go to,° go to! You have known what you
should not.

GENTLEWOMAN  She has spoke what she should not, 50
I am sure of that. Heaven knows what she has known.

LADY MACBETH  Here's the smell of the blood still.
All the perfumes of Arabia will not sweeten this little
hand. Oh, oh, oh!

DOCTOR  What a sigh is there! The heart is sorely 55
charged.°

GENTLEWOMAN  I would not have such a heart in
my bosom for the dignity° of the whole body.

DOCTOR  Well, well, well—

GENTLEWOMAN  Pray God it be, sir.                        60

DOCTOR  This disease is beyond my practice.° Yet I
have known those which have walked in their sleep
who have died holily in their beds.

LADY MACBETH  Wash your hands; put on your
nightgown; look not so pale! I tell you yet again, 65
Banquo's buried. He cannot come out on's° grave.

---

217 **hell-kite** hellish bird of prey  220 **Dispute** counter  225
**Naught** wicked  232 **intermission** interval; **front to front**
forehead to forehead (i.e., face to face)  237 **Our lack . . .
leave** We need only to take our leave  239 **Put . . . instruments** arm themselves (?) urge us, their agents, onward (?)
**V.i.6 closet** chest

11–12 **effects of watching** deeds of one awake  13 **actual
performances** deeds  17 **meet** suitable  21 **guise** custom  22
**close** hidden  27 **sense** i.e., powers of sight  35 **satisfy**
confirm  41 **to accompt** into account  48 **Go to** an exclamation  56 **charged** burdened  58 **dignity** worth, rank  61
**practice** professional skill  66 **on's** of his

DOCTOR   Even so?

LADY MACBETH   To bed, to bed! There's knocking
at the gate. Come, come, come, come, give me your
hand! What's done cannot be undone. To bed, to bed, 70
to bed!          *Exit* LADY [MACBETH].

DOCTOR   Will she go now to bed?

GENTLEWOMAN   Directly.

DOCTOR
Foul whisp'rings are abroad. Unnatural deeds
Do breed unnatural troubles. Infected minds    75
To their deaf pillows will discharge their secrets.
More needs she the divine than the physician.
God, God forgive us all! Look after her;
Remove from her the means of all annoyance,°
And still° keep eyes upon her. So good night.    80
My mind she has mated° and amazed my sight:
I think, but dare not speak.

GENTLEWOMAN          Good night, good doctor.
                          *Exeunt.*

### Scene II. [*The country near Dunsinane.*]

*Drum and colors. Enter* MENTEITH, CAITHNESS,
ANGUS, LENNOX, SOLDIERS.

MENTEITH
The English pow'r° is near, led on by Malcolm,
His uncle Siward and the good Macduff.
Revenges burn in them; for their dear° causes
Would to the bleeding and the grim alarm
Excite the mortified man.°

ANGUS          Near Birnam Wood    5
Shall we well meet them; that way are they coming.

CAITHNESS
Who knows if Donalbain be with his brother?

LENNOX
For certain, sir, he is not. I have a file°
Of all the gentry: there is Siward's son,
And many unrough° youths that even now    10
Protest° their first of manhood.

MENTEITH          What does the tyrant?

CAITHNESS
Great Dunsinane he strongly fortifies.
Some say he's mad; others, that lesser hate him,
Do call it valiant fury: but, for certain,
He cannot buckle his distempered° cause    15
Within the belt of rule.°

ANGUS          Now does he feel
His secret murders sticking on his hands;
Now minutely revolts upbraid° his faith-breach.
Those he commands move only in command,
Nothing in love. Now does he feel his title    20
Hang loose about him, like a giant's robe
Upon a dwarfish thief.

MENTEITH          Who then shall blame
His pestered° senses to recoil and start,

When all that is within him does condemn
Itself for being there?

CAITHNESS        Well, march we on,    25
To give obedience where 'tis truly owed.
Meet we the med'cine° of the sickly weal,°
And with him pour we, in our country's purge,
Each drop of us.°

LENNOX          Or so much as it needs
To dew° the sovereign° flower and drown the weeds. 30
Make we our march towards Birnam.
                     *Exeunt, marching.*

### Scene III. [*Dunsinane. In the castle.*]

*Enter* MACBETH, DOCTOR, *and* ATTENDANTS.

MACBETH
Bring me no more reports; let them fly all!
Till Birnam Wood remove to Dunsinane
I cannot taint° with fear. What's the boy Malcolm?
Was he not born of woman? The spirits that know
All mortal consequences° have pronounced me thus: 5
"Fear not, Macbeth; no man that's born of woman
Shall e'er have power upon thee." Then fly, false
     thanes,
And mingle with the English epicures.
The mind I sway° by and the heart I bear
Shall never sag with doubt nor shake with fear.    10

*Enter* SERVANT.

The devil damn thee black, thou cream-faced loon!°
Where got'st thou that goose look?

SERVANT
There is ten thousand—

MACBETH          Geese, villain?

SERVANT          Soldiers, sir.

MACBETH
Go prick thy face and over-red° thy fear,
Thou lily-livered boy. What soldiers, patch?°    15
Death of° thy soul! Those linen° cheeks of thine
Are counselors to fear. What soldiers, whey-face?

SERVANT
The English force, so please you.

MACBETH
Take thy face hence.        [*Exit* SERVANT.]
         Seyton!—I am sick at heart,
When I behold—Seyton, I say!—This push°    20
Will cheer me ever, or disseat° me now.
I have lived long enough. My way of life
Is fall'n into the sear,° the yellow leaf,
And that which should accompany old age,
As honor, love, obedience, troops of friends,    25
I must not look to have; but, in their stead,
Curses not loud but deep, mouth-honor, breath,

---

**79 annoyance** injury  **80 still** continuously  **81 mated**
baffled
**V.ii.1 pow'r** army  **3 dear** heartfelt  **4–5 Would . . . man**
i.e., would incite a dead man (or a paralyzed man) to join the
bloody and grim call to battle  **8 file** list  **10 unrough** i.e.,
beardless  **11 Protest** assert  **15 distempered** swollen by
dropsy  **16 rule** self-control  **18 minutely revolts upbraid**
rebellions every minute rebuke  **23 pestered** tormented

**27 med'cine** i.e., Malcolm; **weal** commonwealth  **29 Each
. . . us** i.e., every last drop of our blood (?)  **30 dew** bedew,
water (and thus make grow); **sovereign** (1) royal (2) remedial
**V.iii.3 taint** become infected  **5 mortal consequences** future
human events  **9 sway** move  **11 loon** fool  **14 over-red**
cover with red  **15 patch** fool  **16 of** upon; **linen** i.e., pale
**20 push** effort  **21 disseat** i.e., unthrone (with word-play on
"cheer," pronounced "chair")  **23 sear** withered

Which the poor heart would fain deny, and dare not.
Seyton!

*Enter* SEYTON.

SEYTON
What's your gracious pleasure?

MACBETH                          What news more?    30

SEYTON
All is confirmed, my lord, which was reported.

MACBETH
I'll fight, till from my bones my flesh be hacked.
Give me my armor.

SEYTON                    'Tis not needed yet.

MACBETH
I'll put it on.
Send out moe° horses, skirr° the country round.    35
Hang those that talk of fear. Give me mine armor.
How does your patient, doctor?

DOCTOR                          Not so sick, my lord,
As she is troubled with thick-coming fancies
That keep her from her rest.

MACBETH                          Cure her of that.
Canst thou not minister to a mind diseased,    40
Pluck from the memory a rooted sorrow,
Raze out° the written troubles of the brain,
And with some sweet oblivious° antidote
Cleanse the stuffed bosom of that perilous stuff
Which weighs upon the heart?

DOCTOR                          Therein the patient    45
Must minister to himself.

MACBETH
Throw physic° to the dogs, I'll none of it.
Come, put mine armor on. Give me my staff.
Seyton, send out.—Doctor, the thanes fly from me.—
Come, sir, dispatch.° If thou couldst, doctor, cast    50
The water° of my land, find her disease
And purge it to a sound and pristine health,
I would applaud thee to the very echo,
That should applaud again.—Pull't off, I say.—
What rhubarb, senna, or what purgative drug,    55
Would scour these English hence? Hear'st thou of
   them?

DOCTOR
Ay, my good lord; your royal preparation
Makes us hear something.

MACBETH                          Bring it° after me.
I will not be afraid of death and bane°
Till Birnam Forest come to Dunsinane.    60

DOCTOR [*Aside.*]
Were I from Dunsinane away and clear,
Profit again should hardly draw me here.    *Exeunt.*

Scene IV. [*Country near Birnam Wood.*]

*Drum and colors. Enter* MALCOLM, SIWARD, MAC-
DUFF, *Siward's son,* [YOUNG SIWARD], MENTEITH,
CAITHNESS, ANGUS, *and* SOLDIERS, *marching.*

MALCOLM
Cousins, I hope the days are near at hand

35 moe° more; skirr scour    42 Raze out erase    43 oblivious
causing forgetfulness    47 physic medical science    50 dispatch
hurry    50-51 cast The water analyze the urine    58 it i.e., the
armor    59 bane destruction

That chambers will be safe.°

MENTEITH                    We doubt it nothing.°

SIWARD
What wood is this before us?

MENTEITH                    The Wood of Birnam.

MALCOLM
Let every soldier hew him down a bough
And bear't before him. Thereby shall we shadow    5
The numbers of our host, and make discovery°
Err in report of us.

SOLDIERS                    It shall be done.

SIWARD
We learn no other but° the confident tyrant
Keeps still in Dunsinane, and will endure°
Our setting down before't.

MALCOLM                    'Tis his main hope,    10
For where there is advantage to be given°
Both more and less° have given him the revolt,
And none serve with him but constrainèd things
Whose hearts are absent too.

MACDUFF                    Let our just censures
Attend the true event,° and put we on    15
Industrious soldiership.

SIWARD                    The time approaches,
That will with due decision make us know
What we shall say we have and what we owe.°
Thoughts speculative their unsure hopes relate,
But certain issue strokes must arbitrate:°    20
Towards which advance the war.°    *Exeunt, marching.*

Scene V. [*Dunsinane. Within the castle.*]

*Enter* MACBETH, SEYTON, *and* SOLDIERS, *with drum
and colors.*

MACBETH
Hang out our banners on the outward walls.
The cry is still "They come!" Our castle's strength
Will laugh a siege to scorn. Here let them lie
Till famine and the ague° eat them up.
Were they not forced° with those that should be ours,    5
We might have met them dareful,° beard to beard,
And beat them backward home. *A cry within of women.*
                              What is that noise?

SEYTON
It is the cry of women, my good lord.    [*Exit.*]

MACBETH
I have almost forgot the taste of fears:
The time has been, my senses would have cooled    10
To hear a night-shriek, and my fell° of hair
Would at a dismal treatise° rouse and stir
As life were in't. I have supped full with horrors.

V.iv.2 That . . . safe that a man will be safe in his bedroom;
nothing not at all    6 discovery reconnaissance    8 no other
but nothing but that    9 endure allow    11 advantage . . .
given afforded an opportunity    12 more and less high and
low    14-15 just . . . event true judgment await the actual
outcome    18 owe own (the contrast is between "what we
shall say we have" and "what we shall really have")    20
certain . . . arbitrate the definite outcome must be decided
by battle    21 war army
V.v.4 ague fever    5 forced reinforced    6 met them dareful
i.e., met them in the battlefield boldly    11 fell pelt    12 treatise
story

Direness, familiar to my slaughterous thoughts,
Cannot once start° me.

[*Enter* SEYTON.]

                 Wherefore was that cry?     15

SEYTON
The queen, my lord, is dead.

MACBETH
She should° have died hereafter;
There would have been a time for such a word.°
Tomorrow, and tomorrow, and tomorrow
Creeps in this petty pace from day to day,     20
To the last syllable of recorded time;
And all our yesterdays have lighted fools
The way to dusty death. Out, out, brief candle!
Life's but a walking shadow, a poor player
That struts and frets his hour upon the stage     25
And then is heard no more. It is a tale
Told by an idiot, full of sound and fury,
Signifying nothing.

*Enter a* MESSENGER.

Thou com'st to use thy tongue; thy story quickly!

MESSENGER
Gracious my lord,     30
I should report that which I say I saw,
But know not how to do't.

MACBETH              Well, say, sir.

MESSENGER
As I did stand my watch upon the hill,
I looked toward Birnam, and anon, methought,
The wood began to move.

MACBETH            Liar and slave!     35

MESSENGER
Let me endure your wrath, if't be not so.
Within this three mile may you see it coming;
I say a moving grove.

MACBETH          If thou speak'st false,
Upon the next tree shalt thou hang alive,
Till famine cling° thee. If thy speech be sooth,°     40
I care not if thou dost for me as much.
I pull in resolution,° and begin
To doubt° th' equivocation of the fiend
That lies like truth: "Fear not, till Birnam Wood
Do come to Dunsinane!" And now a wood     45
Comes toward Dunsinane. Arm, arm, and out!
If this which he avouches° does appear,
There is nor flying hence nor tarrying here.
I 'gin to be aweary of the sun,
And wish th' estate° o' th' world were now undone.     50
Ring the alarum bell! Blow wind, come wrack!
At least we'll die with harness° on our back.    *Exeunt.*

### Scene VI. [*Dunsinane. Before the castle.*]

*Drum and colors. Enter* MALCOLM, SIWARD, MAC-
DUFF, *and their* ARMY, *with boughs.*

MALCOLM
Now near enough. Your leavy° screens throw down,

And show like those you are. You, worthy uncle,
Shall, with my cousin, your right noble son,
Lead our first battle.° Worthy Macduff and we°
Shall take upon's what else remains to do,     5
According to our order.°

SIWARD              Fare you well.
Do we° but find the tyrant's power° tonight,
Let us be beaten, if we cannot fight.

MACDUFF
Make all our trumpets speak; give them all breath,
Those clamorous harbingers of blood and death.     10

            *Exeunt. Alarums continued.*

### Scene VII. [*Another part of the field.*]

*Enter* MACBETH.

MACBETH
They have tied me to a stake; I cannot fly,
But bearlike I must fight the course.° What's he
That was not born of woman? Such a one
Am I to fear, or none.

*Enter* YOUNG SIWARD.

YOUNG SIWARD
What is thy name?

MACBETH           Thou'lt be afraid to hear it.     5

YOUNG SIWARD
No; though thou call'st thyself a hotter name
Than any is in hell.

MACBETH           My name's Macbeth.

YOUNG SIWARD
The devil himself could not pronounce a title
More hateful to mine ear.

MACBETH           No, nor more fearful.

YOUNG SIWARD
Thou liest, abhorrèd tyrant; with my sword     10
I'll prove the lie thou speak'st.

         *Fight, and* YOUNG SIWARD *slain.*

MACBETH          Thou wast born of woman.
But swords I smile at, weapons laugh to scorn,
Brandished by man that's of a woman born.    *Exit.*

*Alarums. Enter* MACDUFF.

MACDUFF
That way the noise is. Tyrant, show thy face!
If thou be'st slain and with no stroke of mine,     15
My wife and children's ghosts will haunt me still.
I cannot strike at wretched kerns,° whose arms
Are hired to bear their staves.° Either thou, Macbeth,
Or else my sword, with an unbattered edge,
I sheathe again undeeded.° There thou shouldst be;     20
By this great clatter, one of greatest note
Seems bruited.° Let me find him, Fortune!
And more I beg not.             *Exit. Alarums.*

*Enter* MALCOLM *and* SIWARD.

---

15 **start** startle   17 **should** inevitably would (?)   18 **word**
message   40 **cling** wither; **sooth** truth   42 **pull in resolution**
restrain confidence   43 **doubt** suspect   47 **avouches** asserts
50 **th' estate** the orderly condition   52 **harness** armor
V.vi.1 **leavy** leafy

4 **battle** battalion; **we** Malcolm uses the royal "we"
6 **order** plan   7 **Do we** if we do; **power** forces
V.vii.2 **course** bout, round (he has in mind an attack of dogs
or men upon a bear chained to a stake)   17 **kerns** foot soldiers
(contemptuous)   18 **staves** spears   20 **undeeded** i.e., having
done nothing   22 **bruited** reported

SIWARD
This way, my lord. The castle's gently rend'red:°
The tyrant's people on both sides do fight;                    25
The noble thanes do bravely in the war;
The day almost itself professes° yours,
And little is to do.

MALCOLM                    We have met with foes
That strike beside us.°

SIWARD                    Enter, sir, the castle.
                              *Exeunt. Alarum.*

[Scene VIII. *Another part of the field.*]

*Enter* MACBETH.

MACBETH
Why should I play the Roman fool, and die
On mine own sword? Whiles I see lives,° the gashes
Do better upon them.

*Enter* MACDUFF.

MACDUFF                    Turn, hell-hound, turn!

MACBETH
Of all men else I have avoided thee.
But get thee back! My soul is too much charged°      5
With blood of thine already.

MACDUFF                    I have no words:
My voice is in my sword, thou bloodier villain
Than terms can give thee out!° *Fight. Alarum.*

MACBETH                    Thou losest labor:
As easy mayst thou the intrenchant° air
With thy keen sword impress° as make me bleed:      10
Let fall thy blade on vulnerable crests;
I bear a charmèd life, which must not yield
To one of woman born.

MACDUFF                    Despair° thy charm,
And let the angel° whom thou still hast served
Tell thee, Macduff was from his mother's womb      15
Untimely ripped.

MACBETH
Accursèd be that tongue that tells me so,
For it hath cowed my better part of man!°
And be these juggling fiends no more believed,
That palter° with us in a double sense;                    20
That keep the word of promise to our ear,
And break it to our hope. I'll not fight with thee.

MACDUFF
Then yield thee, coward,
And live to be the show and gaze o' th' time:°
We'll have thee, as our rarer monsters° are,      25
Painted upon a pole,° and underwrit,
"Here may you see the tyrant."

MACBETH                    I will not yield,
To kiss the ground before young Malcolm's feet,

And to be baited° with the rabble's curse.
Though Birnam Wood be come to Dunsinane,      30
And thou opposed, being of no woman born,
Yet I will try the last. Before my body
I throw my warlike shield. Lay on, Macduff;
And damned be him that first cries, "Hold, enough!"
                              *Exeunt, fighting. Alarums.*

[Re]*enter fighting, and* MACBETH *slain.* [*Exit* MACDUFF,
*with* MACBETH.] *Retreat and flourish.° Enter, with drum
and colors,* MALCOLM, SIWARD, ROSS, THANES, *and*
SOLDIERS.

MALCOLM
I would the friends we miss were safe arrived.      35

SIWARD
Some must go off;° and yet, by these I see,
So great a day as this is cheaply bought.

MALCOLM
Macduff is missing, and your noble son.

ROSS
Your son, my lord, has paid a soldier's debt:
He only lived but till he was a man;                    40
The which no sooner had his prowess confirmed
In the unshrinking station° where he fought,
But like a man he died.

SIWARD                    Then he is dead?

ROSS
Ay, and brought off the field. Your cause of sorrow
Must not be measured by his worth, for then      45
It hath no end.

SIWARD                    Had he his hurts before?

ROSS
Ay, on the front.

SIWARD                    Why then, God's soldier be he!
Had I as many sons as I have hairs,
I would not wish them to a fairer death:
And so his knell is knolled.

MALCOLM                    He's worth more sorrow,      50
And that I'll spend for him.

SIWARD                    He's worth no more:
They say he parted well and paid his score:°
And so God be with him! Here comes newer comfort.

*Enter* MACDUFF *with Macbeth's head.*

MACDUFF
Hail, king! for so thou art: behold, where stands
Th' usurper's cursèd head. The time is free.°      55
I see thee compassed° with thy kingdom's pearl,
That speak my salutation in their minds,
Whose voices I desire aloud with mine:
Hail, King of Scotland!

ALL                    Hail, King of Scotland!

*Flourish.*

MALCOLM
We shall not spend a large expense of time      60
Before we reckon with your several loves,°

24 **gently rend'red** surrendered without a struggle   27 **itself professes** declares itself   29 **beside us** i.e., deliberately miss us (?) as our comrades (?)
**V.viii.**2 **Whiles . . . lives** so long as I see living men   5 **charged** burdened   8 **terms . . . out** words can describe you   9 **intrenchant** incapable of being cut   10 **impress** make an impression on   13 **Despair** despair of   14 **angel** i.e., fallen angel, fiend   18 **better . . . man** manly spirit   20 **palter** equivocate   24 **gaze . . . time** spectacle of the age   25 **monsters** freaks   26 **Painted . . . pole** i.e., pictured on a banner set by a showman's booth

29 **baited** assailed (like a bear by dogs)   34 s.d. **Retreat and flourish** trumpet call to withdraw, and fanfare   36 **go off** die (theatrical metaphor)   42 **unshrinking station** i.e., place at which he stood firmly   52 **parted . . . score** departed well and settled his account   55 **The time is free** The world is liberated   56 **compassed** surrounded   61 **reckon . . . loves** reward the devotion of each of you

And make us even with you. My thanes and kinsmen,
Henceforth be earls, the first that ever Scotland
In such an honor named. What's more to do,
Which would be planted newly with the time°—          65
As calling home our exiled friends abroad
That fled the snares of watchful tyranny,
Producing forth the cruel ministers°
Of this dead butcher and his fiendlike queen,

Who, as 'tis thought, by self and violent° hands      70
Took off her life—this, and what needful else
That calls upon us,° by the grace of Grace
We will perform in measure, time, and place:°
So thanks to all at once and to each one,
Whom we invite to see us crowned at Scone.            75

*Flourish. Exeunt omnes.*

**64–65 What's . . . time** what else must be done which should
be newly established in this age    **68 ministers** agents

**70 self and violent** her own violent    **72 calls upon us**
demands my attention    **73 in . . . place** fittingly, at the
appropriate time and place

# THE TRAGEDY OF
# ANTONY AND CLEOPATRA

EDITED BY BARBARA EVERETT

## Introduction

*Antony and Cleopatra* was written in 1607, or a little earlier. That is, it probably followed immediately after the four great tragedies, *Hamlet, Othello, King Lear,* and *Macbeth,* all of which were written in the half-dozen years after the turn of the century—the period during which Shakespeare's genius was at its most assured, mature, and profound. And *Antony and Cleopatra* itself witnesses to this authoritative mastery of an artistic maturity: Coleridge, in a fine phrase, spoke of the play as being "in all exhibitions of a giant power in its strength and vigor of maturity, a formidable rival of the *Macbeth, Lear, Othello,* and *Hamlet.*" But whether the play is, in reality, a tragedy, is a more open question: its uniqueness of form and mood is a part of its power, and unique things are not easy to classify. When the Folio editors came to collect the plays together after Shakespeare's death, they named this *The Tragedie of Anthonie, and Cleopatra* (unless the title was Shakespeare's own) and placed it in the "Tragedies" section that closed the Folio. But the play is, in its total effect, so unlike the tragedies that preceded it, that for long now critics have hesitated to group it with them. The words with which Coleridge praises the play are in themselves suggestive of a distinction; Bradley, later, did not include it in his *Shakespearean Tragedy,* and G. Wilson Knight similarly excludes it from his study of the tragedies, *The Wheel of Fire*—though both discuss it elsewhere. New classifications of the play have been made in the attempt to specify its highly individual quality. It is most usually referred to, now, as a "Roman play" and grouped as such with *Julius Caesar* and *Coriolanus:* on the grounds that all three, in taking their materials from North's Plutarch, take also from these "Lives of the Noble Grecians and Romans" an interest that is at least as historical and political as it is tragical, and an ethos that is at least as classical as it is Christian. A recent study has classified it anew as a "problem play," and grouped it as such with *Julius Caesar* and *Measure for Measure,* arguing that all three are alike, and unusual, in presenting a specifically moral problem in such a way as to leave radical indecision about the rights and wrongs of the case. And lastly, though no critic has ever gone so far as to group the play with the comedies, several have pointed out—and with good reason—how comic its effect sometimes is.

Obviously, categorizing a play is not vital to understanding it. Moreover, the exercise of classifying a thing can only aim at the comparative, and hope to create some limited definition within which unlike things may be compared and contrasted, and so throw light on one another. However, the attempts to classify *Antony and Cleopatra*—and the difficulties met with in the process—do have an unusual interest. For it is "uncategorizable" in a new and special way. There are one or two plays of Shakespeare—*Troilus and Cressida* and *Measure for Measure* are probably the best examples—which are similarly hard to classify, but which remain much simpler propositions. Though brilliant and full of interest, they are far from perfect or coherent works of art; and it is therefore easier to see in them (or to imagine one sees) the marks of changing purpose, or of discordances within the given materials, that make the act of classification so difficult. It is possible to suggest that *Measure for Measure* was intended to be a comedy on a not unfamiliar pattern, though in an unfamiliar milieu, but that the development in Shakespeare's artistic vision broke apart the preconceived notion on which the play began. Similarly, it is possible to suggest that *Troilus and Cressida* may have begun as a love tragedy on the same design as *Romeo and Juliet,* but that a greatly changed mood and insight destroyed that simpler romantic formula. Both plays at least offer materials for such hesitant suggestions with their sudden changes of mood, their strange discordances in characterization, their awkward or seemingly patched-up endings. *Antony and Cleopatra,* by contrast, suggests no such change of purpose or uncertainty in handling materials. It is, in final poetic and dramatic effect, one of the most triumphantly harmonious, coherent, and "finished" plays that Shakespeare ever wrote, from first to last line bearing the impress of a unified purpose powerfully carried out. Coleridge, again, seizes on this dominant effect of the play when he points out the degree to which Shakespeare "impresses the notion of giant strength. . . . This [is] owing to the manner in which it is sustained throughout—that he *lives* in and through the play." And yet, though the impression of a unified purpose is so strong, it is far from easy to decide what that unified purpose is.

One of the reasons for this is that the play "works" at many different levels and in many different ways. In it, many different—and even contradictory—kinds of experience are fused together; with the result that the play is continually suggestive of different kinds and categories of drama. Diversity and complexity of experience are of course a part of the strength and power of the preceding tragedies: but in them all diversities are subsumed under a dominating tragic discipline, by which the play moves steadily to its catastrophic climax. *Hamlet's* Gravedigger, *Lear's* Fool, *Macbeth's* Porter do not provide "comic relief," though this phrase is sometimes used of them: rather, they substantiate the tragic experience from a point of view at a large distance from the heroic—and therefore substantiate it the more impressively. In *Antony and Cleopatra*, the tragic and the comic experience coexist, among others. It is tragic not only in the sense of containing the "sad" and the "serious" (for many of Shakespeare's best and truest comedies also do that) but also in the expression of an irremediable loss, incurred consciously and borne responsibly: Antony reaches "the very heart of loss," and knows it. And yet it is also comic, not only in the sense of containing the satirical or the farcical (for Shakespeare's tragedies also do that) but also in the expression of an ineffaceable lightheartedness: as when Cleopatra, preparing for death, says:

> go fetch
> My best attires. I am again for Cydnus,
> To meet Mark Antony. (V.ii.227-29)

and, to the asp that kills her:

> O, couldst thou speak,
> That I might hear thee call great Caesar ass
> Unpolicied! (V.ii.306-08)

"Lighthearted" is not, admittedly, a complete enough word for this: the somewhat old-fashioned word "high-hearted" is perhaps closer to it. But however it is named, the mood evoked here, and elsewhere in the play, is nearer to the experience evoked in the mature comedies than it is to the gravely responsible tone of Hamlet at his death, Othello's solemn bravura, Lear's agonized questioning, or Macbeth's desperate obduracy. The tone and presentation throughout the play is thus so compounded of strangely blended elements as to be elusive of a final classification. The play can be described from several different points of view, and in the terms of several different categories, and each would point to elements really present in it: but none would describe it quite completely enough.

There is, for instance, good reason to call *Antony and Cleopatra* a "Roman play," and to point out the historical and political interest that distinguishes it from the earlier tragedies. As in *Julius Caesar*, which had been written some eight years earlier (that is, just before *Hamlet*, the first of the mature tragedies), Shakespeare has taken his materials from well-known history—so well known, in fact, as in part to circumscribe his treatment of it. The basis of *Hamlet*, *King Lear*, and *Macbeth* is also of course historical, but presented Shakespeare with nothing as radically unalterable as the murder of Julius Caesar, the fate of Antony, or the coming to power of Octavius Caesar.

Shakespeare's Octavius—Caesar, as he is always called in *Antony and Cleopatra*—was to become Augustus, perhaps the greatest of Roman emperors, creator of the Pax Romana that closed the long period of unrest, revolution, and war, with the time of peace in which Christ was to be born. Thus, in the war with Antony, when Antony's allies have deserted and sympathy for him is at its strongest, Caesar redresses the balance by a brief but significant reminder of his future role in history:

> The time of universal peace is near.
> Prove this a prosp'rous day, the three-nooked world
> Shall bear the olive freely. (IV.vi.5-7)

Antony's course is as much a "given factor" as Caesar's. Plutarch's "Life of Antony" (perhaps somewhat romanticizing the case) had established the cause of Antony's downfall: he had lost the world because of his love for Cleopatra. Whether that love were treated with some severity (as Plutarch treated it) or with tender admiration (as Chaucer and many others had treated it), its fatality had become an historical fact.

The political battle, then, is between two men sharply distinguished in their roles: Caesar, the young, sober, peace-loving imperial administrator, and Antony, the middle-aged soldier, orator, and lover, a hardened campaigner in war, politics, and love. And the battle is fought for a large enough issue: the rule of the whole civilized world some forty years before the birth of Christ. For Antony and Caesar are two of the triumvirs who rule the Empire between them, and early in the play it becomes clear that the third, Lepidus, is an insignificant go-between. The scale of the prize that the two men are fighting for is also established at once in the play. Philo bitterly sees Antony as

> The triple pillar of the world transformed
> Into a strumpet's fool. (I.i.12-13)

And Antony himself turns an exhilarated affirmation of his love into a rejection of the whole Empire:

> Let Rome in Tiber melt, and the wide arch
> Of the ranged empire fall! Here is my space. (I.i.33-34)

On Antony's second appearance in the play, he is presented in a scene all the more sharply effective for its contrast with the immediately preceding scene of the fortune-telling, which is slow, sleepy, and casual: he appears as a man facing a rapid and cumulatively urgent succession of news from all over the Empire—the wars of his wife Fulvia and his brother Lucius, their conjunct war against Caesar, the swift and victorious invasions of the Parthian Labienus, Fulvia's death, the threats of Pompey, and the dangerously shifting sympathies of the Roman people. Caesar, in his turn, is presented on his first appearance in an exactly comparable way, as a man habituated to an enormous and urgent sphere of action. Both these scenes are brilliantly effective in their conversion of necessary exposition to purely dramatic purposes: they move with an almost breathless speed and energy, and establish Antony and Caesar as men of affairs at a very high level indeed. This effect is maintained, though by less concentrated means, throughout the play. The action moves rapidly from place to place in the great Empire, from Alexandria to Rome, from Misenum to "a plain in Syria," from Athens to Rome again. The characters think and plan—sometimes rhetorically, sometimes merely with an easy and businesslike precision—in terms of the whole world:

> [his] quality, going on,
> The sides o' th' world may danger.     (I.ii.192–93)
>
> thou, the greatest soldier of the world     (I.iii.38)
>
> The demi-Atlas of this earth     (I.v.23)
>
> The third o' th' world is yours     (II.ii.63)
>
>        To you all three,
> The senators alone of this great world     (II.vi.8–9)
>
> Wilt thou be lord of all the world?     (II.vii.63)
>
> These three world-sharers     (II.vii.71)
>
> Wars 'twixt you twain would be
> As if the world should cleave.     (III.iv.30–31)
>
> The greater cantle of the world is lost
> With very ignorance     (III.x.6–7)

Such language (of which this is only a selection) is the medium of the play, and it establishes the size of the battle-field—real and metaphorical—on which the contest for power is being fought.

The course of this battle for power is simple in outline. The first appearance of Antony and Caesar—Antony in his "Egyptian fetters," though still able to throw them off: Caesar revealing in clear, precise terms his cool disgust at Antony's way of life and aware also of the dangers of such a political associate—presents them as personally incompatible and potentially rivals. As Caesar says:

>        [it] cannot be
> We shall remain in friendship, our conditions
> So diff'ring in their acts.     (II.ii.113–15)

The two are reconciled under the pressure of Pompey's threat to the triumvirate and seal their peace by Antony's marriage to Octavia, Caesar's sister. The desertion of Octavia by Antony gives Caesar the pretext for war, once he has himself gained some advantage in power. After the ruinous defeat at Actium, Antony's fall is rapid: his allies and his armies desert to the more powerful man, and he is lost. Through an apparently leisurely and circuitous stream of events that keeps closely to the historical sequence, there emerges into prominence the political theme: the maneuvers and manipulations, the honors and dishonors, of a battle between incompatible standards for the government of the whole Roman world.

To describe the play in these terms is to give it something of the discipline, and something of the limitation, of any game of power—say, a game of chess played out on the board of the world. And such an image would not be entirely alien to the mood of the play: Antony, for instance, accuses Cleopatra in similar terms, in a moment of despairing anger:

> she, Eros, has
> Packed cards with Caesar, and false-played my glory
> Unto an enemy's triumph.     (IV.xiv.18–20)

And yet to use this image of the game is to realize how much in the play it does not comprehend: indeed, even as Antony uses this image, there is a sudden and significant sense that he has lost even his imaginative command of the full weight of the situation. If the play presents a game of history and politics, it presents also something deeper and more important: a tragedy of human experience. When Antony finds himself at "the very heart of loss," he is maddened at both the loss of the world and the loss of all trust in Cleopatra; but in losing both, he is also crying out at the loss of himself.

It is not enough to say, simply, that Shakespeare is far more interested in the loser, Antony, than he is in the winner, Caesar; or even to say that his interest is with that relation between Antony and Cleopatra that caused the loss of the world. It is rather that the whole situation is presented so that the historical and political interest—the gain or loss of world power—becomes a part or facet of another and greater subject: the ruin of two people, and with them, of a whole sphere of human experience. Any political history may have its "human interest"; Plutarch's "Life of Antony" is vivid, shrewd, and alive in its portraiture, and Shakespeare is largely and unusually indebted to Plutarch's characterization of Antony. What differentiates *Antony and Cleopatra* is not merely a livelier or even a deeper characterization, but a transformation of all action and event into a process of tragic and individual experience.

This touches several characters besides the hero and heroine. The mere opportunist, Pompey, soon to disappear from the play, has a moment of sudden importance, seriousness, and dignity in the galley scene, when he rejects the chance of world power on a point of honor. The tough, cynical, common-sense soldier, Enobarbus (who in Plutarch dies of an ague), dies of a broken heart at his desertion of Antony, and the scene has, again, a weight of dignity and solemnity. Caesar himself, on hearing of the death of Antony, is moved—for the first time in the play—by a sudden access of personal feeling, in the awareness of what he has lost of himself by that death. None of these incidents could have any historical or political importance, though they might, perhaps, be shown as having historical and political effects; their significance and their weight lie in a different sphere of value. It is significant that each of these small incidents has the effect of isolating the person concerned, so that he appears for a moment as detached from, or even alien to, the world around him; for tragedy deals with the experience of a man, or of Man, rather than of men.

The greatest individuals in the play are, of course, Antony and Cleopatra: it is on their absolute selfhood that they base their glory. "We stand up peerless." And it is this arrogant and obdurate sense of themselves that distinguishes them from Caesar—though all three are, in fact, engaged on a quite similar quest for power that makes them, on a detached view, remarkably alike. Caesar can speak as nobly, as authoritatively, and as impressively as the other two; but he speaks a different language. His words have, at their best, the stature of judgment: of a rational social wisdom that takes its force from its generality. To him, Antony is

> A man who is th' abstract of all faults
> That all men follow.     (I.iv.9–10)

He surveys Antony with a level detachment that reduces his actions to caricature, and gives the final condemnation a rigorous justice:

> to confound such time
> That drums him from his sport and speaks as loud
> As his own state and ours, 'tis to be chid
> As we rate boys who, being mature in knowledge,
> Pawn their experience to their present pleasure
> And so rebel to judgment.            (I.iv.28–33)

This is powerfully spoken, and its effect is largely that of the judicial and weighty summary of a situation from outside; it is the voice of common judgment and social wisdom. This voice interposes its realities throughout the play, and is not confined to Caesar alone: Antony too can speak with the voice of "Rome." But the language that Antony and Cleopatra make their own is something very different, and challenges the sober judgment of Rome. It is a language expressive of a whole radically different way of living and feeling: a language of immediate individual experience, sensory in its apprehension, exalted or intense in its tone, and arrogant in its claims. Love or desolation, exhilaration or rage become their own argument, and the intense experience of an exceptional individual becomes its own rationale. So Antony, proclaiming his love for Cleopatra, converts his profession into a challenge of Rome and all that Rome stands for:

> Let Rome in Tiber melt, and the wide arch
> Of the ranged empire fall! Here is my space,
> Kingdoms are clay: our dungy earth alike
> Feeds beast as man. The nobleness of life
> Is to do thus; when such a mutual pair
> And such a twain can do't, in which I bind,
> On pain of punishment, the world to weet
> We stand up peerless.            (I.i.33–40)

So also Cleopatra, exquisitely lamenting the death of Antony, transforms her desolation into a vision of an empty world:

> O, see, my women,
> The crown o' th' earth doth melt. My lord!
> O, withered is the garland of the war,
> The soldier's pole is fall'n: young boys and girls
> Are level now with men. The odds is gone,
> And there is nothing left remarkable
> Beneath the visiting moon.            (IV.xv.62–68)

Both these speeches reveal an element vital to the characterization of Antony and Cleopatra. The first is more than a profession of love—whether we choose to regard that love as the glorification of sensual excitement or as the affirmation of a noble passion; the second is more than a woman's lament for a dead man—whether we choose to regard that lament as profound insight or as delusion. Each is an affirmation of selfhood, and a proclamation that this self is "peerless," "remarkable," incomparable, in its love and in its loss and in its very existence. Antony and Cleopatra are—to put the matter at its simplest—proud: proud of being themselves, and proud of being greater than anyone else in the world. Nor are they monstrous in this, for the whole world of the play is governed by the ideal of pride, and in it "honor" and "nobility," "greatness" and "reputation," are the very fabric of existence. Antony's fame, eminence, and power; Cleopatra's royalty; their love for each other; the admiration of their followers—all these things feed their pride and are fed by it. And all their great and good qualities serve it: Antony's courage and generosity and largeness of spirit, Cleopatra's wit and charm and enormous abundance of life. When their "greatness" is destroyed, the world is empty to them, for the loss of pride is a death:

> The soul and body rive not more in parting
> Than greatness going off.            (IV.xiii.5–6)

The tragedy of Antony and Cleopatra, then, is not simply their loss of the world, nor even their death, but the destruction of pride that accompanies both. All that makes them admirable is inextricably confused with its own corruptions: their energy, vitality, and power are self-defeating. Antony is caught between the dual and mutually destructive sources of his pride, power in Rome and pleasure in Egypt; Cleopatra discovers or proves at Actium her full power over Antony, and in doing so loses both him and the world. Cleopatra fights to hold Antony, and Antony fights to hold the world, and in the process all Antony's courage reveals itself as inextricable from blind and irrational violence, and his generosity from sensual obsession; all Cleopatra's vitality and self-possession reveals itself as wayward, demanding, and treacherous. Caesar sees clearly when he calls Antony "the old ruffian," and Antony knows Cleopatra for a "boggler ever." In defeat—a defeat which is the loss of an ideal, as well as the loss of the world—both grow, paradoxically, more gentle, more human, and more wholly sympathetic. But both choose the "Roman" death of suicide, which is itself a last affirmation of pride in themselves and a refusal of the humiliation of walking in Caesar's triumph. Cleopatra places on her head the crown of a country she no longer rules, prepares to join a husband she never had, and rejects with contempt a world which has humiliated her, dying a death

> fitting for a princess
> Descended of so many royal kings.            (V.ii.326–27)

This tragic subject Shakespeare has created out of his historical and political materials; and it is a subject that merits Caesar's words at the close of the play:

> High events as these
> Strike those that make them; and their story is
> No less in pity, than his glory which
> Brought them to be lamented.            (V.ii.359–62)

Yet there can be a large difference between a play's "subject," summarized in detachment, and the full effect of the play itself; and this is true of *Antony and Cleopatra*. It certainly contains the "high events," the "pity" and "glory" that Caesar suggests as he closes the play on a fittingly high and sober note. But to leave the account of the play here would be as partial as to describe it, simply, as a historical and political drama.

In the first place, Antony's and Cleopatra's fates and fortunes are not presented with the kind of tragic or dramatic intensity that such an outline might suggest. Rather, they and their world are presented in a series of leisurely—at first sight, almost casual—insights, that include in their range the great and the small, the significant and the insignificant: a fortunetelling and a great battle, a political conference and a wild party, a memory of the lovers' first meeting and a death in a monument, a woman slapping a messenger and a countryman giving a lecture on the nature of asps. Instead of the cumulative intensity of the earlier tragedies, which speed and slacken and speed again to their catastrophic climaxes, the play presents something more leisurely, more spacious, and more impassive; its structure lies in the panoramic or kaleidoscopic display of diverse aspects of a world, seen in all its variety. At one moment, we watch a conference of world leaders, attempting with some dignity and seriousness to come to terms with each other—an attempt that justifies Antony's earlier bitter self-accusations; after the briefest of pauses, they are all celebrating in a farcical party that ends with a Bacchic version of ring-a-ring-a-roses. Cleopatra speaks, over the dead Antony, her exquisite lament for the loss of all that is valuable in the world; shortly after, she is doing her best to cheat Caesar of her jewels. The whole play is constructed, in this manner, out of a pattern of juxtapositions and contrasts, with the point of view continually shifting and changing; and the effect is something very different from "tragic" intensity, though full of a complex and absorbing life.

Closely related to this fluid and changing dramatic vision is the presentation of the characters themselves; indeed, it might be more proper to say that the concept of "character" itself is transformed. The earlier tragic heroes change, where they change at all in the course of the play, by a process of development; inner potentialities for good and evil are gradually brought to the view as the play proceeds. This is only very partially true of Antony and Cleopatra. They display, rather, a succession of different moods and impulses, continually changing. This is, of course, most true of Cleopatra, who is "infinite variety" itself; but there is hardly a character in the play who is not capable, to some degree, of being and doing the unexpected. The result is that a quick fluidity and changeableness of character becomes the norm, almost the rule: and in such a world, tragic motivation becomes impossible, and tragic responsibility is largely absent. Men seem to be moved by impulse and instinct, chance and expediency; and the guilts and terrors, shames and miseries of the earlier tragedies are very largely absent.

This is to suggest a world that relatively lacks psychological and metaphysical depth. It would be truer to say that *Antony and Cleopatra* creates a physical rather than a metaphysical world and that its density of substance rather than its depth of treatment commands the attention. It creates a world that is triumphantly "natural" rather than "supernatural"—although the natural, in this play, is not without its mysteries. The soothsayer reads, and reads correctly, in "Nature's infinite book of secrecy"; and when the soldiers, on guard by night in the streets of Alexandria, hear "Music i' th' air," they recognize it as the departure of a god from a defeated man:

'Tis the god Hercules, whom Antony loved,
Now leaves him.                              (IV.iii.15–16)

To say that the world of *Antony and Cleopatra* is "natural" is to say that it presents all experiences and all events as rooted in the "dungy earth" or the "varying tide" of physical existence. And that physical existence is itself a "varying shore," subject to continual change in the battle of the elements. In politics as in love, the procession of times moves in a continual destruction; so Antony, in the proclamation of his love that challenges the power of the great Roman Empire, is making a proclamation and a challenge that time itself will silently verify:

Let Rome in Tiber melt, and the wide arch
Of the ranged empire fall! Here is my space:
Kingdoms are clay.                           (I.i.33–35)

The great lyrical image for the triumph of time is the image of the setting of the sun and the coming on of night; and this image fittingly colors the close of the play. The suicide of both Antony and Cleopatra is prefaced by the same echoing image:

Unarm, Eros. The long day's task is done,
And we must sleep.                           (IV.xiv.35–36)

Finish, good lady, the bright day is done,
And we are for the dark.                     (V.ii.193–94)

Wherever such imagery occurs in the play, it has an effect that is undoubtedly complex. One of the many things it does is to suggest that Antony's political defeat and his and Cleopatra's individual tragedy are both set within the context of a larger process, simpler and more universal. All that happens in the play—the reversals of fortune, the victories and defeats, the alienations and reconciliations—all are a part of the "interchange of state" that rules the whole natural world,

Increasing store with loss, and loss with store. (Sonnet 64)

Antony, in his "dotage," and Cleopatra, "wrinkled deep in time," suffer a defeat at the hands of a power greater than Caesar; and the cold politician Caesar himself has fought his way to the possession of an empire that will crumble in his hands to "dungy earth."

This fact Antony and Cleopatra know, and Caesar does not; their wisdom and their folly derives from their knowledge of it, and Caesar's power and his limitations derive from his ignorance or denial of it. Caesar's ambition is to "possess the time," by possessing the world for a while; Antony and Cleopatra live only in the present instant, and lose the world for good:

There's not a minute of our lives should stretch
Without some pleasure now.                   (I.i.46–47)

To give up the battle with time and live intensely in the present instant; to create a small and circumscribed area in which to exist, in an exhilarated moment of freedom and vitality—this is a way or vision of life more native to comedy than to tragedy. And it is the way of life that Cleopatra, above all, represents.

That time—O, times!—
I laughed him out of patience; and that night
I laughed him into patience; and next morn,

Ere the ninth hour, I drunk him to his bed;
Then put my tires and mantles on him, whilst
I wore his sword Philippan.                    (II.v.18–23)

Cleopatra's world is essentially a world of "play": a world, that is, that studies to find fit expression for the exuberance of natural energies and needs no justification for what it does. Her world is self-justifying, self-delighting, perhaps self-destroying; as such it is a perpetual challenge and threat to Caesar's vision of universal power and universal peace. The two cannot coexist: and in any battle between Cleopatra's devious wits and Caesar's steady will-to-power, the latter must triumph. Yet Cleopatra will live out even defeat on her own terms, as though it were an exuberant and triumphant game, the rules of which are her own and no one else's; her image of the dead Antony is of a god who has eluded, by the play of his intense natural energies, the restraining world of time:

> For his bounty,
> There was no winter in't: an autumn 'twas
> That grew the more by reaping. His delights
> Were dolphinlike, they showed his back above
> The element they lived in.                    (V.ii.86–90)

Just such an image she makes of her own death: she "plays till doomsday," secure and free within the limited dream she has created.

Certainly that dream is a limited one, always circumscribed by the opposed realities of Caesar and of time:

CLEOPATRA
  Think you there was or might be such a man
  As this I dreamt of?
DOLABELLA                    Gentle madam, no.    (V.ii.93–94)

In presenting these realities side by side, and involved with each other—the comic and tragic deeply interfused—*Antony and Cleopatra* creates a world that is as complex as it is profoundly original. One phrase of Cleopatra's—her "Here's sport indeed," as she draws the dying Antony to her—bears all the profound comic pathos and tragic irony that fills and characterizes the play. Yet this mingled experience is as strong as it is complex; it has a power and vitality that is Antony's when, in defeat, he "mocks the midnight bell":

> Let's have one other gaudy night: call to me
> All my sad captains; fill our bowls once more;
> Let's mock the midnight bell.                    (III.xiii.183–85)

### A NOTE ON THE SOURCE

The principal source of *Antony and Cleopatra* is the "Life of Marcus Antonius," in Sir Thomas North's translation of Plutarch's *Lives of the Noble Grecians and Romans* (published 1579). Shakespeare seems to have known parts, at least, of North's Plutarch for some ten years before he wrote *Antony and Cleopatra;* and he had already used the early part of the "Life of Marcus Antonius" when gathering materials for *Julius Caesar,* seven or so years before. The use Shakespeare makes of this "Life" for *Antony and Cleopatra,* however, is far more thorough, more extensive, and more interesting. Considerable insight into Shakespeare's artistry

and method of working may be gained from a comparison of the source with the play: so much does Shakespeare take from Plutarch, and so radically does he transform it. From Plutarch's whole conception of Antony, down to the last few words of his Charmion, Shakespeare borrows heavily and directly, humanizing and deepening all that he borrows; and the process is illuminating.

Shakespeare's handling of his main source may be briefly outlined as follows. Plutarch's life of Antony is full, leisurely, and detailed. Shakespeare takes from Plutarch all the major events of Antony's later life, with one exception: the long and unsuccessful campaign against the Parthians; he also makes use of events that take place before the opening of the play, such as Antony's first meeting with Cleopatra and what ensues from it. In addition, he borrows—sometimes to an exceptional degree—from Plutarch's vivid, pithy, and dignified narration of speeches and events. In each case, the rehandling is instructive.

Two examples of the first kind of borrowing must suffice here. First, the situation at the opening of the play. Plutarch recounts how Antony, while with Cleopatra in Alexandria, hears news both of Fulvia's and Lucius' wars against Caesar, their defeat and expulsion from Italy, and of Labienus' victories in Asia; Antony prepares to meet the Parthians but is recalled to Italy by letters from his wife, and on the journey hears of her death. At a later point, after his marriage to Octavia, the threat from Sextus Pompeius arises. All this Shakespeare compacts into the news brought, with an effect of rapidly mounting disaster, to Antony in Cleopatra's court, violently challenging his former mood of serene and triumphant exhilaration and necessitating his immediate departure. Thus, in the first two scenes of the play, Shakespeare uses Plutarch's materials cogently and with strong effect, establishing thereby the major conflict of the play. For a second example: his handling of the events succeeding Actium. Shakespeare abbreviates and rearranges, so that the defeat's importance and finality (and Cleopatra's blame in it) are accentuated; the desertion of Domitius (a minor character in Plutarch, whom Shakespeare converts into the far more important Enobarbus) is moved from before Actium to after it, accentuating Antony's isolation in defeat, and the deserter dies not of illness but of a broken heart; and the one successful sally against Caesar, Shakespeare places after, instead of before, Antony's farewell to his servants and the departure of Hercules—thus making the isolated Antony's last exhilaration of victory the more ironic and pathetic, and yet paradoxically heroic. In each of these examples, Shakespeare is not merely compacting and rearranging for dramatic purposes; he is making great tragedy out of good history.

The same may be said of some of the passages where the verbal echoes and reminiscences are strongest. For example, Enobarbus' famous "The barge she sat in, like a burnished throne . . ." is extremely close to Plutarch's beautiful description of Cleopatra at Cydnus. But where Plutarch is describing a rich and exquisite scene, Shakespeare is creating—by small additions and alterations—the extraordinary power of Cleopatra that draws the people, the winds, and the water longingly after her. By giving the speech of reminiscence to the tough and common-sense Enobarbus, and touching it with his humor and "Roman" sanity, Shakespeare heightens, by contrast, the hyperbolical praise of Cleopatra; and, more, he brings alive the conflicting values of the play. Antony is about to marry Octavia; Enobarbus' speech revives the full and fatal power of Cleopatra, at her first meeting with Antony. Both the re-creation of the speech and its placing in the play throw the greatest light on Shakespeare's artistic intentions.

A reader interested in the other works that contributed to the play (to a much smaller degree, but still interestingly) will find a discussion of them in Kenneth Muir's useful study, *Shakespeare's Sources* (1957), Vol. I, "Comedies and Tragedies," pp. 201–19.

## A NOTE ON THE TEXT

*Antony and Cleopatra* was entered in the Stationers' Register in May 1608. Though this procedure normally suggested that publication would follow shortly, the play remained, in fact, unprinted until 1623, when it appeared in the "Tragedies" section of the First Folio. This First Folio text of the play is therefore the single authoritative one, and all succeeding editions—including of course the present one—derive from it.

It is widely agreed that the Folio text of *Antony and Cleopatra* was almost certainly printed directly from Shakespeare's own manuscript, and not from a transcript or prompter's copy. The features of the Folio text that suggest a source in Shakespearean manuscript may be briefly summarized as follows. First, it contains unusual spellings and word usages, some of which seem to be peculiar to Shakespeare, and some of which were, at any rate, archaic by the time the Folio was printed. Second, many of the Folio misprints are of the kind (occurring also in other texts of the plays) that would seem to arise from the individual character of Shakespeare's own handwriting. Third, it lacks all act and scene divisions, except for the opening "Actus Primus, Scoena Prima"; a lack that indicates copy prepared primarily for the theater. Fourth, its stage directions are unusually full and detailed, and are often of the nature of an author's "notes on the text"; for example, "Alarum afar off, as at a sea fight." And lastly, the Folio text contains a passage in the first scene at the monument (IV.xv.12–29) that suggests the direct carrying over of the author's deletions and rewritings (see relevant footnote to text). None of this is absolutely conclusive, but taken together the evidence leaves little doubt that the Folio text was printed directly from Shakespeare's manuscript.

As a text, it is relatively good: it contains many slips but few real difficulties. Its major flaw is the occurrence of very frequent mislineation. This has been silently adjusted in the present edition, as the "correct" lineation is either clear, or, where doubtful, immaterial. The present edition also adds a list of dramatis personae, which is lacking in the Folio; and it adds act and scene divisions, and indications of locality, except for the Folio's opening "Actus Primus, Scoena Prima" which is here translated. It also supplements the existing stage directions. All such additions and supplementations are indicated by brackets. The positions of a few stage directions have been slightly altered; speech prefixes and other abbreviations are expanded, punctuation and spelling are modernized. The spelling of proper names is regularized: for example, "Cleopatra" is given, though in F "Cleopater" also appears; again, "Decretas" is given though in F "Decretus" also appears;

"Canidius" is given for F's "Camidius," "Camidias," and "Camindius"; and so forth. (In a few instances, where the change is more marked, the reading is listed below.) All other departures from the Folio text are listed below, and utilize earlier editorial emendations; the adopted reading is given in boldface type, and then the original reading in roman. As in the footnotes to the text, a line number followed by "s.d." indicates the stage direction that follows the given line, or that interrupts it.

**I.i.39 On** One   **50 whose** who
**I.ii.4 charge** change   **41 fertile** foretell   **64 Alexas** [F treats "Alexas" as a speech prefix and gives him the rest of the speech here given to Charmian]   **81 Saw** Saue   **113** [F adds s.d.: "*Enter another Messenger*"]   **114 ho, the news!** how the newes?   **115 First Attendant** 1 Mes   **116 Second Attendant** 2 Mes   **119 Messenger** 3 Mes   **131 Ho now, Enobarbus!** How now Enobarbus **138 occasion** an occasion   **180 leave** loue   **185 Hath** Haue   **194 hair** heire
**I.iii.25 first** fitst   **43 services** Seruicles   **82 by my sword** by Sword
**I.iv.3 Our** One   **8 Vouchsafed** vouchsafe   **9 abstract** abstracts **44 deared** fear'd   **46 lackeying** lacking   **56 wassails** Vassailes **58 Pansa** Pausa   **75 we** me
**I.v.34 s.d. Antony** Caesar   **50 dumbed** dumbe   **61 man** mans
**II.i.16, 18, 38** [F's speech prefix here, as for all speeches in the scene other than those of Pompey and Varrius, is "*Mene.*" But the context clearly indicates that Menas as well as Menecrates speaks in the scene]   **21 waned** wand   **41 warred** wan'd
**II.ii.121 not so** not, say   **122 reproof** proofe   **172 s.d. Exit** Exit omnes. Manet   **206 glow** gloue   **208 gentlewomen** Gentlewoman   **225 heard** hard   **234 pow'r breathe** powr breath
**II.iii.21 afeard** a feare   **29 away** alway
**II.v.12 Tawny-finned** Tawny fine   **43 is** 'tis   **52 jailer** laylor
**II.vi.s.d. Agrippa, with** Agrippa, Menas with   **19 is** his   **58 composition** composion   **66 meanings** meaning   **69 more of** more
**II.vii.1 their** th' their   **4 high-colored** high Conlord   **13 lief** liue   **36 pyramises** Pyramisis   **92 then** then he   **101 grows** grow   **112 bear** beate   **125 Splits** Spleet's   **129 father's** Father **130–34 Take . . . out** [F gives all to Enobarbus, mistaking (?) speech prefix "*Menas*" for vocative]
**III.i.5 Silius** Romaine [so throughout scene]   **8 whither** whether
**III.ii.10 Agrippa** Ant   **16 figures** Figure   **60 wept** weepe
**III.iv.9 took't** look't   **24 yours** your   **30 Your** You   **38 has** he's
**III.v.14 world, thou hast** would thou hadst   **16 the one the other** the other
**III.vi.13 he there** hither;   **kings of kings** King of Kings   **74 Comagene** Comageat
**III.vii.4 it is** it it   **5 Is't** If   **23 Toryne** Troine   **35 muleters** Militers   **51 Actium** Action   **69 led** leade   **72 Canidius** Ven
**III.x.s.d. Enobarbus** Enobarbus and Scarus   **14 June** Inne   **27 he** his
**III.xi.19 that** them   **44 He is** Hee's   **47 seize** cease   **51 whither** whether   **58 tow** stowe   **59 Thy** The
**III.xiii.10 meréd** meered   **55 Caesar** Caesars   **56 embraced** embrace   **74 deputation** disputation   **104 errand** arrant   **162 smite** smile   **165 discandying** discandering   **168 sits** sets   **199 preys on** prayes in   **201 s.d. Exit** Exeunt
**IV.ii.1 Domitius** Domitian
**IV.iii.7 Third Soldier** 1
**IV.iv.5–8 Nay . . . must be** [F gives all to Cleopatra, mistaking (?) speech prefix "Anthony" for vocative, and misplacing (?) it after "help too"]   **8 Sooth, la** Sooth-law   **13 daff't** daft   **24 Captain** Alex
**IV.v.1, 3, 6 Soldier** Eros
**IV.viii.2 gests** guests   **23 favoring** sauoring
**IV.xii.4 augurers** Auguries   **21 spanieled** pannelled
**IV.xiv.4 towered** toward   **10 dislimns** dislimes   **19 Caesar** Caesars   **104 ho!** how
**IV.xv.76 e'en** in   **94 s.d. off** of
**V.i.s.d. Maecenas** Menas   **28, 31 Agrippa** Dol   **59 live** leaue
**V.ii.56 varletry** Varlotarie   **81 little O, th' earth** little o' th' earth **87 autumn 'twas** Antony it was   **104 smites** suites   **216 Ballad** Ballads; **o' tune** a Tune   **228 Cydnus** Cidrus   **318 awry** away **319 s.d. rustling in** rustling in and Dolabella

# THE TRAGEDY OF
# ANTONY AND CLEOPATRA

[Dramatis Personae

MARK ANTONY  
OCTAVIUS CAESAR  } *triumvirs*  
M. AEMILIUS LEPIDUS  
SEXTUS POMPEIUS  
DOMITIUS ENOBARBUS  
VENTIDIUS  
EROS  
SCARUS  } *friends to Antony*  
DECRETAS  
DEMETRIUS  
PHILO  
CANIDIUS *lieutenant general to Antony*  
SILIUS *an officer in Ventidius' army*  
MAECENAS  
AGRIPPA  
DOLABELLA  } *friends to Caesar*  
PROCULEIUS  
THIDIAS  
GALLUS  

TAURUS *lieutenant general to Caesar*  
MENAS  
MENECRATES  } *friends to Pompey*  
VARRIUS  
ROMAN OFFICER *under Ventidius*  
AN AMBASSADOR *from Antony to Caesar*  
ALEXAS  
MARDIAN  
SELEUCUS  } *attendants on Cleopatra*  
DIOMEDES  
A SOOTHSAYER  
A CLOWN  
CLEOPATRA *Queen of Egypt*  
OCTAVIA *sister to Caesar and wife to Antony*  
CHARMIAN  } *attendants on Cleopatra*  
IRAS  
OFFICERS SOLDIERS MESSENGERS  
  ATTENDANTS  

*Scene:* several parts of the Roman Empire]

## ACT I

Scene I. [*Alexandria. Cleopatra's palace.*]

*Enter* DEMETRIUS *and* PHILO.

PHILO  
Nay, but this dotage of our general's  
O'erflows the measure. Those his goodly eyes  
That o'er the files and musters of the war  
Have glowed like plated° Mars, now bend, now turn  
The office° and devotion of their view  5  
Upon a tawny front.° His captain's heart,  

Which in the scuffles of great fights hath burst  
The buckles on his breast, reneges all temper°  
And is become the bellows and the fan  
To cool a gypsy's° lust.  

*Flourish.° Enter* ANTONY, CLEOPATRA, *her* LADIES,  
*the* TRAIN, *with* EUNUCHS *fanning her.*  

                      Look where they come:  10  
Take but good note, and you shall see in him  
The triple pillar° of the world transformed  
Into a strumpet's fool. Behold and see.  
CLEOPATRA  
If it be love indeed, tell me how much.

---

*The decorative border shown above was used in the First Folio edition of Shakespeare's plays, 1623.*  
**I.i.4 plated** armored **5 office** service **6 tawny front** dark face (with a pun on the military sense of *front*, "first line of battle")

**8 reneges all temper** gives up all self-control **10 gypsy's** gypsies were believed to have come from Egypt, hence "gyptians"; they had a reputation for trickery, sorcery, and lechery **10 s.d. Flourish** fanfare of trumpets **12 The triple pillar** i.e., one of the triumvirs who ruled the world

**ANTONY**

There's beggary in the love that can be reckoned. 15

**CLEOPATRA**

I'll set a bourn° how far to be beloved.

**ANTONY**

Then must thou needs find out new heaven, new
earth.

*Enter a* MESSENGER.

**MESSENGER**

News, my good lord, from Rome.

**ANTONY**                                                Grates me! The sum.°

**CLEOPATRA**

Nay, hear them, Antony.
Fulvia° perchance is angry; or who knows          20
If the scarce-bearded Caesar° have not sent
His pow'rful mandate to you, "Do this, or this;
Take in° that kingdom, and enfranchise° that.
Perform't, or else we damn thee."

**ANTONY**                                                How,° my love?

**CLEOPATRA**

Perchance? Nay, and most like:                      25
You must not stay here longer, your dismission°
Is come from Caesar; therefore hear it, Antony.
Where's Fulvia's process?° Caesar's I would say? Both?
Call in the messengers. As I am Egypt's queen,
Thou blushest, Antony, and that blood of thine      30
Is Caesar's homager:° else so° thy cheek pays shame
When shrill-tongued Fulvia scolds. The messengers!

**ANTONY**

Let Rome in Tiber melt, and the wide arch
Of the ranged empire fall! Here is my space,
Kingdoms are clay: our dungy earth alike          35
Feeds beast as man. The nobleness of life
Is to do thus;° when such a mutual pair
And such a twain can do't, in which I bind,
On pain of punishment, the world to weet°
We stand up peerless.

**CLEOPATRA**                          Excellent falsehood!       40
Why did he marry Fulvia, and not love her?
I'll seem the fool I am not. Antony
Will be—himself.°

**ANTONY**                    But stirred° by Cleopatra.
Now for the love of Love and her soft hours,
Let's not confound° the time with conference harsh.  45
There's not a minute of our lives should stretch
Without some pleasure now. What sport tonight?

**CLEOPATRA**

Hear the ambassadors.

**ANTONY**                          Fie, wrangling queen!
Whom everything becomes—to chide, to laugh,
To weep; whose every passion fully° strives       50
To make itself, in thee, fair and admired.

---

16 **bourn** limit  18 **Grates . . . sum** It's irritating!
Be brief  20 **Fulvia** Antony's wife  21 **scarce-bearded
Caesar** Octavius, then twenty-three, was some twenty years
younger than Antony  23 **Take in** occupy; **enfranchise** set
free from slavery  24 **How** a common exclamation, like
"What!"  26 **dismission** dismissal  28 **process** summons
(i.e., to appear in court)  31 **homager** vassal; **else so** or else
37 **thus** perhaps they embrace, but perhaps "thus" alludes to
their way of life  39 **weet** know  43 **himself** (1) the peerless
Antony (2) the fool he is; **stirred** (1) angered (2) inspired,
inflamed  45 **confound** waste  50 **fully** absolutely and successfully

---

No messenger but thine; and all alone
Tonight we'll wander through the streets and note
The qualities of people. Come, my queen;
Last night you did desire it. [*To* ATTENDANTS.] Speak
not to us.          *Exeunt* [ANTONY *and* CLEOPATRA,]   55
                                        *with the* TRAIN.

**DEMETRIUS**

Is Caesar with° Antonius prized so slight?

**PHILO**

Sir, sometimes, when he is not Antony,
He comes too short of that great property°
Which still° should go with Antony.

**DEMETRIUS**                                I am full sorry
That he approves° the common liar, who          60
Thus speaks of him at Rome; but I will hope
Of better deeds tomorrow. Rest you happy! *Exeunt.*

[*Scene II. Alexandria. Cleopatra's palace.*]

*Enter* ENOBARBUS, LAMPRIUS, *a* SOOTHSAYER,
RANNIUS, LUCILLIUS, CHARMIAN, IRAS, MARDIAN
*the eunuch, and* ALEXAS.

CHARMIAN  Lord Alexas, sweet Alexas, most anything Alexas, almost most absolute Alexas, where's the
soothsayer that you praised so to th' queen? O, that I
knew this husband, which, you say, must charge his
horns with garlands!°                                       5

ALEXAS  Soothsayer!

SOOTHSAYER  Your will?

CHARMIAN  Is this the man? Is't you, sir, that know
things?

**SOOTHSAYER**

In Nature's infinite book of secrecy                     10
A little I can read.

ALEXAS  Show him your hand.

**ENOBARBUS**

Bring in the banquet° quickly: wine enough
Cleopatra's health to drink.

CHARMIAN  Good sir, give me good fortune.           15

**SOOTHSAYER**

I make not, but foresee.

CHARMIAN  Pray then, foresee me one.

**SOOTHSAYER**

You shall be yet far fairer° than you are.

CHARMIAN  He means in flesh.

IRAS  No, you shall paint when you are old.           20

CHARMIAN  Wrinkles forbid!

ALEXAS  Vex not his prescience; be attentive.

CHARMIAN  Hush!

**SOOTHSAYER**

You shall be more beloving than beloved.

CHARMIAN  I had rather heat my liver° with drinking.  25

ALEXAS  Nay, hear him.

CHARMIAN  Good now, some excellent fortune! Let

---

56 **with** by  58 **property** quality  59 **still** always  60
**approves** corroborate
I.ii.4–5 **charge . . . garlands** be a blindly happy cuckold of
a husband (*charge* = load; *horns* = symbol of a cuckold;
*garlands* = bridegroom's chaplet, and sign of happy prosperity)  13 **banquet** light refreshment of fruit and wine
18 **fairer** more beautiful (though in the next line Charmian
pretends to take it another way, "plumper")  25 **liver** believed
to be the seat of sexual desire

me be married to three kings in a forenoon and widow
them all; let me have a child at fifty, to whom Herod
of Jewry° may do homage; find me to marry me with 30
Octavius Caesar, and companion me with my mistress.

SOOTHSAYER
You shall outlive the lady whom you serve.

CHARMIAN   O excellent! I love long life better than
figs.°

SOOTHSAYER
You have seen and proved a fairer former fortune   35
Than that which is to approach.

CHARMIAN   Then belike my children shall have no
names.° Prithee, how many boys and wenches must I
have?

SOOTHSAYER
If every of your wishes had a womb,   40
And fertile every wish, a million.

CHARMIAN   Out, fool! I forgive thee for a witch.°

ALEXAS   You think none but your sheets are privy to
your wishes.

CHARMIAN   Nay, come, tell Iras hers.   45

ALEXAS   We'll know all our fortunes.

ENOBARBUS   Mine, and most of our fortunes,
tonight, shall be—drunk to bed.

IRAS   There's a palm presages chastity, if nothing else.

CHARMIAN   E'en as the o'erflowing Nilus presageth   50
famine.

IRAS   Go, you wild bedfellow, you cannot soothsay.

CHARMIAN   Nay, if an oily palm° be not a fruitful
prognostication,° I cannot scratch mine ear. Prithee,
tell her but a workyday° fortune.   55

SOOTHSAYER   Your fortunes are alike.

IRAS   But how, but how? Give me particulars.

SOOTHSAYER   I have said.

IRAS   Am I not an inch of fortune better than she?

CHARMIAN   Well, if you were but an inch of fortune   60
better than I, where would you choose it?

IRAS   Not in my husband's nose.°

CHARMIAN   Our worser thoughts heavens mend!
Alexas—come, his fortune, his fortune! O, let him
marry a woman that cannot go,° sweet Isis,° I beseech   65
thee, and let her die too, and give him a worse, and let
worse follow worse till the worst of all follow him
laughing to his grave, fiftyfold a cuckold! Good Isis,
hear me this prayer, though thou deny me a matter of
more weight: good Isis, I beseech thee!   70

IRAS   Amen. Dear goddess, hear that prayer of the
people! For, as it is a heartbreaking to see a handsome
man loose-wived,° so it is a deadly sorrow to behold a
foul° knave uncuckolded. Therefore, dear Isis, keep
decorum,° and fortune him accordingly!   75

CHARMIAN   Amen.

ALEXAS   Lo, now, if it lay in their hands to make me a
cuckold, they would make themselves whores but
they'd do't.

ENOBARBUS
Hush, here comes Antony.

CHARMIAN              Not he, the queen.   80

*Enter* CLEOPATRA.

CLEOPATRA
Saw you my lord?

ENOBARBUS           No, lady.

CLEOPATRA              Was he not here?

CHARMIAN   No, madam.

CLEOPATRA
He was disposed to mirth; but on the sudden
A Roman thought° hath struck him. Enobarbus!

ENOBARBUS   Madam?   85

CLEOPATRA
Seek him, and bring him hither. Where's Alexas?

ALEXAS
Here at your service. My lord approaches.

*Enter* ANTONY, *with a* MESSENGER [*and* ATTEND-
ANTS].

CLEOPATRA
We will not look upon him. Go with us.
       *Exeunt* [*all but* ANTONY, MESSENGER, *and*
                         ATTENDANTS].

MESSENGER
Fulvia thy wife first came into the field.

ANTONY
Against my brother Lucius?   90

MESSENGER   Ay.
But soon that war had end, and the time's state
Made friends of them, jointing their force 'gainst
    Caesar,
Whose better issue° in the war, from Italy
Upon the first encounter drave them.

ANTONY             Well, what worst?   95

MESSENGER
The nature of bad news infects the teller.

ANTONY
When it concerns the fool or coward. On.
Things that are past are done, with me. 'Tis thus:
Who tells me true, though in his tale lie death,
I hear him as° he flattered.

MESSENGER          Labienus—   100
This is stiff news—hath with his Parthian force
Extended° Asia: from Euphrates°
His conquering banner shook, from Syria
To Lydia and to Ionia,
Whilst—

ANTONY   Antony, thou wouldst say—

MESSENGER            O, my lord.   105

ANTONY
Speak to me home, mince not the general tongue:°
Name Cleopatra as she is called in Rome;
Rail thou in Fulvia's phrase, and taunt my faults
With such full license as both truth and malice

---

**29–30 Herod of Jewry** i.e., even that blustering tyrant who
slaughtered the innocents of Judea   **34 figs** phallic allusion
**37–38 have no names** be bastards   **42 I . . . witch** (1)
You have no power of prophecy, so I absolve you from the
charge of being a witch (2) A sorcerer like you is allowed to be
outspoken   **53 oily palm** sign of a lascivious nature   **53–54
fruitful prognostication** omen of fertility   **55 workyday**
commonplace   **62 husband's nose** bawdy, hence "worser
thoughts" in next line   **65 go** satisfactorily copulate (?) bear
children (?); **Isis** goddess of fertility and the moon   **73 loose-
wived** with a faithless, lecherous wife   **74 foul** ugly   **74–75
keep decorum** i.e., act like a just goddess

**84 Roman thought** (1) thought of Rome (2) serious reflection
**94 better issue** greater success   **100 as** as if   **102 Extended**
seized upon; **Euphrates** accented on first syllable   **106 Speak
. . . tongue** Be blunt, don't diminish what everyone is saying

Have power to utter. O, then we bring forth weeds 110
When our quick winds° lie still, and our ills told us
Is as our earing.° Fare thee well awhile.

MESSENGER
At your noble pleasure. *Exit* MESSENGER.

ANTONY
From Sicyon, ho, the news! Speak there!

FIRST ATTENDANT
The man from Sicyon—is there such an one? 115

SECOND ATTENDANT
He stays upon your will.°

ANTONY Let him appear.
These strong Egyptian fetters I must break
Or lose myself in dotage.

*Enter another* MESSENGER, *with a letter.*

What are you?

MESSENGER
Fulvia thy wife is dead.

ANTONY Where died she?

MESSENGER
In Sicyon. 120
Her length of sickness, with what else more serious
Importeth thee to know, this bears. [*Gives a letter.*]

ANTONY Forbear me.° [*Exit* MESSENGER.]
There's a great spirit gone! Thus did I desire it:
What our contempts doth often hurl from us,
We wish it ours again. The present pleasure, 125
By revolution low'ring,° does become
The opposite of itself: she's good, being gone;
The hand could° pluck her back that shoved her on.
I must from this enchanting° queen break off:
Ten thousand harms, more than the ills I know, 130
My idleness doth hatch. Ho now, Enobarbus!

*Enter* ENOBARBUS.

ENOBARBUS What's your pleasure, sir?
ANTONY I must with haste from hence.
ENOBARBUS Why, then we kill all our women. We
see how mortal an unkindness is to them. If they suffer 135
our departure, death's the word.
ANTONY I must be gone.
ENOBARBUS Under a compelling occasion let women
die.° It were pity to cast them away for nothing,
though between them and a great cause they should 140
be esteemed nothing. Cleopatra, catching but the
least noise of this, dies instantly; I have seen her die
twenty times upon far poorer moment.° I do think
there is mettle° in death, which commits some loving
act upon her, she hath such a celerity in dying. 145
ANTONY She is cunning past man's thought.
ENOBARBUS Alack, sir, no; her passions are made of
nothing but the finest part of pure love. We cannot
call her winds and waters sighs and tears; they are
greater storms and tempests than almanacs can report. 150

This cannot be cunning in her; if it be, she makes a
show'r of rain as well as Jove.
ANTONY Would I had never seen her!
ENOBARBUS O, sir, you had then left unseen a wonderful piece of work, which not to have been blest 155
withal would have discredited your travel.
ANTONY Fulvia is dead.
ENOBARBUS Sir?
ANTONY Fulvia is dead.
ENOBARBUS Fulvia? 160
ANTONY Dead.
ENOBARBUS Why, sir, give the gods a thankful
sacrifice. When it pleaseth their deities to take the wife
of a man from him, it shows to man the tailors of the
earth; comforting therein, that when old robes are 165
worn out, there are members to make new. If there
were no more women but Fulvia, then had you indeed
a cut,° and the case to be lamented. This grief is
crowned with consolation: your old smock brings
forth a new petticoat, and indeed the tears live in an 170
onion that should water this sorrow.
ANTONY
The business she hath broachèd in the state
Cannot endure my absence.
ENOBARBUS And the business you have broached
here cannot be without you; especially that of 175
Cleopatra's, which wholly depends on your abode.°
ANTONY
No more light° answers. Let our° officers
Have notice what we purpose. I shall break°
The cause of our expedience° to the queen
And get her leave to part. For not alone 180
The death of Fulvia, with more urgent touches,°
Do strongly speak to us, but the letters too
Of many our contriving friends° in Rome
Petition us at home. Sextus Pompeius
Hath given the dare to Caesar and commands 185
The empire of the sea. Our slippery people,
Whose love is never linked to the deserver
Till his deserts are past, begin to throw
Pompey the Great and all his dignities
Upon° his son; who, high in name and power, 190
Higher than both in blood and life,° stands up
For the main soldier;° whose quality, going on,
The sides o' th' world may danger.° Much is breeding,
Which, like the courser's hair,° hath yet but life
And not a serpent's poison. Say our pleasure, 195
To such whose places under us require,
Our quick remove from hence.
ENOBARBUS I shall do't. [*Exeunt.*]

---

**168 cut** (1) severe blow (2) pudendum (the entire speech infuses
bawdy meanings [e.g., of "tailors" and "members"] into the
conceit of the world as a tailor's shop, with the gods as tailors
cutting new clothes out of old, replacing old people with new;
the tailor's shop is where men make love and breed) **174–76
And . . . abode** bawdy again **177 light** indecent; **our** royal
plural **178 break** tell **179 expedience** (1) haste (2) expedition **181 more urgent touches** more pressing reasons **183
many . . . friends** many who plot on my behalf **188–90
throw . . . Upon** transfer . . . to **191 blood and life**
courage and energy **191–92 stands . . . soldier** sets himself
up as the greatest soldier in the world **192–93 whose . . .
danger** whose character may, if his fortunes prosper, threaten
the structure of the world **194 courser's hair** a horse's hair
placed in water was thought to turn into a serpent

**111 quick winds** lively winds (that ventilate the soil) **111–12
our ills . . . earing** i.e., when our faults are told to us, it is like
plowing (that makes the ground fertile) **116 stays . . . will**
awaits your pleasure **122 Forbear me** leave me **126 By
revolution low'ring** sinking in our estimation (as the wheel
of time turns and spins the present moment downward) **128
could** would like to **129 enchanting** spellbinding **139 die**
throughout this speech Enobarbus puns on a second meaning
of *die*, "to experience sexual orgasm" **143 moment** cause
**144 mettle** strength

[Scene III. *Alexandria. Cleopatra's palace.*]

*Enter* CLEOPATRA, CHARMIAN, ALEXAS, *and* IRAS.

CLEOPATRA
Where is he?

CHARMIAN    I did not see him since.°

CLEOPATRA
See where he is, who's with him, what he does:
I did not send you. If you find him sad,°
Say I am dancing; if in mirth, report
That I am sudden sick. Quick, and return.    5

                       [*Exit* ALEXAS.]

CHARMIAN
Madam, methinks, if you did love him dearly,
You do not hold the method to enforce
The like from him.

CLEOPATRA        What should I do, I do not?

CHARMIAN
In each thing give him way, cross him in nothing.

CLEOPATRA
Thou teachest like a fool: the way to lose him!    10

CHARMIAN
Tempt° him not so too far. I wish, forbear.
In time we hate that which we often fear.

*Enter* ANTONY.

But here comes Antony.

CLEOPATRA         I am sick and sullen.

ANTONY
I am sorry to give breathing° to my purpose—

CLEOPATRA
Help me away, dear Charmian! I shall fall.    15
It cannot be thus long; the sides of nature
Will not sustain it.°

ANTONY        Now, my dearest queen—

CLEOPATRA
Pray you, stand farther from me.

ANTONY              What's the matter?

CLEOPATRA
I know by that same eye there's some good news.
What, says the married woman you may go?    20
Would she had never given you leave to come!
Let her not say 'tis I that keep you here.
I have no power upon you; hers you are.

ANTONY
The gods best know—

CLEOPATRA        O, never was there queen
So mightily betrayed! Yet at the first    25
I saw the treasons planted.°

ANTONY        Cleopatra—

CLEOPATRA
Why should I think you can be mine, and true
(Though you in swearing shake the thronèd gods)
Who have been false to Fulvia? Riotous madness,
To be entangled with those mouth-made vows    30
Which break themselves in swearing.°

ANTONY         Most sweet queen—

CLEOPATRA
Nay, pray you seek no color° for your going,
But bid farewell, and go. When you sued staying,°
Then was the time for words: no going then;
Eternity was in our lips and eyes,    35
Bliss in our brows' bent,° none our parts so poor
But was a race of heaven;° they are so still,
Or thou, the greatest soldier of the world,
Art turned the greatest liar.

ANTONY              How now, lady?

CLEOPATRA
I would I had thy inches; thou shouldst know    40
There were a heart in Egypt.°

ANTONY          Hear me, queen:
The strong necessity of time commands
Our services awhile; but my full heart
Remains in use with you.° Our Italy
Shines o'er with civil swords;° Sextus Pompeius    45
Makes his approaches to the port of Rome;
Equality of two domestic powers
Breed scrupulous faction;° the hated, grown to
     strength,
Are newly grown to love;° the condemned Pompey,
Rich in his father's honor, creeps apace    50
Into the hearts of such as have not thrived
Upon the present state, whose numbers threaten;
And quietness, grown sick of rest, would purge
By any desperate change.° My more particular,°
And that which most with you should safe my    55
     going,
Is Fulvia's death.

CLEOPATRA
Though age from folly could not give me freedom,
It does from childishness. Can Fulvia die?

ANTONY
She's dead, my queen.
Look here, and at thy sovereign leisure read    60
The garboils° she awaked. At the last, best,°
See when and where she died.

CLEOPATRA        O most false love!
Where be the sacred vials° thou shouldst fill
With sorrowful water? Now I see, I see,
In Fulvia's death, how mine received shall be.    65

ANTONY
Quarrel no more, but be prepared to know
The purposes I bear; which are, or cease,
As you shall give th' advice. By the fire
That quickens Nilus' slime,° I go from hence

---

32 **color** pretext   33 **sued staying** pleaded to stay   36 **brows' bent** eyebrows' arch   37 **race of heaven** (1) of heavenly flavor (2) of heavenly origin, rooted in heaven   41 **Egypt** here, as elsewhere, Cleopatra as well as the country   44 **in . . . you** for you to possess   45 **civil swords** swords drawn in civil war   47–48 **Equality . . . faction** Where the rule at home is equally divided between two, parties grow up, quarreling over tiny points   48–49 **the hated . . . love** The hated begin to be loved as they gain power   53–54 **quietness . . . change** i.e., a long peace has developed disease in the body politic, which demands to be made well by the bloodletting of war and revolution   54 **My more particular** my own more personal reason   61 **garboils** commotion; **best** i.e., best news of all   63 **sacred vials** the bottles of tears supposedly placed by Romans in friends' tombs   68–69 **By . . . slime** by the sun that generates life in the Nile's mud

---

**I.iii.1 since** recently   **3 sad** serious   **11 Tempt** try   **14 breathing** utterance   **16–17 sides . . . it** the human frame will not stand it   **26 planted** like seeds, and like mines   **31 Which . . . swearing** which are broken the second they are uttered

Thy soldier-servant, making peace or war                               70
As thou affects.°

CLEOPATRA        Cut my lace,° Charmian, come—
But let it be: I am quickly ill, and well,
So Antony loves.°

ANTONY            My precious queen, forbear,
And give true evidence to his love, which stands°
An honorable trial.

CLEOPATRA            So Fulvia told me.                                  75
I prithee turn aside and weep for her;
Then bid adieu to me, and say the tears
Belong to Egypt. Good now, play one scene
Of excellent dissembling, and let it look
Like perfect honor.

ANTONY            You'll heat my blood: no more.        80

CLEOPATRA
You can do better yet; but this is meetly.°

ANTONY
Now by my sword—

CLEOPATRA            And target.° Still he mends.
But this is not the best. Look, prithee, Charmian,
How this Herculean Roman does become
The carriage of his chafe.°

ANTONY            I'll leave you, lady.                     85

CLEOPATRA
Courteous lord, one word.
Sir, you and I must part, but that's not it:
Sir, you and I have loved, but there's not it:
That you know well. Something it is I would—
O, my oblivion is a very Antony,                                        90
And I am all forgotten.°

ANTONY            But that your royalty
Holds idleness your subject,° I should take you
For idleness itself.

CLEOPATRA            'Tis sweating labor
To bear° such idleness so near the heart
As Cleopatra this. But, sir, forgive me,                                95
Since my becomings° kill me when they do not
Eye well to you. Your honor calls you hence;
Therefore be deaf to my unpitied folly,
And all the gods go with you. Upon your sword
Sit laurel victory, and smooth success                                 100
Be strewed before your feet!

ANTONY            Let us go. Come:
Our separation so abides and flies
That thou residing here goes yet with me,
And I hence fleeting here remain with thee.
Away!                                                     Exeunt. 105

[Scene IV. *Rome. Caesar's house.*]

*Enter Octavius* [CAESAR], *reading a letter*, LEPIDUS,
*and their* TRAIN.

CAESAR
You may see, Lepidus, and henceforth know
It is not Caesar's natural vice to hate
Our great competitor.° From Alexandria
This is the news: he fishes, drinks, and wastes
The lamps of night in revel; is not more manlike        5
Than Cleopatra, nor the queen of Ptolemy°
More womanly than he; hardly gave audience, or
Vouchsafed to think he had partners. You shall find
    there
A man who is th' abstract of all faults
That all men follow.°

LEPIDUS            I must not think there are        10
Evils enow° to darken all his goodness;
His faults, in him, seem as the spots of heaven,
More fiery by night's blackness, hereditary
Rather than purchased,° what he cannot change
Than what he chooses.                                   15

CAESAR
You are too indulgent. Let's grant it is not
Amiss to tumble on the bed of Ptolemy,
To give a kingdom for a mirth, to sit
And keep the turn of tippling° with a slave,
To reel the streets at noon, and stand the buffet        20
With knaves that smells of sweat. Say this becomes
    him
(As his composure° must be rare indeed
Whom these things cannot blemish); yet must Antony
No way excuse his foils° when we do bear
So great weight in his lightness.° If he filled          25
His vacancy° with his voluptuousness,
Full surfeits and the dryness of his bones
Call on him for't.° But to confound° such time
That drums him from his sport and speaks as loud
As his own state and ours, 'tis to be chid               30
As we rate boys who, being mature in knowledge,
Pawn their experience to their present pleasure
And so rebel to judgment.°

*Enter a* MESSENGER.

LEPIDUS            Here's more news.

MESSENGER
Thy biddings have been done, and every hour,
Most noble Caesar, shalt thou have report                35
How 'tis abroad. Pompey is strong at sea,
And it appears he is beloved of those
That only have feared Caesar: to the ports
The discontents° repair, and men's reports
Give him° much wronged.

CAESAR            I should have known no less.        40
It hath been taught us from the primal state°

---

71 **affects** choosest; **Cut my lace** of her tight bodice, i.e.,
"Give me air"   73 **So Antony loves** (1) if Antony loves
me (2) in just such a changeable way does Antony love me
74 **stands** sustains   81 **meetly** suitable   82 **target** small shield
84–85 **How . . . chafe** how gracefully this descendant of
Hercules acts out his rage   90–91 **my . . . forgotten** (1) My
forgetful memory is like Antony and has deserted me (2) My
forgetfulness even, like my memory, is consumed by the image
of Antony, and my mind is empty of all else   91–92 **But that
. . . subject** if you were not queen over trifling   93–94 **labor
To bear** pun on childbirth   96 **becomings** graces

**I.iv.3 competitor** partner   **6 queen of Ptolemy** Cleopatra
had nominally married her brother Ptolemy, who was only a
child, at the command of Julius Caesar   **9–10 abstract . . .
follow** symbol of universal weakness   **11 enow** enough
**14 purchased** acquired   **19 keep . . . tippling** exchange
toasts   **22 composure** character   **24 foils** stains   **24–25 when
. . . lightness** when his triviality throws such a burden on us
**26 vacancy** leisure   **27–28 Full . . . for't** let him pay the
price in sickness and syphilis   **28 confound** waste   **30–33 'tis
. . . judgment** deserves the considered rebuke we give to
boys who, though old enough to know better, give up all the
wisdom they have learned in exchange for a moment's pleasure
**39 discontents** malcontents   **40 Give him** say he is   **41 from
. . . state** since governments began

That he which is was wished until he were;°
And the ebbed man, ne'er loved till ne'er worth love,
Comes deared by being lacked. This common body,°
Like to a vagabond flag° upon the stream,                    45
Goes to and back, lackeying the varying tide,
To rot itself with motion.
MESSENGER                    Caesar, I bring thee word
Menecrates and Menas, famous pirates,
Makes the sea serve them, which they ear° and wound
With keels of every kind. Many hot inroads                   50
They make in Italy; the borders maritime
Lack blood to think on't, and flush° youth revolt.
No vessel can peep forth but 'tis as soon
Taken as seen; for Pompey's name strikes more
Than could his war resisted.
CAESAR                    Antony,                             55
Leave thy lascivious wassails.° When thou once
Was beaten from Modena,° where thou slew'st
Hirtius and Pansa, consuls, at thy heel
Did famine follow, whom thou fought'st against
(Though daintily brought up) with patience more             60
Than savages could suffer.° Thou didst drink
The stale° of horses and the gilded° puddle
Which beasts would cough at. Thy palate then did
    deign°
The roughest berry on the rudest hedge.
Yea, like the stag when snow the pasture sheets,            65
The barks of trees thou browsed. On the Alps
It is reported thou didst eat strange flesh,
Which some did die to look on. And all this
(It wounds thine honor that I speak it now)
Was borne so like a soldier that thy cheek                  70
So much as lanked° not.
LEPIDUS                    'Tis pity of him.
CAESAR
Let his shames quickly
Drive him to Rome. 'Tis time we twain
Did show ourselves i' th' field; and to that end
Assemble we immediate council. Pompey                       75
Thrives in our idleness.
LEPIDUS                    Tomorrow, Caesar,
I shall be furnished to inform you rightly
Both what by sea and land I can be able°
To front° this present time.
CAESAR                    Till which encounter,
It is my business too. Farewell.                            80
LEPIDUS
Farewell, my lord. What you shall know meantime
Of stirs abroad, I shall beseech you, sir,
To let me be partaker.
CAESAR                    Doubt not, sir;
I knew it for my bond.°                    Exeunt.

[Scene V. Alexandria. Cleopatra's palace.]

Enter CLEOPATRA, CHARMIAN, IRAS, and
MARDIAN.

CLEOPATRA  Charmian!
CHARMIAN  Madam?
CLEOPATRA [Yawning.]
Ha, ha.
Give me to drink mandragora.°
CHARMIAN                    Why, madam?
CLEOPATRA
That I might sleep out this great gap of time              5
My Antony is away.
CHARMIAN                    You think of him too much.
CLEOPATRA
O, 'tis treason!
CHARMIAN                    Madam, I trust, not so.
CLEOPATRA
Thou, eunuch Mardian!
MARDIAN                    What's your highness' pleasure?
CLEOPATRA
Not now to hear thee sing. I take no pleasure
In aught an eunuch has: 'tis well for thee                 10
That, being unseminared,° thy freer thoughts
May not fly forth of Egypt. Hast thou affections?°
MARDIAN  Yes, gracious madam.
CLEOPATRA  Indeed?
MARDIAN
Not in deed, madam; for I can do nothing                   15
But what indeed is honest° to be done:
Yet have I fierce affections, and think
What Venus did with Mars.°
CLEOPATRA                    O, Charmian,
Where think'st thou he is now? Stands he, or sits he?
Or does he walk? Or is he on his horse?                    20
O happy horse, to bear the weight of Antony!
Do bravely, horse, for wot'st° thou whom thou
    mov'st?
The demi-Atlas° of this earth, the arm
And burgonet° of men. He's speaking now,
Or murmuring, "Where's my serpent of old Nile?"           25
(For so he calls me.) Now I feed myself
With most delicious poison. Think on me,
That am with Phoebus'° amorous pinches black
And wrinkled deep in time. Broad-fronted Caesar,°
When thou wast here above the ground, I was               30
A morsel for a monarch; and great Pompey°
Would stand and make his eyes grow in my brow;
There would he anchor his aspect,° and die
With looking on his life.

Enter ALEXAS from Antony.

ALEXAS                    Sovereign of Egypt, hail!

---

42 **That . . . were** that a man in power had supporters until
he gained power  44 **common body** populace  45 **vagabond flag** aimlessly drifting iris  49 **ear** plow  52 **flush**
vigorous, lusty  56 **wassails** revelry  57 **Modena** accented
on second syllable  61 **suffer** summon up  62 **stale** urine;
**gilded** i.e., yellow with scum  63 **deign** not disdain  71
**lanked** thinned  78 **I . . . able** my powers can be  79
**front** confront  84 **bond** duty

I.v.4 **mandragora** mandrake (a strong narcotic)  11 **unseminared** unsexed  12 **affections** passions  16 **honest** chaste
18 **Venus . . . Mars** Venus, goddess of love, and Mars, god
of war, were lovers  22 **wot'st** knowest  23 **demi-Atlas** the
Titan Atlas supported the heavens on his shoulders  24
**burgonet** visored helmet  28 **Phoebus'** the sun's  29 **Broad-
fronted Caesar** wide-browed Caesar (i.e., Julius Caesar,
whose mistress she had been in youth)  31 **great Pompey**
Cnaeus Pompeius (son of Pompey the Great)  33 **aspect** gaze
(accented on second syllable)

**CLEOPATRA**
How much unlike art thou Mark Antony!  35
Yet, coming from him, that great med'cine hath
With his tinct gilded thee.°
How goes it with my brave Mark Antony?

**ALEXAS**
Last thing he did, dear queen,
He kissed—the last of many doubled kisses—  40
This orient° pearl. His speech sticks in my heart.

**CLEOPATRA**
Mine ear must pluck it thence.

**ALEXAS**                                          "Good friend," quoth he,
"Say the firm° Roman to great Egypt sends
This treasure of an oyster; at whose foot,
To mend the petty present, I will piece°  45
Her opulent throne with kingdoms. All the East
(Say thou) shall call her mistress." So he nodded,
And soberly did mount an arm-gaunt° steed,
Who neighed so high that what I would have spoke
Was beastly dumbed° by him.

**CLEOPATRA**                        What was he, sad or merry?  50

**ALEXAS**
Like to the time o' th' year between the extremes
Of hot and cold, he was nor sad nor merry.

**CLEOPATRA**
O well-divided disposition!° Note him,
Note him, good Charmian, 'tis the man;° but note him.
He was not sad, for he would shine on those  55
That make their looks by his; he was not merry,
Which seemed to tell them his remembrance lay
In Egypt with his joy; but between both.
O heavenly mingle! Be'st thou sad or merry,
The violence of either thee becomes,  60
So does it no man else.—Met'st thou my posts?°

**ALEXAS**
Ay, madam, twenty several° messengers.
Why do you send so thick?

**CLEOPATRA**                        Who's born that day
When I forgot to send to Antony
Shall die a beggar. Ink and paper, Charmian.  65
Welcome, my good Alexas. Did I, Charmian,
Ever love Caesar so?

**CHARMIAN**                  O, that brave° Caesar!

**CLEOPATRA**
Be choked with such another emphasis!°
Say "the brave Antony."

**CHARMIAN**                        The valiant Caesar!

**CLEOPATRA**
By Isis, I will give thee bloody teeth  70
If thou with Caesar paragon° again
My man of men.

**CHARMIAN**          By your most gracious pardon,
I sing but after you.

**CLEOPATRA**              My salad days,

When I was green° in judgment, cold in blood,
To say as I said then. But come, away,  75
Get me ink and paper.
He shall have every day a several greeting,
Or I'll unpeople Egypt.                    *Exeunt.*


# [ ACT II ]

### [Scene I. *Messina. Pompey's house.*]

*Enter* POMPEY, MENECRATES, *and* MENAS, *in warlike manner.*

**POMPEY**
If the great gods be just, they shall° assist
The deeds of justest men.

**MENECRATES**                  Know, worthy Pompey,
That what they do delay, they not deny.°

**POMPEY**
Whiles we are suitors to their throne, decays
The thing we sue° for.

**MENECRATES**              We, ignorant of ourselves,  5
Beg often our own harms, which the wise pow'rs
Deny us for our good; so find we profit
By losing of our prayers.

**POMPEY**                      I shall do well:
The people love me, and the sea is mine;
My powers are crescent,° and my auguring° hope  10
Says it will come to th' full. Mark Antony
In Egypt sits at dinner, and will make
No wars without doors.° Caesar gets money where
He loses hearts. Lepidus flatters both,
Of both is flattered, but he neither loves,  15
Nor either cares for him.

**MENAS**                      Caesar and Lepidus
Are in the field;° a mighty strength they carry.

**POMPEY**
Where have you this? 'Tis false.

**MENAS**                              From Silvius, sir.

**POMPEY**
He dreams: I know they are in Rome together,
Looking for Antony. But all the charms° of love,  20
Salt° Cleopatra, soften thy waned° lip!
Let witchcraft join with beauty, lust with both!
Tie up the libertine in a field of feasts,
Keep his brain fuming. Epicurean cooks
Sharpen with cloyless sauce his appetite,  25
That sleep and feeding may prorogue° his honor
Even till a Lethe'd° dullness—

*Enter* VARRIUS.

How now, Varrius?

---

36–37 **that . . . thee** alchemists long tried to make or discover the "philosopher's stone" or *elixir vitae*—known as the "great medicine" and the "tincture"—which had the property of turning base metals to gold, and of restoring youth  41 **orient** eastern, bright  43 **firm** constant  45 **piece** add to  48 **arm-gaunt** battleworn (?) battle-hungry (?)  50 **beastly dumbed** silenced by a beast  53 **disposition** temperament  54 **'tis the man** that's exactly what he is like  61 **posts** messengers  62 **several** separate  67 **brave** splendid, fine  68 **emphasis** forceful statement  71 **paragon** compare

74 **green** young, silly
**II.i.1 shall** surely must  3 **what . . . deny** i.e., delay in performing does not necessarily imply a refusal  5 **sue** beg  10 **crescent** growing (i.e., waxing like the moon—hence the following image); **auguring** prophesying  13 **without doors** out-of-doors (contrasted with the indoor "wars" of love)  17 **in the field** ready for battle  20 **charms** spells  21 **Salt** lustful; **waned** pale and thin (like the old moon)  26 **prorogue** suspend  27 **Lethe'd** oblivious (from Lethe, a river in Hades; those who drank of the water forgot all)

VARRIUS
This is most certain, that I shall deliver:
Mark Antony is every hour in Rome
Expected. Since he went from Egypt 'tis          30
A space for farther travel.°
POMPEY          I could have given less matter
A better ear. Menas, I did not think
This amorous surfeiter would have donned his helm
For such a petty war. His soldiership
Is twice the other twain; but let us rear          35
The higher our opinion,° that our stirring
Can from the lap of Egypt's widow pluck
The ne'er-lust-wearied Antony.
MENAS          I cannot hope°
Caesar and Antony shall well greet° together;
His wife that's dead did trespasses to Caesar;          40
His brother warred upon him—although I think
Not moved° by Antony.
POMPEY          I know not, Menas,
How lesser enmities may give way to greater.
Were't not that we stand up against them all,
'Twere pregnant they should square between them-
selves,°          45
For they have entertainèd cause enough
To draw their swords; but how the fear of us
May cement° their divisions and bind up
The petty difference, we yet not know.
Be't as our gods will have't! It only stands          50
Our lives upon,° to use our strongest hands.
Come, Menas.          *Exeunt.*

[Scene II. *Rome. Lepidus' house.*]

*Enter* ENOBARBUS *and* LEPIDUS.

LEPIDUS
Good Enobarbus, 'tis a worthy deed,
And shall become you well, to entreat your captain
To soft and gentle speech.
ENOBARBUS          I shall entreat him
To answer like himself: if Caesar move° him,
Let Antony look over Caesar's head          5
And speak as loud as Mars. By Jupiter,
Were I the wearer of Antonio's beard,
I would not shave't today!°
LEPIDUS          'Tis not a time
For private stomaching.°
ENOBARBUS          Every time
Serves for the matter that is then born in't.          10
LEPIDUS
But small to greater matters must give way.

30–31 'tis . . . travel there has been time for an even longer journey  35–36 let . . . opinion let us think all the better of ourselves  38 hope believe  39 well greet meet amiably  42 moved encouraged  44–45 Were't . . . themselves Had we not challenged them (and thus united them) they would probably have quarreled among themselves  48 cement accented on first syllable  50–51 It . . . upon only, it is a matter of life and death to us all
II.ii.4 move irritate  8 I . . . today (1) I would not do him the courtesy of clean-shaving (2) I would not remove the temptation of plucking it (an incitement to fight)  9 private stomaching personal resentment

ENOBARBUS
Not if the small come first.
LEPIDUS          Your speech is passion;
But pray you stir no embers up. Here comes
The noble Antony.

*Enter* ANTONY *and* VENTIDIUS [*in conversation*].

ENOBARBUS          And yonder, Caesar.

*Enter* [*from the other side*] CAESAR, MAECENAS, *and* AGRIPPA [*in conversation*].

ANTONY
If we compose° well here, to Parthia.          15
Hark, Ventidius.
CAESAR          I do not know,
Maecenas; ask Agrippa.
LEPIDUS          Noble friends,
That which combined us was most great, and let not
A leaner action rend us. What's amiss,
May it be gently heard. When we debate          20
Our trivial difference loud, we do commit
Murder in healing wounds. Then, noble partners,
The rather for I earnestly beseech,
Touch you the sourest points with sweetest terms,
Nor curstness grow to th' matter.°
ANTONY          'Tis spoken well.          25
Were we before our armies, and to fight,
I should do thus.°          *Flourish.*
CAESAR
Welcome to Rome.
ANTONY          Thank you.
CAESAR          Sit.
ANTONY          Sit, sir.
CAESAR          Nay then.

[*They sit.*]

ANTONY
I learn you take things ill which are not so,
Or being, concern you not.
CAESAR          I must be laughed at          30
If, or for nothing or° a little, I
Should say myself offended, and with you
Chiefly i' th' world; more laughed at that I should
Once name you derogately,° when to sound your
name
It not concerned me.
ANTONY          My being in Egypt, Caesar,          35
What was't to you?
CAESAR
No more than my residing here at Rome
Might be to you in Egypt: yet if you there
Did practice on my state,° your being in Egypt
Might be my question.
ANTONY          How intend you? Practiced?          40
CAESAR
You may be pleased to catch at mine intent
By what did here befall me. Your wife and brother

15 compose come to an agreement  25 Nor . . . matter and do not let ill temper be added to the problem at hand  27 thus perhaps Antony embraces Caesar, but perhaps he means his words would be temperate in any circumstance  31 or . . . or either . . . or  34 derogately disparagingly  39 practice . . . state plot against my rule

Made wars upon me, and their contestation
Was theme for you;° you were the word of war.°

ANTONY
You do mistake your business: my brother never   45
Did urge me° in his act. I did inquire it
And have my learning from some true reports°
That drew their swords with you. Did he not rather
Discredit my authority with yours,
And make the wars alike against my stomach,°   50
Having alike your cause? Of this, my letters
Before did satisfy you. If you'll patch a quarrel,
As matter whole you have to make it with,°
It must not be with this.

CAESAR                        You praise yourself
By laying defects of judgment to me, but   55
You patched up your excuses.

ANTONY                        Not so, not so:
I know you could not lack, I am certain on't,
Very necessity of this thought, that I,
Your partner in the cause 'gainst which he fought,
Could not with graceful eyes attend° those wars   60
Which fronted° mine own peace. As for my wife,
I would you had her spirit in such another;°
The third o' th' world is yours, which with a snaffle
You may pace° easy, but not such a wife.

ENOBARBUS   Would we had all such wives, that the   65
men might go to wars with the women.

ANTONY
So much uncurbable, her garboils, Caesar,
Made out of her impatience—which not wanted
Shrewdness of policy too—I grieving grant
Did you too much disquiet: for that you must   70
But° say, I could not help it.

CAESAR                        I wrote to you;
When rioting in Alexandria you
Did pocket up my letters, and with taunts
Did gibe my missive° out of audience.

ANTONY                        Sir,
He fell upon me, ere admitted, then:   75
Three kings I had newly feasted, and did want
Of what I was i' th' morning; but next day
I told him of myself,° which was as much
As to have asked him pardon. Let this fellow
Be nothing of° our strife: if we contend,   80
Out of our question wipe him.

CAESAR                        You have broken
The article° of your oath, which you shall never
Have tongue to charge me with.

LEPIDUS                        Soft,° Caesar!

ANTONY                        No,
Lepidus; let him speak.
The honor is sacred which he talks on now,   85
Supposing that I lacked it. But on, Caesar,
The article of my oath—

44 **Was . . . you** had you as root cause (?); provided you with a pretext (?); **you . . . war** The war was about you   **46 Did urge me** made use of my name   **47 reports** reporters   **50 stomach** desire   **52–53 If . . . with** if you want to fabricate a quarrel out of odds and ends, though in fact you have more substantial materials for one   **60 with . . . attend** look favorably on   **61 fronted** attacked   **62 I . . . another** I wish you were married to just such a wife   **64 pace** train (used of horses)   **71 But** only   **74 missive** messenger   **78 myself** my condition   **80 Be nothing of** have no place in   **82 article** precise terms   **83 Soft** be careful

CAESAR
To lend me arms and aid when I required them,
The which you both denied.

ANTONY                        Neglected rather:
And then when poisonèd hours had bound me up   90
From mine own knowledge. As nearly as I may,
I'll play the penitent to you: but mine honesty
Shall not make poor my greatness, nor my power
Work without it.° Truth is, that Fulvia,
To have me out of Egypt, made wars here,   95
For which myself, the ignorant motive, do
So far ask pardon as befits mine honor
To stoop in such a case.

LEPIDUS                        'Tis noble spoken.

MAECENAS
If it might please you, to enforce no further
The griefs° between ye: to forget them quite   100
Were to remember that the present need
Speaks to atone you.°

LEPIDUS                        Worthily spoken, Maecenas.

ENOBARBUS   Of, if you borrow one another's love
for the instant, you may, when you hear no more
words of Pompey, return it again: you shall have time   105
to wrangle in when you have nothing else to do.

ANTONY
Thou art a soldier only; speak no more.

ENOBARBUS   That truth should be silent I had almost
forgot.

ANTONY
You wrong this presence;° therefore speak no more.   110

ENOBARBUS   Go to, then; your considerate stone.°

CAESAR
I do not much dislike the matter, but
The manner of his speech; for't cannot be
We shall remain in friendship, our conditions°
So diff'ring in their acts. Yet if I knew   115
What hoop should hold us stanch, from edge to edge
O' th' world I would pursue it.

AGRIPPA                        Give me leave, Caesar.

CAESAR
Speak, Agrippa.

AGRIPPA
Thou hast a sister by the mother's side,°
Admired Octavia: great Mark Antony   120
Is now a widower.

CAESAR                        Say not so, Agrippa:
If Cleopatra heard you, your reproof
Were well deserved of rashness.°

ANTONY
I am not married, Caesar: let me hear
Agrippa further speak.   125

AGRIPPA
To hold you in perpetual amity,
To make you brothers, and to knit your hearts
With an unslipping knot, take Antony
Octavia to his wife; whose beauty claims

94 **it** honesty (?)   **100 griefs** grievances   **102 Speaks . . . you** demands your reconciliation   **110 presence** dignified company   **111 your considerate stone** I will be silent as stone about what I am thinking   **114 conditions** temperaments   **119 by . . . side** i.e., half-sister (though actually Octavia was a full sister of Octavius)   **122–23 your . . . rashness** You would get a deserved reproof for being foolhardy

No worse a husband than the best of men;    130
Whose virtue and whose general graces speak
That which none else can utter. By this marriage
All little jealousies,° which now seem great,
And all great fears, which now import° their dangers,
Would then be nothing: truths would be tales,    135
Where now half-tales be truths:° her love to both
Would each to other, and all loves to both,
Draw after her. Pardon what I have spoke;
For 'tis a studied, not a present° thought,
By duty ruminated.

ANTONY          Will Caesar speak?    140

CAESAR
Not till he hears how Antony is touched°
With what is spoke already.

ANTONY          What power is in Agrippa,
If I would say, "Agrippa, be it so,"
To make this good?

CAESAR          The power of Caesar, and
His power unto Octavia.

ANTONY          May I never    145
To this good purpose, that so fairly shows,
Dream of impediment! Let me have thy hand.
Further this act of grace,° and from this hour
The heart of brothers govern in our loves
And sway our great designs.

CAESAR          There's my hand.    150
A sister I bequeath you, whom no brother
Did ever love so dearly. Let her live
To join our kingdoms and our hearts; and never
Fly off our loves° again.

LEPIDUS          Happily, amen.

ANTONY
I did not think to draw my sword 'gainst Pompey,    155
For he hath laid strange courtesies and great
Of late upon me. I must thank him only,
Lest my remembrance° suffer ill report:
At heel of that,° defy him.

LEPIDUS          Time calls upon's.
Of us must Pompey presently° be sought,    160
Or else he seeks out us.

ANTONY          Where lies he?

CAESAR
About the Mount Mesena.°

ANTONY
What is his strength by land?

CAESAR
Great and increasing; but by sea
He is an absolute master.

ANTONY          So is the fame.°    165
Would we had spoke together! Haste we for it,
Yet, ere we put ourselves in arms, dispatch we
The business we have talked of.

CAESAR          With most gladness;
And do invite you to my sister's view,
Whither straight I'll lead you.

ANTONY          Let us, Lepidus,    170
Not lack your company.

LEPIDUS          Noble Antony,
Not sickness should detain me.
      *Flourish. Exit [all but]* ENOBARBUS,
           AGRIPPA, MAECENAS.

MAECENAS   Welcome from Egypt, sir.

ENOBARBUS   Half the heart° of Caesar, worthy
Maecenas. My honorable friend, Agrippa.    175

AGRIPPA   Good Enobarbus.

MAECENAS   We have cause to be glad that matters are
so well disgested.° You stayed well by't° in Egypt.

ENOBARBUS   Ay, sir, we did sleep day out of counte-
nance° and made the night light with drinking.    180

MAECENAS   Eight wild boars roasted whole at a
breakfast, and but twelve persons there; is this true?

ENOBARBUS   This was but as a fly by° an eagle: we
had much more monstrous matter of feast, which
worthily deserved noting.    185

MAECENAS   She's a most triumphant lady, if report be
square° to her.

ENOBARBUS   When she first met Mark Antony, she
pursed up° his heart, upon the river of Cydnus.

AGRIPPA   There she appeared indeed; or my reporter    190
devised° well for her.

ENOBARBUS
I will tell you.
The barge she sat in, like a burnished throne,
Burned on the water: the poop was beaten gold;
Purple the sails, and so perfumèd that    195
The winds were lovesick with them; the oars were
   silver,
Which to the tune of flutes kept stroke and made
The water which they beat to follow faster,
As amorous of their strokes. For her own person,
It beggared all description: she did lie    200
In her pavilion, cloth-of-gold of tissue,°
O'erpicturing that Venus where we see
The fancy outwork nature:° on each side her
Stood pretty dimpled boys, like smiling Cupids,
With divers-colored fans, whose wind did seem    205
To glow the delicate cheeks which they did cool,
And what they undid did.°

AGRIPPA          O, rare for Antony.

ENOBARBUS
Her gentlewomen, like the Nereides,°
So many mermaids, tended her i' th' eyes,
And made their bends adornings.° At the helm    210
A seeming mermaid steers: the silken tackle
Swell with the touches of those flower-soft hands,

---

**174 Half the heart** dear friend (though possibly the idea is that
Caesar is equally devoted to Agrippa and to Maecenas)   **178
disgested** digested; **stayed well by't** "lived it up.
**179–80 we . . . countenance** We disconcerted the day by
sleeping through it   **183 by** compared with   **187 square** just,
true   **189 pursed up** put in her purse, took possession of
**191 devised** invented   **201 cloth-of-gold of tissue** a rich
fabric interwoven with gold threads   **202–03 O'erpicturing
. . . nature** surpassing that painting of Venus where we
can see the imagination excelling nature itself in creative
ability   **207 And . . . did** i.e., and seemed to produce the
warm color they were cooling   **208 Nereides** sea nymphs
**209–10 tended . . . adornings** stood before her and waited
on her, their bowing movements being works of art in
themselves

---

**133 jealousies** suspicions   **134 import** bring   **135–36 truths
would . . . truths** Things true would be disbelieved, whereas
now half-truths are believed   **139 present** momentary   **141
touched** affected   **148 grace** reconciliation   **154 Fly . . .
loves** May our love for each other desert us   **158 remembrance** memory (of kindnesses done)   **159 At . . . that**
immediately after   **160 presently** at once   **162 Mesena**
Misenum, an Italian port   **165 fame** report

That yarely frame the office.° From the barge
A strange invisible perfume hits the sense
Of the adjacent wharfs.° The city cast                           215
Her people out upon her; and Antony,
Enthroned i' th' marketplace, did sit alone,
Whistling to th' air; which, but for vacancy,°
Had gone to gaze on Cleopatra too,
And made a gap in nature.
AGRIPPA                              Rare Egyptian!          220
ENOBARBUS
Upon her landing, Antony sent to her,
Invited her to supper. She replied,
It should be better he became her guest;
Which she entreated. Our courteous Antony,
Whom ne'er the word of "No" woman heard speak,    225
Being barbered ten times o'er, goes to the feast,
And, for his ordinary,° pays his heart
For what his eyes eat only.
AGRIPPA                              Royal wench!
She made great Caesar lay his sword to bed;
He plowed her, and she cropped.°
ENOBARBUS                            I saw her once           230
Hop forty paces through the public street;
And having lost her breath, she spoke, and panted,
That° she did make defect perfection,
And, breathless, pow'r breathe forth.
MAECENAS
Now Antony must leave her utterly.                              235
ENOBARBUS
Never; he will not:
Age cannot wither her, nor custom stale
Her infinite variety: other women cloy
The appetites they feed, but she makes hungry
Where most she satisfies; for vilest things                      240
Become themselves° in her, that the holy priests
Bless her when she is riggish.°
MAECENAS
If beauty, wisdom, modesty, can settle
The heart of Antony, Octavia is
A blessèd lottery° to him.
AGRIPPA                              Let us go.              245
Good Enobarbus, make yourself my guest
Whilst you abide here.
ENOBARBUS              Humbly, sir, I thank you. *Exeunt.*

[Scene III. *Rome. Caesar's house.*]

*Enter* ANTONY, CAESAR, OCTAVIA *between them.*

ANTONY
The world and my great office will sometimes
Divide me from your bosom.
OCTAVIA                              All which time
Before the gods my knee shall bow my prayers
To them for you.
ANTONY              Good night, sir. My Octavia,
Read not my blemishes in the world's report:                    5

I have not kept my square,° but that to come
Shall all be done by th' rule. Good night, dear lady.
Good night, sir.
CAESAR   Good night.              *Exit, [with* OCTAVIA].

*Enter* SOOTHSAYER.

ANTONY
Now, sirrah: you do wish yourself in Egypt?                     10
SOOTHSAYER
Would I had never come from thence, nor you
thither.
ANTONY
If you can, your reason?
SOOTHSAYER
I see it in my motion,° have it not in my tongue,
But yet hie you to Egypt again.
ANTONY                              Say to me,
Whose fortunes shall rise higher, Caesar's, or mine?    15
SOOTHSAYER   Caesar's.
Therefore, O Antony, stay not by his side.
Thy daemon,° that thy spirit which keeps thee, is
Noble, courageous, high, unmatchable,
Where Caesar's is not. But near him thy angel           20
Becomes afeard, as being o'erpow'red: therefore
Make space enough between you.
ANTONY                              Speak this no more.
SOOTHSAYER
To none but thee; no more but when to thee.
If thou dost play with him at any game,
Thou art sure to lose; and of° that natural luck        25
He beats thee 'gainst the odds. Thy luster thickens°
When he shines by: I say again, thy spirit
Is all afraid to govern thee near him;
But he away, 'tis noble.
ANTONY                              Get thee gone.
Say to Ventidius I would speak with him.                30
                                   *Exit* [SOOTHSAYER].
He shall to Parthia. Be it art or hap,°
He hath spoken true. The very dice obey him,
And in our sports my better cunning faints
Under his chance:° if we draw lots, he speeds;°
His cocks do win the battle still° of mine              35
When it is all to naught,° and his quails ever
Beat mine, inhooped,° at odds. I will to Egypt:
And though I make this marriage for my peace,
I' th' East my pleasure lies.

*Enter* VENTIDIUS.

                                   O, come, Ventidius,
You must to Parthia. Your commission's ready:           40
Follow me, and receive't.                    *Exeunt.*

[Scene IV. *Rome. A street.*]

*Enter* LEPIDUS, MAECENAS, *and* AGRIPPA.

213 yarely . . . office deftly perform the task   215 wharfs banks   218 but for vacancy i.e., but for the law that nature abhors a vacuum   227 ordinary public dinner in a tavern   230 she cropped i.e., had a child (Caesarion)   233 That so that   241 Become themselves are becoming   242 riggish wanton   245 lottery allotment

II.iii.6 kept my square kept straight   13 motion mind   18 daemon guardian angel   25 of by   26 thickens dims   31 art or hap skill or chance   34 chance luck; speeds is successful   35 still always   36 it . . . naught the odds are all to nothing (against him)   37 inhooped confined within a ring

LEPIDUS
Trouble yourselves no further: pray you, hasten
Your generals after.
AGRIPPA                    Sir, Mark Antony
Will e'en but kiss Octavia, and we'll follow.
LEPIDUS
Till I shall see you in your soldier's dress,
Which will become you both, farewell.
MAECENAS                          We shall.     5
As I conceive° the journey, be at Mount°
Before you, Lepidus.
LEPIDUS                    Your way is shorter;
My purposes do draw me much about:°
You'll win two days upon me.
BOTH                          Sir, good success.
LEPIDUS
Farewell.                          Exeunt. 10

[Scene V. Alexandria. Cleopatra's palace.]

Enter CLEOPATRA, CHARMIAN, IRAS, and ALEXAS.

CLEOPATRA
Give me some music: music, moody° food
Of us that trade in love.
OMNES°                    The music, ho!

Enter MARDIAN the eunuch.

CLEOPATRA
Let it alone, let's to billiards: come, Charmian.
CHARMIAN
My arm is sore; best play with Mardian.
CLEOPATRA
As well a woman with an eunuch played     5
As with a woman. Come, you'll play with me, sir?
MARDIAN   As well as I can, madam.
CLEOPATRA
And when good will is showed, though't come too
    short,
The actor may plead pardon. I'll none now.
Give me mine angle,° we'll to th' river: there,     10
My music playing far off, I will betray
Tawny-finned fishes. My bended hook shall pierce
Their slimy jaws; and as I draw them up,
I'll think them every one an Antony,
And say, "Ah, ha! y' are caught!"
CHARMIAN                    'Twas merry when 15
You wagered on your angling, when your diver
Did hang a salt° fish on his hook, which he
With fervency drew up.
CLEOPATRA          That time—O times!—
I laughed him out of patience; and that night
I laughed him into patience; and next morn,     20
Ere the ninth hour, I drunk him to his bed;
Then put my tires° and mantles on him, whilst
I wore his sword Philippan.°

Enter a MESSENGER.

                    O, from Italy!

Ram thou thy fruitful tidings in mine ears,
That long time have been barren.
MESSENGER                    Madam, madam—    25
CLEOPATRA
Antonio's dead! If thou say so, villain,
Thou kill'st thy mistress: but well and free,
If thou so yield him. There is gold and here
My bluest veins to kiss, a hand that kings
Have lipped, and trembled kissing.     30
MESSENGER
First, madam, he is well.
CLEOPATRA          Why, there's more gold.
But, sirrah, mark, we use
To say the dead are well:° bring it to that,
The gold I give thee will I melt and pour
Down thy ill-uttering throat.     35
MESSENGER
Good madam, hear me.
CLEOPATRA          Well, go to, I will:
But there's no goodness in thy face if Antony
Be free and healthful; so tart a favor°
To trumpet such good tidings? If not well,
Thou shouldst come like a Fury crowned with snakes,    40
Not like a formal° man.
MESSENGER          Will't please you hear me?
CLEOPATRA
I have a mind to strike thee ere thou speak'st:
Yet, if thou say Antony lives, is well,
Or friends with Caesar, or not captive to him,
I'll set thee in a shower of gold, and hail     45
Rich pearls upon thee.
MESSENGER          Madam, he's well.
CLEOPATRA                    Well said.
MESSENGER
And friends with Caesar.
CLEOPATRA          Th' art an honest man.
MESSENGER
Caesar and he are greater friends than ever.
CLEOPATRA
Make thee a fortune from me.
MESSENGER                    But yet, madam—
CLEOPATRA
I do not like "But yet"; it does allay     50
The good precedence:° fie upon "But yet";
"But yet" is as a jailer to bring forth
Some monstrous malefactor. Prithee, friend,
Pour out the pack of matter to mine ear,
The good and bad together: he's friends with Caesar,    55
In state of health, thou say'st, and thou say'st, free.
MESSENGER
Free, madam, no: I made no such report;
He's bound unto Octavia.
CLEOPATRA          For what good turn?°
MESSENGER
For the best turn i' th' bed.
CLEOPATRA          I am pale, Charmian.
MESSENGER
Madam, he's married to Octavia.     60

II.iv.6 conceive understand; Mount i.e., Misenum  8 My
. . . about My plans take me the long way around
II.v.1 moody melancholy (with pun on musical mood or key)
2 Omnes all (Latin)  10 angle fishing tackle  17 salt dried
22 tires headdresses  23 Philippan Antony's sword is named
after Philippi, where he conquered Brutus and Cassius

33 well i.e., in having gone to heaven  38 tart a favor
sour an expression  41 formal (1) sane (2) normally shaped
50–51 allay . . . precedence qualify the good news before it
58 For . . . turn she takes his "bound" in the sense "indebted
to"; he then takes up her "turn," or "act," in a sexual sense

CLEOPATRA
The most infectious pestilence upon thee!

*Strikes him down.*

MESSENGER
Good madam, patience.

CLEOPATRA          What say you? *Strikes him.* Hence,
Horrible villain! Or I'll spurn° thine eyes
Like balls before me: I'll unhair thy head,

*She hales him up and down.*

Thou shalt be whipped with wire and stewed in brine, 65
Smarting in ling'ring pickle.°

MESSENGER                    Gracious madam,
I that do bring the news made not the match.

CLEOPATRA
Say 'tis not so, a province I will give thee,
And make thy fortunes proud: the blow thou hadst
Shall make thy peace for moving me to rage,     70
And I will boot thee° with what gift beside
Thy modesty° can beg.

MESSENGER                He's married, madam.

CLEOPATRA
Rogue, thou hast lived too long. *Draw a knife.*

MESSENGER                         Nay, then I'll run.
What mean you, madam? I have made no fault. *Exit.*

CHARMIAN
Good madam, keep yourself within yourself,    75
The man is innocent.

CLEOPATRA
Some innocents 'scape not the thunderbolt.
Melt Egypt into Nile, and kindly creatures
Turn all to serpents! Call the slave again:
Though I am mad, I will not bite him. Call!    80

CHARMIAN
He is afeard to come.

CLEOPATRA            I will not hurt him.

                    [*Exit* CHARMIAN.]

These hands do lack nobility, that they strike
A meaner than myself; since I myself
Have given myself the cause.°

*Enter* [CHARMIAN *and*] *the* MESSENGER *again.*

                         Come hither, sir.
Though it be honest, it is never good         85
To bring bad news: give to a gracious message
An host of tongues, but let ill tidings tell
Themselves, when they be felt.

MESSENGER                    I have done my duty.

CLEOPATRA
Is he married?
I cannot hate thee worser than I do          90
If thou again say, "Yes."

MESSENGER                 He's married, madam.

CLEOPATRA
The gods confound° thee! Dost thou hold there still?

MESSENGER
Should I lie, madam?

CLEOPATRA            O, I would thou didst,

63 **spurn** kick  66 **pickle** pickling solution (of painful salt or acid)  71 **boot thee** compensate you  72 **modesty** humble rank  84 **the cause** i.e., by loving Antony  92 **confound** destroy

So° half my Egypt were submerged and made
A cistern for scaled snakes! Go get thee hence;   95
Hadst thou Narcissus in thy face,° to me
Thou wouldst appear most ugly. He is married?

MESSENGER
I crave your highness' pardon.

CLEOPATRA                    He is married?

MESSENGER
Take no offense that I would not offend you:°
To punish me for what you make me do          100
Seems much unequal:° he's married to Octavia.

CLEOPATRA
O, that his fault should make a knave of thee,
That art not what th' art sure of!° Get thee hence,
The merchandise which thou hast brought from Rome
Are all too dear for me. Lie they upon thy hand, 105
And be undone° by 'em!         [*Exit* MESSENGER.]

CHARMIAN            Good your highness, patience.

CLEOPATRA
In praising Antony I have dispraised Caesar.

CHARMIAN
Many times, madam.

CLEOPATRA          I am paid for't now.
Lead me from hence;
I faint. O, Iras, Charmian! 'Tis no matter.     110
Go to the fellow, good Alexas; bid him
Report the feature° of Octavia: her years,
Her inclination,° let him not leave out
The color of her hair. Bring me word quickly.

                         [*Exit* ALEXAS.]

Let him forever go!—let him not!—Charmian,    115
Though he be painted one way like a Gorgon,
The other way's a Mars.° [*To* MARDIAN.] Bid you
    Alexas
Bring me word how tall she is.—Pity me, Charmian,
But do not speak to me. Lead me to my chamber.

                              *Exeunt.*

[*Scene VI. Near Misenum.*]

*Flourish. Enter* POMPEY [*and* MENAS] *at one door, with
drum and trumpet: at another,* CAESAR, LEPIDUS,
ANTONY, ENOBARBUS, MAECENAS, AGRIPPA, *with*
SOLDIERS *marching.*

POMPEY
Your hostages I have, so have you mine;
And we shall talk before we fight.

CAESAR                           Most meet°
That first we come to words, and therefore have we
Our written purposes before us sent;
Which, if thou hast considered, let us know      5
If 'twill tie up thy discontented sword

94 **So** even if  96 **Hadst . . . face** even if you were as handsome as Narcissus (Greek youth of great beauty)  99 **Take . . . you** Do not be angry at me for hesitating to tell you what I know will anger you  101 **unequal** unjust  103 **That . . . of** who are not really as wicked as the news you insist on  106 **undone** bankrupted  112 **feature** appearance (not limited to facial characteristics)  113 **inclination** character  116–17 **Though . . . Mars** alluding to "perspective" pictures, trick paintings that showed contrasted figures—here a monstrous woman and the god of war—when looked at from opposite sides
**II.vi.2 meet** fit

And carry back to Sicily much tall° youth
That else must perish here.

POMPEY             To you all three,
The senators alone of this great world,
Chief factors° for the gods: I do not know     10
Wherefore my father should revengers want,°
Having a son and friends, since Julius Caesar,
Who at Philippi the good Brutus ghosted,°
There saw you laboring for him. What was't
That moved pale Cassius to conspire? And what    15
Made all-honored, honest, Roman Brutus,
With the armed rest, courtiers of beauteous freedom,
To drench the Capitol—but that they would
Have one man but a man?° And that is it
Hath made me rig my navy, at whose burden    20
The angered ocean foams; with which I meant
To scourge th' ingratitude that despiteful Rome
Cast on my noble father.

CAESAR            Take your time.

ANTONY
Thou canst not fear° us, Pompey, with thy sails.
We'll speak with thee° at sea. At land thou know'st    25
How much we do o'ercount thee.

POMPEY           At land indeed
Thou dost o'ercount° me of my father's house:
But since the cuckoo builds not for himself,
Remain in't as thou mayst.°

LEPIDUS           Be pleased to tell us
(For this is from the present°) how you take    30
The offers we have sent you.

CAESAR           There's the point.

ANTONY
Which do not be entreated to, but weigh
What it is worth embraced.°

CAESAR           And what may follow,
To try a larger fortune.°

POMPEY           You have made me offer
Of Sicily, Sardinia; and I must    35
Rid all the sea of pirates; then, to send
Measures of wheat to Rome; this 'greed upon,
To part with unhacked edges° and bear back
Our targes° undinted.

OMNES°           That's our offer.

POMPEY           Know then
I came before you here a man prepared    40
To take this offer. But Mark Antony
Put me to some impatience. Though I lose
The praise of it by telling, you must know,
When Caesar and your brother were at blows,

Your mother came to Sicily and did find    45
Her welcome friendly.

ANTONY         I have heard it, Pompey,
And am well studied for a liberal thanks,
Which I do owe you.°

POMPEY         Let me have your hand:
I did not think, sir, to have met you here.

ANTONY
The beds i' th' East are soft; and thanks to you,    50
That called me timelier° than my purpose hither;
For I have gained by't.

CAESAR         Since I saw you last
There's a change upon you.

POMPEY         Well, I know not
What counts° harsh Fortune casts° upon my face,
But in my bosom shall she never come    55
To make my heart her vassal.

LEPIDUS         Well met here.

POMPEY
I hope so, Lepidus. Thus we are agreed.
I crave our composition° may be written,
And sealed between us.

CAESAR         That's the next to do.

POMPEY
We'll feast each other ere we part, and let's    60
Draw lots who shall begin.

ANTONY         That will I, Pompey.

POMPEY
No, Antony, take the lot:
But, first or last, your fine Egyptian cookery
Shall have the fame. I have heard that Julius Caesar
Grew fat with feasting there.

ANTONY         You have heard much.    65

POMPEY
I have fair meanings, sir.

ANTONY         And fair words to them.

POMPEY
Then so much have I heard:
And I have heard Apollodorus carried—

ENOBARBUS
No more of that: he did so.

POMPEY         What, I pray you?

ENOBARBUS
A certain queen to Caesar in a mattress.    70

POMPEY
I know thee now; how far'st thou, soldier?

ENOBARBUS         Well;
And well am like to do, for I perceive
Four feasts are toward.°

POMPEY         Let me shake thy hand;
I never hated thee: I have seen thee fight
When I have envied thy behavior.

ENOBARBUS         Sir,    75
I never loved you much; but I ha' praised ye
When you have well deserved ten times as much
As I have said you did.

POMPEY         Enjoy thy plainness,

---

7 **tall** brave   10 **factors** agents   11 **want** lack   13 **ghosted** haunted   19 **but a man** merely a man (and not a king or demigod)   24 **fear** frighten   25 **speak with thee** meet you   27 **o'ercount** cheat (Antony had used it in the sense of "outnumber," but Pompey punningly alludes to a house Antony bought from the elder Pompey but did not pay for)   28–29 **But . . . mayst** But since cuckoos can't build (and therefore have to steal other birds' nests), keep it if you can hold on to it (Pompey includes in this sentence a jeering suggestion that Antony is a cuckold, a lover of a faithless woman)   30 **from the present** beside the point   33 **embraced** if accepted   33–34 **And . . . fortune** (1) and what the result may be, if you try to do better for yourself (i.e., risk war) (2) and the even greater things you may gain, if you join us and our affairs prosper   38 **edges** swords   39 **targes** shields; **Omnes** i.e., Caesar, Antony, Lepidus

47–48 **am . . . you** I am ready indeed to give you the free and full thanks that I owe you   51 **timelier** earlier   54 **counts** reckonings; **casts** (1) throws (2) sums up (the lines and wrinkles resulting from a hard life are compared to a bill of costs written out by a cruelly precise Fortune)   58 **composition** agreement   73 **toward** in the offing (accented "tòward")

It nothing ill becomes thee.°
Aboard my galley I invite you all:      80
Will you lead, lords?
ALL               Show's the way, sir.
POMPEY                      Come.
       *Exeunt. Manet*° ENOBARBUS *and* MENAS.
MENAS [*Aside.*] Thy father, Pompey, would ne'er
have made this treaty.—You and I have known,° sir.
ENOBARBUS    At sea, I think.
MENAS    We have, sir.                 85
ENOBARBUS    You have done well by water.
MENAS    And you by land.
ENOBARBUS    I will praise any man that will praise me;
though it cannot be denied what I have done by land.
MENAS    Nor what I have done by water.      90
ENOBARBUS    Yes, something you can deny for your
own safety: you have been a great thief by sea.
MENAS    And you by land.
ENOBARBUS    There I deny my land service.° But give
me your hand, Menas: if our eyes had authority,°   95
here they might take two thieves kissing.°
MENAS    All men's faces are true,° whatsome'er their
hands are.
ENOBARBUS    But there is never a fair woman has a
true face.                          100
MENAS    No slander; they steal hearts.
ENOBARBUS    We came hither to fight with you.
MENAS    For my part, I am sorry it is turned to a drink-
ing. Pompey doth this day laugh away his fortune.
ENOBARBUS    If he do, sure he cannot weep't back 105
again.
MENAS    Y' have said, sir. We looked not for Mark
Antony here. Pray you, is he married to Cleopatra?
ENOBARBUS    Caesar's sister is called Octavia.
MENAS    True, sir, she was the wife of Caius Marcellus. 110
ENOBARBUS    But she is now the wife of Marcus An-
tonius.
MENAS    Pray ye,° sir?
ENOBARBUS    'Tis true.
MENAS    Then is Caesar and he forever knit together. 115
ENOBARBUS    If I were bound to divine of this unity, I
would not prophesy so.
MENAS    I think the policy° of that purpose made more
in the marriage than the love of the parties.
ENOBARBUS    I think so too. But you shall find the 120
band that seems to tie their friendship together will be
the very strangler of their amity: Octavia is of a holy,
cold, and still conversation.°
MENAS    Who would not have his wife so?
ENOBARBUS    Not he that himself is not so; which is 125
Mark Antony. He will to his Egyptian dish again:
then shall the sighs of Octavia blow the fire up in
Caesar, and, as I said before, that which is the strength

of their amity shall prove the immediate author of
their variance. Antony will use his affection where it is. 130
He married but his occasion° here.
MENAS    And thus it may be. Come, sir, will you
aboard? I have a health for you.
ENOBARBUS    I shall take it, sir: we have used our
throats in Egypt.                  135
MENAS    Come, let's away.           *Exeunt.*

[Scene VII. *On board Pompey's galley, off Misenum.*]

*Music plays. Enter two or three* SERVANTS, *with a
banquet.*

FIRST SERVANT    Here they'll be, man. Some o' their
plants° are ill-rooted already; the least wind i' th'
world will blow them down.
SECOND SERVANT    Lepidus is high-colored.
FIRST SERVANT    They have made him drink alms   5
drink.°
SECOND SERVANT    As they pinch one another by the
disposition, he cries out, "No more";° reconciles them
to his entreaty, and himself to th' drink.
FIRST SERVANT    But it raises the greater war between 10
him and his discretion.
SECOND SERVANT    Why, this it is to have a name in
great men's fellowship. I had as lief have a reed that
will do me no service, as a partisan° I could not heave.
FIRST SERVANT    To be called into a huge sphere,° 15
and not to be seen to move° in't, are the holes where
eyes should be, which pitifully disaster° the cheeks.

*A sennet*° *sounded. Enter* CAESAR, ANTONY, POMPEY,
LEPIDUS, AGRIPPA, MAECENAS, ENOBARBUS,
MENAS, *with other* CAPTAINS.

ANTONY
Thus do they, sir: they take° the flow o' th' Nile
By certain scales i'° th' pyramid. They know
By th' height, the lowness, or the mean, if dearth   20
Or foison° follow. The higher Nilus swells,
The more it promises; as it ebbs, the seedsman
Upon the slime and ooze scatters his grain,
And shortly comes to harvest.
LEPIDUS    Y' have strange serpents there.    25
ANTONY    Ay, Lepidus.
LEPIDUS    Your° serpent of Egypt is bred now of your
mud by the operation of your sun: so is your crocodile.
ANTONY    They are so.
POMPEY    Sit—and some wine! A health to Lepidus! 30
LEPIDUS    I am not so well as I should be, but I'll ne'er
out.°

---

**131 occasion** convenience
**II.vii.2 plants** pun on foot or sole of foot   **5–6 alms drink** (1)
remains of liquor usually saved for alms people (2) drinking
done kindly, i.e., toasts given to smooth over quarrels   **8 No
more** (1) no more quarreling (2) no more to drink   **14 partisan**
great long-handled spear   **15 sphere** (1) area of influence (2)
revolving circle holding a star or planet, in the old astronomy
**16 move** (1) be active, influential (2) circle, like a planet   **17
disaster** ruin (with a suggestion of a star's malignant influence)
**17 s.d. sennet** trumpet call signaling the entrance of a great man
**18 take** measure   **19 scales i'** degree marks on   **20–21 dearth
Or foison** famine or plenty   **27 Your** a colloquialism suggesting casual knowledgeableness   **31–32 I'll ne'er out** I won't
give in

**79 It . . . thee** It suits you very well   **81 s.d. Manet**
Latin for "remains"; the plural is properly *manent*, but the
singular is often used for the plural, just as "exit" is often
used for "exeunt"   **83 known** met   **94 deny . . . service** a
quibble: "I claim exemption from military service" and "I
deny that I have been a thief"   **95 authority** authority to
arrest   **96 two thieves kissing** (1) two crooks fraternizing
(2) two thieving hands clasping   **97 true** (1) honest (2)
natural, without make-up   **113 Pray ye** pardon me (incredulous)   **118 policy** political expediency   **123 still conversation**
quiet manner

ENOBARBUS   Not till you have slept; I fear me you'll be in° till then.

LEPIDUS   Nay, certainly, I have heard the Ptolemies' 35 pyramises° are very goodly things; without contra- diction I have heard that.

MENAS [*Aside to* POMPEY.]
Pompey, a word.

POMPEY [*Aside to* MENAS.] Say in mine ear: what is't?

MENAS [*Aside to* POMPEY.]
Forsake thy seat, I do beseech thee, captain,
And hear me speak a word.

POMPEY [*Aside to* MENAS.] Forbear me till anon.°    40

[MENAS] *whispers in's ear.*

This wine for Lepidus!

LEPIDUS   What manner o' thing is your crocodile?

ANTONY   It is shaped, sir, like itself, and it is as broad as it hath breadth; it is just so high as it is, and moves with it° own organs. It lives by that which nourisheth 45 it, and the elements once out of it, it transmigrates.

LEPIDUS   What color is it of?

ANTONY   Of it own color too.

LEPIDUS   'Tis a strange serpent.

ANTONY   'Tis so; and the tears of it are wet.    50

CAESAR   Will this description satisfy him?

ANTONY   With the health that Pompey gives him; else he is a very epicure.

POMPEY [*Aside to* MENAS.]
Go hang, sir, hang! Tell me of that? Away!
Do as I bid you.—Where's this cup I called for?    55

MENAS [*Aside to* POMPEY.]
If for the sake of merit thou wilt hear me,
Rise from thy stool.

POMPEY [*Aside to* MENAS.]
           I think th' art mad. The matter?

[*Rises and walks aside.*]

MENAS
I have ever held my cap off to° thy fortunes.

POMPEY
Thou hast served me with much faith. What's else to
   say?
Be jolly, lords.

ANTONY        These quicksands, Lepidus,    60
Keep off them, for you sink.

MENAS
Wilt thou be lord of all the world?

POMPEY
                What say'st thou?

MENAS
Wilt thou be lord of the whole world? That's twice.

POMPEY
How should that be?

MENAS          But entertain it,°
And though thou think me poor, I am the man    65
Will give thee all the world.

POMPEY         Hast thou drunk well?

MENAS
No, Pompey, I have kept me from the cup.
Thou art, if thou dar'st be, the earthly Jove:

Whate'er the ocean pales,° or sky inclips,°
Is thine, if thou wilt ha't.

POMPEY         Show me which way.    70

MENAS
These three world-sharers, these competitors,°
Are in thy vessel. Let me cut the cable;
And when we are put off, fall to their throats.
All there is thine.

POMPEY        Ah, this thou shouldst have done,
And not have spoke on't. In me 'tis villainy,    75
In thee't had been good service. Thou must know,
'Tis not my profit that does lead mine honor;
Mine honor, it. Repent that e'er thy tongue
Hath so betrayed thine act. Being done unknown,
I should have found it afterwards well done,    80
But must condemn it now. Desist, and drink.

MENAS [*Aside.*]
For this,
I'll never follow thy palled° fortunes more.
Who seeks, and will not take when once 'tis offered,
Shall never find it more.

POMPEY        This health to Lepidus!    85

ANTONY
Bear him ashore. I'll pledge it for him, Pompey.

ENOBARBUS
Here's to thee, Menas!

MENAS        Enobarbus, welcome.

POMPEY   Fill till the cup be hid.

ENOBARBUS   There's a strong fellow, Menas.

[*Points to the* SERVANT *who carried off* LEPIDUS.]

MENAS   Why?    90

ENOBARBUS   'A° bears the third part of the world, man; see'st not?

MENAS
The third part then is drunk. Would it were all,
That it might go on wheels!°

ENOBARBUS
Drink thou: increase the reels.°    95

MENAS   Come.

POMPEY
This is not yet an Alexandrian feast.

ANTONY
It ripens towards it. Strike the vessels,° ho!
Here's to Caesar!

CAESAR        I could well forbear't.
It's monstrous labor when I wash my brain    100
And it grows fouler.

ANTONY        Be a child o' th' time.

CAESAR
Possess it, I'll make answer;°
But I had rather fast from all, four days,
Than drink so much in one.

ENOBARBUS         Ha, my brave emperor!
Shall we dance now the Egyptian bacchanals°    105
And celebrate our drink?

POMPEY        Let's ha't, good soldier.

---

**69 pales** fences in; **inclips** embraces   **71 competitors** partners
**83 palled** decayed   **91 'A** he   **94 go on wheels** (1) go easily
(2) spin wildly   **95 reels** (1) revels (2) staggering movements
**98 Strike the vessels** broach the casks   **102 Possess . . .**
**answer** Master the time (rather than be mastered by it), is
my answer   **105 bacchanals** riotous salute to Bacchus, god
of wine

---

**34 in** (1) in the game (2) in liquor   **36 pyramises** a false plural made up from the Latin singular; Lepidus is pretentious and drunk   **40 Forbear . . . anon** Leave me alone for a minute   **45 it** its   **58 held . . . to** treated respectfully   **64 But entertain it** only accept it

ANTONY
Come, let's all take hands
Till that the conquering wine hath steeped our sense
In soft and delicate Lethe.°

ENOBARBUS                    All take hands:
Make battery to our ears with the loud music;          110
The while I'll place you; then the boy shall sing.
The holding° every man shall bear as loud
As his strong sides can volley.

*Music plays.* ENOBARBUS *places them hand in hand.*

*The Song.*
      Come, thou monarch of the vine,
      Plumpy Bacchus with pink eyne!°          115
      In thy fats° our cares be drowned,
      With thy grapes our hairs be crowned.
        Cup us till the world go round,
        Cup us till the world go round!

CAESAR
What would you more? Pompey, good night. Good
    brother,          120
Let me request you off:° our graver business
Frowns at this levity. Gentle lords, let's part;
You see we have burnt our cheeks: strong Enobarb
Is weaker than the wine, and mine own tongue
Splits what it speaks: the wild disguise° hath almost   125
Anticked° us all. What needs more words? Good
    night.
Good Antony, your hand.

POMPEY                    I'll try you° on the shore.
ANTONY
And shall, sir. Give's your hand.
POMPEY                    O, Antony,
You have my father's house. But what, we are
    friends!
Come down into the boat.
        [*Exeunt all but* ENOBARBUS *and* MENAS.]

ENOBARBUS [*To* MENAS.] Take heed you fall not.   130
MENAS
I'll not on shore; no, to my cabin!
These drums! These trumpets, flutes! What!
Let Neptune hear we bid a loud farewell
To these great fellows. Sound and be hanged, sound
    out!

*Sound a flourish, with drums.*

ENOBARBUS
Hoo, says 'a. There's my cap.          135

[*Throws his cap in the air.*]

MENAS
Hoa! Noble captain, come.          *Exeunt.*

# [ ACT III ]

[Scene I. *A plain in Syria.*]

*Enter* VENTIDIUS *as it were in triumph, the dead body of*
*Pacorus borne before him;* [*with* SILIUS *and other*
ROMANS].

VENTIDIUS
Now, darting° Parthia, art thou struck; and now
Pleased Fortune does of Marcus Crassus'° death
Make me revenger. Bear the king's son's body
Before our army. Thy Pacorus, Orodes,
Pays this for Marcus Crassus.
SILIUS                    Noble Ventidius,          5
Whilst yet with Parthian blood thy sword is warm,
The fugitive Parthians follow. Spur through Media,
Mesopotamia, and the shelters whither
The routed fly. So thy grand captain, Antony,
Shall set thee on triumphant chariots, and          10
Put garlands on thy head.
VENTIDIUS                    O Silius, Silius,
I have done enough: a lower place,° note well,
May make too great an act. For learn this, Silius,
Better to leave undone, than by our deed
Acquire too high a fame when him we serve's away.   15
Caesar and Antony have ever won
More in their officer than person. Sossius,
One of my place° in Syria, his° lieutenant,
For quick accumulation of renown,
Which he achieved by th' minute,° lost his favor.   20
Who does i' th' wars more than his captain can
Becomes his captain's captain; and ambition
(The soldier's virtue) rather makes choice of loss
Than gain which darkens him.
I could do more to do Antonius good,          25
But 'twould offend him, and in his offense
Should my performance perish.°
SILIUS                    Thou hast, Ventidius, that
Without the which a soldier and his sword
Grants scarce distinction.° Thou wilt write to Antony?
VENTIDIUS
I'll humbly signify what in his name,          30
That magical word of war, we have effected;
How, with his banners and his well-paid ranks,
The ne'er-yet-beaten horse of Parthia
We have jaded° out o' th' field.
SILIUS                    Where is he now?
VENTIDIUS
He purposeth to Athens; whither, with what haste   35
The weight we must convey with's will permit,
We shall appear before him.—On, there; pass along.
                    *Exeunt.*

---

109 **Lethe** forgetfulness   112 **holding** refrain   115 **pink eyne**
half-closed eyes   116 **fats** vats   121 **request you off** beg you
leave the ship with me   125 **disguise** drunken revelry   126
**Anticked** made fools of   127 **try you** test your power (to
hold liquor)

**III.i.1 darting** the Parthians' method of attack was to fling
darts and then retreat swiftly, shooting arrows   **2 Marcus**
**Crassus** treacherously killed by Orodes, King of Parthia and
father of Pacorus   **12 lower place** subordinate   **18 place**
rank; **his** Antony's   **20 by th' minute** every minute, incessantly   **27 perish** i.e., lose its value to me   **27–29 that . . .**
**distinction** that quality (i.e., discretion) without which it is
hard to see any difference between a soldier and his sword
**34 jaded** driven like nags

[Scene II. *Rome. Caesar's house*.]

*Enter* AGRIPPA *at one door*, ENOBARBUS *at another*.

AGRIPPA
What, are the brothers parted?°

ENOBARBUS
They have dispatched with Pompey; he is gone;
The other three are sealing.° Octavia weeps
To part from Rome; Caesar is sad, and Lepidus
Since Pompey's feast, as Menas says, is troubled          5
With the green-sickness.°

AGRIPPA                    'Tis a noble Lepidus.

ENOBARBUS
A very fine one. O, how he loves Caesar!

AGRIPPA
Nay, but how dearly he adores Mark Antony!

ENOBARBUS
Caesar? Why, he's the Jupiter of men.

AGRIPPA
What's Antony? The god of Jupiter.          10

ENOBARBUS
Spake you of Caesar? How! The nonpareil!°

AGRIPPA
O Antony! O thou Arabian bird!°
Would you praise Caesar, say "Caesar": go no
    further.

AGRIPPA
Indeed, he plied them both with excellent praises.

ENOBARBUS
But he loves Caesar best, yet he loves Antony:          15
Hoo! Hearts, tongues, figures, scribes, bards, poets,
    cannot
Think, speak, cast,° write, sing, number—hoo!—
His love to Antony. But as for Caesar,
Kneel down, kneel down, and wonder.

AGRIPPA                              Both he loves.

ENOBARBUS
They are his shards,° and he their beetle. [*Trumpet
    within.*] So—                                        20
This is to horse. Adieu, noble Agrippa.

AGRIPPA
Good fortune, worthy soldier, and farewell!

*Enter* CAESAR, ANTONY, LEPIDUS, *and* OCTAVIA.

ANTONY
No further, sir.

CAESAR
You take from me a great part of myself;
Use me well in't. Sister, prove such a wife          25
As my thoughts make thee, and as my farthest band
Shall pass on thy approof.° Most noble Antony,
Let not the piece° of virtue which is set
Betwixt us as the cement° of our love
To keep it builded, be the ram to batter          30
The fortress of it: for better might we

Have loved without this mean,° if on both parts
This be not cherished.

ANTONY                    Make me not offended
In° your distrust.

CAESAR          I have said.

ANTONY                        You shall not find,
Though you be therein curious,° the least cause          35
For what you seem to fear. So the gods keep you
And make the hearts of Romans serve your ends!
We will here part.

CAESAR
Farewell, my dearest sister, fare thee well.
The elements be kind to thee, and make          40
Thy spirits all of comfort. Fare thee well.

OCTAVIA
My noble brother!

ANTONY
The April's in her eyes: it is love's spring,
And these the showers to bring it on. Be cheerful.

OCTAVIA
Sir, look well to my husband's house; and—

CAESAR                                        What,          45
Octavia?

OCTAVIA   I'll tell you in your ear.

ANTONY
Her tongue will not obey her heart, nor can
Her heart inform her tongue; the swan's-down feather
That stands upon the swell at the full of tide,          50
And neither way inclines.°

ENOBARBUS [*Aside to* AGRIPPA.]
Will Caesar weep?

AGRIPPA [*Aside to* ENOBARBUS.]
                    He has a cloud in's face.

ENOBARBUS [*Aside to* AGRIPPA.]
He were the worse for that, were he a horse;°
So is he, being a man.

AGRIPPA [*Aside to* ENOBARBUS.]   Why, Enobarbus,
When Antony found Julius Caesar dead,          55
He cried almost to roaring; and he wept
When at Philippi he found Brutus slain.

ENOBARBUS [*Aside to* AGRIPPA.]
That year indeed he was troubled with a rheum.°
What willingly he did confound° he wailed,
Believe't, till I wept too.

CAESAR                    No, sweet Octavia,          60
You shall hear from me still: the time shall not
Outgo my thinking on you.

ANTONY                    Come, sir, come,
I'll wrestle with you in my strength of love:
Look, here I have you; thus I let you go,
And give you to the gods.

CAESAR                    Adieu; be happy!          65

LEPIDUS
Let all the number of the stars give light
To thy fair way!

III.ii.1 **parted** departed   3 **sealing** making the last arrangements   6 **green-sickness** anemia supposed to affect lovesick
girls (Lepidus' hangover is attributed to his love of Antony and
Octavius)   11 **nonpareil** unequaled thing   12 **Arabian bird**
phoenix (unique and immortal)   17 **cast** count   20 **shards**
wings   26–27 **As my thoughts . . . approof** as I believe you
to be, and such as I would give my utmost bond that you will
triumphantly prove to be   28 **piece** masterpiece   29 **cement**
accented on first syllable

32 **mean** intermediary   34 **In** by   35 **curious** overscrupulous
49–51 **swan's . . . inclines** pressure of feeling urges Octavia
to speak but prevents her from finding the words; she hesitates
—like a feather held immobile by cross-currents at the turn of
the tide—between husband and brother, love and sorrow,
speech and silence   53 **horse** a horse with a dark face, or
without a white star on its face, was less prized   58 **rheum**
watering at the eyes   59 **confound** destroy

CAESAR        Farewell, farewell! *Kisses* OCTAVIA.
ANTONY                   Farewell!
                *Trumpets sound. Exeunt.*

[Scene III. *Alexandria. Cleopatra's palace.*]

*Enter* CLEOPATRA, CHARMIAN, IRAS, *and* ALEXAS.

CLEOPATRA
   Where is the fellow?
ALEXAS               Half afeard to come.
CLEOPATRA
   Go to, go to.

*Enter the* MESSENGER *as before.*°

           Come hither, sir.
ALEXAS             Good majesty,
   Herod of Jewry° dare not look upon you
   But when you are well pleased.
CLEOPATRA          That Herod's head
   I'll have: but how, when Antony is gone       5
   Through whom I might command it? Come thou
      near.
MESSENGER
   Most gracious majesty!
CLEOPATRA
   Didst thou behold Octavia?
MESSENGER    Ay, dread queen.
CLEOPATRA    Where?                      10
MESSENGER
   Madam, in Rome.
   I looked her in the face, and saw her led
   Between her brother and Mark Antony.
CLEOPATRA
   Is she as tall as me?
MESSENGER        She is not, madam.
CLEOPATRA
   Didst hear her speak? Is she shrill-tongued or low?    15
MESSENGER
   Madam, I heard her speak; she is low-voiced.
CLEOPATRA
   That's not so good.° He cannot like her long.
CHARMIAN
   Like her? O Isis! 'Tis impossible.
CLEOPATRA
   I think so, Charmian. Dull of tongue, and dwarfish.
   What majesty is in her gait? Remember,      20
   If e'er thou look'st on majesty.
MESSENGER           She creeps:
   Her motion and her station are as one.°
   She shows a body rather than a life,
   A statue than a breather.
CLEOPATRA        Is this certain?
MESSENGER
   Or I have no observance.
CHARMIAN          Three in Egypt      25
   Cannot make better note.
CLEOPATRA           He's very knowing,

I do perceive't. There's nothing in her yet.
The fellow has good judgment.
CHARMIAN            Excellent.
CLEOPATRA
Guess at her years, I prithee.
MESSENGER          Madam,
She was a widow—
CLEOPATRA      Widow? Charmian, hark.     30
MESSENGER
And I do think she's thirty.°
CLEOPATRA
Bear'st thou her face in mind? Is't long or round?
MESSENGER
Round, even to faultiness.
CLEOPATRA
For the most part, too, they are foolish that are so.
Her hair, what color?               35
MESSENGER
Brown, madam; and her forehead
As low as she would wish it.°
CLEOPATRA        There's gold for thee.
Thou must not take my former sharpness ill;
I will employ thee back again: I find thee
Most fit for business. Go, make thee ready;     40
Our letters are prepared.     [*Exit* MESSENGER.]
CHARMIAN          A proper° man.
CLEOPATRA
Indeed he is so: I repent me much
That so I harried him. Why, methinks, by him,
This creature's no such thing.°
CHARMIAN          Nothing, madam.
CLEOPATRA
The man hath seen some majesty, and should know.    45
CHARMIAN
Hath he seen majesty? Isis else defend,°
And serving you so long!
CLEOPATRA
I have one thing more to ask him yet, good Charmian;
But 'tis no matter, thou shalt bring him to me
Where I will write. All may be well enough.     50
CHARMIAN
I warrant you, madam.            *Exeunt.*

[Scene IV. *Athens. Antony's house.*]

*Enter* ANTONY *and* OCTAVIA.

ANTONY
Nay, nay, Octavia, not only that,
That were excusable, that and thousands more
Of semblable import°—but he hath waged
New wars 'gainst Pompey; made his will, and read it
To public ear;°                    5
Spoke scantly of me: when perforce he could not
But pay me terms of honor, cold and sickly
He vented them, most narrow measure° lent me;

---

III.iii.2 s.d. **as before** i.e., nervously, as he left her   **3 Herod of Jewry** i.e., even the fiercest of tyrants   **17 That's . . . good** (1) That's a nuisance. Nevertheless . . . (2) That's a bad thing to be   **22 Her motion . . . one** Moving and standing still are the same thing with her

**31 thirty** Cleopatra, being thirty-eight, lets this pass   **37 As low . . . it** colloquial phrase: low enough, and I hope she's pleased with it   **41 proper** excellent   **44 no such thing** nothing very much   **46 Isis else defend** Isis forbid
**III.iv.3 semblable import** similar significance   **4–5 made . . . ear** i.e., like Julius Caesar, made a will benefiting the people and so worked up popular support   **8 narrow measure** little credit

When the best hint was given him, he not took't,
Or did it from his teeth.°
OCTAVIA                    O, my good lord,          10
Believe not all; or, if you must believe,
Stomach° not all. A more unhappy lady,
If this division chance, ne'er stood between,
Praying for both parts.
The good gods will mock me presently°          15
When I shall pray, "O, bless my lord and husband!"—
Undo that prayer by crying out as loud,
"O, bless my brother!" Husband win, win brother,
Prays, and destroys the prayer; no midway
'Twixt these extremes at all.
ANTONY                        Gentle Octavia,          20
Let your best love draw to that point which seeks
Best to preserve it. If I lose mine honor,
I lose myself: better I were not yours
Than yours so branchless.° But, as you requested,
Yourself shall go between's: the meantime, lady,          25
I'll raise the preparation of a war
Shall stain° your brother. Make your soonest haste;
So your desires are yours.
OCTAVIA                    Thanks to my lord.
The Jove of power make me, most weak, most weak,
Your reconciler! Wars 'twixt you twain would be          30
As if the world should cleave, and that slain men
Should solder up the rift.
ANTONY
When it appears to you where this begins,
Turn your displeasure that way, for our faults
Can never be so equal that your love          35
Can equally move with them. Provide your going;
Choose your own company, and command what cost
Your heart has mind to.                    *Exeunt.*

[Scene V. *Athens. Antony's house.*]

*Enter* ENOBARBUS *and* EROS.

ENOBARBUS  How now, friend Eros?
EROS  There's strange news come, sir.
ENOBARBUS  What, man?
EROS  Caesar and Lepidus have made wars upon
Pompey.          5
ENOBARBUS  This is old. What is the success?°
EROS  Caesar, having made use of him in the wars
'gainst Pompey, presently denied him rivality,°
would not let him partake in the glory of the action;
and not resting here, accuses him of letters he had          10
formerly wrote to Pompey; upon his own appeal,°
seizes him; so the poor third is up,° till death enlarge
his confine.
ENOBARBUS
Then, world, thou hast a pair of chaps,° no more;
And throw between them all the food thou hast,          15
They'll grind the one the other.° Where's Antony?

10 **from his teeth** grudgingly  12 **Stomach** resent  15
**presently** immediately  24 **branchless** mutilated  27 **stain**
eclipse (the reputation of)
**III.v.6 success** sequel  8 **rivality** partnership  11 **upon . . .
appeal** on his (Caesar's) own accusation  12 **up** shut up,
imprisoned  14 **chaps** jaws  15–16 **And . . . other** and feed
them with all the victims in the world, they (Caesar and
Antony) will nevertheless meet, and one consume the other

EROS
He's walking in the garden—thus, and spurns
The rush that lies before him; cries "Fool Lepidus!"
And threats the throat of that his officer
That murd'red Pompey.°
ENOBARBUS                    Our great navy's rigged.          20
EROS
For Italy and Caesar. More, Domitius:
My lord desires you presently. My news
I might have told hereafter.
ENOBARBUS                        'Twill be naught;
But let it be. Bring me to Antony.
EROS  Come, sir.                              *Exeunt.* 25

[Scene VI. *Rome. Caesar's house.*]

*Enter* AGRIPPA, MAECENAS, *and* CAESAR.

CAESAR
Contemning° Rome, he has done all this and more
In Alexandria. Here's the manner of't:
I' th' marketplace on a tribunal silvered,
Cleopatra and himself in chairs of gold
Were publicly enthroned; at the feet sat          5
Caesarion, whom they call my father's° son,
And all the unlawful issue that their lust
Since then hath made between them. Unto her
He gave the stablishment° of Egypt; made her
Of lower Syria, Cyprus, Lydia,          10
Absolute queen.
MAECENAS          This in the public eye?
CAESAR
I' th' common showplace, where they exercise.
His sons he there proclaimed the kings of kings:
Great Media, Parthia, and Armenia
He gave to Alexander; to Ptolemy he assigned          15
Syria, Cilicia, and Phoenicia. She
In th' habiliments of the goddess Isis
That day appeared, and oft before gave audience,
As 'tis reported, so.
MAECENAS          Let Rome be thus informed.
AGRIPPA
Who, queasy° with his insolence already,          20
Will their good thoughts call from him.
CAESAR
The people knows it, and have now received
His accusations.
AGRIPPA          Who does he accuse?
CAESAR
Caesar: and that, having in Sicily
Sextus Pompeius spoiled,° we had not rated° him          25
His part o' th' isle. Then does he say he lent me
Some shipping, unrestored. Lastly, he frets
That Lepidus of the triumvirate
Should be deposed; and, being, that we detain
All this revenue.°
AGRIPPA          Sir, this should be answered.          30

20 **Pompey** Pompey has by now been murdered, according
to Plutarch, by Antony's command; Pompey would have
proved useful to Antony in the coming war
**III.vi.1 Contemning** despising  6 **my father** Octavius had
been adopted by Julius Caesar  9 **stablishment** possession  20
**queasy** disgusted  25 **spoiled** despoiled; **rated** allotted  30
**revenue** accented on second syllable

CAESAR
'Tis done already, and the messenger gone.
I have told him Lepidus was grown too cruel,
That he his high authority abused
And did deserve his change; for what I have con-
     quered,
I grant him part; but then in his Armenia,      35
And other of his conquered kingdoms, I
Demand the like.

MAECENAS      He'll never yield to that.

CAESAR
Nor must not then be yielded to in this.

*Enter* OCTAVIA, *with her* TRAIN.

OCTAVIA
Hail, Caesar, and my lord, hail, most dear Caesar!

CAESAR
That ever I should call thee castaway!      40

OCTAVIA
You have not called me so, nor have you cause.

CAESAR
Why have you stol'n upon us thus? You come not
Like Caesar's sister. The wife of Antony
Should have an army for an usher, and
The neighs of horse to tell of her approach      45
Long ere she did appear. The trees by th' way
Should have borne men, and expectation fainted,
Longing for what it had not. Nay, the dust
Should have ascended to the roof of heaven,
Raised by your populous troops. But you are come   50
A market maid to Rome, and have prevented
The ostentation° of our love; which, left unshown,
Is often left unloved.° We should have met you
By sea and land, supplying every stage
With an augmented greeting.

OCTAVIA                        Good my lord,      55
To come thus was I not constrained, but did it
On my free will. My lord, Mark Antony,
Hearing that you prepared for war, acquainted
My grievèd ear withal; whereon I begged
His pardon for return.

CAESAR                  Which soon he granted,   60
Being an abstract° 'tween his lust and him.

OCTAVIA
Do not say so, my lord.

CAESAR                   I have eyes upon him,
And his affairs come to me on the wind.
Where is he now?

OCTAVIA          My lord, in Athens.

CAESAR
No, my most wrongèd sister, Cleopatra      65
Hath nodded him to her. He hath given his empire
Up to a whore, who now° are levying
The kings o' th' earth for war. He hath assembled
Bocchus, the King of Libya; Archelaus,
Of Cappadocia; Philadelphos, King      70
Of Paphlagonia; the Thracian king, Adallas;
King Mauchus of Arabia; King of Pont;
Herod of Jewry; Mithridates, King

Of Comagene; Polemon and Amyntas,
The Kings of Mede and Lycaonia;      75
With a more larger list of scepters.

OCTAVIA                  Ay me most wretched,
That have my heart parted betwixt two friends
That does afflict each other!

CAESAR                      Welcome hither.
Your letters did withhold our breaking forth,
Till we perceived both how you were wrong led   80
And we in negligent danger.° Cheer your heart:
Be you not troubled with the time, which drives
O'er your content these strong necessities;
But let determined things to destiny
Hold unbewailed their way. Welcome to Rome,   85
Nothing more dear to me. You are abused°
Beyond the mark° of thought: and the high gods,
To do you justice, makes his ministers
Of us° and those that love you. Best of comfort,
And ever welcome to us.

AGRIPPA                 Welcome, lady.      90

MAECENAS
Welcome, dear madam.
Each heart in Rome does love and pity you.
Only th' adulterous Antony, most large°
In his abominations, turns you off
And gives his potent regiment to a trull°      95
That noises it° against us.

OCTAVIA                     Is it so, sir?

CAESAR
Most certain. Sister, welcome. Pray you
Be ever known to patience. My dear'st sister! *Exeunt.*

[Scene VII. *Near Actium. Antony's camp.*]

*Enter* CLEOPATRA *and* ENOBARBUS.

CLEOPATRA
I will be even with thee, doubt it not.

ENOBARBUS
But why, why, why?

CLEOPATRA
Thou hast forspoke° my being in these wars,
And say'st it is not fit.

ENOBARBUS            Well, is it, is it?

CLEOPATRA
Is't not denounced against us?° Why should not we   5
Be there in person?

ENOBARBUS [*Aside.*]   Well, I could reply:
If we should serve with horse and mares together,
The horse were merely° lost; the mares would bear
A soldier and his horse.

CLEOPATRA              What is't you say?

ENOBARBUS
Your presence needs must puzzle° Antony;      10
Take from his heart, take from his brain, from's time,

---

52 **ostentation** public display   53 **left unloved** (1) unrequited
(2) thought not to exist   61 **abstract** (1) immaterial, merely
notional thing (2) shortcut (3) symbol (of what prevented him
from indulging his lust)   67 **who now** and they now

81 **in negligent danger** endangered by doing nothing   86
**abused** deceived   87 **mark** reach   88–89 **makes . . . us**
make us their agents of justice   93 **large** loose, licentious   95
**potent . . . trull** powerful authority to a prostitute   96
**noises it** is clamorous
III.vii.3 **forspoke** spoken against   5 **denounced against us**
Caesar had declared, or denounced—the technical term—war
on Cleopatra personally   8 **merely** utterly   10 **puzzle**
bewilder, bring to a standstill

What should not then be spared. He is already
Traduced for levity; and 'tis said in Rome
That Photinus an eunuch and your maids
Manage this war.
CLEOPATRA     Sink Rome, and their tongues rot    15
That speak against us! A charge we bear i' th' war,
And as the president of my kingdom will
Appear there for a man. Speak not against it,
I will not stay behind.

*Enter* ANTONY *and* CANIDIUS.

ENOBARBUS     Nay, I have done.
Here comes the emperor.
ANTONY     Is it not strange, Canidius,    20
That from Tarentum and Brundusium
He could so quickly cut the Ionian sea
And take in° Toryne?—You have heard on't, sweet?
CLEOPATRA
Celerity is never more admired
Than by the negligent.
ANTONY     A good rebuke,    25
Which might have well becomed the best of men
To taunt at slackness. Canidius, we
Will fight with him by sea.
CLEOPATRA     By sea; what else?
CANIDIUS
Why will my lord do so?
ANTONY     For that° he dares us to't.
ENOBARBUS
So hath my lord dared him to single fight.    30
CANIDIUS
Ay, and to wage this battle at Pharsalia,
Where Caesar fought with Pompey: but these offers,
Which serve not for his vantage, he shakes off;
And so should you.
ENOBARBUS     Your ships are not well manned;
Your mariners are muleters,° reapers, people    35
Ingrossed by swift impress.° In Caesar's fleet
Are those that often have 'gainst Pompey fought;
Their ships are yare,° yours, heavy: no disgrace
Shall fall you for refusing him at sea,
Being prepared for land.
ANTONY     By sea, by sea.    40
ENOBARBUS
Most worthy sir, you therein throw away
The absolute soldiership you have by land,
Distract° your army, which doth most consist
Of war-marked footmen, leave unexecuted
Your own renownèd knowledge, quite forgo    45
The way which promises assurance, and
Give up yourself merely to chance and hazard'
From firm security.
ANTONY     I'll fight at sea.
CLEOPATRA
I have sixty sails, Caesar none better.
ANTONY
Our overplus of shipping will we burn,    50
And with the rest full-manned, from th' head of
Actium

Beat th' approaching Caesar. But if we fail,
We then can do't at land.

*Enter a* MESSENGER.

    Thy business?
MESSENGER
The news is true, my lord, he is descried;
Caesar has taken Toryne.    55
ANTONY
Can he be there in person? 'Tis impossible;
Strange that his power° should be. Canidius,
Our nineteen legions thou shalt hold by land
And our twelve thousand horse. We'll to our ship.
Away, my Thetis!°

*Enter a* SOLDIER.

    How now, worthy soldier?    60
SOLDIER
O noble emperor, do not fight by sea,
Trust not to rotten planks. Do you misdoubt
This sword and these my wounds? Let th' Egyptians
And the Phoenicians go a-ducking:° we
Have used to conquer standing on the earth    65
And fighting foot to foot.
ANTONY     Well, well: away!
    *Exit* ANTONY, CLEOPATRA, *and* ENOBARBUS.
SOLDIER
By Hercules, I think I am i' th' right.
CANIDIUS
Soldier, thou art; but his whole action grows
Not in the power on't:° so our leader's led,
And we are women's men.
SOLDIER     You keep by land    70
The legions and the horse whole, do you not?
CANIDIUS
Marcus Octavius, Marcus Justeius,
Publicola, and Caelius are for sea;
But we keep whole by land. This speed of Caesar's
Carries° beyond belief.
SOLDIER     While he was yet in Rome,    75
His power went out in such distractions° as
Beguiled all spies.
CANIDIUS     Who's his lieutenant, hear you?
SOLDIER
They say, one Taurus.
CANIDIUS     Well I know the man.

*Enter a* MESSENGER.

MESSENGER
The emperor calls Canidius.
CANIDIUS
With news the time's with labor, and throws forth    80
Each minute some.°     *Exeunt.*

---

**23 take in** conquer   **29 For that** because   **35 muleters** mule drivers   **36 Ingrossed . . . impress** collected by hasty conscription   **38 yare** swift, nimble   **43 Distract** (1) divide (2) confuse    **57 power** army   **60 Thetis** sea goddess, mother of Achilles   **64 a-ducking** (1) swimming like ducks (2) tipped underwater   **68–69 his . . . on't** his entire plan of action has developed away from its sources of power   **75 Carries** shoots him forward   **76 distractions** divisions   **80–81 With . . . some** More news is born every minute

[Scene VIII. *A plain near Actium.*]

*Enter* CAESAR, *with his* ARMY, *marching.*

CAESAR    Taurus!

TAURUS    My lord?

CAESAR
Strike not by land; keep whole, provoke not battle
Till we have done at sea. Do not exceed
The prescript of this scroll. Our fortune lies                5
Upon this jump.° *Exit,* [*with* TAURUS *and the* ARMY].

[Scene IX. *Another part of the plain.*]

*Enter* ANTONY *and* ENOBARBUS.

ANTONY
Set we our squadrons on yond side o' th' hill
In eye of Caesar's battle;° from which place
We may the number of the ships behold,
And so proceed accordingly. *Exit,* [*with* ENOBARBUS].

[Scene X. *Another part of the plain.*]

CANIDIUS *marcheth with his land* ARMY *one way over
the stage, and* TAURUS, *the lieutenant of Caesar,* [*with his*
ARMY,] *the other way. After their going in is heard the
noise of a sea fight. Alarum. Enter* ENOBARBUS.

ENOBARBUS
Naught,° naught, all naught! I can behold no longer.
Th' *Antoniad,* the Egyptian admiral,°
With all their sixty, fly and turn the rudder:
To see't mine eyes are blasted.

*Enter* SCARUS.

SCARUS                          Gods and goddesses,
All the whole synod° of them!

ENOBARBUS                    What's thy passion?       5

SCARUS
The greater cantle° of the world is lost
With very ignorance;° we have kissed away
Kingdoms and provinces.

ENOBARBUS                  How appears the fight?

SCARUS
On our side like the tokened pestilence,°
Where death is sure. Yon ribaudred° nag of Egypt—      10
Whom leprosy o'ertake!—i' th' midst o' th' fight,
When vantage like a pair of twins appeared,
Both as the same, or rather ours the elder,°
The breese° upon her, like a cow in June,
Hoists sails, and flies.

ENOBARBUS          That I beheld:                    15
Mine eyes did sicken at the sight, and could not
Endure a further view.

SCARUS                          She once being loofed,°
The noble ruin of her magic, Antony,
Claps on his sea wing, and (like a doting mallard°)
Leaving the fight in height, flies after her.            20
I never saw an action of such shame;
Experience, manhood, honor, ne'er before
Did violate so itself.

ENOBARBUS          Alack, alack!

*Enter* CANIDIUS.

CANIDIUS
Our fortune on the sea is out of breath,
And sinks most lamentably. Had our general              25
Been what he knew himself,° it had gone well.
O, he has given example for our flight
Most grossly by his own.

ENOBARBUS              Ay, are you thereabouts?°
Why then, good night indeed.

CANIDIUS
Toward Peloponnesus are they fled.                      30

SCARUS
'Tis easy to't; and there I will attend
What further comes.

CANIDIUS              To Caesar will I render
My legions and my horse; six kings already
Show me the way of yielding.

ENOBARBUS                      I'll yet follow
The wounded chance° of Antony, though my reason         35
Sits in the wind against me.°              [*Exeunt.*]

[Scene XI. *Alexandria. Cleopatra's palace.*]

*Enter* ANTONY, *with* ATTENDANTS.

ANTONY
Hark! The land bids me tread no more upon't,
It is ashamed to bear me. Friends, come hither.
I am so lated° in the world that I
Have lost my way forever. I have a ship
Laden with gold: take that, divide it; fly,              5
And make your peace with Caesar.

OMNES                          Fly? Not we.

ANTONY
I have fled myself, and have instructed cowards
To run and show their shoulders. Friends, be gone.
I have myself resolved upon a course
Which has no need of you. Be gone.                       10
My treasure's in the harbor. Take it. O,
I followed that° I blush to look upon.
My very hairs do mutiny, for the white
Reprove the brown for rashness,° and they them
For fear and doting. Friends, be gone; you shall        15
Have letters from me to some friends that will
Sweep your way for you. Pray you, look not sad,
Nor make replies of loathness; take the hint°

III.viii.6 jump risk
III.ix.2 battle battle line
III.x.1 Naught i.e., all's come to nothing    2 admiral flagship
5 synod assembly    6 cantle segment of a sphere    7 With very
ignorance by utter stupidity    9 tokened pestilence first fatal
symptoms of the plague    10 ribaudred apparently from
*ribald,* but of uncertain meaning; probably just a cursing word;
"filthy"    13 elder greater    14 breese gadfly (with pun on
*breeze, wind*)

17 loofed (1) luffed, i.e., with the head of a ship turned into the
wind (2) aloofed, rapidly departing    19 mallard wild duck
26 Been . . . himself been his true self—and he knew what
that was    28 are you thereabouts Is that where your thoughts
are?    35 wounded chance broken fortunes    36 Sits . . .
me is opposed to me
III.xi.3 lated belated (as of a traveler, caught by the encroaching night)    12 that what    14 rashness foolishness    18 hint
opportunity

Which my despair proclaims. Let that be left
Which leaves itself.° To the seaside straightway!          20
I will possess you of that ship and treasure.
Leave me, I pray, a little: pray you now,
Nay, do so; for indeed I have lost command,°
Therefore I pray you. I'll see you by and by.

*Sits down.*

*Enter* CLEOPATRA *led by* CHARMIAN, [IRAS,] *and*
EROS.

EROS   Nay, gentle madam, to him, comfort him.          25
IRAS   Do, most dear queen.
CHARMIAN   Do: why, what else?
CLEOPATRA   Let me sit down. O, Juno!
ANTONY   No, no, no, no, no.
EROS   See you here, sir?                                30
ANTONY   O, fie, fie, fie!
CHARMIAN   Madam!
IRAS   Madam, O, good empress!
EROS   Sir, sir!
ANTONY
Yes, my lord, yes. He° at Philippi kept                  35
His sword e'en like a dancer,° while I struck
The lean and wrinkled Cassius; and 'twas I
That the mad Brutus ended: he alone
Dealt on lieutenantry,° and no practice had
In the brave squares° of war: yet now—No matter.        40
CLEOPATRA   Ah, stand by.
EROS   The queen, my lord, the queen.
IRAS
Go to him, madam, speak to him;
He is unqualitied° with very shame.
CLEOPATRA
Well then, sustain me. O!                                45
EROS
Most noble sir, arise. The queen approaches.
Her head's declined, and death will seize her, but°
Your comfort makes the rescue.
ANTONY
I have offended reputation,°
A most unnoble swerving.
EROS                          Sir, the queen.            50
ANTONY
O, whither hast thou led me, Egypt? See
How I convey my shame out of thine eyes
By looking back° what I have left behind
'Stroyed in dishonor.
CLEOPATRA            O my lord, my lord,
Forgive my fearful sails! I little thought              55
You would have followed.
ANTONY            Egypt, thou knew'st too well
My heart was to thy rudder tied by th' strings,
And thou shouldst tow me after. O'er my spirit
Thy full supremacy thou knew'st, and that

Thy beck might from the bidding of the gods            60
Command me.
CLEOPATRA        O, my pardon!
ANTONY                      Now I must
To the young man send humble treaties, dodge
And palter in the shifts of lowness,° who
With half the bulk o' th' world played as I pleased,
Making and marring fortunes. You did know             65
How much you were my conqueror, and that
My sword, made weak by my affection,° would
Obey it on all cause.
CLEOPATRA          Pardon, pardon!
ANTONY
Fall° not a tear, I say; one of them rates°
All that is won and lost. Give me a kiss;             70
Even this repays me. We sent our schoolmaster:°
Is 'a come back? Love, I am full of lead.
Some wine, within there, and our viands! Fortune
   knows
We scorn her most when most she offers blows.
                                        *Exeunt.*


[Scene XII. *Egypt. Caesar's camp.*]

*Enter* CAESAR, AGRIPPA, DOLABELLA, [THIDIAS,]
*with others.*

CAESAR
Let him appear that's come from Antony.
Know you him?
DOLABELLA   Caesar, 'tis his schoolmaster:
An argument that he is plucked, when hither
He sends so poor a pinion of his wing,
Which had superfluous kings for messengers          5
Not many moons gone by.

*Enter* AMBASSADOR *from Antony.*

CAESAR                      Approach and speak.
AMBASSADOR
Such as I am, I come from Antony.
I was of late as petty to his ends
As is the morn-dew on the myrtle leaf
To his grand sea.°
CAESAR            Be't so. Declare thine office.      10
AMBASSADOR
Lord of his fortunes he salutes thee, and
Requires° to live in Egypt; which not granted,
He lessons° his requests, and to thee sues
To let him breathe between the heavens and earth,
A private man in Athens: this for him.                15
Next, Cleopatra does confess thy greatness,
Submits her to thy might, and of thee craves
The circle° of the Ptolemies for her heirs,
Now hazarded to thy grace.°
CAESAR                      For Antony,
I have no ears to his request. The queen            20

19–20 Let . . . itself Leave the man who has taken leave of his
senses (?) Leave the man who has given himself up for lost (?)
23 I . . . command (1) My feelings are becoming uncontrollable (2) I have lost the right to order you   35 He Octavius
36 like a dancer i.e., for ornament only   39 Dealt on lieutenantry told his subordinates how to fight   40 squares
squadrons   44 unqualitied beside himself   47 but unless   49
reputation honor   53 By looking back i.e., by averting my
eyes and by lonely meditation on

63 palter . . . lowness employ the tricks of a man brought
low   67 affection love   69 Fall let fall; rates (1) is worth
(2) berates, rebukes as unimportant   71 our schoolmaster
i.e., the tutor of his and Cleopatra's children
III.xii.10 To . . . sea (1) to the great sea that is its source and
end (2) to the great sea that is Antony   12 Requires requests
13 lessons disciplines (though perhaps the word should be
emended to "lessens")   18 circle crown   19 Now . . .
grace now dependent for its fate on your favor

Of audience nor desire shall fail, so° she
From Egypt drive her all-disgracèd friend
Or take his life there. This if she perform,
She shall not sue unheard. So to them both.

AMBASSADOR
Fortune pursue thee!

CAESAR                 Bring him through the bands.    25
                        [*Exit* AMBASSADOR.]

[*To* THIDIAS.]

To try thy eloquence now 'tis time. Dispatch.
From Antony win Cleopatra: promise,
And in our name, what she requires; add more,
From thine invention, offers.° Women are not
In their best fortunes strong, but want will perjure    30
The ne'er-touched vestal.° Try thy cunning, Thidias;
Make thine own edict° for thy pains, which we
Will answer as a law.

THIDIAS                Caesar, I go.

CAESAR
Observe how Antony becomes his flaw,°
And what thou think'st his very action speaks    35
In every power that moves.

THIDIAS            Caesar, I shall.    *Exeunt.*


[Scene XIII. *Alexandria. Cleopatra's palace.*]


Enter CLEOPATRA, ENOBARBUS, CHARMIAN, *and*
IRAS.

CLEOPATRA
What shall we do, Enobarbus?

ENOBARBUS                 Think, and die.

CLEOPATRA
Is Antony, or we, in fault for this?

ENOBARBUS
Antony only, that would make his will°
Lord of his reason. What though you fled
From that great face of war, whose several ranges    5
Frighted each other? Why should he follow?
The itch of his affection° should not then
Have nicked° his captainship, at such a point,
When half to half the world opposed, he being
The merèd question.° 'Twas a shame no less    10
Than was his loss, to course° your flying flags
And leave his navy gazing.

CLEOPATRA               Prithee, peace.

Enter the AMBASSADOR, *with* ANTONY.

ANTONY
Is that his answer?

AMBASSADOR
Ay, my lord.

ANTONY
The queen shall then have courtesy, so° she    15
Will yield us up.

AMBASSADOR     He says so.

ANTONY                 Let her know't.
To the boy Caesar send this grizzled head,
And he will fill thy wishes to the brim
With principalities.

CLEOPATRA            That head, my lord?

ANTONY
To him again! Tell him he wears the rose    20
Of youth upon him; from which the world should
    note
Something particular.° His coin, ships, legions
May be a coward's, whose ministers would prevail
Under the service of a child as soon
As i' th' command of Caesar. I dare him therefore    25
To lay his gay comparisons° apart
And answer me declined,° sword against sword,
Ourselves alone. I'll write it: follow me.
                [*Exeunt* ANTONY *and* AMBASSADOR.]

ENOBARBUS [*Aside.*]
Yes, like enough: high-battled° Caesar will
Unstate his happiness and be staged to th' show    30
Against a sworder!° I see men's judgments are
A parcel° of their fortunes, and things outward
Do draw the inward quality after them
To suffer all alike.° That he should dream,
Knowing all measures,° the full Caesar will    35
Answer his emptiness! Caesar, thou hast subdued
His judgment too.

Enter a SERVANT.

SERVANT         A messenger from Caesar.

CLEOPATRA
What, no more ceremony? See, my women,
Against the blown rose may they stop their nose
That kneeled unto the buds. Admit him, sir.    40
                        [*Exit* SERVANT.]

ENOBARBUS [*Aside.*]
Mine honesty and I begin to square.°
The loyalty well held to fools does make
Our faith° mere folly: yet he that can endure
To follow with allegiance a fall'n lord
Does conquer him that did his master conquer    45
And earns a place i' th' story.

Enter THIDIAS.

CLEOPATRA               Caesar's will?

THIDIAS
Hear it apart.

CLEOPATRA  None but friends: say boldly.

THIDIAS
So, haply,° are they friends to Antony.

---

21 **so** provided that  27–29 **promise . . . offers** possibly corrupt; rearranges to the much more lucid: "promise/What she requires and in our name add more/Offers from thine invention"  30 **perjure** make a perjurer of  31 **ne'er-touched vestal** immaculate virgin  32 **Make . . . edict** decree what you think the right reward  34 **becomes his flaw** takes his fall
**III.xiii.3 will** desire, lust  7 **affection** passion  8 **nicked** (1) maimed (2) got the better of  10 **merèd question** sole ground of dispute  11 **course** pursue

15 **so** if  22 **Something particular** i.e., a fact concerning Caesar  26 **comparisons** i.e., the ships, etc., which make him Antony's superior by comparison  27 **declined** i.e., in years and fortunes  29 **high-battled** elevated high by great armies  30–31 **Unstate . . . sworder** strip his good fortune of all its power, and make a public exhibition of himself against a gladiator  32 **parcel** part  34 **suffer all alike** deteriorate together  35 **knowing all measures** having experienced every measure of fortune  41 **square** quarrel  43 **faith** faithfulness  48 **haply** perhaps

ENOBARBUS
He needs as many, sir, as Caesar has,
Or needs not us. If Caesar please, our master  50
Will leap to be his friend; for us, you know,
Whose he is we are, and that is Caesar's.

THIDIAS                                So.
Thus then, thou most renowned: Caesar entreats
Not to consider in what case thou stand'st
Further than he is Caesar.°

CLEOPATRA              Go on: right royal.  55

THIDIAS
He knows that you embraced not Antony
As you did love, but as you feared him.

CLEOPATRA                              O!

THIDIAS
The scars upon your honor therefore he
Does pity, as constrainèd blemishes,
Not as deserved.

CLEOPATRA        He is a god, and knows  60
What is most right. Mine honor was not yielded,
But conquered merely.°

ENOBARBUS        [Aside.] To be sure of that,
I will ask Antony. Sir, sir, thou art so leaky
That we must leave thee to thy sinking, for
Thy dearest quit thee.        Exit ENOBARBUS.

THIDIAS            Shall I say to Caesar  65
What you require° of him? For he partly begs
To be desired to give. It much would please him
That of his fortunes you should make a staff
To lean upon. But it would warm his spirits
To hear from me you had left Antony,  70
And put yourself under his shroud,°
The universal landlord.

CLEOPATRA            What's your name?

THIDIAS
My name is Thidias.

CLEOPATRA        Most kind messenger,
Say to great Caesar this: in deputation°
I kiss his conqu'ring hand; tell him I am prompt  75
To lay my crown at 's feet, and there to kneel.
Tell him, from his all-obeying° breath I hear
The doom of Egypt.°

THIDIAS            'Tis your noblest course:
Wisdom and fortune combating together,
If that the former dare but what it can,°  80
No chance may shake it. Give me grace to lay
My duty° on your hand.

CLEOPATRA [Giving her hand.] Your Caesar's father oft,
When he hath mused of taking kingdoms in,
Bestowed his lips on that unworthy place,
As° it rained kisses.

Enter ANTONY and ENOBARBUS.

ANTONY            Favors, by Jove that thunders!  85
What art thou, fellow?

THIDIAS            One that but performs

The bidding of the fullest° man, and worthiest
To have command obeyed.

ENOBARBUS            [Aside.] You will be whipped.

ANTONY [Calling for SERVANTS.]
Approach there!—Ah, you kite!° Now, gods and
  devils!
Authority melts from me. Of late, when I cried,
  "Ho!"  90
Like boys unto a muss° kings would start forth,
And cry, "Your will?" Have you no ears? I am
Antony yet.

Enter a SERVANT [followed by others].

            Take hence this Jack° and whip him.

ENOBARBUS [Aside.]
'Tis better playing with a lion's whelp
Than with an old one dying.

ANTONY                Moon and stars!  95
Whip him! Were 't twenty of the greatest tributaries
That do acknowledge Caesar, should I find them
So saucy with the hand of she here—what's her name
Since she was Cleopatra? Whip him, fellows,
Till like a boy you see him cringe his face  100
And whine aloud for mercy. Take him hence.

THIDIAS
Mark Antony—

ANTONY            Tug him away. Being whipped,
Bring him again. The Jack of Caesar's shall
Bear us an errand to him.
            Exeunt [SERVANTS,] with THIDIAS.
You were half blasted° ere I knew you. Ha!  105
Have I my pillow left unpressed in Rome,
Forborne the getting° of a lawful race,
And by a gem of women, to be abused
By one that looks on feeders?°

CLEOPATRA            Good my lord—

ANTONY
You have been a boggler° ever:  110
But when we in our viciousness grow hard
(O misery on 't!) the wise gods seel° our eyes,
In our own filth drop our clear judgments, make us
Adore our errors, laugh at 's while we strut
To our confusion.°

CLEOPATRA        O, is 't come to this?  115

ANTONY
I found you as a morsel cold upon
Dead Caesar's trencher:° nay, you were a fragment°
Of Gneius Pompey's, besides what hotter hours,
Unregist'red in vulgar fame,° you have
Luxuriously picked out.° For I am sure,  120
Though you can guess what temperance should be,
You know not what it is.

CLEOPATRA            Wherefore is this?

---

87 **fullest** greatest (in character and fortunes)  89 **kite** ignoble
bird of prey  91 **muss** scramble, fighting heap of bodies  93
**Jack** fellow, knave  105 **blasted** worn out  107 **getting**
begetting  109 **feeders** servants, parasites  110 **boggler**
waverer  112 **seel** blind (in falconry, a hawk's eyelids are
seeled, or sewn up, before it grows used to being hooded)
115 **confusion** destruction  117 **trencher** wooden dish;
**fragment** leftover  119 **vulgar fame** common knowledge,
popular rumor  120 **Luxuriously picked out** lecherously
selected

---

55 **Caesar** i.e., famous for generosity  62 **merely** utterly  66
**require** request  71 **shroud** protection  74 **in deputation** by
proxy  77 **all-obeying** which all obey  78 **doom of Egypt**
judgment of the Queen of Egypt  80 **If . . . can** if a wise
man has the courage merely to go on being wise  82 **duty**
i.e., a kiss  85 **As** as if

ANTONY
To let a fellow that will take rewards
And say, "God quit° you!" be familiar with
My playfellow, your hand, this kingly seal  125
And plighter of high hearts. O, that I were
Upon the hill of Basan to outroar
The hornèd herd!° For I have savage cause,
And to proclaim it civilly were like
A haltered neck which does the hangman thank  130
For being yare° about him.

*Enter a* SERVANT, *with* THIDIAS.

Is he whipped?
SERVANT
Soundly, my lord.
ANTONY          Cried he? And begged 'a pardon?
SERVANT
He did ask favor.
ANTONY
If that thy father live, let him repent
Thou wast not made his daughter; and be thou sorry  135
To follow Caesar in his triumph, since
Thou hast been whipped for following him. Hence-
forth
The white hand of a lady fever thee,
Shake thou to look on't. Get thee back to Caesar,
Tell him thy entertainment:° look thou say  140
He makes me angry with him; for he seems
Proud and disdainful, harping on what I am,
Not what he knew I was. He makes me angry,
And at this time most easy 'tis to do't,
When my good stars that were my former guides  145
Have empty left their orbs° and shot their fires
Into th' abysm of hell. If he mislike
My speech and what is done, tell him he has
Hipparchus, my enfranchèd° bondman, whom
He may at pleasure whip, or hang, or torture,  150
As he shall like, to quit me. Urge it thou.
Hence with thy stripes, be gone!     *Exit* THIDIAS.
CLEOPATRA
Have you done yet?
ANTONY          Alack, our terrene moon°
Is now eclipsed, and it portends alone
The fall of Antony.
CLEOPATRA          I must stay his time.°  155
ANTONY
To flatter Caesar, would you mingle eyes
With one that ties his points?°
CLEOPATRA          Not know me yet?
ANTONY
Cold-hearted toward me?
CLEOPATRA          Ah, dear, if I be so,
From my cold heart let heaven engender hail,
And poison it in the source, and the first stone  160
Drop in my neck: as it determines,° so

Dissolve my life! The next Caesarion smite,
Till by degrees the memory° of my womb,
Together with my brave Egyptians all,
By the discandying° of this pelleted storm,  165
Lie graveless, till the flies and gnats of Nile
Have buried them for prey!
ANTONY          I am satisfied.
Caesar sits down in Alexandria, where
I will oppose his fate.° Our force by land
Hath nobly held; our severed navy too  170
Have knit again, and fleet,° threat'ning most sealike.
Where hast thou been, my heart?° Dost thou hear, lady?
If from the field I shall return once more
To kiss these lips, I will appear in blood;°
I and my sword will earn our chronicle.°  175
There's hope in't yet.
CLEOPATRA
That's my brave lord!
ANTONY
I will be treble-sinewed, hearted, breathed,°
And fight maliciously; for when mine hours
Were nice° and lucky, men did ransom lives  180
Of me for jests; but now I'll set my teeth
And send to darkness all that stop me. Come,
Let's have one other gaudy° night: call to me
All my sad captains; fill our bowls once more;
Let's mock the midnight bell.
CLEOPATRA          It is my birthday.  185
I had thought t' have held it poor. But since my lord
Is Antony again, I will be Cleopatra.
ANTONY
We will yet do well.
CLEOPATRA
Call all his noble captains to my lord.
ANTONY
Do so, we'll speak to them; and tonight I'll force  190
The wine peep through their scars. Come on, my queen,
There's sap in't yet! The next time I do fight,
I'll make death love me, for I will contend
Even with his pestilent scythe.
          *Exeunt [all but* ENOBARBUS].
ENOBARBUS
Now he'll outstare the lightning. To be furious  195
Is to be frighted out of fear, and in that mood
The dove will peck the estridge;° and I see still
A diminution in our captain's brain
Restores his heart. When valor preys on reason,
It eats the sword it fights with. I will seek  200
Some way to leave him.          *Exit.*

---

124 **quit** reward  126–28 **O . . . herd** i.e., Antony is so well provided with the cuckold's horns that he should be among the "fat bulls of Basan" of Psalm 22  131 **yare** deft  140 **entertainment** reception  146 **orbs** spheres  149 **enfranchèd** freed  153 **terrene moon** earthly Isis (goddess of the moon)  155 **stay his time** i.e., wait till his rage ends  157 **one . . . points** one who laces up his clothes, i.e., a valet  161 **determines** comes to an end, melts

163 **memory** memorials, heirs  165 **discandying** melting  169 **oppose his fate** challenge his destiny  171 **fleet** float  172 **heart** courage  174 **in blood** (1) covered with blood (2) in full vigor  175 **chronicle** place in history  178 **I . . . breathed** I will have the strength, courage, and expertise of three men  180 **nice** delicate, wanton  183 **gaudy** joyful  197 **estridge** goshawk (?) ostrich (?)

# [ A C T  I V ]

[Scene I. *Before Alexandria. Caesar's camp.*]

*Enter* CAESAR, AGRIPPA, *and* MAECENAS, *with his*
ARMY, CAESAR *reading a letter.*

CAESAR
He calls me boy, and chides as he had power
To beat me out of Egypt. My messenger
He hath whipped with rods; dares me to personal
    combat.
Caesar to Antony: let the old ruffian know
I have many other ways to die; meantime        5
Laugh at his challenge.
MAECENAS                    Caesar must think,
When one so great begins to rage,° he's hunted
Even to falling. Give him no breath, but now
Make boot of his distraction:° never anger
Made good guard for itself.
CAESAR              Let our best heads        10
Know that tomorrow the last of many battles
We mean to fight. Within our files° there are,
Of those that served Mark Antony but late,
Enough to fetch him in.° See it done,
And feast the army; we have store to do't,      15
And they have earned the waste. Poor Antony!
                                *Exeunt.*


[Scene II. *Alexandria. Cleopatra's palace.*]

*Enter* ANTONY, CLEOPATRA, ENOBARBUS, CHAR-
MIAN, IRAS, ALEXAS, *with others.*

ANTONY
He will not fight with me, Domitius?
ENOBARBUS                        No.
ANTONY
Why should he not?
ENOBARBUS
He thinks, being twenty times of better fortune,
He is twenty men to one.
ANTONY                Tomorrow, soldier,
By sea and land I'll fight: or° I will live,      5
Or bathe my dying honor in the blood
Shall make it live again. Woo't° thou fight well?
ENOBARBUS
I'll strike, and cry, "Take all!"°
ANTONY                Well said, come on;
Call forth my household servants; let's tonight
Be bounteous at our meal.

*Enter three or four* SERVITORS.

                Give me thy hand,        10
Thou hast been rightly honest—so hast thou—
Thou—and thou—and thou: you have served me well,
And kings have been your fellows.°
CLEOPATRA [*Aside to* ENOBARBUS.] What means this?

ENOBARBUS [*Aside to* CLEOPATRA.]
'Tis one of those odd tricks which sorrow shoots
Out of the mind.
ANTONY          And thou art honest too.        15
I wish I could be made so many men,
And all of you clapped up together in
An Antony, that I might do you service
So good as you have done.
OMNES                The gods forbid!
ANTONY
Well, my good fellows, wait on me tonight:      20
Scant not my cups, and make as much of me
As when mine empire was your fellow too
And suffered my command.°
CLEOPATRA [*Aside to* ENOBARBUS.]
                What does he mean?
ENOBARBUS [*Aside to* CLEOPATRA.]
To make his followers weep.
ANTONY                Tend me tonight;
May be it is the period° of your duty.          25
Haply° you shall not see me more; or if,
A mangled shadow. Perchance tomorrow
You'll serve another master. I look on you
As one that takes his leave. Mine honest friends,
I turn you not away, but like a master          30
Married to your good service; stay till death.
Tend me tonight two hours, I ask no more,
And the gods yield° you for't!
ENOBARBUS                What mean you, sir,
To give them this discomfort? Look, they weep,
And I, an ass, am onion-eyed; for shame,        35
Transform us not to women.
ANTONY                Ho, ho, ho!
Now the witch take me° if I meant it thus!
Grace° grow where those drops fall! My hearty friends,
You take me in too dolorous a sense,
For I spake to you for your comfort, did desire you    40
To burn this night with torches. Know, my hearts,
I hope well of tomorrow, and will lead you
Where rather I'll expect victorious life
Than death and honor.° Let's to supper, come,
And drown consideration.            *Exeunt.*    45


[Scene III. *Alexandria. Before Cleopatra's palace.*]

*Enter a company of* SOLDIERS.

FIRST SOLDIER
Brother, good night: tomorrow is the day.
SECOND SOLDIER
It will determine one way: fare you well.
Heard you of nothing strange about the streets?
FIRST SOLDIER
Nothing. What news?
SECOND SOLDIER
Belike° 'tis but a rumor. Good night to you.    5

---

**IV.i.7 rage** grow mad  **9 Make . . . distraction** profit from
his rage  **12 files** ranks  **14 fetch him in** capture him
**IV.ii.5 or** either  **7 Woo't** wilt  **8 Take all** all or nothing
**13 kings . . . fellows** kings have served me too, but no
better

**23 suffered my command** served under my authority  **25
period** end  **26 Haply** perhaps  **33 yield** reward  **37 the
witch take me** may I be bewitched  **38 Grace** (1) God's
grace, favor (2) herb of grace, rue  **44 death and honor**
honorable death
**IV.iii.5 Belike** probably

**FIRST SOLDIER**
Well, sir, good night. *They meet other* SOLDIERS.
**SECOND SOLDIER**   Soldiers, have careful watch.
**THIRD SOLDIER**
And you. Good night, good night.

*They place themselves in every corner of the stage.*

**SECOND SOLDIER**
Here we;° and if tomorrow
Our navy thrive, I have an absolute hope
Our landmen will stand up.
**FIRST SOLDIER**                'Tis a brave army,                    10
And full of purpose.

*Music of the hautboys is under the stage.*

**SECOND SOLDIER**   Peace! What noise?
**FIRST SOLDIER**                               List, list!
**SECOND SOLDIER**
Hark!
**FIRST SOLDIER**   Music i' th' air.
**THIRD SOLDIER**                Under the earth.
**FOURTH SOLDIER**
It signs° well, does it not?
**THIRD SOLDIER**                No.
**FIRST SOLDIER**                Peace, I say!
What should this mean?
**SECOND SOLDIER**
'Tis the god Hercules, whom Antony loved,            15
Now leaves him.
**FIRST SOLDIER**
Walk; let's see if other watchmen
Do hear what we do.
**SECOND SOLDIER**   How now, masters?
**OMNES** (*Speak together.*)                How now?
How now? Do you hear this?
**FIRST SOLDIER**                Ay. Is't not strange?
**THIRD SOLDIER**
Do you hear, masters? Do you hear?                  20
**FIRST SOLDIER**
Follow the noise so far as we have quarter.
Let's see how it will give off.°
**OMNES**
Content. 'Tis strange.                    *Exeunt.*


[Scene IV. *Alexandria. Cleopatra's palace.*]

*Enter* ANTONY *and* CLEOPATRA, *with* [CHARMIAN
*and*] *others* [*attending*].

**ANTONY**
Eros! Mine armor, Eros!
**CLEOPATRA**                Sleep a little.
**ANTONY**
No, my chuck.° Eros! Come, mine armor, Eros!

*Enter* EROS [*with armor*].

Come, good fellow, put thine iron° on.

---

8 **Here we** here is our post   13 **signs** signifies   22 **give off**
cease
IV.iv.2 **chuck** chick   3 **thine iron** that armor (of mine) you
hold

---

If Fortune be not ours today, it is
Because we brave her.° Come.
**CLEOPATRA**                Nay, I'll help too.        5
What's this for?
**ANTONY**        Ah, let be, let be! Thou art
The armorer of my heart. False,° false; this, this.
**CLEOPATRA**
Sooth, la, I'll help: thus it must be.
**ANTONY**                            Well, well,
We shall thrive now. See'st thou, my good fellow?
Go put on thy defenses.
**EROS**                Briefly,° sir.                    10
**CLEOPATRA**
Is not this buckled well?
**ANTONY**                Rarely, rarely:
He that unbuckles this, till we do please
To daff't° for our repose, shall hear a storm.
Thou fumblest, Eros, and my queen's a squire
More tight° at this than thou. Dispatch. O, love,       15
That thou couldst see my wars today, and knew'st
The royal occupation:° thou shouldst see
A workman° in't.

*Enter an armed* SOLDIER.

                Good morrow to thee; welcome:
Thou look'st like him that knows a warlike charge.°
To business that we love we rise betime              20
And go to't with delight.
**SOLDIER**                A thousand, sir,
Early though't be, have on their riveted trim,°
And at the port° expect you.

*Shout. Trumpets flourish. Enter* CAPTAINS *and*
SOLDIERS.

**CAPTAIN**
The morn is fair. Good morrow, general.
**ALL**
Good morrow, general.
**ANTONY**                'Tis well blown,° lads.        25
This morning, like the spirit of a youth
That means to be of note, begins betimes.
So, so. Come, give me that: this way; well said.°
Fare thee well, dame; whate'er becomes of me,
This is a soldier's kiss. Rebukable                 30
And worthy shameful check° it were to stand
On more mechanic compliment.° I'll leave thee
Now like a man of steel. You that will fight,
Follow me close; I'll bring you to't. Adieu.
                *Exeunt* [*all but* CLEOPATRA *and* CHARMIAN].
**CHARMIAN**
Please you retire to your chamber?
**CLEOPATRA**                Lead me.                    35
He goes forth gallantly. That he and Caesar might
Determine this great war in single fight!
Then Antony—but now—Well, on.                *Exeunt.*

---

4–5 **If . . . her** (1) If Fortune is not friendly to us today,
it will be because we defy her (2) We shall be fortunate today,
or we shall defy Fortune   7 **False** i.e., wrong piece   10
**Briefly** soon   13 **daff't** put it off   15 **tight** skilled   17 **royal**
**occupation** kingly trade   18 **workman** professional   19
**charge** duty   22 **riveted trim** armor   23 **port** gate   25 **well**
**blown** (1) i.e., on the trumpets (2) in full flower (of the morning)   28 **well said** well done   31 **shameful check** shaming
rebuke   31–32 **to . . . compliment** to make a business of
vulgar civilities

[Scene V. *Alexandria. Antony's camp.*]

*Trumpets sound. Enter* ANTONY *and* EROS, [*a* SOLDIER *meeting them*].

SOLDIER
The gods make this a happy° day to Antony!
ANTONY
Would thou and those thy scars had once prevailed
To make me fight at land!
SOLDIER         Hadst thou done so,
The kings that have revolted, and the soldier
That has this morning left thee, would have still    5
Followed thy heels.
ANTONY       Who's gone this morning?
SOLDIER              Who?
One ever near thee: call for Enobarbus,
He shall not hear thee, or from Caesar's camp
Say, "I am none of thine."
ANTONY       What sayest thou?
SOLDIER             Sir,
He is with Caesar.
EROS       Sir, his chests and treasure    10
He has not with him.
ANTONY      Is he gone?
SOLDIER        Most certain.
ANTONY
Go, Eros, send his treasure after; do it;
Detain no jot, I charge thee. Write to him
(I will subscribe°) gentle adieus and greetings;
Say that I wish he never find more cause    15
To change a master. O, my fortunes have
Corrupted honest men! Dispatch. Enobarbus!
           *Exit,* [*with* EROS *and* SOLDIER].

[Scene VI. *Alexandria. Caesar's camp.*]

*Flourish. Enter* AGRIPPA, CAESAR, *with* ENOBARBUS, *and* DOLABELLA.

CAESAR
Go forth, Agrippa, and begin the fight.
Our will is Antony be took alive:
Make it so known.
AGRIPPA
Caesar, I shall.            [*Exit.*]
CAESAR
The time of universal peace is near.    5
Prove this a prosp'rous day, the three-nooked° world
Shall bear the olive freely.

*Enter a* MESSENGER.

MESSENGER       Antony
Is come into the field.
CAESAR       Go charge Agrippa
Plant those that have revolted in the vant,°
That Antony may seem to spend his fury    10
Upon himself.      *Exeunt* [*all but* ENOBARBUS].
ENOBARBUS
Alexas did revolt and went to Jewry on
Affairs of Antony; there did dissuade°

IV.v.1 **happy** fortunate   14 **subscribe** sign
IV.vi.6 **three-nooked** three-cornered (Europe, Asia, Africa)
9 **vant** first lines   13 **dissuade** i.e., persuade to leave Antony

Great Herod to incline himself to Caesar
And leave his master Antony. For this pains    15
Caesar hath hanged him. Canidius and the rest
That fell away have entertainment, but
No honorable trust. I have done ill,
Of which I do accuse myself so sorely
That I will joy no more.

*Enter a* SOLDIER *of Caesar's.*

SOLDIER       Enobarbus, Antony    20
Hath after thee sent all thy treasure, with
His bounty overplus. The messenger
Came on my guard, and at thy tent is now
Unloading of his mules.
ENOBARBUS       I give it you.
SOLDIER
Mock not, Enobarbus:    25
I tell you true: best you safed the bringer
Out of the host;° I must attend mine office
Or would have done't myself. Your emperor
Continues still a Jove.        *Exit.*
ENOBARBUS
I am alone the° villain of the earth,    30
And feel I am so most.° O, Antony,
Thou mine of bounty, how wouldst thou have paid
My better service, when my turpitude
Thou dost so crown with gold! This blows° my
   heart.
If swift thought° break it not, a swifter mean    35
Shall outstrike thought; but thought will do't, I feel.
I fight against thee! No, I will go seek
Some ditch wherein to die: the foul'st best fits
My latter part of life.          *Exit.*

[Scene VII. *Field of battle between the camps.*]

*Alarum. Drums and trumpets. Enter* AGRIPPA [*and* SOLDIERS].

AGRIPPA
Retire; we have engaged ourselves too far:
Caesar himself has work,° and our oppression°
Exceeds what we expected.    *Exit,* [*with* SOLDIERS].

*Alarums. Enter* ANTONY, *and* SCARUS *wounded.*

SCARUS
O my brave emperor, this is fought indeed!
Had we done so at first, we had droven them home    5
With clouts° about their heads.
ANTONY       Thou bleed'st apace.
SCARUS
I had a wound here that was like a T,
But now 'tis made an H.° [*Retreat sounded*] *far off.*
ANTONY       They do retire.

26–27 **best . . . host** you had better see that the man who brought them has safe-conduct through enemy lines   30 **alone the** the only   31 **And . . . most** and no one could be more bitterly aware of it   34 **blows** swells   35 **thought** sorrow
IV.vii.2 **has work** is hard-pressed; **our oppression** the pressure on us   6 **clouts** (1) blows (2) bandages   8 **H** pun on *ache,* pronounced "aitch"

SCARUS
We'll beat 'em into bench holes.° I have yet
Room for six scotches° more.                                            10

*Enter* EROS.

EROS
They are beaten, sir, and our advantage serves
For a fair victory.
SCARUS                    Let us score° their backs
And snatch 'em up, as we take hares, behind:
'Tis sport to maul a runner.
ANTONY                              I will reward thee
Once for thy sprightly° comfort, and tenfold        15
For thy good valor. Come thee on.
SCARUS                                 I'll halt° after. *Exeunt.*

[Scene VIII. *Before Alexandria.*]

*Alarum. Enter* ANTONY *again in a march;* SCARUS,
*with others.*

ANTONY
We have beat him to his camp. Run one before
And let the queen know of our gests.° Tomorrow,
Before the sun shall see's, we'll spill the blood
That has today escaped. I thank you all,
For doughty-handed are you, and have fought        5
Not as you served the cause, but as't had been
Each man's like mine: you have shown all Hectors.
Enter the city, clip° your wives, your friends,
Tell them your feats, whilst they with joyful tears
Wash the congealment from your wounds, and kiss  10
The honored gashes whole.

*Enter* CLEOPATRA.

         [*To* SCARUS.] Give me thy hand;
To this great fairy° I'll commend thy acts,
Make her thanks bless thee.—O thou day o' th' world,
Chain mine armed neck; leap thou, attire and all,
Through proof of harness° to my heart, and there   15
Ride on the pants triumphing.
CLEOPATRA                          Lord of lords!
O infinite virtue,° com'st thou smiling from
The world's great snare uncaught?
ANTONY                                 Mine nightingale,
We have beat them to their beds. What, girl! Though
   gray
Do something mingle with our younger brown, yet
   ha' we                                               20
A brain that nourishes our nerves, and can
Get goal for goal of youth.° Behold this man:
Commend unto his lips thy favoring hand.—
Kiss it, my warrior.—He hath fought today
As if a god in hate of mankind had                    25
Destroyed in such a shape.
CLEOPATRA                    I'll give thee, friend,
An armor all of gold; it was a king's.

ANTONY
He has deserved it, were it carbuncled°
Like holy Phoebus' car.° Give me thy hand.
Through Alexandria make a jolly march;              30
Bear our hacked targets° like the men that owe° them.
Had our great palace the capacity
To camp this host, we all would sup together
And drink carouses to the next day's fate,
Which promises royal peril. Trumpeters,             35
With brazen din blast you the city's ear,
Make mingle with our rattling tabourines,°
That heaven and earth may strike their sounds together,
Applauding our approach.                   *Exeunt.*

[Scene IX. *Caesar's camp.*]

*Enter a* SENTRY *and his* COMPANY. ENOBARBUS
*follows.*

SENTRY
If we be not relieved with this hour,
We must return to th' court of guard. The night
Is shiny, and they say we shall embattle
By th' second hour i' th' morn.
FIRST WATCH                    This last day was
A shrewd° one to's.
ENOBARBUS           O, bear me witness, night—      5
SECOND WATCH
What man is this?
FIRST WATCH        Stand close, and list him.
ENOBARBUS
Be witness to me, O, thou blessèd moon,
When men revolted shall upon record
Bear hateful memory, poor Enobarbus did
Before thy face repent!
SENTRY                     Enobarbus?
SECOND WATCH                          Peace:       10
Hark further.
ENOBARBUS
O sovereign mistress° of true melancholy,
The poisonous damp of night disponge° upon me,
That life, a very rebel to my will,
May hang no longer on me. Throw my heart            15
Against the flint and hardness of my fault,
Which, being dried with grief, will break to powder,
And finish all foul thoughts. O, Antony,
Nobler than my revolt is infamous,
Forgive me in thine own particular,°               20
But let the world rank me in register°
A master-leaver° and a fugitive.
O, Antony! O, Antony!                        [*Dies.*]
FIRST WATCH              Let's speak to him.
SENTRY
Let's hear him, for the things he speaks
May concern Caesar.
SECOND WATCH     Let's do so. But he sleeps.       25

---

9 **bench holes** holes in a privy   10 **scotches** gashes   12
**score** slash   15 **sprightly** high-hearted   16 **halt** limp
**IV.viii.2 gests** deeds   8 **clip** embrace   12 **fairy** enchantress
15 **proof of harness** impenetrable armor   17 **virtue** valor
22 **Get . . . youth** keep pace with every point won by
youth

28 **carbuncled** jeweled   29 **Phoebus' car** the sun god's
chariot   31 **targets** shields; **owe** own   37 **tabourines** small
drums
**IV.ix.5 shrewd** curst, bad   12 **mistress** i.e., the moon   13
**disponge** drip   20 **in . . . particular** yourself   21 **in register** in its records   22 **master-leaver** (1) supreme traitor (2)
runaway servant

SENTRY
Swoons rather, for so bad a prayer as his
Was never yet for° sleep.
FIRST WATCH                    Go we to him.
SECOND WATCH
Awake, sir, awake; speak to us.
FIRST WATCH                    Hear you, sir?
SENTRY
The hand of death hath raught° him. *Drums afar off.*
  Hark! The drums
Demurely° wake the sleepers. Let us bear him          30
To th' court of guard: he is of note. Our hour
Is fully out.
SECOND WATCH
Come on then; he may recover yet.
                              *Exeunt, [with the body].*


[Scene X. *Between the two camps.*]

*Enter* ANTONY *and* SCARUS, *with their* ARMY.

ANTONY
Their preparation is today by sea;
We please them not by land.
SCARUS                    For both, my lord.
ANTONY
I would they'd fight i' th' fire or i' th' air;°
We'd fight there too. But this it is: our foot
Upon the hills adjoining to the city          5
Shall stay with us—order for sea is given;
They have put forth the haven—
Where their appointment we may best discover
And look on their endeavor.          *Exeunt.*


[Scene XI. *Between the two camps.*]

*Enter* CAESAR *and his* ARMY.

CAESAR
But being charged,° we will be still by land—
Which, as I take't, we shall, for his best force
Is forth to man his galleys. To the vales,
And hold our best advantage.°          *Exeunt.*


[Scene XII. *Before Alexandria.*]

*Enter* ANTONY *and* SCARUS.

ANTONY
Yet they are not joined.° Where yond pine does stand
I shall discover all. I'll bring thee word
Straight how 'tis like to go.          *Exit.*


*Alarum afar off, as at a sea fight.*°

SCARUS                    Swallows have built
In Cleopatra's sails their nests. The augurers
Say they know not, they cannot tell, look grimly,          5
And dare not speak their knowledge. Antony
Is valiant, and dejected, and by starts
His fretted° fortunes give him hope and fear
Of what he has, and has not.

*Enter* ANTONY.

ANTONY                    All is lost!
This foul Egyptian hath betrayèd me:          10
My fleet hath yielded to the foe, and yonder
They cast their caps up and carouse together
Like friends long lost. Triple-turned° whore! 'Tis thou
Hast sold me to this novice, and my heart
Makes only wars on thee. Bid them all fly;          15
For when I am revenged upon my charm,°
I have done all. Bid them all fly, be gone.
                              [*Exit* SCARUS.]
O sun, thy uprise shall I see no more.
Fortune and Antony part here, even here
Do we shake hands. All come to this? The hearts          20
That spanieled me at heels, to whom I gave
Their wishes, do discandy,° melt their sweets
On blossoming Caesar; and this pine is barked,°
That overtopped them all. Betrayed I am.
O this false soul of Egypt! This grave charm,°          25
Whose eye becked forth my wars, and called them
  home,
Whose bosom was my crownet, my chief end,°
Like a right° gypsy hath at fast and loose°
Beguiled me, to the very heart of loss.
What, Eros, Eros!

*Enter* CLEOPATRA.

                    Ah, thou spell! Avaunt!°          30
CLEOPATRA
Why is my lord enraged against his love?
ANTONY
Vanish, or I shall give thee thy deserving
And blemish Caesar's triumph. Let him take thee
And hoist thee up to the shouting plebeians;°
Follow his chariot, like the greatest spot°          35
Of all thy sex: most monsterlike be shown
For poor'st diminutives,° for dolts, and let
Patient Octavia plow thy visage up
With her preparèd nails.          *Exit* CLEOPATRA.
                    'Tis well th' art gone,
If it be well to live; but better 'twere          40

3 s.d. Alarum . . . fight the Folio prints this direction just before the entrance of Antony and Scarus; if F's placement is correct, the noise fills the otherwise empty stage for a moment and makes ironic Antony's first line, but probably the direction should be placed either in its present position or in the middle of line 9   8 fretted (1) checkered (2) worn, decayed   13 Triple-turned i.e., from Pompey, from Julius Caesar, from Antony   16 charm witch   22 discandy dissolve   23 barked stripped bare   25 grave charm deadly witch   27 crownet . . . end crown and end of all I did   28 right true; fast and loose a cheating game played by gypsies, in which the dupe inevitably fails to make fast a coiled rope   30 Avaunt Begone!   34 plebeians accented on first syllable   35 spot blemish   37 diminutives little people, i.e., the populace

27 for a prelude to   29 raught reached   30 Demurely soberly, with a low sound
IV.x.3 i' th' fire or i' th' air i.e., as well as the other two elements, earth and water (land and sea)
IV.xi.1 But being charged unless we are attacked   4 hold . . . advantage take up the best position we can
IV.xii.1 joined i.e., in battle

Thou fell'st into my fury, for one death
Might have prevented many. Eros, ho!
The shirt of Nessus is upon me; teach me,
Alcides, thou mine ancestor, thy rage.
Let me lodge Lichas on the horns o' th' moon,°   45
And with those hands that grasped the heaviest club
Subdue my worthiest self. The witch shall die:
To the young Roman boy she hath sold me, and I fall
Under this plot: she dies for't. Eros, ho!        *Exit.*

[Scene XIII. *Alexandria. Cleopatra's palace.*]

*Enter* CLEOPATRA, CHARMIAN, IRAS, MARDIAN.

CLEOPATRA
Help me, my women! O, he's more mad
Than Telamon° for his shield; the boar of Thessaly°
Was never so embossed.°
CHARMIAN                To th' monument:
There lock yourself, and send him word you are dead.
The soul and body rive° not more in parting   5
Than greatness going off.
CLEOPATRA                To th' monument!
Mardian, go tell him I have slain myself:
Say that the last I spoke was "Antony"
And word it, prithee, piteously. Hence, Mardian,
And bring me how he takes my death. To th' monument!               *Exeunt.* 10

[Scene XIV. *Alexandria. Cleopatra's palace.*]

*Enter* ANTONY *and* EROS.

ANTONY
Eros, thou yet behold'st me?
EROS                Ay, noble lord.
ANTONY
Sometime we see a cloud that's dragonish,
A vapor sometime like a bear or lion,
A towered citadel, a pendant rock,
A forkèd mountain, or blue promontory   5
With trees upon't that nod unto the world
And mock our eyes with air. Thou hast seen these signs:
Thy are black vesper's pageants.°
EROS                Ay, my lord.

ANTONY
That which is now a horse, even with a thought
The rack dislimns,° and makes it indistinct   10
As water is in water.
EROS                It does, my lord.
ANTONY
My good knave° Eros, now thy captain is
Even such a body: here I am Antony,
Yet cannot hold this visible shape, my knave.
I made these wars for Egypt; and the queen—   15
Whose heart I thought I had, for she had mine,
Which, whilst it was mine, had annexed unto't
A million moe,° now lost—she, Eros, has
Packed cards with Caesar, and false-played my glory
Unto an enemy's triumph.°   20
Nay, weep not, gentle Eros, there is left us
Ourselves to end ourselves.

*Enter* MARDIAN.

                O, thy vile lady!
She has robbed me of my sword.°
MARDIAN                No, Antony;
My mistress loved thee, and her fortunes mingled
With thine entirely.
ANTONY                Hence, saucy eunuch, peace!   25
She hath betrayed me and shall die the death.
MARDIAN
Death of one person can be paid but once,
And that she has discharged. What thou wouldst do
Is done unto thy hand.° The last she spake
Was "Antony! most noble Antony!"   30
Then in the midst a tearing groan did break
The name of Antony; it was divided
Between her heart and lips: she rend'red° life,
Thy name so buried in her.
ANTONY                Dead, then?
MARDIAN                Dead.
ANTONY
Unarm, Eros. The long day's task is done,   35
And we must sleep. [*To* MARDIAN.] That thou depart'st hence safe
Does pay thy labor richly: go.   *Exit* MARDIAN.
                Off, pluck off:
The sevenfold shield of Ajax° cannot keep
The battery° from my heart. O, cleave, my sides!
Heart, once be stronger than thy continent,°   40
Crack thy frail case! Apace, Eros, apace.
No more a soldier. Bruisèd pieces,° go;
You have been nobly borne.—From me awhile.
                *Exit* EROS.
I will o'ertake thee, Cleopatra, and
Weep for my pardon. So it must be, for now   45
All length° is torture: since the torch is out,
Lie down, and stray no farther. Now all labor

43–45 Nessus . . . moon the death of Antony's ancestor Hercules—called Alcides in line 44—is here recalled; Hercules killed the centaur Nessus with a poisoned arrow, for trying to rape his wife Deianira; the dying Nessus in revenge gave his robe, soaked in poisoned blood, to Deianira, pretending it would act as a love charm; she sent it to her husband for this purpose; in his dying agonies Hercules hurled the bringer of it, Lichas, high in the air
IV.xiii.2 Telamon Ajax, who went mad and killed himself when he lost the contest between himself and Odysseus for the arms and shield of Achilles; boar of Thessaly sent by Artemis to ravage the country of King Oeneus, and killed by his son Meleager   3 embossed (of a hunted animal) foaming at the mouth from fury and exhaustion   5 rive rend
IV.xiv.8 black vesper's pageants evening's brightly colored but unreal scenery ("pageants" = floats of the mystery plays, hence plays, masques, etc.)

9–10 even . . . dislimns as swift as thought the cloud formation ("rack") obliterates   12 knave boy   18 moe more   19–20 Packed . . . triumph stacked the cards to favor herself and Caesar, and so treacherously played her hand as to allow Caesar to trump my glory   23 sword i.e., soldiership, masculinity   29 unto thy hand already for you   33 rend'red surrendered   38 sevenfold . . . Ajax made of brass and lined with seven layers of oxhide   39 battery bombardment   40 thy continent what holds you in   42 pieces armor   46 length length of life

Mars what it does; yea, very force entangles
Itself with strength.° Seal then,° and all is done.
Eros!—I come, my queen.—Eros!—Stay for me.          50
Where souls do couch on flowers, we'll hand in hand,
And with our sprightly° port° make the ghosts gaze:
Dido and her Aeneas° shall want troops,°
And all the haunt be ours.—Come, Eros, Eros!

*Enter* EROS.

EROS
What would my lord?
ANTONY                 Since Cleopatra died,          55
I have lived in such dishonor that the gods
Detest my baseness. I, that with my sword
Quartered° the world and o'er green Neptune's back
With ships made cities, condemn myself to lack°
The courage of a woman; less noble mind          60
Than she which by her death our Caesar tells
"I am conqueror of myself." Thou art sworn, Eros,
That, when the exigent° should come, which now
Is come indeed, when I should see behind me
Th' inevitable prosecution° of          65
Disgrace and horror, that on my command
Thou then wouldst kill me. Do't, the time is come.
Thou strik'st not me, 'tis Caesar thou defeat'st.
Put color in thy cheek.
EROS                 The gods withhold me!
Shall I do that which all the Parthian darts,          70
Though enemy, lost aim and could not?
ANTONY                 Eros,
Wouldst thou be windowed in great Rome and see
Thy master thus: with pleached° arms, bending down
His corrigible° neck, his face subdued
To penetrative shame,° whilst the wheeled seat          75
Of fortunate Caesar, drawn before him, branded
His baseness that ensued?°
EROS                 I would not see't.
ANTONY
Come then; for with a wound I must be cured.
Draw that thy honest sword, which thou hast worn
Most useful for thy country.
EROS                 O, sir, pardon me.          80
ANTONY
When I did make thee free, swor'st thou not then
To do this when I bade thee? Do it at once,
Or thy precedent° services are all
But accidents unpurposed. Draw, and come.
EROS
Turn from me then that noble countenance          85
Wherein the worship of the whole world lies.

ANTONY
Lo thee!°

[*Turns from him.*]

EROS
My sword is drawn.
ANTONY                 Then let it do at once
The thing why thou hast drawn it.
EROS                 My dear master,
My captain, and my emperor, let me say,          90
Before I strike this bloody stroke, farewell.
ANTONY
'Tis said, man, and farewell.
EROS
Farewell, great chief. Shall I strike now?
ANTONY                 Now, Eros.
EROS
Why, there then! Thus I do escape the sorrow
Of Antony's death.                 *Kills himself.*
ANTONY                 Thrice-nobler than myself,          95
Thou teachest me, O valiant Eros, what
I should, and thou couldst not. My queen and Eros
Have by their brave instruction got upon me
A nobleness in record.° But I will be
A bridegroom in my death, and run into't          100
As to a lover's bed. Come then; and, Eros,
Thy master dies thy scholar. To do thus

[*Falls on his sword.*]

I learned of thee. How? Not dead? Not dead?
The guard, ho! O, dispatch me!

*Enter* [DECRETAS *and*] *a* [*company of the*] GUARD.

FIRST GUARD                 What's the noise?
ANTONY
I have done my work ill, friends. O, make an end          105
Of what I have begun.
SECOND GUARD                 The star is fall'n.
FIRST GUARD
And time is at his period.°
ALL                 Alas, and woe!
ANTONY
Let him that loves me strike me dead.
FIRST GUARD
Not I.
SECOND GUARD   Nor I.
THIRD GUARD                 Nor anyone. *Exeunt* [GUARD].
DECRETAS
Thy death and fortunes bid thy followers fly.          110
This sword but shown to Caesar, with this tidings,
Shall enter° me with him.

*Enter* DIOMEDES.

DIOMEDES
Where's Antony?
DECRETAS                 There, Diomed, there.
DIOMEDES                 Lives he?
Wilt thou not answer, man?          [*Exit* DECRETAS.]

---

48–49 **very . . . strength** the image probably is of a creature caught more tightly in a net by the very violence of its struggles   49 **Seal then** finish then (i.e., the final act of sealing a document, especially a will)   52 **sprightly** (1) high-hearted, gay (2) ghostly; **port** bearing   53 **Dido . . . Aeneas** the legendary lovers are brought together, though in Virgil, Dido repulses forever the faithless Aeneas; **want troops** lack retinue   58 **Quartered** (1) covered with troops (2) carved up   59 **to lack** for lacking   63 **exigent** need   65 **inevitable prosecution** unescapable pursuit   73 **pleached** folded (twisted behind?)   74 **corrigible** submissive   74–75 **subdued . . . shame** filled with the humiliation of deepest shame   76–77 **branded . . . ensued** made as hideously clear as the mark branded on a criminal or animal the abject nature of the man who followed   83 **precedent** former

87 **Lo thee** There you are, then!   98–99 **got . . . record** beaten me in achieving a noble place in the story   107 **period** end   112 **enter** recommend

ANTONY
Art thou there, Diomed? Draw thy sword, and give
    me                                                                            115
Sufficing strokes for death.
DIOMEDES                                  Most absolute lord,
My mistress Cleopatra sent me to thee.
ANTONY
When did she send thee?
DIOMEDES                                  Now, my lord.
ANTONY                                                          Where is she?
DIOMEDES
Locked in her monument. She had a prophesying fear
Of what hath come to pass; for when she saw        120
(Which never shall be found) you did suspect
She had disposed° with Caesar, and that your rage
Would not be purged,° she sent you word she was
    dead;
But, fearing since how it might work, hath sent
Me to proclaim the truth, and I am come,                125
I dread, too late.
ANTONY
Too late, good Diomed. Call my guard, I prithee.
DIOMEDES
What ho! The emperor's guard! The guard, what ho!
Come, your lord calls!

*Enter four or five of the* GUARD *of Antony.*

ANTONY
Bear me, good friends, where Cleopatra bides;       130
'Tis the last service that I shall command you.
FIRST GUARD
Woe, woe, are we, sir, you may not live to wear
All your true followers out.°
ALL                                          Most heavy day!
ANTONY
Nay, good my fellows, do not please sharp fate
To grace it with your sorrows. Bid that welcome    135
Which comes to punish us, and we punish it,
Seeming to bear it lightly. Take me up:
I have led you oft; carry me now, good friends,
And have my thanks for all.
              *Exit* [*the* GUARD,] *bearing* ANTONY.

[*Scene XV. Alexandria. The monument.*]

*Enter* CLEOPATRA *and her* MAIDS *aloft,*° *with* CHAR-
MIAN *and* IRAS.

CLEOPATRA
O, Charmian, I will never go from hence.
CHARMIAN
Be comforted, dear madam.
CLEOPATRA                        No, I will not.
All strange and terrible events are welcome,
But comforts we despise. Our size of sorrow,
Proportioned to our cause, must be as great            5
As that which makes it.

*Enter* DIOMED [*below*].

                                   How now? Is he dead?

122 **disposed** settled things   123 **purged** cured   132–33
**live . . . out** outlive all your faithful men
**IV.xv.s.d. aloft** presumably on the upper stage at the back of
the main stage

DIOMEDES
His death's upon him, but not dead.
Look out o' th' other side your monument;
His guard have brought him thither.

*Enter,* [*below,*] ANTONY, *and the* GUARD [*bearing him*].

CLEOPATRA                                  O sun,
Burn the great sphere thou mov'st in: darkling° stand  10
The varying shore o' th' world! O Antony,
Antony, Antony! Help, Charmian, help, Iras, help:
Help, friends below, let's draw him hither.°
ANTONY                                                          Peace!
Not Caesar's valor hath o'erthrown Antony,
But Antony's hath triumphed on itself.                   15
CLEOPATRA
So it should be, that none but Antony
Should conquer Antony, but woe 'tis so!
ANTONY
I am dying, Egypt, dying; only
I here importune° death awhile, until
Of many thousand kisses the poor last                   20
I lay upon thy lips.
CLEOPATRA                        I dare not,° dear;
Dear my lord, pardon: I dare not,
Lest I be taken. Not th' imperious show
Of the full-fortuned Caesar ever shall
Be brooched with me,° if knife, drugs, serpents have   25
Edge, sting, or operation. I am safe:
Your wife Octavia, with her modest eyes
And still conclusion,° shall acquire no honor
Demuring° upon me. But come, come, Antony—
Help me, my women—we must draw thee up:               30
Assist, good friends.
ANTONY                        O, quick, or I am gone.
CLEOPATRA
Here's sport indeed! How heavy weighs my lord!
Our strength is all gone into heaviness,°
That makes the weight. Had I great Juno's power,
The strong-winged Mercury should fetch thee up       35
And set thee by Jove's side. Yet come a little,
Wishers were ever fools. O, come, come, come.

*They heave* ANTONY *aloft to* CLEOPATRA.

And welcome, welcome! Die when thou hast lived,
Quicken° with kissing. Had my lips that power,
Thus would I wear them out.
ALL                                          A heavy sight!       40
ANTONY
I am dying, Egypt, dying.
Give me some wine, and let me speak a little.
CLEOPATRA
No, let me speak, and let me rail so high

10 **darkling** in darkness   12–13 **Help . . . hither** Shakespeare
appears to have made a false start, afterward left uncanceled, in
lines 12–13, or even to line 29; Cleopatra's plan for getting
Antony in is passed over, then repeated, in a curious way; and
Antony's "I am dying" is also repeated   19 **importune** beg
21 **dare not** i.e., dare not descend, or open the gates   25 **Be
. . . me** have me as its ornament   28 **still conclusion** (1)
silent judgment (2) impassive finality   29 **Demuring** looking
soberly   33 **heaviness** (1) weight (2) sorrow   39 **Quicken**
come to life

That the false housewife° Fortune break her wheel,°
Provoked by my offense.°
ANTONY          One word, sweet queen.  45
Of Caesar seek your honor, with your safety. O!
CLEOPATRA
They do not go together.
ANTONY          Gentle, hear me:
None about Caesar trust but Proculeius.
CLEOPATRA
My resolution and my hands I'll trust,
None about Caesar.  50
ANTONY
The miserable change now at my end
Lament nor sorrow at, but please your thoughts
In feeding them with those my former fortunes,
Wherein I lived; the greatest prince o' th' world,
The noblest; and do now not basely die,  55
Not cowardly put off my helmet to
My countryman; a Roman, by a Roman
Valiantly vanquished. Now my spirit is going,
I can no more.
CLEOPATRA    Noblest of men, woo't die?
Hast thou no care of me? Shall I abide  60
In this dull world, which in thy absence is
No better than a sty? O, see, my women,
               [ANTONY dies.]
The crown o' th' earth doth melt. My lord!
O, withered is the garland° of the war,
The soldier's pole° is fall'n: young boys and girls  65
Are level now with men. The odds° is gone,
And there is nothing left remarkable°
Beneath the visiting moon.

[Faints.]

CHARMIAN  O, quietness, lady!
IRAS  She's dead too, our sovereign.  70
CHARMIAN  Lady!
IRAS  Madam!
CHARMIAN  O madam, madam, madam!
IRAS  Royal Egypt! Empress!
CHARMIAN  Peace, peace, Iras!  75
CLEOPATRA
No more but e'en a woman, and commanded
By such poor passion as the maid that milks
And does the meanest chares.° It were for me
To throw my scepter at the injurious gods,
To tell them that this world did equal theirs  80
Till they had stol'n our jewel. All's but naught.
Patience is sottish,° and impatience does
Become a dog that's mad: then is it sin
To rush into the secret house of death
Ere death dare come to us? How do you, women?  85
What, what, good cheer! Why, how now, Charmian?
My noble girls! Ah, women, women, look,
Our lamp is spent, it's out. Good sirs,° take heart:

We'll bury him; and then, what's brave, what's noble,
Let's do't after the high Roman fashion,  90
And make death proud to take us. Come, away.
This case of that huge spirit now is cold.
Ah, women, women! Come; we have no friend
But resolution, and the briefest° end.
          Exeunt, bearing off Antony's body.

# [ACT V]

[Scene I. Alexandria. Caesar's camp.]

Enter CAESAR, AGRIPPA, DOLABELLA, MAECENAS,
[GALLUS, PROCULEIUS,] with his COUNCIL OF WAR.

CAESAR
Go to him, Dolabella, bid him yield:
Being so frustrate, tell him, he mocks
The pauses that he makes.°
DOLABELLA      Caesar, I shall.  [Exit.]

Enter DECRETAS, with the sword of Antony.

CAESAR
Wherefore is that? And what art thou that dar'st
Appear thus° to us?
DECRETAS      I am called Decretas.  5
Mark Antony I served, who best was worthy
Best to be served. Whilst he stood up and spoke,
He was my master, and I wore my life
To spend upon his haters. If thou please
To take me to thee, as I was to him  10
I'll be to Caesar; if thou pleasest not,
I yield thee up my life.
CAESAR      What is't thou say'st?
DECRETAS
I say, O Caesar, Antony is dead.
CAESAR
The breaking° of so great a thing should make
A greater crack.° The round world  15
Should have shook lions into civil° streets
And citizens to their dens. The death of Antony
Is not a single doom; in the name lay
A moiety° of the world.
DECRETAS      He is dead, Caesar,
Not by a public minister of justice  20
Nor by a hirèd knife; but that self° hand
Which writ his honor in the acts it did
Hath, with the courage which the heart did lend it,
Splitted the heart. This is his sword,
I robbed his wound of it: behold it stained  25
With his most noble blood.
CAESAR    [Weeping.] Look you, sad friends.
The gods rebuke me, but it is tidings
To wash the eyes of kings.
AGRIPPA      And strange it is

---

44 **false housewife** treacherous hussy, strumpet; **wheel** (1) spinning wheel (the especial property of a "housewife") (2) wheel of Fortune, whose turns govern the affairs of men  45 **offense** insults  64 **garland** flower, crown  65 **pole** (1) standard (2) polestar (3) Maypole (suggested by 'garland")  66 **odds** measure, distinctive value  67 **remarkable** wonderful  78 **chares** chores  82 **sottish** dully stupid  88 **sirs** used of women, as of men

94 **briefest** swiftest
V.i.2–3 **Being . . . makes** Tell him that, since he is truly defeated, these delays are a mere mockery  5 **thus** i.e., holding a naked sword  14 **breaking** (1) destruction (2) disclosure, report  15 **crack** (1) breach (2) explosive sound  16 **civil** city  19 **moiety** half  21 **self** selfsame

That nature must compel us to lament
Our most persisted° deeds.
MAECENAS                    His taints and honors      30
Waged equal with° him.
AGRIPPA                A rarer spirit never
Did steer humanity; but you gods will give us
Some faults to make us men. Caesar is touched.
MAECENAS
When such a spacious mirror's set before him,
He needs must see himself.
CAESAR                O Antony,      35
I have followed° thee to this. But we do launch°
Diseases in our bodies. I must perforce
Have shown to thee such a declining day
Or look on thine: we could not stall° together
In the whole world. But yet let me lament      40
With tears as sovereign° as the blood of hearts
That thou, my brother, my competitor
In top of all design,° my mate in empire,
Friend and companion in the front of war,
The arm of mine own body, and the heart      45
Where mine his° thoughts did kindle—that our stars,
Unreconciliable, should divide
Our equalness to this. Hear me, good friends—
*Enter an* EGYPTIAN.
But I will tell you at some meeter season.
The business of this man looks out of him;      50
We'll hear him what he says. Whence are you?
EGYPTIAN
A poor Egyptian yet.° The queen my mistress,
Confined in all she has, her monument,
Of thy intents desires instruction,
That she preparèdly may frame herself      55
To th' way she's forced to.
CAESAR                Bid her have good heart:
She soon shall know of us, by some of ours,
How honorable and how kindly we
Determine for her. For Caesar cannot live
To be ungentle.
EGYPTIAN        So the gods preserve thee!      *Exit.* 60
CAESAR
Come hither, Proculeius. Go and say
We purpose her no shame: give her what comforts
The quality of her passion° shall require,
Lest, in her greatness, by some mortal stroke
She do defeat us. For her life in Rome      65
Would be eternal in our triumph.° Go,
And with your speediest bring us what she says
And how you find of her.
PROCULEIUS        Caesar, I shall.
                    *Exit* PROCULEIUS.
CAESAR
Gallus, go you along. [*Exit* GALLUS.] Where's
    Dolabella,
To second Proculeius?
ALL                Dolabella!      70

CAESAR
Let him alone, for I remember now
How he's employed. He shall in time be ready.
Go with me to my tent, where you shall see
How hardly° I was drawn into this war,
How calm and gentle I proceeded still      75
In all my writings. Go with me, and see
What I can show in this.                *Exeunt.*

[Scene II. *Alexandria. The monument.*]

*Enter* CLEOPATRA, CHARMIAN, IRAS, *and* MARDIAN.

CLEOPATRA
My desolation does begin to make
A better life. 'Tis paltry to be Caesar:
Not being Fortune, he's but Fortune's knave,°
A minister of her will. And it is great
To do that thing that ends all other deeds,      5
Which shackles accidents and bolts up change;
Which sleeps, and never palates° more the dung,
The beggar's nurse and Caesar's.°

*Enter,* [*to the gates of the monument,*] PROCULEIUS,
[GALLUS, *and* SOLDIERS].

PROCULEIUS
Caesar sends greeting to the Queen of Egypt,
And bids thee study on what fair demands      10
Thou mean'st to have him grant thee.
CLEOPATRA                What's thy name?
PROCULEIUS
My name is Proculeius.
CLEOPATRA                Antony
Did tell me of you, bade me trust you, but
I do not greatly care to be deceived,°
That have no use for trusting. If your master      15
Would have a queen his beggar, you must tell him
That majesty, to keep decorum, must
No less beg than a kingdom: if he please
To give me conquered Egypt for my son,
He gives me so much of mine own as I      20
Will kneel to him with thanks.
PROCULEIUS                Be of good cheer:
Y' are fall'n into a princely hand, fear nothing.
Make your full reference freely° to my lord,
Who is so full of grace that it flows over
On all that need. Let me report to him      25
Your sweet dependency, and you shall find
A conqueror that will pray in aid for kindness,°
Where he for grace is kneeled to.
CLEOPATRA                Pray you, tell him
I am his fortune's vassal, and I send him
The greatness he has got. I hourly learn      30
A doctrine of obedience, and would gladly
Look him i' th' face.
PROCULEIUS                This I'll report, dear lady.

30 **persisted** persisted in    31 **Waged equal with** were equally matched in    36 **followed** pursued; **launch** lance    39 **stall** dwell    41 **sovereign** potent    42–43 **my competitor . . . design** my partner in noblest enterprise    46 **his** its    52 **yet** still (though Egypt will soon be Roman)    63 **passion** strong emotion (here, grief)    65–66 **For . . . triumph** Alive, in Rome, walking in my triumphal procession, she would manifest my power to the end of time

74 **hardly** reluctantly
**V.ii.3 knave** servant    7 **palates** tastes    7–8 **dung . . . Caesar's** the dungy earth, whose fruits are the source of life to beggar and to emperor    14 **to be deceived** whether or not I am deceived    23 **Make . . . freely** hand your affairs fully    27 **pray . . . kindness** beg you to assist him to be kind to you

Have comfort, for I know your plight is pitied
Of him that caused it.

[*Enter* GALLUS *and* SOLDIERS *behind.*]°

You see how easily she may be surprised.     35

[*They seize* CLEOPATRA.]

Guard her till Caesar come.

IRAS    Royal Queen!

CHARMIAN    O, Cleopatra! Thou art taken, queen.

CLEOPATRA
Quick, quick, good hands! [*Draws a dagger.*]

PROCULEIUS            Hold, worthy lady, hold!

[*Disarms her.*]

Do not yourself such wrong, who are in this    40
Relieved,° but not betrayed.

CLEOPATRA          What, of death too,
That rids our dogs of languish?°

PROCULEIUS           Cleopatra,
Do not abuse my master's bounty by
Th' undoing of yourself: let the world see
His nobleness well acted, which your death    45
Will never let come forth.°

CLEOPATRA          Where art thou, death?
Come hither, come! Come, come, and take a queen
Worth many babes and beggars!

PROCULEIUS          O, temperance, lady!

CLEOPATRA
Sir, I will eat no meat, I'll not drink, sir—
If idle talk will once be necessary—    50
I'll not sleep neither. This mortal house I'll ruin,
Do Caesar what he can. Know, sir, that I
Will not wait pinioned° at your master's court
Nor once be chastised with the sober eye
Of dull Octavia. Shall they hoist me up    55
And show me to the shouting varletry°
Of censuring Rome? Rather a ditch in Egypt
Be gentle grave unto me! Rather on Nilus' mud
Lay me stark nak'd and let the waterflies
Blow° me into abhorring! Rather make    60
My country's high pyramides° my gibbet
And hang me up in chains!

PROCULEIUS          You do extend
These thoughts of horror further than you shall
Find cause in Caesar.

*Enter* DOLABELLA.

DOLABELLA          Proculeius,
What thou hast done, thy master Caesar knows,    65
And he hath sent for thee. For the queen,
I'll take her to my guard.

PROCULEIUS          So, Dolabella,
It shall content me best: be gentle to her

[*To* CLEOPATRA.]

To Caesar I will speak what you shall please,
If you'll employ me to him.

CLEOPATRA          Say, I would die.    70
         *Exit* PROCULEIUS, [*with* SOLDIERS].

DOLABELLA
Most noble empress, you have heard of me?

CLEOPATRA
I cannot tell.

DOLABELLA    Assuredly you know me.

CLEOPATRA
No matter, sir, what I have heard or known.
You laugh when boys or women tell their dreams;
Is't not your trick?°

DOLABELLA          I understand not, madam.    75

CLEOPATRA
I dreamt there was an Emperor Antony.
O, such another sleep, that I might see
But such another man.

DOLABELLA          If it might please ye—

CLEOPATRA
His face was as the heav'ns, and therein stuck
A sun and moon, which kept their course and lighted    80
The little O, th' earth.

DOLABELLA          Most sovereign creature—

CLEOPATRA
His legs bestrid the ocean: his reared arm
Crested the world: his voice was propertied
As all the tunèd spheres,° and that to friends;
But when he meant to quail° and shake the orb,    85
He was as rattling thunder. For his bounty,
There was no winter in't: an autumn 'twas
That grew the more by reaping. His delights
Were dolphinlike, they showed his back above
The element they lived in. In his livery°    90
Walked crowns and crownets:° realms and islands were
As plates° dropped from his pocket.

DOLABELLA          Cleopatra—

CLEOPATRA
Think you there was or might be such a man
As this I dreamt of?

DOLABELLA          Gentle madam, no.

CLEOPATRA
You lie, up to the hearing of the gods.    95
But if there be nor ever were one such,
It's past the size of dreaming;° nature wants stuff
To vie strange forms with fancy, yet t' imagine
An Antony were nature's piece 'gainst fancy,
Condemning shadows quite.°

DOLABELLA          Hear me, good madam.    100

---

**75 trick** way   **83–84 propertied . . . spheres** musical as the spheres (referring to the belief in the music of the spheres, made by the harmonious blend of each planet's "note" and normally too fine for human ears to catch)   **85 quail** make quail   **90 livery** (1) service (2) possession, guardianship (legal term)   **91 crowns and crownets** i.e., kings and princes   **92 plates** silver coins   **96–97 But . . . dreaming** but suppose you were right, and no such man exists, and never did exist, how can I have imagined such a man, for no mere dreaming fantasy could make something so great   **97–100 nature . . . quite** reality lacks the material to compete with imagination in the creation of strange forms, yet the creation of an Antony would be a masterpiece of conception on the part of reality, surpassing and discrediting all the illusions of imagination

---

**34 s.d.** the Folio gives no stage direction here; it was presumably left to the stage performance to decide on the procedure by which the Romans capture the tomb   **41 Relieved** rescued   **42 languish** lingering illness   **46 let come forth** allow to be revealed   **53 pinioned** with clipped wings   **56 varletry** mob   **60 Blow** swell   **61 pyramides** four syllables, accented on second

Your loss is as yourself, great; and you bear it
As answering to the weight. Would I might never
O'ertake pursued success, but I do° feel,
By the rebound of yours, a grief that smites
My very heart at root.

CLEOPATRA                    I thank you, sir.          105
Know you what Caesar means to do with me?

DOLABELLA
I am loath to tell you what I would you knew.

CLEOPATRA
Nay, pray you, sir.

DOLABELLA          Though he be honorable—

CLEOPATRA
He'll lead me, then, in triumph?

DOLABELLA
Madam, he will. I know't.          110

*Flourish. Enter* PROCULEIUS, CAESAR, GALLUS,
MAECENAS, *and others of his* TRAIN.

ALL
Make way there! Caesar!

CAESAR
Which is the Queen of Egypt?

DOLABELLA
It is the emperor, madam.

*Cleopatra kneels.*

CAESAR
Arise! You shall not kneel:
I pray you rise; rise, Egypt.

CLEOPATRA                    Sir, the gods          115
Will have it thus. My master and my lord
I must obey.

CAESAR          Take to you no hard thoughts.
The record of what injuries you did us,
Though written in our flesh, we shall remember
As things but done by chance.

CLEOPATRA                    Sole sir o' th' world,          120
I cannot project° mine own cause so well
To make it clear,° but do confess I have
Been laden with like frailties which before
Have often shamed our sex.

CAESAR                    Cleopatra, know,
We will extenuate rather than enforce.°          125
If you apply° yourself to our intents,
Which towards you are most gentle, you shall find
A benefit in this change; but if you seek
To lay on me a cruelty by taking
Antony's course, you shall bereave yourself          130
Of my good purposes, and put your children
To that destruction which I'll guard them from
If thereon you rely. I'll take my leave.

CLEOPATRA
And may, through all the world: 'tis yours, and we,
Your scutcheons° and your signs of conquest, shall          135
Hang in what place you please. Here, my good lord.

[*Hands him a paper.*]

CAESAR
You shall advise me in all for Cleopatra.

CLEOPATRA
This is the brief° of money, plate, and jewels
I am possessed of. 'Tis exactly valued,
Not petty things admitted. [*Calling.*] Where's Seleucus?          140

[*Enter* SELEUCUS.]

SELEUCUS    Here, madam.

CLEOPATRA
This is my treasurer; let him speak, my lord,
Upon his peril, that I have reserved
To myself nothing. Speak the truth, Seleucus.

SELEUCUS
Madam,          145
I had rather seel° my lips than to my peril
Speak that which is not.

CLEOPATRA                    What have I kept back?

SELEUCUS
Enough to purchase what you have made known.

CAESAR
Nay, blush not, Cleopatra, I approve
Your wisdom in the deed.

CLEOPATRA                    See, Caesar: O, behold,          150
How pomp is followed! Mine° will now be yours,
And should we shift estates, yours would be mine.
The ingratitude of this Seleucus does
Even make me wild. O slave, of no more trust
Than love that's hired! What, goest thou back? Thou shalt          155
Go back, I warrant thee; but I'll catch thine eyes,
Though they had wings. Slave, soulless villain, dog!
O rarely° base!

CAESAR          Good queen, let us entreat you.

CLEOPATRA
O Caesar, what a wounding shame is this,
That thou vouchsafing here to visit me,          160
Doing the honor of thy lordliness
To one so meek, that mine own servant should
Parcel° the sum of my disgraces by
Addition of his envy.° Say, good Caesar,
That I some lady° trifles have reserved,          165
Immoment° toys, things of such dignity
As we greet modern° friends withal; and say
Some nobler token I have kept apart
For Livia° and Octavia, to induce
Their mediation—must I be unfolded          170
With° one that I have bred? The gods! it smites me
Beneath the fall I have. [*To* SELEUCUS.] Prithee go hence,
Or I shall show the cinders° of my spirits
Through th' ashes of my chance.° Wert thou a man,
Thou wouldst have mercy on me.

CAESAR                    Forbear, Seleucus.          175
[*Exit* SELEUCUS.]

CLEOPATRA
Be it known that we, the greatest, are misthought°

103 **but I do** if I do not   121 **project** set forth (accented on
first syllable)   122 **clear** innocent   125 **enforce** emphasize
126 **apply** conform   135 **scutcheons** armorial bearings (alluding to the captured shields displayed by a conqueror)

138 **brief** summary   146 **seel** sew up   151 **Mine** i.e., my
followers   158 **rarely** exceptionally   163 **Parcel** piece out
164 **envy** malice   165 **lady** lady's   166 **Immoment** unimportant   167 **modern** ordinary   169 **Livia** Caesar's wife
170–71 **unfolded With** exposed by   173 **cinders** burning
coals   174 **chance** fortune   176 **misthought** misjudged

For things that others do, and when we fall,
We answer others' merits in our name,°
Are therefore to be pitied.
CAESAR                    Cleopatra,
Not what you have reserved, nor what acknowledged, 180
Put we i' th' roll of conquest: still be't yours,
Bestow it at your pleasure, and believe
Caesar's no merchant, to make prize° with you
Of things that merchants sold. Therefore be cheered,
Make not your thoughts your prisons: no, dear queen, 185
For we intend so to dispose you as
Yourself shall give us counsel. Feed and sleep:
Our care and pity is so much upon you
That we remain your friend; and so adieu.
CLEOPATRA
My master, and my lord!
CAESAR              Not so. Adieu.          190
        *Flourish. Exeunt* CAESAR *and his* TRAIN.
CLEOPATRA
He words me, girls, he words me, that I should not
Be noble to myself! But hark thee, Charmian.

[*Whispers to* CHARMIAN.]

IRAS
Finish, good lady, the bright day is done,
And we are for the dark.
CLEOPATRA              Hie thee again:
I have spoke already, and it is provided;          195
Go put it to the haste.
CHARMIAN              Madam, I will.

*Enter* DOLABELLA.

DOLABELLA
Where is the queen?
CHARMIAN              Behold, sir.          [*Exit.*]
CLEOPATRA              Dolabella!
DOLABELLA
Madam, as thereto sworn, by your command
(Which my love makes religion to obey)
I tell you this: Caesar through Syria          200
Intends his journey, and within three days
You with your children will he send before.
Make your best use of this. I have performed
Your pleasure, and my promise.
CLEOPATRA              Dolabella,
I shall remain your debtor.
DOLABELLA              I, your servant.          205
Adieu, good queen; I must attend on Caesar.
CLEOPATRA
Farewell, and thanks.          *Exit* [DOLABELLA].
              Now, Iras, what think'st thou?
Thou, an Egyptian puppet,° shall be shown
In Rome as well as I: mechanic slaves°
With greasy aprons, rules, and hammers shall          210
Uplift us to the view. In their thick breaths,

Rank of gross diet,° shall we be enclouded,
And forced to drink their vapor.
IRAS                    The gods forbid!
CLEOPATRA
Nay, 'tis most certain, Iras. Saucy lictors°
Will catch at us like strumpets, and scald° rhymers          215
Ballad us out o' tune. The quick comedians
Extemporally will stage us, and present
Our Alexandrian revels: Antony
Shall be brought drunken forth, and I shall see
Some squeaking Cleopatra boy my greatness°          220
I' th' posture of a whore.
IRAS              O, the good gods!
CLEOPATRA
Nay, that's certain.
IRAS
I'll never see't! For I am sure mine nails
Are stronger than mine eyes.
CLEOPATRA              Why, that's the way
To fool their preparation, and to conquer          225
Their most absurd intents.

*Enter* CHARMIAN.

                    Now, Charmian!
Show me, my women, like a queen: go fetch
My best attires. I am again for Cydnus,
To meet Mark Antony. Sirrah° Iras, go.
Now, noble Charmian, we'll dispatch indeed,          230
And when thou hast done this chare,° I'll give thee
    leave
To play till doomsday.—Bring our crown and all.
              [*Exit* IRAS.] *A noise within.*
Wherefore's this noise?

*Enter a* GUARDSMAN.

GUARDSMAN              Here is a rural fellow
That will not be denied your highness' presence:
He brings you figs.          235
CLEOPATRA
Let him come in.              *Exit* GUARDSMAN.
              What poor an° instrument
May do a noble deed! He brings me liberty.
My resolution's placed,° and I have nothing
Of woman in me: now from head to foot
I am marble-constant: now the fleeting moon°          240
No planet is of mine.

*Enter* GUARDSMAN *and* CLOWN° [*with basket*].

GUARDSMAN              This is the man.
CLEOPATRA
Avoid,° and leave him.          *Exit* GUARDSMAN.
Hast thou the pretty worm of Nilus° there,
That kills and pains not?

---

178 **We . . . name** (1) we have to be responsible for faults committed in our name ("merits" = deserts, acts deserving punishment) (2) our name is used to validate the actions of others  183 **make prize** haggle  208 **puppet** she envisages Iras as a doll manipulated by the puppeteer, Octavius—i.e., a figure posed on a float following Caesar in the triumphal procession  209 **mechanic slaves** vulgar workmen

212 **Rank . . . diet** stinking of bad food  214 **Saucy lictors** insolent officers  215 **scald** scurvy  220 **boy my greatness** reduce my greatness to the crude imitation that a boy can manage (in England women's parts were acted by boys or young men)  229 **Sirrah** an address to inferiors, used equally of men or women  231 **chare** chore  236 **What poor an** what a poor  238 **placed** fixed  240 **fleeting moon** a symbol of fickleness, especially in women; and Cleopatra's special symbol, as being Isis or moon goddess  241 s.d. **Clown** rustic  242 **Avoid** depart  243 **worm of Nilus** serpent of Nile, i.e., asp or small viper

CLOWN   Truly I have him; but I would not be the 245
party that should desire you to touch him, for his
biting is immortal:° those that do die of it do seldom
or never recover.

CLEOPATRA   Remember'st thou any that have died
on't?                                                         250

CLOWN   Very many, men and women too. I heard of°
one of them no longer than yesterday; a very honest°
woman, but something given to lie, as a woman
should not do but in the way of honesty; how she died
of the biting of it, what pain she felt; truly, she makes a 255
very good report o' th' worm; but he that will believe
all that they say shall never be saved by half that they
do; but this is most falliable, the worm's an odd worm.

CLEOPATRA   Get thee hence, farewell.

CLOWN   I wish you all joy of the worm.                       260

[Sets down his basket.]

CLEOPATRA   Farewell.

CLOWN   You must think this, look you, that the
worm will do his kind.°

CLEOPATRA   Ay, ay, farewell.

CLOWN   Look you, the worm is not to be trusted but 265
in the keeping of wise people: for indeed there is no
goodness in the worm.

CLEOPATRA   Take thou no care; it shall be heeded.

CLOWN   Very good. Give it nothing, I pray you, for
it is not worth the feeding.                                  270

CLEOPATRA   Will it eat me?

CLOWN   You must not think I am so simple but I
know the devil himself will not eat a woman. I know
that a woman is a dish for the gods, if the devil dress°
her not. But truly, these same whoreson devils do the 275
gods great harm in their women; for in every ten that
they make, the devils mar five.

CLEOPATRA   Well, get thee gone, farewell.

CLOWN   Yes, forsooth. I wish you joy o' th' worm.
                                                       Exit.

[Enter IRAS with a robe, crown, etc.]

CLEOPATRA
Give me my robe, put on my crown, I have          280
Immortal longings° in me. Now no more
The juice of Egypt's grape shall moist this lip.
Yare,° yare, good Iras; quick: methinks I hear
Antony call: I see him rouse himself
To praise my noble act. I hear him mock           285
The luck of Caesar, which the gods give men
To excuse their after wrath.° Husband, I come:
Now to that name my courage prove my title!
I am fire, and air; my other elements
I give to baser life.° So, have you done?         290

Come then, and take the last warmth of my lips.
Farewell, kind Charmian, Iras, long farewell.
           [Kisses them. IRAS falls and dies.]
Have I the aspic° in my lips? Dost fall?
If thou and nature can so gently part,
The stroke of death is as a lover's pinch,         295
Which hurts, and is desired. Dost thou lie still?
If thus thou vanishest, thou tell'st the world
It is not worth leave-taking.

CHARMIAN
Dissolve, thick cloud, and rain, that I may say
The gods themselves do weep.

CLEOPATRA                      This proves me base:  300
If she first meet the curlèd° Antony,
He'll make demand of her, and spend that kiss
Which is my heaven to have. Come, thou mortal
   wretch,°

[To an asp, which she applies to her breast.]

With thy sharp teeth this knot intrinsicate°
Of life at once untie. Poor venomous fool,         305
Be angry, and dispatch.° O, couldst thou speak,
That I might hear thee call great Caesar ass
Unpolicied!°

CHARMIAN   O eastern star!°

CLEOPATRA                      Peace, peace!
Dost thou not see my baby at my breast,
That sucks the nurse asleep?

CHARMIAN              O, break! O, break!          310

CLEOPATRA
As sweet as balm, as soft as air, as gentle—
O, Antony! Nay, I will take thee too:

[Applies another asp to her arm.]

What° should I stay—                          Dies.°

CHARMIAN
In this wild world? So, fare thee well.
Now boast thee, death, in thy possession lies      315
A lass unparalleled. Downy windows, close;
And golden Phoebus° never be beheld
Of eyes again so royal! Your crown's awry;
I'll mend it, and then play—

Enter the GUARD, rustling in.

FIRST GUARD
Where's the queen?

CHARMIAN              Speak softly, wake her not.  320

FIRST GUARD
Caesar hath sent—

CHARMIAN              Too slow a messenger.

[Applies an asp.]

O, come apace, dispatch; I partly feel thee.

FIRST GUARD
Approach, ho! All's not well: Caesar's beguiled.

---

**247 immortal** his blunder for *mortal*   **251 heard of**
heard from   **252 honest** (1) chaste (2) truthful (similar
innuendoes fill the speech, with puns on "lie" and "die")
**263 do his kind** act according to his nature   **274 dress**
(1) prepare (i.e., of food) (2) clothe, equip   **281 Immortal longings** (1) the desires of a goddess (2) longings for
immortality   **283 Yare** quickly   **287 their after wrath** the
retributive punishments heaped by the gods on those who have
been too proud of their good fortune   **289–90 I am . . . life**
man was believed to be made up of four elements, two higher—
fire and air—and two lower or baser—earth and water

**293 aspic** asp   **301 curlèd** freshly barbered   **303 thou mortal
wretch** you deadly little object ("wretch," like "fool" in line
305, is often an affectionate term, used especially of children)
**304 intrinsicate** intricate   **306 dispatch** quickly end it   **308
Unpolicied** lacking statecraft; **eastern star** morning star,
Venus   **313 What** why   **313 s.d. Dies** modern actresses
prefer to die upright, seated regally, but Caesar's penultimate
and final speeches suggest that Cleopatra dies—as in Plutarch—
"upon a bed"   **317 Phoebus** sun god

SECOND GUARD
  There's Dolabella sent from Caesar; call him.

FIRST GUARD
  What work is here! Charmian, is this well done?    325

CHARMIAN
  It is well done, and fitting for a princess
  Descended of so many royal kings.
  Ah, soldier!                CHARMIAN *dies.*

*Enter* DOLABELLA.

DOLABELLA
  How goes it here?

SECOND GUARD   All dead.

DOLABELLA           Caesar, thy thoughts
  Touch their effects° in this: thyself art coming    330
  To see performed the dreaded act which thou
  So sought'st to hinder.

*Enter* CAESAR *and all his* TRAIN, *marching.*

ALL           A way there, a way for Caesar!

DOLABELLA
  O, sir, you are too sure an augurer:
  That you did fear is done.

CAESAR          Bravest at the last,
  She leveled at° our purposes, and being royal,    335
  Took her own way. The manner of their deaths?
  I do not see them bleed.

DOLABELLA        Who was last with them?

FIRST GUARD
  A simple countryman, that brought her figs.
  This was his basket.

CAESAR           Poisoned, then.

FIRST GUARD         O, Caesar,
  This Charmian lived but now, she stood and spake;    340
  I found her trimming up the diadem
  On her dead mistress; tremblingly she stood,
  And on the sudden dropped.

CAESAR         O, noble weakness!
  If they had swallowed poison, 'twould appear
  By external swelling; but she looks like sleep,    345
  As she would catch another Antony
  In her strong toil° of grace.

DOLABELLA       Here, on her breast,
  There is a vent° of blood, and something blown;°
  The like is on her arm.

FIRST GUARD
  This is an aspic's trail; and these fig leaves    350
  Have slime upon them, such as th' aspic leaves
  Upon the caves of Nile.

CAESAR         Most probable
  That so she died: for her physician tells me
  She hath pursued conclusions° infinite
  Of easy ways to die. Take up her bed,    355
  And bear her women from the monument.
  She shall be buried by her Antony.
  No grave upon the earth shall clip° in it
  A pair so famous. High events as these
  Strike° those that make them; and their story is    360
  No less in pity, than his glory which
  Brought them to be lamented. Our army shall
  In solemn show attend this funeral,
  And then to Rome. Come, Dolabella, see
  High order in this great solemnity.     *Exeunt omnes.* 365

---

330 **Touch their effects** meet with realization   **335 leveled at** (1) guessed (2) fought against

347 **toil** snare   **348 vent** discharge; **blown** swollen   **354 conclusions** experiments   **358 clip** clasp   **360 Strike** touch

# THE TRAGEDY OF CORIOLANUS

EDITED BY REUBEN BROWER

## Introduction

The closing speech of *Coriolanus* reminds us of similar speeches at the end of other plays by Shakespeare:

> Take him up.
> Help, three o' th' chiefest soldiers; I'll be one.
> Beat thou the drum, that it speak mournfully;
> Trail your steel pikes. Though in this city he
> Hath widowed and unchilded many a one,
> Which to this hour bewail the injury,
> Yet he shall have a noble memory.
> Assist. *Exeunt, bearing the body of Marcius.*
> *A dead march sounded.*

So *Julius Caesar:*

> According to his virtue, let us use him
> With all respect and rites of burial.
> Within my tent his bones tonight shall lie,
> Most like a soldier, ordered honorably.

And *Hamlet:*

> Let four captains
> Bear Hamlet like a soldier to the stage,
> For he was likely, had he been put on,
> To have proved most royal; and for his passage
> The soldiers' music and the rite of war
> Speak loudly for him.

Though we recognize in all these endings the convention by which the curtainless Elizabethan stage was cleared of its actors, yet we can easily imagine that the convention might have been expressed in different language, and without this special emphasis on the protagonist—borne from the scene "like a soldier," with "music and the rite of war" —particularly when he happened to be Hamlet. It seems certain that the gesture so expressed was more than a stage convention, or rather that it represented another and deeper convention about the nature of the chief actor in a tragedy. The modern reader certainly feels some strain in speaking of *The* Tragedy *of Coriolanus*, particularly if he has just been reading *King Lear* or *Antony and Cleopatra*,

plays that most of us regard as prime examples of that ever-debatable term. George Bernard Shaw has called *Coriolanus* Shakespeare's "finest comedy"; one critic has described it as a satire; another, as debate rather than a tragedy. Most of us will agree that when we speak of *Coriolanus* as a "tragedy," we mean something rather peculiar. But those who admire the play will rejoice in that "peculiarity." The aim of this introductory essay is to give some clue to its essence, to its rare and special value. (The editor assumes that the reader will have read the play at least once before turning to the Introduction.)

The more alert and more literate members of Shakespeare's audience—not to be identified with any one social class—would have recognized that the three processional speeches above marked the death of a hero in a more than modern conventional sense. Even if they were relatively unread, they were literate in a most relevant respect, through hearing in the theater the language of dying heroes in these and in many other plays. They would have sensed much by way of implication in "virtue," "like a soldier," and "a noble memory," just as they would have appreciated the special force of "deeds" in the great speech of Cominius:

COMINIUS
> I shall lack voice: the deeds of Coriolanus
> Should not be uttered feebly. It is held
> That valor is the chiefest virtue and
> Most dignifies the haver. If it be, 85
> The man I speak of cannot in the world
> Be singly counterpoised. At sixteen years,
> When Tarquin made a head for Rome, he fought
> Beyond the mark of others. Our then dictator,
> Whom with all praise I point at, saw him fight, 90
> When with his Amazonian chin he drove
> The bristled lips before him. He bestrid
> An o'erpressed Roman, and i' th' consul's view
> Slew three opposers; Tarquin's self he met,
> And struck him on his knee. In that day's feats, 95
> When he might act the woman in the scene,
> He proved best man i' th' field, and for his meed
> Was brow-bound with the oak. His pupil age

Man-ent'red thus, he waxèd like a sea;
And, in the brunt of seventeen battles since, 100
He lurched all swords of the garland. For this last,
Before and in Corioles, let me say,
I cannot speak him home. He stopped the fliers,
And by his rare example made the coward
Turn terror into sport; as weeds before 105
A vessel under sail, so men obeyed
And fell below his stem. His sword, death's stamp,
Where it did mark, it took; from face to foot
He was a thing of blood, whose every motion
Was timed with dying cries. Alone he ent'red 110
The mortal gate of th' city, which he painted
With shunless destiny; aidless came off,
And with a sudden reinforcement struck
Corioles like a planet. Now all's his,
When by and by the din of war 'gan pierce 115
His ready sense, then straight his doubled spirit
Requick'ned what in flesh was fatigate,
And to the battle came he; where he did
Run reeking o'er the lives of men, as if
'Twere a perpetual spoil; and till we called 120
Both field and city ours, he never stood
To ease his breast with panting.
MENENIUS                        Worthy man!

. . .

COMINIUS            Our spoils he kicked at,
And looked upon things precious as they were 125
The common muck of the world. He covets less
Than misery itself would give, rewards
His deeds with doing them, and is content
To spend the time to end it.
MENENIUS                He's right noble. 129
Let him be called for.            (II.ii.82–122, 124–30)

Consider the growth of the picture of Coriolanus in this speech and, in particular, certain words and phrases important for defining the special character of his tragedy. Menenius' comment at the end, "right noble," is the key to the speech, and also one of the more important thematic expressions for interpreting Coriolanus' whole career. The meaning of "noble"—like "worthy," it is often equivalent in Shakespeare to "heroic"—is summed up in this tremendous survey of the "deeds of Coriolanus." The theme is anticipated at the start by direct statement: "It is held/ That *valor* is the chiefest virtue" (line 84), "valor" being defined here as the ancient Roman "virtue," the Latin *virtus*.

As Cominius' story begins, the stress falls first on Coriolanus as wonder boy ("At sixteen years," line 87), as the beardless youth with "Amazonian chin" (line 91)—a description that reminds us oddly of his potent mother, Volumnia. We next see him crowned, "brow-bound with the oak" (line 98); then we get an impression of boyhood swiftly thrust into manhood: "His pupil age/Man-ent'red thus" (lines 98–99). The brusque compound renews the physical energy of "ent'red" ("initiated into"), especially as it is linked at once with "waxèd like a sea" (line 99), an image that turns the "man" into a vast natural force. Again Coriolanus is crowned: "He lurched all swords of the garland" (line 101); but how oddly this is put, as if men were swords and swords wore garlands,

as if the man himself now wore the ornament of "swords." He stands a "rare example" (line 104) against the "fliers," who appears as mere "weeds before/A vessel" (lines 105–06). With "below his stem" (line 107), the man becomes the "stem," the bow, of a ship. From pointed bow, the image glides in true Shakespearean fashion to "sword," to "stamp" (line 107), a die for stamping a coin or a medal. Where the "stamp" made its "mark," its cutting edge "took" (line 108): it killed. The sword is seen now as a sword-machine coming down on its victims, quite literally "impressing" them. Then Coriolanus himself is dehumanized, turned into a mere blood-thing (line 109), with "every motion . . . timed" (lines 109–10), working with mechanical regularity, yet incongruously dripping with blood.

"Alone"—once more the "rare example"—he entered the "mortal," the fatal, gate by which death comes (lines 110–11). He "painted [it]/With shunless destiny" (lines 111–12): the bloody instrument smeared it with the gore of dying men, made it one with the death of men who could not escape their fate. The abstractness of idiom fits in with the whole style of Shakespeare's vision in the speech and in the play, imparting to the hero the added impersonality of a divine power. We may recall Volumnia's awesome image:

Death, that dark spirit, in's nervy arm doth lie,
Which, being advanced, declines, and then men die.
(II.i.164–65)

She too sees Coriolanus as the great sword-sweeping arm of Death.

He "struck Corioles like a planet" (lines 113–14). Now Coriolanus is a more terrifying force of nature, "striking" with fatal disease as the planets were believed to do, by the death-ray of the Elizabethan cosmos. There is a final impression of swift action and "reeking" gore before Cominius' summing up (lines 124–29). Coriolanus' reward for his "deeds" lies in the pure doing, in "living it up in action." Heroic violence, it is suggested, is self-destructive: in killing time, the hero is killing himself.

Shakespeare's audience—that better part of which we have spoken—would have recognized more quickly and more certainly than a twentieth-century audience that the core of this speech was an epic, or rather, heroic, narrative in the Greco-Roman tradition. Many would have already seen other "noble Roman histories," plays on similar Roman or Greek subjects; and many would have had in grammar school some direct contact with Latin epic and with Greek epic story in Latin versions. They would have caught in "noble" and the "deeds of Coriolanus" an echo of phrases like Homer's *klea andron*, "the glorious deeds of great heroës dead," as Chapman translates it. In "The man I speak of," they would have heard Virgil's *arma virumque cano*, in which *virum* is related to *virtus*, to "valor" as described by Cominius. (Stanyhurst's translation of Virgil [1582] renders *virum* as "manhood," a word that shows the identification, frequent in Shakespeare, of "man" with "hero.") To appreciate more fully the "nobility" of Coriolanus' career and what Shakespeare made of it, we need to have some notion of the heroic ideal implied by Cominius' speech and by Corio-lanus' further history in the play.

Shakespeare himself was familiar with the ancient heroic tradition in various forms. If he knew little Greek, he had access to Latin and French translations of Homer, to Virgil, Ovid, and Seneca in the original and translation, and to the early books of Chapman's *Iliad*, of which he had made use in *Troilus and Cressida* (1601–02). Although Chapman considerably revised his earlier version before publishing his complete *Iliad* in 1611, his translation may serve as a relevant example of the Renaissance remaking of the ancient heroic ideal. Back of Chapman stands the Homeric hero as he is presented in the *Iliad:* he is the man who "goes forward" in battle to display his excellence in fighting, who faces death with clear-eyed awareness and with very human fears, knowing that his lot or *moira* is unchangeable, that his every act is related to divine if only partially understood powers. The greatest of heroes, Achilles, goes well beyond the typical heroic norms, both in the excesses of his wrath and in the assertion of an absolute superheroism that aims at being "godlike" indeed, and that makes him finally a deeply tragic figure. In assert-ing his own will, Achilles ironically brings on himself the death of Patroclus, and in living out the violence of wrath, he comes to recognize the uselessness and the inevitability of all violence. In the scene with Priam near the close of the *Iliad*, he sees that both the hero and his victim are acting parts within a pattern controlled by the gods.

The Renaissance image of the ancient hero, though ultimately inherited from Homer, had been much affected by the two great Roman transformations of Virgil and Seneca, and by the reshaping of the Greco-Roman tradi-tion in the medieval romances. These various traditions were complexly blended in the Renaissance theory of the Heroic Poem, an ideal pattern that attempted to strike a compromise between Romance and ancient epic. (*The Faerie Queene* is the unclassic example of what happened when traditions so opposed were combined in a single work.) But the theory itself was much more classical than romantic and much more Virgilian than Homeric. The true heroic poem was like the *Aeneid*, required to have an abstract subject, preferably Christian and explicitly moral, and a hero who equaled and surpassed Aeneas as an exemplar of virtue.

There are many signs in Chapman's *Iliad* of his re-sponse to this Renaissance theory: for example, his view that the *Iliad* is "the true image of all virtues and humane government." Homer embodies all truth, and the highest truth is "learning," learning in a very special sense:

> this is learning; to have skill to throw
> Reins on your body's powers that nothing know,
> And fills the soul's powers so with act and art
> That she can curb the body's angry part,
> All perturbations; all affects that stray
> From this one object, which is to obey
> Her sovereign empire.        *The Tears of Peace* (1609)

In the first word of the *Iliad*—"wrath"—Homer "con-tracts" his "Proposition," his subject: "predominant perturbation," that is, "the body's fervor and fashion of out-ward fortitude, to all possible height of heroical action." The "affects," the passions when "predominant," do not obey the rule of "the soul," or "reason," as Chapman says elsewhere. We have in Chapman the translator a heroic poet who distrusts heroic passion—since it leads almost inevitably to a failure of "learning"—but who has the wis-dom to admit that this same passion offers the greatest occasions for the exercise of moral control.

Consider now Chapman's version (1611) of the scene in the *Iliad*, Book I, in which Achilles is tempted to draw his sword, but on Athena's advice decides not to:

> Thetis' son at this stood vext. His heart
> Bristled his bosom and two ways drew his discursive
>    part—
> If, from his thigh his sharp sword drawn, he should make
>    room about
> Atrides' person, slaught'ring him, or sit his anger out
> And curb his spirit. While these thoughts strived in his
>    blood and mind
> And he his sword drew, down from heaven Athenia
>    stooped and shined . . .
> He, turning back his eye, amaze struck every faculty,
> Yet straight he knew her by her eyes, so terrible they were
> Sparkling with ardor, and thus spoke: "Thou seed of
>    Jupiter,
> Why com'st thou? To behold his pride, that boasts our
>    empery?
> Then witness, with it, my revenge, and see that insolence
>    die
> That lives to wrong me." She replied: "I come from
>    heaven to see
> Thy anger settled, if thy soul will use her sovereignty
> In fit reflection. I am sent from Juno, whose affects
> Stand heartily inclined to both. Come, give both respects
> And cease contention. Draw no sword. Use words, and
>    such as may
> Be bitter to his pride, but just. For, trust in what I say,
> A time shall come when thrice the worth of that he
>    forceth now
> He shall propose for recompense of these wrongs. There-
>    fore throw
> Reins on thy passions, and serve us."

Chapman, we see, has turned the episode into one of "learning" in his sense. First, the inner action is given much greater importance than in the original. This Achilles is more of a meditator than Homer's: "his heart . . . two ways drew his *discursive* part," that is, the part that reasons. In Homer we have simply a very physical heart in a "shaggy chest," whereas in Chapman we find Hamlet's contrast of man and "beast that wants discourse of reason." The process by which Chapman's Achilles "curbs his spirit" is a good example of how Chapman takes over an elementary form of thought from Homer and gives it a new and complex interpretation. So we hear of various powers of mind: "amaze struck every faculty." More significant is Athena's advice on the right way to settle anger. Homer's goddess says merely, "Stop quarrel-ing; don't draw your sword." But Chapman's says:

> "Therefore throw
> Reins on thy passions, and serve us."

This Athena adds another note; like Hamlet, Achilles is to "speak daggers," but use none: "Draw no sword. Use words . . . but *just*" ones. The addition is important, since Chapman is in fact eager to make Achilles' wrath moral by substituting controlled anger for mere passion. Achilles' reply to Athena is another example of "learning":

> "Though my heart
> Burn in anger, yet my soul must conquer th' angry part
> And yield you conquest. Who subdues his earthly part for
>    heaven,
> Heaven to his prayers subdues his wish."

The basic opposition of passions and soul may be either Platonic or Christian, but Chapman's language is so emphatically Christian that we may wonder whether we are listening to a hero or a saint. (At other points in Chapman's *Iliad*, Achilles is as bloodthirsty and cruel as Homer's hero at his worst.) Whatever Chapman's intention may have been, his true hero seems more often to be Hector, who displays the self-control, the self-knowledge, that Achilles aspires to but rarely achieves.

Although Chapman has so completely reinterpreted the ancient heroic image in Renaissance terms, we can still trace in his heroes the main outlines of the heroic role as it appears in the *Iliad*. But it is the Renaissance transformation of the ancient ideal that is most instructive if we are to understand the heroes of Shakespeare: in particular, Chapman's tendency to regard the heroic career as moral education or as a tragic failure to live up to a moral ideal. Modern readers, it should be added, are in general too prone to see the meditativeness of the Renaissance hero and to miss the complete heroic image as Shakespeare and Chapman understood it.

For a practicing dramatist, this ideal, a blend of the ancient and modern, pagan and Christian, held important possibilities. A Renaissance Achilles or Hector who faced the irony of his situation, who clearly recognized the conflict of allegiances, would be tragic in the fullest sense. He would be, for example, the Antony of *Antony and Cleopatra*. The ideal that Shakespeare had encountered in Chapman's *Iliad* and elsewhere was wonderfully renewed for him by his reading of another ancient classic, one that he read with the closest attention, Plutarch's *Lives of the Noble Grecians and Romans* in North's translation. It is worth noting here that twice in the "Life of Coriolanus" Plutarch illustrates his point by quoting Homer, and especially interesting that in defending Homer's allowance for "our own free will and reason" he quotes, in a fairly lax version, the lines on Achilles' "angry heart."

The concept of the true hero implied in the North-Plutarch "Life," on which Shakespeare's play is largely based, is very close to Chapman's, as may be seen from some of the more general comments on the hero's character:

this Martius' natural wit and great heart did marvelously stir up his courage to do and attempt notable acts. But on the other side, for lack of education, he was so choleric and impatient, that he would yield to no living creature: which made him churlish, uncivil, and altogether unfit for any man's conversation. Yet men marveling much at his constancy, that he was never overcome with pleasure nor money and how he would endure easily all manner of pains and travails, thereupon they well liked and commended his stoutness and temperancy. But for all that, they could not be acquainted with him, as one citizen useth to be with another in the city. His behavior was so unpleasant to them by reason of a certain insolent and stern manner he had, which, because he was too lordly, was disliked. And to say truly, the greatest benefit that learning bringeth unto men is this: that it teacheth men that be rude and rough of nature, by compass and rule of reason, to be civil and courteous, and to like better the mean state than the higher. Now in those days, valiantness was honored in Rome above all other virtues, which they call *virtus*, by the name of virtue itself, as including in that general name all other special virtues besides. So that *virtus* in the Latin was as much as valiantness.

(Plutarch, "Life of Coriolanus")

Note first the high praise of Martius' "great heart" and "notable acts," and more especially what follows: "*But on the other side*"—here North sounds exactly like Chapman—"for lack of education, he was so choleric and impatient, that he would yield to no living creature." North reinforces this with a remark showing clearly that "education" means "learning" in Chapman's sense of the word: "And to say truly, the greatest benefit that learning bringeth into men is this: that it teacheth men that be rude and rough of nature, by compass and rule of reason, to be civil and courteous." But in the next sentence we are reminded that Coriolanus was the pattern of *virtus*. Yet according to North's view—and it would be Chapman's, too—Coriolanus was not fit to be "a prince" or "governor," because he "lacked the gravity and affability that is gotten with judgment of learning and reason." He has another characteristic that is connected with his "choler" and his "self-will and opinion" (we should say, "pride"): "[he] remembered not how willfulness is the thing of the world, which a governor of a commonwealth for pleasing should shun, being that which Plato called solitariness." Note how Coriolanus' obstinacy and pride are described as "solitariness," the uncivil "aloneness" of men "who will never yield to others' reason."

Bearing in mind Plutarch's picture of heroic Coriolanus, and this brief sketch of the ancient hero in Renaissance guise, let us return to the "deeds of Coriolanus" in Shakespeare's play. We can now appreciate more fully certain features of Cominius' narrative: the august and at times coldly Latin style, the *nobility* of this display of *virtue*, the terrifying energy of a hero who is a lone instrument of death and destiny. We see in Coriolanus a figure like Achilles in his most vengeful phrase, hurrying for slaughter, who "did/Run reeking o'er the lives of men." We recall, too, how in earlier scenes Shakespeare has stressed by imagery and stage business the "bloodiness," "aloneness," and other nonhuman qualities underlined also in Cominius' portrait. Coriolanus has been pictured as "mantled," "painted," "smeared," and "masqued" in blood; heard with the "thunder-like percussion" of a cannon; seen swordlike "outdaring his senseless sword" and acting alone, apart from his plebeian followers—both impressions being vividly merged in the scene when his men "*wave their swords*" and "*take him up in their arms*":

O me alone! Make you a sword of me?        (I.vi.76)

Whether these cries are to be read as questions or as exclamations—and there is no certainty—it is clear that in uttering them Coriolanus sees himself in splendid isolation, like a sword swung aloft in battle.

But this very emphasis on a nonhuman aloneness is a sign that Shakespeare was not writing an ancient heroic tragedy, not even of the Renaissance type of *Antony and Cleopatra*. He had seen in Plutarch's "solitariness" another subject and another possible treatment. "Suppose we set Achilles down in the Roman forum—what then?" There are subtle hints in Cominius' speech of this other subject and attitude: "It is *held*/That valor is the chiefest virtue . . . *if it be*. . . ." Menenius' comment, "He's right noble./Let him be called for" is just, but also offhand and curt in Coriolanus' own manner. "Enough of that," Menenius seems to say—and irony breaks in. "Say more," he implies, "and you may remind people of this hero's immense pride," "his haughty obstinate mind," as North puts it, a quality that Shakespeare stresses much more than Plutarch. But Shakespeare does not limit himself, as some critics suppose, to portraying a flawed proud and angry man. He had grasped in the *Lives* and in the Roman historians the importance of the forum, of the Roman state, which he viewed with his contemporaries as an example both of "the mischiefs of discord and civil dissention" and of the well-ordered society, a model of a true commonwealth. Shakespeare sets the "deeds of Coriolanus" against the great parable of Menenius, "the body's members" and their revolt "against the belly" (I.i.97–156). There are many contemporary documents that show a familiarity with this figure and with the related metaphor of the "disease" and "health" of the body politic. To the Elizabethan mind, the state, in more than a modern figurative sense, embodies a natural order: the parts receive from the governing center "that natural competency/Whereby they live." The dramatic point of the brilliantly comic scene in which this fable is presented does not lie in the fable itself, but in the way it is acted out by Menenius in cooperation with the citizens. The good-natured insolence and sturdy candor, the tough repartee of the exchanges, belong to a game played between patrician and people. The "belly-smile" of the patrician, and the "great toe" of the plebeian, help to impart the feeling of healthy relatedness in a civil society. To that, *"Enter Caius Marcius"*—followed by Menenius' greeting:

Hail, noble Marcius!

with the answer:

Thanks. What's the matter, you dissentious rogues
That, rubbing the poor itch of your opinion,
Make yourselves scabs?                    (I.i.165–68)

The "nature" of the state is henceforth counterpoised by the "nature" of Coriolanus: "What he cannot help in his nature," one citizen says to another in the beginning of this same scene, "you account a vice in him." From here to the end of the play Shakespeare keeps dramatizing this clash of natures until Coriolanus, still protesting, hears "great Nature" cry, " 'Deny not.' " and

He bowed his nature, never known before
But to be rough, unswayable, and free.    (V.vi.24–25)

In North's version of the climactic scene where Coriolanus gives in to his mother's pleas (V.iii), there is considerable emphasis on the claims of "nature" and the "natural" in various senses. But there is nothing in the "Life" as a whole like Shakespeare's interweaving throughout his drama of variations on this central theme. The opposition of "natures" in *Coriolanus* produces a continuous play of irony, as every protestation of the hero, or of his friends and enemies, is heard against a suppressed negation.

Again taking a hint from Plutarch—which he develops fully and explicitly—Shakespeare introduces one further strand of ironic ambiguity into his picture of Coriolanus, the link between his heroic energy and his love of his mother. "There's no man in the world," she explains near the end of the play, "More bound to's mother." (Such is the stuff of heroes: Achilles must have his guardian Thetis.) "What he hath done famously," a citizen says, "though soft-conscienced men can be content to say it was for his country, he did it to please his mother and to be partly proud, which he is, even to the altitude of his virtue" (I.i.36–40). More curious still, warmaking, love, and marriage are closely related and almost identified in the minds of Volumnia and her son. Coriolanus has a way of embracing generals as if they were brides of war:

MARCIUS [*To* COMINIUS.]
                              O, let me clip ye
In arms as sound as when I wooed; in heart
As merry as when our nuptial day was done,
And tapers burned to bedward!            (I.vi.29–32)

Much later—with the inevitability ironic echo—Aufidius answers him in kind:

                    that I see thee here,
Thou noble thing, more dances my rapt heart
Than when I first my wedded mistress saw
Bestride my threshold.                    (IV.v.119–22)

If we keep in mind these many contrasts in the nature of Coriolanus, and the heroic image that his role evokes by similarity and by contrast, and if we remember, too, the vision of society symbolized by Menenius' fable, we shall appreciate better the Shakespearean complexity of the climactic scenes of the play. We shall also reach a truer measure of its peculiar flavor as tragedy. Consider first the scene where Coriolanus, about to be made consul, makes his magnificent attack on the tribunes and their officers. To him, the advice to abolish the tribuneship is a call to a godlike "noble life":

                    Therefore, beseech you—
You that will be less fearful than discreet;
That love the fundamental part of state
More than you doubt the change on't; that prefer
A noble life before a long, and wish
To jump a body with a dangerous physic
That's sure of death without it—at once pluck out
The multitudinous tongue; let them not lick
The sweet which is their poison. Your dishonor
Mangles true judgment, and bereaves the state
Of that integrity which should become't;
Not having the power to do the good it would,
For th' ill which doth control't.          (III.i.149–61)

By this point in the play the noble life is not only being equated with the "deeds of Coriolanus," but with the ironic qualifications of his pride. "A 'noble' life" on his lips can be taken by the tribunes and people simply as "the life of the nobles, the Senate." Coriolanus' plea for the "fundamental part of state," his concern for the "integrity" of the body politic, seemingly echoes Menenius' fable; but "to pluck out/The multitudinous tongue," to eliminate the tribunes, is effectively to deny the people any part in the government. Coriolanus does not want a "blended" voice, but only one. He alone, he half implies, is the proper voice of the state. He is making this plea, he says, in the interest of avoiding "confusion." But the hero who pleads for order, who fears revolution, speaks revolutionary doctrines and nearly starts one. He of course intends a counterrevolution; but he very nearly sets a true popular revolution under way.

The metaphor that runs through Coriolanus' speech is the familiar medical one of the play (used once, but only once, by Plutarch): he offers "a dangerous physic," and in his view he is the health of the state. But to the tribune Sicinius, "He's a disease that must be cut away" (III.i.294). Menenius accepts the implication, but proposes "a cure" rather than "surgery." He would proceed by "the humane way" of compromise; that is, by Chapman's (and Plutarch's) way of "humane government." But the fatality of Coriolanus' nature—his pride and "choler," his lack of temperance—carries him on to destroy what he thinks he is saving. "His nature is too noble for the world," says Menenius,

> He would not flatter Neptune for his trident,
> Or Jove for's power to thunder. His heart's his mouth:
> What his breast forges, that his tongue must vent;
> And, being angry, does forget that ever
> He heard the name of death. (III.i.255–59)

Here is the man who will equal the gods, the forgelike machine of war and death, deafened by wrath.

Coriolanus' insistence on being true to his heroic nature is constantly to the fore from this point to the end of the play. So in the next scene with the nobles and Volumnia, a scene that has no parallel in Plutarch, he asks with boyish puzzlement,

> Why did you wish me milder? Would you have me
> False to my nature? Rather say I play
> The man I am. (III.ii.14–16)

Volumnia's sensible advice fits—up to a point—Chapman's and North's concept of "education":

> I have a heart as little apt as yours,
> But yet a brain that leads my use of anger
> To better vantage. (III.ii.29–31)

Menenius comments, "Well said, noble woman!" But this is not Coriolanus' nobility; his is of the pure Homeric type, absolute and without compromise. "You are too absolute," Volumnia well says,

> Though therein you can never be too noble
> But when extremities speak. (III.ii.40–41)

But Volumnia does not altogether understand her son: it is exactly in "extremities" that the hero must be "too noble," that his nature clearly cries out. Coriolanus faces a dilemma similar to Antony's—how to be both noble and politic. Volumnia attempts to make him feel that the politic can be identified at one and the same time with nobility, with loyalty to the better part of the state and to the family, and most significantly, with loyalty to herself:

> I am in this
> Your wife, your son, these senators, the nobles.
> (III.ii.64–65)

Her despairing

> Do as thou list.
> Thy valiantness was mine, thou suck'st it from me,
> But owe thy pride thyself. (III.ii.128–30)

only increases the sense of their likeness, of the physical bond between them: they are one flesh and one blood.

But the physical intensity of the appeal is persuasive for the moment, and for the first time in the scene, Coriolanus calls her "mother":

> Mother, I am going to the marketplace. (III.ii.131)

What this curbing of his nature costs him has been suggested earlier in the same scene, when like Othello he says farewell to arms:

> Away, my disposition, and possess me
> Some harlot's spirit! My throat of war be turned,
> Which quired with my drum, into a pipe
> Small as an eunuch. (III.ii.111–14)

and when he suddenly reverses himself:

> I will not do't;
> Lest I surcease to honor mine own truth,
> And by my body's action teach my mind
> A most inherent baseness. (III.ii.120–23)

Though the words Coriolanus uses are very like Chapman's his actions have really turned the ideal upside down. While everyone is urging him to conquer his body's "angry part" by discipline of "spirit," he sees only a betrayal of spirit by flesh.

He will seek "a world elsewhere," outside state and family, out of the ordered nature he had known in Rome, and fight, now truly "alone,/Like to a lonely dragon, that his fen/Makes feared and talked of more than seen" (IV.i.29–31). With splendid irony he asserts that though outside society he will still be the same noble hero: "you shall/Hear . . . never of me aught/But what is like me formerly" (IV.i.51–53). In the flattering talk of the Volscians he seems to recover his old nobility, "as if he were son and heir to Mars," but this new-found independence is an illusion, as Aufidius' ominous hints make clear. Aufidius' explanation of why Coriolanus was "hated" and "banished"—though it neglects some reasons, and though it is not Shakespeare's "last word" on his hero—does offer one important hypothesis borne out by much of the play:

whether ['twas] *nature*,
Not to be other than one thing, not moving
From th' casque to th' cushion, but commanding peace
Even with the same austerity and garb
As he controlled the war.          (IV.vii.41–45)

In this last phase of Coriolanus' career there is, as in Achilles' last battles, something much more frightening about his pride and his wrath. "He was," says Cominius

a kind of nothing, titleless,
Till he had forged himself a name o' th' fire
Of burning Rome.                     (V.i.13–15)

He harshly rejects his "old father," Menenius,

Away!

       . . .

Wife, mother, child, I know not.     (V.ii.79, 81)

The Second Watch gives one final impression of Coriolanus' dehumanization just before the women come to beg him to save the city: "He's the rock, the oak not to be wind-shaken" (V.ii.110). What then will happen to the man who supposes he is "author of himself," the absolute hero detached from humanity?

As when Menenius pleads with him earlier, he will attempt to separate personal allegiance from allegiance to country. When the women approach, his eye moves quickly from his wife to his mother, who claims and receives his attention during most of the scene. He speaks to her first in the strange impersonal style that others have used of him: "the honored mold/Wherein this trunk was framed" (V.iii.22–23); but at once he is stressing the close physical bond of mother and son: "and in her hand/ The grandchild to her blood." With a typical turn, he at once denies this and all similar bonds: "All bond and privilege of nature, break!" He will be deliberately unnatural; but when he sees those "doves' " eyes, he "melts" —and how wonderfully the imagery recalls the hard god-like self he has tried to be: "I melt, and am not/Of stronger earth"—he is not the metallic machine man of earlier scenes. When his "mother bows," it is indeed a "perturbation" in nature, and "great Nature" cries out against it (V.iii.33). He denies "instinct," innate impulse, and, with consummate irony, declares that he is "author of himself," as it were, self-born!

But soon he is yielding to nature in the sense of family affection, as he gives his wife "a kiss/Long as my exile," while still insisting that he is not yielding to nature in the sense of allegiance to his country. When he sees his mother kneeling, he comes out with great hyperbolic oaths in the best heroic vein:

Then let the pebbles on the hungry beach
Fillip the stars! Then let the mutinous winds
Strike the proud cedars 'gainst the fiery sun.
                                     (V.iii.58–60)

Like Othello and Lear, Coriolanus invokes the very disorder he fears, the disorder of which he is the unconscious instrument. Like Hector, he sees his son as the reincarnation of his own heroism, his words recalling his own nobility and his lonely strength and inhumanity. He prays that the boy may prove

To shame unvulnerable, and stick i' th' wars
Like a great sea-mark, standing every flaw.  (V.iii.73–74)

But he is still trying to hold off the claims of wife and mother: "Tell me not," he shouts, "Wherein I seem unnatural."

Then come Volumnia's two great appeals in answer to his poignantly absurd assertion. The keynote of the first is struck in

thy sight, which should
Make our eyes flow with joy, hearts dance with comforts,
Constrains them weep and shake with fear and sorrow,
Making the mother, wife, and child, to see
The son, the husband, and the father tearing
His country's bowels out.            (V.iii.98–103)

The body of the state, here realized with such physical vividness, is equated with mother, wife, and child, as if to say "tearing that body is tearing us." During the rest of the speech, Volumnia's language intensifies this identification until the climax,

thou shalt no sooner
March to assault thy country than to tread
(Trust to't, thou shalt not) on thy mother's womb
That brought thee to this world.     (V.iii.122–25)

This violent image is Plutarch's, and the identification of the mother with the body of the state is suggested by one of his comments; but the comment shows also the relative simplicity of his analysis, and his unawareness of the emotional confusion that Volumnia is exploiting so successfully:

yet he had no reason for the love of his mother to pardon his country, but rather he should in pardoning his country, have spared his mother, because his mother and wife were members of the body of his country and city, which he did besiege.
(Plutarch, "The Comparison of Alcibiades with
Marcius Coriolanus")

Volumnia's second appeal falls into three distinct phases. First she urges him to reconcile the Romans and the Volsces, offering the same kind of sensible advice she had given earlier when begging him to be "mild" to the tribunes. Next she makes a masterly attack on the very nobility that stands in the way of compromise, pointing out that the only practical "benefit" of being so absolutely noble is to destroy his country and gain a "name . . ./To th' ensuing age abhorred." She enforces her argument with a satirical picture of the godlike role Coriolanus has aimed at, seeking "To imitate the graces of the gods" as if he were to "thunder" like Jove, and yet to "charge" his lightning with a "bolt" that would only split "an oak" (V.iii.140–53). Something, yes, but hardly a cosmic catastrophe. She keeps reminding him that she speaks for wife, son, and mother; and in her final stroke she reinforces all three claims:

This fellow had a Volscian to his mother;
His wife is in Corioles, and his child
Like him by chance.             (V.iii.178–80)

Again she identifies personal and social bonds, as she reads him out of family, Rome, and humanity. His reply is one of the great speaking silences in Shakespeare:

*Holds her by the hand, silent.*
                    O mother, mother!
What have you done? Behold, the heavens do ope,
The gods look down, and this unnatural scene
They laugh at.             (V.iii.182–85)

"Unnatural"—just when he is responding to all these most natural claims. For a moment he seems to see his dilemma more clearly, and to understand that in giving in to his mother he is responding to the demands of his native country and state. But he soon is talking as if all can be well: he can give in to his mother, be false to the Volscians, and "frame convenient peace."

The last scene of the play begins as an ironic repetition of the scene in which he had "mildly" given in to his mother's advice. At that time he had not been able to sustain the part; but now he "bows his nature" and comes "marching" in, "*the commoners being with him.*" In contrast to the usual isolation of his figure from the plebeians, Coriolanus is seen *with* the people, and we catch another ironic reflection from the past: Menenius' easy companionship with the lower orders. Coriolanus seems for once to "belong," and he cries happily, "I am returned your soldier;/No more infected with my country's love" (V.vi.70–71). What was once his health is now disease, and loyalty to the enemies of Rome is his "cure." He is so terribly unaware of what he has been doing that he responds with dreamlike deafness to Aufidius' cry of "traitor"—the exact echo of the tribunes' earlier "H' as spoken like a traitor" (III.i.162).

When he finally takes in Aufidius' cruel caricature of how he had given in to his mother, he can hardly speak: "Hear'st thou, Mars?" His incoherent cry, reminding us of the godlike soldier he had been, is inadequate, but dramatically concentrated in the highest degree. Shakespeare was never more successful than in this brief dialogue in focusing the rich meanings of a whole play in the slightest verbal gestures. To Aufidius' slanderous "boy of tears," he cries:

Cut me to pieces, Volsces, men and lads,
Stain all your edges on me. "Boy"! False hound!
If you have writ your annals true, 'tis there,
That, like an eagle in a dovecote, I
Fluttered your Volscians in Corioles.
Alone I did it. "Boy"?             (V.vi.110–15)

"Alone" and "'Boy'?" carry the weight of his whole dramatic career. In "Alone" we recall his cult of independence, his integrity, his insistence on being "Coriolanus." But we hear also the opposite theme in a play in which wholeness of the state is the public ideal, in which metaphors of the body politic keep reminding us that the great natural order is realized in a whole of which the single man is only a part. This is his final denial of nature's bond, making only clearer his real dependence on Rome, his

mother, Menenius, and now on the Volscians. "'Boy'?" in its scornful tone is Coriolanus' way of saying "*man*-hero." But the hero cannot act in this setting; he can only utter frustrated cries. He *is* in part behaving like a boy, and he *had* responded to his mother. The single word recalls too a long history of boyish irresponsibility and lack of control.

But there is another view, as always in this play: "The man is noble," one of the Volscians says, "and his fame folds in/This orb o' th' earth" (V.vi.123–24). The "deeds of Coriolanus" cannot be forgotten any more than "the impatience" that North finds so dangerous in the "governor of a state." The closing processional speech, with which we began, marks the death of a hero: "Yet he shall have a noble memory."

If we now compare Coriolanus with the model of all Greek and Roman literary heroes, Achilles, and with the Renaissance counterpart in Chapman and North, and finally with the chief characters of other Shakespearean tragedies, we can define more clearly the character of the play—surely the most original of Shakespeare's heroic dramas, whatever we choose to call it. Throughout *Coriolanus* Shakespeare is continually recalling the ancient model in imagery associating his hero with divinities and "shunless destiny." Like Menenius, Shakespeare has "godded him indeed." Perhaps Coriolanus is most like Achilles in his passionate pride, in his "choler," in his shifting from "rage to sorrow," emotions that lie very close together, as Plutarch had noted. But he comes nearest to the essence of Homer's hero in his absoluteness, in his determination to imitate "the graces of the gods," in his will to push the heroic to the limit until he destroys his own society along with his enemy's. In reducing all virtues to *virtus*, he is the Greek hero Romanized, while in his assertion of his own nature in the face of "great Nature," he betrays the Senecan ancestry of the Elizabethan hero. Though many read him lessons in patience, he is incapable of true "learning."

But there is no moment when, like Achilles, he sees his anger and curses it, nothing to correspond to the scene with Priam, no vision of himself and a higher order within which his action and suffering are placed and made more comprehensible. His last gesture is like his first, to "use his lawful sword." He knows little of what Chapman calls the soul's "sovereignty in fit reflection," not to mention "subduing his earthly part for heaven." He is the most Roman, the least Christian, of Shakespeare's major heroes.

This Roman-ness is felt in the austerity of a style that lends itself so well to irony, and that is the best index to the quality of the play. In *Coriolanus*, Shakespeare seems to turn his back on the richness of language in *Antony and Cleopatra*, with the deliberate intention of creating a protagonist who will deny much that is common to his own and the Renaissance heroic ideal. And yet there are in Coriolanus the makings of a tragedy in Shakespeare's more typical manner: he is a man nobly conscious of his role, a "governor" like Lear or Macbeth on whom the health of society depends, a person like Lear and Othello of immense impatience in a situation calling for utmost patience, a man like Antony whose action is godlike and connected with dimly perceived supernatural forces. Both are instruments of the mighty Roman state, for Romans a prime symbol of the directing power of fate.

But there is of course an obvious defect that makes even Macbeth tragic in a sense of the word that does not fit Coriolanus: the lack of the troubled conscience that separates Macbeth from the tyrant he seems to be to his enemies. In the final scene with his mother, Coriolanus is barely conscious that he is betraying the Volscians, just as in his last entrance he does not realize that he has been "infected by his country's love." His whole career is based on an illusion of *aloneness,* the belief that a man, a general, a statesman, can act alone. Hence the bafflement and humiliation when he must bow to others—feelings he can express only in rotelike speeches. It is the spectator, not Coriolanus, who feels the poignancy of this betrayal of others and himself. Like a "dull actor," as he says, he performs dully, and when out of his part, he is completely "out."

For Coriolanus has only one way of meeting the world —assertion of simple soldierly nobility. In this he has much in common with Othello, who also lives by absolutes, whose world collapses at any suggestion that he is *not* a soldier. But there is no terrible recognition by the hero, as there is in the final scenes of *Othello,* that simple soldiery and simple justice have not been enough, that they have indeed brought chaos again. Damnation, which Othello calls on himself, and which presupposes a sense of sin, is incomprehensible to this noble Roman. He is equally incapable of "noble" Antony's "I am so lated in the world that I/Have lost my way for ever."

One last comparison with Achilles is to the point. In comparison with Shakespeare's "men," these two are great boys. Both are strangely allied with their mothers, both produce "confusion" by their overdeveloped sense of self and their disregard of the claims of society. The difference in the result depends on the difference noted earlier: Shakespeare sets his hero in a much more complex social world. The noble voice that calls to battle may no longer sound noble in the Capitol. Though it calls for order, it becomes indistinguishable from the voice of tyrant and traitor. The man who fears innovation, who has no gift for making compromises and dealing "mildly," may prove the most violent of innovators, worse than a mere mob. Shakespeare's picture of the people is not flattering, but not unintelligent: one cannot build an orderly society by following the whims of the many-headed monster. But fixity of principle in a prince can be as dangerous to the state as the fickleness of a mob.

Shakespeare's state is necessarily not that of the Roman Republic, since both society and cosmos have been translated in Elizabethan-Jacobean terms. His subject—apart from the peculiar character of Coriolanus—is implicit in the "degree" speech of *Troilus and Cressida* (I.iii.75 ff.). It should be remembered that Ulysses' speech was occasioned by Achilles' revolt and that Ulysses later tried to show Achilles the evils resulting from his loss of heroic nobility. Shakespeare returns in *Coriolanus* to the subject implied in these scenes of *Troilus and Cressida,* but with a new Achilles and a new certainty of aim, and with a resultant concentration lacking in the earlier play. In *Troilus and Cressida,* Achilles was an ambiguous creature, a lover and a gangster, and the drama of disunity in the state was crossed by a drama of disunity in love. The end, appropriately, is sound and fury, signifying nothing. But in *Coriolanus* Shakespeare limits the social subject more

severely, and though his picture of the social order is highly particularized, it does not lose a large clarity. As in *Antony and Cleopatra,* the "wide arch/Of the ranged" Roman state is never lost from view.

Against that ordered complexity the simple extremism of Coriolanus stands out in all its nobility and absurdity. The noble simplicity of the hero, the certainty with which issues are expressed and arguments are presented by Coriolanus and by his enemies, and the high decorum of the rather chill oratorical style take us in the direction of French classical drama. This is, after *Julius Caesar,* Shakespeare's most *Latin* play.

It was "all in Plutarch," we may be tempted to say. But when we read Plutarch we discover what Shakespeare was capable of learning—how wonderfully he selected and how skillfully he concentrated on his themes, embodying them in particular dramatic expressions. We can almost feel Shakespeare's excitement as he read; his recognition that here was a subject he had wanted to handle as early as when he was writing *Julius Caesar* and *Troilus and Cressida.* What a discovery—after reading late medieval versions of the ancient heroic in which the hero is reduced to a chivalric lover or worse, to find that the hero is a man who has never ceased loving his mother, a man for whom marriage is second to war, whose true love is his own heroic image. Hints of these and other traits of Shakespeare's hero —his nobility and heroic virtue, his obstinate pride and lack of self-control—can be found in the "Life of Coriolanus." Other basic features of Shakespeare's drama—the picture of the Roman state and society, the debate over the claims of nature, great and small—can also be traced to Plutarch's text. But though many separate elements of Shakespeare's grand design are Plutarchan, it is Shakespeare who has "put them together," and the "putting together" is a dramatic and poetic feat. The imagery of Volumnia's appeal, for example, is resonant with the sense of the state and society that Shakespeare had presented early in the play. In reporting Coriolanus' death, Plutarch merely says the conspirators "all fell upon him, and killed him in the marketplace, none of the people once offering to rescue him." There is no speech from Aufidius, and, more notable, none from Coriolanus, nothing to correspond to "Alone I did it. 'Boy'?" Those few words show that Shakespeare had combined perfectly an intense and rich understanding of the hero-boy, mother's son, and noble Roman with his sharply outlined picture of the social and political world, in a total vision that makes the cry so large in reference, so poignantly absurd, so tragic in a curiously ironic sense.

## A NOTE ON THE SOURCE

The main source used by Shakespeare in writing *Coriolanus* is the "Life of Coriolanus" in Sir Thomas North's translation of Plutarch's *Lives of the Noble Grecians and Romans* (first published in 1579). Comparison of the play with the "Life" will remind us that both "source" and "use" are misleading terms for describing what happens when a writer of the first rank makes a new work out of an old one. In writing *Coriolanus,* Shakespeare was not merely borrowing discrete items from Plutarch; he was engaged in a total imaginative act, seeking to satisfy his inner measure of what was right for his own sensibility, for his sense of the hero's character, and for his complex "feel" of the dramatic world that was coming into being as he wrote. Our certainty that the play is one of Shakespeare's "most assured artistic successes," as T. S. Eliot has said, is strengthened when we discover what he accepted and what he rejected, and particularly when we see how he adapted his borrowings to his vision of Coriolanus and the tragedy as a whole.

Shakespeare's vision—though for all time—was not timeless in origin, but shaped in part by the social and literary culture in which he lived and by the audience for which he produced his plays. We have seen in the Introduction (pp. 1313-15) how the Greco-Roman heroic ideal in its Renaissance form had an effect on Coriolanus and on its meaning for contemporary and succeeding audiences. Shakespeare's treatment of civil disorders in Republican Rome was almost certainly affected also by popular protests and uprisings in England during the early 1600's, disturbances brought on by the enclosure of farm lands and by the lack of grain and the consequent "dearth." That Shakespeare takes the famine as the principal cause for the plebeians' complaints, rather than as in Plutarch "the sore oppression of usurers," is almost certainly traceable to the unrest in England, and, more especially, to the Midlands revolt of 1607. The extensive emphasis in the play—as compared with the "Life"—on the body-state metaphor is probably to be explained in part by the contemporary concern with the dangers of insurrection. Shakespeare also elaborated on Plutarch's brief tale of the body and its members by drawing on Sidney's *Apology for Poetry*, Livy's *Roman History*, both in the original and in the translation of Philemon Holland (1600), and William Camden's *Remains of a Greater Work Concerning Britain* (1605).

The main events of Shakespeare's play, including the important scenes of Coriolanus' attack on the tribuneship (III.i), his banishment and his joining Aufidius (IV.i, v), and the climactic scene with his mother (V.iii), are all based on Plutarch. The principal features that Shakespeare stresses in his portrayal of Coriolanus have their origin, at least in an elementary form, in the pages of the "Life." But Shakespeare has given even greater importance than Plutarch to Coriolanus' pride and uncontrollable temper and especially to the close emotional bond to his mother. Some critics have seen in the prominent role of Menenius, of which there is only the slightest hint in Plutarch, Shakespeare's intention of minimizing the social isolation that Plutarch ascribes to his hero, his unfitness for association with other men. But Menenius spends much of his time warning Coriolanus of these deficiencies, and of the likely consequences of his heroically simple and inept behavior. It should also be noted that in spite of his temperamental aloneness, Plutarch's hero, like Shakespeare's, has strong political supporters among the patricians. Where Shakespeare departs, and significantly, is in eliminating all references to political maneuvering by Coriolanus, of which there are fairly many instances in the "Life." Other critics have noted that Plutarch attributes a reputation for eloquence to Coriolanus, whereas Shakespeare seems to stress his lack of ability as a speaker and debater. But the point surely is that Shakespeare, as Menenius explains,

endows Coriolanus with the eloquence of a soldier—violent and powerful, though often tactless, utterance. He has but one style, and hence his calls for the defense of the state sound strangely like his calls to battle. (Compare III.i.149-57 and I.vi.67-75.)

A survey of the principal scenes that are wholly or largely invented by Shakespeare will give some idea of how thoroughly he adapted Plutarch's moral history to fit his peculiar dramatic subject of the Achillean hero exposed to the complexities and necessary compromises of the Roman-Jacobean political world. First, there are all the episodes in which Menenius figures prominently, with the exception of that part of the first scene in which he tells his fable. The occasion for this moral lesson, the retreat to the Sacred Mount, is passed over by Shakespeare, though Plutarch's narrative of it contains his sole mention of Menenius. (In Livy's *History*, Menenius dies soon after this event takes place.) All the other scenes in which Menenius does so much to defend Coriolanus against his enemies, or to enhance his noble exploits, or to temper his wrath, are entirely of Shakespeare's making. In II.i, there is the bitterly comic telling-off of the tribunes, followed by the joyous welcome of the returning hero; in II.iii, the dialogue with Coriolanus and with the tribunes during the election scene; and the further exchanges with the tribunes in III.i, after Coriolanus has been accused of being a traitor. Although in some of these earlier scenes Shakespeare is using Menenius to voice arguments advanced by the more politic patricians of the "Life," he had little basis in Plutarch for the prominent part taken by Menenius in a number of the scenes that follow Coriolanus' banishment. As often in this play, Shakespeare telescopes two or three Plutarchan scenes into one, centering the action on one of his more important characters. The scene in which Menenius begs Coriolanus to spare Rome is—like Cominius' report of his own attempt—a substitution for one of several embassies from Rome described in Plutarch's narrative.

Shakespeare has invented all the scenes in which Volumnia figures, with the exception of the women's embassy of V.iii. The scene that introduces Volumnia, Virgilia, and Valeria (I.iii), in which Volumnia shows that she had indeed made Coriolanus after her own image of "valiantness," grows from a single remark in the "Life" about the "joy his mother did take of him." The later scene in which she and Menenius urge Coriolanus to act "mildly" in answering the tribunes (III.ii) is a brilliant piece of dramatic foreshadowing, preparing for the final submission of son to mother in Act V. (One characteristic of the play is the number of scenes that have close parallels, in which Coriolanus goes through the same routines but under changed circumstances, which he alone seems not to notice. Hence the odd *déjà vu*, almost nightmarish quality of much of the action in the latter part of the play.) Shakespeare also introduces a number of other scenes or episodes in which Volumnia has an important part, such as her rejoicing over her son's return from war (II.i), her farewell at the gate and her railing afterward (IV.i, ii), and her triumphant return from the final embassy (V.v). The speeches and scenes in which Shakespeare builds up the ambiguous hate-love relationship between Aufidius and Coriolanus in anticipation of their meeting in IV.v grow from a single reference to their rivalry in the "Life."

No listing of inventions, or of parallels between *Coriolanus* and Plutarch's narrative, can give a true impression of how wonderfully Shakespeare has transformed the Plutarchan original, even when seeming to follow it closely. The most obvious example, Volumnia's great appeal (V.iii), offers the most telling proof of the art with which Shakespeare adapted North's language to suit the immediate context while keeping in view the larger dramatic and poetic design of the play. A few instances may suggest what can be learned by comparing the scene with the original in North's translation. Where Plutarch's Coriolanus is "overcome with natural affection" even before his mother speaks, Shakespeare's hero is caught in a violently shifting debate between the claims of nature, great and small, a conflict expressed in direct speech wholly invented by Shakespeare (lines 22–37). As we have seen in the Introduction (p. 1316), the debate is not limited to this speech but runs deeply through the play. In the play, in which the bond with the mother is so central to the hero's character, the son is the first to kneel, and in the wholly new passages between Coriolanus and his son, we are reminded of the parallel to Hector (in a domestic and "natural" moment Coriolanus becomes less Achillean); we are reminded too of the early scene in which the boy-killer of butterflies is Coriolanus in miniature. The image he invokes of "a great sea-mark" is rooted in the imagery of natural forces and "things" so characteristic of Shakespeare's awesome and nonhuman hero. An example of where the verbal parallels are closest will indicate the remarkable depth and consistency of Shakespeare's dramatic and poetic art:

VOLUMNIA            thou shalt no sooner
  March to assault thy country than to tread
  (Trust to't, thou shalt not) on thy mother's womb
  That brought thee to this world.        (V.iii.122–25)

thou shalt see, my son, and trust unto it, thou shalt no sooner march forward to assault thy country, but thy foot shall tread upon thy mother's womb that brought thee first into this world.

                              (Plutarch, "Life of Coriolanus")

Shakespeare has closely imitated in his verse the climactic form of North's sentence, with its skillful suspension through well-placed pauses and the repeated "thou shalt"; but by building the whole speech to end at this point, he has exploited the emotional climax much more fully than North, who has Volumnia go straight on with "And I may not defer to see the day . . ." More important, Shakespeare anticipates the image earlier in the speech in a way to make inescapable the identification of the mother's physical self with "mother Rome." North has Volumnia say earlier, "making myself to see my son, and my daughter here her husband, besieging the walls of his native country." Shakespeare brings his triple allegiance home and focuses it in a metaphor of such violence that even Coriolanus must feel the unnaturalness of his behavior and recognize in advance the implication of the final image:

Making the mother, wife, and child, to see
  The son, the husband, and the father, tearing
  His country's bowels out.        (V.iii.101–03)

The identity of "mothers," human and national, is quietly underlined a moment later in Volumnia's passing reference to "The country, our dear nurse." Compare with this North's relatively aloof and cold "the nurse of their native country." But the full impact of the appeal would be lost if we did not feel behind these physical mother-and-country images the recurring metaphors of the body politic and the large dramatic and philosophic premise they express. The personal and the patriotic appeals, which Shakespeare found in Plutarch, have been fused with a local intensity of feeling and with a far-reaching reference to Shakespeare's view, both of his individual characters and of the society in which they act. Dryden once spoke of Shakespeare as having "all the images of Nature . . . present to him" as he wrote. In comparing Volumnia's speech with its "source," we see Shakespeare writing *Coriolanus* with one eye on North, to be sure, but with all the images of the play and all their dramatic values present to his plastic imagination.

## A NOTE ON THE TEXT

The text of *Coriolanus* has survived only in the First Folio (1623), on which the present edition is based. There are no records of performances earlier than 1623, but there is a mocking imitation of the curious phrase, "lurched all swords of the garland" (II.ii.101), in Ben Jonson's *Epicoene, or The Silent Woman* (1609). It is therefore almost certain that the play was written and performed not later than 1609. The use in Menenius' fable of the body and its members and of expressions from William Camden's *Remains* of 1605, and the probable allusion to the Midlands revolt of 1607, point to a date of 1607 or later. (See A Note on the Source.) There is also the possible reference to the Great Frost of 1607–08 in the phrase "the coal of fire upon the ice" (I.i.174). It seems safe to assume that *Coriolanus* was written after *Antony and Cleopatra*, somewhere between 1607 and 1609.

The Folio text of *Coriolanus* might be described, like that of *The Tempest*, as a distinguished one; it was prepared with great care and is especially remarkable for its elaborate stage directions. W. W. Greg's assertion that the text was printed from the author's manuscript is now widely accepted. The stage directions, presumably Shakespeare's own, are those of a man of the theater who has his eye on the stage and the actors. For example: "*Enter Marcius and Aufidius, at several doors*" (I.viii); "*They all bustle about Coriolanus*" (III.i.184); and the most telling gesture of the play, "*Holds her by the hand, silent*" (V.iii.182).

But though the text brings us so close to the practicing hand of the poet-playwright, it was edited and printed by mortal men. It has a fairly high number of errors, and emendations have been found necessary in at least twenty to twenty-five places. One line has been omitted (II.iii.245), and in two passages the style is so cryptic as to seem almost surely corrupt (III.ii.74–80; V.i.67–69). The most disturbing defect of the Folio text of *Coriolanus* is the widespread mislineation. There are many lines that are either too short or too long, as measured by the usual blank-verse norm, and it is often very hard to determine where the line division should occur. Most of these abnormalities, it has been pointed out, come in short speeches, or at the end or beginning of speeches in rapid dialogue. There are a relatively few instances in which speeches are assigned to seemingly inappropriate speakers. There are also variations in the names of speakers, most of them of little significance, and usually in names of minor persons. The town that gives the hero his honorific title is usually called "Corioles," though "Coriolus" and "Corialus" also occur. There is considerable uncertainty as to how both "Corioles" and "Coriolanus" are to be accented. The common reader, like the learned editor, is free to follow his rhythmic sense in particular lines: "Coríoles" or "Corióles"? "Coriolánus" (the usual pronunciation) or "Coríolanus"?

The present edition follows the Folio text closely, but spelling and punctuation are modernized, abbreviations are amplified, names of speakers are regularized, and some stage directions are moved slightly. The act divisions (translated from Latin) are those of the Folio; no scenes, except the first, are indicated in the Folio text. All other scene divisions printed here (in brackets) are those of the Globe edition. The list of readings given below includes only those words in the Folio that have been omitted or emended. The reading adopted in this edition is printed in boldface type, followed by the original reading in roman.

**I.i.7 Marcius** Martius (throughout the play) **16 or** one **28 First Citizen** All **35 Second Citizen** All **57 First Citizen** 2 Cit. (throughout the rest of Scene i) **93 stale't** scale't **112 tauntingly** taintingly **216 Shouting** Shooting **220 unroofed** vnroo'st **228 s.d. Junius** Annius **241 Lartius** Lucius **I.ii.s.d. Corioles** Coriolus **4 on** one **30 They've** Th'haue **I.iii.36 that's** that **43 sword, contemning. Tell** sword. Contenning, tell **82 Virgilia** Vlug, **84 yarn** yearne **85 Ithaca** Athica **98 whom** who **I.iv.s.d., 12 s.d. Corioles** Corialus **31 herd of—boils** Heard of Byles **42 trenches. Follow's** Trenches followes **45 s.d. Enters the gates** Enter the Gati **56 Were** Weare **57 Cato's** Calues **I.vi.21 Who's** Whose **22 flayed** Flead **53 Antiates** Antients **70 Lesser** Lessen **I.viii.7 Holloa** hollow

**I.ix.46 coverture** Ouerture **50 shout** shoot **65 Caius Marcius** Marcus Caius (in this order throughout) **I.x.30 cypress** Cyprus **II.i.24 how are** ho ware **58 cannot** can **63 you you** you **65 bisson** beesome **170 Coriolanus** Martius Caius Coriolanus **182 wear** were **184 Coriolanus** Com. **190 You** yon **207 s.d. Brutus** Enter Brutus **216 flamens** Plamins **237 napless** Naples **258 touch** teach **II.ii.25 ascent** assent **50 state's** states **81 one on's** on ones **91 chin** Shinne **92 bristled** brizled **II.iii.28 wedged** wadg'd **43 all together** altogether **69 Ay, not** I. but **116 hire** higher **117 toge** tongue **245 And Censorinus that was so surnamed** [F omits; this line, invented by N. Delius in his edition of 1872, is indebted to Plutarch **256 Citizens** All

**III.i.33 herd** Heard **48 Coriolanus** Com. **91 good** God! **92 reckless** wreaklesse **126 Their** There **143 Where one** Whereon **185 All** [F has no speech prefix here, but gives "All" before line 187] **214 All Citizens**] All Ple. **228 him!** him. Exeunt. **229 your** our **230 Coriolanus** Com. **236 Cominius** Corio. **237 Coriolanus** Mene. [speech assigned to Menenius through line 241] **239 Menenius** [see preceding note] **287 our** one **323 bring him** bring him in peace **III.ii.21 thwartings** things **32 herd** heart **55 roted** roated **115 lulls** lull **III.iii.32 for th'** fourth **36 Throng** Through **55 accents** Acticns **89 flaying** Fleaing **99 do** doth **110 for** from **136 s.d. The other Senators** Cumalijs **IV.i.24 thee** the **34 Whither wilt** Whether will **IV.iii.33 will** well **IV.iv.23 hate** haue **IV.v.3 master** M. **82 Whooped** Hoop'd **98 Thou'rt** Th'art **113 clip** cleep **183 lief** liue **236 sleepy** sleepe **IV.vi.4 do** do we **34 lamentation** Lamention **90 wi' th'** with **138 one** oue **IV.vii.34 osprey** Aspray **37 'twas** 'was **39 defect** detect **49 virtues** Vertue **55 founder** fouler **V.i.16 wracked fair** wrack'd for **V.ii.s.d. on** or **16 haply** happely **60 errand** arrant **63 but by my** but my **100 swoon** swoond **V.iii.48 prate** pray **63 holp** hope **104 enmity's** enmities **141 war's** Warres **149 fine** fiue **152 charge** change **169 him with** him with **192 stead** steed **V.iv.49 s.d. all together** altogether **V.v.4 Unshout** Vnshoot **V.vi.114 Fluttered** Flatter'd **129 s.d. the Conspirators** both the Conspirators

# THE TRAGEDY OF CORIOLANUS

[Dramatis Personae

CAIUS MARCIUS *afterwards Caius Marcius Coriolanus*
TITUS LARTIUS } *generals against the Volscians*
COMINIUS }
MENENIUS AGRIPPA *friend to Coriolanus*
SICINIUS VELUTUS } *tribunes of the people*
JUNIUS BRUTUS }
YOUNG MARCIUS *son to Coriolanus*
A ROMAN HERALD
A ROMAN *named Nicanor*
TULLUS AUFIDIUS *general of the Volscians*
LIEUTENANT *to Aufidius*
CONSPIRATORS *with Aufidius*

A VOLSCIAN *named Adrian*
A CITIZEN *of Antium*
TWO VOLSCIAN GUARDS
VOLUMNIA *mother to Coriolanus*
VIRGILIA *wife to Coriolanus*
VALERIA *friend to Virgilia*
GENTLEWOMAN *attending on Virgilia*
USHER *attending on Valeria*
ROMAN AND VOLSCIAN SENATORS
PATRICIANS AEDILES LICTORS
SOLDIERS CITIZENS MESSENGERS
SERVANTS *to Aufidius* OTHER
ATTENDANTS

*Scene*: Rome and the neighborhood; Corioli and the neighborhood; Antium]

## ACT I

### Scene I. [*Rome. A street.*]

*Enter a company of mutinous* CITIZENS *with staves, clubs, and other weapons.*

FIRST CITIZEN  Before we proceed any further, hear me speak.
ALL  Speak, speak.
FIRST CITIZEN  You are all resolved rather to die than to famish? 5
ALL  Resolved, resolved.
FIRST CITIZEN  First you know, Caius Marcius is chief enemy to the people.
ALL  We know't, we know't.
FIRST CITIZEN  Let us kill him, and we'll have corn° 10 at our own price. Is't a verdict?

ALL  No more talking on't; let it be done. Away, away!
SECOND CITIZEN  One word, good citizens.
FIRST CITIZEN  We are accounted poor citizens, the 15 patricians good.° What authority surfeits on would relieve us. If they would yield us but the superfluity while it were wholesome, we might guess° they relieved us humanely; but they think we are too dear;° the leanness that afflicts us, the object° of our misery, is 20 as an inventory to particularize their abundance;° our sufferance is a gain to them. Let us revenge this with our pikes° ere we become rakes.° For the gods know I speak this in hunger for bread, not in thirst for revenge. 25
SECOND CITIZEN  Would you proceed especially against Caius Marcius?

---

*The decorative border shown above appeared on the first page of* Coriolanus *in the First Folio edition of Shakespeare's plays, 1623.*

**I.i.10 corn** grain (wheat, barley, etc., not Indian corn)

**16 good** well-off  **18 guess** think  **19 dear** expensive  **20 object** sight  **21 inventory . . . abundance** list in which to read a detailed account of their wealth as compared with our poverty  **23 pikes** pitchforks; **rakes** cf. *lean as a rake*

FIRST CITIZEN　Against him first: he's a very dog to the commonalty.°

SECOND CITIZEN　Consider you what services he 30 has done for his country?

FIRST CITIZEN　Very well, and could be content to give him good report for't, but that he pays himself with being proud.

SECOND CITIZEN　Nay, but speak not maliciously. 35

FIRST CITIZEN　I say unto you, what he hath done famously he did it to that end; though soft-conscienced men can be content to say it was for his country, he did it to please his mother and to be partly proud,° which he is, even to the altitude of his virtue.° 40

SECOND CITIZEN　What he cannot help in his nature you account a vice in him. You must in no way say he is covetous.

FIRST CITIZEN　If I must not, I need not be barren of accusations. He hath faults (with surplus) to tire in 45 repetition. (*Shouts within.*) What shouts are these? The other side o' th' city is risen. Why stay we prating here? To th' Capitol!°

ALL　Come, come.

FIRST CITIZEN　Soft,° who comes here? 50

*Enter* MENENIUS *Agrippa.*

SECOND CITIZEN　Worthy Menenius Agrippa, one that hath always loved the people.

FIRST CITIZEN　He's one honest enough; would all the rest were so!

MENENIUS
What work's, my countrymen, in hand? Where go you 55
With bats and clubs? The matter? Speak, I pray you.

FIRST CITIZEN　Our business is not unknown to th' Senate; they have had inkling this fortnight what we intend to do, which now we'll show 'em in deeds. They say poor suitors have strong breaths; they shall 60 know we have strong arms too.

MENENIUS
Why, masters, my good friends, mine honest neighbors,
Will you undo yourselves?

FIRST CITIZEN　We cannot, sir; we are undone already. 65

MENENIUS
I tell you, friends, most charitable care
Have the patricians of you. For your wants,
Your suffering in this dearth,° you may as well
Strike at the heaven with your staves as lift them
Against the Roman state, whose course will on 70
The way it takes, cracking ten thousand curbs°
Of more strong link asunder than can ever
Appear in your impediment.° For the dearth,
The gods, not the patricians, make it, and
Your knees to them (not arms) must help. Alack, 75
You are transported° by calamity

Thither where more attends you; and you slander
The helms° o' th' state, who care for you like fathers,
When you curse them as enemies.

FIRST CITIZEN　Care for us! True, indeed! They 80 ne'er cared for us yet. Suffer us to famish, and their storehouses crammed with grain; make edicts for usury, to support usurers; repeal daily any wholesome act established against the rich, and provide more piercing statutes daily to chain up and restrain the poor. 85 If the wars eat us not up, they will; and there's all the love they bear us.

MENENIUS
Either you must
Confess yourselves wondrous malicious,
Or be accused of folly. I shall tell you 90
A pretty tale; it may be you have heard it;
But since it serves my purpose, I will venture
To stale't° a little more.

FIRST CITIZEN　Well, I'll hear it, sir. Yet you must not think to fob off° our disgrace° with a tale. But, 95 and't° please you, deliver.

MENENIUS
There was a time when all the body's members
Rebelled against the belly; thus accused it:
That only like a gulf° it did remain
I' th' midst o' th' body, idle and unactive, 100
Still cupboarding the viand,° never bearing
Like labor with the rest; where th' other instruments°
Did see and hear, devise, instruct, walk, feel,
And, mutually participate,° did minister
Unto the appetite and affection° common 105
Of the whole body. The belly answered—

FIRST CITIZEN　Well, sir, what answer made the belly?

MENENIUS
Sir, I shall tell you. With a kind of smile,
Which ne'er came from the lungs, but even thus— 110
For, look you, I may make the belly smile
As well as speak—it tauntingly replied
To th' discontented members, the mutinous parts
That envied his receipt;° even so most fitly
As you malign our senators for that 115
They are not such as you.

FIRST CITIZEN　　　　　　　Your belly's answer—What?
The kingly crownèd head, the vigilant eye,
The counselor heart, the arm our soldier,
Our steed the leg, the tongue our trumpeter,
With other muniments° and petty helps 120
In this our fabric, if that they—

MENENIUS　　　　　　　What then?
'Fore me,° this fellow speaks! What then? What then?

FIRST CITIZEN
Should by the cormorant belly be restrained,
Who is the sink° o' th' body—

MENENIUS　　　　　　　Well, what then?

---

29 **commonalty** common people　39 **to be partly proud** in part from pride　40 **virtue** valor (Latin sense)　48 **Capitol** Capitoline Hill, on which the Temple of Jupiter stood (here and often, for the Senate House nearby)　50 **Soft** stop (an interjection)　68 **dearth** famine　71 **curbs** restraints　73 **in your impediment** in any hindrance you make　76 **transported** carried out of your minds

78 **helms** helmsmen　93 **stale't** make it stale　95 **fob off** set aside with a trick; **disgrace** misfortune　96 **and't** if it　99 **gulf** whirlpool　101 **viand** food　102 **instruments** organs　104 **mutually participate** taking part in common　105 **affection** inclination　114 **his receipt** what he received　120 **muniments** furnishings (fortifications)　122 **'Fore me** by my soul　124 **sink** sewer

FIRST CITIZEN
The former agents, if they did complain,  125
What could the belly answer?

MENENIUS                I will tell you;
If you'll bestow a small (of what you have little)
Patience awhile, you'st° hear the belly's answer.

FIRST CITIZEN
Y' are° long about it.

MENENIUS                Note me this, good friend
Your most grave belly° was deliberate,  130
Not rash like his accusers, and thus answered:
"True is it, my incorporate friends," quoth he,
"That I receive the general food at first,
Which you do live upon; and fit it is,
Because I am the storehouse and the shop°  135
Of the whole body. But, if you do remember,
I send it through the rivers of your blood,
Even to the court, the heart, to th' seat o' th' brain;
And, through the cranks° and offices° of man,
The strongest nerves° and small inferior veins  140
From me receive that natural competency°
Whereby they live; and though that all at once"—
You, my good friends, this says the belly, mark me—

FIRST CITIZEN
Ay, sir; well, well.

MENENIUS            "Though all at once cannot
See what I do deliver out to each,  145
Yet I can make my audit up, that all
From me do back receive the flour of all,
And leave me but the bran." What say you to't?

FIRST CITIZEN
It was an answer. How apply you this?

MENENIUS
The senators of Rome are this good belly,  150
And you the mutinous members. For examine
Their counsels and their cares, disgest° things rightly
Touching the weal o' th' common,° you shall find
No public benefit which you receive
But it proceeds or comes from them to you,  155
And no way from yourselves. What do you think,
You, the great toe of this assembly?

FIRST CITIZEN
I the great toe! Why the great toe?

MENENIUS
For that, being one o' th' lowest, basest, poorest,
Of this most wise rebellion, thou goest foremost.  160
Thou rascal,° that are worst in blood° to run,
Lead'st first to win some vantage.°
But make you ready your stiff° bats and clubs;
Rome and her rats are at the point of battle;
The one side must have bale.°

*Enter Caius* MARCIUS.

Hail, noble Marcius!  165

MARCIUS
Thanks. What's the matter, you dissentious rogues
That, rubbing the poor itch of your opinion,
Make yourselves scabs?°

FIRST CITIZEN            We have ever your good word.

MARCIUS
He that will give good words to thee will flatter
Beneath abhorring. What would you have, you curs,  170
That like nor peace nor war? The one affrights you,
The other makes you proud. He that trusts to you,
Where he should find you lions, finds you hares;
Where foxes, geese. You are no surer, no,
Than is the coal of fire upon the ice,  175
Or hailstone in the sun. Your virtue is
To make him worthy whose offense subdues him°
And curse that justice did it.° Who deserves greatness
Deserves your hate; and your affections° are
A sick man's appetite, who desires most that  180
Which would increase his evil. He that depends
Upon your favors swims with fins of lead
And hews down oaks with rushes. Hang ye! Trust ye!
With every minute you do change a mind,
And call him noble that was now your hate,  185
Him vile that was your garland. What's the matter
That in these several places of the city
You cry against the noble Senate, who
(Under the gods) keep you in awe, which else
Would feed on one another? What's their seeking?  190

MENENIUS
For corn at their own rates, whereof they say
The city is well stored.

MARCIUS                Hang 'em! They say!
They'll sit by th' fire, and presume to know
What's done i' th' Capitol: who's like to rise,
Who thrives and who declines; side factions° and give
out  195
Conjectural marriages, making parties strong,
And feebling° such as stand not in their liking
Below their cobbled shoes. They say there's grain
enough!
Would the nobility lay aside their ruth,°
And let me use my sword, I'd make a quarry°  200
With thousands of these quartered slaves, as high
As I could pick my lance.

MENENIUS
Nay, these are almost thoroughly persuaded;
For thou abundantly they lack discretion,
Yet are they passing° cowardly. But, I beseech you,  205
What says the other troop?

MARCIUS                They are dissolved. Hang 'em!
They said they were an-hungry;° sighed forth prov-
erbs°—
That hunger broke stone walls, that dogs must eat,
That meat was made for mouths, that the gods sent
not

128 **you'st** you'll (for "you shalt")  129 **Y' are** you're  130 **Your . . . belly** this most grave belly we speak of  135 **shop** factory  139 **cranks** winding paths; **offices** parts of a house where household work is done, e.g., kitchen  140 **nerves** tendons  141 **natural competency** supply adequate to their nature  152 **disgest** digest  153 **weal . . . common** welfare of the people  161 **rascal** a lean deer, or a hound; **blood** condition  162 **vantage** advantage  163 **stiff** stout  165 **bale** harm

168 **Make yourselves scabs** make scabs for yourselves (also, "make yourselves into loathsome fellows")  177 **subdues him** lays him low  178 **that . . . it** the justice that punished him  179 **affections** desires  195 **side factions** take sides (form parties)  197 **feebling** weakening (bringing down)  199 **ruth** compassion  200 **quarry** heap of dead (usually of game animals)  205 **passing** exceedingly  207 **an-hungry** hungry; **sighed forth proverbs** implying that they talk like rustics

Corn for the rich men only. With these shreds      210
They vented their complainings, which being an-
    swered,
And a petition granted them, a strange one,
To break the heart of generosity°
And make bold power look pale, they threw their caps
As they would hang them on the horns o' th' moon,   215
Shouting their emulation.°

MENENIUS                    What is granted them?

MARCIUS
Five tribunes to defend their vulgar° wisdoms,
Of their own choice. One's Junius Brutus—
Sicinius Velutus, and—I know not. 'Sdeath!
The rabble should have first unroofed the city,   220
Ere so prevailed with me; it will in time
Win upon power° and throw forth greater themes
For insurrection's arguing.°

MENENIUS                    This is strange.

MARCIUS
Go, get you home, you fragments!

*Enter a* MESSENGER, *hastily.*

MESSENGER
Where's Caius Marcius?

MARCIUS                    Here: what's the matter?   225

MESSENGER
The news is, sir, the Volsces are in arms.

MARCIUS
I am glad on't: then we shall ha' means to vent°
Our musty superfluity. See, our best elders.

*Enter* SICINIUS *Velutus, Junius* BRUTUS, COMINIUS,
TITUS *Lartius, with other* SENATORS.

FIRST SENATOR
Marcius, 'tis true that you have lately told us;
The Volsces are in arms.

MARCIUS                    They have a leader,   230
Tullus Aufidius, that will put you to't.°
I sin in envying his nobility;
And were I anything but what I am,
I would wish me only he.

COMINIUS                    You have fought together.

MARCIUS
Were half to half the world by th' ears, and he   235
Upon my party, I'd revolt, to make
Only my wars with him. He is a lion
That I am proud to hunt.

FIRST SENATOR                    Then, worthy Marcius,
Attend upon Cominius to these wars.

COMINIUS
It is your former promise.

MARCIUS                    Sir, it is,   240
And I am constant.° Titus Lartius, thou
Shalt see me once more strike at Tullus' face.
What, art thou stiff?° Stand'st out?°

TITUS                    No, Caius Marcius;

I'll lean upon one crutch and fight with t' other
Ere stay behind this business.

MENENIUS                    O, true-bred!   245

FIRST SENATOR
Your company to th' Capitol; where I know
Our greatest friends attend us.

TITUS          [*To* COMINIUS.] Lead you on.

[*To* MARCIUS.]

Follow Cominius; we must follow you;
Right worthy you priority.°

COMINIUS                    Noble Marcius!

FIRST SENATOR [*To the* CITIZENS.]
Hence to your homes; begone!

MARCIUS                    Nay, let them follow.   250
The Volsces have much corn; take these rats thither
To gnaw their garners. Worshipful mutineers,
Your valor puts well forth.° Pray, follow.   *Exeunt.*
    CITIZENS *steal away. Manet*° SICINIUS *and* BRUTUS.

SICINIUS
Was ever man so proud as is this Marcius?

BRUTUS
He has no equal.   255

SICINIUS
When we were chosen tribunes for the people—

BRUTUS
Marked you his lip and eyes?

SICINIUS                    Nay, but his taunts.

BRUTUS
Being moved, he will not spare to gird° the gods.

SICINIUS
Bemock the modest moon.

BRUTUS
The present wars devour him; he is grown   260
Too proud to be so valiant.°

SICINIUS                    Such a nature,
Tickled with good success,° disdains the shadow
Which he treads on at noon. But I do wonder
His insolence can brook to be commanded
Under Cominius.

BRUTUS                    Fame, at the which he aims,   265
In whom already he's well graced, cannot
Better be held, nor more attained, than by
A place below the first. For what miscarries
Shall be the general's fault, though he perform
To th' utmost of a man; and giddy censure   270
Will then cry out of Marcius, "O, if he
Had borne the business!"

SICINIUS                    Besides, if things go well,
Opinion, that so sticks on Marcius, shall
Of his demerits° rob Cominius.

BRUTUS                    Come:
Half all Cominius' honors are to Marcius,   275
Though Marcius earned them not; and all his faults
To Marcius shall be honors, though indeed
In aught he merit not.

SICINIUS                    Let's hence, and hear

---

213 **break . . . generosity** give the deathblow to the nobility
216 **Shouting their emulation** expressing envious joy   217
**vulgar** common, plebeian   222 **Win upon power** get the
better of authority   223 **For insurrection's arguing** for rebels
to debate in action (abstract for concrete, as often in *Coriolanus*)
227 **vent** get rid of   231 **put you to't** test you severely
241 **constant** faithful   243 **stiff** obstinate, set (on not fighting);
**Stand'st out** You're staying out of it?

249 **Right . . . priority** you well deserve first place   253 **puts
well forth** gives fair promise (literally, buds)   253 s.d. **Manet**
remains (Latin; although the subject is plural, this form, the
third person singular, commonly appears in Elizabethan stage
directions)   258 **gird** taunt   260–61 **grown . . . valiant** i.e.,
such pride is not permissible in one so warlike (because dangerous)   262 **success** outcome   274 **demerits** deserts

How the dispatch° is made; and in what fashion,
More than his singularity,° he goes                                    280
Upon this present action.
BRUTUS                              Let's along.          *Exeunt.*

[Scene II. *Corioli. The Senate House.*]

*Enter Tullus* AUFIDIUS, *with* SENATORS *of Corioles.*

FIRST SENATOR
So, your opinion is, Aufidius,
That they of Rome are ent'red in° our counsels,
And know how we proceed.
AUFIDIUS                              Is it not yours?
What° ever have been thought on in this state
That could be brought to bodily act ere Rome          5
Had circumvention?° 'Tis not four days gone
Since I heard thence—these are the words—I think
I have the letter here. Yes, here it is:
"They have pressed a power,° but it is not known
Whether for east or west. The dearth is great;       10
The people mutinous; and it is rumored,
Cominius, Marcius your old enemy
(Who is of Rome worse hated than of you),
And Titus Lartius, a most valiant Roman,
These three lead on this preparation°                15
Whither 'tis bent—most likely 'tis for you.
Consider of it."
FIRST SENATOR     Our army's in the field.
We never yet made doubt but Rome was ready
To answer us.
AUFIDIUS          Nor did you think it folly
To keep your great pretenses° veiled till when       20
They needs must show themselves; which in the
   hatching,
It seemed, appeared to Rome. By the discovery
We shall be short'ned in our aim, which was
To take in° many towns ere almost Rome
Should know we were afoot.
SECOND SENATOR          Noble Aufidius,             25
Take your commission; hie you to your bands:
Let us alone to guard Corioles.
If they set down before's,° for the remove°
Bring up your army; but I think you'll find
They've not prepared for us.
AUFIDIUS               O, doubt not that;            30
I speak from certainties. Nay, more,
Some parcels° of their power are forth already,
And only hitherward.° I leave your honors.
If we and Caius Marcius chance to meet,
'Tis sworn between us we shall ever strike           35
Till one can do no more.
ALL                    The gods assist you!

AUFIDIUS
And keep your honors safe!
FIRST SENATOR                    Farewell.
SECOND SENATOR                              Farewell.
ALL   Farewell.                        *Exeunt omnes.*°

[Scene III. *Rome. A room in Marcius' house.*]

*Enter* VOLUMNIA *and* VIRGILIA, *mother and wife to
Marcius. They set them down on two low stools, and sew.*

VOLUMNIA  I pray you, daughter, sing, or express
yourself in a more comfortable° sort. If my son were
my husband, I should freelier rejoice in that absence
wherein he won honor than in the embracements of
his bed where he would show most love. When yet   5
he was but tender-bodied, and the only son of my
womb; when youth with comeliness plucked all gaze°
his way; when, for a day of kings' entreaties, a mother
should not sell him an hour from her beholding; I,
considering how honor would become such a person°—  10
that it was no better than picture-like to hang by th'
wall, if renown made it not stir—was pleased to let
him seek danger where he was like to find fame. To a
cruel war I sent him, from whence he returned, his
brows bound with oak.° I tell thee, daughter, I sprang  15
not more in joy at first hearing he was a man-child
than now in first seeing he had proved himself a man.
VIRGILIA  But had he died in the business, madam,
how then?
VOLUMNIA  Then his good report should have been    20
my son; I therein would have found issue. Hear me
profess° sincerely: had I a dozen sons, each in my love
alike, and none less dear than thine and my good
Marcius, I had rather had eleven die nobly for their
country than one voluptuously surfeit out of action.   25

*Enter a* GENTLEWOMAN.

GENTLEWOMAN
Madam, the Lady Valeria is come to visit you.
VIRGILIA
Beseech° you give me leave to retire myself.
VOLUMNIA
Indeed, you shall not.
Methinks I hear hither your husband's drum;
See him pluck Aufidius down by th' hair—           30
As children from a bear, the Volsces shunning him.
Methinks I see him stamp thus, and call thus:
"Come on, you cowards, you were got° in fear,
Though you were born in Rome." His bloody brow
With his mailed hand then wiping, forth he goes,    35
Like to a harvest-man that's tasked to mow
Or° all or lose his hire.
VIRGILIA
His bloody brow? O Jupiter, no blood!
VOLUMNIA
Away, you fool! It more becomes a man

---

**279 dispatch** execution of the business   **280 More . . .
singularity** apart from his usual peculiarity of manner
**I.ii.2 ent'red in** initiated into (familiar with)   **4 What** plural,
i.e., "counsels," line 2   **6 circumvention** means to circumvent   **9 pressed a power** collected troops   **15 preparation**
force that has been prepared   **20 great pretenses** main intentions (cf. *grand design*)   **24 take in** capture   **28 set down
before's** lay siege to us; **remove** raising of the siege   **32
parcels** portions   **33 hitherward** i.e., to attack Rome

**38 s.d. omnes** all (Latin)
**I.iii.2 comfortable** cheerful   **7 plucked all gaze** drew the
eyes of all   **10 person** handsome figure   **15 oak** "garland"
of honor for saving a fellow Roman in battle   **22 profess**
declare   **27 Beseech** I beg   **33 got** begotten   **37 Or** either

Than gilt his trophy.° The breasts of Hecuba,° 40
When she did suckle Hector, looked not lovelier
Than Hector's forehead when it spit forth blood
At Grecian sword, contemning.° Tell Valeria
We are fit° to bid her welcome.

         *Exit* GENTLEWOMAN.

VIRGILIA
Heavens bless° my lord from fell° Aufidius! 45

VOLUMNIA
He'll beat Aufidius' head below his knee,
And tread upon his neck.

*Enter* VALERIA, *with an* USHER° *and a*
GENTLEWOMAN.

VALERIA My ladies both, good day to you.

VOLUMNIA Sweet madam!

VIRGILIA I am glad to see your ladyship. 50

VALERIA How do you both? You are manifest
housekeepers.° What are you sewing here? A fine
spot,° in good faith. How does your little son?

VIRGILIA I thank your ladyship; well, good madam.

VOLUMNIA He had rather see the swords and hear a 55
drum than look upon his schoolmaster.

VALERIA O' my word, the father's son! I'll swear 'tis
a very pretty boy. O' my troth, I looked upon him
o' Wednesday half an hour together; has such a
confirmed° countenance! I saw him run after a gilded 60
butterfly; and when he caught it, he let it go again;
and after it again; and over and over he comes, and up
again; catched it again; or whether his fall enraged
him, or how 'twas, he did so set his teeth, and tear it.
O, I warrant, how he mammocked° it! 65

VOLUMNIA One on's° father's moods.

VALERIA Indeed, la, 'tis a noble child.

VIRGILIA A crack,° madam.

VALERIA Come, lay aside your stitchery; I must have
you play the idle huswife with me this afternoon. 70

VIRGILIA No, good madam; I will not out of doors.

VALERIA Not out of doors!

VOLUMNIA She shall, she shall.

VIRGILIA Indeed, no, by your patience;° I'll not over
the threshold till my lord return from the wars. 75

VALERIA Fie, you confine yourself most unreasonably; come, you must go visit the good lady that
lies in.

VIRGILIA I will wish her speedy strength, and visit
her with my prayers; but I cannot go thither. 80

VOLUMNIA Why I pray you?

VIRGILIA 'Tis not to save labor, nor that I want° love.

VALERIA You would be another Penelope;° yet, they
say, all the yarn she spun in Ulysses' absence did but
fill Ithaca° full of moths. Come; I would your cambric 85
were sensible° as your finger, that you might leave
pricking it for pity. Come, you shall go with us.

VALERIA No, good madam, pardon me; indeed, I
will not forth.

VALERIA In truth, la, go with me, and I'll tell you ex- 90
cellent news of your husband.

VIRGILIA O, good madam, there can be none yet.

VALERIA Verily, I do not jest with you; there came
news from him last night.

VIRGILIA Indeed, madam? 95

VALERIA In earnest, it's true; I heard a senator speak
it. Thus it is: the Volsces have an army forth; against
whom Cominius the general is gone, with one part of
our Roman power. Your lord and Titus Lartius are
set down before their city Corioles; they nothing 100
doubt prevailing, and to make it brief wars. This is
true, on mine honor; and so, I pray, go with us.

VIRGILIA Give me excuse, good madam; I will obey
you in everything hereafter.

VOLUMNIA Let her alone, lady; as she is now, she will 105
but disease our better mirth.°

VALERIA In troth, I think she would. Fare you well,
then. Come, good sweet lady. Prithee, Virgilia, turn
thy solemness out o' door, and go along with us.

VIRGILIA No, at a word,° madam; indeed, I must not. 110
I wish you much mirth.

VALERIA Well then, farewell.    *Exeunt* LADIES.

[Scene IV. *Before Corioli.*]

*Enter* MARCIUS, *Titus* LARTIUS, *with drum and colors,
with* CAPTAINS *and* SOLDIERS, *as before the city
Corioles. To them a* MESSENGER.

MARCIUS
Yonder comes news: a wager they have met.

LARTIUS
My horse to yours, no.

MARCIUS       'Tis done.

LARTIUS         Agreed.

MARCIUS
Say, has our general met the enemy?

MESSENGER
They lie in view, but have not spoke° as yet.

LARTIUS
So, the good horse is mine.

MARCIUS      I'll buy him of you. 5

LARTIUS
No, I'll nor sell nor give him; lend you him I will
For half a hundred years. Summon the town.

MARCIUS
How far off lie these armies?

MESSENGER      Within this mile and half.

MARCIUS
Then shall we hear their 'larum,° and they ours.
Now, Mars, I prithee, make us quick in work, 10
That we with smoking° swords may march from
  hence
To help our fielded° friends! Come, blow thy blast.

---

**40 trophy** monument; **Hecuba** Queen of Troy and mother
of Hector, who defended the city from the Greeks **43
contemning** in scorn **44 fit** ready **45 bless** guard; **fell**
savage **47 s.d. Usher** servant accompanying a lady **51–52
manifest housekeepers** clearly stay-at-homes **53 spot**
pattern in embroidery **60 confirmed** determined **65
mammocked** tore to pieces **66 on's** of his **68 crack** rascal
**74 patience** leave **82 want** am lacking in **83 Penelope**
Ulysses' faithful wife, who by using her weaving as an excuse,
postponed her answer to offers of marriage **85 Ithaca** Ulysses'
home city **86 sensible** sensitive

**106 disease . . . mirth** spoil our fun, which would be better
(without her) **110 at a word** to put it briefly
**I.iv.4 spoke** engaged **9 'larum** alarum, call to arms **11
smoking** reeking (with blood) **12 fielded** in the field of
battle

*They sound a parley. Enter two* SENATORS, *with others,*
*on the walls of Corioles.*

Tullus Aufidius, is he within your walls?

FIRST SENATOR
No, nor a man that fears you less than he;
That's lesser than a little. (*Drum afar off.*) Hark, our
  drums                                                          15
Are bringing forth our youth. We'll break our walls
Rather than they shall pound us up.° Our gates,
Which yet seem shut, we have but pinned with rushes;
They'll open of themselves. (*Alarum far off.*) Hark you,
  far off!
There is Aufidius. List what work he makes                      20
Amongst your cloven° army.

MARCIUS                            O, they are at it!

LARTIUS
Their noise be our instruction.° Ladders, ho!

*Enter the* ARMY *of the Volsces.*

MARCIUS
They fear us not, but issue forth their city.
Now put your shields before your hearts, and fight
With hearts more proof° than shields. Advance, brave
  Titus.                                                        25
They do disdain us much beyond our thoughts,
Which makes me sweat with wrath. Come on, my
  fellows.
He that retires, I'll take him for a Volsce,
And he shall feel mine edge.

*Alarum. The* ROMANS *are beat back to their trenches.*
*Enter* MARCIUS, *cursing.*

MARCIUS
All the contagion of the south° light on you,                  30
You shames of Rome! You herd of—boils and plagues
Plaster you o'er, that you may be abhorred
Farther than seen, and one infect another
Against the wind a mile!° You souls of geese
That bear the shapes of men, how have you run               35
From slaves that apes would beat! Pluto and hell!
All hurt behind, backs red, and faces pale
With flight and agued° fear! Mend° and charge
  home,°
Or, by the fires of heaven, I'll leave the foe
And make my wars on you. Look to't. Come on;               40
If you'll stand fast, we'll beat them to their wives,
As they us to our trenches. Follow's!°

*Another alarum; and* MARCIUS *follows them° to [the]*
*gates and is shut in.°*

So, now the gates are ope. Now prove good seconds!°

'Tis for the followers° Fortune widens them,
Not for the fliers. Mark me, and do the like.              45
                                            *Enters the gates.*

FIRST SOLDIER
Foolhardiness; not I.
SECOND SOLDIER    Nor I.
FIRST SOLDIER
See, they have shut him in. *Alarum continues.*
ALL                              To th' pot,° I warrant him.

*Enter Titus* LARTIUS.

LARTIUS
What is become of Marcius?
ALL                          Slain, sir, doubtless.
FIRST SOLDIER
Following the fliers at the very heels,
With them he enters; who, upon the sudden,                 50
Clapped to their gates. He is himself alone,
To answer all the city.
LARTIUS                          O noble fellow!
Who sensibly° outdares his senseless sword,
And when it bows stand'st up! Thou art left, Marcius!
A carbuncle° entire, as big as thou art,                   55
Were not so rich a jewel. Thou wast a soldier
Even to Cato's° wish, not fierce and terrible
Only in strokes; but with thy grim looks and
The thunderlike percussion of thy sounds
Thou mad'st thine enemies shake, as if the world           60
Were feverous and did tremble.

*Enter* MARCIUS, *bleeding, assaulted by the enemy.*

FIRST SOLDIER                    Look, sir.
LARTIUS                          O, 'tis Marcius!
Let's fetch him off, or make remain alike.°
                            *They fight, and all enter the city.*


[Scene V. *Within Corioli.*]

*Enter certain* ROMANS, *with spoils.*

FIRST ROMAN    This will I carry to Rome.
SECOND ROMAN    And I this.
THIRD ROMAN    A murrain on't!° I took this for silver.
                                                *Exeunt.*

*Alarum continues still afar off.*
*Enter* MARCIUS *and Titus* LARTIUS, *with a* TRUMPET.°

MARCIUS
See here these movers° that do prize their hours
At a cracked drachma!° Cushions, leaden spoons,            5
Irons of a doit,° doublets that hangmen would
Bury with those that wore them, these base slaves,
Ere yet the fight be done, pack up. Down with them!
And hark, what noise the general makes! To him!
There is the man of my soul's hate, Aufidius,              10

17 **pound us up** shut us in (cf. *dog pound*)    21 **cloven** divided
22 **be our instruction** be a lesson to us    25 **proof** tested (and
so impenetrable)    30 **south** south wind (pestilential)    34
**Against . . . mile** i.e., the infection carrying a mile in the face
of a contrary wind    38 **agued** i.e., shaking as if from an ague-
fit ("ague" = malarial fever);  **Mend** do better (with pun on
the hygienic sense);  **home** i.e., into the heart of the enemy's
forces    42 **Follow's** follow us, i.e., follow me (the Folio gives
"trenches followes"; the adopted reading makes sense out of
the Folio reading, but it is ugly and anticlimactic; perhaps
"followes" is a misplaced stage direction)    42 s.d. **them** the
Volsces;  **is shut in** i.e., at the end of this speech Marcius
enters the gates and is shut in    43 **seconds** helpers

44 **followers** pursuers    47 **To th' pot** to destruction (cf. *gone
to pot*)    53 **sensibly** though subject to feeling    55 **carbuncle**
a red precious stone    57 **Cato** the Censor, stern upholder
of old Roman virtues    62 **make remain alike** stay like
him ("remain," a noun, means "a stay")
**I.v.3 murrain on't** plague on it    3 s.d. **Trumpet** trumpeter
4 **movers** active fellows (ironical)    5 **drachma** Greek coin
6 **of a doit** worth a doit (coin of little value)

Piercing our Romans. Then, valiant Titus, take
Convenient numbers to make good° the city;
Whilst I, with those that have the spirit, will haste
To help Cominius.
LARTIUS            Worthy sir, thou bleed'st;
Thy exercise hath been too violent       15
For a second course° of fight.
MARCIUS           Sir, praise me not;
My work hath yet not warmed me. Fare you well.
The blood I drop is rather physical°
Than dangerous to me. To Aufidius thus
I will appear, and fight.
LARTIUS         Now the fair goddess, Fortune, 20
Fall deep in love with thee; and her great charms
Misguide thy opposers' swords! Bold gentleman,
Prosperity be thy page!°
MARCIUS          Thy friend no less
Than those she placeth highest! So farewell.
LARTIUS
Thou worthiest Marcius!      [*Exit* MARCIUS.] 25
Go, sound thy trumpet in the marketplace;
Call thither all the officers o' th' town,
Where they shall know our mind. Away!     *Exeunt.*

[Scene VI. *Near the camp of Cominius.*]

*Enter* COMINIUS, *as it were in retire, with* SOLDIERS.

COMINIUS
Breathe° you, my friends; well fought; we are come
  off°
Like Romans, neither foolish in our stands
Nor cowardly in retire.° Believe me, sirs,
We shall be charged again. Whiles we have struck,
By interims and conveying gusts° we have heard   5
The charges of our friends. The Roman gods,
Lead their successes° as we wish our own,
That both our powers, with smiling fronts° encoun-
  t'ring,
May give you thankful sacrifice!

*Enter a* MESSENGER.

                 Thy news?
MESSENGER
The citizens of Corioles have issued,        10
And given to Lartius and to Marcius battle.
I saw our party to their trenches driven,
And then I came away.
COMINIUS        Though thou speakest truth,
Methinks thou speak'st not well. How long is't since?
MESSENGER
Above an hour, my lord.               15
COMINIUS
'Tis not a mile; briefly° we heard their drums.
How couldst thou in a mile confound° an hour,
And bring thy news so late?
MESSENGER         Spies of the Volsces

Held me in chase, that I was forced to wheel
Three or four miles about; else had I, sir,       20
Half an hour since brought my report.

*Enter* MARCIUS.

COMINIUS            Who's yonder
That does appear as he were flayed? O gods!
He has the stamp° of Marcius, and I have
Before-time seen him thus.
MARCIUS         Come I too late?
COMINIUS
The shepherd knows not thunder from a tabor°   25
More than I know the sound of Marcius' tongue
From every meaner man.
MARCIUS         Come I too late?
COMINIUS
Ay, if you come not in the blood of others,
But mantled in your own.
MARCIUS       O, let me clip° ye
In arms as sound as when I wooed; in heart      30
As merry as when our nuptial day was done,
And tapers burned to bedward!°
COMINIUS        Flower of warriors!
How is't with Titus Lartius?
MARCIUS
As with a man busied about decrees:
Condemning some to death and some to exile;   35
Ransoming him, or pitying, threat'ning th' other;
Holding Corioles in the name of Rome,
Even like a fawning greyhound in the leash,
To let him slip° at will.
COMINIUS        Where is that slave
Which told me they had beat you to your trenches?   40
Where is he? Call him hither.
MARCIUS         Let him alone;
He did inform° the truth. But for our gentlemen,°
The common file°—a plague! tribunes for them!—
The mouse ne'er shunned the cat as they did budge
From rascals worse than they.
COMINIUS       But how prevailed you? 45
MARCIUS
Will the time serve to tell? I do not think.
Where is the enemy? Are you lords o' th' field?
If not, why cease you till you are so?
COMINIUS             Marcius,
We have at disadvantage fought and did
Retire to win our purpose.                50
MARCIUS
How lies their battle? Know you on which side
They have placed their men of trust?
COMINIUS           As I guess, Marcius,
Their bands i' th' vaward° are the Antiates,
Of their best trust; o'er them Aufidius,
Their very heart of hope.
MARCIUS          I do beseech you,    55
By all the battles wherein we have fought,
By th' blood we have shed together, by th' vows

**12 make good** make sure of   **16 course** bout   **18 physical**
beneficial   **23 page** attendant
**I.vi.1 Breathe** rest; **are come off** leave the field   **3 retire**
retreat   **5 By . . . gusts** at intervals, by gusts of wind
carrying (the sound)   **7 successes** outcomes   **8 fronts** first
lines (also, "faces")   **16 briefly** a short time ago   **17 confound** waste

**23 stamp** characteristic features (metaphor from coining)
**25 tabor** small drum   **29 clip** embrace   **32 burned to bedward** burned low, announcing the time for bed   **39 let him
slip** unleash him   **42 inform** report; **gentlemen** ironical
**43 common file** the plebeian soldiers   **53 vaward** vanguard,
advance troops

We have made to endure friends, that you directly
Set me against Aufidius and his Antiates;
And that you not delay the present,° but,                    60
Filling the air with swords advanced and darts,
We prove° this very hour.
COMINIUS                    Though I could wish
You were conducted to a gentle bath,
And balms applied to you, yet dare I never
Deny your asking. Take your choice of those           65
That best can aid your action.
MARCIUS                    Those are they
That most are willing. If any such be here—
As it were sin to doubt—that love this painting
Wherein you see me smeared; if any fear
Lesser his person° than an ill report;                     70
If any think brave death outweighs bad life,
And that his country's dearer than himself;
Let him alone, or so many so minded,
Wave thus, to express his disposition,°
And follow Marcius.                                        75

*They all shout, and wave their swords; take him up in their
arms, and cast up their caps.*

O me alone! Make you a sword of me?
If these shows be not outward, which of you
But is four Volsces? None of you but is
Able to bear against the great Aufidius
A shield as hard as his. A certain number,              80
Though thanks to all, must I select from all. The rest
Shall bear the business in some other fight,
As cause will be obeyed.° Please you to march;
And four shall quickly draw out my command,
Which men are best inclined.
COMINIUS                    March on, my fellows:   85
Make good this ostentation,° and you shall
Divide in all with us.                          *Exeunt.*

[Scene VII. *The gates of Corioli.*]

*Titus* LARTIUS, *having set a guard upon Corioles, going
with drum and trumpet toward* COMINIUS *and Caius
MARCIUS, enters with a* LIEUTENANT, *other* SOLDIERS,
*and a* SCOUT.

LARTIUS
So, let the ports° be guarded; keep your duties
As I have set them down. If I do send, dispatch
Those centuries° to our aid; the rest will serve
For a short holding. If we lose the field,
We cannot keep the town.
LIEUTENANT                    Fear not our care, sir.   5
LARTIUS
Hence, and shut your gates upon's.
Our guider, come; to th' Roman camp conduct us.
                                    *Exit,* [*with the rest*].

[Scene VIII. *A field of battle.*]

*Alarum as in battle. Enter* MARCIUS *and* AUFIDIUS, *at
several doors.*°

MARCIUS
I'll fight with none but thee, for I do hate thee
Worse than a promise-breaker.
AUFIDIUS                    We hate alike:
Not Afric° owns a serpent I abhor
More than thy fame and envy. Fix thy foot.
MARCIUS
Let the first budger° die the other's slave,            5
And the gods doom him after!
AUFIDIUS                    If I fly, Marcius,
Holloa° me like a hare.
MARCIUS                    Within these hours, Tullus,
Alone I fought in your Corioles walls,
And made what work I pleased. 'Tis not my blood
Wherein thou see'st me masked. For thy revenge   10
Wrench up thy power to th' highest.
AUFIDIUS                    Wert thou the Hector
That was the whip of your bragged progeny,°
Thou shouldst not scape me here.

*Here they fight, and certain* VOLSCES *come in the aid of
Aufidius.* MARCIUS *fights till they be driven in breathless.*

Officious, and not valiant, you have shamed me
In your condemnèd seconds.°                             15

[Scene IX. *The Roman camp.*]

*Flourish. Alarum. A retreat is sounded. Enter at one
door,* COMINIUS *with the* ROMANS; *at another door,*
MARCIUS, *with his arm in a scarf.*

COMINIUS
If I should tell thee o'er this thy day's work,
Thou't° not believe thy deeds. But I'll report it
Where senators shall mingle tears with smiles;
Where great patricians shall attend, and shrug,°
I' th' end admire; where ladies shall be frighted,     5
And, gladly quaked,° hear more; where the dull
     tribunes,
That with the fusty° plebeians hate thine honors,
Shall say against their hearts, "We thank the gods
Our Rome hath such a soldier."
Yet cam'st thou to a morsel of this feast,°            10
Having fully dined before.

*Enter Titus* [LARTIUS], *with his* POWER, *from the
pursuit.*

LARTIUS                    O general,
Here is the steed, we the caparison!°
Hadst thou beheld—
MARCIUS                    Pray now, no more. My mother,
Who has a charter° to extol her blood,

60 **delay the present** put off the present occasion   **62 prove**
make trial of   **69–70 fear . . . person** fear less for his
body   **74 disposition** inclination   **83 cause . . . obeyed**
occasion shall demand   **86 ostentation** display
**I.vii.1 ports** gates   **3 centuries** companies (smallest units of a
Roman legion)

**I.viii.s.d. at several doors** from different entrances   **3 Afric**
Africa   **5 budger** one who moves   **7 Holloa** shout "halloo"
after (in hunting)   **12 whip . . . progeny** the whip used by
your boasted ancestors, the Trojans, against the Greeks   **15 In
. . . seconds** by your damnable help (cf. I.iv.43)
**I.ix.2 Thou't** thou wouldst   **4 shrug** i.e., in disbelief   **6
quaked** made to shake   **7 fusty** moldy   **10 cam'st . . . feast**
refers to Marcius' coming to support Cominius in the latter
part of the battle just ended   **12 caparison** the (mere) trappings   **14 charter** privilege granted her

When she does praise me grieves me. I have done    15
As you have done, that's what I can; induced
As you have been, that's for my country.
He that has but effected his good will°
Hath overta'en° mine act.

COMINIUS              You shall not be
The grave of your deserving; Rome must know    20
The value of her own. 'Twere a concealment
Worse than a theft, no less than a traducement,°
To hide your doings; and to silence that
Which, to the spire and top of praises vouched,°
Would seem but modest. Therefore, I beseech you,    25
In sign of what you are, not to reward
What you have done, before our army hear me.

MARCIUS
I have some wounds upon me, and they smart
To hear themselves rememb'red.

COMINIUS            Should they not,
Well might they fester 'gainst° ingratitude,    30
And tent themselves° with death.° Of all the horses—
Whereof we have ta'en good, and good store°—of all
The treasure in this field achieved and city,
We render you the tenth; to be ta'en forth
Before the common distribution at    35
Your only choice.

MARCIUS        I thank you, general;
But cannot make my heart consent to take
A bribe to pay my sword. I do refuse it,
And stand upon my common part with those
That have beheld the doing.    40

*A long flourish. They all cry, "Marcius! Marcius!"* cast
*up their caps and lances.* COMINIUS *and* LARTIUS *stand
bare.*

MARCIUS
May these same instruments, which you profane,
Never sound more! When drums and trumpets shall
I' th' field prove flatterers, let courts and cities be
Made all of false-faced soothing!°
When steel grows soft as the parasite's silk,    45
Let him° be made a coverture° for th' wars!
No more, I say! For that° I have not washed
My nose that bled, or foiled° some debile° wretch,
Which without note here's many else have done,
You shout me forth    50
In acclamations hyperbolical;
As if I loved my little should be dieted
In° praises sauced with lies.

COMINIUS            Too modest are you;
More cruel to your good report than grateful
To us that give° you truly. By your patience,    55
If 'gainst yourself you be incensed, we'll put you
(Like one that means his proper° harm) in manacles,
Then reason safely with you. Therefore, be it known,
As to us, to all the world, that Caius Marcius

Wears this war's garland: in token of the which,    60
My noble steed, known to the camp, I give him,
With all his trim belonging;° and from this time,
For what he did before Corioles, call him,
With all th' applause and clamor of the host,
Caius Marcius Coriolanus.    65
Bear th' addition° nobly ever!

*Flourish. Trumpets sound, and drums.*

OMNES°
Caius Marcius Coriolanus!

CORIOLANUS
I will go wash:
And when my face is fair, you shall perceive
Whether I blush, or no. Howbeit, I thank you.    70
I mean to stride your steed, and at all times
To undercrest your good addition°
To th' fairness° of my power.

COMINIUS           So, to our tent;
Where, ere we do repose us, we will write
To Rome of our success. You, Titus Lartius,    75
Must to Corioles back; send us to Rome
The best,° with whom we may articulate°
For their own good and ours.

LARTIUS           I shall, my lord.

CORIOLANUS
The gods begin to mock me. I, that now
Refused most princely gifts, am bound to beg    80
Of my lord general.

COMINIUS           Take't; 'tis yours. What is't?

CORIOLANUS
I sometime lay here in Corioles
At a poor man's house; he used me kindly.
He cried to me; I saw him prisoner;
But when Aufidius was within my view,    85
And wrath o'erwhelmed my pity. I request you
To give my poor host freedom.

COMINIUS           O, well begged!
Were he the butcher of my son, he should
Be free as is the wind. Deliver him, Titus.

LARTIUS
Marcius, his name?

CORIOLANUS        By Jupiter, forgot!    90
I am weary; yea, my memory is tired.
Have we no wine here?

COMINIUS           Go we to our tent.
The blood upon your visage dries; 'tis time
It should be looked to. Come.         *Exeunt.*

[Scene X. *The camp of the Volsces.*]

*A flourish. Cornets. Enter Tullus* AUFIDIUS, *bloody,
with two or three* SOLDIERS.

AUFIDIUS
The town is ta'en!

---

18 **good will** firm intention   19 **overta'en** surpassed   22
**traducement** slander   24 **to . . . vouched** though attested
in the highest terms of praise   30 **'gainst** against, in the face of
31 **tent themselves** be cleansed (refers to cleaning a wound
with a linen roll, a "tent"); **death** the "tent" being
"death," the wounds would prove fatal   32 **good store** plenty
44 **soothing** flattery   46 **him** it; **coverture** clothing   47
**For that** because   48 **foiled** defeated; **debile** weak   52–53
**dieted In** fed by   55 **give** report   57 **proper** own

62 **his trim belonging** the equipment that goes with it   66
**addition** title   67 **Omnes** all (Latin)   72 **undercrest . . .
addition** support the fine title you give (a "crest" in heraldry
is a figure above a shield; the suggested image is of a shield
with a man on horseback [line 71], beneath a crest [the
"addition"])   73 **To th' fairness** to the exact measure   77
**best** chief men; **articulate** make terms

FIRST SOLDIER
'Twill be delivered back on good condition.°

AUFIDIUS
Condition!
I would I were a Roman; for I cannot,
Being a Volsce, be that I am. Condition!    5
What good condition° can a treaty find
I' th' part that is at mercy?° Five times, Marcius,
I have fought with thee; so often hast thou beat me;
And wouldst do so, I think, should we encounter
As often as we eat. By th' elements,    10
If e'er again I meet him beard to beard,
He's mine or I am his. Mine emulation
Hath not that honor in't it had; for where
I thought to crush him in an equal force,
True sword to sword, I'll potch° at him some way,    15
Or wrath or craft may get him.

FIRST SOLDIER    He's the devil.

AUFIDIUS
Bolder, though not so subtle. My valor's poisoned
With only suff'ring stain° by him; for him
Shall fly out of itself.° Nor sleep nor sanctuary,
Being naked,° sick, nor fane° nor Capitol,    20
The prayers of priests nor times of sacrifice,
Embarquements° all of fury, shall lift up
Their rotten privilege and custom 'gainst
My hate to Marcius. Where I find him, were it
At home, upon my brother's guard,° even there,    25
Against the hospitable canon,° would I
Wash my fierce hand in's heart. Go you to th' city;
Learn how 'tis held, and what they are that must
Be hostages for Rome.

FIRST SOLDIER    Will not you go?

AUFIDIUS
I am attended° at the cypress grove. I pray you—    30
'Tis south the city mills—bring me word thither
How the world goes, that to the pace of it
I may spur on my journey.

FIRST SOLDIER    I shall, sir.    [*Exeunt.*]

# ACT II

[*Scene I. Rome. A public place.*]

*Enter* MENENIUS, *with the two tribunes of the people,*
SICINIUS *and* BRUTUS.

MENENIUS    The augurer° tells me we shall have news
tonight.

BRUTUS    Good or bad?

MENENIUS    Not according to the prayer of the people,
for they love not Marcius.    5

SICINIUS    Nature teaches beasts to know their friends.

MENENIUS    Pray you, who does the wolf love?

SICINIUS    The lamb.

MENENIUS    Ay, to devour him, as the hungry plebeians would the noble Marcius.    10

BRUTUS    He's a lamb indeed, that baas like a bear.

MENENIUS    He's a bear indeed, that lives like a lamb.
You two are old men: tell me one thing that I shall
ask you.

BOTH    Well, sir.    15

MENENIUS    In what enormity° is Marcius poor in,
that you two have not in abundance?

BRUTUS    He's poor in no one fault, but stored with all.

SICINIUS    Especially in pride.

BRUTUS    And topping all others in boasting.    20

MENENIUS    This is strange now. Do you two know
how you are censured° here in the city—I mean of us
o' th' right-hand file?° Do you?

BOTH    Why, how are we censured?

MENENIUS    Because you talk of pride now—will you    25
not be angry?

BOTH    Well, well, sir, well.

MENENIUS    Why 'tis no great matter; for a very little
thief of occasion° will rob you of a great deal of
patience. Give your dispositions the reins, and be    30
angry at your pleasures; at the least, if you take it as a
pleasure to you in being so. You blame Marcius for
being proud?

BRUTUS    We do it not alone, sir.

MENENIUS    I know you can do very little alone; for    35
your helps are many, or else your actions would grow
wondrous single:° your abilities are too infantlike for
doing much alone. You talk of pride: O that you
could turn your eyes toward the napes of your necks,
and make but an interior survey of your good selves!    40
O that you could!

BOTH    What then, sir?

MENENIUS    Why, then you should discover a brace
of unmeriting, proud, violent, testy° magistrates (alias
fools) as any in Rome.    45

SICINIUS    Menenius, you are known well enough°
too.

MENENIUS    I am known to be a humorous° patrician,
and one that loves a cup of hot wine with not a drop
of allaying° Tiber in't; said to be something imperfect    50
in favoring the first complaint,° hasty and tinderlike
upon too trivial motion;° one that converses° more
with the buttock of the night than with the forehead
of the morning. What I think I utter, and spend my
malice in my breath. Meeting two such wealsmen° as    55
you are—I cannot call you Lycurguses°—if the drink
you give me touch my palate adversely, I make a
crooked face at it. I cannot say your worships have
delivered the matter well, when I find the ass in compound with the major part of your syllables;° and    60

I.x.2 condition terms   6 condition with pun on sense of
"quality"   7 I' . . . mercy on the side that is vanquished (at
the mercy of the victor)   15 potch poke (thrust, in fencing)
18 stain darkening   19 fly . . . itself go out of its natural
course   20 naked unarmed; fane shrine   22 Embarquements
restraints   25 upon . . . guard with my brother on guard
(over him)   26 hospitable canon law of hospitality   30
attended awaited
II.i.1 augurer more correctly "augur," Roman official who
foretold the future

16 enormity fault   22 how . . . censured the opinion held
of you   23 o' . . . file of the upper classes, patricians
28–29 very . . . occasion i.e., a very little occasion is a thief
who   37 single weak, slight   44 testy snappish   46 known
well enough i.e., notorious   48 humorous whimsical   50
allaying diluting   50–51 something . . . complaint somewhat at fault in siding with the party who first puts his
case   52 motion impulse; converses associates   55 wealsmen
statesmen   56 Lycurguses Lycurgus was a Greek lawgiver
59–60 ass . . . syllables pun on overuse of "as-es" in legal
expressions, e.g., "whereas"

though I must be content to bear with those that say
you are reverend grave men, yet they lie deadly that
tell you you have good faces. If you see this in the
map° of my microcosm,° follows it that I am known
well enough too? What harm can your bisson con- 65
spectuities° glean out of this character, if I be known
well enough too?

BRUTUS  Come, sir, come, we know you well
enough.

MENENIUS  You know neither me, yourselves, nor 70
anything. You are ambitious for poor knaves' caps
and legs.° You wear out a good wholesome forenoon
in hearing a cause° between an orange-wife and a
forset-seller,° and then rejourn° the controversy of
threepence to a second day of audience. When you 75
are hearing a matter between party and party, if you
chance to be pinched with the colic, you make faces
like mummers,° set up the bloody flag° against all
patience, and, in roaring for a chamber pot, dismiss the
controversy bleeding, the more entangled by your 80
hearing. All the peace you make in their cause is
calling both the parties knaves. You are a pair of
strange ones.

BRUTUS  Come, come, you are well understood to be
a perfect giber° for the table than a necessary bencher 85
in the Capitol.°

MENENIUS  Our very priests must become mockers, if
they shall encounter such ridiculous subjects as you
are. When you speak best unto the purpose, it is not
worth the wagging of your beards; and your beards 90
deserve not so honorable a grave as to stuff a botcher's°
cushion or to be entombed in an ass's packsaddle. Yet
you must be saying Marcius is proud; who, in a cheap
estimation, is worth all your predecessors since
Deucalion;° though peradventure some of the best of 95
'em were hereditary hangmen. Good-e'en to your
worships. More of your conversation° would infect
my brain, being the herdsmen of the beastly plebeians.
I will be bold to take my leave of you.

              BRUTUS *and* SICINIUS *[step] aside.*

*Enter* VOLUMNIA, VIRGILIA, *and* VALERIA.

How now, my as fair as noble ladies—and the moon, 100
were she earthly, no nobler—whither do you follow
your eyes so fast?

VOLUMNIA  Honorable Menenius, my boy Marcius
approaches; for the love of Juno, let's go.

MENENIUS  Ha? Marcius coming home? 105

VOLUMNIA  Ay, worthy Menenius; and with most
prosperous approbation.°

MENENIUS  Take my cap, Jupiter,° and I thank thee.
Hoo! Marcius coming home!

TWO LADIES  Nay, 'tis true. 110

VOLUMNIA  Look, here's a letter from him; the state
hath another, his wife another; and, I think, there's
one at home for you.

MENENIUS  I will make my very house reel tonight.
A letter for me? 115

VIRGILIA  Yes, certain, there's a letter for you; I saw't.

MENENIUS  A letter for me? It gives me an estate° of
seven years' health; in which time I will make a lip°
at the physician. The most sovereign prescription in
Galen° is but empiricutic,° and, to this preservative, of 120
no better report° than a horse-drench.° Is he not
wounded? He was wont to come home wounded.

VIRGILIA  O, no, no, no.

VOLUMNIA  O, he is wounded; I thank the gods for't.

MENENIUS  So do I too, if it be not too much. Brings 125
'a° victory in his pocket? The wounds become him.

VOLUMNIA  On's brows, Menenius. He comes the
third time home with the oaken garland.

MENENIUS  Has he disciplined Aufidius soundly?

VOLUMNIA  Titus Lartius writes they fought together, 130
but Aufidius got off.

MENENIUS  And 'twas time for him too, I'll warrant
him that. And° he had stayed by him, I would not
have been so fidiused° for all the chests in Corioles,
and the gold that's in them. Is the Senate possessed° of 135
this?

VOLUMNIA  Good ladies, let's go. Yes, yes, yes. The
Senate has letters from the general, wherein he gives
my son the whole name of° the war. He hath in this
action outdone his former deeds doubly. 140

VALERIA  In troth, there's wondrous things spoke of
him.

MENENIUS  Wondrous! Ay, I warrant you, and not
without his true purchasing.°

VIRGILIA  The gods grant them true! 145

VOLUMNIA  True? Pow waw!°

MENENIUS  True! I'll be sworn they are true. Where
is he wounded?—[*To the* TRIBUNES.] God save your
good worships! Marcius is coming home. He has more
cause to be proud.—Where is he wounded? 150

VOLUMNIA  I' th' shoulder and i' th' left arm. There
will be large cicatrices° to show the people, when he
shall stand for his place.° He received in the repulse of
Tarquin seven hurts i' th' body.

MENENIUS  One i' th' neck, and two i' th' thigh— 155
there's nine that I know.

VOLUMNIA  He had before this last expedition twenty-
five wounds upon him.

MENENIUS  Now it's twenty-seven: every gash was
an enemy's grave. (*A shout and flourish.*) Hark! the 160
trumpets.

VOLUMNIA  These are the ushers of Marcius. Before
him he carries noise, and behind him he leaves tears.
Death, that dark spirit, in's nervy° arm doth lie,
Which, being advanced, declines, and then men die. 165

---

**64 map** i.e., face; **microcosm** little world, i.e., body  **65–66
bisson conspectuities** blind visual powers  **71–72 caps
and legs** salutes and bows  **73 cause** case  **74 forset-seller**
seller of taps for wine kegs; **rejourn** adjourn  **78 mummers**
Christmas masquers, who act impromptu plays; **bloody flag**
war flag  **85 giber** joker  **85–86 necessary . . . Capitol**
indispensable judge in the Senate (cf. *the bench* for *court*)
**91 botcher** mender of old clothes  **95 Deucalion** the Noah
of Greek myth  **97 conversation** cf. line 52  **106–07 with
. . . approbation** with signs of the greatest success  **108
Jupiter** god of the sky and upper air

**117 estate** state (fortune?)  **118 make a lip** make a face  **120
Galen** Greek physician; **empiricutic** quackish  **121 report**
reputation; **horse-drench** drink of horse-medicine  **126 'a** he
**133 And if**  **134 fidiused** "Aufidius-ed" (cf. line 129, "disciplined Aufidius soundly")  **135 possessed** duly informed
**139 name of** credit for  **144 true purchasing** really earning
(the praise)  **146 Pow waw** a Volumnian "pooh-pooh"
**152 cicatrices** scars (Latin)  **153 place** the consulship  **164
nervy** sinewy

*A sennet.° Trumpets sound. Enter* COMINIUS *the general
and Titus* LARTIUS; *between them,* CORIOLANUS,
*crowned with an oaken garland; with* CAPTAINS *and*
SOLDIERS, *and a* HERALD.

HERALD
Know, Rome, that all alone Marcius did fight
Within Corioles gates, where he hath won,
With fame, a name to Caius Marcius; these
In honor follows Coriolanus.
Welcome to Rome, renownèd Coriolanus!          170

*Sound. Flourish.*

ALL
Welcome to Rome, renownèd Coriolanus!
CORIOLANUS
No more of this, it does offend my heart;
Pray now, no more.
COMINIUS              Look, sir, your mother!
CORIOLANUS                            O,
You have, I know, petitioned all the gods
For my prosperity! *Kneels.*
VOLUMNIA          Nay, my good soldier, up;      175
My gentle Marcius, worthy Caius, and
By deed-achieving° honor newly named—
What is it?—Coriolanus must I call thee?—
But, O, thy wife!
CORIOLANUS          My gracious silence, hail!
Wouldst thou have laughed had I come coffined home, 180
That weep'st to see me triumph? Ah, my dear,
Such eyes the widows in Corioles wear,
And mothers that lack sons.
MENENIUS                    Now, the gods crown thee!
CORIOLANUS
And live you yet? [*To* VALERIA.] O my sweet lady,
  pardon.
VOLUMNIA
I know not where to turn. O, welcome home!      185
And welcome, general: and y' are welcome all.
MENENIUS
A hundred thousand welcomes. I could weep,
And I could laugh, I am light and heavy.° Welcome!
A curse begin at very root on's heart
That is not glad to see thee! You are three      190
That Rome should dote on. Yet, by the faith of men,
We have some old crab-trees here at home that will
  not
Be grafted° to your relish. Yet welcome, warriors.
We call a nettle but a nettle, and
The faults of fools but folly.
COMINIUS              Ever right.                195
CORIOLANUS
Menenius, ever, ever.
HERALD
Give way there, and go on.
CORIOLANUS [*To* VOLUMNIA *and* VIRGILIA.]
                    Your hand, and yours!
Ere in our own house I do shade my head,
The good patricians must be visited;

From whom I have received not only greetings,    200
But with them change of honors.°
VOLUMNIA                          I have lived
To see inherited° my very wishes
And the buildings of my fancy. Only
There's one thing wanting, which I doubt not but
Our Rome will cast upon thee.
CORIOLANUS                  Know, good mother,   205
I had rather be their servant in my way
Than sway with them in theirs.
COMINIUS                      On, to the Capitol!
        *Flourish. Cornets. Exeunt in state, as before.*

BRUTUS *and* SICINIUS [*come forward*].

BRUTUS
All tongues speak of him, and the blearèd sights
Are spectacled to see him. Your prattling nurse
Into a rapture° lets her baby cry                210
While she chats° him; the kitchen malkin° pins
Her richest lockram° 'bout her reechy° neck,
Clamb'ring the walls to eye him. Stalls, bulks,° win-
  dows,
Are smothered up, leads° filled and ridges horsed°
With variable complexions,° all agreeing          215
In earnestness to see him. Seld-shown flamens°
Do press among the popular throngs, and puff
To win a vulgar station.° Our veiled dames
Commit the war of white and damask in
Their nicely gawded° cheeks to th' wanton spoil   220
Of Phoebus'° burning kisses. Such a pother,°
As if that whatsoever god who leads him
Were slyly crept into his human powers,
And gave him graceful posture.
SICINIUS                      On the sudden,
I warrant him consul.
BRUTUS              Then our office may,         225
During his power, go sleep.
SICINIUS
He cannot temp'rately transport his honors
From where he should begin and end,° but will
Lose those he hath won.
BRUTUS              In that there's comfort.
SICINIUS                              Doubt not
The commoners, for whom we stand, but they       230
Upon° their ancient malice will forget
With the least cause these his new honors; which°
That he will give them make I as little question
As° he is proud to do't.
BRUTUS                  I heard him swear,
Were he to stand for consul, never would he       235
Appear i' th' marketplace, nor on him put
The napless° vesture of humility;

165 s.d. sennet set of notes for trumpet or cornet to herald an
important person, differing from a "flourish" or "fanfare"; cf.
s.d. line 160)    177 deed-achieving achieved by deeds (cf.
"the deeds of Coriolanus," II.ii.82)    188 light and heavy
both merry and sad    193 grafted i.e., improved

201 change of honors fresh honors    202 inherited in my possession    210 rapture fit    211 chats gossips about; malkin slut
212 lockram coarse linen; reechy dirty    213 bulks stalls (stands
for goods to be sold)    214 leads leaded roofs; horsed "ridden"
by viewers    215 variable complexions different physical
types    216 Seld-shown flamens priests rarely seen in public
(each flamen was in charge of the cult of a particular deity)
218 vulgar station place with the common people    220
gawded adorned    221 Phoebus sun god; pother commotion
228 and end i.e., to where he should end    231 Upon on
account of    232 which i.e., "cause"    234 As as that    237
napless threadbare

Nor, showing, as the manner is, his wounds
To th' people, beg their stinking breaths.

SICINIUS                    'Tis right.

BRUTUS
It was his word. O, he would miss it rather      240
Than carry° it but by the suit of the gentry to him
And the desire of the nobles.

SICINIUS             I wish no better
Than have him hold that purpose and to put it
In execution.

BRUTUS          'Tis most like he will.

SICINIUS
It shall be to him then as our good wills:°      245
A sure destruction.

BRUTUS          So it must fall out
To him or our authorities. For an end,°
We must suggest° the people in what hatred
He still° hath held them; that to's power he would
Have made them mules, silenced their pleaders and     250
Dispropertied° their freedoms, holding them,
In human action and capacity,
Of no more soul nor fitness for the world
Than camels in their war, who have their provand°
Only for bearing burdens, and sore blows      255
For sinking under them.

SICINIUS         This, as you say, suggested
At some time when his soaring insolence
Shall touch the people—which time shall not want,°
If he be put upon't,° and that's as easy
As to set dogs on sheep—will be his fire      260
To kindle their dry stubble; and their blaze
Shall darken him forever.

*Enter a* MESSENGER.

BRUTUS           What's the matter?

MESSENGER
You are sent for to the Capitol. 'Tis thought
That Marcius shall be consul.
I have seen the dumb men throng to see him and     265
The blind to hear him speak. Matrons flung gloves,
Ladies and maids their scarfs and handkerchers,
Upon him as he passed; the nobles bended,
As to Jove's statue, and the commons made
A shower and thunder with their caps and shouts.     270
I never saw the like.

BRUTUS         Let's to the Capitol,
And carry with us ears and eyes for th' time,
But hearts for the event.°

SICINIUS         Have with you.°     *Exeunt.*

[Scene II. *Rome. The Senate House.*]

*Enter two* OFFICERS, *to lay cushions,° as it were in the Capitol.*

FIRST OFFICER   Come, come, they are almost here.
How many stand for consulships?

SECOND OFFICER   Three, they say; but 'tis thought
of everyone Coriolanus will carry it.

FIRST OFFICER   That's a brave fellow; but he's ven-   5
geance° proud, and loves not the common people.

SECOND OFFICER   Faith, there hath been many great
men that have flattered the people, who ne'er loved
them; and there be many that they have loved, they
know not wherefore; so that, if they love they know   10
not why, they hate upon no better a ground. Therefore, for Coriolanus neither to care whether they love
or hate him manifests the true knowledge he has in
their disposition,° and out of his noble carelessness lets
them plainly see't.   15

FIRST OFFICER   If he did not care whether he had
their love or no, he waved° indifferently 'twixt doing
them neither good nor harm. But he seeks their hate
with greater devotion than they can render it him,
and leaves nothing undone that may fully discover°   20
him their opposite.° Now, to seem to affect° the
malice° and displeasure of the people is as bad as that
which he dislikes, to flatter them for their love.

SECOND OFFICER   He hath deserved worthily of his
country; and his ascent is not by such easy degrees as   25
those who, having been supple and courteous to the
people, bonneted,° without any further deed to have
them at all into their estimation and report.° But he
hath so planted his honors in their eyes and his actions
in their hearts that for their tongues to be silent and   30
not confess so much were a kind of ingrateful injury;
to report otherwise were a malice° that, giving itself
the lie, would pluck reproof and rebuke from every
ear that heard it.

FIRST OFFICER   No more of him; he's a worthy   35
man. Make way, they are coming.

*A sennet. Enter the* PATRICIANS *and the* TRIBUNES *of the people,* LICTORS° *before them;* CORIOLANUS, MENENIUS, COMINIUS *the consul.* SICINIUS *and* BRUTUS *take their places by themselves.* CORIOLANUS *stands.*

MENENIUS
Having determined of° the Volsces, and
To send for Titus Lartius, it remains,
As the main point of this our after-meeting,
To gratify° his noble service that      40
Hath thus stood for° his country. Therefore, please
   you
Most reverend and grave elders, to desire
The present consul and last° general
In our well-found° successes, to report
A little of that worthy work performed      45
By Caius Marcius Coriolanus; whom
We met here both to thank and to remember°
With honors like himself.

**241 carry** win   **245 as . . . wills** as we strongly desire   **247 For an end** to force the issue (?) finally (?)   **248 suggest** insinuate into the minds of   **249 still** ever   **251 Dispropertied** dispossessed them of   **254 provand** provisions   **258 want** be lacking   **259 put upon't** provoked to it   **273 event** outcome; **Have with you** Coming with you!   **II.ii.s.d. cushions** seats for dignitaries

**5–6 vengeance** frightfully (cf. *with a vengeance*)   **13–14 in their disposition** of their mood   **17 waved** would waver   **20 discover** show   **21 opposite** opponent; **affect** aim at   **22 malice** ill will   **27 bonneted** took off their caps (in flattery) **27–28 to have . . . report** to get themselves at all into (win their way into), their esteem   **32 malice** act of ill will   **36 s.d. Lictors** attendants who preceded Roman officials to announce their approach   **37 determined of** decided concerning   **40 gratify** reward   **41 stood for** defended   **43 last** late   **44 well-found** fortunately met with   **47 remember** distinguish

FIRST SENATOR                    Speak, good Cominius:
Leave nothing out for length, and make us think
Rather our state's defective for requital                50
Than we to stretch it out.° [*To the* TRIBUNES.] Masters
    o' th' people,
We do request your kindest ears; and, after,
Your loving motion toward the common body,°
To yield° what passes here.
SICINIUS                         We are convented°
Upon a pleasing treaty,° and have hearts               55
Inclinable to honor and advance
The theme of our assembly.
BRUTUS                           Which the rather°
We shall be blessed° to do, if he remember
A kinder value° of the people than
He hath hereto prized them at.
MENENIUS                         That's off,° that's off;   60
I would you rather had been silent. Please you
To hear Cominius speak?
BRUTUS                           Most willingly.
But yet my caution was more pertinent
Than the rebuke you give it.
MENENIUS                         He loves your people;
But tie him not to be their bedfellow.                 65
Worthy Cominius, speak.

CORIOLANUS *rises and offers to go away.*

                        Nay, keep your place.
FIRST SENATOR
Sit, Coriolanus; never shame to hear
What you have nobly done.
CORIOLANUS                       Your honors' pardon:
I had rather have my wounds to heal again
Than hear say how I got them.
BRUTUS                           Sir, I hope            70
My words disbenched° you not.
CORIOLANUS                       No, sir. Yet oft,
When blows have made me stay, I fled from words.
You soothed° not, therefore hurt not; but your people,
I love them as they weigh—
MENENIUS                         Pray now, sit down.
CORIOLANUS
I had rather have one scratch my head i' th' sun       75
When the alarum were struck than idly sit
To hear my nothings monstered.° *Exit* CORIOLANUS.
MENENIUS                         Masters of the people,
Your multiplying spawn how can he flatter—
That's thousand to one good one—when you now see
He had rather venture all his limbs for honor          80
Than one on 's ears° to hear it? Proceed, Cominius.
COMINIUS
I shall lack voice: the deeds of Coriolanus
Should not be uttered feebly. It is held
That valor is the chiefest virtue° and

Most dignifies the haver. If it be,                    85
The man I speak of cannot in the world
Be singly counterpoised.° At sixteen years,
When Tarquin° made a head for° Rome, he fought
Beyond the mark of others. Our then dictator,
Whom with all praise I point at, saw him fight,        90
When with his Amazonian° chin he drove
The bristled lips before him. He bestrid
An o'erpressed Roman, and i' th' consul's view
Slew three opposers; Tarquin's self he met,
And struck him on his knee.° In that day's feats,      95
When he might act the woman in the scene,°
He proved best man i' th' field, and for his meed°
Was brow-bound with the oak. His pupil age°
Man-ent'red° thus, he waxèd like a sea;
And, in the brunt of seventeen battles since,          100
He lurched° all swords of the garland. For this last,
Before and in Corioles, let me say,
I cannot speak him home.° He stopped the fliers,
And by his rare example made the coward
Turn terror into sport; as weeds before               105
A vessel under sail, so men obeyed
And fell below his stem.° His sword, death's stamp,°
Where it did mark, it took;° from face to foot
He was a thing of blood, whose every motion
Was timed with dying cries. Alone he ent'red          110
The mortal gate of th' city, which he painted
With shunless destiny;° aidless came off,
And with a sudden reinforcement struck
Corioles like a planet.° Now, all's his,
When by and by the din of war 'gan° pierce            115
His ready° sense, then straight his doubled° spirit
Requick'ned what in flesh was fatigate,°
And to the battle came he; where he did
Run reeking o'er the lives of men, as if
'Twere a perpetual spoil;° and till we called         120
Both field and city ours, he never stood
To ease his breast with panting.
MENENIUS                         Worthy man!
FIRST SENATOR
He cannot but with measure fit° the honors
Which we devise him.
COMINIUS                         Our spoils he kicked at,
And looked upon things precious as they were          125
The common muck of the world. He covets less
Than misery° itself would give, rewards
His deeds with doing them, and is content

---

50–51 **our . . . out** our government (the Senate) is lacking in the resources for reward rather than we in our effort to extend it   53 **motion . . . body** influence with the common people   54 **yield** approve; **convented** convened   55 **treaty** proposal for discussion   57 **rather** sooner   58 **blessed** happy   59 **value** estimate   60 **off** not to the point   71 **disbenched** unseated   73 **soothed** flattered   77 **monstered** turned into marvels   81 **Than . . . ears** than venture one of his ears   84 **virtue** cf. Latin *virtus*, manly strength; on this speech, see Introduction pp. 1312–13

87 **singly counterpoised** matched in value (literally, in weight) by one man   88 **Tarquin** early king of Rome, expelled from the city; **made . . . for** raised a force against   91 **Amazonian** i.e., beardless   95 **on his knee** to his knees   96 **in the scene** on that stage   97 **meed** reward   98 **His pupil age** the years when he was learning (the art of war)   99 **Man-ent'red** having been initiated into manhood   101 **lurched** robbed   103 **speak him home** find words to match his merit   107 **stem** bow; **stamp** a die for stamping a coin or medal   108 **took** made its mark; killed (perhaps also, "infected fatally"; cf. "struck," line 113)   111–12 **painted . . . destiny** smeared with blood of dying men, who could not shun their fate   113–14 **struck . . . planet** planets supposedly had power to "strike," infect with disease   115 **'gan** began to   116 **ready** responsive; **doubled** renewed   117 **fatigate** fatigued   120 **spoil** slaughter   123 **with measure fit** measure up to; or, "bear with self-control" (?)   127 **misery** poverty

To spend the time to end it.°
MENENIUS            He's right noble.
Let him be called for.
FIRST SENATOR      Call Coriolanus.        130
OFFICER
He doth appear.

*Enter* CORIOLANUS.

MENENIUS
The Senate, Coriolanus, are well pleased
To make thee consul.
CORIOLANUS          I do owe them still°
My life and services.
MENENIUS         It then remains
That you do speak to the people.
CORIOLANUS          I do beseech you     135
Let me o'erleap that custom, for I cannot
Put on the gown,° stand naked,° and entreat them,
For my wounds' sake, to give their suffrage. Please you
That I may pass° this doing.
SICINIUS           Sir, the people
Must have their voices;° neither will they bate°    140
One jot of ceremony.
MENENIUS        Put them not to't.°
Pray you, go fit you to the custom, and
Take to you, as your predecessors have,
Your honor with your form.°
CORIOLANUS        It is a part
That I shall blush in acting, and might well    145
Be taken from the people.
BRUTUS   [*To* SICINIUS.] Mark you that.
CORIOLANUS
To brag unto them, "Thus I did, and thus!"
Show them th' unaching scars which I should hide,
As if I had received them for the hire
Of their breath only!
MENENIUS        Do not stand upon't.°    150
We recommend to you, tribunes of the people,
Our purpose° to them; and to our noble consul
Wish we all joy and honor.
SENATORS
To Coriolanus come all joy and honor!
       *Flourish cornets. Then exeunt. Manet*
         SICINIUS *and* BRUTUS.
BRUTUS
You see how he intends to use the people.    155
SICINIUS
May they perceive's intent! He will require° them,
As if he did contemn what he requested
Should be in them to give.
BRUTUS        Come, we'll inform them
Of our proceedings here. On th' marketplace.
I know, they do attend us.      [*Exeunt.*] 160

---

129 **To spend . . . it** to kill it in action ("to live it up in action")   133 **still** always   137 **gown** "vesture of humility" (cf. II.i.237); **naked** i.e., "without any coat underneath" (North)   139 **pass** pass over   140 **voices** votes; **bate** deduct   141 **Put . . . to't** Don't test them (by omitting any part of the ceremony)   144 **Your honor . . . form** the honor with the ceremony it imposes on you   150 **stand upon't** make an issue of it   152 **purpose** proposal   156 **require** ask

---

[*Scene III. Rome. The Forum.*]

*Enter seven or eight* CITIZENS.

FIRST CITIZEN   Once if he° do require our voices, we ought not to deny him.
SECOND CITIZEN   We may, sir, if we will.
THIRD CITIZEN   We have power in ourselves to do it, but it is a power that we have no power to do; for   5
if he show us his wounds and tell us his deeds, we are to put our tongues into those wounds and speak for them; so, if he tell us his noble deeds, we must also tell him our noble acceptance of them. Ingratitude is monstrous; and for the multitude to be ingrateful,   10
were to make a monster of the multitude; of the which we being members, should bring ourselves to be monstrous members.
FIRST CITIZEN   And to make us no better thought of, a little help will serve; for once we stood up° about   15
the corn, he himself stuck not to call us the many-headed multitude.
THIRD CITIZEN   We have been called so of many; not that our heads are some brown, some black, some abram,° some bald, but that our wits are so diversely   20
colored. And truly I think, if all our wits were to issue out of one skull, they would fly east, west, north, south, and their consent of° one direct way should be at once to all the points o' th' compass.
SECOND CITIZEN   Think you so? Which way do   25
you judge my wit would fly?
THIRD CITIZEN   Nay, your wit will not so soon out as another man's will; 'tis strongly wedged up in a blockhead; but if it were at liberty, 'twould, sure, southward.   30
SECOND CITIZEN   Why that way?
THIRD CITIZEN   To lose itself in a fog; where being three parts melted away with rotten° dews, the fourth would return for conscience sake, to help to get thee a wife.°   35
SECOND CITIZEN   You are never without your tricks. You may, you may.°
THIRD CITIZEN   Are you all resolved to give your voices? But that's no matter, the greater part° carries it. I say, if he would incline to the people, there was never   40
a worthier man.

*Enter* CORIOLANUS *in a gown of humility, with* MENENIUS.

Here he comes, and in the gown of humility. Mark his behavior. We are not to stay all together, but to come by him where he stands, by ones, by twos, and by threes. He's to make his requests by particulars;°   45
wherein every one of us has a single honor, in giving him our own voices with our own tongues. Therefore follow me, and I'll direct you how you shall go by him.
ALL   Content, content.      [*Exeunt* CITIZENS.]

---

**II.iii.1 Once if he** if he once   **15 once . . . up** when we took a stand   **20 abram** auburn   **23 consent of** agreement on   **33 rotten** unhealthy   **34–35 for . . . wife** i.e., because of the bastards he had fathered (?)   **37 You may, you may** "O.K., O.K."   **39 greater part** majority   **45 by particulars** to each in turn

MENENIUS

O sir, you are not right. Have you not known             50
The worthiest men have done't?

CORIOLANUS                          What must I say?—
"I pray, sir"—Plague upon't! I cannot bring
My tongue to such a pace. "Look, sir, my wounds!
I got them in my country's service, when
Some certain of your brethren roared and ran             55
From th' noise of our own drums."

MENENIUS                                       O me, the gods!
You must not speak of that. You must desire them
To think upon° you.

CORIOLANUS            Think upon me! Hang 'em!
I would they would forget me, like the virtues
Which our divines lose by 'em.°

MENENIUS                              You'll mar all.           60
I'll leave you. Pray you, speak to 'em, I pray you,
In wholesome° manner.                          *Exit.*

*Enter three of the* CITIZENS.

CORIOLANUS            Bid them wash their faces,
And keep their teeth clean. So, here comes a brace.°
You know the cause, sir, of my standing here.

THIRD CITIZEN  We do, sir; tell us what hath    65
brought you to't.

CORIOLANUS  Mine own desert.

SECOND CITIZEN  Your own desert?

CORIOLANUS  Ay, not mine own desire.

THIRD CITIZEN  How not your own desire?           70

CORIOLANUS  No, sir, 'twas never my desire yet to
trouble the poor with begging.

THIRD CITIZEN  You must think, if we give you
anything, we hope to gain by you.

CORIOLANUS  Well then, I pray, your price o' th'   75
consulship?

FIRST CITIZEN  The price is, to ask it kindly.

CORIOLANUS  Kindly sir, I pray let me ha't. I have
wounds to show you, which shall be yours in private.
Your good voice, sir; what say you?                  80

SECOND CITIZEN  You shall ha't, worthy sir.

CORIOLANUS  A match,° sir. There's in all two worthy
voices begged. I have your alms. Adieu.

THIRD CITIZEN  But this is something° odd.

SECOND CITIZEN  And 'twere to give again—but  85
'tis no matter.                                  *Exeunt.*

*Enter two other* CITIZENS.

CORIOLANUS  Pray you now, if it may stand° with
the tune of your voices that I may be consul, I have
here the customary gown.

FIRST CITIZEN  You have deserved nobly of your  90
country, and you have not deserved nobly.

CORIOLANUS  Your enigma?

FIRST CITIZEN  You have been a scourge to her
enemies, you have been a rod to her friends. You have
not indeed loved the common people.                 95

CORIOLANUS  You should account me the more
virtuous, that I have not been common in my love. I
will, sir, flatter my sworn brother, the people, to earn

a dearer estimation of° them; 'tis a condition° they
account gentle; and since the wisdom of their choice  100
is rather to have my hat than my heart, I will practice
the insinuating nod, and be off° to them most counter-
feitly; that is, sir, I will counterfeit the bewitchment of
some popular man,° and give it bountiful to the
desirers. Therefore, beseech you I may be consul.    105

SECOND CITIZEN  We hope to find you our friend;
and therefore give you our voices heartily.

FIRST CITIZEN  You have received many wounds for
your country.

CORIOLANUS  I will not seal° your knowledge with  110
showing them. I will make much of your voices and
so trouble you no farther.

BOTH  The gods give you joy, sir, heartily! [*Exeunt.*]

CORIOLANUS
Most sweet voices!
Better it is to die, better to starve,                     115
Than crave the hire which first we do deserve.
Why in this woolvish toge° should I stand here,
To beg of Hob° and Dick that does appear°
Their needless vouches?° Custom calls me to't.
What custom wills, in all things should we do't,      120
The dust on antique time would lie unswept,
And mountainous error be too highly heaped
For truth to o'erpeer.° Rather than fool it so,
Let the high office and the honor go
To one that would do thus. I am half through:         125
The one part suffered, the other will I do.

*Enter three* CITIZENS *more.*

Here come moe° voices.
Your voices! For your voices I have fought;
Watched° for your voices; for your voices bear
Of wounds two dozen odd; battles thrice six            130
I have seen, and heard of; for your voices have
Done many things, some less, some more. Your voices!
Indeed, I would be consul.

FIRST CITIZEN  He has done nobly, and cannot go
without any honest man's voice.                       135

SECOND CITIZEN  Therefore let him be consul. The
gods give him joy, and make him good friend to the
people!

ALL  Amen, amen. God save thee, noble consul!
                          [*Exeunt* CITIZENS.]

CORIOLANUS  Worthy voices!                         140

*Enter* MENENIUS, *with* BRUTUS *and* SICINIUS.

MENENIUS
You have stood your limitation;° and the tribunes
Endue you with the people's voice. Remains
That in th' official marks° invested you
Anon do meet the Senate.

CORIOLANUS                        Is this done?

58 **think upon** think well of  60 **lose by 'em** waste on them
in preaching ("pearls before swine")  62 **wholesome** reasonable  63 **brace** pair (of dogs)  82 **A match** agreed  84
**something** somewhat  87 **stand** agree

99 **dearer estimation of** higher valuation from;  **condition**
quality  102 **be off** take my hat off  104 **popular man**
"friend the of people"  110 **seal** make authentic (legal sense)
117 **in . . . toge** i.e., disguising myself (a backhand reference
to "wolf in sheep's clothing"; note that Coriolanus "lives
like a lamb," according to II.i.12)  118 **Hob** nickname of
"Robert"; a country fellow;  **that does appear** i.e., as they
come, one by one  119 **vouches** confirmations  123 **o'erpeer**
rise above  127 **moe** more  129 **Watched** kept watch  141
**limitation** time set for requesting votes  143 **marks** insignia

SICINIUS
The custom of request you have discharged:    145
The people do admit you, and are summoned
To meet anon upon your approbation.°

CORIOLANUS
Where? At the Senate House?

SICINIUS           There, Coriolanus.

CORIOLANUS
May I change these garments?

SICINIUS           You may, sir.

CORIOLANUS
That I'll straight do, and, knowing myself again,    150
Repair° to th' Senate House.

MENENIUS
I'll keep you company. Will you along?°

BRUTUS
We stay here for the people.

SICINIUS           Fare you well.
        *Exeunt* CORIOLANUS *and* MENENIUS.
He has it° now; and, by his looks, methinks
'Tis warm at's° heart.

BRUTUS        With a proud heart he wore    155
His humble weeds. Will you dismiss the people?

*Enter the* PLEBEIANS.

SICINIUS
How now, my masters,° have you chose this man?

FIRST CITIZEN
He has our voices, sir.

BRUTUS
We pray the gods he may deserve your loves.

SECOND CITIZEN
Amen, sir. To my poor unworthy notice,    160
He mocked us when he begged our voices.

THIRD CITIZEN           Certainly;
He flouted us downright.

FIRST CITIZEN
No, 'tis his kind of speech—he did not mock us.

SECOND CITIZEN
Not one amongst us, save yourself, but says
He used us scornfully. He should have showed us    165
His marks of merit, wounds received for's country.

SICINIUS
Why, so he did, I am sure.

ALL           No, no; no man saw 'em.

THIRD CITIZEN
He said he had wounds which he could show in
   private;
And with his hat, thus waving it in scorn,
"I would be consul," says he. "Agèd custom,    170
But by your voices, will not so permit me;
Your voices therefore." When we granted that,
Here was, "I thank you for your voices. Thank you,
Your most sweet voices. Now you have left your
   voices,
I have no further° with you." Was not this mockery?    175

SICINIUS
Why either were you ignorant° to see't,

Or, seeing it, of such childish friendliness
To yield° your voices?

BRUTUS        Could you not have told him
As you were lessoned:° when he had no power,
But was a petty servant to the state,    180
He was your enemy, ever spake against
Your liberties and the charters° that you bear
I' th' body of the weal;° and now, arriving
A place° of potency and sway o' th' state,°
If he should still malignantly remain    185
Fast foe to th' plebeii,° your voices might
Be curses to yourselves? You should have said
That as his worthy deeds did claim no less
Than what he stood for,° so his gracious nature
Would think upon you° for your voices, and    190
Translate° his malice towards you into love,
Standing your friendly lord.

SICINIUS        Thus to have said,
As you were fore-advised, had touched° his spirit
And tried his inclination; from him plucked
Either his gracious promise, which you might,    195
As cause had called you up,° have held him to;
Or else it would have galled his surly nature,
Which easily endures not article°
Tying him to aught. So, putting him to rage,
You should have ta'en th' advantage of his choler,°    200
And passed him unelected.

BRUTUS        Did you perceive
He did solicit you in free° contempt
When he did need your loves; and do you think
That his contempt shall not be bruising to you
When he hath power to crush? Why, had your bodies    205
No heart° among you? Or had you tongues to cry°
Against the rectorship° of judgment?

SICINIUS           Have you
Ere now denied the asker, and now again,
Of° him that did not ask but mock, bestow
Your sued-for tongues?    210

THIRD CITIZEN
He's not confirmed; we may deny him yet.

SECOND CITIZEN
And will deny him.
I'll have five hundred voices of that sound.

FIRST CITIZEN
I twice five hundred, and their friends to piece 'em.°

BRUTUS
Get you hence instantly, and tell those friends    215
They have chose a consul that will from them take
Their liberties, make them of no more voice
Than dogs that are as often beat for barking
As therefor° kept to do so.

SICINIUS        Let them assemble;
And, on a safer° judgment, all revoke    220

---

147 anon . . . approbation at once to confirm your appointment (as consul)   151 Repair return   152 along come too
154 it the emotion that "warms his heart," either the satisfaction of success, or the irritation of offended pride; cf. "his fire,"
II.i.260   155 at's at his   157 my masters gentlemen   175 no
further no more to do   176 ignorant too dull

178 yield give   179 lessoned instructed   182 charters privileges   183 weal commonwealth   184 A place direct object of
"arriving," i.e., "reaching"; potency . . . state power in
managing the state   186 plebeii Latin for "plebeians"   189
what . . . for the office he ran for   190 think upon you
think well of you   191 Translate transform   193 touched
tested   196 As . . . up as an occasion (emergency) would
have roused you   198 article condition   200 choler anger
202 free open   206 heart spirit; cry give your voices   207
rectorship rule   209 Of on   214 piece 'em add to them
(cf. *piece out*)   219 therefor for that reason   220 safer sounder

Your ignorant election.° Enforce° his pride
And his old hate unto you; besides, forget not
With what contempt he wore the humble weed,
How in his suit he scorned you; but your loves,
Thinking upon his services, took from you                          225
Th' apprehension° of his present portance,°
Which most gibingly, ungravely, he did fashion
After the inveterate hate he bears you.
BRUTUS                                       Lay
A fault on us, your tribunes, that we labored,
No impediment between,° but that you must                          230
Cast your election on him.
SICINIUS                        Say you chose him
More after° our commandment than as guided
By your own true affections;° and that your minds,
Preoccupied with what you rather must do
Than what you should, made you against the grain                   235
To voice him consul.° Lay the fault on us.
BRUTUS
Ay, spare us not. Say we read lectures to you,
How youngly he began to serve his country,
How long continued; and what stock he springs of,
The noble house o' th' Marcians, from whence came                  240
That Ancus Marcius, Numa's° daughter's son,
Who after great Hostilius here was king;
Of the same house Publius and Quintus were,
That our best water brought by conduits hither;
[And Censorinus that was so surnamed]°                             245
And nobly namèd so, twice being censor,
Was his great ancestor.
SICINIUS                      One thus descended,
That hath beside well in his person wrought
To be set high in place, we did commend
To your remembrances: but you have found,                          250
Scaling° his present bearing with his past,
That he's your fixèd enemy, and revoke
Your sudden° approbation.
BRUTUS                          Say you ne'er had done't
(Harp on that still) but by our putting on;°
And presently, when you have drawn your number,°                   255
Repair to th' Capitol.
CITIZENS                      We will so. Almost all
Repent in their election.            Exeunt PLEBEIANS.
BRUTUS                      Let them go on;
This mutiny were better put in hazard°
Than stay, past doubt, for greater.
If, as his nature is, he fall in rage                              260
With their refusal, both observe and answer
The vantage of his anger.°
SICINIUS                        To th' Capitol, come.
We will be there before the stream o' th' people;
And this shall seem, as partly 'tis, their own,
Which we have goaded onward.                    Exeunt. 265

221 **ignorant election** choice made in ignorance; **Enforce** urge, insist on  226 **apprehension** perception; **portance** bearing  230 **No impediment between** putting no obstacle in your way (i.e., we have made the way free for you to choose him)  232 **after** following  233 **affections** desires  236 **voice him consul** make him consul by your votes  241 **Numa** second king of Rome  245 **And . . . surnamed** see A Note on the Text, p. 1323  251 **Scaling** weighing  253 **sudden** hasty  254 **putting on** urging  255 **drawn your number** gathered your crowd (of supporters)  258 **This . . . hazard** it would be better to run the risk of this minor disorder  261–62 **answer . . . anger** take advantage of the opportunity his anger affords

# A C T  I I I

[Scene I. Rome. A street.]

*Cornets. Enter* CORIOLANUS, MENENIUS, *all the* GENTRY, COMINIUS, *Titus* LARTIUS, *and other* SENATORS.

CORIOLANUS
Tullus Aufidius then had made new head?°
LARTIUS
He had, my lord; and that it was which caused
Our swifter composition.°
CORIOLANUS
So then the Volsces stand but as at first;
Ready, when time shall prompt them, to make road                   5
Upon's° again.
COMINIUS          They are worn,° lord consul, so
That we shall hardly in our ages° see
Their banners wave again.
CORIOLANUS                        Saw you Aufidius?
LARTIUS
On safeguard° he came to me; and did curse
Against the Volsces, for they had so vilely                        10
Yielded the town. He is retired to Antium.
CORIOLANUS
Spoke he of me?
LARTIUS              He did, my lord.
CORIOLANUS                                  How? What?
LARTIUS
How often he had met you, sword to sword;
That of all things upon the earth he hated
Your person most; that he would pawn his fortunes                  15
To hopeless restitution,° so he might
Be called your vanquisher.
CORIOLANUS                        At Antium lives he?
LARTIUS
At Antium.
CORIOLANUS
I wish I had a cause to seek him there,
To oppose his hatred fully. Welcome home.                          20

*Enter* SICINIUS *and* BRUTUS.

Behold, these are the tribunes of the people,
The tongues o' th' common mouth. I do despise them;
For they do prank them° in authority,
Against all noble sufferance.°
SICINIUS                            Pass no further.
CORIOLANUS
Ha? What is that?                                                  25
BRUTUS
It will be dangerous to go on—no further.
CORIOLANUS
What makes this change?
MENENIUS
The matter?
COMINIUS
Hath he not passed the noble and the common?°

**III.i.1 made new head** raised a new force  **3 swifter composition** coming to terms sooner  **5–6 make road Upon's** invade us  **6 worn** worn out  **7 ages** lifetime  **9 On safeguard** under safe-conduct  **16 To hopeless restitution** without hope of their being redeemed  **23 prank them** dress themselves up  **24 Against . . . sufferance** so that no noble can endure it  **29 noble . . . common** the patricians and the plebeians

BRUTUS
Cominius, no.

CORIOLANUS  Have I had children's voices?                    30

FIRST SENATOR
Tribunes, give way; he shall to th' marketplace.

BRUTUS
The people are incensed against him.

SICINIUS                                   Stop,
Or all will fall in broil.°

CORIOLANUS                    Are these your herd?
Must these have voices, that can yield them now,°
And straight disclaim° their tongues? What are your
    offices?                                              35
You being their mouths, why rule you not their teeth?
Have you not set them on?

MENENIUS                    Be calm, be calm.

CORIOLANUS
It is a purposed thing,° and grows by plot,
To curb the will of the nobility.
Suffer't, and live with such as cannot rule,             40
Nor ever will be ruled.

BRUTUS                    Call't not a plot.
The people cry you mocked them; and of late,
When corn was given them gratis, you repined,°
Scandaled° the suppliants for the people, called them
Time-pleasers, flatterers, foes to nobleness.            45

CORIOLANUS
Why, this was known before.

BRUTUS                    Not to them all.

CORIOLANUS
Have you informed° them sithence?°

BRUTUS                    How! I inform them!

CORIOLANUS
You are like to do such business.

BRUTUS                    Not unlike
Each way to better yours.°

CORIOLANUS
Why then should I be consul? By yond clouds,             50
Let me deserve so ill as you, and make me
Your fellow tribune.

SICINIUS                    You show too much of that
For which the people stir.° If you will pass
To where you are bound, you must inquire your way,
Which you are out of,° with a gentler spirit,            55
Or never be so noble as a consul,
Nor yoke with him for° tribune.

MENENIUS                    Let's be calm.

COMINIUS
The people are abused;° set on.° This palt'ring°
Becomes not Rome; nor has Coriolanus
Deserved this so dishonored rub,° laid falsely°          60
I' th' plain way of his merit.

CORIOLANUS                    Tell me of corn!
This was my speech, and I will speak't again—

MENENIUS
Not now, not now.

FIRST SENATOR        Not in this heat, sir, now.

CORIOLANUS
Now, as I live, I will.
My nobler friends, I crave their pardons.                65
For the mutable, rank-scented meiny,° let them
Regard me as I do not flatter, and
Therein behold themselves. I say again,
In soothing them, we nourish 'gainst our Senate
The cockle° of rebellion, insolence, sedition,          70
Which we ourselves have ploughed for, sowed, and
    scattered,
By mingling them with us, the honored number,
Who lack not virtue, no, nor power, but that
Which they have given to beggars.

MENENIUS                    Well, no more.       75

FIRST SENATOR
No more words, we beseech you.

CORIOLANUS                    How! No more!
As for my country I have shed my blood,
Not fearing outward force, so shall my lungs
Coin words till their decay° against those measles,°
Which we disdain should tetter° us, yet sought
The very way to catch them.

BRUTUS                    You speak o' th' people   80
As if you were a god, to punish, not
A man of their infirmity.°

SICINIUS                    'Twere well
We let the people know't.

MENENIUS                    What, what? His choler?

CORIOLANUS
Choler?
Were I as patient as the midnight sleep,                 85
By Jove, 'twould be my mind!

SICINIUS                    It is a mind
That shall remain a poison where it is,
Not poison any further.

CORIOLANUS                    Shall remain!
Hear you this Triton° of the minnows? Mark you
His absolute "shall"?

COMINIUS                    'Twas from the canon.°

CORIOLANUS                    "Shall"!       90
O good but most unwise patricians! Why,
You grave but reckless senators, have you thus
Given Hydra here° to choose an officer,
That with his peremptory "shall," being but
The horn and noise o' th' monster's, wants not spirit    95
To say he'll turn your current in° a ditch,
And make your channel his? If he have power,
Then vail your ignorance;° if none, awake
Your dangerous lenity. If you are learned,°
Be not as common fools; if you are not,                  100
Let them have cushions° by you. You are plebeians,
If they be senators; and they are no less,°
When, both your voices blended, the great'st taste

33 **in broil** into a riot  34 **now** at one time  35 **disclaim** disown  38 **purposed thing** premeditated affair  43 **repined** regretted it  44 **Scandaled** slandered  47 **informed** instructed; **sithence** since  48–49 **Not . . . yours** likely in every way to do your business better  53 **stir** are rebelling  55 **are out of** are straying from  57 **for** as  58 **abused** deceived; **set on** incited; **palt'ring** cheating  60 **rub** hindrance (in bowling on the green, any roughness of ground); **falsely** treacherously  66 **meiny** crowd  70 **cockle** weed  78 **decay** death; **measles** the disease; and "foul wretches," from *mesel* = leper  79 **tetter** infect with leprous eruption  82 **of their infirmity** having the same weaknesses as they  89 **Triton** sea god, trumpeter of Neptune (cf. "horn," line 95)  90 **from the canon** against the law  93 **Given Hydra here** permitted this many-headed beast  96 **in** (aside) into  98 **vail your ignorance** let your ignorance (that gave the power) bow (to him)  99 **learned** wise  101 **cushions** symbol of senatorial rank; cf. II.ii.s.d.  102 **no less** i.e., no less than senators

Most palates theirs.° They choose their magistrate;
And such a one as he, who puts his "shall," 105
His popular "shall," against a graver bench°
Than ever frowned in Greece. By Jove himself,
It makes the consuls base; and my soul aches
To know, when two authorities are up,°
Neither supreme, how soon confusion° 110
May enter 'twixt the gap of both and take
The one by th' other.°

**COMINIUS**                    Well, on to th' marketplace.

**CORIOLANUS**
Whoever gave that counsel to give forth
The corn o' th' storehouse gratis, as 'twas used
Sometime in Greece—

**MENENIUS**          Well, well, no more of that. 115

**CORIOLANUS**
Though there the people had more absolute pow'r,
I say they nourished disobedience, fed
The ruin of the state.

**BRUTUS**                    Why shall the people give
One that speaks thus their voice?

**CORIOLANUS**                    I'll give my reasons,
More worthier than their voices. They know the corn 120
Was not our recompense,° resting well assured
They ne'er did service for't. Being pressed to° th' war,
Even when the navel° of the state was touched,
They would not thread° the gates; this kind of service
Did not deserve corn gratis. Being i' th' war, 125
Their mutinies and revolts, wherein they showed
Most valor, spoke not for them. Th' accusation
Which they have often made against the Senate,
All cause unborn,° could never be the native°
Of our so frank° donation. Well, what then? 130
How shall this bosom multiplied° digest°
The Senate's courtesy? Let deeds express
What's like to be their words: "We did request it;
We are the greater poll,° and in true fear
They gave us our demands." Thus we debase 135
The nature of our seats, and make the rabble
Call our cares° fears; which will in time
Break ope the locks o' th' Senate and bring in
The crows to peck the eagles.

**MENENIUS**                    Come, enough.

**BRUTUS**
Enough, with over measure.

**CORIOLANUS**                    No, take more. 140
What may be sworn by, both divine and human,
Seal what I end withal!° This double worship,
Where one part does disdain with cause, the other
Insult without° all reason; where gentry,° title,
    wisdom,

Cannot conclude° but by the yea and no 145
Of general ignorance—it must omit°
Real necessities, and give way the while
To unstable slightness.° Purpose so barred,° it follows
Nothing is done to purpose. Therefore, beseech you—
You that will be less fearful than discreet;° 150
That love the fundamental part of state°
More than you doubt° the change on't; that prefer
A noble life before a long, and wish
To jump° a body with a dangerous physic°
That's sure of death without it—at once pluck out 155
The multitudinous tongue;° let them not lick
The sweet which is their poison. Your dishonor
Mangles true judgment, and bereaves the state
Of that integrity° which should become't;
Not having the power to do the good it would, 160
For th' ill which doth control't.°

**BRUTUS**                    H' as said enough.

**SICINIUS**
H' as spoken like a traitor and shall answer°
As traitors do.

**CORIOLANUS** Thou wretch, despite o'erwhelm thee!
What should the people do with these bald° tribunes,
On whom depending, their obedience fails 165
To th' greater bench?° In a rebellion,
When what's not meet, but what must be, was law,
Then were they chosen; in a better hour
Let what is meet be said it must be meet,°
And throw their power i' th' dust. 170

**BRUTUS**
Manifest treason!

**SICINIUS**          This a consul! No.

**BRUTUS**
The aediles,° ho!

*Enter an* AEDILE.

                    Let him be apprehended.

**SICINIUS**
Go, call the people, [*exit* AEDILE] in whose name
    myself
Attach° thee as a traitorous innovator,
A foe to th' public weal. Obey, I charge thee, 175
And follow to thine answer.°

**CORIOLANUS**                    Hence, old goat!°

**ALL** [PATRICIANS]
We'll surety° him.

**COMINIUS**          Aged sir, hands off.

**CORIOLANUS**
Hence, rotten thing, or I shall shake thy bones
Out of thy garments.

**SICINIUS**          Help, ye citizens!

---

103–04 **great'st . . . theirs** the dominant flavor tastes most of them (i.e., they have the most votes) **106 bench** court **109 up** active **110 confusion** violent disorder (in a revolution) **111–12 take . . . other** seize and overthrow one by means of the other **121 recompense** reward for past services **122 pressed to** conscripted for **123 navel** center (cf. Menenius' fable, I.i) **124 thread** pass through **129 All cause unborn** with no cause in existence; **native** original, parent (i.e., their accusation not the origin of our gift) **130 frank** unsolicited **131 bosom multiplied** many-bosomed beast ("Hydra," line 93); **digest** (1) digest (2) understand ("bosom" can mean both "cavity of the stomach" and "heart," i.e., "mind") **134 poll** number **137 cares** concern for the state **142 withal** with **144 without** beyond; **gentry** gentle birth

**145 conclude** decide **146 omit** overlook **148 unstable slightness** unsteady trifling; **Purpose so barred** when the intention (of charting a policy in advance) is so thwarted **150 less . . . discreet** more prudent than fearful (on lines 150–61, see Introduction, p. 1316) **151 fundamental . . . state** basic constitution of the government **152 doubt** fear **154 jump** risk harming; **physic** medicine, treatment **156 multitudinous tongue** the voice of the "Hydra," the tribuneship **159 integrity** wholeness **161 control't** overpower it **162 answer** i.e., in court, be brought to trial; cf. lines 176, 324 **164 bald** trivial (pun) **166 th' greater bench** the Senate **169 it . . . meet** that it *must* be fitting **172 aediles** officers attached to the tribunes **174 Attach** arrest **176 answer** legal term for "meeting a charge"; **goat** evidently the tribunes are bearded; cf. II.i.90 **177 surety** stand surety for

*Enter a rabble of* PLEBEIANS, *with the* AEDILES.

MENENIUS
On both sides more respect.      180

SICINIUS
Here's he that would take from you all your power.

BRUTUS
Seize him, aediles!

ALL [CITIZENS]
Down with him, down with him!

SECOND SENATOR
Weapons, weapons, weapons!

*They all bustle about* CORIOLANUS.

[ALL]
Tribunes!—Patricians!—Citizens!—What, ho!—    185
Sicinius!—Brutus!—Coriolanus!—Citizens!—
Peace, peace, peace!—Stay! Hold! Peace!

MENENIUS
What is about to be? I am out of breath.
Confusion's° near. I cannot speak. You, tribunes
To th' people! Coriolanus, patience!      190
Speak, good Sicinius.

SICINIUS        Hear me, people; peace!

ALL [CITIZENS]
Let's hear our tribune. Peace!—Speak, speak, speak.

SICINIUS
You are at point to lose° your liberties:
Marcius would have all from you; Marcius,
Whom late you have named for consul.

MENENIUS        Fie, fie, fie!    195
This is the way to kindle, not to quench.

FIRST SENATOR
To unbuild the city, and to lay all flat.

SICINIUS
What is the city but the people?

ALL [CITIZENS]        True,
The people are the city.

BRUTUS
By the consent of all, we were established    200
The people's magistrates.

ALL [CITIZENS]        You so remain.

MENENIUS
And so are like to do.

COMINIUS
That is the way to lay the city flat,
To bring the roof to the foundation,
And bury all which yet distinctly ranges,°    205
In heaps and piles of ruin.

SICINIUS        This deserves death.

BRUTUS
Or° let us stand to° our authority,
Or let us lose it. We do here pronounce,
Upon the part o' th' people, in° whose power
We were elected theirs,° Marcius is worthy    210
Of present death.

SICINIUS        Therefore lay hold of him;
Bear him to th' rock Tarpeian,° and from thence

Into destruction cast him.

BRUTUS        Aediles, seize him!

ALL [CITIZENS]
Yield, Marcius, yield!

MENENIUS        Hear me one word;
Beseech you, tribunes, hear me but a word.    215

AEDILES Peace, peace!

MENENIUS [*To* BRUTUS.]
Be that you seem, truly your country's friend,
And temp'rately proceed to what you would
Thus violently redress.

BRUTUS        Sir, those cold ways,
That seem like prudent helps, are very poisonous    220
Where the disease is violent. Lay hands upon him,
And bear him to the rock.

CORIOLANUS *draws his sword.*

CORIOLANUS        No, I'll die here.
There's some among you have beheld me fighting;
Come, try upon yourselves what you have seen me.

MENENIUS
Down with that sword! Tribunes, withdraw awhile.    225

BRUTUS
Lay hands upon him.

MENENIUS        Help Marcius, help,
You that be noble; help him, young and old!

ALL [CITIZENS]
Down with him, down with him!

*In this mutiny,° the* TRIBUNES, *the* AEDILES, *and the*
PEOPLE *are beat in.*

MENENIUS
Go, get you to your house; begone, away!
All will be naught° else.

SECOND SENATOR        Get you gone.

CORIOLANUS        Stand fast;    230
We have as many friends as enemies.

MENENIUS
Shall it be put to that?°

FIRST SENATOR        The gods forbid!
I prithee, noble friend, home to thy house;
Leave us to cure this cause.°

MENENIUS        For 'tis a sore upon us
You cannot tent° yourself. Begone, beseech you.    235

COMINIUS
Come, sir, along with us.

CORIOLANUS
I would they were barbarians, as they are,
Though in Rome littered; not Romans, as they are
not,
Though calved i' th' porch o' th' Capitol.°

MENENIUS        Begone.
Put not your worthy° rage into your tongue:    240
One time will owe another.°

CORIOLANUS        On fair ground
I could beat forty of them.

MENENIUS        I could myself

---

**189 Confusion** ruin (resulting from civil disorder; cf. line 110)
**193 at . . . lose** on point of losing   **205 distinctly ranges**
extends in separate orderly rows (of buildings)   **207 Or** either;
**stand to** stand by   **209 in** by   **210 theirs** i.e., their representatives   **212 rock Tarpeian** from which criminals were
thrown

**228 s.d. mutiny** riot   **230 naught** ruined   **232 put to that**
driven to that extremity   **234 cause** dispute   **235 tent** treat
(cf. I.ix.31)   **239 porch . . . Capitol** portico of the temple of
Jupiter on the Capitoline Hill   **240 worthy** justifiable (?)
noble (?)   **241 One . . . another** one time (the present, when
the people are in revolt) will be compensated by another (when
the people are checked)

Take up a brace° o' th' best of them; yea, the two
  tribunes.

COMINIUS
But now 'tis odds beyond arithmetic;°
And manhood is called foolery when it stands      245
Against a falling fabric.° Will you hence
Before the tag° return? Whose rage doth rend
Like interrupted waters, and o'erbear°
What they are used to bear.

MENENIUS                              Pray you, begone.
I'll try whether my old wit be in request          250
With those that have but little. This must be patched
With cloth of any color.

COMINIUS                    Nay, come away.
             *Exeunt* CORIOLANUS *and* COMINIUS.

PATRICIAN
This man has marred his fortune.

MENENIUS
His nature is too noble for the world:
He would not flatter Neptune for his trident,      255
Or Jove for's power to thunder. His heart's his mouth:
What his breast forges, that his tongue must vent;
And, being angry, does forget that ever
He heard the name of death.

*A noise within.*

Here's goodly work!

PATRICIAN              I would they were abed!      260

MENENIUS
I would they were in Tiber! What the vengeance!°
Could he not speak 'em fair?°

*Enter* BRUTUS *and* SICINIUS, *with the* RABBLE *again.*

SICINIUS                    Where is this viper
That would depopulate the city and
Be every man himself?

MENENIUS          You worthy tribunes—

SICINIUS
He shall be thrown down the Tarpeian rock          265
With rigorous hands. He hath resisted law,
And therefore law shall scorn him further trial
Than the severity of the public power,°
Which he so sets at nought.

FIRST CITIZEN              He shall well know
The noble tribunes are the people's mouths,        270
And we their hands.

ALL [CITIZENS]
He shall, sure on't.

MENENIUS          Sir, sir—

SICINIUS   Peace!

MENENIUS
Do not cry havoc,° where you should but hunt
With modest warrant.°

SICINIUS          Sir, how comes't that you      275
Have holp° to make this rescue?

MENENIUS                    Hear me speak:

As I do know the consul's worthiness,
So can I name his faults.

SICINIUS              Consul! What consul?

MENENIUS
The consul Coriolanus.

BRUTUS              He consul!

ALL [CITIZENS]
No, no, no, no, no.                              280

MENENIUS
If, by the tribunes' leave, and yours, good people,
I may be heard, I would crave a word or two;
The which shall turn you to no further harm
Than so much loss of time.

SICINIUS              Speak briefly then;
For we are peremptory° to dispatch                285
This viperous traitor. To eject him hence
Were but our danger,° and to keep him here
Our certain death. Therefore it is decreed
He dies tonight.

MENENIUS      Now the good gods forbid
That our renownèd Rome, whose gratitude          290
Towards her deservèd° children is enrolled
In Jove's own book, like an unnatural dam
Should now eat up her own!

SICINIUS
He's a disease that must be cut away.

MENENIUS
O, he's a limb that has but a disease;           295
Mortal,° to cut it off; to cure it, easy.
What has he done to Rome that's worthy death?
Killing our enemies, the blood he hath lost
Which I dare vouch is more than that he hath
By many an ounce—he dropped it for his country;  300
And what is left, to lose it by his country
Were to us all that do't and suffer it
A brand° to th' end o' th' world.

SICINIUS              This is clean kam.°

BRUTUS
Merely° awry. When he did love his country,
It honored him.

MENENIUS      The service of the foot            305
Being once gangrened, is not then respected
For what before it was.

BRUTUS              We'll hear no more.
Pursue him to his house and pluck° him thence,
Lest his infection, being of catching nature,
Spread further.

MENENIUS      One word more, one word!          310
This tiger-footed rage, when it shall find
The harm of unscanned° swiftness, will, too late,
Tie leaden pounds° to's° heels. Proceed by process;°
Lest parties (as he is beloved) break out,
And sack great Rome with Romans.

BRUTUS                    If it were so—        315

SICINIUS
What° do ye talk?

---

243 **Take . . . brace** take on a couple   244 **beyond
arithmetic** beyond number   246 **fabric** building   247 **tag**
riffraff ("tag and rag")   248 **o'erbear** overcome   261
**What the vengeance** an emphatic "What!"; cf. *What the
devil!*   262 **speak 'em fair** talk civilly to them (and so flatter)
268 **the public power** the power derived from the people
274 **cry havoc** call for general slaughter   275 **With modest
warrant** with moderate justification   276 **holp** helped

285 **peremptory** resolved   287 **but our danger** only the risk
we now run   291 **deservèd** deserving   296 **Mortal** deadly
303 **brand** mark of disgrace; **clean kam** completely wrong
(literally, "kam" = crooked)   304 **Merely** absolutely   308
**pluck** take   312 **unscanned** thoughtless   313 **pounds** pound-
weights; **to's** to its; **process** due process of law   316 **What**
why

Have we not had a taste of his obedience?
Our aediles smote? Ourselves resisted? Come!

MENENIUS
Consider this: he has been bred i' th' wars
Since 'a could draw a sword, and is ill schooled     320
In bolted° language; meal and brain together
He throws without distinction. Give me leave,
I'll go to him, and undertake to bring him
Where he shall answer, by a lawful form,°
In peace, to his utmost peril.°

FIRST SENATOR          Noble tribunes,     325
It is the humane way. The other course
Will prove too bloody, and the end of it
Unknown to the beginning.

SICINIUS          Noble Menenius,
Be thou then as the people's officer.
Masters, lay down your weapons.

BRUTUS          Go not home.     330

SICINIUS
Meet on the marketplace. We'll attend you there,
Where, if you bring not Marcius, we'll proceed
In our first way.

MENENIUS          I'll bring him to you.

[To the SENATORS.]

Let me desire your company. He must come,
Or what is worst will follow.

SENATORS          Pray you, let's to him.     335
                              *Exeunt omnes.*

[Scene II. *Rome. The house of Coriolanus.*]

*Enter* CORIOLANUS, *with* NOBLES.

CORIOLANUS
Let them pull all about mine ears; present me
Death on the wheel° or at wild horses' heels;
Or pile ten hills on the Tarpeian rock,
That the precipitation° might down stretch
Below the beam of sight;° yet will I still     5
Be thus to them.

A NOBLE          You do the nobler.

CORIOLANUS
I muse° my mother
Does not approve me further, who was wont
To call them woolen vassals,° things created
To buy and sell with groats;° to show bare heads     10
In congregations, to yawn, be still and wonder,
When one but of my ordinance° stood up
To speak of peace or war.

*Enter* VOLUMNIA.

                              I talk of you:
Why did you wish me milder? Would you have me

False to my nature? Rather say I play     15
The man I am.

VOLUMNIA          O, sir, sir, sir,
I would have had you put your power well on,
Before you had worn it out.

CORIOLANUS          Let go.°

VOLUMNIA
You might have been enough the man you are,
With striving less to be so. Lesser had been     20
The thwartings of your dispositions,° if
You had not showed them how ye were disposed
Ere they lacked power to cross you.

CORIOLANUS          Let them hang.

VOLUMNIA
Ay, and burn too.

*Enter* MENENIUS, *with the* SENATORS.

MENENIUS
Come, come, you have been too rough, something°
     too rough;     25
You must return and mend it.

SENATOR          There's no remedy,
Unless, by not so doing, our good city
Cleave in the midst° and perish.

VOLUMNIA          Pray be counseled;
I have a heart as little apt° as yours,
But yet a brain that leads my use of anger     30
To better vantage.

MENENIUS          Well said, noble woman!
Before he should thus stoop to th' herd, but that
The violent fit o' th' time craves it as physic°
For the whole state, I would put mine armor on,
Which I can scarcely bear.

CORIOLANUS          What must I do?     35

MENENIUS
Return to th' tribunes.

CORIOLANUS          Well, what then? What then?

MENENIUS
Repent what you have spoke.

CORIOLANUS
For them! I cannot do it to the gods,
Must I then do't to them?

VOLUMNIA          You are too absolute;
Though therein you can never be too noble     40
But when extremities speak.° I have heard you say,
Honor and policy, like unsevered° friends,
I' th' war do grow together. Grant that, and tell me
In peace what each of them by th' other lose
That they combine not there.

CORIOLANUS          Tush, tush!

MENENIUS          A good demand.     45

VOLUMNIA
If it be honor in your wars to seem
The same you are not, which for your best ends
You adopt° your policy, how is it less or worse
That it° shall hold companionship in peace

321 **bolted** refined (literally, "sifted")   324 **answer . . . form** meet the charges according to the forms of law   325 to . . . **peril** at the risk of the severest penalty
III.ii.2 **the wheel** by being bound to a wheel and beaten to death; an Elizabethan, not Roman, penalty   4 **precipitation** steepness   5 **Below . . . sight** beyond the range of sight ("beam" = a ray passing from the object to the eye)   7 **muse** wonder   9 **woolen vassals** i.e., rough-dressed members of the lowest class   10 **groats** four-penny coins   12 **ordinance** rank

18 **Let go** enough of that   21 **dispositions** inclinations   25 **something** somewhat   26–28 **There's . . . midst** there's no help for it (you must compromise); else, because of your failure to do so, our good city may be split in two   29 **apt** compliant   33 **physic** medical treatment   41 **when extremities speak** when the most critical situations demand (see Introduction, p. 1317)   42 **unsevered** inseparable   48 **adopt** adopt as   49 **it** pretense, "to seem/The same you are not"

With honor as in war; since that to both                                    50
It stands in like request?°

CORIOLANUS                   Why force° you this?

VOLUMNIA
Because that now it lies you on° to speak
To th' people, not by your own instruction,
Nor by th' matter which your heart prompts you,
But with such words that are but roted° in                                  55
Your tongue, though but bastards and syllables
Of no allowance to your bosom's truth.°
Now, this no more dishonors you at all
Than to take in° a town with gentle words,
Which else would put you to your fortune° and                              60
The hazard of much blood.
I would dissemble with my nature, where
My fortunes and my friends at stake required
I should do so in honor.° I am in this°
Your wife, your son, these senators, the nobles;                            65
And you will rather show our general° louts
How you can frown than spend a fawn upon 'em
For the inheritance° of their loves and safeguard
Of what that want° might ruin.

MENENIUS                        Noble lady!
Come, go with us; speak fair; you may salve so,                             70
Not what is dangerous present, but the loss
Of what is past.

VOLUMNIA        I prithee now, my son,
Go to them with this bonnet in thy hand;
And thus far having stretched it (here be with
    them),
Thy knee bussing° the stones (for in such business                         75
Action is eloquence, and the eyes of th' ignorant
More learnèd than the ears), waving° thy head,
Which° often thus correcting thy stout° heart,
Now humble as the ripest mulberry
That will not hold the handling; or° say to them,                          80
Thou art their soldier, and being bred in broils
Hast not the soft way which, thou dost confess,
Were fit for thee to use, as they to claim,
In asking their good loves; but thou wilt frame
Thyself, forsooth,° hereafter theirs, so far                               85
As thou hast power and person.

MENENIUS                        This but done,
Even as she speaks, why, their hearts were yours;
For they have pardons, being asked, as free°
As words to little purpose.

VOLUMNIA                        Prithee now,
Go, and be ruled; although I know thou hadst                               90
    rather
Follow thine enemy in a fiery gulf°

Than flatter him in a bower.°

*Enter* COMINIUS.

                                    Here is Cominius.

COMINIUS
I have been i' th' marketplace;° and, sir, 'tis fit
You make strong party,° or defend yourself
By calmness or by absence. All's in anger.                                 95

MENENIUS
Only fair speech.

COMINIUS        I think 'twill serve, if he
Can thereto frame his spirit.

VOLUMNIA                        He must, and will.
Prithee now, say you will, and go about it.

CORIOLANUS
Must I go show them my unbarbed sconce?° Must I
With my base tongue give to my noble heart                                100
A lie that it must bear? Well, I will do't.
Yet, were there but this single plot° to lose,
This mold° of Marcius, they to dust should grind it,
And throw't against the wind. To th' marketplace!
You have put me now to such a part° which never          105
I shall discharge° to th' life.

COMINIUS        Come, come, we'll prompt you.

VOLUMNIA
I prithee now, sweet son, as thou hast said
My praises made thee first a soldier, so,
To have my praise for this, perform a part
Thou hast not done before.

CORIOLANUS        Well, I must do't.                                       110
Away, my disposition, and possess me
Some harlot's° spirit! My throat of war be turned,
Which quired° with my drum, into a pipe°
Small as an eunuch or the virgin voice
That babies lulls asleep! The smiles of knaves         115
Tent in my cheeks, and schoolboys' tears take up°
The glasses of my sight!° A beggar's tongue
Make motion through my lips, and my armed knees,
Who bowed but in my stirrup, bend like his
That hath received an alms! I will not do't;          120
Lest I surcease° to honor mine own truth,
And by my body's action teach my mind
A most inherent° baseness.

VOLUMNIA                        At thy choice then
To beg of thee, it is my more dishonor
Than thou of them. Come all to ruin! Let              125
Thy mother rather feel thy pride than fear
Thy dangerous stoutness,° for I mock at death
With as big heart as thou. Do as thou list.°
Thy valiantness was mine, thou suck'st it from me,
But owe° thy pride thyself.

CORIOLANUS                        Pray, be content:     130
Mother, I am going to the marketplace;

51 **stands . . . request** is equally in demand; **force** urge 52 **it . . . on** it is your duty  55 **roted** learned by rote  56–57 **but . . . truth** only false expressions wholly unacceptable to your heart's understanding  59 **take in** capture  60 **put . . . fortune** force you to take your chances (in war)  64 **in honor** in honor bound (*not* Coriolanus' understanding of "honor"); **I . . . this** I speak in this for (implying also, "I stand in place of")  66 **general** common  68 **inheritance** possession  69 **that want** i.e., of their loves  74–80 the text may be corrupt  75 **bussing** kissing (touching)  77 **waving** bowing up and down  78 **Which** subject of "correcting" in a nominative absolute; the sentence is urgent; the syntax, sketchy; **stout** proud  80 **or** marks the turn from "action" to "eloquence," line 76  85 **forsooth** in truth  88 **free** liberal (to grant)  91 **in . . . gulf** into an abyss of flame

92 **bower** ladies' chamber  93 **marketplace** Forum of ancient Rome  94 **make strong party** maintain your side strongly  99 **unbarbed sconce** unarmed head ("sconce" often used in comic contexts)  102 **plot** of earth  103 **mold** both "frame" and "earth"; cf. V.iii.22  105 **part** in a play  106 **discharge** perform  112 **harlot** rascal (used of both sexes)  113 **quired** sang harmoniously; **pipe** i.e., voice  116 **take up** possess  117 **glasses . . . sight** my eyeballs  121 **surcease** cease  123 **inherent** firmly settled  126–27 **feel . . . stoutness** suffer the effects of thy pride, but not fear the danger of it ("stoutness" = obstinacy, as in North, nearly equal to "pride"; cf. line 78)  128 **thou list** you please  130 **owe** own, have

Chide me no more. I'll mountebank° their loves,
Cog° their hearts from them, and come home beloved
Of all the trades in Rome. Look, I am going.
Commend me to my wife. I'll return consul;      135
Or never trust to what my tongue can do
I' th' way of flattery further.

VOLUMNIA                    Do your will.

*Exit* VOLUMNIA.

COMINIUS
Away, the tribunes do attend you. Arm yourself
To answer mildly; for they are prepared
With accusations, as I hear, more strong      140
Than are upon you yet.

CORIOLANUS
The word° is "mildly." Pray you, let us go.
Let them accuse me by invention,° I
Will answer in° mine honor.

MENENIUS                    Ay, but mildly.

CORIOLANUS
Well, mildly be it then—mildly.      *Exeunt.* 145


[Scene III. *Rome. The Forum.*]


*Enter* SICINIUS *and* BRUTUS.

BRUTUS
In this point charge him home,° that he affects°
Tyrannical power. If he evade us there,
Enforce him° with his envy° to the people,
And that the spoil got on° the Antiates
Was ne'er distributed.

*Enter an* AEDILE.

                    What, will he come?      5

AEDILE
He's coming.

BRUTUS          How accompanied?

AEDILE
With old Menenius and those senators
That always favored him.

SICINIUS                    Have you a catalog
Of all the voices that we have procured,
Set down by th' poll?°

AEDILE                    I have; 'tis ready.      10

SICINIUS
Have you collected them by tribes?

AEDILE                    I have.

SICINIUS
Assemble presently° the people hither:
And when they hear me say, "It shall be so
I' th' right and strength o' th' commons," be it either
For death, for fine, or banishment, then let them,      15
If I say "Fine," cry "Fine!"—if "Death," cry "Death!"

Insisting on the old prerogative
And power i' th' truth o' th' cause.°

AEDILE                    I shall inform them.

BRUTUS
And when such time° they have begun to cry,
Let them not cease, but with a din confused      20
Enforce° the present execution
Of what we chance to sentence.

AEDILE                    Very well.

SICINIUS
Make them be strong, and ready for this hint,°
When we shall hap to give't them.

BRUTUS                    Go about it. [*Exit* AEDILE.]
Put him to° choler straight. He hath been used      25
Ever to conquer and to have his worth°
Of contradiction. Being once chafed, he cannot
Be reined again to temperance; then he speaks
What's in his heart, and that is there which looks
With us° to break his neck:

*Enter* CORIOLANUS, MENENIUS, *and* COMINIUS,
*with others.*

SICINIUS                    Well, here he comes.      30

MENENIUS
Calmly, I do beseech you.

CORIOLANUS
Ay, as an ostler, that for th' poorest piece°
Will bear the knave by th' volume.° Th' honored gods
Keep Rome in safety, and the chairs of justice
Supplied with worthy men! Plant love among's!      35
Throng our large temples with the shows of peace,
And not our streets with war!

FIRST SENATOR                    Amen, amen.

MENENIUS
A noble wish.

*Enter the* AEDILE, *with the* PLEBEIANS.

SICINIUS
Draw near, ye people.

AEDILE
List to your tribunes. Audience!° peace, I say!      40

CORIOLANUS
First, hear me speak.

BOTH TRIBUNES          Well, say. Peace, ho!

CORIOLANUS
Shall I be charged no further than this present?°
Must all determine° here?

SICINIUS                    I do demand,°
If you submit you to the people's voices,
Allow° their officers, and are content      45
To suffer lawful censure for such faults
As shall be proved upon you.

CORIOLANUS                    I am content.

MENENIUS
Lo, citizens, he says he is content.

---

**132 mountebank** win their loves by tricky actions (cf. a *mountebank*, a quack doctor, who puts on an act to sell his wares)  **133 Cog** cheat  **142 word** password  **143 accuse . . . invention** invent accusations against me  **144 in** in a way consistent with

**III.iii.1 charge him home** press your accusations against him to the limit; **affects** aims at  **3 Enforce him** press him hard; **envy** ill will  **4 got on** won from  **10 by th' poll** by counting heads  **12 presently** at once (cf. line 21)

**18 i' . . . cause** resting in the justice of the case  **19 when such time** at such time when  **21 Enforce** press for  **23 hint** opportunity  **25 Put him to** drive him to  **26 his worth** his pennyworth, i.e., his fill  **29–30 looks With us** promises in harmony with our intent  **32 piece** coin  **33 bear . . . volume** endure being called knave enough times to fill a book  **40 Audience** Give ear!  **42 this present** this immediate occasion  **43 determine** reach a conclusion; **demand** ask  **45 Allow** acknowledge

The warlike service he has done, consider; think
Upon the wounds his body bears, which show 50
Like graves i' th' holy churchyard.

CORIOLANUS Scratches with briers,
Scars to move laughter only.

MENENIUS Consider further,
That when he speaks not like a citizen,
You find him like a soldier.° Do not take
His rougher accents for malicious sounds, 55
But, as I say, such as become a soldier
Rather than envy° you.

COMINIUS Well, well, no more.

CORIOLANUS
What is the matter
That, being passed for consul with full voice,
I am so dishonored that the very hour 60
You take it off again?

SICINIUS Answer to us.

CORIOLANUS
Say, then. 'Tis true, I ought so.

SICINIUS
We charge you, that you have contrived to take
From Rome all seasoned° office, and to wind
Yourself into° a power tyrannical, 65
For which you are a traitor to the people.

CORIOLANUS
How! Traitor!

MENENIUS Nay, temperately! Your promise.

CORIOLANUS
The fires i' th' lowest hell fold in the people!
Call me their traitor, thou injurious° tribune!
Within° thine eyes sat twenty thousand deaths, 70
In thy hands clutched as many millions, in
Thy lying tongue both numbers, I would say
"Thou liest" unto thee with a voice as free°
As I do pray the gods.

SICINIUS Mark you this, people?

ALL [CITIZENS]
To th' rock, to th' rock with him!

SICINIUS Peace! 75
We need not put new matter to his charge.
What you have seen him do and heard him speak,
Beating your officers, cursing yourselves,
Opposing laws with strokes, and here defying
Those whose great power must try him—even this, 80
So criminal and in such capital° kind,
Deserves th' extremest death.

BRUTUS But since he hath
Served well for Rome—

CORIOLANUS What do you prate of service?

BRUTUS
I talk of that that know it.

CORIOLANUS You! 85

MENENIUS
Is this the promise that you made your mother?

COMINIUS
Know, I pray you—

CORIOLANUS I'll know no further.

Let them pronounce the steep Tarpeian death,°
Vagabond exile, flaying, pent° to linger
But with a grain a day, I would not buy 90
Their mercy at the price of one fair word,
Nor check my courage° for what they can give,
To have't with saying "Good morrow."

SICINIUS For that he has
(As much as in him lies°) from time to time
Envied against° the people, seeking means 95
To pluck away their power, as now° at last
Given hostile strokes, and that not° in the presence
Of dreaded justice, but on the ministers
That do distribute it—in the name o' th' people,
And in the power of us the tribunes, we, 100
Even from this instant, banish him our city,
In peril of precipitation
From off the rock Tarpeian, never more
To enter our Rome gates. I' th' people's name,
I say it shall be so. 105

ALL [CITIZENS]
It shall be so, it shall be so! Let him away!
He's banished, and it shall be so.

COMINIUS
Hear me, my masters and my common friends—

SICINIUS
He's sentenced; no more hearing.

COMINIUS Let me speak.
I have been consul, and can show for Rome 110
Her enemies' marks upon me. I do love
My country's good with a respect more tender,
More holy and profound, than mine own life,
My dear wife's estimate,° her womb's increase
And treasure of my loins; then if I would 115
Speak that—

SICINIUS We know your drift. Speak what?

BRUTUS
There's no more to be said, but he is banished
As enemy to the people and his country.
It shall be so.

ALL [CITIZENS]
It shall be so, it shall be so. 120

CORIOLANUS
You common cry° of curs, whose breath I hate
As reek° o' th' rotten fens, whose loves I prize
As the dead carcasses of unburied men
That do corrupt my air, I banish you.
And here remain with your uncertainty! 125
Let every feeble rumor shake your hearts!
Your enemies, with nodding of their plumes,
Fan you into despair! Have the power still
To banish your defenders, till at length
Your ignorance (which finds not till it feels,° 130
Making but reservation of yourselves,°
Still° your own foes) deliver you as most
Abated° captives to some nation

---

54 **like a soldier** see Introduction, p. 1312 57 **envy** express malice towards 64 **seasoned** established (or "moderate," "well moderated") 64–65 **wind Yourself into** make your way by indirect and crooked means 69 **injurious** insulting 70 **Within** if within 73 **free** unrestrained 81 **capital** defined by line 82

88 **steep Tarpeian death** cf. line 103 89 **pent** i.e., "Let them pronounce" the sentence of being "pent," imprisoned 92 **courage** spirit 94 **as . . . lies** as lies in his power 95 **Envied against** shown malice towards 96 **as now** with respect to this occasion (or "now," "as" being redundant) 97 **not** not only 114 **estimate** worth 121 **cry** pack 122 **reek** mist 130 **finds . . . feels** does not understand until it suffers the consequences 131 **Making . . . yourselves** saving only yourselves 132 **Still** ever 133 **Abated** beaten down

That won you without blows! Despising
For you the city, thus I turn my back.                              135
There is a world elsewhere.

*Exeunt* CORIOLANUS, COMINIUS, [MENENIUS,]
*with the other* SENATORS.

AEDILE
The people's enemy is gone, is gone!

ALL [CITIZENS]
Our enemy is banished, he is gone! Hoo—oo!

*They all shout, and throw up their caps.*

SICINIUS
Go see him out at gates, and follow him,
As he hath followed you, with all despite;°                         140
Give him deserved vexation.° Let a guard
Attend us through the city.

ALL [CITIZENS]
Come, come, let's see him out at gates; come!
The gods preserve our noble tribunes! Come. *Exeunt.*


# A C T   I V

[Scene I. *Rome. Before a gate of the city.*]

*Enter* CORIOLANUS, VOLUMNIA, VIRGILIA, MENE-
NIUS, COMINIUS, *with the young* NOBILITY *of Rome.*

CORIOLANUS
Come, leave your tears; a brief farewell. The beast
With many heads butts me away. Nay, mother,
Where is your ancient courage? You were used
To say extremities was° the trier of spirits;
That common chances common men could bear;       5
That when the sea was calm all boats alike
Showed mastership in floating; fortune's blows°
When most struck home, being gentle wounded
   craves
A noble cunning.° You were used to load me
With precepts that would make invincible         10
The heart that conned° them.

VIRGILIA
O heavens! O heavens!

CORIOLANUS                    Nay, I prithee, woman—

VOLUMNIA
Now the red pestilence strike all trades in Rome,
And occupations perish!

CORIOLANUS                    What, what, what!
I shall be loved when I am lacked. Nay, mother,   15
Resume that spirit when you were wont to say,
If you had been the wife to Hercules,
Six of his labors you'd have done, and saved
Your husband so much sweat. Cominius,
Droop not; adieu. Farewell, my wife, my mother.   20
I'll do well yet. Thou old and true Menenius,
Thy tears are salter than a younger man's,

And venomous to thine eyes. My sometime° general,
I have seen thee stern, and thou hast oft beheld
Heart-hard'ning spectacles; tell these sad women   25
'Tis fond° to wail inevitable strokes,
As 'tis to laugh at 'em. My mother, you wot° well
My hazards still have been your solace,° and
Believe't not lightly—though I go alone,
Like to a lonely dragon, that his fen              30
Makes feared and talked of more than seen—your son
Will or exceed the common° or be caught
With cautelous° baits and practice.°

VOLUMNIA                              My first son,
Whither wilt thou go? Take good Cominius
With thee awhile. Determine on some course         35
More than a wild exposure° to each chance
That starts i' th' way before thee.

CORIOLANUS                              O the gods!

COMINIUS
I'll follow thee a month, devise with thee
Where thou shalt rest, that thou mayst hear of us
And we of thee. So, if the time thrust forth       40
A cause for thy repeal,° we shall not send
O'er the vast world to seek a single man,
And lose advantage,° which doth ever cool
I' th' absence of the needer.°

CORIOLANUS                    Fare ye well!
Thou hast years upon thee; and thou art too full   45
Of the wars' surfeits to go rove with one
That's yet unbruised. Bring° me but out at gate.
Come, my sweet wife, my dearest mother, and
My friends of noble touch;° when I am forth,
Bid me farewell, and smile. I pray you, come.      50
While I remain above the ground you shall
Hear from me still, and never of me aught
But what is like me formerly.

MENENIUS                      That's worthily
As any ear can hear. Come, let's not weep.
If I could shake off but one seven years           55
From these old arms and legs, by the good gods,
I'd° with thee every foot.

CORIOLANUS                    Give me thy hand.
Come.                                              *Exeunt.*


[Scene II. *Rome. Near the gate.*]

*Enter the two tribunes,* SICINIUS *and* BRUTUS, *with the*
AEDILE.

SICINIUS
Bid them all° home; he's gone, and we'll no further.
The nobility are vexed, whom we see have sided
In his behalf.

BRUTUS        Now we have shown our power,
Let us seem humbler after it is done
Than when it was a-doing.

SICINIUS                    Bid them home.      5

---

140 despite contempt   141 Give . . . vexation torment him
as he deserves
IV.i.4 extremities was plural subject permissible in Elizabethan usage   7 fortune's blows supply introductory "that"
7–9 fortune's . . . cunning when fortune's blows strike
hardest, to act the gentleman though wounded demands a
noble use of intelligence   11 conned studied

23 sometime former   26 fond foolish   27 wot know   28
solace interest   32 or . . . common either surpass the usual
achievements of men   33 cautelous crafty; practice treachery
36 exposure exposure   41 repeal recall   43 advantage the
opportune moment   44 needer i.e., of "advantage"   47 Bring
conduct   49 noble touch tested nobility (cf. touchstone)   57
I'd I would (go)
IV.ii.1 them all the plebeians

Say their great enemy is gone, and they
Stand in their ancient strength.
BRUTUS                    Dismiss them home. [*Exit* AEDILE.]
Here comes his mother.

*Enter* VOLUMNIA, VIRGILIA, *and* MENENIUS.

SICINIUS                    Let's not meet her.
BRUTUS                                        Why?
SICINIUS
They say she's mad.
BRUTUS
They have ta'en note of us. Keep on your way.     10
VOLUMNIA
O, y' are well met. Th' hoarded° plague o' th' gods
Requite your love!
MENENIUS            Peace, peace, be not so loud.
VOLUMNIA
If that I could for weeping, you should hear—
Nay, and you shall hear some. [*To* BRUTUS.] Will
     you be gone?
VIRGILIA [*To* SICINIUS.]
You shall stay too. I would I had the power     15
To say so to my husband.
SICINIUS                    Are you mankind?°
VOLUMNIA
Ay, fool; is that a shame? Note but this, fool.
Was not a man my father? Hadst thou foxship°
To banish him that struck more blows for Rome
Than thou hast spoken words?
SICINIUS                    O blessed heavens!     20
VOLUMNIA
Moe° noble blows than ever thou wise words;
And for Rome's good. I'll tell thee what—yet go!
Nay, but thou shalt stay too. I would my son
Were in Arabia,° and thy tribe before him,
His good sword in his hand.
SICINIUS                    What then?
VIRGILIA                                    What then!     25
He'd make an end of thy posterity.
VOLUMNIA
Bastards and all.
Good man, the wounds that he does bear for Rome!
MENENIUS
Come, come, peace.
SICINIUS
I would he had continued to his country     30
As he began, and not unknit himself
The noble knot he made.°
BRUTUS                    I would he had.
VOLUMNIA
"I would he had"! 'Twas you incensed the rabble;
Cats, that can judge as fitly of his worth
As I can of those mysteries which heaven     35
Will not have earth to know.
BRUTUS                    Pray, let's go.
VOLUMNIA
Now, pray, sir, get you gone;

You have done a brave deed. Ere you go, hear this:
As far as doth the Capitol exceed
The meanest house in Rome, so far my son—     40
This lady's husband here, this, do you see?—
Whom you have banished—does exceed you all.
BRUTUS
Well, well, we'll leave you.
SICINIUS                    Why stay we to be baited
With° one that wants her wits?     *Exit* TRIBUNES.
VOLUMNIA                    Take my prayers with you.
I would the gods had nothing else to do     45
But to confirm my curses! Could I meet 'em
But once a day, it would unclog my heart
Of what lies heavy to't.
MENENIUS            You have told them home,°
And by my troth you have cause. You'll sup with me?
VOLUMNIA
Anger's my meat; I sup upon myself,     50
And so shall starve with feeding. Come, let's go.
Leave this faint puling,° and lament as I do,
In anger, Juno-like. Come, come, come.
                    *Exeunt* [VOLUMNIA *and* VIRGILIA].
MENENIUS                    Fie, fie, fie! *Exit.*

[*Scene III. Between Rome and Antium.*]

*Enter a* ROMAN *and a* VOLSCE.

ROMAN   I know you well, sir, and you know me: your
name, I think, is Adrian.
VOLSCE   It is so, sir. Truly, I have forgot you.
ROMAN   I am a Roman; and my services are, as you
are, against 'em.° Know you me yet?     5
VOLSCE   Nicanor? No!
ROMAN   The same, sir.
VOLSCE   You had more beard when I last saw you;
but your favor° is well appeared° by your tongue.
What's the news in Rome? I have a note° from the     10
Volscian state to find you out there. You have well
saved me a day's journey.
ROMAN   There hath been in Rome strange insurrec-
tions; the people against the senators, patricians, and
nobles.     15
VOLSCE   Hath been! Is it ended then? Our state thinks
not so; they are in a most warlike preparation, and
hope to come upon them in the heat of their division.
ROMAN   The main blaze of it is past, but a small thing
would make it flame again; for the nobles receive° so     20
to heart the banishment of that worthy Coriolanus,
that they are in a ripe aptness to take all power from
the people and to pluck from them their tribunes
forever. This lies glowing, I can tell you, and is almost
mature for the violent breaking out.     25
VOLSCE   Coriolanus banished!
ROMAN   Banished, sir.
VOLSCE   You will be welcome with this intelligence,
Nicanor.
ROMAN   The day serves well for them° now. I have     30

---

**11 hoarded** stored up (for punishment)   **16 mankind** mad,
of manlike violence (Sicinius' meaning; but Volumnia takes it
in the sense of "human")   **18 foxship** cunning   **21 Moe**
more   **24 Arabia** a desert (outside Roman law and order)
**32 noble . . . made** bond to Rome made by his heroic
deeds.

**44 With** by   **48 told them home** "hit them where it hurts"
**52 puling** whining
**IV.iii.5 'em** the Romans   **9 favor** face; **appeared** made to
appear   **10 a note** instructions   **20 receive** take   **30 them** the
Volscians

heard it said the fittest time to corrupt a man's wife is when she's fall'n out with her husband. Your noble Tullus Aufidius will appear well in these wars, his great opposer, Coriolanus, being now in no request of° his country. 35

VOLSCE He cannot choose.° I am most fortunate thus accidentally to encounter you. You have ended my business, and I will merrily accompany you home.

ROMAN I shall, between this° and supper, tell you most strange things from Rome, all tending to the 40 good of their adversaries. Have you an army ready, say you?

VOLSCE A most royal one; the centurions° and their charges,° distinctly billeted,° already in th' entertainment,° and to be on foot at an hour's warning. 45

ROMAN I am joyful to hear of their readiness, and am the man, I think, that shall set them in present action. So, sir, heartily well met, and most glad of your company.

VOLSCE You take my part from me, sir. I have the 50 most cause to be glad of yours.

ROMAN Well, let us go together. *Exeunt.*

[Scene IV. *Antium. Before Aufidius' house.*]

*Enter* CORIOLANUS *in mean apparel, disguised and muffled.*

CORIOLANUS
A goodly city is this Antium. City,
'Tis I that made thy widows: many an heir
Of these fair edifices 'fore my wars°
Have I heard groan and drop. Then know me not,
Lest that thy wives with spits and boys with stones 5
In puny battle slay me.

*Enter a* CITIZEN.

Save you,° sir.

CITIZEN
And you.

CORIOLANUS Direct me, if it be your will,
Where great Aufidius lies.° Is he in Antium?

CITIZEN
He is, and feasts the nobles of the state
At his house this night.

CORIOLANUS Which is his house, beseech you? 10

CITIZEN
This here before you.

CORIOLANUS Thank you, sir: farewell.
*Exit* CITIZEN.
O world, thy slippery turns! Friends now fast sworn,
Whose double bosoms seems° to wear one heart,
Whose hours, whose bed, whose meal and exercise
Are still together, who twin, as 'twere, in love 15

Unseparable, shall within this hour,
On a dissension of a doit,° break out
To bitterest enmity. So fellest° foes,
Whose passions and whose plots have broke their sleep
To take the one the other, by some chance, 20
Some trick° not worth an egg, shall grow dear friends
And interjoin their issues.° So with me:
My birthplace hate I, and my love's upon
This enemy town. I'll enter. If he slay me,
He does fair justice; if he give me way, 25
I'll do his country service. *Exit.*

[Scene V. *Antium. A hall in Aufidius' house.*]

*Music plays. Enter a* SERVINGMAN.

FIRST SERVINGMAN Wine, wine, wine! What service is here! I think our fellows are asleep. [*Exit.*]

*Enter another* SERVINGMAN.

SECOND SERVINGMAN Where's Cotus? My master calls for him. Cotus! *Exit.*

*Enter* CORIOLANUS.

CORIOLANUS
A goodly house. The feast smells well, but I 5
Appear not like a guest.

*Enter the* FIRST SERVINGMAN.

FIRST SERVINGMAN What would you have, friend? Whence are you? Here's no place for you: pray go to the door!° *Exit.*

CORIOLANUS
I have deserved no better entertainment, 10
In being Coriolanus.

*Enter* SECOND SERVINGMAN.

SECOND SERVINGMAN Whence are you, sir? Has the porter his eyes in his head that he gives entrance to such companions?° Pray get you out.

CORIOLANUS Away! 15

SECOND SERVINGMAN "Away!" Get you away.

CORIOLANUS Now thou'rt troublesome.

SECOND SERVINGMAN Are you so brave?° I'll have you talked with anon.°

*Enter* THIRD SERVINGMAN; *the* FIRST [SERVINGMAN] *meets him.*

THIRD SERVINGMAN What fellow's this? 20

FIRST SERVINGMAN A strange one as ever I looked on! I cannot get him out o' th' house. Prithee call my master to him.

THIRD SERVINGMAN What have you to do here, fellow? Pray you avoid° the house. 25

CORIOLANUS Let me but stand; I will not hurt your hearth.

THIRD SERVINGMAN What are you?

CORIOLANUS A gentleman.

THIRD SERVINGMAN A marv'lous° poor one. 30

CORIOLANUS   True, so I am.

THIRD SERVINGMAN   Pray you, poor gentleman, take up some other station; here's no place for you. Pray you avoid. Come.

CORIOLANUS   Follow your function,° go and batten° 35 on cold bits.

*Pushes him away from him.*

THIRD SERVINGMAN   What, you will not? Prithee, tell my master what a strange guest he has here.

SECOND SERVINGMAN   And I shall.
                              *Exit* SECOND SERVINGMAN.

THIRD SERVINGMAN   Where dwell'st thou?          40

CORIOLANUS   Under the canopy.°

THIRD SERVINGMAN   Under the canopy!

CORIOLANUS   Ay.

THIRD SERVINGMAN   Where's that?

CORIOLANUS   I' th' city of kites and crows.       45

THIRD SERVINGMAN   I' th' city of kites and crows! What an ass it is! Then thou dwell'st with daws° too?

CORIOLANUS   No, I serve not thy master.

THIRD SERVINGMAN   How, sir! Do you meddle with my master?                                          50

CORIOLANUS   Ay; 'tis an honester service than to meddle with thy mistress. Thou prat'st, and prat'st; serve with thy trencher.° Hence!   *Beats him away.*

*Enter* AUFIDIUS *with the* [SECOND] SERVINGMAN.

AUFIDIUS   Where is this fellow?

SECOND SERVINGMAN   Here, sir. I'd have beaten 55 him like a dog, but for disturbing the lords within.

AUFIDIUS
Whence com'st thou? What wouldst thou? Thy name?
Why speak'st not? Speak, man. What's thy name?

CORIOLANUS                    [*Unmuffling.*] If, Tullus,
Not yet thou know'st me, and, seeing me, dost not
Think me° for the man I am, necessity            60
Commands me name myself.

AUFIDIUS                    What is thy name?

CORIOLANUS
A name unmusical to the Volscians' ears,
And harsh in sound to thine.

AUFIDIUS                    Say, what's thy name?
Thou hast a grim appearance, and thy face
Bears a command° in't. Though thy tackle's torn,  65
Thou show'st° a noble vessel. What's thy name?

CORIOLANUS
Prepare thy brow to frown. Know'st thou me yet?

AUFIDIUS
I know thee not. Thy name!

CORIOLANUS
My name is Caius Marcius, who hath done
To thee particularly, and to all the Volsces,       70
Great hurt and mischief;° thereto witness may
My surname, Coriolanus. The painful° service,

The extreme dangers, and the drops of blood
Shed for my thankless country, are requited
But with that surname—a good memory°               75
And witness of the malice and displeasure
Which thou shouldst bear me. Only that name remains.
The cruelty and envy° of the people,
Permitted by our dastard nobles, who
Have all forsook me, hath devoured the rest;       80
And suffered me by th' voice of slaves to be
Whooped out of Rome. Now, this extremity
Hath brought me to thy hearth; not out of hope
(Mistake me not) to save my life; for if
I had feared death, of all the men i' th' world    85
I would have 'voided thee; but in mere spite,
To be full quit of° those my banishers,
Stand I before thee here. Then if thou hast
A heart of wreak° in thee, that wilt revenge
Thine own particular wrongs and stop those maims   90
Of shame° seen through thy country, speed thee straight
And make my misery serve thy turn. So use it
That my revengeful services may prove
As benefits to thee; for I will fight
Against my cank'red° country with the spleen°      95
Of all the under fiends.° But if so be
Thou dar'st not this and that to prove more fortunes°
Thou'rt tired, then, in a word, I also am
Longer to live most weary, and present
My throat to thee and to thy ancient malice;      100
Which not to cut would show thee but a fool,
Since I have ever followed thee with hate,
Drawn tuns° of blood out of thy country's breast,
And cannot live but to thy shame, unless
It be to do thee service.

AUFIDIUS                    O Marcius, Marcius!     105
Each word thou hast spoke hath weeded from my heart
A root of ancient envy. If Jupiter
Should from yond cloud speak divine things,
And say, "'Tis true," I'd not believe them more
Than thee, all noble Marcius. Let me twine         110
Mine arms about that body, where against
My grainèd ash° an hundred times hath broke
And scarred the moon with splinters. Here I clip°
The anvil of my sword, and do contest
As hotly and as nobly with thy love               115
As ever in ambitious strength I did
Contend against thy valor. Know thou first,
I loved the maid I married; never man
Sighed truer breath. But that° I see thee here,
Thou noble thing, more dances my rapt° heart      120
Than when I first my wedded mistress saw
Bestride my threshold. Why, thou Mars, I tell thee,
We have a power on foot,° and I had purpose

IV.v.9 **to the door** out of doors   14 **companions** fellows (in bad sense)   18 **brave** impudent   19 **anon** soon   25 **avoid** leave   30 **marv'lous** strangely   35 **Follow your function** do your regular work;   **batten** grow fat   41 **canopy** sky (cf. *canopy* over a throne)   47 **daws** foolish birds   53 **trencher** wooden plate   60 **Think me** take me   65 **a command** a look of authority   66 **show'st** appear'st   71 **mischief** serious harm   72 **painful** laborious

75 **memory** memorial   78 **envy** ill will   87 **full quit of** fully revenged on   89 **heart of wreak** vengeful heart   90–91 **maims Of shame** shameful wounds (e.g., the Roman occupation of Corioli)   95 **cank'red** corrupted (by ingratitude and envy);   **spleen** rage   96 **under fiends** devils in hell   97 **prove more fortunes** try the chances of fortune further   103 **tuns** casks   112 **grainèd ash** spear of ash, the grain showing   113 **clip** embrace   119 **that** because   120 **rapt** enraptured   123 **power on foot** force in the field

Once more to hew thy target° from thy brawn,°
Or lose mine arm for't. Thou hast beat me out° 125
Twelve several times, and I have nightly since
Dreamt of encounters 'twixt thyself and me.
We have been down together in my sleep,
Unbuckling helms, fisting each other's throat,
And waked° half dead with nothing. Worthy Marcius, 130
Had we no other quarrel else to Rome but that
Thou art thence banished, we would muster all
From twelve to seventy, and pouring war
Into the bowels of ungrateful Rome,
Like a bold flood o'erbeat.° O, come, go in, 135
And take our friendly senators by th' hands,
Who now are here, taking their leaves of me
Who am prepared against your territories,
Though not for Rome itself.
CORIOLANUS    You bless me, gods!
AUFIDIUS
Therefore, most absolute° sir, if thou wilt have 140
The leading of thine own revenges, take
Th' one half of my commission,° and set down°—
As best thou art experienced, since thou know'st
Thy country's strength and weakness—thine own
 ways,
Whether to knock against the gates of Rome, 145
Or rudely visit them in parts remote
To fright them ere destroy. But come in.
Let me commend thee first to those that shall
Say yea to thy desires. A thousand welcomes!
And more a friend than e'er an enemy; 150
Yet, Marcius, that was much. Your hand: most
 welcome!        *Exeunt.*

*Enter*° *two of the* SERVINGMEN.

FIRST SERVINGMAN Here's a strange alteration!
SECOND SERVINGMAN By my hand, I had thought
to have strucken him with a cudgel; and yet my mind
gave me° his clothes made a false report of him. 155
FIRST SERVINGMAN What an arm he has! He turned
me about with his finger and his thumb, as one would
set up a top.
SECOND SERVINGMAN Nay, I knew by his face
that there was something in him; he had, sir, a kind of 160
face, methought—I cannot tell how to term it.
FIRST SERVINGMAN He had so, looking as it were—
would I were hanged, but I thought there was more
in him than I could think.
SECOND SERVINGMAN So did I, I'll be sworn. He is 165
simply the rarest man i' th' world.
FIRST SERVINGMAN I think he is; but a greater
soldier than he, you wot° one.
SECOND SERVINGMAN Who, my master?
FIRST SERVINGMAN Nay, it's no matter for that. 170
SECOND SERVINGMAN Worth six on him.
FIRST SERVINGMAN Nay, not so neither. But I take
him to be the greater soldier.

SECOND SERVINGMAN Faith, look you, one cannot
tell how to say that. For the defense of a town our 175
general is excellent.
FIRST SERVINGMAN Ay, and for an assault too.

*Enter the* THIRD SERVINGMAN.

THIRD SERVINGMAN O slaves, I can tell you news—
news, you rascals!
BOTH [FIRST AND SECOND SERVINGMEN] What, 180
what, what? Let's partake.
THIRD SERVINGMAN I would not be a Roman, of
all nations; I had as lief° be a condemned man.
BOTH Wherefore? Wherefore?
THIRD SERVINGMAN Why here's he that was wont 185
to thwack our general—Caius Marcius.
FIRST SERVINGMAN Why do you say "thwack our
general"?
THIRD SERVINGMAN I do not say "thwack our
general," but he was always good enough for him. 190
SECOND SERVINGMAN Come, we are fellows° and
friends. He was ever too hard for him; I have heard
him say so himself.
FIRST SERVINGMAN He was too hard for him
directly,° to say the troth on't. Before Corioles he 195
scotched° him and notched him like a carbonado.°
SECOND SERVINGMAN And he had been cannibally
given, he might have boiled and eaten him too.
FIRST SERVINGMAN But more of thy news?
THIRD SERVINGMAN Why, he is so made on° here 200
within as if he were son and heir to Mars; set at
upper end o' th' table; no question asked him by any
of the senators but they stand bald° before him. Our
general himself makes a mistress of him; sanctifies
himself with's hand,° and turns up the white o' th' eye° 205
to his discourse. But the bottom° of the news is, our
general is cut i' th' middle and but one half of what he
was yesterday, for the other has half by the entreaty
and grant of the whole table.° He'll go, he says, and
sowl° the porter of Rome gates by th' ears. He will 210
mow all down before him, and leave his passage
polled.°
SECOND SERVINGMAN And he's as like to do't as
any man I can imagine.
THIRD SERVINGMAN Do't! He will do't; for look 215
you, sir, he has as many friends as enemies; which
friends, sir, as it were, durst not (look you, sir) show
themselves (as we term it) his friends whilst he's in
directitude.°
FIRST SERVINGMAN Directitude! What's that? 220
THIRD SERVINGMAN But when they shall see, sir,
his crest up° again and the man in blood,° they will
out of their burrows (like conies° after rain) and revel
all with him.

124 **target** shield; **brawn** brawny arm 125 **out** completely
130 **waked** (I have) awakened 135 **o'erbeat** surge over (the
land) 140 **absolute** perfect 142 **my commission** the forces
under me; **set down** determine 151 **s.d. Enter** perhaps they
come forward from backstage, since neither has been assigned
an "Exit" 154–55 **my mind gave me** I had an idea 167–76
the First Servingman is cautiously and cunningly vague in his
references to the "greater soldier" 168 **wot** know

183 **lief** willingly 191 **fellows** comrades 195 **directly** plainly
196 **scotched** slashed; **carbonado** meat scored with knife,
for broiling 200 **so made on** made so much of 203 **bald**
bareheaded 205 **sanctifies . . . hand** touches his hand as if it
were a holy relic 205 **turns . . . eye** in pious wonder
206 **bottom** last (jokingly for "the climax") 208–09 **has
. . . table** has half because all at the table beg him to take it,
and give it to him 210 **sowl** drag 212 **polled** cleared (used
of cutting hair) 219 **directitude** comic mistake for *discredit* (?)
222 **crest up** like an animal aroused; **in blood** in top condition
223 **conies** rabbits

FIRST SERVINGMAN  But when goes this forward? 225

THIRD SERVINGMAN  Tomorrow, today, presently.° You shall have the drum struck up this afternoon. 'Tis as it were a parcel° of their feast, and to be executed ere they wipe their lips.

SECOND SERVINGMAN  Why, then we shall have a 230 stirring world again. This peace is nothing but to rust iron, increase tailors, and breed balladmakers.

FIRST SERVINGMAN  Let me have war, say I; it exceeds peace as far as day does night; it's sprightly walking, audible,° and full of vent.° Peace is a very 235 apoplexy, lethargy; mulled,° deaf, sleepy, insensible; a getter of more bastard children than war's a destroyer of men.

SECOND SERVINGMAN  'Tis so; and as wars in some sort may be said to be a ravisher, so it cannot be denied 240 but peace is a great maker of cuckolds.

FIRST SERVINGMAN  Ay, and it makes men hate one another.

THIRD SERVINGMAN  Reason: because they then less need one another. The wars for my money. I hope to 245 see Romans as cheap as Volscians. They are rising,° they are rising.

BOTH [FIRST AND SECOND SERVINGMEN]  In, in, in! in, *Exeunt.*

[Scene VI. *Rome. A public place.*]

*Enter the two tribunes,* SICINIUS *and* BRUTUS.

SICINIUS
We hear not of him, neither need we fear him;
His remedies are tame.° The present peace
And quietness of the people, which before
Were in wild hurry,° here do make his friends
Blush that the world goes well; who rather had, 5
Though they themselves did suffer by't, behold
Dissentious numbers pest'ring° streets than see
Our tradesmen singing in their shops, and going
About their functions friendly.

BRUTUS
We stood to't° in good time.

*Enter* MENENIUS.

                                Is this Menenius? 10

SICINIUS
'Tis he, 'tis he. O, he is grown most kind
Of late. Hail, sir!

MENENIUS          Hail to you both!

SICINIUS
Your Coriolanus is not much missed
But with his friends. The commonwealth doth stand,
And so would do, were he more angry at it. 15

MENENIUS
All's well; and might have been much better, if
He could have temporized.

SICINIUS          Where is he, hear you?

MENENIUS
Nay, I hear nothing. His mother and his wife
Hear nothing from him.

*Enter three or four* CITIZENS.

ALL [CITIZENS]
The gods preserve you both!

SICINIUS                Good-e'en,° our neighbors. 20

BRUTUS
Good-e'en to you all, good-e'en to you all.

FIRST CITIZEN
Ourselves, our wives, and children, on our knees,
Are bound to pray for you both.

SICINIUS                          Live, and thrive!

BRUTUS
Farewell, kind neighbors. We wished Coriolanus
Had loved you as we did.

ALL [CITIZENS]          Now the gods keep you! 25

BOTH TRIBUNES
Farewell, farewell.          *Exeunt* CITIZENS.

SICINIUS
This is a happier and more comely° time
Than when these fellows ran about the streets
Crying confusion.°

BRUTUS          Caius Marcius was
A worthy officer i' th' war, but insolent, 30
O'ercome with pride, ambitious past all thinking,
Self-loving—

SICINIUS          And affecting° one sole throne,
Without assistance.°

MENENIUS          I think not so.

SICINIUS
We should by this, to all our lamentation,
If he had gone forth consul, found° it so. 35

BRUTUS
The gods have well prevented it, and Rome
Sits safe and still without him.

*Enter an* AEDILE.

AEDILE                Worthy tribunes,
There is a slave, whom we have put in prison,
Reports the Volsces with two several powers°
Are ent'red in the Roman territories, 40
And with the deepest malice of the war
Destroy what lies before 'em.

MENENIUS                'Tis Aufidius,
Who, hearing of our Marcius' banishment,
Thrusts forth his horns° again into the world,
Which were inshelled when Marcius stood for Rome, 45
And durst not once peep out.

SICINIUS          Come, what talk you
Of Marcius?

BRUTUS
Go see this rumorer whipped. It cannot be
The Volsces dare break with us.

MENENIUS                Cannot be!
We have record that very well it can;
And three examples of the like hath been 50
Within my age. But reason with° the fellow,

226 **presently** now  228 **parcel** part  235 **audible** of good hearing; **full of vent** with plenty of outlets for energy (?; cf.I.i.227)  236 **mulled** dulled (like wine sweetened and heated)  246 **rising** getting up from table  **IV.vi.2 His . . . tame** His attempts to "cure" the state are (now) harmless (cf. "dangerous physic," III.i.154)  4 **hurry** commotion  7 **pest'ring** filling with disturbance  10 **stood to't** made an issue of it

20 **Good-e'en** good evening  27 **comely** respectable  29 **Crying confusion** calling for disorder  32 **affecting** aiming at  33 **Without assistance** not sharing his powers with others  35 **found** have found  39 **several powers** separate forces  44 **horns** like a snail  52 **reason with** talk with

Before you punish him, where he heard this,
Lest you shall chance to whip your information
And beat the messenger who bids beware          55
Of what is to be dreaded.

SICINIUS                          Tell not me:
I know this cannot be.

BRUTUS                          Not possible.

*Enter a* MESSENGER.

MESSENGER
The nobles in great earnestness are going
All to the Senate House. Some news is coming
That turns° their countenances.

SICINIUS                          'Tis this slave—          60
Go whip him 'fore the people's eyes—his raising,°
Nothing but his report.

MESSENGER                    Yes, worthy sir,
The slave's report is seconded;° and more,
More fearful, is delivered.

SICINIUS                    What more fearful?

MESSENGER
It is spoke freely out of many mouths,          65
How probable I do not know, that Marcius,
Joined with Aufidius, leads a power 'gainst Rome,
And vows revenge as spacious as between
The young'st and oldest thing.°

SICINIUS                          This is most likely!

BRUTUS
Raised only that the weaker sort may wish          70
Good Marcius home again.

SICINIUS                    The very trick on't.

MENENIUS
This is unlikely:
He and Aufidius can no more atone°
Than violent'st contrariety.

*Enter [a* SECOND] MESSENGER.

SECOND MESSENGER
You are sent for to the Senate.          75
A fearful army, led by Caius Marcius
Associated with Aufidius, rages
Upon our territories, and have already
O'erborne their way,° consumed with fire, and took
What lay before them.

*Enter* COMINIUS.

COMINIUS                    O, you have made good work! 80

MENENIUS
What news? What news?

COMINIUS
You have holp to ravish your own daughters and
To melt the city leads° upon your pates,
To see your wives dishonored to° your noses—

MENENIUS
What's the news? What's the news?          85

COMINIUS
Your temples burnèd in their cement, and

Your franchises, whereon you stood,° confined
Into an auger's bore.

MENENIUS                    Pray now, your news?—
You have made fair work, I fear me.—Pray, your
news?—
If Marcius should be joined wi' th' Volscians—

COMINIUS                          If!          90
He is their god; he leads them like a thing
Made by some other deity than Nature,
That shapes man better; and they follow him
Against us brats with no less confidence
Than boys pursuing summer butterflies,          95
Or butchers killing flies.

MENENIUS                    You have made good work,
You and your apron-men;° you that stood so much
Upon the voice of occupation° and
The breath of garlic-eaters!

COMINIUS                    He'll shake
Your Rome about your ears.

MENENIUS                    As Hercules          100
Did shake down mellow fruit. You have made fair
work!

BRUTUS
But is this true, sir?

COMINIUS                    Ay; and you'll look pale
Before you find it other. All the regions
Do smilingly revolt, and who resists
Are mocked for valiant ignorance,          105
And perish constant° fools. Who is't can blame him?
Your enemies and his find something in him.

MENENIUS
We are all undone, unless
The noble man have mercy.

COMINIUS                    Who shall ask it?
The tribunes cannot do't for shame; the people          110
Deserve such pity of him as the wolf
Does of the shepherds. For his best friends, if they
Should say, "Be good to Rome," they charged° him
even
As those should do that had deserved his hate,
And therein showed° like enemies.

MENENIUS                    'Tis true:          115
If he were putting to my house the brand
That should consume it, I have not the face
To say, "Beseech you, cease." You have made fair
hands,°
You and your crafts! You have crafted fair!°

COMINIUS                    You have brought
A trembling upon Rome, such as was never          120
S' incapable° of help.

TRIBUNES                    Say not we brought it.

MENENIUS
How! Was't we? We loved him, but, like beasts
And cowardly nobles, gave way unto your clusters,°
Who did hoot him out o' th' city.

COMINIUS                    But I fear

---

**60 turns** changes   **61 his raising** his starting (i.e., the rumor; note comma and the following explanatory phrase)   **63 seconded** confirmed (by further reports)   **68–69 as spacious . . . thing** covering the span between youngest and oldest, i.e., the whole population   **73 atone** be reconciled   **79 O'erborne their way** (like a stream) overflowed everything in their way   **83 leads** roofs   **84 to** before   **87 franchises . . . stood** rights, on which you insisted   **97 apron-men** artisans   **98 occupation** manual workers   **106 constant** loyal   **113 charged** would attack, urge (both senses relevant)   **115 showed** would show   **118 made fair hands** handled matter finely   **119 crafted fair** plied your trade (of cunning) beautifully   **121 S' incapable** so unsusceptible   **123 clusters** crowds

They'll roar him in again. Tullus Aufidius,    125
The second name of men,° obeys his points°
As if he were his officer. Desperation
Is all the policy, strength, and defense,
That Rome can make against them.

*Enter a troop of* CITIZENS.

MENENIUS                      Here come the clusters.
And is Aufidius with him? You are they    130
That made the air unwholesome when you cast
Your stinking greasy caps in hooting at
Coriolanus' exile. Now he's coming,
And not a hair upon a soldier's head
Which will not prove a whip. As many coxcombs°    135
As you threw caps up will he tumble down,
And pay you for your voices.° 'Tis no matter;
If he could burn us all into one coal,°
We have deserved it.

OMNES
Faith, we hear fearful news.

FIRST CITIZEN          For mine own part,    140
When I said banish him, I said 'twas pity.

SECOND CITIZEN   And so did I.

THIRD CITIZEN   And so did I; and, to say the truth,
so did very many of us. That we did, we did for the
best; and though we willingly consented to his banish-    145
ment, yet it was against our will.

COMINIUS
Y' are goodly things, you voices!

MENENIUS                      You have made
Good work, you and your cry!° Shall's° to the
    Capitol?

COMINIUS
O, ay, what else?                      *Exeunt both.*

SICINIUS
Go masters, get you home; be not dismayed;    150
These are a side° that would be glad to have
This true which they so seem to fear. Go home,
And show no sign of fear.

FIRST CITIZEN   The gods be good to us! Come,
masters, let's home. I ever said we were i' th' wrong    155
when we banished him.

SECOND CITIZEN   So did we all. But come, let's
home.                      *Exit* CITIZENS.

BRUTUS
I do not like this news.

SICINIUS                      Nor I.

BRUTUS
Let's to the Capitol. Would half my wealth    160
Would buy this for a lie!

SICINIUS                      Pray, let's go.
                      *Exeunt* TRIBUNES.

[*Scene VII. A camp not far from Rome.*]

*Enter* AUFIDIUS, *with his* LIEUTENANT.

AUFIDIUS
Do they still fly to th' Roman?

LIEUTENANT
I do not know what witchcraft's in him, but
Your soldiers use him as the grace 'fore meat,
Their talk at table and their thanks at end;
And you are dark'ned° in this action sir,    5
Even by your own.°

AUFIDIUS          I cannot help it now,
Unless by using means° I lame the foot
Of our design. He bears himself more proudlier,
Even to my person, than I thought he would
When first I did embrace him; yet his nature    10
In that's no changeling,° and I must excuse
What cannot be amended.

LIEUTENANT          Yet I wish, sir—
I mean for your particular°—you had not
Joined in commission° with him, but either
Have borne the action of yourself, or else    15
To him had left it solely.

AUFIDIUS
I understand thee well; and be thou sure,
When he shall come to his account, he knows not
What I can urge against him. Although it seems,
And so he thinks, and is no less apparent    20
To th' vulgar eye, that he bears all things fairly,
And shows good husbandry° for the Volscian state,
Fights dragonlike, and does achieve as soon
As draw his sword. Yet he hath left undone
That which shall break his neck or hazard mine,    25
Whene'er we come to our account.

LIEUTENANT
Sir, I beseech you, think you he'll carry Rome?

AUFIDIUS
All places yields to him ere he sits down,°
And the nobility of Rome are his;
The senators and patricians love him too.    30
The tribunes are no soldiers, and their people
Will be as rash in the repeal, as hasty
To expel him thence. I think he'll be to Rome
As is the osprey° to the fish, who takes it
By sovereignty of nature.° First he was    35
A noble servant to them, but he could not
Carry his honors even.° Whether 'twas pride,
Which out of daily fortune ever taints°
The happy° man; whether defect of judgment,
To fail in the disposing of those chances    40
Which he was lord of; or whether nature,
Not to be other than one thing, not moving
From th' casque° to th' cushion,° but commanding
    peace
Even with the same austerity and garb
As he controlled the war; but one of these—    45
As he hath spices° of them all—not all,
For I dare so far free him—made him feared,

126 second . . . men second in renown (to Coriolanus);
points directions (?)   135 coxcombs fools' heads (cf. costume
of a fool)   137 voices votes   138 coal piece of burned fuel
148 cry pack; Shall's shall us (we)   151 side faction

IV.vii.5 dark'ned put in the shade   6 your own your own
men   7 using means taking steps   11 no changeling i.e., he
is the selfsame man   13 your particular your own sake   14
Joined in commission shared the command   22 husbandry
management   28 sits down lays siege   34 osprey fish hawk
35 By . . . nature refers to the osprey's supposed power of
subduing its prey before touching it   37 even and keep his
balance   38 daily . . . taints success coming day after day
always infects   39 happy lucky   43 casque helmet, i.e.,
military life; cushion i.e., position of authority in civil life;
cf. III.i.101   46 spices flavors, i.e., traces

So hated, and so banished. But he has a merit
To choke it in the utt'rance.° So our virtues
Lie in th' interpretation of the time;°                           50
And power, unto itself most commendable,
Hath not a tomb so evident as a chair°
T' extol what it hath done.
One fire drives out one fire; one nail, one nail;
Rights by rights founder, strengths by strengths do
    fail.°                                                        55
Come, let's away. When, Caius, Rome is thine,
Thou art poor'st of all; then shortly art thou mine.

                                              *Exeunt.*

# ACT V

[Scene I. *Rome. A public place.*]

*Enter* MENENIUS, COMINIUS, SICINIUS, [*and*]
BRUTUS, *the two tribunes, with others.*

MENENIUS
No, I'll not go. You hear what he hath said
Which was sometime° his general, who loved him
In a most dear particular.° He called me father;
But what o' that? Go you that banished him,
A mile before his tent fall down, and knee          5
The way° into his mercy. Nay, if he coyed°
To hear Cominius speak, I'll keep at home.
COMINIUS
He would not seem to know me.
MENENIUS                           Do you hear?
COMINIUS
Yet one time he did call me by my name.
I urged our old acquaintance, and the drops         10
That we have bled together. Coriolanus
He would not answer to; forbade all names;
He was a kind of nothing, titleless,
Till he had forged himself a name o' th' fire
Of burning Rome.
MENENIUS        Why, so! You have made good work!  15
A pair of tribunes that have wracked° fair Rome
To make coals° cheap! A noble memory!
COMINIUS
I minded° him how royal 'twas to pardon
When it was less expected; he replied,
It was a bare° petition of a state                  20
To one whom they had punished.
MENENIUS                           Very well.
Could he say less?
COMINIUS
I offered° to awaken his regard

For's private friends. His answer to me was,
He could not stay to pick them in a pile           25
Of noisome musty chaff. He said 'twas folly,
For one poor grain or two, to leave unburnt
And still to nose th' offense.°
MENENIUS                    For one poor grain or two!
I am one of those; his mother, wife, his child,
And this brave fellow too, we are the grains;      30
You are the musty chaff, and you are smelt
Above the moon. We must be burnt for you.
SICINIUS
Nay, pray, be patient; if you refuse your aid
In this so never-needed° help, yet do not
Upbraid's with our distress. But, sure, if you     35
Would be your country's pleader, your good tongue,
More than the instant army we can make,°
Might stop our countryman.
MENENIUS                    No, I'll not meddle.
SICINIUS
Pray you, go to him.
MENENIUS              What should I do?
BRUTUS
Only make trial what your love can do              40
For Rome, towards° Marcius.
MENENIUS                    Well, and say that Marcius
Return me, as Cominius is returned,
Unheard—what then?—
But as a discontented friend, grief-shot°
With his unkindness? Say't be so?
SICINIUS                    Yet your good will   45
Must have that thanks from Rome after the measure
As you intended well.°
MENENIUS              I'll undertake't:
I think he'll hear me. Yet to bite his lip
And hum at good Cominius much unhearts° me.
He was not taken well;° he had not dined.          50
The veins unfilled, our blood is cold, and then
We pout upon the morning, are unapt
To give or to forgive; but when we have stuffed
These pipes and these conveyances° of our blood
With wine and feeding, we have suppler souls       55
Than in our priestlike fasts. Therefore I'll watch him
Till he be dieted to° my request,
And then I'll set upon him.
BRUTUS
You know the very road into his kindness,
And cannot lose your way.
MENENIUS              Good faith, I'll prove° him,  60
Speed° how it will. I shall ere long have knowledge
Of my success.                              *Exit.*
COMINIUS    He'll never hear him.
SICINIUS                    Not?
COMINIUS
I tell you he does sit in gold, his eye
Red as 'twould burn Rome, and his injury°

---

48–49 **a merit . . . utt'rance** a merit that is nullified
in the very act of being expressed (because of faults inseparable
from the particular virtues being praised)   50 **the time** the
age (our contemporaries)   52 **chair** of the speaker who praises
the achievements made possible by "power," line 51; probably
with reference to the Roman rostrum, or speakers' platform
54–55 **One fire . . . fail** examples of the self-destructive
process described in lines 48–53
**V.i.2 sometime** formerly   3 **most dear particular** most
precious intimacy   5–6 **knee The way** make your way on
your knees   6 **coyed** showed reluctance   16 **wracked** ruined
17 **coals** charcoal   18 **minded** reminded   20 **bare** mere   23
**offered** tried

28 **nose th' offense** smell the offensive stuff   34 **so never-
needed** never so needed (as now)   37 **instant . . . make**
the army we can raise at this time   41 **towards** in relation
to   44 **grief-shot** struck by grief   46–47 **after . . . well**
in proportion to your good intentions   49 **unhearts**
discourages   50 **taken well** approached at a good time   54
**conveyances** channels   57 **dieted to** prepared for by feeding
60 **prove** make trial of   61 **Speed** turn out   64 **injury** sense
of the wrong done to him

The jailer to his pity. I kneeled before him;                    65
'Twas very faintly he said, "Rise"; dismissed me
Thus with his speechless hand. What he would do
He sent in writing after me, what he would not,
Bound with an oath to yield° to his conditions;
So that all hope is vain,°                                        70
Unless° his noble mother and his wife,
Who (as I hear) mean to solicit him
For mercy to his country. Therefore, let's hence,
And with our fair entreaties haste them on.      *Exeunt.*

[Scene II. *Entrance of the Volscian camp before Rome.*]

*Enter* MENENIUS *to the* WATCH *on guard.*

FIRST WATCH
Stay. Whence are you?
SECOND WATCH              Stand, and go back.
MENENIUS
You guard like men, 'tis well; but, by your leave,
I am an officer of state, and come
To speak with Coriolanus.
FIRST WATCH              From whence?
MENENIUS                              From Rome.
FIRST WATCH
You may not pass, you must return: our general      5
Will no more hear from thence.
SECOND WATCH
You'll see your Rome embraced with fire, before
You'll speak with Coriolanus.
MENENIUS              Good my friends,
If you have heard your general talk of Rome
And of his friends there, it is lots to blanks°      10
My name hath touched your ears: it is Menenius.
FIRST WATCH
Be it so; go back. The virtue of your name
Is not here passable.°
MENENIUS              I tell thee, fellow,
Thy general is my lover. I have been
The book of his good acts whence men have read      15
His fame unparalleled—haply amplified;
For I have ever verified° my friends
(Of whom he's chief) with all the size that verity
Would without lapsing° suffer. Nay, sometimes,
Like a bowl upon a subtle° ground,                   20
I have tumbled past the throw,° and in his praise
Have almost stamped° the leasing.° Therefore, fellow,
I must have leave to pass.
FIRST WATCH      Faith, sir, if you had told as many lies
in his behalf as you have uttered words in your own,      25
you should not pass here; no, though it were as
virtuous to lie as to live chastely. Therefore go back.

MENENIUS      Prithee, fellow, remember my name is
Menenius, always factionary° on the party of your
general.                                                  30
SECOND WATCH      Howsoever you have been his liar,
as you say you have, I am one that, telling true under
him, must say you cannot pass. Therefore go back.
MENENIUS      Has he dined, canst thou tell? For I would
not speak with him till after dinner.                     35
FIRST WATCH      You are a Roman, are you?
MENENIUS      I am, as thy general is.
FIRST WATCH      Then you should hate Rome, as he
does. Can you, when you have pushed out your gates
the very defender of them, and in a violent popular      40
ignorance given your enemy your shield, think to
front° his revenges with the easy groans of old women,
the virginal palms of your daughters, or with the
palsied intercession of such a decayed dotant° as you
seem to be? Can you think to blow out the intended      45
fire your city is ready to flame in, with such weak
breath as this? No, you are deceived; therefore, back
to Rome, and prepare for your execution. You are
condemned; our general has sworn you out of
reprieve and pardon.                                      50
MENENIUS      Sirrah, if thy captain knew I were here, he
would use me with estimation.°
FIRST WATCH      Come, my captain knows you not.
MENENIUS      I mean, thy general.
FIRST WATCH      My general cares not for you. Back, I      55
say; go, lest I let forth your half-pint of blood. Back—
that's the utmost of your having.° Back.
MENENIUS      Nay, but, fellow, fellow—

*Enter* CORIOLANUS, *with* AUFIDIUS.

CORIOLANUS      What's the matter?
MENENIUS      Now, you companion,° I'll say an errand°      60
for you; you shall know now that I am in estimation;
you shall perceive that a Jack guardant° cannot office
me° from my son Coriolanus. Guess but by my enter-
tainment° with him if thou stand'st not i' th' state of
hanging, or of some death more long in spectatorship      65
and crueller in suffering; behold now presently, and
swoon for what's to come upon thee. [*To* CORIO-
LANUS.] The glorious gods sit in hourly synod about
thy particular prosperity, and love thee no worse than
thy old father Menenius does! O my son, my son!      70
Thou art preparing fire for us; look thee, here's water
to quench it. I was hardly° moved to come to thee; but
being assured none but myself could move thee, I have
been blown out of your° gates with sighs; and conjure
thee to pardon Rome and thy petitionary° country-      75
men. The good gods assuage thy wrath, and turn the
dregs of it upon this varlet here; this, who, like a
block,° hath denied my access to thee.
CORIOLANUS      Away!
MENENIUS      How! Away!                                   80
CORIOLANUS
Wife, mother, child, I know not. My affairs

---

67–69 **What . . . yield** He sent a written message saying what
he would do and what he would not, and bound us with an
oath that we should yield (text probably corrupt)   70 **vain**
because the conditions are ruinous   71 **Unless** except for (or
perhaps "solicit him," line 72, is to be understood: "unless his
noble mother and his wife solicit him")
**V.ii.10 lots to blanks** more than an even chance; "lots" refers
to tickets in a lottery taking prizes; "blanks," to those not
taking prizes   13 **passable** current (of money, but with a pun
on *password*)   17 **verified** testified to the merit of   19 **lapsing**
slipping (into error)   20 **subtle** deceptive   21 **tumbled . . .
throw** rolled beyond the proper distance   22 **stamped** given
currency to (cf. *stamp* a coin); **leasing** falsehood

29 **factionary** an active worker   42 **front** face   44 **dotant**
dotard   52 **estimation** esteem   57 **of your having** you can
get   60 **companion** fellow; **say an errand** give a message
62 **Jack guardant** wretch of a sentry   63 **office me** use his
office to keep me   63–64 **entertainment** reception   72 **hardly**
with difficulty   74 **your** of Rome   75 **petitionary** who are
asking for mercy   78 **block** blockhead

Are servanted° to others. Though I owe
My revenge properly,° my remission° lies
In Volscian breasts. That we have been familiar,°
Ingrate forgetfulness° shall poison rather
Than pity note how much.° Therefore be gone.    85
Mine ears against your suits are stronger than
Your gates against my force. Yet, for° I loved thee,
Take this along; I writ it for thy sake,
And would have sent it. Another word, Menenius,    90
I will not hear thee speak. This man, Aufidius,
Was my beloved in Rome; yet thou behold'st.

AUFIDIUS
You keep a constant° temper.

           *Exeunt* [CORIOLANUS *and* AUFIDIUS].
           *Manet the* GUARD *and* MENENIUS.

FIRST WATCH   Now, sir, is your name Menenius?

SECOND WATCH   'Tis a spell, you see, of much   95
power. You know the way home again.

FIRST WATCH   Do you hear how we are shent° for
keeping your greatness back?

SECOND WATCH   What cause, do you think, I have
to swoon!    100

MENENIUS   I neither care for th' world nor your
general. For such things as you, I can scarce think
there's any, y' are so slight. He that hath a will to die
by himself° fears it not from another. Let your general
do his worst. For you, be that you are, long; and your   105
misery increase with your age! I say to you, as I was
said to, "Away!"                    *Exit.*

FIRST WATCH   A noble fellow, I warrant him.

SECOND WATCH   The worthy fellow is our general.
He's the rock, the oak not to be wind-shaken.    110

                   *Exit* WATCH.


       [Scene III. *The tent of Coriolanus.*]

*Enter* CORIOLANUS *and* AUFIDIUS, [*with others*].

CORIOLANUS
We will before the walls of Rome tomorrow
Set down° our host. My partner in this action,
You must report to th' Volscian lords how plainly°
I have borne° this business.

AUFIDIUS           Only their ends
You have respected; stopped your ears against    5
The general suit of Rome; never admitted
A private whisper—no, not with such friends
That thought them sure of you.

CORIOLANUS          This last old man,
Whom with a cracked heart I have sent to Rome,
Loved me above the measure of a father,    10
Nay, godded me° indeed. Their latest refuge°
Was to send him; for whose old love I have
(Though I showed° sourly to him) once more offered
The first conditions, which they did refuse

And cannot now accept; to grace° him only    15
That thought he could do more, a very little
I have yielded to. Fresh embassies and suits,
Nor° from the state nor private friends, hereafter
Will I lend ear to. (*Shout within.*) Ha! What shout is
    this?
Shall I be tempted to infringe my vow    20
In the same time 'tis made? I will not.

*Enter* VIRGILIA, VOLUMNIA, VALERIA, *young*
MARCIUS, *with* ATTENDANTS.

My wife comes foremost; then the honored mold°
Wherein this trunk° was framed, and in her hand
The grandchild to her blood. But out, affection!
All bond and privilege of nature, break!    25
Let it be virtuous to be obstinate.
What is that curtsy worth? Or those doves' eyes,
Which can make gods forsworn? I melt, and am not
Of stronger earth° than others. My mother bows,
As if Olympus° to a molehill should    30
In supplication nod; and my young boy
Hath an aspect of intercession which
Great Nature cries, "Deny not." Let the Volsces
Plough Rome, and harrow Italy! I'll never
Be such a gosling to° obey instinct, but stand    35
As if a man were author of himself
And knew no other kin.

VIRGILIA          My lord and husband!

CORIOLANUS
These eyes are not the same I wore in Rome.

VIRGILIA
The sorrow that delivers° us thus changed
Makes you think so.

CORIOLANUS        Like a dull actor now,    40
I have forgot my part and I am out,°
Even to a full disgrace.—Best of my flesh,
Forgive my tyranny;° but do not say,
For that, "Forgive our Romans." O, a kiss
Long as my exile, sweet as my revenge!    45
Now, by the jealous queen of heaven,° that kiss
I carried from thee, dear, and my true lip
Hath virgined it e'er since. You gods! I prate,°
And the most noble mother of the world
Leave unsaluted. Sink, my knee, i' th' earth;    50

*Kneels.*

Of thy deep duty° more impression° show
Than that of common sons.

VOLUMNIA          O, stand up blest!
Whilst with no softer cushion than the flint
I kneel before thee, and unproperly°
Show duty, as mistaken all this while    55
Between the child and parent. [*Kneels.*]

CORIOLANUS          What's this?

---

**82 servanted** subject (servantlike)   **82–83 I . . . properly** my
revenge belongs to me alone   **83 remission** power to pardon
**84 That . . . familiar** our intimacy in the past   **85 Ingrate
forgetfulness** my ungrateful forgetfulness   **86 how much**
how much "we have been familiar," how great the intimacy
was   **88 for** because   **93 constant** loyal, true   **97 shent**
scolded   **104 by himself** by his own hand
**V.iii.2 Set down** i.e., in a siege   **3 plainly** openly   **4 borne**
conducted   **11 godded me** made me a god; **latest refuge** last
resource   **13 showed** appeared

**15 grace** honor   **18 Nor** neither   **22–37** see Introduction,
p. 1318   **22 mold** form (also "earth")   **23 trunk** body   **28–29
not . . . earth** cf. *our common clay*   **30 Olympus** a mountain, home of the Greek gods   **35 to** as to   **39 delivers** presents
**41 out** speechless ("stuck")   **43 tyranny** cruelty   **46 queen of
heaven** Juno, guardian of marriage   **48 prate** babble   **51
duty** reverence; **impression** i.e., "i' th' earth"   **54 un-
properly** defined by lines 55–56: in a way that does not belong
to me, as though I had always misunderstood the relation
between child and parent

Your knees to me? To your corrected° son?
Then let the pebbles on the hungry° beach
Fillip° the stars! Then let the mutinous winds
Strike the proud cedars 'gainst the fiery sun,                    60
Murd'ring impossibility, to make
What cannot be, slight work.

VOLUMNIA                              Thou art my warrior;
I holp to frame thee. Do you know this lady?

CORIOLANUS
The noble sister of Publicola,
The moon of Rome, chaste as the icicle                           65
That's curdied° by the frost from purest snow
And hangs on Dian's temple—dear Valeria!

VOLUMNIA
This is a poor epitome° of yours,°
Which by th' interpretation of full time°
May show° like all yourself.

CORIOLANUS                            The god of soldiers,°         70
With the consent of supreme Jove, inform°
Thy thoughts with nobleness, that thou mayst prove
To shame unvulnerable, and stick° i' th' wars
Like a great sea-mark,° standing every flaw,°
And saving those that eye thee!

VOLUMNIA                              Your knee, sirrah.°            75

CORIOLANUS
That's my brave boy!

VOLUMNIA
Even he, your wife, this lady, and myself
Are suitors to you.

CORIOLANUS           I beseech you, peace!
Or, if you'd ask, remember this before:
The thing I have forsworn° to grant may never                     80
Be held by you denials.° Do not bid me
Dismiss my soldiers, or capitulate°
Again with Rome's mechanics.° Tell me not
Wherein I seem unnatural. Desire not
T' allay my rages and revenges with                               85
Your colder reasons.

VOLUMNIA             O, no more, no more!
You have said you will not grant us anything;
For we have nothing else to ask but that
Which you deny already. Yet we will ask,
That, if you fail in° our request, the blame                      90
May hang upon your hardness. Therefore hear us.

CORIOLANUS
Aufidius, and you Volsces, mark; for we'll
Hear nought from Rome in private. Your request?

VOLUMNIA
Should we be silent and not speak, our raiment
And state of bodies would bewray° what life                       95
We have led since thy exile. Think with thyself

How more unfortunate than all living women
Are we come hither; since that thy sight, which should
Make our eyes flow with joy, hearts dance with
     comforts,
Constrains them weep and shake with fear and sorrow,   100
Making the mother, wife, and child, to see
The son, the husband, and the father, tearing
His country's bowels out. And to poor we°
Thine enmity's most capital:° thou barr'st us
Our prayers to the gods, which is a comfort               105
That all but we enjoy. For how can we,
Alas, how can we for our country pray,
Whereto we are bound, together with thy victory,
Whereto we are bound? Alack, or° we must lose
The country, our dear nurse, or else thy person,         110
Our comfort in the country. We must find
An evident° calamity, though we had
Our wish, which side should win; for either thou
Must as a foreign recreant° be led
With manacles through our streets, or else             115
Triumphantly tread on thy country's ruin,
And bear the palm for having bravely shed
Thy wife and children's blood. For myself, son,
I purpose not to wait on fortune till
These wars determine.° If I cannot persuade thee       120
Rather to show a noble grace° to both parts°
Than seek the end of one, thou shalt no sooner
March to assault thy country than to tread
(Trust to't, thou shalt not) on thy mother's womb
That brought thee to this world.

VIRGILIA                              Ay, and mine,               125
That brought you forth this boy, to keep your name
Living to time.°

BOY                    'A° shall not tread on me;
I'll run away till I am bigger, but then I'll fight.

CORIOLANUS
Not of a woman's tenderness to be,
Requires nor child nor woman's face to see.              130
I have sat too long.

VOLUMNIA             Nay, go not from us thus.

[Rises.]

If it were so that our request did tend
To save the Romans, thereby to destroy
The Volsces whom you serve, you might condemn us,
As poisonous of your honor. No, our suit                 135
Is that you reconcile them; while the Volsces
May say, "This mercy we have showed," the Romans,
"This we received"; and each in either side
Give the all-hail to thee, and cry," Be blest
For making up this peace!" Thou know'st, great son,      140
The end of war's uncertain; but this certain,
That, if thou conquer Rome, the benefit
Which thou shalt thereby reap is such a name
Whose repetition will be dogged with curses,
Whose chronicle thus writ,° "The man was noble,          145
But with his last attempt° he wiped it° out,

---

57 **corrected** who is corrected (by your kneeling)  58 **hungry**
barren  59 **Fillip** strike  66 **curdied** congealed  68 **epitome**
brief but comprehensive version of a larger work; **of yours,**
belonging to you, of you  69 **time** "time" is compared to a
commentator on a text  70 **show** appear; **god of soldiers**
Mars (Coriolanus' special divinity)  71 **inform** imbue (give an
inner form or character to)  73 **stick** stand out  74 **a great
sea-mark** some prominent object that guides mariners (cf.
*landmark*, the common modern term); **flaw** gust of wind  75
**sirrah** sir (affectionately)  80 **forsworn** sworn not to  81
**denials** i.e., refusals to all of you (therefore, plural)  82
**capitulate** arrange terms  83 **mechanics** manual laborers
90 **fail in** fail to grant  95 **bewray** reveal

103 **we** for "us"  104 **capital** deadly  109 **or** either  112
**evident** certain  114 **recreant** traitor  120 **determine** come
to an end  121 **grace** consideration, favor; **parts** sides (parties)
126-27 **keep . . . time** perpetuate your name (keep it living
as long as time lasts)  127 **'A** he  145 **writ** will be written
146 **attempt** undertaking; **it** his nobility

Destroyed his country, and his name remains
To th' ensuing age abhorred." Speak to me, son.
Thou hast affected the fine strains° of honor,
To imitate the graces of the gods,°                                    150
To tear with thunder the wide cheeks o' th' air,
And yet to charge° thy sulphur° with a bolt
That should but rive an oak. Why dost not speak?
Think'st thou it honorable for a noble man
Still to remember wrongs? Daughter, speak you:         155
He cares not for your weeping. Speak thou, boy:
Perhaps thy childishness will move him more
Than can our reasons. There's no man in the world
More bound to's mother, yet here he lets me prate
Like one i' th' stocks. Thou hast never in thy life       160
Showed thy dear mother any courtesy,
When she (poor hen) fond of° no second brood,
Has clocked° thee to the wars, and safely home
Loaden° with honor. Say my request's unjust,
And spurn me back. But if it be not so,                          165
Thou art not honest,° and the gods will plague thee,
That thou restrain'st from me the duty which
To a mother's part belongs. He turns away.
Down, ladies! Let us shame him with our knees.
To his surname Coriolanus 'longs more pride          170
Than pity to our prayers. Down! An end;
This is the last. So we will home to Rome,
And die among our neighbors. Nay, behold's!°
This boy, that cannot tell what he would have,
But kneels and holds up hands for fellowship,        175
Does reason° our petition with more strength
Than thou hast to deny't. Come, let us go.
This fellow had a Volscian to his mother;
His wife is in Corioles, and his child
Like him by chance. Yet give us our dispatch.°       180
I am hushed until our city be a-fire,
And then I'll speak a little.

CORIOLANUS    *Holds her by the hand, silent.*
                                    O mother, mother!
What have you done? Behold, the heavens do ope,
The gods look down, and this unnatural scene
They laugh at. O my mother, mother! O!                    185
You have won a happy victory to Rome;
But, for your son—believe it, O, believe it!—
Most dangerously you have with him prevailed,
If not most mortal to° him. But let it come.
Aufidius, though I cannot make true wars,                 190
I'll frame convenient° peace. Now, good Aufidius,
Were you in my stead, would you have heard
A mother less? Or granted less, Aufidius?

AUFIDIUS
I was moved withal.°
CORIOLANUS            I dare be sworn you were!
And, sir, it is no little thing to make                             195
Mine eyes to sweat compassion. But, good sir,
What peace you'll make, advise me. For my part,

I'll not to Rome, I'll back with you; and pray you
Stand to° me in this cause. O mother! Wife!
AUFIDIUS [*Aside.*]
I am glad thou hast set thy mercy and thy honor        200
At difference in thee. Out of that I'll work
Myself a former fortune.°
CORIOLANUS [*To* VOLUMNIA *and* VIRGILIA.]
                            Ay, by and by;
But we will drink together; and you shall bear
A better witness back than words, which° we
On like conditions will have countersealed.                205
Come, enter with us. Ladies, you deserve
To have a temple° built you. All the swords
In Italy, and her confederate arms,°
Could not have made this peace.          *Exeunt.*

[*Scene IV. Rome. A public place.*]

*Enter* MENENIUS *and* SICINIUS.

MENENIUS    See you yond coign° o' th' Capitol, yond
cornerstone?
SICINIUS    Why, what of that?
MENENIUS    If it be possible for you to displace it with
your little finger, there is some hope the ladies of    5
Rome, especially his mother, may prevail with him.
But I say there is no hope in't; our throats are sentenced, and stay upon° execution.
SICINIUS    Is't possible that so short a time can alter the
condition of a man?                                                         10
MENENIUS    There is differency between a grub and a
butterfly; yet your butterfly was a grub. This Marcius
is grown from man to dragon: he has wings; he's
more than a creeping thing.
SICINIUS    He loved his mother dearly.                          15
MENENIUS    So did he me; and he no more remembers
his mother now than an eight-year-old horse. The
tartness of his face sours ripe grapes. When he walks,
he moves like an engine° and the ground shrinks before
his treading. He is able to pierce a corslet° with his eye,  20
talks like a knell, and his hum° is a battery.° He sits in
his state° as a thing made for Alexander.° What he bids
be done is finished with his bidding. He wants nothing
of a god but eternity and a heaven to throne in.
SICINIUS    Yes, mercy, if you report him truly.            25
MENENIUS    I paint him in the character. Mark what
mercy his mother shall bring from him. There is no
more mercy in him than there is milk in a male tiger;
that shall our poor city find. And all this is 'long of°
you.                                                                                     30
SICINIUS    The gods be good unto us!
MENENIUS    No, in such a case the gods will not be
good unto us. When we banished him, we respected
not them; and, he returning to break our necks, they
respect not us.                                                                  35

---

149 **affected . . . strains** aimed at the refinements   150
**graces . . . gods** qualities that give the gods splendor and
power; illustrated with irony, lines 151–53   152 **charge** load
(make heavy, or "load," as of a gun); **sulphur** lightning (see
Introduction, p. 1318)   162 **fond of** eager for   163 **clocked**
clucked   164 **Loaden** laden   166 **honest** honorable   173
**behold's** behold us   176 **reason** plead for   180 **dispatch**
dismissal   189 **mortal to** with deadly results for   191 **convenient** fitting   194 **withal** by it (thereby)

199 **Stand to** stand by   201–02 **work . . . fortune** regain
my former position and power   204 **which** i.e., the written
document   207 **temple** of the Fortune of Women; so in
Plutarch   208 **confederate arms** allied powers
V.iv.1 **coign** corner   8 **stay upon** wait for   19 **engine**
machine of war   20 **corslet** body armor   21 **his hum** i.e.,
his saying "Hum!"; **battery** beating of drums for an attack
22 **state** chair of state; **thing . . . Alexander** image of
Alexander the Great   29 **'long of** along of, because of

*Enter a* MESSENGER.

MESSENGER
Sir, if you'd save your life, fly to your house.
The plebeians have got your fellow-tribune,
And hale° him up and down; all swearing if
The Roman ladies bring not comfort home
They'll give him death by inches.

*Enter another* MESSENGER.

SICINIUS                    What's the news?      40
SECOND MESSENGER
Good news, good news! The ladies have prevailed,
The Volscians are dislodged,° and Marcius gone.
A merrier day did never yet greet Rome,
No, not th' expulsion of the Tarquins.
SICINIUS                                Friend,
Art thou certain this is true? Is't most certain?   45
SECOND MESSENGER
As certain as I know the sun is fire.
Where have you lurked,° that you make doubt of it?
Ne'er through an arch so hurried the blown° tide,
As the recomforted through th' gates. Why, hark you!

*Trumpets, hautboys;° drums beat; all together.*

The trumpets, sackbuts,° psalteries,° and fifes,
Tabors° and cymbals, and the shouting Romans,    50
Make the sun dance. Hark you! (*A shout within.*)
MENENIUS                    This is good news.
I will go meet the ladies. This Volumnia
Is worth of consuls, senators, patricians,
A city full; of tribunes such as you,            55
A sea and land full. You have prayed well today.
This morning for ten thousand of your throats
I'd not have given a doit. Hark, how they joy!

*Sound still with the shouts.*

SICINIUS
First, the gods bless you for your tidings; next,
Accept my thankfulness.
SECOND MESSENGER    Sir, we have all          60
Great cause to give great thanks.
SICINIUS                    They are near the city!
SECOND MESSENGER
Almost at point to enter.
SICINIUS                We'll meet them,
And help the joy.
                                    *Exeunt.*

[*Scene V. Rome. Near the gate.*]

*Enter two* SENATORS, *with* LADIES, *passing over the
stage, with other* LORDS.

FIRST SENATOR
Behold our patroness, the life of Rome!
Call all your tribes together, praise the gods,
And make triumphant fires; strew flowers before them.
Unshout the noise that banished Marcius,

Repeal° him with the welcome of his mother.    5
Cry, "Welcome, ladies, welcome!"
ALL                            Welcome, ladies,
Welcome!

*A flourish with drums and trumpets.*

[*Scene VI. Corioli. A public place.*]

*Enter Tullus* AUFIDIUS, *with* ATTENDANTS.

AUFIDIUS
Go tell the lords o' th' city I am here.
Deliver them this paper. Having read it,
Bid them repair to th' marketplace, where I,
Even in theirs and in the commons' ears,
Will vouch the truth of it. Him° I accuse        5
The city ports° by this hath entered, and
Intends t' appear before the people, hoping
To purge himself with words. Dispatch.
                        [*Exeunt* ATTENDANTS.]

*Enter three or four* CONSPIRATORS *of Aufidius' faction.*

                            Most welcome!
FIRST CONSPIRATOR
How is it with our general?
AUFIDIUS                    Even so
As with a man by his own alms empoisoned,°      10
And with° his charity slain.
SECOND CONSPIRATOR    Most noble sir,
If you do hold the same intent wherein
You wished us parties,° we'll deliver you
Of your great danger.
AUFIDIUS            Sir, I cannot tell;
We must proceed as we do find the people.        15
THIRD CONSPIRATOR
The people will remain uncertain whilst
'Twixt you there's difference; but the fall of either
Makes the survivor heir of all.
AUFIDIUS                    I know it,
And my pretext to strike at him admits
A good construction. I raised him, and I pawned°   20
Mine honor for his truth;° who being so heightened,
He watered his new plants with dews of flattery,
Seducing so my friends; and, to this end,
He bowed his nature, never known before
But to be rough, unswayable, and free.           25
THIRD CONSPIRATOR
Sir, his stoutness°
When he did stand for consul, which he lost
By lack of stooping—
AUFIDIUS            That I would have spoke of.
Being banished for't, he came unto my hearth,
Presented to my knife his throat. I took him,
Made him joint-servant with me;° gave him way°   30
In all his own desires; nay, let him choose
Out of my files,° his projects to accomplish,

38 hale haul   42 are dislodged have broken up camp   47
lurked been hiding   48 blown swollen (by wind)   49 s.d.
hautboy original of the modern oboe   50 sackbuts trom-
bones; psalteries harplike stringed instruments   51 Tabors
small drums

V.v.5 Repeal recall
V.vi.5 Him he whom   6 ports gates   10 empoisoned
destroyed   11 with by   13 parties partisans   20 pawned
staked   21 truth loyalty   26 stoutness proud obstinacy   31
joint-servant with me sharer of my service (to the state);
gave him way humored him   33 files ranks

My best and freshest men; served his designments°
In mine own person; holp to reap the fame          35
Which he did end° all his; and took some pride
To do myself this wrong; till at the last
I seemed his follower, not partner; and
He waged me with his countenance,° as if
I had been mercenary.°
FIRST CONSPIRATOR   So he did, my lord.          40
The army marveled at it; and, in the last,°
When he had carried° Rome and that we looked
For no less spoil than glory—
AUFIDIUS                    There was it;°
For which my sinews° shall be stretched upon° him.
At° a few drops of women's rheum,° which are          45
As cheap as lies, he sold the blood and labor
Of our great action. Therefore shall he die,
And I'll renew me in his fall. But hark!

*Drums and trumpets sounds, with great shouts of the people.*

FIRST CONSPIRATOR
Your native town you entered like a post,°
And had no welcomes home; but he returns,          50
Splitting the air with noise.
SECOND CONSPIRATOR   And patient fools,
Whose children he hath slain, their base throats tear
With giving him glory.
THIRD CONSPIRATOR   Therefore, at your vantage,°
Ere he express himself or move the people
With what he would say, let him feel your sword,          55
Which we will second.° When he lies along,°
After your way his tale pronounced° shall bury
His reasons with his body.
AUFIDIUS                    Say no more:
Here come the lords.

*Enter the LORDS of the city.*

ALL LORDS
You are most welcome home.
AUFIDIUS                    I have not deserved it.          60
But, worthy lords, have you with heed perused
What I have written to you?
ALL [LORDS]               We have.
FIRST LORD                    And grieve to hear't.
What faults he made before the last, I think
Might have found easy fines;° but there to end
Where he was to begin, and give away          65
The benefit of our levies,° answering us
With our own charge,° making a treaty where
There was a yielding—this admits no excuse.
AUFIDIUS
He approaches. You shall hear him.

*Enter CORIOLANUS, marching with drum and colors,
the COMMONERS being with him.*

CORIOLANUS
Hail, lords! I am returned your soldier;          70
No more infected° with my country's love
Than when I parted° hence, but still subsisting°
Under your great command. You are to know
That prosperously I have attempted, and
With bloody passage° led your wars even to          75
The gates of Rome. Our spoils we have brought home
Doth more than counterpoise a full third part
The charges° of the action. We have made peace
With no less honor to the Antiates
Than shame to th' Romans; and we here deliver,          80
Subscribed° by th' consuls and patricians,
Together with the seal o' th' Senate, what
We have compounded° on.
AUFIDIUS               Read it not, noble lords;
But tell the traitor in the highest degree
He hath abused your powers.          85
CORIOLANUS
Traitor! How now!
AUFIDIUS               Ay, traitor, Marcius!
CORIOLANUS                         Marcius!
AUFIDIUS
Ay, Marcius, Caius Marcius! Dost thou think
I'll grace° thee with that robbery, thy stol'n name
Coriolanus, in Corioles?
You lords and heads o' th' state, perfidiously          90
He has betrayed your business and given up,
For certain drops of salt, your city Rome,
I say "your city," to his wife and mother;
Breaking his oath and resolution, like
A twist° of rotten silk; never admitting          95
Counsel o' th' war; but at his nurse's tears
He whined and roared away your victory;
That° pages blushed at him, and men of heart°
Looked wond'ring each at others.
CORIOLANUS               Hear'st thou, Mars?
AUFIDIUS
Name not the god, thou boy of tears!
CORIOLANUS                         Ha!
AUFIDIUS                         No more.          100
CORIOLANUS
Measureless liar, thou hast made my heart
Too great for what contains it. "Boy"! O slave!
Pardon me, lords, 'tis the first time that ever
I was forced to scold. Your judgments, my grave lords,
Must give this cur the lie; and his own notion°—          105
Who wears my stripes impressed upon him, that
Must bear my beating to his grave—shall join
To thrust the lie unto him.
FIRST LORD
Peace, both, and hear me speak.
CORIOLANUS
Cut me to pieces, Volsces, men and lads,          110
Stain all your edges on me. "Boy"! False hound!
If you have writ your annals true, 'tis there,°

---

34 **designments** designs   36 **end** get in (of crops)   39 **waged
. . . his countenance** for wages gave me patronizing looks
40 **mercenary** serving for pay   41 **in the last** in the last place,
finally   42 **carried** won   43 **There was it** That was the
crucial thing   44 **sinews** i.e., strength; **upon** against   45 **At**
at the price of; **rheum** tears   49 **post** messenger   53 **at your
vantage** at a moment opportune for you   56 **second** support
(with our swords); **along** stretched at full length   57 **After
. . . pronounced** his story told in your version   64 **fines**
penalties   66 **our levies** the armies we raised   66–67 **answering . . . charge** paying us (only) with our own expenditure

71 **infected** (see Introduction, p. 1319)   72 **parted** departed;
**subsisting** remaining   75 **passage** action   77–78 **more . . .
charges** exceed the costs by a whole third (cf. line 67)   81
**Subscribed** signed   83 **compounded** agreed   88 **grace** honor
95 **twist** thread (made of more than one strand)   98 **That** so
that; **of heart** of spirit   105 **notion** understanding   112
**there** (written) there

That, like an eagle in a dovecote, I
Fluttered your Volscians in Corioles.
Alone I did it. "Boy"?

AUFIDIUS                    Why, noble lords,                    115
Will you be put in mind of his blind fortune,°
Which was your shame, by this unholy braggart,
'Fore your own eyes and ears?

ALL CONSPIRATORS            Let him die for't.

ALL PEOPLE   Tear him to pieces!—Do it presently!°—
He killed my son!—My daughter!—He killed my     120
cousin Marcius!—He killed my father!

SECOND LORD
Peace, ho! no outrage, peace!
The man is noble, and his fame folds in°
This orb o' th' earth. His last offenses to us
Shall have judicious° hearing. Stand,° Aufidius,     125
And trouble not the peace.

CORIOLANUS              O that I had him,
With six Aufidiuses or more—his tribe,
To use my lawful sword!

AUFIDIUS              Insolent villain!

ALL CONSPIRATORS
Kill, kill, kill, kill, kill him!

*Draw the* CONSPIRATORS *and kills* MARCIUS, *who
falls.* AUFIDIUS *stands on him.*

LORDS                    Hold, hold, hold, hold!

AUFIDIUS
My noble masters, hear me speak.

FIRST LORD              O Tullus!              130

SECOND LORD
Thou hast done a deed whereat valor will weep.

THIRD LORD
Tread not upon him. Masters all, be quiet;
Put up your swords.

AUFIDIUS
My lords, when you shall know—as in this rage
Provoked by him, you cannot—the great danger     135
Which this man's life did owe you,° you'll rejoice
That he is thus cut off. Please it your honors
To call me to your senate, I'll deliver°
Myself your loyal servant, or endure
Your heaviest censure.°

FIRST LORD              Bear from hence his body,     140
And mourn you for him. Let him be regarded
As the most noble corse° that ever herald
Did follow to his urn.

SECOND LORD              His own impatience
Takes from Aufidius a great part of blame.
Let's make the best of it.

AUFIDIUS                    My rage is gone,     145
And I am struck with sorrow. Take him up.
Help, three o' th' chiefest soldiers; I'll be one.
Beat thou the drum, that it speak mournfully;
Trail your steel pikes. Though in this city he
Hath widowed and unchilded many a one,     150
Which to this hour bewail the injury,
Yet he shall have a noble memory.°
Assist.                    *Exeunt bearing the body of Marcius.
A dead march sounded.*

116 **blind fortune** mere good luck (Fortune is a blind goddess)
119 **presently** at once   123 **folds in** embraces   125 **judicious**
judicial; **Stand** stop

136 **did owe you** held in payment for you   138 **deliver**
prove   140 **censure** sentence   142 **corse** corpse   152 **memory**
memorial

# THE LIFE OF TIMON OF ATHENS

EDITED BY MAURICE CHARNEY

## Introduction

There is general agreement that *Timon of Athens* is an unfinished play. In an influential article in the *Review of English Studies* (1942), Una Ellis-Fermor described *Timon* as "a play such as a great artist might leave behind him, roughed out, worked over in part and then abandoned; full of inconsistencies in form and presentation, with fragments (some of them considerable) bearing the unmistakable stamp of his workmanship scattered throughout." The roughnesses of the play are obvious to any conscientious reader of Shakespeare. The blank verse is often extremely irregular, with many lines that do not fit into the iambic pentameter pattern. There are strange eruptions of prose in verse passages, and there are many inept repetitions of words and phrases from one line to the next. Characters appear, such as the Fool and Page (II.ii), who are not properly integrated into the action; there are two conflicting epitaphs for Timon in Act V; and the Poet and Painter announced at IV.iii.350 do not arrive until almost two hundred lines later. The subplot of Alcibiades and his revenge on Athens is so loosely related to the main action which it is intended to parallel that some have suspected a lost scene. We know that the murderer for whom Alcibiades is pleading in III.v cannot be Timon, but he is not anyone else in the play, and it is more than an idle curiosity which seeks to know his name.

One detail in the play is the subject of a fascinating study. In "Shakespeare Learns the Value of Money," Terence Spencer discusses the inconsistency in the references to talents. A talent was an ancient coin frequently mentioned in Plutarch and the Bible, and generally taken to be worth half a hundredweight of silver, or well over $1000 in its modern equivalent. The sum of 1000 talents that Timon seeks from the Senators (II.ii) is an absurdly large one (more than $1,000,000), and it is possible that Shakespeare really did not know how much a talent was worth. At some point he learned its true value and corrected the references at the beginning of the play, but left others uncorrected. The request for "fifty five hundred talents" in III.ii seems to mean either fifty or five hundred, depending on how much a talent is worth, and the references to "so many talents" in the same scene should be replaced by actual sums.

This example of the talents is a very neat one for demonstrating that many details in *Timon* need to be revised and corrected and that the play lacks the sort of polishing and tidying up that one would expect from a final draft. The circumstances surrounding the printing of *Timon* (discussed in the Note on the Text) lend further support to this idea. There can be no doubt that the play as it appears in Shakespeare's First Folio of 1623 is unfinished. But Miss Ellis-Fermor's thesis has done great harm to the appreciation of *Timon* because it suggests that the play is not only unfinished (in the sense of lacking any final revision), but that it is a mere collection of jottings and rough sketches without any integral coherence. I would strongly disagree with this point of view. It seems to me that *Timon* is completely finished in conception: its structure makes good sense as a whole, its characters are well adapted to the overall plan, and its style, tone, imagery, and dramatic handling all contribute to a unified imaginative vision.

Because *Timon* is an unusual play, it would be more profitable to try to understand its uniqueness than to compare it unfavorably with the great tragedies that preceded it. The structure of the play is that of a dramatic fable, divided into two sharply contrasted parts. By dramatic fable I mean what other critics have called a morality play or an allegory—that is, a structure that does not proceed rationally and causatively from point to point, but rather one that progresses by a series of unmotivated leaps from one imaginative state to another. We are not meant to examine the credibility of Timon's financial extravagance, or his total unawareness of his bankruptcy, or his sudden discovery of an inexhaustible supply of gold. We accept these improbabilities as part of our willing suspension of disbelief. The testing of the three false friends in Act III moves as in a folk tale to its inevitable conclusion, and the faithful servant who remains true while all others are false is a familiar fairy-tale figure. The exact cause of Timon's death is left poetically obscure, and no attempt at all is made to give his sudden change from philanthropy to misanthropy a psychological basis. The structure of the play is schematic, and the dramatic action separates itself into a series of well-defined episodes related to each other analogically rather than causally. One scene is not the source or cause or motive for another, but is, rather, a parallel to it and serves as a comment on it. I should like to look more closely at the structure of *Timon* in order to show that the play is complete and fully imagined within the meaning of a dramatic fable. For this purpose, I will survey the action scene by scene and offer an account of "what happens in *Timon*."

The first sequence of ninety-four lines before Timon appears is of crucial importance for establishing the tone and mood of the play as well as announcing its major themes. We have a Poet and Painter, a Jeweler and Merchant, who have come to peddle their wares to Timon, as patron of the arts and general connoisseur. None of these characters is named, and they represent, as in an allegory, the type functions of their names. Behind the elaborate compliment and self-deprecation of this scene lies a blatant hucksterism that well expresses the rottenness of Athens. The meretriciousness of the Poet and Painter is particularly disturbing, since we expect them to aim higher than merely "to propagate their states." Shakespeare seems nowhere else to have put artists in such an unfavorable light.

The controlling element in the scene is the Poet's allegory of Fortune, which serves as a central fable for the play. The goddess Fortune and her capricious ways much occupied the minds of men in the Middle Ages and Renaissance, and great efforts were made to reconcile the Roman myth with Christian morality. Wealth and all material benefits are the fortuitous and insubstantial gifts of Fortune, the blindfolded goddess who is forever turning the wheel on which her worshipers are placed (the wheel in a gambling casino derives from this one). Timon's alliance with Fortune early in the play clearly foreshadows his ruin, "When Fortune in her shift and change of mood/ Spurns down her late beloved."

Thus, when Timon enters at line 94 with great ceremony, "*addressing himself courteously to every suitor*," we are already prepared not to accept his munificence at its face value. The pack of suppliants is itself so mixed in degrees of worth that we cannot help agreeing with Dr. Johnson, who said that the play is a "warning against that ostentatious liberality which scatters bounty but confers no benefits, and buys flattery but no friendship." Timon is at his height in this scene, reveling in his philanthropic role. There is, of course, something dreamlike about this early scene, with its mixture of charity, prodigality, and enormous public display. The entrance of Apemantus at line 175 restores some measure of reality, since he at least speaks the truth, however churlish and snarling he may be in his personal manner. He warns Timon of his waste and extravagance, but Apemantus is so unsympathetic in his role of satiric, malcontent railer that he is almost never believed; this is another disturbing element in the play. The young military hero, Alcibiades, also appears in I.i, but aside from his elaborate military costume, he is a colorless figure and, with the single exception of III.v, remains so throughout.

In I.ii, Timon is still high and godlike as he presides over an elaborate banquet for his friends. There is a strong visual emphasis on the fact that Timon's bounty shows itself in hedonism and high living more than in old-fashioned benevolence. His ideal of friendship is inseparable from the clubby atmosphere of good food and drink and the *Gemütlichkeit* of mutual compliment. As Apemantus had said earlier, "He that loves to be flattered is worthy o' th' flatterer." The Masque of Amazons in this scene is an element of spectacle common in Shakespeare's later plays and not very closely related to the action. Incidentally, the only women in the play are those Amazons and the prostitutes, Phrynia and Timandra; the world of Athens is distinctly a man's world.

It is in I.ii that Flavius, the always loyal steward of Timon, tells us that his master is bankrupt, everything is mortgaged, and utter ruin is imminent. Flavius resembles Apemantus in speaking the truth, but he has a fund of compassion for Timon—"I bleed inwardly for my lord"— while Apemantus cynically delights in misfortune.

The first scene of Act II takes us back to the opening of the play, and once again we are plunged into the icy reality of Athens, in which all values are on a strictly cash basis. A Senator who is not named is counting up Timon's debts and is impatiently dispatching his servant to dun him for the money. He loves and honors Timon, of course, "But must not break my back to heal his finger." The most shocking aspect of this scene is the contempt in which the Senator holds Timon for his generosity:

> If I want gold, steal but a beggar's dog
> And give it Timon—why the dog coins gold.    (II.i.5–6)

The Senator is only elaborating on Timon's own formula: "there's none/Can truly say he gives, if he receives." But Timon's rejection of reciprocity in giving leaves him terribly vulnerable.

The next scene (II.ii) marks a new stage in the action, for Timon is now finally aware of his bankruptcy. In an effort to avoid the overwhelming truth, Timon will test his friends by seeking to borrow money from them. This process is accomplished in three satiric scenes in Act III, written in vivid colloquial style. They are all brief vignettes, very different from each other, and designed to show the varieties of evasive ingenuity. The scene with Lucullus (III.i) is so masterfully done that we are almost convinced that "this is no time to lend money, especially upon bare friendship without security." In the next scene (III.ii), three Strangers are introduced to serve as choral commentators on what is happening and to arouse our sympathies for Timon. These Strangers are merely non-Athenians without any further specification (although one of them is called Hostilius); they are in no way connected with the plot and appear only to vindicate Timon.

In III.iv, the creditors' servants are again assembled at the house of Timon as they were in II.ii. When Timon enters "*in a rage*," we have a new development in the action, since Timon now has been stripped of his illusions. His misanthropy proper begins at this point, and he speaks in the highly emotional, freely associative style reserved for those distracted. Timon seems to be on the road to that bitter self-knowledge demanded by tragic recognition, yet he never progresses any further, and the tragedy, at least from the point of view of Aristotle's *Poetics*, remains truncated and fragmentary. In his hysterical, martyrlike sufferings, Timon does not turn inward as do so many of Shakespeare's tragic protagonists; instead, he begins to gloat over the possibility of being brilliantly and histrionically revenged in a mock-banquet.

III.v is the first and only full scene of the subplot. It is well written and fully written, with a carefully developed oration by Alcibiades for a friend and fellow soldier who has killed a man to defend his honor. This speech is, by the way, in the direct tradition of the "mercy" speeches of Portia in *The Merchant of Venice* and Isabella in *Measure for Measure*. Although the scene has no plot links with what precedes, it does have a strong thematic connection with it. The Athenian Senators show the same ingratitude to a benefactor of their state as they did to Timon. This scene plays an important part in developing the tone and mood of Athens, so that when Timon's mock-banquet and revenge follow in the next scene, we are glad to see the tables turned on the greedy, usurious Senators. Alcibiades' banishment in this scene foreshadows the self-exile of Timon at the end of the next scene.

The final scene of Act III is carefully written up to provide an effective climax for the first part of the play: "Uncover, dogs, and lap." This is a memorable line, and the dramatic skill with which the discovery and reversal are managed shows Shakespeare at his best. It is a great moment for Timon, who has once again recovered his former stature. One interesting structural element is that Timon in this scene is beginning to take over the role of Apemantus: his grace echoes Apemantus' bitter benediction in I.ii, and in Acts IV and V the verbal echoes become more marked. Another striking feature is the reaction of the guests to Timon's revenge. Here we have an excellent example of the use of sharp contrast to establish an effect. The friends are as untouched by Timon's towering pronouncements as the dunning servants were in III.iv. After having their souls seared by Timon's revelations of their inner corruption, they respond with utter banality: "Push, did you see my cap?," "I have lost my gown," "He gave me a jewel th' other day, and now he has beat it out of my hat. Did you see my jewel?" This farcical anticlimax of high comedy concludes when the lost items have been recovered.

Timon's soliloquy outside the walls of Athens in the next scene (IV.i) has none of the meditative, soul-searching qualities of the soliloquies in *Hamlet* or *Macbeth*; it is purely an oration by one with no onstage audience. Timon's vision of chaos in this scene is so radical that it fails to be convincing. It is perhaps not more extreme than Lear's speeches on the heath, but it has no psychological terror and passion to support the violent rhetoric, and the intensity of the language seems to be separated from any occasion which might have caused it. This leads to some odd side effects, even to an irreverent feeling of sick humor in some of the most hysterical imprecations:

> Son of sixteen,
> Pluck the lined crutch from thy old limping sire,
> With it beat out his brains.          (IV.i.13–15)

One of the drawbacks in a dramatic fable is that we cannot have the psychological thickness needed to support statements like the above. The fourth and fifth acts of *Timon* are unsuccessful partly because the impassioned rhetoric cannot sustain itself without an impassioned action.

The brief second scene of Act IV shows us Timon's servants, "All broken implements of a ruined house," still faithful to him in adversity. They are the counterparts of the false friends, and they modify our possible contempt

for Timon. Along with the three Strangers of III.ii, they prevent the play from becoming out-and-out satire.

IV.iii, a long and miscellaneous scene, consists chiefly of a series of encounters with Timon. It is worth noting that Timon's cave in the woods seems to be as easily accessible as a good midtown office. These encounters all meet with predictable failure, as we might expect in a dramatic fable, so that their main function seems to be to exhibit Timon's misanthropy in a number of different guises. One new movement, however, is the sense of world-weariness that comes over Timon, accompanied by a desire to die. It begins at line 380 and culminates in the moving speech:

> My long sickness
> Of health and living now begins to mend,
> And nothing brings me all things.          (V.i.186–88)

At the beginning of IV.iii, Timon's parable of the "Twinned brothers of one womb" shows us that he now believes in the Poet's vision of Fortune in the first scene of the play. "All's obliquy," everything is crooked and perverse, and the law of nature no longer rules man. Timon's hate would not be so disturbing if it did not include a petulant self-hate by which he forfeits all neutral ground. He is not the one just man bearing witness against corruption, but as worthless and corrupt as the rest. His primitivism, then, is a mere sham, and there is ironic justification for his finding gold rather than roots. He will use it to fulfill his evil vision and make "Destruction fang mankind."

The appearance of Alcibiades with a brace of whores undercuts his heroic pretensions, and the slangy directness of the whores makes them more interesting than their noble captain. Like other realists in the play, Phrynia and Timandra humor Timon in the hope of gain: "More counsel with more money, bounteous Timon." In their plainspeaking refusal to flatter, they make explicit a theme from the earlier part of the play: "Believe't that we'll do anything for gold."

The word-slinging wit-combat with Apemantus has some of the best and some of the worst speeches in the play. The absolute low point, it seems to me, is the series of insults they hurl at each other. There is not enough inventiveness in either calumniator to go beyond Timon's "Would thou wert clean enough to spit upon"—my entry for the worst line in the play, which gains an added point from Timon's insufferable snobbishness. But the mutual judgments that Timon and Apemantus make of each other are excellently done, and they show an old-fashioned character analysis rare in this play. Apemantus' case against Timon is made so explicitly that we cannot possibly mistake Timon for Shakespeare's mouthpiece. Timon is a naturally disdainful man, who feigns misanthropy out of pique with Fortune; he is an absolutist who cannot make any compromises with the human condition. As Apemantus says, "The middle of humanity thou never knewest, but the extremity of both ends." This hits home, but Timon's account of Apemantus' meanness and envy and essentially servile nature also strikes its mark and draws blood.

The meeting with the anonymous Banditti is full of improbability, and their sententiousness and lack of ferocity are disappointing. The encounter with Flavius that closes the scene shows Timon again at his worst, since he is grudgingly forced to admit that there is one honest man.

Shadwell got around this difficulty in his version of the play (1678) by introducing an honest woman, Evandra, who is able to regenerate Timon. At this point in the structure of Shakespeare's play, it is clear that Timon must soon die, if only to satisfy the exacerbation of the audience. He has reached such an extreme position that he can go no further in negation. Being a static and flat character, he has already involved himself in tedious repetition.

V.i continues the previous scene, with the Poet and Painter forming another exhibit of why Timon took to the woods; we are pleased to see them laboring so hard for rewards they will not receive. The mission from Athens at the end of the scene suggests that some changes have occurred in the city since Timon's departure, although the elaborate, unnecessarily complicated rhetoric of the Senators hints that these changes could not have been very profound. The "heaps and sums" and "figures of their love" inevitably imply that the Senators are ready to offer Timon a handsome bribe. After the announcement of Timon's death and the discovery of his epitaph, the play ends conventionally with a sense of the purgation of evil and the possibility of a new and better life in the once corrupted city.

At the risk of reviewing the plot, I have gone into some detail about the structure of *Timon* in order to show that it is a coherent whole with carefully developed analogies between its parts, and not a mere hodgepodge of first thoughts, jottings, roughings-out, or fragments. Although it has many flaws, it does seem to me a completed play, and one that can satisfactorily be acted in its present form (as it has been in recent years by the Old Vic—twice—the Stratford Festival Company of Canada, and many others). There is no doubt that *Timon* could be improved, but it does make good sense dramatically as it now stands. I would not try to push the argument further than that. A dramatic fable by its very nature has many weaknesses in psychological characterization and tragic development, but it can produce some striking effects of simplicity, symmetry, and dramatic intensity. These excellences of *Timon* have perhaps been best appreciated by William Hazlitt, who in *The Characters of Shakespear's Plays* said that the play

always appeared to us to be written with as intense a feeling of his subject as any one play of Shakespeare. It is one of the few in which he seems to be in earnest throughout, never to trifle nor go out of his way. He does not relax in his efforts, nor lose sight of the unity of his design.

The imagery of *Timon* has an inner consistency that reflects the completeness of the play as a work of the imagination. Images of disease, especially venereal disease, pervade the action, evoking the sort of disgust one finds in *Hamlet* and *Troilus and Cressida*. Man's nature is infected and the soul of the world is sick. Timon's misanthropy itself rages as virulently as any disease. Animal imagery and predatory images of food and eating combine with those of disease to strengthen its negative aspect. In Timon's tirades, especially, all mankind is reduced to Hobbes's fearful state of nature, where the law of the jungle once more prevails. There is much elaborate play on the dog image, since Apemantus was himself a Cynic philosopher, a school derived from the Greek word for dog and thought to

have currish properties. William Empson has discussed some of the overtones of this image in the play, and Caroline Spurgeon has pointed to the typical fawning image-cluster of dogs licking candy. The imagery of gold is too obvious to dwell on, but one should remember its double sense of evil and blessing. There are also traditional themes of winter and summer, cold and hot, constriction and flow, which follow the movement of the dramatic action.

Shakespeare seems to be completely in control of the style of *Timon*, which, if it has rough places that need to be revised, has also some extraordinary felicities. The play is not lyric in intent, so that some of the most vivid lyric effects are used negatively to support Timon's cruel imagination. The best passage of this sort is Timon's advice to Alcibiades to wage total war and spare none, for all are hypocritical dissemblers:

> Let not the virgin's cheek
> Make soft thy trenchant sword: for those milk paps,
> That through the window-bars bore at men's eyes,
> Are not within the leaf of pity writ,
> But set them down horrible traitors.     (IV.iii.115–19)

"Window-bars" has sometimes been interpreted to mean the open-work squares on the bodice of a woman's frock, but its literal reference to the bars outside a window seems more natural. We have the image of a young virgin mewed up in her chamber, whose disturbing sexuality as she stands at her window transfixes men and pierces them through. One must struggle against one's natural instincts to overcome these charms, and the lyric expression is used for derogatory purposes. Another more shocking example of twisted lyricism is Timon's advice to Flavius:

> Hate all, curse all, show charity to none,
> But let the famished flesh slide from the bone
> Ere thou relieve the beggar.     (IV.iii.530–32)

The physical force of the image is not buried in faded metaphor. Its cruelty is stark and unadorned.

One other stylistic excellence in *Timon* is its epigrammatic conciseness, the ability to pack a complex meaning into a brief phrase. There are many examples of this, some of them, as "feast-won, fast-lost," founded on proverbs. Flavius' defense of Timon also suggests a proverb, although it is not a recorded one: "Never mind/Was to be so unwise to be so kind." The effect of compression probably depends upon the multiple connotations of "kind" and "unwise"; a paraphrase would demand a good deal of amplification. The most numerous examples of this kind of writing are, I think, in III.v. Here the conciseness is part of the dramatic plan, and the Senators' brusque questions are ominous in their brevity: "Now, captain?," "What's that?," "How?," "What?," and then the explicit, "Do you dare our anger?" which precedes Alcibiades' banishment. In the carefully articulated rhetoric of Alcibiades' oration, there are many of these pregnant phrases. When the First Senator states as his guiding principle, "He forfeits his own blood that spills another," Alcibiades simply cannot believe what he has heard: "Must it be so? It must not be." The repetition gives special point to the line, as it also does in Alcibiades' final soliloquy:

I'm worse than mad. I have kept back their foes,
While they have told their money, and let out
Their coin upon large interest, I myself
Rich only in large hurts. All those, for this? (III.v.106-09)

The ironic echoing of "large" prepares us for the antithesis of the final question. The deliberate ambiguity of "this" suggests a wide range of meanings: this banishment, this debasement, this travesty of justice, this perversion of honor and merit—in sum, this evil, corrupt, tyrannical city governed by cynically usurious Senators.

*Timon* has many of the qualities of satire and high comedy. In the attempt to depict the sophisticated, morally corrupt, and completely money-oriented life of Athens, Shakespeare uses a sharp realism of style expressed in easy colloquial speech. The scenes with the false friends in Act III (i, ii, iii) are the best sustained examples of this style. Lucullus' reply to Flaminius' request for money shows an unabashed ironic scorn: "La, la, la, la! 'Nothing doubting,' says he? Alas, good lord, a noble gentleman 'tis, if he would not keep so good a house." Lucullus is completely at his ease, and his use of contracted speech forms throughout this scene indicates an assumed and contemptuous familiarity. Another example of Shakespeare's mastery of the colloquial style is Flavius' report of how the Senators reacted to his request for a loan:

They answer in a joint and corporate voice,
That now they are at fall, want treasure, cannot
Do what they would, are sorry; you are honorable,
But yet they could have wished—they know not:
Something hath been amiss—a noble nature
May catch a wrench—would all were well—'tis pity—
And so, intending other serious matters,
After distasteful looks, and these hard fractions,
With certain half-caps and cold-moving nods.
They froze me into silence.    (II.ii.211-20)

"These hard fractions" show Shakespeare's skill at imitating, by syntax and phrase, the halting dishonesty of the Senators. The fragments are those of actual speech, and their disconnectedness is intended to soften the blow on Timon. Even such a glorious spender as Timon "May catch a wrench" and go broke, and, as Lucullus says, "this is no time to lend money, especially upon bare friendship without security."

Another approach to the integrity of *Timon* is to consider the play in the context of Shakespeare's other works. *Timon* has most often been compared with *King Lear*. Coleridge called it an "after vibration" of *King Lear*, and A. C. Bradley compared the two plays extensively in his study of Shakespearean tragedy. Both deal with the theme of ingratitude and its overpowering effects on Lear and Timon, who both react with a fierce indictment of man and society. But in *King Lear* this indictment touches the protagonist, too, and leads him to a bitter self-awareness which is not present in *Timon*. There is no inward-turning in the latter play, no soul-searching of any sort, which gives it the effect of satire rather than tragedy. Both Lear and Timon are first shown in an atmosphere of false flattery and public adoration. They are soon reduced to primitive nature, but in Lear's case this stripping-down has a necessity lacking in Timon's, who chooses self-exile in

the woods and perversely persists in it even after he has found gold. One may also compare Kent and Flavius, the unshakably loyal servants who minister to their masters in adversity, but Kent is individualized as a character by a keen, blunt-speaking wit, whereas Flavius only fulfills a type function. In both plays, the frequent contrast of "nothing" and "all" identifies the extreme nature of the tragic action, which eschews any happy mean between prosperity and adversity.

*Timon* is especially close to those dark, satirical plays that put a strong emphasis on sexual corruption: *Measure for Measure*, *Hamlet*, and *Troilus and Cressida*. While *Timon* conveys the strongest sense of sexual disease, it shares a disillusioned view of human nature and an overpowering sense of deceit and hypocrisy with these other plays. It has been suggested that all these plays (except *Hamlet*) were written for the more fastidious audiences of the Inns of Court or the private theaters. That would help to explain the difficult, closely reasoned, and abstract character of many of their speeches.

There is a specific connection between *Timon* and *Troilus and Cressida* in the characters of Apemantus and Thersites. Both are scurrilous, churlish, and thoroughly unattractive truth-speakers, who, like professional fools, prick the illusions in their plays. Their own reality is never intended to be any alternative to the pretensions they attack, since they are both base and mean-spirited. Perhaps Apemantus, by his profession of Cynic philosophy, is a somewhat more attractive figure than the completely servile Thersites.

The relation of *Timon* to *Coriolanus* is so close that it deserves particular attention. Both plays are based on North's Plutarch for their essential details, and the exile of Alcibiades with his return to conquer his native city is very like the career of Coriolanus. The two are, in fact, parallel lives in Plutarch. The banishment of Alcibiades and Coriolanus is manipulated by a politically and morally corrupt group, whose mediocrity is disturbed by the presence of military heroes. The subsequent plea of the Senators to spare their city is also similar in the two plays. In structure both plays are divided into two distinct parts, one showing the wrong or evil, the other the revenge for it. The opening fable of Fortune's hill in *Timon* parallels the fable of the belly and the members in *Coriolanus*; both provide a convenient set of ideas by which to interpret the action, and both foreshadow what will eventually occur.

One could enumerate many similarities in detail between the two plays, but the larger similarities in conception are more important. *Timon* and *Coriolanus* are both tragedies that cannot be judged by the standards of Aristotle's *Poetics*: in neither play does the tragic protagonist have much awareness of what is happening to him, and there is no tragic recognition at all. Neither Timon nor Coriolanus has any sense of the middle state of man, the mean, the human condition. They are both absolutists, extremists, harsh individualists who wish to be either god or beast, but nothing in between. They are equally insensitive to human failings and weaknesses—even Timon's philanthropy is always public, never personal. Both plays put strong emphasis on public display and have many large scenes of crowded activity. There are very few personal or domestic scenes, and almost no attention at all is devoted to romantic heroines. The soliloquies in both plays are never used for purposes of self-analysis or self-exploration. Stylistically, both plays seem very objective and impersonal, and there are excellent examples in both of a condensed and telegraphic dramatic speech without lyric amplification. Both plays also have a good deal of satire, which draws on an extensive imagery of disease, animals, and food.

In the absence of any external evidence, I agree with E. K. Chambers in placing *Timon* after *Coriolanus* as the last of Shakespeare's tragedies, written sometime around 1608. However, Chambers' dating of *Timon* (in *William Shakespeare*, Vol. I), is based on assumptions about Shakespeare's psychological and physical condition at the time of composition that are difficult to accept:

> Both *King Lear* and *Timon of Athens* seem to show symptoms of mental disturbance. But mental disturbance may come in waves. It may very likely only be a whimsy of my own that during the attempt at *Timon of Athens* a wave broke, then an illness followed, and that when it passed, the breach between the tragic and the romantic period was complete.

*Timon* has always been a favorite candidate for the "mythical sorrows of Shakespeare," and Chambers only echoes more than a century of romantic speculation on the dark corners of Shakespeare's soul. Georg Brandes in his *William Shakespeare* said much the same thing in a more rapturous and unrestrained form:

> all that, in these years, Shakespeare has endured and experienced, thought and suffered, is concentrated into the one great despairing figure of Timon of Athens, "misanthropos," whose savage rhetoric is like a dark secretion of clotted blood and gall, drawn off to assuage pain.

Recently, a number of medical critics have stated that Timon is suffering from the classic symptoms of syphilis, which reach the stage of paresis by Act IV. Perhaps we must then postulate that Shakespeare himself was suffering from the French malady in order to be able to write about it. This is the same order of fallacy as attributing Shakespeare's bird lore and flower lore to his close observation of the Warwickshire countryside, despite the fact that they have figured in literary traditions at least as old as the ancient Greeks.

Shakespeare surely tried to protect himself from being taken for a Timonist by making Timon so unattractive and unsympathetic. "Yond despised and ruinous man" is a lost soul, self-exiled and self-damned by his own evil vision of reality. We cannot have become so uncritically enamored of the power of blackness as not to see the truth of Apemantus' judgment:

> Thou hast cast away thyself, being like thyself:
> A madman so long, now a fool.          (IV.iii.221-22)

We would not want to accept this, however, as a final appraisal of Timon, whose fierce energy and passion redeem him from the pettiness and rancor of his accusers. "Friendship's full of dregs," but to escape the humdrum complications of the common fate by trying to be either god or beast can be a more agonizing experience. Both Shakespeare's and Molière's misanthrope fascinate us and repel us because their attempt is so heroic, so uncompromising, and so inhuman.

## A NOTE ON THE SOURCES

The ultimate source for Shakespeare's play is probably Lucian's satiric dialogue, *Timon*, written in Greek in the second century A.D. It is unlikely that Shakespeare read Lucian in Greek, but the earliest English translation, by Thomas Heywood, was not published until 1637. There may, of course, have been an earlier English translation that has not survived, but a more likely possibility is that Shakespeare used the French translation by Filbert Bretin in 1582 (as Honigmann argues). A number of Italian versions were also available, as well as a Latin translation by Erasmus. The verbal parallels between Shakespeare and Lucian are few, but there is a striking similarity in style and tone. Common sense insists that Lucian must be Shakespeare's ultimate source, even though the exact stages of transmission are not clear to us.

The most direct and commonly agreed-on source for *Timon* is Sir Thomas North's translation of Plutarch, *The Lives of the Noble Grecians and Romans*, first published in 1579 (although Shakespeare probably used the 1595 edition). There is a brief digression in the "Life of Marcus Antonius" that recounts how Antony, despondent after his defeat at the battle of Actium, living apart from men in a house by the sea called Timoneon. Plutarch follows Strabo's version of the story, which represents Antony as deliberately imitating the example of Timon. Timon was apparently an actual person who lived in Athens in the fifth century B.C., and about whose misanthropy many legends arose. He was a favorite butt of the Greek comic dramatists. There are a few further references to Timon in Plutarch's "Life of Alcibiades," which was the Greek life paired with that of the Roman Coriolanus. If *Timon* was written around the time of *Antony and Cleopatra* and *Coriolanus*, it is not surprising that all three plays should draw on North's Plutarch. It is likely that Shakespeare used Plutarch more extensively than the source passages would indicate. Six names in *Timon*, for example, come from the "Life of Marcus Antonius," and the "Life of Lucullus" provides us with an excellent background for the character in Shakespeare's play.

The account of Timon in William Painter's *The Palace of Pleasure*, first published in 1566 (but Shakespeare probably used the 1575 edition), draws on Plutarch for its facts, but orders them with an eye to making a good story. There is perhaps one bit of evidence of Shakespeare's literal use of Painter. Timon's epitaphs in the play are taken over verbatim from North's Plutarch except for one change: Shakespeare uses Painter's phrase, "wicked caitiffs," in place of North's "wicked wretches." Since Shakespeare probably drew on Painter for *All's Well That Ends Well*, and possibly for *Romeo and Juliet*, it is reasonable to suppose that he also read the brief account of Timon. The version of the Timon story given in Sir Richard Barckley, *A Discourse of the Felicity of Man* (1598), is derived almost entirely from Painter.

The most controversial and puzzling source that has been claimed for Shakespeare's play is the anonymous *Timon*, which the Reverend Alexander Dyce in 1842 first published from a manuscript for the Shakespeare Society (now Dyce MS 52.25F in the Victoria and Albert Museum, London). This is an academic play, full of self-consciously learned allusions and quotations. It is based on Lucian, although on at least three occasions it introduces material not in Lucian and also used, in somewhat different form, by Shakespeare: (1) a mock-banquet scene in which Timon serves stones painted to look like artichokes; (2) the faithful Steward Laches, who follows his master in adversity; (3) the burial by Timon of his newly discovered gold. None of these is so distinctive that it can be accounted for only by direct borrowing, but the combination suggests that Shakespeare may have seen a performance of the play, read the manuscript, or heard about the play from someone who had seen or read it. Just how this could have occurred is entirely a matter of speculation.

The date of the "old" *Timon* play (as it is usually called) is very uncertain. It has generally been assigned to the last quarter of the sixteenth century, but recently some scholars have argued that it may just as easily follow Shakespeare's *Timon* as precede it. Bradbrook thinks that it is a burlesque of Shakespeare's play presented by the law students of the Inner Temple at their Christmas revels (see *Renaissance Drama*, IX [1966], 83–103). A late date for the "old" *Timon* play accounts for the similarities with Shakespeare that do not derive from Lucian, but it is difficult to reconstruct how the academic author could have known a Shakespearean play that was presumably never completely finished, never acted, and not published until 1623. The records may, of course, be incomplete, but then the argument has to be founded on a series of negative probabilities. Proponents of a late date for the "old" *Timon* play have heard echoes in it of *King Lear* and *The Merchant of Venice*, but these are questionable. One other explanation for the similarity of *Timon of Athens* to the "old" *Timon* play is that they both drew on a common source now lost. This is a convenient postulate, but not very helpful in the present case, since nothing further is known about this common source.

Two other sources for which claims have been offered have generally been rejected by scholars: Boiardo's *Timone* (1494) and Lyly's *Campaspe* (1584). In the latter play, Diogenes is rather close to Shakespeare's Apemantus, but the malcontent railer was a familiar type, and Shakespeare had already created Jaques in *As You Like It* and Thersites in *Troilus and Cressida*.

There are many allusions to Timon in Renaissance English literature. He was a stock figure for the misanthrope, whose life was often described in animal analogies. Shakespeare refers to Timon in *Love's Labor's Lost*, when Berowne hypocritically berates his companions for being in love:

> O me, with what strict patience have I sat
> To see a king transformèd to a gnat!
> To see great Hercules whipping a gig,
> And profound Solomon to tune a jig,
> And Nestor play at push-pin with the boys,
> And critic Timon laugh at idle toys!          (IV.iii.162–67)

### A NOTE ON THE TEXT

Our sole authority for the text of *Timon of Athens* is the First Folio of Shakespeare, published in 1623. It may only be the result of a lucky accident that the play was printed

at all, since *Troilus and Cressida* was intended to follow *Romeo and Juliet* in the section of Tragedies, and three pages of *Troilus and Cressida* were actually set up and printed. But difficulties over the copyright of *Troilus and Cressida* probably forced Jaggard to stop work on it. He allowed a sufficient number of blank pages for it, and then went on to set up and print *Julius Caesar*. Contrary to Jaggard's expectations, the difficulties with *Troilus and Cressida* were not quickly resolved. Something had to fill the space left for *Troilus and Cressida*, and *Timon* was decided on. It is a relatively short play, so that it only partially fills the allotted pages. Signature ii is omitted and there is an awkward gap between pages 98 and 109 (beginning of *Julius Caesar*), despite the blown-up and elaborately decorated list of actors' names that has a page to itself at the end of *Timon*.

Whether *Timon* would have been printed at all if the difficulties with *Troilus and Cressida* had not occurred is a teasing question, but the condition of its text strongly confirms its role as an afterthought or stopgap. *Timon* is full of the kind of inconsistencies and roughnesses that suggest a play that has not received any final revision (see the Introduction). There is no record of a performance of the play during Shakespeare's lifetime, and the possibility seems unlikely. It is obviously not the sort of play that a business-minded publisher would be eager to include in an expensive and speculative venture like the Shakespeare Folio. The text of *Timon* was set up either directly from Shakespeare's "foul papers" (rough draft), or from a transcript of them made by a scribe.

The state of the text has an important bearing on the editing of the play. If *Timon* is indeed a play that has not received that final revision and polishing necessary to put it into actable (or printable) form, it is not the job of a modern editor to undertake this task for Shakespeare. It is not up to a modern editor, for example, to make the lines scan by piecing them out differently (a formidable task here), or to distribute specific roles to the First, Second, Third, and Fourth Lords, or to make other changes of an essentially "improving" nature. I assume that the present-day reader would like to have the play in a modernized form, but as close as possible to the way Shakespeare left it. I have therefore made very few changes in the Folio text, even at the expense of leaving loose ends or inconsistencies. (It would be wonderfully satisfying to know whom Alcibiades is pleading for in III.v.)

Two matters of special interest are related to the nature of the text: lineation and stage directions. In the text of *Timon* there is either serious mislineation (the printing of blank verse lines in some other form, either broken in two or run together as prose), or a failure in a number of places to write regular, five-beat, iambic lines. That is, either the compositor took wide liberties with the metrics, or the author himself made errors or allowed himself a great deal of freedom. Considering the unrevised state of the text, one is forced to conclude that the printed version is probably an accurate rendering of the copy. "Mislineation" is, therefore, a misleading term. I have generally followed the lineation of the Folio, except where lines are obviously broken into two to fill up the "cast off" space (that is, the amount of space estimated to be needed for a certain quantity of copy), or run together as prose where not enough space was allowed. The Folio lineation usually makes for good speech rhythm, with important pauses at the ends of lines. To run these lines through the blank verse meat grinder would distort their quality as dramatic speech.

How one treats the Folio stage directions of *Timon* also depends upon one's attitude to the text. The indications of action in this play are of the permissive and literary sort characteristic of an author's manuscript. For example, the final part of the stage direction that opens I.ii reads: *"Then comes dropping after all, Apemantus, discontentedly, like himself."* This is a descriptive stage direction, which would have been put into a more practical form in a promptbook prepared by the stage manager. To change this direction to *"Then enter Apemantus, alone and at a distance"* (as Sisson does in his fine text) is to throw away a significant Shakespearean line for the sake of some imagined modern production. In an unrevised play such as *Timon* there is a special sanction for retaining the obviously authorial stage directions of the Folio, which bring us closer to the original manuscript of the play than do the colorless, clarified directions of a modern editor. I have also avoided one other type of correction in the stage directions. When it is not clear who is being addressed, I have not seen fit to supply a name. In V.i, for example, Timon is upbraiding Poet and Painter in turn, but the text never specifies which one. I have simply indicated *"To one"* and *"To the other,"* although in a production it would obviously have to be either to Poet or Painter. Perhaps these two characters are meant to have a Rosencrantz and Guildenstern interchangeability.

In the present text, spelling has been modernized, except that certain older forms have been retained when they are essentially different from their modern counterparts, for example, "vild" (for "vile"), "huswife" (for "housewife"), "a th'" (for "o' th'"). The punctuation has been modernized within limits, but I have generally been wary of introducing changes where the Folio pointing makes good sense. Even editors scrupulous about the language of the Folio seem not to feel bound by the punctuation. Capitalization has been modernized, and contractions not affecting pronunciation have been eliminated (especially in the verb forms). For stylistic reasons, I have omitted

many traditional exclamation marks. The speech prefixes have been expanded and somewhat clarified. The list of actors' names is taken from the Folio, where it is printed (with one name given twice, and with the names in a slightly different order) at the end of the play.

Typographical errors have been corrected, and some stage directions have been slightly moved. Many traditional stage directions, not in the Folio, have been supplied in brackets. The traditional act and scene divisions and scene locations have been indicated for convenience, but the reader should recall that the action of the play was continuous and the scenes often unlocalized. The Folio indicates only "Actus Primus, Scoena Prima."

Other departures from the Folio are listed below. The reading of the present text is given first, in boldface type, and then the reading of the Folio (F) in roman.

**I.i.s.d. Enter Poet, Painter, Jeweler, Merchant** [F adds "and Mercer"]   **21 gum, which oozes** Gowne, which vses   **87 hands** hand; **slip** sit   **166 satiety** society   **215 cost** cast   **282 Come** Comes   **291 I'll keep you company** [in F part of speech of Second Lord]
**I.ii.29 ever** verie   **114 s.d. Sound tucket** [F follows this with another s.d., "Enter the Maskers of Amazons, with Lutes in their hands, dauncing and playing," incorrectly anticipating the entry at line 130; the necessary part of this s.d. is therefore added to that of line 130]   **125 Th' ear** There   **130 First Lord** First Lord Luc.   **152 First Lady** I Lord
**II.ii.4 resumes** resume   **43 of broken** of debt, broken   **78 mistress'** Masters   **107 mistress'** Masters   **135 proposed** propose   **192 Flaminius** Flauius   **192 s.d. Enter Flaminius, Servilius, and Third Servant** Enter three Seruants
**III.i.s.d. with** with a
**III.iii.21 and I** and
**III.iv.s.d. two Servants** man   **50 ate** eate   **87 Hortensius 1.** Var.   **111 Sempronius—all** Sempronius Vllorxa
**III.v.17 An** And   **68 'em** him
**III.vi.92 with your** you with   **116–17** [speech prefixes reversed]
**IV.i.13 Son** Some   **21 let** yet
**IV.iii.12 pasture** Pastour   **13 lean** leaue   **88 tub-fast** fubfast   **117 window-bars** window Barne   **122 thy** the   **157 scolds** scold'st   **255 drudges** drugges   **256 command** command'st   **272 rogue** ragge   **284 my** thy   **397 them** then   **495 mild** wilde   **512 A usuring kindness, as** If not a Vsuring kindnesse, and as
**V.i.5–6 Phrynia and Timandra** Phrinica and Timandylo   **71 men** man   **115 s.d. Beats . . . cave** Exeunt   **126 chance** chanc'd   **133 cauterizing** Cantherizing   **147 sense** since   **182 reverend'st** reuerends
**V.iv.55 Descend** Defend   **64 s.d. Soldier** Messenger

# THE LIFE OF TIMON OF ATHENS

[The Actors' Names

TIMON *of Athens*
LUCIUS *and* } *two flattering lords*
LUCULLUS
SEMPRONIUS *another flattering lord*
VENTIDIUS *one of Timon's false friends*
APEMANTUS *a churlish philosopher*
ALCIBIADES *an Athenian captain*
POET
PAINTER
JEWELER
MERCHANT
[FLAVIUS *steward to Timon*]
FLAMINIUS *one of Timon's servants*
SERVILIUS *another*
[LUCILIUS *another*]

CAPHIS
PHILOTUS
TITUS
HORTENSIUS } *several servants to*
[SERVANT *to*] *Varro*     *usurers*
[SERVANT *to*] *Lucius*
[SERVANT *to Isidore*]
[AN OLD ATHENIAN]
[THREE STRANGERS]
[A PAGE]
[A FOOL]
[PHRYNIA } *mistresses to Alcibiades*]
[TIMANDRA]
*Certain* MASKERS [*as*] *Cupid* [*and Amazons*]
*Certain* SENATORS, *certain* THIEVES, *with divers
other* SERVANTS *and* ATTENDANTS, [LORDS,
OFFICERS, SOLDIERS]

*Scene:* Athens and the neighboring woods]

## ACT I

### Scene I. [*Athens. Timon's house.*]

*Enter* POET, PAINTER, JEWELER, MERCHANT *at
several° doors.*

POET
Good day, sir.
PAINTER          I am glad y' are well.
POET
I have not seen you long; how goes the world?

PAINTER
It wears,° sir, as it grows.
POET                          Ay that's well known.
But what particular rarity? What strange,
Which manifold record° not matches? See,                5
Magic of bounty,° all these spirits thy power
Hath conjured to attend. I know the merchant.
PAINTER
I know them both; th' other's a jeweler.
MERCHANT
O 'tis a worthy lord.
JEWELER              Nay that's most fixed.°
MERCHANT
A most incomparable man, breathed,° as it were,      10

*The decorative border shown above appeared on the first page of*
Timon of Athens *in the First Folio edition of Shakespeare's
plays, 1623.*

**I.i.s.d. several** separate (the Poet and Painter enter at one door,
the Jeweler and Merchant at another)

**3 wears** wears out  **5 manifold record** many and varied
records, history ("record" accented on second syllable)  **6
bounty** generosity  **9 fixed** certain  **10 breathed** exercised,
trained

1375

To an untirable and continuate° goodness.
He passes.°

JEWELER   I have a jewel here—

MERCHANT
O pray let's see't. For the Lord Timon, sir?

JEWELER
If he will touch the estimate.° But for that—

POET [*Aside to* PAINTER.]
When we for recompense have praised the vild,°   15
It stains the glory in that happy° verse
Which aptly sings the good.

MERCHANT [*Looking at the jewel.*]   'Tis a good form.

JEWELER
And rich. Here is a water,° look ye.

PAINTER
You are rapt, sir, in some work, some dedication
To the great lord.

POET                         A thing slipped idly from me.   20
Our poesy is as a gum, which oozes
From whence 'tis nourished. The fire i' th' flint
Shows not till it be struck; our gentle flame
Provokes itself,° and like the current flies
Each bound it chases.° What have you there?   25

PAINTER
A picture, sir. When comes your book forth?

POET
Upon the heels of my presentment,° sir.
Let's see your piece.

PAINTER                         'Tis a good piece.

POET
So 'tis; this comes off well and excellent.

PAINTER
Indifferent.°

POET             Admirable. How this grace   30
Speaks his own standing!° What a mental power
This eye shoots forth! How big° imagination
Moves in this lip! To th' dumbness° of the gesture
One might interpret.°

PAINTER
It is a pretty mocking° of the life.   35
Here is a touch—is't good?

POET                         I will say of it,
It tutors nature; artificial strife°
Lives in these touches, livelier than life.

*Enter certain* SENATORS, [*who pass over the stage and
exeunt*].

PAINTER
How this lord is followed!

POET
The Senators of Athens, happy men!   40

PAINTER
Look, moe!°

POET
You see this confluence, this great flood of visitors:
I have in this rough work shaped out a man
Whom this beneath world° doth embrace and hug
With amplest entertainment. My free drift   45
Halts not particularly,° but moves itself
In a wide sea of wax;° no leveled° malice
Infects one comma in the course I hold,
But flies an eagle flight, bold and forth on,
Leaving no tract° behind.   50

PAINTER
How shall I understand you?

POET                         I will unbolt to you.
You see how all conditions,° how all minds,
As well of glib and slipp'ry creatures as
Of grave and austere quality, tender down°
Their services to Lord Timon. His large fortune,   55
Upon his good and gracious nature hanging,
Subdues and properties° to his love and tendance°
All sorts of hearts; yea, from the glass-faced° flatterer
To Apemantus, that few things loves better
Than to abhor himself—even he drops down   60
The knee before him, and returns in peace
Most rich in Timon's nod.

PAINTER             I saw them speak together.

POET
Sir, I have upon a high and pleasant hill
Feigned° Fortune to be throned. The base o' th' mount
Is ranked with all deserts,° all kind of natures   65
That labor on the bosom of this sphere
To propagate their states.° Amongst them all,
Whose eyes are on this sovereign lady fixed,
One do I personate of Lord Timon's frame,°
Whom Fortune with her ivory hand° wafts to her,   70
Whose present° grace° to present slaves and servants
Translates° his rivals.

PAINTER             'Tis conceived to scope.°
This throne, this Fortune, and this hill, methinks,
With one man beckoned from the rest below,
Bowing his head against the steepy mount   75
To climb his happiness, would be well expressed
In our condition.

POET             Nay, sir, but hear me on.
All those which were his fellows but of late,
Some better than his value, on the moment
Follow his strides, his lobbies fill with tendance,   80
Rain sacrificial whisperings° in his ear,

---

11 **continuate** uninterrupted   12 **passes** surpasses   14 **touch the estimate** offer the expected price   15 **vild** vile   16 **happy** fortunate   18 **water** luster (of a jewel)   23–24 **our . . . itself** the inspiration of poets is spontaneous, not externally provoked like the "fire i' th' flint"   25 **Each . . . chases** i.e., the stream flows towards the shore but rebounds upon contact   27 **presentment** presentation (to Timon)   30 **Indifferent** neither good nor bad   31 **standing** dignity, social status   32 **big** adverb   33 **dumbness** silence (as in a dumb show)   34 **interpret** supply words   35 **mocking** imitation   37 **artificial strife** the striving of art to outdo nature   41 **moe** more

44 **beneath world** sublunary world (Timon as the moon)   46 **particularly** at individuals   47 **sea of wax** either a sea of inspiration as easily molded as wax—not limited to a mere writing tablet of wax—or perhaps a waxing sea swelling with inspiration; **leveled** aimed (at one person)   50 **tract** either "trace" or "track"   52 **conditions** (1) social classes (2) temperaments   54 **tender down** offer (as one offers money)   57 **properties** appropriates; **tendance** attendance   58 **glass-faced** mirror-faced   64 **Feigned** imagined   65 **deserts** degrees of worth   67 **propagate their states** increase their possessions   69 **frame** (1) disposition (2) physical stature   70 **ivory hand** hand white and smooth as ivory (this is the right hand of Fortune, with which she distributes her favors; with the left, or dark, hand she takes them away)   71 **present** (1) existing now (2) immediate; **grace** graciousness, generosity   72 **Translates** transforms; **to scope** to the purpose, just right   81 **sacrificial whisperings** lines 81–83 suggest the hieratic atmosphere surrounding Timon, now high in Fortune's favor

Make sacred even his stirrup, and through him
Drink° the free air.

PAINTER                    Ay marry,° what of these?

POET
When Fortune in her shift and change of mood
Spurns down her late beloved, all his dependants      85
Which labored after him to the mountain's top,
Even on their knees and hands, let him slip down,
Not one accompanying his declining foot.

PAINTER
'Tis common.
A thousand moral paintings° I can show                90
That shall demonstrate° these quick° blows of Fortune's
More pregnantly than words. Yet you do well
To show Lord Timon that mean° eyes have seen
The foot above the head.°

*Trumpets sound. Enter Lord* TIMON, *addressing himself
courteously to every suitor;* [*a* MESSENGER *from Ventidius
talking with him;* LUCILIUS *and other* SERVANTS
*following*].

TIMON                    Imprisoned is he, say you?

MESSENGER
Ay, my good lord; five talents° is his debt,           95
His means most short, his creditors most strait.°
Your honorable letter he desires
To those have shut him up, which failing,
Periods° his comfort.

TIMON                    Noble Ventidius—well.
I am not of that feather° to shake off                100
My friend when he must need me. I do know him
A gentleman that well deserves a help,
Which he shall have. I'll pay the debt and free him.

MESSENGER
Your lordship ever binds° him.

TIMON
Commend me to him; I will send his ransom,            105
And being enfranchised bid him come to me.
'Tis not enough to help the feeble up,
But to support him after. Fare you well.

MESSENGER
All happiness to your honor.                *Exit.*

*Enter an* OLD ATHENIAN.

OLD ATHENIAN
Lord Timon, hear me speak.

TIMON                    Freely, good father.         110

OLD ATHENIAN
Thou hast a servant named Lucilius.

TIMON
I have so. What of him?

OLD ATHENIAN
Most noble Timon, call the man before thee.

TIMON
Attends he here or no? Lucilius!

LUCILIUS
Here at your lordship's service.                       115

OLD ATHENIAN
This fellow° here, Lord Timon, this thy creature,°
By night frequents my house. I am a man
That from my first have been inclined to thrift,
And my estate deserves an heir more raised
Than one which holds a trencher.°

TIMON                           Well; what further?  120

OLD ATHENIAN
One only daughter have I, no kin else,
On whom I may confer what I have got.
The maid is fair, a° th' youngest for a bride,
And I have bred her at my dearest cost
In qualities of the best. This man of thine            125
Attempts her love. I prithee, noble lord,
Join with me to forbid him her resort;°
Myself have spoke in vain.

TIMON                       The man is honest.

OLD ATHENIAN
Therefore he will be,° Timon.
His honesty rewards him in itself;                     130
It must not bear° my daughter.

TIMON                      Does she love him?

OLD ATHENIAN
She is young and apt.
Our own precedent° passions do instruct us
What levity's in youth.

TIMON                    Love you the maid?

LUCILIUS
Ay, my good lord, and she accepts of it.               135

OLD ATHENIAN
If in her marriage my consent be missing,
I call the gods to witness, I will choose
Mine heir from forth the beggars of the world,
And dispossess her all.°

TIMON                     How shall she be endowed,
If she be mated with an equal° husband?                140

OLD ATHENIAN
Three talents on the present;° in future, all.

TIMON
This gentleman of mine hath served me long.
To build his fortune I will strain a little,
For 'tis a bond° in men. Give him thy daughter;
What you bestow, in him I'll counterpoise,°            145
And make him weigh with her.

OLD ATHENIAN             Most noble lord,
Pawn me to this your honor, she is his.

TIMON
My hand to thee, mine honor on my promise.

LUCILIUS
Humbly I thank your lordship; never may

---

83 **Drink** breathe; **marry** indeed (originally "By the Virgin Mary") 90 **moral paintings** allegorical pictures (especially wall hangings) 91 **demonstrate** accented on second syllable; **quick** (1) swift (2) full of life 93 **mean** lowly 94 **foot . . . head** in the quick changes that Fortune brings, the foot of the lowliest may suddenly appear above the head of the highest 95 **five talents** see Introduction, p. 1367 96 **strait** strict 99 **Periods** puts an end to 100 **feather** character 104 **binds** attaches by ties of gratitude (with play on "free" in line 103)

116 **fellow, creature** terms of contempt 120 **trencher** wooden plate or shallow dish on which meat is served (a servant who waits on tables would hold a trencher) 123 **a** a worndown form for "of" 127 **her resort** resort or access to her 129 **Therefore . . . be** since Lucilius *is* honest (or honorable), he will therefore show his honesty by not pursuing the Old Athenian's daughter 131 **bear** carry away 133 **precedent** former (accented on second syllable) 139 **all** completely 140 **equal** either socially or financially 141 **on the present** at once 144 **bond** obligation 145 **counterpoise** counterbalance

That state or fortune fall into my keeping,          150
Which is not owed° to you.

                *Exit* [LUCILIUS, *with* OLD ATHENIAN].

POET
  Vouchsafe° my labor, and long live your lordship.
TIMON
  I thank you; you shall hear from me anon.
  Go not away. What have you there, my friend?
PAINTER
  A piece of painting, which I do beseech          155
  Your lordship to accept.
TIMON                      Painting is welcome.
  The painting is almost the natural man;
  For since dishonor traffics° with man's nature,
  He is but outside.° These penciled° figures are
  Even such as they give out.° I like your work,    160
  And you shall find I like it. Wait attendance
  Till you hear further from me.
PAINTER                        The gods preserve ye.
TIMON
  Well fare you, gentleman. Give me your hand;
  We must needs dine together. Sir, your jewel
  Hath suffered under praise.°
JEWELER                      What, my lord, dispraise?  165
TIMON
  A mere° satiety of commendations.
  If I should pay you for't as 'tis extolled,
  It would unclew° me quite.
JEWELER                    My lord, 'tis rated
  As those which sell would give.° But you well know,
  Things of like value, differing in the owners,   170
  Are prizèd by their masters.° Believe't, dear lord,
  You mend° the jewel by the wearing it.
TIMON  Well mocked.°
MERCHANT
  No, my good lord; he speaks the common tongue°
  Which all men speak with him.                     175

*Enter* APEMANTUS.

TIMON
  Look who comes here; will you be chid?
JEWELER
  We'll bear with your lordship.
MERCHANT                        He'll spare none.
TIMON
  Good morrow to thee, gentle° Apemantus.
APEMANTUS
  Till I be gentle, stay thou for thy good morrow—
  When thou art Timon's dog, and these knaves honest.  180

TIMON
  Why dost thou call them knaves, thou know'st them
    not?
APEMANTUS  Are they not Athenians?
TIMON  Yes.
APEMANTUS  Then I repent not.
JEWELER  You know me, Apemantus?                    185
APEMANTUS  Thou know'st I do, I called thee by thy
  name.
TIMON  Thou art proud, Apemantus.
APEMANTUS  Of nothing so much as that I am not like
  Timon.                                            190
TIMON  Whither art going?
APEMANTUS  To knock out an honest Athenian's
  brains.
TIMON  That's a deed thou't die for.
APEMANTUS  Right, if doing nothing be death by th'   195
  law.
TIMON  How lik'st thou this picture, Apemantus?
APEMANTUS  The best, for the innocence.°
TIMON  Wrought he not well that painted it?
APEMANTUS  He wrought better that made the          200
  painter, and yet he's but a filthy° piece of work.
PAINTER  Y' are a dog.°
APEMANTUS  Thy mother's of my generation.° What's
  she, if I be a dog?
TIMON  Wilt dine with me, Apemantus?                205
APEMANTUS  No. I eat not lords.
TIMON  And° thou shouldst, thou'dst anger ladies.
APEMANTUS  O they eat lords; so they come by great
  bellies.°
TIMON  That's a lascivious apprehension.            210
APEMANTUS  So, thou apprehend'st it, take it for thy
  labor.
TIMON  How dost thou like this jewel, Apemantus?
APEMANTUS  Not so well as plain-dealing, which will
  not cost a man a doit.°                           215
TIMON  What dost thou think 'tis worth?
APEMANTUS  Not worth my thinking. How now,
  poet?
POET  How now, philosopher?
APEMANTUS  Thou liest.                              220
POET  Art not one?
APEMANTUS  Yes.
POET  Then I lie not.
APEMANTUS  Art not a poet?
POET  Yes.                                          225
APEMANTUS  Then thou liest.° Look in thy last work,
  where thou hast feigned him° a worthy fellow.
POET  That's not feigned, he is so.
APEMANTUS  Yes, he is worthy of thee, and to pay
  thee for thy labor. He that loves to be flattered is  230
  worthy o' th' flatterer. Heavens, that I were a lord!
TIMON  What wouldst do then, Apemantus?

---

151 **owed** (1) acknowledged to you as the cause of it
(2) due to you as a debt  152 **Vouchsafe** deign to accept
158 **traffics** deals (pejorative sense)  159 **but outside** merely
external, a false semblance; **penciled** painted  160 **Even
. . . out** i.e., painting, in contrast with human nature,
is honest; it make no pretense to be something other than
what it appears to be  165 **under praise** in being praised,
since the jewel is beyond praise (but the Jeweler takes it in the
sense of "dispraise")  166 **mere** absolute  168 **unclew** undo
169 **As . . . give** i.e., at the wholesale price  171 **Are . . .
masters** are valued according to the social status of their
owners  172 **mend** improve  173 **mocked** simulated (i.e., I
know your flattery is only part of your sales talk)  174 **speaks
. . . tongue** says what everyone is saying  178 **gentle** (1)
well-born (a conventional complimentary epithet) (2) mild

198 **innocence** (1) harmlessness (2) foolishness  201 **filthy** contemptible  202 **dog** Apemantus is a Cynic philosopher;
"cynic" is derived from the Greek word for dog  203 **generation** (1) breed (2) persons born at about the same time
207 **And** if  208–09 **come . . . bellies** become pregnant
215 **doit** a small Dutch coin worth less than a farthing (used
as a type expression for any very small sum)  226 **liest** a play
on the old idea that poetry is a *mimesis*, imitation, mocking, or
feigning of reality and therefore a lie  227 **him** Timon

APEMANTUS   E'en as Apemantus does now: hate a
lord with my heart.

TIMON   What, thyself?                 235

APEMANTUS   Ay.

TIMON   Wherefore?

APEMANTUS   That I had no angry wit to be a lord.°
Art not thou a merchant?

MERCHANT   Ay, Apemantus.            240

APEMANTUS   Traffic° confound thee, if the gods will
not.

MERCHANT   If traffic do it, the gods do it.

APEMANTUS   Traffic's thy god, and thy god confound
thee.                                    245

*Trumpet sounds. Enter a* MESSENGER.

TIMON
What trumpet's that?

MESSENGER
'Tis Alcibiades and some twenty horse,°
All of companionship.°

TIMON
Pray entertain them, give them guide to us.
          [*Exeunt some* ATTENDANTS.]
You must needs dine with me. Go not you hence    250
Till I have thanked you. When dinner's done
Show me this piece. I am joyful of your sights.°

*Enter* ALCIBIADES, *with the rest.*

Most welcome, sir.

APEMANTUS          So, so.
Their° aches° contract and starve° your supple joints!
That there should be small love amongst these sweet
   knaves,                                  255
And all this courtesy! The strain of man's bred out
Into baboon and monkey.

ALCIBIADES
Sir, you have saved° my longing, and I feed
Most hungerly on your sight.

TIMON            Right welcome, sir.
Ere we depart, we'll share a bounteous time      260
In different pleasures. Pray you let us in.
             *Exeunt* [*all but* APEMANTUS].

*Enter two* LORDS.

FIRST LORD   What time a day is't, Apemantus?

APEMANTUS   Time to be honest.

FIRST LORD   That time serves still.°

APEMANTUS   The most accursèd thou that still   265
omit'st° it.

SECOND LORD   Thou art going to Lord Timon's
feast?

APEMANTUS   Ay, to see meat fill knaves and wine
heat fools.                             270

SECOND LORD   Fare thee well, fare thee well.

APEMANTUS   Thou art a fool to bid me farewell twice.

SECOND LORD   Why, Apemantus?

APEMANTUS   Shouldst have kept one to thyself, for I
mean to give thee none.                   275

FIRST LORD   Hang thyself!

APEMANTUS   No, I will do nothing at thy bidding.
Make thy requests to thy friend.

SECOND LORD   Away, unpeaceable° dog, or I'll spurn
thee hence.                              280

APEMANTUS   I will fly like a dog the heels a th' ass.
                                     [*Exit.*]

FIRST LORD
He's opposite to° humanity. Come, shall we in
And taste Lord Timon's bounty? He outgoes
The very heart of kindness.

SECOND LORD
He pours it out. Plutus, the god of gold,      285
Is but his steward; no meed° but he repays
Sevenfold above itself. No gift to him
But breeds the giver a return exceeding
All use of quittance.°

FIRST LORD          The noblest mind he carries°
That ever governed man.

SECOND LORD         Long may he live    290
In fortunes. Shall we in?

FIRST LORD          I'll keep you company. *Exeunt.*


                         [*Scene II. Timon's house.*]

*Hautboys° playing loud music. A great banquet served in;
and then enter Lord* TIMON, *the* STATES,° *the Athenian*
LORDS, VENTIDIUS (*which Timon redeemed from prison*),
[*and* ALCIBIADES. STEWARD *and others attending.*]
*Then comes dropping after all,* APEMANTUS, *discontentedly, like himself.*

VENTIDIUS
Most honored Timon,
It hath pleased the gods to remember my father's age,
And call him to long peace.
He is gone happy, and has left me rich.
Then, as in grateful virtue I am bound        5
To your free° heart, I do return those talents
Doubled with thanks and service, from whose help
I derived liberty.

TIMON          O by no means,
Honest Ventidius. You mistake my love;
I gave it freely ever, and there's none        10
Can truly say he gives, if he receives.
If our betters° play at that game, we must not dare
To imitate them; faults that are rich are fair.°

VENTIDIUS
A noble spirit.

TIMON
Nay, my lords, ceremony° was but devised at first   15

**279 unpeaceable** quarrelsome   **282 opposite to** (1) hostile to
(2) the reverse of   **286 meed** (1) merit, desert (2) gift (?)   **289
All . . . quittance** all the customary returns made in repayment of debts (one meaning of "use" is "interest"); **carries**
bears
**I.ii.s.d. Hautboys** oboes; **the States** persons of state, the
senators   **6 free** generous   **12 our betters** those of higher
rank   **13 faults . . . fair** the faults of rich persons are made to
seem attractive because of their wealth   **15 ceremony** ceremonious attitudes

**238 no . . . lord** no more wit in my anger than to wish
to be a lord (?)   **241 Traffic** trade, business   **247 horse**
horsemen   **248 All of companionship** all of the same party
**252 of your sights** at the sight of you   **254 Their** of Alcibiades
and his soldiers; **aches** the reference is probably to venereal
disease—"aches" is dissyllabic, pronounced "aitches"; **starve**
destroy   **258 saved** anticipated and so prevented   **264 still**
always   **266 omit'st** neglects

To set a gloss on faint deeds, hollow welcomes,
Recanting goodness, sorry ere 'tis shown.
But where there is true friendship, there needs none.
Pray sit; more welcome are ye to my fortunes
Than my fortunes to me. 20

FIRST LORD
My lord, we always have confessed it.°

APEMANTUS
Ho, ho, confessed it? Hanged it,° have you not?

TIMON
O Apemantus, you are welcome.

APEMANTUS
No, you shall not make me welcome.
I come to have thee thrust me out of doors. 25

TIMON
Fie, th' art a churl, y' have got a humor° there
Does not become a man; 'tis much to blame.
They say, my lords, Ira furor brevis est,° but yond
man is ever angry. Go, let him have a table by himself,
for he does neither affect° company, nor is he fit for't 30
indeed.

APEMANTUS Let me stay at thine apperil,° Timon. I
come to observe, I give thee warning on't.

TIMON I take no heed of thee. Th' art an Athenian,
therefore welcome. I myself would have no power;° 35
prithee let my meat make thee silent.

APEMANTUS I scorn thy meat; 'twould choke me,
for I should ne'er flatter thee.° O you gods! What a
number of men eats Timon, and he sees 'em not! It
grieves me to see so many dip their meat in one man's 40
blood, and all the madness is, he cheers them up too.
I wonder men dare trust themselves with men.
Methinks they should invite them without knives:°
Good for their meat, and safer for their lives.
There's much example for't; the fellow that sits next 45
him, now parts bread with him, pledges the breath of
him in a divided draught,° is the readiest man to kill
him. 'T'as been proved. If I were a huge° man, I
should fear to drink at meals,
Lest they should spy my windpipe's dangerous notes;° 50
Great men should drink with harness° on their throats.

TIMON
My lord, in heart;° and let the health go round.

SECOND LORD
Let it flow this way, my good lord.

APEMANTUS Flow this way? A brave° fellow. He
keeps his tides° well. Those healths will make thee and 55
thy state° look ill, Timon.
Here's that which is too weak to be a sinner,
Honest water, which ne'er left man i' th' mire.

This and my food are equals, there's no odds;
Feasts° are too proud to give thanks to the gods. 60
*Apemantus' Grace.*
Immortal gods, I crave no pelf;°
I pray for no man but myself.
Grant I may never prove so fond°
To trust man on his oath or bond,
Or a harlot for her weeping, 65
Or a dog that seems a-sleeping,
Or a keeper° with my freedom,
Or my friends if I should need 'em.
Amen. So fall to't:
Rich men sin, and I eat root. 70

[*Eats and drinks.*]

Much good dich° thy good heart, Apemantus.

TIMON Captain Alcibiades, your heart's in the field
now.

ALCIBIADES My heart is ever at your service, my
lord. 75

TIMON You had rather be at a breakfast of° enemies
than a dinner of friends.

ALCIBIADES So° they were bleeding new, my lord,
there's no meat like 'em; I could wish my best friend
at such a feast. 80

APEMANTUS Would all those flatterers were thine
enemies then, that then thou mightst kill 'em—and
bid° me to 'em.

FIRST LORD Might we but have that happiness, my
lord, that you would once use our hearts,° whereby 85
we might express some part of our zeals, we should
think ourselves for ever perfect.°

TIMON O no doubt, my good friends, but the gods
themselves have provided that I shall have much help
from you: how had you been my friends else? Why 90
have you that charitable° title from° thousands, did
not you chiefly belong to my heart? I have told more
of you to myself than you can with modesty speak in
your own behalf; and thus far I confirm° you. O you
gods, think I, what need we have any friends, if we 95
should ne'er have need of 'em? They were the most
needless creatures living should we ne'er have use for
'em, and would most resemble sweet instruments hung
up in cases, that keeps their sounds to themselves. Why
I have often wished myself poorer that I might come 100
nearer° to you. We are born to do benefits; and what
better or properer can we call our own than the riches
of our friends? O what a precious comfort 'tis to have
so many like brothers commanding one another's
fortunes. O joy's e'en made away ere't can be born.° 105
Mine eyes cannot hold out water,° methinks. To forget their faults,° I drink to you.

---

22 **confessed . . . it** an allusion to the proverb "Confess and be hanged" 26 **humor** temperamental quirk (in the old physiological sense of the four humors) 28 **Ira . . . est** anger is a brief fury or madness (Horace, *Epistles*, I.ii.62) 30 **affect** (1) like (2) seek out 32 **apperil** peril 35 **no power** i.e., to force you to be silent 37–38 **'twould . . . thee** Apemantus would prefer to choke on Timon's meat than to flatter him 43 **knives** dinner guests customarily brought their own knives 47 **a divided draught** a drink from a cup that is passed around the table 48 **huge** important 50 **Lest . . . notes** lest men should cut my throat when my head is tilted backward (with additional allusion to the windpipe as a musical instrument, like a bagpipe) 51 **harness** armor 52 **My . . . heart** a toast 54 **brave** excellent 55 **tides** times (with play on the usual sense, linked to "flow") 56 **state** estate, fortune

60 **Feasts** i.e., those who give feasts 61 **pelf** possessions 63 **fond** foolish 67 **keeper** jailer 71 **dich** may it do (?) 76 **of** consisting of (but later in the sentence it means "with") 78 **So** provided that 83 **bid** invite 85 **use our hearts** i.e., make trial of the feelings in our hearts 87 **perfect** i.e., in our happiness in demonstrating our love for Timon 91 **charitable** loving, kindly; **from** from among 94 **confirm** sanction, corroborate (your claims as friends) 101 **nearer** (1) closer to your hearts (2) closer to your financial status 105 **e'en . . . born** our weeping for joy seems to destroy joy before it properly exists 106 **hold out water** keep out tears 107 **faults** defects

APEMANTUS  Thou weep'st to make them drink,° Timon.

SECOND LORD
Joy had the like conception° in our eyes,          110
And at that instant like a babe sprung up.°

APEMANTUS
Ho, ho! I laugh to think that babe a bastard.

THIRD LORD
I promise you, my lord, you moved me much.

APEMANTUS  Much.

*Sound tucket.°*

TIMON
What means that trump?

*Enter* SERVANT.

How now?          115

SERVANT  Please you, my lord, there are certain ladies most desirous of admittance.

TIMON  Ladies? What are their wills?

SERVANT  There comes with them a forerunner, my lord, which bears that office to signify their pleasures.°          120

TIMON  I pray let them be admitted.

*[Enter* CUPID.]

CUPID
Hail to thee, worthy Timon, and to all
That of his bounties taste. The five best senses
Acknowledge thee their patron, and come freely
To gratulate° thy plenteous bosom. Th' ear,          125
Taste, touch, all, pleased from thy table rise;
They only now come but to feast thine eyes.°

TIMON
They're welcome all; let 'em have kind admittance.
Music° make their welcome.          [*Exit* CUPID.]

FIRST LORD
You see, my lord, how ample y' are beloved.          130

*[Music.] Enter* CUPID, *with the masque*° *of* LADIES [*as*] Amazons,° *with lutes in their hands, dancing and playing.*

APEMANTUS
Hoy-day!°
What a sweep° of vanity comes this way.
They dance? They are madwomen.
Like° madness is the glory° of this life,
As this pomp shows to° a little oil and root.          135
We make ourselves fools to disport° ourselves,
And spend our flatteries to drink° those men

Upon whose age we void° it up again
With poisonous spite and envy.°
Who lives that's not depravèd or depraves?°          140
Who dies that bears not one spurn° to their graves
Of their friends' gift?°
I should fear those that dance before me now
Would one day stamp upon me. 'T'as been done.
Men shut their doors against a setting sun.          145

*The* LORDS *rise from table, with much adoring of*° TIMON, *and to show their loves, each single out an Amazon, and all dance, men with women, a lofty strain or two to the hautboys, and cease.*

TIMON
You have done our pleasures much grace, fair ladies,
Set a fair fashion on° our entertainment,
Which was not half so beautiful and kind.°
You have added worth unto't and luster,
And entertained me with mine own device.°          150
I am to thank you for't.

FIRST LADY
My lord, you take us even at the best.°

APEMANTUS  Faith, for the worst is filthy, and would not hold taking,° I doubt me.°

TIMON
Ladies, there is an idle banquet° attends you,          155
Please you to dispose yourselves.°

ALL LADIES
Most thankfully, my lord.
          *Exeunt* [CUPID *and* LADIES].

TIMON  Flavius.

FLAVIUS
My lord.

TIMON  The little casket bring me hither.

FLAVIUS
Yes, my lord. [*Aside.*] More jewels yet?          160
There is no crossing him in's humor,°
Else I should tell him well, i' faith I should,
When all's spent, he'd be crossed° then, and° he could.
'Tis pity bounty had not eyes behind,
That man might ne'er be wretched for his mind.°          165
          *Exit.*

FIRST LORD
Where be our men?

SERVANT
Here, my lord, in readiness.

SECOND LORD
Our horses.

*Enter* FLAVIUS [*with the casket*].

---

108 **to . . . drink** (1) to provide drink for them (they drink up your tears, and you and your estate, too) (2) to furnish a pretext for their carousing  110 **the like conception** a similar birth (i.e., accompanied with tears)  111 **like . . . up** i.e., the sight of Timon's joy immediately caused the birth of a like joy in the eyes of his friends  114 **s.d. tucket** a flourish on a trumpet  120 **pleasures** wishes  125 **gratulate** (1) greet (2) gratify, please  127 **but . . . eyes** only to appeal to the sense of sight, whereas at Timon's banquet all the senses were gratified  129 **Music** let music  130 **s.d. masque** an elaborate allegorical show or entertainment with emphasis on spectacle, music, and dance; **Amazons** legendary female warriors  131 **Hoy-day** exclamation of surprise  132 **sweep** in reference to the sweeping motion of the dancers  134 **Like** similar; **glory** vainglory  135 **to** compared to  136 **disport** amuse  137 **drink** drink the health of

138 **void** vomit  139 **envy** malice  140 **depravèd or depraves** slandered or a slanderer  141 **spurn** insult  142 **gift** giving  145 **s.d. adoring of** paying homage to  147 **Set . . . on** given a pleasant semblance to  148 **kind** gracious  150 **mine own device** suggests that Timon designed the masque or at least had the idea for it  152 **take . . . best** judge us in the most favorable and complimentary way  153–54 **would . . . taking** sexual "taking" is not possible because of rottenness caused by venereal disease  154 **doubt me** fear, suspect (reflexive)  155 **idle banquet** trifling dessert or light collation  156 **Please . . . yourselves** if you please to take your places  161 **no . . . humor** no thwarting him in his capricious disposition  163 **crossed** (1) thwarted (2) have his debts canceled ("crossed" off a list) (3) be given money (have his palm "crossed"); **and** if  165 **for his mind** for his generous inclinations

TIMON
O my friends,
I have one word to say to you. Look you, my good
    lord,                                                            170
I must entreat you honor me so much
As to advance° this jewel; accept it and wear it,
Kind my lord.

FIRST LORD
I am so far already in your gifts—

ALL
So are we all.                                                       175

*Enter a* SERVANT.

SERVANT My lord, there are certain nobles of the
Senate newly alighted, and come to visit you.

TIMON They are fairly° welcome.

FLAVIUS I beseech your honor, vouchsafe me a word;
it does concern you near.                                           180

TIMON Near? Why then another time I'll hear thee.
I prithee let's be provided to show them entertainment.

FLAVIUS [*Aside.*] I scarce know how.

*Enter another* SERVANT.

SECOND SERVANT
May it please your honor, Lord Lucius,
Out of his free love, hath presented to you                         185
Four milk-white horses, trapped in silver.°

TIMON
I shall accept them fairly. Let the presents
Be worthily entertained.°

*Enter a* THIRD SERVANT.

                            How now? What news?

THIRD SERVANT Please you, my lord, that honorable gentleman Lord Lucullus entreats your company   190
tomorrow to hunt with him, and has sent your honor
two brace° of greyhounds.

TIMON
I'll hunt with him, and let them be received
Not without fair reward.

FLAVIUS              [*Aside.*] What will this come to?
He commands us to provide, and give great gifts,   195
And all out of an empty coffer;
Nor will he know his purse, or yield° me this,
To show him what a beggar his heart is,
Being of no power to make his wishes good.
His promises fly so beyond his state°                                200
That what he speaks is all in debt; he owes for ev'ry
    word.
He is so kind that he now pays interest for't;
His land's put to their books.° Well, would I were
Gently put out of office before I were forced out.
Happier is he that has no friend to feed                             205
Than such that do e'en enemies exceed.°
I bleed inwardly for my lord.                       *Exit.*

TIMON
You do yourselves much wrong,

You bate° too much of your own merits.
Here, my lord, a trifle of our love.                                 210

SECOND LORD
With more than common thanks I will receive it.

THIRD LORD
O he's the very soul of bounty.

TIMON And now I remember, my lord, you gave
good words the other day of a bay courser° I rode on.
'Tis yours because you liked it.                                     215

FIRST LORD
O I beseech you pardon me, my lord, in that.°

TIMON You may take my word, my lord, I know no
man can justly praise but what he does affect.° I weigh°
my friend's affection with° mine own. I'll tell you true,
I'll call to you.°                                                   220

ALL LORDS
O none so welcome.

TIMON
I take all and your several° visitations
So kind to heart, 'tis not enough to give.°
Methinks I could deal° kingdoms to my friends,
And ne'er be weary. Alcibiades,                                      225
Thou art a soldier, therefore seldom rich;
It° comes in charity to thee, for all thy living°
Is 'mongst the dead, and all the lands thou hast
Lie in a pitched field.°

ALCIBIADES
Ay, defiled° land, my lord.                                          230

FIRST LORD
We are so virtuously bound—

TIMON
And so am I to you.

SECOND LORD
So infinitely endeared°—

TIMON
All to you.° Lights, more lights!

FIRST LORD
The best of happiness, honor, and fortunes                           235
Keep with you, Lord Timon.

TIMON
Ready for his friends.                          *Exeunt* LORDS.

APEMANTUS                       What a coil's° here,
Serving of becks° and jutting out of bums!°
I doubt whether their legs° be worth the sums
That are given for 'em. Friendship's full of dregs;                  240
Methinks false hearts should never have sound legs.°
Thus honest fools lay out their wealth on curtsies.°

---

172 **advance** enhance in value (by your wearing it)   178
**fairly** courteously   186 **trapped in silver** with harness
coverings adorned in silver   188 **worthily entertained**
appropriately received   192 **two brace** two pairs   197 **yield**
grant   200 **state** estate, possessions   203 **put . . . books**
mortgaged (entered on creditors' account books)   206 **Than
. . . exceed** (1) than such a number that surpasses the
number of one's enemies (2) than such sort of friends whose
demands go beyond those of one's enemies

209 **bate** abate, undervalue   214 **bay courser** reddish-brown
stallion   216 **in that** in accepting your gift (because I
seemed to solicit it)   218 **affect** like, desire to possess;
**weigh** consider   219 **with** equal with   219–20 **I'll tell . . . you**
I assure you I will call on you   222 **all . . . several** the sum
total (an intensive form)   223 **'tis . . . give** mere gifts, no
matter how great, cannot truly express the feeling in my heart
224 **deal** distribute   227 **It** what you receive, a gift; **living**
(1) existence (2) property (3) livelihood   229 **pitched field**
field prepared for a battle   230 **defiled land** a quibble on the
proverb, "He that toucheth pitch shall be defiled," *Ecclesiasticus*
13:1   233 **endeared** indebted   234 **All to you** I am all these
things to you rather than vice versa   237 **coil** fuss, bustle,
confusion   238 **Serving of becks** offering of nods or
curtsies; **bums** posteriors   239 **legs** (1) bows (cf. "to make
a leg") (2) the limbs themselves   241 **sound legs** legs healthy
enough to make obeisances   242 **curtsies** (1) bows (2)
courtesies (a different spelling of the same word)

TIMON
Now Apemantus, if thou wert not sullen,
I would be good to thee.
APEMANTUS  No, I'll nothing; for if I should be 245
bribed too, there would be none left to rail upon° thee,
and then thou wouldst sin the faster. Thou giv'st so
long, Timon, I fear me thou wilt give away thyself in
paper° shortly. What needs these feasts, pomps, and
vainglories? 250
TIMON  Nay, and you begin to rail on society once, I
am sworn not to give regard to you. Farewell, and
come with better music. _Exit._
APEMANTUS  So. Thou wilt not hear me now, thou
shalt not then.° 255
I'll lock thy heaven° from thee.
O that men's ears should be
To counsel deaf, but not to flattery. _Exit._

## [ACT II]

### [Scene I. _A senator's house._]

_Enter a_ SENATOR.

SENATOR
And late° five thousand. To Varro and to Isidore
He owes nine thousand, besides my former sum,
Which makes it five and twenty. Still° in motion
Of raging waste? It cannot hold,° it will not.
If I want gold, steal but a beggar's dog 5
And give it Timon—why the dog coins gold.
If I would sell my horse and buy twenty moe
Better than he—why give my horse to Timon;
Ask nothing, give it him, it foals me straight,°
And able horses. No porter° at his gate, 10
But rather one that smiles, and still invites
All that pass by. It cannot hold; no reason
Can sound his state in safety.° Caphis, ho!
Caphis, I say!

_Enter_ CAPHIS.

CAPHIS          Here, sir, what is your pleasure?
SENATOR
Get on your cloak, and haste you to Lord Timon; 15
Importune him for my moneys; be not ceased
With slight denial; nor then silenced when
"Commend me to your master" and the cap
Plays in the right hand, thus°—but tell him,
My uses° cry to me; I must serve my turn 20
Out of mine own;° his days and times° are past,

And my reliances on his fracted° dates
Have smit my credit. I love and honor him,
But must not break my back to heal his finger.
Immediate are my needs, and my relief 25
Must not be tossed and turned to me in words,
But find supply immediate. Get you gone;
Put on a most importunate aspect,°
A visage of demand; for I do fear,
When every feather sticks in his own wing,° 30
Lord Timon will be left a naked gull,°
Which flashes now a phoenix.° Get you gone.
CAPHIS
I go, sir.
SENATOR
Ay, go sir! Take the bonds along with you,
And have the dates in.° Come!
CAPHIS                    I will, sir.
SENATOR                         Go! _Exeunt._ 35

### [Scene II. _Timon's house._]

_Enter_ [FLAVIUS, the] _steward, with many bills in his hand._

FLAVIUS
No care, no stop, so senseless of expense
That he will neither know how to maintain it,
Nor cease his flow of riot.° Takes no accompt
How things go from him, nor resumes no care°
Of what is to continue. Never mind 5
Was to be so unwise to be so kind.°
What shall be done he will not hear, till feel.
I must be round° with him, now he comes from
   hunting.
Fie, fie, fie, fie!

_Enter_ CAPHIS, [_with the_ SERVANTS _of_] _Isidore and Varro._

CAPHIS
Good even, Varro. What, you come for money? 10
VARRO'S SERVANT
Is't not your business too?
CAPHIS
It is; and yours too, Isidore?
ISIDORE'S SERVANT  It is so.
CAPHIS
Would we were all discharged.°
VARRO'S SERVANT  I fear it.° 15
CAPHIS
Here comes the lord.

_Enter_ TIMON _and his_ TRAIN, [_and_ ALCIBIADES].

TIMON
So soon as dinner's done, we'll forth again,

**246 rail upon** revile **248–49 in paper** in promissory notes and other paper records of debts **254–55 thou . . . then** you will not be able to listen to me later, when you are bankrupt **256 thy heaven** i.e., the advice by which I might have saved you from ruin
**II.i.1 late** lately **3 Still** always **4 hold** last **9 straight** immediately **10 No porter** because a porter's function is to keep out undesirable persons **12–13 no . . . safety** because Timon is insolvent, no reasonable person can safely fathom or test his estate ("sound" in its nautical sense) **18–19 "Commend . . . thus** examples of anticipated ceremonious delays by Timon **20 uses** financial needs **21 mine own** my own money; **days and times** due dates of his debts

**22 fracted** broken **28 aspect** accented on second syllable **30 sticks . . . wing** is returned to the bird to which it belongs (i.e., when Timon's debts, and the security he has given for them, are settled) **31 gull** (1) unfledged bird (2) credulous dupe **32 phoenix** a rare legendary bird which immolated itself and was reborn from its own ashes; a unique or matchless person **35 have . . . in** put in the exact dates when the bonds fall due **II.ii.3 riot** extravagance, irresponsible reveling **4 resumes no care** has no concern **6 to . . . kind** (1) as to be so generous (2) in order to be so generous **8 round** blunt **14 discharged** paid (of a debt) **15 I fear it** I doubt it

My Alcibiades. [*To* CAPHIS.] With me, what is your
will?

CAPHIS
My lord, here is a note of certain dues.

TIMON
Dues? Whence are you?

CAPHIS                         Of Athens here, my lord.      20

TIMON
Go to my steward.

CAPHIS
Please it your lordship, he hath put me off
To the succession of new days° this month.
My master is awaked by great occasion
To call upon his own, and humbly prays you      25
That with your other noble parts you'll suit°
In giving him his right.

TIMON                         Mine honest friend,
I prithee but repair° to me next morning.

CAPHIS
Nay, good my lord—

TIMON                         Contain thyself, good friend.

VARRO'S SERVANT
One Varro's servant, my good lord—              30

ISIDORE'S SERVANT   From Isidore; he humbly prays
your speedy payment.

CAPHIS   If you did know, my lord, my master's
wants—

VARRO'S SERVANT   'Twas due on° forfeiture, my      35
lord, six weeks and past.

ISIDORE'S SERVANT   Your steward puts me off, my
lord, and I am sent expressly to your lordship.

TIMON
Give me breath.
I do beseech you, good my lords, keep on;°      40
I'll wait upon you instantly.
                 [*Exeunt* ALCIBIADES *and* LORDS.]
                 [*To* FLAVIUS.] Come hither. Pray you,
How goes the world,° that I am thus encount'red
With clamorous demands of broken bonds,
And the detention° of long since due debts
Against my honor?

FLAVIUS                         Please you, gentlemen,      45
The time is unagreeable to this business.
Your importunacy° cease till after dinner,
That I may make his lordship understand
Wherefore you are not paid.

TIMON
Do so, my friends. See them well entertained.      *Exit.* 50

FLAVIUS
Pray draw near.                              [*Exit.*]

*Enter* APEMANTUS *and* FOOL.

CAPHIS
Stay, stay, here comes the fool with Apemantus.
Let's ha' some sport with 'em.

VARRO'S SERVANT   Hang him, he'll abuse us.

ISIDORE'S SERVANT   A plague upon him, dog!      55

VARRO'S SERVANT   How dost, fool?

APEMANTUS   Dost dialogue with thy shadow?

VARRO'S SERVANT   I speak not to thee.

APEMANTUS   No, 'tis to thyself. [*To the* FOOL.] Come
away.                                        60

ISIDORE'S SERVANT   [*To* VARRO'S SERVANT.]
There's the fool hangs on your back already.

APEMANTUS   No, thou stand'st single,° th' art not on
him yet.

CAPHIS   Where's the fool now?

APEMANTUS   He last asked the question. Poor rogues      65
and usurers' men, bawds between gold and want.

ALL SERVANTS   What are we, Apemantus?

APEMANTUS   Asses.

ALL SERVANTS   Why?

APEMANTUS   That you ask me what you are, and do      70
not know yourselves. Speak to 'em, fool.

FOOL   How do you, gentlemen?

ALL SERVANTS   Gramercies,° good fool. How does
your mistress?

FOOL   She's e'en setting on water to scald° such chick-      75
ens as you are. Would we could see you at Corinth.°

APEMANTUS   Good, gramercy.

*Enter* PAGE.

FOOL   Look you, here comes my mistress' page.

PAGE [*To the* FOOL.]   Why, how now, captain? What
do you in this wise company? How dost thou,      80
Apemantus?

APEMANTUS   Would I had a rod° in my mouth, that
I might answer thee profitably.°

PAGE   Prithee, Apemantus, read me the superscrip-
tion° of these letters. I know not which is which.      85

APEMANTUS   Canst not read?

PAGE   No.

APEMANTUS   There will little learning die then that
day thou art hanged. This is to Lord Timon, this to
Alcibiades. Go, thou wast born a bastard, and thou'lt      90
die a bawd.

PAGE   Thou wast whelped a dog, and thou shalt
famish a dog's death.° Answer not, I am gone.   *Exit.*

APEMANTUS   E'en so thou outrun'st grace.° Fool, I
will go with you to Lord Timon's.              95

FOOL   Will you leave me there?

APEMANTUS   If Timon stay at home. You three serve
three usurers?

ALL SERVANTS   Ay; would they served us.

APEMANTUS   So would I—as good a trick as ever      100
hangman served thief.

FOOL   Are you three usurers' men?

ALL SERVANTS   Ay, fool.

FOOL   I think no usurer but has a fool to his servant.
My mistress is one, and I am her fool. When men      105
come to borrow of your masters, they approach sadly,°

---

23 To . . . days from one day to the next   26 That . . . suit
that you will act in accordance with your other noble qualities
28 repair return   35 on on penalty of   40 keep on go ahead
42 How . . . world what is going on   44 detention withholding payment   47 importunacy urgent solicitation

62 single alone   73 Gramercies thanks   75 scald a method
of removing feathers from chickens (with suggestions of
loss of hair in venereal disease, and of sweating in a heated
tub, which was one of the treatments of venereal disease)   76
Corinth ancient city noted for licentiousness (hence a cant
term for brothel or red-light district)   82 rod stick to beat
you with   83 profitably for your profit or improvement
84–85 superscription address   93 famish . . . death die
by famishing, a mean death appropriate for a dog   94
E'en . . . grace By leaving now and not listening to my profitable answer, you will never receive grace   106 sadly gravely

and go away merry; but they enter my mistress' house merrily, and go away sadly. The reason of this?

VARRO'S SERVANT   I could render one.

APEMANTUS   Do it then, that we may account thee a 110 whoremaster and a knave, which notwithstanding, thou shalt be no less esteemed.

VARRO'S SERVANT   What is a whoremaster, fool?

FOOL   A fool in good clothes, and something like thee. 'Tis a spirit; sometime't appears like a lord, 115 sometime like a lawyer, sometime like a philosopher, with two stones° moe than's artificial one.° He is very often like a knight; and generally, in all shapes that man goes up and down in, from fourscore to thirteen, this spirit walks in. 120

VARRO'S SERVANT   Thou are not altogether a fool.

FOOL   Nor thou altogether a wise man. As much foolery as I have, so much wit thou lack'st.

APEMANTUS   That answer might have become Apemantus. 125

*Enter* TIMON *and* [FLAVIUS, *the*] *steward.*

ALL SERVANTS   Aside, aside, here comes Lord Timon.

APEMANTUS   Come with me, fool, come.

FOOL   I do not always follow lover, elder brother, and woman;° sometime the philosopher.

FLAVIUS
Pray you, walk near: I'll speak with you anon.° 130
        *Exeunt* [APEMANTUS, FOOL, *and* SERVANTS].

TIMON
You make me marvel wherefore ere this time
Had you not fully laid my state° before me,
That I might so have rated° my expense
As I had leave of means.°

FLAVIUS                           You would not hear me.
At many leisures° I proposed—

TIMON                           Go to.° 135
Perchance some single vantages° you took
When my indisposition° put you back,
And that unaptness° made your minister°
Thus to excuse yourself.

FLAVIUS                    O my good lord,
At many times I brought in my accompts, 140
Laid them before you; you would throw them off,
And say you found them in mine honesty.
When for some trifling present you have bid me
Return so much, I have shook my head and wept;
Yea 'gainst th' authority of manners,° prayed you 145
To hold your hand more close. I did endure
Not seldom, nor so slight checks,° when I have
Prompted° you in the ebb of your estate
And your great flow of debts. My loved lord,
Though you hear now, too late, yet now's a time: 150

The greatest of your having° lacks a half
To pay your present debts.

TIMON                    Let all my land be sold.

FLAVIUS
'Tis all engaged,° some forfeited and gone,
And what remains will hardly stop the mouth
Of present dues. The future comes apace.° 155
What shall defend the interim? And at length
How goes our reck'ning?

TIMON
To Lacedaemon did my land extend.

FLAVIUS
O my good lord, the world is but a word;
Were it all yours to give it in a breath, 160
How quickly were it gone!

TIMON                    You tell me true.

FLAVIUS
If you suspect my husbandry or falsehood,°
Call me before th' exactest auditors,
And set me on° the proof. So the gods bless me,
When all our offices° have been oppressed° 165
With riotous feeders,° when our vaults° have wept
With drunken spilth° of wine, when every room
Hath blazed with lights and brayed with minstrelsy,
I have retired me to a wasteful cock,°
And set mine eyes at flow.°

TIMON                    Prithee no more. 170

FLAVIUS
Heavens, have I said, the bounty of this lord!
How many prodigal bits° have slaves and peasants
This night englutted!° Who is not Timon's?
What heart, head, sword, force, means, but is Lord
    Timon's?
Great Timon, noble, worthy, royal Timon! 175
Ah, when the means are gone that buy this praise,
The breath is gone whereof this praise is made.
Feast-won, fast-lost;° one cloud of winter show'rs,
These flies are couched.°

TIMON                    Come, sermon me no further.
No villainous bounty° yet hath passed my heart; 180
Unwisely, not ignobly, have I given.
Why dost thou weep? Canst thou the conscience° lack
To think I shall lack friends? Secure° thy heart.
If I would broach the vessels° of my love,
And try the argument° of hearts by borrowing, 185
Men and men's fortunes could I frankly° use
As I can bid thee speak.

FLAVIUS                    Assurance° bless your thoughts.

151 greatest . . . having your worth estimated at the highest possible figure   153 engaged mortgaged   155 apace swiftly   162 suspect . . . falsehood suspect me of false husbandry or dishonest management   164 on to   165 offices service rooms of a household; oppressed crowded   166 feeders servants; vaults wine cellars   167 spilth spilling   169 wasteful cock spigot (of a wine cask) that has not been shut off   170 And . . . flow following the example of the "wasteful cock," I have added my tears to the general riot and superfluity   172 prodigal bits wasteful morsels   173 englutted gulped down   178 Feast-won, fast-lost The friendship that is won by giving feasts is quickly lost (with pun on *fast* as noun and adverb)   179 couched lying hidden   180 villainous bounty generosity for evil purposes   182 conscience reasonableness   183 Secure make free from care or apprehension   184 broach the vessels tap the casks   185 try the argument test the theme or contents   186 frankly freely   187 Assurance may assurance

117 stones testicles; artificial one philosopher's stone (a highly refined substance which could turn base metals into gold)   128–29 lover . . . woman persons who might be expected to be generous   130 anon soon   132 state financial situation   133 rated regulated   134 As . . . means as my means would allow   135 At many leisures when you were at leisure; Go to nonsense (an exclamation of impatience)   136 vantages opportunities   137 indisposition disinclination   138 unaptness unreadiness to listen; minister ministration, prompting   145 authority of manners the dictates of good manners   147 checks rebukes   148 Prompted in its theatrical sense

TIMON
And in some sort these wants of mine are crowned,°
That I account them blessings; for by these
Shall I try friends. You shall perceive how you          190
Mistake my fortunes; I am wealthy in my friends.
Within there! Flaminius! Servilius!

*Enter* [FLAMINIUS, SERVILIUS, *and* THIRD SERVANT].

SERVANTS  My lord, my lord.
TIMON  I will dispatch you severally.° [*To* SERVILIUS.]
You to Lord Lucius, [*to* FLAMINIUS] to Lord Lucullus  195
you; I hunted with his honor today. [*To* THIRD
SERVANT.] You to Sempronius. Commend me to
their loves; and I am proud, say, that my occasions°
have found time to use 'em toward a supply of money.
Let the request be fifty talents.          200
FLAMINIUS  As you have said, my lord.
                              [*Exeunt* SERVANTS.]
FLAVIUS [*Aside.*]  Lord Lucius and Lucullus? Humh!
TIMON
Go you, sir, to the senators,
Of whom, even to the state's best health,° I have
Deserved this hearing. Bid 'em send o' th' instant          205
A thousand talents to me.
FLAVIUS                              I have been bold,
For that I knew it the most general° way,
To them to use your signet° and your name;
But they do shake their heads, and I am here
No richer in return.
TIMON                    Is't true? Can't be?          210
FLAVIUS
They answer in a joint and corporate voice,
That now they are at fall,° want treasure, cannot
Do what they would, are sorry; you are honorable,
But yet they could have wished—they know not;
Something hath been amiss—a noble nature          215
May catch a wrench°—would all were well—'tis
     pity—
And so, intending° other serious matters,
After distasteful looks, and these hard fractions,°
With certain half-caps° and cold-moving° nods,
They froze me into silence.
TIMON                    You gods reward them!          220
Prithee man look cheerly. These old fellows
Have their ingratitude in them hereditary.
Their blood is caked, 'tis cold, it seldom flows;
'Tis lack of kindly° warmth they are not kind;
And nature, as it grows again toward earth,°          225
Is fashioned for the journey, dull and heavy.
Go to Ventidius. Prithee be not sad;
Thou art true and honest; ingeniously° I speak,
No blame belongs to thee. Ventidius lately

Buried his father, by whose death he's stepped          230
Into a great estate. When he was poor,
Imprisoned, and in scarcity of friends,
I cleared him with five talents. Greet him from me,
Bid him suppose some good necessity°
Touches his friend, which craves to be rememb'red          235
With those five talents. That had, give't these fellows
To whom 'tis instant° due. Nev'r speak or think
That Timon's fortunes 'mong° his friends can sink.
FLAVIUS
I would I could not think it; that thought is bounty's
     foe.
Being free° itself, it thinks all others so.          *Exeunt.*  240


# [ A C T   I I I ]

## [Scene I. *Lucullus' house.*]

FLAMINIUS *waiting to speak with Lord* [LUCULLUS]
*from his master, enters a* SERVANT *to him.*

SERVANT  I have told my lord of you; he is coming
down to you.
FLAMINIUS  I thank you, sir.

*Enter* LUCULLUS.

SERVANT  Here's my lord.
LUCULLUS [*Aside.*]  One of Lord Timon's men? A          5
gift I warrant. Why this hits right; I dreamt of a silver
basin and ewer tonight.°—Flaminius, honest Flaminius,
you are very respectively° welcome, sir. Fill me some
wine. [*Exit* SERVANT.] And how does that honorable,
complete,° free-hearted gentleman of Athens, thy very          10
bountiful good lord and master?
FLAMINIUS  His health is well, sir.
LUCULLUS  I am right glad that his health is well, sir.
And what hast thou there under thy cloak, pretty°
Flaminius?          15
FLAMINIUS  Faith, nothing but an empty box, sir,
which in my lord's behalf I come to entreat your
honor to supply;° who, having great and instant
occasion to use fifty talents, hath sent to your lordship
to furnish him, nothing doubting your present°          20
assistance therein.
LUCULLUS  La, la, la, la! "Nothing doubting," says
he? Alas, good lord, a noble gentleman 'tis, if he would
not keep so good a house.° Many a time and often I ha'
dined with him, and told him on't, and come again to          25
supper to him of purpose to have him spend less, and
yet he would embrace no counsel, take no warning by
my coming. Every man has his fault, and honesty° is
his. I ha' told him on't, but I could ne'er get him
from't.          30

*Enter* SERVANT *with wine.*

---

**188 crowned** given a royal dignity  **194 severally** separately
**198 occasions** needs  **204 even . . . health** i.e., Timon,
because of his own generosity to the state in the past, now
deserves a loan from them to the very outermost limit they
can pay (?)  **207 general** usual  **208 signet** signet ring (as
sign of authority to act)  **212 at fall** at ebb tide  **216
catch a wrench** accidentally be twisted from its natural
bent  **217 intending** pretending  **218 hard fractions** harsh
fragments of speech (conveyed in the broken syntax)  **219
half-caps** half-courteous salutations; **cold-moving** producing
cold, frigid  **224 kindly** (1) natural (2) generous  **225 grows
. . . earth** approaches death and the grave  **228 ingeniously**
ingenuously, candidly

**234 good necessity** valid need  **237 instant** instantly, immediately  **238 'mong** in the midst of  **240 free** bounteous
**III.i.7 tonight** last night  **8 respectively** respectfully  **10
complete** fully equipped or endowed, perfect  **14 pretty**
vague epithet of praise  **18 supply** fill  **20 present** immediate
**24 so . . . house** such lavish hospitality  **28 honesty**
generosity

SERVANT  Please your lordship, here is the wine.

LUCULLUS  Flaminius, I have noted thee always wise. Here's to thee.

FLAMINIUS  Your lordship speaks your pleasure.°

LUCULLUS  I have observed thee always for a towardly 35 prompt spirit,° give thee thy due, and one that knows what belongs to reason; and canst use the time well, if the time use thee well.° Good parts° in thee. [*To* SERVANT.] Get you gone, sirrah. [*Exit* SERVANT.] Draw nearer, honest Flaminius. Thy lord's a bountiful 40 gentleman, but thou art wise, and thou know'st well enough, although thou com'st to me, that this is no time to lend money, especially upon bare friendship without security. Here's three solidares° for thee. Good boy, wink° at me, and say thou saw'st me not. Fare 45 thee well.

FLAMINIUS
Is't possible the world should so much differ,°
And we alive that lived?° Fly, damnèd baseness,
To him that worships thee.

[*Throws back the money.*]

LUCULLUS  Ha? Now I see thou art a fool, and fit for 50 thy master.     *Exit.*

FLAMINIUS
May these° add to the number that may scald° thee.
Let molten coin be thy damnation,°
Thou disease of a friend, and not himself.
Has friendship such a faint and milky heart
It turns° in less than two nights? O you gods! 55
I feel my master's passion.° This slave
Unto his honor° has my lord's meat° in him;
Why should it thrive and turn to nutriment
When he is turned to poison?
O may diseases only work upon't, 60
And when he's sick to death, let not that part of nature°
Which my lord paid for be of any power
To expel sickness, but prolong his hour.°     *Exit.*

[*Scene II. A public place.*]

*Enter* LUCIUS, *with three* STRANGERS.°

LUCIUS  Who, the Lord Timon? He is my very good friend and an honorable gentleman.

FIRST STRANGER  We know him for no less, though we are but strangers to him. But I can tell you one thing, my lord, and which I hear from common 5 rumors: now Lord Timon's happy hours are done and past, and his estate shrinks from him.

LUCIUS  Fie, no, do not believe it; he cannot want for money.

SECOND STRANGER  But believe you this, my lord, 10 that not long ago, one of his men was with the Lord Lucullus to borrow so many talents,° nay urged extremely for't, and showed what necessity belonged to't, and yet was denied.

LUCIUS  How? 15

SECOND STRANGER  I tell you, denied, my lord.

LUCIUS  What a strange case was that! Now before the gods I am ashamed on't. Denied that honorable man? There was very little honor showed in't. For my own part, I must needs confess, I have received 20 some small kindnesses from him, as money, plate,° jewels, and suchlike trifles, nothing comparing to his;° yet had he mistook him° and sent to me, I should ne'er have denied his occasion° so many talents.

*Enter* SERVILIUS.

SERVILIUS  See, by good hap, yonder's my lord; I 25 have sweat to see his honor. My honored lord.

LUCIUS  Servilius? You are kindly met, sir. Fare thee well; commend me to thy honorable virtuous lord, my very exquisite friend.

SERVILIUS  May it please your honor, my lord hath 30 sent—

LUCIUS  Ha? What has he sent? I am so much endeared° to that lord; he's ever sending. How shall I thank him, think'st thou? And what has he sent now?

SERVILIUS  Has only sent his present occasion now, 35 my lord, requesting your lordship to supply his instant use with so many talents.

LUCIUS
I know his lordship is but merry with me,
He cannot want° fifty five hundred talents.°

SERVILIUS
But in the meantime he wants less, my lord. 40
If his occasion were not virtuous,
I should not urge it half so faithfully.

LUCIUS
Dost thou speak seriously, Servilius?

SERVILIUS
Upon my soul 'tis true, sir.

LUCIUS  What a wicked beast was I to disfurnish my- 45 self against° such a good time, when I might ha' shown myself honorable! How unluckily it happ'ned that I should purchase the day before for a little part,° and undo a great deal of honor!° Servilius, now before the gods I am not able to do—the more beast, I say! I 50 was sending to use Lord Timon myself, these gentlemen can witness; but I would not for the wealth of

---

34 **speaks your pleasure** is pleased to say so   35–36 **towardly prompt spirit** well-disposed and well-inclined person   37–38 **if . . . well** if you strike good fortune   38 **parts** qualities   44 **solidares** perhaps Shakespeare was referring to the Roman "solidus," which was used in England for a shilling   45 **wink** shut your eyes   47 **differ** change   48 **And . . . lived** i.e., the world changes so swiftly, it is hard to believe that the same people are still alive   52 **these** the rejected coins; **scald** i.e., in hell   53 **thy damnation** the torment you will suffer in hell (perhaps a reference to the pouring of molten gold down the throat of Marcus Crassus by the Parthians, thought of as a punishment in hell for avarice)   56 **turns** curdles   57 **passion** anger, suffering (trisyllabic)   57–58 **slave . . . honor** ironical: "this man who claims to be so devoted to honor"   58 **meat** food (in general, in contradistinction to "drink")   62 **that . . . nature** that part of his body nourished by Timon's food   64 **but . . . hour** may he have a lingering death   III.ii.s.d. **Strangers** foreigners, non-Athenians

12 **so many talents** an indefinite number probably intended to be replaced, in revision, by a definite number   21 **plate** utensils for domestic use, especially of gold or silver   22 **his** Lucullus'   23 **mistook him** made a mistake   24 **occasion** need   32–33 **endeared** indebted   39 **want** (1) be without, lack (2) need, desire; **fifty five hundred talents** a huge sum (see Introduction, p. 1367)   45–46 **disfurnish myself against** to allow myself to be unprovided for   48 **for . . . part** for a little business transaction (deliberately vague)   49 **undo . . . honor** lose the anticipated honor of lending to Timon

Athens I had done't now. Commend me bountifully
to his good lordship, and I hope his honor will conceive the fairest° of me, because I have no power to 55
be kind. And tell him this from me, I count it one of
my greatest afflictions, say, that I cannot pleasure such
an honorable gentleman. Good Servilius, will you
befriend me so far as to use mine own words to him?

SERVILIUS  Yes, sir, I shall.  60

LUCIUS
I'll look you out a good turn, Servilius.

*Exit* SERVILIUS.

True, as you said, Timon is shrunk indeed,
And he that's once denied will hardly speed.°  *Exit.*

FIRST STRANGER
Do you observe this, Hostilius?

SECOND STRANGER  Ay, too well.

FIRST STRANGER
Why this is the world's soul, and just of the same piece° 65
Is every flatterer's sport.° Who can call him his friend
That dips in the same dish? For in my knowing
Timon has been this lord's father,
And kept his° credit with his° purse;
Supported his estate; nay, Timon's money  70
Has paid his men their wages. He ne'er drinks
But Timon's silver treads° upon his lip,
And yet—O see the monstrousness of man
When he looks out in an ungrateful shape°—
He does deny him, in respect of his,°  75
What charitable men afford to beggars.

THIRD STRANGER
Religion groans at it.

FIRST STRANGER  For mine own part,
I never tasted° Timon in my life,
Nor came any of his bounties over me
To mark me for his friend. Yet I protest,  80
For his right° noble mind, illustrious virtue,
And honorable carriage,°
Had his necessity made use of me,
I would have put my wealth into donation,°
And the best half should have returned° to him,  85
So much I love his heart. But I perceive
Men must learn now with pity to dispense,
For policy° sits above conscience.  *Exeunt.*

[Scene III. *Sempronius' house.*]

*Enter a* THIRD SERVANT [*of Timon*], *with* SEMPRO-
NIUS, *another of Timon's friends.*

SEMPRONIUS
Must he needs trouble me in't—humh!—'bove all
others?
He might have tried Lord Lucius or Lucullus,

And now Ventidius is wealthy too,
Whom he redeemed from prison. All these
Owes their estates unto him.

THIRD SERVANT  My lord,  5
They have all been touched° and found base metal,
For they have all denied him.

SEMPRONIUS  How? Have they denied him?
Has Ventidius and Lucullus denied him,
And does he send to me? Three? Humh!
It shows but little love or judgment in him.  10
Must I be his last refuge? His friends, like physicians,
Thrive, give him over.° Must I take th' cure upon me?
Has much disgraced me in't; I'm angry at him
That might have known my place.° I see no sense for't,
But his occasions° might have wooed me first;  15
For, in my conscience, I was the first man
That e'er received gift from him.
And does he think so backwardly° of me now
That I'll requite it last? No.
So it may prove an argument° of laughter  20
To th' rest, and I 'mongst lords be thought a fool.
I'd rather than the worth of thrice the sum,
Had° sent to me first, but for my mind's sake;°
I'd such a courage° to do him good. But now return,
And with their faint reply this answer join:  25
Who bates° mine honor shall not know my coin.

*Exit.*

THIRD SERVANT  Excellent. Your lordship's a goodly
villain. The devil knew not what he did when he
made man politic;° he crossed himself by't;° and I
cannot think but in the end the villainies of man will  30
set him clear.° How fairly° this lord strives to appear
foul!° Takes virtuous copies to be wicked.° Like those°
that under hot ardent zeal would set whole realms on
fire, of such a nature is his politic love.
This was my lord's best hope; now all are fled  35
Save only the gods. Now his friends are dead,
Doors that were ne'er acquainted with their wards°
Many a bounteous year, must be employed
Now to guard sure° their master.
And this is all a liberal° course allows;  40
Who cannot keep his wealth must keep his house.°

*Exit.*

III.iii.6 **touched** tested (by being rubbed on a touchstone; unlike base metals, gold and silver produced the proper colored streak)  12 **Thrive . . . over** prosper on his money while they are giving him up for dead (?)  14 **my place** i.e., before Lucullus, Lucius, and Ventidius  15 **occasions** needs  18 **backwardly** (1) poorly (2) near the end, late  20 **argument** occasion, subject  23 **Had** he had (perhaps "H'ad"?); **but . . . sake** if only to express my good will toward him  24 **courage** desire  26 **bates** abates, undervalues  29 **politic** cunning; **he . . . by't** the devil thwarted his own purposes by making man his rival in shrewdness and guile  30–31 **will . . . clear** will make the devil appear innocent (when compared with the "villainies of man")  31 **How fairly** with what a beautiful appearance  32 **foul** ugly; **Takes . . . wicked** models himself on exemplars of virtue to serve as disguise for his wickedness; **those** religious fanatics (perhaps "zeal" suggests an allusion to Puritans)  37 **wards** locks  39 **sure** securely  40 **liberal** generous  41 **keep his house** remain at home (for fear of being arrested for debt)

54–55 **conceive the fairest** think the best  63 **speed** be successful, prosper  65 **piece** sort, kind  66 **sport** mockery, diversion (as Lucius has just made sport of Timon)  69 **kept his** sustained Lucius'; **his** Timon's  72 **treads** presses  74 **shape** form  75 **in . . . his** in relation to what Lucius is worth  78 **tasted** experienced the qualities of  81 **right** very  82 **carriage** moral conduct  84 **put . . . donation** treated my fortune as a gift from Timon  85 **returned** been given back  88 **policy** cunning

[Scene IV. *Timon's house.*]

*Enter Varro's* [*two* SERVANTS], *meeting others. All* [*the* SERVANTS *of*] *Timon's creditors to wait for his coming out. Then enter* [*the* SERVANT *of*] *Lucius;* [*then* TITUS] *and* HORTENSIUS.

VARRO'S FIRST SERVANT
Well met; good morrow, Titus and Hortensius.
TITUS
The like to you, kind Varro.
HORTENSIUS                              Lucius!
What, do we meet together?
LUCIUS' SERVANT                    Ay, and I think
One business does command us all;
For mine is money.
TITUS                    So is theirs and ours.                    5

*Enter* PHILOTUS.

LUCIUS' SERVANT
And, sir, Philotus' too!
PHILOTUS                    Good day at once.°
LUCIUS' SERVANT
Welcome, good brother. What do you think the hour?
PHILOTUS
Laboring for nine.
LUCIUS' SERVANT
So much?
PHILOTUS    Is not my lord seen yet?
LUCIUS' SERVANT                    Not yet.
PHILOTUS
I wonder on't; he was wont to shine at seven.    10
LUCIUS' SERVANT
Ay, but the days are waxed° shorter with him.
You must consider that a prodigal course
Is like the sun's,
But not like his recoverable,° I fear.
'Tis deepest winter in Lord Timon's purse;    15
That is, one may reach deep enough and yet
Find little.
PHILOTUS    I am of your fear for that.
TITUS
I'll show you how t' observe° a strange event.
Your lord sends now for money?
HORTENSIUS                    Most true, he does.
TITUS
And he wears jewels now of Timon's gift,    20
For which I wait for money.
HORTENSIUS
It is against my heart.°
LUCIUS' SERVANT    Mark how strange it shows,
Timon in this should pay more than he owes;°
And e'en as if your lord should wear rich jewels
And send for money for 'em.    25
HORTENSIUS
I'm weary of this charge,° the gods can witness.
I know my lord hath spent of Timon's wealth,
And now ingratitude makes it worse than stealth.°

VARRO'S FIRST SERVANT
Yes, mine's three thousand crowns. What's yours?
LUCIUS' SERVANT
Five thousand mine.    30
VARRO'S FIRST SERVANT
'Tis much deep, and it should seem by th' sum
Your master's confidence° was above mine,°
Else surely his had equaled.

*Enter* FLAMINIUS.

TITUS    One of Lord Timon's men.
LUCIUS' SERVANT    Flaminius? Sir, a word. Pray is    35
my lord ready to come forth?
FLAMINIUS    No, indeed he is not.
TITUS    We attend his lordship; pray signify so much.
FLAMINIUS    I need not tell him that; he knows you
are too diligent.                    [*Exit.*]    40

*Enter* [FLAVIUS, *the*] *steward, in a cloak, muffled.*°

LUCIUS' SERVANT
Ha! Is not that his steward muffled so?
He goes away in a cloud.° Call him, call him.
TITUS    Do you hear, sir?
VARRO'S SECOND SERVANT    By your leave, sir.
FLAVIUS
What do ye ask of me, my friend?    45
TITUS
We wait for certain money here, sir.
FLAVIUS                    Ay,
If money were as certain as your waiting,
'Twere sure enough.
Why then preferred° you not your sums and bills
When your false masters ate of my lord's meat?    50
Then they could smile, and fawn upon° his debts,
And take down th' int'rest° into their glutt'nous maws.
You do yourselves but wrong to stir me up;
Let me pass quietly.
Believe't, my lord and I have made an end;    55
I have no more to reckon,° he to spend.
LUCIUS' SERVANT
Ay, but this answer will not serve.
FLAVIUS
If 'twill not serve, 'tis not so base as you,
For you serve knaves.                    [*Exit.*]
VARRO'S FIRST SERVANT    How? What does his    60
cashiered° worship mutter?
VARRO'S SECOND SERVANT    No matter what; he's
poor, and that's revenge enough. Who can speak
broader° than he that has no house to put his head in?
Such may rail against great buildings.    65

*Enter* SERVILIUS.

TITUS    O here's Servilius. Now we shall know some
answer.
SERVILIUS    If I might beseech you, gentlemen, to re-
pair° some other hour, I should derive much from't.

---

III.iv.6 **at once** to you all    11 **waxed** grown    12–14 **pro-**
**digal . . . recoverable** the prodigal, like the sun, declines,
but cannot renew himself every day    18 **observe** observe and
interpret    22 **against my heart** contrary to my natural feeling
23 **should . . . owes** he has given the gifts, and now he is
also asked for the money for them    26 **charge** task    28 **stealth**
stealing

32 **confidence** trust; **mine** my master's    40 s.d. **muffled**
wrapped up, especially about the face    42 **in a cloud** (1) in a
state of gloominess and concern (2) covered with a cloud
because he is muffled    49 **preferred** proffered, presented    51
**fawn upon** seek favor by servility (used especially of dogs)
52 **th' int'rest** i.e., what they ate was equivalent to the interest
due on the money owed them by Timon    56 **reckon** keep
account of    61 **cashiered** dismissed from employment    64
**broader** more critically    68–69 **repair** come

For take't of my soul,° my lord leans wondrously to 70
discontent. His comfortable° temper has forsook him,
he's much out of health, and keeps his chamber.
LUCIUS' SERVANT
Many do keep their chambers are not sick;
And if it be so far beyond his health,
Methinks he should the sooner pay his debts, 75
And make a clear° way to the gods.
SERVILIUS                                    Good gods!
TITUS
We cannot take this for answer, sir.
FLAMINIUS (*Within.*)
Servilius, help! My lord, my lord!

*Enter* TIMON *in a rage.*

TIMON
What, are my doors opposed against my passage?
Have I been ever free,° and must my house 80
Be my retentive° enemy? My jail?
The place which I have feasted,° does it now,
Like all mankind, show me an iron heart?
LUCIUS' SERVANT  Put in° now, Titus.
TITUS  My lord, here is my bill. 85
LUCIUS' SERVANT  Here's mine.
HORTENSIUS  And mine, my lord.
BOTH VARRO'S SERVANTS  And ours, my lord.
PHILOTUS  All our bills.
TIMON
Knock me down with 'em, cleave me to the girdle.° 90
LUCIUS' SERVANT  Alas, my lord—
TIMON  Cut my heart in sums.°
TITUS  Mine, fifty talents.
TIMON  Tell out° my blood.
LUCIUS' SERVANT  Five thousand crowns, my lord. 95
TIMON
Five thousand drops pays that. What yours? And
    yours?
VARRO'S FIRST SERVANT  My lord—
VARRO'S SECOND SERVANT  My lord—
TIMON  Tear me, take me, and the gods fall upon you.
                                            *Exit* TIMON.
HORTENSIUS  Faith, I perceive our masters may throw 100
their caps at their money;° these debts may well be
called desperate° ones, for a madman owes 'em.
                                            *Exeunt.*

*Enter* TIMON [*and* FLAVIUS].

TIMON
They have e'en put my breath from me,° the slaves.
Creditors? Devils!

FLAVIUS  My dear lord— 105
TIMON  What if it should be so?
FLAVIUS  My lord—
TIMON  I'll have it so. My steward!
FLAVIUS  Here, my lord.
TIMON
So fitly?° Go, bid° all my friends again, 110
Lucius, Lucullus, and Sempronius—all.
I'll once more feast the rascals.
FLAVIUS                              O my lord,
You only speak from your distracted soul;
There's not so much left to furnish out
A moderate table.
TIMON              Be it not in thy care.° 115
Go, I charge thee, invite them all, let in the tide
Of knaves once more; my cook and I'll provide.
                                            *Exeunt.*

[Scene V. *The Senate House.*]

*Enter three* SENATORS *at one door,* ALCIBIADES *meeting
them with* ATTENDANTS.

FIRST SENATOR
My lord, you have my voice° to't. The fault's
Bloody; 'tis necessary he should die.
Nothing emboldens sin so much as mercy.
SECOND SENATOR
Most true; the law shall bruise 'em.°
ALCIBIADES
Honor, health, and compassion to the Senate. 5
FIRST SENATOR
Now, captain?
ALCIBIADES
I am an humble suitor to your virtues;
For pity is the virtue° of the law,
And none but tyrants use it cruelly.
It pleases time and fortune to lie heavy 10
Upon a friend of mine, who in hot blood
Hath stepped into the law;° which is past depth°
To those that, without heed, do plunge into't.
He is a man, setting his fate° aside,
Of comely virtues; 15
Nor did he soil the fact° with cowardice
(An honor in him which buys out° his fault),
But with a noble fury and fair° spirit,
Seeing his reputation touched to death,
He did oppose his foe; 20
And with such sober and unnoted° passion
He did behove° his anger, ere 'twas spent,
As if he had but proved an argument.°
FIRST SENATOR
You undergo too strict a paradox,°

70 take't . . . soul from my heart (i.e., sincerely)  71 comfortable cheerful  76 clear (1) free from debt (2) innocent, unstained (because he has paid his debts) (3) untrammeled, without the obstacle of debts  80 free (1) generous (2) unrestrained  81 retentive confining  82 place . . . feasted the house itself in which I have given feasts  84 Put in i.e., put in your claim for money  90 Knock . . . girdle Timon chooses to understand "bills" not as "accounts of money due," but as "weapons"—a bill had a long wooden handle with a blade or ax-shaped head at one end, and it was capable of cutting a man through to the belt  92 in sums into sums of money  94 Tell out count out  100–01 may throw . . . money may give up their money for lost  102 desperate beyond hope of recovery (cf. "sperate," recoverable)  103 put . . . me put me out of breath

110 fitly conveniently; bid invite  115 Be . . . care Let the feast be my concern
III.v.1 voice vote  4 bruise 'em crush them (possibly sinners or wrongdoers in general?)  8 virtue characteristic excellence  12 stepped . . . law done something to bring him within the jurisdiction of the law; past depth beyond any measurable depth  14 his fate this one fateful action of his  16 soil the fact sully the deed  17 buys out redeems  18 fair excellent  21 unnoted not notable, i.e., calm  22 behove control  23 argument i.e., a *point d'honneur* rather than a personal passion  24 undergo . . . paradox attempt to argue a position that is excessively paradoxical

Striving to make an ugly deed look fair.                          25
Your words have took such pains as if they labored
To bring manslaughter into form,° and set
Quarreling upon the head of valor, which indeed
Is valor misbegot, and came into the world
When sects and factions° were newly born.          30
He's truly valiant that can wisely suffer
The worst that man can breathe,°
And make his wrongs his outsides,°
To wear them like his raiment, carelessly,
And ne'er prefer° his injuries to his heart,          35
To bring it into danger.
If wrongs be evils and enforce us kill,
What folly 'tis to hazard life for ill.

ALCIBIADES    My lord—

FIRST SENATOR
You cannot make gross sins look clear.°          40
To revenge is no valor, but to bear.°

ALCIBIADES
My lords, then, under favor,° pardon me,
If I speak like a captain.
Why do fond° men expose themselves to battle,
And not endure all threats? Sleep upon't,          45
And let the foes quietly cut their throats
Without repugnancy?° If there be
Such valor in the bearing, what make we
Abroad?° Why then, women are more valiant
That stay at home, if bearing° carry it,°          50
And the ass more captain than the lion, the fellow
Loaden with irons wiser than the judge,
If wisdom be in suffering. O my lords,
As you are great, be pitifully good.°
Who cannot condemn rashness in cold blood?          55
To kill, I grant, is sin's extremest gust,°
But in defense, by mercy,° 'tis most just.
To be in anger is impiety;
But who is man that is not angry?
Weigh but the crime with this.          60

SECOND SENATOR
You breathe in vain.

ALCIBIADES          In vain? His service done
At Lacedaemon and Byzantium
Were a sufficient briber for his life.

FIRST SENATOR
What's that?

ALCIBIADES Why say,° my lords, h' as done fair service,
And slain in fight many of your enemies.          65
How full of valor did he bear himself
In the last conflict, and made plenteous wounds!

SECOND SENATOR
He has made too much plenty with 'em.
He's a sworn rioter;° he has a sin° that often
Drowns him and takes his valor prisoner.          70

If there were no foes, that were enough
To overcome him. In that beastly fury
He has been known to commit outrages,
And cherish factions.° 'Tis inferred° to us
His days are foul and his drink dangerous.          75

FIRST SENATOR
He dies.

ALCIBIADES    Hard fate. He might have died in war.
My lords, if not for any parts° in him—
Though his right arm might purchase his own time,°
And be in debt to none—yet, more to move you,
Take my deserts to his, and join 'em both.          80
And for I know your reverend ages love
Security,° I'll pawn my victories, all
My honor to you, upon his good returns.°
If by this crime he owes the law his life,
Why, let the war receive't in valiant gore,          85
For law is strict, and war is nothing more.

FIRST SENATOR
We are for law. He dies. Urge it no more,
On height of our displeasure. Friend or brother,
He forfeits his own blood that spills another.

ALCIBIADES
Must it be so? It must not be.          90
My lords, I do beseech you know me.

SECOND SENATOR          How?

ALCIBIADES
Call me to your remembrances.

THIRD SENATOR          What?

ALCIBIADES
I cannot think but your age° has forgot me;
It could not else be I should prove so base
To sue° and be denied such common grace.          95
My wounds ache at you.

FIRST SENATOR          Do you dare our anger?
'Tis in few words, but spacious in effect:
We banish thee for ever.

ALCIBIADES          Banish me?
Banish your dotage, vanish usury,
That makes the Senate ugly.          100

FIRST SENATOR
If after two days' shine Athens contain thee,
Attend our weightier judgment.° And, not to swell
    our spirit,°
He shall be executed presently.° Exeunt [SENATORS].

ALCIBIADES
Now the gods keep you old enough, that you may live
Only in bone,° that none may look on you.          105
I'm worse than mad. I have kept back their foes,
While they have told° their money, and let out
Their coin upon large interest, I myself
Rich only in large hurts. All those, for this?
Is this the balsam° that the usuring Senate          110
Pours into captains' wounds? Banishment!

27 form i.e., a legal and acceptable form   30 factions trisyllabic
32 breathe utter   33 outsides mere externals   35 prefer present
40 clear innocent   41 bear tolerate (our wrongs)   42 under
favor by your leave (a formula of politeness)   44 fond foolish
47 repugnancy resistance, fighting back   49 Abroad away
from home, at battle   50 bearing (1) enduring of wrongs (2)
childbearing (3) bearing of men in sexual intercourse; carry it
win the day   54 be pitifully good be good in showing pity
56 gust (1) taste, relish (2) strong wind or storm   57 by mercy
in a merciful interpretation   64 say let us say, let us admit   69
rioter debauchee; sin i.e., drunkenness

74 cherish factions foster dissension; inferred reported   77
parts good qualities   78 his own time i.e., his proper time to
die   82 Security (1) safety, freedom from care or apprehension (2) collateral for a debt   83 good returns profit on an
investment   93 your age i.e., you, because of your age   95
To sue to beg   102 Attend . . . judgment expect a more
severe sentence from us; not . . . spirit not to allow our
anger any further scope   103 presently at once   105 Only in
bone i.e., be mere hideous skeletons   107 told counted   110
balsam balm

It comes not ill. I hate not to be banished;
It is a cause worthy my spleen° and fury,
That I may strike at Athens. I'll cheer up
My discontented troops and lay for hearts.°          115
'Tis honor with most lands to be at odds;
Soldiers should brook° as little wrongs as gods. *Exit.*

[*Scene VI. A banqueting hall in Timon's house.*]

[*Music. Tables set out,* SERVANTS *attending.*] *Enter
divers* FRIENDS [*of Timon*] *at several doors.*

FIRST LORD   The good time of day to you, sir.
SECOND LORD   I also wish it to you. I think this
honorable lord did but try us this other day.
FIRST LORD   Upon that were my thoughts tiring°
when we encount'red. I hope it is not so low with him   5
as he made it seem in the trial of his several friends.
SECOND LORD   It should not be, by the persuasion°
of his new feasting.
FIRST LORD   I should think so. He hath sent me an
earnest inviting, which many my near occasions° did   10
urge me to put off; but he hath conjured me beyond
them, and I must needs appear.
SECOND LORD   In like manner was I in debt to my
importunate business, but he would not hear my
excuse. I am sorry, when he sent to borrow of me,   15
that my provision° was out.
FIRST LORD   I am sick of that grief too, as I understand how all things go.°
SECOND LORD   Every man here's so. What would he
have borrowed of you?          20
FIRST LORD   A thousand pieces.°
SECOND LORD   A thousand pieces?
FIRST LORD   What of you?
SECOND LORD   He sent to me, sir—

*Enter* TIMON *and* ATTENDANTS.

                                   Here he comes.
TIMON   With all my heart, gentlemen both; and how   25
fare you?
FIRST LORD   Ever at the best, hearing well of your
lordship.
SECOND LORD   The swallow° follows not summer
more willing than we your lordship.          30
TIMON [*Aside.*]   Nor more willingly leaves winter,
such summer birds are men.—Gentlemen, our dinner
will not recompense this long stay. Feast your ears
with the music awhile, if they will fare so harshly°
o' th' trumpet's sound; we shall to't presently.°          35
FIRST LORD   I hope it remains not unkindly with
your lordship that I returned you an empty messenger.

TIMON   O sir, let it not trouble you.
SECOND LORD   My noble lord—
TIMON   Ah my good friend, what cheer?          40
SECOND LORD   My most honorable lord, I am e'en
sick of shame that when your lordship this other day
sent to me, I was so unfortunate a beggar.
TIMON   Think not on't, sir.
SECOND LORD   If you had sent but two hours   45
before—
TIMON   Let it not cumber your better remembrance.°

*The banquet brought in.*

Come, bring in all together.
SECOND LORD   All covered dishes.°
FIRST LORD   Royal cheer,° I warrant you.          50
THIRD LORD   Doubt not that, if money and the
season can yield it.
FIRST LORD   How do you? What's the news?
THIRD LORD   Alcibiades is banished. Hear you of it?
FIRST AND SECOND LORDS   Alcibiades banished?   55
THIRD LORD   'Tis so, be sure of it.
FIRST LORD   How? How?
SECOND LORD   I pray you upon what?°
TIMON   My worthy friends, will you draw near?
THIRD LORD   I'll tell you more anon.° Here's a noble   60
feast toward.°
SECOND LORD   This is the old man still.°
THIRD LORD   Will't hold?° Will't hold?
SECOND LORD   It does; but time will°—and so—
THIRD LORD   I do conceive.°          65
TIMON   Each man to his stool, with that spur° as he
would to the lip of his mistress. Your diet° shall be in
all places alike.° Make not a city feast° of it, to let the
meat cool ere we can agree upon the first place. Sit, sit.
The gods require our thanks.          70
  You great benefactors, sprinkle our society with
thankfulness. For your own gifts, make yourselves
praised. But reserve° still to give, lest your deities be
despised. Lend to each man enough that one need not
lend to another; for were your godheads to borrow of   75
men, men would forsake the gods. Make the meat be
beloved more than the man that gives it. Let no
assembly of twenty be without a score of villains. If
there sit twelve women at the table, let a dozen of
them be as they are. The rest of your fees,° O gods—   80
the senators of Athens, together with the common
leg° of people—what is amiss in them, you gods,
make suitable for destruction. For these my present
friends, as they are to me nothing, so in nothing bless
them, and to nothing are they welcome.          85
Uncover, dogs, and lap.

[*The dishes are uncovered and seen to be full of water.*]

113 **spleen** malice, passionate hatred   115 **lay for hearts** i.e.,
try to win their hearts to my cause (or, possibly, try to win
the hearts of new followers)   117 **brook** endure
**III.vi.4 tiring** feeding (especially, to tear flesh in feeding as
does a bird of prey)   7 **by the persuasion** on the evidence
10 **many . . . occasions** my many pressing social obligations
16 **provision** supply (of money)   17–18 **as . . . go** i.e., on
the evidence of his "new feasting," things seem to be picking
up again with Timon   21 **pieces** gold coins worth about a
pound (but probably used vaguely)   29 **swallow** cf. the proverb, "Swallows, like false friends, fly away upon the approach
of winter"   34 **fare so harshly** feed on such rough food
35 **we . . . presently** we shall sit down to eat immediately

47 **cumber . . . remembrance** burden your good memory
49 **covered dishes** signifies food of high quality   50 **Royal
cheer** food fit for a king   58 **upon what** for what cause   60
**anon** soon   61 **toward** forthcoming   62 **still** ever, without
change   63 **Will't hold** Will it last?   64 **time will** presumably
a platitude such as "Time will alter all things"   65 **conceive**
understand   66 **spur** spurring, speed   67 **diet** food   67–68 **in
. . . alike** the same at all places of the table (i.e., no need for
seating according to rank)   68 **city feast** a formal London
banquet (London is the "City")   73 **reserve** keep something
in reserve   80 **fees** property, possessions   82 **leg** limb (as a
literal part of the body politic)

SOME SPEAK   What does his lordship mean?
SOME OTHER   I know not.
TIMON
May you a better feast never behold,
You knot of mouth-friends.° Smoke° and lukewarm
   water                                                                    90
Is your perfection.° This is Timon's last,
Who, stuck and spangled° with your flatteries,
Washes it off and sprinkles in your faces
Your reeking° villainy. [Throws the water in their faces.
   Live loathed and long,
Most smiling, smooth,° detested parasites,                    95
Courteous destroyers, affable wolves, meek bears,
You fools of fortune, trencher-friends, time's flies,
Cap-and-knee slaves, vapors, and minute-jacks.°
Of man and beast the infinite° malady
Crust you quite o'er. What, dost thou go?                     100
Soft, take thy physic° first; thou too, and thou.
Stay, I will lend thee money, borrow° none.

[Drives them out.]

What? All in motion? Henceforth be no feast,
Whereat a villain's not a welcome guest.
Burn house, sink Athens, henceforth hated be       105
Of° Timon man and all humanity.               Exit.

Enter the SENATORS, with other LORDS.

FIRST LORD   How now, my lords?
SECOND LORD   Know you the quality of Lord
   Timon's fury?
THIRD LORD   Push,° did you see my cap?            110
FOURTH LORD   I have lost my gown.
FIRST LORD   He's but a mad lord, and naught but
   humors° sways him. He gave me a jewel th' other day,
   and now he has beat it out of my hat. Did you see my
   jewel?                                                                    115
THIRD LORD   Did you see my cap?
SECOND LORD   Here 'tis.
FOURTH LORD   Here lies my gown.
FIRST LORD   Let's make no stay.
SECOND LORD
   Lord Timon's mad.
THIRD LORD              I feel't upon my bones.       120
FOURTH LORD
   One day he gives us diamonds, next day stones.
              Exeunt the SENATORS [and others].

# [ACT IV]

[Scene I. Outside the walls of Athens.]

Enter TIMON.

TIMON
Let me look back upon thee. O thou wall
That girdles in those wolves, dive in the earth,
And fence not Athens. Matrons, turn incontinent;
Obedience fail in children. Slaves and fools,
Pluck the grave wrinkled Senate from the bench,     5
And minister° in their steads. To general filths°
Convert o' th' instant green° virginity;
Do't in your parents' eyes. Bankrupts, hold fast
Rather than render back;° out with your knives,
And cut your trusters' throats. Bound° servants, steal;   10
Large-handed° robbers your grave masters are,
And pill° by law. Maid, to thy master's bed,
Thy mistress is o' th' brothel. Son of sixteen,
Pluck the lined° crutch from thy old limping sire,
With it beat out his brains. Piety, and fear,          15
Religion to° the gods, peace, justice, truth,
Domestic awe,° night-rest, and neighborhood,°
Instruction, manners, mysteries,° and trades,
Degrees,° observances, customs, and laws,
Decline to your confounding contraries,°              20
And let confusion° live. Plagues incident to° men,
Your potent and infectious fevers heap
On Athens ripe for stroke. Thou cold sciatica,
Cripple our senators, that their limbs may halt°
As lamely as their manners. Lust and liberty°        25
Creep in the minds and marrows of our youth,
That 'gainst the stream of virtue they may strive,
And drown themselves in riot. Itches, blains,°
Sow all th' Athenian bosoms, and their crop
Be general leprosy. Breath infect breath,            30
That their society, as their friendship, may
Be merely° poison. Nothing I'll bear from thee
But nakedness, thou detestable° town;
Take thou that too, with multiplying bans.°
Timon will to the woods, where he shall find        35
Th' unkindest beast more kinder° than mankind.
The gods confound—hear me, you good gods all—
Th' Athenians both within and out that wall.
And grant, as Timon grows, his hate may grow
To the whole race of mankind, high and low.       40
Amen.                                        Exit.

---

90 knot of mouth-friends pack of (1) friends merely in speech (2) friends won through feeding, "trencher-friends"; Smoke (1) insubstantiality (2) mere talk   91 perfection highest excellence (?) perfect likeness of you (?)   92 stuck and spangled bespattered and tricked out (as if with spangles)   94 reeking giving off smoke or fumes, stinking   95 smooth flattering   97–98 You . . . minute-jacks you dupes of fortune, friends won by feeding, insects that appear only in fair weather, servile slaves always kneeling or removing caps in deference, insubstantial creatures, and figures who strike the bell of a clock (i.e., opportunistic persons)   99 infinite unlimited   101 physic medicine   102 borrow i.e., borrow none from others (?) I will borrow none (?)   106 Of by   110 Push an effeminate expression of impatience   113 humors whims, caprices

IV.i.6 minister govern; filths harlots (or, more generally, immoral acts or corruption)   7 green young, inexperienced   9 render back repay debts   10 Bound under obligation to serve for a stated period   11 Large-handed rapacious (usually means "generous")   12 pill steal   14 lined padded   16 Religion to religious concern for   17 Domestic awe the respect appropriate to domestic relations (to parents, home, etc.); neighborhood neighborliness   18 mysteries crafts, callings   19 Degrees social classes   20 confounding contraries opposites that destroy each other and so bring on general chaos   21 confusion ruin; incident to natural to   24 halt limp   25 liberty licentiousness   28 blains blisters   32 merely utterly   33 detestable primary accent on first syllable   34 multiplying bans ever-increasing curses (?) multiple curses (?)   36 more kinder (1) more generous, gracious (2) more natural, closer to the moral law of nature

[Scene II. *Athens. Timon's house.*]

*Enter* [FLAVIUS, *the*] *steward, with two or three*
SERVANTS.

FIRST SERVANT
Hear you, master steward, where's our master?
Are we undone, cast off, nothing remaining?

FLAVIUS
Alack, my fellows, what should I say to you?
Let me be recorded° by the righteous gods,
I am as poor as you.

FIRST SERVANT        Such a house broke?        5
So noble a master fall'n, all gone, and not
One friend to take his fortune° by the arm,
And go along with him?

SECOND SERVANT        As we do turn our backs
From our companion thrown into his grave,
So his familiars to his buried fortunes°        10
Slink all away, leave their false vows with him,
Like empty purses picked; and his poor self,
A dedicated beggar to the air,°
With his disease of all-shunned poverty,
Walks like contempt alone.

*Enter other* SERVANTS.

                    More of our fellows.        15

FLAVIUS
All broken implements of a ruined house.

THIRD SERVANT
Yet do our hearts wear Timon's livery,
That see I by our faces; we are fellows° still,
Serving alike in sorrow. Leaked is our bark,
And we poor mates stand on the dying deck,        20
Hearing the surges threat. We must all part
Into this sea of air.°

FLAVIUS                Good fellows all,
The latest° of my wealth I'll share amongst you.
Wherever we shall meet, for Timon's sake,
Let's yet be fellows. Let's shake our heads and say,        25
As 'twere a knell unto our master's fortunes,
"We have seen better days." Let each take some.

[*Gives money.*]

Nay, put out all your hands. Not one word more;
Thus part we rich in sorrow, parting poor.

                    *Embrace, and part several ways.*
O the fierce wretchedness that glory brings us!        30
Who would not wish to be from wealth exempt,
Since riches point to° misery and contempt?
Who would be so mocked with glory, or to live°
But in a dream of friendship,
To have his pomp and all what state compounds°        35
But only painted,° like his varnished° friends?

Poor honest lord, brought low by his own heart,
Undone by goodness. Strange, unusual blood,°
When man's worst sin is, he does too much good.
Who then dares to be half so kind° again?        40
For bounty, that makes gods, do still mar men.
My dearest lord, blessed to be° most accursed,
Rich only to be wretched, thy great fortunes
Are made thy chief afflictions. Alas, kind lord,
He's flung in rage from this ingrateful seat°        45
Of monstrous friends;
Nor has he with him to supply his life,°
Of that° which can command it.
I'll follow and inquire him out.
I'll ever serve his mind with my best will;        50
Whilst I have gold, I'll be his steward still.        *Exit.*

[Scene III. *Before Timon's cave.*]

*Enter* TIMON *in the woods.*

TIMON
O blessèd breeding sun, draw from the earth
Rotten humidity;° below thy sister's orb°
Infect the air. Twinned brothers of one womb,
Whose procreation, residence, and birth,
Scarce is dividant°—touch° them with several° for-
    tunes,        5
The greater scorns the lesser. Not nature,
To whom all sores lay siege, can bear great fortune
But by contempt of nature.°
Raise me this beggar, and deny't° that lord,
The senators shall bear contempt hereditary,°        10
The beggar native° honor.
It is the pasture lards the brother's sides,
The want that makes him lean.° Who dares? Who
    dares
In purity of manhood stand upright
And say, this man's a flatterer? If one be,        15
So are they all, for every grise° of fortune
Is smoothed° by that below. The learnèd pate°
Ducks to the golden fool.° All's obliquy;°
There's nothing level in our cursèd natures
But direct villainy. Therefore be abhorred        20
All feasts, societies, and throngs of men.
His semblable,° yea himself, Timon disdains;
Destruction fang° mankind. Earth, yield me roots.

**38 blood** disposition    **40 half so kind** i.e., as Timon
was, who came to grief because of it    **42 blessed to be**
blessed with wealth only to be    **45 seat** residence    **47 to
. . . life** i.e., he has no food and drink    **48 that** money
**IV.iii.2 Rotten humidity** humidity that causes things to rot;
**below . . . orb** beneath the moon (i.e., in the middle air
between earth and moon)    **5 dividant** divisible, separable;
**touch** test; **several** different    **6–8 Not . . . nature** Human
nature, which is subjected to all sorts of miseries, when it
encounters good fortune rejects its own natural affection and
despises mankind    **9 deny't** deny to raise    **10 hereditary** as
if they were born that way and not simply victims of fortune's
caprices    **11 native** as if he were born with it    **12–13 It . . .
lean** i.e., the "twinned brothers" (line 3) are distinguished by
their gifts of fortune; the rich pasture, and not any intrinsic
worth, makes one brother fat and the other lean    **16 grise**
step    **17 smoothed** flattered, facilitated by flattery; **pate** head
**18 Ducks . . . fool** inclines in deference to the rich fool;
**obliquy** obliquity, moral crookedness    **22 semblable** anything like himself    **23 fang** (1) seize, as with fangs (2) provide
with fangs

**IV.ii.4 Let . . . recorded** let it be recorded of me    **7 his fortune** i.e., Timon in his ill fortune    **10 his familiars . . .
fortunes** those who were the familiar friends of his now-
buried fortunes (also suggests "familiar spirit," a personal
servant from the spirit world)    **13 dedicated . . . air** a
beggar vowed or doomed to wander about in the open air
**18 fellows** fellow servants    **22 this . . . air** the open air,
which is as comfortless to us as is the sea to sailors on a sinking
ship    **23 latest** last    **32 point to** lead to    **33 to live** i.e., who
would wish to live    **35 all . . . compounds** all that worldly
splendor is composed of    **36 painted** illusory; **varnished** fair-
seeming

[*Digs.*]

Who seeks for better of thee, sauce° his palate
With thy most operant° poison. What is here?                25
Gold? Yellow, glittering, precious gold?
No, gods, I am no idle votarist.°
Roots, you clear° heavens! Thus much of this will
    make
Black, white; foul, fair; wrong, right;
Base, noble; old, young; coward, valiant.                30
Ha, you gods! Why this? What this, you gods? Why
    this
Will lug your priests and servants from your sides;
Pluck stout men's pillows from below their heads.°
This yellow slave
Will knit and break religions, bless th' accursed,        35
Make the hoar° leprosy adored, place° thieves,
And give them title, knee, and approbation
With senators on the bench. This is it
That makes the wappened° widow wed again;
She, whom the spital-house° and ulcerous sores°         40
Would cast the gorge° at, this embalms and spices
To th' April day° again. Come, damned earth,
Thou common whore of mankind, that puts odds
Among the rout of nations,° I will make thee
Do thy right nature.° *March afar off.*
                    Ha? A drum? Th' art quick,°        45
But yet I'll bury thee. Thou't go,° strong thief,
When gouty keepers of thee cannot stand.
Nay, stay thou out for earnest.°

[*Keeps some gold.*]

*Enter* ALCIBIADES, *with drum and fife, in warlike
manner; and* PHRYNIA *and* TIMANDRA.

ALCIBIADES
What art thou there? Speak.
TIMON
A beast as thou art. The canker° gnaw thy heart        50
For showing me again the eyes of man.
ALCIBIADES
What is thy name? Is man so hateful to thee
That art thyself a man?
TIMON
I am Misanthropos° and hate mankind.
For thy part, I do wish thou wert a dog,                55
That I might love thee something.°
ALCIBIADES                        I know thee well,
But in thy fortunes am unlearned and strange.°

TIMON
I know thee too, and more than that I know thee
I not desire to know. Follow thy drum,
With man's blood paint the ground gules,° gules.        60
Religious canons, civil laws are cruel;
Then what should war be? This fell° whore of thine
Hath in her more destruction than thy sword,
For all her cherubin look.
PHRYNIA                        Thy lips rot off.
TIMON
I will not kiss thee; then the rot returns°            65
To thine own lips again.
ALCIBIADES
How came the noble Timon to this change?
TIMON
As the moon does, by wanting° light to give.
But then renew° I could not like the moon;
There were no suns to borrow of.                        70
ALCIBIADES
Noble Timon, what friendship may I do thee?
TIMON
None, but to maintain my opinion.°
ALCIBIADES
What is it, Timon?
TIMON
Promise me friendship, but perform none.
If thou wilt not promise, the gods plague thee,        75
For thou art a man. If thou dost perform,
Confound thee, for thou art a man.
ALCIBIADES
I have heard in some sort of thy miseries.
TIMON
Thou saw'st them when I had prosperity.
ALCIBIADES
I see them now; then was a blessed time.                80
TIMON
As thine is now, held with a brace° of harlots.
TIMANDRA
Is this th' Athenian minion,° whom the world
Voiced so regardfully?°
TIMON                        Art thou Timandra?
TIMANDRA                                    Yes.
TIMON
Be a whore still; they love thee not that use thee.
Give them diseases, leaving° with thee their lust.     85
Make use of thy salt° hours. Season° the slaves
For tubs and baths;° bring down rose-cheeked youth
To the tub-fast and the diet.°
TIMANDRA                        Hang thee, monster!
ALCIBIADES
Pardon him, sweet Timandra, for his wits
Are drowned and lost in his calamities.                 90
I have but little gold of late, brave° Timon,

24 **sauce** season  25 **operant** potent  27 **no idle votarist**
i.e., I have not sworn my vow in an idle or trifling way
28 **clear** pure  33 **Pluck . . . heads** i.e., kill even strong
men by sudden suffocation  36 **hoar** white; **place** elevate
to a place or office of dignity  39 **wappened** sexually
exhausted  40 **spital-house** hospital (especially for the
lower classes and sufferers from loathsome diseases);
**ulcerous sores** i.e., those afflicted with ulcerous sores  41
**cast the gorge** vomit  41-42 **embalms . . . day** i.e.,
preserves, perfumes, and generally revivifies to a springlike and
youthful amorousness  43-44 **puts . . . nations** sets the disorderly mob of nations at strife with one another  45 **Do . . .
nature** i.e., cause strife and dissension; **quick** (1) alive (2)
speedily had and lost  46 **go** walk, move  48 **for earnest** as an
installment  50 **canker** (1) ulcerous sore (2) canker-worm
54 **Misanthropos** the man-hater  56 **something** somewhat
57 **strange** ignorant

60 **gules** red (the heraldic term)  62 **fell** destructive  65 **the
rot returns** based on a prevalent belief that by transmitting a
venereal infection to another, one loses it himself  68 **wanting**
lacking  69 **renew** (1) to become new (2) to extend a loan (as
in the next line)  72 **maintain my opinion** i.e., be a misan-
thropist, too  81 **brace** usually used for a pair of dogs on a
leash  82 **minion** favorite, darling  83 **Voiced so regardfully** spoke of with so much regard  85 **leaving** while they
leave  86 **salt** lustful, salacious; **Season** spice  87 **tubs and
baths** sweating-tubs and hot baths (used to treat venereal
disease)  88 **tub-fast . . . diet** fasting and special diet were
treatments for venereal disease  91 **brave** excellent

The want whereof doth daily make revolt
In my penurious° band. I have heard, and grieved,
How cursèd Athens, mindless of thy worth,
Forgetting thy great deeds, when neighbor states,    95
But for thy sword and fortune, trod° upon them—

TIMON
I prithee beat thy drum° and get thee gone.

ALCIBIADES
I am thy friend and pity thee, dear Timon.

TIMON
How dost thou pity him whom thou dost trouble?
I had rather be alone.

ALCIBIADES                Why fare thee well.    100
Here is some gold for thee.

TIMON                        Keep it, I cannot eat it.

ALCIBIADES
When I have laid proud Athens on a heap—

TIMON
War'st thou 'gainst Athens?

ALCIBIADES              Ay, Timon, and have cause.

TIMON
The gods confound them all in thy conquest,°
And thee after when thou hast conquerèd.    105

ALCIBIADES
Why me, Timon?

TIMON            That by killing of villains
Thou wast born to conquer my country.
Put up° thy gold. Go on, here's gold, go on.
Be as a planetary plague,° when Jove
Will o'er some high-viced city hang his poison    110
In the sick air. Let not thy sword skip one.
Pity not honored age for his white beard:
He is an usurer. Strike me the counterfeit matron:
It is her habit° only that is honest,°
Herself's a bawd. Let not the virgin's cheek    115
Make soft thy trenchant° sword: for those milk paps,
That through the window-bars° bore at men's eyes,
Are not within the leaf of pity writ,°
But set them down horrible traitors. Spare not the babe
Whose dimpled smiles from fools exhaust° their mercy:    120
Think it a bastard, whom the oracle
Hath doubtfully° pronounced thy throat shall cut,
And mince it sans remorse.° Swear against objects.°
Put armor on thine ears and on thine eyes,
Whose proof° nor yells of mothers, maids, nor babes,    125
Nor sight of priests in holy vestments bleeding,
Shall pierce a jot. There's gold to pay thy soldiers.
Make large confusion;° and, thy fury spent,
Confounded be thyself. Speak not, begone.

ALCIBIADES
Hast° thou gold yet, I'll take the gold thou givest me,    130
Not all thy counsel.

TIMON
Dost thou or dost thou not, heaven's curse upon thee.

PHRYNIA AND TIMANDRA
Give us some gold, good Timon; hast thou more?

TIMON
Enough to make a whore forswear her trade,
And to make whores, a bawd.° Hold up, you sluts,    135
Your aprons mountant.° You are not oathable,°
Although I know you'll swear, terribly swear
Into strong shudders and to heavenly agues
Th' immortal gods that hear you. Spare your oaths;
I'll trust to your conditions.° Be whores still,°    140
And he whose pious breath seeks to convert you,
Be strong in whore, allure him, burn him up;
Let your close fire predominate his smoke,°
And be no turncoats. Yet may your pains six months
Be quite contrary.° And thatch    145
Your poor thin roofs with burdens of the dead—°
Some that were hanged, no matter.
Wear them, betray with them; whore still;
Paint till a horse may mire° upon your face.
A pox of wrinkles!°

PHRYNIA AND TIMANDRA
                    Well, more gold. What then?    150
Believe't that we'll do anything for gold.

TIMON
Consumptions° sow
In hollow° bones of man; strike their sharp° shins,
And mar men's spurring. Crack the lawyer's voice,
That he may never more false title plead,    155
Nor sound his quillets° shrilly. Hoar the flamen,°
That scolds against the quality of flesh°
And not believes himself. Down with the nose,°
Down with it flat, take the bridge quite away
Of him, that his particular to foresee,    160
Smells from the general weal.° Make curled-pate ruffians bald,
And let the unscarred braggarts of the war
Derive some pain from you. Plague all,
That your activity may defeat and quell
The source of all erection.° There's more gold.    165

93 penurious needy  96 trod would have trodden  97 beat
thy drum i.e., let thy drummer give the signal for departure
104 in thy conquest in your victory over them  108 Put up
put away  109 planetary plague plague caused by the planets
114 habit dress; honest chaste  116 trenchant cutting  117
window-bars lattice work of a window (?) open-work
squares of the bodice of a woman's frock (?)  118 within . . .
writ written down on the page with the names of those who
are to be pitied and spared  120 exhaust draw out, elicit  122
doubtfully ambiguously  123 mince . . . remorse cut it up
without pity; objects objections, accusations of cruelty  125
proof high quality (of armor), impenetrability  128 confusion destruction  130 Hast if you have

135 And . . . bawd i.e., and enough to make a bawd give up
her trade of making whores (or, perhaps, enough to make a
whore set herself up as a bawd, making whores instead of being
one)  136 aprons mountant rising aprons (a mock-heraldic
phrase with sexual overtones); oathable capable of being placed
under oath  140 conditions dispositions; still always  143 Let
. . . smoke Let the hidden fire of your sexuality or disease
dominate over the smoke of idle words of he who "seeks to
convert you"  144-45 Yet . . . contrary May you spend six
months of the year in being whores and the other six in repairing the physical damage occasioned by your debaucheries (?)
145-46 And . . . dead Wear wigs (or possibly false pubes)
made from loads of hair taken from the dead (venereal disease
was thought to cause loss of hair)  149 mire sink into the mire
or mud (because of the thickness of cosmetics)  150 pox of
wrinkles a pox on wrinkles, away with wrinkles (since they
can be covered with cosmetics  152 Consumptions wasting
diseases (here venereal disease)  153 hollow . . . sharp i.e.,
the disease will make the bones hollow and the shins painful
156 quillets subtle verbal distinctions; Hoar the flamen
whiten the priest with disease, or cause his hair to turn white
(possible pun on whore)  157 quality of flesh the nature of
the flesh, sexual pleasure  158 Down . . . nose an effect of
syphilis  160-61 his particular . . . weal to provide for his
private advantage or profit, he abandons the proper scent that
contributes to the public good or welfare  165 source . . .
erection sexuality itself

Do you damn others, and let this damn you,
And ditches grave° you all.

**PHRYNIA AND TIMANDRA**
More counsel with more money, bounteous Timon.

**TIMON**
More whore, more mischief first; I have given you
     earnest.°

**ALCIBIADES**
Strike up the drum towards Athens. Farewell, Timon.  170
If I thrive well, I'll visit thee again.

**TIMON**
If I hope well,° I'll never see thee more.

**ALCIBIADES**
I never did thee harm.

**TIMON**
Yes, thou spok'st well of me.

**ALCIBIADES**             Call'st thou that harm?

**TIMON**
Men daily find it. Get thee away, and take    175
Thy beagles with thee.

**ALCIBIADES**        We but offend him. Strike!
     [*Drum beats.*] *Exeunt* [ALCIBIADES,
         PHRYNIA, *and* TIMANDRA].

**TIMON**
That nature, being sick of° man's unkindness,
Should yet be hungry! Common mother, thou,

[*Digging*]

Whose womb unmeasurable and infinite breast
Teems° and feeds all; whose selfsame mettle,°    180
Whereof thy proud child, arrogant man, is puffed,°
Engenders the black toad and adder blue,
The gilded newt and eyeless venomed worm,
With all th' abhorrèd births below crisp° heaven
Whereon Hyperion's quick'ning fire° doth shine;   185
Yield him, who all the human sons do hate,
From forth thy plenteous bosom, one poor root.
Ensear° thy fertile and conceptious° womb;
Let it no more bring out ingrateful man.
Go great° with tigers, dragons, wolves, and bears,   190
Teem with new monsters, whom thy upward face
Hath to the marbled mansion all above°
Never presented. O, a root, dear thanks!
Dry up thy marrows,° vines and plough-torn leas,
Whereof ingrateful man, with liquorish draughts   195
And morsels unctious,° greases his pure mind,
That from it all consideration° slips—

*Enter* APEMANTUS.

More man? Plague, plague!

**APEMANTUS**
I was directed hither. Men report
Thou dost affect° my manners, and dost use them.   200

**TIMON**
'Tis then because thou dost not keep a dog
Whom I would imitate. Consumption° catch thee.

**APEMANTUS**
This is in thee a nature but infected,°
A poor unmanly melancholy sprung
From change of future.° Why this spade? This place?  205
This slavelike habit° and these looks of care?
Thy flatterers yet wear silk, drink wine, lie soft,
Hug their diseased perfumes,° and have forgot
That ever Timon was. Shame not these woods
By putting on the cunning of a carper.°   210
Be thou a flatterer now, and seek to thrive
By that which has undone thee. Hinge thy knee,
And let his very breath whom thou'lt observe
Blow off thy cap;° praise his most vicious strain°
And call it excellent. Thou wast told thus.°   215
Thou gav'st thine ears, like tapsters° that bade wel-
     come,
To knaves and all approachers. 'Tis most just
That thou turn rascal; hadst thou wealth again,
Rascals should have't. Do not assume my likeness.

**TIMON**
Were I like thee, I'd throw away myself.   220

**APEMANTUS**
Thou hast cast away thyself, being like thyself:
A madman so long, now a fool. What, think'st
That the bleak air, thy boisterous chamberlain,°
Will put thy shirt on warm? Will these moist° trees,
That have outlived the eagle, page thy heels   225
And skip when thou point'st out?° Will the cold
     brook,
Candied° with ice, caudle° thy morning taste
To cure thy o'er-night's surfeit?° Call the creatures
Whose naked natures live in all the spite
Of wreakful° heaven, whose bare unhousèd trunks,  230
To the conflicting elements exposed,
Answer mere nature.° Bid them flatter thee.
O thou shalt find—

**TIMON**        A fool of thee. Depart.

**APEMANTUS**
I love thee better now than e'er I did.

**TIMON**
I hate thee worse.

**APEMANTUS**    Why?

**TIMON**        Thou flatter'st misery.   235

---

**167 grave** be a grave for, bury  **169 earnest** a partial payment to seal a bargain  **172 If . . . well** if my hopes are realized  **177 of** as a result of  **180 Teems** brings forth; **mettle** (1) substance (2) vigorous spirit  **181 puffed** puffed up with pride  **184 crisp** with curled clouds (?) shining, clear (?)  **185 Hyperion's quick'ning fire** the sun was thought to have the power of generating some of the lower forms of insect life  **188 Ensear** dry up; **conceptious** conceiving, prolific  **190 great** pregnant  **192 above** in heaven  **194 marrows** the type of a rich food, not a necessity of life, produced by the "vines" and "leas"  **196 unctious** an obsolete variant form of *unctuous*  **197 consideration** ability to consider  **200 affect** imitate

**202 Consumption** any wasting disease  **203 infected** (1) affected, factitious (2) caught like an infection from your changed circumstances  **205 change of future** change in your material prospects  **206 habit** dress, garb  **208 diseased perfumes** diseased and perfumed mistresses  **210 By . . . carper** by pretending to the profession of a cynic or railer (which any fool can do)  **213–14 let . . . cap** kneel so obsequiously close to the person you are paying court to that his breath may blow off your cap  **214 strain** quality  **215 Thou . . . thus** in your prosperity others spoke to you in this manner  **216 tapsters** tavern-keepers or bartenders are proverbial for their indiscriminate hospitality  **223 chamberlain** one who waits on a king or lord in his bedchamber  **224 moist** damp  **226 point'st out** indicate your desires  **227 Candied** congealed, encrusted; **caudle** offer a caudle (a warm, spiced, mildly alcoholic drink given to the sick)  **228 o'er-night's surfeit** previous night's indulgence in drink  **230 wreakful** vengeful  **232 Answer mere nature** correspond to or reflect nature in its barest and most rigorous form

APEMANTUS
I flatter not, but say thou art a caitiff.°

TIMON
Why dost thou seek me out?

APEMANTUS                          To vex thee.

TIMON
Always a villain's office° or a fool's.
Dost please thyself in't?

APEMANTUS              Ay.

TIMON                          What, a knave too?

APEMANTUS
If thou didst put this sour cold habit° on          240
To castigate thy pride, 'twere well; but thou
Dost it enforcedly.° Thou'dst courtier be again
Wert thou not beggar. Willing misery°
Outlives incertain pomp, is crowned before.°
The one is filling still,° never complete;          245
The other, at high wish.° Best state, contentless,
Hath a distracted and most wretched being,
Worse than the worst, content.°
Thou shouldst desire to die, being miserable.

TIMON
Not by his breath° that is more miserable.          250
Thou art a slave, whom Fortune's tender arm
With favor never clasped, but bred a dog.
Hadst thou, like us, from our first swath° proceeded
The sweet degrees° that this brief world affords
To such as may the passive drudges° of it          255
Freely command, thou wouldst have plunged thyself
In general riot,° melted down thy youth
In different beds of lust, and never learned
The icy precepts of respect,° but followed
The sug'red game° before thee. But myself—          260
Who had the world as my confectionary,°
The mouths, the tongues, the eyes, and hearts of men
At duty, more than I could frame employment;°
That numberless upon me stuck, as leaves
Do on the oak, have with one winter's brush°          265
Fell° from their boughs, and left me open, bare
For every storm that blows—I to bear this,
That never knew but better, is some burden.
Thy nature did commence in sufferance,° time
Hath made thee hard in't. Why shouldst thou hate
     men?          270
They never flattered thee. What hast thou given?

236 **caitiff** wretch   238 **office** duty   240 **habit** (1) garment
(2) outward manner, bearing   242 **enforcedly** as if you were
being forced to do it   243 **Willing misery** voluntary poverty
244 **is crowned before** comes earlier to the fulfillment of its
desires and wishes   245 **The one . . . still** pomp, like a leaky
vessel, can never be filled (or fulfilled)   246 **The other . . .
wish** "willing misery," because it wishes little, can easily
arrive at the height of its wishes   246–48 **Best . . . content**
A man in even the best material condition, if he is without
content or happiness, is confused and wretched, worse than a
man in the poorest condition who is contented   250 **breath**
voice   253 **swath** swaddling clothes   253–54 **proceeded . . .
degrees** advanced from one stage to the next above it (in
sense of academic "degrees")   255 **passive drudges** submissive menial servants   257 **riot** debauchery   259 **icy . . .
respect** the chilling rules of reason that constitute proper social
conduct   260 **sug'red game** outwardly sweet quarry (probably whores)   261 **confectionary** a place where sweetmeats
are made   263 **frame employment** invent work for   265
**winter's brush** brush of a wintry wind   266 **Fell** fallen   269
**sufferance** suffering

If thou wilt curse, thy father, that poor rogue,
Must be thy subject; who in spite put stuff
To° some she-beggar and compounded thee
Poor rogue hereditary. Hence, begone.          275
If thou hadst not been born the worst° of men,
Thou hadst been a knave and flatterer.

APEMANTUS                          Art thou proud yet?

TIMON
Ay, that I am not thee.

APEMANTUS                  I, that I was
No prodigal.

TIMON          I, that I am one now.
Were all the wealth I have shut up in thee,          280
I'd give thee leave to hang it. Get thee gone.
That° the whole life of Athens were in this!
Thus would I eat it. [*Eats a root.*]

APEMANTUS                  Here, I will mend° thy feast.

[*Offers him food.*]

TIMON
First mend my company, take away thyself.

APEMANTUS
So I shall mend mine own, by th' lack of thine.          285

TIMON
'Tis not well mended so, it is but botched;°
If not, I would it were.

APEMANTUS
What wouldst thou have to° Athens?

TIMON
Thee thither in a whirlwind. If thou wilt,
Tell them there I have gold; look, so I have.          290

APEMANTUS
Here is no use for gold.

TIMON                  The best and truest;
For here it sleeps and does no hirèd harm.

APEMANTUS
Where liest a nights, Timon?

TIMON                  Under that's above me.°
Where feed'st thou a days, Apemantus?

APEMANTUS
Where my stomach finds meat, or rather where I eat it.          295

TIMON
Would poison were obedient and knew my mind!

APEMANTUS
Where wouldst thou send it?

TIMON
To sauce thy dishes.

APEMANTUS   The middle of humanity thou never
knewest, but the extremity of both ends. When thou          300
wast in thy gilt and thy perfume, they mocked thee
for too much curiosity;° in thy rags thou know'st
none, but art despised for the contrary. There's a
medlar° for thee; eat it.

TIMON   On what I hate I feed not.          305

APEMANTUS   Dost hate° a medlar?

273–74 **put stuff To** made pregnant (contemptuous)   276
**worst** i.e., in social and financial position   282 **That** would that
283 **mend** improve   286 **botched** clumsily repaired (because
Apemantus is still present—with himself)   288 **to** in   293
**that's above me** that which is above me, the sky   302 **curiosity** carefulness, fastidiousness   304 **medlar** a fruit like a small
brown-skinned apple, not ready to be eaten until in the early
stages of decay   306 **hate** "eat" and "hate" were pronounced
alike in Elizabethan English

TIMON  Ay, though it look like thee.

APEMANTUS  And° th' hadst hated meddlers° sooner, thou shouldst have loved thyself better now. What man didst thou ever know unthrift° that was beloved 310 after° his means?

TIMON  Who, without those means thou talk'st of, didst thou ever know beloved?

APEMANTUS  Myself.

TIMON  I understand thee; thou hadst some means to 315 keep a dog.°

APEMANTUS  What things in the world canst thou nearest compare to thy flatterers?

TIMON  Women nearest, but men—men are the things themselves. What wouldst thou do with the world, 320 Apemantus, if it lay in thy power?

APEMANTUS  Give it the beasts, to be rid of the men.

TIMON  Wouldst thou have thyself fall in the confusion of men,° and remain a beast with the beasts?

APEMANTUS  Ay, Timon.                                    325

TIMON  A beastly ambition, which the gods grant thee t' attain to. If thou wert the lion, the fox would beguile° thee. If thou wert the lamb, the fox would eat thee. If thou wert the fox, the lion would suspect thee, when peradventure° thou wert accused by the ass. If 330 thou wert the ass, thy dullness would torment thee, and still thou liv'dst but as a breakfast to the wolf. If thou wert the wolf, thy greediness would afflict thee, and oft thou shouldst hazard thy life for thy dinner. Wert thou the unicorn,° pride and wrath would 335 confound° thee, and make thine own self the conquest of thy fury. Wert thou a bear, thou wouldst be killed by the horse. Wert thou a horse, thou wouldst be seized by the leopard. Wert thou a leopard, thou wert german° to the lion, and the spots° of thy kindred 340 were jurors° on thy life. All thy safety were remotion,° and thy defense absence. What beast couldst thou be that were not subject to a beast? And what a beast art thou already, that see'st not thy loss in transformation!°

APEMANTUS  If thou couldst please me with speaking 345 to me, thou mightst have hit upon it here. The commonwealth of Athens is become a forest of beasts.

TIMON  How has the ass broke the wall, that thou art out of the city?

APEMANTUS  Yonder comes a poet and a painter.° 350 The plague of company light upon thee! I will fear to catch it, and give way.° When I know not what else to do, I'll see thee again.

TIMON  When there is nothing living but thee, thou shalt be welcome. I had rather be a beggar's dog than 355 Apemantus.

APEMANTUS
Thou art the cap° of all the fools alive.

TIMON
Would thou wert clean enough to spit upon.

APEMANTUS
A plague on thee, thou art too bad to curse.

TIMON
All villains that do stand by thee° are pure.          360

APEMANTUS
There is no leprosy but what thou speak'st.

TIMON
If I name thee.
I'll beat thee, but I should infect my hands.

APEMANTUS
I would my tongue could rot them off.

TIMON
Away, thou issue of a mangy dog.                       365
Choler° does kill me that thou art alive;
I swound° to see thee.

APEMANTUS  Would thou wouldst burst.

TIMON  Away, thou tedious rogue, I am sorry I shall lose a stone by thee.                                    370

[Throws a stone at him.]

APEMANTUS  Beast!

TIMON  Slave!

APEMANTUS  Toad!

TIMON
Rogue, rogue, rogue!
I am sick of this false world, and will love naught    375
But even the mere necessities upon't.
Then, Timon, presently° prepare thy grave.
Lie where the light foam of the sea may beat
Thy gravestone daily. Make thine epitaph,
That death in me° at others' lives may laugh.          380

[To the gold.]

O thou sweet king-killer, and dear divorce
'Twixt natural° son and sire, thou bright defiler
Of Hymen's° purest bed, thou valiant Mars,
Thou ever young, fresh, loved, and delicate wooer,
Whose blush° doth thaw the consecrated snow          385
That lies on Dian's° lap. Thou visible god,
That sold'rest close impossibilities°
And mak'st them kiss; that speak'st with every tongue
To every purpose. O thou touch° of hearts,
Think thy slave man rebels, and by thy virtue         390
Set them into confounding odds,° that beasts
May have the world in empire.

APEMANTUS               Would 'twere so,

---

**308 And** if; **meddlers** (1) the fruit (2) busybodies, intriguers (3) those who overindulge in sexual intercourse **310 unthrift** prodigal, spendthrift **311 after** in accordance with (i.e., the true love for an "unthrift" is not in proportion with his bounty) **316 a dog** i.e., you had just enough to keep a dog so that something might love you **323–24 confusion of men** the original fall in the Garden of Eden **328 beguile** trick **330 peradventure** perchance **335 unicorn** an untamable beast, who, in his fury to attack the treed lion, runs his horn into the tree and puts himself at the mercy of the lion **336 confound** destroy **340 german** akin; **spots** (1) markings (2) moral stains, vices **341 jurors** witnesses (especially false ones); **remotion** removal of yourself (to a distance), remoteness **344 in transformation** in seeking to be transformed into a beast **350 poet . . . painter** they do not actually enter until the beginning of Act V **352 give way** retire

**357 cap** chief, summit **360 that . . . thee** compared to you **366 Choler** anger **367 swound** swoon **376 But . . . upon't** except the bare necessities of life **377 presently** immediately **380 in me** by my example **382 natural** son by birth (does not mean "illegitimate") **383 Hymen** Greek god of marriage **385 blush** glow **386 Dian** Diana, the virgin huntress, Greek goddess of chastity **387 sold'rest close impossibilities** joins closely together things thought to be irreconcilable **389 touch** touchstone **391 into confounding odds** at ruinous strife

But not till I am dead. I'll say th' hast gold.
Thou wilt be thronged to shortly.

TIMON                    Thronged to?

APEMANTUS                    Ay.

TIMON
Thy back, I prithee.

APEMANTUS        Live, and love thy misery.    395

TIMON
Long live so, and so die. I am quit.°

*Enter the* BANDITTI.

APEMANTUS
Moe things like men! Eat, Timon, and abhor them.
                    *Exit* APEMANTUS.

FIRST BANDIT   Where should he have his gold? It is
some poor fragment, some slender ort° of his remainder. The mere° want of gold, and the falling-from°   400
of his friends, drove him into this melancholy.

SECOND BANDIT   It is noised° he hath a mass of
treasure.

THIRD BANDIT   Let us make the assay° upon him. If
he care not for't, he will supply us easily; if he covet-   405
ously reserve it, how shall's get it?

SECOND BANDIT   True, for he bears it not about
him; 'tis hid.

FIRST BANDIT   Is not this he?

ALL   Where?    410

SECOND BANDIT   'Tis his description.

THIRD BANDIT   He? I know him.

ALL   Save thee,° Timon.

TIMON   Now, thieves?

ALL
Soldiers, not thieves.

TIMON                    Both too, and women's sons.    415

ALL
We are not thieves, but men that much do want.°

TIMON
Your greatest want is, you want much of meat.°
Why should you want? Behold, the earth hath roots;
Within this mile break forth a hundred springs;
The oaks bear mast,° the briers scarlet hips;°    420
The bounteous huswife° Nature on each bush
Lays her full mess° before you. Want? Why want?

FIRST BANDIT
We cannot live on grass, on berries, water,
As beasts and birds and fishes.

TIMON
Nor on the beasts themselves, the birds and fishes;    425
You must eat men. Yet thanks I must you con°
That you are thieves professed, that you work not
In holier shapes; for there is boundless theft
In limited° professions. Rascal thieves,
Here's gold. Go, suck the subtle° blood o' th' grape,    430
Till the high fever° seethe your blood to froth,

And so 'scape hanging. Trust not the physician;
His antidotes are poison, and he slays
Moe° than you rob. Take wealth and lives together,
Do, villain, do, since you protest° to do't.    435
Like workmen, I'll example you with thievery:°
The sun's a thief, and with his great attraction°
Robs the vast sea. The moon's an arrant thief,
And her pale fire she snatches from the sun.
The sea's a thief, whose liquid surge resolves    440
The moon into salt tears.° The earth's a thief,
That feeds and breeds by a composture° stol'n
From gen'ral excrement. Each thing's a thief.
The laws, your curb and whip, in their rough power
Has unchecked theft. Love not yourselves; away,    445
Rob one another. There's more gold; cut throats,
All that you meet are thieves. To Athens go,
Break open shops; nothing can you steal
But thieves do lose it. Steal less for this I give you,°
And gold confound you howsoe'er.° Amen.    450

THIRD BANDIT   Has almost charmed me from my
profession by persuading me to it.

FIRST BANDIT   'Tis in the malice of mankind° that
he thus advises us, not to have us thrive in our
mystery.°    455

SECOND BANDIT   I'll believe him as an enemy,° and
give over° my trade.

FIRST BANDIT   Let us first see peace in Athens; there
is no time so miserable but a man may be true.°
                    *Exit* THIEVES.

*Enter [*FLAVIUS,*] the steward to Timon.*

FLAVIUS
O you gods!    460
Is yond despised and ruinous° man my lord?
Full of decay and failing? O monument
And wonder° of good deeds evilly bestowed!
What an alteration of honor° has desp'rate want
made!
What vilder° thing upon the earth than friends,    465
Who can bring noblest minds to basest ends!
How rarely does it meet with this time's guise,°
When man was wished° to love his enemies!
Grant I may ever love, and rather woo
Those that would mischief me than those that do.°    470
Has caught me in his eye; I will present

---

**434 Moe** more   **435 protest** profess   **436 Like . . . thievery**
As one instructs workmen by practical example, so I will give
you some precedents for your line of work, thievery   **437
attraction** drawing power   **440–41 whose . . . tears** the
idea is that the sea's tides are stolen from the moon's precipitation   **442 composture** compost, manure   **449 Steal . . .
you** even if you steal less because of the gold I am giving you
**450 howsoe'er** nevertheless   **453 in . . . mankind** because
of the malice Timon bears to all mankind   **455 mystery** trade,
profession   **456 I'll . . . enemy** Since he is an enemy, I'll do the
opposite of what he advises   **457 give over** give up   **458–59
there . . . true** You can become an honest man any time you
choose (therefore, why do it now?)   **461 ruinous** ruined   **462–63
monument And wonder** wonderful monument (memorial
or tombstone)   **464 alteration of honor** change (for the
worse) in honor   **465 vilder** viler   **467 How . . . guise** How
excellently does Timon's example fit in with the moral tone of
these times (spoken ironically)   **468 wished** desired (by God)
**470 Those . . . do** I will love those enemies who are direct
and open in their desire to harm me better than those who harm
me under the guise of friendship

---

**396 quit** rid (of Apemantus)   **399 ort** leftover bit   **400 mere**
sheer; **falling-from** falling-off   **402 noised** rumored   **404
make the assay** put it to the test   **413 Save thee** God save
thee (a conventional salutation)   **416 want** need, lack   **417
you . . . meat** you desire (or lack) a good deal of food (i.e.,
if you didn't eat so much your wants would be smaller)   **420
mast** acorns (generally fed to swine); **hips** fruit of the rose
**421 huswife** housewife   **422 mess** meal   **426 con** offer   **429
limited** limited in numbers, restricted (as a guild)   **430 subtle**
treacherous   **431 high fever** i.e., of drunkenness

My honest grief unto him, and as my lord
Still serve him with my life. My dearest master.

TIMON
Away! What art thou?

FLAVIUS                    Have you forgot me, sir?

TIMON
Why dost ask that? I have forgot all men.                    475
Then, if thou grunt'st° th' art a man,
I have forgot thee.

FLAVIUS
An honest poor servant of yours.

TIMON
Then I know thee not.
I never had honest man about me, I; all                    480
I kept were knaves,° to serve in meat to villains.

FLAVIUS
The gods are witness,
Nev'r did poor steward wear a truer grief
For his undone lord than mine eyes for you.

TIMON
What, dost thou weep? Come nearer. Then I love thee 485
Because thou art a woman, and disclaim'st
Flinty° mankind, whose eyes do never give°
But thorough° lust and laughter. Pity's sleeping.
Strange times, that weep with laughing, not with
    weeping!

FLAVIUS
I beg of you to know me, good my lord,                    490
T' accept my grief, and whilst this poor wealth lasts,
To entertain° me as your steward still.

TIMON
Had I a steward
So true, so just, and now so comfortable?°
It almost turns my dangerous nature mild.                    495
Let me behold thy face. Surely, this man
Was born of woman.
Forgive my general and exceptless° rashness,
You perpetual-sober gods. I do proclaim
One honest man. Mistake me not, but one.                    500
No more I pray—and he's a steward.
How fain would I have hated all mankind,
And thou redeem'st thyself. But all save thee
I fell° with curses.
Methinks thou art more honest now than wise;                    505
For, by oppressing° and betraying me,
Thou might'st have sooner got another service.°
For many so arrive at second masters
Upon their first lord's neck.° But tell me true—
For I must ever doubt,° though ne'er so sure—                    510
Is not thy kindness subtle, covetous,
A usuring kindness, as rich men deal° gifts,
Expecting in return twenty for one?

FLAVIUS
No, my most worthy master, in whose breast

Doubt and suspect,° alas, are placed too late.                    515
You should have feared false times when you did feast.
Suspect still° comes where an estate is least.
That which I show, heaven knows, is merely° love,
Duty and zeal to your unmatchèd mind,
Care of your food and living; and believe it,                    520
My most honored lord,
For any benefit that points° to me,
Either in hope or present, I'd exchange
For this one wish, that you had power and wealth
To requite me by making rich yourself.                    525

TIMON
Look thee, 'tis so. Thou singly° honest man,
Here, take. The gods out of my misery
Has sent thee treasure. Go, live rich and happy,
But thus conditioned:° thou shalt build from° men;
Hate all, curse all, show charity to none,                    530
But let the famished flesh slide from the bone
Ere thou relieve the beggar. Give to dogs
What thou deniest to men. Let prisons swallow 'em,
Debts wither 'em to nothing; be men like blasted°
    woods,
And may diseases lick up their false bloods.                    535
And so farewell, and thrive.

FLAVIUS
O let me stay and comfort you, my master.

TIMON
If thou hat'st curses
Stay not; fly, whilst thou art blessed and free.
Ne'er see thou man, and let me ne'er see thee.                    540
            Exit [FLAVIUS; and exit TIMON into his cave].

# [ ACT V ]

[Scene I. *Before Timon's cave*.]

*Enter* POET *and* PAINTER; [TIMON *listens from his cave,
unseen*].

PAINTER  As I took note of the place, it cannot be far
where he abides.

POET  What's to be thought of him? Does the rumor
hold for true that he's so full of gold?

PAINTER  Certain. Alcibiades reports it. Phrynia and 5
Timandra had gold of him. He likewise enriched poor
straggling soldiers° with great quantity. 'Tis said he
gave unto his steward a mighty sum.

POET  Then this breaking° of his has been but a try°
for his friends?                    10

PAINTER  Nothing else. You shall see him a palm° in
Athens again, and flourish with the highest. Therefore
'tis not amiss we tender° our loves to him in this
supposed distress of his. It will show honestly° in us,
and is very likely to load our purposes with what they 15

---

476 **grunt'st** i.e., even your claim to be a man is delivered
in an animal grunt (since all men are bestial)  481 **knaves** (1)
servants (2) villains  487 **Flinty** hardhearted; **give** weep  488
**But thorough** except through  492 **entertain** receive into
service  494 **comfortable** comforting  498 **exceptless** making
no exceptions  504 **fell** cause to fall, strike down  506
**oppressing** distressing  507 **service** position as a servant
509 **Upon . . . neck** by treading down their first master and
mounting on his neck (or shoulders)  510 **doubt** suspect, fear
512 **deal** distribute

515 **suspect** suspicion  517 **still** always  518 **merely** entirely
522 **points** might accrue  526 **singly** (1) uniquely (2) truly
529 **But thus conditioned** with this condition; **from** away
from  534 **blasted** blighted
V.i.7 **soldiers** the banditti, who claimed to be soldiers  9
**breaking** going bankrupt; **try** test  11 **palm** cf. Psalm 92:11,
"The righteous shall flourish like the palm-tree"  13 **tender**
offer  14 **honestly** honorably

travail° for, if it be a just and true report that goes of
his having.°

POET  What have you now to present unto him?

PAINTER  Nothing at this time but my visitation; only
I will promise him an excellent piece.                    20

POET  I must serve him so too, tell him of an intent
that's coming toward him.

PAINTER  Good as the best. Promising is the very air
o' th' time; it opens the eyes of expectation. Performance is ever the duller for his act,° and but in the    25
plainer and simpler kind of people, the deed of saying°
is quite out of use. To promise is most courtly and
fashionable; performance is a kind of will or testament,
which argues a great sickness in his judgment that
makes it.                                                 30

*Enter TIMON from his cave.*

TIMON [*Aside.*]  Excellent workman, thou canst not
paint a man so bad as is thyself.

POET  I am thinking what I shall say I have provided
for him. It must be a personating of himself;° a satire
against the softness° of prosperity, with a discovery°   35
of the infinite flatteries that follow youth and opulency.

TIMON [*Aside.*]  Must thou needs stand for° a villain
in thine own work? Wilt thou whip thine own faults
in other men? Do so, I have gold for thee.

POET  Nay, let's seek him.                                40
Then do we sin against our own estate,°
When we may profit meet, and come too late.

PAINTER  True.
When the day serves, before black-cornered night,°
Find what thou want'st by free and offered light.        45
Come.

TIMON [*Aside.*]
I'll meet you at the turn.°
What a god's gold, that he is worshiped
In a baser temple° than where swine feed!
'Tis thou that rig'st the bark and plough'st the foam,    50
Settlest admirèd reverence° in a slave.
To thee be worshiped and thy saints for aye;°
Be° crowned with plagues that thee alone obey.
Fit I meet them.

[*Comes forward.*]

POET
Hail, worthy Timon.

PAINTER                   Our late noble master.           55

TIMON
Have I once° lived to see two honest men?

POET
Sir,
Having often of your open bounty tasted,

Hearing you were retired,° your friends fall'n off,
Whose thankless natures, O abhorrèd spirits,              60
Not all the whips of heaven are large enough—
What, to you,
Whose star-like nobleness gave life and influence°
To their whole being! I am rapt,° and cannot cover
The monstrous bulk of this ingratitude                   65
With any size° of words.

TIMON                Let it go;
Naked, men may see't the better.
You that are honest, by being what you are,
Make them° best seen and known.

PAINTER                           He and myself
Have traveled in the great show'r of your gifts,         70
And sweetly felt it.

TIMON          Ay, you are honest men.

PAINTER
We are hither come to offer you our service.

TIMON
Most honest men. Why, how shall I requite you?
Can you eat roots and drink cold water? No?

BOTH
What we can do, we'll do to do you service.              75

TIMON
Y' are honest men. Y' have heard that I have gold,
I am sure you have. Speak truth, y' are honest men.

PAINTER
So it is said, my noble lord, but therefore
Came not my friend nor I.

TIMON
Good honest men. Thou draw'st a counterfeit°             80
Best in all Athens. Th' art indeed the best;
Thou counterfeit'st most lively.°

PAINTER                So-so, my lord.

TIMON
E'en so, sir, as I say. And for thy fiction,°
Why thy verse swells with stuff so fine and smooth°
That thou art even natural in thine art.°                85
But for all this, my honest-natured friends,
I must needs say you have a little fault;
Marry,° 'tis not monstrous in you, neither wish I
You take much pains to mend.

BOTH                    Beseech your honor
To make it known to us.

TIMON                You'll take it ill.                  90

BOTH
Most thankfully, my lord.

TIMON                Will you indeed?

BOTH
Doubt it not, worthy lord.

TIMON
There's never a one of you but trusts a knave
That mightily deceives you.

BOTH                    Do we, my lord?

---

16 **travail** (1) labor (2) travel  17 **having** wealth  25 **his
act** its act, its having been put into action  26 **deed of
saying** the doing of what a person says he will do  34
**personating of himself** representation of Timon and his
situation  35 **softness** weakness, flabbiness; **discovery**
revelation (a theatrical term)  37 **stand for** serve as a model for
41 **estate** fortune, material possessions  44 **black-cornered
night** night which creates dark corners and is obscure like them
47 **I'll . . . turn** I will match your tricks with better ones of
my own  49 **baser temple** the human body  51 **Settlest
admirèd reverence** establishes a wondering awe (of his
master)  52 **for aye** forever  53 **Be** may they be  56 **once**
indeed (an intensive)

59 **retired** withdrawn  63 **influence** i.e., astrological influence
64 **rapt** carried away with emotion  66 **size** (1) magnitude
(2) starchlike glue used on cloth, especially before painting
on it  69 **them** the thankless natures of his fair-weather friends
80 **counterfeit** (1) representation, picture (2) false representation  82 **most lively** in a most lifelike manner  83 **fiction**
imaginative feigning  84 **smooth** polished (with implication
of flattery)  85 **thou . . . art** (1) your writings represent a
triumph of nature over art; your art conceals itself (2) you
show your evil natural self in your artful dissimulation  88
**Marry** indeed

**TIMON**
Ay, and you hear him cog,° see him dissemble,     95
Know his gross patchery,° love him, feed him,
Keep° in your bosom, yet remain assured
That he's a made-up° villain.
**PAINTER**
I know none such, my lord.
**POET**                Nor I.
**TIMON**
Look you, I love you well; I'll give you gold:     100
Rid me these villains from your companies.
Hang them, or stab them, drown them in a draught,°
Confound° them by some course, and come to me,
I'll give you gold enough.
**BOTH**
Name them, my lord, let's know them.     105
**TIMON**
You that way, and you this; but two in company.°
Each man apart, all single and alone,
Yet an arch-villain keeps him company.

[*To one.*]

If where thou art, two villains shall not be,
Come not near him. [*To the other.*] If thou wouldst
    not reside     110
But° where one villain is, then him abandon.
Hence, pack,° there's gold; you came for gold, ye
    slaves.

[*To one.*]

You have work for me, there's payment. Hence!

[*To the other.*]

You are an alchemist, make gold of that.
Out, rascal dogs!     115
          [*Beats them out, then retires into his cave.*]

*Enter* [FLAVIUS, *the*] *steward, and two* SENATORS.

**FLAVIUS**
It is vain that you would speak with Timon,
For he is set so only to himself°
That nothing but himself, which looks like man,
Is friendly with him.
**FIRST SENATOR**       Bring us to his cave.
It is our part and promise° to th' Athenians     120
To speak with Timon.
**SECOND SENATOR**       At all times alike
Men are not still the same; 'twas time and griefs
That framed him thus. Time with his fairer hand
Offering the fortunes of his former days,
The former man may make him. Bring us to him,     125
And chance it° as it may.
**FLAVIUS**           Here is his cave.
Peace and content be here. Lord Timon! Timon!
Look out, and speak to friends. Th' Athenians
By two of their most reverend Senate greet thee.
Speak to them, noble Timon.     130

---

*Enter* TIMON *out of his cave.*

**TIMON**
Thou sun that comforts, burn! Speak and be hanged.
For each true word a blister,° and each false
Be as a cauterizing to the root o' th' tongue,
Consuming it with speaking.
**FIRST SENATOR**       Worthy Timon—
**TIMON**
Of none but such as you, and you of Timon.     135
**FIRST SENATOR**
The Senators of Athens greet thee, Timon.
**TIMON**
I thank them, and would send them back the plague,
Could I but catch it for them.
**FIRST SENATOR**       O forget
What we are sorry for ourselves in thee.°
The Senators, with one consent of love,°     140
Entreat thee back to Athens, who have thought
On special dignities, which vacant lie
For thy best use and wearing.°
**SECOND SENATOR**       They confess
Toward thee forgetfulness too general° gross;
Which now the public body,° which doth seldom     145
Play the recanter, feeling in itself
A lack of Timon's aid, hath sense withal°
Of it own fall,° restraining° aid to Timon;
And send forth us to make their sorrowed render,°
Together with a recompense more fruitful°     150
Than their offense can weigh down by the dram°—
Ay, even such heaps and sums of love and wealth
As shall to thee blot out what wrongs were theirs,
And write in thee the figures° of their love,
Ever to read them° thine.
**TIMON**       You witch° me in it;     155
Surprise me to the very brink of tears.
Lend me a fool's heart and a woman's eyes,
And I'll beweep these comforts,° worthy Senators.
**FIRST SENATOR**
Therefore so please thee to return with us,
And of our Athens, thine and ours, to take     160
The captainship, thou shalt be met with thanks,
Allowed° with absolute power, and thy good name
Live with authority. So soon we shall drive back
Of Alcibiades th' approaches wild,
Who like a boar too savage doth root up     165
His country's peace.
**SECOND SENATOR** And shakes his threat'ning sword
Against the walls of Athens.
**FIRST SENATOR**       Therefore, Timon—

---

**95 cog** cheat    **96 patchery** roguery    **97 Keep** let him dwell
**98 made-up** complete    **102 draught** privy, sink    **103 Confound** destroy    **106 but . . . company** i.e., wherever either of them is, there is both a poet (or painter) and a villain    **111 But** except    **112 pack** be off    **117 is . . . himself** is so completely preoccupied with himself    **120 our . . . promise** the role we promised to play    **126 chance it** may it turn out

**132 For . . . blister** an ironic reversal of the proverbial belief that a lie causes a blister on the tongue    **139 in thee** in the wrongs we have caused you    **140 consent of love** harmonious voice of affection    **143 For . . . wearing** only you are suited to fill these dignities with the proper distinction    **144 general** universally    **145 the public body** the Senate as representative of the body politic    **147 withal** at the same time    **148 it own fall** its own fall from grace; **restraining** keeping back    **149 sorrowed render** sorrowful rendering of an account    **150 fruitful** abundant    **151 weigh . . . dram** balance in weight even if measured to the last tiny unit    **154 figures** (1) written characters (2) numerals (as in counting money) (3) images, representations    **155 them** the Athenians as represented in the "figures of their love"; **witch** bewitch    **158 comforts** pleasures    **162 Allowed** endowed

TIMON
Well, sir, I will; therefore I will, sir, thus:
If Alcibiades kill my countrymen,
Let Alcibiades know this of Timon,                        170
That Timon cares not. But if he sack fair Athens,
And take our goodly agèd men by th' beards,
Giving our holy virgins to the stain
Of contumelious,° beastly, mad-brained war,
Then let him know, and tell him Timon speaks it,         175
In pity of our agèd and our youth,
I cannot choose but tell him that I care not,
And let him take't at worst.° For their knives care not
While you have throats to answer.° For myself,
There's not a whittle° in th' unruly camp°              180
But I do prize it at my love° before
The reverend'st throat in Athens. So I leave you
To the protection of the prosperous° gods,
As thieves to keepers.°
FLAVIUS                    Stay not, all's in vain.
TIMON
Why I was writing of my epitaph;                         185
It will be seen tomorrow. My long sickness
Of health and living now begins to mend,
And nothing° brings me all things. Go, live still;
Be Alcibiades your plague, you his,
And last° so long enough.
FIRST SENATOR            We speak in vain.                190
TIMON
But yet I love my country, and am not
One that rejoices in the common wrack,°
As common bruit° doth put it.
FIRST SENATOR               That's well spoke.
TIMON
Commend me to my loving countrymen.
FIRST SENATOR
These words become° your lips as they pass thorough
them.                                                    195
SECOND SENATOR
And enter in our ears like great triumphers°
In their applauding gates.°
TIMON                    Commend me to them,
And tell them that to ease them of their griefs,
Their fears of hostile strokes, their aches,° losses,
Their pangs of love, with other incident throes°        200
That nature's fragile vessel doth sustain
In life's uncertain voyage, I will some kindness do
them;
I'll teach them to prevent° wild Alcibiades' wrath.
FIRST SENATOR
I like this well; he will return again.

TIMON
I have a tree which grows here in my close,°             205
That mine own use invites me to cut down,
And shortly must I fell it. Tell my friends,
Tell Athens, in the sequence of degree,°
From high to low throughout, that whoso please
To stop affliction, let him take his haste;             210
Come hither ere my tree hath felt the ax,
And hang himself. I pray you do my greeting.
FLAVIUS
Trouble him no further; thus you still° shall find him.
TIMON
Come not to me again, but say to Athens,
Timon hath made his everlasting mansion                  215
Upon the beachèd verge of the salt flood,°
Who° once a day with his embossèd° froth
The turbulent surge shall cover. Thither come,
And let my gravestone be your oracle.°
Lips, let four words go by and language end.°            220
What is amiss, plague and infection mend.
Graves only be men's works and death their gain.
Sun, hide thy beams; Timon hath done his reign.
                                            Exit TIMON.
FIRST SENATOR
His discontents are unremovably
Coupled to nature.°                                      225
SECOND SENATOR
Our hope in him is dead. Let us return,
And strain° what other means is left unto us
In our dear° peril.
FIRST SENATOR   It requires swift foot.      Exeunt.


[Scene II. Before the walls of Athens.]

Enter two other SENATORS, with a MESSENGER.

THIRD SENATOR
Thou hast painfully discovered.° Are his files°
As full as thy report?
MESSENGER            I have spoke the least.°
Besides, his expedition° promises
Present° approach.
FOURTH SENATOR
We stand much hazard if they bring not Timon.             5
MESSENGER
I met a courier, one mine ancient° friend,
Whom though in general part° we were opposed,
Yet our old love made a particular° force,

174 contumelious insolent  178 take't at worst put the
worst interpretation he wishes on it  179 throats to answer
throats to be cut by the knives of Alcibiades' soldiers (and
voices to protest for yourselves)  180 whittle small knife; th'
unruly camp (1) the party of those revolting against Athens (2)
the disorderly, turbulent army (of Alcibiades)  181 prize . . .
love value it in my esteem  183 prosperous propitious  184
As . . . keepers as I would leave thieves to the protection
of their jailers  188 nothing nothingness, oblivion  190 last
endure  192 wrack destruction  193 bruit rumor  195
become befit  196 triumphers triumphant marchers  197
applauding gates city gates thronged with those applauding
the triumph  199 aches two syllables, pronounced "aitches"
200 incident throes agonies likely to occur  203 prevent
anticipate (but First Senator interprets "to keep from occurring")

205 close enclosure  208 sequence of degree proper order of
the social hierarchy  213 still always  216 beachèd . . .
flood edge of the sea that forms a beach  217 Who "the
beachèd verge"; embossèd covered with foam (usually from
the mouth of a hunted animal)  219 be your oracle be consulted by you as if it were an oracle (a place where divine
pronouncements are made, or the god making such pronouncements)  220 let . . . end speak only a few more words
("four" is used indefinitely) and then not speak any further
225 Coupled to nature a part of his nature  227 strain exert
to the utmost  228 dear grievous, dire
V.ii.1 Thou . . . discovered (1) Your revelation was painful
to us (2) You have made your revelation in painstaking detail;
files ranks  2 spoke the least reported the minimum  3
expedition speed  4 Present immediate  6 ancient former
7 in general part in matters of general or public interest  8
particular personal

And made us speak like friends. This man was riding
From Alcibiades to Timon's cave      10
With letters of entreaty, which imported°
His fellowship i' th' cause against your city,
In part for his sake moved.°

*Enter the other* SENATORS [*from Timon*].

THIRD SENATOR      Here come our brothers.
FIRST SENATOR
No talk° of Timon, nothing of him expect.
The enemy's drum is heard, and fearful scouring°      15
Doth choke the air with dust. In, and prepare.
Ours is the fall, I fear, our foes the snare.°      *Exeunt.*


[Scene III. *Before Timon's cave.*]

*Enter a* SOLDIER *in the woods, seeking Timon.*

SOLDIER
By all description this should be the place.
Who's here? Speak, ho! No answer? What is this?°
"Timon is dead, who hath outstretched his span.°
Some beast read this; there does not live a man."°
Dead, sure, and this his grave. What's on this tomb      5
I cannot read. The character I'll take with wax;°
Our captain hath in every figure° skill,
An aged° interpreter, though young in days
Before proud Athens he's set down° by this,
Whose fall the mark° of his ambition is.      *Exit.* 10


[Scene IV. *Before the walls of Athens.*]

*Trumpets sound. Enter* ALCIBIADES, *with his* POWERS,
*before Athens.*

ALCIBIADES
Sound to this coward and lascivious town
Our terrible° approach.

*Sounds a parley.° The* SENATORS *appear upon the walls.*°

Till now you have gone on, and filled the time
With all licentious measure,° making your wills
The scope° of justice. Till now, myself and such      5
As slept° within the shadow of your power,

Have wandered with our traversed° arms and breathed
Our sufferance vainly.° Now the time is flush,°
When crouching marrow in the bearer strong°
Cries, of itself, "No more." Now breathless wrong°      10
Shall sit and pant in your great chairs of ease,°
And pursy° insolence shall break his wind
With fear and horrid° flight.
FIRST SENATOR      Noble and young,
When thy first griefs° were but a mere conceit,°
Ere thou hadst power or we had cause of fear,      15
We sent to thee to give thy rages balm,
To wipe out our ingratitude with loves
Above their° quantity.
SECOND SENATOR      So did we woo
Transformèd Timon to our city's love
By humble message and by promised means.°      20
We were not all unkind, nor all deserve
The common stroke of war.
FIRST SENATOR      These walls of ours
Were not erected by their hands from whom
You have received your grief; nor are they such
That these great tow'rs, trophies, and schools° should
     fall      25
For private faults in them.
SECOND SENATOR      Nor are they living
Who were the motives that you first went out.°
Shame that they wanted, cunning in excess
Hath broke their hearts.° March, noble lord,
Into our city with thy banners spread.      30
By decimation and a tithèd death,°
If thy revenges hunger for that food
Which nature loathes, take thou the destined tenth,
And by the hazard of the spotted die,°
Let die the spotted.°
FIRST SENATOR      All have not offended.      35
For those that were, it is not square° to take
On those that are, revenge. Crimes, like lands,
Are not inherited. Then, dear countryman,
Bring in thy ranks, but leave without° thy rage.
Spare thy Athenian cradle and those kin      40
Which in the bluster° of thy wrath must fall
With those that have offended. Like a shepherd,
Approach the fold° and cull th' infected forth,
But kill not all together.
SECOND SENATOR      What thou wilt,

---

**11 imported** bore as their message (with additional suggestion of "importuned" or urged) **13 moved** instigated **14 No talk** let us not talk **15 scouring** scurrying about (in preparation for battle) **17 our . . . snare** our foes are the snare or trap that will cause the downfall of Athens **V.iii.2 What is this** presumably the Soldier finds an inscription or trial epitaph composed by Timon in English, which the Soldier can read, whereas the epitaph on Timon's tomb is in Latin, which the Soldier cannot read **3 outstretched his span** lived beyond his allotted or desired life span **4 there . . . man** all men left alive are merely beasts **6 character . . . wax** I will take a wax impression of the letters **7 figure** written character **8 aged** experienced **9 set down** i.e., in a siege **10 mark** goal **V.iv.2 terrible** terrifying **2 s.d. Sounds a parley** i.e., by a special signal on drum or trumpet, Alcibiades calls for a conference with the enemy to try to make peace; **upon the walls** i.e., upon the upper stage **4 With . . . measure** with all kinds of unbridled conduct **5 scope** extent **6 slept** (1) were asleep, inactive (2) lived

**7 traversed** folded across (in resignation) **7–8 breathed . . . vainly** spoke in vain about our sufferings **8 flush** ripe **9 When . . . strong** when the resolute man's courage is aroused **10 breathless wrong** wrongdoers breathless through fear **11 great . . . ease** comfortably upholstered chairs of state **12 pursy** short-winded **13 horrid** horrible **14 griefs** grievances; **conceit** idea **18 their** the antecedent is either "griefs" or "rages" or both **20 means** conditions of peace (or possibly "riches") **25 trophies, and schools** monuments, and public buildings **27 motives . . . out** instigators or movers of your original banishment **28–29 Shame . . . hearts** i.e., their hearts were broken with remorse for two common moral failings: lack of a sense of disgrace for their wrongdoing and excess of crafty deceit **31 decimation . . . death** the killing of one person in ten **34 by . . . die** by chance, as in dice ("die" is the singular of "dice") **35 spotted** (1) guilty (2) those selected by the "spots" on the dice **36 square** honest **39 without** outside **41 bluster** tempest **43 fold** enclosure for sheep or the flock itself

Thou rather shalt enforce it with thy smile                45
Than hew to't° with thy sword.

FIRST SENATOR                    Set but thy foot
Against our rampired° gates, and they shall ope,
So° thou wilt send thy gentle heart before
To say thou't enter friendly.

SECOND SENATOR              Throw thy glove,
Or any token of thine honor else,                          50
That thou wilt use the wars as thy redress
And not as our confusion.° All thy powers°
Shall make their harbor° in our town till we
Have sealed° thy full desire.

ALCIBIADES                    Then there's my glove.
Descend and open your uncharged ports.°                    55
Those enemies of Timon's and mine own
Whom you yourselves shall set out for reproof,°
Fall, and no more. And to atone° your fears
With my more noble meaning,° not a man
Shall pass his quarter,° or offend the stream              60
Of regular justice in your city's bounds,
But shall be remedied° to your public laws
At heaviest answer.°

BOTH SENATORS       'Tis most nobly spoken.

ALCIBIADES
Descend, and keep your words.

[*The* SENATORS *descend, and open the gates.*]

*Enter a* SOLDIER.

SOLDIER
My noble general, Timon is dead,                           65

**46 hew to't** cut thy way to it    **47 rampired** fortified    **48 So**
provided that    **52 confusion** destruction; **powers** armed
forces    **53 make their harbor** be billeted    **54 sealed** solemnly
ratified (by fulfilling)    **55 uncharged ports** unassailed gates
**57 reproof** shame    **58 atone** appease    **59 meaning** intention
**60 quarter** billet (?) area of duty (?)    **62 remedied** turned
over for remedy    **63 At heaviest answer** for the maximum
punishment

Entombed upon the very hem° o' th' sea,
And on his gravestone this insculpture° which
With wax I brought away, whose soft impression
Interprets° for my poor ignorance.

ALCIBIADES *reads the epitaph.*°

ALCIBIADES
"Here lies a wretched corse,° of wretched soul bereft.  70
Seek not my name. A plague consume you, wicked
     caitiffs° left.
Here lie I, Timon, who alive all living men did hate.
Pass by and curse thy fill, but pass, and stay not here
     thy gait."
These well express in thee thy latter° spirits.
Though thou abhorr'dst in us our human griefs,            75
Scorn'dst our brains' flow,° and those our droplets
     which
From niggard° nature fall; yet rich conceit°
Taught thee to make vast Neptune weep for aye°
On thy low grave, on faults forgiven. Dead
Is noble Timon, of whose memory                           80
Hereafter more. Bring me into your city,
And I will use the olive with my sword,°
Make war breed peace, make peace stint° war, make
     each
Prescribe to other, as each other's leech.°
Let our drums strike.                    *Exeunt.*  85

**66 hem** edge (the "beachèd verge" of V.i.216)    **67 insculpture**
inscription    **69 Interprets** acts as an interpreter    **69 s.d.**
**epitaph** there are two epitaphs here, both from North's *Plutarch*,
and it seems very likely that one of them—probably the first—
was intended to be omitted    **70 corse** corpse    **71 caitiffs**
wretches    **74 latter** later, more recent    **76 brains' flow** tears
**77 niggard** stingy; **rich conceit** fanciful imagination    **78 for
aye** forever    **82 use . . . sword** combine the olive branch of
peace with the sword of war, show mercy even though I enter
your city as a conqueror    **83 stint** cause to stop    **84 leech**
physician

# PERICLES, PRINCE OF TYRE

EDITED BY ERNEST SCHANZER

## Introduction

*Pericles* presents several unique problems. Most critics agree that, while Acts III, IV, and V are substantially Shakespeare's, Acts I and II are not. The questions to be asked, therefore, are: Who is the author of Acts I and II? And, further, how did the non-Shakespearean first two acts come to be joined to the Shakespearean last three acts? As to this there are two main possibilities: (1) that Shakespeare collaborated with another playwright, as he did a few years later with John Fletcher in *Henry VIII*, *The Two Noble Kinsmen*, and the lost *Cardenio*; (2) that Shakespeare came across a complete play on the subject of *Pericles* and began to rewrite it at the point where the subject matter caught his imagination, the point at which Pericles, during a storm at sea, is suddenly confronted with the death of his wife and the birth of his daughter. According to this hypothesis, Shakespeare, being an extremely busy man, did not bother to rewrite the first two acts, except, perhaps, to add a few touches here and there.

Of these two possibilities the latter seems to me by far the more likely. That Shakespeare should have collaborated with the author of the first two acts seems very improbable. To collaborate with John Fletcher is one thing; to collaborate with the exceedingly mediocre talent that could produce Acts I and II of *Pericles*, quite another. It is true that these first two acts must have been a good deal better than they are in the text in which they have come down to us. For the quarto text—and this adds greatly to the intricate problems presented by the play—is very corrupt, not only in Acts I and II, but in the Shakespearean part as well. Whole lines are missing, others are garbled, verse is frequently set out as prose, and occasionally prose as verse. It is, most scholars agree, a text based on a report made from visits to the theater, and bears the usual marks of such a reported text—above all, a large number of auditory errors and mislineation of Shakespeare's blank verse.

The quarto of *Pericles*, then, is, in many ways, very imperfect. But where for other Shakespeare plays with bad quarto texts we also have a good text, for *Pericles* we have only the one text, published for the first time in 1609, in what was, no doubt, a pirated edition (that is, it was printed without the permission of Shakespeare and his company). The problem of the authorship of the first two

acts is therefore made much more difficult by the absence of any good text of the play, and scholars have not been able to agree on the probable identity of the author, though various candidates, such as Thomas Heywood, George Wilkins, and, most recently, John Day, have been put forward.

The whole matter is further complicated by the publication in 1608 of a prose narrative by George Wilkins, entitled *The Painfull Aduentures of Pericles Prince of Tyre*, "being," we are assured on the title page, "the true History of the Play of *Pericles*, as it was lately presented by the worthy and ancient Poet *Iohn Gower*." And in *The Argument of the whole Historie* the reader is entreated "to receiue this Historie in the same maner as it was vnder the habite of ancient *Gower* the famous English Poet, by the Kings Maiesties Players [that is, Shakespeare's company] excellently presented." There is every indication that Wilkins' claim is trustworthy: that he had witnessed one or more performances of Shakespeare's play and had based his novel on this, while also drawing freely (and without acknowledgment) on Laurence Twine's prose version of the same story, *The Patterne of Painefull Aduentures*, which had been reprinted in 1607, and is one of the two chief sources of *Pericles*. In publishing his novel in 1608 Wilkins, no doubt, attempted to exploit the great popularity which the play, according to all indications, enjoyed from the outset.

Wilkins' novel is of great interest and value since, next to the quarto text, it provides the only clue that we possess about the nature of the play as performed by Shakespeare's company. Not only can editors of *Pericles* draw on it in devising their stage directions (as has been done in this edition, for instance, at II.ii.16, where the s.d. "*As each Knight passes, his page, who goes before him, presents his shield to Princess Thaisa*" is based on Wilkins' "their Pages before them bearing their Deuices on their shields . . . which being by the knights Page deliuered to the Lady"), but they can find support in it for emendations of corrupt readings in the quarto text. For example, the change of the quarto's certainly corrupt "untimely" to "uncomely" at I.i.129 is strongly supported by Wilkins' "hee was become both father, sonne, and husband by his vncomely and abhorred actions with his owne child." At one point in the text of this edition (III.ii.84–87) even a whole sentence, which in the quarto is manifestly corrupt, Cerimon's

> I heard of an Egyptian
> That had nine hours lien dead,
> Who was by good appliance recoverèd,

has been replaced by the corresponding sentence in Wilkins' narrative, which, with the words in parentheses omitted, sounds very much like Shakespeare's verse and thus may well reproduce what he had written: "I haue read of some Egyptians, who after foure houres death (if man may call it so) haue raised impouerished bodies, like to this, vnto their former health."

Lastly, there is one scene where the quarto text is undoubtedly deficient, and where Wilkins' novel, even if we cannot draw on it for emendations, affords us glimpses of what the main outline of the Shakespearean original appears to have been. It is the scene between Marina and Lysimachus in the brothel (IV.vi.69–121). In Wilkins' novel, as in the play, Lysimachus is depicted as an old client of the bawd, led to the brothel by lust. But in the novel, as the result of Marina's passionate pleas and reproaches, he undergoes a reformation, declaring: "I hither came with thoughtes intemperate, foule and deformed, the which your paines so well hath laued, that they are now white." It is here that the novel diverges most sharply from the play, where, at the corresponding point, Lysimachus is made to declare:

> For me, be you thoughten
> That I came with no ill intent; for to me
> The very doors and windows savor vilely. (IV.vi.113–15)

This stands, of course, in complete contradiction to what we have been shown in the first part of the scene, where Lysimachus is presented as an old and favorite client. This contradiction has led some scholars to suggest that Lysimachus' later claims reflect a change of mind on Shakespeare's part, a belated attempt to make him a more acceptable husband for Marina. But it seems incredible that Shakespeare should not have bothered to bring the earlier part of the scene into line with this new conception. Furthermore, the writing, which is for the most part Shakespearean up to line 109, ceases to be so at precisely the point at which Lysimachus protests his innocence, and we get such wretched un-Shakespearean stuff as his "For me, be you thoughten. . . ." I believe, then, that lines 109–21 represent the reporter's attempt to reconstruct an only dimly remembered passage, which, for some reason, was missing in his report, and that in doing so he turned Lysimachus from a character somewhat like that of Bertram in *All's Well That Ends Well* into one closer to the duke in *Measure for Measure*. The great value of Wilkins' account of this scene is not only that he preserved for us what I believe to be Shakespeare's version of it, which had been distorted by the reporter, but that he incidentally seems to have kept a good many of Shakespeare's lines which are missing in the quarto text, as the following extract from the dialogue between Marina and Lysimachus will show. The lines which seem to me Shakespearean have been italicized and the blank verse line division has been indicated.

If you take from mee mine honour, *you are like him,/that makes a gappe into forbidden ground*, after whome too many enter, and you are guiltie of all their euilles: my life is yet vnspotted, my chastitie vnstained in thought. *Then if your violence deface this building,/ the workemanship of heauen, made vp for good*, and not to be the exercise of sinnes intemperaunce, you do kill your owne honour, abuse your owne iustice, and impouerish me. Why quoth *Lysimachus, this house wherein thou liuest,/is euen the receptacle of all mens sinnes,/and nurse of wickednesse*, and how canst thou then be otherwise then naught, that liuest in it? It is not good, answered *Marina*, when you that are the Gouernour, who should liue well, *the better to be bolde to punish euill*, doe knowe that there is such a roofe, and yet come vnder it. Is there a necessitie (my yet good Lord) if there be fire before me, that I must strait then thither flie and burne my selfe? Or if suppose this house, (*which too too many feele such houses are)/should be the Doctors patrimony, and Surgeons feeding;* folowes it therefore, that I must needs infect my self to giue them maintenance? O my good Lord, kill me, but not deflower me, punish me how you please, so you spare my chastitie, and since it is all the dowry that both the Gods haue giuen, and men haue left to me, do not you take it from me; make me your seruant, I will willingly obey you; make mee your bondwoman, *I will accompt it freedome; let me be/the worst that is called vile, so I may still/liue honest, I am content:* or if you thinke it is too blessed a happinesse to haue me so, *let me euen now, now in this minute die,* and Ile accompt my death more happy than my birth. With which wordes (being spoken vpon her knees) while her eyes were the glasses that carried the water of her mishap, the good Gentlewoman being mooued, hee lift her vp with his hands, and euen then imbraced her in his hart, saying aside: *Now surely this is Virtues image,/or rather, Vertues selfe, sent downe, from heauen,/a while to raigne on earth,* to teach vs what we should be. So in steede of willing her to drie her eyes, he wiped the wet himselfe off, and could haue found in his heart, with modest thoughts to haue kissed her, but that hee feared the offer would offend her. This onely hee sayde, Lady, for such your vertues are, *a farre more worthy stile your beuty challenges,* and no way lesse your beauty can promise me that you are, *I hither came/ with thoughtes intemperate, foule and deformed,* the which your paines so well hath laued, that they are now white, continue still to all so, and for my parte, *who hither came but to haue payd the price,/a peece of golde for your virginitie,* now giue you twenty to releeue your honesty. *It shall become you still/to be euen as you are, a peece of goodnesse,/the best wrought vppe, that euer Nature made,* and if that any shall inforce you ill, if you but send to me, I am your friend. With which promise, leauing her presence, she most humbly thanked the Gods for the preseruation of of her chastitie, and the reformation of his mind.

I should mention at this point a hypothesis that attempts to account for the stylistic differences between the first two and the last three acts of the play in a radically different way from those mentioned so far. In an important article (*Shakespeare Survey 5*, pp. 25–49) Professor Philip Edwards has suggested that Shakespeare may have been responsible for the entire play, and that the difference in style between the two parts may be due to the different methods adopted by two reporters: the one reporting Acts I and II, the other Acts III–V. The former

> welds into mediocre verse the words, phrases and general sense of the original so far as he can remember them. He is at his best in prose, where remodeling is not attempted. The second reporter, perhaps giving the original very much more faithfully than his predecessor, makes no attempt at rewriting, and after the first scene does not make more than desultory attempts to write down the verse in lines.

This hypothesis is in many ways attractive. For instance, it accounts better than any other for the intermittent occurrence in the first two acts of lines that are manifestly Shakespearean. But there are several grave objections to it, which make it in my view untenable: (1) It seems hard to believe that two men should be willing to adopt such utterly different methods of reporting in order to achieve a composite text. (2) If the first two acts were really by Shakespeare, then those lines in the quarto text that are identical with passages in Wilkins' novel ought to be acceptable Shakespearean verse. But this is clearly not so. For example:

> A gentleman of Tyre; my name Pericles;
> My education been in arts and arms;
> Who, looking for adventures in the world,
> Was by the rough seas reft of ships and men,
> And after shipwrack driven upon this shore. (II.iii.83–87)

agrees almost word for word with the corresponding passage in Wilkins' narrative, but is plainly not Shakespearean. (3) If the report of the last three acts of the play is so much more faithful than that of the first two acts, we ought to find more verbal echoes of the quarto in the part of Wilkins' narrative corresponding to the last three acts than in that corresponding to the first two. In fact, rather the reverse is the case.

The likeliest hypothesis seems to me, then, that late in 1607 or early in 1608, at about the time he was writing *Antony and Cleopatra*, Shakespeare came across a manuscript play on the subject of *Pericles* (which may or may not have been performed on the stage), written by some very minor playwright; that he rewrote entirely the last three acts, and had it performed by his company at the Globe Theatre in the spring of 1608.[1] But it seems that Shakespeare rewrote not only the last three acts, but also occasional lines in the first two acts and, I believe, one whole scene, II.i.

As we read through the wooden, jog-trot, largely end-stopped verse of the first two acts, we come across lines that are late-Shakespearean in diction and movement. The most notable example of this occurs in the play's opening scene, in Pericles' speech to King Antiochus after he has solved the riddle. It begins with the mediocre verse typical of the author of the first two acts:

---

[1] The latest date of composition of the Shakespearean part of *Pericles*, May 1608, seems provided by the play's entry in the Stationers' Register in that month. Its earliest date seems determined chiefly by the style of the verse, which cannot be much earlier than 1607.

> Great king,
> Few love to hear the sins they love to act;
> 'Twould braid yourself too near for me to tell it.
> Who has a book of all that monarchs do,
> He's more secure to keep it shut than shown;
> For vice repeated is like the wand'ring wind
> Blows dust in others' eyes to spread itself;
> And yet the end of all is bought thus dear:
> The breath is gone, and the sore eyes see clear
> To stop the air would hurt them. (I.i.92–101)

Then come a few lines that are unmistakably Shakespearean:

> The blind mole casts
> Copped hills towards heaven, to tell the earth is thronged
> By man's oppression; and the poor worm doth die for't.
> (I.i.101–03)

And then the former verse continues on its jog-trot way.

As for the opening scene of Act II, consisting of a mixture of verse and prose, few commentators have been bold enough to assign it to Shakespeare. But if it is not his work, it is remarkably like it, in both its verse and prose; and it certainly cannot be by the author of the remainder of the first two acts, for it is utterly different in style and manner. If we make allowance for the corruption of the text, there is nothing in the scene that one needs deny to Shakespeare. Pericles' opening speech is quite Shakespearean, though it deteriorates toward the end:

> Yet cease your ire, you angry stars of heaven!
> Wind, rain, and thunder, remember, earthly man
> Is but a substance that must yield to you. (II.i.1–3)

There enter three Fishermen, and the ways in which they are made instantly real and vivid with the greatest economy of means, and in which they dispense their worldly wisdom and witticisms, bear the mark of Shakespeare. The Fishermen's prose is counterpointed by Pericles' verse, and some of this is undoubtedly Shakespearean, for example,

> What I have been I have forgot to know;
> But what I am want teaches me to think on:
> A man thronged up with cold. (II.i.75–77)

and two lines toward the end of the scene, which no one but Shakespeare could have written:

> And spite of all the rapture of the sea,
> This jewel holds his building on my arm. (II.i.161–62)

There remains still the problem of the authorship of the choruses. This is made much more difficult by the fact that they are written in a purposely archaic idiom, to suit their speaker, the poet Gower, a contemporary of Chaucer, whose version of the story in his *Confessio Amantis* served as the play's main source (see A Note on the Sources). Most of the choruses are clearly written in imitation of the octosyllabic couplets in which Gower had told his story. And their archaic idiom also suits the old tale that is the play's subject matter. Ben Jonson referred to *Pericles* contemptuously as a "moldy tale," but the appearance of the mold of antiquity is clearly just what its authors wished to achieve. This is vividly brought home to us by the opening lines of Gower's first chorus (lines 1–10). From the first, the story's antiquity is emphasized as one of its chief virtues.

Which of the choruses are by Shakespeare, and which by the author of Acts I and II? All the indications are that the Shakespearean choruses start precisely where we would expect—at the beginning of Act III. Shakespeare tries to maintain a certain continuity with the earlier choruses in the play by using archaic diction and octosyllabic couplets (though he abandons these for decasyllables after the opening chorus of Act IV). But though written purposely in a naive and simple idiom, the Shakespearean choruses are quite devoid of the clumsy, empty, elliptic diction and lame rhythm of the earlier choruses. The juxtaposition of a few lines from each will make the difference manifest. Here are the opening lines of the chorus at the beginning of Act II:

> Here have you seen a mighty king
> His child iwis to incest bring;
> A better prince and benign lord
> That will prove awful both in deed and word.
> Be quiet, then, as men should be,
> Till he hath passed necessity.
> I'll show you those in trouble's reign
> Losing a mite, a mountain gain.
> The good in conversation,
> To whom I give my benison,
> Is still at Tharsus, where each man
> Thinks all is writ he spoken can;
> And, to remember what he does,
> Build his statue to make him glorious.
> But tidings to the contrary
> Are brought your eyes; what need speak I?

And here, by contrast, are the opening lines of the chorus at the beginning of Act III:

> Now sleep y-slackèd hath the rout;
> No din but snores the house about,
> Made louder by the o'erfed breast
> Of this most pompous marriage feast.
> The cat, with eyne of burning coal,
> Now couches 'fore the mouse's hole;
> And crickets sing at the oven's mouth
> All the blither for their drouth.
> Hymen hath brought the bride to bed,
> Where by the loss of maidenhead
> A babe is molded. Be attent,
> And time that is so briefly spent
> With your fine fancies quaintly eche.
> What's dumb in show I'll plain with speech.

We still have archaisms ("y-slackèd," "eyne"), but the verse is incomparably more vivid, vigorous, and accomplished. Moreover, into these Shakespearean choruses enters an element not found in those of Acts I and II, but familiar to us from the choruses in *Henry V*: the audience is repeatedly asked to use its imagination to eke out what is being presented on the stage (for example, "And time that is so briefly spent/With your fine fancies quaintly eche";

"In your supposing once more put your sight:/Of heavy Pericles think this his bark").

The story of Pericles, or Apollonius of Tyre, as he was called prior to Shakespeare's play, had been one of the most popular tales in the Middle Ages and the Renaissance. Probably it goes back to Hellenistic times, having its origin in some lost Greek romance. Not only the story's names and settings point to this (Pentapolis is located in the play as somewhere in Greece, while Tyre, Ephesus, Antioch, Tharsus, and Mytilene, where the rest of the action takes place, are all on or near the coast of Asia Minor), but the outline of the story is typical of the Greek romances. These are tales of marvelous adventures, marked by an abundance of shipwrecks; hairbreadth escapes from wild beasts, bandits, or pirates; innocent maidens, who preserve their virtue in spite of all assaults; and ending in miraculous reunions of parents and children, brothers and sisters, husbands and wives, long believed dead. The main emotion that the Greek romances set out to arouse in the reader is a sense of wonder at the strange incidents that they describe. And a sense of wonder is also one of the main emotions aroused by Shakespeare's Last Plays; "rare," "strange," "wonderful," "like an old tale," are expressions that characters in these plays use again and again to voice their response to the events they witness, and this response is also shared by the audience.

In the English drama written before Shakespeare there is one type of play which sets out to evoke this response, and which is linked with the Greek romances: the miracle play or dramatized saint's legend, a form of drama highly popular beginning with the twelfth century, and still performed in Shakespeare's youth. Unfortunately, few of these plays have survived, but from these and extant French miracle plays one can infer their nature. Like the Greek romances, they are tales of strange adventures, separations, wanderings across seas and lands, rescues miraculously effected, dangers overcome and trials passed, until the final triumph of reunion with loved relatives or the triumph of martyrdom. It has been claimed—justly, I think—that these miracle plays had a much more profound influence on the development of English Renaissance drama than had the medieval mystery plays. And the editor of the New Arden *Pericles* has suggested that it was from such miracle plays that the broad structural features of the play may be derived.

In its structure *Pericles* is unlike any of Shakespeare's earlier comedies. This can be seen most readily if we compare the handling of time. In the comedies before *Pericles* Shakespeare either observed the most rigorous unity of time, as in *The Comedy of Errors*, or he contained the action within a few days, as in *A Midsummer Night's Dream*, or at most within a few months, as in *All's Well That Ends Well*. But nowhere had he used a time scheme similar to that of *Pericles*, where between Acts III and IV there is a time gap of fourteen years. This time scheme is used once more in *The Winter's Tale*, where between Acts III and IV there is an interval of sixteen years. And in both plays, while in the first three acts our attention centers on the royal father (Pericles, Leontes), in the fourth act his place is taken by his daughter (Marina, Perdita), while the fifth act is given over to the reunion of father and daughter, followed by the reunion of husband and wife. In consequence we have in these two plays a kind of double focus, upon father and daughter, which is quite unlike anything found in Shakespeare's other plays.[2] In the earlier comedies our attention is sometimes divided between different pairs of lovers, as in *The Two Gentlemen of Verona, Love's Labor's Lost,* and *The Taming of the Shrew;* or between different groups of characters, as in *A Midsummer Night's Dream, As You Like It,* and *Twelfth Night.* But nowhere else do we have this shift of focus from father to daughter, and the great gap of time in the middle of the play.

In *The Winter's Tale* this structure is all-important as a vehicle of the play's significances by contrasting the images of wintry barrenness and desolation centering on Leontes with images of spring and fertility centering on Perdita. In *Pericles* the function of the double focus is less immediately obvious. The parallels between the misfortunes that befall father and daughter—in both cases their afflictions begin with a plot to murder them, which they escape, only to be overtaken by further calamities—have a similar effect to the parallels between main plot and subplot in *King Lear* and *Timon of Athens.* The sudden and violent blows of fortune that strike Marina, as they had struck her father, deepen and widen the play's image of the world as a lasting storm, whirring us from our friends (IV.i.19–20). But to this parallel Shakespeare adds a contrast, found in the way in which father and daughter respond to these afflictions.

A number of critics in recent years have claimed that Pericles, as Shakespeare depicts him, is an embodiment of patience in adversity, a kind of male Griselda-figure, and that the play presents an *exemplum* of this virtue of patience that leads to restoration and happiness. Now it is true that, compared to his prototypes in the sources, Pericles behaves under the earlier blows of fortune with much moderation and restraint. For instance, in his reception of the news of his wife's death, where in Gower and Twine he indulges in the most frantic display of grief, in Shakespeare's scene he expresses it much less vehemently. Yet nothing suggests to me here that he is meant to be seen as an embodiment of patience in adversity. The nurse, Lychorida, repeatedly calls upon him to be patient: "Patience, good sir; do not assist the storm" (assist, that is, by his loud cries of grief); "Patience, good sir,/Even for this charge" (III.i.19, 26–27). It would be odd to be preaching patience to a figure embodying that virtue. His reception of the news of Marina's death, as described in dumb show and chorus, suggests even less that Shakespeare thought of Pericles as pre-eminently a patient man. "*Cleon shows Pericles the tomb,*" we are told, "*whereat Pericles makes lamentation, puts on sackcloth, and in a mighty passion departs.*" And Gower comments:

> And Pericles, in sorrow all devoured,
> With sighs shot through and biggest tears o'ershowered,
> Leaves Tharsus and again embarks. He swears
> Never to wash his face, nor cut his hairs.
> He puts on sackcloth, and to sea. He bears
> A tempest, which his mortal vessel tears,
> And yet he rides it out.          (IV.iv.25–31)

The "tempest, which his mortal vessel tears" is, of course, the storm of his "mighty passion" that ravages his mortal body. He does not die ("And yet he rides it out"). But he shuts himself away from all human society, and when Marina visits him, he has not spoken to a living soul for three months. Can Shakespeare really have thought that this is the way in which exemplars of patience accept the blows of fortune? Wilkins certainly thought otherwise, and makes clear his view of Pericles' action of shutting himself away from his fellow men by making Lysimachus declare that "though his misfortunes haue beene great, and by which he hath great cause for this sorrow, it is great pitty he should continue thus peruerse and obstinate, or so noble a gentleman come to so dishonorable a death," and having Marina tell her father that "hee was borne a Prince, whose dignity being to gouerne others, it was most foule in him to misgouerne himselfe."

Neither can I believe in the suggestion made by one of the proponents of this view (J. M. S. Tompkins in *Review of English Studies* [1952], 315 ff.)—a suggestion that has been widely accepted—that Shakespeare called his hero "Pericles" after the Athenian statesman, whose life he could have read in Plutarch, who stresses the patience of his hero at the beginning and end of the "Life." I can perceive no resemblance between the two, apart from the fact that they are both excellent fellows. Previously it had been held—and, I think, rightly—that the name was derived from the *Arcadia,* Sir Philip Sidney's great prose romance, which is full of incidents like those described in *Pericles.* One of its two heroes, called Pyrocles, is depicted as a pattern of all princely virtues. That Shakespeare had Sidney's hero in mind while writing his play seems proved by the fact that Marina's description of her father's behavior during the storm at sea in which she was born closely follows Sidney's account of Pyrocles' behavior during the storm at sea that precedes his shipwreck.[3] Like Sidney's hero, Pericles is depicted as an exemplar not of patience but of all princely excellences. The episodes in the first two acts—often claimed, I believe unjustly, to be insufficiently integrated with the rest of the play—serve not only to present instances of the many blows of fortune that strike Pericles, but also to exhibit his various excellences: his perspicacity in solving Antiochus' riddle (even if it does not seem to *us* a particularly hard one); his loving care of his subjects, which makes him grieve over the danger to which he has unwittingly exposed them; his

---

[2] This double focus is well brought out by the quarto's title page: "The late, And much admired Play, Called Pericles, Prince of Tyre. With the true Relation of the whole Historie, aduentures, and fortunes of the said Prince: As also, The no lesse strange, and worthy accidents, in the Birth and Life, of his Daughter Mariana."

[3] That the author of the first two acts had Pyrocles in mind when writing of his hero's adventures seems indicated by II.i. and II.ii. As J. C. Maxwell has pointed out, there is nothing in previous versions of the story about the fishing up of the rusty armor, or about the hero's participation and victory in a tournament. In Gower he takes part and excels in athletic games held in the presence of the king; in Twine he gains the king's favor by his expertise in playing tennis with him and washing him in his bath. The idea of Pericles entering the lists anonymously, in an old, rusty armor inherited from his father, with a pair of bases made from a fisherman's cloak, and proving victorious over all rivals, would seem to have been suggested by Sidney's description of how Pyrocles, in mean attire, entered the lists and defeated the champion at a tournament at the court of King Basilius: "For he had neither picture, nor device; his armor of as old a fashion (besides the rusty poorness) that it might better seem a monument of his grandfather's courage; about his middle he had, instead of bases, a long cloak of silk, which, as unhandsomely as it needs must, became the wearer . . .' (*Arcadia,* I.17.5).

surpassing excellence in the tournament; his accomplishment in ballroom dancing in full armor (in the *Arcadia* it is
the other hero, Musidorus, who dances featly in armor);
his supreme skill as a musician; and his modesty, courtesy,
and graceful bearing throughout these scenes. Only in his
response to the blows of fortune does he fall short of the
princely ideal, most signally in his self-seclusion from all
human society after being falsely persuaded of the death of
Marina. In this he again resembles Pyrocles, whose only
discernible fault is a lack of patience in adversity, which
culminates in the episode in which he attempts to brain
himself by running his head against the wall, after being
falsely persuaded of the death of his beloved Philoclea.
(The parallel is increased by the resemblance between
Dionyza and Sidney's Cecropia, which has been noted by
commentators.)

Just as Pericles is depicted as the pattern of all princely
excellences, so Marina is shown to be the pattern of all
excellences becoming to a princess. This is made manifest
both in the action and in Gower's commentary upon it,
above all in his opening choruses in Acts IV and V. If we are
looking for a figure in the play exemplifying patience in
adversity, it is here that it is to be found. This is emphasized
in the great recognition scene, when Pericles exlaims:

> Tell thy story.
> If thine, considered, prove the thousandth part
> Of my endurance, thou art a man, and I
> Have suffered like a girl; yet thou dost look
> Like Patience gazing on kings' graves, and smiling
> Extremity out of act. (V.i.138–43)

Her endurance has, in fact, proved much greater than his.
Instead of shutting herself up in her grief, after suffering
a series of afflictions that more than equal his, this fourteen-
year-old girl becomes the admired teacher of many skills
to pupils of noble race. She then endures Pericles' initial
rough reception of her, yet continues to look "Like
Patience gazing on kings' graves, and smiling/Extremity
out of act."

We have seen, then, that the play's double focus on
father and daughter serves to bring out a contrast as well
as a parallel between them, both of which are important
to the play's full effect. Elsewhere, too, in *Pericles* such
basic parallels and contrasts are to be found. In the non-
Shakespearean part there is above all the extended parallel
and contrast between the main action of Act I and Act II.
Having presented in Act I the wicked king with his wicked
daughter, whose hand Pericles tries to gain by solving a
riddle, the playwright presents in Act II the good king
with his good daughter, whose hand Pericles tries to gain
by winning a tournament. Just as he was successful in
solving the riddle, he is successful in winning the tournament. And where the wicked king, Antiochus, pretended
friendship toward him, while actually planning his death,
the good king, Simonides, pretends enmity toward him,
while actually planning to make him his son-in-law.

In the Shakespearean part there is the extended parallel
between Pericles' mistaken belief in the death of his wife
and his mistaken belief in the death of his daughter, and
his final reunion with each. Less obvious is the contrast
between the monstrous incest of father and daughter in
Act I, brought out in such lines of the riddle as

> He's father, son, and husband mild;
> I mother, wife, and yet his child. (I.i.69–70)

and the blessed "incest" of father and daughter in Act V,
suggested by Pericles' words to Marina, "Thou that
beget'st him that did thee beget" (V.i.199).

It is such parallels and contrasts—which are typical both
of Sidney's *Arcadia* and of Shakespeare's previous plays—
that help to give shape and coherence to the episodic and
formless romance material on which *Pericles* is based.

I have taken issue with the view that Pericles is an
exemplar of the virtue of patience in adversity. I find even
more misleading the common assertion that Shakespeare
presents the main events of the play, both the misfortunes
and the reunions, as the work of divine Providence. The
whole pattern of Pericles' painful adventures, as these
critics see it, is a pattern imposed by the gods. But the
notion of a divine Providence that persecutes wholly
virtuous characters so cruelly and for so long is repugnant,
and so several of these critics are driven to discover some
offense in the protagonists for which they are punished.
Such an attempt to find a pattern of sin, punishment,
expiation, and restoration in the play seems to me to violate
and distort its whole spirit. It is to assimilate *Pericles*
to *The Winter's Tale* and *The Tempest*, where sin and
expiation do play an important part. In *Pericles*, as in
the miracle plays, we are confronted with the *undeserved*
sufferings of the wholly innocent and entirely virtuous—of
Pericles, Thaisa, and Marina. And both their misfortunes
and their restorations are shown to be mainly due to
accident, to chance. The goddess who presides over the
play is not Diana but Fortuna. It is by accident that the
waves throw up the coffin containing Thaisa at Ephesus
near the house of Cerimon, just the person who possesses
the rare medical knowledge and skill needed to restore her
to life. It is accident that brings Pericles' ship Mytilene
and Marina on board this ship, thus enabling father and
daughter to be reunited. To see in all this the hand of
Providence is indeed to take away from our sense of wonder. Only once in the play is there any clear evidence of
supernatural intervention: in V.i., where the goddess
Diana appears to Pericles in a vision. Without this vision
the final reunion of Thaisa with her husband and daughter
would have been difficult to bring about. In both Shakespeare's sources this vision is found, though only in
Shakespeare is it the goddess Diana that appears to Pericles.
Gower speaks of a vision sent by "the high god," while in
Twine's version an angel appears to Pericles in his sleep.
But I can find no suggestion in the play that Diana had any
other part in its events.

It is true that, like all Shakespeare's virtuous and noble
characters, Pericles sees the hand of heaven behind all the
accidents that befall him. At the news of Thaisa's death he
cries out,

> O you gods!
> Why do you make us love your goodly gifts,
> And snatch them straight away? (III.i.22–24)

And at the reunion with Thaisa he exclaims:

> You gods, your present kindness
> Makes my past miseries sports. (V.iii.39–40)

But, as with Shakespeare's great tragedies, this view is not imposed by the play upon the audience. It is above all contradicted by the choruses (except for the final moralistic one, of doubtful authorship), for Gower insists repeatedly upon Fortune's responsibility for the events. It is Fortune, he tells us, at the beginning of Act II, that threw Pericles ashore near Pentapolis. It is "Fortune's mood," he remarks at the beginning of Act III, that conjures up the storm during which Marina is born.

> Let Pericles believe his daughter's dead,
> And bear his courses to be orderèd
> By Lady Fortune;         (IV.iv.46–48)

he comments in Act IV. But Lady Fortune is merely the personification of the power of accident in human affairs.

I have spoken of the sense of wonder and amazement that Shakespeare's Last Plays seek to evoke in both characters and audience. It vents itself in a language that is characteristic of these plays, and that has appeared only fitfully before, chiefly in Shakespeare's late tragedies. It is a simple, translucent language, melodious in sound, slow in pace, remote and dreamlike in its effect. Certain images tend to recur, above all images of precious objects: pearls, jewels, silver, and gold. Here are two examples of it from *Pericles*:

>         She is alive! Behold,
> Her eyelids, cases to those heavenly jewels
> Which Pericles hath lost, begin to part
> Their fringes of bright gold; the diamonds
> Of a most praisèd water doth appear
> To make the world twice rich. Live,
> And make us weep to hear your fate, fair creature,
> Rare as you seem to be.     (III.ii.99–106)

> I am great with woe, and shall deliver weeping.
> My dearest wife was like this maid, and such
> My daughter might have been: my queen's square brows;
> Her stature to an inch; as wandlike straight;
> As silver-voiced; her eyes as jewel-like
> And cased as richly; in pace another Juno;
> Who starves the ears she feeds, and makes them hungry
> The more she gives them speech.     (V.i.109–16)

Apart from the more powerful evocation of a sense of wonder, and the style in which it expresses itself, what is it that chiefly marks off *Pericles* from Shakespeare's preceding comedies, and that points forward to the other Last Plays?

Closely related to this increased sense of wonder is a greater predominance of fairy-tale motifs and fairy-tale atmosphere. *Pericles* is full of such motifs, from the opening scene, in which the young prince has to solve a riddle in order to gain the hand of the beautiful princess, to the play's Epilogue, which announces, in the manner of fairy tales, the reward of the virtuous and the cruel punishment of the wicked. This fairy-tale atmosphere makes it easier to accept the improbabilities in the play's action: Pericles' failure to visit his daughter for fourteen years after leaving her with Cleon and Dionyza; Thaisa's decision to lead the life of a vestal because, unaccountably, she will never see her husband again. (This could easily have been motivated, as it is in Gower and Wilkins, by her mistaken belief that

her husband was drowned during the storm at sea. Perhaps some lines to this effect have dropped out of the text).

Allied to the increased predominance of the fairy-tale atmosphere is the intrusion of the supernatural, which does not enter into the earlier comedies, with the single exception of *A Midsummer Night's Dream*. In *Pericles* Diana appears to the hero in a vision; in *Cymbeline* Jupiter descends on his eagle and prophesies; in *The Winter's Tale* we have the oracle of Apollo, and in *The Tempest* Ariel and his fellow spirits.

I have already spoken of the difference of structure that marks off *Pericles* and *The Winter's Tale* from all Shakespeare's other plays. Next, there is the difference in the young heroine. It is partly a difference in age: Marina is fourteen years old, Miranda fifteen, Perdita sixteen, while the young heroines of the preceding comedies, such as Beatrice, Portia, Rosalind, and Viola, seem a good deal older. For a heroine in a previous play who is of Marina's age we have to turn not to a comedy but to an early tragedy. Juliet, too, is fourteen years old. In personality also Marina is more like Juliet, or like Cordelia, than she is like Portia, or Beatrice, or Rosalind, who dazzle us above all by their wit. And unlike all the heroines of the preceding comedies, Marina exists primarily not in relation to a lover but to her father. She is given a husband at the end, but in a most perfunctory way, and we are never even told whether she loves him. Shakespeare is clearly not at all interested in the Marina–Lysimachus relationship. In the other Last Plays there is no parallel to this. While the relation of father and daughter is also of some importance in them, it is the relation of the daughter to her lover, of Perdita to Florizel, of Miranda to Ferdinand, of Imogen to Posthumus, that mainly concerns us.

Finally, these Last Plays differ from the preceding comedies in the weight and scope given to the scenes depicting the reunion of loved relatives long separated and believed dead. This motif is dominant in *Pericles*, *Cymbeline*, and *The Winter's Tale*—much less so in *The Tempest*. It had also occurred in some of Shakespeare's earlier comedies. In *Twelfth Night* and *Measure for Measure* a loved brother, firmly believed dead, suddenly appears alive before his sister. In *Much Ado About Nothing* and *All's Well That Ends Well* a bride believed dead appears alive before her bridegroom or husband. In the final scene of *The Comedy of Errors* Shakespeare staged the biggest reunion of them all: not only two pairs of twin brothers, who had been separated since babyhood, are reunited, but the parents of the one pair with each other as well as with their sons, all after some thirty-three years of separation. It is the perfunctory manner in which these reunions are dramatized, the absence of any expression of their emotional experience, that makes these scenes in the earlier comedies (with the exception of *Twelfth Night*) so different in impact from the reunion scenes especially of *Pericles* and *The Winter's Tale*.

Until the closing of the theaters in 1642 *Pericles* seems to have been one of Shakespeare's greatest stage successes. The fact that the quarto text was reprinted five times between 1609 and 1635 alone bears witness to its popularity. At the Restoration it was the first of Shakespeare's plays to be revived, with Betterton in the title role. But in the two hundred and fifty years from then until the beginning of this century the play fell into disrepute, receiving only a handful of performances, and even these giving the play in a radically altered or mutilated form. Only in the last few decades has it begun again to receive the attention it deserves from producers and critics, who have come to see that, as well as being full of highly effective scenes for the stage, it contains some of Shakespeare's loveliest and most haunting verse.

## A NOTE ON THE SOURCES

The chief literary influence discernible in *Pericles* is Sir Philip Sidney's *Arcadia*. It extends not only to structure, action, treatment of character, themes, and atmosphere (see Introduction, pp. 1411 ff.), but also to a number of verbal echoes in both parts of the play. In the non-Shakespearean part we find such echoes at I.i.11–12 ("The senate house of the planets was at no time so set, for the decreeing of perfection in a man"), and I.i.63–64 ("asking no advise of no thought, but of faithfulness and courage"); in the Shakespearean part the echoes at III.ii.100–04 ("Her faire liddes then hiding her fairer eyes, seemed unto him sweete boxes of mother of pearle, riche in themselves, but contaning in them farre richer Jewells") and at IV.Cho.23–25 ("the cloth loking with many eies upon her, & lovingly embracing the wounds she gave it") are less close but still manifest. The most extensive detailed parallel also belongs to Shakespeare's part: Marina's description of her father's behavior during the storm at sea in which she was born,

> My father, as nurse says, did never fear,
> But cried, "Good seamen!" to the sailors, galling
> His kingly hands haling ropes          (IV.i.52–54)

was closely influenced by the great storm scene in the *Arcadia* (which also seems to have left its mark on the opening scene of *The Tempest*), where we are told of the princes that they "did in their countenances accuse no point of feare, but encouraging them [the sailors] to doo what might be done (putting their handes to everie most painefull office). . . ." While Shakespeare, as was his wont, has made the description far more vivid and dramatic, he retains the order in which the three ingredients—fearlessness, encouragement, painful office—are mentioned in Sidney's account.

The play has two main sources: Book VIII of John Gower's *Confessio Amantis*, written toward the end of the fourteenth century and printed in 1532 and 1554; and Laurence Twine's prose narrative *The Patterne of Painefull Adventures*, registered in 1576, and extant in an undated edition and a reprint in 1607. Though both sources were drawn upon throughout the play, the influence of Gower greatly predominates, so that his spirit is fitly chosen to act as the play's presenter. Not only does it usually follow Gower rather than Twine at points in the plot where the two diverge, but it is also much more under the verbal influence of Gower than of Twine. I have been able to find only one clear verbal echo of Twine (at I.Cho.18), while there are many such echoes of Gower; at III.ii.107 the whole line is taken over from Gower (lines 1206–07, "Ha, wher am I?/Where is my Lord, what world is this?"), and other verbal echoes are found, for instance, at I.i.156; V.Cho.14; and V.i.88.

The names, too, are mainly derived from Gower: Dionyza (*Dionise* in Gower, *Dionisiades* in Twine); Lychorida (*Lichorida* in Gower, *Ligozides* in Twine); Thaisa (derived from *Thaise*, Gower's name for Pericles' daughter, called Tharsia in Twine; Pericles' wife is there called *Lucina* and left nameless in Gower); Leonine (in Gower the name of the pander); Helicanus (from a Tyrian messenger called *Hellican* in Gower's text, but *Helicanus* in one of the Latin glosses; *Elinatus* in Twine); Philoten (*Philomacia* in Twine); Thaliard (*Taliart* in Gower, *Taliarchus* in Twine). Cerimon's name is found in both Gower and Twine. The names Pericles, Marina, Simonides, Lysimachus, Cleon, Escanes, and Boult are not found in any of the sources. They may have been Shakespeare's inventions, or may have been taken over by him from the old play.

The only exception to the predominance of Gower as a source is found in three scenes in Act IV, where Twine is principally drawn on. In IV.i Marina's mourning for her dead nurse, and her intended visit to her grave, are entirely based on Twine, there being no mention of this in Gower; the intervention of the pirates is also much closer to Twine. IV.iii · is entirely based on Twine. There is nothing in Gower to suggest that Cleon in any way disapproves of the murder. In IV.vi the play follows Twine in making Lysimachus visit the brothel as a client, whereas in Gower he is free from any stain, never visits the brothel, and encounters Marina for the first time on board her father's ship.

Readers wishing to study Gower's and Twine's share in each scene of the play should consult the headnotes in J. C. Maxwell's edition. Whether Shakespeare went directly to these sources or depended entirely on the old play which he rewrote—if this is, in fact, what happened—is a moot point. But his use of sources elsewhere suggests that he would not have shunned the labor of reading Gower, Twine, and whatever other version of the story came his way; and it seems probable that the verbal echoes of Gower were derived at first hand. The only indication that any other version of the story has been made use of is the word "bitumed" at III.i.72 and III.ii.57. This word, which is found in neither Gower nor Twine—nor anywhere else in Shakespeare—occurs in its Latin form (*cum bitumine liniri*), in the same context, in the story as told in the *Gesta Romanorum*, the Latin collection of tales, probably compiled around the turn of the thirteenth century, from which Twine's novel, by way of a French translation, is derived.

The Shakespearean part of *Pericles* follows the narrative outline of the sources with a fidelity not found elsewhere in the poet's dramatization of romance material, and this may be taken as a further indication that the scenario is not of his devising. Oddly, the non-Shakespearean part of the play adds more that is not in Gower and Twine than the Shakespearean part. No suggestion in any of the sources is provided for the figure of Helicanus, and his scene with Pericles (I.ii) and with the Tyrian Lords (II.iv); nor for the tournament scene (II.ii; see Introduction, p. 1411, note 3), or for Simonides' faked anger with Pericles (II.v). As G. A. Barker has pointed out in an important article in *English Studies*, XLIV (1963), the main concern of the author of the first two acts seems to have been with political ideas—with what constitutes the good ruler. But this theme is of little importance in Shakespeare's part of the play. And neither he nor the author of the first two acts betrays much concern with what was Gower's avowed purpose in telling the Apollonius story: to make men see that unlawful love, like Antiochus', leads to disaster, whereas lawful, honorable love, like Apollonius', leads eventually to happiness (lines 1993–2019). Much closer to the heart of Shakespeare's presentation seems Twine's view of the story's events; it is well expressed by the title page of his novel, "The Patterne of painefull Aduentures: Containing the most excellent, pleasant and variable Historie of the strange accidents that befell vnto Prince Apollonius, the Lady Lucina his wife, and Tharsia his daughter. Wherein the vncertaintie of this world, and the fickle state of mans life are liuely described." To this Shakespeare adds a concern with the way in which men endure the blows of fortune, expressed by means of the parallels and contrasts discussed in the Introduction (pp. 1411 ff.).

## A NOTE ON THE TEXT

*The booke of Pericles Prynce of Tyre* (i.e., presumably, the promptbook) was entered, together with *Antony and Cleopatra*, in the Stationers' Register on May 20, 1608. Both plays were entered to Edward Blount, and, as neither of them was published by him, it has been supposed that these were "blocking entries," designed to prevent piracy. If so, this proved unsuccessful in the case of *Pericles*, for what is certainly a pirated version of the play was brought out in 1609 by another publisher, Henry Gosson. It proved so popular that a second quarto edition of the play was published by him in the same year, a third appeared in 1611, a fourth in 1619, a fifth in 1630, and a sixth in 1635 (Q2–Q6). As all of these are merely reprints of one another, they have no independent textual authority. *Pericles* was not included in the first collected edition of Shakespeare's plays, the First Folio of 1623, and was not added to any collected edition until the second impression of the Third Folio, in 1664, where it was reprinted from Q6. Varying explanations of the reason for the play's exclusion from the First Folio have been put forward: copyright difficulties; the absence of a good text available to the editors; the fact that the play is only partly Shakespeare's. The last would seem the most probable reason, and is weakened only by the inclusion in the Folio of *Henry VIII*.

The only authoritative text of *Pericles* is therefore that of the first quarto of 1609 (Q). It is unfortunately a very poor text, as the list below of some hundred and eighty corrupt readings makes immediately apparent. At least some twenty of these would seem to be auditory errors, due to a mishearing by the reporter of the words spoken on the stage (apparent instances of this are found at I.i.114; I.ii.86; II.ii.30; IV.Cho.26; IV.iv.24; V.i.229). Most scholars agree that the text derives from a report of the play as performed by Shakespeare's company. It is the degree of badness of the report about which they are divided. Some would group it with the "bad" quartos, such as those of *Romeo and Juliet* and *Hamlet*; others insist that, in spite of numerous corruptions, many of them due to the compositors, the text is basically a good one. My own

view is that the quarto of *Pericles* stands somewhere between the good and the bad quartos: too faithful to its original to be classed as a "bad" quarto; too full of errors (both graphic and auditory), of omissions, and additions, to be accounted a good one.

Next to the errors due to mishearing, the reporter seems responsible for a variety of other deficiencies in the text: (1) In the Shakespearean part, after—for the most part impeccably—setting out the verse of III.i, he apparently found the task too demanding, and wrote out the remaining blank verse as prose; and that is how most of it was set by the compositors. (2) He occasionally seems to have added words, or even whole lines, that can scarcely have been in the Shakespearean original (for example, V.i.241–42). (3) There are two scenes in the play in which an evident gap in the report is to be found: in I.ii, where some diaologue between Pericles and Helicanus is evidently missing (before line 38; see the gloss on line 37); and in IV.vi, where some dialogue between Marina and Lysimachus appears to have been lost (after line 108). In the first case the reporter seems to have made little attempt to fill the gap; in the second case he apparently tried to fill it by reconstructing the missing lines from memory—a memory that must have been exceedingly dim (see Introduction, pp. 1408).

But apart from this instance, there is no indication in the text that—as in all the "bad" quartos proper—the report was a memorial reconstruction. On the contrary—at least in the Shakespearean part—the report must have been made at the theater, probably during repeated visits to performances of the play. Long scenes such as III.i and V.i, in which the text has every appearance of adhering faithfully to the Shakespearean original, cannot have been reported from memory.[4] In the non-Shakespearean part it is much more difficult to be sure of this, and there are some grounds for supposing that its fidelity to the original text is not as great (notably in II.i).

The majority of the corrupt readings in Q seem, in fact, to have been introduced not by the reporter but by the compositors (Philip Edwards has shown them to have been three in number), who were uniformly slovenly and careless at their task (except in II.v, which seems to be free from compositorial errors). They misread words, misassigned speeches, occasionally omitted speech prefixes, sometimes set prose as verse, and made only sporadic—and then quite inept—attempts to reestablish Shakespeare's blank verse division. The occasional omission of words within a line (as at I.iv.13), or of a whole line (as, apparently, after line 14 in IV.iii and probably after line 122 in I.ii), would also seem to be attributable to them rather than to the reporter.

The text of this edition diverges on a number of points from preceding ones:

(1) Where the quarto text is manifestly corrupt and we are left with nonsense, I have not hesitated to emend, even when we cannot be sure that the chosen emendation is necessarily the right one and when previous modern editors have retained the original reading. Instances of this

---

[4] I do not share Philip Edwards' pessimistic view that "we have in these later acts only the *disjecta membra* of once powerful verse," that "we lose sight, presumably forever, of the genuine version of the last three acts, from the opening of III.ii" (*Shakespeare Survey* 5 [1952], 38).

are found at I.iv.13; III.ii.84–87; IV.i.11; and V.i.210. On the other hand, Q readings have, on a very few occasions, been retained where previous editors have emended, for example at III.i.68, where editors have unnecessarily emended Q's "coffin" to "coffer," since the two words were used interchangeably in Shakespeare's day.

(2) Like other editors, I have for the most part followed Malone's relineation of Shakespeare's blank verse in the passages where it was set as prose. But occasionally, where better and more Shakespearean verse seemed to result, I have introduced line divisions not found in previous editions, for example, at III.iii.9–15; IV.i.27–30; V.i.21–22.

(3) Sometimes I have departed from the punctuation adopted by previous editors, and thereby imposed a different meaning on the text. An example of this is found at I.i.7–12:

> Bring in our daughter, clothèd like a bride,
> For the embracements even of Jove himself;
> At whose conception, till Lucina reigned,
> Nature this dowry gave to glad her presence.
> The senate house of planets all did sit,
> To knit in her their best perfections.

The last four lines are a major crux in the play, and have been much emended and discussed. Most editors put a colon in line 10, either after "gave" or after "presence" (Q puts a semicolon after "gave" and a comma after "presence"), thus making the planetary influence itself Nature's dowry. But this does not make astrological sense, as (a) beauty was considered the gift of Nature, not of the planets; (b) planetary influence would be thought of as exerted at birth, not between conception and birth; (c) such planetary influence would not be believed to be in the gift of Nature. By punctuating as above, I have separated Nature's gift from that of the planets, interpreting: "between conception and birth Nature gave her her beauty as dowry ('this dowry': the beauty you are about to behold); then, at her birth, the planets bestowed upon her other, nonphysical, perfections over which they have control." The change in punctuation thus restores sense to the passage, and to Nature and the stars what is the due of each.

(4) Not infrequently the explanations given in the glosses differ from those of previous editors. For example, at I.Cho.42 the word "justify," instead of having its modern meaning is, I believe, one of a series of legal metaphors, and has the archaic meaning of "acquit, absolve" (*Oxford English Dictionary* 4); while at V.i.221 I believe it has another archaic meaning, that of "affirm" (*Oxford English Dictionary* 5b).

(5) I have parted company from previous editors over several stage directions, which they have taken over from Malone's edition, and which seem quite unjustified. There are two chief instances of this. At the opening of III.ii Q's direction reads, "*Enter Lord Cerymon with a seruant.*" Malone, followed by most subsequent editors, added to this "*and some Persons who have been shipwrecked*," because of Cerimon's line, "Get fire and meat for these poor men" (line 3). But to march several characters onto the stage, only to march them off again a few lines later (line 10) without their having uttered a word, would be a most un-Shakespearean piece of dramaturgy. I have, therefore,

adhered to Q's direction, and emended "these" in line 3 to "those," so that Pericles is speaking of some poor men —there is not the slightest indication that they are shipwrecked—who are never brought on stage, but are merely mentioned in order to display Cerimon in his role of benefactor. The other instance occurs at the opening of V.i. We are on board Pericles' ship, having just been told by Gower:

> In your supposing once more put your sight:
> Of heavy Pericles think this his bark.     (V.Cho.21–22)

Malone, with evidently little faith in the audience's capacity for supposing, has added to the required direction ("*On board Pericles' Ship,*" etc.), "*A Barge lying beside the Tyrian Vessel.*" At line 10 he introduced the direction, "*The Gentlemen and the Two Sailors descend, and go on board the Barge. Enter, from thence, Lysimachus and Lords*"; at line 52, "*Exit Lord, in the Barge of Lysimachus*"; and at line 65, "*Enter, from the Barge, Lord, Marina, and a young Lady.*" And all these directions have been taken over by subsequent editors. It is not clear how Malone envisaged the staging of this, but he evidently imagined the barge—by means of some piece of stage machinery—departing, and returning a few minutes later with Marina, all in full view of the audience. There is neither need nor warrant for all this, and in the present edition Malone's barge has been silently dropped.

In the quartos of *Pericles* the text is not divided into acts and scenes. The act division was introduced by the Third Folio, and the scene division by Malone. In the present text spelling and punctuation have been modernized, and speech prefixes expanded and regularized. All additions to Q's stage directions are indicated by brackets. Purely typographical errors have been silently corrected. All other departures from the quarto text are listed below, with the adopted reading given first in boldface type, followed by Q's reading in roman.

**I.Cho.39 a** of
**I.i.8 For the embracements** For embracements   **18 razed** racte **57 Antiochus** [Q omits]   **112 our** your   **114 cancel** counsell **121 s.d. Exeunt . . . Pericles** Manet Pericles solus   **128 you're** you   **129 uncomely** vntimeley   **170 Antiochus** [Q omits] **I.ii.s.d. Enter Pericles** Enter Pericles with his Lords   **4 Be my** By me   **21 honor him** honour   **26 th' ostent** the stint   **31 am** once   **42 blast** sparke   **45 a peace** peace   **66 you** you yourselfe **83 Bethought me** Bethought   **84 fears** feare   **86 doubt** doo't **100 grieve them** griue for them   **122 we'll** will
**I.iii.1 Thaliard** [Q omits]   **27 ears it** seas   **28 seas** Sea   **30 Helicanus** [Q omits]   **34 betook** betake
**I.iv.13 sorrows cease not** sorrowes   **17 helps** helpers   **36 they** thy   **39 two summers** too sauers   **58 thou** thee   **67 Hath** That **74 him's** himnes   **76–77 will, what need we fear?/On ground's the lowest,** will, and what they can,/What need wee leaue our grounds the lowest?
**II.Cho.11 Tharsus** Tharstill   **19 for he strives** for though he striue   **22 Sends word** Sau'd one   **24 hid intent to murder** hid in Tent to murdred [changed in some copies of Q to "had intent to murder"]
**II.i.6 me breath** my breath   **12 What ho, Pilch!** What, to pelch?   **18 fetch thee** fetch'th   **34 devours** deuowre   **42 Third Fisherman.** I.   **57 scratch it** Search   **82 quoth-a** ke-tha   **86 holidays** all day; **moreo'er** more; or   **94 your** you   **103–04 is called Pentapolis** I cald Pantapoles   **126 thy crosses** crosses **134 thee from!—may't** thee, Fame may   **161 rapture** rupture **164 delightful** delight   **171 equal** a Goale

**II.ii.4 daughter** daughter heere   **27 Più per dolcezza che per forza** Pue Per doleera kee per forsa   **28 what's** with   **29 chivalry** Chiually   **30 pompae** Pompey   **56 for** by
**II.iii.3 To** I   **13 yours** your   **26 Envied** Enuies   **29 but** not   **38 Yon** You   **39 tells me** tels   **44 son's** sonne like   **51 stored** stur'd   **52 you do** do you   **114 Simonides** [Q omits]
**II.iv.10 their** those   **33 gives** giue's   **34 leaves** leaue   **35 death's indeed** death in deed   **36 this: kingdoms** this Kingdome is   **42 For** Try   **57 endeavor it** endeauour
**III.Cho.2 the house about** about the house   **6 'fore** from   **7 crickets** Cricket   **8 All** Are   **17 coigns** Crignes   **29 t'** appease t'oppresse   **35 Y-ravishèd** Iranyshed   **46 Fortune's mood** fortune mou'd   **60 sea-tossed** seas tost
**III.i.7 Thou stormest** then storme   **11 midwife** my wife   **26 Vie** Vse   **52 custom** easterne   **53-54 for . . . straight** [In Q this is printed after "meet" in the next line]   **61 in the ooze** in oare   **63 And** The   **66 paper** Taper
**III.ii.3 those** these   **26 held** hold   **37 And I can** and can   **38 gives** doth giue   **41 treasure** pleasure   **48 never raze** neuer   **57 bitumed** bottomed   **77 even** euer   **84-87 I have read/Of some Egyptians, who after four hours' death/Have raised impoverished bodies, like to this,/Unto their former health** I heard of an Egiptian that had 9. howers lien dead,/Who was by good applyaunce recouered   **89 still** rough   **95 Breathes** breath
**III.iii.5 shafts** shakes   **6 hurt** hant   **7 woundingly** wondringly   **29-30 honor all,/Unscissored** honour,/All vnsisterd   **31 ill** will
**III.iv.5 eaning** learning
**IV.Cho.10 her** hie;   **heart** art   **14 Seeks** Seeke   **17 ripe** right;   **rite** sight   **21 she** they   **26 night-bird** night bed   **32 With dove of Paphos might the crow** The Doue of Paphos might with the crow   **47 carry** carried
**IV.i.5-6 or flaming love thy bosom/Enslave** in flaming, thy loue bosome, enflame   **11 weeping her old nurse's** weeping for her onely Mistresse   **19 is as a** is a   **24-25 favor/Is** fauours   **27 On the sea margent** ere the sea marre it   **62 stem** sterne   **92 s.d. They . . . Marina** Exit   **95 she'll** shee will

**IV.ii.4 much** much much   **21 they're too** ther's two   **51 It** I   **67 me to** me, for to   **75 was like to** was to   **107 i' the** ethe   **114 crowns of** crownes in   **128 Bawd.** Mari.
**IV.iii.1 are** ere   **6 A** O   **12 fact** face   **17 pious** impious   **27 prime** prince   **28 sources** courses   **31 distain** disdaine   **33 Marina's** Marianas
**IV.iv.7 scene** sceanes   **8 i' th' gaps** with gappes   **10 the** thy   **12 life's** liues   **16 Tyre** time   **18 his this** his   **19 go on** grone   **24 true-owed** true olde   **29 puts** put   **48 scene** Steare
**IV.vi.s.d. Enter . . . Boult** Enter Bawdes   **3 40 dignifies** dignities   **41 punk** number   **72 name't** name   **92 aloof** aloft   **134 ways** way   **140 She** He   **157 ways** way   **189 I will** will   **198 women** woman
**V.Cho.8 silk, twin** Silke Twine   **13 lost** left   **14 Whence** Where   **16 city's hived** Citie striu'de
**V.i.11 Mytilenian Sailor.** Hell. [changed in some copies of Q to "*I. Say.*"]   **16 you, sir,** to you to   **35-37 Lysimachus. Yet . . . wish./Helicanus. Behold . . . Till** yet . . . wish./Lys. Behold . . . person./Hell. Till   **37 night** wight   **47 ports** parts   **50 And with her fellow maid is now** and her fellow maides, now   **67 presence** present   **71 I'd** I do;   **rarely wed** rarely to wed   **72 Fair one, all** Faire on all;   **bounty** beautie   **74 feat** fate   **82 s.d. They . . . sings** The Song   **83 Marked** Marke   **105 countrywoman** Countrey women   **106 shores? . . . shores** shewes? . . . shewes   **110 such** sucha one   **127 make my senses** make senses   **130 say** stay   **144 thou them?** Thy thou thy   **158 Motion as well?** Motion well   **166-67 be: My daughter's buried.** be my daughter, buried   **184 Pericles** Hell.   **210-11 perfect, and thou art/The** perfit, the   **211 life** like   **217 thou art** th' art   **229 doubt** doat   **236 Pericles. I hear most heavenly music** Lys. I heare./Per. Most heauenly Musicke   **249-50 life./Perform** like, or performe   **264 suit** sleight
**V.iii.6 who** whom   **8 whom** who   **15 nun** mum   **22 one** in   **49 Pericles.** Hell.   **68 I bless** blesse   **69 Nightly** night   **83** [Q has "*FINIS*" after this line, as well as after line 101]   **88 preserved** preferd   **99 punish them** punish

# PERICLES, PRINCE OF TYRE

[Dramatis Personae

GOWER *as Chorus*
ANTIOCHUS *King of Antioch*
PERICLES *Prince of Tyre*
HELICANUS } *two lords of Tyre*
ESCANES
SIMONIDES *King of Pentapolis*
CLEON *Governor of Tharsus*
LYSIMACHUS *Governor of Mytilene*
CERIMON *a lord of Ephesus*
THALIARD *a lord of Antioch*
PHILEMON *servant to Cerimon*
LEONINE *servant to Dionyza*

MARSHAL
A PANDER
BOULT *his servant*
THE DAUGHTER OF ANTIOCHUS
DIONYZA *wife to Cleon*
THAISA *daughter to Simonides*
MARINA *daughter to Pericles and Thaisa*
LYCHORIDA *nurse to Marina*
A BAWD
DIANA
LORDS  LADIES  KNIGHTS  GENTLEMEN
  SAILORS  PIRATES  FISHERMEN
  MESSENGERS

*Scene:* dispersedly in various Mediterranean countries]

## [ACT I]

[*Before the king's palace at Antioch, with heads displayed upon its walls.*]

*Enter* GOWER° [*as Chorus*].

GOWER
To sing a song that old° was sung,
From ashes ancient Gower is come,
Assuming man's infirmities,°
To glad your ear, and please your eyes.
It hath been sung at festivals,                                    5
On ember-eves° and holidays,
And lords and ladies in their lives
Have read it for restoratives.

*The decorative border shown above appeared on the title page of the first quarto edition of* Pericles, *1609.*

**I.Cho.s.d. Gower** John Gower, fourteenth-century poet **1 old** of old  **3 Assuming man's infirmities** putting on man's infirm body  **6 ember-eves** evenings before the fasts known as "ember days"

The purchase° is to make men glorious;
Et bonum quo antiquius eo melius.°                                10
If you, born in those latter times,
When wit's more ripe, accept my rhymes,
And that to hear an old man sing
May to your wishes pleasure bring,
I life would wish, and that I might                              15
Waste it for you, like taper-light.
This Antioch,° then; Antiochus the great
Built up this city for his chiefest seat,
The fairest in all Syria—
I tell you what mine authors say.                                20
This king unto him took a peer,°
Who died, and left a female heir,
So buxom,° blithe, and full of face,°
As heaven had lent her all his grace;
With whom the father liking took,                                25

**9 purchase** gain  **10 Et . . . melius** and the more ancient a good thing is the better it is (Latin)  **17 This Antioch** this is Antioch  **21 peer** companion, consort  **23 buxom** gay, lively; **full of face** beautiful (?) with a round face (?)

1418

And her to incest did provoke.
Bad child, worse father, to entice his own
To evil should° be done by none.
But custom° what they did begin
Was with long use accounted no sin.     30
The beauty of this sinful dame
Made many princes thither frame,°
To seek her as a bedfellow,
In marriage pleasures playfellow;
Which to prevent he made a law,     35
To keep her still, and men in awe:°
That whoso asked her for his wife,
His riddle told° not, lost his life.
So for her many a wight did die,
As yon grim looks do testify.     40

[Points to the heads.]

What now ensues, to the judgment of your eye
I give my cause, who best can justify.°     *Exit.*

[Scene I. *Before the palace of Antioch.*]

*Enter* ANTIOCHUS, *Prince* PERICLES, *and followers.*

ANTIOCHUS
Young Prince of Tyre, you have at large received°
The danger of the task you undertake.
PERICLES
I have, Antiochus, and, with a soul
Embold'ned with the glory of her praise,
Think death no hazard in this enterprise.     5
ANTIOCHUS
Music!

[*Music sounds.*]

Bring in our daughter, clothèd like a bride,
For the embracements even of Jove himself;
At whose conception, till Lucina reigned,°
Nature this dowry° gave to glad her presence.°     10
The senate house of planets all did sit,
To knit in her their best perfections.

*Enter Antiochus'* DAUGHTER.

PERICLES
See where she comes, appareled like the spring,
Graces her subjects, and her thoughts the king
Of every virtue gives° renown to men!     15
Her face the book of praises, where is read
Nothing but curious° pleasures, as from thence
Sorrow were ever razed,° and testy wrath
Could never be her mild companion.°
You gods that made me man, and sway in love;°     20

That have enflamed desire in my breast
To taste the fruit of yon celestial tree
Or die in th' adventure, be my helps,
As° I am son and servant to your will,
To compass such a boundless happiness!     25
ANTIOCHUS
Prince Pericles—
PERICLES
That would be son to great Antiochus.
ANTIOCHUS
Before thee stands this fair Hesperides,°
With golden fruit, but dangerous to be touched;
For deathlike dragons here affright thee hard.     30
Her face like heaven enticeth thee to view
Her countless glory, which desert must gain;
And which without desert, because thine eye
Presumes to reach, all the whole heap° must die.
Yon sometimes° famous princes, like thyself,     35
Drawn by report, advent'rous by desire,
Tell thee, with speechless tongues and semblance pale,
That without covering, save yon field of stars,
Here they stand martyrs slain in Cupid's wars;
And with dead cheeks advise thee to desist     40
For° going on death's net, whom none resist.
PERICLES
Antiochus, I thank thee, who hath taught
My frail mortality to know itself,
And by those fearful objects to prepare
This body, like to them, to what I must;     45
For death remembered should be like a mirror,
Who tells us life's but breath, to trust it error.
I'll make my will, then; and, as sick men do,
Who know the world, see heaven, but, feeling woe,
Gripe° not at earthly joys as erst they did,     50
So I bequeath a happy peace to you
And all good men, as every prince should do;
My riches to the earth from whence they came;

[*To the* PRINCESS.]

But my unspotted fire of love to you.
Thus, ready for the way of life or death,     55
I wait the sharpest blow, Antiochus.
ANTIOCHUS
Scorning advice, read the conclusion° then:

[*He throws down the riddle.*]

Which read and not expounded, 'tis decreed,
As these before thee thou thyself shalt bleed.
DAUGHTER
Of all 'sayed yet,° mayst thou prove prosperous!     60
Of all 'sayed yet, I wish thee happiness.
PERICLES
Like a bold champion I assume the lists,°
Nor ask advice of any other thought
But faithfulness and courage.

28 **should** which should   29 **custom** through custom   32 **frame** direct their course   36 **To . . . awe** to keep her always to himself, and to keep others from demanding her in marriage   38 **told** expounded   41–42 **What . . . justify** In what now ensues I submit my case to the judgment of your eye, as you are best able to acquit me (of the charge of having told an incredible tale)
**I.i.1 at large received** learned fully   9 **till Lucina reigned** i.e., before her birth (Lucina is the goddess of childbirth)   10 **this dowry** i.e., her beauty; **to . . . presence** to make her presence delightful (?)   15 **gives** which gives   17 **curious** exquisite   18 **razed** erased   19 **her mild companion** the companion of her mildness   20 **sway in love** who govern in love

24 **As** as surely as   28 **Hesperides** the daughters of Hesperus, the evening star (but here, by confusion, the garden containing the golden apples, which, with the aid of a dragon, they were appointed to watch)   34 **the whole heap** the whole body   35 **sometimes** once   41 **For** for fear of   50 **gripe** grasp   57 **conclusion** riddle   60 **'sayed yet** who have yet assayed   62 **assume the lists** undertake the contest

*[He reads] the riddle.*

> I am no viper,° yet I feed                                65
> On mother's flesh, which did me breed.
> I sought a husband, in which labor
> I found that kindness° in a father.
> He's father, son, and husband mild;
> I mother, wife, and yet his child.                        70
> How they may be, and yet in two,°
> As you will live, resolve it you.

*[Aside.]*

Sharp physic is the last.° But O, you powers,
That gives° heaven countless eyes to view men's acts:
Why cloud they not their sights perpetually,             75
If this be true which makes me pale to read it?
Fair glass of light,° I loved you, and could still,
Were not this glorious casket stored with ill.
But I must tell you, now my thoughts revolt;
For he's no man on whom perfections wait                 80
That, knowing sin within, will touch the gate.
You are a fair viol, and your sense° the strings;
Who, fingered to make man his lawful music,
Would draw heaven down, and all the gods to
     hearken;
But being played upon before your time,                  85
Hell only danceth at so harsh a chime.
Good sooth,° I care not for you.

*[He turns towards the* PRINCESS.*]*

ANTIOCHUS
Prince Pericles, touch not, upon thy life,
For that's an article within our law
As dangerous° as the rest. Your time's expired.          90
Either expound now, or receive your sentence.

PERICLES
Great king,
Few love to hear the sins they love to act;
'Twould braid° yourself too near° for me to tell it.
Who has a book of all that monarchs do,                  95
He's more secure to keep it shut than shown;
For vice repeated° is like the wand'ring wind
Blows° dust in others' eyes to spread° itself;
And yet the end of all is bought thus dear:
The breath is gone, and the sore eyes see clear         100
To stop the air would hurt them. The blind mole casts
Copped° hills towards heaven, to tell the earth is
     thronged°
By man's oppression; and the poor worm° doth die
     for't.
Kings are earth's gods; in vice their law's their will;
And if Jove stray, who dares say Jove doth ill?         105
It is enough you know; and it is fit,
What being more known grows worse, to smother it.

---

**65 I . . . viper** vipers were believed to be born by eating their way out of the mother's body   **68 kindness** (1) kinship (2) affection   **71 How . . . two** how these things may be, and yet all be found in two persons   **73 Sharp . . . last** The last condition of the riddle is an unpleasant medicine   **74 gives** give (the third person plural in *-s* is not unusual)   **77 glass of light** i.e., one who reflects light, as does a mirror, but does not contain it   **82 sense** senses (?)   **87 Good sooth** truly   **90 dangerous** rigorous   **94 braid** upbraid; **too near** touching you too closely   **97 repeated** talked about   **98 Blows** which blows; **to spread** in spreading   **102 Copped** peaked; **thronged** crushed   **103 worm** creature

---

> All love the womb that their first being bred;
> Then give my tongue like leave to love my head.

ANTIOCHUS *[Aside.]*
Heaven, that I had thy head! He has found the mean-
     ing.                                                 110
But I will gloze° with him. *[Aloud.]* Young Prince of
     Tyre,
Though by the tenor of our strict edict,
Your exposition misinterpreting,
We might proceed to cancel of° your days,
Yet hope, succeeding° from so fair a tree               115
As your fair self, doth tune us otherwise.
Forty days longer we do respite you;
If by which time our secret be undone,°
This mercy shows we'll joy in such a son.
And until then your entertain° shall be                 120
As doth befit our honor and your worth.

*[Exeunt all but* PERICLES.*]*

PERICLES
How courtesy would seem° to cover sin,
When what is done is like an hypocrite,
The which is good in nothing but in sight!°
If it be true that I interpret false,                   125
Then were it certain you were not so bad
As with foul incest to abuse your soul;
Where now you're both a father and a son
By your uncomely° claspings with your child,
Which pleasures fits a husband, not a father;           130
And she an eater of her mother's flesh
By the defiling of her parents' bed;
And both like serpents are, who though they feed
On sweetest flowers, yet they poison breed.
Antioch, farewell, for wisdom sees, those men           135
Blush° not in actions blacker than the night,
Will 'schew° no course to keep them from the
     light.
One sin, I know, another doth provoke;
Murder's as near to lust as flame to smoke.
Poison and treason are the hands of sin,                140
Ay, and the targets,° to put off° the shame.
Then, lest my life be cropped to keep you clear,
By flight I'll shun the danger which I fear.    *Exit.*

*Enter* ANTIOCHUS.

ANTIOCHUS
He hath found the meaning,
For which we mean to have his head. He must            145
Not live to trumpet forth my infamy,
Nor tell the world Antiochus doth sin
In such a loathèd manner.
And therefore instantly this prince must die;
For by his fall my honor must keep high.               150
Who attends us there?

*Enter* THALIARD.

THALIARD               Doth your highness call?

---

**111 gloze** talk speciously   **114 cancel of** the canceling of   **115 succeeding** resulting   **118 secret be undone** riddle be solved   **120 entertain** entertainment, reception   **122 seem** make a specious appearance   **124 sight** outward appearance   **129 uncomely** improper (see Introduction, p. 1407)   **136 Blush** who blush   **137 'schew** eschew, avoid   **141 targets** shields; **put off** avert

ANTIOCHUS
Thaliard,
You are of our chamber,° Thaliard, and our mind
   partakes°
Her private actions to your secrecy;
And for your faithfulness we will advance you.        155
Thaliard, behold, here's poison, and here's gold!
We hate the Prince of Tyre, and thou must kill him.
It fits thee not to ask the reason why.
Because we bid it. Say, is it done?

THALIARD
My lord, 'tis done.

ANTIOCHUS                    Enough.                 160

*Enter a* MESSENGER.

Let your breath cool yourself telling your haste.

MESSENGER
My lord, Prince Pericles is fled.              [*Exit.*]

ANTIOCHUS   As thou wilt live, fly after; and like an
arrow shot from a well-experienced archer hits the
mark his eye doth level° at, so thou never return     165
unless thou say Prince Pericles is dead.

THALIARD   My lord, if I can get him within my pistol's
length, I'll make him sure° enough. So farewell to
your highness.

ANTIOCHUS
Thaliard, adieu! [*Exit* THALIARD.] Till Pericles be
   dead                                               170
My heart can lend no succor to my head.        [*Exit.*]

[*Scene II. Tyre. A room in the palace.*]

*Enter* PERICLES.

PERICLES [*To* SERVANTS *without.*]
Let none disturb us.
Why should this change of thoughts,
The sad companion, dull-eyed melancholy,
Be my so used° a guest as not an hour
In the day's glorious walk or peaceful night,          5
The tomb where grief should sleep, can breed me
   quiet?
Here pleasures court mine eyes, and mine eyes shun
   them,
And danger, which I feared, is at Antioch,
Whose arm seems far too short to hit me here;
Yet neither pleasure's art can joy° my spirits,       10
Nor yet the other's distance comfort me.
Then it is thus: the passions of the mind,
That have their first conception by misdread,°
Have after-nourishment and life by care;
And what was first but fear what might be done,       15
Grows elder now and cares° it be not done.
And so with me: the great Antiochus,
'Gainst whom I am too little to contend,
Since he's so great can° make his will his act,
Will think me speaking, though I swear to silence;    20

Nor boots it me° to say I honor him,
If he suspect I may dishonor him.
And what may make him blush in being known°
He'll stop the course by which it might be known.
With hostile forces he'll o'erspread the land,        25
And with th' ostent° of war will look so huge,
Amazement° shall drive courage from the state,
Our men be vanquished ere they do resist,
And subjects punished that ne'er thought offense;
Which care of them, not pity of myself,               30
Who am no more but as the tops of trees
Which fence° the roots they grow by and defend
   them,
Makes both my body pine and soul to languish,
And punish that before that he would punish.

*Enter* [HELICANUS *and*] *all the* LORDS *to* PERICLES.

FIRST LORD
Joy and all comfort in your sacred breast!            35

SECOND LORD
And keep your mind, till you return to us,
Peaceful and comfortable!°

HELICANUS
Peace, peace, and give experience tongue.°
They do abuse° the king that flatter him,
For flattery is the bellows blows up° sin;            40
The thing the which is flattered but a spark
To which that blast gives heat and stronger glowing;
Whereas reproof, obedient and in order,
Fits kings, as they are men, for they may err.
When Signor Sooth° here does proclaim a peace         45
He flatters you, makes war upon your life.
Prince, pardon me, or strike me, if you please;
I cannot be much lower than my knees.

[*He kneels.*]

PERICLES
All leave us else!° But let your cares o'er-look°
What shipping and what lading's° in our haven,        50
And then return to us. [*Exeunt* LORDS.] Helicanus,
Thou hast moved us. What see'st thou in our looks?

HELICANUS
An angry brow, dread lord.

PERICLES
If there be such a dart in princes' frowns,
How durst thy tongue move anger to our face?          55

HELICANUS
How dares the plants look up to heaven, from whence
They have their nourishment?

PERICLES                    Thou knowest I have power
To take thy life from thee.

---

**21 boots it me** does it avail me   **23 in being known** if
it were known   **26 th' ostent** the display   **27 Amazement** consternation   **32 fence** protect   **36–37 And keep
. . . comfortable** these lines must be either corrupt or
misplaced, as Pericles' decision to leave Tyre is not taken till the
end of the scene   **37 comfortable** cheerful (a passage in which
Helicanus reproves Pericles for wasting "his body there with
pining sorrow, upon whose safety depended the lives and
prosperity of a whole kingdom" [Wilkins] and is sternly rebuked
by him for his presumption, must have preceded the next
speech, but is missing from the text)   **38 give experience
tongue** allow experience to speak   **39 abuse** ill-use   **40
blows up** which fans into flame   **45 Signor Sooth** Sir Flattery
**49 All . . . else** Everybody else leave us; **o'erlook** look into
**50 lading's** cargo's

---

**153 of our chamber** our chamberlain; **partakes** imparts
**165 level** aim   **168 sure** unable to do harm
**I.ii.4 used** customary   **10 joy** give joy to   **13 misdread**
dread of evil   **16 cares** is anxious that   **19 can** that he can

HELICANUS                    I have ground the ax myself;
Do but you strike the blow.
PERICLES                          Rise, prithee, rise.

[*He raises him.*]

Sit down. Thou art no flatterer.                                        60
I thank thee for't; and heaven forbid
That kings should let their ears hear their faults hid!°
Fit counselor and servant for a prince,
Who by thy wisdom makes a prince thy servant,
What wouldst thou have me do?
HELICANUS                    To bear with patience 65
Such griefs as you do lay upon yourself.
PERICLES
Thou speak'st like a physician, Helicanus,
That ministers a potion unto me
That thou wouldst tremble to receive thyself.
Attend° me then: I went to Antioch,                              70
Where, as thou know'st, against the face of death
I sought the purchase° of a glorious beauty,
From whence an issue I might propagate
Are arms° to princes and bring joys to subjects.
Her face was to mine eye beyond all wonder;        75
The rest—hark in thine ear—as black as incest;
Which by my knowledge found, the sinful father
Seemed° not to strike, but smooth;° but thou know'st
   this:
'Tis time to fear when tyrants seems to kiss.
Which fear so grew in me, I hither fled,                      80
Under the covering of a careful° night,
Who seemed my good protector; and, being here,
Bethought me what was past, what might succeed.
I knew him tyrannous; and tyrants' fears
Decrease not, but grow faster than the years;         85
And should he doubt, as no doubt he doth,°
That I should open° to the list'ning air
How many worthy princes' bloods were shed
To keep his bed of blackness unlaid ope,°
To lop that doubt,° he'll fill this land with arms,      90
And make pretense of wrong that I have done him;
When all for mine, if I may call, offense
Must feel war's blow, who° spares not innocence;
Which love to all, of which thyself art one,
Who now° reprovedst me for't—
HELICANUS                              Alas, sir!                        95
PERICLES
Drew sleep out of mine eyes, blood from my cheeks,
Musings into my mind, with thousand doubts
How I might stop this tempest ere it came;
And finding little comfort to relieve them,
I thought it princely charity to grieve them.°          100
HELICANUS
Well, my lord, since you have given me leave to
   speak,
Freely will I speak. Antiochus you fear,
And justly, too, I think, you fear the tyrant

Who either by public war or private treason
Will take away your life.                                                105
Therefore, my lord, go travel for a while,
Till that his rage and anger be forgot,
Or till the Destinies do cut his thread of life.
Your rule direct° to any; if to me,
Day serves not light more faithful° than I'll be.   110
PERICLES
I do not doubt thy faith.
But should he wrong my liberties° in my absence?
HELICANUS
We'll mingle our bloods together in the earth,
From whence we had our being and our birth.
PERICLES
Tyre, I now look from thee then, and to Tharsus   115
Intend° my travel, where I'll hear from thee,
And by whose letters I'll dispose myself.°
The care I had and have of subjects' good
On thee I lay, whose wisdom's strength can bear it.
I'll take thy word for faith, not ask thine oath:      120
Who shuns not to break one° will crack both.
But in our orbs we'll live so round° and safe,°
That time of both this truth shall ne'er convince:°
Thou showed'st a subject's shine, I a true prince.°
                                   *Exit, [with* HELICANUS].

[*Scene III. The palace at Tyre.*]

*Enter* THALIARD *solus,*°

THALIARD   So this is Tyre, and this the court. Here
must I kill King Pericles; and if I do it not, I am sure
to be hanged at home. 'Tis dangerous. Well, I perceive
he was a wise fellow and had good discretion that,
being bid to ask what he would of the king, desired he   5
might know none of his secrets. Now do I see he had
some reason for't: for if a king bid a man be a villain,
he's bound by the indenture° of his oath to be one.
Husht, here comes the lords of Tyre.

*Enter* HELICANUS, ESCANES, *with other* LORDS.

HELICANUS
You shall not need, my fellow peers of Tyre,          10
Further to question me of your king's departure.
His sealed commission left in trust with me
Does speak sufficiently he's gone to travel.
THALIARD [*Aside.*]   How? The king gone?
HELICANUS
If further yet you will be satisfied                                15
Why, as it were, unlicensed of your loves°
He would depart, I'll give some light unto you.
Being at Antioch—
THALIARD [*Aside.*] What from Antioch?

109 **direct** assign  110 **Day . . . faithful** day is not served
by light more faithfully  112 **liberties** prerogatives  116
**Intend** direct  117 **dispose myself** direct my actions  121
**one** pronounced as a disyllable  122 **we'll . . . round**
(1) we'll live so honestly (2) we'll move in such a perfect circle;
**safe** trustworthily  123 **of . . . convince** shall never confute
this truth regarding both of us  124 **Thou . . . prince** You
showed a subject's luster, I showed myself a true prince
**I.iii.s.d. solus** alone (Latin)  8 **indenture** contract binding
servant to master  16 **unlicensed . . . loves** without your
loving assent

62 **hear . . . hid** i.e., hear the flattery that hides their faults
70 **Attend** listen to  72 **purchase** acquisition  74 **Are arms**
which are arms  78 **Seemed** pretended; **smooth** flatter  81
**careful** taking good care  86 **And . . . doth** the first "doubt,"
meaning "fear," is pronounced as a disyllable  87 **open** reveal
89 **unlaid ope** undisclosed  90 **doubt** dread, fear  93 **who**
which  95 **now** just now  100 **grieve them** grieve for them

HELICANUS

Royal Antiochus—on what cause I know not—
Took some displeasure at him; at least he judged so;  20
And doubting lest° he had erred or sinned,
To show his sorrow, he'd correct° himself;
So puts himself unto the shipman's toil,
With whom each minute threatens life or death.

THALIARD [Aside.]

Well, I perceive I shall not be hanged now  25
Although I would.
But since he's gone, the king's ears it must please
He scaped the land, to perish at the seas.
I'll present myself. [Aloud.] Peace to the lords of Tyre!

HELICANUS

Lord Thaliard from Antiochus is welcome.  30

THALIARD

From him I come
With message unto princely Pericles.
But since my landing I have understood
Your lord has betook himself to unknown travels.
Now message must return from whence it came.  35

HELICANUS

We have no reason to desire it,
Commended° to our master, not to us.
Yet, ere you shall depart, this we desire:
As friends to Antioch we may feast in Tyre.

Exit, [with the rest].

[Scene IV. Tharsus.]

Enter CLEON, the Governor of Tharsus, with his wife
[DIONYZA] and others.

CLEON

My Dionyza, shall we rest us here,
And by relating tales of others' griefs,
See if 'twill teach us to forget our own?

DIONYZA

That were to blow at fire in hope to quench it;
For who digs° hills because they do aspire  5
Throws down one mountain to cast up a higher.
O my distressed lord, even such our griefs are;
Here they are but felt and seen with mischief's° eyes,
But like to groves, being topped, they higher rise.

CLEON

O Dionyza,  10
Who wanteth food and will not say he wants it,
Or can conceal his hunger till he famish?
Our tongues and sorrows cease not to sound deep
Our woes into the air, our eyes to weep,°
Till tongues fetch breath that may proclaim them
  louder,  15
That, if heaven slumber while their creatures want,
They may awake their helps to comfort them.
I'll then discourse our woes, felt several years,
And wanting breath to speak help me° with tears.

DIONYZA

I'll do my best, sir.  20

CLEON

This Tharsus. o'er which I have the government,
A city on° whom plenty held full hand,
For riches strewed herself° even in her streets;
Whose towers bore heads so high they kissed the
  clouds,
And strangers ne'er beheld but wond'red at;  25
Whose men and dames so jetted and adorned,°
Like one another's glass to trim them by;°
Their tables were stored full, to glad the sight,
And not so much to feed on as delight;
All poverty was scorned, and pride so great,  30
The name of help grew odious to repeat.°

DIONYZA

O, 'tis too true!

CLEON

But see what heaven can do by this our change:
These mouths who but of late earth, sea, and air
Were all too little to content and please,  35
Although they gave their creatures in abundance,
As houses are defiled for want of use,
They are now starved for want of exercise;
Those palates who, not yet two summers younger,
Must have inventions° to delight the taste,  40
Would now be glad of bread, and beg for it;
Those mothers who, to nuzzle up° their babes,
Thought nought too curious,° are ready now
To eat those little darlings whom they loved.
So sharp are hunger's teeth that man and wife  45
Draw lots who first shall die to lengthen life.
Here stands a lord, and there a lady weeping;
Here many sink, yet those which see them fall
Have scarce strength left to give them burial.
Is not this true?  50

DIONYZA

Our cheeks and hollow eyes do witness it.

CLEON

O, let those cities that of plenty's cup
And her prosperities so largely taste,
With their superfluous riots,° hear these tears!
The misery of Tharsus may be theirs.  55

Enter a LORD.

LORD

Where's the Lord Governor?

CLEON

Here.
Speak out thy sorrows which thou bring'st in haste,
For comfort is too far for us to expect.

LORD

We have descried, upon our neighboring shore,  60
A portly sail° of ships make hitherward.

CLEON

I thought as much.

---

21 **doubting lest** fearing that ("doubting" is here trisyllabic)  22 **he'd correct** he wanted to punish  37 **Commended** since it is commended
**I.iv.5 digs** digs down  8 **mischief's** misfortune's  13–14 **Our tongues . . . weep** let our sorrowful tongues (hendiadys) not cease to . . ., let our eyes not cease to weep  19 **help me** do you help me

22 **on** over  23 **riches strewed herself** "riches" is a feminine singular  26 **jetted and adorned** strutted and dressed themselves up  27 **glass . . . by** pattern according to which to array themselves  31 **repeat** mention  40 **inventions** ingenious novelties  42 **nuzzle up** bring up  43 **curious** exquisite  54 **superfluous riots** inordinate revels  61 **portly sail** stately fleet

One sorrow never comes but brings an heir
That may succeed as his inheritor;
And so in ours: some neighboring nation,  65
Taking advantage of our misery,
Hath stuffed the hollow vessels with their power,°
To beat us down, the which are down already,
And make a conquest of unhappy me,
Whereas° no glory's got to overcome.  70

LORD
That's the least fear; for, by the semblance
Of their white flags displayed, they bring us peace,
And come to us as favorers, not as foes.°

CLEON
Thou speak'st like him's untutored to repeat:°
Who makes the fairest show means most deceit.  75
But bring they what they will, what need we fear?
On ground's the lowest,° and we are halfway there.
Go tell their general we attend° him here,
To know for what he comes, and whence he comes,
And what he craves.°  80

LORD
I go, my lord.  [Exit.]

CLEON
Welcome is peace, if he on peace consist;°
If wars, we are unable to resist.

Enter PERICLES, with ATTENDANTS.

PERICLES
Lord Governor, for so we hear you are,
Let not our ships and number of our men  85
Be like a beacon fired t' amaze your eyes.
We have heard your miseries as far as Tyre,
And seen the desolation of your streets;
Nor come we to add sorrow to your tears,
But to relieve them of their heavy load;  90
And these our ships you happily may think°
Are like the Trojan horse was° stuffed within
With bloody veins expecting overthrow,°
Are stored with corn to make your needy bread,°
And give them life whom hunger starved half dead.  95

ALL
The gods of Greece protect you!
And we'll pray for you. [They kneel.]

PERICLES                         Arise, I pray you, rise;
We do not look for reverence but for love,
And harborage for ourself, our ships, and men.

CLEON
The which when any shall not gratify,°  100
Or pay you with unthankfulness in thought,
Be it our wives, our children, or ourselves,
The curse of heaven and men succeed their evils!
Till when—the which I hope shall ne'er be seen—
Your grace is welcome to our town and us.  105

PERICLES
Which welcome we'll accept; feast here awhile,
Until our stars that frown lend us a smile.  Exeunt.

# [ACT II]

Enter GOWER.

GOWER
Here have you seen a mighty king
His child iwis° to incest bring;
A better prince and benign lord
That will prove awful° both in deed and word.
Be quiet, then, as men should be,  5
Till he hath passed necessity.°
I'll show you those in trouble's reign°
Losing a mite, a mountain gain.
The good in conversation,°
To whom I give my benison,  10
Is still at Tharsus, where each man
Thinks all is writ he spoken can;°
And, to remember° what he does,
Build his statue to make him glorious.
But tidings to the contrary  15
Are brought your eyes; what need speak I?

*Dumb Show.*

Enter at one door PERICLES, *talking with* CLEON; *all
the* TRAIN *with them. Enter at another door a* GENTLE-
MAN *with a letter to* PERICLES; PERICLES *shows the
letter to* CLEON. PERICLES *gives the* MESSENGER *a
reward and knights him. Exit* PERICLES *at one door, and*
CLEON *at another.*

Good Helicane, that stayed at home,
Not to eat honey like a drone
From others' labors, for he strives
To killen bad, keep good alive,  20
And to fulfill his prince' desire,
Sends word of all that haps in Tyre:
How Thaliard came full bent with° sin
And hid intent° to murder him;
And that in Tharsus was not best  25
Longer for him to make his rest.
He, doing so,° put forth to seas,
Where when men been there's seldom ease;
For now the wind begins to blow;
Thunder above and deeps below  30
Makes such unquiet that the ship
Should° house him safe is wracked and split;
And he, good prince, having all lost,
By waves from coast to coast is tossed.
All perishen of man, of pelf,°  35
Ne aught escapend° but himself;
Till fortune, tired with doing bad,
Threw him ashore, to give him glad.°
And here he comes. What shall be next,
Pardon old Gower—this 'longs° the text.  [Exit.]  40

**67 power** armed force  **70 Whereas** where  **74 him's . . .
repeat** him who has never been taught to recite  **77 On . . .
lowest** he who lies upon the ground can fall no lower  **78
attend** await  **80 craves** desires  **82 on peace consist**
stands on peace  **91 you . . . think** you may perhaps think
**92 was** which was  **93 With . . . overthrow** with bloodthirsty warriors waiting for the overthrow (of Troy)  **94
your needy bread** bread for your needy citizens  **100
gratify** show gratitude for

**II.Cho.2 iwis** assuredly  **4 awful** commanding profound
respect  **6 passed necessity** experienced extreme hardship
**7 those . . . reign** those who under the dominion of trouble
**9 conversation** conduct, way of life  **12 all . . . can** all his
words are holy writ  **13 remember** commemorate  **23 bent
with** intent upon  **24 And hid intent** and with hidden
intent  **27 doing so** acting as advised  **32 Should** which
should  **35 pelf** possessions  **36 escapend** escaping  **38 glad**
gladness  **40 'longs** belongs to

[Scene I. *Pentapolis, at the seashore.*]

*Enter* PERICLES, *wet.*

PERICLES
Yet cease your ire, you angry stars of heaven!
Wind, rain, and thunder, remember, earthly man
Is but a substance that must yield to you;
And I, as fits my nature, do obey you.
Alas, the seas hath cast me on the rocks,    5
Washed me from shore to shore, and left me breath
Nothing to think on but ensuing death.
Let it suffice the greatness of your powers
To have bereft a prince of all his fortunes;
And having thrown him from your wat'ry grave,    10
Here to have death in peace is all he'll crave.

*Enter three* FISHERMEN.

FIRST FISHERMAN   What ho, Pilch!°
SECOND FISHERMAN   Ha, come and bring away° the
nets!
FIRST FISHERMAN   What, Patchbreech, I say!    15
THIRD FISHERMAN   What say you, master?
FIRST FISHERMAN   Look how thou stirr'st now!°
Come away,° or I'll fetch thee with a wanion.°
THIRD FISHERMAN   Faith, master, I am thinking of
the poor men that were cast away before us even now.    20
FIRST FISHERMAN   Alas, poor souls, it grieved my
heart to hear what pitiful cries they made to us to help
them, when, well-a-day,° we could scarce help ourselves.
THIRD FISHERMAN   Nay, master, said not I as much    25
when I saw the porpoise how he bounced and tumbled? They say they're half fish, half flesh. A plague
on them! They ne'er come but I look to be washed.
Master, I marvel how the fishes live in the sea.
FIRST FISHERMAN   Why, as men do a-land: the great    30
ones eat up the little ones. I can compare our rich
misers to nothing so fitly as to a whale; 'a° plays and
tumbles, driving the poor fry before him, and at last
devours them all at a mouthful: Such whales have I
heard on a' th' land,° who never leave gaping till they    35
swallowed the whole parish, church, steeple, bells,
and all.
PERICLES [*Aside.*]   A pretty moral.°
THIRD FISHERMAN   But, master, if I had been the
sexton, I would have been that day in the belfry.    40
SECOND FISHERMAN   Why, man?
THIRD FISHERMAN   Because he should have swallowed me too; and when I had been in his belly, I
would have kept such a jangling of the bells that he
should never have left till he cast bells, steeple, church,    45
and parish up again. But if the good King Simonides
were of my mind—
PERICLES [*Aside.*]   Simonides!
THIRD FISHERMAN   We would purge the land of
these drones that rob the bee of her honey.    50

PERICLES [*Aside.*]
How from the finny subject° of the sea
These fishers tell the infirmities of men;
And from their wat'ry empire recollect°
All that may men approve° or men detect!°

[*Aloud.*]

Peace be at your labor, honest fishermen!    55
SECOND FISHERMAN   Honest good fellow, what's
that? If it be a day fits you, scratch it out of the calen-
dar, and nobody look after it.°
PERICLES
May° see the sea hath cast upon your coast—
SECOND FISHERMAN   What a drunken knave was    60
the sea to cast° thee in our way!
PERICLES
A man whom both the waters and the wind
In that vast tennis court hath made the ball
For them to play upon entreats you pity him.
He asks of you that never used to beg.    65
FIRST FISHERMAN   No, friend, cannot you beg?
Here's them in our country of Greece gets more with
begging than we can do with working.
SECOND FISHERMAN   Canst thou catch any fishes,
then?    70
PERICLES   I never practiced it.
SECOND FISHERMAN   Nay, then, thou wilt starve,
sure; for here's nothing to be got nowadays unless thou
canst fish for't.
PERICLES
What I have been I have forgot to know;    75
But what I am want teaches me to think on:
A man thronged up° with cold. My veins are chill,
And have no more of life than may suffice
To give my tongue that heat to ask your help;
Which if you shall refuse, when I am dead,    80
For that° I am a man, pray you see me buried.
FIRST FISHERMAN   Die, quoth-a?° Now gods for-
bid't! And I have a gown here! Come, put it on; keep
thee warm. Now, afore me,° a handsome fellow!
Come, thou shalt go home, and we'll have flesh for    85
holidays, fish for fasting days, and moreo'er puddings
and flapjacks,° and thou shalt be welcome.
PERICLES   I thank you, sir.
SECOND FISHERMAN   Hark you, my friend: you said
you could not beg.    90
PERICLES   I did but crave.
SECOND FISHERMAN   But crave? Then I'll turn craver
too, and so I shall 'scape whipping.°
PERICLES   Why, are your beggars whipped, then?
SECOND FISHERMAN   O, not all, my friend, not all!    95
For if all your beggars were whipped, I would wish

**II.i.12 Pilch** a coarse outer garment made of leather or skin,
here used, like "Patchbreech," jestingly as a name   **13 bring
away** bring here without delay   **17 how . . . now** what a
stock you are!   **18 Come away** come here right away;
**with a wanion** with a vengeance   **23 well-a-day** alas   **32 'a**
he   **35 heard . . . land** heard of on land   **38 moral** tale
conveying a moral lesson   **51 subject** subjects, citizens   **53 recollect** gather up   **54
approve** commend; **detect** expose (in wrongdoing)   **56–58
Honest . . . after it** a lost line in which Pericles wishes
the fishermen a good day appears to have preceded this passage;
the fisherman rudely replies that if the day fitted Pericles'
wretched appearance it ought to be removed from the calendar
  **59 May** you may   **61 cast** (1) cast up, vomit (2) throw   **77
thronged up** overwhelmed   **81 For that** because   **82 quoth-
a** did he say   **84 afore me** upon my word   **87 flapjacks**
pancakes   **92–93 Then . . . whipping** i.e., through not
calling himself a beggar (whipping, administered by the beadle,
was the regular punishment of beggars in Shakespeare's day)

no better office than to be beadle. But, master, I'll go draw up the net.          [*Exit, with* THIRD FISHERMAN.]

PERICLES [*Aside.*]
How well this honest mirth becomes° their labor!

FIRST FISHERMAN   Hark you, sir, do you know 100 where ye are?

PERICLES   Not well.

FIRST FISHERMAN   Why, I'll tell you: this is called Pentapolis, and our king the good Simonides.

PERICLES   The good Simonides do you call him?   105

FIRST FISHERMAN   Ay, sir; and he deserves so to be called, for his peaceable reign and good government.

PERICLES   He is a happy king, since he gains from his subjects the name of good by his government. How far is his court distant from this shore?          110

FIRST FISHERMAN   Marry,° sir, half a day's journey. And I'll tell you, he hath a fair daughter, and tomorrow is her birthday; and there are princes and knights come from all parts of the world to joust and tourney for her love.          115

PERICLES   Were my fortunes equal to my desires, I could wish to make one there.

FIRST FISHERMAN   O, sir, things must be as they may; and what a man cannot get he may lawfully deal for his wife's soul.°          120

*Enter the two* FISHERMEN, *drawing up a net.*

SECOND FISHERMAN   Help, master, help! Here's a fish hangs in the net like a poor man's right° in the law: 'twill hardly come out. Ha, bots on't,° 'tis come at last; and 'tis turned to a rusty armor.

PERICLES
An armor, friends! I pray you, let me see it.   125
Thanks, Fortune, yet, that after all thy crosses
Thou givest me somewhat to repair° myself;
And though it was mine own, part of my heritage
Which my dead father did bequeath to me,
With this strict charge, even as he left his life:   130
"Keep it, my Pericles; it hath been a shield
'Twixt me and death"—and pointed to this brace°—
"For that it saved me, keep it; in like necessity—
The which the gods protect thee from!—may't defend
   thee."
It kept where I kept, I so dearly loved it;   135
Till the rough seas, that spares not any man,
Took it in rage, though calmed have given't again.
I thank thee for't. My shipwrack now's no ill,
Since I have here my father gave° in his will.

FIRST FISHERMAN   What mean you, sir?   140

PERICLES
To beg of you, kind friends, this coat of worth,
For it was sometime target° to a king;
I know it by this mark. He loved me dearly,
And for his sake I wish the having of it;
And that you'd guide me to your sovereign's court,   145
Where with it I may appear a gentleman.

And if that ever my low fortune's better,
I'll pay your bounties; till then rest your debtor.

FIRST FISHERMAN   Why, wilt thou tourney for the lady?          150

PERICLES
I'll show the virtue° I have borne in arms.

FIRST FISHERMAN   Why, d' ye take it, and the gods give thee good on't!

SECOND FISHERMAN   Ay, but hark you, my friend: 'twas we that made up this garment through the 155 rough seams of the waters. There are certain condolements,° certain vails.° I hope, sir, if you thrive, you'll remember from whence you had them.°

PERICLES
Believe't, I will!
By your furtherance I am clothed in steel;   160
And spite of all the rapture° of the sea,
This jewel holds his building° on my arm.
Unto thy value° I will mount myself
Upon a courser, whose delightful steps
Shall make the gazer joy to see him tread.   165
Only, my friend, I yet am unprovided
Of a pair of bases.°

SECOND FISHERMAN   We'll sure provide. Thou shalt have my best gown to make thee a pair; and I'll bring thee to the court myself.          170

PERICLES
Then honor be but equal to my will,
This day I'll rise, or else add ill to ill.          [*Exeunt.*]

[Scene II. *Pentapolis. The court of Simonides. A public way leading to the lists. A pavilion near it.*]

*Enter* SIMONIDES, *with* [LORDS,] ATTENDANTS, *and* THAISA.

SIMONIDES
Are the knights ready to begin the triumph?°

FIRST LORD
They are, my liege,
And stay your coming to present themselves.

SIMONIDES
Return° them we are ready; and our daughter,
In honor of whose birth these triumphs are,   5
Sits here like Beauty's child, whom Nature gat°
For men to see and seeing wonder at. [*Exit a* LORD.]

THAISA
It pleaseth you, my royal father, to express
My commendations great, whose merit's less.

SIMONIDES
It's fit it should be so; for princes are   10
A model° which heaven makes like to itself:
As jewels lose their glory if neglected,
So princes their renowns if not respected.

99 becomes suits with   111 Marry why (a mild oath, from "By the Virgin Mary")   119–20 he . . . soul no sense can be made of the text as it stands, nor has it been plausibly emended   122 right just claim   123 bots on't a plague upon it   127 repair renew, restore   132 brace armor covering the arms   139 my father gave that which my father gave   142 target literally, light shield, hence protection

151 virtue valor   156–57 condolements probably a malapropism through confusion with *dole*, meaning "distribution of gifts"   157 vails perquisites, tips   158 them the armor   161 rapture act of plunder, seizure   162 building fixed place   163 Unto thy value to as high a value (as the jewel will fetch)   167 bases pleated skirt, worn by knights on horseback
II.ii.1 triumph festivity, here tournament   4 Return tell by way of answer   6 gat begat   11 model likeness in little

'Tis now your honor,° daughter, to entertain°
The labor of each knight in his device.°　　　　　　15

**THAISA**
Which, to preserve mine honor, I'll perform.

[SIMONIDES *and* THAISA *take seats in the pavilion.*]
*The* FIRST KNIGHT *passes by.* [*As each knight passes, his*
*page, who goes before him, presents his shield to Princess*
THAISA.]

**SIMONIDES**
Who is the first that doth prefer° himself?

**THAISA**
A knight of Sparta, my renownèd father;
And the device he bears upon his shield
Is a black Ethiop reaching at the sun.　　　　　　20
The word,° Lux tua vita mihi.°

**SIMONIDES**
He loves you well that holds his life of you.

*The* SECOND KNIGHT [*passes*].

Who is the second that presents himself?

**THAISA**
A prince of Macedon, my royal father;
And the device he bears upon his shield　　　　　　25
Is an armed knight that's conquered by a lady;
The motto thus, in Spanish, Più per dolcezza che per
forza.°

[*The*] THIRD KNIGHT [*passes*].

**SIMONIDES**
And what's the third?

**THAISA**　　　　　　　　　The third of Antioch;
And his device a wreath of chivalry.°
The word, Me pompae provexit apex.°　　　　　　30

[*The*] FOURTH KNIGHT [*passes*].

**SIMONIDES**
What is the fourth?

**THAISA**
A burning torch that's turnèd upside down.
The word, Qui me alit me extinguit.°

**SIMONIDES**
Which shows that beauty hath his° power and will,
Which can as well inflame as it can kill.　　　　　　35

[*The*] FIFTH KNIGHT [*passes*].

**THAISA**
The fifth, an hand environèd with clouds,
Holding out gold that's by the touchstone tried.
The motto thus, Sic spectanda fides.°

[*The*] sixth knight, [PERICLES, *passes, without page*].

**SIMONIDES**
And what's the sixth and last, the which the knight
himself
With such a graceful courtesy delivered?°　　　　　　40

**THAISA**
He seems to be a stranger; but his present° is
A withered branch that's only green at top;
The motto, In hac spe vivo.°

**SIMONIDES**
A pretty moral.
From the dejected state wherein he is,　　　　　　45
He hopes by you his fortunes yet may flourish.

**FIRST LORD**
He had need mean better than his outward show
Can any way speak in his just commend;°
For by his rusty outside he appears
To have practiced more the whipstock° than the lance.　50

**SECOND LORD**
He well may be a stranger, for he comes
To an honored triumph strangely furnishèd.

**THIRD LORD**
And on set purpose let his armor rust
Until this day to scour it in the dust.

**SIMONIDES**
Opinion's° but a fool that makes us scan°　　　　　　55
The outward habit for the inward man.
But stay, the knights are coming!
We will withdraw into the gallery.　　　　　[*Exeunt.*]

*Great shouts* [*within*], *and all cry,* "The mean° knight!"

[Scene III. *Pentapolis. A hall of state.*]

*Enter the king* [SIMONIDES, THAISA, MARSHAL,
LORDS, LADIES,] *and* KNIGHTS *from tilting,* [*and*
ATTENDANTS].

**SIMONIDES**
Knights,
To say you're welcome were superfluous.
To place upon the volume of your deeds,
As in a title page, your worth in arms,°
Were more than you expect, or more than's fit,　　　　5
Since every worth in show commends itself.
Prepare for mirth, for mirth becomes a feast.
You are princes and my guests.

**THAISA**
But you my knight and guest;
To whom this wreath of victory I give,　　　　　　10
And crown you king of this day's happiness.

**PERICLES**
'Tis more by fortune, lady, than my merit.

**SIMONIDES**
Call it by what you will, the day is yours;
And here, I hope, is none that envies it.

---

**14 honor** honorable duty; **entertain** receive **15 device**
emblematic figure, accompanied by a motto, inscribed on the
shield **17 prefer** present **21 word** motto; **Lux . . . mihi**
Thy light is life to me (Latin) **27 Più . . . forza** More by
gentleness than by force (Italian) **29 wreath of chivalry** the
twisted band by which, in heraldry, the crest is joined to the
knight's helmet **30 Me . . . apex** The crown of the triumph
has led me on (Latin) **33 Qui . . . extinguit** Who feeds me
puts me out (Latin) **34 his** its **38 Sic spectanda fides** Thus
is faithfulness to be tried (Latin)

**40 delivered** presented **41 present** object presented **43 In
hac spe vivo** In this hope I live (Latin) **48 commend**
commendation **50 To . . . whipstock** to have wielded more
the handle of a whip, i.e., worked as a carter **55 Opinion**
public opinion; **scan** scrutinize, examine **58 s.d. mean** shabby
**II.iii.4 As . . . arms** title pages of early printed books often
proclaimed the excellence of their contents

In framing° an artist, art hath thus decreed:  15
To make some good, but others to exceed;
And you are her labored scholar.° Come, queen o' th'
    feast—
For, daughter, so you are—here take your place.
Marshal, the rest as they deserve their grace.°

KNIGHTS
We are honored much by good Simonides.  20

SIMONIDES
Your presence glads our days. Honor we love;
For who hates honor hates the gods above.

MARSHAL
Sir, yonder is your place.

PERICLES          Some other is more fit.

FIRST KNIGHT
Contend not, sir; for we are gentlemen
Have° neither in our hearts nor outward eyes  25
Envied the great, nor shall the low despise.

PERICLES
You are right courteous knights.

SIMONIDES          Sit, sir, sit.

[Aside.]

By Jove I wonder, that is king of thoughts,
These cates° resist me, he but thought upon.°

THAISA [Aside.]
By Juno, that is queen of marriage,  30
All viands that I eat
Do seem unsavory, wishing him my meat.

[To SIMONIDES.]

Sure he's a gallant gentleman.

SIMONIDES
He's but a country gentleman;
Has done no more than other knights have done;  35
Has broken a staff or so; so let it pass.

THAISA [Aside.]
To me he seems like diamond to glass.

PERICLES [Aside.]
Yon king's to me like to my father's picture,
Which tells me in that glory once he was;
Had princes sit like stars about his throne,  40
And he the sun for them to reverence;
None that beheld him but, like lesser lights,
Did vail° their crowns to his supremacy;
Where now his son's a glowworm in the night,
The which hath fire in darkness, none in light.  45
Whereby I see that Time's the king of men;
He's both their parent and he is their grave,
And gives them what he will, not what they crave.

SIMONIDES
What, are you merry, knights?

KNIGHTS
Who can be other in this royal presence?  50

SIMONIDES
Here, with a cup that's stored unto the brim—
As you do love, fill to° your mistress' lips—
We drink this health to you.

KNIGHTS          We thank your grace.

SIMONIDES
Yet pause awhile.
Yon knight doth sit too melancholy,  55
As if the entertainment in our court
Had not a show might countervail° his worth.
Note it not you, Thaisa?

THAISA
What is't to me, my father?

SIMONIDES
O, attend, my daughter:  60
Princes, in this, should live like gods above,
Who freely give to everyone that come
To honor them.
And princes not doing so are like to gnats,
Which make a sound, but killed are wond'red at.°  65
Therefore, to make his entrance° more sweet,
Here, say we drink this standing-bowl° of wine to him.

THAISA
Alas, my father, it befits not me
Unto a stranger knight to be so bold:
He may my proffer take for an offense,  70
Since men take women's gifts for impudence.

SIMONIDES
How?
Do as I bid you, or you'll move me else!

THAISA [Aside.]
Now, by the gods, he could not please me better.

SIMONIDES
And furthermore tell him we desire to know of him  75
Of whence he is, his name and parentage.

THAISA
The king my father, sir, has drunk to you.

PERICLES
I thank him.

THAISA
Wishing it so much blood unto your life.

PERICLES
I thank both him and you, and pledge him freely.  80

THAISA
And further he desires to know of you
Of whence you are, your name and parentage.

PERICLES
A gentleman of Tyre; my name Pericles;
My education been° in arts and arms;
Who, looking for adventures in the world,  85
Was by the rough seas reft of ships and men,
And after shipwreck driven upon this shore.

THAISA
He thanks your grace; names himself Pericles,
A gentleman of Tyre,
Who only by misfortune of the seas,  90
Bereft of ships and men, cast on this shore.

SIMONIDES
Now, by the gods, I pity his misfortune,
And will awake him from his melancholy.
Come, gentlemen, we sit too long on trifles,
And waste the time which looks for other revels.  95
Even in your armors, as you are addressed,°

---

**15 framing** molding  **17 her labored scholar** the scholar
over whom art took special pains  **19 grace** favor  **25 Have**
that have  **29 cates** delicacies; **resist . . . upon** repel me (?)
when I but think of him  **43 vail** lower  **52 to** in honor of

**57 countervail** be equal to  **65 but . . . at** i.e., when they
are found to be such small animals, after making so great a
noise  **66 entrance** trisyllabic  **67 standing-bowl** bowl resting on a foot  **84 been** has been  **96 addressed** accoutered

Will well° become a soldier's dance.
I will not have excuse with saying this:
Loud music° is too harsh for ladies' heads,
Since they love men in arms° as well as beds.    100

*They dance.*°

So, this was well asked, 'twas so well performed.
Come, sir, here's a lady that wants breathing° too;
And I have heard you knights of Tyre
Are excellent in making ladies trip,°
And that their measures° are as excellent.    105

PERICLES
In those that practice them they are, my lord.

SIMONIDES
O, that's as much as you would be denied
Of your fair courtesy.° *They dance.* Unclasp, unclasp!
Thanks, gentlemen, to all; all have done well,

[*To* PERICLES.]

But you the best. Pages and lights, to conduct    110
These knights unto their several lodgings! Yours, sir,
We have given order be next our own.

PERICLES
I am at your grace's pleasure.

SIMONIDES
Princes, it is too late to talk of love,
And that's the mark I know you level° at.    115
Therefore each one betake him to his rest;
Tomorrow all for speeding° do their best.    [*Exeunt.*]

[Scene IV. *Tyre.*]

*Enter* HELICANUS *and* ESCANES.

HELICANUS
No, Escanes, know this of me:
Antiochus from incest lived not free;
For which, the most high gods not minding° longer
To withhold the vengeance that they had in store,
Due to this heinous capital offense,    5
Even in the height and pride of all his glory,
When he was seated in a chariot
Of an inestimable value, and
His daughter with him, a fire from heaven came,
And shriveled up their bodies, even to loathing.    10
For they so stunk
That all those eyes adored° them ere their fall
Scorn now their hand should give them burial.

ESCANES
'Twas very strange.

HELICANUS
And yet but justice; for though this king were great,    15
His greatness was no guard to bar heaven's shaft,
But sin had his° reward.

ESCANES      'Tis very true.

*Enter two or three* LORDS.

FIRST LORD
See, not a man in private conference
Or council has respect with him but he.

SECOND LORD
It shall no longer grieve° without reproof.    20

THIRD LORD
And cursed be he that will not second it.

FIRST LORD
Follow me then. Lord Helicane, a word.

HELICANUS
With me? And welcome. Happy day, my lords!

FIRST LORD
Know that our griefs° are risen to the top,
And now at length they overflow their banks.    25

HELICANUS
Your griefs, for what? Wrong not your prince you
    love.

FIRST LORD
Wrong not yourself, then, noble Helicane;
But if the prince do live, let us salute him,
Or know what ground's made happy by his breath.
If in the world he live, we'll seek him out;    30
If in his grave he rest, we'll find him there;
And be resolved° he lives to govern us,
Or, dead, gives cause to mourn his funeral,
And leaves us to our free election.

SECOND LORD
Whose death's indeed the strongest in our censure.°    35
And knowing this: kingdoms without a head,
Like goodly buildings left without a roof
Soon fall to ruin, your noble self,
That best know how to rule and how to reign,
We thus submit unto—our sovereign.    40

ALL
Live, noble Helicane!

HELICANUS
For honor's cause, forbear your suffrages.
If that you love Prince Pericles, forbear.
Take I° your wish, I leap into the seas
Where's hourly trouble for a minute's ease.    45
A twelvemonth longer let me entreat you
To forbear° the absence of your king;
If in which time expired he not return,
I shall with aged patience bear your yoke.
But if I cannot win you to this love,°    50
Go search like nobles, like noble subjects,
And in your search spend your adventurous worth;
Whom if you find, and win unto return,
You shall like diamonds sit about his crown.

FIRST LORD
To wisdom he's a fool that will not yield;    55

---

**97 Will well** two such words as "your steps" must have originally preceded this  **99 Loud music** i.e., the loud noise made by the clashing of their armor (?)  **100 arms** a pun is presumably intended  **100 s.d. They dance** most editors assume that the first dance is performed by the Knights alone, the second by the Knights and Ladies. The text, especially line 102, suggests rather that both dances are mixed. In the first dance Thaisa and, perhaps, Pericles do not participate; in the second they dance together  **102 breathing** exercise  **104 trip** dance a light dance (with a double entendre)  **105 measures** dances  **107–08 denied . . . courtesy** refused permission to show your courtesy (by dancing with Thaisa) (?)  **115 level** aim  **117 speeding** success
**II.iv.3 minding** being inclined  **12 adored** that adored

**17 his** its  **20 grieve** be a grievance  **24 griefs** grievances  **32 resolved** satisfied  **35 strongest . . . censure** the more likely supposition in our judgment  **44 Take I** if I should accept  **47 forbear** tolerate, endure  **50 love** act of kindness

And since Lord Helicane enjoineth us,
We with our travels will endeavor it.

HELICANUS
Then you love us, we you, and we'll clasp hands:
When peers thus knit, a kingdom ever stands.

[*Exeunt.*]


[Scene V. *Pentapolis. A room in the palace.*]

*Enter the king* [SIMONIDES] *reading of a letter at one door; the* KNIGHTS *meet him.*

FIRST KNIGHT
Good morrow to the good Simonides.

SIMONIDES
Knights, from my daughter this I let you know:
That for this twelvemonth she'll not undertake
A married life.
Her reason to herself is only known,
Which from her by no means° can I get.                              5

SECOND KNIGHT
May we not get access to her, my lord?

SIMONIDES
Faith, by no means. She hath so strictly tied her
To her chamber that 'tis impossible.
One twelve moons° more she'll wear Diana's livery.°   10
This by the eye of Cynthia° hath she vowed,
And on her virgin honor will not break it.

THIRD KNIGHT
Loath° to bid farewell, we take our leaves.
[*Exeunt* KNIGHTS.]

SIMONIDES
So, they are well dispatched.
Now to my daughter's letter:                                      15
She tells me here she'll wed the stranger knight,
Or never more to view nor day nor light.
'Tis well, mistress; your choice agrees with mine.
I like that well! Nay, how absolute° she's in't,
Not minding whether I dislike or no!                              20
Well, I do commend her choice,
And will no longer have it be delayed.
Soft,° here he comes! I must dissemble it.

*Enter* PERICLES.

PERICLES
All fortune to the good Simonides!

SIMONIDES
To you as much. Sir, I am beholding° to you          25
For your sweet music this last night. I do
Protest my ears were never better fed
With such delightful pleasing harmony.

PERICLES
It is your grace's pleasure to commend;
Not my desert.

SIMONIDES          Sir, you are music's master.         30

PERICLES
The worst of all her scholars, my good lord.

SIMONIDES
Let me ask you one thing: What do you think of
My daughter, sir?

PERICLES          A most virtuous princess.

SIMONIDES
And she is fair, too, is she not?

PERICLES
As a fair day in summer, wondrous fair.              35

SIMONIDES
Sir, my daughter thinks very well of you;
Ay, so well that you must be her master,
And she will be your scholar: therefore look to it.

PERICLES
I am unworthy for her schoolmaster.

SIMONIDES
She thinks not so; peruse this writing else.°        40

PERICLES [*Aside.*]
What's here?
A letter that she loves the knight of Tyre!
'Tis the king's subtlety to have my life.

[*Kneels.*]

O, seek not to entrap me, gracious lord,
A stranger and distressèd gentleman,                 45
That never aimed so high to° love your daughter,
But bent all offices° to honor her.

SIMONIDES
Thou hast bewitched my daughter, and thou art
A villain!

PERICLES By the gods, I have not.
Never did thought of mine levy° offense;             50
Nor never did my actions yet commence
A deed might° gain her love or your displeasure.

SIMONIDES
Traitor, thou liest!

PERICLES          Traitor?

SIMONIDES                    Ay, traitor!

PERICLES
Even in his throat—unless it be the king—
That calls me traitor I return the lie.              55

SIMONIDES [*Aside.*]
Now, by the gods, I do applaud his courage.

PERICLES
My actions are as noble as my thoughts,
That never relished of° a base descent.
I came unto your court for honor's cause,
And not to be a rebel to her state;°                 60
And he that otherwise accounts of me,
This sword shall prove he's honor's enemy.

SIMONIDES
No?
Here comes my daughter, she can witness it.

*Enter* THAISA.

PERICLES
Then, as you are as virtuous as fair,                65
Resolve° your angry father if my tongue
Did e'er solicit, or my hand subscribe
To any syllable that made love to you.

---

II.v.6 means here pronounced as a disyllable   10 One twelve
moons one year; wear Diana's livery i.e., remain a virgin
11 Cynthia the moon   13 Loath here pronounced as a disyllable   19 absolute positive, decided   23 Soft hold (an
interjection)   25 beholding indebted

40 else if you do not believe it   46 to as to   47 bent all
offices turned all my services   50 levy apparently misused for
*level*, i.e., aim   52 might that might   58 relished of had a
trace of   60 her state honor's domain   66 Resolve inform

**THAISA**

Why, sir, say if you had,
Who takes offense at that would° make me glad?    70

**SIMONIDES**

Yea, mistress, are you so peremptory?°

*(Aside.)*

I am glad on't with all my heart.—
I'll tame you; I'll bring you in subjection!
Will you, not having my consent,
Bestow your love and your affections    75
Upon a stranger?—*(aside)* who, for aught I know,
May be, nor can I think the contrary,
As great in blood as I myself—
Therefore hear you, mistress: either frame
Your will to mine—and you, sir, hear you:    80
Either be ruled by me, or I'll make you—
Man and wife.
Nay, come, your hands and lips must seal it too!
And being joined, I'll thus your hopes destroy;
And for further grief—God give you joy!    85
What, are you both pleased?

**THAISA**              Yes, if you love me, sir.

**PERICLES**

Even as my life my blood° that fosters it.

**SIMONIDES**

What, are you both agreed?

**BOTH**

Yes, if't please your majesty.

**SIMONIDES**

It pleaseth me so well that I will see you wed;    90
And then, with what haste you can, get you to bed.
                          *Exeunt.*

# [ A C T   I I I ]

*Enter* GOWER.

**GOWER**

Now sleep y-slackèd° hath the rout;°
No din but snores the house about,
Made louder by the o'erfed breast
Of this most pompous° marriage feast.
The cat, with eyne° of burning coal,    5
Now couches 'fore the mouse's hole;
And crickets sing at the oven's mouth
All the blither for their drouth.°
Hymen° hath brought the bride to bed,
Where by the loss of maidenhead    10
A babe is molded. Be attent,°
And time that is so briefly° spent
With your fine fancies° quaintly° eche.°
What's dumb in show I'll plain° with speech.

*[Dumb Show.]*

*Enter* PERICLES *and* SIMONIDES *at one door, with* ATTENDANTS; *a* MESSENGER *meets them, kneels, and gives* PERICLES *a letter;* PERICLES *shows it* SIMONIDES; *the* LORDS *kneel to him. Then enter* THAISA *with child, with* LYCHORIDA, *a nurse; the king [*SIMONIDES*] shows her the letter; she rejoices; she and* PERICLES *take leave of her father, and depart [with* LYCHORIDA *and their* ATTENDANTS. *Then exeunt* SIMONIDES *and the rest].*

By many a dern° and painful° perch°    15
Of Pericles the careful search
By the four opposing coigns°
Which the world together joins
Is made with all due diligence
That horse and sail and high expense    20
Can stead° the quest. At last from Tyre,
Fame answering the most strange inquire,°
To th' court of King Simonides
Are letters brought, the tenor these:
Antiochus and his daughter dead,    25
The men of Tyrus on the head
Of Helicanus would set on
The crown of Tyre, but he will none.
The mutiny he there hastes t' appease;
Says to 'em, if King Pericles    30
Come not home in twice six moons,
He, obedient to their dooms,°
Will take the crown. The sum° of this,
Brought hither to Pentapolis,
Y-ravishèd° the regions round,    35
And everyone with claps can° sound,°
"Our heir-apparent is a king!
Who dreamt, who thought of such a thing?"
Brief,° he must hence depart to Tyre.
His queen with child makes her desire—    40
Which who shall cross?—along to go.
Omit we all their dole° and woe.
Lychorida, her nurse, she takes,
And so to sea. Their vessel shakes
On Neptune's billow; half the flood    45
Hath their keel cut;° but Fortune's mood
Varies again: the grislèd° north
Disgorges such a tempest forth
That, as a duck for life that dives,
So up and down the poor ship drives.    50
The lady shrieks and, well-a-near,°
Does fall in travail with her fear;
And what ensues in this fell storm
Shall for itself itself perform.
I nill° relate, action° may    55
Conveniently the rest convey;
Which might not what by me is told.

---

70 **would** which would   71 **peremptory** determined   87 **my blood** i.e., loves my blood
III.Cho.1 **y-slackèd** reduced to inactivity; **rout** company of revelers   4 **pompous** magnificent   5 **eyne** eyes (archaic plural)   8 **drouth** dryness   9 **Hymen** the god of marriage   11 **attent** attentive   12 **briefly** quickly   13 **fancies** imaginings; **quaintly** skillfully; **eche** augment (old spelling of *eke*)   14 **plain** explain

15 **dern** wild, drear; **painful** toilsome; **perch** measure of land   17 **opposing coigns** opposite corners   21 **stead** be of use to   22 **Fame . . . inquire** Rumor having responded to inquiries in the most distant regions (?)   32 **dooms** judgments   33 **sum** gist   35 **Y-ravishèd** enraptured   36 **can** began (a Middle English variant of *gan*); **sound** proclaim, declare   39 **Brief** in short   42 **dole** grief   45-46 **half . . . cut** i.e., half the voyage has been completed   47 **grislèd** horrible, grisly   51 **well-a-near** alas   55 **nill** will not (Middle English); **action** here pronounced as a trisyllable

In your imagination hold
This stage the ship, upon whose deck
The sea-tossed Pericles appears to speak.            [*Exit.*] 60


[Scene I.]

*Enter* PERICLES, *a-shipboard.*

PERICLES
The god of this great vast° rebuke these surges,
Which wash both heaven and hell; and thou that hast
Upon the winds command, bind them in brass,
Having called them from the deep! O, still
Thy deaf'ning dreadful thunders; gently quench            5
Thy nimble° sulphurous flashes! O, how, Lychorida,
How does my queen? Thou stormest venomously;
Wilt thou spit all thyself? The seaman's whistle
Is as a whisper in the ears of death,
Unheard. Lychorida!—Lucina,° O            10
Divinest patroness and midwife gentle
To those that cry by night, convey thy deity
Aboard our dancing boat; make swift the pangs
Of my queen's travails! Now, Lychorida!

*Enter* LYCHORIDA, [*with an* INFANT].

LYCHORIDA
Here is a thing too young for such a place,            15
Who, if it had conceit,° would die, as I
Am like to do. Take in your arms this piece
Of your dead queen.
PERICLES                        How? How, Lychorida?
LYCHORIDA
Patience, good sir; do not assist the storm.
Here's all that is left living of your queen—            20
A little daughter. For the sake of it
Be manly, and take comfort.
PERICLES                        O you gods!
Why do you make us love your goodly gifts,
And snatch them straight away? We here below
Recall not what we give, and therein may            25
Vie honor with you.°
LYCHORIDA                Patience, good sir,
Even for this charge.°
PERICLES                Now, mild may be thy life!
For a more blusterous birth had never babe;
Quiet and gentle thy conditions! For
Thou art the rudeliest welcome to this world            30
That ever was prince's child. Happy what follows!
Thou hast as chiding a nativity
As fire, air, water, earth, and heaven can make,
To herald thee from the womb. Even at the first
Thy loss is more than can thy portage quit,°            35
With all thou canst find here. Now the good gods
Throw their best eyes upon't!

*Enter two* SAILORS.

FIRST SAILOR   What courage, sir? God save you!
PERICLES
Courage enough. I do not fear the flaw:°
It hath done to me the worst. Yet, for the love            40
Of this poor infant, this fresh,° new seafarer,
I would it would be quiet.
FIRST SAILOR   Slack the bolins° there! Thou wilt not,
wilt thou? Blow, and split thyself!
SECOND SAILOR   But sea-room, and° the brine and            45
cloudy billow kiss the moon, I care not.
FIRST SAILOR   Sir, your queen must overboard; the
sea works° high, the wind is loud, and will not lie° till
the ship be cleared of the dead.
PERICLES   That's your superstition.            50
FIRST SAILOR   Pardon us, sir; with us at sea it hath
been still° observed; and we are strong in custom.°
Therefore briefly° yield her; for she must overboard
straight.
PERICLES
As you think meet. Most wretched queen!            55
LYCHORIDA   Here she lies, sir.
PERICLES
A terrible childbed hast thou had, my dear;
No light, no fire. Th' unfriendly elements
Forgot thee utterly; nor have I time
To give thee hallowed to thy grave, but straight            60
Must cast thee, scarcely coffined, in the ooze;
Where, for° a monument upon thy bones,
And e'er-remaining lamps, the belching whale
And humming water must o'erwhelm thy corpse,
Lying with simple shells. O Lychorida,            65
Bid Nestor bring me spices, ink and paper,
My casket and my jewels; and bid Nicander
Bring me the satin coffin.° Lay the babe
Upon the pillow. Hie thee, whiles I say
A priestly farewell to her. Suddenly,° woman!            70
                                    [*Exit* LYCHORIDA.]
SECOND SAILOR   Sir, we have a chest beneath the
hatches, Caulked and bitumèd° ready.
PERICLES
I thank thee. Mariner, say, what coast is this?
SECOND SAILOR
We are near Tharsus.
PERICLES                        Thither, gentle mariner,
Alter thy course for Tyre. When canst thou reach it?            75
SECOND SAILOR
By break of day, if the wind cease.
PERICLES
O make for Tharsus!
There will I visit Cleon, for the babe
Cannot hold out to Tyrus. There I'll leave it
At careful° nursing. Go thy ways,° good mariner.            80
I'll bring the body presently.°   *Exit,* [*with* SAILORS].

---

III.i.1 **vast** boundless expanse  **6 nimble** swift  **10 Lucina**
goddess of childbirth  **16 conceit** capacity to understand  **26**
**Vie . . . you** compete with you in respect of honor  **27**
**Even . . . charge** for the sake of the babe left in your care
**35 than . . . quit** than your cargo (i.e., all that you are going
to possess in the course of the voyage of life) can compensate
for (?)  **39 flaw** gust of wind  **41 fresh** raw, inexperienced  **43**
**bolins** ropes from weather-side of square sail to bow  **45**
**and** if  **48 works** rages; **lie** subside  **52 still** always; **strong**
**in custom** steadfast in observing customs  **53 briefly** quickly
**62 for** instead of  **68 coffin** case, box  **70 Suddenly** at once
**72 bitumèd** made watertight with bitumen  **80 careful** full
of good care; **Go thy ways** come along  **81 presently**
immediately

[Scene II. *Ephesus. A room in Cerimon's house.*]

*Enter Lord* CERIMON *with a* SERVANT.

CERIMON
Philemon, ho!

*Enter* PHILEMON.

PHILEMON
Doth my lord call?
CERIMON
Get fire and meat for those poor men:
'T'as been a turbulent and stormy night.
                              [*Exit* PHILEMON.]
SERVANT
I have been in many; but such a night as this      5
Till now I ne'er endured.
CERIMON
Your master will be dead ere you return.
There's nothing can be minist'red to nature
That can recover him. Give this to the 'pothecary,
And tell me how it works.°      [*Exit* SERVANT.]

*Enter two* GENTLEMEN.

FIRST GENTLEMAN          Good morrow.      10
SECOND GENTLEMAN
Good morrow to your lordship.
CERIMON                    Gentlemen,
Why do you stir so early?
FIRST GENTLEMAN
Sir,
Our lodgings, standing bleak upon the sea,
Shook as the earth did quake;      15
The very principals° did seem to rend
And all to topple. Pure surprise and fear
Made me to quit the house.
SECOND GENTLEMAN
That is the cause we trouble you so early;
'Tis not our husbandry.°
CERIMON          O, you say well.      20
FIRST GENTLEMAN
But I much marvel that your lordship, having
Rich tire° about you, should at these early hours
Shake off the golden slumber of repose.
'Tis most strange,
Nature should be so conversant with pain,°      25
Being thereto not compelled.
CERIMON                    I held it ever
Virtue and cunning° were endowments greater
Than nobleness° and riches: careless heirs
May the two latter darken and expend,
But immortality attends° the former,      30
Making a man a god. 'Tis known, I ever
Have studied physic, through which secret art,
By turning o'er authorities, I have,
Together with my practice, made familiar
To me and to my aid° the blest infusions      35

That dwells in vegetives,° in metals, stones;
And I can speak of the disturbances
That nature works, and of her cures; which gives me
A more° content in course of true delight
Than to be thirsty after tottering honor,      40
Or tie my treasure up in silken bags,
To please the Fool and Death.°
SECOND GENTLEMAN
Your honor has through Ephesus poured forth
Your charity, and hundreds call themselves
Your creatures, who by you have been restored;      45
And not° your knowledge, your personal pain,° but
      even
Your purse, still° open, hath built Lord Cerimon
Such strong renown as time shall never raze.

*Enter two or three* [SERVANTS] *with a chest.*

FIRST SERVANT
So; lift there!
CERIMON          What's that?
FIRST SERVANT                    Sir, even now      50
Did the sea toss up upon our shore this chest.
'Tis of some wrack.
CERIMON                    Set't down, let's look upon't.
SECOND GENTLEMAN
'Tis like a coffin, sir.
CERIMON                    Whate'er it be,
'Tis wondrous heavy. Wrench it open straight.°
If the sea's stomach be o'ercharged with gold,
'Tis a good constraint of fortune      55
It belches upon us.°
SECOND GENTLEMAN      'Tis so, my lord.
CERIMON
How close 'tis caulked and bitumed!
Did the sea cast it up?
FIRST SERVANT
I never saw so huge a billow, sir,
As tossed it upon shore.
CERIMON                    Wrench it open: soft! It smells   60
Most sweetly in my sense.
SECOND GENTLEMAN          A delicate odor.
CERIMON
As ever hit my nostril. So; up with it!
O you most potent gods! What's here, a corse!
SECOND GENTLEMAN
Most strange!
CERIMON          Shrouded in cloth of state;°
Balmed,° and entreasured with full bags of spices!   65
A passport too! Apollo, perfect me°
In the characters!°

[*Reads from a scroll.*]

      Here I give to understand,
      If e'er this coffin drives a-land,
      I, King Pericles, have lost      70
      This queen, worth all our mundane cost.°

III.ii.9-10 Give . . . works this prescription must be intended for someone other than the Servant's master  16 principals chief rafters of a house  20 husbandry zeal for work  22 tire belongings  25 pain trouble, labor  27 cunning skill  28 nobleness nobility (i.e., social rank)  30 attends awaits  35 my aid my assistant (?)

36 vegetives vegetables, herbs  39 more greater  42 Fool and Death probably an allusion to the Dance of Death, in which these two figures often appeared as companions  46 not not only; pain trouble  47 still always  53 straight immediately  56 It . . . us that it belches this chest upon us  64 cloth of state magnificent fabric  65 Balmed anointed with fragrant oil  66 perfect me instruct me fully  67 characters writing (the stress falls here on the second syllable)  71 mundane cost worldly riches

Who finds her, give her burying;
She was the daughter of a king.
Besides this treasure for a fee,
The gods requite his charity!       75
If thou livest, Pericles, thou hast a heart
That even cracks for woe! This chanced tonight.°

SECOND GENTLEMAN
Most likely, sir.

CERIMON       Nay, certainly tonight;
For look how fresh she looks! They were too rough
That threw her in the sea. Make a fire within.       80
Fetch hither all my boxes in my closet.

                [*Exit* SERVANT.]

Death may usurp on nature° many hours,
And yet the fire of life kindle again
The o'erpressed spirits. [I have read
Of some Egyptians, who after four hours' death       85
Have raised impoverished° bodies, like to this,
Unto their former health.]°

*Enter one* [SERVANT] *with napkins and fire.*

                Well said,° well said;
The fire and cloths.°
The still and woeful music that we have,
Cause it to sound, beseech you.       90

[*Music.*]

The viol once more! How thou stirr'st,° thou block!
The music there! [*Music.*] I pray you, give her air.
Gentlemen,
This queen will live: nature° awakes; a warmth
Breathes out of her. She hath not been entranced°       95
Above five hours. See how she 'gins to blow°
Into life's flower again!

FIRST GENTLEMAN       The heavens
Through you increase our wonder, and sets up
Your fame forever.

CERIMON       She is alive! Behold,
Her eyelids, cases to those heavenly jewels       100
Which Pericles hath lost, begin to part
Their fringes of bright gold; the diamonds
Of a most praisèd water° doth appear
To make the world twice rich. Live,
And make us weep to hear your fate, fair creature,       105
Rare as you seem to be. *She moves.*

THAISA       O dear Diana,
Where am I? Where's my lord? What world is this?

SECOND GENTLEMAN
Is not this strange?

FIRST GENTLEMAN    Most rare!

CERIMON       Hush, my gentle neighbors!
Lend me your hands; to the next chamber bear her.
Get linen. Now this matter must be looked to,       110
For her relapse is mortal.° Come, come;
And Aesculapius° guide us!

          *They carry her away. Exeunt omnes.*°

[Scene III. *Tharsus.*]

*Enter* PERICLES *at Tharsus with* CLEON *and* DIONYZA,
[*and* LYCHORIDA *with* MARINA *in her arms*].

PERICLES
Most honored Cleon, I must needs be gone:
My twelve months are expired, and Tyrus stands
In a litigious° peace. You and your lady,
Take from my heart all thankfulness! The gods
Make up the rest upon you!

CLEON       Your shafts of fortune,       5
Though they hurt you mortally, yet glance
Full° woundingly on us.

DIONYZA       O your sweet queen!
That the strict fates had pleased you had brought her
    hither
To have blest mine eyes with her!

PERICLES       We cannot but
Obey the powers above us. Could I rage       10
And roar as doth the sea she lies in, yet
The end must be as 'tis. My gentle babe,
Marina, whom, for° she was born at sea,
I have named so, here I charge
Your charity withal,° leaving her       15
The infant of your care; beseeching you
To give her princely training, that she may
Be mannered as she is born.

CLEON       Fear not, my lord, but think
Your grace, that fed my country with your corn,
For which the people's prayers still fall upon you,       20
Must in your child be thought on. If neglection°
Should therein make me vile, the common body,°
By you relieved, would force me to my duty.
But if to that my nature need a spur,
The gods revenge it upon me and mine,       25
To the end of generation!°

PERICLES       I believe you.
Your honor and your goodness teach me to't,
Without your vows. Till she be married, madam,
By bright Diana, whom we honor all,
Unscissored shall this hair of mine remain,       30
Though I show ill in't. So I take my leave.
Good madam, make me blessèd in your care
In bringing up my child.

DIONYZA       I have one myself,
Who shall not be more dear to my respect°
Than yours, my lord.

PERICLES       Madam, my thanks and prayers.   35

CLEON
We'll bring your grace e'en to the edge o' th' shore,
Then give you up to the masked° Neptune and
The gentlest winds of heaven.

PERICLES       I will embrace
Your offer. Come, dearest madam. O, no tears,
Lychorida, no tears!       40
Look to your little mistress, on whose grace°
You may depend hereafter. Come, my lord. [*Exeunt.*]

[Scene IV. *Ephesus.*]

*Enter* CERIMON *and* THAISA.

CERIMON
Madam, this letter, and some certain jewels,
Lay with you in your coffer; which are
At your command. Know you the character?°

THAISA
It is my lord's. That I was shipped at sea
I well remember, even on my eaning time;°          5
But whether there delivered, by the holy gods,
I cannot rightly say. But since King Pericles,
My wedded lord, I ne'er shall see again,
A vestal livery will I take me to,°
And never more have joy.          10

CERIMON
Madam, if this you purpose as ye speak,
Diana's temple is not distant far,
Where you may abide till your date° expire.
Moreover, if you please, a niece of mine
Shall there attend you.          15

THAISA
My recompense is thanks, that's all;
Yet my good will is great, though the gift small.
          *Exit,* [*with* CERIMON].

# [ A C T   I V ]

*Enter* GOWER.

GOWER
Imagine Pericles arrived at Tyre,
Welcomed and settled to his own desire.
His woeful queen we leave at Ephesus,
Unto Diana there's° a votaress.
Now to Marina bend your mind,          5
Whom our fast-growing scene must find
At Tharsus, and by Cleon trained
In music's letters;° who hath gained
Of education all the grace,
Which makes her both the heart and place°          10
Of general wonder. But, alack,
That monster, Envy, oft the wrack°
Of earnèd praise, Marina's life
Seeks to take off by treason's° knife.
And in this kind:° Our Cleon hath          15
One daughter, and a full grown wench,
Even ripe for marriage rite. This maid
Hight° Philoten; and it is said
For certain in our story, she
Would ever with Marina be.          20
Be't when she weaved the sleided° silk
With fingers long, small,° white as milk;
Or when she would with sharp needle° wound

The cambric, which she made more sound
By hurting it; or when to th' lute          25
She sung, and made the night-bird° mute,
That still records with moan;° or when
She would with rich and constant pen
Vail° to her mistress Dian; still
This Philoten contends in skill          30
With absolute° Marina: so
With dove of Paphos° might the crow
Vie° feathers white. Marina gets
All praises, which are paid as debts,
And not as given. This so darks°          35
In Philoten all graceful marks
That Cleon's wife, with envy rare,
A present° murderer does prepare°
For good Marina, that her daughter
Might stand peerless by this slaughter.          40
The sooner her vile thoughts to stead,°
Lychorida, our nurse, is dead;
And cursèd Dionyza hath
The pregnant° instrument of wrath
Prest° for this blow. The unborn event°          45
I do commend to your content;°
Only I carry wingèd time
Post° on the lame feet of my rhyme;
Which never could I so convey
Unless your thoughts went on my way.          50
Dionyza does appear,
With Leonine, a murderer.          *Exit.*

[Scene I. *Tharsus, near the seashore.*]

*Enter* DIONYZA, *with* LEONINE.

DIONYZA
Thy oath remember; thou hast sworn to do't.
'Tis but a blow, which never shall be known.
Thou canst not do a thing in the world so soon
To yield thee so much profit. Let not conscience,
Which is but cold, or flaming love thy bosom          5
Enslave too nicely;° nor let pity, which
Even women have cast off, melt thee, but be
A soldier to° thy purpose.

LEONINE
I will do't. But yet she is a goodly creature!

DIONYZA
The fitter then the gods should have her.          10
Here she comes weeping° her old nurse's death!
Thou art resolved?

LEONINE                    I am resolved.

*Enter* MARINA *with a basket of flowers.*

MARINA
No, I will rob Tellus° of her weed°

III.iv.3 character handwriting 5 eaning time time of childbirth 9 vestal . . . to i.e., I will live the life of a vestal virgin 13 date term of life
IV.Cho.4 there's there as 8 music's letters the study of music 10 place dwelling 12 wrack ruin 14 treason's treachery's 15 in this kind in the following way 18 Hight is named 21 sleided a variant of *sleaved*, i.e., divided into filaments 22 small slender 23 needle here pronounced as a monosyllable
26 night-bird nightingale 27 still . . . moan ever sings dolefully 29 Vail do homage 31 absolute free from imperfection 32 dove of Paphos Venus' dove 33 Vie compete in respect of 35 darks darkens, puts in the shade 38 present speedy; prepare provide 41 stead aid 44 pregnant disposed, inclined 45 Prest ready; event outcome 46 commend . . . content commend to you, hoping that it will please you 48 Post post-haste
IV.i.6 nicely scrupulously 8 A soldier to wholly devoted to 11 weeping lamenting 13 Tellus the earth; weed garment (of flowers)

To strew thy green° with flowers; the yellows, blues,
The purple violets, and marigolds,                                      15
Shall as a carpet° hang upon thy grave,
While summer days doth last. Ay me, poor maid,
Born in a tempest, when my mother died,
This world to me is as a lasting storm,
Whirring° me from my friends.°                                         20

DIONYZA
How now, Marina, why do you keep alone?
How chance my daughter is not with you?
Do not consume your blood with sorrowing.°
Have you a nurse of me! Lord, how your favor°
Is changed with this unprofitable woe!                                  25
Come, give me your flowers.
On the sea margent walk with Leonine.
The air is quick° there and it pierces, and
Sharpens the stomach. Come, Leonine, take
Her by the arm, walk with her.

MARINA                            No, I pray you.                        30
I'll not bereave you of your servant.

DIONYZA                               Come, come!
I love the king your father and yourself
With more than foreign° heart. We every day
Expect him here. When he shall come, and find
Our paragon to° all reports thus blasted,                               35
He will repent the breadth° of his great voyage;
Blame both my lord and me, that we have taken
No care to your best courses.° Go, I pray you,
Walk, and be cheerful once again; reserve°
That excellent complexion, which did steal                              40
The eyes of young and old. Care not for me;
I can go home alone.

MARINA                      Well, I will go;
But yet I have no desire to it.

DIONYZA                         Come, come,
I know 'tis good for you.
Walk half an hour, Leonine, at the least.                               45
Remember what I have said.

LEONINE                       I warrant° you, madam.

DIONYZA
I'll leave you, my sweet lady, for a while.
Pray, walk softly,° do not heat your blood. What!
I must have care of you.

MARINA                    My thanks, sweet madam.
[Exit DIONYZA.]
Is this wind westerly that blows?

LEONINE                            Southwest.                            50

MARINA
When I was born the wind was north.

LEONINE                               Was't so?

MARINA
My father, as nurse says, did never fear,
But cried, "Good seamen!" to the sailors, galling°
His kingly hands haling ropes;
And, clasping° to the mast, endured a sea                               55

That almost burst the deck.

LEONINE                      When was this?

MARINA
When I was born.
Never was waves nor wind more violent;
And from the ladder-tackle washes off
A canvas-climber.° "Ha!" says one, "wolt° out?"                        60
And with a dropping° industry they skip
From stem to stern; the boatswain whistles, and
The master calls and trebles their confusion.

LEONINE
Come, say your prayers!

MARINA
What mean you?                                                          65

LEONINE
If you require a little space for prayer,
I grant it. Pray; but be not tedious, for
The gods are quick of ear, and I am sworn
To do my work with haste.

MARINA                     Why will you kill me?

LEONINE
To satisfy my lady.                                                     70

MARINA
Why would she have me killed?
Now, as° I can remember, by my troth,
I never did her hurt in all my life.
I never spake bad word nor did ill turn
To any living creature. Believe me, la,°                                75
I never killed a mouse, nor hurt a fly;
I trod upon a worm against my will,
But I wept for't. How have I offended,
Wherein my death might yield her any profit,
Or my life imply her any danger?                                        80

LEONINE
My commission
Is not to reason of the deed, but do't.

MARINA
You will not do't for all the world, I hope.
You are well-favored,° and your looks foreshow
You have a gentle heart. I saw you lately,                              85
When you caught hurt in parting two that fought.
Good sooth,° it showed well in you. Do so now.
Your lady seeks my life: come you between,
And save poor me, the weaker!

LEONINE                        I am sworn,
And will dispatch. [Seizes her.]

Enter PIRATES.

FIRST PIRATE    Hold, villain! [LEONINE runs away.]
SECOND PIRATE            A prize! A prize!                               90
THIRD PIRATE    Half-part,° mates, half-part! Come,
let's have her aboard suddenly.°
[They carry off MARINA.]

Enter LEONINE.

LEONINE
These roguing° thieves serve the great pirate Valdes,
And they have seized Marina. Let her go;
There's no hope° she'll return. I'll swear she's dead,                  95

---

14 green i.e., the green turf of Lychorida's grave  16 carpet
piece of tapestry  20 Whirring whirling, hurrying along;
friends relations  23 Do . . . sorrowing alluding to the
ancient notion that each sigh takes a drop of blood from the
heart  24 favor face, looks  28 quick sharp  33 foreign not
of one's family  35 to according to  36 breadth extent  38
to . . . courses to what was best for you  39 reserve preserve, guard  46 warrant promise  48 softly slowly  53
galling making sore by chafing  55 clasping clinging

60 canvas-climber sailor climbing aloft to trim sails;
wolt wilt  61 dropping dripping wet  72 as as far as  75
la exclamation to emphasize a statement  84 well-favored
good-looking  87 good sooth truly  91 Half-part go shares
92 suddenly at once  93 roguing vagrant  95 hope i.e., fear

And thrown into the sea. But I'll see further:
Perhaps they will but please themselves upon her,
Not carry her aboard. If she remain,
Whom they have ravished must by me be slain. *Exit.*

[Scene II. *Mytilene. In front of a brothel.*]

*Enter the three Bawds* [*i.e., a* PANDER, *his servant*
BOULT, *and a* BAWD].

PANDER   Boult!

BOULT   Sir?

PANDER   Search the market narrowly! Mytilene is full
of gallants. We lost too much money this mart° by
being too wenchless.      5

BAWD   We were never so much out of creatures. We
have but poor three, and they can do no more than
they can do; and they with continual action are even
as good as rotten.

PANDER   Therefore let's have fresh ones, whate'er we   10
pay for them. If there be not a conscience to be used
in every trade, we shall never prosper.

BAWD   Thou say'st true: 'tis not our bringing up of
poor bastards—as, I think, I have brought up some
eleven—      15

BOULT   Ay, to eleven;° and brought them down
again.° But shall I search the market?

BAWD   What else, man? The stuff° we have, a strong
wind will blow it to pieces, they are so pitifully
sodden.°      20

PANDER   Thou sayest true; they're too unwholesome,
o' conscience.° The poor Transylvanian is dead that
lay with the little baggage.

BOULT   Ay, she quickly pooped° him; she made him
roast meat for worms. But I'll go search the market.   25
     *Exit.*

PANDER   Three or four thousand chequins° were as
pretty a proportion° to live quietly, and so give over.°

BAWD   Why to give over, I pray you? Is it a shame to
get° when we are old?

PANDER   O, our credit° comes not in like the com-   30
modity,° nor the commodity wages not° with the
danger. Therefore, if in our youths we could pick
up some pretty estate, 'twere not amiss to keep our
door hatched.° Besides, the sore terms we stand upon
with the gods will be strong with us for giving o'er.   35

BAWD   Come, other sorts° offend as well as we.

PANDER   As well as we? Ay, and better too; we offend
worse. Neither is our profession any trade;° it's no
calling. But here comes Boult.

*Enter* BOULT, *with the* PIRATES *and* MARINA.

BOULT   Come your ways,° my masters! You say she's   40
a virgin?

FIRST PIRATE   O, sir, we doubt it not.

BOULT   Master, I have gone through° for this piece°
you see. If you like her, so; if not, I have lost my
earnest.°      45

BAWD   Boult, has she any qualities?°

BOULT   She has a good face, speaks well, and has
excellent good clothes. There's no farther necessity of
qualities can° make her be refused.

BAWD   What's her price, Boult?      50

BOULT   It cannot be bated° one doit° of a thousand
pieces.

PANDER   Well, follow me, my masters; you shall
have your money presently.° Wife, take her in.
Instruct her what she has to do, that she may not be   55
raw° in her entertainment.°

     [*Exeunt* PANDER *and* PIRATES.]

BAWD   Boult, take you the marks of her, the color of
her hair, complexion, height, her age, with warrant
of her virginity; and cry, "He that will give most shall
have her first!" Such a maidenhead were no cheap   60
thing, if men were as they have been. Get this done as
I command you.

BOULT   Performance shall follow.      *Exit.*

MARINA
Alack that Leonine was so slack, so slow!
He should have struck, not spoke; or that these pirates,   65
Not enough barbarous, had not o'erboard
Thrown me to seek my mother!

BAWD   Why lament you, pretty one?

MARINA   That I am pretty.

BAWD   Come, the gods have done their part in you.   70

MARINA   I accuse them not.

BAWD   You are light° into my hands, where you are
like to live.

MARINA
The more my fault
To 'scape his hands where I was like to die.

BAWD   Ay, and you shall live in pleasure.

MARINA   No.

BAWD   Yes, indeed shall you, and taste gentlemen of
all fashions. You shall fare well: you shall have the
difference° of all complexions.° What° do you stop   80
your ears?

MARINA   Are you a woman?

BAWD   What would you have me be, and° I be not a
woman?

MARINA   An honest° woman, or not a woman.      85

BAWD   Marry,° whip thee, gosling!° I think I shall
have something to do with you.° Come, you're a
young foolish sapling, and must be bowed as I would
have you.

MARINA   The gods defend me!      90

BAWD   If it please the gods to defend you by men,

**IV.ii.4 mart** market-time   **16 to eleven** up to the age of
eleven   **16–17 brought . . . again** i.e., by prostituting them
**18 stuff** goods for sale   **20 sodden** grown rotten by soaking
(referring to the treatment of venereal disease by means of the
sweating tub)   **22 o' conscience** on my conscience   **24
pooped** foundered (?)   **26 chequins** sequins, Italian gold
coins   **27 proportion** portion, share; **give over** give up,
retire   **29 get** acquire money   **30 credit** reputation   **30–31
commodity** profit   **31 wages not** is not commensurate   **34
hatched** with the hatch (the lower half of a divided door) shut
**36 sorts** classes of people   **38 trade** recognized business   **40
Come your ways** come along

**43 gone through** completed the process of bargaining (?);
**piece** girl   **45 earnest** money given as a deposit   **46 qualities**
accomplishments   **49 can** that can   **51 bated** reduced; **doit**
smallest coin, worth half a farthing   **54 presently** immediately
**56 raw** inexperienced; **entertainment** manner of reception
**72 are light** have fallen   **80 difference** variety; **complexions**
colors of skin, i.e., men of every race; **What** why   **83 and** if
**85 honest** chaste   **86 Marry** interjection expressing indignation; **whip thee, gosling** hang thee, greenhorn   **87 have
. . . you** have trouble with you

then men must comfort you, men must feed you, men
stir you up.° Boult's returned.

[*Enter* BOULT.]

Now, sir, hast thou cried° her through the market?

BOULT   I have cried her almost to the number of her 95
hairs;° I have drawn her picture with my voice.

BAWD   And I prithee tell me, how dost thou find the
inclination of the people, especially of the younger
sort?

BOULT   Faith, they listened to me as they would have 100
hearkened to their father's testament. There was a
Spaniard's mouth wat'red and° he went to bed to her
very description.

BAWD   We shall have him here tomorrow with his
best ruff on. 105

BOULT   Tonight, tonight. But, mistress, do you know
the French knight that cowers i' the hams?

BAWD   Who, Monsieur Veroles?°

BOULT   Ay, he: he offered° to cut a caper at the
proclamation; but he made a groan at it, and swore 110
he would see her tomorrow.

BAWD   Well, well; as for him, he brought his disease
hither. Here he does but repair° it. I know he will
come in our shadow,° to scatter his crowns of the sun.°

BOULT   Well, if we had of every nation a traveler, we 115
should lodge them with this sign.°

BAWD [*To* MARINA.]   Pray you, come hither awhile.
You have fortunes coming upon you. Mark me: you
must seem to do that fearfully which you commit
willingly; despise profit where you have most gain. 120
To weep that you live as ye do makes pity in your
lovers: seldom but that pity begets you a good
opinion, and that opinion a mere° profit.

MARINA   I understand you not.

BOULT   O, take her home,° mistress, take her home! 125
These blushes of hers must be quenched with some
present° practice.

BAWD   Thou sayest true, i' faith, so they must. For
your bride goes to that with shame which is her way
to go with warrant.° 130

BOULT   Faith, some do, and some do not. But,
mistress, if I have bargained for the joint—

BAWD   Thou mayest cut a morsel off the spit.

BOULT   I may so?

BAWD   Who should deny it? Come, young one, I like 135
the manner of your garments well.

BOULT   Ay, by my faith, they shall not be changed
yet.

BAWD   Boult, spend thou that in the town. Report
what a sojourner we have: you'll lose nothing by 140
custom.° When nature framed° this piece, she meant
thee a good turn. Therefore say what a paragon she is,
and thou hast the harvest out of thine own report.

BOULT   I warrant you, mistress, thunder shall not so
awake the beds of eels° as my giving out her beauty 145
stirs up the lewdly inclined. I'll bring home some
tonight.

BAWD   Come your ways! Follow me.

MARINA
If fires be hot, knives sharp, or waters deep,
Untied I still my virgin knot will keep. 150
Diana aid my purpose!

BAWD   What have we to do with Diana? Pray you,
will you go with us?        *Exit, [with the rest].*

[Scene III. *Tharsus.*]

*Enter* CLEON *and* DIONYZA.

DIONYZA
Why are you foolish? Can it be undone?
CLEON
O Dionyza, such a piece of slaughter
The sun and moon ne'er looked upon!
DIONYZA
I think you'll turn a child again.
CLEON
Were I chief lord of all this spacious world, 5
I'd give it to undo the deed. A lady
Much less in blood than virtue,° yet a princess
To equal any single crown o' th' earth
I' th' justice of compare!° O villain Leonine!
Whom thou hast pois'ned too. 10
If thou hadst drunk to him,° 't had been a kindness°
Becoming° well thy fact.° What canst thou say
When noble Pericles shall demand his child?
DIONYZA
That she is dead. Nurses are not the fates°
To foster it, not ever to preserve. 15
She died at night. I'll say so. Who can cross° it?
Unless you play the pious innocent,
And for an honest attribute° cry out,
"She died by foul play."
CLEON        O, go to.° Well, well.
Of all the faults beneath the heavens the gods 20
Do like this worst.
DIONYZA        Be one of those that thinks
The petty wrens of Tharsus will fly hence
And open this to Pericles.° I do shame
To think of what a noble strain you are,
And of how coward a spirit.
CLEON        To such proceeding 25
Whoever but his approbation added,
Though not his prime° consent, he did not flow°
From honorable sources.

---

**93 stir you up** excite you   **94 cried** (1) advertised by loud
cries (2) extolled   **95–96 almost . . . hairs** any number of
times   **102 and** as if   **108 Veroles** from French *vérole* = pox
**109 offered** attempted   **113 repair** renew   **114 shadow**
shelter; **crowns . . . sun** French gold coins   **116 this sign**
i.e., Marina's charms   **123 mere** downright   **125 take her
home** tell her your mind (?)   **127 present** immediate
**129–30 which . . . warrant** to which she is entitled to go
**140–41 by custom** i.e., by our getting customers   **141 framed**
shaped

**144–45 thunder . . . eels** thunder was supposed to rouse
eels from the mud
**IV.iii.7 Much . . . virtue** even more so in point of virtue
than of descent   **9 I' . . . compare** in a just comparison   **11
If . . . him** i.e., if thou hadst poisoned thyself in pledging him;
**a kindness** (1) a kind action (2) an appropriate action   **12
Becoming** befitting; **fact** deed   **14 fates** a line seems to have
dropped out here, to the effect that the nurse's power over
human life is merely "To foster it . . ."   **16 cross** contradict
**18 an honest attribute** the reputation of honesty   **19 go to** an
expression of disapproval   **22–23 The . . . Pericles** an
allusion to the popular belief in the revelation of hidden
murders by a telltale bird   **27 prime** initial; **flow** issue

DIONYZA                    Be it so, then.
Yet none does know but you how she came dead,
Nor none can know, Leonine being gone.                    30
She did distain° my child, and stood between
Her and her fortunes: none would look on her,
But cast their gazes on Marina's face;
Whilst ours was blurted at,° and held a malkin,°
Not worth the time of day.° It pierced me thorough; 35
And though you call my course unnatural,
You not your child well loving, yet I find
It greets me° as an enterprise of kindness°
Performed to your sole daughter.
CLEON                    Heavens forgive it!
DIONYZA
And as for Pericles, what should he say?                    40
We wept after her hearse, and yet we mourn.
Her monument°
Is almost finished, and her epitaphs
In glitt'ring golden characters° express
A general praise to her, and care in us                    45
At whose expense 'tis done.
CLEON                    Thou art like the harpy,
Which, to betray, dost, with thine angel's face,
Seize with thine eagle's talents.°
DIONYZA
Ye're like one that superstitiously
Do swear to th' gods that winter kills the flies.°    50
But yet I know you'll do as I advise.    [*Exeunt.*]

[*Scene IV. Before Marina's monument at Tharsus.*]

[*Enter* GOWER.]

GOWER
Thus time we waste,° and long leagues make short;
Sail seas in cockles,° have and wish but for't;°
Making,° to take° our imagination,
From bourn to bourn,° region to region.
By you being pardoned, we commit no crime                    5
To use one language in each several clime
Where our scene° seems to live. I do beseech you
To learn of me, who stand i' th' gaps to teach you
The stages of our story. Pericles
Is now again thwarting° the wayward seas,                    10
Attended on by many a lord and knight,
To see his daughter, all his life's delight.
Old Helicanus goes along. Behind
Is left to govern it, you bear in mind,
Old Escanes, whom Helicanus late°                    15
Advanced in Tyre to great and high estate.

Well-sailing ships and bounteous winds have brought
This king to Tharsus—think his pilot thought;°
So with his steerage° shall your thoughts go on—
To fetch his daughter home, who first° is gone.    20
Like motes and shadows see them move awhile.
Your ears unto your eyes I'll reconcile.

[*Dumb Show.*]

*Enter* PERICLES *at one door, with all his* TRAIN; CLEON
*and* DIONYZA *at the other.* CLEON *shows* PERICLES *the
tomb; whereat* PERICLES *makes lamentation, puts on sackcloth, and in a mighty passion departs.* [*Then* CLEON,
DIONYZA, *and the rest go also.*]

See how belief may suffer by foul show!°
This borrowed passion° stands for true-owed° woe.
And Pericles, in sorrow all devoured,                    25
With sighs shot through and biggest tears o'ershow-
    ered,
Leaves Tharsus and again embarks. He swears
Never to wash his face, nor cut his hairs.
He puts on sackcloth, and to sea. He bears
A tempest, which his mortal vessel° tears,                    30
And yet he rides it out.° Now please you wit°
The epitaph is° for Marina writ
By wicked Dionyza.

[*Reads the inscription on Marina's monument.*]

"The fairest, sweetest, and best lies here,
Who withered in her spring of year.                    35
She was of Tyrus the King's daughter,°
On whom foul death hath made this slaughter.
Marina was she called; and at her birth
Thetis,° being proud, swallowed some part o' th' earth.
Therefore the earth, fearing to be o'erflowed,                    40
Hath Thetis' birth-child° on the heavens bestowed;
Wherefore she° does—and swears she'll never stint—
Make raging battery upon shores of flint."
No visor° does become black villainy
So well as soft and tender flattery.                    45
Let Pericles believe his daughter's dead,
And bear his courses to be orderèd°
By Lady Fortune; while our scene° must play
His daughter's woe and heavy well-a-day°
In her unholy service. Patience, then,                    50
And think you now are all in Mytilen.    *Exit.*

[*Scene V. Mytilene. A street before the brothel.*]

*Enter,* [*from the brothel,*] *two* GENTLEMEN.

FIRST GENTLEMAN    Did you ever hear the like?
SECOND GENTLEMAN    No, nor never shall do in
such a place as this, she being once gone.

---

**31 distain** cast a slur on    **34 blurted at** treated with scorn;
**malkin** slut    **35 time of day** a greeting    **38 greets me**
presents itself to me; **kindness** love    **42 monument** probably
a few words, such as "which stands i' the marketplace," have
here dropped out    **44 characters** letters    **47–48 dost . . .
talents** i.e., dost, while smiling at thy victim with thine
angel's face, seize it with thine eagle's talents (a common
variant of *talons*)    **49–50 Ye're . . . flies** You are so much
afraid of divine vengeance that you even swear to the gods
that it is not you but winter which is guilty of the death of flies
**IV.iv.1 waste** annihilate    **2 cockles** cockleshells; **have . . .
for't** have by merely wishing for it    **3 Making** making our
way; **take** captivate, delight    **4 bourn** frontier    **7 scene**
dramatic performance    **10 thwarting** crossing    **15 late**
recently

**18 think . . . thought** think that his pilot is thought    **19 with
his steerage** with the course held by Pericles    **20 first** before
him    **23 suffer . . . show** be abused by hypocrisy    **24 borrowed
passion** counterfeit grief; **true-owed** sincerely owned    **30
vessel** i.e., his body    **31 he . . . out** i.e., he survives it;
**wit** know    **32 is** that is    **36 of . . . daughter** daughter of
the King of Tyrus    **39 Thetis** a sea nymph (here, as commonly
in Elizabethan literature, confused with Tethys, wife of
Oceanus, hence the sea personified)    **41 birth-child** person
born in a particular place    **42 she** the sea    **44 visor** mask,
disguise    **47 bear . . . orderèd** suffer his actions to be regulated    **48 scene** performance    **49 well-a-day** grief

FIRST GENTLEMAN  But to have divinity preached
there! Did you ever dream of such a thing?          5
SECOND GENTLEMAN  No, no. Come, I am for no
more bawdy houses. Shall's go hear the vestals° sing?
FIRST GENTLEMAN  I'll do anything now that is
virtuous; but I am out of the road of rutting° forever.
                              *Exit, [with the other].*

[Scene VI. *Mytilene. A room in the brothel.*

*Enter* PANDER, BAWD, *and* BOULT.]

PANDER  Well, I had rather than twice the worth of
her she had ne'er come here.
BAWD  Fie, fie upon her! She's able to freeze the god
Priapus,° and undo a whole generation. We must
either get her ravished or be rid of her. When she  5
should do for clients her fitment° and do me the
kindness of our profession, she has me° her quirks,
her reasons, her master-reasons, her prayers, her knees;
that she would make a puritan of the devil, if he
should cheapen° a kiss of her.                      10
BOULT  Faith, I must ravish her, or she'll disfurnish°
us of all our cavalleria° and make our swearers priests.
PANDER  Now, the pox upon her green-sickness° for
me!°
BAWD  Faith, there's no way to be rid on't but by the  15
way to the pox.° Here comes the Lord Lysimachus
disguised.
BOULT  We should have both lord and lown,° if the
peevish baggage would but give way to customers.

*Enter* LYSIMACHUS.

LYSIMACHUS  How now! How° a dozen of virgini-  20
ties?
BAWD  Now, the gods to-bless° your honor!
BOULT  I am glad to see your honor in good health.
LYSIMACHUS  You may so; 'tis the better for you that
your resorters stand upon sound legs. How now,  25
wholesome° iniquity, have you that° a man may deal
withal° and defy the surgeon?
BAWD  We have here one, sir, if she would—but there
never came her like in Mytilene.
LYSIMACHUS  If she'd do the deeds of darkness, thou  30
wouldst say.
BAWD  Your honor knows what 'tis to say° well
enough.
LYSIMACHUS  Well, call forth, call forth.
BOULT  For flesh and blood, sir, white and red, you  35
shall see a rose; and she were a rose indeed, if she had
but—
LYSIMACHUS  What, prithee?
BOULT  O, sir, I can be modest.

LYSIMACHUS  That dignifies the renown of a bawd  40
no less than it gives a good report to a punk to be
chaste.°                              [*Exit* BOULT.]
BAWD  Here comes that which grows to° the stalk—
never plucked yet, I can assure you.

[*Enter* BOULT, *with* MARINA.]

Is she not a fair creature?                         45
LYSIMACHUS  Faith, she would serve after a long
voyage at sea. Well, there's for you. Leave us.
BAWD  I beseech your honor, give me leave: a word,
and I'll have done presently.°
LYSIMACHUS  I beseech you, do.                      50
BAWD  [*To* MARINA.]  First, I would have you note,
this is an honorable man.
MARINA  I desire to find him so, that I may worthily
note° him.
BAWD  Next, he's the governor of this country, and  55
a man whom I am bound to.
MARINA  If he govern the country, you are bound° to
him indeed; but how honorable he is in that I know
not.
BAWD  Pray you, without any more virginal fencing,  60
will you use him kindly? He will line your apron with
gold.
MARINA  What he will do graciously, I will thankfully
receive.
LYSIMACHUS  Ha' you done?                           65
BAWD  My lord, she's not paced° yet; you must take
some pains to work her to your manage.° Come, we
will leave his honor and her together. Go thy ways.°
         [*Exeunt* BAWD, PANDER, *and* BOULT.]
LYSIMACHUS  Now, pretty one, how long have you
been at this trade?                                 70
MARINA  What trade, sir?
LYSIMACHUS  Why, I cannot name't but I shall
offend.
MARINA  I cannot be offended with my trade. Please
you to name it.                                     75
LYSIMACHUS  How long have you been of this profes-
sion?
MARINA  E'er since I can remember.
LYSIMACHUS  Did you go to't° so young? Were you a
gamester° at five or at seven?                      80
MARINA  Earlier too, sir, if now I be one.
LYSIMACHUS  Why, the house you dwell in proclaims
you to be a creature of sale.
MARINA  Do you know this house to be a place of
such resort, and will come into't? I hear say you're  85
of honorable parts and are the governor of this place.
LYSIMACHUS  Why, hath your principal° made
known unto you who I am?
MARINA  Who is my principal?
LYSIMACHUS  Why, your herb-woman; she that sets  90
seeds and roots of shame and iniquity. O, you have

IV.v.7 vestals virgin priestesses  9 rutting fornication
IV.vi.4 Priapus the classical god of fertility  6 fitment duty
6–7 do me . . . has me the "ethical dative," frequently used
in narrative by Shakespeare  10 cheapen bargain for  11
disfurnish deprive  12 cavalleria body of gentlemen (Italian)
13 green-sickness squeamishness  13–14 for me say I  16
pox syphilis  18 lown loon, lowborn fellow  20 How at
what price  22 to-bless bless entirely ("to" is an intensive
prefix)  26 wholesome health-giving (used ironically); that
that which  26–27 deal withal have sexual relations with
32 what . . . say how to express my meaning

41–42 it . . . chaste to be chaste gives a good reputation to a
prostitute (the whole speech is ironic)  43 grows to is an
integral part of  49 presently at once  54 note respect
57 bound subject (another example of Marina's "quirks" of
which the bawd complained)  66 paced taught her paces  67
manage action and paces to which a horse is trained  68
Go thy ways Come along  79 go to't copulate  80 gamester
one addicted to amorous sport  87 principal employer

heard something of my power, and so stand aloof for
more serious wooing. But I protest to thee, pretty one,
my authority shall not see thee, or else look friendly
upon thee. Come, bring me to some private place. 95
Come, come.

MARINA
If you were born to honor, show it now;
If put upon you,° make the judgment good
That thought you worthy of it.

LYSIMACHUS
How's this? How's this? Some more; be sage.

MARINA                  For me, 100
That am a maid, though most ungentle fortune
Have placed me in this sty, where, since I came,
Diseases have been sold dearer than physic—
That the gods
Would set me free from this unhallowed place, 105
Though they did change me to the meanest bird
That flies i' th' purer air!

LYSIMACHUS        I did not think
Thou couldst have spoke so well; ne'er dreamt thou
   couldst.
Had I brought hither a corrupted mind,
Thy speech had altered it. Hold, here's gold for thee; 110
Persever in that clear° way thou goest,
And the gods strengthen thee!

MARINA           The good gods preserve you!

LYSIMACHUS
For me, be you thoughten°
That I came with no ill intent; for to me
The very doors and windows savor° vilely. 115
Fare thee well. Thou art a piece of virtue, and
I doubt not but thy training hath been noble.
Hold, here's more gold for thee.
A curse upon him, die he like a thief,
That robs thee of thy goodness! If thou dost 120
Hear from me, it shall be for thy good.

[Enter BOULT.]

BOULT   I beseech your honor, one piece for me.

LYSIMACHUS
Avaunt,° thou damned doorkeeper!°
Your house, but for this virgin that doth prop it,
Would sink, and overwhelm you. Away!    [Exit.] 125

BOULT   How's this? We must take another course
with you. If your peevish° chastity, which is not worth
a breakfast in the cheapest country under the cope,°
shall undo a whole household, let me be gelded like a
spaniel. Come your ways. 130

MARINA   Whither would you have me?

BOULT   I must have your maidenhead taken off, or
the common hangman shall execute it.° Come your
ways. We'll have no more gentlemen driven away.
Come your ways, I say. 135

Enter BAWD.

BAWD   How now! What's the matter?

BOULT   Worse and worse, mistress: she has here
spoken holy words to the Lord Lysimachus.

BAWD   O abominable!

BOULT   She makes our profession as it were to stink 140
afore the face of the gods.

BAWD   Marry, hang her up forever!

BOULT   The nobleman would have dealt with her like
a nobleman, and she sent him away as cold as a snow-
ball; saying his prayers too. 145

BAWD   Boult, take her away! Use her at thy pleasure.
Crack the glass of her virginity, and make the rest
malleable.

BOULT   And if° she were a thornier piece of ground
than she is, she shall be ploughed. 150

MARINA   Hark, hark, you gods!

BAWD   She conjures!° Away with her! Would she
had never come within my doors! Marry, hang you!
She's born to undo us. Will you not go the way of
womenkind? Marry come up,° my dish of chastity 155
with rosemary and bays!°            [Exit.]

BOULT   Come, mistress; come your ways with me.

MARINA   Whither wilt thou have me?

BOULT   To take from you the jewel you hold so dear.

MARINA   Prithee, tell me one thing first. 160

BOULT   Come now, your one thing.

MARINA
What canst thou wish thine enemy to be?

BOULT   Why, I could wish him to be my master, or,
rather, my mistress.

MARINA
Neither of these are so bad as thou art, 165
Since they do better thee in their command.°
Thou hold'st a place for which the pained'st° fiend
Of hell would not in reputation change.
Thou art the damnèd doorkeeper to every
Coistrel° that comes inquiring for his Tib;° 170
To the choleric fisting° of every rogue
Thy ear is liable; thy food is such
As hath been belched on by infected lungs.

BOULT   What would you have me do? Go to the wars,
would you? Where a man may serve seven years for 175
the loss of a leg, and have not money enough in the
end to buy him a wooden one?

MARINA
Do any thing but this thou doest.° Empty
Old receptacles,° or common shores,° of filth;
Serve by indenture° to the common hangman. 180
Any of these ways are yet better than this.
For what thou professest° a baboon, could he speak,
Would own a name too dear.° That the gods

98 If . . . you if honor was bestowed upon you   111 clear
free from blame   113 For . . . thoughten this line, like
much else in this scene, is undoubtedly corrupt, but the true
reading seems irrecoverable; see Introduction, p. 1408   115
savor smell   123 Avaunt be off; doorkeeper pander   127
peevish refractory   128 cope sky   132–33 or . . . execute
it with a play on the "head" of "maidenhead"

149 And if even if   152 conjures invokes supernatural aid
(with the suggestion of black magic)   155 Marry come up
an expression of contempt akin to our "hoity-toity"   155–56
dish . . . bays a gibe at Marina's ostentatious virtue; dishes at
Christmas were thus garnished   166 do . . . command are
superior to you through their position of authority   167
pained'st most tormented   170 Coistrel base fellow; Tib
strumpet   171 fisting punching   178 doest pronounced as a
disyllable   179 receptacles the stress here falls on the first
syllable; common shores i.e., the no-man's-land by the sea,
where filth was allowed to be deposited for the tide to wash
away   180 by indenture i.e., as apprentice   182 thou pro-
fessest you have as an occupation   183 Would . . . dear
would claim to possess too high a reputation

Would safely deliver me from this place!
Here, here's gold for thee.                                    185
If that thy master would gain by me,
Proclaim that I can sing, weave, sew, and dance,
With other virtues° which I'll keep from boast;
And I will undertake all these to teach.
I doubt not but this populous city will                        190
Yield many scholars.
BOULT   But can you teach all this you speak of?
MARINA
Prove that I cannot, take me home again,
And prostitute me to the basest groom°
That doth frequent your house.                                 195
BOULT   Well, I will see what I can do for thee. If I
can place thee, I will.
MARINA   But amongst honest women?
BOULT   Faith, my acquaintance lies little amongst
them. But since my master and mistress hath bought   200
you, there's no going but by their consent. Therefore
I will make them acquainted with your purpose,° and
I doubt not but I shall find them tractable enough.
Come, I'll do for thee what I can; come your ways.
                                              *Exeunt.*

## [ACT V]

*Enter* GOWER.

GOWER
Marina thus the brothel 'scapes, and chances
Into an honest house, our story says.
She sings like one immortal, and she dances
As goddesslike to her admired lays;
Deep clerks° she dumbs, and with her neele° composes  5
Nature's own shape of bud, bird, branch, or berry,
That even her art sisters° the natural roses;
Her inkle,° silk, twin with the rubied cherry;
That pupils lacks she none of noble race,
Who pour their bounty on her; and her gain              10
She gives the cursèd bawd. Here we her place;
And to her father turn our thoughts again,
Where we left him on the sea. We there him lost;
Whence, driven before the winds, he is arrived
Here where his daughter dwells; and on this coast       15
Suppose him now at anchor. The city's hived°
God Neptune's annual feast to keep; from whence
Lysimachus our Tyrian ship espies,
His banners sable, trimmed with rich expense;
And to him° in his barge with fervor hies.              20
In your supposing° once more put your sight:
Of heavy° Pericles think this his bark;
Where what is done in action, more, if might,°
Shall be discovered.° Please you, sit and hark.    *Exit.*

188 **virtues** accomplishments   194 **groom** menial   202 **purpose** proposition
V.Cho.5 **Deep clerks** men of profound learning; **neele** needle   7 **sisters** is exactly like   8 **inkle** linen thread   16 **The city's hived** i.e., the citizens are gathered like bees in a hive   19–20 **His . . . him** its . . . it   21 **In your supposing** under the guidance of your imagination   22 **heavy** sorrowful   23 **more, if might** and more if it were possible   24 **discovered** disclosed

[*Scene I. On board Pericles' ship, off Mytilene. A pavilion on deck, with a curtain before it;* PERICLES *within, unkempt and clad in sackcloth, reclining on a couch.*]

*Enter* HELICANUS, *to him two* SAILORS [*one belonging to the Tyrian vessel, the other of Mytilene*].

TYRIAN SAILOR
Where is Lord Helicanus?
He can resolve° you. O, here he is.
Sir, there is a barge put off from Mytilene,
And in it is Lysimachus, the governor,
Who craves to come aboard. What is your will?          5
HELICANUS
That he have his. Call up some gentlemen.
TYRIAN SAILOR   Ho, gentlemen! my lord calls.

*Enter two or three* GENTLEMEN.

FIRST GENTLEMAN   Doth your lordship call?
HELICANUS
Gentlemen, there is some° of worth would come
  aboard.
I pray, greet him fairly.°   [*Exeunt the* GENTLEMEN.]   10

*Enter* LYSIMACHUS [*and* LORDS, *with the* GENTLE-MEN].

MYTILENIAN SAILOR [*To* LYSIMACHUS.]
Sir,
This is the man that can, in aught you would,
Resolve you.
LYSIMACHUS   Hail, reverend sir! The gods preserve
  you!                                                  15
HELICANUS
And you, sir, to outlive the age I am,
And die as I would do.
LYSIMACHUS               You wish me well.
Being on shore, honoring of Neptune's triumphs,°
Seeing this goodly vessel ride before us,
I made to it, to know of whence you are.               20
HELICANUS
First, what is your place?°
LYSIMACHUS               I am the governor of
This place you lie before.
HELICANUS
Sir,
Our vessel is of Tyre, in it the king;
A man who for this three months hath not spoken        25
To anyone, nor taken sustenance
But to prorogue° his grief.
LYSIMACHUS
Upon what ground is his distemperature?°
HELICANUS
'Twould be too tedious to repeat;
But the main grief springs from the loss               30
Of a belovèd daughter and a wife.
LYSIMACHUS
May we not see him?
HELICANUS
You may;

V.i.2 **resolve** free from uncertainty   9 **some** someone   10 **fairly** courteously   18 **triumphs** festivities   21 **place** official position   27 **prorogue** prolong   28 **distemperature** mental disturbance

But bootless° is your sight; he will not speak
To any.
LYSIMACHUS    Yet let me obtain my wish.     35
HELICANUS [*Draws back the curtain.*]
Behold him. This was a goodly person
Till the disaster that, one mortal° night,
Drove him to this.
LYSIMACHUS
Sir king, all hail! The gods preserve you!
Hail, royal sir!            40
HELICANUS
It is in vain; he will not speak to you.
LORD
Sir,
We have a maid in Mytilene, I durst wager,
Would win some words of him.
LYSIMACHUS          'Tis well bethought.
She questionless, with her sweet harmony,    45
And other chosen° attractions, would allure,
And make a batt'ry through his deafened ports,°
Which now are midway stopped.
She is all happy as the fairest of all,
And with her fellow maid is now upon     50
The leafy shelter that abuts against
The island's side.

[*He whispers to a* LORD, *who leaves.*]

HELICANUS
Sure, all° effectless; yet nothing we'll omit
That bears recovery's name. But since your kindness
We have stretched thus far, let us beseech you   55
That for our gold we may provision have,
Wherein we are not destitute for want,
But weary for the staleness.
LYSIMACHUS      O sir, a courtesy
Which if we should deny, the most just God
For every graff° would send a caterpillar,    60
And so inflict° our province. Yet once more
Let me entreat to know at large° the cause
Of your king's sorrow.
HELICANUS
Sit, sir, I will recount it to you.
But see, I am prevented.°         65

[*Enter* LORD, *with* MARINA *and another* GIRL.]

LYSIMACHUS
O, here's the lady that I sent for.
Welcome, fair one! Is't not a goodly presence?°
HELICANUS
She's a gallant° lady.
LYSIMACHUS
She's such a one that, were I well assured
Came° of a gentle kind° and noble stock,    70
I'd wish no better choice, and think me rarely° wed.

[*To* MARINA.]

Fair one, all goodness that consists in° bounty
Expect even here, where is a kingly patient.

If that thy prosperous° and artificial° feat
Can draw him but to answer thee in aught,    75
Thy sacred physic shall receive such pay
As thy desires can wish.
MARINA          Sir, I will use
My utmost skill in his recovery,
Provided
That none but I and my companion maid    80
Be suffered to come near him.
LYSIMACHUS        Come, let us leave her;
And the gods make her prosperous!

[*They withdraw.* MARINA *sings.*]

LYSIMACHUS
Marked he your music?
MARINA         No, nor looked on us.
LYSIMACHUS    See, she will speak to him.
MARINA
Hail, sir! My lord, lend ear.        85
PERICLES   Hum, ha!

[*He pushes her back.*]

MARINA
I am a maid,
My lord, that ne'er before invited eyes,°
But have been gazed on like a comet. She speaks,
My lord, that may be, hath endured a grief    90
Might equal yours, if both were justly weighed.
Though wayward fortune did malign° my state,
My derivation was from ancestors
Who stood equivalent with mighty kings:
But time hath rooted out my parentage,    95
And to the world and awkward casualties°
Bound me in servitude. [*Aside.*] I will desist.
But there is something glows upon my cheek,
And whispers in mine ear, "Go not till he speak."
PERICLES
My fortunes—parentage—good parentage—    100
To equal mine—was it not thus? What say you?
MARINA
I said, my lord, if you did know my parentage,
You would not do me violence.
PERICLES        I do think so.
Pray you, turn your eyes upon me.
You're like something that—what countrywoman?°   105
Here of these shores?
MARINA       No, nor of any shores.
Yet I was mortally° brought forth, and am
No other than I appear.
PERICLES
I am great° with woe, and shall deliver° weeping.
My dearest wife was like this maid, and such    110
My daughter might have been: my queen's square
   brows;°
Her stature to an inch; as wandlike straight;
As silver-voiced; her eyes as jewel-like
And cased° as richly; in pace° another Juno;

---

34 **bootless** unavailing   37 **mortal** fatal   46 **chosen** choice
47 **ports** inlets   53 **all** entirely   60 **graff** graft, grafted plant
61 **inflict** afflict   62 **at large** in full   65 **prevented** forestalled
67 **presence** person   68 **gallant** excellent   70 **Came** she
came; **kind** family   71 **rarely** splendidly   72 **goodness . . .
in** good things that inhere in

74 **prosperous** successful; **artificial** skillful   88 **invited eyes**
i.e., invited anyone to look at her   92 **malign** treat malignantly
96 **awkward casualties** adverse chances   105 **what countrywoman** of what county?   107 **mortally** humanly   109 **great**
pregnant; **deliver** give birth to   111 **square brows** high
forehead   114 **cased** encased; **pace** gait

Who starves the ears she feeds, and makes them hungry 115
The more she gives them speech. Where do you live?

MARINA
Where I am but a stranger: from the deck
You may discern the place.

PERICLES                    Where were you bred?
And how achieved you these endowments, which
You make more rich to owe?°                              120

MARINA
If I
Should tell my history, it would seem like lies
Disdained in the reporting.°

PERICLES                    Prithee, speak.
Falseness cannot come from thee; for thou lookest
Modest as Justice, and thou seemest a palace        125
For the crowned Truth to dwell in. I will believe thee,
And make my senses credit thy relation
To points that seem impossible; for thou lookest
Like one I loved indeed. What were thy friends?°
Didst thou not say when I did push thee back—       130
Which was when I perceived thee—that thou cam'st
From good descending?°

MARINA                    So indeed I did.

PERICLES
Report thy parentage. I think thou said'st
Thou hadst been tossed from wrong to injury,
And that thou thought'st thy griefs might equal mine, 135
If both were opened.°

MARINA                    Some such thing I said,
And said no more but what my thoughts
Did warrant me was likely.

PERICLES                    Tell thy story.
If thine, considered, prove the thousandth part
Of my endurance,° thou art a man, and I             140
Have suffered like a girl; yet thou dost look
Like Patience gazing on kings' graves, and smiling
Extremity out of act.° What were thy friends?°
How lost thou them? Thy name, my most kind virgin?
Recount, I do beseech thee: come, sit by me.        145

MARINA
My name is Marina.

PERICLES                    O, I am mocked,
And thou by some incensèd god sent hither
To make the world to laugh at me.

MARINA                    Patience, good sir,
Or here I'll cease.

PERICLES                    Nay, I'll be patient.
Thou little know'st how thou dost startle me        150
To call thyself Marina.

MARINA                    The name
Was given me by one that had some power:
My father, and a king.

PERICLES                    How, a king's daughter?
And called Marina?

MARINA                    You said you would believe me;
But, not to be a troubler of your peace,            155
I will end here.

PERICLES                    But are you flesh and blood?
Have you a working pulse, and are no fairy?
Motion° as well? Speak on. Where were you born?
And wherefore called Marina?

MARINA                    Called Marina
For I was born at sea.

PERICLES                    At sea! What mother?      160

MARINA
My mother was the daughter of a king;
Who died the minute I was born,
As my good nurse Lychorida hath oft
Delivered° weeping.

PERICLES                    O, stop there a little!
This is the rarest dream that e'er dulled sleep      165
Did mock sad fools withal.° This cannot be:
My daughter's buried. Well, where were you bred?
I'll hear you more, to th' bottom of your story,
And never interrupt you.

MARINA
You scorn. Believe me, 'twere best I did give o'er.  170

PERICLES
I will believe you by the syllable
Of what you shall deliver. Yet, give me leave:
How came you in these parts? Where were you bred?

MARINA
The king my father did in Tharsus leave me;
Till cruel Cleon, with his wicked wife,              175
Did seek to murder me;
And having wooed a villain to attempt it,
Who having drawn to do't,
A crew of pirates came and rescued me;
Brought me to Mytilene.° But, good sir,             180
Whither will you have me? Why do you weep? It
    may be
You think me an impostor: no, good faith!
I am the daughter to King Pericles,
If good King Pericles be.°

PERICLES                    Ho, Helicanus!

HELICANUS    Calls my lord?                          185

PERICLES
Thou art a grave and noble counselor,
Most wise in general. Tell me, if thou canst,
What this maid is, or what is like° to be,
That thus hath made me weep?

HELICANUS                    I know not;
But here's the regent, sir, of Mytilene             190
Speaks° nobly of her.

LYSIMACHUS                    She never would tell
Her parentage; being demanded that,
She would sit still° and weep.

PERICLES
O Helicanus, strike me, honored sir!
Give me a gash, put me to present pain;             195
Lest this great sea of joys rushing upon me
O'erbear° the shores of my mortality,
And drown me with their sweetness. O, come hither,
Thou that beget'st° him that did thee beget;
Thou that wast born at sea, buried at Tharsus,       200

---

120 to owe by owning them  123 in the reporting in the
very act of utterance  129 friends relations  132 descending
lineage  136 opened disclosed  140 my endurance what
I have endured  143 Extremity . . . act extreme calamity
out of striking (?) extreme despair out of committing
suicide (?); friends relations

158 Motion i.e., the movement of the blood and spirits
through the body  164 Delivered reported  166 withal with
180 Mytilene the final syllable is here sounded  184 be i.e., be
alive  188 like likely  191 Speaks that speaks  193 still always
197 O'erbear overwhelm  199 beget'st i.e., gives new life to

And found at sea again! O Helicanus,
Down on thy knees; thank the holy gods as loud
As thunder threatens us: this is Marina!
What was thy mother's name? Tell me but that,
For truth can never be confirmed enough,     205
Though doubts did ever sleep.

MARINA                First, sir, I pray,
What is your title?

PERICLES
I am Pericles of Tyre: but tell me now
My drowned queen's name, as in the rest you said
Thou hast been godlike perfect, and thou art°     210
The heir of kingdoms and another life
To Pericles, thy father.

MARINA [Kneels.]
Is it no more to be your daughter than
To say my mother's name was Thaisa?
Thaisa was my mother, who did end     215
The minute I began.

PERICLES
Now blessing on thee! Rise; thou art my child.
Give me fresh garments. [To MARINA.] Mine own!
   Helicanus,
She is not dead at Tharsus, as she should have been°
By° savage Cleon. She shall tell thee all;     220
When thou shalt kneel, and justify in knowledge°
She is thy very princess. Who is this?

HELICANUS
Sir, 'tis the Governor of Mytilene,
Who, hearing of your melancholy state,
Did come to see you.

PERICLES          I embrace you.     225
Give me my robes. I am wild in my beholding.°
O heavens bless my girl! [Music.] But hark, what
   music?
Tell Helicanus, my Marina, tell him
O'er, point by point, for yet he seems to doubt,
How sure you are my daughter. But what music?     230

HELICANUS
My lord, I hear none.

PERICLES
None?
The music of the spheres! List, my Marina.

LYSIMACHUS
It is not good to cross him; give him way.

PERICLES
Rarest sounds! Do ye not hear?

LYSIMACHUS         Music, my lord?     235

PERICLES
I hear most heavenly music.
It nips me unto° list'ning, and thick slumber
Hangs upon mine eyes. Let me rest.

[He sleeps.]

LYSIMACHUS
A pillow for his head. So leave him all.
Well, my companion friends,     240

If this but answer to my just belief,
I'll well remember you.°    [Exeunt all but PERICLES.]

DIANA [appears to PERICLES in a vision].

DIANA
My temple stands in Ephesus, Hie thee thither,
And do upon mine altar sacrifice.
There, when my maiden priests are met together,     245
Before the people all,
Reveal how thou at sea didst lose thy wife.
To mourn thy crosses,° with thy daughter's, call,
And give them repetition to the life.°
Perform my bidding, or thou livest in woe;     250
Do't, and happy,° by my silver bow!
Awake, and tell thy dream.      [She vanishes.]

PERICLES
Celestial Dian, goddess argentine,°
I will obey thee. Helicanus!

[Enter HELICANUS, LYSIMACHUS, and MARINA.]

HELICANUS               Sir?

PERICLES
My purpose was for Tharsus, there to strike     255
The inhospitable Cleon; but I am
For other service first: toward Ephesus
Turn our blown° sails; eftsoons° I'll tell thee why.

[To LYSIMACHUS.]

Shall we refresh us, sir, upon your shore,
And give you gold for such provision as     260
Our intents° will need?

LYSIMACHUS
Sir,
With all my heart; and when you come ashore
I have another suit.

PERICLES         You shall prevail,
Were it to woo my daughter; for it seems     265
You have been noble towards her.

LYSIMACHUS
Sir, lend me your arm.

PERICLES           Come, my Marina.     Exeunt.


[Scene II. The temple of Diana at Ephesus; THAISA and
several MAIDENS standing near the altar, all appareled as
priestesses; CERIMON and other inhabitants of Ephesus
attending.]

[Enter GOWER.]

GOWER
Now our sands are almost run;
More a little, and then dumb.
This, my last boon, give me—
For such kindness must relieve me—
That you aptly° will suppose     5

---

210 and thou art these words are missing in the text   219
should have been was said to be   220 By at the hands of
221 justify in knowledge affirm in recognition of her claim
226 beholding appearance, looks (?)   237 nips me unto compels me to

241–42 If . . . you i.e., if Marina is really a princess (and
therefore a fit match for me) I shall well reward you (?) (lines
240–42 read like the reporter's addition and ought, probably,
to be omitted) 248 crosses misfortunes 249 repetition
. . . life lifelike recital 251 happy i.e., thou livest happy
253 argentine silvery 258 blown inflated by the wind;
eftsoons afterward, shortly   261 intents purposes
V.ii.5 aptly readily

What pageantry, what feats, what shows,
What minstrelsy and pretty° din,
The regent made in Mytilin
To greet the king. So he thrived
That he is promised to be wived                                    10
To fair Marina; but in no wise
Till he° had done his sacrifice,
As Dian bade: whereto being bound,°
The interim, pray you, all confound.°
In feathered briefness° sails are filled,                          15
And wishes fall out as they're willed.
At Ephesus the temple° see
Our king and all his company.
That he can hither come so soon
Is by your fancies' thankful doom.°                 [*Exit.*] 20

[*Scene III. The temple of Diana. Enter* PERICLES,
*with* LYSIMACHUS, HELICANUS, *and* MARINA.]

PERICLES
Hail, Dian! To perform thy just command,
I here confess myself the King of Tyre;
Who, frighted from my country, did wed
At Pentapolis the fair Thaisa.
At sea in childbed died she, but brought forth            5
A maid-child called Marina; who, O goddess,
Wears yet thy silver livery.° She at Tharsus
Was nursed with Cleon;° whom at fourteen years
He sought to murder; but her better stars
Brought her to Mytilene; 'gainst whose shore           10
Riding,° her fortunes brought the maid aboard us,
Where, by her own most clear remembrance, she
Made known herself my daughter.
THAISA                                         Voice and favor!°
You are, you are—O royal Pericles!

[*Swoons.*]

PERICLES
What means the nun? She dies! Help, gentlemen!      15
CERIMON
Noble sir,
If you have told Diana's altar true,°
This is your wife.
PERICLES            Reverend appearer,° no.
I threw her overboard with these very arms.
CERIMON
Upon this coast, I warrant you.
PERICLES                        'Tis most certain.     20
CERIMON
Look to the lady. O, she's but overjoyed.
Early one blustering morn this lady
Was thrown upon this shore. I oped the coffin,
Found there rich jewels; recovered her,° and placed her
Here in Diana's temple.
PERICLES               May we see them?         25

**7 pretty** pleasing  **12 he** Pericles, whereas in lines 9–10
Lysimachus is referred to  **13 bound** on his way  **14 all
confound** entirely consume  **15 In feathered briefness** with
winged speed  **17 Ephesus the temple** the temple of Ephesus
**20 your . . . doom** the thanks-deserving verdict of your
imaginations
**V.iii.7 Wears . . . livery** i.e., is still a virgin  **8 with Cleon**
in Cleon's family  **11 Riding** as we rode at anchor  **13 favor**
looks, face  **17 true** the truth  **18 appearer** one who appears
**24 recovered her** restored her to consciousness

CERIMON
Great sir, they shall be brought you to my house,
Whither I invite you. Look, Thaisa is
Recovered.
THAISA       O, let me look!
If he be none of mine, my sanctity
Will to my sense bend no licentious ear,°           30
But curb it, spite of seeing. O, my lord,
Are you not Pericles? Like him you spake,
Like him you are. Did you not name a tempest,
A birth and death?
PERICLES            The voice of dead Thaisa!
THAISA
That Thaisa am I, supposèd dead and drowned.     35
PERICLES
Immortal Dian!
THAISA           Now I know you better.
When we with tears parted° Pentapolis,
The king my father gave you such a ring.

[*Points to his ring.*]

PERICLES
This, this! No more.° You gods, your present kindness
Makes my past miseries sports. You shall do well     40
That° on the touching of her lips I may
Melt and no more be seen. O come, be buried
A second time within these arms.
MARINA                        My heart
Leaps to be gone into my mother's bosom.

[*Kneels to* THAISA.]

PERICLES
Look who kneels here: flesh of thy flesh, Thaisa;    45
Thy burden at the sea, and called Marina,
For she was yielded° there.
THAISA                    Blest, and mine own!
HELICANUS
Hail, madam, and my queen!
THAISA                    I know you not.
PERICLES
You have heard me say, when I did fly from Tyre
I left behind an ancient substitute.                50
Can you remember what I called the man?
I have named him oft.
THAISA                'Twas Helicanus then.
PERICLES
Still confirmation.
Embrace him, dear Thaisa; this is he.
Now do I long to hear how you were found;          55
How possibly preserved; and who to thank,
Besides the gods, for this great miracle.
THAISA
Lord Cerimon, my lord: this man,
Through whom the gods have shown their power;
   that can
From first to last resolve you.°
PERICLES                    Reverend sir,     60

**29–30 If . . . ear** If he is not my husband, my holiness will not
listen licentiously to my desire  **37 parted** departed from
**39 No more** i.e., no more confirmation is needed that you are
Thaisa (alternatively one could punctuate "No more, you
gods!" and interpret: give me no greater happiness, you gods!)
**40–41 You . . . That** you would do well if  **47 yielded**
brought forth  **60 resolve you** free you from doubt

The gods can have no mortal officer
More like a god than you. Will you deliver°
How this dead queen re-lives?

CERIMON       I will, my lord.
Beseech you first, go with me to my house,
Where shall be shown you all was found with her;    65
How she came placed here in the temple;
No needful thing omitted.

PERICLES       Pure Dian,
I bless thee for thy vision, and will offer
Nightly oblations to thee. Thaisa,
This prince, the fair betrothèd of your daughter,    70
Shall marry her at Pentapolis. And now,
This ornament
Makes° me look dismal will I clip to form;°
And what this fourteen years no razor touched,
To grace thy marriage-day I'll beautify.    75

THAISA
Lord Cerimon hath letters of good credit,° sir,
My father's dead.

PERICLES
Heavens make a star of him! Yet there, my queen,
We'll celebrate their nuptials, and ourselves
Will in that kingdom spend our following days.    80
Our son and daughter shall in Tyrus reign.
Lord Cerimon, we do our longing stay°

62 **deliver** relate    73 **Makes** which makes; **form** proper shape
76 **credit** trustworthiness    82 **stay** delay

To hear the rest untold.° Sir, lead's the way. [*Exeunt.*]

[*Enter*] GOWER.

[GOWER]
In Antiochus and his daughter you have heard
Of monstrous lust the due and just reward.    85
In Pericles, his queen and daughter, seen,
Although assailed with fortune fierce and keen,
Virtue preserved from fell destruction's blast,°
Led on by heaven, and crowned with joy at last.
In Helicanus may you well descry    90
A figure of truth, of faith, of loyalty.
In reverent Cerimon there well appears
The worth that learnèd charity aye wears.
For wicked Cleon and his wife, when fame°
Had spread his cursèd deed, the honored name    95
Of Pericles to rage the city turn,°
That him and his° they in his palace burn;
The gods for murder seemèd so content
To punish them, although not done but meant.°
So, on your patience evermore attending,    100
New joy wait on you! Here our play has ending.
                             [*Exit.*]

83 **untold** i.e., that is yet untold   88 **blast** blowing up (?) stroke of lightning (?) blight (?)   94 **fame** report   94–96 **when fame . . . city turn** i.e., holding Pericles' name in such honor, the citizens are enraged by the report of the murder of his child   97 **his** i.e., his family   99 **although . . . meant** although the murder was not carried out but merely intended

# CYMBELINE

## EDITED BY RICHARD HOSLEY

## Introduction

In *Cymbeline* Shakespeare combines three stories which originate at three different points in space (so to speak) and gradually converge toward the end of the play. The first story is of a wife who is separated from and eventually reunited with her husband: Imogen and Posthumus. This constitutes the primary action of the play. It fills the first two acts to the exclusion of all else, and, though subordinated to a secondary and a tertiary action in Acts III and IV, it dominates the last act. Thus it is the major structural entity of the play, giving shape to the whole from beginning to end. The second story is of two sons who have been separated from their father in infancy and who eventually are reunited with him: Guiderius and Arviragus. This constitutes the secondary action of the play. It does not begin, however, in the first act and run in parallel with the primary action, as do the secondary actions of *Twelfth Night*, *The Merchant of Venice*, and *King Lear*. Rather, it begins in the middle of the play (III.iii), is partly joined to the primary action through the sojourn of Imogen with the sons in her assumed identity of Fidele (III.vi–IV.ii), and is fully joined to the primary action in the long last scene of the play (V.v). In this respect it bears a general resemblance to the secondary actions of *Pericles* and *The Winter's Tale* (where the subject is again the reunion of child with parent), the chief difference being that in those plays Shakespeare, having chosen to present the early story of the mother and father together with the story of the loss of the infant child, employed a mid-play lapse of many years during which the child might grow to marriageable age. The third story is of a king who successfully defends his country against invasion: Cymbeline. This, despite the emphasis given it by the play's title and by Cymbeline's presence in the primary action from the start in his role as Imogen's father, constitutes a tertiary action, beginning, like the secondary action, not in the first act but in the middle of the play, when the Roman ambassador Lucius demands tribute of Cymbeline. Gradually the tertiary action approaches the other actions of the play, joining first the primary action when Lucius accepts Fidele as his page, then the secondary when Guiderius and Arviragus decide to take up arms against the Romans. In the last scene the three actions are fused in a brilliant dénouement

in which no fewer than twenty-five plot complications are untied.

Each of the three stories of which *Cymbeline* is composed is itself a combination of various literary elements. The Imogen-Posthumus story is by all odds the most complex of the three. The basic source of this story is the ninth novella of the Second Day of Boccaccio's *Decameron*. (Shakespeare also made some use of a German variant of the Boccaccio novella which had been translated into English under the title of *Frederick of Jennen* early in the sixteenth century.) In the first half of his story Shakespeare is generally faithful to the first half of Boccaccio's story. Like Boccaccio, he presents the husband's wager on the wife's chastity, the villain's stratagem of the trunk, the consequent winning of the wager, and the servant's failure to carry out the husband's order to kill the wife. A significant variation in this part of the story is that Shakespeare's villain actually attempts the seduction of the wife; Boccaccio's villain becomes by common report so convinced of the wife's chastity that he gives up all thought of winning the wager without guile and proceeds immediately to the stratagem of the trunk. Another significant variation is Shakespeare's providing a father for the heroine—and, in fact, a father who is a king. Accordingly the heroine is raised in rank from merchant's wife to princess, the initial separation on which the whole story turns being due not to the husband's casual absence on commerce but to his political exile. Thus a subsequent connection with the political story of Cymbeline is provided for.

For the first half of the Imogen-Posthumus story (and for the second as well) Shakespeare also used as source an anonymous dramatic romance entitled *The Rare Triumphs of Love and Fortune* (acted 1582). (In *Cymbeline* the two sources may be thought of as superimposed one upon the other.) In *Love and Fortune* a princess named Fidelia (compare Imogen's pseudonym, Fidele) is in love with a supposed orphan who, like Posthumus, has been brought up as the king's ward. Fidelia's brother secures the banishment of the lover, who thereupon sends word to Fidelia to run away from court and meet him at a cave. (The plan miscarries and Fidelia, like Imogen, wanders about until she meets an old man who, like Belarius, had been a courtier until unjustly banished by the king and who now lives as a hermit in a cave.) To the basic situation of *Love and Fortune* Shakespeare added the folk-tale motif of the Wicked Stepmother, a significant difference from the usual situation being that Shakespeare's stepmother wishes not to substitute her own child for the father's child but to advance her son by marrying him to the father's daughter, who, in the absence of surviving male issue, is heir to the kingdom. (The queen's motivation becomes more conventional at III.v.64.) Thus a political motive for the banishment of Posthumus is provided. The Physician is an added character required by the plot device of the potion, which Shakespeare made use of later in the play.

In the second half of the Imogen-Posthumus story Shakespeare departed more widely from Boccaccio's story, but he retained its essential framework. In Boccaccio, the wife adopts male disguise, takes service with a merchant, travels with him to Alexandria, passes into the service of the sultan (whose especial favor she comes to enjoy), meets the villain in a shop, and succeeds in bringing him to judgment before the sultan and her husband. The villain is forced to confess, the husband repents of his error, husband and wife are reunited, and the villain is executed. In Shakespeare, the wife adopts male disguise, travels to Wales (where she lives for a time with rustic outlaws), takes service with the general of an invading army, is captured along with the invaders by the king (whose especial favor she comes to enjoy), recognizes the villain among the captives, and succeeds in bringing him to judgment before the king and her husband. The villain repents and confesses, the husband repents of his error, husband and wife are reunited, and the villain is forgiven.

Two variations in this part of the Imogen–Posthumus story have the effect of unifying divergent strands of the triple-action plot. The disguised wife's sojourn with rustic outlaws in the mountains of Wales (apparently suggested by Fidelia's experience in *Love and Fortune*, but perhaps also reflective of Erminia's pastoral sojourn in Book VII of Tasso's *Jerusalem Delivered*) connects the primary action with the secondary action involving Cymbeline's lost sons; and Imogen's acceptance of service with the Roman general Lucius (which is essentially present in Boccaccio) connects the primary action with the tertiary action of the invasion of Britain. Two further variations are of interest. The first, a structural matter, involves the point at which the author begins his story. Boccaccio begins his story at the point of the wager, Shakespeare his at a point shortly after the marriage that will make the wager possible. It is as though *Cymbeline* were the second part of an Elizabethan two-part play of which the first part, a comedy, has ended, as by convention a comedy should, with the marriage of lovers who have succeeded in overcoming all obstacles (parental opposition among them) to their union. In *Othello* Shakespeare had already used this particular starting point for a story of jealousy in marriage, beginning the action with a confrontation of angry father and successful wooer in the presence of the newly married daughter. In *Cymbeline* there is the same initial confrontation, the chief difference being that the father (unlike Brabantio) does not suggest to the husband the possibility of the daughter's infidelity. Another variation from Boccaccio is the strong emphasis Shakespeare gives to the reciprocal themes of repentance and forgiveness. Posthumus, long

before he learns he has been deceived by Iachimo, sincerely repents of, and wishes to die in expiation for, the crime that he supposes he has committed against Imogen; and, as he freely repents, so Imogen freely forgives him. Again, Iachimo, when his plot is exposed, undergoes a "conversion" that may be compared with the conversion of Edmund in *King Lear* ("some good I mean to do,/Despite of mine own nature") and contrasted with the defiant persistence in evil of Iago in *Othello* ("Demand me nothing. What you know, you know"). The sincerity of Iachimo's conversion is proved by his willingness to accept the punishment of death; and, as he freely repents, so Posthumus freely forgives him. Here, as in *The Winter's Tale* and *The Tempest*, Shakespeare echoes themes he had treated more fully in *The Merchant of Venice* and *Measure for Measure*.

In addition to these variations, Shakespeare made four important additions to the latter half of Boccaccio's story: the killing of Cloten, the supposed death of Imogen, Imogen's mistaking Cloten's body for that of Posthumus, and the Vision of Posthumus.

Since there is no character in Boccaccio corresponding to Cloten, his essential character may well have been suggested by Fidelia's villainous brother in *Love and Fortune*. The killing of Cloten by Guiderius is closely connected with Cloten's intention to rape Imogen. This intention makes Cloten an example of lust and villainy to be compared with the example afforded by Iachimo: the one lecherous villain is stupid and boorish, the other subtle and Italianate. The intention also "justifies" the killing of Cloten, for in effect Guiderius, even though unaware of Cloten's intention and Fidele's true identity, acts to protect his sister from rape. The manner of the killing—decapitation, with the severed head being thrown into a stream that will carry it to the sea—appears to echo a folk ritual of some sort. There is a patent allusion to the death of Orpheus, whose severed head was thrown into the river Hebrus, down which it was carried to the sea and eventually to Lesbos; and there was an analogous ritual connected with the worship of Adonis at Alexandria, where "a Head, of papyrus, representing the god, was, with every show of mourning, committed to the waves, and borne within seven days by a current . . . to Byblos . . ." (Jessie L. Weston, *From Ritual to Romance* [1957], p. 47). (These allusions, mock-epic or mock-mythic in relation to Cloten himself, may carry serious meaning in relation to Cloten as a surrogate for Posthumus.) The killing of Cloten may be compared also with the killing of Antigonus in *The Winter's Tale*: in each case a vicious or a flawed character is punished for attempted violence against the heroine, and in each case there seems to be operative a tradition of tragicomedy that goes back ultimately to what Aristotle called "tragedy with a double issue"—that is, a play threatening death which provides a happy ending for "good" characters but the reward of death for "bad." This tradition is involved also in the death of the queen at the end of the play.

The general plot device of the supposed death of a beloved woman (a staple of Greek romance) was one that Shakespeare had already used in *Romeo and Juliet*, *Much Ado About Nothing*, and *Pericles*, and that he was to use again in *The Winter's Tale*; and he had used the particular device of the potion that brings about the supposed death in *Romeo and Juliet*. In *Cymbeline* (IV.ii) the supposed death of Imogen symbolizes the death that Posthumus had commanded, separates Imogen from the rustic outlaws, and emphasizes the operation of Providence in the accident of the malevolent queen's having requested poison of a physician who, because of his wisdom and benevolence, supplied her instead with a harmless sleeping potion.

The killing of Cloten and the supposed death of Imogen lead to the Elizabethan-Gothic grotesquerie of Imogen's mistaking the headless body of Cloten for that of Posthumus. Through this theatrically sensational mistake (so embarrassing to modern audiences) Shakespeare makes the interesting point that Imogen, like Posthumus, can be victimized by circumstance and deceived by appearance— and in a situation outwardly suggestive of sexual compromise, for unwittingly the paragon of virtue lies beside and lovingly embraces the body of a man who is not her husband but her would-have-been rapist. (Even so she has earlier unwittingly spent the night with her would-be seducer, Iachimo.) A possible source of this episode exists in an anonymous dramatic romance entitled *Clyomon and Clamydes*, dating from the 1580's. Here the heroine, Neronis, who has left the court in the disguise of a boy and taken service with a shepherd, comes upon a coffin containing the body of the King of Norway, earlier slain in combat by Neronis's lover Clyomon. Since Clyomon has left his emblazoned shield beside the coffin, Neronis mistakes the body of the King of Norway for that of Clyomon, grieves, despairs, and is on the point of committing suicide. At this moment the personification of Providence descends from heaven, gives Neronis a paper informing her that Clyomon is alive, and returns to heaven. Another possible source of this episode is afforded by the *Ethiopica* of Heliodorus, in which Theagenes embraces the body of a dead woman which he mistakes for that of his beloved, Chariclea.

The Vision of Posthumus (V.iv), in which Jupiter descends from heaven, may have been suggested by the descent of Providence in *Clyomon and Clamydes*. In any case, the Vision involves a literary tradition deriving ultimately from the appearance-of-a-god-in-a-dream of classical epic. Shakespeare had used such a dream theophany in *Pericles*, where the goddess Diana appears to the protagonist in a dream; and he had used the closely allied convention of the appearance-of-a-ghost-in-a-dream in *Richard III*, where the ghosts of Richard's victims appear successively to the dreaming Richard and Richmond. A native stage tradition may also be influential, for the great fifteenth-century scriptural cycles frequently employ the appearance-of-an-angel-in-a-dream. An Elizabethan stage convention is certainly operative, the god who descends from stage cover to stage by means of suspension-gear: Juno in *The Tempest*, Venus in Greene's *Alphonsus King of Aragon*, Providence in the anonymous *Clyomon and Clamydes*, perhaps Diana in *Pericles*. In *Cymbeline*, as Bertrand Evans has pointed out, Jupiter is not a *deus ex machina* in the sense that he resolves a complication of the plot; rather, the theophany focuses our growing awareness that God's providence is indeed at work, even though for a time (during the long and frightening absence of Iachimo, the only person who, by confessing his slander against Imogen, can resolve the major complication of the plot) we may have seen little visible evidence of it. It should be

added that the authenticity of the Vision, frequently called in question by critics of the nineteenth and early twentieth centuries, is now (together with the authenticity of the rest of the play) generally accepted, perhaps largely because of the cogent demonstration by G. Wilson Knight in *The Crown of Life* (1947).

At least one other influence on the Imogen-Posthumus story can be discerned: that of Greek romance. The influence was already present in Boccaccio's story, for Greek romance characteristically involves a separation of lover from beloved (or of husband from wife), consequent wanderings over great distances and for long periods of time, and an eventual reunion of the lovers. *Apollonius of Tyre*, which Shakespeare had dramatized in *Pericles*, is a good example of the type, but an example of specific relevance to *Cymbeline* is afforded by the *Ethiopica* of Heliodorus, of which an Elizabethan translation (the first of three) appeared in 1567. From the Ethiopica (to which he had alluded in *Twelfth Night*, V.i.117) Shakespeare apparently took a suggestion for the striking of the disguised Imogen by Posthumus (V.v). Chariclea, who has been separated from her lover, Theagenes, comes to Memphis and recognizes him. Since she is disguised as a beggar, however, Theagenes does not recognize her.

> Frantically, as if sight of him had stung her, she ran to him, clasped him close, hung upon his neck, and caressed him with inarticulate sighs and tears. When he saw her face, begrimed and purposely discolored, and her torn and tattered garments, he took her for a shameless beggar. He pulled her off and thrust her away, and when she would not let go he struck her for troubling him and blocking his view of Calasiris and his sons. She said to him softly, "Pythias, have you forgotten the lamp?" The words struck Theagenes like a bolt. He remembered that the lamp was a token they had agreed upon and gazed into Chariclea's eyes, whose brilliance broke upon him like the sun's rays through a cloud. He threw his arms about her and embraced her.          (translation by Moses Hadas)

The striking of Imogen by Posthumus may also reflect a device of the romantic epics, the individual combat between two knights in which the lover, ignorant of his opponent's sex and true identity, fights with and sometimes kills his beloved in male disguise. Romantic-epic examples include the combat between Tancred and Clorinda in Book XII of Tasso's *Jerusalem Delivered* and that between Arthegal and Britomart in Book III of Spenser's *Faerie Queene*; and dramatic examples in the same tradition include the combat between the title characters of Kyd's *Soliman and Perseda* and between Amintor and Aspatia in *The Maid's Tragedy* by Beaumont and Fletcher.

The secondary action of the play—consisting of the story of Guiderius and Arviragus—begins in III.iii, although we are warned early to expect it by a reference to Cymbeline's lost sons at I.i.57. The Guiderius-Arviragus story employs that standard device of romance tradition, the "lost child." This is Shakespeare's most important innovation in the "historical" materials available to him. Usually—because of the characteristic concern of romance with love—the lost child is a girl, apparently of low degree, who is enabled to marry her lover of high degree when it is revealed that she also is of gentle birth. This is the situation of the heroine in many of the comedies of Plautus and Terence, and it is a common situation in pastoral romance. (Examples are afforded by Glycerium in the *Andria* of Terence, Pastorella in Book VI of *The Faerie Queene*, and Perdita in *The Winter's Tale*.) Sometimes the lost child is a boy, but in such cases the story does not usually involve a love situation, presumably because the mobility required of the wanderer who comes to the environment of the lost child is unsuited to the decorum of a girl. (Compare the convenience, if not the necessity, of Imogen's male disguise.) Sometimes the lost male child is involved ultimately in a situation in which he unwittingly takes or threatens the life of his father (for example, the *Oedipus* of Sophocles) or in which the father unwittingly takes or threatens the life of his son (for example, *The Captives* of Plautus). Cymbeline's threat to execute the confessed homicide Guiderius, who is actually his own son, seems to echo the oedipal situation of *The Captives*, in which the father, Hegio, threatens to execute the supposed slave, Tyndarus, who is actually his own son.

The Guiderius-Arviragus story includes the corollary story of Belarius: as they are lost children, so he is their supposed father. Belarius is primarily the "rusticated courtier" of pastoral romance: the educated and civilized gentleman or nobleman who lives in isolation or among shepherds and with whom the protagonist passes some time during his wanderings. Sometimes the rusticated courtier's exile is voluntary, the result of an unhappy love affair or some other disillusionment. An example is Philisides in Sidney's *Arcadia*. More frequently the rusticated courtier's exile is enforced, the result of banishment for political reasons. An example is Duke Senior in *As You Like It*. Belarius, an example of the latter type, has an apparent source in Bomelio, the unjustly exiled courtier of *Love and Fortune* who lives in a cave and whom Fidelia meets after running away from court.

Belarius, however, is not only the rusticated courtier, he is also the "shepherd father" of pastoral romance. Usually the shepherd father is only a foster father and the lost child that he rears as his own is a girl. Examples are Melibee, supposed father of Pastorella in Book VI of *The Faerie Queene*, and the Shepherd, supposed father of Perdita in *The Winter's Tale*. Shakespeare makes Belarius not a shepherd but a hunter, because Guiderius and Arviragus must have had the sort of training with weapons that will fit them to fight effectively in defense of their country; and he makes Belarius a mountaineer in order to emphasize the danger of his position as a political outlaw. (Thus Shakespeare, through discarding sheep and shepherds, emphasizes the primitivism that is at the core of most pastoralism.) Nevertheless, it is convenient briefly to regard Belarius as a "shepherd" father in order to understand his relation to tradition. Since the rusticated courtier is rarely a father, Shakespeare seems, in Belarius, to have combined the pastoral character-types of the courtier rusticated for political reasons and the shepherd father. He was to make the same significant combination in amplified and most original form in *The Tempest*, where the only essential departure from the combined traditions (aside from the omission of sheep and shepherds) is that Prospero is not the foster father but the true father of Miranda.

The Guiderius-Arviragus story is amplified and linked to the tertiary action of the play by Shakespeare's use of material from Holinshed's *Chronicles of England, Scotland, and Ireland* (1587): specifically the Scottish victory over Danish invaders at the Battle of Luncarty (near Perth) in 976, which was achieved through the stalwart fighting of the husbandman Hay and his two sons. This joining of the Guiderius-Arviragus story to the Cymbeline story leads to its further joining, in the final scene of the play, to the Imogen-Posthumus story.

The tertiary action of the play—consisting of the Cymbeline story—begins in III.i with the appearance of the Roman ambassador Lucius, although we are warned to expect this action by a reference to Lucius at II.iii.56 and by another to the payment of Roman tribute at II.iv.13. The basic source is *The History of England* in Holinshed's *Chronicles*, but particular details have been traced to other sources. Since Holinshed attributes the denial of tribute to Cymbeline's son Guiderius, Shakespeare may well have followed Spenser in attributing the denial to Cymbeline. Moreover, a number of Shakespearean details appear to derive from Thomas Blenerhasset's "Guidericus" in the 1578 edition of the Second Part of *The Mirror for Magistrates* and from John Higgins' "Guiderius" in the 1587 edition of *The Mirror*. Perhaps the most interesting are the disguising of Posthumus as a British soldier and his fighting against the Romans. These details were apparently suggested by Higgins' account of the Roman captain Hamonius, who disguises himself as a British soldier and pretends to fight against the Romans in order to gain the opportunity of killing Guiderius. One other influence on the Cymbeline story is Shakespeare's own tradition of depicting the invasion of Britain or England, as in *King Lear*, *Richard III*, *3 Henry VI*, and *King John*. In each of these cases, as in *Cymbeline*, the invasion is represented as partly or entirely beneficial to the island kingdom.

The foregoing account stresses the abundance of sources and traditions that Shakespeare characteristically blended into an organic whole in writing *Cymbeline*. The play is extremely complex in its relation to tradition. It is also complex in other respects, posing a number of problems both real and imaginary. The critics have reacted very differently to *Cymbeline*. At one extreme are the Rationalists, chief among them Dr. Johnson (1765):

> To remark the folly of the fiction, the absurdity of the conduct, the confusion of the names and manners of different times, and the impossibility of the events in any system of life, were to waste criticism upon unresisting imbecility, upon faults too evident for detection and too gross for aggravation.

At the other extreme are the Imogenolaters, of whom perhaps the best example is Swinburne (1880):

> The very crown and flower of all her father's daughters— I do not speak here of her human father but her divine— woman above all Shakespeare's women is Imogen. As in Cleopatra we found the incarnate sex, the woman ever-lasting, so in Imogen we find half-glorified already the immortal godhead of womanhood.

Neither critic need now be taken seriously, although it may be observed that Johnson's aversion to the violent yoking together of Roman Britain and Renaissance

Rome reveals a characteristic blindness to the essence of romance.

Many other problems once posed by *Cymbeline* have been solved by recent criticism and scholarship. One such problem has already been mentioned: doubt of the authenticity of certain parts of the play, in particular the Vision of Posthumus. No one now denies that the play is entirely the work of Shakespeare. Another problem has been posed by the suggestion of a lost source-play. The theory, however, is both unnecessary and unsupported by evidence, and it seems to be at variance with what we know of Shakespeare's originality in the handling of multiple sources in such plays as *King Lear*, *The Merchant of Venice*, and *The Taming of the Shrew*. Another problem has been posed by A. H. Thorndike's suggestion that *Cymbeline* reveals the influence of Beaumont and Fletcher's *Philaster*. This theory has now been effectively disposed of by the late Harold S. Wilson in his English Institute lecture of 1951. Another problem has been posed by the complexity of the plot, which, entailing as it does some two dozen separate dénouements, prompted Shaw, in *Cymbeline Refinished*, to rewrite the last act at half the length of the original for a production of 1937. Here Shakespeare's technical virtuosity and its relation to themes of the play have been well expounded by Bertrand Evans. Still another problem has been posed by the character of Posthumus and particularly his motivation in accepting Iachimo's wager. Here W. W. Lawrence has enlightened us by setting Posthumus' action in an appropriate context of Renaissance conceptions of a wife's chastity and her husband's honor. And yet another difficulty is posed by the play's characteristic style, which is heavily metaphorical, often perverse in syntax, and sometimes so elliptical as to raise the question whether we are dealing with a metaphysical toughness of thought and angularity of expression comparable to Donne's, or simply with a corrupt text. In the great majority of cases, surely, the former interpretation is to be preferred, for the style of *Cymbeline* can be paralleled in such near-contemporary plays as *Antony and Cleopatra*, *Coriolanus*, and *The Winter's Tale*.

One teasing problem remains. Modern editors classify *Cymbeline* as a comedy. Why then was the play classified as a tragedy in the Shakespeare Folio of 1623? The classification could be simply an error, Heminges and Condell having forgotten that the play does not end with the death of the title character. Or, as has been suggested, the classification could be due to late receipt of copy in the printing-house, after the comedies (the first of the three genres of the Folio) had been printed off. Neither explanation is very satisfactory. On balance it seems more reasonable to assume that the classification resulted from a deliberate decision on the part of Heminges and Condell. The problem can perhaps be solved by considering two other Folio plays now classified as comedies: *The Winter's Tale* and *Troilus and Cressida*. (All three plays are tragicomedies, the first two of traditional type, the third of nontraditional.) What is the difference between, on the one hand, *The Winter's Tale* (classified as a comedy in the Folio) and, on the other, *Cymbeline* and *Troilus and Cressida* (classified as tragedies in the Folio)? Simply that the first play does not include war in its action, whereas the two latter plays do. In this respect *The Winter's Tale* is like the thirteen other "comedies" of the Folio classification, and *Cymbeline* and *Troilus and Cressida* are like the ten other "tragedies" of the Folio classification. (The distinction does not, to be sure, hold exactly in the case of *All's Well That Ends Well* and *Romeo and Juliet*: in the former play, however, war is not a political matter but a device to expose the braggart soldier Parolles; and in the latter play war is represented by the feud between the rival houses of Capulet and Montague.) Having denied themselves the convenient classification of tragicomedy, Heminges and Condell seem to have made the best of an imperfect bargain by associating *The Winter's Tale* with that Shakespearean genre (comedy) which usually excludes war from the action, *Cymbeline* and *Troilus and Cressida* with that Shakespearean genre (tragedy) which (like history) usually includes war in the action. Some uncertainty about their decision may be reflected in the fact that in the Folio *The Winter's Tale* stands as the very last of the comedies, *Cymbeline* as the very last of the tragedies. *Troilus and Cressida*, for reasons connected with the printing of the Folio, stands by itself between the histories and the tragedies.

*Cymbeline* is generally dated during the theatrical season of 1609–10. It was seen by Simon Forman, presumably at the Globe, sometime before September 12, 1611, when Forman died. (Unfortunately his account of the play merely names the characters and summarizes the plot.) *Cymbeline* may have been designed for original production by the King's Men at their indoor theater, the Blackfriars, or at their outdoor theater, the Globe. The issue is relatively unimportant, however, since the same plays were frequently performed at both kinds of playhouse, public and private. On January 1, 1634, *Cymbeline* was acted "at Court by the King's Players," being "well-liked by the King." Probably the theater was the Cockpit-in-Court at Whitehall, though it may have been the Great Hall of Whitehall Palace. In original production *Cymbeline* was presumably performed on a stage generally similar to the one that appears in the well-known De Witt drawing of the Swan Playhouse—that is to say, without benefit of an "inner stage." The present text has been annotated in accordance with this assumption.

## A NOTE ON THE SOURCES

The sources of *Cymbeline* are discussed in the Introduction. The ninth novella of the Second Day of Boccaccio's *Decameron* is reprinted (in the anonymous translation of 1620), in the individual-volume Signet edition of *Cymbeline*. *Frederick of Jennen* is reprinted in an appendix to the New Arden edition of *Cymbeline* (1955). *The Rare Triumphs of Love and Fortune* is edited by W. W. Greg in the Malone Society Reprints (1931), *Clyomon and Clamydes* by Betty Littleton (1968). The *Ethiopica* of Heliodorus has been translated by Moses Hadas: *Heliodorus: An Ethiopian Romance* (1957). Relevant parts of the *History of England* and the *History of Scotland* in Holinshed's *Chronicles* (1587) are reprinted in the Signet paperback edition of *Cymbeline*. Blenerhasset's "Guidericus" and Higgins's "Guiderius" have been edited by Lily B. Campbell, in *Parts Added to the Mirror for Magistrates* (1946).

## A NOTE ON THE TEXT

There is only one "substantive" edition of *Cymbeline*, the Shakespeare Folio of 1623. Because of incomplete notation of properties and music in the stage directions of F, it seems clear that the printer's copy for F was not a promptbook nor the faithful transcript of one; and several directions are phrased in the "fictive" language characteristic of an author writing his own stage directions. Probably therefore the copy for F consisted of an authorial manuscript or the faithful transcript of one: either (1) "foul papers" (the author's last working draft of the play before preparation of a promptbook) in unusually clean condition (like the copy for *Antony and Cleopatra*); (2) authorial "fair copy" (the author's faithful transcript of his own foul papers); or (3) a faithful scribal transcript of foul papers or authorial fair copy. The type for F was set by a single compositor, Jaggard's Compositor B. (See Charlton Hinman, *The Printing and Proof-Reading of the First Folio of Shakespeare* [1963].) F provides, in general, a good text, correctly lined and with relatively few corruptions. In the present edition "accidental" errors in F have been emended silently; "substantive" errors requiring emendation are listed at the end of this note.

F is divided into acts and scenes. Division into acts presumably derives from original production of the play with four intervals for nondramatic music. (Compare Wilfred T. Jewkes, *Act Division in Elizabethan and Jacobean Plays*, 1958.) Division into scenes presumably derives from annotation of the printer's copy by a Folio editor wishing to give the text a semblance of neoclassical style. The present edition follows the act divisions of F and for convenience of reference, the scene divisions of the Globe edition, although at three points these vary (both correctly and incorrectly) from those of F. Globe I.i combines F I.i and ii, incorrectly since the stage (despite notice by players going off of those coming on) is technically clear at I.i.69 (the "overlap" of players is paralleled at I.ii.117 of *Measure for Measure*). Globe II.iv and v divide F II.iv, correctly since the stage is clear at II.iv.152. And Globe III.vi combines F III.vi and vii, incorrectly since the stage is clear at III.vi.27. Both Globe and F fail to mark a new scene at IV.ii.100, incorrectly since the stage is clear at that point.

F contains no place headings, for the reason that the play was originally produced without changeable scenery. (Compare Richard Southern, *Changeable Scenery: Its Origin and Development in the British Theatre* [1952].) Place headings have been added here in accordance with a general requirement of the present edition, but such headings designate only the three general locales of the action, Britain, Rome, and Wales. A more specific designation is impossible in at least three instances (I.ii,

II.i, II.v); and in any case specific designations are misleading since they suggest a change of scenery for each scene with a particular locale different from that of the preceding scene.

In the following list of substantive emendations the reading of the present edition is given in boldface type, that of F in roman type.

**I.i.4 First Gentleman** 1 [so throughout balance of scene] **10 Second Gentleman** 2 [so throughout balance of scene] **158 Exeunt** Exit
**I.ii.1 First Lord** 1 [so throughout balance of scene and in II.i and II.iii] **7 Second Lord** 2 [so throughout balance of scene and in II.i and II.iii]
**I.iii.9 this** his
**I.iv.48 not** [not in F] **75 Britain** Britanie **77 but believe** beleeue **87–88 purchase** purchases **132 thousand** thousands
**I.v.3 s.d. Exeunt** Exit **75 s.d.** [occurs after line 74 in F] **85 s.d. Exeunt** Exit
**I.vi.7 desire** desires **28 takes** take **104 Fixing** Fiering **109 illustrous** illustrious **168 men's** men **169 descended** defended
**II.i.27 your** you **34 tonight** night **52 s.d. Exeunt** Exit **62 husband, than** Husband. Then **63 make. The** make the **66 s.d. Exit** Exeunt
**II.ii.49 bare** beare **51 s.d. Exeunt** Exit
**II.iii.7 Cloten** [not in F] **29 Cloten** [not in F] **30 vice** voyce **44 out** on't **48 solicits** solicity **138 garment** Garments **155 you** your
**II.iv.6 hopes** hope **18 legions** Legion **24 mingled** wing-led **47 not** note **100–01 that. She** that She **135 the** her
**II.v.16 German** Iarmen **27 have a** [not in F]
**III.i.19 ribbed . . . palèd** ribb'd . . . pal'd **20 rocks** Oakes **53 be. We do say** be, we do. Say
**III.ii.67 score** store **78 here, nor** heere, not
**III.iii.2 Stoop** Sleepe **23 bribe** Babe **28 know** knowes **83 wherein they** whereon the
**III.iv.79 afore't** a-foot **90 make** makes **102 out** [not in F] **124 courtesan** Curtezan? **148 haply** happily
**III.v.17 s.d. Exeunt** Exit **32 looks** looke **40 strokes** stroke **41 s.d. Messenger** a Messenger **55 s.d.** [occurs after "days" in F] **140 insultment** insulment
**III.vi.70 I'ld** I
**III.vii.9 commends** commands
**IV.i.18 her** thy **19 haply** happily
**IV.ii.49** [speech heading Arui. precedes "He" in F] **58 patience** patient **122 thank** thanks **132 humor** Honor **186 ingenious** ingenuous **205 crayer** care **206 Might** Might'st **290 is** are **332 s.d.–333 Enter Lucius and Captains; a Soothsayer to them. Captain. The legions** Enter Lucius, Captaines, and a Soothsayer. Cap. To them, the Legions **336 are in** are heere in
**IV.iv.2 find we** we finde **8 us** v. **17 the** their **27 hard** heard
**V.i.1 wished** am wisht
**V.iii.24 harts** hearts **42 stooped** stopt **43 they** the **84 First Captain** 1 [so throughout balance of scene] **86 Second Captain** 2 [so throughout balance of scene]
**V.iv.s.d. Jailers** Gaoler **1 First Jailer** Gao **51 come** came **57 look** looke, looke **129 are as often** are often **139 sir** Sis **154 on** one **176 s.d. Exit** Exeunt
**V.v.62 Ladies** La **64 heard** heare **126 saw** see **134 On** One **205 it** [not in F] **297 sorry** sorrow **334 mere** neere **378 ye** we **386 brothers** Brother **392 inter'gatories** Interrogatories **405 so** no **435 Soothsayer** [not in F] **445 Leo-natus** Leonatus **449 thy** this **469 this yet** yet this

# CYMBELINE

[Dramatic Personae

CYMBELINE *King of Britain*
IMOGEN *daughter to Cymbeline by a former wife, later disguised under the name of Fidele*
POSTHUMUS LEONATUS *a gentleman, husband to Imogen*
GUIDERIUS
ARVIRAGUS } *sons to Cymbeline, disguised under the names of Polydore and Cadwal, supposed sons to Morgan*
BELARIUS *a banished lord, disguised under the name of Morgan*
QUEEN *wife to Cymbeline*
CLOTEN *son to the queen by a former husband*
CORNELIUS *a physician employed by the queen*
PISANIO *servant to Posthumus*
LORDS *attending on Cymbeline*
LADIES *attending on the queen*
HELEN *a lady attending on Imogen*
TWO LORDS *friends to Cloten*
TWO GENTLEMEN *of Cymbeline's court*
TWO BRITON CAPTAINS
MUSICIANS *employed by Cloten*

MESSENGERS
TWO JAILERS

CAIUS LUCIUS *Roman ambassador, later general of the Roman forces*
TWO ROMAN SENATORS
ROMAN TRIBUNES
ROMAN CAPTAINS
A SOOTHSAYER *named Philharmonus*
PHILARIO *an Italian friend to Posthumus*
IACHIMO *an Italian friend to Philario*
A FRENCHMAN *friend to Philario*

JUPITER
GHOST *of Sicilius Leonatus, father to Posthumus*
GHOST *of the mother to Posthumus*
GHOSTS *of the two young brothers to Posthumus, called Leonati*

BRITON SOLDIERS   ROMAN SOLDIERS
ATTENDANTS   A DUTCHMAN *and*
A SPANIARD (*friends to Philario*)

*Scene:* Britain, Rome, Wales]

# ACT I

## Scene I. [*Britain.*]

*Enter two* GENTLEMEN.

FIRST GENTLEMAN
You do not meet a man but frowns. Our bloods°
No more obey the heavens than our courtiers
Still seem as does the king's.°

SECOND GENTLEMAN    But what's the matter?

FIRST GENTLEMAN
His daughter, and the heir of's kingdom, whom
He purposed to his wife's sole son—a widow    5
That late he married—hath referred° herself
Unto a poor but worthy gentleman. She's wedded,
Her husband banished, she imprisoned. All
Is outward sorrow, though I think the king
Be touched at very heart.

SECOND GENTLEMAN    None but the king?    10

FIRST GENTLEMAN
He that hath lost her too. So is the queen,
That most desired the match. But not a courtier,
Although they wear their faces to the bent°
Of the king's looks, hath a heart that is not
Glad at the thing they scowl at.

SECOND GENTLEMAN    And why so?    15

FIRST GENTLEMAN
He that hath missed the princess is a thing
Too bad for bad report, and he that hath her—
I mean, that married her, alack good man,
And therefore banished—is a creature such
As, to seek through the regions of the earth    20
For one his like, there would be something failing
In him that should compare. I do not think
So fair an outward and such stuff within
Endows a man but he.

SECOND GENTLEMAN    You speak him far.°

FIRST GENTLEMAN
I do extend him, sir, within himself,°    25
Crush him together rather than unfold
His measure duly.

SECOND GENTLEMAN    What's his name and birth?

FIRST GENTLEMAN
I cannot delve him to the root. His father
Was called Sicilius, who did join his honor°
Against the Romans with Cassibelan,    30
But had his titles by Tenantius, whom
He served with glory and admired° success,
So gained the sur-addition° Leonatus;
And had, besides this gentleman in question,
Two other sons, who in the wars o' th' time    35
Died with their swords in hand; for which their father,
Then old and fond of issue,° took such sorrow
That he quit being, and his gentle lady,
Big of this gentleman our theme, deceased

*The decorative border shown on page 1454 appeared on the first
page of* Cymbeline *in the First Folio edition of Shakespeare's plays,
1623.*

**I.i.1 bloods** moods  **3 seem . . . king's** wear expressions like
the king's  **6 referred** given  **13 bent** inclination  **24 speak
him far** praise him much  **25 do . . . himself** i.e., do not
exaggerate his real merit  **29 honor** reputation (as a soldier)
**32 admired** wondered at  **33 sur-addition** additional title
**37 fond of issue** doting on children

As he was born. The king he takes the babe    40
To his protection, calls him Posthumus Leonatus,
Breeds him and makes him of his bedchamber,°
Puts to him° all the learnings that his time°
Could make him the receiver of, which he took
As we do air, fast as 'twas minist'red,    45
And in's spring became a harvest, lived in court—
Which rare it is to do—most praised, most loved,
A sample to the youngest, to th' more mature
A glass that feated them,° and to the graver
A child that guided dotards. To his mistress,    50
For whom he now is banished—her own price°
Proclaims how she esteemed him and his virtue.
By her election° may be truly read
What kind of man he is.

SECOND GENTLEMAN    I honor him
Even out of° your report. But pray you tell me,    55
Is she sole child to th' king?

FIRST GENTLEMAN    His only child.
He had two sons—if this be worth your hearing,
Mark it—the eldest of them at three years old,
I' th' swathing clothes the other, from their nursery
Were stol'n, and to this hour no guess in knowledge    60
Which way they went.

SECOND GENTLEMAN    How long is this ago?

FIRST GENTLEMAN
Some twenty years.

SECOND GENTLEMAN
That a king's children should be so conveyed,°
So slackly guarded, and the search so slow
That could not trace them!

FIRST GENTLEMAN    Howsoe'er 'tis strange,    65
Or that the negligence may well be laughed at,
Yet is it true, sir.

SECOND GENTLEMAN    I do well believe you.

FIRST GENTLEMAN
We must forbear.° Here comes° the gentleman,
The queen, and princess.    *Exeunt.*

*Enter the* QUEEN, POSTHUMUS, *and* IMOGEN.

QUEEN
No, be assured you shall not find me, daughter,    70
After the slander° of most stepmothers,
Evil-eyed unto you. You're my prisoner, but
Your jailer shall deliver you the keys
That lock up your restraint. For you, Posthumus,
So soon as I can win th' offended king,    75
I will be known your advocate. Marry,° yet
The fire of rage is in him, and 'twere good
You leaned unto° his sentence with what patience
Your wisdom may inform you.

POSTHUMUS    Please your highness,
I will from hence today.

QUEEN    You know the peril.    80

**42 of his bedchamber** i.e., a chamberlain  **43 Puts to him**
sets him to work at; **time** age  **49 glass . . . them** mirror
that reflected their features  **51 price** what she is willing to
undergo for his sake  **53 election** choice  **55 out of** beyond
**63 conveyed** stolen  **68 forbear** withdraw; **Here comes**
this entrance-announcement shows that, though the stage is
technically "clear" at line 69 (at which point F marks a new
scene), the oncoming players enter before the offgoing ones
have completed their exit  **71 slander** ill repute  **76 Marry**
indeed (from "By the Virgin Mary")  **78 leaned unto**
deferred to

I'll fetch a turn about the garden, pitying
The pangs of barred affections, though the king
Hath charged you should not speak together. *Exit.*

IMOGEN                                              O
Dissembling courtesy! How fine this tyrant
Can tickle° where she wounds! My dearest husband, 85
I something fear my father's wrath, but nothing—
Always reserved° my holy duty°—what
His rage can do on me. You must be gone,
And I shall here abide the hourly shot
Of angry eyes, not comforted to live                    90
But that there is this jewel in the world
That I may see again.

POSTHUMUS                   My queen, my mistress.
O lady, weep no more, lest I give cause
To be suspected of more tenderness
Than doth become a man. I will remain                   95
The loyal'st husband that did e'er plight troth;
My residence, in Rome at one Philario's,
Who to my father was a friend, to me
Known but by letter. Thither write, my queen,
And with mine eyes I'll drink the words you send,      100
Though ink be made of gall.

*Enter* QUEEN.

QUEEN                            Be brief, I pray you.
If the king come, I shall incur I know not
How much of his displeasure. [*Aside.*] Yet I'll move him
To walk this way. I never do him wrong
But he does buy° my injuries, to be friends;          105
Pays dear for my offenses.              [*Exit.*]

POSTHUMUS              Should we be taking leave
As long a term as yet we have to live,
The loathness to depart would grow. Adieu.

IMOGEN
Nay, stay a little.
Were you but riding forth to air yourself,             110
Such parting were too petty. Look here, love;
This diamond was my mother's. [*Giving a ring.*] Take
   it, heart,
But° keep it till you woo another wife,
When Imogen is dead.

POSTHUMUS              How, how? Another?
You gentle gods, give me but this I have,              115
And cere up° my embracements from a next
With bonds of death! Remain, remain thou here
While sense can keep it on. And, sweetest, fairest,
As I my poor self did exchange for you
To your so infinite loss, so in our trifles           120
I still win of you. For my sake wear this.

[*Giving a bracelet.*]
It is a manacle of love; I'll place it
Upon this fairest prisoner.

IMOGEN                    O the gods!
When shall we see again?

*Enter* CYMBELINE *and* LORDS.

POSTHUMUS                Alack, the king!

CYMBELINE
Thou basest thing, avoid° hence, from my sight!       125

---

If after this command thou fraught° the court
With thy unworthiness, thou diest. Away!
Thou'rt poison to my blood.

POSTHUMUS                  The gods protect you,
And bless the good remainders of° the court.
I am gone.                              *Exit.*

IMOGEN      There cannot be a pinch in death          130
More sharp than this is.

CYMBELINE              O disloyal thing
That shouldst repair° my youth, thou heap'st
A year's age on me.

IMOGEN               I beseech you, sir,
Harm not yourself with your vexation.
I am senseless of° your wrath; a touch more rare°     135
Subdues all pangs, all fears.

CYMBELINE                    Past grace? obedience?

IMOGEN
Past hope, and in despair; that way, past grace.

CYMBELINE
That mightst have had the sole son of my queen.

IMOGEN
O blessed that I might not! I chose an eagle
And did avoid a puttock.°                             140

CYMBELINE
Thou took'st a beggar, wouldst have made my throne
A seat for baseness.

IMOGEN              No, I rather added
A luster to it.

CYMBELINE  O thou vile one!

IMOGEN                      Sir,
It is your fault that I have loved Posthumus.
You bred him as my playfellow, and he is              145
A man worth any woman; overbuys me
Almost the sum he pays.°

CYMBELINE              What, art thou mad?

IMOGEN
Almost, sir. Heaven restore me! Would I were
A neatherd's° daughter, and my Leonatus
Our neighbor shepherd's son.

*Enter* QUEEN.

CYMBELINE              Thou foolish thing!             150
[*To* QUEEN.]
They were again together. You have done
Not after our command. Away with her
And pen her up.

QUEEN           Beseech° your patience. Peace,
Dear lady daughter, peace! Sweet sovereign,
Leave us to ourselves, and make yourself some comfort 155
Out of your best advice.°

CYMBELINE              Nay, let her languish
A drop of blood a day and, being aged,
Die of this folly.    *Exeunt* [CYMBELINE *and* LORDS].

*Enter* PISANIO.

QUEEN           Fie, you must give way.—
Here is your servant. How now, sir? What news?

---

126 fraught freight, burden  129 remainders of those who
remain at  132 repair renew  135 am senseless of do not
feel; touch more rare finer anxiety  140 puttock kite (bird
of prey)  146-47 overbuys . . . pays he exceeds me in worth
by almost the price which he is now called upon to pay, i.e.,
banishment (J. M. Nosworthy)  149 neatherd's cowherd's
153 Beseech I beseech  156 advice consideration

85 tickle (pretend to) please  87 reserved excepting; duty
of child to parent  105 buy gladly accept  113 But only
116 cere up shroud  125 avoid go

PISANIO
My lord your son drew on my master.

QUEEN           Ha!      160
No harm, I trust, is done?

PISANIO          There might have been
But that my master rather played than fought
And had no help of anger. They were parted
By gentlemen at hand.

QUEEN       I am very glad on't.

IMOGEN
Your son's my father's friend; he takes his part°    165
To draw upon an exile. O brave sir!
I would they were in Afric both together,
Myself by with a needle° that I might prick
The goer-back. Why came you from your master?

PISANIO
On his command. He would not suffer me     170
To bring him to the haven, left these notes
Of what commands I should be subject to
When't pleased you to employ me.

QUEEN        This hath been
Your faithful servant. I dare lay° mine honor
He will remain so.

PISANIO     I humbly thank your highness.    175

QUEEN
Pray walk awhile.            [Exit QUEEN.]

IMOGEN
About some half-hour hence, pray you speak with me.
You shall at least go see my lord aboard.
For this time leave me.      Exeunt [severally°].

## Scene II. [Britain.]

*Enter* CLOTEN° *and two* LORDS.

FIRST LORD   Sir, I would advise you to shift a shirt;
the violence of action hath made you reek° as a sacrifice. Where air comes out, air comes in; there's none
abroad so wholesome as that you vent.°

CLOTEN   If my shirt were bloody, then to shift it. 5
Have I hurt him?

SECOND LORD [*Aside.*]   No, faith, not so much as his
patience.

FIRST LORD   Hurt him? His body's a passable°
carcass if he be not hurt. It is a throughfare for steel if 10
it be not hurt.

SECOND LORD [*Aside.*]   His steel was in debt. It went
o' th' backside the town.°

CLOTEN   The villain would not stand° me.

SECOND LORD [*Aside.*]   No, but he fled forward still, 15
toward your face.

FIRST LORD   Stand you? You have land enough of
your own, but he added to your having, gave you
some ground.

SECOND LORD [*Aside.*]   As many inches as you have 20
oceans. Puppies!

CLOTEN   I would they had not come between us.

SECOND LORD [*Aside.*]   So would I, till you had
measured how long a fool you were upon the ground.

CLOTEN   And that she should love this fellow and 25
refuse me!

SECOND LORD [*Aside.*]   If it be a sin to make a true
election,° she is damned.

FIRST LORD   Sir, as I told you always, her beauty and
her brain go not together. She's° a good sign,° but I 30
have seen small reflection of her wit.

SECOND LORD [*Aside.*]   She shines not upon fools,
lest the reflection should hurt her.

CLOTEN   Come, I'll to my chamber. Would there had
been some hurt done!    35

SECOND LORD [*Aside.*]   I wish not so—unless it had
been the fall of an ass, which is no great hurt.

CLOTEN   You'll go with us?

FIRST LORD   I'll attend your lordship.

CLOTEN   Nay, come, let's go together.    40

SECOND LORD   Well, my lord.        *Exeunt.*

## Scene III. [Britain.]

*Enter* IMOGEN *and* PISANIO.

IMOGEN
I would thou grew'st unto the shores o' th' haven
And questioned'st every sail. If he should write,
And I not have it, 'twere a paper lost
As offered mercy is.° What was the last
That he spake to thee?

PISANIO        It was his queen, his queen.    5

IMOGEN
Then waved his handkerchief?

PISANIO           And kissed it, madam.

IMOGEN
Senseless° linen, happier therein than I!
And that was all?

PISANIO       No, madam. For so long
As he could make me with this eye or ear
Distinguish him from others, he did keep    10
The deck, with glove or hat or handkerchief
Still waving, as° the fits and stirs of's mind
Could best express how slow his soul sailed on,
How swift his ship.

IMOGEN      Thou shouldst have made him
As little as a crow or less, ere left    15
To after-eye° him.

PISANIO      Madam, so I did.

IMOGEN
I would have broke mine eyestrings, cracked them but
To look upon him till the diminution
Of space° had pointed him sharp as my needle;
Nay, followed him till he had melted from    20
The smallness of a gnat to air, and then

---

165 **takes his part** plays his usual role    168 **needle** pronounced
"neel"    174 **lay** stake    179 **s.d. severally** by different tiring-
house doors (Imogen follows the queen offstage while Pisanio
exits by the other door)
**I.ii.s.d. Cloten** rhymes with *rotten*; cf. "Cloten's clotpoll,"
IV.ii.184   2 **reek** give off vapors   4 **vent** give off   9 **passable**
affording passage (quibble on the sense of "tolerable")   12–13
**It . . . town** like a debtor avoiding a creditor by taking a
back street (i.e., his rapier missed)   14 **stand** confront

28 **election** choice   30 **She's** she has; **sign** appearance
**I.iii.3–4 'twere . . . is** a letter gone astray would be as great
a loss as mercy that fails to reach its object   7 **Senseless** without
feeling   12 **as** as if   15–16 **ere . . . after-eye** before you
stopped looking after   19 **space** i.e., distance

Have turned mine eye and wept. But, good Pisanio,
When shall we hear from him?

PISANIO                              Be assured, madam,
With his next vantage.°

IMOGEN
I did not take my leave of him, but had                 25
Most pretty things to say. Ere I could tell him
How I would think on him at certain hours
Such thoughts and such; or I could make him swear
The shes of Italy should not betray
Mine interest and his honor; or have charged him       30
At the sixth hour of morn, at noon, at midnight,
T' encounter me with orisons,° for then
I am in heaven for him; or ere I could
Give him that parting kiss which I had set
Betwixt two charming° words—comes in my father,       35
And like the tyrannous breathing of the north
Shakes all our buds from growing.

Enter a LADY.°

LADY                              The queen, madam,
Desires your highness' company.

IMOGEN
Those things I bid you do, get them dispatched.
I will attend the queen.

PISANIO              Madam, I shall.        Exeunt. 40

Scene IV. [Rome.]

Enter PHILARIO, IACHIMO,° a FRENCHMAN, a
DUTCHMAN, and a SPANIARD.

IACHIMO  Believe it, sir, I have seen him in Britain.
He was then of a crescent note,° expected to prove so
worthy as since he hath been allowed the name of.
But I could then have looked on him without the
help of admiration,° though the catalogue of his en-   5
dowments had been tabled° by his side and I to peruse
him by items.

PHILARIO  You speak of him when he was less furnished than now he is with that which makes° him
both without and within.                                10

FRENCHMAN  I have seen him in France. We had very
many there could behold the sun° with as firm eyes as
he.

IACHIMO  This matter of marrying his king's daughter, wherein he must be weighed rather by her value  15
than his own, words him, I doubt not, a great deal
from the matter.°

FRENCHMAN  And then his banishment.

IACHIMO  Ay, and the approbation of those that weep
this lamentable divorce under her colors° are wonder- 20
fully to extend him° be it but to fortify her judgment,

which else an easy battery might lay flat for taking a
beggar without less° quality.° But how comes it he is
to sojourn with you? How creeps acquaintance?

PHILARIO  His father and I were soldiers together, to  25
whom I have been often bound for no less than my life.

Enter POSTHUMUS.

Here comes the Briton. Let him be so entertained°
amongst you as suits, with gentlemen of your knowing, to a stranger° of his quality.° I beseech you all
be better known to this gentleman, whom I commend  30
to you as a noble friend of mine. How worthy he is
I will leave to appear hereafter, rather than story him
in his own hearing.

FRENCHMAN  Sir, we have known together° in
Orleans.                                                35

POSTHUMUS  Since when I have been debtor to you
for courtesies which I will be ever to pay and yet pay
still.

FRENCHMAN  Sir, you o'errate my poor kindness. I
was glad I did atone° my countryman and you. It had  40
been pity you should have been put together° with so
mortal a purpose as then each bore, upon importance°
of so slight and trivial a nature.

POSTHUMUS  By your pardon, sir, I was then a young
traveler; rather shunned to go even° with what I       45
heard than in my every action to be guided by others'
experiences. But upon my mended judgment, if I
offend not to say it is mended, my quarrel was not
altogether slight.

FRENCHMAN  Faith, yes, to be put to the arbitrament  50
of swords, and by such two that would by all likelihood have confounded° one the other or have fall'n
both.

IACHIMO  Can we with manners ask what was the
difference?                                             55

FRENCHMAN  Safely, I think. 'Twas a contention in
public, which may without contradiction° suffer the
report. It was much like an argument that fell out last
night, where each of us fell in praise of our country°
mistresses; this gentleman at that time vouching—and 60
upon warrant of bloody affirmation°—his to be more
fair, virtuous, wise, chaste, constant, qualified,° and
less attemptable than any the rarest of our ladies in
France.

IACHIMO  That lady is not now living, or this gentle-  65
man's opinion, by this,° worn out.

POSTHUMUS  She holds her virtue still, and I my mind.

IACHIMO  You must not so far prefer her 'fore ours of
Italy.

POSTHUMUS  Being so far provoked as I was in        70
France, I would abate° her nothing, though I profess
myself her adorer, not her friend.°

24 vantage opportunity 32 T' encounter . . . orisons
join me in prayers 35 charming protecting from evil 37
s.d. the Lady's message has the theatrical function of motivating Imogen's exit
I.iv.s.d. Iachimo probably pronounced "Yákimo"; cf. "yellow Iachimo," II.v.14; but possibly pronounced "Jáckimo"
since the name is a variant of the Italian Giacomo  2 crescent
note growing reputation  5 admiration wonder  6 tabled
tabulated  9 makes is the making of  12 behold the sun as
the eagle—noblest of birds—was thought to do 16–17
words . . . matter makes him out better than he truly is
20 colors banner  21 extend him enlarge his reputation

23 without less i.e., with less (double negative); quality
inherent worth  27 entertained welcomed  29 stranger
foreigner; quality rank  34 known together been acquainted
40 atone reconcile  41 put together i.e., in a duel  42
importance a matter  45 shunned . . . even refused to agree
52 confounded destroyed  57 contradiction objection
59 country i.e., of our own countries (with bawdy quibble)
61 warrant . . . affirmation pledge to support by shedding
blood (R. B. Heilman)  62 qualified endowed with good
qualities  66 by this by this time  71 abate depreciate  72
friend paramour

IACHIMO   As fair and as good—a kind of hand-in-hand° comparison—had been something too fair and too good for any lady in Britain. If she went before° 75 others I have seen, as that diamond of yours outlusters many I have beheld, I could not but believe she excelled many; but I have not seen the most precious diamond that is, nor you the lady.

POSTHUMUS   I praised her as I rated her. So do I my 80 stone.

IACHIMO   What do you esteem it at?

POSTHUMUS   More than the world enjoys.°

IACHIMO   Either your unparagoned mistress is dead, or she's outprized° by a trifle.       85

POSTHUMUS   You are mistaken. The one may be sold or given, or° if there were wealth enough for the purchase or merit for the gift. The other is not a thing for sale, and only the gift of the gods.

IACHIMO   Which the gods have given you?       90

POSTHUMUS   Which by their graces I will keep.

IACHIMO   You may wear her in title yours, but you know strange fowl light upon neighboring ponds. Your ring may be stol'n too. So your brace of unprizable estimations,° the one is but frail and the other 95 casual.° A cunning thief, or a that-way-accomplished courtier, would hazard the winning both of first and last.

POSTHUMUS   Your Italy contains none so accomplished a courtier to convince the honor° of my 100 mistress, if, in the holding or loss of that, you term her frail. I do nothing doubt you have store of thieves; notwithstanding, I fear not my ring.

PHILARIO   Let us leave° here, gentlemen.

POSTHUMUS   Sir, with all my heart. This worthy 105 signior, I thank him, makes no stranger of me; we are familiar at first.°

IACHIMO   With five times so much conversation I should get ground of° your fair mistress, make her go back even to the yielding, had I admittance, and 110 opportunity to° friend.

POSTHUMUS   No, no.

IACHIMO   I dare thereupon pawn the moiety° of my estate to your ring, which in my opinion o'ervalues it something. But I make my wager rather against 115 your confidence than her reputation; and, to bar your offense herein too, I durst attempt it against any lady in the world.

POSTHUMUS   You are a great deal abused° in too bold a persuasion,° and I doubt not you sustain what y' are 120 worthy of by your attempt.

IACHIMO   What's that?

POSTHUMUS   A repulse—though your attempt, as you call it, deserve more: a punishment too.

PHILARIO   Gentlemen, enough of this. It came in too 125 suddenly; let it die as it was born, and I pray you be better acquainted.

IACHIMO   Would I had put my estate and my neighbor's on th' approbation° of what I have spoke!

POSTHUMUS   What lady would you choose to assail? 130

IACHIMO   Yours, whom in constancy you think stands so safe. I will lay you ten thousand ducats to your ring that, commend me to the court where your lady is, with no more advantage than the opportunity of a second conference, and I will bring from thence 135 that honor of hers which you imagine so reserved.

POSTHUMUS   I will wage° against your gold, gold to it. My ring I hold dear as my finger; 'tis part of it.

IACHIMO   You are a friend, and therein the wiser. If you buy ladies' flesh at a million a dram, you cannot 140 preserve it from tainting. But I see you have some religion in you, that° you fear.

POSTHUMUS   This° is but a custom in your tongue. You bear a graver purpose, I hope.

IACHIMO   I am the master of my speeches, and would 145 undergo° what's spoken, I swear.

POSTHUMUS   Will you? I shall but lend my diamond till your return. Let there be covenants° drawn between's. My mistress exceeds in goodness the hugeness of your unworthy thinking. I dare you to this match: 150 here's my ring.

PHILARIO   I will have it no lay.°

IACHIMO   By the gods, it is one. If I bring you no sufficient testimony that I have enjoyed the dearest bodily part of your mistress, my ten thousand ducats 155 are yours; so is your diamond too. If I come off and leave her in such honor as you have trust in, she your jewel, this your jewel, and my gold are yours— provided I have your commendation° for my more free entertainment.°       160

POSTHUMUS   I embrace these conditions. Let us have articles betwixt us. Only, thus far you shall answer: if you make your voyage upon her and give me directly° to understand you have prevailed, I am no further your enemy; she is not worth our debate. If 165 she remain unseduced, you not making it appear otherwise, for your ill opinion and th' assault you have made to her chastity you shall answer me with your sword.

IACHIMO   Your hand; a covenant. We will have these 170 things set down by lawful counsel, and straight away° for Britain, lest the bargain should catch cold and starve.° I will fetch my gold and have our two wagers recorded.

POSTHUMUS   Agreed.       175

      [*Exeunt* POSTHUMUS *and* IACHIMO.]

FRENCHMAN   Will this hold, think you?

PHILARIO   Signior Iachimo will not from it. Pray let us follow 'em.       *Exeunt.*

Scene V. [*Britain.*]

*Enter* QUEEN, LADIES, *and* CORNELIUS.

---

73–74 **hand-in-hand** claiming equality   **75 went before** excelled   **83 enjoys** possesses   **85 outprized** exceeded in value   **87 or** either   **94–95 unprizable estimations** inestimable values   **96 casual** liable to accident   **100 convince the honor** conquer the chastity   **104 leave** leave off   **107 at first** from the first   **109 get ground of** gain an advantage over (a dueling metaphor followed by bawdy quibbles on "go back" and "yielding")   **111 to** as a   **113 moiety** half   **119 abused** deceived   **120 persuasion** opinion

**129 approbation** proof   **137 wage** wager   **142 that** since **143 This** i.e., what you say   **146 undergo** undertake   **148 covenants** a legal agreement   **152 lay** wager   **159 commendation** introduction to her   **160 entertainment** welcome **164 directly** plainly   **171 straight away** immediately I shall leave   **173 starve** die

QUEEN
Whiles yet the dew's on ground, gather those flowers.
Make haste. Who has the note° of them?

LADY                                            I, madam.

QUEEN
Dispatch.°                          *Exeunt* LADIES.
Now, Master Doctor, have you brought those drugs?

CORNELIUS
Pleaseth your highness, ay. Here they are, madam.      5

[*Presenting a box.*]

But I beseech your grace, without offense—
My conscience bids me ask—wherefore you have
Commanded of me these most poisonous compounds,°
Which are the movers of a languishing death,
But, though slow, deadly.

QUEEN                          I wonder, doctor,      10
Thou ask'st me such a question. Have I not been
Thy pupil long? Hast thou not learned° me how
To make perfumes? distil? preserve? yea, so
That our great king himself doth woo me oft
For my confections?° Having thus far proceeded—      15
Unless thou think'st me devilish—is't not meet
That I did amplify my judgment° in
Other conclusions?° I will try the forces
Of these thy compounds on such creatures as
We count not worth the hanging—but none human—      20
To try the vigor of them and apply
Allayments to their act,° and by them° gather
Their° several virtues and effects.

CORNELIUS                          Your highness
Shall from this practice but make hard your heart.      25
Besides, the seeing these effects will be
Both noisome and infectious.

QUEEN                          O, content thee.

*Enter* PISANIO.

[*Aside.*]

Here comes a flattering rascal. Upon him
Will I first work. He's for his master,
And enemy to my son.—How now, Pisanio?—
Doctor, your service for this time is ended;      30
Take your own way.

CORNELIUS [*Aside.*] I do suspect you, madam,
But you shall do no harm.

QUEEN          [*To* PISANIO.] Hark thee, a word.

CORNELIUS [*Aside.*]
I do not like her. She doth think she has
Strange ling'ring poisons. I do know her spirit
And will not trust one of her malice with      35
A drug of such damned nature. Those she has
Will stupefy and dull the sense awhile,
Which first perchance she'll prove° on cats and dogs,
Then afterwards up higher; but there is
No danger in what show of death it makes,      40
More than the locking up the spirits a time,
To be more fresh, reviving. She is fooled

With a most false effect, and I the truer
So to be false with her.

QUEEN                          No further service, doctor,
Until I send for thee.

CORNELIUS          I humbly take my leave.      *Exit.*      45

QUEEN
Weeps she still, say'st thou? Dost thou think in time
She will not quench° and let instructions enter
Where folly now possesses? Do thou work.
When thou shalt bring me word she loves my son,
I'll tell thee on the instant thou art then      50
As great as is thy master; greater, for
His fortunes all lie speechless and his name
Is at last gasp. Return he cannot nor
Continue where he is. To shift his being°
Is to exchange one misery with another,      55
And every day that comes comes to decay°
A day's work in him. What shalt thou expect
To be depender on a thing that leans,
Who cannot be new built, nor has no friends
So much as but to prop him? [*Dropping the box;*
PISANIO *picks it up.*] Thou tak'st up      60
Thou know'st not what, but take it for thy labor.
It is a thing I made which hath the king
Five times redeemed from death. I do not know
What is more cordial.° Nay, I prithee take it.
It is an earnest° of a farther good      65
That I mean to thee. Tell thy mistress how
The case stands with her; do't as from thyself.
Think what a chance thou changest on,° but think
Thou hast thy mistress still—to boot, my son,
Who shall take notice of thee. I'll move the king      70
To any shape of thy preferment° such
As thou'lt desire; and then myself, I chiefly,
That set thee on to this desert,° am bound
To load thy merit richly. Call my women.
Think on my words. *Exit* PISANIO. A sly and constant
knave,      75
Not to be shaked; the agent for his master,
And the remembrancer° of her to hold
The handfast° to her lord. I have given him that
Which, if he take, shall quite unpeople her
Of liegers° for her sweet,° and which she after,      80
Except she bend her humor,° shall be assured
To haste it too.

*Enter* PISANIO *and* LADIES.

                    So, so. Well done, well done.
The violets, cowslips, and the primroses
Bear to my closet.° Fare thee well, Pisanio.
Think on my words.          *Exeunt* QUEEN *and* LADIES.

PISANIO                          And shall do.      85
But when to my good lord I prove untrue,
I'll choke myself. There's all I'll do for you.      *Exit.*

I.v.2 **note** list  **3 Dispatch** make haste  **8 compounds** drugs
**12 learned** taught  **15 confections** drugs  **17 judgment**
knowledge  **18 conclusions** experiments  **22 Allayments**
. . . **act** antidotes to their action; **them** the experiments  **23**
**Their** of the compounds  **38 prove** test

**47 quench** cool down  **54 being** location  **56 decay** destroy
**64 cordial** restorative  **65 earnest** pledge  **68 chance** . . .
**on** i.e., opportunity you have to change service (?)  **71**
**preferment** advancement  **73 desert** action meriting reward
**77 remembrancer** person employed to remind someone
(legal term)  **78 handfast** marriage contract  **80 liegers**
ambassadors; **sweet** lover  **81 bend her humor** change her
mind  **84 closet** private room

## Scene VI. [*Britain.*]

*Enter* IMOGEN *alone.*

IMOGEN
A father cruel and a stepdame false,
A foolish suitor to a wedded lady
That hath her husband banished. O, that husband,
My supreme crown of grief, and those repeated°
Vexations of it! Had I been thief-stol'n,    5
As my two brothers, happy; but most miserable
Is the desire that's glorious.° Blessed be those,
How mean° soe'er, that have their honest wills,°
Which seasons° comfort. Who may this be? Fie!

*Enter* PISANIO *and* IACHIMO.

PISANIO
Madam, a noble gentleman of Rome,    10
Comes° from my lord with letters.
IACHIMO             Change you,° madam:
The worthy Leonatus is in safety
And greets your highness dearly.    [*Presenting a letter.*]
IMOGEN             Thanks, good sir.
You're kindly welcome.
IACHIMO [*Aside.*]
All of her that is out of door° most rich!    15
If she be furnished with a mind so rare,
She is alone th' Arabian bird,° and I
Have lost the wager. Boldness be my friend!
Arm me, audacity, from head to foot,
Or like the Parthian° I shall flying fight—    20
Rather, directly fly.
IMOGEN (*Reads.*) "He is one of the noblest note,° to
whose kindnesses I am most infinitely tied. Reflect°
upon him accordingly, as you value your trust—
                       *Leonatus.*"    25

So far I read aloud.
But even the very middle of my heart
Is warmed by th' rest and takes it thankfully.
You are as welcome, worthy sir, as I
Have words to bid you, and shall find it so    30
In all that I can do.
IACHIMO          Thanks, fairest lady.
What, are men mad? Hath nature given them eyes
To see this vaulted arch and the rich crop°
Of sea and land, which can distinguish 'twixt
The fiery orbs above and the twinned° stones    35
Upon the numbered° beach, and can we not
Partition° make with spectacles so precious°
'Twixt fair and foul?
IMOGEN         What makes your admiration?°
IACHIMO
It cannot be i' th' eye, for apes and monkeys,

'Twixt two such shes, would chatter this way° and    40
Contemn with mows° the other; nor i' th' judgment,
For idiots, in this case of favor,° would
Be wisely definite;° nor i' th' appetite°—
Sluttery, to such neat excellence opposed,
Should make desire vomit emptiness,°    45
Not so allured to feed.
IMOGEN
What is the matter, trow?°
IACHIMO           The cloyèd will°—
That satiate yet unsatisfied desire, that tub
Both filled and running—ravening first the lamb,
Longs after for the garbage.
IMOGEN          What, dear sir,    50
Thus raps° you? Are you well?
IACHIMO           Thanks, madam, well.

[*To* PISANIO.]

Beseech you, sir, desire
My man's abode° where I did leave him.
He's strange and peevish.°
PISANIO           I was going, sir,
To give him welcome.            *Exit.* 55
IMOGEN
Continues well my lord? His health, beseech you?
IACHIMO
Well, madam.
IMOGEN
Is he disposed to mirth? I hope he is.
IACHIMO
Exceeding pleasant; none a stranger° there
So merry and so gamesome. He is called    60
The Briton reveler.
IMOGEN         When he was here
He did incline to sadness,° and ofttimes
Not knowing why.
IACHIMO        I never saw him sad.
There is a Frenchman his companion, one
An eminent monsieur that, it seems, much loves    65
A Gallian° girl at home. He furnaces°
The thick° sighs from him, whiles the jolly Briton—
Your lord, I mean—laughs from's free lungs, cries, "O,
Can my sides hold to think that man who knows
By history, report, or his own proof°    70
What woman is, yea, what she cannot choose
But must be, will's free hours languish° for
Assurèd bondage?"
IMOGEN        Will my lord say so?
IACHIMO
Ay, madam, with his eyes in flood with laughter.
It is a recreation to be by    75
And hear him mock the Frenchman. But heavens know
Some men are much to blame.
IMOGEN        Not he, I hope.

---

**I.vi.4 repeated** (already) enumerated   **7 desire that's glorious**
i.e., unfulfilled longing that aspires to great things (Nosworthy)
**8 mean** low-ranking; **honest wills** plain desires   **9 seasons**
give relish to   **11 Comes** who comes; **you** i.e., your expression   **15 out of door** external, visible   **17 Arabian bird**
phoenix (of which species only one example existed at a time)
**20 Parthian** mounted archer who shot arrows behind him
while in flight (Iachimo will resort to indirect methods)   **22
note** reputation   **23 Reflect** bestow attention   **33 crop**
harvest   **35 twinned** exactly alike   **36 numbered** abounding (in stones)   **37 Partition** distinction; **spectacles so
precious** i.e., eyesight   **38 admiration** wonder

**40 this way** toward Imogen   **41 mows** grimaces   **42 case of
favor** question of beauty   **43 definite** decisive; **appetite**
physical desire   **45 make . . . emptiness** i.e., destroy
desire   **47 What . . . trow** What are you talking about,
I wonder; **will** sexual desire   **51 raps** transports   **52–53
desire . . . abode** request that my servant remain   **54
strange and peevish** a foreigner and skittish   **59 none a
stranger** there is no foreigner   **62 sadness** seriousness   **66
Gallian** French; **furnaces** exhales like a furnace   **67 thick**
frequent   **70 proof** experience   **72 languish** pass in languishing

IACHIMO
Not he—but yet heaven's bounty towards him might
Be used more thankfully. In himself 'tis° much;
In you, which I account his, beyond all talents.°  80
Whilst I am bound to wonder, I am bound
To pity too.

IMOGEN  What do you pity, sir?

IACHIMO
Two creatures heartily.

IMOGEN  Am I one, sir?
You look on me. What wrack° discern you in me
Deserves your pity?

IACHIMO  Lamentable! What,  85
To hide me from the radiant sun and solace°
I' th' dungeon by a snuff!°

IMOGEN  I pray you, sir,
Deliver with more openness your answers
To my demands. Why do you pity me?

IACHIMO
That others do,  90
I was about to say, enjoy your—but
It is an office° of the gods to venge it,
Not mine to speak on't.

IMOGEN  You do seem to know
Something of me or what concerns me. Pray you,
Since doubting° things go ill often hurts more  95
Than to be sure they do—for certainties
Either are past remedies, or, timely knowing,°
The remedy then born—discover° to me
What° both you spur and stop.

IACHIMO  Had I this cheek
To bathe my lips upon; this hand, whose touch,  100
Whose every touch, would force the feeler's soul
To th' oath of loyalty; this object, which
Takes prisoner the wild motion of mine eye,
Fixing it only here; should I, damned then,
Slaver with lips as common as the stairs  105
That mount the Capitol; join gripes° with hands
Made hard with hourly falsehood (falsehood, as
With labor); then bye-peeping° in an eye
Base and illustrous° as the smoky light
That's fed with stinking tallow—it were fit  110
That all the plagues of hell should at one time
Encounter° such revolt.°

IMOGEN  My lord, I fear,
Has forgot Britain.

IACHIMO  And himself. Not I
Inclined to this intelligence pronounce°
The beggary° of his change, but 'tis your graces  115
That from my mutest conscience° to my tongue
Charms this report out.

IMOGEN  Let me hear no more.

IACHIMO
O dearest soul, your cause doth strike my heart
With pity that doth make me sick. A lady

So fair, and fastened to an empery°  120
Would° make the great'st king double, to be partnered
With tomboys° hired with that self exhibition°
Which your own coffers yield; with diseased ventures°
That play with all infirmities for gold
Which rottenness can lend nature; such boiled stuff°  125
As well might poison poison! Be revenged,
Or she that bore you was no queen, and you
Recoil° from your great stock.

IMOGEN  Revenged?
How should I be revenged? If this be true—
As I have such a heart that both mine ears  130
Must not in haste abuse—if it be true,
How should I be revenged?

IACHIMO  Should he make me
Live like Diana's priest betwixt cold sheets,
Whiles he is vaulting variable ramps,°
In your despite, upon your purse? Revenge it.  135
I dedicate myself to your sweet pleasure,
More noble than that runagate° to your bed,
And will continue fast to your affection,
Still close° as sure.

IMOGEN  What ho, Pisanio!

IACHIMO
Let me my service tender on your lips.  140

IMOGEN
Away, I do condemn mine ears that have
So long attended thee.° If thou wert honorable,
Thou wouldst have told this tale for virtue, not
For such an end thou seek'st, as base as strange.
Thou wrong'st a gentleman who is as far  145
From thy report as thou from honor, and
Solicits here a lady that disdains
Thee and the devil alike. What ho, Pisanio!
The king my father shall be made acquainted
Of thy assault. If he shall think it fit  150
A saucy stranger in his court to mart°
As in a Romish stew° and to expound
His beastly mind to us, he hath a court
He little cares for and a daughter who
He not respects at all. What ho, Pisanio!  155

IACHIMO
O happy Leonatus! I may say
The credit° that thy lady hath of° thee
Deserves thy trust, and thy most perfect goodness
Her assured credit. Blessèd live you long,
A lady to the worthiest sir that ever  160
Country called his,° and you his mistress, only
For the most worthiest fit. Give me your pardon.
I have spoke this to know if your affiance°
Were deeply rooted, and shall make your lord
That which he is, new o'er; and he is one°  165
The truest mannered,° such a holy witch°

79 'tis i.e., heaven's bounty is  80 beyond all talents beyond
all natural endowments, i.e., inestimable  84 wrack disaster
86 solace find pleasure  87 snuff candle-end  92 office duty
95 doubting fearing  97 timely knowing if one knows in
time  98 discover reveal  99 What why  106 gripes grips
108 bye-peeping peeping sidelong  109 illustrous lackluster
112 Encounter confront; revolt inconstancy  113–14 Not
. . . pronounce I, though disinclined to bring this news,
report  115 beggary meanness  116 conscience knowledge

120 empery empire  121 Would which would  122
tomboys whores; self exhibition selfsame allowance  123
ventures whores  125 boiled stuff i.e., women who have
been "sweated" for venereal disease  128 Recoil decline
134 variable ramps fickle whores  137 runagate traitor
139 close secret  142 attended thee listened to you (in anger
Imogen shifts from formal "you" to familiar "thee," thus
treating Iachimo as an inferior; at line 168 she reverts to
"you")  151 to mart should do business  152 Romish stew
Roman bawdyhouse  157 credit trust; of in  161 his its own
163 affiance faith  165 one above all  166 truest mannered
most honestly behaved; witch charmer

That he enchants societies into° him.
Half all men's hearts are his.

IMOGEN            You make amends.

IACHIMO
He sits 'mongst men like a descended god.
He hath a kind of honor sets him off                                170
More than a mortal seeming.° Be not angry,
Most mighty princess, that I have adventured
To try your taking° of a false report, which hath
Honored with confirmation your great judgment
In the election of a sir so rare,                                    175
Which° you know cannot err. The love I bear him
Made me to fan° you thus, but the gods made you,
Unlike all others, chaffless. Pray your pardon.

IMOGEN
All's well, sir. Take my pow'r i' th' court for yours.

IACHIMO
My humble thanks. I had almost forgot
T' entreat your grace but in a small request,                        180
And yet of moment too, for it concerns
Your lord, myself, and other noble friends
Are° partners in the business.

IMOGEN            Pray what is't?

IACHIMO
Some dozen Romans of us and your lord—                              185
The best feather of our wing—have mingled sums
To buy a present for the emperor;
Which I, the factor° for the rest, have done
In France. 'Tis plate of rare device, and jewels
Of rich and exquisite form, their values great,                      190
And I am something curious,° being strange,°
To have them in safe stowage. May it please you
To take them in protection?

IMOGEN            Willingly;
And pawn mine honor for their safety. Since
My lord hath interest in them, I will keep them                      195
In my bedchamber.

IACHIMO            They are in a trunk
Attended by my men. I will make bold
To send them to you, only for this night.
I must aboard tomorrow.

IMOGEN            O, no, no.

IACHIMO
Yes, I beseech, or I shall short° my word                            200
By length'ning my return. From Gallia°
I crossed the seas on purpose and on promise
To see your grace.

IMOGEN            I thank you for your pains.
But not away tomorrow!

IACHIMO            O, I must, madam.
Therefore I shall beseech you, if you please                         205
To greet your lord with writing, do't tonight.
I have outstood my time, which is material
To th' tender° of our present.

IMOGEN            I will write.
Send your trunk to me; it shall safe be kept
And truly yielded you. You're very welcome.                          210

             *Exeunt [severally].*

---

167 **into** to   171 **mortal seeming** human appearance   173
**try your taking** test your reception   176 **Which** who   177
**fan** winnow   184 **Are** i.e., who are   188 **factor** agent   191
**curious** anxious; **strange** a foreigner   200 **short** fall short of
201 **Gallia** France   208 **tender** giving

# ACT II

## Scene I. [Britain.]

*Enter* CLOTEN *and the two* LORDS.

CLOTEN  Was there ever man had such luck? When I
kissed the jack,° upon an upcast° to be hit away! I had
a hundred pound on't. And then a whoreson jackanapes must take me up° for swearing, as if I borrowed
mine oaths of him and might not spend them at my       5
pleasure.

FIRST LORD  What got he by that? You have broke
his pate with your bowl.

SECOND LORD [*Aside.*]  If his wit had been like him
that broke it, it would have run all out.                10

CLOTEN  When a gentleman is disposed to swear, it is
not for any standers-by to curtail his oaths. Ha?

SECOND LORD  No, my lord—[*Aside.*] Nor crop the
ears of them.

CLOTEN  Whoreson dog, I gave him satisfaction!          15
Would he had been one of my rank.°

SECOND LORD [*Aside.*]  To have smelled like a fool.

CLOTEN  I am not vexed more at anything in th'
earth. A pox on't! I had rather not be so noble as I am.
They dare not fight with me because of the queen       20
my mother. Every jack-slave° hath his bellyful of
fighting, and I must go up and down like a cock that
nobody can match.

SECOND LORD [*Aside.*]  You are cock and capon too,
and° you crow, cock, with your comb on.                 25

CLOTEN  Sayest thou?

SECOND LORD  It is not fit your lordship should
undertake° every companion° that you give offense to.

CLOTEN  No, I know that, but it is fit I should commit
offense° to my inferiors.                                30

SECOND LORD  Ay, it is fit for your lordship only.

CLOTEN  Why, so I say.

FIRST LORD  Did you hear of a stranger° that's come
to court tonight?

CLOTEN  A stranger, and I not know on't?                 35

SECOND LORD [*Aside.*]  He's a strange fellow himself,
and knows it not.

FIRST LORD  There's an Italian come, and, 'tis thought,
one of Leonatus' friends.

CLOTEN  Leonatus? A banished rascal, and he's         40
another, whatsoever he be. Who told you of this
stranger?

FIRST LORD  One of your lordship's pages.

CLOTEN  Is it fit I went to look upon him? Is there no
derogation° in't?                                        45

SECOND LORD  You cannot derogate,° my lord.

CLOTEN  Not easily, I think.

SECOND LORD [*Aside.*]  You are a fool, granted;
therefore your issues,° being foolish, do not derogate.

---

**II.i.2 kissed the jack** came close to the target ball (in the game
of bowls); **upcast** chance   4 **take me up** rebuke me   16 **of
my rank** i.e., so I might have challenged him to a duel (the
Second Lord quibbles)   21 **jack-slave** lout   25 **and** if   28
**undertake** take on: **companion** low fellow   29–30 **commit
offense** offer battle   33 **stranger** foreigner   45 **derogation**
loss of dignity   46 **cannot derogate** do anything derogatory
to your rank (with quibble on the sense of "have no dignity
to lose")   49 **issues** deeds

CLOTEN    Come, I'll go see this Italian. What I have    50
lost today at bowls I'll win tonight of him. Come, go.
SECOND LORD    I'll attend your lordship.

*Exeunt* [CLOTEN *and* FIRST LORD].

That such a crafty devil as is his mother
Should yield the world this ass! A woman that
Bears all down° with her brain, and this her son    55
Cannot take two from twenty, for his heart,°
And leave eighteen. Alas, poor princess,
Thou divine Imogen, what thou endur'st,
Betwixt a father by thy stepdame governed,
A mother hourly coining plots, a wooer    60
More hateful than the foul expulsion is
Of thy dear husband, than that horrid act
Of the divorce he'ld make. The heavens hold firm
The walls of thy dear honor, keep unshaked
That temple, thy fair mind, that thou mayst stand,    65
T' enjoy thy banished lord and this great land!    *Exit.*

Scene II. [*Britain.*]

*Enter* IMOGEN *in her bed,*° *and a* LADY.

IMOGEN
Who's there? My woman Helen?
LADY                          Please you, madam.
IMOGEN
What hour is it?
LADY                Almost midnight, madam.
IMOGEN
I have read three hours then. Mine eyes are weak.
Fold down the leaf where I have left. To bed.
Take not away the taper, leave it burning;    5
And if thou canst awake by four o' th' clock,
I prithee call me. Sleep hath seized me wholly.

[*Exit* LADY.]

To your protection I commend me, gods.
From fairies° and the tempters of the night
Guard me, beseech ye!    10

*Sleeps.* IACHIMO [*comes*] *from the trunk.*

IACHIMO
The crickets sing, and man's o'erlabored sense
Repairs itself by rest. Our Tarquin° thus
Did softly press the rushes° ere he wakened
The chastity he wounded. Cytherea,°
How bravely° thou becom'st thy bed, fresh lily,°    15
And whiter than the sheets! That I might touch!
But kiss, one kiss! Rubies unparagoned,
How dearly they do't! 'Tis her breathing that
Perfumes the chamber thus. The flame o' th' taper
Bows toward her and would underpeep her lids    20
To see th' enclosèd lights, now canopied

Under these windows,° white and azure-laced
With blue of heaven's own tinct. But my design:
To note the chamber. I will write all down:
Such and such pictures; there the window; such    25
Th' adornment of her bed; the arras, figures,
Why, such and such; and the contents o' th' story.°
Ah, but some natural notes° about her body
Above ten thousand meaner movables°
Would testify, t' enrich mine inventory.    30
O sleep, thou ape° of death, lie dull° upon her.
And be her sense but as a monument,°
Thus in a chapel lying. Come off, come off—

[*Removing her bracelet.*]

As slippery as the Gordian knot was hard.
'Tis mine, and this will witness outwardly,    35
As strongly as the conscience° does within,
To th' madding of her lord. On her left breast
A mole cinque-spotted,° like the crimson drops
I' th' bottom of a cowslip. Here's a voucher°
Stronger than ever law could make. This secret    40
Will force him think I have picked the lock and ta'en
The treasure of her honor. No more. To what end?
Why should I write this down that's riveted,
Screwed to my memory? She hath been reading late
The tale of Tereus.° Here the leaf's turned down    45
Where Philomel gave up. I have enough.
To th' trunk again, and shut the spring of it.
Swift, swift, you dragons of the night, that dawning
May bare the raven's eye.° I lodge in fear.
Though this a heavenly angel, hell is here.    50

*Clock strikes.*

One, two, three. Time, time! [*Goes into the trunk.*]
                                        *Exeunt.*°

Scene III. [*Britain.*]

*Enter* CLOTEN *and* LORDS.

FIRST LORD    Your lordship is the most patient man in
loss, the most coldest° that ever turned up ace.°
CLOTEN    It would make any man cold° to lose.
FIRST LORD    But not every man patient after the
noble temper of your lordship. You are most hot and    5
furious when you win.
CLOTEN    Winning will put any man into courage. If I
could get this foolish Imogen, I should have gold
enough. It's almost morning, is't not?
FIRST LORD    Day, my lord.    10
CLOTEN    I would this music would come. I am advised
to give her music a-mornings; they say it will penetrate.°

22 **windows** shutters, i.e., eyelids   27 **th' story** the story
depicted on the arras (cf. II.iv.69)   28 **notes** marks   29
**meaner movables** lesser furnishings   31 **ape** mimic; **dull**
heavy   32 **monument** recumbent effigy on a tomb   36 **conscience** knowledge   38 **cinque-spotted** having five spots   39
**voucher** guarantee   45 **Tereus** who raped Philomela;
apparently the book is Ovid's *Metamorphoses*   49 **bare . . .
eye** the raven supposedly being an early bird   51 **s.d. Exeunt**
the bed and trunk are carried offstage or concealed by dropping
the front curtain
**II.iii.2 coldest** calmest; **ace** one, the lowest throw at dice (pun
on *ass*)   3 **cold** gloomy   12–14 **penetrate** affect emotionally
(with bawdy quibble)

55 **Bears all down** overcomes everything   56 **for his heart**
to save his life
**II.ii.s.d. Enter . . . bed** in Elizabethan open-stage production
the bed is "thrust out" upon the stage by attendants and the
trunk is carried on; in modern proscenium-arch production
the bed and trunk are usually "discovered" by raising the front
curtain   9 **fairies** i.e., malignant fairies   12 **Tarquin** who raped
Lucrece   13 **rushes** Elizabethan floor-covering   14 **Cytherea**
Venus   15 **bravely** magnificently; **lily** emblem of chastity

*Enter* MUSICIANS.

Come on, tune. If you can penetrate° her with your
fingering, so; we'll try with tongue too. If none will
do, let her remain, but I'll never give o'er.° First, a very
excellent good-conceited° thing; after, a wonderful
sweet air with admirable rich words to it—and then
let her consider.

                              *Song.*

    Hark, hark, the lark at heaven's gate sings,                    20
        And Phoebus 'gins° arise,
    His steeds to water at those springs
        On chaliced flowers that lies;
    And winking Mary-buds° begin
        To ope their golden eyes.                                   25
    With every thing that pretty is,
        My lady sweet, arise,
            Arise, arise!

CLOTEN     So, get you gone. If this penetrate, I will con-
sider° your music the better; if it do not, it is a vice° in  30
her ears which horsehairs° and calves' guts,° nor the
voice of unpaved° eunuch to boot, can never amend.
                                        [*Exeunt* MUSICIANS.]

*Enter* CYMBELINE *and* QUEEN.

SECOND LORD    Here comes the king.
CLOTEN    I am glad I was up so late, for that's the reason
I was up so early. He cannot choose but take this         35
service I have done fatherly. Good morrow to your
majesty and to my gracious mother.
CYMBELINE    Attend you here the door of our stern
daughter? Will she not forth?
CLOTEN    I have assailed her with musics, but she       40
vouchsafes no notice.
CYMBELINE
    The exile of her minion° is too new;
    She hath not yet forgot him. Some more time
    Must wear the print of his remembrance out,
    And then she's yours.
QUEEN                    You are most bound to th' king,   45
    Who lets go by no vantages° that may
    Prefer° you to his daughter. Frame° yourself
    To order solicits,° and be friended
    With aptness of the season. Make denials
    Increase your services. So seem as if                 50
    You were inspired to do those duties which
    You tender to her; that you in all obey her,
    Save when command to your dismission° tends,
    And therein you are senseless.°
CLOTEN                    Senseless? Not so.

[*Enter a* MESSENGER.]

MESSENGER
    So like you,° sir, ambassadors from Rome.            55
    The one is Caius Lucius.
CYMBELINE                    A worthy fellow,

16 **give o'er** give up   17 **good-conceited** well-devised
21 **Phoebus 'gins** Apollo (the sun) begins to   24 **winking
Mary-buds** closed marigold buds   29–30 **consider** reward
30 **vice** flaw   31 **horsehairs** bowstrings; **calves' guts**
fiddle-strings   32 **unpaved** unstoned (i.e., castrated)   42
**minion** darling   46 **vantages** opportunities   47 **Prefer**
recommend; **Frame** prepare   48 **solicits** solicitations   53
**dismission** rejection   54 **senseless** insensible   55 **So like you**
if you please

Albeit he comes on angry purpose now.
But that's no fault of his. We must receive him
According to the honor of his sender,
And towards himself, his goodness forespent° on us,   60
We must extend our notice. Our dear son,
When you have given good morning to your mistress,
Attend the queen and us. We shall have need
T' employ you towards this Roman. Come, our queen.
                            *Exeunt [all but* CLOTEN].
CLOTEN
    If she be up, I'll speak with her; if not,           65
    Let her lie still and dream. By your leave, ho!

[*Knocks.*]

    I know her women are about her. What
    If I do line° one of their hands? 'Tis gold
    Which buys admittance—oft it doth—yea, and makes
    Diana's rangers° false° themselves, yield up           70
    Their deer to th' stand o' th' stealer;° and 'tis gold
    Which makes the true man killed and saves the thief,
    Nay, sometime hangs both thief and true man. What
    Can it not do and undo? I will make
    One of her women lawyer to° me, for                    75
    I yet not understand° the case myself.
    By your leave.

*Knocks. Enter a* LADY.

LADY
    Who's there that knocks?
CLOTEN                    A gentleman.
LADY                                      No more?
CLOTEN
    Yes, and a gentlewoman's son.
LADY                                That's more
    Than some whose tailors are as dear as yours          80
    Can justly boast of. What's your lordship's pleasure?
CLOTEN
    Your lady's person. Is she ready?°
LADY                                      Ay,
    To keep her chamber.
CLOTEN                    There is gold for you.
    Sell me your good report.
LADY
    How? My good name? Or to report of you               85
    What I shall think is good? The princess!

*Enter* IMOGEN. [*Exit* LADY.]

CLOTEN
    Good morrow, fairest sister. Your sweet hand.
IMOGEN
    Good morrow, sir. You lay out too much pains
    For purchasing but trouble. The thanks I give
    Is telling you that I am poor of thanks               90
    And scarce can spare them.
CLOTEN                    Still I swear I love you.
IMOGEN
    If you but said so, 'twere as deep° with me.

60 **forespent** having earlier been spent   68 **line** i.e., with
money   70 **rangers** gamekeepers; **false** betray   71 **stand
. . . stealer** standing-place of the hunter (quibble on the
sense of "erection of the phallus")   75 **lawyer to** quibble on
*lower to*, i.e., lie down for   76 **understand** quibble on *stand
under*, i.e., penetrate   82 **ready** dressed   92 **deep** effective

If you swear still,° your recompense is still
That I regard it not.

CLOTEN                    This is no answer.

IMOGEN
But° that you shall not say I yield, being silent,          95
I would not speak. I pray you spare me. Faith,
I shall unfold° equal discourtesy°
To your best kindness. One of your great knowing°
Should learn, being taught, forbearance.

CLOTEN
To leave you in your madness, 'twere my sin.          100
I will not.

IMOGEN
Fools are not mad folks.

CLOTEN                    Do you call me fool?

IMOGEN
As I am mad, I do.
If you'll be patient, I'll no more be mad;
That cures us both. I am much sorry, sir,          105
You put me to forget a lady's manners
By being so verbal;° and learn now for all
That I, which know my heart, do here pronounce
By th' very truth of it, I care not for you,
And am so near the lack of charity          110
To accuse myself I hate° you—which I had rather
You felt than make't my boast.

CLOTEN                    You sin against
Obedience, which you owe your father. For
The contract you pretend° with that base wretch,
One bred of alms and fostered with cold dishes,          115
With scraps o' th' court—it is no contract, none.
And though it be allowed in meaner° parties—
Yet who than he more mean?—to knit their souls,
On whom there is no more dependency°
But brats and beggary, in self-figured° knot;          120
Yet you are curbed from that enlargement° by
The consequence° o' th' crown, and must not foil°
The precious note° of it with a base slave,
A hilding for° a livery, a squire's cloth,
A pantler°—not so eminent.

IMOGEN                    Profane fellow!          125
Wert thou the son of Jupiter, and no more
But what thou art besides, thou wert too base
To be his groom. Thou wert dignified° enough,
Even to the point of envy, if 'twere made
Comparative for your virtues to be styled          130
The under-hangman of his kingdom,° and hated
For being preferred° so well.

CLOTEN                    The south fog° rot him!

IMOGEN
He never can meet more mischance than come
To be but named of thee. His meanest garment

That ever hath but clipped° his body is dearer          135
In my respect° than all the hairs above thee,
Were they all made such men. How now, Pisanio?

*Enter* PISANIO.

CLOTEN
"His garment"? Now the devil—

IMOGEN
To Dorothy my woman hie thee presently.°

CLOTEN
"His garment"?

IMOGEN                    I am sprited° with a fool,          140
Frighted, and angered worse. Go bid my woman
Search for a jewel that too casually
Hath left mine arm. It was thy master's. Shrew° me
If I would lose it for a revenue
Of any king's in Europe. I do think          145
I saw't this morning; confident I am
Last night 'twas on mine arm; I kissed it.
I hope it be not gone to tell my lord
That I kiss aught but he.

PISANIO                    'Twill not be lost.

IMOGEN
I hope so.° Go and search.          [*Exit* PISANIO.]

CLOTEN                    You have abused me.          150
"His meanest garment"?

IMOGEN                    Ay, I said so, sir.
If you will make't an action,° call witness to't.

CLOTEN
I will inform your father.

IMOGEN                    Your mother too.
She's my good lady and will conceive,° I hope,
But the worst of me. So I leave you, sir,          155
To th' worst of discontent.          *Exit.*

CLOTEN                    I'll be revenged.
"His meanest garment"? Well.          *Exit.°*


Scene IV. [*Rome.*]

POSTHUMUS
Fear it not, sir. I would I were so sure
To win the king as I am bold° her honor
Will remain hers.

PHILARIO                    What means° do you make to him?

POSTHUMUS
Not any, but abide the change of time,
Quake in the present winter's state, and wish          5
That warmer days would come. In these feared° hopes
I barely gratify° your love; they failing,
I must die much your debtor.

PHILARIO
Your very goodness and your company
O'erpays all I can do. By this,° your king          10
Hath heard of great Augustus; Caius Lucius
Will do's commission throughly. And I think
He'll grant the tribute, send th' arrearages,

---

**93 still** continually  **95 But** so  **97 unfold** display; **equal discourtesy** i.e., discourtesy equal  **98 knowing** knowledge  **107 verbal** talkative  **111 To . . . hate** that I accuse myself of hating  **113–14 For . . . pretend** as for the marriage contract you claim  **117 meaner** lower-ranking  **119 dependency** retinue  **120 self-figured** shaped by one's self  **121 enlargement** freedom  **122 consequence** importance; **foil** defile  **123 note** eminence, importance  **124 hilding for** good-for-nothing fit only for  **125 pantler** pantry-servant  **128 dignified** given honor  **129–31 if . . . kingdom** if, according to the virtue of each of you, you were made under-hangman and he king (Heilman)  **132 preferred** advanced; **south fog** the damp, supposedly unhealthy, south wind

**135 clipped** embraced  **136 respect** regard  **139 presently** immediately  **140 sprited** haunted  **143 Shrew** curse  **150 so** i.e., not  **152 action** lawsuit  **154 conceive** come to believe  **157 s.d. Exit** by the other door
**II.iv.2 bold** confident  **3 means** overtures  **6 feared** fear-laden  **7 gratify** repay  **10 this** this time

Or look upon our Romans, whose remembrance
Is yet fresh in their grief.
POSTHUMUS                    I do believe,          15
Statist° though I am none, nor like to be,
That this will prove a war; and you shall hear
The legions now in Gallia sooner landed
In our not-fearing Britain than have tidings
Of any penny tribute paid. Our countrymen          20
Are men more ordered than when Julius Caesar
Smiled at their lack of skill but found their courage
Worthy his frowning at. Their discipline,
Now mingled with their courages, will make known
To their approvers° they are people such          25
That mend upon° the world.

*Enter* IACHIMO.

PHILARIO                         See, Iachimo!
POSTHUMUS
The swiftest harts have posted° you by land,
And winds of all the corners° kissed your sails
To make your vessel nimble.
PHILARIO                         Welcome, sir.
POSTHUMUS
I hope the briefness of your answer° made          30
The speediness of your return.
IACHIMO                         Your lady
Is one of the fairest that I have looked upon.
POSTHUMUS
And therewithal the best, or let her beauty
Look through a casement to allure false hearts
And be false with them.
IACHIMO                 Here are letters° for you.     35
POSTHUMUS
Their tenor good, I trust.
IACHIMO                         'Tis very like.
POSTHUMUS
Was Caius Lucius in the Briton court
When you were there?
IACHIMO                 He was expected then,
But not approached.
POSTHUMUS                 All is well yet.
Sparkles this stone as it was wont, or is't not          40
Too dull for your good wearing?
IACHIMO                         If I have lost it,
I should have lost the worth of it in gold.
I'll make a journey twice as far t' enjoy
A second night of such sweet shortness which
Was mine in Britain—for the ring is won.          45
POSTHUMUS
The stone's too hard to come by.
IACHIMO                         Not a whit,
Your lady being so easy.
POSTHUMUS                 Make not, sir,
Your loss your sport. I hope you know that we
Must not continue friends.
IACHIMO                 Good sir, we must,
If you keep covenant. Had I not brought          50
The knowledge° of your mistress home, I grant

We were to question° farther, but I now
Profess myself the winner of her honor,
Together with your ring, and not the wronger
Of her or you, having proceeded but          55
By both your wills.
POSTHUMUS         If you can make't apparent
That you have tasted her in bed, my hand
And ring is yours. If not, the foul opinion
You had of her pure honor gains or loses
Your sword or mine, or masterless leave° both          60
To who shall find them.
IACHIMO                 Sir, my circumstances,°
Being so near the truth as I will make them,
Must first induce you to believe; whose strength
I will confirm with oath, which I doubt not
You'll give me leave to spare° when you shall find          65
You need it not.
POSTHUMUS         Proceed.
IACHIMO                 First, her bedchamber—
Where I confess I slept not, but profess
Had that was well worth watching°—it was hanged
With tapestry of silk and silver; the story
Proud Cleopatra, when she met her Roman°          70
And Cydnus swelled above the banks, or° for
The press of boats or pride: a piece of work
So bravely° done, so rich, that it did strive
In workmanship and value;° which I wondered
Could be so rarely and exactly wrought,          75
Since the true life on't was—
POSTHUMUS                 This is true,
And this you might have heard of here, by me
Or by some other.
IACHIMO         More particulars
Must justify° my knowledge.
POSTHUMUS                 So they must,
Or do your honor injury.
IACHIMO                 The chimney°          80
Is south the chamber, and the chimney-piece°
Chaste Dian bathing. Never saw I figures
So likely to report° themselves. The cutter°
Was as another Nature, dumb;° outwent° her,
Motion and breath left out.
POSTHUMUS                 This is a thing          85
Which you might from relation° likewise reap,
Being, as it is, much spoke of.
IACHIMO                 The roof o' th' chamber
With golden cherubins is fretted.° Her andirons—
I had forgot them—were two winking° Cupids
Of silver, each on one foot standing, nicely          90
Depending on their brands.°
POSTHUMUS                 This is her honor!
Let it be granted you have seen all this—and praise

---

16 **Statist** politician  25 **approvers** testers  26 **That mend upon** whose reputation grows with  27 **have posted** must have sped  28 **corners** i.e., of the earth  30 **your answer** the answer you received  35 **are letters** is a letter  51 **knowledge** carnal knowledge

52 **question** dispute (as in a duel)  60 **leave** let it leave  61 **circumstances** details  65 **spare** omit  68 **watching** remaining awake for  70 **Roman** Antony  71 **or** either  73 **bravely** finely  73–74 **it . . . value** it was doubtful whether the workmanship or the intrinsic value was greater  79 **justify** prove  80 **chimney** fireplace  81 **chimney-piece** sculpture placed over the fireplace  83 **likely to report** apt to identify; **cutter** sculptor  84 **as . . . dumb** like Nature in creative power although unable to make the sculpture speak; **outwent** surpassed  86 **relation** report  88 **fretted** carved  89 **winking** with closed eyes, i.e., blind  91 **Depending . . . brands** leaning on their torches

Be given to your remembrance—the description
Of what is in her chamber nothing saves
The wager you have laid.

IACHIMO                    Then, if you can          95

[*Showing the bracelet.*]

Be pale,° I beg but leave to air this jewel. See!
And now 'tis up° again. It must be married
To that your diamond; I'll keep them.

POSTHUMUS                    Jove!
Once more let me behold it. Is it that
Which I left with her?

IACHIMO                    Sir, I thank her, that.          100
She stripped it from her arm; I see her yet.
Her pretty action did outsell° her gift,
And yet enriched it too. She gave it me and said
She prized it once.

POSTHUMUS          May be she plucked it off
To send it me.

IACHIMO          She writes so to you, doth she?          105

POSTHUMUS
O, no, no, no, 'tis true. Here, take this too.

[*Giving the ring.*]

It is a basilisk° unto mine eye,
Kills me to look on't. Let there be no honor
Where there is beauty; truth, where semblance; love,
Where there's another man. The vows of women          110
Of no more bondage be to where they are made
Than they are to their virtues, which is nothing.°
O, above measure false!

PHILARIO                    Have patience, sir,
And take your ring again; 'tis not yet won.
It may be probable° she lost it, or          115
Who knows if one° her women, being corrupted,
Hath stol'n it from her?

POSTHUMUS                    Very true,
And so I hope he came by't. Back my ring;
Render to me some corporal sign about her
More evident° than this, for this was stol'n.          120

IACHIMO
By Jupiter, I had it from her arm.

POSTHUMUS
Hark you, he swears; by Jupiter he swears.
'Tis true—nay, keep the ring—'tis true. I am sure
She would not lose it. Her attendants are
All sworn° and honorable. They induced to steal it?          125
And by a stranger? No, he hath enjoyed her.
The cognizance° of her incontinency
Is this.° She hath bought the name of whore thus
          dearly.
There, take thy hire,° and all the fiends of hell
Divide themselves between you!

PHILARIO                    Sir, be patient.          130

This is not strong enough to be believed
Of one persuaded° well of.

POSTHUMUS                    Never talk on't.
She hath been colted° by him.

IACHIMO                    If you seek
For further satisfying, under her breast—
Worthy the pressing—lies a mole, right proud          135
Of that most delicate lodging. By my life,
I kissed it, and it gave me present° hunger
To feed again, though full. You do remember
This stain° upon her?

POSTHUMUS          Ay, and it doth confirm
Another stain,° as big as hell can hold,          140
Were there no more but it.

IACHIMO                    Will you hear more?

POSTHUMUS
Spare your arithmetic; never count the turns.
Once, and a million!

IACHIMO                    I'll be sworn.

POSTHUMUS                    No swearing.
If you will swear you have not done't, you lie,
And I will kill thee if thou dost deny          145
Thou'st made me cuckold.

IACHIMO                    I'll deny nothing.

POSTHUMUS
O that I had her here, to tear her limb-meal!°
I will go there and do't i' th' court, before
Her father. I'll do something.          *Exit.*

PHILARIO                    Quite besides
The government° of patience! You have won.          150
Let's follow him and pervert° the present wrath
He hath against himself.

IACHIMO                    With all my heart.     *Exeunt.*

[*Scene V. Rome.*]

*Enter* POSTHUMUS.

POSTHUMUS
Is there no way for men to be,° but women
Must be half-workers?° We are all bastards,
And that most venerable man which I
Did call my father was I know not where
When I was stamped.° Some coiner° with his tools          5
Made me a counterfeit; yet my mother seemed
The Dian° of that time. So doth my wife
The nonpareil° of this. O, vengeance, vengeance!
Me of my lawful pleasure she restrained
And prayed me oft forbearance—did it with          10
A pudency° so rosy, the sweet view on't°
Might well have warmed old Saturn°—that I thought
          her
As chaste as unsunned snow. O, all the devils!
This yellow° Iachimo in an hour, was't not?
Or less? At first?° Perchance he spoke not, but,          15

**96 Be pale** remain unflushed, i.e., calm   **97 up** put up,
pocketed   **102 outsell** exceed in value   **107 basilisk** monster
supposedly capable of killing by look   **110–12 The vows
. . . nothing** Let the vows of women be no more binding
to the recipients of them than women are bound to their
own virtues—which is not at all (Nosworthy)   **115 probable**
provable   **116 one** one of   **120 evident** conclusive   **125
sworn** i.e., to loyalty   **127 cognizance** badge   **128 this**
the bracelet   **129 hire** reward

**132 persuaded** that we are persuaded to think   **133 colted**
possessed sexually   **137 present** immediate   **139 stain** mark
**140 stain** corruption   **147 limb-meal** limb from limb
**150 government** control   **151 pervert** divert
**II.v.1 be** exist   **2 half-workers** i.e., in begetting   **5 stamped**
minted; **coiner** counterfeiter   **7 Dian** Diana (goddess of
chastity)   **8 nonpareil** one without equal   **11 pudency**
modesty; **on't** of it   **12 Saturn** considered to be cold and
gloomy   **14 yellow** i.e., of complexion   **15 At first** immediately

Like a full-acorned° boar, a German one,
Cried "O!" and mounted; found no opposition
But what he looked for should oppose and she
Should from encounter guard. Could I find out
The woman's part in me! For there's no motion°    20
That tends to vice in man but I affirm
It is the woman's part. Be it lying, note it,
The woman's; flattering, hers; deceiving, hers;
Lust and rank° thoughts, hers, hers; revenges, hers;
Ambitions, covetings, change of prides,° disdain,    25
Nice° longing, slanders, mutability,°
All faults that have a name, nay, that hell knows,
Why, hers, in part or all, but rather all.
For even to vice
They are not constant, but are changing still    30
One vice but of a minute old for one
Not half so old as that. I'll write against them,
Detest them, curse them. Yet 'tis greater skill°
In a true hate to pray they have their will;
The very devils cannot plague them better.     *Exit.* 35

# ACT III

## Scene I. [*Britain.*]

*Enter in state* CYMBELINE, QUEEN, CLOTEN, *and*
LORDS *at one door and, at another,* Caius LUCIUS *and*
ATTENDANTS.

CYMBELINE
Now say, what would Augustus Caesar with us?
LUCIUS
When Julius Caesar, whose remembrance yet
Lives in men's eyes and will to ears and tongues
Be theme and hearing ever, was in this Britain
And conquered it, Cassibelan thine uncle,    5
Famous in Caesar's praises no whit less
Than in his feats deserving it, for him
And his succession granted Rome a tribute,
Yearly three thousand pounds, which by thee lately
Is left untendered.
QUEEN               And, to kill the marvel,°    10
Shall be so ever.
CLOTEN          There be many Caesars
Ere such another Julius. Britain's a world
By itself, and we will nothing pay
For wearing our own noses.
QUEEN               That opportunity
Which then they had to take from's, to resume    15
We have again. Remember, sir, my liege,
The kings your ancestors, together with
The natural bravery of your isle, which stands
As Neptune's park, ribbèd° and palèd° in
With rocks unscalable and roaring waters,    20
With sands that will not bear your enemies' boats
But suck them up to th' topmast. A kind of conquest

Caesar made here, but made not here his brag
Of "Came and saw and overcame." With shame,
The first that ever touched him, he was carried    25
From off our coast, twice beaten; and his shipping,
Poor ignorant° baubles on our terrible seas,
Like eggshells moved upon their surges, cracked
As easily 'gainst our rocks. For joy whereof
The famed Cassibelan, who was once at point°—    30
O giglot° Fortune!—to master° Caesar's sword,
Made Lud's Town° with rejoicing fires bright
And Britons strut with courage.
CLOTEN   Come, there's no more tribute to be paid.
Our kingdom is stronger than it was at that time, and,    35
as I said, there is no moe° such Caesars. Other of them
may have crooked° noses, but to owe° such straight
arms, none.
CYMBELINE
Son, let your mother end.
CLOTEN   We have yet many among us can gripe° as    40
hard as Cassibelan. I do not say I am one, but I have a
hand. Why tribute? Why should we pay tribute? If
Caesar can hide the sun from us with a blanket or put
the moon in his pocket, we will pay him tribute for
light; else, sir, no more tribute, pray you now.    45
CYMBELINE
You must know,
Till the injurious° Romans did extort
This tribute from us, we were free. Caesar's ambition,
Which swelled so much that it did almost stretch
The sides o' th' world, against all color° here    50
Did put the yoke upon's; which to shake off
Becomes a warlike people, whom we reckon
Ourselves to be. We do say then to Caesar,
Our ancestor was that Mulmutius which
Ordained our laws, whose use the sword of Caesar    55
Hath too much mangled, whose repair and franchise°
Shall, by the power we hold, be our good deed,
Though Rome be therefore angry. Mulmutius made
our laws,
Who was the first of Britain which did put
His brows within a golden crown and called    60
Himself a king.
LUCIUS         I am sorry, Cymbeline,
That I am to pronounce Augustus Caesar—
Caesar, that hath moe kings his° servants than
Thyself domestic officers—thine enemy.
Receive it from me then: war and confusion°    65
In Caesar's name pronounce I 'gainst thee. Look
For fury not to be resisted. Thus defied,
I thank thee for myself.
CYMBELINE        Thou art welcome, Caius.
Thy Caesar knighted me; my youth I spent
Much under him; of him I gathered honor,    70
Which he to seek° of me again, perforce,
Behooves me keep at utterance.° I am perfect°

---

16 **full-acorned** fed full with acorns   20 **motion** impulse
24 **rank** lascivious   25 **change of prides** varying extravagances   26 **Nice** wanton; **mutability** inconstancy   33 **skill**
reason
III.i.10 **kill the marvel** end the astonishment (caused by
nonpayment)   19 **ribbèd** enclosed; **palèd** fenced

27 **ignorant** inexperienced   30 **at point** at the point   31
**giglot** wanton; **to master** of mastering   32 **Lud's Town**
London   36 **moe** more   37 **crooked** i.e., Roman; **owe** own
40 **gripe** grasp   47 **injurious** insulting   50 **against all color**
without any right   56 **franchise** free exercise   63 **his** as
his   65 **confusion** destruction   71 **he to seek** his seeking   72
**keep at utterance** defend to the last ditch; **perfect** well
aware

That the Pannonians and Dalmatians° for
Their liberties are now in arms, a precedent
Which not to read would show the Britons cold.° 75
So Caesar shall not find them.

LUCIUS                          Let proof° speak.

CLOTEN  His majesty bids you welcome. Make pastime
with us a day or two, or longer. If you seek us afterwards in other terms, you shall find us in our salt-
water girdle; if you beat us out of it, it is yours. If you 80
fall in the adventure, our crows shall fare the better
for you, and there's an end.

LUCIUS  So, sir.

CYMBELINE
I know your master's pleasure, and he mine.
All the remain° is, welcome.                    *Exeunt.* 85

Scene II. [*Britain.*]

*Enter* PISANIO, *reading of a letter.*

PISANIO
How? of adultery? Wherefore write you not
What monsters her accuse? Leonatus,
Of master, what a strange° infection
Is fall'n into thy ear! What false Italian,
As poisonous-tongued as handed, hath prevailed          5
On thy too ready hearing? Disloyal? No.
She's punished for her truth° and undergoes,°
More goddesslike than wifelike, such assaults
As would take in° some virtue. O my master,
Thy mind to° her is now as low as were                   10
Thy fortunes. How? That I should murder her,
Upon the love and truth and vows which I
Have made to thy command? I her? Her blood?
If it be so to do good service, never
Let me be counted serviceable. How look I                15
That I should seem to lack humanity
So much as this fact° comes to? [*Reading.*] "Do't! The
    letter
That I have sent her, by her own command
Shall give thee opportunity." O damned paper,
Black as the ink that's on thee! Senseless° bauble,     20
Art thou a fedary for° this act, and look'st
So virginlike without? Lo, here she comes.

*Enter* IMOGEN.

I am ignorant in° what I am commanded.

IMOGEN
How now, Pisanio?

PISANIO
Madam, here is a letter from my lord.                    25

IMOGEN
Who, thy lord? That is my lord Leonatus?
O, learn'd indeed were that astronomer°
That knew the stars as I his characters;°

He'ld lay the future open. You good gods,
Let what is here contained relish of love,              30
Of my lord's health, of his content—yet not°
That we two are asunder; let that grieve him.
Some griefs are med'cinable;° that is one of them,
For it doth physic love°—of his content
All but in that. Good wax, thy leave. Blest be          35
You bees that make these locks of counsel.° Lovers
And men in dangerous bonds° pray not alike;
Though forfeiters° you cast in prison, yet
You clasp young Cupid's tables.° Good news, gods!

[*Reading.*]

"Justice and your father's wrath, should he take me in  40
his dominion, could not be so cruel to me as° you, O
the dearest of creatures, would even renew me with
your eyes. Take notice that I am in Cambria° at
Milford Haven. What your own love will out of this
advise you, follow. So he wishes you all happiness,     45
that remains loyal to his vow, and your increasing in
love.                               *Leonatus Posthumus.*"

O, for a horse with wings! Hear'st thou, Pisanio?
He is at Milford Haven. Read, and tell me
How far 'tis thither. If one of mean affairs°           50
May plod it in a week, why may not I
Glide thither in a day? Then, true Pisanio,
Who long'st like me to see thy lord, who long'st—
O, let me bate°—but not like me, yet long'st,
But in a fainter kind—O, not like me!                   55
For mine's beyond beyond: say, and speak thick°—
Love's counselor should fill the bores of hearing,°
To th' smothering of the sense—how far it is
To this same blessèd Milford. And by th' way°
Tell me how Wales was made so happy as                  60
T' inherit such a haven. But first of all,
How we may steal from hence, and for the gap
That we shall make in time from our hence-going
And our return, to excuse. But first, how get hence?
Why should excuse be born or ere begot?°               65
We'll talk of that hereafter. Prithee speak,
How many score of miles may we well rid°
'Twixt hour and hour?

PISANIO                    One score 'twixt sun and sun,
Madam, 's enough for you, and too much too.

IMOGEN
Why, one that rode to's execution, man,                 70
Could never go so slow. I have heard of riding wagers
Where horses have been nimbler than the sands
That run i' th' clock's behalf.° But this is fool'ry.
Go bid my woman feign a sickness, say
She'll home to her father; and provide me presently°    75
A riding suit, no costlier than would fit

---

**73 Pannonians and Dalmatians** inhabitants of present-day
Hungary and Yugoslavia  **75 cold** deficient in spirit  **76
proof** experience  **85 the remain** that remains
**III.ii.3 strange** foreign  **7 truth** fidelity; **undergoes** endures
**9 take in** conquer  **10 to** compared with  **17 fact** crime  **20
Senseless** inanimate  **21 fedary for** accomplice in  **23 am
ignorant in** will pretend ignorance of  **27 astronomer**
astrologer  **28 characters** handwriting

**31 not** not content  **33 med'cinable** curative  **34 physic love**
keep love healthy  **36 locks of counsel** waxen seals  **37 in
dangerous bonds** under contracts imposing penalties  **38
forfeiters** contract-violators  **39 tables** notebooks  **41 as** but
that  **43 Cambria** Wales  **50 mean affairs** ordinary business
**54 bate** abate, modify (the statement)  **56 thick** profusely
**57 bores of hearing** ears  **59 by th' way** on the way  **65 or
ere begot** i.e., before conception (of the deed that makes
excuse necessary)  **67 rid** cover  **73 i' . . . behalf** in place
of a clock  **75 presently** immediately

A franklin's° housewife.°
ISANIO            Madam, you're best consider.
IMOGEN
I see before me,° man. Nor here, nor here,°
Nor what ensues,° but have a fog in them
That I cannot look through. Away, I prithee;     80
Do as I bid thee. There's no more to say.
Accessible is none but Milford way. *Exeunt [severally].*

### Scene III. [*Wales.*]

*Enter* BELARIUS, GUIDERIUS, *and* ARVIRAGUS.

BELARIUS
A goodly day not to keep house with such
Whose roof's as low as ours! Stoop, boys. This gate°
Instructs you how t' adore the heavens and bows you°
To a morning's holy office. The gates of monarchs
Are arched so high that giants may jet° through     5
And keep their impious turbans on without
Good morrow to the sun. Hail, thou fair heaven!
We house i' th' rock, yet use thee not so hardly°
As prouder livers do.
GUIDERIUS        Hail, heaven!
ARVIRAGUS                 Hail, heaven!
BELARIUS
Now for our mountain sport. Up to yond hill;     10
Your legs are young. I'll tread these flats. Consider,
When you above perceive me like a crow,
That it is place° which lessens and sets off,°
And you may then revolve what tales I have told you
Of courts, of princes, of the tricks in war.     15
This° service is not service, so being done,
But being so allowed.° To apprehend thus
Draws us a profit from all things we see,
And often, to our comfort, shall we find
The sharded° beetle in a safer hold°     20
Than is the full-winged eagle. O, this life
Is nobler than attending for a check,°
Richer than doing nothing for a bribe,
Prouder than rustling in unpaid-for silk:
Such gain the cap° of him that makes him fine°     25
Yet keeps his book uncrossed.° No life to ours.
GUIDERIUS
Out of your proof° you speak. We poor unfledged
Have never winged from view o' th' nest, nor know
not
What air's from home. Haply this life is best
If quiet life be best, sweeter to you     30
That have a sharper known, well corresponding
With your stiff age; but unto us it is
A cell of ignorance, traveling abed,°

A prison, or a debtor that not dares
To stride a limit.°
ARVIRAGUS       What should we speak of     35
When we are old as you? When we shall hear
The rain and wind beat dark December, how
In this our pinching° cave shall we discourse
The freezing hours away? We have seen nothing.
We are beastly:° subtle as the fox for prey,     40
Like° warlike as the wolf for what we eat.
Our valor is to chase what flies. Our cage
We make a choir, as doth the prisoned bird,
And sing our bondage freely.
BELARIUS               How you speak!
Did you but know the city's usuries     45
And felt them knowingly; the art o' th' court,
As hard to leave as keep,° whose top to climb
Is certain falling, or so slipp'ry that
The fear's as bad as falling; the toil o' th' war,
A pain° that only seems to seek out danger     50
I' th' name of fame and honor, which dies i' th' search
And hath as oft a sland'rous epitaph
As record of fair act; nay, many times
Doth ill deserve° by doing well; what's worse,
Must curtsy at the censure. O boys, this story     55
The world may read in me. My body's marked
With Roman swords, and my report° was once
First with the best of note.° Cymbeline loved me,
And when a soldier was the theme, my name
Was not far off. Then was I as a tree     60
Whose boughs did bend with fruit. But in one night
A storm or robbery, call it what you will,
Shook down my mellow hangings,° nay, my leaves,
And left me bare to weather.
GUIDERIUS            Uncertain favor!
BELARIUS
My fault being nothing, as I have told you oft,     65
But that two villains, whose false oaths prevailed
Before my perfect honor, swore to Cymbeline
I was confederate with the Romans. So
Followed my banishment, and this twenty years
This rock and these demesnes have been my world,     70
Where I have lived at honest freedom, paid
More pious debts to heaven than in all
The fore-end° of my time. But up to th' mountains!
This is not hunters' language. He that strikes
The venison first shall be the lord o' th' feast;     75
To him the other two shall minister,
And we will fear no poison, which attends°
In place of greater state. I'll meet you in the valleys.
                *Exeunt* [GUIDERIUS *and* ARVIRAGUS].
How hard it is to hide the sparks of nature!
These boys know little they are sons to th' king,     80
Nor Cymbeline dreams that they are alive.
They think they are mine, and though trained up thus
meanly
I' th' cave wherein they bow, their thoughts do hit
The roofs of palaces, and nature prompts them
In simple and low things to prince it much     85

---

**77 franklin** small landowner; **housewife** pronounced "huzzif"
**78 before me** i.e., what is immediately ahead; **Nor here,
nor here** neither to this side nor that   **79 what ensues** the
eventual outcome
**III.iii.2 This gate** one of the tiring-house doors (representing
the "cave")  **3 bows you** makes you bow  **5 jet** strut  **8
hardly** badly  **13 place** position; **sets off** displays to advantage
**16 This** any particular  **17 allowed** approved  **20 sharded**
provided with wing-cases; **hold** stronghold  **22 attending
. . . check** doing service at court only to receive a rebuke
**25 gain the cap** win approval; **makes him fine** dresses
elegantly  **26 keeps . . . uncrossed** does not cancel the debts
in his account book  **27 proof** experience  **33 abed** i.e., in
imagination

**35 stride a limit** step over a boundary  **38 pinching** distress-
ingly cold  **40 beastly** beastlike  **41 Like** as  **47 keep** remain
at  **50 pain** labor  **54 deserve** earn  **57 report** reputation
**58 note** reputation  **63 hangings** fruit  **73 fore-end** early
part  **77 attends** is present

Beyond the trick° of others. This Polydore,
The heir of Cymbeline and Britain, who
The king his father called Guiderius—Jove!
When on my three-foot stool I sit and tell
The warlike feats I have done, his spirits fly out 90
Into my story; say, "Thus mine enemy fell,
And thus I set my foot on's neck," even then
The princely blood flows in his cheek, he sweats,
Strains his young nerves,° and puts himself in posture
That acts my words. The younger brother Cadwal, 95
Once Arviragus, in as like a figure°
Strikes life into my speech and shows much more

[*Horn.*]

His own conceiving.° Hark, the game is roused!
O Cymbeline, heaven and my conscience knows
Thou didst unjustly banish me; whereon, 100
At three and two years old, I stole these babes,
Thinking to bar thee of succession as
Thou refts° me of my lands. Euriphile,
Thou wast their nurse; they took thee for their mother,
And every day do honor to her grave. 105
Myself, Belarius, that am Morgan called,
They take for natural father. The game is up.° *Exit.*

Scene IV. [*Wales.*]

*Enter* PISANIO *and* IMOGEN.

IMOGEN
Thou told'st me, when we came from horse, the place
Was near at hand. Ne'er longed my mother so
To see me first as I have° now. Pisanio, man,
Where is Posthumus? What is in thy mind
That makes thee stare thus? Wherefore breaks that sigh 5
From th' inward of thee? One but painted thus
Would be interpreted a thing perplexed°
Beyond self-explication. Put thyself
Into a havior° of less fear, ere wildness°
Vanquish my staider senses. What's the matter?° 10
Why tender'st thou that paper to me with
A look untender? If't be summer news,
Smile to't before; if winterly, thou need'st
But keep that count'nance still. My husband's hand?
That drug-damned Italy hath outcraftied° him, 15
And he's at some hard point.° Speak, man! Thy tongue
May take off some extremity,° which to read
Would be even mortal to me.
PISANIO                                     Please you read,
And you shall find me, wretched man, a thing
The most disdained of fortune. 20
IMOGEN (*Reads.*)   "Thy mistress, Pisanio, hath played
the strumpet in my bed, the testimonies whereof lies
bleeding in me. I speak not out of weak surmises, but
from proof as strong as my grief and as certain as I
expect my revenge. That part thou, Pisanio, must act 25

for me, if thy faith be not tainted with the breach of
hers. Let thine own hands take away her life. I shall
give thee opportunity at Milford Haven—she hath my
letter for the purpose—where, if thou fear to strike
and to make me certain it is done, thou art the pander 30
to her dishonor and equally to me disloyal."
PISANIO
What shall I need to draw my sword? The paper
Hath cut her throat already. No, 'tis slander,
Whose edge is sharper than the sword, whose tongue
Outvenoms all the worms° of Nile, whose breath 35
Rides on the posting° winds and doth belie°
All corners of the world. Kings, queens, and states,°
Maids, matrons, nay, the secrets of the grave
This viperous slander enters. What cheer, madam?
IMOGEN
False to his bed? What is it to be false? 40
To lie in watch° there and to think on him?
To weep 'twixt clock and clock?° If sleep charge°
    nature,
To break it with a fearful° dream of him
And cry myself awake? That's false to's bed, is it?
PISANIO
Alas, good lady! 45
IMOGEN
I false? Thy° conscience witness! Iachimo,
Thou didst accuse him of incontinency.
Thou then looked'st like a villain; now, methinks,
Thy favor's° good enough. Some jay° of Italy,
Whose mother was her painting,° hath betrayed him. 50
Poor I am stale, a garment out of fashion,
And, for I am richer than to hang by th' walls,°
I must be ripped. To pieces with me! O,
Men's vows are women's traitors! All good seeming,°
By thy revolt,° O husband, shall be thought 55
Put on for villainy, not born where't grows,°
But worn a bait for ladies.
PISANIO                               Good madam, hear me.
IMOGEN
True honest men, being heard° like false Aeneas,° 60
Were in his time thought false, and Sinon's° weeping
Did scandal° many a holy tear, took pity
From most true wretchedness. So thou, Posthumus,
Wilt lay the leaven on all proper men;°
Goodly° and gallant shall be false and perjured
From thy great fail.° Come, fellow, be thou honest;
Do thou thy master's bidding. When thou see'st him, 65
A little witness my obedience. Look,
I draw the sword myself. Take it, and hit
The innocent mansion of my love, my heart.
Fear not, 'tis empty of all things but grief.
Thy master is not there, who was indeed 70

---

86 **trick** capacity   94 **nerves** sinews   96 **in . . . figure**
playing his part equally well   98 **conceiving** interpretation
103 **refts** robbed   107 **up** roused
**III.iv.3 have** i.e., have longing (to see Posthumus)   7 **perplexed**
troubled   9 **havior** appearance; **wildness** panic   10 **matter**
business   15 **outcraftied** outwitted   16 **at . . . point** in some
difficult situation   17 **take . . . extremity** lessen the shock

35 **worms** serpents   36 **posting** speeding; **belie** fill with lies
37 **states** lords   41 **in watch** awake   42 **'twixt . . . clock**
from hour to hour; **charge** burden   43 **fearful** frightening
46 **Thy** Posthumus'   49 **favor** appearance; **jay** whore   50
**Whose . . . painting** i.e., dependent on make-up   52 **for . . .
walls** i.e., since I am too valuable to be set aside   54 **seeming**
appearance   55 **revolt** turning away   56 **not . . . grows**
i.e., transplanted (hence assumed)   58 **heard** heard to speak;
**Aeneas** who jilted Dido   59 **Sinon** who persuaded Troy to
admit the Trojan horse   60 **scandal** make disreputable   62
**lay . . . men** cause all honorable men to be thought corrupt
63 **Goodly** handsome   64 **fail** failure

The riches of it. Do his bidding, strike!
Thou mayst be valiant in a better cause,
But now thou seem'st a coward.

PISANIO                          Hence, vile instrument!
Thou shalt not damn my hand.

IMOGEN                               Why, I must die,
And if I do not by thy hand, thou art                          75
No servant of thy master's. Against self-slaughter
There is a prohibition so divine
That cravens° my weak hand. Come, here's my heart—
Something's° afore't; soft,° soft, we'll no defense—
Obedient° as the scabbard. What is here?                       80
The scriptures° of the loyal Leonatus
All turned to heresy? Away, away,
Corrupters of my faith! You shall no more
Be stomachers° to my heart. Thus may poor fools
Believe false teachers. Though those that are betrayed 85
Do feel the treason sharply, yet the traitor
Stands in worse case of woe.
And thou, Posthumus, that didst set up
My disobedience 'gainst the king my father
And make me put into contempt the suits                        90
Of princely fellows, shalt hereafter find
It is no act of common passage, but
A strain of rareness;° and I grieve myself
To think, when thou shalt be disedged° by her
That now thou tirest° on, how thy memory                       95
Will then be panged° by me. Prithee dispatch,
The lamb entreats the butcher. Where's thy knife?
Thou art too slow to do thy master's bidding
When I desire it too.

PISANIO              O gracious lady,
Since I received command to do this business                  100
I have not slept one wink.

IMOGEN                            Do't, and to bed then.

PISANIO
I'll wake mine eyeballs out° first.

IMOGEN                                   Wherefore then
Didst undertake it? Why hast thou abused
So many miles with a pretense? This place?
Mine action and thine own? Our horses' labor?                 105
The time inviting thee? The perturbed court
For my being absent? whereunto I never
Purpose return. Why hast thou gone so far,
To be unbent° when thou hast ta'en thy stand,°
Th' elected° deer before thee?

PISANIO                            But to win time            110
To lose so bad employment, in the which
I have considered of a course. Good lady,
Hear me with patience.

IMOGEN                        Talk thy tongue weary, speak.
I have heard I am a strumpet, and mine ear,
Therein false struck, can take no greater wound,              115

Nor tent to bottom that.° But speak.

PISANIO                            Then, madam,
I thought you would not back° again.

IMOGEN                                 Most like,
Bringing me here to kill me.

PISANIO                            Not so, neither.
But if I were as wise as honest, then
My purpose would prove well. It cannot be                     120
But that my master is abused.° Some villain,
Ay, and singular° in his art, hath done you both
This cursèd injury.

IMOGEN
Some Roman courtesan.°

PISANIO                        No, on my life:
I'll give but notice you are dead, and send him               125
Some bloody sign of it,° for 'tis commanded
I should do so. You shall be missed at court,
And that will well confirm it.

IMOGEN                             Why, good fellow,
What shall I do the while? Where bide? How live?
Or in my life what comfort when I am                          130
Dead to my husband?

PISANIO                    If you'll back to th' court—

IMOGEN
No court, no father, nor no more ado
With that harsh, noble, simple nothing,
That Cloten, whose love suit hath been to me
As fearful as a siege.

PISANIO                     If not at court,                  135
Then not in Britain must you bide.

IMOGEN                                Where then?
Hath Britain all the sun that shines? Day, night,
Are they not but° in Britain? I' th' world's volume
Our Britain seems as of it, but not in't;°
In a great pool a swan's nest. Prithee think               140
There's livers out of Britain.

PISANIO                           I am most glad
You think of other place. Th' ambassador,
Lucius the Roman, comes to Milford Haven
Tomorrow. Now if you could wear a mind
Dark° as your fortune is, and but disguise                  145
That° which, t' appear itself,° must not yet be
But by self-danger, you should tread a course
Pretty and full of view;° yea, haply,° near
The residence of Posthumus, so nigh, at least,
That though his actions were not visible, yet             150
Report should render° him hourly to your ear
As truly as he moves.

IMOGEN                       O, for such means,
Though peril to my modesty,° not death on't,
I would adventure.

PISANIO                    Well then, here's the point:
You must forget to be a woman; change                      155
Command° into obedience, fear and niceness°—
The handmaids of all women, or more truly

**78 cravens** makes cowardly  **79 Something** Posthumus'
letter; **soft** wait  **80 Obedient** i.e., as ready to receive the
sword  **81 scriptures** writings  **84 stomachers** ornamental
cloth worn under lacing of the bodice (she has been holding the
letter against her breast)  **92–93 It . . . rareness** i.e., my
choice of you was not an everyday matter but resulted from
rare qualities  **94 be disedged** have lost the edge (of appetite)
**95 tirest** feedest ravenously (hawking term)  **96 panged**
tormented  **102 wake . . . out** remain awake till my eyes
drop out  **109 unbent** with bow unbent, unprepared; **stand**
hunting station  **110 elected** chosen

**116 tent . . . that** probe reaching to bottom of the wound
**117 back** go back  **121 abused** deceived  **122 singular**
unique  **124 courtesan** courtier  **126 it** your death  **138 not
but** only  **139 of . . . in't** i.e., part of the world yet separated
from it  **145 Dark** inscrutable  **146 That** her sex; **itself** as
itself  **148 full of view** with good prospects; **haply** perhaps
**151 render** describe  **153 modesty** chastity  **156 Command**
habit of commanding (as a person of rank); **niceness**
fastidiousness

Woman it° pretty self—into a waggish courage;
Ready in gibes, quick-answered,° saucy, and
As quarrelous° as the weasel. Nay, you must     160
Forget that rarest treasure of your cheek,
Exposing it—but O, the harder° heart!
Alack, no remedy—to the greedy touch
Of common-kissing Titan,° and forget
Your laborsome° and dainty trims,° wherein     165
You made great Juno angry.°

IMOGEN            Nay, be brief.
I see into thy end° and am almost
A man already.

PISANIO       First, make yourself but like one.
Forethinking° this, I have already fit°—
'Tis in my cloak-bag—doublet, hat, hose, all     170
That answer° to them. Would you, in their serving,°
And with what imitation you can borrow
From youth of such a season,° 'fore noble Lucius
Present yourself, desire his service,° tell him
Wherein you're happy,° which will make him know,°     175
If that his head have ear in music; doubtless
With joy he will embrace° you, for he's honorable,
And, doubling that, most holy. Your means° abroad—
You have me, rich, and I will never fail
Beginning nor supplyment.

IMOGEN          Thou art all the comfort     180
The gods will diet me with. Prithee away.
There's more to be considered, but we'll even°
All that good time will give us. This attempt
I am soldier to,° and will abide° it with
A prince's courage. Away, I prithee.     185

PISANIO
Well, madam, we must take a short farewell,
Lest, being missed, I be suspected of
Your carriage° from the court. My noble mistress,
Here is a box; I had it from the queen.
What's in't is precious. If you are sick at sea     190
Or stomach-qualmed at land, a dram of this
Will drive away distemper.° To some shade,
And fit you to your manhood. May the gods
Direct you to the best.

IMOGEN          Amen. I thank thee.

*Exeunt [severally].*

## Scene V. [*Britain.*]

*Enter* CYMBELINE, QUEEN, CLOTEN, LUCIUS, [*a*
MESSENGER, ATTENDANTS,] *and* LORDS.

CYMBELINE
Thus far, and so farewell.

LUCIUS          Thanks, royal sir.

My emperor hath wrote: I must from hence,
And am right sorry that I must report ye
My master's enemy.

CYMBELINE         Our subjects, sir,
Will not endure his yoke, and for ourself     5
To show less sovereignty than they, must needs
Appear unkinglike.

LUCIUS          So, sir. I desire of you
A conduct° overland to Milford Haven.
Madam, all joy befall your grace, and you.°

CYMBELINE
My lords, you are appointed for that office;°     10
The due of honor in no point omit.
So farewell, noble Lucius.

LUCIUS          Your hand, my lord.

CLOTEN
Receive it friendly, but from this time forth
I wear it as your enemy.

LUCIUS          Sir, the event°
Is yet to name the winner. Fare you well.     15

CYMBELINE
Leave not the worthy Lucius, good my lords,
Till he have crossed the Severn. Happiness!

*Exeunt* LUCIUS *et ceteri.*°

QUEEN
He goes hence frowning, but it honors us
That we have given him cause.

CLOTEN          'Tis all the better;
Your valiant Britons have their wishes in it.     20

CYMBELINE
Lucius hath wrote already to the emperor
How it goes here. It fits us therefore ripely°
Our chariots and our horsemen be in readiness.
The pow'rs that he already hath in Gallia
Will soon be drawn to head,° from whence he moves     25
His war for Britain.

QUEEN         'Tis not sleepy business,
But must be looked to speedily and strongly.

CYMBELINE
Our expectation that it would be thus
Hath made us forward. But, my gentle queen,
Where is our daughter? She hath not appeared     30
Before the Roman, nor to us hath tendered
The duty of the day. She looks° us like
A thing more made of malice than of duty.
We have noted it.—Call her before us, for
We have been too slight in sufferance.°

*[Exit* MESSENGER.*]*

QUEEN          Royal sir,     35
Since the exile of Posthumus, most retired
Hath her life been; the cure whereof, my lord,
'Tis time must do. Beseech your majesty,
Forbear sharp speeches to her. She's a lady
So tender of° rebukes that words are strokes,     40
And strokes death to her.

*Enter* MESSENGER.

---

158 **it** its   159 **quick-answered** quick-answering   160
**quarrelous** quarrelsome   162 **harder** too hard   164 **common-kissing Titan** the sun which kisses everything alike   165
**laborsome** elaborate; **trims** apparel   166 **angry** i.e., with
jealousy   167 **end** purpose   169 **Forethinking** planning in
advance for; **fit** prepared   171 **answer** correspond; **in their
serving** with their aid   173 **season** age   174 **his service**
employment as his servant   175 **happy** accomplished; **make
him know** satisfy him   177 **embrace** welcome   178 **means**
i.e., of subsistence   182 **even** keep pace with   184 **soldier to**
brave enough for; **abide** face   188 **Your carriage** removing
you   192 **distemper** illness

**III.v.8 conduct** escort   9 **you** Cymbeline   10 **office** duty
14 **event** outcome   17 **s.d. et ceteri** and others (Attendants
and Lords)   22 **fits . . . ripely** behooves us therefore strongly
25 **drawn to head** gathered into an army   32 **looks** seems to
35 **slight in sufferance** remiss in permissiveness   40 **tender
of** sensitive to

CYMBELINE             Where is she, sir? How
Can her contempt be answered?°
MESSENGER              Please you, sir,
Her chambers are all locked, and there's no answer
That will be given to th' loud of noise we make.
QUEEN
My lord, when last I went to visit her,     45
She prayed me to excuse her keeping close;°
Whereto constrained by her infirmity,
She should that duty leave unpaid to you
Which daily she was bound to proffer. This
She wished me to make known, but our great court°  50
Made me to blame in memory.°
CYMBELINE            Her doors locked?
Not seen of late? Grant, heavens, that which I fear
Prove false!                               *Exit.*
QUEEN      Son, I say, follow the king.
CLOTEN
That man of hers, Pisanio, her old servant,
I have not seen these two days.
QUEEN                Go, look after.    55
                       *Exit* [CLOTEN].
Pisanio, thou that stand'st so for° Posthumus—
He hath a drug of mine. I pray his absence
Proceed° by swallowing that, for he believes
It is a thing most precious. But for her,
Where is she gone? Haply despair hath seized her,  60
Or, winged with fervor of her love, she's flown
To her desired Posthumus. Gone she is
To death or to dishonor, and my end
Can make good use of either. She being down,
I have the placing of the British crown.    65

*Enter* CLOTEN.

How now, my son?
CLOTEN             'Tis certain she is fled.
Go in and cheer the king. He rages; none
Dare come about him.
QUEEN         [*Aside.*] All the better. May
This night forestall° him of the coming day!
                       *Exit* QUEEN.
CLOTEN
I love and hate her, for° she's fair and royal,    70
And that° she hath all courtly parts° more exquisite
Than lady, ladies, woman. From every one
The best she hath, and she, of all compounded,
Outsells° them all. I love her therefore, but
Disdaining me and throwing favors on    75
The low Posthumus slanders° so her judgment
That what's else rare is choked; and in that point
I will conclude to hate her, nay, indeed,
To be revenged upon her. For, when fools
Shall—

*Enter* PISANIO.

          Who is here? What, are you packing,° sirrah?°  80
Come hither. Ah, you precious pander! Villain,

Where is thy lady? In a word, or else
Thou art straightway with the fiends.
PISANIO                O good my lord!
CLOTEN
Where is thy lady? Or, by Jupiter,
I will not ask again. Close° villain,    85
I'll have this secret from thy heart or rip
Thy heart to find it. Is she with Posthumus?
From whose so many weights of baseness cannot
A dram of worth be drawn.
PISANIO            Alas, my lord,
How can she be with him? When was she missed?  90
He is in Rome.
CLOTEN        Where is she, sir? Come nearer.°
No farther halting. Satisfy me home°
What is become of her.
PISANIO
O my all-worthy lord!
CLOTEN            All-worthy villain!
Discover° where thy mistress is at once,    95
At the next word. No more of "worthy lord"!
Speak, or thy silence on the instant is
Thy condemnation and thy death.
PISANIO              Then, sir,
This paper° is the history of my knowledge
Touching her flight. [*Presenting a letter.*]
CLOTEN         Let's see't. I will pursue her  100
Even to Augustus' throne.
PISANIO     [*Aside.*] Or° this, or perish.
She's far enough, and what he learns by this
May prove his travel, not her danger.
CLOTEN                Hum!
PISANIO [*Aside.*]
I'll write to my lord she's dead. O Imogen,
Safe mayst thou wander, safe return again!    105
CLOTEN   Sirrah, is this letter true?
PISANIO   Sir, as I think.
CLOTEN   It is Posthumus' hand, I know't. Sirrah, if
thou wouldst not be a villain, but do me true service,
undergo° those employments wherein I should have  110
cause to use thee with a serious industry—that is, what
villainy soe'er I bid thee do, to perform it directly and
truly—I would think thee an honest man. Thou
shouldst neither want my means for thy relief nor my
voice for thy preferment.°    115
PISANIO   Well, my good lord.
CLOTEN   Wilt thou serve me? For since patiently and
constantly thou hast stuck to the bare fortune of that
beggar Posthumus, thou canst not, in the course of
gratitude, but be a diligent follower of mine. Wilt  120
thou serve me?
PISANIO   Sir, I will.
CLOTEN   Give me thy hand. Here's my purse. Hast any
of thy late master's garments in thy possession?
PISANIO   I have, my lord, at my lodging the same suit  125
he wore when he took leave of my lady and mistress.
CLOTEN   The first service thou dost me, fetch that suit
hither. Let it be thy first service. Go.
PISANIO   I shall, my lord.              *Exit.*

42 **answered** accounted for  46 **close** to herself  50 **our great
court** i.e., state affairs  51 **to . . . memory** fail to remember
56 **stand'st so for** so much supportest  58 **Proceed by** result
from  69 **forestall** deprive  70 **for** because  71 **that** because;
**parts** qualities  74 **Outsells** outvalues  76 **slanders** denigrates
80 **packing** plotting; **sirrah** term of address to an inferior

85 **Close** secretive  91 **nearer** to the point  92 **home** thoroughly  95 **Discover** reveal  99 **This paper** cf. line 130 and
V.v.279  101 **Or** either  110 **undergo** undertake  115 **preferment** advancement

CLOTEN    Meet thee at Milford Haven! I forgot to ask 130
him one thing; I'll remember't anon. Even there, thou
villain Posthumus, will I kill thee. I would these garments were come. She said upon a time—the bitterness
of it I now belch from my heart—that she held the very
garment of Posthumus in more respect than my noble 135
and natural person, together with the adornment of
my qualities. With that suit upon my back will I
ravish her; first kill him, and in her eyes. There shall
she see my valor, which will then be a torment to her
contempt. He on the ground, my speech of insultment° 140
ended on his dead body, and when my lust hath dined
—which, as I say, to vex her I will execute in the
clothes that she so praised—to the court I'll knock her
back,° foot° her home again. She hath despised me
rejoicingly, and I'll be merry in my revenge.          145

*Enter* PISANIO [*with the clothes*].

Be those the garments?
PISANIO    Ay, my noble lord.
CLOTEN    How long is't since she went to Milford
Haven?
PISANIO    She can scarce be there yet.                150
CLOTEN    Bring this apparel to my chamber; that is the
second thing that I have commanded thee. The third
is that thou wilt be a voluntary mute to my design.
Be but duteous, and true preferment shall tender itself
to thee. My revenge is now at Milford. Would I had 155
wings to follow it! Come, and be true.        *Exit.*

PISANIO
Thou bid'st me to my loss,° for true to thee
Were to prove false, which I will never be,
To him° that is most true. To Milford go,
And find not her whom thou pursuest. Flow, flow,   160
You heavenly blessings, on her. This fool's speed
Be crossed° with slowness; labor be his meed.°  *Exit.*


Scene VI. [*Wales.*]

*Enter* IMOGEN *alone* [*in boy's clothes*].

IMOGEN
I see a man's life is a tedious one.
I have tired myself, and for two nights together
Have made the ground my bed. I should be sick
But that my resolution helps me. Milford,
When from the mountain-top Pisanio showed thee,   5
Thou wast within a ken.° O Jove, I think
Foundations° fly the wretched—such, I mean,
Where they should be relieved. Two beggars told me
I could not miss my way. Will poor folks lie,
That have afflictions on them, knowing 'tis       10
A punishment or trial? Yes. No wonder,
When rich ones scarce tell true. To lapse in fulness°
Is sorer° than to lie for need, and falsehood
Is worse in kings than beggars. My dear lord,
Thou art one o' th' false ones. Now I think on thee   15
My hunger's gone, but even° before, I was

At point° to sink for° food. But what is this?
Here is a path to't. 'Tis some savage hold.°
I were best not call; I dare not call. Yet famine,
Ere clean° it o'erthrow nature, makes it valiant.   20
Plenty and peace breeds cowards; hardness° ever
Of hardiness is mother. Ho! Who's here?
If anything that's civil,° speak; if savage,
Take or lend.° Ho! No answer? Then I'll enter.
Best draw my sword, and if mine enemy             25
But fear the sword like me, he'll scarcely look on't.
Such a foe,° good heavens!            *Exit.*°

*Enter* BELARIUS, GUIDERIUS, *and* ARVIRAGUS.

BELARIUS
You, Polydore, have proved best woodman° and
Are master of the feast. Cadwal and I
Will play the cook and servant; 'tis our match.°   30
The sweat of industry would dry and die
But for the end it works to. Come, our stomachs
Will make what's homely° savory. Weariness
Can snore upon the flint when resty° sloth
Finds the down pillow hard. Now peace be here,   35
Poor house, that keep'st thyself.
GUIDERIUS                    I am throughly weary.
ARVIRAGUS
I am weak with toil, yet strong in appetite.
GUIDERIUS
There is cold meat i' th' cave. We'll browse on that
Whilst what we have killed be cooked.
BELARIUS  [*Looking through door.*] Stay, come not in.
But that it eats our victuals, I should think       40
Here were a fairy.
GUIDERIUS           What's the matter,° sir?
BELARIUS
By Jupiter, an angel; or, if not,
An earthly paragon. Behold divineness
No elder than a boy.

*Enter* IMOGEN.

IMOGEN
Good masters, harm me not.                         45
Before I entered here, I called and thought
To have begged or bought what I have took. Good
    troth,°
I have stol'n naught, nor would not, though I had
    found
Gold strewed i' th' floor. Here's money for my meat.
I would have left it on the board so soon          50
As I had made my meal, and parted
With pray'rs for the provider.
GUIDERIUS               Money, youth?
ARVIRAGUS
All gold and silver rather turn to dirt,
As 'tis no better reckoned but of those
Who worship dirty gods.
IMOGEN                  I see you're angry.          55

140 insultment scornful triumph   143–44 knock her back
beat her home   144 foot kick   157 loss i.e., of honor   159
him Posthumus   162 crossed thwarted; meed reward
III.vi.6 a ken view   7 Foundations security (quibble on the
sense of "hospitals")   12 lapse in fulness i.e., lie when
prosperous   13 sorer worse   16 even just

17 At point about; for for lack of   18 hold stronghold   20
clean completely   21 hardness hardship   23 civil civilized
24 Take or lend take (what I have) or give (what you will)
27 Such a foe i.e., may I have (if any) such a foe   27 s.d. Exit
at this point, since the stage is cleared, F marks a new scene
28 woodman hunter   30 match agreement   33 homely
plain   34 resty lazy   41 matter subject (of your remark)   47
Good troth in truth

Know, if you kill me for my fault, I should
Have died had I not made it.

**BELARIUS**               Whither bound?

**IMOGEN**
To Milford Haven.

**BELARIUS**
What's your name?

**IMOGEN**
Fidele, sir. I have a kinsman who       60
Is bound for Italy; he embarked at Milford;
To whom being going, almost spent with hunger,
I am fall'n in this offense.

**BELARIUS**          Prithee, fair youth,
Think us no churls, nor measure our good minds
By this rude place we live in. Well encountered!    65
'Tis almost night; you shall have better cheer°
Ere you depart, and thanks° to stay and eat it.
Boys, bid him welcome.

**GUIDERIUS**          Were you a woman, youth,
I should woo hard but be° your groom in honesty.
I'ld bid for you as I do buy.°

**ARVIRAGUS**            I'll make't my comfort   70
He is a man. I'll love him as my brother,
And such a welcome as I'ld give to him
After long absence, such is yours. Most welcome.
Be sprightly,° for you fall 'mongst friends.

**IMOGEN**              'Mongst friends?
—If brothers.° [Aside.] Would it had been so that they 75
Had been my father's sons! Then had my prize°
Been less,° and so more equal ballasting°
To thee, Posthumus.

**BELARIUS**          He wrings° at some distress.

**GUIDERIUS**
Would I could free't!

**ARVIRAGUS**          Or I, whate'er it be,
What pain it cost, what danger. Gods!

**BELARIUS**          Hark, boys. [Whispers.] 80

**IMOGEN**
Great men
That had a court no bigger than this cave,
That did attend themselves° and had the virtue
Which their own conscience sealed them,° laying by°
That nothing-gift° of differing° multitudes,      85
Could not outpeer° these twain. Pardon me, gods,
I'ld change my sex to be companion with them,
Since Leonatus false.

**BELARIUS**          It shall be so.
Boys, we'll go dress our hunt.° Fair youth, come in.
Discourse is heavy, fasting. When we have supped,   90
We'll mannerly demand thee of thy story,
So far as thou wilt speak it.

**GUIDERIUS**          Pray draw near.

**ARVIRAGUS**
The night to th' owl and morn to th' lark less welcome.

**IMOGEN**
Thanks, sir.

**ARVIRAGUS**
I pray draw near.                *Exeunt.* 95

### Scene VII. [Rome.]

*Enter two Roman* SENATORS *and* TRIBUNES.

**FIRST SENATOR**
This is the tenor of the emperor's writ:°
That since the common men are now in action
'Gainst the Pannonians and Dalmatians,
And that the legions now in Gallia are
Full weak to undertake our wars against        5
The fall'n-off° Britons, that we do incite
The gentry to this business. He creates
Lucius proconsul, and to you the tribunes,
For this immediate levy, he commends°
His absolute commission.° Long live Caesar!     10

**TRIBUNE**
Is Lucius general of the forces?

**SECOND SENATOR**            Ay.

**TRIBUNE**
Remaining now in Gallia?

**FIRST SENATOR**          With those legions
Which I have spoke of, whereunto your levy
Must be supplyant.° The words of your commission
Will tie you to° the numbers and the time      15
Of their dispatch.

**TRIBUNE**          We will discharge our duty. *Exeunt.*

# ACT IV

### Scene I. [Wales.]

*Enter* CLOTEN *alone.*

**CLOTEN**   I am near to th' place where they should meet,
if Pisanio have mapped it truly. How fit° his garments
serve me! Why should his mistress, who was made by
him that made the tailor, not be fit° too? The rather,
saving reverence of° the word, for° 'tis said a woman's   5
fitness° comes by fits. Therein I must play the workman. I dare speak it to myself, for it is not vainglory
for a man and his glass° to confer in his own chamber—
I mean, the lines of my body are as well drawn as his;
no less young, more strong, not beneath him in    10
fortunes, beyond him in the advantage of the time,°
above him in birth, alike conversant in general° services, and more remarkable in single oppositions.° Yet
this imperceiverant° thing loves him in my despite.
What mortality° is! Posthumus, thy head, which now   15
is growing upon thy shoulders, shall within this hour

---

66 **cheer** entertainment   67 **thanks** i.e., our thanks   69 **but be** ere I should fail to be (E. Dowden)   70 **I'ld . . . buy** I'd seek your hand in earnest   74 **sprightly** in good spirits   75 **If brothers** i.e., yes, if we were indeed brothers   76 **prize** price, value (quibble on the sense of "captured ship")   77 **less** since then she would not be heir apparent; **ballasting** weight   78 **wrings** writhes   83 **attend themselves** i.e., get along without attendants   84 **sealed them** authenticated for them (as in affixing a waxen seal to a legal document); **laying by** setting aside   85 **nothing-gift** worthless gift (flattery); **differing** fickle   86 **outpeer** surpass   89 **hunt** quarry

**III.vii.1 writ** dispatch   6 **fall'n-off** revolted   9 **commends** entrusts   10 **absolute commission** full authority   14 **supplyant** supplementary   15 **tie you to** confirm for you   **IV.i.2 fit** suitably   4 **fit** suitable   5 **saving reverence of** begging pardon for; **for** since   6 **fitness** sexual inclination   8 **glass** looking-glass   11 **advantage of the time** social opportunities   12 **general** i.e., military   13 **single oppositions** duels   14 **imperceiverant** imperceptive   15 **mortality** life

be off, thy mistress enforced,° thy garments cut to
pieces before her face; and all this done, spurn her home
to her father, who may haply be a little angry for my
so rough usage; but my mother, having power of° his 20
testiness, shall turn all into my commendations. My
horse is tied up safe. Out, sword, and to a sore° purpose! Fortune put them into my hand. This is the very
description of their meeting place, and the fellow dares
not deceive me.                              *Exit.* 25

Scene II. [*Wales.*]

*Enter* BELARIUS, GUIDERIUS, ARVIRAGUS, *and*
IMOGEN *from the cave.*

BELARIUS
You are not well. Remain here in the cave;
We'll come to you after hunting.
ARVIRAGUS                        Brother, stay here.
Are we not brothers?
IMOGEN                So man and man should be,
But clay and clay° differs in dignity,°
Whose dust° is both alike. I am very sick. 5
GUIDERIUS
Go you to hunting, I'll abide with him.
IMOGEN
So sick I am not, yet I am not well,
But not so citizen° a wanton° as
To seem to die ere sick. So please you, leave me;
Stick to your journal° course; the breach of custom 10
Is breach of all. I am ill, but your being by me
Cannot amend° me; society is no comfort
To one not sociable. I am not very sick,
Since I can reason of it. Pray you trust me here—
I'll rob none but myself—and let me die, 15
Stealing so poorly.°
GUIDERIUS          I love thee—I have spoke it—
How much° the quantity, the weight as much
As I do love my father.
BELARIUS              What? How, how?
ARVIRAGUS
If it be sin to say so, sir, I yoke me
In my good brother's fault. I know not why 20
I love this youth, and I have heard you say
Love's reason's without reason. The bier at door,
And a demand who is't shall die, I'ld say,
"My father, not this youth."
BELARIUS        [*Aside.*] O noble strain!°
O worthiness of nature, breed of greatness! 25
Cowards father cowards and base things sire base;
Nature hath meal and bran, contempt and grace.
I'm not their father; yet who this should be
Doth miracle itself, loved before me.°—
'Tis the ninth hour o' th' morn.
ARVIRAGUS                    Brother, farewell. 30

IMOGEN
I wish ye sport.
ARVIRAGUS        You health.—So please you,° sir.
IMOGEN [*Aside.*]
These are kind creatures. Gods, what lies I have heard!
Our courtiers say all's savage but at court.
Experience, O, thou disprov'st report!
Th' imperious° seas breeds monsters; for the dish 35
Poor tributary rivers as° sweet fish.
I am sick still, heartsick. Pisanio,
I'll now taste of thy drug.
GUIDERIUS              I could not stir him.°
He said he was gentle,° but unfortunate;
Dishonestly afflicted, but yet honest. 40
ARVIRAGUS
Thus did he answer me, yet said hereafter
I might know more.
BELARIUS            To th' field, to th' field.—
We'll leave you for this time; go in and rest.
ARVIRAGUS
We'll not be long away.
BELARIUS              Pray be not sick,
For you must be our housewife.
IMOGEN                        Well or ill, 45
I am bound° to you.                          *Exit.*
BELARIUS            And shalt be ever.
This youth, howe'er distressed, appears° he hath had
Good ancestors.
ARVIRAGUS    How angel-like he sings!
GUIDERIUS
But his neat° cookery! He cut our roots in characters,°
And sauced our broths as Juno had been sick 50
And he her dieter.
ARVIRAGUS        Nobly he yokes
A smiling with a sigh, as if the sigh
Was that° it was for not being such a smile;
The smile mocking the sigh that it would fly
From so divine a temple to commix 55
With winds that sailors rail at.
GUIDERIUS                    I do note
That grief and patience, rooted in them both,
Mingle their spurs° together.
ARVIRAGUS                  Grow patience,
And let the stinking elder,° grief, untwine
His perishing° root with° the increasing vine. 60
BELARIUS
It is great morning.° Come away.—Who's there?

*Enter* CLOTEN.

CLOTEN
I cannot find those runagates.° That villain
Hath mocked me. I am faint.
BELARIUS                  "Those runagates"?
Means he not us? I partly know him. 'Tis
Cloten, the son o' th' queen. I fear some ambush. 65

---

17 **enforced** raped  20 **power of** control over  22 **sore**
causing suffering (quibble on the sense of "wound," i.e., vagina)
**IV.ii.4 clay and clay** one person and another; **dignity** rank
5 **dust** remains after death  8 **citizen** city-bred, bourgeois;
**wanton** spoiled child  10 **journal** daily  12 **amend** cure
16 **poorly** i.e., from myself only  17 **How much** as much
24 **strain** heredity  28–29 **who . . . me** that this person,
whoever he is, should be loved more than I is miraculous

31 **So please you** at your service  35 **imperious** imperial
36 **as** just as  38 **stir him** move him (to tell his story)
39 **gentle** wellborn  46 **bound** indebted (Belarius quibbles on
the sense of "tied by affection")  47 **appears** appears as though
49 **neat** elegant; **characters** designs  53 **that** what  58 **spurs**
chief roots  59 **elder** elder tree  60 **perishing** destructive;
**with** from  61 **great morning** broad daylight  62 **runagates**
runaways

I saw him not these many years, and yet
I know 'tis he. We are held as outlaws. Hence!

GUIDERIUS
He is but one. You and my brother search
What companies° are near. Pray you, away.
Let me alone with him.°
        *[Exeunt* BELARIUS *and* ARVIRAGUS.]

CLOTEN        Soft,° what are you     70
That fly me thus? Some villain° mountaineers?
I have heard of such. What slave art thou?

GUIDERIUS              A thing
More slavish did I ne'er than answering
A "slave" without a knock.

CLOTEN           Thou art a robber,
A lawbreaker, a villain. Yield thee, thief.     75

GUIDERIUS
To who? To thee? What art thou? Have not I
An arm as big as thine? A heart as big?
Thy words, I grant, are bigger, for I wear not
My dagger in my mouth. Say what thou art,
Why I should yield to thee.

CLOTEN         Thou villain base,     80
Know'st me° not by my clothes?

GUIDERIUS        No, nor thy tailor, rascal,
Who is thy grandfather. He made those clothes,
Which, as it seems, make thee.

CLOTEN         Thou precious varlet,°
My tailor made them not.

GUIDERIUS        Hence then, and thank     85
The man that gave them thee. Thou art some fool;
I am loath to beat thee.

CLOTEN        Thou injurious° thief,
Hear but my name and tremble.

GUIDERIUS        What's thy name?

CLOTEN
Cloten, thou villain.

GUIDERIUS
Cloten, thou double villain, be thy name,
I cannot tremble at it. Were it Toad, or Adder, Spider,     90
'Twould move me sooner.

CLOTEN        To thy further fear,
Nay, to thy mere° confusion, thou shalt know
I am son to th' queen.

GUIDERIUS        I am sorry for't; not seeming°
So worthy as thy birth.

CLOTEN        Art not afeard?

GUIDERIUS
Those that I reverence, those I fear—the wise;     95
At fools I laugh, not fear them.

CLOTEN        Die the death!
When I have slain thee with my proper° hand,
I'll follow those that even now fled hence
And on the gates of Lud's Town set your heads.
Yield, rustic mountaineer.        *Fight and exeunt.*   100

*Enter* BELARIUS *and* ARVIRAGUS.

BELARIUS
No company's abroad?°

ARVIRAGUS
None in the world. You did mistake him sure.

BELARIUS
I cannot tell. Long is it since I saw him,
But time hath nothing blurred those lines of favor°
Which then he wore. The snatches° in his voice,     105
And burst of speaking, were as his. I am absolute°
'Twas very Cloten.°

ARVIRAGUS        In this place we left them.
I wish my brother make good time° with him,
You say he is so fell.°

BELARIUS        Being scarce made up,°
I mean to man, he had not apprehension     110
Of roaring terrors; for defect of judgment
Is oft the cause of fear.°

*Enter* GUIDERIUS [*with Cloten's head*].

                 But see, thy brother.

GUIDERIUS
This Cloten was a fool, an empty purse;
There was no money in't. Not Hercules
Could have knocked out his brains, for he had none.   115
Yet I not doing this, the fool had borne
My head as I do his.

BELARIUS        What hast thou done?

GUIDERIUS
I am perfect° what: cut off one Cloten's head,
Son to the queen, after his own report;
Who called me traitor, mountaineer, and swore     120
With his own single hand he'ld take us in,°
Displace our heads where—thank the gods—they grow,
And set them on Lud's Town.

BELARIUS        We are all undone.

GUIDERIUS
Why, worthy father, what have we to lose
But that° he swore to take, our lives? The law     125
Protects not us. Then why should we be tender
To° let an arrogant piece of flesh threat us,
Play judge and executioner all himself,
For° we do fear the law? What company
Discover you abroad?

BELARIUS        No single soul     130
Can we set eye on, but in all safe reason
He must have some attendants. Though his humor°
Was nothing but mutation—ay, and that
From one bad thing to worse—not frenzy, not
Absolute madness could so far have raved     135
To bring him here alone. Although perhaps
It may be heard at court that such as we
Cave here, hunt here, are outlaws, and in time
May make° some stronger head;° the which he hearing—
As it is like him—might break out, and swear     140
He'ld fetch us in; yet is't not probable

---

**69 companies** companions   **70 Let . . . him** Leave him to me; **Soft** wait   **71 villain** lowborn   **81 me** i.e., my rank   **83 precious varlet** egregious knave   **86 injurious** insulting   **92 mere** utter   **93 not seeming** since you do not seem   **97 proper** own   **101 abroad** about

**104 lines of favor** contours of his face   **105 snatches** hesitations   **106 absolute** certain   **107 very Cloten** Cloten himself   **108 make good time** have good fortune   **109 fell** fierce; **made up** grown   **111–12 for . . . fear** sense unclear and frequently emended; Belarius seems to be saying that Cloten lacked the intelligence to be frightened   **118 perfect** well aware   **121 take us in** overcome us   **125 that** what   **126–27 tender To** so considerate as to   **129 For** because   **132 humor** chief characteristic   **139 make** make up; **head** force

To come° alone, either he so undertaking,
Or they so suffering.° Then on good ground we fear,
If we do fear this body hath a tail°
More perilous than the head.

ARVIRAGUS                    Let ordinance°          145
Come as the gods foresay° it. Howsoe'er,
My brother hath done well.

BELARIUS                    I had no mind
To hunt this day. The boy Fidele's sickness
Did make my way long forth.°

GUIDERIUS                    With his own sword,
Which he did wave against my throat, I have ta'en   150
His head from him. I'll throw't into the creek
Behind our rock, and let it to the sea
And tell the fishes he's the queen's son, Cloten.
That's all I reck.°                            *Exit.*

BELARIUS          I fear 'twill be revenged.
Would, Polydore, thou hadst not done't, though valor 155
Becomes thee well enough.

ARVIRAGUS                    Would I had done't,
So° the revenge alone pursued° me. Polydore,
I love thee brotherly, but envy much
Thou hast robbed me of this deed. I would revenges
That possible° strength might meet would seek us
    through°                                    160
And put us to our answer.

BELARIUS                    Well, 'tis done.
We'll hunt no more today, nor seek for danger
Where there's no profit. I prithee, to our rock;
You and Fidele play the cooks. I'll stay
Till hasty Polydore return, and bring him         165
To dinner presently.

ARVIRAGUS                    Poor sick Fidele,
I'll willingly to him. To gain° his color
I'ld let a parish of such Clotens blood°
And praise myself for charity.                 *Exit.*

BELARIUS                    O thou goddess,
Thou divine Nature, thou thyself thou blazon'st°   170
In these two princely boys! They are as gentle
As zephyrs blowing below the violet,
Not wagging his sweet head; and yet as rough,
Their royal blood enchafed,° as the rud'st wind
That by the top doth take the mountain pine       175
And make him stoop to th' vale. 'Tis wonder
That an invisible instinct should frame° them
To royalty° unlearned, honor untaught,
Civility° not seen from other, valor
That wildly grows° in them but yields a crop      180
As if it had been sowed. Yet still it's strange
What Cloten's being here to us portends,
Or what his death will bring us.

*Enter* GUIDERIUS.

GUIDERIUS                    Where's my brother?

I have sent Cloten's clotpoll° down the stream
In embassy to his mother; his body's hostage      185
For his return. *Solemn music.*

BELARIUS          My ingenious° instrument!
Hark, Polydore, it sounds. But what occasion
Hath Cadwal now to give it motion? Hark!

GUIDERIUS
Is he at home?

BELARIUS          He went hence even now.

GUIDERIUS
What does he mean? Since death of my dear'st mother 190
It did not speak before. All solemn things
Should answer° solemn accidents.° The matter?
Triumphs° for nothing and lamenting toys°
Is jollity for apes and grief for boys.
Is Cadwal mad?

*Enter* ARVIRAGUS *with* IMOGEN, *dead, bearing her in
his arms.*

BELARIUS          Look, here he comes,           195
And brings the dire occasion in his arms
Of what we blame him for.

ARVIRAGUS                    The bird is dead
That we have made so much on.° I had rather
Have skipped from sixteen years of age to sixty,
To have turned my leaping time into a crutch,     200
Than have seen this.

GUIDERIUS          O sweetest, fairest lily!
My brother wears thee not the one half so well
As when thou grew'st thyself.

BELARIUS                    O Melancholy,
Who ever yet could sound thy bottom, find
The ooze, to show what coast thy sluggish crayer°  205
Might eas'liest harbor in? Thou blessèd thing,
Jove knows what man thou mightst have made; but I,°
Thou diedst, a most rare boy, of melancholy.
How found you him?

ARVIRAGUS          Stark,° as you see,
Thus smiling, as° some fly had tickled slumber,   210
Not as Death's dart being laughed at;° his right cheek
Reposing on a cushion.

GUIDERIUS          Where?

ARVIRAGUS                    O' th' floor;
His arms thus leagued.° I thought he slept, and put
My clouted brogues° from off my feet, whose rude-
    ness°
Answered my steps too loud.

GUIDERIUS                    Why, he but sleeps.  215
If he be gone, he'll make his grave a bed;
With female fairies will his tomb be haunted,
And worms will not come to thee.

ARVIRAGUS                    With fairest flowers,
Whilst summer lasts and I live here, Fidele,
I'll sweeten thy sad grave. Thou shalt not lack    220
The flower that's like thy face, pale primrose; nor

---

142 **To come** for him to come  143 **suffering** allowing
144 **tail** i.e., followers  145 **ordinance** whatever is ordained
146 **foresay** foretell, determine  149 **way long forth** i.e.,
way forth seem long  154 **reck** care  157 **So** so that; **pursued**
would have pursued  160 **possible** our available; **seek us
through** search thoroughly for us  167 **gain** restore  168 **let
. . . blood** kill a parish-full of Clotens  170 **blazon'st** pro-
claimest  174 **enchafed** heated  177 **frame** dispose  178
**royalty** regal conduct  179 **Civility** civilized behavior  180
**wildly grows** grows wild

184 **clotpoll** blockhead  186 **ingenious** skillfully constructed
192 **answer** correspond to; **accidents** events  193 **Triumphs**
public festivities; **lamenting toys** lamenting over trifles
198 **on** of  205 **crayer** small trading vessel  207 **I** i.e., what I
know is  209 **Stark** stiff (as in death)  210 **as** as if  211 **as
. . . at** as if laughing at Death's arrow  213 **leagued** folded
214 **clouted brogues** heavy, nail-studded shoes; **rudeness**
roughness

The azured harebell,° like thy veins; no, nor
The leaf of eglantine,° whom not to slander,
Outsweet'ned not thy breath. The ruddock° would
With charitable bill—O bill sore shaming                     225
Those rich-left heirs that let their fathers lie
Without a monument!—bring thee all this;
Yea, and furred moss besides, when flow'rs are none,
To winter-ground° thy corse—

GUIDERIUS                            Prithee have done,
And do not play in wench-like words with that                230
Which is so serious. Let us bury him,
And not protract with admiration what
Is now due debt. To th' grave.

ARVIRAGUS                    Say, where shall's° lay him?

GUIDERIUS
By good Euriphile, our mother.

ARVIRAGUS                            Be't so.
And let us, Polydore, though now our voices                   235
Have got the mannish crack, sing him to th' ground,
As once to our mother; use like note and words,
Save that Euriphile must be Fidele.

GUIDERIUS
Cadwal,
I cannot sing. I'll weep, and word° it with thee,            240
For notes of sorrow out of tune are worse
Than priests and fanes° that lie.

ARVIRAGUS                            We'll speak it then.

BELARIUS
Great griefs, I see, med'cine° the less, for Cloten
Is quite forgot. He was a queen's son, boys,
And though he came our enemy, remember                        245
He was paid° for that. Though mean and mighty,
    rotting
Together, have one dust, yet reverence,
That angel of the world, doth make distinction
Of place 'tween high and low. Our foe was princely,
And though you took his life as being° our foe,              250
Yet bury him as° a prince.

GUIDERIUS                    Pray you fetch him hither.
Thersites'° body is as good as Ajax'°
When neither are alive.

ARVIRAGUS                    If you'll go fetch him,
We'll say our song the whilst. Brother, begin.
                            [Exit BELARIUS.]

GUIDERIUS
Nay, Cadwal, we must lay his head to th' east;°             255
My father hath a reason for't.

ARVIRAGUS                            'Tis true.

GUIDERIUS
Come on then and remove him.

ARVIRAGUS                    So. Begin.
                        Song.

GUIDERIUS    Fear no more the heat o' th' sun
                Nor the furious winter's rages;
                Thou thy wordly task hast done,              260
                Home art gone and ta'en thy wages.

Golden lads and girls all must,
As° chimney-sweepers, come to dust.

ARVIRAGUS    Fear no more the frown o' th' great;
                Thou are past the tyrant's stroke.           265
            Care no more to clothe and eat;
                To thee the reed is as the oak.
            The scepter, learning, physic,° must
            All follow this and come to dust.

GUIDERIUS    Fear no more the lightning flash,               270
ARVIRAGUS        Nor th' all-dreaded thunder-stone;
GUIDERIUS    Fear not slander, censure rash;
ARVIRAGUS        Thou hast finished joy and moan.
BOTH         All lovers young, all lovers must
                Consign to° thee and come to dust.           275

GUIDERIUS    No exorciser° harm thee,
ARVIRAGUS    Nor no witchcraft charm thee.
GUIDERIUS    Ghost unlaid forbear thee;°
ARVIRAGUS    Nothing ill come near thee.
BOTH         Quiet consummation° have,                       280
                And renownèd be thy grave.

*Enter* BELARIUS *with the body of Cloten.*

GUIDERIUS
We have done our obsequies. Come, lay him down.

BELARIUS
Here's a few flowers, but 'bout midnight, more.
The herbs that have on them cold dew o' th' night
Are strewings fitt'st for graves. Upon their faces.°         285
You were as flow'rs, now withered; even so
These herblets shall° which we upon you strew.
Come on, away; apart upon our knees.
The ground that gave them first has them again.
Their pleasures here are past, so is their pain.             290
    *Exeunt* [BELARIUS, GUIDERIUS, *and* ARVIRAGUS].
IMOGEN (*Awakes.*)
Yes, sir, to Milford Haven. Which is the way?
I thank you. By yond bush? Pray, how far thither?
'Ods pittikins,° can it be six mile yet?
I have gone° all night. Faith, I'll lie down and sleep.

[*Seeing Cloten.*]

But, soft, no bedfellow! O gods and goddesses!               295
These flow'rs are like the pleasures of the world;
This bloody man, the care on't. I hope I dream,
For so° I thought I was a cave-keeper
And cook to honest creatures. But 'tis not so;
'Twas but a bolt° of nothing, shot at nothing,              300
Which the brain makes of fumes.° Our very eyes
Are sometimes like our judgments, blind. Good faith,
I tremble still with fear, but if there be
Yet left in Heaven as small a drop of pity
As a wren's eye, feared gods, a part° of it!                 305
The dream's here still. Even when I wake it is
Without me, as within me; not imagined, felt.

---

222 **azured harebell** sky-blue wild hyacinth  223 **eglantine** sweetbriar  224 **ruddock** robin  229 **winter-ground** protect in winter (?)  233 **shall's** shall us (we)  240 **word** speak  242 **fanes** temples  243 **med'cine** cure  246 **paid** punished  250 **as being** because he was  251 **as** as being, because he was  252 **Thersites'** the vituperative Greek warrior of the Trojan War; **Ajax'** one of the Greek heroes at Troy  255 **to th' east** the reverse of Christian practice

263 **As** like  268 **scepter, learning, physic** i.e., kings, scholars, physicians  275 **Consign to** co-sign with (i.e., meet the same fate)  276 **exorciser** spirit-raiser  278 **forbear thee** let thee alone  280 **consummation** fulfillment, end  285 **faces** fronts  287 **shall** shall be  293 **'Ods pittikins** God's little pity, God have mercy  294 **gone** walked  298 **so** i.e., while dreaming  300 **bolt** arrow  301 **fumes** bodily vapors thought to rise to the brain and cause dreams  305 **a part** i.e., grant me a part

A headless man? The garments of Posthumus?
I know the shape of's leg; this is his hand,
His foot Mercurial,° his Martial° thigh, 310
The brawns° of Hercules; but his Jovial° face—
Murder in heaven? How? 'Tis gone. Pisanio,
All curses madded° Hecuba° gave the Greeks,
And mine to boot, be darted on thee! Thou,
Conspired° with that irregulous° devil Cloten, 315
Hath here cut off my lord. To write and read
Be henceforth treacherous! Damned Pisanio
Hath with his forgèd letters—damned Pisanio—
From this most bravest vessel of the world
Struck the maintop. O Posthumus, alas, 320
Where is thy head? Where's that? Ay me, where's
 that?
Pisanio might have killed thee at the heart
And left this head on. How should this be? Pisanio?
'Tis he and Cloten. Malice and lucre° in them
Have laid this woe here. O, 'tis pregnant,° pregnant! 325
The drug he gave me, which he said was precious
And cordial° to me, have I not found it
Murd'rous to th' senses? That confirms it home.°
This is Pisanio's deed, and Cloten.° O,
Give color to my pale cheek with thy blood, 330
That we the horrider may seem to those
Which° chance to find us. O my lord, my lord!

[*Falling on the body.*]

*Enter* LUCIUS *and* CAPTAINS; *a* SOOTHSAYER *to
them.*°

CAPTAIN
The legions garrisoned in Gallia
After° your will have crossed the sea, attending°
You here at Milford Haven with your ships. 335
They are in readiness.
LUCIUS                    But what from Rome?
CAPTAIN
The Senate hath stirred up the confiners°
And gentlemen of Italy, most willing spirits
That promise noble service, and they come
Under the conduct of bold Iachimo, 340
Siena's° brother.
LUCIUS          When expect you them?
CAPTAIN
With the next benefit o' th' wind.
LUCIUS                        This forwardness°
Makes our hopes fair. Command our present numbers
Be mustered; bid the captains look to't.—Now, sir,
What have you dreamed of late of this war's purpose? 345
SOOTHSAYER
Last night the very gods showed me a vision—
I fast° and prayed for their intelligence°—thus:
I saw Jove's bird, the Roman eagle, winged

From the spongy° south to this part of the west,
There vanished in the sunbeams; which portends, 350
Unless my sins abuse° my divination,
Success to th' Roman host.
LUCIUS                    Dream often so,
And never false.° Soft, ho, what trunk is here?
Without his top? The ruin speaks that sometime°
It was a worthy building. How, a page? 355
Or° dead or sleeping on him? But dead rather,
For nature doth abhor° to make his bed
With the defunct or sleep upon the dead.
Let's see the boy's face.
CAPTAIN                He's alive, my lord.
LUCIUS
He'll, then, instruct us of this body. Young one, 360
Inform us of thy fortunes, for it seems
They crave to be demanded. Who is this
Thou mak'st thy bloody pillow? Or who was he
That, otherwise than noble nature did,°
Hath altered that good picture? What's thy interest 365
In this sad wrack?° How came't? Who is't? What art
 thou?
IMOGEN
I am nothing, or if not,
Nothing to be were better. This was my master,
A very valiant Briton and a good,
That here by mountaineers lies slain. Alas, 370
There is no more such masters. I may wander
From east to occident, cry out for service,
Try many, all good, serve truly, never
Find such another master.
LUCIUS                      'Lack, good youth,
Thou mov'st no less with thy complaining than 375
Thy master in bleeding. Say his name, good friend.
IMOGEN
Richard du Champ. [*Aside.*] If I do lie and do
No harm by it, though the gods hear, I hope
They'll pardon it.—Say you, sir?
LUCIUS                        Thy name?
IMOGEN Fidele, sir.
LUCIUS
Thou dost approve° thyself the very same; 380
Thy name well fits thy faith, thy faith thy name.
Wilt take thy chance with me? I will not say
Thou shalt be so well mastered, but be sure
No less beloved. The Roman emperor's letters
Sent by a consul to me should not sooner 385
Than thine own worth prefer° thee. Go with me.
IMOGEN
I'll follow, sir. But first, and't please the gods,
I'll hide my master from the flies, as deep
As these poor pickaxes° can dig; and when
With wild wood-leaves and weeds I ha' strewed his
 grave 390
And on it said a century of° prayers,
Such as I can,° twice o'er, I'll weep and sigh,
And leaving so his service, follow you,

---

310 **Mercurial** quick (like Mercury's); **Martial** powerful (like Mars') 311 **brawns** muscles; **Jovial** majestic (like Jove's) 313 **madded** maddened; **Hecuba** wife of Priam, king of Troy 315 **Conspired** having conspired; **irregulous** lawless 324 **lucre** greed 325 **pregnant** evident 327 **cordial** restorative 328 **home** thoroughly 329 **Cloten** i.e., Cloten's 332 **Which** who 332 **s.d. to them** presumably the Soothsayer enters, a moment later, at another door 334 **After** according to; **attending** waiting for 337 **confiners** inhabitants 341 **Siena's** i.e., the Duke of Siena's 342 **forwardness** promptness 347 **fast** fasted; **intelligence** communication

349 **spongy** damp 351 **abuse** render inaccurate 353 **false** falsely 354 **sometime** once 356 **Or** either 357 **nature doth abhor** man naturally abhors (Heilman) 364 **did** i.e., painted (J. C. Maxwell) 366 **wrack** ruin of a man 380 **approve** prove 386 **prefer** recommend 389 **pickaxes** i.e., fingers 391 **century of** hundred 392 **can** know

So° please you entertain° me.

LUCIUS                                    Ay, good youth,
And rather father thee than master thee.          395
My friends,
The boy hath taught us manly duties. Let us
Find out the prettiest daisied plot we can
And make him with our pikes and partisans°
A grave. Come, arm° him. Boy, he's preferred°     400
By thee to us, and he shall be interred
As soldiers can. Be cheerful; wipe thine eyes.
Some falls are means the happier to arise.    *Exeunt.*


Scene III. [*Britain.*]

*Enter* CYMBELINE, LORDS, *and* PISANIO.

CYMBELINE
Again, and bring me word how 'tis with her.
                              [*Exit a* LORD.]
A fever with° the absence of her son,
A madness, of which her life's in danger. Heavens,
How deeply you at once do touch° me! Imogen,
The great part of my comfort, gone; my queen      5
Upon a desperate bed,° and in a time
When fearful wars point at me; her son gone,
So needful for this present. It strikes me past
The hope of comfort.—But for thee, fellow,
Who needs must know of her departure and          10
Dost seem so ignorant, we'll enforce it from thee
By a sharp torture.

PISANIO              Sir, my life is yours,
I humbly set it at your will; but for my mistress,
I nothing° know where she remains, why gone.
Nor when she purposes return. Beseech your highness, 15
Hold me your loyal servant.

LORD                          Good my liege,
The day that she was missing he was here.
I dare be bound he's true and shall perform
All parts of his subjection° loyally. For Cloten,
There wants no diligence in seeking him,          20
And will° no doubt be found.

CYMBELINE              The time is troublesome.°

[*To* PISANIO.]

We'll slip you° for a season, but our jealousy°
Does yet depend.°

LORD              So please your majesty,
The Roman legions, all from Gallia drawn,
Are landed on your coast, with a supply           25
Of Roman gentlemen by the Senate sent.

CYMBELINE
Now for° the counsel of my son and queen!
I am amazed with matter.°

LORD                          Good my liege,

Your preparation° can affront no less°
Than what you hear of. Come more,° for more you're
  ready.                                          30
The want is but° to put those pow'rs in motion
That long to move.

CYMBELINE          I thank you. Let's withdraw,
And meet the time as it seeks us. We fear not
What can from Italy annoy° us, but
We grieve at chances here. Away.                  35
                    *Exeunt* [*all but* PISANIO].

PISANIO
I heard no letter° from my master since
I wrote him Imogen was slain. 'Tis strange.
Nor hear I from my mistress, who did promise
To yield me often tidings. Neither know I
What is betid° to Cloten, but remain             40
Perplexed in all. The heavens still must work.
Wherein I am false I am honest; not true, to be true.
These present wars shall find I love my country,
Even to the note° o' th' king, or I'll fall in them.
All other doubts, by time let them be cleared;    45
Fortune brings in some boats that are not steered.
                                          *Exit.*


Scene IV. [*Wales.*]

*Enter* BELARIUS, GUIDERIUS, *and* ARVIRAGUS.

GUIDERIUS
The noise is round about us.

BELARIUS                    Let us from it.

ARVIRAGUS
What pleasure, sir, find we in life, to lock° it
From action and adventure?

GUIDERIUS                  Nay, what hope
Have we in hiding us? This way° the Romans
Must or° for Britons slay us or receive us        5
For barbarous and unnatural revolts°
During their use,° and slay us after.

BELARIUS                              Sons,
We'll higher to the mountains, there secure us.
To the king's party there's no going. Newness
Of Cloten's death—we being not known, not mustered 10
Among the bands—may drive us to a render°
Where we have lived, and so extort from's that
Which we have done, whose answer° would be death
Drawn on° with torture.

GUIDERIUS              This is, sir, a doubt
In such a time nothing becoming you             15
Nor satisfying us.

ARVIRAGUS          It is not likely
That when they hear the Roman horses neigh,
Behold their quartered fires,° have both their eyes
And ears so cloyed importantly° as now,

---

394 **So** if it; **entertain** employ  399 **partisans** halberds  400
**arm** carry; **preferred** recommended
**IV.iii.2 with** resulting from  4 **touch** wound  6 **Upon . . .**
**bed** desperately ill  14 **nothing** not at all  19 **subjection** duty
as a subject  21 **will** he will; **troublesome** full of troubles
22 **slip you** let you go free; **jealousy** suspicion  23 **depend**
remain  27 **Now for** would I had  28 **amazed with matter**
confounded by business

29 **preparation** armed forces; **affront no less** i.e., face larger
forces  30 **Come more** if more come  31 **The . . . but**
the only thing needed is  34 **annoy** harm  36 **no letter** i.e.,
not at all  40 **is betid** has happened  44 **note** knowledge
**IV.iv.2 lock** preclude  4 **This way** i.e., if we do so  5 **or**
either  6 **revolts** rebels  7 **During their use** while they have
use for us  11 **render** account  13 **answer** requital  14
**Drawn on** brought about  18 **quartered fires** camp fires
19 **cloyed importantly** burdened with important matters

That they will waste their time upon our note,° 20
To know from whence we are.

BELARIUS                    O, I am known
Of many in the army. Many years,
Though Cloten then° but young, you see, not wore
    him
From my remembrance. And besides, the king
Hath not deserved my service nor your loves, 25
Who find in my exile the want of breeding,°
The certainty° of this hard life; aye hopeless
To have the courtesy your cradle promised,
But to be still hot summer's tanlings° and
The shrinking slaves of winter.

GUIDERIUS                    Than be so 30
Better to cease to be. Pray, sir, to th' army.
I and my brother are not known; yourself
So out of thought, and thereto so o'ergrown,°
Cannot be questioned.

ARVIRAGUS              By this sun that shines,
I'll thither. What thing is't that I never 35
Did see man die, scarce ever looked on blood
But that of coward hares, hot° goats, and venison!
Never bestrid a horse, save one that had
A rider like myself, who ne'er wore rowel°
Nor iron on his heel! I am ashamed 40
To look upon the holy sun, to have
The benefit of his blest beams, remaining
So long a poor unknown.

GUIDERIUS              By heavens, I'll go.
If you will bless me, sir, and give me leave,
I'll take the better care, but if you will not, 45
The hazard therefore due° fall on me by
The hands of Romans!

ARVIRAGUS              So say I. Amen.

BELARIUS
No reason I, since of your lives you set
So slight a valuation, should reserve
My cracked° one to more care. Have with you, boys! 50
If in your country° wars you chance to die,
That is my bed too, lads, and there I'll lie.
Lead, lead. [Aside.] The time seems long; their blood
    thinks scorn
Till it fly out and show them princes born.    Exeunt.


# A C T   V

## Scene I. [Britain.]

Enter POSTHUMUS alone [with a bloody handkerchief].

POSTHUMUS
Yea, bloody cloth, I'll keep thee, for I wished
Thou shouldst be colored thus. You married ones,°
If each of you should take this course, how many
Must murder wives much better than themselves

For wrying° but a little! O Pisanio, 5
Every good servant does not all commands;
No bond but° to do just ones. Gods, if you
Should have ta'en vengeance on my faults, I never
Had lived to put on this;° so had you saved
The noble Imogen to repent, and struck 10
Me, wretch more worth your vengeance. But alack,
You snatch some hence for little faults; that's love,
To have them fall° no more; you some permit
To second° ills with ills, each elder° worse,
And make them° dread it,° to the doers' thrift.° 15
But Imogen is your own. Do your best wills,
And make me blest to obey. I am brought hither
Among th' Italian gentry, and to fight
Against my lady's kingdom. 'Tis enough
That, Britain, I have killed thy mistress; peace, 20
I'll give no wound to thee. Therefore, good heavens,
Hear patiently my purpose. I'll disrobe me
Of these Italian weeds and suit myself
As does a Briton peasant. So I'll fight
Against the part° I come with; so I'll die 25
For thee, O Imogen, even for whom my life
Is every breath a death; and thus, unknown,
Pitied nor hated, to the face of peril
Myself I'll dedicate. Let me make men know
More valor in me than my habits° show. 30
Gods, put the strength o' th' Leonati in me.
To shame the guise° o' th' world, I will begin
The fashion, less without and more within.    Exit.


## Scene II. [Britain.]

Enter LUCIUS, IACHIMO, and the ROMAN ARMY at
one door, and the BRITON ARMY at another, Leonatus
POSTHUMUS following like a poor soldier. They march
over and go out.° Then enter again in skirmish IACHIMO
and POSTHUMUS. He vanquisheth and disarmeth
IACHIMO and then leaves him.

IACHIMO
The heaviness and guilt within my bosom
Takes off° my manhood. I have belied° a lady,
The princess of this country, and the air on't°
Revengingly enfeebles me; or° could this carl,°
A very drudge of nature's, have subdued me 5
In my profession? Knighthoods and honors, borne
As I wear mine, are titles but of scorn.
If that thy gentry, Britain, go before°
This lout as he exceeds our lords, the odds
Is that we scarce are men and you are gods.    Exit. 10

The battle continues. The BRITONS fly; CYMBELINE is
taken. Then enter to his rescue BELARIUS, GUIDERIUS,
and ARVIRAGUS.

---

20 **upon our note** on noticing us  23 **then** i.e., was then
26 **Who . . . breeding** you who through sharing my exile
experience a lack of education  27 **certainty** inescapability
29 **tanlings** tanned persons  33 **o'ergrown** replaced in their
thoughts  37 **hot** lecherous  39 **rowel** the wheel on a spur
46 **hazard therefore due** risk attendant upon being unblessed
50 **cracked** i.e., since old  51 **country** country's
**V.i.2 You married ones** he addresses the audience

5 **wrying** deviating, going wrong  7 **No bond but** i.e., he is
bound only  9 **put on this** instigate this crime  13 **fall** i.e.,
from virtue  14 **second** follow up; **elder** i.e., later  15 **them**
the doers; **dread it** repent the evil course; **thrift** profit  25
**part** side  30 **habits** clothes  32 **guise** custom
**V.ii.s.d. They . . . out** each group marches about the stage
and exits by the other door  2 **Takes off** destroys; **belied**
slandered  3 **on't** of it  4 **or** otherwise; **carl** churl  8 **go
before** excel

BELARIUS
Stand, stand! We have th' advantage of the ground.
The lane is guarded. Nothing routs us but
The villainy of our fears.
GUIDERIUS, ARVIRAGUS    Stand, stand, and fight!

*Enter* POSTHUMUS *and seconds the* BRITONS. *They
rescue* CYMBELINE *and exeunt. Then enter* LUCIUS,
IACHIMO, *and* IMOGEN.

LUCIUS
Away, boy, from the troops, and save thyself,
For friends kill friends, and the disorder's such    15
As War were hoodwinked.°
IACHIMO                    'Tis their fresh supplies.
LUCIUS
It is a day turned strangely; or betimes°
Let's reinforce or fly.                    *Exeunt.*

Scene III. [*Britain.*]

*Enter* POSTHUMUS *and a Briton* LORD.

LORD
Cam'st thou from where they made the stand?
POSTHUMUS                        I did;
Though you, it seems, come from the fliers.
LORD                            I did.
POSTHUMUS
No blame be to you, sir, for all was lost,
But that the heavens fought. The king himself
Of his wings destitute, the army broken,    5
And but the backs of Britons seen, all flying
Through a strait° lane; the enemy full-hearted,°
Lolling the tongue with slaught'ring, having work
More plentiful than tools to do't, struck down
Some mortally, some slightly touched,° some falling    10
Merely through fear, that the strait pass was dammed
With dead men hurt behind,° and cowards living
To die with lengthened shame.
LORD                    Where was this lane?
POSTHUMUS
Close by the battle, ditched, and walled with turf;
Which gave advantage to an ancient soldier,    15
An honest one I warrant, who deserved
So long a breeding as his white beard came to,°
In doing this for's country. Athwart the lane
He with two striplings—lads more like to run
The country base° than to commit such slaughter;    20
With faces fit for masks,° or rather fairer
Than those for preservation cased or shame°—
Made good the passage, cried to those that fled,
"Our Britain's harts die flying, not our men.
To darkness fleet° souls that fly backwards. Stand,    25
Or we are Romans° and will give you that

Like beasts which you shun beastly,° and may save
But to look back in frown.° Stand, stand!" These
    three,
Three thousand confident, in act as many—
For three performers are the file° when all    30
The rest do nothing—with this word "Stand, stand,"
Accommodated by the place, more charming°
With their own nobleness, which could have turned
A distaff to a lance, gilded° pale looks,
Part° shame, part spirit renewed; that some, turned
    coward    35
But by example°—O, a sin in war,
Damned in the first beginners!—'gan to look
The way that they° did and to grin° like lions
Upon the pikes o' th' hunters. Then began
A stop i' th' chaser,° a retire; anon°    40
A rout, confusion thick. Forthwith they fly
Chickens, the way which they stooped° eagles; slaves,
The strides they victors made; and now our cowards,
Like fragments° in hard voyages, became
The life o' th' need.° Having found the back door open    45
Of the unguarded hearts, heavens, how they wound!
Some slain before,° some dying, some° their friends
O'erborne i' th' former wave, ten chased by one
Are now each one the slaughterman of twenty.
Those that would die or ere° resist are grown    50
The mortal bugs° o' th' field.°
LORD                    This was strange chance:
A narrow lane, an old man, and two boys.
POSTHUMUS
Nay, do not wonder at it. You are made
Rather to wonder at the things you hear
Than to work any.° Will you rhyme upon't    55
And vent it° for a mock'ry? Here is one:
"Two boys, an old man twice a boy, a lane,
Preserved the Britons, was the Romans' bane."
LORD
Nay, be not angry, sir.
POSTHUMUS            'Lack, to what end?
Who dares not stand° his foe, I'll be his friend;    60
For if he'll do as he is made° to do,
I know he'll quickly fly my friendship too.
You have put° me into rhyme.
LORD                Farewell. You're angry. *Exit.*
POSTHUMUS
Still going?° This is a lord! O noble misery,°
To be i' th' field, and ask "What news?" of me!    65
Today how many would have given their honors
To have saved their carcasses, took heel to do't,
And yet died too! I, in mine own woe charmed,°

16 **hoodwinked** blindfolded   17 **or betimes** either quickly
**V.iii.7 strait** narrow; **full-hearted** full of courage   10
**touched** wounded   12 **behind** i.e., while running away   17
**So . . . to** to live (renowned) as long after this day as he had
lived before in growing his beard   19–20 **run . . . base** play
the game of prisoner's base   21 **masks** for protection from
sunburn (so used by ladies)   22 **for . . . shame** covered for
protection or modesty   25 **fleet** are wafted   26 **are Romans**
i.e., will behave like Romans

27 **beastly** like cowards   27–28 **save . . . frown** prevent
only by looking back defiantly   30 **file** whole force   32
**more charming** i.e., winning over others   34 **gilded**
brought color to   35 **Part** some   36 **by example** by imitating
others   38 **they** the three men; **grin** bare the teeth   40 **stop
. . . chaser** sudden check (as of a horse) on the part of the
pursuer; **anon** soon   42 **stooped** swooped (hawking term)
44 **fragments** scraps (of food)   45 **life . . . need** a source of
life in time of need   47 **slain before** i.e., who had feigned
death; **some** some of   50 **or ere** before   51 **mortal bugs**
deadly terrors; **field** battle   55 **work any** perform any such
deeds   56 **vent it** make it known   60 **stand** withstand   61
**made** naturally inclined   63 **put** forced   64 **going** running
away; **noble misery** wretchedness of false nobility   68
**charmed** preserved as by a charm

Could not find Death where I did hear him groan
Nor feel him where he struck. Being an ugly monster,   70
'Tis strange he hides him in fresh cups, soft beds,
Sweet words, or hath moe ministers than we
That draw his knives i' th' war. Well, I will find him,
For being now a favorer to° the Briton,
No more a Briton.° I have resumed again   75
The part I came in. Fight I will no more,
But yield me to the veriest hind° that shall
Once touch my shoulder.° Great the slaughter is
Here made by th' Roman; great the answer° be
Britons must take. For me, my ransom's death.   80
On either side I come to spend my breath,°
Which neither here I'll keep nor bear again,
But end it by some means for Imogen.

*Enter two [Briton] CAPTAINS and SOLDIERS.*

FIRST CAPTAIN
Great Jupiter be praised, Lucius is taken.
'Tis thought the old man and his sons were angels.   85
SECOND CAPTAIN
There was a fourth man, in a silly habit,°
That gave th' affront° with them.
FIRST CAPTAIN                    So 'tis reported,
But none of 'em can be found. Stand, who's there?
POSTHUMUS
A Roman,
Who had not now been drooping here if seconds°   90
Had answered him.°
SECOND CAPTAIN   Lay hands on him. A dog,
A leg of Rome shall not return to tell
What crows have pecked them here. He brags his service
As if he were of note.° Bring him to th' king.

*Enter CYMBELINE, BELARIUS, GUIDERIUS, ARVIR-*
*AGUS, PISANIO, and Roman CAPTIVES [guarded]. The*
*CAPTAINS present POSTHUMUS to CYMBELINE, who*
*delivers him over to a JAILER.*           [Exeunt.]

### Scene IV. [Britain.]

*Enter° POSTHUMUS and [two] JAILERS.*

FIRST JAILER
You shall not now be stol'n; you have locks upon you.
So graze as you find pasture.
SECOND JAILER          Ay, or a stomach.°
                              [Exeunt JAILERS.]
POSTHUMUS
Most welcome, bondage, for thou art a way,
I think, to liberty. Yet am I better
Than one that's sick o' th' gout, since he had rather   5

Groan so in perpetuity than be cured
By th' sure physician, Death, who is the key
T' unbar these locks. My conscience, thou art fettered
More than my shanks and wrists. You good gods, give me
The penitent instrument to pick that bolt,°   10
Then free° for ever. Is't enough I am sorry?
So children temporal fathers do appease;
Gods are more full of mercy. Must I repent,
I cannot do it better than in gyves,°
Desired more than constrained.° To satisfy,°   15
If of my freedom 'tis the main part,° take
No stricter render° of me than my all.°
I know you are more clement than vile men,
Who of their broken debtors take a third,
A sixth, a tenth, letting them thrive again   20
On their abatement.° That's not my desire.
For Imogen's dear life take mine; and though
'Tis not so dear,° yet 'tis a life; you coined it.
'Tween man and man they weigh not every stamp;°
Though light, take pieces for the figure's° sake;   25
You rather mine, being yours.° And so, great pow'rs,
If you will take this audit,° take this life
And cancel these cold bonds.° O Imogen,
I'll speak to thee in silence.

*[Sleeps.]*

*Solemn music. Enter, as in an apparition, SICILIUS*
*Leonatus, father to POSTHUMUS, an old man attired like*
*a warrior; leading in his hand an ancient MATRON, his*
*wife and mother to POSTHUMUS with MUSIC° before*
*them. Then, after other MUSIC, follows the two young*
*LEONATI, brothers to Posthumus, with wounds as they*
*died in the wars. They circle POSTHUMUS round as he*
*lies sleeping.*

SICILIUS
No more, thou Thunder-master,° show thy spite on mortal flies.   30
With Mars fall out, with Juno chide, that thy adulteries
      Rates° and revenges.
Hath my poor boy done aught but well, whose face I never saw?
I died whilst in the womb he stayed attending°
      Nature's law;
Whose father then, as men report thou orphans' father art,   35
Thou shouldst have been, and shielded him from this earth-vexing smart.°

**74 being . . . to** since he now favors   **75 No . . . Briton**
i.e., I will seek Death among the Romans   **77 hind** peasant
**78 touch my shoulder** as in a formal arrest   **79 answer**
retaliation   **81 spend my breath** give up my life   **86 a silly
habit** lowly clothing   **87 affront** attack   **90 seconds**
supporters   **91 answered him** acted as he did   **94 note**
reputation
**V.iv.s.d. Enter** the action may be continuous from V.iii,
Posthumus and the Jailers remaining on stage after the exit of
Cymbeline at the end of that scene; in any case at the beginning
of V.iv the locale of the action changes from open country to a
prison   **2 stomach** appetite (for grazing)

**10 penitent . . . bolt** tool of repentance which will unfetter
my conscience   **11 free** i.e., in death   **14 gyves** fetters   **15
constrained** forced upon me; **satisfy** make atonement   **16
If . . . part** i.e., if atonement is essential to my freedom of
conscience   **17 stricter render** sterner repayment; **all** i.e., life
**21 abatement** reduced amount   **23 dear** valuable   **24 stamp**
coin   **25 figure** the ruler's image stamped on the "piece"
(coin)   **26 You . . . yours** i.e., you should take my life the
sooner since (though light coin) it is at least stamped in your
image   **27 take this audit** accept this account   **28 cancel
. . . bonds** i.e., remove (through letting me die) these iron
shackles (quibble on the sense of "void these worthless contracts")   **29 s.d. Music** musicians   **30 Thunder-master**
Jupiter   **32 Rates** scolds   **34 Attending** awaiting   **36 earth-
vexing smart** suffering which plagues the life of man

MOTHER
Lucina° lent not me her aid, but took me in my throes,
That from me was Posthumus ripped, came crying
    'mongst his foes,
        A thing of pity.

SICILIUS
Great Nature like his ancestry moulded the stuff° so
    fair          40
That he deserved the praise o' th' world, as great
    Sicilius' heir.

FIRST BROTHER
When once he was mature for man,° in Britain where
    was he
That could stand up his parallel, or fruitful° object be
In eye of Imogen, that best could deem his dignity?°

MOTHER
With marriage wherefore was he mocked, to be exiled
    and thrown          45
From Leonati seat and cast from her his dearest one,
    Sweet Imogen?

SICILIUS
Why did you° suffer Iachimo, slight° thing of Italy,
To taint his nobler heart and brain with needless
    jealousy,
And to become the geck° and scorn o' th' other's
    villainy?          50

SECOND BROTHER
For this from stiller seats° we come, our parents and
    us twain,
That striking in our country's cause fell bravely and
    were slain,
Our fealty and Tenantius'° right with honor to main-
    tain.

FIRST BROTHER
Like hardiment° Posthumus hath to Cymbeline per-
    formed.
Then, Jupiter, thou king of gods, why hast thou thus
    adjourned°          55
The graces for his merits due, being all to dolors
    turned?

SICILIUS
Thy crystal window ope; look out. No longer exercise
Upon a valiant race thy harsh and potent injuries.

MOTHER
Since, Jupiter, our son is good, take off his miseries.

SICILIUS
Peep through thy marble mansion. Help, or we poor
    ghosts will cry          60
To th' shining synod of the rest° against thy deity.

BROTHERS
Help, Jupiter, or we appeal and from thy justice fly.

JUPITER *descends*° *in thunder and lightning, sitting upon
an eagle. He throws a thunderbolt. The* GHOSTS *fall on
their knees.*

JUPITER
No more, you petty spirits of region low,°
    Offend our hearing. Hush! How dare you ghosts
Accuse the Thunderer, whose bolt, you know,      65
    Sky-planted,° batters all rebelling coasts?
Poor shadows of Elysium, hence, and rest
    Upon your never-withering banks of flow'rs.
Be not with mortal accidents° opprest.
    No care of yours it is; you know 'tis ours.      70
Whom best I love I cross;° to make my gift,
    The more delayed, delighted. Be content.
Your low-laid son our godhead will uplift;
    His comforts thrive, his trials well are spent.°
Our Jovial star° reigned at his birth, and in      75
    Our temple was he married. Rise, and fade.
He shall be lord of Lady Imogen,
    And happier much by his affliction made.
This tablet lay upon his breast, wherein
    Our pleasure his full fortune doth confine.°      80
And so, away; no farther with your din
    Express impatience, lest you stir up mine.
Mount, eagle, to my palace crystalline.      *Ascends.*

SICILIUS
He came in thunder; his celestial breath
Was sulphurous to smell; the holy eagle      85
Stooped, as to foot us.° His ascension is
More sweet° than our blest fields;° his royal bird
Prunes° the immortal wing and cloys° his beak,
As when his god is pleased.

ALL                    Thanks, Jupiter.

SICILIUS
The marble pavement closes;° he is entered      90
His radiant roof. Away, and, to be blest,
Let us with care perform his great behest.
               [*The* GHOSTS] *vanish.*°

POSTHUMUS [*Waking.*]
Sleep, thou hast been a grandsire and begot
A father to me, and thou hast created
A mother and two brothers; but, O scorn,°      95
Gone! They went hence so soon as they were born.
Am so I am awake. Poor wretches that depend
On greatness' favor, dream as I have done,
Wake, and find nothing. But, alas, I swerve.°
Many dream not to find, neither deserve,      100
And yet are steeped in favors. So am I,
That have this golden chance and know not why.
What fairies haunt this ground? A book? O rare one,
Be not, as is our fangled° world, a garment
Nobler than that it covers. Let thy effects      105
So follow to° be most unlike our courtiers,
As good as promise.

*Reads.*

"Whenas° a lion's whelp shall, to himself unknown,

---

63 **region low** Hades   66 **Sky-planted** based in the sky   69 **accidents** occurrences   71 **cross** thwart   74 **spent** ended   75 **Jovial star** the planet Jupiter   80 **confine** i.e., state precisely   86 **Stooped . . . us** swooped (hawking term) as if to seize us in his talons   87 **More sweet** in contrast to his angry, sulphurous descent; **our blest fields** the Elysian Fields   88 **Prunes** preens; **cloys** claws   90 **closes** apparently an allusion to the trap door in the underside of the stage cover through which Jupiter has ascended   92 **s.d. vanish** i.e., exit rapidly   95 **scorn** mockery   99 **swerve** err   104 **fangled** addicted to finery   106 **to** as to   108 **Whenas** when

37 **Lucina** Juno Lucina (goddess of childbirth)   40 **stuff** substance   42 **mature for man** fully matured   43 **fruitful** ripe, mature   44 **deem his dignity** judge his worth   48 **you** Jupiter; **slight** worthless   50 **geck** dupe   51 **stiller seats** quieter abodes (in the Elysian Fields)   53 **Tenantius'** Sicilius'   54 **hardiment** bold exploits   55 **adjourned** deferred   61 **the rest** the other gods   62 **s.d. descends** Jupiter is lowered by suspension-gear from stage cover to stage

without seeking find, and be embraced by a piece of
tender air; and when from a stately cedar shall be 110
lopped branches which, being dead many years, shall
after revive, be jointed to the old stock, and freshly
grow; then shall Posthumus end his miseries, Britain
be fortunate and flourish in peace and plenty."
'Tis still a dream, or else such stuff as madmen   115
Tongue,° and brain° not; either, both, or nothing;
Or senseless° speaking, or a speaking such
As sense° cannot untie. Be what it is,
The action of my life is like it,° which
I'll keep, if but for sympathy.°   120

*Enter* JAILER.

JAILER   Come, sir, are you ready for death?
POSTHUMUS   Overroasted rather; ready long ago.
JAILER   Hanging° is the word, sir. If you be ready for
that, you are well cooked.
POSTHUMUS   So, if I prove a good repast to the 125
spectators, the dish pays the shot.°
JAILER   A heavy reckoning for you, sir. But the comfort is, you shall be called to no more payments, fear
no more tavern bills, which are as often the sadness of
parting as the procuring of mirth. You come in faint 130
for want of meat, depart reeling with too much drink;
sorry that you have paid too much, and sorry that you
are paid too much;° purse and brain both empty; the
brain the heavier for being too light, the purse too
light, being drawn° of heaviness. O, of this contradic- 135
tion you shall now be quit. O, the charity of a penny
cord! It sums up thousands in a trice. You have no true
debitor and creditor° but it; of what's past, is, and to
come, the discharge.° Your neck, sir, is pen, book, and
counters;° so the acquittance° follows.   140
POSTHUMUS   I am merrier to die than thou art to live.
JAILER   Indeed, sir, he that sleeps feels not the toothache; but a man that were° to sleep your sleep, and a
hangman to help him to bed, I think he would change
places with his officer;° for, look you, sir, you know 145
not which way you shall go.
POSTHUMUS   Yes indeed do I, fellow.
JAILER   Your death has eyes in's head° then. I have not
seen him so pictured.° You must either be directed by
some that take upon them to know, or to take upon 150
yourself that which I am sure you do not know, or
jump° the after-inquiry on your own peril. And how
you shall speed in° your journey's end, I think you'll
never return to tell on.°
POSTHUMUS   I tell thee, fellow, there are none want 155
eyes to direct them the way I am going but such as
wink° and will not use them.

116 **Tongue** speak; **brain** understand   117 **Or** senseless either irrational   118 **sense** the power of reason   119
**like it** i.e., without meaning or incapable of understanding
120 **sympathy** the resemblance   123 **Hanging** the Jailer,
picking up the metaphor in "Overroasted," quibbles on the
sense of "hanging of meat"   126 **dish . . . shot** the excellence
of the food justifies its cost   133 **are . . . much** have been
subdued by too much liquor   135 **drawn** emptied   138
**debitor and creditor** account book   139 **discharge** payment
140 **counters** used for reckoning; **acquittance** receipt   143
**a man that were** i.e., if a man were destined   145 **officer**
executioner   148 **Your . . . head** i.e., you seem to be informed
about what will happen to you after death   149 **pictured** in
the traditional skull or death's head   152 **jump** gamble on   153
**speed in** fare at   154 **on** of   157 **wink** close

JAILER   What an infinite mock is this, that a man
should have the best use of eyes to see the way of
blindness! I am sure hanging's the way of winking.   160

*Enter a* MESSENGER.

MESSENGER   Knock off his manacles; bring your
prisoner to the king.
POSTHUMUS   Thou bring'st good news; I am called
to be made free.°
JAILER   I'll be hanged then.   165
POSTHUMUS   Thou shalt be then freer than a jailer.
No bolts for the dead.

   [*Exeunt* POSTHUMUS *and* MESSENGER.]

JAILER   Unless a man would marry a gallows and
beget young gibbets, I never saw one so prone.° Yet,
on my conscience, there are verier knaves desire to live, 170
for all° he be a Roman; and there be some of them°
too that die against their wills. So should I, if I were
one. I would we were all of one mind, and one mind
good. O, there were desolation of jailers and gallowses!
I speak against my present profit, but my wish hath a 175
preferment° int'.   *Exit.*

## Scene V. [*Britain.*]

*Enter* CYMBELINE, BELARIUS, GUIDERIUS, ARVIR-
AGUS, PISANIO, *and* LORDS.

CYMBELINE
Stand by my side, you whom the gods have made
Preservers of my throne. Woe is my heart
That the poor soldier that so richly fought,
Whose rags shamed gilded arms, whose naked breast
Stepped before targes of proof,° cannot be found.   5
He shall be happy that can find him, if
Our grace can make him so.
BELARIUS                            I never saw
Such noble fury in so poor a thing,
Such precious deeds in one that promised naught
But beggary and poor looks.
CYMBELINE                  No tidings of him?   10
PISANIO
He hath been searched among the dead and living,
But no trace of him.
CYMBELINE           To my grief, I am
The heir of his reward, which I will add
To you, the liver, heart, and brain° of Britain,
By whom I grant she lives. 'Tis now the time   15
To ask of whence you are. Report it.
BELARIUS                              Sir,
In Cambria are we born, and gentlemen.
Further to boast were neither true nor modest,
Unless I add we are honest.
CYMBELINE                   Bow your knees.
Arise my knights o' th' battle;° I create you   20
Companions to our person and will fit° you
With dignities becoming your estates.°

164 **made free** i.e., by death   169 **prone** eager   171 **for all**
even though; **them** Romans   176 **preferment** promotion
(for myself)
V.v.5 **targes of proof** shields of proven strength   14 **liver
. . . brain** the vital parts—Belarius, Guiderius, and Arviragus
20 **knights . . . battle** knights created on the battlefield
21 **fit** equip   22 **estates** ranks

*Enter* CORNELIUS *and* LADIES.

There's business in these faces. Why so sadly
Greet you our victory? You look like Romans
And not o' th' court of Britain.

CORNELIUS                Hail, great king!    25
To sour your happiness I must report
The queen is dead.

CYMBELINE        Who worse than a physician
Would this report become? But I consider
By med'cine life may be prolonged, yet death
Will seize the doctor too. How ended she?    30

CORNELIUS
With horror, madly dying, like her life,
Which, being cruel to the world, concluded
Most cruel to herself. What she confessed
I will report, so please you. These her women
Can trip me° if I err, who with wet cheeks    35
Were present when she finished.

CYMBELINE             Prithee say.

CORNELIUS
First, she confessed she never loved you, only
Affected° greatness got by you, not you;
Married your royalty, was wife to your place,
Abhorred your person.°

CYMBELINE         She alone knew this,    40
And but° she spoke it dying, I would not
Believe her lips in opening° it. Proceed.

CORNELIUS
Your daughter, whom she bore in hand° to love
With such integrity, she did confess
Was as a scorpion to her sight, whose life,    45
But that her flight prevented it, she had
Ta'en off° by poison.

CYMBELINE        O most delicate° fiend!
Who is't can read a woman? Is there more?

CORNELIUS
More, sir, and worse. She did confess she had
For you a mortal mineral,° which, being took,    50
Should by the minute° feed on life and, ling'ring,
By inches waste you. In which time she purposed,
By watching, weeping, tendance,° kissing, to
O'ercome you with her show° and, in time,
When she had fitted you° with her craft, to work    55
Her son into th' adoption of the crown;
But failing of her end by his strange absence,
Grew shameless desperate, opened, in despite
Of heaven and men, her purposes, repented
The evils she hatched were not effected, so    60
Despairing died.

CYMBELINE      Heard you all this, her women?

LADIES
We did, so please your highness.

CYMBELINE           Mine eyes
Were not in fault, for she was beautiful;
Mine ears, that heard her flattery; nor my heart,

That thought her like her seeming.° It had been
vicious°    65
To have mistrusted her. Yet, O my daughter,
That it° was folly in me thou mayst say,
And prove it in thy feeling.° Heaven mend all!

*Enter* LUCIUS, IACHIMO, [*the* SOOTHSAYER,] *and
other Roman* PRISONERS, [*guarded; the* MESSENGER
*and* POSTHUMUS] *Leonatus behind;*° *and* IMOGEN.

Thou com'st not, Caius, now for tribute. That
The Britons have razed out,° though with the loss    70
Of many a bold one; whose kinsmen have made suit
That their° good souls may be appeased with slaughter
Of you their captives, which ourself have granted.
So think of your estate.°

LUCIUS
Consider, sir, the chance of war. The day    75
Was yours by accident; had it gone with us,
We should not, when the blood was cool, have
threatened
Our prisoners with the sword. But since the gods
Will have it thus, that nothing but our lives
May be called ransom, let it come. Sufficeth    80
A Roman with a Roman's heart can suffer.
Augustus lives to think on't—and so much
For my peculiar° care. This one thing only
I will entreat: my boy, a Briton born,
Let him be ransomed. Never master had    85
A page so kind, so duteous, diligent,
So tender over his occasions,° true,
So feat,° so nurselike. Let his virtue join
With my request, which I'll make bold your highness
Cannot deny. He hath done no Briton harm,    90
Though he have served a Roman. Save him, sir,
And spare no blood beside.

CYMBELINE        I have surely seen him;
His favor° is familiar to me. Boy,
Thou hast looked thyself into° my grace
And art mine own. I know not why, wherefore,    95
To say,° "Live, boy." Ne'er thank thy master. Live,
And ask of Cymbeline what boon thou wilt,
Fitting my bounty and thy state; I'll give it,
Yea, though thou do demand a prisoner,
The noblest ta'en.

IMOGEN        I humbly thank your highness.    100

LUCIUS
I do not bid thee beg my life, good lad,
And yet I know thou wilt.

IMOGEN           No, no, alack,
There's other work in hand. I see a thing°
Bitter to me as death; your life, good master,
Must shuffle° for itself.

LUCIUS          The boy disdains me;    105
He leaves me, scorns me. Briefly° die their joys

---

**35 trip me** expose inaccuracy   **38 Affected** loved   **40 your
person** you as a person   **41 but** except that   **42 opening**
disclosing   **43 bore in hand** pretended   **47 Ta'en off**
destroyed; **delicate** subtle   **50 mortal mineral** deadly poison
**51 by the minute** minute by minute   **53 tendance** attention
**54 show** simulation (of devotion)   **55 fitted you** shaped you
to her purpose

**65 seeming** appearance; **had been vicious** would have
been morally wrong   **67 it** trusting her   **68 prove . . . feeling** experience the effect of my folly in your suffering   **68
s.d. behind** Posthumus remains apart from the main group
of players till line 209   **70 razed out** erased   **72 their** i.e., of
those slain in battle   **74 your estate** the condition of your souls
**83 peculiar** individual   **87 tender . . . occasions** sensitive
to his wants   **88 feat** dexterous   **93 favor** face   **94 looked
thyself into** gained by thy looks   **96 To say** I am saying
**103 thing** the ring on Iachimo's finger   **105 shuffle** shift
**106 Briefly** quickly

That place them on the truth° of girls and boys.
Why stands he so perplexed?
CYMBELINE What wouldst thou, boy?
I love thee more and more. Think more and more
What's best to ask. Know'st him thou look'st on?
  Speak. 110
Wilt have him live? Is he thy kin? Thy friend?
IMOGEN
He is a Roman, no more kin to me
Than I to your highness; who, being born your vassal,
Am something nearer.
CYMBELINE Wherefore ey'st him so?
IMOGEN
I'll tell you, sir, in private, if you please 115
To give me hearing.
CYMBELINE Ay, with all my heart,
And lend my best attention. What's thy name?
IMOGEN
Fidele, sir.
CYMBELINE Thou'rt my good youth, my page;
I'll be thy master. Walk with me; speak freely.
BELARIUS
Is not this boy revived from death?
ARVIRAGUS One sand another 120
Not more resembles that sweet rosy lad
Who died, and was Fidele. What think you?
GUIDERIUS
The same dead thing alive.
BELARIUS
Peace, peace, see further. He eyes us not; forbear.
Creatures may be alike. Were't he, I am sure 125
He would have spoke to us.
GUIDERIUS But we saw him dead.
BELARIUS
Be silent, let's see further.
PISANIO [Aside.] It is my mistress.
Since she is living, let the time run on
To good or bad.
CYMBELINE Come, stand thou by our side;
Make thy demand aloud.—Sir, step you forth, 130
Give answer to this boy, and do it freely;
Or, by our greatness and the grace of it,
Which is our honor, bitter torture shall
Winnow the truth from falsehood.—On, speak to him.
IMOGEN
My boon is that this gentleman may render° 135
Of whom he had this ring.
POSTHUMUS [Aside.] What's that to him?
CYMBELINE
That diamond upon your·finger, say
How came it yours.
IACHIMO
Thou'lt torture me to leave° unspoken that
Which to be spoke would torture thee.
CYMBELINE How? Me? 140
IACHIMO
I am glad to be constrained to utter that
Which torments me to conceal. By villainy
I got this ring. 'Twas Leonatus' jewel,
Whom thou didst banish, and—which more may
  grieve thee,

As it doth me—a nobler sir ne'er lived 145
'Twixt sky and ground. Wilt thou hear more, my lord?
CYMBELINE
All that belongs to this.
IACHIMO That paragon, thy daughter,
For whom my heart drops blood and° my false spirits
Quail to remember—Give me leave, I faint.
CYMBELINE
My daughter? What of her? Renew thy strength. 150
I had rather thou shouldst live while nature will°
Than die ere I hear more. Strive, man, and speak.
IACHIMO
Upon a time—unhappy was the clock
That struck the hour!—it was in Rome—accursed
The mansion where!—'twas at a feast—O, would 155
Our viands had been poisoned, or at least
Those which I heaved to head!°—the good Posthu-
  mus—
What should I say? He was too good to be
Where ill men were, and was the best of all
Amongst the rar'st of good ones—sitting sadly, 160
Hearing us praise our loves of Italy
For beauty that made barren the swelled boast
Of him that best could speak; for feature,° laming
The shrine° of Venus or straight-pight° Minerva,
Postures° beyond brief nature;° for condition,° 165
A shop° of all the qualities that man
Loves woman for; besides that hook° of wiving,
Fairness which strikes the eye—
CYMBELINE I stand on fire.
Come to the matter.°
IACHIMO All too soon I shall,
Unless thou wouldst grieve quickly. This Posthumus, 170
Most like a noble lord in love and one
That had a royal lover, took his hint,°
And not dispraising whom we praised—therein
He was as calm as virtue—he began
His mistress' picture; which by his tongue being made, 175
And then a mind put in't,° either our brags
Were cracked° of kitchen trulls, or his description
Proved us unspeaking sots.°
CYMBELINE Nay, nay, to th' purpose.
IACHIMO
Your daughter's chastity—there it begins.
He spake of her as° Dian had hot dreams 180
And she alone were cold;° whereat I, wretch,
Made scruple of° his praise and wagered with him
Pieces of gold 'gainst this which then he wore
Upon his honored finger, to attain
In suit° the place of's bed and win this ring 185
By hers and mine adultery. He, true knight,
No lesser of her honor confident

107 truth loyalty   135 render state   139 to leave for leaving

148 and and whom   151 while nature will the rest of
your natural life   157 heaved to head lifted to mouth
163 feature shapeliness   163–64 laming The shrine making
deformed (by comparison) the image   164 straight-pight
tall, erect   165 Postures forms; beyond brief nature i.e.,
more richly endowed than mortal beings; condition character
166 shop repository   167 hook fishhook   169 matter point
172 hint opportunity   176 And . . . in't i.e., added to which
was a good mind   177 cracked boasted   178 unspeaking
sots inarticulate fools   180 as as if   181 cold chaste   182
Made scruple of expressed doubt about, disputed   185 suit
amorous solicitation (Maxwell)

Than I did truly find her, stakes this ring;
And would so, had it been a carbuncle°
Of Phoebus' wheel,° and might so safely had it          190
Been all the worth of's car. Away to Britain
Post I in this design. Well may you, sir,
Remember me at court, where I was taught
Of° your chaste daughter the wide difference
'Twixt amorous° and villainous. Being thus quenched  195
Of hope, not longing,° mine Italian brain
'Gan in your duller Britain operate
Most vilely; for my vantage,° excellent.
And, to be brief, my practice° so prevailed
That I returned with simular° proof enough              200
To make the noble Leonatus mad
By wounding his belief in her renown°
With tokens thus and thus; averring° notes
Of chamber hanging, pictures, this her bracelet—
O cunning, how I got it!—nay, some marks                205
Of secret on her person, that he could not
But think her bond of chastity quite cracked,
I having ta'en the forfeit.° Whereupon—
Methinks I see him now—
POSTHUMUS  [Advancing.] Ay, so thou dost,
Italian fiend! Ay me, most credulous fool,              210
Egregious murderer, thief, anything
That's due° to all the villains past, in being,
To come! O, give me cord or knife or poison,
Some upright justicer!° Thou, king, send out
For torturers ingenious. It is I                        215
That all th' abhorrèd things o' th' earth amend°
By being worse than they. I am Posthumus,
That killed thy daughter—villainlike, I lie—
That caused a lesser villain than myself,
A sacrilegious thief, to do't. The temple               220
Of Virtue was she; yea, and she herself.°
Spit, and throw stones, cast mire upon me, set
The dogs o' th' street to bay me; every villain
Be called Posthumus Leonatus, and
Be villainy less° than 'twas! O Imogen!                 225
My queen, my life, my wife! O Imogen,
Imogen, Imogen!
IMOGEN              Peace, my lord. Hear, hear—
POSTHUMUS
Shall's° have a play of this? Thou scornful page,
There lie thy part.° [Striking her; she falls.]
PISANIO              O gentlemen, help!
Mine and your mistress! O my lord Posthumus,            230
You ne'er killed Imogen till now. Help, help!
Mine honored lady!
CYMBELINE          Does the world go round?
POSTHUMUS
How comes these staggers° on me?
PISANIO                        Wake, my mistress!

CYMBELINE
If this be so, the gods do mean to strike me
To death with mortal° joy.
PISANIO                    How fares my mistress?  235
IMOGEN
O, get thee from my sight;
Thou gav'st me poison. Dangerous fellow, hence;
Breathe not where princes are.
CYMBELINE                  The tune° of Imogen!
PISANIO
Lady,
The gods throw stones of sulphur° on me if             240
That box I gave you was not thought by me
A precious° thing; I had it from the queen.
CYMBELINE
New matter still.
IMOGEN          It poisoned me.
CORNELIUS          O gods!
I left out one thing which the queen confessed,
Which must approve° thee honest. "If Pisanio           245
Have," said she, "given his mistress that confection°
Which I gave him for cordial, she is served
As I would serve a rat."
CYMBELINE              What's this, Cornelius?
CORNELIUS
The queen, sir, very oft importuned me
To temper° poisons for her, still pretending°          250
The satisfaction of her knowledge only
In killing creatures vile, as cats and dogs
Of no esteem.° I, dreading that her purpose
Was of more danger, did compound for her
A certain stuff which, being ta'en, would cease°       255
The present pow'r of life, but in short time
All offices of nature° should again
Do their due functions. Have you ta'en of it?
IMOGEN
Most like° I did, for I was dead.°
BELARIUS                      My boys,
There was our error.
GUIDERIUS          This is sure Fidele.              260
IMOGEN
Why did you throw your wedded lady from you?
Think that you are upon a rock,° and now
Throw me again. [Embracing him.]
POSTHUMUS          Hang there like fruit, my soul,
Till the tree die!
CYMBELINE          How now, my flesh, my child?
What, mak'st thou me a dullard° in this act?°          265
Wilt thou not speak to me?
IMOGEN          [Kneeling.] Your blessing, sir.
BELARIUS
Though you did love this youth, I blame ye not;
You had a motive° for't.
CYMBELINE              My tears that fall

189 carbuncle red precious stone  190 Of Phoebus' wheel decorating the sun god's chariot  194 Of by  195 amorous i.e., faithful  195–96 Being . . . longing the fire of hope (though not of desire) being thus put out  198 vantage profit  199 practice plot  200 simular simulated, specious  202 renown good name  203 averring avouching  208 forfeit that which was forfeited for breach of contract  211–21 anything That's due any word that's appropriate  214 justicer judge  216 amend make better (by contrast)  221 she herself Virtue herself  225 less i.e., by comparison with my villainy  228 Shall's shall us (we)  229 There . . . part play your role lying there  233 staggers dizziness

235 mortal deadly, fatal  238 tune voice  240 stones of sulphur thunderbolts  242 precious i.e., beneficial  245 approve prove  246 confection drug  250 temper mix; still pretending always alleging as her purpose  253 esteem value  255 cease suspend  257 offices of nature bodily parts  259 like probably; dead as if dead  262 upon a rock sense unclear; "rock" is sometimes emended to "lock," a hold in wrestling  265 mak'st . . . dullard treat me like a fool (by ignoring me); act action, scene  268 motive cause

Prove holy water on thee. Imogen,
Thy mother's° dead.

IMOGEN                    I am sorry for't, my lord.          270

CYMBELINE
O, she was naught,° and long of° her it was
That we meet here so strangely; but her son
Is gone, we know not how nor where.

PISANIO                              My lord,
Now fear is from me, I'll speak troth.° Lord Cloten,
Upon my lady's missing, came to me          275
With his sword drawn, foamed at the mouth, and
    swore,
If I discovered° not which way she was gone,
It was my instant death. By accident
I had a feignèd letter of my master's
Then in my pocket, which directed him          280
To seek her on the mountains near to Milford;
Where, in a frenzy, in my master's garments,
Which he enforced from me, away he posts
With unchaste purpose and with oath to violate
My lady's honor. What became of him          285
I further know not.

GUIDERIUS          Let me end the story:
I slew him there.

CYMBELINE          Marry,° the gods forfend!°
I would not thy good deeds° should from my lips
Pluck a hard sentence. Prithee, valiant youth,
Deny't again.°

GUIDERIUS    I have spoke it, and I did it.          290

CYMBELINE
He was a prince.

GUIDERIUS
A most incivil° one. The wrongs he did me
Were nothing princelike, for he did provoke me
With language that would make me spurn the sea
If it could so roar to me. I cut off's head,          295
And am right glad he is not standing here
To tell this tale of mine.

CYMBELINE                    I am sorry for thee.
By thine own tongue thou art condemned and must
Endure our law. Thou'rt dead.

IMOGEN                              That headless man
I thought had been my lord.

CYMBELINE                    Bind the offender          300
And take him from our presence.

BELARIUS                    Stay, sir king.
This man is better than the man he slew,
As well descended as thyself, and hath
More of thee merited than a band of Clotens
Had ever scar for.°—Let his arms alone;          305
They were not born for bondage.

CYMBELINE                    Why, old soldier:
Wilt thou undo the worth thou art unpaid for°
By tasting of our wrath? How of descent
As good as we?

ARVIRAGUS    In that he spake too far.

CYMBELINE
And thou° shalt die for't.

BELARIUS                    We will die all three          310
But I will prove° that two on's° are as good
As I have given out him. My sons, I must
For mine own part unfold a dangerous speech,
Though haply well for you.

ARVIRAGUS                    Your danger's ours.

GUIDERIUS
And our good his.

BELARIUS          Have at it then. By leave,°          315
Thou hadst, great king, a subject who
Was called Belarius.

CYMBELINE          What of him? He is
A banished traitor.

BELARIUS          He it is that hath
Assumed° this age; indeed a banished man,
I know not how a traitor.

CYMBELINE          Take him hence.          320
The whole world shall not save him.

BELARIUS                    Not too hot.°
First pay me for the nursing of thy sons,
And let it° be confiscate all, so soon
As I have received it.

CYMBELINE          Nursing of my sons?

BELARIUS
I am too blunt and saucy; here's my knee.          325
Ere I arise I will prefer° my sons;
Then spare not the old father. Mighty sir,
These two young gentlemen that call me father
And think they are my sons are none of mine;
They are the issue of your loins, my liege,          330
And blood of your begetting.

CYMBELINE                    How? My issue?

BELARIUS
So sure as you your father's. I, old Morgan,
Am that Belarius whom you sometime° banished.
Your pleasure was my mere° offense, my punishment
Itself, and all my treason; that I suffered          335
Was all the harm I did. These gentle princes—
For such and so they are—these twenty years
Have I trained up; those arts° they have as I
Could put into them. My breeding was, sir, as
Your highness knows. Their nurse, Euriphile,          340
Whom for the theft I wedded, stole these children
Upon my banishment. I moved° her to't,
Having received the punishment before
For that which I did then. Beaten° for loyalty
Excited me to treason. Their dear loss,          345
The more of° you 'twas felt, the more it shaped
Unto° my end of stealing them. But, gracious sir,
Here are your sons again, and I must lose
Two of the sweet'st companions in the world.
The benediction of these covering heavens          350
Fall on their heads like dew, for they are worthy
To inlay heaven with stars.

CYMBELINE                    Thou weep'st and speak'st.

270 **mother's** stepmother's  271 **naught** wicked; **long of** because of  274 **troth** truth  277 **discovered** revealed  287 **Marry** indeed (from "By the Virgin Mary"); **forfend** forbid  288 **thy good deeds** i.e., in view of the good deeds (in battle) that thou  290 **Deny't again** speak again and deny what you have said (Nosworthy)  292 **incivil** unmannerly  305 **Had . . . for** ever earned by wounds  307 **worth . . . for** thy not yet rewarded esteem (?)

310 **thou** Belarius  311 **But . . . prove** if I do not prove (Maxwell); **on's** of us  315 **By leave** by your permission  319 **Assumed** attained to  321 **hot** fast  323 **it** the payment  326 **prefer** promote (in rank)  333 **sometime** once  334 **mere** entire  338 **arts** accomplishments  342 **moved** incited  344 **Beaten** my having been beaten  346 **of** by  346–47 **shaped Unto** served

The service° that you three have done is more
Unlike° than this thou tell'st. I lost my children;
If these be they, I know not how to wish     355
A pair of worthier sons.

BELARIUS          Be pleased awhile.
This gentleman whom I call Polydore,
Most worthy prince, as yours, is true Guiderius;
This gentleman, my Cadwal, Arviragus,
Your younger princely son. He, sir, was lapped°     360
In a most curious° mantle, wrought by th' hand
Of his queen mother, which for more probation°
I can with ease produce.

CYMBELINE         Guiderius had
Upon his neck a mole, a sanguine° star;
It was a mark of wonder.

BELARIUS          This is he,     365
Who hath upon him still that natural stamp.
It was wise Nature's end° in the donation
To be his evidence now.

CYMBELINE         O, what am I?
A mother to the birth of three? Ne'er mother
Rejoiced deliverance more. Blest pray you be,     370
That, after this strange starting from your orbs,°
You may reign in them now! O Imogen,
Thou hast lost by this a kingdom.

IMOGEN          No, my lord,
I have got two worlds by't. O my gentle brothers,     375
Have we thus met? O, never say hereafter
But I am truest speaker. You called me brother
When I was but your sister, I you brothers
When ye were so indeed.

CYMBELINE         Did you e'er meet?

ARVIRAGUS
Ay, my good lord.

GUIDERIUS       And at first meeting loved,
Continued so until we thought he died.     380

CORNELIUS
By the queen's dram she swallowed.

CYMBELINE          O rare instinct!
When shall I hear all through? This fierce° abridgment
Hath to it circumstantial° branches, which
Distinction should be rich in.° Where, how lived you?
And when came you to serve our Roman captive?     385
How parted with your brothers? How first met them?
Why fled you from the court? And whither? These,
And your three motives° to the battle, with
I know not how much more, should be demanded,
And all the other bye-dependences°     390
From chance° to chance; but nor° the time nor place
Will serve our long inter'gatories. See,
Posthumus anchors upon Imogen,
And she like harmless lightning throws her eye
On him, her brothers, me, her master, hitting     395
Each object with a joy; the counterchange°

Is severally in all.° Let's quit this ground
And smoke° the temple with our sacrifices.
Thou° art my brother; so we'll hold thee ever.

IMOGEN
You° are my father too, and did relieve° me     400
To see this gracious season.°

CYMBELINE         All o'erjoyed
Save these in bonds; let them be joyful too,
For they shall taste our comfort.°

IMOGEN          My good master,
I will yet do you service.

LUCIUS         Happy be you!

CYMBELINE
The forlorn° soldier, that so nobly fought,     405
He would have well becomed this place and graced
The thankings of a king.

POSTHUMUS         I am, sir,
The soldier that did company these three
In poor beseeming;° 'twas a fitment° for
The purpose I then followed. That I was he,     410
Speak, Iachimo. I had you down and might
Have made you finish.°

IACHIMO    [Kneeling.] I am down again,
But now my heavy conscience sinks° my knee,
As then your force did. Take that life, beseech you,
Which I so often° owe; but your ring first,     415
And here the bracelet of the truest princess
That ever swore her faith.

POSTHUMUS         Kneel not to me.
The pow'r that I have on you is to spare you;
The malice towards you to forgive you. Live,
And deal with others better.

CYMBELINE         Nobly doomed!°     420
We'll learn our freeness° of a son-in-law:
Pardon's the word to all.

ARVIRAGUS         You holp us, sir,
As° you did mean indeed to be our brother.
Joyed are we that you are.

POSTHUMUS
Your servant, princes. Good my lord of Rome,     425
Call forth your soothsayer. As I slept, methought
Great Jupiter, upon his eagle backed,°
Appeared to me, with other spritely° shows
Of mine own kindred. When I waked, I found
This label° on my bosom, whose containing°     430
Is so from° sense in hardness that I can
Make no collection of° it. Let him show
His skill in the construction.°

LUCIUS         Philharmonus!

SOOTHSAYER
Here, my good lord.

LUCIUS         Read, and declare the meaning.

SOOTHSAYER (Reads.) "Whenas a lion's whelp shall,     435

---

353 **service** i.e., in battle   354 **Unlike** improbable   360 **lapped** wrapped   361 **curious** elaborately wrought   362 **probation** proof   364 **sanguine** blood-red   367 **end** purpose   371 **orbs** spheres, orbits (of planets)   382 **fierce** drastic   383 **circumstantial** detailed   383–84 **which . . . in** which deserves to be elaborately discriminated (Maxwell)   388 **your three motives** the motives of you three   390 **bye-dependences** connected circumstances   391 **chance** event; **nor** neither   396 **counterchange** exchange

397 **severally in all** in each and in all   398 **smoke** fill with smoke   399 **Thou** Belarius   400 **You** Belarius; **relieve** aid   401 **gracious season** joyful occasion   403 **taste our comfort** share in our joy   405 **forlorn** lost, missing   409 **beseeming** appearance, clothing; **fitment** suitable device   412 **finish** die   413 **sinks** lowers   415 **often** many times over   420 **doomed** judged   421 **freeness** generosity   423 **As** as if   427 **upon . . . backed** upon the back of his eagle   428 **spritely** ghostly   430 **label** piece of paper; **containing** contents   431 **from** remote from   432 **collection of** conclusion about   433 **construction** interpretation

to himself unknown, without seeking find, and be
embraced by a piece of tender air; and when from a
stately cedar shall be lopped branches which, being
dead many years, shall after revive, be jointed to the
old stock, and freshly grow; then shall Posthumus end 440
his miseries, Britain be fortunate and flourish in peace
and plenty."
Thou, Leonatus, art the lion's whelp;
The fit and apt construction of thy name,
Being Leo-natus,° doth import so much.— 445
The piece of tender air, thy virtuous daughter,
Which we call mollis aer,° and mollis aer
We term it mulier.°—Which mulier I divine
Is thy most constant wife, who° even now
Answering the letter of the oracle, 450
Unknown to you, unsought, were clipped° about
With this most tender air.
CYMBELINE                    This hath some seeming.°
SOOTHSAYER
The lofty cedar, royal Cymbeline,
Personates° thee, and thy lopped branches point
Thy two sons forth; who, by Belarius stol'n, 455
For many years thought dead, are now revived,
To the majestic cedar joined, whose issue
Promises Britain peace and plenty.
CYMBELINE                    Well,
My peace we will begin. And, Caius Lucius,

Although the victor, we submit to Caesar 460
And to the Roman empire, promising
To pay our wonted tribute, from the which
We were dissuaded by our wicked queen,
Whom° heavens in justice, both on her and hers,°
Have laid most heavy hand. 465
SOOTHSAYER
The fingers of the pow'rs above do tune
The harmony of this peace. The vision
Which I made known to Lucius ere the stroke
Of this yet scarce-cold battle, at this instant
Is full accomplished; for the Roman eagle, 470
From south to west on wing soaring aloft,
Lessened herself and in the beams o' th' sun
So vanished; which foreshowed our princely eagle,
Th' imperial Caesar, should again unite
His favor with the radiant Cymbeline, 475
Which shines here in the west.
CYMBELINE                    Laud we the gods,
And let our crooked° smokes climb to their nostrils
From our blest altars. Publish we this peace
To all our subjects. Set we forward;° let
A Roman and a British ensign wave 480
Friendly together. So through Lud's Town march,
And in the temple of great Jupiter
Our peace we'll ratify, seal it with feasts.
Set on there!° Never was a war did cease,
Ere bloody hands were washed, with such a peace. 485

*Exeunt.*

445 **Leonatus** lion-born  447 **mollis aer** tender air  448
**mulier** woman (thought to derive from *mollis* = soft)  449
**who** thou who (Posthumus)  451 **clipped** embraced  452
**seeming** plausibility  454 **Personates** represents

464 **Whom** on whom; **hers** Cloten  477 **crooked** curling
479 **Set we forward** let us march  484 **Set on there** Begin
marching

# THE WINTER'S TALE

EDITED BY FRANK KERMODE

## Introduction

*The Winter's Tale* is a very late work of Shakespeare's, probably the last he wrote without a collaborator except for *The Tempest*; and it is universally supposed to be closely associated with *Cymbeline, The Tempest,* and *Pericles* (although *Pericles* probably contains the work of another hand) in a grouping of comedies commonly called the "romances." I have no intention of trying to overthrow this supposition; but it is worth recalling that the friends of Shakespeare who compiled the First Folio in 1623, far from thinking these plays should be read as a group, allowed them to be separated from each other to the limits of physical possibility. *The Tempest* is the first play in the Folio, heading the section of comedies; *The Winter's Tale* is the last of the comedies, and was almost left out altogether; *Cymbeline* comes last among the *tragedies,* and is the final play of the Folio; *Pericles* they did not include at all, and it was left to the editors of the Third Folio (1664) to insert it, together with six other plays that nobody now attributes to Shakespeare. But the long labors of the chronologists have brought together these scattered cousins; it is another "triumph of time," like *The Winter's Tale* itself. And this has prepared the way for much interesting comment on the group and the relations between its members. Still, the indifference or imperceptiveness of Heminges and Condell may at least serve as a caution. Much as the romances resemble one another, they also exhibit striking differences; under the family resemblance, each has its private, personal life. The warning is so obvious as to be often ignored, and some intemperate commentary has resulted. *The Winter's Tale* has suffered with the others.

There is, for instance, the view—less common nowadays, but still to be met with—that these plays share a sort of calm or detached simplicity, as if the author had sought in romance relief from the evils and disasters of the tragedies. Now, the idea of romance, properly understood, implies passion and catastrophe, storm and violence; and Shakespeare's romances not only contain such elements, but often enact them with much turbulence both in the action and in the language. The verse frequently registers not a gentle detachment but rather a remarkable activity of mind. Thus the jealousy of Leontes may in the last

analysis be a less complex matter than that of Othello; but it is less simply expressed. The language that embodies it combines hysterical grossness with suggestions of a mind once habituated to clarity but no longer quite able to declare itself clearly because of emotional pressure:

> Ha' not you seen, Camillo—
> But that's past doubt, you have, or your eyeglass
> Is thicker than a cuckold's horn—or heard—
> For to a vision so apparent, rumor
> Cannot be mute—or thought—for cogitation
> Resides not in that man that does not think—
> My wife is slippery? (I.ii.267–73)

The evidence of Hermione's adultery is so overwhelming, so disgusting, that an intelligent friend's failure to notice it is an additional cause for anger. Leontes, accustomed to putting his thoughts clearly, organizes what he has to say in terms of sight, hearing, and reflection; but it would be equally loathsome to hear Camillo fawningly agree or disagree in order to dissuade Leontes from the course of self-torture to which he has committed himself. Thus contempt and fear join with sexual disgust and an intolerable sense of his own indignity to crowd and crush the speech, and neither Elizabethan nor modern punctuation can cope with its jolting syntax and distorted argument. Measure it against the grave and by no means ill-written opening of Greene's *Pandosto:* "whoso seeks by friendly counsel to raze out this hellish passion, it forthwith suspecteth that he giveth this advice to cover his own guiltiness. Yea, whoso is pained with this restless torment doubteth all, distrusteth himself, is always frozen with fear and fired with suspicion." Leontes in the play is ablaze with the passion of which Greene merely speaks. Or compare the same speech with Othello's after his fall into the same hell of sexual shock, reduced, when his agony is greatest, to broken exclamations: "O blood, blood, blood!" "Goats and monkeys!" Othello is not credited, as Leontes is, with an articulateness that matches his sense of self-destruction; he makes the great gestures appropriate to a noble understanding of what it means for a hero's life to be broken—

"Man but a rush against Othello's breast,/And he retires"
—but escapes the more intellectual torments of Leontes.[1]

Nor is this tumult of passionate meaning confined to
moments of agony. It is a fair criticism of *Cymbeline* that
there are places in it where the language is unnecessarily
opaque, where—to quote Coleridge's definition of
"mental bombast"—there are "thoughts and images too
great for the subject." In *The Tempest* when Prospero tells
Miranda of his brother's treachery, he can scarcely com-
press his meaning in his excited utterance. In *The Winter's
Tale* we feel the pressure of excited intelligence in many
other speakers, as well as in Leontes, notably in Perdita
and Florizel; their language breaks bounds in the quest for
completeness of statement.

> What you do
> Still betters what is done. When you speak, sweet,
> I'd have you do it ever; when you sing,
> I'd have you buy and sell so; so give alms,
> Pray so; and for the ord'ring your affairs,
> To sing them too. When you do dance, I wish you
> A wave o' th' sea, that you might ever do
> Nothing but that—move still, still so,
> And own no other function. Each your doing,
> So singular in each particular,
> Crowns what you are doing in the present deeds,
> That all your acts are queens.          (IV.iv.135–46)

Florizel begins a catalogue of beauties, each more amorously and extravagantly expressed than its predecessor, and
all related to action: "do," "done," "do," "doing,"
"function," "doing," "acts." He is drunk with the exquisite
activity of Perdita. But he has a rhetorical scheme, and
persists in it: each act is in itself perfect, yet each surpasses
the other. This lover's hyperbole might ring out frigidly
from the pages of Greene's novella, but here the whole
scheme is transformed by the figure of the wave, a rich
metaphor that the verse enacts rhythmically: "move still,
still so"; until, at the end, the rhetorician's wit glows with
imaginative solemnity, for "queens" not only concludes
the prescribed scheme but moves us out beyond it, into the
sphere where Perdita, singing and dancing, queen of the
feast and dressed as a goddess of spring's renewal, assumes
the power to end by her action the hard grip of winter on
the lives of her parents.

Such verse makes ridiculous the notion of an author
grown vaguely benign with old age; and it is to be found
in all the romances. There are other common features. In
every play there is a discovery of lost royalty, princesses
who are represented as of almost divine virtue and beauty;
characters near death are restored to life; the breach in
some prince's life is mended, years after the disaster which

caused it, by the agency of young, beautiful, and innocent
people; there are scenes of a pastoral character. All this is
of the nature of romance, and the plays could well be
called romantic tragicomedies. Edwin Greenlaw long ago
pointed out that they derive ultimately from the Greek
novel, especially perhaps from *Daphnis and Chloe*. This
is the world of lost princesses, great storms that sunder
families, lifetimes spent in wandering or suffering, babies
put to sea in little boats (an experience that belonged to
Perdita, in the source story, though Shakespeare saved it
for Miranda) and later recognized by a mole or a jewel.
Greene's *Pandosto*, on which Shakespeare based his *Winter's Tale*, is a typical Elizabethan novel in the same tradition. And these plays are dramatic versions of such stories.

Shakespeare had used elements of romance plot as early
as *The Comedy of Errors*; in returning to it he handles it
with a new simplicity, especially in *The Winter's Tale*. He
has no more compunction than a novelist might have in
allowing sixteen years to pass in the middle of the story.
But this is not because he could not help it, because his
technique had gone soft. Stories of this kind are in their
nature somewhat primitive, and if profundities are to be
found in them it will be by the writer who respects their
nature. It required much lucidity and experience to design
*The Winter's Tale* so simply. "Shakespeare," Northrop
Frye has said, "arrived in his last period at the bedrock of
drama, the romantic spectacle out of which all the more
specialized forms of drama, such as tragedy and social
comedy, have come, and to which they recurrently return."
Of course there are very bad romance plays, some of them
in the repertory of Shakespeare's company at this period.
Merely using an archaic narrative ensures no big bonus of
significance. That is the reward of genius, and of a lifetime
of intelligent practice. I daresay Shakespeare might have
been surprised to read in Frye that his Hermione is a
"Proserpine figure," but not to hear that he had told
his story in such a way that we see human life renewing
itself, as spring follows winter. He even suggests the
relevance of the well-known Proserpine myth in Perdita's
flower speech. He is writing, with very conscious art, about
the destruction and renewal of life, and finds in these
romance stories the pattern he needs; it is his craft to elicit
and enlarge their relevance.

It is perfectly consistent to add that Shakespeare was
probably writing to meet a specific public demand (as the
revival of an old and bad romance, *Mucedorus*, suggests).
With similar opportunism, he probably used in the fourth
act dances that his company had performed under grander
circumstances at court. He may also have had in mind the
Blackfriars, his company's new indoor theater, where from
about 1609 they enjoyed the advantages of a smaller
house with better music, good artificial lighting, scenes and
machines, and an audience willing to pay six times the
price of the cheapest place at the Globe. This was the time
of the spectacular masques at the court of James I; Shakespeare's company were the King's Men; never had relations
between court and stage been closer than now. They
continued to play in the great outdoor theater; but possibly
the Blackfriars, where some of the courtly spectacle could
be reproduced, had something to do with the vogue for
extravagant romance stories.

Yet this is not the most important clue to the nature of
*The Winter's Tale*. For that we should turn to the greatest

---

[1] I am not suggesting that *The Winter's Tale* has the stature of
*Othello*. The tragedy has a different and perhaps a greater design;
its focus is on the hero and the ideas by which he animates and gives
value to his world; whereas the hero of *The Winter's Tale* is Time;
or you might prefer to say that its heroine is Nature. The difference
of emphasis may be suggested by one small indication. The word
"honor" occurs with great frequency in *The Winter's Tale* to show
that its characters are all necessarily concerned with this public
acceptance of their own integrity; but the *idea* of honor is not at all
stressed, as of course it is in *Othello*, and I myself had not noticed
the frequent occurrence of the word until I gave the text slow
editorial scrutiny. The main interests of the play lie in such a way
that "honor" is a marginal, though necessary, consideration.

works in prose and verse of the period, Sidney's *Arcadia* and Spenser's *Faerie Queene*. It is no reflection on Greene to say that his novel cannot live with such romances as these; for they are in intention and performance the profoundest and most serious art of the period (Spenser's book, to risk a comparison for the modern reader, is as complex in plan as *Ulysses*). They nevertheless use romantic themes. They are concerned less with psychological realism than with supernaturally sanctioned reality under human appearances. Shakespeare knew them both, and used them, especially Spenser. Marina is his Florimel, Perdita his Pastorella; in *The Winter's Tale* he transforms Fawnia, Greene's royal changeling, and does so to make her like Spenser's noble shepherdess. And insofar as *The Winter's Tale* is philosophical it is Spenserian too; like Spenser, Shakespeare is preoccupied by Time as destroyer and renewer, that which ruins the work of men but is the father of truth. Just as the sea appears to be aimlessly destructive, tearing apart father and child, husband and wife, but is in the end seen to be "merciful" because it finally brings them together and restores their happiness, so Time only seems to change things because it must renew their truth.

> All things steadfastness do hate
> And changèd be: yet being rightly weighed
> They are not changèd from their first estate,
> But by their change their being do dilate,
> And turning to themselves at length again,
> Do work their own perfection so by fate.
>
> (*Faerie Queene*, VII.vii.515–20)

Whatever else may be added on the point, this is the "philosophy" of *The Winter's Tale* as well as of the Mutability Cantos of Spenser. And Greene, to give him his due, called the novel on which Shakespeare based his play *Pandosto: or, The Triumph of Time*.

One more point before we turn from the romances in general to the specific qualities of *The Winter's Tale*: stories of this kind create for the dramatist peculiar technical problems. Characteristically, they require that there be treated the initial disaster by which the plot gains movement; the intermediate period where people suffer under the consequent wrongs and sorrows; and finally the restoration of happiness, the *recognition*, where all, by the work of time, "turns to itself at length again." Dramatically, the focus of such stories will tend to be the recognition; in *Pericles*, a very straggling play, this climax was what overwhelmingly interested Shakespeare, and he made it a kind of prototype of all the others. In *Cymbeline* he attempted a multiple recognition scene so extraordinary as to be without theatrical parallel. In *The Tempest* he concentrates the whole action at the moment of climax, merely recalling the initial treachery of Antonio. In *The Winter's Tale* he approaches the problem quite differently by dividing the story into three parts: first the Sicilian disaster, the destruction of happiness by Leontes' diseased passion; then the "green world" in which Perdita demonstrates renewed beauty and nobility (these two parts being equally balanced as to length); and finally an act of recognition. Though the great scene in *Pericles* is the ancestor of them all, the recognition scenes of these plays are all very different, and this of course contributes to their individuality, the sense

we have that each grows its own imaginative and philosophical atmosphere. And nowhere is this atmosphere more distinctive, nowhere is the recognition more daringly conceived, than in *The Winter's Tale*.

Some indication of the dramatist's intention, both in this and in other aspects of the play, may be derived from a consideration of the changes he made in his source. The reader of Greene's *Pandosto* may see for himself the extent of both debt and deviation. But on the crucial matter of the great final act something must be said here. The statue scene is without parallel in *Pandosto*; at some stage Shakespeare made the momentous decision to keep Hermione alive, and invented the motif of the statue. It is possible that he did so in the course of writing; as Coleridge early pointed out, it would have been simple enough to provide for her survival by some ambiguity in the oracle, but Shakespeare does not do so, and it is a remarkable instance, the only one in Shakespeare or perhaps in the whole drama of the period, of the playwright's concealing so material a circumstance from the audience. Simon Forman, reporting on a performance of 1611 when the play was still fairly new, did not include in his account of the plot any allusion to the statue scene, so the play may have been without it in its first form. Having preserved Hermione alive, Shakespeare had of course greatly increased his technical problem at the end of the play. Had he followed Greene, the climactic moment would have been the discovery of Perdita's identity, and the scene would have had to be very like that of the reunion of Pericles and Marina. He could hardly have followed this with another scene of rapt verse and music for the reunion of Leontes and his wife; so he boldly throws away the Perdita recognition in a scene of gentlemanly chatter, and saves the great effects for the reunion of father, mother, and daughter at the end. Thus he avoids the anticlimactic conclusion of *Pericles*, where the reunion with Thaisa cannot make much effect after the great scene that precedes it. So Shakespeare solved his technical problem; the question remains, why did he need to create it by forsaking Greene and keeping Hermione alive? Why should the climax of the play be not the restoration of Perdita to her inheritance but the restoration of the queen to life? No one can answer that without looking at the play as a whole.

The whole work is as unorthodox structurally as the final scene. The first part, up to the end of III.ii, is dominated by the insane and tyrannous passion of Leontes. The Sicilian court has been a world of courtesy and innocence; these are virtues of Hermione and also of Polixenes, whose opening speech, with its pastoral figures, merely establishes an intelligent harmony that will be broken by the power of the diseased king. Polixenes remembers the innocence of his childhood friendship with Leontes, and says it resembled that of man before the Fall, when passion overthrew reason; and with the onset of the king's jealousy this overthrow is reenacted. It is clumsy to treat this as pure allegory, though that is a modern fashion; Shakespeare knew very well that there was implied in this narrative an analogy with the Fall, and he lived in an age when biblical typology and allegory were as familiar as they now seem outlandish. But this should lead us to the conclusion, not that he was writing allegory, but that he was recognizing the *typical* quality of this, as of any other story. A powerful mind is disturbed by a passion it is unwilling to control;

suddenly the clear world of honor and courtesy darkens; friends can be Judases, good counselors traitors; what seems to be virtuous is in truth vicious; the gods themselves are liars. Here as elsewhere Shakespeare associates this profound perturbation, this infection of a world with the disease of one mind, with a specifically sexual misery. For Leontes— the word tolls out through these scenes—is diseased, and the air around him is infected, as if by a plague-bearing planet. His very language is hectic. That there is another and purer air we learn from the brief, beautifully placed III.i, when Cleomenes and Dion speak of the delicate climate and sweet air of Apollo's temple. And when, sixteen years later, we breathe the air of Perdita's pastoral Bohemia we recognize once more a purity associated with pure sexuality; as when Perdita wishes her lover "quick, and in mine arms." The country, its healing herbs and prophylactic flowers, is the antithesis of the plague-stricken city. And later, when Perdita arrives in Sicily, Leontes remembers the days of the great infection and prays accordingly:

> The blessèd gods
> Purge all infection from our air whilst you
> Do climate here! (V.i.168–70)

In the dark opening phase, the part of Hermione is that of the victim, Leontes that of the tyrant. Tyranny begins, as Milton says, "when upstart passions catch the government." But he considers and rejects the idea that he is behaving tyrannously; she, at her trial (which must recall the trial of Katherine in *Henry VIII*), argues that he is. His rejection of the oracle is a tyrannous act (Greene's Pandosto accepts it), and he at once suffers the traditional fate of the tyrant, the sudden exemplary punishment of heaven. His son dies, his queen dies; henceforth his life must be only repentance and obloquy. Or so it seems. At the end of III.ii, halfway through the play, we have reached what is practically a full tragic close, and if Leontes were to stab himself at that point there would be little sense of dramatic illogic. He has thrown away the pearl richer than all his tribe. Only the hint of the oracle ("*if* that which is lost be not found") and the fact that in romance castaway children always turn up, exist to make a faint suggestion of a happy issue.

The next scene, III.iii, is crucial, and again extraordinary; Antigonus, having had a vision of the *dead* Hermione, is sacrificed in order to move the play into a fantastic realm; the Clown and his father show us how different is the world we have entered by the unconcerned calm of their talk on the sinking of the ship and the bear's consumption of Antigonus. Then the old man speaks the famous line: "Now bless thyself; thou met'st with things dying, I with things new born." We pass from the world in which happiness and prosperity are destroyed by the storm of passion, to the world where Nature—"great creating Nature," as Shakespeare calls the presiding figure of the Mutability Cantos—reestablishes love and human continuance and proves that time and change are her servants, agents not only of change but of perpetuity, redeemers as well as destroyers.

The central action of Act IV is not complicated, but it is a very long act, and must have been the longer for the various diversions, the "nest of antics" ridiculed by Jonson, the catches and songs. The mood is of innocence (even Autolycus contributes to this, partly by establishing rustic

virtues as opposed to those of the court—an old pastoral theme, and one paralleled by the debates between Corin and Touchstone in *As You Like It*), and Shakespeare wanted this part of the play to have mass enough to balance the Sicilian opening. Essentially, this act establishes a world in which Perdita's inborn nobility can display itself.

Although Shakespeare accepts some of the assumptions of the pastoral genre, it was clearly his effort to avoid urban condescension and sentimentality in this scene. These shepherds and shepherdesses are not the graceful figures of Spenser and Sidney; the young clown has his meanness, the old one his strong sense of self-preservation; Polixenes is charmed by the feast and by Perdita's beauty, but when the holiday is over his exposure of the girl and his judgment of his son are extremely tough. Against this infused realism, the insistence upon Perdita's superiority, her innate nobility and godlike beauty, becomes more remarkable. It is, considered merely as a narrative device, part of the tradition, but it occupied Shakespeare at a very deep level. There are signs of his interest in it at an earlier stage in his career, but in the romances he turned upon it the same deepening attention as we observe him giving such conventions as the twin plot—that which was first only a dramaturgical device becomes an issue for mature meditation. Marina in the brothel and Cymbeline's sons in the Welsh cave have the virtue of high birth, and their hereditary cultivation will show itself even in unfavorable circumstances. In *The Tempest* Caliban is the base natural stock, Miranda (educated with him) has, as part of her inheritance, that "better nature" which places her on the side of mankind toward the gods, as he is on the side toward the beasts.[2] Perdita, like all the romance heroines mistaken for a goddess, is, very remarkably, made the occasion for Shakespeare's fullest exposition of the idea. It is characteristic of Shakespeare's economy that her flower piece, which could have been a moment of pastoral prettiness, modulates into this quasi-philosophical debate with Polixenes:

PERDITA               Sir, the year growing ancient,
Not yet on summer's death, nor on the birth
Of trembling winter, the fairest flow'rs o' th' season
Are our carnations and streaked gillyvors,
Which some call Nature's bastards; of that kind
Our rustic garden's barren; and I care not
To get slips of them.
POLIXENES        Wherefore, gentle maiden,
Do you neglect them?
PERDITA              For I have heard it said,
There is an art, which in their piedness shares
With great creating Nature.
POLIXENES                 Say there be;
Yet Nature is made better by no mean
But Nature makes that mean; so over that art
Which you say adds to Nature, is an art
That Nature makes. You see, sweet maid, we marry
A gentler scion to the wildest stock,
And make conceive a bark of baser kind
By bud of nobler race. This is an art
Which does mend Nature, change it rather; but

[2] This point is discussed and documented in my Arden edition of *The Tempest* (sixth rev. ed., 1958).

The art itself is Nature.

PERDITA              So it is.

POLIXENES

Then make your garden rich in gillyvors,
And do not call them bastards.

PERDITA              I'll not put

The dibble in earth, to set one slip of them;
No more than were I painted, I would wish
This youth should say 'twere well, and only therefore
Desire to breed by me.          (IV.iv.79–103)

In this disagreement Polixenes only *seems* to win, though he has the general weight of contemporary thought on his side; the art of the gardener in improving wild natural stocks was treated as a figure of the distinctive human power to improve and civilize the environment, and it was customary to add that in so doing Art was nevertheless the agent of Nature. Perdita does not know she is herself noble, and is only playing at being a queen, though the audience has already noted strong suggestions of her royalty, indeed of her semidivinity; and there is a purely dramatic irony in the discussion, since Polixenes is to oppose the union of his noble son with a supposedly baseborn girl, thus contradicting his own philosophy; whereas she, baseborn and hoping to marry a prince, resists his horticultural analogy. Her case is precisely that of Marvell in his poem "The Mower against Gardens," in which the gardener is called not an improver of nature but a pander; but Perdita, unable to answer the argument from gardening, produces one from cosmetics ("the gillyvors are like painted women") and so tacitly rejects the implied resemblance between herself and "barks of baser kind." Leaving aside the purely dramatic ironies, this debate is one on which the arguments on both sides were well known, and Shakespeare's purpose is not to identify himself with one side or the other so much as to tell the audience that the great topic of the relations between Art and Nature are relevant to his purposes; to establish in every word as well as every action the "better nature" of Perdita, and to prepare the way for a climactic scene in which, when the statue proves to be powerful and beautiful beyond the scope of art, we shall see finally the incomparable work of "great creating Nature." Whenever he includes discussion of this kind—as he does, for example, in *The Merchant of Venice*, in *Troilus and Cressida*, in *Measure for Measure*—we may expect it to have its repercussions on the action. In this play we find them in the last act.

The pattern of this act is determined, as we have seen, by the need for a double recognition, but nothing at the level of plot required the dramatist to bring Hermione back into the play as a statue. Admittedly the scene lends itself to that tone of exalted joy which distinguishes these late plays of reunion, and is magnificently theatrical; having once committed himself to the situation the old master makes the most of the chance, holds us to the long moment of Hermione's immobility, and when it is over, concludes the play with what must appear unless the director has the necessary sensitivity and tact, unseemly haste. But as usual he makes theatrical effect compatible with thematic interest. Paulina soaks her guests in art by taking them on an extended tour of the gallery before she lets them see the statue. They praise it for its naturalness, its "life," while she protests that the color is still wet and calls it a "poor image." "What was he that did make it?" asks Leontes in unconscious tribute to the god of nature. The work is so "alive," he says, "that we are mocked with art." Slowly the statue moves out of the possibilities of art: "what fine chisel/Could ever yet cut breath?" Then it moves indeed, and the hypothesis that this is art can only be defended by calling that art magic. Finally it speaks, and blesses Perdita, and this no work of art, but only works of great creating Nature, can do.

In its identification of the thematic and the theatrical, this is a true work of Shakespeare's. It is, of course, more complex than my account suggests. The survival of Hermione authenticates Perdita's beauty; Time, which has seemed the destroyer, is a redeemer. At one masterly moment Perdita herself stands like a statue beside the supposed statue of her mother, to remind us that created things work their own perfection and continuance in time, as well as suffer under it. And in the end the play seems to say (I borrow the language of Yeats) that "whatever is begotten, born and dies" is nobler than "monuments of unageing intellect"—and also, when truly considered, more lasting.

Such a formula may justly attract the complaint that it is partial and moralizing. The play is a great one, with a natural energy that supports all it says about natural power; its scheme is deep-laid and its language fertile in suggestion. It will not be trapped by the historian, though he can speak of the vogue of tragicomic romance and compare Perdita with Pastorella. It will not, either, be caught in the net of allegory. To say that Hermione suffers, dies, and is restored to life is not to suggest a parallel that the author missed, but equally not to hit his true intention. All truths, he might argue, are related to the Truth; all good stories will have—to use the term of Erich Auerbach—a "figural" quality. *The Winter's Tale*, like many other stories, deals with sin and forgiveness, and with the triumph of time— also a Christian theme. But we value it not for some hidden truth, but for its power to realize experience, to show something of life that could be shown only by the intense activity of intellect and imagination in the medium of a theatrical form. It is not a great allegory or a great argument, but a great play.

## A NOTE ON THE SOURCE

Shakespeare's source was a novella by his old enemy Robert Greene. The title of the first edition reads:

*Pandosto. The Triumph of Time. Wherein is discouered by a pleasant Historie, that although by the meanes of sinister fortune, Truth may be concealed, yet by Time in spight of fortune it is most manifestly reuealed. Pleasant for age to auoyde drowsie thoughtes, profitable for youth to eschue other wanton pastimes, and bringing to both a desired content. Temporis filia veritas. By Robert Greene, Maister of Artes in Cambridge. Omne tulit punctum qui miscuit vtile dulci.* Imprinted at London by Thomas Orwin for Thomas Cadman, dwelling at the Signe of the Bible, neere vnto the North doore of Paules, 1588.

The Short Title Catalogue records only one copy of this edition, in the British Museum; and that is imperfect. There were subsequent editions in 1592, 1595, 1607, and later. But although there was so recent an edition available, Shakespeare appears to have used the first. He seems for some reason to have been interested in Greene at this time, for he also drew on the pamphleteer's popular studies of the London underworld, especially *The Second Part of Conny-catching* (1592), useful for describing the tricks of Autolycus (especially the cheating of the Clown in IV.iii); and although he rejected Greene's personal names, he replaced "Garinter" by "Mamillius," perhaps remembering Greene's "looking glass for the ladies of England," *Mamillia* (1583).

Shakespeare treats *Pandosto* in his usual way, freely changing it but often echoing its language and incidents. The following very brief summary uses the names Shakespeare gave the characters.

Shakespeare changes the countries about; Leontes is King of Bohemia, Polixenes of Sicily; and it is the wife of Polixenes who is daughter of the Empress of Russia, not Hermione. Greene's Hermione, though perfectly innocent, gives more color to the suspicions of Leontes by the freedom of her conduct toward Polixenes. She does not discover her pregnancy till she is already in prison. Camillo shows more self-interest in the novel, and has no part in the return of Perdita to her father. The jealousy of Leontes, though not well founded, is less of a brainstorm in the original. He sends the new baby to sea in a little boat by herself; there is no Antigonus. After the trial he instantly accepts the word of the oracle, but his son and his wife both die. Perdita is cast ashore in Sicily and reared by shepherds interested in the gold that accompanies her. Years later, she is wooed by Florizel, but here the tone of the novel is very different from that of the play, despite suggestions that Shakespeare used in the sheep-shearing scene. Florizel is much more formal, and the relationship, until Perdita, properly suspicious, alters it by insisting on her virtue, is not much different from an ordinary seduction of a country girl by a courtier. But Florizel, appearing as a shepherd, establishes the honesty of his intentions and plans to amass money to elope with Perdita to Italy. The unhappy old shepherd is tricked into boarding the ship (but not by Autolycus, who does not exist in the novel). When the couple arrives in Bohemia, Leontes conceives a lustful desire for Perdita, and throws Florizel into prison. But when he hears the whole story from the ambassadors of Polixenes (who is alarmed to think of his son in the hands of an enemy), he frees Florizel and condemns Perdita and her father to death. But the old man now tells his tale; Perdita is proved to be Leontes' lost daughter. She returns to Sicily with Florizel, and they are married; but Leontes kills himself from remorse.

I have given no account of many changes that are simply a matter of dramaturgical economy. Despite the strong similarities in plot, there are important alterations in Shakespeare. The greatest of these, if the least tangible, is his substitution of Nature for Fortune as the deity presiding over the original story; and the consequent reconstruction in the statue scene, with Hermione restored and Leontes transported with joy at the recovery of his wife, his daughter, and his friend. For Shakespeare's Perdita and Florizel, Greene affords little more than hints, and the whole pastoral of the fourth act is similarly built on mere suggestions. Greene's Florizel knows better than to speak freely of his love; and Polixenes does not visit the sheep-

fold, let alone converse with Perdita on profound topics. The point at which the two works most closely concur is the scene of Hermione's trial, but other references to Greene's text are fairly frequent, so that it looks as if Shakespeare had the book on his desk. It was the story he wanted, to adapt as freely as he chose, and he shuns the Arcadianism of Greene's dialogue; yet once again the dead author might have found cause to complain, as he had eighteen years earlier, that the "upstart crow" had been "beautified with our feathers."

## A NOTE ON THE TEXT

*The Winter's Tale* was placed at the end of the section of comedies in the Folio of 1623. There was no earlier edition, and so all subsequent editions derive from the Folio text. Bibliographical evidence shows that the play was added to the Folio late, when a number of the history plays had already been printed. Possibly no copy was available until then. The copy that eventually reached the printing house was almost certainly a transcript of the play made by Ralph Crane, whose hand is now well known to scholars. Crane did a good deal for Shakespeare's company, the King's Men, and the Folio texts of *The Tempest* and *The Two Gentlemen of Verona*—and possibly other plays too—are attributable to him. Certain of his characteristics—notably his fondness for brackets and his habit of placing all the entries at the head of the scene, whether or not they are repeated when the character actually comes in—are abundantly in evidence in the Folio text of *The Winter's Tale*.

The text is very deficient in stage directions, and Crane's copy was evidently not made for use in the playhouse. But he was an intelligent scribe, and doubtless gave the compositor clean copy. In fact, this is one of the cleanest of Shakespeare's texts, despite the difficulty of some of the verse. The present edition deletes the superfluous entries at heads of scenes and places them at the appropriate positions, modernizes spelling and punctuation, and translates from Latin into English the Folio's act and scene divisions. The list of characters, here prefixed to the play, in the Folio follows the play. Other material departures from the Folio text are listed below in boldface type, followed by the Folio's reading (F) in roman; in only three or four places is any real difficulty involved.

I.i.29 **have** hath
I.ii.104 **And** A   158 **do** does   208 **you, they say** you say   276 **hobbyhorse** Holy-horse   327–28 **Sully/The purity** Sully the puritie   446–47 **thereon/His execution sworn** Thereon his Execution sworne
II.i.25–26 **I have one/Of** I have one of
II.ii.6 **whom** who   52 **let't** le't
II.iii.39 **What** Who   53 **profess** professes   177 **its** it
III.ii.1 **session** Sessions   10 **Silence** [F italicizes, as if s.d.]   32 **Who** Whom   107 **for** no
III.iii.18 **awaking** a waking   116 **made** mad
IV.iii.10 **With heigh, with heigh** With heigh   58 **offends** offend
IV.iv.2 **Do** Do's   12 **Digest it with** Digest with   13 **swoon** sworne   98 **your** you   160 **out** on't   364 **who** whom   422 **acknowledged** acknowledge   426 **who** whom   431 **shalt see** shalt neuer see   442 **hoop** hope   470 **your** my   493 **hide** hides   502 **whom** who   552 **asks thee, the son, forgiveness** asks thee there Sonne forgiuenesse   708 **know not** know   738 **or toaze** at toaze   846 **Exit** Exeunt
V.i.12 **True, too true** [F places the first "true" at the end of Leontes' previous speech]   61 **just cause** just such cause   75 **I have done** [F gives to Cleomenes]
V.ii.35 **Hermione** Hermiones
V.iii.18 **Lonely** Louely   96 **Or** on

# THE WINTER'S TALE

### The Names of the Actors

LEONTES *King of Sicilia*
MAMILLIUS *young Prince of Sicilia*
CAMILLO
ANTIGONUS
CLEOMENES } *four lords of Sicilia*
DION
HERMIONE *queen to Leontes*
PERDITA *daughter to Leontes and Hermione*
PAULINA *wife to Antigonus*
EMILIA *a lady [attending on Hermione]*
POLIXENES *King of Bohemia*
FLORIZEL *Prince of Bohemia*

OLD SHEPHERD *reputed father of Perdita*
CLOWN *his son*
AUTOLYCUS *a rogue*
ARCHIDAMUS *a lord of Bohemia*
[A MARINER]
[A JAILER]
[MOPSA
DORCAS } *shepherdesses*]
*Other* LORDS *and* GENTLEMEN [LADIES
OFFICERS *of the Court*] SERVANTS
SHEPHERDS SHEPHERDESSES
[TIME *as chorus*]

[*Scene:* Sicilia and Bohemia]

## ACT I

### Scene I. [*Sicilia, the court of Leontes.*]

*Enter* CAMILLO *and* ARCHIDAMUS.

ARCHIDAMUS If you shall chance, Camillo, to visit Bohemia, on the like occasion whereon my services are now on foot, you shall see, as I have said, great difference betwixt our Bohemia and your Sicilia.

CAMILLO I think this coming summer the King of 5 Sicilia means to pay Bohemia the visitation which he justly owes him.

ARCHIDAMUS Wherein our entertainment shall shame us we will be justified in our loves;° for indeed— 10

CAMILLO Beseech you—

ARCHIDAMUS Verily I speak it in the freedom of my knowledge: we cannot with such magnificence—in so rare—I know not what to say. . . . We will give you sleepy drinks, that your senses, unintelligent° of our 15 insufficience, may, though they cannot praise us, as little accuse us.

CAMILLO You pay a great deal too dear for what's given freely.

ARCHIDAMUS Believe me, I speak as my under- 20 standing instructs me, and as mine honesty puts it to utterance.

CAMILLO Sicilia cannot show himself overkind to Bohemia. They were trained together in their childhoods; and there rooted betwixt them then such an 25 affection, which cannot choose but branch° now. Since their more mature dignities and royal necessities made separation of their society,° their encounters though not personal, have been royally attorneyed° with interchange of gifts, letters, loving embassies, 30 that they have seemed to be together, though absent; shook hands, as over a vast;° and embraced as it were

*The decorative border shown above was used in the First Folio edition of Shakespeare's plays, 1623.*

**I.i.8–9 Wherein . . . loves** our entertainment may fall short of yours, but we shall make up for it by the strength of our affection

**15 unintelligent** unaware **26 branch** i.e., flourish **28 society** companionship **29 attorneyed** supplied by substitutes **32 vast** desolate space

from the ends of opposed winds. The heavens continue
their loves!

ARCHIDAMUS  I think there is not in the world either 35
malice or matter to alter it. You have an unspeakable
comfort of your young Prince Mamillius; it is a
gentleman of the greatest promise that ever came into
my note.

CAMILLO  I very well agree with you in the hopes of 40
him. It is a gallant child; one that, indeed, physics the
subject,° makes old hearts fresh; they that went on
crutches ere he was born desire yet their life to see him
a man.

ARCHIDAMUS  Would they else be content to die? 45

CAMILLO  Yes, if there were no other excuse why they
should desire to live.

ARCHIDAMUS  If the king had no son, they would
desire to live on crutches till he had one.    *Exeunt.*


Scene II. [*The court of Leontes.*]


*Enter* LEONTES, HERMIONE, MAMILLIUS, POLI-
XENES, CAMILLO, [*and* ATTENDANTS].

POLIXENES
Nine changes of the wat'ry star° hath been
The shepherd's note since we have left our throne
Without a burden: time as long again
Would be filled up, my brother, with our thanks,
And yet we should for perpetuity                              5
Go hence in debt. And therefore, like a cipher,
Yet standing in rich place, I multiply
With one "We thank you," many thousands moe°
That go before it.°

LEONTES                   Stay your thanks awhile,
And pay them when you part.

POLIXENES                          Sir, that's tomorrow. 10
I am questioned by my fears of what may chance
Or breed upon our absence, that may blow
No sneaping winds at home, to make us say,
"This is put forth too truly."° Besides, I have stayed
To tire your royalty.

LEONTES                   We are tougher, brother,       15
Than you can put us to't.°

POLIXENES                          No longer stay.

LEONTES
One sev'night longer.

POLIXENES                          Very sooth, tomorrow.

LEONTES
We'll part the time between's then; and in that
I'll no gainsaying.°

POLIXENES          Press me not, beseech you, so.
There is no tongue that moves, none, none i' th' world 20

So soon as yours could win me; so it should now,
Were there necessity in your request, although
'Twere needful I denied it. My affairs
Do even drag me homeward; which to hinder
Were, in your love, a whip to me;° my stay,        25
To you a charge and trouble: to save both,
Farewell, our brother.

LEONTES                   Tongue-tied, our queen? Speak you.

HERMIONE
I had thought, sir, to have held my peace until
You had drawn oaths from him not to stay. You, sir,
Charge him too coldly. Tell him you are sure       30
All in Bohemia's well; this satisfaction,
The bygone day proclaimed. Say this to him,
He's beat from his best ward.°

LEONTES                   Well said, Hermione.

HERMIONE
To tell he longs to see his son were strong;
But let him say so then, and let him go;           35
But let him swear so, and he shall not stay,
We'll thwack him hence with distaffs.
Yet of your royal presence, I'll adventure
The borrow of a week. When at Bohemia
You take my lord, I'll give him my commission      40
To let him there a month behind the gest°
Prefixed for's parting, yet, good deed,° Leontes,
I love thee not a jar° o' th' clock behind
What lady she° her lord. You'll stay?

POLIXENES                          No, madam.

HERMIONE
Nay, but you will?

POLIXENES          I may not, verily.                 45

HERMIONE
Verily?
You put me off with limber° vows; but I,
Though you would seek t' unsphere the stars with oaths,
Should yet say, "Sir, no going." Verily,
You shall not go; a lady's "Verily" is              50
As potent as a lord's. Will you go yet?
Force me to keep you as prisoner,
Not like a guest; so you shall pay your fees°
When you depart, and save your thanks. How say you?
My prisoner or my guest? By your dread "Verily,"   55
One of them you shall be.

POLIXENES                   Your guest, then, madam:
To be your prisoner should import offending;°
Which is for me less easy to commit,
Than you to punish.

HERMIONE          Not your jailer, then,
But your kind hostess. Come, I'll question you      60
Of my lord's tricks, and yours, when you were boys:
You were pretty lordings then?

POLIXENES                   We were, fair queen,
Two lads that thought there was no more behind°
But such a day tomorrow as today,
And to be boy eternal.

41–42 **physics the subject** is good medicine for the people
**I.ii.1 wat'ry star** the moon  **8 moe** more  **3–9 time . . .
it** it would take us the same length of time to thank you, and
even then we should leave here forever your debtors. So I offer
you one more thank-you, which, though it is in itself nothing,
works like a zero on the end of a number and multiplies all the
thanks I have given you before (instead of merely adding to
them)  **11–14 I . . . truly** I am worried about what may
happen at home, perhaps as a result of my absence—worried
in case blighting influences may not be at work which we shall
regret, saying "We went away only too well"  **16 put us to't**
drive us to extremities  **19 I'll no gainsaying** I'll not accept a
refusal

**25 Were . . . me** i.e., though doing it out of love, you
would be tormenting me by making me stay in these
circumstances  **33 ward** defensive posture in fencing  **41
gest** stage of royal progress; time allocated to one place on
the route  **42 good deed** indeed, in very deed  **43 jar** tick
**44 lady she** gentlewoman  **47 limber** limp  **53 fees** which
were always due from prisoner to jailer  **57 import offending**
mean that I had committed some crime  **63 behind** to come

HERMIONE                    Was not my lord            65
The verier wag o' th' two?

POLIXENES
We were as twinned lambs, that did frisk i' th' sun,
And bleat the one at th' other; what we changed°
Was innocence for innocence; we knew not
The doctrine of ill-doing, nor dreamed            70
That any did; had we pursued that life,
And our weak spirits ne'er been higher reared
With stronger blood, we should have answered heaven
Boldly, "Not guilty"; the imposition cleared,
Hereditary ours.°

HERMIONE              By this we gather            75
You have tripped since.

POLIXENES                    O my most sacred lady,
Temptations have since then been born to's, for
In those unfledged days was my wife a girl;
Your precious self had then not crossed the eyes
Of my young playfellow.

HERMIONE                    Grace to boot!°            80
Of this make no conclusion,° lest you say
Your queen and I are devils. Yet go on,
Th' offenses we have made you do we'll answer,
If you first sinned with us, and that with us
You did continue fault, and that you slipped not            85
With any but with us.

LEONTES              Is he won yet?

HERMIONE
He'll stay, my lord.

LEONTES                    At my request he would not.
Hermione, my dearest, thou never spok'st
To better purpose.

HERMIONE              Never?

LEONTES                    Never but once.

HERMIONE
What! Have I twice said well? When was't before?            90
I prithee tell me; cram's with praise, and make's
As fat as tame things: one good deed, dying tongueless,
Slaughters a thousand waiting upon that.
Our praises are our wages—you may ride's
With one soft kiss a thousand furlongs, ere            95
With spur we heat an acre.° But to th' goal:
My last good deed was to entreat his stay.
What was my first? It has an elder sister,
Or I mistake you; O, would her name were Grace!
But once before I spoke to th' purpose? When?            100
Nay, let me have't; I long.

LEONTES                    Why, that was when
Three crabbèd months had soured themselves to death,
Ere I could make thee open thy white hand
And clap° thyself my love; then didst thou utter,
"I am yours forever."

HERMIONE                    'Tis Grace indeed.            105
Why, lo you now, I have spoke to th' purpose twice:
The one forever earned a royal husband;
Th' other, for some while a friend.

LEONTES                    [Aside.] Too hot, too hot!
To mingle friendship far is mingling bloods.
I have tremor cordis° on me; my heart dances,            110
But not for joy, not joy. This entertainment
May a free face put on, derive a liberty
From heartiness, from bounty, fertile bosom,°
And well become the agent—'t may, I grant;
But to be paddling palms and pinching fingers,            115
As now they are, and making practiced smiles
As in a looking glass; and then to sigh, as 'twere
The mort o' th' deer°—oh, that is entertainment
My bosom likes not, nor my brows.° Mamillius,
Art thou my boy?

MAMILLIUS                    Ay, my good lord.

LEONTES                    I' fecks!°            120
Why, that's my bawcock.° What, hast smutched thy
    nose?
They say it is a copy out of mine. Come, captain,
We must be neat—not neat,° but cleanly, captain:
And yet the steer, the heifer, and the calf,
Are all called neat. Still virginaling°            125
Upon his palm? How now, you wanton calf,
Art thou my calf?

MAMILLIUS                    Yes, if you will, my lord.

LEONTES
Thou want'st a rough pash,° and the shoots that I have
To be full like me: yet they say we are
Almost as like as eggs; women say so,            130
That will say anything. But were they false
As o'er-dyed blacks,° as wind, as waters; false
As dice are to be wished, by one that fixes
No bourn° 'twixt his and mine—yet were it true
To say this boy were like me. Come, Sir Page,            135
Look on me with your welkin° eye. Sweet villain,
Most dear'st, my collop!° Can thy dam,° may't be?
Affection!° Thy intention° stabs the center.°
Thou dost make possible things not so held,
Communicat'st with dreams—how can this be?—            140
With what's unreal thou coactive art,
And fellow'st nothing. Then 'tis very credent°
Thou mayst co-join with something, and thou dost,
And that beyond commission, and I find it,
And that to the infection of my brains,            145
And hardening of my brows.°

110 **tremor cordis** palpitation of the heart    113 **fertile bosom**
generous affection    117–18 **as 'twere . . . deer** like the horn
call signifying the death of the deer    119 **brows** alluding to the
myth of the horns that grow on the foreheads of cuckolds    120
**fecks** a mild oath, derived from "I' faith"    121 **bawcock** fine
fellow (French = *beau coq*)    123 **neat** Leontes rejects the word
because it also means "horned cattle"    125 **virginaling** i.e., as
if playing the virginals (a small keyboard instrument)    128
**pash** head    132 **o'er-dyed blacks** black garments worn out
by too much dyeing    134 **bourn** boundary    136 **welkin** blue
(like the sky)    137 **collop** a cut off his own flesh; **dam** mother
(Leontes' thoughts still run on cattle)    138 **Affection** passion;
**intention** purpose; **center** of the world(?) of my heart(?)
142 **credent** credible    138–46 **Affection . . . brows** may be
corrupt; paraphrase: "Passion! Your desire for fulfillment can
pierce to the heart of things. You deal with matters normally
thought of as illusory—with dreams and fantasies, impossible
as that sounds. You collaborate with the unreal; so it is not
improbable that you should do so with what really exists;
this is what has happened, as my mental disturbance and
cuckold's horns indicate." The passion is jealousy; Leontes
recognizes that it is sometimes baseless, but argues that it is
not so in his case

68 **changed** exchanged    72–75 **our weak . . . ours** i.e., had
the weakness of our animal spirits not been fortified by the
passionate blood of maturity, our wills would never have been
corrupted, and we should have been able to claim exemption
from the taint of original sin    80 **Grace to boot** Heaven help
me!    81 **make no conclusion** do not pursue that line of
argument    96 **heat an acre** race over a furlong    104 **clap**
offer the handclasp that seals a bargain

POLIXENES                    What means Sicilia?
HERMIONE
  He something seems unsettled.
POLIXENES                         How, my lord?
LEONTES
  What cheer? How is't with you, best brother?
HERMIONE                                You look
  As if you held a brow of much distraction;
  Are you moved, my lord?
LEONTES                    No, in good earnest.          150
  How sometimes nature will betray its folly,
  Its tenderness, and make itself a pastime
  To harder bosoms! Looking on the lines
  Of my boy's face, methoughts I did recoil
  Twenty-three years, and saw myself unbreeched,     155
  In my green velvet coat; my dagger muzzled,
  Lest it should bite its master, and so prove,
  As ornaments oft do, too dangerous.
  How like, methought, I then was to this kernel,
  This squash,° this gentleman. Mine honest friend,   160
  Will you take eggs for money?°
MAMILLIUS
  No, my lord, I'll fight.
LEONTES
  You will? Why, happy man be's dole!° My brother,
  Are you so fond of your young prince as we
  Do seem to be of ours?
POLIXENES               If at home, sir,              165
  He's all my exercise, my mirth, my matter;
  Now my sworn friend, and then mine enemy;
  My parasite, my soldier, statesman, all.
  He makes a July's day short as December,
  And with his varying childness, cures in me         170
  Thoughts that would thick my blood.°
LEONTES                           So stands this squire
  Officed with me.° We two will walk, my lord,
  And leave you to your graver steps. Hermione,
  How thou lov'st us, show in our brother's welcome;
  Let what is dear in Sicily, be cheap;               175
  Next to thyself and my young rover, he's
  Apparent° to my heart.
HERMIONE              If you would seek us,
  We are yours i' th' garden; shall's attend you there?
LEONTES
  To your own bents dispose you; you'll be found,
  Be you beneath the sky. [Aside.] I am angling° now,  180
  Though you perceive me not how I give line.
  Go to, go to!
  How she holds up the neb,° the bill to him!
  And arms her with the boldness of a wife
  To her allowing° husband! [Exeunt POLIXENES,
    HERMIONE, and ATTENDANTS.] Gone already!          185
  Inch-thick, knee-deep, o'er head and ears a forked°
    one!
  Go play, boy, play: thy mother plays, and I

Play too—but so disgraced a part, whose issue°
Will hiss me to my grave; contempt and clamor
Will be my knell. Go play, boy, play. There have been, 190
Or I am much deceived, cuckolds ere now,
And many a man there is, even at this present,
Now, while I speak this, holds his wife by th' arm,
That little thinks she has been sluiced in's absence,
And his pond fished by his next neighbor, by         195
Sir Smile, his neighbor, nay, there's comfort in't,
Whiles other men have gates, and those gates opened,
As mine, against their will. Should all despair,
That have revolted° wives, the tenth of mankind
Would hang themselves. Physic for't there's none;    200
It is a bawdy planet, that will strike
Where 'tis predominant;° and 'tis powerful, think it,
From east, west, north, and south. Be it concluded,
No barricado for a belly. Know't
It will let in and out the enemy,                    205
With bag and baggage. Many thousand on's
Have the disease, and feel't not. How now, boy!
MAMILLIUS
  I am like you, they say.
LEONTES              Why, that's some comfort.
  What! Camillo there?
CAMILLO
  Ay, my good lord.                                  210
LEONTES
  Go play, Mamillius; thou'rt an honest man.
                              [Exit MAMILLIUS.]
  Camillo, this great sir will yet stay longer.
CAMILLO
  You had much ado to make his anchor hold;
  When you cast out, it still came home.
LEONTES                              Didst note it?
CAMILLO
  He would not stay at your petitions, made          215
  His business more material.
LEONTES                   Didst perceive it?
[Aside.]
  They're here with me already:° whispering, round-
    ing:°
  "Sicilia is a so-forth":° 'tis far gone,
  When I shall gust° it last. How came't, Camillo,
  That he did stay?
CAMILLO          At the good queen's entreaty.       220
LEONTES
  "At the queen's" be't: "Good" should be pertinent,
  But so it is, it is not. Was this taken°
  By any understanding pate but thine?
  For thy conceit is soaking,° will draw in
  More than the common blocks.° Not noted, is't,      225
  But of the finer natures? By some severals°
  Of headpiece extraordinary? Lower messes°
  Perchance are to this business purblind? Say.

**160 squash** unripe peapod (young person)   **161 take . . . money** allow yourself to be imposed upon   **163 happy . . . dole** may it be his lot to be a happy man   **171 thick my blood** make me melancholy   **171–72 So . . . me** My son has a similar post in my household   **177 Apparent** heir apparent   **180 angling** giving them scope, "playing" them   **183 neb** beak   **185 allowing** approving   **186 forked** alluding to the branching cuckold's horns

**188 issue** exit (following the idea of the actor not capable of his part)   **199 revolted** unfaithful   **202 predominant** in the ascendant (a technical term in astrology)   **217 They're . . . already** they (onlookers) have already caught on to my situation; **rounding** speaking in secret   **218 so-forth** i.e., they slyly avoid the word "cuckold"   **219 gust** taste, hear of   **222 taken** observed   **224 conceit is soaking** intelligence is absorbent   **225 blocks** blockheads   **226 severals** individuals   **227 Lower messes** inferior people ("mess" in the sense of a group who dine together and would be of the same—low—rank)

CAMILLO
Business, my lord? I think most understand
Bohemia stays here longer.

LEONTES          Ha?

CAMILLO          Stays here longer.    230

LEONTES
Ay, but why?

CAMILLO
To satisfy your highness, and the entreaties
Of our most gracious mistress.

LEONTES          Satisfy
Th' entreaties of your mistress? Satisfy?
Let that suffice. I have trusted thee, Camillo,    235
With all the nearest things to my heart, as well
My chamber-counsels,° wherein, priestlike, thou
Hast cleansed my bosom—ay, from thee departed
Thy penitent reformed; but we have been
Deceived in thy integrity, deceived    240
In that which seems so.

CAMILLO          Be it forbid, my lord!

LEONTES
To bide° upon't. Thou art not honest; or
If thou inclin'st that way, thou art a coward,
Which hoxes° honesty behind, restraining
From course required; or else thou must be counted    245
A servant, grafted in my serious trust,
And therein negligent; or else a fool,
That see'st a game played home, the rich stake drawn,°
And tak'st it all for jest.

CAMILLO          My gracious lord,
I may be negligent, foolish, and fearful,    250
In every one of these no man is free
But that his negligence, his folly, fear,
Among the infinite doings of the world,
Sometime puts forth.° In your affairs, my lord,
If ever I were willful negligent,    255
It was my folly; if industriously
I played the fool, it was my negligence,
Not weighing well the end: if ever fearful
To do a thing, where I the issue doubted,
Whereof the execution did cry out    260
Against the nonperformance, 'twas a fear
Which oft infects the wisest. These, my lord,
Are such allowed infirmities, that honesty
Is never free of. But beseech your grace,
Be plainer with me, let me know my trespass    265
By its own visage;° if I then deny it,
'Tis none of mine.

LEONTES          Ha' not you seen, Camillo—
But that's past doubt, you have, or your eyeglass°
Is thicker than a cuckold's horn—or heard—
For to a vision so apparent, rumor    270
Cannot be mute—or thought—for cogitation
Resides not in that man that does not think—
My wife is slippery?° If thou wilt confess,

Or else be impudently negative,
To have nor eyes, nor ears, nor thought, then say    275
My wife's a hobbyhorse,° deserves a name
As rank as any flax-wench,° that puts to
Before her troth-plight; say't, and justify't.

CAMILLO
I would not be a stander-by to hear
My sovereign mistress clouded so, without    280
My present° vengeance taken; 'shrew my heart,
You never spoke what did become you less
Than this; which to reiterate, were sin
As deep as that, though true.°

LEONTES          Is whispering nothing?
Is leaning cheek to cheek? Is meeting noses?    285
Kissing with inside lip? Stopping the career°
Of laughter with a sigh (a note infallible
Of breaking honesty°)? Horsing foot on foot?
Skulking in corners? Wishing clocks more swift?
Hours, minutes? Noon, midnight? And all eyes    290
Blind with the pin and web,° but theirs; theirs only,
That would unseen be wicked? Is this nothing?
Why, then the world and all that's in't is nothing,
The covering sky is nothing, Bohemia nothing,
My wife is nothing, nor nothing have these nothings,    295
If this be nothing.

CAMILLO          Good my lord, be cured
Of this diseased opinion, and betimes,
For 'tis most dangerous.

LEONTES          Say it be, 'tis true.

CAMILLO
No, no, my lord.

LEONTES          It is; you lie, you lie.
I say thou liest, Camillo, and I hate thee,    300
Pronounce thee a gross lout, a mindless slave,
Or else a hovering° temporizer, that
Canst with thine eyes at once see good and evil,
Inclining to them both. Were my wife's liver°
Infected as her life, she would not live    305
The running of one glass.°

CAMILLO          Who does infect her?

LEONTES
Why, he that wears her like her medal,° hanging
About his neck, Bohemia, who, if I
Had servants true about me, that bare eyes
To see alike mine honor as their profits,    310
Their own particular thrifts,° they would do that
Which should undo more doing. Ay, and thou,
His cupbearer, whom I from meaner form
Have benched° and reared to worship, who mayst see
Plainly as heaven sees earth, and earth see heaven,    315
How I am galled, mightst bespice a cup,
To give mine enemy a lasting wink;°
Which draught to me were cordial.°

---

237 **chamber-counsels** confessions of secret sins   242 **bide** insist   244 **hoxes** hamstrings   248 **played . . . drawn** played earnestly, great stakes being won   254 **puts forth** shows itself   266 **By . . . visage** under its true name   268 **eyeglass** the lens of the eye   267–73 **Ha' not . . . slippery?** Have you not seen—you must have, or your sight is grossly thick—or heard—as you must, since Hermione's conduct is so open that there must be gossip about it—or thought—and unless you have you cannot think at all—that my wife is unfaithful?

276 **hobbyhorse** loose woman   277 **flax-wench** low-bred girl   281 **present** immediate   284 **As deep . . . true** i.e., as wicked as her adultery if it were a fact, which it is not   286 **career** gallop   288 **honesty** chastity   291 **pin and web** cataract   302 **hovering** vacillating   304 **liver** since this was the seat of the passions, it presumably was infected; transposition of "liver" and "life" has been proposed   306 **glass** hourglass   307 **medal** here a portrait miniature worn about the neck   311 **particular thrifts** special gains   314 **benched** raised to place of dignity   317 **give . . . wink** close his eyes forever   318 **cordial** medicine

CAMILLO                         Sir, my lord,
I could do this, and that with no rash potion,
But with a lingering dram° that should not work        320
Maliciously, like poison; but I cannot
Believe this crack to be in my dread mistress,
So sovereignly being honorable.
I have loved thee°—

LEONTES
Make that thy question, and go rot!°        325
Dost think I am so muddy, so unsettled,
To appoint° myself in this vexation? Sully
The purity and whiteness of my sheets—
Which to preserve is sleep; which being spotted,
Is goads, thorns, nettles, tails of wasps—        330
Give scandal to the blood o' th' prince, my son,
Who I do think is mine, and love as mine,
Without ripe° moving to't? Would I do this?
Could man so blench?°

CAMILLO                 I must believe you, sir;
I do, and will fetch off Bohemia for't:        335
Provided that when he's removed, your highness
Will take again your queen as yours at first,
Even for your son's sake, and thereby for sealing
The injury of tongues, in courts and kingdoms
Known and allied to yours.

LEONTES                         Thou dost advise me,        340
Even so as I mine own course have set down.
I'll give no blemish to her honor, none.

CAMILLO
My lord,
Go then; and with a countenance as clear
As friendship wears at feasts, keep with Bohemia,        345
And with your queen: I am his cupbearer;
If from me he have wholesome beverage,
Account me not your servant.

LEONTES                         This is all:
Do't, and thou hast the one half of my heart;
Do't not, thou split'st thine own.

CAMILLO                         I'll do't, my lord.        350

LEONTES
I will seem friendly, as thou hast advised me.    *Exit.*

CAMILLO
O miserable lady! But for me,
What case stand I in? I must be the poisoner
Of good Polixenes, and my ground to do't
Is the obedience to a master—one        355
Who, in rebellion with himself, will have
All that are his so too. To do this deed,
Promotion follows; if I could find example
Of thousands that had struck anointed kings,
And flourished after, I'd not do't; but since        360
Nor brass, nor stone, nor parchment bears not one,
Let villainy itself forswear't.° I must
Forsake the court; to do't, or no, is certain

To me a break-neck. Happy star reign now!
Here comes Bohemia.

*Enter* POLIXENES.

POLIXENES                 This is strange: methinks        365
My favor here begins to warp. Not speak?
Good day, Camillo.

CAMILLO                 Hail, most royal sir.

POLIXENES
What is the news i' th' court?

CAMILLO                         None rare, my lord.

POLIXENES
The king hath on him such a countenance,
As he had lost some province, and a region        370
Loved as he loves himself; even now I met him
With customary compliment, when he,
Wafting his eyes to th' contrary,° and falling
A lip of much contempt, speeds from me, and
So leaves me to consider what is breeding        375
That changes thus his manners.

CAMILLO
I dare not know, my lord.

POLIXENES
How, dare not? Do not? Do you know, and dare not
Be intelligent to me? 'Tis thereabouts;
For to yourself, what you do know, you must,        380
And cannot say you dare not.° Good Camillo,
Your changed complexions are to me a mirror,
Which shows me mine changed too: for I must be
A party in this alteration, finding
Myself thus altered with't.

CAMILLO                         There is a sickness        385
Which puts some of us in distemper; but
I cannot name the disease; and it is caught
Of you, that yet are well.

POLIXENES                 How caught of me?
Make me not sighted like the basilisk.°
I have looked on thousands, who have sped° the better        390
By my regard, but killed none so. Camillo,
As you are certainly a gentleman, thereto
Clerklike experienced,° which no less adorns
Our gentry than our parents' noble names
In whose success° we are gentle:° I beseech you,        395
If you know aught which does behoove my knowledge
Thereof to be informed, imprison't not
In ignorant concealment.

CAMILLO                         I may not answer.

POLIXENES
A sickness caught of me, and yet I well?
I must be answered. Dost thou hear, Camillo,        400
I conjure° thee, by all the parts° of man,
Which honor does acknowledge, whereof the least
Is not this suit of mine, that thou declare
What incidency° thou dost guess of harm

320 lingering dram slow-working dose   324 I . . . thee
difficult to explain; Camillo may be about to protest his long
loyalty, or threaten withdrawal of his love, but he would hardly
address the king as "thou"; some editors give the words to
Leontes, which hardly helps   325 Make . . . rot i.e., If you
doubt the queen's infidelity, go to hell!   327 appoint
establish   333 ripe adequate, matured   334 blench swerve
358–62 if . . . forswear't even if the records showed that
king-killers prospered, I would not do it; but since they prove
the contrary, villainy itself should forswear regicide

373 Wafting . . . contrary looking (contemptuously) away
378–81 How, dare not? . . . you dare not What do you
mean, dare not? That you do not? Can it be that you know,
and dare not tell me? That must be the explanation, since you
cannot say you do not dare tell yourself what you know
389 basilisk a mythical serpent that killed by looking   390
sped prospered   393 Clerklike experienced with the experience of an educated man   395 success succession; gentle wellborn   401 conjure adjure; parts duties, functions   404
incidency threat

Is creeping toward me; how far off, how near,    405
Which way to be prevented, if to be;
If not, how best to bear it.
CAMILLO           Sir, I will tell you,
Since I am charged in honor, and by him
That I think honorable. Therefore mark my counsel,
Which must be ev'n as swiftly followed as    410
I mean to utter it; or both yourself and me
Cry lost, and so good night.
POLIXENES           On, good Camillo.
CAMILLO
I am appointed him° to murder you.
POLIXENES
By whom, Camillo?
CAMILLO           By the king.
POLIXENES           For what?
CAMILLO
He thinks, nay with all confidence he swears,    415
As he had seen't, or been an instrument
To vice° you to't, that you have touched his queen
Forbiddenly.
POLIXENES   Oh then my best blood turn
To an infected jelly, and my name
Be yoked with his, that did betray the Best!°    420
Turn then my freshest reputation to
A savor° that may strike the dullest nostril
Where I arrive, and my approach be shunned,
Nay, hated too, worse than the great'st infection
That e'er was heard, or read!
CAMILLO         Swear his thought over° 425
By each particular star in heaven, and
By all their influences; you may as well
Forbid the sea for to obey the moon,
As or by oath remove or counsel shake
The fabric of his folly, whose foundation    430
Is piled upon his faith, and will continue
The standing of his body.°
POLIXENES         How should this grow?°
CAMILLO
I know not: but I am sure 'tis safer to
Avoid what's grown than question how 'tis born.
If therefore you dare trust my honesty,
That lies enclosèd in this trunk, which you    435
Shall bear along impawned,° away tonight.
Your followers I will whisper to the business,
And will by twos and threes, at several posterns,°
Clear them o' th' city. For myself, I'll put    440
My fortunes to your service, which are here
By this discovery lost. Be not uncertain,
For by the honor of my parents, I
Have uttered truth; which if you seek to prove,°
I dare not stand by; nor shall you be safer,    445

Than one condemned by the king's own mouth, thereon
His execution sworn.°
POLIXENES         I do believe thee:
I saw his heart in's face. Give me thy hand,
Be pilot to me, and thy places° shall
Still° neighbor mine. My ships are ready, and    450
My people did expect my hence departure
Two days ago. This jealousy
Is for a precious creature; as she's rare,
Must it be great; and, as his person's mighty,
Must it be violent: and, as he does conceive,    455
He is dishonored by a man, which ever
Professed° to him, why his revenges must
In that be made more bitter. Fear o'ershades me;
Good expedition° by my friend, and comfort
The gracious queen, part of his theme, but nothing    460
Of his ill-ta'en suspicion.° Come, Camillo,
I will respect thee as a father, if
Thou bear'st my life off hence; let us avoid.°
CAMILLO
It is in mine authority to command
The keys of all the posterns: please your highness    465
To take the urgent hour. Come, sir, away.    *Exeunt.*

# ACT II

## Scene I. [*Sicilia, the court of Leontes.*]

*Enter* HERMIONE, MAMILLIUS, LADIES.

HERMIONE
Take the boy to you; he so troubles me,
'Tis past enduring.
FIRST LADY        Come, my gracious lord,
Shall I be your playfellow?
MAMILLIUS        No, I'll none of you.
FIRST LADY
Why, my sweet lord?
MAMILLIUS
You'll kiss me hard, and speak to me, as if    5
I were a baby still. I love you better.
SECOND LADY
And why so, my lord?
MAMILLIUS        Not for because
Your brows are blacker; yet black brows, they say,
Become some women best, so that there be not
Too much hair there, but in a semicircle,    10
Or a half-moon, made with a pen.
SECOND LADY        Who taught° this?

413 **him** i.e., by Leontes   417 **To vice** to force   420 **that . . . Best** Judas   422 **savor** alluding to the idea that infection (e.g., of the plague) could be smelled (hence the use of flowers in posies as a prophylactic)   425 **Swear . . . over** deny his suspicion with oaths   427–32 **you may . . . body** i.e., you may as well attempt the obviously impossible as try to remove by your oaths or pull down by your advice the structure of his crazy delusion, which has its foundations on settled belief, and will last as long as his life (stand up as long as he can)   432 **How . . . grow** How can this have grown up?   437 **impawned** as a pledge of good faith (Camillo points to his body, which is the "trunk")   439 **posterns** gates   444 **prove** test

446–47 **mouth . . . sworn** i.e., the king, having condemned him, has sworn that the sentence will be death (possibly corrupt; see A Note on the Text, p. 1500)   449 **places** offices, functions, dignities   450 **Still** always   457 **Professed** made professions (of friendship)   459 **expedition** speed   460–61 **part . . . suspicion** obscure; Shakespeare's sense has perhaps not quite got through; a possible paraphrase is, "May my speedy departure also help the queen, who is involved in Leontes' fantasy though she has no rightful place in his suspicions," but this fails to explain why Polixenes thought his departure would help Hermione; perhaps "expedition" is not the subject of "comfort"—then he is merely wishing the queen comfort in the troubles he is leaving her to, and the vagueness of the expression matches the emptiness of the wish   463 **avoid** depart   II.i.11 **taught** taught you

MAMILLIUS
I learned it out of women's faces. Pray now,
What color are your eyebrows?

FIRST LADY                              Blue, my lord.

MAMILLIUS
Nay, that's a mock. I have seen a lady's nose
That has been blue, but not her eyebrows.

FIRST LADY                              Hark ye,  15
The queen, your mother, rounds apace; we shall
Present our services to a fine new prince
One of these days, and then you'd wanton° with us,
If we would have you.

SECOND LADY          She is spread of late
Into a goodly bulk; good time encounter her!  20

HERMIONE
What wisdom stirs amongst you? Come, sir, now
I am for you again; pray you sit by us,
And tell's a tale.

MAMILLIUS          Merry or sad shall't be?

HERMIONE
As merry as you will.

MAMILLIUS
A sad tale's best for winter; I have one  25
Of sprites and goblins.

HERMIONE          Let's have that, good sir.
Come on, sit down; come on, and do your best,
To fright me with your sprites; you're powerful at it.

MAMILLIUS
There was a man.

HERMIONE          Nay, come sit down; then on.

MAMILLIUS
Dwelt by a churchyard—I will tell it softly,  30
Yond crickets° shall not hear it.

HERMIONE
Come on, then, and give't me in mine ear.

[Enter LEONTES, ANTIGONUS, and LORDS.]

LEONTES
Was he met there? His train? Camillo with him?

LORD
Behind the tuft of pines I met them, never
Saw I men scour° so on their way. I eyed them  35
Even to their ships.

LEONTES          How blest am I
In my just censure,° in my true opinion!
Alack, for lesser knowledge! How accursed,
In being so blest! There may be in the cup
A spider° steeped, and one may drink, depart,  40
And yet partake no venom, for his knowledge
Is not infected; but if one present
Th' abhorred ingredient to his eye, make known
How he hath drunk, he cracks his gorge, his sides,
With violent hefts.° I have drunk, and seen the spider.  45
Camillo was his help in this, his pander.
There is a plot against my life, my crown;
All's true that is mistrusted; that false villain,
Whom I employed, was pre-employed by him;

He has discovered° my design, and I  50
Remain a pinched thing;° yea, a very trick
For them to play at will. How came the posterns
So easily open?

LORD          By his great authority;
Which often hath no less prevailed than so
On your command.

LEONTES          I know't too well.  55

[To HERMIONE.]

Give me the boy. I am glad you did not nurse him;
Though he does bear some signs of me, yet you
Have too much blood in him.

HERMIONE          What is this? Sport?

LEONTES
Bear the boy hence, he shall not come about her;
[Exit MAMILLIUS and a LADY.]
Away with him, and let her sport herself  60
With that she's big with; for 'tis Polixenes
Has made thee swell thus.

HERMIONE          But I'd say he had not;
And I'll be sworn you would believe my saying,
Howe'er you lean to th' nayward.°

LEONTES          You, my lords,
Look on her, mark her well; be but about  65
To say, "She is a goodly lady," and
The justice of your hearts will thereto add,
" 'Tis pity she's not honest, honorable";
Praise her but for this her without-door form,°
Which on my faith deserves high speech, and straight  70
The shrug, the hum or ha, these petty brands
That calumny doth use—oh, I am out!°
That mercy does, for calumny will sear
Virtue itself—these shrugs, these hum's and ha's,
When you have said she's goodly, come between,°  75
Ere you can say she's honest. But be't known,
From him that has most cause to grieve it should be,
She's an adult'ress.

HERMIONE          Should a villain say so,
The most replenished° villain in the world,
He were as much more villain; you, my lord,  80
Do but mistake.

LEONTES          You have mistook, my lady,
Polixenes for Leontes. O thou thing,
Which I'll not call a creature of thy place,°
Lest barbarism, making me the precedent,
Should a like language use to all degrees,°  85
And mannerly distinguishment leave out
Betwixt the prince and beggar. I have said
She's an adult'ress, I have said with whom.
More, she's a traitor, and Camillo is
A federary° with her, and one that knows  90
What she should shame to know herself
But with her most vile principal°—that she's
A bed-swerver,° even as bad as those
That vulgars give bold'st titles; ay, and privy

To this their late escape.

HERMIONE                    No, by my life,                    95
Privy to none of this; how will this grieve you,
When you shall come to clearer knowledge, that
You thus have published° me! Gentle my lord,
You scarce can right me throughly then to say
You did mistake.

LEONTES                    No; if I mistake                    100
In those foundations which I build upon,
The center° is not big enough to bear
A schoolboy's top. Away with her to prison.
He who shall speak for her is afar off guilty,
But that he speaks.°

HERMIONE                    There's some ill planet reigns;    105
I must be patient, till the heavens look
With an aspect more favorable. Good my lords,
I am not prone to weeping, as our sex
Commonly are; the want of which vain dew
Perchance shall dry your pities. But I have        110
That honorable grief lodged here which burns
Worse than tears drown. Beseech you all, my lords,
With thoughts so qualified° as your charities
Shall best instruct you, measure me; and so
The king's will be performed!

LEONTES                    Shall I be heard?                   115

HERMIONE
Who is't that goes with me? Beseech your highness
My women may be with me, for you see
My plight requires it. Do not weep, good fools;
There is no cause; when you shall know your mistress
Has deserved prison, then abound in tears,          120
As I come out; this action I now go on
Is for my better grace.° Adieu, my lord.
I never wished to see you sorry; now
I trust I shall. My women come, you have leave.

LEONTES
Go, do our bidding: hence.                          125

[*Exeunt* QUEEN *and* LADIES.]

LORD
Beseech your highness, call the queen again.

ANTIGONUS
Be certain what you do, sir, lest your justice
Prove violence, in the which three great ones suffer,
Yourself, your queen, your son.

LORD                    For her, my lord,
I dare my life lay down, and will do't, sir,        130
Please you t' accept it, that the queen is spotless
I' th' eyes of heaven, and to you—I mean,
In this, which you accuse her.

ANTIGONUS                    If it prove
She's otherwise, I'll keep my stables where
I lodge my wife;° I'll go in couples° with her;    135

Than when I feel and see her, no farther trust her;
For every inch of woman in the world,
Ay, every dram of woman's flesh is false,
If she be.

LEONTES
Hold your peaces.

LORD                    Good my lord.                           140

ANTIGONUS
It is for you we speak, not for ourselves.
You are abused, and by some putter-on°
That will be damned for't. Would I knew the villain,
I would land-damn° him! Be she honor-flawed,
I have three daughters: the eldest is eleven;       145
The second and the third, nine and some five:
If this prove true, they'll pay for't. By mine honor,
I'll geld 'em all; fourteen they shall not see
To bring false generations.° They are co-heirs,
And I had rather glib° myself than they              150
Should not produce fair issue.

LEONTES                    Cease, no more!
You smell this business with a sense as cold
As is a dead man's nose; but I do see't, and feel't,
As you feel doing thus; and see withal
The instruments that feel.°

ANTIGONUS                    If it be so,                       155
We need no grave to bury honesty;
There's not a grain of it the face to sweeten
Of the whole dungy earth.

LEONTES                    What? Lack I credit?°

LORD
I had rather you did lack than I, my lord,
Upon this ground; and more it would content me     160
To have her honor true than your suspicion,
Be blamed for't how you might.

LEONTES                    Why, what need we
Commune with you of this, but rather follow
Our forceful instigation? Our prerogative
Calls not your counsels, but our natural goodness   165
Imparts this;° which, if you, or stupefied,
Or seeming so, in skill,° cannot, or will not,
Relish a truth like us, inform yourselves,
We need no more of your advice. The matter,
The loss, the gain, the ord'ring on't,              170
Is all properly ours.

ANTIGONUS                    And I wish, my liege,
You had only in your silent judgment tried it,
Without more overture.

LEONTES                    How could that be?
Either thou art most ignorant by age,
Or thou wert born a fool. Camillo's flight,         175
Added to their familiarity—
Which was as gross as ever touched conjecture,°

98 published publicly proclaimed or denounced    102 center
of the earth, and so of the universe, i.e., "If I am mistaken, no
foundation can be trusted"    105 But . . . speaks i.e., in
merely speaking he is found guilty as a remote accomplice
113 qualified tempered, moderated    121–22 this . . . grace
by contrast with one who goes to prison to be disgraced, I
embark on this course to add to my honesty and credit    134–35
I'll . . . wife obscure, but certainly coarse: he will keep his
stallions locked up when his wife is near (?)    135 go in
couples be coupled by a leash to her, for safety's sake (of
course, he means that if the queen is unchaste, other women
must be even more so)

142 putter-on plotter, one who instigates    144 land-damn
severely beat (?)    149 false generations illegitimate children
150 glib castrate    153–55 but . . . that feel Leontes here
strikes either Antigonus or himself; "But I see it and feel it with
immediate, vital force, as you do when you strike yourself thus
(or, when I strike you thus)—you feel it and see the hands
that inflicted the pain"    158 Lack I credit Am I not
believed?    164–66 Our prerogative . . . this i.e., I am not
obliged to seek your advice; it is out of the goodness of my
heart that I tell you this (Leontes, on his dignity, uses the royal
"we")    167 skill reason    177 as ever . . . conjecture as
ever conjecture reached to

That lacked sight only, naught for approbation°
But only seeing, all other circumstances
Made up to th' deed—doth push on this proceeding.    180
Yet, for a greater confirmation—
For in an act of this importance, 'twere
Most piteous to be wild°—I have dispatched in post
To sacred Delphos,° to Apollo's temple,
Cleomenes and Dion, whom you know    185
Of stuffed sufficiency.° Now, from the oracle
They will bring all,° whose spiritual counsel had,
Shall stop, or spur me. Have I done well?

LORD
Well done, my lord.

LEONTES
Though I am satisfied, and need no more    190
Than what I know, yet shall the oracle
Give rest to th' minds of others—such as he,°
Whose ignorant credulity will not
Come up to th' truth. So have we thought it good
From our free person she should be confined,    195
Lest that the treachery of the two fled hence
Be left her to perform.° Come, follow us,
We are to speak in public: for this business
Will raise° us all.

ANTIGONUS   [Aside.] To laughter, as I take it,
If the good truth were known.            Exeunt. 200


Scene II. [Sicilia, a prison.]

Enter PAULINA, a GENTLEMAN, [and ATTENDANTS].

PAULINA
The keeper of the prison, call to him;
Let him have knowledge who I am. [Exit GENTLE-
   MAN.] Good lady,
No court in Europe is too good for thee—
What dost thou then in prison?

[Enter GENTLEMAN, with the] JAILER.

                Now, good sir,
You know me, do you not?

JAILER                For a worthy lady,    5
And one whom much I honor.

PAULINA                Pray you, then,
Conduct me to the queen.

JAILER                I may not, madam,
To the contrary I have express commandment.

PAULINA
Here's ado, to lock up honesty and honor from
Th' access of gentle visitors! Is't lawful, pray you,    10
To see her women? Any of them? Emilia?

JAILER
So please you, madam,
To put apart these your attendants, I
Shall bring Emilia forth.

PAULINA                I pray now call her.
Withdraw yourselves.
            [Exeunt GENTLEMAN and ATTENDANTS.]

JAILER                And, madam,    15
I must be present at your conference.

PAULINA
Well, be't so, prithee.            [Exit JAILER.]
Here's such ado to make no stain a stain,
As passes coloring.°

[Enter JAILER, with] EMILIA.

                Dear gentlewoman,
How fares our gracious lady?    20

EMILIA
As well as one so great and so forlorn
May hold together. On her frights and griefs
(Which° never tender lady hath borne greater)
She is, something before her time, delivered.

PAULINA
A boy?

EMILIA   A daughter, and a goodly babe,    25
Lusty, and like to live; the queen receives
Much comfort in't; says, "My poor prisoner,
I am innocent as you."

PAULINA                I dare be sworn.
These dangerous, unsafe lunes° i' th' king, beshrew
   them!
He must be told on't, and he shall; the office    30
Becomes a woman best. I'll take't upon me.
If I prove honey-mouthed, let my tongue blister,°
And never to my red-looked anger be
The trumpet° any more. Pray you, Emilia,
Commend my best obedience to the queen;    35
If she dares trust me with her little babe,
I'll show't the king, and undertake to be
Her advocate to th' loud'st. We do not know
How he may soften at the sight o' th' child;
The silence often of pure innocence    40
Persuades, when speaking fails.

EMILIA                Most worthy madam,
Your honor and your goodness is so evident,
That your free undertaking cannot miss
A thriving issue: there is no lady living
So meet° for this great errand. Please your ladyship    45
To visit the next room, I'll presently°
Acquaint the queen of your most noble offer,
Who but today hammered of° this design,
But durst not tempt° a minister of honor
Lest she should be denied.

PAULINA                Tell her, Emilia,    50
I'll use that tongue I have; if wit° flow from't
As boldness from my bosom, let't not be doubted
I shall do good.

EMILIA                Now be you blest for it!
I'll to the queen. Please you come something nearer.

---

178 **approbation** proof   183 **wild** rash   184 **Delphos** Delos
(Shakespeare mistakenly thought the oracle of Apollo was
there rather than at Delphi; in this error he follows his source,
*Pandosto*   186 **stuffed sufficiency** more than adequate depend-
ability   187 **all** the whole truth   192 **he** Antigonus   196–97
**Lest . . . perform** referring to the "plot against his life and
crown" of which he accuses all three   199 **raise** rouse

II.ii.19 **coloring** the art of dyeing (thus giving a specious
appearance)   23 **Which** than which   29 **lunes** fits of lunacy
32 **tongue blister** because lies were supposed to blister the
tongue   33–34 **red-looked . . . trumpet** the figure is of an
angry face as a herald dressed in red and preceded by a trum-
pet(er)   45 **meet** fitting   46 **presently** immediately   48
**hammered of** deliberated upon   49 **tempt** make trial of   51
**wit** wisdom

JAILER
Madam, if't please the queen to send the babe, 55
I know not what I shall incur to pass it,°
Having no warrant.

PAULINA      You need not fear it, sir:
This child was prisoner to the womb and is
By law and process of great Nature thence
Freed, and enfranchised; not a party to 60
The anger of the king, nor guilty of,
If any be, the trespass of the queen.

JAILER
I do believe it.

PAULINA
Do not you fear—upon mine honor, I
Will stand betwixt you and danger.      *Exeunt.* 65

#### Scene III. [*Sicilia, the court of Leontes.*]

*Enter* LEONTES, SERVANTS, ANTIGONUS, *and*
LORDS.

LEONTES
Nor night nor day no rest: it is but weakness
To bear the matter thus, mere weakness. If
The cause were not in being—part o' th' cause,°
She, th' adult'ress (for the harlot° king
Is quite beyond mine arm, out of the blank 5
And level° of my brain, plot-proof); but she,
I can hook to me—say that she were gone,
Given to the fire, a moiety° of my rest
Might come to me again. Who's there?

SERVANT      My lord!

LEONTES
How does the boy? 10

FIRST ATTENDANT
He took good rest tonight; 'tis hoped
His sickness is discharged.

LEONTES      To see his nobleness!
Conceiving the dishonor of his mother,
He straight declined, drooped, took it deeply,
Fastened, and fixed the shame on't in himself; 15
Threw off his spirit, his appetite, his sleep,
And downright languished. Leave me solely; go,
See how he fares. [*Exit* SERVANT.] Fie, fie, no thought
of him!°
The very thought of my revenges that way
Recoil upon me—in himself too mighty, 20
And in his parties, his alliance; let him be,
Until a time may serve. For present vengeance
Take it on her. Camillo and Polixenes
Laugh at me, make their pastime at my sorrow;
They should not laugh if I could reach them, nor 25
Shall she within my power.

*Enter* PAULINA, [*with the* BABY].

LORD      You must not enter.

PAULINA
Nay, rather, good my lords, be second to° me.
Fear you his tyrannous passion more, alas,
Than the queen's life? A gracious innocent soul,
More free° than he is jealous.

ANTIGONUS      That's enough. 30

SERVANT
Madam, he hath not slept tonight, commanded
None should come at him.

PAULINA      Not so hot, good sir;
I come to bring him sleep. 'Tis such as you
That creep like shadows by him, and do sigh
At each his needless heavings—such as you 35
Nourish the cause of his awaking. I
Do come with words as medicinal as true,
Honest as either, to purge him of that humor°
That presses him from sleep.

LEONTES      What noise there, ho?

PAULINA
No noise, my lord, but needful conference 40
About some gossips° for your highness.

LEONTES      How?
Away with that audacious lady! Antigonus,
I charged thee that she should not come about me;
I knew she would.

ANTIGONUS      I told her so, my lord,
On your displeasure's peril, and on mine, 45
She should not visit you.

LEONTES      What? Canst not rule her?

PAULINA
From all dishonesty he can: in this,
Unless he take the course that you have done—
Commit me for committing° honor, trust it,
He shall not rule me.

ANTIGONUS      La you now, you hear, 50
When she will take the rein, I let her run;
But she'll not stumble.°

PAULINA      Good my liege, I come—
And I beseech you hear me, who profess
Myself your loyal servant, your physician,
Your most obedient counselor; yet that dares 55
Less appear so in comforting° your evils,
Than such as most seem yours°—I say, I come
From your good queen.

LEONTES      Good queen!

PAULINA
Good queen, my lord, good queen, I say good queen,
And would by combat° make her good, so were I 60
A man, the worst° about you.

LEONTES      Force her hence.

PAULINA
Let him that makes but trifles of his eyes
First hand me. On mine own accord I'll off,
But first I'll do my errand. The good queen

---

**56 to pass it** as a result of allowing it to pass
**II.iii.3 th' cause** Leontes interrupts himself, remembering that
Polixenes is inaccessible, so that only part of the cause of his
agony is within his power to destroy   **4 harlot** lewd   **5–6 cut
. . . level** beyond my range ("blank" is the center of the
target; "level" means "aim"; the reference is to archery)   **8
moiety** half   **18 him** Polixenes

**27 be second to** support   **30 free** innocent   **38 humor** illness
**41 gossips** godparents   **49 Commit . . . committing** the
word is used in a punning sense, meaning first "send to prison"
and second "performing"   **51–52 rein . . . run . . . stumble**
Antigonus, as usual, speaks of his wife as if she were a horse
**56 comforting** abetting, countenancing   **57 as . . . yours** as
are nearest to you   **60 by combat** in a trial by combat (which
would, in the code of chivalry, vindicate a lady's honor)   **61
the worst** the lowest in degree

(For she is good) hath brought you forth a daughter; 65
Here 'tis; commends it to your blessing.

*[She lays down the* BABY.]

LEONTES                                    Out!
A mankind° witch! Hence with her, out o' door!
A most intelligencing° bawd!
PAULINA                          Not so;
I am as ignorant in that as you
In so entitling me; and no less honest              70
Than you are mad; which is enough, I'll warrant,
As this world goes, to pass for honest.
LEONTES                              Traitors!
Will you not push her out? [*To* ANTIGONUS.] Give
    her the bastard,
Thou dotard, thou art woman-tired,° unroosted
By thy Dame Partlet° here. Take up the bastard,   75
Take't up, I say; give't to thy crone.
PAULINA                            Forever
Unvenerable be thy hands, if thou
Tak'st up the princess, by that forcèd baseness°
Which he has put upon't!
LEONTES              He dreads his wife.
PAULINA
So I would you did; then 'twere past all doubt     80
You'd call your children yours.
LEONTES                  A nest of traitors.
ANTIGONUS
I am none, by this good light.
PAULINA                      Nor I: nor any
But one that's here, and that's himself; for he,
The sacred honor of himself, his queen's,
His hopeful son's, his babe's, betrays to slander,   85
Whose sting is sharper than the sword's; and will not
(For as the case now stands, it is a curse
He cannot be compelled to't) once remove
The root of his opinion, which is rotten
As ever oak or stone was sound.
LEONTES                      A callat°            90
Of boundless tongue, who late hath beat her husband,
And now baits° me! This brat is none of mine;
It is the issue of Polixenes.
Hence with it, and together with the dam,
Commit them to the fire.
PAULINA              It is yours:                  95
And might we lay th' old proverb° to your charge,
So like you, 'tis the worse. Behold, my lords,
Although the print be little, the whole matter
And copy° of the father: eye, nose, lip,
The trick of's frown, his forehead, nay, the valley,  100
The pretty dimples of his chin and cheek; his smiles;
The very mold and frame of hand, nail, finger.
And thou, good goddess Nature, which hast made it
So like to him that got° it, if thou hast
The ordering of the mind too, 'mongst all colors   105

No yellow° in't, lest she suspect, as he does,
Her children not her husband's.
LEONTES                  A gross hag!
And, lozel,° thou art worthy to be hanged,
That wilt not stay her tongue.
ANTIGONUS              Hang all the husbands
That cannot do that feat, you'll leave yourself      110
Hardly one subject.
LEONTES          Once more, take her hence.
PAULINA
A most unworthy and unnatural lord
Can do no more.
LEONTES          I'll ha' thee burned.
PAULINA                          I care not;
It is an heretic that makes the fire,
Not she which burns in't. I'll not call you tyrant;   115
But this most cruel usage of your queen
(Not able to produce more accusation
Than your own weak-hingèd° fancy) something
    savors
Of tyranny, and will ignoble make you,
Yea, scandalous to the world.
LEONTES              On your allegiance,°        120
Out of the chamber with her! Were I a tyrant,°
Where were her life? She durst not call me so,
If she did know me one. Away with her.
PAULINA
I pray you do not push me, I'll be gone.
Look to your babe, my lord, 'tis yours: Jove send her  125
A better guiding spirit. What needs these hands?
You, that are thus so tender o'er his follies,
Will never do him good, not one of you.
So, so; farewell, we are gone.            *Exit.*
LEONTES
Thou, traitor, hast set on thy wife to this.        130
My child? Away with't! Even thou, that hast
A heart so tender o'er it, take it hence,
And see it instantly consumed with fire.
Even thou, and none but thou. Take it up straight;
Within this hour bring me word 'tis done,          135
And by good testimony, or I'll seize° thy life,
With what thou else call'st thine; if thou refuse,
And wilt encounter with my wrath, say so;
The bastard brains with these my proper° hands
Shall I dash out. Go, take it to the fire,         140
For thou sett'st on thy wife.
ANTIGONUS              I did not, sir;
These lords, my noble fellows, if they please,
Can clear me in't.
LORDS          We can: my royal liege,
He is not guilty of her coming hither.
LEONTES
You're liars all.                                  145
LORD
Beseech your highness, give us better credit.
We have always truly served you, and beseech

67 mankind male, ferocious, violent   68 intelligencing i.e.,
acting as a pander   74 woman-tired henpecked   75 Dame
Partlet traditionally the name of the hen; compare Reynard
the fox, etc.   78 forcèd baseness falsely base name (bastard)
90 callat scold   91–92 beat . . . baits pronounced alike   96
th' old proverb i.e., "They are so like that they are the worse
for it"   98–99 print . . . matter . . . copy the figure is
derived from printing   104 got begot

106 yellow the color of jealousy   108 lozel worthless fellow
118 weak-hinged ill-supported   120 On your allegiance the
ultimate command; to disobey it is treason   121 tyrant
Paulina avoided calling him tyrant, but in coming close to so
doing reminded him that this interpretation might all too easily
be put upon his actions   136 seize confiscate   139 proper
own

So to esteem of us; and on our knees we beg,
As recompense of our dear services
Past, and to come, that you do change this purpose,    150
Which being so horrible, so bloody, must
Lead on to some foul issue. We all kneel.

LEONTES
I am a feather for each wind that blows.
Shall I live on to see this bastard kneel
And call me father? Better burn it now    155
Than curse it then. But be it; let it live.
It shall not neither. You, sir, come you hither:
You that have been so tenderly officious
With Lady Margery,° your midwife there,
To save this bastard's life—for 'tis a bastard,    160
So sure as this beard's gray°—what will you adventure,
To save this brat's life?

ANTIGONUS          Anything, my lord,
That my ability may undergo,
And nobleness impose—at least thus much:
I'll pawn° the little blood which I have left,    165
To save the innocent—anything possible.

LEONTES
It shall be possible. Swear by this sword°
Thou wilt perform my bidding.

ANTIGONUS          I will, my lord.

LEONTES
Mark, and perform it: see'st thou? For the fail°
Of any point in't, shall not only be    170
Death to thyself, but to thy lewd-tongued wife,
Whom for this time we pardon. We enjoin thee,
As thou art liegeman to us, that thou carry
This female bastard hence, and that thou bear it
To some remote and desert place, quite out    175
Of our dominions; and that there thou leave it,
Without more mercy, to its own protection
And favor of the climate. As by strange fortune
It came to us, I do in justice charge thee,
On thy soul's peril, and thy body's torture,    180
That thou commend it strangely° to some place,
Where chance may nurse or end it. Take it up.

ANTIGONUS
I swear to do this, though a present death
Had been more merciful. Come on, poor babe,
Some powerful spirit instruct the kites and ravens    185
To be thy nurses! Wolves and bears, they say,
Casting their savageness aside, have done
Like offices of pity. Sir, be prosperous
In more than this deed does require!° And blessing
Against this cruelty fight on thy side,    190
Poor thing, condemned to loss. *Exit, [with the* BABY].

LEONTES          No, I'll not rear
Another's issue.

*Enter a* SERVANT.

SERVANT      Please your highness, posts
From those you sent to th' oracle are come
An hour since: Cleomenes and Dion,

Being well arrived from Delphos, are both landed,    195
Hasting to th' court.

LORD          So please you, sir, their speed
Hath been beyond accompt.°

LEONTES          Twenty-three days
They have been absent; 'tis good speed; foretells
The great Apollo suddenly will have
The truth of this appear. Prepare you, lords,    200
Summon a session,° that we may arraign
Our most disloyal lady; for as she hath
Been publicly accused, so shall she have
A just and open trial. While she lives,
My heart will be a burden to me. Leave me,    205
And think upon my bidding.      *Exeunt.*


# ACT III

### Scene I. [*Sicilia. On a high road.*]

*Enter* CLEOMENES *and* DION.

CLEOMENES
The climate's delicate, the air most sweet,
Fertile the isle,° the temple much surpassing
The common praise it bears.

DION          I shall report,
For most it caught me, the celestial habits°
(Methinks I so should term them) and the reverence    5
Of the grave wearers. O, the sacrifice,
How ceremonious, solemn, and unearthly
It was i' th' off'ring!

CLEOMENES          But of all, the burst
And the ear-deaf'ning voice o' th' oracle,
Kin to Jove's thunder, so surprised my sense,    10
That I was nothing.

DION          If th' event° o' th' journey
Prove as successful to the queen (O be't so!)
As it hath been to us rare, pleasant, speedy,
The time is worth the use on't.

CLEOMENES          Great Apollo
Turn all to th' best; these proclamations,    15
So forcing faults upon Hermione,
I little like.

DION      The violent carriage° of it
Will clear or end the business when the oracle,
Thus by Apollo's great divine° sealed up,
Shall the contents discover, something rare    20
Even then will rush to knowledge. Go; fresh horses,
And gracious be the issue!      *Exeunt.*


### Scene II. [*Sicilia, a court of justice.*]

*Enter* LEONTES, LORDS, OFFICERS.

LEONTES
This session, to our great grief we pronounce,
Even pushes 'gainst our heart. The party tried,

---

**159 Lady Margery** another facetious name of the hen   **161 this beard's gray** Leontes here, presumably, refers to—perhaps touches—the beard of Antigonus   **165 pawn** pledge   **167 by this sword** by the cross on the handle, or that formed by the hilt and the blade   **169 fail** failure   **181 strangely** as a stranger   **189 require** deserve

**197 beyond accompt** unprecedented   **201 session** judicial trial or investigation
**III.i.2 the isle** i.e., Delos (as in II.i.184; again by mistake for Delphi)   **4 celestial habits** heavenly clothing   **11 event** outcome   **17 carriage** management   **19 great divine** chief priest

The daughter of a king, our wife, and one
Of us too much beloved. Let us be cleared
Of being tyrannous, since we so openly
Proceed in justice, which shall have due course,      5
Even to the guilt or the purgation.°
Produce the prisoner.

OFFICER
It is his highness' pleasure that the queen
Appear in person here in court.

[*Enter*] HERMIONE, *as to her trial*,° [PAULINA, *and*]
LADIES.

                              Silence.°      10

LEONTES
Read the indictment.
OFFICER   "Hermione, queen to the worthy Leontes,
King of Sicilia, thou art here accused and arraigned of
high treason, in committing adultery with Polixenes,
King of Bohemia, and conspiring with Camillo to take   15
away the life of our sovereign lord the king, thy royal
husband; the pretense° whereof being by circumstances
partly laid open, thou, Hermione, contrary to the faith
and allegiance of a true subject, didst counsel and aid
them, for their better safety, to fly away by night."      20

HERMIONE
Since what I am to say must be but that
Which contradicts my accusation, and
The testimony on my part no other
But what comes from myself, it shall scarce boot°
   me
To say, "Not guilty"; mine integrity      25
Being counted falsehood, shall, as I express it,
Be so received. But thus: if powers divine
Behold our human actions—as they do—
I doubt not then, but innocence shall make
False accusation blush, and tyranny      30
Tremble at patience. You, my lord, best know—
Who least will seem to do so—my past life
Hath been as continent, as chaste, as true,
As I am now unhappy; which is more
Than history can pattern,° though devised      35
And played to take° spectators. For behold me,
A fellow of the royal bed, which owe°
A moiety of the throne, a great king's daughter,
The mother to a hopeful prince, here standing
To prate and talk for life and honor, 'fore      40
Who please to come and hear. For life, I prize it
As I weigh grief, which I would spare; for honor,
'Tis a derivative from me to mine,°
And only that I stand for. I appeal
To your own conscience, sir, before Polixenes      45
Came to your court, how I was in your grace,
How merited to be so; since he came,
With what encounter so uncurrent, I
Have strained t' appear thus;° if one jot beyond

The bound of honor, or in act or will      50
That way inclining,° hardened be the hearts
Of all that hear me, and my near'st of kin
Cry fie upon my grave!

LEONTES                  I ne'er heard yet
That any of these bolder vices wanted
Less impudence to gainsay what they did,      55
Than to perform it first.°
HERMIONE                  That's true enough,
Though 'tis a saying, sir, not due to me.
LEONTES
You will not own it.
HERMIONE            More than mistress of
Which comes to me in name of fault, I must not
At all acknowledge.° For Polixenes,      60
With whom I am accused, I do confess
I loved him, as in honor he required;°
With such a kind of love, as might become
A lady like me; with a love, even such,
So, and no other, as yourself commanded;      65
Which not to have done, I think had been in me
Both disobedience and ingratitude
To you, and toward your friend, whose love had
   spoke,
Even since it could speak, from an infant, freely,
That it was yours. Now, for conspiracy,      70
I know not how it tastes, though it be dished°
For me to try how; all I know of it,
Is that Camillo was an honest man;
And why he left your court, the gods themselves,
Wotting° no more than I, are ignorant.      75
LEONTES
You knew of his departure, as you know
What you have underta'en to do in's absence.
HERMIONE                              Sir,
You speak a language that I understand not.
My life stands in the level° of your dreams,
Which I'll lay down.
LEONTES               Your actions are my dreams.      80
You had a bastard by Polixenes,
And I but dreamed it. As you were past all shame—
Those of your fact° are so—so past all truth;
Which to deny concerns more than avails;° for as
Thy brat hath been cast out, like to itself,°      85
No father owning it (which is indeed
More criminal in thee than it) so thou
Shalt feel our justice; in whose easiest passage
Look for no less than death.
HERMIONE                    Sir, spare your threats:
The bug° which you would fright me with, I seek.      90
To me can life be no commodity.°
The crown and comfort of my life, your favor,
I do give° lost, for I do feel it gone,

50–51 **or in . . . inclining** either in performance or intention
approaching the bounds of honor   55–56 **Less . . . first** the
point is that if one is bold enough to commit the crime, one will
be bold enough to deny it; but the expression is not very clear
58–60 **More . . . acknowledge** I must refuse to acknowledge
as my own, faults which I do not in fact possess   62 **required**
was entitled to   71 **dished** served (as of food)   75 **Wotting**
if they know   79 **level** range (archery)   83 **Those . . . fact**
those guilty of your crime   84 **concerns . . . avails** is more
trouble to you than it's worth   85 **like to itself** i.e., appropriately, since it has no father   90 **bug** bogey, bugbear   91
**commodity** advantage, asset   93 **give** reckon as

**III.ii.7 purgation** acquittal   **10 s.d. as to her trial** this direction occurs in the Folio at the head of the scene   **10 Silence**
italic in the Folio, as if a stage direction, but presumably the
Officer calls out the word   **17 pretense** design   **24 boot** assist
**35 can pattern** can offer parallels   **36 take** move   **37 owe**
own   **43 'Tis . . . mine** i.e., it is my son's inheritance
**48–49 With . . . thus** by what outrageous conduct I have
acted so unlike myself as to bring upon myself the ordeal of
this appearance in court

But know not how it went. My second joy,
And first fruits of my body, from his presence              95
I am barred, like one infectious. My third comfort,
Starred° most unluckily, is from my breast,
The innocent milk in its most innocent mouth,
Haled out to murder. Myself on every post°
Proclaimed a strumpet; with immodest hatred              100
The childbed privilege denied, which 'longs°
To women of all fashion.° Lastly, hurried
Here to this place, i' th' open air, before
I have got strength of limit.° Now, my liege,
Tell me, what blessings I have here alive,              105
That I should fear to die? Therefore proceed.
But yet hear this—mistake me not: for life,
I prize it not a straw, but for mine honor,
Which I would free—if I shall be condemned
Upon surmises, all proofs sleeping else              110
But what your jealousies awake, I tell you
'Tis rigor, and not law.° Your honors all,
I do refer me to the oracle:
Apollo be my judge!

LORD                    This your request
Is altogether just; therefore bring forth,              115
And in Apollo's name, his oracle.

[Exeunt OFFICERS.]

HERMIONE
The Emperor of Russia° was my father.
Oh that he were alive, and here beholding
His daughter's trial! That he did but see
The flatness° of my misery; yet with eyes              120
Of pity, not revenge!

[Enter OFFICERS, with] CLEOMENES [and] DION.

OFFICER
You here shall swear upon this sword of justice,
That you, Cleomenes and Dion, have
Been both at Delphos, and from thence have brought
This sealed-up oracle, by the hand delivered              125
Of great Apollo's priest; and that since then
You have not dared to break the holy seal,
Nor read the secrets in't.

CLEOMENES, DION          All this we swear.

LEONTES
Break up the seals and read.

OFFICER          "Hermione is chaste, Polixenes blameless,          130
Camillo a true subject, Leontes a jealous tyrant, his
innocent babe truly begotten, and the king shall live
without an heir, if that which is lost be not found."

LORDS
Now blessèd be the great Apollo!

HERMIONE                    Praised!

LEONTES
Hast thou read truth?

OFFICER                    Ay, my lord, even so              135
As it is here set down.

LEONTES
There is no truth at all i' th' oracle.
The sessions shall proceed; this is mere falsehood.

[Enter a SERVANT.]

SERVANT
My lord, the king, the king!

LEONTES                    What is the business?

SERVANT
O sir, I shall be hated to report it.              140
The prince, your son, with mere conceit° and fear
Of the queen's speed,° is gone.

LEONTES                    How? Gone?

SERVANT                              Is dead.

LEONTES
Apollo's angry, and the heavens themselves
Do strike at my injustice. [HERMIONE faints.] How
now there!

PAULINA
This news is mortal° to the queen—look down              145
And see what death is doing.

LEONTES                    Take her hence;
Her heart is but o'ercharged, she will recover.
I have too much believed mine own suspicion.
Beseech you tenderly apply to her
Some remedies for life. [Exeunt PAULINA and LADIES,
     with HERMIONE.] Apollo, pardon              150
My great profaneness 'gainst thine oracle.
I'll reconcile me to Polixenes,
New woo my queen, recall the good Camillo—
Whom I proclaim a man of truth, of mercy.
For, being transported by my jealousies              155
To bloody thoughts and to revenge, I chose
Camillo for the minister to poison
My friend Polixenes; which had been done,
But that the good mind of Camillo tardied
My swift command, though I with death and with              160
Reward did threaten and encourage him,
Not doing it and being done.° He, most humane,
And filled with honor, to my kingly guest
Unclasped my practice,° quit his fortunes here—
Which you knew great—and to the hazard°              165
Of all incertainties himself commended,
No richer than his honor. How he glisters
Through my rust!° And how his piety
Does my deeds make the blacker!

[Enter PAULINA.]

PAULINA                    Woe the while!
O cut my lace,° lest my heart, cracking it,              170
Break too!

LORD
What fit is this, good lady?

---

97 **Starred** fated  99 **post** on which public notices and advertisements were placed; in Greene's novel the king issues a proclamation concerning his wife's guilt, which is "blazed through the country"  101 **'longs** belongs  102 **fashion** rank  104 **strength of limit** strength to go out  112 **rigor . . . law** tyranny, not justice  117 **Emperor of Russia** in *Pandosto* it is the wife of Polixenes who is daughter of this emperor  120 **flatness** completeness

141 **conceit** concept, thought  142 **speed** fortune, success  145 **mortal** deadly  160–62 **though . . . done** though I threatened him with death for not doing it, and promised him rewards for doing it  164 **Unclasped my practice** revealed my plot  165 **Which . . . hazard** the line apparently lacks a foot, which the Second Folio—with the approval of some editors—supplies by inserting the word "certain" before "hazard"  168 **Through my rust** again, to mend the meter, F2 reads "through my dark rust"; some editors read "Thorough," which is interchangeable with "Through"  170 **cut my lace** to give her more breath

PAULINA
What studied torments, tyrant, hast for me?
What wheels, racks, fires? What flaying, boiling
In leads or oils? What old or newer torture 175
Must I receive, whose every word deserves
To taste of thy most worst. Thy tyranny,
Together working with thy jealousies,
Fancies too weak for boys, too green and idle
For girls of nine—O, think what they have done, 180
And then run mad indeed, stark mad; for all
Thy begone fooleries were but spices° of it.
That thou betrayedst Polixenes, 'twas nothing;
That did but show thee, of a fool,° inconstant,
And damnable ingrateful. Nor was't much 185
Thou wouldst have poisoned good Camillo's honor,
To have him kill a king—poor trespasses,
More monstrous standing by;° whereof I reckon
The casting forth to crows thy baby daughter
To be or none, or little; though a devil 190
Would have shed water out of fire,° ere done't;
Nor is't directly laid to thee the death
Of the young prince, whose honorable thoughts,
Thoughts high for one so tender, cleft the heart
That could conceive a gross and foolish sire 195
Blemished his gracious dam. This is not, no,
Laid to thy answer; but the last—O lords,
When I have said,° cry "woe": the queen, the queen,
The sweet'st, dear'st creature's dead; and vengeance
    for't
Not dropped down yet.
LORDS                         The higher pow'rs forbid! 200
PAULINA
I say she's dead; I'll swear't. If word nor oath
Prevail not, go and see; if you can bring
Tincture or luster in her lip, her eye,
Heat outwardly or breath within, I'll serve you
As I would do the gods. But, O thou tyrant, 205
Do not repent these things, for they are heavier
Than all thy woes can stir;° therefore betake thee
To nothing but despair. A thousand knees,
Ten thousand years together, naked, fasting,
Upon a barren mountain, and still winter° 210
In storm perpetual, could not move the gods
To look that way thou wert.
LEONTES                         Go on, go on;
Thou canst not speak too much, I have deserved
All tongues to talk their bitt'rest.
LORD                         Say no more;
Howe'er the business goes, you have made fault 215
I' th' boldness of your speech.
PAULINA                         I am sorry for't;
All faults I make, when I shall come to know them,
I do repent. Alas, I have showed too much
The rashness of a woman; he is touched
To th' noble heart. What's gone and what's past help 220
Should be past grief; do not receive affliction
At my petition;° I beseech you, rather

Let me be punished that have minded you
Of what you should forget. Now, good my liege,
Sir, royal sir, forgive a foolish woman. 225
The love I bore your queen—lo, fool again!
I'll speak of her no more, nor of your children;
I'll not remember° you of my own lord,
Who is lost too. Take your patience to you,
And I'll say nothing.
LEONTES                         Thou didst speak but well, 230
When most the truth° which I receive much better
Than to be pitied of thee. Prithee bring me
To the dead bodies of my queen and son.
One grave shall be for both; upon them shall
The causes of their death appear, unto 235
Our shame perpetual. Once a day I'll visit
The chapel where they lie, and tears shed there
Shall be my recreation.° So long as nature
Will bear up with this exercise, so long
I daily vow to use it. Come, and lead me 240
To these sorrows.                         Exeunt.


Scene III. [Bohemia,° the seacoast.]

*Enter* ANTIGONUS [*and*] *a* MARINER, [*with a*] BABE.

ANTIGONUS
Thou art perfect° then our ship hath touched upon
The deserts of Bohemia?
MARINER                         Ay, my lord, and fear
We have landed in ill time; the skies look grimly,
And threaten present blusters. In my conscience,°
The heavens with that we have in hand are angry 5
And frown upon's.
ANTIGONUS
Their sacred wills be done! Go get aboard,
Look to thy bark, I'll not be long before
I call upon thee.
MARINER                         Make your best haste, and go not
Too far i' th' land; 'tis like to be loud weather; 10
Besides, this place is famous for the creatures
Of prey that keep° upon't.
ANTIGONUS                         Go thou away,
I'll follow instantly.
MARINER                         I am glad at heart
To be so rid o' th' business.                         *Exit.*
ANTIGONUS                         Come, poor babe;
I have heard, but not believed, the spirits o' th' dead 15
May walk again; if such thing be,° thy mother
Appeared to me last night; for ne'er was dream
So like awaking. To me comes a creature,
Sometimes her head on one side, some another;
I never saw a vessel of like sorrow 20

228 **remember** remind   230–31 **Thou . . . truth** you spoke
well only when most telling the truth   238 **recreation** diversion (to do so will be his only pastime)
**III.iii.s.d. Bohemia** substituted for the Sicily of *Pandosto*;
Bohemia, as is notorious, had no seacoast   **1 perfect** certain
**4 conscience** knowledge, awareness (but with something of
the modern meaning also)   **12 keep** live   **16 if . . . be**
Antigonus takes the skeptical Protestant view as a rule, but is
convinced of the reality of the vision; possibly Shakespeare,
when he wrote this scene, had not yet had the idea of reanimat-
ing Hermione

182 **spices** samples   184 **of a fool** for a fool   188 **standing by**
i.e., and so available for comparison   191 **shed . . . fire** wept
out of burning eyes   198 **said** said it   207 **all . . . stir** all thy
penitence can remove   210 **still winter** forever winter
221–22 **do . . . petition** I would not have you suffer because
I prayed that you should

So filled, and so becoming.° In pure white robes,
Like very sanctity,° she did approach
My cabin° where I lay; thrice bowed before me,
And, gasping to begin some speech, her eyes
Became two spouts; the fury spent, anon    25
Did this break from her: "Good Antigonus,
Since fate, against thy better disposition,
Hath made thy person for the thrower-out
Of my poor babe, according to thine oath,
Places remote enough are in Bohemia,    30
There weep, and leave it crying; and for the babe
Is counted lost forever, Perdita°
I prithee call't. For this ungentle business
Put on thee by my lord, thou ne'er shalt see
Thy wife Paulina more." And so, with shrieks,    35
She melted into air. Affrighted much,
I did in time collect myself, and thought
This was so,° and no slumber. Dreams are toys;°
Yet for this once, yea superstitiously,°
I will be squared° by this. I do believe    40
Hermione hath suffered death, and that
Apollo would (this being indeed the issue
Of King Polixenes) it should here be laid
Either for life, or death, upon the earth
Of its right father. Blossom, speed thee well!    45

[*He lays down the* BABY.]

There lie, and there thy character:° there these,

[*Lays down a bundle.*]

Which may, if Fortune please, both breed thee,° pretty,
And still rest thine.° The storm begins; poor wretch,
That for thy mother's fault art thus exposed
To loss, and what may follow! Weep I cannot,°    50
But my heart bleeds; and most accursed am I
To be by oath enjoined to this. Farewell,
The day frowns more and more; thou'rt like to have
A lullaby too rough; I never saw
The heavens so dim by day. A savage clamor!°    55
Well may I get aboard! This is the chase;°
I am gone forever.      *Exit, pursued by a bear.*

[*Enter*] SHEPHERD.

SHEPHERD  I would there were no age between ten
and three-and-twenty, or that youth would sleep out
the rest; for there is nothing in the between but getting    60
wenches with child, wronging the ancientry, stealing,
fighting. Hark you now! Would any but these boiled°
brains of nineteen and two-and-twenty hunt this
weather? They have scared away two of my best
sheep, which I fear the wolf will sooner find than the    65
master; if anywhere I have them, 'tis by the seaside,
browsing of ivy.° Good luck, an't° be thy will, what

have we here? Mercy on's, a barne!° A very pretty
barne; a boy or a child,° I wonder? A pretty one, a very
pretty one; sure, some scape;° though I am not    70
bookish, yet I can read waiting-gentlewoman in the
scape. This has been some stair-work, some trunk-
work,° some behind-door-work; they were warmer
that got this than the poor thing is here. I'll take it up
for pity; yet I'll tarry till my son come; he hallowed    75
but even now. Whoa-ho-hoa!

*Enter* CLOWN.

CLOWN  Hilloa, loa!
SHEPHERD  What? Art so near? If thou'lt see a thing
to talk on, when thou art dead and rotten, come
hither. What ail'st thou, man?    80
CLOWN  I have seen two such sights, by sea and by
land! But I am not to say it is a sea, for it is now the
sky; betwixt the firmament and it, you cannot thrust a
bodkin's point.
SHEPHERD  Why, boy, how is it?    85
CLOWN  I would you did but see how it chafes, how
it rages, how it takes up° the shore, but that's not to
the point. O, the most piteous cry of the poor souls!
Sometimes to see 'em, and not to see 'em; now the
ship boring the moon with her mainmast, and anon    90
swallowed with yeast and froth, as you'd thrust a cork
into a hogshead. And then for the land-service,° to
see how the bear tore out his shoulder bone, how he
cried to me for help, and said his name was Antigonus,
a nobleman! But to make an end of the ship, to see how    95
the sea flapdragoned° it; but first, how the poor souls
roared, and the sea mocked them; and how the poor
gentleman roared, and the bear mocked him, both
roaring louder than the sea or weather.
SHEPHERD  Name of mercy, when was this, boy?    100
CLOWN  Now, now; I have not winked since I saw
these sights; the men are not yet cold under water, nor
the bear half dined on the gentleman; he's at it now.
SHEPHERD  Would I had been by, to have helped the
old man!    105
CLOWN  I would you had been by the ship's side, to
have helped her; there your charity would have
lacked footing.°
SHEPHERD  Heavy matters, heavy matters! But look
thee here, boy. Now bless thyself; thou met'st with    110
things dying, I with things new born. Here's a sight
for thee; look thee, a bearing-cloth° for a squire's
child; look thee here, take up, take up, boy; open it;
so, let's see; it was told me I should be rich by the fairies.
This is some changeling;° open't; what's within, boy?    115

21 So . . . becoming so filled with sorrow, and so beautiful in sorrow  22 very sanctity sanctity itself  23 cabin berth  32 Perdita meaning "the lost girl"  38 This was so this was real; toys trifles  39 superstitiously again the Protestant view of ghosts  40 squared regulated, ordered  44 character description (by which Perdita is later to be recognized)  47 breed thee raise you, pay for your upbringing  48 And . . . thine there will be something over  50 Weep I cannot though the ghost had told him to  55 savage clamor the noise of the hunters  56 chase the bear  62 boiled seething, hot  67 browsing of ivy "whereon they do greatly feed," according to *Pandosto*; an't if it

68 barne child (cf. modern Scots *bairn*)  69 boy . . . child a boy or a girl ("child" for "girl" is a dialect form and presumably was so in 1610)  70 scape sexual misadventure  72–73 trunk-work clandestine action  87 takes up rebukes  92 land-service i.e., the soldier who serves on land (Antigonus) as opposed to the seamen aboard the ship (perhaps with a pun on *service* meaning "dish"—Antigonus being food for the bear)  96 flapdragoned swallowed down (as drinkers swallowed flapdragons [raisins, etc.] out of burning brandy)  107–08 charity . . . footing alluding to the establishment of charitable foundations  112 bearing-cloth christening robe  115 changeling usually the inferior child left by the fairies; here the child they stole, found with their gold, which must be kept secret

CLOWN   You're a made° old man; if the sins of your youth are forgiven you, you're well to live. Gold, all gold!

SHEPHERD   This is fairy gold, boy, and 'twill prove so; up with't, keep it close;° home, home, the next° 120 way! We are lucky, boy, and to be so still° requires nothing but secrecy. Let my sheep go; come, good boy, the next way home.

CLOWN   Go you the next way with your findings, I'll go see if the bear be gone from the gentleman, and 125 how much he hath eaten. They are never curst° but when they are hungry. If there be any of him left, I'll bury it.

SHEPHERD   That's a good deed. If thou mayest discern by that which is left of him what he is, fetch 130 me to th' sight of him.

CLOWN   Marry° will I; and you shall help to put him i' th' ground.

SHEPHERD   'Tis a lucky day, boy, and we'll do good deeds on't.                          *Exeunt.* 135

# ACT IV

## Scene I.

*Enter* TIME, *the chorus.*

TIME
I that please some, try° all, both joy and terror
Of good and bad; that makes and unfolds error,
Now take upon me, in the name of Time,
To use my wings. Impute it not a crime
To me, or my swift passage, that I slide         5
O'er sixteen years, and leave the growth untried°
Of that wide gap, since it is in my pow'r
To o'erthrow law, and in one self-born hour
To plant, and o'erwhelm custom.° Let me pass;°
The same I am, ere ancient'st order was         10
Or what is now received. I witness to
The times that brought them in; so shall I do
To th' freshest things now reigning, and make stale
The glistering of this present, as my tale
Now seems to it.° Your patience this allowing,  15
I turn my glass, and give my scene such growing
As you had slept between. Leontes leaving—
Th' effects of his fond° jealousies so grieving,
That he shuts up himself—imagine me,
Gentle spectators, that I now may be            20

In fair Bohemia; and remember well,
I mentioned° a son o' th' king's, which Florizel
I now name to you; and with speed so pace
To speak of Perdita, now grown in grace
Equal with wond'ring.° What of her ensues        25
I list not° prophesy; but let Time's news
Be known when 'tis brought forth. A shepherd's daughter,
And what to her adheres,° which follows after,°
Is th' argument° of Time. Of this allow,
If ever you have spent time worse, ere now;      30
If never, yet that Time himself doth say,
He wishes earnestly you never may.      *Exit.*

## Scene II. [*Bohemia, the court of Polixenes.*]

*Enter* POLIXENES *and* CAMILLO.

POLIXENES   I pray thee, good Camillo, be no more importunate. 'Tis a sickness denying thee anything, a death to grant this.

CAMILLO   It is fifteen years since I saw my country; though I have, for the most part, been aired abroad, I 5 desire to lay my bones there. Besides, the penitent king, my master, hath sent for me, to whose feeling sorrows I might be some allay, or I o'erween to° think so, which is another spur to my departure.

POLIXENES   As thou lov'st me, Camillo, wipe not 10 out the rest of thy services by leaving me now. The need I have of thee, thine own goodness hath made. Better not to have had thee, than thus to want° thee; thou, having made me businesses, which none, without thee, can sufficiently manage, must either stay to 15 execute them thyself, or take away with thee the very services thou hast done; which if I have not enough considered—as too much I cannot—to be more thankful to thee shall be my study, and my profit therein the heaping friendships.° Of that fatal country Sicilia, 20 prithee speak no more, whose very naming punishes me with the remembrance of that penitent (as thou call'st him) and reconciled king, my brother, whose loss of his most precious queen and children are even now to be afresh lamented. Say to me, when saw'st 25 thou the Prince Florizel, my son? Kings are no less unhappy, their issue not being gracious, than they are in losing them when they have approved their virtues.°

CAMILLO   Sir, it is three days since I saw the prince. What his happier affairs may be are to me unknown; 30 but I have missingly° noted, he is of late much retired from court, and is less frequent to his princely exercises° than formerly he hath appeared.

**116 made** Folio reads "mad," but this emendation of Theobald is supported by the parallel passage in *Pandosto* **120 close** secret; **next** nearest **121 still** always **126 curst** vicious **132 Marry** indeed (from "By the Virgin Mary") **IV.i.1 try** test **6 growth untried** Time asks to be excused from detailed accounts of the interim and its developments, for instance Perdita's childhood **8–9 law . . . custom** note the distinction: Time "plants" custom but not law; custom lacks the authority of law, and relates to erroneous opinion; hence the contemporary use of the word in attacks on such ceremonies of the Roman Church as seemed to Protestants without scriptural authority **9 Let me pass** not clear in detail, but the sense is, "Let me pass over that gap; I alone remain unchanged from the beginning—and have passed over that far greater gap" **14–15 as . . . it** as my tale seems stale compared with the play it interrupts **18 fond** foolish

**22 mentioned** unless the whole play is thought of as Time's report, this is not so; various emendations have been suggested, of which the best is "A mentioned son . . ." **25 Equal with wond'ring** to a degree demanding admiration **26 I list not** I do not care to **28 adheres** belongs; **after** at this period an acceptable rhyme for "daughter" **29 argument** story

**IV.ii.8 o'erween to** am boastful enough to **13 want** be without **20 friendships** friendly offices **26–28 Kings . . . virtues** It is as hard for kings to bear the disobedience and ill conduct of their children as to lose them when convinced of their virtues **31 missingly** because he noted not the prince but his absence **32–33 exercises** military and sporting activities

POLIXENES  I have considered so much, Camillo, and with some care, so far that I have eyes under my 35 service, which look upon his removedness;° from whom I have this intelligence,° that he is seldom from the house of a most homely shepherd—a man, they say, that from very nothing, and beyond the imagination of his neighbors, is grown into an unspeakable 40 estate.

CAMILLO  I have heard, sir, of such a man, who hath a daughter of most rare note; the report of her is extended more than can be thought to begin from such a cottage. 45

POLIXENES  That's likewise part of my intelligence; but, I fear, the angle° that plucks our son thither. Thou shalt accompany us to the place, where we will, not appearing what we are, have some question° with the shepherd; from whose simplicity I think it not uneasy 50 to get the cause of my son's resort thither. Prithee be my present partner in this business, and lay aside the thoughts of Sicilia.

CAMILLO  I willingly obey your command.

POLIXENES  My best Camillo! We must disguise 55 ourselves. *Exit* [POLIXENES, *with* CAMILLO].

Scene III. [*A road near the Shepherd's cottage.*]

*Enter* AUTOLYCUS, *singing.*

When daffodils begin to peer,
With heigh the doxy° over the dale,
Why, then comes in the sweet o' the year,
For the red blood reigns in the winter's pale.°

The white sheet bleaching on the hedge,    5
With heigh the sweet birds, O how they sing!
Doth set my pugging° tooth an edge,
For a quart of ale is a dish for a king.

The lark, that tirra-lirra chants,
With heigh, with heigh, the thrush and the jay!    10
Are summer songs for me and my aunts°
While we lie tumbling in the hay.

I have served Prince Florizel, and in my time wore
three-pile,° but now I am out of service.

But shall I go mourn for that, my dear?    15
The pale moon shines by night;
And when I wander here and there
I then do most go right.
If tinkers may have leave to live,
And bear the sow-skin budget,°    20
Then my account I well may give,
And in the stocks avouch° it.

My traffic is sheets; when the kite builds, look to lesser linen.° My father named me Autolycus,° who

being, as I am, littered under Mercury,° was likewise a 25 snapper-up of unconsidered trifles. With die and drab,° I purchased this caparison, and my revenue is the silly cheat.° Gallows and knock° are too powerful on the highway. Beating and hanging are terrors to me; for the life to come, I sleep out the thought of it. A prize, 30 a prize.

*Enter* CLOWN.

CLOWN  Let me see, every 'leven wether tods,° every tod yields pound and odd shilling; fifteen hundred shorn, what comes the wool to?

AUTOLYCUS  [*Aside.*]  If the springe° hold, the cock's° 35 mine.

CLOWN  I cannot do't without counters. Let me see, what am I to buy for our sheep-shearing feast? Three pound of sugar, five pound of currants, rice—what will this sister of mine do with rice? But my father 40 hath made her mistress of the feast, and she lays it on. She hath made me four-and-twenty nosegays for the shearers (three-man song-men° all, and very good ones), but they are most of them means° and basses; but one Puritan amongst them, and he sings psalms to 45 hornpipes.° I must have saffron to color the warden pies;° mace;° dates, none, that's out of my note; nutmegs, seven; a race or two of ginger, but that I may beg; four pound of prunes, and as many of raisins o' th' sun.° 50

AUTOLYCUS  Oh, that ever I was born!

CLOWN  I' th' name of me!

AUTOLYCUS  Oh help me, help me; pluck but off these rags; and then, death, death!

CLOWN  Alack, poor soul, thou hast need of more 55 rags to lay on thee, rather than have these off.

AUTOLYCUS  Oh sir, the loathsomeness of them offends me more than the stripes I have received, which are mighty ones and millions.

CLOWN  Alas, poor man, a million of beating may 60 come to a great matter.

AUTOLYCUS  I am robbed, sir, and beaten; my money and apparel ta'en from me, and these detestable things put upon me.

CLOWN  What, by a horseman or a footman?° 65

AUTOLYCUS  A footman, sweet sir, a footman.

CLOWN  Indeed, he should be a footman, by the garments he has left with thee; if this be a horseman's coat, it hath seen very hot service. Lend me thy hand, I'll help thee. Come, lend me thy hand. 70

[*Helps him up.*]

AUTOLYCUS  Oh good sir, tenderly, oh!

CLOWN  Alas, poor soul!

35–36 so . . . removedness to the extent that I am having him watched in the place where he is hiding himself  37 intelligence report  47 angle fishhook  49 question talk  IV.iii.2 doxy beggar's mistress  4 pale (1) enclosure (2) paleness  7 pugging thieving (to "pug" means to "pull off"; perhaps Autolycus is thinking of his sheet-stealing; he is all set to begin snatching them off the hedges)  11 aunts whores  14 three-pile the best velvet  20 sow-skin budget pigskin toolbag  22 avouch corroborate  23–24 when . . . linen this is a warning: the kite will use bits of household linen for its nest; Autolycus will snatch your sheets  24 Autolycus son of Chione by Mercury, grandfather of Ulysses; Homer says he excelled in thieving, and Ovid that "in theft and filching" he "had no peers"

25 under Mercury under the influence of the star Mercury (Mercury was the patron of thieves)  26 die and drab i.e., dice and whores are responsible for my having no clothes but these  27–28 silly cheat simple (petty) theft  28 knock beating (the risks of highway robbery, death, or combat on the road seem too great)  32 every . . . tods every eleven sheep yield a tod (28 pounds) of wool  35 springe snare; cock's woodcock's  43 three-man song-men singers of lively catches for three voices  44 means tenors  45–46 psalms to hornpipes i.e., he is an unusually cheerful Puritan  46–47 warden pies pies made of warden pears; mace spice made of nutmeg  50 o' th' sun sun-dried  65 footman foot soldier

AUTOLYCUS  Oh good sir, softly, good sir; I fear, sir, my shoulder blade is out.

CLOWN  How now? Canst stand?    75

AUTOLYCUS  Softly, dear sir; good sir, softly; you ha' done me a charitable office.

[*Picks his pocket.*]

CLOWN  Dost lack any money? I have a little money for thee.

AUTOLYCUS  No, good sweet sir; no, I beseech you, 80 sir; I have a kinsman not past three-quarters of a mile hence, unto whom I was going. I shall there have money, or anything I want; offer me no money, I pray you; that kills my heart.

CLOWN  What manner of fellow was he that robbed 85 you?

AUTOLYCUS  A fellow, sir, that I have known to go about with troll-my-dames;° I knew him once a servant of the prince. I cannot tell, good sir, for which of his virtues it was, but he was certainly whipped out 90 of the court.

CLOWN  His vices,° you would say; there's no virtue whipped out of the court; they cherish it to make it stay there; and yet it will no more but abide.°

AUTOLYCUS  Vices, I would say, sir. I know this man 95 well; he hath been since an ape-bearer;° then a process-server,° a bailiff: then he compassed a motion° of the Prodigal Son,° and married a tinker's wife within a mile where my land and living° lies; and, having flown over many knavish professions, he settled only in 100 rogue. Some call him Autolycus.

CLOWN  Out upon him! Prig,° for my life, prig! He haunts wakes, fairs, and bear-baitings.

AUTOLYCUS  Very true, sir; he, sir, he; that's the rogue that put me into this apparel.    105

CLOWN  Not a more cowardly rogue in all Bohemia; if you had but looked big, and spit at him, he'd have run.

AUTOLYCUS  I must confess to you, sir, I am no fighter; I am false of heart that way, and that he knew, 110 I warrant him.

CLOWN  How do you now?

AUTOLYCUS  Sweet sir, much better than I was. I can stand and walk. I will even take my leave of you, and pace softly towards my kinsman's.    115

CLOWN  Shall I bring thee on the way?

AUTOLYCUS  No, good-faced sir, no, sweet sir.

CLOWN  Then fare thee well; I must go buy spices for our sheep-shearing.    *Exit.*

AUTOLYCUS  Prosper you, sweet sir! Your purse is 120 not hot enough to purchase your spice. I'll be with you at your sheep-shearing too; if I make not this cheat bring out another, and the shearers prove sheep, let me be unrolled,° and my name put in the book of virtue!    125

*Song.*

Jog on, jog on, the footpath way,
And merrily hent° the stile-a;
A merry heart goes all the day,
Your sad tires in a mile-a.    *Exit.*

Scene IV. [*Bohemia, the Shepherd's cottage.*]

*Enter* FLORIZEL [*and*] PERDITA.

FLORIZEL
These your unusual weeds° to each part of you
Do give a life; no shepherdess, but Flora,°
Peering in April's front.° This your sheep-shearing
Is as a meeting of the petty gods,
And you the queen on't.

PERDITA            Sir, my gracious lord,    5
To chide at your extremes° it not becomes me—
Oh pardon, that I name them! Your high self,
The gracious mark° o' th' land, you have obscured
With a swain's wearing; and me, poor lowly maid,
Most goddesslike pranked up. But that our feasts    10
In every mess have folly, and the feeders
Digest it with a custom,° I should blush
To see you so attired; swoon, I think,
To show myself a glass.

FLORIZEL            I bless the time
When my good falcon made her flight across    15
Thy father's ground.

PERDITA            Now Jove afford you cause!
To me the difference° forges dread; your greatness
Hath not been used to fear. Even now I tremble
To think your father by some accident
Should pass this way, as you did: oh, the fates!    20
How would he look to see his work, so noble,
Vilely bound up?° What would he say? Or how
Should I, in these my borrowed flaunts,° behold
The sternness of his presence?

FLORIZEL            Apprehend
Nothing but jollity. The gods themselves,    25
Humbling their deities to love, have taken
The shapes of beasts upon them. Jupiter
Became a bull, and bellowed; the green Neptune
A ram, and bleated; and the fire-robed god,
Golden Apollo, a poor humble swain,°    30
As I seem now. Their transformations
Were never for a piece° of beauty rarer,
Nor in a way° so chaste, since my desires

127 **hent** take hold of (to leap over)
**IV.iv.1 unusual weeds** unaccustomed garments (Perdita is dressed to be mistress of the feast)  **2 Flora** Perdita's costume may have resembled that of the Roman goddess  **3 Peering . . . front** i.e., Flora in April, when the flowers peep out rather than boldly appear  **6 extremes** exaggerations  **8 mark** the object of everyone's attention  **10–12 our . . . custom** our feasts, at every social level, admit licensed folly, which the guests tolerate, calling it a custom  **17 difference** i.e., in our ranks  **22 Vilely bound up** the analogy is with a good book shabbily bound  **23 flaunts** finery  **27–30 Jupiter . . . swain** Jupiter took the shape of a bull to carry off Europa; Neptune became a ram to woo Theophane; Apollo served as a shepherd to help Admetus win Alcestis  **32 piece** work of art  **33 in a way** he refers to the chastity of his intentions, not to Perdita herself

88 **troll-my-dames** a game played by women, rather like bagatelle  **92 vices** the Clown fails to see Autolycus' little joke  **94 abide** make a brief stay  **96 ape-bearer** one who carries a monkey about for exhibition  **96–97 process-server** server of writs, bailiff  **97 compassed a motion** got possession of a puppet show  **98 Prodigal Son** a favorite theme for representation  **99 land and living** Autolycus refers grandly to his estates  **102 Prig** thief  **124 unrolled** struck off the honorable list of vagabonds

Run not before mine honor, nor my lusts
Burn hotter than my faith.

PERDITA                              Oh, but sir,                    35
Your resolution cannot hold when 'tis
Opposed, as it must be, by th' power of the king.
One of these two must be necessities,
Which then will speak, that you must change this
    purpose,
Or I my life.°

FLORIZEL      Thou dearest Perdita,                    40
With these forced° thoughts, I prithee, darken not
The mirth o' th' feast: or° I'll be thine, my fair,
Or not my father's. For I cannot be
Mine own, nor anything to any, if
I be not thine. To this I am most constant,                    45
Though destiny say no. Be merry, gentle;
Strangle such thoughts as these, with anything
That you behold the while. Your guests are coming;
Lift up your countenance, as it were the day
Of celebration of that nuptial, which                    50
We two have sworn shall come.

PERDITA                              O Lady Fortune,
Stand you auspicious!

FLORIZEL              See, your guests approach.
Address yourself to entertain them sprightly,
And let's be red with mirth.

[*Enter*] SHEPHERD, CLOWN, POLIXENES, CAMILLO
[*disguised*], MOPSA, DORCAS, SERVANTS.

SHEPHERD
Fie, daughter! When my old wife lived, upon                    55
This day, she was both pantler,° butler, cook;
Both dame and servant; welcomed all, served all;
Would sing her song, and dance her turn; now here
At upper end o' th' table, now i' th' middle;
On° his shoulder, and his; her face o' fire                    60
With labor and the thing she took to quench it,
She would to each one sip. You are retired,°
As if you were a feasted one, and not
The hostess of the meeting. Pray you bid
These unknown friends to's welcome, for it is                    65
A way to make us better friends, more known.
Come, quench your blushes, and present yourself
That which you are, mistress o' th' feast. Come on,
And bid us welcome to your sheep-shearing,
As your good flock shall prosper.

PERDITA          [*To* POLIXENES.] Sir, welcome.                    70
It is my father's will I should take on me
The hostess-ship o' th' day. [*To* CAMILLO.] You're
    welcome, sir.
Give me those flow'rs there, Dorcas. Reverend sirs,
For you there's rosemary and rue; these keep
Seeming and savor° all the winter long.                    75
Grace and remembrance° be to you both,
And welcome to our shearing!

POLIXENES                              Shepherdess—
A fair one are you—well you fit our ages

With flow'rs of winter.

PERDITA                  Sir, the year growing ancient,
Not yet on summer's death, nor on the birth                    80
Of trembling winter, the fairest flow'rs o' th' season
Are our carnations, and streaked gillyvors,°
Which some call Nature's bastards;° of that kind
Our rustic garden's barren; and I care not
To get slips of them.

POLIXENES              Wherefore, gentle maiden,                    85
Do you neglect them?

PERDITA                  For I have heard it said,
There is an art, which in their piedness shares
With great creating Nature.

POLIXENES                  Say there be;
Yet Nature is made better by no mean
But Nature makes that mean; so over that art                    90
Which you say adds to Nature, is an art
That Nature makes. You see, sweet maid, we marry
A gentler scion to the wildest stock,
And make conceive a bark of baser kind
By bud of nobler race. This is an art                    95
Which does mend Nature, change it rather; but
The art itself is Nature.°

PERDITA              So it is.

POLIXENES
Then make your garden rich in gillyvors,
And do not call them bastards.

PERDITA                  I'll not put
The dibble° in earth, to set one slip of them;                    100
No more than were I painted, I would wish
This youth should say 'twere well, and only therefore
Desire to breed by me. Here's flow'rs for you:
Hot lavender,° mints, savory, marjoram,
The marigold that goes to bed wi' th' sun,                    105
And with him rises, weeping; these are flow'rs
Of middle summer, and I think they are given
To men of middle age. You're very welcome.

CAMILLO
I should leave grazing, were I of your flock,
And only live by gazing.

PERDITA                  Out, alas!                    110
You'd be so lean that blasts of January
Would blow you through and through. [*To*
    FLORIZEL.] Now, my fair'st friend,
I would I had some flow'rs o' th' spring, that might
Become your time of day—[*to* SHEPHERDESSES] and
    yours, and yours,
That wear upon your virgin branches yet                    115
Your maidenheads growing. O Proserpina,
For the flow'rs now, that, frighted, thou let'st fall
From Dis's wagon!° Daffodils,
That come before the swallow dares, and take°

38–40 One . . . life i.e., the time will come when Florizel will
have to give up his plans, or Perdita will lose her life
41 forced strained, unduly fearful   42 or either   56 pantler
keeper of the pantry   60 On at   62 retired withdrawn
75 Seeming and savor color and scent   76 Grace and remembrance rue is for grace and repentance; rosemary for
remembrance, because the fragrance lasted indefinitely

82 gillyvors pinks (sometimes in modern regional usage, "wall-
flowers"; but here Perdita means carnations, pinks, sweet
william—the blooms have streaks of color, and for this reason
were associated with loose women; the whole debate on the
gillyvors is discussed in the Introduction)   83 Nature's
bastards see Introduction   89–97 Yet Nature . . . is Nature
see Introduction   100 dibble tool for making holes to plant
seeds or cuttings   104 Hot lavender the epithet has not been
satisfactorily explained   116–18 Proserpina . . . wagon the
God of the Underworld bore off Proserpine as she gathered
flowers with her mother, Ceres, in the Vale of Enna; Ovid's
account (*Metamorphoses* V.398–99) mentions that she dropped
the flowers she had picked   119 take charm, captivate

The winds of March with beauty; violets, dim,          120
But sweeter than the lids of Juno's eyes,
Or Cytherea's° breath; pale primroses,
That die unmarried° ere they can behold
Bright Phoebus in his strength (a malady
Most incident to maids); bold oxlips, and          125
The crown imperial; lilies of all kinds,
The flower-de-luce being one. O, these I lack
To make you garlands of, and my sweet friend,
To strew him o'er and o'er!

FLORIZEL                    What, like a corse?°

PERDITA
No, like a bank for Love to lie and play on;          130
Not like a corse; or if, not to be buried,
But quick° and in mine arms. Come, take your flow'rs;
Methinks I play as I have seen them do
In Whitsun pastorals;° sure this robe of mine
Does change my disposition.

FLORIZEL                    What you do          135
Still betters what is done. When you speak, sweet,
I'd have you do it ever; when you sing,
I'd have you buy and sell so; so give alms,
Pray so; and for the ord'ring your affairs,
To sing them too. When you do dance, I wish you          140
A wave o' th' sea, that you might ever do
Nothing but that—move still, still so,
And own no other function. Each your doing,
So singular in each particular,
Crowns what you are doing in the present deeds,          145
That all your acts are queens.°

PERDITA                    O Doricles,°
Your praises are too large; but that your youth
And the true blood which peeps° fairly through't,
Do plainly give you out an unstained shepherd,
With wisdom I might fear, my Doricles,          150
You wooed me the false way.°

FLORIZEL                    I think you have
As little skill° to fear, as I have purpose
To put you to't. But come, our dance, I pray;
Your hand, my Perdita; so turtles° pair
That never mean to part.

PERDITA                    I'll swear for 'em.          155

POLIXENES
This is the prettiest low-born lass that ever
Ran on the greensward; nothing she does or seems
But smacks of something greater than herself,
Too noble for this place.

CAMILLO                    He tells her something
That makes her blood look out;° good sooth° she is          160
The queen of curds and cream.°

CLOWN                    Come on, strike up.

DORCAS
Mopsa must be your mistress; marry, garlic
To mend her kissing with!°

MOPSA                    Now, in good time!°

CLOWN
Not a word, a word, we stand upon our manners.
Come, strike up.          165

*Here a dance of* SHEPHERDS *and* SHEPHERDESSES.

POLIXENES
Pray, good shepherd, what fair swain is this,
Which dances with your daughter?

SHEPHERD
They call him Doricles, and boasts himself
To have a worthy feeding;° but I have it
Upon his own report, and I believe it:          170
He looks like sooth. He says he loves my daughter;
I think so too; for never gazed the moon
Upon the water, as he'll stand and read,
As 'twere, my daughter's eyes; and, to be plain,
I think there is not half a kiss to choose          175
Who loves another° best.

POLIXENES                    She dances featly.°

SHEPHERD
So she does anything, though I report it
That should be silent. If young Doricles
Do light upon her, she shall bring him that
Which he not dreams of.          180

*Enter* SERVANT.

SERVANT   O master, if you did but hear the peddler at
the door, you would never dance again after a tabor°
and pipe; no, the bagpipe could not move you. He
sings several tunes faster than you'll tell° money; he
utters them as he had eaten ballads,° and all men's ears          185
grew to his tunes.

CLOWN   He could never come better; he shall come
in; I love a ballad but even too well, if it be doleful
matter merrily set down; or a very pleasant thing
indeed, and sung lamentably.          190

SERVANT   He hath songs for man or woman of all
sizes; no milliner can so fit his customers with gloves.
He has the prettiest love songs for maids, so without
bawdry, which is strange; with such delicate burdens°
of dildos and fadings:° "Jump her, and thump her";°          195
and where some stretch-mouthed rascal would, as it
were, mean mischief, and break a foul gap° into the
matter, he makes the maid to answer, "Whoop, do
me no harm, good man";° puts him off, slights him,
with "Whoop, do me no harm, good man."          200

POLIXENES   This is a brave fellow.

---

122 **Cytherea's** Venus'   123 **die unmarried** because it grows
in shade, and in spring, Milton has "the rathe primrose that
forsaken dies"   129 **corse** corpse   132 **quick** alive   134
**Whitsun pastorals** Whitsun was the season for games related
to old spring festivals, and Perdita refers probably to the king
and queen in these games—identified with Robin Hood and
Marian   143–46 **Each . . . queens** "Your manner in each act
crowns the act" (Dr. Johnson)   146 **Doricles** Florizel's
pseudonym   148 **peeps** shows   151 **the false way** i.e., by
flattery   152 **skill** reason   154 **turtles** doves   160 **blood look
out** blush; **good sooth** in truth   161 **queen . . . cream**
John Dover Wilson argues that Camillo is calling Perdita a
"white-pot queen"—the name given in some May games to
the queen, by association with a dish called "white-pot," made
of custard, cream, spices, apples, etc.

162–63 **garlic . . . with** use garlic to overcome her bad breath
163 **in good time** expression of indignation   169 **feeding**
landed property   176 **another** the other; **featly** nimbly   182
**tabor** little drum   184 **tell** count   185 **ballads** broadsheet
words and music, to familiar tunes and on topical subjects
194 **burdens** refrains   195 **dildos and fadings** dildos, often
mentioned in ballad refrains, are phalli; fadings are indecent
refrains; **Jump . . . her** familiar ballad refrains   197 **foul
gap** i.e., a break in the song for obscene patter   198–99
**Whoop . . . man** an extant ballad, coarse in character,
has this refrain; the joke in this speech lies in the Servant's
praising Autolycus for the decency of his songs, and simultaneously betraying the fact of their indecency

CLOWN  Believe me, thou talkest of an admirable conceited° fellow. Has he any unbraided° wares?

SERVANT  He hath ribbons of all the colors i' th' rainbow; points,° more than all the lawyers in Bohemia 205 can learnedly handle, though they come to him by th' gross;° inkles,° caddisses,° cambrics, lawns. Why, he sings 'em over, as they were gods or goddesses; you would think a smock were a she-angel, he so chants to the sleevehand,° and the work about the 210 square° on't.

CLOWN  Prithee bring him in, and let him approach singing.

PERDITA  Forewarn him that he use no scurrilous words in's tunes.          [*Exit* SERVANT.] 215

CLOWN  You have of these peddlers° that have more in them than you'd think, sister.

PERDITA  Ay, good brother, or go about to° think.

*Enter* AUTOLYCUS, *singing.*

> Lawn as white as driven snow,
> Cypress° black as e'er was crow,          220
> Gloves as sweet as damask roses,°
> Masks for faces, and for noses;°
> Bugle-bracelet,° necklace-amber,
> Perfume for a lady's chamber;
> Golden quoifs° and stomachers          225
> For my lads to give their dears;
> Pins and poking-sticks° of steel;
> What maids lack from head to heel!
> Come buy of me, come, come buy, come buy,
> Buy lads, or else your lasses cry; come buy!          230

CLOWN  If I were not in love with Mopsa, thou shouldst take no money of me; but being enthralled as I am, it will also be the bondage° of certain ribbons and gloves.

MOPSA  I was promised them against° the feast, but 235 they come not too late now.

DORCAS  He hath promised you more than that, or there be liars.

MOPSA  He hath paid you all he promised you; may be he has paid you more, which will shame you to 240 give him again.°

CLOWN  Is there no manners left among maids? Will they wear their plackets° where they should bear their faces? Is there not milking-time, when you are going to bed, or kiln-hole,° to whistle of these secrets, but 245

you must be tittle-tattling before all our guests? 'Tis well they are whis'pring. Clammer° your tongues, and not a word more.

MOPSA  I have done. Come, you promised me a tawdry-lace,° and a pair of sweet gloves.          250

CLOWN  Have I not told thee how I was cozened by the way, and lost all my money?

AUTOLYCUS  And indeed, sir, there are cozeners abroad; therefore it behooves men to be wary.

CLOWN  Fear not thou, man; thou shalt lose nothing 255 here.

AUTOLYCUS  I hope so, sir, for I have about me many parcels of charge.°

CLOWN  What hast here? Ballads?

MOPSA  Pray now, buy some. I love a ballad in print, 260 a-life,° for then we are sure they are true.

AUTOLYCUS  Here's one to a very doleful tune, how a usurer's wife was brought to bed of twenty money-bags at a burden, and how she longed to eat adders' heads and toads carbonadoed.°          265

MOPSA  Is it true, think you?

AUTOLYCUS  Very true, and but a month old.

DORCAS  Bless me from marrying a usurer!

AUTOLYCUS  Here's the midwife's name to't: one Mistress Taleporter, and five or six honest wives that 270 were present. Why should I carry lies abroad?

MOPSA  Pray you now, buy it.

CLOWN  Come on, lay it by, and let's first see moe° ballads; we'll buy the other things anon.

AUTOLYCUS  Here's another ballad, of a fish° that 275 appeared upon the coast on Wednesday the fourscore of April, forty thousand fathom above water, and sung this ballad against the hard hearts of maids; it was thought she was a woman, and was turned into a cold fish for she would not exchange flesh with one that 280 loved her. The ballad is very pitiful, and as true.

DORCAS  Is it true too, think you?

AUTOLYCUS  Five justices' hands at it, and witnesses more than my pack will hold.

CLOWN  Lay it by too; another.          285

AUTOLYCUS  This is a merry ballad, but a very pretty one.

MOPSA  Let's have some merry ones.

AUTOLYCUS  Why, this is a passing merry one, and goes to the tune of "Two Maids Wooing a Man." 290 There's scarce a maid westward but she sings it; 'tis in request, I can tell you.

MOPSA  We can both sing it. If thou'lt bear a part, thou shalt hear; 'tis in three parts.

DORCAS  We had the tune on't, a month ago.          295

AUTOLYCUS  I can bear my part, you must know 'tis my occupation. Have at it with you.

*Song.*

AUTOLYCUS  Get you hence, for I must go
          Where it fits not you to know.

DORCAS          Whither?          300

203 **conceited** witty; **unbraided** new ("braided wares" are shop-soiled)  205 **points** tagged laces, by which clothes were held up (with a pun on the sense of "arguments")  207 **gross** twelve dozen points (also with reference to clerkly "engrossing," the lawyer's fair copying); **inkles** linen tapes; **caddisses** worsted tapes for garters  210 **sleevehand** cuff  211 **square** embroidered yoke  216 **You . . . peddlers** there are peddlers  218 **go about to** intend to  220 **Cypress** crape  221 **Gloves . . . roses** it was the fashion to perfume gloves  222 **Masks . . . noses** to protect ladies' faces or noses from the sun  223 **Bugle-bracelet** bracelet of beads  225 **quoifs** head scarves  227 **poking-sticks** metal rods used in ironing starched ruffs  233 **bondage** i.e., he is a prisoner of Mopsa, and will take the fairings into captivity with him  235 **against** before  240-41 **paid you more . . . again** this girlish insult means, "Perhaps he has made you pregnant"  243 **plackets** petticoats, or slits in petticoats (often used indecently; here the Clown merely means that they should not as it were wash their dirty linen in public)  245 **kiln-hole** the place containing the fire for malt making (convenient for confidential talk)

247 **Clammer** silence (technical term in bellringing)  250 **tawdry-lace** silk worn around the neck (called after Saint Audrey [Etheldreda], who was punished for youthful ostentation —especially fine necklaces—by a tumor in the throat)  258 **parcels of charge** goods of value  261 **a-life** dearly  265 **carbonadoed** cut up and broiled  273 **moe** more  275 **of a fish** records of very similar ballads survive

MOPSA    O whither?
DORCAS    Whither?
MOPSA    It becomes thy oath full well,
    Thou to me thy secrets tell.
DORCAS    Me too; let me go thither.    305
MOPSA    Or thou go'st to th' grange or mill,
DORCAS    If to either thou dost ill.
AUTOLYCUS    Neither.
DORCAS    What, neither?
AUTOLYCUS    Neither.    310
DORCAS    Thou hast sworn my love to be.
MOPSA    Thou hast sworn it more to me.
    Then whither goest? Say, whither?
CLOWN    We'll have this song out anon by ourselves;
my father and the gentlemen are in sad° talk, and we'll 315
not trouble them. Come bring away thy pack after
me; wenches, I'll buy for you both. Peddler, let's have
the first choice; follow me, girls.
    [*Exeunt* CLOWN, DORCAS, *and* MOPSA.]
AUTOLYCUS    And you shall pay well for 'em.

        *Song.*

Will you buy any tape, or lace for your cape,    320
    My dainty duck, my dear-a?
Any silk, any thread, any toys for your head,
    Of the new'st, and fin'st fin'st wear-a?
Come to the peddler, money's a meddler,
    That doth utter° all men's ware-a.    *Exit.* 325

*Enter* SERVANT.

SERVANT    Master, there is three carters, three shepherds, three neatherds,° three swineherds that have
made themselves all men of hair;° they call themselves
saltiers,° and they have a dance, which the wenches
say is a gallimaufry° of gambols, because they are not 330
in't; but they themselves are o' th' mind, if it be not
too rough for some that know little but bowling,° it
will please plentifully.
SHEPHERD    Away! We'll none on't; here has been too
much homely foolery already. I know, sir, we weary 335
you.
POLIXENES    You weary those that refresh us; pray
let's see these four threes of herdsmen.
SERVANT    One three of them, by their own report, sir,
hath danced before the king;° and not the worst of 340
the three but jumps twelve foot and a half by th'
squier.°
SHEPHERD    Leave your prating; since these good men
are pleased, let them come in; but quickly now.
SERVANT    Why, they stay at door, sir.    [*Exit.*] 345

*Here a dance of twelve* SATYRS.

POLIXENES [*To* SHEPHERD.]
O father, you'll know more of that hereafter.

[*To* CAMILLO.]
Is it not too far gone? 'Tis time to part them.
He's simple and tells much. How now, fair shepherd!
Your heart is full of something that does take
Your mind from feasting. Sooth, when I was young, 350
And handed° love as you do, I was wont
To load my she with knacks; I would have ransacked
The peddler's silken treasury, and have poured it
To her acceptance: you have let him go,
And nothing marted with° him. If your lass    355
Interpretation should abuse,° and call this
Your lack of love or bounty, you were straited°
For a reply, at least if you make a care
Of happy holding her.
FLORIZEL    Old sir, I know
She prizes not such trifles as these are;    360
The gifts she looks from me are packed and locked
Up in my heart, which I have given already,
But not delivered.° O, hear me breathe my life
Before this ancient sir, who, it should seem,
Hath sometime loved: I take thy hand, this hand    365
As soft as dove's down, and as white as it,
Or Ethiopian's tooth, or the fanned snow that's bolted°
By th' northern blasts twice o'er—
POLIXENES    What follows this?
How prettily th' young swain seems to wash
The hand was fair° before! I have put you out;    370
But to your protestation: let me hear
What you profess.
FLORIZEL    Do, and be witness to't.
POLIXENES
And this my neighbor too?
FLORIZEL    And he, and more
Than he, and men; the earth, the heavens, and all:
That were I crowned the most imperial monarch,    375
Thereof most worthy; were I the fairest youth
That ever made eye swerve; had force and knowledge
More than was ever man's, I would not prize them
Without her love; for her, employ them all,
Commend them, and condemn them to her service,    380
Or to their own perdition.°
POLIXENES    Fairly offered.
CAMILLO
This shows a sound affection.
SHEPHERD    But, my daughter,
Say you the like to him?
PERDITA    I cannot speak
So well, nothing so well; no, nor mean better.
By th' pattern of mine own thoughts I cut out    385
The purity of his.
SHEPHERD    Take hands, a bargain;
And friends unknown, you shall bear witness to't:
I give my daughter to him, and will make
Her portion equal his.
FLORIZEL    O, that must be
I' th' virtue of your daughter. One being dead,    390

---

**315 sad** serious  **325 utter** put forth  **327 neatherds** cowherds
**328 men of hair** hairy men, satyrs (or the wild men of medieval
art and entertainment)  **329 saltiers** satyrs (or perhaps leapers,
vaulters, from French *saultier* = vaulter)  **330 gallimaufry**
hodgepodge  **332 bowling** here, a gentle activity, contrasted
with the acrobatic dance  **340 before the king** the performers
of this dance had certainly done so, perhaps in this very dance
**342 squier** rule

**351 handed** dealt with  **355 marted with** bought of
**356 Interpretation should abuse** choose to misunderstand
**357 straited** in difficulties  **362–63 given . . . delivered**
the deal is settled, but the goods not yet handed over
**367 bolted** sifted  **370 was fair** that was fair  **380–81 Commend . . . perdition** commend them to her service, or
condemn them to their own perdition

I shall have more than you can dream of yet,
Enough then for your wonder.° But come on,
Contract us 'fore these witnesses.

SHEPHERD                              Come, your hand;
And, daughter, yours.

POLIXENES                  Soft, swain, awhile, beseech you,
Have you a father?

FLORIZEL          I have; but what of him?                    395

POLIXENES
Knows he of this?

FLORIZEL          He neither does, nor shall.

POLIXENES
Methinks a father
Is at the nuptial of his son a guest
That best becomes the table. Pray you once more,
Is not your father grown incapable                    400
Of reasonable affairs? Is he not stupid
With age and alt'ring rheums?° Can he speak, hear?
Know man from man? Dispute his own estate?
Lies he not bed-rid? And again does nothing
But what he did being childish?

FLORIZEL                              No, good sir;                    405
He has his health, and ampler strength indeed
Than most have of his age.

POLIXENES                  By my white beard,
You offer him, if this be so, a wrong
Something unfilial. Reason my son°
Should choose himself a wife, but as good reason    410
The father, all whose joy is nothing else
But fair posterity, should hold some counsel
In such a business.

FLORIZEL          I yield all this;
But for some other reasons, my grave sir,
Which 'tis not fit you know, I not acquaint          415
My father of this business.

POLIXENES                  Let him know't.

FLORIZEL
He shall not.

POLIXENES  Prithee, let him.

FLORIZEL                  No, he must not.

SHEPHERD
Let him, my son; he shall not need to grieve
At knowing of thy choice.

FLORIZEL                  Come, come, he must not.
Mark our contract.°

POLIXENES [Discovering himself.] Mark your divorce,
    young sir,                    420
Whom son I dare not call; thou art too base
To be acknowledged. Thou, a scepter's heir,
That thus affect'st° a sheep-hook! Thou, old traitor,
I am sorry that by hanging thee, I can
But shorten thy life one week. And thou, fresh piece 425
Of excellent witchcraft, who of force must know
The royal fool thou cop'st with—

SHEPHERD                              O my heart!

POLIXENES
I'll have thy beauty scratched with briers and made
More homely than thy state. For thee, fond° boy,
If I may ever know thou dost but sigh                    430
That thou no more shalt see this knack—as never
I mean thou shalt—we'll bar thee from succession;
Not hold thee of our blood, no not our kin,
Farre than Deucalion off.° Mark thou my words.
Follow us to the court. Thou, churl, for this time,      435
Though full of our displeasure, yet we free thee
From the dead blow of it. And you, enchantment,
Worthy enough a herdsman—yea him, too,
That makes himself, but for our honor therein,
Unworthy thee°—if ever henceforth thou                    440
These rural latches to his entrance open,
Or hoop his body more with thy embraces,
I will devise a death as cruel for thee
As thou art tender to't.                    Exit.

PERDITA                  Even here undone!
I was not much afeard; for once or twice                    445
I was about to speak and tell him plainly,
The selfsame sun that shines upon his court
Hides not his visage from our cottage, but
Locks on alike. [To FLORIZEL.] Will't please you, sir,
    be gone?
I told you what would come of this. Beseech you,       450
Of your own state take care: this dream of mine
Being now awake, I'll queen it no inch farther,
But milk my ewes, and weep.

CAMILLO                  Why, how now, father!
Speak ere thou diest.

SHEPHERD                  I cannot speak nor think,
Nor dare to know that which I know. [To FLORIZEL.]
    O sir,                    455
You have undone a man of fourscore three,
That thought to fill his grave in quiet, yea,
To die upon the bed my father died,
To lie close by his honest bones; but now
Some hangman must put on my shroud, and lay me        460
Where no priest shovels in dust.° Oh cursèd wretch,
That knew'st this was the prince, and wouldst ad-
    venture
To mingle faith with him! Undone, undone!
If I might die within this hour, I have lived
To die when I desire.                    Exit.

FLORIZEL                  Why look you so upon me?      465
I am but sorry, not afeard; delayed,
But nothing altered. What I was, I am;
More straining on, for plucking back; not following
My leash unwillingly.°

CAMILLO                  Gracious my lord,
You know your father's temper; at this time            470
He will allow no speech—which I do guess

---

391–92 I . . . wonder I shall have more than you can at this
time dream of, and enough to amaze you when you know of it
402 alt'ring rheums i.e., rheumatic afflictions which disturb
his judgment    409 Reason my son there is reason that my son
420 contract Wilson in the New Cambridge edition points out
that "we have here a description, all but the final solemn words,
of one of those betrothal ceremonies which were held as legally
binding as marriage in church"    423 affect'st desirest, lovest

429 fond foolish    434 Farre . . . off further back than
Deucalion (legendary ancient king of Thessaly)    438–40
yea . . . thee indeed, you are worthy of Florizel—whose
conduct has made him, save for the fact of his being my
son, unworthy of you    461 Where . . . dust (before the
Reformation, and even in the First Prayer Book of Edward VI,
the priest was directed to do this; felons were buried by the
gallows    468–69 More . . . unwillingly the image is of a
hound; Florizel continues on his chosen course, all the more
strongly for having been dragged back; he is not going to do
as his father says against his will

You do not purpose to him—and as hardly
Will he endure your sight as yet, I fear;
Then, till the fury of his highness settle,
Come not before him.

FLORIZEL                    I not purpose it.                    475
I think, Camillo?

CAMILLO                    Even he, my lord.

PERDITA
How often have I told you 'twould be thus?
How often said my dignity would last
But till 'twere known?

FLORIZEL                    It cannot fail, but by
The violation of my faith, and then                    480
Let Nature crush the sides o' th' earth together,
And mar the seeds within.° Lift up thy looks;
From my succession wipe me, father, I
Am heir to my affection.

CAMILLO                    Be advised.

FLORIZEL
I am, and by my fancy; if my reason                    485
Will thereto be obedient, I have reason;
If not, my senses better pleased with madness,°
Do bid it welcome.

CAMILLO                    This is desperate, sir.

FLORIZEL
So call it, but it does fulfill my vow;
I needs must think it honesty. Camillo,                    490
Not for Bohemia, nor the pomp that may
Be thereat gleaned; for all the sun sees or
The close earth wombs or the profound seas hide
In unknown fathoms, will I break my oath
To this my fair beloved. Therefore, I pray you,                    495
As you have even been my father's honored friend,
When he shall miss me, as in faith I mean not
To see him any more, cast your good counsels
Upon his passion; let myself and Fortune
Tug° for the time to come. This you may know,                    500
And so deliver: I am put to sea
With her whom here I cannot hold on shore;
And most opportune° to her need, I have
A vessel rides fast by, but not prepared
For this design. What course I mean to hold                    505
Shall nothing benefit your knowledge, nor
Concern me the reporting.

CAMILLO                    O my lord,
I would your spirit were easier for advice,
Or stronger for your need.

FLORIZEL                    Hark, Perdita—

[To CAMILLO.]

I'll hear you by and by.

CAMILLO                    He's irremovable,                    510
Resolved for flight. Now were I happy if
His going I could frame to serve my turn,
Save him from danger, do him love and honor,

Purchase the sight again of dear Sicilia,
And that unhappy king, my master, whom                    515
I so much thirst to see.

FLORIZEL                    Now, good Camillo,
I am so fraught with curious° business that
I leave out ceremony.°

CAMILLO                    Sir, I think
You have heard of my poor services i' th' love
That I have borne your father?

FLORIZEL                    Very nobly                    520
Have you deserved; it is my father's music
To speak your deeds, not little of his care
To have them recompensed, as thought on.

CAMILLO                    Well, my lord,
If you may please to think I love the king,
And through him what's nearest to him, which is                    525
Your gracious self, embrace but my direction,°
If your more ponderous and settled project
May suffer alteration. On mine honor,
I'll point you where you shall have such receiving
As shall become your highness, where you may                    530
Enjoy your mistress; from the whom, I see
There's no disjunction to be made, but by—
As heavens forfend—your ruin; marry her;
And with my best endeavors, in your absence,
Your discontenting° father strive to qualify°                    535
And bring him up to liking.

FLORIZEL                    How, Camillo,
May this, almost a miracle, be done?
That I may call thee something more than man,
And after that trust to thee.

CAMILLO                    Have you thought on
A place whereto you'll go?

FLORIZEL                    Not any yet;                    540
But as th' unthought-on accident is guilty
To what we wildly do, so we profess
Ourselves to be the slaves of chance, and flies
Of every wind that blows.°

CAMILLO                    Then list° to me.
This follows, if you will not change your purpose,                    545
But undergo this flight: make for Sicilia,
And there present yourself and your fair princess
(For so I see she must be) 'fore Leontes.
She shall be habited as it becomes
The partner of your bed. Methinks I see                    550
Leontes opening his free arms and weeping
His welcomes forth; asks thee, the son, forgiveness,
As 'twere i' th' father's person; kisses the hands
Of your fresh princess; o'er and o'er divides him
'Twixt his unkindness and his kindness: th' one                    555
He chides to hell, and bids the other grow
Faster° than thought or time.

FLORIZEL                    Worthy Camillo,
What color° for my visitation shall I
Hold up before him?

481–82 Let . . . within for this image of the end of creation compare *Macbeth* IV.i.59 and *King Lear* III.ii.8    485–87 **fancy . . . reason . . . madness** if the fancy, which makes images, is not obedient to the reason—a higher mental power—the result is madness or dream (Florizel wants his reason to obey his fancy; otherwise, he says, he'd rather be mad; for the psychology involved, see *A Midsummer Night's Dream* V.i.2 ff.) **500 Tug** contend, strive    **503 opportune** accent on second syllable

**517 curious** needing great care    **518 ceremony** Florizel is apologizing for having broken away from Camillo to hold his urgent private talk with Perdita    **526 direction** advice    **535 discontenting** displeased; **qualify** appease, moderate (used, for example, of tempering wine with water)    **541–44 But . . . blows** since we are compelled to this wild behavior by a chance we never foresaw, we think of ourselves as the slaves of chance, and will go where it sends us, like flies in a wind    **544 list** listen    **557 Faster** firmer    **558 color** pretext

CAMILLO          Sent by the king your father
To greet him, and to give him comforts. Sir,    560
The manner of your bearing towards him, with
What you, as from your father, shall deliver,
Things known betwixt us three, I'll write you down,
The which shall point you forth at every sitting
What you must say, that he shall not perceive,    565
But that° you have your father's bosom there,
And speak his very heart.
FLORIZEL          I am bound to you;
There is some sap° in this.
CAMILLO          A course more promising
Than a wild dedication of yourselves
To unpathed waters, undreamed shores, most certain    570
To miseries enough: no hope to help you,
But as you shake off one, to take another;
Nothing so certain as your anchors, who
Do their best office if they can but stay° you,
Where you'll be loath to be. Besides, you know,    575
Prosperity's the very bond of love,
Whose fresh complexion and whose heart together
Affliction alters.
PERDITA          One of these is true:
I think affliction may subdue the cheek,
But not take in the mind.
CAMILLO          Yea? Say you so?    580
There shall not at your father's house these seven years°
Be born another such.
FLORIZEL          My good Camillo,
She is as forward of her breeding as
She is i' th' rear 'our birth.°
CAMILLO          I cannot say 'tis pity
She lacks instructions, for she seems a mistress    585
To most that teach.
PERDITA          Your pardon, sir; for this,
I'll blush you thanks.
FLORIZEL          My prettiest Perdita!
But O, the thorns we stand upon! Camillo—
Preserver of my father, now of me,
The medicine° of our house—how shall we do?    590
We are not furnished like Bohemia's son,
Nor shall appear° in Sicilia.
CAMILLO          My lord,
Fear none of this. I think you know my fortunes
Do all lie there; it shall be so my care
To have you royally appointed,° as if    595
The scene you play were mine. For instance, sir,
That you may know you shall not want—one word.

*[They talk aside.]*

*Enter* AUTOLYCUS.

AUTOLYCUS   Ha, ha, what a fool° Honesty is! And
Trust, his sworn brother, a very simple gentleman. I
have sold all my trumpery: not a counterfeit stone,    600
not a ribbon, glass, pomander, brooch, table-book,°
ballad, knife, tape, glove, shoe-tie, bracelet, horn-ring,
to keep my pack from fasting. They throng who
should buy first, as if my trinkets had been hallowed,°
and brought a benediction to the buyer; by which    605
means I saw whose purse was best in picture,° and
what I saw to my good use I remembered. My clown,
who wants but something to be a reasonable man,
grew so in love with the wenches' song, that he would
not stir his pettitoes° till he had both tune and words,    610
which so drew the rest of the herd to me that all their
other senses stuck in ears: you might have pinched a
placket, it was senseless; 'twas nothing to geld a
codpiece of a purse; I would have filed keys off that
hung in chains. No hearing, no feeling, but my sir's°    615
song, and admiring the nothing° of it. So that in this
time of lethargy I picked and cut most of their festival
purses; and had not the old man come in with a
hubbub against his daughter and the king's son, and
scared my choughs° from the chaff, I had not left a    620
purse alive in the whole army.

*[CAMILLO, FLORIZEL, and PERDITA come forward.]*

CAMILLO
Nay, but my letters, by this means being there
So soon as you arrive, shall clear that doubt.
FLORIZEL
And those that you'll procure from King Leontes?
CAMILLO
Shall satisfy your father.
PERDITA          Happy be you!    625
All that you speak shows fair.
CAMILLO *[Seeing* AUTOLYCUS.*]*
Who have we here?
We'll make an instrument of this, omit
Nothing may give us aid.
AUTOLYCUS
If they have overheard me now—why, hanging.    630
CAMILLO
How now, good fellow, why shak'st thou so?
Fear not, man; here's no harm intended to thee.
AUTOLYCUS   I am a poor fellow, sir.
CAMILLO   Why, be so still; here's nobody will steal
that from thee. Yet for the outside of thy poverty we    635
must make an exchange; therefore disease° thee
instantly—thou must think there's a necessity in't—
and change garments with this gentleman; though the
pennyworth on his side be the worst, yet hold thee,
there's some boot.°    640

*[Giving money.]*

AUTOLYCUS   I am a poor fellow, sir. *[Aside.]* I know
ye well enough.
CAMILLO   Nay, prithee dispatch; the gentleman is
half flayed° already.
AUTOLYCUS   Are you in earnest, sir? *[Aside.]* I smell    645
the trick on't.

---

565–66 **perceive, But that** know otherwise than that   **568 sap** life fluid   **574 stay** hold   **581 these seven years** used to signify a long, indefinite period   **583–84 She is as . . . birth** she is as far in advance of the way of life she was reared to as she is inferior to us in birth   **590 medicine** physician   **592 appear** appear so (the second word may have dropped out)   **595 royally appointed** equipped like a prince   **598 Ha, ha, what a fool . . .** these lines echo passages in Greene's *Second Part of Conny-catching* (1592); the character of Autolycus, and the account of the tricks of his trade, is indebted to this book

**601 table-book** notebook   **604 hallowed** sacred   **606 in picture** to look at (?)   **610 pettitoes** toes (especially of a pig)   **615 my sir's** the Clown's   **616 nothing** nothingness, nonsense (with perhaps, as Wilson suggests, a pun on *noting*)   **620 choughs** fools   **636 disease** undress   **640 boot** extra reward   **644 flayed** skinned (undressed)

FLORIZEL  Dispatch, I prithee.

AUTOLYCUS  Indeed, I have had earnest,° but I cannot with conscience take it.

CAMILLO  Unbuckle, unbuckle. 650

[FLORIZEL *and* AUTOLYCUS *exchange garments.*]

Fortunate mistress—let my prophecy°
Come home to ye—you must retire yourself
Into some covert; take your sweetheart's hat
And pluck it o'er your brows, muffle your face,
Dismantle you, and, as you can, disliken 655
The truth of your own seeming,° that you may
(For I do fear eyes over°) to shipboard
Get undescried.

PERDITA  I see the play so lies
That I must bear a part.

CAMILLO  No remedy.
Have you done there?

FLORIZEL  Should I now meet my father, 660
He would not call me son.

CAMILLO  Nay, you shall have no hat.

[*Giving hat to* PERDITA.]

Come, lady, come; farewell, my friend.

AUTOLYCUS  Adieu, sir.

FLORIZEL
O Perdita, what have we twain forgot?
Pray you, a word.

CAMILLO [*Aside.*]
What I do next shall be to tell the king 665
Of this escape, and whither they are bound;
Wherein my hope is, I shall so prevail
To force him after; in whose company
I shall re-view Sicilia, for whose sight
I have a woman's longing.

FLORIZEL  Fortune speed us! 670
Thus we set on, Camillo, to th' seaside.

CAMILLO
The swifter speed, the better.

*Exit* [CAMILLO, *with* FLORIZEL *and* PERDITA].

AUTOLYCUS  I understand the business, I hear it. To
have an open ear, a quick eye, and a nimble hand, is
necessary for a cutpurse; a good nose is requisite also, 675
to smell out work for th' other senses. I see this is the
time that the unjust man doth thrive. What an exchange had this been without boot! What a boot is
here, with this exchange! Sure, the gods do this year
connive at° us, and we may do anything extempore. 680
The prince himself is about a piece of iniquity—stealing
away from his father, with his clog° at his heels; if I
thought it were a piece of honesty to acquaint the
king withal, I would not do't. I hold it the more
knavery to conceal it; and therein am I constant to my 685
profession.

*Enter* CLOWN *and* SHEPHERD.

Aside, aside! Here is more matter for a hot brain.
Every lane's end, every shop, church, session, hanging,
yields a careful man work.

CLOWN  See, see, what a man you are now! There is 690
no other way but to tell the king she's a changeling,
and none of your flesh and blood.

SHEPHERD  Nay, but hear me.

CLOWN  Nay, but hear me.

SHEPHERD  Go to, then. 695

CLOWN  She being none of your flesh and blood, your
flesh and blood has not offended the king, and so your
flesh and blood is not to be punished by him. Show
those things you found about her, those secret things,
all but what she has with her. This being done, let the 700
law go whistle; I warrant you.

SHEPHERD  I will tell the king all, every word, yea,
and his son's pranks too; who, I may say, is no honest
man, neither to his father nor to me, to go about to
make me the king's brother-in-law. 705

CLOWN  Indeed brother-in-law was the farthest off
you could have been to him; and then your blood had
been the dearer by I know not how much an ounce.

AUTOLYCUS [*Aside.*]  Very wisely, puppies!

SHEPHERD  Well, let us to the king; there is that in this 710
fardel° will make him scratch his beard.

AUTOLYCUS [*Aside.*]  I know not what impediment
this complaint may be to the flight of my master.

CLOWN  Pray heartily he be at palace.°

AUTOLYCUS [*Aside.*]  Though I am not naturally 715
honest, I am so sometimes by chance. Let me pocket up
my peddler's excrement.° [*Takes off false beard.*] How
now, rustics, whither are you bound?

SHEPHERD  To th' palace, an it like your worship.

AUTOLYCUS  Your affairs there, what, with whom,° 720
the condition of that fardel, the place of your dwelling,
your names, your ages, of what having,° breeding, and
anything that is fitting to be known, discover.

CLOWN  We are but plain fellows, sir.

AUTOLYCUS  A lie: you are rough, and hairy. Let me 725
have no lying; it becomes none but tradesmen, and
they often give us soldiers the lie, but we pay them for
it with stamped coin, not stabbing steel; therefore they
do not give us the lie.°

CLOWN  Your worship had like to have given us one, 730
if you had not taken yourself with the manner.°

SHEPHERD  Are you a courtier,° an't like you, sir?

AUTOLYCUS  Whether it like me or no, I am a
courtier. See'st thou not the air of the court in these
enfoldings? Hath not my gait in it the measure° of the 735

---

648 **earnest** money paid as installment, "deposit"  651 **prophecy** the prophecy is the form of address, "Fortunate mistress"
655–56 **disliken . . . seeming** a complicated way of saying
"alter your usual appearance," which may indicate Shakespeare's
obsessive interest in problems related to "truth" and "seeming"
657 **eyes over** watching, spying eyes  680 **connive at** close
their eyes to  682 **clog** hindrance (Perdita)

711 **fardel** bundle  714 **at palace** the Clown speaks of the
king being "at palace" as he might of an ordinary man being
"at home" (Cambridge editors)  717 **excrement** i.e., his
beard (hair, beard, and nails were called "excrement," from
Latin *excrescere* = to grow out)  720 **what, with whom**
parodying a form of legal questioning to terrify the rustics
722 **having** property  726–29 **it becomes . . . lie** tradesmen give the lie by giving short measure, but the simple
soldier nevertheless pays them for the lie with money, not
with his sword—so the tradesmen are not, after all, *giving* the
lie; they are selling it (Wilson's explanation)  731 **with the
manner** in the act (at first Autolycus was about to lie by
saying "give" instead of "sell" when speaking of the tradesmen; but he caught himself in the act and changed his statement)  732 **courtier** Autolycus is wearing Florizel's festive
clothes  735 **measure** stately tread

court? Receives not thy nose court-odor from me? Reflect I not on thy baseness court-contempt? Think'st thou, for that I insinuate, or toaze° from thee thy business, I am therefore no courtier? I am courtier cap-a-pé;° and one that will either push on or pluck back thy business there; whereupon I command thee to open thy affair. 740

SHEPHERD   My business, sir, is to the king.

AUTOLYCUS   What advocate hast thou to him?

SHEPHERD   I know not, an't like you. 745

CLOWN   Advocate's the court-word for a pheasant;° say you have none.

SHEPHERD   None, sir; I have no pheasant, cock nor hen.

AUTOLYCUS
How blessed are we that are not simple men! 750
Yet Nature might have made me as these are,
Therefore I will not disdain.

CLOWN   This cannot be but a great courtier.

SHEPHERD   His garments are rich, but he wears them not handsomely. 755

CLOWN   He seems to be the more noble in being fantastical. A great man, I'll warrant; I know by the picking on's teeth.°

AUTOLYCUS   The fardel there? What's i' th' fardel? Wherefore that box? 760

SHEPHERD   Sir, there lies such secrets in this fardel and box, which none must know but the king, and which he shall know within this hour, if I may come to th' speech of him.

AUTOLYCUS   Age, thou hast lost thy labor. 765

SHEPHERD   Why, sir?

AUTOLYCUS   The king is not at the palace; he is gone aboard a new ship, to purge melancholy and air himself; for if thou be'st capable of things serious, thou must know the king is full of grief. 770

SHEPHERD   So 'tis said, sir—about his son, that should have married a shepherd's daughter.

AUTOLYCUS   If that shepherd be not in handfast,° let him fly; the curses he shall have, the tortures he shall feel, will break the back of man, the heart of monster. 775

CLOWN   Think you so, sir?

AUTOLYCUS   Not he alone shall suffer what wit can make heavy, and vengeance bitter; but those that are germane° to him, though removed fifty times, shall all come under the hangman; which, though it be great pity, yet it is necessary. An old sheep-whistling rogue, a ram-tender, to offer to have his daughter come into grace! Some say he shall be stoned; but that death is too soft for him, say I. Draw our throne into a sheep-cote! All deaths are too few, the sharpest too easy. 780 785

CLOWN   Has the old man e'er a son, sir, do you hear, an't like you, sir?

AUTOLYCUS   He has a son—who shall be flayed alive, then 'nointed over with honey, set on the head of a wasp's nest; then stand till he be three-quarters and a dram dead; then recovered again with aqua vitae or 790

some other hot infusion; then, raw as he is, and in the hottest day prognostication° proclaims, shall he be set against a brick wall, the sun looking with a southward eye upon him, where he is to behold him with flies blown to death. But what talk we of these traitorly rascals, whose miseries are to be smiled at, their offenses being so capital? Tell me, for you seem to be honest plain men, what you have to the king; being something gently considered,° I'll bring you where he is aboard, tender° your persons to his presence, whisper him in your behalfs; and if it be in man besides the king to effect your suits, here is man shall do it. 795 800

CLOWN   He seems to be of great authority. Close with him,° give him gold; and though authority be a stubborn bear, yet he is oft led by the nose with gold. Show the inside of your purse to the outside of his hand, and no more ado. Remember—stoned, and flayed alive. 805

SHEPHERD   An't please you, sir, to undertake the business for us, here is that gold I have; I'll make it as much more, and leave this young man in pawn till I bring it you. 810

AUTOLYCUS   After I have done what I promised?

SHEPHERD   Ay, sir. 815

AUTOLYCUS   Well, give me the moiety.° Are you a party in this business?

CLOWN   In some sort, sir; but though my case be a pitiful one, I hope I shall not be flayed° out of it.

AUTOLYCUS   Oh, that's the case of the shepherd's son: hang him, he'll be made an example. 820

CLOWN   Comfort, good comfort! We must to the king, and show our strange sights; he must know 'tis none of your daughter, nor my sister; we are gone else. Sir, I will give you as much as this old man does when the business is performed, and remain, as he says, your pawn till it be brought you. 825

AUTOLYCUS   I will trust you. Walk before toward the seaside, go on the right hand; I will but look upon the hedge,° and follow you. 830

CLOWN   We are blessed, in this man, as I may say, even blessed.

SHEPHERD   Let's before, as he bids us. He was provided to do us good.     [*Exeunt* SHEPHERD *and* CLOWN.]

AUTOLYCUS   If I had a mind to be honest, I see Fortune would not suffer me: she drops booties in my mouth. I am courted now with a double occasion— gold, and a means to do the prince, my master, good; which who knows how that may turn back° to my advancement? I will bring these two moles, these blind ones, aboard him. If he think it fit to shore them again, and that the complaint they have to the king concerns him nothing, let him call me rogue for being so far officious; for I am proof against that title, and what shame else belongs to't. To him will I present them, there may be matter in it.     *Exit.* 835 840 845

---

738 **toaze** tease, worry, comb out   740 **cap-a-pé** head-to-foot (of armor; here, thorough, complete)   746 **Advocate's . . . pheasant** the Clown, misunderstanding the word, thinks Autolycus is referring to the practice of bribing the judge with a bird   758 **picking on's teeth** regarded as an elegant practice   773 **handfast** custody   779 **germane** related

793 **prognostication** weather forecast in the almanac for the year   799–800 **being . . . considered** if you bribe me like a gentleman (handsomely)   801 **tender** present   804–05 **Close with him** accept his offer   816 **moiety** half   818–19 **case . . . flayed** punning on *case* = skin   829–30 **look . . . hedge** i.e., relieve himself   839 **turn back** redound

# ACT V

Scene I. [*Sicilia, the court of Leontes.*]

*Enter* LEONTES, CLEOMENES, DION, PAULINA,
SERVANTS.

CLEOMENES
Sir, you have done enough, and have performed
A saintlike sorrow. No fault could you make
Which you have not redeemed; indeed paid down
More penitence than done trespass. At the last,
Do as the heavens have done: forget your evil;            5
With them forgive yourself.

LEONTES                                    Whilst I remember
Her and her virtues, I cannot forget
My blemishes in them, and so still think of
The wrong I did myself; which was so much,
That heirless it hath made my kingdom, and              10
Destroyed the sweet'st companion that e'er man
Bred his hopes out of.

PAULINA                                True, too true, my lord.
If one by one you wedded all the world,
Or from the all that are took something good
To make a perfect woman, she you killed                 15
Would be unparalleled.

LEONTES                                I think so. Killed?
She I killed! I did so; but thou strik'st me
Sorely, to say I did—it is as bitter
Upon thy tongue as in my thought. Now, good now,
Say so but seldom.

CLEOMENES          Not at all, good lady:                20
You might have spoken a thousand things that would
Have done the time more benefit, and graced°
Your kindness better.

PAULINA                            You are one of those
Would have him wed again.

DION                                If you would not so,
You pity not the state, nor the remembrance°            25
Of his most sovereign name; consider little
What dangers, by his highness' fail° of issue,
May drop upon his kingdom, and devour
Incertain lookers-on.° What were more holy
Than to rejoice the former queen is well?               30
What holier than, for royalty's repair,
For present comfort, and for future good,
To bless the bed of majesty again
With a sweet fellow to't?

PAULINA                            There is none worthy,
Respecting her that's gone; besides, the gods           35
Will have fulfilled their secret purposes;
For has not the divine Apollo said—
Is't not the tenor of his oracle—
That King Leontes shall not have an heir
Till his lost child be found? Which that it shall,      40
Is all as monstrous to our human reason
As my Antigonus to break his grave,
And come again to me; who, on my life,
Did perish with the infant. 'Tis your counsel

My lord should to the heavens be contrary,              45
Oppose against their wills. [*To* LEONTES.] Care not
    for issue,
The crown will find an heir. Great Alexander
Left his to th' worthiest: so his successor
Was like to be the best.

LEONTES                            Good Paulina,
Who hast the memory of Hermione,                        50
I know, in honor: O, that ever I
Had squared me to° thy counsel! Then, even now,
I might have looked upon my queen's full eyes,
Have taken treasure from her lips—

PAULINA                                    And left them
More rich for what they yielded.

LEONTES                                Thou speak'st truth;  55
No more such wives, therefore no wife. One worse,
And better used, would make her sainted spirit
Again possess her corpse, and on this stage,
Where we offenders now appear,° soul-vexed,
And begin, "Why to me?"°

PAULINA                            Had she such power,       60
She had just cause.

LEONTES                  She had, and would incense me
To murder her I married.

PAULINA                        I should so.
Were I the ghost that walked. I'd bid you mark
Her eye, and tell me for what dull part in't
You chose her; then I'd shriek, that even your ears     65
Should rift to hear me, and the words that followed
Should be, "Remember mine."

LEONTES                            Stars, stars,
And all eyes else, dead coals! Fear thou no wife;
I'll have no wife, Paulina.

PAULINA                        Will you swear
Never to marry, but by my free leave?                   70

LEONTES
Never, Paulina, so be blessed my spirit.

PAULINA
Then, good my lords, bear witness to his oath.

CLEOMENES
You tempt him overmuch.

PAULINA                        Unless another,
As like Hermione as is her picture,
Affront° his eye.

CLEOMENES        Good madam—

PAULINA                                I have done;          75
Yet if my lord will marry, if you will, sir—
No remedy but you will—give me the office
To choose you a queen; she shall not be so young
As was your former, but she shall be such
As, walked your first queen's ghost, it should take joy  80
To see her in your arms.

LEONTES                        My true Paulina,
We shall not marry till thou bidd'st us.

PAULINA                                That

---

**V.i.22 graced** suited  **25 remembrance** he means the perpet-
uation of the king's name in a son  **27 fail** failure  **29 Incertain lookers-on** bystanders whose uncertainty makes them
incapable of action

**52 squared me to** regulated myself by  **59 Where . . .
appear** many attempts to emend this passage have given no
better sense than the Folio: the verb "appear" is needed both
for the offenders and for the ghost of Hermione; the obscurity
arises from its doing duty for both; compare the famous
difficulty in *Hamlet* IV.iv.53: "Rightly to be great/Is not to stir
without great argument . . . ," where "not" stands for "not
not"  **60 Why to me** why do you offer such treatment to me?
**75 Affront** confront

Shall be when your first queen's again in breath;
Never till then.

*Enter a* SERVANT.

SERVANT
One that gives out himself Prince Florizel,        85
Son of Polixenes, with his princess—she
The fairest I have yet beheld—desires access
To your high presence.

LEONTES        What with him? He comes not
Like to his father's greatness; his approach,
So out of circumstance,° and sudden, tells us        90
'Tis not a visitation framed,° but forced
By need and accident. What train?°

SERVANT        But few,
And those but mean.

LEONTES        His princess, say you, with him?

SERVANT
Ay, the most peerless piece of earth, I think,
That e'er the sun shone bright on.

PAULINA        O Hermione,        95
As every present time doth boast itself
Above a better, gone, so must thy grave
Give way to what's seen now. Sir, you yourself
Have said, and writ so; but your writing now
Is colder than that theme:° "She had not been,        100
Nor was not to be equaled"; thus your verse°
Flowed with her beauty once; 'tis shrewdly ebbed,
To say you have seen a better.

SERVANT        Pardon, madam:
The one I have almost forgot—your pardon—
The other, when she has obtained your eye,        105
Will have your tongue too. This is a creature,
Would she begin a sect, might quench the zeal
Of all professors° else; make proselytes
Of who she but bid follow.

PAULINA        How! Not women?

SERVANT
Women will love her that she is a woman        110
More worth than any man; men, that she is
The rarest of all women.

LEONTES        Go, Cleomenes,
Yourself, assisted with your honored friends,
Bring them to our embracement. *Exit* [CLEOMENES,
    *with others*]. Still, 'tis strange,
He should thus steal upon us.

PAULINA        Had our prince,        115
Jewel of children, seen this hour, he had paired
Well with this lord; there was not full a month
Between their births.

LEONTES
Prithee no more; cease; thou know'st
He dies to me again, when talked of. Sure        120
When I shall see this gentleman, thy speeches
Will bring me to consider that which may
Unfurnish me of reason. They are come.

*Enter* FLORIZEL, PERDITA, CLEOMENES, *and others*.

Your mother was most true to wedlock, prince,
For she did print your royal father off,        125
Conceiving you. Were I but twenty-one,
Your father's image is so hit in you,
His very air, that I should call you brother,
As I did him, and speak of something wildly
By us performed before. Most dearly welcome!        130
And your fair princess—goddess! Oh, alas!
I lost a couple that 'twixt heaven and earth
Might thus have stood begetting wonder as
You, gracious couple, do. And then I lost—
All mine own folly—the society,        135
Amity too, of your brave father, whom,
Though bearing misery, I desire my life
Once more to look on him.°

FLORIZEL        By his command
Have I here touched Sicilia, and from him
Give you all greetings that a king, at friend,°        140
Can send his brother; and but infirmity,
Which waits upon worn times,° hath something
    seized°
His wished ability, he had himself
The lands and waters 'twixt your throne and his
Measured to look upon you; whom he loves        145
(He bade me say so) more than all the scepters
And those that bear them living.

LEONTES        Oh, my brother—
Good gentleman!—the wrongs I have done thee stir
Afresh within me; and these thy offices,°
So rarely kind, are as interpreters        150
Of my behindhand slackness.° Welcome hither,
As is the spring to th' earth! And hath he too
Exposed this paragon to th' fearful usage,
At least ungentle, of the dreadful Neptune,
To greet a man not worth her pains, much less        155
Th' adventure° of her person?

FLORIZEL        Good my lord,
She came from Libya.

LEONTES        Where the warlike Smalus,
That noble honored lord, is feared and loved?

FLORIZEL
Most royal sir, from thence; from him, whose daughter
His tears proclaimed his, parting with her; thence,        160
A prosperous south wind friendly, we have crossed,
To execute the charge my father gave me,
For visiting your highness. My best train
I have from your Sicilian shores dismissed;
Who, for Bohemia bend, to signify        165
Not only my success in Libya, sir,
But my arrival and my wife's in safety
Here where we are.

LEONTES        The blessèd gods
Purge all infection from our air whilst you
Do climate° here! You have a holy father,        170
A graceful° gentleman, against whose person,
So sacred as it is, I have done sin;

---

90 **out of circumstance** lacking ceremony  91 **framed** planned  92 **train** attendants  100 **theme** Hermione herself  101 **verse** he had presumably written verses of compliment to Hermione  108 **professors** those who profess zeal for religion (especially Puritans)

136–38 **whom . . . him** I wish to go on living, however miserably, in order to look on him again (the final "him" is dispensable, but the construction is not unique in Shakespeare)  140 **at friend** being in friendship with  142 **worn times** advanced years; **seized** arrested  149 **offices** kindnesses, compliments  150–51 **interpreters . . . slackness** put into words feelings I have been too slow in expressing  156 **adventure** risk  170 **climate** reside  171 **graceful** virtuous

For which, the heavens, taking angry note,
Have left me issueless; and your father's blessed,
As he from heaven merits it, with you, 175
Worthy his goodness. What might I have been,
Might I a son and daughter now have looked on,
Such goodly things as you!

*Enter a* LORD.

LORD                              Most noble sir,
That which I shall report will bear no credit,
Were not the proof so nigh. Please you, great sir, 180
Bohemia greets you from himself, by me;
Desires you to attach° his son, who has—
His dignity and duty both cast off—
Fled from his father, from his hopes, and with
A shepherd's daughter.
LEONTES                    Where's Bohemia? Speak. 185
LORD
Here in your city; I now came from him.
I speak amazedly, and it becomes
My marvel° and my message. To your court
Whiles he was hast'ning—in the chase, it seems,
Of this fair couple—meets he on the way 190
The father of this seeming lady, and
Her brother, having both their country quitted,
With this young prince.
FLORIZEL                    Camillo has betrayed me;
Whose honor and whose honesty till now
Endured all weathers.
LORD                        Lay't so to his charge; 195
He's with the king your father.
LEONTES                        Who? Camillo?
LORD
Camillo, sir; I spake with him; who now
Has these poor men in question.° Never saw I
Wretches so quake; they kneel, they kiss the earth;
Forswear° themselves as often as they speak. 200
Bohemia stops his ears, and threatens them
With divers deaths in death.°
PERDITA                    Oh my poor father!
The heaven sets spies upon us, will not have
Our contract celebrated.
LEONTES                    You are married?
FLORIZEL
We are not, sir, nor are we like to be; 205
The stars, I see, will kiss the valleys first;
The odds for high and low's alike.°
LEONTES                        My lord,
Is this the daughter of a king?
FLORIZEL                        She is,
When once she is my wife.
LEONTES
That once, I see by your good father's speed, 210
Will come on very slowly. I am sorry,
Most sorry, you have broken from his liking,
Where you were tied in duty; and as sorry
Your choice is not so rich in worth° as beauty,

That you might well enjoy her.
FLORIZEL                    Dear, look up. 215
Though Fortune, visible an enemy,
Should chase° us, with my father, power no jot
Hath she to change our loves. Beseech you, sir,
Remember since you owed no more to Time
Than I do now; with thought of such affections, 220
Step forth mine advocate; at your request
My father will grant precious things as trifles.
LEONTES
Would he do so, I'd beg your precious mistress,
Which he counts but a trifle.
PAULINA                    Sir, my liege,
Your eye hath too much youth in't; not a month 225
'Fore your queen died, she was more worth such gazes
Than what you look on now.
LEONTES                    I thought of her,
Even in these looks I made. But your petition
Is yet unanswered. I will to your father.
Your honor not o'erthrown by your desires,° 230
I am friend to them and you: upon which errand
I now go toward him. Therefore follow me,
And mark what way I make.° Come, good my lord.
                                        *Exeunt.*

Scene II. [*Sicilia, before the palace of Leontes.*]

*Enter* AUTOLYCUS *and a* GENTLEMAN.

AUTOLYCUS Beseech you, sir, were you present at
this relation?
FIRST GENTLEMAN I was by at the opening of the
fardel, heard the old shepherd deliver the manner how
he found it; whereupon, after a little amazedness, we 5
were all commanded out of the chamber; only this,
methought I heard the shepherd say, he found the
child.
AUTOLYCUS I would most gladly know the issue of it.
FIRST GENTLEMAN I make a broken delivery of the 10
business, but the changes I perceived in the king and
Camillo were very notes of admiration.° They
seemed almost, with staring on one another, to tear
the cases of their eyes.° There was speech in their
dumbness, language in their very gesture; they looked 15
as they had heard of a world ransomed, or one
destroyed. A notable passion of wonder appeared in
them; but the wisest beholder that knew no more but
seeing° could not say if th' importance° were joy, or
sorrow—but in the extremity of the one it must 20
needs be.

*Enter another* GENTLEMAN.

Here comes a gentleman that happily° knows more:
the news, Rogero?
SECOND GENTLEMAN Nothing but bonfires. The
oracle is fulfilled; the king's daughter is found; such a 25

182 **attach** arrest  187–88 **becomes My marvel** suits my
bewilderment  198 **in question** in talk, in conference  200
**Forswear** deny on oath  202 **divers . . . death** various
tortures  207 **odds . . . alike** dicing terms; "Fortune is a
cheater who beguiles princes and shepherds alike with his false
dice" (Wilson)  214 **worth** rank
217 **chase** persecute  230 **Your . . . desires** a certain insistence
on this point of prenuptial chastity is observable both in this
play and in *The Tempest*  233 **what . . . make** how far I
succeed
**V.ii.12 notes of admiration** exclamation points  14 **cases
. . . eyes** eyelids  18–19 **but seeing** but what he saw  19
**importance** significance  22 **happily** haply, perhaps

deal of wonder is broken out within this hour that balladmakers cannot be able to express it.

*Enter another* GENTLEMAN.

Here comes the Lady Paulina's steward; he can deliver you more. How goes it now, sir? This news, which is called true, is so like an old tale that the verity of it is in 30 strong suspicion. Has the king found his heir?

THIRD GENTLEMAN  Most true, if ever truth were pregnant by circumstance;° that which you hear you'll swear you see, there is such unity in the proofs. The mantle of Queen Hermione; her jewel about the neck 35 of it; the letters of Antigonus found with it, which they know to be his character;° the majesty of the creature, in resemblance of the mother; the affection° of nobleness, which nature shows above her breeding and many other evidences—proclaim her, with all 40 certainty, to be the king's daughter. Did you see the meeting of the two kings?

SECOND GENTLEMAN  No.

THIRD GENTLEMAN  Then have you lost a sight which was to be seen, cannot be spoken of. There might you 45 have beheld one joy crown another, so and in such manner that it seemed Sorrow wept to take leave of them; for their joy waded in tears. There was casting up of eyes, holding up of hands, with countenance° of such distraction that they were to be known by 50 garment, not by favor.° Our king, being ready to leap out of himself for joy of his found daughter, as if that joy were now become a loss, cries, "Oh, thy mother, thy mother"; then asks Bohemia forgiveness, then embraces his son-in-law; then again worries he his 55 daughter with clipping° her. Now he thanks the old shepherd, which stands by, like a weather-bitten conduit° of many kings' reigns. I never heard of such another encounter, which lames report to follow it, and undoes description to do it.° 60

SECOND GENTLEMAN  What, pray you, became of Antigonus, that carried hence the child?

THIRD GENTLEMAN  Like an old tale still, which will have matter to rehearse, though credit° be asleep, and not an ear open: he was torn to pieces with° a bear. 65 This avouches the shepherd's son, who has not only his innocence° (which seems much) to justify him, but a handkerchief and rings of his that Paulina knows.

FIRST GENTLEMAN  What became of his bark and his followers? 70

THIRD GENTLEMAN  Wracked the same instant of their master's death, and in the view of the shepherd: so that all the instruments which aided to expose the child were even then lost when it was found. But oh, the noble combat, that 'twixt joy and sorrow was fought 75 in Paulina! She had one eye declined for the loss of her husband, another elevated that the oracle was fulfilled. She lifted the princess from the earth, and so locks her

in embracing as if she would pin her to her heart, that she might no more be in danger of losing.° 80

FIRST GENTLEMAN  The dignity of this act was worth the audience of kings and princes, for by such was it acted.

THIRD GENTLEMAN  One of the prettiest touches of all, and that which angled for mine eyes—caught the 85 water though not the fish—was, when at the relation of the queen's death, with the manner how she came to't bravely confessed and lamented by the king, how attentiveness wounded his daughter; till, from one sign of dolor to another, she did, with an "Alas"—I 90 would fain say—bleed tears; for I am sure my heart wept blood. Who was most marble there changed color; some swooned, all sorrowed. If all the world could have seen't, the woe had been universal.

FIRST GENTLEMAN  Are they returned to the court? 95

THIRD GENTLEMAN  No, the princess, hearing of her mother's statue, which is in the keeping of Paulina— a piece many years in doing and now newly performed° by that rare Italian master, Julio Romano,° who, had he himself eternity and could put breath into his work, 100 would beguile Nature of her custom, so perfectly he is her ape:° he so near to Hermione hath done Hermione, that they say one would speak to her and stand in hope of answer. Thither with all greediness of affection are they gone, and there they intend to sup. 105

SECOND GENTLEMAN  I thought she had some great matter there in hand, for she hath privately, twice or thrice a day, ever since the death of Hermione, visited that removed house. Shall we thither, and with our company piece° the rejoicing? 110

FIRST GENTLEMAN  Who would be thence that has the benefit of access? Every wink of an eye some new grace will be born. Our absence makes us unthrifty to our knowledge.° Let's along.

*Exit, [with the other* GENTLEMEN].

AUTOLYCUS  Now, had I not the dash of my former 115 life in me, would preferment drop on my head. I brought the old man and his son aboard the prince; told him I heard them talk of a fardel and I know not what; but he at that time overfond of the shepherd's daughter (so he then took her to be), who began to be 120 much seasick, and himself little better, extremity of weather continuing, this mystery remained undiscovered. But 'tis all one to me; for had I been the finder-out of this secret, it would not have relished° among my other discredits. 125

*Enter* SHEPHERD *and* CLOWN.

Here come those I have done good to against my will, and already appearing in the blossoms of their fortune.

32–33 truth . . . circumstance made evident by, filled out by circumstances  37 character handwriting  38 affection natural disposition  49 countenance probably meant as a plural; a common orthographical feature in Shakespearean texts  51 favor features  56 clipping embracing  57–58 weather-bitten conduit weatherworn fountain (the old man's tears make him resemble a fountain in human shape)  60 do it describe it  64 credit belief  65 with by  67 innocence simplicity

80 losing being lost  98 performed completed  99 Julio Romano Italian painter (1492–1546); this allusion has caused much debate, because of the anachronism, and because Julio is remembered not as a sculptor but as a painter, though he probably practiced sculpture as well  99–102 had . . . ape had he this other attribute of God and could put breath into his statues, he would cheat Nature of her trade, so closely can he imitate her (the sentiment is a little confused)  110 piece i.e., add to  113–14 unthrifty . . . knowledge careless in the accumulation of knowledge  124 relished proved tasteful, acceptable

SHEPHERD  Come, boy, I am past moe children; but thy sons and daughters will be all gentlemen born.

CLOWN  You are well met, sir. You denied to fight 130 with me this other day, because I was no gentleman born. See you these clothes? Say you see them not and think me still no gentleman born; you were best say these robes are not gentlemen born. Give me the lie, do; and try whether I am not now a gentleman 135 born.

AUTOLYCUS  I know you are now, sir, a gentleman born.

CLOWN  Ay, and have been so any time these four hours.                                                                        140

SHEPHERD  And so have I, boy.

CLOWN  So you have; but I was a gentleman born before my father; for the king's son took me by the hand and called me brother; and then the two kings called my father brother; and then the prince, (my 145 brother) and the princess (my sister) called my father father; and so we wept; and there was the first gentlemanlike tears that ever we shed.

SHEPHERD  We may live, son, to shed many more.

CLOWN  Ay; or else 'twere hard luck, being in so 150 preposterous° estate as we are.

AUTOLYCUS  I humbly beseech you, sir, to pardon me all the faults I have committed to your worship, and to give me your good report to the prince, my master.                                                                              155

SHEPHERD  Prithee, son, do: for we must be gentle, now we are gentlemen.

CLOWN  Thou wilt amend thy life?

AUTOLYCUS  Ay, an it like° your good worship.

CLOWN  Give me thy hand. I will swear to the prince 160 thou art as honest a true° fellow as any is in Bohemia.

SHEPHERD  You may say it, but not swear it.

CLOWN  Not swear it, now I am a gentleman? Let boors and franklins° say it, I'll swear it.

SHEPHERD  How if it be false, son?                                165

CLOWN  If it be ne'er so false, a true gentleman may swear it in the behalf of his friend; and I'll swear to the prince thou art a tall fellow of thy hands,° and that thou wilt not be drunk; but I know thou art no tall fellow of thy hands, and that thou wilt be drunk; but 170 I'll swear it, and I would thou wouldst be a tall fellow of thy hands.

AUTOLYCUS  I will prove so, sir, to my power.°

CLOWN  Ay, by any means prove a tall fellow. If I do not wonder how thou dar'st venture to be drunk, not 175 being a tall fellow, trust me not. Hark, the kings and the princes, our kindred, are going to see the queen's picture. Come, follow us; we'll be thy good masters.

*Exeunt.*

Scene III. [*Sicilia, a chapel in Paulina's house.*]

*Enter* LEONTES, POLIXENES, FLORIZEL, PERDITA, CAMILLO, PAULINA, LORDS, &c.

LEONTES
O grave and good Paulina, the great comfort
That I have had of thee!

151 **preposterous** malapropism for *prosperous*  159 **an it like** if it please  161 **true** honest (as opposed to thieving)  164 **boors and franklins** peasants and yeomen  168 **tall . . . hands** man of courage  173 **to my power** as far as I am able

PAULINA                          What, sovereign sir,
I did not well, I meant well. All my services
You have paid home.° But that you have vouchsafed,
With your crowned brother and these your contracted°                                                                        5
Heirs of your kingdoms, my poor house to visit,
It is a surplus of your grace, which never
My life may last to answer.

LEONTES                          O Paulina,
We honor you with trouble; but we came
To see the statue of our queen. Your gallery               10
Have we passed through, not without much content
In many singularities;° but we saw not
That which my daughter came to look upon,
The statue of her mother.

PAULINA                          As she lived peerless,
So her dead likeness I do well believe                      15
Excels whatever yet you looked upon,
Or hand of man hath done; therefore I keep it
Lonely, apart. But here it is; prepare
To see the life as lively mocked, as ever
Still sleep mocked death: behold, and say 'tis well.        20

[PAULINA *draws a curtain and discovers*] HERMIONE [*standing*] *like a statue.*

I like your silence; it the more shows off
Your wonder; but yet speak, first you, my liege.
Comes it not something near?

LEONTES                          Her natural posture!
Chide me, dear stone, that I may say indeed
Thou art Hermione; or rather, thou art she             25
In thy not chiding; for she was as tender
As infancy and grace. But yet, Paulina,
Hermione was not so much wrinkled, nothing
So agèd as this seems.

POLIXENES                          Oh, not by much.

PAULINA
So much the more our carver's excellence,                  30
Which lets go by some sixteen years, and makes her
As she lived° now.

LEONTES                 As now she might have done,
So much to my good comfort, as it is
Now piercing to my soul. Oh, thus she stood,
Even with such life of majesty—warm life,                  35
As now it coldly stands—when first I wooed her.
I am ashamed: does not the stone rebuke me,
For being more stone than it? O royal piece!
There's magic in thy majesty, which has
My evils conjured to remembrance,° and                     40
From thy admiring daughter took the spirits,
Standing like stone with thee.

PERDITA                          And give me leave,
And do not say 'tis superstition that
I kneel, and then implore her blessing. Lady,
Dear queen, that ended when I but began,                   45
Give me that hand of yours to kiss.

V.iii.4 **paid home** paid in full  5 **your contracted** this "your" should possibly be omitted; the compositor could have caught it from "your crowned" or from the next line  12 **singularities** varieties  32 **As she lived** as if she lived  39–40 **magic . . . conjured . . . remembrance** the sight of the statue has called up his sins into his mind as a magician summons demons

PAULINA                              O, patience!
The statue is but newly fixed, the color's
Not dry.

CAMILLO
My lord, your sorrow was too sore laid on,
Which sixteen winters cannot blow away,                50
So many summers dry. Scarce any joy
Did ever so long live; no sorrow
But killed itself much sooner.

POLIXENES                         Dear my brother,
Let him that was the cause of this have power
To take off so much grief from you as he              55
Will piece up° in himself.

PAULINA                             Indeed, my lord,
If I had thought the sight of my poor image
Would thus have wrought you—for the stone is
    mine—
I'd not have showed it.

LEONTES                 Do not draw the curtain.

PAULINA
No longer shall you gaze on't, lest your fancy         60
May think anon it moves.

LEONTES                    Let be, let be!
Would I were dead, but that methinks already°—
What was he that did make it? See, my lord,
Would you not deem it breathed? And that those
    veins
Did verily bear blood?

POLIXENES            Masterly done!                    65
The very life seems warm upon her lip.

LEONTES
The fixure° of her eye has motion in't,
As we are mocked with art.

PAULINA                      I'll draw the curtain;
My lord's almost so far transported that
He'll think anon it lives.

LEONTES               O sweet Paulina,                  70
Make me to think so twenty years together!
No settled° senses of the world can match
The pleasure of that madness. Let't alone.

PAULINA
I am sorry, sir, I have thus far stirred you; but
I could afflict you farther.

LEONTES                 Do, Paulina;                    75
For this affliction has a taste as sweet
As any cordial° comfort. Still, methinks,
There is an air comes from her. What fine chisel
Could ever yet cut breath? Let no man mock me,
For I will kiss her.

PAULINA           Good my lord, forbear!               80
The ruddiness upon her lip is wet;
You'll mar it if you kiss it; stain your own
With oily painting. Shall I draw the curtain?

LEONTES
No, not these twenty years.

PERDITA                     So long could I
Stand by, a looker-on.

PAULINA             Either forbear,                     85
Quit presently the chapel, or resolve you

For more amazement. If you can behold it,
I'll make the statue move indeed, descend,
And take you by the hand—but then you'll think,
Which I protest against, I am assisted                 90
By wicked powers.

LEONTES              What you can make her do,
I am content to look on; what to speak,
I am content to hear; for 'tis as easy
To make her speak, as move.

PAULINA                    It is required
You do awake your faith; then, all stand still.         95
Or those that think it is unlawful business
I am about, let them depart.

LEONTES                       Proceed.
No foot shall stir.

PAULINA             Music, awake her: strike.
'Tis time; descend; be stone no more; approach;
Strike all that look upon with marvel; come;           100
I'll fill your grave up. Stir; nay, come away;
Bequeath to death your numbness, for from him
Dear life redeems you. You perceive she stirs.

[HERMIONE comes down.]

Start not; her actions shall be holy as
You hear my spell is lawful. Do not shun her           105
Until you see her die again, for then
You kill her double. Nay, present your hand.
When she was young, you wooed her; now, in age,
Is she become the suitor?

LEONTES                  Oh, she's warm!
If this be magic, let it be an art                     110
Lawful as eating.

POLIXENES           She embraces him.

CAMILLO
She hangs about his neck;
If she pertain to life, let her speak too.

POLIXENES
Ay, and make it manifest where she has lived,
Or how stol'n from the dead.

PAULINA                        That she is living,     115
Were it but told you, should be hooted at
Like an old tale; but it appears she lives,
Though yet she speak not. Mark a little while:
Please you to interpose, fair madam; kneel,
And pray your mother's blessing; turn, good lady,     120
Our Perdita is found.

HERMIONE            You gods look down,
And from your sacred vials pour your graces
Upon my daughter's head! Tell me, mine own,
Where hast thou been preserved? Where lived? How
    found
Thy father's court? For thou shalt hear that I,       125
Knowing by Paulina that the oracle
Gave hope thou wast in being,° have preserved
Myself to see the issue.

PAULINA               There's time enough for that,
Lest they desire upon this push° to trouble
Your joys with like relation. Go together,            130
You precious winners all; your exultation
Partake° to every one. I, an old turtle,

56 piece up make his own   62 Would . . . already may I
die if I do not think it moves already (Staunton)   67 fixure
early form of fixture   72 settled sane   77 cordial heart-
warming

Will wing me to some withered bough, and there
My mate, that's never to be found again,
Lament till I am lost.
LEONTES                O peace, Paulina!          135
Thou shouldst a husband take by my consent,
As I by thine a wife. This is a match,
And made between's by vows. Thou hast found mine,
But how, is to be questioned; for I saw her,
As I thought, dead; and have in vain said many          140
A prayer upon her grave. I'll not seek farre,°
For him, I partly know his mind, to find thee
An honorable husband. Come, Camillo,
And take her by the hand, whose° worth and honesty

141 **farre** farther   144 **whose** Camillo's

Is richly noted, and here justified          145
By us, a pair of kings. Let's from this place.
What! Look upon my brother.° Both your pardons,
That e'er I put between your holy looks
My ill suspicion. This your son-in-law,
And son unto the king, whom, heavens directing,          150
Is troth-plight to your daughter. Good Paulina,
Lead us from hence, where we may leisurely
Each one demand and answer to his part
Performed in this wide gap of time since first
We were dissevered. Hastily lead away.          *Exeunt.*  155

147 **Look . . . brother** Hermione has presumably shown
some natural embarrassment about greeting Polixenes

# THE TEMPEST

EDITED BY ROBERT LANGBAUM

## Introduction

*The Tempest* is probably the last play wholly written by Shakespeare. Generations of readers have for this reason been tempted to see it as a culmination of Shakespeare's vision, to identify Prospero with Shakespeare, and to read the famous speech in which Prospero breaks his magic wand as Shakespeare's farewell to his art. Although critics nowadays hesitate to identify Prospero with Shakespeare, those of us who love *The Tempest* cannot help feeling that it represents a culmination—that Shakespeare could not have written it without the wisdom and technique he had accumulated through writing all his other plays.

We get this impression because the characterizations, for example, are so simple—Prospero is wise, Miranda is pure, Caliban is base, Antonio is wicked. Yet these are not the simple characters of a playwright who cannot do any better. They are the simple characters of the playwright who has already created Hamlet and Macbeth and Lear. And we feel this; we feel we are in touch, through the characters of *The Tempest*, with very real and very powerful forces. Caliban, who speaks one of the most beautiful passages of poetry in the play, is enigmatic enough. But where will you come to an end of understanding Ariel? Ariel's complexity certainly does not lie in his characterization. It lies, you may say, in the poetry he speaks. But that is to beg the question.

It is the deliberate return to naiveté, after the tragic complexity, that makes us feel there is something special about the four plays of Shakespeare's final period. The special effect is most apparent in *The Tempest*, because it is the lightest in surface of the four. It is presented to us as a gorgeous bubble, which is blown up for our entertainment like the masque Prospero conjures for Ferdinand and Miranda, and which is just as easily dispelled in the end. Yet *The Tempest* contains the subject matter of tragedy, and it gives us throughout the sense of omniscience, of surveying all life, that we get only at the highest points of illumination in the tragedies. No wonder then that *The Tempest* seems the appropriate statement of age, of the man who, having seen it all, can teach us that the profoundest statement is the lightest and that life, when we see through it, is gay, is tragicomically gay—

that the evil, the violence, the tragedy are all part of a providential design.

*The Tempest* was probably written during the fall and winter of 1610–11. It was produced at court in the fall of 1611, and again during the winter of 1612–13 as part of the festivities that preceded the marriage of the king's daughter Elizabeth to the Elector Palatine. The First Folio probably gives us the play as it was acted at court during the winter. But there is insufficient evidence to support the contention of some scholars that the play was radically revised for the wedding festivities and that the wedding masque in Act IV was inserted in honor of the betrothed couple. Some scholars have even, in their disappointment with the verse of the wedding masque, supposed that the masque was not written by Shakespeare. But Shakespeare always uses a deliberately stilted style for a play within a play; and the masque depends for its effectiveness on spectacle rather than language. Unless new external evidence turns up, there is no reason to look outside the play itself for an explanation of the wedding masque, since the masque fits in subject matter and form into the very texture of *The Tempest*.

The masque brings to a climax the theme of nature versus art that is central to *The Tempest*. For Heaven and Earth, Juno and Ceres, unite in the masque to pronounce a blessing on the union of Ferdinand and Miranda, and to connect sexual union with nature's fruitfulness as seen in its ideal aspect. Venus and her son Cupid are, however, as representatives of lawless passion, specifically excluded from the natural force celebrated in the masque. This fits in with Prospero's severe warning to Ferdinand not to "break" Miranda's "virgin knot" before marriage. Nature is celebrated in the masque as a principle of order. And it is shown to be, as a principle of order, inextricably intertwined with art, civilization, idea.

There is good reason to believe that Shakespeare had in mind, when he wrote *The Tempest*, the reports that first reached England in September 1610 of the miraculous deliverance of the crew and passengers of a ship that had been lost the year before in a terrible tempest off the Bermudas—those stormy islands that Shakespeare refers to in *The Tempest* as "the still-vexed Bermoothes." The

1537

written accounts of the survivors emphasize the providential quality of their deliverance, for the castaways were saved by the magically beneficent nature of the island on which they found themselves. These so-called Bermuda pamphlets (named in A Note on the Source) go on to see the very storm and shipwreck as providential, since they enabled the castaways to discover for the benefit of mankind that the islands that mariners had shunned as inhabited by devils were actually an island paradise.

In exclaiming over the ways of providence, the Bermuda pamphlets offer those paradoxes that are at the heart of the tragicomic vision—the sort of paradoxes Shakespeare uses in *The Tempest*. "Though the seas threaten, they are merciful," says Ferdinand in the end. And Gonzalo sums up the meaning of the play through a series of paradoxes. "Was Milan thrust from Milan, that his issue/Should become kings of Naples?" he asks.

> In one voyage
> Did Claribel her husband find at Tunis,
> And Ferdinand her brother found a wife
> Where he himself was lost; Prospero his dukedom
> In a poor isle; and all of us ourselves
> When no man was his own.          (V.i.208–13)

This is the essential message of tragicomedy—that we lose in order to recover something greater, that we die in order to be reborn to a better life. One of the Bermuda pamphlets, *The True Declaration of the Estate of the Colonie in Virginia*, speaks paradoxically of "those infortunate (yet fortunate) islands," and even calls the shipwreck and deliverance "this tragical comedy."

The Bermuda episode must have raised again for Shakespeare the perennial question that became particularly pertinent after the discovery of the New World—the question whether nature is not superior to art, and whether man is not nobler in a state of nature than in a state of civilization. It is not surprising that Shakespeare had also in mind, when he wrote *The Tempest*, the essay "Of the Caniballes," in which Montaigne praises the American Indians in terms that helped establish the ideal of the Noble Savage. Gonzalo's description of his ideal commonwealth is a close paraphrase of Montaigne's essay.

The island of *The Tempest* is in the Mediterranean, somewhere between Tunis and Naples; yet it seems more magically remote and unlocated than if it had been given a specific location, even one so far as the Bermudas. By setting his island in the Mediterranean, Shakespeare is able to bring the European tradition to bear on the question of nature versus art. He can assimilate the latest ideas about the New World to traditional ideas of the Golden Age and the Garden of Eden. He can remind us of Aeneas, who lost Troy that he might found Rome. Aeneas was driven by a storm to Carthage (specifically associated here with Tunis), from whence he sailed to Italy. In fulfilling his destiny, he underwent wanderings and ordeals analogous to those of the court party in *The Tempest*, including a banquet involving harpies. It is worth mentioning, in connection with the enigmatic references to "widow Dido" and "widower Aeneas," that two of the Bermuda pamphlets compare Dido and Aeneas, as colonizers of new territories, to the colonists of the New World. (Dido was the Phoenician princess who founded Carthage.)

Shakespeare addresses himself to the question of nature versus art by ringing all possible changes on the meaning of "nature." Caliban is natural in that he is earthy and earthbound, low, material. But Ariel is just as natural in that he represents the fluid elements of water and air and also those bodiless energies of nature that strike us as "spiritual." Caliban, whose name may derive from "cannibal," is the natural man seen in one aspect. But Miranda is also natural, and the two are contrasted throughout. Both were brought up in a state of nature; and if Miranda never saw a man other than her father, Caliban never saw a woman other than his mother. Caliban is natural in the sense that nature is rudimentary and mindless; he cannot be educated. Miranda is natural in the sense that we take the Golden Age or the Garden of Eden to be our natural condition. She has been superbly educated by Prospero, but education has with her been absorbed in the natural; knowledge has not lost her the Garden.

The case of Caliban is complex, because we cannot be certain that he is human. He was begotten by a devil on the witch Sycorax, and he is spoken of either as something between an animal and a man, or as something between a sea and a land animal. All the ironic changes on the meaning of "nature" can be heard in Trinculo's remark about Caliban: "That a monster should be such a natural!"—in which "natural" means "idiot." If we take nature to be a principle of order, then the primitive Caliban is a monster, a piece of disorder or deformity.

Trinculo's remark contrasts with Miranda's, when she thinks Ferdinand must be a god, "for nothing natural/I ever saw so noble." Ferdinand, too, and in the end Alonso think for the same reason that Miranda must be a goddess. Shakespeare would seem to be telling us that your view of the natural depends on your view of the supernatural—on whether you see behind natural phenomena the evil machinations of the witch Sycorax and her devil-god Setebos, or whether you see at work a rational and benevolent Providence. He seems to be telling us that every creature can be judged by its potential metamorphoses, be what it is capable of becoming. Miranda sees all the human beings in the play as godlike. But Caliban, who constantly shifts before our eyes between human and animal, fears that he and his drunken co-conspirators will turn into apes or into barnacles, geese believed to be the product of metamorphosis from shellfish.

There is no question as to which view of nature Shakespeare adheres to. He presents here, as in the history plays and the tragedies, a grand vision of order in nature and society; only the emphasis here, far more than in his other plays, is on nature. The fact that Caliban takes the drunken butler, Stephano, for a god is a sign of how high man ranks on the scale of life. It is because we recognize the differences of degree within the human scale that we laugh at Caliban's illusion, but give our poetic faith to the illusion of Ferdinand and Miranda when they take each other for divine. Caliban's crime in conspiring against Prospero is a sin against degree—like the plot of Antonio and Sebastian against Alonso, and Antonio's usurpation of Prospero's throne. Prospero erred in attempting to educate Caliban, just as he erred in allowing Antonio to play the duke in Milan. In both cases, he blurred distinctions of degree and helped create the disorder that followed.

Caliban is evil only when judged by human standards,

or when he himself aspires to get above his place. In attempting to be "free," he only exchanges masters; for a slave he is and should be, as he himself recognizes in the end. Ariel, on the other hand, is by nature a free spirit (he seems free enough even in the bondage of which he complains), and he is therefore appropriately freed in the end. There is a connection in Shakespeare's world view between biological and social rank and moral obligation. Thus, Antonio's crime against his brother and sovereign is also spoken of as "unnatural." But Antonio is much worse than Caliban, because much higher up on the scale. For the same reason, Stephano and Trinculo seem even baser than Caliban and even more ridiculous in their aspiration to get above themselves.

With the exception of Antonio, all the characters in the play are saved in the end according to their degree. They undergo a ritual temptation and punishment. Caliban, Stephano, and Trinculo are befouled in a horsepond for their temptation to murder Prospero; and when Stephano and Trinculo are tempted to steal the clothes left out for them as bait, all three conspirators are chased away by spirits in the shape of dogs. These punishments are appropriate to the level of their moral life.

The court party are ritualistically tempted and punished by the banquet that disappears when they start to eat of it. Antonio and Sebastian have also been tempted to murder Alonso; and Alonso has been ritualistically punished by the supposed loss of his son and by his brother's temptation to do to him what he helped Antonio do to Prospero. When Ariel, who is invisible to everyone except Prospero, accuses Alonso, Antonio, and Sebastian of being "three men of sin," his voice comes to them as an inner voice. Alonso's subsequent attack of conscience comes as a total illumination. He now understands the union of the natural and moral order:

Methought the billows spoke and told me of it;
The winds did sing it to me; and the thunder,

. . .

            did bass my trespass.
Therefore my son i' th' ooze is bedded.
                                        (III.iii.96–97, 99–100)

Since Ferdinand and Miranda start without guilt, their development is mystical rather than moral. Ferdinand's ordeal prepares him to share with Miranda the vision of heaven on earth that Prospero sets before them in the wedding masque. They themselves appear in a masquelike vision of perfection, when Prospero draws a curtain to reveal them to the court party. Note that Ferdinand repeats in his ordeal the bondage of Caliban. But bondage at the lovers' high level of existence is transformed into freedom and happiness.

Prospero himself is, I think, tempted, when he remembers Caliban's conspiracy against him, to take revenge against the court party; for Caliban's conspiracy reminds him of the conspiracy of Antonio and Alonso. It is inconsistent with Prospero's role of a providence in the play to suppose that he did not from the start plan for events to work out as they do, and that he is actually converted from some original purpose of revenge by Ariel's remark that he would pity the court party were he human. Since Prospero obviously planned the marriage of Ferdinand and Miranda, it is likely that he also planned to be reconciled with Alonso and the others and that Ariel recalls him to his purpose. The point where, at the thought of Caliban, Prospero interrupts the masque, and is shaken by emotion, is the one point where he seems fallible like the other human beings in the play. We seem to be getting, in his lapse from and return to his purpose, the repetition of a moral conversion from thoughts of revenge that took place before the play begins. All the tragic events of Prospero's earlier life are portrayed for us through such repetitions; so that the tragic events appear to us in a comic perspective, since we now see how well everything turned out.

Almost all the characters pair off. As sovereign and father, Prospero pairs off with Alonso; and as magician, he pairs off with Caliban's mother, the witch Sycorax, who practiced black magic on the island as against Prospero's white magic. Ferdinand pairs off with Miranda; Antonio with Sebastian; Stephano with Trinculo; Caliban with Ariel. In his role of providence, Prospero stands alone at the top of the design. Such symmetries are at the heart of comic technique, perhaps because they make us feel we are seeing events from above, as part of a pattern, and can therefore restrain sympathy in the confidence that all is well. The design also explains the sense in which Shakespeare is not realistic in *The Tempest*. He is dealing in simplifications like those of the mathematician. He is giving us a diagram of the order of things.

The play begins with a scene of disorder—a tempest at sea that renders meaningless the usual social order. The sailors are disrespectful to the aristocrats, who in trying to assert authority get in the way of the ship's organization. The good-humored courage of Gonzalo stands out against the irrationality of Antonio and Sebastian, who scream abuse at the sailors—though they are later in the play to think themselves very rational in plotting social disorder. The storm gives the boatswain a chance to display a natural superiority that has nothing to do with rank.

In the next scene, we learn that the tempest is an illusion created to regenerate the social order—to restore a reformed Prospero to the throne of Milan, and to lead Ferdinand and Miranda to the throne of Naples. Ariel turns the noise and confusion of the tempest into music, the music that leads Ferdinand to Miranda. The play is pervaded, as G. Wilson Knight has shown in *The Shakespearian Tempest*, by the imagery of tempest, sea, natural noise, and music. This imagery sets the play in a world where disorder is seen to be not merely at the service of order, but inextricably intertwined, indeed identical, with it. It requires only a transformation of perception to recognize order in disorder.

It is, I think, because Ariel makes music out of the natural noises of the island that there is an undersong of animal noises behind one of his songs, and the sound of the sea behind another. When Caliban says, "Be not afeard; the isle is full of noises,/Sounds and sweet airs that give delight and hurt not," he catches the world of nature between metamorphoses, between noise and music, sleep and waking. We say he renders the magical atmosphere of the island. We mean by this that, like Ariel in his songs, Caliban in this lovely speech shows the appearances of things as fluid and ever-changing aspects of a single force—

a force that is beneficent, though it may seem in certain aspects evil.

This force is represented by the sea that washes through every nook and cranny of the play, moving the characters to their destiny both by carrying them there and by washing right up into their consciousness. When Prospero tells Miranda of the "sea sorrow" that brought them to the island, he describes the sea as both threatening and loving. We were cast adrift, he says,

> To cry to th' sea that roared to us; to sigh
> To th' winds, whose pity, sighing back again,
> Did us but loving wrong.          (I.ii.149–51)

The supposed drowning of Ferdinand is spoken of in attractive images. And when one of Alonso's courtiers suggests that Ferdinand may have made it to land, he makes us see that, by struggling against the waves, Ferdinand actually rode them to shore as you ride a fiery steed.

> I saw him beat the surges under him
> And ride upon their backs. He trod the water,
> Whose enmity he flung aside, and breasted
> The surge most swol'n that met him. His bold head
> 'Bove the contentious waves he kept, and oared
> Himself with his good arms in lusty stroke
> To th' shore . . .          (II.i.119–25)

The passage—which is, in its complexity of implication and its metrical suppleness, a good example of Shakespeare's late style—turns violence into harmony. It is but a step away from the song in which Ariel makes drowning seem so desirable, because it is, like all aspects of existence in this play, "a sea change/Into something rich and strange"—into the one force that moves all things. Prospero's magic is a portion of nature's; his providential design is a portion of God's.

Antonio, when he tempts Sebastian to murder the king, uses sea imagery, connecting it with the imagery of sleep and dream to signify the force of Sebastian's real desire. Antonio speaks, through his imagery, truer than he knows; for even his plot is necessary to the providential design of the play. Antonio is an effective villain, because he manipulates real, which is to say magical, forces. Prospero uses the imagery of metamorphosis when he tells Miranda how Antonio so transformed the Milanese court as to make real Antonio's appearance of being duke. The wild sounds of sea and tempest turn for Alonso into rational music that tells him of his crime. And Prospero brings the sea imagery to a climax when he says in the end of the court party,

> Their understanding
> Begins to swell, and the approaching tide
> Will shortly fill the reasonable shore,
> That now lies foul and muddy.          (V.i.79–82)

The sea is now identified with rationality.

The most admirable characters are those who can perceive order in disorder, because they have the capacity for wonder. When Ferdinand says "Admired Miranda," he is playing on the meaning of her name; he is saying, "O wonderful woman, who is to be wondered at." And when, during the masque, he calls Prospero "So rare a wond'red father" (a father possessed of wonders and therefore to be wondered at), it is a sign that he now sees Prospero rightly. There is an irony in Miranda's famous remark at the end, when she first beholds the court party:

> O, wonder!
> How many goodly creatures are there here!
> How beauteous mankind is! O brave new world
> That has such people in't!          (V.i.181–84)

Nevertheless, it is the whole point of the play to make us feel that Miranda is right—that she, in her innocence, sees all these people as they really are, as through all their metamorphoses they are tending to be.

It is to Caliban's credit that he exhibits a capacity for wonder lacking in Stephano and Trinculo and in Antonio and Sebastian. That is because Caliban is natural. His faults do not stem from a perversion of reason, as do those of the four witty characters who do not exhibit a capacity for wonder. Only Gonzalo combines both wit and wonder. In the first appearance of the court party, we see how differently the same phenomena may strike different people. For only Gonzalo sees that their deliverance was miraculous and that the island is a paradise. To be in the Garden of Eden is, we are to understand, a matter of perception. Antonio and Sebastian are with their witty quibbling—their quibble, for example, over the few miles that separate modern Tunis from ancient Carthage—merely destructive.

The effect of wonder is created in *The Tempest* through a combination of several genres—tragicomedy, pastoral, romance, and masque. Antonio's temptation of Sebastian has been compared to the temptation of Macbeth by Lady Macbeth; it is the stuff of tragedy. Our view of it, however, is comic, because we know that Ariel is watching over the scene and has brought it about as part of Prospero's design. The whole action is comic in this sense. The abbreviation of time (*The Tempest* and *The Comedy of Errors* are the only plays in which Shakespeare observes the classical unity of time) enables us to see even Prospero's tragedy in Milan as, in restrospect, for the best. The comic perspective does not, however, make us laugh. It makes us marvel.

Not only the tragedy, but the comedy, too, is dissolved in wonder. Bernard Knox has, in "*The Tempest* and the Ancient Comic Tradition," connected *The Tempest* with Roman comedies about slaves. Nevertheless, Caliban and Ariel are too marvelous to be laughed at as we laugh at the slaves in Roman comedies. Stephano and Trinculo seem a kind of comic relief, just because we do so little laughing at the main action of *The Tempest*. Through Prospero's eyes, *The Tempest* shows us life as God must see it. God could not view life tragically, because He knows that all is for the best. God also knows, as Prospero knows of Ferdinand, that the ordeals He sets for us are for our own good and are not so hard or serious as we think them. Neither, however, could God laugh at us as we laugh at the characters in comedies; for He would not ridicule us, or be dazzled by our wit.

Prospero's view of life is set forth in the famous speech in which he says, after dispelling the wedding masque, "We are such stuff/As dreams are made on." He is, I think, recovering his perspective in this speech after the relapse into thoughts of revenge. The speech is, like

Miranda's exclamations, an expression of the marvelous quality of life. Prospero implies, in consoling Ferdinand for the disappearance of the masque, that if life is as illusory as the masque, it is also as gorgeously illusory. He implies also that there is a reality behind life just as there is Prospero behind the masque.

In his detachment from the appearances of life, Prospero regains an innocence of vision analogous to Miranda's. It is the vision of pastoral, the genre that deals with man and nature in their unfallen state. By swiftly recapitulating all the facts of life, tragicomedy leads us to see through life with the eyes of Miranda, who never left the Garden. Tragicomedy uses to this end the devices of romance. For romance deals in marvelous events and solves its problems through metamorphoses and recognition scenes—through, in other words, transformations of perception. When Alonso recognizes Prospero and Ferdinand, both of whom he had thought dead, he recognizes their magical precious- ness and thus really *sees* them for the first time. The same is true of the crew's response to the ship, when it is magically restored to them. The recognized objects are transformed through the transformed eyes of the beholders; so that more is restored than has been lost.

The masque, with its emphasis on spectacle and surprise, subordinates all other effects to the effect of wonder. "The fringèd curtains of thine eye advance," says Prospero to Miranda when the spectacle of Ferdinand is about to break upon her. It is as though a theater curtain were to be raised; as, indeed, it is raised or drawn when the spectacle of the lovers breaks upon the court party. All the scenes that offer the characters illumination are masquelike and illusory. Yet it is through these illusions that the characters come to understand reality. We all found ourselves, says Gonzalo in the end, "when no man was his own."

Art is just such an experience of enchantment. The speech in which Prospero breaks his magic wand is not so much Shakespeare's farewell to his art as it is his com- ment on the relation between art and life. For in breaking his wand and taking himself and the others back to Italy, Prospero seems to be saying that the enchanted island is no abiding place, but rather a place through which we pass in order to renew and strengthen our sense of reality.

In spite of its fantastic elements, *The Tempest*, as F. R. Leavis has pointed out, never confuses but rather clarifies our sense of reality. That is no small part of its achievement —though it is characteristic of our time that Leavis prefers *The Winter's Tale* just because it is less realistic than *The Tempest*. With its bias against realism, and its interest in a symbolic art, our time is better equipped than any time since Shakespeare's to appreciate the last plays. The seven- teenth and eighteenth centuries liked Shakespeare's early comedies best of all. The nineteenth century liked the tragedies best, and on the whole we still do. But it may be that the last plays—and especially *The Tempest*, which is as I see it the best of them—will in future have most to say to us. Certainly the interest in them has risen steadily in the last generation.

#### A NOTE ON THE SOURCE

There is no known source for the plot of *The Tempest*. As far as we know, *The Tempest* and *Love's Labor's Lost* are Shakespeare's two original plots. Attempts have been made to locate the source of *The Tempest* in the German comedy *Die Schöne Sidea* by Jakob Ayrer, who died in 1605;[1] in certain scenarios of the Italian *commedia dell' arte*;[2] in two Spanish romances.[3] The differences, however, between these plots and the plot of *The Tempest* seem more significant than the similarities. The things these plots have in common with one another and with the plot of *The Tempest* are folk-tale motifs that have long been the common property of storytellers and playwrights.[4]

If there is no source for *The Tempest*, there are documents that are relevant to it. The names of many of the characters probably derive from Thomas' *History of Italy* (1549), and the name "Setebos" derives from Robert Eden's *History of Travaile* (1577), which mentions the "great devill Setebos" worshiped by the Patagonians. In Gonzalo's speech on the ideal commonwealth (II.i.148–73), Shakespeare paraphrases a discussion on nature versus art from John Florio's transla- tion (1603) of Montaigne's essay on the American Indians, "Of the Caniballes" (Caliban's name may derive from "cannibal"). And in Prospero's farewell to his art (V.i.33– 57), Shakespeare paraphrases a speech of the witch Medea, on magic and metamorphosis, from Ovid's *Metamorphoses* —using Arthur Golding's translation (1567), which he apparently checked against the Latin original. As was mentioned in the Introduction, there is good reason to believe that Shakespeare had in mind, and may even have had on his desk, when he wrote *The Tempest*, certain reports that appeared in 1610 of a tempest and a shipwreck that took place off the Bermudas in 1609. These so-called Bermuda pamphlets require a word of explanation.

On June 2, 1609, a fleet of nine ships set sail from Plymouth for Virginia, carrying more than five hundred colonists. On July 24, a tempest off the Bermudas separated from the rest of the fleet the flagship, the *Sea-Venture*, which carried the admiral, Sir George Somers, and the new governor of the colony, Sir Thomas Gates. In the course of the next several weeks, the other ships straggled into the port at Jamestown, but the occupants of the *Sea- Venture* were given up for lost. Then, miraculously, almost a year later, on May 23, 1610, the castaways arrived in Jamestown in two small ships they had built for the journey. Their deliverance, when the news of it reached London in September, was regarded as providential. But the beneficent hand of Providence emerged even more clearly when the reports of the shipwreck began to appear. For the reports showed the stormy Bermudas, which mariners had shunned as an "Ile of Divels," to be actually an island paradise.

Since Shakespeare was closely connected with the leaders of the Virginia Company (for example, the Earls of Southampton and Pembroke), which had sponsored the expedition, he would have had good reason to read the

[1] See H. H. Furness' Variorum Edition of *The Tempest* (1897), pp. 324–43, which includes a translation of Ayrer's comedy.
[2] See H. D. Gray, "The Sources of *The Tempest*," *Modern Language Notes*, XXXV (1920), 321–30.
[3] Antonio de Eslava's *Noches de Invierno* (1609), Chap. IV (see Hardin Craig, *Interpretation of Shakespeare* [1948], pp. 344–45), and Diego Ortuñez de Calahorra's *Espejo de Príncipes y Caballeros* (1562; English translation, 1578–1601) (see Joseph de Perott, "The Probable Source of the Plot of Shakespeare's *Tempest*," *Publications of the Clark University Library*, I [1903–05], 209–16).
[4] See W. W. Newell, "Sources of Shakespeare's *Tempest*," *Journal of American Folk-Lore*, XVI (1905), 234–57.

reports of the shipwreck that appeared in 1610. The first to appear was *A Discovery of the Barmudas, otherwise called the Ile of Divels,* by Sylvester Jourdain,[5] who was with Somers. A month later there appeared *The True Declaration of the estate of the Colonie in Virginia,* which was the report of the Virginia Company.[6] Most important for our purposes is a long letter by William Strachey, who was also with Somers, which is dated July 15, 1610, but which doubtless came over to London with Gates in September. Strachey's letter was not published until 1625, in *Purchas His Pilgrimes.*[7] But it seems to have circulated in manuscript among the leaders of the Virginia Company, and we may be reasonably sure that Shakespeare read it, since it bears most closely of all the reports on *The Tempest.* It is called *A true repertory of the wracke, and redemption of Sir Thomas Gates Knight; upon, and from the Ilands of the Bermudas: his comming to Virginia, and the estate of that Colonie then, and after.*

Strachey's description of the tempest ("our clamors drowned in the winds, and the winds in thunder. Prayers might well be in the heart and lips, but drowned in the outcries of the officers") pinpoints details of Shakespeare's opening scene. And the wrecking of the *Sea-Venture* (we "gave her now up, rent in pieces, and absolutely lost") recalls Shakespeare's "All lost!" . . . "We split, we split!" (I.i.51, 60). Caliban's mysterious "Young scamels from the rock" (II.ii.174) may refer to the "webfooted fowl," which the castaways named "sea owls" and which came miraculously when called, allowing themselves to be weighed and selected for slaughter. When Strachey says the providential deliverance teaches "that Truth is the daughter of Time, and that men ought not to deny everything which is not subject to their own sense," we are reminded of Gonzalo's speech on travelers' tales (III.iii.43–49). In spite of the deliverance, there were attempted mutinies against Sir Thomas Gates that parallel the attempted mutinies against Prospero and the King of Naples. And Sir Thomas' failure, after the arrival in Virginia, to tame the Indians—

making him realize "how little a fair and noble entreaty works upon a barbarous disposition"—resembles Prospero's failure with Caliban, "on whose nature/Nurture can never stick (IV.i.188–89).

## A NOTE ON THE TEXT

*The Tempest* was first printed in the Folio of 1623, the First Folio. The Folio text has been carefully edited and punctuated, and it has unusually complete stage directions that are probably Shakespeare's own. *The Tempest* is perhaps the finest text in the Folio, which may be why the Folio editors placed it first in the volume.

The present division into acts and scenes is that of the Folio. The present edition silently modernizes spelling and punctuation, regularizes speech prefixes, translates into English the Folio's Latin designations of act and scene, and makes certain changes in lineation in the interest either of meter, meaning, or a consistent format. The list of "Names of the Actors," which appears at the end of the play in the Folio, is here given at the beginning. Other departures from the Folio are listed below, including changes in lineation that bear upon the meaning. The reading of the present text is given first, in boldface type, and then the reading of the Folio (F) in roman.

[5] Facsimile edition, ed. J. Q. Adams (1940).
[6] Reprinted in *Tracts and Other Papers,* Vol. III (1844), collected by Peter Force.
[7] Vol. XIX (1906).

**The Scene: An uninhabited island**/Names of the Actors [appears at the end of play in F]
**I.i.37 s.d. Enter Sebastian, Antonio, and Gonzalo** [in F occurs after "plague," line 36]
**I.ii.173 princess'** Princesse **201 lightnings** Lightning **272 wast** was **283 she** he **382 the burden bear** beare/the burthen
**II.i.5 master** Masters **38–39 Antonio . . . Sebastian** [speakers reversed in F]
**III.i.2 sets** set **15 busiest** busie lest **93 withal** with all
**III.ii.125 scout** cout
**III.iii.17 Sebastian   I say tonight. No more** [appears in F after s.d.] **29 islanders** Islands
**IV.i.9 off** of **13 gift** guest **124 s.d. Juno and . . . employment** [follows line 127 in F] **193 them on** on them **231 Let't** let's
**V.i. 60 boiled** boile **72 Didst** Did **75 entertained** entertaine **82 lies** ly **199 remembrance** remembrances

# THE TEMPEST

The Scene: An uninhabited island

Names of the Actors

ALONSO *King of Naples*
SEBASTIAN *his brother*
PROSPERO *the right Duke of Milan*
ANTONIO *his brother, the usurping Duke of Milan*
FERDINAND *son to the King of Naples*
GONZALO *an honest old councilor*
ADRIAN *and* FRANCISCO *lords*
CALIBAN *a savage and deformed slave*
TRINCULO *a jester*
STEPHANO *a drunken butler*

MASTER *of a ship*
BOATSWAIN
MARINERS
MIRANDA *daughter to Prospero*
ARIEL *an airy spirit*
IRIS
CERES
JUNO      } *[presented by] spirits*
NYMPHS
REAPERS

*[Other* SPIRITS *attending on Prospero]*

## ACT I

### Scene I. [*On a ship at sea.*]

*A tempestuous noise of thunder and lightning heard. Enter
a* SHIPMASTER *and a* BOATSWAIN.

MASTER  Boatswain!
BOATSWAIN  Here, master. What cheer?
MASTER  Good,° speak to th' mariners! Fall to't
yarely,° or we run ourselves aground. Bestir, bestir!
*Exit.*

*Enter* MARINERS.

BOATSWAIN  Heigh, my hearts! Cheerly, cheerly, my 5
hearts! Yare, yare! Take in the topsail! Tend to th'
master's whistle! Blow till thou burst thy wind, if
room enough!°

*The decorative border shown above appeared on the first page of*
The Tempest *in the First Folio edition of Shakespeare's plays, 1623.*
**I.i.3 Good** good fellow  **4 yarely** briskly  **7–8 Blow . . .
enough** The storm can blow and split itself as long as there is
open sea, without rocks, to maneuver in

*Enter* ALONSO, SEBASTIAN, ANTONIO,
FERDINAND, GONZALO, *and others.*

ALONSO  Good boatswain, have care. Where's the
master? Play the men.°                               10
BOATSWAIN  I pray now, keep below.
ANTONIO  Where is the master, bos'n?
BOATSWAIN  Do you not hear him? You mar our
labor. Keep your cabins; you do assist the storm.
GONZALO  Nay, good, be patient.                      15
BOATSWAIN  When the sea is. Hence! What cares
these roarers for the name of king? To cabin! Silence!
Trouble us not!
GONZALO  Good, yet remember whom thou hast
aboard.                                              20
BOATSWAIN  None that I more love than myself. You
are a councilor; if you can command these elements to
silence and work the peace of the present,° we will not
hand° a rope more. Use your authority. If you cannot,
give thanks you have lived so long, and make yourself 25

**10 Play the men** Act like men  **23 work . . . present** restore
the present to peace (since as a councilor his job is to quell
disorder)  **24 hand** handle

ready in your cabin for the mischance of the hour, if it so hap. Cheerly, good hearts! Out of our way, I say.

*Exit.*

GONZALO  I have great comfort from this fellow. Methinks he hath no drowning mark upon him; his complexion is perfect gallows.° Stand fast, good Fate, 30 to his hanging! Make the rope of his destiny our cable, for our own doth little advantage.° If he be not born to be hanged, our case is miserable.

*Exit, [with the rest].*

*Enter* BOATSWAIN.

BOATSWAIN  Down with the topmast! Yare! Lower, lower! Bring her to try with main course!° (*A cry* 35 *within.*) A plague upon this howling! They are louder than the weather or our office.°

*Enter* SEBASTIAN, ANTONIO, *and* GONZALO.

Yet again? What do you here? Shall we give o'er° and drown? Have you a mind to sink?

SEBASTIAN  A pox o' your throat, you bawling, 40 blasphemous, incharitable dog!

BOATSWAIN  Work you, then.

ANTONIO  Hang, cur! Hang, you whoreson, insolent noisemaker! We are less afraid to be drowned than thou art.                                                        45

GONZALO  I'll warrant him for° drowning, though the ship were no stronger than a nutshell and as leaky as an unstanched° wench.

BOATSWAIN  Lay her ahold, ahold! Set her two courses!° Off to sea again! Lay her off!°            50

*Enter* MARINERS *wet.*

MARINERS  All lost! To prayers, to prayers! All lost!

*[Exeunt.]*

BOATSWAIN  What, must our mouths be cold?

GONZALO
The king and prince at prayers! Let's assist them,
For our case is as theirs.

SEBASTIAN                    I am out of patience.

ANTONIO
We are merely° cheated of our lives by drunkards.  55
This wide-chopped° rascal—would thou mightst lie drowning
The washing of ten tides!°

GONZALO                    He'll be hanged yet,
Though every drop of water swear against it
And gape at wid'st to glut him.

*A confused noise within:* "Mercy on us!"—
"We split, we split!"—"Farewell, my wife and children!"                                                        60

"Farewell, brother!"—"We split, we split, we split!"

*[Exit* BOATSWAIN.*]*

ANTONIO
Let's all sink wi' th' king.

SEBASTIAN                    Let's take leave of him.

*Exit, [with* ANTONIO*].*

GONZALO  Now would I give a thousand furlongs of sea for an acre of barren ground—long heath,° brown furze, anything. The wills above be done, but I would 65 fain die a dry death.                                *Exit.*

Scene II. [*The island. In front of Prospero's cell.*]

*Enter* PROSPERO *and* MIRANDA.

MIRANDA
If by your art, my dearest father, you have
Put the wild waters in this roar, allay them.
The sky, it seems, would pour down stinking pitch
But that the sea, mounting to th' welkin's cheek,°
Dashes the fire out. O, I have suffered              5
With those that I saw suffer! A brave° vessel
(Who had no doubt some noble creature in her)
Dashed all to pieces! O, the cry did knock
Against my very heart! Poor souls, they perished!
Had I been any god of power, I would           10
Have sunk the sea within the earth or ere
It should the good ship to have swallowed and
The fraughting° souls within her.

PROSPERO                    Be collected.
No more amazement.° Tell your piteous heart
There's no harm done.

MIRANDA                    O, woe the day!

PROSPERO                    No harm.    15
I have done nothing but in care of thee,
Of thee my dear one, thee my daughter, who
Art ignorant of what thou art, naught knowing
Of whence I am, nor that I am more better
Than Prospero, master of a full poor cell,      20
And thy no greater father.°

MIRANDA                    More to know
Did never meddle° with my thoughts.

PROSPERO                                'Tis time
I should inform thee farther. Lend thy hand
And pluck my magic garment from me. So.

*[Lays down his robe.]*

Lie there, my art. Wipe thou thine eyes; have comfort.  25
The direful spectacle of the wrack, which touched
The very virtue° of compassion in thee,
I have with such provision° in mine art
So safely ordered that there is no soul—
No, not so much perdition° as an hair         30
Betid° to any creature in the vessel
Which thou heard'st cry, which thou saw'st sink. Sit down;
For thou must now know farther.

---

**29–30 no drowning . . . gallows** alluding to the proverb, "He that's born to be hanged need fear no drowning"  **32 doth little advantage** gives us little advantage  **35 Bring . . . course** Heave to, under the mainsail  **36–37 They . . . office** These passengers make more noise than the tempest or than we do at our work  **38 give o'er** give up trying to run the ship  **46 warrant him for** guarantee him against  **48 unstanched** wide-open  **49–50 Lay . . . courses** the ship is still being blown dangerously to shore, so the boatswain orders that the foresail be set in addition to the mainsail; but the ship still moves toward shore  **50 Lay her off** i.e., away from the shore  **55 merely** completely  **56 wide-chopped** big-mouthed  **57 ten tides** pirates were hanged on the shore and left there until three tides had washed over them

**64 heath** heather
**I.ii.4 welkin's cheek** face of the sky  **6 brave** fine, gallant (the word often has this meaning in the play)  **13 fraughting** forming her freight  **14 amazement** consternation  **21 thy . . . father** thy father, no greater than the Prospero just described  **22 meddle** mingle  **27 virtue** essence  **28 provision** foresight  **30 perdition** loss  **31 Betid** happened

MIRANDA                 You have often
Begun to tell me what I am; but stopped
And left me to a bootless inquisition,           35
Concluding, "Stay; not yet."
PROSPERO            The hour's now come;
The very minute bids thee ope thine ear.
Obey, and be attentive. Canst thou remember
A time before we came unto this cell?
I do not think thou canst, for then thou wast not   40
Out° three years old.
MIRANDA             Certainly, sir, I can.
PROSPERO
By what? By any other house or person?
Of anything the image tell me that
Hath kept with thy remembrance.
MIRANDA              'Tis far off,
And rather like a dream than an assurance      45
That my remembrance warrants.° Had I not
Four or five women once that tended me?
PROSPERO
Thou hadst, and more, Miranda. But how is it
That this lives in thy mind? What see'st thou else
In the dark backward and abysm of time?        50
If thou rememb'rest aught ere thou cam'st here,
How thou cam'st here thou mayst.
MIRANDA             But that I do not.
PROSPERO
Twelve year since, Miranda, twelve year since,
Thy father was the Duke of Milan° and
A prince of power.
MIRANDA          Sir, are not you my father?   55
PROSPERO
Thy mother was a piece° of virtue, and
She said thou wast my daughter; and thy father
Was Duke of Milan; and his only heir
And princess, no worse issued.°
MIRANDA             O the heavens!
What foul play had we that we came from thence?   60
Or blessèd was't we did?
PROSPERO          Both, both, my girl!
By foul play, as thou say'st, were we heaved thence,
But blessedly holp° hither.
MIRANDA            O, my heart bleeds
To think o' th' teen that I have turned you to,°
Which is from° my remembrance! Please you, farther. 65
PROSPERO
My brother and thy uncle, called Antonio—
I pray thee mark me—that a brother should
Be so perfidious—he whom next thyself
Of all the world I loved, and to him put
The manage of my state,° as at that time       70
Through all the signories° it was the first,
And Prospero the prime duke, being so reputed
In dignity, and for the liberal arts
Without a parallel. Those being all my study,
The government I cast upon my brother        75
And to my state grew stranger, being transported

And rapt in secret studies. Thy false uncle—
Dost thou attend me?
MIRANDA          Sir, most heedfully.
PROSPERO
Being once perfected° how to grant suits,
How to deny them, who t' advance, and who      80
To trash for overtopping,° new-created
The creatures that were mine, I say—or changed 'em,
Or else new-formed 'em°—having both the key°
Of officer and office, set all hearts i' th' state
To what tune pleased his ear, that now he was     85
The ivy which had hid my princely trunk
And sucked my verdure out on't. Thou attend'st not?
MIRANDA
O, good sir, I do.
PROSPERO        I pray thee mark me.
I thus neglecting worldly ends, all dedicated
To closeness° and the bettering of my mind—     90
With that which, but by being so retired,
O'erprized all popular rate, in my false brother
Awaked an evil nature,° and my trust,
Like a good parent,° did beget of him
A falsehood in its contrary as great          95
As my trust was, which had indeed no limit,
A confidence sans bound. He being thus lorded—
Not only with what my revenue° yielded
But what my power might else exact, like one
Who having into truth—by telling of it°—      100
Made such a sinner of his memory
To° credit his own lie, he did believe
He was indeed the duke, out o' th' substitution
And executing th' outward face of royalty
With all prerogative.° Hence his ambition growing— 105
Dost thou hear?
MIRANDA        Your tale, sir, would cure deafness.
PROSPERO
To have no screen between this part he played
And him he played it for, he needs will be
Absolute Milan.° Me (poor man) my library
Was dukedom large enough. Of temporal royalties 110
He thinks me now incapable; confederates
(So dry° he was for sway) wi' th' King of Naples
To give him annual tribute, do him homage,
Subject his coronet to his crown, and bend
The dukedom, yet unbowed (alas, poor Milan!),    115
To most ignoble stooping.
MIRANDA          O the heavens!

**79 perfected** grown skillful   **81 trash for overtopping** (1)
check the speed of (as of hounds) (2) cut down to size (as of over-
tall trees) the aspirants for political favor who are growing too
bold   **81–83 new-created . . . 'em** he recreated my following
—either exchanging my adherents for his own, or else transforming my adherents into different people   **83 key** a pun leading
to the musical metaphor   **90 closeness** seclusion   **91–93 With
. . . nature** with that dedication to the mind which, were it
not that it kept me from exercising the duties of my office
would surpass in value all ordinary estimate, I awakened evil
in my brother's nature   **94 good parent** alluding to the proverb cited by Miranda in line 120   **98 revenue** pronounced
"revènue"   **99–100 like . . . it** like one who really had these
things—by repeatedly saying he had them ("into" = unto)
**102 To** as to   **103–05 out . . . prerogative** as a result of his
acting as my substitute and performing the outward functions
of royalty with all its prerogatives   **109 Absolute Milan** Duke
of Milan in fact   **112 dry** thirsty

**41 Out** fully   **46 remembrance warrants** memory guarantees   **54 Milan** pronounced "Mílan"   **56 piece** masterpiece
**59 no worse issued** of no meaner lineage than he   **63 holp**
helped   **64 teen . . . to** sorrow I have caused you to remember
**65 from** out of   **70 manage . . . state** management of my
domain   **71 signories** lordships (of Italy)

PROSPERO
Mark his condition,° and th' event;° then tell me
If this might be a brother.

MIRANDA              I should sin
To think but nobly of my grandmother.
Good wombs have borne bad sons.

PROSPERO            Now the condition. 120
This King of Naples, being an enemy
To me inveterate, hearkens my brother's suit;
Which was, that he, in lieu o' th' premises°
Of homage and I know not how much tribute,
Should presently extirpate me and mine 125
Out of the dukedom and confer fair Milan,
With all the honors, on my brother. Whereon,
A treacherous army levied, one midnight
Fated to th' purpose, did Antonio open
The gates of Milan; and, i' th' dead of darkness, 130
The ministers° for th' purpose hurried thence
Me and thy crying self.

MIRANDA          Alack, for pity!
I, not rememb'ring how I cried out then,
Will cry it o'er again; it is a hint°
That wrings mine eyes to't.

PROSPERO         Hear a little further, 135
And then I'll bring thee to the present business
Which now's upon's; without the which this story
Were most impertinent.°

MIRANDA          Wherefore did they not
That hour destroy us?

PROSPERO         Well demanded, wench.
My tale provokes that question. Dear, they durst not, 140
So dear the love my people bore me; nor set
A mark so bloody on the business; but,
With colors fairer, painted their foul ends.
In few,° they hurried us aboard a bark;
Bore us some leagues to sea, where they prepared 145
A rotten carcass of a butt,° not rigged,
Nor tackle, sail, nor mast; the very rats
Instinctively have quit it. There they hoist us,
To cry to th' sea that roared to us; to sigh
To th' winds, whose pity, sighing back again, 150
Did us but loving wrong.

MIRANDA          Alack, what trouble
Was I then to you!

PROSPERO        O, a cherubin
Thou wast that did preserve me! Thou didst smile,
Infused with a fortitude from heaven,
When I have decked° the sea with drops full salt, 155
Under my burden groaned; which° raised in me
An undergoing stomach,° to bear up
Against what should ensue.

MIRANDA         How came we ashore?

PROSPERO
By providence divine.
Some food we had, and some fresh water, that 160
A noble Neapolitan, Gonzalo,
Out of his charity, who being then appointed

Master of this design, did give us, with
Rich garments, linens, stuffs, and necessaries
Which since have steaded° much. So, of his gentleness, 165
Knowing I loved my books, he furnished me
From mine own library with volumes that
I prize above my dukedom.

MIRANDA          Would I might
But ever see that man!

PROSPERO        Now I arise.
Sit still, and hear the last of our sea sorrow. 170
Here in this island we arrived; and here
Have I, thy schoolmaster, made thee more profit
Than other princess' can,° that have more time
For vainer hours, and tutors not so careful.

MIRANDA
Heavens thank you for't! And now I pray you, sir— 175
For still 'tis beating in my mind—your reason
For raising this sea storm?

PROSPERO        Know thus far forth.
By accident most strange, bountiful Fortune
(Now my dear lady)° hath mine enemies
Brought to this shore; and by my prescience 180
I find my zenith° doth depend upon
A most auspicious star, whose influence
If now I court not, but omit,° my fortunes
Will ever after droop. Here cease more questions.
Thou art inclined to sleep. 'Tis a good dullness, 185
And give it way. I know thou canst not choose.

[MIRANDA *sleeps.*]

Come away,° servant, come! I am ready now.
Approach, my Ariel! Come!

*Enter* ARIEL.

ARIEL
All hail, great master! Grave sir, hail! I come
To answer thy best pleasure; be't to fly, 190
To swim, to dive into the fire, to ride
On the curled clouds. To thy strong bidding task°
Ariel and all his quality.°

PROSPERO        Hast thou, spirit,
Performed, to point,° the tempest that I bade thee?

ARIEL
To every article. 195
I boarded the king's ship. Now on the beak,°
Now in the waist,° the deck,° in every cabin,
I flamed amazement.° Sometime I'd divide
And burn in many places; on the topmast,
The yards, and boresprit° would I flame distinctly,° 200
Then meet and join. Jove's lightnings, the precursors
O' th' dreadful thunderclaps, more momentary
And sight-outrunning were not. The fire and cracks
Of sulfurous roaring the most mighty Neptune
Seem to besiege, and make his bold waves tremble; 205
Yea, his dread trident shake.

**117 condition** terms of his pact with Naples; **event** outcome
**123 in . . . premises** in return for the guarantees **131
ministers** agents **134 hint** occasion **138 impertinent**
inappropriate **144 few** few words **146 butt** tub **155 decked**
covered (wept salt tears into the sea) **156 which** Miranda's
smile **157 undergoing stomach** spirit of endurance

**165 steaded** been of use **173 princess' can** princesses can
have **179 Now . . . lady** i.e., formerly my foe, now my
patroness **181 zenith** apex of fortune **183 omit** neglect
**187 Come away** come from where you are; come here **192
task** tax to the utmost **193 quality** cohorts (Ariel is leader of
a band of spirits) **194 to point** in every detail **196 beak**
prow **197 waist** amidships; **deck** poop **198 flamed amazement** struck terror by appearing as (Saint Elmo's) fire **200
boresprit** bowsprit; **distinctly** in different places

PROSPERO                    My brave spirit!
Who was so firm, so constant, that this coil°
Would not infect his reason?

ARIEL                            Not a soul
But felt a fever of the mad and played
Some tricks of desperation. All but mariners          210
Plunged in the foaming brine and quit the vessel,
Then all afire with me. The king's son Ferdinand,
With hair up-staring° (then like reeds, not hair),
Was the first man that leapt; cried, "Hell is empty,
And all the devils are here!"

PROSPERO                        Why, that's my spirit!  215
But was not this nigh shore?

ARIEL                            Close by, my master.

PROSPERO
But are they, Ariel, safe?

ARIEL                         Not a hair perished.
On their sustaining° garments not a blemish,
But fresher than before; and as thou bad'st me,
In troops I have dispersed them 'bout the isle.        220
The king's son have I landed by himself,
Whom I left cooling of the air with sighs
In an odd angle of the isle, and sitting,
His arms in this sad knot.

[Illustrates with a gesture.]

PROSPERO                        Of the king's ship,
The mariners, say how thou hast disposed,              225
And all the rest o' th' fleet.

ARIEL                            Safely in harbor
Is the king's ship; in the deep nook where once
Thou call'dst me up at midnight to fetch dew
From the still-vexed Bermoothes,° there she's hid;
The mariners all under hatches stowed,                 230
Who, with a charm joined to their suff'red° labor,
I have left asleep. And for the rest o'th' fleet,
Which I dispersed, they all have met again,
And are upon the Mediterranean flote°
Bound sadly home for Naples,                           235
Supposing that they saw the king's ship wracked
And his great person perish.

PROSPERO                        Ariel, thy charge
Exactly is performed; but there's more work.
What is the time o' th' day?

ARIEL                         Past the mid season.°

PROSPERO
At least two glasses.° The time 'twixt six and now    240
Must by us both be spent most preciously.

ARIEL
Is there more toil? Since thou dost give me pains,°
Let me remember° thee what thou hast promised,
Which is not yet performed me.

PROSPERO                        How now? Moody?
What is't thou canst demand?

ARIEL                         My liberty.              245

PROSPERO
Before the time be out? No more!

ARIEL                            I prithee,
Remember I have done thee worthy service,

Told thee no lies, made thee no mistakings, served
Without or grudge or grumblings. Thou did promise
To bate me° a full year.

PROSPERO                    Dost thou forget            250
From what a torment I did free thee?

ARIEL                                        No.

PROSPERO
Thou dost; and think'st it much to tread the ooze
Of the salt deep,
To run upon the sharp wind of the North,
To do me business in the veins° o' th' earth          255
When it is baked° with frost.

ARIEL                            I do not, sir.

PROSPERO
Thou liest, malignant thing! Hast thou forgot
The foul witch Sycorax,° who with age and envy°
Was grown into a hoop? Hast thou forgot her?

ARIEL
No, sir.

PROSPERO      Thou hast. Where was she born? Speak!    260
Tell me!

ARIEL
Sir, in Argier.°

PROSPERO      O, was she so? I must
Once in a month recount what thou hast been,
Which thou forget'st. This damned witch Sycorax,
For mischiefs manifold, and sorceries terrible         265
To enter human hearing, from Argier,
Thou know'st, was banished. For one thing she did
They would not take her life. Is not this true?

ARIEL
Ay, sir.

PROSPERO
This blue-eyed° hag was hither brought with child     270
And here was left by th' sailors. Thou, my slave,
As thou report'st thyself, wast then her servant.
And, for thou wast a spirit too delicate
To act her earthy and abhorred commands,
Refusing her grand hests,° she did confine thee,      275
By help of her more potent ministers,°
And in her most unmitigable rage,
Into a cloven pine; within which rift
Imprisoned thou didst painfully remain
A dozen years; within which space she died            280
And left thee there, where thou didst vent thy groans
As fast as millwheels strike. Then was this island
(Save for the son that she did litter here,
A freckled whelp, hagborn) not honored with
A human shape.

ARIEL              Yes, Caliban her son.              285

PROSPERO
Dull thing, I say so! He, that Caliban
Whom now I keep in service. Thou best know'st
What torment I did find thee in; thy groans
Did make wolves howl and penetrate the breasts
Of ever-angry bears. It was a torment                 290

207 coil uproar  213 up-staring standing on end  218 sustaining buoying them up  229 Bermoothes Bermudas  231
suff'red undergone  234 flote sea  239 mid season noon
240 two glasses two o'clock  242 pains hard tasks  243
remember remind

250 bate me reduce my term of service  255 veins streams
256 baked caked  258 Sycorax name not found elsewhere;
probably derived from Greek sys, "sow," and korax, which
means both "raven"—see line 324—and "hook"—hence perhaps
"hoop"; envy malice  262 Argier Algiers  270 blue-eyed
referring to the livid color of the eyelid, a sign of pregnancy
275 hests commands  276 her . . . ministers her agents,
spirits more powerful than thou

To lay upon the damned, which Sycorax
Could not again undo. It was mine art,
When I arrived and heard thee, that made gape
The pine, and let thee out.

ARIEL                                I thank thee, master.

PROSPERO
If thou more murmur'st, I will rend an oak          295
And peg thee in his° knotty entrails till
Thou hast howled away twelve winters.

ARIEL                                Pardon, master.
I will be correspondent° to command
And do my spriting gently.°

PROSPERO                        Do so; and after two days
I will discharge thee.

ARIEL                        That's my noble master!       300
What shall I do? Say what? What shall I do?

PROSPERO
Go make thyself like a nymph o' th' sea. Be subject
To no sight but thine and mine, invisible
To every eyeball else.° Go take this shape
And hither come in't. Go! Hence with diligence!    305
                                        *Exit* [ARIEL].
Awake, dear heart, awake! Thou hast slept well.
Awake!

MIRANDA
The strangeness of your story put
Heaviness in me.

PROSPERO        Shake it off. Come on.
We'll visit Caliban, my slave, who never          310
Yields us kind answer.

MIRANDA                'Tis a villain, sir,
I do not love to look on.

PROSPERO                But as 'tis,
We cannot miss° him. He does make our fire,
Fetch in our wood, and serves in offices
That profit us. What, ho! Slave! Caliban!         315
Thou earth, thou! Speak!

CALIBAN        (*Within.*) There's wood enough within.

PROSPERO
Come forth, I say! There's other business for thee.
Come, thou tortoise! When?°

*Enter* ARIEL *like a water nymph.*

Fine apparition! My quaint° Ariel,
Hark in thine ear. [*Whispers.*]

ARIEL            My lord, it shall be done.      *Exit.* 320

PROSPERO
Thou poisonous slave, got by the devil himself
Upon thy wicked dam, come forth!

*Enter* CALIBAN.

CALIBAN
As wicked dew as e'er my mother brushed
With raven's feather from unwholesome fen
Drop on you both! A southwest blow on ye          325
And blister you all o'er!

PROSPERO
For this, be sure, tonight thou shalt have cramps,
Side-stitches that shall pen thy breath up. Urchins°
Shall, for that vast of night that they may work,°
All exercise on thee; thou shalt be pinched        330
As thick as honeycomb, each pinch more stinging
Than bees that made 'em.

CALIBAN                I must eat my dinner.
This island's mine by Sycorax my mother,
Which thou tak'st from me. When thou cam'st first,
Thou strok'st me and made much of me; wouldst give
  me                                               335
Water with berries in't; and teach me how
To name the bigger light, and how the less,
That burn by day and night. And then I loved thee
And showed thee all the qualities o' th' isle,
The fresh springs, brine pits, barren place and fertile. 340
Cursed be I that did so! All the charms
Of Sycorax—toads, beetles, bats, light on you!
For I am all the subjects that you have,
Which first was mine own king; and here you sty me
In this hard rock, whiles you do keep from me      345
The rest o' th' island.

PROSPERO                Thou most lying slave,
Whom stripes° may move, not kindness! I have used
  thee
(Filth as thou art) with humane care, and lodged thee
In mine own cell till thou didst seek to violate
The honor of my child.                             350

CALIBAN
O ho, O ho! Would't had been done!
Thou didst prevent me; I had peopled else
This isle with Calibans.

MIRANDA°                Abhorrèd slave,
Which any print of goodness wilt not take,
Being capable of all ill!° I pitied thee,          355
Took pains to make thee speak, taught thee each hour
One thing or other. When thou didst not, savage,
Know thine own meaning, but wouldst gabble like
A thing most brutish, I endowed thy purposes
With words that made them known. But thy vile race, 360
Though thou didst learn, had that in't which good
  natures
Could not abide to be with. Therefore wast thou
Deservedly confined into this rock, who hadst
Deserved more than a prison.

CALIBAN
You taught me language, and my profit on't         365
Is, I know how to curse. The red plague rid° you
For learning me your language!

PROSPERO                        Hagseed, hence!
Fetch us in fuel. And be quick, thou'rt best,°
To answer other business. Shrug'st thou, malice?
If thou neglect'st or dost unwillingly             370
What I command, I'll rack thee with old° cramps,

**296 his** its   **298 correspondent** obedient   **299 do . . . gently**
render graciously my services as a spirit   **303–04 invisible
. . . else** Ariel is invisible to everyone in the play except
Prospero; Henslowe's *Diary*, an Elizabethan stage account, lists
"a robe for to go invisible"   **313 miss** do without   **318 When**
expression of impatience   **319 quaint** ingenious

**328 Urchins** goblins in the shape of hedgehogs   **329 vast
. . . work** the long, empty stretch of night during which
malignant spirits are allowed to be active   **347 stripes** lashes
**353 Miranda** many editors transfer this speech to Prospero
as inappropriate to Miranda   **355 capable . . . ill** susceptible
only to evil impressions   **366 rid** destroy   **368 thou'rt best**
you'd better   **371 old** plenty of (with an additional suggestion, "such as old people have")

Fill all thy bones with aches,° make thee roar
That beasts shall tremble at thy din.

CALIBAN                                    No, pray thee.

[*Aside*.]

I must obey. His art is of such pow'r
It would control my dam's god, Setebos,                    375
And make a vassal of him.

PROSPERO                          So, slave; hence!

*Exit* CALIBAN.

*Enter* FERDINAND; *and* ARIEL (*invisible*), *playing and
singing.*

                    *Ariel's song.*
          Come unto these yellow sands,
               And then take hands.
          Curtsied when you have and kissed
               The wild waves whist,°                    380
          Foot it featly° here and there;
          And, sweet sprites, the burden bear.
               Hark, hark!

*Burden, dispersedly.*° Bow, wow!

               The watchdogs bark.                    385

*Burden, dispersedly.* Bow, wow!

          Hark, hark! I hear
          The strain of strutting chanticleer
               Cry cock-a-diddle-dow.

FERDINAND
Where should this music be? I' th' air or th' earth?    390
It sounds no more; and sure it waits upon
Some god o' th' island. Sitting on a bank,
Weeping again the King my father's wrack,
This music crept by me upon the waters,
Allaying both their fury and my passion°                395
With its sweet air. Thence I have followed it,
Or it hath drawn me rather; but 'tis gone.
No, it begins again.
                    *Ariel's song.*
          Full fathom five thy father lies;
               Of his bones are coral made;            400
          Those are pearls that were his eyes;
               Nothing of him that doth fade
          But doth suffer a sea change
          Into something rich and strange.
          Sea nymphs hourly ring his knell:            405

*Burden.* Ding-dong.

          Hark! Now I hear them—ding-dong bell.

FERDINAND
The ditty does remember my drowned father.
This is no mortal business, nor no sound
That the earth owes.° I hear it now above me.          410

PROSPERO
The fringèd curtains of thine eye advance°
And say what thou see'st yond.

MIRANDA                          What is't? A spirit?
Lord, how it looks about! Believe me, sir,
It carries a brave form. But 'tis a spirit.

PROSPERO
No, wench; it eats, and sleeps, and hath such senses    415
As we have, such. This gallant which thou see'st
Was in the wrack; and, but he's something stained
With grief (that's beauty's canker), thou mightst call
     him
A goodly person. He hath lost his fellows
And strays about to find 'em.

MIRANDA                     I might call him            420
A thing divine; for nothing natural
I ever saw so noble.

PROSPERO    [*Aside*.] It goes on, I see,
As my soul prompts it. Spirit, fine spirit, I'll free thee
Within two days for this.

FERDINAND               Most sure, the goddess
On whom these airs attend! Vouchsafe my prayer          425
May know if you remain° upon this island,
And that you will some good instruction give
How I may bear me° here. My prime request,
Which I do last pronounce, is (O you wonder!)
If you be maid or no?

MIRANDA               No wonder, sir,                   430
But certainly a maid.

FERDINAND            My language? Heavens!
I am the best of them that speak this speech,
Were I but where 'tis spoken.

PROSPERO                     How? The best?
What wert thou if the King of Naples heard thee?

FERDINAND
A single° thing, as I am now, that wonders              435
To hear thee speak of Naples. He does hear me;
And that he does I weep. Myself am Naples,
Who with mine eyes, never since at ebb, beheld
The king my father wracked.

MIRANDA                     Alack, for mercy!

FERDINAND
Yes, faith, and all his lords, the Duke of Milan        440
And his brave son° being twain.°

PROSPERO              [*Aside*.] The Duke of Milan
And his more braver daughter could control° thee,
If now 'twere fit to do't. At the first sight
They have changed eyes.° Delicate Ariel,
I'll set thee free for this. [*To* FERDINAND.] A word,
     good sir.                                          445
I fear you have done yourself some wrong.° A word!

MIRANDA
Why speaks my father so ungently? This
Is the third man that e'er I saw; the first
That e'er I sighed for. Pity move my father
To be inclined my way!

FERDINAND               O, if a virgin,                 450
And your affection not gone forth, I'll make you
The queen of Naples.

PROSPERO               Soft, sir! One word more.

---

**372 aches** pronounced "aitches"  **379–80 kissed . . . whist**
when you have, through the harmony of kissing in the dance,
kissed the wild waves into silence (?) when you have kissed
in the dance, the wild waves being silenced (?)  **381 featly**
nimbly  **384 Burden, dispersedly** an undersong, coming from
all parts of the stage; it imitates the barking of dogs and
perhaps at the end the crowing of a cock  **395 passion** grief
**410 owes** owns  **411 advance** raise

**425–26 Vouchsafe . . . remain** may my prayer induce you to
inform me whether you dwell  **428 bear me** conduct myself
**435 single** (1) solitary (2) helpless  **441 son** the only time
Antonio's son is mentioned; **twain** two (of these lords)  **442
control** refute  **444 changed eyes** i.e., fallen in love  **446
done . . . wrong** said what is not so

*[Aside.]*
They are both in either's pow'rs. But this swift business
I must uneasy make, lest too light winning
Make the prize light. *[To* FERDINAND.*]* One word
    more! I charge thee                                          455
That thou attend me. Thou dost here usurp
The name thou ow'st° not, and hast put thyself
Upon this island as a spy, to win it
From me, the lord on't.

FERDINAND                        No, as I am a man!

MIRANDA
There's nothing ill can dwell in such a temple.             460
If the ill spirit have so fair a house,
Good things will strive to dwell with't.

PROSPERO                              Follow me.

*[To* MIRANDA.*]*

Speak not you for him; he's a traitor. *[To* FERDI-
    NAND.*]* Come!
I'll manacle thy neck and feet together;
Sea water shalt thou drink; thy food shall be              465
The fresh-brook mussels, withered roots, and husks
Wherein the acorn cradled. Follow!

FERDINAND                        No.
I will resist such entertainment till
Mine enemy has more pow'r.

*He draws, and is charmed from moving.*

MIRANDA                        O dear father,
Make not too rash a trial of him, for                      470
He's gentle and not fearful.°

PROSPERO                        What, I say,
My foot my tutor?° *[To* FERDINAND.*]* Put thy sword
    up, traitor—
Who mak'st a show but dar'st not strike, thy conscience
Is so possessed with guilt! Come, from thy ward!°
For I can here disarm thee with this stick°                475
And make thy weapon drop.

MIRANDA                        Beseech you, father!

PROSPERO
Hence! Hang not on my garments.

MIRANDA                              Sir, have pity.
I'll be his surety.

PROSPERO        Silence! One word more
Shall make me chide thee, if not hate thee. What,
An advocate for an impostor? Hush!                         480
Thou think'st there is no more such shapes as he,
Having seen but him and Caliban. Foolish wench!
To th' most of men this is a Caliban,
And they to him are angels.

MIRANDA                        My affections
Are then most humble. I have no ambition                   485
To see a goodlier man.

PROSPERO *[To* FERDINAND.*]*
Come on, obey!
Thy nerves° are in their infancy again
And have no vigor in them.

FERDINAND                        So they are.
My spirits, as in a dream, are all bound up.               490

My father's loss, the weakness which I feel,
The wrack of all my friends, not this man's threats
To whom I am subdued, are but light to me,
Might I but through my prison once a day
Behold this maid. All corners else o' th' earth            495
Let liberty make use of. Space enough
Have I in such a prison.

PROSPERO *[Aside.]*
It works. *[To* FERDINAND.*]* Come on.

*[To* ARIEL.*]*

Thou hast done well, fine Ariel! *[To* FERDINAND.*]*
    Follow me.

*[To* ARIEL.*]* Hark what thou else shalt do me.

MIRANDA                              Be of comfort.   500
My father's of a better nature, sir,
Than he appears by speech. This is unwonted
Which now came from him.

PROSPERO                        Thou shalt be as free
As mountain winds; but then° exactly do
All points of my command.

ARIEL                        To th' syllable.        505

PROSPERO *[To* FERDINAND.*]*
Come, follow. *[To* MIRANDA.*]* Speak not for him.
                                        *Exeunt.*

# ACT II

Scene I. *[Another part of the island.]*

*Enter* ALONSO, SEBASTIAN, ANTONIO, GONZALO,
ADRIAN, FRANCISCO, *and others.*

GONZALO
Beseech you, sir, be merry. You have cause
(So have we all) of joy; for our escape
Is much beyond our loss. Our hint of° woe
Is common; every day some sailor's wife,
The master of some merchant,° and the merchant,
Have just our theme of woe. But for the miracle,
I mean our preservation, few in millions
Can speak like us. Then wisely, good sir, weigh
Our sorrow with° our comfort.

ALONSO                        Prithee, peace.

SEBASTIAN *[Aside to* ANTONIO.*]*   He receives comfort   10
like cold porridge.°

ANTONIO *[Aside to* SEBASTIAN.*]*   The visitor° will not
give him o'er so.°

SEBASTIAN   Look, he's winding up the watch of his
wit; by and by it will strike.                             15

GONZALO   Sir—

SEBASTIAN *[Aside to* ANTONIO.*]*   One. Tell.°

GONZALO
When every grief is entertained, that's° offered
Comes to th' entertainer—

---

**504 then** till then
**II.i.3 hint of** occasion for   **5 master . . . merchant** captain
of some merchant ship   **9 with** against   **10–11 He . . .
porridge** "He" is Alonso; pun on "peace," since porridge
contained peas   **12 visitor** spiritual comforter   **13 give . . .
so** release him so easily   **17 One. Tell** He has struck one. Keep
count   **18 that's** that which is

**457 ow'st** ownest   **471 gentle . . . fearful** of noble birth and
no coward   **472 My . . . tutor** am I to be instructed by my
inferior   **474 ward** fighting posture   **475 stick** his wand
**488 nerves** sinews

SEBASTIAN   A dollar.  20

GONZALO   Dolor comes to him, indeed. You have spoken truer than you purposed.

SEBASTIAN   You have taken it wiselier° than I meant you should.

GONZALO   Therefore, my lord—  25

ANTONIO   Fie, what a spendthrift is he of his tongue!

ALONSO   I prithee, spare.°

GONZALO   Well, I have done. But yet—

SEBASTIAN   He will be talking.

ANTONIO   Which, of he or Adrian, for a good wager, 30 first° begins to crow?

SEBASTIAN   The old cock.°

ANTONIO   The cock'rel.°

SEBASTIAN   Done! The wager?

ANTONIO   A laughter.°  35

SEBASTIAN   A match!

ADRIAN   Though this island seem to be desert—

ANTONIO   Ha, ha, ha!

SEBASTIAN   So, you're paid.

ADRIAN   Uninhabitable and almost inaccessible—  40

SEBASTIAN   Yet—

ADRIAN   Yet—

ANTONIO   He could not miss't.

ADRIAN   It must needs be of subtle, tender, and delicate temperance.°  45

ANTONIO   Temperance was a delicate wench.

SEBASTIAN   Ay, and a subtle, as he most learnedly delivered.

ADRIAN   The air breathes upon us here most sweetly.

SEBASTIAN   As if it had lungs, and rotten ones.  50

ANTONIO   Or as 'twere perfumed by a fen.

GONZALO   Here is everything advantageous to life.

ANTONIO   True; save means to live.

SEBASTIAN   Of that there's none, or little.

GONZALO   How lush and lusty the grass looks! How 55 green!

ANTONIO   The ground indeed is tawny.

SEBASTIAN   With an eye° of green in't.

ANTONIO   He misses not much.

SEBASTIAN   No; he doth but mistake the truth totally.  60

GONZALO   But the rarity of it is—which is indeed almost beyond credit—

SEBASTIAN   As many vouched rarities are.

GONZALO   That our garments, being, as they were, drenched in the sea, hold, notwithstanding, their 65 freshness and glosses, being rather new-dyed than stained with salt water.

ANTONIO   If but one of his pockets could speak, would it not say he lies?°

SEBASTIAN   Ay, or very falsely pocket up his report.°  70

GONZALO   Methinks our garments are now as fresh as when we put them on first in Afric, at the marriage of the king's fair daughter Claribel to the King of Tunis.

SEBASTIAN   'Twas a sweet marriage, and we prosper well in our return.  75

ADRIAN   Tunis was never graced before with such a paragon to° their queen.

GONZALO   Not since widow Dido's time.

ANTONIO   Widow? A pox o' that! How came that "widow" in? Widow Dido!  80

SEBASTIAN   What if he had said "widower Aeneas"° too? Good Lord, how you take it!

ADRIAN   "Widow Dido," said you? You make me study of that. She was of Carthage, not of Tunis.

GONZALO   This Tunis, sir, was Carthage.  85

ADRIAN   Carthage?

GONZALO   I assure you, Carthage.

ANTONIO   His word is more than the miraculous harp.°

SEBASTIAN   He hath raised the wall and houses too.  90

ANTONIO   What impossible matter will he make easy next?

SEBASTIAN   I think he will carry this island home in his pocket and give it his son for an apple.

ANTONIO   And, sowing the kernels of it in the sea, 95 bring forth more islands.

GONZALO   Ay!

ANTONIO   Why, in good time.°

GONZALO   [To ALONSO.] Sir, we were talking that our garments seem now as fresh as when we were at 100 Tunis at the marriage of your daughter, who is now queen.

ANTONIO   And the rarest that e'er came there.

SEBASTIAN   Bate,° I beseech you, widow Dido.

ANTONIO   O, widow Dido? Ay, widow Dido!  105

GONZALO   Is not, sir, my doublet as fresh as the first day I wore it? I mean, in a sort.°

ANTONIO   That "sort" was well fished for.

GONZALO   When I wore it at your daughter's marriage.  110

ALONSO
You cram these words into mine ears against
The stomach of my sense.° Would I had never
Married my daughter there! For, coming thence,
My son is lost; and, in my rate,° she too,
Who is so far from Italy removed  115
I ne'er again shall see her. O thou mine heir
Of Naples and of Milan, what strange fish
Hath made his meal on thee?

FRANCISCO                         Sir, he may live.
I saw him beat the surges under him
And ride upon their backs. He trod the water,  120
Whose enmity he flung aside, and breasted
The surge most swol'n that met him. His bold head
'Bove the contentious waves he kept, and oared

---

23 **wiselier** i.e., understood my pun   27 **spare** spare your words   30–31 **Which . . . first** let's wager which of the two, Gonzalo or Adrian, will first   32 **old cock** Gonzalo   33 **cock'rel** young cock; i.e., Adrian   35 **laughter** the winner will have the laugh on the loser   45 **temperance** climate (in the next line, a girl's name)   58 **eye** spot (also perhaps Gonzalo's eye)   68–69 **If . . . lies** i.e., the insides of Gonzalo's pockets are stained   70 **Ay . . . report** unless the pocket were, like a false knave, to receive without resentment the imputation that it is unstained

77 **to** for   80–81 **Widow Dido . . . "widower Aeneas"** the point of the joke is that Dido was a widow, but one does not ordinarily think of her that way; and the same with Aeneas   88–89 **miraculous harp** of Amphion, which raised only the *walls* of Thebes; whereas Gonzalo has rebuilt the whole ancient city of Carthage by identifying it mistakenly with modern Tunis   98 **Why . . . time** hearing Gonzalo reaffirm his false statement about Tunis and Carthage, Antonio suggests that Gonzalo will indeed, at the first opportunity, carry this island home in his pocket   104 **Bate** except   107 **in a sort** so to speak   111–12 **against . . . sense** though my mind (or feelings) have no appetite for them   114 **rate** opinion

Himself with his good arms in lusty stroke
To th' shore, that o'er his° wave-worn basis bowed,° 125
As stooping to relieve him. I not doubt
He came alive to land.

ALONSO                    No, no, he's gone.

SEBASTIAN [*To* ALONSO.]
Sir, you may thank yourself for this great loss,
That would not bless our Europe with your daughter,
But rather loose her to an African,          130
Where she, at least, is banished from your eye
Who hath cause to wet the grief on't.

ALONSO                    Prithee, peace.

SEBASTIAN
You were kneeled to and importuned otherwise
By all of us; and the fair soul herself
Weighed, between loathness and obedience, at   135
Which end o' th' beam should bow.° We have lost
      your son,
I fear, forever. Milan and Naples have
Moe° widows in them of this business' making
Than we bring men to comfort them.
The fault's your own.

ALONSO            So is the dear'st° o' th' loss.   140

GONZALO
My Lord Sebastian,
The truth you speak doth lack some gentleness,
And time to speak it in. You rub the sore
When you should bring the plaster.

SEBASTIAN                    Very well.

ANTONIO
And most chirurgeonly.°                    145

GONZALO [*To* ALONSO.]
It is foul weather in us all, good sir,
When you are cloudy.

SEBASTIAN [*Aside to* ANTONIO.]   Foul weather?

ANTONIO [*Aside to* SEBASTIAN.]          Very foul.

GONZALO
Had I plantation° of this isle, my lord—

ANTONIO
He'd sow 't with nettle seed.

SEBASTIAN                    Or docks, or mallows.

GONZALO
And were the king on't, what would I do?    150

SEBASTIAN
Scape being drunk for want of wine.

GONZALO
I' th' commonwealth I would by contraries°
Execute all things. For no kind of traffic°
Would I admit; no name of magistrate;
Letters° should not be known; riches, poverty,   155
And use of service,° none; contract, succession,°
Bourn,° bound of land, tilth,° vineyard, none;
No use of metal, corn, or wine, or oil;
No occupation; all men idle, all;

And women too, but innocent and pure;      160
No sovereignty.

SEBASTIAN          Yet he would be king on't.

ANTONIO The latter end of his commonwealth forgets the beginning.

GONZALO
All things in common nature should produce
Without sweat or endeavor. Treason, felony,   165
Sword, pike, knife, gun, or need of any engine°
Would I not have; but nature should bring forth,
Of it° own kind, all foison,° all abundance,
To feed my innocent people.

SEBASTIAN   No marrying 'mong his subjects?   170

ANTONIO   None, man, all idle—whores and knaves.

GONZALO
I would with such perfection govern, sir,
T' excel the Golden Age.

SEBASTIAN          [*Loudly.*] Save his majesty!

ANTONIO [*Loudly.*]
Long live Gonzalo!

GONZALO          And—do you mark me, sir?

ALONSO
Prithee, no more. Thou dost talk nothing to me.   175

GONZALO   I do well believe your highness; and did it
to minister occasion° to these gentlemen, who are of
such sensible° and nimble lungs that they always use to
laugh at nothing.

ANTONIO   'Twas you we laughed at.      180

GONZALO   Who in this kind of merry fooling am
nothing to you; so you may continue, and laugh at
nothing still.

ANTONIO   What a blow was there given!

SEBASTIAN   And° it had not fall'n flatlong.°   185

GONZALO   You are gentlemen of brave mettle; you
would lift the moon out of her sphere if she would
continue in it five weeks without changing.

*Enter* ARIEL [*invisible*] *playing solemn music.*

SEBASTIAN   We would so, and then go a-batfowling.°

ANTONIO   Nay, good my lord, be not angry.      190

GONZALO   No, I warrant you; I will not adventure
my discretion so weakly.° Will you laugh me asleep?
For I am very heavy.

ANTONIO   Go sleep, and hear us.

[*All sleep except* ALONSO, SEBASTIAN, *and* ANTONIO.]

ALONSO
What, all so soon asleep? I wish mine eyes      195
Would, with themselves, shut up my thoughts. I find
They are inclined to do so.

SEBASTIAN          Please you, sir,
Do not omit° the heavy offer of it.
It seldom visits sorrow; when it doth,
It is a comforter.

---

125 **his** its; **wave-worn basis bowed** the image is of a guardian cliff on the shore   135–36 **Weighed . . . bow** Claribel's
unwillingness to marry was outweighed by her obedience to
her father   138 **Moe** more   140 **dear'st** intensifies the meaning
of the noun   145 **chirurgeonly** like a surgeon   148 **plantation**
colonization (Antonio then puns by taking the word in its other
sense)   152 **contraries** in contrast to the usual customs   153
**traffic** trade   155 **Letters** learning   156 **service** servants;
**succession** inheritance   157 **Bourn** boundary; **tilth** agriculture

166 **engine** weapon   168 **it** its; **foison** abundance   177
**minister occasion** afford opportunity   178 **sensible** sensitive
185 **And** if; **flatlong** with the flat of the sword   189 **We
. . . a-batfowling** We would use the moon for a lantern
in order to hunt birds at night by attracting them with a light
and beating them down with bats; i.e., in order to gull simpletons like you (?)   191–92 **adventure . . . weakly** risk my
reputation for good sense because of your weak wit   198 **omit**
neglect

ANTONIO     We two, my lord,          200
Will guard your person while you take your rest,
And watch your safety.

ALONSO          Thank you. Wondrous heavy.
          [ALONSO *sleeps. Exit* ARIEL.]

SEBASTIAN
What a strange drowsiness possesses them!

ANTONIO
It is the quality o' th' climate.

SEBASTIAN          Why
Doth it not then our eyelids sink? I find not     205
Myself disposed to sleep.

ANTONIO          Nor I: my spirits are nimble.
They fell together all, as by consent.
They dropped as by a thunderstroke. What might,
Worthy Sebastian—O, what might?—No more!
And yet methinks I see it in thy face,          210
What thou shouldst be. Th' occasion speaks° thee, and
My strong imagination sees a crown
Dropping upon thy head.

SEBASTIAN          What? Art thou waking?

ANTONIO
Do you not hear me speak?

SEBASTIAN          I do; and surely
It is a sleepy language, and thou speak'st          215
Out of thy sleep. What is it thou didst say?
This is a strange repose, to be asleep
With eyes wide open; standing, speaking, moving,
And yet so fast asleep.

ANTONIO          Noble Sebastian,
Thou let'st thy fortune sleep—die, rather; wink'st°     220
Whiles thou art waking.

SEBASTIAN          Thou dost snore distinctly;
There's meaning in thy snores.

ANTONIO
I am more serious than my custom. You
Must be so too, if heed° me; which to do
Trebles thee o'er.°

SEBASTIAN          Well, I am standing water.     225

ANTONIO
I'll teach you how to flow.

SEBASTIAN          Do so. To ebb
Hereditary sloth instructs me.

ANTONIO          O,
If you but knew how you the purpose cherish
Whiles thus you mock it; how, in stripping it,
You more invest it!° Ebbing men, indeed,          230
Most often do so near the bottom run
By their own fear or sloth.

SEBASTIAN          Prithee, say on.
The setting of thine eye and cheek proclaim
A matter° from thee; and a birth, indeed,
Which throes thee much° to yield.

ANTONIO          Thus, sir:     235
Although this lord of weak remembrance,° this
Who shall be of as little memory°

When he is earthed,° hath here almost persuaded
(For he's a spirit of persuasion, only
Professes to persuade°) the king his son's alive,     240
'Tis as impossible that he's undrowned
As he that sleeps here swims.

SEBASTIAN          I have no hope
That he's undrowned.

ANTONIO          O, out of that no hope
What great hope have you! No hope that way is
Another way so high a hope that even          245
Ambition cannot pierce a wink beyond,
But doubt discovery there.° Will you grant with me
That Ferdinand is drowned?

SEBASTIAN          He's gone.

ANTONIO          Then tell me,
Who's the next heir of Naples?

SEBASTIAN          Claribel.

ANTONIO
She that is Queen of Tunis; she that dwells          250
Ten leagues beyond man's life;° she that from Naples
Can have no note—unless the sun were post;°
The man i' th' moon's too slow—till newborn chins
Be rough and razorable;° she that from whom
We all were sea-swallowed,° though some cast° again,     255
And, by that destiny, to perform an act
Whereof what's past is prologue, what to come,
In yours and my discharge.

SEBASTIAN          What stuff is this? How say you?
'Tis true my brother's daughter's Queen of Tunis;
So is she heir of Naples; 'twixt which regions     260
There is some space.

ANTONIO          A space whose ev'ry cubit
Seems to cry out, "How shall that Claribel
Measure us back to Naples? Keep in Tunis,
And let Sebastian wake!" Say this were death
That now hath seized them, why, they were no worse     265
Than now they are. There be that can rule Naples
As well as he that sleeps; lords that can prate
As amply and unnecessarily
As this Gonzalo; I myself could make
A chough° of as deep chat. O, that you bore          270
The mind that I do! What a sleep were this
For your advancement! Do you understand me?

SEBASTIAN
Methinks I do.

ANTONIO          And how does your content
Tender° your own good fortune?

SEBASTIAN          I remember
You did supplant your brother Prospero.

ANTONIO          True.     275
And look how well my garments sit upon me,

**238 earthed** buried  **239–40 only . . . persuade** his only profession is to persuade  **246–47 Ambition . . . there** the eye of ambition can reach no farther, but must even doubt the reality of what it discerns thus far  **251 Ten . . . life** it would take a lifetime to get within ten leagues of the place  **252 post** messenger  **253–54 till . . . razorable** till babies just born be ready to shave  **254–55 she . . . sea-swallowed** she who is separated from Naples by so dangerous a sea that we were ourselves swallowed up by it  **255 cast** cast upon the shore (with a suggestion of its theatrical meaning that leads to the next metaphor)  **270 chough** jackdaw (a bird that can be taught to speak a few words)  **274 Tender** regard (i.e., Do you like your good fortune?)

**211 speaks** speaks to  **220 wink'st** dost shut thine eyes  **224 if heed** if you heed  **225 Trebles thee o'er** makes thee three times what thou now art  **229–30 in stripping . . . invest it** in stripping the purpose off you, you clothe yourself with it all the more  **234 matter** matter of importance  **235 throes thee much** costs thee much pain  **236 remembrance** memory  **237 of . . . memory** as little remembered

Much feater° than before. My brother's servants
Were then my fellows; now they are my men.

SEBASTIAN
But, for your conscience—

ANTONIO
Ay, sir, where lies that? If 'twere a kibe,°  280
'Twould put me to my slipper; but I feel not
This deity in my bosom. Twenty consciences
That stand 'twixt me and Milan, candied be they
And melt, ere they molest! Here lies your brother,
No better than the earth he lies upon—  285
If he were that which now he's like, that's dead°—
Whom I with this obedient steel (three inches of it)
Can lay to bed forever; whiles you, doing thus,
To the perpetual wink° for aye might put
This ancient morsel, this Sir Prudence, who  290
Should not upbraid our course. For all the rest,
They'll take suggestion as a cat laps milk;
They'll tell the clock° to any business that
We say befits the hour.

SEBASTIAN                    Thy case, dear friend,
Shall be my precedent. As thou got'st Milan,  295
I'll come by Naples. Draw thy sword. One stroke
Shall free thee from the tribute which thou payest,
And I the king shall love thee.

ANTONIO                    Draw together;
And when I rear my hand, do you the like,
To fall it on Gonzalo. [*They draw.*]

SEBASTIAN                O, but one word!  300

*Enter* ARIEL [*invisible*] *with music and song.*

ARIEL
My master through his art foresees the danger
That you, his friend, are in, and sends me forth
(For else his project dies) to keep them living.

*Sings in Gonzalo's ear.*

While you here do snoring lie,
Open-eyed conspiracy  305
His time doth take.
If of life you keep a care,
Shake off slumber and beware.
Awake, awake!

ANTONIO
Then let us both be sudden.

GONZALO          [*Wakes.*] Now good angels  310
Preserve the king!

[*The others wake.*]

ALONSO
Why, how now? Ho, awake! Why are you drawn?
Wherefore this ghastly looking?

GONZALO                    What's the matter?

SEBASTIAN
Whiles we stood here securing your repose,
Even now, we heard a hollow burst of bellowing  315
Like bulls, or rather lions. Did't not wake you?
It struck mine ear most terribly.

ALONSO                    I heard nothing.

ANTONIO
O, 'twas a din to fright a monster's ear,
To make an earthquake! Sure it was the roar
Of a whole herd of lions.

ALONSO          Heard you this, Gonzalo?  320

GONZALO
Upon mine honor, sir, I heard a humming,
And that a strange one too, which did awake me.
I shaked you, sir, and cried. As mine eyes opened,
I saw their weapons drawn. There was a noise,
That's verily.° 'Tis best we stand upon our guard,  325
Or that we quit this place. Let's draw our weapons.

ALONSO
Lead off this ground, and let's make further search
For my poor son.

GONZALO          Heavens keep him from these beasts!
For he is, sure, i' th' island.

ALONSO                    Lead away.

ARIEL
Prospero my lord shall know what I have done.  330
So, king, go safely on to seek thy son.          *Exeunt.*

Scene II. [*Another part of the island.*]

*Enter* CALIBAN *with a burden of wood. A noise of thunder
heard.*

CALIBAN
All the infections that the sun sucks up
From bogs, fens, flats, on Prosper fall, and make him
By inchmeal° a disease! His spirits hear me,
And yet I needs must curse. But they'll nor pinch,
Fright me with urchin shows,° pitch me i' th' mire,  5
Nor lead me, like a firebrand,° in the dark
Out of my way, unless he bid 'em. But
For every trifle are they set upon me;
Sometime like apes that mow° and chatter at me,
And after bite me; then like hedgehogs which  10
Lie tumbling in my barefoot way and mount
Their pricks at my footfall; sometime am I
All wound with adders, who with cloven tongues
Do hiss me into madness.

*Enter* TRINCULO.

                    Lo, now, lo!
Here comes a spirit of his, and to torment me  15
For bringing wood in slowly. I'll fall flat.
Perchance he will not mind me.

[*Lies down.*]

TRINCULO  Here's neither bush nor shrub to bear off°
any weather at all, and another storm brewing; I
hear it sing i' th' wind. Yond same black cloud,  20
yond huge one, looks like a foul bombard° that
would shed his liquor. If it should thunder as it did
before, I know not where to hide my head. Yond
same cloud cannot choose but fall by pailfuls. What
have we here? A man or a fish? Dead or alive? A  25

---

325 **verily** the truth
**II.ii.3 By inchmeal** inch by inch  **5 urchin shows** impish
apparitions  **6 like a firebrand** in the form of a will-o'-the-
wisp  **9 mow** make faces  **18 bear off** ward off  **21 bombard** large leather jug

277 **feater** more becomingly  280 **kibe** chilblain on the heel
286 **that's dead** that is, if he were dead  289 **wink** eye-shut
293 **tell the clock** say yes

fish! He smells like a fish; a very ancient and fishlike smell; a kind of not of the newest Poor John.° A strange fish! Were I in England now, as once I was, and had but this fish painted,° not a holiday fool there but would give a piece of silver. There would this monster make a man;° any strange beast there makes a man. When they will not give a doit° to relieve a lame beggar, they will lay out ten to see a dead Indian. Legged like a man! And his fins like arms! Warm, o' my troth! I do now let loose my opinion, hold it no longer. This is no fish, but an islander, that hath lately suffered by a thunderbolt. [*Thunder.*] Alas, the storm is come again! My best way is to creep under his gaberdine; there is no other shelter hereabout. Misery acquaints a man with strange bedfellows. I will here shroud till the dregs of the storm be past. 30 35 40

*[Creeps under Caliban's garment.]*

*Enter* STEPHANO, *singing,* [*a bottle in his hand.*]

STEPHANO I shall no more to sea, to sea;
  Here shall I die ashore.
This is a very scurvy tune to sing at a man's funeral. Well, here's my comfort. 45

*Drinks.*

  The master, the swabber, the boatswain, and I,
    The gunner, and his mate,
  Loved Mall, Meg, and Marian, and Margery,
    But none of us cared for Kate.
  For she had a tongue with a tang,
    Would cry to a sailor, "Go hang!"
She loved not the savor of tar nor of pitch;
  Yet a tailor might scratch her where'er she did itch.
  Then to sea, boys, and let her go hang!
This is a scurvy tune too; but here's my comfort. 50 55

*Drinks.*

CALIBAN Do not torment me! O!
STEPHANO What's the matter? Have we devils here? Do you put tricks upon's with savages and men of Inde, ha? I have not 'scaped drowning to be afeard now of your four legs. For it hath been said, "As proper a man as ever went on four legs cannot make him give ground"; and it shall be said so again, while Stephano breathes at' nostrils.° 60
CALIBAN The spirit torments me. O!
STEPHANO This is some monster of the isle, with four legs, who hath got, as I take it, an ague. Where the devil should he learn our language? I will give him some relief, if it be but for that. If I can recover° him, and keep him tame, and get to Naples with him, he's a present for any emperor that ever trod on neat's leather.° 65 70
CALIBAN Do not torment me, prithee; I'll bring my wood home faster.
STEPHANO He's in his fit now and does not talk after the wisest. He shall taste of my bottle; if he have never drunk wine afore, it will go near to remove his 75

fit. If I can recover him and keep him tame, I will not take too much° for him. He shall pay for him that hath him, and that soundly.
CALIBAN Thou dost me yet but little hurt. Thou wilt anon;° I know it by thy trembling.° Now Prosper works upon thee. 80
STEPHANO Come on your ways, open your mouth; here is that which will give language to you, cat.° Open your mouth. This will shake your shaking, I can tell you, and that soundly. [*Gives* CALIBAN *drink.*] You cannot tell who's your friend. Open your chaps° again. 85
TRINCULO I should know that voice. It should be— but he is drowned; and these are devils. O, defend me! 90
STEPHANO Four legs and two voices—a most delicate monster! His forward voice now is to speak well of his friend; his backward voice is to utter foul speeches and to detract. If all the wine in my bottle will recover him, I will help his ague. Come! [*Gives drink.*] Amen! I will pour some in thy other mouth. 95
TRINCULO Stephano!
STEPHANO Doth thy other mouth call me? Mercy, mercy! This is a devil, and no monster. I will leave him; I have no long spoon.° 100
TRINCULO Stephano! If thou beest Stephano, touch me and speak to me; for I am Trinculo—be not afeard —thy good friend Trinculo.
STEPHANO If thou beest Trinculo, come forth. I'll pull thee by the lesser legs. If any be Trinculo's legs, these are they. [*Draws him out from under Caliban's garment.*] Thou art very Trinculo indeed! How cam'st thou to be the siege° of this mooncalf?° Can he vent Trinculos? 105
TRINCULO I took him to be killed with a thunder-stroke. But art thou not drowned, Stephano? I hope now thou art not drowned. Is the storm overblown? I hid me under the dead mooncalf's gaberdine for fear of the storm. And art thou living, Stephano? O Stephano, two Neapolitans scaped! 110
STEPHANO Prithee do not turn me about; my stomach is not constant. 115
CALIBAN [*Aside.*]
These be fine things, and if° they be not sprites.
That's a brave god and bears celestial liquor.
I will kneel to him.
STEPHANO How didst thou scape? How cam'st thou hither? Swear by this bottle how thou cam'st hither. I escaped upon a butt of sack which the sailors heaved o'erboard—by this bottle which I made of the bark of a tree with mine own hands since I was cast ashore. 120
CALIBAN I'll swear upon that bottle to be thy true subject, for the liquor is not earthly. 125
STEPHANO Here! Swear then how thou escap'dst.
TRINCULO Swum ashore, man, like a duck. I can swim like a duck, I'll be sworn.
STEPHANO Here, kiss the book. [*Gives him drink.*] Though thou canst swim like a duck, thou art made like a goose. 130

**77–78 not . . . much** too much will not be enough **81 anon** soon; **trembling** Trinculo is shaking with fear **84 cat** alluding to the proverb "Liquor will make a cat talk" **87 chaps** jaws **100 long spoon** alluding to the proverb "He who sups with (i.e., from the same dish as) the devil must have a long spoon" **108 siege** excrement; **mooncalf** monstrosity **117 and if** if

**27 Poor John** dried hake **29 painted** i.e., as a sign hung outside a booth at a fair **31 make a man** pun: make a man's fortune **32 doit** smallest coin **63 at' nostrils** at the nostrils **68 recover** cure **70–71 neat's leather** cowhide

TRINCULO   O Stephano, hast any more of this?

STEPHANO   The whole butt, man. My cellar is in a rock by th' seaside, where my wine is hid. How now, 135 mooncalf? How does thine ague?

CALIBAN   Hast thou not dropped from heaven?

STEPHANO   Out o' th' moon, I do assure thee. I was the Man i' th' Moon when time was.°

CALIBAN
I have seen thee in her, and I do adore thee.       140
My mistress showed me thee, and thy dog, and thy bush.°

STEPHANO   Come, swear to that; kiss the book. [*Gives him drink.*] I will furnish it anon with new contents. Swear.

[CALIBAN *drinks.*]

TRINCULO   By this good light, this is a very shallow 145 monster! I afeard of him? A very weak monster! The Man i' th' Moon? A most poor credulous monster! Well drawn,° monster, in good sooth!

CALIBAN
I'll show thee every fertile inch o' th' island;
And I will kiss thy foot. I prithee, be my god.       150

TRINCULO,   By this light, a most perfidious and drunken monster! When's god's asleep, he'll rob his bottle.

CALIBAN
I'll kiss thy foot. I'll swear myself thy subject.

STEPHANO   Come on then. Down, and swear!       155

TRINCULO   I shall laugh myself to death at this puppy-headed monster. A most scurvy monster! I could find in my heart to beat him—

STEPHANO   Come, kiss.

TRINCULO   But that the poor monster's in drink. An 160 abominable monster!

CALIBAN
I'll show thee the best springs; I'll pluck thee berries;
I'll fish for thee, and get thee wood enough.
A plague upon the tyrant that I serve!
I'll bear him no more sticks, but follow thee,       165
Thou wondrous man.

TRINCULO   A most ridiculous monster, to make a wonder of a poor drunkard!

CALIBAN
I prithee let me bring thee where crabs° grow;
And I with my long nails will dig thee pignuts,°       170
Show thee a jay's nest, and instruct thee how
To snare the nimble marmoset. I'll bring thee
To clust'ring filberts, and sometimes I'll get thee
Young scamels° from the rock. Wilt thou go with me?

STEPHANO   I prithee now, lead the way without any 175 more talking. Trinculo, the king and all our company else being drowned, we will inherit here. Here, bear my bottle. Fellow Trinculo, we'll fill him by and by again.

CALIBAN *sings drunkenly.*

CALIBAN   Farewell, master; farewell, farewell!       180

TRINCULO   A howling monster! A drunken monster!

CALIBAN
No more dams° I'll make for fish,
    Nor fetch in firing
    At requiring,
Nor scrape trenchering,° nor wash dish.       185
    'Ban, 'Ban, Ca—Caliban
    Has a new master. Get a new man!
Freedom, high day! High day, freedom! Freedom, high day, freedom!

STEPHANO   O brave monster! Lead the way. *Exeunt.* 190

# ACT III

Scene I. [*In front of Prospero's cell.*]

*Enter* FERDINAND, *bearing a log.*

FERDINAND
There be some sports are painful, and their labor
Delight in them sets off;° some kinds of baseness
Are nobly undergone, and most poor matters
Point to rich ends. This my mean task
Would be as heavy to me as odious, but       5
The mistress which I serve quickens° what's dead
And makes my labors pleasures. O, she is
Ten times more gentle than her father's crabbed;
And he's composed of harshness. I must remove
Some thousands of these logs and pile them up,       10
Upon a sore injunction.° My sweet mistresss
Weeps when she sees me work, and says such baseness
Had never like executor. I forget;°
But these sweet thoughts do even refresh my labors,
Most busiest when I do it.°

*Enter* MIRANDA; *and* PROSPERO [*behind, unseen*].

MIRANDA                Alas, now pray you,       15
Work not so hard! I would the lightning had
Burnt up those logs that you are enjoined to pile!
Pray set it down and rest you. When this burns,
'Twill weep° for having wearied you. My father
Is hard at study; pray now rest yourself;       20
He's safe for these three hours.

FERDINAND                O most dear mistress,
The sun will set before I shall discharge
What I must strive to do.

MIRANDA                If you'll sit down,
I'll bear your logs the while. Pray give me that;
I'll carry it to the pile.

FERDINAND                No, precious creature,       25
I had rather crack my sinews, break my back,
Than you should such dishonor undergo
While I sit lazy by.

---

**139 when time was** once upon a time   **141–42 thee . . . bush** the Man in the Moon was banished there, according to legend, for gathering brushwood with his dog on Sunday   **148 Well drawn** a good pull at the bottle   **169 crabs** crab-apples   **170 pignuts** earthnuts   **174 scamels** perhaps a misprint for "seamels" or "seamews," a kind of sea bird

**182 dams** to catch fish and keep them   **185 trenchering** trenchers, wooden plates   **III.i.2 sets off** cancels   **6 quickens** brings to life   **11 sore injunction** severe command   **13 forget** i.e., my task   **15 Most . . . it** i.e., my thoughts are busiest when I am (the Folio's "busie lest" has been variously emended; "it" may refer to "task," line 4, the understood object in line 13)   **19 weep** i.e., exude resin

MIRANDA                    It would become me
As well as it does you; and I should do it
With much more ease; for my good will is to it,     30
And yours it is against.

PROSPERO          [*Aside.*] Poor worm, thou art infected!
This visitation° shows it.

MIRANDA                    You look wearily.

FERDINAND
No, noble mistress, 'tis fresh morning with me
When you are by at night.° I do beseech you,
Chiefly that I might set it in my prayers,     35
What is your name?

MIRANDA                    Miranda. O my father,
I have broke your hest° to say so!

FERDINAND                    Admired Miranda!°
Indeed the top of admiration, worth
What's dearest to the world! Full many a lady
I have eyed with best regard, and many a time     40
Th' harmony of their tongues hath into bondage
Brought my too diligent ear. For several virtues
Have I liked several women; never any
With so full soul but some defect in her
Did quarrel with the noblest grace she owed,°     45
And put it to the foil.° But you, O you,
So perfect and so peerless, are created
Of every creature's best.

MIRANDA                    I do not know
One of my sex; no woman's face remember,
Save, from my glass, mine own. Nor have I seen     50
More that I may call men than you, good friend,
And my dear father. How features are abroad
I am skilless° of; but, by my modesty
(The jewel in my dower), I would not wish
Any companion in the world but you;     55
Nor can imagination form a shape,
Besides yourself, to like of.° But I prattle
Something too wildly, and my father's precepts
I therein do forget.

FERDINAND          I am, in my condition,
A prince, Miranda; I do think, a king     60
(I would not so), and would no more endure
This wooden slavery than to suffer
The fleshfly blow my mouth. Hear my soul speak!
The very instant that I saw you, did
My heart fly to your service; there resides,     65
To make me slave to it; and for your sake
Am I this patient log-man.

MIRANDA                    Do you love me?

FERDINAND
O heaven, O earth, bear witness to this sound,
And crown what I profess with kind event°
If I speak true! If hollowly, invert     70
What best is boded me° to mischief! I,
Beyond all limit of what else i' th' world,
Do love, prize, honor you.

MIRANDA                    I am a fool
To weep at what I am glad of.

PROSPERO          [*Aside.*] Fair encounter
Of two most rare affections! Heavens rain grace     75
On that which breeds between 'em!

FERDINAND                    Wherefore weep you?

MIRANDA
At mine unworthiness, that dare not offer
What I desire to give, and much less take
What I shall die to want.° But this is trifling;°
And all the more it seeks to hide itself,     80
The bigger bulk it shows. Hence, bashful cunning,
And prompt me, plain and holy innocence!
I am your wife, if you will marry me;
If not, I'll die your maid. To be your fellow°
You may deny me; but I'll be your servant,     85
Whether you will or no.

FERDINAND                    My mistress, dearest,
And I thus humble ever.

MIRANDA                    My husband then?

FERDINAND
Ay, with a heart as willing
As bondage e'er of freedom.° Here's my hand.

MIRANDA
And mine, with my heart in't; and now farewell     90
Till half an hour hence.

FERDINAND                    A thousand thousand!

*Exeunt* [FERDINAND *and* MIRANDA *in different
directions*].

PROSPERO
So glad of this as they I cannot be,
Who are surprised withal;° but my rejoicing
At nothing can be more. I'll to my book;
For yet ere suppertime must I perform     95
Much business appertaining.°          *Exit.*

Scene II. [*Another part of the island.*]

*Enter* CALIBAN, STEPHANO, *and* TRINCULO.

STEPHANO  Tell not me! When the butt is out, we
will drink water; not a drop before. Therefore bear up
and board 'em!° Servant monster, drink to me.

TRINCULO  Servant monster? The folly of this island!
They say there's but five upon this isle; we are three     5
of them. If th' other two be brained like us, the state
totters.

STEPHANO  Drink, servant monster, when I bid thee;
thy eyes are almost set in thy head.

TRINCULO  Where should they be set else? He were a     10
brave monster indeed if they were set in his tail.

STEPHANO  My man-monster hath drowned his
tongue in sack. For my part, the sea cannot drown me.
I swam, ere I could recover the shore, five-and-thirty
leagues off and on, by this light. Thou shalt be my     15
lieutenant, monster, or my standard.°

TRINCULO  Your lieutenant, if you list;° he's no
standard.

STEPHANO  We'll not run,° Monsieur Monster.

32 **visitation** (1) visit (2) attack of plague (referring to metaphor of "infected")  34 **at night** i.e., even at night when I am
very tired  37 **hest** command; **Admired Miranda** *admired*
means "to be wondered at"; the Latin *Miranda* means "wonderful"  45 **owed** owned  46 **put . . . foil** defeated it  53
**skilless** ignorant  57 **like of** like  69 **event** outcome  71
**What . . . me** whatever good fortune fate has in store for me

79 **to want** if I lack; **trifling** i.e., to speak in riddles like this
84 **fellow** equal  89 **of freedom** i.e., to win freedom  93
**withal** by it  96 **appertaining** i.e., to my plan
**III.ii.2–3 bear . . . 'em** i.e., drink up  16 **standard** standard-
bearer, ensign (pun, since Caliban is so drunk he cannot stand)
17 **if you list** if it please you (with pun on *list* as pertaining
to a ship that leans over to one side)

TRINCULO   Nor go° neither; but you'll lie° like dogs, 20
and yet say nothing neither.
STEPHANO   Mooncalf, speak once in thy life, if thou
beest a good mooncalf.
CALIBAN   How does thy honor? Let me lick thy shoe.
I'll not serve him; he is not valiant.                          25
TRINCULO   Thou liest, most ignorant monster; I am
in case° to justle° a constable. Why, thou deboshed°
fish thou, was there ever man a coward that hath
drunk so much sack as I today? Wilt thou tell a
monstrous lie, being but half a fish and half a monster? 30
CALIBAN   Lo, how he mocks me! Wilt thou let him,
my lord?
TRINCULO   "Lord" quoth he? That a monster should
be such a natural!°
CALIBAN
Lo, lo, again! Bite him to death, I prithee.            35
STEPHANO   Trinculo, keep a good tongue in your
head. If you prove a mutineer—the next tree!° The
poor monster's my subject, and he shall not suffer
indignity.
CALIBAN
I thank my noble lord. Wilt thou be pleased      40
To hearken once again to the suit I made to thee?
STEPHANO   Marry,° will I. Kneel and repeat it; I will
stand, and so shall Trinculo.

*Enter* ARIEL, *invisible.*

CALIBAN
As I told thee before, I am subject to a tyrant,
A sorcerer, that by his cunning hath                    45
Cheated me of the island.
ARIEL
Thou liest.
CALIBAN   Thou liest, thou jesting monkey thou!
I would my valiant master would destroy thee.
I do not lie.
STEPHANO   Trinculo, if you trouble him any more 50
in's tale, by this hand, I will supplant some of your
teeth.
TRINCULO   Why, I said nothing.
STEPHANO   Mum then, and no more. Proceed.
CALIBAN
I say by sorcery he got this isle;                          55
From me he got it. If thy greatness will
Revenge it on him—for I know thou dar'st,
But this thing° dare not—
STEPHANO   That's most certain.
CALIBAN
Thou shalt be lord of it, and I'll serve thee.      60
STEPHANO
How now shall this be compassed?
Canst thou bring me to the party?
CALIBAN
Yea, yea, my lord! I'll yield him thee asleep,
Where thou mayst knock a nail into his head.
ARIEL   Thou liest; thou canst not.                        65

CALIBAN
What a pied° ninny's this! Thou scurvy patch!°
I do beseech thy greatness, give him blows
And take his bottle from him. When that's gone,
He shall drink naught but brine, for I'll not show him
Where the quick freshes° are.                             70
STEPHANO   Trinculo, run into no further danger!
Interrupt the monster one word further and, by this
hand, I'll turn my mercy out o' doors and make a
stockfish° of thee.
TRINCULO   Why, what did I? I did nothing. I'll go 75
farther off.
STEPHANO   Didst thou not say he lied?
ARIEL   Thou liest.
STEPHANO   Do I so? Take thou that! [*Strikes* TRIN-
CULO.] As you like this, give me the lie another time. 80
TRINCULO   I did not give the lie. Out o' your wits,
and hearing too? A pox o' your bottle! This can sack
and drinking do. A murrain° on your monster, and
the devil take your fingers!
CALIBAN   Ha, ha, ha!                                          85
STEPHANO   Now forward with your tale. [*To*
TRINCULO.] Prithee, stand further off.
CALIBAN
Beat him enough. After a little time
I'll beat him too.
STEPHANO                Stand farther. Come, proceed.
CALIBAN
Why, as I told thee, 'tis a custom with him      90
I' th' afternoon to sleep. There thou mayst brain him,
Having first seized his books, or with a log
Batter his skull, or paunch° him with a stake,
Or cut his wezand° with thy knife. Remember
First to possess his books; for without them      95
He's but a sot,° as I am, nor hath not
One spirit to command. They all do hate him
As rootedly as I. Burn but his books.
He has brave utensils° (for so he calls them)
Which, when he has a house, he'll deck withal.  100
And that most deeply to consider is
The beauty of his daughter. He himself
Calls her a nonpareil. I never saw a woman
But only Sycorax my dam and she;
But she as far surpasseth Sycorax                     105
As great'st does least.
STEPHANO                Is it so brave a lass?
CALIBAN
Ay, lord. She will become thy bed, I warrant,
And bring thee forth brave brood.
STEPHANO   Monster, I will kill this man. His daughter
and I will be king and queen—save our graces!—and 110
Trinculo and thyself shall be viceroys. Dost thou like
the plot, Trinculo?
TRINCULO   Excellent.
STEPHANO   Give me thy hand. I am sorry I beat thee;
but while thou liv'st, keep a good tongue in thy head. 115

---

19–20 **run, lie** with puns on secondary meanings: "make
water," "excrete"  20 **go** walk  27 **case** fit condition; **justle**
jostle; **deboshed** debauched  34 **natural** idiot  37 **the next
tree** i.e., you will be hanged  42 **Marry** an expletive, from
"By the Virgin Mary"  58 **this thing** Trinculo

66 **pied** referring to Trinculo's parti-colored jester's costume;
**patch** clown  70 **quick freshes** living springs of fresh water
74 **stockfish** dried cod, softened by beating  83 **murrain**
plague (that infects cattle)  93 **paunch** stab in the belly  94
**wezand** windpipe  96 **sot** fool  99 **brave utensils** fine
furnishings (pronounced "útensils")

CALIBAN
Within this half hour will he be asleep.
Wilt thou destroy him then?
STEPHANO              Ay, on mine honor.
ARIEL
This will I tell my master.
CALIBAN
Thou mak'st me merry; I am full of pleasure.
Let us be jocund. Will you troll the catch°     120
You taught me but whilere?°
STEPHANO    At thy request, monster, I will do reason,
any reason.° Come on, Trinculo, let us sing.

*Sings.*

       Flout 'em and scout° 'em
       And scout 'em and flout 'em!     125
       Thought is free.
CALIBAN
That's not the tune.

ARIEL *plays the tune on a tabor° and pipe.*

STEPHANO    What is this same?
TRINCULO    This is the tune of our catch, played by the
picture of Nobody.°     130
STEPHANO    If thou beest a man, show thyself in thy
likeness. If thou beest a devil, take't as thou list.
TRINCULO    O, forgive me my sins!
STEPHANO    He that dies pays all debts. I defy thee.
Mercy upon us!     135
CALIBAN
Art thou afeard?
STEPHANO    No, monster, not I.
CALIBAN
Be not afeard; the isle is full of noises,
Sounds and sweet airs that give delight and hurt not.
Sometimes a thousand twangling instruments     140
Will hum about mine ears; and sometime voices
That, if I then had waked after long sleep,
Will make me sleep again; and then, in dreaming,
The clouds methought would open and show riches
Ready to drop upon me, that, when I waked,     145
I cried to dream again.
STEPHANO    This will prove a brave kingdom to me,
where I shall have my music for nothing.
CALIBAN
When Prospero is destroyed.
STEPHANO    That shall be by and by; I remember the    150
story.
TRINCULO    The sound is going away; let's follow it,
and after do our work.
STEPHANO    Lead, monster; we'll follow. I would I
could see this taborer; he lays it on.     155
TRINCULO [*To* CALIBAN.]    Wilt come?° I'll follow
Stephano.                    *Exeunt.*

Scene III. [*Another part of the island.*]

*Enter* ALONSO, SEBASTIAN, ANTONIO, GONZALO,
ADRIAN, FRANCISCO, &c.

GONZALO
By'r Lakin,° I can go no further, sir;
My old bones aches. Here's a maze trod indeed
Through forthrights and meanders.° By your patience,
I needs must rest me.
ALONSO           Old lord, I cannot blame thee,
Who am myself attached° with weariness     5
To th' dulling of my spirits. Sit down and rest.
Even here I will put off my hope, and keep it
No longer for my flatterer. He is drowned
Whom thus we stray to find; and the sea mocks
Our frustrate search on land. Well, let him go.     10
ANTONIO [*Aside to* SEBASTIAN.]
I am right glad that he's so out of hope.
Do not for one repulse forgo the purpose
That you resolved t' effect.
SEBASTIAN [*Aside to* ANTONIO.]    The next advantage
Will we take throughly.°
ANTONIO [*Aside to* SEBASTIAN.]    Let it be tonight;
For, now they are oppressed with travel, they     15
Will not nor cannot use such vigilance
As when they are fresh.
SEBASTIAN [*Aside to* ANTONIO.]    I say tonight. No
    more.

*Solemn and strange music; and* PROSPERO *on the top*°
*(invisible). Enter several strange* SHAPES, *bringing in a
banquet; and dance about it with gentle actions of salutations;
and, inviting the king [*ALONSO] &c. to eat, they depart.*

ALONSO
What harmony is this? My good friends, hark!
GONZALO
Marvelous sweet music!
ALONSO
Give us kind keepers,° heavens! What were these?     20
SEBASTIAN
A living drollery.° Now I will believe
That there are unicorns; that in Arabia
There is one tree, the phoenix' throne; one phoenix
At this hour reigning there.
ANTONIO          I'll believe both;
And what does else want credit,° come to me,     25
And I'll be sworn 'tis true. Travelers ne'er did lie,
Though fools at home condemn 'em.
GONZALO            If in Naples
I should report this now, would they believe me
If I should say I saw such islanders?
(For certes these are people of the island)     30
Who, though they are of monstrous shape, yet note,
Their manners are more gentle, kind, than of
Our human generation you shall find
Many—nay, almost any.
PROSPERO        [*Aside.*] Honest lord,

---

120 **troll the catch** sing the round    121 **but whilere** just now
122–23 **reason, any reason** i.e., anything within reason    124
**scout** jeer at    127 **s.d. tabor** small drum worn at the side
130 **Nobody** alluding to the picture of No-body—a man all
head, legs, and arms, but without trunk—on the title page of
the anonymous comedy *No-body and Some-body*    156 **Wilt
come** Caliban lingers because the other two are being
distracted from his purpose by the music

**III.iii.1 By'r Lakin** by our Lady    3 **forthrights and meanders** straight and winding paths    5 **attached** seized    14
**throughly** thoroughly    17 **s.d. the top** upper stage (or perhaps
a playing area above it)    20 **kind keepers** guardian angels
21 **drollery** puppet show    25 **credit** believing

Thou hast said well; for some of you there present 35
Are worse than devils.

ALONSO                                   I cannot too much muse°
Such shapes, such gesture, and such sound, expressing
(Although they want the use of tongue) a kind
Of excellent dumb discourse.

PROSPERO          [*Aside.*] Praise in departing.°

FRANCISCO
They vanished strangely.

SEBASTIAN                           No matter, since 40
They have left their viands behind; for we have
    stomachs.
Will't please you taste of what is here?

ALONSO                                        Not I.

GONZALO
Faith, sir, you need not fear. When we were boys,
Who would believe that there were mountaineers
Dewlapped° like bulls, whose throats had hanging at
    'em 45
Wallets of flesh? Or that there were such men
Whose heads stood in their breasts? Which now we
    find
Each putter-out of five for one° will bring us
Good warrant of.

ALONSO                         I will stand to, and feed;
Although my last, no matter, since I feel 50
The best is past. Brother, my lord the duke,
Stand to, and do as we.

*Thunder and lightning. Enter* ARIEL, *like a harpy; claps
his wings upon the table; and with a quaint device*° *the
banquet vanishes.*

ARIEL
You are three men of sin, whom destiny—
That hath to instrument° this lower world
And what is in't—the never-surfeited sea 55
Hath caused to belch up you and on this island,
Where man doth not inhabit, you 'mongst men
Being most unfit to live. I have made you mad;
And even with suchlike valor° men hang and drown
Their proper selves. [ALONSO, SEBASTIAN, *&c. draw
    their swords.*] You fools! I and my fellows 60
Are ministers of Fate. The elements,
Of whom your swords are tempered,° may as well
Wound the loud winds, or with bemocked-at stabs
Kill the still-closing° waters, as diminish
One dowle° that's in my plume.° My fellow ministers 65
Are like invulnerable. If you could hurt,°
Your swords are now too massy° for your strengths
And will not be uplifted. But remember
(For that's my business to you) that you three
From Milan did supplant good Prospero; 70

Exposed unto the sea, which hath requit it,°
Him and his innocent child; for which foul deed
The pow'rs, delaying, not forgetting, have
Incensed the seas and shores, yea, all the creatures,
Against your peace. Thee of thy son, Alonso, 75
They have bereft; and do pronounce by me
Ling'ring perdition (worse than any death
Can be at once) shall step by step attend
You and your ways; whose wraths to guard you from,
Which here, in this most desolate isle, else falls 80
Upon your heads, is nothing but heart's sorrow°
And a clear life ensuing.

*He vanishes in thunder; then, to soft music, enter the*
SHAPES *again, and dance with mocks and mows,*° *and
carrying out the table.*

PROSPERO
Bravely the figure of this harpy hast thou
Performed, my Ariel; a grace it had, devouring.°
Of my instruction hast thou nothing bated° 85
In what thou hadst to say. So, with good life°
And observation strange,° my meaner ministers°
Their several kinds have done.° My high charms work,
And these, mine enemies, are all knit up
In their distractions. They now are in my pow'r; 90
And in these fits I leave them, while I visit
Young Ferdinand, whom they suppose is drowned,
And his and mine loved darling.          [*Exit above.*]

GONZALO
I' th' name of something holy, sir, why stand you
In this strange stare?

ALONSO                         O, it is monstrous, monstrous! 95
Methought the billows spoke and told me of it;
The winds did sing it to me; and the thunder,
That deep and dreadful organ pipe, pronounced
The name of Prosper; it did bass my trespass.°
Therefore my son i' th' ooze is bedded; and 100
I'll seek him deeper than e'er plummet sounded
And with him there lie mudded.                    *Exit.*

SEBASTIAN                              But one fiend at a time,
I'll fight their legions o'er!°

ANTONIO                              I'll be thy second.

                    *Exeunt* [SEBASTIAN *and* ANTONIO].

GONZALO
All three of them are desperate; their great guilt,
Like poison given to work a great time after, 105
Now 'gins to bite the spirits. I do beseech you,
That are of suppler joints, follow them swiftly
And hinder them from what this ecstasy°
May now provoke them to.

ADRIAN                              Follow, I pray you.

                              *Exeunt omnes.*

---

**36 muse** wonder at   **39 Praise in departing** Save your
praise for the end   **45 Dewlapped** with skin hanging from
the neck (like mountaineers with goiter)   **48 putter-out . . .
one** traveler who insures himself by depositing a sum of
money to be repaid fivefold if he returns safely (i.e., any
ordinary traveler will confirm nowadays those reports we used
to think fanciful)   **52 s.d. quaint device** ingenious device (of
stage mechanism)   **54 to instrument** as its instrument   **59
suchlike valor** i.e., the courage that comes of madness   **62
tempered** composed   **64 still-closing** ever closing again (as
soon as wounded)   **65 dowle** bit of down; **plume** plumage
**66 If . . . hurt** even if you could hurt us   **67 massy** heavy

**71 requit it** avenged that crime   **81 nothing . . . sorrow**
only repentance (will protect you from the wrath of these
powers)   **82 s.d. mocks and mows** mocking gestures and
grimaces   **84 devouring** i.e., in making the banquet disappear
**85 bated** omitted   **86 good life** good lifelike acting   **87
observation strange** remarkable attention to my wishes;
**meaner ministers** i.e., inferior to Ariel   **88 Their . . . done**
have acted the parts their natures suited them for   **99 bass my
trespass** i.e., made me understand my trespass by turning it
into music for which the thunder provided the bass part   **103
o'er** one after another to the last   **108 ecstasy** madness

# ACT IV

## Scene I. [*In front of Prospero's cell.*]

*Enter* PROSPERO, FERDINAND, *and* MIRANDA.

PROSPERO
If I have too austerely punished you,
Your compensation makes amends; for I
Have given you here a third of mine own life,
Or that for which I live; who once again
I tender to thy hand. All thy vexations                    5
Were but my trials of thy love, and thou
Hast strangely° stood the test. Here, afore heaven,
I ratify this my rich gift. O Ferdinand,
Do not smile at me that I boast her off,°
For thou shalt find she will outstrip all praise          10
And make it halt° behind her.

FERDINAND                          I do believe it
Against an oracle.°

PROSPERO
Then, as my gift, and thine own acquisition
Worthily purchased, take my daughter. But
If thou dost break her virgin-knot before                 15
All sanctimonious° ceremonies may
With full and holy rite be minist'red,
No sweet aspersion° shall the heavens let fall
To make this contract grow;° but barren hate,
Sour-eyed disdain, and discord shall bestrew             20
The union of your bed with weeds so loathly
That you shall hate it both. Therefore take heed,
As Hymen's lamps shall light you.°

FERDINAND                          As I hope
For quiet days, fair issue, and long life,
With such love as 'tis now, the murkiest den,            25
The most opportune° place, the strong'st suggestion
Our worser genius can,° shall never melt
Mine honor into lust, to take away
The edge° of that day's celebration
When I shall think or Phoebus' steeds are foundered°     30
Or Night kept chained below.°

PROSPERO                          Fairly spoke.
Sit then and talk with her; she is thine own.
What, Ariel! My industrious servant, Ariel!

*Enter* ARIEL.

ARIEL
What would my potent master? Here I am.

PROSPERO
Thou and thy meaner fellows your last service            35
Did worthily perform; and I must use you
In such another trick. Go bring the rabble,°
O'er whom I give thee pow'r, here to this place.

Incite them to quick motion; for I must
Bestow upon the eyes of this young couple               40
Some vanity of° mine art. It is my promise,
And they expect it from me.

ARIEL                              Presently?

PROSPERO
Ay, with a twink.

ARIEL
Before you can say "Come" and "Go,"
And breathe twice and cry, "So, so,"                    45
Each one, tripping on his toe,
Will be here with mop and mow.°
Do you love me, master? No?

PROSPERO
Dearly, my delicate Ariel. Do not approach
Till thou dost hear me call.

ARIEL                          Well; I conceive.°  *Exit.*  50

PROSPERO
Look thou be true.° Do not give dalliance
Too much the rein; the strongest oaths are straw
To th' fire i' th' blood. Be more abstemious,
Or else good night your vow!

FERDINAND                          I warrant you, sir.
The white cold virgin snow upon my heart°              55
Abates the ardor of my liver.°

PROSPERO                          Well.
Now come, my Ariel; bring a corollary°
Rather than want a spirit. Appear, and pertly!
No tongue! All eyes! Be silent.

*Soft music. Enter* IRIS.°

IRIS
Ceres, most bounteous lady, thy rich leas°             60
Of wheat, rye, barley, fetches,° oats, and peas;
Thy turfy mountains, where live nibbling sheep,
And flat meads thatched with stover,° them to keep;
Thy banks with pionèd and twillèd brims,°
Which spongy April at thy hest betrims                  65
To make cold nymphs chaste crowns; and thy broom
   groves,
Whose shadow the dismissèd bachelor loves,
Being lasslorn; thy pole-clipt vineyard;°
And thy sea-marge, sterile and rocky-hard,
Where thou thyself dost air°—the queen o' th' sky,°    70
Whose wat'ry arch and messenger am I,
Bids thee leave these, and with her sovereign grace,

JUNO *descends.*°

Here on this grass plot, in this very place,

To come and sport; her peacocks fly amain.°
Approach, rich Ceres, her to entertain.                                75

*Enter* CERES.

CERES
Hail, many-colored messenger, that ne'er
Dost disobey the wife of Jupiter,
Who, with thy saffron wings, upon my flow'rs
Diffusest honey drops, refreshing show'rs,
And with each end of thy blue bow dost crown          80
My bosky° acres and my unshrubbed down,
Rich scarf to my proud earth. Why hath thy queen
Summoned me hither to this short-grassed green?

IRIS
A contract of true love to celebrate
And some donation freely to estate°                         85
On the blessed lovers.

CERES                            Tell me, heavenly bow,
If Venus or her son, as thou dost know,
Do now attend the queen? Since they did plot
The means that dusky Dis my daughter got,°
Her and her blind boy's scandaled° company             90
I have forsworn.

IRIS                        Of her society
Be not afraid; I met her deity
Cutting the clouds towards Paphos,° and her son
Dove-drawn with her. Here thought they to have done
Some wanton charm upon this man and maid,             95
Whose vows are, that no bed-right shall be paid
Till Hymen's torch be lighted. But in vain;
Mars's hot minion is returned again;°
Her waspish-headed son° has broke his arrows,
Swears he will shoot no more, but play with sparrows 100
And be a boy right out.°

[JUNO *alights*.]

CERES                            Highest queen of state,
Great Juno, comes; I know her by her gait.

JUNO
How does my bounteous sister? Go with me
To bless this twain, that they may prosperous be
And honored in their issue.                               105

*They sing.*

JUNO        Honor, riches, marriage blessing,
            Long continuance, and increasing,
            Hourly joys be still° upon you!
            Juno sings her blessings on you.
[CERES] Earth's increase, foison° plenty,           110
            Barns and garners never empty,
            Vines with clust'ring bunches growing,
            Plants with goodly burden bowing;
            Spring come to you at the farthest
            In the very end of harvest.°                115
            Scarcity and want shall shun you,
            Ceres' blessing so is on you.

FERDINAND
This is a most majestic vision, and
Harmonious charmingly. May I be bold
To think these spirits?

PROSPERO                    Spirits, which by mine art  120
I have from their confines called to enact
My present fancies.

FERDINAND            Let me live here ever!
So rare a wond'red° father and a wise
Makes this place Paradise.

JUNO *and* CERES *whisper, and send* IRIS *on employment.*

PROSPERO                        Sweet now, silence!
Juno and Ceres whisper seriously.                      125
There's something else to do. Hush and be mute,
Or else our spell is marred.

IRIS
You nymphs, called Naiades, of the windring° brooks,
With your sedged crowns and ever-harmless looks,
Leave your crisp° channels, and on this green land  130
Answer your summons; Juno does command.
Come, temperate nymphs, and help to celebrate
A contract of true love; be not too late.

*Enter certain* NYMPHS.

You sunburned sicklemen, of August weary,
Come hither from the furrow and be merry.            135
Make holiday; your rye-straw hats put on,
And these fresh nymphs encounter everyone
In country footing.°

*Enter certain* REAPERS, *properly habited. They join with
the* NYMPHS *in a graceful dance; towards the end whereof*
PROSPERO *starts suddenly and speaks;° after which, to a
strange, hollow, and confused noise, they heavily° vanish.*

PROSPERO [*Aside*.]
I had forgot that foul conspiracy
Of the beast Caliban and his confederates            140
Against my life. The minute of their plot
Is almost come. [*To the* SPIRITS.] Well done! Avoid!°
    No more!

FERDINAND
This is strange. Your father's in some passion
That works him strongly.

MIRANDA                        Never till this day
Saw I him touched with anger so distempered.°       145

PROSPERO
You do look, my son, in a movèd sort,°
As if you were dismayed; be cheerful, sir.
Our revels now are ended. These our actors,
As I foretold you, were all spirits and
Are melted into air, into thin air;                     150
And, like the baseless fabric of this vision,
The cloud-capped towers, the gorgeous palaces,
The solemn temples, the great globe itself,
Yea, all which it inherit,° shall dissolve,

74 amain swiftly (peacocks, sacred to Juno, drew her chariot)
81 bosky shrubbed   85 estate bestow   89 dusky . . . got
alluding to the abduction of Proserpine by Pluto (Dis), god of
the underworld   90 scandaled scandalous   93 Paphos in
Cyprus, center of Venus' cult   98 Mars's . . . again Mars's
lustful mistress (Venus) is on her way back to Paphos   99
waspish-headed son Cupid is irritable and stings with his
arrows   101 boy right out an ordinary boy   108 still ever
110 foison abundance   114–15 Spring . . . harvest i.e.,
May there be no winter in your lives

123 wond'red possessed of wonders; i.e., both wonderful and
wonder-working, and therefore to be wondered at   128
windring winding and wandering (?)   130 crisp rippling
138 footing dance   138 s.d. speaks breaking the spell, which
depends on silence; heavily reluctantly   142 Avoid Begone!
145 distempered violent   146 movèd sort troubled state
154 it inherit occupy it

And, like this insubstantial pageant faded,                        155
Leave not a rack° behind. We are such stuff
As dreams are made on, and our little life
Is rounded with a sleep. Sir, I am vexed.
Bear with my weakness; my old brain is troubled.
Be not disturbed with my infirmity.                                160
If you be pleased, retire into my cell
And there repose. A turn or two I'll walk
To still my beating mind.
FERDINAND, MIRANDA  We wish your peace.
                    *Exit* [FERDINAND, *with* MIRANDA].
PROSPERO
Come with a thought! I thank thee,° Ariel. Come.

*Enter* ARIEL.

ARIEL
Thy thoughts I cleave to. What's thy pleasure?
PROSPERO                                    Spirit,    165
We must prepare to meet with Caliban.
ARIEL
Ay, my commander. When I presented° Ceres,
I thought to have told thee of it, but I feared
Lest I might anger thee.
PROSPERO
Say again, where didst thou leave these varlets?°  170
ARIEL
I told you, sir, they were red-hot with drinking;
So full of valor that they smote the air
For breathing in their faces, beat the ground
For kissing of their feet; yet always bending°
Towards their project. Then I beat my tabor;         175
At which like unbacked° colts they pricked their ears,
Advanced° their eyelids, lifted up their noses
As they smelt music. So I charmed their ears
That calflike they my lowing followed through
Toothed briers, sharp furzes, pricking goss,° and    180
    thorns,
Which ent'red their frail shins. At last I left them
I' th' filthy mantled° pool beyond your cell,
There dancing up to th' chins, that the foul lake
O'erstunk their feet.
PROSPERO            This was well done, my bird.
Thy shape invisible retain thou still.               185
The trumpery° in my house, go bring it hither
For stale° to catch these thieves.
ARIEL                    I go, I go.           *Exit.*
PROSPERO
A devil, a born devil, on whose nature
Nurture can never stick; on whom my pains,
Humanely taken, all, all lost, quite lost!           190
And as with age his body uglier grows,
So his mind cankers. I will plague them all,
Even to roaring.

*Enter* ARIEL, *loaden with glistering apparel, &c.*

        Come, hang them on this line.°

[PROSPERO *and* ARIEL *remain, invisible.*] *Enter* CALI-
BAN, STEPHANO, *and* TRINCULO, *all wet.*

CALIBAN
Pray you tread softly, that the blind mole may not
Hear a foot fall. We now are near his cell.          195
STEPHANO  Monster, your fairy, which you say is a
harmless fairy, has done little better than played the
Jack° with us.
TRINCULO  Monster, I do smell all horse piss, at which
my nose is in great indignation.                     200
STEPHANO  So is mine. Do you hear, monster? If I
should take a displeasure against you, look you—
TRINCULO  Thou wert but a lost monster.
CALIBAN
Good my lord, give me thy favor still.
Be patient, for the prize I'll bring thee to         205
Shall hoodwink° this mischance. Therefore speak
    softly.
All's hushed as midnight yet.
TRINCULO  Ay, but to lose our bottles in the pool—
STEPHANO  There is not only disgrace and dishonor in
that, monster, but an infinite loss.                 210
TRINCULO  That's more to me than my wetting. Yet
this is your harmless fairy, monster.
STEPHANO  I will fetch off my bottle, though I be o'er
ears° for my labor.
CALIBAN
Prithee, my king, be quiet. See'st thou here?        215
This is the mouth o' th' cell. No noise, and enter.
Do that good mischief which may make this island
Thine own forever, and I, thy Caliban,
For aye thy footlicker.
STEPHANO  Give me thy hand. I do begin to have       220
bloody thoughts.
TRINCULO  O King Stephano! O peer!° O worthy
Stephano, look what a wardrobe here is for thee!
CALIBAN
Let it alone, thou fool! It is but trash.
TRINCULO  O, ho, monster! We know what belongs      225
to a frippery.° O King Stephano!
STEPHANO  Put off that gown, Trinculo! By this
hand, I'll have that gown!
TRINCULO  Thy grace shall have it.
CALIBAN
The dropsy drown this fool! What do you mean         230
To dote thus on such luggage?° Let't alone,
And do the murder first. If he awake,
From toe to crown he'll fill our skins with pinches,
Make us strange stuff.
STEPHANO  Be you quiet, monster. Mistress line, is not 235
this my jerkin?° [*Takes it down.*] Now is the jerkin
under the line.° Now, jerkin, you are like to lose your
hair and prove a bald jerkin.°

---

156 **rack** wisp of cloud   164 **I thank thee** i.e., for the masque
(?)   167 **presented** acted the part of (?) introduced (?)   170
**varlets** ruffians   174 **bending** directing their steps   176
**unbacked** unbroken   177 **Advanced** lifted up   180 **goss** gorse
182 **filthy mantled** covered with filthy scum   186 **trumpery**
the "glistering apparel" mentioned in the next stage direction
187 **stale** decoy   193 **line** lime tree (linden)

198 **Jack** (1) knave (2) jack-o'-lantern, will-o'-the-wisp   206
**hoodwink** put out of sight   213–14 **o'er ears** i.e., over
my ears in water   222 **peer** alluding to the song "King Stephen
was and a worthy peer;/His breeches cost him but a crown,"
quoted in *Othello* II.iii   226 **frippery** old-clothes shop; i.e.,
we are good judges of castoff clothes   231 **luggage** useless
encumbrances   236 **jerkin** kind of jacket   237 **under the
line** pun: (1) under the lime tree (2) under the equator   238
**bald jerkin** sailors proverbially lost their hair from fevers
contracted while crossing the equator

TRINCULO  Do, do!° We steal by line and level,°
and't like° your grace.                                          240

STEPHANO  I thank thee for that jest. Here's a garment
for't. Wit shall not go unrewarded while I am king of
this country. "Steal by line and level" is an excellent
pass of pate.° There's another garment for't.

TRINCULO  Monster, come put some lime° upon your  245
fingers, and away with the rest.

CALIBAN
I will have none on't. We shall lose our time
And all be turned to barnacles,° or to apes
With foreheads villainous low.

STEPHANO  Monster, lay-to your fingers; help to bear  250
this away where my hogshead of wine is, or I'll turn
you out of my kingdom. Go to, carry this.

TRINCULO  And this.

STEPHANO  Ay, and this.

*A noise of hunters heard. Enter divers* SPIRITS *in shape of
dogs and hounds, hunting them about;* PROSPERO *and*
ARIEL *setting them on.*

PROSPERO  Hey, Mountain, hey!                              255

ARIEL  Silver! There it goes, Silver!

PROSPERO
Fury, Fury! There, Tyrant, there! Hark, hark!
[CALIBAN, STEPHANO, *and* TRINCULO *are driven out.*]
Go, charge my goblins that they grind their joints
With dry convulsions,° shorten up their sinews
With agèd° cramps, and more pinch-spotted make
them                                                                260
Than pard or cat o' mountain.°

ARIEL                                      Hark, they roar!

PROSPERO
Let them be hunted soundly. At this hour
Lies at my mercy all mine enemies.
Shortly shall all my labors end, and thou
Shalt have the air at freedom. For a little,              265
Follow, and do me service.                        *Exeunt.*

# ACT V

Scene I. [*In front of Prospero's cell.*]

*Enter* PROSPERO *in his magic robes, and* ARIEL.

PROSPERO
Now does my project gather to a head.
My charms crack not, my spirits obey, and Time
Goes upright with his carriage.° How's the day?

ARIEL
On the sixth hour, at which time, my lord,
You said our work should cease.

PROSPERO                          I did say so       5

When first I raised the tempest. Say, my spirit,
How fares the king and's followers?

ARIEL                              Confined together
In the same fashion as you gave in charge,
Just as you left them—all prisoners, sir,
In the line grove which weather-fends° your cell.       10
They cannot budge till your release.° The king,
His brother, and yours abide all three distracted,
And the remainder mourning over them,
Brimful of sorrow and dismay; but chiefly
Him that you termed, sir, the good old Lord Gonzalo.   15
His tears runs down his beard like winter's drops
From eaves of reeds.° Your charm so strongly works
'em,
That if you now beheld them, your affections
Would become tender.

PROSPERO               Dost thou think so, spirit?

ARIEL
Mine would, sir, were I human.

PROSPERO                    And mine shall.        20
Hast thou, which art but air, a touch, a feeling
Of their afflictions, and shall not myself
One of their kind, that relish all as sharply,
Passion° as they, be kindlier moved than thou art?
Though with their high wrongs I am struck to th'
quick,                                                            25
Yet with my nobler reason 'gainst my fury
Do I take part. The rarer action is
In virtue than in vengeance. They being penitent,
The sole drift of my purpose doth extend
Not a frown further. Go, release them, Ariel.          30
My charms I'll break, their senses I'll restore,
And they shall be themselves.

ARIEL                        I'll fetch them, sir. *Exit.*

PROSPERO
Ye elves of hills, brooks, standing lakes, and groves,
And ye that on the sands with printless foot
Do chase the ebbing Neptune, and do fly him°          35
When he comes back; you demi-puppets that
By moonshine do the green sour ringlets° make,
Whereof the ewe not bites; and you whose pastime
Is to make midnight mushrumps,° that rejoice
To hear the solemn curfew; by whose aid                40
(Weak masters° though ye be) I have bedimmed
The noontide sun, called forth the mutinous winds,
And 'twixt the green sea and the azured vault
Set roaring war; to the dread rattling thunder
Have I given fire and rifted Jove's stout oak          45
With his own bolt; the strong-based promontory
Have I made shake and by the spurs° plucked up
The pine and cedar; graves at my command
Have waked their sleepers, oped, and let 'em forth
By my so potent art. But this rough magic              50
I here abjure; and when I have required°
Some heavenly music (which even now I do)
To work mine end upon their senses that°

239 **Do, do** Fine, fine!; **by . . . level** by plumb line and carpenter's level; i.e., according to rule (with pun on *line*)  240
**and't like** if it please  244 **pass of pate** sally of wit  245
**lime** bird lime (which is sticky; thieves have sticky fingers)
248 **barnacles** kind of geese supposed to have developed from
shellfish  259 **dry convulsions** such as come when the joints
are dry from old age  260 **agèd** i.e., such as old people have
261 **pard . . . mountain** leopard or catamount
**V.i.2–3 Time . . . carriage** time does not stoop under his
burden (because there is so little left to do)

10 **weather-fends** protects from the weather  11 **till your
release** until released by you  17 **eaves of reeds** i.e., a thatched
roof  24 **Passion** verb  35 **fly him** fly with him  37 **green
sour ringlets** "fairy rings," little circles of rank grass supposed
to be formed by the dancing of fairies  39 **mushrumps**
mushrooms  41 **masters** masters of supernatural power  47
**spurs** roots  51 **required** asked for  53 **their senses that** the
senses of those whom

This airy charm is for, I'll break my staff,
Bury it certain fathoms in the earth,    55
And deeper than did ever plummet sound
I'll drown my book.

*Solemn music.*

*Here enters* ARIEL *before; then* ALONSO, *with a frantic gesture, attended by* GONZALO; SEBASTIAN *and* ANTONIO *in like manner, attended by* ADRIAN *and* FRANCISCO. *They all enter the circle which* PROSPERO *had made, and there stand charmed; which* PROSPERO *observing, speaks.*

A solemn air, and° the best comforter
To an unsettled fancy, cure thy brains,
Now useless, boiled within thy skull! There stand,    60
For you are spell-stopped.
Holy Gonzalo, honorable man,
Mine eyes, ev'n sociable to the show of thine,
Fall fellowly drops.° The charm dissolves apace;
And as the morning steals upon the night,    65
Melting the darkness, so their rising senses
Begin to chase the ignorant fumes that mantle
Their clearer reason. O good Gonzalo,
My true preserver, and a loyal sir
To him thou follow'st, I will pay thy graces    70
Home° both in word and deed. Most cruelly
Didst thou, Alonso, use me and my daughter.
Thy brother was a furtherer in the act.
Thou art pinched for't now, Sebastian. Flesh and blood,
You, brother mine, that entertained ambition,    75
Expelled remorse° and nature;° whom, with Sebastian
(Whose inward pinches therefore are most strong),
Would here have killed your king, I do forgive thee,
Unnatural though thou art. Their understanding
Begins to swell, and the approaching tide    80
Will shortly fill the reasonable shore,
That now lies foul and muddy. Not one of them
That yet looks on me or would know me. Ariel,
Fetch me the hat and rapier in my cell.
I will discase° me, and myself present    85
As I was sometime Milan. Quickly, spirit!
Thou shalt ere long be free.

          [*Exit* ARIEL *and returns immediately.*]

ARIEL *sings and helps to attire him.*

   Where the bee sucks, there suck I;
   In a cowslip's bell I lie;
   There I couch when owls do cry.    90
   On the bat's back I do fly
   After summer merrily.
   Merrily, merrily shall I live now
   Under the blossom that hangs on the bough.

PROSPERO
Why, that's my dainty Ariel! I shall miss thee,    95
But yet thou shalt have freedom; so, so, so.
To the king's ship, invisible as thou art!
There shalt thou find the mariners asleep

Under the hatches. The master and the boatswain
Being awake, enforce them to this place,    100
And presently,° I prithee.

ARIEL
I drink the air before me, and return
Or ere your pulse twice beat.        *Exit.*

GONZALO
All torment, trouble, wonder, and amazement
Inhabits here. Some heavenly power guide us    105
Out of this fearful country!

PROSPERO           Behold, sir king,
The wrongèd Duke of Milan, Prospero.
For more assurance that a living prince
Does now speak to thee, I embrace thy body,
And to thee and thy company I bid    110
A hearty welcome.

ALONSO           Whe'r° thou be'st he or no,
Or some enchanted trifle° to abuse me,
As late I have been, I not know. Thy pulse
Beats, as of flesh and blood; and, since I saw thee,
Th' affliction of my mind amends, with which,    115
I fear, a madness held me. This must crave°
(And if this be at all)° a most strange story.
Thy dukedom I resign and do entreat
Thou pardon me my wrongs. But how should Prospero
Be living and be here?

PROSPERO           First, noble friend,    120
Let me embrace thine age, whose honor cannot
Be measured or confined.

GONZALO           Whether this be
Or be not, I'll not swear.

PROSPERO           You do yet taste
Some subtleties° o' th' isle, that will not let you
Believe things certain. Welcome, my friends all.    125

[*Aside to* SEBASTIAN *and* ANTONIO.]

But you, my brace of lords, were I so minded,
I here could pluck his highness' frown upon you,
And justify° you traitors. At this time
I will tell no tales.

SEBASTIAN   [*Aside.*] The devil speaks in him.

PROSPERO           No.
For you, most wicked sir, whom to call brother    130
Would even infect my mouth, I do forgive
Thy rankest fault—all of them; and require
My dukedom of thee, which perforce I know
Thou must restore.

ALONSO           If thou beest Prospero,
Give us particulars of thy preservation;    135
How thou hast met us here, whom three hours since
Were wracked upon this shore; where I have lost
(How sharp the point of this remembrance is!)
My dear son Ferdinand.

PROSPERO           I am woe° for't, sir.

ALONSO
Irreparable is the loss, and Patience    140
Says it is past her cure.

---

**58 and** which is   **63–64 sociable . . . drops** associating themselves with the (tearful) appearance of your eyes, shed tears in sympathy   **70–71 pay . . . Home** repay thy favors thoroughly   **76 remorse** pity; **nature** natural feeling   **85 discase** disrobe

**101 presently** immediately   **111 Whe'r** whether   **112 trifle** apparition   **116 crave** require (to account for it)   **117 And . . . all** if this is really happening   **124 subtleties** deceptions (referring to pastries made to look like something else—e.g., castles made out of sugar)   **128 justify** prove   **139 woe** sorry

PROSPERO                I rather think
You have not sought her help, of whose soft grace
For the like loss I have her sovereign aid
And rest myself content.
ALONSO                      You the like loss?
PROSPERO
As great to me, as late,° and supportable°                    145
To make the dear° loss, have I means much weaker
Than you may call to comfort you; for I
Have lost my daughter.
ALONSO                    A daughter?
O heavens, that they were living both in Naples,
The king and queen there! That they were, I wish    150
Myself were mudded in that oozy bed
Where my son lies. When did you lose your daughter?
PROSPERO
In this last tempest. I perceive these lords
At this encounter do so much admire°
That they devour their reason, and scarce think      155
Their eyes do offices° of truth, their words
Are natural breath. But, howsoev'r you have
Been justled from your senses, know for certain
That I am Prospero, and that very duke
Which was thrust forth of Milan, who most strangely  160
Upon this shore, where you were wracked, was
   landed
To be the lord on't. No more yet of this;
For 'tis a chronicle of day by day,
Not a relation for a breakfast, nor
Befitting this first meeting. Welcome, sir;           165
This cell's my court. Here have I few attendants,
And subjects none abroad.° Pray you look in.
My dukedom since you have given me again,
I will requite you with as good a thing,
At least bring forth a wonder to content ye           170
As much as me my dukedom.

*Here* PROSPERO *discovers°* FERDINAND *and* MIRANDA
*playing at chess.*

MIRANDA
Sweet lord, you play me false.
FERDINAND                        No, my dearest love,
I would not for the world.
MIRANDA
Yes, for a score of kingdoms you should wrangle,
And I would call it fair play.°
ALONSO                          If this prove         175
A vision of the island, one dear son
Shall I twice lose.
SEBASTIAN          A most high miracle!
FERDINAND
Though the seas threaten, they are merciful.
I have cursed them without cause. [*Kneels.*]
ALONSO                          Now all the blessings
Of a glad father compass thee about!                  180

Arise, and say how thou cam'st here.
MIRANDA                          O, wonder!
How many goodly creatures are there here!
How beauteous mankind is! O brave new world
That has such people in't!
PROSPERO                    'Tis new to thee.
ALONSO
What is this maid with whom thou wast at play?        185
Your eld'st° acquaintance cannot be three hours.
Is she the goddess that hath severed us
And brought us thus together?
FERDINAND                    Sir, she is mortal;
But by immortal providence she's mine.
I chose her when I could not ask my father            190
For his advice, nor thought I had one. She
Is daughter to this famous Duke of Milan,
Of whom so often I have heard renown
But never saw before; of whom I have
Received a second life; and second father             195
This lady makes him to me.
ALONSO                      I am hers.
But, O, how oddly will it sound that I
Must ask my child forgiveness!
PROSPERO                        There, sir, stop.
Let us not burden our remembrance with
A heaviness that's gone.
GONZALO                  I have inly wept,            200
Or should have spoke ere this. Look down, you gods,
And on this couple drop a blessèd crown!
For it is you that have chalked forth the way
Which brought us hither.
ALONSO                    I say amen, Gonzalo.
GONZALO
Was Milan thrust from Milan that his issue            205
Should become kings of Naples? O, rejoice
Beyond a common joy, and set it down
With gold on lasting pillars. In one voyage
Did Claribel her husband find at Tunis,
And Ferdinand her brother found a wife                210
Where he himself was lost; Prospero his dukedom
In a poor isle; and all of us ourselves
When no man was his own.
ALONSO [*To* FERDINAND *and* MIRANDA.]  Give me
   your hands.
Let grief and sorrow still° embrace his heart
That doth not wish you joy.
GONZALO                    Be it so! Amen!           215

*Enter* ARIEL, *with the* MASTER *and* BOATSWAIN
*amazedly following.*

O, look, sir; look, sir! Here is more of us!
I prophesied if a gallows were on land,
This fellow could not drown. Now, blasphemy,
That swear'st grace o'erboard,° not an oath on shore?
Hast thou no mouth by land? What is the news?        220
BOATSWAIN
The best news is that we have safely found
Our king and company; the next, our ship,
Which, but three glasses° since, we gave out split,

---

145 **As . . . late** as great to me as your loss, and as recent;
**supportable** pronounced "súpportable"  146 **dear** intensifies
the meaning of the noun  154 **admire** wonder  156 **do
offices** perform services  167 **abroad** i.e., on the island
171 **s.d. discovers** reveals (by opening a curtain at the back of
the stage)  174–75 **for . . . play** i.e., if we were playing for
stakes just short of the world, you would protest as now; but
then, the issue being important, I would call it fair play, so
**much** do I love you (?)

186 **eld'st** longest  214 **still** forever  219 **That . . . o'erboard** that (at sea) swearest enough to cause grace to be withdrawn from the ship  223 **glasses** hours

Is tight and yare° and bravely rigged as when
We first put out to sea.

ARIEL  [*Aside to* PROSPERO.] Sir, all this service          225
Have I done since I went.

PROSPERO  [*Aside to* ARIEL.] My tricksy spirit!

ALONSO
These are not natural events; they strengthen
From strange to stranger. Say, how came you hither?

BOATSWAIN
If I did think, sir, I were well awake,
I'd strive to tell you. We were dead of sleep          230
And (how we know not) all clapped under hatches;
Where, but even now, with strange and several° noises
Of roaring, shrieking, howling, jingling chains,
And moe° diversity of sounds, all horrible,
We were awaked; straightway at liberty;          235
Where we, in all our trim, freshly beheld
Our royal, good, and gallant ship, our master
Cap'ring to eye° her. On a trice, so please you,
Even in a dream, were we divided from them
And were brought moping° hither.

ARIEL          [*Aside to* PROSPERO.] Was't well done?          240

PROSPERO [*Aside to* ARIEL.]
Bravely, my diligence. Thou shalt be free.

ALONSO
This is as strange a maze as e'er men trod,
And there is in this business more than nature
Was ever conduct° of. Some oracle
Must rectify our knowledge.

PROSPERO                    Sir, my liege,          245
Do not infest your mind with beating on
The strangeness of this business. At picked leisure,
Which shall be shortly, single I'll resolve you
(Which to you shall seem probable) of every
These happened accidents;° till when, be cheerful          250
And think of each thing well. [*Aside to* ARIEL.] Come
   hither, spirit.
Set Caliban and his companions free.
Untie the spell. [*Exit* ARIEL.] How fares my gracious
   sir?
There are yet missing of your company
Some few odd lads that you remember not.          255

*Enter* ARIEL, *driving in* CALIBAN, STEPHANO, *and*
TRINCULO, *in their stolen apparel.*

STEPHANO  Every man shift for all the rest, and let no
man take care for himself; for all is but fortune.
Coragio,° bully-monster, coragio!

TRINCULO  If these be true spies which I wear in my
head, here's a goodly sight.          260

CALIBAN
O Setebos,° these be brave spirits indeed!
How fine my master is! I am afraid
He will chastise me.

SEBASTIAN          Ha, ha!
What things are these, my Lord Antonio?
Will money buy 'em?

ANTONIO                    Very like. One of them          265
Is a plain fish and no doubt marketable.

PROSPERO
Mark but the badges° of these men, my lords,
Then say if they be true.° This misshapen knave,
His mother was a witch, and one so strong
That could control the moon, make flows and ebbs,          270
And deal in her command without her power.°
These three have robbed me, and this demi-devil
(For he's a bastard one) had plotted with them
To take my life. Two of these fellows you
Must know and own; this thing of darkness I          275
Acknowledge mine.

CALIBAN                    I shall be pinched to death.

ALONSO
Is not this Stephano, my drunken butler?

SEBASTIAN
He is drunk now. Where had he wine?

ALONSO
And Trinculo is reeling ripe. Where should they
Find this grand liquor that hath gilded 'em?          280
How cam'st thou in this pickle?

TRINCULO  I have been in such a pickle, since I saw
you last, that I fear me will never out of my bones. I
shall not fear flyblowing.°

SEBASTIAN  Why, how now, Stephano?          285

STEPHANO  O, touch me not! I am not Stephano, but
a cramp.

PROSPERO  You'd be king o' the isle, sirrah?

STEPHANO  I should have been a sore° one then.

ALONSO
This is a strange thing as e'er I looked on.          290

PROSPERO
He is as disproportioned in his manners
As in his shape. Go, sirrah, to my cell;
Take with you your companions. As you look
To have my pardon, trim it handsomely.

CALIBAN
Ay, that I will; and I'll be wise hereafter,          295
And seek for grace. What a thrice-double ass
Was I to take this drunkard for a god
And worship this dull fool!

PROSPERO                    Go to! Away!

ALONSO
Hence, and bestow your luggage where you found it.

SEBASTIAN  Or stole it rather.          300
     [*Exeunt* CALIBAN, STEPHANO, *and* TRINCULO.]

PROSPERO
Sir, I invite your highness and your train
To my poor cell, where you shall take your rest
For this one night; which, part of it, I'll waste°
With such discourse as, I not doubt, shall make it
Go quick away—the story of my life,          305
And the particular accidents° gone by
Since I came to this isle. And in the morn
I'll bring you to your ship, and so to Naples,

---

**224 yare** shipshape  **232 several** various  **234 moe** more
**238 Cap'ring to eye** dancing to see  **240 moping** in a daze
**244 conduct** conductor  **248–50 single . . . accidents** I myself will solve the problems (and my story will make sense to
you) concerning each and every incident that has happened
**258 Coragio** courage (Italian)  **261 Setebos** the god of
Caliban's mother

**267 badges** worn by servants to indicate to whose service they
belong; in this case, the stolen clothes are badges of their
rascality  **268 true** honest  **271 deal . . . . power** i.e.,
dabble in the moon's realm without the moon's legitimate
authority  **284 flyblowing** pickling preserves meat from flies
**289 sore** (1) tyrannical (2) aching  **303 waste** spend  **306
accidents** incidents

Where I have hope to see the nuptial
Of these our dear-beloved solemnizèd;°                310
And thence retire me to my Milan, where
Every third thought shall be my grave.

ALONSO                                   I long
To hear the story of your life, which must
Take° the ear strangely.

PROSPERO                        I'll deliver° all;
And promise you calm seas, auspicious gales,         315
And sail so expeditious that shall catch°
Your royal fleet far off. [*Aside to* ARIEL.] My Ariel,
   chick,
That is thy charge. Then to the elements
Be free, and fare thou well! [*To the others.*] Please you,
   draw near.                              *Exeunt omnes.*

310 **solemnizèd** pronounced "solémnizèd"   314 **Take** captivate; **deliver** tell   316 **catch** catch up with

# EPILOGUE

*Spoken by* PROSPERO.

Now my charms are all o'erthrown,
And what strength I have's mine own,
Which is most faint. Now 'tis true
I must be here confined by you,
Or sent to Naples. Let me not,                        5
Since I have my dukedom got
And pardoned the deceiver, dwell
In this bare island by your spell;
But release me from my bands°
With the help of your good hands.°                    10
Gentle breath° of yours my sails
Must fill, or else my project fails,
Which was to please. Now I want°
Spirits to enforce, art to enchant;
And my ending is despair                              15
Unless I be relieved by prayer,°
Which pierces so that it assaults
Mercy itself and frees all faults.
As you from crimes would pardoned be,
Let your indulgence set me free.          *Exit.*   20

**Epi.9 bands** bonds   **10 hands** i.e., applause to break the spell
**11 Gentle breath** i.e., favorable comment   **13 want** lack
**16 prayer** i.e., this petition

# THE LIFE OF

# KING HENRY THE EIGHTH

EDITED BY S. SCHOENBAUM

## Introduction

Although *The Life of King Henry VIII* has for more than a century given rise to vigorous, sometimes heated, discussion, it has received much less interpretative consideration than any other of Shakespeare's dramatizations of English history; the two best-known books on the subject, Lily B. Campbell's *Shakespeare's Histories* and E. M. W. Tillyard's *Shakespeare's History Plays*, ignore it. Attention has focused instead on a single great problem unrelated in any direct way to the play's meaning or worth. In the title of his celebrated essay, first published in 1850, James Spedding asked, "Who Wrote Shakespeare's *Henry VIII?*" and scholars have raised the same question ever since.[1] Indeed, a great Shakespearean of our century, John Dover Wilson, confessed with engaging candor that the chief interest of the play for him lay in the authorship problem. That problem is the most vexing to the editor of *Henry VIII*. While he may be permitted to regret the disproportionate attention lavished on a single specialized issue of scholarship, he must nevertheless recognize that it can scarcely be disregarded in a responsible Introduction. He will do well to confront it straightaway.

Spedding argued that *Henry VIII* represents not Shakespeare's unaided work but, rather, a collaborative effort in which he was joined by an inferior writer who composed the greater part and was responsible for the general design, which Spedding found incoherent. This inferior playwright he identified as John Fletcher. Although some earlier scholars had expressed doubts about the homogeneity of *Henry VIII*, no one had previously developed a reasoned case for Fletcher's part-authorship. Spedding's evidence is internal. In the scenes attributed to Shakespeare he finds vigor, reality, impassioned language, and figurative richness; the Fletcher portions are conventional, diffuse, and languid. These stylistic impressions Spedding reinforces with metrical statistics: the scenes assigned to Fletcher are distinguished by a preponderance of feminine endings (an extra unstressed syllable terminating the blank-verse line) normal for Fletcher but excessive for Shakespeare. Spedding's argument was not universally accepted—Swinburne early demurred—but it has proved enormously influential: so influential that the theory of Shakespeare-Fletcher collaboration is even today not infrequently stated as a fact.

The great drawback to stylistic evidence is its subjectivity, which resides to a degree even in the seemingly mechanical metrical tests that Spedding, along with most nineteenth-century scholars, found persuasive. But additional evidence of a more objective nature has been forthcoming. In an important monograph, *The Problem of Henry VIII Reopened* (1949), A. C. Partridge offered linguistic data based on the use of expletive *do* in affirmative statements (favored by Shakespeare), *-th* inflectional endings in the third person singular present indicative of notional and auxiliary verbs (also favored by Shakespeare), and colloquial clippings of personal pronouns (favored by Fletcher). These linguistic characteristics essentially confirm Spedding's division of the play. Partridge's evidence has been supplemented by Cyrus Hoy in his recent painstaking investigation of the entire Fletcher canon. Hoy finds in the Folio text of *Henry VIII* "two distinct linguistic patterns: one [Fletcher's] marked by the occurrence of *ye* in eleven of the play's sixteen scenes, to a total of 71 times, and a distinct preference for the contraction '*em* to the expanded pronominal form *them*; the second pattern [Shakespeare's] is marked by the absence of *ye*, a preference for *them* to '*em*, and the frequent use of *hath* which, with one exception (I.i) is never found in a scene containing *ye*."[2] (The present edition differs from most modern-spelling texts in retaining contracted forms as they appear in the Folio.)

For the reader's convenience, the customary scene allocation made by those who view the play as a Fletcher-Shakespeare collaboration is summarized in the following table:

---

[1] The essay, which first appeared in *The Gentleman's Magazine* (August 1850), is more conveniently accessible in *Transactions of the New Shakspere Society* (1874), Appendix, pp. 1*–18*. For my discussion of the authorship question in this Introduction I am obliged to Northwestern University Press for permission to include materials from my book, *Internal Evidence and Elizabethan Dramatic Authorship* (1966), in which the principal contributions to the controversy are evaluated.

[2] Cyrus Hoy, "The Shares of Fletcher and His Collaborators in the Beaumont and Fletcher Canon (VII)," *Studies in Bibliography*, XV (1962), 77. Hoy's discussion of the play occupies pp. 76–85; a statistical table of his findings appears on p. 90.

| Prologue | | Fletcher |
|---|---|---|
| Act I, | sc. i–ii | Shakespeare |
| | sc. iii–iv | Fletcher |
| Act II, | sc. i–ii | Fletcher |
| | sc. iii–iv | Shakespeare |
| Act III, | sc. i | Fletcher |
| | sc. ii (lines 1–204) | Shakespeare |
| | sc. ii (remainder) | Fletcher |
| Act IV, | sc. i–ii | Fletcher |
| Act V, | sc. i | Shakespeare |
| | sc. ii–v | Fletcher |
| Epilogue | | Fletcher |

The dual-authorship hypothesis is, moreover, attractive on other than linguistic or stylistic grounds. Around 1609, Shakespeare's company began performing in the enclosed Blackfriars Theatre, the lease to which it had recently acquired. Although the open-air Globe remained in use (indeed, *Henry VIII* was written for that house), it was gradually supplanted in importance by the new theater, which catered to a select, well-to-do clientele. At about the same time as this crucial change in operations, the premier theatrical company of the age was faced with the problem of the imminent retirement of the playwright largely responsible for its overwhelming preeminence. How, after all, does one go about replacing Shakespeare? The King's Men could not very well avoid pondering this unenviable question. Their crisis was resolved—successfully by the criterion of box-office receipts—when the company arranged for Fletcher to succeed Shakespeare as their principal dramatist. And what could be a more natural procedure during the transitional phase than that Shakespeare should collaborate with the brilliant young playwright destined to replace him?[3]

Yet it is a hypothesis, not a certainty, that *Henry VIII* is the end product of such a partnership. A distinguished minority of scholars—among them Peter Alexander, Hardin Craig, R. A. Foakes, G. Wilson Knight, and Geoffrey Bullough—have remained unconvinced despite the cumulative weight of stylistic, linguistic, and historical probabilities. They have, furthermore, discerned in the play an organic unity which they regard as more compatible with single than with divided authorship. The concrete evidence for collaboration is, after all, entirely internal and, in the nature of things, inconclusive without external support. Even the welcome linguistic data do not always provide so clearcut a pattern as one might wish, and there is always the danger that scribes or compositors did not consistently follow such minutiae in the manuscripts which they transmitted. It is a fact that Heminges and Condell, the earliest editors of Shakespeare, printed *Henry VIII* in the First Folio without any hint that another writer had a share in the play. Whether they did or did not know the circumstances of composition we cannot definitely say; but, as they were Shakespeare's friends and professional colleagues at the time, the likelihood is that they did. But would they have omitted the work from the Folio even if they understood it to be in large measure another's? Again we cannot positively say. It is also a fact, though, that they failed to include *Sir Thomas More*,

*Pericles*, and *The Two Noble Kinsmen:* works of collaborative or doubtful status. It is true, too, that they printed a text of *Macbeth* with the non-Shakespearean Hecate scenes; but these amount only to a small portion of the whole play. The external evidence thus points to single jurisdiction, yet not with such force as to dismay those maintaining the contrary view.

After working closely with the text of *Henry VIII* over a fairly long period, and after weighing the arguments of his predecessors, the present editor is satisfied that two styles indeed coexist in the play, that Shakespeare and Fletcher are the authors indicated by those styles, and that the traditional distribution of scenes is by and large correct. He also believes, however, that Hoy may be right in detecting Shakespeare's presence in several scenes usually attributed to Fletcher alone (II.ii, III.ii.204–460, and IV.ii), although he would not venture upon any line-by-line allocation.[4] Because the Prologue and Epilogue are such short passages, he doubts that a persuasive case can be made for ascription to either Shakespeare or Fletcher. The view, maintained by the anticollaborationists, that *Henry VIII* possesses a structure of imagery and other features reflecting careful planning does not for this reader carry any great evidential significance as regards authorship. Such interpretive considerations inevitably have a subjective aspect: there are competent critics who do not find in the work the unity claimed for it by other competent critics. And even granting the existence of such unity, it does not necessarily follow that it could have been achieved only by an artist working on his own. There are sufficient instances of dramatists who have pooled their talents to produce integrated works, sometimes attaining (as in the case of Jonson, Chapman, and Marston's *Eastward Ho*) remarkable consistency of texture; just as there are instances of totally incoherent plays composed by one individual. The hypothesis of Shakespeare-Fletcher collaboration on *Henry VIII* is reasonable and better supported by tangible evidence than most such hypotheses, and it is probable that the majority of students will continue to support it. At the same time it remains a hypothesis, and there will probably always be some dissenters. For better or for worse, this editor is unstirred by the partisan fervor that the debate has aroused; his firmest conviction is that the problem admits of no ultimate solution.

If the authorship question presents notorious difficulties, the very existence of the play is in some respects awkward. For many, one suspects, it would have been much more satisfying had Shakespeare concluded his playwriting career with *The Tempest*, a drama as magically evocative as the island on which its action takes place. The great themes of forgiveness and reconciliation achieve (so it seems) final form: it is the culmination of the artist's vision. Understandably, readers and audiences have found irresistible the temptation to identify the creator with his creation, and to see in Prospero's abjuration of his magic the dramatist's farewell to the stage:

> I'll break my staff,
> Bury it certain fathoms in the earth,
> And deeper than did ever plummet sound
> I'll drown my book.               (V.i.54–57)

[3] For an excellent discussion of these questions see Gerald E. Bentley, "Shakespeare and the Blackfriars Theatre," *Shakespeare Survey I*, ed. Allardyce Nicoll (1948), pp. 38–50.

[4] This editor would not, however, join Hoy in also crediting Shakespeare with a share in II.i and IV.i.

And then how anticlimactic, after the revels have been declared ended, for their master to return a couple of years later with yet another revel! To complicate matters further, the play in which the timeless artificer now had at least a hand was quite possibly topical in its inspiration, and certainly it was spectacular (in the showy theatrical sense) in its design. If the composition of *Henry VIII* testifies to anything, it is to the committed professionalism of its author: the supreme poet was yet a shareholder in a company of players and not unwilling to emerge from semiretirement in Stratford to provide his London colleagues with a vehicle admirably suited to catching the popular fancy in a moment of national rejoicing.

The occasion for rejoicing was the marriage on Saint Valentine's Day, 1613, of Princess Elizabeth, daughter of James I, to Prince Frederick, the Elector Palatine and champion of the Protestant cause in Germany. During the previous autumn Prince Henry, the heir to the throne, had died, and the nation had been plunged into grief; now the period of mourning was over, and the lavish wedding celebrations—including masques, feasts, and fireworks—signalized the change of mood. A play extolling the reign of England's first Protestant defender of the faith, and doing so in scenes of pomp and pageantry, would be in harmony with the occasion. Act V of *Henry VIII* celebrates the birth of Princess Elizabeth of glorious memory, and (as R. A. Foakes has observed) the identity of name between the young bride and the great queen did not escape notice at the time. "How much are we, the inhabitants of this whole isle, bound unto our good God, that hath lent us such a princess," declared George Webbe in *The Bride Royal* (1613), "and in her hath renewed and revived the name and nature of our late deceased, ever to be remembered, happy Queen Elizabeth!" Cranmer's speech (V.v.14–62), prophesying the peace and prosperity of Elizabeth's reign and alluding flatteringly to their continuance under James, resembles in phrasing and imagery what was being said in the marriage tracts and sermons.[5]

To suggest, however, that *Henry VIII* was composed specifically for the royal festivities would be to stretch the evidence, for no court performance of the play is mentioned in the Lord Treasurer's accounts for this period, although we know that five other works of Shakespeare were acted before the newlyweds. Possibly *Henry VIII* was the "stage play to be acted in the Great Hall by the King's players" which aroused "much expectation" on February 16, but which was canceled in favor of a masque; but this is mere speculation.

In identifying *Henry VIII* with *All Is True*, a play about the same monarch's reign known only from a single contemporary reference, we are on surer ground: *All Is True* would be an appropriate alternative title for *Henry VIII*, in view of the Prologue's emphasis on "our chosen truth" (line 18). A performance of *All Is True* at the Globe Theatre on June 29, 1613, was the occasion of the most sensational occurrence in the history of that playhouse. The event is described in a letter, dated July 2, 1613, written by Sir Henry Wotton to Sir Edmund Bacon:

The King's players had a new play called *All Is true*, representing some principal pieces of the reign of Henry VIII, which was set forth with many extraordinary circumstances of pomp and majesty, even to the matting of the stage; the Knights of the Order with their Georges and garters, the Guards with their embroidered coats, and the like: sufficient in truth within a while to make greatness very familiar, if not ridiculous. Now, King Henry making a masque at the Cardinal Wolsey's house, and certain chambers being shot off at his entry, some of the paper, or other stuff, wherewith one of them was stopped, did light on the thatch, where being thought at first but an idle smoke, and their eyes more attentive to the show, it kindled inwardly, and ran round like a train, consuming within less than an hour the whole house to the very grounds.

This was the fatal period of that virtuous fabric, wherein yet nothing did perish but wood and straw, and a few forsaken cloaks; only one man had his breeches set on fire, that would perhaps have broiled him, if he had not by the benefit of a provident wit put it out with bottle ale.[6]

Thus did the Globe perish; but (as Stow's *Annals*, 1631 ed., records) "the next spring it was new builded in far fairer manner than before."

We need feel no surprise that the patrician Wotton should express tolerant disapproval at the public staging of the ceremonies and pastimes of the great before the heterogeneous multitude that frequented the Globe. More suggestive is his tacit admission that he has been impressed, if reluctantly, by "the many extraordinary circumstances of pomp and majesty"—impressed at second hand, for he was not an eyewitness to the performance he recounts. Whatever deeper resonances are implied, *Henry VIII* on the stage was the super-spectacle of its own day. In an Introduction to the play this aspect calls for special emphasis, as it is least likely to come through adequately on the printed page: the life of a spectacle, appealing as it does directly to eye and ear, is in the presentation.

How deliberately does the play dwell on awesome princely occasions! Sometimes these are depicted through the resources of language alone, as in Norfolk's description of the Field of the Cloth of Gold (I.i), or in the account by the two Gentlemen of the trial of "the great Duke of Buckingham" by his peers at Westminster Hall (II.i), or in the Third Gentleman's narration of the solemn ritual at the coronation of Queen Anne in Westminster Abbey (IV.i). But, where possible, stirring events are dramatized. We attend Wolsey's splendid banquet and masque; we witness Katherine's vision of dancing, white-robed spirits; we become bystanders when Anne returns with her retinue from the Abbey. The dramatis personae for *Henry VIII* is the largest for any play in the canon, and for such episodes as the procession in Act IV the company must have pressed into service all of its available personnel. The extended stage directions, authorial in origin, show an unusual regard for the proper disposition of the players in the big scenes. For Katherine's trial

[5] The correspondences are described and documented by R. A. Foakes in his Introduction to the New Arden edition of *Henry VIII* (1957), pp. xxxi–xxxii. I owe my reference to *The Bride Royal* to this edition, p. xxx.

[6] *The Life and Letters of Sir Henry Wotton*, edited by L. Pearsall Smith (1907), II, pp. 32–33.

*The King takes place under the cloth of state; the two Cardinals
sit under him as judges. The Queen takes place some distance
from the King. The Bishops place themselves on each side the
court, in manner of a consistory; below them, the Scribes. The
Lords sit next the Bishops. The rest of the Attendants stand in
convenient order about the stage.*                    (II.iv.s.d.)

The gorgeous costumes of princes, prelates, and function-
aries contributed to the visual magnificence of these
scenes, as did the impressive assortment of stage properties,
including the purse with the Great Seal, the silver cross,
silver mace, and silver pillars, the gold scepter and collars
of S's, the gilt copper crown, gold crown, and gold
coronals and demicoronals.

These visual effects were complemented and enhanced
by sound, which is called for throughout. Patience, Queen
Katherine's woman, sings of the miraculous powers of
"sweet music" as she accompanies herself on the lute.
Such soothing moments, however, are rare: on other
occasions we hear the blended voices of the choristers, the
sound of oboes and cornets, the sterner notes of drum and
trumpet, the roar of the cannon. *Henry VIII* is an un-
abashedly noisy play, guaranteed to keep even the drowsiest
spectator awake. "Some come to take their ease," the
Epilogue declares,

And sleep an act or two; but those, we fear,
W' have frighted with our trumpets.          (Epi.3–4)

Of the several companies performing in London at the
time, only the King's Men had the resources to do justice
to such a play. The destruction of the theater during what
was possibly the premier performance is not without a
certain ironic fitness: it was the spectacular effect to end
(literally) all spectacular effects.

In the most notable modern revival of *Henry VIII*,
produced by Tyrone Guthrie at Stratford-on-Avon in
1949–50, the director fully exploited the opportunities for
processional pageantry, display, and crowd movement.
For such exploitation the earliest theatrical precedents and
the text itself (as we have noted) afford ample warrant.
These features of the play have contributed to the dissatisfaction with it expressed by some commentators:
spectacle, being nonverbal, has always prompted condescension or worse on the part of critics whose orientation
is literary or philosophical rather than theatrical. "The
Spectacle," Aristotle observed in the *Poetics*, "has, indeed,
an emotional attraction of its own, but, of all the parts, it
is the least artistic, and connected least with the art of
poetry." Even granting the validity of the judgment, the
propriety of applying to another genre the criteria Aristotle
formulated for tragedy may be doubtful. For although
*Henry VIII* dramatizes several individual tragedies—
Buckingham's, Katherine's, Wolsey's—it is not itself a
tragedy but a history play concerned more with the public
conduct of its personages than with their buried lives; its
intention is to stage, in Wotton's words, "some principal
pieces of the reign of Henry VIII."

Clowning and buffoonery of the kind found in Samuel
Rowley's *When You See Me You Know Me* (1605), which
deals with the same reign, are rejected in favor of an
appropriate seriousness and dignity of tone, although the
rejection is fortunately not so sweeping as to exclude humor

altogether: witness the bawdry of the old Lady (II.iii) and
the low comedy of the Porter and his man (V.iv). The
repeated stress in the Prologue is on the historical genuine-
ness of the play's people and events, their reality:

Think ye see
The very persons of our noble story
As they were living.                    (Pro.25–27)

The pursuit of historical verisimilitude (whether achieved
or not) obviously limits the playwright's freedom to select,
shape, and explore events. It cannot be claimed that the
genre represents the highest form to which dramatic art
may aspire, but there can be no denying its perennial
appeal to theatergoers; of plays produced in recent years,
Peter Shaffer's spectacular dramatization of Pizarro's
conquest of Peru, *The Royal Hunt of the Sun*, perhaps
most closely approximates the type. *Henry VIII* is best
understood—and appreciated—on its own terms.

Those terms are not, however, confined to spectacle.
Again the Prologue helpfully gives a clue to purpose. The
audience is instructed in how to respond to the calamities
befalling the eminent personages whose careers will unfold
before it:

Think you see them great,
And followed with the general throng and sweat
Of thousand friends. Then, in a moment, see
How soon this mightiness meets misery;
And if you can be merry then, I'll say
A man may weep upon his wedding day.     (Pro.27–32)

These lines suggest the evanescence of worldly glory.
Fortune, the blind goddess, raises her favorites high upon
her wheel, then capriciously flings them to earth. It is an
old theme; in the permutations of Fortune's wheel medieval
writers discerned the quintessential tragic pattern. According to Chaucer's Monk, in *The Canterbury Tales*,

Tragedie is to seyn a certeyn storie,
As olde bookes maken us memorie,
Of hym that stood in greet prosperitee,
And is yfallen out of heigh degree
Into myserie, and endeth wrecchedly.
                    (Prologue, Monk's Tale, 1973–77)

*Henry VIII* presents, in the context of Renaissance court
life, a trio of such falls from high degree.

The victims, so different in their characters and lives,
share not only a common fortune but also, at the last, a
common pathos, which they fully savor. Buckingham's
stoic forbearance in the face of death gives place in his final
words to a self-pitying note, however sober and controlled:

All good people,
Pray for me! I must now forsake ye; the last hour
Of my long weary life is come upon me.
Farewell!
And when you would say something that is sad,
Speak how I fell. I have done, and God forgive me.
                    (II.i.131–36)

No sooner has he departed the scene than the two Gentlemen, having lamented his passing, discuss the impending fall of Katherine in almost identical terms (" 'Tis woeful"). The discarded queen, "sick to death," is granted a dream of eternal happiness to come. In a last assertion of regal greatness, she dismisses an unintentionally negligent messenger, then prepares for the end. "I must to bed," she cries to Patience;

> Call in more women. When I am dead, good wench,
> Let me be used with honor. Strew me over
> With maiden flowers, that all the world may know
> I was a chaste wife to my grave. Embalm me,
> Then lay me forth. Although unqueened, yet like
> A queen and daughter to a king, inter me.
> I can no more.                    (IV.ii.167–73)

It is perhaps the play's most affecting moment.

The most stunning of the three downfalls, however, is that of Wolsey. For a suitable epitaph we may turn to a contemporary of Shakespeare who suffered a fate analogous to that of the cardinal. "The rising unto place is laborious," Francis Bacon wrote in his essay "Of Great Place,"

> and by pains men come to greater pains; and it is sometimes base; and by indignities men come to dignities. The standing is slippery, and the regress is either a downfall or at least an eclipse, which is a melancholy thing.

Although the cardinal is not the play's protagonist, his cold presence dominates the first three acts. Somehow he must be humanized in defeat, and in the space of a hundred lines the arrogant prince of the church is humbled and reconciled to his new condition. Like Katherine and Buckingham, he prays for his king. He also shows solicitude for the future of his servant Cromwell, and for the first time we do not suspect a selfish motive lurking behind the apparent altruism. Wolsey weeps—the scene is frankly sentimental—and repents (a trifle smugly) his worldliness:

> O Cromwell, Cromwell,
> Had I but served my God with half the zeal
> I served my king, he would not in mine age
> Have left me naked to mine enemies.    (III.ii.455–58)

There is only slight foreshadowing (in II.ii) of Wolsey's fall, and the transformation itself, read in the study, seems somewhat abrupt; but in a spectacular drama of comparatively external nature, subtle nuances of character portrayal are hardly required. The scene has worked superbly on the stage, as is attested by the fact that the role of Wolsey has attracted a number of great actors, among them Kemble, Macready, and Kean.

If the three successive falls from greatness are well contrived to move an audience to generous sympathy, they do not engage the deeper tragic emotions, nor were they intended to do so, as the larger pattern of the play makes clear. Scenes of calamity alternate throughout with happier occasions. The splendid festivities in York House (I.iv), for example, follow hard upon the Surveyor's devastating testimony against Buckingham; the gaiety of the masque is in turn succeeded by the somber episode of the duke's entry after his arraignment. At the same time that Katherine's misfortunes press in upon her, we watch Ann Bullen's star rise. And so on. Such juxtapositions are not unusual in Elizabethan plays, nor, for that matter, in dramatic art generally, but in this case the total effect is of a complex tonal and thematic orchestration.

In the concluding movement of *Henry VIII*, in which the grand design stands fully revealed, the joyous strain triumphs. The fourth—and last—of the threatened falls does not come to pass. Cranmer, who never aspired to greatness, is tested in the crucible of courtly intrigue. Like his predecessors, he is the object of plots, but he undergoes special humiliations: the Archbishop of Canterbury is made to cool his heels outside the council chamber door with grooms and lackeys. Yet he emerges unscathed, and no heads roll as a result. Instead there is forgiveness and reconciliation, in which Cranmer, his accusers, and the king all participate. The archbishop can then go on to officiate at the christening of Princess Elizabeth and to utter the speeches of prophetic rapture in the final scene. Machinations have ceased. Some private individuals, most notably Katherine, have in the course of the drama suffered unjust deprivations, but the commonwealth has prospered. A newborn infant symbolizes happier days to come.

*Henry VIII* is unique among Shakespeare's histories in not depicting an England at war or under the threat of war. Thematically the play has closer links with the immediately preceding romances than with the two historical tetralogies of a previous decade. We are not so far removed after all from the world of *The Tempest*, in which sinister plots are thwarted, enemies are reconciled, and hopeful auguries attend a younger generation. In the character of Henry, who presides over the action by exercising the quasi-magical prerogatives of kingship, we have a figure in some ways analogous to Prospero.[7]

The destinies of all the principal personages lie in Henry's hands. A Buckingham or a Wolsey or a Katherine may absorb attention for a time, but they all pass from the stage, not to return; Henry abides, and his presence gives a measure of narrative unity to heterogeneous events. Yet his actual role is limited—he speaks fewer than 450 lines—and the king makes no appearance whatever in Act IV. No very searching portrayal of him is attempted in the play that bears his name. For a modern audience he must present difficulties: the figure cut by Shakespeare's Henry differs so strikingly from the popular image derived from more recent histories or from films and stage plays. In the Jacobean Henry we do not see the insatiable thirster after sovereignty or the profligate who squandered his parsimonious father's treasure in pursuit of the sport of kings. Nor do we see the gourmand and sensualist, the devourer of drumsticks and wives. Great events associated with Henry's reign lie outside the scope of the action: the Reformation and the dissolution of the monasteries, the martyrdom of Sir Thomas More, the execution of Anne Boleyn three brief years after the christening celebrated in the play.

The Henry of *The Life of King Henry the Eighth* wears the

---

7 The relationship of *Henry VIII* to Shakespeare's last plays is explored with penetrating subtlety (occasionally oversubtlety) by Foakes in the New Arden edition, Introduction, pp. xxxvii–lxii. Foakes also deals perceptively with the themes and structure of the play.

mantle of royalty securely. At first, it is true, his exalted position shields him from knowledge of the intrigues in his own court; he has never heard of Wolsey's oppressive tax scheme for which (as a matter of historical fact) Henry himself was responsible. But as the action unfolds, his awareness, and hence his authority, increase. Once he knows about Wolsey's perfidy, he rejects the cardinal decisively. In the Cranmer episode, Henry controls all the strings, but the manipulation serves national interests rather than any need for self-aggrandizement. Thus he would appear to approximate closely enough the popular patriot-monarch lauded by Holinshed and the other Tudor apologists.

But what are we to make of the divorce? Much attention is given in the play to the king's conscientious scruple— after more than twenty years of wedlock!—about the propriety of his marriage to the widow of his own brother. On this issue of a wounded conscience Henry meditates privately, expatiates at length in public, and seeks counsel from the most learned scholars in Christendom. Yet before any divorce is bruited, we see him evidently attracted to the woman who will become his next wife. And before Katherine's trial—the results of which are a foregone conclusion—there is Suffolk's cynically revealing aside:

CHAMBERLAIN
    It seems the marriage with his brother's wife
    Has crept too near his conscience.
SUFFOLK                    [*Aside.*] No, his conscience
    Has crept too near another lady.          (II.ii.16–18)

Historically Henry's reasons for a divorce were several, but the overriding consideration was his need to continue the succession with a male heir, which Katherine had failed to produce and was no longer capable of producing. This motive is not glossed over in the play—indeed, Henry dwells on it at length (II.iv.184–97)—but the force of the point is blunted by the weight given to the king's scruple.

The problem is further complicated by the fact that the dramatists provide Henry with no self-revelatory soliloquies and by the related fact that his public pronouncements cannot always be taken at face value. In open court he declares:

    Prove but our marriage lawful, by my life
    And kingly dignity, we are contented
    To wear our mortal state to come with her,
    Katherine our queen, before the primest creature
    That's paragoned o' th' world.          (II.iv. 224–28)

This does not sound insincere, but hard upon Henry's tribute to his sweet bedfellow comes an aside (233–38) in which he expresses impatience with the "dilatory sloth and tricks of Rome" that hinder the divorce; and in the next scene we have Katherine's complaint that he has long ceased to love her. It is as though the dramatists, having set out to extol Henry and, through him, England, were nevertheless unable—or unwilling—entirely to suppress undercurrents of motive and policy inconsistent with so simplified a view of him. The effect is of a disturbing ambiguity of character.

It is not the play's only ambiguity. Buckingham presents a similar problem, although to a lesser degree. Is he in fact a traitor or is he a wholly innocent sacrifice to Wolsey's malice? Our first inclination is to regard the duke simply as the victim of a frame-up, and certainly much weight is given to his wrongs. In the sympathetically conceived Katherine he has a stalwart defender. The chief witness against him bears, we know, a personal grudge, and Buckingham protests his innocence in moving terms as he goes to the block. Yet the king's anger in I.ii has a righteous accent, and if he is responsible, however unwittingly, for a judicial murder, he is not afterward disturbed by it. The Surveyor's testimony is never rebutted. Buckingham himself admits that, "upon the premises," he has been justly tried by his peers, and the Second Gentleman's last remark about him has a proviso: "If the duke be guiltless. . . ." After Buckingham's last exit, fairly early in the play, little is made of the matter apart from an inconclusive exchange between Surrey and Wolsey in III.ii. The "woefulness" of Buckingham's fall we do not question, but his degree of actual guilt—if any—remains in doubt. A faint unease persists in the reader's mind.

Such puzzlements, which have prompted reservations about the play on the part of some critics, loom larger in the study than on the stage. In the theater attention focuses first on the splendor and fanfare of the grand processional entries and the ceremonies of public life. The contrastingly intimate scenes, in which a young maid of honor is shown royal favor while her defeated elders confront isolation and imminent death, appeal more directly to the emotions, if on no very profound level. Then there are the great set speeches: we are stirred by the eloquence—impassioned or elegiac—of Buckingham's apologia, Katherine's defense of the sanctity of her marriage, and Wolsey's long farewell to all his greatness. And finally, along with the multitude on the stage and in the audience, we are swept up in the visionary ecstasy of the ritualistic episode of the christening. *Henry VIII* is Shakespeare's festive history. It is appropriate that the play was chosen for performance at the Old Vic in London in 1953 to celebrate the coronation of Queen Elizabeth II.

## A NOTE ON THE SOURCES

The chief sources for the play, as for Shakespeare's great earlier cycle of historical dramas on the reigns of the English monarchs from Richard II through Richard III, is Raphael Holinshed's *Chronicles of England, Scotland, and Ireland* (second ed., 1587). It is depended upon throughout, except for the story of the plot against Cranmer, and his vindication, in Act V; here the authority, closely followed, is John Foxe's *Acts and Monuments,* the enlarged 1570 version of which went through a number of editions before the close of the century. Whether the playwright(s) also profited from other narrative chronicles is a matter for speculation: the phraseological parallels adduced by scholars are often less than striking, and it is well known that the chroniclers themselves borrowed from one another freely. But Edward Hall's *Union of the Two Noble and Illustre Families of Lancaster and York* (1542) may have been consulted, and it is possible—althought not demonstrable— that Wolsey's images of the star past its meridian and of the bladder of pride (III.ii.224–28, 359–62) derive from John Speed's *History of Great Britain* (1611). More persuasive is the evidence that the author(s) knew Samuel Rowley's boisterously farcical and blithely anachronistic drama on Henry's reign, *When You See Me You Know Me*, printed in 1605 and perhaps revived before being reprinted in 1613—the probable year of first performance for *Henry VIII*. The sneering references in the latter to "a merry bawdy play" consisting of "fool and fight" (Pro.14–19) may allude to *When You See Me*, which nevertheless seems to have provided some minor inspiration, most notably in Henry's persistent ejaculation, "Ha!," used in both works. A significant indirect source is George Cavendish's *Life of Wolsey*, which, although not published until 1641, was utilized by the chroniclers from Stow (1565) onward.

But of the direct and continuous dependence on Holinshed in *Henry VIII* there can be no question. The historical events of the play, from the Field of the Cloth of Gold in 1520 to the christening of Princess Elizabeth in 1533, cover roughly a third of Henry's long reign (1509–47). Four great episodes dominate this segment of Holinshed's narrative: Buckingham's fall, the divorce, Wolsey's disgrace, and the king's remarriage, culminating in the christening of the future queen. So too do they dominate the play. The source was evidently read with great care. At times, as in Katherine's long speech (II.iv.11–55), the dramatic blank verse is the prose of the *Chronicles* paraphrased (although even here there are significant additions). Holinshed is levied upon also for the elaborate stage directions for the ceremonial entries and processions in II.iv, IV.i, and V.v.

If adherence to the source was close, it was not, however, slavish. The abundant material of the *Chronicles* is winnowed, rearranged, and combined in accordance with the necessities of the dramatic design. Certain changes were dictated by limitations of stage personnel: the pageantry of the coronation, calling for a multitude of supernumeraries, had to be reduced. Other alterations are more substantive. Holinshed's account of the unfortunate Bishop of Durham who mistakenly sent the king a book documenting his private affairs, and thus enabled Wolsey to destroy him, is transferred to the cardinal himself (III.ii.121 ff.). In the play the first hint of the king's attraction to Anne Bullen precedes Buckingham's execution, and is manifested at a feast which, with nice artistic economy, also illustrates the lavish scale on which Wolsey lives (I.iv). Historically, the king set his affections on Anne eight years after the execution, and she does not appear in Holinshed's description of the revel at York House that provides the basis for this scene.

Perhaps the most interesting transformations involve the portrayal of character. It is true that the king remains, in play as in chronicle, the exemplary monarch whose motives, unlike those of lesser mortals, are never critically examined. But on the stage his moments of anger or of withdrawal into pensiveness reveal facets of the smiling or stern public figure that Holinshed does not attempt to suggest. So, too, the Henry of the play gains in authority in the course of the action; hoodwinked by Wolsey in the earlier scenes, he is nobody's fool in Act V. Again the source offers no precedent. In the play the fallen Wolsey is invested with a pathos and dignity only barely hinted at in the chronicle. Katherine is endowed by the dramatist(s)

with greater strength and regality than she displays in Holinshed, an effect in part achieved by such devices as her fearless—if unavailing—defense of Buckingham and accusations against the cardinal in the king's presence (I.ii.9 ff.).

By such means are the prosaic historical narratives of Holinshed and Foxe transformed into complex poetic drama.

## A NOTE ON THE TEXT

*The Famous History of the Life of King Henry the Eighth* did not achieve publication until seven years after Shakespeare's death, when it appeared in the collected First Folio of his works as the last of the history plays. The 1623 Folio furnishes the only authoritative early edition of *Henry VIII*. Fortunately it is a very good one: behind the Folio text apparently lies a careful scribal transcription of the authors'—or author's—own manuscript. To the playwright(s), rather than the prompter, we presumably owe the very full stage directions called for by a spectacular historical drama. With few exceptions, entrances and exits are fully indicated. Speech prefixes are throughout correct and unambiguous, except for confusion of the First and Second Gentleman at IV.i.20–23 and 55, and of the Lord Chamberlain with the Lord Chancellor at V.iii.85 and 87. Indeed, the text as a whole is very clean and straightforward, with relatively little corruption or error of any kind, although the language—often complex in Shakespeare's mature manner—not surprisingly presents a number of interpretative problems.

The Folio text directly or indirectly provides the basis for all subsequent editions of *Henry VIII*. Wherever possible the present edition reproduces it, modernizing spelling and altering punctuation and verse lineations where the editor's sense of literary and dramatic fitness dictated. The Latin act and scene divisions of the Folio have been translated, and a new division (as in the Globe text) is introduced after V.ii.35. Consequently, in the fifth act the Folio's "Scena Tertia" and "Scena Quarta" are rendered as V.iv and V.v respectively. Abbreviations have been expanded and speech prefixes regularized. Stage directions have been amplified where necessary, such additions being printed within brackets. Obvious typographical errors have been corrected and eccentric spellings regularized where appropriate without notice, but all significant emendations are noted below. In this list the adopted reading is given in boldface type, followed by the rejected Folio reading in roman type or a note of the Folio's omission within brackets.

I.i.42–45 **All . . . function** [F assigns to Buckingham] **47 as you guess** [F assigns to Norfolk] **63 web, 'a** Web. O **69–70 that? . . . hell,** that, . . . Hell? **183 He** [F omits] **200 Hereford** Hertford **219 Parke** Pecke **221 Nicholas** Michaell **226 lord** Lords
I.ii.157 **feared** feare **165 confession's** Commissions **171 win** F omits] **181 To** For this to **191 Bulmer** Blumer
I.iii.12 **saw** see **13 Or** A **59 wherewithal. In him** wherewithall in him
II.i.20 **Parke** Pecke **86 mark** make
II.iii.14 **quarrel** quarrell **61 you** you, to you
II.iv.172 **A** And **217 summons. Unsolicited** Summons unsolicited

III.i.21 **coming, now I think on't** comming; now I thinke on't 23 s.d. **Campeius** Campian 61 **your** our
III.ii.143 **glad** gald 172 **filed** fill'd 293 **Who** Whom 344 **Chattels** Castles
IV.i.20–23 **I thank . . . business?** [F assigns to First Gentleman] 34 **Kimbolton** Kymmalton 55 **And sometimes falling ones.** [F assigns to Second Gentleman] 101 **Stokesly** Stokeley
IV.ii.7 **think** thanke 50 **honor from** Honor. From

V.i.24 **thee** the 37 **time** Lime 140 **precipice** Precepit 177 s.d. **[Exeunt.]** Exit Ladie
V.ii.8 **piece** Peere
V.iii.85–86 **This . . . lords.** [F assigns to Lord Chamberlain] 87–91 **Then . . . agreed, lords?** [F assigns to Lord Chamberlain] 125 **bare** base 133 **this** his 174 **heart** hearts
V.v.37 **ways** way 70 **your** you

# THE LIFE OF
# KING HENRY THE EIGHTH

[Dramatis Personae

KING HENRY THE EIGHTH
CARDINAL WOLSEY
CARDINAL CAMPEIUS
CAPUCIUS *ambassador from the Emperor Charles V*
CRANMER *Archbishop of Canterbury*
DUKE OF NORFOLK
DUKE OF BUCKINGHAM
DUKE OF SUFFOLK
EARL OF SURREY
LORD CHAMBERLAIN
LORD CHANCELLOR
GARDINER *Bishop of Winchester*
BISHOP OF LINCOLN
LORD ABERGAVENNY
LORD SANDS
SIR HENRY GUILDFORD
SIR THOMAS LOVELL
SIR ANTHONY DENNY
SIR NICHOLAS VAUX
SECRETARIES *to Wolsey*
CROMWELL *servant to Wolsey*

GRIFFITH *gentleman usher to Queen Katherine*
THREE GENTLEMEN
DOCTOR BUTTS *physician to the king*
GARTER KING-AT-ARMS
SURVEYOR *to the Duke of Buckingham*
BRANDON *and a Sergeant-at-Arms*
DOOR-KEEPER *of the council chamber*
PAGE *to Gardiner* A CRIER
PORTER *and his* MAN

QUEEN KATHERINE *wife to King Henry, after-ward divorced*
ANNE BULLEN *her maid of honor, afterward queen*
AN OLD LADY *friend to Anne Bullen*
PATIENCE *woman to Queen Katherine*

*Several* LORDS *and* LADIES *in the dumb shows* WOMEN *attending upon the queen* SCRIBES OFFICERS GUARDS OTHER ATTENDANTS SPIRITS

*Scene:* London; Westminster; Kimbolton]

## THE PROLOGUE

I come no more to make you laugh.° Things now
That bear a weighty and a serious brow,
Sad, high, and working,° full of state° and woe,
Such noble scenes as draw the eye to flow,
We now present. Those that can pity, here      5
May, if they think it well, let fall a tear:
The subject will deserve it. Such as give
Their money out of hope they may believe
May here find truth° too. Those that come to see
Only a show or two, and so agree               10
The play may pass, if they be still and willing,
I'll undertake may see away their shilling°
Richly in two short hours.° Only they
That come to hear a merry bawdy play,
A noise of targets,° or to see a fellow         15
In a long motley coat guarded with yellow,°

*The decorative border shown above appeared on the first page of Henry VIII in the First Folio edition of Shakespeare's plays, 1623.*
**Pro.1 no . . . laugh** the previous play was presumably a comedy **3 Sad . . . woe king** serious, elevated, and moving; **state** dignity

**9 truth** possibly alluding to the play's alternative title, *All Is True* **12 shilling** the admission price for an expensive seat near the stage **13 two short hours** a conventional reference to performance duration; not to be taken literally **15 targets** shields **16 In . . . yellow** in the parti-colored costume of the professional fool, trimmed ("guarded") in yellow

Will be deceived;° for, gentle hearers, know,
To rank our chosen truth with such a show
As fool and fight is, beside forfeiting
Our own brains and the opinion that we bring     20
To make that only true we now intend,°
Will leave us never an understanding friend.°
Therefore, for goodness' sake, and as you are known
The first and happiest hearers of the town,°
Be sad, as we would make ye. Think ye see     25
The very persons of our noble story
As° they were living. Think you see them great,
And followed with the general throng and sweat
Of thousand friends. Then, in a moment, see
How soon this mightiness meets misery;     30
And if you can be merry then, I'll say
A man may weep upon his wedding day.

# A C T  I

Scene I. [*London. An antechamber in the palace.*]

*Enter the Duke of* NORFOLK *at one door; at the other the Duke of* BUCKINGHAM *and the Lord* ABERGAVENNY.

BUCKINGHAM
Good morrow, and well met. How have ye done
Since last we saw° in France?
NORFOLK           I thank your grace,
Healthful, and ever since a fresh° admirer
Of what I saw there.
BUCKINGHAM       An untimely ague°
Stayed me a prisoner in my chamber when     5
Those suns of glory,° those two lights of men,
Met in the vale of Andren.
NORFOLK          'Twixt Guynes and Arde.°
I was then present; saw them salute on horseback;
Beheld them when they lighted,° how they clung
In their embracement, as° they grew together;     10
Which had they, what four throned ones could have
     weighed°
Such a compounded one?
BUCKINGHAM       All the whole time
I was my chamber's prisoner.°
NORFOLK         Then you lost
The view of earthly glory. Men might say,
Till this time pomp was single,° but now married     15
To one above itself.° Each following day
Became the next day's master,° till the last

Made former wonders its. Today the French,
All clinquant,° all in gold, like heathen gods,
Shone down the English; and tomorrow they     20
Made Britain India:° every man that stood
Showed like a mine. Their dwarfish pages were
As cherubins, all gilt. The madams° too,
Not used to toil, did almost sweat to bear
The pride° upon them, that their very labor     25
Was to them as a painting.° Now this masque°
Was cried° incomparable, and th' ensuing night
Made it a fool and beggar. The two kings,
Equal in luster, were now best, now worst,
As presence° did present them: him in eye     30
Still him in praise;° and being present both,
'Twas said they saw but one, and no discerner
Durst wag his tongue in censure.° When these suns
(For so they phrase° 'em) by their heralds challenged
The noble spirits to arms, they did perform     35
Beyond thought's compass, that former fabulous
     story,°
Being now seen possible enough, got credit,
That Bevis° was believed.
BUCKINGHAM        O, you go far.
NORFOLK
As I belong to worship,° and affect
In honor honesty,° the tract of everything     40
Would by a good discourser lose some life
Which action's self was tongue to.° All was royal;
To the disposing of it nought rebelled.°
Order gave each thing view;° the office° did
Distinctly° his full function.
BUCKINGHAM       Who did guide—     45
I mean, who set the body and the limbs
Of this great sport° together, as you guess?
NORFOLK
One, certes,° that promises no element°
In such a business.
BUCKINGHAM     I pray you, who, my lord?
NORFOLK
All this was ord'red° by the good discretion     50
Of the right reverend Cardinal of York.
BUCKINGHAM
The devil speed him!° No man's pie is freed
From his ambitious finger. What had he
To do in these fierce° vanities? I wonder

---

17 **deceived** disappointed   19–21 **beside . . . intend** besides abandoning any claims to intelligence and our reputation for aiming to present only the truth   22 **an understanding friend** perhaps alluding to the groundlings—spectators standing under the stage—who were sometimes ironically praised for their "understanding"   24 **first . . . town** the best and most favorably disposed audience in London   27 **As** as if
**I.i.2 saw** saw one another   3 **fresh** ready, eager   4 **ague** fever   6 **suns of glory** i.e., Henry VIII and Francis I (with perhaps a quibble on *suns* = sons)   7 **Guynes and Arde** towns in Picardy lying on either side of the valley of Andren; Guynes was in English, Arde in French hands   9 **lighted** alighted   10 **as** as if   11 **weighed** equaled in weight   12–13 **All . . . prisoner** historically, he was in fact present, whereas Norfolk was in England at the time   15 **single** i.e. relatively modest   15–16 **married . . . itself** united to constitute a greater pomp   16–17 **Each . . . master** each day taught something to the next, which superseded it ("master" = teacher)

9 **clinquant** glittering   21 **India** probably not India; but the New World, whose gold mines yielded fabulous wealth   23 **madams** ladies   25 **pride** finery   25–26 **their . . . painting** their very exertion made them flushed, as if rouged   26 **masque** courtly spectacle   27 **cried** declared   30 **presence** being in public   30–31 **him in eye . . . praise** The one seen was always the one praised   32–33 **no discerner . . . censure** no beholder dared choose one above the other   34 **phrase** describe   36 **that . . . story** so that stories formerly thought incredible   38 **Bevis** Bevis of Hampton, the legendary Saxon knight celebrated in medieval romance   39 **worship** the nobility   39–40 **affect . . . honesty** love truth as a point of honor   40–42 **the tract . . . tongue to** the course of all these events, however well narrated, would in the description lose some of the color and spark of the actuality   43 **rebelled** jarred   44 **Order . . . view** Everything was arranged so that it could easily be viewed; **office** official, or officials as a group   45 **Distinctly** i.e., without confusion   47 **sport** entertainment   48 **certes** certainly; **promises no element** would not be expected to share   50 **ord'red** arranged   52 **The devil speed him** The devil (rather than God) prosper him!   54 **fierce** extravagant

That such a keech° can with his very bulk      55
Take up° the rays o' th' beneficial sun,°
And keep it from the earth.
NORFOLK             Surely, sir,
There's in him stuff° that puts him to these ends;
For, being not propped by ancestry, whose grace
Chalks successors their way,° nor called upon      60
For high feats done to th' crown,° neither allied
To eminent assistants,° but spiderlike,
Out of his self-drawing° web, 'a gives us note,°
The force of his own merit makes his way°—
A gift° that heaven gives for him, which buys      65
A place next to the king.
ABERGAVENNY         I cannot tell
What heaven hath given him: let some graver eye
Pierce into that. But I can see his pride
Peep through each part of him. Whence has he that?
If not from hell, the devil is a niggard,°      70
Or has given all before, and he begins
A new hell in himself.
BUCKINGHAM         Why the devil,
Upon this French going out,° took he upon him
(Without the privity° o' th' king) t' appoint
Who should attend on him? He makes up the file°      75
Of all the gentry, for the most part such
To whom as great a charge° as little honor
He meant to lay upon; and his own letter,
The honorable board of council out,°
Must fetch him in he papers.°
ABERGAVENNY         I do know      80
Kinsmen of mine, three at the least, that have
By this so sickened their estates that never
They shall abound° as formerly.
BUCKINGHAM         O, many
Have broke their backs with laying manors on 'em°
For this great journey. What did this vanity°      85
But minister communication of
A most poor issue?°
NORFOLK         Grievingly I think,
The peace between the French and us not values°
The cost that did conclude it.
BUCKINGHAM         Every man,
After the hideous storm that followed, was      90
A thing inspired, and, not consulting,° broke
Into a general prophecy:° that this tempest,
Dashing the garment of this peace, aboded°

The sudden breach on't.
NORFOLK         Which is budded out;
For France hath flawed the league, and hath attached°    95
Our merchants' goods at Bordeaux.
ABERGAVENNY         Is it therefore
Th' ambassador is silenced?
NORFOLK         Marry,° is't.
ABERGAVENNY
A proper title of a peace,° and purchased
At a superfluous rate!°
BUCKINGHAM         Why, all this business
Our reverend cardinal carried.°
NORFOLK         Like it° your grace,      100
The state takes notice of the private difference°
Betwixt you and the cardinal. I advise you
(And take it from a heart that wishes towards you
Honor and plenteous° safety) that you read°
The cardinal's malice and his potency°      105
Together; to consider further that
What his high hatred would effect wants not
A minister° in his power. You know his nature,
That he's revengeful, and I know his sword
Hath a sharp edge. It's long and't may be said      110
It reaches far, and where 'twill not extend,°
Thither he darts it. Bosom up° my counsel;
You'll find it wholesome.° Lo, where comes that rock
That I advise your shunning.

*Enter Cardinal* WOLSEY, *the purse° borne before him,
certain of the* GUARD, *and two* SECRETARIES *with
papers. The cardinal* [WOLSEY] *in his passage fixeth his
eye on* BUCKINGHAM, *and* BUCKINGHAM *on him, both
full of disdain.*

WOLSEY
The Duke of Buckingham's surveyor,° ha?      115
Where's his examination?°
FIRST SECRETARY         Here, so please you.
WOLSEY
Is he in person ready?
FIRST SECRETARY         Aye, please your grace.
WOLSEY
Well, we shall then know more, and Buckingham
Shall lessen his big° look.
          *Exeunt Cardinal* [WOLSEY] *and his* TRAIN.
BUCKINGHAM
This butcher's cur° is venomed-mouthed, and I      120
Have not the power to muzzle him. Therefore best
Not wake him in his slumber. A beggar's book
Outworths a noble's blood.°
NORFOLK         What, are you chafed?°

---

**55 keech** animal fat rolled into a lump (with a sneer at Wolsey's reputed origin as a butcher's son; cf. line 120) **56 Take up** obstruct; **sun** i.e., the king **58 stuff** qualities, capabilities **59–60 whose . . . way** whose special excellence marks a path for followers **60–61 called . . . crown** chosen in recognition of lofty exploits in behalf of the crown **62 assistants** (1) public officials (2) supporters **63 self-drawing** self-spinning; **'a . . . note** he lets us know **64 makes his way** wins him preferment **65 gift** i.e., merit **70 If . . . niggard** the devil is the source of pride, the sin for which Lucifer fell and hell was created **73 going out** expedition **74 privity** confidential participation **75 file** list **77 charge** expense **79 out** unconsulted **80 fetch . . . papers** fetch in whom he puts on his list **83 abound** prosper **84 broke . . . 'em** ruined themselves by pawning their estates to outfit themselves **85 vanity** extravagance **86–87 minister . . . issue** furnish occasion for unproductive talk (with a possible quibble on *poor issue* = impoverished heirs) **88 not values** is not worth **91 not consulting** i.e., one another **92 a general prophecy** i.e., all prophesied the same **93 aboded** foretold

**95 flawed . . . attached** broken the treaty and confiscated **97 Marry** indeed (a mild oath, from "By the Virgin Mary") **98 A proper . . . peace** an excellent contract of peace (ironic) **99 superfluous rate** excessive cost **100 carried** managed; **Like it** if it please (a courteous formula for volunteering unasked information) **101 difference** disagreement **104 plenteous** ample; **read** construe **105 potency** power **107–08 wants . . . minister** does not lack an agent **111 extend** reach **112 Bosom up** conceal within your bosom **113 wholesome** sound **114 s.d. purse** bag containing the Great Seal that is the insignia of the Lord Chancellor's office **115 surveyor** overseer of an estate; Charles Knyvet, Buckingham's cousin **116 examination** deposition **119 big** haughty **120 butcher's cur** referring to Wolsey's parentage **122–23 A beggar's . . . blood** A beggar's book-learning is more esteemed than nobility of descent **123 chafed** angry

Ask God for temp'rance; that's th' appliance only°
Which your disease requires.

**BUCKINGHAM**            I read in's looks    125
Matter against me, and his eye reviled
Me as his abject object.° At this instant
He bores° me with some trick. He's gone to th'
     king;
I'll follow and outstare him.

**NORFOLK**            Stay, my lord,
And let your reason with your choler question°    130
What 'tis you go about. To climb steep hills
Requires slow pace at first. Anger is like
A full hot° horse who, being allowed his way,
Self-mettle° tires him. Not a man in England
Can advise me like you; be to yourself    135
As you would to your friend.

**BUCKINGHAM**          I'll to the king,
And from a mouth of honor° quite cry down
This Ipswich° fellow's° insolence, or proclaim
There's difference in no persons.°

**NORFOLK**           Be advised.°
Heat not a furnace for your foe so hot    140
That it do singe yourself. We may outrun
By violent swiftness that which we run at,
And lose by overrunning.° Know you not
The fire that mounts the liquor° till't run o'er
In seeming to augment it wastes it? Be advised.    145
I say again there is no English soul
More stronger° to direct you than yourself,
If with the sap° of reason you would quench,
Or but allay, the fire of passion.

**BUCKINGHAM**            Sir,
I am thankful to you, and I'll go along    150
By your prescription; but this top-proud° fellow
(Whom from the flow of gall I name not, but
From sincere motions)° by intelligence°
And proofs as clear as founts in July° when
We see each grain of gravel, I do know    155
To be corrupt and treasonous.

**NORFOLK**           Say not "treasonous."

**BUCKINGHAM**
To th' king I'll say't, and make my vouch° as strong
As shore of rock. Attend.° This holy fox,
Or wolf, or both (for he is equal rav'nous
As he is subtle, and as prone to mischief    160
As able to perform't, his mind and place°
Infecting one another, yea, reciprocally)
Only to show his pomp° as well in France

As here at home, suggests° the king our master
To this last costly treaty, th' interview,°    165
That swallowed so much treasure, and like a glass
Did break i' th' wrenching.°

**NORFOLK**           Faith, and so it did.

**BUCKINGHAM**
Pray give me favor,° sir. This cunning cardinal
The articles o' th' combination drew°
As himself pleased; and they were ratified    170
As he cried, "Thus let be," to as much end
As give a crutch to th' dead. But our count-cardinal
Has done this, and 'tis well; for worthy Wolsey,
Who cannot err, he did it. Now this follows
(Which, as I take it, is a kind of puppy    175
To th' old dam,° treason) Charles the emperor,
Under pretense to see the queen his aunt
(For 'twas indeed his color,° but he came
To whisper Wolsey) here makes visitation.°
His fears were that the interview betwixt    180
England and France might through their amity
Breed him some prejudice, for from this league
Peeped harms that menaced him. He privily°
Deals with our cardinal; and, as I trow°
(Which I do well, for I am sure the emperor    185
Paid ere he promised, whereby his suit was granted
Ere it was asked) but when the way was made
And paved with gold, the emperor thus desired,
That he would please to alter the king's course
And break the foresaid peace. Let the king know,    190
As soon he shall by me, that thus the cardinal
Does buy and sell° his honor as he pleases,
And for his own advantage.

**NORFOLK**           I am sorry
To hear this of him, and could wish he were
Something mistaken° in't.

**BUCKINGHAM**        No, not a syllable:    195
I do pronounce° him in that very shape
He shall appear in proof.°

*Enter* BRANDON, *a* SERGEANT-AT-ARMS *before him,
and two or three of the* GUARD.

**BRANDON**
Your office, sergeant: execute it.

**SERGEANT**           Sir,
My lord the Duke of Buckingham, and Earl
Of Hereford, Stafford, and Northampton, I    200
Arrest thee of high treason, in the name
Of our most sovereign king.

**BUCKINGHAM**          Lo you,° my lord,
The net has fall'n upon me! I shall perish
Under device and practice.°

---

**124 appliance only** only remedy   **127 abject object** object of contempt   **128 bores** cheats   **130 with . . . question** dispute with your anger   **133 full hot** high-spirited   **134 Self-mettle** his own natural vigor   **137 from . . . honor** speaking as a nobleman   **138 Ipswich** Wolsey's birthplace; **fellow's** usually applied to inferiors; cf. III.ii.280 and IV.ii.100   **139 There's . . . persons** distinctions of rank no longer matter; **Be advised** Take care   **143 overrunning** running beyond   **144 mounts the liquor** causes the liquor to rise   **147 More stronger** better qualified (double comparatives, and also superlatives, are frequent in Shakespeare)   **148 sap** juice, fluid   **151 top-proud** excessively proud   **152–53 Whom . . . motions** of whom I thus speak not out of spite but from sincere motives   **153 intelligence** intelligence reports   **154 founts in July** i.e., streams no longer muddied by spring floods ("July" is accented on the first syllable)   **157 vouch** allegation   **158 Attend** Listen   **161 mind and place** inclinations and position   **163 pomp** magnificence

**164 suggests** prompts (used of the devil)   **165 interview** "ceremonial meeting of princes" (Foakes)   **167 wrenching** rinsing   **168 Pray . . . favor** Please hear me out   **169 articles . . . drew** drew up the terms of the peace treaty   **176 dam** mother   **178 color** pretext   **179 makes visitation** pays a visit   **183 privily** secretly   **184 as I trow** as I believe (the principal clause required after the parenthetical comment does not appear; grammar has yielded to the speaker's emotion, but the sense of the passage is clear)   **192 buy and sell** traffic in   **195 Something mistaken** to some extent misinterpreted   **196 pronounce** declare   **197 He . . . proof** experience will reveal him   **202 Lo you** behold   **204 device and practice** plots and intrigues

BRANDON                I am sorry
To see you ta'en from liberty, to look on       205
The business present.° 'Tis his highness' pleasure
You shall to th' Tower.°

BUCKINGHAM          It will help me nothing
To plead mine innocence, for that due is on me
Which makes my whit'st part black. The will of heav'n
Be done in this and all things! I obey.        210
O my Lord Aberga'ny, fare you well!

BRANDON
Nay, he must bear you company. [*To* ABERGA-
    VENNY.] The king
Is pleased you shall to th' Tower, till you know
How he determines further.

ABERGAVENNY          As the duke said,
The will of heaven be done, and the king's pleasure    215
By me obeyed!

BRANDON      Here is a warrant from
The king t' attach° Lord Montacute, and the bodies°
Of the duke's confessor, John de la Car,
One Gilbert Parke, his councillor—

BUCKINGHAM              So, so;
These are the limbs o' th' plot. No more, I hope.     220

BRANDON
A monk o' th' Chartreux.°

BUCKINGHAM         O, Nicholas Hopkins?

BRANDON                           He.

BUCKINGHAM
My surveyor is false; the o'er-great cardinal
Hath showed him gold. My life is spanned° already.
I am the shadow of poor Buckingham,
Whose figure even this instant cloud puts on,      225
By dark'ning my clear sun.° My lord, farewell.

                             *Exeunt.*

Scene II. [*The same. The council chamber.*]

*Cornets. Enter* KING *Henry, leaning on the cardinal's
shoulder; the* NOBLES, [*a* SECRETARY *of the cardinal's,*]
*and Sir Thomas* LOVELL. *The cardinal* [WOLSEY]
*places himself under the king's feet° on his right side.*

KING
My life itself, and the best heart° of it,
Thanks you for this great care. I stood i' th' level°
Of a full-charged confederacy,° and give thanks
To you that choked it. Let be called before us
That gentleman of Buckingham's.° In person      5
I'll hear him his confessions justify,°
And point by point the treasons of his master
He shall again relate.

*A noise within, crying* "Room for the queen!"

[KATHERINE, *who is*] *ushered by the Duke of* NORFOLK.
*Enter the* QUEEN, [*Duke of*] NORFOLK *and* [*Duke of*]
SUFFOLK. *She kneels.* KING *riseth from his state, takes her
up, kisses and placeth her by him.*

QUEEN KATHERINE
Nay, we must longer kneel: I am a suitor.

KING
Arise, and take place° by us. Half your suit      10
Never name to us: you have half our power.
The other moiety° ere you ask is given.
Repeat your will,° and take it.

QUEEN KATHERINE          Thank your majesty.
That you would love yourself, and in that love
Not unconsiderèd leave your honor nor        15
The dignity of your office, is the point
Of my petition.

KING            Lady mine, proceed.

QUEEN KATHERINE
I am solicited,° not by a few,
And those of true condition,° that your subjects
Are in great grievance. There have been commissions   20
Sent down among 'em, which hath flawed° the heart
Of all their loyalties; wherein although,
My good Lord Cardinal, they vent reproaches
Most bitterly on you as putter-on°
Of these exactions, yet the king our master—     25
Whose honor heaven shield from soil!—even he
    escapes not
Language unmannerly; yea, such which breaks
The sides of loyalty, and almost appears
In loud rebellion.

NORFOLK          Not almost appears—
It doth appear. For, upon these taxations,      30
The clothiers all, not able to maintain
The many to them 'longing,° have put off
The spinsters, carders, fullers,° weavers, who,
Unfit for other life, compelled by hunger
And lack of other means, in desperate manner    35
Daring th' event to th' teeth,° are all in uproar,
And danger serves among them.°

KING          Taxation?
Wherein? And what taxation? My Lord Cardinal,
You that are blamed for it alike with us,
Know you of this taxation?

WOLSEY          Please you, sir,      40
I know but of a single part° in aught
Pertains to th' state, and front but in that file
Where others tell steps with me.°

QUEEN KATHERINE          No, my lord?
You know no more than others? But you frame
Things that are known alike,° which are not whole-
    some                                  45

**205–06 to look . . . present** (1) and to see what is now happening (2) to be involved in the present affair   **207 Tower** the Tower of London (where suspected traitors were imprisoned) **217 attach** arrest; **bodies** persons **221 Chartreux** Charterhouse (i.e., a Carthusian) **223 spanned** measured out **225–26 Whose . . . sun** whose form is at this instant clouded by misfortune that dims my glory and alienates me from my king ("sun" may refer to both Buckingham and Henry) **I.ii.s.d. under . . . feet** at the feet of the king, who is seated on a raised and canopied "state," or throne   **1 best heart** very core   **2 i' th' level** in direct range   **3 full-charged confederacy** fully loaded conspiracy   **5 That . . . Buckingham's** the surveyor referred to at I.i.222   **6 justify** confirm

**10 take place** be seated   **12 moiety** half   **13 Repeat your will** state your wish   **18 solicited** informed by petitioners   **19 true condition** loyal disposition   **21 flawed** broken   **24 putter-on** instigator   **32 to them 'longing** employed by them   **33 spinsters, carders, fullers** "spinsters" = spinners (usually female); carders combed out impurities from the wool; fullers cleansed the cloth by beating   **36 Daring . . . teeth** defiantly daring the worst   **37 serves among them** is welcomed as a comrade   **41 a single part** i.e., my own individual share **42–43 front . . . me** only march in the front rank of those who keep in step with me, i.e., share my responsibility   **44–45 frame . . . alike** devise measures known to all alike (in the council)

To° those which would not know them, and yet must
Perforce be their acquaintance.° These exactions
(Whereof my sovereign would have note),° they are
Most pestilent° to th' hearing; and to bear 'em
The back is sacrifice to th' load. They say                        50
They are devised by you, or else you suffer
Too hard an exclamation.°

KING                            Still exaction!
The nature of it? In what kind, let's know,
Is this exaction?

QUEEN KATHERINE
I am much too venturous                                            55
In tempting of your patience, but am boldened
Under your promised pardon. The subject's grief°
Comes through commissions, which compels from
     each
The sixth part of his substance, to be levied
Without delay; and the pretense° for this                         60
Is named your wars in France. This makes bold
     mouths.
Tongues spit their duties out, and cold hearts freeze
Allegiance° in them. Their curses now
Live where their prayers did, and it's come to pass,
This tractable obedience is a slave                                65
To each incensèd will.° I would your highness
Would give it quick consideration, for
There is no primer baseness.°

KING                            By my life,
This is against our pleasure.

WOLSEY                          And for me,
I have no further gone in this than by                            70
A single voice,° and that not passed me but
By learned approbation of the judges. If I am
Traduced by ignorant tongues, which neither know
My faculties° nor person, yet will be
The chronicles of my doing, let me say                            75
'Tis but the fate of place,° and the rough brake°
That virtue must go through. We must not stint
Our necessary actions in the fear
To cope° malicious censurers, which ever,
As rav'nous fishes, do a vessel follow                            80
That is new-trimmed,° but benefit no further
Than vainly longing. What we oft do best,
By sick° interpreters (once° weak ones) is
Not ours or not allowed;° what worst, as oft,
Hitting a grosser quality,° is cried up                           85
For our best act. If we shall stand still,
In fear our motion° will be mocked or carped at,
We should take root here where we sit,
Or sit state-statues only.°

KING                            Things done well,
And with a care, exempt themselves from fear.                     90

Things done without example,° in their issue°
Are to be feared. Have you a precedent
Of this commission? I believe, not any.
We must not rend° our subjects from our laws,
And stick them in our will.° Sixth part of each?                  95
A trembling° contribution! Why, we take
From every tree lop,° bark, and part o' th' timber,
And though we leave it with a root, thus hacked,°
The air will drink the sap. To every county
Where this is questioned° send our letters with                   100
Free pardon to each man that has denied
The force° of this commission. Pray look to't;
I put it to your care.

WOLSEY [To the SECRETARY.] A word with you.
Let there be letters writ to every shire
Of the king's grace and pardon. The grievèd commons  105
Hardly conceive° of me: let it be noised
That through our° intercession this revokement
And pardon comes. I shall anon° advise you
Further in the proceeding.          Exit SECRETARY.

Enter SURVEYOR.

QUEEN KATHERINE
I am sorry that the Duke of Buckingham                            110
Is run in° your displeasure.

KING                            It grieves many.
The gentleman is learned and a most rare° speaker;
To Nature none more bound;° his training such
That he may furnish and instruct great teachers,
And never seek for aid out of° himself. Yet see,                 115
When these so noble benefits° shall prove
Not well disposed,° the mind growing once corrupt,
They turn to vicious forms, ten times more ugly
Than ever they were fair. This man so complete,
Who was enrolled 'mongst wonders, and when we,                    120
Almost with ravished listening,° could not find
His hour of speech a minute—he, my lady,
Hath into monstrous habits° put the graces
That once were his, and is become as black
As if besmeared in hell. Sit by us. You shall hear—              125
This was his gentleman in trust°—of him
Things to strike honor sad. Bid him recount
The fore-recited practices,° whereof
We cannot feel too little, hear too much.

WOLSEY
Stand forth, and with bold spirit relate what° you,              130
Most like a careful subject, have collected°
Out of the Duke of Buckingham.

KING                            Speak freely.

SURVEYOR
First, it was usual with him—every day

45–46 wholesome To (1) beneficial to (2) approved by
47 their acquaintance acquainted with them   48 note
knowledge   49 pestilent offensive   52 exclamation reproach
57 grief grievance   60 pretense pretext   63 Allegiance four
syllables   65–66 This . . . will this willing obedience of theirs
has given way to angry passion   68 primer baseness "mischief more urgently in need of redress" (Foakes)   71 voice
vote   74 faculties qualities   76 place high office; brake thicket
79 cope encounter   81 new-trimmed newly made sea-
worthy   83 sick unsound; once in short   84 Not . . .
allowed denied us or condemned   85 Hitting . . . quality
appealing to the baser sort   87 motion (1) movement (2)
proposal   89 state-statues only mere replicas of statesmen

91 example precedent; issue consequences   94 rend pluck
95 stick . . . will i.e., make them creatures of our arbitrary
power   96 trembling accompanied by, or causing, trembling
97 lop smaller branches and twigs   98 thus hacked when it is
thus hacked   100 questioned disputed   102 force validity
106 Hardly conceive (1) think harshly (2) scarcely have any
conception   107 our note his use of the royal pronoun   108
anon soon   111 Is run in has incurred   112 rare accomplished
113 bound indebted (for his endowments)   115 out of from
outside   116 benefits natural gifts   117 disposed applied
121 Almost . . . listening listening almost spellbound   123
habits garments   126 in trust trusted   128 fore-recited
practices already revealed plots   130 what i.e., what information   131 collected gathered (by spying)

It would infect his speech—that if the king
Should without issue die, he'll carry it° so    135
To make the scepter his. These very words
I've heard him utter to his son-in-law,
Lord Aberga'ny, to whom by oath he menaced
Revenge upon the cardinal.
WOLSEY             Please your highness, note
This dangerous conception° in this point.    140
Not friended by his wish,° to your high person
His will is most malignant, and it stretches
Beyond you to your friends.
QUEEN KATHERINE        My learned Lord Cardinal,
Deliver all with charity.
KING             Speak on.
How grounded he his title to the crown    145
Upon our fail?° To this point hast thou heard him
At any time speak aught?
SURVEYOR        He was brought to this
By a vain prophecy of Nicholas Henton.°
KING
What was that Henton?
SURVEYOR        Sir, a Chartreux friar,
His confessor, who fed him every minute    150
With words of sovereignty.°
KING             How know'st thou this?
SURVEYOR
Not long before your highness sped to° France,
The duke being at the Rose,° within the parish
Saint Lawrence Poultney, did of me demand
What was the speech° among the Londoners    155
Concerning the French journey. I replied
Men feared the French would prove perfidious,
To the king's danger. Presently° the duke
Said 'twas the fear indeed and that he doubted°
'Twould prove the verity of certain words    160
Spoke by a holy monk "that oft," says he,
"Hath sent to me, wishing me to permit
John de la Car, my chaplain, a choice° hour
To hear from him a matter of some moment;
Whom after under the confession's seal    165
He solemnly had sworn that what he spoke
My chaplain to no creature living but
To me should utter, with demure° confidence
This pausingly ensued: 'Neither the king nor's heirs
(Tell you the duke) shall prosper. Bid him strive    170
To win the love o' th' commonalty.° The duke
Shall govern England.'"
QUEEN KATHERINE        If I know you well,
You were the duke's surveyor, and lost your office
On the complaint o' th' tenants. Take good heed
You charge not in your spleen° a noble person,    175
And spoil° your nobler soul.° I say, take heed;

Yes, heartily beseech you.
KING             Let him on.
Go forward.
SURVEYOR    On my soul, I'll speak but truth.
I told my lord the duke, by th' devil's illusions
The monk might be deceived, and that 'twas dangerous    180
To ruminate on this so far, until
It forged him° some design, which,° being believed,
It was much like to do. He answered, "Tush,
It can do me no damage"; adding further,
That, had the king in his last sickness failed,°    185
The cardinal's and Sir Thomas Lovell's heads
Should have gone off.
KING             Ha! What, so rank?° Ah, ha!
There's mischief in this man. Canst thou say further?
SURVEYOR
I can, my liege.
KING             Proceed.
SURVEYOR        Being at Greenwich,
After your highness had reproved the duke    190
About Sir William Bulmer—
KING             I remember
Of such a time: being my sworn° servant,
The duke retained him his. But on. What hence?
SURVEYOR
"If" (quoth he), "I for this had been committed,
As to the Tower I thought, I would have played    195
The part my father meant to act upon
Th' usurper Richard, who, being at Salisbury,
Made suit to come in's presence; which if granted,
As he made semblance° of his duty, would
Have put his knife into him."
KING             A giant traitor!    200
WOLSEY
Now, madam, may his highness live in freedom,
And this man out of prison?
QUEEN KATHERINE        God mend all!
KING
There's something more would out of thee. What
   say'st?
SURVEYOR
After "the duke his father," with the "knife,"
He stretched him,° and with one hand on his dagger,    205
Another spread on's breast, mounting° his eyes,
He did discharge a horrible oath whose tenor
Was, were he evil used,° he would outgo
His father by as much as a performance
Does an irresolute° purpose.
KING             There's his period,°    210
To sheathe his knife in us. He is attached.°
Call him to present° trial. If he may
Find mercy in the law, 'tis his; if none,
Let him not seek't of us. By day and night!
He's traitor to th' height.°          *Exeunt.*    215

---

**135 carry it** manage things   **140 conception** design   **141 Not . . . wish** not granted his wish (that the king should die childless)   **146 fail** (1) failure to beget an heir (2) death   **148 Henton** his name was in fact Nicholas Hopkins, Henton being the name of his priory   **151 sovereignty** i.e., relating to his accession to the throne   **152 sped to** set out for   **153 the Rose** a manor house belonging to Buckingham   **155 speech** report   **158 Presently** instantly   **159 doubted** suspected   **163 choice** suitable   **168 demure** solemn   **171 commonalty** common people   **175 spleen** malice   **176 spoil** destroy; **nobler soul** moral nobility taking precedence over the nobility of rank mentioned in the previous line

**182 forged him** caused him to fashion; **which** the monk's words   **185 failed** died   **187 rank** (1) corrupt (2) full grown (the plot)   **192 sworn** two syllables   **199 semblance** pretense   **205 stretched him** stretched himself to his full height   **206 mounting** raising   **208 evil used** badly treated   **210 irresolute** unfulfilled; **period** goal   **211 attached** arrested   **212 present** immediate   **215 height** utmost degree

Scene III. [*An antechamber in the palace.*]

*Enter Lord* CHAMBERLAIN *and Lord* SANDS.

CHAMBERLAIN
Is't possible the spells of France should juggle
Men into such strange mysteries?°

SANDS            New customs,
Though they be never so ridiculous
(Nay, let 'em be unmanly) yet are followed.

CHAMBERLAIN
As far as I see, all the good our English     5
Have got by the late voyage is but merely
A fit or two o' th' face;° but they are shrewd° ones,
For when they hold 'em,° you would swear directly
Their very noses had been counsellors
To Pepin or Clotharius,° they keep state° so.     10

SANDS
They have all new legs,° and lame ones; one would take it,
That never saw 'em pace° before, the spavin
Or springhalt° reigned among 'em.

CHAMBERLAIN          Death! My lord,
Their clothes are after such a pagan cut to't,°
That, sure, th' have worn out Christendom.°

*Enter Sir Thomas* LOVELL.

                     How now? 15
What news, Sir Thomas Lovell?

LOVELL            Faith, my lord,
I hear of none but the new proclamation
That's clapped° upon the court gate.

CHAMBERLAIN          What is't for?

LOVELL
The reformation of our traveled gallants
That fill the court with quarrels, talk, and tailors.     20

CHAMBERLAIN
I'm glad 'tis there. Now I would pray our monsieurs
To think an English courtier may be wise,
And never see the Louvre.°

LOVELL            They must either
(For so run the conditions) leave those remnants
Of fool and feather° that they got in France,     25
With all their honorable points of ignorance°
Pertaining thereunto, as fights and fireworks,°
Abusing° better men than they can be
Out of a foreign wisdom, renouncing clean
The faith they have in tennis and tall stockings,     30
Short blist'red° breeches, and those types° of travel,

And understand° again like honest men,
Or pack° to their old playfellows. There, I take it,
They may, cum privilegio,° "oui" away
The lag-end° of their lewdness, and be laughed at.     35

SANDS
'Tis time to give 'em physic,° their diseases
Are grown so catching.

CHAMBERLAIN        What a loss our ladies
Will have of these trim vanities!°

LOVELL             Aye, marry,
There will be woe indeed, lords. The sly whoresons
Have got a speeding° trick to lay down ladies.     40
A French song and a fiddle has no fellow.°

SANDS
The devil fiddle 'em! I am glad they are going,
For, sure, there's no converting of 'em. Now
An honest country lord, as I am, beaten
A long time out of play, may bring his plain-song,°     45
And have an hour of hearing; and, by'r Lady,°
Held current music° too.

CHAMBERLAIN        Well said, Lord Sands.
Your colt's tooth° is not cast yet?

SANDS            No, my lord,
Nor shall not while I have a stump.°

CHAMBERLAIN          Sir Thomas,
Whither were you a-going?

LOVELL            To the cardinal's.     50
Your lordship is a guest too.

CHAMBERLAIN         O, 'tis true.
This night he makes a supper, and a great one,
To many lords and ladies. There will be
The beauty of this kingdom, I'll assure you.

LOVELL
That churchman bears a bounteous mind indeed,     55
A hand as fruitful as the land that feeds us.
His dews fall everywhere.

CHAMBERLAIN        No doubt he's noble.
He had a black° mouth that said other of him.

SANDS
He may, my lord; has wherewithal. In him
Sparing° would show a worse sin than ill doctrine.     60
Men of his way° should be most liberal;
They are set here for examples.

CHAMBERLAIN           True, they are so,
But few now give so great ones. My barge stays;
Your lordship shall along. Come, good Sir Thomas,
We shall be late else, which I would not be,     65
For I was spoke to,° with Sir Henry Guildford
This night to be comptrollers.°

SANDS           I am your lordship's. *Exeunt.*

---

**I.iii.1–2 juggle . . . mysteries** trick men into into such oddly mysterious behavior **7 fit . . . face** a grimace or two; **shrewd** nasty **8 hold 'em** i.e., screw up their faces in this way **10 Pepin or Clotharius** sixth- and seventh-century kings of the Franks; **keep state** affect grandeur **11 new legs** new fashions in walking or bowing **12 pace** walk (suggesting horse references that follow) **12–13 spavin Or springhalt** diseases affecting horses' legs **14 to't** as well **15 worn out Christendom** used up Christian fashions **18 clapped** fastened **23 Louvre** palace of the French kings in Paris; now the art museum **25 fool and feather** foolish fashions (alluding to the feathers worn by some gallants in their hats) **26 honorable . . . ignorance** ignorant conceptions of honorable conduct **27 fights and fireworks** i.e., duelling and whoring (with a possible reference to venereal disease as the outcome) **28 Abusing** goes with "points of ignorance," and is not parallel with "renouncing" in the next line, which continues the thought indicated by "leave" in line 24 **31 blist'red** puffed; **types** insignia

**32 understand** comprehend things, in general (with a possible quibble on *stand under* [i.e., clothes]) **33 pack** clear out **34 cum privilegio** with license **35 lag-end** latter part **36 physic** medical treatment **38 trim vanities** spruce fops **40 speeding** effective **41 fellow** equal **45 plain-song** simple melody **46 by'r Lady** i.e., by the Virgin Mary (a mild oath) **47 Held current music** have it accepted as good music **48 colt's tooth** i.e., youthful lustiness **49 stump** with a bawdy double meaning **58 black** evil **60 Sparing** frugality **61 way** i.e., of life **66 spoke to** asked **67 comptrollers** household officers in charge of the festivities

#### Scene IV. [*A hall in York Place.*]

*Hautboys.° A small table under a state° for the cardinal, a longer table for the guests. Then enter* ANNE *Bullen and divers other* LADIES *and* GENTLEMEN *as guests, at one door; at another door, enter Sir Henry* GUILDFORD.

GUILDFORD
Ladies, a general welcome from his grace
Salutes ye all. This night he dedicates
To fair content and you. None here, he hopes,
In all this noble bevy,° has brought with her
One care abroad. He would have all as merry    5
As, first, good company, good wine, good welcome,
Can make good people.

*Enter Lord* CHAMBERLAIN, *Lord* SANDS, *and* [*Sir Thomas*] LOVELL.

                 O, my lord, y' are tardy.
The very thought of this fair company
Clapped wings to me.

CHAMBERLAIN
You are young, Sir Harry Guildford.    10

SANDS
Sir Thomas Lovell, had the cardinal
But half my lay thoughts in him, some of these
Should find a running banquet,° ere they rested,
I think would better please 'em. By my life,
They are a sweet society° of fair ones.    15

LOVELL
O, that your lordship were but now confessor
To one or two of these!

SANDS         I would I were;
They should find easy penance.

LOVELL            Faith, how easy?

SANDS
As easy as a down bed would afford it.

CHAMBERLAIN
Sweet ladies, will it please you sit? Sir Harry,    20
Place you° that side; I'll take the charge of this.
His grace is ent'ring. Nay, you must not freeze.
Two women placed together makes cold weather.
My Lord Sands, you are one will keep 'em waking:
Pray, sit between these ladies.

SANDS            By my faith,    25
And thank your lordship. By your leave, sweet ladies.
If I chance to talk a little wild, forgive me;
I had it from my father.

ANNE            Was he mad, sir?

SANDS
O, very mad, exceeding mad, in love too;
But he would bite none. Just as I do now,    30
He would kiss you twenty with a breath.°

[*Kisses her.*]

CHAMBERLAIN           Well said,° my lord.
So, now y' are fairly° seated. Gentlemen,
The penance lies on you if these fair ladies

Pass away° frowning.

SANDS           For my little cure,°
Let me alone.    35

*Hautboys. Enter Cardinal* WOLSEY, *and takes his state.°*

WOLSEY
Y' are welcome, my fair guests. That noble lady
Or gentleman that is not freely merry
Is not my friend. This, to confirm my welcome;
And to you all, good health. [*Drinks.*]

SANDS           Your grace is noble.
Let me have such a bowl may hold my thanks,    40
And save me so much talking.

WOLSEY           My Lord Sands,
I am beholding° to you. Cheer your neighbors.
Ladies, you are not merry. Gentlemen,
Whose fault is this?

SANDS           The red wine first must rise
In their fair cheeks, my lord. Then we shall have 'em    45
Talk us to silence.

ANNE           You are a merry gamester,°
My Lord Sands.

SANDS          Yes, if I make my play.°
Here's to your ladyship; and pledge it, madam,
For 'tis to such a thing—

ANNE           You cannot show me.

SANDS
I told your grace they would talk anon.

*Drum and trumpet; chambers° discharged.*

WOLSEY               What's that?    50

CHAMBERLAIN
Look out there, some° of ye. [*Exit* SERVANT.]

WOLSEY           What warlike voice,
And to what end, is this? Nay, ladies, fear not;
By all the laws of war y' are privileged.°

[*Re*]*enter a* SERVANT.

CHAMBERLAIN
How now, what is't?

SERVANT         A noble troop of strangers,
For so they seem. Th' have left their barge, and landed,    55
And hither make,° as great ambassadors
From foreign princes.

WOLSEY         Good Lord Chamberlain,
Go, give 'em welcome: you can speak the French tongue;
And pray receive 'em nobly and conduct 'em
Into our presence, where this heaven of beauty    60
Shall shine at full upon them. Some attend him.
           [*Exit* CHAMBERLAIN, *attended.*]

*All rise, and tables removed.*

You have now a broken° banquet, but we'll mend it.
A good digestion to you all; and once more
I show'r a welcome on ye: welcome all.

---

34 **Pass away** leave; **cure** (1) charge, parish (continuing the ecclesiastical metaphor of lines 16 ff.) (2) remedy   35 **s.d. state** chair of state   42 **beholding** beholden   46 **gamester** playful person   47 **make my play** win my game   50 **s.d. chambers** small cannon used for ceremonial purposes   51 **some** some one (cf. also line 61)   53 **privileged** entitled to immunity   56 **make** make their way   62 **broken** interrupted, with a possible pun on "poor remains" (of a feast)

I.iv.s.d. **Hautboys** oboes; **state** canopy   4 **bevy** company (of ladies)   13 **running banquet** hasty repast (with a bawdy double meaning)   15 **society** assembly   21 **Place you** i.e., place the guests   31 **kiss . . . breath** kiss twenty in one breath; **said** done   32 **fairly** properly

*Hautboys. Enter* KING *and others, as* MASQUERS,°
*habited° like shepherds, ushered by the Lord* CHAMBER-
LAIN. *They pass directly before the cardinal* [WOLSEY],
*and gracefully salute him.*

A noble company! What are their pleasures?            65
CHAMBERLAIN
Because they speak no English, thus they prayed
To tell your grace: that having heard by fame°
Of this so noble and so fair assembly
This night to meet here, they could do no less
(Out of the great respect they bear to beauty)        70
But leave their flocks and, under your fair conduct,°
Crave leave to view these ladies and entreat
An hour of revels with 'em.
WOLSEY                         Say, Lord Chamberlain,
They have done my poor house grace; for which I
      pay 'em
A thousand thanks and pray 'em take their pleasures.  75

*Choose ladies;* KING *and* ANNE *Bullen.*

KING
The fairest hand I ever touched! O beauty,
Till now I never knew thee!

*Music. Dance.*

WOLSEY
My lord!
CHAMBERLAIN   Your grace?
WOLSEY                   Pray tell 'em thus much from me:
There should be one amongst 'em, by his person,
More worthy this place than myself, to whom          80
(If I but knew him) with my love and duty
I would surrender it.°
CHAMBERLAIN         I will, my lord.

*Whisper[s with the* MASQUERS].

WOLSEY
What say they?
CHAMBERLAIN   Such a one, they all confess,
There is indeed, which they would have your grace
Find out, and he will take it.
WOLSEY                    Let me see then.         85
By all your good leaves, gentlemen; here I'll make
My royal choice.°
KING [*Unmasking.*] Ye have found him, cardinal.
You hold a fair assembly; you do well, lord.
You are a churchman, or, I'll tell you, cardinal,
I should judge now unhappily.°
WOLSEY              I am glad               90
Your grace is grown so pleasant.°
KING                        My Lord Chamberlain,
Prithee come hither. What fair lady's that?
CHAMBERLAIN
An't please your grace, Sir Thomas Bullen's daughter,
The Viscount Rochford, one of her highness' women.
KING
By heaven, she is a dainty one. Sweetheart,       95

I were unmannerly to take you out°
And not to kiss you.° A health, gentlemen!
Let it go round.
WOLSEY
Sir Thomas Lovell, is the banquet ready
I' th' privy chamber?
LOVELL              Yes, my lord.
WOLSEY                          Your grace,   100
I fear, with dancing is a little heated.
KING
I fear, too much.
WOLSEY          There's fresher air, my lord,
In the next chamber.
KING
Lead in your ladies, every one. Sweet partner,
I must not yet forsake you. Let's be merry,          105
Good my Lord Cardinal. I have half a dozen healths
To drink to these fair ladies, and a measure°
To lead 'em once again; and then let's dream
Who's best in favor.° Let the music knock it.°
                              *Exeunt with trumpets.*

# ACT II

Scene I. [*Westminster. A street.*]

*Enter two* GENTLEMEN *at several° doors.*

FIRST GENTLEMAN
Whither away so fast?
SECOND GENTLEMAN   O, God save ye!
Ev'n to the Hall,° to hear what shall become
Of the great Duke of Buckingham.
FIRST GENTLEMAN                I'll save you
That labor, sir. All's now done but the ceremony
Of bringing back the prisoner.
SECOND GENTLEMAN           Were you there?     5
FIRST GENTLEMAN
Yes, indeed was I.
SECOND GENTLEMAN Pray speak what has happened.
FIRST GENTLEMAN
You may guess quickly what.
SECOND GENTLEMAN          Is he found guilty?
FIRST GENTLEMAN
Yes, truly is he, and condemned upon't.
SECOND GENTLEMAN
I am sorry for't.
FIRST GENTLEMAN   So are a number more.
SECOND GENTLEMAN
But, pray, how passed it?°                      10
FIRST GENTLEMAN
I'll tell you in a little.° The great duke
Came to the bar, where to his accusations
He pleaded still not guilty, and allegèd°
Many sharp reasons to defeat° the law.

**64 s.d. masquers** i.e., disguised and vizarded as for a court
masque; **habited** dressed   **67 fame** report   **71 under . . .
conduct** with your kind permission   **82 it** the place of honor
**87 royal choice** choice of a king   **90 unhappily** unfavorably
**91 pleasant** merry

**96 take you out** i.e., invite you to dance   **97 to kiss you**
customary following a dance   **107 measure** stately dance   **109
best in favor** (1) prettiest (2) most favored (by the ladies);
**knock it** strike up
**II.i.s.d. several** different   **2 Hall** Westminster Hall   **10 how
passed it** i.e., what happened at the trial?   **11 in a little** in
brief   **13 allegèd** put forward   **14 defeat** frustrate

The king's attorney° on the contrary°                    15
Urged on° the examinations, proofs,° confessions
Of divers witnesses; which the duke desired
To him brought viva voce to his face;
At which appeared against him his surveyor;
Sir° Gilbert Parke, his councillor; and John Car,   20
Confessor to him; with that devil monk,
Hopkins, that made this mischief.

SECOND GENTLEMAN                    That was he
That fed him with his prophecies?

FIRST GENTLEMAN                       The same.
All these accused him strongly, which° he fain°
Would have flung from him; but indeed he could not.  25
And so his peers upon his evidence
Have found him guilty of high treason. Much
He spoke, and learnedly, for life, but all
Was either pitied in him or forgotten.°

SECOND GENTLEMAN
After all this, how did he bear himself?            30

FIRST GENTLEMAN
When he was brought again to th' bar, to hear
His knell rung out, his judgment,° he was stirred
With such an agony he sweat extremely
And something spoke in choler, ill and hasty.
But he fell to himself again, and sweetly           35
In all the rest showed a most noble patience.

SECOND GENTLEMAN
I do not think he fears death.

FIRST GENTLEMAN                 Sure,° he does not;
He never was so womanish. The cause
He may a little grieve at.

SECOND GENTLEMAN    Certainly
The cardinal is the end° of this.

FIRST GENTLEMAN                   'Tis likely,      40
By all conjectures: first, Kildare's attainder,°
Then Deputy of Ireland, who removed,
Earl Surrey was sent thither, and in haste too,
Lest he should help his father.°

SECOND GENTLEMAN      That trick of state
Was a deep envious° one.

FIRST GENTLEMAN        At his return               45
No doubt he will requite it. This is noted,
And generally:° whoever the king favors,
The card'nal instantly will find employment,
And far enough from court too.

SECOND GENTLEMAN            All the commons
Hate him perniciously,° and, o' my conscience,     50
Wish him ten fathom deep. This duke as much
They love and dote on; call him bounteous Bucking-
    ham,
The mirror of all courtesy—

*Enter* BUCKINGHAM *from his arraignment, tipstaves*°

before him, the ax with the edge towards him, halberds°
on each side, accompanied with Sir Thomas LOVELL, Sir
Nichclas VAUX, Sir Walter SANDS,° and common
people, &c.

FIRST GENTLEMAN                    Stay there, sir,
And see the noble ruined man you speak of.

SECOND GENTLEMAN
Let's stand close,° and behold him.

BUCKINGHAM                        All good people,   55
You that thus far have come to pity me,
Hear what I say, and then go home and lose° me.
I have this day received a traitor's judgment,
And by that name must die. Yet, heaven bear witness,
And if I have a conscience, let it sink° me         60
Even as the ax falls, if I be not faithful!
The law I bear no malice for my death:
'T has done, upon the premises,° but justice.
But those that sought it I could wish more° Christians.
Be what they will,° I heartily forgive 'em.        65
Yet let 'em look° they glory not in mischief
Nor build their evils° on the graves of great men,°
For then my guiltless blood must cry against 'em.
For further life in this world I ne'er hope,
Nor will I sue, although the king have mercies      70
More than I dare make faults. You few that loved me
And dare be bold to weep for Buckingham,
His noble friends and fellows, whom to leave
Is only bitter° to him, only dying,
Go with me like good angels to my end;             75
And as the long divorce of steel° falls on me,
Make of your prayers one sweet sacrifice,°
And lift my soul to heaven. Lead on, o' God's name.

LOVELL
I do beseech your grace, for charity,
If ever any malice in your heart                    80
Were hid against me, now to forgive me frankly.°

BUCKINGHAM
Sir Thomas Lovell, I as free forgive you
As I would be forgiven. I forgive all.
There cannot be those numberless offenses
'Gainst me that I cannot take° peace with. No black
    envy°                                          85
Shall mark my grave. Commend me to his grace,
And if he speak of Buckingham, pray tell him
You met him half in heaven. My vows and prayers
Yet are the king's and, till my soul forsake,°
Shall cry for blessings on him. May he live        90
Longer than I have time to tell° his years!
Ever beloved and loving may his rule be,
And when old time shall lead him to his end,
Goodness and he fill up one monument!°

15 **king's attorney** John Fitz-James, afterward Chief Justice of the King's Bench; **contrary** contrary side   16 **Urged on** (1) argued on the evidence of (intransitive) (2) pressed the evidence of (transitive); **examinations, proofs** depositions, statements   20 **Sir** a courtesy title for a cleric   24 **which** i.e., which accusations; **fain** gladly   29 **Was . . . forgotten** either aroused only unavailing pity or had no effect   32 **judgment** sentence (also in line 58)   37 **Sure** surely   40 **the end** at the root   41 **attainder** disgrace   44 **father** father-in-law (cf. III.ii.261–65)   45 **envious** malicious   47 **generally** by all   50 **perniciously** mortally   53 **s.d. tipstaves** bailiffs, so called because they carried silver-tipped staffs

53 **s.d. halberds** halberdiers (officers bearing long-handled weapons with ax-and-spear points); **Sir Walter Sands** Sir William Sands in Holinshed   55 **close** (1) out of view (2) silent   57 **lose** forget   60 **sink** destroy   63 **premises** (1) circumstances (2) proceedings   64 **more** i.e., more sincere   65 **Be . . . will** whoever they may be   66 **look** look to it   67 **evils** privies (?); **great men** noblemen   74 **only bitter** the only bitterness   76 **divorce of steel** separation of body and soul caused by the ax   77 **sacrifice** offering   81 **frankly** freely (for Lovell's reference see I.ii.186–87)   85 **take** make; **envy** malice   89 **forsake** i.e., part from my body   91 **tell** count   94 **monument** grave

LOVELL
To th' waterside I must conduct your grace,       95
Then give my charge up to Sir Nicholas Vaux,
Who undertakes° you to your end.

VAUX                                      Prepare there;
The duke is coming. See the barge be ready,
And fit it with such furniture° as suits
The greatness of his person.

BUCKINGHAM                     Nay, Sir Nicholas,       100
Let it alone; my state now will but mock me.
When I came hither, I was Lord High Constable
And Duke of Buckingham; now, poor Edward
     Bohun.°
Yet I am richer than my base accusers
That never knew what truth meant. I now seal° it,       105
And with that blood will make 'em one day groan for't.
My noble father, Henry of Buckingham,
Who first raised head° against usurping Richard,°
Flying for succor to his servant Banister,
Being distressed, was by that wretch betrayed,       110
And without trial fell. God's peace be with him!
Henry the Seventh succeeding, truly pitying
My father's loss, like a most royal prince,
Restored me to my honors, and out of ruins
Made my name once more noble. Now his son,       115
Henry the Eighth, life, honor, name, and all
That made me happy, at one stroke has taken
Forever from the world. I had my trial,
And must needs say a noble one; which makes me
A little happier than my wretched father.       120
Yet thus far we are one in fortunes: both
Fell by our servants, by those men we loved most—
A most unnatural and faithless service!
Heaven has an end° in all. Yet, you that hear me,
This from a dying man receive as certain:       125
Where you are liberal of your loves and counsels
Be sure you be not loose.° For those you make friends
And give your hearts to, when they once perceive
The least rub° in your fortunes, fall away
Like water from ye, never found again       130
But where they mean to sink° ye. All good people,
Pray for me! I must now forsake ye; the last hour
Of my long weary life° is come upon me.
Farewell!
And when you would say something that is sad,       135
Speak how I fell. I have done, and God forgive me.
                              *Exeunt* DUKE *and* TRAIN.

FIRST GENTLEMAN
O, this is full of pity! Sir, it calls,
I fear, too many curses on their heads
That were the authors.°

SECOND GENTLEMAN  If the duke be guiltless,
'Tis full of woe. Yet I can give you inkling       140
Of an ensuing evil, if it fall,
Greater than this.

FIRST GENTLEMAN  Good angels keep it from us!
What may it be? You do not doubt my faith,° sir?

SECOND GENTLEMAN
This secret is so weighty, 'twill require
A strong faith to conceal it.

FIRST GENTLEMAN          Let me have it;       145
I do not talk much.

SECOND GENTLEMAN  I am confident;°
You shall,° sir. Did you not of late days hear
A buzzing° of a separation
Between the king and Katherine?

FIRST GENTLEMAN                  Yes, but it held° not;
For when the king once heard it, out of anger       150
He sent command to the Lord Mayor straight
To stop the rumor and allay° those tongues
That durst disperse it.

SECOND GENTLEMAN  But that slander, sir,
Is found a truth now, for it grows again
Fresher than e'er it was, and held for certain       155
The king will venture at it. Either the cardinal
Or some about him near have, out of malice
To the good queen, possessed him with a scruple°
That will undo her. To confirm this too,
Cardinal Campeius is arrived, and lately;°       160
As all think, for this business.

FIRST GENTLEMAN              'Tis the cardinal;
And merely to revenge him on the emperor°
For not bestowing on him at his asking
The archbishopric of Toledo, this is purposed.

SECOND GENTLEMAN
I think you have hit the mark. But is't not cruel       165
That she should feel the smart of this? The cardinal
Will have his will, and she must fall.

FIRST GENTLEMAN              'Tis woeful.
We are too open° here to argue this;
Let's think in private more.          *Exeunt.*


Scene II. [*An antechamber in the palace.*]

*Enter Lord* CHAMBERLAIN, *reading this letter.*

CHAMBERLAIN  "My lord, the horses your lordship
sent for, with all the care I had, I saw well chosen,
ridden,° and furnished.° They were young and handsome, and of the best breed in the north. When they
were ready to set out for London, a man of my Lord       5
Cardinal's, by commission and main power,° took
'em from me, with this reason: his master would be
served before a subject, if not before the king; which
stopped our mouths, sir."
I fear he will indeed. Well, let him have them.       10
He will have all, I think.

*Enter to the Lord* CHAMBERLAIN, *the Dukes of* NOR-
FOLK *and* SUFFOLK.

---

97 **undertakes** has charge of  99 **furniture** equipment  103
**Bohun** his family name was actually Stafford, although in the
female line he was descended from the Bohuns  105 **seal** ratify
108 **raised head** gathered troops; **Richard** Richard III  124
**end** purpose  127 **loose** careless  129 **rub** check  131 **sink**
destroy  133 **long weary life** he was forty-three  139
**authors** originators  143 **faith** trustworthiness

146 **confident** i.e., of your discretion  147 **shall** i.e., shall
have it  148 **buzzing** rumor  149 **held** lasted  152 **allay**
silence  158 **possessed . . . scruple** put a doubt in his
mind  160 **Cardinal . . . lately** Lorenzo Campeggio, or
Campeius, did not actually arrive from Rome until 1528,
seven years after Buckingham's execution  162 **emperor**
Charles V, Holy Roman Emperor and King of Spain;
nephew to Katherine; (see I.i.176–90 and II.ii.25)  168 **open**
(1) public (2) indiscreet
**II.ii.3 ridden** broken in; **furnished** outfitted  6 **commission
. . . power** warrant and sheer force

**NORFOLK**
Well met, my Lord Chamberlain.

**CHAMBERLAIN**
Good day to both your graces.

**SUFFOLK**
How is the king employed?

**CHAMBERLAIN**      I left him private,°
Full of sad° thoughts and troubles.

**NORFOLK**      What's the cause?   15

**CHAMBERLAIN**
It seems the marriage with his brother's wife
Has crept too near his conscience.

**SUFFOLK**      [Aside.] No, his conscience
Has crept too near another lady.

**NORFOLK**      'Tis so.
This is the cardinal's doing; the king-cardinal,
That blind priest, like the eldest son of Fortune,   20
Turns what he list.° The king will know° him one day.

**SUFFOLK**
Pray God he do! He'll never know himself else.

**NORFOLK**
How holily he works in all his business,
And with what zeal! For, now he has cracked the
    league
Between us and the emperor, the queen's great
    nephew,   25
He dives into the king's soul, and there scatters
Dangers, doubts, wringing° of the conscience,
Fears and despairs; and all these for° his marriage.
And out of all these to restore the king,
He counsels a divorce, a loss of her   30
That like a jewel has hung twenty years
About his neck, yet never lost her luster;
Of her that loves him with that excellence
That angels love good men with, even of her
That, when the greatest stroke of fortune falls,   35
Will bless the king. And is not this course pious?

**CHAMBERLAIN**
Heaven keep me from such counsel! 'Tis most true
These news are everywhere; every tongue speaks 'em,
And every true heart weeps for't. All that dare
Look into these affairs see this main end,   40
The French king's sister.° Heaven will one day open
The king's eyes, that so long have slept upon°
This bold bad man.

**SUFFOLK**      And free us from his slavery.

**NORFOLK**
We had need pray,
And heartily, for our deliverance,   45
Or this imperious man will work us all
From princes into pages. All men's honors
Lie like one lump° before him, to be fashioned
Into what pitch° he please.

**SUFFOLK**      For me, my lords,
I love him not, nor fear him—there's my creed.   50

As I am made without him, so I'll stand,
If the king please. His curses and his blessings
Touch me alike; th' are breath I not believe in.
I knew him, and I know him; so I leave him
To him that made him proud—the pope.°   55

**NORFOLK**      Let's in,
And with some other business put the king
From these sad thoughts that work too much upon
    him.
My lord, you'll bear us company?

**CHAMBERLAIN**      Excuse me,
The king has sent me otherwere. Besides,
You'll find a most unfit time to disturb him.   60
Health to your lordships.

**NORFOLK**      Thanks, my good Lord Chamberlain.
*Exit Lord* CHAMBERLAIN, *and the* KING *draws
the curtain° and sits reading pensively.*

**SUFFOLK**
How sad he looks; sure, he is much afflicted.°

**KING**
Who's there, ha?

**NORFOLK**      Pray God he be not angry.

**KING**
Who's there, I say? How dare you thrust yourselves
Into my private meditations?   65
Who am I, ha?

**NORFOLK**
A gracious king that pardons all offenses
Malice ne'er meant. Our breach of duty this way°
Is business of estate,° in which we come
To know your royal pleasure.

**KING**      Ye are too bold.   70
Go to;° I'll make ye know your times of business.
Is this an hour for temporal affairs, ha?
*Enter* WOLSEY *and* CAMPEIUS *with a commission.*
Who's there? My good Lord Cardinal? O my Wolsey,
The quiet of my wounded conscience,
Thou art a cure fit for a king. [To CAMPEIUS.] You're
    welcome,   75
Most learnèd reverend sir, into our kingdom:
Use us and it. [To WOLSEY.] My good lord, have
    great care
I be not found a talker.°

**WOLSEY**      Sir, you cannot.
I would your grace would give us but an hour
Of private conference.

**KING** [To NORFOLK and SUFFOLK.] We are busy; go.   80

**NORFOLK** [Aside to SUFFOLK.]
This priest has no pride in him?

**SUFFOLK** [Aside to NORFOLK.]
Not to speak of.
I would not be so sick though for his place.°
But this cannot continue.

**NORFOLK**      [Aside to SUFFOLK.] If it do,
I'll venture one have-at-him.°

---

14 **private** alone   15 **sad** grave (also in lines 57, 62)   20–21 **That . . . list** i.e., he takes after Fortune in his disregard for others and his capriciousness (Fortune was depicted as blind and turning a wheel; eldest sons had special privileges)   21 **know** understand (also in next line)   27 **wringing** torture   28 **for** because of   41 **French king's sister** the Duchess of Alençon (see III.ii.86–87)   42 **slept upon** been blind to   48 **lump** i.e., of clay (cf. Romans 9:21)   49 **pitch** height (figurative), i.e., rank or degree of dignity

55 **the pope** the expected reference would be to the devil   61 s.d. **draws the curtain** the king is thus revealed seated within a curtained booth or recess; see the General Introduction, p. 7   62 **afflicted** disturbed   68 **this way** in this respect   69 **estate** state   71 **Go to** an exclamation of impatience or disapproval   78 **talker** i.e., rather than a doer   83 **so . . . place** so sick with pride even if it meant having his position   85 **have-at-him** thrust (the phrase "Have at you," meaning "Here goes!" or "Watch out!" signaled an attack)

SUFFOLK  [*Aside to* NORFOLK.] I another.                    85
               *Exeunt* NORFOLK *and* SUFFOLK.

WOLSEY
Your grace has given a precedent of wisdom
Above all princes, in committing freely
Your scruple to the voice of Christendom.
Who can be angry now? What envy° reach you?
The Spaniard,° tied by blood and favor to her,        90
Must now confess, if they have any goodness,
The trial just and noble. All the clerks°
(I mean the learnèd ones) in Christian kingdoms
Have their free voices.° Rome, the nurse of judgment,
Invited by your noble self, hath sent                 95
One general tongue° unto us, this good man,
This just and learnèd priest, Card'nal Campeius,
Whom once more I present unto your highness.

KING
And once more in mine arms I bid him welcome,
And thank the holy conclave° for their loves.         100
They have sent me such a man I would have wished
   for.

CAMPEIUS
Your grace must needs deserve all strangers'° loves,
You are so noble. To your highness' hand
I tender my commission; by whose virtue,
The court of Rome commanding, you, my Lord           105
Cardinal of York, are joined with me their servant
In the unpartial° judging of this business.

KING
Two equal° men. The queen shall be acquainted
Forthwith for what you come. Where's Gardiner?

WOLSEY
I know your majesty has always loved her              110
So dear in heart not to deny her that°
A woman of less place might ask by law:
Scholars allowed freely to argue for her.

KING
Aye, and the best she shall have, and my favor
To him that does best—God forbid else. Cardinal,    115
Prithee call Gardiner to me, my new secretary;
I find him a fit fellow.

[WOLSEY *beckons.*] *Enter* GARDINER.

WOLSEY [*Aside to* GARDINER.]
Give me your hand: much joy and favor to you.
You are the king's now.

GARDINER [*Aside to* WOLSEY.] But to be commanded
Forever by your grace, whose hand has raised me.      120

KING
Come hither, Gardiner.

*Walks and whispers.*

CAMPEIUS
My Lord of York, was not one Doctor Pace
In this man's place before him?

WOLSEY                          Yes, he was.

CAMPEIUS
Was he not held a learnèd man?

WOLSEY                          Yes, surely.

CAMPEIUS
Believe me, there's an ill opinion spread then,       125
Even of yourself, Lord Cardinal.

WOLSEY                          How? Of me?

CAMPEIUS
They will not stick° to say you envied him
And, fearing he would rise (he was so virtuous),
Kept him a foreign man still;° which so grieved him
That he ran mad and died.°

WOLSEY              Heaven's peace be with him!       130
That's Christian care enough. For living murmurers°
There's places of rebuke. He was a fool,
For he would needs be virtuous. That good fellow,
If I command him, follows my appointment;°
I will have none so near else. Learn this, brother,   135
We live not to be griped° by meaner persons.

KING
Deliver° this with modesty to th' queen.
                              *Exit* GARDINER.
The most convenient place that I can think of
For such receipt° of learning is Blackfriars;°
There ye shall meet about this weighty business.      140
My Wolsey, see it furnished.° O, my lord,
Would it not grieve an able° man to leave
So sweet a bedfellow? But, conscience, conscience!
O, 'tis a tender place, and I must leave her.    *Exeunt.*


Scene III. [*An antechamber of the queen's apartments.*]

*Enter* ANNE *Bullen and an* OLD LADY.

ANNE
Not for that neither. Here's the pang that pinches:°
His highness having lived so long with her, and she
So good a lady that no tongue could ever
Pronounce° dishonor of her—by my life,
She never knew harmdoing—O, now, after               5
So many courses of the sun° enthronèd,
Still growing in a majesty and pomp, the which
To leave a thousandfold more bitter than
'Tis sweet at first t' acquire—after this process,°
To give her the avaunt,° it is a pity                10
Would move a monster.

OLD LADY              Hearts of most hard temper
Melt and lament for her.

ANNE              O, God's will! Much better
She ne'er had known pomp; though't be temporal,°
Yet, if that quarrel,° Fortune, do divorce
It from the bearer, 'tis a sufferance panging°       15
As soul and body's severing.

OLD LADY              Alas, poor lady!
She's a stranger° now again.

**127 stick** scruple **129 foreign man still** continually on
missions abroad  **130 died** Pace in fact outlived Wolsey by six
years  **131 murmurers** grumblers  **134 appointment** direction  **136 griped** clutched familiarly  **137 Deliver** relate
**139 receipt** accommodation; **Blackfriars** Dominican monastery buildings in London  **141 furnished** fitted up  **142 able**
vigorous
**II.iii.1 pinches** torments  **4 Pronounce** utter  **6 courses
. . . sun** years  **9 this process** what has passed  **10 give . . .
avaunt** order her to go  **13 temporal** worldly  **14 quarrel**
quarreler (abstract for concrete)  **15 sufferance panging**
suffering as agonizing  **17 stranger** foreigner

**89 envy** malice  **90 Spaniard** Spaniards (Katherine was
daughter to Ferdinand of Spain)  **92 clerks** scholars  **94 Have
. . . voices** may freely express their opinions  **96 One
general tongue** one spokesman for all  **100 holy conclave**
College of Cardinals  **102 strangers'** foreigners'  **107 unpar-
tial** impartial  **108 equal** just, impartial  **111 that** that which

ANNE            So much the more
Must pity drop upon her. Verily,
I swear, 'tis better to be lowly born
And range with humble livers° in content       20
Than to be perked up° in a glist'ring° grief
And wear a golden sorrow.
OLD LADY           Our content
Is our best having.°
ANNE         By my troth and maidenhead,
I would not be a queen.
OLD LADY           Beshrew me,° I would,
And venture maidenhead for't; and so would you,    25
For all this spice° of your hypocrisy.
You that have so fair parts° of woman on you,
Have too a woman's heart, which ever yet
Affected° eminence, wealth, sovereignty;
Which, to say sooth,° are blessings; and which gifts    30
(Saving your mincing)° the capacity
Of your soft cheveril° conscience would receive,
If you might please to stretch it.
ANNE           Nay, good troth.°
OLD LADY
Yes, troth, and troth. You would not be a queen?
ANNE
No, not for all the riches under heaven.       35
OLD LADY
'Tis strange. A threepence bowed° would hire me,
Old as I am, to queen° it. But, I pray you,
What think you of a duchess? Have you limbs
To bear that load of title?
ANNE           No, in truth.
OLD LADY
Then you are weakly made. Pluck off° a little;    40
I would not be a young count° in your way,°
For more than blushing comes to. If your back
Cannot vouchsafe° this burden, 'tis too weak
Ever to get a boy.
ANNE       How you do talk!
I swear again, I would not be a queen       45
For all the world.
OLD LADY      In faith, for little England°
You'd venture an emballing.° I myself
Would for Caernarvonshire,° although there 'longed
No more to th' crown but that. Lo, who comes here?

*Enter Lord* CHAMBERLAIN.

CHAMBERLAIN
Good morrow, ladies. What were't worth to know    50
The secret of your conference?°
ANNE           My good lord,
Not your demand; it values not° your asking.
Our mistress' sorrows we were pitying.
CHAMBERLAIN
It was a gentle business, and becoming
The action of good women. There is hope       55
All will be well.
ANNE       Now, I pray God, amen!
CHAMBERLAIN
You bear a gentle mind, and heav'nly blessings
Follow such creatures. That you may, fair lady,
Perceive I speak sincerely, and high note's
Ta'en of your many virtues, the king's majesty    60
Commends his good opinion of you,° and
Does purpose honor to you no less flowing°
Than Marchioness of Pembroke; to which title
A thousand pound a year, annual support,
Out of his grace he adds.
ANNE           I do not know       65
What kind° of my obedience I should tender.
More than my all is nothing; nor my prayers
Are not° words duly hallowed, nor my wishes
More worth than empty vanities. Yet prayers and
    wishes
Are all I can return. Beseech your lordship,       70
Vouchsafe° to speak my thanks and my obedience,
As from a blushing handmaid, to his highness,
Whose health and royalty I pray for.
CHAMBERLAIN           Lady,
I shall not fail t' approve the fair conceit°
The king hath of you. [*Aside.*] I have perused her well.   75
Beauty and honor in her are so mingled
That they have caught the king; and who knows yet
But from this lady may proceed a gem
To lighten all this isle?—I'll to the king,
And say I spoke with you.
ANNE           My honored lord.     80
                  *Exit Lord* CHAMBERLAIN.
OLD LADY
Why, this it is:° see, see!
I have been begging sixteen years in court,
Am yet a courtier beggarly,° nor could
Come pat betwixt too early and too late
For any suit of pounds;° and you (O fate!)       85
A very fresh fish here—fie, fie, fie upon
This compelled° fortune!—have your mouth filled up
Before you open it.
ANNE       This is strange to me.
OLD LADY
How tastes it? Is it bitter? Forty pence, no.
There was a lady once ('tis an old story)       90
That would not be a queen, that would she not,
For all the mud in Egypt.° Have you heard it?

**20 range . . . livers** rank with humble folk   **21 perked up**
decked out; **glist'ring** glittering   **23 having** possession   **24
Beshrew me** may evil befall me (a mild imprecation)   **26
spice** dash, sample   **27 parts** qualities (of mind and person)
**29 Affected** aspired to   **30 say sooth** tell the truth   **31
Saving your mincing** despite your coyness   **32 cheveril**
kidskin   **33 troth** faith   **36 bowed** bent (and therefore worthless); with a possible quibble on *bawd*   **37 queen** with a pun
on *quean* = bawd   **40 Pluck off** come down in rank   **41
count** with a bawdy double meaning; **way** (1) path (2)
virginal condition   **43 vouchsafe** deign to accept   **46 little
England** perhaps with a reference to Pembrokeshire, called
"little England beyond Wales"; word follows (line 63) of
Anne's promotion to Marchioness—historically, to Marquess—
of Pembroke   **47 emballing** investment with the ball as
emblem of sovereignty (with a bawdy pun)   **48 Caernarvonshire** a poor Welsh county

**51 conference** conversation   **52 values not** is not worth
**61 Commends . . . you** presents his compliments   **62
flowing** abundant   **66 kind** expression   **67–68 nor . . .
not** the double negative lends emphasis   **71 Vouchsafe** be
good enough   **74 approve . . . conceit** confirm the good
opinion   **81 this it is** so it goes   **83 beggarly** (1) poor (2)
begging   **85 suit of pounds** i.e., petition for money   **87
compelled** i.e., forced upon her   **92 mud in Egypt** riches of
Egypt (the mud being the source of its fertility)

ANNE
Come, you are pleasant.

OLD LADY                    With your theme, I could
O'ermount° the lark. The Marchioness of Pembroke?
A thousand pounds a year for pure respect?°        95
No other obligation? By my life,
That promises moe° thousands: honor's train
Is longer than his foreskirt. By this time
I know your back will bear a duchess. Say,
Are you not stronger than you were?

ANNE                            Good lady,        100
Make yourself mirth with your particular fancy,
And leave me out on't. Would I had no being,
If this salute my blood° a jot. It faints me°
To think what follows.
The queen is comfortless, and we forgetful        105
In our long absence. Pray, do not deliver°
What here y' have heard to her.

OLD LADY            What do you think me?—*Exeunt.*

Scene IV. [*A hall in Blackfriars.*]

*Trumpets, sennet,° and cornets. Enter two* VERGERS, *with
short silver wands; next them, two* SCRIBES, *in the habit
of doctors;° after them, the [Arch]bishop of* CANTERBURY
*alone; after him, the Bishops of* LINCOLN, ELY, ROCH-
ESTER, *and* SAINT ASAPH. *Next them, with some small
distance, follows a* GENTLEMAN *bearing the purse, with
the Great Seal, and a cardinal's hat; then two* PRIESTS,
*bearing each a silver cross; then [*GRIFFITH,*] a gentleman
usher bareheaded, accompanied with a* SERGEANT-AT-
ARMS *bearing a silver mace; then two* GENTLEMEN
*bearing two great silver pillars;° after them, side by side,
the two* CARDINALS; *two* NOBLEMEN *with the sword
and mace. The* KING *takes place° under the cloth of state;°
the two* CARDINALS *sit under him as judges. The* QUEEN
*takes place some distance from the* KING. *The* BISHOPS
*place themselves on each side the court, in manner of a
consistory;° below them, the* SCRIBES. *The* LORDS *sit
next the* BISHOPS. *The rest of the* ATTENDANTS *stand
in convenient order about the stage.*

WOLSEY
Whilst our commission from Rome is read,
Let silence be commanded.

KING                        What's the need?
It hath already publicly been read,
And on all sides th' authority allowed.
You may then spare that time.

WOLSEY                        Be't so. Proceed.        5

SCRIBE
Say "Henry King of England, come into the court."

CRIER
Henry King of England, &c.

KING
Here.

SCRIBE
Say "Katherine Queen of England, come into the
court."

CRIER
Katherine Queen of England, &c.        10

*The* QUEEN *makes no answer, rises out of her chair, goes
about the court, comes to the* KING, *and kneels at his feet;
then speaks.*

QUEEN KATHERINE
Sir, I desire you do me right and justice,
And to bestow your pity on me; for
I am a most poor woman and a stranger,
Born out of your dominions; having here
No judge indifferent,° nor no more assurance        15
Of equal friendship and proceeding.° Alas, sir,
In what have I offended you? What cause
Hath my behavior given to your displeasure
That thus you should proceed to put me off°
And take your good grace° from me? Heaven witness,        20
I have been to you a true and humble wife,
At all times to your will conformable,
Ever in fear to kindle your dislike,
Yea, subject to your countenance, glad or sorry
As I saw it inclined. When was the hour        25
I ever contradicted your desire,
Or made it not mine too? Or which of your friends
Have I not strove to love, although I knew
He were mine enemy? What friend of mine
That had to him derived° your anger did I        30
Continue in my liking? Nay, gave° notice
He was from thence discharged? Sir, call to mind
That I have been your wife in this obedience
Upward of twenty years, and have been blessed
With many children by you. If, in the course        35
And process of this time, you can report,
And prove it too, against mine honor aught,
My bond to wedlock or my love and duty,
Against° your sacred person, in God's name,
Turn me away, and let the foul'st contempt        40
Shut door upon me, and so give me up
To the sharp'st kind of justice. Please you, sir,
The king, your father, was reputed for
A prince most prudent, of an excellent
And unmatched wit° and judgment. Ferdinand,        45
My father, King of Spain, was reckoned one
The wisest° prince that there had reigned by many
A year before. It is not to be questioned
That they had gathered a wise council to them
Of every realm, that did debate this business,        50
Who deemed our marriage lawful. Wherefore I
humbly
Beseech you, sir, to spare me, till I may
Be by my friends in Spain advised, whose counsel
I will implore. If not, i' th' name of God,
Your pleasure be fulfilled!

WOLSEY            You have here, lady,        55
And of your choice, these reverend fathers, men

94 O'ermount fly higher than   95 for pure respect simply
out of esteem   97 moe more   103 salute my blood exhila-
rates me; faints me makes me faint   106 deliver report
II.iv.s.d. sennet trumpet fanfare; habit of doctors i.e.,
capped and gowned as doctors of law; two . . . pillars
Wolsey's insignia; takes place takes his seat; cloth of state
canopy; consistory College of Cardinals

15 indifferent unbiased   16 equal . . . proceeding impartial
friendship and proceedings   19 put me off discard me   20
grace (1) self (2) favor   30 derived incurred   31 gave i.e.,
gave not   39 Against (1) i.e., or aught against (?) (2) toward
(?)   45 wit intelligence   46–47 one The wisest the very
wisest

Of singular integrity and learning,
Yea, the elect o' th' land, who are assembled
To plead your cause. It shall be therefore bootless°
That longer you desire the court,° as well                        60
For your own quiet,° as to rectify
What is unsettled in the king.

CAMPEIUS                          His grace
Hath spoken well and justly. Therefore, madam,
It's fit this royal session do proceed,
And that without delay their arguments                            65
Be now produced and heard.

QUEEN KATHERINE                          Lord Cardinal,
To you I speak.

WOLSEY          Your pleasure, madam?

QUEEN KATHERINE                          Sir,
I am about to weep; but, thinking that
We are a queen, or long have dreamed so, certain°
The daughter of a king, my drops of tears                         70
I'll turn to sparks of fire.

WOLSEY          Be patient yet.

QUEEN KATHERINE
I will, when you are humble; nay, before,
Or God will punish me. I do believe
(Induced by potent circumstances)° that
You are mine enemy, and make my challenge°                        75
You shall not be my judge; for it is you
Have blown this coal° betwixt my lord and me—
Which God's dew quench! Therefore I say again,
I utterly abhor,° yea, from my soul
Refuse you for my judge, whom, yet once more,                     80
I hold my most malicious foe, and think not
At all a friend to truth.

WOLSEY                          I do profess
You speak not like yourself, who ever yet
Have stood to° charity and displayed th' effects
Of disposition gentle and of wisdom                               85
O'ertopping woman's pow'r. Madam, you do me
          wrong:
I have no spleen° against you, nor injustice
For you or any. How far I have proceeded,
Or how far further shall, is warranted
By a commission from the consistory,                              90
Yea, the whole consistory of Rome. You charge me
That I have blown this coal. I do deny it.
The king is present. If it be known to him
That I gainsay my deed,° how may he wound,
And worthily, my falsehood—yea, as much                           95
As you have done my truth. If he know
That I am free of your report,° he knows
I am not of your wrong.° Therefore in him
It lies to cure me, and the cure is to
Remove these thoughts from you; the which before                 100
His highness shall speak in,° I do beseech
You, gracious madam, to unthink your speaking

And to say so no more.

QUEEN KATHERINE          My lord, my lord,
I am a simple woman, much too weak
T' oppose your cunning. Y' are meek and humble-
          mouthed.                                                105
You sign your place and calling, in full seeming,
With meekness and humility,° but your heart
Is crammed with arrogancy, spleen, and pride.
You have by fortune and his highness' favors
Gone slightly° o'er low steps, and now are mounted  110
Where pow'rs° are your retainers, and your words
(Domestics to you) serve your will as't please
Yourself pronounce their office.° I must tell you,
You tender° more your person's honor than
Your high profession spiritual; that again          115
I do refuse you for my judge, and here,
Before you all, appeal unto the pope,
To bring my whole cause 'fore his holiness,
And to be judged by him.

*She curtsies to the* KING, *and offers to depart.*

CAMPEIUS                          The queen is obstinate,
Stubborn° to justice, apt to accuse it,° and         120
Disdainful to be tried by't. 'Tis not well.
She's going away.

KING
Call her again.

CRIER
Katherine Queen of England, come into the court.

GRIFFITHS
Madam, you are called back.                          125

QUEEN KATHERINE
What need you note it? Pray you keep your way;°
When you are called, return. Now the Lord help!
They vex me past my patience. Pray you, pass on.
I will not tarry; no, nor ever more
Upon this business my appearance make               130
In any of their courts.

                          *Exit* QUEEN, *and her* ATTENDANTS.

KING                          Go thy ways, Kate.
The man i' th' world who shall report he has
A better wife, let him in naught be trusted,
For speaking false in that. Thou art, alone°—
If thy rare qualities, sweet gentleness,             135
Thy meekness saintlike, wifelike government,°
Obeying in commanding,° and thy parts
Sovereign and pious else, could speak thee out°—
The queen of earthly queens. She's noble born,
And like her true nobility she has                   140
Carried herself towards me.

WOLSEY                          Most gracious sir,
In humblest manner I require° your highness,
That it shall please you to declare in hearing

---

59 **bootless** profitless  60 **longer . . . court** longer you
draw out the business of the court (by pleading for a postponement)  61 **quiet** i.e., of mind  69 **certain** certainly  74
**Induced . . . circumstances** persuaded by strong reasons
75 **challenge** objection (legal term)  77 **blown this coal** stirred
up this strife (proverbial)  79 **abhor** protest against (legal term)
84 **stood to** supported  87 **spleen** malice  94 **gainsay my
deed** now deny what I have done  97 **free . . . report**
innocent of your charges  98 **I . . . wrong** i.e., I have been
wronged by you  101 **in** regarding

106–07 **You . . . humility** to all outward appearances you
set a stamp of meekness and humility on your high spiritual
office  110 **slightly** easily  111 **pow'rs** those in power  111–13
**your words . . . office** i.e., your words are your servants, and
you need only speak in order for your will to be done  114
**tender** value  120 **Stubborn** unpliant; **apt . . . it** prone to
call it in question  126 **keep your way** keep going  134
**alone** without rival  136 **government** self-control  137
**Obeying in commanding** self-restrained when giving orders
137–38 **thy parts . . . out** your other excellent and pious
qualities could describe you fully  142 **require** beg

Of all these ears—for where I am robbed and bound,
There must I be unloosed, although not there          145
At once and fully satisfied—whether ever I
Did broach this business to your highness, or
Laid any scruple in your way which might
Induce you to the question on't? Or ever
Have to you, but with thanks to God for such          150
A royal lady, spake one the least° word that might
Be to the prejudice of her present state,
Or touch° of her good person?
KING                        My Lord Cardinal,
I do excuse you; yea, upon mine honor,
I free you from't. You are not to be taught°          155
That you have many enemies that know not
Why they are so, but, like to village curs,
Bark when their fellows do. By some of these
The queen is put in anger. Y' are excused.
But will you be more justified? You ever          160
Have wished the sleeping of this business, never desired
It to be stirred, but oft have hind'red, oft,
The passages° made toward it. On my honor
I speak° my good Lord Cardinal to this point,
And thus far clear him. Now, what moved me to't,          165
I will be bold with time and your attention.
Then mark th' inducement. Thus it came; give heed
   to't:
My conscience first received a tenderness,
Scruple, and prick, on certain speeches uttered
By th' Bishop of Bayonne, then French ambassador,          170
Who had been hither sent on the debating
A marriage 'twixt the Duke of Orleans and
Our daughter Mary. I' th' progress of this business,
Ere a determinate resolution,° he
(I mean the bishop) did require a respite,          175
Wherein he might the king his lord advertise°
Whether our daughter were legitimate,
Respecting this our marriage with the dowager,
Sometimes° our brother's wife. This respite shook
The bosom of my conscience, entered me,          180
Yea, with a spitting° power, and made to tremble
The region of my breast; which forced such way
That many mazed considerings° did throng,
And pressed in with this caution. First, methought
I stood not in the smile of heaven, who had          185
Commanded nature that my lady's womb,
If it conceived a male child by me, should
Do no more offices of life to't than
The grave does to th' dead; for her male issue
Or° died where they were made, or shortly after          190
This world had aired them. Hence I took a thought
This was a judgment on me, that my kingdom,
Well worthy the best heir o' th' world, should not
Be gladded in't by me. Then follows that
I weighed the danger which my realms stood in          195
By this my issue's fail,° and that gave to me
Many a groaning throe. Thus hulling° in

The wild sea of my conscience, I did steer
Toward this remedy whereupon we are
Now present here together. That's to say,          200
I meant to rectify° my conscience, which
I then did feel full sick, and yet° not well,
By all the reverend fathers of the land
And doctors learned. First I began in private
With you, my Lord of Lincoln. You remember          205
How under my oppression° I did reek,°
When I first moved° you.
LINCOLN                    Very well, my liege.
KING
I have spoke long. Be pleased yourself to say
How far you satisfied me.
LINCOLN               So please your highness,
The question did at first so stagger me,          210
Bearing a state of mighty moment in't
And consequence of dread, that I committed
The daring'st counsel which I had to doubt,°
And did entreat your highness to this course
Which you are running here.
KING                      I then moved you,          215
My Lord of Canterbury, and got your leave
To make this present summons.° Unsolicited
I left no reverend person in this court,
But by particular consent proceeded
Under your hands and seals.° Therefore, go on;          220
For no dislike i' th' world against the person
Of the good queen, but the sharp thorny points
Of my allegèd° reasons, drives this forward.
Prove but our marriage lawful, by my life
And kingly dignity, we are contented          225
To wear our mortal state to come with her,
Katherine our queen, before the primest° creature
That's paragoned° o' th' world.
CAMPEIUS                  So please your highness,
The queen being absent, 'tis a needful fitness
That we adjourn this court till further° day.          230
Meanwhile must be an earnest motion°
Made to the queen to call back her appeal
She intends unto his holiness.
KING              [Aside.] I may perceive
These cardinals trifle with me. I abhor
This dilatory sloth and tricks of Rome.          235
My learned and well-belovèd servant, Cranmer,
Prithee return; with thy approach, I know,
My comfort comes along.—Break up the court;
I say, set on.          Exeunt, in manner as they entered.

151 on the least a single   153 touch sullying   155 You . . .
taught you do not have to be told   163 passages proceedings
164 speak bear witness for   174 determinate resolution
final decision   176 advertise inform (accent on second syllable)
179 Sometimes formerly   181 spitting transfixing, as though
impaled on a spit   183 mazed considerings perplexed thoughts
190 Or either   196 issue's fail i.e., failure to have a son   197
hulling drifting with sail furled

201 rectify set right (cf. line 61)   202 yet now still   206
oppression heavy burden; reek sweat (literally, smoke with
heat)   207 moved proposed the matter   211-13 Bearing
. . . doubt concerning so momentous a state of affairs, with
consequences so dreadful to contemplate, that I did not trust
myself to give the boldest advice (i.e., that the marriage be
dissolved)   217 summons i.e., of the queen   220 Under . . .
seals with your signed and sealed consent   223 allegèd stated
227 primest foremost   228 paragoned held up as a paragon
230 further a more distant   231 motion appeal

# A C T  I I I

Scene I. [*London. The queen's apartments.*]

*Enter* QUEEN *and her* WOMEN, *as at work.*

QUEEN KATHERINE
Take thy lute, wench. My soul grows sad with
   troubles;
Sing and disperse 'em, if thou canst. Leave° working.

              *Song.*
Orpheus° with his lute made trees,
And the mountain tops that freeze,
   Bow themselves when he did sing.         5
To his music plants and flowers
Ever sprung, as sun and showers
   There had made a lasting spring.

Everything that heard him play,
Even the billows of the sea,
   Hung their heads, and then lay by.°      10
In sweet music is such art,
Killing care and grief of heart
   Fall asleep, or hearing die.

*Enter a* GENTLEMAN.

QUEEN KATHERINE
How now?                        15
GENTLEMAN
And't° please your grace, the two great cardinals
Wait in the presence.°
QUEEN KATHERINE   Would they speak with me?
GENTLEMAN
They willed me say so, madam.
QUEEN KATHERINE        Pray their graces
To come near. [*Exit* GENTLEMAN.] What can be their
   business
With me, a poor weak woman, fall'n from favor?   20
I do not like their coming, now I think on't.
They should be good men, their affairs as righteous;°
But all hoods make not monks.

*Enter the two cardinals,* WOLSEY *and* CAMPEIUS.

WOLSEY             Peace to your highness!
QUEEN KATHERINE
Your graces find me here part of° a housewife.
I would be all, against the worst may happen.°   25
What are your pleasures with me, reverend lords?
WOLSEY
May it please you, noble madam, to withdraw
Into your private chamber, we shall give you
The full cause of our coming.
QUEEN KATHERINE        Speak it here;
There's nothing I have done yet, o' my conscience,   30
Deserves a corner. Would all other women
Could speak this with as free a soul as I do!
My lords, I care not (so much I am happy

Above a number) if my actions
Were tried by every tongue, every eye saw 'em,   35
Envy and base opinion° set against 'em,
I know my life so even.° If your business
Seek me out, and that way I am wife in,°
Out with it boldly: truth loves open dealing.
WOLSEY  Tanta est erga te mentis integritas, regina  40
  serenissima°—
QUEEN KATHERINE
O, good my lord, no Latin;
I am not such a truant since my coming,
As not to know the language I have lived in.
A strange tongue makes my cause more strange,
   suspicious;°               45
Pray speak in English. Here are some will thank you,
If you speak truth, for their poor mistress' sake.
Believe me, she has had much wrong. Lord Cardinal,
The willing'st° sin I ever yet committed
May be absolved in English.
WOLSEY           Noble lady,   50
I am sorry my integrity should breed
(And service to his majesty and you)
So deep suspicion, where all° faith was meant.
We come not by the way of accusation,
To taint that honor every good tongue blesses,   55
Nor to betray you any way to sorrow—
You have too much, good lady—but to know
How you stand minded in the weighty difference
Between the king and you, and to deliver,
Like free and honest men, our just opinions   60
And comforts to your cause.
CAMPEIUS         Most honored madam,
My Lord of York, out of his noble nature,
Zeal and obedience he still bore° your grace,
Forgetting, like a good man, your late censure
Both of his truth and him (which was too far°)   65
Offers, as I do, in° a sign of peace,
His service and his counsel.
QUEEN KATHERINE [*Aside.*] To betray me.—
My lords, I thank you both for your good wills.
Ye speak like honest men; pray God ye prove so!   70
But how to make ye suddenly° an answer,
In such a point of weight, so near° mine honor,
More near my life, I fear, with my weak wit.°
And to such men of gravity and learning,
In truth I know not. I was set° at work   75
Among my maids, full little, God knows, looking
Either for such men or such business.
For her sake that I have been°—for I feel
The last fit° of my greatness—good your graces,
Let me have time and counsel for my cause.
Alas, I am a woman friendless, hopeless!   80
WOLSEY
Madam, you wrong the king's love with these fears.
Your hopes and friends are infinite.

---

**III.i.2 Leave** leave off  **3 Orpheus** in mythology the music
of his lyre tamed wild beasts and entranced even inanimate
nature  **11 lay by** subsided  **16 And't** if it  **17 presence** presence chamber  **22 their . . . righteous** i.e., their business
should be as righteous as they themselves good  **24 part of**
to some extent (because she is sewing)  **25 I . . . happen** I
would like to be a complete one, in preparation for the worst
(i.e., in case I am divorced and left nothing else)

**36 Envy . . . opinion** malice and unworthy gossip  **37 even**
equable  **38 Seek . . . in** concerns me, and my behavior as
a wife  **40–41 Tanta . . . serenissima** So unprejudiced are we
toward you, most serene queen  **45 strange, suspicious**
foreign, and hence suspicious  **49 willing'st** most deliberate
**53 all** only  **63 still bore** has always borne  **65 far** extreme
**66 in** as  **70 suddenly** on the spur of the moment  **71 near**
closely affecting  **72 wit** intelligence  **74 set** seated  **77 For
. . . been** for what I once was  **78 fit** seizure (as in an illness)

QUEEN KATHERINE                    In England
But little for my profit. Can you think, lords,
That any Englishman dare give me counsel
Or be a known friend, 'gainst his highness' pleasure— 85
Though he be grown so desperate to be honest°—
And live a subject? Nay, forsooth, my friends,
They that must weigh out° my afflictions,
They that my trust must grow to, live not here.
They are, as all my other comforts, far hence    90
In mine own country, lords.
CAMPEIUS                     I would your grace
Would leave your griefs, and take my counsel.
QUEEN KATHERINE                  How, sir?
CAMPEIUS
Put your main cause into the king's protection;
He's loving and most gracious. 'Twill be much
Both for your honor better and your cause,°    95
For if the trial of the law o'ertake ye,
You'll part away° disgraced.
WOLSEY                  He tells you rightly.
QUEEN KATHERINE
Ye tell me what ye wish for both—my ruin.
Is this your Christian counsel? Out upon ye!
Heaven is above all yet; there sits a judge    100
That no king can corrupt.
CAMPEIUS            Your rage mistakes us.
QUEEN KATHERINE
The more shame for ye. Holy men I thought ye,
Upon my soul, two reverend cardinal virtues;°
But cardinal sins° and hollow hearts I fear ye.
Mend 'em, for shame, my lords. Is this your comfort? 105
The cordial that ye bring a wretched lady,
A woman lost among ye, laughed at, scorned?
I will not wish ye half my miseries:
I have more charity. But say I warned ye.
Take heed, for heaven's sake, take heed, lest at once° 110
The burden of my sorrows fall upon ye.
WOLSEY
Madam, this is a mere distraction.°
You turn the good we offer into envy.°
QUEEN KATHERINE
Ye turn me into nothing. Woe upon ye,
And all such false professors!° Would you have me    115
(If you have any justice, any pity,
If ye be anything but churchmen's habits°)
Put my sick cause into his hands that hates me?
Alas, has banished me his bed already;
His love, too long ago! I am old,° my lords,    120
And all the fellowship I hold now with him
Is only my obedience. What can happen
To me above this wretchedness? All your studies
Make me a curse like this!°

CAMPEIUS                    Your fears are worse.°
QUEEN KATHERINE
Have I lived thus long (let me speak° myself,    125
Since virtue finds no friends) a wife, a true one?
A woman, I dare say without vainglory,
Never yet branded with suspicion?
Have I with all my full affections
Still met the king? Loved him next heaven? Obeyed
him?    130
Been, out of fondness, superstitious to him?°
Almost forgot my prayers to content him?
And am I thus rewarded? 'Tis not well, lords.
Bring me a constant woman° to her husband,
One that ne'er dreamed a joy beyond his pleasure,°    135
And to that woman, when she has done most,
Yet will I add an honor: a great patience.
WOLSEY
Madam, you wander from the good we aim at.
QUEEN KATHERINE
My lord, I dare not make myself so guilty
To give up willingly that noble title    140
Your master wed me to. Nothing but death
Shall e'er divorce my dignities.
WOLSEY                  Pray hear me.
QUEEN KATHERINE
Would I had never trod this English earth,
Or felt the flatteries that grow upon it!
Ye have angels' faces, but heaven knows your hearts.°    145
What will become of me now, wretched lady!
I am the most unhappy woman living.
Alas, poor wenches, where are now your fortunes?
Shipwracked upon a kingdom, where no pity,
No friends, no hope; no kindred weep for me;    150
Almost no grave allowed me. Like the lily,
That once was mistress of the field, and flourished,
I'll hang my head and perish.
WOLSEY                  If your grace
Could but be brought to know our ends are honest,°
You'd feel more comfort. Why should we, good lady,    155
Upon what cause, wrong you? Alas, our places,
The way of our profession is against it.
We are to cure such sorrows, not to sow 'em.
For goodness' sake, consider what you do;
How you may hurt yourself, aye, utterly    160
Grow° from the king's acquaintance, by this carriage.°
The hearts of princes kiss obedience,
So much they love it; but to stubborn spirits
They swell, and grow as terrible as storms.
I know you have a gentle, noble temper,    165
A soul as even as a calm. Pray think us
Those we profess, peacemakers, friends, and servants.
CAMPEIUS
Madam, you'll find it so. You wrong your virtues
With these weak women's fears. A noble spirit,
As yours was put into you, ever casts    170
Such doubts, as false coin, from it. The king loves you;
Beware you lose it not. For us, if you please

86 so . . . honest so reckless as to come out honestly
in my support   88 weigh out attach full weight to   95
Both . . . cause better for both your honor and your cause
97 part away depart   103 cardinal virtues the essential virtues (comprising fortitude, justice, prudence, and temperance);
with a pun on the visitors' station   104 cardinal sins alluding
to the seven deadly sins; with pun on carnal, the Elizabethan
pronunciation of cardinal   110 at once all at once   112 mere
distraction sheer madness   113 envy malice   115 professors
i.e., of Christianity   117 habits garb   120 old she was forty-
three   123–24 All . . . this Let all your learned efforts make
my life any more wretched than it already is

124 worse i.e., than your actual situation   125 speak describe
131 superstitious to him his idolator   134 constant woman
woman faithful   135 pleasure (1) enjoyment (2) wishes
145 Ye . . . hearts alluding to the proverb "Fair face, foul
heart"   154 ends are honest intentions are honorable   161
Grow be estranged; carriage conduct

To trust us in your business, we are ready
To use our utmost studies° in your service.

QUEEN KATHERINE
Do what ye will, my lords; and pray forgive me.    175
If I have used myself° unmannerly,
You know I am a woman, lacking wit
To make a seemly answer to such persons.
Pray do my service° to his majesty.
He has my heart yet, and shall have my prayers    180
While I shall have my life. Come, reverend fathers,
Bestow your counsels on me. She now begs
That little thought, when she set footing° here,
She should have bought her dignities so dear. *Exeunt.*


Scene II. [*Antechamber to the king's apartment.*]

*Enter the Duke of* NORFOLK, *Duke of* SUFFOLK, *Lord*
SURREY, *and Lord* CHAMBERLAIN.

NORFOLK
If you will now unite in your complaints
And force them with a constancy,° the cardinal
Cannot stand under them. If you omit
The offer of this time,° I cannot promise
But that you shall sustain moe new disgraces,    5
With these you bear already.

SURREY           I am joyful
To meet the least occasion that may give me
Remembrance of my father-in-law, the duke,°
To be revenged on him.

SUFFOLK           Which of the peers
Have uncontemned° gone by him, or at least°    10
Strangely neglected? When did he regard
The stamp of nobleness in any person
Out of° himself?

CHAMBERLAIN   My lords, you speak your pleasures.°
What he deserves of you and me I know;
What we can do to him, though now the time    15
Gives way° to us, I much fear.° If you cannot
Bar his access to th' king, never attempt
Anything on him, for he hath a witchcraft
Over the king in's tongue.

NORFOLK           O, fear him not;
His spell in that is out.° The king hath found    20
Matter against him that forever mars
The honey of his language. No, he's settled,
Not to come off, in his displeasure.°

SURREY           Sir,
I should be glad to hear such news as this
Once every hour.

NORFOLK           Believe it, this is true.    25

In the divorce his contrary proceedings°
Are all unfolded; wherein he appears
As I would wish mine enemy.

SURREY           How came
His practices° to light?

SUFFOLK           Most strangely.

SURREY           O, how? How?

SUFFOLK
The cardinal's letters to the pope miscarried,    30
And came to th' eye o' th' king; wherein was read
How that the cardinal did entreat his holiness
To stay the judgment o' th' divorce. For if
It did take place, "I do" (quoth he), "perceive
My king is tangled in affection to    35
A creature° of the queen's, Lady Anne Bullen."

SURREY
Has the king this?

SUFFOLK           Believe it.

SURREY           Will this work?

CHAMBERLAIN
The king in this perceives him how he coasts
And hedges his own way.° But in this point
All his tricks founder, and he brings his physic    40
After his patient's death: the king already
Hath married the fair lady.

SURREY           Would he had!

SUFFOLK
May you be happy in your wish, my lord!
For, I profess, you have it.

SURREY           Now, all my joy
Trace the conjunction!°

SUFFOLK           My amen to't!

NORFOLK           All men's!    45

SUFFOLK
There's order given for her coronation.
Marry, this is yet but young, and may be left
To some ears unrecounted. But, my lords,
She is a gallant creature and complete°
In mind and feature. I persuade me, from her    50
Will fall some blessing to this land, which shall
In it be memorized.°

SURREY           But will the king
Digest° this letter of the cardinal's?
The Lord forbid!

NORFOLK           Marry, amen!

SUFFOLK           No, no.
There be moe wasps that buzz about his nose    55
Will make this sting the sooner. Cardinal Campeius
Is stol'n away to Rome; hath ta'en no leave;
Has left the cause o' th' king unhandled, and
Is posted° as the agent of our cardinal
To second all his plot. I do assure you    60
The king cried "Ha!" at this.

CHAMBERLAIN           Now God incense him,
And let him cry "Ha!" louder!

---

**174 studies** endeavors   **176 used myself** behaved   **179 do
my service** offer my respects   **183 footing** foot
**III.ii.2 force . . . constancy** urge them with determination
**3–4 omit . . . time** neglect this opportunity   **8 my . . .
duke** Buckingham; see II.i.43–44   **10 uncontemned** un-
despised; **at least** i.e., have not at least been   **13 Out of**
besides; **speak your pleasures** are free to say what you
care to   **16 way** scope; **fear** doubt   **20 His . . . out** His
influence that way is finished   **22–23 he's . . . displeasure**
he (Wolsey) is fixed, not to escape, in his (the king's) displeasure
(but "he" could possibly refer to the king, in which case "come
off" = desist)

**26 contrary proceedings** (1) proceedings contradicting their
outward appearance (2) adverse proceedings   **29 practices** plots
**36 creature** dependent   **38–39 coasts . . . way** moves circuitously and stealthily (i.e., as by coasts and hedgerows) toward his own goals   **44–45 all . . . conjunction** all the joy I
can wish follow the marriage   **49 complete** fully endowed
**52 memorized** made memorable   **53 Digest** stomach   **59
posted** hastened

NORFOLK                           But, my lord,
When returns Cranmer?
SUFFOLK
He is returned in his opinions,° which
Have satisfied the king for his divorce,                    65
Together with all famous colleges
Almost in Christendom. Shortly, I believe,
His second marriage shall be published,° and
Her coronation. Katherine no more
Shall be called queen, but princess dowager            70
And widow to Prince Arthur.
NORFOLK                         This same Cranmer's
A worthy fellow, and hath ta'en much pain
In the king's business.
SUFFOLK                    He has, and we shall see him
For it an archbishop.
NORFOLK             So I hear.
SUFFOLK                                    'Tis so.

*Enter* WOLSEY *and* CROMWELL.

The cardinal!                                                        75
NORFOLK
Observe, observe, he's moody.
WOLSEY
The packet,° Cromwell,
Gave't you the king?
CROMWELL                To his own hand, in's bedchamber.
WOLSEY
Looked he o' th' inside of the paper?°
CROMWELL                                        Presently°
He did unseal them, and the first he viewed,            80
He did it with a serious mind; a heed
Was in his countenance. You he bade
Attend him here this morning.
WOLSEY                              Is he ready
To come abroad?
CROMWELL        I think by this he is.
WOLSEY
Leave me awhile.                        *Exit* CROMWELL. 85

[*Aside.*]
It shall be to the Duchess of Alençon,
The French king's sister; he shall marry her.
Anne Bullen? No. I'll no Anne Bullens for him;
There's more in't than fair visage. Bullen?
No, we'll no Bullens. Speedily I wish                      90
To hear from Rome. The Marchioness of Pembroke!°
NORFOLK
He's discontented.
SUFFOLK              Maybe he hears the king
Does whet his anger to° him.
SURREY                              Sharp enough,
Lord, for thy justice!
WOLSEY [*Aside.*]
The late queen's gentlewoman, a knight's daughter,  95
To be her mistress' mistress? The queen's queen?

This candle burns not clear. 'Tis I must snuff it;
Then out it goes.° What though I know her virtuous
And well deserving? Yet I know her for
A spleeny° Lutheran, and not wholesome to          100
Our cause that she should lie i' th' bosom of
Our hard-ruled° king. Again, there is sprung up
An heretic, an arch one, Cranmer, one
Hath° crawled into the favor of the king,
And is his oracle.
NORFOLK            He is vexed at something.        105

*Enter* KING, *reading of a schedule,* [*and* LOVELL].

SURREY
I would 'twere something that would fret the string,°
The master-cord on's° heart.
SUFFOLK                        The king, the king!
KING
What piles of wealth hath he accumulated
To his own portion! And what expense by th' hour
Seems to flow from him! How, i' th' name of thrift,  110
Does he rake this together? Now, my lords,
Saw you the cardinal?°
NORFOLK                My lord, we have
Stood here observing him. Some strange commotion°
Is in his brain. He bites his lip, and starts;
Stops on a sudden, looks upon the ground,           115
Then lays his finger on his temple; straight
Springs out into fast gait; then stops again,
Strikes his breast hard, and anon he casts
His eye against° the moon. In most strange postures
We have seen him set himself.
KING                            It may well be             120
There is a mutiny in's mind. This morning
Papers of state he sent me to peruse,
As I required. And wot° you what I found
There, on my conscience, put unwittingly?
Forsooth, an inventory, thus importing:°              125
The several parcels° of his plate,° his treasure,
Rich stuffs,° and ornaments of household, which
I find at such proud rate° that it outspeaks
Possession of a subject.°
NORFOLK                    It's heaven's will;
Some spirit put this paper in the packet             130
To bless your eye withal.
KING                        If we did think
His contemplation were above the earth,
And fixed on spiritual object,° he should still
Dwell in his musings; but I am afraid
His thinkings are below the moon,° not worth        135
His serious considering.

97–98 This . . . goes i.e., I will be called on to clear away the
impediments to this marriage, but instead will use the opportunity to quash it altogether ("snuff" = trim the wick)  100
spleeny (1) staunch (2) splenetic  102 hard-ruled difficult to
manage  104 Hath that hath  106 fret the string gnaw
through the tendon  107 on's of his  112 Saw . . . cardinal
the king, engrossed in the schedule, has not noticed Wolsey's
presence  113 commotion turmoil, mutiny (see line 121)
119 against toward  123 wot know  125 thus importing
conveying this information  126 several parcels various
particulars; plate gold and silver household plate  127 stuffs
cloths  128 proud rate high value  128–29 outspeaks . . .
subject describes more than a subject should own  133
spiritual object a spiritual objective  135 below the moon
worldly

64 returned . . . opinions i.e., not in person, but in that the
opinions have been received from him  68 published proclaimed
77 packet parcel of state papers  79 paper wrapper; Presently
immediately  91 Marchioness of Pembroke Anne did not
in fact receive the title until 1532, three years after the events
of this scene  93 to against

KING *takes his seat; whispers* LOVELL, *who goes to the cardinal* [WOLSEY].

WOLSEY                          Heaven forgive me!
Ever God bless your highness!
KING                          Good my lord,
You are full of heavenly stuff,° and bear the inventory
Of your best graces in your mind; the which
You were now running o'er. You have scarce time          140
To steal from spiritual leisure° a brief span
To keep your earthly audit. Sure, in that
I deem you an ill husband,° and am glad
To have you therein my companion.
WOLSEY                                                   Sir,
For holy offices I have a time; a time                   145
To think upon the part of business which
I bear i' th' state; and Nature does require
Her times of preservation, which perforce
I, her frail son, amongst my brethren mortal,°
Must give my tendance° to.
KING                          You have said well.         150
WOLSEY
And ever may your highness yoke together,
As I will lend you cause, my doing well
With my well saying!
KING                          'Tis well said again,
And 'tis a kind of good deed to say well.
And yet words are no deeds. My father loved you;         155
He said he did, and with his deed did crown°
His word upon you. Since I had my office
I have kept you next my heart; have not alone
Employed you where high profits might come home,
But pared my present havings,° to bestow                 160
My bounties upon you.
WOLSEY          [*Aside.*] What should this mean?
SURREY [*Aside.*]
The Lord increase this business!
KING                          Have I not made you
The prime man of the state? I pray you tell me
If what I now pronounce you have found true;
And, if you may confess it, say withal,                  165
If you are bound to us or no. What say you?
WOLSEY
My sovereign, I confess your royal graces,
Showered on me daily, have been more than could
My studied purposes requite,° which went
Beyond all man's endeavors. My endeavors                 170
Have ever come too short of my desires,
Yet filed° with my abilities. Mine own ends
Have been mine so that° evermore they pointed
To th' good of your most sacred person and
The profit of the state. For your great graces          175
Heaped upon me, poor undeserver, I
Can nothing render but allegiant° thanks,
My prayers to heaven for you, my loyalty,
Which ever has and ever shall be growing

Till death, that winter, kill it.
KING                          Fairly answered;           180
A loyal and obedient subject is
Therein illustrated. The honor of it
Does pay the act of it, as, i' th' contrary,
The foulness is the punishment.° I presume
That, as my hand has opened bounty to you,               185
My heart dropped love, my pow'r rained honor, more
On you than any,° so your hand and heart,
Your brain and every function of your power,
Should, notwithstanding that° your bond of duty,
As 'twere in love's particular,° be more                 190
To me, your friend, than any.
WOLSEY                          I do profess
That for your highness' good I ever labored
More° than mine own; that am, have,° and will be—
Though all the world should crack their duty to you
And throw it from their soul; though perils did          195
Abound as thick as thought could make 'em, and
Appear in forms more horrid—yet my duty,
As doth a rock against the chiding° flood,
Should the approach of this wild river break,°
And stand unshaken yours.
KING                          'Tis nobly spoken.         200
Take notice, lords, he has a loyal breast,
For you have seen him open't. [*Giving him papers.*]
     Read o'er this;
And after, this; and then to breakfast with
What appetite you have.
     *Exit* KING, *frowning upon the cardinal* [WOLSEY];
     *the* NOBLES *throng after him, smiling and whispering.*
WOLSEY                          What should this mean?
What sudden anger's this? How have I reaped it?          205
He parted frowning from me, as if ruin
Leaped from his eyes. So looks the chafèd° lion
Upon the daring huntsman that has galled° him,
Then makes him nothing.° I must read this paper;
I fear, the story of his anger. 'Tis so;                 210
This paper has undone me. 'Tis th' account
Of all that world of wealth I have drawn together
For mine own ends; indeed, to gain the popedom,
And fee my friends in Rome. O negligence,
Fit for a fool to fall by! What cross° devil             215
Made me put this main° secret in the packet
I sent the king? Is there no way to cure this?
No new device to beat this from his brains?
I know 'twill stir him strongly; yet I know
A way, if it take right,° in spite of fortune            220
Will bring me off° again. What's this? "To th' pope"?
The letter, as I live, with all the business
I writ to's holiness. Nay then, farewell!
I have touched the highest point of all my greatness,

---

**182–84 The honor . . . punishment** i.e., Virtue is its own reward, just as evil is its own punishment   **187 any** on anyone   **189 notwithstanding that** over and above   **190 in love's particular** out of personal affection   **193 More** as in Buckingham's speech, I.i.184 ff., the speaker's emotion overcomes the restraints of normal syntax in the rest of this speech, but the sense is clear; **have** have been   **198 chiding** tumultuous   **199 break** check   **207 chafèd** angry   **208 galled** wounded   **209 makes him nothing** annihilates him   **215 cross** thwarting, perverse   **216 main** crucial   **220 take right** succeed   **221 bring me off** rescue me

---

**138 stuff** concerns (with a possible quibble on the household stuff referred to in line 127)   **141 spiritual leisure** religious occupations   **143 husband** manager   **149 amongst . . . mortal** i.e., in my human (as distinguished from divine) capacity   **150 tendance** attention   **156 crown** confirm   **160 havings** possessions   **168–69 more . . . requite** more than I could with diligent endeavors repay   **172 filed** kept pace   **173 so that** only to the extent that   **177 allegiant** loyal

And from that full meridian° of my glory 225
I haste now to my setting. I shall fall
Like a bright exhalation° in the evening,
And no man see me more.

*Enter to* WOLSEY *the Dukes of* NORFOLK *and* SUFFOLK,
*the Earl of* SURREY, *and the Lord* CHAMBERLAIN.

NORFOLK
Hear the king's pleasure, cardinal, who commands you
To render up the Great Seal° presently° 230
Into our hands, and to confine yourself
To Asher House, my Lord of Winchester's,°
Till you hear further from his highness.
WOLSEY                                   Stay:
Where's your commission, lords? Words cannot carry
Authority so weighty.
SUFFOLK                    Who dare cross° 'em, 235
Bearing the king's will from his mouth expressly?
WOLSEY
Till I find more than will or words to do it°—
I mean your malice—know, officious lords,
I dare, and must deny it. Now I feel
Of what coarse metal ye are molded—envy; 240
How eagerly ye follow my disgraces,
As if it fed ye! And how sleek and wanton°
Ye appear in everything may bring my ruin!
Follow your envious courses, men of malice;
You have Christian warrant° for 'em, and no doubt 245
In time will find their fit rewards. That seal
You ask with such a violence, the king,
Mine and your master, with his own hand gave me;
Bade me enjoy it, with the place and honors,
During my life; and, to confirm his goodness, 250
Tied it by letters-patents.° Now, who'll take it?
SURREY
The king, that gave it.
WOLSEY                 It must be himself, then.
SURREY
Thou art a proud traitor, priest.
WOLSEY                           Proud lord, thou liest.
Within these forty hours Surrey durst better
Have burnt that tongue than said so.
SURREY                              Thy ambition, 255
Thou scarlet sin,° robbed this bewailing land
Of noble Buckingham, my father-in-law.
The heads of all thy brother cardinals,
With thee and all thy best parts° bound together,
Weighed° not a hair of his. Plague of your policy! 260
You sent me Deputy for Ireland;°
Far from his succor, from the king, from all
That might have mercy on the fault thou gav'st him,

Whilst your great goodness, out of holy pity,
Absolved him with an ax.
WOLSEY                    This, and all else 265
This talking lord can lay upon my credit,°
I answer, is most false. The duke by law
Found his deserts. How innocent I was
From any private malice in his end,
His noble jury and foul cause can witness. 270
If I loved many words, lord, I should tell you
You have as little honesty as honor,
That° in the way of loyalty and truth
Toward the king, my ever royal master,
Dare mate° a sounder man than Surrey can be, 275
And all that love his follies.
SURREY                    By my soul,
Your long coat, priest, protects you; thou shouldst feel
My sword i' th' lifeblood of thee else. My lords,
Can ye endure to hear this arrogance?
And from this fellow? If we live thus tamely, 280
To be thus jaded° by a piece of scarlet,
Farewell nobility. Let his grace go forward,
And dare us with his cap, like larks.°
WOLSEY                              All goodness
Is poison to thy stomach.
SURREY                  Yes, that goodness
Of gleaning all the land's wealth into one, 285
Into your own hands, card'nal, by extortion;
The goodness of your intercepted packets
You writ to th' pope against the king. Your goodness,
Since you provoke me, shall be most notorious.
My Lord of Norfolk,° as you are truly noble, 290
As you respect the common good, the state
Of our despised nobility, our issues,°
Who, if he live, will scarce be gentlemen,
Produce the grand sum of his sins, the articles°
Collected from his life. I'll startle you 295
Worse than the sacring bell,° when the brown wench
Lay kissing in your arms, Lord Cardinal.
WOLSEY
How much, methinks, I could despise this man,
But that I am bound in charity against it!
NORFOLK
Those articles, my lord, are in the king's hand; 300
But, thus much,° they are foul ones.
WOLSEY                              So much fairer
And spotless shall mine innocence arise,
When the king knows my truth.
SURREY                        This cannot save you.
I thank my memory I yet remember
Some of these articles, and out they shall. 305
Now, if you can blush and cry "guilty," cardinal,
You'll show a little honesty.
WOLSEY                      Speak on, sir;
I dare your worst objections. If I blush,
It is to see a nobleman want° manners.

---

**225 meridian** a star's highest point  **227 exhalation** meteor
**230 Great Seal** insignia of the Lord Chancellor's office; see note
to I.i.114 s.d.; **presently** at once  **232 Lord of Winchester's**
as Wolsey was himself still Bishop of Winchester, we are perhaps meant to think of his successor, Stephen Gardiner  **235
cross** oppose  **237 do it** (1) "render up the Great Seal" (line
230) (2) carry such great authority  **242 wanton** unrestrained
**245 Christian warrant** justification by Christian principles
(ironic)  **251 Tied . . . letters-patents** confirmed it by
documents of formal conveyance  **256 scarlet sin** referring to
the color of his cassock, and also the traditional idea of scarlet
sins, as in Isaiah 1:18  **259 parts** qualities  **260 Weighed**
equaled in weight  **261 Ireland** three syllables

**266 credit** reputation  **273 That** the antecedent is "I," line 271
**275 mate** match  **281 jaded** intimidated  **283 dare . . . larks**
i.e., dazzle us with his cardinal's hat, as larks were dazed and
caught by means of a mirror and piece of red cloth  **290 Lord
of Norfolk** Norfolk was actually Surrey's father  **292 issues**
children  **294 articles** charges in an indictment  **296 sacring
bell** the consecrating bell rung at the elevation of the Host, the
most solemn portion of the Mass  **301 thus much** i.e., so much
I can say  **309 want** lack

**SURREY**
I had rather want those than my head. Have at you!° 310
First that, without the king's assent or knowledge,
You wrought to be a legate;° by which power
You maimed the jurisdiction of all bishops.

**NORFOLK**
Then that in all you writ to Rome, or else
To foreign princes, "Ego et Rex meus"° 315
Was still inscribed; in which you brought the king
To be your servant.

**SUFFOLK**        Then, that without the knowledge
Either of king or council, when you went
Ambassador to the emperor,° you made bold
To carry into Flanders the Great Seal.° 320

**SURREY**
Item, you sent a large commission
To Gregory de Cassado, to conclude,
Without the king's will or the state's allowance,
A league between his highness and Ferrara.

**SUFFOLK**
That out of mere° ambition you have caused 325
Your holy hat to be stamped on the king's coin.°

**SURREY**
Then that you have sent innumerable substance°
(By what means got, I leave to your own conscience)
To furnish° Rome and to prepare the ways
You have for dignities, to the mere undoing 330
Of all the kingdom. Many more there are,
Which, since they are of you and odious,
I will not taint my mouth with.

**CHAMBERLAIN**        O my lord,
Press not a falling man too far: 'tis virtue.°
His faults lie open to the laws; let them, 335
Not you, correct him. My heart weeps to see him
So little of his great self.

**SURREY**        I forgive him.

**SUFFOLK**
Lord Cardinal, the king's further pleasure is—
Because all those things you have done of late,
By your power legative,° within this kingdom, 340
Fall into th' compass of a praemunire°—
That therefore such a writ be sued° against you:
To forfeit all your goods, lands, tenements,
Chattels, and whatsoever, and to be
Out of the king's protection. This is my charge. 345

**NORFOLK**
And so we'll leave you to your meditations
How to live better. For your stubborn answer
About the giving back the Great Seal to us,
The king shall know it, and no doubt shall thank you.

So fare you well, my little good Lord Cardinal. 350
*Exeunt all but* WOLSEY.

**WOLSEY**
So farewell to the little good you bear me.
Farewell! A long farewell to all my greatness!
This is the state of man: today he puts forth
The tender leaves of hopes; tomorrow blossoms,
And bears his blushing honors thick upon him. 355
The third day comes a frost, a killing frost,
And, when he thinks, good easy° man, full surely
His greatness is aripening, nips his root,
And then he falls, as I do. I have ventured,
Like little wanton° boys that swim on bladders, 360
This many summers in a sea of glory,
But far beyond my depth. My high-blown pride
At length broke under me and now has left me,
Weary and old with service, to the mercy
Of a rude° stream that must forever hide me. 365
Vain pomp and glory of this world, I hate ye.
I feel my heart new opened. O, how wretched
Is that poor man that hangs on princes' favors!
There is betwixt that smile we would aspire to,
That sweet aspect of princes, and their ruin,° 370
More pangs and fears than wars or women have.
And when he falls, he falls like Lucifer,°
Never to hope again.

*Enter* CROMWELL, *standing amazed.*

       Why, how now, Cromwell?

**CROMWELL**
I have no power to speak, sir.

**WOLSEY**        What, amazed
At my misfortunes? Can thy spirit wonder 375
A great man should decline? Nay, and° you weep,
I am fall'n indeed.

**CROMWELL**        How does your grace?

**WOLSEY**        Why, well;
Never so truly happy, my good Cromwell.
I know myself° now, and I feel within me
A peace above all earthly dignities, 380
A still and quiet conscience. The king has cured me,
I humbly thank his grace; and from these shoulders,
These ruined pillars, out of pity, taken
A load would sink a navy—too much honor.
O, 'tis a burden, Cromwell, 'tis a burden 385
Too heavy for a man that hopes for heaven!

**CROMWELL**
I am glad your grace has made that right use of° it.

**WOLSEY**
I hope I have. I am able now, methinks,
Out of a fortitude of soul I feel,
To endure more miseries and greater far 390
Than my weak-hearted enemies dare offer.
What news abroad?

**CROMWELL**        The heaviest and the worst
Is your displeasure° with the king.

**WOLSEY**        God bless him!

---

**310 Have at you** Here goes; cf. II.ii.85 (the six charges that follow are the most serious of the nine leveled against Wolsey) **312 legate** i.e., the papal representative in England **315 Ego . . . meus** my king and I (the normal Latin word order, although Shakespeare followed the chroniclers in taking it to imply that Wolsey put himself before the king) **319 emperor** Charles V; see I.i.176–90 **320 To . . . Seal** the Seal, and thus the Lord Chancellor, were not supposed to leave the country **325 mere** sheer **326 Your . . . coin** a usurpation of royal prerogative **327 innumerable substance** countless treasure **329 furnish** supply **334 virtue** i.e., to relent **340 legative** as a papal legate **341 Fall . . . praemunire** come within the penalties—forfeiture of goods and outlawry—prescribed by the Statute of Praemunire, which limited papal authority in England **342 sued** moved

**357 easy** easygoing **360 wanton** playful **365 rude** turbulent **370 their ruin** the ruin they cause **372 he . . . Lucifer** cf. Isaiah 14:12: "How art thou fallen from Heaven, O Lucifer, son of the morning" **376 and if** **379 know myself** i.e., "recognize my limitations and my sins and am able to transcend them" (Foakes) **387 made . . . of** derived that benefit from **393 displeasure** loss of favor

CROMWELL
The next is, that Sir Thomas More is chosen
Lord Chancellor in your place.

WOLSEY                               That's somewhat sudden. 395
But he's a learnèd man. May he continue
Long in his highness' favor and do justice
For truth's sake and his conscience, that his bones,
When he has run his course and sleeps in blessings,
May have a tomb of orphans' tears wept on him!    400
What more?

CROMWELL    That Cranmer is returned with welcome,
Installed Lord Archbishop of Canterbury.

WOLSEY
That's news indeed.

CROMWELL              Last, that the Lady Anne,
Whom the king hath in secrecy long married,
This day was viewed in open as his queen,            405
Going to chapel; and the voice° is now
Only about her coronation.

WOLSEY
There was the weight that pulled me down. O
    Cromwell,
The king has gone beyond° me. All my glories
In that one woman I have lost forever.               410
No sun shall ever usher forth mine honors,
Or gild again the noble troops that waited
Upon my smiles. Go get thee from me, Cromwell;
I am a poor fall'n man, unworthy now
To be thy lord and master. Seek the king          415
(That sun I pray may never set!)—I have told him
What and how true thou art. He will advance thee;
Some little memory of me will stir him
(I know his noble nature) not to let
Thy hopeful service perish too. Good Cromwell,      420
Neglect him not; make use° now, and provide
For thine own future safety.

CROMWELL                      O my lord,
Must I then leave you? Must I needs forgo°
So good, so noble, and so true a master?
Bear witness, all that have not hearts of iron,      425
With what a sorrow Cromwell leaves his lord.
The king shall have my service, but my prayers
Forever and forever shall be yours.

WOLSEY
Cromwell, I did not think to shed a tear
In all my miseries, but thou hast forced me,        430
Out of thy honest truth,° to play the woman.
Let's dry our eyes—and thus far hear me, Cromwell,
And when I am forgotten, as I shall be,
And sleep in dull° cold marble where no mention
Of me more must be heard of, say I taught thee,     435
Say, Wolsey, that once trod the ways of glory,
And sounded all the depths and shoals of honor,
Found thee a way, out of his wrack, to rise in:
A sure and safe one, though thy master missed it.
Mark but my fall and that that ruined me.           440
Cromwell, I charge thee, fling away ambition.
By that sin fell the angels. How can man then,
The image of his Maker, hope to win° by it?
Love thyself last; cherish those hearts that hate thee;

Corruption wins not more than honesty.               445
Still° in thy right hand carry gentle peace
To silence envious tongues. Be just, and fear not.
Let all the ends thou aim'st at be thy country's,
Thy God's, and truth's. Then if thou fall'st, O Crom-
    well,
Thou fall'st a blessed martyr.° Serve the king;     450
And prithee, lead me in.
There take an inventory of all I have
To the last penny; 'tis the king's. My robe,°
And my integrity to heaven, is all
I dare now call mine own. O Cromwell, Cromwell,     455
Had I but served my God with half the zeal
I served my king, he would not in mine age
Have left me naked to mine enemies.

CROMWELL
Good sir, have patience.

WOLSEY                     So I have. Farewell
The hopes of court! My hopes in heaven do dwell.    460
                                          *Exeunt.*


# A C T   I V

### Scene I. [*A street in Westminster.*]

*Enter two* GENTLEMEN, *meeting one another.*

FIRST GENTLEMAN
Y' are well met once again.°

SECOND GENTLEMAN         So are you.

FIRST GENTLEMAN
You come to take your stand here, and behold
The Lady Anne pass from her coronation?

SECOND GENTLEMAN
'Tis all my business. At our last encounter
The Duke of Buckingham came from his trial.          5

FIRST GENTLEMAN
'Tis very true. But that time offered sorrow;
This, general joy.

SECOND GENTLEMAN    'Tis well. The citizens,
I am sure, have shown at full their royal° minds—
As, let 'em have their rights, they are ever forward°—
In celebration of this day with shows,              10
Pageants, and sights of honor.

FIRST GENTLEMAN               Never greater,
Nor, I'll assure you, better taken,° sir.

SECOND GENTLEMAN
May I be bold to ask what that contains,
That paper in your hand?

FIRST GENTLEMAN          Yes. 'Tis the list
Of those that claim their offices this day          15
By custom° of the coronation.
The Duke of Suffolk is the first, and claims
To be High Steward; next, the Duke of Norfolk,
He to be Earl Marshal. You may read the rest.

406 **voice** talk   409 **gone beyond** overreached   421 **make
use** take advantage   423 **forgo** forsake   431 **truth** faith   434
**dull** (1) inanimate (2) cheerless   443 **win** profit

446 **Still** always   448–50 **Let . . . martyr** after becoming
Earl of Essex and Lord Great Chamberlain, Cromwell fell
from favor and was beheaded in 1540   453 **robe** cardinal's habit
**IV.i.1 again** they met previously in II.i   8 **royal** i.e., well disposed to the king   9 **let . . . forward** to give them their due,
they are always eager to do   12 **taken** received   16 **By custom**
i.e., in accordance with hereditary privilege

SECOND GENTLEMAN
I thank you, sir; had I not known those customs,    20
I should have been beholding° to your paper.
But, I beseech you, what's become of Katherine,
The princess dowager? How goes her business?

FIRST GENTLEMAN
That I can tell you too. The Archbishop
Of Canterbury, accompanied with other    25
Learnèd and reverend fathers of his order,
Held a late° court at Dunstable, six miles off
From Ampthill, where the princess lay; to which
She was often cited° by them, but appeared not.
And, to be short, for not appearance and    30
The king's late scruple, by the main assent°
Of all these learnèd men she was divorced,
And the late marriage made of none effect;°
Since which she was removed to Kimbolton,
Where she remains now sick.

SECOND GENTLEMAN       Alas, good lady!    35

[*Trumpets.*]

The trumpets sound: stand close, the queen is coming.

*Hautboys.*

      THE ORDER OF THE CORONATION.
   1. *A lively flourish° of trumpets.*
   2. *Then two* JUDGES.
   3. LORD CHANCELLOR, *with purse and mace before
     him.*
   4. CHORISTERS, *singing. Music.°*
   5. MAYOR *of London, bearing the mace. Then* GARTER,
     *in his coat of arms, and on his head he wore a gilt
     copper crown.*
   6. *Marquess* DORSET, *bearing a scepter of gold, on his
     head a demicoronal° of gold. With him, the Earl of
    * SURREY, *bearing the rod of silver with the dove,
     crowned with an earl's coronet. Collars of S's.°*
   7. *Duke of* SUFFOLK, *in his robe of estate,° his coronet
     on his head, bearing a long white wand, as High
     Steward. With him, the Duke of* NORFOLK, *with the
     rod of marshalship, a coronet on his head. Collars of S's.*
   8. *A canopy borne by four of the* CINQUE-PORTS;°
     *under it, the* QUEEN *in her robe, in her hair,° richly
     adorned with pearl, crowned. On each side her, the
     Bishops of* LONDON *and* WINCHESTER.
   9. *The old* DUCHESS *of Norfolk, in a coronal of gold,
     wrought with flowers, bearing the* QUEEN'S *train.*
   10. *Certain ladies or* COUNTESSES, *with plain circlets
     of gold without flowers.*
*Exeunt, first passing over the stage in order and state, and
then a great flourish of trumpets. [As the procession passes,
      the two* GENTLEMEN *comment upon it.*]

SECOND GENTLEMAN
A royal train,° believe me. These I know.
Who's that that bears the scepter?

FIRST GENTLEMAN       Marquess Dorset;
And that the Earl of Surrey, with the rod.

SECOND GENTLEMAN
A bold brave gentleman. That should be    40
The Duke of Suffolk?

FIRST GENTLEMAN    'Tis the same: High Steward.

SECOND GENTLEMAN
And that my Lord of Norfolk?

FIRST GENTLEMAN       Yes.

SECOND GENTLEMAN    [*Looking on the* QUEEN.]
           Heaven bless thee!
Thou hast the sweetest face I ever looked on.
Sir, as I have a soul, she is an angel;
Our king has all the Indies° in his arms,    45
And more and richer, when he strains° that lady.
I cannot blame his conscience.

FIRST GENTLEMAN       They that bear
The cloth of honor over her, are four barons
Of the Cinque-ports.

SECOND GENTLEMAN
Those men are happy, and so are all are near her.    50
I take it, she that carries up the train
Is that old noble lady, Duchess of Norfolk.

FIRST GENTLEMAN
It is, and all the rest are countesses.

SECOND GENTLEMAN
Their coronets say so. These are stars indeed.

FIRST GENTLEMAN
And sometimes falling° ones.

SECOND GENTLEMAN       No more of that.    55
      [*The last of the procession exits; trumpets sound.*]

*Enter a third* GENTLEMAN.

FIRST GENTLEMAN
God save you, sir! Where have you been broiling?

THIRD GENTLEMAN
Among the crowd i' th' abbey, where a finger
Could not be wedged in more: I am stifled
With the mere rankness° of their joy.

SECOND GENTLEMAN       You saw
The ceremony?

THIRD GENTLEMAN    That I did.

FIRST GENTLEMAN       How was it?    60

THIRD GENTLEMAN
Well worth the seeing.

SECOND GENTLEMAN Good sir, speak° it to us.

THIRD GENTLEMAN
As well as I am able. The rich stream
Of lords and ladies, having brought the queen
To a prepared place in the choir, fell off°
A distance from her, while her grace sat down    65
To rest awhile, some half an hour or so,
In a rich chair of state, opposing° freely
The beauty of her person to the people.
Believe me, sir, she is the goodliest woman
That ever lay by man; which when the people    70
Had the full view of, such a noise arose

---

**21 beholding** beholden    **27 late** recent    **29 cited** summoned
**31 main assent** general agreement    **33 late . . . effect** former
marriage annulled    **36 s.d. flourish** fanfare;  **Music** musicians;
**Garter** i.e., Garter King-at-Arms; **demicoronal** small coronet;
**Collars of S's** gold chains of office fashioned of S-shaped
links; **estate** state; **four . . . Cinque-ports** i.e., four barons
of the channel ports (the ports, five in all, were Dover, Hastings,
Hythe, Romney, and Sandwich); **in her hair** with her hair
hanging loosely (the custom for brides)    **37 train** retinue

**45 all the Indies** i.e., the East and the West (the Indies were
celebrated for their riches)    **46 strains** clasps    **55 falling** with
a double meaning; "falling" = surrendering chastity    **59
mere rankness** sheer stink    **61 speak** describe    **64 off** back
**67 opposing** exposing

As the shrouds° make at sea in a stiff tempest,
As loud and to as many tunes; hats, cloaks—
Doublets,° I think—flew up, and had their faces
Been loose, this day they had been lost. Such joy    75
I never saw before. Great-bellied° women
That had not half a week to go, like rams°
In the old time of war, would shake the press,°
And make 'em reel before 'em. No man living
Could say "This is my wife" there, all were woven    80
So strangely in one piece.

SECOND GENTLEMAN    But what followed?

THIRD GENTLEMAN
At length her grace rose, and with modest paces
Came to the altar, where she kneeled and saintlike
Cast her fair eyes to heaven and prayed devoutly;
Then rose again and bowed her to the people;    85
When by the Archbishop of Canterbury
She had all the royal makings of° a queen,
As° holy oil, Edward Confessor's crown,
The rod, and bird of peace, and all such emblems
Laid nobly on her; which performed, the choir,    90
With all the choicest music° of the kingdom,
Together sung "Te Deum." So she parted,°
And with the same full state° paced back again
To York Place, where the feast is held.°

FIRST GENTLEMAN    Sir,
You must no more call it York Place; that's past.    95
For, since the cardinal fell, that title's lost:°
'Tis now the king's, and called Whitehall.

THIRD GENTLEMAN    I know it,
But 'tis so lately altered that the old name
Is fresh about me.

SECOND GENTLEMAN    What two reverend bishops
Were those that went on each side of the queen?    100

THIRD GENTLEMAN
Stokesly and Gardiner; the one of Winchester,
Newly preferred from° the king's secretary,
The other, London.

SECOND GENTLEMAN    He of Winchester
Is held no great good lover of the archbishop's,
The virtuous Cranmer.

THIRD GENTLEMAN    All the land knows that;    105
However, yet there is no great breach. When it comes,
Cranmer will find a friend will° not shrink from him.

SECOND GENTLEMAN
Who may that be, I pray you?

THIRD GENTLEMAN    Thomas Cromwell,
A man in much esteem with th' king, and truly
A worthy friend. The king has made him Master    110
O' th' Jewel House,
And one, already, of the Privy Council.

SECOND GENTLEMAN
He will deserve more.

THIRD GENTLEMAN    Yes, without all doubt.
Come, gentlemen, ye shall go my way,

Which is to th' court, and there ye shall be my guests;    115
Something° I can command. As I walk thither,
I'll tell ye more.

BOTH    You may command us, sir.    Exeunt.

Scene II. [Kimbolton.]

*Enter* KATHERINE, *dowager, sick; led between* GRIFFITH,
*her gentleman usher, and* PATIENCE, *her woman.*

GRIFFITH
How does your grace?

KATHERINE    O Griffith, sick to death.
My legs like loaden branches bow to th' earth,
Willing to leave their burden. Reach a chair.
So—now, methinks, I feel a little ease.
Didst thou not tell me, Griffith, as thou led'st me,    5
That the great child of honor, Cardinal Wolsey,
Was dead?°

GRIFFITH    Yes, madam; but I think your grace,
Out of the pain you suffered, gave no ear to't.

KATHERINE
Prithee, good Griffith, tell me how he died.
If well, he stepped before me happily°    10
For my example.

GRIFFITH    Well, the voice goes,° madam.
For after the stout Earl Northumberland
Arrested him at York, and brought him forward,
As a man sorely tainted,° to his answer,
He fell sick suddenly, and grew so ill    15
He could not sit his mule.

KATHERINE    Alas, poor man!

GRIFFITH
At last, with easy roads,° he came to Leicester,
Lodged in the abbey; where the reverend abbot,
With all his covent,° honorably received him;
To whom he gave these words: "O father abbot,    20
An old man broken with the storms of state
Is come to lay his weary bones among ye;
Give him a little earth for charity."
So went to bed, where eagerly° his sickness
Pursued him still; and three nights after this,    25
About the hour of eight, which he himself
Foretold should be his last, full of repentance,
Continual meditations, tears, and sorrows,
He gave his honors to the world again,
His blessèd part° to heaven, and slept in peace.    30

KATHERINE
So may he rest. His faults lie gently on him!
Yet thus far, Griffith, give me leave to speak° him,
And yet with charity. He was a man
Of an unbounded stomach,° ever ranking
Himself with princes; one that by suggestion    35
Tied° all the kingdom. Simony° was fair play;

---

His own opinion was his law. I' th' presence°
He would say untruths and be ever double°
Both in his words and meaning. He was never,
But where he meant to ruin, pitiful.     40
His promises were, as he then was, mighty,
But his performance, as he is now, nothing.
Of his own body he was ill,° and gave
The clergy ill example.

GRIFFITH            Noble madam,
Men's evil manners live in brass; their virtues     45
We write in water. May it please your highness
To hear me speak his good° now?

KATHERINE            Yes, good Griffith;
I were malicious else.

GRIFFITH            This cardinal,
Though from an humble stock, undoubtedly
Was fashioned to much honor from his cradle.     50
He was a scholar, and a ripe and good one;
Exceeding wise, fair-spoken, and persuading;
Lofty and sour to them that loved him not,
But to those men that sought him, sweet as summer.
And though he were unsatisfied in getting,°     55
Which was a sin, yet in bestowing, madam,
He was most princely: ever witness for him
Those twins of learning that he raised in you,°
Ipswich and Oxford; one of which fell with him,
Unwilling to outlive the good° that did it;     60
The other,° though unfinished, yet so famous,
So excellent in art,° and still so rising,
That Christendom shall ever speak his virtue.
His overthrow heaped happiness upon him,
For then, and not till then, he felt himself,°     65
And found the blessedness of being little.
And, to add greater honors to his age
Than man could give him, he died fearing God.

KATHERINE
After my death I wish no other herald,
No other speaker of my living actions,°     70
To keep mine honor from corruption,
But such an honest chronicler as Griffith.
Whom° I most hated living, thou hast made me,
With thy religious truth and modesty,°
Now in his ashes honor. Peace be with him!     75
Patience, be near me still, and set me lower:
I have not long to trouble thee. Good Griffith,
Cause the musicians play me that sad note°
I named my knell, whilst I sit meditating
On that celestial harmony° I go to.     80

*Sad and solemn music.*

GRIFFITH
She is asleep. Good wench, let's sit down quiet,
For fear we wake her. Softly, gentle Patience.

---

**37 presence** presence chamber, i.e., before the king   **38 double** deceitful   **43 Of . . . ill** i.e., he was depraved in his sexual conduct   **47 speak his good** describe his good qualities   **55 unsatisfied in getting** insatiably acquisitive   **58 raised in you** i.e., erected in your cities   **60 good** goodness   **61 other** i.e., Christ Church, Oxford   **62 art** learning   **65 felt himself** truly knew himself   **70 living actions** actions during my life   **73 Whom** object of "hated"; also of "honor" in line 75   **74 religious . . . modesty** strict truth and moderation   **78 note** tune   **80 celestial harmony** the heavenly spheres in their revolutions were thought to produce a music accessible only to the liberated soul

*The Vision.*

*Enter, solemnly tripping° one after another, six personages, clad in white robes, wearing on their heads garlands of bays,° and golden vizards° on their faces; branches of bays or palm in their hands. They first congee° unto her, then dance; and, at certain changes,° the first two hold a spare garland over her head; at which the other four make reverent curtsies. Then the two that held the garland deliver the same to the other next two, who observe the same order in their changes, and holding the garland over her head; which done, they deliver the same garland to the last two, who likewise observe the same order; at which, as it were by inspiration, she makes in her sleep signs of rejoicing, and holdeth up her hands to heaven. And so in their dancing vanish, carrying the garland with them. The music continues.*

KATHERINE
Spirits of peace, where are ye? Are ye all gone,
And leave me here in wretchedness behind ye?

GRIFFITH
Madam, we are here.

KATHERINE        It is not you I call for.     85
Saw ye none enter since I slept?

GRIFFITH            None, madam.

KATHERINE
No? Saw you not even now a blessèd troop
Invite me to a banquet, whose bright faces
Cast thousand beams upon me, like the sun?
They promised me eternal happiness,     90
And brought me garlands, Griffith, which I feel
I am not worthy yet to wear. I shall, assuredly.

GRIFFITH
I am most joyful, madam, such good dreams
Possess your fancy.

KATHERINE        Bid the music leave;°
They are harsh and heavy to me. *Music ceases.*

PATIENCE        Do you note     95
How much her grace is altered on the sudden?
How long her face is drawn? How pale she looks,
And of an earthy cold? Mark her eyes.

GRIFFITH
She is going, wench. Pray, pray.

PATIENCE        Heaven comfort her!

*Enter a* MESSENGER.

MESSENGER
And't like° your grace—

KATHERINE        You are a saucy fellow!     100
Deserve we no more reverence?

GRIFFITH        You are to blame,
Knowing she will not lose° her wonted greatness,
To use so rude behavior. Go to, kneel.

MESSENGER
I humbly do entreat your highness' pardon:
My haste made me unmannerly. There is staying°     105
A gentleman, sent from the king, to see you.

KATHERINE
Admit him entrance, Griffith; but this fellow
Let me ne'er see again.        *Exit* MESSENGER.

---

**82 s.d. tripping** with light steps; **bays** bay leaves (symbolic of triumph); **vizards** masks (probably to indicate that they are spirits); **congee** bow ceremoniously; **changes** movements in the dance   **94 music leave** musicians stop   **100 And't like** if it please   **102 lose** give up   **105 staying** waiting

*Enter Lord* CAPUCIUS.°

                    If my sight fail not,
You should be Lord Ambassador from the emperor,
My royal nephew, and your name Capucius.          110

CAPUCIUS
Madam, the same. Your servant.

KATHERINE                    O, my lord,
The times and titles now are altered strangely
With me since first you knew me. But I pray you,
What is your pleasure with me?

CAPUCIUS                    Noble lady,
First, mine own service to your grace; the next,     115
The king's request that I would visit you,
Who grieves much for your weakness, and by me
Sends you his princely commendations,°
And heartily entreats you take good comfort.

KATHERINE
O my good lord, that comfort comes too late;       120
'Tis like a pardon after execution.°
That gentle physic,° given in time, had cured me,
But now I am past all comforts here° but prayers.
How does his highness?

CAPUCIUS                    Madam, in good health.

KATHERINE
So may he ever do, and ever flourish,              125
When I shall dwell with worms, and my poor name
Banished the kingdom! Patience, is that letter
I caused you write yet sent away?

PATIENCE                    No, madam.

[*Giving it to* KATHERINE.]

KATHERINE
Sir, I most humbly pray you to deliver
This to my lord the king.

CAPUCIUS                    Most willing, madam.     130

KATHERINE
In which I have commended to his goodness
The model° of our chaste loves, his young daughter°—
The dews of heaven fall thick in blessings on her!—
Beseeching him to give her virtuous breeding°—
She is young, and of a noble modest nature;        135
I hope she will deserve well—and a little
To love her for her mother's sake that loved him
Heaven knows how dearly. My next poor petition
Is that his noble grace would have some pity
Upon my wretched women that so long              140
Have followed both my fortunes° faithfully;
Of which there is not one, I dare avow
(And now° I should not lie), but will deserve,
For virtue and true beauty of the soul,
For honesty and decent carriage,                  145
A right good husband, let him be° a noble;
And, sure, those men are happy that shall have 'em.
The last is, for my men—they are the poorest,

But poverty could never draw 'em from me—
That they may have their wages duly paid 'em,      150
And something over to remember me by.
If heaven had pleased to have given me longer life
And able° means, we had not parted thus.
These are the whole contents; and, good my lord,
By that you love the dearest in this world,        155
As you wish Christian peace to souls departed,
Stand these poor people's friend, and urge the king
To do me this last right.

CAPUCIUS                    By heaven, I will,
Or let me lose the fashion° of a man!

KATHERINE
I thank you, honest lord. Remember me             160
In all humility unto his highness.
Say his long trouble now is passing
Out of this world. Tell him in death I blessed him,
For so I will. Mine eyes grow dim. Farewell,
My lord. Griffith, farewell. Nay, Patience,        165
You must not leave me yet. I must to bed;
Call in more women. When I am dead, good wench,
Let me be used with honor. Strew me over
With maiden flowers,° that all the world may know
I was a chaste wife to my grave. Embalm me,        170
Then lay me forth. Although unqueened, yet like
A queen and daughter to a king, inter me.
I can° no more.              *Exeunt, leading* KATHERINE.

# A C T   V

## Scene I. [*London. A gallery in the palace.*]

*Enter* GARDINER, *Bishop of Winchester, a* PAGE *with a
torch before him, met by Sir Thomas* LOVELL.

GARDINER
It's one o'clock, boy, is't not?

BOY                        It hath struck.

GARDINER
These should be hours for necessities,
Not for delights; times to repair our nature
With comforting repose, and not for us
To waste these times. Good hour of night, Sir Thomas!  5
Whither so late?

LOVELL          Came you from the king, my lord?

GARDINER
I did, Sir Thomas, and left him at primero°
With the Duke of Suffolk.

LOVELL                    I must to him too
Before he go to bed. I'll take my leave.

GARDINER
Not yet, Sir Thomas Lovell. What's the matter?    10
It seems you are in haste; and if there be
No great offense belongs to't, give your friend
Some touch° of your late business. Affairs that walk
(As they say spirits do) at midnight have
In them a wilder nature than the business          15

---

108 **s.d. Exit . . . Capucius** most editors have Griffith
exit with the messenger and reenter with Capucius, but
he need not leave the stage in order to usher in the visitor
118 **commendations** greetings  121 **execution** "-tion" is
disyllabic  122 **physic** healing art  123 **here** in this world
132 **model** image; **daughter** Mary, afterward queen (1553–
58)  134 **breeding** upbringing  141 **both my fortunes** my
good fortune and bad  143 **now** at the point of death  146
**let him be** i.e., even

153 **able** sufficient  159 **fashion** form, nature  169 **maiden
flowers** flowers appropriate to one who was chaste  173 **can**
can do
**V.i.7 primero** a card game  13 **touch** inkling

That seeks dispatch by day.

LOVELL              My lord, I love you,
And durst commend a secret to your ear
Much weightier than this work. The queen's in labor,
They say, in great extremity, and feared
She'll with the labor end.

GARDINER           The fruit she goes with     20
I pray for heartily, that it may find
Good time,° and live; but for the stock,° Sir Thomas,
I wish it grubbed up now.

LOVELL             Methinks I could
Cry thee amen,° and yet my conscience says
She's a good creature and, sweet lady, does     25
Deserve our better wishes.

GARDINER           But, sir, sir,
Hear me, Sir Thomas. Y' are a gentleman
Of mine own way;° I know you wise, religious;
And, let me tell you, it will ne'er be well—
'Twill not, Sir Thomas Lovell, take't of me—     30
Till Cranmer, Cromwell (her two hands°) and she
Sleep in their graves.

LOVELL         Now, sir, you speak of two
The most remarked° i' th' kingdom. As for Cromwell,
Beside that of the Jewel House, is made Master
O' th' Rolls,° and the king's secretary; further, sir,     35
Stands in the gap and trade° of moe preferments,
With which the time° will load him. Th' archbishop
Is the king's hand and tongue, and who dare speak
One syllable against him?

GARDINER           Yes, yes, Sir Thomas,
There are that dare, and I myself have ventured     40
To speak my mind of him. And indeed this day,
Sir, I may tell it you, I think I have
Insensed° the lords o' th' council that he is
(For, so I know he is, they know he is)°
A most arch heretic, a pestilence     45
That does infect the land; with which they moved°
Have broken with° the king, who hath so far
Given ear to our complaint, of his great grace
And princely care foreseeing those fell° mischiefs
Our reasons° laid before him, hath° commanded     50
Tomorrow morning to the council board
He be convented.° He's a rank weed, Sir Thomas,
And we must root him out. From your affairs
I hinder you too long. Good night, Sir Thomas.

*Exit GARDINER and PAGE.*

LOVELL
Many good nights, my lord; I rest your servant.     55

*Enter KING and SUFFOLK.*

KING
Charles, I will play no more tonight.
My mind's not on't; you are too hard for me.

SUFFOLK
Sir, I did never win of you before.

KING
But little, Charles,
Nor shall not, when my fancy's on my play.     60
Now, Lovell, from the queen what is the news?

LOVELL
I could not personally deliver to her
What you commanded me, but by her woman
I sent your message; who° returned her thanks
In the great'st humbleness, and desired your highness     65
Most heartily to pray for her.

KING           What say'st thou, ha?
To pray for her? What, is she crying out?

LOVELL
So said her woman, and that her suff'rance° made
Almost each pang a death.

KING           Alas, good lady!

SUFFOLK
God safely quit° her of her burden, and     70
With gentle travail, to the gladding of
Your highness with an heir!

KING           'Tis midnight, Charles;
Prithee, to bed, and in thy prayers remember
Th' estate° of my poor queen. Leave me alone,
For I must think of that which company     75
Would not be friendly to.°

SUFFOLK           I wish your highness
A quiet night, and my good mistress will
Remember in my prayers.

KING           Charles, good night. *Exit* SUFFOLK.

*Enter Sir Anthony DENNY.*

Well, sir, what follows?

DENNY
Sir, I have brought my lord the archbishop,     80
As you commanded me.

KING           Ha? Canterbury?

DENNY
Aye, my good lord.

KING           'Tis true: where is he, Denny?

DENNY
He attends your highness' pleasure.

KING           Bring him to us.
[*Exit* DENNY.]

LOVELL [*Aside.*]
This is about that which the bishop° spake;
I am happily° come hither.     85

*Enter CRANMER and DENNY.*

KING
Avoid° the gallery. (LOVELL *seems to stay.*) Ha! I have
said.° Be gone.
What!           *Exeunt* LOVELL *and* DENNY.

CRANMER [*Aside.*] I am fearful.° Wherefore frowns he
thus?
'Tis his aspect° of terror. All's not well.

---

22 **Good time** i.e., a safe delivery; **stock** trunk (of a tree),
i.e., the queen   24 **Cry thee amen** i.e., second you   28 **way**
i.e., religious persuasion (anti-Lutheran)   31 **hands** supporters
33 **remarked** in the public eye   34–35 **Master . . . Rolls** Keeper
of the Records   36 **gap and trade** entrance and beaten path
37 **time** i.e., the trend of the times   43 **Insensed** (1) informed
(2) stirred up ("insensed" = incensed)   44 **For . . . they
know he is** for if I know he is, then I can make them know
46 **moved** angered   47 **broken with** broken the information
to   49 **fell** terrible   50 **reasons** account, explanation; **hath**
i.e., that he has   52 **convented** summoned

64 **who** and who (i.e., the queen)   68 **suff'rance** suffering
70 **quit** release   74 **estate** condition   75–76 **that . . . to** i.e.,
matters for which company would not be helpful   84 **bishop**
Gardiner   85 **happily** opportunely   86 **Avoid** leave; **said**
spoken   87 **fearful** afraid   88 **aspect** expression (accent on
second syllable)

KING
How now, my lord? You do desire to know
Wherefore I sent for you.

CRANMER      [*Kneeling.*] It is my duty     90
T' attend your highness' pleasure.

KING            Pray you, arise,
My good and gracious Lord of Canterbury.
Come, you and I must walk a turn together;
I have news to tell you. Come, come, give me your
    hand.
Ah, my good lord, I grieve at what I speak,     95
And am right sorry to repeat what follows.
I have, and most unwillingly, of late
Heard many grievous, I do say, my lord,
Grievous complaints of you; which, being considered,
Have moved° us and our council, that you shall     100
This morning come before us; where I know
You cannot with such freedom purge° yourself
But that, till further trial in those charges
Which will require your answer, you must take
Your patience to you and be well contented     105
To make your house our Tow'r.° You a brother of us,°
It fits we thus proceed, or else no witness
Would come against you.

CRANMER [*Kneeling.*]
I humbly thank your highness,
And am right glad to catch this good occasion     110
Most throughly° to be winnowèd, where my chaff
And corn° shall fly asunder; for I know
There's none stands under° more calumnious tongues
Than I myself, poor man.

KING          Stand up, good Canterbury;
Thy truth and thy integrity is rooted     115
In us, thy friend. Give me thy hand; stand up.
Prithee, let's walk. Now, by my holidame,°
What manner of man are you? My lord, I looked
You would have given me your petition, that
I should have ta'en some pains to bring together     120
Yourself and your accusers, and to have heard you,
Without indurance further.°

CRANMER        Most dread liege,
The good I stand on is my truth and honesty.
If they shall fail, I with mine enemies
Will triumph o'er my person; which I weigh not,     125
Being of those virtues vacant.° I fear nothing°
What can be said against me.

KING         Know you not
How your state stands i' th' world, with the whole
    world?
Your enemies are many, and not small. Their practices
Must bear the same proportion,° and not ever°     130
The justice and the truth o' th' question carries
The due° o' th' verdict with it. At what ease°

Might corrupt minds procure knaves as corrupt
To swear against you? Such things have been done.
You are potently opposed, and with a malice     135
Of as great size. Ween you of° better luck—
I mean, in perjured witness°—than your master,°
Whose minister you are, awhiles here he lived
Upon this naughty° earth? Go to, go to;
You take a precipice for no leap of danger,     140
And woo your own destruction.

CRANMER         God and your majesty
Protect mine innocence, or I fall into
The trap is° laid for me!

KING        Be of good cheer;
They shall no more prevail than we give way° to.
Keep comfort to you, and this morning see     145
You do appear before them. If they shall chance,
In charging you with matters, to commit you,°
The best persuasions to the contrary
Fail not to use, and with what vehemency
Th' occasion shall instruct you. If entreaties     150
Will render you no remedy, this ring
Deliver them, and your appeal to us
There make before them. Look, the good man weeps!
He's honest, on mine honor. God's blest mother,
I swear he is true-hearted, and a soul     155
None better in my kingdom. Get you gone,
And do as I have bid you. (*Exit* CRANMER.) He has
    strangled
His language in his tears.

*Enter* OLD LADY; [LOVELL *following*].

GENTLEMAN     (*Within.*) Come back: what mean you?
OLD LADY
I'll not come back; the tidings that I bring
Will make my boldness manners. Now, good angels     160
Fly o'er thy royal head, and shade thy person
Under their blessed wings!

KING         Now by thy looks
I guess thy message. Is the queen delivered?
Say "aye," and of a boy.

OLD LADY        Aye, aye, my liege,
And of a lovely boy. The God of heaven     165
Both now and ever bless her! 'Tis a girl
Promises boys hereafter. Sir, your queen
Desires your visitation, and to be
Acquainted with this stranger. 'Tis as like you
As cherry is to cherry.

KING        Lovell!
LOVELL        Sir?     170
KING
Giver her an hundred marks.° I'll to the queen.
                    *Exit* KING.
OLD LADY
An hundred marks? By this light, I'll ha' more.
An ordinary groom is for° such payment.
I will have more, or scold it out of him.

---

100 **moved** persuaded   102 **purge** i.e., of guilt   106 **make**
. . . **Tow'r** be housed in the Tower (cf. I.i.207); **You**
. . . **us** i.e., you being a member of the council   111
**throughly** thoroughly   112 **corn** wheat   113 **stands under**
subject to   117 **by my holidame** by my holiness (a formula of
protestation)   122 **indurance further** (1) imprisonment in
addition (2) further hardship   125–26 **I weigh . . . vacant** I
do not value if it is devoid of those virtues (i.e., truth and
honesty)   126 **nothing** not at all   129–30 **Their . . . proportion** their plots must correspond in number and scope
130 **ever** always   132 **due** fit reward; **At what ease** how easily

136 **Ween you of** do you reckon on   137 **witness** evidence;
**master** Christ   139 **naughty** wicked   143 **is** that is   144
**way** scope   147 **commit you** i.e., to imprisonment in the
Tower   171 **an hundred marks** one mark = 67 pence (two-
thirds of a pound); a hundred marks = £66.67, a substantial
sum   173 **for** entitled to

Said I for this, the girl was like to him? I'll     175
Have more, or else unsay't; and now, while 'tis hot,
I'll put it to the issue.        [Exeunt.]


Scene II. [Before the entrance to the council chamber.]

Enter CRANMER, Archbishop of Canterbury; [PURSUI-
VANTS,° PAGES, &c., attending at the door].

CRANMER
I hope I am not too late; and yet the gentleman
That was sent to me from the council prayed me
To make great haste. All fast?° What means this? Ho!
Who waits there? Sure, you know me?

Enter KEEPER.

KEEPER               Yes, my lord,
But yet I cannot help you.        5
CRANMER
Why?
KEEPER
Your grace must wait till you be called for.

Enter Doctor BUTTS.

CRANMER             So.
BUTTS [Aside.]
This is a piece of malice. I am glad
I came this way so happily. The king
Shall understand it presently.°      Exit BUTTS.
CRANMER       [Aside.] 'Tis Butts,    10
The King's physician. As he passed along,
How earnestly he cast his eyes upon me.
Pray heaven he sound° not my disgrace! For certain,
This is of purpose laid by some that hate me
(God turn° their hearts! I never sought their malice)   15
To quench mine honor. They would shame to make
    me
Wait else at door, a fellow-councillor,
'Mong boys, grooms, and lackeys. But their pleasures
Must be fulfilled, and I attend with patience.

Enter the KING and BUTTS at a window above.°

BUTTS
I'll show your grace the strangest sight—
KING            What's that, Butts? 20
BUTTS
I think your highness saw this many a day.
KING
Body o' me, where is it?
BUTTS          There, my lord:
The high promotion of his Grace of Canterbury.
Who holds his state° at door 'mongst pursuivants,
Pages, and footboys.
KING       Ha? 'Tis he, indeed.    25
Is this the honor they do one another?
'Tis well there's one above 'em yet. I had thought

They had parted so much honesty° among 'em,
At least good manners, as not thus to suffer
A man of his place and so near our favor      30
To dance attendance on their lordships' pleasures,
And at the door too, like a post with packets.°
By holy Mary, Butts, there's knavery.
Let 'em alone, and draw the curtain close;
We shall hear more anon.      35
     [They retire behind the curtain; CRANMER
                   remains waiting outside.]


[Scene III. The council chamber.]

A council table brought in with chairs and stools, and placed
under the state.° Enter Lord CHANCELLOR, places himself
at the upper end of the table on the left hand; a seat being left
void° above him, as for Canterbury's seat. Duke of
SUFFOLK, Duke of NORFOLK, SURREY, Lord CHAM-
BERLAIN, GARDINER, seat themselves in order on each
side. CROMWELL at lower end, as secretary. [KEEPER at
the door.]

CHANCELLOR
Speak to the business, master secretary.
Why are we met in council?
CROMWELL        Please your honors,
The chief cause concerns his grace of Canterbury.
GARDINER
Has he had knowledge° of it?
CROMWELL        Yes.
NORFOLK             Who waits there?
KEEPER
Without,° my noble lords?
GARDINER          Yes.
KEEPER           My Lord Archbishop;   5
And has done half an hour, to know your pleasures.
CHANCELLOR
Let him come in.
KEEPER       Your grace may enter now.

CRANMER [enters and] approaches the council table.

CHANCELLOR
My good Lord Archbishop, I'm very sorry
To sit here at this present° and behold
That chair stand empty. But we all are men,    10
In our own natures frail and capable
Of° our flesh; few are angels: out of which frailty
And want of wisdom, you, that best should teach us,
Have misdemeaned yourself, and not a little,
Toward the king first, then his laws, in filling   15
The whole realm, by your teaching and your chap-
    lains'—
For so we are informed—with new opinions,
Divers and dangerous; which are heresies,
And, not reformed, may prove pernicious.°
GARDINER
Which reformation must be sudden too,      20

---

V.ii.s.d. pursuivants junior officers attendant upon the heralds
3 fast shut   10 understand it presently know about it at
once   13 sound (1) fathom (2) make known   15 turn convert
19 s.d. above i.e., on the upper stage; note the reference to a
curtain, line 34   24 holds his state maintains the dignity of
his position

28 parted . . . honesty shared enough decency   32 post
with packets courier with letters
V.iii.s.d. state canopy; void empty   4 had knowledge been
informed   5 Without outside the door   9 at this present
now   11–12 capable Of susceptible to the weaknesses of   19
pernicious ruinous

My noble lords; for those that tame wild horses
Pace 'em not in their hands° to make 'em gentle,
But stop their mouths with stubborn° bits and spur 'em
Till they obey the manage.° If we suffer,
Out of our easiness and childish pity                                    25
To one man's honor, this contagious sickness,
Farewell all physic. And what follows then?
Commotions, uproars, with a general taint°
Of the whole state; as of late days our neighbors,
The upper Germany,° can dearly witness,                          30
Yet freshly pitied in our memories.

CRANMER
My good lords, hitherto, in all the progress
Both of my life and office, I have labored,
And with no little study, that my teaching
And the strong course of my authority                              35
Might go one way, and safely; and the end
Was ever to do well. Nor is there living
(I speak it with a single heart,° my lords)
A man that more detests, more stirs° against,
Both in his private conscience and his place,                      40
Defacers of a public peace, than I do.
Pray heaven, the king may never find a heart
With less allegiance in it! Men that make
Envy and crookèd malice nourishment°
Dare bite the best. I do beseech your lordships               45
That, in this case of° justice, my accusers,
Be what they will, may stand forth face to face,
And freely urge° against me.

SUFFOLK                            Nay, my lord,
That cannot be. You are a councillor,
And, by that virtue,° no man dare accuse you.                  50

GARDINER
My lord, because we have business of more moment,
We will be short with you. 'Tis his highness' pleasure,
And our consent,° for better trial of you,
From hence you be committed to the Tower;
Where, being but a private man° again,                             55
You shall know many dare accuse you boldly,
Mcre than, I fear, you are provided for.

CRANMER
Ah, my good Lord of Winchester, I thank you;
You are always my good friend. If your will pass,°
I shall both find your lordship° judge and juror,             60
You are so merciful. I see your end:
'Tis my undoing. Love and meekness, lord,
Become a churchman better than ambition.
Win straying souls with modesty° again;
Cast none away. That I shall clear myself,                        65
Lay all the weight ye can upon my patience,
I make as little doubt as you do conscience°
In doing daily wrongs. I could say more,
But reverence to your calling makes me modest.

22 **Pace . . . hands** do not lead them by hand through their
paces  23 **stubborn** stiff, inflexible  24 **manage** training  28
**taint** corruption  30 **upper Germany** possibly referring to
the peasants' uprising in Saxony in 1521–22 or to other insur-
rections in 1524 and 1535  38 **with . . . heart** i.e., without
duplicity  39 **stirs** bestirs himself  43–44 **make . . . nourishment** "make nourishment" = feed on  46 **of** involving  48
**urge** press their charges  50 **that virtue** virtue of that  53
**our consent** what we have consented to  55 **private man**
i.e., without public office  59 **pass** prevail  60 **both . . . lordship** find your lordship both  64 **modesty** moderation  67
**I . . . conscience** I have as little doubt as you have scruples

GARDINER
My lord, my lord, you are a sectary;°                               70
That's the plain truth. Your painted gloss discovers,°
To men that understand you, words° and weakness.

CROMWELL
My Lord of Winchester, y' are a little,
By your good favor, too sharp. Men so noble,
However faulty, yet should find respect                           75
For what they have been; 'tis a cruelty
To load° a falling man.

GARDINER                         Good master secretary,
I cry your honor mercy;° you may, worst°
Of all this table, say so.

CROMWELL                    Why, my lord?

GARDINER
Do not I know you for a favorer                                     80
Of this new sect? Ye are not sound.°

CROMWELL                              Not sound?

GARDINER
Not sound, I say.

CROMWELL          Would you were half so honest!
Men's prayers then would seek you, not their fears.

GARDINER
I shall remember this bold language.

CROMWELL                              Do.
Remember your bold life too.

CHANCELLOR                     This is too much;               85
Forbear, for shame, my lords.

GARDINER                   I have done.

CROMWELL                              And I.

CHANCELLOR
Then thus for you, my lord: it stands agreed,
I take it, by all voices, that forthwith
You be conveyed to th' Tower a prisoner,
There to remain till the king's further pleasure           90
Be known unto us. Are you all agreed, lords?

ALL
We are.

CRANMER  Is there no other way of mercy,
But I must needs to th' Tower, my lords?

GARDINER                                  What other
Would you expect? You are strangely° troublesome.
Let some o' th' guard be ready there.

*Enter the* GUARD.

CRANMER                                 For me?               95
Must I go like a traitor thither?

GARDINER                       Receive him,
And see him safe i' th' Tower.

CRANMER                    Stay, good my lords,
I have a little yet to say. Look there, my lords.           100
By virtue of that ring, I take my cause
Out of the gripes° of cruel men, and give it
To a most noble judge, the king my master.

CHAMBERLAIN
This is the king's ring.

SURREY                    'Tis no counterfeit.

70 **sectary** follower of a (heretical) sect  71 **painted gloss discovers** deceitful appearance (or speech) reveals  72 **words**
i.e., rather than content  77 **load** oppress  78 **cry . . . mercy**
beg your honor's pardon; **worst** with least justification
81 **sound** loyal  94 **strangely** uncommonly  100 **gripes**
clutches

SUFFOLK
'Tis the right ring, by heaven. I told ye all,
When we first put this dangerous stone a-rolling,
'Twould fall upon ourselves.
NORFOLK                          Do you think, my lords,   105
The king will suffer but° the little finger
Of this man to be vexed?
CHAMBERLAIN              'Tis now too certain.
How much more is his life in value with° him?
Would I were fairly out on't!
CROMWELL                 My mind gave° me,
In seeking tales and informations                       110
Against this man, whose honesty the devil
And his disciples only envy at,°
Ye blew the fire that burns ye. Now have at ye!

*Enter* KING, *frowning on them; takes his seat.*

GARDINER
Dread sovereign, how much are we bound to heaven
In daily thanks, that gave us such a prince,          115
Not only good and wise, but most religious;
One that in all obedience makes the church
The chief aim of his honor, and, to strengthen
That holy duty, out of dear respect,°
His royal self in judgment comes to hear             120
The cause betwixt her and this great offender.
KING
You were ever good at sudden commendations,°
Bishop of Winchester. But know, I come not
To hear such flattery now, and in my presence
They are too thin and bare to hide offenses.        125
To me you cannot reach. You play the spaniel,
And think with wagging of your tongue to win me;
But, whatsoe'er thou tak'st me for, I'm sure
Thou hast a cruel nature and a bloody.

[*To* CRANMER.]

Good man, sit down. Now let me see the proudest,  130
He that dares most, but wag his finger at thee.
By all that's holy, he had better starve°
Than but once think this place becomes thee not.
SURREY
May it please your grace—
KING                      No, sir, it does not please me.
I had thought I had had men of some understanding  135
And wisdom of my council, but I find none.
Was it discretion, lords, to let this man,
This good man—few of you deserve that title—
This honest man, wait like a lousy° footboy
At chamber door? And one as great as you are?      140
Why, what a shame was this! Did my commission
Bid ye so far forget yourselves? I gave ye
Power as he was a councillor to try him,
Not as a groom. There's some of ye, I see,
More out of malice than integrity,                        145
Would try him to the utmost, had ye mean;°
Which ye shall never have while I live.

CHANCELLOR                              Thus far,
My most dread sovereign, may it like° your grace
To let my tongue excuse all. What was purposed
Concerning his imprisonment was rather,            150
If there be faith in men, meant for his trial
And fair purgation° to the world, than malice,
I'm sure, in me.
KING             Well, well, my lords, respect him.
Take him and use him well; he's worthy of it.
I will say thus much for him, if a prince              155
May be beholding to a subject, I
Am, for his love and service, so to him.
Make me no more ado, but all embrace him.
Be friends, for shame, my lords! My Lord of Canter-
   bury,
I have a suit which you must not deny me:          160
That is, a fair young maid that yet wants° baptism;
You must be godfather, and answer for her.
CRANMER
The greatest monarch now alive may glory
In such an honor. How may I deserve it,
That am a poor and humble subject to you?        165
KING Come, come, my lord, you'd spare your
   spoons.° You shall have two noble partners° with you:
   the old Duchess of Norfolk, and Lady Marquess
   Dorset. Will these please you?
Once more, my Lord of Winchester, I charge you,  170
Embrace and love this man.
GARDINER                   With a true heart
And brother-love I do it.
CRANMER              And let heaven
Witness how dear I hold this confirmation.
KING
Good man, those joyful tears show thy true heart.
The common voice,° I see, is verified                   175
Of thee, which says thus: "Do my Lord of Canterbury
A shrewd° turn, and he's your friend forever."
Come, lords, we trifle time away. I long
To have this young one made a Christian.
As I have made ye one, lords, one remain;         180
So I grow stronger, you more honor gain.      *Exeunt.*


Scene [IV. *The palace yard.*]

*Noise and tumult within. Enter* PORTER *and his* MAN.

PORTER  You'll leave your noise anon, ye rascals. Do
   you take the court for Parish Garden?° Ye rude° slaves,
   leave your gaping.°

(*Within.*) Good master porter, I belong to th' larder.°

PORTER  Belong to th' gallows, and be hanged, ye   5
   rogue! Is this a place to roar in? Fetch me a dozen

---

106 **suffer but** allow even   108 **in value with** esteemed by
109 **gave** told   112 **envy at** hate   119 **dear respect** heartfelt
care (for the church)   122 **sudden commendations** extemporaneous compliments   132 **starve** die   139 **lousy** lice-
infested   146 **mean** means

148 **like** please   152 **purgation** vindication   161 **wants** lacks
166–67 **spare your spoons** save the expense of giving spoons
(traditional christening gifts)   167 **partners** co-sponsors   175
**common voice** popular report   177 **shrewd** nasty
V.iv.2 **Parish Garden** Paris Garden, a boisterous bearbaiting
arena on the Bankside; **rude** uncivilized   3 **leave your gaping**
stop your bawling   4 **belong . . . larder** am employed in the
(palace) pantry

crab-tree staves, and strong ones: these are but switches
to 'em.° I'll scratch your heads. You must be seeing
christenings? Do you look for ale and cakes° here, you
rude rascals?                                                    10

MAN
Pray, sir, be patient. 'Tis as much impossible,
Unless we sweep 'em from the door with cannons,
To scatter 'em, as 'tis to make 'em sleep
On May Day° morning, which will never be.
We may as well push against Paul's° as stir 'em.             15

PORTER   How got they in, and be hanged?

MAN
Alas, I know not. How gets the tide in?
As much as one sound cudgel of four foot
(You see the poor remainder) could distribute,
I made no° spare, sir.

PORTER                    You did nothing, sir.          20

MAN
I am not Samson, nor Sir Guy, nor Colbrand,°
To mow 'em down before me; but if I spared any
That had a head to hit, either young or old,
He or she, cuckold or cuckold-maker,
Let me ne'er hope to see a chine° again;                     25
And that I would not for a cow, God save her!°

(Within.) Do you hear, master porter?

PORTER   I shall be with you° presently, good master
puppy. Keep the door close, sirrah.°

MAN   What would you have me do?                             30

PORTER   What should you do, but knock 'em down by
th' dozens? Is this Moorfields° to muster in? Or have
we some strange Indian with the great tool° come
to court, the women so besiege us? Bless me, what
a fry of fornication° is at door! On my Christian con-      35
science, this one christening will beget a thousand; here
will be father, godfather, and all together.

MAN   The spoons° will be the bigger, sir. There is a
fellow somewhat near the door, he should be a brazier
by his face,° for, o' my conscience, twenty of the dog      40
days° now reign in's nose. All that stand about him are
under the line;° they need no other penance. That fire-
drake° did I hit three times on the head, and three times
was his nose discharged against me; he stands there,
like a mortarpiece,° to blow us.° There was a haber-        45
dasher's wife of small wit near him, that railed upon

me till her pinked porringer° fell off her head, for
kindling such a combustion in the state. I missed the
meteor once, and hit that woman, who cried out
"Clubs!"° when I might see from far some forty            50
truncheoners° draw to her succor, which were the
hope o' th' Strand,° where she was quartered. They fell
on; I made good° my place. At length they came to th'
broomstaff° to me. I defied 'em still; when suddenly a
file° of boys behind 'em, loose shot,° delivered such a    55
show'r of pebbles, that I was fain° to draw mine honor
in and let 'em win the work.° The devil was amongst
'em, I think, surely.

PORTER   These are the youths that thunder at a playhouse and fight for bitten apples; that no audience but   60
the tribulation° of Tower Hill° or the limbs° of Limehouse,° their dear brothers, are able to endure. I have
some of 'em in Limbo Patrum,° and there they are like
to dance these three days; besides the running banquet
of two beadles° that is to come.                             65

*Enter Lord* CHAMBERLAIN.

CHAMBERLAIN
Mercy o' me, what a multitude are here!
They grow still too; from all parts they are coming,
As if we kept a fair here. Where are these porters,
These lazy knaves? Y' have made a fine hand, fellows;
There's a trim° rabble let in. Are all these              70
Your faithful friends o' th' suburbs?° We shall have
Great store of room, no doubt, left for the ladies,
When they pass back from the christening.

PORTER                    And't please your honor,
We are but men; and what so many may do,
Not being torn apieces, we have done.                       75
An army cannot rule 'em.

CHAMBERLAIN              As I live,
If the king blame me for't, I'll lay ye all
By th' heels, and suddenly;° and on your heads
Clap round° fines for neglect. Y' are lazy knaves,
And here ye lie baiting of bombards° when             80
Ye should do service. Hark! The trumpets sound;
Th' are come already from the christening.
Go, break among the press,° and find a way out
To let the troop pass fairly, or I'll find
A Marshalsea° shall hold ye play these two months.     85

PORTER
Make way there for the princess.

---

7–8 **switches to 'em** twigs in comparison   **9 ale and cakes**
traditional fare at christenings and other celebrations   **14 May
Day** a holiday the celebration of which began before sunrise
**15 Paul's** Saint Paul's Cathedral   **20 made no** did not   **21
Samson . . . Colbrand** all three possessed legendary strength;
Guy of Warwick was celebrated in romance for slaying the
Danish giant Colbrand   **25 see a chine** i.e., eat beef   **26 for
. . . her** a current expression of doubtful import; perhaps
meaningless   **28 I . . . you** I'll trounce you (Maxwell)   **29
sirrah** term of address used to inferiors   **32 Moorfields** a
recreation field on the London outskirts   **33 some . . . tool**
American Indians were exhibited at court; "tool" = penis   **35
fry of fornication** (1) swarm of would-be fornicators (2)
swarming offspring of fornication   **38 spoons** cf. V.iii.166–67
**39–40 brazier . . . face** brassworker by his (red) face
**40–41 dog days** the period from about July 3 to August 15,
when Sirius, the Dog Star, rises at almost the same time as the
sun; regarded as the hottest and most unwholesome season of
the year   **42 line** equator   **42–43 firedrake** (1) fiery dragon
(2) meteor   **45 mortarpiece** squat cannon with a large bore;
**blow us** blow us up

47 **pinked porringer** round cap with scalloped edge or
ornamental perforations   **50 Clubs** the rallying cry of the
London apprentices   **51 truncheoners** truncheon (or cudgel)
bearers   **51–52 were . . . Strand** i.e., belonged to the shops
in the Strand, in Jacobean times a fashionable street   **52–53
They . . . good** they attacked; I defended   **53–54 to th'
broomstaff** i.e., to close quarters   **55 file** small company;
**loose shot** unaffiliated marksmen   **56 fain** obliged   **57 work**
fort   **61 tribulation** troublemakers; **Tower Hill** an unruly
district; **limbs** inhabitants, with a possible reference to the
limbs of the devil   **61–62 Limehouse** the rough dockyard area
**63 Limbo Patrum** i.e., prison (literally, the underworld abode
of the souls of the just who died before Christ's coming)   **64–65
running . . . beadles** i.e., a public whipping, as a dessert to
the "feast" of their confinement   **70 trim** fine   **71 suburbs**
disreputable districts outside city jurisdiction   **77–78 I'll . . .
suddenly** I'll have you all put straightaway into fetters   **79
round** stiff   **80 baiting of bombards** drinking from leather
jugs   **83 press** throng   **85 Marshalsea** prison in Southwark

MAN                          You great fellow,
Stand close up, or I'll make your head ache.

PORTER
You i' th' camlet,° get up o' th' rail:
I'll peck you o'er the pales° else.              *Exeunt.*

Scene [V. *The palace.*]

*Enter trumpets, sounding; then two* ALDERMEN, LORD
MAYOR, GARTER,° CRANMER, *Duke of* NORFOLK
*with his marshal's staff, Duke of* SUFFOLK, *two* NOBLE-
MEN *bearing great standing-bowls° for the christening gifts;
then four* NOBLEMEN *bearing a canopy, under which the*
DUCHESS *of Norfolk, godmother, bearing the* CHILD
*richly habited in a mantle, &c., train borne by a* LADY.
*Then follows the Marchioness* DORSET, *the other godmother, and* LADIES. *The troop pass once about the stage,
and* GARTER *speaks.*

GARTER   Heaven, from thy endless goodness, send
prosperous life, long, and ever happy, to the high and
mighty Princess of England, Elizabeth!

*Flourish. Enter* KING *and* GUARD.

CRANMER [*Kneeling.*]
And to your royal grace and the good queen.
My noble partners° and myself thus pray:                5
All comfort, joy, in this most gracious lady
Heaven ever laid up to make parents happy
May hourly fall upon ye!
KING                 Thank you, good Lord Archbishop.
What is her name?
CRANMER          Elizabeth.
KING                      Stand up, lord.

[*The* KING *kisses the* CHILD.]

With this kiss take my blessing: God protect thee!    10
Into whose hand I give thy life.
CRANMER                       Amen.
KING
My noble gossips,° y' have been too prodigal.°
I thank ye heartily; so shall this lady,
When she has so much English.
CRANMER               Let me speak, sir,
For heaven now bids me; and the words I utter        15
Let none think flattery, for they'll find 'em truth.
This royal infant—heaven still° move about her!—
Though in her cradle, yet now promises
Upon this land a thousand thousand blessings,
Which time shall bring to ripeness. She shall be      20
(But few now living can behold that goodness)
A pattern to all princes living with her
And all that shall succeed. Saba° was never
More covetous of wisdom and fair virtue
Than this pure soul shall be. All princely graces     25
That mold up such a mighty piece° as this is,
With all the virtues that attend the good,

Shall still be doubled on her. Truth shall nurse her,
Holy and heavenly thoughts still counsel her.
She shall be loved and feared. Her own° shall bless her;  30
Her foes shake like a field of beaten corn,°
And hang their heads with sorrow. Good grows with
   her;
In her days every man shall eat in safety
Under his own vine what he plants, and sing
The merry songs of peace to all his neighbors.         35
God shall be truly known, and those about her
From her shall read° the perfect ways of honor,
And by those claim their greatness, not by blood.
Nor shall this peace sleep with her; but as when
The bird of wonder dies, the maiden phoenix,°          40
Her ashes new create another heir
As great in admiration° as herself,
So shall she leave her blessedness to one°
(When heaven shall call her from this cloud of dark-
   ness)
Who from the sacred ashes of her honor                45
Shall starlike rise, as great in fame as she was,
And so stand fixed.° Peace, plenty, love, truth, terror,
That were the servants to this chosen infant,
Shall then be his, and like a vine grow to him.
Wherever the bright sun of heaven shall shine,         50
His honor and the greatness of his name
Shall be, and make new nations. He shall flourish,
And like a mountain cedar reach his branches
To all the plains about him.° Our children's children
Shall see this, and bless heaven.
KING                      Thou speakest wonders.  55
CRANMER
She shall be, to the happiness of England,
An agèd princess; many days shall see her,
And yet no day without a deed to crown it.
Would I had known no more! But she must die:
She must, the saints must have her. Yet a virgin,      60
A most unspotted lily, shall she pass
To th' ground, and all the world shall mourn her.
KING
O Lord Archbishop,
Thou hast made me now a man; never before
This happy child did I get° anything.                 65
This oracle of comfort has so pleased me
That when I am in heaven I shall desire
To see what this child does, and praise my Maker.
I thank ye all. To you, my good Lord Mayor,
And your good brethren, I am much beholding;          70
I have received much honor by your presence,
And ye shall find me thankful. Lead the way, lords.
Ye must all see the queen, and she must thank ye;
She will be sick else. This day, no man think°
H'as° business at his house; for all shall stay:°     75
This little one shall make it holiday.        *Exeunt.*

88 camlet a rich fabric made of Angora wool and other
materials  89 peck . . . pales pitch you over the palings
V.v.s.d. Garter see IV.i.36 s.d. and note; standing-bowls
bowls with supporting legs or base  5 partners co-sponsors
12 gossips godparents; prodigal generous with gifts  17 still
always  23 Saba the Queen of Sheba  26 mold . . . piece
go to form so great a personage

30 own i.e., own people    31 corn wheat   37 read learn   40
phoenix the fabled Arabian bird—unique in all the world—
that after a life of 660 years rises anew from the ashes in which
it has consumed itself   42 admiration "ability to excite
wonder" (Foakes)   43 one James I   47 fixed i.e., as a fixed
star  50–54 Wherever . . . about him inspired by a prophecy in Genesis 17:4–6 which was often cited in connection
with Princess Elizabeth's marriage in 1613 (Foakes); the "new
nations" may allude to the colonization of Virginia  65 get beget
74 no man think let no man think  75 H'as he has; stay stop

# E P I L O G U E

'Tis ten to one this play can never please
All that are here. Some come to take their ease,
And sleep an act or two; but those, we fear,
W' have frighted with our trumpets; so, 'tis clear,
They'll say 'tis naught;° others, to hear the city          5
Abused extremely, and to cry, "That's witty!"°

Which we have not done neither; that,° I fear,
All the expected good w' are like to hear
For this play at this time, is only in
The merciful construction° of good women,          10
For such a one we showed 'em. If they smile
And say 'twill do, I know, within a while
All the best men are ours; for 'tis ill hap°
If they hold when their ladies bid 'em clap.

**Epi.5 naught** worthless   **5–6 others . . . witty** a glance at
the vogue for satirical comedies of London life

**7 that** so that   **10 construction** interpretation   **13 hap** luck

# THE TWO NOBLE KINSMEN

## EDITED BY CLIFFORD LEECH

## Introduction

The Two Noble Kinsmen was first published in a quarto edition of 1634, with statements on its title page that it had been "Presented at the Blackfriers by the Kings Maiesties servants, with great applause" and that it was "Written by the memorable Worthies of their time; Mr. *John Fletcher*, and Mr. *William Shakespeare*, Gent." The publisher was John Waterson, a reputable figure who brought out other plays belonging to the King's Men, the company with which Shakespeare and Fletcher had been intimately associated. Although in 1646, when Waterson assigned to Humphrey Moseley his rights in the play, it was included with two others as simply the work of "Mr. Flesher," there is an immediately strong case for accepting the title page's statement of authorship. If Waterson were looking for a way of attracting custom, it would have been at least as effective in 1634 to attribute the play to Beaumont and Fletcher. Moreover, it appears that the manuscript from which he printed had been used in the theater itself[1] and that Waterson had bought it from the players in the normal way of business. And we shall see that the probable date of composition and first performance was 1613, when we have other evidence that Shakespeare and Fletcher were working in close association.

It is true, on the other hand, that Heminges and Condell did not include The Two Noble Kinsmen in the Shakespeare Folio of 1623, where in the preliminary address "To the great Variety of Readers" there is an implication that all of Shakespeare's plays were being published in the collection. But it appears that *Timon of Athens* was not originally included in their plans for the volume, and we know that *Troilus and Cressida*, probably through difficulties over copyright, was almost left out. And they did omit *Pericles*. That The Two Noble Kinsmen was included in the 1679 Folio of "Beaumont and Fletcher" plays is also not substantial evidence against Shakespeare's part-authorship, for that volume brought together many plays in which Fletcher collaborated with various dramatists of his time, the linking of his name with Beaumont's on the title page (as in the earlier Beaumont and Fletcher Folio of 1647) being merely a tribute to the brief association of the two men which laid the basis for Fletcher's fame and established

a mode of dramatic writing that was long influential in the English theater.

Nevertheless, the publishing history of the play belongs far more with Beaumont and Fletcher than with Shakespeare. It has been regularly included in collected editions of Beaumont and Fletcher since their Folio of 1679, from Tonson's edition of 1711 to the Cambridge edition of Arnold Glover and A. R. Waller of 1905-12. It did not appear in a collected Shakespeare until 1841, when Charles Knight (who believed that Fletcher's collaborator here was George Chapman) yielded to the extent of including it in a volume of "Doubtful Plays" appended to his *Pictorial Shakespeare*. By then, though dissentient voices were not infrequently raised, the case for Shakespeare's part-authorship had become more than formidable. Pope, in his *Shakespeare* of 1725, thought the play contained "more of our author than some of those which have been received as genuine," and Lamb and Coleridge and De Quincey were all convinced of Shakespeare's presence, though Hazlitt and Shelley could find nothing of it. William Spalding, however, in his *Letter on Shakspere's Authorship of The Two Noble Kinsmen* (Edinburgh, 1833; reprinted in the *Transactions of the New Shakspere Society*, 1874), Samuel Hickson in his article "The Shares of Shakspere and Fletcher in The Two Noble Kinsmen" (*Westminster Review*, 1847; reprinted in the *Transactions of the New Shakspere Society*, 1874), and above all Harold Littledale in the introduction to his edition of the play for the New Shakspere Society (1876-85) brought the techniques of nineteenth-century scholarship to bear on the problem and, though they differed to some extent in assigning to the two dramatists their respective shares, they left little doubt in most readers' minds that here was a collaboration between the leading dramatist of the King's Men and the writer who succeeded him in that role in 1613.

Yet is is still exceptional to find The Two Noble Kinsmen in a collected edition of Shakespeare's plays. Most of its readers during this century have come to know it through its inclusion in C. F. Tucker Brooke's *The Shakespeare Apocrypha* (Oxford, 1908). G. L. Kittredge has it in his *Complete Works of Shakespeare* (Boston, 1936); it is planned

[1] See A Note on the Text, p. 1623.

for inclusion in the New Cambridge edition; and it is now presented as part of the Signet Classic Shakespeare.

The elder dramatist's authorship is commonly recognized most surely in the first and fifth acts, particularly in the first three scenes of Act I and the first, third, and fourth scenes of Act V: that is, the solemn approach of the three Queens to Theseus on his wedding day, the conversation of Palamon and Arcite while they are still in Thebes, the scene where Emilia and Hippolyta talk of friendship, the invocations addressed to Mars and Venus and Diana, and the conclusion of the whole story in Arcite's victory and death. In addition, Shakespeare has been generally found in the opening lines of II.i, where the Jailer's Daughter makes her first appearance, and in III.i, where the escaped Palamon meets the disguised Arcite. In the rest of the play there are frequent echoes of other plays by Shakespeare: the madness of the Jailer's Daughter has obvious associations with Ophelia's madness, and later in this Introduction it will be suggested that Fletcher for special purposes was drawing upon his intimate knowledge of his collaborator's work. If we accept the commonly held view of the two writers' shares (and there is little reason to be skeptical about it), it was Shakespeare who wrote the beginning and the ending and introduced all the major characters and strands of action. But by the time this play was composed he may have been less regularly in attendance at the playhouse than formerly, and it seems likely enough that the final putting together of the manuscript was left to Fletcher. Indeed, more than one scholar has come to the conclusion that he made some insertions in the Shakespeare scenes.

It will be convenient to set out the probable authorship of the play's various scenes thus:

| | | |
|---|---|---|
| Prologue | | Fletcher? |
| Act I, | sc. i–iii | Shakespeare |
| | sc. iv–v | Shakespeare? |
| Act II, | sc. i (lines 1–59) | Shakespeare |
| | sc. i (remainder), ii–v | Fletcher |
| Act III, | sc. i | Shakespeare |
| | sc. ii–vi | Fletcher |
| Act IV, | sc. i–iii | Fletcher |
| Act V, | sc. i | Shakespeare |
| | sc. ii | Fletcher |
| | sc. iii–iv | Shakespeare |
| Epilogue | | Fletcher? |

The dividing of the play between Shakespeare and Fletcher has been worked out by scholars primarily on the basis of the stylistic differences between their writing. Certainly even a casual reading of the play will show that certain scenes have a complex, "knotted" verse that is close to Shakespeare's in his later years, while others belong clearly with the open-textured, casual style that Beaumont and Fletcher developed in manifest reaction against the involutions of the earliest Jacobeans. The difference has been brought home forcibly to the present editor through the process of annotation. If one compares the scenes where Palamon and Arcite talk together, putting I.ii and III.i on one side and II.i (from the exit of the Jailer, his Daughter, and her Wooer), III.iii, and III.vi on the other, one sees immediately that the first group requires continuous attention from the reader, and probably

frequent recourse to the annotations, while the second group has nearly the familiarity of the English now current. When the editor was preparing the annotations, it was with no thought of giving fuller comment on Shakespeare's portion than on Fletcher's, but in the event it proved that in Shakespeare's the proportion of notes to lines was 51 percent in the scenes just indicated while in Fletcher's the proportion of notes to lines was 25 percent. Elsewhere in Fletcher's part of the play the figure is higher, as the terms used in connection with the morris dance of III.v needed comment, and Fletcher can use a more elaborate vocabulary for special purposes (as in the description of the knights in IV.ii and in the account of madness in IV.iii). Nevertheless, the presence of the two hands is obvious almost throughout, and evident at a glance in scenes where the basic material (Palamon and Arcite talking together) is similar.

The time of composition is hardly in dispute. The entertainment which the country Schoolmaster presents to Theseus and his court in III.v is taken over from an antimasque in Francis Beaumont's *Masque of the Inner Temple and Gray's Inn*, presented at Whitehall on February 20, 1613. In the published book of the masque we learn that this part of the entertainment was so well liked by the king that he asked to have it danced again at the end of the whole performance. Such antimasques at court were commonly entrusted to professional players, and it would be an easy matter for Fletcher, with his friend and former collaborator Beaumont's permission, to make further use of what had already proved successful. But clearly this would not be likely except soon after the original performance. The date 1613 for *The Two Noble Kinsmen* is confirmed by the reference in Jonson's *Bartholomew Fair* (1614) to "Palamon" as a character in a play (IV.iii): this is not certain evidence, for the name also occurs in Samuel Daniel's *The Queen's Arcadia* (1605), but Daniel's work was a university play and was already some years old in 1614; Jonson is far more likely to have had a more recent and better-known play in mind. Moreover, 1613 was the year in which a lost play called *Cardenio*[2] (which in 1653 was attributed to Fletcher and Shakespeare by the publisher Humphrey Moseley) was twice acted at court, and it was also the year in which *Henry VIII* was almost certainly acted for the first time. Although by no means all Shakespeare scholars are agreed on the double authorship of *Henry VIII*, there is strong cumulative evidence that in 1613, after Shakespeare had written the last of his series of romances and was about to retire from the stage, and when Beaumont on his marriage had broken with the theater and thus terminated the short but highly profitable collaboration that he and Fletcher had known for some five years, a new and brief association was established between Fletcher and Shakespeare, and that *The Two Noble Kinsmen* was one of its fruits.

In these circumstances, and with the assumption that the main planning of the play was, as has seemed likely, Shakespeare's, we should expect to find a clear enough relationship to the romances that Shakespeare had been writing since *Pericles* (c. 1609) and that he had brought to a conclusion in *The Tempest* (1611). And resemblances are hardly to be missed. In *Pericles* he had gone to Gower's

---

[2] It may exist in an altered form in Lewis Theobald's version of the story, called *Double Falsehood* and published in 1728.

*Confessio Amantis* for his story; here he goes to Gower's contemporary, Chaucer. *Pericles* and *The Winter's Tale* have Hellenistic settings; *The Two Noble Kinsmen* takes us to Athens and briefly to Thebes. The romances present a world where the gods are freely invoked and where they play a direct part in the action—Diana appearing to Pericles in a dream and sending him to Ephesus so that he may find his lost wife Thaisa, Jupiter appearing to Posthumus Leonatus in prison and offering a riddling promise of good fortune to him and of a happy ending to the strife between Rome and Britain, Apollo being consulted on the question of Hermione's guilt and striking Mamillius dead when his father, Leontes, rejects the message from the oracle. In *The Tempest* there are, it is true, no gods—they would be out of place in a drama where a human character has unlimited control over events (though not over the human will)—but there are spirits who represent Juno and Ceres and Iris and who offer divine blessings and admonitions. *The Two Noble Kinsmen* keeps the gods off the stage too, but their altars are there, they are solemnly invoked, and tokens of their favor are given. At the play's end Theseus marvels how the apparently contradictory promises of Mars and Venus have both been fulfilled. More obviously—indeed, more disturbingly—than in the previous plays the human characters of *The Two Noble Kinsmen* are subject to divine power. Theseus can devise a plan for finding out Emilia's husband and for ending the strife between the knights, but it is the gods who circuitously determine things, to the wonder and embarrassment of those concerned.

In some striking features this play has a special relationship with *Pericles*. That had a detachable first act (which was omitted at a Stratford-on-Avon revival in 1947), with formal speechmaking in a context of love and death: so has *The Two Noble Kinsmen*, which could easily have been adjusted to begin with Palamon and Arcite already in prison. Then Arcite's encounter in II.ii with the countrymen who will take part in the games for Emilia's birthday resembles Pericles' encounter with the fishermen in II.i, where he learns there are games to be held in Thaisa's honor: both Pericles and Arcite are victors and are received into the lady's favor. But in *Pericles* the games are a formal tournament, which takes place in an atmosphere of high ceremony, while in *The Two Noble Kinsmen* it is a matter of simple running and wrestling. The tournament, however, is not forgotten and occurs offstage in the final encounter between Palamon and Arcite, each aided by three knights. The cry of "The mean knight!" that indicates at the end of II.ii that Pericles has been victorious anticipates the cries of "Palamon!" and "Arcite!" and "Victory!" that Emilia hears in V.iii. Here the influence of one of Shakespeare's romances is seen operative on a Fletcher portion of the later play.

But there is a more subtle echo of *The Winter's Tale*. Commentators have sometimes seen there a suggestion that Leontes, believing his wife is being unfaithful to him with his best friend, is unconsciously more deeply outraged by the breach in friendship than by the breach in marriage. Certainly the nostalgic reminiscences of Leontes and Polixenes in I.ii, their sense that an Eden was lost when they grew up and took wives, is to be linked with the passage in *The Two Noble Kinsmen*, I.iii, where Emilia and Hippolyta talk of the friendship between Theseus and

Pirithous and the friendship between Emilia and the dead girl Flavina: Hippolyta is not sure even now that she has the first place in Theseus' heart; Emilia has no thought that a husband can be as near to her as Flavina was. In the center of the later play, moreover, there is the friendship of Palamon and Arcite: it is broken when they both love Emilia, but even as they plan to fight to the death (in III.iii) they look back with some longing on their earlier and lighter loves, which did not harm their friendship. That is a brief respite, for Palamon is soon asserting his claim again, but the scene where they help to arm each other (III.vi) is strong in its suggestion of enduring affection. They embrace solemnly before the invocation of their respective divine patrons (V.i), and Arcite's words to Emilia when he appears to have won her are heavily charged with a sense of the price he has paid:

Emily,
To buy you I have lost what's dearest to me
Save what is bought, and yet I purchase cheaply
As I do rate your value. (V.iii.111-14)

Shakespeare's romances are, among other things, love stories, but they are not simple exaltations of the bond that ties most men to women.

This indeed suggests a connection with his earliest plays. *The Two Gentlemen of Verona* was also a play about friendship, and it is difficult not to believe that its very title was echoed in that of *The Two Noble Kinsmen*. There Valentine and Proteus were firm friends until Proteus fell in love with the girl his friend loved. The right and wrong of the matter were simple; Proteus is thoroughly treacherous and gets to the point of attempting rape. When he repents, Valentine has so high a sense of what friendship demands that he is willing to let Proteus have the girl, not thinking even of consulting her. At that time Shakespeare could make discreet fun of the friendship idea and could quickly make all things come right. Moreover, it was Proteus' villainy and Valentine's simple faith that caused the trouble, while in *The Two Noble Kinsmen* Palamon and Arcite love Emilia because they have to, and Arcite dies because the gods have determined so. That Shakespeare thought back to *The Two Gentlemen* is, I think, indubitable, just as he thought back to *The Comedy of Errors* in the final turn of events in *Pericles*, just as he remembered the rambling romantic plays of the popular theater he first knew when he wrote *Pericles* and *Cymbeline* and *The Winter's Tale*. In going back to beginnings, *The Two Noble Kinsmen* is of a piece with the romances, though it has a formality of structure, as we shall see, that links it with *The Tempest* more than with the plays that immediately preceded that play.

It is, however, another early play that is here most prominently in his mind, and again the resemblance goes along with contrast and deliberate reconsideration. Like *The Two Noble Kinsmen*, *A Midsummer Night's Dream* begins with preparations for the wedding of Theseus and Hippolyta, it is partly concerned with an amateur performance given before the duke by his subjects, and it shows the court during a May-morning ceremony coming upon two men who have fallen out through rivalry in love. In the earlier play the wedding is not interrupted, there being merely a planned delay before it takes place; the play-within-the-play occurs at the end, not the middle; the rivals in love have had their quarrel already sorted out by Puck and Oberon before Theseus arrives. And it is not quite the same Theseus in the two plays. The earlier duke has the authority of the later one, but he is ever sanguine and relaxed: he will not believe the "story of the night," and he is patronizing toward play-acting and somewhat ill-mannered during the performance. The duke of *The Two Noble Kinsmen* may finally attempt to console himself by marveling at the divine legerdemain, but there is an unrelaxed seriousness in him and a continuing puzzlement. The man who at first decrees perpetual imprisonment for Palamon and Arcite, and later death for them both, and after that death for the loser (and his supporters) in the tournament, is a shrewd realist very different from the man who told Hermia he could not bend the law for her sake —her father's authority being supreme—and finally acquiesced in her marriage with Lysander and told Egeus he must accept the situation. We can see a similar change, along with a resemblance, in the later play's echoing of Helena's account of her girlhood friendship with Hermia (III.ii): when Emilia speaks of the relationship between herself and Flavina, Shakespeare is no longer offering merely a gentle picture of two girls together.

Shakespeare, then, using a well-known story that had been prominently in his mind when he wrote *A Midsummer Night's Dream* (circa 1595–96), helped to compose a play that had strong links both with the late romances and with early comedies that he had already shown a disposition to recall and to look upon with a changed vision. The reunions at the ends of *The Comedy of Errors* and *Pericles* are as different as can be imagined; the spanning of the years in *Pericles* and *The Winter's Tale* does not make those plays similar in spirit to the romances of the 1570's (and the following decade or so) that Sidney made fun of in *An Apology for Poetry;* magic has a different look in *The Tempest* when we compare that play with *A Midsummer Night's Dream*. There is a certain casualness of manner in *The Two Noble Kinsmen*, such indeed as Lytton Strachey saw in the late romances as a whole, but it goes along with a reserving of judgment about human beings and the conditions under which they live.

And in this situation Fletcher was no longer with Beaumont but with an elder dramatist whose plays were always strongly in his mind, to the point where he would deliberately modify an initial Shakespeare situation and then work out the pattern of events that would result. He and Beaumont had done that with *Philaster* (circa 1609), taking the *Hamlet* situation without the ghost, as later—on his own— he was to write a sequel to *The Taming of the Shrew* in *The Woman's Prize or The Tamer Tamed* (circa 1611) and, probably along with Massinger, to invert the *Lear* situation in *Thierry and Theodoret* (circa 1617). With Beaumont he had shared a lodging and had developed a dramatic mode in which their two minds functioned, it seemed, as one: though we may perhaps be able to differentiate his verse from Beaumont's, we do not get the feeling in their joint plays that two diverse attitudes are alternating as each in his turn pushes his pen. Fletcher's later collaboration with Massinger resembles his collaboration with Shakespeare in *The Two Noble Kinsmen* to the extent that we feel the characterization and the march of event are seen through different eyes in different parts of

the play. If we are correct, as many people have thought, in assuming that Shakespeare put his scenes into Fletcher's hands and let him do the job of conflating the two shares, this was a situation new to this dramatist. That the story would have attracted him is understandable: the clash between love and friendship in Palamon and Arcite has some similarity to that between friendship and honor in Melantius and Amintor in *The Maid's Tragedy* (circa 1610) and would similarly lend itself to the patterned alternations of conduct that Fletcher delighted in; and there must have been a piquancy in working in association with Shakespeare, to whom he owed much, whose work, however, must have seemed old-fashioned, imperfectly sophisticated. He and Beaumont had pulled Hamlet down to the comic level of Philaster; now Shakespeare's Palamon and Arcite could be irreverently handled in the same play as Shakespeare was presenting them.

It is not that Fletcher makes the kinsmen directly absurd (though coming near it in their exchange of sentiments, followed at once by their quarrel, in II.i), and he clearly has some partiality for Arcite; but he does take a feline pleasure in the way love holds them, in the way they try to live up to the friendship code at the same time as they are protesting their separate devotions to Emilia. And this goes along with a special fluency in his writing (seen, for example, in the prison-and-garden sequence of II.i), and a fondness for setting the story in brakes and flowers. Nature is never ominous for Fletcher, but its presence as a framework for strife is always ironic.

In one place the work of Fletcher's deflating hand reminds us of an effect found in Shakespeare's own *The Winter's Tale*, V.ii, and in scenes frequently ascribed to Fletcher in *Henry VIII* (II.i, IV.i). The Messenger in *The Two Noble Kinsmen*, IV.ii, seems to the present editor's ear to be intentionally comic, with his ecstatic praise of the attendant knights, his overreadiness to speak at line 72, his general extravagance of imagery, and in particular the doting on one knight's freckles and the ludicrous comparison of his sinews to the bodily shape of a pregnant woman (lines 128–29). Here I believe we have Fletcher taking up what he found in *The Winter's Tale*, and pushing it much further both in *Henry VIII* and in *The Two Noble Kinsmen*.

If general opinion is right in assigning the opening of II.i to Shakespeare, it was he who introduced the Jailer's Daughter. But the use made of her is characteristically Fletcher's. First we should note his boldness in giving her so many scenes alone (II.iii, II.v, III.ii, III.iv): the contrast with Emilia's safe establishment in Theseus' court is striking; and while Emilia is always herself, never in love, protesting yet acquiescent, grieved rather than disturbed, the Jailer's Daughter moves from lighthearted romance—

> Out upon't,
> What pushes are we wenches driven to
> When fifteen once has found us!     (II.iii.5–7)

—to fear and hunger, and thence to a sense of exposure—

> I am very cold, and all the stars are out too,
> The little stars and all, that look like aglets.
> The sun has seen my folly.     (III.iv.1–3)

—and thence to madness. The descent is not merely pathetic: it is comic, as we see in her taking part in the morris dance of III.v, and it is powerfully suggestive of the casual destructiveness of the love impulse. Aspatia in *The Maid's Tragedy* is too often seen as a merely pathetic figure: there is destructiveness there too, for herself and for Amintor. Fletcher had a strong sense of how disintegration worked, most brilliantly realized in his Maximus in *Valentinian* (circa 1614). And we may, I think, assume that it was Fletcher's idea to have the girl in *The Two Noble Kinsmen* "cured" by making her take her humble Wooer for Palamon, and thus in imagination lie with the man she loved. At the end of the play Emilia is almost on the point of marrying Arcite; the gods intervene, and she is in Palamon's arms. Neither girl has choice, neither girl has, ultimately it seems, the power to differentiate. Moreover, they are linked in that the Jailer's Daughter has to play her part in the morris dance, her madness making her, in the opinion of the Countrymen, the more apt for the grotesque gambols required, while Emilia, trying to preserve neutrality and sobriety, is nevertheless shuttled from one knight's arms to the other's. This gives the country entertainment of III.v a function in the play: it is a comic counterpart to, and an anticipation of, the final tournament, and their respective roles in the two spectacles bring together the girl who loves Palamon and the girl who weds him. In his development of the subplot, Fletcher seems thus to have continued his work of deflation.

Here, however, it is necessary to distinguish with some care. Shakespeare's handling of Palamon and Arcite and Theseus and Emilia is no simple romancing, as we have seen. They are powerless human beings manipulated by the gods, and in a measure comic in their subjection. But the comedy is wry and serious, nowhere more so than in Palamon's invocation of Venus in V.i.[3] Fletcher's comedy is much more self-conscious, more obviously grotesque, and though it too is wry there is laughter in it.

Not only deflation of the elder dramatist can be seen, but a measure of parody too. The Jailer's Daughter echoes Ophelia; Emilia brooding over the pictures of Palamon and Arcite in IV.ii echoes the Gertrude who was made to look on pictures of Claudius and the elder Hamlet; even the Doctor's bed trick in V.ii (for it is substantially that) may echo Shakespeare's elaborate employments of the device. And again and again there are tricks of wording— for example, the Doctor's "I think she has a perturbed mind, which I cannot minister to" (IV.iii.58–59)—that take up phrases which Fletcher knew from Shakespeare. The parodying is not hostile or unadmiring. We can remember that in 1613 Shakespeare was forty-nine and Fletcher thirty-four, that we have strong evidence that they worked together on two, perhaps on three, plays: the relationship must have been a complex one. Through the remaining twelve years of Fletcher's career his predecessor's work was never far from his mind, but he enjoyed it without a total reverence. That in writing his share of *The Two Noble Kinsmen* he made the play something of a medley would not deeply disturb him. He did not bring to the writing of any play a sense of full commitment.

A court record suggests that Shakespeare's and Fletcher's play was given there in 1619,[4] and the occurrence in the text of two actors' names[5] enables us to deduce that the play was revived about 1625–26. The title page of 1634 is perhaps deliberately ambiguous in its "Presented at the Blackfriers": this could imply, but need not, that the play was still in the repertory. But after 1642 for a very long time the stage had almost no use for the play.[6] In 1664 Pepys saw at Lincoln's Inn Fields Theatre *The Rivals* (not a new play then), which is a free adaptation of *The Two Noble Kinsmen* and, though it was published anonymously in 1668, can be safely attributed to Sir William Davenant. He was a dramatist of experience and some note in Charles I's reign, he was largely responsible for the restarting of theater performances in London during the Interregnum (his operatic *The Siege of Rhodes* being acted in 1656), and he was one of the two London theater managers in the earliest Restoration years. He made free use of pre-1642 drama, adapting *Macbeth* and (with Dryden) *The Tempest* for current taste. In *The Rivals* he contrived a version of the story he found in Shakespeare and Fletcher, with no Theseus, no petitioning Queens, no invocation of the gods, no tournament, and a happy ending. Though he occasionally keeps to the words he found, he uses none of the old names and changes the place of action to Arcadia. Heraclea, corresponding to Emilia, cannot make up her mind between Theocles and Philander, but finds that Philander is loved by Celania, the daughter of the Provost (no mere jailer): therefore she decides to take Theocles, and Philander consents to love Celania. Davenant wanted to make a refined comedy, and to do it he had to remove most of the action and all the grossness. Celania does go distracted for a while, but only in a polite way. The play is of no importance, but so far as is known it provided the occasion for the only contact with the stage that *The Two Noble Kinsmen* had between the early seventeenth century and the early twentieth century. Not even William Poel is on record as having thought of a revival.

Then in March 1928 the Old Vic staged it, with Ernest Milton as Palamon, Eric Portman as Arcite, Jean Forbes-Robertson as the Jailer's Daughter, and Barbara Everest as Emilia. Writing in *The London Mercury* for April 1928, A. G. MacDonell praised Jean Forbes-Robertson, and noted that Palamon was done comically, in a red wig. This reviewer was much taken with the realistic playing of the mad scenes, and grateful that he did not have to endure simple nobility in two kinsmen. The only other productions I have been able to trace are one at the Antioch Area

---

[3] See A Note on the Source, pp. 1621–23.

[4] E. K. Chambers, *William Shakespeare: A Study of Facts and Problems* (1930), II, p. 346.

[5] See A Note on the Text, pp. 1623–25.

[6] The almost complete disregard of our play in the late seventeenth century is indicated by Dryden's failure to mention it in his Preface to his volume of *Fables* (1700) or to give in his *Palamon and Arcite*, included in that volume, any clear indication that he had read it. He does, when writing of Emilia at Book I, line 175, use the phrase "To do the observance due to sprightly May," which is a little nearer to "to do observance/To flow'ry May" (*The Two Noble Kinsmen*, II.iv.50–51) than to Chaucer's "to have remembraunce/To don honour to May" (*The Knight's Tale*, lines 188–89), but Chaucer in another context has "to doon his observaunce to May" (line 642). Dryden also makes a little more of the freckled face of one of the kinsmen's supporters (Book III, lines 76, 475) than Chaucer does (lines 1311–12), which could be due to the stress on this feature in *The Two Noble Kinsmen*, IV.ii.120–23. Neither of these points can make us firmly deduce that Dryden gave the play a thought as he adapted Chaucer.

Theater, Antioch College, Ohio, which was given eight times in August and September 1955 under the direction of Arthur Lithgow, and one at the Department of Drama, University of Bristol, England. I am most grateful to Mr. Lithgow, now of the McCarter Theater at Princeton, and to Miss Marcia Overstreet and Miss Ernestine C. Brecht of Antioch College, for writing to me about the productions there, and to Professor Glynne Wickham, Head of the Department of Drama at Bristol, for his information concerning the Bristol performance. Mr. Lithgow reports that the play proved "very stage-worthy," particularly the scenes involving the Jailer's Daughter, and that Mr. Ellis Rabb was "very grand" as Palamon. Some cutting had to be done of "repetitive passages," but Shakespeare's hand was felt in the "high imagery."

This is a relatively inglorious stage history for a play in which Shakespeare was concerned, and we must honor the Old Vic, Antioch College, and the University of Bristol for going against the current. Despite the coldness of the London reviewers (MacDonell was typical), it is evident that something happened to the Jailer's Daughter scenes when they got on the stage, and this was confirmed at Antioch College, where indeed the play as a whole seems to have found itself at home. It is more than time that a further attempt was made to see it in action. It does, after all, contain the invocations to the gods in V.i, passages of dramatic verse outstanding even in 1613, a good time for dramatic verse; it contains some of Fletcher's most skillful and characteristic writing; it will one day, perhaps, come to be recognized as throwing a new kind of light on Shakespeare's concluding work in the theater. It needs a large and flexible stage: there is a most suitable one at Stratford, Ontario, another at Chichester in England, and others—both indoor and outdoor—easily found in the United States. One of these might well meet the challenge of what was perhaps Shakespeare's (though only partly Shakespeare's) last play.

It has some good verse and a fairly realistic picture of the onset of madness, but the director contemplating a revival will want to be assured of more than that. It is true that he must face difficulties. The play has the appearance of a romantic story, as Beaumont and Fletcher's *Philaster* has, but in neither instance does the romantic effect work properly. With *Philaster* that was because Beaumont and Fletcher were determined on a sophisticated undercutting of the romantic gesture; with *The Two Noble Kinsmen* there is the complication that two men of widely differing temperaments shared the writing. Shakespeare had used romance with high authority in *The Winter's Tale* and *The Tempest*, involving his audience in a love story in a setting that was both natural and strange, and at the same time making them feel that they were in the presence of stern and unknowable powers. But now he was working with Fletcher, whose sights were lower, essentially those that had characterized *Philaster*. For Shakespeare, we can assume it was the sense of the inscrutable that made the story attractive to him; for Fletcher, it was its essential, often painful, but never overwhelming absurdity. Because it seems likely that Fletcher had the task of putting together his and Shakespeare's work on the play, the overriding effect is Fletcherian: we are taken to high realms of thought, and deliberately let down, as we are so often, but less extravagantly, in the other plays in which Fletcher had

a main hand. It is a paradox that Shakespeare seems to have planned *The Two Noble Kinsmen* and that Fletcher gave it its dominant tone. But that tone is dominant, not exclusive: from Shakespeare we get the solemn pageant of the Queens' mission in I.i, the sage talk of Emilia and Hippolyta in I.iii, the sharp magniloquence of the prayers in V.i; and Fletcher's deflations do not take them from our memory.

But what has probably put off most readers and potential directors has been the nature of the characterization. Shakespeare's handling of character from *Pericles* onward was lacking in the complexity and verisimilitude that had marked the comedies and frequently the tragedies of his middle and mature years. But audiences have been ready to accept Leontes in place of Othello, Miranda in place of Rosalind, Prospero in place of Hamlet, because in these plays they are led consistently toward the idea of "great creating Nature," toward a sense of epiphany, toward an austere assertion that to accept what is remains the best hope, the highest wisdom, we have. But Fletcher has been little more successful on the stage from the eighteenth to the twentieth century, either alone or in collaboration with Beaumont, than he has been in association with Shakespeare. Reviewing the Old Vic performance of *The Two Noble Kinsmen* in 1928, James Agate asked how any actress could make anything of Emilia, passed from hero to hero as from pillar to post.[7] A. G. MacDonell, we have seen, found even one manifestly noble kinsman enough to bear. Fletcher offers nothing in the way of obvious compensation for his stereotyping of human characters; these are, he suggests, the types that men fall into, or imagine they fall into, or try to live up to the idea of falling into. The Fletcherian drama is a drama about men's refusal to live as individuals. In his plays, men avoid nakedness by doing what they feel the codes and traditions of society demand from them. We may differentiate Palamon from Arcite: one is more rough, the other ready to see himself as sinning because he devoted himself to Emilia a few seconds after his friend did. But each keeps within a stereotype, a notion that belongs to the playhouse of the mind that men are always imagining for themselves: they are alike victims and worshipers of Bacon's Idols of the Theater. It is a kind of characterization that in recent years Brecht has familiarized us with, and we should now therefore be the more fitted to respond to the mode and to see what the play as a whole is saying.

It is indeed a well-arranged play, despite the duality of authorship and the dichotomy of attitude that in this instance is thus imposed. Instead of the loose storytelling we might expect, we have a fairly tight structure, and in A Note on the Source (p. 1621) we shall see that this has been achieved partly through the changes made in adapting Chaucer. The action involves three interwoven strands: (1) the prologue action, as we may call it, concerning the conflict between Athens and Thebes; (2) the story of the rivalry for Emilia; (3) the story of the Jailer's Daughter. The first makes the play begin in a manner of high seriousness and formal rhetoric, and it is in manifest contrast with the slighter, more personal stories of the knights and the girls. The subplot, as we have seen, reflects ironically on the plot of the knights.

7 *Brief Chronicles* (1943), pp. 53–56.

The act division throughout is firm, and is related to the play's changes of locality. Act I concerns itself with the conflict between Athens (chivalrous) and Thebes (ignoble), ending with the imprisonment of the nearly dead Palamon and Arcite (noble on the wrong side). Act II gives us their falling in love and release from prison, and introduces the subplot. Act III is wholly outside the town: it shows how Palamon and Arcite meet again, how the Jailer's Daughter loses Palamon, how Theseus and his court are entertained by a group of rustics including the Daughter, and finally how the duke comes upon the kinsmen and decrees their final trial. Act IV, which is briefly and quietly indeterminate, makes toward the cure of the Daughter and emphasizes the perplexity of Emilia it is, as often with a fourth act, a halting place before the catastrophe. Act V gives us the tournament and its curious consequences, with both girls in some sense pledged to Palamon. Athens and Thebes are the localities of Act I, Athens and the country nearby those of Act II, the country consistently is the place of action in Act III, the city of Athens (but alternating between palace and prison) in Acts IV and V. As the play progresses its range of locality shrinks, so that what begins as an opposition of Thebes and Athens ends as an opposition of palace and prison within a single city. The point of rest toward which we move is marked by death and bereavement and acquiescence: the Jailer who freed Arcite in Act II, and put Palamon under further restraint, is prominently in the stage picture when Palamon is prepared for execution and then, at the news of Arcite's death, for marriage.

The play's recurrent irony is supported by other details of the planning. Theseus is ceremoniously petitioned by the Queens in I.i and by Hippolyta, Emilia, and Pirithous in III.vi: he yields in both instances, though with eloquence in the earlier, Shakespearean passage and with the cleverness of compromise in Fletcher's III.vi. The talk between Palamon and Arcite in I.ii, where they show their wish to leave a corrupt Thebes, becomes ironic when in fighting for Thebes they come near death and are sentenced to life imprisonment. The discussion of friendship by Hippolyta and Emilia in I.iii not only anticipates the dominant friendship motif in the play as a whole, but casts an ironic light on the knights' subsequent devotion to Emilia. And just as the subplot as a whole reflects on Emilia and her ultimate disposal, so the entertainment devised by the Schoolmaster, which brings Theseus and the Jailer's Daughter together on the stage for the only time, is not only a contrast to and an anticipation of the wryly presented tournament of Act V: it also gives a distorted image of the entertainment that the kinsmen and the duke and his ladies offer to the audience in the theater.

Of course, this is a Blackfriars play. The King's Men had taken over that "private" theater (previously used by the child actors) around 1610 and had begun by using it as their winter house, keeping the Globe for the summer. The title page of 1634 mentions only the Blackfriars, and we may assume that at least by the 1620's this play had found its right home there. It is a sophisticated—even, we have seen, a dislocated—play, not firm, ultimately, in its implications but surely fascinating, if disturbing and at times irritating, to watch. Its epilogue calls it "the tale we have told—/For 'tis no other." That was what Shakespeare had insistently, in the text as well as in the title, called The

*Winter's Tale*. *The Two Noble Kinsmen*, like that earlier romance, is a strange story with many reversals of fortune, but like that too it has its unromantic aftertaste and is more carefully structured than a casual glance suggests. The Blackfriars audience was at times most gullible, ready to lose itself in a merely romanticized wonderland, but it could rise to the appreciation of something complex: it welcomed Fletcher's masterpiece in comedy, *The Humorous Lieutenant* (circa 1619–20), and, though we cannot be sure that it much liked the experience, it saw Ford's *The Broken Heart* some dozen years after that. There were doubtless moments of puzzlement with *The Two Noble Kinsmen* in 1613 and the following years, but at least some of the spectators must have noticed that the supreme dramatist and his more than clever successor were not failing them.

Nor would they, I think, fail us now if we again put their joint play on the stage.[8]

## A NOTE ON THE SOURCE

The source of *The Two Noble Kinsmen*, as we have seen, is *The Knight's Tale*, which was most easily available to the collaborators in Speght's edition of Chaucer, published in 1598 (reprinted three times by 1602). In the dramatization a considerable number of changes were made. We may notice them under several heads:

(1) The action throughout is compressed. In Chaucer there is a time lapse between the first seeing of Emilia by the kinsmen and the release of Arcite. Then Arcite spends some years in Thebes before returning to Athens to see Emilia again. Meanwhile Palamon has seven years in prison. When Theseus has arranged the tournament, the kinsmen are to return to Athens in a year's time. Arcite takes some time to die after the horse has thrown

---

[8] Since this Introduction was written, Paul Bertram has published a substantial book with the title *Shakespeare and The Two Noble Kinsmen* (1965), arguing that Shakespeare was the sole author of the play. It is a piece of well-informed writing, and Bertram has scored some good points in showing how the nineteenth-century scholars seized on the idea of dual authorship because of a reluctance to imagine Shakespeare writing the franker sections of the play. He argues, moreover, that the play has unity in its plotting (as indeed it has) and that throughout there is the same full use of Chaucer. Less successfully, he disposes of the evidence of verse tests by insisting that some of the scenes treated by the editors as verse are really in prose (as they are presented in the quarto): this is, I think, to disregard the strong blank-verse character of much of the writing. The reader of the present edition will be able to decide whether the scenes involving the Countrymen and the Jailer and his Daughter (apart from the beginning of II.i and the whole of IV.iii) are legitimately printed as verse. Moreover, Bertram is one of the, alas, many who have a low regard for Fletcher: he insists on Shakespeare's sole authorship of *Henry VIII* and *The Two Noble Kinsmen*, but will let Fletcher have *Cardenio*, which seems to him of minor weight. And he does not successfully meet the evidence of the 1634 title page. It is possible to quote, as he does, the statement of Leonard Digges, in the 1640 edition of Shakespeare's *Poems*, that Shakespeare did not bed "from each witty friend a Scene/To peece his Acts with," but that is another matter than the frank and equal sharing of a play with his obvious successor in 1613. It used to be necessary to argue for Shakespeare's participation in *The Two Noble Kinsmen;* now we have to safeguard Fletcher's right to a part of it. And the argument of this Introduction is that there are, despite close cooperation, a difference of view and a difference of style that indicate two authors, one of them supreme and the other at least major in his time.

him, and it is a matter of years before Emilia brings herself to marry Palamon. In the play we are not told how long Palamon and Arcite are in prison, but there is no suggestion that it is a great while. Clearly Palamon escapes soon after Arcite has entered Emilia's service. The time lapse before the tournament is a single month. Arcite dies almost immediately, and Emilia is to marry Palamon, it appears, the next day.

These changes are partly to give an effect of tighter structure to what is in Chaucer a diffuse narrative, but they also increase the sense of divine manipulation. The kinsmen in II.i look forward to a slow lifetime in prison; instead, they are whirled through a series of events, and at the end of the play Emilia is passed from arm to arm in a manner that suggests no cosmic concern for her dignity.

(2) There are also changes for the sake of obvious dramatic effectiveness. In the poem Theseus' wedding is not interrupted by the mission of the Queens. There are not three Queens but a crowd of queens and duchesses. Emilia has no attendant in the garden with whom she can talk informally and lightly. Palamon is not removed from the garden room after Arcite's departure. At the tournament each of the kinsmen is to be accompanied by a hundred knights. The invocations to the gods are in the order Venus, Diana, Mars, which has not the climactic effect secured in the play by Emilia's prayer coming last. The falling of the single rose from the tree brings the whole scene to a striking (and disturbing) conclusion.

(3) Other changes increase this sense of disturbance. Most obvious among these is the decree of Theseus that the knights defeated in the tournament shall die. Of course, this allows the theatrically effective saving of Palamon from the block, and it puts more at stake than the disposal of Emilia's person. Shakespeare may have thought of this change because in *Pericles* the unsuccessful suitors of Antiochus' daughter were similarly vowed to death. In any event, it is an element in the play that links it with the dangers and actual deaths that are found in the preceding romances. Moreover, there is nothing in the invocation of Venus in *The Knight's Tale* that resembles the words on the goddess' power that Palamon speaks. He hails her as

> sovereign queen of secrets,
>
> . . . .
>
> that canst make
> A cripple flourish with his crutch, and cure him
> Before Apollo; that mayst force the king
> To be his subject's vassal, and induce
> Stale Gravity to dance: the pollèd bachelor
> Whose youth like wanton boys through bonfires
> Have skipped thy flame, at seventy thou canst catch
> And make him, to the scorn of his hoarse throat,
> Abuse young lays of love. (V.i.77, 81–89)

The images of the cripple grotesquely cured, of authority submissive and dancing, of old age straining its throat with a love song, contribute powerfully to that harsh strain in Shakespeare's section of the play that has been noted in the Introduction. And then we find Palamon seeking favor by boasting of his own credulity, and doing it in terms that, for an audience, are surely meant to be repellent:

> I knew a man
> Of eighty winters, this I told them, who
> A lass of fourteen brided. 'Twas thy power
> To put life into dust: the aged cramp
> Had screwed his square foot round,
> The gout had knit his fingers into knots,
> Torturing convulsions from his globy eyes
> Had almost drawn their spheres, that what was life
> In him seemed torture. This anatomy
> Had by his young fair fere a boy, and I
> Believed it was his, for she swore it was,
> And who would not believe her? (V.i.107–18)

We may think back to Antony's concern with his gray hairs, to Leontes' finding wrinkles in what he thinks is Hermione's statue, but the degree of frankness is new. Palamon, the servant of Venus, puts himself side by side with the other victims he describes.[9]

(4) Nothing in Chaucer corresponds to the Jailer's Daughter plot. We are simply told that Palamon escaped with the help of a friend. In the Introduction (p. 1617) we have seen how Shakespeare and Fletcher use the subplot to affect the audience's response to the story of the knights and their love.

(5) In Chaucer the gods are at odds with each other, and the quarrel is settled by the ingenuity of Saturn, so that all promises can be kept. In the play we are rather made to feel that a single power speaks through the gods, that the matter is predetermined, that all that the gods do is to give hints of a future that neither prayer nor divine intervention can modify.

In a few places the play includes some quite incidental echoes of Chaucer. Thus Arcas, one of the Countrymen named at II.ii.37 and III.v.47, is the name of the son of Callisto, who, as "Calystope," is referred to in *The Knight's Tale*, line 1198. The Schoolmaster mentions the story of Meleager and Atalanta at III.v.18; Chaucer mentions it at *The Knight's Tale*, lines 1212–13. In the play the tournament is held in the place where Theseus found the knights fighting (III.vi.293): in *The Knight's Tale*, lines 1999–2006, we learn that it is Arcite's funeral pyre that is to be erected in that place. The consolation that Palamon offers to his friends as they are about to submit themselves to the block (V.iv.1–13), although altogether sharper in its comments on the nature of life, bears an obvious relation to the arguments that Theseus uses in *The Knight's Tale*, lines 2189–98, in order to persuade Palamon and Emilia to give up their mourning for Arcite and enter into marriage. Such points of casual resemblance between play and poem, with the dramatists freely manipulating the words and images they found in Chaucer, show the intimacy of their acquaintance with the source.

*The Knight's Tale* had been twice dramatized before 1613. In 1566 Richard Edwardes' *Palamon and Arcite* was acted at Christ Church, Oxford, before Elizabeth, and Henslowe's *Diary* registers a *Palamon and Arcite* acted in 1594, probably as a new play. Neither of these is extant, but there is no reason to believe that they had any connection with *The Two Noble Kinsmen*.

[9] In his Introduction to Shakespeare's *Sonnets* (see page 1728), W. H. Auden comments on this passage's choice of "humiliating or horrid" examples of the power of Venus and on "the intensity of the disgust at masculine sexual vanity."

In the Introduction (pp. 1617–18) we have seen that Shakespeare and Fletcher were dependent also on their memories of several earlier Shakespeare plays, ranging from *The Two Gentlemen of Verona* to the late romances, and that this has helped to make the play into something very different from a straightforward dramatization of Chaucer.

## A NOTE ON THE TEXT

There is no doubt that the text used by the printer of the quarto of 1634 had been in the hands of a prompter (presumably of the Blackfriars Theater). The most obvious evidence of this is the appearance in the margin of three "warnings"—that is, reminders that preparation must be made for an ensuing entry. These are noted below in the list of places where the present edition varies from the quarto, but it will be useful to bring them together here:

(1) On C3$^v$ of the quarto, in the left margin opposite I.iii.58–64:

> 2. Hearses rea-/dy with Pala-/mon: and Arci-/te: the 3./Queenes./Theseus: and/his Lordes/ready.

At this point the scene has more than thirty lines to run: the "warning" is of what will be required at the beginning of I.iv, which comes on C4$^r$.

(2) On C4$^v$, in the left margin opposite I.iv.26–27:

> 3. Hearses rea-/dy.

These hearses are for the bodies of the three kings slain at Thebes and will be brought on at the beginning of I.v twenty lines later, on the same page of the quarto.

(3) On G2$^v$, in the left margin opposite III.v.65–66:

> Chaire and/stooles out.

These properties are required for Theseus and his company to sit on to watch the Schoolmaster's entertainment: the dialogue indicates that they sit some thirty lines later, at III.v.98.

Further evidence of theater use of the copy behind the quarto is in the appearance of actors' names in the entries. At IV.ii.69 the quarto stage direction reads "*Enter Messengers. Curtis.*" ("*Messengers*" being clearly an error for "*Messenger*"), and the entry which opens V.iii reads ". . . *and/some Attendants, T. Tucke: Curtis.*" The actors referred to can be identified as Curtis Greville, who was a hired man in the King's Company in 1626, probably having joined them the preceding year, and Thomas Tuckfield, whose name appears in a list of "Musitions and other necessary attendantes" of the King's Company in 1624.[10] From these dates it is clear that the actors' names were inserted on the occasion of a revival in the 1620's, not for the original performance of 1613.

Actors' names appearing in a text may be due to an author who has a particular member of the company in mind for a part, but this could not be the case with the two names in *The Two Noble Kinsmen*. For one thing, Greville and Tuckfield were not with the company when Shakespeare and Fletcher were writing the play; for

another, the messenger of IV.ii and the attendants of V.iii are characterless parts: an author would have no views on who should play them, but a prompter might wish to remind himself of the actors' identities.

The quarto contains further indications of playhouse use. Act IV ends with the stage direction "*Florish. Exeunt,*" the "*Florish*" obviously being wrongly placed: it is needed for the entry of Theseus and the rest at the beginning of Act V. The same thing occurs at the end of V.ii. In these instances we can deduce that "Florish" was added in the margin between IV.iii and V.i and between V.ii and V.iii respectively, and the printer took it as going with the exits and not with the following entries. Then we have several marginal stage directions printed, like the "warnings" noted above, in roman type—one at the beginning of II.iv:

> This short flo-/rish of Cor-/nets and/Showtes with-/in.

and another opposite the heading "*Actus Tertius.*":

> Cornets in/sundry places./Noise and/hallowing as/people a May-/ing:

The marginal placing, the use of roman type, and the curious phrasing "This short florish" all suggest that here we have prompter's additions to the manuscript. A third instance of this is at III.v.134–37, where the text in the quarto is as follows:

|  | *Per. Produce.* |  | *Musicke Dance.* |
|---|---|---|---|
| Knocke for | I*ntrate filii*, Come forth, and foot it, |  |  |
| Schoole. Enter | *Ladies, if we have been merry* |  |  |
| The Dance. | *And have pleased thee with a derry,* |  |  |

The italic stage direction can be taken as at least possibly authorial. In the original manuscript there could have been a marginal speech heading "*Sch.*" (the quarto's regular form) before "Intrate. . . ." A prompter, however, might see no clearly marked entry for the dancers or cue for their entry, and might insert these in the left margin, running the insertion together with "*Sch.*" Conceivably "for" was added during preparation for printing in an attempt to make sense of "Knocke./Sch./Enter The Dance." Alternatively the manuscript as altered by the prompter read thus:

> Knocke for
>
>    Sch.
>
> The Dance.

and the printer moved "Sch[oole]." to the left and added "Enter" in an attempt to make sense of it. It would be good theatrical usage to have a "knock" (striking the floor of the stage with a staff) as a signal. But at III.v.17 the agreed signal was to be his flinging up his cap: the author of the scene would not be likely to forget this so quickly, but a prompter might at first reading. Like the two previously noted stage directions, this one is in roman.

One other stage direction is marginal and in roman. This occurs at III.vi.93:

> They bow se-/verall wayes:/then advance/and stand.

An asterisk is inserted in III.vi.93 after Arcite has said "And me my love!" and before he continues "Is there ought else to say?" This is, I think, likely to be an authorial addition: it is literary in character, and the placing of the asterisk looks like an author's wish to indicate that the action must come between the two halves of Arcite's speech. But for the printer it would appear in the margin along with the prompter's additional stage directions and warnings, so he has used roman type for this as for those.

Even so, the evidence for the presence of the prompter's hand is fairly plentiful, and he may also have been responsible for all the indications of sound effects (horns, cornets, flourishes), not merely for those noted above. Yet it does not seem very likely that in 1634 the printer had in front of him a promptbook actually used in performance. Sir Walter Greg drew attention to the possibility that even "warnings" could appear in a manuscript which was merely annotated by a prompter before the promptbook itself was made.[11] And it is evident that the "warnings" here given are not complete: an executioner's block would be needed for V.iv, and a chair for Arcite at V.iv.84. Also, some of the entries are incomplete: Artesius and Attendants must be added at I.i.s.d. (though we can assume that the printer is responsible for the apparent omission of Pirithous); a Herald, Lords, Attendants, Palamon and Arcite must be added at I.iv.s.d.; at III.v.s.d. the entry includes "2. or 3 wenches," but five are needed for the dance; at IV.i.102 the vague "and others," though possible in a prompt copy, may be an additional sign of authorial inexactitude.

Our text also contains certain things that might well have been eliminated in a prompt copy. At I.i.217 there is the stage direction "Exeunt towards the Temple." This indicates that Hippolyta, Emilia, Pirithous, and the Attendants begin to move toward the stage door that here represents the temple entrance, but Theseus has still an exchange with Pirithous (I.i.219–24) before the procession has left the stage. This is clear enough to a reader, but a prompter would be likely to tidy it up. Then at II.i.50 there is the direction "Enter Palamon and Arcite, above." The Jailer and his Daughter comment from below and then leave the stage. The quarto marks a general "Exeunt." and then gives a new scene heading:

Scæna 2. Enter Palamon, and Arcite in prison.

The action is surely continuous, and in the present edition a new scene is not started at this point. The kinsmen need to remain above, as the later part of the scene will be more effective if they look down to the garden to see Emilia, as they do in Chaucer: moreover, the "leap the garden . . . and pitch between her arms" of II.i.275–76 strongly suggests that Arcite is above. The explanation of the condition of the text here is probably that II.i.1–57 are by Shakespeare and the rest of the scene by Fletcher: they had worked out in advance that Shakespeare would introduce the new characters (Jailer, Daughter, Wooer) and Fletcher would do the kinsmen's first encounters with Emilia. So the two sections of the scene would be separate: II.i.60 would start a new sheet of paper. In other words, this suggests that the printer in 1634 had in front of him

either the holograph manuscript of Shakespeare and Fletcher or a transcript faithful to it. It should also be noted that the quarto is unusual in its indications of locality: in addition to the "Temple" and "prison" already noted, we have "Enter Palamon as out of a bush" at III.i.30 s.d. and "Enter Palamon from the bush" at III.vi.s.d. Such indications of locality are of course rare in seventeenth-century play texts: those in our play are similar to "Enter Timon in the woods" and "Enter Timon from his Caue" in the Folio text Timon of Athens, IV.iii.s.d. and V.i.30 s.d. Timon was almost certainly printed either from Shakespeare's own manuscript or from a faithful transcript of it.

Now it must be remembered that we know of performances of The Two Noble Kinsmen in 1613, probably in 1619, and around 1625.[12] The printer's copy in 1634 has some relation to the last of these (from the evidence of the two actors' names), but it is puzzling to think of the prompter on that occasion annotating the authors' original manuscript if a prompt copy for 1613 (and 1619) were available. It could of course have been lost or not immediately available. And we cannot be sure that all the prompter's additions were made at the same time: the "warnings" and additional stage directions could have been inserted in 1613 and the actors' names in 1625. Nevertheless, there is a good case for believing that the quarto is directly based on the author's manuscript (or a faithful transcript of it), which the prompter had annotated before the making of a promptbook. When the play came to be printed, the company would be more likely to give such a manuscript to the publisher rather than the promptbook itself, which would be needed at the theater if the play were to be acted again.[13]

When the play was reprinted in the Beaumont and Fletcher Folio of 1679, the text was based on that of the quarto. This is firmly established not only by the statement in the Folio itself but by the frequent agreement between the texts in accidentals. Although the 1679 printing shows a considerable number of variants, they have no independent authority and are mainly corrections of misprints, new misprints, and casual changes in accidentals. For the present edition, therefore, the Folio readings have been treated in the same way as those of all subsequent texts: that is, they have been regarded as editorial emendations or errors, to be taken into account in emending the quarto text but not recorded where they have not been accepted by the present editor.

All substantive departures from the quarto are recorded below, with the reading of the present edition in boldface type followed by the quarto reading in roman. It will be seen that the prompter's "warnings" have been transposed into stage directions and inserted in brackets at the appropriate places. The stage directions that have been noted above as almost certainly the prompter's are, however,

---

[11] The Shakespeare First Folio (1955), p. 141.

[12] See Introduction, p. 1619.

[13] F. O. Waller in his article "Printer's Copy for The Two Noble Kinsmen," Studies in Bibliography, XI (1958), pp. 61–84, has argued along these lines. This article incorporates material in Waller's unpublished Chicago dissertation of 1958, A Critical, Old-spelling Edition of "The Two Noble Kinsmen": the fullest textual studies so far made of the play are to be found in this thesis and in Paul Bertram's Shakespeare and The Two Noble Kinsmen (1965). Bertram, however, takes the view that the printer in 1634 had before him a holograph Shakespeare manuscript that had been used as a promptbook.

printed in this edition in the same way as other stage directions (which may of course be either author's or prompter's).

It may be noted that, unlike most of his predecessors, the present editor accepts Skeat's emendation "harebells" at I.i.9, and that he is the first to take the quarto speech heading "*All*" at IV.i.145 as part of the Jailer's Daughter's speech.

In this edition italic type is used for stage directions (as generally in the quarto), roman type is used for all dialogue and songs (in place of the quarto's italic for proper names in the dialogue and for the songs), and small capitals are used for speech headings (in place of the quarto's italics). Punctuation and spelling have been modernized, obvious typographical errors have been silently corrected, and the quarto's Latin headings for acts and scenes are given in English. The quarto's "nev'r," "ev'r," "ev'n" spellings are here rendered as "ne'er," "e'er," "e'en," whenever the meter seems to require a monosyllable; elsewhere the full spellings of these words are used. When a quarto reading exists in two states, corrected and uncorrected, the list below indicates the uncorrected state by a raised "a" after the reading given, the corrected state by a raised "b."

In a number of places the quarto prints lines as prose which there seems to be good reason to take as blank verse. Decisions in such cases are always difficult, but the present edition follows several of its predecessors in printing as verse where a blank verse rhythm seems to underlie, and sometimes clearly to emerge from, the fairly free dialogue pattern.

In conformity with the practice of the present edition, localities have been inserted in scene headings, but these and all other editorial additions to the quarto are given in brackets.

**Pro.19 writer** wrighter **25 water, do** water. Do **26 tack** take **29 travail** travell

**I.i.s.d. Pirithous** Theseus **9 harebells** her bels **16 angel** angle **20 chough** hoar Clough hee **59 lord. The day** Lord the day **61 groom.** Groome, **68 Nemean** Nenuan **83 'stilled** stilde [Folio "stil'd"] **90 thy** the **99 blood-sized** blood cizd **112 glassy** glasse **125 sister** sifter **138 move** mooves **155 Rinsing** Wrinching **210 soldier, as before.** Soldier (as before) **211 Aulis** Anly **217 s.d. Hippolyta . . . towards** Exeunt towards

**I.ii.65 power there's nothing; almost puts** power: there's nothing, almost puts **70 glory; one** glory on;[b] glory on[a]

**I.iii.22 brine** brine, **31 one** ore **54 eleven a** eleven; Flavina Flauia **58–64** [note in quarto margin: "2. Hearses rea-/dy with Palamon: and Arci-/te: the 3./Queenes./Theseus: and/his Lordes/ready."] **79 every innocent** fury-innocent **82 dividual** individuall

**I.iv.18 smeared** smeard[b] succard[a] **22 We 'lieve** We leave **26–27** [note in quarto margin: "3. Hearses rea-/dy."] **40 friends' behests** friends, beheastes **41 Love's provocations** Loves, provocations **45 O'er-wrestling** Or wrastling **49 'fore** for

**II.i.1 little . . . live:** little, . . . live, **19–20 that now.** So that. Now, so **50 s.d.** [in quarto, after "night" in line 49] **57** [in quarto, new scene heading: "Scæna 2. Enter Palamon, and Arcite in prison."] **60 war. Yet** warre yet, **78 wore** were **79 Ravished** Bravishd **124 could.** could, **175** [quarto makes this the

last line of Arcite's speech] **207 mere** neere **214 have.** have, **259 be,** be. **260 Arcite;** Arcite, **275 s.d.** [and throughout rest of scene] **Jailer** Keeper **319 life?** life.

**II.ii** [quarto marks as "Scæna 3."] **39 ye** yet **52 means.** meanes; **says** sees **74 him!** him

**II.iii** [quarto marks as "Scæna 4."]

**II.iv.s.d. Short . . . within.** This short . . . within [in margin] **19 I believe** Beleeve,

**II.v** [quarto marks as "Scæna 6."]

**III.i.s.d. Cornets . . . a-Maying** [in quarto, in margin] **2 laund** land; **rite** Right **10 place** pace **36 looked, the void'st** lookd the voydes **94 only, sir. Your** onely, Sir your **95 Wind horns off** Winde hornes of Cornets **97 musit** Musicke **107 not.** nor;

**III.ii.1 brake** Beake **7 reck** wreake **19 fed** feed **28 brine** bine

**III.iii.23 them** then **50 armor?** Armour.

**III.iv.9 Spoon** Vpon **10 tack** take

**III.v** [quarto marks as "Scæna 6."] **s.d. Bavian** Baum five [italic] **2. or 3.** jave **47 once! You** once, you can tell Arcas **65–67** [note in quarto margin: "Chaire and/stooles out."] **67 Till we** till **91 Wind horns** [in quarto after "I'll lead"] **93 Exeunt . . . Schoolmaster** [in quarto, after "boys," line 92] **97 Theseus** Per. **135 s.d. Knock** Knocke for Schoole [in margin] **135** [quarto omits speech heading] **137 ye** the **140 thee** three **155 Wind horns** [in quarto, after "made," line 156]

**III.vi** [quarto marks as "Scæna 7."] **28 man. When** man, when **39 spared. Your** spard, your **68 I warrant** Ile warrant **86 strait** streight **111 safety,** safely **146 thy** this **175 us;** us, **176 valiant,** valiant; **243 prune** proyne **290 again, it** againe it

**IV.i.45–46 Wooer. No, sir . . . 'Tis—** Wooer [italic] No Sir not well./Woo. [speech heading] Tis **48 have told** told **84 wreath** wreake **110 rearly** rarely **120 Far** For **141 Second Friend** 1. Fr. **145 cheerly all!** O, O, O cheerely./All. [speech heading] Owgh, owgh, owgh **149 Tack** take

**IV.ii.16 Jove** Love **37 pardon, Palamon:** pardon: Palamon, **54 s.d. Enter a Gentleman** Enter Emil. and Gent. **69 s.d. Enter a Messenger** Enter Messengers, Curtis **76 first** fitst **81 fire** faire **86–87 baldric, . . . with:** Bauldricke; . . . with, **104 tods** tops **109 court** corect

**IV.iii.8 s.d.** [in quarto, after "business," line 8] **31 i' th' other** i'th/Thother **86 carve** crave

**V.i.s.d. Flourish** [in quarto, precedes "*Exeunt.*" of IV.iii] **7 s.d. Flourish of cornets** [in quarto, at line 5] **50 whose approach** [first added by Seward in 1750: the words, or something like them, seem necessary] **54 armipotent** armenypotent **68 design march boldly.** designe; march boldly, **91 his;** his **118–21 Brief, I . . . done no companion;/To . . . not a defier;/To . . . rejoicer.** briefe I . . . done; no Companion/To . . . not; a defyer/To . . . cannct; a Rejoycer, **130** [quarto inserts speech heading "Pal."] **136 s.d. They bow** [in quarto, after line 134] **151 'pointed** pointed **152 him; out of two** him out of two, **154 election. Of mine eyes** election of mine eyes,

**V.ii.34 Videlicet, the way of flesh** [quarto has "Videlicet" in roman and "way of flesh" in italic, doubtless through a casual error] **39 humor** honour **53 tune** turne

**V.iii.s.d. Flourish** [in quarto, precedes "*Exeunt*" of V.ii] **Attendants** [quarto adds "T. Tucke: Curtis."] **13 well, penciled** well pencild **54 him** them **66 s.d. Cornets . . . "A Palamon!"** [in quarto, at line 64]; **Enter a Servant** [may be erroneous, as there were attendants on stage, and the Servant brings no news] **75 in't else:** in't; else **77 s.d.** [in quarto, at line 75] **92 s.d.** [in quarto, at line 91] **121 to th' all** I to'th all; I

**V.iv.1** [quarto omits speech heading] **5–6 pity; to live still . . . wishes;** pitty. To live still, . . . wishes, **39 Second and Third Knights** 1. 2. K **46 dearly** early **76 On end he stands** [in quarto, printed at the end of the line, perhaps indicating that it was preceded by some illegible words in the manuscript] **78 victor's** victoros **86–87 mighty! . . . unbroken,** mightie . . . unbroken: **106 Hath** Hast **132 sorry; still** sorry still,

# THE TWO NOBLE KINSMEN

[Dramatis Personae

THESEUS *Duke of Athens*
PIRITHOUS *friend to Theseus*
ARTESIUS *an Athenian*
PALAMON ⎫ *kinsmen, nephews to Creon, King of*
ARCITE ⎭ *Thebes*
VALERIUS *a Theban*
SIX KNIGHTS
JAILER
WOOER *to the Jailer's Daughter*
DOCTOR
BROTHER ⎫ *to the Jailer*
TWO FRIENDS ⎭

SCHOOLMASTER
A HERALD   MESSENGERS   COUNTRYMEN
  HYMEN   A BOY   AN EXECUTIONER
  GUARD   TABORER   BAVIAN *or Fool*
  LORDS   ATTENDANTS
HIPPOLYTA *an Amazon, bride to Theseus*
EMILIA *her sister*
THREE QUEENS
THE JAILER'S DAUGHTER
WAITING-WOMAN *to Emilia*
MAIDS   COUNTRY WENCHES   NYMPHS

*Scene:* Athens and the country nearby; Thebes]

## PROLOGUE

*Flourish.*°

New plays and maidenheads are near akin:
Much followed° both, for both much money gi'en,
If they stand sound and well. And a good play—
Whose modest scenes blush on his marriage day,
And shake to lose his honor—is like her                    5
That after holy tie and first night's stir
Yet still is modesty, and still retains
More of the maid to sight than husband's pains.°
We pray our play may be so, for I am sure
It has a noble breeder, and a pure,                        10
A learnèd, and a poet never went
More famous yet 'twixt Po and silver Trent.
Chaucer, of all admired, the story gives:
There constant to eternity it lives.
If we let fall° the nobleness of this,°                    15

And the first sound this child hear be a hiss,
How will it shake the bones of that good man,
And make him cry from under ground, "O fan
From me the witless chaff of such a writer°
That blasts my bays, and my famed works makes
    lighter                                                 20
Than Robin Hood!" This is the fear we bring;
For, to say truth, it were an endless° thing,
And too ambitious, to aspire to him.
Weak as we are, and almost breathless 'swim
In this deep water, do but you hold out                    25
Your helping hands, and we shall tack about,°
And something do to save us. You shall hear
Scenes, though below his art, may yet appear
Worth two hours' travail.° To his bones sweet sleep;
Content to you. If this play do not keep                   30
A little dull time from us, we perceive
Our losses fall so thick we must needs leave.°
*Flourish.*

---

*The decorative border shown above appeared on the first page of the quarto edition of* The Noble Kinsmen, *1634*.
**Pro.s.d. Flourish** trumpet fanfare  **2 followed** pursued, cultivated  **8 pains** endeavors  **15 let fall** fail to maintain; **this** Chaucer's poem

**19 such a writer** the singular is notable, but by no means decisive on the question of authorship  **22 endless** purposeless, vain  **26 tack about** change direction  **29 travail** labor (with a suggestion of *travel*, as the play's action moves from place to place)  **32 leave** give up acting

1626

# ACT I

## [Scene I. *Athens. Before a temple.*]

*Enter* HYMEN° *with a torch burning; a* BOY *in a white robe before, singing and strewing flowers; after* HYMEN, *a* NYMPH, *encompassed in her tresses,° bearing a wheaten garland;° then* THESEUS *between two other* NYMPHS *with wheaten chaplets° on their heads; then* HIPPOLYTA *the bride, led by* PIRITHOUS, *and another holding a garland over her head, her tresses likewise hanging; after her,* EMILIA *holding up her train;* [ARTESIUS *and* ATTENDANTS]. *Music.*

#### The Song.

Roses, their sharp spines being gone,
Not royal in their smells alone,
But in their hue;
Maiden pinks, of odor faint,
Daisies smell-less, yet most quaint,°          5
And sweet thyme true;

Primrose, first-born child of Ver,°
Merry spring-time's harbinger,
With harebells dim;
Oxlips, in their cradles growing,          10
Marigolds, on death-beds blowing,°
Lark's-heels trim;°

All dear Nature's children sweet
Lie 'fore bride and bridegroom's feet,

*Strew flowers.*

Blessing their sense;          15
Not an angel° of the air,
Bird melodious, or bird fair,
Is° absent hence;

The crow, the sland'rous cuckoo, nor
The boding raven, nor chough hoar,          20
Nor chatt'ring pie,
May on our bridehouse° perch or sing,
Or with them any discord bring,
But from it fly.

*Enter three* QUEENS *in black, with veils stained, with imperial crowns. The* FIRST QUEEN *falls down at the foot of* THESEUS; *the* SECOND *falls down at the foot of* HIPPOLYTA; *the* THIRD *before* EMILIA.

FIRST QUEEN
For pity's sake and true gentility's,°          25
Hear and respect° me.
SECOND QUEEN          For your mother's sake,
And as you wish your womb may thrive with fair ones,
Hear and respect me.

THIRD QUEEN
Now for the love of him whom Jove hath marked
The honor of your bed,° and for the sake          30
Of clear° virginity, be advocate
For us, and our distresses. This good deed
Shall raze you° out o' th' Book of Trespasses°
All you are set down there.
THESEUS
Sad lady, rise.
HIPPOLYTA    Stand up.
EMILIA                    No knees to me.          35
What woman I may stead° that is distressed
Does bind me to her.
THESEUS
What's your request? Deliver you for all.
FIRST QUEEN
We are three queens, whose sovereigns fell before
The wrath of cruel Creon;° who endured°          40
The beaks of ravens, talons of the kites,
And pecks of crows, in the foul fields of Thebes.
He will not suffer us to burn their bones,
To urn their ashes, nor to take th' offense
Of mortal loathsomeness from the blest eye          45
Of holy Phoebus,° but infects the winds
With stench of our slain lords. O pity, duke,
Thou purger of the earth, draw thy feared sword
That does good turns to th' world; give us the bones
Of our dead kings, that we may chapel° them;          50
And of thy boundless goodness take some note
That for our crownèd heads we have no roof,
Save this which is the lion's and the bear's,
And vault° to everything.
THESEUS                    Pray you kneel not.
I was transported with your speech, and suffered          55
Your knees to wrong themselves. I have heard the fortunes
Of your dead lords, which gives me such lamenting
As wakes my vengeance and revenge for 'em.
King Capaneus° was your lord. The day
That he should° marry you, at such a season          60
As now it is with me, I met your groom.
By Mars' altar, you were that time fair:
Not Juno's mantle° fairer than your tresses,
Nor in more bounty spread her; your wheaten wreath
Was then nor threshed° nor blasted;° Fortune at you          65
Dimpled her cheek with smiles. Hercules our kinsman,°
Then weaker than your eyes, laid by his club:

---

**I.i.s.d. Hymen** god of marriage; **encompassed in her tresses** with hair loose, in token of virginity; **wheaten garland** a symbol of fertility and peace; **chaplets** wreaths  **5 quaint** pretty  **7 Ver** spring  **11 on death-beds blowing** blooming on graves  **12 trim** neat  **16 angel** here a synonym for "bird"  **18 Is** often emended to "Be," but the indicative seems acceptable  **22 bridehouse** house where a wedding is celebrated  **25 gentility** nobleness  **26 respect** give attention to

**29–30 whom . . . bed** for whom Jove has destined the honor of wedding you  **31 clear** pure  **33 raze you** delete for you; **Book of Trespasses** recording angel's register of sins  **36 stead** help  **40 Creon** King of Thebes after Oedipus; **endured** have endured  **45–46 blest . . . Phoebus** the sun  **50 chapel** bury in a chapel  **54 vault** arched roof (here the sky)  **59 Capaneus** here four syllables, though classically three  **60 should** was to  **63 Juno's mantle** Juno was goddess of marriage and her mantle is described in *Iliad*, XIV; but the peacock was sacred to Juno, and "mantle" also suggests the bird's spread tail  **65 threshed** beaten so as to separate grain from husks (here an image for fertilizing: cf. I.i.s.d.); **blasted** i.e., by widowhood  **66 kinsman** according to Plutarch's "Life of Theseus," both he and Hercules were descended on their mothers' side from Pelops; moreover, Theseus as alleged son of Poseidon could claim kinship with Hercules, son of Zeus

He tumbled down upon his Nemean hide°
And swore his sinews thawed. O grief and time,
Fearful consumers, you will all devour.                              70

FIRST QUEEN
O I hope some god,
Some god hath put his mercy in your manhood,
Whereto he'll infuse pow'r, and press you forth
Our undertaker.°

THESEUS                              O no knees, none, widow,
Unto the helmeted Bellona° use them,                                 75
And pray for me your soldier.
Troubled I am. *Turns away.* [*The* QUEENS *rise.*]

SECOND QUEEN   Honored Hippolyta,
Most dreaded Amazonian, that hast slain
The scythe-tusked boar, that with thy arm as strong
As it is white, wast near to make the male                          80
To thy sex captive, but that this thy lord,
Born to uphold creation in that honor
First Nature 'stilled it in,° shrunk thee into
The bound° thou wast o'erflowing, at once subduing
Thy force and thy affection; soldieress,                            85
That equally canst poise° sternness with pity,
Whom° now I know hast much more power on him
Than ever he had on thee, who ow'st° his strength
And his love too, who is a servant for
The tenor of thy speech;° dear glass of° ladies,                    90
Bid him that we whom flaming war doth scorch
Under the shadow of his sword may cool us;
Require him he advance it o'er our heads;
Speak't in a woman's key, like such a woman
As any of us three; weep ere you fail;                              95
Lend us a knee;
But° touch the ground for us no longer time
Than a dove's motion when the head's plucked off;
Tell him if he i' th' blood-sized° field lay swoll'n,
Showing the sun his teeth, grinning at the moon,                    100
What you would do.

HIPPOLYTA                              Poor lady, say no more.
I had as lief trace° this good action with you
As that whereto I am going, and never yet
Went I so willing way.° My lord is taken
Heart-deep with your distress. Let him consider.                    105
I'll speak anon.

THIRD QUEEN (*Kneel*[s] *to* EMILIA.) O my petition was
Set down in ice, which by hot grief uncandied°
Melts into drops, so sorrow wanting form
Is pressed with deeper matter.°

EMILIA                              Pray stand up,
Your grief is written in your cheek.

THIRD QUEEN                              O woe,                      110

You cannot read it there; there through my tears,°
Like wrinkled pebbles in a glassy stream
You may behold 'em.° Lady, lady, alack!
He that will all the treasure know o' th' earth
Must know the center° too; he that will fish                        115
For my least minnow, let him lead his line°
To catch one at my heart. O pardon me,
Extremity that sharpens sundry wits
Makes me a fool. [*She rises.*]

EMILIA                              Pray you say nothing, pray you.
Who cannot feel nor see the rain, being in't,                       120
Knows neither wet nor dry. If that you were
The ground-piece° of some painter, I would buy you
T' instruct me 'gainst a capital grief indeed
Such heart-pierced° demonstration.° But alas,
Being a natural sister of our sex,°                                 125
Your sorrow beats so ardently upon me
That it shall make a counter-reflect° 'gainst
My brother's heart, and warm it to some pity
Though it were made of stone. Pray have good com-
    fort.

THESEUS
Forward to th' temple, leave not out a jot                          130
O' th' sacred ceremony.

FIRST QUEEN                              O this celebration
Will long last, and be more costly than
Your suppliants' war. Remember that your fame
Knolls in the ear o' th' world; what you do quickly
Is not done rashly; your first thought is more                      135
Than others' labored meditance,° your premeditating
More than their actions. But O Jove, your actions,
Soon as they move, as ospreys do the fish,°
Subdue before they touch. Think, dear duke, think
What beds our slain kings have.

SECOND QUEEN                              What griefs our beds       140
That our dear lords have none.

THIRD QUEEN                              None fit for th' dead.
Those that with cords, knives, drams' precipitance,°
Weary of this world's light, have to themselves
Been death's most horrid agents, human grace°
Affords them dust and shadow.°

FIRST QUEEN                              But our lords                145
Lie blist'ring 'fore the visitating° sun,
And were good kings when living.

THESEUS                              It is true,
And I will give you comfort, to give° your dead lords
    graves.
The which to do, must make some work with Creon.

FIRST QUEEN
And that work presents itself to th' doing.°                        150

68 **Nemean hide** Hercules customarily wore the hide of the lion of Nemea, which he had slain   73–74 **press . . . undertaker** impel you to champion our cause   75 **Bellona** goddess of war   83 **'stilled it in** instilled in it   84 **bound** limit, as bank of a river   86 **equally canst poise** canst justly balance   87 **Whom** usual in seventeenth century before a parenthetic clause   88 **ow'st** possessest   89–90 **who . . . speech** who is obedient to everything you say   90 **glass of** mirror for (as in "mirror for magistrates," etc.)   97 **But** only   99 **blood-sized** spread with blood   102 **trace** pursue   104 **so willing way** any way so willingly   106–09 **O . . . matter** i.e., the formality of her previous speech (lines 29–34) now melts into tears, but grief in its formlessness can receive the imprint of a "deeper matter" (in this instance the desire for funeral rites and vengeance)   107 **uncandied** dissolved

111 **there . . . tears** i.e., in her eyes   113 **'em** i.e., her eyes, where her grief is imaged   115 **center** i.e., of the earth   116 **lead his line** weight it with lead   122 **ground-piece** flat representation (?)   124 **heart-pierced** heart-piercing; **demonstration** i.e., your demonstration of grief would instruct me how to bear any great grief   125 **Being . . . sex** since you are a woman like me (but "sifter" may be the right reading: see A Note on the Text)   127 **counter-reflect** reflection   136 **meditance** meditation, planning   138 **ospreys . . . fish** the osprey was believed to fascinate the fish before catching it   142 **drams' precipitance** suicide by taking poison   144 **grave** mercy   145 **shadow** shelter   146 **visitating** inflicting harm (?)   148 **to give** by giving   150 **presents . . . doing** offers itself to be done at once

Now 'twill take form,° the heats are gone tomorrow.
Then bootless toil must recompense itself
With its own sweat. Now he's secure,°
Not dreams we stand before your puissance,
Rinsing our holy begging in our eyes     155
To make petition clear.

SECOND QUEEN     Now you may take him,
Drunk with his victory.

THIRD QUEEN     And his army full
Of bread° and sloth.

THESEUS     Artesius, that best knowest
How to draw out° fit to this enterprise
The prim'st for this proceeding, and the number     160
To carry° such a business, forth and levy
Our worthiest instruments, whilst we dispatch
This grand act of our life, this daring deed
Of fate° in wedlock.

FIRST QUEEN     Dowagers, take hands,
Let us be widows to our woes,° delay     165
Commends us to a famishing hope.

ALL [QUEENS]     Farewell.

SECOND QUEEN
We come unseasonably, but when could grief
Cull forth,° as unpanged° judgment can, fitt'st time
For best solicitation?

THESEUS     Why, good ladies,
This is a service whereto I am going     170
Greater than any was; it more imports me
Than all the actions that I have foregone°
Or futurely° can cope.

FIRST QUEEN     The more proclaiming
Our suit shall be neglected. When her arms,
Able to lock Jove from a synod,° shall     175
By warranting° moonlight corslet thee, O when
Her twining cherries shall their sweetness fall°
Upon thy tasteful° lips, what wilt thou think
Of rotten kings or blubbered queens, what care
For what thou feel'st not, what thou feel'st being able     180
To make Mars spurn his drum? O if thou couch
But one night with her, every hour in't will
Take hostage of thee for a hundred,° and
Thou shalt remember nothing more than what
That banquet bids thee to.

HIPPOLYTA     [Kneels.] Though much unlike     185
You should be so transported, as much sorry
I should be such a suitor;° yet I think,
Did I not by th' abstaining of my joy,
Which breeds a deeper longing, cure their surfeit
That craves a present med'cine, I should pluck     190
All ladies' scandal° on me. Therefore, sir,
As I shall here make trial of my pray'rs,
Either presuming them to have some force

Or sentencing for aye their vigor dumb,°
Prorogue° this business we are going about, and hang     195
Your shield afore your heart, about that neck
Which is my fee,° and which I freely lend
To do these poor queens service.

ALL QUEENS     [To EMILIA.] O help now,
Our cause cries for your knee.

EMILIA     [Kneels.] If you grant not
My sister her petition in that force,°     200
With that celerity and nature which
She makes it in,° from henceforth I'll not dare
To ask you anything, nor be so hardy°
Ever to take a husband.

THESEUS     Pray stand up.

[HIPPOLYTA and EMILIA rise.]

I am entreating of myself to do     205
That which you kneel to have me. Pirithous,
Lead on the bride; get you and pray the gods
For success, and return; omit not anything
In the pretended° celebration. Queens,
Follow your soldier, as before.° [To ARTESIUS.] Hence
you,     210
And at the banks of Aulis° meet us with
The forces you can raise, where we shall find
The moiety of a number for a business
More bigger-looked.°     [Exit ARTESIUS.]
    Since that our theme is haste,
I stamp this kiss upon thy current° lip.     215
Sweet, keep it as my token. [Kisses HIPPOLYTA.] Set
you forward,
For I will see you gone.

[HIPPOLYTA, EMILIA, PIRITHOUS, and ATTEND
ANTS begin to move] towards the temple.

Farewell, my beauteous sister. Pirithous,
Keep the feast full,° bate not an hour on't.

PIRITHOUS     Sir,
I'll follow you at heels. The feast's solemnity     220
Shall want° til your return.

THESEUS     Cousin, I charge you
Budge not from Athens. We shall be returning
Ere you can end this feast, of which I pray you
Make no abatement. Once more, farewell all.

[The procession enters the temple.]

FIRST QUEEN
Thus dost thou still make good the tongue o' th'
world.°     225

SECOND QUEEN
And earn'st a deity equal with Mars.

---

151 **form** shape   153 **secure** confident   158 **bread** food, feasting   159 **draw out** select   161 **carry** carry out   163–64 **daring . . . fate** deed challenging fate   165 **be . . . woes** live without woes like widows (as we are)   168 **Cull forth** choose   **unpanged** untormented   172 **foregone** previously experienced   173 **futurely** in the future   175 **synod** council   176 **warranting** authorizing   177 **fall** let fall   178 **tasteful** tasting   183 **Take . . . hundred** i.e., you will feel committed to spend a hundred more with her   185–87 **Though . . . suitor** my reluctance to ask this is as great as my doubt that you would be so moved by our love-making   191 **scandal** disgrace

194 **sentencing . . . dumb** declaring that they shall never be uttered again   195 **Prorogue** postpone   197 **fee** property   200 **in that force** with that vigor   201–02 **nature . . . it in** condition of mind in which she makes it   203 **hardy** bold   209 **pretended** intended   210 **as before** as I have already declared myself   211 **banks of Aulis** see A Note on the Text: Aulis was a seaport, but "banks" could refer to the shore; however, this was an odd way to proceed from Athens to Thebes   212–14 **where . . . bigger-looked** where I shall gather the other half of a force that would serve for a larger undertaking than this   215 **current** fleeting (transferred from Theseus, who is in haste), with a suggestion also of putting his royal stamp on her lip as on a coin   219 **full** fully   221 **want** be incomplete   225 **make . . . world** justify what the world says of you

THIRD QUEEN
If not above him, for
Thou being but mortal makest affections bend
To godlike honors.° They themselves,° some say,
Groan under such a mast'ry.°

THESEUS                          As we are men,                    230
Thus should we do. Being sensually subdued,
We lose our human title.° Good cheer, ladies.
Now turn we towards your comforts.

*Flourish. Exeunt.*

Scene II. [*Thebes.*]

*Enter* PALAMON *and* ARCITE.

ARCITE
Dear Palamon, dearer in love than blood°
And our prime° cousin, yet° unhardened in
The crimes of nature, let us leave the city
Thebes, and the temptings in't, before we further
Sully our gloss of youth;                                              5
And here to keep in abstinence we shame
As in incontinence:° for not to swim
I' th' aid o'° th' current were almost to sink,
At least to frustrate striving;° and to follow
The common stream, 'twould bring us to an eddy      10
Where we should turn° or drown; if labor through,
Our gain but life and weakness.

PALAMON                          Your advice
Is cried up° with example: what strange ruins
Since first we went to school may we perceive
Walking in Thebes? Scars and bare weeds               15
The gain o' th' Martialist,° who did propound
To his bold ends honor and golden ingots,
Which though he won he had not, and now flirted°
By peace for whom he fought: who then shall offer
To Mars's so scorned altar? I do bleed                    20
When such I meet, and wish great Juno would
Resume her ancient fit of jealousy°
To get the soldier work, that peace might purge
For her repletion,° and retain° anew
Her charitable heart, now hard and harsher            25
Than strife or war could be.

ARCITE                          Are you not out?°
Meet you no ruin but the soldier in
The cranks and turns° of Thebes? You did begin
As if you met decays of many kinds.

Perceive you none that do arouse your pity          30
But th' unconsidered° soldier?

PALAMON                          Yes, I pity
Decays where'er I find them, but such most
That sweating in an honorable toil
Are paid with ice° to cool 'em.

ARCITE                          'Tis not this
I did begin to speak of: this is virtue                    35
Of no respect in Thebes. I spake of Thebes,
How dangerous if we will keep our honors
It is for our residing, where every evil
Hath a good color,° where every seeming good's
A certain evil, where not to be ev'n jump°             40
As they° are, here were to be° strangers, and
Such things to be,° mere° monsters.

PALAMON                          'Tis in our power
(Unless we fear that apes can tutor's) to
Be masters of our manners. What need I
Affect° another's gait, which is not catching         45
Where there is faith, or to be fond upon
Another's way of speech, when by mine own
I may be reasonably conceived°—saved too,
Speaking it truly?° Why am I bound
By any generous bond° to follow him                    50
Follows his tailor,° haply so long until
The followed make pursuit?° Or let me know
Why mine own barber is unblest, with him
My poor chin too, for° 'tis not scissored just
To such a favorite's glass.° What canon° is there    55
That does command my rapier from my hip
To dangle't in my hand, or to go tiptoe
Before the street be foul?° Either I am
The fore-horse in the team, or I am none
That draw i' th' sequent trace.° These poor slight sores   60
Need not a plantain.° That which rips my bosom
Almost to th' heart's—

ARCITE                          Our uncle Creon.

PALAMON                          He,
A most unbounded tyrant, whose successes
Makes heaven unfeared, and villainy assured
Beyond its power there's nothing; almost puts       65
Faith in a fever, and deifies alone
Voluble° chance; who° only attributes
The faculties of other instruments
To his own nerves and act;° commands men service,

---

228–29 **makest . . . honors** turn your natural inclinations toward the winning of divine honors  **229 They themselves** the gods  **230 such a mast'ry** i.e., as yours  **231–32 Being . . . title** By yielding to our senses we lose our claim to be considered men
**I.ii.1 blood** kinship  **2 prime** closest; **yet** as yet  **6–7 here . . . incontinence** here it is as shameful to abstain from vice as (elsewhere) to indulge in it  **8 I' . . . o'** with  **9 frustrate striving** make our efforts useless  **11 turn** i.e., turn and begin to swim with the current  **13 cried up** supported  **16 Martialist** follower of Mars (i.e., soldier)  **18 flirted** mocked  **21–22 Juno . . . jealousy** Juno's jealousy was a contributing factor to the Trojan War  **23–24 peace . . . repletion** a common image: war was seen as a recurrent necessity so that society might "purge" itself of the results of too self-indulgent living: "for" here means "as a remedy for"  **24 retain** take into service  **26 Are . . . out** Are you not mistaking the matter?  **28 cranks and turns** winding streets and passages

**31 unconsidered** neglected  **34 Are . . . ice** i.e., are treated coolly (ironically appropriate, because they have been sweating)  **39 color** appearance  **40 jump** exactly  **41 they** the Thebans; **were to be** would be  **42 Such . . . be** to be such things as they (the Thebans) are; **mere** absolute  **45 Affect** imitate  **48 conceived** understood  **49 Speaking it truly** i.e., if I speak the truth  **50 generous bond** nobleman's obligation  **50–51 follow . . . tailor** imitate a man who takes instruction about conduct from his tailor  **51–52 until . . . pursuit** until the tailor, not having been paid, pursues his client to dun him  **54 for** because  **54–55 just . . . glass** exactly in the fashion affected by such-and-such a favored person  **55 canon** law (particularly divine or ecclesiastical law)  **57–58 go . . . foul** suggestive either of a mincing gait or of a way of walking so as to avoid noise, for purposes of surprise attack  **58–60 Either . . . trace** Either I shall lead or I shall refuse to be one that merely follows (the image being from a team of horses)  **61 plantain** the leaves of the plantain herb were much used for treating wounds, stanching blood, etc.  **67 Voluble** inconstant; **who** the "tyrant" of line 63  **67–69 who . . . act** who takes what his subjects do as his own achievement

And what they win in't, boot° and glory; one                    70
That fears not to do harm; good, dares not.° Let
The blood of mine that's sib° to him be sucked
From me with leeches, let them break and fall
Off me with that corruption.

ARCITE                          Clear-spirited° cousin,
Let's leave his court, that we may nothing share     75
Of his loud infamy; for our milk
Will relish of the pasture,° and we must
Be vile or disobedient, not his kinsmen
In blood unless in quality.°

PALAMON                          Nothing truer.
I think the echoes of his shames have deafed          80
The ears of heav'nly justice: widows' cries
Descend again into their throats, and have not
Due audience of° the gods.

*Enter* VALERIUS.

                                Valerius!

VALERIUS
The king calls for you; yet be leaden-footed°
Till his great rage be off him. Phoebus, when        85
He broke his whipstock° and exclaimed against
The horses of the sun, but whispered to°
The loudness of his fury.

PALAMON                          Small winds shake him,
But what's the matter?°

VALERIUS
Theseus, who where he threats appalls, hath sent     90
Deadly defiance to him and pronounces
Ruin to Thebes, who is at hand to seal
The promise of his wrath.°

ARCITE                          Let him approach.
But that we fear the gods in him,° he brings not
A jot of terror to us. Yet what° man                  95
Thirds° his own worth (the case is each of ours)
When that his action's dregged,° with mind assured
'Tis bad he goes about.

PALAMON                          Leave that unreasoned.°
Our services stand now for Thebes, not Creon.
Yet to be neutral to him were dishonor,              100
Rebellious to oppose: therefore we must
With him stand to the mercy of our Fate,
Who hath bounded our last minute.°

ARCITE                          So we must.
Is't said this war's afoot, or it shall be
On fail of some condition?°

VALERIUS                          'Tis in motion:     105

The intelligence of state came in the instant
With the defier.°

PALAMON                Let's to the king, who were he
A quarter carrier of that honor which
His enemy come in, the blood we venture
Should be as for our health, which were not spent,   110
Rather laid out for purchase.° But alas,
Our hands advanced before our hearts,° what will
The fall o' th' stroke do damage?

ARCITE                          Let th' event,°
That never erring arbitrator, tell us
When we know all ourselves, and let us follow        115
The becking of our chance.           *Exeunt.*

## Scene III. [*Athens.*]

*Enter* PIRITHOUS, HIPPOLYTA, EMILIA.

PIRITHOUS
No further.

HIPPOLYTA   Sir, farewell. Repeat my wishes
To our great lord, of whose success I dare not
Make any timorous question, yet I wish him
Excess and overflow of power, and't might be
To dure° ill-dealing Fortune. Speed° to him:          5
Store never hurts good governors.°

PIRITHOUS                          Though I know
His ocean needs not my poor drops, yet they
Must yield their tribute there. [*To* EMILIA.] My pre-
cious maid,
Those best affections° that the heavens infuse
In their best-tempered pieces,° keep enthroned        10
In your dear heart.

EMILIA                Thanks, sir. Remember me
To our all-royal brother, for whose speed°
The great Bellona I'll solicit; and
Since in our terrene° state petitions are not
Without gifts understood, I'll offer to her           15
What I shall be advised° she likes: our hearts
Are in his army, in his tent.

HIPPOLYTA                In's bosom.
We have been soldiers, and we cannot weep
When our friends don their helms, or put to sea,
Or tell of babes broached on the lance, or women     20
That have sod° their infants in—and after eat them—
The brine they wept at killing 'em.° Then if
You stay to see of us such spinsters,° we
Should hold you here forever.

PIRITHOUS                Peace be to you
As I pursue this war, which shall be then            25
Beyond further requiring.°           *Exit* PIRITHOUS.

---

70 boot profit, booty  71 good, dares not dares not do
good  72 sib related  74 Clear-spirited noble-spirited
76–77 our . . . pasture what we produce will be affected by
our environment  78–79 not . . . quality we must not hold
the position of members of his family unless we are like him in
character  83 Due audience of fitting attention from  84
be leaden-footed do not hasten  86 whipstock here, whip
87 to in comparison with  89 the matter the cause of disturbance  92–93 seal . . . wrath confirm what his angry words
have spoken  94 fear . . . him fear him as an emissary of the
gods  95 what here equivalent to "every"  96 Thirds reduces
to a third of its former strength  97 dregged accompanied by
dross matter  98 unreasoned unspoken, not argued about
103 Who . . . minute who has already settled the time when
our lives end  105 On . . . condition if stated terms of peace
are not agreed to

106–07 The intelligence . . . defier The news that the war
had started came at the same time as the declaration  111
laid . . . purchase invested for profit  112 Our . . . hearts
our hands being engaged rather than our desires  113 event
result
I.iii.4–5 and't . . . dure in case it were necessary to undergo
5 Speed hasten  6 Store . . . governors Plenty is never
a handicap to good leaders  9 affections inclinations
10 best-tempered pieces most harmoniously wrought
creatures  12 speed success  14 terrene earthly  16 shall be
advised am told  21 sod boiled  22 brine . . . 'em tears
they shed as they killed them  23 spinsters i.e., weak women
25–26 which . . . requiring i.e., peace will be ensured

EMILIA                          How his longing
Follows his friend! Since his depart,° his sports,
Though craving seriousness and skill, passed slightly
His careless execution,° where nor gain
Made him regard, or loss consider, but                    30
Playing one business in his hand, another
Directing in his head—his mind nurse equal
To these so diff'ring twins.° Have you observed him,
Since our great lord departed?

HIPPOLYTA                       With much labor;°
And I did love him for't. They two have cabined°         35
In many as dangerous as poor a corner,
Peril and want contending.° They have skiffed
Torrents whose roaring tyranny and power
I' th' least of these° was dreadful; and they have
Fought out together where Death's self was lodged,       40
Yet Fate hath brought them off.° Their knot of love,
Tied, weaved, entangled, with so true, so long,
And with a finger of so deep a cunning,
May be outworn, never undone.° I think
Theseus cannot be umpire to himself,                      45
Cleaving his conscience° into twain and doing
Each side like° justice, which he loves best.°

EMILIA                                    Doubtless
There is a best, and Reason has no manners
To say it is not you.° I was acquainted
Once with a time when I enjoyed a playfellow.            50
You were at wars, when she the grave enriched
Who made too proud the bed, took leave o' th' moon
(Which then looked pale at parting) when our count°
Was each eleven.

HIPPOLYTA        'Twas Flavina.

EMILIA                          Yes.
You talk of Pirithous' and Theseus' love.               55
Theirs has more ground,° is more maturely seasoned,
More buckled° with strong judgment, and their needs
The one of th' other may be said to water
Their intertangled roots of love. But I
And she I sigh and spoke of were things innocent,       60
Loved for we did,° and like the elements
That know not what, nor why, yet do effect
Rare issues by their operance,° our souls
Did so to one another: what she liked
Was then of me approved, what not condemned—             65
No more arraignment;° the flow'r that I would pluck

And put between my breasts, O then but beginning
To swell about the blossom, she would long
Till she had such another, and commit it
To the like innocent cradle, where phoenixlike           70
They died in perfume;° on my head no toy
But was her pattern;° her affections°—pretty
Though happily her careless were°—I followed
For my most serious decking;° had mine ear
Stol'n some new air, or at adventure hummed on           75
From musical coinage,° why, it was a note
Whereon her spirits would sojourn, rather dwell on,
And sing it in her slumbers. This rehearsal,°
Which—every innocent° wots well—comes in
Like old importment's bastard,° has this end            80
That the true love 'tween maid and maid may be
More than in sex dividual.°

HIPPOLYTA                     Y' are out of breath,
And this high-speeded pace is but to say
That you shall never, like the maid Flavina,
Love any that's called man.

EMILIA                       I am sure I shall not.       85

HIPPOLYTA
Now alack, weak sister,
I must no more believe thee in this point,
Though in't I know thou dost believe thyself,
That I will trust a sickly appetite
That loathes even as it longs. But sure, my sister,      90
If I were ripe for your persuasion, you
Have said enough to shake me from the arm
Of the all-noble Theseus, for whose fortunes
I will now in and kneel, with great assurance
That we, more than his Pirithous, possess               95
The high throne in his heart.

EMILIA                         I am not against
Your faith, yet I continue mine.              Exeunt.

Scene IV. [Thebes.]

Cornets. A battle struck° within. Then a retreat. Flourish.
Then enter THESEUS (victor) [with a HERALD, LORDS,
and ATTENDANTS and with PALAMON and ARCITE
carried on hearses].° The three QUEENS meet him, and
fall on their faces before him.

FIRST QUEEN
To thee no star be dark!°

SECOND QUEEN           Both heaven and earth
Friend° thee forever!

THIRD QUEEN           All the good that may
Be wished upon thy head, I cry "amen" to't!

THESEUS
Th' impartial gods, who from the mounted° heavens

27 **depart** departure   28–29 **passed . . . execution** were
given only slight and careless attention   32–33 **his mind . . .
twins** i.e., his mind was equally concerned with what he was
doing and with what he was imagining (fighting with Theseus)
34 **labor** attention   35 **cabined** lodged together   37 **contending** i.e., being comparable in degree   39 **I' . . . these** referring
either to "Peril and want," line 37, or to "tyranny and power,"
line 38   41 **brought them off** brought them to safety   44
**May . . . undone** may be worn out by death, not unknotted
before   45–47 **Theseus . . . best** even Theseus cannot judge
whether he loves best himself or Pirithous   46 **conscience**
consciousness   47 **like** equal   49 **To . . . you** Emilia, taking
Hippolyta's remark in a different way from that intended, suggests that Theseus must love Hippolyta best of all; lines 95–96
make it less likely that "you" is indefinite, meaning that
Theseus must in reason love himself better than his friend   53
**our count** the number of our years   56 **ground** foundation
57 **buckled** supported   61 **for we did** merely because we
did   62–63 **effect . . . operance** produce strange happenings through their operation   65–66 **what . . . arraignment**
what she did not like was condemned by me, without further
consideration of the case

70–71 **phoenixlike . . . perfume** referring to the legendary
phoenix, from whose fragrant funeral pyre the next phoenix
was born   71 **toy** trifling ornament   72 **pattern** i.e., for
imitation; **affections** inclinations, preferences   73 **Though
. . . were** though her preferences might be carelessly made
74 **decking** adornment   75–76 **hummed . . . coinage** i.e.,
improvised   78 **rehearsal** recital   79 **innocent** child   80
**Like . . . bastard** like a feeble imitation of the experience
itself   81–82 **That . . . dividual** that their love may be greater
than the love of those different in sex
**I.iv.s.d. struck** sounded; **hearses** carriages   1 **To . . . dark**
Let all stars be favorable to you   2 **Friend** befriend   4
**mounted** high (with a suggestion of the gods on horseback
looking down on men as beasts under their control)

View us their mortal herd, behold who err    5
And in their time chastise. Go and find out
The bones of your dead lords, and honor them
With treble ceremony; rather than a gap
Should be in their dear° rites, we would supply't.
But those we will depute which shall invest    10
You in your dignities, and even° each thing
Our haste does leave imperfect. So adieu,
And heaven's good eyes look on you. *Exeunt* QUEENS
     What are those?

HERALD
Men of great quality, as may be judged
By their appointment.° Some of Thebes have told's    15
They are sisters' children, nephews to the king.

THESEUS
By th' helm of Mars, I saw them in the war,
Like to a pair of lions smeared with prey,
Make lanes in troops aghast. I fixed my note°
Constantly on them, for they were a mark    20
Worth a god's view. What prisoner was't that told
     me°
When I enquired their names?

HERALD            We 'lieve° they're called
     Arcite and Palamon.

THESEUS            'Tis right: those, those;
     They are not dead?

HERALD
Nor in a state of life: had they been taken    25
When their last hurts were given, 'twas possible
They might have been recovered. Yet they breathe
And have the name of men.°

THESEUS            Then like men use 'em.
The very lees of such—millions of rates°—
Exceed the wine of others. All our surgeons    30
Convent° in their behoof, our richest balms,
Rather than niggard, waste. Their lives concern us
Much more than Thebes is worth. Rather than have
     'em
Freed of this plight and in their morning state,°
Sound and at liberty, I would 'em dead,°    35
But forty-thousandfold we had rather have 'em
Prisoners to us than Death.° Bear 'em speedily
From our kind air, to them unkind,° and minister
What man to man may do—for our sake more,
Since I have known frights, fury, friends' behests,    40
Love's provocations, zeal, a mistress' task,
Desire of liberty, a fever, madness,
Hath set a mark which Nature could not reach to
Without some imposition—sickness in will
O'er-wrestling strength in reason.° For our love    45
And great Apollo's° mercy, all our best

Their best skill tender.° Lead into the city,
Where, having bound things scattered, we will post
To Athens 'fore our army.      *Flourish. Exeunt.*

## Scene V. [*Thebes.*]

*Music. Enter the* QUEENS *with the hearses of their knights,
in a funeral solemnity, &c.*

          [*Song.*]
Urns and odors bring away,°
Vapors, sighs, darken the day;
Our dole more deadly looks than dying:
Balms and gums° and heavy cheers,°
Sacred vials filled with tears,    5
And clamors through the wild air flying.

Come, all sad and solemn shows
That are quick-eyed Pleasure's foes:
We convent° nought else but woes,
We convent, &c.    10

THIRD QUEEN [*To* SECOND QUEEN.]
This funeral path brings° to your household's grave.
Joy seize on you again. Peace sleep with him.

SECOND QUEEN [*To* FIRST QUEEN.]
And this to yours.°

FIRST QUEEN [*To* THIRD QUEEN.] Yours this way.
     Heavens lend°
A thousand differing ways to one sure end.

THIRD QUEEN
This world's a city full of straying° streets,    15
And death's the market place where each one meets.
          *Exeunt severally.°*

# A C T  I I

## Scene I. [*Athens. A garden with a room in a prison above.*]

*Enter* JAILER *and* WOOER.

JAILER   I may depart with° little while I live: something I may cast to you, not much. Alas, the prison I keep, though it be for great ones, yet they seldom come. Before one salmon you shall take a number of minnows. I am given out to be better lined than it can   5 appear to me report is a true speaker.° I would I were really that I am delivered° to be. Marry,° what I have, be it what it will, I will assure° upon my daughter at the day of my death.

WOOER   Sir, I demand no more than your own offer,   10 and I will estate° your daughter in what I have promised.

JAILER   Well, we will talk more of this when the solemnity° is passed. But have you a full promise of her?   15

**9 dear** valued   **11 even** make right   **15 appointment** accouterment   **19 fixed my note** directed my attention   **21 What . . . me** i.e., what was it that a prisoner told me   **22 'lieve** believe   **28 have . . . men** can still be called men   **29 millions of rates** millions of times   **31 Convent** summon   **34 in . . . state** as they were this morning   **35 would 'em dead** would rather they were dead   **37 Death** i.e., prisoners to Death   **38 kind . . . unkind** i.e., the open air is healthy to us but not to them   **40–45 Since . . . reason** i.e., since I have known cases where unusual physical or emotional disturbance has produced results that Nature could not produce without some special stimulus ("imposition"), this disturbance being able to overcome what could be reasonably expected   **46 Apollo** as god of healing

**47 tender** minister
**I.v.1 bring away** accompany us   **4 gums** used for perfume at the funeral rites; **heavy cheers** sad faces   **9 convent** summon, bring together   **11 brings** leads   **13 this to yours** the Queens now take their different paths home; **lend** provide   **15 straying** winding   **16 s.d. severally** separately
**II.i.1 depart with** give   **5–6 I . . . speaker** I am generally believed to be better off than there seems to me cause for rumor to assert   **7 delivered** said; **Marry** indeed   **8 assure** i.e., bestow   **11 estate** endow   **14 solemnity** i.e., wedding

*Enter* DAUGHTER.

When that shall be seen, I tender my consent.

WOOER   I have, sir. Here she comes.

JAILER   Your friend and I have chanced to name you
here, upon the old business; but no more of that now.
So soon as the court-hurry° is over, we will have an   20
end of it. I' th' meantime look tenderly to the two
prisoners. I can tell you they are princes.

DAUGHTER   These strewings° are for their chamber.
'Tis pity they are in prison, and 'twere pity they
should be out. I do think they have patience to make   25
any adversity ashamed: the prison itself is proud of
'em, and they have all the world in their chamber.°

JAILER   They are famed to be a pair of absolute° men.

DAUGHTER   By my troth, I think Fame but stammers
'em:° they stand a grize° above the reach of report.   30

JAILER   I heard them reported in the battle to be the
only doers.°

DAUGHTER   Nay, most likely, for they are noble
suff'rers. I marvel how they would have looked had
they been victors, that with such a constant nobility   35
enforce a freedom out of bondage, making misery
their mirth, and affliction a toy to jest at.

JAILER   Do they so?

DAUGHTER   It seems to me they have no more sense
of their captivity than I of ruling Athens. They eat   40
well, look merrily, discourse of many things, but
nothing of their own restraint° and disasters. Yet
sometimes a divided° sigh, martyred as 'twere i' th'
deliverance, will break from one of them—when the
other presently° gives it so sweet a rebuke that I could   45
wish myself a sigh to be so chid, or at least a sigher to
be comforted.

WOOER   I never saw 'em.

JAILER   The duke himself came privately in the night,
and so did they:° what the reason of it is I know not.   50

*Enter* PALAMON *and* ARCITE *above.*

Look, yonder they are. That's Arcite looks out.

DAUGHTER   No, sir, no! That's Palamon! Arcite is the
lower° of the twain. You may perceive a part of him.

JAILER   Go to, leave your pointing. They would not
make us their object.° Out of their sight!   55

DAUGHTER   It is a holiday to look on them. Lord, the
diff'rence of men!

*Exeunt* [JAILER, WOOER, DAUGHTER].

PALAMON
How do you, noble cousin?

ARCITE                   How do you, sir?

PALAMON
Why, strong enough to laugh at misery,
And bear the chance of war. Yet we are prisoners   60
I fear forever, cousin.

ARCITE                   I believe it,
And to that destiny have patiently
Laid up my hour to come.°

PALAMON               O cousin Arcite,
Where is Thebes now? Where is our noble country?
Where are our friends, and kindreds?° Never more   65
Must we behold those comforts, never see
The hardy youths strive for the games of honor,
Hung with painted favors of their ladies,
Like tall ships under sail; then start amongst 'em
And as an east wind leave 'em all behind us,   70
Like lazy clouds, whilst Palamon and Arcite,
Even in the wagging of a wanton leg,°
Outstripped the people's praises, won the garlands
Ere they have time to wish 'em ours. O never
Shall we two exercise, like twins of Honor,   75
Our arms again, and feel our fiery horses
Like proud seas under us! Our good swords now—
Better the red-eyed god of war ne'er wore!—
Ravished our sides, like age must run to rust
And deck the temples of those gods that hate us.   80
These hands shall never draw 'em out like lightning
To blast whole armies more.

ARCITE                   No, Palamon,
Those hopes are prisoners with us: here we are
And here the graces of our youths must wither
Like a too timely° spring; here age must find us,   85
And which is heaviest, Palamon, unmarried;
The sweet embraces of a loving wife,
Loaden with kisses, armed with thousand Cupids,
Shall never clasp our necks, no issue° know us,
No figures of ourselves shall we e'er see,   90
To glad our age, and like young eagles teach 'em
Boldly to gaze against bright arms,° and say:
"Remember what your fathers were, and conquer."
The fair-eyed maids shall weep our banishments,
And in their songs curse ever-blinded Fortune   95
Till she for shame see what a wrong she has done
To youth and nature. This is all our world:
We shall know nothing here but one another,
Hear nothing but the clock that tells° our woes.
The vine shall grow, but we shall never see it;   100
Summer shall come, and with her all delights;
But dead-cold winter must inhabit here still.

PALAMON
'Tis too true, Arcite. To our Theban hounds,
That shook the agèd forest with their echoes
No more now must we halloo, no more shake   105
Our pointed javelins, whilst the angry swine°
Flies like a Parthian quiver° from our rages,
Struck with our well-steeled darts. All valiant uses,°
The food and nourishment of noble minds,
In us two here shall perish. We shall die—   110

20 court-hurry celebrations at court (?)   23 strewings rushes
27 they . . . chamber their nobility makes their chamber
into a whole world (?) everyone visits them (?)   28 absolute
complete   29–30 Fame . . . 'em i.e., their reputation falls
short of their worth   30 grize step   32 only doers unique
performers   42 restraint imprisonment   43 divided broken
off   45 presently at once   49–50 The duke . . . they i.e.,
Theseus brought the princes secretly to the prison   53 lower
shorter   54–55 They . . . object They would not point at us

63 Laid . . . come i.e., resolved myself   64–65 Where is
Thebes . . . kindreds these references to Thebes are very
different from those in the princes' conversation of I.ii
72 Even . . . leg as quickly as a leg might be wantonly, or
idly, moved   85 too timely too early   89 issue children
92 arms weapons and armor (with an allusion to the eagle's
ability to look directly at the sun)   99 tells counts   106 angry
swine wild boar   107 Parthian quiver the Parthian bowman
was famed for shooting his arrows while retreating: here
the fleeing boar, with the arrows stuck in it, is seen as the
Parthian's quiver   108 uses customs, practices

Which is the curse of honor—lastly,°
Children of grief and ignorance.
ARCITE                 Yet, cousin,
Even from the bottom of these miseries,
From all that Fortune can inflict upon us,
I see two comforts rising, two mere° blessings,    115
If the gods please: to hold here a brave patience,
And the enjoying of our griefs together.
Whilst Palamon is with me, let me perish
If I think this our prison.
PALAMON             Certainly,
'Tis a main° goodness, cousin, that our fortunes    120
Were twined together. 'Tis most true, two souls
Put in two noble bodies, let 'em suffer
The gall of hazard,° so° they grow together,
Will never sink; they must not, say° they could.
A willing man dies sleeping, and all's done.°    125
ARCITE
Shall we make worthy uses of this place
That all men hate so much?
PALAMON            How, gentle cousin?
ARCITE
Let's think this prison holy sanctuary,
To keep us from corruption of worse men.
We are young and yet desire the ways of honor    130
That liberty and common conversation,
The poison of pure spirits, might like women
Woo us to wander from. What worthy blessing
Can be but our imaginations
May make it ours? And here being thus together,    135
We are an endless mine° to one another;
We are one another's wife, ever begetting
New births of love; we are father, friends, acquain-
     tance;
We are in one another families;
I am your heir, and you are mine. This place    140
Is our inheritance; no hard oppressor
Dare take this from us; here with a little patience
We shall live long, and loving; no surfeits seek us;
The hand of war hurts none here, nor the seas
Swallow their youth. Were we at liberty,    145
A wife might part us lawfully, or business,
Quarrels consume us, envy of ill men
Crave our acquaintance.° I might sicken, cousin,
Where you should never know it, and so perish
Without your noble hand to close mine eyes,    150
Or prayers to the gods. A thousand chances,
Were we from hence, would sever us.
PALAMON          You have made me—
I thank you, cousin Arcite—almost wanton°
With my captivity. What a misery
It is to live abroad, and everywhere!    155
'Tis like a beast, methinks. I find the court here,
I am sure a more content,° and all those pleasures
That woo the wills of men to vanity

I see through now, and am sufficient°
To tell the world 'tis but a gaudy shadow    160
That old Time, as he passes by, takes with him.
What had we been old° in the court of Creon,
Where sin is justice, lust and ignorance
The virtues of the great ones! Cousin Arcite,
Had not the loving gods found this place for us,    165
We had died as they do, ill old men, unwept,
And had their epitaphs, the people's curses.
Shall I say more?
ARCITE          I would hear you still.
PALAMON                 Ye shall.
Is there record of any two that loved
Better than we do, Arcite?
ARCITE           Sure there cannot.    170
PALAMON
I do not think it possible our friendship
Should ever leave us.
ARCITE          Till our deaths it cannot,

*Enter* EMILIA *and her* WOMEN [*below*].

And after death our spirits shall be led
To those that love eternally.° Speak on, sir.

[PALAMON *sees* EMILIA.]

EMILIA
This garden has a world of pleasures in't.    175
What flow'r is this?
WOMAN          'Tis called Narcissus, madam.
EMILIA
That was a fair boy certain, but a fool
To love himself:° were there not maids enough?
ARCITE
Pray, forward.°
PALAMON     Yes.
EMILIA          Or were they all hard-hearted?
WOMAN
They could not be to one so fair.
EMILIA               Thou wouldst not.    180
WOMAN
I think I should not, madam.
EMILIA              That's a good wench;
But take heed to your kindness, though.
WOMAN             Why, madam?
EMILIA
Men are mad things.
ARCITE        Will ye go forward, cousin?
EMILIA
Canst not thou work such flowers in silk, wench?
WOMAN             Yes.
EMILIA
I'll have a gown full of 'em and of these.    185
This is a pretty color, will't not do
Rarely upon a skirt, wench?
WOMAN          Dainty, madam.
ARCITE
Cousin, cousin, how do you, sir? Why, Palamon!

---

111 **lastly** three syllables   115 **mere** pure   120 **main** principal
123 **gall of hazard** bitterness of misadventure; **so** provided
that   124 **say** even if   125 **A . . . done** A man resigned to his
fate dies as gently as falling asleep (but the tone of this line is
not resigned)   136 **mine** source of wealth   148 **Crave our
acquaintance** i.e., contaminate by impact on us (editors have
variously emended—e.g., to "Grave" = bury, "Cleave" =
separate)   153 **wanton** i.e., delighted   157 **a more content**
i.e., a court more contented than the real one

159 **sufficient** able   162 **What . . . old** what if we had been
old (editors have emended to "What had we been, old . . .")
173–74 **our . . . eternally** our souls shall be with famous lovers
in Elysium   176–78 **Narcissus . . . himself** Narcissus fell in
love with his own reflection in water, and drowned in trying to
embrace it   179 **forward** i.e., continue

PALAMON
Never till now I was in prison, Arcite.
ARCITE
Why, what's the matter, man?
PALAMON                    Behold, and wonder.   190
By heaven, she is a goddess.
ARCITE  [*Seeing* EMILIA.] Ha!
PALAMON                    Do reverence.
She is a goddess, Arcite.
EMILIA                    Of all flow'rs
Methinks a rose is best.
WOMAN                    Why, gentle madam?
EMILIA
It is the very emblem of a maid.
For when the west wind courts her gently°        195
How modestly she blows,° and paints° the sun
With her chaste blushes! When the north comes near
     her,
Rude and impatient, then like chastity
She locks her beauties in her bud again,
And leaves him to base briers.°
WOMAN                    Yet, good madam,   200
Sometimes her modesty will blow so far
She falls for't:° a maid,
If she have any honor, would be loath
To take example by her.
EMILIA                    Thou art wanton.
ARCITE
She is wondrous fair.
PALAMON          She is all the beauty extant.°   205
EMILIA
The sun grows high, let's walk in. Keep these flowers:
We'll see how mere art can come near their colors.
I am wondrous merry-hearted, I could laugh now.
WOMAN
I could lie down,° I am sure.
EMILIA                    And take one with you?°
WOMAN
That's as we bargain,° madam.
EMILIA                    Well, agree° then.   210
               *Exeunt* EMILIA *and* WOMAN.
PALAMON
What think you of this beauty?
ARCITE                    'Tis a rare one.
PALAMON
Is't but a rare one?
ARCITE          Yes, a matchless beauty.
PALAMON
Might not a man well lose himself and love her?
ARCITE
I cannot tell what you have done. I have.
Beshrew mine eyes for't, now I feel my shackles.   215
PALAMON
You love her, then?
ARCITE          Who would not?
PALAMON                    And desire her?

ARCITE
Before my liberty.
PALAMON          I saw her first.
ARCITE
That's nothing.
PALAMON          But it shall be.
ARCITE                    I saw her too.
PALAMON
Yes, but you must not love her.
ARCITE
I will not as you do, to worship her,             220
As she is heavenly and a blessèd goddess:
I love her as a woman, to enjoy her.
So both may love.
PALAMON
You shall not love at all.
ARCITE                    Not love at all?
Who shall deny me?                                225
PALAMON
I that first saw her, I that took possession
First with mine eye of all those beauties
In her revealed to mankind. If thou lov'st her,
Or entertain'st a hope to blast my wishes,
Thou art a traitor, Arcite, and a fellow°        230
False as thy title to her. Friendship, blood,°
And all the ties between us I disclaim
If thou once think upon her.
ARCITE                    Yes, I love her,
And if the lives of all my name° lay on it,
I must do so, I love her with my soul.            235
If that will lose ye,° farewell, Palamon:
I say again, I love, and in loving her maintain
I am as worthy and as free a lover
And have as just a title to her beauty
As any Palamon or any living                      240
That is a man's son.
PALAMON          Have I called thee friend?
ARCITE
Yes, and have found me so; why are you moved thus?
Let me deal coldly° with you: am not I
Part of your blood, part of your soul? You have told
     me
That I was Palamon and you were Arcite.           245
PALAMON
Yes.
ARCITE  Am not I liable to those affections,°
Those joys, griefs, angers, fears, my friend shall suffer?
PALAMON
Ye may be.
ARCITE          Why then would you deal so cunningly,
So strangely, so unlike a noble kinsman,
To love alone? Speak truly, do you think me       250
Unworthy of her sight?
PALAMON                    No, but unjust,
If thou pursue that sight.
ARCITE                    Because another
First sees the enemy, shall I stand still
And let mine honor down, and never charge?
PALAMON
Yes, if he be but one.

195 gently three syllables  196 blows opens into flower;
paints gives an image of  200 leaves . . . briers leaves only
base briers for him  202 for't as a result of it  205 extant in
existence  208–09 laugh . . . down the Woman turns
Emilia's merriment into an allusion to the proverb "Laugh
and lie down"  209 And . . . you i.e., lie down with a (male)
companion  210 bargain, agree come to terms

230 fellow often used contemptuously at this time  231
blood kinship  234 name family  236 lose ye make me lose
you  243 coldly rationally  246 affections emotions

ARCITE          But say that one          255
Had rather combat me?
PALAMON          Let that one say so,
And use thy freedom; else if thou pursuest her,
Be as that cursèd man that hates his country,
A branded villain.
ARCITE          You are mad.
PALAMON          I must be,
Till thou art worthy, Arcite: it concerns me.°          260
And in this madness if I hazard thee°
And take thy life, I deal but truly.
ARCITE          Fie, sir.
You play the child extremely. I will love her,
I must, I ought to do so, and I dare,
And all this justly.
PALAMON          O that now, that now          265
Thy false self and thy friend had but this fortune
To be one hour at liberty, and grasp
Our good swords in our hands, I would quickly teach
          thee
What 'twere to filch affection from another.
Thou art baser in it than a cutpurse.          270
Put but thy head out of this window more,
And as I have a soul, I'll nail thy life to't.
ARCITE
Thou dar'st not, fool, thou canst not, thou art feeble.
Put my head out? I'll throw my body out,
And leap° the garden, when I see her next          275

*Enter* JAILER [*above*].

And pitch° between her arms to anger thee.
PALAMON
No more; the keeper's coming; I shall live
To knock thy brains out with my shackles.
ARCITE          Do.
JAILER
By your leave, gentlemen.
PALAMON          Now, honest keeper?
JAILER
Lord Arcite, you must presently° to th' duke;          280
The cause I know not yet.
ARCITE          I am ready, keeper.
JAILER
Prince Palamon, I must awhile bereave you
Of your fair cousin's company.
          *Exeunt* ARCITE *and* JAILER.
PALAMON          And me too,
Even when you please, of life. Why is he sent for?
It may be he shall marry her, he's goodly,°          285
And like enough the duke hath taken notice
Both of his blood and body. But his falsehood—
Why should a friend be treacherous? If that
Get him a wife so noble and so fair,
Let honest men ne'er love again. Once more          290
I would but see this fair one. Blessed garden,
And fruit, and flowers more blessed that still° blossom
As her bright eyes shine on ye! Would I were
For° all the fortune of my life hereafter

Yon little tree, yon blooming apricock!          295
How I would spread, and fling my wanton arms
In at her window! I would bring her fruit
Fit for the gods to feed on; youth and pleasure
Still as she tasted should be doubled on her,
And if she be not heavenly I would make her          300
So near the gods in nature, they should fear her.

*Enter* JAILER [*above*].

And then I am sure she would love me. How now,
          keeper,
Where's Arcite?
JAILER          Banished. Prince Pirithous
Obtained his liberty; but never more
Upon his oath and life must he set foot          305
Upon this kingdom.
PALAMON          [*Aside.*] He's a blessed man,
He shall see Thebes again, and call to arms
The bold young men, that when he bids 'em charge
Fall on like fire. Arcite shall have a fortune,°
If he dare make himself a worthy lover,          310
Yet in the field to strike a battle° for her,
And if he lose her then, he's a cold coward.
How bravely may he bear himself to win her
If he be noble Arcite! Thousand ways.°
Were I at liberty, I would do things          315
Of such a virtuous greatness that this lady,
This blushing virgin, should take manhood to her
And seek to ravish me.
JAILER          My lord, for you
I have this charge too.
PALAMON          To discharge my life?
JAILER
No, but from this place to remove your lordship:          320
The windows are too open.°
PALAMON          Devils take 'em
That are so envious° to me! Prithee kill me.
JAILER
And hang for't afterward.
PALAMON          By this good light,
Had I a sword I would kill thee.
JAILER          Why, my lord?
PALAMON
Thou bring'st such pelting° scurvy news continually          325
Thou art not worthy life. I will not go.
JAILER
Indeed you must, my lord.
PALAMON          May I see the garden?
JAILER
No.
PALAMON          Then I am resolved, I will not go.
JAILER
I must constrain you then; and for you are dangerous,
I'll clap more irons on you.
PALAMON          Do, good keeper.          330
I'll shake 'em so, ye shall not sleep,
I'll make ye a new morris.° Must I go?

---

**260 it concerns me** It is of importance to me  **261 hazard thee** put your life in danger (?) risk losing your friendship (?)  **275 leap** leap down into  **276 pitch** plant myself  **280 presently** immediately  **285 goodly** handsome  **292 still** ever  **294 For** in exchange for

**309 a fortune** a chance  **311 strike a battle** sound a call to battle  **316 Thousand ways** i.e., there are a thousand ways in which he may show himself brave  **321 open** easy to escape from  **322 envious** malicious  **325 pelting** paltry, contemptible  **332 make . . . morris** dance a new morris dance for you (in which bells would jingle on the dancer's coat)

JAILER
There is no remedy.
PALAMON  Farewell, kind window.
May rude wind never hurt thee. O my lady,
If ever thou hast felt what sorrow was,  335
Dream how I suffer. Come; now bury me.
*Exeunt* PALAMON *and* JAILER.

Scene II. [*The open country.*]

*Enter* ARCITE.

ARCITE
Banished the kingdom! 'Tis a benefit,
A mercy I must thank 'em for; but banished
The free enjoying of that face I die for,
O 'twas a studied punishment, a death
Beyond imagination! Such a vengeance  5
That, were I old and wicked, all my sins
Could never pluck upon me. Palamon,
Thou has the start now, thou shalt stay and see
Her bright eyes break each morning 'gainst thy
   window,
And let in life into thee; thou shalt feed  10
Upon the sweetness of a noble beauty
That Nature ne'er exceeded, nor ne'er shall.
Good gods! What happiness has Palamon!
Twenty to one, he'll come to speak to her,
And if she be as gentle as she's fair,  15
I know she's his: he has a tongue will tame
Tempests, and make the wild rocks wanton. Come
   what can come,
The worst is death. I will not leave the kingdom.
I know mine own° is but a heap of ruins,
And no redress there. If I go, he has her.  20
I am resolved another shape° shall make me,°
Or end my fortunes. Either way I am happy:
I'll see her and be near her, or no more.

*Enter four* COUNTRY PEOPLE, *and one with a garland
before them.*

FIRST COUNTRYMAN
My masters, I'll be there, that's certain.
SECOND COUNTRYMAN
And I'll be there.  25
THIRD COUNTRYMAN
And I.
FOURTH COUNTRYMAN
Why, then, have with ye,° boys. 'Tis but a chiding.°
Let the plough play today; I'll tickle't out
Of the jades'° tails tomorrow.
FIRST COUNTRYMAN  I am sure
To have my wife as jealous as a turkey,  30
But that's all one.° I'll go through,° let her mumble.
SECOND COUNTRYMAN
Clap her aboard° tomorrow night, and stow° her,
And all's made up again.

II.ii.19 **mine own** Thebes  21 **another shape** a disguise;
**make me** bring good fortune to me  27 **have with ye** i.e.,
I'll be there too; **'Tis . . . chiding** The worst that can happen
is a chiding  29 **jades'** nags'  31 **that's all one** that's a matter
of indifference; **go through** i.e., go through with it  32 **Clap
her aboard** board her (as a conquered ship); **stow** fill the hold
with cargo (continuing the metaphor)

THIRD COUNTRYMAN  Aye, do but put
A fescue in her fist,° and you shall see her
Take a new lesson out° and be a good wench.  35
Do we all hold,° against° the Maying?
FOURTH COUNTRYMAN  Hold?
What should ail us?°
THIRD COUNTRYMAN  Arcas will be there.
SECOND COUNTRYMAN  And Sennois
And Rycas, and three better lads ne'er danced
Under green tree; and ye know what wenches, ha?
But will the dainty dominie,° the schoolmaster,  40
Keep touch,° do you think? For he does all,° ye know.
THIRD COUNTRYMAN
He'll eat a hornbook° ere he fail. Go to,
The matter's too far driven between
Him and the tanner's daughter to let slip now,°
And she must see the duke, and she must dance too.  45
FOURTH COUNTRYMAN
Shall we be lusty!°
SECOND COUNTRYMAN [*Dances.*]
All the boys in Athens
Blow wind i' th' breech on's,° and here I'll be
And there I'll be, for our town, and here again
And there again! Ha, boys, hey for the weavers!°  50
FIRST COUNTRYMAN
This must be done i' th' woods.
FOURTH COUNTRYMAN  O pardon me.°
SECOND COUNTRYMAN
By any means.° Our thing of learning° says so,
Where he himself will edify the duke
Most parlously° in our behalfs. He's excellent i' th'
   woods;
Bring him to th' plains,° his learning makes no cry.°  55
THIRD COUNTRYMAN
We'll see the sports, then every man to's tackle.°
And, sweet companions, let's rehearse by any means
Before the ladies see us, and do sweetly,°
And God knows what may come on't.
FOURTH COUNTRYMAN  Content;
The sports once ended, we'll perform. Away, boys,
   and hold!°  60
ARCITE [*Comes forward.*]
By your leaves, honest friends. Pray you, whither go
   you?

33–34 **put . . . fist** a "fescue" was a small stick, etc., which
a teacher used as a pointer; here it indicates a penis, the idea
being "give *her* something to point with"  35 **Take . . .
out** learn a new lesson (continuing the metaphor)  36 **hold**
hold to our purposes; **against** in regard to  37 **ail us** make
us incapable  40 **dainty dominie** fine schoolmaster  41
**Keep touch** hold to his word; **does all** i.e., is indispensable
42 **hornbook** sheet of paper protected by a sheet of transparent
horn, used in teaching the alphabet, etc.  43–44 **The matter's
. . . now** i.e., their love affair cannot fail to lead to marriage
46 **lusty** vigorous  47–48 **All . . . on's** i.e., all the boys in
Athens are supporting us (literally, are helping us to dance by
blowing us from the ground)  50 **hey . . . weavers** the
Second Countryman, like Bottom, is a weaver and will dance
in honor of his craft  51 **pardon me** indicating dissent  52
**By any means** in any case; **Our . . . learning** i.e., the
Schoolmaster  54 **parlously** amazingly  54–55 **He's . . .
plains** a *double-entendre* is fairly obvious, implying that the
Schoolmaster is better in the earlier than in the later stages
of sexual activity  55 **makes no cry** wins no applause (and,
continuing the metaphor, he will not make a girl cry out)  56
**every . . . tackle** let every man keep his engagement  58
**sweetly** delectably  60 **hold** hold to your purposes

FOURTH COUNTRYMAN
Whither? Why, what a question's that!

ARCITE
Yes, 'tis a question to me that know not.

THIRD COUNTRYMAN
To the games, my friend.

SECOND COUNTRYMAN
Where were you bred you know it not?

ARCITE             Not far, sir.   65
Are there such games today?

FIRST COUNTRYMAN      Yes, marry are there,
And such as you never saw. The duke himself
Will be in person there.

ARCITE           What pastimes are they?

SECOND COUNTRYMAN
Wrestling and running. [*Aside.*] 'Tis a pretty fellow.

THIRD COUNTRYMAN
Thou wilt not go along?

ARCITE         Not yet, sir.

FOURTH COUNTRYMAN       Well, sir,   70
Take your own time. Come, boys.

FIRST COUNTRYMAN     My mind misgives me
This fellow has a vengeance° trick o' th' hip:
Mark how his body's made for't.°

SECOND COUNTRYMAN     I'll be hanged, though
If he dare venture. Hang him! Plum porridge,°
He wrestle? He roast eggs!° Come, let's be gone, lads   75
             *Exeunt [the] four [*COUNTRYMEN*]*

ARCITE
This is an offered opportunity
I durst not wish for. Well, I could have wrestled,°
The best men called it excellent, and run
Swifter than wind upon a field of corn,
Curling the wealthy ears, never flew.° I'll venture   80
And in some poor disguise be there. Who knows
Whether my brows may not be girt with garlands,
And happiness° prefer me to a place
Where I may ever dwell in sight of her?

                *Exit* ARCITE

### Scene III. [*The prison.*]

*Enter Jailer's* DAUGHTER *alone.*

DAUGHTER
Why should I love this gentleman? 'Tis odds
He never will affect° me; I am base,°
My father the mean keeper of his prison,
And he a prince; to marry him is hopeless,
To be his whore is witless. Out upon't,
What pushes° are we wenches driven to   5
When fifteen once has found us!° First I saw him:

I, seeing, thought he was a goodly man:
He has as much to please a woman in him,
If he please to bestow it so, as ever   10
These eyes yet looked on. Next, I pitied him,
And so would any young wench o' my conscience
That ever dreamed, or vowed her maidenhead
To a young handsome man. Then I loved him,
Extremely loved him, infinitely loved him.   15
And yet he had a cousin, fair as he too.
But in my heart was Palamon, and there,
Lord, what a coil he keeps!° To hear him
Sing in an evening, what a heaven it is!
And yet his songs are sad ones. Fairer spoken   20
Was never gentleman. When I come in
To bring him water in a morning, first
He bows his noble body, then salutes me thus:
"Fair, gentle maid, good-morrow, may thy goodness
Get thee a happy husband." Once he kissed me.   25
I loved my lips the better ten days after—
Would he would do so ev'ry day! He grieves much,
And me as much to see his misery.
What should I do to make him know I love him,
For I would fain enjoy him? Say I ventured   30
To set him free? What says the law then? Thus much
For law, or kindred!° I will do it,
And this night, or tomorrow, he shall love me.   *Exit.*

### Scene IV. [*At the games.*]

*Short flourish of cornets,° and shouts within. Enter*
THESEUS, HIPPOLYTA, PIRITHOUS, EMILIA,
ARCITE [*disguised*] *with a garland, &c.*

THESEUS
You have done worthily. I have not seen,
Since Hercules, a man of tougher sinews.
Whate'er you are, you run the best and wrestle
That these times can allow.°

ARCITE          I am proud to please you.

THESEUS
What country bred you?

ARCITE          This; but far off, prince.   5

THESEUS
Are you a gentleman?

ARCITE          My father said so,
And to those gentle uses gave me life.°

THESEUS
Are you his heir?

ARCITE        His youngest, sir.

THESEUS           Your father
Sure is a happy sire, then. What proves you?°

ARCITE
A little of all noble qualities:°   10
I could have kept° a hawk, and well have halloo'd

---

72 **vengeance** confounded   73 **for't** i.e., for wrestling   74 **Plum porridge** dish made of plums thickened with barley, etc. (here used as a term of contempt for one not likely to excel in wrestling)   75 **He roast eggs** i.e., he would be more capable of cooking an egg   77 **could have wrestled** used to be able to wrestle   79–80 **Swifter . . . flew** swifter than wind . . . ever flew (the illogical negative "never" was idiomatic in the seventeenth century, but editors have frequently emended)   83 **happiness** good fortune
**II.iii.2 affect** love; **base** of low birth   6 **pushes** shifts   7 **When . . . us** when we have reached the age of fifteen

18 **coil he keeps** disturbance he makes   31–32 **Thus . . . kindred** we can imagine her clicking her fingers, thus filling out line 32
**II.iv.s.d. cornets** hunting horns   4 **allow** acknowledge, praise   7 **to . . . life** brought me up to practice such noble customs   9 **What proves you** What can you show for yourself?   10 **qualities** abilities   11 **could have kept** was able to keep

To a deep cry° of dogs; I dare not praise
My feat in horsemanship, yet they that knew me
Would say it was my best piece;° last, and greatest,
I would be thought a soldier.

THESEUS　　　　　　　　You are perfect.　15

PIRITHOUS
Upon my soul, a proper man.

EMILIA　　　　　　　He is so.

PIRITHOUS
How do you like him, lady?

HIPPOLYTA　　　　　I admire° him:
I have not seen so young a man so noble,
If he say true, of his sort.

EMILIA　　　　　　　I believe
His mother was a wondrous handsome woman:　20
His face methinks goes that way.°

HIPPOLYTA　　　　　　But his body
And fiery mind illustrate° a brave father.

PIRITHOUS
Mark how his virtue,° like a hidden sun,
Breaks through his baser garments.

HIPPOLYTA　　　　　　He's well got,° sure.

THESEUS
What made you seek this place, sir?

ARCITE　　　　　　　Noble Theseus,　25
To purchase name,° and do my ablest service
To such a well-found° wonder as thy worth,
For only in thy court, of all the world,
Dwells fair-eyed Honor.

PIRITHOUS　　　　All his words are worthy.

THESEUS
Sir, we are much indebted to your travel,°　30
Nor shall you lose your wish. Pirithous,
Dispose of° this fair gentleman.

PIRITHOUS　　　　　Thanks, Theseus.

[To ARCITE.]

Whate'er you are y' are mine, and I shall give you
To a most noble service, to this lady,
This bright young virgin; pray observe her goodness;　35
You have honored her fair birthday with your virtues,
And as your due y' are hers. Kiss her fair hand, sir.

ARCITE
Sir, y' are a noble giver. Dearest beauty,
Thus let me seal my vowed faith. [Kisses her hand.]
　When your servant,
Your most unworthy creature, but offends you,　40
Command him die: he shall.

EMILIA　　　　　　That were too cruel.
If you deserve well, sir, I shall soon see't.
Y' are mine, and somewhat better than your rank I'll
　use you.

PIRITHOUS
I'll see you furnished,° and because you say
You are a horseman, I must needs entreat you　45
This afternoon to ride, but 'tis a rough one.°

ARCITE
I like him better, prince: I shall not then
Freeze in my saddle.

THESEUS　　　　　Sweet, you must be ready,
And you, Emilia, and you, friend, and all,
Tomorrow by the sun° to do observance
To flow'ry May in Dian's wood. Wait well, sir,
Upon your mistress. Emily, I hope　50
He shall not go afoot.

EMILIA　　　　　　That were a shame, sir,
While I have horses. [To ARCITE.] Take your choice,
　and what
You want at any time, let me but know it.　55
If you serve faithfully, I dare assure you
You'll find a loving mistress.

ARCITE　　　　　　If I do not,
Let me find that my father ever hated,
Disgrace and blows.

THESEUS　　　　Go, lead the way: you have won it.°
It shall be so; you shall receive all dues　60
Fit for the honor you have won; 'twere wrong else.
Sister, beshrew my heart, you have a servant
That, if I were a woman, would be master.
But you are wise.

EMILIA　　　I hope too wise for that,° sir.
　　　　　　　Flourish. Exeunt omnes.


## Scene V. [The prison.]

Enter Jailer's DAUGHTER alone.

DAUGHTER
Let all the dukes, and all the devils, roar:
He is at liberty. I have ventured for him,
And out I have brought him to a little wood
A mile hence. I have sent him where a cedar,
Higher than all the rest, spreads like a plane　5
Fast by a brook, and there he shall keep close°
Till I provide him files and food, for yet
His iron bracelets are not off. O Love,
What a stout-hearted child thou art! My father
Durst better have endured cold iron° than done it.　10
I love him, beyond love and beyond reason,
Or wit,° or safety: I have made him know it.
I care not, I am desperate. If the law
Find me,° and then condemn me for't, some wenches,
Some honest-hearted maids, will sing my dirge,　15
And tell to memory my death was noble,
Dying almost a martyr. That way he takes
I purpose is my way too. Sure he cannot
Be so unmanly as to leave me here.
If he do, maids will not so easily　20
Trust men again. And yet he has not thanked me
For what I have done—no, not so much as kissed me,
And that methinks is not so well. Nor scarcely
Could I persuade him to become a freeman,
He made such scruples of the wrong he did　25

12 **deep cry** loud pack　14 **piece** feature, accomplishment　17 **admire** wonder at　21 **goes that way** suggests that　22 **illustrate** confer honor on (stressed on second syllable)　23 **virtue** nobility　24 **well got** nobly descended　26 **purchase name** win reputation　27 **well-found** well-reputed　30 **travel** journey (or, perhaps, labor)　32 **Dispose of** take charge of　44 **furnished** provided (with what you need)　46 **a rough one** i.e., an untrained or unruly horse

50 **by the sun** by sunrise　59 **you . . . it** i.e., your success in the games makes you deserve to lead the way　64 **I . . . that** Emilia rejects Theseus' suggestion of marriage
**II.v.6 keep close** stay in hiding　10 **endured cold iron** suffered death with sword or ax　12 **wit** good sense　14 **Find me** bring me to judgment

To me, and to my father. Yet I hope,
When he considers more, this love of mine
Will take more root within him. Let him do
What he will with me, so he use me kindly,
For use me so he shall, or I'll proclaim him,    30
And to his face, no man.° I'll presently°
Provide him necessaries, and pack my clothes up,
And where there is a path of ground° I'll venture,
So° he be with me. By him, like a shadow,
I'll ever dwell. Within this hour the hubbub    35
Will be all o'er the prison: I am then
Kissing the man they look for. Farewell, father;
Get many more such prisoners, and such daughters,
And shortly you may keep yourself.° Now to him.

                           [*Exit.*]

# ACT III

## Scene I. [*The open country.*]

*Cornets in sundry places. Noise and hallooing° as people a-
Maying. Enter* ARCITE *alone.*

ARCITE

The duke has lost Hippolyta; each took
A several° laund.° This is a solemn rite
They owe bloomed May, and the Athenians pay it
To th' heart of ceremony.° O Queen Emilia,
Fresher than May, sweeter                  5
Than her gold buttons° on the boughs or all
Th' enameled knacks° o' th' mead or garden—yea,
We challenge too the bank of any nymph
That makes the stream seem flowers!° Thou, O jewel
O' th' wood, o' th' world, hast likewise° blest a place   10
With thy sole presence, in thy rumination,°
That I, poor man, might eftsoons° come between
And chop on some cold thought.° Thrice blessed
    chance
To drop on° such a mistress, expectation
Most guiltless on't!° Tell me, O lady Fortune,    15
Next after Emily my sovereign, how far
I may be proud. She takes strong note of° me,
Hath made me near her;° and this beauteous morn,
The prim'st° of all the year, presents me with
A brace of horses: two such steeds might well    20

Be by a pair of kings backed, in a field
That their crowns' titles tried.° Alas, alas,
Poor cousin Palamon, poor prisoner, thou
So little dream'st upon my fortune that
Thou think'st thyself the happier thing, to be    25
So near Emilia! Me thou deem'st at Thebes,
And therein wretched, although free. But if
Thou knew'st my mistress breathed on me, and that
I eared° her language, lived in her eye°—O coz,°
What passion would enclose thee!°                           

*Enter* PALAMON *as out of a bush, with his shackles.* [*He*]
*bends his fist at* ARCITE.

PALAMON                            Traitor kinsman,    30
Thou shouldst perceive my passion, if these signs
Of prisonment were off me, and this hand
But owner of a sword. By all oaths in one,
I and the justice of my love would make thee
A confessed traitor, O thou most perfidious    35
That ever gently° looked, the void'st of honor
That e'er bore gentle token!° Falsest cousin
That ever blood made kin, call'st thou her thine?
I'll prove it in my shackles, with these hands
Void of appointment,° that thou liest, and art    40
A very thief in love, a chaffy° lord,
Nor worth the name of villain—had I a sword,
And these house-clogs° away.

ARCITE                          Dear cousin Palamon—

PALAMON

Cozener Arcite, give me language such
As thou hast showed me feat.°

ARCITE                        Not finding in    45
The circuit of my breast any gross stuff
To form me like your blazon,° holds me to
This gentleness of answer: 'tis your passion
That thus mistakes, the which to you being enemy
Cannot to me be kind;° honor and honesty    50
I cherish, and depend on, howsoe'er
You skip° them in me, and with them, fair coz,
I'll maintain my proceedings. Pray be pleased
To show in generous° terms your griefs,° since that
Your question's° with your equal, who professes    55
To clear his own way,° with the mind and sword
Of a true gentleman.

PALAMON                  That thou durst, Arcite!

ARCITE

My coz, my coz, you have been well advertised°
How much I dare. Y' have seen me use my sword

---

**31 no man** impotent; **presently** at once   **33 path of ground** way through woods, etc. (some editors emend to "patch of ground")   **34 So** provided that   **39 shortly . . . yourself** i.e., you will soon lose all of them and will have only yourself to look after
**III.i.s.d. hallooing** cries of people calling to each other from a distance, or urging dogs in the chase   **2 several** different; **laund** open space among woods (obsolete form of *lawn*)   **4 To . . . ceremony** most ceremoniously   **6 buttons** buds   **7 enameled knacks** trifles of various colors   **8–9 bank . . . flowers** i.e., by the stream reflecting the flowers on its bank   **10 likewise** like the "nymph" of line 8   **11 in thy rumination** as you meditate there   **12 eftsoons** quickly   **12–13 come . . . thought** "chop" was a hunting term meaning to seize prey before it was away from cover: here the idea is apparently that Arcite hopes merely to come into Emilia's chaste ("cold") thoughts   **14 drop on** come upon   **14–15 expectation . . . on't** i.e., without at all expecting it   **17 takes . . . of** observes closely   **18 made . . . her** made me attend on her   **19 prim'st** supreme

**22 That . . . tried** where their claims to the crowns were being decided   **29 eared** listened to, with also a suggestion of "ear" = to plow; **in her eye** where she can see me, but with the suggestion of being so close as to see his reflection in her eye; **coz** cousin   **30 enclose thee** i.e., imprison you (doubly ironic in that Arcite thinks Palamon physically in prison while he is actually free but is "enclosed" by the passion indicated)   **36 gently** nobly   **37 bore gentle token** showed outward sign of nobility   **40 Void of appointment** without weapons to fight with   **41 chaffy** worthless   **43 house-clogs** i.e., his shackles   **44–45 give . . . feat** i.e., let your language correspond with your actions   **47 your blazon** your description of me   **49–50 the which . . . kind** as your passion is your enemy, it cannot be kind to me, your friend and other self   **52 skip** overlook   **54 generous** noble; **griefs** grievances   **55 question's** quarrel's   **55–56 professes . . . way** claims to justify his conduct   **58 advertised** informed (stressed on second syllable)

Against th' advice° of fear. Sure° of another          60
You would not hear me doubted, but your silence
Should break out, though i' th' sanctuary.°

PALAMON                                    Sir,
I have seen you move in such a place° which well
Might justify your manhood: you were called
A good knight and a bold. But the whole week's not
    fair                                              65
If any day it rain. Their valiant temper°
Men lose when they incline° to treachery,
And then they fight like compelled° bears, would fly
Were they not tied.

ARCITE              Kinsman, you might as well
Speak this and act it in your glass, as to          70
His ear which now disdains you.

PALAMON                        Come up to me,
Quit me of these cold gyves,° give me a sword,
Though it be rusty, and the charity
Of one meal lend me. Come before me then,
A good sword in thy hand, and do but say          75
That Emily is thine, I will forgive
The trespass thou hast done me, yea my life
If then thou carry't;° and brave souls in shades
That have died manly, which will seek of me
Some news from earth, they shall get none but this,   80
That thou art brave and noble.

ARCITE                          Be content.
Again betake you to your hawthorn house.°
With counsel of the night,° I will be here
With wholesome viands. These impediments°
Will I file off. You shall have garments, and          85
Perfumes to kill the smell o' th' prison. After,
When you shall stretch yourself and say but "Arcite,
I am in plight,"° there shall be at your choice
Both sword and armor.

PALAMON              O you heavens, dares any
So noble bear° a guilty business? None          90
But only Arcite. Therefore none but Arcite
In this kind is so bold.

ARCITE          Sweet Palamon!

PALAMON
I do embrace you and your offer. For
Your offer do't I only, sir. Your person
Without hypocrisy I may not wish          95

*Wind horns off.*

More than my sword's edge on't.

ARCITE                        You hear the horns.
Enter your musit° lest this match between's
Be crossed ere met.° Give me your hand. Farewell.
I'll bring you every needful thing. I pray you
Take comfort and be strong.

PALAMON                Pray hold your promise,   100

And do the deed with a bent brow°—most certain
You love me not; be rough with me, and pour
This oil° out of your language. By this air,
I could for each word give a cuff,° my stomach°
Not reconciled by reason.

ARCITE              Plainly spoken,          105
Yet pardon me hard language.° When I spur

*Wind horns.*

My horse, I chide him not. Content and anger
In me have but one face.° Hark, sir, they call
The scattered to the banquet:° you must guess
I have an office° there.

PALAMON          Sir, your attendance          110
Cannot please heaven, and I know your office
Unjustly is achieved.°

ARCITE              If a good title°—
I am persuaded this question, sick between's,
By bleeding must be cured.° I am a suitor
That to your sword you will bequeath this plea,°   115
And talk of it no more.

PALAMON              But this one word:
You are going now to gaze upon my mistress,
For, note you, mine she is.

ARCITE              Nay, then.

PALAMON                        Nay, pray you,
You talk of feeding me to breed me strength.
You are going now to look upon a sun          120
That strengthens what it looks on: there you have
A vantage o'er me, but enjoy't till
I may enforce my remedy. Farewell.

                              *Exeunt [severally].*


Scene II. [*The open country.*]

*Enter Jailer's* DAUGHTER *alone.*

DAUGHTER
He has mistook the brake° I meant, is gone
After his fancy.° 'Tis now well nigh morning.
No matter, would it were perpetual night,
And darkness lord o' th' world. Hark! 'Tis a wolf!
In me hath grief slain fear, and but for one thing   5
I care for nothing, and that's Palamon.
I reck not if the wolves would jaw me, so
He had this file. What if I halloo'd for him?
I cannot halloo. If I whooped, what then?
If he not answered, I should call a wolf          10
And do him but that service.° I have heard
Strange howls this live-long night: why may't not be
They have made prey of him? He has no weapons,
He cannot run, the jingling of his gyves

60 **advice** warning; **Sure** surely  62 **i' th' sanctuary** in a church, but also with the suggestion of breaking out of "sanctuary" (a place of safety) for the sake of righting his friend  63 **in . . . place** in battle or tournament  66 **temper** character  67 **incline** yield  68 **compelled** i.e., in bear-baiting (stressed on first syllable here)  72 **gyves** fetters  78 **If . . . carry't** if you then kill me  82 **hawthorn house** shelter in the hawthorn bush  83 **With . . . night** with only night as my confidant  84 **These impediments** Palamon's shackles  88 **in plight** in good condition, ready  90 **bear** carry out  97 **musit** gap in a hedge through which a hare, etc., might pass when hunted  98 **crossed ere met** prevented before begun

101 **with . . . brow** sternly  103 **oil** courtesy, gentleness  104 **cuff** blow; **stomach** anger  106 **pardon . . . language** allow me not to use hostile language  108 **one face** the same outward manifestation  109 **banquet** light repast, as for a hunting party  110 **office** duty to perform  112 **Unjustly is achieved** has been unfairly won; **If . . . title** either Arcite interrupts himself or, as some editors have done, we should emend "If" to "I've"  113–14 **this . . . cured** Arcite sees the quarrel as a sick person standing between them: they must cure the sickness by letting blood from it  115 **plea** lawsuit  III.ii.1 **brake** thicket  2 **After his fancy** where his fancy has led him  11 **do . . . service** i.e., (ironically) bring a wolf to him

Might call fell° things to listen, who have in them    15
A sense to know a man unarmed, and can
Smell where resistance° is. I'll set it down°
He's torn to pieces: they howled many together
And then they fed on him. So much for that;
Be bold to ring the bell.° How stand I then?    20
All's chared° when he is gone. No, no, I lie.
My father's to be hanged for his escape,
Myself to beg, if I prized life so much
As to deny my act, but that I would not,
Should I try death by dozens.° I am moped:°    25
Food took I none these two days,
Sipped some water. I have not closed mine eyes
Save when my lids scoured off their brine.° Alas,
Dissolve my life, let not my sense unsettle,
Lest I should drown, or stab, or hang myself.    30
O state of nature,° fail together° in me,
Since thy best props are warped! So which way now?
The best way is the next° way to a grave:
Each errant step beside° is torment. Lo,
The moon is down, the crickets chirp, the screech-owl    35
Calls in° the dawn. All offices° are done
Save what I fail in. But the point is this:
An end, and that is all.°                    *Exit.*

Scene III. [*The open country.*]

*Enter* ARCITE *with meat, wine, and files.*

ARCITE
I should be near the place. Ho, cousin Palamon!

*Enter* PALAMON.

PALAMON
Arcite?
ARCITE The same. I have brought you food and files.
Come forth and fear not; here's no Theseus.
PALAMON
Nor none so honest, Arcite.
ARCITE                    That's no matter,
We'll argue that hereafter. Come, take courage,    5
You shall not die thus beastly;° here, sir, drink,
I know you are faint; then I'll talk further with you.
PALAMON
Arcite, thou mightst now poison me.
ARCITE                    I might;
But I must° fear you first. Sit down, and good now,°
No more of these vain parleys: let us not,    10
Having our ancient reputation with us,
Make talk for fools and cowards.° To your health, &c.

[*He drinks.*]
PALAMON
Do.°
ARCITE    Pray sit down then, and let me entreat you,
By all the honesty and honor in you,
No mention of this woman, 'twill disturb us;    15
We shall have time enough.
PALAMON                    Well, sir, I'll pledge you.
[*He drinks.*]
ARCITE
Drink a good hearty draught, it breeds good blood, man.
Do not you feel it thaw you?
PALAMON                    Stay, I'll tell you
After a draught or two more.
ARCITE                    Spare it not,
The duke has more, coz. Eat now.
PALAMON                    Yes. [*He eats.*]
ARCITE                    I am glad    20
You have so good a stomach.°
PALAMON                    I am gladder
I have so good meat to't.
ARCITE                    Is't not mad° lodging
Here in the wild woods, cousin?
PALAMON                    Yes, for them
That have wild° consciences.
ARCITE                    How tastes your victuals?
Your hunger needs no sauce, I see.
PALAMON                    Not much.    25
But if it did, yours° is too tart. Sweet cousin,
What is this?
ARCITE    Venison.
PALAMON                    'Tis a lusty° meat.
Give me more wine. [ARCITE *gives him the wine.*]
     Here, Arcite, to the wenches
We have known in our days. The Lord Steward's daughter,
Do you remember her? [*He offers the wine to* ARCITE.]
ARCITE                    After you, coz.    30
PALAMON
She loved a black-haired man.
ARCITE                    She did so. Well, sir?
PALAMON
And I have heard some call him Arcite, and—
ARCITE
Out with't, 'faith.
PALAMON                    She met him in an arbor:
What did she there, coz? Play o' th' virginals?°
ARCITE
Something she did, sir.
PALAMON                    Made her groan a month for't;    35
Or two, or three, or ten.°
ARCITE                    The Marshal's sister
Had her share too, as I remember, cousin,
Else there be tales° abroad. You'll pledge her?
PALAMON                    Yes.

15 **fell** savage    17 **resistance** the power to resist; **set it down** take it as settled    20 **ring the bell** i.e., toll the bell for his death    21 **All's chared** all tasks are ended    25 **Should . . . dozens** should I have to die many times or in many ways; **moped** bewildered, numbed    28 **when . . . brine** when I closed them to get rid of my tears    31 **state of nature** condition of being alive; **together** altogether    33 **next** nearest    34 **Each . . . beside** i.e., each step that does not lead directly to my grave    36 **Calls in** summons (the owl, doing duty for the cock, indicates the upside-downness of her world); **offices** tasks    38 **An end . . . all** i.e., only death is to come
**III.iii.6 thus beastly** in your present beastlike condition    9 **must** should have to; **good now** please    12 **Make . . . cowards** give matter for fools and cowards to talk about

13 **Do** i.e., do drink    21 **stomach** appetite    22 **mad** fantastic    24 **wild** disordered    26 **yours** i.e., the sauce you bring in your words and presence    27 **lusty** hearty, invigorating    34 **Play . . . virginals** "virginals" was the name of a small instrument like a spinet; here punningly used with reference to sexual intercourse    35–36 **groan . . . ten** Palamon leads archly to the idea of gestation    38 **tales** false reports

[*He drinks.*]

ARCITE
A pretty brown wench 'tis. There was a time
When young men went a-hunting—and a wood,     40
And a broad beech, and thereby hangs a tale,
Heigh ho!
PALAMON   For Emily, upon my life! Fool,
Away with this strained mirth! I say again
That sigh was breathed for Emily. Base cousin,
Dar'st thou break° first?
ARCITE          You are wide.°
PALAMON             By heaven and earth,   45
There's nothing in thee honest.
ARCITE            Then I'll leave you:
You are a beast° now.
PALAMON        As thou mak'st me, traitor.
ARCITE
There's all things needful: files and shirts and perfumes.
I'll come again some two hours hence, and bring
That that shall quiet all.
PALAMON        A sword and armor?     50
ARCITE
Fear me not; you are now too foul;° farewell.
Get off your trinkets,° you shall want nought.
PALAMON                Sirrah°—
ARCITE
I'll hear no more.                *Exit.*
PALAMON     If he keep touch,° he dies for't. *Exit.*

Scene IV. [*The open country.*]

*Enter Jailer's* DAUGHTER.

DAUGHTER
I am very cold, and all the stars are out too,
The little stars and all, that look like aglets.°
The sun has seen my folly. Palamon!
Alas, no, he's in heaven. Where am I now?
Yonder's the sea, and there's a ship: how't tumbles,   5
And there's a rock lies watching under water;
Now, now, it beats upon it;° now, now, now!
There's a leak sprung, a sound° one; how they cry!
Spoon° her before the wind, you'll lose all else!
Up with a course° or two, and tack about,° boys!    10
Good night, good night, y' are gone. I am very
    hungry.
Would I could find a fine frog; he would tell me
News from all parts o' th' world; then would I make
A carack° of a cockleshell, and sail
By east and north-east to the King of Pigmies,    15
For he tells fortunes rarely. Now my father
Twenty to one is trussed up in a trice°
Tomorrow morning. I'll say never a word.

(*Sing[s].*)
For I'll cut my green coat, a foot above my knee,
And I'll clip my yellow locks, an inch below mine eye.   20
    Hey, nonny, nonny, nonny!
He's° buy me a white cut,° forth for to ride,
And I'll go seek him, through the world that is so wide.
    Hey, nonny, nonny, nonny!
O for a prick now like a nightingale,         25
To put my breast against!° I shall sleep like a top else.
                              *Exit.*

Scene V. [*The open country.*]

*Enter a* SCHOOLMASTER, *four* COUNTRYMEN *and*
BAVIAN,° *five* WENCHES, *with a* TABORER.°

SCHOOLMASTER
Fie, fie,
What tediosity and disensanity°
Is here among ye? Have my rudiments
Been labored so long with ye, milked unto ye,
And, by a figure,° even the very plumbroth°    5
And marrow of my understanding laid upon ye?
And do you still cry "where" and "how" and "where-
    fore"?
You most coarse frieze° capacities, ye jean° judgments,
Have I said "thus let be," and "there let be,"
And "then let be," and no man understand me?    10
Proh deum, medius fidius,° ye are all dunces!
For why, here stand I. Here the duke comes; there are
    you
Close° in the thicket; the duke appears; I meet him
And unto him I utter learnèd things,
And many figures; he hears, and nods, and hums,    15
And then cries "Rare!," and I go forward; at length
I fling my cap up—mark there—then do you,
As once did Meleager and the boar,°
Break comely° out before him—like true lovers,°
Cast yourselves in a body° decently,        20
And sweetly, by a figure, trace and turn,° boys.
FIRST COUNTRYMAN
And sweetly we will do it, Master Gerald.
SECOND COUNTRYMAN
Draw up the company. Where's the taborer?
THIRD COUNTRYMAN
Why, Timothy!
TABORER       Here, my mad boys, have at ye!°
SCHOOLMASTER
But, I say, where's their women?

---

45 **break** break our agreement not to refer to Emilia (but also with a suggestion of emotion breaking out); **wide** wide of the mark   47 **beast** i.e., not fit for conversation   51 **foul** unwashed, etc.   52 **trinkets** i.e., shackles; **Sirrah** contemptuous form of address   53 **keep touch** keep his promise
**III.iv.2 aglets** jewels used as hair ornaments and for tags to laces   7 **it beats upon it** i.e., the ship strikes the rock   8 **sound** great   9 **Spoon** scud   10 **course** sail attached to the lower yards of a ship; **tack about** change direction   14 **carack** ship of large burden   17 **trussed . . . trice** hanged immediately

22 **He's** vulgar form of "He'll"; **cut** laboring horse, so called because either with docked tail or gelded   25–26 **prick . . . against** alluding to the common belief that the nightingale presses against a thorn in order to stay awake and sing
**III.v.s.d. Bavian** the fool in the morris dance (the word signifying either "driveler" or "baboon"; **Taborer** one who plays a small drum   2 **disensanity** insanity ("dis-" here being intensive)   5 **figure** i.e., of speech; **plumbroth** as "plum porridge," II.ii.74   8 **frieze** rough woollen cloth; **jean** a kind of fustian (also spelled *jane*)   11 **Proh . . . fidius** O God, most certainly   13 **Close** secretly   18 **Meleager . . . boar** alluding to Meleager's killing the Calydonian boar, and his bringing the boar's head to Atalanta   19 **comely** fittingly; **lovers** i.e., of Theseus   20 **Cast . . . body** arrange yourselves in a group for the dance   21 **trace and turn** dance and revolve   24 **have at ye** i.e., I am ready for you

FOURTH COUNTRYMAN          Here's Friz and Maudlin. 25

SECOND COUNTRYMAN
And little Luce with the white legs, and bouncing°
   Barbary.

FIRST COUNTRYMAN
And freckled Nell, that never failed her master.°

SCHOOLMASTER
Where be your ribands, maids? Swim° with your
   bodies,
And carry it° sweetly and deliverly,°
And now and than a favor,° and a frisk.°          30

NELL
Let us alone,° sir.

SCHOOLMASTER Where's the rest o' th' music?°

THIRD COUNTRYMAN
Dispersed° as you commanded.

SCHOOLMASTER                    Couple° then,
And see what's wanting. Where's the Bavian?
My friend, carry your tail without offense
Or scandal to the ladies; and be sure          35
You tumble with audacity, and manhood,
And when you bark do it with judgment.

BAVIAN                    Yes, sir.

SCHOOLMASTER
Quo usque tandem?° Here is a woman wanting.°

FOURTH COUNTRYMAN
We may go whistle.° All the fat's i' th' fire.

SCHOOLMASTER
We have,                                          40
As learnèd authors utter, washed a tile,°
We have been fatuus,° and labored vainly.

SECOND COUNTRYMAN
This is that scornful piece,° that scurvy hilding,°
That gave her promise faithfully she would be here,
Cicely the sempster's° daughter.               45
The next gloves that I give her shall be dogskin.
Nay, and° she fail me once! You can tell, Arcas,°
She swore by wine and bread she would not break.°

SCHOOLMASTER
An eel and woman,
A learnèd poet says,° unless by th' tail          50
And with thy teeth thou hold, will either° fail.
In manners this was false position.°

FIRST COUNTRYMAN
A fire ill° take her! Does she flinch now?

THIRD COUNTRYMAN                    What
Shall we determine,° sir?

SCHOOLMASTER                    Nothing.
Our business is become a nullity,               55
Yea, and a woeful, and a piteous nullity.

FOURTH COUNTRYMAN
Now when the credit of our town lay on it,
Now to be frampel,° now to piss o' th' nettle!°
Go thy ways, I'll remember thee, I'll fit thee!°

*Enter Jailer's* DAUGHTER.

DAUGHTER [*Sings.*]
   The *George Alow*° came from the south,     60
     From the coast of Barbary-a,
   And there he met with brave gallants of war,
     By one, by two, by three-a.
   Well hailed, well hailed, you jolly gallants,
     And whither now are you bound-a?           65
   O let me have your company
     Till we come to the sound-a.
There was three fools fell out about an owlet.
     The one said it was an owl;
     The other he said nay;                     70
     The third he said it was a hawk,
     And her bells° were cut away.

THIRD COUNTRYMAN
There's a dainty° mad woman, master,
Comes i' th' nick,° as mad as a march hare.
If we can get her dance, we are made again:°   75
I warrant her, she'll do the rarest° gambols.

FIRST COUNTRYMAN
A mad woman? We are made, boys.

SCHOOLMASTER
And are you mad, good woman?

DAUGHTER                    I would be sorry else.
Give me your hand.

SCHOOLMASTER          Why?

DAUGHTER                    I can tell your fortune.
You are a fool. Tell ten. I have posed him.° Buzz.°   80
Friend, you must eat no white bread; if you do,
Your teeth will bleed extremely. Shall we dance, ho?
I know you, y' are a tinker: sirrah tinker,
Stop no more holes but what you should.°

SCHOOLMASTER                    Dii boni!°
A tinker, damsel?

DAUGHTER          Or a conjuror.                85
Raise me a devil now, and let him play
Qui passa,° o' th' bells and bones.°

SCHOOLMASTER                    Go take her,
And fluently° persuade her to a peace.

---

26 **bouncing** large of body  27 **that . . . master** i.e.,
did whatever he wanted of her  28 **Swim** move flowingly
29 **carry it** i.e., perform the dance; **deliverly** nimbly
30 **favor** presumably a kiss; **frisk** caper  31 **Let us alone**
Leave it to us; **music** musicians  32 **Dispersed** i.e.,
scattered in arranged places; **Couple** take your partners  38
**Quo usque tandem** how long now; **wanting** missing  39
**We . . . whistle** We have occupied ourselves to no purpose
41 **washed a tile** labored in vain (Latin *laterem lavare*)  42
**fatuus** foolish  43 **piece** creature; **hilding** good-for-nothing
45 **sempster's** probably = sempstress's  47 **and** if;
**Arcas** the name of one of the Countrymen: cf. II.ii.37  48
**break** break her word  50 **learnèd poet** no one has identified
the "poet," if he existed; but Fletcher used the proverb in other
plays  51 **either** both  52 **position** statement of a proposition,
affirmation (the Schoolmaster means that Cicely's breaking her
word was the equivalent in manners to the stating of a false
proposition in logic)  53 **fire ill** perhaps equivalent to "pox,"
or "ill" may be adverbial  54 **determine** decide to do

58 **frampel** peevish, froward; **piss . . . nettle** give herself
occasion to show bad temper  59 **fit thee** punish you as you
deserve  60 **George Alow** this was the name of a ship in a
ballad published in 1611  72 **bells** used on a hawk for ease in
tracing it  73 **dainty** fine  74 **i' th' nick** i.e., just when we need
her  75 **we . . . again** our fortune is once more secure  76
**rarest** finest  80 **Tell . . . him** counting on one's fingers was a
common method of testing idiocy; the Jailer's Daughter decides
the Schoolmaster cannot pass the test; **Buzz** exclamation commanding
silence  84 **Stop . . . should** alluding to the proverb
"A tinker stops one hole and makes others"; but with an
obvious double meaning here; **Dii boni** Good gods!  87 **Qui**
**passa** the song "*Chi passa per questa strada*"; **bells and bones**
similar to Bottom's "the tongs and the bones," *A Midsummer
Night's Dream*, IV.i.30: "bones" were bone clappers held
between the fingers  88 **fluently** quickly

Et opus exegi, quod nec Iovis ira, nec ignis.°
Strike up,° and lead her in.°

SECOND COUNTRYMAN   Come, lass, let's trip it.   90

DAUGHTER
I'll lead.

THIRD COUNTRYMAN   Do, do.

SCHOOLMASTER   Persuasively, and cunningly!°

*Wind horns.*

Away, boys! I hear the horns.
Give me some meditation,° and mark your cue.
                              *Exeunt all but* SCHOOLMASTER.
Pallas° inspire me!

*Enter* THESEUS, PIRITHOUS, HIPPOLYTA, EMILIA,
ARCITE, *and* TRAIN. [*A chair and stools are brought out.*]°

THESEUS              This way the stag took.

SCHOOLMASTER
Stay, and edify!°

THESEUS              What have we here?   95

PIRITHOUS
Some country sport, upon my life, sir.

THESEUS
Well, sir, go forward, we will edify.
Ladies, sit down; we'll stay it.°

[*They sit.*]

SCHOOLMASTER
Thou doughty duke, all hail! All hail, sweet ladies!

THESEUS
This is a cold beginning.°   100

SCHOOLMASTER
If you but favor, our country pastime made is.
We are a few of those collected here
That ruder tongues distinguish° villager.
And to say verity, and not to fable,
We are a merry rout, or else a rabble   105
Or company, or by a figure Chorus,°
That 'fore thy dignity will dance a morris.
And I that am the rectifier° of all,
By title Pedagogus, that let fall
The birch upon the breeches of the small ones,   110
And humble with a ferula° the tall ones,
Do here present this machine,° or this frame;°
And dainty duke, whose doughty dismal fame
From Dis to Daedalus,° from post to pillar°

Is blown abroad, help me, thy poor well-willer,   115
And with thy twinkling eyes look right and straight
Upon this mighty "Morr," of mickle weight;
"Is" now comes in—which being glued together
Makes "Morris,"° and the cause that we came hither,
The body of our sport of no small study.   120
I first appear, though rude, and raw, and muddy,
To speak before thy noble grace this tenor,°
At whose great feet I offer up my penner;°
The next° the Lord of May, and Lady bright,
The Chambermaid and Servingman by night   125
That seek out silent hanging;° then mine Host
And his fat Spouse, that welcomes to their° cost
The gallèd° Traveler, and with a beck'ning
Informs the Tapster to inflame the reck'ning;
Then the beest-eating° Clown, and next the Fool,   130
The Bavian with long tail, and eke long tool,°
Cum multis aliis° that make a dance.
Say "Aye," and all shall presently advance.

THESEUS
Aye, aye, by any means, dear dominie.

PIRITHOUS                              Produce.°

SCHOOLMASTER
Intrate, filii!° Come forth and foot it.   135

*Knock.° Enter the* DANCE. *Music.* [*They*] *dance.*

Ladies, if we have been merry
And have pleased ye with a derry,
And a derry, and a down,
Say the Schoolmaster's no Clown.
Duke, if we have pleased thee too   140
And have done as good boys should do,
Give us but a tree or twain
For a maypole, and again,
Ere another year run out,
We'll make thee laugh and all this rout.°   145

THESEUS
Take twenty, dominie. [*To* HIPPOLYTA.] How does
   my sweetheart?

HIPPOLYTA
Never so pleased, sir.

EMILIA                    'Twas an excellent dance,
And for a preface I never heard a better.

THESEUS
Schoolmaster, I thank you. One see 'em all rewarded.

PIRITHOUS [*Gives money.*]
And here's something to paint your pole withal.   150

THESEUS
Now to our sports again.

---

**89 Et . . . ignis** I have achieved something which neither
Jove's anger nor fire . . . (from Ovid's *Metamorphoses,*
xv. 871, where it reads "*Jamque opus . . . nec ignes*")   **90
Strike up** begin the music;  **in** offstage, into the thicket
where the dancers will wait   **91 cunningly** skillfully   **93
meditation** time for meditation (?) attention (?)   **94 Pallas**
as goddess of learning   **94 s.d. A chair . . . out** see
A Note on the Text for III.v.65–67   **95 edify** the Schoolmaster's English for "profit mentally," "be edified"   **98 stay
it** wait here for it   **100 cold beginning** deliberately taking
"hail" for a reference to the weather   **103 distinguish** classify
**106 by . . . Chorus** the Schoolmaster's "figure" allows him to
compare the morris dancers with the chorus of a classical play
**108 rectifier** pedant's word for "director"   **111 ferula** cane
**112 machine** structure, device (stressed on first syllable); **frame**
contrivance   **114 Dis to Daedalus** Dis was the Greek god of
the underworld, Daedalus the maker of the Labyrinth in Crete;
the Schoolmaster's use of learning is indiscriminate; **from
. . . pillar** from one resource to another (the Schoolmaster is
desperate for a rhyme)

**117–19 Morr . . . Morris** perhaps the Schoolmaster holds
up two boards in turn, with the syllables "Morr" and "is"
on them, and then puts them together; but the first board
could show a picture of a Moor   **122 tenor** properly,
the wording of a document; drift   **123 penner** pen case
(offered as a token of his services to Theseus)   **124 next**
i.e., next to appear   **126 seek . . . hanging** i.e., seek out a
curtain or tapestry behind which they can make love   **127 their**
perhaps plural because "Traveler" is so understood   **128
gallèd** distressed   **130 beest-eating** probably indicates the
Clown's partiality for "beest," the milk of a cow soon after
calving, used in making puddings   **131 tool** sexual organ
**132 Cum multis aliis** with many others   **134 Produce** bring
forth   **135 Intrate, filii** Enter, my sons!   **135 s.d. Knock** the
Schoolmaster gives a signal for the entry; but see A Note on
the Text, p. 1623   **145 rout** company

**SCHOOLMASTER**

May the stag thou hunt'st stand° long,
And thy dogs be swift and strong,
May they kill him without lets,°
And the ladies eat his dowsets!°                                  155

*Wind horns.*

[*To the* DANCERS.]

Come, we are all made. Dii deaeque omnes!°
Ye have danced rarely, wenches.          *Exeunt.*

Scene VI. [*The open country.*]

*Enter* PALAMON *from the bush.*

**PALAMON**

About this hour my cousin gave his faith
To visit me again, and with him bring
Two swords and two good armors: if he fail,
He's neither man nor soldier. When he left me,
I did not think a week could have restored            5
My lost strength to me, I was grown so low
And crestfall'n with my wants. I thank thee, Arcite,
Thou art yet a fair foe, and I feel myself,
With this refreshing, able once again
To outdure° danger. To delay it longer              10
Would make the world think when it comes to hearing
That I lay fatting like a swine to fight,°
And not a soldier. Therefore this blest morning
Shall be the last; and that sword he refuses,°
If it but hold,° I kill him with: 'tis justice.          15
So love and fortune for me!

*Enter* ARCITE *with armors and swords.*

                              O good-morrow!

**ARCITE**

Good-morrow, noble kinsman.

**PALAMON**                    I have put you
To too much pains, sir.

**ARCITE**              That too much, fair cousin,
Is but a debt to honor, and my duty.

**PALAMON**

Would you were so in all, sir! I could wish ye        20
As kind a kinsman as you force me find
A beneficial foe, that my embraces
Might thank ye, not my blows.

**ARCITE**              I shall think either,
Well done, a noble recompense.

**PALAMON**                    Then I shall quit° you.

**ARCITE**

Defy me in these fair terms, and you show°         25
More than a mistress to me. No more anger,
As you love anything that's honorable!
We were not bred° to talk, man. When we are armed
And both upon our guards, then let our fury,
Like meeting of two tides, fly strongly from us,     30

And then to whom the birthright° of this beauty
Truly pertains—without upbraidings, scorns,
Despisings of our persons, and such poutings
Fitter for girls and schoolboys—will be seen,
And quickly, yours or mine. Will't please you arm,
  sir?                                                            35
Or if you feel yourself not fitting yet
And furnished with your old strength, I'll stay,°
  cousin,
And ev'ry day discourse you into health,
As I am spared.° Your person I am friends with,
And I could wish I had not said I loved her,         40
Though I had died.° But loving such a lady
And justifying° my love, I must not fly from't.

**PALAMON**

Arcite, thou art so brave an enemy
That no man but thy cousin's fit to kill thee.
I am well and lusty.° Choose your arms.

**ARCITE**                              Choose you, sir.  45

**PALAMON**

Wilt thou exceed in all, or dost thou do it
To make me spare thee?

**ARCITE**              If you think so, cousin,
You are deceived, for as I am a soldier
I will not spare you.

**PALAMON**              That's well said.

**ARCITE**                              You'll find it.°

**PALAMON**

Then as I am an honest man and love,                50
With all the justice of affection°
I'll pay thee soundly.° This I'll take.

                              [*Chooses an armor.*]

**ARCITE**                    That's mine then.

[*Takes the other.*]

I'll arm you first.

**PALAMON**         Do. [ARCITE *arms him.*] Pray thee tell
  me, cousin,
Where gott'st thou this good armor?

**ARCITE**                    'Tis the duke's,
And to say true, I stole it. Do I pinch you?         55

**PALAMON**

No.

**ARCITE**   Is't not too heavy?

**PALAMON**                    I have worn a lighter,
But I shall make it serve.

**ARCITE**              I'll buckle't close.

**PALAMON**

By any means.°

**ARCITE**         You care not for a grand guard?°

**PALAMON**

No, no, we'll use no horses. I perceive
You would fain be at that fight.°

**ARCITE**              I am indifferent.°   60

31 **birthright** the right to possess her, given to one of
us at birth  37 **stay** wait  39 **As . . . spared** as long as I
am alive  41 **Though . . . died** i.e., as a result of my silence
42 **justifying** affirming, defending  45 **lusty** vigorous  49
**find it** i.e., find it so  51 **justice of affection** justice
administered by one who loves the offender  52 **soundly**
fully, strongly  58 **By any means** Please do; **grand guard**
part of the armor worn by a knight on horseback  60 **at that
fight** i.e., fight on horseback; **indifferent** i.e., as to how we
fight

152 **stand** endure  154 **lets** hindrances  155 **dowsets** testicles
156 **Dii deaeque omnes** All gods and goddesses!
**III.vi.10 outdure** survive  12 **fatting . . . fight** being fattened to fight as a swine is fattened to be eaten  14 **that . . .
refuses** Palamon will give Arcite his choice  15 **If . . . hold**
if it does not break  24 **quit** requite  25 **show** appear  28
**bred** brought up

PALAMON
'Faith, so am I. Good cousin, thrust the buckle
Through far enough.

ARCITE                    I warrant you.

PALAMON                              My casque° now.

ARCITE
Will you fight bare-armed?

PALAMON                    We shall be the nimbler.

ARCITE
But use your gauntlets, though. Those are o' th' least:°
Prithee take mine, good cousin.

PALAMON                    Thank you, Arcite.    65
How do I look, am I fall'n much away?°

ARCITE
'Faith, very little: love has used you kindly.

PALAMON
I warrant thee, I'll strike home.

ARCITE                    Do, and spare not;
I'll give you cause, sweet cousin.

PALAMON                    Now to you, sir.

[*He arms* ARCITE.]

Methinks this armor's very like that, Arcite,    70
Thou wor'st that day the three kings fell, but lighter.

ARCITE
That was a very good one, and that day
I well remember you outdid me, cousin.
I never saw such valor: when you charged
Upon the left wing of the enemy,    75
I spurred hard to come up, and under me
I had a right good horse.

PALAMON                    You had indeed:
A bright bay, I remember.

ARCITE                    Yes, but all
Was vainly labored in me: you outwent me,
Nor could my wishes reach you.° Yet a little    80
I did by imitation.

PALAMON                    More by virtue;°
You are modest, cousin.

ARCITE                    When I saw you charge first,
Methought I heard a dreadful clap of thunder
Break from the troop.

PALAMON                    But still before that flew
The lightning of your valor. Stay a little,    85
Is not this piece too strait?°

ARCITE                    No, no, 'tis well.

PALAMON
I would have nothing hurt thee but my sword,
A bruise would be dishonor.

ARCITE                    Now I am perfect.°

PALAMON
Stand off° then.

ARCITE                    Take my sword, I hold° it better.

PALAMON
I thank ye. No, keep it, your life lies° on it.    90
Here's one: if it but hold, I ask no more
For all my hopes. My cause and honor guard me!

ARCITE
And me my love! *They bow several ways;° then advance
and stand.* Is there aught else to say?

PALAMON
This only, and no more. Thou art mine aunt's son,
And that blood we desire to shed is mutual,    95
In me thine, and in thee mine. My sword
Is in my hand, and if thou kill'st me
The gods and I forgive thee. If there be
A place prepared for those that sleep in honor,
I wish his weary soul that falls may win it.    100
Fight bravely, cousin. Give me thy noble hand.

ARCITE
Here, Palamon. [*They take hands.*] This hand shall
never more
Come near thee with such friendship.

PALAMON                              I commend° thee.

ARCITE
If I fall, curse me, and say I was a coward,
For none but such dare die in these just trials.    105
Once more farewell, my cousin.

PALAMON                              Farewell, Arcite.

[*They*] *fight. Horns within; they stand.*

ARCITE
Lo, cousin, lo, our folly has undone us.

PALAMON
Why?

ARCITE
This is the duke, a-hunting as I told you:
If we be found, we are wretched. O retire    110
For honor's sake, and safety, presently°
Into your bush again. Sir, we shall find
Too many hours to die in, gentle cousin.
If you be seen, you perish instantly
For breaking prison, and I, if you reveal me,    115
For my contempt;° then all the world will scorn us,
And say we had a noble difference,°
But base disposers° of it.

PALAMON                    No, no, cousin,
I will no more be hidden, nor put off
This great adventure to a second trial.    120
I know your cunning, and I know your cause.°
He that faints° now, shame take him: put thyself
Upon thy present guard.°

ARCITE                    You are not mad?

PALAMON
Or I will make th' advantage of this hour
Mine own, and what to come shall threaten me    125
I fear less than my fortune.° Know, weak cousin,
I love Emilia, and in that I'll bury
Thee, and all crosses° else.

ARCITE                    Then come what can come,
Thou shalt know, Palamon, I dare as well
Die as discourse or sleep. Only this fears me:°    130

---

62 **casque** helmet  64 **Those . . . least** those you have are the
smallest possible  66 **am . . . away** have I got much thinner
80 **Nor . . . you** i.e., my wish to be by your side could not
put me there  81 **virtue** natural talent  86 **strait** tight  88
**perfect** ready  89 **Stand off** stand away; **hold** think  90 **lies**
depends

93 s.d. **bow several ways** bow formally in different directions, as in the lists  103 **commend** praise, honor  111 **presently** at once  116 **contempt** i.e., of Theseus' banishment
of him  117 **difference** quarrel  118 **disposers** controllers
121 **your cause** i.e., why you wish to postpone the fight  122
**faints** draws back  123 **Upon . . . guard** on guard at once
126 **my fortune** i.e., in this fight  128 **crosses** obstacles  130
**fears me** makes me fear

The law will have the honor of our ends.
Have at thy life!

PALAMON          Look to thine own well, Arcite.

[*They*] *fight again. Horns. Enter* THESEUS, HIPPOLYTA,
EMILIA, PIRITHOUS *and* TRAIN.

THESEUS
What ignorant and mad malicious° traitors
Are you, that 'gainst the tenor° of my laws
Are making battle, thus like knights appointed,          135
Without my leave, and officers of arms?°
By Castor,° both shall die.

PALAMON                    Hold° thy word, Theseus.
We are certainly both traitors, both despisers
Of thee, and of thy goodness. I am Palamon
That cannot love thee, he that broke thy prison:          140
Think well what that deserves; and this is Arcite:
A bolder traitor never trod thy ground,
A falser ne'er seemed friend. This is the man
Was begged° and banished, this is he contemns thee
And what thou dar'st do; and in this disguise          145
Against thy own edict follows thy sister,
That fortunate bright star,° the fair Emilia,
Whose servant—if there be a right in seeing,
And first bequeathing of the soul to—justly
I am, and which is more, dares think her his.          150
This treachery, like a most trusty lover,
I called him now to answer. If thou be'st
As thou art spoken, great and virtuous,
The true decider of all injuries,
Say "Fight again," and thou shalt see me, Theseus.          155
Do such a justice thou thyself wilt envy.
Then take my life, I'll woo thee to't.

PIRITHOUS                    O heaven,
What more than man is this!

THESEUS                    I have sworn.

ARCITE                    We seek not
Thy breath of mercy, Theseus: 'tis to me
A thing as soon to die as thee to say it,          160
And no more moved. Where° this man calls me traitor,
Let me say thus much: if in love be treason
In service of so excellent a beauty,
As I love most, and in that faith will perish,
As I have brought my life here to confirm it,          165
As I have served her truest, worthiest,
As I dare kill this cousin that denies it,
So let me be most traitor, and ye please me.
For° scorning thy edict, duke, ask that lady
Why she is fair, and why her eyes command me          170
Stay here to love her; and if she say "traitor,"
I am a villain fit to lie unburied.

PALAMON
Thou shalt have pity of us both, O Theseus,
If unto neither thou show mercy. Stop,
As thou art just, thy noble ear against us;          175
As thou art valiant, for thy cousin's soul
Whose twelve strong labors crown his memory,°

Let's die together, at one instant, duke:
Only a little let him fall before me,
That I may tell my soul he shall not have her.          180

THESEUS
I grant your wish, for to say true your cousin
Has ten times more offended, for I gave him
More mercy than you found, sir, your offenses
Being no more than his. None here speak for 'em,
For ere the sun set both shall sleep forever.          185

HIPPOLYTA
Alas the pity! Now or never, sister,
Speak not to be denied: that face of yours
Will bear the curses else of after ages
For these lost cousins.

EMILIA                    In my face, dear sister,
I find no anger to 'em, nor no ruin:          190
The misadventure of their own eyes kill° 'em.
Yet that I will be woman, and have pity,
My knees shall grow to th' ground but° I'll get mercy.
Help me, dear sister; in a deed so virtuous
The powers of all women will be with us.          195

[*They kneel.*]

Most royal brother!

HIPPOLYTA          Sir, by our tie of marriage!

EMILIA
By your own spotless honor!

HIPPOLYTA                    By that faith,
That fair hand, and that honest heart you gave me!

EMILIA
By that you would have pity° in another,
By your own virtues infinite!

HIPPOLYTA                    By valor,          200
By all the chaste nights I have ever pleased you!

THESEUS
These are strange conjurings.°

PIRITHOUS                    Nay, then I'll in too:

[*He kneels.*]

By all our friendship, sir, by all our dangers,
By all you love most—wars, and this sweet lady!

EMILIA
By that you would have trembled to deny          205
A blushing maid!°

HIPPOLYTA          By your own eyes; by strength,
In which you swore I went beyond all women,
Almost all men, and yet I yielded, Theseus.

PIRITHOUS
To crown all this: by your most noble soul,
Which cannot want° due mercy! I beg first.          210

HIPPOLYTA
Next hear my prayers.

EMILIA                    Last let me entreat, sir.

PIRITHOUS
For mercy!

HIPPOLYTA    Mercy!

EMILIA                    Mercy on these princes!

---

**133 malicious** evilly disposed  **134 tenor** purport  **136 officers
of arms** officials formally appointed to supervise a fight  **137
Castor** son of Zeus by Leda, twin brother to Pollux; **Hold** keep
**144 begged** petitioned for  **147 fortunate bright star** star
bringing good fortune  **161 Where** whereas  **169 For** as for
**176–77 thy cousin's . . . memory** i.e., the soul of Hercules,
who legendarily performed twelve great labors

**191 kill** plural verb through association with "eyes," despite
the singular subject  **193 but** unless (or until)  **199 By . . .
pity** by whatever you would have pity on  **202 conjurings**
conjurations  **205–06 that . . . maid** presumably, the love
the maid asked for  **210 want** fail to get (?) lack the power to
feel (?)

THESEUS
Ye make my faith° reel. [*They rise.*] Say I felt
Compassion to 'em both, how would you place it?°

EMILIA
Upon their lives—but with their banishments.    215

THESEUS
You are a right° woman, sister. You have pity,
But want the understanding where to use it.
If you desire their lives, invent a way
Safer than banishment. Can these two live
And have the agony of love about 'em,    220
And not kill one another? Every day
They'd fight about you, hourly bring your honor
In public question with their swords. Be wise then,
And here forget 'em. It concerns your credit,
And my oath equally. I have said they die:    225
Better they fall by th' law than one another.
Bow° not my honor.

EMILIA                    O my noble brother,
That oath was rashly made, and in your anger;
Your reason will not hold° it. If such vows
Stand for express will,° all the world must perish.    230
Beside, I have another oath, 'gainst yours,
Of more authority, I am sure more love,
Not made in passion neither, but good heed.

THESEUS
What is it, sister?

PIRITHOUS          Urge it home, brave lady.

EMILIA
That you would ne'er deny me anything    235
Fit for my modest suit, and your free granting.
I tie you to your word now: if ye fall in't,°
Think how you maim your honor—
For now I am set a-begging, sir, I am deaf
To all but your compassion—how their lives    240
Might breed the ruin of my name, opinion.°
Shall anything that loves me perish for me?
That were a cruel wisdom. Do men prune
The straight young boughs that blush with thousand
    blossoms
Because they may be rotten?° O duke Theseus,    245
The goodly mothers that have groaned for these,
And all the longing maids that ever loved,
If your vow stand, shall curse me and my beauty,
And in their funeral songs for these two cousins
Despise my cruelty, and cry woe worth° me,    250
Till I am nothing but the scorn of women.
For heaven's sake save their lives, and banish 'em.

THESEUS
On what conditions?

EMILIA                    Swear 'em never more
To make me their contention, or to know me,°
To tread upon thy dukedom, and to be,    255
Wherever they shall travel, ever strangers

To one another.

PALAMON          I'll be cut a-pieces
Before I take this oath: forget I love her?
O all ye gods despise me then! Thy banishment
I not mislike, so° we may fairly carry    260
Our swords and cause along. Else never trifle,
But make our lives, duke: I must love and will,
And for that love must and dare kill this cousin
On any piece° the earth has.

THESEUS                    Will you, Arcite,
Take these conditions?

PALAMON          He's a villain then.    265

PIRITHOUS
These are men.°

ARCITE
No, never, duke. 'Tis worse to me than begging
To take my life so basely. Though I think
I never shall enjoy her, yet I'll preserve
The honor of affection, and die for her,    270
Make° death a devil.

THESEUS
What may be done? For now I feel compassion.

PIRITHOUS
Let it not fall° again, sir.

THESEUS                    Say, Emilia,
If one of them were dead, as one must, are you
Content to take th' other to your husband?    275
They cannot both enjoy you. They are princes
As goodly as your own eyes, and as noble
As ever fame yet spoke of. Look upon 'em,
And if you can love, end this difference.
I give consent; are you content too, princes?    280

BOTH [COUSINS]
With all our souls.

THESEUS          He that she refuses
Must die then.

BOTH [COUSINS]   Any death thou canst invent, duke.

PALAMON
If I fall from that mouth,° I fall with favor,
And lovers yet unborn shall bless my ashes.

ARCITE
If she refuse me, yet my grave will wed me,    285
And soldiers sing my epitaph.

THESEUS                    Make choice, then.

EMILIA
I cannot, sir, they are both too excellent:
For me, a hair shall never fall of these men.°

HIPPOLYTA
What will become of 'em?

THESEUS                    Thus I ordain it,
And by mine honor, once again, it stands,    290
Or both shall die. You shall both to your country,
And each within this month, accompanied
With three fair knights, appear again in this place,
In which I'll plant a pyramid;° and whether,°
Before us that are here, can force his cousin    295
By fair and knightly strength to touch the pillar,

---

213 **faith** i.e., in his own judgment    214 **how . . . it** i.e., in
what way would you have it bestowed    216 **right** true, typical
227 **Bow** humiliate, bring disgrace on    229 **hold** hold to
230 **express will** unshakable resolve    237 **fall in't** renege on it
240–41 **how . . . opinion** i.e., how the taking away of their
lives might lead to the ruin of my name and reputation (some
editors emend to "name's opinion"; some take "opinion" as
an exclamation of contempt)    245 **Because . . . rotten**
because they may later become rotten    250 **woe worth** woe
befall    254 **know me** hold me in their minds

---

260 **so** provided that    264 **piece** i.e., of ground    266 **men** i.e.,
complete men    271 **Make** though you make    273 **fall** weaken
283 **from that mouth** i.e., the sentence being spoken by her
288 **For . . . men** it will not be because of me that a hair of
either shall perish    294 **pyramid** obelisk; **whether** which of
the two

He shall enjoy her; the other lose his head,
And all his friends.° Nor shall he grudge to fall,
Nor think he dies with interest in this lady.
Will this content ye?
PALAMON          Yes. Here, cousin Arcite,          300
I am friends again, till that hour.
ARCITE          I embrace ye.
THESEUS
Are you content, sister?
EMILIA          Yes, I must, sir,
Else both miscarry.
THESEUS          Come, shake hands again, then,
And take heed, as you are gentlemen, this quarrel
Sleep till the hour prefixed,° and hold your course.°          305
PALAMON
We dare not fail thee, Theseus.
THESEUS          Come, I'll give ye
Now usage like to princes, and to friends.
When ye return, who wins I'll settle here,°
Who loses—°yet I'll weep upon his bier.          *Exeunt.*

# ACT IV

## Scene I. [*The prison.*]

*Enter* JAILER *and his* FRIEND.

JAILER
Hear you no more, was nothing said of me
Concerning the escape of Palamon?
Good sir, remember.
FIRST FRIEND          Nothing that I heard,
For I came home before the business°
Was fully ended. Yet I might perceive,          5
Ere I departed, a great likelihood
Of both their pardons. For Hippolyta
And fair-eyed Emily upon their knees
Begged with such handsome pity that the duke
Methought stood staggering, whether he should follow          10
His rash oath or the sweet compassion
Of those two ladies; and to second them
That truly noble prince Pirithous,
Half his own heart,° set in too,° that° I hope
All shall be well. Neither heard I one question          15
Of your name, or his 'scape.

*Enter* SECOND FRIEND.

JAILER          Pray heaven it hold so.
SECOND FRIEND
Be of good comfort, man; I bring you news,
Good news.
JAILER          They are welcome.
SECOND FRIEND          Palamon has cleared you,

And got your pardon, and discovered° how
And by whose means he escaped, which was your          20
daughter's,
Whose pardon is procured too, and the prisoner,
Not to be held ungrateful to her goodness,
Has given a sum of money to her marriage,
A large one I'll assure you.
JAILER          Ye are a good man
And ever bring good news.
FIRST FRIEND          How was it ended?          25
SECOND FRIEND
Why, as it should be: they that never begged
But they prevailed had their suits fairly granted.
The prisoners have their lives.
FIRST FRIEND          I knew 'twould be so.
SECOND FRIEND
But there be new conditions, which you'll hear of
At better time.
JAILER          I hope they are good.
SECOND FRIEND          They are honorable;          30
How good they'll prove I know not.

*Enter* WOOER.

FIRST FRIEND          'Twill be known.
WOOER
Alas, sir, where's your daughter?
JAILER          Why do you ask?
WOOER
O sir, when did you see her?
SECOND FRIEND          How he looks!
JAILER
This morning.
WOOER          Was she well? Was she in health?
Sir, when did she sleep?
FIRST FRIEND          These are strange questions.          35
JAILER
I do not think she was very well, for now
You make me mind her,° but° this very day
I asked her questions, and she answered me
So far from what she was, so childishly,
So sillily, as if she were a fool,          40
An innocent,° and I was very angry.
But what of her, sir?
WOOER          Nothing but my pity;°
But you must know it, and as good by me
As by another that less loves her.
JAILER          Well, sir?
FIRST FRIEND
Not right?°
SECOND FRIEND          Not well?
WOOER          No, sir, not well.          45
'Tis too true, she is mad.
FIRST FRIEND          It cannot be.
WOOER
Believe you'll find it so.
JAILER          I half suspected
What you have told me: the gods comfort her!
Either this was her love to Palamon,
Or fear of my miscarrying° on his 'scape,          50

---

298 **And all his friends** i.e., they shall lose their heads too
305 **prefixed** arranged; **hold your course** keep to your resolve
308 **settle here** give him a home in Athens   309 **Who loses—**
Theseus, by changing the construction, shows his realization
that the second half of the antithesis must be anticlimactic
IV.i.4 **business** three syllables   14 **Half . . . heart** i.e., the
possessor of half of Theseus' heart; **set it too** joined in as well;
**that** so that

19 **discovered** revealed   37 **mind her** call her to mind; **but**
only   41 **innocent** idiot   42 **Nothing . . . pity** it is only
pity that makes me speak   45 **Not right** i.e., in the head   50
**miscarrying** dying

Or both.

**WOOER** 'Tis likely.

**JAILER**                    But why all this haste,° sir?

**WOOER**
I'll tell you quickly. As I late was angling
In the great lake that lies behind the palace,
From the far shore, thick set with reeds and sedges,
As patiently I was attending sport,                                          55
I heard a voice, a shrill one, and attentive
I gave my ear, when I might well perceive
'Twas one that sung, and by the smallness of it
A boy or woman. I then left my angle
To his own skill, came near, but yet perceived not        60
Who made the sound, the rushes and the reeds
Had so encompassed it.° I laid me down
And listened to the words she sung, for then,
Through a small glade cut by the fishermen,
I saw it was your daughter.

**JAILER**                    Pray go on, sir.            65

**WOOER**
She sung much, but no sense. Only I heard her
Repeat this often: "Palamon is gone,
Is gone to th' wood to gather mulberries;
I'll find him out tomorrow."

**FIRST FRIEND**                    Pretty soul!

**WOOER**
"His shackles will betray him, he'll be taken,            70
And what shall I do then? I'll bring a bevy,
A hundred black-eyed maids, that love as I do,
With chaplets° on their heads of daffadillies,
With cherry lips, and cheeks of damask roses,
And all we'll dance an antic° 'fore the duke,           75
And beg his° pardon." Then she talked of you, sir,
That you must lose your head tomorrow morning,
And she must gather flowers to bury you,
And see the house made handsome. Then she sung
Nothing but "Willow, willow, willow,"° and between   80
Ever was "Palamon, fair Palamon,"
And "Palamon was a tall young man."° The place
Was knee-deep where she sat; her careless tresses
A wreath of bullrush rounded; about her stuck
Thousand fresh water flowers of several colors—        85
That methought she appeared like the fair nymph
That feeds the lake with waters, or as Iris°
Newly dropped down from heaven. Rings she made
Of rushes that grew by, and to 'em spoke
The prettiest posies:° "Thus our true love's tied,"      90
"This you may loose,° not me," and many a one.
And then she wept, and sung again, and sighed,
And with the same breath smiled, and kissed her hand.

**SECOND FRIEND**
Alas, what pity it is!

**WOOER**                    I made in to her.°
She saw me, and straight sought the flood; I saved her, 95

And set her safe to land—when presently°
She slipped away, and to the city made,
With such a cry, and swiftness, that believe me
She left me far behind her. Three or four
I saw from far off cross° her: one of 'em              100
I knew to be your brother; where she stayed,°
And fell, scarce to be got away. I left them with her,

*Enter* BROTHER, DAUGHTER, *and others.*

And hither came to tell you. Here they are.

**DAUGHTER** [*Sings.*]
May you never more enjoy the light, &c.
Is not this a fine song?

**BROTHER**                    O, a very fine one.       105

**DAUGHTER**
I can sing twenty more.

**BROTHER**                    I think you can.

**DAUGHTER**
Yes, truly can I. I can sing "The Broom"°
And "Bonny Robin."° Are not you a tailor?

**BROTHER**
Yes.

**DAUGHTER** Where's my wedding gown?

**BROTHER**                    I'll bring it tomorrow.

**DAUGHTER**
Do, very rearly,° I must be abroad else°              110
To call the maids, and pay the minstrels,
For I must lose my maidenhead by cocklight:°
'Twill never thrive else.°

*(Sings.)*

O fair, O sweet,° &c.

**BROTHER**
You must e'en take it patiently.

**JAILER**                    'Tis true.            115

**DAUGHTER**
Good e'en, good men, pray did you ever hear
Of one young Palamon?

**JAILER**                    Yes, wench, we know him.

**DAUGHTER**
Is't not a fine young gentleman?

**JAILER**                    'Tis, love.

**BROTHER**
By no mean cross her, she is then distempered
Far worse than now she shows.

**FIRST FRIEND**                    Yes, he's a fine man.   120

**DAUGHTER**
O, is he so? You have a sister?

**FIRST FRIEND**                    Yes.

**DAUGHTER**
But she shall never have him, tell her so,
For a trick that I know.° Y' had best look to her,

---

51 **haste** the Wooer's haste in coming to tell the Jailer
62 **it** the place   73 **chaplets** wreaths   75 **antic** grotesque
dance, as in an antimasque   76 **his** Palamon's   80 **Willow,
willow, willow** Desdemona's song in *Othello*, IV.iii   82
**Palamon . . . man** a variant of the song "When Samson
was a tall young man," possibly referred to in *Love's Labor's
Lost*, I.ii.169   87 **Iris** goddess of the rainbow   90 **posies**
mottoes engraved on rings   91 **loose** may have the meaning
"lose," the two words being commonly spelled *loose*   94 **made
. . . her** forced my way through the rushes to her

96 **presently** at once   100 **cross** intercept   101 **stayed** stopped
107 **The Broom** a popular song quoted in W. Wager's play
*The Longer thou livest the more Fool thou art* (c. 1559) and elsewhere: "broom" here is the shrub of that name   108 **Bonny
Robin** a song preserved in Queen Elizabeth's Virginal Book
and in William Ballet's Lute Book: Ophelia sings a line of it in
*Hamlet*, IV.v, where, as here, it may imply a sexual meaning
for "Robin"   110 **rearly** early; **I . . . else** otherwise I shall be
away from home   112 **by cocklight** before dawn   113
**'Twill . . . else** otherwise things will never prosper with me
114 **O fair, O sweet** a song included among "Certaine Sonets"
in Sidney's 1598 Folio   123 **For . . . know** because of a
stratagem that I know

For if she see him once, she's gone, she's done,
And undone in an hour. All the young maids    125
Of our town are in love with him, but I laugh at 'em
And let 'em all alone.° Is't not a wise course?

FIRST FRIEND                      Yes.

DAUGHTER
There is at least two hundred now with child by him,
There must be four; yet I keep close° for all this,
Close as a cockle;° and all these must be boys—    130
He has the trick° on't—and at ten years old
They must be all gelt for musicians,
And sing the wars of Theseus.

SECOND FRIEND           This is strange.

DAUGHTER
As ever you heard, but say nothing.

FIRST FRIEND                No.

DAUGHTER
They come from all parts of the dukedom to him.    135
I'll warrant ye, he had not so few last night
As twenty to dispatch: he'll tickle't up°
In two hours, if his hand be in.°

JAILER                 She's lost
Past all cure.

BROTHER     Heaven forbid, man.

DAUGHTER
Come hither, you are a wise man.

FIRST FRIEND           Does she know him?   140

SECOND FRIEND
No, would she did.

DAUGHTER       You are master of a ship?°

JAILER
Yes.

DAUGHTER   Where's your compass?

JAILER                Here.

DAUGHTER            Set it to th' north.
And now direct your course to th' wood, where
    Palamon
Lies longing for me. For the tackling let me alone.
Come° weigh, my hearts, cheerly all! O, O, O, 'tis
    up!°                             145
The wind's fair: top the bowling!° Out with the
    mainsail!
Where's your whistle, master?

BROTHER          Let's get her in.

JAILER
Up to the top, boy!

BROTHER       Where's the pilot?

FIRST FRIEND                Here.

DAUGHTER
What ken'st° thou?

SECOND FRIEND   A fair wood.

DAUGHTER          Bear for° it, master! Tack about!

(*Sings.*)

When Cynthia with her borrowed light, &c.  *Exeunt.*   150

## Scene II. [*The palace of Theseus.*]

*Enter* EMILIA *alone, with two pictures.*

EMILIA
Yet I may bind those wounds up,° that must open
And bleed to death for my sake else: I'll choose,
And end their strife. Two such young handsome men
Shall never fall for me; their weeping mothers,
Following the dead cold ashes of their sons,    5
Shall never curse my cruelty. Good heaven,
What a sweet face has Arcite! If wise Nature
With all her best endowments, all those beauties
She sows into the births of noble bodies,
Were here a mortal woman, and had in her    10
The coy denials of young maids, yet doubtless
She would run mad for this man. What an eye,
Of what a fiery sparkle, and quick° sweetness,
Has this young prince! Here° Love himself sits smiling:
Just such another° wanton Ganymede    15
Set Jove a-fire with and enforced the god
Snatch up the goodly boy° and set him by him,
A shining constellation. What a brow
Of what a spacious majesty he carries—
Arched like the great-eyed Juno's, but far sweeter,    20
Smoother than Pelops' shoulder!° Fame and Honor
Methinks from hence,° as from a promontory
Pointed° in heaven, should clap their wings and sing
To all the under-world° the loves and fights
Of gods and such men near 'em.° Palamon    25
Is but his foil, to him a mere dull shadow:
He's swarth,° and meager, of an eye as heavy
As if he had lost his mother; a still temper,°
No stirring in him, no alacrity,
Of all this spritely sharpness not a smile.°    30
Yet these that we count errors may become him:
Narcissus° was a sad boy, but a heavenly.
O who can find the bent of woman's fancy?
I am a fool, my reason is lost in me,
I have no choice,° and I have lied so lewdly°    35
That women ought to beat me. On my knees
I ask thy pardon, Palamon: thou art alone,°
And only beautiful, and these the eyes,

---

**127 let . . . alone** pay no attention to them   **129 keep close** maintain secrecy   **130 Close as a cockle** the proverb occurs also in Shirley's *The School of Compliment* (1625): "cockle" here indicates "cockleshell," formerly used for the shells of mollusks generally   **131 trick** method   **137 tickle't up** i.e., finish the task (with a strong suggestion of sexual pleasure)   **138 if . . . in** if he is in good form   **141 master . . . ship** the Daughter has taken the Schoolmaster for a tinker, III.v.83, and the Brother for a tailor, IV.i.108; Palamon is always a soldier, and she completes the proverbial four occupations by taking her father for a sailor   **145 Come** lines 145–49 are hardly verse, and the 1634 quarto prints mainly as prose; but a faint sense of line breaks seems to lie behind the Daughter's staccato phrases; **'tis up** i.e., the tackling; the "O, O, O" indicates the Daughter's imaginary exertions   **146 top the bowling** slant the bowline (rope run from the middle of the perpendicular of the weather side of a sail to the larboard or starboard bow, for the purpose of keeping the sail steady in a wind)

**149 ken'st** see'st; **Bear for** sail toward
**IV.ii.1 bind . . . up** proleptic for "prevent those wounds from being given"   **13 quick** vital   **14 Here** i.e., in his eye   **15 another** i.e., another smile (or eye?)   **17 the goodly boy** Ganymede   **21 Pelops' shoulder** Pelops was son of Tantalus and father of Atreus: Marlowe, *Hero and Leander*, i.65, mentions his shoulder as a standard of whiteness   **22 from hence** i.e., from Arcite's brow   **23 Pointed** coming to its point   **24 the under-world** the earth   **25 such . . . 'em** demigods, etc.   **27 swarth** dark-complexioned   **28 still temper** placid disposition   **30 smile** trace (with an echo of Arcite's smiling mentioned in lines 14–15)   **32 Narcissus** cf. II.i.176–78   **35 choice** ability to choose; **lewdly** grossly   **37 alone** unique, supreme

These the bright lamps of beauty, that command
And threaten Love, and what young maid dare cross°
  'em?                                40
What a bold gravity, and yet inviting,
Has this brown manly face! O Love, this only
From this hour is complexion.° Lie there, Arcite,
Thou art a changeling° to him, a mere gipsy,
And this the noble body. I am sotted,°      45
Utterly lost, my virgin's faith has fled me!
For if my brother but even now had asked me
Whether° I loved, I had run mad for Arcite;
Now if my sister, more for Palamon.
Stand both together:° now come ask me, brother.  50
Alas, I know not. Ask me now, sweet sister.
I may go look.° What a mere child is Fancy,
That having two fair gawds° of equal sweetness
Cannot distinguish, but must cry for both!

*Enter [a]* GENTLEMAN.

How now, sir?
GENTLEMAN  From the noble duke your brother,  55
Madam, I bring you news: the knights are come.
EMILIA
To end the quarrel?
GENTLEMAN        Yes.
EMILIA                Would I might end first!
What sins have I committed, chaste Diana,°
That my unspotted youth must now be soiled
With blood of princes, and my chastity  60
Be made the altar where the lives of lovers,
Two greater and two better never yet
Made mothers joy, must be the sacrifice
To my unhappy beauty?

*Enter* THESEUS, HIPPOLYTA, PIRITHOUS, *and*
ATTENDANTS.

THESEUS             Bring 'em in
Quickly: by any means,° I long to see 'em.  65
Your two contending lovers are returned,
And with them their fair knights. Now, my fair sister,
You must love one of them.
EMILIA            I had rather both,
So° neither for my sake should fall untimely.

*Enter [a]* MESSENGER.

THESEUS
Who saw 'em?
PIRITHOUS    I a while.°
GENTLEMAN        And I.  70
THESEUS
From whence come you, sir?
MESSENGER        From the knights.
THESEUS              Pray speak,
You that have seen them, what they are.
MESSENGER          I will, sir,

And truly what I think. Six braver spirits
Than these they have brought, if we judge by the
  outside,
I never saw nor read of. He that stands  75
In the first place with Arcite, by his seeming
Should be a stout° man, by his face a prince.
His very looks so say him: his complexion
Nearer a brown than black; stern, and yet noble,
Which shows him hardy, fearless, proud of dangers;  80
The circles of his eyes show fire within him,
And as a heated° lion so he looks;
His hair hangs long behind him, black and shining
Like ravens' wings; his shoulders broad and strong,
Armed long and round,° and on his thigh a sword  85
Hung by a curious baldric,° when he frowns
To seal his will with:° better o' my conscience
Was never soldier's friend.°
THESEUS
Thou hast well described him.
PIRITHOUS          Yet a great deal short,
Methinks, of him that's first with Palamon.  90
THESEUS
Pray speak him, friend.
PIRITHOUS        I guess he is a prince too,
And if it may be, greater;° for his show°
Has all the ornament of honor in't.
He's somewhat bigger than the knight he° spoke of,
But of a face far sweeter. His complexion  95
Is, as a ripe grape, ruddy. He has felt
Without doubt what he fights for,° and so apter
To make this cause his own. In's face appears
All the fair hopes of what he undertakes,°
And when he's angry, then a settled° valor,  100
Not tainted with extremes, runs through his body
And guides his arm to brave things. Fear he cannot,
He shows no such soft temper. His head's yellow,
Hard-haired, and curled, thick twined like ivy tods,°
Not to undo° with thunder. In his face  105
The livery of the warlike maid° appears,
Pure red and white, for yet no beard has blest him;
And in his rolling eyes sits Victory,
As if she ever meant to court his valor.°
His nose stands high, a character° of honor;  110
His red lips, after fights,° are fit for ladies.
EMILIA
Must these men die too?
PIRITHOUS         When he speaks, his tongue
Sounds like a trumpet. All his lineaments
Are as a man would wish 'em, strong and clean.
He wears a well-steeled ax, the staff of gold.  115
His age some five and twenty.

---

**77 stout** bold, strong  **82 heated** enraged (with perhaps a suggestion of "in heat")  **85 Armed . . . round** with long, round arms  **86 baldric** belt  **86–87 when . . . with** to effect his desire with when he is angry  **87–88 better . . . friend** no soldier has had a better, more trustworthy sword  **92 greater** i.e., more than a prince; **show** appearance  **94 he** the Messenger  **97 what . . . for** i.e., love  **98–99 In's . . . undertakes** he shows great hope of success  **100 settled** steady  **104 ivy tods** ivy bushes  **105 Not to undo** not to be undone, not disheveled  **106 the warlike maid** the goddess of war, Bellona  **109 court his valor** if "court" is right—see A Note on the Text—the image is strained: the look in his eyes seems in love with his own valor  **110 character** token  **111 after fights** when fighting is over

---

**40 cross** gainsay  **42–43 this only . . . complexion** i.e., only this complexion is acceptable  **44 changeling** child left by the fairies in place of another  **45 sotted** reduced to stupidity  **48 Whether** which of the two  **50 Stand both together** she puts the two pictures side by side  **52 I . . . look** i.e., I may go seek (for I do not yet know)  **53 gawds** toys, trifles  **58 Diana** appropriately invoked by Emilia, as in V.i, as Diana was the patron of Amazons  **65 by any means** indeed  **69 So** provided that  **70 a while** briefly

MESSENGER                              There's another,
A little man, but of a tough soul, seeming
As great as any: fairer promises
In such a body yet I never looked on.

PIRITHOUS
O, he that's freckle-faced?

MESSENGER                         The same, my lord.           120
Are they° not sweet ones?

PIRITHOUS                    Yes, they are well.

MESSENGER                                    Methinks,
Being so few and well disposed,° they show
Great and fine art in nature. He's white-haired,°
Not wanton white, but such a manly color
Next to an auburn;° tough, and nimble set,          125
Which shows an active soul. His arms are brawny,
Lined with strong sinews: to the shoulder-piece
Gently they swell, like women new-conceived,°
Which speaks him prone to labor,° never fainting
Under the weight of arms; stout-hearted, still,°     130
But when he stirs, a tiger. He's gray-eyed,
Which yields compassion where he conquers;° sharp
To spy advantages, and where he finds 'em
He's swift to make 'em his. He does no wrongs,
Nor takes none.° He's round-faced, and when he
    smiles                                          135
He shows° a lover, when he frowns a soldier.
About his head he wears the winner's oak,°
And in it stuck the favor of his lady.
His age some six and thirty. In his hand
He bears a charging staff,° embossed with silver.   140

THESEUS
Are they all thus?

PIRITHOUS          They are all the sons of Honor.

THESEUS
Now as I have a soul I long to see 'em!
Lady, you shall see men fight now.°

HIPPOLYTA                              I wish it,
But not the cause, my lord. They would show
Bravely about the titles of two kingdoms;°          145
'Tis pity Love should be so tyrannous.
O my soft-hearted sister, what think you?
Weep not till they weep blood. Wench, it must be.

THESEUS
You have steeled 'em with your beauty. Honored
    friend,
To you I give the field:° pray order it             150
Fitting the persons that must use it.

PIRITHOUS                              Yes, sir.

THESEUS
Come, I'll go visit 'em: I cannot stay,°

---

Their fame has fired me so. Till they appear,
Good friend, be royal.°

PIRITHOUS          There shall want no bravery.°

EMILIA
Poor wench, go weep, for whosoever wins            155
Loses a noble cousin, for thy sins.       *Exeunt.*

## Scene III. [*The prison.*]

*Enter* JAILER, WOOER, DOCTOR.

DOCTOR  Her distraction is more at some time of the
moon than at other some, is it not?

JAILER  She is continually in a harmless distemper,
sleeps little, altogether without appetite, save often
drinking, dreaming of another world, and a better;   5
and what broken° piece of matter soe'er she's about,
the name Palamon lards it,° that she farces° ev'ry
business withal, fits it to every question.

*Enter* DAUGHTER.

Look where she comes, you shall perceive her behavior.

DAUGHTER  I have forgot it quite. The burden° on't  10
was "Down-a down-a," and penned by no worse man
than Geraldo, Emilia's schoolmaster.° He's as fantas-
tical° too, as ever he may go upon's legs,° for in the
next world will Dido see Palamon, and then will she
be out of love with Aeneas.°                         15

DOCTOR  What stuff's here? Poor soul!

JAILER  E'en thus all day long.

DAUGHTER  Now for this charm that I told you of,
you must bring a piece of silver on the tip of your
tongue, or no ferry.° Then if it be your chance to come  20
where the blessed spirits—as there's a sight now°—we
maids that have our livers perished,° cracked to pieces
with love, we shall come there, and do nothing all day
long but pick flowers with Proserpine.° Then will I
make Palamon a nosegay, then let him mark me°—    25
then!

DOCTOR  How prettily she's amiss! Note her a little
further.

DAUGHTER  'Faith, I'll tell you, sometime we go to
barley-break,° we of the blessed. Alas, 'tis a sore life  30
they have i' th' other place, such burning, frying,
boiling, hissing, howling, chatt'ring, cursing—O they
have shrewd measure;° take heed! If one be mad, or
hang or drown themselves, thither they go, Jupiter

---

154 **be royal** make the arrangements with magnificence;
**bravery** splendor
**IV.iii.6 broken** disconnected   **7 lards it** fills it (is rubbed into
it like lard); **farces** stuffs   **10 burden** refrain   **12 Emilia's
schoolmaster** the Daughter is of course mistaken   **12–13
fantastical** fanciful   **13 as . . . legs** as he could possibly be
**13–15 for . . . Aeneas** she imagines that the Schoolmaster has
taught her a song about Dido after death loving Palamon, now
dead too, instead of Aeneas   **20 no ferry** Charon, the ferryman of the underworld, will not take you across the Styx   **21
as . . . now** as I can see them now ("as" may be merely
exclamatory, and possibly "sight" here means "great number")
**22 perished** shriveled up (the liver was believed to be the seat
of the affections)   **24 pick . . . Proserpine** Proserpine was
picking flowers when Pluto carried her off to be queen of the
underworld   **25 mark me** pay attention to me   **30 barley-
break** a game played by six persons in couples, in which
one couple occupies a marked space called "hell"   **33
shrewd measure** harsh punishment

---

121 **they** the freckles   122 **disposed** arranged   123 **white-
haired** blond   125 **auburn** yellowish white   128 **new-
conceived** recently made pregnant   129 **labor** toil (but continuing the image of "new-conceived")   130 **still** quiet   131–
32 **gray-eyed . . . conquers** apparently gray eyes were considered a sign of mercy   134–35 **He . . . none** He neither
inflicts nor submits to an unfair attack   136 **shows** appears
137 **winner's oak** wreath of oak leaves bestowed for valor
140 **charging staff** spear used in charging an enemy   143
**you . . . now** (Hippolyta, as an Amazon, would have a
prejudice in favor of women as fighters; Theseus assures her she
will now see fighting on a higher level than she has known)
144–45 **would . . . kingdoms** would be good to watch if they
were fighting to win each other's kingdoms   150 **give the
field** assign the task of arranging the tournament   152 **stay** wait

bless us, and there shall we be put in a cauldron of lead 35
and usurers' grease,° amongst a whole million of cutpurses, and there boil like a gammon of bacon that will
never be enough.°                                          *Exit.*

DOCTOR   How her brain coins!°

[*Enter* DAUGHTER.]

DAUGHTER   Lords and courtiers, that have got maids 40
with child, they are in this place, they shall stand in
fire up to the navel, and in ice up to th' heart, and there
th' offending part burns, and the deceiving part
freezes: in troth a very grievous punishment, as one
would think, for such a trifle. Believe me, one would 45
marry a leprous witch to be rid on't, I'll assure you.

DOCTOR   How she continues this fancy! 'Tis not an
engraffed° madness, but a most thick and profound
melancholy.°

DAUGHTER   To hear there a proud lady, and a proud 50
city wife, howl together! I were a beast and° I'd call
it good sport. One cries "O this smoke!," another
"This fire!" One cries "O that ever I did it behind the
arras!" and then howls; th' other curses a suing fellow°
and her garden house.°                                     55

(*Sings.*)

I will be true, my stars, my fate, &c.
                                  *Exit* DAUGHTER.

JAILER   What think you of her, sir?

DOCTOR   I think she has a perturbed mind, which I
cannot minister to.

JAILER   Alas, what then?                                  60

DOCTOR   Understand you she ever affected any man
ere she beheld Palamon?

JAILER   I was once, sir, in great hope she had fixed her
liking on this gentleman my friend.

WOOER   I did think so too, and would account I had a 65
great penn'orth° on't, to give half my 'state° that both
she and I at this present stood unfeignedly on the same
terms.

DOCTOR   That intemperate surfeit of her eye° hath distempered the other senses: they may return and settle 70
again to execute their preordained faculties, but they
are now in a most extravagant vagary. This you must
do: confine her to a place where the light may rather
seem to steal in than be permitted; take upon you,
young sir her friend, the name of Palamon; say you 75
come to eat with her, and to commune of love. This
will catch her attention, for this her mind beats upon:°
other objects that are inserted 'tween her mind and eye
becoming the pranks and friskins° of her madness. Sing
to her such green° songs of love as she says Palamon 80
hath sung in prison. Come to her, stuck in° as sweet
flowers as the season is mistress of, and thereto make an
addition of some other compounded° odors, which are

grateful° to the sense. All this shall become° Palamon,
for Palamon can sing, and Palamon is sweet and ev'ry 85
good thing. Desire to eat with her, carve her,° drink to
her, and, still among,° intermingle your petition of
grace and acceptance into her favor. Learn what maids
have been her companions and play-feres,° and let
them repair to her with "Palamon" in their mouths, 90
and appear with tokens, as if they suggested° for him.
It is a falsehood she is in, which is with falsehoods to be
combated. This may bring her to eat, to sleep, and
reduce° what's now out of square° in her into their
former law and regiment.° I have seen it approved,° 95
how many times I know not, but to make the number
more I have great hope in this. I will between the
passages° of this project come in with my appliance.°
Let us put it in execution and hasten the success,°
which doubt not will bring forth comfort.   *Exeunt.* 100

# ACT V

Scene I. [*Before the altars of Mars, Venus, and Diana.*]

*Flourish. Enter* THESEUS, PIRITHOUS, HIPPOLYTA,
ATTENDANTS.

THESEUS
Now let 'em enter, and before the gods
Tender their holy prayers. Let the temples
Burn bright with sacred fires, and the altars
In hallowed clouds commend their swelling incense°
To those above us. Let no due be wanting:              5
They have a noble work in hand, will honor°
The very powers that love 'em.

*Flourish of cornets. Enter* PALAMON *and* ARCITE *and
their* KNIGHTS.

PIRITHOUS                          Sir, they enter.
THESEUS
You valiant and strong-hearted enemies,
You royal german-foes,° that this day come
To blow that nearness° out that flames between ye,    10
Lay by your anger for an hour, and dovelike
Before the holy altars of your helpers,
The all-feared gods, bow down your stubborn bodies.
Your ire is more than mortal: so your help be;
And as the gods regard ye,° fight with justice.       15
I'll leave you to your prayers, and betwixt ye
I part° my wishes.
PIRITHOUS              Honor crown the worthiest!
                          *Exit* THESEUS *and his* TRAIN.

---

36 **usurers' grease** fat sweated by usurers   38 **enough** done,
cooked   39 **coins** spins fancies   48 **engraffed** implanted,
firmly planted   48–49 **thick . . . melancholy** morbid condition known as "melancholy," to be distinguished from the
normal "melancholy" humor   51 **and** if   54 **suing fellow**
persistent wooer   55 **garden house** notoriously used for
assignations   66 **penn'orth** bargain; **'state** property   69
**intemperate . . . eye** i.e., by seeing Palamon   77 **beats
upon** is preoccupied with   79 **friskins** vagaries   80 **green**
youthful   81 **stuck in** adorned with   83 **compounded** mixed
84 **grateful** pleasing; **become** be suitable for   86 **carve
her** carve for her   87 **still among** ever betweenwhiles
89 **play-feres** playfellows   91 **suggested** interceded   94
**reduce** bring back; **out of square** irregular   95 **regiment**
government, order; **approved** confirmed   98 **passages** separate stages; **appliance** device, stratagem (presumably his
device of making the disguised Wooer sleep with her)   99
**success** result
V.i.4 **swelling incense** incense that swells into clouds   6 **will
honor** i.e., which will honor   9 **german-foes** foes who are of
the same family   10 **nearness** kinship and friendship (editors
have suggested "furnace" and "fierceness" as emendations)
15 **as . . . ye** i.e., as they are just to you   17 **part** divide

PALAMON

The glass° is running now that cannot finish
Till one of us expire. Think you but thus,
That were there aught in me which strove to show°          20
Mine enemy in this business, were't one eye
Against another, arm oppressed by arm,°
I would destroy th' offender, coz, I would
Though parcel° of myself. Then from this gather
How I should tender° you.

ARCITE                          I am in labor°          25
To push your name, your ancient love, our kindred
Out of my memory, and i' th' selfsame place
To seat something I would confound.° So hoist we°
The sails that must these vessels° port° even where
The heavenly limiter° pleases.

PALAMON                          You speak well.          30
Before I turn,° let me embrace thee, cousin.

[They embrace.]

This I shall never do again.

ARCITE                          One farewell.

PALAMON

Why, let it be so: farewell, coz.

                    Exeunt PALAMON and his KNIGHTS.

ARCITE                          Farewell, sir.
Knights, kinsmen, lovers, yea my sacrifices,
True worshippers of Mars—whose spirit in you          35
Expels the seeds of fear, and th' apprehension,
Which still is farther off it°—go with me
Before the god of our profession. There
Require of him the hearts of lions, and
The breath of tigers, yea the fierceness too,          40
Yea the speed also—to go on,° I mean,
Else wish we to be snails. You know my prize
Must be dragged out of blood, force and great feat
Must put my garland on, where she sticks
The queen of flowers:° our intercession then          45
Must be to him that makes the camp a cistern
Brimmed with the blood of men. Give me your aid
And bend your spirits towards him.

They [prostrate themselves and then] kneel [before Mars'
altar].

Thou mighty one, that with thy power hast turned
Green Neptune° into purple, [whose approach]          50
Comets prewarn,° whose havoc in vast field
Unearthèd skulls proclaim, whose breath blows down
The teeming Ceres' foison,° who dost pluck
With hand armipotent from forth blue clouds°
The masoned turrets, that both mak'st and break'st          55
The stony girths° of cities! Me thy pupil,
Youngest follower of thy drum, instruct this day
With military skill, that to thy laud
I may advance my streamer,° and by thee
Be styled the lord o' th' day! Give me, great Mars,          60
Some token of thy pleasure.

Here they fall on their faces as formerly,° and there is heard
clanging of armor, with a short thunder as the burst of a
battle, whereupon they all rise and bow to the altar.

O great corrector of enormous° times,
Shaker of o'er-rank° states, thou grand decider
Of dusty and old titles, that heal'st with blood
The earth when it is sick, and cur'st the world          65
O' th' plurisy° of people! I do take
Thy signs auspiciously and, in thy name,
To my design° march boldly. Let us go.          Exeunt.

Enter PALAMON and his KNIGHTS, with the former
observance.°

PALAMON

Our stars must glister with new fire, or be
Today extinct. Our argument is love,          70
Which if the goddess of it grant, she gives
Victory too: then blend your spirits with mine,
You whose free nobleness do make my cause
Your personal hazard; to the goddess Venus
Commend we our proceeding, and implore          75
Her power unto our party.

Here they kneel as formerly° [to Venus' altar].

Hail, sovereign queen of secrets, who hast power
To call the fiercest tyrant from his rage
And weep unto a girl;° that hast the might
Even with an eye-glance to choke Mars' drum          80
And turn th' alarm to whispers; that canst make
A cripple flourish with° his crutch, and cure him
Before Apollo;° that mayst force the king
To be his subject's vassal, and induce
Stale Gravity to dance: the pollèd° bachelor          85
Whose youth like wanton boys through bonfires
Have° skipped thy flame, at seventy thou canst catch
And make him, to the scorn of his hoarse throat,°
Abuse° young lays of love; what godlike power
Hast thou not power upon? To Phoebus° thou          90
Add'st flames, hotter than his; the heavenly fires
Did scorch his mortal son,° thine him;° the huntress,°

81 glass hourglass   20 show i.e., show itself   22 arm oppressed
by arm if one of my arms were tyrannized over by the other
24 parcel part   25 tender treat (with an ironical suggestion of
the adjectival sense); in labor endeavoring (as a woman in
childbed endeavors to give birth)   28 confound destroy;
hoist we let us hoist   29 these vessels our fortunes and persons; port bring to port   30 limiter the god who sets limits
to things   31 turn turn away   37 farther off it the idea of
fear is farther from fear itself than its "seeds," or first beginnings, are   41 go on advance   44-45 where . . . flowers
where Emilia places her favor (the queen of flowers because it
is hers)   50 Green Neptune i.e., the sea (as the Note on the
Text explains, the bracketed words at the end of this line are
not in the quarto, but some such words seem necessary)   51
prewarn give warning of   53 teeming Ceres' foison the
harvest (Ceres was goddess of the harvest)

54 from . . . clouds from their height in the sky   56 stony
girths walls   59 streamer banner, pennon   61 s.d. as
formerly (suggesting they had done so at line 48)   62
enormous monstrous, degenerate   63 o'er-rank overripe
66 plurisy plethora   68 design goal   68 s.d. former observance the prostration and kneeling used by Arcite and his
Knights, but paid now to Venus's altar, at line 76   76 s.d. as
formerly again referring to Arcite and his Knights   79 weep
. . . girl i.e., make him weep like a girl   82 flourish with
brandish   83 Before Apollo sooner than Apollo (the god of
healing)   85 pollèd bald   87 Have plural through the influence
of "boys"   88 to . . . throat so that his hoarseness is mocked
89 Abuse employ in a ludicrous fashion   90 Phoebus as sun
god   92 his mortal son Phaëthon, who was destroyed when
Phoebus allowed him to drive the sun chariot; thine him
Phoebus was made to feel the heat of love; huntress Diana,
who loved Endymion

All moist and cold, some say began to throw
Her bow away, and sigh. Take to thy grace
Me thy vowed soldier, who do bear thy yoke                95
As 'twere a wreath of roses, yet is heavier
Than lead itself, stings more than nettles.
I have never been foul-mouthed against thy law,
Ne'er revealed secret, for I knew none; would not,
Had I kenned all that were;° I never practiced°         100
Upon man's wife, nor would the libels read
Of liberal wits;° I never at great feasts
Sought to betray a beauty,° but have blushed
At simp'ring sirs that did. I have been harsh
To large confessors,° and have hotly asked them         105
If they had mothers: I had one, a woman,
And women 'twere they wronged. I knew a man
Of eighty winters, this I told them, who
A lass of fourteen brided. 'Twas thy power
To put life into dust: the agèd cramp                   110
Had screwed his square foot round,°
The gout had knit his fingers into knots,
Torturing convulsions from his globy eyes
Had almost drawn their spheres,° that what was life
In him seemed torture. This anatomy°                    115
Had by his young fair fere° a boy, and I
Believed it was his, for she swore it was,
And who would not believe her? Brief,° I am
To those that prate and have done no companion;
To those that boast and have not a defier;              120
To those that would and cannot a rejoicer.
Yea, him I do not love, that tells close offices°
The foulest way, nor names concealments° in
The boldest language. Such a one I am,
And vow that lover never yet made sigh                  125
Truer than I. O then, most soft sweet goddess,
Give me the victory of this question, which
Is true love's merit,° and bless me with a sign
Of thy great pleasure.

*Here music is heard, doves° are seen to flutter; they fall
again upon their faces, then on their knees.*

O thou that from eleven to ninety reign'st              130
In mortal bosoms, whose chase° is this world
And we in herds thy game,° I give thee thanks
For this fair token, which being laid unto
Mine innocent true heart, arms in assurance
My body to this business. Let us rise                   135
And bow before the goddess. *They bow.* Time comes
on.                                             *Exeunt.*

*Still° music of records.° Enter* EMILIA *in white, her hair*

*about her shoulders, a wheaten wreath;° one in white
holding up her train, her hair stuck° with flowers; one before
her carrying a silver hind,° in which is conveyed incense and
sweet odors, which being set upon the altar [of Diana], her*
MAIDS *standing aloof, she sets fire to it; then they curtsy
and kneel.*

EMILIA

O sacred, shadowy, cold and constant queen,
Abandoner of revels, mute contemplative,
Sweet, solitary, white as chaste, and pure
As wind-fanned snow, who to thy female knights          140
Allow'st no more blood than will make a blush,
Which is their order's robe! I here thy priest
Am humbled 'fore thine altar. O vouchsafe
With that thy rare green eye, which never yet
Beheld thing maculate, look on thy virgin;              145
And sacred silver mistress, lend thine ear—
Which ne'er heard scurrile term, into whose port°
Ne'er entered wanton sound—to my petition
Seasoned with holy fear. This is my last
Of vestal office: I am bride-habited,                   150
But maiden-hearted; a husband I have 'pointed,°
But do not know him; out of two I should
Choose one, and pray for his success, but I
Am guiltless of election.° Of mine eyes
Were I to lose one, they are equal precious,            155
I could doom neither: that which perished should
Go to't unsentenced. Therefore, most modest queen,
He of the two pretenders° that best loves me
And has the truest title° in't, let him
Take off my wheaten garland, or else grant              160
The file and quality° I hold I may
Continue° in thy band.

*Here the hind vanishes under the altar, and in the place
ascends a rose tree, having one rose upon it.*

See what our general of ebbs and flows°
Out from the bowels of her holy altar
With sacred act advances: but one rose.                 165
If well inspired,° this battle shall confound°
Both these brave knights, and I a virgin flow'r
Must grow alone, unplucked.

*Here is heard a sudden twang of instruments, and the rose
falls from the tree.*

The flow'r is fall'n, the tree descends. O mistress,
Thou here dischargest me, I shall be gathered.          170
I think so, but I know not thine own will:
Unclasp thy mystery.
I hope she's pleased, her signs were gracious.
                                *They curtsy and exeunt.*

---

100 **all that were** all secrets in existence; **practiced** entered into
designs    101–02 **libels . . . wits** read the abusive writings of
licentious wits    103 **betray a beauty** i.e., reveal her frailty    105
**large confessors** those who boasted much of their love conquests
111 **screwed . . . round** the play on "square" and "round"
makes the image more grotesque    113–14 **globy . . . spheres**
"globy" suggests "swollen," and here "spheres" must be the
eyes themselves, drawn from their sockets; but there is a suggestion of the spheres of the Ptolemaic universe being distorted
through pain    115 **anatomy** skeleton    116 **fere** mate    118
**Brief** in brief    122 **close offices** secret actions    123 **concealments** things that should be concealed    128 **merit** reward
129 s.d. **doves** birds sacred to Venus    131 **chase** place of
hunting    132 **in . . . game** cf. the similar image at I.iv.5
136 s.d. **Still** soft; **records** recorders

136 s.d. **her hair . . . wreath** cf. I.i.s.d.; **stuck** adorned; **hind**
female red deer, emblem of virginity, sacred to Diana    147
**port** portal    151 **'pointed** had appointed for me    154 **Am
. . . election** have made no choice (with the suggestion that
she would betray Diana if she made a choice)    158 **pretenders**
claimants    159 **truest title** best claim    161 **file and quality**
station and character    162 **Continue** continue to have    163
**general . . . flows** Diana as goddess of the moon    166 **well
inspired** prompted by the goddess; **confound** destroy

Scene II. [*The prison.*]

*Enter* DOCTOR, JAILER, *and* WOOER (*in habit of Pala-mon*).

DOCTOR
Has this advice I told you done any good upon her?

WOOER
O very much. The maids that kept her company
Have half-persuaded her that I am Palamon.
Within this half-hour she came smiling to me,
And asked me what I would eat, and when I would kiss
    her.                                                        5
I told her presently,° and kissed her twice.

DOCTOR
'Twas well done. Twenty times had been far better,
For there the cure lies mainly.

WOOER                                        Then she told me
She would watch° with me tonight, for well she knew
What hour my fit would take me.

DOCTOR                                        Let her do so,      10
And when your fit comes, fit her home,° and presently.

WOOER
She would have me sing.

DOCTOR
You did so?

WOOER                No.

DOCTOR                        'Twas very ill done, then:
You should observe° her ev'ry way.

WOOER                                                Alas,
I have no voice, sir, to confirm° her that way.               15

DOCTOR
That's all one,° if ye make a noise.
If she entreat again, do anything:
Lie with her if she ask you.

JAILER                                Ho° there, doctor!

DOCTOR
Yes, in the way of cure.

JAILER                        But first, by your leave,
I' th' way of honesty.°

DOCTOR                        That's but a niceness:°         20
Ne'er cast your child away for honesty;
Cure her first this way, then if she will be honest,
She has the path before her.°

JAILER                                Thank ye, doctor.

DOCTOR
Pray bring her in and let's see how she is.

JAILER
I will, and tell her her Palamon stays for her.              25
But, doctor, methinks you are i' th' wrong still.
                                        *Exit* JAILER.
                                        Go, go.

DOCTOR
You fathers are fine fools! Her honesty?
And° we should give her physic till we find that—

WOOER
Why, do you think she is not honest, sir?

DOCTOR
How old is she?

WOOER                She's eighteen.

DOCTOR                                She may be,            30
But that's all one, 'tis nothing to our purpose.
Whate'er her father says, if you perceive
Her mood inclining that way that I spoke of,
Videlicet,° the way of flesh—you have me?°

WOOER
Yet very well, sir.

DOCTOR                Please her appetite                    35
And do it home:° it cures her° ipso facto°
The melancholy humor that infects her.

WOOER
I am of your mind, doctor.

*Enter* JAILER, DAUGHTER, MAID.

DOCTOR
You'll find it so. She comes: pray humor her.

JAILER
Come, your love Palamon stays° for you, child,              40
And has done this long hour, to visit you.

DAUGHTER
I thank him for his gentle patience.
He's a kind gentleman, and I am much bound to him.
Did you ne'er see the horse he gave me?

JAILER                                                Yes.

DAUGHTER
How do you like him?

JAILER                        He's a very fair° one.         45

DAUGHTER
You never saw him dance?

JAILER                                No.

DAUGHTER                                I have often.
He dances very finely, very comely,
And for a jig°—come cut and long tail to him°—
He turns ye like a top.

JAILER                        That's fine indeed.

DAUGHTER
He'll dance the morris twenty mile an hour,                  50
And that will founder the best hobby-horse,
If I have any skill,° in all the parish;
And gallops to the tune of "Light o' Love."°
What think you of this horse?

JAILER                                Having these virtues,
I think he might be brought to play at tennis.              55

DAUGHTER
Alas, that's nothing.

JAILER                        Can he write and read too?

DAUGHTER
A very fair hand, and casts° himself th' accounts
Of all his hay and provender: that ostler
Must rise betime that cozens him. You know
The chestnut mare the duke has?

JAILER                                Very well.            60

**V.ii.6 presently** at once  **9 watch** stay awake  **11 fit her home** give her the right treatment (lie with her)  **14 observe** humor  **15 confirm** convince  **16 That's all one** that is a matter of indifference  **18 Ho** hold, stop  **20 honesty** chastity (i.e., in marriage; **niceness** overscrupulousness  **23 has . . . her** i.e., can marry afterward  **28 And** if

**34 Videlicet** namely; **have me** understand me  **36 do it home** do it thoroughly; **her** an "ethic" dative; **ipso facto** in itself, through its own power  **40 stays** waits  **45 fair** fine  **48 jig** a boisterous dance, often accompanied by song and used after a play; **come . . . him** i.e., whatever the competition ("cut and long tail," derived from the practice of docking horses' and dogs' tails, means "all kinds," "everybody")  **52 have any skill** know anything about it  **53 Light o' Love** a well-known song, referred to in *The Two Gentlemen of Verona*, I.ii.83  **57 casts** makes up

DAUGHTER
She is horribly in love with him, poor beast,
But he is like his master, coy and scornful.
JAILER
What dowry has she?
DAUGHTER                Some two hundred bottles,°
And twenty strike° of oats; but he'll ne'er have her.
He lisps in's neighing able to entice                65
A miller's mare:° he'll be the death of her.°
DOCTOR
What stuff she utters!
JAILER
Make curtsy, here your love comes.
WOOER                [Comes forward.] Pretty soul,
How do ye? That's a fine maid! There's a curtsy!
DAUGHTER
Yours to command i' th' way of honesty.                70
How far is't now to th' end o' th' world, my masters?
DOCTOR
Why, a day's journey, wench.
DAUGHTER        [To WOOER.] Will you go with me?
WOOER
What shall we do there, wench?
DAUGHTER                Why, play at stool-ball.°
What is there else to do?
WOOER                I am content,
If we shall keep our wedding there.
DAUGHTER                'Tis true,                75
For there, I will assure you, we shall find
Some blind° priest for the purpose, that will venture
To marry us, for here they are nice° and foolish.
Besides, my father must be hanged tomorrow,
And that would be a blot i' th' business.                80
Are not you Palamon?
WOOER                Do not you know me?
DAUGHTER
Yes, but you care not for me. I have nothing
But this poor petticoat and two coarse smocks.°
WOOER
That's all one, I will have you.
DAUGHTER                Will you surely?
WOOER
Yes, by this fair hand will I. [Takes her hand.]
DAUGHTER                We'll to bed, then.                85
WOOER
E'en when you will. [Kisses her.]
DAUGHTER                O sir, you would fain be nibbling.
WOOER
Why do you rub my kiss off?
DAUGHTER                'Tis a sweet one,
And will perfume me finely against the wedding.
Is not this your cousin Arcite?
DOCTOR                Yes, sweetheart,

And I am glad my cousin Palamon                90
Has made so fair a choice.
DAUGHTER                Do you think he'll have me?
DOCTOR
Yes, without doubt.
DAUGHTER                Do you think so too?
JAILER                Yes.
DAUGHTER
We shall have many children. [To the DOCTOR.]
     Lord, how y' are grown!°
My Palamon I hope will grow, too, finely
Now he's at liberty. Alas, poor chicken,°                95
He was kept down with hard meat° and ill lodging,
But I'll kiss him up again.°

Enter a MESSENGER.

MESSENGER
What do you here? You'll lose the noblest sight
That e'er was seen.
JAILER                Are they i' th' field?
MESSENGER                They are.
You bear a charge° there, too.
JAILER                I'll away straight.                100
I must e'en leave you here.
DOCTOR                Nay, we'll go with you:
I will not lose the fight.°
JAILER                How did you like her?°
DOCTOR
I'll warrant you within these three or four days
I'll make her right again. [To WOOER.] You must not
     from her,
But still preserve her in this way.
WOOER                I will.                105
DOCTOR
Let's get her in.
WOOER                Come, sweet, we'll go to dinner,
And then we'll play at cards.
DAUGHTER                And shall we kiss too?
WOOER
A hundred times.
DAUGHTER                And twenty?
WOOER                Aye, and twenty.
DAUGHTER
And then we'll sleep together?
DOCTOR                Take her offer.
WOOER
Yes, marry will we.
DAUGHTER                But you shall not hurt me.                110
WOOER
I will not, sweet.
DAUGHTER                If you do, love, I'll cry.        Exeunt.

Scene III. [Near the place of the tournament.]

Flourish. Enter THESEUS, HIPPOLYTA, EMILIA,
PIRITHOUS, and some ATTENDANTS.

---

63 **bottles** bundles    64 **strike** measure usually equivalent to
the bushel    66 **miller's mare** a mare used for turning a mill
wheel would be the least likely to behave wantonly; **he'll . . .
her** this passage on a wonderful horse, lines 44–66, looks back
to the famous horse of John Banks, whose tricks and apparent
intelligence are frequently referred to in Elizabethan literature;
it performed at least between 1588 and 1600, and was remembered    73 **stool-ball** ball game played most often by women,
and requiring a stool or stools    77 **blind** so that he should not
recognize them    78 **nice** overscrupulous    83 **smocks** under-
garments, shifts

93 **how . . . grown** she noted that Arcite was shorter
than Palamon at II.i.52–53    95 **chicken** child    96 **hard meat**
coarse food    97 **kiss . . . again** make him grow with kissing
(with a phallic suggestion)    100 **bear a charge** have a duty
102 **fight** the emendation "sight" has been suggested and may
be right: cf. line 98 and V.iii.1; **How . . . her** What did
you think of her condition?

EMILIA
I'll no step further.

PIRITHOUS                    Will you lose this sight?

EMILIA
I had rather see a wren hawk at a fly
Than this decision: ev'ry blow that falls
Threats a brave life, each stroke laments the place
Whereon it falls, and sounds more like a bell°          5
Than blade. I will stay here. It is enough
My hearing shall be punishèd with what
Shall happen, 'gainst the which there is
No deafing°—but to hear, not taint mine eye
With dread sights it may shun.

PIRITHOUS                    Sir, my good lord,          10
Your sister will no further.

THESEUS                    O she must.
She shall see deeds of honor in their kind,°
Which sometime show well, penciled.° Nature now
Shall make and act the story, the belief
Both sealed with eye and ear.° [*To* EMILIA.] You
    must be present.                                     15
You are the victor's meed,° the price,° and garland
To crown the question's title.°

EMILIA                    Pardon me.
If I were there, I'd wink.°

THESEUS                    You must be there:
This trial is as 'twere i' th' night, and you
The only star to shine.

EMILIA                    I am extinct.°                 20
There is but envy° in that light which shows
The one the other: Darkness, which ever was
The dam° of Horror, who does stand accursed
Of many mortal millions, may even now,
By casting her black mantle over both,                   25
That° neither could find other, get herself
Some part of a good name,° and many a murder
Set off° whereto she's guilty.

HIPPOLYTA                    You must go.

EMILIA
In faith, I will not.

THESEUS                    Why, the knights must kindle
Their valor at your eye. Know of this war                30
You are the treasure, and must needs be by
To give the service pay.°

EMILIA                    Sir, pardon me,
The title of a kingdom may be tried
Out of itself.°

THESEUS                    Well, well, then, at your pleasure.
Those that remain with you could wish their office      35
To any of their enemies.

HIPPOLYTA                    Farewell, sister.
I am like to know your husband 'fore yourself

By some small start of time. He whom the gods
Do of the two know best,° I pray them he
Be made your lot.                                        40

*Exeunt* THESEUS, HIPPOLYTA, PIRITHOUS, &c.

EMILIA
Arcite is gently visaged; yet his eye
Is like an engine° bent, or a sharp weapon
In a soft sheath: mercy and manly courage
Are bedfellows in his visage. Palamon
Has a most menacing aspect,° his brow                    45
Is graved,° and seems to bury what it frowns on;
Yet sometime 'tis not so, but alters to
The quality of his thoughts:° long time his eye
Will dwell upon his object; melancholy
Becomes him nobly. So does Arcite's mirth,               50
But Palamon's sadness is a kind of mirth,
So mingled° as if mirth did make him sad,
And sadness merry. Those darker humors that
Stick misbecomingly on others, on him
Live in fair dwelling.                                   55

*Cornets. Trumpets sound as to a charge.*

Hark how yon spurs to spirit do incite
The princes to their proof!° Arcite may win me,
And yet may Palamon wound Arcite to
The spoiling of his figure.° O what pity
Enough for such a chance?° If I were by,                 60
I might do hurt, for they would glance their eyes
Toward my seat, and in that motion might
Omit a ward,° or forfeit an offense°
Which craved that very time. It is much better
I am not there. O better never born
Than minister to such harm!

*Cornets. A great cry and noise within, crying* "A Palamon!" *Enter [a]* SERVANT.

                                        What is the chance?

SERVANT
The cry's "A Palamon!"

EMILIA
Then he has won: 'twas ever likely.
He looked all grace° and success, and he is
Doubtless the prim'st of men. I prithee run            70
And tell me how it goes.

*Shout, and cornets. Crying* "A Palamon!"

SERVANT                    Still "Palamon!"

EMILIA
Run and inquire. [*Exit* SERVANT.] Poor servant,° thou
    hast lost!
Upon my right side still° I wore thy picture,
Palamon's on the left. Why so I know not,
I had no end in't else:° chance would have it so.       75

---

On the sinister° side the heart lies: Palamon
Had the best boding chance.° *Another cry, and shout
within, and cornets.* This burst of clamor
Is sure th' end o' th' combat.

*Enter* SERVANT.

SERVANT
They said that Palamon had Arcite's body
Within an inch o' th' pyramid, that the cry          80
Was general "A Palamon!" But anon
Th' assistants° made a brave redemption,° and
The two bold titlers° at this instant are
Hand-to-hand at it.

EMILIA                    Were° they metamorphosed
Both into one! O why? There were no woman          85
Worth so composed a man:° their single share,°
Their nobleness peculiar to them, gives
The prejudice of disparity, value's shortness,°
To any lady breathing.

*Cornets. Cry within:* "Arcite! Arcite!"

                    More exulting?
"Palamon" still?

SERVANT          Nay, now the sound is "Arcite!"     90
EMILIA
I prithee lay attention to the cry.
Set both thine ears to th' business.

*Cornets. A great shout and cry:* "Arcite! Victory!"

SERVANT                    The cry is
"Arcite!" and "Victory!" Hark! "Arcite! Victory!"
The combat's consummation is proclaimed
By the wind instruments.

EMILIA                    Half-sights° saw          95
That Arcite was no babe. God's lid,° his richness
And costliness° of spirit looked through him:° it could
No more be hid in him than fire in flax,
Than humble banks can go to law° with waters
That drift° winds force to raging. I did think        100
Good Palamon would miscarry, yet I knew not
Why I did think so: our reasons are not prophets
When oft our fancies are. They are coming off.°
Alas, poor Palamon!

*Cornets. Enter* THESEUS, HIPPOLYTA, PIRITHOUS,
ARCITE *as victor, and* ATTENDANTS, *&c.*

THESEUS
Lo, where our sister is in expectation,               105
Yet quaking and unsettled!° Fairest Emily,
The gods by their divine arbitrament
Have given you this knight: he is a good one
As ever struck at head. Give me your hands.
Receive you her, you him; be plighted with            110
A love that grows as you decay.

ARCITE                    Emily,
To buy you I have lost what's dearest to me
Save what is bought, and yet I purchase cheaply
As I do rate your value.

THESEUS                    O loved sister,
He speaks now of as brave a knight as e'er            115
Did spur a noble steed. Surely the gods
Would have him die a bachelor, lest his race
Should show i' th' world too godlike! His behavior
So charmed me that methought Alcides° was
To him a sow° of lead. If I could praise              120
Each part of him to th' all I have spoke,° your Arcite
Did° not lose by't, for he that was thus good
Encount'red yet his better. I have heard
Two emulous Philomels° beat the ear o' th' night
With their contentious throats, now one the higher,    125
Anon the other, then again the first,
And by and by outbreasted,° that the sense°
Could not be judge between 'em: so it fared
Good space between these kinsmen, till heavens did
Make hardly° one the winner. Wear the garland         130
With joy that you have won. For the subdued,
Give them our present justice,° since I know
Their lives but pinch° 'em. Let it here be done.
The scene's not for our seeing: go we hence
Right joyful, with some sorrow. [*To* ARCITE.] Arm
  your prize:°                                         135
I know you will not loose her. Hippolyta,
I see one eye of yours conceives a tear
The which it will deliver. *Flourish.*

EMILIA                    Is this winning?
O all you heavenly powers, where is your mercy?
But that your wills have said it must be so,           140
And charge me live to comfort this unfriended,
This miserable prince, that cuts away
A life more worthy from him than all women,
I should, and would, die too.

HIPPOLYTA                    Infinite pity
That four such eyes should be so fixed on one          145
That two must needs be blind for't!°

THESEUS                    So it is. *Exeunt.*

Scene IV. [*The same.*]

*Enter* PALAMON *and his* KNIGHTS *pinioned,* JAILER,
EXECUTIONER, *&c.,* GUARD.

PALAMON
There's many a man alive that hath outlived
The love o' th' people, yea i' th' selfsame state°
Stands many a father with his child: some comfort
We have by so considering. We expire,
And not without men's pity; to live still               5
Have their good wishes;° we prevent

76 **sinister** left   77 **best boding chance** i.e., the most favorable omen   82 **assistants** Arcite's knights; **redemption** rescue   83 **titlers** claimants to the title   84 **Were** O that they were   86 **so . . . man** a man so compounded   **their single share** the share of virtue that each has singly   88 **prejudice . . . shortness** i.e., the disadvantage of inequality, the state of inferiority   95 **Half-sights** glimpses   96 **lid** eyelid   97 **costliness** rareness; **looked through him** was apparent in him   99 **go to law** engage in conflict   100 **drift** driving   103 **coming off** leaving the place of tournament   106 **unsettled** uncertain, still disturbed

119 **Alcides** Hercules   120 **sow** mass of solidified metal taken from a furnace   120–21 **If . . . spoke** if I were to praise his every quality in the same way as I have praised him in general terms   122 **Did** would   124 **Philomels** nightingales   127 **outbreasted** outsung; **that the sense** so that the hearing   130 **hardly** with difficulty   132 **present justice** i.e., immediate execution   133 **pinch** irk   135 **Arm your prize** i.e., take Emilia to your arms   146 **That . . . for't** i.e., that one of the men must die
V.iv.2 **state** condition   5–6 **to . . . wishes** have their good wishes that we should still live

The loathsome misery of age, beguile
The gout and rheum that in lag° hours attend
For gray approachers.° We come towards the gods
Young and unwappered,° not halting under crimes    10
Many and stale:° that sure shall please the gods
Sooner than such,° to give° us nectar with 'em,
For we are more clear° spirits. My dear kinsmen,
Whose lives for this poor comfort° are laid down,
You have sold 'em too cheap.

FIRST KNIGHT          What ending could be    15
Of more content? O'er us the victors have
Fortune, whose title° is as momentary
As to us death is certain. A grain of honor
They not o'er-weigh us.

SECOND KNIGHT       Let us bid farewell,
And with our patience anger tott'ring Fortune,    20
Who at her certain'st° reels.

THIRD KNIGHT          Come, who begins?

PALAMON
E'en he that led you to this banquet shall
Taste to you all.° [To JAILER.] Ah, ha, my friend, my
    friend,
Your gentle daughter gave me freedom once:
You'll see't done now forever.° Pray, how does she?    25
I heard she was not well. Her kind of ill°
Gave me some sorrow.

JAILER          Sir, she's well restored,
And to be married shortly.

PALAMON         By my short life,
I am most glad on't: 'tis the latest thing
I shall be glad of, prithee tell her so.    30
Commend me to her, and to piece° her portion
Tender her this. [Gives him a purse.]

FIRST KNIGHT    Nay, let's be offerers all.

SECOND KNIGHT
Is it a maid?

PALAMON    Verily I think so,
A right good creature, more to me° deserving
Than I can 'quite° or speak of.

ALL KNIGHTS          Commend us to her.    35

*They give their purses.*

JAILER
The gods requite you all, and make her thankful.

PALAMON
Adieu; and let my life be now as short
As my leave-taking. *Lies on the block.*

FIRST KNIGHT        Lead, courageous cousin.

SECOND AND THIRD KNIGHTS
We'll follow cheerfully.

*A great noise within, crying* "Run! Save! Hold!" *Enter
in haste a* MESSENGER.

MESSENGER        Hold, hold, O hold, hold, hold!

*Enter* PIRITHOUS *in haste.*

PIRITHOUS
Hold, ho! It is a cursèd haste you made    40
If you have done° so quickly. Noble Palamon,
The gods will show their glory in a life°
That thou art yet to lead.

PALAMON         Can that be,
When Venus I have said° is false? How do things fare?°

PIRITHOUS
Arise, great sir, and give the tidings ear    45
That are most dearly° sweet and bitter.

PALAMON          What
Hath waked us from our dream?°

PIRITHOUS       List then. Your cousin,
Mounted upon a steed that Emily
Did first bestow on him, a black one, owing°
Not a hair-worth of white, which some will say    50
Weakens his price, and many will not buy
His goodness with this note°—which superstition
Here finds allowance°—on this horse is Arcite
Trotting the stones of Athens, which the calkins°
Did rather tell° than trample, for the horse    55
Would make his length a mile,° if't pleased his rider
To put pride in him. As he thus went counting
The flinty pavement, dancing as 'twere to th' music
His own hoofs made—for as they say from iron
Came music's origin—what envious flint,    60
Cold as old Saturn, and like him possessed
With fire malevolent, darted a spark,
Or what fierce sulphur else to this end made,
I comment not: the hot horse, hot as fire,
Took toy° at this, and fell to what disorder    65
His power could give his will, bounds, comes on end,
Forgets school-doing,° being therein trained
And of kind manage;° piglike he whines
At the sharp rowel, which he frets at rather
Than any jot obeys; seeks all foul means    70
Of boist'rous and rough jadery to dis-seat
His lord, that kept it° bravely. When nought served,
When neither curb would crack, girth break, nor
    diff'ring° plunges
Dis-root his rider whence he grew, but that
He kept him 'tween his legs, on his hind hoofs    75
On end he stands,
That Arcite's legs being higher than his head
Seemed with strange art to hang; his victor's wreath
Even then fell off his head; and presently°
Backward the jade comes o'er, and his full poise°    80
Becomes the rider's load. Yet is he living,
But such a vessel 'tis that floats but for

---

8 **lag** last   9 **gray approachers** gray-haired men approaching death   10 **unwappered** unwearied (perhaps with a suggestion of sexual excess)   11 **stale** of long standing   12 **such** men such as described; **to give** so that they will give   13 **clear** noble, unstained   14 **this poor comfort** Palamon admits the puniness of his own consolation   17 **title** i.e., favor   21 **at her certain'st** when she seems most stable   23 **Taste . . . all** act as taster at a banquet for you   25 **You'll . . . forever** i.e., you will see me win a final freedom   26 **kind of ill** i.e., madness   31 **piece** contribute to   34 **to me** i.e., from me   35 **'quite** requite

41 **done** finished   42 **show . . . life** i.e., through your life (as their creature) their glory will be manifested   44 **I have said** i.e., as I have said; **How . . . fare** What has happened?   46 **dearly** intensely   47 **dream** i.e., of death   49 **owing** possessing   52 **with this note** because of this peculiarity   53 **Here finds allowance** is here confirmed   54 **calkins** parts of a horseshoe turned down to prevent slipping   55 **tell** count   56 **make . . . mile** take mile-long paces   65 **toy** fright, exception   67 **school-doing** training   68 **of kind manage** well disciplined   72 **it** his seat   73 **diff'ring** varying   79 **presently** at once   80 **poise** weight

The surge that next approaches. He much desires
To have some speech with you. Lo, he appears.

*Enter* THESEUS, HIPPOLYTA, EMILIA, ARCITE *in a chair.*

PALAMON
O miserable end of our alliance!                                    85
The gods are mighty! Arcite, if thy heart,
Thy worthy, manly heart be yet unbroken,
Give me thy last words: I am Palamon,
One that yet loves thee dying.
ARCITE                                    Take Emilia,
And with her all the world's joy. Reach° thy hand.    90
Farewell. I have told° my last hour. I was false,
Yet never treacherous.° Forgive me, cousin.
One kiss from fair Emilia. [*She kisses him.*] 'Tis done.
Take her. I die.                                    [*Dies.*]
PALAMON            Thy brave soul seek Elysium!
EMILIA
I'll close thine eyes, prince. Blessed souls be with thee!°  95
Thou art a right good man, and while I live
This day° I give to tears.
PALAMON                                    And I to honor.°
THESEUS
In this place first you fought: e'en very here
I sund'red you. Acknowledge to the gods
Our thanks that you are living.°                          100
His part is played, and though it were too short
He did it well. Your day is lengthened, and
The blissful dew of heaven does arrouse° you.
The powerful Venus well hath graced her altar,
And given you your love. Our master Mars    105
Hath vouched his oracle, and to Arcite gave
The grace of the contention.° So the deities
Have showed due justice. Bear this° hence.
PALAMON                                    O cousin,
That we should things desire which do cost us
The loss of our desire!° That nought could buy    110
Dear love but loss of dear love!°
THESEUS                                    Never Fortune
Did play a subtler game. The conquered triumphs,
The victor has the loss; yet in the passage°
The gods have been most equal.° Palamon,
Your kinsman hath confessed the right o' th' lady    115

Did lie in you, for you first saw her, and
Even then proclaimed your fancy. He restored her
As your stol'n jewel, and desired your spirit
To send him hence forgiven. The gods my justice
Take from my hand,° and they themselves become    120
The executioners. Lead your lady off,
And call your lovers° from the stage of death,°
Whom I adopt my friends. A day or two
Let us look sadly, and give grace unto
The funeral of Arcite, in whose end°                    125
The visages of bridegrooms we'll put on
And smile with Palamon; for whom an hour,
But one hour since, I was as dearly sorry
As glad of Arcite; and am now as glad
As for him sorry. O you heavenly charmers,°        130
What things you make of us! For what we lack,
We laugh;° for what we have, are sorry;° still
Are children in some kind. Let us be thankful
For that which is, and with you leave° dispute
That are above our question. Let's go off,        135
And bear us like the time.°            *Flourish. Exeunt.*

# EPILOGUE

I would now ask ye how ye like the play,
But, as it is with schoolboys, cannot say.°
I am cruel° fearful. Pray yet stay a while,
And let me look upon ye. No man smile?
Then it goes hard, I see. He that has                      5
Loved a young handsome wench, then, show his face—
'Tis strange if none be here—and if he will
Against his conscience, let him hiss, and kill
Our market. 'Tis in vain, I see, to stay° ye.
Have at the worst can come,° then! Now what say ye?    10
And yet mistake me not: I am not bold;
We have no such cause. If the tale° we have told—
For 'tis no other—any way content ye,
For to that honest purpose it was meant ye,°
We have our end; and ye shall have ere long        15
I dare say many a better, to prolong
Your old loves to us. We, and all our might,
Rest at your service. Gentlemen, good night.

*Flourish.*

90 **Reach** i.e., give me   91 **told** counted, lived through
91–92 **false . . . treacherous** Arcite admits Palamon's
greater right to Emilia in seeing her first, but declares he took
no unfair advantage   95 **Blessed . . . thee** i.e., May you
be with the blessed souls   97 **This day** i.e., the anniversaries
of this day; **to honor** i.e., to honoring Arcite's memory
99–100 **Acknowledge . . . living** Declare to the gods that
we rejoice in your being alive (the emendation of "Our" to
"Your" has been suggested)   103 **arrouse** sprinkle   107 **grace
. . . contention** good fortune in the contest   108 **this** Arcite's
body   109–10 **That . . . desire** i.e., alas that the winning of
what we want takes away our desire for it   110–11 **That . . .
love** i.e., that one love (Emilia) could be won only by losing
another (Arcite)   113 **passage** course of events   114 **equal**
just

120 **Take . . . hand** i.e., take away from me   122 **lovers** his
Knights; **stage of death** scaffold   125 **in whose end** at the
conclusion of which   130 **you heavenly charmers** the Fates
(who control us with their charms or magic)   131–32 **For
. . . laugh** we feel pleasure at the thought of the thing we do
not possess   132 **for . . . sorry** we are sad to have what we
do possess   134 **leave** cease to   136 **bear . . . time** conduct
ourselves appropriately to the occasion
**Ep.2 say** speak   3 **cruel** dreadfully   9 **stay** i.e., try to prevent
10 **Have . . . come** let us face the worst event possible   12
**tale** alluding to the title of the source   14 **meant ye** intended
for you

# THE
# POEMS AND SONNETS

# THE POEMS

INTRODUCTION BY WILLIAM EMPSON

EDITED BY WILLIAM BURTO

## Introduction

The poems of Shakespeare have great ability and moments of genius, but we need not labor to praise them, since we must rejoice that he went back to the theater—recognizing perhaps that they were in some way inadequate for him. Nonetheless, they saved his career at the one crucial time, and they record (though mainly in the *Sonnets*) an experience so formative that the plays echo it for the rest of his life. No other playwright known to us worked regularly for the public theaters both before and after their long shutdown because of the plague in 1592–94, after which new companies of actors had to be formed; to survive it was an achievement. At this time a patron was essential for him, whereas afterward (apart from one graceful kindness) he seems to have avoided writing for patrons. His early life is obscure but two facts stand out like rocks: he dedicated to the Earl of Southampton (born October 1573) both *Venus and Adonis* (1593) and *The Rape of Lucrece* (1594), sounding much more intimate on the second occasion. Our first record of Shakespeare as a member of the Lord Chamberlain's Company, in which he stayed for the rest of his working life—indeed our first record of it performing at a London theater—is dated just after the earl's coming of age. The earl became liable to a heavy fine for rejecting a marriage arranged during his minority, so perhaps did not pay very much, but did agree to help get the company launched. By writing for a patron, Shakespeare met the crisis in an accepted manner, as a modern author might apply for "relief"; the playwright Marlowe, born in the same year, was also at this time writing a mythological narrative poem, though it happened to be interrupted by his murder; maybe they pretended to one another that this was a tiresome chore. Shakespeare's meter had been made the fashionable one for the purpose by Lodge in 1589; and may I at once refer anybody who wants further information of this scholarly kind to the excellent New Cambridge edition of the *Poems* by J. C. Maxwell (1966). I want in this Introduction to concentrate on what may be called the human or experiential reality of the poems, presenting such evidence as I have about that with decent care.

It is a startling initial fact that *Venus and Adonis*, his first publication, appears in the Stationers' Register as licensed by the Archbishop of Canterbury in person. The poem soon made its impact, and libidinous undergraduates are said to have slept with it under their pillows. The fact that Shakespeare bearded and won over the "little black husband" of Elizabeth, a particularly grim member of her court, argues that the Bard was in great nerve and good spirits. Shakespeare was not yet thirty, and few of the people who had enjoyed his plays would remember his name, but that is a time when authors need to make contacts. One can glean a little from the Register itself about the conditions of his problem. The *Dictionary of National Biography* reports that John Whitgift (1530–1604) accepted the theories of Calvin throughout his career, sometimes to the annoyance of the queen, but denied their application to Church Government, so that he was free to persecute Calvinists as well as Papists, bringing them ruin by repeated fines; at this work he showed "brutal insolence in examining prisoners, and invariably argued for the severest penalties." Having a private fortune, he maintained a troop in his own livery, and it was this troop that arrested Essex and his followers during their attempt at rebellion. Soon after his appointment in 1583 he secured a tightening-up of the licensing system: for example, the ballads on separate sheets had now to be approved; and, unlike his predecessor, he would license a few books under his own name every year. Nearly all of them were pamphlets on current theological controversies, for which his decision would anyway be needed, but he also showed a creditable interest in the advancement of learning; for example, he licensed books purporting to teach the Welsh language and the history of China. The Bishop of London, who was another established licensing authority, also adopted the custom of giving his own name to a few books each year; most of them dealt with political news from Western Europe. He worked closely with the archbishop but seems to have had no literary leanings, though he had of course social ones.

Thus in February 1591 the archbishop and the bishop together licensed the rather perfunctory translation of the *Orlando Furioso* by Sir John Harrington. The queen (so people said at the time) had found her maids of honor giggling over his translation of a sexy canto, and had ordered him to go and stay in his country house until he had translated the whole epic. Both his parents had been with her during her imprisonment in the Tower, when she was almost without hope, and she had made him her godson. It was agreed that the English badly needed to be raised to the cultural level of the Italians somehow, and yet admittedly, on the moral side, such a poem needed thorough sanctification by the Church of England. Thus the occasion had every claim upon the assistance of the hierarchy. I count about 180 entries in the Register for 1590, 40 of them by the bishop and 8 by the archbishop; these proportions are fairly steady for the next two years. In 1592 the archbishop licensed a book of love poems, though in Latin—the *Amintae Gaudia* of Thomas Watson (1557?-92). Watson was a classical scholar of good family, and he had just died; he had assisted the poverty of better poets, and his verses were sure not to excite desire. The archbishop entered the fatal year 1593 by licensing Hooker's *Ecclesiastical Polity* and on April 9 he licensed Churchyard's *Challenge*. The book is a final miscellany by a sturdy, loyal old chap, then about seventy-three, who died soon after; it calls the queen a phoenix on several occasions. Nobody could blame the archbishop, but he was perhaps starting to go a little out of his way, as Churchyard had no social claims. Within three weeks he had licensed the indecent *Venus and Adonis*. There was no immediate sign of trouble; it was the only year he reached double figures, ending in September with Nashe—*Christ's Tears over Jerusalem* and *The Unfortunate Traveler* (Nashe had defended the Anglican hierarchy in comic pamphlets, and the first of these books is a work of penitence). But in the following year, 1594, only one publication was licensed by the archbishop himself: "The Table of Ten Commandments, with the Pictures of Moses and Aaron"—a poster, no doubt, for display in all churches; the queen felt she had to let him keep up appearances so far. In the following year he appears to have been forgiven, signing for works of theological controversy at a merry pace, but never again did he license anything even appearing to be a work of literature.

When the poem became notorious, somebody would look it up in the Register hoping to find an irregularity; and, when the truth got about, the queen evidently told the archbishop that he must stop making a fool of himself for at least a year. We may be sure he said, as a number of modern critics would say, that these randy students were the ones who had got the poem wrong; probably he could also claim that the author had told him so. A letter from Southampton would be needed for Shakespeare to get an interview, but it would cut little ice with the archbishop, and Shakespeare would then have to rely on his own eloquence. The apology of Chettle shows that he was socially adroit.[1] He would be found to share the anxieties of the archbishop about the petulant earl, regarding him with grave pity. His own little poem, designed as a warning for the young man, carried a peculiarly high and severe moral allegory; and might he perhaps illustrate

the point by quotation? (He would read from the final curse of Venus, saying that all loves on earth will in future be upset by parents arranging marriages and suchlike.) Whitgift had almost certainly ruined Shakespeare's father, whether the father was a Papist or a Puritan; it gives a welcome feeling of reality to see an author of revenge plays actually taking a quiet civil revenge. I doubt whether he felt this as a duty, but it might seem an excuse for letting himself be pushed forward by the giggling Southampton. He would enjoy the scene chiefly as a test of skill.

C. S. Lewis found the poem disgusting, mainly because Venus sweats, and J. C. Maxwell writes very sensibly here (his edition, p. xii): Shakespeare, he finds, is "exploiting . . . the sheer comedy of sexuality" in lines 230–40, where we meet the "sweet bottom-grass" of the erotic landscape. This explanation is rather too disinfectant; there is a joke, sure enough, based on evasion of a censorship, but a young man who felt prepared to take this Venus on would find the description positively exciting. We recognize Venus as divine because she is free not merely from bodily shame but even from social precaution; that Adonis is snubbing her just cannot enter her mind. But also the modern conventions about sweat are sharply different from the Elizabethan ones. Many love poems of the time regard the sweat of a lady as somehow a proof of her elegance and refinement; the smell is not recommended as an excitement for our lower nature, the only way it could be praised in a modern novel. In *The Rape of Lucrece* we find the sweat of the chaste Lucrece while she is peacefully asleep singled out for praise; one hand is

On the green coverlet; whose perfect white
Showed like an April daisy on the grass,
With pearly sweat resembling dew of night. (lines 394–96)

I do not know that any poet before Andrew Marvell praised the smell of the sweat of male farmhands, but I expect someone did. Spenser would have blamed Lewis here for being "nice," meaning squeamish and proud of it, an unsoldierly trait. And indeed the impressiveness, the final solidity, of *Venus and Adonis* does turn upon not being "nice," partly from its firm show of acquaintance with country sport, partly from not even caring whether you find the details funny or not. And then, in his own mind, the story would have some bearing on his marriage to a woman of twenty-six when he was eighteen. No doubt it all took a bit of nerve.

At the end of the poem (line 1166) the corpse of Adonis is "melted like a vapor" and a flower springs up from his blood; Venus plucks it, saying that it smells like Adonis, though not as nice, and that the sap dripping from the break is like the tears that he shed too readily:

this was thy father's guise—
Sweet issue of a more sweet-smelling sire—
For every little grief to wet his eyes;
To grow unto himself was his desire,
And so 'tis thine; but know, it is as good
To wither in my breast as in his blood. (lines 1177–82)

The earlier sonnets frequently blame the man addressed for trying to live to himself like a flower, and for resisting a marriage; the personal application was easy enough to

---

[1] Chettle had published the dying pamphlet of Greene, which contained various libels on authors—some of them justified, says Chettle (December 1592); but he has now met Shakespeare and found "his demeanour no less excellent than the quality he professes. Besides, divers of worship have reported his uprightness of dealing, which argues his honesty, and his facetious grace in writing, which approves his art."

recognize. But people in the know were meant to regard this as only incidental to the structure. The poem recounts a Myth of Origin, like "how the Elephant got its Trunk," a form that scholars, both in Shakespeare's time and our own, revere to a rather surprising degree. (The genuinely ancient examples are believed to have been designed to support the practice of some already existing ritual or custom.) Shakespeare meant his poem to be classically respectable, unlike the plays which he could make a living from, and the motto on his title page boasts of it; but he is not hampered by the form, spurred by it rather. The terrible prophecy of Venus, at the end, at least seems to tell a general truth and thereby give the poem a universal "significance." Also, I have come to think, he extracted from the Myth of Origin a new literary device, very important in the seventeenth century, though hardly ever employed by himself in its pure form except for *The Phoenix and the Turtle*.

The central trope of John Donne, the only bit of metaphysics in Metaphysical Poetry, runs as follows: a ruler or mistress or saint is being praised, for Justice, Beauty, Holiness, or what not, and this is done by saying, "You are the Platonic Idea, in person, of Justice or what not"; in the same way, Venus had always been Love walking about in person. Elizabeth Drury has to hold this position in the *Anniversaries*, or they are mere nonsense. Only Jesus Christ (an individual who was also the Logos) had ever deserved such praise, but the literary acceptance of classical deities meant that it could be used without feeling blasphemous. It has become an arid formula when Donne writes to the Countess of Bedford:

Your (or You) Virtue two vast uses serves;
It ransoms one sex, and one Court preserves.

The two words in parentheses have to mean "or perhaps Virtue *is* you," but probably poor Donne is just hammering out the formula to try and get some of his wife's grocery bills paid. When I was a student, people thought that he had imported this trick from Spain, but Professor Edward Wilson kindly tells me that there is at least no prominent use of it in sixteenth-century Spanish poetry. Some recent critic has named the trick "inverted Platonism," and it certainly needs to be distinguished from Platonism. It is rather silly, though there were some splendid uses of it, so perhaps I will not seem too patriotic when claiming it as a home product.

No one will be surprised that Shakespeare could see the dramatic or "quibbling" possibilities of his story, as when saying of Venus, "She's Love, she loves, and yet she is not loved" (line 610), or when the irritated Adonis, like C. S. Lewis, says that what she calls love is really "sweating Lust" (line 794). But Venus at line 12 is already saying it about Adonis, who is merely human—at any rate, until after he is dead. In the full "metaphysical" trope, it is standard to say that the death of the individual entails a universal absence of the abstraction—after Punctuality Smith has died, nobody can ever catch a train again. But why should this be true of Adonis, unless because Venus will go off in a huff? Her presentiment of his death, she says, cannot be true because the consequences of it would be too awful:

"O Jove," quoth she, "how much a fool was I
To be of such a weak and silly mind
To wail his death who lives, and must not die
Till mutual overthrow of mortal kind!
  For he being dead, with him is beauty slain,
  And, beauty dead, black chaos comes again."

(lines 1015–20)

She already expects the race of man to destroy itself; and the last two hundred lines of the poem, after she has found him dead, are loaded with her despairing insistence that there is no love left in the world.[2] The conception is not a minor decoration in the poem.

Shakespeare did not need to invent it here because he had already used it superbly in *Titus Andronicus* (V.ii), published in 1594 to help launch the company but probably written about 1590. The Empress Tamora, who has done great wrong to Titus, believes him to be in consequence so mad that he can be tricked into facilitating the murder of his surviving son Lucius. She therefore visits him disguised as Revenge-in-Person, bringing her two sons disguised as Rape and Murder. An Elizabethan spectator was of course thoroughly accustomed to allegorical pageants and charades; he too could if necessary have disguised himself as Revenge. Titus cannot help behaving queerly, but uses this weakness to further his revenge, like Hieronymo in *The Spanish Tragedy* of Kyd, and the eventual Hamlet of Shakespeare. He plays up to her with eerie glee and magnificent rhetoric:

Look round about the wicked streets of Rome,
And when thou find'st a man that's like thyself,
Good Murder, stab him; he's a murderer.   (V.ii.98–100)

After a good deal of this, she is so certain he is mad that he can easily deceive her into eating her two sons, disguised as a pie. It is wild but not irrelevant, indeed simply true, because the practical trouble with revenge is that it does not finish, but produces blood feuds. Shakespeare is always prepared to think, "Why are we interested in the story?" and then say the reason why on the stage. The poem about Venus offered a very different opportunity for the technique, but one can see that his mind would take to it readily. I do not know that anybody else was already using it so early.

We need not doubt that Shakespeare considered the end of the poem dignified, and half believed what he told the archbishop. But the dedication of it already envisages that a "graver labor" will come next, so there was no change of plan before setting out on *The Rape of Lucrece*. This too is a Myth of Origin; to insist upon it, the death of Lucrece causes an absurd change in human blood (line 1750). A hero did not need to be a god before such things

---

[2] A footnote by F. T. Prince at line 1020 of *Venus and Adonis*, in his New Arden edition of *The Poems*, may seem all that is needed to destroy my position. It is true that T. W. Baldwin, in *On the Literary Genetics of Shakspere's Poems and Sonnets* (pp. 39–52), claims to find the sources of such phrases in recent Latin poetry; and he may well be right. But he seems unable to tell the difference between making the general remark: "Without beauty, there would be chaos," and saying: "Because this individual man is dead, all human love affairs will in future be chaotic." He offers no quotation of this second type. Nor can any be extracted from the *Four Hymns* of Spenser, mentioned by F. T. Prince.

could happen; one could easily have a historical Myth of Origin (for example, *Macbeth* is about how the Scots, thanks to the Stuarts, took to civilized hereditary rule instead of tribal warfare). The story of Lucrece was an exciting and dangerous example because it explained how Rome threw off her kings and thus acquired an almost superhuman virtue; though somewhat obscurely, this gave its justifying importance to the heroine's choice of suicide. Both the Bible (I Samuel 12:12–25) and the classics (in practice, Plutarch) disapproved of royalty; the institution could be defended only as a necessity for our fallen natures. Also, Brutus had a mysterious importance for a patriot and a dramatist. No other great period of drama, anywhere in the world, had so much interest in madmen as the Elizabethan one. This apparently derived from the Hamlet of Kyd, whose story came from a twelfth-century historian of Denmark, "the Saxon who knew Latin." But the story had classical authority from Livy's brief remarks on Lucius Junius Brutus, who pretended imbecility in order to be safe till he could take revenge; indeed, Saxo has been suspected of imitating Livy to provide elegance for his savage material, so that Hamlet, whose basic trouble in the fairy tale was that he could not tell a lie, was truthful as ever when he said "I am more an antique Roman than a Dane." The Brutus who killed Caesar was his bastard, as Shakespeare remarks in *1 Henry VI* (IV.i), though he kept it out of *Julius Caesar;* and a more antique Brutus, a parricide as usual, had been the first to civilize Britain; hence the name. Now, it was Brutus who plucked the dagger from Lucrece's body and championed the expulsion of the kings. He had pretended imbecility up to that very moment,

> Burying in Lucrece' wound his folly's show.
> He with the Romans was esteemèd so
> As seely jeering idiots are with kings,
> For sportive words and utt'ring foolish things;
>
> But now he throws that shallow habit by
> Wherein deep policy did him disguise.     (lines 1810–15)

The Romans take an oath, and the last line of the poem says that the Tarquins were banished forever. J. C. Maxwell says in his note:

> It is curious that Shakespeare makes no mention here (though the Argument concludes with it) of the historical importance of this, as involving the abolition of the monarchy (unless "everlasting" glances at it); this tells heavily against the view . . . that the popularity of the poem owed much to its bearing on political issues.

It is curious that the scholars of our age, though geared up as never before, are unable to imagine living under a censorship or making an effort to avoid trouble with thought police; these unpleasant features of current experience were also familiar in most historical periods, so that the disability must regularly prevent scholars from understanding what they read. Southampton, who seemed fated to irritate the queen, might well be inclined to cool thoughts about royalty; and Shakespeare would be wise to hesitate as to how far one might go. Though never very republican, you would think, he was certainly interested in Brutus; he had already, in *Titus Andronicus*, written better than any other Eliza-

bethan the part of the half-genuine madman. Yet both themes are subdued to the decorum of his poem.

The resulting work is hard to read straight through, but one should realize that Shakespeare has made it static by deliberate choice. Francis Berry pointed out in *The Shakespeare Inset* that, although both these poems contain a high proportion of dialogue, the reader does not remember them so, because all the harangues might just as well be soliloquies. Indeed the silent colloquy between Lucrece and the low-class messenger, blushing together at cross-purposes (line 1339), stands out because it is as near as we get to any contact between two minds. In a play the audience wants the story to go forward, but here the Bard could practice rhetoric like five-finger exercises on the piano. Also, the rhetoric works mainly by calling up parallel cases, so that here again the figure of myth becomes a sort of generalization. Even this perhaps hardly excuses the long stretch of looking at tapestries of the Fall of Troy, which one may suspect was written later as a substitute for dangerous thoughts about royalty; Lucrece when appealing to Tarquin flatters his assumptions by recalling the virtues of royalty, and the highly formal structure of the work demands that she should recognize the inadequacy of such ideals after her appeal has failed. It would be sensible to have an unpublished version suited to the patron, who contributed a great deal more than the buyers would; and besides, it would give the welcome feeling of conspiracy. But anyhow the poem needs here a feeling of grim delay—she has already decided upon suicide, but has to wait for the arrival of the proper witnesses.

Whether she was right to kill herself has been long discussed, and Shakespeare was probably not so absurd as we think to let her review the Christian objection to suicide—its origins are hard to trace. Saint Augustine, caddish as usual, had written "if adulterous, why praised? if chaste, why killed?"; and one might suspect that the romantic rhetoric of Shakespeare is used only to evade this old dilemma. But he is interested in the details of the case, and probably had in mind a solution, though he did not care to express it grossly. Livy already has Tarquin force her by an inherently social threat; if she rejects him, he will stab both her and a male servant in the same bed and claim afterward that he had been righteously indignant at finding them there (line 670). It is assumed that her reputation has a political importance for her aristocratic family, which she puts before everything else; he gags her with her bedclothes, but not because she is expected to resist. Immediately after the rape, and till her death, she speaks of herself as guilty, and Shakespeare concurs. However, just before she stabs herself the assembled lords protest that she is still innocent, and she does not deny this, but brushes it aside as unimportant beside a social consequence:

> "No, no!" quoth she, "no dame hereafter living
> By my excuse shall claim excuse's giving."
>
>                                         (lines 1714–15)

Coleridge in a famous passage derided Beaumont and Fletcher because the ladies in their plays regard chastity as a costly trinket which they are liable to mislay, and it is not obvious why Shakespeare is different here. When Tarquin slinks from her bed, he says, "She bears the load of lust he left behind"; "She desperate with her nails her flesh doth tear"; she "there remains a hopeless castaway" (lines 734, 739, 744). Perhaps, he reflects, the instability of women is an excuse for her: they have "waxen minds. . . . Then call them not the authors of their ill" (lines 1240, 1244). Just before killing herself, she speaks to her husband and the assembled lords of her "gross blood" and its "accessary yieldings" (lines 1655, 1658); one could hardly ask her to be much plainer. She was no virgin, having several children; and it is a basic fact about the young Shakespeare that he considers young men in general overwhelmingly desirable to women, let alone brave young lords. Thus she took an involuntary pleasure in the rape, though she would have resisted it in any way possible; that is why she felt guilty, and why some of her blood turned black, making a precedent for all future corrupted blood (line 1750). The reader perhaps is also guilty, having taken a sexual pleasure in these descriptions of sexual wrong—as much at least as the "homely villain" who wondered how she was making him blush. But we are not told that she would have killed herself for this private shame; she considers the suicide useful for public reasons. Saint Augustine would conclude that she deserved death for enjoying the rape and hell for her suicide afterward; but the dramatist is sure that all her reactions, in this tricky situation, do her the greatest credit and are enough to explain the permanent majesty of Rome.

The Passionate Pilgrim (1599) is a cheat, by a pirate who is very appreciative of the work of Shakespeare. It starts with two genuine sonnets (138 and 144), each of them implying plenty of story and giving a smart crack at the end; and the third item, a sonnet extracted from Love's Labor's Lost, follows quite naturally. Paging ahead in the bookshop, one found poems that might easily be Shakespeare's, though most of them are now generally considered not to be; it would be sensible to buy at once. What we learn from this is that Shakespeare had become news, a personality exciting curiosity, and there are other signs of it. In the previous year, for the first time, a play had been printed with his name on the title page ("Love's Labor's Lost, as it was presented before her Highness this last Christmas"), and the absurd Palladis Tamia by Meres had at least treated his work as deserving scholarly attention. The Shakespeare Allusion Book finds many more references to Falstaff than to any other character (Hamlet comes second, with the others far behind him). Thus in 1598 his reputation came to the boil, so to speak; this was why his public was willing to trust him through his tragic period, though they did not like it as much.

The editor would have printed more sonnets if he could, and yet the ones chosen are well suited to his purpose—how could that happen? John Dover Wilson in his Introduction to the Sonnets of Shakespeare thought that the Dark Woman (he will not call her a lady) had allowed a publisher two specimens with a view to raising the price of her whole collection. But this ignores the state of the market; she would have succeeded in publishing her collection and would not have needed to offer bait. I think that a visitor was left to wait in a room where a cabinet had been left unlocked—rather carelessly, but the secret poems were about five years old; he saw at once that they would sell, but did not know how much time was available. Thumbing through the notebook (the poems cannot have been on separate sheets, or he could have

taken more without being noticed), he chose two with saucy last couplets for hurried copying. In one of the variants, the 1609 edition has a simple misprint, but as a rule it has the slightly better text—either because the thief miscopied or because Shakespeare had second thoughts. I think that one of these cases allows us to decide the alternative:

> I smiling credit her false-speaking tongue,
> Outfacing faults in love with love's ill rest. (Sonnet 138)

In 1609 the second line has become: "On both sides thus is simple truth suprest." J. C. Maxwell gives an admirable gloss for the pirate version: "With (the help of) the ill-grounded sense of security that is characteristic of love," and plainly this is more like Shakespeare. But it is rather out of place; the poem has very little to do with his private experience or sensibility, commenting with sad good humor on almost universal departures from truth. The duller line is more good-mannered in a way, and he would not give his first draft of a sonnet to his "private friends" (as Meres wrote), or even, one would think, to the Dark Lady. Poets of our own time have been known to add in the desired obscurity when they rewrite, but Shakespeare is more likely to have removed it. So probably he was the one who left the cabinet unlocked.

This publication also refutes the Herbert Theory of the Sonnets, for a reason that its supporters have been too high-minded to observe. William Herbert, later Earl of Pembroke, became eighteen in April 1598 and was hardly allowed to come to London earlier, as he was a sickly lad, addicted to headaches (John Dover Wilson, op. cit., p. 66); though later, I do not deny, an honest man and a useful patron, who deserved to have the First Folio dedicated to him in 1623. But this would mean that the sonnet about letting Shakespeare's boy patron borrow his mistress, when the pirate got it into print, would be hot news. The Elizabethans would call the incident thorough toad-eating, and it would be sure to get mentioned in some of the letters of gossip. I am not saying that Shakespeare would not have done it, though I think it was outside his mode of life at this date, but that he could not have hushed it up, in these circumstances. Consider what moral Ben Jonson would find to say (whereas, in 1594, moral Ben Jonson had not yet poked his nose above the boards). The first soliloquy of Prince Hal, assuring the audience that he will betray Falstaff, has close verbal echoes of the first of the pathetic sonnets ("Full many a glorious morning") trying to defend the patron for a betrayal of Shakespeare. But this does not mean that they were written at the same time; the implications would be horrible. The joke of Falstaff largely turns on the repeated bite of his self-defense, and Shakespeare may well be drawing a good deal upon his own humiliations when the servant of a patron, in his twenties. But he would need to use these memories in the assurance of secrecy, feeling them distant, feeling that they could be laughed over.

The reader should be warned of a slight change of idiom in the couplet of Sonnet 144:

> The truth I shall not know, but live in doubt
> Till my bad angel fire my good one out.

The Variorum edition gives a list of references to periodicals, mainly Victorian, and until I looked them up I imagined they proved that the Dark Lady is accused of having gonorrhea. They merely show that the phrase *fire out* was then used as we use *fire*, to mean "dismiss a person from a job"; it did not then, as now, inevitably suggest firing something from a gun. Shakespeare need only be saying: "I will not know whether the Dark Lady has seduced the patron till she gets bored and dismisses him; then no doubt both will come round to me with indignant stories." We may be sure he did realize that an explosive insult was in the background, because he had a complex verbal awareness, as when he left his wife his second-best bed; but if the Dark Lady had really caught the disease we would hear more about it in his personal poems. A labored epigram by Edward Guilpin, published in 1598, is I think simply a crude imitation of Shakespeare's joke here; he must have been one of the "private friends" who were allowed (says Meres) to read some of the "sugared Sonnets." It would be pretty sad to believe that Shakespeare copied the merry thought from Guilpin as soon as he read his book, and had it stolen at once.

One has to try to make sense of these dates; it is fundamental to the understanding of Shakespeare's development, I think, that the relations with a patron come in 1592–95, when a patron was needed. Leslie Hotson, indeed, put the *Sonnets* five years earlier, in an entertaining book that proposed a new addressee for them (*Mr. W. H.*, 1964); he laughs at the scholars for viewing Shakespeare as Little Dopey, shambling along in the rear of Marlowe and the rest, "a remarkably late developer." But his development really is unusual; usually the lyrical power comes earlier than the constructive one. Reading through the plays in the generally accepted order—*The Comedy of Errors, 1, 2, and 3 Henry VI, The Taming of the Shrew, Titus Andronicus*—one gets hardly a breath of poetry so far, though plenty of vigorous rhetoric, and a clear mind at work making the best of the plots. A little poetry comes in with *Richard III*, so that he was just beginning to be a poet, aged twenty-seven or so, when the plague forced him to rely on it for survival. After two years, when the theaters open again, he seems essentially a poetic dramatist. Another contrast, though more trivial, is perhaps more striking. Bernard Shaw remarked that Shakespeare must have suffered torture if he ever rose over his comedies after he had grown up—assuming, I think, that any adult feels an obscure personal shame when he hears another man boast of being a gentleman. Probably the boasting of lads together is much the same in all classes, but it is true that an entry of three young lords, swanking by making jokes that are assumed to be top-class, occurs in all his comedies between 1594 and 1598, whereas the characters in the early comedies are mostly traders, and the lords in *Henry VI* simply murderers. One might perhaps blame Shakespeare for choosing to write about aristocrats, but not, having chosen to, for doing some fieldwork on how they actually talked. It is not what is now called snobbery, because he could not pretend to be anything but the servant of his earl. Probably he would be allowed to hand around drinks at a party given by the earl for young men of standing—listening with all his ears, though, as one gathers from the plays, much more free to make jokes himself than a modern servant is. In private he seems to have scolded his lord unreasonably, as privileged servants often do. C. S. Lewis, in *English Literature in the Sixteenth*

*Century* (1954), spoke of "the self-abnegation, the 'naughting,'" of the sonnets, more like a parent than a lover: "In certain senses of the word 'love,' Shakespeare is not so much our best as our only love-poet" (p. 505). This is noble, but it is perhaps only the other side of a feeling that the gratitude is overstrained. And yet, the sonnets thank the patron because

> thou . . . dost advance
> As high as learning my rude ignorance.    (Sonnet 78)

The actual teaching of the earl can hardly have been more than a few social tips, but as a window upon the great world Shakespeare had been feeling the need of him badly. The feelings seem better grounded if we realize that the childish patron was giving far more than he knew. And, unless we redate the plays as a whole, remembering that the evidence is quite an elaborate structure, there is only one plausible time for fitting in this bit of education.

*A Lover's Complaint* was printed at the end of the sonnets in 1609, but many critics have denied that Shakespeare wrote it—chiefly on grounds of vocabulary and imagery, but also by calling lines bad when they are simply dramatic, imagined as by another speaker (for example, lines 106–11). Much of it, he would consider, had needed correcting before it was published, as indeed do many of the sonnets themselves; he forces the words into his rhyme scheme and general intention so hurriedly that our textual notes sometimes only amount to lame excuses (for example, around line 235). But at least Kenneth Muir has now proved Shakespeare's authorship, by "clusters" (*William Shakespeare 1564–1964*, ed. E. A. Bloom); the principle is that if an author happens to use one word of a cluster his mind drags in most of the others soon after, and this process is not conscious or noticeable enough for an admirer to imitate it, nor is it affected, as imagery in general can be, by a change of subject matter or recent experience. I think the poem is evidently by Shakespeare on psychological grounds, and a kind of echo of the sonnets (this of course is why they were kept together, and eventually pirated together); but I am confronted by an agreement among the scholars (Mazwell's edition, p. xxxv) that it must have been written after 1600. Similar arguments have been used to maintain that the sonnets themselves were written late; the explanation, I think, is that Shakespeare often first tried out a novelty of style in his private poetry. I ask for only two years; the poem was written in 1598, with tranquility, looking back with tender humor at his relations with Southampton, and just after killing off Falstaff. There would be no intention of publication; perhaps he wrote it in the evenings of a solitary journey. It would at any rate be a change, after seeing himself as Falstaff, to become the traditional forsaken damsel (forsaken, because by 1596 the earl had become absorbed in his dangerous life; we need not look for a specific ground of quarrel, though we may expect that Shakespeare did, at the time). Shakespeare, like other authors, often used poetry to scold himself out of a bad state of mind, and took for granted that no one would realize he was doing it. He knew it was a delusion that the earl had betrayed him, and writing about Falstaff had aggravated the sentiment, so he wrote a parody. Or perhaps he merely felt it was delightful to carry the belief to a wild extreme. These conjectures have the merit of explaining why the poem was written at all, though (fairly clearly) not intended for publication. Most people find that working for a repertory company is exhausting in itself, especially if they have part responsibility for the management; a man who also gives the company two masterpieces a year, as regular as clockwork, with a good deal of reading behind them, is not looking around for something to do. It is thus in order to suppose an internal reason for undertaking this quite lengthy bit of work, since there is no external one.

The first ten verses set the scene, and the rest is all spoken by the ruined girl; as many critics have remarked, the best and most Shakespearean lines express reproach:

Thus merely with the garment of a Grace,
The naked and concealèd fiend he covered. (lines 316–17)

O father, what a hell of witchcraft lies
In the small orb of one particular tear! (lines 288–89)

All the same, the girl firmly asserts in the last words of the poem that she would have him ruin her again if she got the chance:

O, all that borrowed motion, seeming owed,
Would yet again betray the fore-betrayed
And new-pervert a reconcilèd maid! (lines 327–30)

No other author would do this; one man would bewail the seduction and another treat it jovially, but not both at once. Indeed, rather few male poets seem convinced that young men in general are irresistible to women. A reader of novels will rightly feel baffled at not knowing the social arrangements of this village, where many people write sonnets expounding the suitability of the rich jewels that they are presenting to the young man (line 210); is it in Arcadia or Warwickshire? is he the son of a laborer, or the heir to a hundred acres, say?

He had the dialect and different skill,
Catching all passions in his craft of will,

That he did in the general bosom reign
Of young, of old, and sexes both enchanted,
To dwell with him in thoughts, or to remain
In personal duty, following where he haunted. (lines 125–30)

The magical picture applies to only one person, who had been already an earl when still a child; no wonder, after puzzling their heads, they decided that he was the one who was clever, and not just his horse (lines 114–19). In all the undramatic poems Shakespeare is deliberately holding back the power to be funny, which was considered when he wrote A Lover's Complaint to be much his greatest power; but he knew a joke when he saw one, even if he had just written it down himself. But perhaps when I say "funny" I would be more intelligible to young people (who have such grim ideas now of what makes a joke) if I said "charming." The chief merit of Alfred L. Rowse's account, on the other hand (William Shakespeare, 1964), was in its powerful presentation of Southampton as a typical neurotic invert, intolerably disagreeable, who could only regard the queen as a personal rival. Under James, after he had unexpectedly won back his life, he played a considerable part in founding the English colonies in America, and the only picture that conveys his charm

shows him as an elder statesman. (It is in C. C. Stopes's Life, p. 449.) But we have a glimpse of him when twenty in the Valentine of the Two Gentlemen of Verona. This figure is bustling along, with a rope ladder hidden under his cloak, to abduct the daughter of the Duke of Milan, but the duke accosts him and asks his advice—how is one to abduct a lady who is kept locked up in a high bedroom? Why, with a rope ladder, of course, equipped with grappling irons but light enough to carry under one's cloak; Valentine feels he is cleverly secret because he just manages to restrain himself from offering to share the use of his rope ladder with the outraged father, but so far from that, he and his cloak are farcically transparent. The brash informative practicality of this does not feel to me neurotic at all, and I expect that many of his servants were in love with him when he was twenty, not only Shakespeare. Plainly he seemed very young to Shakespeare, who was not only ten years older but had had a harder time. The Bard could not be considered low; as heir to an ex-mayor of Stratford he would become entitled to gentility. But the social ladder was long and steep, and the expense of the clothes the earl wore all the time would alone be enough to make him seem legendary—though he did not seem another breed from common men, the title being a recent creation.

A grave change in the whole tone of Shakespeare's writing arrives at the time of Hamlet (1600), the first major tragedy, and here it would be fussy to suppose that he was even remembering his relations with the patron. Critics since A. C. Bradley have pretty well agreed that "sex-horror" is prominent all through the tragic period (perhaps burning itself out in the unfinished Timon of Athens, before Antony and Cleopatra). I do not understand this change, though I expect there is a simple answer if we knew it. The reason why The Lover's Complaint must have been written earlier is simply that otherwise it would have been much grimmer. The change I think is prominent even in the parallels to Hamlet that give Muir his main evidence; The Lover's Complaint is regularly less fierce than the echoes of it that convey the doom of Ophelia. We have no non-dramatic poems to guide us after the tragic period has set in.

Only one remains to be considered, and it is short; but it has come to seem the only very good narrative poem, exquisite, baffling, and exalted: The Phoenix and the Turtle.[3]

[3] There has been a recent move in favor of saying The Phoenix and Turtle instead of The Phoenix and the Turtle. It is true that the title pages of Chester speak of "The Phoenix and Turtle," and Shakespeare's poem as first printed has no title. But his way of regarding this pair has long been recognized as slightly different from Chester's. A social column will report the presence at a party of "The Earl and Countess of X" because they are expected to go together, and that is how Chester feels about his Phoenix and Turtle, but Shakespeare, whatever else he feels, always regards their co-presence with a touch of surprise. A critic may write about a poem: "The familiar lion and unicorn serve to emphasize the wholly conventional character of the imagery," but they become "the lion and the unicorn" when they are fighting for the crown. Shakespeare's poem really is a bit like "The Walrus and the Carpenter," and cannot be properly appreciated unless that is seen. Looking now for evidence to support the traditional preference (though it is apparently no older than a Boston edition of 1805), I find the poem grants it repeatedly: "Phoenix and the turtle fled," "this turtle and his queen," "the turtle saw his right," "it made this threne,/To the phoenix and the dove," "And the turtle's loyal breast/To eternity doth rest." In effect, The Phoenix and the Turtle emerges as a habitual rhythm of Shakespeare's poem, and an illogical pedantry ought not to be allowed to destroy so natural a title.

It is much better, I think, if viewed less portentously than has become usual. The occasion for Shakespeare's agreeing to write this bit of praise, in late 1598 or early 1599, was a humane and domestic one, though socially rather smart. I have no impulse to deny that vast and fundamental meanings derive or arise from the poem, such as were adumbrated when C. S. Lewis said that reading it was like entering the secret origins of creation, or at least of the creation of the heroines of Shakespeare's plays. But it does not tell Queen Elizabeth to produce an heir by the Earl of Essex, nor even mutter about the marital secrets of the Countess of Bedford. If Shakespeare had been prone to say things like that, he would not have stayed afloat for long upon the smoking waters of the court. It may be hoped that such theories are going out of fashion, but what we are regularly told now, though it sounds more modest, is quite as damaging to the poem. J. C. Maxwell takes it for granted when he remarks that Shakespeare's poem "contradicts the personal allegory of Chester's poem," so that "our interpretation must be from within the poem itself." He seems to feel that this makes it pure. But Shakespeare would have been abominably rude if he had behaved like that, after agreeing to take part in the social event of offering a volume of congratulation to Sir John Salisbury. The whole book was about the birth of a new Phoenix from the ashes of the old one, a story that every reader had been taught at school, and here it was somehow in praise of Salisbury's marriage; but Shakespeare is presumed to say: "No, of course the new Phoenix wasn't born. When you burned the old one you simply killed it, as anybody could have told you you would." But, even if he had tried to offer this rudeness, it would not have been printed. The immense indulgences nowadays offered to the avant-garde are not in question here. Salisbury was a forthright and decisive man, brought up to advance the glory of his house, and we know he made Ben Jonson rewrite one of the poems for his book; he would no more have allowed Shakespeare to palm off on him a subjective poem than a seditious one.

Verses by Shakespeare, Marston, Chapman, and Jonson, and also by an anonymous poet who seems to be Jonson again (probably one of his team had backed out from fear of ridicule) are added at the end of a long allegorical poem, *Love's Martyr*, by Robert Chester (unregistered, 1601); a separate title page assures us that these too are "never before extant, and (now first) consecrated to the love and merit of the thrice-noble knight, Sir John Salisbury." The book appeared at the height of the War of the Theaters, when several of the contributors were quarreling, and soon after the execution of Essex, when it was very dangerous to print a riddle that might arouse the suspicions of the queen. Surely it is natural to expect that the poems were written earlier.

The introduction to an edition by Carleton Brown (1914) of *Poems by Sir John Salusbury and Robert Chester* (Early English Text Society, 113) is a mine of information and entertainment about these characters, and ought I think to have settled the question. Salisbury (we may use the ordinary spelling because Chester's book does) was squire of Lleweny in north Wales, and had married in 1586 at the age of twenty an illegitimate but recognized daughter of the King of Man (or Earl of Derby); some verses written for the wedding already call her a royal bird. In 1595 he came to London as a law student and was made squire of the body to the queen; he was her cousin, and a determined Anglican (having got the estate when his Papist brother was executed for the Babington Plot), and had a standing quarrel in Denbighshire with supporters of the Essex faction. This last would be no help until the execution of Essex, early in 1601, but in June of that year he was knighted by the queen herself. By October he was back home being elected to Parliament as Knight of the Shire, with scandalous disorders, so he must have moved fast. Clearly, the poem was hurried out to celebrate the knighthood, unregistered to save time and because the queen would not suspect a man she was rewarding for his loyalty; but the writing would have been done beforehand, to wait for the occasion. A line from Jonson's "Epode" here is quoted in *England's Parnassus* (1600) showing that at least some of these poems were ready about two years before publication. Also an autograph copy of Jonson's "Enthusiastic Ode" survives, inscribed to the Countess of Bedford. The squire would show round all the poems at court, as soon as they were ready; and the ever-helpful countess might be expected to want her own copy of Jonson's contribution, as it was not yet to be available in print. In this poem he was evidently struggling to be as jolly about the Phoenix as the Turtle demanded. Clumsy as Jonson was, he would not have given it to the countess as direct praise of her own charms; or at least, she would not have kept it, if he had.

In 1597 the squire had printed some poems at the end of *Sinetes Passion* by Robert Parry, who calls him "the Patron"; they make very elaborate anagrams (in easy singing lines) on the names of three adored ladies, one of them his wife's sister. While very pugnacious, he was what a later age called "a martyr to the fair," attentive to the ladies, so it had seemed all right at the time of the wedding to make him a sacrifice as Turtle beside the semi-royal bride as Phoenix. In 1598 he would be a very useful patron for the young Ben Jonson, who was in desperate need of one, and he seems to have told Jonson to whip up a chorus of London poets. Shakespeare's company was giving Jonson a production, and it would be consistent to help him here too—assuming that Shakespeare had no objections to the general plan. So far from that, Shakespeare was amused or charmed by both the squire and his poet—as is clear once we admit that he wrote his tribute, not while Hamlet was saying he could not bear to think what his mother did in bed, but while Henry V was saying,

Though it appear a little out of fashion,
There is much care and valor in this Welshman.

(IV.i.83–84)

Shakespeare made it part of his business to keep an eye on these pushful Welsh cousins of the queen, and he recommended them to his audiences without hiding their absurdity.

Chester, says Brown, was probably the resident chaplain in the big house at Lleweny, anyway a dependent who praised the family by an allegory at the time of the grand wedding. Later he was induced to add a lot of tedious padding (Nature takes the Phoenix on a grand tour), but the basic allegory is quite short and readable, though radically absurd. A marriage does indeed require mutual accommodation, and love may genuinely receive "a mystical reinforcement" on the birth of a child; but to praise a grand marriage by calling it a martyrdom is a gaffe, all the more absurd because sure to be suspected of being true. Chester evidently came to feel this during the years while he was adding the encyclopedia verses, and when at last he had to tell the London poets what the whole thing meant, so that they could reinforce it, he said it meant "married chastity." This idea had not been prominent when he began, though the intention was already high and pure. When Nature at last leads the Phoenix to the Turtle, she asks whether he has been chaste, and, on being reassured, explains that for her to produce issue requires burning alive; both birds at once collect twigs, so there is no long period of married chastity. (This of course is *why* you sometimes see birds carrying about twigs.) The main poem by Ben Jonson puzzles about his set theme, in a plain-man way; it seems a new idea to him. Trying to isolate the ideal, he appears to describe a man who spares his wife the act of sex in order not to offend her delicacy. We should welcome any sign of readiness among men of that age to treat their wives more considerately, especially if it meant spacing out the child-births; but the refined thoughts expressed by Jonson here are remote from his tastes and convictions as otherwise known. He is not a hypocrite, because he is writing to a set theme; but his modern admirers should not praise him for his nobility. Rather out of the side of his mouth, he lets drop that one need not praise a husband who chose this course merely to hide impotence:

> We do not number here
> Such spirits as are only continent
> Because lust's means are spent.

Oddly enough, Shakespeare manages to work the same reflection into his mood of total praise; the reproduction of the Phoenix, he surmises, has failed only because of the married chastity of the couple: " 'Twas not their infirmity." Various modern critics have explained that Shakespeare could not bear the thought of reproduction when he wrote the poem; but nobody has yet ascribed quite so much delicacy to Ben Jonson.

*The Mutual Flame* by G. Wilson Knight (1955) shows that the Phoenix legend had often been used to symbolize a love denied bodily consummation, because that would be adulterous or homosexual or politically disruptive, so that the love is driven to more spiritual courses. He suggests that the poem may be about the squire's love for his wife's sister, which would at least avoid absurdity. One should remember here an epigram of C. S. Lewis, that Spenser was the first poet to have the nerve to say it is convenient for a man to be in love with his own wife. There had been a change of feeling since the Middle Ages, a thing so general that poor Chester, in the backwoods, around 1587, was running Spenser close for the priority. Salisbury of course really did consider himself ready for heroic self-sacrifice whenever that became necessary; the idea was basic to his status, and had to be expressed firmly in his book; but otherwise he wanted the book to be as jolly as possible, and his pride in his wife had better be expressed in a firmly sexy manner—that was a point where he could take over from his chaplain. His marriage had produced four children

in the first four years, six in the next ten (no twins), and one of his bastards had been baptized in the parish church in 1597. No wonder Jonson argued about what Chester could have meant. The Phoenix herself will not have come to London, with all those ailing children, but a few vigorous comments survive from her and she apparently lived to be seventy-five.[4] Shakespeare might genuinely have supposed it to be an ideal though perhaps barbaric marriage.

The Wilson Knight thesis does have a secondary truth; what keeps the long absurd poem sweet is Chester's love for his master. This kind of love was avowable and not usually tormented, but when Chester comes to present himself as the Pelican, who gazes upon the burning, he positively claims a share in the honors of sacrifice; both the Phoenix and the Turtle become the "young ones" of this Pelican and feed their "hungry fancies" on her breast. He has been underrated, I think; so long as he is praising his dear Lion (the coat of arms of Salisbury was a white lion) he has any amount of limpid depth. And why should not his absurdity (though he fears it) express something profound? If anything seems wrong with his poem, he says as he lumbers toward the end, abandoning for a moment the disguise of the Pelican,

> 'tis lameness of the mind
> That had no better skill; yet let it pass,
> For burdenous loads are set upon an ass.

This is the royal generosity of the Shakespearean clown, and Shakespeare was quite right to salute it.

Once the general tone has been grasped, of slightly fuddled good humor, the dramatic placing of the piece by Shakespeare can be seen as reasonably good. The two first additional poems are subscribed "Vatum Chorus" (all the poets) and praise the virtues of Salisbury only, not his wife or family; then two poems subscribed "Ignoto" (Unknown, by the starving but invincible Ben Jonson again, of course), without pretending not to know the Phoenix legend (which would be too absurd) manage to direct our attention to the sacrifice of the old Phoenix, not presenting it as repaid by the birth of a new one. Such is the purpose of the phrasing, "One Phoenix born, another Phoenix burn." The build-up is only rough, but it is an intentional preparation for what Shakespeare is going to do. Shakespeare then presents himself as one of the spectators after the burning, among the nonpredatory birds who are the voice of Reason, and they fall into despair because the result of the experiment is delayed. I gather from J. C. Maxwell's edition that it was traditional to allow a period of dramatic suspense. Shakespeare ingeniously fits in the set theme of "married chastity" as an excuse for the failure of the experiment. But what follows his noble resignation, what holds the opposite page, is the astonishment of a birth from the ashes. It begins:

---

[4] Carleton Brown, *Poems by Sir John Salusbury and Robert Chester* (1914), p. xxvi. Chester's poem says that the Phoenix had been anxious before meeting the Turtle, being of ripe age and fearing to have no offspring. No doubt it was often a tricky business to find a good enough marriage for the bastard daughter of an earl. I expect she was twenty-five when the elder brother of young John was hanged, so that he inherited the estate and became free to marry her in what would be considered the nick of time. It does not mean that she was the queen, who would be sixty-five.

O 'twas a moving epicidium!
Can Fire? Can Time? Can blackest Fate consume
So rare Creation? No, 'tis thwart to sense;
Corruption quakes to touch such excellence.

The recent scholarly edition of Marston's *Poems* (1961, ed. Davenport) says firmly that the word *epicidium* (poem about death) means the poem by Shakespeare just concluded. Marston snatches a moment to compliment Shakespeare, as he bounds onto the stage to describe the event in an entirely different literary style; and his only objection is that the forecast in Shakespeare's poem has, astoundingly, turned out wrong:

Let me stand numbed with wonder; never came
So strong amazement on astonished eye
As this, this measureless pure rarity.

I consider that very good poetry. The subsequent poems all deal with Salisbury's domestic life, wife or child being mentioned every time, so that Shakespeare's poem acts as a watershed. Anyhow, he could not have intended to spoil the show because of his neuroses; that would be quite outside his habits and training. He was acting as a good trouper when he left the climax to Marston, and he seems to have remembered Marston's bit long afterward for the last scene of *The Winter's Tale*.

Having thus restored the poem to decency, one may consider its use of "inverted Platonism." It says that, because these two ideal lovers are dead, there will never be real lovers again, anywhere:

Truth may seem, but cannot be;
Beauty brag, but 'tis not she;
Truth and Beauty buried be.                (lines 62–64)

However, the next and final verse abandons this high extremity of nonsense:

To this urn let those repair
That are either true or fair;
For these dead birds sigh a prayer.        (lines 65–67)

I suppose the reason why Shakespeare can afford to be lax about it in this curious way, which allows him a graceful ending to the poem, is that he is working in an accepted mode. All the poets in the book seem in command of the trick, even Robert Chester; he uses it when the Pelican rejoices that the Turtle chose to burn alive, though the Phoenix tried to spare him (the experience turned out to be a pleasure, according to the Pelican's eye-witness account). Otherwise, he says:

Love had been murdered in the infancy;
Without these two, no love at all can be.

It is clear then that Chester was writing another Myth of Origin. But can he have had the whole machine ready in 1587, a homely author, remotely secluded? This seemed to me a great puzzle, and I am glad to have it removed by W. H. Matchett's recent book on the poem (1965). He explains that Chester added the Pelican section, at the end of his first draft, when the squire took him to London

to negotiate with the poets (the squire would not himself have demanded to be praised for married chastity). In a way, Chester must have known the idea from the start because it is inherent in this use of myth, but he had become uneasy about the absurdity of his whole plan; so that it would be a great relief when the smart poets, though they did laugh at him as he had expected, told him that his absurdity had become the height of fashion. He was inspired to add what is the most eloquent and personal section of the whole work.

Matchett has a very welcome energy of logic and research; what other critics limply assume, he follows up.[5] I hope his book will drive out of people's minds the main idea which he champions, that Shakespeare was writing about the loves of Elizabeth and Essex; when he says that Shakespeare refers to the queen as already dead in order to rebuke her for not having followed his previous advice, whereas in fact the exasperated and appalling old woman had become dangerous to anybody who had to approach her, surely this is enough to act as a purge. But I think he is right (for instance) in saying that Jonson became frightened on hearing that the poems would appear during 1601, when they were likely to be supposed to be about Essex; he made some baffling remarks in his plays of that year, hoping to offset the publication. Matchett also gets his teeth into "inverted Platonism," as one might expect, and it is a great comfort to find a critic who is prepared to attend to the words. Somehow he contrives to denounce Marston and not Shakespeare for using this trope:

Against Shakespeare's materialistic basis for negative judgment, he asserts a pseudo-Platonic basis for positive judgment. As an exposition of Platonic abstractions, Marston's poem is an awkward melange; as a compliment to an allegorized individual—claiming that this person is himself the Idea upon which all else depends—his poem further degrades the very idealism it pretends to express.

Marston says he had been wondering why all the young girls were so ugly and stupid nowadays until he saw the new Phoenix, and then he realized that Nature had just been saving up, so as to give her everything. The eldest Salisbury child, a daughter, would have been about twelve when this was written for her, and it seems well enough calculated for her age-group; she would think it rather fun. If anything, I should call it science fiction, not Platonism; it does not deserve to be rebuked as false philosophy, because it scarcely even pretends to be philosophy. But somebody else deserves the rebuke; why do modern critics invariably write down that the trope is neo-platonic? Its effects, very various, are nearly always broader and more imaginative than would be gathered from this docketing.

Elizabethan jokes are notoriously confusing, but it would be wrong to think that the Welsh squire was being fooled by the city slickers. He wanted his book as jolly as was compatible with having it sustain the glory of his house, and he rejected the first draft of Ben Jonson's

---

[5] He remarks that a scribe may write the name of the author after copying a poem without intending a signature, and this would destroy a good deal of the edifice of Carleton Brown. But if you wrote a name with set formal flourishes, surely that implied it was your signature.

Invocation"; at least, there is no other reason why this much more solemn version in Jonson's handwriting should have been kept among the Salisbury papers. And he must have strained the good will of his chaplain when he inserted his own "Cantos" at the end of the allegory, celebrating his delight in the beauty of the Phoenix in a very unsacrificial manner (only the first is announced as written by the Turtle, but they all have his very recognizable facility and ingenuity, and the printer might well get confused among the stage directions and acknowledgments). The celebration of his knighthood positively required family jollity; indeed, one can understand that Shakespeare, though willing to assist, felt he would avoid strain if he joined them only in their darkest hour. Even so, what he was joining was a kind of domestic game.

An important idea is at work in such love poetry, though admittedly one that was ridiculous in the eyes of the world; it forbade a husband to claim marital rights through his legal superiority, and such is the point of Shakespeare's ninth verse. We know that Chapman thought the affair funny, though in a grave pedantic manner, because he headed his piece (which praised the knight who has learned his virtues by serving his lady) "Peristeros, or the male Turtle." He has had to invent a masculine form for the word, since the Greeks considered all doves female; however monogamous they may be, the creatures do not know which sex they are, but try out the alternatives (Sir Julian Huxley, in *Essays of a Biologist*, reports this of various water birds). A female Phoenix had been invented by the Renaissance to gratify a taste for Amazons —till then its secret sex had been "known to God alone"; but a Turtle wearing the trousers does seem to have been a real novelty, not only for a classicist. It proved the grandeur of the Lion, as his poet almost says in the *Epistle Dedicatory*, that he was safe from ridicule even when presented as a Turtle. The Latin "Tur tur" no doubt gave to the cooing of the pets of Venus, in the minds of the poets, a deeper note of sultry passion; to make them into symbols of chastity thus put an extra strain upon the gravity of the reader—it had been the charm of the silly creatures that no frustration attended their single-minded desires. Shakespeare's poem is a wide valley brimful of an unspecified sorrow, but one should also feel, before hearing any explanation, the gaiety inherent in its effects of sound. As the anthem of the birds reaches its severest exultation, their tweeting modulates into the arch baby-talk of a dandling nurse; as we soar heavenward between the Co-supremes, we mysteriously almost graze the Cow that jumped over the Moon;

> To themselves yet either neither,
> Simple were so well compounded. (lines 43–44)

It does seem rather odd, in a way, that he went straight on from this to his great tragic period.

## A NOTE ON THE TEXT

THE CANONICAL POEMS. Three nondramatic poems (other than the sonnets) are regularly attributed to Shakespeare: *Venus and Adonis*, *The Rape of Lucrece*, and *The Phoenix and the Turtle*. *Venus and Adonis* was first published in a quarto dated 1593, *Lucrece* (thus the title page, but the heading at the beginning of the poem, and on all the following pages, is *The Rape of Lucrece*) in a quarto dated 1594. Both quartos are dedicated to Shakespeare's patron, the Earl of Southampton. These two books were Shakespeare's first publications, and they were destined for a nobleman's eye; Shakespeare apparently read the proofs, and the texts are remarkably clean. There is no reason to believe that he had anything to do with the later quartos, which introduce numerous changes.

The third canonical poem, *The Phoenix and the Turtle*, appears (without a title) attributed to Shakespeare in a quarto (1601) whose title page reads in part: "*Love's Martyr* . . . allegorically shadowing the truth of Love, in the constant fate of the phoenix and turtle. . . . A poem . . . by Robert Chester. . . . To these [Chester's poem and other materials] are added some new compositions, of several modern writers, whose names are subscribed to their several works, upon the first subject, viz. the phoenix and turtle."

THE APOCRYPHAL POEMS. *A Lover's Complaint* appears at the end of the 1609 volume of Shakespeare's sonnets, published by Thomas Thorpe. No one doubts that the sonnets are Shakespeare's, but many doubt that *A Lover's Complaint* is his. The usual view is that the poem does not sound like Shakespeare, and that the publisher's ascription is of no value. The poem does not do Shakespeare great credit, and a fair number of its words do not appear elsewhere in Shakespeare; still, there is no evidence that anyone else wrote it. Thorpe's attribution is not compelling, but it is all the evidence there is.

In 1599 a dishonest publisher named William Jaggard issued *The Passionate Pilgrim. By W. Shakespeare.* The book contains twenty poems, of which five are certainly by Shakespeare and four are certainly not by Shakespeare. The remaining eleven are of uncertain authorship, but there is no reason (other than Jaggard's dubious word) to believe that Shakespeare wrote any of these, though of course he may have written one or more of them. The five poems by Shakespeare are numbered I, II, III, V, and XVI (I and II are versions of sonnets 138 and 144; III and V are versions of sonnets in *Love's Labor's Lost*, IV.iii.57–70 and IV.ii.107–20; XVI is a version of a short poem in *Love's Labor's Lost*, IV.iii.98–117). These five poems are given in the present volume in the *Sonnets* and *Love's Labor's Lost*. The four poems that are not by Shakespeare are VIII (by Richard Barnfield), XI (by Bartholomew Griffin), XIX (really two poems, probably one by Marlowe and one by Raleigh), and XX (by Richard Barnfield). The remaining eleven poems are presented here, though few people would care to claim them all for Shakespeare. They are for the most part competent, but only number XII has aroused much enthusiasm.

Departures from the copy texts are listed below. The adopted reading is given first in boldface type, followed by the original reading in roman. The copy text for *Venus and Adonis* and *The Rape of Lucrece* is of course the first quarto of each poem. The copy text of *The Phoenix and the Turtle* is *Love's Martyr* (1601), that of *A Lover's Complaint* is the quarto of 1609. The earliest known complete text of *The Passionate Pilgrim* is the second edition (1599), but some pages of the first edition (perhaps also 1599) survive at the

Folger Library. This earlier edition provides texts of three (IV, XVII, and XVIII) of the eleven doubtful poems. The copy text for the other eight doubtful poems is necessarily the second edition.

**Venus and Adonis  19 satiety** sacietie  **231, 239 deer** deare  **432 Ear's** Eares  **616 javelin's** iauelings  **644 Saw'st** Sawest  **680 overshoot** ouer-shut  **748 th'** the th'  **754 sons** suns  **873 twine** twin'd  **940 dost** doest  **1031 as** are  **1054 was** had
**The Rape of Lucrece  550 blows** blow  **883 mak'st** makest  **884 blow'st** blowest  **1227 flower** flowre  **1312 schedule** Cedule  **1662 wreathèd** wretched  **1680 one woe** on woe  **1713 in it** it in
**A Lover's Complaint  14 lattice** lettice  **80 Of** O  **95 wear** were  **112 manage** mannad'g  **118 Came** Can  **182 woo** vow  **241 Paling** Playing  **252 procured** procure  **260 nun** Sunne  **293 O** Or  **311 as** is[6]

---

[6] William Empson suggests emending *A Lover's Complaint*, line 311, which reads: "Showing fair nature is both kind and tame." Mr. Empson writes: "It seems better, though not necessary, to

**The Passionate Pilgrim IV  5 ear** eares  **10 her** his
**VII 11 midst** mids
**X 8, 9 left'st** lefts
**XIV 24 sighed** sight  **27 a moon** an houre
**XV 3 fair'st** fairest
**XVII 28 back** blacke  **33 lass** loue  **34 moan** woe
**XVIII 4 fancy's partial might** fancy (partyall might)  **12 thy** her; **sell** sale  **22 Press** Prease  **26, 29 ere** yer  **45 be** by  **51 ear** are

---

emend *is* to *as*, an easy change in itself. Otherwise *kind and tame* has to mean 'the fact that he could seduce *any* virgin makes them all look like sheep.' Maybe this was Shakespeare's opinion, but he does not express it so bleakly. Besides, *them* in the next line has to refer back to *strange forms* (line 303), the pretenses of tenderness which the seducer was skilled at adopting; if your mind is cluttered with tame ladies you miss the grammar. *Nature* here is chiefly the sexual experience, and he shows it to the virgins *as* not alarming; it really is *fair*, we are told by the author and the wronged lady, and this should content us. They can hardly want to assert that it is always *tame*."

# VENUS AND ADONIS

*Vilia miretur vulgus: mihi flavus Apollo*
*Pocula Castalia plena ministret aqua.°*

TO THE RIGHT HONORABLE
HENRY WRIOTHESLEY°
*Earl of Southampton and Baron of Titchfield*

RIGHT HONORABLE,
I know not how I shall offend in dedicating my unpolished lines to your lordship, nor how the world    5
will censure me for choosing so strong a prop to support so weak a burden; only, if your honor seem
but pleased, I account myself highly praised, and vow to take advantage of all idle hours, till I have
honored you with some graver labor. But if the first heir of my invention° prove deformed, I shall be
sorry it had so noble a godfather, and never after ear° so barren a land, for fear it yield me still so bad
a harvest. I leave it to your honorable survey, and your honor to your heart's content; which I wish    10
may always answer your own wish and the world's hopeful expectation.

Your honor's in all duty,
WILLIAM SHAKESPEARE.

Even as the sun with purple-colored° face
Had ta'en his last leave of the weeping morn,
Rose-cheeked Adonis hied him to the chase;
Hunting he loved, but love he laughed to scorn.
　Sick-thoughted° Venus makes amain° unto him,    5
　And like a bold-faced suitor 'gins to woo him.

"Thrice fairer than myself," thus she began,
"The field's chief flower, sweet above compare,
Stain to all nymphs,° more lovely than a man,
More white and red than doves or roses are,    10
　Nature that made thee, with herself at strife,
　Saith that the world hath ending with thy life.

"Vouchsafe, thou wonder, to alight thy steed,
And rein his proud head to the saddlebow.
If thou wilt deign this favor, for thy meed°    15
A thousand honey° secrets shalt thou know.
　Here come and sit, where never serpent hisses,
　And being set, I'll smother thee with kisses.

"And yet not cloy thy lips with loathed satiety,
But rather famish them amid their plenty,    20
Making them red and pale with fresh variety:
Ten kisses short as one, one long as twenty.
　A summer's day will seem an hour but short,
　Being wasted° in such time-beguiling sport."

With this she seizeth on his sweating palm,    25
The precedent of pith and livelihood,°
And trembling in her passion, calls it balm,
Earth's sovereign salve to do a goddess good:
　Being so enraged,° desire doth lend her force
　Courageously to pluck him from his horse.    30

*The decorative border shown above appeared on the title page of the
quarto edition of* The Rape of Lucrece, *1594.*
**Vilia . . . aqua** from Ovid, *Amores*, I.xv.35–36: "Let the mob
admire base things; may golden Apollo serve me full cups from
the Castalian spring" **2 Henry Wriothesley** third Earl of
Southampton, 1573–1624, thought to be Shakespeare's patron
**8 first . . . invention** my first work brought to publication
(a number of plays had already been written and produced
but were unpublished; and plays were usually considered
not worth publishing) **9 ear** plow, till
**1 purple-colored** crimson **5 Sick-thoughted** lovesick;
**amain** swiftly, strongly **9 Stain . . . nymphs** i.e., by his
surpassing beauty he eclipses them

**15 meed** reward **16 honey** sweet **24 wasted** spent **26
precedent . . . livelihood** sign of strength and energy
**29 enraged** aroused

Over one arm the lusty courser's rein,
Under her other was the tender boy,
Who blushed and pouted in a dull disdain,
With leaden appetite, unapt to toy;°
    She red and hot as coals of glowing fire,    35
    He red for shame, but frosty in desire.

The studded bridle on a ragged bough
Nimbly she fastens. O, how quick is love!
The steed is stallèd up, and even now
To tie the rider she begins to prove.°    40
    Backward she pushed him, as she would be thrust,
    And governed him in strength, though not in lust.

So soon was she along° as he was down,
Each leaning on their elbows and their hips.
Now doth she stroke his cheek, now doth he frown    45
And 'gins to chide, but soon she stops his lips,
    And kissing speaks, with lustful language broken,
    "If thou wilt chide, thy lips shall never open."

He burns with bashful shame; she with her tears
Doth quench the maiden burning of his cheeks;    50
Then with her windy sighs and golden hairs
To fan and blow them dry again she seeks.
    He saith she is immodest, blames her miss;°
    What follows more, she murders with a kiss.

Even as an empty eagle, sharp by fast,°    55
Tires° with her beak on feathers, flesh, and bone,
Shaking her wings, devouring all in haste,
Till either gorge be stuffed or prey be gone—
    Even so she kissed his brow, his cheek, his chin,
    And where she ends she doth anew begin.    60

Forced to content,° but never to obey,
Panting he lies and breatheth in her face.
She feedeth on the steam as on a prey
And calls it heavenly moisture, air of grace,
    Wishing her cheeks were gardens full of flowers,    65
    So they were dewed with such distilling showers.

Look how° a bird lies tangled in a net,
So fastened in her arms Adonis lies.
Pure shame and awed° resistance made him fret,
Which bred more beauty in his angry eyes:    70
    Rain added to a river that is rank°
    Perforce will force it overflow the bank.

Still she entreats, and prettily entreats,
For to a pretty ear° she tunes her tale.
Still is he sullen, still he low'rs and frets,    75
'Twixt crimson shame and anger ashy-pale.
    Being red, she loves him best; and being white,
    Her best is bettered with a more° delight.

Look how he can, she cannot choose but love;
And by her fair immortal hand she swears    80
From his soft bosom never to remove
Till he take truce with her contending tears,
    Which long have rained, making her cheeks all wet;
    And one sweet kiss shall pay this comptless° debt.

Upon this promise did he raise his chin,    85
Like a divedapper° peering through a wave,
Who, being looked on, ducks as quickly in:
So offers her to give what she did crave,
    But when her lips were ready for his pay,
    He winks,° and turns his lips another way.    90

Never did passenger° in summer's heat
More thirst for drink than she for this good turn.
Her help she sees, but help she cannot get;
She bathes in water, yet her fire must burn.
    "O, pity," 'gan she cry, "flint-hearted boy!    95
    'Tis but a kiss I beg—why art thou coy?

"I have been wooed as I entreat thee now,
Even by the stern and direful god of war,
Whose sinewy neck in battle ne'er did bow,
Who conquers where he comes in every jar;°    100
    Yet hath he been my captive and my slave,
    And begged for that which thou unasked shalt have.

"Over my altars hath he hung his lance,
His batt'red shield, his uncontrollèd crest,°
And for my sake hath learned to sport and dance,    105
To toy, to wanton, dally, smile, and jest,
    Scorning his churlish drum and ensign red,
    Making my arms his field, his tent my bed.

"Thus he that overruled I overswayèd,
Leading him prisoner in a red-rose chain.    110
Strong-tempered steel his stronger strength obeyèd;
Yet was he servile to my coy disdain.
    O, be not proud, nor brag not of thy might,
    For mast'ring her that foiled the god of fight!

"Touch but my lips with those fair of thine—    115
Though mine be not so fair, yet are they red—
The kiss shall be thine own as well as mine.
What see'st thou in the ground? Hold up thy head,
    Look in mine eyeballs, there thy beauty lies,
    Then why not lips on lips, since eyes in eyes?    120

"Art thou ashamed to kiss? Then wink° again,
And I will wink; so shall the day seem night.
Love keeps his revels where there are but twain.
Be bold to play; our sport is not in sight.
    These blue-veined violets whereon we lean    125
    Never can blab, nor know not what we mean.

---

34 **unapt to toy** not ready for love's play  **40 prove** try
43 **along** stretched out  **53 miss** misbehavior  **55 sharp by
fast** hungry from fasting  **56 Tires** tears  **61 content** endure
**67 Look how** just as  **69 awed** intimidated  **71 rank** full  **74
ear** pun on *air*  **78 more** greater

84 **comptless** countless  **86 divedapper** small waterbird  **90
winks** (1) winces (2) shuts his eyes  **91 passenger** traveler
**100 jar** fight  **104 uncontrollèd crest** unbowed helmet  **121
wink** close your eyes

"The tender spring° upon thy tempting lip
Shows thee unripe; yet mayst thou well be tasted.
Make use of time, let not advantage slip;
Beauty within itself should not be wasted.          130
    Fair flowers that are not gath'red in their prime
    Rot and consume themselves in little time.

"Were I hard-favored, foul, or wrinkled old,
Ill-nurtured, crooked, churlish, harsh in voice,
O'erworn, despisèd, rheumatic, and cold,          135
Thick-sighted,° barren, lean, and lacking juice,
    Then mightst thou pause, for then I were not for
      thee;
    But having no defects, why dost abhor me?

"Thou canst not see one wrinkle in my brow;
Mine eyes are gray and bright and quick in turning.          140
My beauty as the spring doth yearly grow,
My flesh is soft and plump, my marrow burning;
    My smooth moist hand, were it with thy hand felt,
    Would in thy palm dissolve, or seem to melt.

"Bid me discourse, I will enchant thine ear,          145
Or like a fairy trip upon the green,
Or like a nymph with long dishevelled hair,
Dance on the sands, and yet no footing seen.
    Love is a spirit all compact° of fire,
    Not gross to sink, but light, and will aspire.°          150

"Witness this primrose bank whereon I lie;°
These forceless° flowers like sturdy trees support me.
Two strengthless doves will draw me through the sky
From morn till night, even where I list to sport me.
    Is love so light, sweet boy, and may it be          155
    That thou should think it heavy unto thee?

"Is thine own heart to thine own face affected?°
Can thy right hand seize love upon thy left?
Then woo thyself, be of thyself rejected;
Steal thine own freedom, and complain on theft.          160
    Narcissus° so himself himself forsook,
    And died to kiss his shadow in the brook.

"Torches are made to light, jewels to wear,
Dainties to taste, fresh beauty for the use,
Herbs for their smell, and sappy plants to bear.          165
Things growing to themselves are growth's abuse.
    Seeds spring from seeds, and beauty breedeth beauty.
    Thou wast begot; to get it is thy duty.

"Upon the earth's increase° why shouldst thou feed
Unless the earth with thy increase be fed?          170
By law of nature thou art bound to breed,
That thine may live when thou thyself art dead;
    And so in spite of death thou dost survive,
    In that thy likeness still is left alive."

By this° the lovesick queen began to sweat,          175
For where they lay the shadow had forsook them,
And Titan,° tired in the midday heat,
With burning eye did hotly overlook them,
    Wishing Adonis had his team to guide,
    So he were like him, and by Venus' side.          180

And now Adonis, with a lazy sprite,°
And with a heavy, dark, disliking eye,
His low'ring brows o'erwhelming his fair sight,
Like misty vapors when they blot the sky,
    Souring his cheeks, cries, "Fie, no more of love!          185
    The sun doth burn my face—I must remove."

"Ay me," quoth Venus, "young, and so unkind?
What bare° excuses mak'st thou to be gone!
I'll sigh celestial breath, whose gentle wind
Shall cool the heat of this descending sun.          190
    I'll make a shadow for thee of my hairs;
    If they burn too, I'll quench them with my tears.

"The sun that shines from heaven shines but warm,
And, lo, I lie between that sun and thee:
The heat I have from thence doth little harm,          195
Thine eye darts forth the fire that burneth me;
    And were I not immortal, life were done
    Between this heavenly and earthly sun.

"Art thou obdurate, flinty, hard as steel?
Nay, more than flint, for stone at rain relenteth.°          200
Art thou a woman's son, and canst not feel
What 'tis to love? how want of love tormenteth?
    O, had thy mother borne so hard a mind,
    She had not brought forth thee, but died unkind.

"What am I that thou shouldst contemn me this?°          205
Or what great danger dwells upon my suit?
What were thy lips the worse for one poor kiss?
Speak, fair,° but speak fair words or else be mute.
    Give me one kiss, I'll give it thee again,
    And one for int'rest, if thou wilt have twain.          210

"Fie, lifeless picture, cold and senseless stone,
Well-painted idol, image dull and dead,
Statue contenting but the eye alone,
Thing like a man, but of no woman bred!
    Thou art no man, though of a man's complexion,°          215
    For men will kiss even by their own direction."°

This said, impatience chokes her pleading tongue,
And swelling passion doth provoke a pause.
Red cheeks and fiery eyes blaze forth her wrong;
Being judge in love, she cannot right her cause.°          220
    And now she weeps, and now she fain° would speak,
    And now her sobs do her intendments break.°

127 **tender spring** young growth (that will become a beard)
136 **Thick-sighted** with poor eyesight 149 **compact** composed 150 **aspire** rise up, float 151 **Witness . . . lie** let
this bank whereon I lie bear witness 152 **forceless** frail, without strength 157 **to . . . affected** in love with thine own face
161 **Narcissus** a beautiful youth who fell in love with his
own reflection 169 **increase** produce 175 **By this** by this time, now 177 **Titan** the sun god 181
**lazy sprite** dull spirit 188 **bare** inadequate 200 **relenteth**
i.e., is worn away 205 **this** thus 208 **fair** fair one 215
**complexion** external appearance 216 **direction** volition
220 **Being . . . cause** i.e., though Venus is the judge in all
disputes of love, she cannot obtain justice for herself 221 **fain**
gladly 222 **intendments break** intentions (i.e., what she
was going to say) interrupt

Sometime she shakes her head, and then his hand,
Now gazeth she on him, now on the ground.
Sometime her arms infold him like a band:                    225
She would, he will not in her arms be bound.
    And when from thence he struggles to be gone,
    She locks her lily fingers one in one.

"Fondling,"° she saith, "since I have hemmed thee here
Within the circuit of this ivory pale,°                       230
I'll be a park, and thou shalt be my deer:
Feed where thou wilt, on mountain or in dale;
    Graze on my lips; and if those hills be dry,
    Stray lower, where the pleasant fountains lie.

"Within this limit is relief° enough,                         235
Sweet bottom-grass,° and high delightful plain,
Round rising hillocks, brakes° obscure and rough,
To shelter thee from tempest and from rain.
    Then be my deer since I am such a park;
    No dog shall rouse° thee though a thousand bark."         240

At this Adonis smiles as in disdain,
That° in each cheek appears a pretty dimple;
Love made those hollows, if° himself were slain,
He might be buried in a tomb so simple,
    Foreknowing well, if there he came to lie,               245
    Why, there Love lived, and there he could not die.

These lovely caves, these round enchanting pits,
Opened their mouths to swallow Venus' liking.°
Being mad before, how doth she now for wits?
Struck dead at first, what needs a second striking?          250
    Poor queen of love, in thine own law forlorn,
    To love a cheek that smiles at thee in scorn!

Now which way shall she turn? What shall she say?
Her words are done, her woes the more increasing;
The time is spent, her object will away,                      255
And from her twining arms doth urge releasing.
    "Pity!" she cries, "some favor, some remorse!"°
    Away he springs and hasteth to his horse.

But, lo, from forth a copse that neighbors by
A breeding jennet,° lusty, young, and proud,                  260
Adonis' trampling courser doth espy,
And forth she rushes, snorts, and neighs aloud.
    The strong-necked steed, being tied unto a tree,
    Breaketh his rein, and to her straight goes he.

Imperiously he leaps, he neighs, he bounds,                   265
And now his woven girths he breaks asunder;
The bearing° earth with his hard hoof he wounds,
Whose hollow womb resounds like heaven's thunder;
    The iron bit he crusheth 'tween his teeth,
    Controlling what he was controllèd with.                  270

His ears up-pricked, his braided hanging mane
Upon his compassed crest° now stand on end;
His nostrils drink the air, and forth again,
As from a furnace, vapors doth he send;
    His eye, which scornfully glisters like fire,             275
    Shows his hot courage° and his high desire.

Sometime he trots, as if he told° the steps,
With gentle majesty and modest pride;
Anon he rears upright, curvets,° and leaps,
As who should say, "Lo, thus my strength is tried,           280
    And this I do to captivate the eye
    Of the fair breeder that is standing by."

What recketh he his rider's angry stir,°
His flattering° "Holla" or his "Stand, I say"?
What cares he now for curb or pricking spur,                  285
For rich caparisons or trappings gay?
    He sees his love, and nothing else he sees,
    For nothing else with his proud sight agrees.

Look when° a painter would surpass the life
In limning° out a well-proportioned steed,                    290
His art with nature's workmanship at strife,
As if the dead the living should exceed—
    So did this horse excel a common one
    In shape, in courage, color, pace, and bone.°

Round-hoofed, short-jointed, fetlocks shag and long,    295
Broad breast, full eye, small head, and nostril wide,
High crest, short ears, straight legs and passing strong,
Thin mane, thick tail, broad buttock, tender hide:
    Look what° a horse should have he did not lack,
    Save a proud rider on so proud a back.                    300

Sometimes he scuds far off, and there he stares;
Anon he starts at stirring of a feather.
To bid the wind a base° he now prepares,
And whe'r° he run or fly they know not whether,
    For through his mane and tail the high wind sings,        305
    Fanning the hairs, who wave like feath'red wings.

He looks upon his love and neighs unto her;
She answers him, as if she knew his mind.
Being proud, as females are, to see him woo her,
She puts on outward strangeness,° seems unkind,              310
    Spurns at his love and scorns the heat he feels,
    Beating his kind embracements with her heels.

Then, like a melancholy malcontent,
He vails° his tail, that, like a falling plume,
Cool shadow to his melting buttock lent;                      315
He stamps, and bites the poor flies in his fume.°
    His love, perceiving how he was enraged,
    Grew kinder, and his fury was assuaged.

---

229 **Fondling** little fool (affectionate)  230 **pale** fence (here,
her arms)  235 **relief** (1) topography, as on a relief-map (2)
(sexual) satisfaction  236 **bottom-grass** valley-grass  237
**brakes** thickets  240 **rouse** drive from cover  242 **That** so
that  243 **if** so that if he  248 **liking** desire  257 **remorse**
mercy  260 **jennet** small Spanish horse  267 **bearing**
receiving

272 **compassed crest** arched ridge of the neck  276 **courage** lust  277 **told** counted  279 **curvets** hops  283 **stir**
excitement  284 **flattering** calming  289 **Look when**
just as  290 **limning out** drawing  294 **bone** frame  299
**Look what** whatever  303 **bid . . . base** challenge the
wind to a chase  304 **whe'r** whether  310 **outward strangeness** show of indifference  314 **vails** lowers  316 **fume** rage

His testy master goeth about to take him,
When, lo, the unbacked° breeder, full of fear,                    320
Jealous of catching,° swiftly doth forsake him,
With her the horse,° and left Adonis there.
  As they were mad unto the wood they hie them,
  Outstripping crows that strive to overfly them.

All swol'n with chafing, down Adonis sits,                        325
Banning° his boist'rous and unruly beast;
And now the happy season once more fits
That lovesick Love° by pleading may be blest;
  For lovers say the heart hath treble wrong
  When it is barred the aidance of the tongue.                    330

An oven that is stopped, or river stayed,
Burneth more hotly, swelleth with more rage;
So of concealèd sorrow may be said
Free vent of words love's fire doth assuage;
  But when the heart's attorney° once is mute,                    335
  The client breaks,° as desperate in his suit.

He sees her coming and begins to glow,
Even as a dying coal revives with wind,
And with his bonnet hides his angry brow,
Looks on the dull earth with disturbèd mind,                     340
  Taking no notice that she is so nigh,
  For all askance he holds her in his eye.

O, what a sight it was, wistly° to view
How she came stealing to the wayward° boy!
To note the fighting conflict of her hue,                        345
How white and red each other did destroy!
  But now her cheek was pale, and by and by°
  It flashed forth fire, as lightning from the sky.

Now was she just before him as he sat,
And like a lowly lover down she kneels;                          350
With one fair hand she heaveth up his hat,
Her other tender hand his fair cheek feels.
  His tend'rer cheek receives her soft hand's print
  As apt as new-fall'n snow takes any dint.°

O, what a war of looks was then between them,                    355
Her eyes petitioners to his eyes suing!
His eyes saw her eyes as° they had not seen them;
Her eyes wooed still, his eyes disdained the wooing;
  And all this dumb play° had his° acts made plain
  With tears which choruslike° her eyes did rain.                 360

Full gently now she takes him by the hand,
A lily prisoned in a jail of snow,
Or ivory in an alablaster band:
So white a friend engirts so white a foe.
  This beauteous combat, willful and unwilling,                  365
  Showed like two silver doves that sit a-billing.

Once more the engine of her thoughts° began:
"O fairest mover on this mortal round,°
Would thou wert as I am, and I a man,
My heart all whole as thine, thy heart my wound!°               370
  For one sweet look thy help I would assure thee,
  Though nothing but my body's bane° would cure thee."

"Give me my hand," saith he. "Why dost thou feel it?"
"Give me my heart," saith she, "and thou shalt have it.
O, give it me lest thy hard heart do steel° it,                  375
And being steeled, soft sighs can never grave° it.
  Then love's deep groans I never shall regard,
  Because Adonis' heart hath made mine hard."

"For shame!" he cries. "Let go, and let me go:
My day's delight is past, my horse is gone,                      380
And 'tis your fault I am bereft him so.
I pray you hence, and leave me here alone;
  For all my mind, my thought, my busy care
  Is how to get my palfrey from the mare."

Thus she replies: "Thy palfrey, as he should,                    385
Welcomes the warm approach of sweet desire.
Affection° is a coal that must be cooled;
Else, suffered,° it will set the heart on fire.
  The sea hath bounds, but deep desire hath none;
  Therefore no marvel though thy horse be gone.                  390

"How like a jade° he stood, tied to the tree,
Servilely mastered with a leathern rein;
But when he saw his love, his youth's fair fee,°
He held such petty bondage in disdain,
  Throwing the base thong from his bending crest,                395
  Enfranchising° his mouth, his back, his breast.

"Who sees his true-love in her naked° bed,
Teaching the sheets a whiter hue than white,
But, when his glutton eye so full hath fed,
His other agents° aim at like delight?                           400
  Who is so faint that dares not be so bold
  To touch the fire, the weather being cold?

"Let me excuse thy courser, gentle boy;
And learn of him, I heartily beseech thee,
To take advantage on° presented joy.                             405
Though I were dumb, yet his proceedings teach thee.
  O, learn to love! The lesson is but plain,
  And once made perfect, never lost again."

"I know not love," quoth he, "nor will not know it,
Unless it be a boar, and then I chase it.                        410
'Tis much to borrow, and I will not owe° it:
My love to love is love but to disgrace it;°
  For I have heard it is a life in death,
  That laughs and weeps, and all but with a° breath.

367 **engine . . . thoughts** her tongue  368 **mover . . .
round** living creature on earth  370 **my wound** i.e., wounded
like mine  372 **bane** ruin  375 **steel** turn to steel  376 **grave**
engrave  387 **Affection** passion  388 **suffered** tolerated
391 **jade** contemptuous term for horse  393 **fair fee** due
reward  396 **Enfranchising** setting free  397 **naked** modifies
"true-love," not "bed"  400 **agents** organs  405 **on** of  411
**owe** own  412 **My . . . it** my only attitude toward love is a
desire to discredit it  414 **but with a** in the same

320 **unbacked** unbroken  321 **Jealous of catching** afraid of
being caught  322 **horse** i.e., stallion  326 **Banning** cursing
328 **Love** Venus  335 **the heart's attorney** the tongue
336 **breaks** goes bankrupt  343 **wistly** attentively  344 **wayward** willful  347 **by and by** quickly  354 **dint** impression
357 **as** as if  359 **dumb play** dumb show, pantomime; **his** its
360 **choruslike** i.e., served as a commentator

"Who wears a garment shapeless and unfinished? 415
Who plucks the bud before one leaf put forth?
If springing things be any jot diminished,
They wither in their prime, prove nothing worth.
　The colt that's backed° and burdened being young
　Loseth his pride, and never waxeth strong. 420

"You hurt my hand with wringing; let us part,
And leave this idle theme, this bootless° chat;
Remove your siege from my unyielding heart;
To love's alarms° it will not ope the gate.
　Dismiss your vows, your feignèd tears, your flatt'ry; 425
　For where a heart is hard they make no batt'ry."°

"What! canst thou talk?" quoth she. "Hast thou a
　　tongue?
O, would thou hadst not, or I had no hearing!
Thy mermaid's° voice hath done me double wrong;
I had my load before, now pressed° with bearing: 430
　Melodious discord, heavenly tune harsh sounding,
　Ear's deep-sweet music, and heart's deep-sore
　　wounding.

"Had I no eyes but ears, my ears would love
That inward beauty and invisible;
Or were I deaf, thy outward parts would move 435
Each part in me that were but sensible.°
　Though neither eyes nor ears, to hear nor see,
　Yet should I be in love by touching thee.

"Say that the sense of feeling were bereft me,
And that I could not see, nor hear, nor touch, 440
And nothing but the very smell were left me,
Yet would my love to thee be still as much;
　For from the stillitory° of thy face excelling
　Comes breath perfumed that breedeth love by
　　smelling.

"But, O, what banquet wert thou to the taste, 445
Being nurse and feeder to the other four!
Would they not wish the feast might ever last
And bid Suspicion double-lock the door,
　Lest Jealousy, that sour unwelcome guest,
　Should by his stealing in disturb the feast?" 450

Once more the ruby-colored portal opened
Which to his speech did honey passage yield;
Like a red morn that ever yet betokened
Wrack° to the seaman, tempest to the field,
　Sorrow to shepherds, woe unto the birds, 455
　Gusts and foul flaws° to herdmen and to herds.

This ill presage advisedly she marketh.
Even as the wind is hushed before it raineth,
Or as the wolf doth grin° before he barketh,
Or as the berry breaks before it staineth, 460
　Or like the deadly bullet of a gun,
　His meaning struck her ere his words begun.

And at his look she flatly falleth down,
For looks kill love, and love by looks reviveth;
A smile recures° the wounding of a frown. 465
But blessèd bankrout° that by love so thriveth!
　The silly° boy, believing she is dead,
　Claps her pale cheek, till clapping makes it red,

And all amazed brake off his late intent,
For sharply he did think to reprehend her, 470
Which cunning love did wittily° prevent.
Fair fall° the wit that can so well defend her!
　For on the grass she lies as she were slain
　Till his breath breatheth life in her again.

He wrings her nose, he strikes her on the cheeks, 475
He bends her fingers, holds her pulses hard,
He chafes her lips; a thousand ways he seeks
To mend the hurt that his unkindness marred.°
　He kisses her; and she, by her good will,°
　Will never rise, so he will kiss her still. 480

The night of sorrow now is turned to day:
Her two blue windows° faintly she upheaveth,
Like the fair sun when in his fresh array
He cheers the morn and all the earth relieveth;
　And so the bright sun glorifies the sky, 485
　So is her face illumined with her eye;

Whose beams upon his hairless face are fixed,
As if from thence they borrowed all their shine.
Were never four such lamps together mixed,
Had not his clouded with his brow's repine;° 490
　But hers, which through the crystal tears gave light,
　Shone like the moon in water seen by night.

"O, where am I?" quoth she, "in earth or heaven,
Or in the ocean drenched, or in the fire?
What hour is this? or morn or° weary even? 495
Do I delight to die, or life desire?
　But now I lived, and life was death's annoy;°
　But now I died, and death was lively joy.

"O, thou didst kill me, kill me once again!
Thy eyes' shrewd° tutor, that hard heart of thine, 500
Hath taught them scornful tricks, and such disdain
That they have murd'red this poor heart of mine;
　And these mine eyes, true leaders to their queen,°
　But for thy piteous lips no more had seen.

"Long may they kiss each other, for this cure! 505
O, never let their crimson liveries wear;°
And as they last, their verdure° still endure,
To drive infection from the dangerous year;
　That the stargazers, having writ on death,°
　May say the plague is banished by thy breath. 510

**419 backed** broken in　**422 bootless** useless　**424 alarms**
attacks　**426 batt'ry** successful entry　**429 mermaid's** siren's
**430 pressed** oppressed　**436 sensible** able to receive any other
sensations　**443 stillitory** distilling plant　**454 Wrack** wreck
**456 flaws** blasts of wind　**459 grin** bare its fangs

**465 recures** heals　**466 bankrout** bankrupt　**467 silly** innocent　**471 wittily** cleverly　**472 Fair fall** prosperity befall
**478 marred** inflicted　**479 by . . . will** willingly　**482 blue
windows** her eyelids　**490 repine** vexation　**495 or . . . or**
either . . . or　**497 annoy** torment　**500 shrewd** harsh　**503
their queen** the heart　**506 crimson liveries wear** red colors
wear out　**507 verdure** freshness　**509 stargazers . . . death**
astrologers, who have predicted an epidemic

"Pure lips, sweet seals in my soft lips imprinted,
What bargains may I make, still° to be sealing?°
To sell myself I can be well contented,
So thou wilt buy, and pay, and use good dealing;
    Which purchase if thou make, for fear of slips°    515
    Set thy seal manual° on my wax-red lips.

"A thousand kisses buys my heart from me;
And pay them at thy leisure, one by one.
What is ten hundred touches° unto thee?
Are they not quickly told° and quickly gone?    520
    Say for nonpayment that the debt should double,
    Is twenty hundred kisses such a trouble?"

"Fair queen," quoth he, "if any love you owe° me,
Measure my strangeness with my unripe years.°
Before I know myself, seek not to know me:    525
No fisher but the ungrown fry° forbears;
    The mellow plum doth fall, the green sticks fast,
    Or being early plucked is sour to taste.

"Look, the world's comforter, with weary gait,
His day's hot task hath ended in the west;    530
The owl, night's herald, shrieks; 'tis very late;
The sheep are gone to fold, birds to their nest,
    And coal-black clouds that shadow heaven's light
    Do summon us to part, and bid good night.

"Now let me say good night, and so say you.    535
If you will say so, you shall have a kiss."
"Good night," quoth she; and, ere he says "Adieu,"
The honey fee of parting tend'red is:
    Her arms do lend his neck a sweet embrace;
    Incorporate° then they seem; face grows to face;    540

Till breathless he disjoined, and backward drew
The heavenly moisture, that sweet coral mouth,
Whose precious taste her thirsty lips well knew,
Whereon they surfeit, yet complain on drouth.
    He with her plenty pressed,° she faint with dearth,    545
    Their lips together glued, fall to the earth.

Now quick desire hath caught the yielding prey,
And gluttonlike she feeds, yet never filleth.
Her lips are conquerors, his lips obey,
Paying what ransom the insulter° willeth;    550
    Whose vulture thought doth pitch the price so high
    That she will draw his lips' rich treasure dry.

And having felt the sweetness of the spoil,
With blindfold fury she begins to forage;
Her face doth reek° and smoke, her blood doth boil,    555
And careless lust stirs up a desperate courage,
    Planting oblivion, beating reason back,
    Forgetting shame's pure blush and honor's wrack.

Hot, faint, and weary with her hard embracing,
Like a wild bird being tamed with too much handling,    560
Or as the fleet-foot roe that's tired with chasing,
Or like the froward° infant stilled with dandling,
    He now obeys and now no more resisteth,
    While she takes all she can, not all she listeth.°

What wax so frozen but dissolves with temp'ring    565
And yields at last to every light impression?
Things out of° hope are compassed oft with vent'ring,°
Chiefly in love, whose leave exceeds commission.°
    Affection° faints not like a pale-faced coward,
    But then woos best when most his choice is froward.°    570

When he did frown, O, had she then gave over,
Such nectar from his lips she had not sucked.
Foul° words and frowns must not repel a lover.
What though the rose have prickles, yet 'tis plucked.
    Were beauty under twenty locks kept fast,    575
    Yet love breaks through and picks them all at last.

For pity now she can no more detain him;
The poor fool° prays her that he may depart.
She is resolved no longer to restrain him;
Bids him farewell, and look well to her heart,    580
    The which, by Cupid's bow she doth protest,
    He carries thence incaged in his breast.

"Sweet boy," she says, "this night I'll waste° in sorrow,
For my sick heart commands mine eyes to watch.°
Tell me, love's master, shall we meet tomorrow?    585
Say, shall we? shall we? wilt thou make the match?"
    He tells her no; tomorrow he intends
    To hunt the boar with certain of his friends.

"The boar!" quoth she; whereat a sudden pale,°
Like lawn° being spread upon the blushing rose,    590
Usurps her cheek; she trembles at his tale,
And on his neck her yoking arms she throws.
    She sinketh down, still hanging by his neck,
    He on her belly falls, she on her back.

Now is she in the very lists° of love,    595
Her champion mounted for the hot encounter.
All is imaginary she doth prove,°
He will not manage° her, although he mount her;
    That worse than Tantalus' is her annoy,°
    To clip° Elysium and to lack her joy.    600

---

**512 still** always; **sealing** i.e., kissing  **515 slips** errors  **516 seal manual** signet ring (i.e., lips)  **519 touches** i.e., kisses **520 told** counted  **523 owe** bear  **524 Measure . . . years** account for my shyness by my youth  **526 fry** young fish **540 Incorporate** joined into one body  **545 pressed** oppressed **550 insulter** exultant winner  **555 reek** i.e., steam **562 froward** fretful  **564 listeth** wants  **567 out of** beyond; **compassed . . . vent'ring** achieved often by venturing  **568 leave exceeds commission** liberty goes beyond what was permitted  **569 Affection** passion, desire  **570 when . . . froward** when the object of his passion is most obstinate  **573 Foul** unpleasant  **578 poor fool** expression of tenderness  **583 waste** spend  **584 watch** stay open  **589 pale** pallor  **590 lawn** a fine linen  **595 lists** field of combat  **597 prove** experience (i.e., all that she experiences is in her imagination) **598 manage** ride  **599 That . . . annoy** so that her torment is worse than that of Tantalus (in Hades, Tantalus was surrounded by food and drink that he could never touch)  **600 clip** embrace

Even so poor birds, deceived with painted grapes,
Do surfeit by the eye and pine the maw;°
Even so she languisheth in her mishaps
As those poor birds that helpless berries saw.
   The warm effects° which she in him finds missing   605
   She seeks to kindle with continual kissing.

But all in vain; good queen, it will not be!
She hath assayed° as much as may be proved:°
Her pleading hath deserved a greater fee;
She's Love, she loves, and yet she is not loved.   610
   "Fie, fie!" he says. "You crush me; let me go!
   You have no reason to withhold me so."

"Thou hadst been gone," quoth she, "sweet boy, ere
   this,
But that thou told'st me thou wouldst hunt the boar.
O, be advised, thou know'st not what it is   615
With javelin's point a churlish swine to gore,
   Whose tushes° never sheathed he whetteth still,
   Like to a mortal° butcher bent to kill.

"On his bow-back he hath a battle set
Of bristly pikes that ever threat his foes;   620
His eyes like glowworms shine when he doth fret;°
His snout digs sepulchers where'er he goes;
   Being moved,° he strikes whate'er is in his way,
   And whom he strikes his crooked tushes slay.

"His brawny sides, with hairy bristles armèd,   625
Are better proof° than thy spear's point can enter;
His short thick neck cannot be easily harmèd;
Being ireful, on the lion he will venter.°
   The thorny brambles and embracing bushes,
   As fearful of him, part; through whom he rushes.   630

"Alas, he naught esteems that face of thine,
To which Love's eyes pays tributary gazes;
Nor thy soft hands, sweet lips, and crystal eyne,°
Whose full perfection all the world amazes;
   But having thee at vantage (wondrous dread!)   635
   Would root° these beauties as he roots the mead.

"O, let him keep his loathsome cabin° still:
Beauty hath naught to do with such foul fiends.
Come not within his danger° by thy will.
They that thrive well take counsel of their friends.   640
   When thou didst name the boar, not to dissemble,°
   I feared thy fortune, and my joints did tremble.

"Didst thou not mark my face? Was it not white?
Saw'st thou not signs of fear lurk in mine eye?
Grew I not faint? and fell I not downright?°   645
Within my bosom, whereon thou dost lie,
   My boding heart pants, beats, and takes no rest,
   But, like an earthquake, shakes thee on my breast.

"For where Love reigns, disturbing Jealousy°
Doth call himself Affection's sentinel,   650
Gives false alarms, suggesteth° mutiny,
And in a peaceful hour doth cry, 'Kill, kill!'
   Distemp'ring° gentle Love in his desire,
   As air and water do abate the fire.

"This sour informer, this bate-breeding° spy,   655
This canker° that eats up Love's tender spring,°
This carry-tale, dissentious Jealousy,
That sometime true news, sometime false doth bring,
   Knocks at my heart, and whispers in mine ear
   That if I love thee, I thy death should fear.   660

"And more than so, presenteth to mine eye
The picture of an angry-chafing boar,
Under whose sharp fangs on his back doth lie
An image like thyself, all stained with gore;
   Whose blood upon the fresh flowers being shed   665
   Doth make them droop with grief and hang the head.

"What should I do, seeing thee so indeed,
That tremble at th' imagination?
The thought of it doth make my faint heart bleed,
And fear doth teach it divination.   670
   I prophesy thy death, my living sorrow,
   If thou encounter with the boar tomorrow.

"But if thou needs wilt hunt, be ruled by me:
Uncouple at° the timorous flying hare,
Or at the fox which lives by subtlety,   675
Or at the roe which no encounter dare.
   Pursue these fearful° creatures o'er the downs,
   And on thy well-breathed° horse keep with thy
   hounds.

"And when thou hast on foot° the purblind° hare,
Mark the poor wretch, to overshoot° his troubles,   680
How he outruns the wind, and with what care
He cranks° and crosses with a thousand doubles.
   The many musits° through the which he goes
   Are like a labyrinth to amaze° his foes.

Sometime he runs among a flock of sheep,   685
To make the cunning hounds mistake their smell,
And sometime where earth-delving conies keep,°
To stop the loud pursuers in their yell;°
   And sometime sorteth° with a herd of deer.
   Danger deviseth shifts,° wit waits on° fear;   690

---

602 **pine the maw** starve the stomach  605 **effects** consequences  608 **assayed** tried; **proved** tried  617 **tushes** tusks  618 **mortal** deadly  621 **fret** rage  623 **moved** angered  626 **better proof** stronger armor  628 **venter** venture  633 **eyne** eyes  636 **root** uproot  637 **cabin** i.e., sty  639 **within his danger** within distance of his power to harm  641 **not to dissemble** to tell the truth  645 **downright** directly

649 **Jealousy** anxiety  651 **suggesteth** incites  653 **Distemp-'ring** decreasing  655 **bate-breeding** strife-creating  656 **canker** worm (that preys on blossoms); **spring** bud  674 **Uncouple at** loose your hounds upon  677 **fearful** timid  678 **well-breathed** well-conditioned  679 **on foot** in chase; **purblind** weak-sighted  680 **overshoot** run beyond  682 **cranks** turns  683 **musits** gaps in a hedge or fence  684 **amaze** confuse  687 **earth-delving conies keep** rabbits that dig burrows dwell  688 **in their yell** i.e., in full cry  689 **sorteth** mingles  690 **shifts** tricks; **waits on** goes with

For there his smell with others being mingled,
The hot scent-snuffing hounds are driven to doubt,
Ceasing their clamorous cry, till they have singled
With much ado the cold fault° cleanly out.
    Then do they spend their mouths;° echo replies,   695
    As if another chase were in the skies.

"By this, poor Wat,° far off upon a hill,
Stands on his hinder legs with list'ning ear,
To hearken if his foes pursue him still.
Anon their loud alarums he doth hear,   700
    And now his grief may be comparèd well
    To one sore sick that hears the passing° bell.

"Then shalt thou see the dew-bedabbled wretch
Turn, and return, indenting° with the way.
Each envious° brier his weary legs do scratch;   705
Each shadow makes him stop, each murmur stay;
    For misery is trodden on by many
    And, being low, never relieved by any.

"Lie quietly and hear a little more.
Nay, do not struggle, for thou shalt not rise.   710
To make thee hate the hunting of the boar,
Unlike myself thou hear'st me moralize,
    Applying this to that, and so to so,
    For love can comment upon every woe.

"Where did I leave?" "No matter where," quoth he;   715
"Leave me, and then the story aptly ends.
The night is spent." "Why, what of that?" quoth she.
"I am," quoth he, "expected of my friends;
    And now 'tis dark, and going I shall fall."
    "In night," quoth she, "desire sees best of all.   720

"But if thou fall, O, then imagine this:
The earth, in love with thee, thy footing trips,
And all is but to rob thee of a kiss.
Rich preys° make true° men thieves. So do thy lips
    Make modest Dian° cloudy° and forlorn,   725
    Lest she should steal a kiss and die forsworn.°

"Now of this dark night I perceive the reason:
Cynthia° for shame obscures her silver shine,
Till forging° Nature be condemned of treason
For stealing molds from heaven that were divine;   730
    Wherein she framed thee, in high heaven's despite,
    To shame the sun by day, and her° by night.

"And therefore hath she bribed the Destinies
To cross° the curious° workmanship of Nature,
To mingle beauty with infirmities   735
And pure perfection with impure defeature,°
    Making it subject to the tyranny
    Of mad mischances and much misery;

"As burning fevers, agues pale and faint,
Life-poisoning pestilence, and frenzies wood,°   740
The marrow-eating sickness° whose attaint°
Disorder breeds by heating of the blood,
    Surfeits, imposthumes,° grief, and damned despair
    Swear Nature's death for framing thee so fair.

"And not the least of all these maladies   745
But in one minute's fight brings beauty under;°
Both favor,° savor, hue,° and qualities,
Whereat th' impartial gazer late did wonder,
    Are on the sudden wasted, thawed, and done,
    As mountain snow melts with the midday sun.   750

"Therefore, despite of fruitless chastity,
Love-lacking vestals, and self-loving nuns,
That on the earth would breed a scarcity
And barren dearth of daughters and of sons,
    Be prodigal; the lamp that burns by night   755
    Dries up his oil to lend the world his light.

"What is thy body but a swallowing grave,
Seeming to bury that posterity
Which by the rights of time thou needs must have
If thou destroy them not in dark obscurity?   760
    If so, the world will hold thee in disdain,
    Sith° in thy pride so fair a hope is slain.

"So in thyself thyself art made away,
A mischief worse than civil home-bred strife,
Or theirs whose desperate hands themselves do slay,   765
Or butcher sire that reaves° his son of life.
    Foul cank'ring rust the hidden treasure frets,°
    But gold that's put to use more gold begets."

"Nay, then," quoth Adon, "you will fall again
Into your idle over-handled theme.   770
The kiss I gave you is bestowed in vain,
And all in vain you strive against the stream;
    For by this black-faced night, desire's foul nurse,
    Your treatise° makes me like you worse and worse.

"If love have lent you twenty thousand tongues,   775
And every tongue more moving than your own,
Bewitching like the wanton mermaid's songs,
Yet from mine ear the tempting tune is blown;
    For know, my heart stands armed in mine ear
    And will not let a false sound enter there,   780

"Lest the deceiving harmony should run
Into the quiet closure° of my breast;
And then my little heart were quite undone,
In his bedchamber to be barred of rest.
    No, lady, no; my heart longs not to groan,   785
    But soundly sleeps while now it sleeps alone.

694 **cold fault** lost scent  695 **spend their mouths** yelp  697 **Wat** traditional name for a hare  702 **passing** funeral  704 **indenting** zigzagging  705 **envious** malicious  724 **preys** booty; **true** honest  725 **Dian** Diana (goddess of chastity and of the hunt); **cloudy** gloomy  726 **forsworn** i.e., having broken her vow of chastity  728 **Cynthia** the moon, i.e., Diana  729 **forging** counterfeiting  732 **her** the moon  734 **cross** thwart; **curious** elaborate  736 **defeature** disfigurement

740 **wood** mad  741 **marrow-eating sickness** syphilis (?); **attaint** infection  743 **imposthumes** abscesses  745–46 **And . . . under** even the least of these maladies in one minute can destroy beauty  747 **favor** features; **hue** complexion  762 **Sith** since  766 **reaves** deprives  767 **frets** erodes  774 **treatise** discourse  782 **closure** enclosure

"What have you urged that I cannot reprove?°
The path is smooth that leadeth on to danger.
I hate not love, but your device° in love,
That lends embracements unto every stranger.          790
    You do it for increase. O strange excuse,
    When reason is the bawd to lust's abuse!

"Call it not love, for Love to heaven is fled
Since sweating Lust on earth usurped his name;
Under whose simple semblance he hath fed          795
Upon fresh beauty, blotting it with blame;
    Which the hot tyrant° stains and soon bereaves,°
    As caterpillars do the tender leaves.

"Love comforteth like sunshine after rain,
But Lust's effect is tempest after sun.          800
Love's gentle spring doth always fresh remain;
Lust's winter comes ere summer half be done.
    Love surfeits not, Lust like a glutton dies;
    Love is all truth, Lust full of forgèd lies.

"More I could tell, but more I dare not say:          805
The text is old, the orator too green.°
Therefore in sadness° now I will away.
My face is full of shame, my heart of teen;°
    Mine ears, that to your wanton talk attended,
    Do burn themselves for having so offended."          810

With this he breaketh from the sweet embrace
Of those fair arms which bound him to her breast
And homeward through the dark laund° runs apace;
Leaves Love upon her back, deeply distressed.
    Look how° a bright star shooteth from the sky,          815
    So glides he in the night from Venus' eye;

Which after him she darts, as one on shore
Gazing upon a late-embarkèd friend
Till the wild waves will have him seen no more,
Whose ridges with the meeting clouds contend.          820
    So did the merciless and pitchy night
    Fold in the object that did feed her sight.

Whereat amazed, as one that unaware
Hath dropped a precious jewel in the flood,
Or 'stonished° as night-wand'rers often are,          825
Their light blown out in some mistrustful° wood,
    Even so confounded in the dark she lay,
    Having lost the fair discovery of her way.

And now she beats her heart, whereat it groans,
That all the neighbor caves, as seeming troubled,          830
Make verbal repetition of her moans.
Passion° on passion deeply is redoubled;
    "Ay me!" she cries, and twenty times, "Woe, woe!"
    And twenty echoes twenty times cry so.

She, marking them, begins a wailing note          835
And sings extemporally a woeful ditty:
How love makes young men thrall,° and old men dote;
How love is wise in folly, foolish-witty.
    Her heavy anthem still concludes in woe,
    And still the choir of echoes answer so.          840

Her song was tedious and outwore the night,
For lovers' hours are long, though seeming short.
If pleased themselves, others, they think, delight
In suchlike circumstance, with suchlike sport.
    Their copious stories, oftentimes begun,          845
    End without audience, and are never done.

For who hath she to spend the night withal
But idle sounds resembling parasits,°
Like shrill-tongued tapsters answering every call,
Soothing the humor of fantastic wits?          850
    She says, " 'Tis so." They answer all, " 'Tis so,"
    And would say after her if she said "No."

Lo, here the gentle lark, weary of rest,
From his moist cabinet° mounts up on high
And wakes the morning, from whose silver breast          855
The sun ariseth in his majesty;
    Who doth the world so gloriously behold
    That cedar tops and hills seem burnished gold.

Venus salutes him with this fair good-morrow:
"O thou clear god, and patron of all light,          860
From whom each lamp and shining star doth borrow
The beauteous influence that makes him bright;
    There lives a son that sucked an earthly mother
    May lend thee light, as thou dost lend to other."

This said, she hasteth to a myrtle grove,          865
Musing the morning is so much o'erworn
And yet she hears no tidings of her love.
She hearkens for his hounds and for his horn.
    Anon she hears them chant it lustily,
    And all in haste she coasteth° to the cry.          870

And as she runs, the bushes in the way
Some catch her by the neck, some kiss her face,
Some twine about her thigh to make her stay.
She wildly breaketh from their strict° embrace,
    Like a milch doe, whose swelling dugs do ache,          875
    Hasting to feed her fawn, hid in some brake.°

By this she hears the hounds are at a bay;°
Whereat she starts, like one that spies an adder
Wreathed up in fatal folds just in his way,
The fear whereof doth make him shake and shudder.          880
    Even so the timorous yelping of the hounds
    Appals her senses and her spirit confounds.

---

787 **reprove** refute   789 **device** cunning   797 **hot tyrant** lust; **bereaves** spoils   806 **green** young   807 **in sadness** in all seriousness   808 **teen** sorrow   813 **laund** open space in a forest   815 **Look how** just as   825 **'stonished** bewildered   826 **mistrustful** feared   332 **Passion** lamentation

837 **thrall** captive   848 **parasits** i.e., flatterers   854 **cabinet** i.e., nest   870 **coasteth** approaches   874 **strict** tight   876 **brake** thicket   877 **at a bay** the moment during a hunt when an animal is forced to turn against its pursuers

For now she knows it is no gentle chase,
But the blunt° boar, rough bear, or lion proud,
Because the cry remaineth in one place,                     885
Where fearfully the dogs exclaim aloud;
    Finding their enemy to be so curst,°
    They all strain court'sy° who shall cope him first.

This dismal cry rings sadly in her ear,
Through which it enters to surprise her heart,             890
Who, overcome by doubt and bloodless fear,
With cold-pale weakness numbs each feeling part:
    Like soldiers when their captain once doth yield,
    They basely fly, and dare not stay the field.

Thus stands she in a trembling ecstasy,°                    895
Till cheering up her senses all dismayed,
She tells them 'tis a causeless fantasy,
And childish error that they are afraid;
    Bids them leave quaking, bids them fear no more;
    And with that word she spied the hunted boar,          900

Whose frothy mouth, bepainted all with red,
Like milk and blood being mingled both togither,
A second fear through all her sinews spread,
Which madly hurries her she knows not whither.
    This way she runs, and now she will no further,        905
    But back retires, to rate the boar for murther.

A thousand spleens° bear her a thousand ways;
She treads the path that she untreads again;
Her more than haste is mated with° delays,
Like the proceedings of a drunken brain,                   910
    Full of respects,° yet naught at all respecting,
    In hand° with all things, naught at all effecting.

Here kennelled in a brake she finds a hound
And asks the weary caitiff° for his master;
And there another licking of his wound,                    915
'Gainst venomed sores the only sovereign plaster;
    And here she meets another sadly scowling,
    To whom she speaks, and he replies with howling.

When he hath ceased his ill-resounding noise,
Another flap-mouthed° mourner, black and grim,            920
Against the welkin° volleys out his voice;
Another and another answer him,
    Clapping their proud tails to the ground below,
    Shaking their scratched ears, bleeding as they go.

Look how the world's poor people are amazèd°              925
At apparitions, signs, and prodigies,
Whereon with fearful eyes they long have gazèd,
Infusing them with dreadful prophecies:
    So she at these sad signs draws up her breath
    And sighing it again, exclaims on° Death.              930

"Hard-favored tyrant, ugly, meager, lean,
Hateful divorce of love!" (thus chides she Death)
"Grim-grinning ghost, earth's worm, what dost thou
    mean,
To stifle beauty and to steal his breath
    Who, when he lived, his breath and beauty set        935
    Gloss on the rose, smell to the violet?

"If he be dead—O no, it cannot be,
Seeing his beauty, thou shouldst strike at it!
O yes, it may; thou hast no eyes to see,
But hatefully at randon° dost thou hit;                   940
    Thy mark is feeble age, but thy false dart
    Mistakes that aim, and cleaves an infant's heart.

"Hadst thou but bid beware, then he had spoke,
And hearing him, thy power had lost his° power.
The Destinies will curse thee for this stroke:            945
They bid thee crop a weed; thou pluck'st a flower.
    Love's golden arrow at him should have fled,
    And not Death's ebon° dart to strike him dead.

"Dost thou drink tears, that thou provok'st such
    weeping?
What may a heavy groan advantage° thee?                   950
Why hast thou cast into eternal sleeping
Those eyes that taught all other eyes to see?
    Now Nature cares not for thy mortal vigor,°
    Since her best work is ruined with thy rigor."

Here overcome, as one full of despair,                    955
She vailed° her eyelids, who like sluices stopped°
The crystal tide that from her two cheeks fair
In the sweet channel of her bosom dropped;
    But through the floodgates breaks the silver rain
    And with his strong course opens them again.          960

O, how her eyes and tears did lend and borrow,
Her eye seen in the tears, tears in her eye,
Both crystals,° where they viewed each other's sorrow—
Sorrow that friendly sighs sought still to dry;
    But like a stormy day, now wind, now rain,            965
    Sighs dry her cheeks, tears make them wet again.

Variable passions throng her constant woe,
As striving who° should best become her grief.
All entertained,° each passion labors so
That every present sorrow seemeth chief,                   970
    But none is best; then join they all together
    Like many clouds consulting° for foul weather.

By this far off she hears some huntsman halloa.
A nurse's song ne'er pleased her babe so well.
The dire imagination she did follow                        975
This sound of hope doth labor to expel;
    For now reviving joy bids her rejoice
    And flatters her it is Adonis' voice.

---

884 **blunt** rough   887 **curst** savage   888 **They . . . court'sy**
i.e., each holds back to allow the other to go first   895 **ecstasy**
fit   907 **spleens** impulses   909 **mated with** checked by   911
**respects** considerations   912 **In hand** occupied   914 **caitiff**
wretch   920 **flap-mouthed** loose-lipped   921 **welkin** sky
925 **amazèd** perplexed   930 **exclaims on** denounces

940 **randon** random   944 **his** its   948 **ebon** black   950
**advantage** profit   953 **mortal vigor** deadly power   956
**vailed** lowered; **who . . . stopped** which, like floodgates,
dammed   963 **crystals** i.e., mirrors   968 **striving who**
competing which   969 **entertained** admitted   972 **consulting** plotting

Whereat her tears began to turn their tide,°
Being prisoned in her eye like pearls in glass;                   980
Yet sometimes falls an orient° drop beside,
Which her cheek melts, as scorning it should pass
    To wash the foul face of the sluttish ground,
    Who is but drunken when she seemeth drowned.

O hard-believing° love, how strange it seems            985
Not to believe, and yet too credulous!
Thy weal and woe are both of them extremes;
Despair and hope makes thee ridiculous:
    The one doth flatter thee in thoughts unlikely,
    In likely thoughts the other kills thee quickly.          990

Now she unweaves the web that she hath wrought:
Adonis lives, and Death is not to blame;
It was not she that called him all to naught.°
Now she adds honors to his hateful name:
    She clepes° him king of graves, and grave for kings, 995
    Imperious supreme° of all mortal things.

"No, no," quoth she, "sweet Death, I did but jest;
Yet pardon me I felt a kind of fear
When as I met the boar, that bloody beast
Which knows no pity but is still severe.                          1000
    Then, gentle shadow° (truth I must confess),
    I railed on thee, fearing my love's decesse.°

" 'Tis not my fault the boar provoked my tongue;
Be wreaked° on him, invisible commander.
'Tis he, foul creature, that hath done thee wrong;      1005
I did but act; he's author of thy slander.
    Grief hath two tongues, and never woman yet
    Could rule them both, without ten women's wit."

Thus hoping that Adonis is alive,
Her rash suspect° she doth extenuate;                          1010
And that his beauty may the better thrive,
With Death she humbly doth insinuate;°
    Tells him of trophies, statues, tombs; and stories°
    His victories, his triumphs, and his glories.

"O Jove," quoth she, "how much a fool was I          1015
To be of such a weak and silly mind
To wail his death who lives, and must not die
Till mutual overthrow of mortal kind!
    For he being dead, with him is beauty slain,
    And, beauty dead, black chaos comes again.              1020

"Fie, fie, found love, thou art as full of fear
As one with treasure laden, hemmed with thieves.
Trifles, unwitnessèd with° eye, or ear,
Thy coward heart with false bethinking grieves."
    Even at this word she hears a merry horn,               1025
    Whereat she leaps that was but late forlorn.

As falcons to the lure, away she flies;
The grass stoops not, she treads on it so light,
And in her haste unfortunately spies
The foul boar's conquest on her fair delight;               1030
    Which seen, her eyes, as murd'red with the view,
    Like stars ashamed of° day, themselves withdrew;

Or as the snail, whose tender horns being hit,
Shrinks backward in his shelly cave with pain,
And there, all smoth'red up, in shade doth sit,            1035
Long after fearing to creep forth again;
    So at his bloody view her eyes are fled
    Into the deep-dark cabins of her head;

Where they resign their office and their light
To the disposing of her troubled brain,                        1040
Who bids them still consort° with ugly night
And never wound the heart with looks again;
    Who,° like a king perplexèd in his throne,
    By their suggestion gives a deadly groan,

Whereat each tributary subject quakes,                       1045
As when the wind, imprisoned in the ground,
Struggling for passage, earth's foundation shakes,
Which with cold terror doth men's minds confound.
    This mutiny each part doth so surprise
    That from their dark beds once more leap her eyes,    1050

And, being opened, threw unwilling light
Upon the wide wound that the boar had trenched°
In his soft flank, whose wonted lily white
With purple tears that his wound wept was drenched.
    No flow'r was nigh, no grass, herb, leaf, or weed,   1055
    But stole his blood and seemed with him to bleed.

This solemn sympathy poor Venus noteth.
Over one shoulder doth she hang her head.
Dumbly she passions,° franticly she doteth:
She thinks he could not die, he is not dead;               1060
    Her voice is stopped, her joints forget to bow;
    Her eyes are mad° that they have wept till° now.

Upon his hurt she looks so steadfastly
That her sight dazzling makes the wound seem three;
And then she reprehends her mangling eye,                1065
That makes more gashes where no breach should be.
    His face seems twain, each several limb is doubled;
    For oft the eye mistakes, the brain being troubled.

"My tongue cannot express my grief for one,
And yet," quoth she, "behold two Adons dead!         1070
My sighs are blown away, my salt tears gone,
Mine eyes are turned to fire, my heart to lead.
    Heavy heart's lead, melt at mine eyes' red fire!
    So shall I die by drops of hot desire.

979 **turn their tide** ebb   981 **orient** bright   985 **hard-believing** skeptical   993 **all to naught** worthless   995 **clepes** names   996 **Imperious supreme** imperial ruler   1001 **shadow** specter   1002 **decesse** decease   1004 **wreaked** revenged   1010 **suspect** suspicion   1012 **insinuate** ingratiate herself   1013 **stories** relates   1023 **unwitnessèd with** unperceived by

1032 **ashamed of** put to shame by   1041 **still consort** always keep company   1043 **Who** which   1052 **trenched** cut   1059 **passions** grieves   1062 **mad** distracted; **till** before

"Alas, poor world, what treasure hast thou lost!    1075
What face remains alive that's worth the viewing?
Whose tongue is music now? What canst thou boast
Of things long since, or any thing ensuing?
    The flowers are sweet, their colors fresh and trim,
    But true sweet beauty lived and died with him.    1080

"Bonnet nor veil henceforth no creature wear;
Nor sun nor wind will ever strive to kiss you.
Having no fair° to lose, you need not fear:
The sun doth scorn you, and the wind doth hiss you.
    But when Adonis lived, sun and sharp air    1085
    Lurked like two thieves, to rob him of his fair;

"And therefore would he put his bonnet on,
Under those brim the gaudy° sun would peep;
The wind would blow it off, and being gone,
Play with his locks; then would Adonis weep;    1090
    And straight, in pity of his tender years,
    They both would strive who first should dry his tears.

"To see his face the lion walked along,
Behind some hedge, because he would not fear° him.
To recreate himself when he hath song,    1095
The tiger would be tame, and gently hear him.
    If he had spoke, the wolf would leave his prey
    And never fright the silly° lamb that day.

"When he beheld his shadow in the brook,
The fishes spread on it their golden gills;    1100
When he was by, the birds such pleasure took
That some would sing, some other in their bills
    Would bring him mulberries and ripe-red cherries:
    He fed them with his sight, they him with berries.

"But this foul, grim, and urchin-snouted° boar,    1105
Whose downward eye still looketh for a grave,
Ne'er saw the beauteous livery that he wore;
Witness the entertainment° that he gave.
    If he did see his face, why then I know
    He thought to kiss him, and hath killed him so.    1110

" 'Tis true, 'tis true! thus was Adonis slain:
He ran upon the boar with his sharp spear,
Who did not whet his teeth at him again,
But by a kiss thought to persuade him there;
    And nuzzling in his flank, the loving swine    1115
    Sheathed unaware the tusk in his soft groin.

"Had I been toothed like him, I must confess,
With kissing him I should have killed him first;
But he is dead, and never did he bless
My youth with his; the more am I accurst."    1120
    With this she falleth in the place she stood
    And stains her face with his congealèd blood.

She looks upon his lips, and they are pale;
She takes him by the hand, and that is cold;
She whispers in his ears a heavy tale,    1125
As if they heard the woeful words she told.
    She lifts the coffer-lids° that close his eyes,
    Where lo, two lamps burnt out in darkness lies;

Two glasses, where herself herself beheld
A thousand times, and now no more reflect;    1130
Their virtue lost wherein they late excelled,
And every beauty robbed of his effect.
    "Wonder of time," quoth she, "this is my spite,°
    That thou being dead, the day should yet be light.

"Since thou art dead, lo here I prophesy,    1135
Sorrow on love hereafter shall attend.
It shall be waited on with jealousy,
Find sweet beginning, but unsavory end,
    Ne'er settled equally, but high or low,
    That all love's pleasure shall not match his woe.    1140

"It shall be fickle, false, and full of fraud;
Bud, and be blasted, in a breathing while;°
The bottom poison, and the top o'erstrawed°
With sweets that shall the truest sight beguile.
    The strongest body shall it make most weak,    1145
    Strike the wise dumb, and teach the fool to speak.

"It shall be sparing, and too full of riot,
Teaching decrepit age to tread the measures;
The staring ruffian shall it keep in quiet,
Pluck down the rich, enrich the poor with treasures;    1150
    It shall be raging mad, and silly mild,
    Make the young old, the old become a child.

"It shall suspect where is no cause of fear;
It shall not fear where it should most mistrust;
It shall be merciful, and too severe,    1155
And most deceiving when it seems most just;
    Perverse it shall be where it shows most toward;°
    Put fear to valor, courage to the coward.

"It shall be cause of war and dire events
And set dissension 'twixt the son and sire,    1160
Subject and servile to all discontents,
As dry combustious matter is to fire.
    Sith in his prime death doth my love destroy,
    They that love best their loves shall not enjoy."

By this the boy that by her side lay killed    1165
Was melted like a vapor from her sight,
And in his blood, that on the ground lay spilled,
A purple flower° sprung up, check'red with white,
    Resembling well his pale cheeks and the blood
    Which in round drops upon their whiteness stood.    1170

---

**1083 fair** beauty  **1088 gaudy** bright  **1094 fear** frighten
**1098 silly** innocent  **1105 urchin-snouted** hedgehog-
snouted  **1108 entertainment** reception

**1127 coffer-lids** lids to treasure chests  **1133 spite** grief
**1142 in . . . while** in one breath  **1143 o'erstrawed** strewn
**1157 toward** docile  **1168 purple flower** i.e., the anemone

She bows her head the new-sprung flower to smell,
Comparing it to her Adonis' breath,
And says within her bosom it shall dwell,
Since he himself is reft from her by death;
   She crops the stalk, and in the breach° appears    1175
   Green-dropping sap, which she compares to tears.

"Poor flow'r," quoth she, "this was thy father's
   guise°—
Sweet issue of a more sweet-smelling sire—
For every little grief to wet his eyes;
To grow unto himself was his desire,    1180
   And so 'tis thine; but know, it is as good
   To wither in my breast as in his blood.

"Here was thy father's bed, here in my breast;
Thou art the next of blood, and 'tis thy right.
Lo in this hollow cradle take thy rest;    1185
My throbbing heart shall rock thee day and night:
   There shall not be one minute in an hour
   Wherein I will not kiss my sweet love's flow'r."

Thus weary of the world, away she hies,
And yokes her silver doves, by whose swift aid    1190
Their mistress, mounted, through the empty skies
In her light chariot quickly is conveyed,
   Holding their course to Paphos,° where their queen
   Means to immure herself and not be seen.

1175 **breach** break (in the stalk)    1177 **guise** custom

1193 **Paphos** where Venus dwells in Cyprus

# THE RAPE OF LUCRECE

TO THE RIGHT HONORABLE
HENRY WRIOTHESLEY
*Earl of Southampton, and Baron of Titchfield*

The love I dedicate to your lordship is without end; whereof this pamphlet without beginning° is but a
superfluous moiety.° The warrant I have of your honorable disposition, not the worth of my untutored 5
lines, makes it assured of acceptance. What I have done is yours; what I have to do is yours; being part
in all I have, devoted yours. Were my worth greater, my duty would show greater; meantime, as it is,
it is bound to your lordship, to whom I wish long life still lengthened with all happiness.

Your lordship's in all duty,
WILLIAM SHAKESPEARE    10

### The Argument

Lucius Tarquinius (for his excessive pride surnamed
Superbus), after he had caused his own father-in-law
Servius Tullius to be cruelly murdered, and, contrary
to the Roman laws and customs, not requiring or staying for the people's suffrages, had possessed himself 5
of the kingdom, went, accompanied with his sons and
other noblemen of Rome, to besiege Ardea; during
which siege the principal men of the army meeting
one evening at the tent of Sextus Tarquinius, the
king's son, in their discourses after supper every one 10
commended the virtues of his own wife; among whom
Collatinus extolled the incomparable chastity of his
wife Lucretia. In that pleasant humor they all posted
to Rome; and intending by their secret and sudden
arrival to make trial of that which every one had 15
before avouched, only Collatinus finds his wife (though
it were late in the night) spinning amongst her maids;
the other ladies were all found dancing and reveling,
or in several disports. Whereupon the noblemen

yielded Collatinus the victory, and his wife the fame. 20
At that time Sextus Tarquinius being inflamed with
Lucrece' beauty, yet smothering his passions for the
present, departed with the rest back to the camp; from
whence he shortly after privily withdrew himself, and
was (according to his estate) royally entertained and 25
lodged by Lucrece at Collatium. The same night he
treacherously stealeth into her chamber, violently
ravished her, and early in the morning speedeth away.
Lucrece, in this lamentable plight, hastily dispatcheth
messengers, one to Rome for her father, another to 30
the camp for Collatine. They came, the one accompanied with Junius Brutus, the other with Publius
Valerius; and finding Lucrece attired in mourning
habit, demanded the cause of her sorrow. She, first
taking an oath of them for her revenge, revealed the 35
actor and whole manner of his dealing, and withal
suddenly stabbed herself. Which done, with one consent they all vowed to root out the whole hated family
of the Tarquins; and bearing the dead body to Rome,
Brutus acquainted the people with the doer and manner 40
of the vile deed, with a bitter invective against the
tyranny of the king; wherewith the people were so
moved that with one consent and a general acclamation
the Tarquins were all exiled, and the state government
changed from kings to consuls. 45

*The decorative border shown above appeared on the title page of the
quarto edition of* The Rape of Lucrece, 1594.
**4 without beginning** i.e., the narrative begins *in medias res*
**5 moiety** small part

From the besiegèd Ardea all in post,°
Borne by the trustless° wings of false desire,
Lust-breathèd° Tarquin leaves the Roman host
And to Collatium bears the lightless° fire
Which, in pale embers hid, lurks to aspire°     5
   And girdle with embracing flames the waist
   Of Collatine's fair love, Lucrece the chaste.

Haply° that name of "chaste" unhap'ly set
This bateless° edge on his keen appetite;°
When Collatine unwisely did not let°     10
To praise the clear unmatchèd red and white
Which triumphed in that sky of his delight,°
   Where mortal stars,° as bright as heaven's beauties,
   With pure aspects° did him peculiar° duties.

For he the night before, in Tarquin's tent,     15
Unlocked the treasure of his happy state:
What priceless wealth the heavens had him lent
In the possession of his beauteous mate;
Reck'ning his fortune at such high proud rate
   That kings might be espousèd to more fame,     20
   But king nor peer to such a peerless dame.

O happiness enjoyed but of° a few,
And if possessed, as soon decayed and done°
As is the morning's silver-melting dew
Against the golden splendor of the sun!     25
An expired date,° canceled ere well begun.
   Honor and beauty, in the owner's arms,
   Are weakly fortressed from a world of harms.

Beauty itself doth of itself persuade
The eyes of men without an orator.     30
What needeth then apologies° be made
To set forth that which is so singular?
Or why is Collatine the publisher°
   Of that rich jewel he should keep unknown
   From thievish ears, because it is his own?     35

Perchance his boast of Lucrece' sov'reignty
Suggested° this proud issue° of a king;
For by our ears our hearts oft tainted be.
Perchance that envy of so rich a thing,
Braving compare,° disdainfully did sting     40
   His high-pitched thoughts, that meaner men should vaunt
   That golden hap° which their superiors want.°

But some untimely thought did instigate
His all too timeless° speed, if none of those.
His honor, his affairs, his friends, his state,°     45
Neglected all, with swift intent he goes
To quench the coal which in his liver° glows.
   O rash false heat, wrapped in repentant cold,
   Thy hasty spring still blasts° and ne'er grows old!

When at Collatium this false lord arrivèd,     50
Well was he welcomed by the Roman dame,
Within whose face Beauty and Virtue strivèd
Which of them both should underprop her fame.
When Virtue bragged, Beauty would blush for shame;
   When Beauty boasted blushes, in despite     55
   Virtue would stain that o'er with silver white.

But Beauty in that white entitulèd°
From Venus' doves, doth challenge that fair field;°
Then Virtue claims from Beauty Beauty's red,
Which Virtue gave the Golden Age to gild°     60
Their silver cheeks, and called it then their shield,
   Teaching them thus to use it in the fight,
   When shame assailed, the red should fence° the white.

This heraldry in Lucrece' face was seen,
Argued° by Beauty's red and Virtue's white;     65
Of either's color was the other queen,
Proving from world's minority° their right.
Yet their ambition makes them still to fight,
   The sovereignty of either being so great
   That oft they interchange each other's seat.     70

This silent war of lilies and of roses,
Which Tarquin viewed in her fair face's field,
In their pure ranks his traitor eye encloses;
Where, lest between them both it should be killed,
The coward captive vanquishèd doth yield     75
   To those two armies that would let him go
   Rather than triumph in so false a foe.

Now thinks he that her husband's shallow tongue,
The niggard prodigal that praised her so,
In that high task hath done her beauty wrong,     80
Which far exceeds his barren skill to show.
Therefore that praise which Collatine doth owe
   Enchanted Tarquin answers° with surmise,°
   In silent wonder of still-gazing eyes.

This earthly saint, adorèd by this devil,     85
Little suspecteth the false worshipper;
For unstained thoughts do seldom dream on evil;
Birds never limed° no secret bushes fear.
So guiltless she securely° gives good cheer
   And reverend° welcome to her princely guest,     90
   Whose inward ill no outward harm expressed;

---

**1 all in post** in great haste   **2 trustless** treacherous   **3 Lust-breathèd** inspired by lust   **4 lightless** smoldering   **5 aspire** ascend   **8 Haply** perhaps   **9 bateless** unbated; **appetite** lust   **10 let** forbear   **12 that . . . delight** Lucrece's face   **13 mortal stars** Lucrece's eyes   **14 aspects** (1) looks (2) astrological influences; **peculiar** private   **22 of** by   **23 done** consumed   **26 date** lease   **31 apologies** i.e., vindications   **33 publisher** proclaimer   **37 Suggested** prompted; **issue** i.e., son   **40 Braving compare** challenging comparison   **42 hap** luck; **want** lack

**44 timeless** untimely   **45 state** status, estate   **47 liver** thought to be the seat of sexual desire   **49 still blasts** always is blasted   **57 entitulèd** having a claim   **58 field** (1) field of battle (2) ground of a shield   **60 gild** color (with a blush)   **63 fence** defend   **65 Argued** expressed   **67 minority** youth (i.e., the Golden Age of line 60)   **83 answers** pays; **surmise** amazement   **88 limed** caught by bird lime (a sticky substance smeared upon branches)   **89 securely** unsuspectingly   **90 reverend** reverent

For that he colored° with his high estate,
Hiding base sin in pleats of majesty;
That° nothing in him seemed inordinate,
Save sometime too much wonder in his eye,                    95
Which, having all, all could not satisfy;
  But poorly rich, so wanteth in his store°
  That, cloyed with much, he pineth still for more.

But she, that never coped with° stranger° eyes,
Could pick no meaning from their parling° looks,            100
Nor read the subtle shining secrecies
Writ in the glassy margents° of such books.
She touched no unknown baits, nor feared no hooks;
  Nor could she moralize° his wanton sight,°
  More than his eyes were opened to the light.            105

He stories to her ears her husband's fame,
Won in the fields of fruitful Italy;
And decks with praises Collatine's high name,
Made glorious by his manly chivalry,
With bruisèd arms° and wreaths of victory.                   110
  Her joy with heaved-up° hand she doth express,
  And wordless so greets heaven for his success.

Far from the purpose of his coming thither
He makes excuses for his being there.
No cloudy show of stormy blust'ring weather                  115
Doth yet in his fair welkin° once appear,
Till sable Night, mother of dread and fear,
  Upon the world dim darkness doth display
  And in her vaulty prison stows the day.

For then is Tarquin brought unto his bed,                    120
Intending° weariness with heavy sprite;°
For, after supper, long he questionèd°
With modest Lucrece, and wore out the night.
Now leaden slumber with life's strength doth fight,
  And everyone to rest himself betakes,                   125
  Save thieves, and cares, and troubled minds that
    wakes.

As one of which doth Tarquin lie revolving
The sundry dangers of his will's obtaining;
Yet ever to obtain his will resolving,
Though weak-built hopes persuade him to abstaining.          130
Despair to gain doth traffic° oft for gaining;
  And when great treasure is the meed° proposed,
  Though death be adjunct,° there's no death supposèd.

Those that much covet are with gain so fond°
That what they have not, that which they possess             135
They scatter and unloose it from their bond,
And so by hoping more they have but less;
Or, gaining more, the profit of excess
  Is but to surfeit, and such griefs sustain
  That they prove bankrout° in this poor rich gain.        140

The aim of all is but to nurse the life
With honor, wealth, and ease in waning age;
And in this aim there is such thwarting strife
That one for all, or all for one we gage:°
As° life for honor in fell° battle's rage;                   145
  Honor for wealth; and oft that wealth doth cost
  The death of all, and all together lost;

So that in vent'ring° ill we leave° to be
The things we are for that which we expect;
And this ambitious foul infirmity,                           150
In having much, torments us with defect°
Of that we have: so then we do neglect
  The thing we have, and all for want of wit,
  Make something nothing by augmenting it.

Such hazard now must doting Tarquin make,                    155
Pawning his honor to obtain his lust;
And for himself himself he must forsake.
Then where is truth, if there be no self-trust?
When shall he think to find a stranger just,
  When he himself himself confounds,° betrays             160
  To sland'rous tongues and wretched hateful days?

Now stole upon the time the dead of night,
When heavy sleep had closed up mortal eyes.
No comfortable° star did lend his light,
No noise but owls, and wolves' death-boding cries;           165
Now serves the season that they may surprise
  The silly° lambs: pure thoughts are dead and still,
  While lust and murder wakes to stain and kill.

And now this lustful lord leapt from his bed,
Throwing his mantle rudely o'er his arm;                     170
Is madly tossed between desire and dread:
Th' one sweetly flatters, th' other feareth harm;
But honest fear, bewitched with lust's foul charm,
  Doth too too oft betake him to retire,
  Beaten away by brainsick° rude desire.                   175

His falchion° on a flint he softly° smiteth,
That from the cold stone sparks of fire do fly;
Whereat a waxen torch forthwith he lighteth,
Which must be lodestar° to his lustful eye;
And to the flame thus speaks advisedly:°                     180
  "As from this cold flint I enforced this fire,
  So Lucrece must I force to my desire."

Here pale with fear he doth premeditate
The dangers of his loathsome enterprise,
And in his inward mind he doth debate                        185
What following sorrow may on this arise;
Then looking scornfully, he doth despise
  His naked armor of still-slaught'red lust°
  And justly thus controls his thoughts unjust:

92 colored cloaked   94 That so that   97 store wealth   99 coped with encountered; stranger i.e., strangers'   100 parling speaking   102 glassy margents margins (of his eyes) 104 moralize interpret; sight glance   110 bruisèd arms battered armor   111 heaved-up uplifted   116 welkin sky   121 Intending pretending; sprite spirit   122 questionèd talked 131 traffic trade   132 meed reward   133 adjunct i.e., the consequence   134 fond infatuated   140 bankrout bankrupt

144 gage pledge   145 As for example; fell fierce   148 vent'-ring risking; leave cease   151 defect the insufficiency   160 confounds destroys   164 comfortable comforting   167 silly innocent   175 brainsick mad   176 falchion curved sword; softly silently   179 lodestar guiding star   180 advisedly deliberately   188 His . . . lust i.e., his armor, lust, is no armor, for when lust is fulfilled it is killed

"Fair torch, burn out thy light, and lend it not          190
To darken her whose light excelleth thine;
And die, unhallowed thoughts, before you blot
With your uncleannness that which is divine.
Offer pure incense to so pure a shrine.
   Let fair humanity abhor the deed          195
   That spots and stains love's modest snow-white
      weed.°

"O shame to knighthood and to shining arms!
O foul dishonor to my household's grave!°
O impious act including all foul garms!
A martial man to be soft fancy's° slave!          200
True valor still° a true respect° should have;
   Then my digression is so vile, so base,
   That it will live engraven in my face.

"Yea, though I die, the scandal will survive
And be an eyesore in my golden coat.°          205
Some loathsome dash° the herald will contrive
To cipher° me how fondly° I did dote;
That my posterity, shamed with the note,
   Shall curse my bones, and hold it for no sin
   To wish that I their father had not been.          210

"What win I if I gain the thing I seek?
A dream, a breath, a froth of fleeting joy.
Who buys a minute's mirth to wail a week?
Or sells eternity to get a toy?
For one sweet grape who will the vine destroy?          215
   Or what fond beggar, but to touch the crown,
   Would with the scepter straight be stroken down?

"If Collatinus dream of my intent,
Will he not wake, and in a desp'rate rage
Post hither this vile purpose to prevent?          220
This siege that hath engirt° his marriage,
This blur to youth, this sorrow to the sage,
   This dying virtue, this surviving shame,
   Whose crime will bear an ever-during° blame?

"O, what excuse can my invention make          225
When thou shalt charge me with so black a deed?
Will not my tongue be mute, my frail joints shake,
Mine eyes forgo their light, my false heart bleed?
The guilt being great, the fear doth still exceed;
   And extreme fear can neither fight nor fly,          230
   But cowardlike with trembling terror die.

"Had Collatinus killed my son or sire,
Or lain in ambush to betray my life,
Or were he not my dear friend, this desire
Might have excuse to work upon his wife,          235
As in revenge or quittal° of such strife;
   But as he is my kinsman, my dear friend,
   The shame and fault finds no excuse nor end.

"Shameful it is—ay, if the fact be known.
Hateful it is—there is no hate in loving.          240
I'll beg her love—but she is not her own.
The worst is but denial and reproving.
My will° is strong, past reason's weak removing.°
   Who fears a sentence° or an old man's saw°
   Shall by a painted cloth° be kept in awe."          245

Thus graceless holds he disputation
'Tween frozen conscience and hot-burning will,
And with good thoughts makes dispensation,°
Urging the worser sense for vantage° still;
Which in a moment doth confound and kill          250
   All pure effects,° and doth so far proceed
   That what is vile shows like a virtuous deed.

Quoth he, "She took me kindly by the hand
And gazed for tidings in my eager eyes,
Fearing some hard news from the warlike band          255
Where her belovèd Collatinus lies.
O, how her fear did make her color rise!
   First red as roses that on lawn° we lay,
   Then white as lawn, the roses took away.

"And how her hand, in my hand being locked,          260
Forced it to tremble with her loyal fear!
Which° strook her sad, and then it° faster rocked
Until her husband's welfare she did hear;
Whereat she smilèd with so sweet a cheer
   That, had Narcissus° seen her as she stood,          265
   Self-love had never drowned him in the flood.

"Why hunt I then for color° or excuses?
All orators are dumb when beauty pleadeth;
Poor wretches have remorse in poor abuses;°
Love thrives not in the heart that shadows dreadeth.°          270
Affection° is my captain, and he leadeth;
   And when his gaudy banner is displayed,
   The coward° fights and will not be dismayed.

"Then childish fear avaunt, debating die!
Respect° and reason wait on° wrinkled age!          275
My heart shall never countermand mine eye.
Sad° pause and deep regard beseems the sage;
My part is youth, and beats these from the stage.
   Desire my pilot is, beauty my prize;
   Then who fears sinking where such treasure lies?"          280

---

**196 weed** garment, i.e., chastity **198 my household's grave** the tomb of my ancestors **200 soft fancy's** i.e., love's **201 still** always; **respect** regard **205 coat** coat of arms **206 loathsome dash** i.e., a mark of disgrace **207 cipher** show; **fondly** foolishly **221 engirt** surrounded to attack **224 ever-during** ever-enduring **236 quittal** requital

**243 will** desire; **removing** dissuasion **244 sentence** moral judgment; **saw** moral saying **245 painted cloth** wall-hanging on which were painted moral texts and illustrative biblical and classical subjects **248 makes dispensation** dispenses **249 vantage** advantage **251 effects** emotions **258 lawn** (fine) linee **262 Which** i.e., the fact that his hand trembled; **it** her heart **265 Narcissus** a beautiful youth who fell in love with his own reflection **267 color** pretext **269 Poor . . . abuses** remorse is felt only by lesser men in their petty transgressions **270 shadows dreadeth** i.e., has scruples **271 Affection** desire **273 The coward** i.e., even the coward **275 Respect** prudence; **wait on** attend **277 Sad** serious

As corn° o'ergrown by weeds, so heedful fear
Is almost choked by unresisted lust.
Away he steals with open list'ning ear,
Full of foul hope and full of fond mistrust;
Both which, as servitors to the unjust,          285
  So cross° him with their opposite persuasion
  That now he vows a league,° and now invasion.

Within his thought her heavenly image sits,
And in the selfsame seat sits Collatine.
That eye which looks on her confounds his wits;    290
That eye which him beholds, as more divine,
Unto a view so false will not incline;
  But with a pure appeal seeks to° the heart,
  Which once corrupted takes the worser part;

And therein heartens up his servile powers,°       295
Who, flatt'red by their leader's jocund show,
Stuff up his lust, as minutes fill up hours;
And as their captain, so their pride doth grow,
Paying more slavish tribute than they owe.
  By reprobate desire thus madly led,              300
  The Roman lord marcheth to Lucrece' bed.

The locks between her chamber and his will,
Each one by him enforced, retires his ward;°
But as they open, they all rate his ill,°
Which drives the creeping thief to some regard.°   305
The threshold grates the door to have him heard;
  Night-wand'ring weasels° shriek to see him
    there;
  They fright him, yet he still pursues his fear.

As each unwilling portal yields him way,
Through little vents and crannies of the place     310
The wind wars with his torch to make him stay,
And blows the smoke of it into his face,
Extinguishing his conduct° in this case;
  But his hot heart, which fond desire doth
    scorch,
  Puffs forth another wind that fires the torch;    315

And being lighted, by the light he spies
Lucretia's glove, wherein her needle sticks;
He takes it from the rushes° where it lies,
And griping it, the needle his finger pricks,
As who should say, "This glove to wanton tricks    320
  Is not inured;° return again in haste;
  Thou see'st our mistress' ornaments are chaste."

But all these poor forbiddings could not stay him;
He in the worst sense consters° their denial:
The doors, the wind, the glove, that did delay him,    325
He takes for accidental things of trial;°
Or as those bars° which stop the hourly dial,
  Who° with a ling'ring stay his course doth let,°
  Till every minute pays the hour his debt.

"So, so," quoth he, "these lets° attend the time,      330
Like little frosts that sometime threat the spring
To add a more rejoicing to the prime°
And give the sneapèd° birds more cause to sing.
Pain pays the income° of each precious thing:
  Huge rocks, high winds, strong pirates, shelves and
    sands,                                          335
  The merchant fears ere rich at home he lands."

Now is he come unto the chamber door
That shuts him from the heaven of his thought,
Which with a yielding latch, and with no more,
Hath barred him from the blessèd thing he sought.     340
So from himself impiety hath wrought°
  That for his prey to pray he doth begin,
  As if the heavens should countenance his sin.

But in the midst of his unfruitful prayer,
Having solicited th' eternal power                     345
That his foul thoughts might compass his fair fair,°
And they would stand auspicious to the hour,
Even there he starts; quoth he, "I must deflow'r.
  The powers to whom I pray abhor this fact;
  How can they then assist me in the act?              350

"Then Love and Fortune be my gods, my guide:
My will is backed with resolution.
Thoughts are but dreams till their effects be tried;
The blackest sin is cleared with absolution;
Against love's fire fear's frost hath dissolution.    355
  The eye of heaven is out, and misty night
  Covers the shame that follows sweet delight."

This said, his guilty hand plucked up the latch,
And with his knee the door he opens wide.
The dove sleeps fast that this night owl will catch.  360
Thus treason works ere traitors be espied.
Who sees the lurking serpent steps aside;
  But she, sound sleeping, fearing no such thing,
  Lies at the mercy of his mortal sting.°

Into the chamber wickedly he stalks                    365
And gazeth on her yet unstainèd bed.
The curtains being close, about he walks,
Rolling his greedy eyeballs in his head.
By their high treason is his heart misled,
  Which gives the watchword to his hand full soon     370
  To draw the cloud that hides the silver moon.

---

**281 corn** grain  **286 cross** thwart  **287 league** peace  **293
seeks to** applies to  **295 his servile powers** i.e., the senses
**303 retires his ward** draws back its bolt  **304 rate his ill**
condemn his evil intentions (by creaking)  **305 regard** caution
**307 weasels** kept in Roman houses in place of cats to catch rats
**313 conduct** conductor (i.e., the torch)  **318 rushes** used as
floor coverings  **321 inured** accustomed

**324 consters** construes  **326 accidental . . . trial** chance
happenings  **327 bars** lines on the face of a clock  **328 Who**
which; **let** delay  **330 lets** hindrances  **332 prime** spring
**333 sneapèd** chilled  **334 income** harvest, gain  **341 wrought**
i.e., wrought him  **346 compass . . . fair** possess his virtuous
beauty  **364 sting** (1) lust (2) penis

Look as° the fair and fiery-pointed sun,
Rushing from forth a cloud, bereaves° our sight,
Even so, the curtain drawn, his eyes begun
To wink,° being blinded with a greater light.      375
Whether it is that she reflects so bright
   That dazzleth them, or else some shame supposed;°
   But blind they are, and keep themselves enclosèd.

O, had they in that darksome prison died,
Then had they seen the period° of their ill!°       380
Then Collatine again by Lucrece' side
In his clear° bed might have reposèd still.
But they must ope, this blessèd league to kill,
   And holy-thoughted Lucrece to their sight
   Must sell her joy, her life, her world's delight.      385

Her lily hand her rosy cheek lies under,
Coz'ning° the pillow of a lawful kiss:
Who, therefore angry, seems to part in sunder,
Swelling on either side to want his bliss;
Between whose hills her head entombèd is;      390
   Where like a virtuous monument she lies,
   To be admired of lewd unhallowed eyes.

Without the bed her other fair hand was,
On the green coverlet; whose perfect white
Showed like an April daisy on the grass,      395
With pearly sweat resembling dew of night.
Her eyes like marigolds had sheathed their light,
   And canopied in darkness sweetly lay
   Till they might open to adorn the day.

Her hair like golden threads played with her breath—      400
O modest wantons, wanton modesty—
Showing life's triumph in the map° of death,
And death's dim look in life's mortality.
Each in her sleep themselves so beautify
   As if between them twain there were no strife,      405
   But that life lived in death, and death in life.

Her breasts like ivory globes circled with blue,
A pair of maiden worlds unconquerèd,
Save of their lord no bearing yoke they knew,
And him by oath they truly honorèd.      410
These worlds in Tarquin new ambition bred,
   Who like a foul usurper went about
   From this fair throne to heave the owner out.

What could he see but mightily he noted?
What did he note but strongly he desirèd?      415
What he beheld, on that he firmly doted,
And in his will° his willful eye he tirèd.
With more than admiration he admirèd
   Her azure veins, her alablaster skin,
   Her coral lips, her snow-white dimpled chin.      420

As the grim lion fawneth° o'er his prey,
Sharp hunger by the conquest satisfied,
So o'er this sleeping soul doth Tarquin stay,
His rage of lust by gazing qualified;
Slacked, not suppressed; for, standing by her side,      425
   His eye, which late this mutiny restrains,
   Unto a greater uproar tempts his veins.

And they, like straggling slaves for pillage fighting,
Obdurate vassals fell exploits effecting,
In bloody death and ravishment delighting,      430
Nor children's tears nor° mothers' groans respecting,
Swell in their pride,° the onset still expecting.
   Anon his beating heart, alarum° striking,
   Gives the hot charge and bids them do their liking.

His drumming heart cheers up° his burning eye,      435
His eye commends° the leading to his hand;
His hand, as proud of such a dignity,
Smoking with pride, marched on to make his stand
On her bare breast, the heart of all her land;
   Whose ranks of blue veins, as his hand did scale,      440
   Left their round turrets destitute and pale.

They, must'ring° to the quiet cabinet°
Where their dear governess and lady lies,
Do tell her she is dreadfully beset
And fright her with confusion of their cries.      445
She, much amazed, breaks ope her locked-up eyes,
   Who, peeping forth this tumult to behold,
   Are by his flaming torch dimmed and controlled.°

Imagine her as one in dead of night,
From forth dull sleep by dreadful fancy waking,      450
That thinks she hath beheld some ghastly sprite,
Whose grim aspect sets every joint a-shaking.
What terror 'tis! but she, in worser taking,°
   From sleep disturbèd, heedfully doth view
   The sight which makes supposèd terror true.      455

Wrapped and confounded in a thousand fears,
Like to a new-killed bird she trembling lies.
She dares not look; yet winking there appears
Quick-shifting antics,° ugly in her eyes.
Such shadows° are the weak brain's forgeries,      460
   Who, angry that the eyes fly from their lights,
   In darkness daunts them with more dreadful sights.

His hand, that yet remains upon her breast
(Rude ram,° to batter such an ivory wall!),
May feel her heart (poor citizen) distressed,      465
Wounding itself to death, rise up and fall,
Beating her bulk,° that his hand shakes withal.
   This moves in him more rage and lesser pity,
   To make the breach and enter this sweet city.

---

**372 Look as** as   **373 bereaves** takes away   **375 wink** close
**377 supposèd** imagined   **380 period** end; **ill** evil   **382 clear**
unstained   **387 Coz'ning** cheating   **402 map** image   **417**
**will** lust

**421 fawneth** rejoices   **431 Nor . . . nor** neither . . . nor
**432 pride** lust   **433 alarum** call to attack in battle   **435 cheers**
**up** encourages   **436 commends** entrusts   **442 must'ring**
rallying; **the quiet cabinet** the heart   **448 controlled** overpowered   **453 taking** fear   **459 antics** grotesque figures   **460**
**shadows** shapes   **464 ram** battering ram   **467 bulk** body

First like a trumpet doth his tongue begin                    470
To sound a parley to his heartless° foe;
Who o'er the white sheet peers her whiter chin,
The reason of this rash alarm to know,
Which he by dumb demeanor° seeks to show;
  But she with vehement prayers urgeth still           475
  Under what color° he commits this ill.

Thus he replies: "The color in thy face,
That even for anger makes the lily pale
And the red rose blush at her own disgrace,
Shall plead for me and tell my loving tale.                   480
Under that color am I come to scale
  Thy never-conquered fort; the fault is thine,
  For those thine eyes betray thee unto mine.

"Thus I forestall thee, if thou mean to chide:
Thy beauty hath ensnared thee to this night,°               485
Where thou with patience must my will° abide,
My will that marks thee for my earth's delight,
Which I to conquer sought with all my might;
  But as reproof and reason beat it dead,
  By thy bright beauty was it newly bred.                490

"I see what crosses my attempt will bring,
I know what thorns the growing rose defends,
I think the honey guarded with a sting:
All this beforehand counsel comprehends.
But Will is deaf, and hears no heedful friends;             495
  Only he hath an eye to gaze on Beauty,
  And dotes on what he looks, 'gainst law or duty.

"I have debated even in my soul,
What wrong, what shame, what sorrow I shall breed;
But nothing can affection's° course control                 500
Or stop the headlong fury of his speed.
I know repentant tears ensue the deed,
  Reproach, disdain, and deadly enmity;
  Yet strive I to embrace mine infamy."

This said, he shakes aloft his Roman blade,                 505
Which, like a falcon tow'ring in the skies,
Coucheth° the fowl below with his wings' shade,
Whose crooked beak threats if he mount he dies.
So under his insulting falchion° lies
  Harmless Lucretia, marking what he tells               510
  With trembling fear, as fowl hear falcons' bells.

"Lucrece," quoth he, "this night I must enjoy thee.
If thou deny, then force must work my way;
For in thy bed I purpose to destroy thee.
That done, some worthless slave of thine I'll slay,         515
To kill thine honor with thy life's decay;
  And in thy dead arms do I mean to place him,
  Swearing I slew him, seeing thee embrace him.

"So thy surviving husband shall remain
The scornful mark of every open eye;                        520
Thy kinsmen hang their heads at this disdain,°
Thy issue blurred with nameless bastardy;
And thou, the author of their obloquy,
  Shalt have thy trespass cited up in rhymes
  And sung by children in succeeding times.             525

"But if thou yield, I rest thy secret friend;
The fault unknown is as a thought unacted.
A little harm done to a great good end
For lawful policy remains enacted.°
The poisonous simple° sometime is compacted°               530
  In a pure compound; being so applied,
  His venom in effect is purified.

"Then, for thy husband and thy children's sake,
Tender° my suit; bequeath not to their lot
The shame that from them no device can take,               535
The blemish that will never be forgot;
Worse than a slavish wipe° or birth-hour's blot;°
  For marks descried in men's nativity
  Are nature's faults, not their own infamy."

Here with a cockatrice'° dead-killing eye                   540
He rouseth up himself and makes a pause;
While she, the picture of pure piety,
Like a white hind° under the gripe's° sharp claws,
Pleads, in a wilderness where are no laws,
  To the rough beast that knows no gentle right         545
  Nor aught obeys but his foul appetite.

But when a black-faced cloud the world doth threat,
In his dim mist th' aspiring mountains hiding,
From earth's dark womb some gentle gust doth get,°
Which blows these pitchy vapors from their biding,         550
Hind'ring their present° fall by this dividing,
  So his unhallowed haste her words delays,
  And moody Pluto winks while Orpheus° plays.

Yet, foul night-waking cat, he doth but dally,
While in his hold-fast foot the weak mouse panteth.        555
Her sad behavior feeds his vulture folly,°
A swallowing gulf that even in plenty wanteth.°
His ear her prayers admits, but his heart granteth
  No penetrable entrance to her plaining.°
  Tears harden lust, though marble wear with raining.  560

---

471 **heartless** frightened  474 **dumb demeanor** dumb show
476 **color** (1) pretext (2) flag (3) anger (choler)  485 **to this
night** i.e., tonight  486 **will** sexual desire  500 **affection's**
passion's  507 **Coucheth** makes cower  509 **falchion** curved
sword (with play on "falcon")

---

521 **disdain** disgrace  529 **enacted** recorded  530 **simple**
medicine; **compacted** compounded  534 **Tender** regard
537 **slavish wipe** i.e., brand mark on a slave; **birth-hour's
blot** birthmark  540 **cockatrice'** basilisk's (mythical serpent
that killed with a glance)  543 **hind** doe; **gripe's** griffin's (?)
eagle's (?)  549 **doth get** makes its way  551 **present** immediate  553 **Pluto . . . Orpheus** Pluto, the ruler of the
underworld, charmed by Orpheus' music, shut his eyes and
allowed Orpheus to lead his wife, Eurydice, back toward
the world  556 **vulture folly** ravenous madness  557 **wanteth**
hungers  599 **plaining** lament

Her pity-pleading eyes are sadly fixèd
In the remorseless wrinkles° of his face.
Her modest eloquence with sighs is mixèd,
Which to her oratory adds more grace.
She puts the period often from his place,°      565
　And midst the sentence to her accent° breaks
　That twice she doth begin ere once she speaks.

She conjures him by high almighty Jove,
By knighthood, gentry, and sweet friendship's oath,
By her untimely tears, her husband's love,      570
By holy human law and common troth,
By heaven and earth, and all the power of both,
　That to his borrowed bed he make retire
　And stoop to° honor, not to foul desire.

Quoth she, "Reward not hospitality            575
With such black payment as thou hast pretended;°
Mud not the fountain that gave drink to thee;
Mar not the thing that cannot be amended.
End thy ill aim before thy shoot° be ended.
　He is no woodman° that doth bend his bow      580
　To strike a poor unseasonable doe.

"My husband is thy friend; for his sake spare me.
Thyself art mighty; for thine own sake leave me.
Myself a weakling; do not then ensnare me.
Thou look'st not like deceit; do not deceive me.  585
My sighs like whirlwinds labor hence to heave° thee.
　If ever man were moved with woman's moans,
　Be movèd with my tears, my sighs, my groans;

"All which together, like a troubled ocean,
Beat at thy rocky and wrack-threat'ning heart,  590
To soften it with their continual motion;
For stones dissolved to water do convert.°
O, if no harder than a stone thou art,
　Melt at my tears and be compassionate!
　Soft pity enters at an iron gate.            595

"In Tarquin's likeness I did entertain thee;
Hast thou put on his shape to do him shame?
To all the host of heaven I complain me.
Thou wrong'st his honor, wound'st his princely name.
Thou art not what thou seem'st; and if the same,  600
　Thou seem'st not what thou art, a god, a king;
　For kings like gods should govern everything.

"How will thy shame be seeded° in thine age
When thus thy vices bud before thy spring?
If in thy hope thou dar'st do such outrage,    605
What dar'st thou not when once thou art a king?
O, be rememb'red, no outrageous thing
　From vassal actors° can be wiped away;
　Then kings' misdeeds cannot be hid in clay.°

"This deed will make thee only loved for fear;    610
But happy monarchs still are feared for love.
With foul offenders thou perforce must bear
When they in thee the like offenses prove.
If but for° fear of this, thy will remove;°
　For princes are the glass,° the school, the book,  615
　Where subjects' eyes do learn, do read, do look.

"And wilt thou be the school where Lust shall learn?
Must he in thee read lectures of such shame?
Wilt thou be glass wherein it shall discern
Authority for sin, warrant for blame,        620
To privilege dishonor in thy name?
　Thou back'st° reproach against long-living laud°
　And mak'st fair reputation but a bawd.

"Hast thou command? By Him that gave it thee,
From a pure heart command thy rebel will!      625
Draw not thy sword to guard iniquity,
For it was lent thee all that brood to kill.
Thy princely office how canst thou fulfill
　When, patterned by thy fault, foul Sin may say,
　He learned to sin, and thou didst teach the way?  630

"Think but how vile a spectacle it were
To view thy present trespass in another.
Men's faults do seldom to themselves appear;
Their own transgressions partially they smother.
This guilt would seem death-worthy in thy brother.  635
　O, how are they wrapped in with infamies
　That from their own misdeeds askaunce° their eyes!

"To thee, to thee, my heaved-up hands appeal,
Not to seducing lust, thy rash relier.°
I sue for exiled majesty's repeal;°           640
Let him return, and flatt'ring thoughts retire.
His true respect° will prison° false desire.
　And wipe the dim mist from thy doting eyne,°
　That thou shalt see thy state, and pity mine."

"Have done," quoth he. "My uncontrollèd tide    645
Turns not, but swells the higher by this let.°
Small lights are soon blown out; huge fires abide
And with the wind in greater fury fret.
The petty streams that pay a daily debt
　To their salt sovereign° with their fresh falls'° haste,  650
　Add to his flow, but alter not his taste."

"Thou art," quoth she, "a sea, a sovereign king;
And, lo, there falls into thy boundless flood
Black lust, dishonor, shame, misgoverning,
Who seek to stain the ocean of thy blood.      655
If all these petty ills shall change thy good,
　Thy sea within a puddle's womb is hearsèd,°
　And not the puddle in thy sea dispersèd.

**562 remorseless wrinkles** pitiless frowns   **565 She . . . place**
she often makes a pause in the middle of a sentence   **566 accent**
speech   **574 stoop to** submit to   **576 pretended** proposed
**579 shoot** act of shooting (with pun on *suit?*)   **580 woodman**
hunter   **586 heave** move   **592 convert** change   **603 seeded**
matured   **608 vassal actors** i.e., subjects, acting on orders   **609
in clay** i.e., in death

**614 If but for** if only for; **thy will remove** dissuade your
lust   **615 glass** looking-glass   **622 Thou back'st** you support;
**laud** praise   **637 askaunce** turn aside   **639 lust . . . relier** i.e.,
lust, which you rashly rely on   **640 repeal** return from exile
**642 respect** respectfulness; **prison** imprison   **643 eyne** eyes
**646 let** hindrance   **650 salt sovereign** the ocean; **falls'** flows'
**657 hearsèd** entombed

"So shall these slaves be king, and thou their slave;
Thou nobly base, they basely dignified;   660
Thou their fair life, and they thy fouler grave;
Thou loathèd in their shame, they in thy pride.
The lesser thing should not the greater hide.
  The cedar stoops not to the base shrub's foot,
  But low shrubs wither at the cedar's root.   665

"So let thy thoughts, low vassals to thy state"—
"No more," quoth he. "By heaven, I will not hear thee!
Yield to my love; if not, enforcèd hate,
Instead of love's coy° touch, shall rudely tear thee.
That done, despitefully° I mean to bear thee   670
  Unto the base bed of some rascal groom,
  To be thy partner in this shameful doom."

This said, he sets his foot upon the light,
For light and lust are deadly enemies;
Shame folded up in blind concealing night,   675
When most unseen, then most doth tyrannize.
The wolf hath seized his prey; the poor lamb cries,
  Till with her own white fleece° her voice controlled°
  Entombs her outcry in her lips' sweet fold;

For with the nightly linen° that she wears   680
He pens her piteous clamors in her head,
Cooling his hot face in the chastest tears
That ever modest eyes with sorrow shed.
O, that prone° lust should stain so pure a bed,
  The spots whereof, could weeping purify,   685
  Her tears should drop on them perpetually!

But she hath lost a dearer thing than life,
And he hath won what he would lose again.
This forcèd league doth force a further strife;
This momentary joy breeds months of pain;   690
This hot desire converts to cold disdain;
  Pure Chastity is rifled of her store,
  And Lust, the thief, far poorer than before.

Look as the full-fed hound or gorgèd hawk,
Unapt for tender smell° or speedy flight,   695
Make slow pursuit, or altogether balk°
The prey wherein by nature they delight,
So surfeit-taking Tarquin fares this night:
  His taste delicious, in digestion souring,
  Devours his will, that lived by foul devouring.   700

O, deeper sin than bottomless conceit°
Can comprehend in still imagination!
Drunken Desire must vomit his receipt°
Ere he can see his own abomination.
While Lust is in his pride, no exclamation°   705
  Can curb his heat or rein his rash desire
  Till, like a jade, Self-will himself doth tire.

And then with lank and lean discolored cheek,
With heavy eye, knit brow, and strengthless pace,
Feeble Desire, all recreant,° poor, and meek,   710
Like to a bankrout beggar wails his case.
The flesh being proud, Desire doth fight with Grace,
  For there it revels; and when that° decays,
  The guilty rebel for remission prays.

So fares it with this fault-full lord of Rome,   715
Who this accomplishment so hotly chasèd;
For now against himself he sounds this doom,
That through the length of times he stands disgracèd.
Besides, his soul's fair temple is defacèd;
  To whose weak ruins muster troops of cares,   720
  To ask the spotted princess° how she fares.

She says her subjects° with foul insurrection
Have battered down her consecrated wall,
And by their mortal° fault brought in subjection
Her immortality and made her thrall   725
To living death and pain perpetual;
  Which° in her prescience° she controllèd still,
  But her foresight could not forestall their will.

Ev'n in this thought through the dark night he stealeth,
A captive victor that hath lost in gain;   730
Bearing away the wound that nothing healeth,
The scar that will despite of cure remain;
Leaving his spoil° perplexed in greater pain.
  She bears the load of lust he left behind,
  And he the burden of a guilty mind.   735

He like a thievish dog creeps sadly thence;
She like a wearied lamb lies panting there.
He scowls, and hates himself for his offense;
She desperate with her nails her flesh doth tear.
He faintly flies, sweating with guilty fear;   740
  She stays, exclaiming on the direful night;
  He runs, and chides his vanished loathed delight.

He thence departs a heavy convertite;°
She there remains a hopeless castaway.°
He in his speed looks for the morning light;   745
She prays she never may behold the day,
"For day," quoth she, "night's scapes° doth open lay,
  And my true eyes have never practiced how
  To cloak offenses with a cunning brow.

"They think not but that every eye can see   750
The same disgrace which they themselves behold;
And therefore would they still in darkness be,
To have their unseen sin remain untold,
For they their guilt with weeping will unfold
  And grave,° like water° that doth eat in steel,   755
  Upon my cheeks what helpless shame I feel."

**669 coy** gentle  **670 despitefully** cruelly  **678 white fleece** i.e., bedclothes; **controlled** overwhelmed  **680 nightly linen** turban (?)  **684 prone** (1) impulsive (2) prostrate  **695 tender smell** weak scent  **696 balk** neglect to pursue  **701 bottomless conceit** infinite imagination  **703 his receipt** what it has received  **705 exclamation** exhortation

**710 recreant** cowed  **713 that** lust  **721 the spotted princess** Tarquin's defiled soul  **722 her subjects** the senses  **724 mortal** deadly  **727 Which** her subjects; **prescience** foreknowledge (i.e., in theory)  **733 spoil** victim  **743 heavy convertite** sad penitent  **744 castaway** lost soul  **747 scapes** transgressions  **755 grave** engrave; **water** i.e., acid

Here she exclaims against repose and rest,
And bids her eyes hereafter still be blind.
She wakes her heart by beating on her breast,
And bids it leap from thence, where it may find          760
Some purer chest to close° so pure a mind.
  Frantic with grief thus breathes she forth her spite
  Against the unseen secrecy of night:

"O comfort-killing Night, image of hell,
Dim register and notary° of shame,          765
Black stage for tragedies and murders fell,
Vast sin-concealing chaos, nurse of blame,
Blind muffled bawd, dark harbor for defame!°
  Grim cave of death, whisp'ring conspirator
  With close-tongued° treason and the ravisher!          770

"O hateful, vaporous, and foggy Night,
Since thou art guilty of my cureless crime,
Muster thy mists to meet the eastern light,
Make war against proportioned° course of time;
Or if thou wilt permit the sun to climb          775
  His wonted height, yet ere he go to bed,
  Knit poisonous clouds about his golden head.

"With rotten damps ravish the morning air;
Let their exhaled unwholesome breaths make sick
The life of purity, the supreme fair,°          780
Ere he arrive his weary noontide prick;°
And let thy musty vapors march so thick
  That in their smoky ranks his smoth'red light
  May set at noon and make perpetual night.

"Were Tarquin Night, as he is but Night's child,°          785
The silver-shining queen he would distain;°
Her twinkling handmaids too, by him defiled,
Through Night's black bosom should not peep
  again.
So should I have co-partners in my pain;
  And fellowship in woe doth woe assuage,          790
  As palmers'° chat makes short their pilgrimage;

"Where now° I have no one to blush with me,
To cross their arms° and hang their heads with mine,
To mask their brows° and hide their infamy;
But I alone, alone must sit and pine,          795
Seasoning the earth with show'rs of silver brine,
  Mingling my talk with tears, my grief with
    groans,
  Poor wasting monuments of lasting moans.

"O Night, thou furnace of foul reeking smoke,
Let not the jealous° Day behold that face          800
Which underneath thy black all-hiding cloak
Immodestly lies martyred with disgrace!
Keep still possession of thy gloomy place,
  That all the faults which in thy reign are made
  May likewise be sepulchered in thy shade!          805

"Make me not object to the telltale Day.
The light will show, charactered° in my brow,
The story of sweet chastity's decay,
The impious breach of holy wedlock vow.
Yea, the illiterate, that know not how          810
  To cipher° what is writ in learnèd books,
  Will quote° my loathsome trespass in my looks.

"The nurse to still her child will tell my story
And fright her crying babe with Tarquin's name.
The orator to deck his oratory          815
Will couple my reproach to Tarquin's shame.
Feast-finding minstrels, tuning my defame,
  Will tie° the hearers to attend each line,
  How Tarquin wrongèd me, I Collatine.

"Let my good name, that senseless° reputation,          820
For Collatine's dear love be kept unspotted.
If that be made a theme for disputation,
The branches of another root are rotted,
And undeserved reproach to him allotted
  That is as clear from this attaint° of mine          825
  As I ere this was pure to Collatine.

"O unseen shame, invisible disgrace!
O unfelt sore, crest-wounding° private scar!
Reproach is stamped in Collatinus' face,
And Tarquin's eye may read the mot° afar,          830
How he in peace is wounded, not in war.
  Alas, how many bear such shameful blows
  Which not themselves, but he that gives them knows!

"If, Collatine, thine honor lay in me,
From me by strong assault it is bereft;          835
My honey lost, and I, a dronelike bee,
Have no perfection of my summer left,
But robbed and ransacked by injurious theft.
  In thy weak hive a wand'ring wasp hath crept
  And sucked the honey which thy chaste bee kept.          840

"Yet am I guilty of thy honor's wrack;
Yet for thy honor did I entertain him:
Coming from thee, I could not put him back,
For it had been dishonor to disdain him.
Besides, of weariness he did complain him          845
  And talked of virtue: O unlooked-for evil,
  When virtue is profaned in such a devil!

**761 close** enclose   **765 notary** recorder   **768 defame** disgrace
**770 close-tongued** secretive   **774 proportioned** orderly
**780 the supreme fair** the sun   **781 Ere . . . prick** before
he arrives wearied at the point of noon (on a sundial)   **785
Night's child** i.e., wicked   **786 distain** defile   **791 palmers'**
pilgrims' (those who had been to the Holy Land wore a palm
leaf)   **792 Where now** whereas   **793 To . . . arms** folded
arms were a sign of melancholy   **794 To . . . brows** a hat
pulled down over one's face was a sign of melancholy

**800 jealous** watchful   **807 charactered** lettered (accent on
second syllable)   **811 cipher** decipher   **812 quote** mark   **818
tie** hold   **820 senseless** (1) impalpable (2) free from sensuality   **825 attaint** disgrace   **828 crest-wounding** i.e., disgraceful to the family crest   **830 mot** motto (with allusion to
the parable of the mote and the beam, Matthew 7:3)

"Why should the worm intrude the maiden bud?
Or hateful cuckoo hatch in sparrows' nests?
Or toads infect fair founts with venom mud?    850
Or tyrant folly lurk in gentle breasts?
Or kings be breakers of their own behests?°
     But no perfection is so absolute
     That some impurity doth not pollute.

"The agèd man that coffers up his gold    855
Is plagued with cramps and gouts and painful fits,
And scarce hath eyes his treasure to behold,
But like still-pining Tantalus° he sits
And useless barns° the harvest of his wits,
     Having no other pleasure of his gain    860
     But torment that it cannot cure his pain.

"So then he hath it when he cannot use it,
And leaves it to be mast'red by his young,
Who in their pride do presently° abuse it;
Their father was too weak, and they too strong,    865
To hold their cursèd-blessèd fortune long.
     The sweets we wish for turn to loathèd sours
     Even in the moment that we call them ours.

"Unruly blasts wait on the tender spring;
Unwholesome weeds take root with precious flow'rs;   870
The adder hisses where the sweet birds sing;
What virtue breeds iniquity devours.
We have no good that we can say is ours,
     But ill-annexèd opportunity°
     Or kills his life or else his quality.°    875

"O Opportunity, thy guilt is great!
'Tis thou that execut'st the traitor's treason;
Thou sets the wolf where he the lamb may get;
Whoever plots the sin, thou point'st the season.
'Tis thou that spurn'st at right, at law, at reason;    880
     And in thy shady cell, where none may spy him,
     Sits Sin, to seize the souls that wander by him.

"Thou mak'st the vestal violate her oath;
Thou blow'st the fire when temperance is thawed;
Thou smother'st honesty, thou murd'rest troth.    885
Thou foul abettor, thou notorious bawd,
Thou plantest scandal and displacest laud.°
     Thou ravisher, thou traitor, thou false thief,
     Thy honey turns to gall, thy joy to grief.

"Thy secret pleasure turns to open shame,    890
Thy private feasting to a public fast,
Thy smoothing° titles to a ragged name,
Thy sug'red tongue to bitter wormwood taste:
Thy violent vanities can never last.
     How comes it then, vile Opportunity,    895
     Being so bad, such numbers seek for thee?

"When wilt thou be the humble suppliant's friend
And bring him where his suit may be obtainèd?
When wilt thou sort° an hour great strifes to end?
Or free that soul which wretchedness hath chainèd?    900
Give physic to the sick, ease to the painèd?
     The poor, lame, blind, halt, creep, cry out for thee;
     But they ne'er meet with Opportunity.

"The patient dies while the physician sleeps;
The orphan pines while the oppressor feeds;    905
Justice is feasting while the widow weeps;
Advice° is sporting while infection breeds.
Thou grant'st no time for charitable deeds:
     Wrath, envy, treason, rape, and murder's rages,
     Thy heinous hours wait on them as their pages.    910

"When Truth and Virtue have to do with thee,
A thousand crosses° keep them from thy aid.
They buy thy help; but Sin ne'er gives a fee,
He gratis comes; and thou art well apaid
As well to hear as grant what he hath said.    915
     My Collatine would else have come to me
     When Tarquin did, but he was stayed by thee.

"Guilty thou art of murder and of theft,
Guilty of perjury and subornation,°
Guilty of treason, forgery, and shift,°    920
Guilty of incest, that abomination:
An accessary by thine inclination
     To all sins past and all that are to come,
     From the creation to the general doom.

"Misshapen Time, copesmate° of ugly Night,    925
Swift subtle post,° carrier of grisly care,
Eater of youth, false slave to false delight,
Base watch° of woes, sin's packhorse, virtue's snare!
Thou nursest all, and murd'rest all that are.
     O, hear me then, injurious shifting Time;    930
     Be guilty of my death, since of my crime.

"Why hath thy servant Opportunity
Betrayed the hours thou gav'st me to repose?
Canceled my fortunes, and enchainèd me
To endless date of never-ending woes?    935
Time's office is to fine° the hate of foes,
     To eat up errors by opinion bred,
     Not spend the dowry of a lawful bed.

"Time's glory is to calm contending kings,
To unmask falsehood and bring truth to light,    940
To stamp the seal of time in agèd things,
To wake the morn and sentinel° the night,
To wrong the wronger till he render right,
     To ruinate° proud buildings with thy hours,
     And smear with dust their glitt'ring golden tow'rs;    945

---

**852 behests** commands   **858 Tantalus** in Hades, Tantalus was surrounded by food and drink that he could never touch   **859 barns** stores   **864 presently** immediately   **874 ill-annexèd opportunity** disastrously connected chance   **875 Or . . . quality** either kills its (good's) life or its nature   **887 laud** praise   **892 smoothing** flattering

**899 sort** choose   **907 Advice** (medical) knowledge   **912 crosses** hindrances   **919 subornation** bribing someone to commit a crime   **920 shift** cheating   **925 copesmate** companion, paramour   **926 subtle post** sly post-rider   **928 watch** watchman   **936 fine** end   **942 sentinel** guard   **944 ruinate** reduce to ruin

"To fill with wormholes stately monuments,
To feed oblivion with decay of things,
To blot old books and alter their contents,
To pluck the quills from ancient ravens' wings,
To dry the old oak's sap and cherish springs,°    950
   To spoil antiquities of hammered steel
   And turn the giddy round of Fortune's wheel;

"To show the beldame° daughters of her daughter,
To make the child a man, the man a child,
To slay the tiger that doth live by slaughter,    955
To tame the unicorn and lion wild,
To mock the subtle in themselves beguiled,
   To cheer the ploughman with increaseful crops
   And waste° huge stones with little water-drops.

"Why work'st thou mischief in thy pilgrimage,    960
Unless thou couldst return to make amends?
One poor retiring° minute in an age
Would purchase thee a thousand thousand friends,
Lending him wit that to bad debtors lends.
   O this dread night, wouldst thou one hour come
     back,    965
   I could prevent this storm and shun thy wrack!

"Thou ceaseless lackey° to Eternity,
With some mischance cross Tarquin in his flight.
Devise extremes beyond extremity
To make him curse this cursèd crimeful night.    970
Let ghastly shadows his lewd eyes affright,
   And the dire thought of his committed evil
   Shape every bush a hideous shapeless devil.

"Disturb his hours of rest with restless trances;
Afflict him in his bed with bedrid groans;    975
Let there bechance him pitiful mischances
To make him moan, but pity not his moans.
Stone him with hard'ned hearts harder than stones,
   And let mild women to him lose their mildness,
   Wilder to him than tigers in their wildness.    980

"Let him have time to tear his curlèd hair,
Let him have time against himself to rave,
Let him have time of Time's help to despair,
Let him have time to live a loathèd slave,
Let him have time a beggar's orts° to crave,    985
   And time to see one that by alms doth live
   Disdain to him disdainèd scraps to give.

"Let him have time to see his friends his foes
And merry fools to mock at him resort;
Let him have time to mark how slow time goes    990
In time of sorrow, and how swift and short
His time of folly and his time of sport;
   And ever let his unrecalling° crime
   Have time to wail th' abusing of his time.

"O Time, thou tutor both to good and bad,    995
Teach me to curse him that thou taught'st this ill.
At his own shadow let the thief run mad,
Himself himself seek every hour to kill.
Such wretched hands such wretched blood should spill,
   For who so base would such an office have    1000
   As sland'rous deathsman° to so base a slave?

"The baser is he, coming from a king,
To shame his hope° with deeds degenerate.
The mightier man, the mightier is the thing
That makes him honored or begets him hate;    1005
For greatest scandal waits on greatest state.
   The moon being clouded presently is missed,
   But little stars may hide them when they list.

"The crow may bathe his coal-black wings in mire
And unperceived fly with the filth away;    1010
But if the like the snow-white swan desire,
The stain upon his silver down will stay.
Poor grooms° are sightless° night, kings glorious day;
   Gnats are unnoted wheresoe'er they fly,
   But eagles gazed upon with every eye.    1015

"Out, idle words, servants to shallow fools,
Unprofitable sounds, weak arbitrators!°
Busy yourselves in skill-contending schools;°
Debate where leisure serves with dull debaters;
To trembling clients° be you mediators:    1020
   For me, I force not argument a straw,°
   Since that my case is past the help of law.

"In vain I rail at Opportunity,
At Time, at Tarquin, and uncheerful Night;
In vain I cavil with mine infamy;    1025
In vain I spurn° at my confirmed despite:°
This helpless smoke of words° doth me no right.
   The remedy indeed to do me good
   Is to let forth my foul defilèd blood.

"Poor hand, why quiver'st thou at this decree?    1030
Honor thyself to rid me of this shame;
For if I die, my honor lives in thee;
But if I live, thou liv'st in my defame.
Since thou couldst not defend thy loyal dame
   And wast afeared to scratch her wicked foe,    1035
   Kill both thyself and her for yielding so."

This said, from her betumbled couch she starteth,
To find some desp'rate instrument of death;
But this no slaughterhouse no tool imparteth°
To make more vent for passage of her breath,    1040
Which, thronging through her lips, so vanisheth
   As smoke from Aetna that in air consumes
   Or that which from dischargèd cannon fumes.

---

950 **cherish springs** renew (1) the water of springs, or (2) young saplings (i.e., new growth of any kind)   953 **beldame** old woman   959 **waste** wear away   962 **retiring** returning 967 **ceaseless lackey** ever-present servant   985 **orts** scraps 993 **unrecalling** irrevocable

1001 **sland'rous deathsman** disgraced executioner   1003 **hope** expectations (as heir)   1013 **grooms** servants; **sightless** invisible   1017 **arbitrators** arbiters (or compromisers)   1018 **in skill-contending schools** i.e., in mere debates   1020 **clients** suitors at law   1021 **force . . . straw** care not a straw for argument   1026 **spurn** kick; **despite** wrong   1027 **smoke of words** mere talk   1039 **imparteth** provides

"In vain," quoth she, "I live, and seek in vain
Some happy mean to end a hapless life.　　　1045
I feared by Tarquin's falchion to be slain,
Yet for the selfsame purpose seek a knife;
But when I feared I was a loyal wife.
　So am I now—O no, that cannot be:
　Of that true type° hath Tarquin rifled me.　　1050

"O, that is gone for which I sought to live,
And therefore now I need not fear to die.
To clear this spot by death, at least I give
A badge° of fame to slander's livery,°
A dying life to living infamy.　　　1055
　Poor helpless help, the treasure stol'n away,
　To burn the guiltless casket where it lay!

"Well, well, dear Collatine, thou shalt not know
The stainèd taste of violated troth.
I will not wrong thy true affection so,　　　1060
To flatter thee with an infringèd oath.
This bastard graff° shall never come to growth:
　He shall not boast who did thy stock pollute
　That thou art doting father of his fruit.

"Nor shall he smile at thee in secret thought,　　1065
Nor laugh with his companions at thy state;
But thou shalt know thy int'rest° was not bought
Basely with gold, but stol'n from forth thy gate.
For me, I am the mistress of my fate,
　And with my trespass never will dispense°　　1070
　Till life to death acquit my forced offense.

"I will not poison thee with my attaint
Nor fold my fault in cleanly coined excuses;
My sable° ground of sin I will not paint
To hide the truth of this false night's abuses.　1075
My tongue shall utter all; mine eyes, like sluices,
　As from a mountain spring that feeds a dale,
　Shall gush pure streams to purge my impure tale."

By this lamenting Philomel° had ended
The well-tuned warble of her nightly sorrow,　1080
And solemn night with slow sad gait descended
To ugly hell; when, lo, the blushing morrow
Lends light to all fair eyes that light will borrow;
　But cloudy Lucrece shames herself to see
　And therefore still in night would cloist'red be.　1085

Revealing day through every cranny spies
And seems to point her out where she sits weeping;
To whom she sobbing speaks, "O eye of eyes
Why pry'st thou through my window? Leave thy
　　peeping.
Mock with thy tickling° beams eyes that are sleeping.　1090
　Brand not my forehead with thy piercing light.
　For day hath naught to do what's done by night."

Thus cavils she with everything she sees.
True grief is fond and testy° as a child,
Who wayward once,° his mood with naught agrees.　1095
Old woes, not infant sorrows, bear them° mild:
Continuance tames the one; the other wild,
　Like an unpracticed swimmer plunging still,
　With too much labor drowns for want of skill.

So she, deep drenchèd in a sea of care,　　　1100
Holds disputation with each thing she views,
And to herself all sorrow doth compare;
No object but her passion's strength renews;
And as one shifts, another straight ensues.°
　Sometime her grief is dumb and hath no words;　1105
　Sometime 'tis mad and too much talk affords.

The little birds that tune° their morning's joy
Make her moans mad with their sweet melody:
For mirth doth search the bottom of annoy;°
Sad souls are slain in merry company;　　　1110
Grief best is pleased with grief's society:
　True sorrow then is feelingly sufficed°
　When with like semblance it is sympathized.

'Tis double death to drown in ken° of shore;
He ten times pines that pines beholding food;　1115
To see the salve doth make the wound ache more;
Great grief grieves most at that would do it good;
Deep woes roll forward like a gentle flood,
　Who, being stopped, the bounding banks o'erflows;
　Grief dallied° with, nor law nor limit knows.　　1120

"You mocking birds," quoth she, "your tunes entomb
Within your hollow swelling feath'red breasts,
And in my hearing be you mute and dumb;
My restless discord loves no stops° nor rests.°
A woeful hostess brooks not merry guests.　　1125
　Relish° your nimble notes to pleasing ears;
　Distress likes dumps° when time is kept with tears.

"Come, Philomel, that sing'st of ravishment,
Make thy sad grove in my disheveled hair.
As the dank earth weeps at thy languishment,　1130
So I at each sad strain will strain a tear
And with deep groans the diapason° bear;
　For burden-wise° I'll hum on Tarquin still,
　While thou on Tereus descants better skill.°

---

**1050 true type** stamp **1054 badge** mark (crest, coat of arms) worn on a servant's sleeve; **livery** garment **1062 graff** graft, shoot **1067 int'rest** property **1070 dispense** pardon **1074 sable** black **1079 Philomel** the nightingale (who, according to legend, had originally been a woman, ravished by Tereus; see lines 1128–34) **1090 tickling** lightly touching

**1094 fond and testy** foolish and irritable **1095 wayward once** once becoming angry **1096 them** themselves **1104 straight ensues** straightway follows **1107 tune** sing **1109 search . . . annoy** pierce to the depths of grief **1112 sufficed** contented **1114 ken** sight **1120 dallied** trifled **1124 stops, rests** (1) cessation of discord (2) musical pauses **1126 Relish** make pleasant (literally, sauce) **1127 dumps** slow mournful tunes **1132 diapason** bass accompaniment **1133 burden-wise** a burden was (1) a bass accompaniment (2) the refrain of a song **1134 descants better skill** (1) sings better (2) sings more intricately

"And whiles against a thorn thou bear'st thy part          1135
To keep thy sharp woes waking, wretched I,
To imitate thee well, against my heart
Will fix a sharp knife to affright mine eye,
Who° if it wink° shall thereon fall and die.
　　These means, as frets° upon an instrument,          1140
　　Shall tune our heartstrings to true languishment.

"And for,° poor bird, thou sing'st not in the day,
As shaming° any eye should thee behold,
Some dark deep desert, seated from the way,°
That knows not parching heat nor freezing cold,          1145
Will we find out; and there we will unfold
　　To creatures stern sad tunes, to change their kinds.°
　　Since men prove beasts, let beasts bear gentle minds."

As the poor frighted deer that stands at gaze,°
Wildly determining which way to fly,          1150
Or one encompassed with a winding maze,
That cannot tread the way out readily;
So with herself is she in mutiny,
　　To live or die which of the twain were better,
　　When life is shamed and death reproach's debtor.°          1155

"To kill myself," quoth she, "alack, what were it
But with my body my poor soul's pollution?
They that lose half with greater patience bear it
Than they whose whole is swallowed in confusion.°
That mother tries a merciless conclusion°          1160
　　Who, having two sweet babes, when death takes one,
　　Will slay the other and be nurse to none.

"My body or my soul, which was the dearer
When the one pure, the other made divine?
Whose love of either to myself was nearer          1165
When both were kept for heaven and Collatine?
Ay me, the bark pilled° from the lofty pine,
　　His leaves will wither and his sap decay:
　　So must my soul, her bark being pilled away.

"Her house is sacked, her quiet interrupted,          1170
Her mansion battered by the enemy;
Her sacred temple spotted, spoiled, corrupted,
Grossly engirt° with daring infamy.
Then let it not be called impiety
　　If in this blemished fort° I make some hole          1175
　　Through which I may convey this troubled soul.

"Yet die I will not till my Collatine
Have heard the cause of my untimely death,
That he may vow, in that sad hour of mine,
Revenge on him that made me stop my breath.          1180
My stainèd blood to Tarquin I'll bequeath,
　　Which, by him tainted, shall for him be spent
　　And as his due writ in my testament.

"My honor I'll bequeath unto the knife
That wounds my body so dishonorèd.          1185
'Tis honor to deprive° dishonored life:
The one will live, the other being dead.
So of shame's ashes shall my fame be bred,
　　For in my death I murder shameful scorn;
　　My shame so dead, mine honor is new born.          1190

"Dear lord of that dear jewel I have lost,
What legacy shall I bequeath to thee?
My resolution, love, shall be thy boast,
By whose example thou revenged mayst be.
How Tarquin must be used, read it in me:          1195
　　Myself thy friend will kill myself thy foe,
　　And for my sake serve thou false Tarquin so.

"This brief abridgment of my will I make:
My soul and body to the skies and ground;
My resolution, husband, do thou take;          1200
Mine honor be the knife's that makes my wound;
My shame be his that did my fame confound;
　　And all my fame that lives disbursèd be
　　To those that live and think no shame of me.

"Thou, Collatine, shalt oversee° this will.          1205
How was I overseen° that thou shalt see it!
My blood shall wash° the slander of mine ill;°
My life's foul deed my life's fair end shall free it.
Faint not, faint heart, but stoutly say, 'So be it.'
　　Yield to my hand, my hand shall conquer thee:          1210
　　Thou dead, both die, and both shall victors be."

This plot of death when sadly she had laid
And wiped the brinish pearl from her bright eyes,
With untuned° tongue she hoarsely calls her maid,
Whose swift obedience to her mistress hies;          1215
For fleet-winged duty with thought's feathers flies.
　　Poor Lucrece' cheeks unto her maid seem so
　　As winter meads when sun doth melt their snow.

Her mistress she doth give demure° good-morrow
With soft-slow tongue, true mark of modesty,          1220
And sorts° a sad look to her lady's sorrow,
For why° her face wore sorrow's livery;
But durst not ask of her audaciously
　　Why her two suns were cloud-eclipsèd so,
　　Nor why her fair cheeks overwashed with woe.          1225

But as the earth doth weep, the sun being set,
Each flower moist'ned like a melting eye,
Even so the maid with swelling drops 'gan wet
Her circled eyne,° enforced by sympathy
Of those fair suns set in her mistress' sky,          1230
　　Who in a salt-waved ocean quench their light,
　　Which makes the maid weep like the dewy night.

---

1139 **Who** which (i.e., her heart); **it wink** i.e., her eye closes
1140 **frets** ridges fastened across the fingerboard of a stringed
instrument to regulate fingering    1142 **for** because    1143
**shaming** being ashamed    1144 **desert . . . way** deserted
place situated away from a path    1147 **kinds** natures    1149
**at gaze** i.e., bewildered    1155 **death reproach's debtor**
i.e., her death (suicide) would be the occasion of reproach
1159 **confusion** destruction    1160 **conclusion** experiment
1167 **pilled** peeled    1173 **engirt** besieged    1175 **fort** her body

1186 **deprive** take away    1205 **oversee** execute    1206 **overseen** deceived    1207 **wash** wash away; **ill** sin    1214 **untuned**
discordant    1219 **demure** modest    1221 **sorts** fits    1222
**For why** because    1229 **circled eyne** rounded eyes (?) eyes
encircled with dark rings (?)

A pretty while these pretty creatures stand,
Like ivory conduits coral cisterns° filling.
One justly weeps, the other takes in hand° 1235
No cause, but company, of her drops spilling.
Their gentle sex to weep are often willing,
    Grieving themselves to guess at others' smarts,
    And then they drown their eyes or break their hearts.

For men have marble, women waxen minds, 1240
And therefore are they formed as marble will;°
The weak oppressed, th' impression of strange kinds
Is formed in them by force, by fraud, or skill.
Then call them not the authors of their ill,
    No more than wax shall be accounted evil 1245
    Wherein is stamped the semblance of a devil.

Their smoothness, like a goodly champain° plain,
Lays open° all the little worms that creep;
In men, as in a rough-grown grove, remain
Cave-keeping° evils that obscurely sleep. 1250
Through crystal walls each little mote° will peep.
    Though men can cover crimes with bold stern looks,
    Poor women's faces are their own faults' books.

No man° inveigh against the with'red flow'r,
But chide rough winter that the flow'r hath killed. 1255
Nor that devoured, but that which doth devour,
Is worthy blame; O, let it not be hild°
Poor women's faults that they are so fulfilled°
    With men's abuses! those proud lords to blame
    Make weak-made women tenants to their shame. 1260

The precedent° whereof in Lucrece view,
Assailed by night with circumstances strong
Of present death, and shame that might ensue
By that her death, to do her husband wrong.
Such danger to resistance did belong 1265
    That dying° fear through all her body spread;
    And who cannot abuse a body dead?

By this, mild patience bid fair Lucrece speak
To the poor counterfeit° of her complaining.
"My girl," quoth she, "on what occasion break 1270
Those tears from thee that down thy cheeks are raining?
If thou dost weep for grief of my sustaining,
    Know, gentle wench, it small avails my mood;°
    If tears could help, mine own would do me good.

"But tell me, girl, when went" (and there she stayed 1275
Till after a deep groan) "Tarquin from hence?"
"Madam, ere I was up," replied the maid,
"The more to blame my sluggard negligence.
Yet with the fault I thus far can dispense:
    Myself was stirring ere the break of day, 1280
    An ere I rose was Tarquin gone away.

"But, lady, if your maid may be so bold,
She would request to know your heaviness."°
"O, peace," quoth Lucrece. "If it should be told,
The repetition cannot make it less; 1285
For more it is than I can well express,
    And that deep torture may be called a hell
    When more is felt than one hath power to tell.

"Go get me hither paper, ink, and pen;
Yet save that labor, for I have them here. 1290
What should I say? One of my husband's men
Bid thou be ready by and by° to bear
A letter to my lord, my love, my dear.
    Bid him with speed prepare to carry it;
    The cause craves haste, and it will soon be writ." 1295

Her maid is gone, and she prepares to write,
First hovering o'er the paper with her quill.
Conceit° and grief an eager combat fight;
What wit sets down is blotted straight with will.
This is too curious° good, this blunt and ill. 1300
    Much like a press of people at a door,
    Throng her inventions, which shall go before.°

At last she thus begins: "Thou worthy lord
Of that unworthy wife that greeteth thee,
Health to thy person! next vouchsafe t' afford 1305
(If ever, love, thy Lucrece thou wilt see)
Some present speed to come and visit me.
    So I commend me, from our house in grief.
    My woes are tedious, though my words are brief."

Here folds she up the tenure° of her woe, 1310
Her certain sorrow writ uncertainly.
By this short schedule° Collatine may know
Her grief, but not her grief's true quality;
She dares not thereof make discovery,
    Lest he should hold it her own gross abuse 1315
    Ere she with blood had stained her stained excuse.°

Besides, the life and feeling of her passion°
She hoards, to spend when he is by to hear her,
When sighs and groans and tears may grace the fashion
Of her disgrace, the better so to clear her 1320
From that suspicion which the world might bear her.
    To shun this blot, she would not blot the letter
    With words till action might become them better.

To see sad sights moves more than hear them told,
For then the eye interprets to the ear 1325
The heavy motion° that it doth behold
When every part a part of woe doth bear.
'Tis but a part of sorrow that we hear.
    Deep sounds° make lesser noise than shallow fords,
    And sorrow ebbs, being blown with wind of words. 1330

---

**1234 coral cisterns** their reddened eyes (?) **1235 takes in
hand** acknowledges **1241 will** i.e., will have them formed
**1247 champain** level **1248 Lays open** reveals **1250 Cave-
keeping** dwelling in caves **1251 mote** speck **1254 No man**
let no man **1257 hild** held **1258 fulfilled** filled **1261 precedent** example **1266 dying** i.e., unnerving **1269 counterfeit** image **1272 of my sustaining** that I sustain **1273
mood** grief

**1283 heaviness** cause of grief **1292 by and by** immediately
**1298 Conceit** thought **1300 curious** cleverly **1302 which
. . . before** which one shall enter first **1310 tenure** statement **1312 schedule** summary **1316 her stained excuse** her
account of her stain **1317 passion** suffering **1326 heavy
motion** melancholy action **1329 sounds** soundings (naval
term)

Her letter now is sealed, and on it writ,
"At Ardea to my lord with more than haste."
The post attends, and she delivers it,
Charging the sour-faced° groom to hie as fast
As lagging fowls before the northern blast;                    1335
    Speed more than speed but dull and slow she deems:
    Extremity still urgeth such extremes.

The homely villain cursies° to her low;
And, blushing on her,° with a steadfast eye,
Receives the scroll without or yea or no                       1340
And forth with bashful innocence doth hie.
But they whose guilt within their bosoms lie
    Imagine every eye beholds their blame,
    For Lucrece thought he blushed to see her shame,

When, seely° groom (God wot°), it was defect                   1345
Of spirit, life,° and bold audacity;
Such harmless creatures have a true respect°
To talk in deeds,° while others saucily
Promise more speed, but do it leisurely.
    Even so this pattern of the worn-out° age                  1350
    Pawned° honest looks, but laid no words to gage.°

His kindled duty kindled her mistrust,
That two red fires in both their faces blazèd.
She thought he blushed as knowing Tarquin's lust,
And, blushing with him, wistly° on him gazèd;                  1355
Her earnest eye did make him more amazèd.
    The more she saw the blood his cheeks replenish,
    The more she thought he spied in her some blemish.

But long she thinks° till he return again,
And yet the duteous vassal scarce is gone;                     1360
The weary time she cannot entertain,°
For now 'tis stale to sigh, to weep and groan:
So woe hath wearied woe, moan tirèd moan,
    That she her plaints a little while doth stay,°
    Pausing for means to mourn some newer way.                 1365

At last she calls to mind where hangs a piece
Of skillful painting, made for° Priam's Troy,°
Before the which is drawn the power of Greece,°
For Helen's rape° the city to destroy,
Threat'ning cloud-kissing Ilion° with annoy;°                  1370
    Which the conceited° painter drew so proud
    As° heaven, it seemed, to kiss the turrets bowed.

A thousand lamentable objects there,
In scorn of° nature, art gave lifeless life;
Many a dry drop seemed a weeping tear                          1375
Shed for the slaught'red husband by the wife.
The red blood reeked, to show the painter's strife,°
    And dying eyes gleamed forth their ashy lights,
    Like dying coals burnt out in tedious nights.

There might you see the laboring pioner°                       1380
Begrimed with sweat, and smearèd all with dust;
And from the tow'rs of Troy there would appear
The very eyes of men through loopholes thrust,
Gazing upon the Greeks with little lust:°
    Such sweet observance° in this work was had                1385
    That one might see those far-off eyes look sad.

In great commanders grace and majesty
You might behold triumphing in their faces;
In youth, quick° bearing and dexterity;
And here and there the painter interlaces                      1390
Pale cowards marching on with trembling paces,
    Which heartless° peasants did so well resemble
    That one would swear he saw them quake and
      tremble.

In Ajax and Ulysses,° O, what art
Of physiognomy might one behold!                               1395
The face of either ciphered° either's heart;
Their face their manners most expressly told:
In Ajax' eyes blunt rage and rigor rolled;
    But the mild glance that sly Ulysses lent
    Showed deep regard and smiling government.°               1400

There pleading might you see grave Nestor° stand,
As 'twere encouraging the Greeks to fight,
Making such sober action with his hand
That it beguiled attention, charmed the sight.
In speech it seemed his beard, all silver white,               1405
    Wagged up and down, and from his lips did fly
    Thin winding breath which purled° up to the sky.

About him were a press of gaping faces,
Which seemed to swallow up his sound advice,
All jointly list'ning, but with several° graces,              1410
As if some mermaid did their ears entice,
Some high, some low—the painter was so nice.°
    The scalps of many, almost hid behind,
    To jump up higher seemed, to mock the mind.

---

1334 **sour-faced** sad-faced (?) long-faced (out of respect)
1338 **homely villain cursies** simple servant bows   1339
**blushing on her** i.e., blushing toward her   1345 **seely**
simple; **wot** knows   1346 **life** liveliness   1347 **respect** aspect
1348 **To . . . deeds** to act and not to talk   1350 **worn-
out** past   1351 **Pawned** pledged; **gage** i.e., to bind him (as
by an oath)   1355 **wistly** earnestly   1359 **long she thinks**
i.e., she thinks time passes slowly   1361 **entertain** occupy
1364 **stay** stop   1367 **made for** depicting; **Priam's Troy**
Priam was King of Troy during the Trojan War   1368 **is . . .
Greece** the Greek army is assembled   1369 **Helen's rape** the
abduction of Helen   1370 **Ilion** Troy; **annoy** destruction
1371 **conceited** ingenious   1372 **As** that

1374 **In scorn of** to rival   1377 **strife** effort   1380 **pioner**
engineer   1384 **lust** pleasure   1385 **sweet observance** loving
accuracy   1389 **quick** lively   1392 **heartless** cowardly   1394
**Ajax and Ulysses** Greek leaders   1396 **ciphered** depicted
1400 **deep . . . government** profound wisdom and successful
rule   1401 **Nestor** an aged Greek leader   1407 **purled** curled
1410 **several** distinct   1412 **nice** precise

Here one man's hand leaned on another's head, 1415
His nose being shadowed by his neighbor's ear;
Here one, being thronged,° bears back, all boll'n° and
    red;
Another, smothered, seems to pelt° and swear;
And in their rage such signs of rage they bear
  As, but for loss of Nestor's golden words, 1420
  It seemed they would debate with angry swords.

For much imaginary work was there;
Conceit° deceitful, so compact, so kind,°
That for Achilles'° image stood his spear,
Griped in an armèd hand; himself behind 1425
Was left unseen, save to the eye of mind:
  A hand, a foot, a face, a leg, a head
  Stood for the whole to be imaginèd.

And from the walls of strong-besiegèd Troy
When their brave hope, bold Hector,° marched to field, 1430
Stood many Troyan mothers, sharing joy
To see their youthful sons bright weapons wield;
And to their hope they such odd action yield°
  That through their light joy seemèd to appear
  (Like bright things stained) a kind of heavy fear. 1435

And from the strond of Dardan,° where they fought,
To Simois'° reedy banks the red blood ran,
Whose waves to imitate the battle sought
With swelling ridges, and their ranks began
To break upon the gallèd° shore, and than° 1440
  Retire again, till, meeting greater ranks,
  They join, and shoot their foam at Simois' banks.

To this well-painted piece is Lucrece come,
To find a face where all distress is stelled.°
Many she sees where cares have carvèd some, 1445
But none where all distress and dolor dwelled
Till she despairing Hecuba° beheld,
  Staring on Priam's wounds with her old eyes,
  Which bleeding under Pyrrhus'° proud foot lies.

In her the painter had anatomized° 1450
Time's ruin, beauty's wrack, and grim care's reign;
Her cheeks with chops° and wrinkles were disguised;°
Of what she was no semblance did remain.
Her blue blood, changed to black in every vein,
  Wanting the spring that those shrunk pipes had fed, 1455
  Showed life imprisoned in a body dead.

On this sad shadow Lucrece spends her eyes
And shapes her sorrow to the beldame's woes,
Who nothing wants to answer her but cries
And bitter words to ban° her cruel foes. 1460
The painter was no god to lend her those;
  And therefore Lucrece swears he did her wrong
  To give her so much grief and not a tongue.

"Poor instrument," quoth she, "without a sound:
I'll tune° thy woes with my lamenting tongue, 1465
And drop sweet balm in Priam's painted wound,
And rail on Pyrrhus that hath done him wrong,
And with my tears quench Troy that burns so long,
  And with my knife scratch out the angry eyes
  Of all the Greeks that are thine enemies. 1470

"Show me the strumpet that began this stir,°
That with my nails her beauty I may tear.
Thy heat of lust, fond Paris, did incur
This load of wrath that burning Troy doth bear.
Thy eye kindled the fire that burneth here, 1475
  And here in Troy, for trespass of thine eye,
  The sire, the son, the dame and daughter die.

"Why should the private pleasure of some one
Become the public plague of many moe?°
Let sin, alone committed, light alone 1480
Upon his head that hath transgressèd so;
Let guiltless souls be freed from guilty woe:
  For one's offense why should so many fall,
  To plague a private sin in general?°

"Lo, here weeps Hecuba, here Priam dies, 1485
Here manly Hector faints, here Troilus° sounds,°
Here friend by friend in bloody channel lies,
And friend to friend gives unadvised° wounds,
And one man's lust these many lives confounds.°
  Had doting Priam checked his son's desire, 1490
  Troy had been bright with fame, and not with fire."

Here feelingly she weeps Troy's painted woes,
For sorrow, like a heavy hanging bell,
Once set on ringing, with his own weight goes;
Then little strength rings out the doleful knell. 1495
So Lucrece, set awork, sad tales doth tell
  To penciled° pensiveness and colored° sorrow:
  She lends them words, and she their looks doth
    borrow.

She throws her eyes about the painting round,°
And who she finds forlorn, she doth lament. 1500
At last she sees a wretched image° bound
That piteous looks to Phrygian shepherds lent.°
His face, though full of cares, yet showed content;
  Onward to Troy with the blunt° swains he goes,
  So mild that patience° seemed to scorn his woes. 1505

---

1417 **thronged** crushed in the crowd; **boll'n** swollen 1418
**pelt** scold 1423 **Conceit** conception; **kind** natural 1424
**Achilles** chief warrior of the Greeks 1430 **Hector** son of
Priam and chief warrior of the Trojans 1433 **odd action
yield** contrary gestures express 1436 **strond of Dardan** shore
of Troas (the country of which Troy was the chief city) 1437
**Simois** river near Troy 1440 **gallèd** eroded; **than** then
1444 **stelled** portrayed 1447 **Hecuba** wife of Priam 1449
**Pyrrhus** Greek warrior, slayer of Priam 1450 **anatomized**
dissected 1452 **chops** cracks; **disguised** disfigured

1460 **ban** curse 1465 **tune** sing 1471 **stir** action (i.e., war)
1479 **moe** more 1484 **in general** on the general public 1486
**Troilus** a son of Priam; **sounds** swoons 1488 **unadvisèd**
unintentional 1489 **confounds** destroys 1497 **penciled,
colored** painted 1499 **round** all around 1501 **wretched
image** i.e., Sinon, the Trojan traitor 1502 **piteous . . .
lent** i.e., aroused compassionate looks from the Phrygian
shepherds 1504 **blunt** simple 1505 **patience** i.e., his patience

In him the painter labored with his skill
To hide deceit, and give the harmless show°
An humble gait, calm looks, eyes wailing still,
A brow unbent° that seemed to welcome woe,
Cheeks neither red nor pale, but mingled so          1510
   That blushing red no guilty instance gave
   Nor ashy pale the fear that false hearts have;

But, like a constant and confirmèd devil,
He entertained a show° so seeming just,
And therein so ensconced his secret evil,          1515
That jealousy° itself could not mistrust
False creeping craft and perjury should thrust
   Into so bright a day such black-faced storms
   Or blot with hell-born sin such saintlike forms.

The well-skilled workman this mild image drew          1520
For perjured Sinon, whose enchanting story°
The credulous old Priam after slew;
Whose words like wildfire burnt the shining glory
Of rich-built Ilion, that the skies were sorry,
   And little stars shot from their fixèd places          1525
   When their glass° fell, wherein they viewed their
    faces.

This picture she advisedly° perused
And chid the painter for his wondrous skill,
Saying, some shape in Sinon's was abused;°
So fair a form lodged not a mind so ill.          1530
And still on him she gazed, and gazing still,
   Such signs of truth in his plain face she spied,
   That she concludes the picture was belied.°

"It cannot be," quoth she, "that so much guile"—
She would have said "can lurk in such a look";          1535
But Tarquin's shape came in her mind the while,
And from her tongue "can lurk" from "cannot" took.
"It cannot be" she in that sense forsook
   And turned it thus: "It cannot be, I find,
   But such a face should bear a wicked mind;          1540

"For even as subtile Sinon here is painted,
So sober-sad, so weary, and so mild
(As if with grief or travail he had fainted),
To me came Tarquin armèd, to beguiled°
With outward honesty, but yet defiled          1545
   With inward vice. As Priam him did cherish,
   So did I Tarquin; so my Troy did perish.

"Look, look, how list'ning Priam wets his eyes,
To see those borrowed° tears that Sinon sheeds!°
Priam, why art thou old, and yet not wise?          1550
For every tear he falls° a Troyan bleeds.
His eye drops fire, no water thence proceeds:
   Those round clear pearls of his that move thy pity
   Are balls of quenchless fire to burn thy city.

"Such devils steal effects from lightless hell,          1555
For Sinon in his fire doth quake with cold,
And in that cold hot burning fire doth dwell.
These contraries such unity do hold
Only to flatter° fools and make them bold.°
   So Priam's trust false Sinon's tears doth flatter          1560
   That he finds means to burn his Troy with water."

Here, all enraged, such passion her assails
That patience is quite beaten from her breast.
She tears the senseless Sinon with her nails,
Comparing him to that unhappy° guest          1565
Whose deed hath made herself herself detest.
   At last she smilingly with this gives o'er:°
   "Fool, fool!" quoth she, "his wounds will not be sore."

Thus ebbs and flows the current of her sorrow,
And time doth weary time with her complaining.          1570
She looks for night, and then she longs for morrow,
And both she thinks too long with her remaining.
Short time seems long in sorrow's sharp sustaining;
   Though woe be heavy,° yet it seldom sleeps,
   And they that watch see time how slow it creeps;          1575

Which all this time hath overslipped her thought°
That she with painted images hath spent,
Being from the feeling of her own grief brought
By deep surmise° of others' detriment,
Losing her woes in shows° of discontent.          1580
   It easeth some, though none it ever curèd,
   To think their dolor others have endurèd.

But now the mindful messenger, come back,
Brings home his lord and other company;
Who finds his Lucrece clad in mourning black,          1585
And round about her tear-distainèd° eye
Blue circles streamed, like rainbows in the sky.
   These water-galls° in her dim element°
   Foretell new storms to those already spent.

Which when her sad-beholding husband saw,          1590
Amazedly in her sad face he stares.
Her eyes, though sod° in tears, looked red and raw,
Her lively color killed with deadly cares.
He hath no power to ask her how she fares;
   Both stood like old acquaintance in a trance,          1595
   Met far from home, wond'ring each other's chance.°

At last he takes her by the bloodless hand,
And thus begins: "What uncouth° ill event
Hath thee befall'n, that thou dost trembling stand?
Sweet love, what spite° hath thy fair color spent?          1600
Why art thou thus attired in discontent?
   Unmask,° dear dear, this moody heaviness,
   And tell thy grief, that we may give redress."

---

**1507 show** appearance   **1509 unbent** unfurrowed   **1514
entertained a show** kept up an appearance   **1516 jealousy**
suspicion   **1521 enchanting story** i.e., bewitching lie   **1526
glass** mirror (i.e., shining Troy)   **1527 advisedly** thoughtfully
**1529 some . . . abused** some other person's form had been
falsely represented as Sinon's   **1533 belied** proved false   **1544
beguiled** beguile   **1549 borrowed** i.e., false; **sheeds** sheds
**1551 falls** lets fall

**1559 flatter** deceive; **make them bold** give them confidence
**1565 unhappy** unfortunate   **1567 gives o'er** ceases   **1574
heavy** (1) distressing (2) sleepy   **1576 overslipped her
thought** gone unnoticed   **1579 surmise** contemplation   **1580
shows** representations   **1586 tear-distainèd** tearstained   **1588
water-galls** atmospheric conditions attendant upon rainbows;
**element** sky   **1592 sod** sodden   **1596 chance** fortune   **1598
uncouth** unknown   **1600 spite** feeling of annoyance   **1602
Unmask** disclose

Three times with sighs she gives her sorrow fire,°
Ere once she can discharge one word of woe.          1605
At length addressed° to answer his desire,
She modestly prepares to let them know
Her honor is ta'en prisoner by the foe,
　While Collatine and his consorted° lords
　With sad attention long to hear her words.          1610

And now this pale swan in her wat'ry nest
Begins the sad dirge of her certain ending:°
"Few words," quoth she, "shall fit the trespass best,
Where no excuse can give the fault amending.
In me moe° woes than words are now depending,°          1615
　And my laments would be drawn out too long
　To tell them all with one poor tirèd tongue.

"Then be this all the task it hath to say:
Dear husband, in the interest° of thy bed
A stranger came and on that pillow lay          1620
Where thou wast wont to rest thy weary head;
And what wrong else may be imaginèd
　By foul enforcement might be done to me,
　From that, alas, thy Lucrece is not free.

"For in the dreadful dead of dark midnight,          1625
With shining falchion in my chamber came
A creeping creature with a flaming light
And softly cried, 'Awake, thou Roman dame,
And entertain° my love; else lasting shame
　On thee and thine this night I will inflict,          1630
　If thou my love's desire do contradict.

"'For some hard-favored groom of thine,' quoth he,
'Unless thou yoke° thy liking to my will,
I'll murder straight, and then I'll slaughter thee
And swear I found you where you did fulfill          1635
The loathsome act of lust, and so did kill
　The lechers in their deed: this act will be
　My fame and thy perpetual infamy.'

"With this I did begin to start and cry;
And then against my heart he set his sword,          1640
Swearing, unless I took all patiently,
I should not live to speak another word.
So should my shame still rest upon record,
　And never be forgot in mighty Rome
　Th' adulterate death of Lucrece and her groom.          1645

"Mine enemy was strong, my poor self weak
And far the weaker with so strong a fear.
My bloody judge forbod° my tongue to speak;
No rightful plea might plead for justice there.
His scarlet lust came evidence to swear          1650
　That my poor beauty had purloined his eyes;
　And when the judge is robbed, the prisoner dies.

"O, teach me how to make mine own excuse,
Or (at the least) this refuge let me find:
Though my gross blood be stained with this abuse,          1655
Immaculate and spotless is my mind;
That was not forced, that never was inclined
　To accessary yieldings, but still pure
　Doth in her poisoned closet yet endure."

Lo, here, the hopeless merchant° of this loss,          1660
With head declined and voice dammed up with woe,
With sad-set eyes and wreathèd arms° across,
From lips new-waxen pale begins to blow
The grief away that stops his answer so.
　But, wretched as he is, he strives in vain;          1665
　What he breathes out his breath drinks up again.

As through an arch the violent roaring tide
Outruns the eye that doth behold his haste,
Yet in the eddy boundeth in his pride
Back to the strait that forced him on so fast;          1670
In rage sent out, recalled in rage being past:
　Even so his sighs, his sorrows, make a saw,°
　To push grief on, and back the same grief draw.

Which speechless woe of his poor she attendeth
And his untimely frenzy° thus awaketh:          1675
"Dear lord, thy sorrow to my sorrow lendeth
Another power; no flood by raining slaketh;
My woe too sensible° thy passion maketh
　More feeling-painful. Let it then suffice
　To drown one woe, one pair of weeping eyes.          1680

"And for my sake when I might charm thee so,°
For she that was thy Lucrece (now attend me)
Be suddenly revengèd on my foe—
Thine, mine, his own. Suppose thou dost defend me
From what is past; the help that thou shalt lend me          1685
　Comes all too late, yet let the traitor die;
　For sparing justice feeds iniquity.

"But ere I name him, you fair lords," quoth she,
Speaking to those that came with Collatine,
"Shall plight your honorable faiths to me          1690
With swift pursuit to 'venge this wrong of mine;
For 'tis a meritorious fair design
　To chase injustice with revengeful arms:
　Knights by their oaths should right poor ladies' harms."

At this request, with noble disposition          1695
Each present lord began to promise aid,
As bound in knighthood to her imposition,
Longing to hear the hateful foe bewrayed.°
But she, that yet her sad task hath not said,
　The protestation stops. "O, speak!" quoth she,          1700
　"How may this forcèd stain be wiped from me?

---

1604 fire i.e., fire to ignite a discharge (from a cannon) 1606
addressed prepared 1609 consorted associated 1612 ending
death 1615 moe more; depending impending 1619
interest possession 1629 entertain receive 1633 yoke submit 1648 forbod forbade

1660 merchant Collatine 1662 wreathèd arms arms folded
(a sign of melancholy) 1672 saw i.e., sawlike motion 1675
frenzy trance 1678 sensible sensitive 1681 so in such things
1698 bewrayed revealed

"What is the quality° of my offense,
Being constrained with dreadful circumstance?
May my pure mind with the foul act dispense,°
My low-declinèd honor to advance?°                    1705
May any terms acquit me from this chance?
    The poisoned fountain clears itself again;
    And why not I from this compellèd stain?"

With this they all at once began to say,
Her body's stain her mind untainted clears;           1710
While with a joyless smile she turns away
The face, that map which deep impression bears
Of hard misfortune, carved in it with tears.
    "No, no!" quoth she, "no dame hereafter living
    By my excuse shall claim excuse's giving."        1715

Here with a sigh as if her heart would break
She throws forth Tarquin's name: "He, he!" she says,
But more than "he" her poor tongue could not speak,
Till after many accents° and delays,
Untimely breathings, sick and short assays,°          1720
    She utters this: "He, he! fair lords, 'tis he
    That guides this hand to give this wound to me."

Even here she sheathèd in her harmless° breast
A harmful knife, that thence her soul unsheathèd.
That blow did bail° it from the deep unrest           1725
Of that polluted prison where it breathèd.
Her contrite sighs unto the clouds bequeathèd
    Her wingèd sprite, and through her wounds doth fly
    Life's lasting date from canceled destiny.°

Stone-still, astonished with this deadly deed,        1730
Stood Collatine and all his lordly crew,
Till Lucrece' father, that beholds her bleed,
Himself on her self-slaught'red body threw,
And from the purple fountain Brutus drew
    The murd'rous knife, and as it left the place,    1735
    Her blood, in poor revenge, held it in chase;

And bubbling from her breast, it doth divide
In two slow rivers, that the crimson blood
Circles her body in on every side,
Who like a late-sacked island vastly° stood          1740
Bare and unpeopled in this fearful flood.
    Some of her blood still pure and red remained,
    And some looked black, and that false Tarquin
        stained.

About the mourning and congealèd face
Of that black blood a wat'ry rigoll° goes,            1745
Which seems to weep upon the tainted place;
And ever since, as pitying Lucrece' woes,
Corrupted blood some watery token shows,
    And blood untainted still doth red abide,
    Blushing at that which is so putrefied.           1750

"Daughter, dear daughter!" old Lucretius cries,
"That life was mine which thou hast here deprivèd;
If in the child the father's image lies,
Where shall I live now Lucrece is unlived?
Thou wast not to this end from me derivèd.            1755
    If children predecease progenitors,
    We are their offspring, and they none of ours.

"Poor broken glass,° I often did behold
In thy sweet semblance my old age new born;
But now that fair fresh mirror, dim and old,          1760
Shows me a bare-boned death° by time outworn.
O, from thy cheeks my image thou hast torn
    And shivered° all the beauty of my glass,
    That I no more can see what once I was.

"O time, cease thou thy course, and last no longer,   1765
If they surcease° to be that should survive.
Shall rotten death make conquest of the stronger
And leave the falt'ring feeble souls alive?
The old bees die, the young possess their hive;
    Then live, sweet Lucrece, live again and see      1770
    Thy father die, and not thy father thee."

By this, starts Collatine as from a dream
And bids Lucretius give his sorrow place;
And then in key-cold° Lucrece' bleeding stream
He falls, and bathes the pale fear in his face,       1775
And counterfeits to die° with her a space;
    Till manly shame bids him possess his breath,
    And live to be revengèd on her death.

The deep vexation of his inward soul
Hath served a dumb arrest° upon his tongue;           1780
Who, mad that sorrow should his use control,
Or keep him from heart-easing words so long,
Begins to talk; but through his lips do throng
    Weak words, so thick° come in his poor heart's aid
    That no man could distinguish what he said.       1785

Yet sometime "Tarquin" was pronouncèd plain,
But through his teeth, as if the name he tore.
This windy tempest, till it blow up rain,
Held back his sorrow's tide, to make it more.
At last it rains, and busy winds give o'er;           1790
    Then son and father weep with equal strife
    Who should weep most, for daughter or for wife.

The one doth call her his, the other his;
Yet neither may possess the claim they lay.
The father says, "She's mine." "O, mine, she is!"     1795
Replies her husband, "Do not take away
My sorrow's interest;° let no mourner say
    He weeps for her, for she was only mine,
    And only must be wailed by Collatine."

1702 **quality** nature  1704 **dispense** be reconciled  1705 **advance** raise  1719 **accents** emphasized sounds  1720 **assays** attempts  1723 **harmless** innocent  1725 **bail** release  1729 **Life's . . . destiny** i.e., eternal life is freed ("canceled") by flying from life on earth ("destiny")  1740 **vastly** like a waste  1745 **wat'ry rigoll** when blood coagulates it separates into a congealed clot and a serum, "wat'ry rigoll"

1758 **glass** mirror  1761 **death** skull  1763 **shivered** shattered  1766 **surcease** cease  1774 **key-cold** i.e., cold as metal  1776 **counterfeits to die** swoons (and seems transported as by an orgasm)  1780 **served . . . arrest** enforced a silence (as if by a warrant)  1784 **thick** quickly  1797 **sorrow's interest** right to sorrow

"O," quoth Lucretius, "I did give that life    1800
Which she too early and too late° hath spilled."
"Woe, woe!" quoth Collatine, "she was my wife,
I owed° her, and 'tis mine that she hath killed."
"My daughter" and "my wife" with clamors filled
　The dispersed air,° who, holding Lucrece' life,    1805
　Answered their cries, "my daughter" and "my wife."

Brutus, who plucked the knife from Lucrece' side,
Seeing such emulation in their woe,
Began to clothe his wit in state and pride,
Burying in Lucrece' wound his folly's show.°    1810
He with the Romans was esteemèd so
　As seely° jeering idiots are with kings,
　For sportive° words and utt'ring foolish things;

But now he throws that shallow habit° by
Wherein deep policy° did him disguise,    1815
And armed his long-hid wits advisedly
To check the tears in Collatinus' eyes.
"Thou wrongèd lord of Rome," quoth he, "arise!
　Let my unsounded° self, supposed a fool,
　Now set thy long-experienced wit to school.    1820

"Why,° Collatine, is woe the cure for woe?
Do wounds help wounds, or grief help grievous deeds?
Is it revenge to give thyself a blow
For his foul act by whom thy fair wife bleeds?
Such childish humor from weak minds proceeds;    1825
　Thy wretched wife mistook the matter so,
　To slay herself that should have slain her foe.

"Courageous Roman, do not steep thy heart
In such relenting° dew of lamentations;
But kneel with me, and help to bear thy part    1830
To rouse our Roman gods with invocations
That they will suffer° these abominations
　(Since Rome herself in them doth stand disgracèd)
　By our strong arms from forth her fair streets chasèd.°

"Now, by the Capitol that we adore,    1835
And by this chaste blood so unjustly stained,
By heaven's fair sun that breeds the fat earth's store,°
By all our country rights in Rome maintainèd,
And by chaste Lucrece' soul that late complainèd
　Her wrongs to us, and by this bloody knife,    1840
　We will revenge the death of this true wife."

This said, he strook° his hand upon his breast
And kissed the fatal knife to end his vow;
And to his protestation° urged the rest,
Who, wond'ring at him, did his words allow.°    1845
Then jointly to the ground their knees they bow,
　And that deep vow which Brutus made before,
　He doth again repeat, and that they swore.

When they had sworn to this advisèd doom,°
They did conclude to bear dead Lucrece thence,    1850
To show her bleeding body thorough Rome,
And so to publish Tarquin's foul offense;
Which being done with speedy diligence,
　The Romans plausibly° did give consent
　To Tarquin's everlasting banishment.    1855

1801 **late** recently　1803 **owed** owned　1805 **The dispersed air** i.e., the boundless air (which has received Lucrece's "life," or spirit, upon her death)　1810 **folly's show** appearance of folly　1812 **seely** simple　1813 **sportive** merry　1814 **habit** cloak (here, of a king's jester)　1815 **policy** calculation　1819 **unsounded** unplumbed　1821 **Why** exclamation of impatience

1829 **relenting** melting　1832 **suffer** allow　1834 **chasèd** i.e., to be chased　1837 **fat earth's store** fertile earth's abundance　1842 **strook** struck　1844 **protestation** vow　1845 **allow** approve　1849 **advisèd doom** considered judgment　1854 **plausibly** with applause (i.e., with a "general acclamation"; see Argument, line 43)

# THE PHOENIX AND THE TURTLE°

Let the bird of loudest lay°
On the sole° Arabian tree
Herald sad° and trumpet° be,
To whose sound chaste wings° obey.

But thou shrieking harbinger,°  5
Foul precurrer° of the fiend,
Augur of the fever's end,°
To this troop come thou not near.

From this session° interdict°
Every fowl of tyrant wing,°  10
Save the eagle, feath'red king:
Keep the obsequy° so strict.

Let the priest in surplice white,
That defunctive music can,°
Be the death-divining° swan,  15
Lest the requiem lack his right.°

And thou treble-dated° crow,
That thy sable gender mak'st
With the breath thou giv'st and tak'st,°
'Mongst our mourners shalt thou go.  20

Here the anthem doth commence:
Love and constancy is dead,
Phoenix and the turtle fled
In a mutual flame from hence.

So they loved, as° love in twain  25
Had the essence° but in one;
Two distincts,° division none:
Number there in love was slain.°

Hearts remote,° yet not asunder;
Distance and no space was seen  30
'Twixt this turtle and his queen;
But in them it were a wonder.°

So between them love did shine
That the turtle saw his right°
Flaming in the phoenix' sight:  35
Either was the other's mine.°

Property° was thus appallèd,
That the self was not the same;
Single nature's double name
Neither two nor one was callèd.  40

Reason, in itself confounded,°
Saw division grow together,
To themselves yet either neither,
Simple° were so well compounded;°

That it° cried, "How true a twain  45
Seemeth this concordant one!
Love hath reason, reason none,
If what parts can so remain."°

Whereupon it made this threne°
To the phoenix and the dove,  50
Co-supremes° and stars of love,
As chorus to their tragic scene.

### Threnos

Beauty, truth, and rarity,°
Grace in all simplicity,
Here enclosed, in cinders° lie.  55

Death is now the phoenix' nest,
And the turtle's loyal breast
To eternity doth rest,

Leaving no posterity:
'Twas not their infirmity,  60
It was married chastity.°

Truth may seem, but cannot be;
Beauty brag, but 'tis not she:°
Truth and Beauty buried be.

To this urn let those repair  65
That are either true or fair;
For these dead birds sigh a prayer.

*The decorative border shown above appeared with* The Phoenix and the Turtle *in Robert Chester's* Love's Martyr, 1601.

**The Phoenix and the Turtle** the Phoenix, a unique legendary bird, was said to fly periodically to Arabia, where, after building a nest of spices, it was consumed in flame, and from its ashes a new Phoenix arose; it is a symbol of immortality. The Turtle, i.e., the turtledove, is a symbol of true love   **1 lay** song   **2 sole** unique   **3 sad** serious; **trumpet** trumpeter   **4 chaste wings** i.e., other good birds   **5 shrieking harbinger** screech owl (?)   **6 precurrer** precursor (apparently Shakespeare's coinage)   **7 Augur . . . end** prophet of death   **9 session** formal gathering, as of a parliament or a court; **interdict** ban   **10 fowl . . . wing** bird of prey, unsocial bird (in contrast to those of "chaste wings," line 4)   **12 obsequy** funeral rite   **14 defunctive music can** is skilled in funeral music   **15 death-divining** foretelling death (the swan allegedly sang only once, just before it died)   **16 his right** its due (?) his (the swan's) rite of requiem (?)   **17 treble-dated** long-lived   **18–19 That . . . tak'st** that breeds your black offspring with the breath you exhale and inhale (alluding to a belief that some birds conceived and laid eggs at the bill)   **25 as** that   **26 essence** nature   **27 distincts** distinct or separate things   **28 Number . . . slain** i.e., because the two were one, and Elizabethan proverbial lore held that "one is no number"

**29 remote** apart   **32 But . . . wonder** i.e., in any others except them it would have been a marvel   **34 his right** what was due to him   **36 mine** (1) my own property (2) source of precious metals   **37 Property** essential nature, peculiar quality   **41 confounded** perplexed   **44 Simple** i.e., simples, elementary elements (?) individual ingredients (?); **compounded** made into a new unity   **45 it** Reason   **48 If . . . remain** i.e., if what divides into two can remain one   **49 threne** funeral song (Greek *threnos*)   **51 Co-supremes** joint rulers   **53 rarity** excellence   **55 cinders** ashes   **61 married chastity** faithful married love (?) abstinence (?)   **63 she** true Beauty

# A LOVER'S COMPLAINT

From off a hill whose concave womb reworded°
A plaintful story from a sist'ring° vale,
My spirits t' attend this double voice accorded,°
And down I laid to list the sad-tuned tale;
Ere long espied a fickle° maid full pale, 5
Tearing of papers,° breaking rings atwain,
Storming her world with sorrow's wind and rain.

Upon her head a platted hive° of straw,
Which fortified her visage from the sun,
Whereon the thought° might think sometime it saw 10
The carcass of a beauty spent and done.
Time had not scythèd° all that youth begun,
Nor youth all quit;° but, spite of heaven's fell° rage,
Some beauty peeped through lattice° of seared age.

Oft did she heave her napkin to her eyne,° 15
Which on it had conceited° characters,
Laund'ring the silken figures in the brine
That seasoned° woe had pelleted° in tears,
And often reading what contents it bears;
As often shrieking undistinguished woe,° 20
In clamors of all size, both high and low.

Sometimes her leveled° eyes their carriage ride,
As they did batt'ry to the spheres intend;°
Sometime diverted their poor balls are tied
To th' orbèd earth; sometimes they do extend 25
Their view right on; anon their gazes lend
To every place at once, and, nowhere fixed,
The mind and sight distractedly commixed.

Her hair, nor loose nor° tied in formal plat,°
Proclaimed in her a careless hand of pride;° 30
For some, untucked, descended her sheaved° hat,
Hanging her pale and pinèd cheek beside;
Some in her threaden fillet° still did bide
And, true to bondage, would not break from thence,
Though slackly braided in loose negligence. 35

A thousand favors from a maund° she drew,
Of amber, crystal, and of bedded° jet,

*The decorative border shown above appeared on the title page of the
first quarto edition of the Sonnets, 1609, in which* A Lover's
Complaint *first appeared.*

Which one by one she in a river threw,
Upon whose weeping margent° she was set,
Like usury,° applying wet to wet, 40
Or monarch's hands that lets not bounty fall
Where want cries some° but where excess begs all.

Of folded schedules° had she many a one
Which she perused, sighed, tore, and gave the flood;
Cracked many a ring of posied° gold and bone, 45
Bidding them find their sepulchers in mud;
Found yet moe° letters sadly penned in blood,
With sleided° silk feat and affectedly
Enswathed° and sealed to curious° secrecy.

These often bathed she in her fluxive° eyes, 50
And often kissed, and often gave to tear;
Cried, "O false blood, thou register of lies,
What unapprovèd° witness dost thou bear!
Ink would have seemed more black and damnèd here!"
This said, in top of rage the lines she rents, 55
Big discontent so breaking their contents.

A reverend° man that grazed his cattle nigh,
Sometime a blusterer that the ruffle° knew
Of court, of city, and had let go by
The swiftest hours, observèd as they flew,° 60
Towards this afflicted fancy° fastly° drew,
And, privileged by age, desires to know
In brief the grounds and motives of her woe.

So slides he down upon his grainèd bat,°
And comely-distant° sits he by her side; 65
When he again desires her, being sat,
Her grievance with his hearing to divide:
If that from him there may be aught applied
Which may her suffering ecstasy° assuage,
'Tis promised in the charity of age. 70

"Father," she says, "though in me you behold
The injury of many a blasting hour,
Let it not tell your judgment I am old;
Not age, but sorrow, over me hath power.
I might as yet have been a spreading flower, 75
Fresh to myself, if I had self-applied
Love to myself, and to no love beside.

1 womb reworded i.e., valley echoed  2 sist'ring nearby (?)
similar (?)  3 accorded agreed (?) inclined (?)  5 fickle unstable  6 papers love letters  8 platted hive woven hat  10
thought mind  12 scythèd cut down  13 all quit entirely
gone; fell deadly  14 lattice i.e., wrinkles  15 heave . . .
eyne lift her handkerchief to her eyes  16 conceited ingenious,
fanciful  18 seasoned (1) matured (2) salted (playing on
"brine" in previous line); pelleted made round (i.e., like hailstones or like pellets of meat or dough)  20 undistinguished
woe incoherent cries  22 leveled aimed (the image is of a fire-
arm on a gun-carriage)  23 As . . . intend as if they intended to
direct their fire against the stars  29 nor . . . nor neither . . .
nor; plat knot  30 careless . . . pride hand indifferent to show
31 sheaved straw  33 threaden fillet headband  36 maund
basket  37 bedded inlaid (emendation to "beaded" is plausible)

39 weeping margent wet bank  40 Like usury i.e.,
adding to the original amount  42 cries some cries out for
some  43 schedules papers with writing  45 posied inscribed
with mottoes  47 moe more  48 sleided raveled  48–49
feat . . . Enswathed tied neatly and elaborately (or
neatly and lovingly)  49 curious painstaking  50 fluxive
flowing  53 unapprovèd unconfirmed, not proved by deeds
57 reverend aged  58 ruffle bustle  59–60 had . . . flew
i.e., had learned about the world through observation during
the busy days of youth  61 fancy love-sick lady; fastly near
(?) quickly (?)  64 grainèd bat shepherd's staff on which
the grain was showing  65 comely-distant at an appropriate
distance  69 ecstasy fit, passion

1715

"But, woe is me, too early I attended°
A youthful suit—it was to gain my grace—
Of one by nature's outwards so commended,
That maidens' eyes stuck over all his face:     80
Love lacked a dwelling, and made him her place;
And when in his fair parts she did abide,
She was new lodged and newly deified.

"His browny locks did hang in crooked curls,     85
And every light occasion° of the wind
Upon his lips their silken parcels hurls.
What's sweet to do, to do will aptly find;
Each eye that saw him did enchant the mind,
For on his visage was in little drawn     90
What largeness thinks in Paradise was sawn.°

"Small show of man was yet upon his chin;
His phoenix down° began but to appear,
Like unshorn velvet, on that termless° skin
Whose bare out-bragged the web it seemed to wear.°     95
Yet showed his visage by that cost° more dear;
And nice affections° wavering stood in doubt
If best were as it was, or best without.

"His qualities were beauteous as his form,
For maiden-tongued° he was, and thereof free;°     100
Yet, if men moved him, was he such a storm
As oft 'twixt May and April is to see,
When winds breathe sweet, unruly though they be.
His rudeness so with his authorized youth
Did livery falseness in a pride of truth.°     105

"Well could he ride, and often men would say,
'That horse his mettle from his rider takes.
Proud of subjection, noble by the sway,
What rounds, what bounds, what course, what stop° he
    makes!'
And controversy hence a question takes,     110
Whether the horse by him became his deed,
Or he his manage by th' well-doing steed.°

"But quickly on this° side the verdict went:
His real habitude° gave life and grace
To appertainings and to ornament,     115
Accomplished in himself, not in his case.°
All aids, themselves made fairer by their place,
Came for° additions; yet their purposed trim
Pieced not° his grace but were all graced by him.

"So on the tip of his subduing tongue     120
All kind of arguments and question deep,
All replication° prompt and reason strong,
For his advantage still did wake and sleep.
To make the weeper laugh, the laugher weep,
He had the dialect and different skill,     125
Catching all passions in his craft of will,°

"That° he did in the general bosom reign
Of young, of old, and sexes both enchanted
To dwell with him in thoughts, or to remain
In personal duty,° following where he haunted.°     130
Consents bewitched, ere he desire, have granted,
And dialogued for him what he would say,
Asked their own wills and made their wills obey.

"Many there were that did his picture get,
To serve their eyes, and in it put their mind,     135
Like fools that in th' imagination set
The goodly objects which abroad they find
Of lands and mansions, theirs in thought assigned,
And laboring in moe pleasures to bestow them
Than the true gouty° landlord which doth owe° them.     140

"So many have, that never touched his hand,
Sweetly supposed them mistress of his heart.
My woeful self, that did in freedom stand
And was my own fee-simple, not in part,°
What with his art in youth and youth in art,     145
Threw my affections in his charmèd° power,
Reserved the stalk and gave him all my flower.

"Yet did I not, as some my equals° did,
Demand of him, nor being desirèd yielded;
Finding myself in honor so forbid,     150
With safest distance I mine honor shielded.
Experience° for me many bulwarks builded
Of proofs new-bleeding,° which remained the foil°
Of this false jewel, and his amorous spoil.

"But, ah, who ever shunned by precedent     155
The destined ill she must herself assay?°
Or forced examples,° 'gainst her own content,
To put the by-past perils in her way?
Counsel may stop awhile what will not stay;
For when we rage,° advice is often seen     160
By blunting us to make our wits more keen.

---

78 **attended** heeded  86 **occasion** chance movement  91 **What . . . sawn** what was seen (or possibly "sown") in large in paradise  93 **phoenix down** i.e., newborn fuzz  94 **termless** young (?) indescribable (?)  95 **Whose . . . wear** i.e., the skin excelled the covering (?)  96 **cost** display, ornament  97 **nice affections** delicate tastes  100 **maiden-tongued** modestly spoken; **thereof free** not shy in speaking  104–05 **His rudeness . . . truth** His agitated behavior, with his privilege of youth, covered falseness with the appearance of honesty  109 **rounds, bounds, stop** terms of horsemanship, or "manage"  111–12 **Whether . . . steed** whether the horse showed his good qualities because of the man, or whether the man showed his skill at horsemanship ("manage") because of the horse's skill  113 **this** i.e., the following  114 **real habitude** true character  116 **case** outside, belongings  118 **for** as  119 **Pieced not** did not add to

122 **replication** reply, repartee  126 **craft of will** skill to persuade  127 **That** so that  130 **In personal duty** i.e., as servants to him; **haunted** frequented  140 **gouty** rheumatic, i.e., old; **owe** own  144 **fee-simple . . . part** absolute possession, without restriction  146 **charmèd** enchanting  148 **my equals** i.e., girls of my age  152 **Experience** knowledge  153 **proofs new-bleeding** examples of others newly ruined; **foil** dark background (to display a jewel)  156 **assay** experience  157 **forced examples** comparisons with her own case which seem to her far-fetched, though she is made to consider them  160 **rage** are impassioned

"Nor gives it satisfaction to our blood,°
That we must curb it upon others' proof,°
To be forbod° the sweets that seems so good
For fear of harms that preach in our behoof.                    165
O appetite, from judgment stand aloof!
The one a palate hath that needs will taste,
Though Reason weep and cry, 'It is thy last.'

"For further I could say this man's untrue,°
And knew the patterns of his foul beguiling;                    170
Heard where his plants in others' orchards grew;
Saw how deceits were gilded in his smiling;
Knew vows were ever brokers° to defiling;
Thought characters and words° merely but art,
And bastards of his foul adulterate heart.                      175

"And long upon these terms I held my city,
Till thus he 'gan besiege me: 'Gentle maid,
Have of my suffering youth some feeling pity
And be not of my holy vows afraid.
That's° to ye sworn to none was ever said;                      180
For feasts of love I have been called unto,
Till now did ne'er invite nor never woo.

"'All my offenses that abroad you see
Are errors of the blood,° none of the mind.
Love made them not. With acture° they may be,                   185
Where neither party is nor true nor kind.
They sought their shame that so their shame did find,
And so much less of shame in me remains
By how much of me their reproach contains.

"'Among the many that mine eyes have seen,                      190
Not one whose flame my heart so much as warmèd,
Or my affection put to th' smallest teen,°
Or any of my leisures ever charmèd.
Harm have I done to them, but ne'er was harmèd;
Kept hearts in liveries,° but mine own was free                 195
And reigned commanding in his monarchy.

"'Look here what tributes wounded fancies sent me
Of pallid pearls and rubies red as blood,
Figuring that they their passions likewise lent me
Of grief and blushes, aptly understood                          200
In bloodless white and the encrimsoned mood;°
Effects of terror and dear modesty,
Encamped in hearts, but fighting outwardly.

"'And, lo, behold these talents° of their hair,
With twisted metal amorously empleached,°                       205
I have received from many a several fair,°
Their kind acceptance weepingly beseeched,
With th' annexions° of fair gems enriched,
And deep-brained sonnets that did amplify
Each stone's dear° nature, worth, and quality.                  210

"'The diamond, why, 'twast beautiful and hard,
Whereto his invised° properties did tend;
The deep-green em'rald, in whose fresh regard
Weak sights their sickly radiance° do amend;
The heaven-hued sapphire, and the opal blend                    215
With objects manifold:° each several° stone,
With wit well blazoned,° smiled or made some moan.

"'Lo, all these trophies of affections hot,
Of pensived and subdued desires the tender,°
Nature hath charged me that I hoard them not,                   220
But yield them up where I myself must render,
That is, to you, my origin and ender.
For these of force must your oblations° be,
Since I their altar, you enpatron me.°

"'O, then, advance of yours that phraseless° hand,              225
Whose white weighs down the airy scale of praise!
Take all these similes° to your own command,
Hollowed° with sighs that burning lungs did raise.
What me, your minister, for you obeys,°
Works under you; and to your audit° comes                       230
Their distract parcels° in combinèd sums.

"'Lo, this device was sent me from a nun,
Or sister sanctified, of holiest note,
Which late her noble suit° in court did shun,
Whose rarest havings° made the blossoms° dote;                  235
For she was sought by spirits of richest coat,°
But kept cold distance, and did thence remove
To spend her living in eternal love.°

"'But, O my sweet, what labor is't to leave
The thing we have not, mast'ring what not strives,              240
Paling° the place° which did no form receive,
Playing patient sports in unconstrainèd gyves?°
She that her fame so to herself contrives,°
The scars of battle 'scapeth by the flight
And makes her absence valiant, not her might.°                  245

---

212 **invised** inward-looking, self-regarding (?) (Latin *invisus* = secret)   214 **radiance** power of vision   215–16 **opal . . . manifold** blended opal, with many other objects (?)   216 **several** separate   217 **blazoned** proclaimed   219 **tender** offering   223 **oblations** offerings   224 **Since . . . me** i.e., I am the altar at which they are offered to you, my patron saint   225 **phraseless** indescribable   227 **similes** love-tokens (jewels and sonnets)   228 **Hollowed** (1) blown up, shaped (2) hallowed   229 **What . . . obeys** whatever obeys me, your servant ("minister")   230 **audit** accounting   231 **distract parcels** separate items   234 **suit** wooing   235 **havings** personal qualities; **blossoms** i.e., flower of the nobility   236 **coat** coats of arms   238 **eternal love** love of things heavenly   241 **Paling** fencing (but "Paling" is an emendation for "Playing"; "Leaving" and "Flying" have also been suggested); **the place** i.e., the nun's heart, which had never received the impression of love   242 **unconstrainèd gyves** fetters that do not constrain (because willingly put on)   243 **her . . . contrives** creates for herself a reputation (for renouncing love)   245 **might** power

---

162 **blood** passion   163 **others' proof** the experience of others   164 **forbod** forbidden   169 **say . . . untrue** tell of this man's untruth   173 **brokers** panders   174 **characters and words** written and spoken words   180 **That's** what's   184 **blood** lust   185 **acture** action (as opposed to volition)   192 **teen** distress   195 **in liveries** as servants   201 **mood** mode   204 **talents** treasures   205 **empleached** intertwined   206 **several fair** different lady   208 **annexions** additions   210 **dear** valuable

" 'O, pardon me, in that my boast is true:
The accident which brought me to her eye
Upon the moment did her force subdue,
And now she would the cagèd cloister fly.
Religious° love put out religion's eye.　　　　　　250
Not to be tempted, would she be inured,°
And now, to tempt all, liberty procured.°

" 'How mighty then you are, O hear me tell:
The broken bosoms° that to me belong
Have emptied all their fountains in my well,　　　255
And mine I pour your ocean all among.
I strong o'er them, and you o'er me being strong,
Must for your victory us all congest,°
As compound love to physic° your cold breast.

" 'My parts had pow'r to charm a sacred nun,　　260
Who, disciplined, ay, dieted in grace,
Believed her eyes when they t' assail begun,°
All vows and consecrations giving place.
O most potential° love! vow, bond, nor space
In thee hath neither sting, knot, nor confine,　　265
For thou art all, and all things else are thine.

" 'When thou impressest,° what are precepts worth
Of stale example? When thou wilt inflame,
How coldly those impediments stand forth
Of wealth, of filial fear, law, kindred, fame!　　270
Love's arms are° peace, 'gainst rule, 'gainst sense, 'gainst
　　shame;
And sweetens, in the suff'ring pangs it bears,
The aloes° of all forces, shocks, and fears.

" 'Now all these hearts that do on mine depend,
Feeling it break, with bleeding groans° they pine;　275
And supplicant their sighs to you extend,
To leave the batt'ry that you make 'gainst mine,
Lending soft audience to my sweet design,
And credent° soul to that strong-bonded oath
That shall prefer° and undertake my troth.'°　　280

"This said, his wat'ry eyes he did dismount,°
Whose sights till then were leveled on my face;
Each cheek a river running from a fount
With brinish current downward flowed apace.
O, how the channel to the stream gave grace!　　285
Who° glazed with crystal gate° the glowing roses
That flame through water which their hue encloses.

"O father, what a hell of witchcraft lies
In the small orb of one particular tear!
But with the inundation of the eyes　　　　　　290
What rocky heart to water will not wear?
What breast so cold that is not warmèd here?
O cleft° effect! Cold modesty, hot wrath,
Both fire from hence and chill extincture hath.

"For, lo, his passion, but an art of craft,　　　295
Even there resolved° my reason into tears;
There my white stole of chastity I daffed,°
Shook off my sober guards and civil° fears;
Appear° to him as he to me appears,
All melting, though our drops° this diff'rence bore:　300
His poisoned me, and mine did him restore.

"In him a plenitude of subtle matter,
Applied to cautels,° all strange forms receives,
Of burning blushes, or of weeping water,
Or sounding° paleness; and he takes and leaves,°　305
In either's aptness,° as it best deceives,
To blush at speeches rank,° to weep at woes,
Or to turn white and sound° at tragic shows;

"That not a heart which in his level° came
Could 'scape the hail° of his all-hurting aim,　　310
Showing fair nature as both kind and tame;°
And, veiled in them,° did win whom he would maim.
Against the thing he sought he would exclaim:
When he most burned in heart-wished luxury,°
He preached pure maid and praised cold chastity.　315

"Thus merely with the garment of a Grace,
The naked and concealèd fiend he covered,
That th' unexperient° gave the tempter place,
Which,° like a cherubin, above them hovered.
Who, young and simple, would not be so lovered?　320
Ay me! I fell, and yet do question make
What I should do again for such a sake.

"O, that infected° moisture of his eye,
O, that false fire which in his cheek so glowed,
O, that forced thunder from his heart did fly,　　325
O, that sad breath his spongy lungs bestowed,
O, all that borrowed motion, seeming owed,°
Would yet again betray the fore-betrayed
And new-pervert a reconcilèd° maid!"

# THE PASSIONATE PILGRIM

## IV

Sweet Cytherea,° sitting by a brook
With young Adonis, lovely, fresh, and green,°
Did court the lad with many a lovely° look,
Such looks as none could look but beauty's queen.
She told him stories, to delight his ear;          5
She showed him favors, to allure his eye;
To win his heart she touched him here and there—
Touches so soft still conquer chastity.
But whether unripe years did want conceit,°
Or he refused to take her figured proffer,          10
The tender nibbler would not touch the bait,
But smile and jest at every gentle offer.
    Then fell she on her back, fair queen, and toward.°
    He rose and ran away. Ah, fool too froward!°

## VI

Scarce had the sun dried up the dewy morn,
And scarce the herd gone to the hedge for shade,
When Cytherea° (all in love forlorn),
A longing tarriance° for Adonis made
Under an osier° growing by a brook,          5
A brook where Adon used to cool his spleen.°
Hot was the day; she hotter that did look
For his approach that often there had been.
Anon he comes, and throws his mantle by,
And stood stark naked on the brook's green brim.          10
The sun looked on the world with glorious eye,
Yet not so wistly° as this queen on him.
    He, spying her, bounced in whereas° he stood.
    "O Jove," quoth she, "why was not I a flood!"

## VII

Fair is my love, but not so fair as fickle;
Mild as a dove, but neither true nor trusty;
Brighter than glass, and yet as glass is, brittle;
Softer than wax, and yet as iron rusty:
    A lily pale, with damask° dye to grace her;          5
    None fairer, nor none falser to deface her.°

*The decorative border shown above is a repeated ornament which appeared on the title page of the second octavo edition of* The Passionate Pilgrim, *1599.*

**IV 1 Cytherea** Venus  **2 green** young  **3 lovely** loving  **9 conceit** understanding  **13 toward** willing  **14 froward** refractory
**VI 3 Cytherea** Venus  **4 tarriance** awaiting  **5 osier** willow  **6 spleen** hot temper  **12 wistly** eagerly  **13 whereas** where
**VII 5 damask** pale red  **6 to deface her** to her discredit

Her lips to mine how often hath she joined,
Between each kiss her oaths of true love swearing!
How many tales to please me hath she coined,°
Dreading my love, the loss whereof still fearing!          10
    Yet, in the midst of all her pure protestings,
    Her faith, her oaths, her tears, and all were jestings.

She burnt with love, as straw with fire° flameth;
She burnt out love, as soon as straw outburneth;
She framed° the love, and yet she foiled° the framing;          15
She bade love last, and yet she fell a-turning.°
    Was this a lover, or a lecher, whether?°
    Bad in the best, though excellent in neither.°

## IX

Fair was the morn when the fair queen of love,
°
Paler for sorrow than her milk-white dove,
For Adon's sake, a youngster proud and wild,
Her stand she takes upon a steep-up hill.          5
Anon Adonis comes with horn and hounds.
She, silly queen, with more than love's good will,
Forbade the boy he should not pass those grounds.
"Once," quoth she, "did I see a fair sweet youth
Here in these brakes deep-wounded with a boar,          10
Deep in the thigh, a spectacle of ruth!°
See, in my thigh," quoth she, "here was the sore."
    She showèd hers; he saw more wounds than one,
    And blushing fled and left her all alone.

## X

Sweet rose, fair flower, untimely plucked, soon vaded,°
Plucked in the bud, and vaded° in the spring!
Bright orient pearl, alack, too timely° shaded!
Fair creature, killed too soon by death's sharp sting!
    Like a green plum that hangs upon a tree,          5
    And falls, through wind, before the fall should be.

I weep for thee, and yet no cause I have;
For why,° thou left'st me nothing in thy will.
And yet thou left'st me more than I did crave,          10
For why,° I cravèd nothing of thee still.
    O yes, dear friend, I pardon crave of thee:
    Thy discontent thou didst bequeath to me.

**9 coinèd** counterfeited  **13 fire** two syllables  **15 framed** formed; **foiled** thwarted  **16 fell a-turning** i.e., turned to others (for sex)  **17 whether** which of the two  **18 neither** also, the sexual organs are "nether" parts
**IX 2** a line rhyming with "wild" is lost  **11 ruth** pity
**X 1, 2 vaded** (1) departed (2) faded  **3 timely** soon  **8, 10 For why** because

## XII

Crabbèd age and youth cannot live together:
Youth is full of pleasance,° age is full of care;
Youth like summer morn, age like winter weather;
Youth like summer brave,° age like winter bare.
Youth is full of sport, age's breath is short; 5
Youth is nimble, age is lame;
Youth is hot and bold, age is weak and cold;
Youth is wild, and age is tame.
Age, I do abhor thee; youth, I do adore thee:
O, my love, my love is young! 10
Age, I do defy° thee. O sweet shepherd hie thee,°
For methinks thou stays too long.

## XIII

Beauty is but a vain and doubtful good;
A shining gloss that vadeth° suddenly;
A flower that dies when first it 'gins to bud;
A brittle glass that's broken presently:°
  A doubtful good, a gloss, a glass, a flower, 5
  Lost, vaded, broken, dead within an hour.

And as goods lost are seld° or never found,
As vaded gloss no rubbing will refresh,
As flowers dead lie witherèd on the ground,
As broken glass no cement° can redress: 10
  So beauty blemished once, for ever lost,
  In spite of physic,° painting, pain, and cost.°

## XIV

Good night, good rest; ah, neither be my share!
She bade good night that kept my rest away,
And daffed me° to a cabin hanged with care
To descant° on the doubts of my decay.
  "Farewell," quoth she, "and come again tomorrow." 5
  Fare well I could not, for I supped with sorrow.

Yet at my parting sweetly did she smile,
In scorn or friendship, nill I conster whether.°
'T may be she joyed to jest at my exile;
'T may be, again to make me wander thither: 10
  "Wander"—a word for shadows like myself
  As° take the pain but cannot pluck the pelf.°

Lord, how mine eyes throw gazes to the east!
My heart doth charge the watch;° the morning rise
Doth cite° each moving sense from idle rest, 15
Not daring trust the office of mine eyes,

While Philomela° sits and sings, I sit and mark,
And wish her lays° were tunèd like the lark;

For she doth welcome daylight with her ditty
And drives away dark dreaming night. 20
The night so packed,° I post° unto my pretty;
Heart hath his hope, and eyes their wishèd sight;
  Sorrow changed to solace and solace mixed with
    sorrow;
  For why,° she sighed and bade me come tomorrow.

Were I with her, the night would post too soon, 25
But now are minutes added to° the hours;
To spite me now, each minute seems a moon:°
Yet not for me, shine sun to succor flowers!
  Pack night, peep day! Good day, of night now
    borrow:
  Short, night, tonight, and length° thyself tomorrow. 30

## XV

It was a lording's° daughter, the fairest one of three,
That likèd of her master° as well as well might be,
Till looking on an Englishman, the fair'st that eye
    could see,
  Her fancy fell a-turning.
Long was the combat doubtful that love with love did
    fight, 5
To leave the master loveless, or kill the gallant knight:
To put in practice either, alas, it was a spite
  Unto the silly° damsel!
But one must be refusèd; more mickle° was the pain
That nothing could be usèd to turn them both to gain, 10
For of the two the trusty knight was wounded with
    disdain:
  Alas, she could not help it!
Thus art° with arms contending was victor of the day,
Which by a gift of learning did bear the maid away:
Then, lullaby, the learned man hath got the lady gay; 15
  For now my song is ended.

## XVII

My flocks feed not, my ewes breed not,
My rams speed not, all is amiss:
Love is dying, faith's defying,°
Heart's denying,° causer of this.
All my merry jigs° are quite forgot, 5
All my lady's love is lost, God wot.°
Where her faith was firmly fixed in love,
There a nay° is placed without remove.
One silly cross° wrought all my loss.
  O frowning Fortune, cursèd fickle dame! 10

XII 2 **pleasance** gaiety  4 **brave** splendid  11 **defy** reject;
**hie thee** hurry
XIII 2 **vadeth** (1) departs (2) fades  4 **presently** soon  7 **seld**
seldom  10 **cement** stress on first syllable  12 **physic** medicine; **cost** expenditure
XIV 3 **daffed me** sent me off  4 **descant** lament (literally,
compose musical variations)  8 **nill . . . whether** I do not
know which  12 **As** who; **pelf** reward  14 **charge the watch**
order the watchman to proclaim day (?)  15 **cite** summon

17 **Philomela** the nightingale  18 **lays** songs  21 **packed** disposed of; **post** hurry  24 **For why** because  26 **added to**
i.e., like  27 **moon** month  30 **Short . . . length** shorten
. . . lengthen
XV 1 **lording's** lord's  2 **master** teacher  8 **silly** inexperienced  9 **more mickle** greater  13 **art** learning
XVII 3 **defying** rejection  4 **denying** perhaps it should be
emended to "renying" = disowning  5 **jigs** songs or dance
tunes  6 **wot** knows  8 **nay** denial  9 **cross** misfortune

For now I see inconstancy
  More in women than in men remain.

In black mourn I, all fears scorn I,
Love hath forlorn me, living in thrall.
Heart is bleeding, all help needing—          15
O cruel speeding,° fraughted° with gall!
My shepherd's pipe can sound no deal;°
My wether's bell rings doleful knell;
My curtail dog,° that wont to have played,
Plays not at all, but seems afraid;          20
With sighs so deep procures to weep,
  In howling wise, to see my doleful plight.
How sighs resound through heartless° ground,
  Like a thousand vanquished men in bloody fight!

Clear wells spring not, sweet birds sing not,      25
Green plants bring not forth their dye.
Herds stand weeping, flocks all sleeping,
Nymphs back peeping fearfully.
All our pleasure known to us poor swains,
All our merry meetings on the plains,          30
All our evening sport from us is fled,
All our love is lost, for Love is dead.
Farewell, sweet lass! Thy like ne'er was
  For a sweet content, the cause of all my moan.
Poor Corydon must live alone.          35
  Other help for him I see that there is none.

## XVIII

When as thine eye hath chose the dame
And stalled the deer° that thou shouldst strike,
Let reason rule things worthy blame,
As well as fancy's partial might;°
  Take counsel of some wiser head,          5
  Neither too young, nor yet unwed.

And when thou com'st thy tale to tell,
Smooth not thy tongue with filèd° talk,
Lest she some subtile practice° smell—
A cripple soon can find a halt;°          10

**16 speeding** lot; **fraughted** laden   **17 no deal** not at all   **19 curtail dog** dog with docked tail   **23 heartless** (1) pitiless (2) cowardly

**XVIII 2 stalled the deer** got the deer within range (with pun on *dear*)   **4 fancy's partial might** a desperate emendation for the text's "fancy (partyall might)," which seems meaningless; the emendation, and its context, means that sexual behavior ("things worthy blame") should be governed by impartial reason and by the partial power of love ("fancy")   **8 filèd** polished   **9 practice** deception   **10 A cripple . . . halt** a cripple knows a limp (and so a woman can recognize a deceiver)

But plainly say thou lov'st her well,
And set thy person forth to sell.

And to her will frame all thy ways.
Spare not to spend, and chiefly there
Where thy desert may merit praise          15
By ringing in thy lady's ear.
  The strongest castle, tower, and town,
  The golden bullet beats it down.

Serve always with assurèd trust
And in thy suit be humble-true.          20
Unless thy lady prove unjust,
Press never thou to choose a new.
  When time shall serve, be thou not slack
  To proffer, though she put thee back.

What though her frowning brows be bent,      25
Her cloudy looks will calm ere night;
And then too late she will repent
That thus dissembled her delight.
  And twice desire, ere it be day,
  That which with scorn she put away.          30

What though she strive to try her strength,
And ban° and brawl and say thee nay,
Her feeble force will yield at length,
When craft hath taught her thus to say:
  "Had women been so strong as men,          35
  In faith, you had not had it then."

The wiles and guiles that women work,
Dissembled with an outward show,
The tricks and toys that in them lurk,
The cock that treads them shall not know.      40
  Have you not heard it said full oft,
  A woman's nay doth stand for naught?

Think women still to strive with men
To sin and never for to saint.
There is no heaven:° be holy then          45
When time with age shall them attaint.
  Were kisses all the joys in bed,
  One woman would another wed.

But soft,° enough! too much, I fear,
Lest that my mistress hear my song.          50
She will not stick to round me on th' ear,°
To teach my tongue to be so long.
  Yet will she blush, here be it said,
  To hear her secrets so bewrayed.°

**32 ban** curse   **45 There . . . heaven** i.e., there is no heavenly bliss in serving women (?)   **49 soft** stop   **51 stick . . . ear** hesitate to scold me   **54 bewrayed** revealed

# THE SONNETS

INTRODUCTION BY W. H. AUDEN

EDITED BY WILLIAM BURTO

## Introduction

Probably, more nonsense has been talked and written, more intellectual and emotional energy expended in vain, on the sonnets of Shakespeare than on any other literary work in the world. Indeed, they have become the best touchstone I know of for distinguishing the sheep from the goats, that is, those who love poetry for its own sake and understand its nature from those who value poems only either as historical documents or because they express feelings or beliefs of which the reader happens to approve.

It so happens that we know almost nothing about the historical circumstances under which Shakespeare wrote these sonnets: we do not know to whom they are addressed or exactly when they were written, and, unless entirely new evidence should turn up, which is unlikely, we never shall.

This has not prevented many very learned gentlemen from displaying their scholarship and ingenuity in conjecture. Though it seems to me rather silly to spend much time upon conjectures that cannot be proved true or false, that is not my real objection to their efforts. What I really object to is their illusion that, if they were successful, if the identity of the Friend, the Dark Lady, the Rival Poet, and so on, could be established beyond doubt, this would in any way illuminate our understanding of the sonnets themselves.

Their illusion seems to me to betray either a complete misunderstanding of the nature of the relation between art and life or an attempt to rationalize and justify plain vulgar idle curiosity.

Idle curiosity is an ineradicable vice of the human mind. All of us like to discover the secrets of our neighbors, particularly the ugly ones. This has always been so, and, probably, always will be. What is relatively new, however —it is scarcely to be found before the latter half of the eighteenth century—is a blurring of the borderline between the desire for truth and idle curiosity, until, today, it has been so thoroughly erased that we can indulge in the latter without the slightest pangs of conscience. A great deal of what today passes for scholarly research is an activity no different from that of reading somebody's private correspondence when he is out of the room, and it does not really make it morally any better if he is out of the room because he is in his grave.

In the case of a man of action—a ruler, a statesman, a general—the man is identical with his biography. In the case of any kind of artist, however, who is a maker not a doer, his biography—the story of his life—and the history of his works are distinct. In the case of a man of action, we can distinguish in a rough and ready way between his private personal life and his public life, but both are lives of action and, therefore, capable of affecting each other. The political interests of a king's mistress, for example, may influence his decisions on national policy. Consequently, the historian, in his search for truth, is justified in investigating the private life of a man of action to the degree that such discoveries throw light upon the history of his times which he had a share in shaping, even if the victim would prefer such secrets not to be known.

The case of any artist is quite different. Art history, the comparison of one work with another, one artistic epoch with another, the study of influences and changes of style, is a legitimate study. The late J. B. Leishman's book, *Themes and Variations in Shakespeare's Sonnets*, is an admirable example of such an enquiry. Even the biography of an artist, if his life as a man was sufficiently interesting, is permissible, provided that the biographer and his readers realize that such an account throws no light whatsoever upon the artist's work. The relation between his life and his works is at one and the same time too self-evident to require comment—every work of art is, in one sense, a self-disclosure—and too complicated ever to unravel. Thus, it is self-evident that Catullus' love for Lesbia was the experience that inspired his love poems, and that, if either of them had had a different character, the poems would have been different; but no amount of research into their lives can tell us why Catullus wrote the actual poems he did, instead of an infinite number of similar poems he might have written instead, why, indeed, he wrote any, or why those he did are good. Even if one could question a poet himself about the relation between some poem of his and the events that provoked him to write it, he could not give a satisfactory answer, because even the most "occasional" poem, in the Goethean sense, involves not only the occasion but the whole life experience of the poet, and he himself cannot identify all the contributing elements.

Further, it should be borne in mind that most genuine artists would prefer that no biography be written. A genuine artist believes he has been put on earth to fulfill a certain function determined by the talent with which he has been entrusted. His personal life is, naturally, of concern to himself and, he hopes, to his personal friends, but he does not think it is or ought to be of any concern to the public. The one thing a writer, for example, hopes for is attentive readers of his writings. He hopes they will study the text closely enough to spot misprints. Shakespeare would be grateful to many scholars, beginning with Malone, who have suggested sensible emendations to the Q text. And he hopes that they will read with patience and intelligence so as to extract as much meaning from the text as possible. If the shade of Shakespeare has read William Empson's explication of "They that have pow'r to hurt and will do none" (Sonnet 94), he may have wondered to himself, "Now, did I *really* say all that?," but he will certainly be grateful to Mr. Empson for his loving care.

Not only would most genuine writers prefer to have no biography written; they would also prefer, were it feasible, that their writings be published anonymously.

Shakespeare is in the singularly fortunate position of being, for all intents and purposes, anonymous. Hence the existence of persons who spend their lives trying to prove that his plays were written by someone else. (How odd it is that Freud should have been a firm believer in the Earl of Oxford theory.)

So far as the sonnets are concerned, the certain facts are just two in number. Two of the sonnets, "When my love swears that she is made of truth" (138), and "Two loves I have, of comfort and despair" (144), appeared in *The Passionate Pilgrim*, a poetic miscellany printed in 1599, and the whole collection was published by G. Eld for T. T. in 1609 with a dedication "To.The.Onlie.Begetter.Of. These.Insuing.Sonnets. Mr. W.H." Meres's reference in 1598 to "sugred Sonnets" by Shakespeare is inconclusive: the word *sonnet* was often used as a general term for a lyric, and even if Meres was using it in the stricter sense, we do not know if the sonnets he was referring to are the ones we have.

Aside from the text itself, this is all we know for certain and all we are ever likely to know. On philological grounds, I am inclined to agree with those scholars who take the word *begetter* to mean procurer, so that Mr. W.H. is not the friend who inspired most of the sonnets, but the person who secured the manuscript for the publisher.

So far as the date of their composition is concerned, all we know for certain is that the relation between Shakespeare and the Friend lasted at least three years:

Three April perfumes in three hot Junes burned,
Since first I saw you fresh, which yet are green.     (104)

The fact that the style of the sonnets is nearer to that of the earlier plays than the later is not conclusive proof that their composition was contemporary with the former, because a poet's style is always greatly influenced by the particular verse form he is employing. As C. S. Lewis has said: "If Shakespeare had taken an hour off from the composition of *Lear* to write a sonnet, the sonnet might not have been in the style of *Lear*." On the whole, I think an early date is a more plausible conjecture than a late one,

because the experiences the sonnets describe seem to me to be more likely to befall a younger man than an older.

Let us, however, forget all about Shakespeare the man, leave the speculations about the persons involved, the names, already or in the future to be put forward, Southampton, Pembroke, Hughes, and so on, to the foolish and the idle, and consider the sonnets themselves.

The first thing that is obvious after reading through the one hundred and fifty-four sonnets as we have them, is that they are not in any kind of planned sequence. The only semblance of order is a division into two unequal heaps—Sonnets 1 to 126 are addressed to a young man, assuming, which is probable but not certain, that there is only one young man addressed, and Sonnets 127–154 are addressed to a dark-haired woman. In both heaps, a triangle situation is referred to in which Shakespeare's friend and his mistress betray him by having an affair together, which proves that the order is not chronological. Sonnets 40 and 42, "Take all my loves, my love, yea take them all," "That thou hast her, it is not all my grief," must be more or less contemporary with 144 and 152, "Two loves I have, of comfort and despair," "In loving thee thou know'st I am forsworn."

Nor in the two sets considered separately is it possible to believe that the order is chronological. Sometimes batches of sonnets occur that clearly belong together—for example, the opening series 1–17, in which the friend is urged to marry, though, even here, 15 seems not to belong, for marriage is not mentioned in it. At other times, sonnets that are similar in theme are widely separated. To take a very trivial example: in 77 Shakespeare speaks of giving his friend a commonplace book.

Look what thy memory cannot contain,
Commit to these waste blanks.

And in 122, he speaks of a similar gift from his friend to him, "Thy gift, thy tables, are within my brain." Surely, it is probable that they exchanged gifts and that these sonnets belong together.

The serious objection, however, to the order of Sonnets 1–126 as the Q text prints them is psychological. Sonnets expressing feelings of unalloyed happiness and devotion are mixed with others expressing grief and estrangement. Some speak of injuries done to Shakespeare by his friend, others of some scandal in which the friend was involved, others again of some infidelity on Shakespeare's part in a succession that makes no kind of emotional sense.

Any passionate relationship can go through and survive painful crises, and become all the stronger for it. As Shakespeare writes in Sonnet 119:

O, benefit of ill: now I find true
That better is by evil still made better;
And ruined love, when it is built anew,
Grows fairer than at first, more strong, far greater.

But forgiveness and reconciliation do not obliterate memory of the past. It is not possible to return to the innocent happiness expressed before any cloud appeared on the sky. It is not, it seems to me, possible to believe that, *after* going through the experiences described in Sonnets 40–42, Shakespeare would write either Sonnet 53,

In all external grace you have some part,
But you like none, none you, for constant heart,

or 105,

Let not my love be called idolatry,
Nor my belovèd as an idol show,
Since all alike my songs and praises be
To one, of one, still such, and ever so.
Kind is my love today, tomorrow kind,
Still constant in a wondrous excellence.

If the order is not chronological, it cannot, either, be a sequence planned by Shakespeare for publication. Any writer with an audience in mind knows that a sequence of poems must climax with one of the best. Yet the sequence as we have it concludes with two of the worst of the sonnets, trivial conceits about, apparently, going to Bath to take the waters. Nor, when preparing for publication, will an author leave unrevised what is obviously a first draft, like Sonnet 99 with its fifteen lines.

A number of scholars have tried to rearrange the sonnets into some more logical order, but such efforts can never be more than conjecture, and it is best to accept the jumble we have been given.

If the first impression made by the sonnets is of their haphazard order, the second is of their extremely uneven poetic value.

After the 1609 edition, the sonnets were pretty well forgotten for more than a century and a half. In 1640 Benson produced an extraordinary hodgepodge in which one hundred and forty-six of them were arranged into seventy-two poems with invented titles, and some of the *he*'s and *him*'s changed to *she*'s and *her*'s. It was not until 1780 that a significant critical text was made by Malone. This happened to be a period when critics condemned the sonnet as a form. Thus Steevens could write in 1766:

Quaintness, obscurity, and tautology are to be regarded as the constituent parts of this exotic species of composition. . . . I am one of those who should have wished it to have expired in the country where it was born. . . . [A sonnet] is composed in the highest strain of affectation, pedantry, circumlocution, and nonsense.

And of Shakespeare's essays in this form:

The strongest act of Parliament that could be framed would fail to compel readers unto their service.

Even when this prejudice against the sonnet as such had begun to weaken, and even after Bardolatry had begun, adverse criticism of the sonnets continued.

Thus Wordsworth, who was as responsible as anyone for rehabilitating the sonnet as a form (though he employed the Petrarchan, not the Shakespearean, kind), remarked:

These sonnets beginning at CXXVII to his mistress are worse than a puzzle-peg. They are abominably harsh, obscure, and worthless. The others are for the most part much better, have many fine lines and passages. They are also in many places warm with passion. Their chief faults —and heavy ones they are—are sameness, tediousness, quaintness, and elaborate obscurity.

Hazlitt:

If Shakespeare had written nothing but his sonnets . . . he would . . . have been assigned to the class of cold, artificial writers, who had no genuine sense of nature or passion.

Keats:

They seem to be full of fine things said unintentionally— in the intensity of working out conceits.

Landor:

Not a single one is very admirable. . . . They are hot and pothery: there is much condensation, little delicacy; like raspberry jam without cream, without crust, without bread; to break its viscidity.

In this century we have reacquired a taste for the conceit, as we have for baroque architecture, and no longer think that artifice is incompatible with passion. Even so, no serious critic of poetry can possibly think that all the sonnets are equally good.

On going through the hundred and fifty-four of them, I find forty-nine that seem to me excellent throughout, and a good number of the rest have one or two memorable lines, but there are also several that I can read only out of a sense of duty. For the inferior ones we have no right to condemn Shakespeare unless we are prepared to believe—a belief for which there is no evidence—that he prepared or intended them all to be published.

Considered in the abstract, as if they were Platonic Ideas, the Petrarchan sonnet seems to be a more esthetically satisfying form than the Shakespearean. Having only two different rhymes in the octave and two in the sestet, each is bound by rhyme into a closed unity, and the asymmetrical relation of 8 to 6 is pleasing. The Shakespearean form, on the other hand, with its seven different rhymes, almost inevitably becomes a lyric of three symmetrical quatrains, finished off with an epigrammatic couplet. As a rule Shakespeare shapes his rhetorical argument in conformity with this, that is to say, there is usually a major pause after the fourth, the eighth, and the twelfth line. Only in one case, Sonnet 86, "Was it the proud full sail of his great verse," does the main pause occur in the middle of the second quatrain, so that the sonnet divides into 6.6.2.

It is the concluding couplet in particular which, in the Shakespearean form, can be a snare. The poet is tempted to use it either to make a summary of the preceding twelve lines that is unnecessary, or to draw a moral that is too glib and trite. In the case of Shakespeare himself, though there are some wonderful couplets, for example the conclusion of 61,

For thee watch I, whilst thou dost wake elsewhere,
From me far off, with others all too near,

or 87,

Thus have I had thee as a dream doth flatter,
In sleep a king, but waking no such matter,

all too often, even in some of the best, the couplet lines are the weakest and dullest in the sonnet, and because they come at the end, the reader has the sense of a disappointing anticlimax.

Despite all this, it seems to me wise of Shakespeare to have chosen the form he did rather than the Petrarchan. Compared with Italian, English is so poor in rhymes that it is almost impossible to write a Petrarchan sonnet in it that sounds effortless throughout. In even the best examples from Milton, Wordsworth, and Rossetti, for instance, one is almost sure to find at least one line the concluding word of which does not seem inevitable, the only word that could accurately express the poet's meaning; one feels it is there only because the rhyme demanded it.

In addition, there are certain things that can be done in the Shakespearean form that the Petrarchan, with its sharp division between octave and sestet, cannot do. In Sonnet 66, "Tired with all these, for restful death I cry," and 129, "Th' expense of spirit in a waste of shame," Shakespeare is able to give twelve single-line *exempla* of the wretchedness of this world and the horrors of lust, with an accumulative effect of great power.

In their style, two characteristics of the sonnets stand out. Firstly, their *cantabile*. They are the work of someone whose ear is unerring. In his later blank verse, Shakespeare became a master of highly complicated effects of sound and rhythm, and the counterpointing of these with the sense, but in the sonnets he is intent upon making his verse as melodious, in the simplest and most obvious sense of the word, as possible, and there is scarcely a line, even in the dull ones, that sounds harsh or awkward. Occasionally, there are lines that foreshadow the freedom of his later verse. For example:

Not mine own fears nor the prophetic soul
Of the wide world dreaming on things to come.    (107)

But, as a rule, he keeps the rhythm pretty close to the metrical base. Inversion, except in the first foot, is rare, and so is trisyllabic substitution. The commonest musical devices are alliteration—

Then, were not summer's distillation left
A liquid prisoner pent in walls of glass    (5)

Let me not to the marriage of true minds
Admit impediments    (116)

—and the careful patterning of long and short vowels—

How many a holy and obsequious tear    (31)

Nor think the bitterness of absence sour    (57)

So far from home into my deeds to pry.    61)

The second characteristic they display is a mastery of every possible rhetorical device—for example, the reiteration of words with either an identical or a different meaning—

love is not love
Which alters when it alteration finds,
Or bends with the remover to remove.    (116)

—or the avoidance of monotony by an artful arithmetical variation of theme or illustration.

Here, I cannot do better than to quote (interpolating lines where appropriate) C. S. Lewis on Sonnet 18. "As often," he says, "the theme begins at line 9,

But thy eternal summer shall not fade,

occupying four lines, and the application is in the couplet:

So long as men can breathe or eyes can see,
So long lives this, and this gives life to thee.

Line 1

Shall I compare thee to a summer's day?

proposes a simile. Line 2

Thou art more lovely and more temperate

corrects it. Then we have two one-line *exempla* justifying the correction

Rough winds do shake the darling buds of May,
And summer's lease hath all too short a date:

then a two-line *exemplum* about the sun

Sometime too hot the eye of heaven shines,
And often is his gold complexion dimmed;

then two more lines

And every fair from fair sometime declines,
By chance, or nature's changing course, untrimmed;

which do not, as we had expected, add a fourth *exemplum* but generalize. Equality of length in the two last variations is thus played off against difference of function."[1]

The visual imagery is usually drawn from the most obviously beautiful natural objects, but, in a number, a single metaphorical conceit is methodically worked out, as in 87, "Farewell, thou art too dear for my possessing," where the character of an emotional relationship is worked out in terms of a legal contract.

In the inferior sonnets, such devices may strike the reader as artificial, but he must reflect that, without the artifice, they might be much worse than they are. The worst one can say, I think, is that rhetorical skill enables a poet to write a poem for which genuine inspiration is lacking that, had he lacked such skill, he would not have written at all.

On the other hand, those sonnets that express passionate emotions, whether of adoration or anger or grief or disgust, owe a very great deal of their effect precisely to Shakespeare's artifice, for without the restraint and distancing that the rhetorical devices provide, the intensity and immediacy of the emotion might have produced, not a poem, but an embarrassing "human document." Wordsworth defined poetry as emotion recollected in tranquility. It seems highly unlikely that Shakespeare wrote many of these sonnets out of recollected emotion. In his case, it is the artifice that makes up for the lack of tranquility.

[1] *English Literature in the Sixteenth Century* (1954), p. 507.

If the vagueness of the historical circumstances under which the sonnets were written has encouraged the goats of idle curiosity, their matter has given the goats of ideology a wonderful opportunity to display their love of simplification at the expense of truth. Confronted with the extremely odd story they tell, with the fact that, in so many of them, Shakespeare addresses a young man in terms of passionate devotion, the sound and sensible citizen, alarmed at the thought that our Top-Bard could have had any experience with which he is unfamiliar, has either been shocked and wished that Shakespeare had never written them, or, in defiance of common sense, tried to persuade himself that Shakespeare was merely expressing in somewhat hyperbolic terms, such as an Elizabethan poet might be expected to use, what any normal man feels for a friend of his own sex. The homosexual reader, on the other hand, determined to secure our Top-Bard as a patron saint of the Homintern, has been uncritically enthusiastic about the first one hundred and twenty-six of the sonnets, and preferred to ignore those to the Dark Lady in which the relationship is unequivocally sexual, and the fact that Shakespeare was a married man and a father.

Dag Hammarskjöld, in a diary found after his death and just recently published in Sweden, makes an observation to which both the above types would do well to listen.

How easy Psychology has made it for us to dismiss the perplexing mystery with a label which assigns it a place in the list of common aberrations.

That we are confronted in the sonnets by a mystery rather than by an aberration is evidenced for me by the fact that men and women whose sexual tastes are perfectly normal, but who enjoy and understand poetry, have always been able to read them as expressions of what they understand by the word *love*, without finding the masculine pronoun an obstacle.

I think that the *primary* experience—complicated as it became later—out of which the sonnets to the friend spring was a mystical one.

All experiences that may be called mystical have certain characteristics in common.

(1) The experience is "given." That is to say, it cannot be induced or prolonged by an effort of will, though the openness of any individual to receive it is partly determined by his age, his psychophysical make-up, and his cultural milieu.

(2) Whatever the contents of the experience, the subject is absolutely convinced that it is a revelation of reality. When it is over, he does not say, as one says when one awakes from a dream, "Now I am awake and conscious again of the real world." He says, rather, "For a while the veil was lifted and a reality revealed which in my 'normal' state is hidden from me."

(3) With whatever the vision is concerned—things, human beings, or God—they are experienced as numinous, clothed in glory, charged with an intense being-thereness.

(4) Confronted by the vision, the attention of the subject, in awe, joy, dread, is absolutely absorbed in contemplation and, while the vision lasts, his self, its desires and needs, are completely forgotten.

Natural mystical experiences, visions that is to say, concerned with created beings, not with a creator God, and without overt religious content, are of two kinds,

which one might call the Vision of Dame Kind and the Vision of Eros.

The classic descriptions of the first are to be found, of course, in certain of Wordsworth's poems, like *The Prelude*, the Immortality Ode, "Tintern Abbey," and "The Ruined Cottage." It is concerned with a multiplicity of creatures, inanimate and animate, but not with persons, though it may include human artifacts. If human beings do appear in it, they are always, I believe, total strangers to the subject, so that, so far as he is concerned, they are not persons. It would seem that, in our culture, this vision is not uncommon in childhood, but rare in adults.

The Vision of Eros, on the other hand, is concerned with a single person, who is revealed to the subject as being of infinite sacred importance. The classic descriptions of it are to be found in Plato's *Symposium*, Dante's *La Vita Nuova*, and some of these sonnets by Shakespeare.

It can, it seems, be experienced before puberty. If it occurs later, though the subject is aware of its erotic nature, his own desire is always completely subordinate to the sacredness of the beloved person, who is felt to be infinitely superior to the lover. Before anything else, the lover desires the happiness of the beloved.

The Vision of Eros is probably a much rarer experience than most people in our culture suppose, but, when it is genuine, I do not think it makes any sense to apply to it terms like *heterosexual* or *homosexual*. Such terms can be legitimately applied only to the profane erotic experiences with which we are all familiar, to lust, for example, an interest in another solely as a sexual object, and that combination of sexual desire and *philia*, affection based upon mutual interests, values, and shared experiences, which is the securest basis for a happy marriage.

That, in the Vision of Eros, the erotic is the medium, not the cause, is proved, I think, by the fact, on which all who have written about it with authority agree, that it cannot long survive an actual sexual relationship. Indeed, it is very doubtful if the Vision can ever be mutual: the story of Tristan and Isolde is a myth, not an instance of what can historically occur. To be receptive to it, it would seem that the subject must be exceptionally imaginative. Class feelings also seem to play a role; no one, apparently, can have such a vision about an individual who belongs to a social group that he has been brought up to regard as inferior to his own, so that its members are not, for him, fully persons.

The medium of the Vision is, however, undoubtedly erotic. Nobody who was unconscious of an erotic interest on his part would use the frank, if not brutal, sexual image that Shakespeare employs in speaking of his friend's exclusive interest in women.

But since she pricked thee out for women's pleasure,
Mine be thy love, and thy love's use their treasure.    (20)

The beloved is always beautiful in the impersonal sense of the word as well as the personal. It is unfortunate that we have to use the same words, *beauty* and *beautiful*, to mean two quite different things. If I say, "Elizabeth has a beautiful figure" or "a beautiful profile," I am referring to an objective, publicly recognizable property, and, so long as the objects are members of the same class, I can compare one with another and arrange them along a scale of beauty. That is why it is possible to hold dog shows, beauty competitions, and so on, or for a sculptor to state in mathematical terms the proportions of the ideal male or female figure. This kind of beauty is a gift of Nature's, depending upon a lucky combination of genes and the luck of good health, and a gift that Nature can, and in due time always does, take away. The reaction of the spectator to it is either impersonal admiration or impersonal sexual desire. Moral approval is not involved. It is perfectly possible for me to say, "Elizabeth has a beautiful figure, but she is a monster."

If, on the other hand, I say, "Elizabeth has a beautiful face or a beautiful expression," though I am still referring to something physical—I could not make the statement if I were blind—I am speaking of something that is personal, a unique face that cannot be compared with that of anyone else, and for which I hold Elizabeth personally responsible. Nature has had nothing to do with it. This kind of beauty is always associated with the notion of moral goodness. It is impossible to imagine circumstances in which I could say, "Elizabeth has a beautiful expression, but she is a monster." And it is this kind of beauty that arouses in the beholder feelings, not of impersonal admiration or lust, but of personal love.

The Petrarchan distinction, employed by Shakespeare in a number of his sonnets, between the love of the eye and the love of the heart, is an attempt, I think, to express the difference between these two kinds of beauty and our response to them.

In the Vision of Eros, both are always present. The beloved is always beautiful in both the public and the personal sense. But, to the lover, the second is more important. Dante certainly thought that Beatrice was a girl whose beauty everybody would admire, but it would not have entered his head to compare her for beauty with other Florentine girls of the same age.

Both Plato and Dante attempt to give a religious explanation of the Vision. Both, that is, regard the love inspired by a created human being as intended to lead the lover toward the love of the uncreated source of all beauty. The difference between them is that Plato is without any notion of what we mean by a person, whether human or Divine; he can think only in terms of the individual and the universal, and beauty for him is always beauty in the impersonal sense. Consequently, on the Platonic ladder, the love of an individual must be forgotten in the love of the universal; what we would call infidelity becomes a moral duty. How different is Dante's interpretation. Neither he nor Beatrice tells us exactly what he had done that had led him to the brink of perdition, but both speak of it as a lack of fidelity on Dante's part to his love for Beatrice. In Paradise, she is with him until the final moment when he turns from her toward "The Eternal Fountain," and even then he knows that her eyes are turned in the same direction. Instead of the many rungs of the Platonic ladder, there is only one step for the lover to take, from the person of the beloved creature to the Person of their common Creator.

It is consistent with Shakespeare's cast of mind as we meet it in the plays, where it is impossible to be certain what his personal beliefs were on any subject, that the sonnets should contain no theory of love: Shakespeare contents himself with simply describing the experience.

Though the primary experience from which they started was, I believe, the Vision of Eros, that is, of course, not all they are about. For the Vision to remain undimmed, it is probably necessary that the lover have very little contact with the beloved, however nice a person she (or he) may be. Dante, after all saw Beatrice only once or twice, and she probably knew little about him. The story of the sonnets seems to me to be the story of an agonized struggle by Shakespeare to preserve the glory of the vision he had been granted in a relationship, lasting at least three years, with a person who seemed intent by his actions upon covering the vision with dirt.

As outsiders, the impression we get of his friend is one of a young man who was not really very nice, very conscious of his good looks, able to switch on the charm at any moment, but essentially frivolous, cold-hearted, and self-centered, aware, probably, that he had some power over Shakespeare—if he thought about it at all, no doubt he gave it a cynical explanation—but with no conception of the intensity of the feelings he had, unwittingly, aroused. Somebody, in fact, rather like Bassanio in *The Merchant of Venice*.

The sonnets addressed to the Dark Lady are concerned with that most humiliating of all erotic experiences, sexual infatuation—*Vénus toute entière à sa proie attachée*.

Simple lust is impersonal; that is to say, the pursuer regards himself as a person but the object of his pursuit as a thing, to whose personal qualities, if she has any, he is indifferent, and, if he succeeds, he expects to be able to make a safe getaway as soon as he becomes bored. Sometimes, however, he gets trapped. Instead of becoming bored, he becomes sexually obsessed, and the girl, instead of conveniently remaining an object, becomes a real person to him, but a person whom he not only does not love, but actively dislikes.

No other poet, not even Catullus, has described the anguish, self-contempt, and rage produced by this unfortunate condition so well as Shakespeare in some of these sonnets, for example, 141, "In faith I do not love thee with my eyes," or 151, "Love is too young to know what conscience is."

Aside from the opening sixteen sonnets urging his friend to marry—which may well, as some scholars have suggested, have been written at the suggestion of some member of the young man's family—aside from these, and half a dozen elegant trifles, what is astonishing about the sonnets, especially when one remembers the age in which they were written, is the impression they make of naked autobiographical confession. The Elizabethans were not given to writing their autobiographies or to "unlocking their hearts." Donne's love poems were no doubt inspired by a personal passion, but this is hidden behind the public performance. It was not until Rousseau and the age of *Sturm und Drang* that confession became a literary genre. After the sonnets, I cannot think of anything in English poetry so seemingly autobiographical until Meredith's *Modern Love*, and even then, the personal events seem to be very carefully "posed."

It is impossible to believe either that Shakespeare wished them to be published or that he can have shown most of them to the young man and woman, whoever they were, to whom they are addressed. Suppose you had written Sonnet 57.

Being your slave, what should I do but tend
Upon the hours and times of your desire?

Can you imagine showing it to the person you were
thinking of? Vice versa, what on earth would you feel,
supposing someone you knew handed you the sonnet and
said, "This is about you"?

Though Shakespeare may have shown the sonnets to
one or two intimate literary friends—it would appear that
he must have—he wrote them, I am quite certain, as one
writes a diary, for himself alone, with no thought of a
public.

When the sonnets are really obscure, they are obscure
in the way that a diary can be, in which the writer does
not bother to explain references that are obvious to him but
that an outsider cannot know. For example, in the opening
lines of Sonnet 125,

Were't aught to me I bore the canopy,
With my extern the outward honoring,

it is impossible for the reader to know whether Shakespeare
is simply being figurative or whether he is referring to some
ceremony in which he actually took part, or, if he is,
what that ceremony can have been. Again, the concluding
couplet of 124 remains impenetrable.

To this I witness call the fools of Time,
Which die for goodness, who have lived for crime.

Some critics have suggested that this is a cryptic reference
to the Jesuits who were executed on charges of high
treason. This may be so, but there is nothing in the text to
prove it, and even if it is so, I fail to understand their
relevance as witnesses to Shakespeare's love, which no
disaster or self-interest can affect.

How the sonnets came to be published—whether
Shakespeare gave copies to some friend who then betrayed
him, or whether some enemy stole them—we shall
probably never know. Of one thing I am certain: Shakespeare must have been horrified when they were published.

The Elizabethan age was certainly as worldly-wise and
no more tolerant, perhaps less, than our own. After all,
sodomy was still a capital offense. The poets of the period,
like Marlowe and Barnfield, whom we know to have been
homosexual, were very careful not to express their feelings
in the first person, but in terms of classical mythology.
Renaissance Italy had the reputation for being tolerant on
this subject, yet when Michelangelo's nephew published
his sonnets to Tomasso de Cavalieri, which are much more
restrained than Shakespeare's, for the sake of his uncle's
reputation he altered the sex, just as Benson was to do with
Shakespeare in 1640.

Shakespeare must have known that his sonnets would
be read by many readers in 1609 as they are read by many
today—with raised eyebrows. Though I believe such a
reaction to be due to a misunderstanding, one cannot say
that it is not understandable.

In our culture, we have good reason to be skeptical when
anyone claims to have experienced the Vision of Eros, and
even to doubt if it ever occurs, because half our literature,
popular and highbrow, ever since the Provençal poets
made the disastrous mistake of trying to turn a mystical

experience into a social cult, is based on the assumption
that what is, probably, a rare experience, is one that
almost everybody has or ought to have; if they do not,
then there must be something wrong with them. We know
only too well how often, when a person speaks of having
"fallen in love" with X, what he or she really feels could be
described in much cruder terms. As La Rochefoucauld
observed, "True love is like seeing ghosts: we all talk about
it, but few of us have ever seen one." It does not follow,
however, that true love or ghosts cannot exist. Perhaps
poets are more likely to experience it than others, or become poets because they have. Perhaps Hannah Arendt is
right: "Poets are the only people to whom love is not only
a crucial but an indispensable experience, which entitles
them to mistake it for a universal one." In Shakespeare's
case, what happened to his relations with his friend and his
mistress, whether they were abruptly broken off in a
quarrel, or slowly faded into indifference, is anybody's
guess. Did Shakespeare later feel that the anguish at the
end was not too great a price to pay for the glory of the
initial vision? I hope so and believe so. Anyway, poets are
tough and can profit from the most dreadful experiences.

There is a scene in *The Two Noble Kinsmen* that most
scholars believe to have been written by Shakespeare and
that, if he did, may very well be the last thing he wrote.
In it there is a speech by Palamon in which he prays to
Venus for her aid. The speech is remarkable, first in its
choice of examples of the power of the goddess—nearly all
are humiliating or horrid—and second for the intensity of
the disgust expressed at masculine sexual vanity.

Hail, sovereign queen of secrets, who hast power
To call the fiercest tyrant from his rage
And weep unto a girl; that hast the might
Even with an eye-glance to choke Mars's drum
And turn th' alarm to whispers; that canst make
A cripple flourish with his crutch, and cure him
Before Apollo; that mayst force the king
To be his subject's vassal, and induce
Stale Gravity to dance; the polled bachelor
Whose youth like wanton boys through bonfires
Have skipped thy flame, at seventy thou canst catch
And make him, to the scorn of his hoarse throat,
Abuse young lays of love; what godlike power
Hast thou not power upon?
                                    Take to thy grace
Me thy vowed soldier, who do bear thy yoke
As 'twere a wreath of roses, yet is heavier
Than lead itself, stings more than nettles.
I have never been foul-mouthed against thy law,
Ne'er revealed secret, for I knew none; would not,
Had I kenned all that were; I never practiced
Upon man's wife, nor would the libels read
Of liberal wits; I never at great feasts
Sought to betray a beauty, but have blushed
At simp'ring sirs that did. I have been harsh
To large confessors, and have hotly asked them
If they had mothers: I had one, a woman,
And women 'twere they wronged. I knew a man
Of eighty winters, this I told them, who
A lass of fourteen brided. 'Twas thy power
To put life into dust: the aged cramp

Had screwed his square foot round,
The gout had knitted his fingers into knots,
Torturing convulsions from his globy eyes
Had almost drawn their spheres, that what was life
In him seemed torture. This anatomy
Had by his young fair fere a boy, and I
Believed it was his, for she swore it was,
And who would not believe her? Brief, I am
To those that prate and have done no companion;
To those that boast and have not a defier;
To those that would and cannot a rejoicer.
Yea, him I do not love, that tells close offices
The foulest way, nor names concealments in
The boldest language. Such a one I am,
And vow that lover never yet made sigh
Truer than I. O then, most soft sweet goddess,
Give me the victory of this question, which
Is true love's merit, and bless me with a sign
Of thy great pleasure.

*Here music is heard, doves are seen to flutter; they fall again*
*upon their faces, then on their knees.*

O thou that from eleven to ninety reign'st
In mortal bosoms, whose chase is this world
And we in herds thy game, I give thee thanks
For this fair token, which being laid unto
Mine innocent true heart, arms in assurance
My body to this business. Let us rise
And bow before the goddess. Time comes on.

                           (V.i.77-90, 94-136)

## A NOTE ON THE TEXT

The present text of the sonnets is based on the quarto of 1609, the only edition of any authority; all subsequent editions of the sonnets derive from that of 1609. Two of the sonnets (138 and 144) had been published, in slightly different versions, in a volume of poems entitled *The Passionate Pilgrim* (1599); quite possibly all or almost all of the sonnets were written in the middle 1590's, though it is equally possible that some were written only shortly before Thorpe issued his quarto with 154 sonnets. There is no evidence that Shakespeare oversaw the publication; probably the order in which the sonnets are presented is the publisher's rather than the author's. In 1640 John Benson issued a second edition. He dropped Thorpe's dedication and eight sonnets, rearranged the order of the remaining ones, made numerous verbal changes to suggest that the sonnets were written to a woman and not to a man, and implied in a preface that the sonnets had never before been published.

The present edition keeps the arrangement of the 1609 quarto, but corrects obvious typographical errors and modernizes spelling and punctuation. Other departures from the quarto are listed below, the present reading first, in boldface type, and then the reading of the quarto in roman.

The textual editor wishes to acknowledge his indebtedness, especially in the glosses, to his late teacher, Hyder Edward Rollins, whose indispensable *New Variorum Edition* is as likely as any scholarly book to bear it out to the edge of doom.

**12.4 are** or  **13.7 Yourself** You selfe  **19.3 jaws** yawes  **19.5 fleets** fleet'st  **25.9 might** worth  **26.12 thy** their  **27.10 thy** their  **34.12 cross** losse  **35.8 thy . . . thy** their . . . their  **41.8 she** he  **43.11 thy** their  **44.13 naught** naughts  **45.12 thy** their  **46.3 thy** their;  **8 thy** their;  **9 'cide** side;  **14 thy** their  **47.11 not** nor  **50.6 dully** duly  **51.10 perfect'st** perfects  **55.1 monuments** monument  **56.13 Or** As  **65.12 of** or  **69.3 due** end;  **5 Thy** Their  **70.1 art** are  **70.6 Thy** Their  **74.12 rememberèd** remembred  **76.7 tell** fel  **77.10 blanks** blacks  **90.11 shall** stall  **91.8 better** bitter  **99.9 One** Our  **102.8 her** his  **111.1 with** wish  **112.14 are** y'are  **113.6 latch** lack;  **14 mine eye** mine  **126.8 minutes** mynuit  **128.11 thy** their;  **14 thy** their  **129.11 proved, a** proud and  **132.6 of the** of th';  **9 mourning** morning  **138.12 to have** t' haue  **144.6 side** sight;  **9 fiend** finde  **153.14 eyes** eye

# THE SONNETS

TO THE ONLY BEGETTER OF
THESE ENSUING SONNETS
MR. W. H. ALL HAPPINESS
AND THAT ETERNITY
PROMISED
BY
OUR EVER-LIVING POET
WISHETH
THE WELL-WISHING
ADVENTURER IN
SETTING
FORTH

T.T.

### 1

From fairest creatures we desire increase,
That thereby beauty's rose might never die,
But as the riper should by time decease,
His tender heir might bear his memory; 4
But thou contracted° to thine own bright eyes,
Feed'st thy light's flame with self-substantial fuel,°
Making a famine where abundance lies,
Thyself thy foe, to thy sweet self too cruel. 8
Thou that art now the world's fresh ornament,
And only° herald to the gaudy spring,
Within thine own bud buriest thy content,°
And, tender churl, mak'st waste in niggarding.° 12
   Pity the world, or else this glutton be,
   To eat the world's due,° by the grave and thee.°

1: **5 contracted** betrothed  **6 self-substantial fuel** fuel of your own substance  **10 only** chief  **11 thy content** what you contain, i.e., potential fatherhood  **12 niggarding** hoarding  **14 world's due** i.e., propagation of the species; **by . . . thee** i.e., by dying without children

*The decorative border shown above appeared on the title page of the first quarto edition of the* Sonnets, *1609.*

The initials concluding the dedication are those of Thomas Thorpe, the publisher of the volume. The identity of Mr. W. H. is uncertain. Most persons who write on the subject have felt it too prosaic to hold that Mr. W. H. was simply a person who brought the poems into the publisher's hands; rather, they have sought to identify him with the friend to whom many of the poems are addressed. The favorite candidates are William Herbert, Earl of Pembroke (and one of the dedicatees of the

### 2

When forty winters shall besiege thy brow,
And dig deep trenches° in thy beauty's field,
Thy youth's proud livery,° so gazed on now,
Will be a tottered weed° of small worth held: 4
Then being asked where all thy beauty lies,
Where all the treasure of thy lusty° days,
To say within thine own deep-sunken eyes,
Were an all-eating shame and thriftless° praise. 8
How much more praise deserved thy beauty's use,°
If thou couldst answer, "This fair child of mine
Shall sum my count,° and make my old excuse,"°
Proving his beauty by succession thine. 12
   This were to be new made when thou art old,
   And see thy blood warm when thou feel'st it cold.

2: **2 trenches** i.e., wrinkles  **3 livery** outward appearance  **4 tottered weed** tattered garment  **6 lusty** vigorous  **8 thriftless** unprofitable  **9 use** investment  **11 sum my count** even out my account; **my old excuse** excuse when I am old

First Folio), and Henry Wriothesley, Earl of Southampton (to whom Shakespeare dedicated *Venus and Adonis* and *The Rape of Lucrece*). But it is unlikely that an earl would be addressed as "Mr." Yet another candidate is Sir William Hervey, third husband of Southampton's mother; his advocates say that Hervey was the "begetter" in the sense that he may have encouraged Shakespeare to write the sonnets urging the young man (allegedly Southampton) to wed.

## 3

Look in thy glass and tell the face thou viewest
Now is the time that face should form another,
Whose fresh repair° if now thou not renewest,
Thou dost beguile the world, unbless some mother.°      4
For where is she so fair whose uneared° womb
Disdains the tillage of thy husbandry?
Or who is he so fond° will be the tomb
Of° his self-love to stop posterity?      8
Thou art thy mother's glass, and she in thee
Calls back the lovely April of her prime;
So thou through windows of thine age shalt see,
Despite of wrinkles, this thy golden time.      12
   But if thou live rememb'red not to be,°
   Die single and thine image dies with thee.

## 4

Unthrifty loveliness, why dost thou spend
Upon thyself thy beauty's legacy?°
Nature's bequest gives nothing but doth lend,
And being frank° she lends to those are free.°      4
Then, beauteous niggard,° why dost thou abuse
The bounteous largess given thee to give?
Profitless usurer, why dost thou use°
So great a sum of sums yet canst not live?°      8
For having traffic° with thyself alone,
Thou of thyself thy sweet self dost deceive.
Then how when Nature calls thee to be gone,
What acceptable audit canst thou leave?      12
   Thy unused beauty must be tombed with thee,
   Which, usèd, lives° th' executor to be.

## 5

Those hours° that with gentle work did frame
The lovely gaze° where every eye doth dwell
Will play the tyrants to the very same
And that unfair° which fairly° doth excel;      4
For never-resting Time leads summer on
To hideous winter and confounds° him there,
Sap checked with frost and lusty leaves quite gone,
Beauty o'ersnowed and bareness everywhere.      8
Then, were not summer's distillation° left
A liquid prisoner pent in walls of glass,
Beauty's effect° with beauty were bereft,
Nor it nor° no remembrance what it was.      12
   But flowers distilled though they with winter meet,
   Leese but their show,° their substance still lives sweet.

## 6

Then let not winter's ragged° hand deface
In thee thy summer ere thou be distilled.
Make sweet some vial; treasure° thou some place
With beauty's treasure ere it be self-killed.      4
That use° is not forbidden usury
Which happies those that pay the willing loan;°
That's for thyself to breed another thee,
Or ten times happier be it ten for one.      8
Ten times thyself were happier° than thou art,
If ten of thine ten times refigured° thee:
Then what could death do if thou shouldst depart,
Leaving thee living in posterity?      12
   Be not self-willed, for thou art much too fair,
   To be death's conquest and make worms thine heir.

## 7

Lo, in the orient° when the gracious light°
Lifts up his burning head, each under° eye
Doth homage to his new-appearing sight,
Serving with looks his sacred majesty;      4
And having climbed the steep-up heavenly hill,
Resembling strong youth in his middle age,
Yet mortal looks° adore his beauty still,
Attending on his golden pilgrimage;      8
But when from highmost pitch,° with weary car,°
Like feeble age he reeleth from the day,
The eyes, 'fore duteous, now converted° are
From his low tract° and look another way:      12
   So thou, thyself outgoing in thy noon,
   Unlooked on diest unless thou get° a son.

## 8

Music to hear,° why hear'st thou music sadly?°
Sweets with sweets war not, joy delights in joy.
Why lov'st thou that which thou receiv'st not gladly,
Or else receiv'st with pleasure thine annoy?      4
If the true concord of well-tunèd sounds,
By unions married, do offend thine ear,
They do but sweetly chide thee, who confounds
In singleness the parts that thou shouldst bear.°      8
Mark how one string, sweet husband to another,°
Strikes each in each by mutual ordering;
Resembling sire, and child, and happy mother,
Who all in one, one pleasing note do sing;      12
   Whose speechless song, being many, seeming one,
   Sings this to thee, "Thou single wilt prove none."°

---

3: **3 fresh repair** youthful state  **4 unbless some mother** leave some woman unblessed with motherhood  **5 uneared** untilled  **7 fond** foolish  **8 Of** because of  **13 rememb'red . . . be** only to be forgotten
4: **2 beauty's legacy** inheritance of beauty  **4 frank, free** generous  **5 niggard** miser  **7 use** (1) invest (2) use up  **8 live** (1) make a living (2) endure  **9 traffic** commerce  **14 lives** i.e., in a son
5: **1 hours** disyllabic  **2 gaze** object gazed on  **4 unfair** make ugly; **fairly** in beauty  **6 confounds** destroys  **9 summer's distillation** perfumes made from flowers  **11 Beauty's effect** i.e., the perfume  **12 Nor . . . nor** (there would be) neither . . . nor  **14 Leese . . . show** lose only their outward form

6: **1 ragged** rough  **3 treasure** enrich  **5 use** lending money at interest  **6 happies . . . loan** makes happy those who willingly pay the loan  **9 happier** luckier  **10 refigured** represented
7: **1 orient** east; **light** sun  **2 under** i.e., earthly  **7 looks** onlookers  **9 highmost pitch** zenith; **car** chariot (of Phoebus)  **11 converted** turned away  **12 tract** track  **14 get** beget
8: **1 Music to hear** you are music to hear; **sadly** gravely  **7–8 confounds . . . bear** i.e., destroys by playing singly the multiple role (of husband and father) that you should play  **9 sweet . . . another** i.e., tuned in unison (so that when struck, its partner vibrates)  **14 none** nothing

## 9

Is it for fear to wet a widow's eye
That thou consum'st thyself in single life?
Ah, if thou issueless° shalt hap° to die,
The world will wail thee like a makeless° wife;                    4
The world will be thy widow and still° weep,
That thou no form of thee hast left behind,
When every private° widow well may keep,
By children's eyes, her husband's shape in mind.                    8
Look what° an unthrift° in the world doth spend,
Shifts but his° place, for still the world enjoys it;
But beauty's waste hath in the world an end,
And kept unused, the user so destroys it:                    12
   No love toward others in that bosom sits
   That on himself such murd'rous shame° commits.

## 10

For shame, deny that thou bear'st love to any
Who for thyself art so unprovident.
Grant if thou wilt, thou art beloved of many,
But that thou none lov'st is most evident;                    4
For thou art so possessed with murd'rous hate,
That 'gainst thyself thou stick'st° not to conspire,
Seeking that beauteous roof° to ruinate,
Which to repair should be thy chief desire.                    8
O, change thy thought, that I may change my mind.
Shall hate be fairer lodged than gentle love?
Be as thy presence° is, gracious and kind,
Or to thyself at least kind-hearted prove.                    12
   Make thee another self for love of me,
   That beauty still° may live in thine or thee.

## 11

As fast as thou shalt wane, so fast thou grow'st
In one of thine, from that which thou departest;
And that fresh blood which youngly° thou bestow'st
Thou mayst call thine, when thou from youth con-
    vertest.°                    4
Herein lives wisdom, beauty, and increase;
Without this,° folly, age, and cold decay.
If all were minded so, the times° should cease,
And threescore year would make the world away.                    8
Let those whom Nature hath not made for store,°
Harsh, featureless, and rude,° barrenly perish.
Look whom° she best endowed, she gave the more;
Which bounteous gift thou shouldst in bounty cherish.                    12
   She carved thee for her seal,° and meant thereby
   Thou shouldst print more, not let that copy die.

## 12

When I do count the clock that tells the time,
And see the brave° day sunk in hideous night;
When I behold the violet past prime,
And sable° curls are silvered o'er with white;                    4
When lofty trees I see barren of leaves,
Which erst° from heat did canopy the herd,
And summer's green, all girded up in sheaves,
Borne on the bier with white and bristly beard;                    8
Then of thy beauty do I question make,°
That thou among the wastes of time must go,
Since sweets and beauties do themselves forsake,
And die as fast as they see others grow,                    12
   And nothing 'gainst Time's scythe can make defense,
   Save breed, to brave° him when he takes thee hence.

## 13

O, that you were yourself, but, love, you are
No longer yours than you yourself here live;
Against° this coming end you should prepare,
And your sweet semblance to some other give.                    4
So should that beauty which you hold in lease°
Find no determination,° then you were
Yourself again after your self's decease,
When your sweet issue° your sweet form should bear.                    8
Who lets so fair a house fall to decay,
Which husbandry° in honor might uphold
Against the stormy gusts of winter's day
And barren rage of death's eternal cold?                    12
   O, none but unthrifts!° Dear my love, you know,
   You had a father; let your son say so.

## 14

Not from the stars do I my judgment pluck,°
And yet methinks I have astronomy;°
But not to tell of good or evil luck,
Of plagues, of dearths, or seasons' quality;                    4
Nor can I fortune to brief minutes tell,°
Pointing° to each his° thunder, rain, and wind,
Or say with princes if it shall go well
By oft predict that° I in heaven find.                    8
But from thine eyes my knowledge I derive,
And, constant stars, in them I read such art°
As° truth and beauty shall together thrive
If from thyself to store° thou wouldst convert:°                    12
   Or else of thee this I prognosticate,
   Thy end is truth's and beauty's doom and date.°

9: 3 **issueless** childless; **hap** happen, chance  4 **makeless** mateless  5 **still** always  7 **private** individual  9 **Look what** whatever; **unthrift** prodigal  10 **his** its  14 **murd'rous shame** shameful murder
10: 6 **stick'st** scruple  7 **roof** i.e., body (which houses the spirit)  11 **presence** appearance  14 **still** always
11: 3 **youngly** in youth  4 **convertest** change  6 **Without this** beyond this course of action  7 **times** generations of men  9 **for store** as stock to draw upon  10 **featureless, and rude** ugly and unrefined  11 **Look whom** whomever  13 **seal** stamp

12: 2 **brave** splendid  4 **sable** black  6 **erst** formerly  9 **question make** entertain doubt  14 **Save . . . brave** except offspring, to defy
13: 3 **Against** in expectation of  5 **in lease** i.e., for a term  6 **determination** end  8 **issue** offspring  10 **husbandry** (1) thrift (2) marriage  13 **unthrifts** prodigals
14: 1 **pluck** derive  2 **astronomy** astrology  5 **fortune . . . tell** i.e., predict the exact time of each happening  6 **Pointing** appointing; **his** its  8 **oft predict that** frequent prediction of what  10 **art** knowledge  11 **As** as that  12 **store** fertility; **convert** turn  14 **doom and date** end, Judgment Day

## 15

When I consider everything that grows
Holds in perfection but a little moment,
That this huge stage presenteth naught but shows
Whereon the stars in secret influence comment;°          4
When I perceive that men as plants increase,
Cheerèd and checked° even by the selfsame sky,
Vaunt° in their youthful sap, at height decrease,
And wear their brave state out of memory;°              8
Then the conceit° of this inconstant stay°
Sets you most rich in youth before my sight,
Where wasteful Time debateth° with Decay,
To change your day of youth to sullied night;          12
   And, all in war with Time for love of you,
   As he takes from you, I engraft° you new.

## 16

But wherefore do not you a mightier way
Make war upon this bloody tyrant Time?
And fortify yourself in your decay
With means more blessèd than my barren rhyme?          4
Now stand you on the top of happy hours,
And many maiden gardens, yet unset,°
With virtuous wish would bear your living flowers,
Much liker than your painted counterfeit.°             8
So should the lines of life° that life repair,
Which this time's pencil,° or my pupil pen,
Neither in inward worth nor outward fair°
Can make you live yourself in eyes of men.             12
   To give away yourself° keeps° yourself still,
   And you must live, drawn by your own sweet skill.

## 17

Who will believe my verse in time to come
If it were filled with your most high deserts?°
Though yet heaven knows it is but as a tomb
Which hides your life and shows not half your parts.°  4
If I could write the beauty of your eyes,
And in fresh numbers° number all your graces,
The age to come would say, "This poet lies,
Such heavenly touches° ne'er touched earthly faces."   8
So should my papers, yellowed with their age,
Be scorned, like old men of less truth than tongue,
And your true rights° be termed a poet's rage°
And stretchèd meter° of an antique song:               12
   But were some child of yours alive that time,
   You should live twice, in it and in my rhyme.

## 18

Shall I compare thee to a summer's day?
Thou art more lovely and more temperate.
Rough winds do shake the darling buds of May,
And summer's lease° hath all too short a date.°        4
Sometime too hot the eye of heaven shines,
And often is his gold complexion dimmed;
And every fair from fair° sometime declines,
By chance, or nature's changing course, untrimmed;°    8
But thy eternal summer shall not fade,
Nor lose possession of that fair thou ow'st,°
Nor shall Death brag thou wand'rest in his shade,
When in eternal lines to time thou grow'st.            12
   So long as men can breathe or eyes can see,
   So long lives this, and this gives life to thee.

## 19

Devouring Time, blunt thou the lion's paws,
And make the earth devour her own sweet brood;
Pluck the keen teeth from the fierce tiger's jaws,
And burn the long-lived phoenix° in her blood;°        4
Make glad and sorry seasons as thou fleets,
And do whate'er thou wilt, swift-footed Time,
To the wide world and all her fading sweets;
But I forbid thee one most heinous crime,              8
O, carve not with thy hours my love's fair brow,
Nor draw no lines there with thine antique° pen.
Him in thy course untainted° do allow,
For beauty's pattern to succeeding men.                12
   Yet do thy worst, old Time; despite thy wrong,
   My love shall in my verse ever live young.

## 20

A woman's face, with Nature's° own hand painted,
Hast thou, the master mistress° of my passion;°
A woman's gentle heart, but not acquainted
With shifting change, as is false women's fashion;     4
An eye more bright than theirs, less false in rolling,°
Gilding the object whereupon it gazeth;
A man in hue° all hues in his controlling,
Which steals men's eyes and women's souls amazeth.     8
And for a woman wert thou first created,
Till Nature as she wrought thee fell a-doting,
And by addition me of thee defeated,°
By adding one thing to my purpose nothing.             12
   But since she pricked thee out° for women's pleasure,
   Mine be thy love, and thy love's use their treasure.

---

**15: 4 in . . . comment** i.e., exert a silent influence  **6 Cheerèd and checked** encouraged and rebuked  **7 Vaunt** boast  **8 wear . . . memory** wear out their handsome condition until it is forgotten  **9 conceit** idea; **stay** duration  **11 debateth** contends  **14 engraft** i.e., with eternizing poetry
**16: 6 unset** unplanted  **8 counterfeit** portrait  **9 lines of life** lineal descendants  **10 time's pencil** artist of the present day  **11 fair** beauty  **13 give away yourself** i.e., to beget children; **keeps** preserves
**17: 2 deserts** rhymes with "parts"  **4 parts** good qualities  **6 numbers** verses  **8 touches** (1) strokes of pencil or brush (2) traits  **11 true rights** due praise; **rage** inspiration  **12 stretchèd meter** poetic exaggeration

**18: 4 lease** allotted time; **date** duration  **7 fair from fair** beautiful thing from beauty  **8 untrimmed** divested of ornament  **10 thou ow'st** you possess
**19: 4 phoenix** mythical bird that periodically is consumed in flames and arises renewed (symbol of immortality); **in her blood** alive  **10 antique** (1) old (2) grotesque, antic  **11 untainted** untouched
**20: 1 Nature's** i.e., not Art's  **2 master mistress** supreme mistress (some editors hyphenate, indicating that in this case the "mistress" is a "master"); **passion** love (or possibly love poems)  **5 rolling** i.e., roving from one to another  **7 hue** appearance (both complexion and form)  **11 defeated** defrauded  **13 pricked thee out** (1) marked you out (2) added a phallus (cf. line 12)

### 21

So is it not with me as with that Muse,°
Stirred° by a painted beauty to his verse,
Who heaven itself for ornament doth use,
And every fair° with his fair doth rehearse;° 4
Making a couplement° of proud compare°
With sun and moon, with earth and sea's rich gems,
With April's first-born flowers, and all things rare
That heaven's air in this huge rondure° hems.° 8
O, let me true in love but truly write,
And then believe me, my love is as fair
As any mother's child, though not so bright
As those gold candles fixed in heaven's air: 12
   Let them say more that like of hearsay well;°
   I will not praise that° purpose not to sell.

### 22

My glass shall not persuade me I am old,
So long as youth and thou are of one date,°
But when in thee Time's furrows I behold,
Then look I death my days should expiate.° 4
For all that beauty that doth cover thee
Is but the seemly raiment of my heart,
Which in thy breast doth live, as thine in me.
How can I then be elder than thou art? 8
O, therefore, love, be of thyself so wary
As I, not for myself, but for thee will,
Bearing thy heart, which I will keep so chary°
As tender nurse her babe from faring ill. 12
   Presume not on° thy heart when mine is slain;
   Thou gav'st me thine, not to give back again.

### 23

As an unperfect actor on the stage,
Who with his fear is put besides his part,
Or some fierce thing replete with too much rage,
Whose strength's abundance weakens his own heart; 4
So I, for fear of trust,° forget to say
The perfect ceremony of love's right,°
And in mine own love's strength seem to decay,
O'ercharged with burden of mine own love's might. 8
O, let my books° be then the eloquence
And dumb presagers° of my speaking breast,
Who plead for love, and look for recompense,
More than that tongue that more hath more expressed.° 12
   O, learn to read what silent love hath writ.
   To hear with eyes belongs to love's fine wit.°

### 24

Mine eye hath played the painter and hath steeled°
Thy beauty's form in table° of my heart;
My body is the frame wherein 'tis held,
And perspective° it is best painter's art, 4
For through the painter must you see his skill,
To find where your true image pictured lies,
Which in my bosom's shop is hanging still,
That hath his° windows glazèd° with thine eyes. 8
Now see what good turns eyes for eyes have done:
Mine eyes have drawn thy shape, and thine for me
Are windows to my breast, wherethrough the sun
Delights to peep, to gaze therein on thee. 12
   Yet eyes this cunning° want° to grace their art,
   They draw but what they see, know not the heart.

### 25

Let those who are in favor with their stars
Of public honor and proud titles boast,
Whilst I whom fortune of such triumph bars,
Unlooked for joy in that° I honor most. 4
Great princes' favorites their fair leaves spread
But° as the marigold at the sun's eye,
And in themselves their pride lies burièd,
For at a frown they in their glory die. 8
The painful° warrior famousèd for might, (worth)
After a thousand victories once foiled,
Is from the book of honor rasèd quite,°
And all the rest forgot for which he toiled. 12
   Then happy I that love and am beloved
   Where I may not remove, nor be removed.

### 26

Lord of my love, to whom in vassalage
Thy merit hath my duty strongly knit,
To thee I send this written ambassage,°
To witness duty, not to show my wit.° 4
Duty so great, which wit so poor as mine
May make seem bare, in wanting° words to show it,
But that I hope some good conceit° of thine
In thy soul's thought, all naked, will bestow it;° 8
Till whatsoever star that guides my moving°
Points on me graciously with fair aspect,°
And puts apparel on my tottered° loving
To show me worthy of thy sweet respect. 12
   Then may I dare to boast how I do love thee;
   Till then, not show my head where thou mayst prove°
      me.

21: 1 Muse poet  2 Stirred inspired  4 fair beautiful thing;
rehearse mention, i.e., compare  5 couplement combination;
compare comparison  8 rondure sphere, world; hems en-
circles  13 that . . . well who delight in empty talk  14 that
who
22: 2 of one date of the same age  4 expiate end  11 chary
carefully  13 Presume not on do not lay claim to
23: 5 for . . . trust fearing to trust myself  6 right pun on
rite  9 books possibly it should be emended to "looks," i.e.,
though silent, he hopes his looks will speak for him  10 dumb
presagers silent foretellers  12 more expressed more often
expressed  14 wit intelligence

24: 1 steeled engraved  2 table tablet, picture  4 perspective
perhaps the idea is that the "frame," in line 3, contributes to the
perspective of the picture it encloses; some editors put a colon
after "perspective"  8 his its; glazèd covered as with glass
13 cunning ability; want lack
25: 4 Unlooked . . . that unexpectedly enjoy that which  6
But only  9 painful painstaking  11 rasèd quite erased
entirely
26: 3 written ambassage message  4 wit mental powers  6
wanting lacking  7 conceit thought  8 all . . . it will accept
(give lodging to) my bare statement  9 moving life  10 aspect
astrological influence  11 tottered tattered  14 prove test

### 27

Weary with toil, I haste me to my bed,
The dear repose for limbs with travel° tired,
But then begins a journey in my head
To work° my mind when body's work's expired;          4
For then my thoughts, from far where I abide,
Intend° a zealous pilgrimage to thee,
And keep my drooping eyelids open wide,
Looking on darkness which the blind do see;          8
Save that my soul's imaginary° sight
Presents thy shadow° to my sightless view,
Which like a jewel hung in ghastly night,
Makes black night beauteous and her old face new.     12
   Lo, thus, by day my limbs, by night my mind,
   For thee, and for myself, no quiet find.

### 28

How can I then return in happy plight
That am debarred the benefit of rest,
When day's oppression is not eased by night,
But day by night and night by day oppressed,          4
And each, though enemies to either's reign,
Do in consent shake hands° to torture me,
The one by toil, the other to complain°
How far I toil, still farther off from thee?          8
I tell the day, to please him, thou art bright
And dost him grace° when clouds do blot the heaven;
So flatter I the swart-complexioned° night,
When sparkling stars twire° not, thou gild'st the even.°  12
   But day doth daily draw my sorrows longer,
   And night doth nightly make grief's length seem
     stronger.

### 29

When, in disgrace° with Fortune and men's eyes,
I all alone beweep my outcast state,
And trouble deaf heaven with my bootless° cries,
And look upon myself and curse my fate,               4
Wishing me like to one more rich in hope,
Featured like him, like him° with friends possessed,
Desiring this man's art,° and that man's scope,°
With what I most enjoy contented least;               8
Yet in these thoughts myself almost despising,
Haply° I think on thee, and then my state,°
Like to the lark at break of day arising
From sullen° earth, sings hymns at heaven's gate;     12
   For thy sweet love rememb'red such wealth brings,
   That then I scorn to change my state with kings.

### 30

When to the sessions° of sweet silent thought
I summon up remembrance of things past,
I sigh the lack of many a thing I sought,
And with old woes new wail° my dear Time's waste.°    4
Then can I drown an eye, unused to flow,
For precious friends hid in death's dateless° night,
And weep afresh love's long since canceled° woe,
And moan th' expense° of many a vanished sight;       8
Then can I grieve at grievances foregone,°
And heavily from woe to woe tell° o'er
The sad account of fore-bemoanèd moan,
Which I new pay as if not paid before.                12
   But if the while I think on thee, dear friend,
   All losses are restored and sorrows end.

### 31

Thy bosom is endearèd° with all hearts
Which I by lacking have supposèd dead;
And there reigns love and all love's loving parts,
And all those friends which I thought burièd.         4
How many a holy and obsequious° tear
Hath dear religious° love stol'n from mine eye,
As interest° of the dead, which° now appear
But things removed that hidden in there lie.          8
Thou art the grave where buried love doth live,
Hung with the trophies° of my lovers gone,
Who all their parts° of me to thee did give;
That due of many° now is thine alone.                 12
   Their images I loved I view in thee,
   And thou, all they, hast all the all of me.

### 32

If thou survive my well-contented day,°
When that churl Death my bones with dust shall cover,
And shalt by fortune once more resurvey
These poor rude lines of thy deceasèd lover,          4
Compare them with the bett'ring° of the time,
And though they be outstripped by every pen,
Reserve° them for my love, not for their rhyme,
Exceeded by the height of happier° men.               8
O, then vouchsafe me but this loving thought:
"Had my friend's Muse grown with this growing age,
A dearer birth than this his love had brought,
To march in ranks of better equipage;°               12
   But since he died, and poets better prove,
   Theirs for their style I'll read, his for his love."

27: 2 travel (1) labor (2) journeying   4 To work to set at work
6 Intend set out upon   9 imaginary imaginative   10 shadow
image
28: 6 shake hands unite   7 the other to complain i.e., the
night causes me to complain   10 dost him grace i.e., shine for
him   11 swart-complexioned dark-complexioned   12 twire
twinkle (?); thou . . . even you brighten the evening
29: 1 disgrace disfavor   3 bootless useless   6 like him, like
him like a second man, like a third man   7 art skill; scope
mental power   10 Haply perchance; state condition   12
sullen gloomy

30: 1 sessions sittings of a court or council   4 new wail newly
bewail; my . . . waste Time's destruction of things dear to me
6 dateless endless   7 canceled i.e., because paid in full   8 expense loss   9 foregone former   10 tell count
31: 1 endearèd made more precious   5 obsequious funereal
6 religious worshipful   7 interest right; which who   10
trophies memorials   11 parts shares   12 That . . . many
that which was due to many
32: 1 my well-contented day i.e., my day of death, whose
arrival will content me   5 bett'ring improved poetry   7
Reserve preserve   8 happier more gifted   12 of better
equipage better equipped

### 33

Full many a glorious morning have I seen
Flatter the mountain tops with sovereign eye,°
Kissing with golden face the meadows green,
Gilding pale streams with heavenly alchemy;     4
Anon° permit the basest° clouds to ride
With ugly rack° on his celestial face,
And from the forlorn° world his visage hide,
Stealing unseen to west with this disgrace.     8
Even so my sun one early morn did shine,
With all triumphant splendor on my brow;
But out alack,° he was but one hour mine,
The region cloud° hath masked him from me now.     12
   Yet him for this my love no whit disdaineth;
   Suns of the world may stain° when heaven's sun
    staineth.

### 34

Why didst thou promise such a beauteous day,
And make me travel forth without my cloak,
To let base° clouds o'ertake me in my way,
Hiding thy brav'ry° in their rotten smoke?°     4
'Tis not enough that through the cloud thou break,
To dry the rain on my storm-beaten face,
For no man well of such a salve can speak,
That heals the wound, and cures not the disgrace.     8
Nor can thy shame give physic° to my grief;
Though thou repent, yet I have still the loss.
Th' offender's sorrow lends but weak relief
To him that bears the strong offense's cross.     12
   Ah, but those tears are pearl which thy love sheeds,°
   And they are rich and ransom° all ill deeds.

### 35

No more be grieved at that which thou hast done:
Roses have thorns, and silver fountains mud,
Clouds and eclipses stain° both moon and sun,
And loathsome canker° lives in sweetest bud.     4
All men make faults, and even I in this,
Authorizing° thy trespass with compare,°
Myself corrupting, salving thy amiss,°
Excusing thy sins more than thy sins are;°     8
For to thy sensual fault I bring in sense°—
Thy adverse party is thy advocate—
And 'gainst myself a lawful plea commence.
Such civil war is in my love and hate     12
   That I an accessory° needs must be
   To that sweet thief which sourly° robs from me.

### 36

Let me confess that we two must be twain,
Although our undivided loves are one.
So shall those blots that do with me remain,
Without thy help, by me be borne alone.     4
In our two loves there is but one respect,°
Though in our lives a separable spite,°
Which though it alter not love's sole° effect,
Yet doth it steal sweet hours from love's delight.     8
I may not evermore acknowledge thee,
Lest my bewailèd guilt should do thee shame;
Nor thou with public kindness honor me,
Unless thou take that honor from thy name.     12
   But do not so; I love thee in such sort
   As, thou being mine, mine is thy good report.°

### 37

As a decrepit father takes delight
To see his active child do deeds of youth,
So I, made lame by Fortune's dearest° spite,
Take all my comfort of° thy worth and truth.     4
For whether beauty, birth, or wealth, or wit,°
Or any of these all, or all, or more,
Entitled in their parts do crownèd sit,°
I make my love engrafted to this store.°     8
So then I am not lame, poor, nor despised
Whilst that this shadow doth such substance give
That I in thy abundance am sufficed
And by a part of all thy glory live.     12
   Look what° is best, that best I wish in thee.
   This wish I have, then ten times happy me!

### 38

How can my Muse want subject to invent,°
While thou dost breathe, that° pour'st into my verse
Thine own sweet argument,° too excellent
For every vulgar paper° to rehearse?°     4
O, give thyself the thanks, if aught in me°
Worthy perusal stand against thy sight;°
For who's so dumb° that cannot write to thee
When thou thyself dost give invention° light?     8
Be thou the tenth Muse, ten times more in worth
Than those old nine which rhymers invocate;°
And he that calls on thee, let him bring forth
Eternal numbers° to outlive long date.°     12
   If my slight Muse do please these curious° days,
   The pain° be mine, but thine shall be the praise.

**33: 2 Flatter . . . eye** i.e., the sun, like a monarch's eye, flatters all that it rests upon  **5 Anon** soon; **basest** darkest  **6 rack** vapory clouds  **7 forlorn** forsaken;  **11 out alack** alas  **12 region cloud** clouds of the upper air  **14 stain** grow dim
**34: 3 base** dark  **4 brav'ry** finery: **rotten smoke** unwholesome vapors  **9 physic** remedy  **13 sheeds** sheds  **14 ransom** atone for
**35: 3 stain** darken  **4 canker** canker worm (that destroys flowers)  **6 Authorizing** justifying; **with compare** by comparison  **7 salving thy amiss** palliating your misbehavior  **8 Excusing . . . are** i.e., offering excuses more abundant than your sins (?)  **9 to . . . sense** perhaps: to your physical fault I add reason ("sense"); possibly, however, "in sense" is a pun on *incense*, i.e., my reason sweetens your sins  **13 accessory** accomplice  **14 sourly** bitterly

**36: 5 but one respect** only one regard  **6 separable spite** spiteful separation  **7 sole** unique  **13–14 But . . . report** this couplet is repeated in Sonnet 96  **14 report** reputation
**37: 3 dearest** most grievous  **4 of** from  **5 wit** intelligence  **7 Entitled . . . sit** sit as king entitled to their places  **8 engrafted . . . store** i.e., fused with and nourished by this abundance  **13 Look what** whatever
**38: 1 want . . . invent** lack subject matter for creation  **2 that** who  **3 argument** subject  **4 vulgar paper** ordinary composition; **rehearse** repeat  **5 in me** of my writings  **6 stand . . . sight** meet your eyes, i.e., be written for you  **7 dumb** mute  **8 invention** imagination  **10 invocate** invoke  **12 numbers** verses; **long date** a distant era  **13 curious** critical  **14 pain** trouble

### 39

O, how thy worth with manners° may I sing,
When thou art all the better part of me?
What can mine own praise to mine own self bring,
And what is't but mine own when I praise thee?      4
Even for° this, let us divided live,
And our dear love lose name of single one,
That by this separation I may give
That due to thee which thou deserv'st alone.      8
O absence, what a torment wouldst thou prove,
Were it not thy sour leisure gave sweet leave
To entertain° the time with thoughts of love,
Which time and thoughts so sweetly dost deceive,      12
  And that thou teachest how to make one twain
  By praising him here who doth hence remain.

### 40

Take all my loves, my love, yea take them all;
What hast thou then more than thou hadst before?
No love, my love, that thou mayst true love call;
All mine was thine, before thou hadst this more.      4
Then if for my love thou my love receivest,
I cannot blame thee for° my love thou usest;°
But yet be blamed, if thou this self° deceivest
By willful taste° of what thyself refusest.      8
I do forgive thy robb'ry, gentle thief,
Although thou steal thee all my poverty;°
And yet love knows it is a greater grief
To bear love's wrong than hate's known° injury.      12
  Lascivious grace,° in whom all ill well shows,
  Kill me with spites; yet we must not be foes.

### 41

Those pretty° wrongs that liberty° commits,
When I am sometime absent from thy heart,
Thy beauty and thy years full well befits,
For still° temptation follows where thou art.      4
Gentle thou art, and therefore to be won;
Beauteous thou art, therefore to be assailed;
And when a woman woos, what woman's son
Will sourly leave her till she have prevailed?      8
Ay me, but yet thou mightst my seat° forbear,
And chide thy beauty and thy straying youth,
Who° lead thee in their riot° even there
Where thou art forced to break a twofold truth:°      12
  Hers, by thy beauty tempting her to thee,
  Thine, by thy beauty being false to me.

### 42

That thou hast her, it is not all my grief,
And yet it may be said I loved her dearly;
That she hath thee is of my wailing chief,°
A loss in love that touches me more nearly.°      4
Loving offenders, thus I will excuse ye:
Thou dost love her, because thou know'st I love her,
And for my sake even so doth she abuse° me,
Suff'ring my friend for my sake to approve° her.      8
If I lose thee, my loss is my love's° gain,
And losing her, my friend hath found that loss:
Both find each other, and I lose both twain,
And both for my sake lay on me this cross.      12
  But here's the joy: my friend and I are one;
  Sweet flattery! Then she loves but me alone.

### 43

When most I wink,° then do mine eyes best see,
For all the day they view things unrespected,°
But when I sleep, in dreams they look on thee
And, darkly bright, are bright in dark directed.      4
Then thou, whose shadow shadows° doth make bright,
How would thy shadow's form° form happy show
To the clear day with thy much clearer light,
When to unseeing eyes thy shade shines so!      8
How would, I say, mine eyes be blessèd made,
By looking on thee in the living day,
When in dead night thy fair imperfect shade
Through heavy sleep on sightless eyes doth stay!      12
  All days are nights to see° till I see thee,
  And nights bright days when dreams do show thee
  me.

###  44

If the dull substance° of my flesh were thought,
Injurious° distance should not stop my way,
For then despite of space I would be brought,
From limits° far remote, where° thou dost stay.      4
No matter then although my foot did stand
Upon the farthest earth removed° from thee;
For nimble thought can jump both sea and land,
As soon as think the place where he° would be.      8
But, ah, thought kills me that I am not thought,
To leap large lengths of miles when thou art gone,
But that so much of earth and water wrought,°
I must attend° time's leisure with my moan,      12
  Receiving naught by elements so slow
  But heavy tears, badges of either's woe.°

42: 3 of . . . chief chief cause of my grief  4 nearly closely
7 abuse deceive  8 approve test, experience sensually  9
love's mistress'
43: 1 wink close my eyes, i.e., sleep  2 unrespected unregarded  5 shadow shadows image darkness  6 thy shadow's
form the body that casts your shadow  13 are . . . see look
like nights
44: 1 dull substance i.e., earth and water (in contrast to air and
fire)  2 Injurious malicious  4 limits districts; where to
where  6 farthest earth removed earth farthest removed  8
he it  11 wrought compounded  12 attend await  14
badges . . . woe i.e., earth's because heavy, water's because
wet (and perhaps because salty)

39: 1 with manners i.e., without self-praise  5 for because of
11 entertain pass
40: 6 for because; thou usest you are intimate with  7 this
self i.e., your other self, the poet ("this self" is, however, often
emended to "thy self")  8 willful taste capricious enjoyment
10 my poverty the little I have  12 known open  13
Lascivious grace i.e., you who have such grace even when
lascivious
41: 1 pretty petty (?); liberty licentiousness  4 still always
9 seat place  11 Who which; riot revels  12 truth duty

The other two,° slight° air and purging fire,
Are both with thee, wherever I abide;
The first my thought, the other my desire,
These present-absent° with swift motion slide.     4
For when these quicker elements are gone
In tender embassy of love to thee,
My life, being made of four, with two alone°
Sinks down to death, oppressed with melancholy;     8
Until life's composition be recured°
By those swift messengers° returned from thee,
Who even but now come back again, assured
Of thy fair health, recounting it to me.     12
 This told, I joy, but then no longer glad,
 I send them back again, and straight grow sad.

Mine eye and heart are at a mortal war
How to divide the conquest of thy sight;°
Mine eye my heart thy picture's sight would bar,
My heart mine eye the freedom of that right.     4
My heart doth plead that thou in him dost lie—
A closet never pierced with crystal eyes;
But the defendant doth that plea deny,
And says in him thy fair appearance lies.     8
To 'cide this title is impanelèd
A quest° of thoughts, all tenants to the heart;
And by their verdict is determinèd
The clear eye's moiety,° and the dear heart's part:     12
 As thus—mine eye's due is thy outward part,
 And my heart's right thy inward love of heart.

Betwixt mine eye and heart a league is took,°
And each doth good turns now unto the other.
When that mine eye is famished for a look,
Or heart in love with sighs himself doth smother,     4
With my love's picture then my eye doth feast,
And to the painted banquet bids my heart.
Another time mine eye is my heart's guest
And in his° thoughts of love doth share a part.     8
So, either by thy picture or my love,
Thyself away are present still with me;
For thou not farther than my thoughts canst move,
And I am still° with them, and they with thee;     12
 Or, if thy sleep, thy picture in my sight
 Awakes my heart to heart's and eye's delight.

48

How careful was I, when I took my way,
Each trifle° under truest° bars to thrust,
That to my use it might unusèd stay
From hands of falsehood, in sure wards° of trust!     4
But thou, to° whom my jewels trifles are,
Most worthy comfort, now my greatest grief,
Thou best of dearest, and mine only care,
Art left the prey of every vulgar° thief.     8
Thee have I not locked up in any chest,°
Save where thou art not, though I feel thou art,
Within the gentle closure of my breast,
From whence at pleasure thou mayst come and part;     12
 And even thence thou wilt be stol'n, I fear,
 For truth° proves thievish for a prize so dear.

49

Against° that time, if ever that time come,
When I shall see thee frown on my defects,
Whenas thy love hath cast his utmost sum,°
Called to that audit by advised respects;°     4
Against that time when thou shalt strangely° pass,
And scarcely greet me with that sun, thine eye,
When love, converted from the thing it was,
Shall reasons find of settled gravity.     8
Against that time do I ensconce me° here
Within the knowledge of mine own desart,°
And this my hand against myself uprear,°
To guard the lawful reasons on thy part.     12
 To leave poor me thou hast the strength of laws,
 Since why to love I can allege no cause.

How heavy° do I journey on the way
When what I seek, my weary travel's end,
Doth teach that ease and that repose to say,
"Thus far the miles are measured from thy friend."     4
The beast that bears me, tired with my woe,
Plods dully on, to bear that weight in me,
As if by some instinct the wretch did know
His rider loved not speed, being made from thee.     8
The bloody spur cannot provoke him on,
That sometimes anger thrusts into his hide,
Which heavily he answers with a groan,
More sharp to me than spurring to his side;     12
 For that same groan doth put this in my mind:
 My grief lies onward and my joy behind.

45: 1 two i.e., of the four elements (see note on the first line of Sonnet 44); slight insubstantial   4 present-absent now here, now gone   7 two alone i.e., earth and water   9 recured restored to health   10 messengers i.e., fire and air
46: 2 conquest . . . sight i.e., the right to gaze on you   10 quest inquest, jury   12 moiety portion
47: 1 league is took agreement is made   8 his the heart's   12 still always

48: 2 trifle i.e., in comparison with the person addressed; truest most trusty   4 wards cells   5 to in comparison with   8 vulgar common   9 chest (1) coffer (2) breast   14 truth honesty
49: 1 Against in preparation for   3 cast . . . sum computed its final reckoning   4 advised respects well-considered reasons   5 strangely with a reserved manner (like a stranger)   9 ensconce me fortify myself   10 desart desert   11 uprear raise as a witness
50: 1 heavy sadly

## 51

Thus can my love excuse the slow offense°
Of my dull bearer, when from thee I speed:
From where thou art why should I haste me thence?
Till I return, of posting° is no need.        4
O, what excuse will my poor beast then find
When swift extremity° can seem but slow?
Then should I spur, though mounted on the wind,
In wingèd speed no motion shall I know.        8
Then can no horse with my desire keep pace;
Therefore desire, of perfect'st love being made,
Shall neigh,° no dull flesh in his fiery race;
But love, for love, thus shall excuse my jade:°        12
    Since from thee going he went willful slow,
    Towards thee I'll run and give him leave to go.°

## 52

So am I as the rich, whose blessèd key°
Can bring him to his sweet up-lockèd treasure,
The which he will not ev'ry hour survey,
For° blunting the fine point of seldom pleasure.°        4
Therefore are feasts so solemn and so rare,
Since, seldom coming, in the long year set,
Like stones of worth they thinly placèd are,
Or captain° jewels in the carcanet.°        8
So is the time that keeps you as my chest,
Or as the wardrobe which the robe doth hide,
To make some special instant special blest,
By new unfolding his° imprisoned pride.        12
    Blessèd are you whose worthiness gives scope,
    Being had, to triumph, being lacked, to hope.

## 53

What is your substance, whereof are you made,
That millions of strange shadows° on you tend?°
Since everyone hath, every one, one shade,°
And you, but one, can every shadow lend.°        4
Describe Adonis, and the counterfeit°
Is poorly imitated after you;
On Helen's cheek all art of beauty set,
And you in Grecian tires° are painted new.        8
Speak of the spring and foison° of the year;
The one doth shadow of your beauty show,
The other as your bounty doth appear,
And you in every blessèd shape we know.        12
    In all external grace you have some part,
    But you like none, none you, for constant heart.

## 54

O, how much more doth beauty beauteous seem,
By that sweet ornament which truth° doth give!
The rose looks fair, but fairer we it deem
For that sweet odor which doth in it live.        4
The canker blooms° have full as deep a dye,
As the perfumèd tincture° of the roses,
Hang on such thorns, and play as wantonly,°
When summer's breath their maskèd° buds discloses;°        8
But, for° their virtue only° is their show,
They live unwooed and unrespected° fade,
Die to themselves. Sweet roses do not so;
Of their sweet deaths are sweetest odors made.°        12
    And so of you, beauteous and lovely youth,
    When that shall vade,° by verse distills your truth.°

## 55

Nor marble, nor the gilded monuments
Of princes, shall outlive this pow'rful rhyme,
But you shall shine more bright in these contents°
Than° unswept stone,° besmeared with sluttish time.        4
When wasteful war shall statues overturn,
And broils° root out the work of masonry,
Nor Mars his° sword nor° war's quick fire shall burn°
The living record of your memory.        8
'Gainst death and all oblivious enmity°
Shall you pace forth; your praise shall still find room
Even in the eyes of all posterity
That wear this world out° to the ending doom.        12
    So, till the judgment that° yourself arise,
    You live in this, and dwell in lovers'° eyes.

---

**51: 1 slow offense** offense of slowness   **4 posting** riding hastily   **6 swift extremity** extreme swiftness   **11 neigh** i.e., in exultation in its ethereal speed (?) (some editors emend to "weigh" with the meaning that desire refuses to keep to the slow pace of the horse and will not weigh down the horse's "dull flesh")   **12 jade** nag   **14 go** walk
**52: 1 key** rhymes with "survey"   **4 For** for fear of; **seldom pleasure** pleasure infrequently enjoyed   **8 captain** chief; **carcanet** collar of jewels   **12 his** its
**53: 2 strange shadows** images not your own (the images of Adonis, Helen, spring, and autumn in the following lines); **tend** wait on   **3 shade** shadow   **4 And . . . lend** and you, though one, can provide a variety of good traits (?)   **5 counterfeit** picture   **8 tires** attire   **9 foison** rich harvest

**54: 2 truth** fidelity   **5 canker blooms** dog roses (which lack the perfume of the damask rose)   **6 tincture** color   **7 wantonly** unrestrainedly   **8 maskèd** hidden; **discloses** opens   **9 for** because; **virtue only** only merit   **10 unrespected** unregarded   **12 are . . . made** perfumes are made   **14 vade** depart, perish; **by . . . truth** by means of verse your essence is distilled ("by" is often emended to "my")
**55: 3 these contents** i.e., the contents of this poem   **4 Than** than in; **stone** memorial tablet in the floor of a church   **6 broils** skirmishes   **7 Nor . . . nor** neither . . . nor; **Mars his** Mars'; **burn** either metaphorically governs "Mars his sword" as well as "war's quick fire," or the verb governing "Mars his sword" is omitted   **9 all oblivious enmity** all enmity that brings oblivion (?) enmity that brings oblivion to all (?)   **12 wear . . . out** outlasts this world   **13 judgment that** Judgment Day when   **14 lovers'** admirers'

## 56

Sweet love,° renew thy force; be it not said
Thy edge° should blunter be than appetite,°
Which but today by feeding is allayed,
Tomorrow sharp'ned in his former might.                    4
So, love, be thou; although today thou fill
Thy hungry eyes even till they wink° with fullness,
Tomorrow see again, and do not kill
The spirit of love with a perpetual dullness.              8
Let this sad int'rim° like the ocean be
Which parts the shore where two contracted new°
Come daily to the banks, that, when they see
Return of love, more blest may be the view;                12
   Or call it winter, which being full of care,
   Makes summer's welcome thrice more wished, more
      rare.

## 57

Being your slave, what should I do but tend°
Upon the hours and times of your desire?
I have no precious time at all to spend,
Nor services to do till you require.                       4
Nor dare I chide the world-without-end° hour
Whilst I, my sovereign, watch the clock for you,
Nor think° the bitterness of absence sour
When you have bid your servant once adieu.                 8
Nor dare I question° with my jealous thought
Where you may be, or your affairs suppose,°
But, like a sad slave, stay and think of naught
Save where you are how happy you make those.               12
   So true a fool is love that in your will,°
   Though you do anything, he thinks no ill.

## 58

That god forbid that made me first your slave
I should in thought control your times of pleasure,
Or at your hand th' account of hours to crave,
Being your vassal bound to stay your leisure.°             4
O, let me suffer, being at your beck,
Th' imprisoned absence of your liberty;°
And patience, tame to sufferance, bide each check,°
Without accusing you of injury.°                           8
Be where you list,° your charter° is so strong
That you yourself may privilege° your time
To what you will; to you it doth belong
Yourself to pardon of self-doing° crime.                   12
   I am to° wait, though waiting so be hell,
   Not blame your pleasure, be it ill or well.

## 59

If there be nothing new, but that which is
Hath been before, how are our brains beguiled,
Which, laboring for invention,° bear amiss
The second burden of a former child!°                      4
O, that record° could with a backward look,
Even of five hundred courses of the sun,°
Show me your image in some antique book,
Since mind at first in character was done;°               8
That I might see what the old world could say
To this composèd wonder° of your frame;
Whether we are mended,° or whe'r° better they,
Or whether revolution be the same.°                        12
   O, sure I am the wits° of former days
   To subjects worse have given admiring praise.

## 60

Like as the waves make towards the pebbled shore,
So do our minutes hasten to their end;
Each changing place with that which goes before,
In sequent° toil all forwards do contend.                  4
Nativity, once in the main of light,°
Crawls to maturity, wherewith being crowned,
Crooked° eclipses 'gainst his glory fight,
And Time that gave doth now his gift confound.°            8
Time doth transfix° the flourish set on youth,
And delves the parallels° in beauty's brow,
Feeds on the rarities of nature's truth,
And nothing stands but for his scythe to mow:              12
   And yet to times in hope° my verse shall stand,
   Praising thy worth, despite his cruel hand.

## 61

Is it thy will thy image should keep open
My heavy eyelids to the weary night?
Dost thou desire my slumbers should be broken
While shadows° like to thee do mock my sight?             4
Is it thy spirit that thou send'st from thee
So far from home into my deeds to pry,
To find out shames and idle hours in me,
The scope and tenure of thy jealousy?°                     8
O no, thy love, though much, is not so great.
It is my love that keeps mine eye awake,
Mine own true love that doth my rest defeat,°
To play the watchman ever for thy sake.                    12
   For thee watch° I, whilst thou dost wake° elsewhere,
   From me far off, with others all too near.

**56: 1 love** spirit of love, i.e., not the beloved **2 edge** keenness;
**appetite** lust **6 wink** shut in sleep **9 sad int'rim** period of
estrangement (?) **10 contracted new** newly betrothed
**57: 1 tend** wait **5 world-without-end** seemingly endless **7
Nor think** nor dare I think **9 question** dispute **10 suppose**
guess at **13 will** desire (with pun on Shakespeare's first name)
**58: 4 stay your leisure** wait until you are unoccupied **6 imprisoned . . . liberty** imprisonment brought to me by your
freedom to absent yourself **7 And . . . check** and patience,
disciplined to accept suffering, endures every rebuke **8 injury**
injustice **9 list** wish; **charter** privilege **10 privilege**
authorize **12 self-doing** (1) done by one's self (2) done to one's
self **13 am to** must

**59: 3 for invention** i.e., to create something new **3-4 bear
. . . child** futilely bring forth only a reproduction of what had
already been created **5 record** memory **6 courses . . . sun**
years **8 Since . . . done** since thought was first expressed in
writing **10 composèd wonder** wonderful composition **11
mended** bettered; **whe'r** whether **12 revolution . . . same**
i.e., cycles are repeated **13 wits** men of intellect
**60: 4 sequent** successive **5 Nativity . . . light** i.e., the newborn, at first in the ocean (metaphorical for "great expanse" or
"flood") of light **7 Crooked** malignant **8 confound**
destroy **9 transfix** destroy **10 delves the parallels** i.e., digs
wrinkles **13 times in hope** future times
**61: 4 shadows** images **8 scope . . . jealousy** aim and meaning of your suspicion **11 defeat** destroy **13 watch** keep
awake; **wake** revel at night (with pun on the sense of "wake up
in bed")

## 62

Sin of self-love possesseth all mine eye
And all my soul and all my every part;
And for this sin there is no remedy,
It is so grounded inward in my heart.                                    4
Methinks no face so gracious° is as mine,
No shape so true, no truth of such account,
And for myself mine own worth do define,
As° I all other° in all worths surmount.                                 8
But when my glass shows me myself indeed,
Beated and chopped° with tanned antiquity,°
Mine own self-love quite contrary I read;
Self so self-loving were iniquity.                                       12
   'Tis thee, myself,° that for° myself I praise,
   Painting my age with beauty of thy days.°

## 63

Against° my love shall be as I am now,
With Time's injurious hand crushed and o'erworn;
When hours have drained his blood and filled his brow
With lines and wrinkles, when his youthful morn                         4
Hath traveled on to Age's steepy night,°
And all those beauties whereof now he's king
Are vanishing, or vanished out of sight,
Stealing away the treasure of his spring;                               8
For such a time do I now fortify°
Against confounding° Age's cruel knife,°
That he shall never cut from memory
My sweet love's beauty, though my lover's life.°                        12
   His beauty shall in these black lines be seen,
   And they shall live, and he in them still green.

## 64

When I have seen by Time's fell° hand defaced
The rich proud cost° of outworn buried age,°
When sometime° lofty towers I see down-razed,
And brass eternal° slave to mortal rage;°                               4
When I have seen the hungry ocean gain
Advantage° on the kingdom of the shore,
And the firm soil win of the wat'ry main,
Increasing store with loss and loss with store;°                        8
When I have seen such interchange of state,°
Or state itself confounded° to decay,
Ruin hath taught me thus to ruminate,
That Time will come and take my love away.                              12
   This thought is as a death, which cannot choose
   But weep to have° that which it fears to lose.

## 65

Since° brass, nor stone, nor earth, nor boundless sea,
But sad mortality o'ersways their power,
How with this rage° shall beauty hold° a plea,
Whose action° is no stronger than a flower?                             4
O, how shall summer's honey breath hold out
Against the wrackful° siege of batt'ring days,
When rocks impregnable are not so stout,
Nor gates of steel so strong but Time decays?°                          8
O, fearful meditation, where, alack,
Shall Time's best jewel from Time's chest lie hid?°
Or what strong hand can hold his swift foot back,
Or who his spoil° of beauty can forbid?                                 12
   O, none, unless this miracle have might,
   That in black ink my love° may still shine bright.

## 66

Tired with all these, for restful death I cry,
As,° to behold desert° a beggar born,
And needy nothing trimmed in jollity,°
And purest faith unhappily forsworn,°                                   4
And gilded° honor shamefully misplaced,
And maiden virtue rudely strumpeted,
And right perfection wrongfully disgraced,°
And strength by limping sway° disabled,                                 8
And art made tongue-tied by authority,
And folly (doctorlike°) controlling skill,
And simple° truth miscalled simplicity,°
And captive good attending° captain ill.                                12
   Tired with all these, from these would I be gone,
   Save that to die, I leave my love alone.

---

**62: 5 gracious** attractive  **8 As** as though; **other** others  **10 chopped** creased; **antiquity** old age  **13 myself** my alter ego; **that for** whom as  **14 days** i.e., youth
**63: 1 Against** in expectation of the time when  **5 Age's steepy night** i.e., old age, which precipitously leads to the darkness of death  **9 fortify** build defenses  **10 confounding** destructive; **knife** i.e., Time's scythe  **12 my lover's life** (1) the life of my lover (2) the life of me, the lover
**64: 1 fell** cruel  **2 cost** splendor; **age** past times  **3 sometime** once  **4 brass eternal** everlasting brass; **mortal rage** the rage of mortality  **6 Advantage** i.e., inroads  **8 Increasing . . . store** i.e., now one increases in abundance ("store") with the other's loss, now one repairs its loss with abundance taken from the other  **9 state** condition (but in line 10 "state" = greatness)  **10 confounded** destroyed  **14 to have** because it has

**65: 1 Since** since there is neither  **3 rage** fury; **hold** maintain  **4 action** case, suit  **6 wrackful** destructive  **8 decays** causes them to decay  **10 from . . . hid** i.e., conceal itself to avoid being enclosed in Time's coffer  **12 spoil** plundering  **14 my love** my beloved
**66: 2 As** for instance; **desert** a deserving person  **3 needy . . . jollity** i.e., a nonentity, who is poor in virtues, festively attired  **4 unhappily forsworn** miserably perjured  **5 gilded** golden  **7 disgraced** disfigured  **8 limping sway** i.e., incompetent authority  **10 doctorlike** with the air of a learned man  **11 simple** pure; **simplicity** stupidity  **12 attending** subordinated to

### 67

Ah, wherefore with infection° should he live,
And with his presence grace impiety,
That sin by him advantage should achieve
And lace° itself with his society?                                                4
Why should false painting° imitate his cheek
And steal dead seeing° of his living hue?
Why should poor° beauty indirectly° seek
Roses of shadow,° since his rose is true?                                8
Why should he live, now Nature bankrout° is,
Beggared of blood to blush through lively veins,°
For she hath no exchequer° now but his,
And, proud° of many, lives upon his gains?               12
   O, him she stores, to show what wealth she had,
   In days long since, before these last so bad.

### 68

Thus is his cheek the map° of days outworn,°
When beauty lived and died as flowers do now,
Before these bastard signs of fair° were born,°
Or durst inhabit on a living brow;                                            4
Before the golden tresses of the dead,
The right of sepulchers, were shorn away
To live a second life on second head,
Ere beauty's dead fleece made another gay.                        8
In him those holy antique hours° are seen,
Without all° ornament, itself and true,
Making no summer of another's green,
Robbing no old to dress his beauty new;                          12
   And him as for a map doth Nature store,°
   To show false Art what beauty was of yore.

### 69

Those parts° of thee that the world's eye doth view
Want° nothing that the thought of hearts can mend;
All tongues, the voice of souls, give thee that due,
Utt'ring bare truth, even so as foes commend.°               4
Thy outward thus with outward praise is crowned,
But those same tongues that give thee so thine own°
In other accents do this praise confound°
By seeing farther than the eye hath shown.                      8
They look into the beauty of thy mind,
And that in guess they measure by thy deeds;
Then, churls, their thoughts, although their eyes were
   kind,
To thy fair flower add the rank smell of weeds;          12
   But why thy odor matcheth not thy show,
   The soil° is this, that thou dost common grow.

### 70

That thou art blamed shall not be thy defect,
For slander's mark was ever yet the fair;
The ornament of beauty is suspect,°
A crow that flies in heaven's sweetest air.                        4
So° thou be good, slander doth but approve°
Thy worth the greater, being wooed of time;°
For canker vice° the sweetest buds doth love,
And thou present'st a pure unstainèd prime.                   8
Thou hast passed by the ambush of young days,°
Either not assailed, or victor being charged;°
Yet this thy praise cannot be so thy praise
To tie up envy,° evermore enlarged.°                              12
   If some suspect of ill masked not thy show,°
   Then thou alone kingdoms of hearts shouldst owe.°

### 71

No longer mourn for me when I am dead
Than you shall hear the surly sullen bell
Give warning to the world that I am fled
From this vile world with vilest worms to dwell.            4
Nay, if you read this line, remember not
The hand that writ it, for I love you so
That I in your sweet thoughts would be forgot,
If thinking on me then should make you woe.                 8
O, if, I say, you look upon this verse,
When I, perhaps, compounded am with clay,
Do not so much as my poor name rehearse,
But let your love even with my life decay,                      12
   Lest the wise world should look into your moan,
   And mock you with me after I am gone.

---

**67: 1 infection** an age of corruption  **4 lace** adorn  **5 false painting** the reference is possibly to the use of cosmetics or possibly to portraiture  **6 dead seeing** the lifeless appearance (though perhaps "seeing" should be emended to "seeming")  **7 poor** second-rate; **indirectly** by imitation  **8 of shadow** painted (?)  **9 bankrout** bankrupt  **10 Beggared . . . veins** i.e., so impoverished that it can blush only with the aid of cosmetics  **11 exchequer** treasury (of natural beauty)  **12 proud** perhaps "falsely proud," but possibly should be emended to " 'prived," i.e., deprived
**68: 1 map** representation, picture; **days outworn** past times  **3 bastard . . . fair** false appearances (cosmetics, wigs) of beauty; **born** with pun on *borne*  **9 antique hours** ancient times  **10 all** any  **13 store** preserve

**69: 1 parts** outward qualities  **2 Want** lack  **4 even . . . commend** i.e., without exaggeration  **6 so thine own** i.e., your due  **7 confound** destroy  **14 soil** (1) ground (2) blemish
**70: 3 ornament . . . suspect** suspicion (because it always seeks out the beautiful) is an ornament of beauty  **5 So** provided that; **approve** prove  **6 wooed of time** i.e., tempted to evil by the present times  **7 canker vice** vice like a canker worm (which preys on buds)  **9 ambush . . . days** snares of youth  **10 charged** attacked  **12 tie up envy** overcome malice; **enlarged** at liberty  **13 If . . . show** i.e., if some suspicion of evil did not surround you  **14 owe** own

## 72

O, lest the world should task you to recite°
What merit lived in me that you should love
After my death, dear love, forget me quite,
For you in me can nothing worthy prove;°          4
Unless you would devise some virtuous lie,
To do more for me than mine own desert,°
And hang more praise upon deceasèd I
Than niggard° truth would willingly impart.       8
O, lest your true love may seem false in this,
That you for love speak well of me untrue,°
My name be° buried where my body is,
And live no more to shame nor me nor° you:        12
  For I am shamed by that which I bring forth,
  And so should you, to love things nothing worth.

## 73

That time of year thou mayst in me behold
When yellow leaves, or none, or few, do hang
Upon those boughs which shake against the cold,
Bare ruined choirs° where late the sweet birds sang.   4
In me thou see'st the twilight of such day
As after sunset fadeth in the west,
Which by and by° black night doth take away,
Death's second self,° that seals up° all in rest.      8
In me thou see'st the glowing of such fire
That° on the ashes of his youth doth lie,
As the deathbed whereon it must expire,
Consumed with that which it was nourished by.         12
  This thou perceiv'st, which makes thy love more
      strong,
  To love that° well which thou must leave ere long.

## 74

But be contented. When that fell° arrest
Without all bail° shall carry me away,
My life hath in this line° some interest°
Which for memorial still° with thee shall stay.    4
When thou reviewest this, thou dost review
The very part was consecrate to thee.
The earth can have but earth, which is his° due;
My spirit is thine, the better part of me.         8
So then thou hast but lost the dregs of life,
The prey of worms, my body being dead;
The coward conquest° of a wretch's° knife,
Too base of thee to be rememberèd.                 12
  The worth of that is that which it contains,
  And that is this, and this with thee remains.°

## 75

So are you to my thoughts as food to life,
Or as sweet-seasoned° showers are to the ground;
And for the peace of you° I hold such strife
As 'twixt a miser and his wealth is found;         4
Now proud as an enjoyer,° and anon°
Doubting° the filching age will steal his treasure;
Now counting best to be with you alone,
Then bettered° that the world may see my pleasure;  8
Sometime all full with feasting on your sight,
And by and by° clean° starvèd for a look;
Possessing or pursuing no delight
Save what is had or must from you be took.         12
  Thus do I pine and surfeit day by day,
  Or gluttoning on all, or° all away.

## 76

Why is my verse so barren of new pride,°
So far from variation or quick change?
Why with the time° do I not glance aside
To new-found methods and to compounds° strange?   4
Why write I still all one,° ever the same,
And keep invention° in a noted weed,°
That every word doth almost tell my name,
Showing their birth, and where° they did proceed?  8
O, know, sweet love, I always write of you,
And you and love are still my argument.°
So all my best is dressing old words new,
Spending again what is already spent:             12
  For as the sun is daily new and old,
  So is my love still telling what is told.

## 77

Thy glass will show thee how thy beauties wear,
Thy dial° how thy precious minutes waste;
The vacant leaves° thy mind's imprint will bear,
And of this book this learning mayst thou taste.   4
The wrinkles which thy glass will truly show,
Of mouthèd° graves, will give thee memory;°
Thou by thy dial's shady stealth° mayst know
Time's thievish progress to eternity.              8
Look what° thy memory cannot contain,
Commit to these waste blanks,° and thou shalt find
Those children° nursed, delivered from thy brain,
To take a new acquaintance of thy mind.           12
  These offices,° so oft as thou wilt look,
  Shall profit thee, and much enrich thy book.

**72: 1 recite** tell **4 prove** find **6 desert** rhymes with "impart" **8 niggard** miserly **10 untrue** untruly **11 My name be** let my name be **12 nor . . . nor** neither . . . nor
**73: 4 choirs** the part of the chancel in which the service is performed **7 by and by** shortly **8 Death's second self** i.e., sleep; **seals up** encloses (with a suggestion of sealing a coffin) **10 That** as **14 that** i.e., that substance, the poet
**74: 1 fell** cruel **2 Without all bail** i.e., without any possibility of release **3 line** verse; **interest** part **4 still** always **7 his** its **11 The coward conquest** i.e., conquest that even a coward can make; **wretch's** Death's (or possibly Time's) **13–14 The . . . remains** i.e., The value of the body is in the spirit it contains, and this spirit is in the poem and remains with you

**75: 2 sweet-seasoned** of the sweet season, spring **3 peace of you** i.e., the peace I find because of you **5 enjoyer** possessor; **anon** soon **6 Doubting** fearing **8 bettered** made happier **10 by and by** soon; **clean** wholly **14 Or . . . or** either . . . or
**76: 1 pride** adornment **3 with the time** (1) following the present fashion (2) with the passage of time **4 compounds** (1) compositions (2) compound words **5 still all one** always one way **6 invention** imaginative creation; **noted weed** well-known dress **8 where** whence **10 argument** theme
**77: 2 dial** sundial **3 vacant leaves** i.e., the blank leaves (of a memorandum book, or "table" as in Sonnet 122) **6 mouthèd** i.e., gaping, openmouthed; **give thee memory** remind you **7 shady stealth** slowly moving shadow **9 Look what** whatever **10 waste blanks** blank pages **11 children** i.e., your thoughts **13 offices** duties (of looking at the mirror, the sundial, and the thoughts in the book)

### 78

So oft have I invoked thee for my Muse
And found such fair assistance in my verse
As° every alien pen° hath got my use°
And under thee° their poesy disperse.    4
Thine eyes, that taught the dumb on high° to sing
And heavy ignorance aloft to fly,
Have added feathers to the learnèd's wing,
And given grace° a double majesty.    8
Yet be most proud of that which I compile,°
Whose influence° is thine, and born of thee.
In others' works thou dost but mend the style,
And arts with thy sweet graces gracèd be;    12
    But thou art all my art and dost advance
    As high as learning my rude° ignorance.

### 79

Whilst I alone did call upon thy aid,
My verse alone had all thy gentle grace;
But now my gracious numbers° are decayed,
And my sick Muse doth give another place.°    4
I grant, sweet love, thy lovely argument°
Deserves the travail of a worthier pen,
Yet what of thee thy poet doth invent
He robs thee of, and pays it thee again.    8
He lends thee virtue, and he stole that word
From thy behavior; beauty doth he give,
And found it in thy cheek; he can afford°
No praise to thee but what in thee doth live.    12
    Then thank him not for that which he doth say,
    Since what he owes° thee thou thyself dost pay.

### 80

O, how I faint° when I of you do write,
Knowing a better spirit° doth use your name,
And in the praise thereof spends all his might,
To make me tongue-tied speaking of your fame.    4
But since your worth, wide as the ocean is,
The humble° as° the proudest sail doth bear,
My saucy bark, inferior far to his,
On your broad main doth willfully° appear.    8
Your shallowest help will hold me up afloat
Whilst he upon your soundless° deep doth ride;
Or, being wracked,° I am a worthless boat,°
He of tall building,° and of goodly pride.°    12
    Then if he thrive, and I be cast away,
    The worst was this: my love was my decay.°

### 81

Or° I shall live your epitaph to make,
Or you survive when I in earth am rotten.
From hence° your memory death cannot take,
Although in me each part° will be forgotten.    4
Your name from hence° immortal life shall have,
Though I, once gone, to all the world must die.
The earth can yield me but a common grave,
When you entombèd in men's eyes shall lie.    8
Your monument shall be my gentle verse,
Which eyes not yet created shall o'erread,
And tongues to be your being shall rehearse°
When all the breathers of this world are dead.    12
    You still shall live—such virtue° hath my pen—
    Where breath° most breathes, even in the mouths of
    men.

### 82

I grant thou wert not married to° my Muse,
And therefore mayst without attaint° o'erlook°
The dedicated° words which writers use
Of their fair subject, blessing every book.    4
Thou art as fair in knowledge as in hue,°
Finding thy worth a limit° past my praise;
And therefore art enforced to seek anew
Some fresher stamp° of the time-bettering° days.    8
And do so, love; yet when they have devised
What strainèd touches rhetoric can lend,
Thou, truly fair,° wert truly sympathized°
In true plain words by thy true-telling friend:    12
    And their gross painting might be better used
    Where cheeks need blood; in thee it is abused.

### 83

I never saw that you did painting need,
And therefore to your fair° no painting set;
I found, or thought I found, you did exceed
The barren tender of a poet's debt;°    4
And therefore have I slept in your report,°
That you yourself, being extant, well might show
How far a modern° quill doth come too short,
Speaking of worth, what worth in you doth grow.    8
This silence for my sin you did impute,
Which shall be most my glory, being dumb;
For I impair not beauty, being mute,
When others would give life and bring a tomb.    12
    There lives more life in one of your fair eyes
    Than both your poets can in praise devise.

---

**78: 3 As** that; **alien pen** pen belonging to others; **got my use** adopted my practice (either style or subject matter) **4 under thee** i.e., with you as patron **5 on high** (1) aloud (2) loftily **8 grace** excellence **9 compile** write **10 influence** inspiration **14 rude** unrefined
**79: 3 gracious numbers** pleasing verses **4 give another place** yield to another **5 thy lovely argument** the theme of your loveliness **11 afford** offer **14 owes** poems are regarded as the poet's repayment of obligation; see Sonnet 83, line 4
**80: 1 faint** waver **2 better spirit** greater genius **6 humble** humblest; **as** as well as **8 willfully** boldly **10 soundless** bottomless **11 wracked** wrecked; **boat** small vessel (in contrast to a ship) **12 tall building** sturdy construction; **pride** magnificence **14 decay** cause of ruin

**81: 1 Or** either **3 From hence** from these poems (?) from the earth (?) **4 in . . . part** all of my qualities **5 from hence** from these poems **11 rehearse** repeat **13 virtue** power **14 breath** life
**82: 1 married to** closely joined to **2 attaint** dishonor; **o'erlook** read over **3 dedicated** devoted (with a pun on dedications prefixed to books) **5 hue** (1) complexion (2) figure **6 limit** reach **8 stamp** impression; **time-bettering** improving **11 fair** beautiful; **truly sympathized** represented to the life
**83: 2 fair** beauty **4 The . . . debt** i.e., the worthless offer that the poet is obliged to make **5 slept . . . report** refrained from praising you **7 modern** trivial

## 84

Who is it that says most, which can say more°
Than this rich praise, that you alone are you,
In whose confine immurèd is the store
Which should example where your equal grew?°    4
Lean penury within that pen doth dwell,
That to his° subject lends not some small glory,
But he that writes of you, if he can tell
That you are you, so dignifies his story.    8
Let him but copy what in you is writ,
Not making worse what nature made so clear,°
And such a counterpart shall fame his wit,°
Making his style admirèd everywhere.    12
   You to your beauteous blessings add a curse,
   Being fond on° praise, which makes your praises
    worse.

## 85

My tongue-tied Muse in manners holds her still°
While comments of your praise, richly compiled,
Reserve their character with golden quill°
And precious phrase by all the Muses filed.°    4
I think good thoughts whilst other° write good words,
And, like unlettered clerk, still° cry "Amen"
To every hymn that able spirit affords°
In polished form of well-refinèd pen.    8
Hearing you praised, I say, " 'Tis so, 'tis true,"
And to the most° of praise add something more;
But that is in my thought, whose love to you,
Though words come hindmost, holds his rank before.    12
   Then others for the breath of words respect,
   Me for my dumb thoughts, speaking in effect.°

## 86

Was it the proud full sail of his° great verse,
Bound for the prize of all too precious you,
That did my ripe thoughts in my brain inhearse,°
Making their tomb the womb wherein they grew?    4
Was it his spirit, by spirits taught to write
Above a mortal pitch, that struck me dead?°
No, neither he, nor his compeers by night
Giving him aid, my verse astonishèd.°    8
He, nor that affable familiar ghost°
Which nightly gulls him with intelligence,°
As victors, of my silence cannot boast;
I was not sick of any fear from thence.    12
   But when your countenance filled up his line,°
   Then lacked I matter, that enfeebled mine.

## 87

Farewell, thou art too dear for my possessing,
And like enough thou know'st thy estimate.°
The charter° of thy worth gives thee releasing;
My bonds in° thee are all determinate.°    4
For how do I hold thee but by thy granting,
And for that riches where is my deserving?
The cause of this fair gift in me is wanting,°
And so my patent° back again is swerving.°    8
Thyself thou gav'st, thy own worth then not knowing,
Or me, to whom thou gav'st it, else mistaking;
So thy great gift, upon misprision growing,°
Comes home again, on better judgment making.    12
   Thus have I had thee as a dream doth flatter,
   In sleep a king, but waking no such matter.

## 88

When thou shalt be disposed to set me light°
And place my merit in the eye of scorn,
Upon thy side against myself I'll fight
And prove thee virtuous, though thou art forsworn.    4
With mine own weakness being best acquainted,
Upon thy part I can set down a story
Of faults concealed wherein I am attainted,
That° thou in losing me shalt win much glory.    8
And I by this will be a gainer too,
For, bending all my loving thoughts on thee,
The injuries that to myself I do,
Doing thee vantage,° double-vantage me.    12
   Such is my love, to thee I so belong,
   That for thy right° myself will bear all wrong.

84: **1 Who . . . more** i.e., who, having said the utmost, can say more   **3–4 In . . . grew** in whom is stored all the abundance which would have to serve as a model for any equal   **6 his** its   **10 clear** radiant   **11 fame his wit** make famous his mind   **14 fond on** foolishly enamored of (but the sense seemed called for here is that the patron's excellence is such that it wreaks havoc with the poets who seek to praise him)
85: **1 in . . . still** is politely silent   **2–3 While . . . quill** while comments in your praise, richly composed with golden pen, preserve their features ("character" means both "writing" and "traits," "features")   **4 filed** polished   **5 other** others   **6 still** always   **7 able spirit affords** i.e., competent poets write   **10 most** utmost   **13–14 Then . . . effect** i.e., then take notice of other poets for their spoken words (but in "breath" there is a suggestion of their insubstantiality), and of me for my silent thoughts, which, by their silence, speak

86: **1 his** a rival poet's   **3 inhearse** enclose as in a coffin   **6 dead** silent   **8 astonishèd** struck dumb   **9 familiar ghost** assisting spirit   **10 gulls . . . intelligence** deceives him with rumors (?)   **13 countenance . . . line** (1) beauty was the subject of his verse (2) approval polished his verse (if the quarto's "fild" is printed "filed" instead of "filled")
87: **2 estimate** value   **3 charter** privilege   **4 bonds in** claims on; **determinate** expired   **7 wanting** lacking   **8 patent** privilege; **back . . . swerving** returns (to you)   **11 upon misprision growing** arising from a mistake
88: **1 set me light** value me little   **8 That** so that   **12 vantage** advantage   **14 right** (1) good (2) privilege

## 89

Say° that thou didst forsake me for some fault,
And I will comment upon that offense.
Speak of my lameness, and I straight will halt,°
Against thy reasons° making no defense. 4
Thou canst not, love, disgrace° me half so ill,
To set a form upon desirèd change,°
As I'll myself disgrace,° knowing thy will.
I will acquaintance° strangle and look strange; 8
Be absent from thy walks, and in my tongue
Thy sweet belovèd name no more shall dwell,
Lest I, too much profane, should do it wrong
And haply° of our old acquaintance tell. 12
  For thee, against myself I'll vow debate,°
  For I must ne'er love him whom thou dost hate.

## 90

Then hate me when thou wilt; if ever, now;
Now, while the world is bent my deeds to cross,
Join with the spite of fortune, make me bow,
And do not drop in for an after-loss.° 4
Ah, do not, when my heart hath 'scaped this sorrow,
Come in the rearward of a conquered woe;°
Give not a windy night a rainy morrow,
To linger out° a purposed° overthrow. 8
If thou wilt leave me, do not leave me last,
When other petty griefs have done their spite,
But in the onset come; so shall I taste
At first the very worst of fortune's might, 12
  And other strains° of woe, which now seem woe,
  Compared with loss of thee will not seem so.

## 91

Some glory in their birth, some in their skill,
Some in their wealth, some in their body's force,
Some in their garments, though newfangled ill,°
Some in their hawks and hounds, some in their horse;° 4
And every humor° hath his° adjunct pleasure,
Wherein it finds a joy above the rest,
But these particulars are not my measure;°
All these I better in one general best. 8
Thy love is better than high birth to me,
Richer than wealth, prouder than garments' cost,
Of more delight than hawks or horses be;
And having thee, of all men's pride° I boast: 12
  Wretched in this alone, that thou mayst take
  All this away, and me most wretched make.

## 92

But do thy worst to steal thyself away,
For term of life thou art assurèd mine,
And life no longer than thy love will stay,
For it depends upon that love of thine. 4
Then need I not to fear the worst of wrongs,
When in the least of them° my life hath end.
I see a better state to me belongs
Than that which on thy humor° doth depend. 8
Thou canst not vex me with inconstant mind,
Since that my life on thy revolt doth lie.°
O, what a happy title° do I find,
Happy to have thy love, happy to die! 12
  But what's so blessèd-fair that fears no blot?
  Thou mayst be false, and yet I know it not.

## 93

So shall I live, supposing thou art true,
Like a deceivèd husband; so love's face
May still seem love to me, though altered new,
Thy looks with me, thy heart in other place. 4
For there can live no hatred in thine eye;
Therefore in that I cannot know thy change.
In many's looks, the false heart's history
Is writ in moods and frowns and wrinkles strange, 8
But heaven in thy creation did decree
That in thy face sweet love should ever dwell;
Whate'er thy thoughts or thy heart's workings be,
Thy looks should nothing thence but sweetness tell. 12
  How like Eve's apple doth thy beauty grow
  If thy sweet virtue answer not thy show.

## 94

They that have pow'r to hurt and will do none,
That do not do the thing they most do show,°
Who, moving others, are themselves as stone,
Unmovèd, cold, and to temptation slow; 4
They rightly do inherit heaven's graces
And husband° nature's riches from expense;°
They are the lords and owners of their faces,
Others but stewards° of their excellence. 8
The summer's flow'r is to the summer sweet,
Though to itself it only live and die;
But if that flow'r with base infection meet,
The basest weed outbraves his° dignity: 12
  For sweetest things turn sourest by their deeds;
  Lilies that fester smell far worse than weeds.

89: 1 Say i.e., assume  3 halt limp  4 reasons arguments  5 disgrace discredit  6 To . . . change to give a good appearance to the change you desire (?)  7 disgrace disfigure  8 acquaintance i.e., familiarity  12 haply by chance  13 debate contention
90: 4 after-loss later loss  6 Come . . . woe i.e., come belatedly when I have conquered my sorrow  8 linger out prolong; purposed intended  13 strains kinds
91: 3 newfangled ill fashionably ugly  4 horse horses  5 humor temperament; his its  7 measure standard (of happiness)  12 all men's pride all that men take pride in
92: 6 the . . . them i.e., any sign that the friend's love is cooling  8 humor caprice  10 Since . . . lie since my life ends if you desert me  11 happy title title to happiness
94: 2 do show (1) seem to do (?) (2) show they could do (?)  6 husband manage prudently; expense loss  8 stewards custodians  12 outbraves his surpasses its

## 95

How sweet and lovely dost thou make the shame
Which, like a canker° in the fragrant rose,
Doth spot the beauty of thy budding name!
O, in what sweets dost thou thy sins enclose!          4
That tongue that tells the story of thy days,
Making lascivious comments on thy sport,°
Cannot dispraise, but in a kind of praise;
Naming thy name blesses an ill report.          8
O, what a mansion have those vices got
Which for their habitation chose out thee,
Where beauty's veil doth cover every blot,
And all things turns to fair that eyes can see!          12
    Take heed, dear heart, of this large privilege;
    The hardest knife ill-used doth lose his° edge.

## 96

Some say thy fault is youth, some wantonness,
Some say thy grace is youth and gentle sport;°
Both grace and faults are loved of more and less;°
Thou mak'st faults graces that to thee resort.          4
As on the finger of a thronèd queen
The basest jewel will be well esteemed,
So are those errors that in thee are seen
To truths translated° and for true things deemed.          8
How many lambs might the stern° wolf betray,
If like a lamb he could his looks translate;
How many gazers mightst thou lead away,
If thou wouldst use the strength of all thy state!°          12
    But do not so; I love thee in such sort
    As, thou being mine, mine is thy good report.

## 97

How like a winter hath my absence been
From thee, the pleasure of the fleeting year!°
What freezings have I felt, what dark days seen,
What old December's bareness everywhere!          4
And yet this time removed was summer's time,
The teeming° autumn, big with rich increase,
Bearing the wanton burden of the prime,°
Like widowed wombs after their lords' decease.          8
Yet this abundant issue° seemed to me
But hope of orphans and unfathered fruit;
For summer and his° pleasures wait on thee,
And, thou away, the very birds are mute;          12
    Or, if they sing, 'tis with so dull a cheer,
    That leaves look pale, dreading the winter's near.

## 98

From you have I been absent in the spring,
When proud-pied° April, dressed in all his trim,°
Hath put a spirit of youth in everything,
That° heavy Saturn° laughed and leaped with him,          4
Yet nor the lays° of birds, nor° the sweet smell
Of different flowers in odor and in hue,
Could make me any summer's story° tell,
Or from their proud lap pluck them where they grew.          8
Nor did I wonder at the lily's white,
Nor praise the deep vermilion in the rose;
They were but sweet, but figures of delight,
Drawn after you, you pattern of all those.          12
    Yet seemed it winter still, and, you away,
    As with your shadow° I with these did play.

## 99

The forward° violet thus did I chide:
Sweet thief, whence didst thou steal thy sweet that
    smells
If not from my love's breath? The purple° pride°
Which on thy soft cheek for complexion dwells          4
In my love's veins thou hast too grossly dyed.
The lily I condemnèd for thy hand,°
And buds of marjoram had stol'n thy hair;
The roses fearfully° on thorns did stand,          8
One blushing shame, another white despair;
A third, nor red nor white, had stol'n of both,
And to his robb'ry had annexed thy breath;
But for his theft, in pride of all his growth          12
A vengeful canker eat° him up to death.
    More flowers I noted, yet I none could see,
    But sweet or color it had stol'n from thee.

## 100

Where art thou, Muse, that thou forget'st so long
To speak of that which gives thee all thy might?
Spend'st thou thy fury° on some worthless song,
Dark'ning thy pow'r to lend base subjects light?          4
Return, forgetful Muse, and straight redeem
In gentle numbers° time so idly spent,
Sing to the ear that doth thy lays° esteem,
And gives thy pen both skill and argument.°          8
Rise, resty° Muse, my love's sweet face survey,
If° Time have any wrinkle graven there;
If any, be a satire to decay°
And make Time's spoils despisèd everywhere.          12
    Give my love fame faster than Time wastes life;
    So thou prevent'st his scythe and crooked knife.

95: 2 **canker** canker worm (that feeds on blossoms)   **6 sport** amorous dalliance   **14 his** its
96: 2 **gentle sport** amorous dalliance (a more favorable interpretation of the "wantonness" of line 1)   **3 of . . . less** by people high and low   **8 translated** transformed   **9 stern** cruel   **12 state** eminent position   **13–14** this couplet ends Sonnet 36   **14 report** reputation
97: 2 **pleasure . . . year** i.e., the summer (normally the pleasant part of the year, but like a winter because of the friend's absence)   **6 teeming** pregnant   **7 Bearing . . . prime** i.e., bearing the load conceived in the wantonness of the spring ("prime" = spring)   **9 issue** offspring   **11 his** its
98: 2 **proud-pied** gorgeously variegated; **trim** ornamental dress   **4 That** so that; **heavy Saturn** the planet Saturn was thought to cause gloominess   **5 lays** songs; **nor . . . nor** neither . . . nor   **7 summer's story** i.e., pleasant stories suitable for summer ("a sad tale's best for winter")   **14 shadow** portrait
99: 1 **forward** early   **3 purple** Shakespeare often does not distinguish between purple and crimson; **pride** splendor   **6 condemnèd . . . hand** condemned for stealing the whiteness of your hand   **8 fearfully** uneasily   **13 canker eat** canker worm ate
100: 3 **fury** poetic enthusiasm   **6 numbers** verses   **7 lays** songs   **8 argument** subject   **9 resty** torpid   **10 If** to see if   **11 be . . . decay** satirize decay

## 101

O truant Muse, what shall be thy amends
For thy neglect of truth in beauty dyed?
Both truth and beauty on my love° depends;
So dost thou too, and therein dignified.°          4
Make answer, Muse, wilt thou not haply° say,
"Truth needs no color,° with his color fixed,°
Beauty no pencil, beauty's truth to lay;°
But best is best, if never intermixed?"°          8
Because he needs no praise, wilt thou be dumb?
Excuse not silence so, for't lies in thee
To make him much outlive a gilded tomb,
And to be praised of ages yet to be.          12
     Then do thy office,° Muse; I teach thee how
     To make him seem, long hence, as he shows now.

## 102

My love is strength'ned, though more weak in seeming;
I love not less, though less the show° appear.
That love is merchandized° whose rich esteeming°
The owner's tongue doth publish everywhere.          4
Our love was new, and then but in the spring,
When I was wont to greet it with my lays,°
As Philomel° in summer's front° doth sing
And stops her pipe in growth of riper° days.          8
Not that the summer is less pleasant now
Than when her mournful hymns did hush the night,
But that° wild music burdens every bough,
And sweets grown common lose their dear delight.          12
     Therefore, like her, I sometime hold my tongue,
     Because I would not dull you with my song.

## 103

Alack, what poverty° my Muse brings forth,
That, having such a scope to show her pride,°
The argument° all bare° is of more worth
Than when it hath my added praise beside.          4
O, blame me not if I no more can write!
Look in your glass, and there appears a face
That overgoes my blunt invention° quite,
Dulling my lines and doing me disgrace.°          8
Were it not sinful then, striving to mend,°
To mar the subject that before was well?
For to no other pass° my verses tend
Than of your graces and your gifts to tell;          12
     And more, much more, than in my verse can sit
     Your own glass shows you when you look in it.

## 104

To me, fair friend, you never can be old,
For as you were when first your eye I eyed,
Such seems your beauty still. Three winters cold
Have from the forests shook three summers' pride,°          4
Three beauteous springs to yellow autumn turned
In process of the seasons have I seen,
Three April perfumes in three hot Junes burned,
Since first I saw you fresh, which yet are green.          8
Ah, yet doth beauty, like a dial hand,
Steal from his figure,° and no pace perceived;
So your sweet hue,° which methinks still° doth stand,
Hath motion, and mine eye may be deceived;          12
     For fear of which, hear this, thou age unbred:°
     Ere you were born was beauty's summer dead.

## 105

Let not my love be called idolatry,
Nor my belovèd as an idol show,
Since all alike my songs and praises be
To one, of one, still° such, and ever so.          4
Kind° is my love today, tomorrow kind,
Still constant in a wondrous excellence;
Therefore my verse, to constancy confined,
One thing expressing, leaves out difference.°          8
Fair,° kind, and true is all my argument,°
Fair, kind, and true, varying to other words;
And in this change is my invention spent,°
Three themes in one, which wondrous scope affords.          12
     Fair, kind, and true have often lived alone,
     Which three till now never kept seat in one.

## 106

When in the chronicle of wasted° time
I see descriptions of the fairest wights,°
And beauty making beautiful old rhyme
In praise of ladies dead and lovely° knights;          4
Then, in the blazon° of sweet beauty's best,
Of hand, of foot, of lip, of eye, of brow,
I see their antique pen would have expressed
Even such a beauty as you master now.          8
So all their praises are but prophecies
Of this our time, all you prefiguring,
And, for° they looked but with divining° eyes,
They had not still° enough your worth to sing:          12
     For° we, which now behold these present days,
     Have eyes to wonder, but lack tongues to praise.

---

101: **3 love** beloved   **4 dignified** you are dignified   **5 haply** perchance   **6 color** artificial color, disguise; **his color fixed** its unchangeable color   **7 to lay** i.e., to put on canvas   **8 intermixed** i.e., with the inadequate words of the Muse   **13 do thy office** perform your duty
102: **2 show** outward manifestation   **3 merchandized** offered for sale, hawked; **esteeming** value   **6 lays** songs   **7 Philomel** the nightingale; **front** forefront   **8 riper** later   **11 But that** i.e., but it seems so because
103: **1 poverty** inferior matter   **2 pride** splendor   **3 argument** theme; **all bare** i.e., of itself   **7 overgoes . . . invention** exceeds my awkward creation   **8 disgrace** discredit   **9 mend** improve   **11 pass** purpose

104: **4 pride** splendor   **10 his figure** its numeral (with a pun on *figure* = the friend's appearance)   **11 sweet hue** fair appearance; **still** (1) motionless (2) always, forever   **13 unbred** unborn
105: **4 still** always   **5 Kind** naturally benevolent   **8 difference** variety   **9 Fair** beautiful; **argument** theme   **11 And . . . spent** i.e., and in variations on this theme I expend all my imagination
106: **1 wasted** past   **2 wights** people   **4 lovely** attractive   **5 blazon** commemorative description   **11 for** because; **divining** guessing   **12 still** yet (the common emendation to "skill" is unnecessary)   **13 For** for even

## 107

Not mine own fears nor the prophetic soul
Of the wide world dreaming on things to come
Can yet the lease° of my true love control,
Supposed as forfeit to a confined doom.°         4
The mortal moon hath her eclipse endured,°
And the sad augurs mock their own presage,
Incertainties now crown themselves assured,°
And peace proclaims olives of endless age.        8
Now with the drops of this most balmy time
My love looks fresh, and Death to me subscribes,°
Since, spite of him, I'll live in this poor rhyme,
While he insults° o'er dull and speechless tribes:   12
   And thou in this shalt find thy monument,
   When tyrants' crests and tombs of brass are spent.°

## 108

What's in the brain that ink may character°
Which hath not figured° to thee my true spirit?
What's new to speak, what now to register,
That may express my love or thy dear merit?       4
Nothing, sweet boy, but yet, like prayers divine,
I must each day say o'er the very same;
Counting no old thing old, thou mine, I thine,
Even as when first I hallowed thy fair name.        8
So that eternal love in love's fresh case°
Weighs not° the dust and injury of age,
Nor gives to necessary wrinkles place,
But makes antiquity for aye his page,°              12
   Finding the first conceit° of love there bred
   Where time and outward form would show it dead.

## 109

O, never say that I was false of heart,
Though absence seemed my flame to qualify.°
As easy might I from myself depart
As from my soul, which in thy breast doth lie.      4
That is my home of love; if I have ranged,°
Like him that travels, I return again,
Just° to the time, not with the time exchanged,°
So that myself bring water for my stain.            8
Never believe, though in my nature reigned
All frailties that besiege all kinds of blood,°
That it could so preposterously be stained
To leave for nothing all thy sum of good;           12
   For nothing this wide universe I call
   Save thou, my rose; in it thou art my all.

## 110

Alas, 'tis true I have gone here and there
And made myself a motley° to the view,
Gored° mine own thoughts, sold cheap what is most dear,
Made old offenses of affections° new.               4
Most true it is that I have looked on truth°
Askance and strangely;° but, by all above,
These blenches° gave my heart another youth,
And worse essays° proved thee my best of love.       8
Now all is done, have what shall have no end.°
Mine appetite I never more will grind
On newer proof,° to try° an older friend,
A god in love, to whom I am confined.               12
   Then give me welcome, next° my heaven the best,
   Even to thy pure and most most loving breast.

## 111

O, for my sake do you with Fortune chide,
The guilty goddess of my harmful deeds,
That° did not better for my life° provide
Than public means which public manners breeds.°      4
Thence comes it that my name receives a brand,°
And almost thence my nature is subdued°
To what it works in, like the dyer's hand.
Pity me then, and wish I were renewed,              8
Whilst, like a willing patient, I will drink
Potions of eisel° 'gainst my strong infection;
No bitterness that I will bitter think,
Nor double penance, to correct correction.          12
   Pity me then, dear friend, and I assure ye
   Even that your pity is enough to cure me.

## 112

Your love and pity doth th' impression fill,°
Which vulgar scandal stamped° upon my brow;
For what care I who calls me well or ill,
So you o'er-green my bad, my good allow?°            4
You are my all the world, and I must strive
To know my shames° and praises from your tongue;
None else to me, nor I to none alive,
That my steeled sense or changes right or wrong.°    8
In so profound° abysm I throw all care
Of others' voices, that my adder's sense°
To critic and to flatterer stoppèd are.
Mark how with my neglect I do dispense:°             12
   You are so strongly in my purpose bred,°
   That all the world besides methinks are dead.°

**107: 3 lease** allotted time **4 Supposed . . . doom** i.e., though it is thought doomed to expire after a limited time **5 The . . . endured** numerous commentators claim that this line dates the sonnet; among interpretations are: 1588, when the Spanish Armada, thought to have assumed a crescent formation, was destroyed; 1595, when the moon underwent a total eclipse; 1595, when Queen Elizabeth I survived a critical period in her horoscope; 1599, when Queen Elizabeth survived an illness **6–7 And . . . assured** and the prophets of gloom are mocked by their own predictions now that uncertainties yield to assurance (?) **10 to me subscribes** acknowledges me as his superior **12 insults** triumphs **14 spent** consumed **108: 1 character** write **2 figured** shown **9 fresh case** youthful appearance **10 Weighs not** cares not for **12 for . . . page** forever his servant **13 conceit** conception **109: 2 qualify** moderate **5 ranged** wandered **7 Just** punctual; **exchanged** changed **10 blood** flesh, temperament

**110: 2 motley** jester **3 Gored** wounded **4 affections** passions **5 truth** fidelity **6 strangely** in a reserved manner **7 blenches** side glances (?) **8 worse essays** trials of worse friendships (?) **9 have what . . . end** take what shall be eternal **11 proof** experiment; **try** test **13 next** next to **111: 3 That** who; **life** livelihood **4 Than . . . breeds** than earning a livelihood by satisfying the public, which engenders vulgar manners **5 brand** stigma **6 subdued** subjected **10 eisel** vinegar (used as a preventative against the plague) **112: 1 doth . . . fill** effaces the scar **2 stamped** allusion to branding felons **4 allow** approve **6 shames** faults **7–8 None else . . . wrong** only you can change my sense of what is right and wrong (?) **9 profound** deep **10 adder's sense** i.e., deaf ears (adders were thought to be deaf) **12 Mark . . . dispense** listen to how I excuse ("dispense with") my neglect (i.e., of others) **13 in . . . bred** grown in my mind **14 That . . . dead** that I think only you have life

### 113

Since I left you, mine eye is in my mind,
And that which governs me to go about
Doth part his° function and is partly blind,°
Seems seeing, but effectually° is out;                    4
For it no form delivers to the heart
Of bird, of flow'r, or shape, which it doth latch.°
Of his° quick° objects hath the mind no part,
Nor his° own vision holds what it doth catch;            8
For if it see the rud'st or gentlest sight,
The most sweet favor° or deformèd'st creature,
The mountain, or the sea, the day, or night,
The crow, or dove, it shapes them to your feature.       12
    Incapable of° more, replete with you,
    My most true° mind thus maketh mine eye untrue.

### 114

Or whether° doth my mind, being crowned with you,°
Drink up the monarch's plague, this flattery?°
Or whether° shall I say mine eye saith true,
And that your love taught it this alchemy,                4
To make of monsters, and things indigest,°
Such cherubins° as your sweet self resemble,
Creating every bad a perfect best
As fast as objects to his beams assemble?°               8
O, 'tis the first, 'tis flatt'ry in my seeing,
And my great mind most kingly drinks it up.
Mine eye well knows what with his gust is 'greeing,°
And to his palate doth prepare the cup.                  12
    If it be poisoned, 'tis the lesser sin
    That° mine eye loves it and doth first begin.

### 115

Those lines that I before have writ to lie,
Even those that said I could not love you dearer.
Yet then my judgment knew no reason why
My most full flame should afterwards burn clearer.        4
But reckoning Time, whose millioned accidents°
Creep in 'twixt vows and change decrees of kings,
Tan° sacred beauty, blunt the sharp'st intents,
Divert° strong minds to th' course of alt'ring things.    8
Alas, why, fearing of Time's tyranny,
Might I not then say, "Now I love you best,"
When I was certain o'er incertainty,
Crowning° the present, doubting of the rest?             12
    Love is a babe; then° might I not say so,°
    To give full growth to that which still doth grow.

### 116

Let me not to the marriage of true minds
Admit impediments;° love is not love
Which alters when it alteration finds,
Or bends with the remover to remove.                      4
O, no, it is an ever-fixèd mark°
That looks on tempests and is never shaken;
It is the star° to every wand'ring bark,
Whose worth's unknown, although his height be taken.°     8
Love's not Time's fool,° though rosy lips and cheeks
Within his bending sickle's compass° come;
Love alters not with his° brief hours and weeks,
But bears it out° even to the edge of doom.°            12
    If this be error and upon° me proved,
    I never writ, nor no man ever loved.

### 117

Accuse me thus: that I have scanted all°
Wherein I should your great deserts repay,
Forgot upon your dearest love to call,
Whereto all bonds do tie me day by day;                   4
That I have frequent° been with unknown minds,°
And given to time° your own dear-purchased right;
That I have hoisted sail to all the winds
Which should transport me farthest from your sight.       8
Book° both my willfulness and errors down,
And on just proof surmise accumulate;°
Bring me within the level° of your frown,
But shoot not at me in your wakened hate;                12
    Since my appeal° says I did strive to prove°
    The constancy and virtue of your love.

---

113: **3 Doth . . . blind** i.e., performs only part of its function,
receiving images but not conveying them to the mind or
"heart"   **3, 7, 8 his** its   **4 effectually** in reality   **6 latch** catch
sight of   **7 quick** fleeting   **10 favor** face   **13 Incapable of**
unable to take in   **14 true** faithful
114: **1, 3 Or whether** indicates alternative questions   **1 being
. . . you** made a king by possessing you   **2 this flattery** i.e.,
false appearances (such as surround a monarch) as specified in
Sonnet 113   **5 indigest** formless   **6 cherubins** angelic
creatures   **8 to . . . assemble** appear to his eye (the eye was
thought to cast beams; see Sonnet 20, line 6)   **11 with . . .
'greeing** agrees with the mind's taste   **14 That** since
115: **5 millioned accidents** innumerable happenings   **7 Tan**
i.e., darken, coarsen   **8 Divert** alter   **12 Crowning** glorifying
**13 then** therefore; **so** i.e., "Now I love you best" (line 10)

116: **2 impediments** an echo of the marriage service in the
Book of Common Prayer: "If any of you know cause or just
impediment . . ."   **5 mark** seamark   **7 the star** the North
Star   **8 Whose . . . taken** whose value (e.g., to mariners) is
inestimable although the star's altitude has been determined   **9
fool** plaything   **10 compass** range, circle   **11 his** Time's   **12
bears it out** survives; **edge of doom** Judgment Day   **13
upon** against
117: **1 scanted all** given only grudgingly   **5 frequent** intimate; **unknown minds** i.e., nonentities   **6 given to time**
squandered on other people of the time   **9 Book** write down
in a book   **10 surmise accumulate** add suspicions   **11 level**
range, aim   **13 appeal** plea; **prove** test

## 118

Like as to make our appetites more keen
With eager compounds° we our palate urge,°
As to prevent° our maladies unseen,
We sicken to shun sickness when we purge;    4
Even so, being full of your ne'er-cloying sweetness,
To bitter sauces° did I frame° my feeding;
And, sick of welfare,° found a kind of meetness°
To be diseased ere that there was true needing.    8
Thus policy° in love, t' anticipate
The ills that were not, grew to faults assured,
And brought to medicine° a healthful state,
Which, rank of° goodness, would by ill be cured.    12
   But thence I learn, and find the lesson true,
   Drugs poison him that so fell sick of you.

## 119

What potions have I drunk of Siren tears
Distilled from limbecks° foul as hell within,
Applying° fears to hopes and hopes to fears,
Still° losing when I saw myself to win!    4
What wretched errors hath my heart committed,
Whilst it hath thought itself so blessèd never!°
How have mine eyes out of their spheres° been fitted°
In the distraction of this madding fever!    8
O, benefit of ill: now I find true
That better is by evil still made better;
And ruined love, when it is built anew,
Grows fairer than at first, more strong, far greater.    12
   So I return rebuked to my content,
   And gain by ills thrice more than I have spent.

## 120

That you were once unkind befriends me now,
And for° that sorrow which I then did feel
Needs must I under my transgression bow,
Unless my nerves° were brass or hammered steel.    4
For if you were by my unkindness shaken,
As I by yours, y' have passed a hell of time,
And I, a tyrant, have no leisure taken
To weigh° how once I suffered in your crime.    8
O, that our night of woe° might have rememb'red°
My deepest sense how hard true sorrow hits,
And soon° to you, as you to me then, tend'red°
The humble salve° which wounded bosoms fits!°    12
   But that your trespass° now becomes a fee;°
   Mine ransoms° yours, and yours must ransom me.

## 121

'Tis better to be vile than vile esteemed
When not to be receives reproach of being,°
And the just° pleasure lost, which is so° deemed
Not by our feeling, but by others' seeing.    4
For why should others' false adulterate eyes
Give salutation to° my sportive° blood?
Or on my frailties why are frailer spies,
Which in their wills° count bad what I think good?    8
No, I am that° I am, and they that level°
At my abuses° reckon up their own;
I may be straight though they themselves be bevel.°
By their rank° thoughts my deeds must not be shown,    12
   Unless this general evil they maintain:
   All men are bad and in their badness reign.

## 122

Thy gift, thy tables,° are within my brain
Full charactered° with lasting memory,
Which shall above that idle rank° remain
Beyond all date, even to eternity;    4
Or, at the least, so long as brain and heart
Have faculty by nature to subsist,
Till each to rased oblivion° yield his° part
Of thee, thy record never can be missed.    8
That poor retention° could not so much hold,
Nor need I tallies° thy dear love to score.
Therefore to give them from me was I bold,
To trust those tables° that receive thee more.    12
   To keep an adjunct to remember thee
   Were to import° forgetfulness in me.

##  123

No, Time, thou shalt not boast that I do change.
Thy pyramids° built up with newer might
To me are nothing novel, nothing strange;
They are but dressings of a former sight.    4
Our dates° are brief, and therefore we admire°
What thou dost foist upon us that is old,
And rather make them born to our desire°
Than think that we before have heard them told.    8
Thy registers° and thee I both defy,
Not wond'ring at the present, nor the past;
For thy records and what we see doth lie,
Made more or less by thy continual haste.    12
   This I do vow, and this shall ever be:
   I will be true despite thy scythe and thee.

**118: 2 eager compounds** tart sauces; **urge** stimulate **3 prevent** forestall **6 bitter sauces** i.e., undesirable people; **frame** direct **7 sick of welfare** gorged with well-being; **meetness** fitness **9 policy** prudence **11 medicine** i.e., the need of medicine **12 rank of** gorged with
**119: 2 limbecks** alembics **3 Applying** i.e., as an ointment **4 Still** always **6 so blessèd never** never so blessed **7 spheres** sockets; **fitted** forced by fits
**120: 2 for** because of **4 nerves** sinews **7–8 no . . . weigh** not taken the time to consider **9 night of woe** i.e., estrangement; **rememb'red** reminded **11 soon** as soon; **tend'red** offered **12 humble salve** balm of humility; **fits** suits **13 that your trespass** that trespass of yours; **fee** compensation **14 ransoms** atones for

**121: 2 being** i.e., being vile **3 just** legitimate; **so** i.e., vile **6 Give salutation to** act on; **sportive** wanton **8 in their wills** willfully (?) **9 that** who (an echo of Exodus 3:14); **level** aim **10 abuses** transgressions **11 bevel** i.e., crooked **12 rank** corrupt
**122: 1 tables** memorandum books **2 charactered** written **3 that idle rank** that useless series of leaves **7 rased oblivion** oblivion that erases; **his** its **9 That poor retention** i.e., the memorandum books **10 tallies** accounting devices **12 those tables** i.e., the mind **14 import** imply
**123: 2 pyramids** possibly an allusion to Egyptian obelisks erected in Rome by Pope Sextus 1586–89; more likely an allusion to triumphal structures erected in London to welcome James I in 1603; most likely a reference to all monuments **5 dates** allotted times; **admire** regard with wonder **7 born . . . desire** turn them into the new things we wish to see **9 registers** records

## 124

If my dear love° were but° the child of state,°
It might for Fortune's bastard be unfathered,°
As subject to Time's love, or to Time's hate,
Weeds among weeds, or flowers with flowers gathered. 4
No, it was builded far from accident;°
It suffers not in smiling pomp, nor falls
Under the blow of thrallèd discontent,°
Whereto th' inviting time our fashion calls. 8
It fears not Policy, that heretic,°
Which works on leases of short-numb'red hours,
But all alone stands hugely politic,°
That it nor grows with heat, nor° drowns with showers. 12
    To this I witness call the fools of Time,°
    Which die for goodness, who have lived for crime.°

## 125

Were't aught° to me I bore the canopy,°
With my extern° the outward honoring,
Or laid great bases for eternity,
Which proves more short than waste or ruining? 4
Have I not seen dwellers on form and favor°
Lose all and more by paying too much rent,°
For compound sweet forgoing simple° savor,
Pitiful thrivers, in their gazing spent?° 8
No, let me be obsequious° in thy heart,
And take thou my oblation, poor but free,
Which is not mixed with seconds,° knows no art,°
But mutual render,° only me for thee. 12
    Hence, thou suborned informer!° A true soul
    When most impeached° stands least in thy control.

## 126

O thou, my lovely boy, who in thy power
Dost hold Time's fickle glass,° his sickle hour,°
Who hast by waning grown,° and therein show'st
Thy lovers withering, as thy sweet self grow'st; 4
If Nature, sovereign mistress over wrack,°
As thou goest onwards, still° will pluck thee back,
She keeps thee to this purpose, that her skill
May Time disgrace and wretched minutes kill. 8
Yet fear her, O thou minion° of her pleasure;
She may detain, but not still° keep her treasure.
    Her audit,° though delayed, answered° must be,
    And her quietus° is to render° thee. 12

## 127

In the old age° black° was not counted fair,°
Or, if it were, it bore not beauty's name.
But now is black beauty's successive heir,°
And beauty slandered with a bastard shame;° 4
For since each hand hath put on° nature's power,
Fairing the foul with art's false borrowed face,°
Sweet° beauty hath no name, no holy bower,
But is profaned, if not lives in disgrace. 8
Therefore my mistress' eyes are raven black,
Her eyes so suited, and they mourners seem,
At° such who, not born fair, no beauty lack,
Sland'ring creation with a false esteem: 12
    Yet so they mourn, becoming of° their woe,
    That every tongue says beauty should look so.

**124: 1 love** the emotion, not the person; **but** only; **child of state** i.e., product of externals such as wealth and power **2 for . . . unfathered** i.e., be marked as the bastard son of Fortune **5 accident** chance **7 thrallèd discontent** discontent of persons oppressed **9 Policy, that heretic** i.e., unprincipled self-interest, which is faithless **11 all . . . politic** i.e., only love is infinitely prudent **12 That it nor . . . nor** since it neither . . . nor **13 fools of Time** playthings of Time (?) time-servers (?) **14 Which . . . crime** i.e., who at the last minute repent their criminal lives
**125: 1 Were't aught** would it be anything; **canopy** borne over an eminent person **2 extern** outward action **5 dwellers . . . favor** i.e., those who make much of appearance and external beauty **6 paying . . . rent** i.e., obsequiousness **7 simple** pure **8 Pitiful . . . spent** pitiable creatures who use themselves up in looking at outward honor **9 obsequious** devoted **11 seconds** i.e., baser matter; **art** artifice **12 render** surrender **13 suborned informer** perjured witness **14 impeached** accused

**126:** Note that this poem consists of six couplets, rather than of the usual three quatrains and a couplet **2 glass** mirror; **hour** hourglass **3 by waning grown** i.e., by growing older growing more beautiful **5 wrack** destruction **6, 10 still** always **9 minion** favorite **11 audit** final account; **answered** paid **12 quietus** final settlement; **render** surrender
**127: 1 old age** i.e., age of chivalry; **black** i.e., brunette; **fair** beautiful (with a pun on the obvious meaning) **3 successive heir** legitimate heir **4 And . . . shame** blond beauty is defamed as illegitimate **5 put on** taken over **6 art's . . . face** i.e., cosmetics **7 Sweet** natural, i.e., blond **11 At** for **13 becoming of** gracing

## 128

How oft, when thou, my music, music play'st
Upon that blessèd wood° whose motion° sounds
With thy sweet fingers when thou gently sway'st°
The wiry concord° that mine ear confounds,°              4
Do I envy those jacks° that nimble leap
To kiss the tender inward of thy hand,°
Whilst my poor lips, which should that harvest reap,
At the wood's boldness by thee blushing stand.           8
To be so tickled, they° would change their state
And situation with those dancing chips
O'er whom thy fingers walk with gentle gait,
Making dead wood more blest than living lips.            12
  Since saucy jacks so happy are in this,
  Give them thy fingers, me thy lips to kiss.

## 129

*Sermon against lust*

Th' expense° of spirit° in a waste of shame
Is lust in action; and, till action, lust
Is perjured, murd'rous, bloody, full of blame,
Savage, extreme, rude, cruel, not to trust;             4
Enjoyed no sooner but despisèd straight;
Past° reason hunted, and no sooner had,
Past° reason hated as a swallowed bait
On purpose laid to make the taker mad;                  8
Made° in pursuit, and in possession so;
Had, having, and in quest to have, extreme;
A bliss in proof,° and proved,° a very woe,
Before, a joy proposed; behind, a dream.°               12
  All this the world well knows, yet none knows well
  To shun the heaven° that leads men to this hell.

## 130

My mistress' eyes are nothing like the sun;
Coral is far more red than her lips' red;
If snow be white, why then her breasts are dun;
If hairs be wires, black wires grow on her head.        4
I have seen roses damasked,° red and white,
But no such roses see I in her cheeks,
And in some perfumes is there more delight
Than in the breath that from my mistress reeks.°        8
I love to hear her speak, yet well I know
That music hath a far more pleasing sound.
I grant I never saw a goddess go;°
My mistress when she walks treads on the ground.        12
  And yet, by heaven, I think my love as rare
  As any she° belied with false compare.°

## 131

Thou art as tyrannous, so as thou art,°
As those whose beauties proudly make them cruel;
For well thou know'st to my dear° doting heart
Thou art the fairest and most precious jewel.           4
Yet, in good faith, some say that thee behold,
Thy face hath not the power to make love groan;
To say they err I dare not be so bold,
Although I swear it to myself alone.                     8
And, to be sure that is not false I swear,
A thousand groans, but thinking on° thy face,
One on another's neck,° do witness bear
Thy black is fairest in my judgment's place.°           12
  In nothing art thou black° save in thy deeds,
  And thence this slander, as I think, proceeds.

## 132

Thine eyes I love, and they, as pitying me,
Knowing thy heart torment° me with disdain,
Have put on black and loving mourners be,
Looking with pretty ruth° upon my pain.                 4
And truly not the morning sun of heaven
Better becomes the gray cheeks of the east,
Nor that full star that ushers in the even°
Doth half that glory to the sober west                  8
As those two mourning° eyes become thy face.
O, let it then as well beseem thy heart
To mourn for me, since mourning doth thee grace,
And suit thy pity like° in every part.                  12
  Then will I swear beauty herself is black,
  And all they foul° that thy complexion lack.

128: **2 wood** keys (of the spinet or virginal); **motion** movement **3 thou gently sway'st** you gently direct **4 wiry concord** harmony of the strings; **confounds** delightfully overcomes **5 jacks** devices that pluck the strings, but here probably misused for keys; in line 13, there is a pun on the meaning "fellows" **5–6** There are always some who cannot bear to think that the Swan of Avon could ever make a mistake about anything. A certain E. W. Naylor explains these lines as follows: "The lady, having removed the rail which ordinarily stops the 'jacks' from jumping right out of the instrument when the keys are struck, was leaning over her work, testing it by striking the defective note, and holding the 'tender inward' of her hand over the 'jack' to prevent it from flying to the other end of the room."—W.H.A. **9 they** the poet's lips
129: **1 expense** expenditure; **spirit** vital power, semen **6, 7 Past** beyond **9 Made** i.e., made mad (most editors emend to "Mad") **11 in proof** while being experienced; **proved** i.e., when experienced **12 dream** nightmare (?) **14 heaven** the sensation (or place?) of bliss

130: **5 damasked** mingled red and white **8 reeks** emanates **11 go** walk **14 she** woman; **compare** comparison
131: **1 so . . . art** i.e., even though you are dark and not considered beautiful **3 dear** loving **10 but thinking on** when I but think of **11 One . . . neck** i.e., in quick succession **12 in . . . place** in the place assigned it by my judgment **13 black** foul
132: **2 torment** to torment **4 ruth** pity **7 even** evening **9 mourning** with a pun on *morning* **12 suit . . . like** clothe thy pity alike **14 foul** ugly

**133**

Beshrew° that heart that makes my heart to groan
For° that deep wound it gives my friend and me.
Is't not enough to torture me alone,
But slave to slavery my sweet'st friend must be?          4
Me from myself thy cruel eye hath taken,
And my next self° thou harder hast engrossed.°
Of him, myself, and thee, I am forsaken;
A torment thrice threefold thus to be crossed.°          8
Prison my heart in thy steel bosom's ward,°
But then my friend's heart let my poor heart bail;°
Whoe'er keeps° me, let my heart be his guard;°
Thou canst not then use rigor° in my jail.°          12
    And yet thou wilt, for I, being pent in thee,
    Perforce am thine, and all that is in me.

**134**

So, now I have confessed that he is thine
And I myself am mortgaged to thy will,°
Myself I'll forfeit, so° that other mine°
Thou wilt restore to be my comfort still.°          4
But thou wilt not, nor he will not be free,
For thou art covetous, and he is kind;
He learned but surety-like to write for me
Under that bond that him as fast doth bind.°          8
The statute° of thy beauty thou wilt take,
Thou usurer that put'st forth all to use,°
And sue a friend came° debtor for my sake;
So him I lose through my unkind abuse.°          12
    Him have I lost, thou hast both him and me;
    He pays the whole, and yet am I not free.

**135**

Whoever hath her wish, thou hast thy *Will*,°
And *Will* to boot, and *Will* in overplus;
More than enough am I that vex thee still,°
To thy sweet will making addition thus.°          4
Wilt thou, whose will is large and spacious,°
Not once vouchsafe° to hide my will in thine?
Shall will in others seem right gracious,°
And in my will no fair acceptance shine?          8
The sea, all water, yet receives rain still°
And in abundance addeth to his° store;
So thou being rich in *Will* add to thy *Will*
One will of mine, to make thy large *Will* more.          12
    Let no unkind,° no fair beseechers° kill;°
    Think all but one, and me in that one *Will*.°

**136**

If thy soul check° thee that I come so near,°
Swear to thy blind soul that I was thy *Will*,
And will, thy soul knows, is admitted there;
Thus far for love my love-suit, sweet, fulfill.          4
*Will* will fulfill the treasure° of thy love,
Ay, fill it full with wills, and my will one.°
In things of great receipt° with ease we prove.
Among a number one is reckoned none.°          8
Then in the number let me pass untold,°
Though in thy store's account° I one must be;
For nothing hold me, so it please thee hold
That nothing me, a something, sweet, to thee.          12
    Make but my name° thy love, and love that still,°
    And then thou lovest me for my name is *Will*.

133: 1 **Beshrew** curse (a mild imprecation)   2 **For** because of
6 **my next self** i.e., my friend; **engrossed** captured   8
**crossed** thwarted   9 **ward** cell   10 **bail** go bail for, i.e., free
11 **keeps** guards; **guard** guardhouse   12 **rigor** cruelty; **my
jail** i.e., my heart
134: 2 **will** (1) purpose (2) carnal desire (perhaps with puns on
Shakespeare's name and the name of the friend)   3 **so** provided
that; **other mine** i.e., my friend   4 **still** always   7–8 **He . . .
bind** perhaps the idea is that the friend, as proxy, wooed the
woman for the poet but is now in her bondage   9 **statute**
security   10 **use** usury   11 **came** who became (?)   12 **my
unkind abuse** unkind deception of me

135: 1 **Will** (1) a person named Will (perhaps the poet, perhaps
the friend, perhaps the woman's husband, perhaps all; *Will* is
capitalized and italicized in this and in the next sonnet wherever
it so appears in the quarto) (2) desire, volition   3, 9 **still** always
4 **making addition thus** i.e., by adding myself   5, 7 rhyming
words are trisyllabic   6 **vouchsafe** consent   10 **his** its   13 **no
unkind** no unkind act, word, or person; **no fair beseechers**
i.e., any applicants for your favors (?)   13 So in Q and a perfectly possible reading. Personally, however, I am inclined to
accept Malone's emendation, "Let no unkind No fair beseechers
kill," which makes "No" a noun and "fair beseechers" the
object of the verb "kill."—W.H.A.   14 **Think . . . Will**
think all Wills as one and include me in that one
136: 1 **check** rebuke; **come so near** (1) touch to the quick (2)
come so near to your bed   5 **fulfill the treasure** fill the
treasury   6 **one** one of them   7 **things . . . receipt** i.e., large
matters   8 **Among . . . none** "One is no number" was an
Elizabethan saying   9 **untold** uncounted   10 **thy store's
account** i.e., the inventory of your supply (of lovers)   13 **my
name** i.e., will, carnal desire (?); **still** always

## 137

Thou blind fool, Love, what dost thou to mine eyes
That they behold and see not what they see?
They know what beauty is, see where it lies,°
Yet what the best is take the worst to be.                    4
If eyes, corrupt° by overpartial looks,
Be anchored in the bay where all men ride,°
Why of eyes' falsehood has thou forgèd hooks,
Whereto the judgment of my heart is tied?                    8
Why should my heart think that a several plot,°
Which my heart knows the wide world's common
      place?°
Or mine eyes seeing this, say this is not,
To° put fair truth upon so foul a face?                      12
   In things right true my heart and eyes have erred,
   And to this false plague° are they now transferred.

## 138

When my love swears that she is made of truth,°
I do believe her though I know she lies,
That° she might think me some untutored youth,
Unlearnèd in the world's false subtleties.                   4
Thus vainly thinking that she thinks me young,
Although she knows my days are past the best,
Simply° I credit° her false-speaking tongue;
On both sides thus is simple truth suppressed.               8
But wherefore says she not she is unjust?°
And wherefore say not I that I am old?
O, love's best habit° is in seeming trust,°
And age in love loves not to have years told.°              12
   Therefore I lie with° her, and she with me,
   And in our faults by lies we flattered be.

## 139

O, call not me to justify the wrong
That thy unkindness lays upon my heart;
Wound me not with thine eye but with thy tongue;
Use power with power° and slay me not by art.°             4
Tell me thou lov'st elsewhere; but in my sight,
Dear heart, forbear to glance thine eye aside;
What need'st thou wound with cunning when thy
      might
Is more than my o'erpressed° defense can bide?              8
Let me excuse thee; ah, my love well knows
Her pretty looks have been mine enemies,
And therefore from my face she turns my foes,°
That they elsewhere might dart their injuries.              12
   Yet do not so; but since I am near slain,
   Kill me outright with looks and rid my pain.

## 140

Be wise as thou art cruel; do not press°
My tongue-tied patience with too much disdain,
Lest sorrow lend me words, and words express
The manner° of my pity-wanting° pain.                       4
If I might teach thee wit,° better it were,
Though not to love, yet love, to tell me so;°
As testy° sick men, when their deaths be near,
No news but health from their physicians know.              8
For if I should despair, I should grow mad,
And in my madness might speak ill of thee.
Now this ill-wresting° world is grown so bad
Mad slanderers by mad ears believèd be.                    12
   That I may not be so,° nor thou belied,
   Bear thine eyes straight, though thy proud heart go
      wide.°

## 141

In faith I do not love thee with mine eyes,
For they in thee a thousand errors note;
But 'tis my heart that loves what they despise,
Who in despite of view° is pleased to dote.                 4
Nor are mine ears with thy tongue's tune delighted,
Nor tender feeling to base touches° prone,
Nor taste, nor smell, desire to be invited
To any sensual feast with thee alone.                       8
But° my five wits° nor my five senses can
Dissuade one foolish heart from serving° thee,
Who leaves unswayed the likeness of a man,°
Thy proud heart's slave and vassal wretch to be.           12
   Only my plague thus far I count my gain,
   That she that makes me sin awards me pain.

## 142

Love is my sin, and thy dear° virtue hate,
Hate of my sin, grounded on sinful loving.
O, but with mine compare thou thine own state,
And thou shalt find it° merits not reproving,               4
Or if it do, not from those lips of thine,
That have profaned their scarlet ornaments°
And sealed false bonds of love as oft as mine,
Robbed others' beds' revenues of their rents.°             8
Be it° lawful I love thee as thou lov'st those
Whom thine eyes woo as mine importune thee.
Root pity in thy heart, that, when it grows,
Thy pity may deserve to pitied be.                         12
   If thou dost seek to have what° thou dost hide,
   By self-example mayst thou be denied.

140: **1 press** oppress  **4 manner** nature; **pity-wanting** unpitied  **5 wit** wisdom  **6 so** i.e., that you love me  **7 testy** fretful  **11 ill-wresting** i.e., misinterpreting everything for the worse  **13 so** (1) a "mad slanderer" (2) so believed  **14 wide** wide of the mark
141: **4 Who . . . view** which in spite of what they see  **6 base touches** sexual contact  **9 But** but neither; **five wits** common wit, imagination, fantasy, estimation, memory  **10 serving** loving  **11 Who . . . man** i.e., which ceases to rule and so leaves me what is only the semblance of a man
142: **1 dear** inmost  **4 it** my state  **6 scarlet ornaments** i.e., lips (compared to scarlet wax that seals documents)  **8 Robbed . . . rents** i.e., has robbed wives of what their husbands owed them  **9 Be it** let it be  **13 what** that which, i.e., pity

137: **3 lies** inhabits  **5 corrupt** corrupted  **6 ride** pun on the sense "to mount sexually"  **9 that . . . plot** that place a private field  **10 common place** open field (with a pun on *common* = promiscuous)  **12 To** so as to  **14 plague** (1) plague of falseness (2) mistress
138: **1 truth** fidelity  **3 That** so that  **7 Simply** (1) foolishly (2) pretending to be simple; **credit** believe  **9 unjust** unfaithful  **11 habit** appearance; **seeming trust** the appearance of truth  **12 told** counted  **13 lie with** (1) lie to (2) sleep with
139: **4 with power** i.e., openly, directly; **art** artful means  **8 o'erpressed** overpowered  **11 my foes** i.e., her looks

*[handwritten: only Theological]*    *[handwritten: only a few that are Impersonal, one of]*

## 143

Lo, as a careful housewife runs to catch
One of her feathered creatures broke away,
Sets down her babe, and makes all swift dispatch
In pursuit of the thing she would have stay;   4
Whilst her neglected child holds her in chase,°
Cries to catch her whose busy care is bent
To follow that which flies before her face,
Not prizing° her poor infant's discontent:   8
So run'st thou after that which flies from thee,
Whilst I, thy babe, chase thee afar behind;
But if thou catch thy hope, turn back to me
And play the mother's part, kiss me, be kind.   12
    So will I pray that thou mayst have thy *Will*,
    If thou turn back and my loud crying still.°

## 144

Two loves I have, of comfort and despair,°
Which like two spirits do suggest me still;°
The better angel is a man right fair,
The worser spirit a woman colored ill.°   4
To win me soon to hell, my female evil
Tempteth my better angel from my side,
And would corrupt my saint to be a devil,
Wooing his purity with her foul pride.   8
And whether that my angel be turned fiend
Suspect I may, yet not directly° tell;
But being both from° me, both to each° friend,
I guess one angel in another's hell.°   12
    Yet this shall I ne'er know, but live in doubt,
    Till my bad angel fire my good one out.°

## 145

Those lips that Love's own hand did make
Breathed forth the sound that said, "I hate"
To me that languished for her sake.
But when she saw my woeful state,   4
Straight in her heart did mercy come,
Chiding that tongue that ever sweet
Was used in giving gentle doom,°
And taught it thus anew to greet:   8
"I hate," she altered with an end°
That followed it as gentle day
Doth follow night, who, like a fiend,
From heaven to hell is flown away.   12
    "I hate" from hate away she threw,
    And saved my life, saying, "not you."

## 146

Poor soul, the center of my sinful earth,°
My sinful earth° these rebel pow'rs that thee array,
Why dost thou pine within and suffer dearth,
Painting° thy outward walls so costly gay?   4
Why so large cost,° having so short a lease,
Dost thou upon thy fading mansion spend?
Shall worms, inheritors of this excess,°
Eat up thy charge?° Is this thy body's end?   8
Then, soul, live thou upon thy servant's loss,
And let that° pine to aggravate° thy store;
Buy terms divine° in selling hours of dross;
Within be fed, without be rich no more:   12
    So shalt thou feed on Death, that feeds on men,
    And Death once dead, there's no more dying then.

## 147

My love is as a fever, longing still°
For that which longer nurseth the disease,
Feeding on that which doth preserve the ill,°
Th' uncertain sickly appetite to please.   4
My reason, the physician to my love,
Angry that his prescriptions are not kept,
Hath left me, and I desperate now approve
Desire is death, which physic did except.°   8
Past cure I am, now reason is past care,
And frantic-mad with evermore unrest;
My thoughts and my discourse as madmen's are,
At random from the truth vainly expressed:   12
    For I have sworn thee fair, and thought thee bright,
    Who art as black as hell, as dark as night.

## 148

O me, what eyes hath Love put in my head,
Which have no correspondence with true sight!
Or, if they have, where is my judgment fled,
That censures° falsely what they see aright?   4
If that be fair whereon my false eyes dote,
What means the world to say it is not so?
If it be not, then love doth well denote
Love's eye° is not so true as all men's no.   8
How can it? O, how can Love's eye be true,
That is so vexed with watching° and with tears?
No marvel then though I mistake my view;°
The sun itself sees not till heaven clears.   12
    O cunning Love, with tears thou keep'st me blind,
    Lest eyes well-seeing thy foul faults should find.

---

**143: 5 holds . . . chase** chases her   **8 prizing** regarding
**13–14** Some scholarly follies are so extraordinary that they
deserve to be immortalized. Gregor Sarrazin, a German-Swiss,
emended these lines as follows: "So will I pray that thou may'est
have thy Hen, [short for Henry]/If thou turn back and my loud
crying pen."—W.H.A.
**144: 1 of . . . despair** i.e., one offering heavenly mercy, the
other offering hellish despair   **2 suggest me still** always urge
me   **4 colored ill** i.e., dark   **10 directly** precisely   **11 from**
away from; **each** each other   **12 in another's hell** with an
allusion to the female sexual organ   **14 fire . . . out** i.e., communicate venereal disease
**145: 7 doom** judgment   **9 end** ending

**146: 1 sinful earth** i.e., body   **2 My sinful earth** obviously
the printer mistakenly repeated here words of the previous line;
among suggested emendations are: "Thrall to," "Fooled by,"
"Rebuke," and "Leagued with"   **4 Painting** i.e., adorning
**5 cost** expense   **7 excess** extravagant expenditure   **8 charge**
(1) expense (2) burden, i.e., the body   **10 that** i.e., the body;
**aggravate** increase   **11 terms divine** ages of immortality
**147: 1 still** always   **3 preserve the ill** prolong the illness   **7–8
approve . . . except** find by experience that Desire, which
refused medicine, is death (?)
**148: 4 censures** judges   **8 eye** with a pun on *aye* in contrast
with "all men's no"   **10 watching** wakefulness   **11 mistake
my view** err in what I see

## 149

Canst thou, O cruel, say I love thee not,
When I against myself with thee partake?°
Do I not think on thee when I forgot
Am of° myself, all tyrant° for thy sake? 4
Who hateth thee that I do call my friend?
On whom frown'st thou that I do fawn upon?
Nay, if thou lour'st on me, do I not spend
Revenge upon myself with present moan?° 8
What merit do I in myself respect
That is so proud thy service to despise,
When all my best doth worship thy defect,°
Commanded by the motion of thine eyes? 12
　But, love, hate on, for now I know thy mind:
　Those that can see thou lov'st, and I am blind.

## 150

O, from what pow'r hast thou this pow'rful might
With insufficiency° my heart to sway?°
To make me give the lie to my true sight°
And swear that brightness doth not grace the day? 4
Whence hast thou this becoming of things ill°
That in the very refuse of thy deeds
There is such strength and warrantize of skill°
That in my mind thy worst all best exceeds? 8
Who taught thee how to make me love thee more,
The more I hear and see just cause of hate?
O, though I love what others do abhor,
With others thou shouldst not abhor my state: 12
　If thy unworthiness raised° love in me,
　More worthy I to be beloved of thee.

## 151

Love is too young to know what conscience is,
Yet who knows not conscience is born of love?
Then, gentle cheater, urge not my amiss,°
Lest guilty of my faults thy sweet self prove. 4
For, thou betraying me, I do betray
My nobler part to my gross body's treason;
My soul doth tell my body that he may
Triumph in love; flesh° stays° no farther reason,° 8
But, rising° at thy name, doth point out thee,
As his triumphant prize. Proud of° this pride,
He is contented thy poor drudge to be,
To stand in thy affairs, fall by thy side. 12
　No want of conscience hold it that I call
　Her "love" for whose dear love I rise and fall.

## 152

In loving thee thou know'st I am forsworn,°
But thou art twice forsworn, to me love swearing;
In act thy bed-vow broke, and new faith torn
In vowing new hate after new love bearing. 4
But why of two oaths' breach do I accuse thee,
When I break twenty? I am perjured most,
For all my vows are oaths but to misuse° thee,
And all my honest faith in thee is lost; 8
For I have sworn deep oaths of thy deep kindness,
Oaths of thy love, thy truth, thy constancy;
And, to enlighten thee,° gave eyes to blindness,°
Or made them swear against the thing they see; 12
　For I have sworn thee fair; more perjured eye,°
　To swear against the truth so foul a lie.

*Translation #1 of Greek Poetry* 153

Cupid laid by his brand° and fell asleep.
A maid of Dian's° this advantage° found,
And his love-kindling fire did quickly steep
In a cold valley-fountain of that ground; 4
Which borrowed from this holy fire of Love
A dateless lively° heat, still° to endure,
And grew a seething° bath, which yet men prove°
Against strange maladies a sovereign° cure. 8
But at my mistress' eye Love's brand new-fired,
The boy for trial needs would° touch my breast;
I, sick withal,° the help of bath° desired,
And thither hied, a sad distempered° guest, 12
　But found no cure; the bath for my help lies
　Where Cupid got new fire—my mistress' eyes.

*Translation #2 of Greek Poetry* 154

The little Love-god° lying once asleep
Laid by his side his heart-inflaming brand,°
Whilst many nymphs that vowed chaste life to keep
Came tripping by, but in her maiden hand 4
The fairest votary° took up that fire,
Which many legions of true hearts had warmed;
And so the general° of hot desire
Was, sleeping, by a virgin hand disarmed. 8
This brand she quenchèd in a cool well by,
Which from Love's fire took heart perpetual,
Growing a bath and healthful remedy
For men diseased; but I, my mistress' thrall,° 12
　Came there for cure, and this by that I prove:
　Love's fire heats water, water cools not love.

---

149: 2 partake unite　3–4 forgot Am of forget　4 all tyrant
i.e., having become altogether a tyrant　8 present moan
immediate grief　11 defect lack of good qualities
150: 2 insufficiency unworthiness; sway rule　3 give . . .
sight accuse my true sight of lying　5 becoming . . . ill i.e.,
power to make evil look attractive　7 warrantize of skill
guarantee of mental power　13 raised sexual innuendo (?)
151: 3 urge . . . amiss stress not my sinfulness　8 flesh the
penis; stays awaits; reason talk　9 rising rebelling (with a
sexual pun, as in "point," line 9; "stand" and "fall," line 12;
and "rise and fall," line 14)　10 Proud of swelling with

152: 1 am forsworn i.e., have broken (my marriage) vows　7
but to misuse merely to misrepresent　11 enlighten thee
make you shine; gave . . . blindness i.e., caused my eyes not
to see the truth　13 eye eyes (with a pun on I)
153: 1 brand torch　2 Dian Diana, goddess of chastity;
advantage opportunity　6 dateless lively eternal living;
still always　7 seething boiling; prove find by experience
8 sovereign potent　10 for . . . would as a test had to　11
withal with it; bath possibly an allusion to the city of Bath,
famous for its curative waters　12 distempered diseased
154: 1 Love-god Cupid　2 brand torch　5 votary one
vowed to chastity　7 general leader, i.e., Cupid　12 thrall
slave

# SUGGESTED REFERENCES

The number of possible references is vast and grows alarmingly. Though no works are indispensable, those listed below have been found helpful. The arrangement is as follows:

1. Reference Works (bibliographies, dictionaries, concordances, encyclopedias, sources, facsimiles, miscellaneous)
2. Biographies
3. The Elizabethan Age
4. Style; Shakespeare's English
5. Textual Matters
6. English Drama Before Shakespeare
7. The Theater and the Actors
8. Studies of Many or All of the Works
9. The Comedies (general studies)
10. The Histories (general studies)
11. The Tragedies (general studies)
12. Individual Plays (listed alphabetically)
13. The Nondramatic Works (general studies, followed by studies of the poems and sonnets)

## 1. REFERENCE WORKS

*Bibliographies.* The most detailed annual bibliographies are published in *Shakespeare Quarterly, Bibliography of English Language and Literature, Studies in Philology,* and *PMLA.* Useful annual reviews of research, sometimes with evaluative comments, are published in *Shakespeare Survey, The Year's Work in English Studies,* and *Shakespeare Studies. Shakespeare Research Opportunities,* No. 3, ed. W. R. Elton (1968), introduces the practice of giving annotated annual bibliographies of "Shakespeare and Renaissance intellectual contexts." Each issue of *Shakespeare Newsletter* synopsizes some recent criticism. Ronald Berman, *A Reader's Guide to Shakespeare's Plays* (1965), is a valuable short guide to about 3,000 pieces of writing on Shakespeare; for more comprehensive (and less selective) listings, see Walther Ebisch and Levin L. Schücking, *A Shakespeare Bibliography* (1931), with a *Supplement for the Years 1930–1935* (1937), and Gordon Ross Smith, *A Classified Shakespeare Bibliography 1936–1958* (1963).

*Dictionaries.* Useful dictionaries include Alexander Schmidt, *Shakespeare-Lexicon* (2 vols., 1874–75, 1886; 5th ed., 1962), and C. T. Onions, *A Shakespeare Glossary* (2nd rev. ed., 1919; 1953). More specialized are Eric Partridge, *Shakespeare's Bawdy* (rev. ed., 1955), on bawdy words and phrases, and Helge Kökeritz, *Shakespeare's Names* (1959), on the pronunciation of proper nouns. See also the titles listed below on Shakespeare's English, section 4.

*Concordances.* John Bartlett, *A New and Complete Concordance . . . to . . . Shakespeare* (1894), is an index to most of the words in Shakespeare; it probably will be displaced by Marvin Spevack, *A Complete and Systematic Concordance to the Works of Shakespeare* (8 vols. projected, 1967– ). Spevack's first volume is an index to words in the comedies, the second to words in the histories and nondramatic works, the third to words in the tragedies and *Pericles, The Two Noble Kinsmen,* and part of *Sir Thomas More.* These volumes include lists of words occurring only in a given play and lists of words by the character who speaks them. The remaining five volumes will contain, in addition to a concordance to the complete works, further statistical information, an index of words arranged according to frequency, a concordance to stage directions, and a list of significant textual variants. Bartlett's *Concordance,* though often inaccurate and devoid of statistical details, still is of some use, however, because Spevack occasionally gives a word only under its old spelling. For example, because his copy-text retains "ambassy" in *Merry Wives of Windsor,* this occurrence of the word is not listed under "embassy," the spelling under which a reader would naturally look for it, and which Bartlett gives. Old-spelling concordances to each play, preserving the spelling of the early texts, are being edited by Trevor Howard-Hill.

*Encyclopedias.* The best Shakespeare encyclopedia is edited by Oscar James Campbell and Edward G. Quinn, *The Reader's Encyclopedia of Shakespeare* (1966), an invaluable work with several thousand entries, many of which are excellent short essays; F. E. Halliday, *A Shakespeare Companion, 1564–1964* (rev. ed., 1964), is also of use, though the entries tend to be very brief. *A New Companion to Shakespeare Studies* (1971), edited by Kenneth Muir and S. Schoenbaum, comprises eighteen chapters on Elizabethan actors and theaters, the social background, Shakespeare's reading, the plays, and so on.

*Sources.* The fullest collection is in Geoffrey Bullough (ed.), *Narrative and Dramatic Sources of Shakespeare* (6 vols., 1957– ; Vol. 7 in preparation). More limited books reprinting material that Shakespeare used are: Richard Hosley (ed.), *Shakespeare's Holinshed* (1968); W. G. Boswell-Stone (ed.), *Shakespeare's Holinshed: The Chronicle and the Historical Plays Compared* (1896); T. J. B. Spencer (ed.), *Shakespeare's Plutarch* (1964); T. J. B. Spencer (ed.), *Elizabethan Love Stories* (1968). Virgil K. Whitaker, *Shakespeare's Use of Learning* (1953), discusses the major debts; Kenneth Muir, *Shakespeare's Sources,* Vol. 1 (1957), discusses the sources of the comedies and the tragedies.

*Facsimiles.* The best facsimile of the Shakespeare First Folio is The Norton Facsimile of *The First Folio of Shakespeare,* prepared by Charlton Hinman (1968). W. W. Greg edited facsimiles of the following quartos: *Hamlet* (Q1), *Hamlet* (Q2), *Henry V, 1 Henry IV, 3 Henry VI, King Lear, Love's Labor's Lost, The Merchant of Venice, The Merry Wives of Windsor, Pericles, Richard III, Romeo and Juliet,* and *Troilus and Cressida.* Joseph Quincy Adams edited a quarto of *Titus Andronicus,* and Charlton Hinman edited a quarto of *Richard II.* The Clarendon Press promises others. Facsimiles of all the nondramatic works have been brought together in a Yale University Press volume entitled *Shakespeare's Poems, A Facsimile of the Earliest Editions* (1964). Inexpensive Xerox facsimiles of any text may be obtained from University Microfilms, Ann Arbor, Michigan.

*Miscellaneous Reference Works.* Robert Kilburn Root, *Classical Mythology in Shakespeare* (1903); Richmond Noble, *Shakespeare's Biblical Knowledge and Use of the Book of Common Prayer* (1935); Peter J. Seng, *The Vocal Songs in the Plays of Shakespeare* (1967); Alfred Harbage, *Annals of English Drama, 975–1700,* revised by S. Schoenbaum (1964); *The Shakespere Allusion Book: A Collection of Allusions to Shakespere from 1591 to 1700,* compiled by C. M. Engleby, reedited by John Monro (1909), reissued with a preface by E. K. Chambers (1932).

## 2. BIOGRAPHIES

E. K. Chambers, *William Shakespeare: A Study of Facts and Problems* (2 vols., 1930), is an invaluable reference work; other massive works are Edgar I. Fripp, *Shakespeare, Man and Artist* (2 vols., 1938), and B. Roland Lewis, *The Shakespeare Documents* (2 vols., 1940). But for a readable biography, with portraits of Stratford and London life, see Marchette Chute, *Shakespeare of London* (1949). Gerald E. Bentley, *Shakespeare: A Biographical Handbook* (1961), is a spare account of the facts, with virtually no conjecture intermingled. Other useful biographies are F. E. Halliday, *Shakespeare: A Pictorial Biography* (new ed., 1964), and Mark Eccles, *Shakespeare in Warwickshire* (1961). S. Schoenbaum, *Shakespeare's Lives* (1970), is a history of biographical scholarship, covering not only books and articles on Shakespeare's life but also such things as the Folio engraving and the Stratford bust, the sonnets and plays as spiritual autobiography, and Shakespeare as a character in plays and novels. The anti-Stratfordians are discussed in Frank W. Wadsworth, *The Poacher from Stratford* (1958); H. N. Gibson, *The Shakespeare Claimants* (1962); William F. and Elizabeth S. Friedman, *The Shakespearean Ciphers Examined* (1957). Some anti-Stratfordian writing is anthologized by George McMichael and Edgar M. Glenn, *Shakespeare and His Rivals* (1962). Shakespeare's reputation is chronicled in Louis Marder, *His Exits and His Entrances* (1963); *The Persistence of Shakespeare Idolatry,* edited by Herbert M. Schueller (1964), has chapters on Shakespeare's reputation in France, Germany, and England.

## 3. ELIZABETHAN AGE

Lacey Baldwin Smith, *The Horizon Book of the Elizabethan World* (1967), is readable and well illustrated. Among other useful historical and political studies are: S. T. Bindoff, *Tudor England* (1959); G. R. Elton, *England Under the Tudors* (1955); S. T. Bindoff, J. Hurstfield, and C. H. Williams (eds.), *Elizabethan Government and Society* (1961); Wallace MacCaffrey, *The Shaping of the Elizabethan Regime* (1968); Alfred L. Rowse, *The England of Elizabeth* (1950); and John B. Black, *The Reign of Elizabeth, 1558–1603* (2nd ed., 1959).

Elizabethan thought is discussed in E. M. W. Tillyard, *The Elizabethan World Picture* (1943); Herschel Clay Baker, *The Dignity of Man: Studies in the Persistence of an Idea* (1947; reprinted in 1961 as *The Image of Man*); Hardin Craig, *The Enchanted Glass: The Elizabethan Mind in Literature* (1936); Douglas Bush, *The Renaissance and English Humanism* (1939); Theodore Spencer, *Shakespeare and the Nature of Man* (1942); and David L. Stevenson (ed.), *The Elizabethan Age.* More specialized studies are: Don Cameron Allen on astrology, *The Star-Crossed Renaissance* (1941); F. R. Johnson, *Astronomical Thought in Renaissance England* (1937); Paul Kocher, *Science and Religion in Renaissance England* (1953); Ernst Cassirer, *The Platonic Renaissance in England* (1954); Ernest William Talbert, *The Problem of Order* (1962); and F. J. Levy, *Tudor Historical Thought* (1967).

On Elizabethan life, in addition to Lacey Baldwin Smith, above, see two books with chapters on a wide variety of topics, W. Raleigh *et al.* (eds.), *Shakespeare's England: An Account of the Life and Manners of His Age* (2 vols., 1916), and Allardyce Nicoll, (ed.), *Shakespeare in His Own Age* (1964; identical with *Shakespeare Survey 17*). Also valuable are: Louis B. Wright and Virginia La Mar (eds.), *Life and Letters in Tudor and Stuart England: First Series* (1962); Muriel St. Clare Byrne, *Elizabethan Life in Town and Country* (7th ed., 1954); Martin Holmes, *Elizabethan London* (1969). John Dover Wilson (ed.), *Life in Shakespeare's England* (2nd ed., 1913), is an anthology of Elizabethan writings on the countryside, superstition, the court, and so on; Allardyce Nicoll (ed.), *The Elizabethans* (1957), has bits of Elizabethan writing and attractive pictures. More specialized studies are: Kenneth Charlton, *Education in Renaissance England* (1965); Joan Simon, *Education and Society in Tudor England* (1966); T. W. Baldwin, *William Shakspere's Small Latine and Lesse Greeke* (2 vols., 1944); Louis B. Wright, *Middle-Class Culture in Elizabethan England* (1935); and John Buxton, *Elizabethan Taste* (1963).

The literature of the period (dramatic and non-dramatic) is studied in Boris Ford (ed.), *The Age of Shakespeare* (1956). Specialized studies of the literature are given elsewhere in this bibliography.

## 4. STYLE; SHAKESPEARE'S ENGLISH

M. C. Bradbrook has a short survey of writings on Shakespeare's style in *Shakespeare Survey 7,* edited by Allardyce Nicoll (1954). On Shakespeare's prose, see Milton Crane, *Shakespeare's Prose* (1951); Jonas A. Barish, *Ben Jonson and the Language of Prose Comedy* (1960); Brian Vickers, *The Artistry of Shakespeare's Prose* (1968); F. P. Wilson, *Shakespeare and the Diction of Common Life* (1941; reprinted in Wilson's *Shakespearian and Other Studies* [1969]); and Morris Palmer Tilley, *A Dictionary of the Proverbs in England in the Sixteenth and Seventeenth Centuries* (1950).

Three general studies are Patrick Cruttwell, *The Shakespearean Moment and Its Place in the Poetry of the Seventeenth Century* (1954); Benjamin Ifor Evans, *The Language of Shakespeare's Plays* (1952); and F. E. Halliday, *The Poetry of Shakespeare's Plays* (1954). Rhyme is discussed by Frederic W. Ness, *The Use of Rhyme in Shakespeare's Plays* (1941); blank verse and imagery are discussed by Moody Prior, *The Language of Tragedy* (1947). On imagery see especially Wolfgang H. Clemen, *The Development of Shakespeare's Imagery* (1951; originally published in German, 1936); also of use are Caroline Spurgeon, *Shakespeare's Imagery and What It Tells Us* (1935); Edward A. Armstrong, *Shakespeare's Imagination* (rev. ed., 1963); and F. R. Johnson, "Shakespearian Imagery and Senecan Imitation," in *Joseph Quincy Adams Memorial Studies* (1948). Kenneth Muir, "Shakespeare's Imagery—Then and Now," in *Shakespeare Survey 18,* edited by Allardyce Nicoll (1965), is an appraisal of scholarship on the subject.

Maurice Charney, *Shakespeare's Roman Plays* (1961), relates imagery to what is seen as well as heard; in *Style in Hamlet* (1969), Charney goes further, discussing, for example, not only imagery of animals, disease, food, and gardens, but also gestures, properties, and sound effects. Sister Miriam Joseph, *Shakespeare's Use of the Arts of Language* (1947; reprinted in part as *Rhetoric in Shakespeare's Time: Literary Theory of Renaissance Europe* [1962]) catalogs Shakespeare's figures; Wilbur Samuel Howell, *Logic and Rhetoric in England, 1500–1700* (1956), is also of interest.

Matters of stage business, dramatic illusion, and so on are discussed in S. L. Bethell, *Shakespeare and the Popular Dramatic Tradition* (1944), and in J. L. Styan, *Shakespeare's Stagecraft* (1967), as well as in Maurice Charney's *Style in Hamlet* (1969). (See also works on acting and costume, listed below in section 7.)

On character see Arthur Sewell, *Character and Society in Shakespeare* (1951). On the construction of the plots, an old book, Richard G. Moulton's *Shakespeare as a Dramatic Artist* (3rd ed., 1893; rev. and enl. ed., 1966), remains one of the best, but see also Harley Granville-Barker, *Prefaces to Shakespeare* (2 vols., 1946–47; four vols. in paperback, 1965); Madeleine Doran, *Endeavors of Art* (1954); Nevill Coghill, *Shakespeare's Professional Skills* (1964); Hereward Price, *Construction in Shakespeare* (1951); and the works listed in the second paragraph of section 11.

On Shakespeare's English, in addition to the dictionaries by Schmidt, Onions, and Partridge mentioned in section 1, and the titles mentioned in the first paragraph of this section, the following are useful: E. A. Abbott, *A Shakespearian Grammar* (new ed., 1886); Henry Cecil Wyld, *A History of Modern Colloquial English* (3rd ed., 1936); Albert C. Baugh, *A History of the English Language* (2nd ed., 1957); Thomas Pyles, *The Origins and Development of the English Language* (1964); L. M. Myers, *The Roots of Modern English* (1966); and A. C. Partridge, *Tudor to Augustan English* (1969). On pronunciation see Helge Kökeritz, *Shakespeare's Pronunciation* (1953), and his *Shakespeare's Names* (1959); and Eric J. Dobson, *English Pronunciation, 1500–1700* (2 vols., 1957). Columbia Records, Inc., has issued a long-playing record of Kökeritz illustrating Shakespeare's pronunciation. M. M. Mahood, *Shakespeare's Wordplay* (1957), contains ingenious discussions of puns, as does Kökeritz' *Shakespeare's Pronunciation.*

## 5. TEXTUAL MATTERS

Fredson Bowers' article on "Textual Criticism" in *The Reader's Encyclopedia of Shakespeare,* edited by Oscar James Campbell and Edward G. Quinn (1966), is a good introduction. Bowers' *Textual and Literary Criticism* (1959) and his *On Editing Shakespeare* (1966) are also useful. Fuller discussions include Ronald B. McKerrow, *An Introduction to Bibliography for Literary Students* (1927); Ronald B. McKerrow, *Prolegomena for the Oxford Shakespeare: A Study in Editorial Method* (1939); W. W. Greg, *The Editorial Problem in Shakespeare: A Survey of the Foundations of the Text* (1942); W. W. Greg, *The Shakespeare First Folio, Its Bibliographical and Textual History* (1955); and Charlton Hinman, *The Printing and Proof-Reading of the First Folio of Shakespeare* (2 vols., 1963).

## 6. ENGLISH DRAMA BEFORE SHAKESPEARE

E. K. Chambers, *The Medieval Stage* (2 vols., 1903), is a compendious account; for a short general introduction to early English drama see A. P. Rossiter, *English Drama from Early Times to the Elizabethans* (1950). Also valuable are V. A. Kolve, *The Play Called "Corpus Christi"* (1966); Frederick M. Salter, *Mediaeval Drama in Chester* (1955); David M. Bevington, *From "Mankind" to Marlowe; Growth of Structure in the Popular Drama of Tudor England* (1962); and, for the development of the medieval Vice to one kind of Elizabethan villain, Bernard Spivack, *Shakespeare and the Allegory of Evil* (1958).

The best general treatment of Shakespeare's immediate dramatic heritage is F. P. Wilson and G. K. Hunter, *The English Drama, 1485–1585* (1969). More specialized studies are Frederick Boas, *University Drama in the Tudor Age* (1914); Thomas W. Craik, *The Tudor Interlude: Stage, Costume, and Acting* (1958); Willard Farnham, *The Medieval Heritage of Elizabethan Tragedy* (1936); Wolfgang H. Clemen, *English Tragedy Before Shakespeare: The Development of Dramatic Speech,* tr. T. S. Dorsch (1961). On the court and the drama

see E. K. Chambers, *The Elizabethan Stage* (4 vols., 1923); Enid Welsford, *The Court Masque* (1927); Marion Jones, "The Court and the Dramatists," *Stratford-upon-Avon Studies 9: Elizabethan Theatre,* edited by John Russell Brown and Bernard Harris (1967); *A Book of Masques; in Honor of Allardyce Nicoll* (1967).

## 7. THE THEATER AND THE ACTORS

The most inclusive work (except for its relative neglect of acting) is E. K. Chambers, *The Elizabethan Stage* (4 vols., 1923). For the influence of earlier staging, see George R. Kernodle, *From Art to Theatre: Form and Convention in the Renaissance* (1944) and Glynne Wickham, *Early English Stages, 1300 to 1660* (3 vols. projected, 1959– ).

For a short account of the public playhouse see Alois M. Nagler, *Shakespeare's Stage* (1958); longer accounts are in C. Walter Hodges, *The Globe Restored* (2nd ed., 1968), and in Bernard Beckerman, *Shakespeare at the Globe, 1599–1609* (1962). Frances Yates, in *Theatre of the World* (1969), argues that the "symbolic geometry" of the Globe, relating the microcosm to the macrocosm, is indebted to a tradition that goes back to Roman theatrical architecture. *Shakespeare Survey 12,* edited by Allardyce Nicoll (1959), in part devoted to the Elizabethan playhouse, includes Richard Hosley's important article on the discovery-space behind the stage doors. Hosley also has articles on the gallery over the stage, in *Shakespeare Quarterly,* VIII (1957), and on the music-room, in *Shakespeare Survey 13,* edited by Allardyce Nicoll (1960). Alfred Harbage, *Shakespeare's Audience* (1941), discusses the size and social composition of the popular audience. Irwin Smith offers a detailed conjecture in *Shakespeare's Blackfriars Playhouse* (1964), reviewed in *Journal of English and Germanic Philology,* LXV (1966), 178–82.

W. W. Greg, *Dramatic Documents from the Elizabethan Playhouses; Stage Plots; Actors' Parts; Prompt Books* (2 vols., 1931), reproduces the basic materials. On acting styles see Alfred Harbage, "Elizabethan Acting," *PMLA,* LIV (1939), reprinted in his *Theatre for Shakespeare* (1955); Bertram L. Joseph, *Acting Shakespeare* (1960); B. L. Joseph, *Elizabethan Acting* (2nd ed., 1964); Chapter 2 of John Russell Brown, *Shakespeare's Plays in Performance* (1966); Daniel Seltzer, "Elizabethan Acting in Othello," *Shakespeare Quarterly,* X (1959); and Daniel Seltzer, "The Staging of the Last Plays," *Stratford-upon-Avon Studies 8: Later Shakespeare,* edited by John Russell Brown and Bernard Harris (1966). See also the works by Charney, Bethell, and Styan mentioned in section 4. On post-Elizabethan acting see Arthur Colby Sprague, *Shakespeare and the Actors: The Stage Business in His Plays (1660–1905)* (1944). On costume and spectacle see Marie C. Linthicum, *Costume in the Drama of Shakespeare and His Contemporaries* (1936); Hal H. Smith, "Some Principles of Elizabethan Stage Costume," *Journal of the Warburg and Courtauld Institutes,* XXV (1962); and Alice S. Venezky, *Pageantry on the Shakespearean Stage* (1951).

## 8. STUDIES OF MANY OR ALL OF THE WORKS

Hardin Craig, *An Interpretation of Shakespeare* (1948), is a solid study of most aspects of the works. Mark Van Doren, *Shakespeare* (1939); Donald A. Stauffer, *Shakespeare's World of Images; The Development of his Moral Ideas* (1949); Derek Traversi, *An Approach to Shakespeare* (2 vols.; 3rd rev. ed., 1968–69); Francis Fergusson, *Shakespeare: The Pattern in His Carpet* (1970); and Norman Rabkin, *Shakespeare and the Common Understanding* (1967), are primarily critical studies. Alfred Harbage, *William Shakespeare: A Reader's Guide* (1963), has a discussion of style and discussions of most of the major plays. Harley Granville-Barker, *Prefaces to Shakespeare* (2 vols., 1946–47; four vols. in paperback, 1965), examines ten plays: the first of the two volumes is on *Hamlet, King Lear, The Merchant of Venice, Antony and Cleopatra,* and *Cymbeline;* the second volume is on *Othello, Coriolanus, Julius Caesar, Romeo and Juliet,* and *Love's Labor's Lost.* M. C. Bradbrook, *Shakespeare and Elizabethan Poetry: A Study of His Earlier Work in Relation to the Poetry of the Time* (1951), discusses the poems and the plays to about 1602. Three valuable books on specific themes that run through many plays are Geoffrey Bush, *Shakespeare and the Natural Condition* (1956); Anne Righter, *Shakespeare and the Idea of the Play* (1962); and Roland Mushat Frye, *Shakespeare and Christian Doctrine* (1963).

Older major criticism includes *Johnson on Shakespeare,* edited by Arthur Sherbo (2 vols., 1968); August Wilhelm von Schlegel, *A Course of Lectures on Dramatic Art and Literature* (1815; tr. J. Black, 1846); William Hazlitt, *Characters of Shakespear's Plays* (1817); and Samuel Taylor Coleridge, *Shakespearean Criticism,* edited by Thomas Middleton Raysor (2 vols., 2nd ed., 1960). Anthologies of older criticism are: D. Nichol Smith (ed.), *Shakespeare Criticism: A Selection* (1916), containing material from 1623 to 1840, and Anne Bradby (ed.), *Shakespeare Criticism, 1919–1935* (1936). F. E. Halliday (ed.), *Shakespeare and His Critics* (rev. ed., 1958), and Frank Kermode (ed.), *Four Centuries of Shakespearian Criticism* (1965), span the entire period. Anthologies of recent criticism include Anne Bradby Ridler (ed.), *Shakespeare Criticism, 1935–1960* (1963); Norman Rabkin, *Approaches to Shakespeare* (1964); Leonard F. Dean (ed.), *Shakespeare: Modern Essays in Criticism* (rev. ed., 1967); James L. Calderwood and Harold E. Toliver (eds.), *Essays in Shakespearean Criticism* (1970); and Alvin B. Kernan, *Modern Shakespearean Criticism* (1970).

### 9. THE COMEDIES

Northrop Frye has written two seminal essays and a book on the comedies: "The Argument of Comedy," *English Institute Essays 1948,* edited by D. A. Robertson (1949); "Characterization in Shakespearian Comedy," *Shakespeare Quarterly,* IV (1953), 271–77; and *A Natural Perspective: The Development of Shakespearean Comedy and Romance* (1965). Frye's *Anatomy of Criticism* also has much valuable material on comedy. Books on most or all of the comedies are: John Russell Brown, *Shakespeare and His Comedies* (2nd ed., 1962); Larry S. Champion, *The Evolution of Shakespeare's Comedy* (1970); H. B. Charlton, *Shakespearian Comedy* (1938); Bertrand Evans, *Shakespeare's Comedies* (1960); and Robert Grams Hunter, *Shakespeare and the Comedy of Forgiveness* (1965). Thomas Marc Parrott, *Shakespearean Comedy* (1949), examines comic elements in all of Shakespeare's plays. Nevill Coghill, "The Basis of Shakespearian Comedy," *Shakespeare Criticism, 1935–1960,* edited by Anne Bradby Ridler (1963), pp. 201–27, examines some of the plays against the inherited critical background. Kenneth Muir (ed.), *Shakespeare: The Comedies* (1965), is an anthology of recent criticism. *Shakespeare Survey 8,* edited by Allardyce Nicoll (1955), and *Shakespeare Survey 22,* edited by Kenneth Muir (1969), are largely devoted to the comedies. M. C. Bradbrook, *The Growth and Structure of Elizabethan Comedy* (1955), is especially good on pre-Shakespearean comedy. David L. Stevenson, *The Love-Game Comedy* (1946), discusses the witty lovers and the traditions behind them. Three specialized studies are O. J. Campbell, *Shakespeare's Satire* (1943; 1963); R. H. Goldsmith, *Wise Fools in Shakespeare* (1955); C. Gesner, *Shakespeare and Greek Romances* (1970). On the earlier comedies see E. M. W. Tillyard, *Shakespeare's Early Comedies* (1965); F. P. Wilson, *Shakespearian*

*and Other Studies* (1969); John Dover Wilson, *Shakespeare's Happy Comedies* (1963); and C. L. Barber, *Shakespeare's Festive Comedy* (1959), which examines *Love's Labor's Lost, A Midsummer Night's Dream, The Merchant of Venice, As You Like It,* and *Twelfth Night* against a background of social festivities (and also discusses *1* and *2 Henry IV*). On the "problem" comedies see W. W. Lawrence, *Shakespeare's Problem Comedies* (1931); E. M. W. Tillyard, *Shakespeare's Problem Plays* (1949); and Ernest Schanzer, *The Problem Plays of Shakespeare* (1963), which seeks to define the term and then studies *Measure for Measure* as well as two tragedies, *Julius Caesar* and *Antony and Cleopatra.* Much has been written on the last plays, the romances. See Derek Traversi, *Shakespeare: The Last Phase* (1954); G. Wilson Knight, *The Crown of Life: Essays in Interpretation of Shakespeare's Final Plays* (1947); and E. M. W. Tillyard, *Shakespeare's Last Plays* (1938; 6th ed., 1964). *Shakespeare Survey 11,* edited by Allardyce Nicoll (1958), contains several important articles on the romances. See also Stanley Wells, "Shakespeare and Romance," *Stratford-upon-Avon Studies 8: Later Shakespeare,* edited by John Russell Brown and Bernard Harris (1966).

### 10. THE HISTORIES

F. P. Wilson has a masterful essay on "The English History Play" in his *Shakespearian and Other Studies* (1969), and A. P. Rossiter has three relevant essays in his *"Angel with Horns" and Other Shakespeare Lectures,* edited by Graham Storey (1961). Valuable longer accounts are E. M. W. Tillyard, *Shakespeare's History Plays* (1944; 1962); Irving Ribner, *The English History Play in the Age of Shakespeare* (1957; rev. ed., 1965); and Max Meredith Reese, *The Cease of Majesty: A Study of Shakespeare's History Plays* (1961). Northrop Frye has many illuminating comments on the histories in *Fools of Time: Studies in Shakespearean Tragedy* (1967). Eugene M. Waith (ed.), *Shakespeare: The Histories* (1965), is a collection of fairly recent essays on these plays; *Shakespeare Survey 6,* edited by Allardyce Nicoll (1953), is largely devoted to the histories. On the second tetralogy see Derek Traversi, *Shakespeare: From "Richard II" to "Henry V"* (1957), and Alvin B. Kernan, "The Henriad: Shakespeare's Major History Plays," *Modern Shakespearean Criticism,* edited by Alvin B. Kernan (1970).

### 11. THE TRAGEDIES

The books by Clemen, Farnham, Spivack, and Wilson and Hunter mentioned in section 6 are highly relevant. Howard Baker, *Induction to Tragedy: A Study in a Development of Form in "Gorboduc," "The Spanish Tragedy,"* and *"Titus Andronicus"* (1939), is also useful, but it is excessive in its rejection of Seneca as a considerable influence. See also F. L. Lucas, *Seneca and Elizabethan Tragedy* (1922); S. F. Johnson, "The Tragic Hero in Early Elizabethan Drama," *Studies in Renaissance Drama,* edited by J. W. Bennett, O. Cargill, and V. Hall (1959); D. J. Palmer, "Elizabethan Tragic Heroes," *Stratford-upon-Avon Studies 9: Elizabethan Theatre,* edited by John Russell Brown and Bernard Harris (1967); and J. M. R. Margeson, *The Origins of English Tragedy* (1967). J. V. Cunningham, *Woe or Wonder: The Emotional Effect of Shakespearean Tragedy* (1951; reprinted in Cunningham's *Tradition and Poetic Structure: Essays in Literary History and Criticism* [1960]), is valuable both for its main thesis and for its readings of particular passages.

A. C. Bradley, *Shakespearean Tragedy* (1904; 1965), on *Hamlet, Othello, King Lear,* and *Macbeth,* remains a work of first importance, although its emphasis on character is now unfashionable; Maynard Mack offers valuable notes toward a different approach in "The Jacobean Shakespeare: Some Observations on the Construction of the Tragedies," *Stratford-upon-Avon Studies 1: Jacobean Theatre*, edited by John Russell Brown and Bernard Harris (1960), pp. 11–41. Helpful general studies include G. B. Harrison, *Shakespeare's Tragedies* (1951); John Holloway, *The Story of the Night* (1961); Irving Ribner, *Patterns in Shakespearian Tragedy* (1960); and Harold S. Wilson, *On the Design of Shakespearean Tragedy* (1957). William Rosen, *Shakespeare and the Craft of Tragedy* (1960), also deals with construction; Brents Stirling, *Unity in Shakespearian Tragedy: The Interplay of Theme and Character* (1956), is largely concerned with unifying images; Northrop Frye, *Fools of Time: Studies in Shakespearean Tragedy* (1967), is perhaps less valuable to the student than is his *Anatomy of Criticism* (1957). G. Wilson Knight's *The Wheel of Fire: Essays in Interpretation of Shakespeare's Sombre Tragedies* (1930; 5th rev. ed., 1957) is chiefly devoted to the tragedies. Alfred Harbage (ed.), *Shakespeare: The Tragedies* (1964), is a useful collection of modern essays.

Specialized studies covering several plays include: Nicholas Brooke, *Shakespeare's Early Tragedies* (1968); Frederick W. Sternfeld, *Music in Shakespearean Tragedy* (1963); M. M. MacCallum, *Shakespeare's Roman Plays and Their Background* (1910); *Shakespeare Survey 10*, edited by Allardyce Nicoll (1957), also on the Roman plays; and Maurice Charney, *Shakespeare's Roman Plays: The Function of Imagery in the Drama* (1961). R. A. Brower, *Hero and Saint: Shakespeare and the Greco-Roman Heroic Tradition* (1970), discusses the classical plays and *Hamlet*, *Othello*, and *King Lear*.

## 12. INDIVIDUAL PLAYS

*All's Well That Ends Well*

Arthos, John. *The Art of Shakespeare* (1964).
Calderwood, James Lee. "Styles of Knowing in *All's Well*," *Modern Language Quarterly*, XXV (1964), 272–94.
Halio, Jay L. "*All's Well That Ends Well*," *Shakespeare Quarterly*, XV (1964), 33–43.
Hunter, G. K. (ed.). *The Arden Shakespeare: All's Well That Ends Well* (3rd ed., 1959).
Hunter, Robert Grams. *Shakespeare and the Comedy of Forgiveness* (1965).
Knight, G. Wilson. *The Sovereign Flower: On Shakespeare as the Poet of Royalism* (1958).
Lawrence, W. W. *Shakespeare's Problem Comedies* (1931; 1960).
Price, Joseph G. *The Unfortunate Comedy: A Study of "All's Well That Ends Well" and Its Critics* (1968).
Rossiter, A. P. "*Angels with Horns*" *and Other Shakespeare Lectures*, ed. Graham Storey (1961).
Schoff, Francis G. "Claudio, Bertram, and a Note on Interpretation," *Shakespeare Quarterly*, X (1959), 11–23.
Stoll, Elmer Edgar. *From Shakespeare to Joyce* (1946).
Tillyard, E. M. W. *Shakespeare's Problem Plays* (1949).

*Antony and Cleopatra*

Barnet, Sylvan. "Recognition and Reversal in *Antony and Cleopatra*," *Shakespeare Quarterly*, VIII (1957), 331–34.
Bradley, A. C. *Oxford Lectures on Poetry* (1909).
Cecil, David. *Antony and Cleopatra*, W. P. Ker Memorial Lecture No. 4 (1943). Reprinted in *Poets and Story-Tellers* (1949; 1961).
Coleridge, Samuel Taylor. *Shakespearean Criticism*, ed. Thomas Middleton Raysor (2 vols.; 2nd ed., 1960).
Danby, John F. *Poets on Fortune's Hill* (1952).
Farnham, Willard. *Shakespeare's Tragic Frontier* (1950).

Goldberg, S. L. "The Tragedy of the Imagination: A Reading of *Antony and Cleopatra*," *The Melbourne Critical Review*, IV (1961), 41–64.
Granville-Barker, Harley. *Prefaces to Shakespeare* (2 vols., 1946–47), Vol. 1.
Holloway, John. *The Story of the Night* (1961).
Kaula, David. "The Time Sense of *Antony and Cleopatra*," *Shakespeare Quarterly*, XV (1964), 211–23.
Knight, G. Wilson. *The Imperial Theme: Further Interpretations of Shakespeare's Tragedies Including the Roman Plays* (1931; 3rd ed., 1953).
Knights, L. C. *Some Shakespearean Themes* (1959).
Leavis, F. R. "*Antony and Cleopatra* and *All for Love*: A Critical Exercise," *Scrutiny*, V (1936–37), 158–69.
Lloyd, Michael. "Cleopatra as Isis," *Shakespeare Survey 12*, ed. Allardyce Nicoll (1959), pp. 88–94.
MacCallum, M. M. W. *Shakespeare's Roman Plays and Their Background* (1910).
Mack, Maynard. "The Jacobean Shakespeare: Some Observations on the Construction of the Tragedies," *Stratford-upon-Avon Studies 1: Jacobean Theatre*, eds. John Russell Brown and Bernard Harris (1960), pp. 11–41.
Maxwell, J. C. "Shakespeare's Roman Plays: 1900–56," *Shakespeare Survey 10*, ed. Allardyce Nicoll (1957), pp. 1–11.
Ornstein, Robert. "The Ethic of the Imagination: Love and Art in *Antony and Cleopatra*," *Stratford-upon-Avon Studies 8: Later Shakespeare*, eds. John Russell Brown and Bernard Harris (1966), pp. 31–46.
Schanzer, Ernest. *The Problem Plays of Shakespeare: A Study of "Julius Caesar," "Measure for Measure," and "Antony and Cleopatra"* (1963).
Spencer, T. J. B. "Shakespeare and the Elizabethan Romans," *Shakespeare Survey 10*, ed. Allardyce Nicoll (1957), pp. 27–38.
Stewart, J. I. M. *Character and Motive in Shakespeare* (1949).
Traversi, Derek. *Shakespeare: The Roman Plays* (1963).

*As You Like It*

Barber, C. L. *Shakespeare's Festive Comedy* (1959).
Barnet, Sylvan. "Strange Events: Improbability in *As You Like It*," *Shakespeare Studies 4*, ed. J. Leeds Barroll (1969), pp. 119–31.
Brown, John Russell. *Shakespeare and His Comedies* (1957; 2nd ed., 1962).
Campbell, Oscar James. *Shakespeare's Satire* (1943).
Charlton, H. B. *Shakespearian Comedy* (1938).
Gardner, Helen. "*As You Like It*," *More Talking of Shakespeare*, ed. John W. P. Garrett (1959), pp. 17–32.
Goldsmith, Robert H. *Wise Fools in Shakespeare* (1955).
Halio, Jay L. "'No Clock in the Forest': Time in *As You Like It*," *Studies in English Literature: 1500–1900*, II (1962), 197–207.
Hunter, G. K. *Shakespeare: The Late Comedies* (1962).
Jenkins, H. "*As You Like It*," *Shakespeare Survey 8*, ed. Allardyce Nicoll (1955), pp. 40–51.
Knowles, Richard. "Myth and Type in *As You Like It*," *ELH; A Journal of English Literary History*, XXXIII (1966), 1–22.
Lascelles, M. "Shakespeare's Pastoral Comedy," *More Talking of Shakespeare*, ed. John W. P. Garrett (1959), pp. 70–86.
McIntosh, Angus. "*As You Like It*: A Grammatical Clue to Character," *A Review of English Literature*, IV, No. 2 (April 1963), 68–81.
Mincoff, Marco. "What Shakespeare Did to *Rosalynde*," *Shakespeare Jahrbuch*, XCVI (1960), 78–89.
Shaw, John. "Fortune and Nature in *As You Like It*," *Shakespeare Quarterly*, VI (1955), 45–50.
Smith, James. "*As You Like It*," *Scrutiny*, IX (1940), 9–32.
Stevenson, David L. *The Love-Game Comedy* (1946).

*The Comedy of Errors*

Baldwin, T. W. *On the Compositional Genetics of "The Comedy of Errors"* (1965).

Barber, C. L. "Shakespearian Comedy in *The Comedy of Errors*," *College English*, XXV (1964), 493–97.

Brooks, Harold F. "Themes and Structure in *The Comedy of Errors*," *Stratford-upon-Avon Studies 3: Early Shakespeare*, eds. John Russell Brown and Bernard Harris (1961), pp. 55–71.

Brown, John Russell. *Shakespeare and His Comedies* (1957; 2nd ed., 1962).

Clubb, L. G. "Italian Comedy and *The Comedy of Errors*," *Comparative Literature*, XIX, 3 (1967), 240–51.

Evans, Bertrand. *Shakespeare's Comedies* (1960).

Fergusson, Francis. "Two Comedies," *The Human Image in Dramatic Literature* (1957), pp. 144–57.

Foakes, R. A. (ed.). *The Arden Shakespeare: The Comedy of Errors* (1962).

Hamilton, A. C. *The Early Shakespeare* (1967).

Lea, K. M. *Italian Popular Comedy: A Study of the Commedia dell' Arte, 1560–1620, with Special Reference to the English Stage* (1934).

Masefield, John. *William Shakespeare* (1911; rev. ed., 1954).

Segal, Erich. *Roman Laughter: The Comedy of Plautus* (1968).

Traversi, Derek. *Shakespeare: The Early Comedies* (1960).

Williams, Gwyn. "*The Comedy of Errors* Rescued from Tragedy," *A Review of English Literature*, V (1964), 63–71.


*Coriolanus*

Bradley, A. C. *A Miscellany* (1929).

Browning, I. R. "Coriolanus—'A Boy of Tears,' " *Essays in Criticism*, V (1955), 18–31.

Burke, Kenneth. "Coriolanus and the Delights of Faction," *Hudson Review*, XIX (1966–67), 185–201.

Charney, Maurice (ed.). *Discussions of Shakespeare's Roman Plays* (1964). Selections by Samuel Johnson, Paul A. Jorgensen, Willard Farnham, and D. J. Enright.

Ellis-Fermor, Una. *Shakespeare the Dramatist*, ed. Kenneth Muir (1961).

Farnham, Willard. *Shakespeare's Tragic Frontier* (1950).

Gordon, D. J. "Name and Fame: Shakespeare's *Coriolanus*," *Papers Mainly Shakespearian*, ed. G. I. Duthie (1964).

Heuer, Herman. "From Plutarch to Shakespeare: A Study of *Coriolanus*," *Shakespeare Survey 10*, ed. Allardyce Nicoll (1957), pp. 50–59.

Holloway, John. *The Story of the Night* (1961).

Kitto, H. D. F. *Poiesis, Structure and Thought* (1966).

Knight, G. Wilson. *The Imperial Theme: Further Interpretations of Shakespeare's Tragedies Including the Roman Plays* (1931; 3rd ed., 1953).

Knights, L. C. *Some Shakespearean Themes* (1959).

Lewis, Wyndham. *The Lion and the Fox* (1951).

MacCallum, M. W. *Shakespeare's Roman Plays and Their Background* (1910).

MacLure, Millar. "Shakespeare and the Lonely Dragon," *University of Toronto Quarterly*, XXIV (1955), 109–20.

Maxwell, J. C. "Animal Imagery in *Coriolanus*," *Modern Language Review*, XLII (1947), 417–21.

Murry, John Middleton. *John Clare and Other Studies* (1950).

Oliver, H. J. "Coriolanus as Tragic Hero," *Shakespeare Quarterly*, X (1959), 53–60.

Palmer, John. *Political Characters of Shakespeare* (1945).

Proser, Matthew. *The Heroic Image in Shakespeare's Tragedies* (1965).

Siegel, Paul N. "Shakespeare and the Neo-chivalric Cult of Honor," *The Centennial Review*, VIII (1964), 39–70.

Spencer, T. J. B. *Shakespeare: The Roman Plays* (1963).

Traversi, Derek. *Shakespeare: The Roman Plays* (1963).

Waith, Eugene. *The Herculean Hero* (1962).


*Cymbeline*

Brockbank, J. P. "History and Histrionics in *Cymbeline*," *Shakespeare Survey 11*, ed. Allardyce Nicoll (1958), pp. 42–49.

Edwards, Philip. "Shakespeare's Romances: 1900–1957," *Shakespeare Survey 11*, ed. Allardyce Nicoll (1958), pp. 1–18.

Evans, Bertrand. "*Cymbeline*," *Shakespeare's Comedies* (1960), pp. 245–89.

Frye, Northrop. *A Natural Perspective: The Development of Shakespearean Comedy and Romance* (1965).

Gesner, Carol. "*Cymbeline* and the Greek Romance: A Study in Genre," *Studies in English Renaissance Literature*, ed. W. F. McNeir (1962), pp. 105–31.

Greenlaw, Edwin. "Shakespeare's Pastorals," *Studies in Philology*, XIII (1916), 122–54.

Hoeniger, F. D. "Irony and Romance in *Cymbeline*," *Studies in English Literature*, II (1962), 219–28.

Jones, Emrys. "Stuart Cymbeline," *Essays in Criticism*, XI (1961), 84–99.

Knight, G. Wilson. "*Cymbeline*," *The Crown of Life: Essays in Interpretation of Shakespeare's Final Plays* (1947), pp. 129–202.

Lawrence, W. W. "The Wager in *Cymbeline*," *Shakespeare's Problem Comedies* (1931), pp. 174–205.

Maxwell, J. C. (ed.). *The New Cambridge Shakespeare: Cymbeline* (1960).

Nosworthy, J. M. "The Sources of the Wager Plot in *Cymbeline*," *Notes and Queries*, CXCVII (1952), 93–96.

———— (ed.). *The Arden Shakespeare: Cymbeline* (1955).

Ribner, Irving. "Shakespeare and Legendary History: *Lear* and *Cymbeline*," *Shakespeare Quarterly*, VII (1956), 47–52.

Stauffer, Donald A. "*Cymbeline*," *Shakespeare's World of Images: The Development of His Moral Ideas* (1949), pp. 278–91.

Stephenson, A. A. "The Significance of *Cymbeline*," *Scrutiny*, X (1942), 329–38.

Thrall, William F. "*Cymbeline*, Boccaccio, and the Wager Story in England," *Studies in Philology*, XXVIII (1931), 639–51.

Wilson, Harold S. "*Philaster* and *Cymbeline*," *English Institute Essays 1951*, ed. Alan S. Downer (1952), pp. 146–67.


*Hamlet*

Alexander, Peter. *Hamlet: Father and Son* (1955).

Bevington, David (ed.). *Twentieth Century Interpretations of "Hamlet"* (1968).

Bradley, A. C. *Shakespearean Tragedy* (1904; 1965).

Brown, John Russell, and Bernard Harris (eds.). *Stratford-upon-Avon Studies 5: "Hamlet"* (1963).

Charney, Maurice. *Style in "Hamlet"* (1969).

Driver, Tom F. *The Sense of History in Greek and Shakespearean Drama* (1960).

Elliott, G. R. *Scourge and Minister: A Study of "Hamlet" as a Tragedy of Revengefulness and Justice* (1951).

Granville-Barker, Harley. *Prefaces to Shakespeare* (2 vols., 1946–47).

Jones, Ernest. *Hamlet and Oedipus* (1954).

Kitto, H. D. F. *Form and Meaning in Drama* (1956).

Levin, Harry. *The Question of Hamlet* (1959).

Mack, Maynard. "The World of *Hamlet*," *Yale Review*, XLI (1952), 502–23.

Mahood, M. M. *Shakespeare's Wordplay* (1957).

Mander, Raymond, and Joe Mitchenson (comps.). *Hamlet Through the Ages: A Pictorial Record from 1709* (1952).

Muir, Kenneth. *Shakespeare's "Hamlet"* (1963).

Nicoll, Allardyce (ed.). *Shakespeare Survey 9* (1956).

Ornstein, Robert. *The Moral Vision of Jacobean Tragedy* (1960).

Prosser, Eleanor. *Hamlet and Revenge* (1967).

Stoll, Elmer Edgar. *Art and Artifice in Shakespeare* (1933; 1962).

Walker, Roy. "*The Time Is Out of Joint*": *A Study of* "*Hamlet*" (1948).

Williamson, Claude C. H. (comp.). *Readings on the Character of Hamlet, 1661–1947* (1951).

Wilson, John Dover. *What Happens in "Hamlet"* (1935; 3rd ed., 1951).

### Henry IV, Part One

Auden, W. H. "*The Dyer's Hand" and Other Essays* (1962), pp. 182–208.

Barber, C. L. *Shakespeare's Festive Comedy* (1959).

Bradley, A. C. *Oxford Lectures on Poetry* (1909).

Brooks, Cleanth, and R. B. Heilman. *Understanding Drama* (1945).

Charlton, H. B. "Falstaff," *Shakespearian Comedy* (1938).

Dickinson, Hugh. "The Reformation of Prince Hal," *Shakespeare Quarterly*, XII (1961), 33–46.

Doran, Madeleine. "Imagery in *Richard II* and in *Henry IV*," *Modern Language Review*, XXXVII (1942), 113–22.

Evans, Gareth Lloyd. "The Comical-Tragical-Historical Method—*Henry IV*," *Stratford-upon-Avon Studies 3. Early Shakespeare*, eds. John Russell Brown and Bernard Harris (1961), pp. 145–63.

Hemingway, Samuel B. "On Behalf of That Falstaff," *Shakespeare Quarterly*, III (1952), 307–11.

Jenkins, Harold. *The Structural Problem in Shakespeare's "Henry the Fourth"* (1956).

Kris, Ernst. "Prince Hal's Conflict," *Psychoanalytic Quarterly*, XVII (1948), 487–505. Reprinted in *Psychoanalytic Explorations in Art* (1962).

McLuhan, Herbert Marshall. "*Henry IV*, a Mirror for Magistrates," *University of Toronto Quarterly*, XVII (1948), 152–60.

Spivack, Bernard. "Falstaff and the Psychomachia," *Shakespeare Quarterly*, VIII (1957), 449–59.

Sprague, Arthur Colby. "Gadshill Revisited," *Shakespeare Quarterly*, IV (1953), 125–37.

Stoll, Elmer Edgar. *Shakespeare Studies: Historical and Comparative in Method* (1927).

Tillyard, E. M. W. *Shakespeare's History Plays* (1944; 1962).

Traversi, Derek. *Shakespeare: From "Richard II" to "Henry V"* (1957).

Unger, Leonard. *The Man in the Name* (1956).

Waldock, A. J. A. "The Men in Buckram," *Review of English Studies*, XXIII (1947), 16–23.

Wilson, John Dover. *The Fortunes of Falstaff* (1943).

### Henry IV, Part Two

Barber, C. L. "Rule and Misrule in *Henry IV*," *Shakespeare's Festive Comedy* (1959).

Barish, Jonas A. "The Turning Away of Prince Hal," *Shakespeare Studies 1*, ed. J. Leeds Barroll (1965), pp. 9–17.

Bradley, A. C. "The Rejection of Falstaff," *Oxford Lectures on Poetry* (1909).

Freud, Sigmund. *Jokes and Their Relation to the Unconscious* (1905), *The Standard Edition of the Complete Psychological Works*, eds. James Strachey *et al.* (24 vols., 1953– ), Vol. 8, pp. 231–32.

Jenkins, Harold. "Shakespeare's History Plays: 1900–1951," *Shakespeare Survey 6*, ed. Allardyce Nicoll (1953), pp. 1–15.

————. *The Structural Problem in Shakespeare's "Henry the Fourth"* (1956).

Jorgensen, Paul A. "The 'Dastardly Treachery' of Prince John of Lancaster," *PMLA*, LXXVI (1961), 488–92.

Kaiser, Walter. "Shakespeare's Falstaff," *Praisers of Folly* (1963).

Knights, L. C. "Time's Subjects: The Sonnets and *King Henry IV, Part II*," *Some Shakespearean Themes* (1959).

Knowles, Richard. "Unquiet and the Double Plot of *2 Henry IV*," *Shakespeare Studies 2*, ed. J. Leeds Barroll (1967), pp. 133–40.

Kris, Ernst. "Prince Hal's Conflict," *Psychoanalytic Quarterly*, XVII (1948), 487–505. Reprinted in *Psychoanalytic Explorations in Art* (1962).

Leech, Clifford. "The Unity of *2 Henry IV*," *Shakespeare Survey 6*, ed. Allardyce Nicoll (1953), pp. 16–24.

Shaaber, M. A. "The Unity of *Henry IV*," *Joseph Quincy Adams Memorial Studies*, eds. James G. McManaway, G. E. Dawson, and E. E. Willoughby (1948), pp. 217–27.

————. (ed.). *A New Variorum Edition of the Second Part of Henry the Fourth* (1941).

Spivack, Bernard. "Falstaff and the Psychomachia," *Shakespeare Quarterly*, VIII (1957), 449–59.

Spurgeon, Caroline. "Note on Images as a Revelation of Character in the Drama," *Shakespeare's Imagery and What It Tells Us* (1935; 1958).

Tillyard, E. M. W. "*Henry IV*," *Shakespeare's History Plays* (1944; 1962).

Traversi, Derek. "*Henry the Fourth, Part II*," *Shakespeare: From "Richard II" to "Henry V"* (1957).

Williams, Philip. "The Birth and Death of Falstaff Reconsidered," *Shakespeare Quarterly*, VIII (1957), 359–65.

Wilson, John Dover. *The Fortunes of Falstaff* (1943).

Young, David P. (ed.). *Twentieth Century Interpretations of "Henry IV, Part Two"* (1968).

### Henry V

Braddy, Haldeen. "Shakespeare's *Henry V* and the French Nobility," *Texas Studies in Literature and Language*, III (1961), 189–96.

Campbell, Lily B. *Shakespeare's "Histories": Mirrors of Elizabethan Policy* (1947).

Ellis-Fermor, Una. *Frontiers of Drama* (1945).

Granville-Barker, Harley. "From *Henry V* to *Hamlet*," *The Annual Shakespeare Lecture* (1925). Reprinted, with revisions, in *Studies in Shakespeare*, ed. Peter Alexander (1964).

Hobday, C. H. "Imagery and Irony in *Henry V*," *Shakespeare Survey 21*, ed. Kenneth Muir (1968), pp. 107–13.

Jorgensen, Paul A. *Shakespeare's Military World* (1956).

Knights, L. C. *Shakespeare: The Histories* (1962).

Matthews, Honor. *Character and Symbol in Shakespeare's Plays* (1962).

Palmer, John. *Political Characters of Shakespeare* (1945).

Reese, Max Meredith. *The Cease of Majesty: A Study of Shakespeare's History Plays* (1961).

Ribner, Irving. *The English History Play in the Age of Shakespeare* (1957; rev. ed., 1965).

Tillyard, E. M. W. *Shakespeare's History Plays* (1944; 1962).

Traversi, Derek. *Shakespeare: From "Richard II" to "Henry V"* (1957).

Walter, J. H. (ed.). *The Arden Shakespeare: King Henry V* (1954).

Wilson, John Dover (ed.). *The New Cambridge Shakespeare: King Henry V* (1947).

Yeats, W. B. "Ideas of Good and Evil" (1903), *Essays and Introductions* (1961).

### Henry VI, Part One

Alexander, Peter. *Shakespeare's "Henry VI" and "Richard III"* (1929).

Bevington, David M. "The Domineering Female in *1 Henry VI*," *Shakespeare Studies 2*, ed. J. Leeds Barroll (1967), pp. 51–58.

Brockbank, J. P. "The Frame of Disorder—*Henry VI*," *Stratford-upon-Avon Studies 3: Early Shakespeare*, eds. John Russell Brown and Bernard Harris (1961), pp. 73–99.

Cairncross, Andrew S. (ed.). *The Arden Shakespeare: The First Part of King Henry VI* (1962).

Campbell, Lily B. *Shakespeare's "Histories": Mirrors of Elizabethan Policy* (1947).

Clemen, Wolfgang H. "Anticipation and Foreboding in Shakespeare's Early Histories," *Shakespeare Survey 6*, ed. Allardyce Nicoll (1953), pp. 23–35.

Gaw, Allison. *The Origin and Development of "1 Henry VI" in Relation to Shakespeare, Marlowe, Peele, and Green* (1926).

Jackson, Barry. "On Producing *Henry VI*," *Shakespeare Survey 6*, ed. Allardyce Nicoll (1953), pp. 49–52.

Jorgensen, Paul A. *Shakespeare's Military World* (1956).

Kirschbaum, Leo. "The Authorship of *1 Henry VI*," *PMLA*, LXVII (1952), 809–22.

Mincoff, Marco. "The Composition of *Henry VI, Part I*," *Shakespeare Quarterly*, XVI (1965), 279–87.

Price, Hereward T. *Construction in Shakespeare* (1951).

Reese, Max Meredith. *The Cease of Majesty: A Study of Shakespeare's History Plays* (1961).

Ribner, Irving. *The English History Play in the Age of Shakespeare* (1957; rev. ed., 1965).

Talbert, Ernest William. *Elizabethan Drama and Shakespeare's Early Plays: An Essay in Historical Criticism* (1963).

Tillyard, E. M. W. *Shakespeare's History Plays* (1944; 1962).

Wilson, John Dover (ed.). *The New Cambridge Shakespeare: The First Part of King Henry VI* (1952).

### Henry VI, Part Two

Alexander, Peter. *Shakespeare's "Henry VI" and "Richard III"* (1929).

Berman, Ronald S. "Fathers and Sons in the Henry VI Plays," *Shakespeare Quarterly*, XIII (1962), 487–97.

Brockbank, J. P. "The Frame of Disorder—*Henry VI*," *Stratford-upon-Avon Studies 3: Early Shakespeare*, eds. John Russell Brown and Bernard Harris (1961), pp. 73–99.

Cairncross, Andrew S. (ed.). *The Arden Shakespeare: The Second Part of King Henry VI* (1957).

Campbell, Lily B. *Shakespeare's "Histories": Mirrors of Elizabethan Policy* (1947).

Doran, Madeleine. *"Henry VI," Parts II and III, Their Relation to "The Contention" and "The True Tragedy,"* University of Iowa Humanistic Studies, Vol. 4, No. 4 (1928).

Greg, W. W. *The Book of Sir Thomas More* (1911).

Jackson, Barry. "On Producing *Henry VI*," *Shakespeare Survey 6*, ed. Allardyce Nicoll (1953), pp. 49–52.

Jordan, John E. "The Reporter of *Henry VI, Part II*," *PMLA*, LXIV (1949), 1089–1113.

Leech, Clifford. "The Two-Part Play: Marlowe and the Early Shakespeare," *Shakespeare Jahrbuch*, XCII (1958), 90–106.

Malone, Edmond. *A Dissertation on the Three Parts of "King Henry VI," Tending to Show that those Plays Were Not Originally Written by Shakespeare* (1787).

Prouty, Charles T. *"The Contention" and Shakespeare's "2 Henry VI": A Comparative Study* (1954).

Ribner, Irving. *The English History Play in the Age of Shakespeare* (1957; rev. ed., 1965).

Sandoe, James. *"King Henry the Sixth, Part II:* Notes During Production," *Theatre Annual*, XIII (1955), 32–48.

Tillyard, E. M. W. *Shakespeare's History Plays* (1944; 1962).

Turner, Robert Y. "Shakespeare and the Public Confrontation Scene in Early History Plays," *Modern Philology*, LXXII (1964), 1–12.

Wilson, John Dover (ed.). *The New Cambridge Shakespeare: The Second Part of King Henry VI* (1952).

### Henry VI, Part Three

Alexander, Peter. *Shakespeare's "Henry VI" and "Richard III"* (1929).

Berman, Ronald S. "Fathers and Sons in the Henry VI Plays," *Shakespeare Quarterly*, XIII (1962), 487–97.

Brockbank, J. P. "The Frame of Disorder—*Henry VI*," *Stratford-upon-Avon Studies 3: Early Shakespeare*, eds. John Russell Brown and Bernard Harris (1961), pp. 73–99.

Cairncross, Andrew S. (ed.). *The Arden Shakespeare: The Third Part of King Henry VI* (1964).

Campbell, Lily B. *Shakespeare's "Histories": Mirrors of Elizabethan Policy* (1947).

Doran, Madeleine. *"Henry VI," Parts II and III, Their Relation to "The Contention" and "The True Tragedy,"* University of Iowa Humanistic Studies, Vol. 4, No. 4 (1928).

Greg, W. W. (ed.). *The True Tragedy of Richard Duke of York (Henry the Sixth, Part III)*, 1595. Shakespeare Quarto Facsimiles, No. 11 (1958).

Jackson, Barry. "On Producing *Henry VI*," *Shakespeare Survey 6*, ed. Allardyce Nicoll (1953), pp. 49–52.

Leech, Clifford. *Shakespeare: The Chronicles* (1962).

Reese, Max Meredith. *The Cease of Majesty: A Study of Shakespeare's History Plays* (1961).

Ribner, Irving. *The English History Play in the Age of Shakespeare* (1957; rev. ed., 1965).

Tillyard, E. M. W. *Shakespeare's History Plays* (1944; 1962).

Wilson, John Dover (ed.). *The New Cambridge Shakespeare: The Third Part of King Henry VI* (1952).

### Henry VIII

Alexander, Peter. "Conjectural History, or Shakespeare's *Henry VIII*," *Essays and Studies*, XVI (1930), 85–120.

Bertram, Paul. *"Henry VIII:* The Consequences of a Problem of Authorship," *Shakespeare and "The Two Noble Kinsmen"* (1965).

Byrne, Muriel St. Clare. "A Stratford Production: *Henry VIII*," *Shakespeare Survey 3*, ed. Allardyce Nicoll (1950), pp. 120–29. A review of the 1949 Guthrie performance.

Felperin, Howard. "Shakespeare's *Henry VIII:* History as Myth," *Studies in English Literature: 1500–1900*, VI (1966), 225–46.

Foakes, R. A. (ed.). *The Arden Shakespeare: King Henry VIII* (1957).

Kermode, Frank. "What Is Shakespeare's *Henry VIII* About?" *Durham University Journal*, N.S., IX (1947–48), 48–55.

Knight, G. Wilson. *The Crown of Life: Essays in Interpretation of Shakespeare's Final Plays* (1947).

Leech, Clifford. "The Structure of the Last Plays," *Shakespeare Survey 11*, ed. Allardyce Nicoll (1958), pp. 19–30.

Maxwell, J. C. (ed.). *The New Cambridge Shakespeare: King Henry the Eighth* (1962).

Mincoff, Marco. "*Henry VIII* and Fletcher," *Shakespeare Quarterly*, XII (1961), 239–60.

Reese, Max Meredith. *The Cease of Majesty: A Study of Shakespeare's History Plays* (1961).

Ribner, Irving. *The English History Play in the Age of Shakespeare* (1957; rev. ed., 1965).

Wasson, John. "In Defense of *King Henry VIII*," *Research Studies*, Washington State University (1964), 261–76.

### Julius Caesar

Ayres, H. M. "Shakespeare's *Julius Caesar* in the Light of Some Other Versions," *PMLA*, XXV (1910), 183–227.

Bonjour, Adrien. *The Structure of "Julius Caesar"* (1958).

Bullough, Geoffrey. *Narrative and Dramatic Sources of Shakespeare*, Vol. 5 (1964).

Charlton, H. B. *Shakespearian Tragedy* (1948).

Charney, Maurice. *Shakespeare's Roman Plays: The Function of Imagery in the Drama* (1961).

Dean, Leonard F. "*Julius Caesar* and Modern Criticism," *The English Journal* (1961), 451–56.

——— (ed.). *Twentieth Century Interpretations of "Julius Caesar"* (1968).

Dorsch, T. S. (ed.). *The Arden Shakespeare: Julius Caesar* (1955; 1970).

Foakes, R. A. "An Approach to *Julius Caesar*," *Shakespeare Quarterly*, V (1954), 259–70.

Granville-Barker, Harley. *Prefaces to Shakespeare* (2 vols., 1946–47), Vol. 2.

Knight, G. Wilson. *The Imperial Theme: Further Interpretations of Shakespeare's Tragedies Including the Roman Plays* (1931; 3rd ed., 1953).

MacCallum, M. W. *Shakespeare's Roman Plays and Their Background* (1910).

Muir, Kenneth. *Shakespeare's Sources*, Vol. 1 (1957).

Palmer, John. *Political Characters of Shakespeare* (1945).

Rabkin, Norman. *Shakespeare and the Common Understanding* (1967).

Schanzer, Ernest. *The Problem Plays of Shakespeare: A Study of "Julius Caesar," "Measure for Measure," and "Antony and Cleopatra"* (1963).

Smith, Gordon Ross. "Brutus, Virtue, and Will," *Shakespeare Quarterly*, X (1959), 367–79.

Smith, Warren D. "The Duplicate Revelation of Portia's Death," *Shakespeare Quarterly*, IV (1953), 153–61.

Stewart, J. I. M. *Character and Motive in Shakespeare* (1949).

Stirling, Brents. *Unity in Shakespearian Tragedy: The Interplay of Theme and Character* (1956).

Walker, Roy. "Unto Caesar: A Review of Recent Productions," *Shakespeare Survey 11*, ed. Allardyce Nicoll (1958), pp. 132–35.

Whitaker, Virgil K. *Shakespeare's Use of Learning* (1953).

### King John

Alexander, Peter. *Shakespeare's Life and Art* (1938).

Berman, Ronald. "Anarchy and Order in *Richard III* and *King John*," *Shakespeare Survey 20*, ed. Kenneth Muir (1967), pp. 51–59.

Boklund, Gunnar. "The Troublesome Ending of *King John*," *Studia Neophilologica*, XL (1968), 175–84.

Bonjour, Adrien. "The Road to Swinstead Abbey: A Study of the Sense and Structure of *King John*," *ELH; A Journal of English Literary History*, XVIII (1951), 253–74.

———. "Bastinado for the Bastard?" *English Studies*, XLV Supplement (1964), 169–76.

Calderwood, James L. "Commodity and Honor in *King John*," *University of Toronto Quarterly*, XXIX (1960), 341–56.

Campbell, Lily B. *Shakespeare's "Histories": Mirrors of Elizabethan Policy* (1947).

Elliott, John R. "Shakespeare and the Double Image of *King John*," *Shakespeare Studies 1*, ed. J. Leeds Barroll (1965), pp. 64–84.

Goddard, Harold C. *The Meaning of Shakespeare* (1951).

Honigmann, E. A. J. (ed.). *The Arden Shakespeare: King John* (4th ed., 1954).

Palmer, John. *Political Characters of Shakespeare* (1945).

Pettet, E. C. "Hot Irons and Fever: A Note on Some Imagery of *King John*," *Essays in Criticism*, IV (1954), 128–44.

Rossiter, A. P. "Ambivalence: The Dialectic of the Histories," *"Angel with Horns" and Other Shakespeare Lectures* (1961).

Stauffer, Donald A. *Shakespeare's World of Images: The Development of His Moral Ideas* (1949).

Tillyard, E. M. W. *Shakespeare's History Plays* (1944; 1962).

Wilson, John Dover (ed.). *The New Cambridge Shakespeare: King John* (1936).

### King Lear

Bradley, A. C. *Shakespearean Tragedy* (1904; 1965).

Campbell, Lily B. *Shakespeare's Tragic Heroes* (1930).

Cunningham, J. V. *Woe or Wonder: The Emotional Effect of Shakespearean Tragedy* (1951). Reprinted in *Tradition and Poetic Structure: Essays in Literary History and Criticism* (1960).

Dowden, Edward. *Shakspere: A Critical Study of His Mind and Art* (1875; 3rd. ed., 1962).

Elton, William R. *King Lear and the Gods* (1966).

Fraser, Russell A. *Shakespeare's Poetics in Relation to "King Lear"* (1962).

Granville-Barker, Harley. *Prefaces to Shakespeare* (2 vols., 1946–47).

Heilman, Robert B. *This Great Stage: Image and Structure in "King Lear"* (1948).

Holloway, John. *The Story of the Night* (1961).

Knight, G. Wilson. *The Wheel of Fire: Essays in Interpretation of Shakespeare's Sombre Tragedies* (1930; 5th rev. ed., 1957).

Leech, Clifford. *Shakespeare's Tragedies* (1950).

Lewis, Wyndham. *The Lion and the Fox* (1927).

Mack, Maynard. "*King Lear*" in Our Time (1965).

Moulton, Richard G. *Shakespeare as a Dramatic Artist* (3rd ed., 1893; rev. and enl. ed., 1966). Especially Part First, Chapter X: "How Climax Meets Climax in the Centre of *Lear*."

Nicoll, Allardyce (ed.). *Shakespeare Survey 13* (1960). Volume devoted to *King Lear*.

Perrett, Wilfrid. *The Story of "King Lear" from Geoffrey of Monmouth to Shakespeare* (1904).

Sewell, Arthur. *Character and Society in Shakespeare* (1951).

Stoll, Elmer Edgar. *Art and Artifice in Shakespeare* (1933; 1962).

Tannenbaum, Samuel A. *Shakespeare's "Lear": A Concise Bibliography* (1940).

Welsford, Enid. *The Fool, His Social and Literary History* (1935).

### Love's Labor's Lost

Baldwin, T. W. *Shakspere's Five-Act Structure: Shakspere's Early Plays on the Background of Renaissance Theories of Five-Act Structure from 1470* (1947).

Barber, C. L. *Shakespeare's Festive Comedy* (1959).

Bradbrook, M. C. *The School of Night: Study in the Literary Relationships of Sir Walter Raleigh* (1936).

Campbell, Oscar James. "*Love's Labour's Lost* Restudied," *Studies in Shakespeare, Milton and Donne by Members of the English Department of the University of Michigan* (1925).

Charlton, H. B. "The Date of *Loves Labours Lost*," *Modern Language Review*, XIII (1918), 257–66, 387–400.

———. *Shakespearian Comedy* (1938).

David, Richard. "Shakespeare's Comedies and the Modern Stage," *Shakespeare Survey 4*, ed. Allardyce Nicoll (1951), pp. 129–35.

Gittings, Robert. *Shakespeare's Rival* (1960).

Granville-Barker, Harley. *Prefaces to Shakespeare* (2 vols., 1946–47), Vol. 2.

Hoy, Cyrus. *The Hyacinth Room* (1964).

Kirschbaum, Leo. "Is *The Spanish Tragedy* a Leading Case? Did a Bad Quarto of *Love's Labour's Lost* Ever Exist?" *Journal of English and Germanic Philology*, XXXVII (1938), 501–12.

Lambrechts, G. " 'The Brief and the Tedious of It': Note sur le Texte de 'Love's Labour's Lost,' " *Études Anglaises*, XVII (1964), 269–83.

Lefranc, Abel. *Sous le Masque de "William Shakespeare"* (1919).

Oakeshott, W. F. *The Queen and the Poet* (1960).

Palmer, John. *Comic Characters of Shakespeare* (1946).

Pater, Walter. "Love's Labour's Lost," *Appreciations* (1889).

Roesen, Bobbyann. "Love's Labour's Lost," *Shakespeare Quarterly*, IV (1953), 411–26.

Schrickx, W. *Shakespeare's Early Contemporaries* (1956).

Stratton, L. D. "The Nine Worthies," *Ashland Studies in Shakespeare*, Ashland, Orgeon, Institute of Renaissance Studies (1965), 67–97.

Vyvyan, John. *Shakespeare and the Rose of Love* (1960).

Westlund, Joseph. "Fancy and Achievement in *Love's Labour's Lost*," *Shakespeare Quarterly*, XVIII (1967), 37–46.

Wilson, John Dover. *Shakespeare's Happy Comedies* (1962).

Yates, F. A. *A Study of "Love's Labour's Lost"* (1936).

———. *Giordano Bruno and the Hermetic Tradition* (1964).


*Macbeth*

Blissett, William. " 'The Secret'st Man of Blood': A Study of Dramatic Irony in *Macbeth*," *Shakespeare Quarterly*, X (1959), 397–408.

Bradley, A. C. *Shakespearean Tragedy* (1904; 1965).

Charlton, H. B. *Shakespearian Tragedy* (1948).

Driver, Tom F. *The Sense of History in Greek and Shakespearean Drama* (1960).

Elliott, G. R. *Dramatic Providence in "Macbeth"* (1958).

Farnham, Willard. *Shakespeare's Tragic Frontier* (1950).

Knights, L. C. *Some Shakespearean Themes* (1959).

Muir, Kenneth (ed.). *Shakespeare Survey 19* (1966). Contains nine essays on *Macbeth*.

Paul, Henry N. *The Royal Play of Macbeth* (1950).

Rosen, William. *Shakespeare and the Craft of Tragedy* (1960).

Stirling, Brents. *Unity in Shakespearian Tragedy: The Interplay of Theme and Character* (1956).

Walker, Roy. *The Time Is Free* (1949).


*Measure for Measure*

Battenhouse, R. W. "*Measure for Measure* and the Christian Doctrine of the Atonement," *PMLA*, LXI (1946), 1029–59.

Bradbrook, M. C. "Authority, Truth, and Justice in *Measure for Measure*," *Review of English Studies*, XVII (1941), 385–99.

Chambers, R. W. *Man's Unconquerable Mind* (1952).

Coghill, Nevill. "Comic Form in *Measure for Measure*," *Shakespeare Survey 8*, ed. Allardyce Nicoll (1955), pp. 14–26.

———. *Shakespeare's Professional Skills* (1964).

Empson, William. *The Structure of Complex Words* (1951).

Fergusson, Francis. *The Human Image in Dramatic Literature* (1957).

Geckle, George L. (ed.). *Twentieth Century Interpretations of "Measure for Measure"* (1970).

Holland, Norman. *The Shakespearean Imagination* (1963).

Knight, G. Wilson. *The Wheel of Fire: Essays in Interpretation of Shakespeare's Sombre Tragedies* (1930; 5th rev. ed., 1957).

Lascelles, Mary. *Shakespeare's "Measure for Measure"* (1953).

Lawrence, W. W. *Shakespeare's Problem Comedies* (1931; 1960).

———. "*Measure for Measure* and Lucio," *Shakespeare Quarterly*, IX (1958), 443–53.

Leavis, F. R. *The Common Pursuit* (1952; 1962).

Leech, Clifford. "The Meaning of *Measure for Measure*," *Shakespeare Survey 3*, ed. Allardyce Nicoll (1950), pp. 66–73.

Maxwell, J. C. "*Measure for Measure*: A Footnote to Recent Criticism," *The Downside Review*, LXV (1947), 45–59.

Merchant, W. Moelwyn. *Shakespeare and the Artist* (1959).

Nagarajan, S. "*Measure for Measure* and Elizabethan Betrothals," *Shakespeare Quarterly*, XIX (1963), 115–19.

Pope, Elizabeth M. "The Renaissance Background of *Measure for Measure*," *Shakespeare Survey 2*, ed. Allardyce Nicoll (1949), pp. 66–82.

Rossiter, A. P. "Angel with Horns" and Other Shakespeare Lectures, ed. Graham Storey (1961).

Schanzer, Ernest. *The Problem Plays of Shakespeare: A Study of "Julius Caesar," "Measure for Measure," and "Antony and Cleopatra"* (1963).

———. "Marriage Contracts in *Measure for Measure*," *Shakespeare Survey 13*, ed. Allardyce Nicoll (1960), pp. 81–89.

Sewell, Arthur. *Character and Society in Shakespeare* (1951).

Sisson, C. J. *The Mythical Sorrows of Shakespeare* (1934).

Stevenson, David L. *The Achievement of "Measure for Measure"* (1966).

Tillyard, E. M. W. *Shakespeare's Problem Plays* (1949).

Wiles, R. W. "*Measure for Measure*: Failure in the Study, Triumph on the Stage," *Transactions of the Royal Society of Canada*, Fourth Series, II (1964), 181–93.


*The Merchant of Venice*

Barber, C. L. *Shakespeare's Festive Comedy* (1959).

Barnet, Sylvan (ed.). *Twentieth Century Interpretations of "The Merchant of Venice"* (1970).

———. "Prodigality and Time in *The Merchant of Venice*," *PMLA*, LXXXVII (1972).

Brown, John Russell (ed.). *The Arden Shakespeare: The Merchant of Venice* (7th rev. ed., 1955).

———. "The Realization of Shylock: A Theatrical Criticism," *Stratford-upon-Avon Studies 3: Early Shakespeare*, eds. John Russell Brown and Bernard Harris (1961), pp. 187–209.

Charlton, H. B. *Shakespearian Comedy* (1938).

Draper, John W. *Stratford to Dogberry* (1961).

Granville-Barker, Harley. *Prefaces to Shakespeare* (2 vols., 1946–47), Vol. I.

Grebanier, Bernard. *The Truth About Shylock* (1962).

Lewalski, Barbara K. "Biblical Allusion and Allegory in *The Merchant of Venice*," *Shakespeare Quarterly*, XIII (1962), 327–43.

Palmer, John. *Comic Characters of Shakespeare* (1946).

Sprague, Arthur Colby. *Shakespeare and the Actors* (1944).

Stauffer, Donald A. *Shakespeare's World of Images: The Development of His Moral Ideas* (1949).


*The Merry Wives of Windsor*

Campbell, Oscar James. "The Italianate Background of *The Merry Wives of Windsor*," *Essays and Studies in English and Comparative Literature*, University of Michigan Publications in Language and Literature, Vol. 8 (1932), 81–117.

Charlton, H. B. "Falstaff," *Shakespearian Comedy* (1938).

Crofts, John. *Shakespeare and the Post Horses* (1937).

Evans, Bertrand. *Shakespeare's Comedies* (1960).

Green, William. *Shakespeare's "Merry Wives of Windsor"* (1962).

Hotson, Leslie. *Shakespeare Versus Shallow* (1931).

Nosworthy, J. M. *Shakespeare's Occasional Plays: Their Origin and Transmission* (1965).

Parrott, Thomas Marc. *Shakespearean Comedy* (1949).

Rosenberg, S. L. Millard. "Duke Friedrich of Württemberg," *Shakespeare Association Bulletin*, VIII (1933), 92–93.

Rye, William Brenchley (ed.). *England as Seen by Foreigners in the Days of Elizabeth and James the First* (1865).

Tighe, Robert Richard, and James Edward Davis. *Annals of Windsor, being a History of the Castle and Town* (2 vols., 1858).

Van Doren, Mark. *Shakespeare* (1939; 1953).

White, David Manning. "An Explanation of the Brocke-Broome Question in Shakespeare's *Merry Wives*," *Philological Quarterly*, XXV (1946), 280–83.

### A Midsummer Night's Dream

Barber, C. L. *Shakespeare's Festive Comedy* (1959).

Bonnard, Georges A. "Shakespeare's Purpose in *Midsummer-Night's Dream*," *Shakespeare Jahrbuch*, XCII (1956). 268–79.

Briggs, K. M. *The Anatomy of Puck* (1959).

Brown, John Russell. *Shakespeare and His Comedies* (1957).

Cody, Richard. *The Landscape of the Mind: Pastoralism and the Platonic Theory in Tasso's "Aminta" and Shakespeare's Early Comedies* (1969).

Dent, R. W. "Imagination in *A Midsummer Night's Dream*," *Shakespeare Quarterly*, XV (1964), 115–29.

Doran, Madeleine. "Pyramus and Thisbe Once More," *Essays on Shakespeare and Elizabethan Drama in Honor of Hardin Craig*, ed. Richard Hosley (1962), pp. 149–62.

Dowden, Edward. *Shakspere: A Critical Study of His Mind and Art* (1875; 3rd ed., 1962).

Evans, Bertrand. *Shakespeare's Comedies* (1960).

Fender, Stephen. *Shakespeare's "A Midsummer Night's Dream." Studies in English Literature*, No. 35 (1968).

Hunter, G. K. *Shakespeare: The Late Comedies* (1962).

Kermode, Frank. "The Mature Comedies," *Stratford-upon-Avon Studies 3: Early Shakespeare*, eds. John Russell Brown and Bernard Harris (1961), pp. 211–27.

Myers, Henry A. "*Romeo and Juliet* and *A Midsummer Night's Dream*: Tragedy and Comedy," *Tragedy: A View of Life* (1956).

Nemerov, Howard. "The Marriage of Theseus and Hippolyta," *Kenyon Review*, XVIII (1956), 633–41.

Olsen, Paul A. "*A Midsummer Night's Dream* and the Meaning of Court Marriage," *ELH; A Journal of English Literary History*, XXIV (1957), 95–119.

Schanzer, Ernest. "The Moon and the Fairies in *A Midsummer-Night's Dream*," *University of Toronto Quarterly*, XXIV (1955), 234–46.

Siegel, Paul N. "*A Midsummer-Night's Dream* and the Wedding Guests," *Shakespeare Quarterly*, IV (1953), 139–44.

Watkins, Ronald. *Moonlight at the Globe: An Essay in Shakespeare Production Based on Performance of "A Midsummer-Night's Dream" at Harrow School* (1946).

Welsford, Enid. *The Court Masque* (1927).

Wickham, Glynne. "*A Midsummer Night's Dream*: The Setting and the Text," *Shakespeare's Dramatic Heritage: Collected Studies in Medieval, Tudor and Shakespearean Drama* (1969), pp. 180–90.

Young, David P. *Something of Great Constancy: The Art of "A Midsummer Night's Dream"* (1966).

### Much Ado About Nothing

Craik, T. W. "*Much Ado About Nothing*," *Scrutiny*, XIX (1953), 297–316.

Davis, Walter R. (ed.). *Twentieth Century Interpretations of "Much Ado About Nothing"* (1969).

Evans, Bertrand. *Shakespeare's Comedies* (1960).

Everett, Barbara. "*Much Ado About Nothing*," *Critical Quarterly*, III (1961), 319–35.

Mulryne, J. R. *Shakespeare: "Much Ado About Nothing"* (1965).

Phialas, Peter G. *Shakespeare's Romantic Comedies: The Development of Their Form and Meaning* (1966).

Prouty, Charles T. *The Sources of "Much Ado About Nothing"* (1950).

Rossiter, A. P. "*Angel with Horns*" *and Other Shakespeare Lectures*, ed. Graham Storey (1961).

Stevenson, David L. *The Love-Game Comedy* (1946).

### Othello

Bayley, John. *The Characters of Love* (1961).

Bradley, A. C. *Shakespearean Tragedy* (1904; 1965).

Clemen, Wolfgang H. *The Development of Shakespeare's Imagery* (1951; originally published in German, 1936).

Eliot, T. S. "Shakespeare and the Stoicism of Seneca," *Selected Essays, 1917–1932* (1932).

Elliott, G. R. *Flaming Minister: A Study of "Othello" as Tragedy of Love and Hate* (1953).

Frye, Northrop. *Fools of Time: Studies in Shakespearean Tragedy* (1967).

Granville-Barker, Harley. "Preface to *Othello*," *Prefaces to Shakespeare* (2 vols., 1946–47), Vol. 2.

Heilman, Robert B. *Magic in the Web: Action and Language in "Othello"* (1956).

Kirschbaum, Leo. "The Modern *Othello*," *ELH; A Journal of English Literary History*, II (1944), 233–96.

Knight, G. Wilson. "The *Othello* Music," *The Wheel of Fire: Essays in Interpretation of Shakespeare's Sombre Tragedies* (1930; 5th rev. ed., 1957), pp. 97–119.

Lawlor, John. *The Tragic Sense in Shakespeare* (1960).

Mack, Maynard. "The Jacobean Shakespeare: Some Observations on the Construction of the Tragedies," *Stratford-upon-Avon Studies 1: Jacobean Theatre*, eds. John Russell Brown and Bernard Harris (1960), pp. 11–41.

Nowottny, Winifred M. T. "Justice and Love in *Othello*," *University of Toronto Quarterly*, XXI (1951–52), 330–44.

Rosenberg, Marvin. *The Masks of "Othello"* (1961).

Sedgewick, G. G. *Of Irony, Especially in Drama* (2nd ed., 1948).

Seltzer, Daniel. "Elizabethan Acting in *Othello*," *Shakespeare Quarterly*, X (1959), 201–1C.

Sewell, Arthur. *Character and Society in Shakespeare* (1951).

Siegel, Paul N. *Shakespearean Tragedy and the Elizabethan Compromise* (1957).

Stoll, Elmer Edgar. "*Othello*, Tragedy of Effect," *From Shakespeare to Joyce* (1944).

Traversi, Derek. *An Approach to Shakespeare* (2 vols.; 3rd rev. ed., 1968–69).

Wilson, Harold S. *On the Design of Shakespearian Tragedy* (1957).

### Pericles

Arthos, John. "*Pericles, Prince of Tyre*: A Study in the Dramatic Use of Romantic Narrative," *Shakespeare Quarterly*, IV (1953), 257–70.

Barker, G. A. "Themes and Variations in Shakespeare's *Pericles*," *English Studies*, XLIV (1963), 401–14.

Danby, John F. "Sidney and the Late-Shakespearian Romance," *Poets on Fortune's Hill* (1952).

Edwards, Philip. "An Approach to the Problem of *Pericles*," *Shakespeare Survey 5*, ed. Allardyce Nicoll (1952), pp. 25–49.

———. "Shakespeare's Romances: 1900–1957," *Shakespeare Survey 11*, ed. Allardyce Nicoll (1958), pp. 1–18.

Felperin, Howard. "Shakespeare's Miracle Play," *Shakespeare Quarterly*, XVIII (1967), 363–74.

Hoeniger, F. D. (ed.). *The Arden Shakespeare: Pericles* (1963).

James, David G. "The Failure of the Ballad-Makers," *Skepticism and Poetry* (1937; 1960).

Knight, G. Wilson. *The Crown of Life: Essays in Interpretation of Shakespeare's Final Plays* (1947).

Maxwell, J. C. (ed.). *The New Cambridge Shakespeare: Pericles* (1956).

Muir, Kenneth. *Shakespeare as Collaborator* (1960).

Tillyard, E. M. W. *Shakespeare's Last Plays* (1938; 6th ed., 1964).

Tompkins, J. M. S. "Why Pericles?" *Review of English Studies*, III (1952), 315–24.

Traversi, Derek. *Shakespeare: The Last Phase* (1954).

### Richard II

Altick, Richard D. "Symphonic Imagery in *Richard II*," *PMLA*, LXII (1947), 339–65.

Black, Matthew W. (ed.). *A New Variorum Edition of Shakespeare: The Life and Death of King Richard the Second* (1956).

Bogard, Travis. "Shakespeare's Second Richard," *PMLA*, LXX (1955), 192–209.

Campbell, Lily B. *Shakespeare's "Histories": Mirrors of Elizabethan Policy* (1947).

Dean, Leonard F. "*Richard II*: The State and the Image of the Theater," *PMLA*, LXVII (1952), 211–18.

Humphreys, A. R. *Shakespeare: "Richard II"* (1967).

Palmer, John. *Political Characters of Shakespeare* (1945).

Pater, Walter. "Shakespeare's English Kings," *Appreciations* (1889).

Reese, Max Meredith. *The Cease of Majesty: A Study of Shakespeare's History Plays* (1961).

Rossiter, A. P. *"Angel with Horns" and Other Shakespeare Lectures*, ed. Graham Storey (1961).

Stirling, Brents. *Unity in Shakespearian Tragedy: The Interplay of Theme and Character* (1956).

Swinburne, A. C. *Three Plays of Shakespeare* (1909).

Tillyard, E. M. W. *Shakespeare's History Plays* (1944; 1962).

Traversi, Derek. *Shakespeare: From "Richard II" to "Henry V"* (1957).

Ure, Peter (ed.). *The Arden Shakespeare: King Richard II* (4th rev. ed., 1956).

Wilson, John Dover (ed.). *The New Cambridge Shakespeare: King Richard II* (1939).

Yeats, W. B. *Ideas of Good and Evil* (1903; 1967).


### Richard III

Boyer, Clarence V. *The Villain as Hero in Elizabethan Tragedy* (1914; 1964).

Campbell, Lily B. *Shakespeare's "Histories": Mirrors of Elizabethan Policy* (1947).

Churchill, George B. *Richard the Third up to Shakespeare* (Palaestra, X) (1900).

Clemen, Wolfgang H. *A Commentary on Shakespeare's "Richard III,"* tr. Jean Bonheim (1968; originally published in German, 1957).

Driver, Tom F. *The Sense of History in Greek and Shakespearean Drama* (1960).

Kendall, Paul Murray. *Richard the Third* (1955).

Krieger, Murray. "The Dark Generations of *Richard III*," *Criticism*, I (1959), 32–48.

More, Sir Thomas. *The History of King Richard III*, ed. Richard S. Sylvester (1963).

Moulton, Richard G. *Shakespeare as a Dramatic Artist* (3rd ed., 1893; rev. and enl. ed., 1966).

Palmer, John. *Political Characters of Shakespeare* (1945).

Ribner, Irving. *The English History Play in the Age of Shakespeare* (1957; rev. ed., 1965).

Rossiter, A. P. *"Angel with Horns" and Other Shakespeare Lectures*, ed. Graham Storey (1961).

Tillyard, E. M. W. *Shakespeare's History Plays* (1944; 1962).

Wilson, John Dover (ed.). *The New Cambridge Shakespeare: Richard III* (1954).

Wood, Alice I. Perry. *The Stage History of Shakespeare's "King Richard the Third"* (1909).


### Romeo and Juliet

Charlton, H. B. *Shakespearian Tragedy* (1948).

Cole, Douglas (ed.). *Twentieth Century Interpretations of "Romeo and Juliet"* (1970).

Hoppe, Harry R. *The Bad Quarto of "Romeo and Juliet": A Bibliography and Textual Study* (1948).

Hosley, Richard (ed.). *The Tragedy of Romeo and Juliet* (1954).

Knight, G. Wilson. *Principles of Shakespearian Production, with Especial Reference to the Tragedies* (1949).

Lawlor, John. "*Romeo and Juliet*," *Stratford-upon-Avon Studies 3: Early Shakespeare*, eds. John Russell Brown and Bernard Harris (1961), pp. 123–45.

Levin, Harry. "Form and Formality in *Romeo and Juliet*," *Shakespeare Quarterly*, XI (1960), 3–11.

Mahood, M. M. *Shakespeare's Wordplay* (1957).

Moore, Olin H. *The Legend of Romeo and Juliet* (1950).

Myers, Henry A. *Tragedy: A View of Life* (1956).

Spurgeon, Caroline. *Leading Motives in the Imagery of Shakespeare's Tragedies*, Shakespeare Association Lecture (1930), pp. 1–17.

Stoll, Elmer Edgar. *Shakespeare's Young Lovers* (1937).

Vyvyan, John. *Shakespeare and the Rose of Love* (1960).

Williams, George Walton (ed.). *The Most Excellent and Lamentable Tragedie of Romeo and Juliet: A Critical Edition* (1964).


### The Taming of the Shrew

Brown, John Russell. *Shakespeare and His Comedies* (1957).

Brunvand, Jan H. "The Folktale Origin of *The Taming of the Shrew*," *Shakespeare Quarterly*, XVII (1966), 345–59.

Charlton, H. B. *Shakespearian Comedy* (1938).

Child, Harold. "The Stage History of *The Taming of the Shrew*," *The New Cambridge Shakespeare: The Taming of the Shrew*, eds. Sir Arthur Quiller-Couch and John Dover Wilson (1928, 1953).

Coghill, Nevill. "The Basis of Shakespearian Comedy," *Essays and Studies*, III (1950); reprinted, in revised form, in *Shakespeare Criticism 1935–1960*, selected with an Introduction by Anne Bradby Ridler (1963), pp. 201–27.

Crane, Milton. "Shakespeare's Comedies and the Critics," *Shakespeare 400*, ed. James G. McManaway (1964), pp. 67–73.

Cutts, John P. *The Shattered Glass: A Dramatic Pattern in Shakespeare's Early Plays* (1968).

Evans, Bertrand. *Shakespeare's Comedies* (1960).

Frey, Albert R. *The Bankside Shakespeare: The Taming of the Shrew* (1888). Prints *A Shrew* and *The Shrew* on opposite pages, so arranged as to call attention to identical and similar passages.

Goddard, Harold C. *The Meaning of Shakespeare* (1951).

Heilman, Robert B. "*The Taming* Untamed, or, The Return of the Shrew," *Modern Language Quarterly*, XXVII (1966), 147–61.

Hosley, Richard. "Sources and Analogues of *The Taming of the Shrew*," *Huntington Library Quarterly*, XXVII (1963–64), 289–308.

Jayne, Sears. "The Dreaming of *The Taming of the Shrew*," *Shakespeare Quarterly*, XXVII (1966), 41–56.

Mack, Maynard. "Engagement and Detachment in Shakespeare's Plays," *Essays on Shakespeare and Elizabethan Drama in Honor of Hardin Craig*, ed. Richard Hosley (1962), pp. 275–96.

Murphy, G. N. "Christopher Sly and the Pronoun-Game in *The Taming of the Shrew*," *Papers on Language and Literature*, II (1966), 67–70.

Orange, L. E. "The Punning of *The Shrew*," *The Southern Quarterly*, III (1965), 293–305.

Phialas, Peter G. *Shakespeare's Romantic Comedies: The Development of Their Form and Meaning* (1966).

Ribner, Irving. "The Morality of Farce: *The Taming of the Shrew*," *Essays in English and American Literature Presented to Robert Bruce McElderry, Jr.*, eds. Max F. Schulz with William D. Templeman and Charles R. Metzger (1967), pp. 165–76.

Stauffer, Donald A. *Shakespeare's World of Images* (1949).

Thorne, W. B. "Folk Elements in *The Taming of the Shrew*," *Queen's Quarterly*, LXXV (1968), 482–96.

Tillyard, E. M. W. "The Fairy-Tale Element in *The Taming of the Shrew*," *Shakespeare 1564–1964: A Collection of Modern Essays by Various Hands*, ed. Edward A. Bloom (1964), pp. 110–14.
———. *Shakespeare's Early Comedies* (1965).

## The Tempest

Auden, W. H. "The Sea and the Mirror: A Commentary on Shakespeare's *The Tempest*," *The Collected Poetry* (1945).
———. *"The Dyer's Hand" and Other Essays* (1962), pp. 128–34, 524–27.
Brower, R. A. "The Mirror of Analogy: *The Tempest*," *The Fields of Light* (1951).
Brown, John Russell, and Bernard Harris (eds.). *Stratford-upon-Avon Studies 8: Later Shakespeare* (1966).
Coleridge, Samuel Taylor. Lecture IX, *The Lectures of 1811–1812*. Reprinted in *Shakespearean Criticism*, ed. Thomas Middleton Raysor (2 vols.; 2nd ed., 1960).
Frye, Northrop. *A Natural Perspective: The Development of Shakespearean Comedy and Romance* (1965).
Gilbert, Allan H. "*The Tempest*: Parallelism in Characters and Situations," *The Journal of English and Germanic Philology*, XIV (1915), 63–74.
Hazlitt, William. "*The Tempest*," *Characters of Shakespear's Plays* (1817). Reprinted in *The Round Table [and] Characters of Shakespear's Plays* (1957).
James, David G. "The Failure of the Ballad-Makers," *Skepticism and Poetry* (1937; 1960).
Knight, G. Wilson. *The Crown of Life: Essays in Interpretation of Shakespeare's Final Plays* (1947).
———. *The Shakespearian Tempest: With a Chart of Shakespeare's Dramatic Universe* (1932; 3rd rev. ed., 1953).
Knox, Bernard. "*The Tempest* and the Ancient Comic Tradition," *English Stage Comedy* (English Institute Essays, 1954), ed. W. K. Wimsatt, Jr. (1955).
Leavis, F. R. "A Criticism of Shakespeare's Last Plays," *Scrutiny*, X (1942), 339–45. Reprinted in *The Common Pursuit* (1952; 1962).
Murry, John Middleton. *Shakespeare* (1936).
Palmer, D. J. (ed.). *Shakespeare, "The Tempest": A Casebook* (1968).
Smith, Hallett (ed.). *Twentieth Century Interpretations of "The Tempest"* (1969).
Spencer, Theodore. "Appearance and Reality in Shakespeare's Last Plays," *Modern Philology*, XXXIX (1942), 265–74.
Still, Colin. *Shakespeare's Mystery Play: A Study of "The Tempest"* (1921). Revised as *The Timeless Theme* (1936).
Strachey, Lytton. "Shakespeare's Final Period," *Books and Characters* (1922). Reprinted in *Literary Essays* (1948).
Tillyard, E. M. W. *Shakespeare's Last Plays* (1938; 6th ed., 1964).
Traversi, Derek. *Shakespeare: The Last Phase* (1954).
William, David. "*The Tempest* on the Stage," *Stratford-upon-Avon Studies 1: Jacobean Theatre*, eds. John Russell Brown and Bernard Harris (1960), pp. 133–57.
Wilson, John Dover. *The Meaning of "The Tempest,"* Robert Spence Watson Memorial Lecture (1936).

## Timon of Athens

Bradbrook, M. C. "The Tragic Pageant of *Timon of Athens*," *Shakespeare the Craftsman* (1969).
Campbell, Oscar James. *Shakespeare's Satire* (1943; 1963).
Collins, A. S. "*Timon of Athens*: A Reconsideration," *Review of English Studies*, XXII (1946), 96–108.
Cook, David. "*Timon of Athens*," *Shakespeare Survey 16*, ed. Allardyce Nicoll (1963), pp. 83–94.
Dowden, Edward. *Shakspere: A Critical Study of His Mind and Art* (1875; 3rd ed., 1962).

Ellis-Fermor, Una. "*Timon of Athens*: An Unfinished Play," *Review of English Studies*, XVIII (1942), 270–83. Reprinted in *Shakespeare the Dramatist*, ed. Kenneth Muir (1961).
Empson, William. *The Structure of Complex Words* (1951).
Farnham, Willard. *Shakespeare's Tragic Frontier* (1950).
Hazlitt, William. *Liber Amoris [1823] and Dramatic Criticisms* (1948).
———. *Characters of Shakespear's Plays* (1817). Reprinted in *The Round Table [and] Characters of Shakespear's Plays* (1957).
Honigmann, E. A. J. "*Timon of Athens*," *Shakespeare Quarterly* XII (1961), 3–20.
Knight, G. Wilson. *The Wheel of Fire: Essays in Interpretation of Shakespeare's Sombre Tragedies* (1930; 5th rev. ed., 1957).
Maxwell, J. C. (ed.). *The New Cambridge Shakespeare: Timon of Athens* (1957).
Oliver, H. J. (ed.). *The Arden Shakespeare: Timon of Athens* (1959).
Richardson, William. *Essays on Shakespeare's Dramatic Characters* (2 vols., 1784–89).
Spencer, Terence. "Shakespeare Learns the Value of Money: The Dramatist at Work on *Timon of Athens*," *Shakespeare Survey 6*, ed. Allardyce Nicoll (1953), pp. 75–78.

## Titus Andronicus

Baker, Howard. *Induction to Tragedy: A Study in a Development of Form in "Gorboduc," "The Spanish Tragedy," and "Titus Andronicus"* (1939).
Brooke, Nicholas. *Shakespeare's Early Tragedies* (1968).
Charlton, H. B. *Shakespearian Tragedy* (1948).
Findlater, Richard. "Shakespearean Atrocities," *Twentieth Century*, CLVIII (1955), 364–72.
Hamilton, A. C. "*Titus Andronicus*; The Form of Shakespearian Tragedy," *Shakespeare Quarterly*, XIV (1963), 201–13.
Hill, R. F. "The Composition of *Titus Andronicus*," *Shakespeare Survey 10*, ed. Allardyce Nicoll (1957), pp. 60–70.
Price, H. T. "The Authorship of *Titus Andronicus*," *Journal of English and Germanic Philology*, XLII (1943), 55–81.
Ribner, Irving. *Patterns in Shakespearean Tragedy* (1960).
Sargent, Ralph M. "The Source of *Titus Andronicus*," *Studies in Philology*, XLVI (1949), 167–83.
Sommers, Alan. "'Wilderness of Tigers': Structure and Symbolism in *Titus Andronicus*," *Essays in Criticism*, X (1960), 275–89.
Spencer, T. J. B. *Shakespeare: The Roman Plays* (1963).
Spivack, Bernard. *Shakespeare and the Allegory of Evil* (1958).
Tynan, Kenneth. *Curtains* (1961).
Waith, Eugene M. "The Metamorphosis of Violence in *Titus Andronicus*," *Shakespeare Survey 10*, ed. Allardyce Nicoll (1957), pp. 39–49.

## Troilus and Cressida

Alexander, Peter. "*Troilus and Cressida*, 1609," *The Library*, Ser. 4, IX (1928), 267–86.
Bethell, S. L. *Shakespeare and the Popular Dramatic Tradition* (1944).
Bradbrook, M. C. "What Shakespeare Did to Chaucer's *Troilus and Criseyde*," *Shakespeare Quarterly*, IX (1958), 311–19.
Brooke, C. F. Tucker. "Shakespeare's Study in Culture and Anarchy," *Yale Review*, XVII (1928), 571–77.
Brower, R. A. *Hero and Saint: Shakespeare and the Greco-Roman Heroic Tradition* (1970).
Campbell, Oscar James. *Comicall Satyre and Shakespeare's "Troilus and Cressida"* (1938).
Chapman, John Jay. *Selected Writings*, ed. Jacques Barzun (1959).

Charlton, H. B. "The Dark Comedies," *Bulletin of the John Rylands Library*, XXI (1937), 78–128.

Coleridge, Samuel Taylor. *Coleridge's Writings on Shakespeare*, ed. Terence Hawkes, intro. Alfred B. Harbage (1959).

Ellis-Fermor, Una. *The Frontiers of Drama* (1945; rev. ed., 1948).

Foakes, R. A. "*Troilus and Cressida* Reconsidered," *University of Toronto Quarterly*, XXXII (1963), 142–54.

Gérard, Albert. "Meaning and Structure in *Troilus and Cressida*," *English Studies*, XL (1959), 148–51, 156–57.

Harrier, R. C. "*Troilus Divided*," *Studies in the English Renaissance Drama in Memory of Karl Julius Holzknecht*, eds. Josephine W. Bennett et al. (1959).

Kaula, David. "Will and Reason in *Troilus and Cressida*," *Shakespeare Quarterly*, XII (1961), 271–83.

Kendall, P. M. "Inaction and Ambivalence in *Troilus and Cressida*," *English Studies in Honor of James Southall Wilson*, ed. Fredson Bowers (1951).

Kimbrough, Robert. *Shakespeare's "Troilus and Cressida" and Its Setting* (1964).

Knight, G. Wilson. *The Wheel of Fire: Essays in Interpretation of Shakespeare's Sombre Tragedies* (1930; 5th rev. ed., 1957).

Knights, L. C. "*Troilus and Cressida* Again," *Scrutiny*, XVIII (1951), 144–57.

Lawrence, W. W. *Shakespeare's Problem Comedies* (1931; 1960).

Muir, Kenneth. "*Troilus and Cressida*," *Shakespeare Survey 8*, ed. Allardyce Nicoll (1955), pp. 28–38.

Nowottny, Winifred M. T. "'Opinion' and 'Value' in *Troilus and Cressida*," *Essays in Criticism*, IV (1954), 282–96.

Reynolds, George F. "*Troilus and Cressida* on the Elizabethan Stage," *Joseph Quincy Adams Memorial Studies*, eds. J. G. McManaway, G. E. Dawson, and E. E. Willoughby (1948).

Richards, I. A. *Speculative Instruments* (1955).

Rollins, Hyder E. "The Troilus-Cressida Story from Chaucer to Shakespeare," *PMLA*, XXXII (1917), 383–429.

Spencer, Theodore. *Shakespeare and the Nature of Man* (1942).

Tillyard, E. M. W. *Shakespeare's Problem Plays* (1949).

Traversi, Derek. *An Approach to Shakespeare* (2 vols.; 3rd rev. ed., 1968–69).

Walker, Alice. *Textual Problems of the First Folio* (1953).


### Twelfth Night

Barber, C. L. *Shakespeare's Festive Comedy* (1959).

Bradley, A. C. "Feste the Jester," *A Miscellany* (1929).

Brown, John Russell. *Shakespeare and His Comedies* (1957).

Furness, Horace Howard (ed.). *A New Variorum Edition of Shakespeare: Twelfe Night, or, What You Will* (1901).

Hollander, John. "*Twelfth Night* and the Morality of Indulgence," *Sewanee Review*, LXVII (1959), 220–38.

Hotson, Leslie. *The First Night of Twelfth Night* (1954).

Jenkins, Harold. "Shakespeare's *Twelfth Night*," *Rice Institute Pamphlet*, XLV (1959), iv, 19–42.

Kermode, Frank. "The Mature Comedies," *Stratford-upon-Avon Studies 3: Early Shakespeare*, eds. John Russell Brown and Bernard Harris (1961), pp. 211–27.

King, Walter N. *Twentieth Century Interpretations of "Twelfth Night"* (1968).

Knight, G. Wilson. *The Shakespearian Tempest: With a Chart of Shakespeare's Dramatic Universe* (1932; 3rd rev. ed., 1953).

Leech, Clifford. *"Twelfth Night" and Shakespearian Comedy* (1965).

Lewalski, Barbara K. "Thematic Patterns in *Twelfth Night*," *Shakespeare Studies 1*, ed. J. Leeds Barroll (1965), pp. 168–81.

Mueschke, Paul, and Jeannette Fleisher. "Jonsonian Elements in the Comic Underplot of *Twelfth Night*," *PMLA*, XLVIII (1933), 722–40.

Pettet, E. C. *Shakespeare and the Romance Tradition* (1950).

Rich, Barnabe. *Rich's "Apolonius & Silla," an Original of Shakespeare's "Twelfth Night,"* ed. Morton Luce (1912).

——. *Rich's Farewell to Military Profession 1581*, ed. Thomas Mabry Cranfill (1959).

Salingar, L. D. "The Design of *Twelfth Night*," *Shakespeare Quarterly*, IX (1958), 117–39.

Summers, Joseph H. "The Masks of *Twelfth Night*," *Shakespeare: Modern Essays in Criticism*, ed. Leonard F. Dean (1961).


### The Two Gentlemen of Verona

Brooks, Harold F. "Two Clowns in a Comedy (to Say Nothing of the Dog): Speed, Launce (and Crab) in *The Two Gentlemen of Verona*," *Essays and Studies 1963*, ed. S. Gorley Putt (1963), pp. 91–100.

Charlton, H. B. *Shakespearian Comedy* (1938).

Danby, John F. "Shakespeare Criticism and *Two Gentlemen of Verona*," *Critical Quarterly*, II (1960), 309–21.

Harrison, Thomas Perrin. "Concerning *The Two Gentlemen of Verona* and Montemayor's *Diana*," *Modern Language Notes*, XLI (1926), 251–52.

Latham, Grace. "On Julia, Silvia, Hero and Viola," *Transactions of the New Shakspere Society*, Part IV (1887–92), 319–50.

Leech, Clifford (ed.). *The Arden Shakespeare: The Two Gentlemen of Verona* (1969).

Nemerov, Howard. *Poetry and Fiction: Essays* (1963).

Parks, George B. "The Development of *The Two Gentlemen of Verona*," *Huntington Library Bulletin*, No. 11 (1937), 1–11.

Parrott, Thomas Marc. *Shakespearean Comedy* (1949).

Pettet, E. C. *Shakespeare and the Romance Tradition* (1950).

Small, Samuel Asa. "The Ending of *The Two Gentlemen of Verona*," *PMLA*, XLVIII (1933), 767–76.

Vyvyan, John. *Shakespeare and the Rose of Love* (1960).

Wells, Stanley. "The Failure of *The Two Gentlemen of Verona*," *Shakespeare Jahrbuch*, XCIX (1963), 161–73.

Wilson, John Dover. *Shakespeare's Happy Comedies* (1962).


### The Two Noble Kinsmen

Agate, James. *Brief Chronicles, a Survey of the Plays of Shakespeare and the Elizabethans in Actual Performance* (1943).

Bentley, Gerald E. "Shakespeare and the Blackfriars Theatre," *Shakespeare Survey 1*, ed. Allardyce Nicoll (1948), pp. 38–50. Reprinted in a modified form in *Shakespeare and His Theatre* (1964), pp. 65–99.

Bertram, Paul. *Shakespeare and "The Two Noble Kinsmen"* (1965).

Edwards, Philip. "On the Design of *The Two Noble Kinsmen*," *A Review of English Literature*, V, No. 4 (October 1964), 89–105.

Hart, Alfred. "Shakespeare and the Vocabulary of *The Two Noble Kinsmen*," *The Review of English Studies*, X (1934), 274–87. Reprinted in *Shakespeare and the Homilies* (1935).

Kermode, Frank. *William Shakespeare: The Final Plays* (1963).

Leech, Clifford. *The John Fletcher Plays* (1962).

Littledale, Harold (ed.). *The Two Noble Kinsmen*, The New Shakspere Society (1876–85).

Mincoff, Marco. "The Authorship of *The Two Noble Kinsmen*," *English Studies*, XXXIII (1952), 97–115.

Muir, Kenneth. *Shakespeare as Collaborator* (1960).

Spalding, W. *A Letter on Shakspere's Authorship of The Two Noble Kinsmen* (1838). Reprinted in *Transactions of the New Shakspere Society* (1876).

Spencer, Theodore. "*The Two Noble Kinsmen*," *Modern Philology*, XXXVI (1939), 255–76.

Waller, Frederick O. "Printer's Copy for *The Two Noble Kinsmen*," *Studies in Bibliography*, XI (1958), 61–84.

*The Winter's Tale*

Bentley, Gerald E. "Shakespeare and the Blackfriars Theatre," *Shakespeare Survey 1*, ed. Allardyce Nicoll (1948), pp. 38–50. Reprinted in a modified form in *Shakespeare and His Theatre* (1964), pp. 65–99.

Bethell, S. L. *The Winter's Tale: A Study* (1947).

Bryant, J. A., Jr. "Shakespeare's Allegory: *The Winter's Tale*," *Sewanee Review*, LXIII (1955), 202–22.

Coghill, Nevill. "Six Points of Stage-Craft in *The Winter's Tale*," *Shakespeare Survey 11*, ed. Allardyce Nicoll (1958), pp. 31–41.

Danby, John F. *Poets on Fortune's Hill* (1952).

Edwards, Philip. "Shakespeare's Romances: 1900–1957," *Shakespeare Survey 11*, ed. Allardyce Nicoll (1958), pp. 1–18.

Ewbank, Inga-Stiner. "The Triumph of Time in *The Winter's Tale*," *A Review of English Literature*, V, No. 2 (April 1964), 83–100.

Frye, Northrop. "The Argument of Comedy," *English Institute Essays, 1948* (1949).

———. *Anatomy of Criticism* (1957).

———. "Recognition in *The Winter's Tale*," *Essays on Shakespeare and Elizabethan Drama*, ed. Richard Hosley (1962).

———. *A Natural Perspective: The Development of Shakespearean Comedy and Romance* (1965).

Greenlaw, E. "Shakespeare's Pastorals," *Studies in Philology*, XIII (1916), 122–54.

Hoeniger, F. D. "The Meaning of *The Winter's Tale*," *University of Toronto Quarterly*, XX (1950), 11–26.

James, D. G. *Skepticism and Poetry* (1937; 1960).

Knight, G. Wilson. *The Crown of Life: Essays in Interpretation of Shakespeare's Final Plays* (1947).

———. *The Shakespearian Tempest: With a Chart of Shakespeare's Dramatic Universe* (1932; 3rd rev. ed., 1953).

Lawlor, John. "*Pandosto* and the Nature of Dramatic Romance," *Philological Quarterly*, XLI (1962), 96–113.

Leavis, F. R. "A Criticism of Shakespeare's Last Plays," *Scrutiny*, X (1942), 339–45. Reprinted in *The Common Pursuit* (1952; 1962).

Pafford, J. H. P. (ed.). *The Arden Shakespeare: The Winter's Tale* (1963).

Pettet, E. C. *Shakespeare and the Romance Tradition* (1950).

Pyle, Fitzroy. "*The Winter's Tale*": *A Commentary on the Structure* (1969).

Schanzer, Ernest. "The Structural Pattern of *The Winter's Tale*," *A Review of English Literature*, V, No. 2 (April 1964), 72–82.

Spencer, Theodore. "Appearance and Reality in Shakespeare's Last Plays," *Modern Philology*, XXXIX (1942), 265–74.

Strachey, Lytton. "Shakespeare's Final Period," *Books and Characters* (1922). Reprinted in *Literary Essays* (1948).

Tillyard, E. M. W. *Shakespeare's Last Plays* (1938; 6th ed., 1964).

Tinkler, F. C. "*The Winter's Tale*," *Scrutiny*, V (1937), 344–64.

Traversi, Derek. *Shakespeare: The Last Phase* (1954).

**13. THE NONDRAMATIC WORKS**

C. S. Lewis, *English Literature in the Sixteenth Century* (1954), and Hallet Smith, *Elizabethan Poetry; A Study in Conventions, Meaning, and Expression* (1952), are interesting histories of the nondramatic literature of the period. There is much on the poems and the earlier plays in M. C. Bradbrook, *Shakespeare and Elizabethan Poetry* (1951). For a review of scholarship on the sonnets and other poems, see *Shakespeare Survey 15*, edited by Allardyce Nicoll (1962), which also contains some essays on the nondramatic works.

*The Poems*

Alvarez, A. "William Shakespeare: *The Phoenix and the Turtle*," *Interpretations*, ed. John Wain (1955).

Bradbrook, M. C. *Shakespeare and Elizabethan Poetry* (1951).

Bush, Douglas. *Mythology and the Renaissance Tradition* (rev. ed., 1963).

Cunningham, J. V. *Tradition and Poetic Structure* (1960).

Empson, William. "*The Phoenix and the Turtle*," *Essays in Criticism*, XVI (1966), 147–53.

Hamilton, A. C. "*Venus and Adonis*," *Studies in English Literature 1500–1900*, I (1961), 1–15.

Knight, G. Wilson. *The Mutual Flame: On Shakespeare's Sonnets and "The Phoenix and the Turtle"* (1955).

Lewis, C. S. *English Literature in the Sixteenth Century* (1954).

Matchett, William H. "*The Phoenix and the Turtle*"; *Shakespeare's Poem and Chester's "Loues martyr"* (1965).

Maxwell, J. C. (ed.). *The New Cambridge Shakespeare: The Poems* (1966).

Muir, Kenneth. "'A Lover's Complaint': A Reconsideration," *Shakespeare 1564–1964* (1964).

Nicoll, Allardyce (ed.). *Shakespeare Survey 15* (1962). This volume has several articles on the poems, including a useful review of scholarship.

Prince, F. T. *Shakespeare: The Poems* (1963).

Rollins, Hyder E. (ed.). *A New Variorum Edition of Shakespeare: The Poems* (1938).

Watkins, W. B. C. *Shakespeare and Spenser* (1961).

*The Sonnets*

Booth, Stephen. *An Essay on Shakespeare's Sonnets* (1969).

Cruttwell, Patrick. *The Shakespearean Moment and Its Place in the Poetry of the Seventeenth Century* (1953).

Herrnstein, Barbara (ed.). *Discussions of Shakespeare's Sonnets* (1964).

Hubler, Edward. *The Sense of Shakespeare's Sonnets* (1952).

———, Northrop Frye, Leslie A. Fiedler, Stephen Spender, and R. P. Blackmur. *The Riddle of Shakespeare's Sonnets* (1962).

Ingram, W. G., and Theodore Redpath (eds.). *Shakespeare's Sonnets* (1964).

Knight, G. Wilson. *The Mutual Flame: On Shakespeare's Sonnets and "The Phoenix and the Turtle"* (1955).

Krieger, Murray. *A Window to Criticism: Shakespeare's Sonnets and Modern Poetics* (1964).

Landry, Hilton. *Interpretations in Shakespeare's Sonnets* (1963).

Leishman, J. B. *Themes and Variations in Shakespeare's Sonnets* (1961).

Lever, J. W. *The Elizabethan Love Sonnet* (1956).

Nicoll, Allardyce (ed.). *Shakespeare Survey 15* (1962).

Ransom, John Crowe. *The World's Body* (1938).

Rollins, Hyder E. (ed.). *A New Variorum Edition of Shakespeare: The Sonnets* (2 vols., 1944).

Wilson, John Dover. *Shakespeare's Sonnets: An Introduction for Historians and Others* (1963).

# INDEX TO FIRST LINES OF THE SONNETS

So is it not with me as with that Muse, 21
Some glory in their birth, some in their skill, 91
Some say thy fault is youth, some wantonness, 96
So, now I have confessed that he is thine, 134
So oft have I invoked thee for my Muse, 78
So shall I live, supposing thou art true, 93
Sweet love, renew thy force; be it not said, 56

Take all my loves, my love, yea take them all, 40
That god forbid that made me first your slave, 58
That thou art blamed shall not be thy defect, 70
That thou hast her, it is not all my grief, 42
That time of year thou mayst in me behold, 73
That you were once unkind befriends me now, 120
The forward violet thus did I chide, 99
The little Love-god lying once asleep, 154
Then hate me when thou wilt; if ever, now, 90
Then let not winter's ragged hand deface, 6
The other two, slight air and purging fire, 45
Th' expense of spirit in a waste of shame, 129
They that have pow'r to hurt and will do none, 94
Thine eyes I love, and they, as pitying me, 132
Those hours that with gentle work did frame, 5
Those lines that I before have writ do lie, 115
Those lips that Love's own hand did make, 145
Those parts of thee that the world's eye doth view, 69
Those pretty wrongs that liberty commits, 41
Thou art as tyrannous, so as thou art, 131
Thou blind fool, Love, what dost thou to mine eyes, 137
Thus can my love excuse the slow offense, 51
Thus is his cheek the map of days outworn, 68
Thy bosom is endearèd with all hearts, 31
Thy gift, thy tables, are within my brain, 122

Thy glass will show thee how thy beauties wear, 77
Tired with all these, for restful death I cry, 66
'Tis better to be vile than vile esteemed, 121
To me, fair friend, you never can be old, 104
Two loves I have, of comfort and despair, 144

Unthrifty loveliness, why dost thou spend, 4

Was it the proud full sail of his great verse, 86
Weary with toil, I haste me to my bed, 27
Were't aught to me I bore the canopy, 125
What is your substance, whereof are you made, 53
What potions have I drunk of Siren tears, 119
What's in the brain that ink may character, 108
When forty winters shall besiege thy brow, 2
When I consider everything that grows, 15
When I do count the clock that tells the time, 12
When I have seen by Time's fell hand defaced, 64
When, in disgrace with Fortune and men's eyes, 29
When in the chronicle of wasted time, 106
When most I wink, then do mine eyes best see, 43
When my love swears that she is made of truth, 138
When thou shalt be disposed to set me light, 88
When to the sessions of sweet silent thought, 30
Where art thou, Muse, that thou forget'st so long, 100
Whilst I alone did call upon thy aid, 79
Whoever hath her wish, thou hast thy *Will*, 135
Who is it that says most, which can say more, 84
Who will believe my verse in time to come, 17
Why didst thou promise such a beauteous day, 34
Why is my verse so barren of new pride, 76

Your love and pity doth th' impression fill, 112

A B C D E F G H I J
1 2 3 4 5 6 7 8 9 0